THE OFFICIAL® 1998 PRICE GUIDE TO BASEBALL CARDS

BY
DR. JAMES BECKETT

SEVENTEENTH EDITION

HOUSE OF COLLECTIBLES • NEW YORK

Important Notice: All of the information, including valuations, in this book has been compiled from the most reliable sources, and every effort has been made to eliminate errors and questionable data. Nevertheless, the possibility of error in a work of such scope always exists. The publisher will not be held responsible for losses which may occur in the purchase, sale or other transaction of items because of information contained herein. Readers who feel they have discovered errors are invited to *write* and inform us, so that they may be corrected in subsequent editions. Those seeking further information on the topics covered in this book are advised to refer to the complete line of *Official Price Guides* published by the House of Collectibles.

Published by:
House of Collectibles
201 East 50th Street
New York, New York 10022

Distributed by Ballantine Books, a division of Random House, Inc.,
New York, and simultaneously in Canada by
Random House of Canada Limited, Toronto.

Manufactured in the United States of America

ISSN: 1062-7138

ISBN: 0-676-60050-6

Seventeenth Edition: April 1997

10 9 8 7 6 5 4 3 2 1

Table of Contents

About the Author

Jim Beckett, the leading authority on sport card values in the United States, maintains a wide range of activities in the world of sports. He possesses one of the finest collections of sports cards and autographs in the world, has made numerous appearances on radio and television, and has been frequently cited in many national publications. He was awarded the first "Special Achievement Award" for Contributions to the Hobby by the National Sports Collectors Convention in 1980, the "Jock-Jaspersen Award" for Hobby Dedication in 1983, and the "Buck Barker, Spirit of the Hobby" Award in 1991.

Dr. Beckett is the author of *Beckett Baseball Card Price Guide, The Official Price Guide to Baseball Cards, The Sport Americana Price Guide to Baseball Collectibles, The Sport Americana Baseball Memorabilia and Autograph Price Guide, Beckett Football Card Price Guide, The Official Price Guide to Football Cards, Beckett Hockey Card Price Guide, The Official Price Guide to Hockey Cards, Beckett Basketball Card Price Guide, The Official Price Guide to Basketball Cards,* and *The Sport Americana Baseball Card Alphabetical Checklist.* In addition, he is the founder, publisher, and editor of *Beckett Baseball Card Monthly, Beckett Basketball Monthly, Beckett Football Card Monthly, Beckett Hockey Monthly, Beckett Future Stars, Beckett Racing Monthly,* and *Beckett Tribute* magazines.

Jim Beckett received his Ph.D. in Statistics from Southern Methodist University in 1975. Prior to starting Beckett Publications in 1984, Dr. Beckett served as an Associate Professor of Statistics at Bowling Green State University and as a vice president of a consulting firm in Dallas, Texas. He currently resides in Dallas with his wife, Patti, and their daughters, Christina, Rebecca, and Melissa.

How to Use This Book

Isn't it great? Every year this book gets bigger and bigger with all the new sets coming out. But even more exciting is that every year there are more collectors, more shows, more stores, and more interest in the cards we love so much. This edition has been enhanced and expanded from the previous edition. The cards you collect — who appears on them, what they look like, where they are from, and (most important to most of you) what their current values are — are enumerated within. Many of the features contained in the other *Beckett Price Guides* have been incorporated into this volume since condition grading, terminology, and many other aspects of collecting are common to the card hobby in general. We hope you find the book both interesting and useful in your collecting pursuits.

The *Beckett Guide* has been successful where other attempts have failed because it is complete, current, and valid. This Price Guide contains not just one, but three prices by condition for all the baseball cards listed. The prices were added to the card lists just prior to printing and reflect not the author's opinions or desires but the going retail prices for each card, based on the marketplace (sports memorabilia conventions and shows, sports card shops, hobby papers, current mail-order catalogs, local club meetings, auction results, and other firsthand reportings of actually realized prices).

What is the best price guide available on the market today? Of course, card sellers prefer the price guide with the highest prices, while card buyers naturally prefer the one with the lowest prices. Accuracy, however, is the true test. Use the price guide trusted by more collectors and dealers than all the others combined. Look for the *Beckett®* name. I won't put my name on anything I won't stake my reputation on. Not the lowest and not the highest — but the most accurate, with integrity.

To facilitate your use of this book, read the complete introductory section on the following pages before going to the pricing pages. Every collectible field has its own terminology; we've tried to capture most of these terms and definitions in our glossary. Please read carefully the section on grading and the condition of your cards, as you cannot determine which price column is appropriate for a given card without first knowing its condition.

Welcome to the world of baseball cards.

How to Collect

Each collection is personal and reflects the individuality of its owner. There are no set rules on how to collect cards. Since card collecting is a hobby or leisure pastime, what you collect, how much you collect, and how much time and money you spend collecting are entirely up to you. The funds you have available for collecting and your own personal taste should determine how you collect. Information and ideas presented here are intended to help you get the most enjoyment from this hobby.

It is impossible to collect every card ever produced. Therefore, beginners as well as intermediate and advanced collectors usually specialize in some way. One of the reasons this hobby is popular is that individual collectors can define and tailor their collecting methods to match their own tastes. To give you some ideas of the various approaches to collecting, we will list some of the more popular areas of specialization.

Many collectors select complete sets from particular years. For example, they may concentrate on assembling complete sets from all the years since their birth or since they became avid sports fans. They may try to collect a card for every player during that specified period of time.

Many others wish to acquire only certain players. Usually such players are the superstars of the sport, but occasionally collectors will specialize in all the cards of players who attended a particular college or came from a certain town. Some collectors are only interested in the first cards or Rookie Cards of certain players. A handy guide for collectors interested in pursuing the hobby this way is the *Sport Americana Baseball Card Alphabetical Checklist.*

Another fun way to collect cards is by team. Most fans have a favorite team, and it is natural for that loyalty to be translated into a desire for cards of the players on that favorite team. For most of the recent years, team sets (all the cards from a given team for that year) are readily available at a reasonable price. *The Sport Americana Team Baseball Card Checklist* will open up this field to the collector.

Obtaining Cards

Several avenues are open to card collectors. Cards still can be purchased in the traditional way: by the pack at the local candy, grocery, drug or major discount stores.

But there are also thousands of card shops across the country that specialize in selling cards individually or by the pack, box, or set. Another alternative is the thousands of card shows held each month around the country, which feature anywhere from eight to 800 tables of sports cards and memorabilia for sale.

For many years, it has been possible to purchase complete sets of baseball cards through mail-order advertisers found in traditional sports media publications, such as *The Sporting News, Baseball Digest, Street & Smith* yearbooks, and others. These sets also are advertised in the card collecting periodicals. Many collectors will begin by subscribing to at least one of the hobby periodicals, all with good up-to-date information. In fact, subscription offers can be found in the advertising section of this book.

Most serious card collectors obtain old (and new) cards from one or more of several main sources: (1) trading or buying from other collectors or dealers; (2) responding to sale or auction ads in the hobby publications; (3) buying at a local hobby store; and/or (4) attending sports collectibles shows or conventions.

We advise that you try all four methods since each has its own distinct advantages: (1) trading is a great way to make new friends; (2) hobby periodicals help you keep up with what's going on in the hobby (including when and where the conventions are happening); (3) stores provide the opportunity to enjoy personalized service and consider a great diversity of material in a relaxed sports-oriented atmosphere; and (4) shows allow you to choose from multiple dealers and thousands of cards under one roof in a competitive situation.

Preserving Your Cards

Cards are fragile. They must be handled properly in order to retain their value. Careless handling can easily result in creased or bent cards. It is, however, not recommended that tweezers or tongs be used to pick up your cards since such utensils might mar or indent card surfaces and thus reduce those cards' conditions and values.

In general, your cards should be handled directly as little as possible. This is sometimes easier to say than to do.

Although there are still many who use custom boxes, storage trays, or even shoe boxes, plastic sheets are the preferred method of many collectors for storing cards.

A collection stored in plastic pages in a three-ring album allows you to view your collection at any time without the need to touch the card itself. Cards can also be kept in single holders (of various types and thickness) designed for the enjoyment of each card individually.

For a large collection, some collectors may use a combination of the above methods. When purchasing plastic sheets for your cards, be sure that you find the pocket size that fits the cards snugly. Don't put your 1951 Bowman in a sheet designed to fit 1981 Topps.

Most hobby and collectibles shops and virtually all collectors' conventions will have these plastic pages available in quantity for the various sizes offered, or you can purchase them directly from the advertisers in this book.

Also, remember that pocket size isn't the only factor to consider when looking for plastic sheets. Other factors such as safety, economy, appearance, availability, or personal preference also may indicate which types of sheets a collector may want to buy.

Damp, sunny and/or hot conditions — no, this is not a weather forecast — are three elements to avoid in extremes if you are interested in preserving your collection. Too much (or too little) humidity can cause the gradual deterioration of a card. Direct, bright sun (or fluorescent light) over time will bleach out the color of a card. Extreme heat accelerates the decomposition of the card. On the other hand, many cards have lasted more than 75 years without much scientific intervention. So be cautious, even if the above factors typically present a problem only when present in the extreme. It never hurts to be prudent.

Collecting vs. Investing

Collecting individual players and collecting complete sets are both popular vehicles for investment and speculation.

Most investors and speculators stock up on complete sets or on quantities of players they think have good investment potential.

There is obviously no guarantee in this book, or anywhere else for that matter, that cards will outperform the stock market or other investment alternatives in the future. After all, baseball cards do not pay quarterly dividends and cards cannot be sold at their "current values" as easily as stocks or bonds.

Nevertheless, investors have noticed a favorable long-term trend in the past performance of baseball and other sports collectibles, and certain cards and sets have outperformed just about any other investment in some years.

Many hobbyists maintain that the best investment is and always will be the building of a collection, which traditionally has held up better than outright speculation.

Some of the obvious questions are: Which cards? When to buy? When to sell? The best investment you can make is in your own education.

The more you know about your collection and the hobby, the more informed the decisions you will be able to make. We're not selling investment tips. We're selling information about the current value of baseball cards. It's up to you to use that information to your best advantage.

Terminology

Each hobby has its own language to describe its area of interest. The nomenclature traditionally used for trading cards is derived from the American Card Catalog, published in 1960 by Nostalgia Press. That catalog, written by Jefferson Burdick (who is called the "Father of Card Collecting" for his pioneering work), uses letter and number designations for each separate set of cards. The letter used in the ACC designation refers to the generic type of card. While both sport and non-sport issues are classified in the ACC, we shall confine ourselves to the sport issues. The following list defines the letters and their meanings as used by the American Card Catalog.

(none) or N - 19th Century U.S. Tobacco
B - Blankets
D - Bakery Inserts Including Bread
E - Early Candy and Gum
F - Food Inserts
H - Advertising
M - Periodicals
PC - Postcards
R - Candy and Gum since 1930

Following the letter prefix and an optional hyphen are one-, two-, or three-digit numbers, R(-)999. These typically represent the company or entity issuing the cards. In several cases, the ACC number is extended by an additional hyphen and another one- or two-digit numerical suffix. For example, the 1957 Topps regular-series baseball card issue carries an ACC designation of R414-11. The "R" indicates a Candy or Gum card produced since 1930. The "414" is the ACC designation for Topps Chewing Gum baseball card issues, and the "11" is the ACC designation for the 1957 regular issue (Topps' eleventh baseball set). Like other traditional methods of identification, this system provides order to the process of cataloging cards; however, most serious collectors learn the ACC designation of the popular sets by repetition and familiarity, rather than by attempting to "figure out" what they might or should be. From 1948 forward, collectors and dealers commonly refer to all sets by their year, maker, type of issue, and any other distinguishing characteristic. For example, such a characteristic could be an unusual issue or one of several regular issues put out by a specific maker in a single year. Regional issues are usually referred to by year, maker, and sometimes by title or theme of the set.

Glossary/Legend

Our glossary defines terms used in the card collecting hobby and in this book. Many of these terms are also common to other types of sports memorabilia collecting. Some terms may have several meanings depending on use and context.

ACC - Acronym for American Card Catalog.

ACETATE - A transparent plastic.

ANN- Announcer.

AS - All-Star card. A card portraying an All-Star Player of the previous year that says "All-Star" on its face.

ATG - All-Time Great card.

ATL - All-Time Leaders card.

AU(TO) - Autographed card.

BC - Bonus Card.

BL - Blue letters.

BLANKET - A felt square (normally 5 to 6 inches) portraying a baseball player.

BOX CARD - Card issued on a box (i.e., 1987 Topps Box Bottoms).

BRICK - A group of 50 or more cards having common characteristics that is intended to be bought, sold or traded as a unit.

CABINETS - Popular and highly valuable photographs on thick card stock produced in the 19th and early 20th century.

CHECKLIST - A list of the cards contained in a particular set. The list is always in numerical order if the cards are numbered. Some unnumbered sets are artificially numbered in alphabetical order, by team and alphabetically within the team, or by uniform number for convenience.

CL - Checklist card. A card that lists in order the cards and players in the set or series. Older checklist cards in Mint condition that have not been marked are very desirable and command premiums.

CO - Coach.

COIN - A small disc of metal or plastic portraying a player in its center.

COLLECTOR ISSUE - A set produced for the sake of the card itself with no product or service sponsor. It derives its name from the fact that most of these sets are produced for sale directly to the hobby market.

COM - Card issued by the Post Cereal Company through their mail-in offer.

COMM - Commissioner.

COMMON CARD - The typical card of any set; it has no premium value accruing from subject matter, numerical scarcity, popular demand, or anomaly.

CONVENTION - A gathering of dealers and collectors at a single location for the purpose of buying, selling, and trading sports memorabilia items. Conventions are open to the public and sometimes feature autograph guests, door prizes, contests, seminars, etc. They are frequently referred to simply as "shows."

COOP - Cooperstown.

COR - Corrected card.

COUPON - See Tab.

CY - Cy Young Award.

DEALER - A person who engages in buying, selling, and trading sports collectibles or supplies. A dealer may also be a collector, but as a dealer, his main goal is to earn a profit.

DIE-CUT - A card with part of its stock partially cut, allowing one or more parts to be folded or removed. After removal or appropriate folding, the remaining part of the card can frequently be made to stand up.

DISC - A circular-shaped card.

DISPLAY CARD - A sheet, usually containing three to nine cards, that is printed and used by the manufacturer to advertise and/or display the packages containing his products and cards. The backs of display cards are blank or contain advertisements.

DK - Diamond King.

DL - Division Leaders.

DP - Double Print (a card that was printed in double the quantity compared to the other cards in the same series) or a Draft Pick card.

DUFEX - A method of card manufacturing technology patented by Pinnacle Brands, Inc. It involves a refractive quality to a card with a foil coating.

EMBOSSED - A raised surface; features of a card that are projected from a flat background.

ERA - Earned Run Average.

ERR - Error card. A card with erroneous information, spelling, or depiction on either side of the card. Most errors are not corrected by the producing card company.

ETCHED - Impressions within the surface of a card.

EXHIBIT - The generic name given to thick-stock, postcard-size cards with single color obverse pictures. The name is derived from the Exhibit Supply Co. of Chicago, the principal manufacturer of this type of card. These also are known as Arcade cards since they were found in many arcades.

FDP - First or First Round Draft Pick.

FOIL - Foil embossed stamp on card.

FOLD - Foldout.

FS - Father/son card.

FULL BLEED - A borderless card; a card containing a photo that encompasses the entire card.

FULL SHEET - A complete sheet of cards that has not been cut up into individual cards by the manufacturer. Also called an uncut sheet.

FUN - Fun Cards.

GL - Green letters.

GLOSS - A card with luster; a shiny finish as in a card with UV coating.

HIGH NUMBER - The cards in the last series of numbers in a year in which such higher-numbered cards were printed or distributed in significantly lesser amounts than the lower-numbered cards. The high-number designation refers to a scarcity of the high-numbered cards. Not all years have high numbers in terms of this definition.

HL - Highlight card.

HOF - Hall of Fame, or a card that portrays a Hall of Famer (HOFer).

HOLOGRAM - A three-dimensional photographic image.

HOR - Horizontal pose on card as opposed to the standard vertical orientation found on most cards.

IA - In Action card.

IF - Infielder.

INSERT - A card of a different type or any other sports collectible (typically a poster or sticker) contained and sold in the same package along with a card or cards of a major set. An insert card is either unnumbered or not numbered in the same sequence as the major set. Sometimes the inserts are randomly distributed and are not found in every pack.

INTERACTIVE - A concept that involves collector participation.

ISSUE - Synonymous with set, but usually used in conjunction with a manufacturer, e.g., a Topps issue.

KARAT - A unit of measure for the fineness of gold; i.e. 24K.

LAYERING - The separation or peeling of one or more layers of the card stock, usually at the corner of the card.

LEGITIMATE ISSUE - A set produced to promote or boost sales of a product or service, e.g., bubblegum, cereal, cigarettes, etc. Most collector issues are not legitimate issues in this sense.

LHP - Lefthanded pitcher.

LID - A circular-shaped card (possibly with tab) that forms the top of the container for the product being promoted.

LL - League leaders or large letters on card.

MAJOR SET - A set produced by a national manufacturer of cards containing a large number of cards. Usually 100 or more different cards comprise a major set.

MEM - Memorial card. For example, the 1990 Donruss and Topps Bart Giamatti cards.

METALLIC - A glossy design method that enhances card features.

MG - Manager.

MINI - A small card; for example, a 1975 Topps card of identical design but smaller dimensions than the regular Topps issue of 1975.

ML - Major League.

MULTI-PLAYER CARD - A single card depicting two or more players (but not a team card).

MVP - Most Valuable Player.

NAU - No autograph on card.

NH - No-Hitter.

NNOF - No Name on Front.

NOF - Name on Front.

NON-SPORT CARD - A card from a set whose major theme is a subject other than a sports subject. A card of a sports figure or event that is part of a non-sport set is still a non-sport card, e.g., while the "Look 'N' See" non-sport card set contains a card of Babe Ruth, a sports figure, that card is a non-sport card.

NOTCHING - The grooving of the card, usually caused by fingernails, rubber bands, or bumping card edges against other objects.

OF - Outfield or Outfielder.

OLY - Olympics Card.

ORG - Organist.

P - Pitcher or Pitching pose.

P1 - First Printing.

P2 - Second Printing.

P3 - Third Printing.

PACKS - A means with which cards are issued in terms of pack type (wax, cello, foil, rack, etc.) and channels of distribution (hobby, retail, etc.).

PANEL - An extended card that is composed of two or more individual cards. Often the panel forms the back part of the container for the product being promoted, e.g., a Hostess panel, a Bazooka panel, an Esskay Meat panel.

PARALLEL- A card that is similar in design to its counterpart from a basic set, but offers a distinguishing quality.

PCL - Pacific Coast League.

PF - Profiles.

PLASTIC SHEET - A clear, plastic page that is punched for insertion into a binder (with standard three-ring spacing) containing pockets for displaying cards. Many different styles of sheets exist with pockets of varying sizes to hold the many differing card formats. Also called a display sheet or storage sheet.

PLATINUM - A metallic element used in the process of creating a glossy card.

PR - Printed name on back.

PREMIUM - A card, sometimes on photographic stock, that is purchased or obtained in conjunction with, or redemption for, another card or product. The premium is not packaged in the same unit as the primary item.

PRES - President.

PRISMATIC/PRISM - A glossy or bright design that refracts or disperses light.

PUZZLE CARD - A card whose back contains a part of a picture which, when joined correctly with other puzzle cards, forms the completed picture.

PUZZLE PIECE - A die-cut piece designed to interlock with similar pieces (e.g., early 1980's Donruss).

PVC - Polyvinyl Chloride, a substance used to make many of the popular card display protective sheets. Non-PVC sheets are considered preferable for long-term storage of cards by many.

RARE - A card or series of cards of very limited availability. Unfortunately, "rare" is a subjective term frequently used indiscriminately to hype value. "Rare" cards are harder to obtain than "scarce" cards.

RB - Record Breaker.

REDEMPTION- A program established by multiple card manufacturers that allows collectors to mail in a special card (usually a random insert) in return for special cards, sets or other prizes not available through conventional channels.

REFRACTORS - A card that features a design element which enhances (distorts) its color/appearance through deflecting light.

REGIONAL - A card or set of cards issued and distributed only in a limited geographical area of the country.

REPLICA - An identical copy or reproduction.

REV NEG - Reversed or flopped photo side of the card. This is a major type of error card, but only some are corrected.

RHP - Righthanded pitcher.

ROY - Rookie of the Year.

RP - Relief pitcher.

SA - Super Action card.

SASE - Self-Addressed, Stamped Envelope.

SB - Stolen Bases.

SCARCE - A card or series of cards of limited availability. This subjective term is sometimes used indiscriminately to hype value. "Scarce" cards are not as difficult to obtain as "rare" cards.

SCR - Script name on back.

SD - San Diego Padres.

SEMI-HIGH - A card from the next to last series of a sequentially issued set. It has more value than an average card and generally less value than a high number. A card is not called a semi-high unless the next to last series in which it exists has an additional premium attached to it.

SERIES - The entire set of cards issued by a particular producer in a particular year; e.g., the 1971 Topps series. Also, within a particular set, series can refer to a group of (consecutively numbered) cards printed at the same time; e.g., the first series of the 1957 Topps issue (#1 through #88).

SET - One each of the entire run of cards of the same type produced by a particular manufacturer during a single year. In other words, if you have a complete set of 1976 Topps then you have every card from #1 up to and including #660, i.e., all the different cards that were produced.

SF - Starflics.

SHEEN - Brightness or luster emitted by a card.

SKIP-NUMBERED - A set that has many unissued card numbers between the lowest number in the set and the highest number in the set; e.g., the 1948 Leaf baseball set contains 98 cards skip-numbered from #1 to #168. A major set in which a few numbers were not printed is not considered to be skip-numbered.

SP - Single or Short Print (a card which was printed in lesser quantity compared to the other cards in the same series; see also DP and TP).

SPECIAL CARD - A card that portrays something other than a single player or team; for example, a card that portrays the previous year's statistical leaders or the results from the previous year's World Series.

SS - Shortstop.

STAMP - Adhesive-backed papers depicting a player. The stamp may be individual or in a sheet of many stamps. Moisture must be applied to the adhesive in order for the stamp to be attached to another surface.

STANDARD SIZE - Most modern sports cards measure 2-1/2 by 3-1/2 inches. Exceptions are noted in card descriptions throughout this book.

STAR CARD - A card that portrays a player of some repute, usually determined by his ability, however, sometimes referring to sheer popularity.

STICKER - A card with a removable layer that can be affixed to (stuck onto) another surface.

STOCK - The cardboard or paper on which the card is printed.

STRIP CARDS - A sheet or strip of cards, particularly popular in the 1920s and 1930s, with the individual cards usually separated by broken or dotted lines.

SUPERIMPOSED - To be affixed on top of something, i.e., a player photo over a solid background.

SUPERSTAR CARD - A card that portrays a superstar; e.g., a Hall of Famer or player with strong Hall of Fame potential.

TAB - A card portion set off from the rest of the card, usually with perforations, that may be removed without damaging the central character or event depicted by the card.

TC - Team Checklist.

TEAM CARD - A card that depicts an entire team.

TEST SET - A set, usually containing a small number of cards, issued by a national card producer and distributed in a limited section or sections of the country. Presumably, the purpose of a test set is to test market appeal for a particular type of card.

THREE-DIMENSIONAL (3D) - A visual image that provides an illusion of depth and perspective.

TOPICAL - a subset or group of cards that have a common theme (e.g., MVP award winners).

TP - Triple Print (a card that was printed in triple the quantity compared to the other cards in the same series).

TRANSPARENT - Clear, see through.

TR - Trade reference on card.

TRIMMED - A card cut down from its original size. Trimmed cards are undesirable to most collectors.

UDCA - Upper Deck Classic Alumni.

UER - Uncorrected Error.

UMP - Umpire.

USA - Team USA.

UV - Ultraviolet, a glossy coating used in producing cards.

VAR - Variation card. One of two or more cards from the same series with the same number (or player with identical pose if the series is unnumbered) differing from one another by some aspect, the different feature stemming from the printing or stock of the card. This can be caused when the manufacturer of the cards notices an error in one or more of the cards, makes the changes, and then resumes the print run. In this case there will be two versions or variations of the same card. Sometimes one of the variations is relatively scarce.

VERT - Vertical pose on card.

WAS - Washington National League (1974 Topps).

WC - What's the Call?

WL - White letter on front.

WS - World Series card.

YL - Yellow letters on front

YT - Yellow team name on front.

***** - to denote multi-sport sets.

Understanding Card Values

Determining Value

Why are some cards more valuable than others? Obviously, the economic laws of supply and demand are applicable to card collecting just as they are to any other field where a commodity is bought, sold or traded in a free, unregulated market.

Supply (the number of cards available on the market) is less than the total number of cards originally produced since attrition diminishes that original quantity. Each year a percentage of cards is typically thrown away, destroyed or otherwise lost to collectors. This percentage is much, much smaller today than it was in the past because more and more people have become increasingly aware of the value of their cards.

For those who collect only Mint condition cards, the supply of older cards can be quite small indeed. Until recently, collectors were not so conscious of the need to preserve the condition of their cards. For this reason, it is difficult to know exactly how many 1953 Topps are currently available, Mint or otherwise. It is generally accepted that there are fewer 1953 Topps available than 1963, 1973 or 1983 Topps cards. If demand were equal for each of these sets, the law of supply and demand would increase the price for the least available sets. Demand, however, is never equal for all sets, so price correlations can be complicated. The demand for a card is influenced by many factors. These include: (1) the age of the card; (2) the number of cards printed; (3) the player(s) portrayed on the card; (4) the attractiveness and popularity of the set; and (5) the physical condition of the card.

In general, (1) the older the card, (2) the fewer the number of the cards printed, (3) the more famous, popular and talented the player, (4) the more attractive and popular the set, and (5) the better the condition of the card, the higher the value of the card will be. There are exceptions to all but one of these factors: the condition of the card. Given two cards similar in all respects except condition, the one in the best condition will always be valued higher.

While those guidelines help to establish the value of a card, the countless exceptions and peculiarities make any simple, direct mathematical formula to determine card values impossible.

Regional Variation

Since the market varies from region to region, card prices of local players may be higher. This is known as a regional premium. How significant the premium is — and if there is any premium at all — depends on the local popularity of the team and the player.

The largest regional premiums usually do not apply to superstars, who often are so well-known nationwide that the prices of their key cards are too high for local dealers to realize a premium.

Lesser stars often command the strongest premiums. Their popularity is concentrated in their home region, creating local demand that greatly exceeds overall demand.

Regional premiums can apply to popular retired players and sometimes can be found in the areas where the players grew up or starred in college.

A regional discount is the converse of a regional premium. Regional discounts occur when a player has been so popular in his region for so long that local collectors and dealers have accumulated quantities of his key cards. The abundant supply may make the cards available in that area at the lowest prices anywhere.

Set Prices

A somewhat paradoxical situation exists in the price of a complete set vs. the combined cost of the individual cards in the set. In nearly every case, the sum of the prices for the individual cards is higher than the cost for the complete set. This is prevalent especially in the cards of the last few years. The reasons for this apparent anomaly stem from the habits of collectors and from the carrying costs to dealers. Today, each card in a set normally is produced in the same quantity as all other cards in its set.

Many collectors pick up only stars, superstars and particular teams. As a result, the dealer is left with a shortage of certain player cards and an abundance of others. He therefore incurs an expense in simply "carrying" these less desirable cards in stock. On the other hand, if he sells a complete set, he gets rid of large numbers of cards at one time. For this reason, he generally is willing to receive less money for a complete set. By doing this, he recovers all of his costs and also makes a profit.

The disparity between the price of the complete set and the sum of the individual cards also has been influenced by the fact that some of the major manufacturers now are pre-collating card sets. Since "pulling" individual cards from the sets involves a specific type of labor (and cost), the singles or star card market is not affected significantly by pre-collation.

Set prices also do not include rare card varieties, unless specifically stated. Of course, the prices for sets do include one example of each type for the given set, but this is the least expensive variety.

Scarce Series

Scarce series occur because cards issued before 1974 were made available to the public each year in several series of finite numbers of cards, rather than all cards of the set being available for purchase at one time. At some point during the year, usually toward the end of the baseball season, interest in current year baseball cards waned. Consequently, the manufacturers produced smaller numbers of these later-series cards.

Nearly all nationwide issues from post-World War II manufacturers (1948 to 1973) exhibit these series variations. In the past, Topps, for example, may have issued series consisting of many different numbers of cards, including 55, 66, 80, 88 and others. Recently, Topps has settled on what is now its standard sheet size of 132 cards, six of which comprise its 792-card set.

While the number of cards within a given series is usually the same as the number of cards on one printed sheet, this is not always the case. For example, Bowman used 36 cards on its standard printed sheets, but in 1948 substituted 12 cards during later print runs of that year's baseball cards. Twelve of the cards from the initial sheet of 36 cards were removed and replaced by 12 different cards giving, in effect, a first series of 36 cards and a second series of 12 new cards. This replacement produced a scarcity of 24 cards — the 12 cards removed from the original sheet and the 12 new cards added to the sheet. A full sheet of 1948 Bowman cards (second printing) shows that card numbers 37 through 48 have replaced 12 of the cards on the first printing sheet.

The Topps Company also has created scarcities and/or excesses of certain cards in many of its sets. Topps, however, has most frequently gone the other direction by double printing some of the cards. Double printing causes an abundance of cards of the players who are on the same sheet more than one time. During the years from 1978 to 1981, Topps double printed 66 cards out of their large 726-card set. The Topps practice of double printing cards in earlier years is the most logical explanation for the known scarcities of particular cards in some of these Topps sets.

From 1988 through 1990, Donruss short printed and double printed certain cards in its major sets. Ostensibly this was because of its addition of bonus team MVP cards in its regular-issue wax packs.

We are always looking for information or photographs of printing sheets of cards for research. Each year, we try to update the hobby's knowledge of distribution anomalies. Please let us know at the address in this book if you have first-hand knowledge that would be helpful in this pursuit.

Grading Your Cards

Each hobby has its own grading terminology — stamps, coins, comic books, record collecting, etc. Collectors of sports cards are no exception. The one invariable criterion for determining the value of a card is its condition: The better the condition of the card, the more valuable it is. Condition grading, however, is subjective. Individual card dealers and collectors differ in the strictness of their grading, but the stated condition of a card should be determined without regard to whether it is being bought or sold.

No allowance is made for age. A 1952 card is judged by the same standards as a 1992 card. But there are specific sets and cards that are condition sensitive (marked with "!" in the Price Guide) because of their border color, consistently poor centering, etc. Such cards and sets sometimes command premiums above the listed percentages in Mint condition.

Centering

Current centering terminology uses numbers representing the percentage of border on either side of the main design. Obviously, centering is diminished in importance for borderless cards such as Stadium Club.

Slightly Off-Center (60/40): A slightly off-center card is one that, upon close inspection, is found to have one border bigger than the opposite border. This degree once was offensive to only purists, but now some hobbyists try to avoid cards that are anything other than perfectly centered.

Off-Center (70/30): An off-center card has one border that is noticeably more than twice as wide as the opposite border.

Badly Off-Center (80/20 or worse): A badly off-center card has virtually no border on one side of the card.

Miscut: A miscut card actually shows part of the adjacent card in its larger border and consequently a corresponding amount of its card is cut off.

Corner Wear

Corner wear is the most scrutinized grading criteria in the hobby. These are the major categories of corner wear:

Corner with a slight touch of wear: The corner still is sharp, but there is a slight touch of wear showing. On a dark-bordered card, this shows as a dot of white.

Fuzzy corner: The corner still comes to a point, but the point has just begun to fray. A slightly "dinged" corner is considered the same as a fuzzy corner.

Slightly rounded corner: The fraying of the corner has increased to where there is only a hint of a point. Mild layering may be evident. A "dinged" corner is considered the same as a slightly rounded corner.

Rounded corner: The point is completely gone. Some layering is noticeable.

Badly rounded corner: The corner is completely round and rough. Severe layering is evident.

Creases

A third common defect is the crease. The degree of creasing in a card is difficult to show in a drawing or picture. On giving the specific condition of an expensive card for sale, the seller should note any creases additionally. Creases can be categorized as to severity according to the following scale:

Light Crease: A light crease is a crease that is barely noticeable upon close inspection. In fact, when cards are in plastic sheets or holders, a light crease may not be seen (until the card is taken out of the holder). A light crease on the front is much more serious than a light crease on the card back only.

Medium Crease: A medium crease is noticeable when held and studied at arm's length by the naked eye, but does not overly detract from the appearance of the card. It is an obvious crease, but not one that breaks the picture surface of the card.

Heavy Crease: A heavy crease is one that has torn or broken through the card's picture surface, e.g., puts a tear in the photo surface.

Alterations

Deceptive Trimming: This occurs when someone alters the card in order (1) to shave off edge wear, (2) to improve the sharpness of the corners, or (3) to improve centering — obviously their objective is to falsely increase the perceived value of the card to an unsuspecting buyer. The shrinkage usually is evident only if the trimmed card is compared to an adjacent full-sized card or if the trimmed card is itself measured.

Obvious Trimming: Obvious trimming is noticeable and unfortunate. It is usually performed by non-collectors who give no thought to the present or future value of their cards.

Deceptively Retouched Borders: This occurs when the borders (especially on those cards with dark borders) are touched up on the edges and corners with magic marker or crayons of appropriate color in order to make the card appear Mint.

Categorization of Defects—Miscellaneous Flaws

The following are common minor flaws that, depending on severity, lower a card's condition by one to four grades and often render it no better than Excellent-Mint: bubbles (lumps in surface), gum and wax stains, diamond cutting (slanted borders), notching, off-centered backs, paper wrinkles, scratched-off cartoons or puzzles on back, rubber band marks, scratches, surface impressions and warping.

The following are common serious flaws that, depending on severity, lower a card's condition at least four grades and often render it no better than Good: chemical or sun fading, erasure marks, mildew, miscutting (severe off-centering), holes, bleached or re-touched borders, tape marks, tears, trimming, water or coffee stains and writing.

Condition Guide

Grades

Mint (Mt) - A card with no flaws or wear. The card has four perfect corners, 60/40 or better centering from top to bottom and from left to right, original gloss, smooth edges and original color borders. A Mint card does not have print spots, color or focus imperfections.

Near Mint-Mint (NrMt-Mt) - A card with one minor flaw. Any one of the following would lower a Mint card to Near Mint-Mint: one corner with a slight touch of wear, barely noticeable print spots, color or focus imperfections. The card must have 60/40 or better centering in both directions, original gloss, smooth edges and original color borders.

Near Mint (NrMt) - A card with one minor flaw. Any one of the following would lower a Mint card to Near Mint: one fuzzy corner or two to four corners with slight touches of wear, 70/30 to 60/40 centering, slightly rough edges, minor print spots, color or focus imperfections. The card must have original gloss and original color borders.

Excellent-Mint (ExMt) - A card with two or three fuzzy, but not rounded, corners and centering no worse than 80/20. The card may have no more than two of the following: slightly rough edges, very slightly discolored borders, minor print spots, color or focus imperfections. The card must have original gloss.

Excellent (Ex) - A card with four fuzzy but definitely not rounded corners and centering no worse than 80/20. The card may have a small amount of original gloss lost, rough edges, slightly discolored borders and minor print spots, color or focus imperfections.

Very Good (Vg) - A card that has been handled but not abused: slightly rounded corners with slight layering, slight notching on edges, a significant amount of gloss lost from the surface but no scuffing and moderate discoloration of borders. The card may have a few light creases.

Good (G), Fair (F), Poor (P) - A well-worn, mishandled or abused card: badly rounded and layered corners, scuffing, most or all original gloss missing,

Centering

Well-centered

Slightly Off-centered

Off-centered

Badly Off-centered

Miscut

Corner Wear

The partial cards here have been photographed at 300%. This was done in order to magnify each card's corner wear to such a degree that differences could be shown on a printed page.

The 1962 Topps Mickey Mantle card definitely has a rounded corner. Some may say that this card is badly rounded, but that is a judgement call.

The 1962 Topps Hank Aaron card has a slightly rounded corner. Note that there is definite corner wear evident by the fraying and that there is no longer a sharp point to which the corner converges.

The 1962 Topps Gil Hodges card has corner wear; it is slightly better than the Aaron card above. Nevertheless, some collectors might classify this Hodges corner as slightly rounded.

The 1962 Topps Manager's Dream card showing Mantle and Mays has slight corner wear. This is not a fuzzy corner as very slight wear is noticeable on the card's photo surface.

The 1962 Topps Don Mossi card has very slight corner wear such that it might be called a fuzzy corner. A close look at the original card shows that the corner is not perfect, but almost. However, note that coner wear is somewhat academic on this card. As you can plainly see, the heavy crease going across his name breaks through the photo surface.

seriously discolored borders, moderate or heavy creases, and one or more serious flaws. The grade of Good, Fair or Poor depends on the severity of wear and flaws. Good, Fair and Poor cards generally are used only as fillers.

The most widely used grades are defined above. Obviously, many cards will not perfectly fit one of the definitions.

Therefore, categories between the major grades known as in-between grades are used, such as Good to Very Good (G-Vg), Very Good to Excellent (VgEx), and Excellent-Mint to Near Mint (ExMt-NrMt). Such grades indicate a card with all qualities of the lower category but with at least a few qualities of the higher category.

The Official Price Guide to Baseball Cards lists each card and set in three grades, with the middle grade valued at about 40-45% of the top grade, and the bottom grade valued at about 10-15% of the top grade.

The value of cards that fall between the listed columns can also be calculated using a percentage of the top grade. For example, a card that falls between the top and middle grades (Ex, ExMt or NrMt in most cases) will generally be valued at anywhere from 50% to 90% of the top grade.

Similarly, a card that falls between the middle and bottom grades (G-Vg, Vg or VgEx in most cases) will generally be valued at anywhere from 20% to 40% of the top grade.

There are also cases where cards are in better condition than the top grade or worse than the bottom grade. Cards that grade worse than the lowest grade are generally valued at 5-10% of the top grade.

When a card exceeds the top grade by one — such as NrMt-Mt when the top grade is NrMt, or Mint when the top grade is NrMt-Mt — a premium of up to 50% is possible, with 10-20% the usual norm.

When a card exceeds the top grade by two — such as Mint when the top grade is NrMt, or NrMt-Mt when the top grade is ExMt — a premium of 25-50% is the usual norm. But certain condition sensitive cards or sets, particularly those from the pre-war era, can bring premiums of up to 100% or even more.

Unopened packs, boxes and factory-collated sets are considered Mint in their unknown (and presumed perfect) state. Once opened, however, each card can be graded (and valued) in its own right by taking into account any defects that may be present in spite of the fact that the card has never been handled.

Selling Your Cards

Just about every collector sells cards or will sell cards eventually. Someday you may be interested in selling your duplicates or maybe even your whole collection. You may sell to other collectors, friends or dealers. You may even sell cards you purchased from a certain dealer back to that same dealer. In any event, it helps to know some of the mechanics of the typical transaction between buyer and seller.

Dealers will buy cards in order to resell them to other collectors who are interested in the cards. Dealers will always pay a higher percentage for items that (in their opinion) can be resold quickly, and a much lower percentage for those items that are perceived as having low demand and hence are slow moving. In either case, dealers must buy at a price that allows for the expense of doing business and a margin for profit.

If you have cards for sale, the best advice we can give is that you get several offers for your cards — either from card shops or at a card show — and take the best offer, all things considered. Note, the "best" offer may not be the one for the highest amount. And remember, if a dealer really wants your cards, he won't let you get away without making his best competitive offer. Another alternative is to place your cards in an auction as one or several lots.

Many people think nothing of going into a department store and paying $15 for an item of clothing for which the store paid $5. But if you were selling your $15 card to a dealer and he offered you $5 for it, you might consider his mark-up unreasonable. To complete the analogy: Most department stores (and card dealers) that consistently pay $10 for $15 items eventually go out of business. An exception is when the dealer has lined up a willing buyer for the item(s) you are attempting to sell, or if the cards are so Hot that it's likely he'll likely have to hold the cards for just a short period of time.

In those cases, an offer of up to 75 percent of book value still will allow the dealer to make a reasonable profit considering the short time he will need to hold the merchandise. In general, however, most cards and collections will bring offers in the range of 25 to 50 percent of retail price. Also consider that most material from the last five to 10 years is plentiful. If that's what you're selling, don't be surprised if your best offer is well below that range.

Interesting Notes

The first card numerically of an issue is the single card most likely to obtain excessive wear.

Consequently, you typically will find the price on the #1 card (in NrMt or Mint condition) somewhat higher than might otherwise be the case.

Similarly, but to a lesser extent (because normally the less important, reverse side of the card is the one exposed), the last card numerically in an issue also is prone to abnormal wear. This extra wear and tear occurs because the first and last cards are exposed to the elements (human element included) more than any of the other cards. They are generally end cards in any brick formations, rubber bandings, stackings on wet surfaces and like activities.

Sports cards have no intrinsic value. The value of a card, like the value of other collectibles, can be determined only by you and your enjoyment in viewing and possessing these cardboard treasures.

Remember, the buyer ultimately determines the price of each baseball card. You are the determining price factor because you have the ability to say "No" to the price of any card by not exchanging your hard-earned money for a given issue. When the cost of a trading card exceeds the enjoyment you will receive from it, your answer should be "No." We assess and report the prices. You set them!

We are always interested in receiving the price input of collectors and dealers. We happily credit major contributors.

We welcome your opinions, since your contributions assist us in ensuring a better guide each year.

If you would like to join our survey list for the next editions of this book and others authored by Dr. Beckett, please send your name and address to Dr. James Beckett, 15850 Dallas Parkway, Dallas, TX 75248.

History of Baseball Cards

Today's version of the baseball card, with its colorful and oft times high-tech fronts and backs, is a far cry from its earliest predecessors. The issue remains cloudy as to which was the very first baseball card ever produced, but the institution of baseball cards dates from the latter half of the 19th century, more than 100 years ago. Early issues, generally printed on heavy cardboard, were of poor quality, with photographs, drawings, and printing far short of today's standards.

Goodwin & Co., of New York, makers of Gypsy Queen, Old Judge, and other cigarette brands, is considered by many to be the first issuer of baseball and other sports cards. Its issues, predominantly sized 1-1/2 by 2-1/2 inches, generally consisted of photographs of baseball players, boxers, wrestlers, and other subjects mounted on stiff cardboard. More than 2,000 different photos of baseball players alone have been identified. These "Old Judges," a collective name commonly used for the Goodwin & Co. cards, were issued from 1886 to 1890 and are treasured parts of many collections today.

Among the other cigarette companies that issued baseball cards still attracting attention today are Allen & Ginter, D. Buchner & Co. (Gold Coin Chewing Tobacco), and P.H. Mayo & Brother. Cards from the first two companies bear colored line drawings, while the Mayos are sepia photographs on black cardboard. In addition to the small-size cards from this era, several tobacco companies issued cabinet-size baseball cards. These "cabinets" were considerably larger than the small cards, usually about 4-1/4 by 6-1/2 inches, and were printed on heavy stock. Goodwin & Co.'s Old Judge cabinets and the National Tobacco Works' "Newsboy" baseball photos are two that remain popular today.

By 1895, the American Tobacco Company began to dominate its competition. They discontinued baseball card inserts in their cigarette packages (actually slide boxes in those days). The lack of competition in the cigarette market had made these inserts unnecessary. This marked the end of the first era of baseball cards. At the dawn of the 20th century, few baseball cards were being issued. But once again, it was the cigarette companies — particularly, the American Tobacco Company — followed to a lesser extent by the candy and gum makers that revived the practice of including baseball cards with their products. The bulk of these cards, identified in the American Card Catalog (designated hereafter as ACC) as T or E cards for 20th century "Tobacco" or "Early Candy and Gum" issues, respectively, were released from 1909 to 1915.

This romantic and popular era of baseball card collecting produced many desirable items. The most outstanding is the fabled T-206 Honus Wagner card. Other perennial favorites among collectors are the T-206 Eddie Plank card, and the T-206 Magee error card. The former was once the second most valuable card and only recently relinquished that position to a more distinctive and aesthetically pleasing Napoleon Lajoie card from the 1933-34 Goudey Gum series. The latter misspells the player's name as "Magie," the most famous and most valuable blooper card.

The ingenuity and distinctiveness of this era has yet to be surpassed. Highlights include:

- the T-202 Hassan triple-folders, one of the best looking and the most distinctive cards ever issued;
- the durable T-201 Mecca double-folders, one of the first sets with players' records on the reverse;
- the T-3 Turkey Reds, the hobby's most popular cabinet card;
- the E-145 Cracker Jacks, the only major set containing Federal League player cards;
- the T-204 Ramlys, with their distinctive black-and-white oval photos and ornate gold borders.

These are but a few of the varieties issued during this period.

Increasing Popularity

While the American Tobacco Company dominated the field, several other tobacco companies, as well as clothing manufacturers, newspapers and periodicals, game makers, and companies whose identities remain anonymous, also issued cards during this period. In fact, the Collins-McCarthy Candy Company, makers of Zeenuts Pacific Coast League baseball cards, issued cards yearly from 1911 to 1938. Its record for continuous annual card production has been exceeded only by the Topps Chewing Gum Company. The era of the tobacco card issues closed with the onset of World War I, with the exception of the Red Man chewing tobacco sets produced from 1952 to 1955.

The next flurry of card issues broke out in the roaring and prosperous 1920s, the era of the E card. The caramel companies (National Caramel, American Caramel, York Caramel) were the leading distributors of these E cards. In addition, the strip card, a continous strip with several cards divided by dotted lines or other sectioning features, flourished during this time. While the E cards and the strip cards generally are considered less imaginative than the T cards or the recent candy and gum issues, they still are pursued by many advanced collectors.

Another significant event of the 1920s was the introduction of the arcade card. Taking its designation from its issuer, the Exhibit Supply Company of Chicago, it is usually known as the "Exhibit" card. Once a trademark of the penny arcades, amusement parks and county fairs across the country, Exhibit machines dispensed nearly postcard-size photos on thick stock for one penny. These picture cards bore likenesses of a favorite cowboy, actor, actress or baseball player. Exhibit Supply and its associated companies produced baseball cards during a longer time span, although discontinuous, than any other manufacturer. Its first cards appeared in 1921, while its last issue was in 1966. In 1979, the Exhibit Supply Company was bought and somewhat revived by a collector/dealer who has since reprinted Exhibit photos of the past.

If the T card period, from 1909 to 1915, can be designated the "Golden Age" of baseball card collecting, then perhaps the "Silver Age" commenced with the introduction of the Big League Gum series of 239 cards in 1933 (a 240th card was added in 1934). These are the forerunners of today's baseball gum cards, and the Goudey Gum Company of Boston is responsible for their success. This era spanned the period from the Depression days of 1933 to America's formal involvement in World War II in 1941.

Goudey's attractive designs, with full-color line drawings on thick card stock, greatly influenced other cards being issued at that time. As a result, the most attractive and popular vintage cards in history were produced in this "Silver Age." The 1933 Goudey Big League Gum series also owes its popularity to the more than 40 Hall of Fame players in the set. These include four cards of Babe Ruth and two of Lou Gehrig. Goudey's reign continued in 1934, when it issued a 96-card set in color, together with the single remaining card from the 1933 series, #106, the Napoleon Lajoie card.

In addition to Goudey, several other bubblegum manufacturers issued baseball cards during this era. DeLong Gum Company issued an extremely attractive set in 1933. National Chicle Company's 192-card "Batter-Up" series of 1934-1936 became the largest die-cut set in card history. In addition, that company offered the popular "Diamond Stars" series during the same period. Other popular sets included the "Tattoo Orbit" set of 60 color cards issued in 1933 and Gum Products' 75-card "Double Play" set, featuring sepia depictions of two players per card.

In 1939, Gum Inc., which later became Bowman Gum, replaced Goudey Gum as the leading baseball card producer. In 1939 and the following year, it issued two important sets of black-and-white cards. In 1939, its "Play Ball America" set consisted of 162 cards. The larger, 240-card "Play Ball" set of 1940 still is considered by many to be the most attractive black-and-white cards ever produced. That firm introduced its only color set in 1941, consisting of 72 cards titled "Play Ball Sports Hall of Fame." Many of these were colored repeats of poses from the black-and-white 1940 series.

In addition to regular gum cards, many manufacturers distributed premium issues during the 1930s. These premiums were printed on paper or photographic stock, rather than card stock. They were much larger than the regular cards and were sold for a penny across the counter with gum (which was packaged separately from the premium). They often were redeemed at the store or through the mail in exchange for the wrappers of previously purchased gum cards, like proof-of-purchase box-top premiums today. The gum premiums are scarcer than the card issues of the 1930s and in most cases no manufacturer's name is present.

World War II brought an end to this popular era of card collecting when paper and rubber shortages curtailed the production of bubblegum baseball cards. They were resurrected again in 1948 by the Bowman Gum Company (the direct descendent of Gum, Inc.). This marked the beginning of the modern era of card collecting.

In 1948, Bowman Gum issued a 48-card set in black and white consisting of one card and one slab of gum in every 1 cent pack. That same year, the Leaf Gum Company also issued a set of cards. Although rather poor in quality, these cards were issued in color. A squabble over the rights to use players' pictures developed between Bowman and Leaf. Eventually Leaf dropped out of the card market, but not before it had left a lasting heritage to the hobby by issuing some of the rarest cards now in existence. Leaf's baseball card series of 1948-49 contained 98 cards, skip numbered to #168 (not all numbers were printed). Of these 98 cards, 49 are relatively plentiful; the other 49, however, are rare and quite valuable.

Bowman continued its production of cards in 1949 with a color series of 240 cards. Because there are many scarce "high numbers," this series remains the most difficult Bowman regular issue to complete. Although the set was printed in color and commands great interest due to its scarcity, it is considered aesthetically inferior to the Goudey and National Chicle issues of the 1930s. In addition to the regular issue of 1949, Bowman also produced a set of 36 Pacific Coast League players. While this was not a regular issue, it still is prized by collectors. In fact, it has become the most valuable Bowman series.

In 1950 (representing Bowman's one-year monopoly of the baseball card market), the company began a string of top quality cards that continued until its demise in 1955. The 1950 series was itself something of an oddity because the low numbers, rather than the traditional high numbers, were the more difficult cards to obtain.

The year 1951 marked the beginning of the most competitive and perhaps the highest quality period of baseball card production. In that year, Topps Chewing Gum Company of Brooklyn entered the market. Topps' 1951 series consisted of two sets of 52 cards each, one set with red backs and the other with blue backs. In addition, Topps also issued 31 insert cards, three of which remain the rarest Topps cards ("Current All-Stars" Konstanty, Roberts and Stanky). The 1951 Topps cards were unattractive and paled in comparison to the 1951 Bowman issues. They were successful, however, and Topps has continued to produce cards ever since.

Intensified Competition

Topps issued a larger and more attractive card set in 1952. This larger size became standard for the next five years. (Bowman followed with larger-size baseball cards in 1953.) This 1952 Topps set has become, like the 1933

Goudey series and the T-206 white border series, the classic set of its era. The 407-card set is a collector's dream of scarcities, rarities, errors and variations. It also contains the first Topps issues of Mickey Mantle and Willie Mays.

As with Bowman and Leaf in the late 1940s, competition over player rights arose. Ensuing court battles occurred between Topps and Bowman. The market split due to stiff competition, and in January 1956, Topps bought out Bowman. (Topps, using the Bowman name, resurrected Bowman as a later label in 1989.) Topps remained essentially unchallenged as the primary producer of baseball cards through 1980. So, the story of major baseball card sets from 1956 through 1980 is by and large the story of Topps' issues. Notable exceptions include the small sets produced by Fleer Gum in 1959, 1960, 1961 and 1963, and the Kellogg's Cereal and Hostess Cakes baseball cards issued to promote their products.

A court decision in 1980 paved the way for two other large gum companies to enter (or reenter, in Fleer's case) the baseball card arena. Fleer, which had last made photo cards in 1963, and the Donruss Company (then a division of General Mills) secured rights to produce baseball cards of current players, thus breaking Topps' monopoly. Each company issued major card sets in 1981 with bubblegum products.

Then a higher court decision in that year overturned the lower court ruling against Topps. It appeared that Topps had regained its sole position as a producer of baseball cards. Undaunted by the revocation ruling, Fleer and Donruss continued to issue cards in 1982 but without bubblegum or any other edible product. Fleer issued its current player baseball cards with "team logo stickers," while Donruss issued its cards with a piece of a baseball jigsaw puzzle.

Sharing the Pie

Since 1981, these three major baseball card producers all have thrived, sharing relatively equal recognition. Each has steadily increased its involvement in terms of numbers of issues per year. To the delight of collectors, their competition has generated novel, and in some cases exceptional, issues of current Major League Baseball players. Collectors also eagerly accepted the debut efforts of Score (1988) and Upper Deck (1989), the newest companies to enter the baseball card producing derby.

Upper Deck's successful entry into the market turned out to be very important. The company's card stock, photography, packaging and marketing gave baseball cards a new standard for quality, and began the "premium card" trend that continues today. The second premium baseball card set to be issued was the 1990 Leaf set, named for and issued by the parent company of Donruss. To gauge the significance of the premium card trend, one need only note that two of the most valuable post-1986 regular-issue cards in the hobby are the 1989 Upper Deck Ken Griffey Jr. and 1990 Leaf Frank Thomas Rookie Cards.

The impressive debut of Leaf in 1990 was followed by Studio, Ultra, and Stadium Club in 1991. Of those, Stadium Club made the biggest impact. In 1992, Bowman, and Pinnacle joined the premium fray. In 1992, Donruss and Fleer abandoned the traditional 50-cent pack market and instead produced premium sets comparable to (and presumably designed to compete against) Upper Deck's set. Those moves, combined with the almost instantaneous spread of premium cards to the other major team sports cards, serve as strong indicators that premium cards were here to stay. Bowman had been a lower-level product from 1989 to '91.

In 1993, Fleer, Topps and Upper Deck produced the first "super premium" cards with Flair, Finest and SP, respectively. The success of all three products was an indication the baseball card market was headed toward even higher price levels, and that turned out to be the case in 1994 with the introduction of Topps' Bowman's Best (a hybrid of prospect-oriented Bowman and the superpremium Finest) and Leaf Limited. Other 1994 debuts included Upper Deck's entry-level Collector's Choice and Pinnacle's hobby-only Select.

Overall, inserts continued to dominate the hobby scene. Specifically, the parallel chase cards first introduced in 1992 with Topps Gold became the latest major hobby trend. Topps Gold was followed by 1993 Finest Refractors (at the time the scarcest insert ever produced and still a landmark set), and the one-per-box Stadium Club First Day Issue.

Of course, the biggest on-field news of 1994 was the owner-provoked players strike that halted the season prematurely. While the baseball card hobby suffered noticeably from the strike, there was no catastrophic market crash as some had feared. However, the strike pulled the plug on a market that was both strong and growing, and contributed to a serious hobby contraction that continues to this day.

By 1995, parallel insert sets were commonplace and had taken on a new complexion: the most popular ones were those that had announced (or at least suspected) print runs of 500 or less, such as Finest Refractors and Select Artist's Proofs.

This trend continued in 1996, with several parallel inserts that were printed in quantities of 250 or less such as Finest Gold Refractors, Fleer Circa Rave, Studio Silver Press Proofs and three of the six Select Certified parallels. It could be argued that the high price tags on these extremely limited parallel cards (many exceeded the $1000 plateau) were driving many single-player collectors to frustration, and even completely out of the hobby. At the same time, average pack prices soared while average number of cards per pack dropped, making the baseball card hobby increasingly more expensive.

On the positive side, two trends from 1996 clearly brought in new collectors: Topps' Mickey Mantle retrospective inserts in both series of Topps and Stadium Club; and Leaf's Signature Series, which included one certified autograph per pack. While the Mantle craze following his passing seemed to be a short-term phenomenon, the inclusion of autographs in packs seemed to have more long-term significance.

Unfortunately, such positives were clearly overshadowed by the industry's overriding problem: too many products costing too much money, with fewer and fewer buyers willing to ante up. The result? Many dealers going out of business, and a buyer's market in which new products usually were available cheaper to the consumer than original dealer cost from the factory. The hobby still faces this very complex problem with no easy solutions in sight.

Finding Out More

The above has been a thumbnail sketch of card collecting from its inception in the 1880s to the present. It is difficult to tell the whole story in just a few pages — there are several other good sources of information. Serious collectors should subscribe to at least one of the excellent hobby periodicals. We also suggest that collectors visit their local card shop(s) and also attend a sports collectibles show in their area. Card collecting is still a young and informal hobby. You can learn more about it in either place. After all, smart dealers realize that spending a few minutes teaching beginners about the hobby often pays off in the long run.

Additional Reading

Each year Beckett Publications produces comprehensive annual price guides for each of the four major sports: *Beckett Baseball Card Price Guide, Beckett Football Card Price Guide, Beckett Basketball Card Price Guide*, and *Beckett Hockey Card Price Guide*. The aim of these annual guides is to provide information and accurate pricing on a wide array of sports cards, ranging from main issues by the major card manufacturers to various regional, promotional, and food issues. Also alphabetical checklists, such as *Sport Americana Baseball Card Alphabetical Checklist #6*, are published to assist the collector in identifying all the cards of any particular player. The seasoned collector will find these tools valuable sources of information that will enable him to pursue his hobby interests.

In addition, abridged editions of the Beckett Price Guides have been published for each of the four major sports as part of the House of Collectibles series: *The Official Price Guide to Baseball Cards, The Official Price Guide to Football Cards, The Official Price Guide to Basketball Cards*, and *The Official Price Guide to Hockey Cards*. Published in a convenient mass-market paperback format, these price guides provide information and accurate pricing on all the main issues by the major card manufacturers.

Advertising

Within this Price Guide you will find advertisements for sports memorabilia material, mail order, and retail sports collectibles establishments. All advertisements were accepted in good faith based on the reputation of the advertiser; however, neither the author, the publisher, the distributors, nor the other advertisers in this Price Guide accept any responsibility for any particular advertiser not complying with the terms of his or her ad.

Readers also should be aware that prices in advertisements are subject to change over the annual period before a new edition of this volume is issued each spring. When replying to an advertisement late in the baseball year, the reader should take this into account, and contact the dealer by phone or in writing for up-to-date price information. Should you come into contact with any of the advertisers in this guide as a result of their advertisement herein, please mention this source as your contact.

Prices in this Guide

Prices found in this guide reflect current retail rates just prior to the printing of this book. They do not reflect the FOR SALE prices of the author, the publisher, the distributors, the advertisers, or any card dealers associated with this guide. No one is obligated in any way to buy, sell or trade his or her cards based on these prices. The price listings were compiled by the author from actual buy/sell transactions at sports conventions, sports card shops, buy/sell advertisements in the hobby papers, for sale prices from dealer catalogs and price lists, and discussions with leading hobbyists in the U.S. and Canada. All prices are in U.S. dollars.

Acknowledgments

A great deal of diligence, hard work, and dedicated effort went into this year's volume. The high standards to which we hold ourselves, however, could not have been met without the expert input and generous amount of time contributed by many people. Our sincere thanks are extended to each and every one of you.

A complete list of these invaluable contributors appears after the Price Guide section.

1995 Bazooka

This 132-card standard-size set was issued by Topps. For the previous 35 years, Topps had used the Bazooka label to issue various cards, but this was the first time a mainstream set was issued in pack form. The five-card packs, with a suggested retail price of 50 cents, included an info card as well as a piece of bubble gum. The fronts have an action photo surrounded by white borders. The "Bazooka" label is in the upper left corner, while the player's name and team are on the bottom of the card. The player's position is identified on the right. The backs have a game as well as his previous season and career stats. There are no Rookie Cards in this set. Factory sets included five Red Hots.

	MINT	NRMT	EXC
COMPLETE SET (132)	10.00	4.50	1.25
COMPLETE FACT.SET (137)	15.00	6.75	1.85
COMMON CARD (1-132)	.05	.02	.01
SEMISTARS	.15	.07	.02
STARS	.30	.14	.04

□ 1	Greg Maddux	1.25	.55	.16
□ 2	Cal Ripken Jr.	1.50	.70	.19
□ 3	Lee Smith	.15	.07	.02
□ 4	Sammy Sosa	.30	.14	.04
□ 5	Jason Bere	.05	.02	.01
□ 6	David Justice	.30	.14	.04
□ 7	Kevin Mitchell	.15	.07	.02
□ 8	Ozzie Guillen	.05	.02	.01
□ 9	Roger Clemens	.30	.14	.04
□ 10	Mike Mussina	.40	.18	.05
□ 11	Sandy Alomar Jr.	.05	.02	.01
□ 12	Cecil Fielder	.15	.07	.02
□ 13	Dennis Martinez	.15	.07	.02
□ 14	Randy Myers	.05	.02	.01
□ 15	Jay Buhner	.30	.14	.04
□ 16	Ivan Rodriguez	.40	.18	.05
□ 17	Mo Vaughn	.50	.23	.06
□ 18	Ryan Klesko	.40	.18	.05
□ 19	Chuck Finley	.15	.07	.02
□ 20	Barry Bonds	.50	.23	.06
□ 21	Dennis Eckersley	.15	.07	.02
□ 22	Kenny Lofton	.50	.23	.06
□ 23	Rafael Palmeiro	.30	.14	.04
□ 24	Mike Stanley	.05	.02	.01
□ 25	Gregg Jefferies	.15	.07	.02
□ 26	Robin Ventura	.15	.07	.02
□ 27	Mark McGwire	.60	.25	.07
□ 28	Ozzie Smith	.40	.18	.05
□ 29	Troy Neel	.05	.02	.01
□ 30	Tony Gwynn	.75	.35	.09
□ 31	Ken Griffey Jr.	2.00	.90	.25
□ 32	Will Clark	.30	.14	.04
□ 33	Craig Biggio	.30	.14	.04
□ 34	Shawon Dunston	.05	.02	.01
□ 35	Wilson Alvarez	.15	.07	.02
□ 36	Bobby Bonilla	.15	.07	.02
□ 37	Marquis Grissom	.30	.14	.04
□ 38	Ben McDonald	.05	.02	.01
□ 39	Delino DeShields	.05	.02	.01
□ 40	Barry Larkin	.30	.14	.04
□ 41	John Olerud	.05	.02	.01
□ 42	Jose Canseco	.30	.14	.04
□ 43	Greg Vaughn	.15	.07	.02
□ 44	Gary Sheffield	.30	.14	.04
□ 45	Paul O'Neill	.15	.07	.02
□ 46	Bob Hamelin	.05	.02	.01
□ 47	Don Mattingly	1.00	.45	.12
□ 48	John Franco	.05	.02	.01
□ 49	Bret Boone	.15	.07	.02
□ 50	Rick Aguilera	.05	.02	.01
□ 51	Tim Wallach	.05	.02	.01
□ 52	Roberto Kelly	.05	.02	.01
□ 53	Danny Tartabull	.05	.02	.01
□ 54	Randy Johnson	.30	.14	.04
□ 55	Greg McMichael	.05	.02	.01
□ 56	Bip Roberts	.05	.02	.01
□ 57	David Cone	.15	.07	.02
□ 58	Raul Mondesi	.30	.14	.04
□ 59	Travis Fryman	.15	.07	.02
□ 60	Jeff Conine	.30	.14	.04
□ 61	Jeff Bagwell	.75	.35	.09
□ 62	Rickey Henderson	.30	.14	.04
□ 63	Fred McGriff	.30	.14	.04
□ 64	Matt Williams	.30	.14	.04
□ 65	Rick Wilkins	.05	.02	.01
□ 66	Eric Karros	.15	.07	.02
□ 67	Mel Rojas	.05	.02	.01
□ 68	Juan Gonzalez	1.00	.45	.12
□ 69	Chuck Carr	.05	.02	.01
□ 70	Moises Alou	.15	.07	.02
□ 71	Mark Grace	.30	.14	.04
□ 72	Alex Fernandez	.15	.07	.02
□ 73	Rod Beck	.05	.02	.01
□ 74	Ray Lankford	.30	.14	.04
□ 75	Dean Palmer	.15	.07	.02
□ 76	Joe Carter	.30	.14	.04
□ 77	Mike Piazza	1.25	.55	.16
□ 78	Eddie Murray	.50	.23	.06
□ 79	Dave Nilsson	.15	.07	.02
□ 80	Brett Butler	.15	.07	.02
□ 81	Roberto Alomar	.50	.23	.06
□ 82	Jeff Kent	.05	.02	.01
□ 83	Andres Galarraga	.30	.14	.04
□ 84	Brady Anderson	.30	.14	.04
□ 85	Jimmy Key	.15	.07	.02
□ 86	Bret Saberhagen	.15	.07	.02
□ 87	Chili Davis	.15	.07	.02
□ 88	Jose Rijo	.05	.02	.01
□ 89	Wade Boggs	.30	.14	.04
□ 90	Len Dykstra	.15	.07	.02
□ 91	Steve Howe	.05	.02	.01
□ 92	Hal Morris	.05	.02	.01
□ 93	Larry Walker	.30	.14	.04
□ 94	Jeff Montgomery	.15	.07	.02
□ 95	Wil Cordero	.05	.02	.01
□ 96	Jay Bell	.15	.07	.02
□ 97	Tom Glavine	.30	.14	.04
□ 98	Chris Hoiles	.05	.02	.01
□ 99	Steve Avery	.15	.07	.02
□ 100	Ruben Sierra	.15	.07	.02
□ 101	Mickey Tettleton	.05	.02	.01
□ 102	Paul Molitor	.40	.18	.05
□ 103	Carlos Baerga	.30	.14	.04
□ 104	Walt Weiss	.05	.02	.01
□ 105	Darren Daulton	.15	.07	.02
□ 106	Jack McDowell	.15	.07	.02
□ 107	Doug Drabek	.05	.02	.01
□ 108	Mark Langston	.05	.02	.01
□ 109	Manny Ramirez	.50	.23	.06
□ 110	Kevin Appier	.15	.07	.02
□ 111	Andy Benes	.05	.02	.01
□ 112	Chuck Knoblauch	.30	.14	.04
□ 113	Kirby Puckett	.60	.25	.07
□ 114	Dante Bichette	.30	.14	.04
□ 115	Deion Sanders	.30	.14	.04
□ 116	Albert Belle	1.00	.45	.12
□ 117	Todd Zeile	.05	.02	.01
□ 118	Devon White	.15	.07	.02
□ 119	Tim Salmon	.30	.14	.04
□ 120	Frank Thomas	2.00	.90	.25
□ 121	John Wetteland	.15	.07	.02
□ 122	James Mouton	.05	.02	.01
□ 123	Javier Lopez	.30	.14	.04
□ 124	Carlos Delgado	.30	.14	.04
□ 125	Cliff Floyd	.15	.07	.02
□ 126	Alex Gonzalez	.05	.02	.01
□ 127	Billy Ashley	.05	.02	.01
□ 128	Rondell White	.30	.14	.04
□ 129	Rico Brogna	.05	.02	.01
□ 130	Melvin Nieves	.15	.07	.02

□ 131 Jose Oliva	.05	.02	.01
□ 132 J.R. Phillips	.05	.02	.01

1995 Bazooka Red Hot

This 22-card standard-size set, featuring some of the most popular players, is similar to the regular issue. Differences between these cards and the regular issue include the photo being shaded in a red background, the position is also in red and the player's name is stamped in gold foil. The backs are numbered with an "RH" prefix. Bazooka factory sets included five Red Hots.

	MINT	NRMT	EXC
COMPLETE SET (22)	20.00	9.00	2.50
COMMON CARD (1-22)	.15	.07	.02
SEMISTARS	.30	.14	.04
STARS	.60	.25	.07
RANDOM INSERTS IN PACKS			
FIVE PER FACTORY SET			

□ RH1 Greg Maddux	2.50	1.10	.30
□ RH2 Cal Ripken Jr.	3.00	1.35	.35
□ RH3 Barry Bonds	1.00	.45	.12
□ RH4 Kenny Lofton	1.00	.45	.12
□ RH5 Mike Stanley	.15	.07	.02
□ RH6 Tony Gwynn	1.50	.70	.19
□ RH7 Ken Griffey Jr.	4.00	1.80	.50
□ RH8 Barry Larkin	.60	.25	.07
□ RH9 Jose Canseco	.60	.25	.07
□ RH10 Paul O'Neill	.30	.14	.04
□ RH11 Randy Johnson	.60	.25	.07
□ RH12 David Cone	.60	.25	.07
□ RH13 Jeff Bagwell	1.50	.70	.19
□ RH14 Matt Williams	.60	.25	.07
□ RH15 Mike Piazza	2.50	1.10	.30
□ RH16 Roberto Alomar	1.00	.45	.12
□ RH17 Jimmy Key	.15	.07	.02
□ RH18 Wade Boggs	.60	.25	.07
□ RH19 Paul Molitor	.75	.35	.09
□ RH20 Carlos Baerga	.60	.25	.07
□ RH21 Albert Belle	2.00	.90	.25
□ RH22 Frank Thomas	4.00	1.80	.50

1996 Bazooka

The 1996 Bazooka standard-size set was issued in one series totalling 132 cards. The 5-card packs retail for $.50 each. The set contains baseball's best rookies, rising stars and veterans. The card fronts feature an exciting full-color photo of the player. The back of each card contains one of five different Bazooka Joe characters, along with the Bazooka Ball flipping game, the player's biographical data and 1995 career statistics. Additionally, every card contains a Funny Fortune, which predicts the fate of each player on a particular date. Packs contain five cards plus one chunk of Bazooka gum.

	MINT	NRMT	EXC
COMP.FACT.SET (133)	14.00	6.25	1.75
COMPLETE SET (132)	10.00	4.50	1.25
COMMON CARD (1-132)	.05	.02	.01
SEMISTARS	.15	.07	.02
STARS	.30	.14	.04
ONE 59 MANTLE PER FACT.SET			
PRODUCED BY TOPPS			

□ 1 Ken Griffey, Jr.	2.00	.90	.25
□ 2 J.T. Snow	.05	.02	.01
□ 3 Rondell White	.30	.14	.04
□ 4 Reggie Sanders	.30	.14	.04
□ 5 Jeff Montgomery	.05	.02	.01
□ 6 Mike Stanley	.05	.02	.01
□ 7 Bernie Williams	.30	.14	.04
□ 8 Mike Piazza	1.25	.55	.16
□ 9 Brian L.Hunter	.05	.02	.01
□ 10 Len Dykstra	.15	.07	.02
□ 11 Ray Lankford	.30	.14	.04
□ 12 Kenny Lofton	.50	.23	.06
□ 13 Robin Ventura	.30	.14	.04
□ 14 Devon White	.05	.02	.01
□ 15 Cal Ripken	1.50	.70	.19
□ 16 Heathcliff Slocumb	.05	.02	.01
□ 17 Ryan Klesko	.40	.18	.05
□ 18 Terry Steinbach	.15	.07	.02
□ 19 Travis Fryman	.30	.14	.04
□ 20 Sammy Sosa	.30	.14	.04
□ 21 Jim Thome	.40	.18	.05
□ 22 Kenny Rogers	.05	.02	.01
□ 23 Don Mattingly	1.00	.45	.12
□ 24 Kirby Puckett	.60	.25	.07
□ 25 Matt Williams	.30	.14	.04
□ 26 Larry Walker	.30	.14	.04
□ 27 Tim Wakefield	.05	.02	.01
□ 28 Greg Vaughn	.30	.14	.04
□ 29 Denny Neagle	.15	.07	.02
□ 30 Ken Caminiti	.30	.14	.04
□ 31 Garret Anderson	.30	.14	.04
□ 32 Brady Anderson	.30	.14	.04
□ 33 Carlos Baerga	.30	.14	.04
□ 34 Wade Boggs	.30	.14	.04
□ 35 Roberto Alomar	.50	.23	.06
□ 36 Eric Karros	.30	.14	.04
□ 37 Jay Buhner	.30	.14	.04
□ 38 Dante Bichette	.30	.14	.04
□ 39 Darren Daulton	.15	.07	.02
□ 40 Jeff Bagwell	.75	.35	.09
□ 41 Jay Bell	.05	.02	.01
□ 42 Dennis Eckersley	.30	.14	.04
□ 43 Will Clark	.30	.14	.04
□ 44 Tom Glavine	.30	.14	.04
□ 45 Rick Aguilera	.05	.02	.01
□ 46 Kevin Seitzer	.05	.02	.01
□ 47 Bret Boone	.05	.02	.01
□ 48 Mark Grace	.30	.14	.04
□ 49 Ray Durham	.30	.14	.04
□ 50 Rico Brogna	.05	.02	.01
□ 51 Kevin Appier	.15	.07	.02
□ 52 Moises Alou	.15	.07	.02
□ 53 Jeff Conine	.30	.14	.04
□ 54 Marty Cordova	.30	.14	.04
□ 55 Jose Mesa	.15	.07	.02
□ 56 Rod Beck	.15	.07	.02
□ 57 Marquis Grissom	.30	.14	.04
□ 58 David Cone	.30	.14	.04
□ 59 Albert Belle	1.00	.45	.12
□ 60 Lee Smith	.30	.14	.04
□ 61 Frank Thomas	2.00	.90	.25
□ 62 Roger Clemens	.30	.14	.04
□ 63 Bobby Bonilla	.30	.14	.04
□ 64 Paul Molitor	.40	.18	.05
□ 65 Chuck Knoblauch	.30	.14	.04
□ 66 Steve Finley	.30	.14	.04
□ 67 Craig Biggio	.30	.14	.04
□ 68 Ramon Martinez	.15	.07	.02

□ 69 Jason Isringhausen	.05	.02	.01
□ 70 Mark Wohlers	.30	.14	.04
□ 71 Vinny Castilla	.30	.14	.04
□ 72 Ron Gant	.30	.14	.04
□ 73 Juan Gonzalez	1.00	.45	.12
□ 74 Mark McGwire	.60	.25	.07
□ 75 Jeff King	.05	.02	.01
□ 76 Pedro Martinez	.30	.14	.04
□ 77 Chad Curtis	.05	.02	.01
□ 78 John Olerud	.05	.02	.01
□ 79 Greg Maddux	1.25	.55	.16
□ 80 Derek Jeter	1.25	.55	.16
□ 81 Mike Mussina	.40	.18	.05
□ 82 Gregg Jefferies	.30	.14	.04
□ 83 Jim Edmonds	.30	.14	.04
□ 84 Carlos Perez	.05	.02	.01
□ 85 Mo Vaughn	.50	.23	.06
□ 86 Todd Hundley	.30	.14	.04
□ 87 Roberto Hernandez	.15	.07	.02
□ 88 Derek Bell	.15	.07	.02
□ 89 Andres Galarraga	.30	.14	.04
□ 90 Brian McRae	.05	.02	.01
□ 91 Joe Carter	.30	.14	.04
□ 92 Orlando Merced	.05	.02	.01
□ 93 Cecil Fielder	.30	.14	.04
□ 94 Dean Palmer	.30	.14	.04
□ 95 Randy Johnson	.30	.14	.04
□ 96 Chipper Jones	1.25	.55	.16
□ 97 Barry Larkin	.30	.14	.04
□ 98 Hideo Nomo	.50	.23	.06
□ 99 Gary Gaetti	.15	.07	.02
□ 100 Edgar Martinez	.30	.14	.04
□ 101 John Wetteland	.15	.07	.02
□ 102 Rafael Palmeiro	.30	.14	.04
□ 103 Chuck Finley	.05	.02	.01
□ 104 Ivan Rodriguez	.40	.18	.05
□ 105 Shawn Green	.05	.02	.01
□ 106 Manny Ramirez	.50	.23	.06
□ 107 Lance Johnson	.15	.07	.02
□ 108 Jose Canseco	.30	.14	.04
□ 109 Fred McGriff	.30	.14	.04
□ 110 David Segui	.05	.02	.01
□ 111 Tim Salmon	.30	.14	.04
□ 112 Hal Morris	.05	.02	.01
□ 113 Tino Martinez	.30	.14	.04
□ 114 Bret Saberhagen	.05	.02	.01
□ 115 Brian Jordan	.30	.14	.04
□ 116 David Justice	.15	.07	.02
□ 117 Jack McDowell	.30	.14	.04
□ 118 Barry Bonds	.50	.23	.06
□ 119 Mark Langston	.05	.02	.01
□ 120 John Valentin	.15	.07	.02
□ 121 Raul Mondesi	.30	.14	.04
□ 122 Quilvio Veras	.05	.02	.01
□ 123 Randy Myers	.05	.02	.01
□ 124 Tony Gwynn	.75	.35	.09
□ 125 Johnny Damon	.15	.07	.02
□ 126 Doug Drabek	.05	.02	.01
□ 127 Bill Pulsipher	.15	.07	.02
□ 128 Paul O'Neill	.05	.02	.01
□ 129 Rickey Henderson	.30	.14	.04
□ 130 Deion Sanders	.30	.14	.04
□ 131 Orel Hershiser	.15	.07	.02
□ 132 Gary Sheffield	.30	.14	.04
□ NNO 59 Bazooka Mantle	4.00	1.80	.50

1948 Bowman

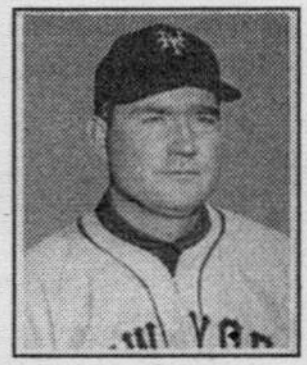

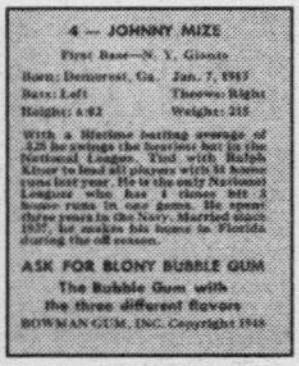

The 48-card Bowman set of 1948 was the first major set of the post-war period. Each 2 1/16" by 2 1/2" card had a black and white photo of a current player, with his biographical information printed in black ink on a gray back. Due to the printing process and the 36-card sheet size upon which Bowman was then printing, the 12 cards marked with an SP in the checklist are scarcer numerically, as they were removed from the printing sheet in order to make room for the 12 high numbers (37-48). Cards were issued in one-card penny packs. Many cards are found with over-printed, transposed, or blank backs. The set features the Rookie Cards of Hall of Famers Yogi Berra, Ralph Kiner, Stan Musial, Red Schoendienst, and Warren Spahn. Half of the cards in the set feature New York players (Yankees or Giants).

	NRMT	VG-E	GOOD
COMPLETE SET (48)	3400.00	1500.00	425.00
COMMON CARD (1-36)	20.00	9.00	2.50
COMMON CARD (37-48)	30.00	13.50	3.70
SP (13/16/20/24/28/34)	40.00	18.00	5.00
SP (22/26)	50.00	22.00	6.25
COMMON DODGERS: 1.5X COM. VALUE			
COMMON YANKEES: 1.5X COM. VALUE			
CARDS PRICED IN NM CONDITION !			
□ 1 Bob Elliott	80.00	12.00	4.00
□ 2 Ewell Blackwell	40.00	18.00	5.00
□ 3 Ralph Kiner	150.00	70.00	19.00
□ 4 Johnny Mize	100.00	45.00	12.50
□ 5 Bob Feller	225.00	100.00	28.00
□ 6 Yogi Berra	450.00	200.00	55.00
□ 7 Pete Reiser SP	120.00	55.00	15.00
□ 8 Phil Rizzuto SP	300.00	135.00	38.00
□ 14 Allie Reynolds	50.00	22.00	6.25
□ 17 Enos Slaughter	100.00	45.00	12.50
□ 18 Warren Spahn	350.00	160.00	45.00
□ 19 Tommy Henrich	40.00	18.00	5.00
□ 29 Joe Page SP	75.00	34.00	9.50
□ 30 Whitey Lockman SP	50.00	22.00	6.25
□ 36 Stan Musial	850.00	375.00	105.00
□ 38 Red Schoendienst	150.00	70.00	19.00
□ 40 Marty Marion	75.00	34.00	9.50
□ 45 Hank Sauer	50.00	22.00	6.25
□ 47 Bobby Thomson	100.00	45.00	12.50
□ 48 Dave Koslo	60.00	14.50	4.10

1949 Bowman

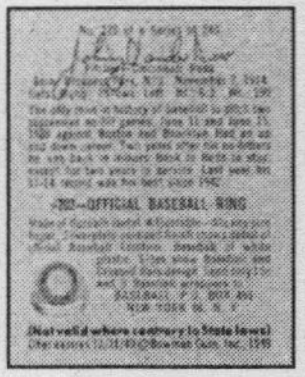

The cards in this 240-card set measure approximately 2 1/16" by 2 1/2". In 1949 Bowman took an intermediate step between black and white and full color with this set of tinted photos on colored backgrounds. Collectors should note the series price variations, which reflect some inconsistencies in the printing process. There are four major varieties in name printing, which are noted in the checklist below: NOF: name on front; NNOF: no name on front; PR: printed name on back; and SCR: script name on back. Cards were issued in five card nickle packs. These variations resulted when Bowman used twelve of the lower numbers to fill out the last press sheet of 36 cards, adding to numbers 217-240. Cards 1-3 and 5-73 can be found with either gray or white backs. The set features the Rookie Cards of Hall of Famers Roy Campanella, Bob Lemon, Robin Roberts, Duke

Snider, and Early Wynn as well as Rookie Cards of Richie Ashburn and Gil Hodges.

	NRMT	VG-E	GOOD
COMPLETE SET (240)	13000.00	5800.00	1600.00
COMMON CARD (1-144)	15.00	6.75	1.85
COMMON CARD (145-240)	50.00	22.00	6.25
LO SEMISTARS	25.00	11.00	3.10
HI SEMISTARS	75.00	34.00	9.50
NOF (4B/78B/83B/88B)	40.00	18.00	5.00
PR (109B/124B/126B)	40.00	18.00	5.00
PR (127B/132B/143B)	40.00	18.00	5.00
COMMON DODGERS: 1.5X COM. VALUE			
COMMON YANKEES: 1.5X COM. VALUE			
CARDS PRICED IN NM CONDITION			

	NRMT	VG-E	GOOD
□ 1 Vern Bickford	80.00	16.00	4.80
□ 11 Lou Boudreau	60.00	27.00	7.50
□ 14 Curt Simmons	35.00	16.00	4.40
□ 18 Bobby Thomson	35.00	16.00	4.40
□ 19 Bobby Brown	35.00	16.00	4.40
□ 23 Bobby Doerr	60.00	27.00	7.50
□ 24 Stan Musial	500.00	220.00	60.00
□ 26 George Kell	60.00	27.00	7.50
□ 27 Bob Feller	175.00	80.00	22.00
□ 29 Ralph Kiner	125.00	55.00	15.50
□ 33 Warren Spahn	175.00	80.00	22.00
□ 35 Vic Raschi	55.00	25.00	7.00
□ 36 Pee Wee Reese	175.00	80.00	22.00
□ 46 Robin Roberts	200.00	90.00	25.00
□ 47 Johnny Sain	40.00	18.00	5.00
□ 50 Jackie Robinson	900.00	400.00	110.00
□ 60 Yogi Berra	275.00	125.00	34.00
□ 64 Dom DiMaggio	35.00	16.00	4.40
□ 65 Enos Slaughter	70.00	32.00	8.75
□ 67 Alvin Dark	35.00	16.00	4.40
□ 69 Tommy Henrich	35.00	16.00	4.40
□ 70 Carl Furillo	100.00	45.00	12.50
□ 73 Billy Cox	35.00	16.00	4.40
□ 84 Roy Campanella	700.00	325.00	90.00
□ 85A Johnny Mize NNOF	80.00	36.00	10.00
□ 85B Johnny Mize NOF	150.00	70.00	19.00
□ 94 Mickey Vernon	35.00	16.00	4.40
□ 98A Phil Rizzuto NNOF	125.00	55.00	15.50
□ 98B Phil Rizzuto NOF	200.00	90.00	25.00
□ 100 Gil Hodges	250.00	110.00	31.00
□ 104 Eddie Stanky	35.00	16.00	4.40
□ 110 Early Wynn	125.00	55.00	15.50
□ 111 Red Schoendienst	70.00	32.00	8.75
□ 114 Allie Reynolds	40.00	18.00	5.00
□ 162 Preacher Roe	125.00	55.00	15.50
□ 174 Terry Moore	100.00	45.00	12.50
□ 175 Luke Appling	125.00	55.00	15.50
□ 185 Pete Reiser	100.00	45.00	12.50
□ 194 Ralph Branca	100.00	45.00	12.50
□ 209 Charlie Keller	100.00	45.00	12.50
□ 210 Joe Gordon	100.00	45.00	12.50
□ 214 Richie Ashburn	550.00	250.00	70.00
□ 224 Satchell Paige	1000.00	450.00	125.00
□ 225 Jerry Coleman	100.00	45.00	12.50
□ 226 Duke Snider	850.00	375.00	105.00
□ 229 Ed Lopat	125.00	55.00	15.50
□ 233 Larry Doby	150.00	70.00	19.00
□ 238 Bob Lemon	200.00	90.00	25.00
□ 240 Babe Young UER (Photo actually Bobby Young)	100.00	20.00	6.00

1950 Bowman

The cards in this 252-card set measure approximately 2 1/16" by 2 1/2". This set, marketed in 1950 by Bowman, represented a major improvement in terms of quality over their previous efforts. Each card was a beautifully colored line drawing developed from a simple photograph. The first 72 cards are the scarcest in the set, while the final 72 cards may be found with or without the copyright line. This was the only Bowman sports set to carry the famous "5-Star" logo. Cards were issued in five-card nickle packs. Key rookies in this set are Hank Bauer, Don Newcombe, and Al Rosen.

	NRMT	VG-E	GOOD
COMPLETE SET (252)	8500.00	3800.00	1050.00
COMMON CARD (1-72)	50.00	22.00	6.25
COMMON CARD (73-252)	16.00	7.25	2.00
LO SEMISTARS	60.00	27.00	7.50
HI SEMISTARS	25.00	11.00	3.10
COMMON DODGERS: 1.5X COM. VALUE			
COMMON YANKEES: 1.5X COM. VALUE			
CARDS PRICED IN NM CONDITION			

	NRMT	VG-E	GOOD
□ 1 Mel Parnell	150.00	30.00	9.00
□ 3 Dom DiMaggio	65.00	29.00	8.00
□ 6 Bob Feller	225.00	100.00	28.00
□ 8 George Kell	75.00	34.00	9.50
□ 10 Tommy Henrich	90.00	40.00	11.00
□ 11 Phil Rizzuto	225.00	100.00	28.00
□ 16 Roy Sievers	65.00	29.00	8.00
□ 19 Warren Spahn	225.00	100.00	28.00
□ 21 Pee Wee Reese	225.00	100.00	28.00
□ 22 Jackie Robinson	750.00	350.00	95.00
□ 23 Don Newcombe	150.00	70.00	19.00
□ 28 Bobby Thomson	65.00	29.00	8.00
□ 31 Del Ennis	65.00	29.00	8.00
□ 32 Robin Roberts	150.00	70.00	19.00
□ 33 Ralph Kiner	100.00	45.00	12.50
□ 35 Enos Slaughter	100.00	45.00	12.50
□ 37 Luke Appling	75.00	34.00	9.50
□ 39 Larry Doby	65.00	29.00	8.00
□ 40 Bob Lemon	75.00	34.00	9.50
□ 43 Bobby Doerr	75.00	34.00	9.50
□ 46 Yogi Berra	325.00	145.00	40.00
□ 58 Carl Furillo	90.00	40.00	11.00
□ 62 Ted Kluszewski	100.00	45.00	12.50
□ 71 Red Schoendienst	75.00	34.00	9.50
□ 74 Johnny Antonelli	35.00	16.00	4.40
□ 75 Roy Campanella	275.00	125.00	34.00
□ 77 Duke Snider	275.00	125.00	34.00
□ 84 Richie Ashburn	100.00	45.00	12.50
□ 94 Lou Boudreau	60.00	27.00	7.50
□ 98 Ted Williams	825.00	375.00	105.00
□ 100 Vic Raschi	35.00	16.00	4.40
□ 101 Bobby Brown	35.00	16.00	4.40
□ 112 Gil Hodges	100.00	45.00	12.50
□ 138 Allie Reynolds	35.00	16.00	4.40
□ 139 Johnny Mize	75.00	34.00	9.50
□ 148 Early Wynn	75.00	34.00	9.50
□ 167 Preacher Roe	35.00	16.00	4.40
□ 215 Ed Lopat	35.00	16.00	4.40
□ 217 Casey Stengel MG	125.00	55.00	15.50
□ 219 Hank Bauer	65.00	29.00	8.00
□ 220 Leo Durocher MG	60.00	27.00	7.50
□ 226 Jim Konstanty	40.00	18.00	5.00
□ 229 Frank Frisch MG	40.00	18.00	5.00
□ 232 Al Rosen	40.00	18.00	5.00
□ 234 Bobby Shantz	40.00	18.00	5.00
□ 248 Sam Jethroe	40.00	18.00	5.00
□ 252 Billy DeMars	35.00	9.50	3.50

1951 Bowman

The cards in this 324-card set measure approximately 2 1/16" by 3 1/8". Many of the obverses of the cards appearing in the 1951 Bowman set are enlargements of those appearing in the previous year. The high number series (253-324) is highly valued and contains the true "Rookie" cards of Mickey Mantle and Willie Mays. Card number 195 depicts Paul Richards in caricature. George Kell's card (number 46) incorrectly lists him as being in the "1941" Bowman series.

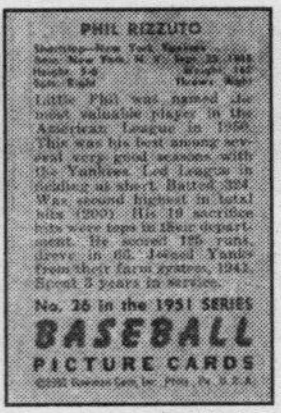

Cards were issued either in one card penny packs or in five card nickle packs. Player names are found printed in a panel on the front of the card. These cards were supposedly also sold in sheets in variety stores in the Philadelphia area.

	NRMT	VG-E	GOOD
COMPLETE SET (324)	16000.00	7200.00	2000.00
COMMON CARD (1-252)	18.00	8.00	2.20
COMMON CARD (253-324)	50.00	22.00	6.25
LO SEMISTARS	25.00	11.00	3.10
HI SEMISTARS	60.00	27.00	7.50
COMMON DODGERS: 1.5X COM. VALUE			
COMMON YANKEES: 1.5X COM. VALUE			
CARDS PRICED IN NM CONDITION			

□ 1 Whitey Ford	800.00	200.00	65.00
□ 2 Yogi Berra	275.00	125.00	34.00
□ 3 Robin Roberts	75.00	34.00	9.50
□ 6 Don Newcombe	50.00	22.00	6.25
□ 7 Gil Hodges	90.00	40.00	11.00
□ 10 Red Schoendienst	55.00	25.00	7.00
□ 14 Alvin Dark	30.00	13.50	3.70
□ 25 Vic Raschi	35.00	16.00	4.40
□ 26 Phil Rizzuto	125.00	55.00	15.50
□ 30 Bob Feller	125.00	55.00	15.50
□ 31 Roy Campanella	225.00	100.00	28.00
□ 32 Duke Snider	225.00	100.00	28.00
□ 40 Gus Bell	35.00	16.00	4.40
□ 46 George Kell 1941 UER	55.00	25.00	7.00
□ 50 Johnny Mize	55.00	25.00	7.00
□ 53 Bob Lemon	55.00	25.00	7.00
□ 54 Ray Boone	35.00	16.00	4.40
□ 56 Ralph Branca	30.00	13.50	3.70
□ 58 Enos Slaughter	55.00	25.00	7.00
□ 60 Chico Carrasquel	30.00	13.50	3.70
□ 62 Lou Boudreau	55.00	25.00	7.00
□ 78 Early Wynn	55.00	25.00	7.00
□ 80 Pee Wee Reese	125.00	55.00	15.50
□ 81 Carl Furillo	50.00	22.00	6.25
□ 109 Allie Reynolds	35.00	16.00	4.40
□ 118 Preacher Roe	35.00	16.00	4.40
□ 122 Joe Garagiola	75.00	34.00	9.50
□ 126 Bobby Thomson	30.00	13.50	3.70
□ 127 Sal Maglie	55.00	25.00	7.00
□ 134 Warren Spahn	125.00	55.00	15.50
□ 143 Ted Kluszewski	40.00	18.00	5.00
□ 151 Larry Doby	35.00	16.00	4.40
□ 165 Ted Williams	700.00	325.00	90.00
□ 181 Casey Stengel MG	75.00	34.00	9.50
□ 183 Hank Bauer	30.00	13.50	3.70
□ 186 Richie Ashburn	90.00	40.00	11.00
□ 196 Billy Pierce	35.00	16.00	4.40
□ 198 Monte Irvin	100.00	45.00	12.50
□ 203 Vernon Law	30.00	13.50	3.70
□ 218 Ed Lopat	35.00	16.00	4.40
□ 219 Gene Woodling	40.00	18.00	5.00
□ 232 Nelson Fox	150.00	70.00	19.00
□ 233 Leo Durocher MG	60.00	27.00	7.50
□ 245 John Berardino	30.00	13.50	3.70
□ 253 Mickey Mantle	8000.00	3600.00	1000.00
□ 254 Jackie Jensen	100.00	45.00	12.50
□ 260 Carl Erskine	100.00	45.00	12.50
□ 282 Frank Frisch MG	75.00	34.00	9.50
□ 290 Bill Dickey CO	100.00	45.00	12.50
□ 295 Al Lopez MG	120.00	55.00	15.00
□ 305 Willie Mays	3200.00	1450.00	400.00
□ 306 Jim Piersall	90.00	40.00	11.00
□ 317 Smoky Burgess	75.00	34.00	9.50
□ 323 Joe Adcock	75.00	34.00	9.50
□ 324 Johnny Pramesa	90.00	27.00	9.00

1952 Bowman

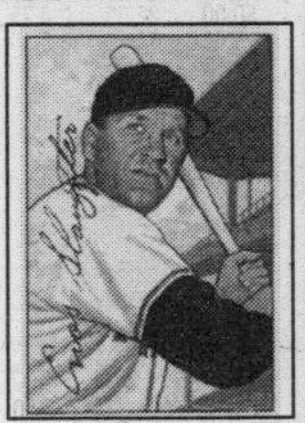

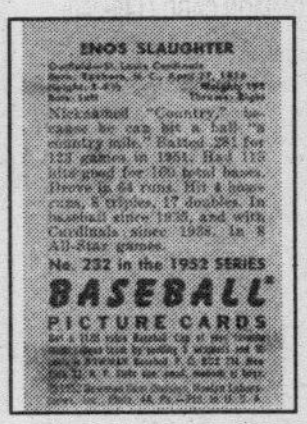

The cards in this 252-card set measure approximately 2 1/16" by 3 1/8". While the Bowman set of 1952 retained the card size introduced in 1951, it employed a modification of color tones from the two preceding years. The cards also appeared with a facsimile autograph on the front and, for the first time since 1949, premium advertising on the back. The 1952 set was apparently sold in sheets as well as in gum packs. Artwork for 15 cards that were never issued was discovered in the early 1980s. Cards ere issued in one card penny packs or five card nickle packs. Notable Rookie Cards in this set are Lew Burdette, Gil McDougald, and Minnie Minoso.

	NRMT	VG-E	GOOD
COMPLETE SET (252)	7500.00	3400.00	950.00
COMMON CARD (1-216)	16.00	7.25	2.00
COMMON CARD (217-252)	40.00	18.00	5.00
LO SEMISTARS	25.00	11.00	3.10
HI SEMISTARS	50.00	22.00	6.25
COMMON DODGERS: 1.5X COM. VALUE			
COMMON YANKEES: 1.5X COM. VALUE			
CARDS PRICED IN NM CONDITION			

□ 1 Yogi Berra	400.00	125.00	40.00
□ 2 Bobby Thomson	40.00	18.00	5.00
□ 4 Robin Roberts	60.00	27.00	7.50
□ 5 Minnie Minoso	125.00	55.00	15.50
□ 8 Pee Wee Reese	125.00	55.00	15.50
□ 11 Ralph Kiner	50.00	22.00	6.25
□ 17 Ed Lopat	40.00	18.00	5.00
□ 21 Nellie Fox	60.00	27.00	7.50
□ 23 Bob Lemon	50.00	22.00	6.25
□ 24 Carl Furillo	40.00	18.00	5.00
□ 27 Joe Garagiola	50.00	22.00	6.25
□ 30 Red Schoendienst	50.00	22.00	6.25
□ 33 Gil McDougald	80.00	36.00	10.00
□ 43 Bob Feller	125.00	55.00	15.50
□ 44 Roy Campanella	225.00	100.00	28.00
□ 52 Phil Rizzuto	125.00	55.00	15.50
□ 53 Richie Ashburn	90.00	40.00	11.00
□ 70 Carl Erskine	35.00	16.00	4.40
□ 75 George Kell	50.00	22.00	6.25
□ 80 Gil Hodges	90.00	40.00	11.00
□ 101 Mickey Mantle	2500.00	1100.00	300.00
□ 115 Larry Doby	35.00	16.00	4.40
□ 116 Duke Snider	200.00	90.00	25.00
□ 128 Don Newcombe	35.00	16.00	4.40
□ 142 Early Wynn	50.00	22.00	6.25
□ 145 Johnny Mize	50.00	22.00	6.25
□ 146 Leo Durocher MG	50.00	22.00	6.25
□ 156 Warren Spahn	125.00	55.00	15.50
□ 161 Jackie Jensen	35.00	16.00	4.40
□ 162 Monte Irvin	50.00	22.00	6.25
□ 191 Bob Friend	40.00	18.00	5.00
□ 196 Stan Musial	600.00	275.00	75.00
□ 217 Casey Stengel MG	150.00	70.00	19.00
□ 218 Willie Mays	1200.00	550.00	150.00
□ 232 Enos Slaughter	90.00	40.00	11.00
□ 244 Lew Burdette	50.00	22.00	6.25
□ 252 Frank Crosetti CO	100.00	25.00	8.00

1953 Bowman B/W

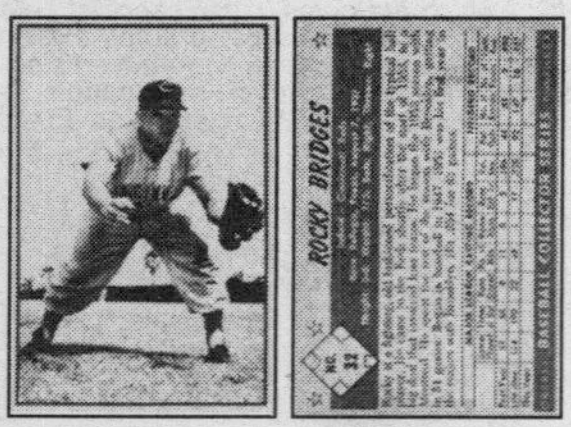

The cards in this 64-card set measure approximately 2 1/2" by 3 3/4". Some collectors believe that the high cost of producing the 1953 color series forced Bowman to issue this set in black and white, since the two sets are identical in design except for the element of color. This set was also produced in fewer numbers than its color counterpart, and is popular among collectors for the challenge involved in completing it. Cards were issued in five-card nickle packs. There are no key Rookie Cards in this set.

	NRMT	VG-E	GOOD
COMPLETE SET (64)	2400.00	1100.00	300.00
COMMON CARD (1-64)	35.00	16.00	4.40
SEMISTARS	50.00	22.00	6.25
COMMON DODGERS: 1.5X COM. VALUE			
COMMON YANKEES: 1.5X COM. VALUE			
CARDS PRICED IN NM CONDITION !			

□ 1 Gus Bell	110.00	22.00	8.75
□ 15 Johnny Mize	125.00	55.00	15.50
□ 25 Johnny Sain	60.00	27.00	7.50
□ 26 Preacher Roe	60.00	27.00	7.50
□ 27 Bob Lemon	125.00	55.00	15.50
□ 28 Hoyt Wilhelm	125.00	55.00	15.50
□ 31 Gene Woodling	60.00	27.00	7.50
□ 36 Jim Piersall	60.00	27.00	7.50
□ 39 Casey Stengel MG	325.00	145.00	40.00
□ 46 Bucky Harris MG	60.00	27.00	7.50
□ 51 Lou Burdette	60.00	27.00	7.50
□ 64 Andy Hansen	50.00	15.00	3.70

1953 Bowman Color

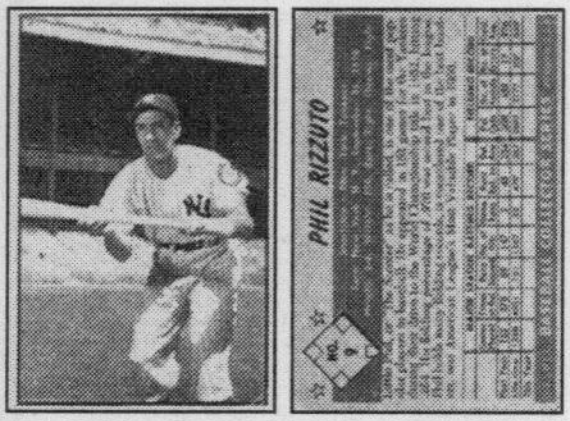

The cards in this 160-card set measure approximately 2 1/2" by 3 3/4". The 1953 Bowman Color set, considered by many to be the best looking set of the modern era, contains Kodachrome photographs with no names or facsimile autographs on the face. Cards were issued in five-card nickle packs. Numbers 113 to 160 are somewhat more difficult to obtain, with numbers 113 to 128 being the most difficult. There are two cards of Al Corwin (126 and 149). There are no key Rookie Cards in this set.

	NRMT	VG-E	GOOD
COMPLETE SET (160)	12000.00	5400.00	1500.00
COMMON CARD (1-112)	30.00	13.50	3.70
COMMON CARD (113-128)	70.00	32.00	8.75
COMMON CARD (129-160)	60.00	27.00	7.50
LO SEMISTARS	40.00	18.00	5.00
COMMON DODGERS: 1.5X COM. VALUE			
COMMON YANKEES: 1.5X COM. VALUE			
CARDS PRICED IN NM CONDITION !			

□ 1 Dave Williams	100.00	20.00	6.00
□ 9 Phil Rizzuto	160.00	70.00	20.00
□ 10 Richie Ashburn	160.00	70.00	20.00
□ 18 Nellie Fox	80.00	36.00	10.00
□ 21 Joe Garagiola	50.00	22.00	6.25
□ 32 Stan Musial	700.00	325.00	90.00
□ 33 Pee Wee Reese HOR	825.00	375.00	105.00
□ 36 Minnie Minoso	60.00	27.00	7.50
□ 40 Larry Doby	50.00	22.00	6.25
□ 44 Yogi Berra Hank Bauer Mickey Mantle	675.00	300.00	85.00
□ 46 Roy Campanella	275.00	125.00	34.00
□ 51 Monte Irvin	60.00	27.00	7.50
□ 55 Leo Durocher MG	70.00	32.00	8.75
□ 57 Lou Boudreau MG	50.00	22.00	6.25
□ 59 Mickey Mantle	3000.00	1350.00	375.00
□ 61 George Kell	70.00	32.00	8.75
□ 62 Ted Kluszewski	60.00	27.00	7.50
□ 63 Gil McDougald	60.00	27.00	7.50
□ 65 Robin Roberts	80.00	36.00	10.00
□ 80 Ralph Kiner	70.00	32.00	8.75
□ 81 Enos Slaughter	70.00	32.00	8.75
□ 92 Gil Hodges	175.00	80.00	22.00
□ 93 Phil Rizzuto and Billy Martin	250.00	110.00	31.00
□ 97 Eddie Mathews	275.00	125.00	34.00
□ 99 Warren Spahn	225.00	100.00	28.00
□ 101 Red Schoendienst	70.00	32.00	8.75
□ 114 Bob Feller	300.00	135.00	38.00
□ 117 Duke Snider	550.00	250.00	70.00
□ 118 Billy Martin	300.00	135.00	38.00
□ 121 Yogi Berra	575.00	250.00	70.00
□ 146 Early Wynn	125.00	55.00	15.50
□ 153 Whitey Ford	500.00	220.00	60.00
□ 160 Cal Abrams	100.00	34.00	9.25

1954 Bowman

The cards in this 224-card set measure approximately 2 1/2" by 3 3/4". A contractual problem apparently resulted in the deletion of the number 66 Ted Williams card from this Bowman set, thereby creating a scarcity that is highly valued among collectors. The set price below does NOT include number 66 Williams but does include number 66 Jim Piersall, the apparent replacement for Williams in spite of the fact that Piersall was already number 210 to appear later in the set. Many errors in players' statistics exist (and some were corrected) while a few players' names were printed on the front, instead of appearing as a facsimile autograph. Most of these differences are so minor that there is no price differential for either card. The cards which changes were made on are #'s 12, 22,25,26,35,38, 41, 43, 47, 53, 61, 67, 80, 81, 82, 85, 93, 94, 99, 103, 105, 124, 138, 139, 140, 145, 153, 156, 174, 179, 185, 212, 216 and 217. The set was issued in seven-card nickle packs. The notable Rookie Cards in this set are Harvey Kuenn and Don Larsen.

	NRMT	VG-E	GOOD
COMPLETE SET (224)	4000.00	1800.00	500.00
COMMON CARD (1-128)	12.00	5.50	1.50
COMMON CARD (129-224)	14.00	6.25	1.75
SEMISTARS	18.00	8.00	2.20
COMMON DODGERS: 1.5X COM. VALUE			
COMMON YANKEES: 1.5X COM. VALUE			
CARDS PRICED IN NM CONDITION !			

	NRMT	VG-E	GOOD
□ 1 Phil Rizzuto	150.00	45.00	15.00
□ 6 Nellie Fox	30.00	13.50	3.70
□ 15 Richie Ashburn	75.00	34.00	9.50
□ 23 Harvey Kuenn	35.00	16.00	4.40
□ 33A Vic Raschi (No mention of trade on back)	20.00	9.00	2.50
□ 33B Vic Raschi (Traded to St.Louis)	35.00	16.00	4.40
□ 38 Minnie Minoso	20.00	9.00	2.50
□ 45 Ralph Kiner	40.00	18.00	5.00
□ 50 George Kell	40.00	18.00	5.00
□ 57 Hoyt Wilhelm	35.00	16.00	4.40
□ 58 Pee Wee Reese	75.00	34.00	9.50
□ 62 Enos Slaughter	40.00	18.00	5.00
□ 64 Eddie Mathews	50.00	22.00	6.25
□ 65 Mickey Mantle	1300.00	575.00	160.00
□ 66A Ted Williams	4600.00	2100.00	575.00
□ 66B Jim Piersall	75.00	34.00	9.50
□ 74 Jim Gilliam	30.00	13.50	3.70
□ 84 Larry Doby	20.00	9.00	2.50
□ 89 Willie Mays	400.00	180.00	50.00
□ 90 Roy Campanella	175.00	80.00	22.00
□ 95 Robin Roberts	50.00	22.00	6.25
□ 97 Gil McDougald	20.00	9.00	2.50
□ 101 Don Larsen	50.00	22.00	6.25
□ 110 Red Schoendienst	35.00	16.00	4.40
□ 122 Carl Furillo	25.00	11.00	3.10
□ 132 Bob Feller	75.00	34.00	9.50
□ 138 Gil Hodges	75.00	34.00	9.50
□ 141 Joe Garagiola	30.00	13.50	3.70
□ 144 Ernie Johnson	25.00	11.00	3.10
□ 145 Billy Martin	60.00	27.00	7.50
□ 154 Don Newcombe	30.00	13.50	3.70
□ 155 Frank Thomas	20.00	9.00	2.50
□ 161 Yogi Berra	175.00	80.00	22.00
□ 163A Dave Philley (No mention of trade on back)	20.00	9.00	2.50
□ 163B Dave Philley (Traded to Cleveland)	36.00	16.00	4.50
□ 164 Early Wynn	50.00	22.00	6.25
□ 170 Duke Snider	125.00	55.00	15.50
□ 177 Whitey Ford	100.00	45.00	12.50
□ 192 Lou Burdette	20.00	9.00	2.50
□ 196 Bob Lemon	40.00	18.00	5.00
□ 201 Bobby Thomson	25.00	11.00	3.10
□ 210 Jim Piersall	20.00	9.00	2.50
□ 218 Preacher Roe	25.00	11.00	3.10
□ 224 Bill Bruton	30.00	5.50	1.50

1955 Bowman

The cards in this 320-card set measure approximately 2 1/2" by 3 3/4". The Bowman set of 1955 is known as the "TV set" because each player photograph is cleverly shown within a television set design. The set contains umpire cards, some transposed pictures (e.g., Johnsons and Bollings), an incorrect spelling for Harvey Kuenn, and a traded line for Palica (all of which are noted in the checklist below). Some three-card advertising strips exist, the backs of these panels contain advertising for Bowman products. Advertising panels seen include Nellie Fox/Carl Furillo/Carl Erskine, Hank Aaron/Johnny Logan/Eddie Miksis, and a panel including Early Wynn and Pee Wee Reese. Cards were issued either in 9-card nickel packs or one card penny packs. The notable Rookie Cards in this set are Elston Howard and Don Zimmer. Hall of Fame umpires pictured in the set are Al Barlick, Jocko Conlon and Cal Hubbard.

	NRMT	VG-E	GOOD
COMPLETE SET (320)	4600.00	2100.00	575.00
COMMON CARD (1-96)	12.00	5.50	1.50
COMMON CARD (97-224)	10.00	4.50	1.25
COMMON CARD (225-320)	16.00	7.25	2.00
UMP (226/235/239/250/258)	30.00	13.50	3.70
UMP (260/272/275/279)	30.00	13.50	3.70
UMP (281/283/284/286)	30.00	13.50	3.70
UMP (289/291/295/297)	30.00	13.50	3.70
UMP (301/305/309/311)	30.00	13.50	3.70
UMP (277/293/299/307/317)	35.00	16.00	4.40
ERR (48A/101A/157A/204A)	10.00	4.50	1.25
COR (48B/101B/157B/204B)	30.00	13.50	3.70
LO SEMISTARS	14.00	6.25	1.75
COMMON DODGERS: 1.5X COM. VALUE			
COMMON YANKEES: 1.5X COM. VALUE			
CARDS PRICED IN NM CONDITION !			

	NRMT	VG-E	GOOD
□ 1 Hoyt Wilhelm	100.00	22.00	6.50
□ 9 Gil McDougald	20.00	9.00	2.50
□ 10 Phil Rizzuto	65.00	29.00	8.00
□ 22 Roy Campanella	125.00	55.00	15.50
□ 23 Al Kaline	150.00	70.00	19.00
□ 25 Minnie Minoso	20.00	9.00	2.50
□ 29 Red Schoendienst	30.00	13.50	3.70
□ 33 Nellie Fox	35.00	16.00	4.40
□ 37 Pee Wee Reese	65.00	29.00	8.00
□ 38 Early Wynn	30.00	13.50	3.70
□ 59 Whitey Ford	75.00	34.00	9.50
□ 60 Enos Slaughter	30.00	13.50	3.70
□ 65 Don Zimmer	25.00	11.00	3.10
□ 67 Don Larsen	20.00	9.00	2.50
□ 68 Elston Howard	75.00	34.00	9.50
□ 89 Lou Boudreau MG	30.00	13.50	3.70
□ 97 Johnny Podres	20.00	9.00	2.50
□ 98 Jim Gilliam	25.00	11.00	3.10
□ 103 Eddie Mathews	50.00	22.00	6.25
□ 130 Richie Ashburn	45.00	20.00	5.50
□ 132A Harvey Kueen ERR (Sic, Kuenn)	20.00	9.00	2.50
□ 132B Harvey Kuenn COR	30.00	13.50	3.70
□ 134 Bob Feller	70.00	32.00	8.75
□ 143 Don Newcombe	25.00	11.00	3.10
□ 158 Gil Hodges	45.00	20.00	5.50
□ 160 Bill Skowron	25.00	11.00	3.10
□ 167 Bob Grim	25.00	11.00	3.10
□ 168 Yogi Berra	90.00	40.00	11.00
□ 169 Carl Furillo	20.00	9.00	2.50
□ 170 Carl Erskine	20.00	9.00	2.50
□ 171 Robin Roberts	35.00	16.00	4.40
□ 179 Hank Aaron	200.00	90.00	25.00
□ 184 Willie Mays	225.00	100.00	28.00
□ 191 Bob Lemon	30.00	13.50	3.70
□ 195B Erv Palica (With trade)	30.00	13.50	3.70
□ 197 Ralph Kiner	30.00	13.50	3.70
□ 202 Mickey Mantle UER Birthdate listed as 10/30/31 Should be 10/20/31	900.00	400.00	110.00
□ 213 George Kell	30.00	13.50	3.70
□ 229 Jim Brosnan	20.00	9.00	2.50
□ 242 Ernie Banks	350.00	160.00	45.00
□ 246 Hank Bauer	25.00	11.00	3.10
□ 259 Don Mossi	25.00	11.00	3.10
□ 265 Albert Barlick UMP	75.00	34.00	9.50
□ 267 Jim Honochick UMP	75.00	34.00	9.50
□ 278 Charlie Neal	35.00	16.00	4.40
□ 296 Bill Virdon	35.00	16.00	4.40
□ 302 Frank Malzone	30.00	13.50	3.70
□ 303 Jocko Conlan UMP	75.00	34.00	9.50

□ 308 Al Lopez MG	50.00	22.00	6.25
□ 313 Augie Donatelli UMP	50.00	22.00	6.25
□ 315 Cal Hubbard UMP	75.00	34.00	9.50
□ 320 George Susce Jr.	45.00	9.00	2.70

1989 Bowman

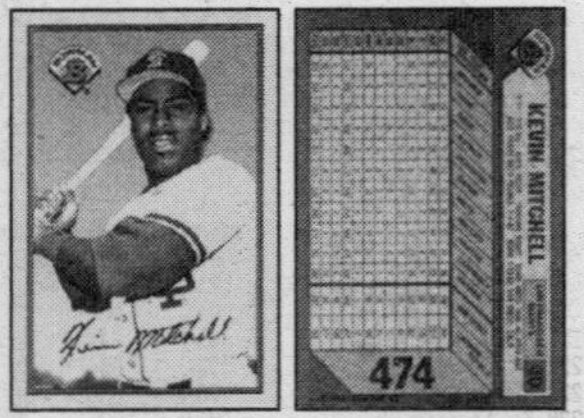

The 1989 Bowman set, produced by Topps, contains 484 slightly oversized cards (measuring 2 1/2" by 3 3/4"). The cards were released in midseason 1989 in wax, rack, and cello pack formats. The fronts have white-bordered color photos with facsimile autographs and small Bowman logos. The backs feature charts detailing 1988 player performances vs. each team. The cards are ordered alphabetically according to teams in the AL and NL. Cards 258-261 form a father/son subset. Rookie Cards in this set include Andy Benes, Ken Griffey Jr., Tino Martinez, Charles Nagy, Gary Sheffield, John Smoltz and Robin Ventura.

	MINT	NRMT	EXC
COMPLETE SET (484)	12.00	5.50	1.50
COMPLETE FACT.SET (484)	12.00	5.50	1.50
COMMON CARD (1-484)	.05	.02	.01
SEMISTARS	.10	.05	.01
STARS	.15	.07	.02
COMPLETE REPRINT SET (11)	2.00	.90	.25
REPRINTS: RANDOM INSERTS IN PACKS...			

□ 1 Oswald Peraza	.05	.02	.01
□ 2 Brian Holton	.05	.02	.01
□ 3 Jose Bautista	.05	.02	.01
□ 4 Pete Harnisch	.10	.05	.01
□ 5 Dave Schmidt	.05	.02	.01
□ 6 Gregg Olson	.10	.05	.01
□ 7 Jeff Ballard	.05	.02	.01
□ 8 Bob Melvin	.05	.02	.01
□ 9 Cal Ripken	.75	.35	.09
□ 10 Randy Milligan	.05	.02	.01
□ 11 Juan Bell	.05	.02	.01
□ 12 Billy Ripken	.05	.02	.01
□ 13 Jim Traber	.05	.02	.01
□ 14 Pete Stanicek	.05	.02	.01
□ 15 Steve Finley	.25	.11	.03
□ 16 Larry Sheets	.05	.02	.01
□ 17 Phil Bradley	.05	.02	.01
□ 18 Brady Anderson	.60	.25	.07
□ 19 Lee Smith	.15	.07	.02
□ 20 Tom Fischer	.05	.02	.01
□ 21 Mike Boddicker	.05	.02	.01
□ 22 Rob Murphy	.05	.02	.01
□ 23 Wes Gardner	.05	.02	.01
□ 24 John Dopson	.05	.02	.01
□ 25 Bob Stanley	.05	.02	.01
□ 26 Roger Clemens	.15	.07	.02
□ 27 Rich Gedman	.05	.02	.01
□ 28 Marty Barrett	.05	.02	.01
□ 29 Luis Rivera	.05	.02	.01
□ 30 Jody Reed	.05	.02	.01
□ 31 Nick Esasky	.05	.02	.01
□ 32 Wade Boggs	.15	.07	.02
□ 33 Jim Rice	.15	.07	.02
□ 34 Mike Greenwell	.05	.02	.01
□ 35 Dwight Evans	.10	.05	.01
□ 36 Ellis Burks	.15	.07	.02
□ 37 Chuck Finley	.10	.05	.01
□ 38 Kirk McCaskill	.05	.02	.01
□ 39 Jim Abbott	.15	.07	.02
□ 40 Bryan Harvey	.10	.05	.01
□ 41 Bert Blyleven	.10	.05	.01
□ 42 Mike Witt	.05	.02	.01
□ 43 Bob McClure	.05	.02	.01
□ 44 Bill Schroeder	.05	.02	.01
□ 45 Lance Parrish	.05	.02	.01
□ 46 Dick Schofield	.05	.02	.01
□ 47 Wally Joyner	.10	.05	.01
□ 48 Jack Howell	.05	.02	.01
□ 49 Johnny Ray	.05	.02	.01
□ 50 Chili Davis	.10	.05	.01
□ 51 Tony Armas	.05	.02	.01
□ 52 Claudell Washington	.05	.02	.01
□ 53 Brian Downing	.05	.02	.01
□ 54 Devon White	.10	.05	.01
□ 55 Bobby Thigpen	.05	.02	.01
□ 56 Bill Long	.05	.02	.01
□ 57 Jerry Reuss	.05	.02	.01
□ 58 Shawn Hillegas	.05	.02	.01
□ 59 Melido Perez	.05	.02	.01
□ 60 Jeff Bittiger	.05	.02	.01
□ 61 Jack McDowell	.15	.07	.02
□ 62 Carlton Fisk	.15	.07	.02
□ 63 Steve Lyons	.05	.02	.01
□ 64 Ozzie Guillen	.05	.02	.01
□ 65 Robin Ventura	.40	.18	.05
□ 66 Fred Manrique	.05	.02	.01
□ 67 Dan Pasqua	.05	.02	.01
□ 68 Ivan Calderon	.05	.02	.01
□ 69 Ron Kittle	.05	.02	.01
□ 70 Daryl Boston	.05	.02	.01
□ 71 Dave Gallagher	.05	.02	.01
□ 72 Harold Baines	.10	.05	.01
□ 73 Charles Nagy	.60	.25	.07
□ 74 John Farrell	.05	.02	.01
□ 75 Kevin Wickander	.05	.02	.01
□ 76 Greg Swindell	.05	.02	.01
□ 77 Mike Walker	.05	.02	.01
□ 78 Doug Jones	.05	.02	.01
□ 79 Rich Yett	.05	.02	.01
□ 80 Tom Candiotti	.05	.02	.01
□ 81 Jesse Orosco	.05	.02	.01
□ 82 Bud Black	.05	.02	.01
□ 83 Andy Allanson	.05	.02	.01
□ 84 Pete O'Brien	.05	.02	.01
□ 85 Jerry Browne	.05	.02	.01
□ 86 Brook Jacoby	.05	.02	.01
□ 87 Mark Lewis	.15	.07	.02
□ 88 Luis Aguayo	.05	.02	.01
□ 89 Cory Snyder	.05	.02	.01
□ 90 Oddibe McDowell	.05	.02	.01
□ 91 Joe Carter	.15	.07	.02
□ 92 Frank Tanana	.05	.02	.01
□ 93 Jack Morris	.10	.05	.01
□ 94 Doyle Alexander	.05	.02	.01
□ 95 Steve Searcy	.05	.02	.01
□ 96 Randy Bockus	.05	.02	.01
□ 97 Jeff M. Robinson	.05	.02	.01
□ 98 Mike Henneman	.05	.02	.01
□ 99 Paul Gibson	.05	.02	.01
□ 100 Frank Williams	.05	.02	.01
□ 101 Matt Nokes	.05	.02	.01
□ 102 Rico Brogna UER (Misspelled Ricco on card back)	.40	.18	.05
□ 103 Lou Whitaker	.15	.07	.02
□ 104 Al Pedrique	.05	.02	.01
□ 105 Alan Trammell	.15	.07	.02
□ 106 Chris Brown	.05	.02	.01
□ 107 Pat Sheridan	.05	.02	.01
□ 108 Chet Lemon	.05	.02	.01
□ 109 Keith Moreland	.05	.02	.01
□ 110 Mel Stottlemyre Jr.	.05	.02	.01
□ 111 Bret Saberhagen	.10	.05	.01
□ 112 Floyd Bannister	.05	.02	.01
□ 113 Jeff Montgomery	.10	.05	.01
□ 114 Steve Farr	.05	.02	.01
□ 115 Tom Gordon UER (Front shows autograph of Don Gordon)	.10	.05	.01
□ 116 Charlie Leibrandt	.05	.02	.01
□ 117 Mark Gubicza	.05	.02	.01
□ 118 Mike Macfarlane	.10	.05	.01
□ 119 Bob Boone	.10	.05	.01
□ 120 Kurt Stillwell	.05	.02	.01

☐ 121	George Brett	.40	.18	.05
☐ 122	Frank White	.10	.05	.01
☐ 123	Kevin Seitzer	.05	.02	.01
☐ 124	Willie Wilson	.05	.02	.01
☐ 125	Pat Tabler	.05	.02	.01
☐ 126	Bo Jackson	.15	.07	.02
☐ 127	Hugh Walker	.05	.02	.01
☐ 128	Danny Tartabull	.05	.02	.01
☐ 129	Teddy Higuera	.05	.02	.01
☐ 130	Don August	.05	.02	.01
☐ 131	Juan Nieves	.05	.02	.01
☐ 132	Mike Birkbeck	.05	.02	.01
☐ 133	Dan Plesac	.05	.02	.01
☐ 134	Chris Bosio	.05	.02	.01
☐ 135	Bill Wegman	.05	.02	.01
☐ 136	Chuck Crim	.05	.02	.01
☐ 137	B.J. Surhoff	.15	.07	.02
☐ 138	Joey Meyer	.05	.02	.01
☐ 139	Dale Sveum	.05	.02	.01
☐ 140	Paul Molitor	.20	.09	.03
☐ 141	Jim Gantner	.05	.02	.01
☐ 142	Gary Sheffield	.75	.35	.09
☐ 143	Greg Brock	.05	.02	.01
☐ 144	Robin Yount	.15	.07	.02
☐ 145	Glenn Braggs	.05	.02	.01
☐ 146	Rob Deer	.05	.02	.01
☐ 147	Fred Toliver	.05	.02	.01
☐ 148	Jeff Reardon	.10	.05	.01
☐ 149	Allan Anderson	.05	.02	.01
☐ 150	Frank Viola	.05	.02	.01
☐ 151	Shane Rawley	.05	.02	.01
☐ 152	Juan Berenguer	.05	.02	.01
☐ 153	Johnny Ard	.05	.02	.01
☐ 154	Tim Laudner	.05	.02	.01
☐ 155	Brian Harper	.05	.02	.01
☐ 156	Al Newman	.05	.02	.01
☐ 157	Kent Hrbek	.10	.05	.01
☐ 158	Gary Gaetti	.05	.02	.01
☐ 159	Wally Backman	.05	.02	.01
☐ 160	Gene Larkin	.05	.02	.01
☐ 161	Greg Gagne	.05	.02	.01
☐ 162	Kirby Puckett	.30	.14	.04
☐ 163	Dan Gladden	.05	.02	.01
☐ 164	Randy Bush	.05	.02	.01
☐ 165	Dave LaPoint	.05	.02	.01
☐ 166	Andy Hawkins	.05	.02	.01
☐ 167	Dave Righetti	.05	.02	.01
☐ 168	Lance McCullers	.05	.02	.01
☐ 169	Jimmy Jones	.05	.02	.01
☐ 170	Al Leiter	.10	.05	.01
☐ 171	John Candelaria	.05	.02	.01
☐ 172	Don Slaught	.05	.02	.01
☐ 173	Jamie Quirk	.05	.02	.01
☐ 174	Rafael Santana	.05	.02	.01
☐ 175	Mike Pagliarulo	.05	.02	.01
☐ 176	Don Mattingly	.50	.23	.06
☐ 177	Ken Phelps	.05	.02	.01
☐ 178	Steve Sax	.05	.02	.01
☐ 179	Dave Winfield	.15	.07	.02
☐ 180	Stan Jefferson	.05	.02	.01
☐ 181	Rickey Henderson	.15	.07	.02
☐ 182	Bob Brower	.05	.02	.01
☐ 183	Roberto Kelly	.10	.05	.01
☐ 184	Curt Young	.05	.02	.01
☐ 185	Gene Nelson	.05	.02	.01
☐ 186	Bob Welch	.05	.02	.01
☐ 187	Rick Honeycutt	.05	.02	.01
☐ 188	Dave Stewart	.10	.05	.01
☐ 189	Mike Moore	.05	.02	.01
☐ 190	Dennis Eckersley	.10	.05	.01
☐ 191	Eric Plunk	.05	.02	.01
☐ 192	Storm Davis	.05	.02	.01
☐ 193	Terry Steinbach	.10	.05	.01
☐ 194	Ron Hassey	.05	.02	.01
☐ 195	Stan Royer	.05	.02	.01
☐ 196	Walt Weiss	.05	.02	.01
☐ 197	Mark McGwire	.30	.14	.04
☐ 198	Carney Lansford	.10	.05	.01
☐ 199	Glenn Hubbard	.05	.02	.01
☐ 200	Dave Henderson	.05	.02	.01
☐ 201	Jose Canseco	.15	.07	.02
☐ 202	Dave Parker	.10	.05	.01
☐ 203	Scott Bankhead	.05	.02	.01
☐ 204	Tom Niedenfuer	.05	.02	.01
☐ 205	Mark Langston	.10	.05	.01
☐ 206	Erik Hanson	.15	.07	.02
☐ 207	Mike Jackson	.05	.02	.01
☐ 208	Dave Valle	.05	.02	.01
☐ 209	Scott Bradley	.05	.02	.01
☐ 210	Harold Reynolds	.05	.02	.01
☐ 211	Tino Martinez	.40	.18	.05
☐ 212	Rich Renteria	.05	.02	.01
☐ 213	Rey Quinones	.05	.02	.01
☐ 214	Jim Presley	.05	.02	.01
☐ 215	Alvin Davis	.05	.02	.01
☐ 216	Edgar Martinez	.25	.11	.03
☐ 217	Darnell Coles	.05	.02	.01
☐ 218	Jeffrey Leonard	.05	.02	.01
☐ 219	Jay Buhner	.25	.11	.03
☐ 220	Ken Griffey Jr.	5.00	2.20	.60
☐ 221	Drew Hall	.05	.02	.01
☐ 222	Bobby Witt	.05	.02	.01
☐ 223	Jamie Moyer	.05	.02	.01
☐ 224	Charlie Hough	.10	.05	.01
☐ 225	Nolan Ryan	.75	.35	.09
☐ 226	Jeff Russell	.05	.02	.01
☐ 227	Jim Sundberg	.05	.02	.01
☐ 228	Julio Franco	.10	.05	.01
☐ 229	Buddy Bell	.10	.05	.01
☐ 230	Scott Fletcher	.05	.02	.01
☐ 231	Jeff Kunkel	.05	.02	.01
☐ 232	Steve Buechele	.05	.02	.01
☐ 233	Monty Fariss	.05	.02	.01
☐ 234	Rick Leach	.05	.02	.01
☐ 235	Ruben Sierra	.15	.07	.02
☐ 236	Cecil Espy	.05	.02	.01
☐ 237	Rafael Palmeiro	.15	.07	.02
☐ 238	Pete Incaviglia	.10	.05	.01
☐ 239	Dave Stieb	.05	.02	.01
☐ 240	Jeff Musselman	.05	.02	.01
☐ 241	Mike Flanagan	.05	.02	.01
☐ 242	Todd Stottlemyre	.10	.05	.01
☐ 243	Jimmy Key	.10	.05	.01
☐ 244	Tony Castillo	.05	.02	.01
☐ 245	Alex Sanchez	.05	.02	.01
☐ 246	Tom Henke	.05	.02	.01
☐ 247	John Cerutti	.05	.02	.01
☐ 248	Ernie Whitt	.05	.02	.01
☐ 249	Bob Brenly	.05	.02	.01
☐ 250	Rance Mulliniks	.05	.02	.01
☐ 251	Kelly Gruber	.05	.02	.01
☐ 252	Ed Sprague	.25	.11	.03
☐ 253	Fred McGriff	.20	.09	.03
☐ 254	Tony Fernandez	.05	.02	.01
☐ 255	Tom Lawless	.05	.02	.01
☐ 256	George Bell	.05	.02	.01
☐ 257	Jesse Barfield	.05	.02	.01
☐ 258	Roberto Alomar Sandy Alomar	.25	.11	.03
☐ 259	Ken Griffey Jr. Ken Griffey Sr.	1.00	.45	.12
☐ 260	Cal Ripken Jr. Cal Ripken Sr.	.30	.14	.04
☐ 261	Mel Stottlemyre Jr. Mel Stottlemyre Sr.	.05	.02	.01
☐ 262	Zane Smith	.05	.02	.01
☐ 263	Charlie Puleo	.05	.02	.01
☐ 264	Derek Lilliquist	.05	.02	.01
☐ 265	Paul Assenmacher	.05	.02	.01
☐ 266	John Smoltz	.75	.35	.09
☐ 267	Tom Glavine	.25	.11	.03
☐ 268	Steve Avery	.40	.18	.05
☐ 269	Pete Smith	.05	.02	.01
☐ 270	Jody Davis	.05	.02	.01
☐ 271	Bruce Benedict	.05	.02	.01
☐ 272	Andres Thomas	.05	.02	.01
☐ 273	Gerald Perry	.05	.02	.01
☐ 274	Ron Gant	.15	.07	.02
☐ 275	Darrell Evans	.10	.05	.01
☐ 276	Dale Murphy	.15	.07	.02
☐ 277	Dion James	.05	.02	.01
☐ 278	Lonnie Smith	.05	.02	.01
☐ 279	Geronimo Berroa	.10	.05	.01
☐ 280	Steve Wilson	.05	.02	.01
☐ 281	Rick Sutcliffe	.05	.02	.01
☐ 282	Kevin Coffman	.05	.02	.01
☐ 283	Mitch Williams	.05	.02	.01
☐ 284	Greg Maddux	.75	.35	.09
☐ 285	Paul Kilgus	.05	.02	.01
☐ 286	Mike Harkey	.05	.02	.01
☐ 287	Lloyd McClendon	.05	.02	.01
☐ 288	Damon Berryhill	.05	.02	.01

□ 289	Ty Griffin	.05	.02	.01
□ 290	Ryne Sandberg	.25	.11	.03
□ 291	Mark Grace	.20	.09	.03
□ 292	Curt Wilkerson	.05	.02	.01
□ 293	Vance Law	.05	.02	.01
□ 294	Shawon Dunston	.05	.02	.01
□ 295	Jerome Walton	.10	.05	.01
□ 296	Mitch Webster	.05	.02	.01
□ 297	Dwight Smith	.10	.05	.01
□ 298	Andre Dawson	.15	.07	.02
□ 299	Jeff Sellers	.05	.02	.01
□ 300	Jose Rijo	.05	.02	.01
□ 301	John Franco	.05	.02	.01
□ 302	Rick Mahler	.05	.02	.01
□ 303	Ron Robinson	.05	.02	.01
□ 304	Danny Jackson	.05	.02	.01
□ 305	Rob Dibble	.10	.05	.01
□ 306	Tom Browning	.05	.02	.01
□ 307	Bo Diaz	.05	.02	.01
□ 308	Manny Trillo	.05	.02	.01
□ 309	Chris Sabo	.05	.02	.01
□ 310	Ron Oester	.05	.02	.01
□ 311	Barry Larkin	.20	.09	.03
□ 312	Todd Benzinger	.05	.02	.01
□ 313	Paul O'Neill	.15	.07	.02
□ 314	Kal Daniels	.05	.02	.01
□ 315	Joel Youngblood	.05	.02	.01
□ 316	Eric Davis	.10	.05	.01
□ 317	Dave Smith	.05	.02	.01
□ 318	Mark Portugal	.05	.02	.01
□ 319	Brian Meyer	.05	.02	.01
□ 320	Jim Deshaies	.05	.02	.01
□ 321	Juan Agosto	.05	.02	.01
□ 322	Mike Scott	.05	.02	.01
□ 323	Rick Rhoden	.05	.02	.01
□ 324	Jim Clancy	.05	.02	.01
□ 325	Larry Andersen	.05	.02	.01
□ 326	Alex Trevino	.05	.02	.01
□ 327	Alan Ashby	.05	.02	.01
□ 328	Craig Reynolds	.05	.02	.01
□ 329	Bill Doran	.05	.02	.01
□ 330	Rafael Ramirez	.05	.02	.01
□ 331	Glenn Davis	.05	.02	.01
□ 332	Willie Ansley	.05	.02	.01
□ 333	Gerald Young	.05	.02	.01
□ 334	Cameron Drew	.05	.02	.01
□ 335	Jay Howell	.05	.02	.01
□ 336	Tim Belcher	.05	.02	.01
□ 337	Fernando Valenzuela	.10	.05	.01
□ 338	Ricky Horton	.05	.02	.01
□ 339	Tim Leary	.05	.02	.01
□ 340	Bill Bene	.05	.02	.01
□ 341	Orel Hershiser	.10	.05	.01
□ 342	Mike Scioscia	.05	.02	.01
□ 343	Rick Dempsey	.05	.02	.01
□ 344	Willie Randolph	.10	.05	.01
□ 345	Alfredo Griffin	.05	.02	.01
□ 346	Eddie Murray	.25	.11	.03
□ 347	Mickey Hatcher	.05	.02	.01
□ 348	Mike Sharperson	.05	.02	.01
□ 349	John Shelby	.05	.02	.01
□ 350	Mike Marshall	.05	.02	.01
□ 351	Kirk Gibson	.10	.05	.01
□ 352	Mike Davis	.05	.02	.01
□ 353	Bryn Smith	.05	.02	.01
□ 354	Pascual Perez	.05	.02	.01
□ 355	Kevin Gross	.05	.02	.01
□ 356	Andy McGaffigan	.05	.02	.01
□ 357	Brian Holman	.05	.02	.01
□ 358	Dave Wainhouse	.05	.02	.01
□ 359	Dennis Martinez	.10	.05	.01
□ 360	Tim Burke	.05	.02	.01
□ 361	Nelson Santovenia	.05	.02	.01
□ 362	Tim Wallach	.05	.02	.01
□ 363	Spike Owen	.05	.02	.01
□ 364	Rex Hudler	.05	.02	.01
□ 365	Andres Galarraga	.15	.07	.02
□ 366	Otis Nixon	.05	.02	.01
□ 367	Hubie Brooks	.05	.02	.01
□ 368	Mike Aldrete	.05	.02	.01
□ 369	Tim Raines	.15	.07	.02
□ 370	Dave Martinez	.05	.02	.01
□ 371	Bob Ojeda	.05	.02	.01
□ 372	Ron Darling	.05	.02	.01
□ 373	Wally Whitehurst	.05	.02	.01
□ 374	Randy Myers	.10	.05	.01
□ 375	David Cone	.15	.07	.02
□ 376	Dwight Gooden	.10	.05	.01
□ 377	Sid Fernandez	.05	.02	.01
□ 378	Dave Proctor	.05	.02	.01
□ 379	Gary Carter	.15	.07	.02
□ 380	Keith Miller	.05	.02	.01
□ 381	Gregg Jefferies	.15	.07	.02
□ 382	Tim Teufel	.05	.02	.01
□ 383	Kevin Elster	.10	.05	.01
□ 384	Dave Magadan	.05	.02	.01
□ 385	Keith Hernandez	.10	.05	.01
□ 386	Mookie Wilson	.10	.05	.01
□ 387	Darryl Strawberry	.10	.05	.01
□ 388	Kevin McReynolds	.05	.02	.01
□ 389	Mark Carreon	.05	.02	.01
□ 390	Jeff Parrett	.05	.02	.01
□ 391	Mike Maddux	.05	.02	.01
□ 392	Don Carman	.05	.02	.01
□ 393	Bruce Ruffin	.05	.02	.01
□ 394	Ken Howell	.05	.02	.01
□ 395	Steve Bedrosian	.05	.02	.01
□ 396	Floyd Youmans	.05	.02	.01
□ 397	Larry McWilliams	.05	.02	.01
□ 398	Pat Combs	.05	.02	.01
□ 399	Steve Lake	.05	.02	.01
□ 400	Dickie Thon	.05	.02	.01
□ 401	Ricky Jordan	.05	.02	.01
□ 402	Mike Schmidt	.20	.09	.03
□ 403	Tom Herr	.05	.02	.01
□ 404	Chris James	.05	.02	.01
□ 405	Juan Samuel	.05	.02	.01
□ 406	Von Hayes	.05	.02	.01
□ 407	Ron Jones	.05	.02	.01
□ 408	Curt Ford	.05	.02	.01
□ 409	Bob Walk	.05	.02	.01
□ 410	Jeff D. Robinson	.05	.02	.01
□ 411	Jim Gott	.05	.02	.01
□ 412	Scott Medvin	.05	.02	.01
□ 413	John Smiley	.05	.02	.01
□ 414	Bob Kipper	.05	.02	.01
□ 415	Brian Fisher	.05	.02	.01
□ 416	Doug Drabek	.10	.05	.01
□ 417	Mike LaValliere	.05	.02	.01
□ 418	Ken Oberkfell	.05	.02	.01
□ 419	Sid Bream	.05	.02	.01
□ 420	Austin Manahan	.05	.02	.01
□ 421	Jose Lind	.05	.02	.01
□ 422	Bobby Bonilla	.10	.05	.01
□ 423	Glenn Wilson	.05	.02	.01
□ 424	Andy Van Slyke	.10	.05	.01
□ 425	Gary Redus	.05	.02	.01
□ 426	Barry Bonds	.40	.18	.05
□ 427	Don Heinkel	.05	.02	.01
□ 428	Ken Dayley	.05	.02	.01
□ 429	Todd Worrell	.05	.02	.01
□ 430	Brad DuVall	.05	.02	.01
□ 431	Jose DeLeon	.05	.02	.01
□ 432	Joe Magrane	.05	.02	.01
□ 433	John Ericks	.05	.02	.01
□ 434	Frank DiPino	.05	.02	.01
□ 435	Tony Pena	.05	.02	.01
□ 436	Ozzie Smith	.20	.09	.03
□ 437	Terry Pendleton	.10	.05	.01
□ 438	Jose Oquendo	.05	.02	.01
□ 439	Tim Jones	.05	.02	.01
□ 440	Pedro Guerrero	.10	.05	.01
□ 441	Milt Thompson	.05	.02	.01
□ 442	Willie McGee	.05	.02	.01
□ 443	Vince Coleman	.05	.02	.01
□ 444	Tom Brunansky	.05	.02	.01
□ 445	Walt Terrell	.05	.02	.01
□ 446	Eric Show	.05	.02	.01
□ 447	Mark Davis	.05	.02	.01
□ 448	Andy Benes	.15	.07	.02
□ 449	Ed Whitson	.05	.02	.01
□ 450	Dennis Rasmussen	.05	.02	.01
□ 451	Bruce Hurst	.05	.02	.01
□ 452	Pat Clements	.05	.02	.01
□ 453	Benito Santiago	.10	.05	.01
□ 454	Sandy Alomar Jr.	.20	.09	.03
□ 455	Garry Templeton	.05	.02	.01
□ 456	Jack Clark	.10	.05	.01
□ 457	Tim Flannery	.05	.02	.01
□ 458	Roberto Alomar	.50	.23	.06
□ 459	Carmelo Martinez	.05	.02	.01
□ 460	John Kruk	.10	.05	.01

□ 461 Tony Gwynn	.40	.18	.05
□ 462 Jerald Clark	.05	.02	.01
□ 463 Don Robinson	.05	.02	.01
□ 464 Craig Lefferts	.05	.02	.01
□ 465 Kelly Downs	.05	.02	.01
□ 466 Rick Reuschel	.05	.02	.01
□ 467 Scott Garrelts	.05	.02	.01
□ 468 Wil Tejada	.05	.02	.01
□ 469 Kirt Manwaring	.05	.02	.01
□ 470 Terry Kennedy	.05	.02	.01
□ 471 Jose Uribe	.05	.02	.01
□ 472 Royce Clayton	.20	.09	.03
□ 473 Robby Thompson	.05	.02	.01
□ 474 Kevin Mitchell	.10	.05	.01
□ 475 Ernie Riles	.05	.02	.01
□ 476 Will Clark	.20	.09	.03
□ 477 Donell Nixon	.05	.02	.01
□ 478 Candy Maldonado	.05	.02	.01
□ 479 Tracy Jones	.05	.02	.01
□ 480 Brett Butler	.10	.05	.01
□ 481 Checklist 1-121	.05	.02	.01
□ 482 Checklist 122-242	.05	.02	.01
□ 483 Checklist 243-363	.05	.02	.01
□ 484 Checklist 364-484	.05	.02	.01

1990 Bowman

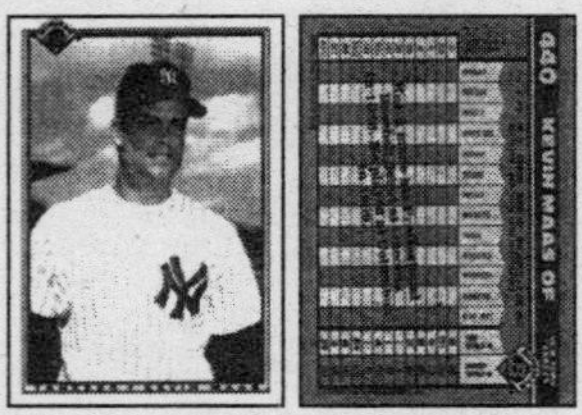

The 1990 Bowman set (produced by Topps) consists of 528 standard-size cards. The cards were issued in wax packs and factory sets. Each wax pack contained one of 11 different 1950's retro art cards. Unlike most sets, player selection focused primarily on rookies instead of proven major leaguers. The cards feature a white border with the player's photo inside and the Bowman logo on top. The card numbering is in team order with the teams themselves being ordered alphabetically within each league. Notable Rookie Cards include Moises Alou, Carlos Baerga, Travis Fryman, Juan Gonzalez, Marquis Grissom, Chuck Knoblauch, Ray Lankford, Ben McDonald, Sammy Sosa, Frank Thomas, Mo Vaughn, Larry Walker, and Bernie Williams.

	MINT	NRMT	EXC
COMPLETE SET (528)	10.00	4.50	1.25
COMPLETE FACT.SET (528)	10.00	4.50	1.25
COMMON CARD (1-528)	.05	.02	.01
SEMISTARS	.10	.05	.01
STARS	.15	.07	.02
COMPLETE ART SET (11)	2.00	.90	.25
ART CARDS: RANDOM INSERTS IN PACKS			

□ 1 Tommy Greene	.05	.02	.01
□ 2 Tom Glavine	.15	.07	.02
□ 3 Andy Nezelek	.05	.02	.01
□ 4 Mike Stanton	.10	.05	.01
□ 5 Rick Luecken	.05	.02	.01
□ 6 Kent Mercker	.10	.05	.01
□ 7 Derek Lilliquist	.05	.02	.01
□ 8 Charlie Leibrandt	.05	.02	.01
□ 9 Steve Avery	.15	.07	.02
□ 10 John Smoltz	.25	.11	.03
□ 11 Mark Lemke	.10	.05	.01
□ 12 Lonnie Smith	.05	.02	.01
□ 13 Oddibe McDowell	.05	.02	.01
□ 14 Tyler Houston	.15	.07	.02
□ 15 Jeff Blauser	.10	.05	.01
□ 16 Ernie Whitt	.05	.02	.01
□ 17 Alexis Infante	.05	.02	.01
□ 18 Jim Presley	.05	.02	.01
□ 19 Dale Murphy	.15	.07	.02
□ 20 Nick Esasky	.05	.02	.01
□ 21 Rick Sutcliffe	.05	.02	.01
□ 22 Mike Bielecki	.05	.02	.01
□ 23 Steve Wilson	.05	.02	.01
□ 24 Kevin Blankenship	.05	.02	.01
□ 25 Mitch Williams	.05	.02	.01
□ 26 Dean Wilkins	.05	.02	.01
□ 27 Greg Maddux	.60	.25	.07
□ 28 Mike Harkey	.05	.02	.01
□ 29 Mark Grace	.15	.07	.02
□ 30 Ryne Sandberg	.25	.11	.03
□ 31 Greg Smith	.05	.02	.01
□ 32 Dwight Smith	.05	.02	.01
□ 33 Damon Berryhill	.05	.02	.01
□ 34 Earl Cunningham UER (Errant * by the word "in")	.05	.02	.01
□ 35 Jerome Walton	.05	.02	.01
□ 36 Lloyd McClendon	.05	.02	.01
□ 37 Ty Griffin	.05	.02	.01
□ 38 Shawon Dunston	.05	.02	.01
□ 39 Andre Dawson	.15	.07	.02
□ 40 Luis Salazar	.05	.02	.01
□ 41 Tim Layana	.05	.02	.01
□ 42 Rob Dibble	.05	.02	.01
□ 43 Tom Browning	.05	.02	.01
□ 44 Danny Jackson	.05	.02	.01
□ 45 Jose Rijo	.05	.02	.01
□ 46 Scott Scudder	.05	.02	.01
□ 47 Randy Myers UER (Career ERA .274, should be 2.74)	.10	.05	.01
□ 48 Brian Lane	.05	.02	.01
□ 49 Paul O'Neill	.10	.05	.01
□ 50 Barry Larkin	.15	.07	.02
□ 51 Reggie Jefferson	.15	.07	.02
□ 52 Jeff Branson	.05	.02	.01
□ 53 Chris Sabo	.05	.02	.01
□ 54 Joe Oliver	.05	.02	.01
□ 55 Todd Benzinger	.05	.02	.01
□ 56 Rolando Roomes	.05	.02	.01
□ 57 Hal Morris	.10	.05	.01
□ 58 Eric Davis	.10	.05	.01
□ 59 Scott Bryant	.05	.02	.01
□ 60 Ken Griffey Sr.	.05	.02	.01
□ 61 Darryl Kile	.10	.05	.01
□ 62 Dave Smith	.05	.02	.01
□ 63 Mark Portugal	.05	.02	.01
□ 64 Jeff Juden	.05	.02	.01
□ 65 Bill Gullickson	.05	.02	.01
□ 66 Danny Darwin	.05	.02	.01
□ 67 Larry Andersen	.05	.02	.01
□ 68 Jose Cano	.05	.02	.01
□ 69 Dan Schatzeder	.05	.02	.01
□ 70 Jim Deshaies	.05	.02	.01
□ 71 Mike Scott	.05	.02	.01
□ 72 Gerald Young	.05	.02	.01
□ 73 Ken Caminiti	.15	.07	.02
□ 74 Ken Oberkfell	.05	.02	.01
□ 75 Dave Rohde	.05	.02	.01
□ 76 Bill Doran	.05	.02	.01
□ 77 Andujar Cedeno	.05	.02	.01
□ 78 Craig Biggio	.15	.07	.02
□ 79 Karl Rhodes	.05	.02	.01
□ 80 Glenn Davis	.05	.02	.01
□ 81 Eric Anthony	.10	.05	.01
□ 82 John Wetteland	.10	.05	.01
□ 83 Jay Howell	.05	.02	.01
□ 84 Orel Hershiser	.10	.05	.01
□ 85 Tim Belcher	.05	.02	.01
□ 86 Kiki Jones	.05	.02	.01
□ 87 Mike Hartley	.05	.02	.01
□ 88 Ramon Martinez	.15	.07	.02
□ 89 Mike Scioscia	.05	.02	.01
□ 90 Willie Randolph	.10	.05	.01
□ 91 Juan Samuel	.05	.02	.01
□ 92 Jose Offerman	.10	.05	.01
□ 93 Dave Hansen	.05	.02	.01
□ 94 Jeff Hamilton	.05	.02	.01
□ 95 Alfredo Griffin	.05	.02	.01

□ 96 Tom Goodwin	.20	.09	.03
□ 97 Kirk Gibson	.10	.05	.01
□ 98 Jose Vizcaino	.15	.07	.02
□ 99 Kal Daniels	.05	.02	.01
□ 100 Hubie Brooks	.05	.02	.01
□ 101 Eddie Murray	.25	.11	.03
□ 102 Dennis Boyd	.05	.02	.01
□ 103 Tim Burke	.05	.02	.01
□ 104 Bill Sampen	.05	.02	.01
□ 105 Brett Gideon	.05	.02	.01
□ 106 Mark Gardner	.05	.02	.01
□ 107 Howard Farmer	.05	.02	.01
□ 108 Mel Rojas	.15	.07	.02
□ 109 Kevin Gross	.05	.02	.01
□ 110 Dave Schmidt	.05	.02	.01
□ 111 Denny Martinez	.10	.05	.01
□ 112 Jerry Goff	.05	.02	.01
□ 113 Andres Galarraga	.15	.07	.02
□ 114 Tim Wallach	.05	.02	.01
□ 115 Marquis Grissom	.60	.25	.07
□ 116 Spike Owen	.05	.02	.01
□ 117 Larry Walker	.50	.23	.06
□ 118 Tim Raines	.15	.07	.02
□ 119 Delino DeShields	.10	.05	.01
□ 120 Tom Foley	.05	.02	.01
□ 121 Dave Martinez	.05	.02	.01
□ 122 Frank Viola UER (Career ERA .384, should be 3.84)	.05	.02	.01
□ 123 Julio Valera	.05	.02	.01
□ 124 Alejandro Pena	.05	.02	.01
□ 125 David Cone	.15	.07	.02
□ 126 Dwight Gooden	.10	.05	.01
□ 127 Kevin D. Brown	.05	.02	.01
□ 128 John Franco	.05	.02	.01
□ 129 Terry Bross	.05	.02	.01
□ 130 Blaine Beatty	.05	.02	.01
□ 131 Sid Fernandez	.05	.02	.01
□ 132 Mike Marshall	.05	.02	.01
□ 133 Howard Johnson	.05	.02	.01
□ 134 Jaime Roseboro	.05	.02	.01
□ 135 Alan Zinter	.05	.02	.01
□ 136 Keith Miller	.05	.02	.01
□ 137 Kevin Elster	.05	.02	.01
□ 138 Kevin McReynolds	.05	.02	.01
□ 139 Barry Lyons	.05	.02	.01
□ 140 Gregg Jefferies	.15	.07	.02
□ 141 Darryl Strawberry	.10	.05	.01
□ 142 Todd Hundley	.60	.25	.07
□ 143 Scott Service	.05	.02	.01
□ 144 Chuck Malone	.05	.02	.01
□ 145 Steve Ontiveros	.05	.02	.01
□ 146 Roger McDowell	.05	.02	.01
□ 147 Ken Howell	.05	.02	.01
□ 148 Pat Combs	.05	.02	.01
□ 149 Jeff Parrett	.05	.02	.01
□ 150 Chuck McElroy	.05	.02	.01
□ 151 Jason Grimsley	.05	.02	.01
□ 152 Len Dykstra	.10	.05	.01
□ 153 Mickey Morandini	.10	.05	.01
□ 154 John Kruk	.10	.05	.01
□ 155 Dickie Thon	.05	.02	.01
□ 156 Ricky Jordan	.05	.02	.01
□ 157 Jeff Jackson	.05	.02	.01
□ 158 Darren Daulton	.10	.05	.01
□ 159 Tom Herr	.05	.02	.01
□ 160 Von Hayes	.05	.02	.01
□ 161 Dave Hollins	.15	.07	.02
□ 162 Carmelo Martinez	.05	.02	.01
□ 163 Bob Walk	.05	.02	.01
□ 164 Doug Drabek	.05	.02	.01
□ 165 Walt Terrell	.05	.02	.01
□ 166 Bill Landrum	.05	.02	.01
□ 167 Scott Ruskin	.05	.02	.01
□ 168 Bob Patterson	.05	.02	.01
□ 169 Bobby Bonilla	.10	.05	.01
□ 170 Jose Lind	.05	.02	.01
□ 171 Andy Van Slyke	.10	.05	.01
□ 172 Mike LaValliere	.05	.02	.01
□ 173 Willie Greene	.15	.07	.02
□ 174 Jay Bell	.10	.05	.01
□ 175 Sid Bream	.05	.02	.01
□ 176 Tom Prince	.05	.02	.01
□ 177 Wally Backman	.05	.02	.01
□ 178 Moises Alou	.20	.09	.03
□ 179 Steve Carter	.05	.02	.01
□ 180 Gary Redus	.05	.02	.01
□ 181 Barry Bonds	.25	.11	.03
□ 182 Don Slaught UER (Card back shows headings for a pitcher)	.05	.02	.01
□ 183 Joe Magrane	.05	.02	.01
□ 184 Bryn Smith	.05	.02	.01
□ 185 Todd Worrell	.05	.02	.01
□ 186 Jose DeLeon	.05	.02	.01
□ 187 Frank DiPino	.05	.02	.01
□ 188 John Tudor	.05	.02	.01
□ 189 Howard Hilton	.05	.02	.01
□ 190 John Ericks	.05	.02	.01
□ 191 Ken Dayley	.05	.02	.01
□ 192 Ray Lankford	.50	.23	.06
□ 193 Todd Zeile	.10	.05	.01
□ 194 Willie McGee	.05	.02	.01
□ 195 Ozzie Smith	.20	.09	.03
□ 196 Milt Thompson	.05	.02	.01
□ 197 Terry Pendleton	.10	.05	.01
□ 198 Vince Coleman	.05	.02	.01
□ 199 Paul Coleman	.05	.02	.01
□ 200 Jose Oquendo	.05	.02	.01
□ 201 Pedro Guerrero	.05	.02	.01
□ 202 Tom Brunansky	.05	.02	.01
□ 203 Roger Smithberg	.05	.02	.01
□ 204 Eddie Whitson	.05	.02	.01
□ 205 Dennis Rasmussen	.05	.02	.01
□ 206 Craig Lefferts	.05	.02	.01
□ 207 Andy Benes	.15	.07	.02
□ 208 Bruce Hurst	.05	.02	.01
□ 209 Eric Show	.05	.02	.01
□ 210 Rafael Valdez	.05	.02	.01
□ 211 Joey Cora	.15	.07	.02
□ 212 Thomas Howard	.05	.02	.01
□ 213 Rob Nelson	.05	.02	.01
□ 214 Jack Clark	.10	.05	.01
□ 215 Garry Templeton	.05	.02	.01
□ 216 Fred Lynn	.05	.02	.01
□ 217 Tony Gwynn	.40	.18	.05
□ 218 Benito Santiago	.05	.02	.01
□ 219 Mike Pagliarulo	.05	.02	.01
□ 220 Joe Carter	.15	.07	.02
□ 221 Roberto Alomar	.30	.14	.04
□ 222 Bip Roberts	.05	.02	.01
□ 223 Rick Reuschel	.05	.02	.01
□ 224 Russ Swan	.05	.02	.01
□ 225 Eric Gunderson	.05	.02	.01
□ 226 Steve Bedrosian	.05	.02	.01
□ 227 Mike Remlinger	.05	.02	.01
□ 228 Scott Garrelts	.05	.02	.01
□ 229 Ernie Camacho	.05	.02	.01
□ 230 Andres Santana	.05	.02	.01
□ 231 Will Clark	.15	.07	.02
□ 232 Kevin Mitchell	.10	.05	.01
□ 233 Robby Thompson	.05	.02	.01
□ 234 Bill Bathe	.05	.02	.01
□ 235 Tony Perezchica	.05	.02	.01
□ 236 Gary Carter	.15	.07	.02
□ 237 Brett Butler	.10	.05	.01
□ 238 Matt Williams	.15	.07	.02
□ 239 Earnie Riles	.05	.02	.01
□ 240 Kevin Bass	.05	.02	.01
□ 241 Terry Kennedy	.05	.02	.01
□ 242 Steve Hosey	.05	.02	.01
□ 243 Ben McDonald	.15	.07	.02
□ 244 Jeff Ballard	.05	.02	.01
□ 245 Joe Price	.05	.02	.01
□ 246 Curt Schilling	.05	.02	.01
□ 247 Pete Harnisch	.05	.02	.01
□ 248 Mark Williamson	.05	.02	.01
□ 249 Gregg Olson	.05	.02	.01
□ 250 Chris Myers	.05	.02	.01
□ 251A David Segui ERR (Missing vital stats at top of card back under name)	.15	.07	.02
□ 251B David Segui COR	.15	.07	.02
□ 252 Joe Orsulak	.05	.02	.01
□ 253 Craig Worthington	.05	.02	.01
□ 254 Mickey Tettleton	.10	.05	.01
□ 255 Cal Ripken	.75	.35	.09
□ 256 Billy Ripken	.05	.02	.01
□ 257 Randy Milligan	.05	.02	.01
□ 258 Brady Anderson	.15	.07	.02
□ 259 Chris Hoiles UER	.15	.07	.02

Baltimore is spelled Balitmore			
□ 260 Mike Devereaux	.05	.02	.01
□ 261 Phil Bradley	.05	.02	.01
□ 262 Leo Gomez	.10	.05	.01
□ 263 Lee Smith	.10	.05	.01
□ 264 Mike Rochford	.05	.02	.01
□ 265 Jeff Reardon	.10	.05	.01
□ 266 Wes Gardner	.05	.02	.01
□ 267 Mike Boddicker	.05	.02	.01
□ 268 Roger Clemens	.15	.07	.02
□ 269 Rob Murphy	.05	.02	.01
□ 270 Mickey Pina	.05	.02	.01
□ 271 Tony Pena	.05	.02	.01
□ 272 Jody Reed	.05	.02	.01
□ 273 Kevin Romine	.05	.02	.01
□ 274 Mike Greenwell	.05	.02	.01
□ 275 Maurice Vaughn	1.50	.70	.19
□ 276 Danny Heep	.05	.02	.01
□ 277 Scott Cooper	.05	.02	.01
□ 278 Greg Blosser	.05	.02	.01
□ 279 Dwight Evans UER (* by "1990 Team Breakdown")	.10	.05	.01
□ 280 Ellis Burks	.15	.07	.02
□ 281 Wade Boggs	.15	.07	.02
□ 282 Marty Barrett	.05	.02	.01
□ 283 Kirk McCaskill	.05	.02	.01
□ 284 Mark Langston	.10	.05	.01
□ 285 Bert Blyleven	.10	.05	.01
□ 286 Mike Fetters	.05	.02	.01
□ 287 Kyle Abbott	.05	.02	.01
□ 288 Jim Abbott	.10	.05	.01
□ 289 Chuck Finley	.10	.05	.01
□ 290 Gary DiSarcina	.15	.07	.02
□ 291 Dick Schofield	.05	.02	.01
□ 292 Devon White	.10	.05	.01
□ 293 Bobby Rose	.05	.02	.01
□ 294 Brian Downing	.05	.02	.01
□ 295 Lance Parrish	.05	.02	.01
□ 296 Jack Howell	.05	.02	.01
□ 297 Claudell Washington	.05	.02	.01
□ 298 John Orton	.05	.02	.01
□ 299 Wally Joyner	.10	.05	.01
□ 300 Lee Stevens	.05	.02	.01
□ 301 Chili Davis	.10	.05	.01
□ 302 Johnny Ray	.05	.02	.01
□ 303 Greg Hibbard	.05	.02	.01
□ 304 Eric King	.05	.02	.01
□ 305 Jack McDowell	.15	.07	.02
□ 306 Bobby Thigpen	.05	.02	.01
□ 307 Adam Peterson	.05	.02	.01
□ 308 Scott Radinsky	.05	.02	.01
□ 309 Wayne Edwards	.05	.02	.01
□ 310 Melido Perez	.05	.02	.01
□ 311 Robin Ventura	.15	.07	.02
□ 312 Sammy Sosa	.75	.35	.09
□ 313 Dan Pasqua	.05	.02	.01
□ 314 Carlton Fisk	.15	.07	.02
□ 315 Ozzie Guillen	.05	.02	.01
□ 316 Ivan Calderon	.05	.02	.01
□ 317 Daryl Boston	.05	.02	.01
□ 318 Craig Grebeck	.05	.02	.01
□ 319 Scott Fletcher	.05	.02	.01
□ 320 Frank Thomas	4.00	1.80	.50
□ 321 Steve Lyons	.05	.02	.01
□ 322 Carlos Martinez	.05	.02	.01
□ 323 Joe Skalski	.05	.02	.01
□ 324 Tom Candiotti	.05	.02	.01
□ 325 Greg Swindell	.05	.02	.01
□ 326 Steve Olin	.10	.05	.01
□ 327 Kevin Wickander	.05	.02	.01
□ 328 Doug Jones	.05	.02	.01
□ 329 Jeff Shaw	.05	.02	.01
□ 330 Kevin Bearse	.05	.02	.01
□ 331 Dion James	.05	.02	.01
□ 332 Jerry Browne	.05	.02	.01
□ 333 Joey Belle	1.00	.45	.12
□ 334 Felix Fermin	.05	.02	.01
□ 335 Candy Maldonado	.05	.02	.01
□ 336 Cory Snyder	.05	.02	.01
□ 337 Sandy Alomar Jr.	.10	.05	.01
□ 338 Mark Lewis	.10	.05	.01
□ 339 Carlos Baerga	.50	.23	.06
□ 340 Chris James	.05	.02	.01
□ 341 Brook Jacoby	.05	.02	.01
□ 342 Keith Hernandez	.10	.05	.01
□ 343 Frank Tanana	.05	.02	.01
□ 344 Scott Aldred	.05	.02	.01
□ 345 Mike Henneman	.05	.02	.01
□ 346 Steve Wapnick	.05	.02	.01
□ 347 Greg Gohr	.05	.02	.01
□ 348 Eric Stone	.05	.02	.01
□ 349 Brian DuBois	.05	.02	.01
□ 350 Kevin Ritz	.05	.02	.01
□ 351 Rico Brogna	.15	.07	.02
□ 352 Mike Heath	.05	.02	.01
□ 353 Alan Trammell	.15	.07	.02
□ 354 Chet Lemon	.05	.02	.01
□ 355 Dave Bergman	.05	.02	.01
□ 356 Lou Whitaker	.15	.07	.02
□ 357 Cecil Fielder UER (* by "1990 Team Breakdown")	.10	.05	.01
□ 358 Milt Cuyler	.05	.02	.01
□ 359 Tony Phillips	.15	.07	.02
□ 360 Travis Fryman	.50	.23	.06
□ 361 Ed Romero	.05	.02	.01
□ 362 Lloyd Moseby	.05	.02	.01
□ 363 Mark Gubicza	.05	.02	.01
□ 364 Bret Saberhagen	.10	.05	.01
□ 365 Tom Gordon	.05	.02	.01
□ 366 Steve Farr	.05	.02	.01
□ 367 Kevin Appier	.15	.07	.02
□ 368 Storm Davis	.05	.02	.01
□ 369 Mark Davis	.05	.02	.01
□ 370 Jeff Montgomery	.10	.05	.01
□ 371 Frank White	.10	.05	.01
□ 372 Brent Mayne	.05	.02	.01
□ 373 Bob Boone	.10	.05	.01
□ 374 Jim Eisenreich	.05	.02	.01
□ 375 Danny Tartabull	.05	.02	.01
□ 376 Kurt Stillwell	.05	.02	.01
□ 377 Bill Pecota	.05	.02	.01
□ 378 Bo Jackson	.15	.07	.02
□ 379 Bob Hamelin	.10	.05	.01
□ 380 Kevin Seitzer	.05	.02	.01
□ 381 Rey Palacios	.05	.02	.01
□ 382 George Brett	.40	.18	.05
□ 383 Gerald Perry	.05	.02	.01
□ 384 Teddy Higuera	.05	.02	.01
□ 385 Tom Filer	.05	.02	.01
□ 386 Dan Plesac	.05	.02	.01
□ 387 Cal Eldred	.10	.05	.01
□ 388 Jaime Navarro	.05	.02	.01
□ 389 Chris Bosio	.05	.02	.01
□ 390 Randy Veres	.05	.02	.01
□ 391 Gary Sheffield	.25	.11	.03
□ 392 George Canale	.05	.02	.01
□ 393 B.J. Surhoff	.10	.05	.01
□ 394 Tim McIntosh	.05	.02	.01
□ 395 Greg Brock	.05	.02	.01
□ 396 Greg Vaughn	.15	.07	.02
□ 397 Darryl Hamilton	.10	.05	.01
□ 398 Dave Parker	.10	.05	.01
□ 399 Paul Molitor	.20	.09	.03
□ 400 Jim Gantner	.05	.02	.01
□ 401 Rob Deer	.05	.02	.01
□ 402 Billy Spiers	.05	.02	.01
□ 403 Glenn Braggs	.05	.02	.01
□ 404 Robin Yount	.15	.07	.02
□ 405 Rick Aguilera	.10	.05	.01
□ 406 Johnny Ard	.05	.02	.01
□ 407 Kevin Tapani	.10	.05	.01
□ 408 Park Pittman	.05	.02	.01
□ 409 Allan Anderson	.05	.02	.01
□ 410 Juan Berenguer	.05	.02	.01
□ 411 Willie Banks	.05	.02	.01
□ 412 Rich Yett	.05	.02	.01
□ 413 Dave West	.05	.02	.01
□ 414 Greg Gagne	.05	.02	.01
□ 415 Chuck Knoblauch	.75	.35	.09
□ 416 Randy Bush	.05	.02	.01
□ 417 Gary Gaetti	.10	.05	.01
□ 418 Kent Hrbek	.10	.05	.01
□ 419 Al Newman	.05	.02	.01
□ 420 Danny Gladden	.05	.02	.01
□ 421 Paul Sorrento	.15	.07	.02
□ 422 Derek Parks	.05	.02	.01
□ 423 Scott Leius	.05	.02	.01
□ 424 Kirby Puckett	.30	.14	.04
□ 425 Willie Smith	.05	.02	.01
□ 426 Dave Righetti	.05	.02	.01

☐ 427 Jeff D. Robinson	.05	.02	.01
☐ 428 Alan Mills	.05	.02	.01
☐ 429 Tim Leary	.05	.02	.01
☐ 430 Pascual Perez	.05	.02	.01
☐ 431 Alvaro Espinoza	.05	.02	.01
☐ 432 Dave Winfield	.15	.07	.02
☐ 433 Jesse Barfield	.05	.02	.01
☐ 434 Randy Velarde	.05	.02	.01
☐ 435 Rick Cerone	.05	.02	.01
☐ 436 Steve Balboni	.05	.02	.01
☐ 437 Mel Hall	.05	.02	.01
☐ 438 Bob Geren	.05	.02	.01
☐ 439 Bernie Williams	.75	.35	.09
☐ 440 Kevin Maas	.05	.02	.01
☐ 441 Mike Blowers	.15	.07	.02
☐ 442 Steve Sax	.05	.02	.01
☐ 443 Don Mattingly	.50	.23	.06
☐ 444 Roberto Kelly	.10	.05	.01
☐ 445 Mike Moore	.05	.02	.01
☐ 446 Reggie Harris	.05	.02	.01
☐ 447 Scott Sanderson	.05	.02	.01
☐ 448 Dave Otto	.05	.02	.01
☐ 449 Dave Stewart	.10	.05	.01
☐ 450 Rick Honeycutt	.05	.02	.01
☐ 451 Dennis Eckersley	.10	.05	.01
☐ 452 Carney Lansford	.10	.05	.01
☐ 453 Scott Hemond	.05	.02	.01
☐ 454 Mark McGwire	.30	.14	.04
☐ 455 Felix Jose	.05	.02	.01
☐ 456 Terry Steinbach	.10	.05	.01
☐ 457 Rickey Henderson	.15	.07	.02
☐ 458 Dave Henderson	.05	.02	.01
☐ 459 Mike Gallego	.05	.02	.01
☐ 460 Jose Canseco	.15	.07	.02
☐ 461 Walt Weiss	.05	.02	.01
☐ 462 Ken Phelps	.05	.02	.01
☐ 463 Darren Lewis	.10	.05	.01
☐ 464 Ron Hassey	.05	.02	.01
☐ 465 Roger Salkeld	.05	.02	.01
☐ 466 Scott Bankhead	.05	.02	.01
☐ 467 Keith Comstock	.05	.02	.01
☐ 468 Randy Johnson	.25	.11	.03
☐ 469 Erik Hanson	.10	.05	.01
☐ 470 Mike Schooler	.05	.02	.01
☐ 471 Gary Eave	.05	.02	.01
☐ 472 Jeffrey Leonard	.05	.02	.01
☐ 473 Dave Valle	.05	.02	.01
☐ 474 Omar Vizquel	.10	.05	.01
☐ 475 Pete O'Brien	.05	.02	.01
☐ 476 Henry Cotto	.05	.02	.01
☐ 477 Jay Buhner	.15	.07	.02
☐ 478 Harold Reynolds	.05	.02	.01
☐ 479 Alvin Davis	.05	.02	.01
☐ 480 Darnell Coles	.05	.02	.01
☐ 481 Ken Griffey Jr.	1.50	.70	.19
☐ 482 Greg Briley	.05	.02	.01
☐ 483 Scott Bradley	.05	.02	.01
☐ 484 Tino Martinez	.15	.07	.02
☐ 485 Jeff Russell	.05	.02	.01
☐ 486 Nolan Ryan	.75	.35	.09
☐ 487 Robb Nen	.15	.07	.02
☐ 488 Kevin Brown	.10	.05	.01
☐ 489 Brian Bohanon	.05	.02	.01
☐ 490 Ruben Sierra	.10	.05	.01
☐ 491 Pete Incaviglia	.05	.02	.01
☐ 492 Juan Gonzalez	2.00	.90	.25
☐ 493 Steve Buechele	.05	.02	.01
☐ 494 Scott Coolbaugh	.05	.02	.01
☐ 495 Geno Petralli	.05	.02	.01
☐ 496 Rafael Palmeiro	.15	.07	.02
☐ 497 Julio Franco	.10	.05	.01
☐ 498 Gary Pettis	.05	.02	.01
☐ 499 Donald Harris	.05	.02	.01
☐ 500 Monty Fariss	.05	.02	.01
☐ 501 Harold Baines	.10	.05	.01
☐ 502 Cecil Espy	.05	.02	.01
☐ 503 Jack Daugherty	.05	.02	.01
☐ 504 Willie Blair	.05	.02	.01
☐ 505 Dave Stieb	.05	.02	.01
☐ 506 Tom Henke	.05	.02	.01
☐ 507 John Cerutti	.05	.02	.01
☐ 508 Paul Kilgus	.05	.02	.01
☐ 509 Jimmy Key	.10	.05	.01
☐ 510 John Olerud	.15	.07	.02
☐ 511 Ed Sprague	.15	.07	.02
☐ 512 Manuel Lee	.05	.02	.01
☐ 513 Fred McGriff	.15	.07	.02
☐ 514 Glenallen Hill	.10	.05	.01
☐ 515 George Bell	.05	.02	.01
☐ 516 Mookie Wilson	.05	.02	.01
☐ 517 Luis Sojo	.05	.02	.01
☐ 518 Nelson Liriano	.05	.02	.01
☐ 519 Kelly Gruber	.05	.02	.01
☐ 520 Greg Myers	.05	.02	.01
☐ 521 Pat Borders	.05	.02	.01
☐ 522 Junior Felix	.05	.02	.01
☐ 523 Eddie Zosky	.05	.02	.01
☐ 524 Tony Fernandez	.05	.02	.01
☐ 525 Checklist 1-132 UER (No copyright mark on the back)	.05	.02	.01
☐ 526 Checklist 133-264	.05	.02	.01
☐ 527 Checklist 265-396	.05	.02	.01
☐ 528 Checklist 397-528	.05	.02	.01

1991 Bowman

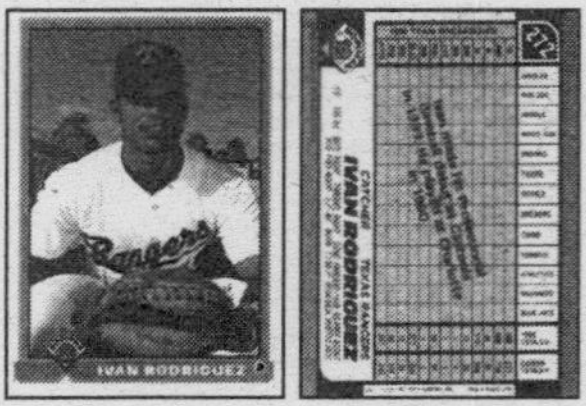

This single-series 704-card standard-size set marked the third straight year that Topps issued a set weighted towards prospects using the Bowman name. Cards were issued in wax packs and factory sets. The cards share a design very similar to the 1990 Bowman set with white borders enframing a color photo. The player name, however, is more prominent than in the previous year set. The cards are arranged in team order by division as follows: AL East, AL West, NL East, and NL West. Subsets include Rod Carew Tribute (1-5), Minor League MVP's (180-185/693-698), AL Silver Sluggers (367-375), NL Silver Sluggers (376-384) and checklists (699-704). Rookie Cards in this set include Jeff Bagwell, Jeff Conine, Carlos Garcia, Pat Hentgen, Chipper Jones, Eric Karros, Ryan Klesko, Kenny Lofton, Javier Lopez, Brian McRae, Raul Mondesi, Mike Mussina, Ivan "Pudge" Rodriguez, Tim Salmon, Reggie Sanders, Jim Thome, Rondell White and Mark Wohlers. There are two instances of misnumbering in the set; Ken Griffey (should be 255) and Ken Griffey Jr. are both numbered 246 and Donovan Osborne (should be 406) and Thomson/Branca share number 410.

	MINT	NRMT	EXC
COMPLETE SET (704)	30.00	13.50	3.70
COMPLETE FACT.SET (704)	30.00	13.50	3.70
COMMON CARD (1-704)	.05	.02	.01
SEMISTARS	.10	.05	.01
STARS	.15	.07	.02

☐ 1 Rod Carew I	.15	.07	.02
☐ 2 Rod Carew II	.15	.07	.02
☐ 3 Rod Carew III	.15	.07	.02
☐ 4 Rod Carew IV	.15	.07	.02
☐ 5 Rod Carew V	.15	.07	.02
☐ 6 Willie Fraser	.05	.02	.01
☐ 7 John Olerud	.10	.05	.01
☐ 8 William Suero	.05	.02	.01
☐ 9 Roberto Alomar	.25	.11	.03
☐ 10 Todd Stottlemyre	.10	.05	.01
☐ 11 Joe Carter	.15	.07	.02
☐ 12 Steve Karsay	.10	.05	.01
☐ 13 Mark Whiten	.10	.05	.01

☐ 14 Pat Borders	.05	.02	.01
☐ 15 Mike Timlin	.05	.02	.01
☐ 16 Tom Henke	.05	.02	.01
☐ 17 Eddie Zosky	.05	.02	.01
☐ 18 Kelly Gruber	.05	.02	.01
☐ 19 Jimmy Key	.10	.05	.01
☐ 20 Jerry Schunk	.05	.02	.01
☐ 21 Manuel Lee	.05	.02	.01
☐ 22 Dave Stieb	.05	.02	.01
☐ 23 Pat Hentgen	.50	.23	.06
☐ 24 Glenallen Hill	.05	.02	.01
☐ 25 Rene Gonzales	.05	.02	.01
☐ 26 Ed Sprague	.10	.05	.01
☐ 27 Ken Dayley	.05	.02	.01
☐ 28 Pat Tabler	.05	.02	.01
☐ 29 Denis Boucher	.05	.02	.01
☐ 30 Devon White	.10	.05	.01
☐ 31 Dante Bichette	.15	.07	.02
☐ 32 Paul Molitor	.20	.09	.03
☐ 33 Greg Vaughn	.15	.07	.02
☐ 34 Dan Plesac	.05	.02	.01
☐ 35 Chris George	.05	.02	.01
☐ 36 Tim McIntosh	.05	.02	.01
☐ 37 Franklin Stubbs	.05	.02	.01
☐ 38 Bo Dodson	.05	.02	.01
☐ 39 Ron Robinson	.05	.02	.01
☐ 40 Ed Nunez	.05	.02	.01
☐ 41 Greg Brock	.05	.02	.01
☐ 42 Jaime Navarro	.05	.02	.01
☐ 43 Chris Bosio	.05	.02	.01
☐ 44 B.J. Surhoff	.10	.05	.01
☐ 45 Chris Johnson	.05	.02	.01
☐ 46 Willie Randolph	.10	.05	.01
☐ 47 Narciso Elvira	.05	.02	.01
☐ 48 Jim Gantner	.05	.02	.01
☐ 49 Kevin Brown	.10	.05	.01
☐ 50 Julio Machado	.05	.02	.01
☐ 51 Chuck Crim	.05	.02	.01
☐ 52 Gary Sheffield	.15	.07	.02
☐ 53 Angel Miranda	.05	.02	.01
☐ 54 Teddy Higuera	.05	.02	.01
☐ 55 Robin Yount	.15	.07	.02
☐ 56 Cal Eldred	.05	.02	.01
☐ 57 Sandy Alomar Jr.	.10	.05	.01
☐ 58 Greg Swindell	.05	.02	.01
☐ 59 Brook Jacoby	.05	.02	.01
☐ 60 Efrain Valdez	.05	.02	.01
☐ 61 Ever Magallanes	.05	.02	.01
☐ 62 Tom Candiotti	.05	.02	.01
☐ 63 Eric King	.05	.02	.01
☐ 64 Alex Cole	.05	.02	.01
☐ 65 Charles Nagy	.10	.05	.01
☐ 66 Mitch Webster	.05	.02	.01
☐ 67 Chris James	.05	.02	.01
☐ 68 Jim Thome	1.50	.70	.19
☐ 69 Carlos Baerga	.15	.07	.02
☐ 70 Mark Lewis	.05	.02	.01
☐ 71 Jerry Browne	.05	.02	.01
☐ 72 Jesse Orosco	.05	.02	.01
☐ 73 Mike Huff	.05	.02	.01
☐ 74 Jose Escobar	.05	.02	.01
☐ 75 Jeff Manto	.05	.02	.01
☐ 76 Turner Ward	.05	.02	.01
☐ 77 Doug Jones	.05	.02	.01
☐ 78 Bruce Egloff	.05	.02	.01
☐ 79 Tim Costo	.05	.02	.01
☐ 80 Beau Allred	.05	.02	.01
☐ 81 Albert Belle	.60	.25	.07
☐ 82 John Farrell	.05	.02	.01
☐ 83 Glenn Davis	.05	.02	.01
☐ 84 Joe Orsulak	.05	.02	.01
☐ 85 Mark Williamson	.05	.02	.01
☐ 86 Ben McDonald	.10	.05	.01
☐ 87 Billy Ripken	.05	.02	.01
☐ 88 Leo Gomez UER	.05	.02	.01
Baltimore is spelled Balitmore			
☐ 89 Bob Melvin	.05	.02	.01
☐ 90 Jeff M. Robinson	.05	.02	.01
☐ 91 Jose Mesa	.10	.05	.01
☐ 92 Gregg Olson	.05	.02	.01
☐ 93 Mike Devereaux	.05	.02	.01
☐ 94 Luis Mercedes	.05	.02	.01
☐ 95 Arthur Rhodes	.10	.05	.01
☐ 96 Juan Bell	.05	.02	.01
☐ 97 Mike Mussina	1.25	.55	.16
☐ 98 Jeff Ballard	.05	.02	.01
☐ 99 Chris Hoiles	.05	.02	.01
☐ 100 Brady Anderson	.15	.07	.02
☐ 101 Bob Milacki	.05	.02	.01
☐ 102 David Segui	.10	.05	.01
☐ 103 Dwight Evans	.10	.05	.01
☐ 104 Cal Ripken	.75	.35	.09
☐ 105 Mike Linskey	.05	.02	.01
☐ 106 Jeff Tackett	.05	.02	.01
☐ 107 Jeff Reardon	.10	.05	.01
☐ 108 Dana Kiecker	.05	.02	.01
☐ 109 Ellis Burks	.15	.07	.02
☐ 110 Dave Owen	.05	.02	.01
☐ 111 Danny Darwin	.05	.02	.01
☐ 112 Mo Vaughn	.50	.23	.06
☐ 113 Jeff McNeely	.05	.02	.01
☐ 114 Tom Bolton	.05	.02	.01
☐ 115 Greg Blosser	.05	.02	.01
☐ 116 Mike Greenwell	.05	.02	.01
☐ 117 Phil Plantier	.10	.05	.01
☐ 118 Roger Clemens	.15	.07	.02
☐ 119 John Marzano	.05	.02	.01
☐ 120 Jody Reed	.05	.02	.01
☐ 121 Scott Taylor	.05	.02	.01
☐ 122 Jack Clark	.10	.05	.01
☐ 123 Derek Livernois	.05	.02	.01
☐ 124 Tony Pena	.05	.02	.01
☐ 125 Tom Brunansky	.05	.02	.01
☐ 126 Carlos Quintana	.05	.02	.01
☐ 127 Tim Naehring	.10	.05	.01
☐ 128 Matt Young	.05	.02	.01
☐ 129 Wade Boggs	.15	.07	.02
☐ 130 Kevin Morton	.05	.02	.01
☐ 131 Pete Incaviglia	.05	.02	.01
☐ 132 Rob Deer	.05	.02	.01
☐ 133 Bill Gullickson	.05	.02	.01
☐ 134 Rico Brogna	.10	.05	.01
☐ 135 Lloyd Moseby	.05	.02	.01
☐ 136 Cecil Fielder	.10	.05	.01
☐ 137 Tony Phillips	.10	.05	.01
☐ 138 Mark Leiter	.05	.02	.01
☐ 139 John Cerutti	.05	.02	.01
☐ 140 Mickey Tettleton	.10	.05	.01
☐ 141 Milt Cuyler	.05	.02	.01
☐ 142 Greg Gohr	.05	.02	.01
☐ 143 Tony Bernazard	.05	.02	.01
☐ 144 Dan Gakeler	.05	.02	.01
☐ 145 Travis Fryman	.15	.07	.02
☐ 146 Dan Petry	.05	.02	.01
☐ 147 Scott Aldred	.05	.02	.01
☐ 148 John DeSilva	.05	.02	.01
☐ 149 Rusty Meacham	.05	.02	.01
☐ 150 Lou Whitaker	.15	.07	.02
☐ 151 Dave Haas	.05	.02	.01
☐ 152 Luis de los Santos	.05	.02	.01
☐ 153 Ivan Cruz	.05	.02	.01
☐ 154 Alan Trammell	.15	.07	.02
☐ 155 Pat Kelly	.10	.05	.01
☐ 156 Carl Everett	.15	.07	.02
☐ 157 Greg Cadaret	.05	.02	.01
☐ 158 Kevin Maas	.05	.02	.01
☐ 159 Jeff Johnson	.05	.02	.01
☐ 160 Willie Smith	.05	.02	.01
☐ 161 Gerald Williams	.05	.02	.01
☐ 162 Mike Humphreys	.05	.02	.01
☐ 163 Alvaro Espinoza	.05	.02	.01
☐ 164 Matt Nokes	.05	.02	.01
☐ 165 Wade Taylor	.05	.02	.01
☐ 166 Roberto Kelly	.05	.02	.01
☐ 167 John Habyan	.05	.02	.01
☐ 168 Steve Farr	.05	.02	.01
☐ 169 Jesse Barfield	.05	.02	.01
☐ 170 Steve Sax	.05	.02	.01
☐ 171 Jim Leyritz	.10	.05	.01
☐ 172 Robert Eenhoorn	.05	.02	.01
☐ 173 Bernie Williams	.25	.11	.03
☐ 174 Scott Lusader	.05	.02	.01
☐ 175 Torey Lovullo	.05	.02	.01
☐ 176 Chuck Cary	.05	.02	.01
☐ 177 Scott Sanderson	.05	.02	.01
☐ 178 Don Mattingly	.50	.23	.06
☐ 179 Mel Hall	.05	.02	.01
☐ 180 Juan Gonzalez	.75	.35	.09
☐ 181 Hensley Meulens	.05	.02	.01
☐ 182 Jose Offerman	.05	.02	.01
☐ 183 Jeff Bagwell	2.50	1.10	.30
☐ 184 Jeff Conine	.50	.23	.06

□	185 Henry Rodriguez	.40	.18	.05
□	186 Jimmie Reese CO	.10	.05	.01
□	187 Kyle Abbott	.05	.02	.01
□	188 Lance Parrish	.05	.02	.01
□	189 Rafael Montalvo	.05	.02	.01
□	190 Floyd Bannister	.05	.02	.01
□	191 Dick Schofield	.05	.02	.01
□	192 Scott Lewis	.05	.02	.01
□	193 Jeff D. Robinson	.05	.02	.01
□	194 Kent Anderson	.05	.02	.01
□	195 Wally Joyner	.10	.05	.01
□	196 Chuck Finley	.10	.05	.01
□	197 Luis Sojo	.05	.02	.01
□	198 Jeff Richardson	.05	.02	.01
□	199 Dave Parker	.10	.05	.01
□	200 Jim Abbott	.10	.05	.01
□	201 Junior Felix	.05	.02	.01
□	202 Mark Langston	.10	.05	.01
□	203 Tim Salmon	1.00	.45	.12
□	204 Cliff Young	.05	.02	.01
□	205 Scott Bailes	.05	.02	.01
□	206 Bobby Rose	.05	.02	.01
□	207 Gary Gaetti	.10	.05	.01
□	208 Ruben Amaro	.05	.02	.01
□	209 Luis Polonia	.05	.02	.01
□	210 Dave Winfield	.15	.07	.02
□	211 Bryan Harvey	.05	.02	.01
□	212 Mike Moore	.05	.02	.01
□	213 Rickey Henderson	.15	.07	.02
□	214 Steve Chitren	.05	.02	.01
□	215 Bob Welch	.05	.02	.01
□	216 Terry Steinbach	.10	.05	.01
□	217 Earnest Riles	.05	.02	.01
□	218 Todd Van Poppel	.10	.05	.01
□	219 Mike Gallego	.05	.02	.01
□	220 Curt Young	.05	.02	.01
□	221 Todd Burns	.05	.02	.01
□	222 Vance Law	.05	.02	.01
□	223 Eric Show	.05	.02	.01
□	224 Don Peters	.05	.02	.01
□	225 Dave Stewart	.10	.05	.01
□	226 Dave Henderson	.05	.02	.01
□	227 Jose Canseco	.15	.07	.02
□	228 Walt Weiss	.05	.02	.01
□	229 Dann Howitt	.05	.02	.01
□	230 Willie Wilson	.05	.02	.01
□	231 Harold Baines	.10	.05	.01
□	232 Scott Hemond	.05	.02	.01
□	233 Joe Slusarski	.05	.02	.01
□	234 Mark McGwire	.30	.14	.04
□	235 Kirk Dressendorfer	.05	.02	.01
□	236 Craig Paquette	.15	.07	.02
□	237 Dennis Eckersley	.10	.05	.01
□	238 Dana Allison	.05	.02	.01
□	239 Scott Bradley	.05	.02	.01
□	240 Brian Holman	.05	.02	.01
□	241 Mike Schooler	.05	.02	.01
□	242 Rich DeLucia	.05	.02	.01
□	243 Edgar Martinez	.15	.07	.02
□	244 Henry Cotto	.05	.02	.01
□	245 Omar Vizquel	.15	.07	.02
□	246 Ken Griffey Jr. (See also 255)	1.50	.70	.19
□	247 Jay Buhner	.15	.07	.02
□	248 Bill Krueger	.05	.02	.01
□	249 Dave Fleming	.10	.05	.01
□	250 Patrick Lennon	.05	.02	.01
□	251 Dave Valle	.05	.02	.01
□	252 Harold Reynolds	.05	.02	.01
□	253 Randy Johnson	.15	.07	.02
□	254 Scott Bankhead	.05	.02	.01
□	255 Ken Griffey Sr. UER (Card number is 246)	.05	.02	.01
□	256 Greg Briley	.05	.02	.01
□	257 Tino Martinez	.15	.07	.02
□	258 Alvin Davis	.05	.02	.01
□	259 Pete O'Brien	.05	.02	.01
□	260 Erik Hanson	.05	.02	.01
□	261 Bret Boone	.15	.07	.02
□	262 Roger Salkeld	.05	.02	.01
□	263 Dave Burba	.05	.02	.01
□	264 Kerry Woodson	.05	.02	.01
□	265 Julio Franco	.10	.05	.01
□	266 Dan Peltier	.05	.02	.01
□	267 Jeff Russell	.05	.02	.01
□	268 Steve Buechele	.05	.02	.01
□	269 Donald Harris	.05	.02	.01
□	270 Robb Nen	.10	.05	.01
□	271 Rich Gossage	.10	.05	.01
□	272 Ivan Rodriguez	1.25	.55	.16
□	273 Jeff Huson	.05	.02	.01
□	274 Kevin Brown	.10	.05	.01
□	275 Dan Smith	.05	.02	.01
□	276 Gary Pettis	.05	.02	.01
□	277 Jack Daugherty	.05	.02	.01
□	278 Mike Jeffcoat	.05	.02	.01
□	279 Brad Arnsberg	.05	.02	.01
□	280 Nolan Ryan	.75	.35	.09
□	281 Eric McCray	.05	.02	.01
□	282 Scott Chiamparino	.05	.02	.01
□	283 Ruben Sierra	.10	.05	.01
□	284 Geno Petralli	.05	.02	.01
□	285 Monty Fariss	.05	.02	.01
□	286 Rafael Palmeiro	.15	.07	.02
□	287 Bobby Witt	.05	.02	.01
□	288 Dean Palmer UER (Photo actually Dan Peltier)	.10	.05	.01
□	289 Tony Scruggs	.05	.02	.01
□	290 Kenny Rogers	.05	.02	.01
□	291 Bret Saberhagen	.10	.05	.01
□	292 Brian McRae	.25	.11	.03
□	293 Storm Davis	.05	.02	.01
□	294 Danny Tartabull	.05	.02	.01
□	295 David Howard	.05	.02	.01
□	296 Mike Boddicker	.05	.02	.01
□	297 Joel Johnston	.05	.02	.01
□	298 Tim Spehr	.05	.02	.01
□	299 Hector Wagner	.05	.02	.01
□	300 George Brett	.40	.18	.05
□	301 Mike Macfarlane	.05	.02	.01
□	302 Kirk Gibson	.10	.05	.01
□	303 Harvey Pulliam	.05	.02	.01
□	304 Jim Eisenreich	.10	.05	.01
□	305 Kevin Seitzer	.05	.02	.01
□	306 Mark Davis	.05	.02	.01
□	307 Kurt Stillwell	.05	.02	.01
□	308 Jeff Montgomery	.10	.05	.01
□	309 Kevin Appier	.10	.05	.01
□	310 Bob Hamelin	.05	.02	.01
□	311 Tom Gordon	.05	.02	.01
□	312 Kerwin Moore	.05	.02	.01
□	313 Hugh Walker	.05	.02	.01
□	314 Terry Shumpert	.05	.02	.01
□	315 Warren Cromartie	.05	.02	.01
□	316 Gary Thurman	.05	.02	.01
□	317 Steve Bedrosian	.05	.02	.01
□	318 Danny Gladden	.05	.02	.01
□	319 Jack Morris	.10	.05	.01
□	320 Kirby Puckett	.30	.14	.04
□	321 Kent Hrbek	.10	.05	.01
□	322 Kevin Tapani	.05	.02	.01
□	323 Denny Neagle	.40	.18	.05
□	324 Rich Garces	.05	.02	.01
□	325 Larry Casian	.05	.02	.01
□	326 Shane Mack	.05	.02	.01
□	327 Allan Anderson	.05	.02	.01
□	328 Junior Ortiz	.05	.02	.01
□	329 Paul Abbott	.05	.02	.01
□	330 Chuck Knoblauch	.25	.11	.03
□	331 Chili Davis	.10	.05	.01
□	332 Todd Ritchie	.05	.02	.01
□	333 Brian Harper	.05	.02	.01
□	334 Rick Aguilera	.10	.05	.01
□	335 Scott Erickson	.10	.05	.01
□	336 Pedro Munoz	.10	.05	.01
□	337 Scott Leius	.05	.02	.01
□	338 Greg Gagne	.05	.02	.01
□	339 Mike Pagliarulo	.05	.02	.01
□	340 Terry Leach	.05	.02	.01
□	341 Willie Banks	.05	.02	.01
□	342 Bobby Thigpen	.05	.02	.01
□	343 Roberto Hernandez	.15	.07	.02
□	344 Melido Perez	.05	.02	.01
□	345 Carlton Fisk	.15	.07	.02
□	346 Norberto Martin	.05	.02	.01
□	347 Johnny Ruffin	.05	.02	.01
□	348 Jeff Carter	.05	.02	.01
□	349 Lance Johnson	.10	.05	.01
□	350 Sammy Sosa	.25	.11	.03
□	351 Alex Fernandez	.15	.07	.02
□	352 Jack McDowell	.10	.05	.01

□	353 Bob Wickman	.05	.02	.01
□	354 Wilson Alvarez	.15	.07	.02
□	355 Charlie Hough	.05	.02	.01
□	356 Ozzie Guillen	.05	.02	.01
□	357 Cory Snyder	.05	.02	.01
□	358 Robin Ventura	.15	.07	.02
□	359 Scott Fletcher	.05	.02	.01
□	360 Cesar Bernhardt	.05	.02	.01
□	361 Dan Pasqua	.05	.02	.01
□	362 Tim Raines	.15	.07	.02
□	363 Brian Drahman	.05	.02	.01
□	364 Wayne Edwards	.05	.02	.01
□	365 Scott Radinsky	.05	.02	.01
□	366 Frank Thomas	2.00	.90	.25
□	367 Cecil Fielder SLUG	.10	.05	.01
□	368 Julio Franco SLUG	.10	.05	.01
□	369 Kelly Gruber SLUG	.05	.02	.01
□	370 Alan Trammell SLUG	.15	.07	.02
□	371 Rickey Henderson SLUG	.15	.07	.02
□	372 Jose Canseco SLUG	.15	.07	.02
□	373 Ellis Burks SLUG	.10	.05	.01
□	374 Lance Parrish SLUG	.05	.02	.01
□	375 Dave Parker SLUG	.10	.05	.01
□	376 Eddie Murray SLUG	.15	.07	.02
□	377 Ryne Sandberg SLUG	.15	.07	.02
□	378 Matt Williams SLUG	.15	.07	.02
□	379 Barry Larkin SLUG	.15	.07	.02
□	380 Barry Bonds SLUG	.15	.07	.02
□	381 Bobby Bonilla SLUG	.10	.05	.01
□	382 Darryl Strawberry SLUG	.10	.05	.01
□	383 Benny Santiago SLUG	.05	.02	.01
□	384 Don Robinson SLUG	.05	.02	.01
□	385 Paul Coleman	.05	.02	.01
□	386 Milt Thompson	.05	.02	.01
□	387 Lee Smith	.10	.05	.01
□	388 Ray Lankford	.15	.07	.02
□	389 Tom Pagnozzi	.05	.02	.01
□	390 Ken Hill	.15	.07	.02
□	391 Jamie Moyer	.05	.02	.01
□	392 Greg Carmona	.05	.02	.01
□	393 John Ericks	.05	.02	.01
□	394 Bob Tewksbury	.05	.02	.01
□	395 Jose Oquendo	.05	.02	.01
□	396 Rheal Cormier	.05	.02	.01
□	397 Mike Milchin	.05	.02	.01
□	398 Ozzie Smith	.20	.09	.03
□	399 Aaron Holbert	.05	.02	.01
□	400 Jose DeLeon	.05	.02	.01
□	401 Felix Jose	.05	.02	.01
□	402 Juan Agosto	.05	.02	.01
□	403 Pedro Guerrero	.05	.02	.01
□	404 Todd Zeile	.10	.05	.01
□	405 Gerald Perry	.05	.02	.01
□	406 Donovan Osborne UER (Card number is 410)	.15	.07	.02
□	407 Bryn Smith	.05	.02	.01
□	408 Bernard Gilkey	.15	.07	.02
□	409 Rex Hudler	.05	.02	.01
□	410 Thomson/Branca Shot Bobby Thomson Ralph Branca (See also 406)	.15	.07	.02
□	411 Lance Dickson	.05	.02	.01
□	412 Danny Jackson	.05	.02	.01
□	413 Jerome Walton	.05	.02	.01
□	414 Sean Cheetham	.05	.02	.01
□	415 Joe Girardi	.10	.05	.01
□	416 Ryne Sandberg	.25	.11	.03
□	417 Mike Harkey	.05	.02	.01
□	418 George Bell	.05	.02	.01
□	419 Rick Wilkins	.05	.02	.01
□	420 Earl Cunningham	.05	.02	.01
□	421 Heathcliff Slocumb	.15	.07	.02
□	422 Mike Bielecki	.05	.02	.01
□	423 Jessie Hollins	.05	.02	.01
□	424 Shawon Dunston	.05	.02	.01
□	425 Dave Smith	.05	.02	.01
□	426 Greg Maddux	.60	.25	.07
□	427 Jose Vizcaino	.05	.02	.01
□	428 Luis Salazar	.05	.02	.01
□	429 Andre Dawson	.15	.07	.02
□	430 Rick Sutcliffe	.05	.02	.01
□	431 Paul Assenmacher	.05	.02	.01
□	432 Erik Pappas	.05	.02	.01
□	433 Mark Grace	.15	.07	.02
□	434 Dennis Martinez	.10	.05	.01
□	435 Marquis Grissom	.15	.07	.02
□	436 Wil Cordero	.15	.07	.02
□	437 Tim Wallach	.05	.02	.01
□	438 Brian Barnes	.05	.02	.01
□	439 Barry Jones	.05	.02	.01
□	440 Ivan Calderon	.05	.02	.01
□	441 Stan Spencer	.05	.02	.01
□	442 Larry Walker	.15	.07	.02
□	443 Chris Haney	.05	.02	.01
□	444 Hector Rivera	.05	.02	.01
□	445 Delino DeShields	.05	.02	.01
□	446 Andres Galarraga	.15	.07	.02
□	447 Gilberto Reyes	.05	.02	.01
□	448 Willie Greene	.10	.05	.01
□	449 Greg Colbrunn	.10	.05	.01
□	450 Rondell White	.50	.23	.06
□	451 Steve Frey	.05	.02	.01
□	452 Shane Andrews	.10	.05	.01
□	453 Mike Fitzgerald	.05	.02	.01
□	454 Spike Owen	.05	.02	.01
□	455 Dave Martinez	.05	.02	.01
□	456 Dennis Boyd	.05	.02	.01
□	457 Eric Bullock	.05	.02	.01
□	458 Reid Cornelius	.05	.02	.01
□	459 Chris Nabholz	.05	.02	.01
□	460 David Cone	.15	.07	.02
□	461 Hubie Brooks	.05	.02	.01
□	462 Sid Fernandez	.05	.02	.01
□	463 Doug Simons	.05	.02	.01
□	464 Howard Johnson	.05	.02	.01
□	465 Chris Donnels	.05	.02	.01
□	466 Anthony Young	.05	.02	.01
□	467 Todd Hundley	.15	.07	.02
□	468 Rick Cerone	.05	.02	.01
□	469 Kevin Elster	.05	.02	.01
□	470 Wally Whitehurst	.05	.02	.01
□	471 Vince Coleman	.05	.02	.01
□	472 Dwight Gooden	.10	.05	.01
□	473 Charlie O'Brien	.05	.02	.01
□	474 Jeromy Burnitz	.10	.05	.01
□	475 John Franco	.05	.02	.01
□	476 Daryl Boston	.05	.02	.01
□	477 Frank Viola	.05	.02	.01
□	478 D.J. Dozier	.05	.02	.01
□	479 Kevin McReynolds	.05	.02	.01
□	480 Tom Herr	.05	.02	.01
□	481 Gregg Jefferies	.15	.07	.02
□	482 Pete Schourek	.15	.07	.02
□	483 Ron Darling	.05	.02	.01
□	484 Dave Magadan	.05	.02	.01
□	485 Andy Ashby	.15	.07	.02
□	486 Dale Murphy	.15	.07	.02
□	487 Von Hayes	.05	.02	.01
□	488 Kim Batiste	.05	.02	.01
□	489 Tony Longmire	.05	.02	.01
□	490 Wally Backman	.05	.02	.01
□	491 Jeff Jackson	.05	.02	.01
□	492 Mickey Morandini	.05	.02	.01
□	493 Darrel Akerfelds	.05	.02	.01
□	494 Ricky Jordan	.05	.02	.01
□	495 Randy Ready	.05	.02	.01
□	496 Darrin Fletcher	.05	.02	.01
□	497 Chuck Malone	.05	.02	.01
□	498 Pat Combs	.05	.02	.01
□	499 Dickie Thon	.05	.02	.01
□	500 Roger McDowell	.05	.02	.01
□	501 Len Dykstra	.10	.05	.01
□	502 Joe Boever	.05	.02	.01
□	503 John Kruk	.10	.05	.01
□	504 Terry Mulholland	.05	.02	.01
□	505 Wes Chamberlain	.05	.02	.01
□	506 Mike Lieberthal	.10	.05	.01
□	507 Darren Daulton	.10	.05	.01
□	508 Charlie Hayes	.05	.02	.01
□	509 John Smiley	.05	.02	.01
□	510 Gary Varsho	.05	.02	.01
□	511 Curt Wilkerson	.05	.02	.01
□	512 Orlando Merced	.15	.07	.02
□	513 Barry Bonds	.25	.11	.03
□	514 Mike LaValliere	.05	.02	.01
□	515 Doug Drabek	.05	.02	.01
□	516 Gary Redus	.05	.02	.01
□	517 William Pennyfeather	.05	.02	.01
□	518 Randy Tomlin	.05	.02	.01
□	519 Mike Zimmerman	.05	.02	.01
□	520 Jeff King	.10	.05	.01

☐ 521	Kurt Miller	.05	.02	.01
☐ 522	Jay Bell	.10	.05	.01
☐ 523	Bill Landrum	.05	.02	.01
☐ 524	Zane Smith	.05	.02	.01
☐ 525	Bobby Bonilla	.10	.05	.01
☐ 526	Bob Walk	.05	.02	.01
☐ 527	Austin Manahan	.05	.02	.01
☐ 528	Joe Ausanio	.05	.02	.01
☐ 529	Andy Van Slyke	.10	.05	.01
☐ 530	Jose Lind	.05	.02	.01
☐ 531	Carlos Garcia	.15	.07	.02
☐ 532	Don Slaught	.05	.02	.01
☐ 533	Gen.Colin Powell	.75	.35	.09
☐ 534	Frank Bolick	.05	.02	.01
☐ 535	Gary Scott	.05	.02	.01
☐ 536	Nikco Riesgo	.05	.02	.01
☐ 537	Reggie Sanders	.50	.23	.06
☐ 538	Tim Howard	.05	.02	.01
☐ 539	Ryan Bowen	.05	.02	.01
☐ 540	Eric Anthony	.05	.02	.01
☐ 541	Jim Deshaies	.05	.02	.01
☐ 542	Tom Nevers	.05	.02	.01
☐ 543	Ken Caminiti	.15	.07	.02
☐ 544	Karl Rhodes	.05	.02	.01
☐ 545	Xavier Hernandez	.05	.02	.01
☐ 546	Mike Scott	.05	.02	.01
☐ 547	Jeff Juden	.05	.02	.01
☐ 548	Darryl Kile	.05	.02	.01
☐ 549	Willie Ansley	.05	.02	.01
☐ 550	Luis Gonzalez	.15	.07	.02
☐ 551	Mike Simms	.05	.02	.01
☐ 552	Mark Portugal	.05	.02	.01
☐ 553	Jimmy Jones	.05	.02	.01
☐ 554	Jim Clancy	.05	.02	.01
☐ 555	Pete Harnisch	.05	.02	.01
☐ 556	Craig Biggio	.15	.07	.02
☐ 557	Eric Yelding	.05	.02	.01
☐ 558	Dave Rohde	.05	.02	.01
☐ 559	Casey Candaele	.05	.02	.01
☐ 560	Curt Schilling	.05	.02	.01
☐ 561	Steve Finley	.15	.07	.02
☐ 562	Javier Ortiz	.05	.02	.01
☐ 563	Andujar Cedeno	.05	.02	.01
☐ 564	Rafael Ramirez	.05	.02	.01
☐ 565	Kenny Lofton	2.00	.90	.25
☐ 566	Steve Avery	.15	.07	.02
☐ 567	Lonnie Smith	.05	.02	.01
☐ 568	Kent Mercker	.05	.02	.01
☐ 569	Chipper Jones	4.00	1.80	.50
☐ 570	Terry Pendleton	.10	.05	.01
☐ 571	Otis Nixon	.05	.02	.01
☐ 572	Juan Berenguer	.05	.02	.01
☐ 573	Charlie Leibrandt	.05	.02	.01
☐ 574	David Justice	.15	.07	.02
☐ 575	Keith Mitchell	.05	.02	.01
☐ 576	Tom Glavine	.15	.07	.02
☐ 577	Greg Olson	.05	.02	.01
☐ 578	Rafael Belliard	.05	.02	.01
☐ 579	Ben Rivera	.05	.02	.01
☐ 580	John Smoltz	.15	.07	.02
☐ 581	Tyler Houston	.05	.02	.01
☐ 582	Mark Wohlers	.40	.18	.05
☐ 583	Ron Gant	.15	.07	.02
☐ 584	Ramon Caraballo	.05	.02	.01
☐ 585	Sid Bream	.05	.02	.01
☐ 586	Jeff Treadway	.05	.02	.01
☐ 587	Javier Lopez	.75	.35	.09
☐ 588	Deion Sanders	.15	.07	.02
☐ 589	Mike Heath	.05	.02	.01
☐ 590	Ryan Klesko	1.50	.70	.19
☐ 591	Bob Ojeda	.05	.02	.01
☐ 592	Alfredo Griffin	.05	.02	.01
☐ 593	Raul Mondesi	1.00	.45	.12
☐ 594	Greg Smith	.05	.02	.01
☐ 595	Orel Hershiser	.10	.05	.01
☐ 596	Juan Samuel	.05	.02	.01
☐ 597	Brett Butler	.10	.05	.01
☐ 598	Gary Carter	.15	.07	.02
☐ 599	Stan Javier	.05	.02	.01
☐ 600	Kal Daniels	.05	.02	.01
☐ 601	Jamie McAndrew	.05	.02	.01
☐ 602	Mike Sharperson	.05	.02	.01
☐ 603	Jay Howell	.05	.02	.01
☐ 604	Eric Karros	.50	.23	.06
☐ 605	Tim Belcher	.05	.02	.01
☐ 606	Dan Opperman	.05	.02	.01
☐ 607	Lenny Harris	.05	.02	.01
☐ 608	Tom Goodwin	.10	.05	.01
☐ 609	Darryl Strawberry	.10	.05	.01
☐ 610	Ramon Martinez	.10	.05	.01
☐ 611	Kevin Gross	.05	.02	.01
☐ 612	Zakary Shinall	.05	.02	.01
☐ 613	Mike Scioscia	.05	.02	.01
☐ 614	Eddie Murray	.25	.11	.03
☐ 615	Ronnie Walden	.05	.02	.01
☐ 616	Will Clark	.15	.07	.02
☐ 617	Adam Hyzdu	.05	.02	.01
☐ 618	Matt Williams	.15	.07	.02
☐ 619	Don Robinson	.05	.02	.01
☐ 620	Jeff Brantley	.05	.02	.01
☐ 621	Greg Litton	.05	.02	.01
☐ 622	Steve Decker	.05	.02	.01
☐ 623	Robby Thompson	.05	.02	.01
☐ 624	Mark Leonard	.05	.02	.01
☐ 625	Kevin Bass	.05	.02	.01
☐ 626	Scott Garrelts	.05	.02	.01
☐ 627	Jose Uribe	.05	.02	.01
☐ 628	Eric Gunderson	.05	.02	.01
☐ 629	Steve Hosey	.05	.02	.01
☐ 630	Trevor Wilson	.05	.02	.01
☐ 631	Terry Kennedy	.05	.02	.01
☐ 632	Dave Righetti	.05	.02	.01
☐ 633	Kelly Downs	.05	.02	.01
☐ 634	Johnny Ard	.05	.02	.01
☐ 635	Eric Christopherson	.05	.02	.01
☐ 636	Kevin Mitchell	.10	.05	.01
☐ 637	John Burkett	.10	.05	.01
☐ 638	Kevin Rogers	.05	.02	.01
☐ 639	Bud Black	.05	.02	.01
☐ 640	Willie McGee	.05	.02	.01
☐ 641	Royce Clayton	.15	.07	.02
☐ 642	Tony Fernandez	.05	.02	.01
☐ 643	Ricky Bones	.05	.02	.01
☐ 644	Thomas Howard	.05	.02	.01
☐ 645	Dave Staton	.05	.02	.01
☐ 646	Jim Presley	.05	.02	.01
☐ 647	Tony Gwynn	.40	.18	.05
☐ 648	Marty Barrett	.05	.02	.01
☐ 649	Scott Coolbaugh	.05	.02	.01
☐ 650	Craig Lefferts	.05	.02	.01
☐ 651	Eddie Whitson	.05	.02	.01
☐ 652	Oscar Azocar	.05	.02	.01
☐ 653	Wes Gardner	.05	.02	.01
☐ 654	Bip Roberts	.05	.02	.01
☐ 655	Robbie Beckett	.05	.02	.01
☐ 656	Benito Santiago	.05	.02	.01
☐ 657	Greg W.Harris	.05	.02	.01
☐ 658	Jerald Clark	.05	.02	.01
☐ 659	Fred McGriff	.15	.07	.02
☐ 660	Larry Andersen	.05	.02	.01
☐ 661	Bruce Hurst	.05	.02	.01
☐ 662	Steve Martin UER Card said he pitched at Waterloo He's an outfielder	.05	.02	.01
☐ 663	Rafael Valdez	.05	.02	.01
☐ 664	Paul Faries	.05	.02	.01
☐ 665	Andy Benes	.05	.02	.01
☐ 666	Randy Myers	.10	.05	.01
☐ 667	Rob Dibble	.05	.02	.01
☐ 668	Glenn Sutko	.05	.02	.01
☐ 669	Glenn Braggs	.05	.02	.01
☐ 670	Billy Hatcher	.05	.02	.01
☐ 671	Joe Oliver	.05	.02	.01
☐ 672	Freddy Benavides	.05	.02	.01
☐ 673	Barry Larkin	.15	.07	.02
☐ 674	Chris Sabo	.05	.02	.01
☐ 675	Mariano Duncan	.05	.02	.01
☐ 676	Chris Jones	.05	.02	.01
☐ 677	Gino Minutelli	.05	.02	.01
☐ 678	Reggie Jefferson	.10	.05	.01
☐ 679	Jack Armstrong	.05	.02	.01
☐ 680	Chris Hammond	.05	.02	.01
☐ 681	Jose Rijo	.05	.02	.01
☐ 682	Bill Doran	.05	.02	.01
☐ 683	Terry Lee	.05	.02	.01
☐ 684	Tom Browning	.05	.02	.01
☐ 685	Paul O'Neill	.10	.05	.01
☐ 686	Eric Davis	.10	.05	.01
☐ 687	Dan Wilson	.25	.11	.03
☐ 688	Ted Power	.05	.02	.01
☐ 689	Tim Layana	.05	.02	.01
☐ 690	Norm Charlton	.05	.02	.01

□ 691 Hal Morris	.05	.02	.01
□ 692 Rickey Henderson	.15	.07	.02
□ 693 Sam Militello	.05	.02	.01
□ 694 Matt Mieske	.05	.02	.01
□ 695 Paul Russo	.05	.02	.01
□ 696 Domingo Mota	.05	.02	.01
□ 697 Todd Guggiana	.05	.02	.01
□ 698 Marc Newfield	.15	.07	.02
□ 699 Checklist 1-122	.05	.02	.01
□ 700 Checklist 123-244	.05	.02	.01
□ 701 Checklist 245-366	.05	.02	.01
□ 702 Checklist 367-471	.05	.02	.01
□ 703 Checklist 472-593	.05	.02	.01
□ 704 Checklist 594-704	.05	.02	.01

1992 Bowman

This 705-card standard-size set was issued in one comprehensive series. Unlike the previous Bowman issues, the 1992 set was radically upgraded to slick stock with gold foil subset cards in an attempt to reposition the brand as a premium level product. It initially stumbled out of the gate, but it's superior selection of prospects enabled it to eventually gain acceptance in the hobby and now stands as one of the more important issues of the 1990's. Cards were distributed in plastic wrap packs, retail jumbo packs and special 80-card retail carton packs. Card fronts feature posed and action color player photos on a UV-coated white card face. A gradated orange bar accented with black diagonal stripes carries the player's name at the bottom right corner. Interspersed throughout the set are 45 special cards with an identical front design except for a textured gold-foil border. The foil cards were inserted one per wax pack and two per jumbo (23 regular cards) pack. These foil cards feature past and present Team USA players and minor league POY Award winners. Each foil card has an extremely slight variation in that the photos are cropped differently. There is no additional value to either version. Some of the regular and special cards picture players in civilian clothing who are still in the farm system. Rookie Cards in this set include Garret Anderson, Carlos Delgado, Alex Gonzalez, Brian Jordan, Alex Ochoa, Mike Piazza, Manny Ramirez, Mariano Rivera and Michael Tucker.

	MINT	NRMT	EXC
COMPLETE SET (705)	300.00	135.00	38.00
COMMON CARD (1-705)	.15	.07	.02
SEMISTARS	.30	.14	.04
STARS	.60	.25	.07
ONE FOIL PER PACK/TWO PER JUMBO			
FIVE FOILS PER 80-CARD CARTON			

□ 1 Ivan Rodriguez	2.50	1.10	.30
□ 2 Kirk McCaskill	.15	.07	.02
□ 3 Scott Livingstone	.15	.07	.02
□ 4 Salomon Torres	.30	.14	.04
□ 5 Carlos Hernandez	.15	.07	.02
□ 6 Dave Hollins	.15	.07	.02
□ 7 Scott Fletcher	.15	.07	.02
□ 8 Jorge Fabregas	.30	.14	.04
□ 9 Andujar Cedeno	.15	.07	.02
□ 10 Howard Johnson	.15	.07	.02
□ 11 Trevor Hoffman	1.50	.70	.19
□ 12 Roberto Kelly	.15	.07	.02
□ 13 Gregg Jefferies	.60	.25	.07
□ 14 Marquis Grissom	1.00	.45	.12
□ 15 Mike Ignasiak	.15	.07	.02
□ 16 Jack Morris	.30	.14	.04
□ 17 William Pennyfeather	.15	.07	.02
□ 18 Todd Stottlemyre	.30	.14	.04
□ 19 Chito Martinez	.15	.07	.02
□ 20 Roberto Alomar	2.00	.90	.25
□ 21 Sam Militello	.15	.07	.02
□ 22 Hector Fajardo	.15	.07	.02
□ 23 Paul Quantrill	.15	.07	.02
□ 24 Chuck Knoblauch	2.00	.90	.25
□ 25 Reggie Jefferson	.30	.14	.04
□ 26 Jeremy McGarity	.15	.07	.02
□ 27 Jerome Walton	.15	.07	.02
□ 28 Chipper Jones	40.00	18.00	5.00
□ 29 Brian Barber	.30	.14	.04
□ 30 Ron Darling	.15	.07	.02
□ 31 Roberto Petagine	.30	.14	.04
□ 32 Chuck Finley	.15	.07	.02
□ 33 Edgar Martinez	.75	.35	.09
□ 34 Napoleon Robinson	.15	.07	.02
□ 35 Andy Van Slyke	.30	.14	.04
□ 36 Bobby Thigpen	.15	.07	.02
□ 37 Travis Fryman	1.25	.55	.16
□ 38 Eric Christopherson	.15	.07	.02
□ 39 Terry Mulholland	.15	.07	.02
□ 40 Darryl Strawberry	.30	.14	.04
□ 41 Manny Alexander	.30	.14	.04
□ 42 Tracy Sanders	.15	.07	.02
□ 43 Pete Incaviglia	.15	.07	.02
□ 44 Kim Batiste	.15	.07	.02
□ 45 Frank Rodriguez	.75	.35	.09
□ 46 Greg Swindell	.15	.07	.02
□ 47 Delino DeShields	.15	.07	.02
□ 48 John Ericks	.15	.07	.02
□ 49 Franklin Stubbs	.15	.07	.02
□ 50 Tony Gwynn	3.00	1.35	.35
□ 51 Clifton Garrett	.15	.07	.02
□ 52 Mike Gardella	.15	.07	.02
□ 53 Scott Erickson	.30	.14	.04
□ 54 Gary Caraballo	.15	.07	.02
□ 55 Jose Oliva	.30	.14	.04
□ 56 Brook Fordyce	.15	.07	.02
□ 57 Mark Whiten	.30	.14	.04
□ 58 Joe Slusarski	.15	.07	.02
□ 59 J.R. Phillips	.30	.14	.04
□ 60 Barry Bonds	2.00	.90	.25
□ 61 Bob Milacki	.15	.07	.02
□ 62 Keith Mitchell	.15	.07	.02
□ 63 Angel Miranda	.15	.07	.02
□ 64 Raul Mondesi	10.00	4.50	1.25
□ 65 Brian Koelling	.15	.07	.02
□ 66 Brian McRae	.60	.25	.07
□ 67 John Patterson	.15	.07	.02
□ 68 John Wetteland	.30	.14	.04
□ 69 Wilson Alvarez	.60	.25	.07
□ 70 Wade Boggs	.60	.25	.07
□ 71 Darryl Ratliff	.15	.07	.02
□ 72 Jeff Jackson	.15	.07	.02
□ 73 Jeremy Hernandez	.15	.07	.02
□ 74 Darryl Hamilton	.15	.07	.02
□ 75 Rafael Belliard	.15	.07	.02
□ 76 Rick Trlicek	.15	.07	.02
□ 77 Felipe Crespo	.30	.14	.04
□ 78 Carney Lansford	.30	.14	.04
□ 79 Ryan Long	.15	.07	.02
□ 80 Kirby Puckett	2.50	1.10	.30
□ 81 Earl Cunningham	.15	.07	.02
□ 82 Pedro Martinez	2.50	1.10	.30
□ 83 Scott Hatteberg	.15	.07	.02
□ 84 Juan Gonzalez UER (65 doubles vs. Tigers)	5.00	2.20	.60
□ 85 Robert Nutting	.15	.07	.02
□ 86 Calvin Reese	.50	.23	.06
□ 87 Dave Silvestri	.15	.07	.02
□ 88 Scott Ruffcorn	.30	.14	.04
□ 89 Rick Aguilera	.15	.07	.02
□ 90 Cecil Fielder	.30	.14	.04
□ 91 Kirk Dressendorfer	.15	.07	.02
□ 92 Jerry DiPoto	.15	.07	.02
□ 93 Mike Felder	.15	.07	.02
□ 94 Craig Paquette	.30	.14	.04
□ 95 Elvin Paulino	.15	.07	.02

☐ 96	Donovan Osborne	.30	.14	.04
☐ 97	Hubie Brooks	.15	.07	.02
☐ 98	Derek Lowe	.30	.14	.04
☐ 99	David Zancanaro	.15	.07	.02
☐ 100	Ken Griffey Jr.	12.00	5.50	1.50
☐ 101	Todd Hundley	1.50	.70	.19
☐ 102	Mike Trombley	.15	.07	.02
☐ 103	Ricky Gutierrez	.15	.07	.02
☐ 104	Braulio Castillo	.15	.07	.02
☐ 105	Craig Lefferts	.15	.07	.02
☐ 106	Rick Sutcliffe	.15	.07	.02
☐ 107	Dean Palmer	.30	.14	.04
☐ 108	Henry Rodriguez	2.00	.90	.25
☐ 109	Mark Clark	.50	.23	.06
☐ 110	Kenny Lofton	12.00	5.50	1.50
☐ 111	Mark Carreon	.15	.07	.02
☐ 112	J.T. Bruett	.15	.07	.02
☐ 113	Gerald Williams	.15	.07	.02
☐ 114	Frank Thomas	12.00	5.50	1.50
☐ 115	Kevin Reimer	.15	.07	.02
☐ 116	Sammy Sosa	1.50	.70	.19
☐ 117	Mickey Tettleton	.15	.07	.02
☐ 118	Reggie Sanders	3.00	1.35	.35
☐ 119	Trevor Wilson	.15	.07	.02
☐ 120	Cliff Brantley	.15	.07	.02
☐ 121	Spike Owen	.15	.07	.02
☐ 122	Jeff Montgomery	.30	.14	.04
☐ 123	Alex Sutherland	.15	.07	.02
☐ 124	Brien Taylor	.30	.14	.04
☐ 125	Brian Williams	.15	.07	.02
☐ 126	Kevin Seitzer	.15	.07	.02
☐ 127	Carlos Delgado	10.00	4.50	1.25
☐ 128	Gary Scott	.15	.07	.02
☐ 129	Scott Cooper	.15	.07	.02
☐ 130	Domingo Jean	.15	.07	.02
☐ 131	Pat Mahomes	.15	.07	.02
☐ 132	Mike Boddicker	.15	.07	.02
☐ 133	Roberto Hernandez	.75	.35	.09
☐ 134	Dave Valle	.15	.07	.02
☐ 135	Kurt Stillwell	.15	.07	.02
☐ 136	Brad Pennington	.30	.14	.04
☐ 137	Jermaine Swinton	.30	.14	.04
☐ 138	Ryan Hawblitzel	.15	.07	.02
☐ 139	Tito Navarro	.15	.07	.02
☐ 140	Sandy Alomar	.30	.14	.04
☐ 141	Todd Benzinger	.15	.07	.02
☐ 142	Danny Jackson	.15	.07	.02
☐ 143	Melvin Nieves	2.00	.90	.25
☐ 144	Jim Campanis	.15	.07	.02
☐ 145	Luis Gonzalez	.30	.14	.04
☐ 146	Dave Doorneweerd	.15	.07	.02
☐ 147	Charlie Hayes	.15	.07	.02
☐ 148	Greg Maddux	6.00	2.70	.75
☐ 149	Brian Harper	.15	.07	.02
☐ 150	Brent Miller	.15	.07	.02
☐ 151	Shawn Estes	1.00	.45	.12
☐ 152	Mike Williams	.15	.07	.02
☐ 153	Charlie Hough	.15	.07	.02
☐ 154	Randy Myers	.30	.14	.04
☐ 155	Kevin Young	.15	.07	.02
☐ 156	Rick Wilkins	.15	.07	.02
☐ 157	Terry Shumpert	.15	.07	.02
☐ 158	Steve Karsay	.30	.14	.04
☐ 159	Gary DiSarcina	.15	.07	.02
☐ 160	Deion Sanders	1.50	.70	.19
☐ 161	Tom Browning	.15	.07	.02
☐ 162	Dickie Thon	.15	.07	.02
☐ 163	Luis Mercedes	.15	.07	.02
☐ 164	Riccardo Ingram	.15	.07	.02
☐ 165	Tavo Alvarez	.30	.14	.04
☐ 166	Rickey Henderson	.60	.25	.07
☐ 167	Jaime Navarro	.15	.07	.02
☐ 168	Billy Ashley	1.00	.45	.12
☐ 169	Phil Dauphin	.15	.07	.02
☐ 170	Ivan Cruz	.15	.07	.02
☐ 171	Harold Baines	.30	.14	.04
☐ 172	Bryan Harvey	.15	.07	.02
☐ 173	Alex Cole	.15	.07	.02
☐ 174	Curtis Shaw	.30	.14	.04
☐ 175	Matt Williams	1.25	.55	.16
☐ 176	Felix Jose	.15	.07	.02
☐ 177	Sam Horn	.15	.07	.02
☐ 178	Randy Johnson	1.25	.55	.16
☐ 179	Ivan Calderon	.15	.07	.02
☐ 180	Steve Avery	.30	.14	.04
☐ 181	William Suero	.15	.07	.02
☐ 182	Bill Swift	.15	.07	.02
☐ 183	Howard Battle	.30	.14	.04
☐ 184	Ruben Amaro	.15	.07	.02
☐ 185	Jim Abbott	.15	.07	.02
☐ 186	Mike Fitzgerald	.15	.07	.02
☐ 187	Bruce Hurst	.15	.07	.02
☐ 188	Jeff Juden	.15	.07	.02
☐ 189	Jeromy Burnitz	.30	.14	.04
☐ 190	Dave Burba	.15	.07	.02
☐ 191	Kevin Brown	.30	.14	.04
☐ 192	Patrick Lennon	.15	.07	.02
☐ 193	Jeff McNeely	.15	.07	.02
☐ 194	Wil Cordero	.75	.35	.09
☐ 195	Chili Davis	.30	.14	.04
☐ 196	Milt Cuyler	.15	.07	.02
☐ 197	Von Hayes	.15	.07	.02
☐ 198	Todd Revenig	.15	.07	.02
☐ 199	Joel Johnston	.15	.07	.02
☐ 200	Jeff Bagwell	5.00	2.20	.60
☐ 201	Alex Fernandez	.60	.25	.07
☐ 202	Todd Jones	.75	.35	.09
☐ 203	Charles Nagy	.30	.14	.04
☐ 204	Tim Raines	.60	.25	.07
☐ 205	Kevin Maas	.15	.07	.02
☐ 206	Julio Franco	.30	.14	.04
☐ 207	Randy Velarde	.15	.07	.02
☐ 208	Lance Johnson	.30	.14	.04
☐ 209	Scott Leius	.15	.07	.02
☐ 210	Derek Lee	.15	.07	.02
☐ 211	Joe Sondrini	.15	.07	.02
☐ 212	Royce Clayton	.30	.14	.04
☐ 213	Chris George	.15	.07	.02
☐ 214	Gary Sheffield	1.25	.55	.16
☐ 215	Mark Gubicza	.15	.07	.02
☐ 216	Mike Moore	.15	.07	.02
☐ 217	Rick Huisman	.15	.07	.02
☐ 218	Jeff Russell	.15	.07	.02
☐ 219	D.J. Dozier	.15	.07	.02
☐ 220	Dave Martinez	.15	.07	.02
☐ 221	Alan Newman	.15	.07	.02
☐ 222	Nolan Ryan	6.00	2.70	.75
☐ 223	Teddy Higuera	.15	.07	.02
☐ 224	Damon Buford	.30	.14	.04
☐ 225	Ruben Sierra	.30	.14	.04
☐ 226	Tom Nevers	.15	.07	.02
☐ 227	Tommy Greene	.15	.07	.02
☐ 228	Nigel Wilson	.30	.14	.04
☐ 229	John DeSilva	.15	.07	.02
☐ 230	Bobby Witt	.15	.07	.02
☐ 231	Greg Cadaret	.15	.07	.02
☐ 232	John Vander Wal	.15	.07	.02
☐ 233	Jack Clark	.30	.14	.04
☐ 234	Bill Doran	.15	.07	.02
☐ 235	Bobby Bonilla	.30	.14	.04
☐ 236	Steve Olin	.15	.07	.02
☐ 237	Derek Bell	2.00	.90	.25
☐ 238	David Cone	.60	.25	.07
☐ 239	Victor Cole	.15	.07	.02
☐ 240	Rod Bolton	.15	.07	.02
☐ 241	Tom Pagnozzi	.15	.07	.02
☐ 242	Rob Dibble	.15	.07	.02
☐ 243	Michael Carter	.15	.07	.02
☐ 244	Don Peters	.15	.07	.02
☐ 245	Mike LaValliere	.15	.07	.02
☐ 246	Joe Perona	.15	.07	.02
☐ 247	Mitch Williams	.15	.07	.02
☐ 248	Jay Buhner	.75	.35	.09
☐ 249	Andy Benes	.15	.07	.02
☐ 250	Alex Ochoa	8.00	3.60	1.00
☐ 251	Greg Blosser	.15	.07	.02
☐ 252	Jack Armstrong	.15	.07	.02
☐ 253	Juan Samuel	.15	.07	.02
☐ 254	Terry Pendleton	.30	.14	.04
☐ 255	Ramon Martinez	.30	.14	.04
☐ 256	Rico Brogna	.30	.14	.04
☐ 257	John Smiley	.15	.07	.02
☐ 258	Carl Everett	.30	.14	.04
☐ 259	Tim Salmon	8.00	3.60	1.00
☐ 260	Will Clark	.75	.35	.09
☐ 261	Ugueth Urbina	1.50	.70	.19
☐ 262	Jason Wood	.15	.07	.02
☐ 263	Dave Magadan	.15	.07	.02
☐ 264	Dante Bichette	.75	.35	.09
☐ 265	Jose DeLeon	.15	.07	.02
☐ 266	Mike Neill	.15	.07	.02
☐ 267	Paul O'Neill	.30	.14	.04

□ 268 Anthony Young	.15	.07	.02
□ 269 Greg W. Harris	.15	.07	.02
□ 270 Todd Van Poppel	.15	.07	.02
□ 271 Pedro Castellano	.15	.07	.02
□ 272 Tony Phillips	.30	.14	.04
□ 273 Mike Gallego	.15	.07	.02
□ 274 Steve Cooke	.30	.14	.04
□ 275 Robin Ventura	.60	.25	.07
□ 276 Kevin Mitchell	.30	.14	.04
□ 277 Doug Linton	.15	.07	.02
□ 278 Robert Eenhoorn	.15	.07	.02
□ 279 Gabe White	.30	.14	.04
□ 280 Dave Stewart	.30	.14	.04
□ 281 Mo Sanford	.15	.07	.02
□ 282 Greg Perschke	.15	.07	.02
□ 283 Kevin Flora	.15	.07	.02
□ 284 Jeff Williams	.15	.07	.02
□ 285 Keith Miller	.15	.07	.02
□ 286 Andy Ashby	.30	.14	.04
□ 287 Doug Dascenzo	.15	.07	.02
□ 288 Eric Karros	3.00	1.35	.35
□ 289 Glenn Murray	.30	.14	.04
□ 290 Troy Percival	2.00	.90	.25
□ 291 Orlando Merced	.30	.14	.04
□ 292 Peter Hoy	.15	.07	.02
□ 293 Tony Fernandez	.15	.07	.02
□ 294 Juan Guzman	.30	.14	.04
□ 295 Jesse Barfield	.15	.07	.02
□ 296 Sid Fernandez	.15	.07	.02
□ 297 Scott Cepicky	.15	.07	.02
□ 298 Garret Anderson	4.00	1.80	.50
□ 299 Cal Eldred	.15	.07	.02
□ 300 Ryne Sandberg	2.00	.90	.25
□ 301 Jim Gantner	.15	.07	.02
□ 302 Mariano Rivera	6.00	2.70	.75
□ 303 Ron Lockett	.15	.07	.02
□ 304 Jose Offerman	.15	.07	.02
□ 305 Denny Martinez	.30	.14	.04
□ 306 Luis Ortiz	.30	.14	.04
□ 307 David Howard	.15	.07	.02
□ 308 Russ Springer	.15	.07	.02
□ 309 Chris Howard	.15	.07	.02
□ 310 Kyle Abbott	.15	.07	.02
□ 311 Aaron Sele	1.00	.45	.12
□ 312 David Justice	.75	.35	.09
□ 313 Pete O'Brien	.15	.07	.02
□ 314 Greg Hansell	.15	.07	.02
□ 315 Dave Winfield	.75	.35	.09
□ 316 Lance Dickson	.15	.07	.02
□ 317 Eric King	.15	.07	.02
□ 318 Vaughn Eshelman	.30	.14	.04
□ 319 Tim Belcher	.15	.07	.02
□ 320 Andres Galarraga	.60	.25	.07
□ 321 Scott Bullett	.15	.07	.02
□ 322 Doug Strange	.15	.07	.02
□ 323 Jerald Clark	.15	.07	.02
□ 324 Dave Righetti	.15	.07	.02
□ 325 Greg Hibbard	.15	.07	.02
□ 326 Eric Hillman	.15	.07	.02
□ 327 Shane Reynolds	3.00	1.35	.35
□ 328 Chris Hammond	.15	.07	.02
□ 329 Albert Belle	5.00	2.20	.60
□ 330 Rich Becker	1.00	.45	.12
□ 331 Eddie Williams	.15	.07	.02
□ 332 Donald Harris	.15	.07	.02
□ 333 Dave Smith	.15	.07	.02
□ 334 Steve Fireovid	.15	.07	.02
□ 335 Steve Buechele	.15	.07	.02
□ 336 Mike Schooler	.15	.07	.02
□ 337 Kevin McReynolds	.15	.07	.02
□ 338 Hensley Meulens	.15	.07	.02
□ 339 Benji Gil	.50	.23	.06
□ 340 Don Mattingly	4.00	1.80	.50
□ 341 Alvin Davis	.15	.07	.02
□ 342 Alan Mills	.15	.07	.02
□ 343 Kelly Downs	.15	.07	.02
□ 344 Leo Gomez	.15	.07	.02
□ 345 Tarrik Brock	.15	.07	.02
□ 346 Ryan Turner	.15	.07	.02
□ 347 John Smoltz	1.25	.55	.16
□ 348 Bill Sampen	.15	.07	.02
□ 349 Paul Byrd	.15	.07	.02
□ 350 Mike Bordick	.30	.14	.04
□ 351 Jose Lind	.15	.07	.02
□ 352 David Wells	.15	.07	.02
□ 353 Barry Larkin	1.00	.45	.12
□ 354 Bruce Ruffin	.15	.07	.02
□ 355 Luis Rivera	.15	.07	.02
□ 356 Sid Bream	.15	.07	.02
□ 357 Julian Vasquez	.15	.07	.02
□ 358 Jason Bere	1.00	.45	.12
□ 359 Ben McDonald	.15	.07	.02
□ 360 Scott Stahoviak	.75	.35	.09
□ 361 Kirt Manwaring	.15	.07	.02
□ 362 Jeff Johnson	.15	.07	.02
□ 363 Rob Deer	.15	.07	.02
□ 364 Tony Pena	.15	.07	.02
□ 365 Melido Perez	.15	.07	.02
□ 366 Clay Parker	.15	.07	.02
□ 367 Dale Sveum	.15	.07	.02
□ 368 Mike Scioscia	.15	.07	.02
□ 369 Roger Salkeld	.15	.07	.02
□ 370 Mike Stanley	.15	.07	.02
□ 371 Jack McDowell	.30	.14	.04
□ 372 Tim Wallach	.15	.07	.02
□ 373 Billy Ripken	.15	.07	.02
□ 374 Mike Christopher	.15	.07	.02
□ 375 Paul Molitor	1.50	.70	.19
□ 376 Dave Stieb	.15	.07	.02
□ 377 Pedro Guerrero	.15	.07	.02
□ 378 Russ Swan	.15	.07	.02
□ 379 Bob Ojeda	.15	.07	.02
□ 380 Donn Pall	.15	.07	.02
□ 381 Eddie Zosky	.15	.07	.02
□ 382 Darnell Coles	.15	.07	.02
□ 383 Tom Smith	.15	.07	.02
□ 384 Mark McGwire	2.50	1.10	.30
□ 385 Gary Carter	.60	.25	.07
□ 386 Rich Amaral	.15	.07	.02
□ 387 Alan Embree	.15	.07	.02
□ 388 Jonathan Hurst	.15	.07	.02
□ 389 Bobby Jones	2.00	.90	.25
□ 390 Rico Rossy	.15	.07	.02
□ 391 Dan Smith	.15	.07	.02
□ 392 Terry Steinbach	.30	.14	.04
□ 393 Jon Farrell	.15	.07	.02
□ 394 Dave Anderson	.15	.07	.02
□ 395 Benny Santiago	.15	.07	.02
□ 396 Mark Wohlers	1.50	.70	.19
□ 397 Mo Vaughn	4.00	1.80	.50
□ 398 Randy Kramer	.15	.07	.02
□ 399 John Jaha	1.50	.70	.19
□ 400 Cal Ripken	6.00	2.70	.75
□ 401 Ryan Bowen	.15	.07	.02
□ 402 Tim McIntosh	.15	.07	.02
□ 403 Bernard Gilkey	.30	.14	.04
□ 404 Junior Felix	.15	.07	.02
□ 405 Cris Colon	.15	.07	.02
□ 406 Marc Newfield	2.00	.90	.25
□ 407 Bernie Williams	2.50	1.10	.30
□ 408 Jay Howell	.15	.07	.02
□ 409 Zane Smith	.15	.07	.02
□ 410 Jeff Shaw	.15	.07	.02
□ 411 Kerry Woodson	.15	.07	.02
□ 412 Wes Chamberlain	.15	.07	.02
□ 413 Dave Mlicki	.15	.07	.02
□ 414 Benny Distefano	.15	.07	.02
□ 415 Kevin Rogers	.15	.07	.02
□ 416 Tim Naehring	.30	.14	.04
□ 417 Clemente Nunez	.50	.23	.06
□ 418 Luis Sojo	.15	.07	.02
□ 419 Kevin Ritz	.15	.07	.02
□ 420 Omar Olivares	.15	.07	.02
□ 421 Manuel Lee	.15	.07	.02
□ 422 Julio Valera	.15	.07	.02
□ 423 Omar Vizquel	.60	.25	.07
□ 424 Darren Burton	.30	.14	.04
□ 425 Mel Hall	.15	.07	.02
□ 426 Dennis Powell	.15	.07	.02
□ 427 Lee Stevens	.15	.07	.02
□ 428 Glenn Davis	.15	.07	.02
□ 429 Willie Greene	.30	.14	.04
□ 430 Kevin Wickander	.15	.07	.02
□ 431 Dennis Eckersley	.30	.14	.04
□ 432 Joe Orsulak	.15	.07	.02
□ 433 Eddie Murray	2.00	.90	.25
□ 434 Matt Stairs	.15	.07	.02
□ 435 Wally Joyner	.30	.14	.04
□ 436 Rondell White	6.00	2.70	.75
□ 437 Rob Maurer	.15	.07	.02
□ 438 Joe Redfield	.15	.07	.02
□ 439 Mark Lewis	.15	.07	.02

□	440	Darren Daulton	.30	.14	.04
□	441	Mike Henneman	.15	.07	.02
□	442	John Cangelosi	.15	.07	.02
□	443	Vince Moore	.15	.07	.02
□	444	John Wehner	.15	.07	.02
□	445	Kent Hrbek	.30	.14	.04
□	446	Mark McLemore	.15	.07	.02
□	447	Bill Wegman	.15	.07	.02
□	448	Robby Thompson	.15	.07	.02
□	449	Mark Anthony	.15	.07	.02
□	450	Archi Cianfrocco	.15	.07	.02
□	451	Johnny Ruffin	.15	.07	.02
□	452	Javier Lopez	8.00	3.60	1.00
□	453	Greg Gohr	.15	.07	.02
□	454	Tim Scott	.15	.07	.02
□	455	Stan Belinda	.15	.07	.02
□	456	Darrin Jackson	.15	.07	.02
□	457	Chris Gardner	.15	.07	.02
□	458	Esteban Beltre	.15	.07	.02
□	459	Phil Plantier	.30	.14	.04
□	460	Jim Thome	15.00	6.75	1.85
□	461	Mike Piazza	60.00	27.00	7.50
□	462	Matt Sinatro	.15	.07	.02
□	463	Scott Servais	.15	.07	.02
□	464	Brian Jordan	5.00	2.20	.60
□	465	Doug Drabek	.15	.07	.02
□	466	Carl Willis	.15	.07	.02
□	467	Bret Barberie	.15	.07	.02
□	468	Hal Morris	.15	.07	.02
□	469	Steve Sax	.15	.07	.02
□	470	Jerry Willard	.15	.07	.02
□	471	Dan Wilson	.75	.35	.09
□	472	Chris Hoiles	.15	.07	.02
□	473	Rheal Cormier	.15	.07	.02
□	474	John Morris	.15	.07	.02
□	475	Jeff Reardon	.30	.14	.04
□	476	Mark Leiter	.15	.07	.02
□	477	Tom Gordon	.15	.07	.02
□	478	Kent Bottenfield	.15	.07	.02
□	479	Gene Larkin	.15	.07	.02
□	480	Dwight Gooden	.30	.14	.04
□	481	B.J. Surhoff	.30	.14	.04
□	482	Andy Stankiewicz	.15	.07	.02
□	483	Tino Martinez	.60	.25	.07
□	484	Craig Biggio	.60	.25	.07
□	485	Denny Neagle	1.50	.70	.19
□	486	Rusty Meacham	.15	.07	.02
□	487	Kal Daniels	.15	.07	.02
□	488	Dave Henderson	.15	.07	.02
□	489	Tim Costo	.15	.07	.02
□	490	Doug Davis	.15	.07	.02
□	491	Frank Viola	.15	.07	.02
□	492	Cory Snyder	.15	.07	.02
□	493	Chris Martin	.15	.07	.02
□	494	Dion James	.15	.07	.02
□	495	Randy Tomlin	.15	.07	.02
□	496	Greg Vaughn	.60	.25	.07
□	497	Dennis Cook	.15	.07	.02
□	498	Rosario Rodriguez	.15	.07	.02
□	499	Dave Staton	.15	.07	.02
□	500	George Brett	3.00	1.35	.35
□	501	Brian Barnes	.15	.07	.02
□	502	Butch Henry	.15	.07	.02
□	503	Harold Reynolds	.15	.07	.02
□	504	David Nied	.30	.14	.04
□	505	Lee Smith	.30	.14	.04
□	506	Steve Chitren	.15	.07	.02
□	507	Ken Hill	.60	.25	.07
□	508	Robbie Beckett	.15	.07	.02
□	509	Troy Afenir	.15	.07	.02
□	510	Kelly Gruber	.15	.07	.02
□	511	Bret Boone	.60	.25	.07
□	512	Jeff Branson	.15	.07	.02
□	513	Mike Jackson	.15	.07	.02
□	514	Pete Harnisch	.15	.07	.02
□	515	Chad Kreuter	.15	.07	.02
□	516	Joe Vitko	.15	.07	.02
□	517	Orel Hershiser	.30	.14	.04
□	518	John Doherty	.15	.07	.02
□	519	Jay Bell	.30	.14	.04
□	520	Mark Langston	.30	.14	.04
□	521	Dann Howitt	.15	.07	.02
□	522	Bobby Reed	.15	.07	.02
□	523	Roberto Munoz	.15	.07	.02
□	524	Todd Ritchie	.30	.14	.04
□	525	Bip Roberts	.15	.07	.02
□	526	Pat Listach	.30	.14	.04
□	527	Scott Brosius	.50	.23	.06
□	528	John Roper	.30	.14	.04
□	529	Phil Hiatt	.30	.14	.04
□	530	Denny Walling	.15	.07	.02
□	531	Carlos Baerga	1.25	.55	.16
□	532	Manny Ramirez	25.00	11.00	3.10
□	533	Pat Clements UER	.15	.07	.02
		(Mistakenly numbered 553)			
□	534	Ron Gant	.60	.25	.07
□	535	Pat Kelly	.15	.07	.02
□	536	Billy Spiers	.15	.07	.02
□	537	Darren Reed	.15	.07	.02
□	538	Ken Caminiti	.60	.25	.07
□	539	Butch Huskey	2.50	1.10	.30
□	540	Matt Nokes	.15	.07	.02
□	541	John Kruk	.30	.14	.04
□	542	John Jaha FOIL	.60	.25	.07
□	543	Justin Thompson	1.25	.55	.16
□	544	Steve Hosey	.15	.07	.02
□	545	Joe Kmak	.15	.07	.02
□	546	John Franco	.15	.07	.02
□	547	Devon White	.30	.14	.04
□	548	Elston Hansen FOIL	.15	.07	.02
□	549	Ryan Klesko	15.00	6.75	1.85
□	550	Danny Tartabull	.15	.07	.02
□	551	Frank Thomas FOIL	15.00	6.75	1.85
□	552	Kevin Tapani	.15	.07	.02
□	553	Willie Banks	.15	.07	.02
		(See also 533)			
□	554	B.J. Wallace FOIL	.30	.14	.04
□	555	Orlando Miller	.50	.23	.06
□	556	Mark Smith	.30	.14	.04
□	557	Tim Wallach FOIL	.15	.07	.02
□	558	Bill Gullickson	.15	.07	.02
□	559	Derek Bell FOIL	.75	.35	.09
□	560	Joe Randa FOIL	.60	.25	.07
□	561	Frank Seminara	.15	.07	.02
□	562	Mark Gardner	.15	.07	.02
□	563	Rick Greene FOIL	.15	.07	.02
□	564	Gary Gaetti	.30	.14	.04
□	565	Ozzie Guillen	.15	.07	.02
□	566	Charles Nagy FOIL	.30	.14	.04
□	567	Mike Milchin	.15	.07	.02
□	568	Ben Shelton	.15	.07	.02
□	569	Chris Roberts FOIL	.30	.14	.04
□	570	Ellis Burks	.60	.25	.07
□	571	Scott Scudder	.15	.07	.02
□	572	Jim Abbott FOIL	.15	.07	.02
□	573	Joe Carter	.75	.35	.09
□	574	Steve Finley	.60	.25	.07
□	575	Jim Olander FOIL	.15	.07	.02
□	576	Carlos Garcia	.30	.14	.04
□	577	Gregg Olson	.15	.07	.02
□	578	Greg Swindell FOIL	.15	.07	.02
□	579	Matt Williams FOIL	1.25	.55	.16
□	580	Mark Grace	.60	.25	.07
□	581	Howard House FOIL	.15	.07	.02
□	582	Luis Polonia	.15	.07	.02
□	583	Erik Hanson	.15	.07	.02
□	584	Salomon Torres FOIL	.30	.14	.04
□	585	Carlton Fisk	.60	.25	.07
□	586	Bret Saberhagen	.30	.14	.04
□	587	Chad McConnell FOIL	.30	.14	.04
□	588	Jimmy Key	.30	.14	.04
□	589	Mike Macfarlane	.15	.07	.02
□	590	Barry Bonds FOIL	2.00	.90	.25
□	591	Jamie McAndrew	.15	.07	.02
□	592	Shane Mack	.15	.07	.02
□	593	Kerwin Moore	.15	.07	.02
□	594	Joe Oliver	.15	.07	.02
□	595	Chris Sabo	.15	.07	.02
□	596	Alex Gonzalez	4.00	1.80	.50
□	597	Brett Butler	.30	.14	.04
□	598	Mark Hutton	.15	.07	.02
□	599	Andy Benes FOIL	.15	.07	.02
□	600	Jose Canseco	.75	.35	.09
□	601	Darryl Kile	.15	.07	.02
□	602	Matt Stairs FOIL	.15	.07	.02
□	603	Robert Butler FOIL	.30	.14	.04
□	604	Willie McGee	.15	.07	.02
□	605	Jack McDowell FOIL	.30	.14	.04
□	606	Tom Candiotti	.15	.07	.02
□	607	Ed Martel	.15	.07	.02
□	608	Matt Mieske FOIL	.30	.14	.04
□	609	Darrin Fletcher	.15	.07	.02

□ 610 Rafael Palmeiro	.75	.35	.09
□ 611 Bill Swift FOIL	.15	.07	.02
□ 612 Mike Mussina	2.50	1.10	.30
□ 613 Vince Coleman	.15	.07	.02
□ 614 Scott Cepicky FOIL UER (Bats: LEFLT)	.15	.07	.02
□ 615 Mike Greenwell	.15	.07	.02
□ 616 Kevin McGehee	.15	.07	.02
□ 617 Jeffrey Hammonds FOIL	2.00	.90	.25
□ 618 Scott Taylor	.15	.07	.02
□ 619 Dave Otto	.15	.07	.02
□ 620 Mark McGwire FOIL	2.50	1.10	.30
□ 621 Kevin Tatar	.15	.07	.02
□ 622 Steve Farr	.15	.07	.02
□ 623 Ryan Klesko FOIL	4.00	1.80	.50
□ 624 Dave Fleming	.15	.07	.02
□ 625 Andre Dawson	.60	.25	.07
□ 626 Tino Martinez FOIL	.60	.25	.07
□ 627 Chad Curtis	.60	.25	.07
□ 628 Mickey Morandini	.15	.07	.02
□ 629 Gregg Olson FOIL	.15	.07	.02
□ 630 Lou Whitaker	.60	.25	.07
□ 631 Arthur Rhodes	.15	.07	.02
□ 632 Brandon Wilson	.15	.07	.02
□ 633 Lance Jennings	.15	.07	.02
□ 634 Allen Watson	.30	.14	.04
□ 635 Len Dykstra	.30	.14	.04
□ 636 Joe Girardi	.15	.07	.02
□ 637 Kiki Hernandez FOIL	.15	.07	.02
□ 638 Mike Hampton	1.00	.45	.12
□ 639 Al Osuna	.15	.07	.02
□ 640 Kevin Appier	.75	.35	.09
□ 641 Rick Helling FOIL	.30	.14	.04
□ 642 Jody Reed	.15	.07	.02
□ 643 Ray Lankford	1.25	.55	.16
□ 644 John Olerud	.30	.14	.04
□ 645 Paul Molitor FOIL	1.50	.70	.19
□ 646 Pat Borders	.15	.07	.02
□ 647 Mike Morgan	.15	.07	.02
□ 648 Larry Walker	.75	.35	.09
□ 649 Pedro Castellano FOIL	.15	.07	.02
□ 650 Fred McGriff	1.00	.45	.12
□ 651 Walt Weiss	.15	.07	.02
□ 652 Calvin Murray FOIL	.30	.14	.04
□ 653 Dave Nilsson	.60	.25	.07
□ 654 Greg Pirkl	.15	.07	.02
□ 655 Robin Ventura FOIL	.60	.25	.07
□ 656 Mark Portugal	.15	.07	.02
□ 657 Roger McDowell	.15	.07	.02
□ 658 Rick Hirtensteiner FOIL	.15	.07	.02
□ 659 Glenallen Hill	.15	.07	.02
□ 660 Greg Gagne	.15	.07	.02
□ 661 Charles Johnson FOIL	5.00	2.20	.60
□ 662 Brian Hunter	.15	.07	.02
□ 663 Mark Lemke	.15	.07	.02
□ 664 Tim Belcher FOIL	.15	.07	.02
□ 665 Rich DeLucia	.15	.07	.02
□ 666 Bob Walk	.15	.07	.02
□ 667 Joe Carter FOIL	.75	.35	.09
□ 668 Jose Guzman	.15	.07	.02
□ 669 Otis Nixon	.15	.07	.02
□ 670 Phil Nevin FOIL	.30	.14	.04
□ 671 Eric Davis	.30	.14	.04
□ 672 Damion Easley	.30	.14	.04
□ 673 Will Clark FOIL	.75	.35	.09
□ 674 Mark Kiefer	.15	.07	.02
□ 675 Ozzie Smith	1.50	.70	.19
□ 676 Manny Ramirez FOIL	6.00	2.70	.75
□ 677 Gregg Olson	.15	.07	.02
□ 678 Cliff Floyd	2.50	1.10	.30
□ 679 Duane Singleton	.30	.14	.04
□ 680 Jose Rijo	.15	.07	.02
□ 681 Willie Randolph	.30	.14	.04
□ 682 Michael Tucker FOIL	2.50	1.10	.30
□ 683 Darren Lewis	.15	.07	.02
□ 684 Dale Murphy	.60	.25	.07
□ 685 Mike Pagliarulo	.15	.07	.02
□ 686 Paul Miller	.15	.07	.02
□ 687 Mike Robertson	.15	.07	.02
□ 688 Mike Devereaux	.15	.07	.02
□ 689 Pedro Astacio	.30	.14	.04
□ 690 Alan Trammell	.60	.25	.07
□ 691 Roger Clemens	.75	.35	.09
□ 692 Bud Black	.15	.07	.02
□ 693 Turk Wendell	.30	.14	.04
□ 694 Barry Larkin FOIL	1.00	.45	.12
□ 695 Todd Zeile	.15	.07	.02
□ 696 Pat Hentgen	2.50	1.10	.30
□ 697 Eddie Taubensee	.15	.07	.02
□ 698 Guillermo Velasquez	.15	.07	.02
□ 699 Tom Glavine	.75	.35	.09
□ 700 Robin Yount	1.00	.45	.12
□ 701 Checklist 1-141	.15	.07	.02
□ 702 Checklist 142-282	.15	.07	.02
□ 703 Checklist 283-423	.15	.07	.02
□ 704 Checklist 424-564	.15	.07	.02
□ 705 Checklist 565-705	.15	.07	.02

1993 Bowman

This 708-card standard-size set was issued in one series and features one of the more comprehensive selection of prospects and rookies available that year. Cards were distributed in 14-card plastic wrapped packs and jumbo packs. Each 14-card pack contained one silver foil bordered subset card. The basic issue card fronts feature white-bordered color action player photos. The player's name appears in white lettering at the bottom right, with his last name printed on an ocher rectangle. The 48 foil subset cards (339-374 and 693-704) feature sixteen 1992 MVPs of the Minor Leagues, top prospects and a few father/son combinations. Rookie Cards in this set include James Baldwin, Trey Beamon, Roger Cedeno, Danny Clyburn, Marty Cordova, Brian L. Hunter, Derek Jeter, Jason Kendall and Andy Pettite.

	MINT	NRMT	EXC
COMPLETE SET (708)	60.00	27.00	7.50
COMMON CARD (1-708)	.10	.05	.01
SEMISTARS	.25	.11	.03
STARS	.50	.23	.06
ONE FOIL PER PACK/2 PER JUMBO			

□ 1 Glenn Davis	.10	.05	.01
□ 2 Hector Roa	.10	.05	.01
□ 3 Ken Ryan	.10	.05	.01
□ 4 Derek Wallace	.10	.05	.01
□ 5 Jorge Fabregas	.25	.11	.03
□ 6 Joe Oliver	.10	.05	.01
□ 7 Brandon Wilson	.10	.05	.01
□ 8 Mark Thompson	.25	.11	.03
□ 9 Tracy Sanders	.10	.05	.01
□ 10 Rich Renteria	.10	.05	.01
□ 11 Lou Whitaker	.50	.23	.06
□ 12 Brian Hunter	2.00	.90	.25
□ 13 Joe Vitiello	.25	.11	.03
□ 14 Eric Karros	.50	.23	.06
□ 15 Joe Kmak	.10	.05	.01
□ 16 Tavo Alvarez	.10	.05	.01
□ 17 Steve Dunn	.25	.11	.03
□ 18 Tony Fernandez	.10	.05	.01
□ 19 Melido Perez	.10	.05	.01
□ 20 Mike Lieberthal	.10	.05	.01
□ 21 Terry Steinbach	.25	.11	.03
□ 22 Stan Belinda	.10	.05	.01
□ 23 Jay Buhner	.50	.23	.06
□ 24 Allen Watson	.10	.05	.01
□ 25 Daryl Henderson	.10	.05	.01
□ 26 Ray McDavid	.25	.11	.03
□ 27 Shawn Green	1.00	.45	.12
□ 28 Bud Black	.10	.05	.01

□ 29	Sherman Obando	.10	.05	.01
□ 30	Mike Hostetler	.10	.05	.01
□ 31	Nate Minchey	.25	.11	.03
□ 32	Randy Myers	.25	.11	.03
□ 33	Brian Grebeck	.10	.05	.01
□ 34	John Roper	.10	.05	.01
□ 35	Larry Thomas	.10	.05	.01
□ 36	Alex Cole	.10	.05	.01
□ 37	Tom Kramer	.10	.05	.01
□ 38	Matt Whisenant	.10	.05	.01
□ 39	Chris Gomez	.25	.11	.03
□ 40	Luis Gonzalez	.10	.05	.01
□ 41	Kevin Appier	.25	.11	.03
□ 42	Omar Daal	.25	.11	.03
□ 43	Duane Singleton	.10	.05	.01
□ 44	Bill Risley	.10	.05	.01
□ 45	Pat Meares	.25	.11	.03
□ 46	Butch Huskey	.25	.11	.03
□ 47	Bobby Munoz	.10	.05	.01
□ 48	Juan Bell	.10	.05	.01
□ 49	Scott Lydy	.10	.05	.01
□ 50	Dennis Moeller	.10	.05	.01
□ 51	Marc Newfield	.25	.11	.03
□ 52	Tripp Cromer	.10	.05	.01
□ 53	Kurt Miller	.10	.05	.01
□ 54	Jim Pena	.10	.05	.01
□ 55	Juan Guzman	.25	.11	.03
□ 56	Matt Williams	.50	.23	.06
□ 57	Harold Reynolds	.10	.05	.01
□ 58	Donnie Elliott	.10	.05	.01
□ 59	Jon Shave	.10	.05	.01
□ 60	Kevin Roberson	.10	.05	.01
□ 61	Hilly Hathaway	.10	.05	.01
□ 62	Jose Rijo	.10	.05	.01
□ 63	Kerry Taylor	.10	.05	.01
□ 64	Ryan Hawblitzel	.10	.05	.01
□ 65	Glenallen Hill	.10	.05	.01
□ 66	Ramon Martinez	.25	.11	.03
□ 67	Travis Fryman	.50	.23	.06
□ 68	Tom Nevers	.10	.05	.01
□ 69	Phil Hiatt	.10	.05	.01
□ 70	Tim Wallach	.10	.05	.01
□ 71	B.J. Surhoff	.25	.11	.03
□ 72	Rondell White	.60	.25	.07
□ 73	Denny Hocking	.25	.11	.03
□ 74	Mike Oquist	.10	.05	.01
□ 75	Paul O'Neill	.25	.11	.03
□ 76	Willie Banks	.10	.05	.01
□ 77	Bob Welch	.10	.05	.01
□ 78	Jose Sandoval	.10	.05	.01
□ 79	Bill Haselman	.10	.05	.01
□ 80	Rheal Cormier	.10	.05	.01
□ 81	Dean Palmer	.25	.11	.03
□ 82	Pat Gomez	.10	.05	.01
□ 83	Steve Karsay	.25	.11	.03
□ 84	Carl Hanselman	.10	.05	.01
□ 85	T.R. Lewis	.10	.05	.01
□ 86	Chipper Jones	4.00	1.80	.50
□ 87	Scott Hatteberg	.10	.05	.01
□ 88	Greg Hibbard	.10	.05	.01
□ 89	Lance Painter	.10	.05	.01
□ 90	Chad Mottola	.25	.11	.03
□ 91	Jason Bere	.25	.11	.03
□ 92	Dante Bichette	.50	.23	.06
□ 93	Sandy Alomar Jr.	.25	.11	.03
□ 94	Carl Everett	.25	.11	.03
□ 95	Danny Bautista	.25	.11	.03
□ 96	Steve Finley	.50	.23	.06
□ 97	David Cone	.50	.23	.06
□ 98	Todd Hollandsworth	2.00	.90	.25
□ 99	Matt Mieske	.25	.11	.03
□ 100	Larry Walker	.50	.23	.06
□ 101	Shane Mack	.10	.05	.01
□ 102	Aaron Ledesma	.10	.05	.01
□ 103	Andy Pettitte	6.00	2.70	.75
□ 104	Kevin Stocker	.25	.11	.03
□ 105	Mike Mohler	.10	.05	.01
□ 106	Tony Menendez	.10	.05	.01
□ 107	Derek Lowe	.25	.11	.03
□ 108	Basil Shabazz	.10	.05	.01
□ 109	Dan Smith	.10	.05	.01
□ 110	Scott Sanders	.10	.05	.01
□ 111	Todd Stottlemyre	.25	.11	.03
□ 112	Benji Simonton	.10	.05	.01
□ 113	Rick Sutcliffe	.10	.05	.01
□ 114	Lee Heath	.10	.05	.01
□ 115	Jeff Russell	.10	.05	.01
□ 116	Dave Stevens	.25	.11	.03
□ 117	Mark Holzemer	.10	.05	.01
□ 118	Tim Belcher	.10	.05	.01
□ 119	Bobby Thigpen	.10	.05	.01
□ 120	Roger Bailey	.10	.05	.01
□ 121	Tony Mitchell	.10	.05	.01
□ 122	Junior Felix	.10	.05	.01
□ 123	Rich Robertson	.10	.05	.01
□ 124	Andy Cook	.10	.05	.01
□ 125	Brian Bevil	.25	.11	.03
□ 126	Darryl Strawberry	.25	.11	.03
□ 127	Cal Eldred	.10	.05	.01
□ 128	Cliff Floyd	.25	.11	.03
□ 129	Alan Newman	.10	.05	.01
□ 130	Howard Johnson	.10	.05	.01
□ 131	Jim Abbott	.10	.05	.01
□ 132	Chad McConnell	.10	.05	.01
□ 133	Miguel Jimenez	.25	.11	.03
□ 134	Brett Backlund	.10	.05	.01
□ 135	John Cummings	.10	.05	.01
□ 136	Brian Barber	.10	.05	.01
□ 137	Rafael Palmeiro	.50	.23	.06
□ 138	Tim Worrell	.10	.05	.01
□ 139	Jose Pett	.50	.23	.06
□ 140	Barry Bonds	.75	.35	.09
□ 141	Damon Buford	.10	.05	.01
□ 142	Jeff Blauser	.10	.05	.01
□ 143	Frankie Rodriguez	.25	.11	.03
□ 144	Mike Morgan	.10	.05	.01
□ 145	Gary DiSarcina	.10	.05	.01
□ 146	Calvin Reese	.50	.23	.06
□ 147	Johnny Ruffin	.10	.05	.01
□ 148	David Nied	.10	.05	.01
□ 149	Charles Nagy	.25	.11	.03
□ 150	Mike Myers	.10	.05	.01
□ 151	Kenny Carlyle	.10	.05	.01
□ 152	Eric Anthony	.10	.05	.01
□ 153	Jose Lind	.10	.05	.01
□ 154	Pedro Martinez	.50	.23	.06
□ 155	Mark Kiefer	.10	.05	.01
□ 156	Tim Laker	.10	.05	.01
□ 157	Pat Mahomes	.10	.05	.01
□ 158	Bobby Bonilla	.25	.11	.03
□ 159	Domingo Jean	.10	.05	.01
□ 160	Darren Daulton	.25	.11	.03
□ 161	Mark McGwire	1.00	.45	.12
□ 162	Jason Kendall	3.00	1.35	.35
□ 163	Desi Relaford	.25	.11	.03
□ 164	Ozzie Canseco	.10	.05	.01
□ 165	Rick Helling	.25	.11	.03
□ 166	Steve Pegues	.10	.05	.01
□ 167	Paul Molitor	.60	.25	.07
□ 168	Larry Carter	.10	.05	.01
□ 169	Arthur Rhodes	.10	.05	.01
□ 170	Damon Hollins	.50	.23	.06
□ 171	Frank Viola	.10	.05	.01
□ 172	Steve Trachsel	.25	.11	.03
□ 173	J.T. Snow	.50	.23	.06
□ 174	Keith Gordon	.10	.05	.01
□ 175	Carlton Fisk	.50	.23	.06
□ 176	Jason Bates	.25	.11	.03
□ 177	Mike Crosby	.10	.05	.01
□ 178	Benny Santiago	.10	.05	.01
□ 179	Mike Moore	.10	.05	.01
□ 180	Jeff Juden	.10	.05	.01
□ 181	Darren Burton	.10	.05	.01
□ 182	Todd Williams	.10	.05	.01
□ 183	John Jaha	.25	.11	.03
□ 184	Mike Lansing	.25	.11	.03
□ 185	Pedro Grifol	.10	.05	.01
□ 186	Vince Coleman	.10	.05	.01
□ 187	Pat Kelly	.10	.05	.01
□ 188	Clemente Alvarez	.25	.11	.03
□ 189	Ron Darling	.10	.05	.01
□ 190	Orlando Merced	.25	.11	.03
□ 191	Chris Bosio	.10	.05	.01
□ 192	Steve Dixon	.10	.05	.01
□ 193	Doug Dascenzo	.10	.05	.01
□ 194	Ray Holbert	.10	.05	.01
□ 195	Howard Battle	.25	.11	.03
□ 196	Willie McGee	.10	.05	.01
□ 197	John O'Donoghue	.10	.05	.01
□ 198	Steve Avery	.25	.11	.03
□ 199	Greg Blosser	.10	.05	.01
□ 200	Ryne Sandberg	.75	.35	.09

□	201	Joe Grahe	.10	.05	.01
□	202	Dan Wilson	.25	.11	.03
□	203	Domingo Martinez	.10	.05	.01
□	204	Andres Galarraga	.50	.23	.06
□	205	Jamie Taylor	.10	.05	.01
□	206	Darrell Whitmore	.10	.05	.01
□	207	Ben Blomdahl	.10	.05	.01
□	208	Doug Drabek	.10	.05	.01
□	209	Keith Miller	.10	.05	.01
□	210	Billy Ashley	.10	.05	.01
□	211	Mike Farrell	.10	.05	.01
□	212	John Wetteland	.25	.11	.03
□	213	Randy Tomlin	.10	.05	.01
□	214	Sid Fernandez	.10	.05	.01
□	215	Quilvio Veras	.25	.11	.03
□	216	Dave Hollins	.10	.05	.01
□	217	Mike Neill	.10	.05	.01
□	218	Andy Van Slyke	.25	.11	.03
□	219	Bret Boone	.25	.11	.03
□	220	Tom Pagnozzi	.10	.05	.01
□	221	Mike Welch	.10	.05	.01
□	222	Frank Seminara	.10	.05	.01
□	223	Ron Villone	.25	.11	.03
□	224	D.J. Thielen	.10	.05	.01
□	225	Cal Ripken	2.50	1.10	.30
□	226	Pedro Borbon Jr.	.25	.11	.03
□	227	Carlos Quintana	.10	.05	.01
□	228	Tommy Shields	.10	.05	.01
□	229	Tim Salmon	.75	.35	.09
□	230	John Smiley	.10	.05	.01
□	231	Ellis Burks	.50	.23	.06
□	232	Pedro Castellano	.10	.05	.01
□	233	Paul Byrd	.10	.05	.01
□	234	Bryan Harvey	.10	.05	.01
□	235	Scott Livingstone	.10	.05	.01
□	236	James Mouton	.25	.11	.03
□	237	Joe Randa	.25	.11	.03
□	238	Pedro Astacio	.10	.05	.01
□	239	Darryl Hamilton	.10	.05	.01
□	240	Joey Eischen	.25	.11	.03
□	241	Edgar Herrera	.25	.11	.03
□	242	Dwight Gooden	.25	.11	.03
□	243	Sam Militello	.10	.05	.01
□	244	Ron Blazier	.25	.11	.03
□	245	Ruben Sierra	.25	.11	.03
□	246	Al Martin	.25	.11	.03
□	247	Mike Felder	.10	.05	.01
□	248	Bob Tewksbury	.10	.05	.01
□	249	Craig Lefferts	.10	.05	.01
□	250	Luis Lopez	.10	.05	.01
□	251	Devon White	.10	.05	.01
□	252	Will Clark	.50	.23	.06
□	253	Mark Smith	.25	.11	.03
□	254	Terry Pendleton	.25	.11	.03
□	255	Aaron Sele	.25	.11	.03
□	256	Jose Viera	.25	.11	.03
□	257	Damion Easley	.10	.05	.01
□	258	Rod Lofton	.10	.05	.01
□	259	Chris Snopek	.50	.23	.06
□	260	Quinton McCracken	.25	.11	.03
□	261	Mike Matthews	.25	.11	.03
□	262	Hector Carrasco	.25	.11	.03
□	263	Rick Greene	.25	.11	.03
□	264	Chris Holt	.10	.05	.01
□	265	George Brett	1.25	.55	.16
□	266	Rick Gorecki	.10	.05	.01
□	267	Francisco Gamez	.10	.05	.01
□	268	Marquis Grissom	.50	.23	.06
□	269	Kevin Tapani UER (Misspelled Tapan on card front)	.10	.05	.01
□	270	Ryan Thompson	.10	.05	.01
□	271	Gerald Williams	.10	.05	.01
□	272	Paul Fletcher	.10	.05	.01
□	273	Lance Blankenship	.10	.05	.01
□	274	Marty Neff	.10	.05	.01
□	275	Shawn Estes	.10	.05	.01
□	276	Rene Arocha	.10	.05	.01
□	277	Scott Eyre	.10	.05	.01
□	278	Phil Plantier	.10	.05	.01
□	279	Paul Spoljaric	.25	.11	.03
□	280	Chris Gambs	.10	.05	.01
□	281	Harold Baines	.25	.11	.03
□	282	Jose Oliva	.10	.05	.01
□	283	Matt Whiteside	.10	.05	.01
□	284	Brant Brown	.10	.05	.01
□	285	Russ Springer	.10	.05	.01
□	286	Chris Sabo	.10	.05	.01
□	287	Ozzie Guillen	.10	.05	.01
□	288	Marcus Moore	.10	.05	.01
□	289	Chad Ogea	.25	.11	.03
□	290	Walt Weiss	.10	.05	.01
□	291	Brian Edmondson	.10	.05	.01
□	292	Jimmy Gonzalez	.10	.05	.01
□	293	Danny Miceli	.25	.11	.03
□	294	Jose Offerman	.10	.05	.01
□	295	Greg Vaughn	.50	.23	.06
□	296	Frank Bolick	.10	.05	.01
□	297	Mike Maksudian	.10	.05	.01
□	298	John Franco	.10	.05	.01
□	299	Danny Tartabull	.10	.05	.01
□	300	Len Dykstra	.25	.11	.03
□	301	Bobby Witt	.10	.05	.01
□	302	Trey Beamon	1.25	.55	.16
□	303	Tino Martinez	.25	.11	.03
□	304	Aaron Holbert	.25	.11	.03
□	305	Juan Gonzalez	1.50	.70	.19
□	306	Billy Hall	.10	.05	.01
□	307	Duane Ward	.10	.05	.01
□	308	Rod Beck	.25	.11	.03
□	309	Jose Mercedes	.10	.05	.01
□	310	Otis Nixon	.10	.05	.01
□	311	Gettys Glaze	.10	.05	.01
□	312	Candy Maldonado	.10	.05	.01
□	313	Chad Curtis	.25	.11	.03
□	314	Tim Costo	.10	.05	.01
□	315	Mike Robertson	.10	.05	.01
□	316	Nigel Wilson	.10	.05	.01
□	317	Greg McMichael	.25	.11	.03
□	318	Scott Pose	.10	.05	.01
□	319	Ivan Cruz	.10	.05	.01
□	320	Greg Swindell	.10	.05	.01
□	321	Kevin McReynolds	.10	.05	.01
□	322	Tom Candiotti	.10	.05	.01
□	323	Rob Wishnevski	.10	.05	.01
□	324	Ken Hill	.25	.11	.03
□	325	Kirby Puckett	1.00	.45	.12
□	326	Tim Bogar	.10	.05	.01
□	327	Mariano Rivera	.60	.25	.07
□	328	Mitch Williams	.10	.05	.01
□	329	Craig Paquette	.10	.05	.01
□	330	Jay Bell	.25	.11	.03
□	331	Jose Martinez	.10	.05	.01
□	332	Rob Deer	.10	.05	.01
□	333	Brook Fordyce	.10	.05	.01
□	334	Matt Nokes	.10	.05	.01
□	335	Derek Lee	.10	.05	.01
□	336	Paul Ellis	.10	.05	.01
□	337	Desi Wilson	.10	.05	.01
□	338	Roberto Alomar	.75	.35	.09
□	339	Jim Tatum FOIL	.10	.05	.01
□	340	J.T. Snow FOIL	.50	.23	.06
□	341	Tim Salmon FOIL	.75	.35	.09
□	342	Russ Davis FOIL	.25	.11	.03
□	343	Javier Lopez FOIL	.75	.35	.09
□	344	Troy O'Leary FOIL	.50	.23	.06
□	345	Marty Cordova FOIL	2.50	1.10	.30
□	346	Bubba Smith FOIL	.10	.05	.01
□	347	Chipper Jones FOIL	4.00	1.80	.50
□	348	Jessie Hollins FOIL	.10	.05	.01
□	349	Willie Greene FOIL	.25	.11	.03
□	350	Mark Thompson FOIL	.25	.11	.03
□	351	Nigel Wilson FOIL	.10	.05	.01
□	352	Todd Jones FOIL	.25	.11	.03
□	353	Raul Mondesi FOIL	1.00	.45	.12
□	354	Cliff Floyd FOIL	.25	.11	.03
□	355	Bobby Jones FOIL	.25	.11	.03
□	356	Kevin Stocker FOIL	.25	.11	.03
□	357	Midre Cummings FOIL	.25	.11	.03
□	358	Allen Watson FOIL	.10	.05	.01
□	359	Ray McDavid FOIL	.10	.05	.01
□	360	Steve Hosey FOIL	.10	.05	.01
□	361	Brad Pennington FOIL	.10	.05	.01
□	362	Frankie Rodriguez FOIL	.25	.11	.03
□	363	Troy Percival FOIL	.25	.11	.03
□	364	Jason Bere FOIL	.25	.11	.03
□	365	Manny Ramirez FOIL	2.00	.90	.25
□	366	Justin Thompson FOIL	.25	.11	.03
□	367	Joe Vitiello FOIL	.25	.11	.03
□	368	Tyrone Hill FOIL	.10	.05	.01
□	369	David McCarty FOIL	.10	.05	.01
□	370	Brien Taylor FOIL	.10	.05	.01

□	371	Todd Van Poppel FOIL	.10	.05	.01
□	372	Marc Newfield FOIL	.25	.11	.03
□	373	Terrell Lowery FOIL	.10	.05	.01
□	374	Alex Gonzalez FOIL	.50	.23	.06
□	375	Ken Griffey Jr.	3.00	1.35	.35
□	376	Donovan Osborne	.10	.05	.01
□	377	Ritchie Moody	.10	.05	.01
□	378	Shane Andrews	.25	.11	.03
□	379	Carlos Delgado	.75	.35	.09
□	380	Bill Swift	.10	.05	.01
□	381	Leo Gomez	.10	.05	.01
□	382	Ron Gant	.50	.23	.06
□	383	Scott Fletcher	.10	.05	.01
□	384	Matt Walbeck	.10	.05	.01
□	385	Chuck Finley	.10	.05	.01
□	386	Kevin Mitchell	.25	.11	.03
□	387	Wilson Alvarez UER (Misspelled Alverez on card front)	.25	.11	.03
□	388	John Burke	.10	.05	.01
□	389	Alan Embree	.10	.05	.01
□	390	Trevor Hoffman	.25	.11	.03
□	391	Alan Trammell	.50	.23	.06
□	392	Todd Jones	.25	.11	.03
□	393	Felix Jose	.10	.05	.01
□	394	Orel Hershiser	.25	.11	.03
□	395	Pat Listach	.10	.05	.01
□	396	Gabe White	.25	.11	.03
□	397	Dan Serafini	.50	.23	.06
□	398	Todd Hundley	.50	.23	.06
□	399	Wade Boggs	.50	.23	.06
□	400	Tyler Green	.10	.05	.01
□	401	Mike Bordick	.10	.05	.01
□	402	Scott Bullett	.10	.05	.01
□	403	LaGrande Russell	.10	.05	.01
□	404	Ray Lankford	.50	.23	.06
□	405	Nolan Ryan	2.50	1.10	.30
□	406	Robbie Beckett	.10	.05	.01
□	407	Brent Bowers	.25	.11	.03
□	408	Adell Davenport	.10	.05	.01
□	409	Brady Anderson	.50	.23	.06
□	410	Tom Glavine	.50	.23	.06
□	411	Doug Hecker	.10	.05	.01
□	412	Jose Guzman	.10	.05	.01
□	413	Luis Polonia	.10	.05	.01
□	414	Brian Williams	.10	.05	.01
□	415	Bo Jackson	.50	.23	.06
□	416	Eric Young	.50	.23	.06
□	417	Kenny Lofton	1.25	.55	.16
□	418	Orestes Destrade	.10	.05	.01
□	419	Tony Phillips	.25	.11	.03
□	420	Jeff Bagwell	1.25	.55	.16
□	421	Mark Gardner	.10	.05	.01
□	422	Brett Butler	.25	.11	.03
□	423	Graeme Lloyd	.10	.05	.01
□	424	Delino DeShields	.10	.05	.01
□	425	Scott Erickson	.10	.05	.01
□	426	Jeff Kent	.25	.11	.03
□	427	Jimmy Key	.25	.11	.03
□	428	Mickey Morandini	.10	.05	.01
□	429	Marcos Armas	.10	.05	.01
□	430	Don Slaught	.10	.05	.01
□	431	Randy Johnson	.50	.23	.06
□	432	Omar Olivares	.10	.05	.01
□	433	Charlie Leibrandt	.10	.05	.01
□	434	Kurt Stillwell	.10	.05	.01
□	435	Scott Brow	.10	.05	.01
□	436	Robby Thompson	.10	.05	.01
□	437	Ben McDonald	.10	.05	.01
□	438	Deion Sanders	.50	.23	.06
□	439	Tony Pena	.10	.05	.01
□	440	Mark Grace	.50	.23	.06
□	441	Eduardo Perez	.10	.05	.01
□	442	Tim Pugh	.10	.05	.01
□	443	Scott Ruffcorn	.10	.05	.01
□	444	Jay Gainer	.10	.05	.01
□	445	Albert Belle	1.50	.70	.19
□	446	Bret Barberie	.10	.05	.01
□	447	Justin Mashore	.10	.05	.01
□	448	Pete Harnisch	.10	.05	.01
□	449	Greg Gagne	.10	.05	.01
□	450	Eric Davis	.25	.11	.03
□	451	Dave Mlicki	.10	.05	.01
□	452	Moises Alou	.50	.23	.06
□	453	Rick Aguilera	.10	.05	.01
□	454	Eddie Murray	.75	.35	.09
□	455	Bob Wickman	.10	.05	.01
□	456	Wes Chamberlain	.10	.05	.01
□	457	Brent Gates	.25	.11	.03
□	458	Paul Wagner	.10	.05	.01
□	459	Mike Hampton	.10	.05	.01
□	460	Ozzie Smith	.60	.25	.07
□	461	Tom Henke	.10	.05	.01
□	462	Ricky Gutierrez	.10	.05	.01
□	463	Jack Morris	.25	.11	.03
□	464	Joel Chimelis	.10	.05	.01
□	465	Gregg Olson	.10	.05	.01
□	466	Javier Lopez	.75	.35	.09
□	467	Scott Cooper	.10	.05	.01
□	468	Willie Wilson	.10	.05	.01
□	469	Mark Langston	.25	.11	.03
□	470	Barry Larkin	.50	.23	.06
□	471	Rod Bolton	.10	.05	.01
□	472	Freddie Benavides	.10	.05	.01
□	473	Ken Ramos	.10	.05	.01
□	474	Chuck Carr	.10	.05	.01
□	475	Cecil Fielder	.25	.11	.03
□	476	Eddie Taubensee	.10	.05	.01
□	477	Chris Eddy	.10	.05	.01
□	478	Greg Hansell	.10	.05	.01
□	479	Kevin Reimer	.10	.05	.01
□	480	Denny Martinez	.25	.11	.03
□	481	Chuck Knoblauch	.50	.23	.06
□	482	Mike Draper	.10	.05	.01
□	483	Spike Owen	.10	.05	.01
□	484	Terry Mulholland	.10	.05	.01
□	485	Dennis Eckersley	.25	.11	.03
□	486	Blas Minor	.10	.05	.01
□	487	Dave Fleming	.10	.05	.01
□	488	Dan Cholowsky	.10	.05	.01
□	489	Ivan Rodriguez	.60	.25	.07
□	490	Gary Sheffield	.50	.23	.06
□	491	Ed Sprague	.25	.11	.03
□	492	Steve Hosey	.10	.05	.01
□	493	Jimmy Haynes	.50	.23	.06
□	494	John Smoltz	.50	.23	.06
□	495	Andre Dawson	.50	.23	.06
□	496	Rey Sanchez	.10	.05	.01
□	497	Ty Van Burkleo	.10	.05	.01
□	498	Bobby Ayala	.25	.11	.03
□	499	Tim Raines	.50	.23	.06
□	500	Charlie Hayes	.10	.05	.01
□	501	Paul Sorrento	.10	.05	.01
□	502	Richie Lewis	.10	.05	.01
□	503	Jason Pfaff	.10	.05	.01
□	504	Ken Caminiti	.50	.23	.06
□	505	Mike Macfarlane	.10	.05	.01
□	506	Jody Reed	.10	.05	.01
□	507	Bobby Hughes	.10	.05	.01
□	508	Wil Cordero	.25	.11	.03
□	509	George Tsamis	.10	.05	.01
□	510	Bret Saberhagen	.25	.11	.03
□	511	Derek Jeter	8.00	3.60	1.00
□	512	Gene Schall	.10	.05	.01
□	513	Curtis Shaw	.10	.05	.01
□	514	Steve Cooke	.10	.05	.01
□	515	Edgar Martinez	.50	.23	.06
□	516	Mike Milchin	.10	.05	.01
□	517	Billy Ripken	.10	.05	.01
□	518	Andy Benes	.10	.05	.01
□	519	Juan de la Rosa	.10	.05	.01
□	520	John Burkett	.10	.05	.01
□	521	Alex Ochoa	.50	.23	.06
□	522	Tony Tarasco	.25	.11	.03
□	523	Luis Ortiz	.10	.05	.01
□	524	Rick Wilkins	.10	.05	.01
□	525	Chris Turner	.10	.05	.01
□	526	Rob Dibble	.10	.05	.01
□	527	Jack McDowell	.25	.11	.03
□	528	Daryl Boston	.10	.05	.01
□	529	Bill Wertz	.10	.05	.01
□	530	Charlie Hough	.10	.05	.01
□	531	Sean Bergman	.10	.05	.01
□	532	Doug Jones	.10	.05	.01
□	533	Jeff Montgomery	.25	.11	.03
□	534	Roger Cedeno	1.25	.55	.16
□	535	Robin Yount	.50	.23	.06
□	536	Mo Vaughn	.75	.35	.09
□	537	Brian Harper	.10	.05	.01
□	538	Juan Castillo	.10	.05	.01
□	539	Steve Farr	.10	.05	.01
□	540	John Kruk	.25	.11	.03

□	541 Troy Neel	.10	.05	.01
□	542 Danny Clyburn	1.00	.45	.12
□	543 Jim Converse	.10	.05	.01
□	544 Gregg Jefferies	.50	.23	.06
□	545 Jose Canseco	.50	.23	.06
□	546 Julio Bruno	.10	.05	.01
□	547 Rob Butler	.10	.05	.01
□	548 Royce Clayton	.25	.11	.03
□	549 Chris Hoiles	.10	.05	.01
□	550 Greg Maddux	2.00	.90	.25
□	551 Joe Ciccarella	.10	.05	.01
□	552 Ozzie Timmons	.50	.23	.06
□	553 Chili Davis	.25	.11	.03
□	554 Brian Koelling	.10	.05	.01
□	555 Frank Thomas	3.00	1.35	.35
□	556 Vinny Castilla	.50	.23	.06
□	557 Reggie Jefferson	.25	.11	.03
□	558 Rob Natal	.10	.05	.01
□	559 Mike Henneman	.10	.05	.01
□	560 Craig Biggio	.50	.23	.06
□	561 Billy Brewer	.10	.05	.01
□	562 Dan Melendez	.10	.05	.01
□	563 Kenny Felder	.10	.05	.01
□	564 Miguel Batista	.25	.11	.03
□	565 Dave Winfield	.50	.23	.06
□	566 Al Shirley	.25	.11	.03
□	567 Robert Eenhoorn	.10	.05	.01
□	568 Mike Williams	.10	.05	.01
□	569 Tanyon Sturtze	.25	.11	.03
□	570 Tim Wakefield	.25	.11	.03
□	571 Greg Pirkl	.10	.05	.01
□	572 Sean Lowe	.25	.11	.03
□	573 Terry Burrows	.10	.05	.01
□	574 Kevin Higgins	.10	.05	.01
□	575 Joe Carter	.50	.23	.06
□	576 Kevin Rogers	.10	.05	.01
□	577 Manny Alexander	.10	.05	.01
□	578 David Justice	.50	.23	.06
□	579 Brian Conroy	.10	.05	.01
□	580 Jessie Hollins	.10	.05	.01
□	581 Ron Watson	.10	.05	.01
□	582 Bip Roberts	.10	.05	.01
□	583 Tom Urbani	.10	.05	.01
□	584 Jason Hutchins	.10	.05	.01
□	585 Carlos Baerga	.50	.23	.06
□	586 Jeff Mutis	.10	.05	.01
□	587 Justin Thompson	.25	.11	.03
□	588 Orlando Miller	.25	.11	.03
□	589 Brian McRae	.25	.11	.03
□	590 Ramon Martinez	.25	.11	.03
□	591 Dave Nilsson	.25	.11	.03
□	592 Jose Vidro	.50	.23	.06
□	593 Rich Becker	.50	.23	.06
□	594 Preston Wilson	.50	.23	.06
□	595 Don Mattingly	1.50	.70	.19
□	596 Tony Longmire	.10	.05	.01
□	597 Kevin Seitzer	.10	.05	.01
□	598 Midre Cummings	.25	.11	.03
□	599 Omar Vizquel	.50	.23	.06
□	600 Lee Smith	.25	.11	.03
□	601 David Hulse	.10	.05	.01
□	602 Darrell Sherman	.10	.05	.01
□	603 Alex Gonzalez	.50	.23	.06
□	604 Geronimo Pena	.10	.05	.01
□	605 Mike Devereaux	.10	.05	.01
□	606 Sterling Hitchcock	.50	.23	.06
□	607 Mike Greenwell	.10	.05	.01
□	608 Steve Buechele	.10	.05	.01
□	609 Troy Percival	.25	.11	.03
□	610 Roberto Kelly	.10	.05	.01
□	611 James Baldwin	2.00	.90	.25
□	612 Jerald Clark	.10	.05	.01
□	613 Albie Lopez	.25	.11	.03
□	614 Dave Magadan	.10	.05	.01
□	615 Mickey Tettleton	.10	.05	.01
□	616 Sean Runyan	.10	.05	.01
□	617 Bob Hamelin	.10	.05	.01
□	618 Raul Mondesi	1.00	.45	.12
□	619 Tyrone Hill	.10	.05	.01
□	620 Darrin Fletcher	.10	.05	.01
□	621 Mike Trombley	.10	.05	.01
□	622 Jeromy Burnitz	.10	.05	.01
□	623 Bernie Williams	.50	.23	.06
□	624 Mike Farmer	.10	.05	.01
□	625 Rickey Henderson	.50	.23	.06
□	626 Carlos Garcia	.10	.05	.01
□	627 Jeff Darwin	.10	.05	.01
□	628 Todd Zeile	.10	.05	.01
□	629 Benji Gil	.25	.11	.03
□	630 Tony Gwynn	1.25	.55	.16
□	631 Aaron Small	.10	.05	.01
□	632 Joe Rosselli	.25	.11	.03
□	633 Mike Mussina	.60	.25	.07
□	634 Ryan Klesko	1.50	.70	.19
□	635 Roger Clemens	.50	.23	.06
□	636 Sammy Sosa	.50	.23	.06
□	637 Orlando Palmeiro	.10	.05	.01
□	638 Willie Greene	.25	.11	.03
□	639 George Bell	.10	.05	.01
□	640 Garvin Alston	.10	.05	.01
□	641 Pete Janicki	.10	.05	.01
□	642 Chris Sheff	.10	.05	.01
□	643 Felipe Lira	.25	.11	.03
□	644 Roberto Petagine	.25	.11	.03
□	645 Wally Joyner	.25	.11	.03
□	646 Mike Piazza	3.00	1.35	.35
□	647 Jaime Navarro	.10	.05	.01
□	648 Jeff Hartsock	.10	.05	.01
□	649 David McCarty	.10	.05	.01
□	650 Bobby Jones	.25	.11	.03
□	651 Mark Hutton	.10	.05	.01
□	652 Kyle Abbott	.10	.05	.01
□	653 Steve Cox	.75	.35	.09
□	654 Jeff King	.25	.11	.03
□	655 Norm Charlton	.10	.05	.01
□	656 Mike Gulan	.10	.05	.01
□	657 Julio Franco	.25	.11	.03
□	658 Cameron Cairncross	.10	.05	.01
□	659 John Olerud	.10	.05	.01
□	660 Salomon Torres	.25	.11	.03
□	661 Brad Pennington	.10	.05	.01
□	662 Melvin Nieves	.50	.23	.06
□	663 Ivan Calderon	.10	.05	.01
□	664 Turk Wendell	.10	.05	.01
□	665 Chris Pritchett	.10	.05	.01
□	666 Reggie Sanders	.50	.23	.06
□	667 Robin Ventura	.25	.11	.03
□	668 Joe Girardi	.10	.05	.01
□	669 Manny Ramirez	2.00	.90	.25
□	670 Jeff Conine	.50	.23	.06
□	671 Greg Gohr	.10	.05	.01
□	672 Andujar Cedeno	.10	.05	.01
□	673 Les Norman	.10	.05	.01
□	674 Mike James	.10	.05	.01
□	675 Marshall Boze	.25	.11	.03
□	676 B.J. Wallace	.10	.05	.01
□	677 Kent Hrbek	.25	.11	.03
□	678 Jack Voigt	.10	.05	.01
□	679 Brien Taylor	.10	.05	.01
□	680 Curt Schilling	.10	.05	.01
□	681 Todd Van Poppel	.10	.05	.01
□	682 Kevin Young	.10	.05	.01
□	683 Tommy Adams	.10	.05	.01
□	684 Bernard Gilkey	.50	.23	.06
□	685 Kevin Brown	.10	.05	.01
□	686 Fred McGriff	.50	.23	.06
□	687 Pat Borders	.10	.05	.01
□	688 Kirt Manwaring	.10	.05	.01
□	689 Sid Bream	.10	.05	.01
□	690 John Valentin	.50	.23	.06
□	691 Steve Olsen	.10	.05	.01
□	692 Roberto Mejia	.10	.05	.01
□	693 Carlos Delgado FOIL	.75	.35	.09
□	694 Steve Gibralter FOIL	.50	.23	.06
□	695 Gary Mota FOIL	.25	.11	.03
□	696 Jose Malave FOIL	.25	.11	.03
□	697 Larry Sutton FOIL	.25	.11	.03
□	698 Dan Frye FOIL	.25	.11	.03
□	699 Tim Clark FOIL	.25	.11	.03
□	700 Brian Rupp FOIL	.25	.11	.03
□	701 Felipe Alou FOIL Moises Alou	.25	.11	.03
□	702 Barry Bonds FOIL Bobby Bonds	.50	.23	.06
□	703 Ken Griffey Sr. FOIL Ken Griffey Jr.	1.00	.45	.12
□	704 Brian McRae FOIL Hal McRae	.25	.11	.03
□	705 Checklist 1	.10	.05	.01
□	706 Checklist 2	.10	.05	.01
□	707 Checklist 3	.10	.05	.01
□	708 Checklist 4	.10	.05	.01

1994 Bowman Previews

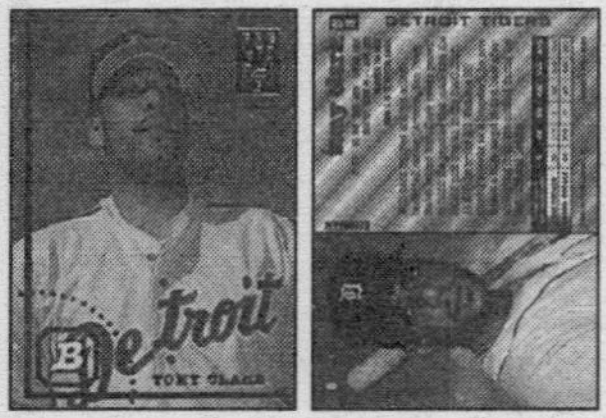

This 10-card standard-size set served as a preview to the 1994 Bowman set. The cards were randomly inserted in Stadium Club second series packs. Card fronts are similar to the full-bleed basic issue. The differences are a multi-colored foil stripe up the left-hand border with a red stripe at bottom. Red foil also surrounds the Bowman logo. In the upper right-hand corner is a blue foil Bowman Preview logo.The backs are identical to the basic issue with a horizontal layout containing a player photo, text and statistics.

	MINT	NRMT	EXC
COMPLETE SET (10)	40.00	18.00	5.00
COMMON CARD (1-10)	1.00	.45	.12
INSERTS IN SER.2 STAD.CLUB PACKS	2.00	.90	.25
□ 1 Frank Thomas	20.00	9.00	2.50
□ 2 Mike Piazza	12.00	5.50	1.50
□ 3 Albert Belle	10.00	4.50	1.25
□ 4 Javier Lopez	2.50	1.10	.30
□ 5 Cliff Floyd	1.00	.45	.12
□ 6 Alex Gonzalez	1.00	.45	.12
□ 7 Ricky Bottalico	1.50	.70	.19
□ 8 Tony Clark	5.00	2.20	.60
□ 9 Mac Suzuki	1.00	.45	.12
□ 10 James Mouton Foil	1.00	.45	.12

1994 Bowman

The 1994 Bowman set consists of 682 standard-size, full-bleed cards primarily distributed in plastic wrap packs and jumbo packs. In addition to a color photo on the front, there is a line of gold foil that runs up the far left side and across the bottom of the card. The player's name is also in gold foil at bottom and the Bowman logo at bottom left is enclosed in gold foil. Horizontal backs contain a player photo on the left and statistics and highlights on the right. There are 51 Foil cards (337-388) that include a number of top young stars and prospects. These foil cards were issued one per foil pack and two per jumbo. Rookie Cards of note include Alan Benes, Tony Clark, Jermaine Dye, Jason Isringhausen, Derrek Lee, Chan Ho Park, Edgar Renteria and Ruben Rivera.

	MINT	NRMT	EXC
COMPLETE SET (682)	110.00	50.00	14.00
COMMON CARD (1-682)	.10	.05	.01
SEMISTARS	.25	.11	.03
STARS	.50	.23	.06
ONE FOIL PER PACK/TWO PER JUMBO			
□ 1 Joe Carter	.50	.23	.06
□ 2 Marcus Moore	.10	.05	.01
□ 3 Doug Creek	.10	.05	.01
□ 4 Pedro Martinez	.50	.23	.06
□ 5 Ken Griffey Jr.	4.00	1.80	.50
□ 6 Greg Swindell	.10	.05	.01
□ 7 J.J. Johnson	.25	.11	.03
□ 8 Homer Bush	.25	.11	.03
□ 9 Arquimedez Pozo	.50	.23	.06
□ 10 Bryan Harvey	.10	.05	.01
□ 11 J.T. Snow	.25	.11	.03
□ 12 Alan Benes	1.50	.70	.19
□ 13 Chad Kreuter	.10	.05	.01
□ 14 Eric Karros	.25	.11	.03
□ 15 Frank Thomas	4.00	1.80	.50
□ 16 Bret Saberhagen	.25	.11	.03
□ 17 Terrell Lowery	.10	.05	.01
□ 18 Rod Bolton	.10	.05	.01
□ 19 Harold Baines	.25	.11	.03
□ 20 Matt Walbeck	.10	.05	.01
□ 21 Tom Glavine	.50	.23	.06
□ 22 Todd Jones	.10	.05	.01
□ 23 Alberto Castillo	.25	.11	.03
□ 24 Ruben Sierra	.25	.11	.03
□ 25 Don Mattingly	2.00	.90	.25
□ 26 Mike Morgan	.10	.05	.01
□ 27 Jim Musselwhite	.25	.11	.03
□ 28 Matt Brunson	.25	.11	.03
□ 29 Adam Meinershagen	.10	.05	.01
□ 30 Joe Girardi	.10	.05	.01
□ 31 Shane Halter	.10	.05	.01
□ 32 Jose Paniagua	.25	.11	.03
□ 33 Paul Perkins	.10	.05	.01
□ 34 John Hudek	.10	.05	.01
□ 35 Frank Viola	.10	.05	.01
□ 36 David Lamb	.10	.05	.01
□ 37 Marshall Boze	.10	.05	.01
□ 38 Jorge Posada	.25	.11	.03
□ 39 Brian Anderson	.25	.11	.03
□ 40 Mark Whiten	.10	.05	.01
□ 41 Sean Bergman	.25	.11	.03
□ 42 Jose Parra	.25	.11	.03
□ 43 Mike Robertson	.10	.05	.01
□ 44 Pete Walker	.10	.05	.01
□ 45 Juan Gonzalez	2.00	.90	.25
□ 46 Cleveland Ladell	.25	.11	.03
□ 47 Mark Smith	.10	.05	.01
□ 48 Kevin Jarvis UER (team listed as Yankees on back)	.10	.05	.01
□ 49 Amaury Telemaco	1.00	.45	.12
□ 50 Andy Van Slyke	.25	.11	.03
□ 51 Rikkert Faneyte	.10	.05	.01
□ 52 Curtis Shaw	.10	.05	.01
□ 53 Matt Drews	.50	.23	.06
□ 54 Wilson Alvarez	.25	.11	.03
□ 55 Manny Ramirez	1.25	.55	.16
□ 56 Bobby Munoz	.10	.05	.01
□ 57 Ed Sprague	.25	.11	.03
□ 58 Jamey Wright	1.00	.45	.12
□ 59 Jeff Montgomery	.25	.11	.03
□ 60 Kirk Rueter	.10	.05	.01
□ 61 Edgar Martinez	.50	.23	.06
□ 62 Luis Gonzalez	.10	.05	.01
□ 63 Tim Vanegmond	.10	.05	.01
□ 64 Bip Roberts	.10	.05	.01
□ 65 John Jaha	.25	.11	.03
□ 66 Chuck Carr	.10	.05	.01
□ 67 Chuck Finley	.10	.05	.01
□ 68 Aaron Holbert	.25	.11	.03
□ 69 Cecil Fielder	.25	.11	.03
□ 70 Tom Engle	.10	.05	.01
□ 71 Ron Karkovice	.10	.05	.01
□ 72 Joe Orsulak	.10	.05	.01
□ 73 Duff Brumley	.10	.05	.01
□ 74 Craig Clayton	.10	.05	.01
□ 75 Cal Ripken	3.00	1.35	.35
□ 76 Brad Fulmer	.75	.35	.09
□ 77 Tony Tarasco	.10	.05	.01
□ 78 Terry Farrar	.10	.05	.01

□ 79	Matt Williams	.50	.23	.06
□ 80	Rickey Henderson	.50	.23	.06
□ 81	Terry Mulholland	.10	.05	.01
□ 82	Sammy Sosa	.60	.25	.07
□ 83	Paul Sorrento	.10	.05	.01
□ 84	Pete Incaviglia	.10	.05	.01
□ 85	Darren Hall	.10	.05	.01
□ 86	Scott Klingenbeck	.25	.11	.03
□ 87	Dario Perez	.10	.05	.01
□ 88	Ugueth Urbina	.25	.11	.03
□ 89	Dave Vanhof	.10	.05	.01
□ 90	Domingo Jean	.10	.05	.01
□ 91	Otis Nixon	.10	.05	.01
□ 92	Andres Berumen	.10	.05	.01
□ 93	Jose Valentin	.25	.11	.03
□ 94	Edgar Renteria	2.50	1.10	.30
□ 95	Chris Turner	.10	.05	.01
□ 96	Ray Lankford	.50	.23	.06
□ 97	Danny Bautista	.10	.05	.01
□ 98	Chan Ho Park	1.00	.45	.12
□ 99	Glenn DiSarcina	.25	.11	.03
□ 100	Butch Huskey	.25	.11	.03
□ 101	Ivan Rodriguez	.75	.35	.09
□ 102	Johnny Ruffin	.10	.05	.01
□ 103	Alex Ochoa	.25	.11	.03
□ 104	Torii Hunter	.25	.11	.03
□ 105	Ryan Klesko	1.00	.45	.12
□ 106	Jay Bell	.25	.11	.03
□ 107	Kurt Peltzer	.10	.05	.01
□ 108	Miguel Jimenez	.10	.05	.01
□ 109	Russ Davis	.25	.11	.03
□ 110	Derek Wallace	.10	.05	.01
□ 111	Keith Lockhart	.10	.05	.01
□ 112	Mike Lieberthal	.10	.05	.01
□ 113	Dave Stewart	.25	.11	.03
□ 114	Tom Schmidt	.10	.05	.01
□ 115	Brian McRae	.25	.11	.03
□ 116	Moises Alou	.25	.11	.03
□ 117	Dave Fleming	.10	.05	.01
□ 118	Jeff Bagwell	1.50	.70	.19
□ 119	Luis Ortiz	.10	.05	.01
□ 120	Tony Gwynn	1.50	.70	.19
□ 121	Jaime Navarro	.10	.05	.01
□ 122	Benny Santiago	.10	.05	.01
□ 123	Darrell Whitmore	.10	.05	.01
□ 124	John Mabry	.75	.35	.09
□ 125	Mickey Tettleton	.10	.05	.01
□ 126	Tom Candiotti	.10	.05	.01
□ 127	Tim Raines	.50	.23	.06
□ 128	Bobby Bonilla	.25	.11	.03
□ 129	John Dettmer	.10	.05	.01
□ 130	Hector Carrasco	.10	.05	.01
□ 131	Chris Hoiles	.10	.05	.01
□ 132	Rick Aguilera	.10	.05	.01
□ 133	David Justice	.50	.23	.06
□ 134	Esteban Loaiza	.25	.11	.03
□ 135	Barry Bonds	1.00	.45	.12
□ 136	Bob Welch	.10	.05	.01
□ 137	Mike Stanley	.10	.05	.01
□ 138	Roberto Hernandez	.25	.11	.03
□ 139	Sandy Alomar	.25	.11	.03
□ 140	Darren Daulton	.25	.11	.03
□ 141	Angel Martinez	.25	.11	.03
□ 142	Howard Johnson	.10	.05	.01
□ 143	Bob Hamelin UER (name and card number colors don't match)	.10	.05	.01
□ 144	J.J. Thobe	.10	.05	.01
□ 145	Roger Salkeld	.10	.05	.01
□ 146	Orlando Miller	.10	.05	.01
□ 147	Dmitri Young	.75	.35	.09
□ 148	Tim Hyers	.10	.05	.01
□ 149	Mark Loretta	.10	.05	.01
□ 150	Chris Hammond	.10	.05	.01
□ 151	Joel Moore	.10	.05	.01
□ 152	Todd Zeile	.10	.05	.01
□ 153	Wil Cordero	.25	.11	.03
□ 154	Chris Smith	.10	.05	.01
□ 155	James Baldwin	.75	.35	.09
□ 156	Edgardo Alfonzo	.50	.23	.06
□ 157	Kym Ashworth	.25	.11	.03
□ 158	Paul Bako	.10	.05	.01
□ 159	Rick Krivda	.10	.05	.01
□ 160	Pat Mahomes	.10	.05	.01
□ 161	Damon Hollins	.10	.05	.01
□ 162	Felix Martinez	.25	.11	.03
□ 163	Jason Myers	.25	.11	.03
□ 164	Izzy Molina	.25	.11	.03
□ 165	Brien Taylor	.10	.05	.01
□ 166	Kevin Orie	.75	.35	.09
□ 167	Casey Whitten	.25	.11	.03
□ 168	Tony Longmire	.10	.05	.01
□ 169	John Olerud	.10	.05	.01
□ 170	Mark Thompson	.25	.11	.03
□ 171	Jorge Fabregas	.10	.05	.01
□ 172	John Wetteland	.25	.11	.03
□ 173	Dan Wilson	.25	.11	.03
□ 174	Doug Drabek	.10	.05	.01
□ 175	Jeffrey McNeely	.10	.05	.01
□ 176	Melvin Nieves	.25	.11	.03
□ 177	Doug Glanville	.25	.11	.03
□ 178	Javier De La Hoya	.10	.05	.01
□ 179	Chad Curtis	.10	.05	.01
□ 180	Brian Barber	.10	.05	.01
□ 181	Mike Henneman	.10	.05	.01
□ 182	Jose Offerman	.10	.05	.01
□ 183	Robert Ellis	.10	.05	.01
□ 184	John Franco	.10	.05	.01
□ 185	Benji Gil	.10	.05	.01
□ 186	Hal Morris	.10	.05	.01
□ 187	Chris Sabo	.10	.05	.01
□ 188	Blaise Ilsley	.10	.05	.01
□ 189	Steve Avery	.25	.11	.03
□ 190	Rick White	.10	.05	.01
□ 191	Rod Beck	.25	.11	.03
□ 192	Mark McGwire UER (No card number on back)	1.25	.55	.16
□ 193	Jim Abbott	.10	.05	.01
□ 194	Randy Myers	.10	.05	.01
□ 195	Kenny Lofton	1.25	.55	.16
□ 196	Mariano Duncan	.10	.05	.01
□ 197	Lee Daniels	.10	.05	.01
□ 198	Armando Reynoso	.10	.05	.01
□ 199	Joe Randa	.25	.11	.03
□ 200	Cliff Floyd	.50	.23	.06
□ 201	Tim Harkrider	.10	.05	.01
□ 202	Kevin Gallaher	.10	.05	.01
□ 203	Scott Cooper	.10	.05	.01
□ 204	Phil Stidham	.10	.05	.01
□ 205	Jeff D'Amico	1.00	.45	.12
□ 206	Matt Whisenant	.10	.05	.01
□ 207	De Shawn Warren	.25	.11	.03
□ 208	Rene Arocha	.10	.05	.01
□ 209	Tony Clark	2.50	1.10	.30
□ 210	Jason Jacome	.25	.11	.03
□ 211	Scott Christman	.25	.11	.03
□ 212	Bill Pulsipher	.25	.11	.03
□ 213	Dean Palmer	.25	.11	.03
□ 214	Chad Mottola	.10	.05	.01
□ 215	Manny Alexander	.10	.05	.01
□ 216	Rich Becker	.25	.11	.03
□ 217	Andre King	.25	.11	.03
□ 218	Carlos Garcia	.10	.05	.01
□ 219	Ron Pezzoni	.10	.05	.01
□ 220	Steve Karsay	.10	.05	.01
□ 221	Jose Musset	.10	.05	.01
□ 222	Karl Rhodes	.10	.05	.01
□ 223	Frank Cimorelli	.10	.05	.01
□ 224	Kevin Jordan	.10	.05	.01
□ 225	Duane Ward	.10	.05	.01
□ 226	John Burke	.10	.05	.01
□ 227	Mike Macfarlane	.10	.05	.01
□ 228	Mike Lansing	.25	.11	.03
□ 229	Chuck Knoblauch	.50	.23	.06
□ 230	Ken Caminiti	.50	.23	.06
□ 231	Gar Finnvold	.10	.05	.01
□ 232	Derrek Lee	2.50	1.10	.30
□ 233	Brady Anderson	.50	.23	.06
□ 234	Vic Darensbourg	.25	.11	.03
□ 235	Mark Langston	.25	.11	.03
□ 236	T.J. Mathews	.25	.11	.03
□ 237	Lou Whitaker	.50	.23	.06
□ 238	Roger Cedeno	.50	.23	.06
□ 239	Alex Fernandez	.50	.23	.06
□ 240	Ryan Thompson	.10	.05	.01
□ 241	Kerry Lacy	.10	.05	.01
□ 242	Reggie Sanders	.50	.23	.06
□ 243	Brad Pennington	.10	.05	.01
□ 244	Bryan Eversgerd	.10	.05	.01
□ 245	Greg Maddux	2.50	1.10	.30
□ 246	Jason Kendall	1.00	.45	.12
□ 247	J.R. Phillips	.10	.05	.01
□ 248	Bobby Witt	.10	.05	.01

□ 249 Paul O'Neill	.25	.11	.03
□ 250 Ryne Sandberg	1.00	.45	.12
□ 251 Charles Nagy	.25	.11	.03
□ 252 Kevin Stocker	.10	.05	.01
□ 253 Shawn Green	.25	.11	.03
□ 254 Charlie Hayes	.10	.05	.01
□ 255 Donnie Elliott	.10	.05	.01
□ 256 Rob Fitzpatrick	.10	.05	.01
□ 257 Tim Davis	.10	.05	.01
□ 258 James Mouton	.25	.11	.03
□ 259 Mike Greenwell	.10	.05	.01
□ 260 Ray McDavid	.25	.11	.03
□ 261 Mike Kelly	.10	.05	.01
□ 262 Andy Larkin	.25	.11	.03
□ 263 Marquis Riley UER	.10	.05	.01
(No card number on back)			
□ 264 Bob Tewksbury	.10	.05	.01
□ 265 Brian Edmondson	.10	.05	.01
□ 266 Eduardo Lantigua	.25	.11	.03
□ 267 Brandon Wilson	.10	.05	.01
□ 268 Mike Welch	.10	.05	.01
□ 269 Tom Henke	.10	.05	.01
□ 270 Calvin Reese	.25	.11	.03
□ 271 Greg Zaun	.25	.11	.03
□ 272 Todd Ritchie	.10	.05	.01
□ 273 Javier Lopez	.50	.23	.06
□ 274 Kevin Young	.10	.05	.01
□ 275 Kirt Manwaring	.10	.05	.01
□ 276 Bill Taylor	.10	.05	.01
□ 277 Robert Eenhoorn	.10	.05	.01
□ 278 Jessie Hollins	.10	.05	.01
□ 279 Julian Tavarez	.25	.11	.03
□ 280 Gene Schall	.25	.11	.03
□ 281 Paul Molitor	.75	.35	.09
□ 282 Neifi Perez	1.00	.45	.12
□ 283 Greg Gagne	.10	.05	.01
□ 284 Marquis Grissom	.50	.23	.06
□ 285 Randy Johnson	.60	.25	.07
□ 286 Pete Harnisch	.10	.05	.01
□ 287 Joel Bennett	.10	.05	.01
□ 288 Derek Bell	.25	.11	.03
□ 289 Darryl Hamilton	.10	.05	.01
□ 290 Gary Sheffield	.60	.25	.07
□ 291 Eduardo Perez	.10	.05	.01
□ 292 Basil Shabazz	.10	.05	.01
□ 293 Eric Davis	.25	.11	.03
□ 294 Pedro Astacio	.10	.05	.01
□ 295 Robin Ventura	.25	.11	.03
□ 296 Jeff Kent	.10	.05	.01
□ 297 Rick Helling	.10	.05	.01
□ 298 Joe Oliver	.10	.05	.01
□ 299 Lee Smith	.25	.11	.03
□ 300 Dave Winfield	.50	.23	.06
□ 301 Deion Sanders	.50	.23	.06
□ 302 Ravelo Manzanillo	.10	.05	.01
□ 303 Mark Portugal	.10	.05	.01
□ 304 Brent Gates	.10	.05	.01
□ 305 Wade Boggs	.50	.23	.06
□ 306 Rick Wilkins	.10	.05	.01
□ 307 Carlos Baerga	.50	.23	.06
□ 308 Curt Schilling	.10	.05	.01
□ 309 Shannon Stewart	.25	.11	.03
□ 310 Darren Holmes	.10	.05	.01
□ 311 Robert Toth	.25	.11	.03
□ 312 Gabe White	.10	.05	.01
□ 313 Mac Suzuki	.25	.11	.03
□ 314 Alvin Morman	.10	.05	.01
□ 315 Mo Vaughn	1.00	.45	.12
□ 316 Bryce Florie	.10	.05	.01
□ 317 Gabby Martinez	.25	.11	.03
□ 318 Carl Everett	.10	.05	.01
□ 319 Kerwin Moore	.10	.05	.01
□ 320 Tom Pagnozzi	.10	.05	.01
□ 321 Chris Gomez	.10	.05	.01
□ 322 Todd Williams	.10	.05	.01
□ 323 Pat Hentgen	.50	.23	.06
□ 324 Kirk Presley	.50	.23	.06
□ 325 Kevin Brown	.10	.05	.01
□ 326 Jason Isringhausen	4.00	1.80	.50
□ 327 Rick Forney	.10	.05	.01
□ 328 Carlos Pulido	.10	.05	.01
□ 329 Terrell Wade	.75	.35	.09
□ 330 Al Martin	.10	.05	.01
□ 331 Dan Carlson	.10	.05	.01
□ 332 Mark Acre	.10	.05	.01
□ 333 Sterling Hitchcock	.25	.11	.03
□ 334 Jon Ratliff	.25	.11	.03
□ 335 Alex Ramirez	1.00	.45	.12
□ 336 Phil Geisler	.10	.05	.01
□ 337 Eddie Zambrano FOIL	.10	.05	.01
□ 338 Jim Thome FOIL	1.00	.45	.12
□ 339 James Mouton FOIL	.25	.11	.03
□ 340 Cliff Floyd FOIL	.50	.23	.06
□ 341 Carlos Delgado FOIL	.60	.25	.07
□ 342 Roberto Petagine FOIL	.25	.11	.03
□ 343 Tim Clark FOIL	.10	.05	.01
□ 344 Bubba Smith FOIL	.10	.05	.01
□ 345 Randy Curtis FOIL	.10	.05	.01
□ 346 Joe Biasucci FOIL	.10	.05	.01
□ 347 D.J. Boston FOIL	.25	.11	.03
□ 348 Ruben Rivera FOIL	8.00	3.60	1.00
□ 349 Bryan Link FOIL	.10	.05	.01
□ 350 Mike Bell FOIL	.75	.35	.09
□ 351 Marty Watson FOIL	.10	.05	.01
□ 352 Jason Myers FOIL	.25	.11	.03
□ 353 Chipper Jones FOIL	3.00	1.35	.35
□ 354 Brooks Kieschnick FOIL	.75	.35	.09
□ 355 Calvin Reese FOIL	.25	.11	.03
□ 356 John Burke FOIL	.10	.05	.01
□ 357 Kurt Miller FOIL	.10	.05	.01
□ 358 Orlando Miller FOIL	.10	.05	.01
□ 359 Todd Hollandsworth FOIL	1.00	.45	.12
□ 360 Rondell White FOIL	.50	.23	.06
□ 361 Bill Pulsipher FOIL	.25	.11	.03
□ 362 Tyler Green FOIL	.10	.05	.01
□ 363 Midre Cummings FOIL	.10	.05	.01
□ 364 Brian Barber FOIL	.10	.05	.01
□ 365 Melvin Nieves FOIL	.25	.11	.03
□ 366 Salomon Torres FOIL	.10	.05	.01
□ 367 Alex Ochoa FOIL	.25	.11	.03
□ 368 Frankie Rodriguez FOIL	.25	.11	.03
□ 369 Brian Anderson FOIL	.25	.11	.03
□ 370 James Baldwin FOIL	.75	.35	.09
□ 371 Manny Ramirez FOIL	1.25	.55	.16
□ 372 Justin Thompson FOIL	.25	.11	.03
□ 373 Johnny Damon FOIL	.60	.25	.07
□ 374 Jeff D'Amico FOIL	1.00	.45	.12
□ 375 Rich Becker FOIL	.25	.11	.03
□ 376 Derek Jeter FOIL	3.00	1.35	.35
□ 377 Steve Karsay FOIL	.10	.05	.01
□ 378 Mac Suzuki FOIL	.25	.11	.03
□ 379 Benji Gil FOIL	.10	.05	.01
□ 380 Alex Gonzalez FOIL	.25	.11	.03
□ 381 Jason Bere FOIL	.25	.11	.03
□ 382 Brett Butler FOIL	.25	.11	.03
□ 383 Jeff Conine FOIL	.50	.23	.06
□ 384 Darren Daulton FOIL	.25	.11	.03
□ 385 Jeff Kent FOIL	.10	.05	.01
□ 386 Don Mattingly FOIL	2.00	.90	.25
□ 387 Mike Piazza FOIL	2.50	1.10	.30
□ 388 Ryne Sandberg FOIL	1.00	.45	.12
□ 389 Rich Amaral	.10	.05	.01
□ 390 Craig Biggio	.50	.23	.06
□ 391 Jeff Suppan	1.50	.70	.19
□ 392 Andy Benes	.25	.11	.03
□ 393 Cal Eldred	.10	.05	.01
□ 394 Jeff Conine	.50	.23	.06
□ 395 Tim Salmon	.60	.25	.07
□ 396 Ray Suplee	.10	.05	.01
□ 397 Tony Phillips	.25	.11	.03
□ 398 Ramon Martinez	.25	.11	.03
□ 399 Julio Franco	.25	.11	.03
□ 400 Dwight Gooden	.25	.11	.03
□ 401 Kevin Lomon	.10	.05	.01
□ 402 Jose Rijo	.10	.05	.01
□ 403 Mike Devereaux	.10	.05	.01
□ 404 Mike Zolecki	.10	.05	.01
□ 405 Fred McGriff	.50	.23	.06
□ 406 Danny Clyburn	.25	.11	.03
□ 407 Robby Thompson	.10	.05	.01
□ 408 Terry Steinbach	.25	.11	.03
□ 409 Luis Polonia	.10	.05	.01
□ 410 Mark Grace	.50	.23	.06
□ 411 Albert Belle	2.00	.90	.25
□ 412 John Kruk	.25	.11	.03
□ 413 Scott Spiezio	.50	.23	.06
□ 414 Ellis Burks UER	.25	.11	.03
(Name spelled Elkis on front)			
□ 415 Joe Vitiello	.25	.11	.03
□ 416 Tim Costo	.10	.05	.01
□ 417 Marc Newfield	.25	.11	.03
□ 418 Oscar Henriquez	.10	.05	.01

419	Matt Perisho	.75	.35	.09
420	Julio Bruno	.10	.05	.01
421	Kenny Felder	.10	.05	.01
422	Tyler Green	.10	.05	.01
423	Jim Edmonds	.75	.35	.09
424	Ozzie Smith	.75	.35	.09
425	Rick Greene	.10	.05	.01
426	Todd Hollandsworth	1.00	.45	.12
427	Eddie Pearson	.50	.23	.06
428	Quilvio Veras	.25	.11	.03
429	Kenny Rogers	.10	.05	.01
430	Willie Greene	.25	.11	.03
431	Vaughn Eshelman	.10	.05	.01
432	Pat Meares	.10	.05	.01
433	Jermaine Dye	8.00	3.60	1.00
434	Steve Cooke	.10	.05	.01
435	Bill Swift	.10	.05	.01
436	Fausto Cruz	.10	.05	.01
437	Mark Hutton	.10	.05	.01
438	Brooks Kieschnick	.75	.35	.09
439	Yorkis Perez	.10	.05	.01
440	Len Dykstra	.25	.11	.03
441	Pat Borders	.10	.05	.01
442	Doug Walls	.10	.05	.01
443	Wally Joyner	.25	.11	.03
444	Ken Hill	.10	.05	.01
445	Eric Anthony	.10	.05	.01
446	Mitch Williams	.10	.05	.01
447	Cory Bailey	.10	.05	.01
448	Dave Staton	.10	.05	.01
449	Greg Vaughn	.50	.23	.06
450	Dave Magadan	.10	.05	.01
451	Chili Davis	.25	.11	.03
452	Gerald Santos	.10	.05	.01
453	Joe Perona	.10	.05	.01
454	Delino DeShields	.10	.05	.01
455	Jack McDowell	.25	.11	.03
456	Todd Hundley	.50	.23	.06
457	Ritchie Moody	.10	.05	.01
458	Bret Boone	.25	.11	.03
459	Ben McDonald	.10	.05	.01
460	Kirby Puckett	1.25	.55	.16
461	Gregg Olson	.10	.05	.01
462	Rich Aude	.25	.11	.03
463	John Burkett	.10	.05	.01
464	Troy Neel	.10	.05	.01
465	Jimmy Key	.25	.11	.03
466	Ozzie Timmons	.25	.11	.03
467	Eddie Murray	1.00	.45	.12
468	Mark Tranberg	.10	.05	.01
469	Alex Gonzalez	.25	.11	.03
470	David Nied	.10	.05	.01
471	Barry Larkin	.50	.23	.06
472	Brian Looney	.10	.05	.01
473	Shawn Estes	.10	.05	.01
474	A.J. Sager	.10	.05	.01
475	Roger Clemens	.50	.23	.06
476	Vince Moore	.10	.05	.01
477	Scott Karl	.25	.11	.03
478	Kurt Miller	.10	.05	.01
479	Garret Anderson	.50	.23	.06
480	Allen Watson	.10	.05	.01
481	Jose Lima	.25	.11	.03
482	Rick Gorecki	.10	.05	.01
483	Jimmy Hurst	.25	.11	.03
484	Preston Wilson	.25	.11	.03
485	Will Clark	.50	.23	.06
486	Mike Ferry	.10	.05	.01
487	Curtis Goodwin	.25	.11	.03
488	Mike Myers	.10	.05	.01
489	Chipper Jones	3.00	1.35	.35
490	Jeff King	.25	.11	.03
491	William VanLandingham	.25	.11	.03
492	Carlos Reyes	.10	.05	.01
493	Andy Pettitte	2.00	.90	.25
494	Brant Brown	.10	.05	.01
495	Daron Kirkreit	.25	.11	.03
496	Ricky Bottalico	.50	.23	.06
497	Devon White	.10	.05	.01
498	Jason Johnson	.10	.05	.01
499	Vince Coleman	.10	.05	.01
500	Larry Walker	.50	.23	.06
501	Bobby Ayala	.10	.05	.01
502	Steve Finley	.50	.23	.06
503	Scott Fletcher	.10	.05	.01
504	Brad Ausmus	.10	.05	.01
505	Scott Talanoa	.10	.05	.01
506	Orestes Destrade	.10	.05	.01
507	Gary DiSarcina	.10	.05	.01
508	Willie Smith	.10	.05	.01
509	Alan Trammell	.50	.23	.06
510	Mike Piazza	2.50	1.10	.30
511	Ozzie Guillen	.10	.05	.01
512	Jeromy Burnitz	.10	.05	.01
513	Darren Oliver	.50	.23	.06
514	Kevin Mitchell	.25	.11	.03
515	Rafael Palmeiro	.50	.23	.06
516	David McCarty	.10	.05	.01
517	Jeff Blauser	.10	.05	.01
518	Trey Beamon	.50	.23	.06
519	Royce Clayton	.25	.11	.03
520	Dennis Eckersley	.25	.11	.03
521	Bernie Williams	.60	.25	.07
522	Steve Buechele	.10	.05	.01
523	Denny Martinez	.25	.11	.03
524	Dave Hollins	.10	.05	.01
525	Joey Hamilton	.75	.35	.09
526	Andres Galarraga	.50	.23	.06
527	Jeff Granger	.25	.11	.03
528	Joey Eischen	.10	.05	.01
529	Desi Relaford	.10	.05	.01
530	Roberto Petagine	.25	.11	.03
531	Andre Dawson	.50	.23	.06
532	Ray Holbert	.10	.05	.01
533	Duane Singleton	.10	.05	.01
534	Kurt Abbott	.25	.11	.03
535	Bo Jackson	.50	.23	.06
536	Gregg Jefferies	.50	.23	.06
537	David Mysel	.10	.05	.01
538	Raul Mondesi	.60	.25	.07
539	Chris Snopek	.10	.05	.01
540	Brook Fordyce	.10	.05	.01
541	Ron Frazier	.10	.05	.01
542	Brian Koelling	.10	.05	.01
543	Jimmy Haynes	.25	.11	.03
544	Marty Cordova	.75	.35	.09
545	Jason Green	.25	.11	.03
546	Orlando Merced	.25	.11	.03
547	Lou Pote	.10	.05	.01
548	Todd Van Poppel	.10	.05	.01
549	Pat Kelly	.10	.05	.01
550	Turk Wendell	.10	.05	.01
551	Herbert Perry	.25	.11	.03
552	Ryan Karp	.25	.11	.03
553	Juan Guzman	.25	.11	.03
554	Bryan Rekar	.25	.11	.03
555	Kevin Appier	.25	.11	.03
556	Chris Schwab	.50	.23	.06
557	Jay Buhner	.50	.23	.06
558	Andujar Cedeno	.10	.05	.01
559	Ryan McGuire	.25	.11	.03
560	Ricky Gutierrez	.10	.05	.01
561	Keith Kimsey	.10	.05	.01
562	Tim Clark	.10	.05	.01
563	Damion Easley	.10	.05	.01
564	Clint Davis	.10	.05	.01
565	Mike Moore	.10	.05	.01
566	Orel Hershiser	.25	.11	.03
567	Jason Bere	.25	.11	.03
568	Kevin McReynolds	.10	.05	.01
569	Leland Macon	.25	.11	.03
570	John Courtright	.10	.05	.01
571	Sid Fernandez	.10	.05	.01
572	Chad Roper	.10	.05	.01
573	Terry Pendleton	.25	.11	.03
574	Danny Miceli	.10	.05	.01
575	Joe Rosselli	.10	.05	.01
576	Mike Bordick	.10	.05	.01
577	Danny Tartabull	.10	.05	.01
578	Jose Guzman	.10	.05	.01
579	Omar Vizquel	.50	.23	.06
580	Tommy Greene	.10	.05	.01
581	Paul Spoljaric	.10	.05	.01
582	Walt Weiss	.10	.05	.01
583	Oscar Jimenez	.10	.05	.01
584	Rod Henderson	.10	.05	.01
585	Derek Lowe	.10	.05	.01
586	Richard Hidalgo	2.00	.90	.25
587	Shayne Bennett	.25	.11	.03
588	Tim Belk	.25	.11	.03
589	Matt Mieske	.10	.05	.01
590	Nigel Wilson	.10	.05	.01

□ 591 Jeff Knox	.25	.11	.03
□ 592 Bernard Gilkey	.25	.11	.03
□ 593 David Cone	.50	.23	.06
□ 594 Paul LoDuca	.25	.11	.03
□ 595 Scott Ruffcorn	.10	.05	.01
□ 596 Chris Roberts	.25	.11	.03
□ 597 Oscar Munoz	.10	.05	.01
□ 598 Scott Sullivan	.25	.11	.03
□ 599 Matt Jarvis	.10	.05	.01
□ 600 Jose Canseco	.50	.23	.06
□ 601 Tony Graffanino	.25	.11	.03
□ 602 Don Slaught	.10	.05	.01
□ 603 Brett King	.25	.11	.03
□ 604 Jose Herrera	.50	.23	.06
□ 605 Melido Perez	.10	.05	.01
□ 606 Mike Hubbard	.10	.05	.01
□ 607 Chad Ogea	.25	.11	.03
□ 608 Wayne Gomes	.25	.11	.03
□ 609 Roberto Alomar	1.00	.45	.12
□ 610 Angel Echevarria	.50	.23	.06
□ 611 Jose Lind	.10	.05	.01
□ 612 Darrin Fletcher	.10	.05	.01
□ 613 Chris Bosio	.10	.05	.01
□ 614 Darryl Kile	.10	.05	.01
□ 615 Frankie Rodriguez	.25	.11	.03
□ 616 Phil Plantier	.10	.05	.01
□ 617 Pat Listach	.10	.05	.01
□ 618 Charlie Hough	.10	.05	.01
□ 619 Ryan Hancock	.25	.11	.03
□ 620 Darrel Deak	.10	.05	.01
□ 621 Travis Fryman	.50	.23	.06
□ 622 Brett Butler	.25	.11	.03
□ 623 Lance Johnson	.25	.11	.03
□ 624 Pete Smith	.10	.05	.01
□ 625 James Hurst	.10	.05	.01
□ 626 Roberto Kelly	.10	.05	.01
□ 627 Mike Mussina	.75	.35	.09
□ 628 Kevin Tapani	.10	.05	.01
□ 629 John Smoltz	.60	.25	.07
□ 630 Midre Cummings	.10	.05	.01
□ 631 Salomon Torres	.10	.05	.01
□ 632 Willie Adams	.10	.05	.01
□ 633 Derek Jeter	3.00	1.35	.35
□ 634 Steve Trachsel	.25	.11	.03
□ 635 Albie Lopez	.25	.11	.03
□ 636 Jason Moler	.10	.05	.01
□ 637 Carlos Delgado	.60	.25	.07
□ 638 Roberto Mejia	.10	.05	.01
□ 639 Darren Burton	.10	.05	.01
□ 640 B.J. Wallace	.10	.05	.01
□ 641 Brad Clontz	.25	.11	.03
□ 642 Billy Wagner	1.00	.45	.12
□ 643 Aaron Sele	.25	.11	.03
□ 644 Cameron Cairncross	.10	.05	.01
□ 645 Brian Harper	.10	.05	.01
□ 646 Marc Valdes UER (No card number on back)	.25	.11	.03
□ 647 Mark Ratekin	.10	.05	.01
□ 648 Terry Bradshaw	.25	.11	.03
□ 649 Justin Thompson	.25	.11	.03
□ 650 Mike Busch	.25	.11	.03
□ 651 Joe Hall	.10	.05	.01
□ 652 Bobby Jones	.25	.11	.03
□ 653 Kelly Stinnett	.10	.05	.01
□ 654 Rod Steph	.10	.05	.01
□ 655 Jay Powell	.25	.11	.03
□ 656 Keith Garagozzo UER (No card number on back)	.10	.05	.01
□ 657 Todd Dunn	.25	.11	.03
□ 658 Charles Peterson	.50	.23	.06
□ 659 Darren Lewis	.10	.05	.01
□ 660 John Wasdin	.50	.23	.06
□ 661 Tate Seefried	.25	.11	.03
□ 662 Hector Trinidad	.25	.11	.03
□ 663 John Carter	.10	.05	.01
□ 664 Larry Mitchell	.10	.05	.01
□ 665 David Catlett	.25	.11	.03
□ 666 Dante Bichette	.50	.23	.06
□ 667 Felix Jose	.10	.05	.01
□ 668 Rondell White	.50	.23	.06
□ 669 Tino Martinez	.25	.11	.03
□ 670 Brian L. Hunter	.60	.25	.07
□ 671 Jose Malave	.25	.11	.03
□ 672 Archi Cianfrocco	.10	.05	.01
□ 673 Mike Matheny	.10	.05	.01
□ 674 Bret Barberie	.10	.05	.01
□ 675 Andrew Lorraine	.10	.05	.01
□ 676 Brian Jordan	.50	.23	.06
□ 677 Tim Belcher	.10	.05	.01
□ 678 Antonio Osuna	.25	.11	.03
□ 679 Checklist	.10	.05	.01
□ 680 Checklist	.10	.05	.01
□ 681 Checklist	.10	.05	.01
□ 682 Checklist	.10	.05	.01

1995 Bowman

Cards from this 439-card standard-size prsopect-oriented set were primarily issued in plastic wrapped packs and jumbo packs. Card fronts feature white broders enframing full color photos. The left border is a reversed negative of the photo. The set includes 54 silver foil subset cards (221-274). The foil subset, largely comprising of minor league stars, have embossed borders and are found one per pack. Rookie Cards of note include Bartolo Colon, Karim Garcia, Derrick Gibson, Vladmir Guerrero, Andruw Jones, Hideo Nomo, Jay Payton and Scott Rolen.

	MINT	NRMT	EXC
COMPLETE SET (439)	150.00	70.00	19.00
COMMON CARD (1-439)	.15	.07	.02
SEMISTARS	.30	.14	.04
STARS	.60	.25	.07
ONE SILVER FOIL PER PACK/TWO PER RACK			

□ 1 Billy Wagner	.30	.14	.04
□ 2 Chris Widger	.15	.07	.02
□ 3 Brent Bowers	.15	.07	.02
□ 4 Bob Abreu	2.50	1.10	.30
□ 5 Lou Collier	.50	.23	.06
□ 6 Juan Acevedo	.15	.07	.02
□ 7 Jason Kelley	.15	.07	.02
□ 8 Brian Sackinsky	.15	.07	.02
□ 9 Scott Christman	.15	.07	.02
□ 10 Damon Hollins	.30	.14	.04
□ 11 Willis Otanez	.30	.14	.04
□ 12 Jason Ryan	.30	.14	.04
□ 13 Jason Giambi	1.00	.45	.12
□ 14 Andy Taulbee	.15	.07	.02
□ 15 Mark Thompson	.15	.07	.02
□ 16 Hugo Pivaral	.30	.14	.04
□ 17 Brien Taylor	.15	.07	.02
□ 18 Antonio Osuna	.15	.07	.02
□ 19 Edgardo Alfonzo	.30	.14	.04
□ 20 Carl Everett	.15	.07	.02
□ 21 Matt Drews	.30	.14	.04
□ 22 Bartolo Colon	4.00	1.80	.50
□ 23 Andruw Jones	40.00	18.00	5.00
□ 24 Robert Person	.15	.07	.02
□ 25 Derrek Lee	1.25	.55	.16
□ 26 John Ambrose	.30	.14	.04
□ 27 Eric Knowles	.30	.14	.04
□ 28 Chris Roberts	.15	.07	.02
□ 29 Don Wengert	.15	.07	.02
□ 30 Marcus Jensen	.30	.14	.04
□ 31 Brian Barber	.15	.07	.02
□ 32 Kevin Brown C	.75	.35	.09
□ 33 Benji Gil	.15	.07	.02
□ 34 Mike Hubbard	.15	.07	.02
□ 35 Bart Evans	.15	.07	.02
□ 36 Enrique Wilson	1.25	.55	.16
□ 37 Brian Buchanan	.30	.14	.04

□	38 Ken Ray	.15	.07	.02
□	39 Micah Franklin	.30	.14	.04
□	40 Ricky Otero	.15	.07	.02
□	41 Jason Kendall	.30	.14	.04
□	42 Jimmy Hurst	.30	.14	.04
□	43 Jerry Wolak	.15	.07	.02
□	44 Jayson Peterson	.30	.14	.04
□	45 Allen Battle	.15	.07	.02
□	46 Scott Stahoviak	.15	.07	.02
□	47 Steve Schrenk	.15	.07	.02
□	48 Travis Miller	.30	.14	.04
□	49 Eddie Rios	.15	.07	.02
□	50 Mike Hampton	.15	.07	.02
□	51 Chad Frontera	.15	.07	.02
□	52 Tom Evans	.15	.07	.02
□	53 C.J. Nitkowski	.30	.14	.04
□	54 Clay Caruthers	.30	.14	.04
□	55 Shannon Stewart	.15	.07	.02
□	56 Jorge Posada	.15	.07	.02
□	57 Aaron Holbert	.15	.07	.02
□	58 Harry Berrios	.15	.07	.02
□	59 Steve Rodriguez	.15	.07	.02
□	60 Shane Andrews	.15	.07	.02
□	61 Will Cunnane	.40	.18	.05
□	62 Richard Hidalgo	.75	.35	.09
□	63 Bill Selby	.15	.07	.02
□	64 Jay Cranford	.15	.07	.02
□	65 Jeff Suppan	.60	.25	.07
□	66 Curtis Goodwin	.30	.14	.04
□	67 John Thomson	.50	.23	.06
□	68 Justin Thompson	.30	.14	.04
□	69 Troy Percival	.15	.07	.02
□	70 Matt Wagner	.30	.14	.04
□	71 Terry Bradshaw	.15	.07	.02
□	72 Greg Hansell	.15	.07	.02
□	73 John Burke	.15	.07	.02
□	74 Jeff D'Amico	.30	.14	.04
□	75 Ernie Young	.30	.14	.04
□	76 Jason Bates	.15	.07	.02
□	77 Chris Stynes	.15	.07	.02
□	78 Cade Gaspar	.30	.14	.04
□	79 Melvin Nieves	.30	.14	.04
□	80 Rick Gorecki	.15	.07	.02
□	81 Felix Rodriguez	.30	.14	.04
□	82 Ryan Hancock	.15	.07	.02
□	83 Chris Carpenter	1.50	.70	.19
□	84 Ray McDavid	.30	.14	.04
□	85 Chris Wimmer	.15	.07	.02
□	86 Doug Glanville	.15	.07	.02
□	87 DeShawn Warren	.15	.07	.02
□	88 Damian Moss	2.00	.90	.25
□	89 Rafael Orellano	.30	.14	.04
□	90 Vladimir Guerrero	15.00	6.75	1.85
□	91 Raul Casanova	1.25	.55	.16
□	92 Karim Garcia	6.00	2.70	.75
□	93 Bryce Florie	.15	.07	.02
□	94 Kevin Orie	.30	.14	.04
□	95 Ryan Nye	.30	.14	.04
□	96 Matt Sachse	.40	.18	.05
□	97 Ivan Arteaga	.15	.07	.02
□	98 Glenn Murray	.15	.07	.02
□	99 Stacy Hollins	.15	.07	.02
□	100 Jim Pittsley	.30	.14	.04
□	101 Craig Mattson	.15	.07	.02
□	102 Neifi Perez	.30	.14	.04
□	103 Keith Williams	.15	.07	.02
□	104 Roger Cedeno	.30	.14	.04
□	105 Tony Terry	.30	.14	.04
□	106 Jose Malave	.15	.07	.02
□	107 Joe Rosselli	.15	.07	.02
□	108 Kevin Jordan	.15	.07	.02
□	109 Sid Roberson	.15	.07	.02
□	110 Alan Embree	.15	.07	.02
□	111 Terrell Wade	.30	.14	.04
□	112 Bob Wolcott	.30	.14	.04
□	113 Carlos Perez	.30	.14	.04
□	114 Mike Bovee	.30	.14	.04
□	115 Tommy Davis	.30	.14	.04
□	116 Jeremey Kendall	.15	.07	.02
□	117 Rich Aude	.15	.07	.02
□	118 Rick Huisman	.15	.07	.02
□	119 Tim Belk	.15	.07	.02
□	120 Edgar Renteria	1.00	.45	.12
□	121 Calvin Maduro	.50	.23	.06
□	122 Jerry Martin	.15	.07	.02
□	123 Ramon Fermin	.15	.07	.02

□	124 Kimera Bartee	.30	.14	.04
□	125 Mark Farris	.30	.14	.04
□	126 Frank Rodriguez	.30	.14	.04
□	127 Bobby Higginson	1.00	.45	.12
□	128 Bret Wagner	.30	.14	.04
□	129 Edwin Diaz	.75	.35	.09
□	130 Jimmy Haynes	.30	.14	.04
□	131 Chris Weinke	.15	.07	.02
□	132 Damian Jackson	.30	.14	.04
□	133 Felix Martinez	.15	.07	.02
□	134 Edwin Hurtado	.15	.07	.02
□	135 Matt Raleigh	.15	.07	.02
□	136 Paul Wilson	1.25	.55	.16
□	137 Ron Villone	.15	.07	.02
□	138 Eric Stuckenschneider	.15	.07	.02
□	139 Tate Seefried	.15	.07	.02
□	140 Rey Ordonez	4.00	1.80	.50
□	141 Eddie Pearson	.15	.07	.02
□	142 Kevin Gallaher	.15	.07	.02
□	143 Torii Hunter	.30	.14	.04
□	144 Daron Kirkreit	.15	.07	.02
□	145 Craig Wilson	.15	.07	.02
□	146 Ugueth Urbina	.15	.07	.02
□	147 Chris Snopek	.15	.07	.02
□	148 Kym Ashworth	.30	.14	.04
□	149 Wayne Gomes	.15	.07	.02
□	150 Mark Loretta	.15	.07	.02
□	151 Ramon Morel	.40	.18	.05
□	152 Trot Nixon	.30	.14	.04
□	153 Desi Relaford	.30	.14	.04
□	154 Scott Sullivan	.15	.07	.02
□	155 Marc Barcelo	.15	.07	.02
□	156 Willie Adams	.15	.07	.02
□	157 Derrick Gibson	5.00	2.20	.60
□	158 Brian Meadows	.50	.23	.06
□	159 Julian Tavarez	.15	.07	.02
□	160 Bryan Rekar	.15	.07	.02
□	161 Steve Gibralter	.30	.14	.04
□	162 Esteban Loaiza	.15	.07	.02
□	163 John Wasdin	.15	.07	.02
□	164 Kirk Presley	.30	.14	.04
□	165 Mariano Rivera	.60	.25	.07
□	166 Andy Larkin	.15	.07	.02
□	167 Sean Whiteside	.15	.07	.02
□	168 Matt Apana	.15	.07	.02
□	169 Shawn Senior	.15	.07	.02
□	170 Scott Gentile	.15	.07	.02
□	171 Quilvio Veras	.15	.07	.02
□	172 Elieser Marrero	.50	.23	.06
□	173 Mendy Lopez	.50	.23	.06
□	174 Homer Bush	.15	.07	.02
□	175 Brian Stephenson	.30	.14	.04
□	176 Jon Nunnally	.30	.14	.04
□	177 Jose Herrera	.15	.07	.02
□	178 Corey Avrard	.40	.18	.05
□	179 David Bell	.15	.07	.02
□	180 Jason Isringhausen	1.50	.70	.19
□	181 Jamey Wright	.30	.14	.04
□	182 Lonell Roberts	.15	.07	.02
□	183 Marty Cordova	.75	.35	.09
□	184 Amaury Telemaco	.15	.07	.02
□	185 John Mabry	.60	.25	.07
□	186 Andrew Vessel	.30	.14	.04
□	187 Jim Cole	.15	.07	.02
□	188 Marquis Riley	.15	.07	.02
□	189 Todd Dunn	.30	.14	.04
□	190 John Carter	.15	.07	.02
□	191 Donnie Sadler	.75	.35	.09
□	192 Mike Bell	.30	.14	.04
□	193 Chris Cumberland	.30	.14	.04
□	194 Jason Schmidt	.30	.14	.04
□	195 Matt Brunson	.15	.07	.02
□	196 James Baldwin	.60	.25	.07
□	197 Bill Simas	.15	.07	.02
□	198 Gus Gandarillas	.15	.07	.02
□	199 Mac Suzuki	.30	.14	.04
□	200 Rick Holifield	.15	.07	.02
□	201 Fernando Lunar	.30	.14	.04
□	202 Kevin Jarvis	.15	.07	.02
□	203 Everett Stull	.15	.07	.02
□	204 Steve Wojciechowski	.15	.07	.02
□	205 Shawn Estes	.15	.07	.02
□	206 Jermaine Dye	4.00	1.80	.50
□	207 Marc Kroon	.15	.07	.02
□	208 Peter Munro	.40	.18	.05
□	209 Pat Watkins	.30	.14	.04

□ 210	Matt Smith	.30	.14	.04
□ 211	Joe Vitiello	.15	.07	.02
□ 212	Gerald Witasick Jr.	.15	.07	.02
□ 213	Freddy Garcia	.30	.14	.04
□ 214	Glenn Dishman	.30	.14	.04
□ 215	Jay Canizaro	.30	.14	.04
□ 216	Angel Martinez	.15	.07	.02
□ 217	Yamil Benitez	.50	.23	.06
□ 218	Fausto Macey	.40	.18	.05
□ 219	Eric Owens	.30	.14	.04
□ 220	Checklist	.15	.07	.02
□ 221	Dwayne Hosey FOIL	.30	.14	.04
□ 222	Brad Woodall FOIL	.15	.07	.02
□ 223	Billy Ashley FOIL	.15	.07	.02
□ 224	Mark Grudzielanek FOIL	1.50	.70	.19
□ 225	Mark Johnson FOIL	.30	.14	.04
□ 226	Tim Unroe FOIL	.30	.14	.04
□ 227	Todd Greene FOIL	.60	.25	.07
□ 228	Larry Sutton FOIL	.15	.07	.02
□ 229	Derek Jeter FOIL	4.00	1.80	.50
□ 230	Sal Fasano FOIL	.30	.14	.04
□ 231	Ruben Rivera FOIL	3.00	1.35	.35
□ 232	Chris Truby FOIL	.30	.14	.04
□ 233	John Donati FOIL	.15	.07	.02
□ 234	Decomba Conner FOIL	.40	.18	.05
□ 235	Sergio Nunez FOIL	.75	.35	.09
□ 236	Ray Brown FOIL	.30	.14	.04
□ 237	Juan Melo FOIL	.75	.35	.09
□ 238	Hideo Nomo FOIL	6.00	2.70	.75
□ 239	Jamie Bluma FOIL	.30	.14	.04
□ 240	Jay Payton FOIL	4.00	1.80	.50
□ 241	Paul Konerko FOIL	6.00	2.70	.75
□ 242	Scott Elarton FOIL	.75	.35	.09
□ 243	Jeff Abbott FOIL	1.25	.55	.16
□ 244	Jim Brower FOIL	.30	.14	.04
□ 245	Geoff Blum FOIL	.40	.18	.05
□ 246	Aaron Boone FOIL	1.00	.45	.12
□ 247	J.R. Phillips FOIL	.15	.07	.02
□ 248	Alex Ochoa FOIL	.60	.25	.07
□ 249	Nomar Garciaparra FOIL	4.00	1.80	.50
□ 250	Garret Anderson FOIL	.30	.14	.04
□ 251	Ray Durham FOIL	.30	.14	.04
□ 252	Paul Shuey FOIL	.15	.07	.02
□ 253	Tony Clark FOIL	1.00	.45	.12
□ 254	Johnny Damon FOIL	.60	.25	.07
□ 255	Duane Singleton FOIL	.15	.07	.02
□ 256	LaTroy Hawkins FOIL	.15	.07	.02
□ 257	Andy Pettitte FOIL	2.50	1.10	.30
□ 258	Ben Grieve FOIL	3.00	1.35	.35
□ 259	Marc Newfield FOIL	.30	.14	.04
□ 260	Terrell Lowery FOIL	.15	.07	.02
□ 261	Shawn Green FOIL	.60	.25	.07
□ 262	Chipper Jones FOIL	3.00	1.35	.35
□ 263	Brooks Kieschnick FOIL	.30	.14	.04
□ 264	Calvin Reese FOIL	.15	.07	.02
□ 265	Doug Million FOIL	.30	.14	.04
□ 266	Marc Valdes FOIL	.15	.07	.02
□ 267	Brian L.Hunter FOIL	.60	.25	.07
□ 268	Todd Hollandsworth FOIL	1.00	.45	.12
□ 269	Rod Henderson FOIL	.15	.07	.02
□ 270	Bill Pulsipher FOIL	.30	.14	.04
□ 271	Scott Rolen FOIL	10.00	4.50	1.25
□ 272	Trey Beamon FOIL	.30	.14	.04
□ 273	Alan Benes FOIL	1.00	.45	.12
□ 274	Dustin Hermanson FOIL	.30	.14	.04
□ 275	Ricky Bottalico	.30	.14	.04
□ 276	Albert Belle	2.50	1.10	.30
□ 277	Deion Sanders	.60	.25	.07
□ 278	Matt Williams	.60	.25	.07
□ 279	Jeff Bagwell	2.00	.90	.25
□ 280	Kirby Puckett	1.50	.70	.19
□ 281	Dave Hollins	.15	.07	.02
□ 282	Don Mattingly	2.50	1.10	.30
□ 283	Joey Hamilton	.30	.14	.04
□ 284	Bobby Bonilla	.30	.14	.04
□ 285	Moises Alou	.30	.14	.04
□ 286	Tom Glavine	.60	.25	.07
□ 287	Brett Butler	.30	.14	.04
□ 288	Chris Hoiles	.15	.07	.02
□ 289	Kenny Rogers	.15	.07	.02
□ 290	Larry Walker	.60	.25	.07
□ 291	Tim Raines	.60	.25	.07
□ 292	Kevin Appier	.30	.14	.04
□ 293	Roger Clemens	.60	.25	.07
□ 294	Chuck Carr	.15	.07	.02
□ 295	Randy Myers	.15	.07	.02
□ 296	Dave Nilsson	.30	.14	.04
□ 297	Joe Carter	.60	.25	.07
□ 298	Chuck Finley	.30	.14	.04
□ 299	Ray Lankford	.60	.25	.07
□ 300	Roberto Kelly	.15	.07	.02
□ 301	Jon Lieber	.15	.07	.02
□ 302	Travis Fryman	.30	.14	.04
□ 303	Mark McGwire	1.50	.70	.19
□ 304	Tony Gwynn	2.00	.90	.25
□ 305	Kenny Lofton	1.25	.55	.16
□ 306	Mark Whiten	.15	.07	.02
□ 307	Doug Drabek	.15	.07	.02
□ 308	Terry Steinbach	.30	.14	.04
□ 309	Ryan Klesko	1.00	.45	.12
□ 310	Mike Piazza	3.00	1.35	.35
□ 311	Ben McDonald	.15	.07	.02
□ 312	Reggie Sanders	.30	.14	.04
□ 313	Alex Fernandez	.30	.14	.04
□ 314	Aaron Sele	.30	.14	.04
□ 315	Gregg Jefferies	.30	.14	.04
□ 316	Rickey Henderson	.60	.25	.07
□ 317	Brian Anderson	.15	.07	.02
□ 318	Jose Valentin	.30	.14	.04
□ 319	Rod Beck	.15	.07	.02
□ 320	Marquis Grissom	.60	.25	.07
□ 321	Ken Griffey Jr.	5.00	2.20	.60
□ 322	Bret Saberhagen	.30	.14	.04
□ 323	Juan Gonzalez	2.50	1.10	.30
□ 324	Paul Molitor	1.00	.45	.12
□ 325	Gary Sheffield	.75	.35	.09
□ 326	Darren Daulton	.30	.14	.04
□ 327	Bill Swift	.15	.07	.02
□ 328	Brian McRae	.30	.14	.04
□ 329	Robin Ventura	.30	.14	.04
□ 330	Lee Smith	.30	.14	.04
□ 331	Fred McGriff	.60	.25	.07
□ 332	Delino DeShields	.15	.07	.02
□ 333	Edgar Martinez	.60	.25	.07
□ 334	Mike Mussina	1.00	.45	.12
□ 335	Orlando Merced	.15	.07	.02
□ 336	Carlos Baerga	.60	.25	.07
□ 337	Wil Cordero	.15	.07	.02
□ 338	Tom Pagnozzi	.15	.07	.02
□ 339	Pat Hentgen	.30	.14	.04
□ 340	Chad Curtis	.15	.07	.02
□ 341	Darren Lewis	.15	.07	.02
□ 342	Jeff Kent	.15	.07	.02
□ 343	Bip Roberts	.15	.07	.02
□ 344	Ivan Rodriguez	1.00	.45	.12
□ 345	Jeff Montgomery	.30	.14	.04
□ 346	Hal Morris	.15	.07	.02
□ 347	Danny Tartabull	.15	.07	.02
□ 348	Raul Mondesi	.60	.25	.07
□ 349	Ken Hill	.15	.07	.02
□ 350	Pedro Martinez	.30	.14	.04
□ 351	Frank Thomas	5.00	2.20	.60
□ 352	Manny Ramirez	1.25	.55	.16
□ 353	Tim Salmon	.60	.25	.07
□ 354	W. VanLandingham	.15	.07	.02
□ 355	Andres Galarraga	.60	.25	.07
□ 356	Paul O'Neill	.30	.14	.04
□ 357	Brady Anderson	.60	.25	.07
□ 358	Ramon Martinez	.30	.14	.04
□ 359	John Olerud	.15	.07	.02
□ 360	Ruben Sierra	.30	.14	.04
□ 361	Cal Eldred	.15	.07	.02
□ 362	Jay Buhner	.60	.25	.07
□ 363	Jay Bell	.30	.14	.04
□ 364	Wally Joyner	.30	.14	.04
□ 365	Chuck Knoblauch	.60	.25	.07
□ 366	Len Dykstra	.30	.14	.04
□ 367	John Wetteland	.30	.14	.04
□ 368	Roberto Alomar	1.25	.55	.16
□ 369	Craig Biggio	.60	.25	.07
□ 370	Ozzie Smith	1.00	.45	.12
□ 371	Terry Pendleton	.30	.14	.04
□ 372	Sammy Sosa	.75	.35	.09
□ 373	Carlos Garcia	.15	.07	.02
□ 374	Jose Rijo	.15	.07	.02
□ 375	Chris Gomez	.15	.07	.02
□ 376	Barry Bonds	1.25	.55	.16
□ 377	Steve Avery	.30	.14	.04
□ 378	Rick Wilkins	.15	.07	.02
□ 379	Pete Harnisch	.15	.07	.02
□ 380	Dean Palmer	.30	.14	.04
□ 381	Bob Hamelin	.15	.07	.02

□ 382 Jason Bere	.15	.07	.02
□ 383 Jimmy Key	.30	.14	.04
□ 384 Dante Bichette	.60	.25	.07
□ 385 Rafael Palmeiro	.60	.25	.07
□ 386 David Justice	.60	.25	.07
□ 387 Chili Davis	.30	.14	.04
□ 388 Mike Greenwell	.15	.07	.02
□ 389 Todd Zeile	.15	.07	.02
□ 390 Jeff Conine	.60	.25	.07
□ 391 Rick Aguilera	.15	.07	.02
□ 392 Eddie Murray	1.25	.55	.16
□ 393 Mike Stanley	.15	.07	.02
□ 394 Cliff Floyd UER (numbered 294)	.30	.14	.04
□ 395 Randy Johnson	.75	.35	.09
□ 396 David Nied	.15	.07	.02
□ 397 Devon White	.30	.14	.04
□ 398 Royce Clayton	.15	.07	.02
□ 399 Andy Benes	.15	.07	.02
□ 400 John Hudek	.15	.07	.02
□ 401 Bobby Jones	.30	.14	.04
□ 402 Eric Karros	.30	.14	.04
□ 403 Will Clark	.60	.25	.07
□ 404 Mark Langston	.15	.07	.02
□ 405 Kevin Brown	.30	.14	.04
□ 406 Greg Maddux	3.00	1.35	.35
□ 407 David Cone	.30	.14	.04
□ 408 Wade Boggs	.60	.25	.07
□ 409 Steve Trachsel	.15	.07	.02
□ 410 Greg Vaughn	.30	.14	.04
□ 411 Mo Vaughn	1.25	.55	.16
□ 412 Wilson Alvarez	.30	.14	.04
□ 413 Cal Ripken	4.00	1.80	.50
□ 414 Rico Brogna	.15	.07	.02
□ 415 Barry Larkin	.60	.25	.07
□ 416 Cecil Fielder	.30	.14	.04
□ 417 Jose Canseco	.60	.25	.07
□ 418 Jack McDowell	.30	.14	.04
□ 419 Mike Lieberthal	.15	.07	.02
□ 420 Andrew Lorraine	.30	.14	.04
□ 421 Rich Becker	.15	.07	.02
□ 422 Tony Phillips	.30	.14	.04
□ 423 Scott Ruffcorn	.15	.07	.02
□ 424 Jeff Granger	.15	.07	.02
□ 425 Greg Pirkl	.15	.07	.02
□ 426 Dennis Eckersley	.30	.14	.04
□ 427 Jose Lima	.15	.07	.02
□ 428 Russ Davis	.15	.07	.02
□ 429 Armando Benitez	.15	.07	.02
□ 430 Alex Gonzalez	.15	.07	.02
□ 431 Carlos Delgado	.60	.25	.07
□ 432 Chan Ho Park	.60	.25	.07
□ 433 Mickey Tettleton	.15	.07	.02
□ 434 Dave Winfield	.60	.25	.07
□ 435 John Burkett	.30	.14	.04
□ 436 Orlando Miller	.15	.07	.02
□ 437 Rondell White	.60	.25	.07
□ 438 Jose Oliva	.15	.07	.02
□ 439 Checklist	.15	.07	.02

1995 Bowman Gold Foil

Numbered 221-274, this 54-card standard-size set is the gold insert parallel version of the silver foil subset found in the basic issue. The odds of finding a gold foil version are one in six packs.

	MINT	NRMT	EXC
COMPLETE SET (54)	200.00	90.00	25.00
COMMON CARD (221-274)	2.00	.90	.25
SEMISTARS	5.00	2.20	.60
RANDOM INSERTS IN PACKS			

□ 229 Derek Jeter	25.00	11.00	3.10
□ 231 Ruben Rivera	15.00	6.75	1.85
□ 238 Hideo Nomo	20.00	9.00	2.50
□ 240 Jay Payton	12.00	5.50	1.50
□ 241 Paul Konerko	25.00	11.00	3.10
□ 249 Nomar Garciaparra	15.00	6.75	1.85
□ 257 Andy Pettitte	15.00	6.75	1.85
□ 258 Ben Grieve	10.00	4.50	1.25
□ 262 Chipper Jones	25.00	11.00	3.10
□ 271 Scott Rolen	30.00	13.50	3.70

1996 Bowman

The 1996 Bowman set was issued in one series totalling 385 cards. The 11-card packs retail for $2.50 each. The fronts feature color action player photos in a tan-checkered frame with the player's name printed in silver foil at the bottom. The backs carry another color player photo with player information, 1995 and career player statistics. Each pack contained 10 regular issue cards plus either one foil parallel or an insert card. In a special promotional program, Topps offered collector's a $100 guarantee on complete sets. To get the guarantee, collector's had to mail in a Guaranteed Value Certificate request form, found in packs, along with a $5 processing and registration fee before the December 31st, 1996 deadline. Collectors would then receive a $100 Guaranteed Value Certificate, of which they could mail back to Topps between August 31st, 1999 and December 31st, 1999, along with their complete set, to receive $100.

	MINT	NRMT	EXC
COMPLETE SET (385)	110.00	50.00	14.00
COMMON CARD (1-385)	.15	.07	.02
SEMISTARS	.30	.14	.04
STARS	.60	.25	.07
COMPLETE FOIL SET (385)	350.00	160.00	45.00
COMMON FOIL (1-385)	.40	.18	.05
FOIL SEMISTARS	2.50	1.10	.30
*FOIL STARS: 2X to 4X BASIC CARD			
*FOIL YOUNG STARS: 1.5X to 3X BASIC CARDS			
ONE FOIL OR INSERT PER PACK			
TWO FOILS PER RETAIL PACK			

□ 1 Cal Ripken	4.00	1.80	.50
□ 2 Ray Durham	.60	.25	.07
□ 3 Ivan Rodriguez	1.00	.45	.12
□ 4 Fred McGriff	.60	.25	.07
□ 5 Hideo Nomo	1.25	.55	.16
□ 6 Troy Percival	.30	.14	.04
□ 7 Moises Alou	.15	.07	.02
□ 8 Mike Stanley	.15	.07	.02
□ 9 Jay Buhner	.15	.07	.02
□ 10 Shawn Green	.15	.07	.02
□ 11 Ryan Klesko	1.00	.45	.12
□ 12 Andres Galarraga	.60	.25	.07
□ 13 Dean Palmer	.15	.07	.02
□ 14 Jeff Conine	.15	.07	.02
□ 15 Brian L.Hunter	.15	.07	.02
□ 16 J.T. Snow	.15	.07	.02
□ 17 Larry Walker	.15	.07	.02
□ 18 Barry Larkin	.30	.14	.04
□ 19 Alex Gonzalez	.15	.07	.02
□ 20 Edgar Martinez	.15	.07	.02
□ 21 Mo Vaughn	1.25	.55	.16
□ 22 Mark McGwire	1.50	.70	.19
□ 23 Jose Canseco	.30	.14	.04
□ 24 Jack McDowell	.15	.07	.02
□ 25 Dante Bichette	.30	.14	.04
□ 26 Wade Boggs	.30	.14	.04
□ 27 Mike Piazza	3.00	1.35	.35
□ 28 Ray Lankford	.15	.07	.02
□ 29 Craig Biggio	.30	.14	.04
□ 30 Rafael Palmeiro	.30	.14	.04
□ 31 Ron Gant	.15	.07	.02
□ 32 Javy Lopez	.15	.07	.02

□ 33 Brian Jordan	.30	.14	.04
□ 34 Paul O'Neill	.15	.07	.02
□ 35 Mark Grace	.15	.07	.02
□ 36 Matt Williams	.30	.14	.04
□ 37 Pedro Martinez	.15	.07	.02
□ 38 Rickey Henderson	.15	.07	.02
□ 39 Bobby Bonilla	.60	.25	.07
□ 40 Todd Hollandsworth	.30	.14	.04
□ 41 Jim Thome	1.00	.45	.12
□ 42 Gary Sheffield	.30	.14	.04
□ 43 Tim Salmon	.30	.14	.04
□ 44 Gregg Jefferies	.15	.07	.02
□ 45 Roberto Alomar	1.25	.55	.16
□ 46 Carlos Baerga	.30	.14	.04
□ 47 Mark Grudzielanek	.15	.07	.02
□ 48 Randy Johnson	.30	.14	.04
□ 49 Tino Martinez	.15	.07	.02
□ 50 Robin Ventura	.30	.14	.04
□ 51 Ryne Sandberg	1.25	.55	.16
□ 52 Jay Bell	.15	.07	.02
□ 53 Jason Schmidt	.15	.07	.02
□ 54 Frank Thomas	5.00	2.20	.60
□ 55 Kenny Lofton	1.25	.55	.16
□ 56 Ariel Prieto	.15	.07	.02
□ 57 David Cone	.15	.07	.02
□ 58 Reggie Sanders	.15	.07	.02
□ 59 Michael Tucker	.15	.07	.02
□ 60 Vinny Castilla	.15	.07	.02
□ 61 Len Dykstra	.15	.07	.02
□ 62 Todd Hundley	.30	.14	.04
□ 63 Brian McRae	.15	.07	.02
□ 64 Dennis Eckersley	.15	.07	.02
□ 65 Rondell White	.30	.14	.04
□ 66 Eric Karros	.30	.14	.04
□ 67 Greg Maddux	3.00	1.35	.35
□ 68 Kevin Appier	.15	.07	.02
□ 69 Eddie Murray	1.25	.55	.16
□ 70 John Olerud	.15	.07	.02
□ 71 Tony Gwynn	2.00	.90	.25
□ 72 David Justice	.30	.14	.04
□ 73 Ken Caminiti	.30	.14	.04
□ 74 Terry Steinbach	.15	.07	.02
□ 75 Alan Benes	.60	.25	.07
□ 76 Chipper Jones	3.00	1.35	.35
□ 77 Jeff Bagwell	2.00	.90	.25
□ 78 Barry Bonds	1.25	.55	.16
□ 79 Ken Griffey Jr.	5.00	2.20	.60
□ 80 Roger Cedeno	.15	.07	.02
□ 81 Joe Carter	.15	.07	.02
□ 82 Henry Rodriguez	.15	.07	.02
□ 83 Jason Isringhausen	.30	.14	.04
□ 84 Chuck Knoblauch	.30	.14	.04
□ 85 Manny Ramirez	1.25	.55	.16
□ 86 Tom Glavine	.15	.07	.02
□ 87 Jeffrey Hammonds	.15	.07	.02
□ 88 Paul Molitor	1.00	.45	.12
□ 89 Roger Clemens	.15	.07	.02
□ 90 Greg Vaughn	.15	.07	.02
□ 91 Marty Cordova	.15	.07	.02
□ 92 Albert Belle	2.50	1.10	.30
□ 93 Mike Mussina	1.00	.45	.12
□ 94 Garret Anderson	.15	.07	.02
□ 95 Juan Gonzalez	2.50	1.10	.30
□ 96 John Valentin	.15	.07	.02
□ 97 Jason Giambi	.30	.14	.04
□ 98 Kirby Puckett	1.50	.70	.19
□ 99 Jim Edmonds	.15	.07	.02
□ 100 Cecil Fielder	.15	.07	.02
□ 101 Mike Aldrete	.15	.07	.02
□ 102 Marquis Grissom	.15	.07	.02
□ 103 Derek Bell	.15	.07	.02
□ 104 Raul Mondesi	.15	.07	.02
□ 105 Sammy Sosa	.30	.14	.04
□ 106 Travis Fryman	.30	.14	.04
□ 107 Rico Brogna	.15	.07	.02
□ 108 Will Clark	.30	.14	.04
□ 109 Bernie Williams	.60	.25	.07
□ 110 Brady Anderson	.30	.14	.04
□ 111 Torii Hunter	.30	.14	.04
□ 112 Derek Jeter	3.00	1.35	.35
□ 113 Mike Kusiewicz	.50	.23	.06
□ 114 Scott Rolen	2.50	1.10	.30
□ 115 Ramon Castro	.30	.14	.04
□ 116 Jose Guillen	2.50	1.10	.30
□ 117 Wade Walker	.15	.07	.02
□ 118 Shawn Senior	.15	.07	.02
□ 119 Onan Masaoka	.50	.23	.06
□ 120 Marlon Anderson	.50	.23	.06
□ 121 Katsuhiro Maeda	.50	.23	.06
□ 122 Garrett Stephenson	.15	.07	.02
□ 123 Butch Huskey	.15	.07	.02
□ 124 D'Angelo Jimenez	.50	.23	.06
□ 125 Tony Mounce	.50	.23	.06
□ 126 Jay Canizaro	.15	.07	.02
□ 127 Juan Melo	.30	.14	.04
□ 128 Steve Gibralter	.15	.07	.02
□ 129 Freddy Garcia	.30	.14	.04
□ 130 Julio Santana UER Card has him born in 1993	.15	.07	.02
□ 131 Richard Hidalgo	.30	.14	.04
□ 132 Jermaine Dye	1.25	.55	.16
□ 133 Willie Adams	.15	.07	.02
□ 134 Everett Stull	.15	.07	.02
□ 135 Ramon Morel	.15	.07	.02
□ 136 Chan Ho Park	.30	.14	.04
□ 137 Jamey Wright	.15	.07	.02
□ 138 Luis Garcia	.15	.07	.02
□ 139 Dan Serafini	.30	.14	.04
□ 140 Ryan Dempster	.60	.25	.07
□ 141 Tate Seefried	.15	.07	.02
□ 142 Jimmy Hurst	.15	.07	.02
□ 143 Travis Miller	.15	.07	.02
□ 144 Curtis Goodwin	.15	.07	.02
□ 145 Rocky Coppinger	1.00	.45	.12
□ 146 Enrique Wilson	.30	.14	.04
□ 147 Jaime Bluma	.15	.07	.02
□ 148 Andrew Vessel	.30	.14	.04
□ 149 Damian Moss	1.00	.45	.12
□ 150 Shawn Gallagher	.40	.18	.05
□ 151 Pat Watkins	.30	.14	.04
□ 152 Jose Paniagua	.30	.14	.04
□ 153 Danny Graves	.30	.14	.04
□ 154 Bryon Gainey	.60	.25	.07
□ 155 Steve Soderstrom	.15	.07	.02
□ 156 Cliff Brumbaugh	.15	.07	.02
□ 157 Eugene Kingsale	.50	.23	.06
□ 158 Lou Collier	.15	.07	.02
□ 159 Todd Walker	4.00	1.80	.50
□ 160 Kris Detmers	.75	.35	.09
□ 161 Josh Booty	1.50	.70	.19
□ 162 Greg Whiteman	.15	.07	.02
□ 163 Damian Jackson	.30	.14	.04
□ 164 Tony Clark	.30	.14	.04
□ 165 Jeff D'Amico	.30	.14	.04
□ 166 Johnny Damon	.30	.14	.04
□ 167 Rafael Orellano	.30	.14	.04
□ 168 Ruben Rivera	1.00	.45	.12
□ 169 Alex Ochoa	.30	.14	.04
□ 170 Jay Powell	.15	.07	.02
□ 171 Tom Evans	.15	.07	.02
□ 172 Ron Villone	.15	.07	.02
□ 173 Shawn Estes	.15	.07	.02
□ 174 John Wasdin	.15	.07	.02
□ 175 Bill Simas	.15	.07	.02
□ 176 Kevin Brown	.30	.14	.04
□ 177 Shannon Stewart	.15	.07	.02
□ 178 Todd Greene	.30	.14	.04
□ 179 Bob Wolcott	.15	.07	.02
□ 180 Chris Snopek	.15	.07	.02
□ 181 Nomar Garciaparra	1.25	.55	.16
□ 182 Cameron Smith	.15	.07	.02
□ 183 Matt Drews	.30	.14	.04
□ 184 Jimmy Haynes	.15	.07	.02
□ 185 Chris Carpenter	.30	.14	.04
□ 186 Desi Relaford	.15	.07	.02
□ 187 Ben Grieve	1.00	.45	.12
□ 188 Mike Bell	.30	.14	.04
□ 189 Luis Castillo	.75	.35	.09
□ 190 Ugueth Urbina	.15	.07	.02
□ 191 Paul Wilson	.60	.25	.07
□ 192 Andruw Jones	10.00	4.50	1.25
□ 193 Wayne Gomes	.15	.07	.02
□ 194 Craig Counsell	.15	.07	.02
□ 195 Jim Cole	.15	.07	.02
□ 196 Brooks Kieschnick	.15	.07	.02
□ 197 Trey Beamon	.15	.07	.02
□ 198 Marino Santana	.15	.07	.02
□ 199 Bob Abreu	.60	.25	.07
□ 200 Calvin Reese	.15	.07	.02
□ 201 Dante Powell	2.00	.90	.25
□ 202 George Arias	.30	.14	.04
□ 203 Jorge Velandia	.15	.07	.02

□ 204 George Lombard	1.25	.55	.16
□ 205 Byron Browne	.15	.07	.02
□ 206 John Frascatore	.15	.07	.02
□ 207 Terry Adams	.15	.07	.02
□ 208 Wilson Delgado	.15	.07	.02
□ 209 Billy McMillon	.15	.07	.02
□ 210 Jeff Abbott	.15	.07	.02
□ 211 Trot Nixon	.15	.07	.02
□ 212 Amaury Telemaco	.15	.07	.02
□ 213 Scott Sullivan	.15	.07	.02
□ 214 Justin Thompson	.15	.07	.02
□ 215 Decomba Conner	.15	.07	.02
□ 216 Ryan McGuire	.15	.07	.02
□ 217 Matt Luke	.15	.07	.02
□ 218 Doug Million	.30	.14	.04
□ 219 Jason Dickson	.30	.14	.04
□ 220 Ramon Hernandez	.60	.25	.07
□ 221 Mark Bellhorn	.50	.23	.06
□ 222 Eric Ludwick	.15	.07	.02
□ 223 Luke Wilcox	.15	.07	.02
□ 224 Marty Malloy	.15	.07	.02
□ 225 Gary Coffee	.50	.23	.06
□ 226 Wendell Magee	.50	.23	.06
□ 227 Brett Tomko	.50	.23	.06
□ 228 Derek Lowe	.15	.07	.02
□ 229 Jose Rosado	.75	.35	.09
□ 230 Steve Bourgeois	.15	.07	.02
□ 231 Neil Weber	.15	.07	.02
□ 232 Jeff Ware	.15	.07	.02
□ 233 Edwin Diaz	.30	.14	.04
□ 234 Greg Norton	.15	.07	.02
□ 235 Aaron Boone	.30	.14	.04
□ 236 Jeff Suppan	.30	.14	.04
□ 237 Bret Wagner	.15	.07	.02
□ 238 Elieser Marrero	.15	.07	.02
□ 239 Will Cunnane	.15	.07	.02
□ 240 Brian Barkley	.40	.18	.05
□ 241 Jay Payton	.75	.35	.09
□ 242 Marcus Jensen	.15	.07	.02
□ 243 Ryan Nye	.15	.07	.02
□ 244 Chad Mottola	.15	.07	.02
□ 245 Scott McClain	.15	.07	.02
□ 246 Jessie Ibarra	.30	.14	.04
□ 247 Mike Darr	.50	.23	.06
□ 248 Bobby Estalella	.75	.35	.09
□ 249 Michael Barrett	.15	.07	.02
□ 250 Jamie Lopiccolo	.40	.18	.05
□ 251 Shane Spencer	.15	.07	.02
□ 252 Ben Petrick	.75	.35	.09
□ 253 Jason Bell	.40	.18	.05
□ 254 Arnold Gooch	.50	.23	.06
□ 255 T.J. Mathews	.15	.07	.02
□ 256 Jason Ryan	.15	.07	.02
□ 257 Pat Cline	.75	.35	.09
□ 258 Rafael Carmona	.15	.07	.02
□ 259 Carl Pavano	2.00	.90	.25
□ 260 Ben Davis	.75	.35	.09
□ 261 Matt Lawton	.15	.07	.02
□ 262 Kevin Sefcik	.15	.07	.02
□ 263 Chris Fussell	.75	.35	.09
□ 264 Mike Cameron	1.50	.70	.19
□ 265 Marty Janzen	.50	.23	.06
□ 266 Livan Hernandez	.75	.35	.09
□ 267 Raul Ibanez	.30	.14	.04
□ 268 Juan Encarnacion	.30	.14	.04
□ 269 David Yocum	.40	.18	.05
□ 270 Jonathan Johnson	.50	.23	.06
□ 271 Reggie Taylor	.30	.14	.04
□ 272 Danny Buxbaum	.15	.07	.02
□ 273 Jacob Cruz	.30	.14	.04
□ 274 Bobby Morris	.15	.07	.02
□ 275 Andy Fox	.15	.07	.02
□ 276 Greg Keagle	.15	.07	.02
□ 277 Charles Peterson	.15	.07	.02
□ 278 Derrek Lee	.75	.35	.09
□ 279 Bryant Nelson	.40	.18	.05
□ 280 Antone Williamson	.75	.35	.09
□ 281 Scott Elarton	.30	.14	.04
□ 282 Shad Williams	.15	.07	.02
□ 283 Rich Hunter	.40	.18	.05
□ 284 Chris Sheff	.15	.07	.02
□ 285 Derrick Gibson	1.00	.45	.12
□ 286 Felix Rodriguez	.15	.07	.02
□ 287 Brian Banks	.15	.07	.02
□ 288 Jason McDonald	.15	.07	.02
□ 289 Glendon Rusch	.50	.23	.06
□ 290 Gary Rath	.15	.07	.02
□ 291 Peter Munro	.15	.07	.02
□ 292 Tom Fordham	.30	.14	.04
□ 293 Jason Kendall	.30	.14	.04
□ 294 Russ Johnson	.75	.35	.09
□ 295 Joe Long	.15	.07	.02
□ 296 Robert Smith	.60	.25	.07
□ 297 Jarrod Washburn	.50	.23	.06
□ 298 Dave Coggin	.50	.23	.06
□ 299 Jeff Yoder	.40	.18	.05
□ 300 Jed Hansen	.15	.07	.02
□ 301 Matt Morris	.75	.35	.09
□ 302 Josh Bishop	.40	.18	.05
□ 303 Dustin Hermanson	.15	.07	.02
□ 304 Mike Gulan	.15	.07	.02
□ 305 Felipe Crespo	.15	.07	.02
□ 306 Quinton McCracken	.15	.07	.02
□ 307 Jim Bonnici	.15	.07	.02
□ 308 Sal Fasano	.15	.07	.02
□ 309 Gabe Alvarez	.75	.35	.09
□ 310 Heath Murray	.40	.18	.05
□ 311 Jose Valentin	1.50	.70	.19
□ 312 Bartolo Colon	1.00	.45	.12
□ 313 Olmedo Saenz	.15	.07	.02
□ 314 Norm Hutchins	.40	.18	.05
□ 315 Chris Holt	.15	.07	.02
□ 316 David Doster	.15	.07	.02
□ 317 Robert Person	.15	.07	.02
□ 318 Donne Wall	.15	.07	.02
□ 319 Adam Riggs	.30	.14	.04
□ 320 Homer Bush	.15	.07	.02
□ 321 Brad Rigby	.15	.07	.02
□ 322 Lou Merloni	.15	.07	.02
□ 323 Neifi Perez	.30	.14	.04
□ 324 Chris Cumberland	.15	.07	.02
□ 325 Alvie Shepherd	.50	.23	.06
□ 326 Jarrod Patterson	.15	.07	.02
□ 327 Ray Ricken	.15	.07	.02
□ 328 Danny Klassen	.15	.07	.02
□ 329 David Miller	.40	.18	.05
□ 330 Chad Alexander	.75	.35	.09
□ 331 Matt Beaumont	.30	.14	.04
□ 332 Damon Hollins	.15	.07	.02
□ 333 Todd Dunn	.15	.07	.02
□ 334 Mike Sweeney	1.00	.45	.12
□ 335 Richie Sexson	.30	.14	.04
□ 336 Billy Wagner	.15	.07	.02
□ 337 Ron Wright	5.00	2.20	.60
□ 338 Paul Konerko	2.00	.90	.25
□ 339 Tommy Phelps	.40	.18	.05
□ 340 Karim Garcia	1.00	.45	.12
□ 341 Mike Grace	.15	.07	.02
□ 342 Russell Branyan	3.00	1.35	.35
□ 343 Randy Winn	.40	.18	.05
□ 344 A.J. Pierzynski	.60	.25	.07
□ 345 Mike Busby	.15	.07	.02
□ 346 Matt Beech	.40	.18	.05
□ 347 Jose Cepeda	.40	.18	.05
□ 348 Brian Stephenson	.15	.07	.02
□ 349 Rey Ordonez	1.00	.45	.12
□ 350 Rich Aurilla	.15	.07	.02
□ 351 Edgard Velazquez	1.50	.70	.19
□ 352 Raul Casanova	.30	.14	.04
□ 353 Carlos Guillen	.15	.07	.02
□ 354 Bruce Aven	.30	.14	.04
□ 355 Ryan Jones	.75	.35	.09
□ 356 Derek Aucoin	.15	.07	.02
□ 357 Brian Rose	1.00	.45	.12
□ 358 Richard Almanzar	.30	.14	.04
□ 359 Fletcher Bates	.40	.18	.05
□ 360 Russ Ortiz	.15	.07	.02
□ 361 Wilton Guerrero	1.00	.45	.12
□ 362 Geoff Jenkins	1.00	.45	.12
□ 363 Pete Janicki	.15	.07	.02
□ 364 Yamil Benitez	.15	.07	.02
□ 365 Aaron Holbert	.15	.07	.02
□ 366 Tim Belk	.15	.07	.02
□ 367 Terrell Wade	.15	.07	.02
□ 368 Terrence Long	.30	.14	.04
□ 369 Brad Fullmer	.30	.14	.04
□ 370 Matt Wagner	.15	.07	.02
□ 371 Craig Wilson	.15	.07	.02
□ 372 Mark Loretta	.15	.07	.02
□ 373 Eric Owens	.15	.07	.02
□ 374 Vladimir Guerrero	3.00	1.35	.35
□ 375 Tommy Davis	.15	.07	.02

□ 376 Donnie Sadler	.30	.14	.04
□ 377 Edgar Renteria	.75	.35	.09
□ 378 Todd Helton	3.00	1.35	.35
□ 379 Ralph Milliard	.15	.07	.02
□ 380 Darin Blood	1.25	.55	.16
□ 381 Shayne Bennett	.15	.07	.02
□ 382 Mark Redman	.30	.14	.04
□ 383 Felix Martinez	.15	.07	.02
□ 384 Sean Watkins	.75	.35	.09
□ 385 Oscar Henriquez	.15	.07	.02
□ NNO 1952 Bowman Mantle Reprint	10.00	4.50	1.25
□ NNO Unnumbered Checklists	.10	.05	.01

1996 Bowman Minor League POY

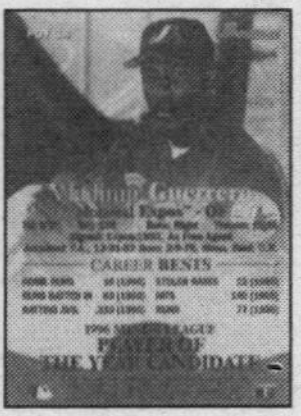

Randomly inserted in packs at a rate of one in 12, this 15-card set features top minor league prospects for Player of the Year Candidates. The fronts carry a color player photo with red-and-silver foil printing. The backs display player information including his career bests.

	MINT	NRMT	EXC
COMPLETE SET (15)	60.00	27.00	7.50
COMMON CARD (1-15)	1.50	.70	.19
RANDOM INSERTS IN PACKS			

□ 1 Andruw Jones	25.00	11.00	3.10
□ 2 Derrick Gibson	3.00	1.35	.35
□ 3 Bob Abreu	2.00	.90	.25
□ 4 Todd Walker	8.00	3.60	1.00
□ 5 Jamey Wright	1.50	.70	.19
□ 6 Wes Helms	6.00	2.70	.75
□ 7 Karim Garcia	4.00	1.80	.50
□ 8 Bartolo Colon	2.50	1.10	.30
□ 9 Alex Ochoa	1.50	.70	.19
□ 10 Mike Sweeney	3.00	1.35	.35
□ 11 Ruben Rivera	4.00	1.80	.50
□ 12 Gabe Alvarez	2.00	.90	.25
□ 13 Billy Wagner	1.50	.70	.19
□ 14 Vladimir Guerrero	12.00	5.50	1.50
□ 15 Edgard Velazquez	4.00	1.80	.50

1994 Bowman's Best

This 200-card standard-size set consists of 90 veteran stars, 90 rookies and prospects and 20 Mirror Image cards. The veteran cards have red backs and are designated 1R-90R. The rookies and prospects cards have blue backs and are designated 1B-90B. The Mirror Image cards feature a veteran star and a prospect matched by position. These cards are numbered 91-110. Subsets featured are Super Vet (1R-6R), Super Rookie (82R-90R), and Blue Chip (1B-11B). Rookie Cards include Alan Benes, Brooks Kieschnick, Chan Ho Park and Ruben Rivera.

	MINT	NRMT	EXC
COMPLETE SET (200)	80.00	36.00	10.00
COMMON BLUE CARD (B1-B90)	.25	.11	.03
COMMON RED CARD (R1-R90)	.25	.11	.03
COMMON MIR.IMAGE (X91-X110)	.25	.11	.03
SEMISTARS	.50	.23	.06
STARS	1.00	.45	.12

□ B1 Chipper Jones	6.00	2.70	.75
□ B2 Derek Jeter	6.00	2.70	.75
□ B3 Bill Pulsipher	.50	.23	.06
□ B4 James Baldwin	1.50	.70	.19
□ B5 Brooks Kieschnick	1.50	.70	.19
□ B6 Justin Thompson	.50	.23	.06
□ B7 Midre Cummings	.25	.11	.03
□ B8 Joey Hamilton	1.50	.70	.19
□ B9 Calvin Reese	.50	.23	.06
□ B10 Brian Barber	.25	.11	.03
□ B11 John Burke	.25	.11	.03
□ B12 DeShawn Warren	.25	.11	.03
□ B13 Edgardo Alfonzo	1.00	.45	.12
□ B14 Eddie Pearson	1.00	.45	.12
□ B15 Jimmy Haynes	.50	.23	.06
□ B16 Danny Bautista	.25	.11	.03
□ B17 Roger Cedeno	1.00	.45	.12
□ B18 Jon Lieber	.25	.11	.03
□ B19 Billy Wagner	2.00	.90	.25
□ B20 Tate Seefried	.50	.23	.06
□ B21 Chad Mottola	.25	.11	.03
□ B22 Jose Malave	.50	.23	.06
□ B23 Terrell Wade	1.50	.70	.19
□ B24 Shane Andrews	.50	.23	.06
□ B25 Chan Ho Park	2.00	.90	.25
□ B26 Kirk Presley	1.00	.45	.12
□ B27 Robbie Beckett	.25	.11	.03
□ B28 Orlando Miller	.25	.11	.03
□ B29 Jorge Posada	.50	.23	.06
□ B30 Frankie Rodriguez	.50	.23	.06
□ B31 Brian L.Hunter	1.25	.55	.16
□ B32 Billy Ashley	.25	.11	.03
□ B33 Rondell White	1.00	.45	.12
□ B34 John Roper	.25	.11	.03
□ B35 Marc Valdes	.50	.23	.06
□ B36 Scott Ruffcorn	.25	.11	.03
□ B37 Rod Henderson	.25	.11	.03
□ B38 Curtis Goodwin	.50	.23	.06
□ B39 Russ Davis	.50	.23	.06
□ B40 Rick Gorecki	.25	.11	.03
□ B41 Johnny Damon	1.25	.55	.16
□ B42 Roberto Petagine	.50	.23	.06
□ B43 Chris Snopek	.25	.11	.03
□ B44 Mark Acre	.25	.11	.03
□ B45 Todd Hollandsworth	2.00	.90	.25
□ B46 Shawn Green	.50	.23	.06
□ B47 John Carter	.25	.11	.03
□ B48 Jim Pittsley	1.00	.45	.12
□ B49 John Wasdin	1.00	.45	.12
□ B50 D.J.Boston	.25	.11	.03
□ B51 Tim Clark	.25	.11	.03
□ B52 Alex Ochoa	.50	.23	.06
□ B53 Chad Roper	.25	.11	.03
□ B54 Mike Kelly	.25	.11	.03
□ B55 Brad Fullmer	1.50	.70	.19
□ B56 Carl Everett	.25	.11	.03
□ B57 Tim Belk	.50	.23	.06
□ B58 Jimmy Hurst	.50	.23	.06
□ B59 Mac Suzuki	.50	.23	.06
□ B60 Michael Moore	.25	.11	.03
□ B61 Alan Benes	3.00	1.35	.35
□ B62 Tony Clark	5.00	2.20	.60
□ B63 Edgar Renteria	5.00	2.20	.60
□ B64 Trey Beamon	1.00	.45	.12
□ B65 LaTroy Hawkins	.50	.23	.06
□ B66 Wayne Gomes	.50	.23	.06
□ B67 Ray McDavid	.50	.23	.06
□ B68 John Dettmer	.25	.11	.03
□ B69 Willie Greene	.50	.23	.06

□	B70	Dave Stevens	.25	.11	.03
□	B71	Kevin Orie	1.50	.70	.19
□	B72	Chad Ogea	.50	.23	.06
□	B73	Ben Van Ryn	.25	.11	.03
□	B74	Kym Ashworth	.50	.23	.06
□	B75	Dmitri Young	1.50	.70	.19
□	B76	Herbert Perry	.50	.23	.06
□	B77	Joey Eischen	.25	.11	.03
□	B78	Arquimedez Pozo	1.00	.45	.12
□	B79	Ugueth Urbina	.50	.23	.06
□	B80	Keith Williams	.50	.23	.06
□	B81	John Frascatore	.25	.11	.03
□	B82	Garey Ingram	.25	.11	.03
□	B83	Aaron Small	.25	.11	.03
□	B84	Olmedo Saenz	.25	.11	.03
□	B85	Jesus Tavarez	.25	.11	.03
□	B86	Jose Silva	.50	.23	.06
□	B87	Jay Witasick	.50	.23	.06
□	B88	Jay Maldonado	.25	.11	.03
□	B89	Keith Heberling	.25	.11	.03
□	B90	Rusty Greer	3.00	1.35	.35
□	R1	Paul Molitor	1.50	.70	.19
□	R2	Eddie Murray	2.00	.90	.25
□	R3	Ozzie Smith	1.50	.70	.19
□	R4	Rickey Henderson	1.00	.45	.12
□	R5	Lee Smith	.50	.23	.06
□	R6	Dave Winfield	1.00	.45	.12
□	R7	Roberto Alomar	2.00	.90	.25
□	R8	Matt Williams	1.00	.45	.12
□	R9	Mark Grace	1.00	.45	.12
□	R10	Lance Johnson	.50	.23	.06
□	R11	Darren Daulton	.50	.23	.06
□	R12	Tom Glavine	1.00	.45	.12
□	R13	Gary Sheffield	1.00	.45	.12
□	R14	Rod Beck	.50	.23	.06
□	R15	Fred McGriff	1.00	.45	.12
□	R16	Joe Carter	1.00	.45	.12
□	R17	Dante Bichette	1.00	.45	.12
□	R18	Danny Tartabull	.25	.11	.03
□	R19	Juan Gonzalez	4.00	1.80	.50
□	R20	Steve Avery	.50	.23	.06
□	R21	John Wetteland	.50	.23	.06
□	R22	Ben McDonald	.25	.11	.03
□	R23	Jack McDowell	.50	.23	.06
□	R24	Jose Canseco	1.00	.45	.12
□	R25	Tim Salmon	1.25	.55	.16
□	R26	Wilson Alvarez	.50	.23	.06
□	R27	Gregg Jefferies	1.00	.45	.12
□	R28	John Burkett	.25	.11	.03
□	R29	Greg Vaughn	1.00	.45	.12
□	R30	Robin Ventura	.50	.23	.06
□	R31	Paul O'Neill	.50	.23	.06
□	R32	Cecil Fielder	.50	.23	.06
□	R33	Kevin Mitchell	.50	.23	.06
□	R34	Jeff Conine	1.00	.45	.12
□	R35	Carlos Baerga	1.00	.45	.12
□	R36	Greg Maddux	5.00	2.20	.60
□	R37	Roger Clemens	1.00	.45	.12
□	R38	Deion Sanders	1.00	.45	.12
□	R39	Delino DeShields	.25	.11	.03
□	R40	Ken Griffey Jr.	8.00	3.60	1.00
□	R41	Albert Belle	4.00	1.80	.50
□	R42	Wade Boggs	1.00	.45	.12
□	R43	Andres Galarraga	1.00	.45	.12
□	R44	Aaron Sele	.50	.23	.06
□	R45	Don Mattingly	4.00	1.80	.50
□	R46	David Cone	1.00	.45	.12
□	R47	Len Dykstra	.50	.23	.06
□	R48	Brett Butler	.50	.23	.06
□	R49	Bill Swift	.25	.11	.03
□	R50	Bobby Bonilla	.50	.23	.06
□	R51	Rafael Palmeiro	1.00	.45	.12
□	R52	Moises Alou	.50	.23	.06
□	R53	Jeff Bagwell	3.00	1.35	.35
□	R54	Mike Mussina	1.50	.70	.19
□	R55	Frank Thomas	8.00	3.60	1.00
□	R56	Jose Rijo	.25	.11	.03
□	R57	Ruben Sierra	.50	.23	.06
□	R58	Randy Myers	.25	.11	.03
□	R59	Barry Bonds	2.00	.90	.25
□	R60	Jimmy Key	.50	.23	.06
□	R61	Travis Fryman	1.00	.45	.12
□	R62	John Olerud	.25	.11	.03
□	R63	David Justice	1.00	.45	.12
□	R64	Ray Lankford	1.00	.45	.12
□	R65	Bob Tewksbury	.25	.11	.03
□	R66	Chuck Carr	.25	.11	.03
□	R67	Jay Buhner	1.00	.45	.12
□	R68	Kenny Lofton	2.50	1.10	.30
□	R69	Marquis Grissom	1.00	.45	.12
□	R70	Sammy Sosa	1.00	.45	.12
□	R71	Cal Ripken	6.00	2.70	.75
□	R72	Ellis Burks	.50	.23	.06
□	R73	Jeff Montgomery	.50	.23	.06
□	R74	Julio Franco	.50	.23	.06
□	R75	Kirby Puckett	2.50	1.10	.30
□	R76	Larry Walker	1.00	.45	.12
□	R77	Andy Van Slyke	.50	.23	.06
□	R78	Tony Gwynn	3.00	1.35	.35
□	R79	Will Clark	1.00	.45	.12
□	R80	Mo Vaughn	2.00	.90	.25
□	R81	Mike Piazza	5.00	2.20	.60
□	R82	James Mouton	.50	.23	.06
□	R83	Carlos Delgado	1.25	.55	.16
□	R84	Ryan Klesko	2.00	.90	.25
□	R85	Javier Lopez	1.00	.45	.12
□	R86	Raul Mondesi	1.25	.55	.16
□	R87	Cliff Floyd	1.00	.45	.12
□	R88	Manny Ramirez	2.50	1.10	.30
□	R89	Hector Carrasco	.25	.11	.03
□	R90	Jeff Granger	.50	.23	.06
□	X91	Frank Thomas Dmitri Young	4.00	1.80	.50
□	X92	Fred McGriff Brooks Kieschnick	1.00	.45	.12
□	X93	Matt Williams Shane Andrews	.25	.11	.03
□	X94	Cal Ripken Kevin Orie	3.00	1.35	.35
□	X95	Barry Larkin Derek Jeter	3.00	1.35	.35
□	X96	Ken Griffey Jr. Johnny Damon	4.00	1.80	.50
□	X97	Barry Bonds Rondell White	1.00	.45	.12
□	X98	Albert Belle Jimmy Hurst	2.00	.90	.25
□	X99	Raul Mondesi Ruben Rivera	8.00	3.60	1.00
□	X100	Roger Clemens Scott Ruffcorn	.50	.23	.06
□	X101	Greg Maddux John Wasdin	2.50	1.10	.30
□	X102	Tim Salmon Chad Mottola	.50	.23	.06
□	X103	Carlos Baerga Arquimedez Pozo	.50	.23	.06
□	X104	Mike Piazza Bobby Hughes	2.50	1.10	.30
□	X105	Carlos Delgado Melvin Nieves	1.00	.45	.12
□	X106	Javier Lopez Jorge Posada	.50	.23	.06
□	X107	Manny Ramirez Jose Malave	1.25	.55	.16
□	X108	Travis Fryman Chipper Jones	3.00	1.35	.35
□	X109	Steve Avery Bill Pulsipher	.50	.23	.06
□	X110	John Olerud Shawn Green	1.00	.45	.12

1994 Bowman's Best Refractors

This 200-card standard-size set is a parallel to the basic Bowman's Best issue. The cards were randomly inserted in packs at a rate of one in nine Bowman's Best packs. The only difference is the refractive coating that allows for a brighter, shinier appearance.

	MINT	NRMT	EXC
COMPLETE SET (200)	1200.00	550.00	150.00
COMMON CARD	3.00	1.35	.35
SEMISTARS	6.00	2.70	.75
STARS	12.00	5.50	1.50
*RED STARS: 6X to 12X BASIC CARDS			
*BLUE STARS: 4X to 8X BASIC CARDS			

*MIRROR IMAGE STARS: 3X to 6X BASIC CARDS
RANDOM INSERTS IN PACKS......................

□ B1 Chipper Jones	80.00	36.00	10.00
□ B2 Derek Jeter	70.00	32.00	8.75
□ B4 James Baldwin	15.00	6.75	1.85
□ B5 Brooks Kieschnick	15.00	6.75	1.85
□ B8 Joey Hamilton	15.00	6.75	1.85
□ B19 Billy Wagner	15.00	6.75	1.85
□ B25 Chan Ho Park	15.00	6.75	1.85
□ B41 Johnny Damon	20.00	9.00	2.50
□ B45 Todd Hollandsworth	25.00	11.00	3.10
□ B55 Brad Fullmer	15.00	6.75	1.85
□ B61 Alan Benes	25.00	11.00	3.10
□ B62 Tony Clark	30.00	13.50	3.70
□ B63 Edgar Renteria	30.00	13.50	3.70
□ B71 Kevin Orie	15.00	6.75	1.85
□ B75 Dmitri Young	20.00	9.00	2.50
□ B90 Rusty Greer	25.00	11.00	3.10
□ R1 Paul Molitor	20.00	9.00	2.50
□ R2 Eddie Murray	25.00	11.00	3.10
□ R3 Ozzie Smith	20.00	9.00	2.50
□ R7 Roberto Alomar	25.00	11.00	3.10
□ R19 Juan Gonzalez	50.00	22.00	6.25
□ R25 Tim Salmon	15.00	6.75	1.85
□ R36 Greg Maddux	60.00	27.00	7.50
□ R40 Ken Griffey Jr.	100.00	45.00	12.50
□ R41 Albert Belle	50.00	22.00	6.25
□ R45 Don Mattingly	50.00	22.00	6.25
□ R53 Jeff Bagwell	40.00	18.00	5.00
□ R54 Mike Mussina	20.00	9.00	2.50
□ R55 Frank Thomas	100.00	45.00	12.50
□ R59 Barry Bonds	25.00	11.00	3.10
□ R68 Kenny Lofton	30.00	13.50	3.70
□ R71 Cal Ripken	80.00	36.00	10.00
□ R75 Kirby Puckett	30.00	13.50	3.70
□ R78 Tony Gwynn	40.00	18.00	5.00
□ R80 Mo Vaughn	25.00	11.00	3.10
□ R81 Mike Piazza	60.00	27.00	7.50
□ R84 Ryan Klesko	25.00	11.00	3.10
□ R86 Raul Mondesi	15.00	6.75	1.85
□ R88 Manny Ramirez	30.00	13.50	3.70
□ X91 Frank Thomas Dmitri Young	30.00	13.50	3.70
□ X94 Cal Ripken Kevin Orie	25.00	11.00	3.10
□ X95 Barry Larkin Derek Jeter	20.00	9.00	2.50
□ X96 Ken Griffey Jr. Johnny Damon	40.00	18.00	5.00
□ X98 Albert Belle Jimmy Hurst	15.00	6.75	1.85
□ X99 Ruben Rivera Raul Mondesi	40.00	18.00	5.00
□ X101 Greg Maddux John Wasdin	20.00	9.00	2.50
□ X104 Mike Piazza Bobby Hughes	20.00	9.00	2.50
□ X108 Travis Fryman Chipper Jones	20.00	9.00	2.50

1995 Bowman's Best

This 195 card standard-size set consists of 90 veteran stars, 90 rookies and prospects and 15 Mirror Image cards. The veteran cards have red backs and are designated R1-R90. Cards of rookies and prospects have blue backs and are designated B1-B90. The Mirror Image cards feature a veteran star and a prospect matched by position. These cards are numbered X1-X15. The fronts have an action photo with the background in silver-foil with the team names at the top and red or blue at the bottom corresponding to the back. The packs contain seven cards and the suggested retail price was $5. The backs have a head shot along with player statistics and information. Rookie Cards include Bartolo Colon, Karim Garcia, Corey Jenkins, Andruw Jones, Hideo Nomo, Jay Payton and Richie Sexson.

	MINT	NRMT	EXC
COMPLETE SET (195)	175.00	80.00	22.00
COMMON BLUE CARD (B1-B90)	.25	.11	.03
COMMON RED CARD (R1-R90)	.25	.11	.03
COMMON CARD (X1-X15)	1.00	.45	.12
SEMISTARS	.50	.23	.06
STARS	1.00	.45	.12
□ B1 Derek Jeter	5.00	2.20	.60
□ B2 Vladimir Guerrero	20.00	9.00	2.50
□ B3 Bob Abreu	3.00	1.35	.35
□ B4 Chan Ho Park	1.00	.45	.12
□ B5 Paul Wilson	1.50	.70	.19
□ B6 Chad Ogea	.25	.11	.03
□ B7 Andruw Jones	50.00	22.00	6.25
□ B8 Brian Barber	.25	.11	.03
□ B9 Andy Larkin	.25	.11	.03
□ B10 Richie Sexson	3.00	1.35	.35
□ B11 Everett Stull	.25	.11	.03
□ B12 Brooks Kieschnick	.50	.23	.06
□ B13 Matt Murray	.25	.11	.03
□ B14 John Wasdin	.25	.11	.03
□ B15 Shannon Stewart	.25	.11	.03
□ B16 Luis Ortiz	.25	.11	.03
□ B17 Marc Kroon	.25	.11	.03
□ B18 Todd Greene	1.25	.55	.16
□ B19 Juan Acevedo	.25	.11	.03
□ B20 Tony Clark	2.00	.90	.25
□ B21 Jermaine Dye	5.00	2.20	.60
□ B22 Derrek Lee	1.50	.70	.19
□ B23 Pat Watkins	.50	.23	.06
□ B24 Calvin Reese	.25	.11	.03
□ B25 Ben Grieve	4.00	1.80	.50
□ B26 Julio Santana	.25	.11	.03
□ B27 Felix Rodriguez	.50	.23	.06
□ B28 Paul Konerko	8.00	3.60	1.00
□ B29 Nomar Garciaparra	5.00	2.20	.60
□ B30 Pat Ahearne	.25	.11	.03
□ B31 Jason Schmidt	.50	.23	.06
□ B32 Billy Wagner	.50	.23	.06
□ B33 Rey Ordonez RC	5.00	2.20	.60
□ B34 Curtis Goodwin	.50	.23	.06
□ B35 Sergio Nunez	1.00	.45	.12
□ B36 Tim Belk	.25	.11	.03
□ B37 Scott Elarton	1.00	.45	.12
□ B38 Jason Isringhausen	2.00	.90	.25
□ B39 Trot Nixon	.50	.23	.06
□ B40 Sid Roberson	.25	.11	.03
□ B41 Ron Villone	.25	.11	.03
□ B42 Ruben Rivera	4.00	1.80	.50
□ B43 Rick Huisman	.25	.11	.03
□ B44 Todd Hollandsworth	1.25	.55	.16
□ B45 Johnny Damon	1.00	.45	.12
□ B46 Garret Anderson	1.00	.45	.12
□ B47 Jeff D'Amico	.50	.23	.06
□ B48 Dustin Hermanson	.50	.23	.06
□ B49 Juan Encarnacion	1.50	.70	.19

□ B50	Andy Pettitte	3.00	1.35	.35
□ B51	Chris Stynes	.25	.11	.03
□ B52	Troy Percival	.25	.11	.03
□ B53	LaTroy Hawkins	.25	.11	.03
□ B54	Roger Cedeno	.50	.23	.06
□ B55	Alan Benes	1.25	.55	.16
□ B56	Karim Garcia	8.00	3.60	1.00
□ B57	Andrew Lorraine	.50	.23	.06
□ B58	Gary Rath	.25	.11	.03
□ B59	Bret Wagner	.50	.23	.06
□ B60	Jeff Suppan	1.00	.45	.12
□ B61	Bill Pulsipher	.50	.23	.06
□ B62	Jay Payton	5.00	2.20	.60
□ B63	Alex Ochoa	1.00	.45	.12
□ B64	Ugueth Urbina	.25	.11	.03
□ B65	Armando Benitez	.25	.11	.03
□ B66	George Arias	1.00	.45	.12
□ B67	Raul Casanova	1.50	.70	.19
□ B68	Matt Drews	.50	.23	.06
□ B69	Jimmy Haynes	.50	.23	.06
□ B70	Jimmy Hurst	.50	.23	.06
□ B71	C.J. Nitkowski	.50	.23	.06
□ B72	Tommy Davis	.50	.23	.06
□ B73	Bartolo Colon	5.00	2.20	.60
□ B74	Chris Carpenter	2.00	.90	.25
□ B75	Trey Beamon	.50	.23	.06
□ B76	Bryan Rekar	.25	.11	.03
□ B77	James Baldwin	1.00	.45	.12
□ B78	Marc Valdes	.25	.11	.03
□ B79	Tom Fordham	.50	.23	.06
□ B80	Marc Newfield	.25	.11	.03
□ B81	Angel Martinez	.25	.11	.03
□ B82	Brian L. Hunter	1.00	.45	.12
□ B83	Jose Herrera	.25	.11	.03
□ B84	Glenn Dishman	.50	.23	.06
□ B85	Jacob Cruz	1.50	.70	.19
□ B86	Paul Shuey	.25	.11	.03
□ B87	Scott Rolen	12.00	5.50	1.50
□ B88	Doug Million	.50	.23	.06
□ B89	Desi Relaford	.50	.23	.06
□ B90	Michael Tucker	.50	.23	.06
□ R1	Randy Johnson	1.25	.55	.16
□ R2	Joe Carter	1.00	.45	.12
□ R3	Chili Davis	.50	.23	.06
□ R4	Moises Alou	.50	.23	.06
□ R5	Gary Sheffield	1.25	.55	.16
□ R6	Kevin Appier	.50	.23	.06
□ R7	Denny Neagle	.50	.23	.06
□ R8	Ruben Sierra	.50	.23	.06
□ R9	Darren Daulton	.50	.23	.06
□ R10	Cal Ripken	6.00	2.70	.75
□ R11	Bobby Bonilla	.50	.23	.06
□ R12	Manny Ramirez	2.00	.90	.25
□ R13	Barry Bonds	2.00	.90	.25
□ R14	Eric Karros	.50	.23	.06
□ R15	Greg Maddux	5.00	2.20	.60
□ R16	Jeff Bagwell	3.00	1.35	.35
□ R17	Paul Molitor	1.50	.70	.19
□ R18	Ray Lankford	1.00	.45	.12
□ R19	Mark Grace	1.00	.45	.12
□ R20	Kenny Lofton	2.00	.90	.25
□ R21	Tony Gwynn	3.00	1.35	.35
□ R22	Will Clark	1.00	.45	.12
□ R23	Roger Clemens	1.00	.45	.12
□ R24	Dante Bichette	1.00	.45	.12
□ R25	Barry Larkin	1.00	.45	.12
□ R26	Wade Boggs	1.00	.45	.12
□ R27	Kirby Puckett	2.50	1.10	.30
□ R28	Cecil Fielder	.50	.23	.06
□ R29	Jose Canseco	1.00	.45	.12
□ R30	Juan Gonzalez	4.00	1.80	.50
□ R31	David Cone	.50	.23	.06
□ R32	Craig Biggio	1.00	.45	.12
□ R33	Tim Salmon	1.00	.45	.12
□ R34	David Justice	1.00	.45	.12
□ R35	Sammy Sosa	1.25	.55	.16
□ R36	Mike Piazza	5.00	2.20	.60
□ R37	Carlos Baerga	1.00	.45	.12
□ R38	Jeff Conine	1.00	.45	.12
□ R39	Rafael Palmeiro	1.00	.45	.12
□ R40	Bret Saberhagen	.50	.23	.06
□ R41	Len Dykstra	.50	.23	.06
□ R42	Mo Vaughn	2.00	.90	.25
□ R43	Wally Joyner	.50	.23	.06
□ R44	Chuck Knoblauch	1.00	.45	.12
□ R45	Robin Ventura	.50	.23	.06
□ R46	Don Mattingly	4.00	1.80	.50
□ R47	Dave Hollins	.25	.11	.03
□ R48	Andy Benes	.25	.11	.03
□ R49	Ken Griffey Jr.	8.00	3.60	1.00
□ R50	Albert Belle	4.00	1.80	.50
□ R51	Matt Williams	1.00	.45	.12
□ R52	Rondell White	1.00	.45	.12
□ R53	Raul Mondesi	1.00	.45	.12
□ R54	Brian Jordan	1.00	.45	.12
□ R55	Greg Vaughn	.50	.23	.06
□ R56	Fred McGriff	1.00	.45	.12
□ R57	Roberto Alomar	2.00	.90	.25
□ R58	Dennis Eckersley	.50	.23	.06
□ R59	Lee Smith	.50	.23	.06
□ R60	Eddie Murray	2.00	.90	.25
□ R61	Kenny Rogers	.25	.11	.03
□ R62	Ron Gant	.50	.23	.06
□ R63	Larry Walker	1.00	.45	.12
□ R64	Chad Curtis	.25	.11	.03
□ R65	Frank Thomas	8.00	3.60	1.00
□ R66	Paul O'Neill	.50	.23	.06
□ R67	Kevin Seitzer	.25	.11	.03
□ R68	Marquis Grissom	1.00	.45	.12
□ R69	Mark McGwire	2.50	1.10	.30
□ R70	Travis Fryman	.50	.23	.06
□ R71	Andres Galarraga	1.00	.45	.12
□ R72	Carlos Perez	.50	.23	.06
□ R73	Tyler Green	.25	.11	.03
□ R74	Marty Cordova	1.25	.55	.16
□ R75	Shawn Green	.50	.23	.06
□ R76	Vaughn Eshelman	.25	.11	.03
□ R77	John Mabry	1.00	.45	.12
□ R78	Jason Bates	.25	.11	.03
□ R79	Jon Nunnally	.50	.23	.06
□ R80	Ray Durham	.50	.23	.06
□ R81	Edgardo Alfonzo	.50	.23	.06
□ R82	Esteban Loaiza	.25	.11	.03
□ R83	Hideo Nomo	8.00	3.60	1.00
□ R84	Orlando Miller	.25	.11	.03
□ R85	Alex Gonzalez	.25	.11	.03
□ R86	Mark Grudzielanek	2.00	.90	.25
□ R87	Julian Tavarez	.25	.11	.03
□ R88	Benji Gil	.25	.11	.03
□ R89	Quilvio Veras	.25	.11	.03
□ R90	Ricky Bottalico	.50	.23	.06
□ X1	Ben Davis	1.50	.70	.19
	Ivan Rodriguez			
□ X2	Mark Redman	1.00	.45	.12
	Manny Ramirez			
□ X3	Reggie Taylor	1.50	.70	.19
	Deion Sanders			
□ X4	Ryan Jaroncyk	1.25	.55	.16
	Shawn Green			
□ X5	Juan LeBron	2.00	.90	.25
	Juan Gonzalez			
□ X6	Toby McKnight	1.25	.55	.16
	Craig Biggio			
□ X7	Michael Barrett	1.25	.55	.16
	Travis Fryman			
□ X8	Corey Jenkins	2.50	1.10	.30
	Mo Vaughn			
□ X9	Ruben Rivera	5.00	2.20	.60
	Frank Thomas			
□ X10	Curtis Goodwin	1.00	.45	.12
	Kenny Lofton			
□ X11	Brian L. Hunter	1.50	.70	.19
	Tony Gwynn			
□ X12	Todd Greene	4.00	1.80	.50
	Ken Griffey Jr.			
□ X13	Karim Garcia	2.00	.90	.25
	Matt Williams			
□ X14	Billy Wagner	1.00	.45	.12
	Randy Johnson			
□ X15	Pat Watkins	1.50	.70	.19
	Jeff Bagwell			

1995 Bowman's Best Refractors

Randomly inserted at a rate of one in six packs, this set is a parallel to the basic Bowman's Best issue. As far as the refractive qualities, the final 15 Mirror Image cards (X1-X15) are considered diffractors which reflects light in a differ-

ent manner than the typical refractor. The veteran refractor cards have been seen with or without the word refractor on the back. So far, there is no difference in pricing for either variation.

	MINT	NRMT	EXC
COMPLETE SET (195)	2500.00	1100.00	300.00
COMMON BLUE (B1-B90)	4.00	1.80	.50
COMMON RED (R1-R90)	4.00	1.80	.50
COMMON MIR.IMAGE (X1-X15)	5.00	2.20	.60
SEMISTARS	8.00	3.60	1.00
STARS	15.00	6.75	1.85

*STARS: 10X to 16X BASIC CARDS
*YOUNG STARS: 6X TO 12X BASIC CARDS
*RCs: 4X TO 8X BASIC CARDS
*MIRROR IMAGE DIFFRACTION: 2.5X TO 5X BASIC CARDS
RANDOM INSERTS IN PACKS

	MINT	NRMT	EXC
□ B1 Derek Jeter	80.00	36.00	10.00
□ B2 Vladimir Guerrero	150.00	70.00	19.00
□ B3 Bob Abreu	15.00	6.75	1.85
□ B5 Paul Wilson	25.00	11.00	3.10
□ B7 Andruw Jones	300.00	135.00	38.00
□ B10 Richie Sexson	25.00	11.00	3.10
□ B18 Todd Greene	15.00	6.75	1.85
□ B20 Tony Clark	20.00	9.00	2.50
□ B21 Jermaine Dye	50.00	22.00	6.25
□ B22 Derrek Lee	20.00	9.00	2.50
□ B25 Ben Grieve	30.00	13.50	3.70
□ B28 Paul Konerko	60.00	27.00	7.50
□ B29 Nomar Garciaparra	50.00	22.00	6.25
□ B33 Rey Ordonez	40.00	18.00	5.00
□ B38 Jason Isringhausen	25.00	11.00	3.10
□ B42 Ruben Rivera	40.00	18.00	5.00
□ B44 Todd Hollandsworth	15.00	6.75	1.85
□ B45 Johnny Damon	25.00	11.00	3.10
□ B50 Andy Pettitte	50.00	22.00	6.25
□ B55 Alan Benes	15.00	6.75	1.85
□ B56 Karim Garcia	60.00	27.00	7.50
□ B62 Jay Payton	40.00	18.00	5.00
□ B73 Bartolo Colon	30.00	13.50	3.70
□ B87 Scott Rolen	80.00	36.00	10.00
□ R1 Randy Johnson	20.00	9.00	2.50
□ R5 Gary Sheffield	20.00	9.00	2.50
□ R10 Cal Ripken	100.00	45.00	12.50
□ R12 Manny Ramirez	30.00	13.50	3.70
□ R13 Barry Bonds	30.00	13.50	3.70
□ R15 Greg Maddux	80.00	36.00	10.00
□ R16 Jeff Bagwell	50.00	22.00	6.25
□ R17 Paul Molitor	25.00	11.00	3.10
□ R20 Kenny Lofton	30.00	13.50	3.70
□ R21 Tony Gwynn	50.00	22.00	6.25
□ R27 Kirby Puckett	40.00	18.00	5.00
□ R30 Juan Gonzalez	60.00	27.00	7.50
□ R35 Sammy Sosa	20.00	9.00	2.50
□ R36 Mike Piazza	80.00	36.00	10.00
□ R42 Mo Vaughn	30.00	13.50	3.70
□ R46 Don Mattingly	60.00	27.00	7.50
□ R49 Ken Griffey Jr.	125.00	55.00	15.50
□ R50 Albert Belle	60.00	27.00	7.50
□ R57 Roberto Alomar	30.00	13.50	3.70
□ R60 Eddie Murray	30.00	13.50	3.70
□ R65 Frank Thomas	125.00	55.00	15.50
□ R69 Mark McGwire	40.00	18.00	5.00
□ R83 Hideo Nomo	60.00	27.00	7.50
□ X9 Ruben Rivera Frank Thomas	25.00	11.00	3.10
□ X12 Todd Greene Ken Griffey Jr.	20.00	9.00	2.50

1996 Bowman's Best Previews

Printed with Finest technology, this 30-card set features the hottest 15 top prospects and 15 veterans and was randomly inserted in 1996 Bowman packs at the rate of one in 12. The fronts display a color action player photo. The backs carry player information.

	MINT	NRMT	EXC
COMPLETE SET (30)	200.00	90.00	25.00
COMMON CARD (BBP1-BBP30)	2.00	.90	.25
SEMISTARS	3.00	1.35	.35

*REFRACTORS: 1X BASIC CARDS
*ATOMIC STARS: 2X BASIC CARDS
RANDOM INSERTS IN BOWMAN PACKS

	MINT	NRMT	EXC
□ BBP1 Chipper Jones	15.00	6.75	1.85
□ BBP2 Alan Benes	2.50	1.10	.30
□ BBP3 Brooks Kieschnick	2.00	.90	.25
□ BBP4 Barry Bonds	6.00	2.70	.75
□ BBP5 Rey Ordonez	5.00	2.20	.60
□ BBP6 Tim Salmon	3.00	1.35	.35
□ BBP7 Mike Piazza	15.00	6.75	1.85
□ BBP8 Billy Wagner	2.00	.90	.25
□ BBP9 Andruw Jones	25.00	11.00	3.10
□ BBP10 Tony Gwynn	10.00	4.50	1.25
□ BBP11 Paul Wilson	4.00	1.80	.50
□ BBP12 Calvin Reese	2.00	.90	.25
□ BBP13 Frank Thomas	25.00	11.00	3.10
□ BBP14 Greg Maddux	15.00	6.75	1.85
□ BBP15 Derek Jeter	15.00	6.75	1.85
□ BBP16 Jeff Bagwell	10.00	4.50	1.25
□ BBP17 Barry Larkin	3.00	1.35	.35
□ BBP18 Todd Greene	2.50	1.10	.30
□ BBP19 Ruben Rivera	6.00	2.70	.75
□ BBP20 Richard Hidalgo	4.00	1.80	.50
□ BBP21 Larry Walker	2.00	.90	.25
□ BBP22 Carlos Baerga	2.00	.90	.25
□ BBP23 Derrick Gibson	4.00	1.80	.50
□ BBP24 Richie Sexson	3.00	1.35	.35
□ BBP25 Mo Vaughn	6.00	2.70	.75
□ BBP26 Hideo Nomo	6.00	2.70	.75
□ BBP27 Nomar Garciaparra	6.00	2.70	.75
□ BBP28 Cal Ripken	20.00	9.00	2.50
□ BBP29 Karim Garcia	6.00	2.70	.75
□ BBP30 Ken Griffey Jr.	25.00	11.00	3.10

1996 Bowman's Best

This 180-card set was issued in packs of six cards at the cost of $4.99 per pack. The fronts feature a color action player cutout of 90 outstanding veteran players on a chromium classic gold background design and 90 up and coming prospects and rookies on a silver design. The backs carry a color player portrait, player information and statistics. A reprint of the 1952 Mickey Mantle card #20 was inserted at the rate of one in 24 packs. A Refractor version of the Mantle was seeded at 1:96 packs and an Atomic Refractor version was seeded at 1:192.

	MINT	NRMT	EXC
COMPLETE SET (180)	100.00	45.00	12.50
COMMON GOLD (1-90)	.25	.11	.03
COMMON SILVER (91-180)	.25	.11	.03
SEMISTARS	.50	.23	.06
STARS	.75	.35	.09
NUMBER 33 NEVER ISSUED			
CLEMENS AND PALMEIRO NUMBERED 32.			

	MINT	NRMT	EXC
□ 1 Hideo Nomo	2.00	.90	.25
□ 2 Edgar Martinez	.75	.35	.09
□ 3 Cal Ripken	6.00	2.70	.75
□ 4 Wade Boggs	.75	.35	.09
□ 5 Cecil Fielder	.50	.23	.06
□ 6 Albert Belle	4.00	1.80	.50
□ 7 Chipper Jones	5.00	2.20	.60
□ 8 Ryne Sandberg	2.00	.90	.25
□ 9 Tim Salmon	.75	.35	.09
□ 10 Barry Bonds	2.00	.90	.25
□ 11 Ken Caminiti	.75	.35	.09
□ 12 Ron Gant	.50	.23	.06
□ 13 Frank Thomas	8.00	3.60	1.00
□ 14 Dante Bichette	.75	.35	.09
□ 15 Jason Kendall	.50	.23	.06
□ 16 Mo Vaughn	2.00	.90	.25
□ 17 Rey Ordonez	1.50	.70	.19
□ 18 Henry Rodriguez	.25	.11	.03
□ 19 Ryan Klesko	1.50	.70	.19
□ 20 Jeff Bagwell	3.00	1.35	.35
□ 21 Randy Johnson	.75	.35	.09
□ 22 Jim Edmonds	.75	.35	.09
□ 23 Kenny Lofton	2.00	.90	.25
□ 24 Andy Pettitte	2.50	1.10	.30
□ 25 Brady Anderson	.75	.35	.09
□ 26 Mike Piazza	5.00	2.20	.60
□ 27 Greg Vaughn	.50	.23	.06
□ 28 Joe Carter	.75	.35	.09
□ 29 Jason Giambi	.75	.35	.09
□ 30 Ivan Rodriguez	1.50	.70	.19
□ 31 Jeff Conine	.50	.23	.06
□ 32 Rafael Palmeiro	.75	.35	.09
□ 33 Roger Clemens	.75	.35	.09
□ 34 Chuck Knoblauch	.75	.35	.09
□ 35 Reggie Sanders	.50	.23	.06
□ 36 Andres Galarraga	.75	.35	.09
□ 37 Paul O'Neill	.25	.11	.03
□ 38 Tony Gwynn	3.00	1.35	.35
□ 39 Paul Wilson	.50	.23	.06
□ 40 Garret Anderson	.50	.23	.06
□ 41 David Justice	.75	.35	.09
□ 42 Eddie Murray	2.00	.90	.25
□ 43 Mike Grace	.50	.23	.06
□ 44 Marty Cordova	.75	.35	.09
□ 45 Kevin Appier	.25	.11	.03
□ 46 Raul Mondesi	.75	.35	.09
□ 47 Jim Thome	1.50	.70	.19
□ 48 Sammy Sosa	1.25	.55	.16
□ 49 Craig Biggio	.75	.35	.09
□ 50 Marquis Grissom	.50	.23	.06
□ 51 Alan Benes	.75	.35	.09
□ 52 Manny Ramirez	2.00	.90	.25
□ 53 Gary Sheffield	1.25	.55	.16
□ 54 Mike Mussina	1.50	.70	.19
□ 55 Robin Ventura	.50	.23	.06
□ 56 Johnny Damon	.50	.23	.06
□ 57 Jose Canseco	.75	.35	.09
□ 58 Juan Gonzalez	4.00	1.80	.50
□ 59 Tino Martinez	.25	.11	.03
□ 60 Brian Hunter	.50	.23	.06
□ 61 Fred McGriff	.75	.35	.09
□ 62 Jay Buhner	.75	.35	.09
□ 63 Carlos Delgado	.50	.23	.06
□ 64 Moises Alou	.25	.11	.03
□ 65 Roberto Alomar	2.00	.90	.25
□ 66 Barry Larkin	.75	.35	.09
□ 67 Vinny Castilla	.25	.11	.03
□ 68 Ray Durham	.50	.23	.06
□ 69 Travis Fryman	.50	.23	.06
□ 70 Jason Isringhausen	.50	.23	.06
□ 71 Ken Griffey Jr.	8.00	3.60	1.00
□ 72 John Smoltz	1.25	.55	.16
□ 73 Matt Williams	.75	.35	.09
□ 74 Chan Ho Park	.50	.23	.06
□ 75 Mark McGwire	2.50	1.10	.30
□ 76 Jeffrey Hammonds	.25	.11	.03
□ 77 Will Clark	.75	.35	.09
□ 78 Kirby Puckett	2.50	1.10	.30
□ 79 Derek Jeter	5.00	2.20	.60
□ 80 Derek Bell	.50	.23	.06
□ 81 Eric Karros	.50	.23	.06
□ 82 Len Dykstra	.50	.23	.06
□ 83 Larry Walker	.75	.35	.09
□ 84 Mark Grudzielanek	.25	.11	.03
□ 85 Greg Maddux	5.00	2.20	.60
□ 86 Carlos Baerga	.75	.35	.09
□ 87 Paul Molitor	1.50	.70	.19
□ 88 John Valentin	.25	.11	.03
□ 89 Mark Grace	.75	.35	.09
□ 90 Ray Lankford	.50	.23	.06
□ 91 Andruw Jones	15.00	6.75	1.85
□ 92 Nomar Garciaparra	2.00	.90	.25
□ 93 Alex Ochoa	.50	.23	.06
□ 94 Derrick Gibson	1.25	.55	.16
□ 95 Jeff D'Amico	.50	.23	.06
□ 96 Ruben Rivera	1.50	.70	.19
□ 97 Vladimir Guerrero	5.00	2.20	.60
□ 98 Calvin Reese	.25	.11	.03
□ 99 Richard Hidalgo	.50	.23	.06
□ 100 Bartolo Colon	.50	.23	.06
□ 101 Karim Garcia	1.50	.70	.19
□ 102 Ben Davis	1.00	.45	.12
□ 103 Jay Powell	.25	.11	.03
□ 104 Chris Snopek	.25	.11	.03
□ 105 Glendon Rusch	.50	.23	.06
□ 106 Enrique Wilson	.50	.23	.06
□ 107 Antonio Alfonseca	.25	.11	.03
□ 108 Wilton Guerrero	1.50	.70	.19
□ 109 Jose Guillen	4.00	1.80	.50
□ 110 Miguel Mejia	.25	.11	.03
□ 111 Jay Payton	1.00	.45	.12
□ 112 Scott Elarton	.50	.23	.06
□ 113 Brooks Kieschnick	.25	.11	.03
□ 114 Dustin Hermanson	.25	.11	.03
□ 115 Roger Cedeno	.50	.23	.06
□ 116 Matt Wagner	.25	.11	.03
□ 117 Lee Daniels	.25	.11	.03
□ 118 Ben Grieve	1.50	.70	.19
□ 119 Ugueth Urbina	.25	.11	.03
□ 120 Danny Graves	.50	.23	.06
□ 121 Dan Donato	.25	.11	.03
□ 122 Matt Ruebel	.25	.11	.03
□ 123 Mark Sievert	.25	.11	.03
□ 124 Chris Stynes	.25	.11	.03
□ 125 Jeff Abbott	.50	.23	.06
□ 126 Rocky Coppinger	1.50	.70	.19
□ 127 Jermaine Dye	2.00	.90	.25
□ 128 Todd Greene	.50	.23	.06
□ 129 Chris Carpenter	.50	.23	.06
□ 130 Edgar Renteria	1.00	.45	.12
□ 131 Matt Drews	.25	.11	.03
□ 132 Edgard Velazquez	2.50	1.10	.30
□ 133 Casey Whitten	.25	.11	.03
□ 134 Ryan Jones	1.00	.45	.12
□ 135 Todd Walker	6.00	2.70	.75
□ 136 Geoff Jenkins	1.25	.55	.16
□ 137 Matt Morris	1.00	.45	.12
□ 138 Richie Sexson	.50	.23	.06
□ 139 Todd Dunwoody	2.00	.90	.25
□ 140 Gabe Alvarez	1.00	.45	.12
□ 141 J.J. Johnson	.25	.11	.03
□ 142 Shannon Stewart	.25	.11	.03
□ 143 Brad Fullmer	.50	.23	.06
□ 144 Julio Santana	.25	.11	.03
□ 145 Scott Rolen	4.00	1.80	.50
□ 146 Amaury Telemaco	.25	.11	.03
□ 147 Trey Beamon	.25	.11	.03
□ 148 Billy Wagner	.25	.11	.03
□ 149 Todd Hollandsworth	.75	.35	.09
□ 150 Doug Million	.50	.23	.06
□ 151 Jose Valentin	2.50	1.10	.30
□ 152 Wes Helms	4.00	1.80	.50
□ 153 Jeff Suppan	.50	.23	.06
□ 154 Luis Castillo	1.00	.45	.12
□ 155 Bob Abreu	.75	.35	.09
□ 156 Paul Konerko	3.00	1.35	.35
□ 157 Jamey Wright	.25	.11	.03
□ 158 Eddie Pearson	.25	.11	.03
□ 159 Jimmy Haynes	.25	.11	.03
□ 160 Derrek Lee	1.00	.45	.12
□ 161 Damian Moss	1.25	.55	.16
□ 162 Carlos Guillen	.25	.11	.03
□ 163 Chris Fussell	1.00	.45	.12

		MINT	NRMT	EXC
□ 164	Mike Sweeney	1.50	.70	.19
□ 165	Donnie Sadler	.50	.23	.06
□ 166	Desi Relaford	.25	.11	.03
□ 167	Steve Gibralter	.25	.11	.03
□ 168	Neifi Perez	.25	.11	.03
□ 169	Antone Williamson	1.00	.45	.12
□ 170	Marty Janzen	.25	.11	.03
□ 171	Todd Helton	5.00	2.20	.60
□ 172	Raul Ibanez	.25	.11	.03
□ 173	Bill Selby	.25	.11	.03
□ 174	Shane Monahan	1.50	.70	.19
□ 175	Robin Jennings	.25	.11	.03
□ 176	Bobby Chouinard	.25	.11	.03
□ 177	Einar Diaz	.25	.11	.03
□ 178	Jason Thompson	.25	.11	.03
□ 179	Rafael Medina	1.00	.45	.12
□ 180	Kevin Orie	.50	.23	.06
□ NNO	1952 Mantle Refractor	30.00	13.50	3.70
□ NNO	1952 Mantle Chrome	8.00	3.60	1.00
□ NNO	1952 Mantle Atomic Refractor	60.00	27.00	7.50

1996 Bowman's Best Atomic Refractors

Inserted one in every 48 packs, this 180-card set is parallel to the 1996 Bowman's Best set. It is similar in design to the regular set but was printed with the newest sparkling refractor technology.

	MINT	NRMT	EXC
COMPLETE SET (180)	6000.00	2700.00	750.00
COMMON CARD (1-180)	10.00	4.50	1.25
SEMISTARS	20.00	9.00	2.50
STARS	30.00	13.50	3.70
*STARS: 18X to 30X BASIC CARDS			
*YOUNG STARS: 15X to 25X BASIC CARDS			
RANDOM INSERTS IN PACKS			

		MINT	NRMT	EXC
□ 3	Cal Ripken	200.00	90.00	25.00
□ 6	Albert Belle	120.00	55.00	15.00
□ 7	Chipper Jones	150.00	70.00	19.00
□ 13	Frank Thomas	250.00	110.00	31.00
□ 20	Jeff Bagwell	100.00	45.00	12.50
□ 26	Mike Piazza	150.00	70.00	19.00
□ 38	Tony Gwynn	100.00	45.00	12.50
□ 58	Juan Gonzalez	120.00	55.00	15.00
□ 71	Ken Griffey Jr.	250.00	110.00	31.00
□ 78	Kirby Puckett	80.00	36.00	10.00
□ 79	Derek Jeter	125.00	55.00	15.50
□ 85	Greg Maddux	150.00	70.00	19.00
□ 91	Andruw Jones	300.00	135.00	38.00
□ 97	Vladimir Guerrero	120.00	55.00	15.00
□ 135	Todd Walker	150.00	70.00	19.00
□ 171	Todd Helton	120.00	55.00	15.00

1996 Bowman's Best Refractors

This 180-card set is parallel to the regular 1996 Bowman Best set and is similar in design. The difference is in the refractive quality of the cards. The cards were inserted at the rate of one in every 12 packs.

	MINT	NRMT	EXC
COMPLETE SET (180)	2000.00	900.00	250.00
COMMON CARD (1-180)	4.00	1.80	.50
SEMISTARS	8.00	3.60	1.00
STARS	12.00	5.50	1.50
*STARS: 7X to 12X BASIC CARDS			
*YOUNG STARS: 6X to 10X BASIC CARDS			
RANDOM INSERTS IN PACKS			

		MINT	NRMT	EXC
□ 3	Cal Ripken	80.00	36.00	10.00
□ 6	Albert Belle	50.00	22.00	6.25
□ 7	Chipper Jones	60.00	27.00	7.50
□ 13	Frank Thomas	100.00	45.00	12.50
□ 20	Jeff Bagwell	40.00	18.00	5.00
□ 26	Mike Piazza	60.00	27.00	7.50
□ 38	Tony Gwynn	40.00	18.00	5.00
□ 58	Juan Gonzalez	50.00	22.00	6.25
□ 71	Ken Griffey Jr.	100.00	45.00	12.50
□ 75	Mark McGwire	30.00	13.50	3.70
□ 78	Kirby Puckett	30.00	13.50	3.70
□ 79	Derek Jeter	60.00	27.00	7.50
□ 85	Greg Maddux	60.00	27.00	7.50
□ 91	Andruw Jones	125.00	55.00	15.50
□ 97	Vladimir Guerrero	50.00	22.00	6.25
□ 135	Todd Walker	60.00	27.00	7.50
□ 171	Todd Helton	50.00	22.00	6.25

1996 Bowman's Best Cuts

Randomly inserted in packs at a rate of one in 24, this chromium card diecut set features 15 of the most collectible players. The fronts display color action player cutouts over the team name and a background of swinging bars. The backs carry player information.

	MINT	NRMT	EXC
COMPLETE SET (15)	225.00	100.00	28.00
COMMON CARD (1-15)	6.00	2.70	.75
*REFRACTORS: 2X BASIC CARDS			
*ATOMIC REFRACTORS: 4X BASIC CARDS.			
RANDOM INSERTS IN PACKS			

		MINT	NRMT	EXC
□ 1	Ken Griffey Jr.	40.00	18.00	5.00
□ 2	Jason Isringhausen	6.00	2.70	.75
□ 3	Derek Jeter	25.00	11.00	3.10
□ 4	Andruw Jones	50.00	22.00	6.25
□ 5	Chipper Jones	25.00	11.00	3.10
□ 6	Ryan Klesko	8.00	3.60	1.00
□ 7	Raul Mondesi	6.00	2.70	.75
□ 8	Hideo Nomo	10.00	4.50	1.25
□ 9	Mike Piazza	25.00	11.00	3.10
□ 10	Manny Ramirez	10.00	4.50	1.25
□ 11	Cal Ripken	30.00	13.50	3.70
□ 12	Ruben Rivera	8.00	3.60	1.00
□ 13	Tim Salmon	6.00	2.70	.75
□ 14	Frank Thomas	40.00	18.00	5.00
□ 15	Jim Thome	8.00	3.60	1.00

1996 Bowman's Best Mirror Image

Randomly inserted in packs at a rate of one in 48, this 10-card set features four top players on a single card at one of ten different positions. The fronts display a color photo of an AL veter-

an with a semicircle containing a color portrait of a prospect who plays the same position. The backs carry a color photo of a NL veteran with a semicircle color portrait of a prospect.

	MINT	NRMT	EXC
COMPLETE SET (10)	250.00	110.00	31.00
COMMON CARD (1-10)	20.00	9.00	2.50
*REFRACTORS: 2X BASIC CARDS			
*ATOMIC REFRACTORS: 4X BASIC CARDS.			
RANDOM INSERTS IN PACKS			

□ 1 Jeff Bagwell	40.00	18.00	5.00
Todd Helton			
Frank Thomas			
Richie Sexson			
□ 2 Craig Biggio	20.00	9.00	2.50
Luis Castillo			
Roberto Alomar			
Desi Relaford			
□ 3 Chipper Jones	30.00	13.50	3.70
Scott Rolen			
Wade Boggs			
George Arias			
□ 4 Barry Larkin	30.00	13.50	3.70
Neifi Perez			
Cal Ripken			
Mark Bellhorn			
□ 5 Larry Walker	20.00	9.00	2.50
Karim Garcia			
Albert Belle			
Ruben Rivera			
□ 6 Barry Bonds	50.00	22.00	6.25
Andruw Jones			
Kenny Lofton			
Donnie Sadler			
□ 7 Tony Gwynn	40.00	18.00	5.00
Vladimir Guerrero			
Ken Griffey			
Ben Grieve			
□ 8 Mike Piazza	25.00	11.00	3.10
Ben Davis			
Ivan Rodriguez			
Jose Valentin			
□ 9 Greg Maddux	25.00	11.00	3.10
Jamey Wright			
Mike Mussina			
Bartolo Colon			
□ 10 Tom Glavine	20.00	9.00	2.50
Billy Wagner			
Randy Johnson			
Jarrod Washburn			

1994 Collector's Choice

Issued by Upper Deck, this 670 standard-size card set was issued in two series of 320 and 350. Factory sets contain five Gold Signature cards for a total of 675 cards. Card fronts feature color player action photos with white borders that are highlighted by vertical gray pinstripes. The player's name and team appear in white lettering at the bottom of the picture. The player's position appears within a black oval beneath an action player icon in a lower corner. The pinstripe border design reappears on the back, which carries another color player action photo in its upper portion. The player's name and position appear vertically within a team color-coded stripe along the photo's right side. A team logo appears at the lower left corner of the photo. Beneath the picture appear the player's biography and stats. Subsets include Rookie Class (1-20), First Draft Picks (21-30), Top Performers (306-315), Up Close (631-640) and Future Foundation (641-650). Rookie Cards include Brian Anderson, Matt Drews, Michael Jordan, Brooks Kieschnick, Derrek Lee, Trot Nixon, Alex Rodriguez, Jose Silva and Terrell Wade.

	MINT	NRMT	EXC
COMPLETE SET (670)	30.00	13.50	3.70
COMPLETE FACT.SET (675)	32.00	14.50	4.00
COMPLETE SERIES 1 (320)	12.00	5.50	1.50
COMPLETE SERIES 2 (350)	18.00	8.00	2.20
COMMON CARD (1-670)	.05	.02	.01
SEMISTARS	.15	.07	.02
STARS	.30	.14	.04
COMP.SILV.SIG.SET (670)	200.00	90.00	25.00
COMP.SILV.SIG.SER.1 (320)	90.00	40.00	11.00
COMP.SILV.SIG.SER.2 (350)	110.00	50.00	14.00
COMMON SILV.SIG (1-670)	.10	.05	.01
SILV.SIG.SEMISTARS	.25	.11	.03
*SILV.SIG.STARS: 2.5X to 5X HI COLUMN			
*SILV.SIG.YOUNG STARS: 1.5X to 3X HI			
ONE SILVER SIGNATURE PER PACK			
COMP.GOLD SIG SET (670)	3000.00	1350.00	375.00
COMP.GOLD SERIES 1 (320)	1500.00	700.00	190.00
COMP.GOLD SERIES 2 (350)	1500.00	700.00	190.00
COMMON GOLD SIG (1-670)	1.50	.70	.19
SEMISTAR GOLD SIG	3.00	1.35	.35
*GOLD VET.STARS: 25X TO 50X HI			
*GOLD YOUNG STARS: 15X TO 30X HI			
*GOLD RCs: 10X TO 20X HI			
GOLD SIG: RANDOM INSERTS IN PACKS			

□ 1 Rich Becker	.15	.07	.02
□ 2 Greg Blosser	.05	.02	.01
□ 3 Midre Cummings	.05	.02	.01
□ 4 Carlos Delgado	.30	.14	.04
□ 5 Steve Dreyer	.05	.02	.01
□ 6 Carl Everett	.05	.02	.01
□ 7 Cliff Floyd	.30	.14	.04
□ 8 Alex Gonzalez	.15	.07	.02
□ 9 Shawn Green	.15	.07	.02
□ 10 Butch Huskey	.15	.07	.02
□ 11 Mark Hutton	.05	.02	.01
□ 12 Miguel Jimenez	.05	.02	.01
□ 13 Steve Karsay	.05	.02	.01
□ 14 Marc Newfield	.15	.07	.02
□ 15 Luis Ortiz	.05	.02	.01
□ 16 Manny Ramirez	.60	.25	.07
□ 17 Johnny Ruffin	.05	.02	.01
□ 18 Scott Stahoviak	.05	.02	.01
□ 19 Salomon Torres	.05	.02	.01
□ 20 Gabe White	.05	.02	.01
□ 21 Brian Anderson	.15	.07	.02
□ 22 Wayne Gomes	.15	.07	.02
□ 23 Jeff Granger	.15	.07	.02
□ 24 Steve Soderstrom	.15	.07	.02
□ 25 Trot Nixon	.30	.14	.04
□ 26 Kirk Presley	.30	.14	.04
□ 27 Matt Brunson	.15	.07	.02
□ 28 Brooks Kieschnick	.40	.18	.05
□ 29 Billy Wagner	.50	.23	.06
□ 30 Matt Drews	.25	.11	.03
□ 31 Kurt Abbott	.15	.07	.02
□ 32 Luis Alicea	.05	.02	.01
□ 33 Roberto Alomar	.50	.23	.06
□ 34 Sandy Alomar Jr.	.15	.07	.02
□ 35 Moises Alou	.15	.07	.02
□ 36 Wilson Alvarez	.15	.07	.02
□ 37 Rich Amaral	.05	.02	.01
□ 38 Eric Anthony	.05	.02	.01
□ 39 Luis Aquino	.05	.02	.01
□ 40 Jack Armstrong	.05	.02	.01
□ 41 Rene Arocha	.05	.02	.01
□ 42 Rich Aude	.15	.07	.02
□ 43 Brad Ausmus	.05	.02	.01
□ 44 Steve Avery	.15	.07	.02
□ 45 Bob Ayrault	.05	.02	.01
□ 46 Willie Banks	.05	.02	.01
□ 47 Bret Barberie	.05	.02	.01
□ 48 Kim Batiste	.05	.02	.01

□ 49 Rod Beck	.15	.07	.02
□ 50 Jason Bere	.15	.07	.02
□ 51 Sean Berry	.05	.02	.01
□ 52 Dante Bichette	.30	.14	.04
□ 53 Jeff Blauser	.05	.02	.01
□ 54 Mike Blowers	.05	.02	.01
□ 55 Tim Bogar	.05	.02	.01
□ 56 Tom Bolton	.05	.02	.01
□ 57 Ricky Bones	.05	.02	.01
□ 58 Bobby Bonilla	.15	.07	.02
□ 59 Bret Boone	.15	.07	.02
□ 60 Pat Borders	.05	.02	.01
□ 61 Mike Bordick	.05	.02	.01
□ 62 Daryl Boston	.05	.02	.01
□ 63 Ryan Bowen	.05	.02	.01
□ 64 Jeff Branson	.05	.02	.01
□ 65 George Brett	.75	.35	.09
□ 66 Steve Buechele	.05	.02	.01
□ 67 Dave Burba	.05	.02	.01
□ 68 John Burkett	.05	.02	.01
□ 69 Jeromy Burnitz	.05	.02	.01
□ 70 Brett Bulter	.15	.07	.02
□ 71 Rob Butler	.05	.02	.01
□ 72 Ken Caminiti	.30	.14	.04
□ 73 Cris Carpenter	.05	.02	.01
□ 74 Vinny Castilla	.30	.14	.04
□ 75 Andujar Cedeno	.05	.02	.01
□ 76 Wes Chamberlain	.05	.02	.01
□ 77 Archi Cianfrocco	.05	.02	.01
□ 78 Dave Clark	.05	.02	.01
□ 79 Jerald Clark	.05	.02	.01
□ 80 Royce Clayton	.15	.07	.02
□ 81 David Cone	.30	.14	.04
□ 82 Jeff Conine	.30	.14	.04
□ 83 Steve Cooke	.05	.02	.01
□ 84 Scott Cooper	.05	.02	.01
□ 85 Joey Cora	.05	.02	.01
□ 86 Tim Costo	.05	.02	.01
□ 87 Chad Curtis	.05	.02	.01
□ 88 Ron Darling	.05	.02	.01
□ 89 Danny Darwin	.05	.02	.01
□ 90 Rob Deer	.05	.02	.01
□ 91 Jim Deshaies	.05	.02	.01
□ 92 Delino DeShields	.05	.02	.01
□ 93 Rob Dibble	.05	.02	.01
□ 94 Gary DiSarcina	.05	.02	.01
□ 95 Doug Drabek	.05	.02	.01
□ 96 Scott Erickson	.05	.02	.01
□ 97 Rikkert Faneyte	.05	.02	.01
□ 98 Jeff Fassero	.05	.02	.01
□ 99 Alex Fernandez	.30	.14	.04
□ 100 Cecil Fielder	.15	.07	.02
□ 101 Dave Fleming	.05	.02	.01
□ 102 Darrin Fletcher	.05	.02	.01
□ 103 Scott Fletcher	.05	.02	.01
□ 104 Mike Gallego	.05	.02	.01
□ 105 Carlos Garcia	.05	.02	.01
□ 106 Jeff Gardner	.05	.02	.01
□ 107 Brent Gates	.05	.02	.01
□ 108 Benji Gil	.05	.02	.01
□ 109 Bernard Gilkey	.15	.07	.02
□ 110 Chris Gomez	.05	.02	.01
□ 111 Luis Gonzalez	.05	.02	.01
□ 112 Tom Gordon	.05	.02	.01
□ 113 Jim Gott	.05	.02	.01
□ 114 Mark Grace	.30	.14	.04
□ 115 Tommy Greene	.05	.02	.01
□ 116 Willie Greene	.15	.07	.02
□ 117 Ken Griffey Jr.	2.00	.90	.25
□ 118 Bill Gullickson	.05	.02	.01
□ 119 Ricky Gutierrez	.05	.02	.01
□ 120 Juan Guzman	.15	.07	.02
□ 121 Chris Gwynn	.05	.02	.01
□ 122 Tony Gwynn	.75	.35	.09
□ 123 Jeffrey Hammonds	.15	.07	.02
□ 124 Erik Hanson	.05	.02	.01
□ 125 Gene Harris	.05	.02	.01
□ 126 Greg W. Harris	.05	.02	.01
□ 127 Bryan Harvey	.05	.02	.01
□ 128 Billy Hatcher	.05	.02	.01
□ 129 Hilly Hathaway	.05	.02	.01
□ 130 Charlie Hayes	.05	.02	.01
□ 131 Rickey Henderson	.30	.14	.04
□ 132 Mike Henneman	.05	.02	.01
□ 133 Pat Hentgen	.30	.14	.04
□ 134 Roberto Hernandez	.15	.07	.02
□ 135 Orel Hershiser	.15	.07	.02
□ 136 Phil Hiatt	.05	.02	.01
□ 137 Glenallen Hill	.05	.02	.01
□ 138 Ken Hill	.05	.02	.01
□ 139 Eric Hillman	.05	.02	.01
□ 140 Chris Hoiles	.05	.02	.01
□ 141 Dave Hollins	.05	.02	.01
□ 142 David Hulse	.05	.02	.01
□ 143 Todd Hundley	.30	.14	.04
□ 144 Pete Incaviglia	.05	.02	.01
□ 145 Danny Jackson	.05	.02	.01
□ 146 John Jaha	.15	.07	.02
□ 147 Domingo Jean	.05	.02	.01
□ 148 Gregg Jefferies	.30	.14	.04
□ 149 Reggie Jefferson	.15	.07	.02
□ 150 Lance Johnson	.15	.07	.02
□ 151 Bobby Jones	.15	.07	.02
□ 152 Chipper Jones	1.50	.70	.19
□ 153 Todd Jones	.05	.02	.01
□ 154 Brian Jordan	.30	.14	.04
□ 155 Wally Joyner	.15	.07	.02
□ 156 David Justice	.30	.14	.04
□ 157 Ron Karkovice	.05	.02	.01
□ 158 Eric Karros	.15	.07	.02
□ 159 Jeff Kent	.05	.02	.01
□ 160 Jimmy Key	.15	.07	.02
□ 161 Mark Kiefer	.05	.02	.01
□ 162 Darryl Kile	.05	.02	.01
□ 163 Jeff King	.15	.07	.02
□ 164 Wayne Kirby	.05	.02	.01
□ 165 Ryan Klesko	.50	.23	.06
□ 166 Chuck Knoblauch	.30	.14	.04
□ 167 Chad Kreuter	.05	.02	.01
□ 168 John Kruk	.15	.07	.02
□ 169 Mark Langston	.15	.07	.02
□ 170 Mike Lansing	.15	.07	.02
□ 171 Barry Larkin	.30	.14	.04
□ 172 Manuel Lee	.05	.02	.01
□ 173 Phil Leftwich	.05	.02	.01
□ 174 Darren Lewis	.05	.02	.01
□ 175 Derek Lilliquist	.05	.02	.01
□ 176 Jose Lind	.05	.02	.01
□ 177 Albie Lopez	.15	.07	.02
□ 178 Javier Lopez	.30	.14	.04
□ 179 Torey Lovullo	.05	.02	.01
□ 180 Scott Lydy	.05	.02	.01
□ 181 Mike Macfarlane	.05	.02	.01
□ 182 Shane Mack	.05	.02	.01
□ 183 Greg Maddux	1.25	.55	.16
□ 184 Dave Magadan	.05	.02	.01
□ 185 Joe Magrane	.05	.02	.01
□ 186 Kirk Manwaring	.05	.02	.01
□ 187 Al Martin	.05	.02	.01
□ 188 Pedro A. Martinez	.05	.02	.01
□ 189 Pedro J. Martinez	.30	.14	.04
□ 190 Ramon Martinez	.15	.07	.02
□ 191 Tino Martinez	.15	.07	.02
□ 192 Don Mattingly	1.00	.45	.12
□ 193 Derrick May	.05	.02	.01
□ 194 David McCarty	.05	.02	.01
□ 195 Ben McDonald	.05	.02	.01
□ 196 Roger McDowell	.05	.02	.01
□ 197 Fred McGriff UER (Stats on back have 73 stolen bases for 1989; should be 7)	.30	.14	.04
□ 198 Mark McLemore	.05	.02	.01
□ 199 Greg McMichael	.05	.02	.01
□ 200 Jeff McNeely	.05	.02	.01
□ 201 Brian McRae	.15	.07	.02
□ 202 Pat Meares	.05	.02	.01
□ 203 Roberto Mejia	.05	.02	.01
□ 204 Orlando Merced	.15	.07	.02
□ 205 Jose Mesa	.15	.07	.02
□ 206 Blas Minor	.05	.02	.01
□ 207 Angel Miranda	.05	.02	.01
□ 208 Paul Molitor	.40	.18	.05
□ 209 Raul Mondesi	.30	.14	.04
□ 210 Jeff Montgomery	.15	.07	.02
□ 211 Mickey Morandini	.05	.02	.01
□ 212 Mike Morgan	.05	.02	.01
□ 213 Jamie Moyer	.05	.02	.01
□ 214 Bobby Munoz	.05	.02	.01
□ 215 Troy Neel	.05	.02	.01
□ 216 Dave Nilsson	.15	.07	.02
□ 217 John O'Donoghue	.05	.02	.01

□ 218 Paul O'Neill	.15	.07	.02
□ 219 Jose Offerman	.05	.02	.01
□ 220 Joe Oliver	.05	.02	.01
□ 221 Greg Olson	.05	.02	.01
□ 222 Donovan Osborne	.05	.02	.01
□ 223 J. Owens	.05	.02	.01
□ 224 Mike Pagliarulo	.05	.02	.01
□ 225 Craig Paquette	.05	.02	.01
□ 226 Roger Pavlik	.05	.02	.01
□ 227 Brad Pennington	.05	.02	.01
□ 228 Eduardo Perez	.05	.02	.01
□ 229 Mike Perez	.05	.02	.01
□ 230 Tony Phillips	.15	.07	.02
□ 231 Hipolito Pichardo	.05	.02	.01
□ 232 Phil Plantier	.05	.02	.01
□ 233 Curtis Pride	.15	.07	.02
□ 234 Tim Pugh	.05	.02	.01
□ 235 Scott Radinsky	.05	.02	.01
□ 236 Pat Rapp	.05	.02	.01
□ 237 Kevin Reimer	.05	.02	.01
□ 238 Armando Reynoso	.05	.02	.01
□ 239 Jose Rijo	.05	.02	.01
□ 240 Cal Ripken	1.50	.70	.19
□ 241 Kevin Roberson	.05	.02	.01
□ 242 Kenny Rogers	.05	.02	.01
□ 243 Kevin Rogers	.05	.02	.01
□ 244 Mel Rojas	.05	.02	.01
□ 245 John Roper	.05	.02	.01
□ 246 Kirk Rueter	.05	.02	.01
□ 247 Scott Ruffcorn	.05	.02	.01
□ 248 Ken Ryan	.05	.02	.01
□ 249 Nolan Ryan	1.50	.70	.19
□ 250 Bret Saberhagen	.15	.07	.02
□ 251 Tim Salmon	.30	.14	.04
□ 252 Reggie Sanders	.30	.14	.04
□ 253 Curt Schilling	.05	.02	.01
□ 254 David Segui	.05	.02	.01
□ 255 Aaron Sele	.15	.07	.02
□ 256 Scott Servais	.05	.02	.01
□ 257 Gary Sheffield	.30	.14	.04
□ 258 Ruben Sierra	.15	.07	.02
□ 259 Don Slaught	.05	.02	.01
□ 260 Lee Smith	.15	.07	.02
□ 261 Cory Snyder	.05	.02	.01
□ 262 Paul Sorrento	.05	.02	.01
□ 263 Sammy Sosa	.30	.14	.04
□ 264 Bill Spiers	.05	.02	.01
□ 265 Mike Stanley	.05	.02	.01
□ 266 Dave Staton	.05	.02	.01
□ 267 Terry Steinbach	.15	.07	.02
□ 268 Kevin Stocker	.05	.02	.01
□ 269 Todd Stottlemyre	.05	.02	.01
□ 270 Doug Strange	.05	.02	.01
□ 271 Bill Swift	.05	.02	.01
□ 272 Kevin Tapani	.05	.02	.01
□ 273 Tony Tarasco	.05	.02	.01
□ 274 Julian Tavarez	.15	.07	.02
□ 275 Mickey Tettleton	.05	.02	.01
□ 276 Ryan Thompson	.05	.02	.01
□ 277 Chris Turner	.05	.02	.01
□ 278 John Valentin	.15	.07	.02
□ 279 Todd Van Poppel	.05	.02	.01
□ 280 Andy Van Slyke	.15	.07	.02
□ 281 Mo Vaughn	.50	.23	.06
□ 282 Robin Ventura	.15	.07	.02
□ 283 Frank Viola	.05	.02	.01
□ 284 Jose Vizcaino	.05	.02	.01
□ 285 Omar Vizquel	.30	.14	.04
□ 286 Larry Walker	.30	.14	.04
□ 287 Duane Ward	.05	.02	.01
□ 288 Allen Watson	.05	.02	.01
□ 289 Bill Wegman	.05	.02	.01
□ 290 Turk Wendell	.05	.02	.01
□ 291 Lou Whitaker	.30	.14	.04
□ 292 Devon White	.05	.02	.01
□ 293 Rondell White	.30	.14	.04
□ 294 Mark Whiten	.05	.02	.01
□ 295 Darrel Whitmore	.05	.02	.01
□ 296 Bob Wickman	.05	.02	.01
□ 297 Rick Wilkins	.05	.02	.01
□ 298 Bernie Williams	.30	.14	.04
□ 299 Matt Williams	.30	.14	.04
□ 300 Woody Williams	.05	.02	.01
□ 301 Nigel Wilson	.05	.02	.01
□ 302 Dave Winfield	.30	.14	.04
□ 303 Anthony Young	.05	.02	.01

□ 304 Eric Young	.15	.07	.02
□ 305 Todd Zeile	.05	.02	.01
□ 306 Jack McDowell TP John Burkett Tom Glavine	.15	.07	.02
□ 307 Randy Johnson TP	.15	.07	.02
□ 308 Randy Myers TP	.05	.02	.01
□ 309 Jack McDowell TP	.05	.02	.01
□ 310 Mike Piazza TP	.60	.25	.07
□ 311 Barry Bonds TP	.30	.14	.04
□ 312 Andres Galarraga TP	.30	.14	.04
□ 313 Juan Gonzalez TP Barry Bonds	.50	.23	.06
□ 314 Albert Belle TP	.50	.23	.06
□ 315 Kenny Lofton TP	.30	.14	.04
□ 316 Barry Bonds CL	.30	.14	.04
□ 317 Ken Griffey Jr. CL	.50	.23	.06
□ 318 Mike Piazza CL	.30	.14	.04
□ 319 Kirby Puckett CL	.30	.14	.04
□ 320 Nolan Ryan CL	.50	.23	.06
□ 321 Roberto Alomar CL	.30	.14	.04
□ 322 Roger Clemens CL	.30	.14	.04
□ 323 Juan Gonzalez CL	.30	.14	.04
□ 324 Ken Griffey Jr. CL	.50	.23	.06
□ 325 David Justice CL	.15	.07	.02
□ 326 John Kruk CL	.05	.02	.01
□ 327 Frank Thomas CL	.50	.23	.06
□ 328 Tim Salmon TC	.15	.07	.02
□ 329 Jeff Bagwell TC	.40	.18	.05
□ 330 Mark McGwire TC	.30	.14	.04
□ 331 Roberto Alomar TC	.30	.14	.04
□ 332 David Justice TC	.15	.07	.02
□ 333 Pat Listach TC	.05	.02	.01
□ 334 Ozzie Smith TC	.30	.14	.04
□ 335 Ryne Sandberg TC	.30	.14	.04
□ 336 Mike Piazza TC	.60	.25	.07
□ 337 Cliff Floyd TC	.15	.07	.02
□ 338 Barry Bonds TC	.30	.14	.04
□ 339 Albert Belle TC	.50	.23	.06
□ 340 Ken Griffey Jr. TC	1.00	.45	.12
□ 341 Gary Sheffield TC	.30	.14	.04
□ 342 Dwight Gooden TC	.05	.02	.01
□ 343 Cal Ripken TC	.75	.35	.09
□ 344 Tony Gwynn TC	.40	.18	.05
□ 345 Lenny Dykstra TC	.05	.02	.01
□ 346 Andy Van Slyke TC	.05	.02	.01
□ 347 Juan Gonzalez TC	.50	.23	.06
□ 348 Roger Clemens TC	.30	.14	.04
□ 349 Barry Larkin TC	.30	.14	.04
□ 350 Andres Galarraga TC	.30	.14	.04
□ 351 Kevin Appier TC	.05	.02	.01
□ 352 Cecil Fielder TC	.05	.02	.01
□ 353 Kirby Puckett TC	.30	.14	.04
□ 354 Frank Thomas TC	1.00	.45	.12
□ 355 Don Mattingly TC	.50	.23	.06
□ 356 Bo Jackson	.30	.14	.04
□ 357 Randy Johnson	.30	.14	.04
□ 358 Darren Daulton	.15	.07	.02
□ 359 Charlie Hough	.05	.02	.01
□ 360 Andres Galarraga	.30	.14	.04
□ 361 Mike Felder	.05	.02	.01
□ 362 Chris Hammond	.05	.02	.01
□ 363 Shawon Dunston	.05	.02	.01
□ 364 Junior Felix	.05	.02	.01
□ 365 Ray Lankford	.30	.14	.04
□ 366 Darryl Strawberry	.15	.07	.02
□ 367 Dave Magadan	.05	.02	.01
□ 368 Gregg Olson	.05	.02	.01
□ 369 Lenny Dykstra	.15	.07	.02
□ 370 Darrin Jackson	.05	.02	.01
□ 371 Dave Stewart	.15	.07	.02
□ 372 Terry Pendleton	.15	.07	.02
□ 373 Arthur Rhodes	.05	.02	.01
□ 374 Benito Santiago	.05	.02	.01
□ 375 Travis Fryman	.30	.14	.04
□ 376 Scott Brosius	.05	.02	.01
□ 377 Stan Belinda	.05	.02	.01
□ 378 Derek Parks	.05	.02	.01
□ 379 Kevin Seitzer	.05	.02	.01
□ 380 Wade Boggs	.30	.14	.04
□ 381 Wally Whitehurst	.05	.02	.01
□ 382 Scott Leius	.05	.02	.01
□ 383 Danny Tartabull	.05	.02	.01
□ 384 Harold Reynolds	.05	.02	.01
□ 385 Tim Raines	.30	.14	.04
□ 386 Darryl Hamilton	.05	.02	.01

□ 387 Felix Fermin	.05	.02	.01
□ 388 Jim Eisenreich	.05	.02	.01
□ 389 Kurt Abbott	.15	.07	.02
□ 390 Kevin Appier	.15	.07	.02
□ 391 Chris Bosio	.05	.02	.01
□ 392 Randy Tomlin	.05	.02	.01
□ 393 Bob Hamelin	.05	.02	.01
□ 394 Kevin Gross	.05	.02	.01
□ 395 Wil Cordero	.15	.07	.02
□ 396 Joe Girardi	.05	.02	.01
□ 397 Orestes Destrade	.05	.02	.01
□ 398 Chris Haney	.05	.02	.01
□ 399 Xavier Hernandez	.05	.02	.01
□ 400 Mike Piazza	1.25	.55	.16
□ 401 Alex Arias	.05	.02	.01
□ 402 Tom Candiotti	.05	.02	.01
□ 403 Kirk Gibson	.15	.07	.02
□ 404 Chuck Carr	.05	.02	.01
□ 405 Brady Anderson	.30	.14	.04
□ 406 Greg Gagne	.05	.02	.01
□ 407 Bruce Ruffin	.05	.02	.01
□ 408 Scott Hemond	.05	.02	.01
□ 409 Keith Miller	.05	.02	.01
□ 410 John Wetteland	.15	.07	.02
□ 411 Eric Anthony	.05	.02	.01
□ 412 Andre Dawson	.30	.14	.04
□ 413 Doug Henry	.05	.02	.01
□ 414 John Franco	.05	.02	.01
□ 415 Julio Franco	.15	.07	.02
□ 416 Dave Hansen	.05	.02	.01
□ 417 Mike Harkey	.05	.02	.01
□ 418 Jack Armstrong	.05	.02	.01
□ 419 Joe Orsulak	.05	.02	.01
□ 420 John Smoltz	.30	.14	.04
□ 421 Scott Livingstone	.05	.02	.01
□ 422 Darren Holmes	.05	.02	.01
□ 423 Ed Sprague	.15	.07	.02
□ 424 Jay Buhner	.30	.14	.04
□ 425 Kirby Puckett	.60	.25	.07
□ 426 Phil Clark	.05	.02	.01
□ 427 Anthony Young	.05	.02	.01
□ 428 Reggie Jefferson	.15	.07	.02
□ 429 Mariano Duncan	.05	.02	.01
□ 430 Tom Glavine	.30	.14	.04
□ 431 Dave Henderson	.05	.02	.01
□ 432 Melido Perez	.05	.02	.01
□ 433 Paul Wagner	.05	.02	.01
□ 434 Tim Worrell	.05	.02	.01
□ 435 Ozzie Guillen	.05	.02	.01
□ 436 Mike Butcher	.05	.02	.01
□ 437 Jim Deshaies	.05	.02	.01
□ 438 Kevin Young	.05	.02	.01
□ 439 Tom Browning	.05	.02	.01
□ 440 Mike Greenwell	.05	.02	.01
□ 441 Mike Stanton	.05	.02	.01
□ 442 John Doherty	.05	.02	.01
□ 443 John Dopson	.05	.02	.01
□ 444 Carlos Baerga	.30	.14	.04
□ 445 Jack McDowell	.15	.07	.02
□ 446 Kent Mercker	.05	.02	.01
□ 447 Ricky Jordan	.05	.02	.01
□ 448 Jerry Browne	.05	.02	.01
□ 449 Fernando Vina	.05	.02	.01
□ 450 Jim Abbott	.05	.02	.01
□ 451 Teddy Higuera	.05	.02	.01
□ 452 Tim Naehring	.05	.02	.01
□ 453 Jim Leyritz	.05	.02	.01
□ 454 Frank Castillo	.05	.02	.01
□ 455 Joe Carter	.30	.14	.04
□ 456 Craig Biggio	.30	.14	.04
□ 457 Geronimo Pena	.05	.02	.01
□ 458 Alejandro Pena	.05	.02	.01
□ 459 Mike Moore	.05	.02	.01
□ 460 Randy Myers	.05	.02	.01
□ 461 Greg Myers	.05	.02	.01
□ 462 Greg Hibbard	.05	.02	.01
□ 463 Jose Guzman	.05	.02	.01
□ 464 Tom Pagnozzi	.05	.02	.01
□ 465 Marquis Grissom	.30	.14	.04
□ 466 Tim Wallach	.05	.02	.01
□ 467 Joe Grahe	.05	.02	.01
□ 468 Bob Tewksbury	.05	.02	.01
□ 469 B.J. Surhoff	.05	.02	.01
□ 470 Kevin Mitchell	.15	.07	.02
□ 471 Bobby Witt	.05	.02	.01
□ 472 Milt Thompson	.05	.02	.01
□ 473 John Smiley	.05	.02	.01
□ 474 Alan Trammell	.30	.14	.04
□ 475 Mike Mussina	.40	.18	.05
□ 476 Rick Aguilera	.05	.02	.01
□ 477 Jose Valentin	.15	.07	.02
□ 478 Harold Baines	.15	.07	.02
□ 479 Bip Roberts	.05	.02	.01
□ 480 Edgar Martinez	.30	.14	.04
□ 481 Rheal Cormier	.05	.02	.01
□ 482 Hal Morris	.05	.02	.01
□ 483 Pat Kelly	.05	.02	.01
□ 484 Roberto Kelly	.05	.02	.01
□ 485 Chris Sabo	.05	.02	.01
□ 486 Kent Hrbek	.15	.07	.02
□ 487 Scott Kamieniecki	.05	.02	.01
□ 488 Walt Weiss	.05	.02	.01
□ 489 Karl Rhodes	.05	.02	.01
□ 490 Derek Bell	.15	.07	.02
□ 491 Chili Davis	.15	.07	.02
□ 492 Brian Harper	.05	.02	.01
□ 493 Felix Jose	.05	.02	.01
□ 494 Trevor Hoffman	.15	.07	.02
□ 495 Dennis Eckersley	.15	.07	.02
□ 496 Pedro Astacio	.05	.02	.01
□ 497 Jay Bell	.15	.07	.02
□ 498 Randy Velarde	.05	.02	.01
□ 499 David Wells	.05	.02	.01
□ 500 Frank Thomas	2.00	.90	.25
□ 501 Mark Lemke	.05	.02	.01
□ 502 Mike Devereaux	.05	.02	.01
□ 503 Chuck McElroy	.05	.02	.01
□ 504 Luis Polonia	.05	.02	.01
□ 505 Damion Easley	.05	.02	.01
□ 506 Greg A. Harris	.05	.02	.01
□ 507 Chris James	.05	.02	.01
□ 508 Terry Mulholland	.05	.02	.01
□ 509 Pete Smith	.05	.02	.01
□ 510 Rickey Henderson	.30	.14	.04
□ 511 Sid Fernandez	.05	.02	.01
□ 512 Al Leiter	.15	.07	.02
□ 513 Doug Jones	.05	.02	.01
□ 514 Steve Farr	.05	.02	.01
□ 515 Chuck Finley	.05	.02	.01
□ 516 Bobby Thigpen	.05	.02	.01
□ 517 Jim Edmonds	.40	.18	.05
□ 518 Graeme Lloyd	.05	.02	.01
□ 519 Dwight Gooden	.15	.07	.02
□ 520 Pat Listach	.05	.02	.01
□ 521 Kevin Bass	.05	.02	.01
□ 522 Willie Banks	.05	.02	.01
□ 523 Steve Finley	.30	.14	.04
□ 524 Delino DeShields	.05	.02	.01
□ 525 Mark McGwire	.60	.25	.07
□ 526 Greg Swindell	.05	.02	.01
□ 527 Chris Nabholz	.05	.02	.01
□ 528 Scott Sanders	.05	.02	.01
□ 529 David Segui	.05	.02	.01
□ 530 Howard Johnson	.05	.02	.01
□ 531 Jaime Navarro	.05	.02	.01
□ 532 Jose Vizcaino	.05	.02	.01
□ 533 Mark Lewis	.05	.02	.01
□ 534 Pete Harnisch	.05	.02	.01
□ 535 Robby Thompson	.05	.02	.01
□ 536 Marcus Moore	.05	.02	.01
□ 537 Kevin Brown	.05	.02	.01
□ 538 Mark Clark	.05	.02	.01
□ 539 Sterling Hitchcock	.15	.07	.02
□ 540 Will Clark	.30	.14	.04
□ 541 Denis Boucher	.05	.02	.01
□ 542 Jack Morris	.15	.07	.02
□ 543 Pedro Munoz	.05	.02	.01
□ 544 Bret Boone	.15	.07	.02
□ 545 Ozzie Smith	.40	.18	.05
□ 546 Dennis Martinez	.15	.07	.02
□ 547 Dan Wilson	.15	.07	.02
□ 548 Rick Sutcliffe	.05	.02	.01
□ 549 Kevin McReynolds	.05	.02	.01
□ 550 Roger Clemens	.30	.14	.04
□ 551 Todd Benzinger	.05	.02	.01
□ 552 Bill Haselman	.05	.02	.01
□ 553 Bobby Munoz	.05	.02	.01
□ 554 Ellis Burks	.15	.07	.02
□ 555 Ryne Sandberg	.50	.23	.06
□ 556 Lee Smith	.15	.07	.02
□ 557 Danny Bautista	.05	.02	.01
□ 558 Rey Sanchez	.05	.02	.01

□ 559 Norm Charlton	.05	.02	.01
□ 560 Jose Canseco	.30	.14	.04
□ 561 Tim Belcher	.05	.02	.01
□ 562 Denny Neagle	.15	.07	.02
□ 563 Eric Davis	.15	.07	.02
□ 564 Jody Reed	.05	.02	.01
□ 565 Kenny Lofton	.60	.25	.07
□ 566 Gary Gaetti	.15	.07	.02
□ 567 Todd Worrell	.05	.02	.01
□ 568 Mark Portugal	.05	.02	.01
□ 569 Dick Schofield	.05	.02	.01
□ 570 Andy Benes	.15	.07	.02
□ 571 Zane Smith	.05	.02	.01
□ 572 Bobby Ayala	.05	.02	.01
□ 573 Chip Hale	.05	.02	.01
□ 574 Bob Welch	.05	.02	.01
□ 575 Deion Sanders	.30	.14	.04
□ 576 Dave Nied	.05	.02	.01
□ 577 Pat Mahomes	.05	.02	.01
□ 578 Charles Nagy	.15	.07	.02
□ 579 Otis Nixon	.05	.02	.01
□ 580 Dean Palmer	.15	.07	.02
□ 581 Roberto Petagine	.15	.07	.02
□ 582 Dwight Smith	.05	.02	.01
□ 583 Jeff Russell	.05	.02	.01
□ 584 Mark Dewey	.05	.02	.01
□ 585 Greg Vaughn	.30	.14	.04
□ 586 Brian Hunter	.05	.02	.01
□ 587 Willie McGee	.05	.02	.01
□ 588 Pedro J. Martinez	.30	.14	.04
□ 589 Roger Salkeld	.05	.02	.01
□ 590 Jeff Bagwell	.75	.35	.09
□ 591 Spike Owen	.05	.02	.01
□ 592 Jeff Reardon	.15	.07	.02
□ 593 Erik Pappas	.05	.02	.01
□ 594 Brian Williams	.05	.02	.01
□ 595 Eddie Murray	.50	.23	.06
□ 596 Henry Rodriguez	.30	.14	.04
□ 597 Erik Hanson	.05	.02	.01
□ 598 Stan Javier	.05	.02	.01
□ 599 Mitch Williams	.05	.02	.01
□ 600 John Olerud	.05	.02	.01
□ 601 Vince Coleman	.05	.02	.01
□ 602 Damon Berryhill	.05	.02	.01
□ 603 Tom Brunansky	.05	.02	.01
□ 604 Robb Nen	.15	.07	.02
□ 605 Rafael Palmeiro	.30	.14	.04
□ 606 Cal Eldred	.05	.02	.01
□ 607 Jeff Brantley	.05	.02	.01
□ 608 Alan Mills	.05	.02	.01
□ 609 Jeff Nelson	.05	.02	.01
□ 610 Barry Bonds	.50	.23	.06
□ 611 Carlos Pulido	.05	.02	.01
□ 612 Tim Hyers	.05	.02	.01
□ 613 Steve Howe	.05	.02	.01
□ 614 Brian Turang	.05	.02	.01
□ 615 Leo Gomez	.05	.02	.01
□ 616 Jesse Orosco	.05	.02	.01
□ 617 Dan Pasqua	.05	.02	.01
□ 618 Marvin Freeman	.05	.02	.01
□ 619 Tony Fernandez	.05	.02	.01
□ 620 Albert Belle	1.00	.45	.12
□ 621 Eddie Taubensee	.05	.02	.01
□ 622 Mike Jackson	.05	.02	.01
□ 623 Jose Bautista	.05	.02	.01
□ 624 Jim Thome	.50	.23	.06
□ 625 Ivan Rodriguez	.40	.18	.05
□ 626 Ben Rivera	.05	.02	.01
□ 627 Dave Valle	.05	.02	.01
□ 628 Tom Henke	.05	.02	.01
□ 629 Omar Vizquel	.30	.14	.04
□ 630 Juan Gonzalez	1.00	.45	.12
□ 631 Roberto Alomar UP	.30	.14	.04
□ 632 Barry Bonds UP	.30	.14	.04
□ 633 Juan Gonzalez UP	.50	.23	.06
□ 634 Ken Griffey Jr. UP	1.00	.45	.12
□ 635 Michael Jordan UP	4.00	1.80	.50
□ 636 David Justice UP	.15	.07	.02
□ 637 Mike Piazza UP	.60	.25	.07
□ 638 Kirby Puckett UP	.30	.14	.04
□ 639 Tim Salmon UP	.15	.07	.02
□ 640 Frank Thomas UP	1.00	.45	.12
□ 641 Alan Benes FF	.75	.35	.09
□ 642 Johnny Damon FF	.30	.14	.04
□ 643 Brad Fullmer FF	.40	.18	.05
□ 644 Derek Jeter FF	1.50	.70	.19
□ 645 Derrek Lee FF	1.25	.55	.16
□ 646 Alex Ochoa FF	.15	.07	.02
□ 647 Alex Rodriguez FF	6.00	2.70	.75
□ 648 Jose Silva FF	.15	.07	.02
□ 649 Terrell Wade FF	.40	.18	.05
□ 650 Preston Wilson FF	.15	.07	.02
□ 651 Shane Andrews	.15	.07	.02
□ 652 James Baldwin	.30	.14	.04
□ 653 Ricky Bottalico	.25	.11	.03
□ 654 Tavo Alvarez	.05	.02	.01
□ 655 Donnie Elliott	.05	.02	.01
□ 656 Joey Eischen	.05	.02	.01
□ 657 Jason Giambi	.50	.23	.06
□ 658 Todd Hollandsworth	.50	.23	.06
□ 659 Brian L. Hunter	.30	.14	.04
□ 660 Charles Johnson	.30	.14	.04
□ 661 Michael Jordan	6.00	2.70	.75
□ 662 Jeff Juden	.05	.02	.01
□ 663 Mike Kelly	.05	.02	.01
□ 664 James Mouton	.15	.07	.02
□ 665 Ray Holbert	.05	.02	.01
□ 666 Pokey Reese	.15	.07	.02
□ 667 Ruben Santana	.05	.02	.01
□ 668 Paul Spoljaric	.05	.02	.01
□ 669 Luis Lopez	.05	.02	.01
□ 670 Matt Walbeck	.05	.02	.01

1994 Collector's Choice Home Run All-Stars

This 15-card standard-size set served as the eighth place prize in the Crash the Game contest, which was a promotion in both series of Collector's Choice. The series 1 expiration was May 18, 1994; series 2 was Oct. 31, 1994. Horizontal fronts feature holographic images of the player that breaks through a brick wall. A small color photo of the player appears at left or right. The backs, outlined with bricks, features a small photo and text that appears over a stadium background. The cards are numbered with an "HA" prefix.

	MINT	NRMT	EXC
COMPLETE SET (8)	5.00	2.20	.60
COMMON CARD (HA1-HA8)	.25	.11	.03
SETS DIST. w/SERIES 1/2 8TH PRIZE			
□ HA1 Juan Gonzalez	1.50	.70	.19
□ HA2 Ken Griffey Jr.	3.00	1.35	.35
□ HA3 Barry Bonds	.75	.35	.09
□ HA4 Bobby Bonilla	.25	.11	.03
□ HA5 Cecil Fielder UER (Card number is HA4)	.50	.23	.06
□ HA6 Albert Belle	1.50	.70	.19
□ HA7 David Justice	.50	.23	.06
□ HA8 Mike Piazza	2.00	.90	.25

1994 Collector's Choice Team vs. Team

Issued one per second series pack, these 15 foldout, scratch-off game cards feature one team's lineup against the other. Various prizes were available through these game cards. The most plentiful was the eighth place Home Run

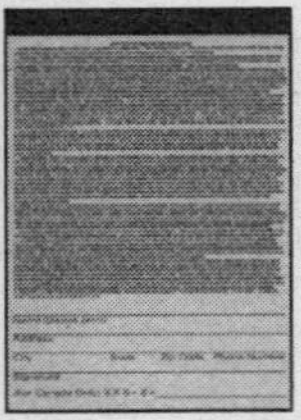

All-Stars hologram set. Prizes were redeemable through October 31, 1994. Scratch-off rules and two small player photos are on the front with complete rules and provisions on the back. The cards fold out to expose the game portion. Cards that are scratched are half the values below.

	MINT	NRMT	EXC
COMPLETE SET (15)	4.00	1.80	.50
COMMON FOLDOUT (1-15)	.25	.11	.03
SEMISTARS	.40	.18	.05
ONE UNNUMBERED CARD PER SER.2 PACK			
*PRIZE BOX SCRATCHED: HALF VALUE......			

	MINT	NRMT	EXC
□ 1 Roberto Alomar / Frank Thomas	1.00	.45	.12
□ 2 Barry Bonds / Ken Griffey Jr.	1.00	.45	,12
□ 3 Roger Clemens / Don Mattingly	.50	.23	.06
□ 4 Lenny Dykstra / David Justice	.25	.11	.03
□ 5 Andres Galarraga / Tony Gwynn	.40	.18	.05
□ 6 Dwight Gooden / Gary Sheffield	.40	.18	.05
□ 7 Ken Griffey Jr. / Juan Gonzalez	1.00	.45	.12
□ 8 Barry Larkin / Jeff Bagwell	.40	.18	.05
□ 9 Pat Listach / Albert Belle	.25	.11	.03
□ 10 Mark McGwire / Tim Salmon	.40	.18	.05
□ 11 Mike Piazza / Barry Bonds	.60	.25	.07
□ 12 Kirby Puckett / Brian McRae	.40	.18	.05
□ 13 Cal Ripken / Cecil Fielder	.75	.35	.09
□ 14 Ryne Sandberg / Ozzie Smith	.50	.23	.06
□ 15 Andy Van Slyke / Cliff Floyd	.25	.11	.03

1995 Collector's Choice

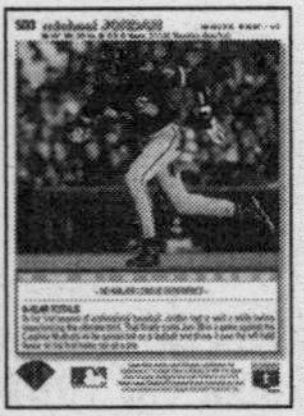

This set contains 530 standard-size cards issued in packs that were sold in 12-card foil hobby and retail foil-packs for a suggested price of 99 cents. The fronts have a color photo with a white border and the player's last name at the bottom in his team's color. The backs have an action photo at the top with statistics and information at the bottom with a silver Upper Deck hologram below that. Subsets featured are Rookie Class (1-27), Future Foundation (28-45), Best of the '90s (51-65) and Whatís the Call? (86-90). Key Rookie Cards in this set include Raul Casanova and Karim Garcia. The 55-card Trade set represents the cards a collector received when the five trade cards were redeemed. They are numbered in continuation of the regular Collector's Choice cards but have a "T" suffix. The cards numbered 542-552 were also issued as a bonus to dealers who ordered collector's choice factory sets. The trade cards offer expired on February 1, 1996.

	MINT	NRMT	EXC
COMPLETE SET (530)	20.00	9.00	2.50
COMPLETE FACT.SET (545)	30.00	13.50	3.70
COMMON CARD (1-530)	.05	.02	.01
SEMISTARS	.15	.07	.02
STARS	.30	.14	.04
COMPLETE TRADE SET (55)	10.00	4.50	1.25
COMMON TRADE (531-585)	.10	.05	.01
COMMON TRADE DP (542-552)	.05	.02	.01
TEN TRADE VIA MAIL PER TRD.EXCH.CARD			
ONE 542-552 RUN PER DLR.FACT.SET ORDER			
COMP.TRD.EXCH.SET (5)	4.00	1.80	.50
COMMON TRD.EXCH. (TC1-TC5)	1.00	.45	.12
COMP.SILVER SIG.SET (530)	75.00	34.00	9.50
COMMON SILVER (1-530)	.10	.05	.01
SILVER SIG.SEMISTARS	.20	.09	.03
SILVER SIG.STARS	.40	.18	.05
*SILV.SIG.STARS: 2X to 4X HI COLUMN.....			
*SILV.SIG.YOUNG STARS: 1.5X to 3X HI			
ONE SILVER SIGNATURE PER PACK...........			
COMP.GOLD SIG SET (530)	1000.00	450.00	125.00
COMMON GOLD SIG (1-530)	1.00	.45	.12
GOLD SIG SEMISTARS	2.50	1.10	.30
*GOLD VETERAN STARS: 10X TO 20X HI....			
*GOLD YOUNG STARS: 7.5 TO 15X HI			
GOLD: RANDOM INSERTS IN PACKS			
GOLD: 12 PER SUPER PACK/15 PER FACT.SET			

	MINT	NRMT	EXC
□ 1 Charles Johnson	.15	.07	.02
□ 2 Scott Ruffcorn	.05	.02	.01
□ 3 Ray Durham	.15	.07	.02
□ 4 Armando Benitez	.05	.02	.01
□ 5 Alex Rodriguez	2.50	1.10	.30
□ 6 Julian Tavarez	.05	.02	.01
□ 7 Chad Ogea	.05	.02	.01
□ 8 Quilvio Veras	.05	.02	.01
□ 9 Phil Nevin	.05	.02	.01
□ 10 Michael Tucker	.15	.07	.02
□ 11 Mark Thompson	.05	.02	.01
□ 12 Rod Henderson	.05	.02	.01
□ 13 Andrew Lorraine	.15	.07	.02
□ 14 Joe Randa	.05	.02	.01
□ 15 Derek Jeter	1.25	.55	.16
□ 16 Tony Clark	.30	.14	.04
□ 17 Juan Castillo	.05	.02	.01
□ 18 Mark Acre	.05	.02	.01
□ 19 Orlando Miller	.05	.02	.01
□ 20 Paul Wilson	.40	.18	.05
□ 21 John Mabry	.30	.14	.04
□ 22 Garey Ingram	.05	.02	.01
□ 23 Garret Anderson	.30	.14	.04
□ 24 Dave Stevens	.05	.02	.01
□ 25 Dustin Hermanson	.15	.07	.02
□ 26 Paul Shuey	.05	.02	.01
□ 27 J.R. Phillips	.05	.02	.01
□ 28 Ruben Rivera FF	1.00	.45	.12
□ 29 Nomar Garciaparra FF	1.00	.45	.12
□ 30 John Wasdin FF	.05	.02	.01
□ 31 Jim Pittsley FF	.15	.07	.02
□ 32 Scott Elarton FF	.40	.18	.05
□ 33 Raul Casanova FF	.50	.23	.06
□ 34 Todd Greene FF	.30	.14	.04
□ 35 Bill Pulsipher FF	.15	.07	.02
□ 36 Trey Beamon FF	.15	.07	.02
□ 37 Curtis Goodwin FF	.15	.07	.02
□ 38 Doug Million FF	.15	.07	.02
□ 39 Karim Garcia FF	2.00	.90	.25
□ 40 Ben Grieve FF	.75	.35	.09

□ 41 Mark Farris FF	.15	.07	.02
□ 42 Juan Acevedo FF	.05	.02	.01
□ 43 C.J. Nitkowski FF	.15	.07	.02
□ 44 Travis Miller FF	.15	.07	.02
□ 45 Reid Ryan FF	.30	.14	.04
□ 46 Nolan Ryan	1.25	.55	.16
□ 47 Robin Yount	.30	.14	.04
□ 48 Ryne Sandberg	.40	.18	.05
□ 49 George Brett	.50	.23	.06
□ 50 Mike Schmidt	.40	.18	.05
□ 51 Cecil Fielder B90	.15	.07	.02
□ 52 Nolan Ryan B90	.60	.25	.07
□ 53 Rickey Henderson B90	.15	.07	.02
□ 54 George Brett B90	.40	.18	.05
Robin Yount			
Dave Winfield			
□ 55 Sid Bream B90	.05	.02	.01
□ 56 Carlos Baerga B90	.15	.07	.02
□ 57 Lee Smith B90	.05	.02	.01
□ 58 Mark Whiten B90	.05	.02	.01
□ 59 Joe Carter B90	.15	.07	.02
□ 60 Barry Bonds B90	.30	.14	.04
□ 61 Tony Gwynn B90	.40	.18	.05
□ 62 Ken Griffey Jr. B90	1.00	.45	.12
□ 63 Greg Maddux B90	.60	.25	.07
□ 64 Frank Thomas B90	1.00	.45	.12
□ 65 Dennis Martinez B90	.05	.02	.01
Kenny Rogers			
□ 66 David Cone	.15	.07	.02
□ 67 Greg Maddux	1.25	.55	.16
□ 68 Jimmy Key	.15	.07	.02
□ 69 Fred McGriff	.30	.14	.04
□ 70 Ken Griffey Jr.	2.00	.90	.25
□ 71 Matt Williams	.30	.14	.04
□ 72 Paul O'Neill	.15	.07	.02
□ 73 Tony Gwynn	.75	.35	.09
□ 74 Randy Johnson	.30	.14	.04
□ 75 Frank Thomas	2.00	.90	.25
□ 76 Jeff Bagwell	.75	.35	.09
□ 77 Kirby Puckett	.60	.25	.07
□ 78 Bob Hamelin	.05	.02	.01
□ 79 Raul Mondesi	.30	.14	.04
□ 80 Mike Piazza	1.25	.55	.16
□ 81 Kenny Lofton	.50	.23	.06
□ 82 Barry Bonds	.50	.23	.06
□ 83 Albert Belle	1.00	.45	.12
□ 84 Juan Gonzalez	1.00	.45	.12
□ 85 Cal Ripken Jr.	1.50	.70	.19
□ 86 Barry Bonds WC	.30	.14	.04
□ 87 Mike Piazza WC	.60	.25	.07
□ 88 Ken Griffey Jr. WC	1.00	.45	.12
□ 89 Frank Thomas WC	1.00	.45	.12
□ 90 Juan Gonzalez WC	.50	.23	.06
□ 91 Jorge Fabregas	.05	.02	.01
□ 92 J.T. Snow	.15	.07	.02
□ 93 Spike Owen	.05	.02	.01
□ 94 Eduardo Perez	.05	.02	.01
□ 95 Bo Jackson	.30	.14	.04
□ 96 Damion Easley	.05	.02	.01
□ 97 Gary DiSarcina	.05	.02	.01
□ 98 Jim Edmonds	.30	.14	.04
□ 99 Chad Curtis	.05	.02	.01
□ 100 Tim Salmon	.30	.14	.04
□ 101 Chili Davis	.15	.07	.02
□ 102 Chuck Finley	.15	.07	.02
□ 103 Mark Langston	.05	.02	.01
□ 104 Brian Anderson	.05	.02	.01
□ 105 Lee Smith	.15	.07	.02
□ 106 Phil Leftwich	.05	.02	.01
□ 107 Chris Donnels	.05	.02	.01
□ 108 John Hudek	.05	.02	.01
□ 109 Craig Biggio	.30	.14	.04
□ 110 Luis Gonzalez	.05	.02	.01
□ 111 Brian L. Hunter	.30	.14	.04
□ 112 James Mouton	.05	.02	.01
□ 113 Scott Servais	.05	.02	.01
□ 114 Tony Eusebio	.05	.02	.01
□ 115 Derek Bell	.15	.07	.02
□ 116 Doug Drabek	.05	.02	.01
□ 117 Shane Reynolds	.05	.02	.01
□ 118 Darryl Kile	.05	.02	.01
□ 119 Greg Swindell	.05	.02	.01
□ 120 Phil Plantier	.05	.02	.01
□ 121 Todd Jones	.05	.02	.01
□ 122 Steve Ontiveros	.05	.02	.01
□ 123 Bobby Witt	.05	.02	.01
□ 124 Brent Gates	.05	.02	.01
□ 125 Rickey Henderson	.30	.14	.04
□ 126 Scott Brosius	.05	.02	.01
□ 127 Mike Bordick	.05	.02	.01
□ 128 Fausto Cruz	.05	.02	.01
□ 129 Stan Javier	.05	.02	.01
□ 130 Mark McGwire	.60	.25	.07
□ 131 Geronimo Berroa	.05	.02	.01
□ 132 Terry Steinbach	.15	.07	.02
□ 133 Steve Karsay	.05	.02	.01
□ 134 Dennis Eckersley	.15	.07	.02
□ 135 Ruben Sierra	.15	.07	.02
□ 136 Ron Darling	.05	.02	.01
□ 137 Todd Van Poppel	.05	.02	.01
□ 138 Alex Gonzalez	.05	.02	.01
□ 139 John Olerud	.05	.02	.01
□ 140 Roberto Alomar	.50	.23	.06
□ 141 Darren Hall	.05	.02	.01
□ 142 Ed Sprague	.15	.07	.02
□ 143 Devon White	.15	.07	.02
□ 144 Shawn Green	.15	.07	.02
□ 145 Paul Molitor	.40	.18	.05
□ 146 Pat Borders	.05	.02	.01
□ 147 Carlos Delgado	.30	.14	.04
□ 148 Juan Guzman	.15	.07	.02
□ 149 Pat Hentgen	.15	.07	.02
□ 150 Joe Carter	.30	.14	.04
□ 151 Dave Stewart	.15	.07	.02
□ 152 Todd Stottlemyre	.05	.02	.01
□ 153 Dick Schofield	.05	.02	.01
□ 154 Chipper Jones	1.25	.55	.16
□ 155 Ryan Klesko	.40	.18	.05
□ 156 David Justice	.30	.14	.04
□ 157 Mike Kelly	.05	.02	.01
□ 158 Roberto Kelly	.05	.02	.01
□ 159 Tony Tarasco	.05	.02	.01
□ 160 Javier Lopez	.30	.14	.04
□ 161 Steve Avery	.15	.07	.02
□ 162 Greg McMichael	.05	.02	.01
□ 163 Kent Mercker	.05	.02	.01
□ 164 Mark Lemke	.05	.02	.01
□ 165 Tom Glavine	.30	.14	.04
□ 166 Jose Oliva	.05	.02	.01
□ 167 John Smoltz	.30	.14	.04
□ 168 Jeff Blauser	.05	.02	.01
□ 169 Troy O'Leary	.05	.02	.01
□ 170 Greg Vaughn	.15	.07	.02
□ 171 Jody Reed	.05	.02	.01
□ 172 Kevin Seitzer	.05	.02	.01
□ 173 Jeff Cirillo	.15	.07	.02
□ 174 B.J. Surhoff	.15	.07	.02
□ 175 Cal Eldred	.05	.02	.01
□ 176 Jose Valentin	.15	.07	.02
□ 177 Turner Ward	.05	.02	.01
□ 178 Darryl Hamilton	.05	.02	.01
□ 179 Pat Listach	.05	.02	.01
□ 180 Matt Mieske	.15	.07	.02
□ 181 Brian Harper	.05	.02	.01
□ 182 Dave Nilsson	.15	.07	.02
□ 183 Mike Fetters	.05	.02	.01
□ 184 John Jaha	.15	.07	.02
□ 185 Ricky Bones	.05	.02	.01
□ 186 Geronimo Pena	.05	.02	.01
□ 187 Bob Tewksbury	.05	.02	.01
□ 188 Todd Zeile	.05	.02	.01
□ 189 Danny Jackson	.05	.02	.01
□ 190 Ray Lankford	.30	.14	.04
□ 191 Bernard Gilkey	.15	.07	.02
□ 192 Brian Jordan	.30	.14	.04
□ 193 Tom Pagnozzi	.05	.02	.01
□ 194 Rick Sutcliffe	.05	.02	.01
□ 195 Mark Whiten	.05	.02	.01
□ 196 Tom Henke	.05	.02	.01
□ 197 Rene Arocha	.05	.02	.01
□ 198 Allen Watson	.05	.02	.01
□ 199 Mike Perez	.05	.02	.01
□ 200 Ozzie Smith	.40	.18	.05
□ 201 Anthony Young	.05	.02	.01
□ 202 Rey Sanchez	.05	.02	.01
□ 203 Steve Buechele	.05	.02	.01
□ 204 Shawon Dunston	.05	.02	.01
□ 205 Mark Grace	.30	.14	.04
□ 206 Glenallen Hill	.05	.02	.01
□ 207 Eddie Zambrano	.05	.02	.01
□ 208 Rick Wilkins	.05	.02	.01
□ 209 Derrick May	.05	.02	.01

□ 210	Sammy Sosa	.30	.14	.04
□ 211	Kevin Roberson	.05	.02	.01
□ 212	Steve Trachsel	.05	.02	.01
□ 213	Willie Banks	.05	.02	.01
□ 214	Kevin Foster	.05	.02	.01
□ 215	Randy Myers	.05	.02	.01
□ 216	Mike Morgan	.05	.02	.01
□ 217	Rafael Bournigal	.05	.02	.01
□ 218	Delino DeShields	.05	.02	.01
□ 219	Tim Wallach	.05	.02	.01
□ 220	Eric Karros	.15	.07	.02
□ 221	Jose Offerman	.05	.02	.01
□ 222	Tom Candiotti	.05	.02	.01
□ 223	Ismael Valdes	.15	.07	.02
□ 224	Henry Rodriguez	.30	.14	.04
□ 225	Billy Ashley	.05	.02	.01
□ 226	Darren Dreifort	.05	.02	.01
□ 227	Ramon Martinez	.15	.07	.02
□ 228	Pedro Astacio	.05	.02	.01
□ 229	Orel Hershiser	.15	.07	.02
□ 230	Brett Butler	.15	.07	.02
□ 231	Todd Hollandsworth	.30	.14	.04
□ 232	Chan Ho Park	.30	.14	.04
□ 233	Mike Lansing	.05	.02	.01
□ 234	Sean Berry	.05	.02	.01
□ 235	Rondell White	.30	.14	.04
□ 236	Ken Hill	.05	.02	.01
□ 237	Marquis Grissom	.30	.14	.04
□ 238	Larry Walker	.30	.14	.04
□ 239	John Wetteland	.15	.07	.02
□ 240	Cliff Floyd	.15	.07	.02
□ 241	Joey Eischen	.05	.02	.01
□ 242	Lou Frazier	.05	.02	.01
□ 243	Darrin Fletcher	.05	.02	.01
□ 244	Pedro J. Martinez	.15	.07	.02
□ 245	Wil Cordero	.05	.02	.01
□ 246	Jeff Fassero	.05	.02	.01
□ 247	Butch Henry	.05	.02	.01
□ 248	Mel Rojas	.05	.02	.01
□ 249	Kirk Rueter	.05	.02	.01
□ 250	Moises Alou	.15	.07	.02
□ 251	Rod Beck	.05	.02	.01
□ 252	John Patterson	.05	.02	.01
□ 253	Robby Thompson	.05	.02	.01
□ 254	Royce Clayton	.05	.02	.01
□ 255	Wm. VanLandingham	.05	.02	.01
□ 256	Darren Lewis	.05	.02	.01
□ 257	Kirt Manwaring	.05	.02	.01
□ 258	Mark Portugal	.05	.02	.01
□ 259	Bill Swift	.05	.02	.01
□ 260	Rikkert Faneyte	.05	.02	.01
□ 261	Mike Jackson	.05	.02	.01
□ 262	Todd Benzinger	.05	.02	.01
□ 263	Bud Black	.05	.02	.01
□ 264	Salomon Torres	.05	.02	.01
□ 265	Eddie Murray	.30	.14	.04
□ 266	Mark Clark	.05	.02	.01
□ 267	Paul Sorrento	.05	.02	.01
□ 268	Jim Thome	.40	.18	.05
□ 269	Omar Vizquel	.30	.14	.04
□ 270	Carlos Baerga	.30	.14	.04
□ 271	Jeff Russell	.05	.02	.01
□ 272	Herbert Perry	.05	.02	.01
□ 273	Sandy Alomar Jr.	.05	.02	.01
□ 274	Dennis Martinez	.15	.07	.02
□ 275	Manny Ramirez	.50	.23	.06
□ 276	Wayne Kirby	.05	.02	.01
□ 277	Charles Nagy	.15	.07	.02
□ 278	Albie Lopez	.05	.02	.01
□ 279	Jeromy Burnitz	.05	.02	.01
□ 280	Dave Winfield	.30	.14	.04
□ 281	Tim Davis	.05	.02	.01
□ 282	Marc Newfield	.15	.07	.02
□ 283	Tino Martinez	.15	.07	.02
□ 284	Mike Blowers	.05	.02	.01
□ 285	Goose Gossage	.15	.07	.02
□ 286	Luis Sojo	.05	.02	.01
□ 287	Edgar Martinez	.30	.14	.04
□ 288	Rich Amaral	.05	.02	.01
□ 289	Felix Fermin	.05	.02	.01
□ 290	Jay Buhner	.30	.14	.04
□ 291	Dan Wilson	.15	.07	.02
□ 292	Bobby Ayala	.05	.02	.01
□ 293	Dave Fleming	.05	.02	.01
□ 294	Greg Pirkl	.05	.02	.01
□ 295	Reggie Jefferson	.15	.07	.02
□ 296	Greg Hibbard	.05	.02	.01
□ 297	Yorkis Perez	.05	.02	.01
□ 298	Kurt Miller	.05	.02	.01
□ 299	Chuck Carr	.05	.02	.01
□ 300	Gary Sheffield	.30	.14	.04
□ 301	Jerry Browne	.05	.02	.01
□ 302	Dave Magadan	.05	.02	.01
□ 303	Kurt Abbott	.05	.02	.01
□ 304	Pat Rapp	.05	.02	.01
□ 305	Jeff Conine	.30	.14	.04
□ 306	Benito Santiago	.05	.02	.01
□ 307	Dave Weathers	.05	.02	.01
□ 308	Robb Nen	.05	.02	.01
□ 309	Chris Hammond	.05	.02	.01
□ 310	Bryan Harvey	.05	.02	.01
□ 311	Charlie Hough	.05	.02	.01
□ 312	Greg Colbrunn	.05	.02	.01
□ 313	David Segui	.05	.02	.01
□ 314	Rico Brogna	.05	.02	.01
□ 315	Jeff Kent	.05	.02	.01
□ 316	Jose Vizcaino	.05	.02	.01
□ 317	Jim Lindeman	.05	.02	.01
□ 318	Carl Everett	.05	.02	.01
□ 319	Ryan Thompson	.05	.02	.01
□ 320	Bobby Bonilla	.15	.07	.02
□ 321	Joe Orsulak	.05	.02	.01
□ 322	Pete Harnisch	.05	.02	.01
□ 323	Doug Linton	.05	.02	.01
□ 324	Todd Hundley	.15	.07	.02
□ 325	Bret Saberhagen	.15	.07	.02
□ 326	Kelly Stinnett	.05	.02	.01
□ 327	Jason Jacome	.05	.02	.01
□ 328	Bobby Jones	.15	.07	.02
□ 329	John Franco	.05	.02	.01
□ 330	Rafael Palmeiro	.30	.14	.04
□ 331	Chris Hoiles	.05	.02	.01
□ 332	Leo Gomez	.05	.02	.01
□ 333	Chris Sabo	.05	.02	.01
□ 334	Brady Anderson	.30	.14	.04
□ 335	Jeffrey Hammonds	.15	.07	.02
□ 336	Dwight Smith	.05	.02	.01
□ 337	Jack Voigt	.05	.02	.01
□ 338	Harold Baines	.15	.07	.02
□ 339	Ben McDonald	.05	.02	.01
□ 340	Mike Mussina	.40	.18	.05
□ 341	Bret Barberie	.05	.02	.01
□ 342	Jamie Moyer	.05	.02	.01
□ 343	Mike Oquist	.05	.02	.01
□ 344	Sid Fernandez	.05	.02	.01
□ 345	Eddie Williams	.05	.02	.01
□ 346	Joey Hamilton	.15	.07	.02
□ 347	Brian Williams	.05	.02	.01
□ 348	Luis Lopez	.05	.02	.01
□ 349	Steve Finley	.15	.07	.02
□ 350	Andy Benes	.05	.02	.01
□ 351	Andujar Cedeno	.05	.02	.01
□ 352	Bip Roberts	.05	.02	.01
□ 353	Ray McDavid	.15	.07	.02
□ 354	Ken Caminiti	.30	.14	.04
□ 355	Trevor Hoffman	.05	.02	.01
□ 356	Mel Nieves	.15	.07	.02
□ 357	Brad Ausmus	.05	.02	.01
□ 358	Andy Ashby	.15	.07	.02
□ 359	Scott Sanders	.05	.02	.01
□ 360	Gregg Jefferies	.15	.07	.02
□ 361	Mariano Duncan	.05	.02	.01
□ 362	Dave Hollins	.05	.02	.01
□ 363	Kevin Stocker	.05	.02	.01
□ 364	Fernando Valenzuela	.15	.07	.02
□ 365	Lenny Dykstra	.15	.07	.02
□ 366	Jim Eisenreich	.05	.02	.01
□ 367	Ricky Bottalico	.15	.07	.02
□ 368	Doug Jones	.05	.02	.01
□ 369	Ricky Jordan	.05	.02	.01
□ 370	Darren Daulton	.15	.07	.02
□ 371	Mike Lieberthal	.05	.02	.01
□ 372	Bobby Munoz	.05	.02	.01
□ 373	John Kruk	.15	.07	.02
□ 374	Curt Schilling	.05	.02	.01
□ 375	Orlando Merced	.05	.02	.01
□ 376	Carlos Garcia	.05	.02	.01
□ 377	Lance Parrish	.05	.02	.01
□ 378	Steve Cooke	.05	.02	.01
□ 379	Jeff King	.15	.07	.02
□ 380	Jay Bell	.15	.07	.02
□ 381	Al Martin	.15	.07	.02

□ 382 Paul Wagner	.05	.02	.01
□ 383 Rick White	.05	.02	.01
□ 384 Midre Cummings	.05	.02	.01
□ 385 Jon Lieber	.05	.02	.01
□ 386 Dave Clark	.05	.02	.01
□ 387 Don Slaught	.05	.02	.01
□ 388 Denny Neagle	.15	.07	.02
□ 389 Zane Smith	.05	.02	.01
□ 390 Andy Van Slyke	.15	.07	.02
□ 391 Ivan Rodriguez	.40	.18	.05
□ 392 David Hulse	.05	.02	.01
□ 393 John Burkett	.15	.07	.02
□ 394 Kevin Brown	.15	.07	.02
□ 395 Dean Palmer	.15	.07	.02
□ 396 Otis Nixon	.05	.02	.01
□ 397 Rick Helling	.05	.02	.01
□ 398 Kenny Rogers	.05	.02	.01
□ 399 Darren Oliver	.15	.07	.02
□ 400 Will Clark	.30	.14	.04
□ 401 Jeff Frye	.05	.02	.01
□ 402 Kevin Gross	.05	.02	.01
□ 403 John Dettmer	.05	.02	.01
□ 404 Manny Lee	.05	.02	.01
□ 405 Rusty Greer	.30	.14	.04
□ 406 Aaron Sele	.15	.07	.02
□ 407 Carlos Rodriguez	.05	.02	.01
□ 408 Scott Cooper	.05	.02	.01
□ 409 John Valentin	.15	.07	.02
□ 410 Roger Clemens	.30	.14	.04
□ 411 Mike Greenwell	.05	.02	.01
□ 412 Tim Vanegmond	.05	.02	.01
□ 413 Tom Brunansky	.05	.02	.01
□ 414 Steve Farr	.05	.02	.01
□ 415 Jose Canseco	.30	.14	.04
□ 416 Joe Hesketh	.05	.02	.01
□ 417 Ken Ryan	.05	.02	.01
□ 418 Tim Naehring	.05	.02	.01
□ 419 Frank Viola	.05	.02	.01
□ 420 Andre Dawson	.30	.14	.04
□ 421 Mo Vaughn	.50	.23	.06
□ 422 Jeff Brantley	.05	.02	.01
□ 423 Pete Schourek	.15	.07	.02
□ 424 Hal Morris	.05	.02	.01
□ 425 Deion Sanders	.30	.14	.04
□ 426 Brian R. Hunter	.05	.02	.01
□ 427 Bret Boone	.15	.07	.02
□ 428 Willie Greene	.05	.02	.01
□ 429 Ron Gant	.15	.07	.02
□ 430 Barry Larkin	.30	.14	.04
□ 431 Reggie Sanders	.15	.07	.02
□ 432 Eddie Taubensee	.05	.02	.01
□ 433 Jack Morris	.30	.14	.04
□ 434 Jose Rijo	.05	.02	.01
□ 435 Johnny Ruffin	.05	.02	.01
□ 436 John Smiley	.05	.02	.01
□ 437 John Roper	.05	.02	.01
□ 438 Dave Nied	.05	.02	.01
□ 439 Roberto Mejia	.05	.02	.01
□ 440 Andres Galarraga	.30	.14	.04
□ 441 Mike Kingery	.05	.02	.01
□ 442 Curt Leskanic	.05	.02	.01
□ 443 Walt Weiss	.05	.02	.01
□ 444 Marvin Freeman	.05	.02	.01
□ 445 Charlie Hayes	.05	.02	.01
□ 446 Eric Young	.15	.07	.02
□ 447 Ellis Burks	.30	.14	.04
□ 448 Joe Girardi	.05	.02	.01
□ 449 Lance Painter	.05	.02	.01
□ 450 Dante Bichette	.30	.14	.04
□ 451 Bruce Ruffin	.05	.02	.01
□ 452 Jeff Granger	.05	.02	.01
□ 453 Wally Joyner	.15	.07	.02
□ 454 Jose Lind	.05	.02	.01
□ 455 Jeff Montgomery	.15	.07	.02
□ 456 Gary Gaetti	.15	.07	.02
□ 457 Greg Gagne	.05	.02	.01
□ 458 Vince Coleman	.05	.02	.01
□ 459 Mike Macfarlane	.05	.02	.01
□ 460 Brian McRae	.15	.07	.02
□ 461 Tom Gordon	.05	.02	.01
□ 462 Kevin Appier	.15	.07	.02
□ 463 Billy Brewer	.05	.02	.01
□ 464 Mark Gubicza	.05	.02	.01
□ 465 Travis Fryman	.15	.07	.02
□ 466 Danny Bautista	.05	.02	.01
□ 467 Sean Bergman	.05	.02	.01

□ 468 Mike Henneman	.05	.02	.01
□ 469 Mike Moore	.05	.02	.01
□ 470 Cecil Fielder	.15	.07	.02
□ 471 Alan Trammell	.30	.14	.04
□ 472 Kirk Gibson	.15	.07	.02
□ 473 Tony Phillips	.15	.07	.02
□ 474 Mickey Tettleton	.05	.02	.01
□ 475 Lou Whitaker	.30	.14	.04
□ 476 Chris Gomez	.05	.02	.01
□ 477 John Doherty	.05	.02	.01
□ 478 Greg Gohr	.05	.02	.01
□ 479 Bill Gullickson	.05	.02	.01
□ 480 Rick Aguilera	.05	.02	.01
□ 481 Matt Walbeck	.05	.02	.01
□ 482 Kevin Tapani	.05	.02	.01
□ 483 Scott Erickson	.05	.02	.01
□ 484 Steve Dunn	.05	.02	.01
□ 485 David McCarty	.05	.02	.01
□ 486 Scott Leius	.05	.02	.01
□ 487 Pat Meares	.05	.02	.01
□ 488 Jeff Reboulet	.05	.02	.01
□ 489 Pedro Munoz	.05	.02	.01
□ 490 Chuck Knoblauch	.30	.14	.04
□ 491 Rich Becker	.05	.02	.01
□ 492 Alex Cole	.05	.02	.01
□ 493 Pat Mahomes	.05	.02	.01
□ 494 Ozzie Guillen	.05	.02	.01
□ 495 Tim Raines	.30	.14	.04
□ 496 Kirk McCaskill	.05	.02	.01
□ 497 Olmedo Saenz	.05	.02	.01
□ 498 Scott Sanderson	.05	.02	.01
□ 499 Lance Johnson	.15	.07	.02
□ 500 Michael Jordan	2.50	1.10	.30
□ 501 Warren Newson	.05	.02	.01
□ 502 Ron Karkovice	.05	.02	.01
□ 503 Wilson Alvarez	.15	.07	.02
□ 504 Jason Bere	.05	.02	.01
□ 505 Robin Ventura	.15	.07	.02
□ 506 Alex Fernandez	.15	.07	.02
□ 507 Roberto Hernandez	.05	.02	.01
□ 508 Norberto Martin	.05	.02	.01
□ 509 Bob Wickman	.05	.02	.01
□ 510 Don Mattingly	1.00	.45	.12
□ 511 Melido Perez	.05	.02	.01
□ 512 Pat Kelly	.05	.02	.01
□ 513 Randy Velarde	.05	.02	.01
□ 514 Tony Fernandez	.05	.02	.01
□ 515 Jack McDowell	.15	.07	.02
□ 516 Luis Polonia	.05	.02	.01
□ 517 Bernie Williams	.30	.14	.04
□ 518 Danny Tartabull	.05	.02	.01
□ 519 Mike Stanley	.05	.02	.01
□ 520 Wade Boggs	.30	.14	.04
□ 521 Jim Leyritz	.05	.02	.01
□ 522 Steve Howe	.05	.02	.01
□ 523 Scott Kamieniecki	.05	.02	.01
□ 524 Russ Davis	.05	.02	.01
□ 525 Jim Abbott	.05	.02	.01
□ 526 Eddie Murray CL	.30	.14	.04
□ 527 Alex Rodriguez CL	1.25	.55	.16
□ 528 Jeff Bagwell CL	.40	.18	.05
□ 529 Joe Carter CL	.15	.07	.02
□ 530 Fred McGriff CL	.15	.07	.02
□ 531T Tony Phillips TRADE	.10	.05	.01
□ 532T Dave Magadan TRADE	.10	.05	.01
□ 533T Mike Gallego TRADE	.10	.05	.01
□ 534T Dave Stewart TRADE	.15	.07	.02
□ 535T Todd Stottlemyre TRADE	.15	.07	.02
□ 536T David Cone TRADE	.15	.07	.02
□ 537T Marquis Grissom TRADE	.30	.14	.04
□ 538T Derrick May TRADE	.10	.05	.01
□ 539T Joe Oliver TRADE	.10	.05	.01
□ 540T Scott Cooper TRADE	.10	.05	.01
□ 541T Ken Hill TRADE	.15	.07	.02
□ 542T Howard Johnson TRADE DP	.05	.02	.01
□ 543T Brian McRae TRADE DP	.10	.05	.01
□ 544T Jaime Navarro TRADE DP	.05	.02	.01
□ 545T Ozzie Timmons TRADE DP	.05	.02	.01
□ 546T Roberto Kelly TRADE DP	.05	.02	.01
□ 547T Hideo Nomo TRADE DP	4.00	1.80	.50
□ 548T Shane Andrews TRADE DP	.10	.05	.01
□ 549T M.Grudzielanek TRADE DP	1.00	.45	.12
□ 550T Carlos Perez TRADE DP	.10	.05	.01
□ 551T Henry Rodriguez TRADE DP	.30	.14	.04
□ 552T Tony Tarasco TRADE DP	.05	.02	.01
□ 553T Glenallen Hill TRADE	.10	.05	.01

□	554T Terry Mulholland TRADE	.10	.05	.01
□	555T Orel Hershiser TRADE	.15	.07	.02
□	556T Darren Bragg TRADE	.10	.05	.01
□	557T John Burkett TRADE	.15	.07	.02
□	558T Bobby Witt TRADE	.10	.05	.01
□	559T Terry Pendleton TRADE	.10	.05	.01
□	560T Andre Dawson TRADE	.30	.14	.04
□	561T Brett Butler TRADE	.15	.07	.02
□	562T Kevin Brown TRADE	.10	.05	.01
□	563T Doug Jones TRADE	.10	.05	.01
□	564T Andy Van Slyke TRADE	.15	.07	.02
□	565T Jody Reed TRADE	.10	.05	.01
□	566T Fernando Valenzuela TRADE	.15	.07	.02
□	567T Charlie Hayes TRADE	.10	.05	.01
□	568T Benji Gil TRADE	.10	.05	.01
□	569T Mark McLemore TRADE	.10	.05	.01
□	570T Mickey Tettleton TRADE	.15	.07	.02
□	571T Bob Tewksbury TRADE	.10	.05	.01
□	572T Rheal Cormier TRADE	.10	.05	.01
□	573T Vaughn Eshelman TRADE	.10	.05	.01
□	574T Mike Macfarlane TRADE	.10	.05	.01
□	575T Bill Swift TRADE	.10	.05	.01
□	576T Mark Whiten TRADE	.10	.05	.01
□	577T Benito Santiago TRADE	.10	.05	.01
□	578T Jason Bates TRADE	.10	.05	.01
□	579T Larry Walker TRADE	.30	.14	.04
□	580T Chad Curtis TRADE	.10	.05	.01
□	581T Bobby Higginson	.75	.35	.09
□	582T Marty Cordova TRADE	.50	.23	.06
□	583T Mike Devereaux TRADE	.10	.05	.01
□	584T John Kruk TRADE	.15	.07	.02
□	585T John Wetteland TRADE	.15	.07	.02
□	TC1 Larry Walker	1.00	.45	.12
□	TC2 David Cone	1.00	.45	.12
□	TC3 Marquis Grissom	1.00	.45	.12
□	TC4 Terry Pendleton	1.00	.45	.12
□	TC5 Fernando Valenzuela	1.00	.45	.12

1995 Collector's Choice Crash the Game

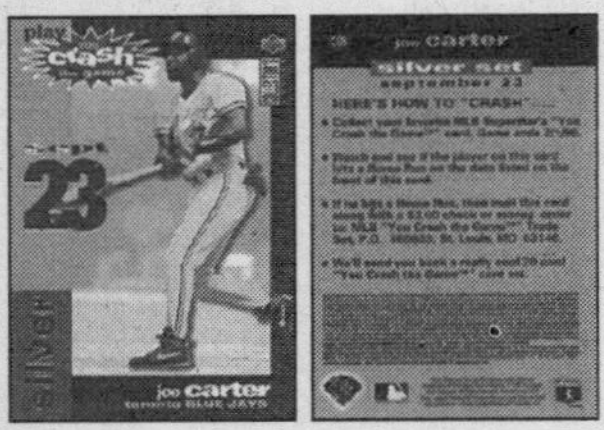

This 60-card standard-size set was randomly inserted in packs at a rate of one in five. The set is an interactive set in which all 20 players have three cards with a date on it. If the player hit a home run on that date, the collector could redeem the card for a complete enhanced set of all 20 players. The fronts have a color-action photo with the game background in yellow. The date the home run needs to be hit is on the left side in silver-foil and the word "silver" (also in silver foil) is at the bottom. The back has information on the game and has the player's name at the bottom with "silver set" below it and the date below that. Prices below are for any of the three dates of said player. However, the complete set price includes all 60 cards. The expiration date for redeeming these cards was February 1, 1996.

	MINT	NRMT	EXC
COMPLETE SET (60)	50.00	22.00	6.25
COMMON CARD (CG1-CG20)	.25	.11	.03
COMPLETE GOLD SET (60)	250.00	110.00	31.00
*GOLD CARDS: 5X VALUE			
GOLD/SILVER: 3 DATES PER PLAYER			
RANDOM INSERTS IN SER.1 PACKS			
COMP.SILVER EXCH.SET (20)	10.00	4.50	1.25
*SILVER EXCH.CARDS: HALF VALUE			
COMP.GOLD EXCH.SET (20)	50.00	22.00	6.25
*GOLD EXCH.CARDS: 4X VALUE			

□	CG1 Jeff Bagwell	.75	.35	.09
□	CG2 Albert Belle	1.00	.45	.12
□	CG3 Barry Bonds	.50	.23	.06
□	CG4 Jose Canseco	.25	.11	.03
□	CG5 Joe Carter	.25	.11	.03
□	CG6 Cecil Fielder	.25	.11	.03
□	CG7 Juan Gonzalez	1.00	.45	.12
□	CG8 Ken Griffey Jr.	2.00	.90	.25
□	CG9 Bob Hamelin	.25	.11	.03
□	CG10 David Justice	.25	.11	.03
□	CG11 Ryan Klesko	.40	.18	.05
□	CG12 Fred McGriff	.25	.11	.03
□	CG13 Mark McGwire	.60	.25	.07
□	CG14 Raul Mondesi	.25	.11	.03
□	CG15 Mike Piazza	1.25	.55	.16
□	CG16 Manny Ramirez	.50	.23	.06
□	CG17 Alex Rodriguez	2.00	.90	.25
□	CG18 Gary Sheffield	.25	.11	.03
□	CG19 Frank Thomas	2.00	.90	.25
□	CG20 Matt Williams	.25	.11	.03

1996 Collector's Choice

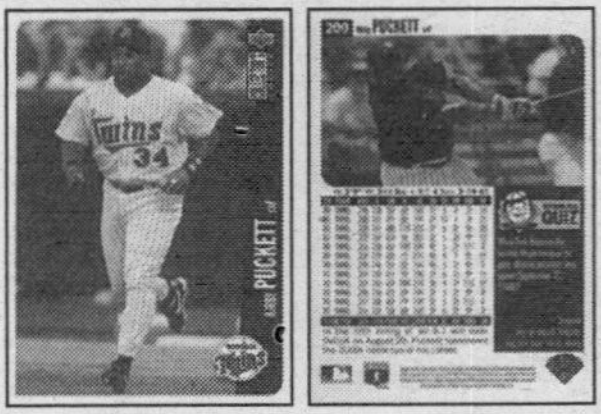

This 365-card standard-size set was issued in 12-card packs with 36 packs per box and 20 boxes per case. Suggested retail price on these packs was 99 cents. Postseason Trade cards were inserted one every 11 packs. These cards had an ordering deadline of May 13 and were each redeemable for 10 cards depicting highlights from the playoffs and World Series, resulting in a 30-card redemption set. The fronts of the regular set feature a player photo, his name and team logo. Super packs were made again in 1996. The backs feature another photo, vital stats and a baseball quiz. The set is broken down thusly: 1995 Stat Leaders (2-9), Rookie Class (10-39), Atlanta Braves (40-49), Baltimore Orioles (50-58), Boston Red Sox (59-68), California Angels (69-78), Chicago Cubs (79-88), Chicago White Sox (89-98), Cincinnati Reds (99, 109-117), Traditional Threads (100-108), Cleveland Indians (118-127), Colorado Rockies (128-137), Detroit Tigers (138-147), Florida Marlins (148-157), Houston Astros (158-167), Kansas City Royals (168-177), Los Angeles Dodgers (178-187), Milwaukee Brewers (188-197), Minnesota Twins (198-207), Montreal Expos (208-217), New York Mets (218-227), New York Yankees (228-237), Oakland A's (238-247), Philadelphia Phillies (248-257), Pittsburgh Pirates (258-267), Fantasy Team (268-279), St. Louis Cardinals (280-289), San Diego Padres (290-299), San Francisco Giants (300-309), Seattle Mariners (310-319), Texas Rangers (320-324, 343-347), International Flavor (325-342), Toronto Blue Jays (348-357), and Checklists (358-365).

	MINT	NRMT	EXC
COMP.FACT.SET (790)	40.00	18.00	5.00
COMPLETE SET (730)	30.00	13.50	3.70
COMPLETE SERIES 1 (365)	16.00	7.25	2.00
COMPLETE SERIES 2 (365)	14.00	6.25	1.75
COMMON CARD (1-360/396-760)	.05	.02	.01

SEMISTARS	.15	.07	.02
STARS	.30	.14	.04
COMP.UPDATE SET (30)	8.00	3.60	1.00
COMMON UPDATE (761-790)	.25	.11	.03
UPDATE SEMISTARS	.50	.23	.06
ONE UPDATE SET PER FACTORY SET			
OR VIA SER.2 WRAPPER OFFER			
COMPLETE TRADE SET (30)	15.00	6.75	1.85
COMMON TRADE (366T-395T)	.15	.07	.02
TRADE SEMISTARS	.50	.23	.06
TEN TRADE CARDS PER TRADE EXCH.CARD			
TRADE EXCH: RANDOM INS.IN SER.1 PACKS			
COMP.SILVER SIG.SET (730)	110.00	50.00	14.00
COMP.SILV.SIG.SER.1 (365)	60.00	27.00	7.50
COMP.SILV.SIG.SER.2 (365)	50.00	22.00	6.25
COMMON SILV. (1-365/396-760)	.10	.05	.01
SILVER SIG.SEMISTARS	.20	.09	.03
*SILVER STARS: 2X to 4X BASIC CARDS			
*SILVER SIG.YOUNG STARS: 1.5X to 3X BASIC CARDS			
ONE SILVER SIGNATURE PER PACK			
COMP.GRIFFEY ACA SET (10)	8.00	3.60	1.00
COMMON GRIFF.(CA1-CA10)	1.00	.45	.12
GRIFFEY ACA: ONE PER SPEC.RETAIL PACK			
COMPLETE NOMO SET (5)	6.00	2.70	.75
COMMON NOMO (1-5)	1.50	.70	.19
NOMO: RANDOM INSERTS IN SER.2 PACKS			

□ 1 Cal Ripken	1.50	.70	.19
□ 2 Edgar Martinez SL Tony Gwynn	.30	.14	.04
□ 3 Albert Belle SL Dante Bichette	.30	.14	.04
□ 4 Albert Belle SL Mo Vaughn Dante Bichette	.30	.14	.04
□ 5 Kenny Lofton SL Quilvio Veras	.15	.07	.02
□ 6 Mike Mussina SL Greg Maddux	.50	.23	.06
□ 7 Randy Johnson SL Hideo Nomo	.30	.14	.04
□ 8 Randy Johnson SL Greg Maddux	.50	.23	.06
□ 9 Jose Mesa SL Randy Myers	.05	.02	.01
□ 10 Johnny Damon	.30	.14	.04
□ 11 Rick Krivda	.05	.02	.01
□ 12 Roger Cedeno	.30	.14	.04
□ 13 Angel Martinez	.05	.02	.01
□ 14 Ariel Prieto	.05	.02	.01
□ 15 John Wasdin	.15	.07	.02
□ 16 Edwin Hurtado	.05	.02	.01
□ 17 Lyle Mouton	.05	.02	.01
□ 18 Chris Snopek	.05	.02	.01
□ 19 Mariano Rivera	.30	.14	.04
□ 20 Ruben Rivera	.40	.18	.05
□ 21 Juan Castro	.30	.14	.04
□ 22 Jimmy Haynes	.30	.14	.04
□ 23 Bob Wolcott	.05	.02	.01
□ 24 Brian Barber	.05	.02	.01
□ 25 Frank Rodriguez	.30	.14	.04
□ 26 Jesus Tavarez	.15	.07	.02
□ 27 Glenn Dishman	.15	.07	.02
□ 28 Jose Herrera	.15	.07	.02
□ 29 Chan Ho Park	.30	.14	.04
□ 30 Jason Isringhausen	.15	.07	.02
□ 31 Doug Johns	.05	.02	.01
□ 32 Gene Schall	.05	.02	.01
□ 33 Kevin Jordan	.05	.02	.01
□ 34 Matt Lawton	.05	.02	.01
□ 35 Karim Garcia	.40	.18	.05
□ 36 George Williams	.05	.02	.01
□ 37 Orlando Palmeiro	.05	.02	.01
□ 38 Jamie Brewington	.05	.02	.01
□ 39 Robert Person	.05	.02	.01
□ 40 Greg Maddux	1.25	.55	.16
□ 41 Marquis Grissom	.30	.14	.04
□ 42 Chipper Jones	1.25	.55	.16
□ 43 David Justice	.15	.07	.02
□ 44 Mark Lemke	.05	.02	.01
□ 45 Fred McGriff	.30	.14	.04
□ 46 Javier Lopez	.30	.14	.04
□ 47 Mark Wohlers	.15	.07	.02
□ 48 Jason Schmidt	.15	.07	.02
□ 49 John Smoltz	.30	.14	.04
□ 50 Curtis Goodwin	.05	.02	.01
□ 51 Greg Zaun	.05	.02	.01
□ 52 Armando Benitez	.05	.02	.01
□ 53 Manny Alexander	.05	.02	.01
□ 54 Chris Hoiles	.05	.02	.01
□ 55 Harold Baines	.15	.07	.02
□ 56 Ben McDonald	.05	.02	.01
□ 57 Scott Erickson	.05	.02	.01
□ 58 Jeff Manto	.05	.02	.01
□ 59 Luis Alicea	.05	.02	.01
□ 60 Roger Clemens	.30	.14	.04
□ 61 Rheal Cormier	.05	.02	.01
□ 62 Vaughn Eshelman	.05	.02	.01
□ 63 Zane Smith	.05	.02	.01
□ 64 Mike Macfarlane	.05	.02	.01
□ 65 Erik Hanson	.05	.02	.01
□ 66 Tim Naehring	.15	.07	.02
□ 67 Lee Tinsley	.05	.02	.01
□ 68 Troy O'Leary	.15	.07	.02
□ 69 Garret Anderson	.30	.14	.04
□ 70 Chili Davis	.05	.02	.01
□ 71 Jim Edmonds	.30	.14	.04
□ 72 Troy Percival	.15	.07	.02
□ 73 Mark Langston	.05	.02	.01
□ 74 Spike Owen	.05	.02	.01
□ 75 Tim Salmon	.30	.14	.04
□ 76 Brian Anderson	.05	.02	.01
□ 77 Lee Smith	.30	.14	.04
□ 78 Jim Abbott	.30	.14	.04
□ 79 Jim Bullinger	.05	.02	.01
□ 80 Mark Grace	.30	.14	.04
□ 81 Todd Zeile	.15	.07	.02
□ 82 Kevin Foster	.05	.02	.01
□ 83 Howard Johnson	.05	.02	.01
□ 84 Brian McRae	.05	.02	.01
□ 85 Randy Myers	.05	.02	.01
□ 86 Jaime Navarro	.05	.02	.01
□ 87 Luis Gonzalez	.05	.02	.01
□ 88 Ozzie Timmons	.05	.02	.01
□ 89 Wilson Alvarez	.30	.14	.04
□ 90 Frank Thomas	2.00	.90	.25
□ 91 James Baldwin	.30	.14	.04
□ 92 Ray Durham	.30	.14	.04
□ 93 Alex Fernandez	.30	.14	.04
□ 94 Ozzie Guillen	.05	.02	.01
□ 95 Tim Raines	.30	.14	.04
□ 96 Roberto Hernandez	.15	.07	.02
□ 97 Lance Johnson	.15	.07	.02
□ 98 John Kruk	.15	.07	.02
□ 99 Mark Portugal	.05	.02	.01
□ 100 Don Mattingly TT	.50	.23	.06
□ 101 Roger Clemens TT	.30	.14	.04
□ 102 Raul Mondesi TT	.15	.07	.02
□ 103 Cecil Fielder TT	.30	.14	.04
□ 104 Ozzie Smith TT	.30	.14	.04
□ 105 Frank Thomas TT	1.00	.45	.12
□ 106 Sammy Sosa TT	.30	.14	.04
□ 107 Fred McGriff TT	.30	.14	.04
□ 108 Barry Bonds TT	.30	.14	.04
□ 109 Thomas Howard	.05	.02	.01
□ 110 Ron Gant	.30	.14	.04
□ 111 Eddie Taubensee	.05	.02	.01
□ 112 Hal Morris	.05	.02	.01
□ 113 Jose Rijo	.05	.02	.01
□ 114 Pete Schourek	.15	.07	.02
□ 115 Reggie Sanders	.30	.14	.04
□ 116 Benito Santiago	.05	.02	.01
□ 117 Jeff Brantley	.05	.02	.01
□ 118 Julian Tavarez	.05	.02	.01
□ 119 Carlos Baerga	.30	.14	.04
□ 120 Jim Thome	.40	.18	.05
□ 121 Jose Mesa	.15	.07	.02
□ 122 Dennis Martinez	.15	.07	.02
□ 123 Dave Winfield	.30	.14	.04
□ 124 Eddie Murray	.50	.23	.06
□ 125 Manny Ramirez	.50	.23	.06
□ 126 Paul Sorrento	.05	.02	.01
□ 127 Kenny Lofton	.50	.23	.06
□ 128 Eric Young	.05	.02	.01
□ 129 Jason Bates	.05	.02	.01
□ 130 Bret Saberhagen	.05	.02	.01
□ 131 Andres Galarraga	.30	.14	.04
□ 132 Joe Girardi	.05	.02	.01
□ 133 John VanderWal	.05	.02	.01
□ 134 David Nied	.05	.02	.01
□ 135 Dante Bichette	.30	.14	.04
□ 136 Vinny Castilla	.30	.14	.04

☐ 137	Kevin Ritz	.05	.02	.01
☐ 138	Felipe Lira	.05	.02	.01
☐ 139	Joe Boever	.05	.02	.01
☐ 140	Cecil Fielder	.30	.14	.04
☐ 141	John Flaherty	.05	.02	.01
☐ 142	Kirk Gibson	.30	.14	.04
☐ 143	Brian Maxcy	.05	.02	.01
☐ 144	Lou Whitaker	.30	.14	.04
☐ 145	Alan Trammell	.30	.14	.04
☐ 146	Bobby Higginson	.30	.14	.04
☐ 147	Chad Curtis	.05	.02	.01
☐ 148	Quilvio Veras	.05	.02	.01
☐ 149	Jerry Browne	.05	.02	.01
☐ 150	Andre Dawson	.30	.14	.04
☐ 151	Robb Nen	.05	.02	.01
☐ 152	Greg Colbrunn	.05	.02	.01
☐ 153	Chris Hammond	.05	.02	.01
☐ 154	Kurt Abbott	.05	.02	.01
☐ 155	Charles Johnson	.15	.07	.02
☐ 156	Terry Pendleton	.15	.07	.02
☐ 157	Dave Weathers	.05	.02	.01
☐ 158	Mike Hampton	.05	.02	.01
☐ 159	Craig Biggio	.30	.14	.04
☐ 160	Jeff Bagwell	.75	.35	.09
☐ 161	Brian L.Hunter	.05	.02	.01
☐ 162	Mike Henneman	.05	.02	.01
☐ 163	Dave Magadan	.05	.02	.01
☐ 164	Shane Reynolds	.15	.07	.02
☐ 165	Derek Bell	.30	.14	.04
☐ 166	Orlando Miller	.05	.02	.01
☐ 167	James Mouton	.05	.02	.01
☐ 168	Melvin Bunch	.05	.02	.01
☐ 169	Tom Gordon	.05	.02	.01
☐ 170	Kevin Appier	.15	.07	.02
☐ 171	Tom Goodwin	.15	.07	.02
☐ 172	Greg Gagne	.05	.02	.01
☐ 173	Gary Gaetti	.15	.07	.02
☐ 174	Jeff Montgomery	.05	.02	.01
☐ 175	Jon Nunnally	.05	.02	.01
☐ 176	Michael Tucker	.15	.07	.02
☐ 177	Joe Vitiello	.05	.02	.01
☐ 178	Billy Ashley	.05	.02	.01
☐ 179	Tom Candiotti	.05	.02	.01
☐ 180	Hideo Nomo	.50	.23	.06
☐ 181	Chad Fonville	.05	.02	.01
☐ 182	Todd Hollandsworth	.30	.14	.04
☐ 183	Eric Karros	.30	.14	.04
☐ 184	Roberto Kelly	.05	.02	.01
☐ 185	Mike Piazza	1.25	.55	.16
☐ 186	Ramon Martinez	.15	.07	.02
☐ 187	Tim Wallach	.05	.02	.01
☐ 188	Jeff Cirillo	.05	.02	.01
☐ 189	Sid Roberson	.05	.02	.01
☐ 190	Kevin Seitzer	.05	.02	.01
☐ 191	Mike Fetters	.05	.02	.01
☐ 192	Steve Sparks	.05	.02	.01
☐ 193	Matt Mieske	.05	.02	.01
☐ 194	Joe Oliver	.05	.02	.01
☐ 195	B.J. Surhoff	.05	.02	.01
☐ 196	Alberto Reyes	.05	.02	.01
☐ 197	Fernando Vina	.05	.02	.01
☐ 198	LaTroy Hawkins	.05	.02	.01
☐ 199	Marty Cordova	.30	.14	.04
☐ 200	Kirby Puckett	.60	.25	.07
☐ 201	Brad Radke	.05	.02	.01
☐ 202	Pedro Munoz	.05	.02	.01
☐ 203	Scott Klingenbeck	.05	.02	.01
☐ 204	Pat Meares	.05	.02	.01
☐ 205	Chuck Knoblauch	.30	.14	.04
☐ 206	Scott Stahoviak	.05	.02	.01
☐ 207	Dave Stevens	.05	.02	.01
☐ 208	Shane Andrews	.05	.02	.01
☐ 209	Moises Alou	.15	.07	.02
☐ 210	David Segui	.05	.02	.01
☐ 211	Cliff Floyd	.05	.02	.01
☐ 212	Carlos Perez	.05	.02	.01
☐ 213	Mark Grudzielanek	.05	.02	.01
☐ 214	Butch Henry	.05	.02	.01
☐ 215	Rondell White	.30	.14	.04
☐ 216	Mel Rojas	.15	.07	.02
☐ 217	Ugueth Urbina	.05	.02	.01
☐ 218	Edgardo Alfonzo	.15	.07	.02
☐ 219	Carl Everett	.05	.02	.01
☐ 220	John Franco	.05	.02	.01
☐ 221	Todd Hundley	.30	.14	.04
☐ 222	Bobby Jones	.05	.02	.01
☐ 223	Bill Pulsipher	.15	.07	.02
☐ 224	Rico Brogna	.05	.02	.01
☐ 225	Jeff Kent	.05	.02	.01
☐ 226	Chris Jones	.05	.02	.01
☐ 227	Butch Huskey	.15	.07	.02
☐ 228	Robert Eenhoorn	.05	.02	.01
☐ 229	Sterling Hitchcock	.05	.02	.01
☐ 230	Wade Boggs	.30	.14	.04
☐ 231	Derek Jeter	1.25	.55	.16
☐ 232	Tony Fernandez	.05	.02	.01
☐ 233	Jack McDowell	.30	.14	.04
☐ 234	Andy Pettitte	.60	.25	.07
☐ 235	David Cone	.30	.14	.04
☐ 236	Mike Stanley	.05	.02	.01
☐ 237	Don Mattingly	1.00	.45	.12
☐ 238	Geronimo Berroa	.15	.07	.02
☐ 239	Scott Brosius	.15	.07	.02
☐ 240	Rickey Henderson	.30	.14	.04
☐ 241	Terry Steinbach	.15	.07	.02
☐ 242	Mike Gallego	.05	.02	.01
☐ 243	Jason Giambi	.15	.07	.02
☐ 244	Steve Ontiveros	.05	.02	.01
☐ 245	Dennis Eckersley	.30	.14	.04
☐ 246	Dave Stewart	.15	.07	.02
☐ 247	Don Wengert	.05	.02	.01
☐ 248	Paul Quantrill	.05	.02	.01
☐ 249	Ricky Bottalico	.05	.02	.01
☐ 250	Kevin Stocker	.05	.02	.01
☐ 251	Lenny Dykstra	.15	.07	.02
☐ 252	Tony Longmire	.05	.02	.01
☐ 253	Tyler Green	.05	.02	.01
☐ 254	Mike Mimbs	.05	.02	.01
☐ 255	Charlie Hayes	.05	.02	.01
☐ 256	Mickey Morandini	.05	.02	.01
☐ 257	Heathcliff Slocumb	.05	.02	.01
☐ 258	Jeff King	.05	.02	.01
☐ 259	Midre Cummings	.05	.02	.01
☐ 260	Mark Johnson	.05	.02	.01
☐ 261	Freddy Garcia	.05	.02	.01
☐ 262	Jon Lieber	.05	.02	.01
☐ 263	Esteban Loaiza	.05	.02	.01
☐ 264	Dan Miceli	.05	.02	.01
☐ 265	Orlando Merced	.15	.07	.02
☐ 266	Denny Neagle	.15	.07	.02
☐ 267	Steve Parris	.05	.02	.01
☐ 268	Greg Maddux FT	.60	.25	.07
☐ 269	Randy Johnson FT	.30	.14	.04
☐ 270	Hideo Nomo FT	.30	.14	.04
☐ 271	Jose Mesa FT	.05	.02	.01
☐ 272	Mike Piazza FT	.60	.25	.07
☐ 273	Mo Vaughn FT	.30	.14	.04
☐ 274	Craig Biggio FT	.30	.14	.04
☐ 275	Edgar Martinez FT	.15	.07	.02
☐ 276	Barry Larkin FT	.30	.14	.04
☐ 277	Sammy Sosa FT	.30	.14	.04
☐ 278	Dante Bichette FT	.30	.14	.04
☐ 279	Albert Belle FT	.50	.23	.06
☐ 280	Ozzie Smith	.40	.18	.05
☐ 281	Mark Sweeney	.05	.02	.01
☐ 282	Terry Bradshaw	.05	.02	.01
☐ 283	Allen Battle	.05	.02	.01
☐ 284	Danny Jackson	.05	.02	.01
☐ 285	Tom Henke	.15	.07	.02
☐ 286	Scott Cooper	.05	.02	.01
☐ 287	Tripp Cromer	.05	.02	.01
☐ 288	Bernard Gilkey	.15	.07	.02
☐ 289	Brian Jordan	.30	.14	.04
☐ 290	Tony Gwynn	.75	.35	.09
☐ 291	Brad Ausmus	.05	.02	.01
☐ 292	Bryce Florie	.05	.02	.01
☐ 293	Andres Berumen	.05	.02	.01
☐ 294	Ken Caminiti	.30	.14	.04
☐ 295	Bip Roberts	.05	.02	.01
☐ 296	Trevor Hoffman	.15	.07	.02
☐ 297	Roberto Petagine	.05	.02	.01
☐ 298	Jody Reed	.05	.02	.01
☐ 299	Fernando Valenzuela	.15	.07	.02
☐ 300	Barry Bonds	.50	.23	.06
☐ 301	Mark Leiter	.05	.02	.01
☐ 302	Mark Carreon	.05	.02	.01
☐ 303	Royce Clayton	.05	.02	.01
☐ 304	Kirt Manwaring	.05	.02	.01
☐ 305	Glenallen Hill	.15	.07	.02
☐ 306	Deion Sanders	.30	.14	.04
☐ 307	Joe Rosselli	.05	.02	.01
☐ 308	Robby Thompson	.05	.02	.01

☐	309	W. VanLandingham	.05	.02	.01
☐	310	Ken Griffey Jr.	2.00	.90	.25
☐	311	Bobby Ayala	.05	.02	.01
☐	312	Joey Cora	.05	.02	.01
☐	313	Mike Blowers	.05	.02	.01
☐	314	Darren Bragg	.05	.02	.01
☐	315	Randy Johnson	.50	.23	.06
☐	316	Alex Rodriguez	2.00	.90	.25
☐	317	Andy Benes	.05	.02	.01
☐	318	Tino Martinez	.30	.14	.04
☐	319	Dan Wilson	.05	.02	.01
☐	320	Will Clark	.30	.14	.04
☐	321	Jeff Frye	.05	.02	.01
☐	322	Benji Gil	.05	.02	.01
☐	323	Rick Helling	.05	.02	.01
☐	324	Mark McLemore	.05	.02	.01
☐	325	Dave Nilsson IF	.05	.02	.01
☐	326	Larry Walker IF	.15	.07	.02
☐	327	Jose Canseco IF	.30	.14	.04
☐	328	Raul Mondesi IF	.15	.07	.02
☐	329	Manny Ramirez IF	.15	.07	.02
☐	330	Robert Eenhoorn IF	.05	.02	.01
☐	331	Chili Davis IF	.05	.02	.01
☐	332	Hideo Nomo IF	.30	.14	.04
☐	333	Benji Gil IF	.05	.02	.01
☐	334	Fernando Valenzuela IF	.15	.07	.02
☐	335	Dennis Martinez IF	.05	.02	.01
☐	336	Roberto Kelly IF	.05	.02	.01
☐	337	Carlos Baerga IF	.30	.14	.04
☐	338	Juan Gonzalez IF	.50	.23	.06
☐	339	Roberto Alomar IF	.30	.14	.04
☐	340	Chan Ho Park IF	.30	.14	.04
☐	341	Andres Galarraga IF	.15	.07	.02
☐	342	Midre Cummings IF	.05	.02	.01
☐	343	Otis Nixon	.05	.02	.01
☐	344	Jeff Russell	.05	.02	.01
☐	345	Ivan Rodriguez	.40	.18	.05
☐	346	Mickey Tettleton	.15	.07	.02
☐	347	Bob Tewksbury	.05	.02	.01
☐	348	Domingo Cedeno	.05	.02	.01
☐	349	Lance Parrish	.15	.07	.02
☐	350	Joe Carter	.30	.14	.04
☐	351	Devon White	.05	.02	.01
☐	352	Carlos Delgado	.30	.14	.04
☐	353	Alex Gonzalez	.05	.02	.01
☐	354	Darren Hall	.05	.02	.01
☐	355	Paul Molitor	.40	.18	.05
☐	356	Al Leiter	.05	.02	.01
☐	357	Randy Knorr	.05	.02	.01
☐	358	Ken Caminiti CL	.05	.02	.01
		Steve Finley			
		Brian Williams			
		Roberto Petagine			
		Andujar Cedeno			
		Phil Plantier			
		Derek Bell			
		Pedro A. Martinez			
		Doug Brocail			
		Craig Shipley			
		Ricky Gutierrez			
☐	359	Hideo Nomo CL	.30	.14	.04
☐	360	Ramon A.Martinez CL	.05	.02	.01
		Ramon J.Martinez			
☐	361	Robin Ventura CL	.15	.07	.02
☐	362	Cal Ripken CL	.75	.35	.09
☐	363	Ken Caminiti CL	.15	.07	.02
☐	364	Albert Belle CL	.50	.23	.06
		Eddie Murray			
☐	365	Randy Johnson CL	.30	.14	.04
☐	366T	Tony Pena TRADE	.15	.07	.02
☐	367T	Jim Thome TRADE	.75	.35	.09
☐	368T	Don Mattingly TRADE	2.00	.90	.25
☐	369T	Jim Leyritz TRADE	.15	.07	.02
☐	370T	Ken Griffey Jr. TRADE	4.00	1.80	.50
☐	371T	Edgar Martinez TRADE	.30	.14	.04
☐	372T	Pete Schourek TRADE	.15	.07	.02
☐	373T	Mark Lewis TRADE	.15	.07	.02
☐	374T	Chipper Jones TRADE	2.50	1.10	.30
☐	375T	Fred McGriff TRADE	.30	.14	.04
☐	376T	Javy Lopez TRADE	.30	.14	.04
☐	377T	Fred McGriff TRADE	.30	.14	.04
☐	378T	Charlie O'Brien TRADE	.15	.07	.02
☐	379T	Mike Devereaux TRADE	.15	.07	.02
☐	380T	Mark Wohlers TRADE	.30	.14	.04
☐	381T	Bob Wolcott TRADE	.15	.07	.02
☐	382T	Manny Ramirez TRADE	1.00	.45	.12

☐	383T	Jay Buhner TRADE	.30	.14	.04
☐	384T	Orel Hershiser TRADE	.30	.14	.04
☐	385T	Kenny Lofton TRADE	1.00	.45	.12
☐	386T	Greg Maddux TRADE	2.50	1.10	.30
☐	387T	Javier Lopez TRADE	.30	.14	.04
☐	388T	Kenny Lofton TRADE	1.00	.45	.12
☐	389T	Eddie Murray TRADE	1.00	.45	.12
☐	390T	Luis Polonia TRADE	.15	.07	.02
☐	391T	Pedro Borbon TRADE	.15	.07	.02
☐	392T	Jim Thome TRADE	.75	.35	.09
☐	393T	Orel Hershiser TRADE	.15	.07	.02
☐	394T	David Justice TRADE	.30	.14	.04
☐	395T	Tom Glavine TRADE	.30	.14	.04
☐	396	Greg Maddux TC	.60	.25	.07
☐	397	Darren Daulton TC	.15	.07	.02
☐	398	Rico Brogna TC	.05	.02	.01
☐	399	Gary Sheffield TC	.30	.14	.04
☐	400	Moises Alou TC	.05	.02	.01
☐	401	Barry Larkin TC	.30	.14	.04
☐	402	Jeff Bagwell TC	.40	.18	.05
☐	403	Sammy Sosa TC	.30	.14	.04
☐	404	Ozzie Smith TC	.30	.14	.04
☐	405	Jay Bell TC	.05	.02	.01
☐	406	Mike Piazza TC	.60	.25	.07
☐	407	Dante Bichette TC	.30	.14	.04
☐	408	Tony Gwynn TC	.40	.18	.05
☐	409	Barry Bonds TC	.30	.14	.04
☐	410	Kenny Lofton TC	.30	.14	.04
☐	411	Johnny Damon TC	.05	.02	.01
☐	412	Frank Thomas TC	1.00	.45	.12
☐	413	Greg Vaughn TC	.15	.07	.02
☐	414	Paul Molitor TC	.30	.14	.04
☐	415	Ken Griffey Jr. TC	1.00	.45	.12
☐	416	Tim Salmon TC	.15	.07	.02
☐	417	Juan Gonzalez TC	.50	.23	.06
☐	418	Mark McGwire TC	.30	.14	.04
☐	419	Roger Clemens TC	.30	.14	.04
☐	420	Wade Boggs TC	.30	.14	.04
☐	421	Cal Ripken TC	.75	.35	.09
☐	422	Cecil Fielder TC	.30	.14	.04
☐	423	Joe Carter TC	.30	.14	.04
☐	424	Osvaldo Fernandez	.30	.14	.04
☐	425	Billy Wagner	.05	.02	.01
☐	426	George Arias	.05	.02	.01
☐	427	Mendy Lopez	.05	.02	.01
☐	428	Jeff Suppan	.15	.07	.02
☐	429	Rey Ordonez	.40	.18	.05
☐	430	Brooks Kieschnick	.05	.02	.01
☐	431	Raul Ibanez	.15	.07	.02
☐	432	Livan Hernandez	.30	.14	.04
☐	433	Shannon Stewart	.05	.02	.01
☐	434	Steve Cox	.05	.02	.01
☐	435	Trey Beamon	.15	.07	.02
☐	436	Sergio Nunez	.05	.02	.01
☐	437	Jermaine Dye	.30	.14	.04
☐	438	Mike Sweeney	.40	.18	.05
☐	439	Richard Hidalgo	.15	.07	.02
☐	440	Todd Greene	.15	.07	.02
☐	441	Robert Smith	.40	.18	.05
☐	442	Rafael Orellano	.05	.02	.01
☐	443	Wilton Guerrero	.40	.18	.05
☐	444	David Doster	.05	.02	.01
☐	445	Jason Kendall	.30	.14	.04
☐	446	Edgar Renteria	.30	.14	.04
☐	447	Scott Spiezio	.05	.02	.01
☐	448	Jay Canizaro	.05	.02	.01
☐	449	Enrique Wilson	.05	.02	.01
☐	450	Bob Abreu	.30	.14	.04
☐	451	Dwight Smith	.05	.02	.01
☐	452	Jeff Blauser	.05	.02	.01
☐	453	Steve Avery	.05	.02	.01
☐	454	Brad Clontz	.05	.02	.01
☐	455	Tom Glavine	.30	.14	.04
☐	456	Mike Mordecai	.05	.02	.01
☐	457	Rafael Belliard	.05	.02	.01
☐	458	Greg McMichael	.05	.02	.01
☐	459	Pedro Borbon	.05	.02	.01
☐	460	Ryan Klesko	.40	.18	.05
☐	461	Terrell Wade	.30	.14	.04
☐	462	Brady Anderson	.30	.14	.04
☐	463	Roberto Alomar	.60	.25	.07
☐	464	Bobby Bonilla	.30	.14	.04
☐	465	Mike Mussina	.40	.18	.05
☐	466	Cesar Devarez	.05	.02	.01
☐	467	Jeffrey Hammonds	.05	.02	.01
☐	468	Mike Devereaux	.05	.02	.01

□ 469 B.J. Surhoff	.05	.02	.01
□ 470 Rafael Palmeiro	.30	.14	.04
□ 471 John Valentin	.15	.07	.02
□ 472 Mike Greenwell	.05	.02	.01
□ 473 Dwayne Hosey	.05	.02	.01
□ 474 Tim Wakefield	.05	.02	.01
□ 475 Jose Canseco	.30	.14	.04
□ 476 Aaron Sele	.05	.02	.01
□ 477 Stan Belinda	.05	.02	.01
□ 478 Mike Stanley	.05	.02	.01
□ 479 Jamie Moyer	.05	.02	.01
□ 480 Mo Vaughn	.50	.23	.06
□ 481 Randy Velarde	.05	.02	.01
□ 482 Gary DiSarcina	.05	.02	.01
□ 483 Jorge Fabregas	.05	.02	.01
□ 484 Rex Hudler	.05	.02	.01
□ 485 Chuck Finley	.05	.02	.01
□ 486 Tim Wallach	.05	.02	.01
□ 487 Eduardo Perez	.05	.02	.01
□ 488 Scott Sanderson	.05	.02	.01
□ 489 J.T. Snow	.15	.07	.02
□ 490 Sammy Sosa	.30	.14	.04
□ 491 Terry Adams	.05	.02	.01
□ 492 Matt Franco	.05	.02	.01
□ 493 Scott Servais	.05	.02	.01
□ 494 Frank Castillo	.05	.02	.01
□ 495 Ryne Sandberg	.50	.23	.06
□ 496 Rey Sanchez	.05	.02	.01
□ 497 Steve Trachsel	.05	.02	.01
□ 498 Jose Hernandez	.05	.02	.01
□ 499 Dave Martinez	.05	.02	.01
□ 500 Babe Ruth FC	.50	.23	.06
□ 501 Ty Cobb FC	.40	.18	.05
□ 502 Walter Johnson FC	.30	.14	.04
□ 503 Christy Mathewson FC	.30	.14	.04
□ 504 Honus Wagner FC	.40	.18	.05
□ 505 Robin Ventura	.30	.14	.04
□ 506 Jason Bere	.05	.02	.01
□ 507 Mike Cameron	.60	.25	.07
□ 508 Ron Karkovice	.05	.02	.01
□ 509 Matt Karchner	.05	.02	.01
□ 510 Harold Baines	.15	.07	.02
□ 511 Kirk McCaskill	.05	.02	.01
□ 512 Larry Thomas	.05	.02	.01
□ 513 Danny Tartabull	.05	.02	.01
□ 514 Steve Gilbralter	.05	.02	.01
□ 515 Bret Boone	.05	.02	.01
□ 516 Jeff Branson	.05	.02	.01
□ 517 Kevin Jarvis	.05	.02	.01
□ 518 Xavier Hernandez	.05	.02	.01
□ 519 Eric Owens	.05	.02	.01
□ 520 Barry Larkin	.30	.14	.04
□ 521 Dave Burba	.05	.02	.01
□ 522 John Smiley	.05	.02	.01
□ 523 Paul Assenmacher	.05	.02	.01
□ 524 Chad Ogea	.05	.02	.01
□ 525 Orel Hershiser	.15	.07	.02
□ 526 Alan Embree	.05	.02	.01
□ 527 Tony Pena	.05	.02	.01
□ 528 Omar Vizquel	.05	.02	.01
□ 529 Mark Clark	.05	.02	.01
□ 530 Albert Belle	1.00	.45	.12
□ 531 Charles Nagy	.05	.02	.01
□ 532 Herbert Perry	.05	.02	.01
□ 533 Darren Holmes	.05	.02	.01
□ 534 Ellis Burks	.30	.14	.04
□ 535 Billy Swift	.05	.02	.01
□ 536 Armando Reynoso	.05	.02	.01
□ 537 Curtis Leskanic	.05	.02	.01
□ 538 Quinton McCracken	.05	.02	.01
□ 539 Steve Reed	.05	.02	.01
□ 540 Larry Walker	.30	.14	.04
□ 541 Walt Weiss	.05	.02	.01
□ 542 Bryan Rekar	.05	.02	.01
□ 543 Tony Clark	.30	.14	.04
□ 544 Steve Rodriguez	.05	.02	.01
□ 545 C.J. Nitkowski	.05	.02	.01
□ 546 Todd Steverson	.05	.02	.01
□ 547 Jose Lima	.05	.02	.01
□ 548 Phil Nevin	.05	.02	.01
□ 549 Chris Gomez	.05	.02	.01
□ 550 Travis Fryman	.30	.14	.04
□ 551 Mark Lewis	.05	.02	.01
□ 552 Alex Arias	.05	.02	.01
□ 553 Marc Valdes	.05	.02	.01
□ 554 Kevin Brown	.15	.07	.02
□ 555 Jeff Conine	.30	.14	.04
□ 556 John Burkett	.05	.02	.01
□ 557 Devon White	.05	.02	.01
□ 558 Pat Rapp	.05	.02	.01
□ 559 Jay Powell	.05	.02	.01
□ 560 Gary Sheffield	.30	.14	.04
□ 561 Jim Dougherty	.05	.02	.01
□ 562 Todd Jones	.05	.02	.01
□ 563 Tony Eusebio	.05	.02	.01
□ 564 Darryl Kile	.05	.02	.01
□ 565 Doug Drabek	.05	.02	.01
□ 566 Mike Simms	.05	.02	.01
□ 567 Derrick May	.05	.02	.01
□ 568 Donne Wall	.05	.02	.01
□ 569 Greg Swindell	.05	.02	.01
□ 570 Jim Pittsley	.05	.02	.01
□ 571 Bob Hamelin	.05	.02	.01
□ 572 Mark Gubicza	.05	.02	.01
□ 573 Chris Haney	.05	.02	.01
□ 574 Keith Lockhart	.05	.02	.01
□ 575 Mike Macfarlane	.05	.02	.01
□ 576 Les Norman	.05	.02	.01
□ 577 Joe Randa	.05	.02	.01
□ 578 Chris Stynes	.05	.02	.01
□ 579 Greg Gagne	.05	.02	.01
□ 580 Raul Mondesi	.30	.14	.04
□ 581 Delino DeShields	.05	.02	.01
□ 582 Pedro Astacio	.05	.02	.01
□ 583 Antonio Osuna	.05	.02	.01
□ 584 Brett Butler	.05	.02	.01
□ 585 Todd Worrell	.15	.07	.02
□ 586 Mike Blowers	.05	.02	.01
□ 587 Felix Rodriguez	.05	.02	.01
□ 588 Ismael Valdes	.15	.07	.02
□ 589 Ricky Bones	.05	.02	.01
□ 590 Greg Vaughn	.30	.14	.04
□ 591 Mark Loretta	.05	.02	.01
□ 592 Cal Eldred	.05	.02	.01
□ 593 Chuck Carr	.05	.02	.01
□ 594 Dave Nilsson	.15	.07	.02
□ 595 John Jaha	.05	.02	.01
□ 596 Scott Karl	.05	.02	.01
□ 597 Pat Listach	.05	.02	.01
□ 598 Jose Valentin	.05	.02	.01
□ 599 Mike Trombley	.05	.02	.01
□ 600 Paul Molitor	.40	.18	.05
□ 601 Dave Hollins	.05	.02	.01
□ 602 Ron Coomer	.05	.02	.01
□ 603 Matt Walbeck	.05	.02	.01
□ 604 Roberto Kelly	.05	.02	.01
□ 605 Rick Aguilera	.05	.02	.01
□ 606 Pat Mahomes	.05	.02	.01
□ 607 Jeff Reboulet	.05	.02	.01
□ 608 Rich Becker	.15	.07	.02
□ 609 Tim Scott	.05	.02	.01
□ 610 Pedro J. Martinez	.15	.07	.02
□ 611 Kirk Rueter	.05	.02	.01
□ 612 Tavo Alvarez	.05	.02	.01
□ 613 Yamil Benitez	.05	.02	.01
□ 614 Darrin Fletcher	.05	.02	.01
□ 615 Mike Lansing	.05	.02	.01
□ 616 Henry Rodriguez	.30	.14	.04
□ 617 Tony Tarasco	.05	.02	.01
□ 618 Alex Ochoa	.15	.07	.02
□ 619 Tim Bogar	.05	.02	.01
□ 620 Bernard Gilkey	.15	.07	.02
□ 621 Dave Mlicki	.05	.02	.01
□ 622 Brent Mayne	.05	.02	.01
□ 623 Ryan Thompson	.05	.02	.01
□ 624 Pete Harnisch	.05	.02	.01
□ 625 Lance Johnson	.15	.07	.02
□ 626 Jose Vizcaino	.05	.02	.01
□ 627 Doug Henry	.05	.02	.01
□ 628 Scott Kamieniecki	.05	.02	.01
□ 629 Jim Leyritz	.05	.02	.01
□ 630 Ruben Sierra	.05	.02	.01
□ 631 Pat Kelly	.05	.02	.01
□ 632 Joe Girardi	.05	.02	.01
□ 633 John Wetteland	.15	.07	.02
□ 634 Melido Perez	.05	.02	.01
□ 635 Paul O'Neill	.05	.02	.01
□ 636 Jorge Posada	.05	.02	.01
□ 637 Bernie Williams	.30	.14	.04
□ 638 Mark Acre	.05	.02	.01
□ 639 Mike Bordick	.15	.07	.02
□ 640 Mark McGwire	.60	.25	.07

☐ 641	Fausto Cruz	.05	.02	.01
☐ 642	Ernie Young	.05	.02	.01
☐ 643	Todd Van Poppel	.05	.02	.01
☐ 644	Craig Paquette	.05	.02	.01
☐ 645	Brent Gates	.05	.02	.01
☐ 646	Pedro Munoz	.05	.02	.01
☐ 647	Andrew Lorraine	.05	.02	.01
☐ 648	Sid Fernandez	.05	.02	.01
☐ 649	Jim Eisenreich	.05	.02	.01
☐ 650	Johnny Damon	.30	.14	.04
☐ 651	Dustin Hermanson	.15	.07	.02
☐ 652	Joe Randa	.05	.02	.01
☐ 653	Michael Tucker	.30	.14	.04
☐ 654	Alan Benes	.30	.14	.04
☐ 655	Chad Fonville	.05	.02	.01
☐ 656	David Bell	.05	.02	.01
☐ 657	Jon Nunnally	.05	.02	.01
☐ 658	Chan Ho Park	.30	.14	.04
☐ 659	LaTroy Hawkins	.05	.02	.01
☐ 660	Jamie Brewington	.05	.02	.01
☐ 661	Quinton McCracken	.05	.02	.01
☐ 662	Tim Unroe	.05	.02	.01
☐ 663	Jeff Ware	.05	.02	.01
☐ 664	Todd Greene	.30	.14	.04
☐ 665	Andrew Lorraine	.05	.02	.01
☐ 666	Ernie Young	.05	.02	.01
☐ 667	Toby Borland	.05	.02	.01
☐ 668	Lenny Webster	.05	.02	.01
☐ 669	Benito Santiago	.05	.02	.01
☐ 670	Gregg Jefferies	.30	.14	.04
☐ 671	Darren Daulton	.15	.07	.02
☐ 672	Curt Schilling	.05	.02	.01
☐ 673	Mark Whiten	.05	.02	.01
☐ 674	Todd Zeile	.15	.07	.02
☐ 675	Jay Bell	.05	.02	.01
☐ 676	Paul Wagner	.05	.02	.01
☐ 677	Dave Clark	.05	.02	.01
☐ 678	Nelson Liriano	.05	.02	.01
☐ 679	Ramon Morel	.05	.02	.01
☐ 680	Charlie Hayes	.05	.02	.01
☐ 681	Angelo Encarnacion	.05	.02	.01
☐ 682	Al Martin	.05	.02	.01
☐ 683	Jacob Brumfield	.05	.02	.01
☐ 684	Mike Kingery	.05	.02	.01
☐ 685	Carlos Garcia	.05	.02	.01
☐ 686	Tom Pagnozzi	.05	.02	.01
☐ 687	David Bell	.05	.02	.01
☐ 688	Todd Stottleymyre	.05	.02	.01
☐ 689	Jose Oliva	.05	.02	.01
☐ 690	Ray Lankford	.30	.14	.04
☐ 691	Mike Morgan	.05	.02	.01
☐ 692	John Frascatore	.05	.02	.01
☐ 693	John Mabry	.30	.14	.04
☐ 694	Mark Petkovsek	.05	.02	.01
☐ 695	Alan Benes	.30	.14	.04
☐ 696	Steve Finley	.30	.14	.04
☐ 697	Marc Newfield	.15	.07	.02
☐ 698	Andy Ashby	.05	.02	.01
☐ 699	Marc Kroon	.05	.02	.01
☐ 700	Wally Joyner	.05	.02	.01
☐ 701	Joey Hamilton	.15	.07	.02
☐ 702	Dustin Hermanson	.15	.07	.02
☐ 703	Scott Sanders	.05	.02	.01
☐ 704	Marty Cordova ROY	.15	.07	.02
☐ 705	Hideo Nomo ROY	.30	.14	.04
☐ 706	Mo Vaughn MVP	.30	.14	.04
☐ 707	Barry Larkin MVP	.30	.14	.04
☐ 708	Randy Johnson CY	.30	.14	.04
☐ 709	Greg Maddux CY	.60	.25	.07
☐ 710	Mark McGwire CB	.30	.14	.04
☐ 711	Ron Gant CB	.15	.07	.02
☐ 712	Andujar Cedeno	.05	.02	.01
☐ 713	Brian Johnson	.05	.02	.01
☐ 714	J.R. Phillips	.05	.02	.01
☐ 715	Rod Beck	.05	.02	.01
☐ 716	Sergio Valdez	.05	.02	.01
☐ 717	Marvin Benard	.05	.02	.01
☐ 718	Steve Scarsone	.05	.02	.01
☐ 719	Rich Aurilia	.05	.02	.01
☐ 720	Matt Williams	.30	.14	.04
☐ 721	John Patterson	.05	.02	.01
☐ 722	Shawn Estes	.05	.02	.01
☐ 723	Russ Davis	.05	.02	.01
☐ 724	Rich Amaral	.05	.02	.01
☐ 725	Edgar Martinez	.30	.14	.04
☐ 726	Norm Charlton	.05	.02	.01
☐ 727	Paul Sorrento	.05	.02	.01
☐ 728	Luis Sojo	.05	.02	.01
☐ 729	Arquimedez Pozo	.05	.02	.01
☐ 730	Jay Buhner	.30	.14	.04
☐ 731	Chris Bosio	.05	.02	.01
☐ 732	Chris Widger	.05	.02	.01
☐ 733	Kevin Gross	.05	.02	.01
☐ 734	Darren Oliver	.05	.02	.01
☐ 735	Dean Palmer	.30	.14	.04
☐ 736	Matt Whiteside	.05	.02	.01
☐ 737	Luis Ortiz	.05	.02	.01
☐ 738	Roger Pavlik	.05	.02	.01
☐ 739	Damon Buford	.05	.02	.01
☐ 740	Juan Gonzalez	1.00	.45	.12
☐ 741	Rusty Greer	.30	.14	.04
☐ 742	Lou Frazier	.05	.02	.01
☐ 743	Pat Hentgen	.30	.14	.04
☐ 744	Tomas Perez	.05	.02	.01
☐ 745	Juan Guzman	.05	.02	.01
☐ 746	Otis Nixon	.05	.02	.01
☐ 747	Robert Perez	.05	.02	.01
☐ 748	Ed Sprague	.15	.07	.02
☐ 749	Tony Castillo	.05	.02	.01
☐ 750	John Olerud	.05	.02	.01
☐ 751	Shawn Green	.05	.02	.01
☐ 752	Jeff Ware	.05	.02	.01
☐ 753	Dante Bichette CL Vinny Castilla Andres Galarraga Larry Walker	.15	.07	.02
☐ 754	Greg Maddux CL	.60	.25	.07
☐ 755	Marty Cordova CL	.15	.07	.02
☐ 756	Ozzie Smith CL	.30	.14	.04
☐ 757	John Vanderwal CL	.05	.02	.01
☐ 758	Andres Galarraga CL	.15	.07	.02
☐ 759	Frank Thomas CL	1.00	.45	.12
☐ 760	Tony Gwynn CL	.40	.18	.05
☐ 761	Randy Myers UPD	.40	.18	.05
☐ 762	Kent Mercker UPD	.25	.11	.03
☐ 763	David Wells UPD	.25	.11	.03
☐ 764	Tom Gordon UPD	.25	.11	.03
☐ 765	Wil Cordero UPD	.25	.11	.03
☐ 766	Dave Magadan UPD	.25	.11	.03
☐ 767	Doug Jones UPD	.25	.11	.03
☐ 768	Kevin Tapani UPD	.40	.18	.05
☐ 769	Curtis Goodwin UPD	.25	.11	.03
☐ 770	Julio Franco UPD	.40	.18	.05
☐ 771	Jack McDowell UPD	.75	.35	.09
☐ 772	Al Leiter UPD	.40	.18	.05
☐ 773	Sean Berry UPD	.25	.11	.03
☐ 774	Bip Roberts UPD	.40	.18	.05
☐ 775	Jose Offerman UPD	.25	.11	.03
☐ 776	Ben McDonald UPD	.40	.18	.05
☐ 777	Dan Serafini UPD	.25	.11	.03
☐ 778	Ryan McGuire UPD	.40	.18	.05
☐ 779	Tim Raines UPD	.75	.35	.09
☐ 780	Tino Martinez UPD	.75	.35	.09
☐ 781	Kenny Rogers UPD	.25	.11	.03
☐ 782	Bob Tewksbury UPD	.25	.11	.03
☐ 783	Rickey Henderson UPD	1.00	.45	.12
☐ 784	Ron Gant UPD	.75	.35	.09
☐ 785	Gary Gaetti UPD	.40	.18	.05
☐ 786	Andy Benes UPD	.40	.18	.05
☐ 787	Royce Clayton UPD	.40	.18	.05
☐ 788	Darryl Hamilton UPD	.25	.11	.03
☐ 789	Ken Hill UPD	.25	.11	.03
☐ 790	Erik Hanson UPD	.25	.11	.03

1996 Collector's Choice Gold Signature

This 730-card set parallels the basic Collector's Choice issue. These cards were inserted approximately one every 35 packs. Cards 1-365 were issued in first series and 396-730 in second series. The cards are similar to the regular issue except they have gold borders and a gold facsimile player's signature on front.

	MINT	NRMT	EXC
COMPLETE SET (730)	1500.00	700.00	190.00
COMPLETE SERIES 1 (365)	800.00	350.00	100.00
COMPLETE SERIES 2 (365)	700.00	325.00	90.00
COMMON CARD (1-360/396-760)	1.00	.45	.12

SEMISTARS	2.50	1.10	.30
STARS	6.00	2.70	.75
*VETERAN STARS: 12.5X TO 25X BASIC CARDS			
*YOUNG STARS: 10X TO 20X BASIC CARDS			
RANDOM INSERTS IN PACKS			

□ 1 Cal Ripken	40.00	18.00	5.00
□ 40 Greg Maddux	30.00	13.50	3.70
□ 42 Chipper Jones	30.00	13.50	3.70
□ 90 Frank Thomas	50.00	22.00	6.25
□ 105 Frank Thomas TT	25.00	11.00	3.10
□ 160 Jeff Bagwell	18.00	8.00	2.20
□ 185 Mike Piazza	30.00	13.50	3.70
□ 231 Derek Jeter	30.00	13.50	3.70
□ 237 Don Mattingly	25.00	11.00	3.10
□ 290 Tony Gwynn	20.00	9.00	2.50
□ 310 Ken Griffey Jr.	50.00	22.00	6.25
□ 316 Alex Rodriguez	40.00	18.00	5.00
□ 362 Cal Ripken CL	20.00	9.00	2.50
□ 412 Frank Thomas TC	25.00	11.00	3.10
□ 415 Ken Griffey Jr. TC	25.00	11.00	3.10
□ 421 Cal Ripken TC	20.00	9.00	2.50
□ 530 Albert Belle	25.00	11.00	3.10
□ 740 Juan Gonzalez	25.00	11.00	3.10
□ 759 Frank Thomas CL	25.00	11.00	3.10

1996 Collector's Choice Crash the Game

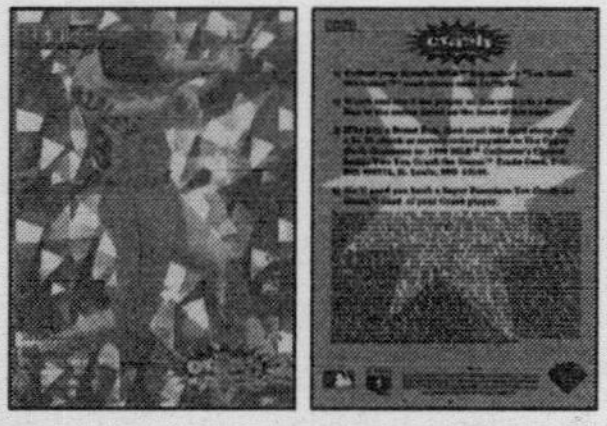

Randomly inserted into one in every five packs, silver Crash the Game interactive cards feature a selection of thirty of baseball's top stars. If the featured player hit a home run during the series specified on the card, it was then eligible to be redeemed for a super premium Cell Card of the same player. Randomly inserted into one in every 50 packs was a parallel gold Crash the Game card. These scarce gold cards were redeemable for super premium Wood Cell Cards. The postmark expiration date for exchanging winning cards was November 18th, 1996.

	MINT	NRMT	EXC
COMPLETE SILVER SET (90)	50.00	22.00	6.25
COMMON SILVER (CG1-CG30)	.40	.18	.05
*GOLD: 5X SILVER VALUE			
*EXCHANGE CARDS: EQUAL VALUE			
*SILVER EXCHANGE: 5X VALUE			
THREE SERIES PER PLAYER			
EXCHANGE REDEEMED w/WINNERS			
EXPIRATION DATE: 11/18/96			
RANDOM INSERTS IN SER.2 PACKS			

□ CG1 Chipper Jones 7/11	2.00	.90	.25
□ CG2 Fred McGriff 7/1	.40	.18	.05
□ CG3 Rafael Palmeiro 7/4	.40	.18	.05
□ CG4 Cal Ripken 6/27	2.50	1.10	.30
□ CG5 Jose Canseco 6/27	.40	.18	.05
□ CG6 Mo Vaughn 6/21	.75	.35	.09
□ CG7 Jim Edmonds 7/18	.40	.18	.05
□ CG8 Tim Salmon 6/20	.40	.18	.05
□ CG9 Sammy Sosa 7/4	.40	.18	.05
□ CG10 Frank Thomas 6/27	3.00	1.35	.35
□ CG11 Albert Belle 6/25	1.50	.70	.19
□ CG12 Manny Ramirez 7/18	.75	.35	.09
□ CG13 Jim Thome 6/27	.60	.25	.07
□ CG14 Dante Bichette 7/11	.40	.18	.05
□ CG15 Vinny Castilla 7/1	.40	.18	.05
□ CG16 Larry Walker 6/24	.40	.18	.05
□ CG17 Cecil Fielder 6/27	.40	.18	.05
□ CG18 Gary Sheffield 7/4	.40	.18	.05
□ CG19 Jeff Bagwell 7/4	1.25	.55	.16
□ CG20 Eric Karros 7/4	.40	.18	.05
□ CG21 Mike Piazza 6/27	2.00	.90	.25
□ CG22 Ken Caminiti 7/11	.40	.18	.05
□ CG23 Barry Bonds 6/27	.75	.35	.09
□ CG24 Matt Williams 7/11	.40	.18	.05
□ CG25 Jay Buhner 6/20	.40	.18	.05
□ CG26 Ken Griffey Jr. 7/18	3.00	1.35	.35
□ CG27 Ron Gant 6/24	.40	.18	.05
□ CG28 Juan Gonzalez 6/28	1.50	.70	.19
□ CG29 Mickey Tettleton 7/4	.40	.18	.05
□ CG30 Joe Carter 6/25	.40	.18	.05

1996 Collector's Choice You Make the Play

This 45-card set was inserted one per pack. Dealers also were offered extra You Make the Play cards depending on how many cases ordered. A dealer who ordered one case received two 12-card packs of these cards for a total of 24 cards. Meanwhile, a dealer who ordered two cases received six 12-card packs for a total of 72 packs. Customers could also receive a 12 of these cards by sending 10 wrappers and $2 to an a mail-in order. This offer expired on May 15, 1996. The cards measure just about the standard-size but have rounded corners. Each player has two results on each card but the value is the same for either result.

	MINT	NRMT	EXC
COMPLETE SET (90)	15.00	6.75	1.85
COMMON CARD (1-45)	.15	.07	.02
*GOLD STARS: 15X TO X BASIC CARDS			
TWO OUTCOMES PER PLAYER			
ONE BASIC CARD PER SER.1 PACK			
GOLD: RANDOM INSERTS IN SER.1 PACKS			

□ 1 Kevin Appier	.15	.07	.02
□ 2 Carlos Baerga	.25	.11	.03
□ 3 Jeff Bagwell	.75	.35	.09
□ 4 Jay Bell	.15	.07	.02
□ 5 Albert Belle	1.00	.45	.12
□ 6 Craig Biggio	.25	.11	.03
□ 7 Wade Boggs	.25	.11	.03
□ 8 Barry Bonds	.50	.23	.06
□ 9 Bobby Bonilla	.25	.11	.03
□ 10 Jose Canseco	.25	.11	.03
□ 11 Joe Carter	.25	.11	.03
□ 12 Darren Daulton	.15	.07	.02
□ 13 Cecil Fielder	.25	.11	.03
□ 14 Ron Gant	.25	.11	.03
□ 15 Juan Gonzalez	1.00	.45	.12
□ 16 Ken Griffey Jr.	2.00	.90	.25
□ 17 Tony Gwynn	.75	.35	.09
□ 18 Randy Johnson	.25	.11	.03
□ 19 Chipper Jones	1.25	.55	.16
□ 20 Barry Larkin	.25	.11	.03
□ 21 Kenny Lofton	.50	.23	.06
□ 22 Greg Maddux	1.25	.55	.16
□ 23 Don Mattingly	1.00	.45	.12
□ 24 Fred McGriff	.25	.11	.03
□ 25 Mark McGwire	.60	.25	.07

□ 26 Paul Molitor	.40	.18	.05
□ 27 Raul Mondesi	.25	.11	.03
□ 28 Eddie Murray	.50	.23	.06
□ 29 Hideo Nomo	.50	.23	.06
□ 30 Jon Nunnally	.15	.07	.02
□ 31 Mike Piazza	1.25	.55	.16
□ 32 Kirby Puckett	.60	.25	.07
□ 33 Cal Ripken	1.50	.70	.19
□ 34 Alex Rodriguez	2.00	.90	.25
□ 35 Tim Salmon	.25	.11	.03
□ 36 Gary Sheffield	.25	.11	.03
□ 37 Lee Smith	.25	.11	.03
□ 38 Ozzie Smith	.40	.18	.05
□ 39 Sammy Sosa	.25	.11	.03
□ 40 Frank Thomas	2.00	.90	.25
□ 41 Greg Vaughn	.25	.11	.03
□ 42 Mo Vaughn	.50	.23	.06
□ 43 Larry Walker	.25	.11	.03
□ 44 Rondell White	.25	.11	.03
□ 45 Matt Williams	.25	.11	.03

1995 Collector's Choice SE

The 1995 Collector's Choice SE set consists of 265 standard-size cards. One in every 216 packs was a Silver Super Pack, containing 12 silver signature cards. One in every 720 packs was a Gold Super Pack, containing 12 gold signature cards. The fronts feature color action player photos with blue borders. The player's name, position and the team name are printed on the bottom of the photo. The SE logo in blue-foil appears in a top corner. On a white background, the backs carry another color player photo with a short player biography, career stats and 1994 highlights. Subsets featured include Rookie Class (1-25), Record Pace (26-30), Stat Leaders (137-144), Fantasy Team (249-260). There are no Rookie Cards in this set.

	MINT	NRMT	EXC
COMPLETE SET (265)	20.00	9.00	2.50
COMMON CARD (1-265)	.10	.05	.01
SEMISTARS	.25	.11	.03
STARS	.50	.23	.06
COMP.SILV.SIG.SET (265)	60.00	27.00	7.50
COMMON SILV.SIG. (1-265)	.20	.09	.03
SILV.SIG.SEMISTARS	.30	.14	.04
*SILV.SIG.STARS: 2X to 4X HI COLUMN			
*SILV.SIG.YOUNG STARS: 1.5X to 3X HI			
ONE SILVER SIGNATURE PER PACK			
12 SILVER SIGNATURES PER SUPER PACK			
COMP.GOLD SIG SET (265)	1500.00	700.00	190.00
COMMON GOLD SIG (1-265)	2.50	1.10	.30
GOLD SIG SEMISTARS	5.00	2.20	.60
*GOLD VETERAN STARS: 18X TO 30X HI			
*GOLD YOUNG STARS: 15X TO 25X HI			
GOLD: RANDOM INSERTS IN PACKS			
GOLD: 12 PER GOLD SUPER PACK			

□ 1 Alex Rodriguez	4.00	1.80	.50
□ 2 Derek Jeter	2.00	.90	.25
□ 3 Dustin Hermanson	.25	.11	.03
□ 4 Bill Pulsipher	.25	.11	.03
□ 5 Terrell Wade	.25	.11	.03
□ 6 Darren Dreifort	.10	.05	.01
□ 7 LaTroy Hawkins	.10	.05	.01
□ 8 Alex Ochoa	.50	.23	.06
□ 9 Paul Wilson	.60	.25	.07
□ 10 Rod Henderson	.10	.05	.01
□ 11 Alan Benes	.50	.23	.06
□ 12 Garret Anderson	.50	.23	.06
□ 13 Armando Benitez	.10	.05	.01
□ 14 Mark Thompson	.10	.05	.01
□ 15 Andrew Lorraine	.25	.11	.03
□ 16 Jose Silva	.10	.05	.01
□ 17 Orlando Miller	.10	.05	.01
□ 18 Russ Davis	.10	.05	.01
□ 19 Jason Isringhausen	.75	.35	.09
□ 20 Ray McDavid	.25	.11	.03
□ 21 Tim VanEgmond	.10	.05	.01
□ 22 Paul Shuey	.10	.05	.01
□ 23 Steve Dunn	.10	.05	.01
□ 24 Mike Lieberthal	.10	.05	.01
□ 25 Chan Ho Park	.50	.23	.06
□ 26 Ken Griffey Jr. RP	1.50	.70	.19
□ 27 Tony Gwynn RP	.60	.25	.07
□ 28 Chuck Knoblauch RP	.50	.23	.06
□ 29 Frank Thomas RP	1.50	.70	.19
□ 30 Matt Williams RP	.25	.11	.03
□ 31 Chili Davis	.25	.11	.03
□ 32 Chad Curtis	.10	.05	.01
□ 33 Brian Anderson	.10	.05	.01
□ 34 Chuck Finley	.25	.11	.03
□ 35 Tim Salmon	.50	.23	.06
□ 36 Bo Jackson	.50	.23	.06
□ 37 Doug Drabek	.10	.05	.01
□ 38 Craig Biggio	.50	.23	.06
□ 39 Ken Caminiti	.50	.23	.06
□ 40 Jeff Bagwell	1.25	.55	.16
□ 41 Darryl Kile	.10	.05	.01
□ 42 John Hudek	.10	.05	.01
□ 43 Brian L. Hunter	.50	.23	.06
□ 44 Dennis Eckersley	.25	.11	.03
□ 45 Mark McGwire	1.00	.45	.12
□ 46 Brent Gates	.10	.05	.01
□ 47 Steve Karsay	.10	.05	.01
□ 48 Rickey Henderson	.50	.23	.06
□ 49 Terry Steinbach	.25	.11	.03
□ 50 Ruben Sierra	.25	.11	.03
□ 51 Roberto Alomar	.75	.35	.09
□ 52 Carlos Delgado	.50	.23	.06
□ 53 Alex Gonzalez	.10	.05	.01
□ 54 Joe Carter	.50	.23	.06
□ 55 Paul Molitor	.60	.25	.07
□ 56 Juan Guzman	.25	.11	.03
□ 57 John Olerud	.10	.05	.01
□ 58 Shawn Green	.25	.11	.03
□ 59 Tom Glavine	.50	.23	.06
□ 60 Greg Maddux	2.00	.90	.25
□ 61 Roberto Kelly	.10	.05	.01
□ 62 Ryan Klesko	.60	.25	.07
□ 63 Javier Lopez	.50	.23	.06
□ 64 Jose Oliva	.10	.05	.01
□ 65 Fred McGriff	.50	.23	.06
□ 66 Steve Avery	.25	.11	.03
□ 67 David Justice	.50	.23	.06
□ 68 Ricky Bones	.10	.05	.01
□ 69 Cal Eldred	.10	.05	.01
□ 70 Greg Vaughn	.25	.11	.03
□ 71 Dave Nilsson	.25	.11	.03
□ 72 Jose Valentin	.25	.11	.03
□ 73 Matt Mieske	.25	.11	.03
□ 74 Todd Zeile	.10	.05	.01
□ 75 Ozzie Smith	.60	.25	.07
□ 76 Bernard Gilkey	.25	.11	.03
□ 77 Ray Lankford	.50	.23	.06
□ 78 Bob Tewksbury	.10	.05	.01
□ 79 Mark Whiten	.10	.05	.01
□ 80 Gregg Jefferies	.25	.11	.03
□ 81 Randy Myers	.10	.05	.01
□ 82 Shawon Dunston	.10	.05	.01
□ 83 Mark Grace	.50	.23	.06
□ 84 Derrick May	.10	.05	.01
□ 85 Sammy Sosa	.50	.23	.06
□ 86 Steve Trachsel	.10	.05	.01
□ 87 Brett Butler	.25	.11	.03
□ 88 Delino DeShields	.10	.05	.01
□ 89 Orel Hershiser	.25	.11	.03
□ 90 Mike Piazza	2.00	.90	.25
□ 91 Todd Hollandsworth	.50	.23	.06
□ 92 Eric Karros	.25	.11	.03
□ 93 Ramon Martinez	.25	.11	.03
□ 94 Tim Wallach	.10	.05	.01

□ 95 Raul Mondesi	.50	.23	.06
□ 96 Larry Walker	.50	.23	.06
□ 97 Wil Cordero	.10	.05	.01
□ 98 Marquis Grissom	.50	.23	.06
□ 99 Ken Hill	.10	.05	.01
□ 100 Cliff Floyd	.25	.11	.03
□ 101 Pedro J. Martinez	.25	.11	.03
□ 102 John Wetteland	.25	.11	.03
□ 103 Rondell White	.50	.23	.06
□ 104 Moises Alou	.25	.11	.03
□ 105 Barry Bonds	.75	.35	.09
□ 106 Darren Lewis	.10	.05	.01
□ 107 Mark Portugal	.10	.05	.01
□ 108 Matt Williams	.50	.23	.06
□ 109 William VanLandingham	.10	.05	.01
□ 110 Bill Swift	.10	.05	.01
□ 111 Robby Thompson	.10	.05	.01
□ 112 Rod Beck	.10	.05	.01
□ 113 Darryl Strawberry	.25	.11	.03
□ 114 Jim Thome	.60	.25	.07
□ 115 Dave Winfield	.50	.23	.06
□ 116 Eddie Murray	.75	.35	.09
□ 117 Manny Ramirez	.75	.35	.09
□ 118 Carlos Baerga	.50	.23	.06
□ 119 Kenny Lofton	.75	.35	.09
□ 120 Albert Belle	1.50	.70	.19
□ 121 Mark Clark	.10	.05	.01
□ 122 Dennis Martinez	.25	.11	.03
□ 123 Randy Johnson	.50	.23	.06
□ 124 Jay Buhner	.50	.23	.06
□ 125 Ken Griffey Jr.	3.00	1.35	.35
□ 126 Goose Gossage	.25	.11	.03
□ 127 Tino Martinez	.25	.11	.03
□ 128 Reggie Jefferson	.25	.11	.03
□ 129 Edgar Martinez	.50	.23	.06
□ 130 Gary Sheffield	.50	.23	.06
□ 131 Pat Rapp	.10	.05	.01
□ 132 Bret Barberie	.10	.05	.01
□ 133 Chuck Carr	.10	.05	.01
□ 134 Jeff Conine	.50	.23	.06
□ 135 Charles Johnson	.25	.11	.03
□ 136 Benito Santiago	.10	.05	.01
□ 137 Matt Williams STL	.25	.11	.03
□ 138 Jeff Bagwell STL	.60	.25	.07
□ 139 Kenny Lofton STL	.50	.23	.06
□ 140 Tony Gwynn STL	.60	.25	.07
□ 141 Jimmy Key STL	.10	.05	.01
□ 142 Greg Maddux STL	1.00	.45	.12
□ 143 Randy Johnson STL	.50	.23	.06
□ 144 Lee Smith STL	.10	.05	.01
□ 145 Bobby Bonilla	.25	.11	.03
□ 146 Jason Jacome	.10	.05	.01
□ 147 Jeff Kent	.10	.05	.01
□ 148 Ryan Thompson	.10	.05	.01
□ 149 Bobby Jones	.25	.11	.03
□ 150 Bret Saberhagen	.25	.11	.03
□ 151 John Franco	.10	.05	.01
□ 152 Lee Smith	.25	.11	.03
□ 153 Rafael Palmeiro	.50	.23	.06
□ 154 Brady Anderson	.50	.23	.06
□ 155 Cal Ripken Jr.	2.50	1.10	.30
□ 156 Jeffrey Hammonds	.25	.11	.03
□ 157 Mike Mussina	.60	.25	.07
□ 158 Chris Hoiles	.10	.05	.01
□ 159 Ben McDonald	.10	.05	.01
□ 160 Tony Gwynn	1.25	.55	.16
□ 161 Joey Hamilton	.25	.11	.03
□ 162 Andy Benes	.10	.05	.01
□ 163 Trevor Hoffman	.10	.05	.01
□ 164 Phil Plantier	.10	.05	.01
□ 165 Derek Bell	.25	.11	.03
□ 166 Bip Roberts	.10	.05	.01
□ 167 Eddie Williams	.10	.05	.01
□ 168 Fernando Valenzuela	.25	.11	.03
□ 169 Mariano Duncan	.10	.05	.01
□ 170 Lenny Dykstra	.25	.11	.03
□ 171 Darren Daulton	.25	.11	.03
□ 172 Danny Jackson	.10	.05	.01
□ 173 Bobby Munoz	.10	.05	.01
□ 174 Doug Jones	.10	.05	.01
□ 175 Jay Bell	.25	.11	.03
□ 176 Zane Smith	.10	.05	.01
□ 177 Jon Lieber	.10	.05	.01
□ 178 Carlos Garcia	.10	.05	.01
□ 179 Orlando Merced	.10	.05	.01
□ 180 Andy Van Slyke	.25	.11	.03
□ 181 Rick Helling	.10	.05	.01
□ 182 Rusty Greer	.50	.23	.06
□ 183 Kenny Rogers UER (shows 110 wins in 1990)	.10	.05	.01
□ 184 Will Clark	.50	.23	.06
□ 185 Jose Canseco	.50	.23	.06
□ 186 Juan Gonzalez	1.50	.70	.19
□ 187 Dean Palmer	.25	.11	.03
□ 188 Ivan Rodriguez	.60	.25	.07
□ 189 John Valentin	.25	.11	.03
□ 190 Roger Clemens	.50	.23	.06
□ 191 Aaron Sele	.25	.11	.03
□ 192 Scott Cooper	.10	.05	.01
□ 193 Mike Greenwell	.10	.05	.01
□ 194 Mo Vaughn	.75	.35	.09
□ 195 Andre Dawson	.50	.23	.06
□ 196 Ron Gant	.25	.11	.03
□ 197 Jose Rijo	.10	.05	.01
□ 198 Bret Boone	.25	.11	.03
□ 199 Deion Sanders	.50	.23	.06
□ 200 Barry Larkin	.50	.23	.06
□ 201 Hal Morris	.10	.05	.01
□ 202 Reggie Sanders	.25	.11	.03
□ 203 Kevin Mitchell	.25	.11	.03
□ 204 Marvin Freeman	.10	.05	.01
□ 205 Andres Galarraga	.50	.23	.06
□ 206 Walt Weiss	.10	.05	.01
□ 207 Charlie Hayes	.10	.05	.01
□ 208 Dave Nied	.10	.05	.01
□ 209 Dante Bichette	.50	.23	.06
□ 210 David Cone	.25	.11	.03
□ 211 Jeff Montgomery	.25	.11	.03
□ 212 Felix Jose	.10	.05	.01
□ 213 Mike Macfarlane	.10	.05	.01
□ 214 Wally Joyner	.25	.11	.03
□ 215 Bob Hamelin	.10	.05	.01
□ 216 Brian McRae	.25	.11	.03
□ 217 Kirk Gibson	.25	.11	.03
□ 218 Lou Whitaker	.50	.23	.06
□ 219 Chris Gomez	.10	.05	.01
□ 220 Cecil Fielder	.25	.11	.03
□ 221 Mickey Tettleton	.10	.05	.01
□ 222 Travis Fryman	.25	.11	.03
□ 223 Tony Phillips	.25	.11	.03
□ 224 Rick Aguilera	.10	.05	.01
□ 225 Scott Erickson	.10	.05	.01
□ 226 Chuck Knoblauch	.50	.23	.06
□ 227 Kent Hrbek	.25	.11	.03
□ 228 Shane Mack	.10	.05	.01
□ 229 Kevin Tapani	.10	.05	.01
□ 230 Kirby Puckett	1.00	.45	.12
□ 231 Julio Franco	.25	.11	.03
□ 232 Jack McDowell	.25	.11	.03
□ 233 Jason Bere	.10	.05	.01
□ 234 Alex Fernandez	.25	.11	.03
□ 235 Frank Thomas	3.00	1.35	.35
□ 236 Ozzie Guillen	.10	.05	.01
□ 237 Robin Ventura	.25	.11	.03
□ 238 Michael Jordan	4.00	1.80	.50
□ 239 Wilson Alvarez	.25	.11	.03
□ 240 Don Mattingly	1.50	.70	.19
□ 241 Jim Abbott	.10	.05	.01
□ 242 Jim Leyritz	.10	.05	.01
□ 243 Paul O'Neill	.25	.11	.03
□ 244 Melido Perez	.10	.05	.01
□ 245 Wade Boggs	.50	.23	.06
□ 246 Mike Stanley	.10	.05	.01
□ 247 Danny Tartabull	.10	.05	.01
□ 248 Jimmy Key	.25	.11	.03
□ 249 Greg Maddux FT	1.00	.45	.12
□ 250 Randy Johnson FT	.50	.23	.06
□ 251 Bret Saberhagen FT	.10	.05	.01
□ 252 John Wetteland FT	.10	.05	.01
□ 253 Mike Piazza FT	1.00	.45	.12
□ 254 Jeff Bagwell FT	.60	.25	.07
□ 255 Craig Biggio FT	.25	.11	.03
□ 256 Matt Williams FT	.25	.11	.03
□ 257 Wil Cordero FT	.10	.05	.01
□ 258 Kenny Lofton FT	.50	.23	.06
□ 259 Barry Bonds FT	.50	.23	.06
□ 260 Dante Bichette FT	.50	.23	.06
□ 261 Ken Griffey Jr. CL	1.00	.45	.12
□ 262 Goose Gossage CL	.10	.05	.01
□ 263 Cal Ripken CL	1.00	.45	.12
□ 264 Kenny Rogers CL	.10	.05	.01
□ 265 John Valentin CL	.25	.11	.03

1981 Donruss

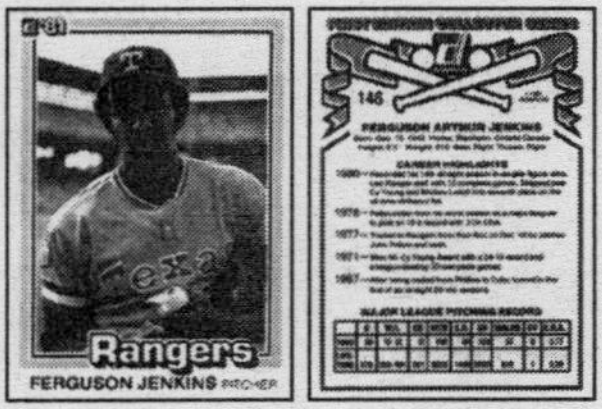

In 1981 Donruss launched itself into the baseball card market with a 600-card set. Wax packs contained 15 cards as well as a piece of gum. This would be the only year that Donruss was allowed to have any confectionary product in their packs. The standard-size cards are printed on thin stock and more than one pose exists for several popular players. Numerous errors of the first print run were later corrected by the company. These are marked P1 and P2 in the checklist below. The key Rookie Cards in this set are Danny Ainge, Tim Raines, and Jeff Reardon.

	MINT	NRMT	EXC
COMPLETE SET (605)	40.00	18.00	5.00
COMMON CARD (1-605)	.10	.05	.01
SEMISTARS	.25	.11	.03
STARS	.50	.23	.06

	MINT	NRMT	EXC
☐ 1 Ozzie Smith	4.00	1.80	.50
☐ 2 Rollie Fingers	.50	.23	.06
☐ 3 Rick Wise	.10	.05	.01
☐ 4 Gene Richards	.10	.05	.01
☐ 5 Alan Trammell	1.25	.55	.16
☐ 6 Tom Brookens	.10	.05	.01
☐ 7A Duffy Dyer P1 (1980 batting average has decimal point)	.25	.11	.03
☐ 7B Duffy Dyer P2 (1980 batting average has no decimal point)	.10	.05	.01
☐ 8 Mark Fidrych	.50	.23	.06
☐ 9 Dave Rozema	.10	.05	.01
☐ 10 Ricky Peters	.10	.05	.01
☐ 11 Mike Schmidt	2.00	.90	.25
☐ 12 Willie Stargell	.60	.25	.07
☐ 13 Tim Foli	.10	.05	.01
☐ 14 Manny Sanguillen	.25	.11	.03
☐ 15 Grant Jackson	.10	.05	.01
☐ 16 Eddie Solomon	.10	.05	.01
☐ 17 Omar Moreno	.10	.05	.01
☐ 18 Joe Morgan	.60	.25	.07
☐ 19 Rafael Landestoy	.10	.05	.01
☐ 20 Bruce Bochy	.10	.05	.01
☐ 21 Joe Sambito	.10	.05	.01
☐ 22 Manny Trillo	.10	.05	.01
☐ 23A Dave Smith P1 (Line box around stats is not complete)	.25	.11	.03
☐ 23B Dave Smith P2 (Box totally encloses stats at top)	.25	.11	.03
☐ 24 Terry Puhl	.10	.05	.01
☐ 25 Bump Wills	.10	.05	.01
☐ 26A John Ellis P1 ERR (Photo on front shows Danny Walton)	.50	.23	.06
☐ 26B John Ellis P2 COR	.25	.11	.03
☐ 27 Jim Kern	.10	.05	.01
☐ 28 Richie Zisk	.10	.05	.01
☐ 29 John Mayberry	.10	.05	.01
☐ 30 Bob Davis	.10	.05	.01
☐ 31 Jackson Todd	.10	.05	.01
☐ 32 Alvis Woods	.10	.05	.01
☐ 33 Steve Carlton	1.00	.45	.12
☐ 34 Lee Mazzilli	.10	.05	.01
☐ 35 John Stearns	.10	.05	.01
☐ 36 Roy Lee Jackson	.10	.05	.01
☐ 37 Mike Scott	.25	.11	.03
☐ 38 Lamar Johnson	.10	.05	.01
☐ 39 Kevin Bell	.10	.05	.01
☐ 40 Ed Farmer	.10	.05	.01
☐ 41 Ross Baumgarten	.10	.05	.01
☐ 42 Leo Sutherland	.10	.05	.01
☐ 43 Dan Meyer	.10	.05	.01
☐ 44 Ron Reed	.10	.05	.01
☐ 45 Mario Mendoza	.10	.05	.01
☐ 46 Rick Honeycutt	.10	.05	.01
☐ 47 Glenn Abbott	.10	.05	.01
☐ 48 Leon Roberts	.10	.05	.01
☐ 49 Rod Carew	.75	.35	.09
☐ 50 Bert Campaneris	.25	.11	.03
☐ 51A Tom Donahue P1 ERR (Name on front misspelled Donahue)	.25	.11	.03
☐ 51B Tom Donohue P2 COR	.10	.05	.01
☐ 52 Dave Frost	.10	.05	.01
☐ 53 Ed Halicki	.10	.05	.01
☐ 54 Dan Ford	.10	.05	.01
☐ 55 Garry Maddox	.10	.05	.01
☐ 56A Steve Garvey P1 ("Surpassed 25 HR")	.50	.23	.06
☐ 56B Steve Garvey P2 ("Surpassed 21 HR")	.50	.23	.06
☐ 57 Bill Russell	.25	.11	.03
☐ 58 Don Sutton	.50	.23	.06
☐ 59 Reggie Smith	.25	.11	.03
☐ 60 Rick Monday	.25	.11	.03
☐ 61 Ray Knight	.25	.11	.03
☐ 62 Johnny Bench	1.25	.55	.16
☐ 63 Mario Soto	.10	.05	.01
☐ 64 Doug Bair	.10	.05	.01
☐ 65 George Foster	.25	.11	.03
☐ 66 Jeff Burroughs	.10	.05	.01
☐ 67 Keith Hernandez	.50	.23	.06
☐ 68 Tom Herr	.25	.11	.03
☐ 69 Bob Forsch	.10	.05	.01
☐ 70 John Fulgham	.10	.05	.01
☐ 71A Bobby Bonds P1 ERR (986 lifetime HR)	.50	.23	.06
☐ 71B Bobby Bonds P2 COR (326 lifetime HR)	.25	.11	.03
☐ 72A Rennie Stennett P1 ("Breaking broke leg")	.25	.11	.03
☐ 72B Rennie Stennett P2 (Word "broke" deleted)	.10	.05	.01
☐ 73 Joe Strain	.10	.05	.01
☐ 74 Ed Whitson	.10	.05	.01
☐ 75 Tom Griffin	.10	.05	.01
☐ 76 Billy North	.10	.05	.01
☐ 77 Gene Garber	.10	.05	.01
☐ 78 Mike Hargrove	.25	.11	.03
☐ 79 Dave Rosello	.10	.05	.01
☐ 80 Ron Hassey	.10	.05	.01
☐ 81 Sid Monge	.10	.05	.01
☐ 82A Joe Charboneau P1 ('78 highlights, "For some reason")	.25	.11	.03
☐ 82B Joe Charboneau P2 (Phrase "For some reason" deleted)	.25	.11	.03
☐ 83 Cecil Cooper	.25	.11	.03
☐ 84 Sal Bando	.25	.11	.03
☐ 85 Moose Haas	.10	.05	.01
☐ 86 Mike Caldwell	.10	.05	.01
☐ 87A Larry Hisle P1 ('77 highlights, line ends with "28 RBI")	.25	.11	.03
☐ 87B Larry Hisle P2 (Correct line "28 HR")	.10	.05	.01
☐ 88 Luis Gomez	.10	.05	.01
☐ 89 Larry Parrish	.10	.05	.01
☐ 90 Gary Carter	.50	.23	.06
☐ 91 Bill Gullickson	.50	.23	.06
☐ 92 Fred Norman	.10	.05	.01
☐ 93 Tommy Hutton	.10	.05	.01
☐ 94 Carl Yastrzemski	1.00	.45	.12
☐ 95 Glenn Hoffman	.10	.05	.01
☐ 96 Dennis Eckersley	.75	.35	.09
☐ 97A Tom Burgmeier P1	.25	.11	.03

	No.	Player			
		ERR (Throws: Right)			
□	97B	Tom Burgmeier P2	.10	.05	.01
		COR (Throws: Left)			
□	98	Win Remmerswaal	.10	.05	.01
□	99	Bob Horner	.25	.11	.03
□	100	George Brett	4.00	1.80	.50
□	101	Dave Chalk	.10	.05	.01
□	102	Dennis Leonard	.10	.05	.01
□	103	Renie Martin	.10	.05	.01
□	104	Amos Otis	.25	.11	.03
□	105	Graig Nettles	.25	.11	.03
□	106	Eric Soderholm	.10	.05	.01
□	107	Tommy John	.50	.23	.06
□	108	Tom Underwood	.10	.05	.01
□	109	Lou Piniella	.25	.11	.03
□	110	Mickey Klutts	.10	.05	.01
□	111	Bobby Murcer	.25	.11	.03
□	112	Eddie Murray	4.00	1.80	.50
□	113	Rick Dempsey	.25	.11	.03
□	114	Scott McGregor	.10	.05	.01
□	115	Ken Singleton	.25	.11	.03
□	116	Gary Roenicke	.10	.05	.01
□	117	Dave Revering	.10	.05	.01
□	118	Mike Norris	.10	.05	.01
□	119	Rickey Henderson	3.00	1.35	.35
□	120	Mike Heath	.10	.05	.01
□	121	Dave Cash	.10	.05	.01
□	122	Randy Jones	.10	.05	.01
□	123	Eric Rasmussen	.10	.05	.01
□	124	Jerry Mumphrey	.10	.05	.01
□	125	Richie Hebner	.10	.05	.01
□	126	Mark Wagner	.10	.05	.01
□	127	Jack Morris	.50	.23	.06
□	128	Dan Petry	.25	.11	.03
□	129	Bruce Robbins	.10	.05	.01
□	130	Champ Summers	.10	.05	.01
□	131	Pete Rose P1	1.50	.70	.19
		(Last line ends with "see card 251")			
□	131B	Pete Rose P2	1.50	.70	.19
		(Last line corrected "see card 371")			
□	132	Willie Stargell	.60	.25	.07
□	133	Ed Ott	.10	.05	.01
□	134	Jim Bibby	.10	.05	.01
□	135	Bert Blyleven	.50	.23	.06
□	136	Dave Parker	.50	.23	.06
□	137	Bill Robinson	.25	.11	.03
□	138	Enos Cabell	.10	.05	.01
□	139	Dave Bergman	.10	.05	.01
□	140	J.R. Richard	.25	.11	.03
□	141	Ken Forsch	.10	.05	.01
□	142	Larry Bowa UER	.25	.11	.03
		(Shortshop on front)			
□	143	Frank LaCorte UER	.10	.05	.01
		(Photo actually Randy Niemann)			
□	144	Denny Walling	.10	.05	.01
□	145	Buddy Bell	.25	.11	.03
□	146	Ferguson Jenkins	.50	.23	.06
□	147	Dannny Darwin	.10	.05	.01
□	148	John Grubb	.10	.05	.01
□	149	Alfredo Griffin	.10	.05	.01
□	150	Jerry Garvin	.10	.05	.01
□	151	Paul Mirabella	.10	.05	.01
□	152	Rick Bosetti	.10	.05	.01
□	153	Dick Ruthven	.10	.05	.01
□	154	Frank Taveras	.10	.05	.01
□	155	Craig Swan	.10	.05	.01
□	156	Jeff Reardon	1.00	.45	.12
□	157	Steve Henderson	.10	.05	.01
□	158	Jim Morrison	.10	.05	.01
□	159	Glenn Borgmann	.10	.05	.01
□	160	LaMarr Hoyt	.25	.11	.03
□	161	Rich Wortham	.10	.05	.01
□	162	Thad Bosley	.10	.05	.01
□	163	Julio Cruz	.10	.05	.01
□	164A	Del Unser P1	.25	.11	.03
		(No "3B" heading)			
□	164B	Del Unser P2	.10	.05	.01
		(Batting record on back corrected ("3B")			
□	165	Jim Anderson	.10	.05	.01
□	166	Jim Beattie	.10	.05	.01
□	167	Shane Rawley	.10	.05	.01
□	168	Joe Simpson	.10	.05	.01

	No.	Player			
□	169	Rod Carew	.75	.35	.09
□	170	Fred Patek	.10	.05	.01
□	171	Frank Tanana	.25	.11	.03
□	172	Alfredo Martinez	.10	.05	.01
□	173	Chris Knapp	.10	.05	.01
□	174	Joe Rudi	.25	.11	.03
□	175	Greg Luzinski	.25	.11	.03
□	176	Steve Garvey	.50	.23	.06
□	177	Joe Ferguson	.10	.05	.01
□	178	Bob Welch	.25	.11	.03
□	179	Dusty Baker	.50	.23	.06
□	180	Rudy Law	.10	.05	.01
□	181	Dave Concepcion	.25	.11	.03
□	182	Johnny Bench	1.25	.55	.16
□	183	Mike LaCoss	.10	.05	.01
□	184	Ken Griffey	.25	.11	.03
□	185	Dave Collins	.10	.05	.01
□	186	Brian Asselstine	.10	.05	.01
□	187	Garry Templeton	.10	.05	.01
□	188	Mike Phillips	.10	.05	.01
□	189	Pete Vuckovich	.25	.11	.03
□	190	John Urrea	.10	.05	.01
□	191	Tony Scott	.10	.05	.01
□	192	Darrell Evans	.25	.11	.03
□	193	Milt May	.10	.05	.01
□	194	Bob Knepper	.10	.05	.01
□	195	Randy Moffitt	.10	.05	.01
□	196	Larry Herndon	.10	.05	.01
□	197	Rick Camp	.10	.05	.01
□	198	Andre Thornton	.25	.11	.03
□	199	Tom Veryzer	.10	.05	.01
□	200	Gary Alexander	.10	.05	.01
□	201	Rick Waits	.10	.05	.01
□	202	Rick Manning	.10	.05	.01
□	203	Paul Molitor	1.50	.70	.19
□	204	Jim Gantner	.25	.11	.03
□	205	Paul Mitchell	.10	.05	.01
□	206	Reggie Cleveland	.10	.05	.01
□	207	Sixto Lezcano	.10	.05	.01
□	208	Bruce Benedict	.10	.05	.01
□	209	Rodney Scott	.10	.05	.01
□	210	John Tamargo	.10	.05	.01
□	211	Bill Lee	.25	.11	.03
□	212	Andre Dawson UER	1.25	.55	.16
		(Middle name Fernando, should be Nolan)			
□	213	Rowland Office	.10	.05	.01
□	214	Carl Yastrzemski	1.00	.45	.12
□	215	Jerry Remy	.10	.05	.01
□	216	Mike Torrez	.10	.05	.01
□	217	Skip Lockwood	.10	.05	.01
□	218	Fred Lynn	.25	.11	.03
□	219	Chris Chambliss	.25	.11	.03
□	220	Willie Aikens	.10	.05	.01
□	221	John Wathan	.10	.05	.01
□	222	Dan Quisenberry	.25	.11	.03
□	223	Willie Wilson	.25	.11	.03
□	224	Clint Hurdle	.10	.05	.01
□	225	Bob Watson	.25	.11	.03
□	226	Jim Spencer	.10	.05	.01
□	227	Ron Guidry	.25	.11	.03
□	228	Reggie Jackson	1.25	.55	.16
□	229	Oscar Gamble	.10	.05	.01
□	230	Jeff Cox	.10	.05	.01
□	231	Luis Tiant	.25	.11	.03
□	232	Rich Dauer	.10	.05	.01
□	233	Dan Graham	.10	.05	.01
□	234	Mike Flanagan	.25	.11	.03
□	235	John Lowenstein	.10	.05	.01
□	236	Benny Ayala	.10	.05	.01
□	237	Wayne Gross	.10	.05	.01
□	238	Rick Langford	.10	.05	.01
□	239	Tony Armas	.25	.11	.03
□	240A	Bob Lacey P1 ERR	.50	.23	.06
		(Name misspelled Bob "Lacy")			
□	240B	Bob Lacey P2 COR	.10	.05	.01
□	241	Gene Tenace	.25	.11	.03
□	242	Bob Shirley	.10	.05	.01
□	243	Gary Lucas	.10	.05	.01
□	244	Jerry Turner	.10	.05	.01
□	245	John Wockenfuss	.10	.05	.01
□	246	Stan Papi	.10	.05	.01
□	247	Milt Wilcox	.10	.05	.01
□	248	Dan Schatzeder	.10	.05	.01
□	249	Steve Kemp	.10	.05	.01

□ 250 Jim Lentine	.10	.05	.01
□ 251 Pete Rose	1.50	.70	.19
□ 252 Bill Madlock	.25	.11	.03
□ 253 Dale Berra	.10	.05	.01
□ 254 Kent Tekulve	.25	.11	.03
□ 255 Enrique Romo	.10	.05	.01
□ 256 Mike Easler	.10	.05	.01
□ 257 Chuck Tanner MG	.25	.11	.03
□ 258 Art Howe	.10	.05	.01
□ 259 Alan Ashby	.10	.05	.01
□ 260 Nolan Ryan	5.00	2.20	.60
□ 261A Vern Ruhle P1 ERR	.50	.23	.06
(Photo on front			
actually Ken Forsch)			
□ 261B Vern Ruhle P2 COR	.25	.11	.03
□ 262 Bob Boone	.25	.11	.03
□ 263 Cesar Cedeno	.25	.11	.03
□ 264 Jeff Leonard	.25	.11	.03
□ 265 Pat Putnam	.10	.05	.01
□ 266 Jon Matlack	.10	.05	.01
□ 267 Dave Rajsich	.10	.05	.01
□ 268 Billy Sample	.10	.05	.01
□ 269 Damaso Garcia	.10	.05	.01
□ 270 Tom Buskey	.10	.05	.01
□ 271 Joey McLaughlin	.10	.05	.01
□ 272 Barry Bonnell	.10	.05	.01
□ 273 Tug McGraw	.25	.11	.03
□ 274 Mike Jorgensen	.10	.05	.01
□ 275 Pat Zachry	.10	.05	.01
□ 276 Neil Allen	.10	.05	.01
□ 277 Joel Youngblood	.10	.05	.01
□ 278 Greg Pryor	.10	.05	.01
□ 279 Britt Burns	.10	.05	.01
□ 280 Rich Dotson	.10	.05	.01
□ 281 Chet Lemon	.10	.05	.01
□ 282 Rusty Kuntz	.10	.05	.01
□ 283 Ted Cox	.10	.05	.01
□ 284 Sparky Lyle	.25	.11	.03
□ 285 Larry Cox	.10	.05	.01
□ 286 Floyd Bannister	.10	.05	.01
□ 287 Byron McLaughlin	.10	.05	.01
□ 288 Rodney Craig	.10	.05	.01
□ 289 Bobby Grich	.25	.11	.03
□ 290 Dickie Thon	.25	.11	.03
□ 291 Mark Clear	.10	.05	.01
□ 292 Dave Lemanczyk	.10	.05	.01
□ 293 Jason Thompson	.10	.05	.01
□ 294 Rick Miller	.10	.05	.01
□ 295 Lonnie Smith	.25	.11	.03
□ 296 Ron Cey	.25	.11	.03
□ 297 Steve Yeager	.10	.05	.01
□ 298 Bobby Castillo	.10	.05	.01
□ 299 Manny Mota	.25	.11	.03
□ 300 Jay Johnstone	.25	.11	.03
□ 301 Dan Driessen	.10	.05	.01
□ 302 Joe Nolan	.10	.05	.01
□ 303 Paul Householder	.10	.05	.01
□ 304 Harry Spilman	.10	.05	.01
□ 305 Cesar Geronimo	.10	.05	.01
□ 306A Gary Mathews P1 ERR	.50	.23	.06
(Name misspelled)			
□ 306B Gary Matthews P2	.25	.11	.03
COR			
□ 307 Ken Reitz	.10	.05	.01
□ 308 Ted Simmons	.25	.11	.03
□ 309 John Littlefield	.10	.05	.01
□ 310 George Frazier	.10	.05	.01
□ 311 Dane Iorg	.10	.05	.01
□ 312 Mike Ivie	.10	.05	.01
□ 313 Dennis Littlejohn	.10	.05	.01
□ 314 Gary Lavelle	.10	.05	.01
□ 315 Jack Clark	.25	.11	.03
□ 316 Jim Wohlford	.10	.05	.01
□ 317 Rick Matula	.10	.05	.01
□ 318 Toby Harrah	.25	.11	.03
□ 319A Dwane Kuiper P1 ERR	.25	.11	.03
(Name misspelled)			
□ 319B Duane Kuiper P2 COR	.10	.05	.01
□ 320 Len Barker	.10	.05	.01
□ 321 Victor Cruz	.10	.05	.01
□ 322 Dell Alston	.10	.05	.01
□ 323 Robin Yount	1.50	.70	.19
□ 324 Charlie Moore	.10	.05	.01
□ 325 Lary Sorensen	.10	.05	.01
□ 326A Gorman Thomas P1	.50	.23	.06
(2nd line on back:			
"30 HR mark 4th")			
□ 326B Gorman Thomas P2	.25	.11	.03
30 HR mark 3rd			
□ 327 Bob Rodgers MG	.10	.05	.01
□ 328 Phil Niekro	.50	.23	.06
□ 329 Chris Speier	.10	.05	.01
□ 330A Steve Rodgers P1	.25	.11	.03
ERR (Name misspelled)			
□ 330B Steve Rogers P2 COR	.10	.05	.01
□ 331 Woodie Fryman	.10	.05	.01
□ 332 Warren Cromartie	.10	.05	.01
□ 333 Jerry White	.10	.05	.01
□ 334 Tony Perez	.50	.23	.06
□ 335 Carlton Fisk	1.25	.55	.16
□ 336 Dick Drago	.10	.05	.01
□ 337 Steve Renko	.10	.05	.01
□ 338 Jim Rice	.50	.23	.06
□ 339 Jerry Royster	.10	.05	.01
□ 340 Frank White	.25	.11	.03
□ 341 Jamie Quirk	.10	.05	.01
□ 342A Paul Spittorff P1 ERR	.25	.11	.03
(Name misspelled)			
□ 342B Paul Splittorff	.10	.05	.01
P2 COR			
□ 343 Marty Pattin	.10	.05	.01
□ 344 Pete LaCock	.10	.05	.01
□ 345 Willie Randolph	.25	.11	.03
□ 346 Rick Cerone	.10	.05	.01
□ 347 Rich Gossage	.50	.23	.06
□ 348 Reggie Jackson	1.25	.55	.16
□ 349 Ruppert Jones	.10	.05	.01
□ 350 Dave McKay	.10	.05	.01
□ 351 Yogi Berra CO	.50	.23	.06
□ 352 Doug DeCinces	.25	.11	.03
□ 353 Jim Palmer	.60	.25	.07
□ 354 Tippy Martinez	.10	.05	.01
□ 355 Al Bumbry	.25	.11	.03
□ 356 Earl Weaver MG	.50	.23	.06
□ 357A Bob Picciolo P1 ERR	.25	.11	.03
(Name misspelled)			
□ 357B Rob Picciolo P2 COR	.10	.05	.01
□ 358 Matt Keough	.10	.05	.01
□ 359 Dwayne Murphy	.10	.05	.01
□ 360 Brian Kingman	.10	.05	.01
□ 361 Bill Fahey	.10	.05	.01
□ 362 Steve Mura	.10	.05	.01
□ 363 Dennis Kinney	.10	.05	.01
□ 364 Dave Winfield	1.50	.70	.19
□ 365 Lou Whitaker	1.00	.45	.12
□ 366 Lance Parrish	.50	.23	.06
□ 367 Tim Corcoran	.10	.05	.01
□ 368 Pat Underwood	.10	.05	.01
□ 369 Al Cowens	.10	.05	.01
□ 370 Sparky Anderson MG	.25	.11	.03
□ 371 Pete Rose	1.50	.70	.19
□ 372 Phil Garner	.25	.11	.03
□ 373 Steve Nicosia	.10	.05	.01
□ 374 John Candelaria	.25	.11	.03
□ 375 Don Robinson	.10	.05	.01
□ 376 Lee Lacy	.10	.05	.01
□ 377 John Milner	.10	.05	.01
□ 378 Craig Reynolds	.10	.05	.01
□ 379A Luis Pujols P1 ERR	.25	.11	.03
Name misspelled Pujois			
□ 379B Luis Pujols P2 COR	.10	.05	.01
□ 380 Joe Niekro	.25	.11	.03
□ 381 Joaquin Andujar	.25	.11	.03
□ 382 Keith Moreland	.25	.11	.03
□ 383 Jose Cruz	.25	.11	.03
□ 384 Bill Virdon MG	.10	.05	.01
□ 385 Jim Sundberg	.25	.11	.03
□ 386 Doc Medich	.10	.05	.01
□ 387 Al Oliver	.25	.11	.03
□ 388 Jim Norris	.10	.05	.01
□ 389 Bob Bailor	.10	.05	.01
□ 390 Ernie Whitt	.10	.05	.01
□ 391 Otto Velez	.10	.05	.01
□ 392 Roy Howell	.10	.05	.01
□ 393 Bob Walk	.25	.11	.03
□ 394 Doug Flynn	.10	.05	.01
□ 395 Pete Falcone	.10	.05	.01
□ 396 Tom Hausman	.10	.05	.01
□ 397 Elliott Maddox	.10	.05	.01
□ 398 Mike Squires	.10	.05	.01
□ 399 Marvis Foley	.10	.05	.01
□ 400 Steve Trout	.10	.05	.01

□ 401 Wayne Nordhagen	.10	.05	.01
□ 402 Tony LaRussa MG	.25	.11	.03
□ 403 Bruce Bochte	.10	.05	.01
□ 404 Bake McBride	.10	.05	.01
□ 405 Jerry Narron	.10	.05	.01
□ 406 Rob Dressler	.10	.05	.01
□ 407 Dave Heaverlo	.10	.05	.01
□ 408 Tom Paciorek	.10	.05	.01
□ 409 Carney Lansford	.25	.11	.03
□ 410 Brian Downing	.10	.05	.01
□ 411 Don Aase	.10	.05	.01
□ 412 Jim Barr	.10	.05	.01
□ 413 Don Baylor	.50	.23	.06
□ 414 Jim Fregosi MG	.10	.05	.01
□ 415 Dallas Green MG	.10	.05	.01
□ 416 Dave Lopes	.25	.11	.03
□ 417 Jerry Reuss	.25	.11	.03
□ 418 Rick Sutcliffe	.50	.23	.06
□ 419 Derrel Thomas	.10	.05	.01
□ 420 Tom Lasorda MG	.25	.11	.03
□ 421 Charlie Leibrandt	.50	.23	.06
□ 422 Tom Seaver	1.25	.55	.16
□ 423 Ron Oester	.10	.05	.01
□ 424 Junior Kennedy	.10	.05	.01
□ 425 Tom Seaver	1.25	.55	.16
□ 426 Bobby Cox MG	.25	.11	.03
□ 427 Leon Durham	.25	.11	.03
□ 428 Terry Kennedy	.10	.05	.01
□ 429 Silvio Martinez	.10	.05	.01
□ 430 George Hendrick	.10	.05	.01
□ 431 Red Schoendienst MG	.50	.23	.06
□ 432 Johnnie LeMaster	.10	.05	.01
□ 433 Vida Blue	.25	.11	.03
□ 434 John Montefusco	.10	.05	.01
□ 435 Terry Whitfield	.10	.05	.01
□ 436 Dave Bristol MG	.10	.05	.01
□ 437 Dale Murphy	.75	.35	.09
□ 438 Jerry Dybzinski	.10	.05	.01
□ 439 Jorge Orta	.10	.05	.01
□ 440 Wayne Garland	.10	.05	.01
□ 441 Miguel Dilone	.10	.05	.01
□ 442 Dave Garcia MG	.10	.05	.01
□ 443 Don Money	.10	.05	.01
□ 444A Buck Martinez P1 ERR (Reverse negative)	.25	.11	.03
□ 444B Buck Martinez P2 COR	.10	.05	.01
□ 445 Jerry Augustine	.10	.05	.01
□ 446 Ben Oglivie	.25	.11	.03
□ 447 Jim Slaton	.10	.05	.01
□ 448 Doyle Alexander	.10	.05	.01
□ 449 Tony Bernazard	.10	.05	.01
□ 450 Scott Sanderson	.10	.05	.01
□ 451 David Palmer	.10	.05	.01
□ 452 Stan Bahnsen	.10	.05	.01
□ 453 Dick Williams MG	.10	.05	.01
□ 454 Rick Burleson	.10	.05	.01
□ 455 Gary Allenson	.10	.05	.01
□ 456 Bob Stanley	.10	.05	.01
□ 457A John Tudor P1 ERR (Lifetime W-L "9.7")	.25	.11	.03
□ 457B John Tudor P2 COR (Corrected "9-7")	.25	.11	.03
□ 458 Dwight Evans	.50	.23	.06
□ 459 Glenn Hubbard	.10	.05	.01
□ 460 U.L. Washington	.10	.05	.01
□ 461 Larry Gura	.10	.05	.01
□ 462 Rich Gale	.10	.05	.01
□ 463 Hal McRae	.50	.23	.06
□ 464 Jim Frey MG	.10	.05	.01
□ 465 Bucky Dent	.25	.11	.03
□ 466 Dennis Werth	.10	.05	.01
□ 467 Ron Davis	.10	.05	.01
□ 468 Reggie Jackson UER (32 HR in 1970, should be 23)	1.25	.55	.16
□ 469 Bobby Brown	.10	.05	.01
□ 470 Mike Davis	.10	.05	.01
□ 471 Gaylord Perry	.50	.23	.06
□ 472 Mark Belanger	.25	.11	.03
□ 473 Jim Palmer	.60	.25	.07
□ 474 Sammy Stewart	.10	.05	.01
□ 475 Tim Stoddard	.10	.05	.01
□ 476 Steve Stone	.25	.11	.03
□ 477 Jeff Newman	.10	.05	.01
□ 478 Steve McCatty	.10	.05	.01
□ 479 Billy Martin MG	.50	.23	.06
□ 480 Mitchell Page	.10	.05	.01
□ 481 Steve Carlton CY	1.00	.45	.12
□ 482 Bill Buckner	.25	.11	.03
□ 483A Ivan DeJesus P1 ERR (Lifetime hits "702")	.25	.11	.03
□ 483B Ivan DeJesus P2 COR (Lifetime hits "642")	.10	.05	.01
□ 484 Cliff Johnson	.10	.05	.01
□ 485 Lenny Randle	.10	.05	.01
□ 486 Larry Milbourne	.10	.05	.01
□ 487 Roy Smalley	.10	.05	.01
□ 488 John Castino	.10	.05	.01
□ 489 Ron Jackson	.10	.05	.01
□ 490A Dave Roberts P1 (Career Highlights: "Showed pop in")	.25	.11	.03
□ 490B Dave Roberts P2 ("Declared himself")	.10	.05	.01
□ 491 George Brett MVP	2.50	1.10	.30
□ 492 Mike Cubbage	.10	.05	.01
□ 493 Rob Wilfong	.10	.05	.01
□ 494 Danny Goodwin	.10	.05	.01
□ 495 Jose Morales	.10	.05	.01
□ 496 Mickey Rivers	.25	.11	.03
□ 497 Mike Edwards	.10	.05	.01
□ 498 Mike Sadek	.10	.05	.01
□ 499 Lenn Sakata	.10	.05	.01
□ 500 Gene Michael MG	.10	.05	.01
□ 501 Dave Roberts	.10	.05	.01
□ 502 Steve Dillard	.10	.05	.01
□ 503 Jim Essian	.10	.05	.01
□ 504 Rance Mulliniks	.10	.05	.01
□ 505 Darrell Porter	.10	.05	.01
□ 506 Joe Torre MG	.25	.11	.03
□ 507 Terry Crowley	.10	.05	.01
□ 508 Bill Travers	.10	.05	.01
□ 509 Nelson Norman	.10	.05	.01
□ 510 Bob McClure	.10	.05	.01
□ 511 Steve Howe	.25	.11	.03
□ 512 Dave Rader	.10	.05	.01
□ 513 Mick Kelleher	.10	.05	.01
□ 514 Kiko Garcia	.10	.05	.01
□ 515 Larry Biittner	.10	.05	.01
□ 516A Willie Norwood P1 (Career Highlights "Spent most of")	.25	.11	.03
□ 516B Willie Norwood P2 ("Traded to Seattle")	.10	.05	.01
□ 517 Bo Diaz	.10	.05	.01
□ 518 Juan Beniquez	.10	.05	.01
□ 519 Scot Thompson	.10	.05	.01
□ 520 Jim Tracy	.10	.05	.01
□ 521 Carlos Lezcano	.10	.05	.01
□ 522 Joe Amalfitano MG	.10	.05	.01
□ 523 Preston Hanna	.10	.05	.01
□ 524A Ray Burris P1 (Career Highlights: "Went on ...")	.25	.11	.03
□ 524B Ray Burris P2 ("Drafted by ...")	.10	.05	.01
□ 525 Broderick Perkins	.10	.05	.01
□ 526 Mickey Hatcher	.25	.11	.03
□ 527 John Goryl MG	.10	.05	.01
□ 528 Dick Davis	.10	.05	.01
□ 529 Butch Wynegar	.10	.05	.01
□ 530 Sal Butera	.10	.05	.01
□ 531 Jerry Koosman	.25	.11	.03
□ 532A Geoff Zahn P1 (Career Highlights: "Was 2nd in")	.25	.11	.03
□ 532B Geoff Zahn P2 ("Signed a 3 year")	.10	.05	.01
□ 533 Dennis Martinez	.25	.11	.03
□ 534 Gary Thomasson	.10	.05	.01
□ 535 Steve Macko	.10	.05	.01
□ 536 Jim Kaat	.50	.23	.06
□ 537 Best Hitters (George Brett, Rod Carew)	2.50	1.10	.30
□ 538 Tim Raines	4.00	1.80	.50
□ 539 Keith Smith	.10	.05	.01
□ 540 Ken Macha	.10	.05	.01
□ 541 Burt Hooton	.10	.05	.01
□ 542 Butch Hobson	.10	.05	.01
□ 543 Bill Stein	.10	.05	.01

□ 544 Dave Stapleton	.10	.05	.01
□ 545 Bob Pate	.10	.05	.01
□ 546 Doug Corbett	.10	.05	.01
□ 547 Darrell Jackson	.10	.05	.01
□ 548 Pete Redfern	.10	.05	.01
□ 549 Roger Erickson	.10	.05	.01
□ 550 Al Hrabosky	.10	.05	.01
□ 551 Dick Tidrow	.10	.05	.01
□ 552 Dave Ford	.10	.05	.01
□ 553 Dave Kingman	.25	.11	.03
□ 554A Mike Vail P1 (Career Highlights: "After two ...")	.25	.11	.03
□ 554B Mike Vail P2 ("Traded to ...")	.10	.05	.01
□ 555A Jerry Martin P1 (Career Highlights: "Overcame a ...")	.25	.11	.03
□ 555B Jerry Martin P2 ("Traded to ...")	.10	.05	.01
□ 556A Jesus Figueroa P1 (Career Highlights: "Had an ...")	.25	.11	.03
□ 556B Jesus Figueroa P2 ("Traded to ...")	.10	.05	.01
□ 557 Don Stanhouse	.10	.05	.01
□ 558 Barry Foote	.10	.05	.01
□ 559 Tim Blackwell	.10	.05	.01
□ 560 Bruce Sutter	.25	.11	.03
□ 561 Rick Reuschel	.25	.11	.03
□ 562 Lynn McGlothen	.10	.05	.01
□ 563A Bob Owchinko P1 (Career Highlights: "Traded to ...")	.25	.11	.03
□ 563B Bob Owchinko P2 ("Involved in a ...")	.10	.05	.01
□ 564 John Verhoeven	.10	.05	.01
□ 565 Ken Landreaux	.10	.05	.01
□ 566A Glen Adams P1 ERR (Name misspelled)	.25	.11	.03
□ 566B Glenn Adams P2 COR	.10	.05	.01
□ 567 Hosken Powell	.10	.05	.01
□ 568 Dick Noles	.10	.05	.01
□ 569 Danny Ainge	3.00	1.35	.35
□ 570 Bobby Mattick MG	.10	.05	.01
□ 571 Joe Lefebvre	.10	.05	.01
□ 572 Bobby Clark	.10	.05	.01
□ 573 Dennis Lamp	.10	.05	.01
□ 574 Randy Lerch	.10	.05	.01
□ 575 Mookie Wilson	.50	.23	.06
□ 576 Ron LeFlore	.25	.11	.03
□ 577 Jim Dwyer	.10	.05	.01
□ 578 Bill Castro	.10	.05	.01
□ 579 Greg Minton	.10	.05	.01
□ 580 Mark Littell	.10	.05	.01
□ 581 Andy Hassler	.10	.05	.01
□ 582 Dave Stieb	.25	.11	.03
□ 583 Ken Oberkfell	.10	.05	.01
□ 584 Larry Bradford	.10	.05	.01
□ 585 Fred Stanley	.10	.05	.01
□ 586 Bill Caudill	.10	.05	.01
□ 587 Doug Capilla	.10	.05	.01
□ 588 George Riley	.10	.05	.01
□ 589 Willie Hernandez	.25	.11	.03
□ 590 Mike Schmidt MVP	1.50	.70	.19
□ 591 Steve Stone CY	.10	.05	.01
□ 592 Rick Sofield	.10	.05	.01
□ 593 Bombo Rivera	.10	.05	.01
□ 594 Gary Ward	.10	.05	.01
□ 595A Dave Edwards P1 (Career Highlights: "Sidelined the")	.25	.11	.03
□ 595B Dave Edwards P2 ("Traded to ...")	.10	.05	.01
□ 596 Mike Proly	.10	.05	.01
□ 597 Tommy Boggs	.10	.05	.01
□ 598 Greg Gross	.10	.05	.01
□ 599 Elias Sosa	.10	.05	.01
□ 600 Pat Kelly	.10	.05	.01
□ 601A Checklist 1-120 P1 ERR Unnumbered (51 Donahue)	.25	.11	.03
□ 601B Checklist 1-120 P2 COR Unnumbered (51 Donohue)	.50	.23	.06
□ 602 Checklist 121-240 Unnumbered	.25	.11	.03
□ 603A Checklist 241-360 P1 ERR Unnumbered (306 Mathews)	.25	.11	.03
□ 603B Checklist 241-360 P2 COR Unnumbered (306 Matthews)	.25	.11	.03
□ 604A Checklist 361-480 P1 ERR Unnumbered (379 Pujois)	.25	.11	.03
□ 604B Checklist 361-480 P2 COR Unnumbered (379 Pujols)	.25	.11	.03
□ 605A Checklist 481-600 P1 ERR Unnumbered (566 Glen Adams)	.25	.11	.03
□ 605B Checklist 481-600 P2 COR Unnumbered (566 Glenn Adams)	.25	.11	.03

1982 Donruss

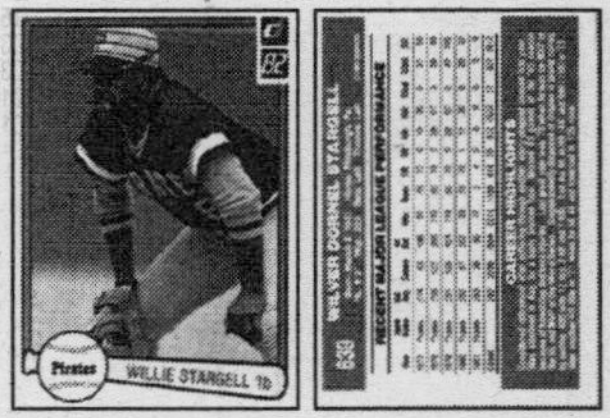

The 1982 Donruss set contains 653 numbered standard-size cards and seven unnumbered checklists. The first 26 cards of this set are entitled Diamond Kings (DK) and feature the artwork of Dick Perez of Perez-Steele Galleries. The set was marketed with puzzle pieces in 15-card packs rather than with bubble gum. There are 63 pieces to the puzzle, which, when put together, make a collage of Babe Ruth entitled "Hall of Fame Diamond King." The card stock in this year's Donruss cards is considerably thicker than the 1981 cards. The seven unnumbered checklist cards are arbitrarily assigned numbers 654 through 660 and are listed at the end of the list below. Notable Rookie Cards in this set include Brett Butler, Cal Ripken Jr., Lee Smith and Dave Stewart.

	MINT	NRMT	EXC
COMPLETE SET (660)	70.00	32.00	8.75
COMPLETE FACT.SET (660)	80.00	36.00	10.00
COMMON CARD (1-660)	.10	.05	.01
SEMISTARS	.20	.09	.03
STARS	.40	.18	.05
□ 1 Pete Rose DK	2.00	.90	.25
□ 2 Gary Carter DK	.40	.18	.05
□ 3 Steve Garvey DK	.40	.18	.05
□ 4 Vida Blue DK	.20	.09	.03
□ 5 Alan Trammell DK COR	.50	.23	.06
□ 5A Alan Trammel DK ERR (Name misspelled)	.50	.23	.06
□ 6 Len Barker DK	.20	.09	.03
□ 7 Dwight Evans DK	.40	.18	.05
□ 8 Rod Carew DK	.60	.25	.07
□ 9 George Hendrick DK	.20	.09	.03
□ 10 Phil Niekro DK	.40	.18	.05
□ 11 Richie Zisk DK	.20	.09	.03
□ 12 Dave Parker DK	.40	.18	.05
□ 13 Nolan Ryan DK	4.00	1.80	.50
□ 14 Ivan DeJesus DK	.20	.09	.03
□ 15 George Brett DK	2.00	.90	.25
□ 16 Tom Seaver DK	.75	.35	.09
□ 17 Dave Kingman DK	.20	.09	.03
□ 18 Dave Winfield DK	1.50	.70	.19
□ 19 Mike Norris DK	.20	.09	.03

□	20 Carlton Fisk DK	.40	.18	.05
□	21 Ozzie Smith DK	2.00	.90	.25
□	22 Roy Smalley DK	.20	.09	.03
□	23 Buddy Bell DK	.20	.09	.03
□	24 Ken Singleton DK	.20	.09	.03
□	25 John Mayberry DK	.20	.09	.03
□	26 Gorman Thomas DK	.20	.09	.03
□	27 Earl Weaver MG	.40	.18	.05
□	28 Rollie Fingers	.40	.18	.05
□	29 Sparky Anderson MG	.20	.09	.03
□	30 Dennis Eckersley	.40	.18	.05
□	31 Dave Winfield	1.50	.70	.19
□	32 Burt Hooton	.10	.05	.01
□	33 Rick Waits	.10	.05	.01
□	34 George Brett	3.50	1.55	.45
□	35 Steve McCatty	.10	.05	.01
□	36 Steve Rogers	.10	.05	.01
□	37 Bill Stein	.10	.05	.01
□	38 Steve Renko	.10	.05	.01
□	39 Mike Squires	.10	.05	.01
□	40 George Hendrick	.10	.05	.01
□	41 Bob Knepper	.10	.05	.01
□	42 Steve Carlton	.75	.35	.09
□	43 Larry Biittner	.10	.05	.01
□	44 Chris Welsh	.10	.05	.01
□	45 Steve Nicosia	.10	.05	.01
□	46 Jack Clark	.20	.09	.03
□	47 Chris Chambliss	.20	.09	.03
□	48 Ivan DeJesus	.10	.05	.01
□	49 Lee Mazzilli	.10	.05	.01
□	50 Julio Cruz	.10	.05	.01
□	51 Pete Redfern	.10	.05	.01
□	52 Dave Stieb	.20	.09	.03
□	53 Doug Corbett	.10	.05	.01
□	54 Jorge Bell	.75	.35	.09
□	55 Joe Simpson	.10	.05	.01
□	56 Rusty Staub	.20	.09	.03
□	57 Hector Cruz	.10	.05	.01
□	58 Claudell Washington	.10	.05	.01
□	59 Enrique Romo	.10	.05	.01
□	60 Gary Lavelle	.10	.05	.01
□	61 Tim Flannery	.10	.05	.01
□	62 Joe Nolan	.10	.05	.01
□	63 Larry Bowa	.20	.09	.03
□	64 Sixto Lezcano	.10	.05	.01
□	65 Joe Sambito	.10	.05	.01
□	66 Bruce Kison	.10	.05	.01
□	67 Wayne Nordhagen	.10	.05	.01
□	68 Woodie Fryman	.10	.05	.01
□	69 Billy Sample	.10	.05	.01
□	70 Amos Otis	.20	.09	.03
□	71 Matt Keough	.10	.05	.01
□	72 Toby Harrah	.20	.09	.03
□	73 Dave Righetti	.40	.18	.05
□	74 Carl Yastrzemski	.75	.35	.09
□	75 Bob Welch	.20	.09	.03
□	76 Alan Trammell COR	1.00	.45	.12
□	76A Alan Trammel ERR (Name misspelled)	1.00	.45	.12
□	77 Rick Dempsey	.20	.09	.03
□	78 Paul Molitor	1.25	.55	.16
□	79 Dennis Martinez	.20	.09	.03
□	80 Jim Slaton	.10	.05	.01
□	81 Champ Summers	.10	.05	.01
□	82 Carney Lansford	.20	.09	.03
□	83 Barry Foote	.10	.05	.01
□	84 Steve Garvey	.40	.18	.05
□	85 Rick Manning	.10	.05	.01
□	86 John Wathan	.10	.05	.01
□	87 Brian Kingman	.10	.05	.01
□	88 Andre Dawson UER (Middle name Fernando, should be Nolan)	1.00	.45	.12
□	89 Jim Kern	.10	.05	.01
□	90 Bobby Grich	.20	.09	.03
□	91 Bob Forsch	.10	.05	.01
□	92 Art Howe	.10	.05	.01
□	93 Marty Bystrom	.10	.05	.01
□	94 Ozzie Smith	3.00	1.35	.35
□	95 Dave Parker	.40	.18	.05
□	96 Doyle Alexander	.10	.05	.01
□	97 Al Hrabosky	.10	.05	.01
□	98 Frank Taveras	.10	.05	.01
□	99 Tim Blackwell	.10	.05	.01
□	100 Floyd Bannister	.10	.05	.01
□	101 Alfredo Griffin	.10	.05	.01
□	102 Dave Engle	.10	.05	.01
□	103 Mario Soto	.10	.05	.01
□	104 Ross Baumgarten	.10	.05	.01
□	105 Ken Singleton	.20	.09	.03
□	106 Ted Simmons	.20	.09	.03
□	107 Jack Morris	.40	.18	.05
□	108 Bob Watson	.20	.09	.03
□	109 Dwight Evans	.40	.18	.05
□	110 Tom Lasorda MG	.20	.09	.03
□	111 Bert Blyleven	.40	.18	.05
□	112 Dan Quisenberry	.20	.09	.03
□	113 Rickey Henderson	2.50	1.10	.30
□	114 Gary Carter	.40	.18	.05
□	115 Brian Downing	.10	.05	.01
□	116 Al Oliver	.20	.09	.03
□	117 LaMarr Hoyt	.10	.05	.01
□	118 Cesar Cedeno	.20	.09	.03
□	119 Keith Moreland	.10	.05	.01
□	120 Bob Shirley	.10	.05	.01
□	121 Terry Kennedy	.10	.05	.01
□	122 Frank Pastore	.10	.05	.01
□	123 Gene Garber	.10	.05	.01
□	124 Tony Pena	.20	.09	.03
□	125 Allen Ripley	.10	.05	.01
□	126 Randy Martz	.10	.05	.01
□	127 Richie Zisk	.10	.05	.01
□	128 Mike Scott	.20	.09	.03
□	129 Lloyd Moseby	.10	.05	.01
□	130 Rob Wilfong	.10	.05	.01
□	131 Tim Stoddard	.10	.05	.01
□	132 Gorman Thomas	.20	.09	.03
□	133 Dan Petry	.10	.05	.01
□	134 Bob Stanley	.10	.05	.01
□	135 Lou Piniella	.20	.09	.03
□	136 Pedro Guerrero	.20	.09	.03
□	137 Len Barker	.10	.05	.01
□	138 Rich Gale	.10	.05	.01
□	139 Wayne Gross	.10	.05	.01
□	140 Tim Wallach	.50	.23	.06
□	141 Gene Mauch MG	.10	.05	.01
□	142 Doc Medich	.10	.05	.01
□	143 Tony Bernazard	.10	.05	.01
□	144 Bill Virdon MG	.10	.05	.01
□	145 John Littlefield	.10	.05	.01
□	146 Dave Bergman	.10	.05	.01
□	147 Dick Davis	.10	.05	.01
□	148 Tom Seaver	.75	.35	.09
□	149 Matt Sinatro	.10	.05	.01
□	150 Chuck Tanner MG	.10	.05	.01
□	151 Leon Durham	.20	.09	.03
□	152 Gene Tenace	.20	.09	.03
□	153 Al Bumbry	.20	.09	.03
□	154 Mark Brouhard	.10	.05	.01
□	155 Rick Peters	.10	.05	.01
□	156 Jerry Remy	.10	.05	.01
□	157 Rick Reuschel	.20	.09	.03
□	158 Steve Howe	.10	.05	.01
□	159 Alan Bannister	.10	.05	.01
□	160 U.L. Washington	.10	.05	.01
□	161 Rick Langford	.10	.05	.01
□	162 Bill Gullickson	.10	.05	.01
□	163 Mark Wagner	.10	.05	.01
□	164 Geoff Zahn	.10	.05	.01
□	165 Ron LeFlore	.20	.09	.03
□	166 Dane Iorg	.10	.05	.01
□	167 Joe Niekro	.20	.09	.03
□	168 Pete Rose	1.50	.70	.19
□	169 Dave Collins	.10	.05	.01
□	170 Rick Wise	.10	.05	.01
□	171 Jim Bibby	.10	.05	.01
□	172 Larry Herndon	.10	.05	.01
□	173 Bob Horner	.20	.09	.03
□	174 Steve Dillard	.10	.05	.01
□	175 Mookie Wilson	.20	.09	.03
□	176 Dan Meyer	.10	.05	.01
□	177 Fernando Arroyo	.10	.05	.01
□	178 Jackson Todd	.10	.05	.01
□	179 Darrell Jackson	.10	.05	.01
□	180 Alvis Woods	.10	.05	.01
□	181 Jim Anderson	.10	.05	.01
□	182 Dave Kingman	.20	.09	.03
□	183 Steve Henderson	.10	.05	.01
□	184 Brian Asselstine	.10	.05	.01
□	185 Rod Scurry	.10	.05	.01
□	186 Fred Breining	.10	.05	.01
□	187 Danny Boone	.10	.05	.01

□ 188	Junior Kennedy	.10	.05	.01
□ 189	Sparky Lyle	.20	.09	.03
□ 190	Whitey Herzog MG	.20	.09	.03
□ 191	Dave Smith	.10	.05	.01
□ 192	Ed Ott	.10	.05	.01
□ 193	Greg Luzinski	.20	.09	.03
□ 194	Bill Lee	.20	.09	.03
□ 195	Don Zimmer MG	.10	.05	.01
□ 196	Hal McRae	.20	.09	.03
□ 197	Mike Norris	.10	.05	.01
□ 198	Duane Kuiper	.10	.05	.01
□ 199	Rick Cerone	.10	.05	.01
□ 200	Jim Rice	.40	.18	.05
□ 201	Steve Yeager	.10	.05	.01
□ 202	Tom Brookens	.10	.05	.01
□ 203	Jose Morales	.10	.05	.01
□ 204	Roy Howell	.10	.05	.01
□ 205	Tippy Martinez	.10	.05	.01
□ 206	Moose Haas	.10	.05	.01
□ 207	Al Cowens	.10	.05	.01
□ 208	Dave Stapleton	.10	.05	.01
□ 209	Bucky Dent	.20	.09	.03
□ 210	Ron Cey	.20	.09	.03
□ 211	Jorge Orta	.10	.05	.01
□ 212	Jamie Quirk	.10	.05	.01
□ 213	Jeff Jones	.10	.05	.01
□ 214	Tim Raines	1.50	.70	.19
□ 215	Jon Matlack	.10	.05	.01
□ 216	Rod Carew	.75	.35	.09
□ 217	Jim Kaat	.20	.09	.03
□ 218	Joe Pittman	.10	.05	.01
□ 219	Larry Christenson	.10	.05	.01
□ 220	Juan Bonilla	.10	.05	.01
□ 221	Mike Easler	.10	.05	.01
□ 222	Vida Blue	.20	.09	.03
□ 223	Rick Camp	.10	.05	.01
□ 224	Mike Jorgensen	.10	.05	.01
□ 225	Jody Davis	.10	.05	.01
□ 226	Mike Parrott	.10	.05	.01
□ 227	Jim Clancy	.10	.05	.01
□ 228	Hosken Powell	.10	.05	.01
□ 229	Tom Hume	.10	.05	.01
□ 230	Britt Burns	.10	.05	.01
□ 231	Jim Palmer	.60	.25	.07
□ 232	Bob Rodgers MG	.10	.05	.01
□ 233	Milt Wilcox	.10	.05	.01
□ 234	Dave Revering	.10	.05	.01
□ 235	Mike Torrez	.10	.05	.01
□ 236	Robert Castillo	.10	.05	.01
□ 237	Von Hayes	.20	.09	.03
□ 238	Renie Martin	.10	.05	.01
□ 239	Dwayne Murphy	.10	.05	.01
□ 240	Rodney Scott	.10	.05	.01
□ 241	Fred Patek	.10	.05	.01
□ 242	Mickey Rivers	.10	.05	.01
□ 243	Steve Trout	.10	.05	.01
□ 244	Jose Cruz	.20	.09	.03
□ 245	Manny Trillo	.10	.05	.01
□ 246	Lary Sorensen	.10	.05	.01
□ 247	Dave Edwards	.10	.05	.01
□ 248	Dan Driessen	.10	.05	.01
□ 249	Tommy Boggs	.10	.05	.01
□ 250	Dale Berra	.10	.05	.01
□ 251	Ed Whitson	.10	.05	.01
□ 252	Lee Smith	6.00	2.70	.75
□ 253	Tom Paciorek	.10	.05	.01
□ 254	Pat Zachry	.10	.05	.01
□ 255	Luis Leal	.10	.05	.01
□ 256	John Castino	.10	.05	.01
□ 257	Rich Dauer	.10	.05	.01
□ 258	Cecil Cooper	.20	.09	.03
□ 259	Dave Rozema	.10	.05	.01
□ 260	John Tudor	.20	.09	.03
□ 261	Jerry Mumphrey	.10	.05	.01
□ 262	Jay Johnstone	.20	.09	.03
□ 263	Bo Diaz	.10	.05	.01
□ 264	Dennis Leonard	.10	.05	.01
□ 265	Jim Spencer	.10	.05	.01
□ 266	John Milner	.10	.05	.01
□ 267	Don Aase	.10	.05	.01
□ 268	Jim Sundberg	.20	.09	.03
□ 269	Lamar Johnson	.10	.05	.01
□ 270	Frank LaCorte	.10	.05	.01
□ 271	Barry Evans	.10	.05	.01
□ 272	Enos Cabell	.10	.05	.01
□ 273	Del Unser	.10	.05	.01
□ 274	George Foster	.20	.09	.03
□ 275	Brett Butler	2.00	.90	.25
□ 276	Lee Lacy	.10	.05	.01
□ 277	Ken Reitz	.10	.05	.01
□ 278	Keith Hernandez	.40	.18	.05
□ 279	Doug DeCinces	.20	.09	.03
□ 280	Charlie Moore	.10	.05	.01
□ 281	Lance Parrish	.40	.18	.05
□ 282	Ralph Houk MG	.20	.09	.03
□ 283	Rich Gossage	.40	.18	.05
□ 284	Jerry Reuss	.20	.09	.03
□ 285	Mike Stanton	.10	.05	.01
□ 286	Frank White	.20	.09	.03
□ 287	Bob Owchinko	.10	.05	.01
□ 288	Scott Sanderson	.10	.05	.01
□ 289	Bump Wills	.10	.05	.01
□ 290	Dave Frost	.10	.05	.01
□ 291	Chet Lemon	.10	.05	.01
□ 292	Tito Landrum	.10	.05	.01
□ 293	Vern Ruhle	.10	.05	.01
□ 294	Mike Schmidt	2.00	.90	.25
□ 295	Sam Mejias	.10	.05	.01
□ 296	Gary Lucas	.10	.05	.01
□ 297	John Candelaria	.10	.05	.01
□ 298	Jerry Martin	.10	.05	.01
□ 299	Dale Murphy	.40	.18	.05
□ 300	Mike Lum	.10	.05	.01
□ 301	Tom Hausman	.10	.05	.01
□ 302	Glenn Abbott	.10	.05	.01
□ 303	Roger Erickson	.10	.05	.01
□ 304	Otto Velez	.10	.05	.01
□ 305	Danny Goodwin	.10	.05	.01
□ 306	John Mayberry	.10	.05	.01
□ 307	Lenny Randle	.10	.05	.01
□ 308	Bob Bailor	.10	.05	.01
□ 309	Jerry Morales	.10	.05	.01
□ 310	Rufino Linares	.10	.05	.01
□ 311	Kent Tekulve	.20	.09	.03
□ 312	Joe Morgan	.60	.25	.07
□ 313	John Urrea	.10	.05	.01
□ 314	Paul Householder	.10	.05	.01
□ 315	Garry Maddox	.10	.05	.01
□ 316	Mike Ramsey	.10	.05	.01
□ 317	Alan Ashby	.10	.05	.01
□ 318	Bob Clark	.10	.05	.01
□ 319	Tony LaRussa MG	.20	.09	.03
□ 320	Charlie Lea	.10	.05	.01
□ 321	Danny Darwin	.10	.05	.01
□ 322	Cesar Geronimo	.10	.05	.01
□ 323	Tom Underwood	.10	.05	.01
□ 324	Andre Thornton	.10	.05	.01
□ 325	Rudy May	.10	.05	.01
□ 326	Frank Tanana	.20	.09	.03
□ 327	Dave Lopes	.20	.09	.03
□ 328	Richie Hebner	.20	.09	.03
□ 329	Mike Flanagan	.20	.09	.03
□ 330	Mike Caldwell	.10	.05	.01
□ 331	Scott McGregor	.10	.05	.01
□ 332	Jerry Augustine	.10	.05	.01
□ 333	Stan Papi	.10	.05	.01
□ 334	Rick Miller	.10	.05	.01
□ 335	Graig Nettles	.20	.09	.03
□ 336	Dusty Baker	.40	.18	.05
□ 337	Dave Garcia MG	.10	.05	.01
□ 338	Larry Gura	.10	.05	.01
□ 339	Cliff Johnson	.10	.05	.01
□ 340	Warren Cromartie	.10	.05	.01
□ 341	Steve Comer	.10	.05	.01
□ 342	Rick Burleson	.10	.05	.01
□ 343	John Martin	.10	.05	.01
□ 344	Craig Reynolds	.10	.05	.01
□ 345	Mike Proly	.10	.05	.01
□ 346	Ruppert Jones	.10	.05	.01
□ 347	Omar Moreno	.10	.05	.01
□ 348	Greg Minton	.10	.05	.01
□ 349	Rick Mahler	.10	.05	.01
□ 350	Alex Trevino	.10	.05	.01
□ 351	Mike Krukow	.10	.05	.01
□ 352A	Shane Rawley ERR (Photo actually Jim Anderson)	.40	.18	.05
□ 352B	Shane Rawley COR	.10	.05	.01
□ 353	Garth Iorg	.10	.05	.01
□ 354	Pete Mackanin	.10	.05	.01
□ 355	Paul Moskau	.10	.05	.01
□ 356	Richard Dotson	.10	.05	.01

□	357 Steve Stone	.20	.09	.03
□	358 Larry Hisle	.10	.05	.01
□	359 Aurelio Lopez	.10	.05	.01
□	360 Oscar Gamble	.10	.05	.01
□	361 Tom Burgmeier	.10	.05	.01
□	362 Terry Forster	.10	.05	.01
□	363 Joe Charboneau	.10	.05	.01
□	364 Ken Brett	.10	.05	.01
□	365 Tony Armas	.10	.05	.01
□	366 Chris Speier	.10	.05	.01
□	367 Fred Lynn	.20	.09	.03
□	368 Buddy Bell	.20	.09	.03
□	369 Jim Essian	.10	.05	.01
□	370 Terry Puhl	.10	.05	.01
□	371 Greg Gross	.10	.05	.01
□	372 Bruce Sutter	.20	.09	.03
□	373 Joe Lefebvre	.10	.05	.01
□	374 Ray Knight	.20	.09	.03
□	375 Bruce Benedict	.10	.05	.01
□	376 Tim Foli	.10	.05	.01
□	377 Al Holland	.10	.05	.01
□	378 Ken Kravec	.10	.05	.01
□	379 Jeff Burroughs	.10	.05	.01
□	380 Pete Falcone	.10	.05	.01
□	381 Ernie Whitt	.10	.05	.01
□	382 Brad Havens	.10	.05	.01
□	383 Terry Crowley	.10	.05	.01
□	384 Don Money	.10	.05	.01
□	385 Dan Schatzeder	.10	.05	.01
□	386 Gary Allenson	.10	.05	.01
□	387 Yogi Berra CO	.50	.23	.06
□	388 Ken Landreaux	.10	.05	.01
□	389 Mike Hargrove	.20	.09	.03
□	390 Darryl Motley	.10	.05	.01
□	391 Dave McKay	.10	.05	.01
□	392 Stan Bahnsen	.10	.05	.01
□	393 Ken Forsch	.10	.05	.01
□	394 Mario Mendoza	.10	.05	.01
□	395 Jim Morrison	.10	.05	.01
□	396 Mike Ivie	.10	.05	.01
□	397 Broderick Perkins	.10	.05	.01
□	398 Darrell Evans	.20	.09	.03
□	399 Ron Reed	.10	.05	.01
□	400 Johnny Bench	.75	.35	.09
□	401 Steve Bedrosian	.20	.09	.03
□	402 Bill Robinson	.10	.05	.01
□	403 Bill Buckner	.20	.09	.03
□	404 Ken Oberkfell	.10	.05	.01
□	405 Cal Ripken	50.00	22.00	6.25
□	406 Jim Gantner	.20	.09	.03
□	407 Kirk Gibson	.75	.35	.09
□	408 Tony Perez	.40	.18	.05
□	409 Tommy John UER (Text says 52-56 as Yankee, should be 52-26)	.40	.18	.05
□	410 Dave Stewart	1.50	.70	.19
□	411 Dan Spillner	.10	.05	.01
□	412 Willie Aikens	.10	.05	.01
□	413 Mike Heath	.10	.05	.01
□	414 Ray Burris	.10	.05	.01
□	415 Leon Roberts	.10	.05	.01
□	416 Mike Witt	.20	.09	.03
□	417 Bob Molinaro	.10	.05	.01
□	418 Steve Braun	.10	.05	.01
□	419 Nolan Ryan UER (Nisnumbering of Nolan's no-hitters on card back)	5.00	2.20	.60
□	420 Tug McGraw	.20	.09	.03
□	421 Dave Concepcion	.20	.09	.03
□	422A Juan Eichelberger ERR (Photo actually Gary Lucas)	.40	.18	.05
□	422B Juan Eichelberger COR	.10	.05	.01
□	423 Rick Rhoden	.10	.05	.01
□	424 Frank Robinson MG	.40	.18	.05
□	425 Eddie Miller	.10	.05	.01
□	426 Bill Caudill	.10	.05	.01
□	427 Doug Flynn	.10	.05	.01
□	428 Larry Andersen UER (Misspelled Anderson on card front)	.10	.05	.01
□	429 Al Williams	.10	.05	.01
□	430 Jerry Garvin	.10	.05	.01
□	431 Glenn Adams	.10	.05	.01
□	432 Barry Bonnell	.10	.05	.01
□	433 Jerry Narron	.10	.05	.01
□	434 John Stearns	.10	.05	.01
□	435 Mike Tyson	.10	.05	.01
□	436 Glenn Hubbard	.10	.05	.01
□	437 Eddie Solomon	.10	.05	.01
□	438 Jeff Leonard	.10	.05	.01
□	439 Randy Bass	.20	.09	.03
□	440 Mike LaCoss	.10	.05	.01
□	441 Gary Matthews	.20	.09	.03
□	442 Mark Littell	.10	.05	.01
□	443 Don Sutton	.40	.18	.05
□	444 John Harris	.10	.05	.01
□	445 Vada Pinson CO	.20	.09	.03
□	446 Elias Sosa	.10	.05	.01
□	447 Charlie Hough	.20	.09	.03
□	448 Willie Wilson	.20	.09	.03
□	449 Fred Stanley	.10	.05	.01
□	450 Tom Veryzer	.10	.05	.01
□	451 Ron Davis	.10	.05	.01
□	452 Mark Clear	.10	.05	.01
□	453 Bill Russell	.20	.09	.03
□	454 Lou Whitaker	.40	.18	.05
□	455 Dan Graham	.10	.05	.01
□	456 Reggie Cleveland	.10	.05	.01
□	457 Sammy Stewart	.10	.05	.01
□	458 Pete Vuckovich	.10	.05	.01
□	459 John Wockenfuss	.10	.05	.01
□	460 Glenn Hoffman	.10	.05	.01
□	461 Willie Randolph	.20	.09	.03
□	462 Fernando Valenzuela	.40	.18	.05
□	463 Ron Hassey	.10	.05	.01
□	464 Paul Splittorff	.10	.05	.01
□	465 Rob Picciolo	.10	.05	.01
□	466 Larry Parrish	.10	.05	.01
□	467 Johnny Grubb	.10	.05	.01
□	468 Dan Ford	.10	.05	.01
□	469 Silvio Martinez	.10	.05	.01
□	470 Kiko Garcia	.10	.05	.01
□	471 Bob Boone	.20	.09	.03
□	472 Luis Salazar	.10	.05	.01
□	473 Randy Niemann	.10	.05	.01
□	474 Tom Griffin	.10	.05	.01
□	475 Phil Niekro	.40	.18	.05
□	476 Hubie Brooks	.20	.09	.03
□	477 Dick Tidrow	.10	.05	.01
□	478 Jim Beattie	.10	.05	.01
□	479 Damaso Garcia	.10	.05	.01
□	480 Mickey Hatcher	.10	.05	.01
□	481 Joe Price	.10	.05	.01
□	482 Ed Farmer	.10	.05	.01
□	483 Eddie Murray	3.50	1.55	.45
□	484 Ben Oglivie	.20	.09	.03
□	485 Kevin Saucier	.10	.05	.01
□	486 Bobby Murcer	.20	.09	.03
□	487 Bill Campbell	.10	.05	.01
□	488 Reggie Smith	.20	.09	.03
□	489 Wayne Garland	.10	.05	.01
□	490 Jim Wright	.10	.05	.01
□	491 Billy Martin MG	.20	.09	.03
□	492 Jim Fanning MG	.10	.05	.01
□	493 Don Baylor	.40	.18	.05
□	494 Rick Honeycutt	.10	.05	.01
□	495 Carlton Fisk	.75	.35	.09
□	496 Denny Walling	.10	.05	.01
□	497 Bake McBride	.10	.05	.01
□	498 Darrell Porter	.20	.09	.03
□	499 Gene Richards	.10	.05	.01
□	500 Ron Oester	.10	.05	.01
□	501 Ken Dayley	.10	.05	.01
□	502 Jason Thompson	.10	.05	.01
□	503 Milt May	.10	.05	.01
□	504 Doug Bird	.10	.05	.01
□	505 Bruce Bochte	.10	.05	.01
□	506 Neil Allen	.10	.05	.01
□	507 Joey McLaughlin	.10	.05	.01
□	508 Butch Wynegar	.10	.05	.01
□	509 Gary Roenicke	.10	.05	.01
□	510 Robin Yount	1.50	.70	.19
□	511 Dave Tobik	.10	.05	.01
□	512 Rich Gedman	.20	.09	.03
□	513 Gene Nelson	.10	.05	.01
□	514 Rick Monday	.10	.05	.01
□	515 Miguel Dilone	.10	.05	.01
□	516 Clint Hurdle	.10	.05	.01

□ 517 Jeff Newman	.10	.05	.01
□ 518 Grant Jackson	.10	.05	.01
□ 519 Andy Hassler	.10	.05	.01
□ 520 Pat Putnam	.10	.05	.01
□ 521 Greg Pryor	.10	.05	.01
□ 522 Tony Scott	.10	.05	.01
□ 523 Steve Mura	.10	.05	.01
□ 524 Johnnie LeMaster	.10	.05	.01
□ 525 Dick Ruthven	.10	.05	.01
□ 526 John McNamara MG	.10	.05	.01
□ 527 Larry McWilliams	.10	.05	.01
□ 528 Johnny Ray	.20	.09	.03
□ 529 Pat Tabler	.20	.09	.03
□ 530 Tom Herr	.20	.09	.03
□ 531 San Diego Chicken COR (With TM)	.75	.35	.09
□ 531B San Diego Chicken ERR (Without TM)	.75	.35	.09
□ 532 Sal Butera	.10	.05	.01
□ 533 Mike Griffin	.10	.05	.01
□ 534 Kelvin Moore	.10	.05	.01
□ 535 Reggie Jackson	1.00	.45	.12
□ 536 Ed Romero	.10	.05	.01
□ 537 Derrel Thomas	.10	.05	.01
□ 538 Mike O'Berry	.10	.05	.01
□ 539 Jack O'Connor	.10	.05	.01
□ 540 Bob Ojeda	.40	.18	.05
□ 541 Roy Lee Jackson	.10	.05	.01
□ 542 Lynn Jones	.10	.05	.01
□ 543 Gaylord Perry	.40	.18	.05
□ 544A Phil Garner ERR (Reverse negative)	.40	.18	.05
□ 544B Phil Garner COR	.20	.09	.03
□ 545 Garry Templeton	.10	.05	.01
□ 546 Rafael Ramirez	.10	.05	.01
□ 547 Jeff Reardon	.40	.18	.05
□ 548 Ron Guidry	.20	.09	.03
□ 549 Tim Laudner	.10	.05	.01
□ 550 John Henry Johnson	.10	.05	.01
□ 551 Chris Bando	.10	.05	.01
□ 552 Bobby Brown	.10	.05	.01
□ 553 Larry Bradford	.10	.05	.01
□ 554 Scott Fletcher	.40	.18	.05
□ 555 Jerry Royster	.10	.05	.01
□ 556 Shooty Babitt UER (Spelled Babbitt on front)	.10	.05	.01
□ 557 Kent Hrbek	1.00	.45	.12
□ 558 Yankee Winners Ron Guidry Tommy John	.20	.09	.03
□ 559 Mark Bomback	.10	.05	.01
□ 560 Julio Valdez	.10	.05	.01
□ 561 Buck Martinez	.10	.05	.01
□ 562 Mike A. Marshall	.20	.09	.03
□ 563 Rennie Stennett	.10	.05	.01
□ 564 Steve Crawford	.10	.05	.01
□ 565 Bob Babcock	.10	.05	.01
□ 566 Johnny Podres CO	.20	.09	.03
□ 567 Paul Serna	.10	.05	.01
□ 568 Harold Baines	.40	.18	.05
□ 569 Dave LaRoche	.10	.05	.01
□ 570 Lee May	.20	.09	.03
□ 571 Gary Ward	.10	.05	.01
□ 572 John Denny	.10	.05	.01
□ 573 Roy Smalley	.10	.05	.01
□ 574 Bob Brenly	.10	.05	.01
□ 575 Bronx Bombers Reggie Jackson Dave Winfield	1.50	.70	.19
□ 576 Luis Pujols	.10	.05	.01
□ 577 Butch Hobson	.10	.05	.01
□ 578 Harvey Kuenn MG	.20	.09	.03
□ 579 Cal Ripken Sr. CO	.20	.09	.03
□ 580 Juan Berenguer	.10	.05	.01
□ 581 Benny Ayala	.10	.05	.01
□ 582 Vance Law	.10	.05	.01
□ 583 Rick Leach	.10	.05	.01
□ 584 George Frazier	.10	.05	.01
□ 585 Phillies Finest Pete Rose Mike Schmidt	1.50	.70	.19
□ 586 Joe Rudi	.10	.05	.01
□ 587 Juan Beniquez	.10	.05	.01
□ 588 Luis DeLeon	.10	.05	.01
□ 589 Craig Swan	.10	.05	.01
□ 590 Dave Chalk	.10	.05	.01
□ 591 Billy Gardner MG	.10	.05	.01
□ 592 Sal Bando	.20	.09	.03
□ 593 Bert Campaneris	.20	.09	.03
□ 594 Steve Kemp	.10	.05	.01
□ 595A Randy Lerch ERR (Braves)	.40	.18	.05
□ 595B Randy Lerch COR (Brewers)	.10	.05	.01
□ 596 Bryan Clark	.10	.05	.01
□ 597 Dave Ford	.10	.05	.01
□ 598 Mike Scioscia	.20	.09	.03
□ 599 John Lowenstein	.10	.05	.01
□ 600 Rene Lachemann MG	.10	.05	.01
□ 601 Mick Kelleher	.10	.05	.01
□ 602 Ron Jackson	.10	.05	.01
□ 603 Jerry Koosman	.20	.09	.03
□ 604 Dave Goltz	.10	.05	.01
□ 605 Ellis Valentine	.10	.05	.01
□ 606 Lonnie Smith	.20	.09	.03
□ 607 Joaquin Andujar	.20	.09	.03
□ 608 Garry Hancock	.10	.05	.01
□ 609 Jerry Turner	.10	.05	.01
□ 610 Bob Bonner	.10	.05	.01
□ 611 Jim Dwyer	.10	.05	.01
□ 612 Terry Bulling	.10	.05	.01
□ 613 Joel Youngblood	.10	.05	.01
□ 614 Larry Milbourne	.10	.05	.01
□ 615 Gene Roof UER (Name on front is Phil Roof)	.10	.05	.01
□ 616 Keith Drumwright	.10	.05	.01
□ 617 Dave Rosello	.10	.05	.01
□ 618 Rickey Keeton	.10	.05	.01
□ 619 Dennis Lamp	.10	.05	.01
□ 620 Sid Monge	.10	.05	.01
□ 621 Jerry White	.10	.05	.01
□ 622 Luis Aguayo	.10	.05	.01
□ 623 Jamie Easterly	.10	.05	.01
□ 624 Steve Sax	.40	.18	.05
□ 625 Dave Roberts	.10	.05	.01
□ 626 Rick Bosetti	.10	.05	.01
□ 627 Terry Francona	.10	.05	.01
□ 628 Pride of Reds Tom Seaver Johnny Bench	1.00	.45	.12
□ 629 Paul Mirabella	.10	.05	.01
□ 630 Rance Mulliniks	.10	.05	.01
□ 631 Kevin Hickey	.10	.05	.01
□ 632 Reid Nichols	.10	.05	.01
□ 633 Dave Geisel	.10	.05	.01
□ 634 Ken Griffey	.20	.09	.03
□ 635 Bob Lemon MG	.40	.18	.05
□ 636 Orlando Sanchez	.10	.05	.01
□ 637 Bill Almon	.10	.05	.01
□ 638 Danny Ainge	1.00	.45	.12
□ 639 Willie Stargell	.40	.18	.05
□ 640 Bob Sykes	.10	.05	.01
□ 641 Ed Lynch	.10	.05	.01
□ 642 John Ellis	.10	.05	.01
□ 643 Ferguson Jenkins	.40	.18	.05
□ 644 Lenn Sakata	.10	.05	.01
□ 645 Julio Gonzalez	.10	.05	.01
□ 646 Jesse Orosco	.10	.05	.01
□ 647 Jerry Dybzinski	.10	.05	.01
□ 648 Tommy Davis CO	.20	.09	.03
□ 649 Ron Gardenhire	.10	.05	.01
□ 650 Felipe Alou CO	.20	.09	.03
□ 651 Harvey Haddix CO	.20	.09	.03
□ 652 Willie Upshaw	.10	.05	.01
□ 653 Bill Madlock	.20	.09	.03
□ 654A DK Checklist 1-26 ERR (Unnumbered) (With Trammel)	.40	.18	.05
□ 654B DK Checklist 1-26 COR (Unnumbered) (With Trammell)	.20	.09	.03
□ 655 Checklist 27-130 (Unnumbered)	.20	.09	.03
□ 656 Checklist 131-234 (Unnumbered)	.20	.09	.03
□ 657 Checklist 235-338 (Unnumbered)	.20	.09	.03
□ 658 Checklist 339-442 (Unnumbered)	.20	.09	.03
□ 659 Checklist 443-544	.20	.09	.03

		MINT	NRMT	EXC
	(Unnumbered)			
□ 660	Checklist 545-653	.20	.09	.03
	(Unnumbered)			

1983 Donruss

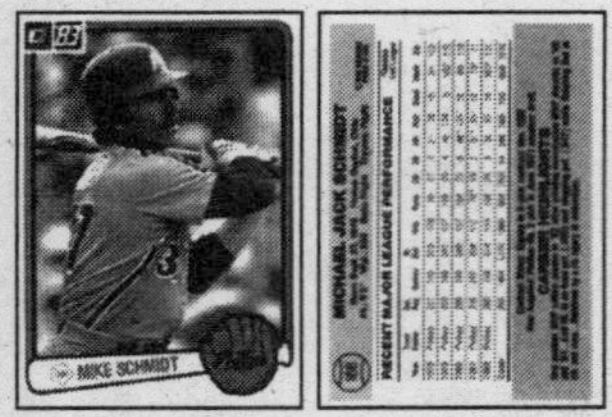

The 1983 Donruss baseball set leads off with a 26-card Diamond Kings (DK) series. Of the remaining 634 standard-size cards, two are combination cards, one portrays the San Diego Chicken, one shows the completed Ty Cobb puzzle, and seven are unnumbered checklist cards. The seven unnumbered checklist cards are arbitrarily assigned numbers 654 through 660 and are listed at the end of the list below. All cards measure the standard size. Card fronts feature full color photos around a framed white broder. Several printing variations are available but the complete set price below includes only the more common of each variation pair. Cards were issued in 15-card packs which included a three-piece Ty Cobb puzzle panel (21 different panels were needed to complete the puzzle). Notable Rookie Cards include Wade Boggs, Tony Gwynn and Ryne Sandberg.

	MINT	NRMT	EXC
COMPLETE SET (660)	90.00	40.00	11.00
COMPLETE FACT.SET (660)	100.00	45.00	12.50
COMMON CARD (1-660)	.10	.05	.01
SEMISTARS	.20	.09	.03
STARS	.40	.18	.05

□ 1	Fernando Valenzuela DK	.40	.18	.05
□ 2	Rollie Fingers DK	.40	.18	.05
□ 3	Reggie Jackson DK	.75	.35	.09
□ 4	Jim Palmer DK	.40	.18	.05
□ 5	Jack Morris DK	.40	.18	.05
□ 6	George Foster DK	.20	.09	.03
□ 7	Jim Sundberg DK	.20	.09	.03
□ 8	Willie Stargell DK	.40	.18	.05
□ 9	Dave Stieb DK	.20	.09	.03
□ 10	Joe Niekro DK	.20	.09	.03
□ 11	Rickey Henderson DK	1.25	.55	.16
□ 12	Dale Murphy DK	.40	.18	.05
□ 13	Toby Harrah DK	.20	.09	.03
□ 14	Bill Buckner DK	.20	.09	.03
□ 15	Willie Wilson DK	.20	.09	.03
□ 16	Steve Carlton DK	.40	.18	.05
□ 17	Ron Guidry DK	.20	.09	.03
□ 18	Steve Rogers DK	.20	.09	.03
□ 19	Kent Hrbek DK	.20	.09	.03
□ 20	Keith Hernandez DK	.20	.09	.03
□ 21	Floyd Bannister DK	.20	.09	.03
□ 22	Johnny Bench DK	.40	.18	.05
□ 23	Britt Burns DK	.20	.09	.03
□ 24	Joe Morgan DK	.40	.18	.05
□ 25	Carl Yastrzemski DK	.40	.18	.05
□ 26	Terry Kennedy DK	.20	.09	.03
□ 27	Gary Roenicke	.10	.05	.01
□ 28	Dwight Bernard	.10	.05	.01
□ 29	Pat Underwood	.10	.05	.01
□ 30	Gary Allenson	.10	.05	.01
□ 31	Ron Guidry	.20	.09	.03
□ 32	Burt Hooton	.10	.05	.01
□ 33	Chris Bando	.10	.05	.01
□ 34	Vida Blue	.20	.09	.03
□ 35	Rickey Henderson	1.50	.70	.19
□ 36	Ray Burris	.10	.05	.01
□ 37	John Butcher	.10	.05	.01
□ 38	Don Aase	.10	.05	.01
□ 39	Jerry Koosman	.20	.09	.03
□ 40	Bruce Sutter	.20	.09	.03
□ 41	Jose Cruz	.20	.09	.03
□ 42	Pete Rose	1.25	.55	.16
□ 43	Cesar Cedeno	.20	.09	.03
□ 44	Floyd Chiffer	.10	.05	.01
□ 45	Larry McWilliams	.10	.05	.01
□ 46	Alan Fowlkes	.10	.05	.01
□ 47	Dale Murphy	.40	.18	.05
□ 48	Doug Bird	.10	.05	.01
□ 49	Hubie Brooks	.20	.09	.03
□ 50	Floyd Bannister	.10	.05	.01
□ 51	Jack O'Connor	.10	.05	.01
□ 52	Steve Senteney	.10	.05	.01
□ 53	Gary Gaetti	.75	.35	.09
□ 54	Damaso Garcia	.10	.05	.01
□ 55	Gene Nelson	.10	.05	.01
□ 56	Mookie Wilson	.20	.09	.03
□ 57	Allen Ripley	.10	.05	.01
□ 58	Bob Horner	.10	.05	.01
□ 59	Tony Pena	.20	.09	.03
□ 60	Gary Lavelle	.10	.05	.01
□ 61	Tim Lollar	.10	.05	.01
□ 62	Frank Pastore	.10	.05	.01
□ 63	Garry Maddox	.10	.05	.01
□ 64	Bob Forsch	.10	.05	.01
□ 65	Harry Spilman	.10	.05	.01
□ 66	Geoff Zahn	.10	.05	.01
□ 67	Salome Barojas	.10	.05	.01
□ 68	David Palmer	.10	.05	.01
□ 69	Charlie Hough	.20	.09	.03
□ 70	Dan Quisenberry	.20	.09	.03
□ 71	Tony Armas	.10	.05	.01
□ 72	Rick Sutcliffe	.20	.09	.03
□ 73	Steve Balboni	.10	.05	.01
□ 74	Jerry Remy	.10	.05	.01
□ 75	Mike Scioscia	.20	.09	.03
□ 76	John Wockenfuss	.10	.05	.01
□ 77	Jim Palmer	.50	.23	.06
□ 78	Rollie Fingers	.40	.18	.05
□ 79	Joe Nolan	.10	.05	.01
□ 80	Pete Vuckovich	.10	.05	.01
□ 81	Rick Leach	.10	.05	.01
□ 82	Rick Miller	.10	.05	.01
□ 83	Graig Nettles	.20	.09	.03
□ 84	Ron Cey	.20	.09	.03
□ 85	Miguel Dilone	.10	.05	.01
□ 86	John Wathan	.10	.05	.01
□ 87	Kelvin Moore	.10	.05	.01
□ 88A	Byrn Smith ERR	.20	.09	.03
	(Sic, Bryn)			
□ 88B	Bryn Smith COR	.40	.18	.05
□ 89	Dave Hostetler	.10	.05	.01
□ 90	Rod Carew	.60	.25	.07
□ 91	Lonnie Smith	.10	.05	.01
□ 92	Bob Knepper	.10	.05	.01
□ 93	Marty Bystrom	.10	.05	.01
□ 94	Chris Welsh	.10	.05	.01
□ 95	Jason Thompson	.10	.05	.01
□ 96	Tom O'Malley	.10	.05	.01
□ 97	Phil Niekro	.40	.18	.05
□ 98	Neil Allen	.10	.05	.01
□ 99	Bill Buckner	.20	.09	.03
□ 100	Ed VandeBerg	.10	.05	.01
□ 101	Jim Clancy	.10	.05	.01
□ 102	Robert Castillo	.10	.05	.01
□ 103	Bruce Berenyi	.10	.05	.01
□ 104	Carlton Fisk	.75	.35	.09
□ 105	Mike Flanagan	.20	.09	.03
□ 106	Cecil Cooper	.20	.09	.03
□ 107	Jack Morris	.40	.18	.05
□ 108	Mike Morgan	.10	.05	.01
□ 109	Luis Aponte	.10	.05	.01
□ 110	Pedro Guerrero	.20	.09	.03
□ 111	Len Barker	.10	.05	.01
□ 112	Willie Wilson	.20	.09	.03
□ 113	Dave Beard	.10	.05	.01
□ 114	Mike Gates	.10	.05	.01
□ 115	Reggie Jackson	1.00	.45	.12
□ 116	George Wright	.10	.05	.01
□ 117	Vance Law	.10	.05	.01
□ 118	Nolan Ryan	4.00	1.80	.50
□ 119	Mike Krukow	.10	.05	.01

□ 120 Ozzie Smith	2.00	.90	.25
□ 121 Broderick Perkins	.10	.05	.01
□ 122 Tom Seaver	.75	.35	.09
□ 123 Chris Chambliss	.20	.09	.03
□ 124 Chuck Tanner MG	.20	.09	.03
□ 125 Johnnie LeMaster	.10	.05	.01
□ 126 Mel Hall	.20	.09	.03
□ 127 Bruce Bochte	.10	.05	.01
□ 128 Charlie Puleo	.10	.05	.01
□ 129 Luis Leal	.10	.05	.01
□ 130 John Pacella	.10	.05	.01
□ 131 Glenn Gulliver	.10	.05	.01
□ 132 Don Money	.10	.05	.01
□ 133 Dave Rozema	.10	.05	.01
□ 134 Bruce Hurst	.20	.09	.03
□ 135 Rudy May	.10	.05	.01
□ 136 Tom Lasorda MG	.20	.09	.03
□ 137 Dan Spillner UER (Photo actually Ed Whitson)	.10	.05	.01
□ 138 Jerry Martin	.10	.05	.01
□ 139 Mike Norris	.10	.05	.01
□ 140 Al Oliver	.20	.09	.03
□ 141 Daryl Sconiers	.10	.05	.01
□ 142 Lamar Johnson	.10	.05	.01
□ 143 Harold Baines	.40	.18	.05
□ 144 Alan Ashby	.10	.05	.01
□ 145 Garry Templeton	.10	.05	.01
□ 146 Al Holland	.10	.05	.01
□ 147 Bo Diaz	.10	.05	.01
□ 148 Dave Concepcion	.20	.09	.03
□ 149 Rick Camp	.10	.05	.01
□ 150 Jim Morrison	.10	.05	.01
□ 151 Randy Martz	.10	.05	.01
□ 152 Keith Hernandez	.40	.18	.05
□ 153 John Lowenstein	.10	.05	.01
□ 154 Mike Caldwell	.10	.05	.01
□ 155 Milt Wilcox	.10	.05	.01
□ 156 Rich Gedman	.10	.05	.01
□ 157 Rich Gossage	.40	.18	.05
□ 158 Jerry Reuss	.20	.09	.03
□ 159 Ron Hassey	.10	.05	.01
□ 160 Larry Gura	.10	.05	.01
□ 161 Dwayne Murphy	.10	.05	.01
□ 162 Woodie Fryman	.10	.05	.01
□ 163 Steve Comer	.10	.05	.01
□ 164 Ken Forsch	.10	.05	.01
□ 165 Dennis Lamp	.10	.05	.01
□ 166 David Green	.10	.05	.01
□ 167 Terry Puhl	.10	.05	.01
□ 168 Mike Schmidt (Wearing 37 rather than 20)	1.50	.70	.19
□ 169 Eddie Milner	.10	.05	.01
□ 170 John Curtis	.10	.05	.01
□ 171 Don Robinson	.10	.05	.01
□ 172 Rich Gale	.10	.05	.01
□ 173 Steve Bedrosian	.20	.09	.03
□ 174 Willie Hernandez	.20	.09	.03
□ 175 Ron Gardenhire	.10	.05	.01
□ 176 Jim Beattie	.10	.05	.01
□ 177 Tim Laudner	.10	.05	.01
□ 178 Buck Martinez	.10	.05	.01
□ 179 Kent Hrbek	.40	.18	.05
□ 180 Alfredo Griffin	.10	.05	.01
□ 181 Larry Andersen	.10	.05	.01
□ 182 Pete Falcone	.10	.05	.01
□ 183 Jody Davis	.10	.05	.01
□ 184 Glenn Hubbard	.10	.05	.01
□ 185 Dale Berra	.10	.05	.01
□ 186 Greg Minton	.10	.05	.01
□ 187 Gary Lucas	.10	.05	.01
□ 188 Dave Van Gorder	.10	.05	.01
□ 189 Bob Dernier	.10	.05	.01
□ 190 Willie McGee	.40	.18	.05
□ 191 Dickie Thon	.10	.05	.01
□ 192 Bob Boone	.20	.09	.03
□ 193 Britt Burns	.10	.05	.01
□ 194 Jeff Reardon	.20	.09	.03
□ 195 Jon Matlack	.10	.05	.01
□ 196 Don Slaught	.40	.18	.05
□ 197 Fred Stanley	.10	.05	.01
□ 198 Rick Manning	.10	.05	.01
□ 199 Dave Righetti	.20	.09	.03
□ 200 Dave Stapleton	.10	.05	.01
□ 201 Steve Yeager	.10	.05	.01
□ 202 Enos Cabell	.10	.05	.01
□ 203 Sammy Stewart	.10	.05	.01
□ 204 Moose Haas	.10	.05	.01
□ 205 Lenn Sakata	.10	.05	.01
□ 206 Charlie Moore	.10	.05	.01
□ 207 Alan Trammell	.40	.18	.05
□ 208 Jim Rice	.40	.18	.05
□ 209 Roy Smalley	.10	.05	.01
□ 210 Bill Russell	.20	.09	.03
□ 211 Andre Thornton	.10	.05	.01
□ 212 Willie Aikens	.10	.05	.01
□ 213 Dave McKay	.10	.05	.01
□ 214 Tim Blackwell	.10	.05	.01
□ 215 Buddy Bell	.20	.09	.03
□ 216 Doug DeCinces	.20	.09	.03
□ 217 Tom Herr	.20	.09	.03
□ 218 Frank LaCorte	.10	.05	.01
□ 219 Steve Carlton	.75	.35	.09
□ 220 Terry Kennedy	.10	.05	.01
□ 221 Mike Easler	.10	.05	.01
□ 222 Jack Clark	.20	.09	.03
□ 223 Gene Garber	.10	.05	.01
□ 224 Scott Holman	.10	.05	.01
□ 225 Mike Proly	.10	.05	.01
□ 226 Terry Bulling	.10	.05	.01
□ 227 Jerry Garvin	.10	.05	.01
□ 228 Ron Davis	.10	.05	.01
□ 229 Tom Hume	.10	.05	.01
□ 230 Marc Hill	.10	.05	.01
□ 231 Dennis Martinez	.20	.09	.03
□ 232 Jim Gantner	.20	.09	.03
□ 233 Larry Pashnick	.10	.05	.01
□ 234 Dave Collins	.10	.05	.01
□ 235 Tom Burgmeier	.10	.05	.01
□ 236 Ken Landreaux	.10	.05	.01
□ 237 John Denny	.10	.05	.01
□ 238 Hal McRae	.20	.09	.03
□ 239 Matt Keough	.10	.05	.01
□ 240 Doug Flynn	.10	.05	.01
□ 241 Fred Lynn	.20	.09	.03
□ 242 Billy Sample	.10	.05	.01
□ 243 Tom Paciorek	.10	.05	.01
□ 244 Joe Sambito	.10	.05	.01
□ 245 Sid Monge	.10	.05	.01
□ 246 Ken Oberkfell	.10	.05	.01
□ 247 Joe Pittman UER (Photo actually Juan Eichelberger)	.10	.05	.01
□ 248 Mario Soto	.10	.05	.01
□ 249 Claudell Washington	.10	.05	.01
□ 250 Rick Rhoden	.10	.05	.01
□ 251 Darrell Evans	.20	.09	.03
□ 252 Steve Henderson	.10	.05	.01
□ 253 Manny Castillo	.10	.05	.01
□ 254 Craig Swan	.10	.05	.01
□ 255 Joey McLaughlin	.10	.05	.01
□ 256 Pete Redfern	.10	.05	.01
□ 257 Ken Singleton	.20	.09	.03
□ 258 Robin Yount	1.25	.55	.16
□ 259 Elias Sosa	.10	.05	.01
□ 260 Bob Ojeda	.10	.05	.01
□ 261 Bobby Murcer	.20	.09	.03
□ 262 Candy Maldonado	.20	.09	.03
□ 263 Rick Waits	.10	.05	.01
□ 264 Greg Pryor	.10	.05	.01
□ 265 Bob Owchinko	.10	.05	.01
□ 266 Chris Speier	.10	.05	.01
□ 267 Bruce Kison	.10	.05	.01
□ 268 Mark Wagner	.10	.05	.01
□ 269 Steve Kemp	.10	.05	.01
□ 270 Phil Garner	.20	.09	.03
□ 271 Gene Richards	.10	.05	.01
□ 272 Renie Martin	.10	.05	.01
□ 273 Dave Roberts	.10	.05	.01
□ 274 Dan Driessen	.10	.05	.01
□ 275 Rufino Linares	.10	.05	.01
□ 276 Lee Lacy	.10	.05	.01
□ 277 Ryne Sandberg	15.00	6.75	1.85
□ 278 Darrell Porter	.10	.05	.01
□ 279 Cal Ripken	16.00	7.25	2.00
□ 280 Jamie Easterly	.10	.05	.01
□ 281 Bill Fahey	.10	.05	.01
□ 282 Glenn Hoffman	.10	.05	.01
□ 283 Willie Randolph	.20	.09	.03
□ 284 Fernando Valenzuela	.20	.09	.03
□ 285 Alan Bannister	.10	.05	.01

□ 286	Paul Splittorff	.10	.05	.01
□ 287	Joe Rudi	.10	.05	.01
□ 288	Bill Gullickson	.20	.09	.03
□ 289	Danny Darwin	.10	.05	.01
□ 290	Andy Hassler	.10	.05	.01
□ 291	Ernesto Escarrega	.10	.05	.01
□ 292	Steve Mura	.10	.05	.01
□ 293	Tony Scott	.10	.05	.01
□ 294	Manny Trillo	.10	.05	.01
□ 295	Greg Harris	.10	.05	.01
□ 296	Luis DeLeon	.10	.05	.01
□ 297	Kent Tekulve	.20	.09	.03
□ 298	Atlee Hammaker	.10	.05	.01
□ 299	Bruce Benedict	.10	.05	.01
□ 300	Fergie Jenkins	.40	.18	.05
□ 301	Dave Kingman	.20	.09	.03
□ 302	Bill Caudill	.10	.05	.01
□ 303	John Castino	.10	.05	.01
□ 304	Ernie Whitt	.10	.05	.01
□ 305	Randy Johnson	.10	.05	.01
□ 306	Garth Iorg	.10	.05	.01
□ 307	Gaylord Perry	.40	.18	.05
□ 308	Ed Lynch	.10	.05	.01
□ 309	Keith Moreland	.10	.05	.01
□ 310	Rafael Ramirez	.10	.05	.01
□ 311	Bill Madlock	.20	.09	.03
□ 312	Milt May	.10	.05	.01
□ 313	John Montefusco	.10	.05	.01
□ 314	Wayne Krenchicki	.10	.05	.01
□ 315	George Vukovich	.10	.05	.01
□ 316	Joaquin Andujar	.10	.05	.01
□ 317	Craig Reynolds	.10	.05	.01
□ 318	Rick Burleson	.10	.05	.01
□ 319	Richard Dotson	.10	.05	.01
□ 320	Steve Rogers	.10	.05	.01
□ 321	Dave Schmidt	.10	.05	.01
□ 322	Bud Black	.20	.09	.03
□ 323	Jeff Burroughs	.10	.05	.01
□ 324	Von Hayes	.20	.09	.03
□ 325	Butch Wynegar	.10	.05	.01
□ 326	Carl Yastrzemski	.75	.35	.09
□ 327	Ron Roenicke	.10	.05	.01
□ 328	Howard Johnson	.50	.23	.06
□ 329	Rick Dempsey UER (Posing as a left-handed batter)	.20	.09	.03
□ 330A	Jim Slaton (Bio printed black on white)	.10	.05	.01
□ 330B	Jim Slaton (Bio printed black on yellow)	.20	.09	.03
□ 331	Benny Ayala	.10	.05	.01
□ 332	Ted Simmons	.20	.09	.03
□ 333	Lou Whitaker	.40	.18	.05
□ 334	Chuck Rainey	.10	.05	.01
□ 335	Lou Piniella	.20	.09	.03
□ 336	Steve Sax	.20	.09	.03
□ 337	Toby Harrah	.10	.05	.01
□ 338	George Brett	3.00	1.35	.35
□ 339	Dave Lopes	.20	.09	.03
□ 340	Gary Carter	.40	.18	.05
□ 341	John Grubb	.10	.05	.01
□ 342	Tim Foli	.10	.05	.01
□ 343	Jim Kaat	.20	.09	.03
□ 344	Mike LaCoss	.10	.05	.01
□ 345	Larry Christenson	.10	.05	.01
□ 346	Juan Bonilla	.10	.05	.01
□ 347	Omar Moreno	.10	.05	.01
□ 348	Chili Davis	.40	.18	.05
□ 349	Tommy Boggs	.10	.05	.01
□ 350	Rusty Staub	.20	.09	.03
□ 351	Bump Wills	.10	.05	.01
□ 352	Rick Sweet	.10	.05	.01
□ 353	Jim Gott	.10	.05	.01
□ 354	Terry Felton	.10	.05	.01
□ 355	Jim Kern	.10	.05	.01
□ 356	Bill Almon UER (Expos/Mets in 1983, not Padres/Mets)	.10	.05	.01
□ 357	Tippy Martinez	.10	.05	.01
□ 358	Roy Howell	.10	.05	.01
□ 359	Dan Petry	.10	.05	.01
□ 360	Jerry Mumphrey	.10	.05	.01
□ 361	Mark Clear	.10	.05	.01
□ 362	Mike Marshall	.10	.05	.01
□ 363	Lary Sorensen	.10	.05	.01
□ 364	Amos Otis	.20	.09	.03
□ 365	Rick Langford	.10	.05	.01
□ 366	Brad Mills	.10	.05	.01
□ 367	Brian Downing	.10	.05	.01
□ 368	Mike Richardt	.10	.05	.01
□ 369	Aurelio Rodriguez	.10	.05	.01
□ 370	Dave Smith	.10	.05	.01
□ 371	Tug McGraw	.20	.09	.03
□ 372	Doug Bair	.10	.05	.01
□ 373	Ruppert Jones	.10	.05	.01
□ 374	Alex Trevino	.10	.05	.01
□ 375	Ken Dayley	.10	.05	.01
□ 376	Rod Scurry	.10	.05	.01
□ 377	Bob Brenly	.10	.05	.01
□ 378	Scot Thompson	.10	.05	.01
□ 379	Julio Cruz	.10	.05	.01
□ 380	John Stearns	.10	.05	.01
□ 381	Dale Murray	.10	.05	.01
□ 382	Frank Viola	.50	.23	.06
□ 383	Al Bumbry	.20	.09	.03
□ 384	Ben Oglivie	.10	.05	.01
□ 385	Dave Tobik	.10	.05	.01
□ 386	Bob Stanley	.10	.05	.01
□ 387	Andre Robertson	.10	.05	.01
□ 388	Jorge Orta	.10	.05	.01
□ 389	Ed Whitson	.10	.05	.01
□ 390	Don Hood	.10	.05	.01
□ 391	Tom Underwood	.10	.05	.01
□ 392	Tim Wallach	.20	.09	.03
□ 393	Steve Renko	.10	.05	.01
□ 394	Mickey Rivers	.10	.05	.01
□ 395	Greg Luzinski	.20	.09	.03
□ 396	Art Howe	.10	.05	.01
□ 397	Alan Wiggins	.10	.05	.01
□ 398	Jim Barr	.10	.05	.01
□ 399	Ivan DeJesus	.10	.05	.01
□ 400	Tom Lawless	.10	.05	.01
□ 401	Bob Walk	.10	.05	.01
□ 402	Jimmy Smith	.10	.05	.01
□ 403	Lee Smith	2.00	.90	.25
□ 404	George Hendrick	.10	.05	.01
□ 405	Eddie Murray	2.50	1.10	.30
□ 406	Marshall Edwards	.10	.05	.01
□ 407	Lance Parrish	.20	.09	.03
□ 408	Carney Lansford	.20	.09	.03
□ 409	Dave Winfield	1.25	.55	.16
□ 410	Bob Welch	.20	.09	.03
□ 411	Larry Milbourne	.10	.05	.01
□ 412	Dennis Leonard	.10	.05	.01
□ 413	Dan Meyer	.10	.05	.01
□ 414	Charlie Lea	.10	.05	.01
□ 415	Rick Honeycutt	.10	.05	.01
□ 416	Mike Witt	.10	.05	.01
□ 417	Steve Trout	.10	.05	.01
□ 418	Glenn Brummer	.10	.05	.01
□ 419	Denny Walling	.10	.05	.01
□ 420	Gary Matthews	.20	.09	.03
□ 421	Charlie Leibrandt UER (Liebrandt on front of card)	.10	.05	.01
□ 422	Juan Eichelberger UER (Photo actually Joe Pittman)	.10	.05	.01
□ 423	Cecilio Guante UER (Listed as Matt on card)	.20	.09	.03
□ 424	Bill Laskey	.10	.05	.01
□ 425	Jerry Royster	.10	.05	.01
□ 426	Dickie Noles	.10	.05	.01
□ 427	George Foster	.20	.09	.03
□ 428	Mike Moore	.20	.09	.03
□ 429	Gary Ward	.10	.05	.01
□ 430	Barry Bonnell	.10	.05	.01
□ 431	Ron Washington	.10	.05	.01
□ 432	Rance Mulliniks	.10	.05	.01
□ 433	Mike Stanton	.10	.05	.01
□ 434	Jesse Orosco	.10	.05	.01
□ 435	Larry Bowa	.20	.09	.03
□ 436	Biff Pocoroba	.10	.05	.01
□ 437	Johnny Ray	.10	.05	.01
□ 438	Joe Morgan	.40	.18	.05
□ 439	Eric Show	.10	.05	.01
□ 440	Larry Biittner	.10	.05	.01
□ 441	Greg Gross	.10	.05	.01
□ 442	Gene Tenace	.20	.09	.03

□ 443	Danny Heep	.10	.05	.01
□ 444	Bobby Clark	.10	.05	.01
□ 445	Kevin Hickey	.10	.05	.01
□ 446	Scott Sanderson	.10	.05	.01
□ 447	Frank Tanana	.20	.09	.03
□ 448	Cesar Geronimo	.10	.05	.01
□ 449	Jimmy Sexton	.10	.05	.01
□ 450	Mike Hargrove	.20	.09	.03
□ 451	Doyle Alexander	.10	.05	.01
□ 452	Dwight Evans	.20	.09	.03
□ 453	Terry Forster	.10	.05	.01
□ 454	Tom Brookens	.10	.05	.01
□ 455	Rich Dauer	.10	.05	.01
□ 456	Rob Picciolo	.10	.05	.01
□ 457	Terry Crowley	.10	.05	.01
□ 458	Ned Yost	.10	.05	.01
□ 459	Kirk Gibson	.40	.18	.05
□ 460	Reid Nichols	.10	.05	.01
□ 461	Oscar Gamble	.10	.05	.01
□ 462	Dusty Baker	.20	.09	.03
□ 463	Jack Perconte	.10	.05	.01
□ 464	Frank White	.20	.09	.03
□ 465	Mickey Klutts	.10	.05	.01
□ 466	Warren Cromartie	.10	.05	.01
□ 467	Larry Parrish	.10	.05	.01
□ 468	Bobby Grich	.20	.09	.03
□ 469	Dane Iorg	.10	.05	.01
□ 470	Joe Niekro	.20	.09	.03
□ 471	Ed Farmer	.10	.05	.01
□ 472	Tim Flannery	.10	.05	.01
□ 473	Dave Parker	.40	.18	.05
□ 474	Jeff Leonard	.10	.05	.01
□ 475	Al Hrabosky	.10	.05	.01
□ 476	Ron Hodges	.10	.05	.01
□ 477	Leon Durham	.10	.05	.01
□ 478	Jim Essian	.10	.05	.01
□ 479	Roy Lee Jackson	.10	.05	.01
□ 480	Brad Havens	.10	.05	.01
□ 481	Joe Price	.10	.05	.01
□ 482	Tony Bernazard	.10	.05	.01
□ 483	Scott McGregor	.10	.05	.01
□ 484	Paul Molitor	1.00	.45	.12
□ 485	Mike Ivie	.10	.05	.01
□ 486	Ken Griffey	.10	.05	.01
□ 487	Dennis Eckersley	.40	.18	.05
□ 488	Steve Garvey	.40	.18	.05
□ 489	Mike Fischlin	.10	.05	.01
□ 490	U.L. Washington	.10	.05	.01
□ 491	Steve McCatty	.10	.05	.01
□ 492	Roy Johnson	.10	.05	.01
□ 493	Don Baylor	.40	.18	.05
□ 494	Bobby Johnson	.10	.05	.01
□ 495	Mike Squires	.10	.05	.01
□ 496	Bert Roberge	.10	.05	.01
□ 497	Dick Ruthven	.10	.05	.01
□ 498	Tito Landrum	.10	.05	.01
□ 499	Sixto Lezcano	.10	.05	.01
□ 500	Johnny Bench	.75	.35	.09
□ 501	Larry Whisenton	.10	.05	.01
□ 502	Manny Sarmiento	.10	.05	.01
□ 503	Fred Breining	.10	.05	.01
□ 504	Bill Campbell	.10	.05	.01
□ 505	Todd Cruz	.10	.05	.01
□ 506	Bob Bailor	.10	.05	.01
□ 507	Dave Stieb	.20	.09	.03
□ 508	Al Williams	.10	.05	.01
□ 509	Dan Ford	.10	.05	.01
□ 510	Gorman Thomas	.10	.05	.01
□ 511	Chet Lemon	.10	.05	.01
□ 512	Mike Torrez	.10	.05	.01
□ 513	Shane Rawley	.10	.05	.01
□ 514	Mark Belanger	.10	.05	.01
□ 515	Rodney Craig	.10	.05	.01
□ 516	Onix Concepcion	.10	.05	.01
□ 517	Mike Heath	.10	.05	.01
□ 518	Andre Dawson UER (Middle name Fernando, should be Nolan)	.75	.35	.09
□ 519	Luis Sanchez	.10	.05	.01
□ 520	Terry Bogener	.10	.05	.01
□ 521	Rudy Law	.10	.05	.01
□ 522	Ray Knight	.20	.09	.03
□ 523	Joe Lefebvre	.10	.05	.01
□ 524	Jim Wohlford	.10	.05	.01
□ 525	Julio Franco	2.00	.90	.25
□ 526	Ron Oester	.10	.05	.01
□ 527	Rick Mahler	.10	.05	.01
□ 528	Steve Nicosia	.10	.05	.01
□ 529	Junior Kennedy	.10	.05	.01
□ 530A	Whitey Herzog MG (Bio printed black on white)	.20	.09	.03
□ 530B	Whitey Herzog MG (Bio printed black on yellow)	.20	.09	.03
□ 531A	Don Sutton (Blue border on photo)	.40	.18	.05
□ 531B	Don Sutton (Green border on photo)	.40	.18	.05
□ 532	Mark Brouhard	.10	.05	.01
□ 533A	Sparky Anderson MG (Bio printed black on white)	.20	.09	.03
□ 533B	Sparky Anderson MG (Bio printed black on yellow)	.20	.09	.03
□ 534	Roger LaFrancois	.10	.05	.01
□ 535	George Frazier	.10	.05	.01
□ 536	Tom Niedenfuer	.10	.05	.01
□ 537	Ed Glynn	.10	.05	.01
□ 538	Lee May	.20	.09	.03
□ 539	Bob Kearney	.10	.05	.01
□ 540	Tim Raines	.50	.23	.06
□ 541	Paul Mirabella	.10	.05	.01
□ 542	Luis Tiant	.20	.09	.03
□ 543	Ron LeFlore	.20	.09	.03
□ 544	Dave LaPoint	.10	.05	.01
□ 545	Randy Moffitt	.10	.05	.01
□ 546	Luis Aguayo	.10	.05	.01
□ 547	Brad Lesley	.20	.09	.03
□ 548	Luis Salazar	.10	.05	.01
□ 549	John Candelaria	.10	.05	.01
□ 550	Dave Bergman	.10	.05	.01
□ 551	Bob Watson	.20	.09	.03
□ 552	Pat Tabler	.10	.05	.01
□ 553	Brent Gaff	.10	.05	.01
□ 554	Al Cowens	.10	.05	.01
□ 555	Tom Brunansky	.20	.09	.03
□ 556	Lloyd Moseby	.10	.05	.01
□ 557A	Pascual Perez ERR (Twins in glove)	2.00	.90	.25
□ 557B	Pascual Perez COR (Braves in glove)	.20	.09	.03
□ 558	Willie Upshaw	.10	.05	.01
□ 559	Richie Zisk	.10	.05	.01
□ 560	Pat Zachry	.10	.05	.01
□ 561	Jay Johnstone	.20	.09	.03
□ 562	Carlos Diaz	.10	.05	.01
□ 563	John Tudor	.10	.05	.01
□ 564	Frank Robinson MG	.40	.18	.05
□ 565	Dave Edwards	.10	.05	.01
□ 566	Paul Householder	.10	.05	.01
□ 567	Ron Reed	.10	.05	.01
□ 568	Mike Ramsey	.10	.05	.01
□ 569	Kiko Garcia	.10	.05	.01
□ 570	Tommy John	.40	.18	.05
□ 571	Tony LaRussa MG	.20	.09	.03
□ 572	Joel Youngblood	.10	.05	.01
□ 573	Wayne Tolleson	.10	.05	.01
□ 574	Keith Creel	.10	.05	.01
□ 575	Billy Martin MG	.20	.09	.03
□ 576	Jerry Dybzinski	.10	.05	.01
□ 577	Rick Cerone	.10	.05	.01
□ 578	Tony Perez	.40	.18	.05
□ 579	Greg Brock	.10	.05	.01
□ 580	Glenn Wilson	.20	.09	.03
□ 581	Tim Stoddard	.10	.05	.01
□ 582	Bob McClure	.10	.05	.01
□ 583	Jim Dwyer	.10	.05	.01
□ 584	Ed Romero	.10	.05	.01
□ 585	Larry Herndon	.10	.05	.01
□ 586	Wade Boggs	10.00	4.50	1.25
□ 587	Jay Howell	.20	.09	.03
□ 588	Dave Stewart	.40	.18	.05
□ 589	Bert Blyleven	.40	.18	.05
□ 590	Dick Howser MG	.20	.09	.03
□ 591	Wayne Gross	.10	.05	.01
□ 592	Terry Francona	.10	.05	.01
□ 593	Don Werner	.10	.05	.01
□ 594	Bill Stein	.10	.05	.01

□ 595 Jesse Barfield	.20	.09	.03
□ 596 Bob Molinaro	.10	.05	.01
□ 597 Mike Vail	.10	.05	.01
□ 598 Tony Gwynn	20.00	9.00	2.50
□ 599 Gary Rajsich	.10	.05	.01
□ 600 Jerry Ujdur	.10	.05	.01
□ 601 Cliff Johnson	.10	.05	.01
□ 602 Jerry White	.10	.05	.01
□ 603 Bryan Clark	.10	.05	.01
□ 604 Joe Ferguson	.10	.05	.01
□ 605 Guy Sularz	.10	.05	.01
□ 606A Ozzie Virgil (Green border on photo)	.20	.09	.03
□ 606B Ozzie Virgil (Orange border on photo)	.20	.09	.03
□ 607 Terry Harper	.10	.05	.01
□ 608 Harvey Kuenn MG	.20	.09	.03
□ 609 Jim Sundberg	.20	.09	.03
□ 610 Willie Stargell	.40	.18	.05
□ 611 Reggie Smith	.20	.09	.03
□ 612 Rob Wilfong	.10	.05	.01
□ 613 The Niekro Brothers Joe Niekro Phil Niekro	.40	.18	.05
□ 614 Lee Elia MG	.10	.05	.01
□ 615 Mickey Hatcher	.10	.05	.01
□ 616 Jerry Hairston	.10	.05	.01
□ 617 John Martin	.10	.05	.01
□ 618 Wally Backman	.10	.05	.01
□ 619 Storm Davis	.10	.05	.01
□ 620 Alan Knicely	.10	.05	.01
□ 621 John Stuper	.10	.05	.01
□ 622 Matt Sinatro	.10	.05	.01
□ 623 Geno Petralli	.20	.09	.03
□ 624 Duane Walker	.10	.05	.01
□ 625 Dick Williams MG	.10	.05	.01
□ 626 Pat Corrales MG	.10	.05	.01
□ 627 Vern Ruhle	.10	.05	.01
□ 628 Joe Torre MG	.20	.09	.03
□ 629 Anthony Johnson	.10	.05	.01
□ 630 Steve Howe	.10	.05	.01
□ 631 Gary Woods	.10	.05	.01
□ 632 LaMarr Hoyt	.20	.09	.03
□ 633 Steve Swisher	.10	.05	.01
□ 634 Terry Leach	.10	.05	.01
□ 635 Jeff Newman	.10	.05	.01
□ 636 Brett Butler	.40	.18	.05
□ 637 Gary Gray	.10	.05	.01
□ 638 Lee Mazzilli	.10	.05	.01
□ 639A Ron Jackson ERR (A's in glove)	10.00	4.50	1.25
□ 639B Ron Jackson COR (Angels in glove, red border on photo)	.10	.05	.01
□ 639C Ron Jackson COR (Angels in glove, green border on photo)	.40	.18	.05
□ 640 Juan Beniquez	.10	.05	.01
□ 641 Dave Rucker	.10	.05	.01
□ 642 Luis Pujols	.10	.05	.01
□ 643 Rick Monday	.10	.05	.01
□ 644 Hosken Powell	.10	.05	.01
□ 645 The Chicken	.40	.18	.05
□ 646 Dave Engle	.10	.05	.01
□ 647 Dick Davis	.10	.05	.01
□ 648 Frank Robinson Vida Blue Joe Morgan	.20	.09	.03
□ 649 Al Chambers	.10	.05	.01
□ 650 Jesus Vega	.10	.05	.01
□ 651 Jeff Jones	.10	.05	.01
□ 652 Marvis Foley	.10	.05	.01
□ 653 Ty Cobb Puzzle Card	.40	.18	.05
□ 654A Dick Perez/Diamond King Checklist 1-26 (Unnumbered) ERR (Word "checklist" omitted from back)	.40	.18	.05
□ 654B Dick Perez/Diamond King Checklist 1-26 (Unnumbered) COR (Word "checklist" is on back)	.40	.18	.05
□ 655 Checklist 27-130 (Unnumbered)	.20	.09	.03
□ 656 Checklist 131-234 (Unnumbered)	.20	.09	.03
□ 657 Checklist 235-338 (Unnumbered)	.20	.09	.03
□ 658 Checklist 339-442 (Unnumbered)	.20	.09	.03
□ 659 Checklist 443-544 (Unnumbered)	.20	.09	.03
□ 660 Checklist 545-653 (Unnumbered)	.20	.09	.03

1984 Donruss

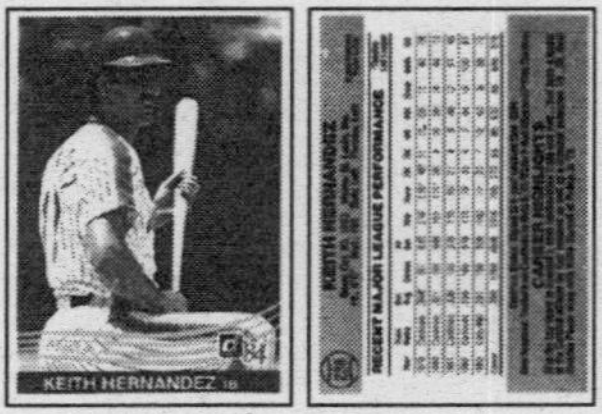

The 1984 Donruss set contains a total of 660 standard-size cards; however, only 658 are numbered. The first 26 cards in the set are again Diamond Kings (DK). A new feature, Rated Rookies (RR), was introduced with this set with Bill Madden's 20 selections comprising numbers 27 through 46. Two "Living Legend" cards designated A (featuring Gaylord Perry and Rollie Fingers) and B (featuring Johnny Bench and Carl Yastrzemski) were issued as bonus cards in wax packs, but were not issued in the factory sets sold to hobby dealers. The seven unnumbered checklist cards are arbitrarily assigned numbers 652 through 658 and are listed at the end of the list below. The attractive card front designs changed considerably from the previous two years. The backs contain statistics and are printed in green and black ink. The cards were distributed with a 3-piece puzzle panel of Duke Snider. There are no extra variation cards included in the complete set price below. The variation cards apparently resulted from a different printing for the factory sets as the Darling and Stenhouse no number variations as well as the Perez-Steele errors were corrected in the factory sets which were released later in the year. Cards found in packs spelled Perez-Steele as Perez-Steel. Notable Rookie Cards in this set include Joe Carter, Don Mattingly, Tony Phillips, Darryl Strawberry, and Andy Van Slyke. The Joe Carter card is almost never found well centered.

	MINT	NRMT	EXC
COMPLETE SET (660)	225.00	100.00	28.00
COMPLETE FACT.SET (658)	250.00	110.00	31.00
COMMON CARD (1-658)	.25	.11	.03
SEMISTARS	.50	.23	.06
STARS	1.00	.45	.12
DIAMOND KING ERR: 80% VALUE OF COR.			
BEWARE OF COUNTERFEITS			

□ 1 Robin Yount DK COR	5.00	2.20	.60
□ 1A Robin Yount DK ERR	5.00	2.20	.60
□ 2 Dave Concepcion DK COR	1.00	.45	.12
□ 2A Dave Concepcion DK ERR	.50	.23	.06
□ 3 Dwayne Murphy DK COR	.40	.18	.05

□ 3A Dwayne Murphy DK ERR	.25	.11	.03
□ 4 John Castino DK COR	.40	.18	.05
□ 4A John Castino DK ERR	.25	.11	.03
□ 5 Leon Durham DK COR	.40	.18	.05
□ 5A Leon Durham DK ERR	.25	.11	.03
□ 6 Rusty Staub DK COR	.50	.23	.06
□ 6A Rusty Staub DK ERR	.40	.18	.05
□ 7 Jack Clark DK COR	.50	.23	.06
□ 7A Jack Clark DK ERR	.40	.18	.05
□ 8 Dave Dravecky DK COR	.50	.23	.06
□ 8A Dave Dravecky DK ERR	.40	.18	.05
□ 9 Al Oliver DK COR	.50	.23	.06
□ 9A Al Oliver DK ERR	.40	.18	.05
□ 10 Dave Righetti DK COR	.50	.23	.06
□ 10A Dave Righetti DK ERR	.40	.18	.05
□ 11 Hal McRae DK COR	.50	.23	.06
□ 11A Hal McRae DK ERR	.40	.18	.05
□ 12 Ray Knight DK COR	.50	.23	.06
□ 12A Ray Knight DK ERR	.40	.18	.05
□ 13 Bruce Sutter DK COR	.50	.23	.06
□ 13A Bruce Sutter DK ERR	.40	.18	.05
□ 14 Bob Horner DK COR	.50	.23	.06
□ 14A Bob Horner DK ERR	.40	.18	.05
□ 15 Lance Parrish DK COR	1.00	.45	.12
□ 15A Lance Parrish DK ERR	.50	.23	.06
□ 16 Matt Young DK COR	.40	.18	.05
□ 16A Matt Young DK ERR	.25	.11	.03
□ 17 Fred Lynn DK COR	.50	.23	.06
□ 17A Fred Lynn DK ERR	.40	.18	.05
□ 18 Ron Kittle DK COR	.40	.18	.05
□ 18A Ron Kittle DK ERR	.25	.11	.03
□ 19 Jim Clancy DK COR	.40	.18	.05
□ 19A Jim Clancy DK ERR	.25	.11	.03
□ 20 Bill Madlock DK COR	.50	.23	.06
□ 20A Bill Madlock DK ERR	.40	.18	.05
□ 21 Larry Parrish DK COR	.40	.18	.05
□ 21A Larry Parrish DK ERR	.25	.11	.03
□ 22 Eddie Murray DK COR	3.00	1.35	.35
□ 22A Eddie Murray DK ERR	3.00	1.35	.35
□ 23 Mike Schmidt DK COR	5.00	2.20	.60
□ 23A Mike Schmidt DK ERR	5.00	2.20	.60
□ 24 Pedro Guerrero DK COR	.50	.23	.06
□ 24A Pedro Guerrero DK ERR	.40	.18	.05
□ 25 Andre Thornton DK COR	.50	.23	.06
□ 25A Andre Thornton DK ERR	.40	.18	.05
□ 26 Wade Boggs DK COR	3.50	1.55	.45
□ 26A Wade Boggs DK ERR	3.50	1.55	.45
□ 27 Joel Skinner RR	.25	.11	.03
□ 28 Tommy Dunbar RR	.25	.11	.03
□ 29A Mike Stenhouse RR ERR (No number on back)	.25	.11	.03
□ 29B Mike Stenhouse RR COR (Numbered on back)	2.00	.90	.25
□ 30A Ron Darling RR ERR (No number on back)	.75	.35	.09
□ 30B Ron Darling RR COR (Numbered on back)	3.00	1.35	.35
□ 31 Dion James RR	.40	.18	.05
□ 32 Tony Fernandez RR	1.00	.45	.12
□ 33 Angel Salazar RR	.25	.11	.03
□ 34 Kevin McReynolds RR	1.00	.45	.12
□ 35 Dick Schofield RR	.40	.18	.05
□ 36 Brad Komminsk RR	.25	.11	.03
□ 37 Tim Teufel RR	.25	.11	.03
□ 38 Doug Frobel RR	.25	.11	.03
□ 39 Greg Gagne RR	.50	.23	.06
□ 40 Mike Fuentes RR	.25	.11	.03
□ 41 Joe Carter RR	45.00	20.00	5.50
□ 42 Mike Brown RR (Angels OF)	.25	.11	.03
□ 43 Mike Jeffcoat RR	.25	.11	.03
□ 44 Sid Fernandez RR	1.00	.45	.12
□ 45 Brian Dayett RR	.25	.11	.03
□ 46 Chris Smith RR	.25	.11	.03
□ 47 Eddie Murray	8.00	3.60	1.00
□ 48 Robin Yount	5.00	2.20	.60
□ 49 Lance Parrish	.40	.18	.05
□ 50 Jim Rice	.50	.23	.06
□ 51 Dave Winfield	5.00	2.20	.60
□ 52 Fernando Valenzuela	.40	.18	.05
□ 53 George Brett	10.00	4.50	1.25
□ 54 Rickey Henderson	5.00	2.20	.60
□ 55 Gary Carter	1.00	.45	.12
□ 56 Buddy Bell	.40	.18	.05
□ 57 Reggie Jackson	4.00	1.80	.50
□ 58 Harold Baines	.50	.23	.06
□ 59 Ozzie Smith	7.00	3.10	.85
□ 60 Nolan Ryan UER (Text on back refers to 1972 as the year he struck out 383; the year was 1973)	20.00	9.00	2.50
□ 61 Pete Rose	5.00	2.20	.60
□ 62 Ron Oester	.25	.11	.03
□ 63 Steve Garvey	1.00	.45	.12
□ 64 Jason Thompson	.25	.11	.03
□ 65 Jack Clark	.40	.18	.05
□ 66 Dale Murphy	1.00	.45	.12
□ 67 Leon Durham	.25	.11	.03
□ 68 Darryl Strawberry	12.00	5.50	1.50
□ 69 Richie Zisk	.25	.11	.03
□ 70 Kent Hrbek	1.00	.45	.12
□ 71 Dave Stieb	.25	.11	.03
□ 72 Ken Schrom	.25	.11	.03
□ 73 George Bell	.40	.18	.05
□ 74 John Moses	.25	.11	.03
□ 75 Ed Lynch	.25	.11	.03
□ 76 Chuck Rainey	.25	.11	.03
□ 77 Biff Pocoroba	.25	.11	.03
□ 78 Cecilio Guante	.25	.11	.03
□ 79 Jim Barr	.25	.11	.03
□ 80 Kurt Bevacqua	.25	.11	.03
□ 81 Tom Foley	.25	.11	.03
□ 82 Joe Lefebvre	.25	.11	.03
□ 83 Andy Van Slyke	2.50	1.10	.30
□ 84 Bob Lillis MG	.25	.11	.03
□ 85 Ricky Adams	.25	.11	.03
□ 86 Jerry Hairston	.25	.11	.03
□ 87 Bob James	.25	.11	.03
□ 88 Joe Altobelli MG	.25	.11	.03
□ 89 Ed Romero	.25	.11	.03
□ 90 John Grubb	.25	.11	.03
□ 91 John Henry Johnson	.25	.11	.03
□ 92 Juan Espino	.25	.11	.03
□ 93 Candy Maldonado	.25	.11	.03
□ 94 Andre Thornton	.25	.11	.03
□ 95 Onix Concepcion	.25	.11	.03
□ 96 Donnie Hill UER (Listed as P, should be 2B)	.40	.18	.05
□ 97 Andre Dawson UER (Wrong middle name, should be Nolan)	4.00	1.80	.50
□ 98 Frank Tanana	.40	.18	.05
□ 99 Curt Wilkerson	.25	.11	.03
□ 100 Larry Gura	.25	.11	.03
□ 101 Dwayne Murphy	.25	.11	.03
□ 102 Tom Brennan	.25	.11	.03
□ 103 Dave Righetti	.40	.18	.05
□ 104 Steve Sax	.40	.18	.05
□ 105 Dan Petry	.40	.18	.05
□ 106 Cal Ripken	30.00	13.50	3.70
□ 107 Paul Molitor UER ('83 stats should say .270 BA, 608 AB, and 164 hits)	5.00	2.20	.60
□ 108 Fred Lynn	.40	.18	.05
□ 109 Neil Allen	.25	.11	.03
□ 110 Joe Niekro	.40	.18	.05
□ 111 Steve Carlton	3.00	1.35	.35
□ 112 Terry Kennedy	.25	.11	.03
□ 113 Bill Madlock	.25	.11	.03
□ 114 Chili Davis	.50	.23	.06
□ 115 Jim Gantner	.40	.18	.05
□ 116 Tom Seaver	4.00	1.80	.50
□ 117 Bill Buckner	.40	.18	.05
□ 118 Bill Caudill	.25	.11	.03
□ 119 Jim Clancy	.25	.11	.03

□ 120 John Castino	.25	.11	.03
□ 121 Dave Concepcion	.40	.18	.05
□ 122 Greg Luzinski	.40	.18	.05
□ 123 Mike Boddicker	.25	.11	.03
□ 124 Pete Ladd	.25	.11	.03
□ 125 Juan Berenguer	.25	.11	.03
□ 126 John Montefusco	.25	.11	.03
□ 127 Ed Jurak	.25	.11	.03
□ 128 Tom Niedenfuer	.25	.11	.03
□ 129 Bert Blyleven	.40	.18	.05
□ 130 Bud Black	.25	.11	.03
□ 131 Gorman Heimueller	.25	.11	.03
□ 132 Dan Schatzeder	.25	.11	.03
□ 133 Ron Jackson	.25	.11	.03
□ 134 Tom Henke	1.00	.45	.12
□ 135 Kevin Hickey	.25	.11	.03
□ 136 Mike Scott	.40	.18	.05
□ 137 Bo Diaz	.25	.11	.03
□ 138 Glenn Brummer	.25	.11	.03
□ 139 Sid Monge	.25	.11	.03
□ 140 Rich Gale	.25	.11	.03
□ 141 Brett Butler	.50	.23	.06
□ 142 Brian Harper	.50	.23	.06
□ 143 John Rabb	.25	.11	.03
□ 144 Gary Woods	.25	.11	.03
□ 145 Pat Putnam	.25	.11	.03
□ 146 Jim Acker	.25	.11	.03
□ 147 Mickey Hatcher	.25	.11	.03
□ 148 Todd Cruz	.25	.11	.03
□ 149 Tom Tellmann	.25	.11	.03
□ 150 John Wockenfuss	.25	.11	.03
□ 151 Wade Boggs UER 1983 runs 10; should be 100	7.00	3.10	.85
□ 152 Don Baylor	.50	.23	.06
□ 153 Bob Welch	.25	.11	.03
□ 154 Alan Bannister	.25	.11	.03
□ 155 Willie Aikens	.25	.11	.03
□ 156 Jeff Burroughs	.25	.11	.03
□ 157 Bryan Little	.25	.11	.03
□ 158 Bob Boone	.40	.18	.05
□ 159 Dave Hostetler	.25	.11	.03
□ 160 Jerry Dybzinski	.25	.11	.03
□ 161 Mike Madden	.25	.11	.03
□ 162 Luis DeLeon	.25	.11	.03
□ 163 Willie Hernandez	.40	.18	.05
□ 164 Frank Pastore	.25	.11	.03
□ 165 Rick Camp	.25	.11	.03
□ 166 Lee Mazzilli	.25	.11	.03
□ 167 Scot Thompson	.25	.11	.03
□ 168 Bob Forsch	.25	.11	.03
□ 169 Mike Flanagan	.25	.11	.03
□ 170 Rick Manning	.25	.11	.03
□ 171 Chet Lemon	.40	.18	.05
□ 172 Jerry Remy	.25	.11	.03
□ 173 Ron Guidry	.40	.18	.05
□ 174 Pedro Guerrero	.40	.18	.05
□ 175 Willie Wilson	.25	.11	.03
□ 176 Carney Lansford	.40	.18	.05
□ 177 Al Oliver	.40	.18	.05
□ 178 Jim Sundberg	.40	.18	.05
□ 179 Bobby Grich	.40	.18	.05
□ 180 Rich Dotson	.25	.11	.03
□ 181 Joaquin Andujar	.25	.11	.03
□ 182 Jose Cruz	.40	.18	.05
□ 183 Mike Schmidt	8.00	3.60	1.00
□ 184 Gary Redus	.25	.11	.03
□ 185 Garry Templeton	.25	.11	.03
□ 186 Tony Pena	.25	.11	.03
□ 187 Greg Minton	.25	.11	.03
□ 188 Phil Niekro	1.00	.45	.12
□ 189 Ferguson Jenkins	1.00	.45	.12
□ 190 Mookie Wilson	.40	.18	.05
□ 191 Jim Beattie	.25	.11	.03
□ 192 Gary Ward	.25	.11	.03
□ 193 Jesse Barfield	.40	.18	.05
□ 194 Pete Filson	.25	.11	.03
□ 195 Roy Lee Jackson	.25	.11	.03
□ 196 Rick Sweet	.25	.11	.03
□ 197 Jesse Orosco	.25	.11	.03
□ 198 Steve Lake	.25	.11	.03
□ 199 Ken Dayley	.25	.11	.03
□ 200 Manny Sarmiento	.25	.11	.03
□ 201 Mark Davis	.25	.11	.03
□ 202 Tim Flannery	.25	.11	.03
□ 203 Bill Scherrer	.25	.11	.03
□ 204 Al Holland	.25	.11	.03
□ 205 Dave Von Ohlen	.25	.11	.03
□ 206 Mike LaCoss	.25	.11	.03
□ 207 Juan Beniquez	.25	.11	.03
□ 208 Juan Agosto	.25	.11	.03
□ 209 Bobby Ramos	.25	.11	.03
□ 210 Al Bumbry	.40	.18	.05
□ 211 Mark Brouhard	.25	.11	.03
□ 212 Howard Bailey	.25	.11	.03
□ 213 Bruce Hurst	.25	.11	.03
□ 214 Bob Shirley	.25	.11	.03
□ 215 Pat Zachry	.25	.11	.03
□ 216 Julio Franco	1.00	.45	.12
□ 217 Mike Armstrong	.25	.11	.03
□ 218 Dave Beard	.25	.11	.03
□ 219 Steve Rogers	.25	.11	.03
□ 220 John Butcher	.25	.11	.03
□ 221 Mike Smithson	.25	.11	.03
□ 222 Frank White	.40	.18	.05
□ 223 Mike Heath	.25	.11	.03
□ 224 Chris Bando	.25	.11	.03
□ 225 Roy Smalley	.25	.11	.03
□ 226 Dusty Baker	.50	.23	.06
□ 227 Lou Whitaker	1.00	.45	.12
□ 228 John Lowenstein	.25	.11	.03
□ 229 Ben Oglivie	.25	.11	.03
□ 230 Doug DeCinces	.25	.11	.03
□ 231 Lonnie Smith	.25	.11	.03
□ 232 Ray Knight	.40	.18	.05
□ 233 Gary Matthews	.25	.11	.03
□ 234 Juan Bonilla	.25	.11	.03
□ 235 Rod Scurry	.25	.11	.03
□ 236 Atlee Hammaker	.25	.11	.03
□ 237 Mike Caldwell	.25	.11	.03
□ 238 Keith Hernandez	.50	.23	.06
□ 239 Larry Bowa	.40	.18	.05
□ 240 Tony Bernazard	.25	.11	.03
□ 241 Damaso Garcia	.25	.11	.03
□ 242 Tom Brunansky	.40	.18	.05
□ 243 Dan Driessen	.25	.11	.03
□ 244 Ron Kittle	.25	.11	.03
□ 245 Tim Stoddard	.25	.11	.03
□ 246 Bob L. Gibson (Brewers Pitcher)	.25	.11	.03
□ 247 Marty Castillo	.25	.11	.03
□ 248 Don Mattingly UER ("Traiing" on back)	50.00	22.00	6.25
□ 249 Jeff Newman	.25	.11	.03
□ 250 Alejandro Pena	.40	.18	.05
□ 251 Toby Harrah	.40	.18	.05
□ 252 Cesar Geronimo	.25	.11	.03
□ 253 Tom Underwood	.25	.11	.03
□ 254 Doug Flynn	.25	.11	.03
□ 255 Andy Hassler	.25	.11	.03
□ 256 Odell Jones	.25	.11	.03
□ 257 Rudy Law	.25	.11	.03
□ 258 Harry Spilman	.25	.11	.03
□ 259 Marty Bystrom	.25	.11	.03
□ 260 Dave Rucker	.25	.11	.03
□ 261 Ruppert Jones	.25	.11	.03
□ 262 Jeff R. Jones (Reds OF)	.25	.11	.03
□ 263 Gerald Perry	.40	.18	.05
□ 264 Gene Tenace	.40	.18	.05
□ 265 Brad Wellman	.25	.11	.03
□ 266 Dickie Noles	.25	.11	.03
□ 267 Jamie Allen	.25	.11	.03
□ 268 Jim Gott	.25	.11	.03
□ 269 Ron Davis	.25	.11	.03
□ 270 Benny Ayala	.25	.11	.03
□ 271 Ned Yost	.25	.11	.03
□ 272 Dave Rozema	.25	.11	.03
□ 273 Dave Stapleton	.25	.11	.03
□ 274 Lou Piniella	.40	.18	.05
□ 275 Jose Morales	.25	.11	.03
□ 276 Broderick Perkins	.25	.11	.03
□ 277 Butch Davis	.25	.11	.03
□ 278 Tony Phillips	4.00	1.80	.50
□ 279 Jeff Reardon	.50	.23	.06
□ 280 Ken Forsch	.25	.11	.03
□ 281 Pete O'Brien	.40	.18	.05
□ 282 Tom Paciorek	.25	.11	.03
□ 283 Frank LaCorte	.25	.11	.03
□ 284 Tim Lollar	.25	.11	.03
□ 285 Greg Gross	.25	.11	.03
□ 286 Alex Trevino	.25	.11	.03
□ 287 Gene Garber	.25	.11	.03

□ 288 Dave Parker	.50	.23	.06
□ 289 Lee Smith	2.00	.90	.25
□ 290 Dave LaPoint	.25	.11	.03
□ 291 John Shelby	.25	.11	.03
□ 292 Charlie Moore	.25	.11	.03
□ 293 Alan Trammell	1.00	.45	.12
□ 294 Tony Armas	.25	.11	.03
□ 295 Shane Rawley	.25	.11	.03
□ 296 Greg Brock	.25	.11	.03
□ 297 Hal McRae	.40	.18	.05
□ 298 Mike Davis	.25	.11	.03
□ 299 Tim Raines	1.00	.45	.12
□ 300 Bucky Dent	.40	.18	.05
□ 301 Tommy John	.50	.23	.06
□ 302 Carlton Fisk	3.00	1.35	.35
□ 303 Darrell Porter	.25	.11	.03
□ 304 Dickie Thon	.25	.11	.03
□ 305 Garry Maddox	.25	.11	.03
□ 306 Cesar Cedeno	.40	.18	.05
□ 307 Gary Lucas	.25	.11	.03
□ 308 Johnny Ray	.25	.11	.03
□ 309 Andy McGaffigan	.25	.11	.03
□ 310 Claudell Washington	.25	.11	.03
□ 311 Ryne Sandberg	15.00	6.75	1.85
□ 312 George Foster	.40	.18	.05
□ 313 Spike Owen	.40	.18	.05
□ 314 Gary Gaetti	.40	.18	.05
□ 315 Willie Upshaw	.25	.11	.03
□ 316 Al Williams	.25	.11	.03
□ 317 Jorge Orta	.25	.11	.03
□ 318 Orlando Mercado	.25	.11	.03
□ 319 Junior Ortiz	.25	.11	.03
□ 320 Mike Proly	.25	.11	.03
□ 321 Randy Johnson UER ('72-'82 stats are from Twins' Randy Johnson, '83 stats are from Braves' Randy Johnson)	.25	.11	.03
□ 322 Jim Morrison	.25	.11	.03
□ 323 Max Venable	.25	.11	.03
□ 324 Tony Gwynn	20.00	9.00	2.50
□ 325 Duane Walker	.25	.11	.03
□ 326 Ozzie Virgil	.25	.11	.03
□ 327 Jeff Lahti	.25	.11	.03
□ 328 Bill Dawley	.25	.11	.03
□ 329 Rob Wilfong	.25	.11	.03
□ 330 Marc Hill	.25	.11	.03
□ 331 Ray Burris	.25	.11	.03
□ 332 Allan Ramirez	.25	.11	.03
□ 333 Chuck Porter	.25	.11	.03
□ 334 Wayne Krenchicki	.25	.11	.03
□ 335 Gary Allenson	.25	.11	.03
□ 336 Bobby Meacham	.25	.11	.03
□ 337 Joe Beckwith	.25	.11	.03
□ 338 Rick Sutcliffe	.40	.18	.05
□ 339 Mark Huismann	.25	.11	.03
□ 340 Tim Conroy	.25	.11	.03
□ 341 Scott Sanderson	.25	.11	.03
□ 342 Larry Biittner	.25	.11	.03
□ 343 Dave Stewart	.50	.23	.06
□ 344 Darryl Motley	.25	.11	.03
□ 345 Chris Codiroli	.25	.11	.03
□ 346 Rich Behenna	.25	.11	.03
□ 347 Andre Robertson	.25	.11	.03
□ 348 Mike Marshall	.25	.11	.03
□ 349 Larry Herndon	.40	.18	.05
□ 350 Rich Dauer	.25	.11	.03
□ 351 Cecil Cooper	.40	.18	.05
□ 352 Rod Carew	2.00	.90	.25
□ 353 Willie McGee	.40	.18	.05
□ 354 Phil Garner	.40	.18	.05
□ 355 Joe Morgan	1.50	.70	.19
□ 356 Luis Salazar	.25	.11	.03
□ 357 John Candelaria	.25	.11	.03
□ 358 Bill Laskey	.25	.11	.03
□ 359 Bob McClure	.25	.11	.03
□ 360 Dave Kingman	.40	.18	.05
□ 361 Ron Cey	.40	.18	.05
□ 362 Matt Young	.25	.11	.03
□ 363 Lloyd Moseby	.25	.11	.03
□ 364 Frank Viola	.50	.23	.06
□ 365 Eddie Milner	.25	.11	.03
□ 366 Floyd Bannister	.25	.11	.03
□ 367 Dan Ford	.25	.11	.03
□ 368 Moose Haas	.25	.11	.03
□ 369 Doug Bair	.25	.11	.03

□ 370 Ray Fontenot	.25	.11	.03
□ 371 Luis Aponte	.25	.11	.03
□ 372 Jack Fimple	.25	.11	.03
□ 373 Neal Heaton	.25	.11	.03
□ 374 Greg Pryor	.25	.11	.03
□ 375 Wayne Gross	.25	.11	.03
□ 376 Charlie Lea	.25	.11	.03
□ 377 Steve Lubratich	.25	.11	.03
□ 378 Jon Matlack	.25	.11	.03
□ 379 Julio Cruz	.25	.11	.03
□ 380 John Mizerock	.25	.11	.03
□ 381 Kevin Gross	.40	.18	.05
□ 382 Mike Ramsey	.25	.11	.03
□ 383 Doug Gwosdz	.25	.11	.03
□ 384 Kelly Paris	.25	.11	.03
□ 385 Pete Falcone	.25	.11	.03
□ 386 Milt May	.25	.11	.03
□ 387 Fred Breining	.25	.11	.03
□ 388 Craig Lefferts	.25	.11	.03
□ 389 Steve Henderson	.25	.11	.03
□ 390 Randy Moffitt	.25	.11	.03
□ 391 Ron Washington	.25	.11	.03
□ 392 Gary Roenicke	.25	.11	.03
□ 393 Tom Candiotti	1.00	.45	.12
□ 394 Larry Pashnick	.25	.11	.03
□ 395 Dwight Evans	.40	.18	.05
□ 396 Goose Gossage	.50	.23	.06
□ 397 Derrel Thomas	.25	.11	.03
□ 398 Juan Eichelberger	.25	.11	.03
□ 399 Leon Roberts	.25	.11	.03
□ 400 Dave Lopes	.40	.18	.05
□ 401 Bill Gullickson	.25	.11	.03
□ 402 Geoff Zahn	.25	.11	.03
□ 403 Billy Sample	.25	.11	.03
□ 404 Mike Squires	.25	.11	.03
□ 405 Craig Reynolds	.25	.11	.03
□ 406 Eric Show	.25	.11	.03
□ 407 John Denny	.25	.11	.03
□ 408 Dann Bilardello	.25	.11	.03
□ 409 Bruce Benedict	.25	.11	.03
□ 410 Kent Tekulve	.40	.18	.05
□ 411 Mel Hall	.40	.18	.05
□ 412 John Stuper	.25	.11	.03
□ 413 Rick Dempsey	.25	.11	.03
□ 414 Don Sutton	.50	.23	.06
□ 415 Jack Morris	.50	.23	.06
□ 416 John Tudor	.25	.11	.03
□ 417 Willie Randolph	.40	.18	.05
□ 418 Jerry Reuss	.25	.11	.03
□ 419 Don Slaught	.40	.18	.05
□ 420 Steve McCatty	.25	.11	.03
□ 421 Tim Wallach	.40	.18	.05
□ 422 Larry Parrish	.25	.11	.03
□ 423 Brian Downing	.25	.11	.03
□ 424 Britt Burns	.25	.11	.03
□ 425 David Green	.25	.11	.03
□ 426 Jerry Mumphrey	.25	.11	.03
□ 427 Ivan DeJesus	.25	.11	.03
□ 428 Mario Soto	.25	.11	.03
□ 429 Gene Richards	.25	.11	.03
□ 430 Dale Berra	.25	.11	.03
□ 431 Darrell Evans	.40	.18	.05
□ 432 Glenn Hubbard	.25	.11	.03
□ 433 Jody Davis	.25	.11	.03
□ 434 Danny Heep	.25	.11	.03
□ 435 Ed Nunez	.25	.11	.03
□ 436 Bobby Castillo	.25	.11	.03
□ 437 Ernie Whitt	.25	.11	.03
□ 438 Scott Ullger	.25	.11	.03
□ 439 Doyle Alexander	.25	.11	.03
□ 440 Domingo Ramos	.25	.11	.03
□ 441 Craig Swan	.25	.11	.03
□ 442 Warren Brusstar	.25	.11	.03
□ 443 Len Barker	.25	.11	.03
□ 444 Mike Easler	.25	.11	.03
□ 445 Renie Martin	.25	.11	.03
□ 446 Dennis Rasmussen	.25	.11	.03
□ 447 Ted Power	.25	.11	.03
□ 448 Charles Hudson	.25	.11	.03
□ 449 Danny Cox	.25	.11	.03
□ 450 Kevin Bass	.25	.11	.03
□ 451 Daryl Sconiers	.25	.11	.03
□ 452 Scott Fletcher	.25	.11	.03
□ 453 Bryn Smith	.25	.11	.03
□ 454 Jim Dwyer	.25	.11	.03
□ 455 Rob Picciolo	.25	.11	.03

□ 456	Enos Cabell	.25	.11	.03
□ 457	Dennis Boyd	.40	.18	.05
□ 458	Butch Wynegar	.25	.11	.03
□ 459	Burt Hooton	.25	.11	.03
□ 460	Ron Hassey	.25	.11	.03
□ 461	Danny Jackson	1.00	.45	.12
□ 462	Bob Kearney	.25	.11	.03
□ 463	Terry Francona	.25	.11	.03
□ 464	Wayne Tolleson	.25	.11	.03
□ 465	Mickey Rivers	.25	.11	.03
□ 466	John Wathan	.25	.11	.03
□ 467	Bill Almon	.25	.11	.03
□ 468	George Vukovich	.25	.11	.03
□ 469	Steve Kemp	.25	.11	.03
□ 470	Ken Landreaux	.25	.11	.03
□ 471	Milt Wilcox	.25	.11	.03
□ 472	Tippy Martinez	.25	.11	.03
□ 473	Ted Simmons	.40	.18	.05
□ 474	Tim Foli	.25	.11	.03
□ 475	George Hendrick	.25	.11	.03
□ 476	Terry Puhl	.25	.11	.03
□ 477	Von Hayes	.25	.11	.03
□ 478	Bobby Brown	.25	.11	.03
□ 479	Lee Lacy	.25	.11	.03
□ 480	Joel Youngblood	.25	.11	.03
□ 481	Jim Slaton	.25	.11	.03
□ 482	Mike Fitzgerald	.25	.11	.03
□ 483	Keith Moreland	.25	.11	.03
□ 484	Ron Roenicke	.25	.11	.03
□ 485	Luis Leal	.25	.11	.03
□ 486	Bryan Oelkers	.25	.11	.03
□ 487	Bruce Berenyi	.25	.11	.03
□ 488	LaMarr Hoyt	.25	.11	.03
□ 489	Joe Nolan	.25	.11	.03
□ 490	Marshall Edwards	.25	.11	.03
□ 491	Mike Laga	.40	.18	.05
□ 492	Rick Cerone	.25	.11	.03
□ 493	Rick Miller UER (Listed as Mike on card front)	.25	.11	.03
□ 494	Rick Honeycutt	.25	.11	.03
□ 495	Mike Hargrove	.40	.18	.05
□ 496	Joe Simpson	.25	.11	.03
□ 497	Keith Atherton	.25	.11	.03
□ 498	Chris Welsh	.25	.11	.03
□ 499	Bruce Kison	.25	.11	.03
□ 500	Bobby Johnson	.25	.11	.03
□ 501	Jerry Koosman	.40	.18	.05
□ 502	Frank DiPino	.25	.11	.03
□ 503	Tony Perez	1.00	.45	.12
□ 504	Ken Oberkfell	.25	.11	.03
□ 505	Mark Thurmond	.25	.11	.03
□ 506	Joe Price	.25	.11	.03
□ 507	Pascual Perez	.25	.11	.03
□ 508	Marvell Wynne	.25	.11	.03
□ 509	Mike Krukow	.25	.11	.03
□ 510	Dick Ruthven	.25	.11	.03
□ 511	Al Cowens	.25	.11	.03
□ 512	Cliff Johnson	.25	.11	.03
□ 513	Randy Bush	.25	.11	.03
□ 514	Sammy Stewart	.25	.11	.03
□ 515	Bill Schroeder	.25	.11	.03
□ 516	Aurelio Lopez	.40	.18	.05
□ 517	Mike G. Brown	.25	.11	.03
□ 518	Graig Nettles	.40	.18	.05
□ 519	Dave Sax	.25	.11	.03
□ 520	Jerry Willard	.25	.11	.03
□ 521	Paul Splittorff	.25	.11	.03
□ 522	Tom Burgmeier	.25	.11	.03
□ 523	Chris Speier	.25	.11	.03
□ 524	Bobby Clark	.25	.11	.03
□ 525	George Wright	.25	.11	.03
□ 526	Dennis Lamp	.25	.11	.03
□ 527	Tony Scott	.25	.11	.03
□ 528	Ed Whitson	.25	.11	.03
□ 529	Ron Reed	.25	.11	.03
□ 530	Charlie Puleo	.25	.11	.03
□ 531	Jerry Royster	.25	.11	.03
□ 532	Don Robinson	.25	.11	.03
□ 533	Steve Trout	.25	.11	.03
□ 534	Bruce Sutter	.40	.18	.05
□ 535	Bob Horner	.25	.11	.03
□ 536	Pat Tabler	.25	.11	.03
□ 537	Chris Chambliss	.25	.11	.03
□ 538	Bob Ojeda	.25	.11	.03
□ 539	Alan Ashby	.25	.11	.03
□ 540	Jay Johnstone	.40	.18	.05
□ 541	Bob Dernier	.25	.11	.03
□ 542	Brook Jacoby	.40	.18	.05
□ 543	U.L. Washington	.25	.11	.03
□ 544	Danny Darwin	.25	.11	.03
□ 545	Kiko Garcia	.25	.11	.03
□ 546	Vance Law UER (Listed as P on card front)	.25	.11	.03
□ 547	Tug McGraw	.40	.18	.05
□ 548	Dave Smith	.25	.11	.03
□ 549	Len Matuszek	.25	.11	.03
□ 550	Tom Hume	.25	.11	.03
□ 551	Dave Dravecky	.40	.18	.05
□ 552	Rick Rhoden	.25	.11	.03
□ 553	Duane Kuiper	.25	.11	.03
□ 554	Rusty Staub	.40	.18	.05
□ 555	Bill Campbell	.25	.11	.03
□ 556	Mike Torrez	.25	.11	.03
□ 557	Dave Henderson	.40	.18	.05
□ 558	Len Whitehouse	.25	.11	.03
□ 559	Barry Bonnell	.25	.11	.03
□ 560	Rick Lysander	.25	.11	.03
□ 561	Garth Iorg	.25	.11	.03
□ 562	Bryan Clark	.25	.11	.03
□ 563	Brian Giles	.25	.11	.03
□ 564	Vern Ruhle	.25	.11	.03
□ 565	Steve Bedrosian	.25	.11	.03
□ 566	Larry McWilliams	.25	.11	.03
□ 567	Jeff Leonard UER (Listed as P on card front)	.25	.11	.03
□ 568	Alan Wiggins	.25	.11	.03
□ 569	Jeff Russell	.50	.23	.06
□ 570	Salome Barojas	.25	.11	.03
□ 571	Dane Iorg	.25	.11	.03
□ 572	Bob Knepper	.25	.11	.03
□ 573	Gary Lavelle	.25	.11	.03
□ 574	Gorman Thomas	.25	.11	.03
□ 575	Manny Trillo	.25	.11	.03
□ 576	Jim Palmer	2.00	.90	.25
□ 577	Dale Murray	.25	.11	.03
□ 578	Tom Brookens	.40	.18	.05
□ 579	Rich Gedman	.25	.11	.03
□ 580	Bill Doran	.40	.18	.05
□ 581	Steve Yeager	.25	.11	.03
□ 582	Dan Spillner	.25	.11	.03
□ 583	Dan Quisenberry	.25	.11	.03
□ 584	Rance Mulliniks	.25	.11	.03
□ 585	Storm Davis	.25	.11	.03
□ 586	Dave Schmidt	.25	.11	.03
□ 587	Bill Russell	.25	.11	.03
□ 588	Pat Sheridan	.25	.11	.03
□ 589	Rafael Ramirez UER (A's on front)	.25	.11	.03
□ 590	Bud Anderson	.25	.11	.03
□ 591	George Frazier	.25	.11	.03
□ 592	Lee Tunnell	.25	.11	.03
□ 593	Kirk Gibson	1.00	.45	.12
□ 594	Scott McGregor	.25	.11	.03
□ 595	Bob Bailor	.25	.11	.03
□ 596	Tommy Herr	.40	.18	.05
□ 597	Luis Sanchez	.25	.11	.03
□ 598	Dave Engle	.25	.11	.03
□ 599	Craig McMurtry	.25	.11	.03
□ 600	Carlos Diaz	.25	.11	.03
□ 601	Tom O'Malley	.25	.11	.03
□ 602	Nick Esasky	.25	.11	.03
□ 603	Ron Hodges	.25	.11	.03
□ 604	Ed VandeBerg	.25	.11	.03
□ 605	Alfredo Griffin	.25	.11	.03
□ 606	Glenn Hoffman	.25	.11	.03
□ 607	Hubie Brooks	.25	.11	.03
□ 608	Richard Barnes UER (Photo actually Neal Heaton)	.25	.11	.03
□ 609	Greg Walker	.40	.18	.05
□ 610	Ken Singleton	.25	.11	.03
□ 611	Mark Clear	.25	.11	.03
□ 612	Buck Martinez	.25	.11	.03
□ 613	Ken Griffey	.40	.18	.05
□ 614	Reid Nichols	.25	.11	.03
□ 615	Doug Sisk	.25	.11	.03
□ 616	Bob Brenly	.25	.11	.03
□ 617	Joey McLaughlin	.25	.11	.03
□ 618	Glenn Wilson	.40	.18	.05

□ 619 Bob Stoddard	.25	.11	.03
□ 620 Lenn Sakata UER (Listed as Len on card front)	.25	.11	.03
□ 621 Mike Young	.25	.11	.03
□ 622 John Stefero	.25	.11	.03
□ 623 Carmelo Martinez	.25	.11	.03
□ 624 Dave Bergman	.25	.11	.03
□ 625 Runnin' Reds UER (Sic, Redbirds) David Green Willie McGee Lonnie Smith Ozzie Smith	1.50	.70	.19
□ 626 Rudy May	.25	.11	.03
□ 627 Matt Keough	.25	.11	.03
□ 628 Jose DeLeon	.25	.11	.03
□ 629 Jim Essian	.25	.11	.03
□ 630 Darnell Coles	.25	.11	.03
□ 631 Mike Warren	.25	.11	.03
□ 632 Del Crandall MG	.25	.11	.03
□ 633 Dennis Martinez	.40	.18	.05
□ 634 Mike Moore	.40	.18	.05
□ 635 Lary Sorensen	.25	.11	.03
□ 636 Ricky Nelson	.25	.11	.03
□ 637 Omar Moreno	.25	.11	.03
□ 638 Charlie Hough	.40	.18	.05
□ 639 Dennis Eckersley	2.50	1.10	.30
□ 640 Walt Terrell	.25	.11	.03
□ 641 Denny Walling	.25	.11	.03
□ 642 Dave Anderson	.25	.11	.03
□ 643 Jose Oquendo	.40	.18	.05
□ 644 Bob Stanley	.25	.11	.03
□ 645 Dave Geisel	.25	.11	.03
□ 646 Scott Garrelts	.25	.11	.03
□ 647 Gary Pettis	.25	.11	.03
□ 648 Duke Snider Puzzle Card	.50	.23	.06
□ 649 Johnnie LeMaster	.25	.11	.03
□ 650 Dave Collins	.25	.11	.03
□ 651 The Chicken	1.00	.45	.12
□ 652 DK Checklist 1-26 (Unnumbered)	.40	.18	.05
□ 653 Checklist 27-130 (Unnumbered)	.40	.18	.05
□ 654 Checklist 131-234 (Unnumbered)	.40	.18	.05
□ 655 Checklist 235-338 (Unnumbered)	.40	.18	.05
□ 656 Checklist 339-442 (Unnumbered)	.40	.18	.05
□ 657 Checklist 443-546 (Unnumbered)	.40	.18	.05
□ 658 Checklist 547-651 (Unnumbered)	.40	.18	.05
□ A Living Legends A Gaylord Perry Rollie Fingers	4.00	1.80	.50
□ B Living Legends B Carl Yastrzemski Johnny Bench	8.00	3.60	1.00

1985 Donruss

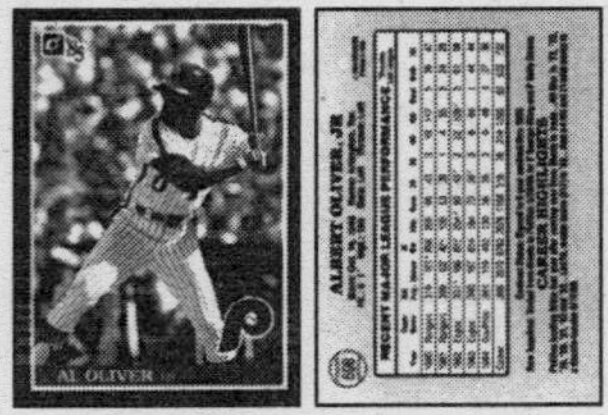

The 1985 Donruss set consists of 660 standard-size cards. Wax packs contained 15 cards and a Lou Gehrig puzzle panel. The fronts feature full color photos framed by jet black borders (making the cards condition sensitive). The first 26 cards of the set feature Diamond Kings (DK), for the fourth year in a row; the artwork on the Diamond Kings was again produced by the Perez-Steele Galleries. Cards 27-46 feature Rated Rookies (RR). The unnumbered checklist cards are arbitrarily numbered below as numbers 654 through 660. Rookie Cards in this set include Roger Clemens, Eric Davis, Shawon Dunston, Dwight Gooden, Orel Hershiser, Jimmy Key, Mark Langston, Terry Pendleton, Kirby Puckett, Jose Rijo, Bret Saberhagen, and Danny Tartabull.

	MINT	NRMT	EXC
COMPLETE SET (660)	120.00	55.00	15.00
COMPLETE FACT.SET (660)	140.00	65.00	17.50
COMMON CARD (1-660)	.10	.05	.01
SEMISTARS	.20	.09	.03
STARS	.40	.18	.05
CONDITION SENSITIVE SET			

□ 1 Ryne Sandberg DK	2.50	1.10	.30
□ 2 Doug DeCinces DK	.10	.05	.01
□ 3 Richard Dotson DK	.10	.05	.01
□ 4 Bert Blyleven DK	.20	.09	.03
□ 5 Lou Whitaker DK	.40	.18	.05
□ 6 Dan Quisenberry DK	.10	.05	.01
□ 7 Don Mattingly DK	4.00	1.80	.50
□ 8 Carney Lansford DK	.20	.09	.03
□ 9 Frank Tanana DK	.10	.05	.01
□ 10 Willie Upshaw DK	.10	.05	.01
□ 11 Claudell Washington DK	.10	.05	.01
□ 12 Mike Marshall DK	.10	.05	.01
□ 13 Joaquin Andujar DK	.10	.05	.01
□ 14 Cal Ripken DK	5.00	2.20	.60
□ 15 Jim Rice DK	.20	.09	.03
□ 16 Don Sutton DK	.20	.09	.03
□ 17 Frank Viola DK	.20	.09	.03
□ 18 Alvin Davis DK	.10	.05	.01
□ 19 Mario Soto DK	.10	.05	.01
□ 20 Jose Cruz DK	.10	.05	.01
□ 21 Charlie Lea DK	.10	.05	.01
□ 22 Jesse Orosco DK	.10	.05	.01
□ 23 Juan Samuel DK	.10	.05	.01
□ 24 Tony Pena DK	.10	.05	.01
□ 25 Tony Gwynn DK	3.00	1.35	.35
□ 26 Bob Brenly DK	.10	.05	.01
□ 27 Danny Tartabull RR	1.00	.45	.12
□ 28 Mike Bielecki RR	.10	.05	.01
□ 29 Steve Lyons RR	.20	.09	.03
□ 30 Jeff Reed RR	.10	.05	.01
□ 31 Tony Brewer RR	.10	.05	.01
□ 32 John Morris RR	.10	.05	.01
□ 33 Daryl Boston RR	.10	.05	.01
□ 34 Al Pulido RR	.10	.05	.01
□ 35 Steve Kiefer RR	.10	.05	.01
□ 36 Larry Sheets RR	.10	.05	.01
□ 37 Scott Bradley RR	.10	.05	.01
□ 38 Calvin Schiraldi RR	.10	.05	.01
□ 39 Shawon Dunston RR	1.00	.45	.12
□ 40 Charlie Mitchell RR	.10	.05	.01
□ 41 Billy Hatcher RR	.40	.18	.05
□ 42 Russ Stephans RR	.10	.05	.01
□ 43 Alejandro Sanchez RR	.10	.05	.01
□ 44 Steve Jeltz RR	.10	.05	.01
□ 45 Jim Traber RR	.10	.05	.01
□ 46 Doug Loman RR	.10	.05	.01
□ 47 Eddie Murray	3.00	1.35	.35
□ 48 Robin Yount	2.00	.90	.25
□ 49 Lance Parrish	.20	.09	.03
□ 50 Jim Rice	.20	.09	.03
□ 51 Dave Winfield	1.50	.70	.19
□ 52 Fernando Valenzuela	.20	.09	.03
□ 53 George Brett	4.00	1.80	.50
□ 54 Dave Kingman	.20	.09	.03
□ 55 Gary Carter	.40	.18	.05
□ 56 Buddy Bell	.20	.09	.03
□ 57 Reggie Jackson	1.50	.70	.19
□ 58 Harold Baines	.20	.09	.03
□ 59 Ozzie Smith	2.50	1.10	.30
□ 60 Nolan Ryan UER (Set strikeout record in 1973, not 1972)	8.00	3.60	1.00
□ 61 Mike Schmidt	2.50	1.10	.30
□ 62 Dave Parker	.40	.18	.05
□ 63 Tony Gwynn	6.00	2.70	.75

☐ 64 Tony Pena	.10	.05	.01
☐ 65 Jack Clark	.20	.09	.03
☐ 66 Dale Murphy	.40	.18	.05
☐ 67 Ryne Sandberg	5.00	2.20	.60
☐ 68 Keith Hernandez	.20	.09	.03
☐ 69 Alvin Davis	.20	.09	.03
☐ 70 Kent Hrbek	.20	.09	.03
☐ 71 Willie Upshaw	.10	.05	.01
☐ 72 Dave Engle	.10	.05	.01
☐ 73 Alfredo Griffin	.10	.05	.01
☐ 74A Jack Perconte (Career Highlights takes four lines)	.10	.05	.01
☐ 74B Jack Perconte (Career Highlights takes three lines)	.10	.05	.01
☐ 75 Jesse Orosco	.10	.05	.01
☐ 76 Jody Davis	.10	.05	.01
☐ 77 Bob Horner	.10	.05	.01
☐ 78 Larry McWilliams	.10	.05	.01
☐ 79 Joel Youngblood	.10	.05	.01
☐ 80 Alan Wiggins	.10	.05	.01
☐ 81 Ron Oester	.10	.05	.01
☐ 82 Ozzie Virgil	.10	.05	.01
☐ 83 Ricky Horton	.10	.05	.01
☐ 84 Bill Doran	.10	.05	.01
☐ 85 Rod Carew	.60	.25	.07
☐ 86 LaMarr Hoyt	.10	.05	.01
☐ 87 Tim Wallach	.20	.09	.03
☐ 88 Mike Flanagan	.10	.05	.01
☐ 89 Jim Sundberg	.10	.05	.01
☐ 90 Chet Lemon	.10	.05	.01
☐ 91 Bob Stanley	.10	.05	.01
☐ 92 Willie Randolph	.20	.09	.03
☐ 93 Bill Russell	.10	.05	.01
☐ 94 Julio Franco	.40	.18	.05
☐ 95 Dan Quisenberry	.20	.09	.03
☐ 96 Bill Caudill	.10	.05	.01
☐ 97 Bill Gullickson	.10	.05	.01
☐ 98 Danny Darwin	.10	.05	.01
☐ 99 Curtis Wilkerson	.10	.05	.01
☐ 100 Bud Black	.10	.05	.01
☐ 101 Tony Phillips	.40	.18	.05
☐ 102 Tony Bernazard	.10	.05	.01
☐ 103 Jay Howell	.10	.05	.01
☐ 104 Burt Hooton	.10	.05	.01
☐ 105 Milt Wilcox	.10	.05	.01
☐ 106 Rich Dauer	.10	.05	.01
☐ 107 Don Sutton	.40	.18	.05
☐ 108 Mike Witt	.10	.05	.01
☐ 109 Bruce Sutter	.20	.09	.03
☐ 110 Enos Cabell	.10	.05	.01
☐ 111 John Denny	.10	.05	.01
☐ 112 Dave Dravecky	.20	.09	.03
☐ 113 Marvell Wynne	.10	.05	.01
☐ 114 Johnnie LeMaster	.10	.05	.01
☐ 115 Chuck Porter	.10	.05	.01
☐ 116 John Gibbons	.10	.05	.01
☐ 117 Keith Moreland	.10	.05	.01
☐ 118 Darnell Coles	.10	.05	.01
☐ 119 Dennis Lamp	.10	.05	.01
☐ 120 Ron Davis	.10	.05	.01
☐ 121 Nick Esasky	.10	.05	.01
☐ 122 Vance Law	.10	.05	.01
☐ 123 Gary Roenicke	.10	.05	.01
☐ 124 Bill Schroeder	.10	.05	.01
☐ 125 Dave Rozema	.10	.05	.01
☐ 126 Bobby Meacham	.10	.05	.01
☐ 127 Marty Barrett	.10	.05	.01
☐ 128 R.J. Reynolds	.10	.05	.01
☐ 129 Ernie Camacho UER (Photo actually Rich Thompson)	.10	.05	.01
☐ 130 Jorge Orta	.10	.05	.01
☐ 131 Lary Sorensen	.10	.05	.01
☐ 132 Terry Francona	.10	.05	.01
☐ 133 Fred Lynn	.20	.09	.03
☐ 134 Bob Jones	.10	.05	.01
☐ 135 Jerry Hairston	.10	.05	.01
☐ 136 Kevin Bass	.10	.05	.01
☐ 137 Garry Maddox	.10	.05	.01
☐ 138 Dave LaPoint	.10	.05	.01
☐ 139 Kevin McReynolds	.20	.09	.03
☐ 140 Wayne Krenchicki	.10	.05	.01
☐ 141 Rafael Ramirez	.10	.05	.01
☐ 142 Rod Scurry	.10	.05	.01
☐ 143 Greg Minton	.10	.05	.01
☐ 144 Tim Stoddard	.10	.05	.01
☐ 145 Steve Henderson	.10	.05	.01
☐ 146 George Bell	.20	.09	.03
☐ 147 Dave Meier	.10	.05	.01
☐ 148 Sammy Stewart	.10	.05	.01
☐ 149 Mark Brouhard	.10	.05	.01
☐ 150 Larry Herndon	.10	.05	.01
☐ 151 Oil Can Boyd	.10	.05	.01
☐ 152 Brian Dayett	.10	.05	.01
☐ 153 Tom Niedenfuer	.10	.05	.01
☐ 154 Brook Jacoby	.10	.05	.01
☐ 155 Onix Concepcion	.10	.05	.01
☐ 156 Tim Conroy	.10	.05	.01
☐ 157 Joe Hesketh	.10	.05	.01
☐ 158 Brian Downing	.10	.05	.01
☐ 159 Tommy Dunbar	.10	.05	.01
☐ 160 Marc Hill	.10	.05	.01
☐ 161 Phil Garner	.10	.05	.01
☐ 162 Jerry Davis	.10	.05	.01
☐ 163 Bill Campbell	.10	.05	.01
☐ 164 John Franco	1.00	.45	.12
☐ 165 Len Barker	.10	.05	.01
☐ 166 Benny Distefano	.10	.05	.01
☐ 167 George Frazier	.10	.05	.01
☐ 168 Tito Landrum	.10	.05	.01
☐ 169 Cal Ripken	8.00	3.60	1.00
☐ 170 Cecil Cooper	.20	.09	.03
☐ 171 Alan Trammell	.40	.18	.05
☐ 172 Wade Boggs	2.50	1.10	.30
☐ 173 Don Baylor	.40	.18	.05
☐ 174 Pedro Guerrero	.20	.09	.03
☐ 175 Frank White	.20	.09	.03
☐ 176 Rickey Henderson	1.50	.70	.19
☐ 177 Charlie Lea	.10	.05	.01
☐ 178 Pete O'Brien	.10	.05	.01
☐ 179 Doug DeCinces	.10	.05	.01
☐ 180 Ron Kittle	.10	.05	.01
☐ 181 George Hendrick	.10	.05	.01
☐ 182 Joe Niekro	.10	.05	.01
☐ 183 Juan Samuel	.10	.05	.01
☐ 184 Mario Soto	.10	.05	.01
☐ 185 Goose Gossage	.20	.09	.03
☐ 186 Johnny Ray	.10	.05	.01
☐ 187 Bob Brenly	.10	.05	.01
☐ 188 Craig McMurtry	.10	.05	.01
☐ 189 Leon Durham	.10	.05	.01
☐ 190 Dwight Gooden	4.00	1.80	.50
☐ 191 Barry Bonnell	.10	.05	.01
☐ 192 Tim Teufel	.10	.05	.01
☐ 193 Dave Stieb	.20	.09	.03
☐ 194 Mickey Hatcher	.10	.05	.01
☐ 195 Jesse Barfield	.10	.05	.01
☐ 196 Al Cowens	.10	.05	.01
☐ 197 Hubie Brooks	.10	.05	.01
☐ 198 Steve Trout	.10	.05	.01
☐ 199 Glenn Hubbard	.10	.05	.01
☐ 200 Bill Madlock	.10	.05	.01
☐ 201 Jeff D. Robinson	.10	.05	.01
☐ 202 Eric Show	.10	.05	.01
☐ 203 Dave Concepcion	.20	.09	.03
☐ 204 Ivan DeJesus	.10	.05	.01
☐ 205 Neil Allen	.10	.05	.01
☐ 206 Jerry Mumphrey	.10	.05	.01
☐ 207 Mike C. Brown	.10	.05	.01
☐ 208 Carlton Fisk	.75	.35	.09
☐ 209 Bryn Smith	.10	.05	.01
☐ 210 Tippy Martinez	.10	.05	.01
☐ 211 Dion James	.10	.05	.01
☐ 212 Willie Hernandez	.10	.05	.01
☐ 213 Mike Easler	.10	.05	.01
☐ 214 Ron Guidry	.20	.09	.03
☐ 215 Rick Honeycutt	.10	.05	.01
☐ 216 Brett Butler	.40	.18	.05
☐ 217 Larry Gura	.10	.05	.01
☐ 218 Ray Burris	.10	.05	.01
☐ 219 Steve Rogers	.10	.05	.01
☐ 220 Frank Tanana UER (Bats Left listed twice on card back)	.10	.05	.01
☐ 221 Ned Yost	.10	.05	.01
☐ 222 Bret Saberhagen UER (18 career IP on back)	1.50	.70	.19
☐ 223 Mike Davis	.10	.05	.01
☐ 224 Bert Blyleven	.40	.18	.05
☐ 225 Steve Kemp	.10	.05	.01

□ 226	Jerry Reuss	.10	.05	.01
□ 227	Darrell Evans UER (80 homers in 1980)	.20	.09	.03
□ 228	Wayne Gross	.10	.05	.01
□ 229	Jim Gantner	.10	.05	.01
□ 230	Bob Boone	.20	.09	.03
□ 231	Lonnie Smith	.10	.05	.01
□ 232	Frank DiPino	.10	.05	.01
□ 233	Jerry Koosman	.10	.05	.01
□ 234	Graig Nettles	.20	.09	.03
□ 235	John Tudor	.10	.05	.01
□ 236	John Rabb	.10	.05	.01
□ 237	Rick Manning	.10	.05	.01
□ 238	Mike Fitzgerald	.10	.05	.01
□ 239	Gary Matthews	.10	.05	.01
□ 240	Jim Presley	.20	.09	.03
□ 241	Dave Collins	.10	.05	.01
□ 242	Gary Gaetti	.20	.09	.03
□ 243	Dann Bilardello	.10	.05	.01
□ 244	Rudy Law	.10	.05	.01
□ 245	John Lowenstein	.10	.05	.01
□ 246	Tom Tellmann	.10	.05	.01
□ 247	Howard Johnson	.20	.09	.03
□ 248	Ray Fontenot	.10	.05	.01
□ 249	Tony Armas	.10	.05	.01
□ 250	Candy Maldonado	.10	.05	.01
□ 251	Mike Jeffcoat	.10	.05	.01
□ 252	Dane Iorg	.10	.05	.01
□ 253	Bruce Bochte	.10	.05	.01
□ 254	Pete Rose	2.00	.90	.25
□ 255	Don Aase	.10	.05	.01
□ 256	George Wright	.10	.05	.01
□ 257	Britt Burns	.10	.05	.01
□ 258	Mike Scott	.10	.05	.01
□ 259	Len Matuszek	.10	.05	.01
□ 260	Dave Rucker	.10	.05	.01
□ 261	Craig Lefferts	.10	.05	.01
□ 262	Jay Tibbs	.10	.05	.01
□ 263	Bruce Benedict	.10	.05	.01
□ 264	Don Robinson	.10	.05	.01
□ 265	Gary Lavelle	.10	.05	.01
□ 266	Scott Sanderson	.10	.05	.01
□ 267	Matt Young	.10	.05	.01
□ 268	Ernie Whitt	.10	.05	.01
□ 269	Houston Jimenez	.10	.05	.01
□ 270	Ken Dixon	.10	.05	.01
□ 271	Pete Ladd	.10	.05	.01
□ 272	Juan Berenguer	.10	.05	.01
□ 273	Roger Clemens	18.00	8.00	2.20
□ 274	Rick Cerone	.10	.05	.01
□ 275	Dave Anderson	.10	.05	.01
□ 276	George Vukovich	.10	.05	.01
□ 277	Greg Pryor	.10	.05	.01
□ 278	Mike Warren	.10	.05	.01
□ 279	Bob James	.10	.05	.01
□ 280	Bobby Grich	.20	.09	.03
□ 281	Mike Mason	.10	.05	.01
□ 282	Ron Reed	.10	.05	.01
□ 283	Alan Ashby	.10	.05	.01
□ 284	Mark Thurmond	.10	.05	.01
□ 285	Joe Lefebvre	.10	.05	.01
□ 286	Ted Power	.10	.05	.01
□ 287	Chris Chambliss	.10	.05	.01
□ 288	Lee Tunnell	.10	.05	.01
□ 289	Rich Bordi	.10	.05	.01
□ 290	Glenn Brummer	.10	.05	.01
□ 291	Mike Boddicker	.10	.05	.01
□ 292	Rollie Fingers	.40	.18	.05
□ 293	Lou Whitaker	.40	.18	.05
□ 294	Dwight Evans	.20	.09	.03
□ 295	Don Mattingly	8.00	3.60	1.00
□ 296	Mike Marshall	.10	.05	.01
□ 297	Willie Wilson	.10	.05	.01
□ 298	Mike Heath	.10	.05	.01
□ 299	Tim Raines	.40	.18	.05
□ 300	Larry Parrish	.10	.05	.01
□ 301	Geoff Zahn	.10	.05	.01
□ 302	Rich Dotson	.10	.05	.01
□ 303	David Green	.10	.05	.01
□ 304	Jose Cruz	.20	.09	.03
□ 305	Steve Carlton	.75	.35	.09
□ 306	Gary Redus	.10	.05	.01
□ 307	Steve Garvey	.40	.18	.05
□ 308	Jose DeLeon	.10	.05	.01
□ 309	Randy Lerch	.10	.05	.01
□ 310	Claudell Washington	.10	.05	.01
□ 311	Lee Smith	1.00	.45	.12
□ 312	Darryl Strawberry	1.00	.45	.12
□ 313	Jim Beattie	.10	.05	.01
□ 314	John Butcher	.10	.05	.01
□ 315	Damaso Garcia	.10	.05	.01
□ 316	Mike Smithson	.10	.05	.01
□ 317	Luis Leal	.10	.05	.01
□ 318	Ken Phelps	.10	.05	.01
□ 319	Wally Backman	.10	.05	.01
□ 320	Ron Cey	.20	.09	.03
□ 321	Brad Komminsk	.10	.05	.01
□ 322	Jason Thompson	.10	.05	.01
□ 323	Frank Williams	.10	.05	.01
□ 324	Tim Lollar	.10	.05	.01
□ 325	Eric Davis	1.50	.70	.19
□ 326	Von Hayes	.10	.05	.01
□ 327	Andy Van Slyke	.60	.25	.07
□ 328	Craig Reynolds	.10	.05	.01
□ 329	Dick Schofield	.10	.05	.01
□ 330	Scott Fletcher	.10	.05	.01
□ 331	Jeff Reardon	.20	.09	.03
□ 332	Rick Dempsey	.10	.05	.01
□ 333	Ben Oglivie	.10	.05	.01
□ 334	Dan Petry	.10	.05	.01
□ 335	Jackie Gutierrez	.10	.05	.01
□ 336	Dave Righetti	.20	.09	.03
□ 337	Alejandro Pena	.10	.05	.01
□ 338	Mel Hall	.10	.05	.01
□ 339	Pat Sheridan	.10	.05	.01
□ 340	Keith Atherton	.10	.05	.01
□ 341	David Palmer	.10	.05	.01
□ 342	Gary Ward	.10	.05	.01
□ 343	Dave Stewart	.20	.09	.03
□ 344	Mark Gubicza	.40	.18	.05
□ 345	Carney Lansford	.20	.09	.03
□ 346	Jerry Willard	.10	.05	.01
□ 347	Ken Griffey	.20	.09	.03
□ 348	Franklin Stubbs	.10	.05	.01
□ 349	Aurelio Lopez	.10	.05	.01
□ 350	Al Bumbry	.10	.05	.01
□ 351	Charlie Moore	.10	.05	.01
□ 352	Luis Sanchez	.10	.05	.01
□ 353	Darrell Porter	.10	.05	.01
□ 354	Bill Dawley	.10	.05	.01
□ 355	Charles Hudson	.10	.05	.01
□ 356	Garry Templeton	.10	.05	.01
□ 357	Cecilio Guante	.10	.05	.01
□ 358	Jeff Leonard	.10	.05	.01
□ 359	Paul Molitor	2.00	.90	.25
□ 360	Ron Gardenhire	.10	.05	.01
□ 361	Larry Bowa	.20	.09	.03
□ 362	Bob Kearney	.10	.05	.01
□ 363	Garth Iorg	.10	.05	.01
□ 364	Tom Brunansky	.20	.09	.03
□ 365	Brad Gulden	.10	.05	.01
□ 366	Greg Walker	.10	.05	.01
□ 367	Mike Young	.10	.05	.01
□ 368	Rick Waits	.10	.05	.01
□ 369	Doug Bair	.10	.05	.01
□ 370	Bob Shirley	.10	.05	.01
□ 371	Bob Ojeda	.10	.05	.01
□ 372	Bob Welch	.10	.05	.01
□ 373	Neal Heaton	.10	.05	.01
□ 374	Danny Jackson UER (Photo actually Frank Wills)	.10	.05	.01
□ 375	Donnie Hill	.10	.05	.01
□ 376	Mike Stenhouse	.10	.05	.01
□ 377	Bruce Kison	.10	.05	.01
□ 378	Wayne Tolleson	.10	.05	.01
□ 379	Floyd Bannister	.10	.05	.01
□ 380	Vern Ruhle	.10	.05	.01
□ 381	Tim Corcoran	.10	.05	.01
□ 382	Kurt Kepshire	.10	.05	.01
□ 383	Bobby Brown	.10	.05	.01
□ 384	Dave Van Gorder	.10	.05	.01
□ 385	Rick Mahler	.10	.05	.01
□ 386	Lee Mazzilli	.10	.05	.01
□ 387	Bill Laskey	.10	.05	.01
□ 388	Thad Bosley	.10	.05	.01
□ 389	Al Chambers	.10	.05	.01
□ 390	Tony Fernandez	.20	.09	.03
□ 391	Ron Washington	.10	.05	.01
□ 392	Bill Swaggerty	.10	.05	.01
□ 393	Bob L. Gibson	.10	.05	.01
□ 394	Marty Castillo	.10	.05	.01

□ 395 Steve Crawford	.10	.05	.01
□ 396 Clay Christiansen	.10	.05	.01
□ 397 Bob Bailor	.10	.05	.01
□ 398 Mike Hargrove	.20	.09	.03
□ 399 Charlie Leibrandt	.10	.05	.01
□ 400 Tom Burgmeier	.10	.05	.01
□ 401 Razor Shines	.10	.05	.01
□ 402 Rob Wilfong	.10	.05	.01
□ 403 Tom Henke	.40	.18	.05
□ 404 Al Jones	.10	.05	.01
□ 405 Mike LaCoss	.10	.05	.01
□ 406 Luis DeLeon	.10	.05	.01
□ 407 Greg Gross	.10	.05	.01
□ 408 Tom Hume	.10	.05	.01
□ 409 Rick Camp	.10	.05	.01
□ 410 Milt May	.10	.05	.01
□ 411 Henry Cotto	.10	.05	.01
□ 412 David Von Ohlen	.10	.05	.01
□ 413 Scott McGregor	.10	.05	.01
□ 414 Ted Simmons	.20	.09	.03
□ 415 Jack Morris	.40	.18	.05
□ 416 Bill Buckner	.20	.09	.03
□ 417 Butch Wynegar	.10	.05	.01
□ 418 Steve Sax	.20	.09	.03
□ 419 Steve Balboni	.10	.05	.01
□ 420 Dwayne Murphy	.10	.05	.01
□ 421 Andre Dawson	1.25	.55	.16
□ 422 Charlie Hough	.20	.09	.03
□ 423 Tommy John	.40	.18	.05
□ 424A Tom Seaver ERR (Photo actually Floyd Bannister)	1.25	.55	.16
□ 424B Tom Seaver COR	25.00	11.00	3.10
□ 425 Tommy Herr	.20	.09	.03
□ 426 Terry Puhl	.10	.05	.01
□ 427 Al Holland	.10	.05	.01
□ 428 Eddie Milner	.10	.05	.01
□ 429 Terry Kennedy	.10	.05	.01
□ 430 John Candelaria	.10	.05	.01
□ 431 Manny Trillo	.10	.05	.01
□ 432 Ken Oberkfell	.10	.05	.01
□ 433 Rick Sutcliffe	.10	.05	.01
□ 434 Ron Darling	.20	.09	.03
□ 435 Spike Owen	.10	.05	.01
□ 436 Frank Viola	.20	.09	.03
□ 437 Lloyd Moseby	.10	.05	.01
□ 438 Kirby Puckett	30.00	13.50	3.70
□ 439 Jim Clancy	.10	.05	.01
□ 440 Mike Moore	.10	.05	.01
□ 441 Doug Sisk	.10	.05	.01
□ 442 Dennis Eckersley	.40	.18	.05
□ 443 Gerald Perry	.10	.05	.01
□ 444 Dale Berra	.10	.05	.01
□ 445 Dusty Baker	.20	.09	.03
□ 446 Ed Whitson	.10	.05	.01
□ 447 Cesar Cedeno	.20	.09	.03
□ 448 Rick Schu	.10	.05	.01
□ 449 Joaquin Andujar	.10	.05	.01
□ 450 Mark Bailey	.10	.05	.01
□ 451 Ron Romanick	.10	.05	.01
□ 452 Julio Cruz	.10	.05	.01
□ 453 Miguel Dilone	.10	.05	.01
□ 454 Storm Davis	.10	.05	.01
□ 455 Jaime Cocanower	.10	.05	.01
□ 456 Barbaro Garbey	.10	.05	.01
□ 457 Rich Gedman	.10	.05	.01
□ 458 Phil Niekro	.40	.18	.05
□ 459 Mike Scioscia	.10	.05	.01
□ 460 Pat Tabler	.10	.05	.01
□ 461 Darryl Motley	.10	.05	.01
□ 462 Chris Codiroli	.10	.05	.01
□ 463 Doug Flynn	.10	.05	.01
□ 464 Billy Sample	.10	.05	.01
□ 465 Mickey Rivers	.10	.05	.01
□ 466 John Wathan	.10	.05	.01
□ 467 Bill Krueger	.10	.05	.01
□ 468 Andre Thornton	.10	.05	.01
□ 469 Rex Hudler	.10	.05	.01
□ 470 Sid Bream	.40	.18	.05
□ 471 Kirk Gibson	.40	.18	.05
□ 472 John Shelby	.10	.05	.01
□ 473 Moose Haas	.10	.05	.01
□ 474 Doug Corbett	.10	.05	.01
□ 475 Willie McGee	.20	.09	.03
□ 476 Bob Knepper	.10	.05	.01
□ 477 Kevin Gross	.10	.05	.01

□ 478 Carmelo Martinez	.10	.05	.01
□ 479 Kent Tekulve	.10	.05	.01
□ 480 Chili Davis	.20	.09	.03
□ 481 Bobby Clark	.10	.05	.01
□ 482 Mookie Wilson	.20	.09	.03
□ 483 Dave Owen	.10	.05	.01
□ 484 Ed Nunez	.10	.05	.01
□ 485 Rance Mulliniks	.10	.05	.01
□ 486 Ken Schrom	.10	.05	.01
□ 487 Jeff Russell	.20	.09	.03
□ 488 Tom Paciorek	.10	.05	.01
□ 489 Dan Ford	.10	.05	.01
□ 490 Mike Caldwell	.10	.05	.01
□ 491 Scottie Earl	.10	.05	.01
□ 492 Jose Rijo	1.00	.45	.12
□ 493 Bruce Hurst	.10	.05	.01
□ 494 Ken Landreaux	.10	.05	.01
□ 495 Mike Fischlin	.10	.05	.01
□ 496 Don Slaught	.10	.05	.01
□ 497 Steve McCatty	.10	.05	.01
□ 498 Gary Lucas	.10	.05	.01
□ 499 Gary Pettis	.10	.05	.01
□ 500 Marvis Foley	.10	.05	.01
□ 501 Mike Squires	.10	.05	.01
□ 502 Jim Pankovits	.10	.05	.01
□ 503 Luis Aguayo	.10	.05	.01
□ 504 Ralph Citarella	.10	.05	.01
□ 505 Bruce Bochy	.10	.05	.01
□ 506 Bob Owchinko	.10	.05	.01
□ 507 Pascual Perez	.10	.05	.01
□ 508 Lee Lacy	.10	.05	.01
□ 509 Atlee Hammaker	.10	.05	.01
□ 510 Bob Dernier	.10	.05	.01
□ 511 Ed VandeBerg	.10	.05	.01
□ 512 Cliff Johnson	.10	.05	.01
□ 513 Len Whitehouse	.10	.05	.01
□ 514 Dennis Martinez	.20	.09	.03
□ 515 Ed Romero	.10	.05	.01
□ 516 Rusty Kuntz	.10	.05	.01
□ 517 Rick Miller	.10	.05	.01
□ 518 Dennis Rasmussen	.10	.05	.01
□ 519 Steve Yeager	.10	.05	.01
□ 520 Chris Bando	.10	.05	.01
□ 521 U.L. Washington	.10	.05	.01
□ 522 Curt Young	.10	.05	.01
□ 523 Angel Salazar	.10	.05	.01
□ 524 Curt Kaufman	.10	.05	.01
□ 525 Odell Jones	.10	.05	.01
□ 526 Juan Agosto	.10	.05	.01
□ 527 Denny Walling	.10	.05	.01
□ 528 Andy Hawkins	.10	.05	.01
□ 529 Sixto Lezcano	.10	.05	.01
□ 530 Skeeter Barnes	.10	.05	.01
□ 531 Randy Johnson	.10	.05	.01
□ 532 Jim Morrison	.10	.05	.01
□ 533 Warren Brusstar	.10	.05	.01
□ 534A Jeff Pendleton ERR (Wrong first name)	1.50	.70	.19
□ 534B Terry Pendleton COR	8.00	3.60	1.00
□ 535 Vic Rodriguez	.10	.05	.01
□ 536 Bob McClure	.10	.05	.01
□ 537 Dave Bergman	.10	.05	.01
□ 538 Mark Clear	.10	.05	.01
□ 539 Mike Pagliarulo	.10	.05	.01
□ 540 Terry Whitfield	.10	.05	.01
□ 541 Joe Beckwith	.10	.05	.01
□ 542 Jeff Burroughs	.10	.05	.01
□ 543 Dan Schatzeder	.10	.05	.01
□ 544 Donnie Scott	.10	.05	.01
□ 545 Jim Slaton	.10	.05	.01
□ 546 Greg Luzinski	.20	.09	.03
□ 547 Mark Salas	.10	.05	.01
□ 548 Dave Smith	.10	.05	.01
□ 549 John Wockenfuss	.10	.05	.01
□ 550 Frank Pastore	.10	.05	.01
□ 551 Tim Flannery	.10	.05	.01
□ 552 Rick Rhoden	.10	.05	.01
□ 553 Mark Davis	.10	.05	.01
□ 554 Jeff Dedmon	.10	.05	.01
□ 555 Gary Woods	.10	.05	.01
□ 556 Danny Heep	.10	.05	.01
□ 557 Mark Langston	1.25	.55	.16
□ 558 Darrell Brown	.10	.05	.01
□ 559 Jimmy Key	1.00	.45	.12
□ 560 Rick Lysander	.10	.05	.01
□ 561 Doyle Alexander	.10	.05	.01

□ 562 Mike Stanton	.10	.05	.01
□ 563 Sid Fernandez	.40	.18	.05
□ 564 Richie Hebner	.10	.05	.01
□ 565 Alex Trevino	.10	.05	.01
□ 566 Brian Harper	.20	.09	.03
□ 567 Dan Gladden	.20	.09	.03
□ 568 Luis Salazar	.10	.05	.01
□ 569 Tom Foley	.10	.05	.01
□ 570 Larry Andersen	.10	.05	.01
□ 571 Danny Cox	.10	.05	.01
□ 572 Joe Sambito	.10	.05	.01
□ 573 Juan Beniquez	.10	.05	.01
□ 574 Joel Skinner	.10	.05	.01
□ 575 Randy St.Claire	.10	.05	.01
□ 576 Floyd Rayford	.10	.05	.01
□ 577 Roy Howell	.10	.05	.01
□ 578 John Grubb	.10	.05	.01
□ 579 Ed Jurak	.10	.05	.01
□ 580 John Montefusco	.10	.05	.01
□ 581 Orel Hershiser	2.50	1.10	.30
□ 582 Tom Waddell	.10	.05	.01
□ 583 Mark Huismann	.10	.05	.01
□ 584 Joe Morgan	.50	.23	.06
□ 585 Jim Wohlford	.10	.05	.01
□ 586 Dave Schmidt	.10	.05	.01
□ 587 Jeff Kunkel	.10	.05	.01
□ 588 Hal McRae	.20	.09	.03
□ 589 Bill Almon	.10	.05	.01
□ 590 Carmen Castillo	.10	.05	.01
□ 591 Omar Moreno	.10	.05	.01
□ 592 Ken Howell	.10	.05	.01
□ 593 Tom Brookens	.10	.05	.01
□ 594 Joe Nolan	.10	.05	.01
□ 595 Willie Lozado	.10	.05	.01
□ 596 Tom Nieto	.10	.05	.01
□ 597 Walt Terrell	.10	.05	.01
□ 598 Al Oliver	.20	.09	.03
□ 599 Shane Rawley	.10	.05	.01
□ 600 Denny Gonzalez	.10	.05	.01
□ 601 Mark Grant	.10	.05	.01
□ 602 Mike Armstrong	.10	.05	.01
□ 603 George Foster	.20	.09	.03
□ 604 Dave Lopes	.20	.09	.03
□ 605 Salome Barojas	.10	.05	.01
□ 606 Roy Lee Jackson	.10	.05	.01
□ 607 Pete Filson	.10	.05	.01
□ 608 Duane Walker	.10	.05	.01
□ 609 Glenn Wilson	.10	.05	.01
□ 610 Rafael Santana	.10	.05	.01
□ 611 Roy Smith	.10	.05	.01
□ 612 Ruppert Jones	.10	.05	.01
□ 613 Joe Cowley	.10	.05	.01
□ 614 Al Nipper UER (Photo actually Mike Brown)	.10	.05	.01
□ 615 Gene Nelson	.10	.05	.01
□ 616 Joe Carter	6.00	2.70	.75
□ 617 Ray Knight	.20	.09	.03
□ 618 Chuck Rainey	.10	.05	.01
□ 619 Dan Driessen	.10	.05	.01
□ 620 Daryl Sconiers	.10	.05	.01
□ 621 Bill Stein	.10	.05	.01
□ 622 Roy Smalley	.10	.05	.01
□ 623 Ed Lynch	.10	.05	.01
□ 624 Jeff Stone	.10	.05	.01
□ 625 Bruce Berenyi	.10	.05	.01
□ 626 Kelvin Chapman	.10	.05	.01
□ 627 Joe Price	.10	.05	.01
□ 628 Steve Bedrosian	.10	.05	.01
□ 629 Vic Mata	.10	.05	.01
□ 630 Mike Krukow	.10	.05	.01
□ 631 Phil Bradley	.20	.09	.03
□ 632 Jim Gott	.10	.05	.01
□ 633 Randy Bush	.10	.05	.01
□ 634 Tom Browning	.40	.18	.05
□ 635 Lou Gehrig Puzzle Card	.50	.23	.06
□ 636 Reid Nichols	.10	.05	.01
□ 637 Dan Pasqua	.20	.09	.03
□ 638 German Rivera	.10	.05	.01
□ 639 Don Schulze	.10	.05	.01
□ 640A Mike Jones (Career Highlights, takes five lines)	.10	.05	.01
□ 640B Mike Jones (Career Highlights, takes four lines)	.10	.05	.01
□ 641 Pete Rose	2.50	1.10	.30
□ 642 Wade Rowdon	.10	.05	.01
□ 643 Jerry Narron	.10	.05	.01
□ 644 Darrell Miller	.10	.05	.01
□ 645 Tim Hulett	.10	.05	.01
□ 646 Andy McGaffigan	.10	.05	.01
□ 647 Kurt Bevacqua	.10	.05	.01
□ 648 John Russell	.10	.05	.01
□ 649 Ron Robinson	.10	.05	.01
□ 650 Donnie Moore	.10	.05	.01
□ 651A Two for the Title Dave Winfield Don Mattingly (Yellow letters)	3.00	1.35	.35
□ 651B Two for the Title Dave Winfield Don Mattingly (White letters)	8.00	3.60	1.00
□ 652 Tim Laudner	.10	.05	.01
□ 653 Steve Farr	.20	.09	.03
□ 654 DK Checklist 1-26 (Unnumbered)	.20	.09	.03
□ 655 Checklist 27-130 (Unnumbered)	.20	.09	.03
□ 656 Checklist 131-234 (Unnumbered)	.20	.09	.03
□ 657 Checklist 235-338 (Unnumbered)	.20	.09	.03
□ 658 Checklist 339-442 (Unnumbered)	.20	.09	.03
□ 659 Checklist 443-546 (Unnumbered)	.20	.09	.03
□ 660 Checklist 547-653 (Unnumbered)	.20	.09	.03

1986 Donruss

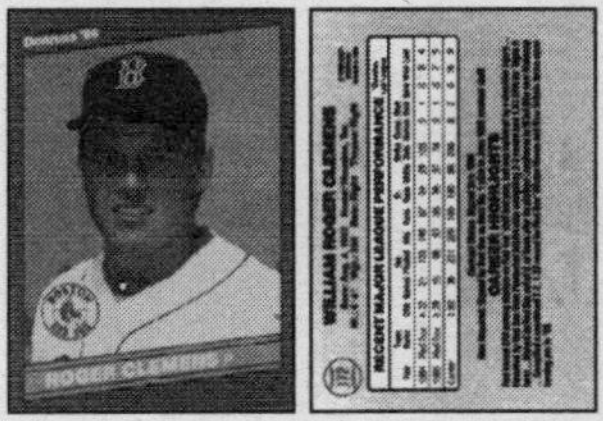

The 1986 Donruss set consists of 660 standard-size cards. Wax packs contained 15 cards plus a Hank Aaron puzzle panel. The card fronts feature blue borders, the standard team logo, player's name, position, and Donruss logo. The first 26 cards of the set are Diamond Kings (DK), for the fifth year in a row; the artwork on the Diamond Kings was again produced by the Perez-Steele Galleries. Cards 27-46 again feature Rated Rookies (RR). The unnumbered checklist cards are arbitrarily numbered below as numbers 654 through 660. Rookie Cards in this set include Jose Canseco, Darren Daulton, Len Dykstra, Cecil Fielder, Andres Galarraga, Fred McGriff, Paul O'Neill, and Mickey Tettleton.

	MINT	NRMT	EXC
COMPLETE SET (660)	70.00	32.00	8.75
COMPLETE FACT.SET (660)	80.00	36.00	10.00
COMMON CARD (1-660)	.10	.05	.01
SEMISTARS	.20	.09	.03
STARS	.40	.18	.05
BEWARE CANSECO COUNTERFEITS			
1986-PRESENT PRICED IN MINT CONDITION			

□ 1 Kirk Gibson DK	.20	.09	.03
□ 2 Goose Gossage DK	.40	.18	.05
□ 3 Willie McGee DK	.10	.05	.01
□ 4 George Bell DK	.10	.05	.01
□ 5 Tony Armas DK	.10	.05	.01

□ 6 Chili Davis DK	.40	.18	.05
□ 7 Cecil Cooper DK	.10	.05	.01
□ 8 Mike Boddicker DK	.10	.05	.01
□ 9 Dave Lopes DK	.10	.05	.01
□ 10 Bill Doran DK	.10	.05	.01
□ 11 Bret Saberhagen DK	.40	.18	.05
□ 12 Brett Butler DK	.20	.09	.03
□ 13 Harold Baines DK	.40	.18	.05
□ 14 Mike Davis DK	.10	.05	.01
□ 15 Tony Perez DK	.40	.18	.05
□ 16 Willie Randolph DK	.20	.09	.03
□ 17 Bob Boone DK	.20	.09	.03
□ 18 Orel Hershiser DK	.40	.18	.05
□ 19 Johnny Ray DK	.10	.05	.01
□ 20 Gary Ward DK	.10	.05	.01
□ 21 Rick Mahler DK	.10	.05	.01
□ 22 Phil Bradley DK	.10	.05	.01
□ 23 Jerry Koosman DK	.20	.09	.03
□ 24 Tom Brunansky DK	.10	.05	.01
□ 25 Andre Dawson DK	.40	.18	.05
□ 26 Dwight Gooden DK	.20	.09	.03
□ 27 Kal Daniels RR	.20	.09	.03
□ 28 Fred McGriff RR	15.00	6.75	1.85
□ 29 Cory Snyder RR	.10	.05	.01
□ 30 Jose Guzman RR	.10	.05	.01
□ 31 Ty Gainey RR	.10	.05	.01
□ 32 Johnny Abrego RR	.10	.05	.01
□ 33 Andres Galarraga RR (No accent)	6.00	2.70	.75
□ 33B Andrés Galarraga RR (Accent over e)	6.00	2.70	.75
□ 34 Dave Shipanoff RR	.10	.05	.01
□ 35 Mark McLemore RR	.50	.23	.06
□ 36 Marty Clary RR	.10	.05	.01
□ 37 Paul O'Neill RR	2.50	1.10	.30
□ 38 Danny Tartabull RR	.20	.09	.03
□ 39 Jose Canseco RR	12.00	5.50	1.50
□ 40 Juan Nieves RR	.10	.05	.01
□ 41 Lance McCullers RR	.10	.05	.01
□ 42 Rick Surhoff RR	.10	.05	.01
□ 43 Todd Worrell RR	.40	.18	.05
□ 44 Bob Kipper RR	.10	.05	.01
□ 45 John Habyan RR	.10	.05	.01
□ 46 Mike Woodard RR	.10	.05	.01
□ 47 Mike Boddicker	.10	.05	.01
□ 48 Robin Yount	.75	.35	.09
□ 49 Lou Whitaker	.40	.18	.05
□ 50 Oil Can Boyd	.10	.05	.01
□ 51 Rickey Henderson	.75	.35	.09
□ 52 Mike Marshall	.10	.05	.01
□ 53 George Brett	2.00	.90	.25
□ 54 Dave Kingman	.20	.09	.03
□ 55 Hubie Brooks	.10	.05	.01
□ 56 Oddibe McDowell	.10	.05	.01
□ 57 Doug DeCinces	.10	.05	.01
□ 58 Britt Burns	.10	.05	.01
□ 59 Ozzie Smith	1.00	.45	.12
□ 60 Jose Cruz	.10	.05	.01
□ 61 Mike Schmidt	1.00	.45	.12
□ 62 Pete Rose	.75	.35	.09
□ 63 Steve Garvey	.40	.18	.05
□ 64 Tony Pena	.10	.05	.01
□ 65 Chili Davis	.40	.18	.05
□ 66 Dale Murphy	.40	.18	.05
□ 67 Ryne Sandberg	2.00	.90	.25
□ 68 Gary Carter	.40	.18	.05
□ 69 Alvin Davis	.10	.05	.01
□ 70 Kent Hrbek	.20	.09	.03
□ 71 George Bell	.20	.09	.03
□ 72 Kirby Puckett	5.00	2.20	.60
□ 73 Lloyd Moseby	.10	.05	.01
□ 74 Bob Kearney	.10	.05	.01
□ 75 Dwight Gooden	.60	.25	.07
□ 76 Gary Matthews	.10	.05	.01
□ 77 Rick Mahler	.10	.05	.01
□ 78 Benny Distefano	.10	.05	.01
□ 79 Jeff Leonard	.10	.05	.01
□ 80 Kevin McReynolds	.20	.09	.03
□ 81 Ron Oester	.10	.05	.01
□ 82 John Russell	.10	.05	.01
□ 83 Tommy Herr	.10	.05	.01
□ 84 Jerry Mumphrey	.10	.05	.01
□ 85 Ron Romanick	.10	.05	.01
□ 86 Daryl Boston	.10	.05	.01
□ 87 Andre Dawson	.40	.18	.05
□ 88 Eddie Murray	1.25	.55	.16
□ 89 Dion James	.10	.05	.01
□ 90 Chet Lemon	.10	.05	.01
□ 91 Bob Stanley	.10	.05	.01
□ 92 Willie Randolph	.20	.09	.03
□ 93 Mike Scioscia	.10	.05	.01
□ 94 Tom Waddell	.10	.05	.01
□ 95 Danny Jackson	.10	.05	.01
□ 96 Mike Davis	.10	.05	.01
□ 97 Mike Fitzgerald	.10	.05	.01
□ 98 Gary Ward	.10	.05	.01
□ 99 Pete O'Brien	.10	.05	.01
□ 100 Bret Saberhagen	.40	.18	.05
□ 101 Alfredo Griffin	.10	.05	.01
□ 102 Brett Butler	.20	.09	.03
□ 103 Ron Guidry	.10	.05	.01
□ 104 Jerry Reuss	.10	.05	.01
□ 105 Jack Morris	.20	.09	.03
□ 106 Rick Dempsey	.10	.05	.01
□ 107 Ray Burris	.10	.05	.01
□ 108 Brian Downing	.10	.05	.01
□ 109 Willie McGee	.10	.05	.01
□ 110 Bill Doran	.10	.05	.01
□ 111 Kent Tekulve	.10	.05	.01
□ 112 Tony Gwynn	2.50	1.10	.30
□ 113 Marvell Wynne	.10	.05	.01
□ 114 David Green	.10	.05	.01
□ 115 Jim Gantner	.10	.05	.01
□ 116 George Foster	.20	.09	.03
□ 117 Steve Trout	.10	.05	.01
□ 118 Mark Langston	.40	.18	.05
□ 119 Tony Fernandez	.10	.05	.01
□ 120 John Butcher	.10	.05	.01
□ 121 Ron Robinson	.10	.05	.01
□ 122 Dan Spillner	.10	.05	.01
□ 123 Mike Young	.10	.05	.01
□ 124 Paul Molitor	1.00	.45	.12
□ 125 Kirk Gibson	.20	.09	.03
□ 126 Ken Griffey	.10	.05	.01
□ 127 Tony Armas	.10	.05	.01
□ 128 Mariano Duncan	.40	.18	.05
□ 129 Pat Tabler	.10	.05	.01
□ 130 Frank White	.20	.09	.03
□ 131 Carney Lansford	.20	.09	.03
□ 132 Vance Law	.10	.05	.01
□ 133 Dick Schofield	.10	.05	.01
□ 134 Wayne Tolleson	.10	.05	.01
□ 135 Greg Walker	.10	.05	.01
□ 136 Denny Walling	.10	.05	.01
□ 137 Ozzie Virgil	.10	.05	.01
□ 138 Ricky Horton	.10	.05	.01
□ 139 LaMarr Hoyt	.10	.05	.01
□ 140 Wayne Krenchicki	.10	.05	.01
□ 141 Glenn Hubbard	.10	.05	.01
□ 142 Cecilio Guante	.10	.05	.01
□ 143 Mike Krukow	.10	.05	.01
□ 144 Lee Smith	.40	.18	.05
□ 145 Edwin Nunez	.10	.05	.01
□ 146 Dave Stieb	.10	.05	.01
□ 147 Mike Smithson	.10	.05	.01
□ 148 Ken Dixon	.10	.05	.01
□ 149 Danny Darwin	.10	.05	.01
□ 150 Chris Pittaro	.10	.05	.01
□ 151 Bill Buckner	.20	.09	.03
□ 152 Mike Pagliarulo	.10	.05	.01
□ 153 Bill Russell	.10	.05	.01
□ 154 Brook Jacoby	.10	.05	.01
□ 155 Pat Sheridan	.10	.05	.01
□ 156 Mike Gallego	.20	.09	.03
□ 157 Jim Wohlford	.10	.05	.01
□ 158 Gary Pettis	.10	.05	.01
□ 159 Toby Harrah	.10	.05	.01
□ 160 Richard Dotson	.10	.05	.01
□ 161 Bob Knepper	.10	.05	.01
□ 162 Dave Dravecky	.20	.09	.03
□ 163 Greg Gross	.10	.05	.01
□ 164 Eric Davis	.40	.18	.05
□ 165 Gerald Perry	.10	.05	.01
□ 166 Rick Rhoden	.10	.05	.01
□ 167 Keith Moreland	.10	.05	.01
□ 168 Jack Clark	.20	.09	.03
□ 169 Storm Davis	.10	.05	.01
□ 170 Cecil Cooper	.20	.09	.03
□ 171 Alan Trammell	.40	.18	.05
□ 172 Roger Clemens	2.50	1.10	.30
□ 173 Don Mattingly	3.00	1.35	.35
□ 174 Pedro Guerrero	.20	.09	.03

□ 175	Willie Wilson	.10	.05	.01
□ 176	Dwayne Murphy	.10	.05	.01
□ 177	Tim Raines	.40	.18	.05
□ 178	Larry Parrish	.10	.05	.01
□ 179	Mike Witt	.10	.05	.01
□ 180	Harold Baines	.40	.18	.05
□ 181	Vince Coleman UER	.40	.18	.05
	(BA 2.67 on back)			
□ 182	Jeff Heathcock	.10	.05	.01
□ 183	Steve Carlton	.50	.23	.06
□ 184	Mario Soto	.10	.05	.01
□ 185	Goose Gossage	.20	.09	.03
□ 186	Johnny Ray	.10	.05	.01
□ 187	Dan Gladden	.10	.05	.01
□ 188	Bob Horner	.10	.05	.01
□ 189	Rick Sutcliffe	.10	.05	.01
□ 190	Keith Hernandez	.20	.09	.03
□ 191	Phil Bradley	.10	.05	.01
□ 192	Tom Brunansky	.10	.05	.01
□ 193	Jesse Barfield	.10	.05	.01
□ 194	Frank Viola	.10	.05	.01
□ 195	Willie Upshaw	.10	.05	.01
□ 196	Jim Beattie	.10	.05	.01
□ 197	Darryl Strawberry	.40	.18	.05
□ 198	Ron Cey	.20	.09	.03
□ 199	Steve Bedrosian	.10	.05	.01
□ 200	Steve Kemp	.10	.05	.01
□ 201	Manny Trillo	.10	.05	.01
□ 202	Garry Templeton	.10	.05	.01
□ 203	Dave Parker	.40	.18	.05
□ 204	John Denny	.10	.05	.01
□ 205	Terry Pendleton	.40	.18	.05
□ 206	Terry Puhl	.10	.05	.01
□ 207	Bobby Grich	.20	.09	.03
□ 208	Ozzie Guillen	.40	.18	.05
□ 209	Jeff Reardon	.20	.09	.03
□ 210	Cal Ripken	4.00	1.80	.50
□ 211	Bill Schroeder	.10	.05	.01
□ 212	Dan Petry	.10	.05	.01
□ 213	Jim Rice	.40	.18	.05
□ 214	Dave Righetti	.10	.05	.01
□ 215	Fernando Valenzuela	.20	.09	.03
□ 216	Julio Franco	.40	.18	.05
□ 217	Darryl Motley	.10	.05	.01
□ 218	Dave Collins	.10	.05	.01
□ 219	Tim Wallach	.10	.05	.01
□ 220	George Wright	.10	.05	.01
□ 221	Tommy Dunbar	.10	.05	.01
□ 222	Steve Balboni	.10	.05	.01
□ 223	Jay Howell	.10	.05	.01
□ 224	Joe Carter	2.50	1.10	.30
□ 225	Ed Whitson	.10	.05	.01
□ 226	Orel Hershiser	.40	.18	.05
□ 227	Willie Hernandez	.10	.05	.01
□ 228	Lee Lacy	.10	.05	.01
□ 229	Rollie Fingers	.40	.18	.05
□ 230	Bob Boone	.20	.09	.03
□ 231	Joaquin Andujar	.10	.05	.01
□ 232	Craig Reynolds	.10	.05	.01
□ 233	Shane Rawley	.10	.05	.01
□ 234	Eric Show	.10	.05	.01
□ 235	Jose DeLeon	.10	.05	.01
□ 236	Jose Uribe	.10	.05	.01
□ 237	Moose Haas	.10	.05	.01
□ 238	Wally Backman	.10	.05	.01
□ 239	Dennis Eckersley	.20	.09	.03
□ 240	Mike Moore	.10	.05	.01
□ 241	Damaso Garcia	.10	.05	.01
□ 242	Tim Teufel	.10	.05	.01
□ 243	Dave Concepcion	.20	.09	.03
□ 244	Floyd Bannister	.10	.05	.01
□ 245	Fred Lynn	.20	.09	.03
□ 246	Charlie Moore	.10	.05	.01
□ 247	Walt Terrell	.10	.05	.01
□ 248	Dave Winfield	.60	.25	.07
□ 249	Dwight Evans	.20	.09	.03
□ 250	Dennis Powell	.10	.05	.01
□ 251	Andre Thornton	.10	.05	.01
□ 252	Onix Concepcion	.10	.05	.01
□ 253	Mike Heath	.10	.05	.01
□ 254A	David Palmer ERR	.10	.05	.01
	(Position 2B)			
□ 254B	David Palmer COR	.40	.18	.05
	(Position P)			
□ 255	Donnie Moore	.10	.05	.01
□ 256	Curtis Wilkerson	.10	.05	.01
□ 257	Julio Cruz	.10	.05	.01
□ 258	Nolan Ryan	4.00	1.80	.50
□ 259	Jeff Stone	.10	.05	.01
□ 260	John Tudor	.10	.05	.01
□ 261	Mark Thurmond	.10	.05	.01
□ 262	Jay Tibbs	.10	.05	.01
□ 263	Rafael Ramirez	.10	.05	.01
□ 264	Larry McWilliams	.10	.05	.01
□ 265	Mark Davis	.10	.05	.01
□ 266	Bob Dernier	.10	.05	.01
□ 267	Matt Young	.10	.05	.01
□ 268	Jim Clancy	.10	.05	.01
□ 269	Mickey Hatcher	.10	.05	.01
□ 270	Sammy Stewart	.10	.05	.01
□ 271	Bob L. Gibson	.10	.05	.01
□ 272	Nelson Simmons	.10	.05	.01
□ 273	Rich Gedman	.10	.05	.01
□ 274	Butch Wynegar	.10	.05	.01
□ 275	Ken Howell	.10	.05	.01
□ 276	Mel Hall	.10	.05	.01
□ 277	Jim Sundberg	.10	.05	.01
□ 278	Chris Codiroli	.10	.05	.01
□ 279	Herm Winningham	.10	.05	.01
□ 280	Rod Carew	.50	.23	.06
□ 281	Don Slaught	.10	.05	.01
□ 282	Scott Fletcher	.10	.05	.01
□ 283	Bill Dawley	.10	.05	.01
□ 284	Andy Hawkins	.10	.05	.01
□ 285	Glenn Wilson	.10	.05	.01
□ 286	Nick Esasky	.10	.05	.01
□ 287	Claudell Washington	.10	.05	.01
□ 288	Lee Mazzilli	.10	.05	.01
□ 289	Jody Davis	.10	.05	.01
□ 290	Darrell Porter	.20	.09	.03
□ 291	Scott McGregor	.10	.05	.01
□ 292	Ted Simmons	.20	.09	.03
□ 293	Aurelio Lopez	.10	.05	.01
□ 294	Marty Barrett	.10	.05	.01
□ 295	Dale Berra	.10	.05	.01
□ 296	Greg Brock	.10	.05	.01
□ 297	Charlie Leibrandt	.10	.05	.01
□ 298	Bill Krueger	.10	.05	.01
□ 299	Bryn Smith	.10	.05	.01
□ 300	Burt Hooton	.10	.05	.01
□ 301	Stu Cliburn	.10	.05	.01
□ 302	Luis Salazar	.10	.05	.01
□ 303	Ken Dayley	.10	.05	.01
□ 304	Frank DiPino	.10	.05	.01
□ 305	Von Hayes	.10	.05	.01
□ 306	Gary Redus	.10	.05	.01
□ 307	Craig Lefferts	.10	.05	.01
□ 308	Sammy Khalifa	.10	.05	.01
□ 309	Scott Garrelts	.10	.05	.01
□ 310	Rick Cerone	.10	.05	.01
□ 311	Shawon Dunston	.20	.09	.03
□ 312	Howard Johnson	.20	.09	.03
□ 313	Jim Presley	.10	.05	.01
□ 314	Gary Gaetti	.20	.09	.03
□ 315	Luis Leal	.10	.05	.01
□ 316	Mark Salas	.10	.05	.01
□ 317	Bill Caudill	.10	.05	.01
□ 318	Dave Henderson	.10	.05	.01
□ 319	Rafael Santana	.10	.05	.01
□ 320	Leon Durham	.10	.05	.01
□ 321	Bruce Sutter	.20	.09	.03
□ 322	Jason Thompson	.10	.05	.01
□ 323	Bob Brenly	.10	.05	.01
□ 324	Carmelo Martinez	.10	.05	.01
□ 325	Eddie Milner	.10	.05	.01
□ 326	Juan Samuel	.10	.05	.01
□ 327	Tom Nieto	.10	.05	.01
□ 328	Dave Smith	.10	.05	.01
□ 329	Urbano Lugo	.10	.05	.01
□ 330	Joel Skinner	.10	.05	.01
□ 331	Bill Gullickson	.10	.05	.01
□ 332	Floyd Rayford	.10	.05	.01
□ 333	Ben Oglivie	.10	.05	.01
□ 334	Lance Parrish	.20	.09	.03
□ 335	Jackie Gutierrez	.10	.05	.01
□ 336	Dennis Rasmussen	.10	.05	.01
□ 337	Terry Whitfield	.10	.05	.01
□ 338	Neal Heaton	.10	.05	.01
□ 339	Jorge Orta	.10	.05	.01
□ 340	Donnie Hill	.10	.05	.01
□ 341	Joe Hesketh	.10	.05	.01
□ 342	Charlie Hough	.20	.09	.03

□ 343 Dave Rozema	.10	.05	.01
□ 344 Greg Pryor	.10	.05	.01
□ 345 Mickey Tettleton	2.00	.90	.25
□ 346 George Vukovich	.10	.05	.01
□ 347 Don Baylor	.40	.18	.05
□ 348 Carlos Diaz	.10	.05	.01
□ 349 Barbaro Garbey	.10	.05	.01
□ 350 Larry Sheets	.10	.05	.01
□ 351 Ted Higuera	.20	.09	.03
□ 352 Juan Beniquez	.10	.05	.01
□ 353 Bob Forsch	.10	.05	.01
□ 354 Mark Bailey	.10	.05	.01
□ 355 Larry Andersen	.10	.05	.01
□ 356 Terry Kennedy	.10	.05	.01
□ 357 Don Robinson	.10	.05	.01
□ 358 Jim Gott	.10	.05	.01
□ 359 Earnie Riles	.10	.05	.01
□ 360 John Christensen	.10	.05	.01
□ 361 Ray Fontenot	.10	.05	.01
□ 362 Spike Owen	.10	.05	.01
□ 363 Jim Acker	.10	.05	.01
□ 364 Ron Davis	.10	.05	.01
□ 365 Tom Hume	.10	.05	.01
□ 366 Carlton Fisk	.40	.18	.05
□ 367 Nate Snell	.10	.05	.01
□ 368 Rick Manning	.10	.05	.01
□ 369 Darrell Evans	.20	.09	.03
□ 370 Ron Hassey	.10	.05	.01
□ 371 Wade Boggs	1.00	.45	.12
□ 372 Rick Honeycutt	.10	.05	.01
□ 373 Chris Bando	.10	.05	.01
□ 374 Bud Black	.10	.05	.01
□ 375 Steve Henderson	.10	.05	.01
□ 376 Charlie Lea	.10	.05	.01
□ 377 Reggie Jackson	.75	.35	.09
□ 378 Dave Schmidt	.10	.05	.01
□ 379 Bob James	.10	.05	.01
□ 380 Glenn Davis	.20	.09	.03
□ 381 Tim Corcoran	.10	.05	.01
□ 382 Danny Cox	.10	.05	.01
□ 383 Tim Flannery	.10	.05	.01
□ 384 Tom Browning	.10	.05	.01
□ 385 Rick Camp	.10	.05	.01
□ 386 Jim Morrison	.10	.05	.01
□ 387 Dave LaPoint	.10	.05	.01
□ 388 Dave Lopes	.20	.09	.03
□ 389 Al Cowens	.10	.05	.01
□ 390 Doyle Alexander	.10	.05	.01
□ 391 Tim Laudner	.10	.05	.01
□ 392 Don Aase	.10	.05	.01
□ 393 Jaime Cocanower	.10	.05	.01
□ 394 Randy O'Neal	.10	.05	.01
□ 395 Mike Easler	.10	.05	.01
□ 396 Scott Bradley	.10	.05	.01
□ 397 Tom Niedenfuer	.10	.05	.01
□ 398 Jerry Willard	.10	.05	.01
□ 399 Lonnie Smith	.10	.05	.01
□ 400 Bruce Bochte	.10	.05	.01
□ 401 Terry Francona	.10	.05	.01
□ 402 Jim Slaton	.10	.05	.01
□ 403 Bill Stein	.10	.05	.01
□ 404 Tim Hulett	.10	.05	.01
□ 405 Alan Ashby	.10	.05	.01
□ 406 Tim Stoddard	.10	.05	.01
□ 407 Garry Maddox	.10	.05	.01
□ 408 Ted Power	.10	.05	.01
□ 409 Len Barker	.10	.05	.01
□ 410 Denny Gonzalez	.10	.05	.01
□ 411 George Frazier	.10	.05	.01
□ 412 Andy Van Slyke	.20	.09	.03
□ 413 Jim Dwyer	.10	.05	.01
□ 414 Paul Householder	.10	.05	.01
□ 415 Alejandro Sanchez	.10	.05	.01
□ 416 Steve Crawford	.10	.05	.01
□ 417 Dan Pasqua	.10	.05	.01
□ 418 Enos Cabell	.10	.05	.01
□ 419 Mike Jones	.10	.05	.01
□ 420 Steve Kiefer	.10	.05	.01
□ 421 Tim Burke	.10	.05	.01
□ 422 Mike Mason	.10	.05	.01
□ 423 Ruppert Jones	.10	.05	.01
□ 424 Jerry Hairston	.10	.05	.01
□ 425 Tito Landrum	.10	.05	.01
□ 426 Jeff Calhoun	.10	.05	.01
□ 427 Don Carman	.10	.05	.01
□ 428 Tony Perez	.40	.18	.05

□ 429 Jerry Davis	.10	.05	.01
□ 430 Bob Walk	.10	.05	.01
□ 431 Brad Wellman	.10	.05	.01
□ 432 Terry Forster	.10	.05	.01
□ 433 Billy Hatcher	.20	.09	.03
□ 434 Clint Hurdle	.10	.05	.01
□ 435 Ivan Calderon	.20	.09	.03
□ 436 Pete Filson	.10	.05	.01
□ 437 Tom Henke	.20	.09	.03
□ 438 Dave Engle	.10	.05	.01
□ 439 Tom Filer	.10	.05	.01
□ 440 Gorman Thomas	.10	.05	.01
□ 441 Rick Aguilera	.50	.23	.06
□ 442 Scott Sanderson	.10	.05	.01
□ 443 Jeff Dedmon	.10	.05	.01
□ 444 Joe Orsulak	.10	.05	.01
□ 445 Atlee Hammaker	.10	.05	.01
□ 446 Jerry Royster	.10	.05	.01
□ 447 Buddy Bell	.20	.09	.03
□ 448 Dave Rucker	.10	.05	.01
□ 449 Ivan DeJesus	.10	.05	.01
□ 450 Jim Pankovits	.10	.05	.01
□ 451 Jerry Narron	.10	.05	.01
□ 452 Bryan Little	.10	.05	.01
□ 453 Gary Lucas	.10	.05	.01
□ 454 Dennis Martinez	.20	.09	.03
□ 455 Ed Romero	.10	.05	.01
□ 456 Bob Melvin	.10	.05	.01
□ 457 Glenn Hoffman	.10	.05	.01
□ 458 Bob Shirley	.10	.05	.01
□ 459 Bob Welch	.10	.05	.01
□ 460 Carmen Castillo	.10	.05	.01
□ 461 Dave Leeper	.10	.05	.01
□ 462 Tim Birtsas	.10	.05	.01
□ 463 Randy St.Claire	.10	.05	.01
□ 464 Chris Welsh	.10	.05	.01
□ 465 Greg Harris	.10	.05	.01
□ 466 Lynn Jones	.10	.05	.01
□ 467 Dusty Baker	.20	.09	.03
□ 468 Roy Smith	.10	.05	.01
□ 469 Andre Robertson	.10	.05	.01
□ 470 Ken Landreaux	.10	.05	.01
□ 471 Dave Bergman	.10	.05	.01
□ 472 Gary Roenicke	.10	.05	.01
□ 473 Pete Vuckovich	.10	.05	.01
□ 474 Kirk McCaskill	.20	.09	.03
□ 475 Jeff Lahti	.10	.05	.01
□ 476 Mike Scott	.10	.05	.01
□ 477 Darren Daulton	2.50	1.10	.30
□ 478 Graig Nettles	.20	.09	.03
□ 479 Bill Almon	.10	.05	.01
□ 480 Greg Minton	.10	.05	.01
□ 481 Randy Ready	.10	.05	.01
□ 482 Len Dykstra	2.00	.90	.25
□ 483 Thad Bosley	.10	.05	.01
□ 484 Harold Reynolds	.50	.23	.06
□ 485 Al Oliver	.20	.09	.03
□ 486 Roy Smalley	.10	.05	.01
□ 487 John Franco	.20	.09	.03
□ 488 Juan Agosto	.10	.05	.01
□ 489 Al Pardo	.10	.05	.01
□ 490 Bill Wegman	.10	.05	.01
□ 491 Frank Tanana	.10	.05	.01
□ 492 Brian Fisher	.10	.05	.01
□ 493 Mark Clear	.10	.05	.01
□ 494 Len Matuszek	.10	.05	.01
□ 495 Ramon Romero	.10	.05	.01
□ 496 John Wathan	.10	.05	.01
□ 497 Rob Picciolo	.10	.05	.01
□ 498 U.L. Washington	.10	.05	.01
□ 499 John Candelaria	.10	.05	.01
□ 500 Duane Walker	.10	.05	.01
□ 501 Gene Nelson	.10	.05	.01
□ 502 John Mizerock	.10	.05	.01
□ 503 Luis Aguayo	.10	.05	.01
□ 504 Kurt Kepshire	.10	.05	.01
□ 505 Ed Wojna	.10	.05	.01
□ 506 Joe Price	.10	.05	.01
□ 507 Milt Thompson	.20	.09	.03
□ 508 Junior Ortiz	.10	.05	.01
□ 509 Vida Blue	.20	.09	.03
□ 510 Steve Engel	.10	.05	.01
□ 511 Karl Best	.10	.05	.01
□ 512 Cecil Fielder	6.00	2.70	.75
□ 513 Frank Eufemia	.10	.05	.01
□ 514 Tippy Martinez	.10	.05	.01

□ 515 Billy Joe Robidoux	.10	.05	.01
□ 516 Bill Scherrer	.10	.05	.01
□ 517 Bruce Hurst	.10	.05	.01
□ 518 Rich Bordi	.10	.05	.01
□ 519 Steve Yeager	.10	.05	.01
□ 520 Tony Bernazard	.10	.05	.01
□ 521 Hal McRae	.20	.09	.03
□ 522 Jose Rijo	.40	.18	.05
□ 523 Mitch Webster	.10	.05	.01
□ 524 Jack Howell	.10	.05	.01
□ 525 Alan Bannister	.10	.05	.01
□ 526 Ron Kittle	.10	.05	.01
□ 527 Phil Garner	.10	.05	.01
□ 528 Kurt Bevacqua	.10	.05	.01
□ 529 Kevin Gross	.10	.05	.01
□ 530 Bo Diaz	.10	.05	.01
□ 531 Ken Oberkfell	.10	.05	.01
□ 532 Rick Reuschel	.10	.05	.01
□ 533 Ron Meridith	.10	.05	.01
□ 534 Steve Braun	.10	.05	.01
□ 535 Wayne Gross	.10	.05	.01
□ 536 Ray Searage	.10	.05	.01
□ 537 Tom Brookens	.10	.05	.01
□ 538 Al Nipper	.10	.05	.01
□ 539 Billy Sample	.10	.05	.01
□ 540 Steve Sax	.10	.05	.01
□ 541 Dan Quisenberry	.10	.05	.01
□ 542 Tony Phillips	.40	.18	.05
□ 543 Floyd Youmans	.10	.05	.01
□ 544 Steve Buechele	.20	.09	.03
□ 545 Craig Gerber	.10	.05	.01
□ 546 Joe DeSa	.10	.05	.01
□ 547 Brian Harper	.10	.05	.01
□ 548 Kevin Bass	.10	.05	.01
□ 549 Tom Foley	.10	.05	.01
□ 550 Dave Van Gorder	.10	.05	.01
□ 551 Bruce Bochy	.10	.05	.01
□ 552 R.J. Reynolds	.10	.05	.01
□ 553 Chris Brown	.10	.05	.01
□ 554 Bruce Benedict	.10	.05	.01
□ 555 Warren Brusstar	.10	.05	.01
□ 556 Danny Heep	.10	.05	.01
□ 557 Darnell Coles	.10	.05	.01
□ 558 Greg Gagne	.20	.09	.03
□ 559 Ernie Whitt	.10	.05	.01
□ 560 Ron Washington	.10	.05	.01
□ 561 Jimmy Key	.40	.18	.05
□ 562 Billy Swift	.20	.09	.03
□ 563 Ron Darling	.10	.05	.01
□ 564 Dick Ruthven	.10	.05	.01
□ 565 Zane Smith	.10	.05	.01
□ 566 Sid Bream	.10	.05	.01
□ 567A Joel Youngblood ERR (Position P)	.10	.05	.01
□ 567B Joel Youngblood COR (Position IF)	.40	.18	.05
□ 568 Mario Ramirez	.10	.05	.01
□ 569 Tom Runnells	.10	.05	.01
□ 570 Rick Schu	.10	.05	.01
□ 571 Bill Campbell	.10	.05	.01
□ 572 Dickie Thon	.10	.05	.01
□ 573 Al Holland	.10	.05	.01
□ 574 Reid Nichols	.10	.05	.01
□ 575 Bert Roberge	.10	.05	.01
□ 576 Mike Flanagan	.10	.05	.01
□ 577 Tim Leary	.10	.05	.01
□ 578 Mike Laga	.10	.05	.01
□ 579 Steve Lyons	.10	.05	.01
□ 580 Phil Niekro	.40	.18	.05
□ 581 Gilberto Reyes	.10	.05	.01
□ 582 Jamie Easterly	.10	.05	.01
□ 583 Mark Gubicza	.20	.09	.03
□ 584 Stan Javier	.20	.09	.03
□ 585 Bill Laskey	.10	.05	.01
□ 586 Jeff Russell	.10	.05	.01
□ 587 Dickie Noles	.10	.05	.01
□ 588 Steve Farr	.20	.09	.03
□ 589 Steve Ontiveros	.20	.09	.03
□ 590 Mike Hargrove	.20	.09	.03
□ 591 Marty Bystrom	.10	.05	.01
□ 592 Franklin Stubbs	.10	.05	.01
□ 593 Larry Herndon	.10	.05	.01
□ 594 Bill Swaggerty	.10	.05	.01
□ 595 Carlos Ponce	.10	.05	.01
□ 596 Pat Perry	.10	.05	.01
□ 597 Ray Knight	.20	.09	.03

□ 598 Steve Lombardozzi	.10	.05	.01
□ 599 Brad Havens	.10	.05	.01
□ 600 Pat Clements	.10	.05	.01
□ 601 Joe Niekro	.10	.05	.01
□ 602 Hank Aaron Puzzle Card	.30	.14	.04
□ 603 Dwayne Henry	.10	.05	.01
□ 604 Mookie Wilson	.20	.09	.03
□ 605 Buddy Biancalana	.10	.05	.01
□ 606 Rance Mulliniks	.10	.05	.01
□ 607 Alan Wiggins	.10	.05	.01
□ 608 Joe Cowley	.10	.05	.01
□ 609 Tom Seaver (Green borders on name)	.50	.23	.06
□ 609B Tom Seaver (Yellow borders on name)	2.00	.90	.25
□ 610 Neil Allen	.10	.05	.01
□ 611 Don Sutton	.40	.18	.05
□ 612 Fred Toliver	.10	.05	.01
□ 613 Jay Baller	.10	.05	.01
□ 614 Marc Sullivan	.10	.05	.01
□ 615 John Grubb	.10	.05	.01
□ 616 Bruce Kison	.10	.05	.01
□ 617 Bill Madlock	.10	.05	.01
□ 618 Chris Chambliss	.20	.09	.03
□ 619 Dave Stewart	.20	.09	.03
□ 620 Tim Lollar	.10	.05	.01
□ 621 Gary Lavelle	.10	.05	.01
□ 622 Charles Hudson	.10	.05	.01
□ 623 Joel Davis	.10	.05	.01
□ 624 Joe Johnson	.10	.05	.01
□ 625 Sid Fernandez	.20	.09	.03
□ 626 Dennis Lamp	.10	.05	.01
□ 627 Terry Harper	.10	.05	.01
□ 628 Jack Lazorko	.10	.05	.01
□ 629 Roger McDowell	.20	.09	.03
□ 630 Mark Funderburk	.10	.05	.01
□ 631 Ed Lynch	.10	.05	.01
□ 632 Rudy Law	.10	.05	.01
□ 633 Roger Mason	.10	.05	.01
□ 634 Mike Felder	.10	.05	.01
□ 635 Ken Schrom	.10	.05	.01
□ 636 Bob Ojeda	.10	.05	.01
□ 637 Ed VandeBerg	.10	.05	.01
□ 638 Bobby Meacham	.10	.05	.01
□ 639 Cliff Johnson	.10	.05	.01
□ 640 Garth Iorg	.10	.05	.01
□ 641 Dan Driessen	.10	.05	.01
□ 642 Mike Brown OF	.10	.05	.01
□ 643 John Shelby	.10	.05	.01
□ 644 Pete Rose (Ty-Breaking)	.60	.25	.07
□ 645 The Knuckle Brothers Phil Niekro Joe Niekro	.20	.09	.03
□ 646 Jesse Orosco	.10	.05	.01
□ 647 Billy Beane	.10	.05	.01
□ 648 Cesar Cedeno	.20	.09	.03
□ 649 Bert Blyleven	.40	.18	.05
□ 650 Max Venable	.10	.05	.01
□ 651 Fleet Feet Vince Coleman Willie McGee	.20	.09	.03
□ 652 Calvin Schiraldi	.10	.05	.01
□ 653 King of Kings (Pete Rose)	1.00	.45	.12
□ 654 Diamond Kings CL 1-26 (Unnumbered)	.20	.09	.03
□ 655A CL 1: 27-130 (Unnumbered) (45 Beane ERR)	.20	.09	.03
□ 655B CL 1: 27-130 (Unnumbered) (45 Habyan COR)	.20	.09	.03
□ 656 CL 2: 131-234 (Unnumbered)	.20	.09	.03
□ 657 CL 3: 235-338 (Unnumbered)	.20	.09	.03
□ 658 CL 4: 339-442 (Unnumbered)	.20	.09	.03
□ 659 CL 5: 443-546 (Unnumbered)	.20	.09	.03
□ 660 CL 6: 547-653 (Unnumbered)	.20	.09	.03

1986 Donruss Rookies

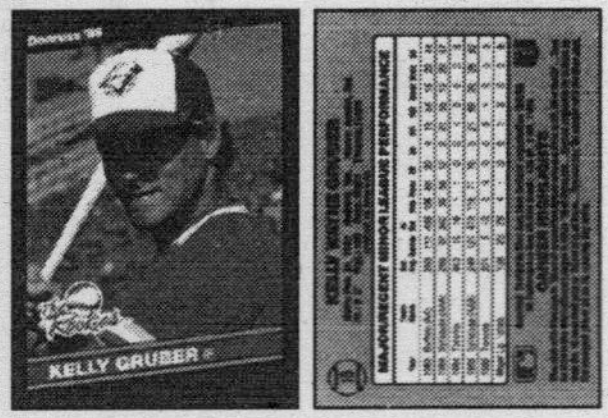

The 1986 Donruss "The Rookies" set features 56 full-color standard-size cards plus a 15-piece puzzle of Hank Aaron. The set was distributed through hobby dealers in a small green, cellophane wrapped factory box. Although the set was wrapped in cellophane, the top card was number 1 Joyner, resulting in a percentage of the Joyner cards arriving in less than perfect condition. Donruss fixed the problem after it was called to their attention and even went so far as to include a customer service phone number in their second printing. Card fronts are similar in design to the 1986 Donruss regular issue except for the presence of "The Rookies" logo in the lower left corner and a bluish green border instead of a blue border. The key extended Rookie Cards in this set are Barry Bonds, Bobby Bonilla, Will Clark, Bo Jackson, Wally Joyner, John Kruk, Kevin Mitchell, and Ruben Sierra.

	MINT	NRMT	EXC
COMPLETE FACT.SET (56)	25.00	11.00	3.10
COMMON CARD (1-56)	.10	.05	.01

	MINT	NRMT	EXC
□ 1 Wally Joyner	1.00	.45	.12
□ 2 Tracy Jones	.10	.05	.01
□ 3 Allan Anderson	.10	.05	.01
□ 4 Ed Correa	.10	.05	.01
□ 5 Reggie Williams	.10	.05	.01
□ 6 Charlie Kerfeld	.10	.05	.01
□ 7 Andres Galarraga	3.00	1.35	.35
□ 8 Bob Tewksbury	.25	.11	.03
□ 9 Al Newman	.25	.11	.03
□ 10 Andres Thomas	.10	.05	.01
□ 11 Barry Bonds	7.00	3.10	.85
□ 12 Juan Nieves	.10	.05	.01
□ 13 Mark Eichhorn	.10	.05	.01
□ 14 Dan Plesac	.10	.05	.01
□ 15 Cory Snyder	.10	.05	.01
□ 16 Kelly Gruber	.10	.05	.01
□ 17 Kevin Mitchell	.40	.18	.05
□ 18 Steve Lombardozzi	.10	.05	.01
□ 19 Mitch Williams	.25	.11	.03
□ 20 John Cerutti	.10	.05	.01
□ 21 Todd Worrell	.40	.18	.05
□ 22 Jose Canseco	4.00	1.80	.50
□ 23 Pete Incaviglia	.40	.18	.05
□ 24 Jose Guzman	.10	.05	.01
□ 25 Scott Bailes	.10	.05	.01
□ 26 Greg Mathews	.10	.05	.01
□ 27 Eric King	.10	.05	.01
□ 28 Paul Assenmacher	.10	.05	.01
□ 29 Jeff Sellers	.10	.05	.01
□ 30 Bobby Bonilla	1.50	.70	.19
□ 31 Doug Drabek	.60	.25	.07
□ 32 Will Clark UER (Listed as throwing right, should be left)	3.00	1.35	.35
□ 33 Bip Roberts	.40	.18	.05
□ 34 Jim Deshaies	.10	.05	.01
□ 35 Mike LaValliere	.10	.05	.01
□ 36 Scott Bankhead	.10	.05	.01
□ 37 Dale Sveum	.10	.05	.01
□ 38 Bo Jackson	2.00	.90	.25
□ 39 Robby Thompson	.25	.11	.03
□ 40 Eric Plunk	.10	.05	.01
□ 41 Bill Bathe	.10	.05	.01
□ 42 John Kruk	1.00	.45	.12
□ 43 Andy Allanson	.10	.05	.01
□ 44 Mark Portugal	.25	.11	.03
□ 45 Danny Tartabull	.25	.11	.03
□ 46 Bob Kipper	.10	.05	.01
□ 47 Gene Walter	.10	.05	.01
□ 48 Rey Quinones UER (Misspelled Quinonez)	.10	.05	.01
□ 49 Bobby Witt	.25	.11	.03
□ 50 Bill Mooneyham	.10	.05	.01
□ 51 John Cangelosi	.10	.05	.01
□ 52 Ruben Sierra	2.50	1.10	.30
□ 53 Rob Woodward	.10	.05	.01
□ 54 Ed Hearn	.10	.05	.01
□ 55 Joel McKeon	.10	.05	.01
□ 56 Checklist 1-56	.10	.05	.01

1987 Donruss

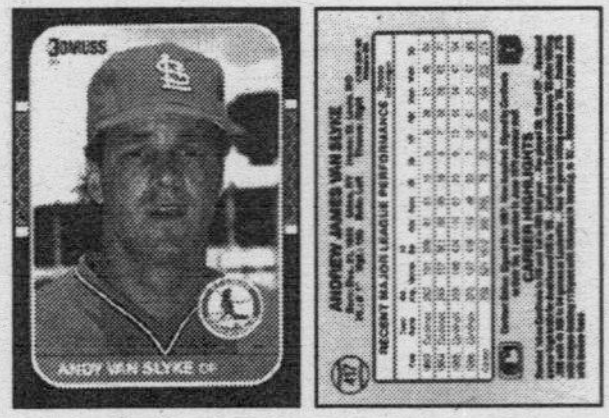

This set consists of 660 standard-size cards. Cards were primarily distributed in 15-card wax packs, rack packs and a factory set. All packs included a Roberto Clemente puzzle panel and the factory sets contained a complete puzzle. The regular-issue cards feature a black and gold border on the front. The backs of the cards in the factory sets are oriented differently than cards taken from wax packs, giving the appearance that one version or the other is upside down when sorting from the card backs. There are no premiums or discounts for either version. The popular Diamond King subset returns for the sixth consecutive year. Some of the Diamond King (1-26) selections are repeats from prior years; Perez-Steele Galleries had indicated in 1987 that a five-year rotation would be maintained in order to avoid depleting the pool of available worthy "kings" on some of the teams. Rookie Cards in this set include Barry Bonds, Bobby Bonilla, Kevin Brown, Will Clark, David Cone, Chuck Finley, Mike Greenwell, Bo Jackson, Wally Joyner, Barry Larkin, Greg Maddux, Kevin Mitchell, Rafael Palmeiro, Ruben Sierra, and Devon White. The Greg Maddux card has been noted to have a premium for perfectly centered copies.

	MINT	NRMT	EXC
COMPLETE SET (660)	32.00	14.50	4.00
COMPLETE FACT.SET (660)	32.00	14.50	4.00
COMMON CARD (1-660)	.05	.02	.01
SEMISTARS	.15	.07	.02
STARS	.30	.14	.04

	MINT	NRMT	EXC
□ 1 Wally Joyner DK	.30	.14	.04
□ 2 Roger Clemens DK	.30	.14	.04
□ 3 Dale Murphy DK	.30	.14	.04
□ 4 Darryl Strawberry DK	.30	.14	.04
□ 5 Ozzie Smith DK	.30	.14	.04
□ 6 Jose Canseco DK	.50	.23	.06
□ 7 Charlie Hough DK	.05	.02	.01
□ 8 Brook Jacoby DK	.05	.02	.01
□ 9 Fred Lynn DK	.05	.02	.01
□ 10 Rick Rhoden DK	.05	.02	.01
□ 11 Chris Brown DK	.05	.02	.01
□ 12 Von Hayes DK	.05	.02	.01
□ 13 Jack Morris DK	.15	.07	.02
□ 14A Kevin McReynolds DK	.30	.14	.04

	ERR (Yellow strip missing on back)			
□ 14B	Kevin McReynolds DK COR	.05	.02	.01
□ 15	George Brett DK	.40	.18	.05
□ 16	Ted Higuera DK	.05	.02	.01
□ 17	Hubie Brooks DK	.05	.02	.01
□ 18	Mike Scott DK	.05	.02	.01
□ 19	Kirby Puckett DK	.75	.35	.09
□ 20	Dave Winfield DK	.30	.14	.04
□ 21	Lloyd Moseby DK	.05	.02	.01
□ 22A	Eric Davis DK ERR (Yellow strip missing on back)	.30	.14	.04
□ 22B	Eric Davis DK COR	.15	.07	.02
□ 23	Jim Presley DK	.05	.02	.01
□ 24	Keith Moreland DK	.05	.02	.01
□ 25A	Greg Walker DK ERR (Yellow strip missing on back)	.30	.14	.04
□ 25B	Greg Walker DK COR	.05	.02	.01
□ 26	Steve Sax DK	.05	.02	.01
□ 27	DK Checklist 1-26	.15	.07	.02
□ 28	B.J. Surhoff RR	.40	.18	.05
□ 29	Randy Myers RR	.40	.18	.05
□ 30	Ken Gerhart RR	.05	.02	.01
□ 31	Benito Santiago RR	.15	.07	.02
□ 32	Greg Swindell RR	.30	.14	.04
□ 33	Mike Birkbeck RR	.05	.02	.01
□ 34	Terry Steinbach RR	.40	.18	.05
□ 35	Bo Jackson RR	1.00	.45	.12
□ 36	Greg Maddux UER (middle name misspelled "Allen")	20.00	9.00	2.50
□ 37	Jim Lindeman RR	.05	.02	.01
□ 38	Devon White RR	.40	.18	.05
□ 39	Eric Bell RR	.05	.02	.01
□ 40	Willie Fraser RR	.05	.02	.01
□ 41	Jerry Browne RR	.15	.07	.02
□ 42	Chris James RR	.05	.02	.01
□ 43	Rafael Palmeiro RR	2.50	1.10	.30
□ 44	Pat Dodson RR	.05	.02	.01
□ 45	Duane Ward RR	.15	.07	.02
□ 46	Mark McGwire RR	4.00	1.80	.50
□ 47	Bruce Fields RR UER (Photo actually Darnell Coles)	.05	.02	.01
□ 48	Eddie Murray	.50	.23	.06
□ 49	Ted Higuera	.05	.02	.01
□ 50	Kirk Gibson	.15	.07	.02
□ 51	Oil Can Boyd	.05	.02	.01
□ 52	Don Mattingly	1.00	.45	.12
□ 53	Pedro Guerrero	.15	.07	.02
□ 54	George Brett	.75	.35	.09
□ 55	Jose Rijo	.05	.02	.01
□ 56	Tim Raines	.15	.07	.02
□ 57	Ed Correa	.05	.02	.01
□ 58	Mike Witt	.05	.02	.01
□ 59	Greg Walker	.05	.02	.01
□ 60	Ozzie Smith	.40	.18	.05
□ 61	Glenn Davis	.05	.02	.01
□ 62	Glenn Wilson	.05	.02	.01
□ 63	Tom Browning	.05	.02	.01
□ 64	Tony Gwynn	.75	.35	.09
□ 65	R.J. Reynolds	.05	.02	.01
□ 66	Will Clark	2.00	.90	.25
□ 67	Ozzie Virgil	.05	.02	.01
□ 68	Rick Sutcliffe	.05	.02	.01
□ 69	Gary Carter	.30	.14	.04
□ 70	Mike Moore	.05	.02	.01
□ 71	Bert Blyleven	.15	.07	.02
□ 72	Tony Fernandez	.05	.02	.01
□ 73	Kent Hrbek	.30	.14	.04
□ 74	Lloyd Moseby	.05	.02	.01
□ 75	Alvin Davis	.05	.02	.01
□ 76	Keith Hernandez	.15	.07	.02
□ 77	Ryne Sandberg	.50	.23	.06
□ 78	Dale Murphy	.30	.14	.04
□ 79	Sid Bream	.05	.02	.01
□ 80	Chris Brown	.05	.02	.01
□ 81	Steve Garvey	.30	.14	.04
□ 82	Mario Soto	.05	.02	.01
□ 83	Shane Rawley	.05	.02	.01
□ 84	Willie McGee	.05	.02	.01
□ 85	Jose Cruz	.05	.02	.01
□ 86	Brian Downing	.05	.02	.01
□ 87	Ozzie Guillen	.30	.14	.04
□ 88	Hubie Brooks	.05	.02	.01
□ 89	Cal Ripken	1.50	.70	.19
□ 90	Juan Nieves	.05	.02	.01
□ 91	Lance Parrish	.15	.07	.02
□ 92	Jim Rice	.30	.14	.04
□ 93	Ron Guidry	.05	.02	.01
□ 94	Fernando Valenzuela	.15	.07	.02
□ 95	Andy Allanson	.05	.02	.01
□ 96	Willie Wilson	.05	.02	.01
□ 97	Jose Canseco	1.00	.45	.12
□ 98	Jeff Reardon	.15	.07	.02
□ 99	Bobby Witt	.15	.07	.02
□ 100	Checklist 28-133	.15	.07	.02
□ 101	Jose Guzman	.05	.02	.01
□ 102	Steve Balboni	.05	.02	.01
□ 103	Tony Phillips	.30	.14	.04
□ 104	Brook Jacoby	.05	.02	.01
□ 105	Dave Winfield	.30	.14	.04
□ 106	Orel Hershiser	.30	.14	.04
□ 107	Lou Whitaker	.30	.14	.04
□ 108	Fred Lynn	.05	.02	.01
□ 109	Bill Wegman	.05	.02	.01
□ 110	Donnie Moore	.05	.02	.01
□ 111	Jack Clark	.15	.07	.02
□ 112	Bob Knepper	.05	.02	.01
□ 113	Von Hayes	.05	.02	.01
□ 114	Bip Roberts	.30	.14	.04
□ 115	Tony Pena	.05	.02	.01
□ 116	Scott Garrelts	.05	.02	.01
□ 117	Paul Molitor	.40	.18	.05
□ 118	Darryl Strawberry	.30	.14	.04
□ 119	Shawon Dunston	.15	.07	.02
□ 120	Jim Presley	.05	.02	.01
□ 121	Jesse Barfield	.05	.02	.01
□ 122	Gary Gaetti	.05	.02	.01
□ 123	Kurt Stillwell	.05	.02	.01
□ 124	Joel Davis	.05	.02	.01
□ 125	Mike Boddicker	.05	.02	.01
□ 126	Robin Yount	.30	.14	.04
□ 127	Alan Trammell	.30	.14	.04
□ 128	Dave Righetti	.05	.02	.01
□ 129	Dwight Evans	.15	.07	.02
□ 130	Mike Scioscia	.05	.02	.01
□ 131	Julio Franco	.15	.07	.02
□ 132	Bret Saberhagen	.15	.07	.02
□ 133	Mike Davis	.05	.02	.01
□ 134	Joe Hesketh	.05	.02	.01
□ 135	Wally Joyner	.50	.23	.06
□ 136	Don Slaught	.05	.02	.01
□ 137	Daryl Boston	.05	.02	.01
□ 138	Nolan Ryan	1.50	.70	.19
□ 139	Mike Schmidt	.40	.18	.05
□ 140	Tommy Herr	.05	.02	.01
□ 141	Garry Templeton	.05	.02	.01
□ 142	Kal Daniels	.05	.02	.01
□ 143	Billy Sample	.05	.02	.01
□ 144	Johnny Ray	.05	.02	.01
□ 145	Rob Thompson	.15	.07	.02
□ 146	Bob Dernier	.05	.02	.01
□ 147	Danny Tartabull	.15	.07	.02
□ 148	Ernie Whitt	.05	.02	.01
□ 149	Kirby Puckett	1.50	.70	.19
□ 150	Mike Young	.05	.02	.01
□ 151	Ernest Riles	.05	.02	.01
□ 152	Frank Tanana	.05	.02	.01
□ 153	Rich Gedman	.05	.02	.01
□ 154	Willie Randolph	.15	.07	.02
□ 155	Bill Madlock	.05	.02	.01
□ 156	Joe Carter	.40	.18	.05
□ 157	Danny Jackson	.05	.02	.01
□ 158	Carney Lansford	.15	.07	.02
□ 159	Bryn Smith	.05	.02	.01
□ 160	Gary Pettis	.05	.02	.01
□ 161	Oddibe McDowell	.05	.02	.01
□ 162	John Cangelosi	.05	.02	.01
□ 163	Mike Scott	.05	.02	.01
□ 164	Eric Show	.05	.02	.01
□ 165	Juan Samuel	.05	.02	.01
□ 166	Nick Esasky	.05	.02	.01
□ 167	Zane Smith	.05	.02	.01
□ 168	Mike C. Brown OF	.05	.02	.01
□ 169	Keith Moreland	.05	.02	.01
□ 170	John Tudor	.05	.02	.01
□ 171	Ken Dixon	.05	.02	.01
□ 172	Jim Gantner	.05	.02	.01
□ 173	Jack Morris	.15	.07	.02

□ 174	Bruce Hurst	.05	.02	.01
□ 175	Dennis Rasmussen	.05	.02	.01
□ 176	Mike Marshall	.05	.02	.01
□ 177	Dan Quisenberry	.05	.02	.01
□ 178	Eric Plunk	.05	.02	.01
□ 179	Tim Wallach	.05	.02	.01
□ 180	Steve Buechele	.05	.02	.01
□ 181	Don Sutton	.30	.14	.04
□ 182	Dave Schmidt	.05	.02	.01
□ 183	Terry Pendleton	.15	.07	.02
□ 184	Jim Deshaies	.05	.02	.01
□ 185	Steve Bedrosian	.05	.02	.01
□ 186	Pete Rose	.40	.18	.05
□ 187	Dave Dravecky	.15	.07	.02
□ 188	Rick Reuschel	.05	.02	.01
□ 189	Dan Gladden	.05	.02	.01
□ 190	Rick Mahler	.05	.02	.01
□ 191	Thad Bosley	.05	.02	.01
□ 192	Ron Darling	.05	.02	.01
□ 193	Matt Young	.05	.02	.01
□ 194	Tom Brunansky	.05	.02	.01
□ 195	Dave Stieb	.05	.02	.01
□ 196	Frank Viola	.05	.02	.01
□ 197	Tom Henke	.05	.02	.01
□ 198	Karl Best	.05	.02	.01
□ 199	Dwight Gooden	.30	.14	.04
□ 200	Checklist 134-239	.15	.07	.02
□ 201	Steve Trout	.05	.02	.01
□ 202	Rafael Ramirez	.05	.02	.01
□ 203	Bob Walk	.05	.02	.01
□ 204	Roger Mason	.05	.02	.01
□ 205	Terry Kennedy	.05	.02	.01
□ 206	Ron Oester	.05	.02	.01
□ 207	John Russell	.05	.02	.01
□ 208	Greg Mathews	.05	.02	.01
□ 209	Charlie Kerfeld	.05	.02	.01
□ 210	Reggie Jackson	.40	.18	.05
□ 211	Floyd Bannister	.05	.02	.01
□ 212	Vance Law	.05	.02	.01
□ 213	Rich Bordi	.05	.02	.01
□ 214	Dan Plesac	.05	.02	.01
□ 215	Dave Collins	.05	.02	.01
□ 216	Bob Stanley	.05	.02	.01
□ 217	Joe Niekro	.05	.02	.01
□ 218	Tom Niedenfuer	.05	.02	.01
□ 219	Brett Butler	.15	.07	.02
□ 220	Charlie Leibrandt	.05	.02	.01
□ 221	Steve Ontiveros	.05	.02	.01
□ 222	Tim Burke	.05	.02	.01
□ 223	Curtis Wilkerson	.05	.02	.01
□ 224	Pete Incaviglia	.15	.07	.02
□ 225	Lonnie Smith	.05	.02	.01
□ 226	Chris Codiroli	.05	.02	.01
□ 227	Scott Bailes	.05	.02	.01
□ 228	Rickey Henderson	.30	.14	.04
□ 229	Ken Howell	.05	.02	.01
□ 230	Darnell Coles	.05	.02	.01
□ 231	Don Aase	.05	.02	.01
□ 232	Tim Leary	.05	.02	.01
□ 233	Bob Boone	.15	.07	.02
□ 234	Ricky Horton	.05	.02	.01
□ 235	Mark Bailey	.05	.02	.01
□ 236	Kevin Gross	.05	.02	.01
□ 237	Lance McCullers	.05	.02	.01
□ 238	Cecilio Guante	.05	.02	.01
□ 239	Bob Melvin	.05	.02	.01
□ 240	Billy Joe Robidoux	.05	.02	.01
□ 241	Roger McDowell	.05	.02	.01
□ 242	Leon Durham	.05	.02	.01
□ 243	Ed Nunez	.05	.02	.01
□ 244	Jimmy Key	.15	.07	.02
□ 245	Mike Smithson	.05	.02	.01
□ 246	Bo Diaz	.05	.02	.01
□ 247	Carlton Fisk	.30	.14	.04
□ 248	Larry Sheets	.05	.02	.01
□ 249	Juan Castillo	.05	.02	.01
□ 250	Eric King	.05	.02	.01
□ 251	Doug Drabek	.40	.18	.05
□ 252	Wade Boggs	.30	.14	.04
□ 253	Mariano Duncan	.05	.02	.01
□ 254	Pat Tabler	.05	.02	.01
□ 255	Frank White	.15	.07	.02
□ 256	Alfredo Griffin	.05	.02	.01
□ 257	Floyd Youmans	.05	.02	.01
□ 258	Rob Wilfong	.05	.02	.01
□ 259	Pete O'Brien	.05	.02	.01
□ 260	Tim Hulett	.05	.02	.01
□ 261	Dickie Thon	.05	.02	.01
□ 262	Darren Daulton	.15	.07	.02
□ 263	Vince Coleman	.05	.02	.01
□ 264	Andy Hawkins	.05	.02	.01
□ 265	Eric Davis	.15	.07	.02
□ 266	Andres Thomas	.05	.02	.01
□ 267	Mike Diaz	.05	.02	.01
□ 268	Chili Davis	.15	.07	.02
□ 269	Jody Davis	.05	.02	.01
□ 270	Phil Bradley	.05	.02	.01
□ 271	George Bell	.05	.02	.01
□ 272	Keith Atherton	.05	.02	.01
□ 273	Storm Davis	.05	.02	.01
□ 274	Rob Deer	.05	.02	.01
□ 275	Walt Terrell	.05	.02	.01
□ 276	Roger Clemens	.75	.35	.09
□ 277	Mike Easler	.05	.02	.01
□ 278	Steve Sax	.05	.02	.01
□ 279	Andre Thornton	.05	.02	.01
□ 280	Jim Sundberg	.05	.02	.01
□ 281	Bill Bathe	.05	.02	.01
□ 282	Jay Tibbs	.05	.02	.01
□ 283	Dick Schofield	.05	.02	.01
□ 284	Mike Mason	.05	.02	.01
□ 285	Jerry Hairston	.05	.02	.01
□ 286	Bill Doran	.05	.02	.01
□ 287	Tim Flannery	.05	.02	.01
□ 288	Gary Redus	.05	.02	.01
□ 289	John Franco	.05	.02	.01
□ 290	Paul Assenmacher	.05	.02	.01
□ 291	Joe Orsulak	.05	.02	.01
□ 292	Lee Smith	.30	.14	.04
□ 293	Mike Laga	.05	.02	.01
□ 294	Rick Dempsey	.15	.07	.02
□ 295	Mike Felder	.05	.02	.01
□ 296	Tom Brookens	.05	.02	.01
□ 297	Al Nipper	.05	.02	.01
□ 298	Mike Pagliarulo	.05	.02	.01
□ 299	Franklin Stubbs	.05	.02	.01
□ 300	Checklist 240-345	.15	.07	.02
□ 301	Steve Farr	.05	.02	.01
□ 302	Bill Mooneyham	.05	.02	.01
□ 303	Andres Galarraga	.50	.23	.06
□ 304	Scott Fletcher	.05	.02	.01
□ 305	Jack Howell	.05	.02	.01
□ 306	Russ Morman	.05	.02	.01
□ 307	Todd Worrell	.15	.07	.02
□ 308	Dave Smith	.05	.02	.01
□ 309	Jeff Stone	.05	.02	.01
□ 310	Ron Robinson	.05	.02	.01
□ 311	Bruce Bochy	.05	.02	.01
□ 312	Jim Winn	.05	.02	.01
□ 313	Mark Davis	.05	.02	.01
□ 314	Jeff Dedmon	.05	.02	.01
□ 315	Jamie Moyer	.15	.07	.02
□ 316	Wally Backman	.05	.02	.01
□ 317	Ken Phelps	.05	.02	.01
□ 318	Steve Lombardozzi	.05	.02	.01
□ 319	Rance Mulliniks	.05	.02	.01
□ 320	Tim Laudner	.05	.02	.01
□ 321	Mark Eichhorn	.05	.02	.01
□ 322	Lee Guetterman	.05	.02	.01
□ 323	Sid Fernandez	.05	.02	.01
□ 324	Jerry Mumphrey	.05	.02	.01
□ 325	David Palmer	.05	.02	.01
□ 326	Bill Almon	.05	.02	.01
□ 327	Candy Maldonado	.05	.02	.01
□ 328	John Kruk	.50	.23	.06
□ 329	John Denny	.05	.02	.01
□ 330	Milt Thompson	.05	.02	.01
□ 331	Mike LaValliere	.05	.02	.01
□ 332	Alan Ashby	.05	.02	.01
□ 333	Doug Corbett	.05	.02	.01
□ 334	Ron Karkovice	.15	.07	.02
□ 335	Mitch Webster	.05	.02	.01
□ 336	Lee Lacy	.05	.02	.01
□ 337	Glenn Braggs	.05	.02	.01
□ 338	Dwight Lowry	.05	.02	.01
□ 339	Don Baylor	.30	.14	.04
□ 340	Brian Fisher	.05	.02	.01
□ 341	Reggie Williams	.05	.02	.01
□ 342	Tom Candiotti	.05	.02	.01
□ 343	Rudy Law	.05	.02	.01
□ 344	Curt Young	.05	.02	.01
□ 345	Mike Fitzgerald	.05	.02	.01

□	346 Ruben Sierra	1.00	.45	.12
□	347 Mitch Williams	.15	.07	.02
□	348 Jorge Orta	.05	.02	.01
□	349 Mickey Tettleton	.15	.07	.02
□	350 Ernie Camacho	.05	.02	.01
□	351 Ron Kittle	.05	.02	.01
□	352 Ken Landreaux	.05	.02	.01
□	353 Chet Lemon	.05	.02	.01
□	354 John Shelby	.05	.02	.01
□	355 Mark Clear	.05	.02	.01
□	356 Doug DeCinces	.05	.02	.01
□	357 Ken Dayley	.05	.02	.01
□	358 Phil Garner	.05	.02	.01
□	359 Steve Jeltz	.05	.02	.01
□	360 Ed Whitson	.05	.02	.01
□	361 Barry Bonds	4.00	1.80	.50
□	362 Vida Blue	.15	.07	.02
□	363 Cecil Cooper	.15	.07	.02
□	364 Bob Ojeda	.05	.02	.01
□	365 Dennis Eckersley	.15	.07	.02
□	366 Mike Morgan	.05	.02	.01
□	367 Willie Upshaw	.05	.02	.01
□	368 Allan Anderson	.05	.02	.01
□	369 Bill Gullickson	.05	.02	.01
□	370 Bobby Thigpen	.15	.07	.02
□	371 Juan Beniquez	.05	.02	.01
□	372 Charlie Moore	.05	.02	.01
□	373 Dan Petry	.05	.02	.01
□	374 Rod Scurry	.05	.02	.01
□	375 Tom Seaver	.30	.14	.04
□	376 Ed VandeBerg	.05	.02	.01
□	377 Tony Bernazard	.05	.02	.01
□	378 Greg Pryor	.05	.02	.01
□	379 Dwayne Murphy	.05	.02	.01
□	380 Andy McGaffigan	.05	.02	.01
□	381 Kirk McCaskill	.05	.02	.01
□	382 Greg Harris	.05	.02	.01
□	383 Rich Dotson	.05	.02	.01
□	384 Craig Reynolds	.05	.02	.01
□	385 Greg Gross	.05	.02	.01
□	386 Tito Landrum	.05	.02	.01
□	387 Craig Lefferts	.05	.02	.01
□	388 Dave Parker	.30	.14	.04
□	389 Bob Horner	.05	.02	.01
□	390 Pat Clements	.05	.02	.01
□	391 Jeff Leonard	.05	.02	.01
□	392 Chris Speier	.05	.02	.01
□	393 John Moses	.05	.02	.01
□	394 Garth Iorg	.05	.02	.01
□	395 Greg Gagne	.05	.02	.01
□	396 Nate Snell	.05	.02	.01
□	397 Bryan Clutterbuck	.05	.02	.01
□	398 Darrell Evans	.15	.07	.02
□	399 Steve Crawford	.05	.02	.01
□	400 Checklist 346-451	.05	.02	.01
□	401 Phil Lombardi	.05	.02	.01
□	402 Rick Honeycutt	.05	.02	.01
□	403 Ken Schrom	.05	.02	.01
□	404 Bud Black	.05	.02	.01
□	405 Donnie Hill	.05	.02	.01
□	406 Wayne Krenchicki	.05	.02	.01
□	407 Chuck Finley	.40	.18	.05
□	408 Toby Harrah	.05	.02	.01
□	409 Steve Lyons	.05	.02	.01
□	410 Kevin Bass	.05	.02	.01
□	411 Marvell Wynne	.05	.02	.01
□	412 Ron Roenicke	.05	.02	.01
□	413 Tracy Jones	.05	.02	.01
□	414 Gene Garber	.05	.02	.01
□	415 Mike Bielecki	.05	.02	.01
□	416 Frank DiPino	.05	.02	.01
□	417 Andy Van Slyke	.15	.07	.02
□	418 Jim Dwyer	.05	.02	.01
□	419 Ben Oglivie	.05	.02	.01
□	420 Dave Bergman	.05	.02	.01
□	421 Joe Sambito	.05	.02	.01
□	422 Bob Tewksbury	.15	.07	.02
□	423 Len Matuszek	.05	.02	.01
□	424 Mike Kingery	.15	.07	.02
□	425 Dave Kingman	.15	.07	.02
□	426 Al Newman	.05	.02	.01
□	427 Gary Ward	.05	.02	.01
□	428 Ruppert Jones	.05	.02	.01
□	429 Harold Baines	.15	.07	.02
□	430 Pat Perry	.05	.02	.01
□	431 Terry Puhl	.05	.02	.01
□	432 Don Carman	.05	.02	.01
□	433 Eddie Milner	.05	.02	.01
□	434 LaMarr Hoyt	.05	.02	.01
□	435 Rick Rhoden	.05	.02	.01
□	436 Jose Uribe	.05	.02	.01
□	437 Ken Oberkfell	.05	.02	.01
□	438 Ron Davis	.05	.02	.01
□	439 Jesse Orosco	.05	.02	.01
□	440 Scott Bradley	.05	.02	.01
□	441 Randy Bush	.05	.02	.01
□	442 John Cerutti	.05	.02	.01
□	443 Roy Smalley	.05	.02	.01
□	444 Kelly Gruber	.05	.02	.01
□	445 Bob Kearney	.05	.02	.01
□	446 Ed Hearn	.05	.02	.01
□	447 Scott Sanderson	.05	.02	.01
□	448 Bruce Benedict	.05	.02	.01
□	449 Junior Ortiz	.05	.02	.01
□	450 Mike Aldrete	.15	.07	.02
□	451 Kevin McReynolds	.05	.02	.01
□	452 Rob Murphy	.05	.02	.01
□	453 Kent Tekulve	.05	.02	.01
□	454 Curt Ford	.05	.02	.01
□	455 Dave Lopes	.15	.07	.02
□	456 Bob Grich	.15	.07	.02
□	457 Jose DeLeon	.05	.02	.01
□	458 Andre Dawson	.30	.14	.04
□	459 Mike Flanagan	.05	.02	.01
□	460 Joey Meyer	.05	.02	.01
□	461 Chuck Cary	.05	.02	.01
□	462 Bill Buckner	.15	.07	.02
□	463 Bob Shirley	.05	.02	.01
□	464 Jeff Hamilton	.05	.02	.01
□	465 Phil Niekro	.30	.14	.04
□	466 Mark Gubicza	.05	.02	.01
□	467 Jerry Willard	.05	.02	.01
□	468 Bob Sebra	.05	.02	.01
□	469 Larry Parrish	.05	.02	.01
□	470 Charlie Hough	.05	.02	.01
□	471 Hal McRae	.15	.07	.02
□	472 Dave Leiper	.05	.02	.01
□	473 Mel Hall	.05	.02	.01
□	474 Dan Pasqua	.05	.02	.01
□	475 Bob Welch	.05	.02	.01
□	476 Johnny Grubb	.05	.02	.01
□	477 Jim Traber	.05	.02	.01
□	478 Chris Bosio	.15	.07	.02
□	479 Mark McLemore	.05	.02	.01
□	480 John Morris	.05	.02	.01
□	481 Billy Hatcher	.05	.02	.01
□	482 Dan Schatzeder	.05	.02	.01
□	483 Rich Gossage	.15	.07	.02
□	484 Jim Morrison	.05	.02	.01
□	485 Bob Brenly	.05	.02	.01
□	486 Bill Schroeder	.05	.02	.01
□	487 Mookie Wilson	.15	.07	.02
□	488 Dave Martinez	.15	.07	.02
□	489 Harold Reynolds	.05	.02	.01
□	490 Jeff Hearron	.05	.02	.01
□	491 Mickey Hatcher	.05	.02	.01
□	492 Barry Larkin	2.50	1.10	.30
□	493 Bob James	.05	.02	.01
□	494 John Habyan	.05	.02	.01
□	495 Jim Adduci	.05	.02	.01
□	496 Mike Heath	.05	.02	.01
□	497 Tim Stoddard	.05	.02	.01
□	498 Tony Armas	.05	.02	.01
□	499 Dennis Powell	.05	.02	.01
□	500 Checklist 452-557	.05	.02	.01
□	501 Chris Bando	.05	.02	.01
□	502 David Cone	1.50	.70	.19
□	503 Jay Howell	.05	.02	.01
□	504 Tom Foley	.05	.02	.01
□	505 Ray Chadwick	.05	.02	.01
□	506 Mike Loynd	.05	.02	.01
□	507 Neil Allen	.05	.02	.01
□	508 Danny Darwin	.05	.02	.01
□	509 Rick Schu	.05	.02	.01
□	510 Jose Oquendo	.05	.02	.01
□	511 Gene Walter	.05	.02	.01
□	512 Terry McGriff	.05	.02	.01
□	513 Ken Griffey	.05	.02	.01
□	514 Benny Distefano	.05	.02	.01
□	515 Terry Mulholland	.15	.07	.02
□	516 Ed Lynch	.05	.02	.01
□	517 Bill Swift	.05	.02	.01

□ 518	Manny Lee	.05	.02	.01
□ 519	Andre David	.05	.02	.01
□ 520	Scott McGregor	.05	.02	.01
□ 521	Rick Manning	.05	.02	.01
□ 522	Willie Hernandez	.05	.02	.01
□ 523	Marty Barrett	.05	.02	.01
□ 524	Wayne Tolleson	.05	.02	.01
□ 525	Jose Gonzalez	.05	.02	.01
□ 526	Cory Snyder	.05	.02	.01
□ 527	Buddy Biancalana	.05	.02	.01
□ 528	Moose Haas	.05	.02	.01
□ 529	Wilfredo Tejada	.05	.02	.01
□ 530	Stu Cliburn	.05	.02	.01
□ 531	Dale Mohorcic	.05	.02	.01
□ 532	Ron Hassey	.05	.02	.01
□ 533	Ty Gainey	.05	.02	.01
□ 534	Jerry Royster	.05	.02	.01
□ 535	Mike Maddux	.05	.02	.01
□ 536	Ted Power	.05	.02	.01
□ 537	Ted Simmons	.15	.07	.02
□ 538	Rafael Belliard	.05	.02	.01
□ 539	Chico Walker	.05	.02	.01
□ 540	Bob Forsch	.05	.02	.01
□ 541	John Stefero	.05	.02	.01
□ 542	Dale Sveum	.05	.02	.01
□ 543	Mark Thurmond	.05	.02	.01
□ 544	Jeff Sellers	.05	.02	.01
□ 545	Joel Skinner	.05	.02	.01
□ 546	Alex Trevino	.05	.02	.01
□ 547	Randy Kutcher	.05	.02	.01
□ 548	Joaquin Andujar	.05	.02	.01
□ 549	Casey Candaele	.05	.02	.01
□ 550	Jeff Russell	.05	.02	.01
□ 551	John Candelaria	.05	.02	.01
□ 552	Joe Cowley	.05	.02	.01
□ 553	Danny Cox	.05	.02	.01
□ 554	Denny Walling	.05	.02	.01
□ 555	Bruce Ruffin	.05	.02	.01
□ 556	Buddy Bell	.15	.07	.02
□ 557	Jimmy Jones	.05	.02	.01
□ 558	Bobby Bonilla	.75	.35	.09
□ 559	Jeff D. Robinson	.05	.02	.01
□ 560	Ed Olwine	.05	.02	.01
□ 561	Glenallen Hill	.30	.14	.04
□ 562	Lee Mazzilli	.05	.02	.01
□ 563	Mike G. Brown P	.05	.02	.01
□ 564	George Frazier	.05	.02	.01
□ 565	Mike Sharperson	.05	.02	.01
□ 566	Mark Portugal	.15	.07	.02
□ 567	Rick Leach	.05	.02	.01
□ 568	Mark Langston	.15	.07	.02
□ 569	Rafael Santana	.05	.02	.01
□ 570	Manny Trillo	.05	.02	.01
□ 571	Cliff Speck	.05	.02	.01
□ 572	Bob Kipper	.05	.02	.01
□ 573	Kelly Downs	.05	.02	.01
□ 574	Randy Asadoor	.05	.02	.01
□ 575	Dave Magadan	.15	.07	.02
□ 576	Marvin Freeman	.15	.07	.02
□ 577	Jeff Lahti	.05	.02	.01
□ 578	Jeff Calhoun	.05	.02	.01
□ 579	Gus Polidor	.05	.02	.01
□ 580	Gene Nelson	.05	.02	.01
□ 581	Tim Teufel	.05	.02	.01
□ 582	Odell Jones	.05	.02	.01
□ 583	Mark Ryal	.05	.02	.01
□ 584	Randy O'Neal	.05	.02	.01
□ 585	Mike Greenwell	.30	.14	.04
□ 586	Ray Knight	.15	.07	.02
□ 587	Ralph Bryant	.05	.02	.01
□ 588	Carmen Castillo	.05	.02	.01
□ 589	Ed Wojna	.05	.02	.01
□ 590	Stan Javier	.05	.02	.01
□ 591	Jeff Musselman	.05	.02	.01
□ 592	Mike Stanley	.30	.14	.04
□ 593	Darrell Porter	.05	.02	.01
□ 594	Drew Hall	.05	.02	.01
□ 595	Rob Nelson	.05	.02	.01
□ 596	Bryan Oelkers	.05	.02	.01
□ 597	Scott Nielsen	.05	.02	.01
□ 598	Brian Holton	.05	.02	.01
□ 599	Kevin Mitchell	.30	.14	.04
□ 600	Checklist 558-660	.05	.02	.01
□ 601	Jackie Gutierrez	.05	.02	.01
□ 602	Barry Jones	.05	.02	.01
□ 603	Jerry Narron	.05	.02	.01
□ 604	Steve Lake	.05	.02	.01
□ 605	Jim Pankovits	.05	.02	.01
□ 606	Ed Romero	.05	.02	.01
□ 607	Dave LaPoint	.05	.02	.01
□ 608	Don Robinson	.05	.02	.01
□ 609	Mike Krukow	.05	.02	.01
□ 610	Dave Valle	.05	.02	.01
□ 611	Len Dykstra	.15	.07	.02
□ 612	Roberto Clemente PUZ	.40	.18	.05
□ 613	Mike Trujillo	.05	.02	.01
□ 614	Damaso Garcia	.05	.02	.01
□ 615	Neal Heaton	.05	.02	.01
□ 616	Juan Berenguer	.05	.02	.01
□ 617	Steve Carlton	.30	.14	.04
□ 618	Gary Lucas	.05	.02	.01
□ 619	Geno Petralli	.05	.02	.01
□ 620	Rick Aguilera	.15	.07	.02
□ 621	Fred McGriff	1.50	.70	.19
□ 622	Dave Henderson	.05	.02	.01
□ 623	Dave Clark	.15	.07	.02
□ 624	Angel Salazar	.05	.02	.01
□ 625	Randy Hunt	.05	.02	.01
□ 626	John Gibbons	.05	.02	.01
□ 627	Kevin Brown	.75	.35	.09
□ 628	Bill Dawley	.05	.02	.01
□ 629	Aurelio Lopez	.05	.02	.01
□ 630	Charles Hudson	.05	.02	.01
□ 631	Ray Soff	.05	.02	.01
□ 632	Ray Hayward	.05	.02	.01
□ 633	Spike Owen	.05	.02	.01
□ 634	Glenn Hubbard	.05	.02	.01
□ 635	Kevin Elster	.30	.14	.04
□ 636	Mike LaCoss	.05	.02	.01
□ 637	Dwayne Henry	.05	.02	.01
□ 638	Rey Quinones	.05	.02	.01
□ 639	Jim Clancy	.05	.02	.01
□ 640	Larry Andersen	.05	.02	.01
□ 641	Calvin Schiraldi	.05	.02	.01
□ 642	Stan Jefferson	.05	.02	.01
□ 643	Marc Sullivan	.05	.02	.01
□ 644	Mark Grant	.05	.02	.01
□ 645	Cliff Johnson	.05	.02	.01
□ 646	Howard Johnson	.05	.02	.01
□ 647	Dave Sax	.05	.02	.01
□ 648	Dave Stewart	.15	.07	.02
□ 649	Danny Heep	.05	.02	.01
□ 650	Joe Johnson	.05	.02	.01
□ 651	Bob Brower	.05	.02	.01
□ 652	Rob Woodward	.05	.02	.01
□ 653	John Mizerock	.05	.02	.01
□ 654	Tim Pyznarski	.05	.02	.01
□ 655	Luis Aquino	.05	.02	.01
□ 656	Mickey Brantley	.05	.02	.01
□ 657	Doyle Alexander	.05	.02	.01
□ 658	Sammy Stewart	.05	.02	.01
□ 659	Jim Acker	.05	.02	.01
□ 660	Pete Ladd	.05	.02	.01

1987 Donruss Rookies

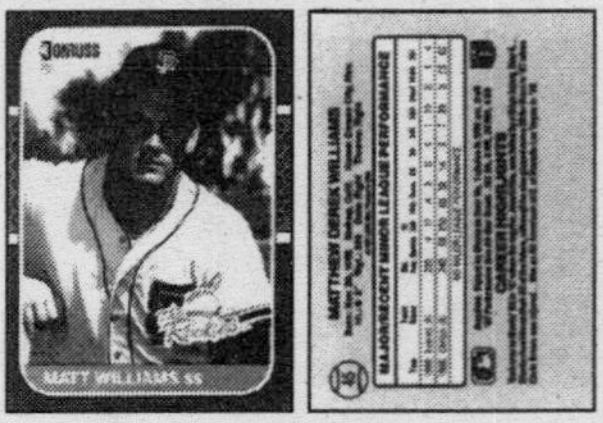

The 1987 Donruss "The Rookies" set features 56 full-color standard-size cards plus a 15-piece puzzle of Roberto Clemente. The set was distributed in factory set form packaged in a small green and black box through hobby dealers. Card fronts are similar in design to the 1987 Donruss regular issue except for the presence of "The Rookies" logo in the lower left corner and a green border instead of a black bor-

der. The key extended Rookie Cards in this set are Ellis Burks and Matt Williams. The second Donruss-issued cards of Greg Maddux and Rafael Palmeiro are also in this set.

	MINT	NRMT	EXC
COMPLETE FACT.SET (56)	20.00	9.00	2.50
COMMON CARD (1-56)	.10	.05	.01
SEMISTARS	.15	.07	.02
□ 1 Mark McGwire	3.00	1.35	.35
□ 2 Eric Bell	.10	.05	.01
□ 3 Mark Williamson	.10	.05	.01
□ 4 Mike Greenwell	.20	.09	.03
□ 5 Ellis Burks	1.50	.70	.19
□ 6 DeWayne Buice	.10	.05	.01
□ 7 Mark McLemore	.10	.05	.01
□ 8 Devon White	.20	.09	.03
□ 9 Willie Fraser	.10	.05	.01
□ 10 Les Lancaster	.10	.05	.01
□ 11 Ken Williams	.10	.05	.01
□ 12 Matt Nokes	.15	.07	.02
□ 13 Jeff M. Robinson	.10	.05	.01
□ 14 Bo Jackson	1.00	.45	.12
□ 15 Kevin Seitzer	.30	.14	.04
□ 16 Billy Ripken	.10	.05	.01
□ 17 B.J. Surhoff	.20	.09	.03
□ 18 Chuck Crim	.10	.05	.01
□ 19 Mike Birkbeck	.10	.05	.01
□ 20 Chris Bosio	.15	.07	.02
□ 21 Les Straker	.10	.05	.01
□ 22 Mark Davidson	.10	.05	.01
□ 23 Gene Larkin	.10	.05	.01
□ 24 Ken Gerhart	.10	.05	.01
□ 25 Luis Polonia	.20	.09	.03
□ 26 Terry Steinbach	.20	.09	.03
□ 27 Mickey Brantley	.10	.05	.01
□ 28 Mike Stanley	.20	.09	.03
□ 29 Jerry Browne	.10	.05	.01
□ 30 Todd Benzinger	.10	.05	.01
□ 31 Fred McGriff	2.50	1.10	.30
□ 32 Mike Henneman	.20	.09	.03
□ 33 Casey Candaele	.10	.05	.01
□ 34 Dave Magadan	.15	.07	.02
□ 35 David Cone	1.50	.70	.19
□ 36 Mike Jackson	.15	.07	.02
□ 37 John Mitchell	.10	.05	.01
□ 38 Mike Dunne	.10	.05	.01
□ 39 John Smiley	.15	.07	.02
□ 40 Joe Magrane	.10	.05	.01
□ 41 Jim Lindeman	.10	.05	.01
□ 42 Shane Mack	.15	.07	.02
□ 43 Stan Jefferson	.10	.05	.01
□ 44 Benito Santiago	.15	.07	.02
□ 45 Matt Williams	5.00	2.20	.60
□ 46 Dave Meads	.10	.05	.01
□ 47 Rafael Palmeiro	2.50	1.10	.30
□ 48 Bill Long	.10	.05	.01
□ 49 Bob Brower	.10	.05	.01
□ 50 James Steels	.10	.05	.01
□ 51 Paul Noce	.10	.05	.01
□ 52 Greg Maddux	14.00	6.25	1.75
□ 53 Jeff Musselman	.10	.05	.01
□ 54 Brian Holton	.10	.05	.01
□ 55 Chuck Jackson	.10	.05	.01
□ 56 Checklist 1-56	.10	.05	.01

1988 Donruss

This set consists of 660 standard-size cards. For the seventh straight year, wax packs consisted of 15 cards plus a puzzle panel (featuring Stan Musial this time around). Cards were also distributed in rack packs and retail and hobby factory sets. Card fronts feature a distinctive black and blue border on the front. The card front border design pattern of the factory set card fronts is oriented differently from that of the regular wax pack cards. No premium or discount exists for either version. Subsets include Diamond Kings (1-27) and Rated Rookies (28-47). Cards marked as SP (short printed) from 648-660 are more difficult to find than the other 13 SP's in the lower 600s. These 26 cards listed as SP were apparently pulled

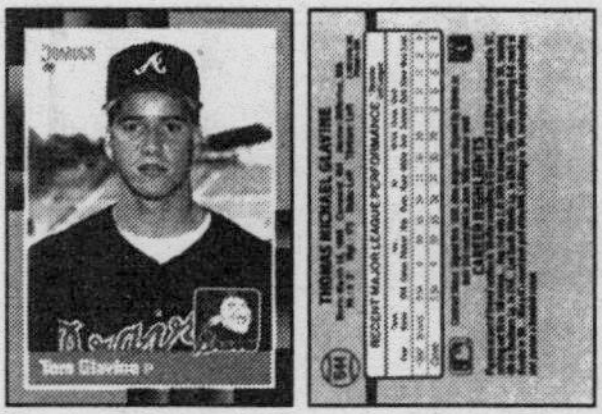

from the printing sheet to make room for the 26 Bonus MVP cards. Numbered with the prefix "BC" for bonus card, this 26-card set featuring the most valuable player from each of the 26 teams was randomly inserted in the wax and rack packs. The cards are distinguished by the MVP logo in the upper left corner of the obverse, and cards BC14-BC26 are considered to be more difficult to find than cards BC1-BC13. Six of the checklist cards were done two different ways to reflect the inclusion or exclusion of the Bonus MVP cards in the wax packs. In the checklist below, the A variations (for the checklist cards) are from the wax packs and the B variations are from the factory-collated sets. The key Rookie Cards in this set are Roberto Alomar, Jay Bell, Jay Buhner, Ellis Burks, Ken Caminiti, Ron Gant, Tom Glavine, Mark Grace, Gregg Jefferies, Jack McDowell, and Matt Williams. There was also a Kirby Puckett card issued as the package back of Donruss blister packs; it uses a different photo from both of Kirby's regular and Bonus MVP cards and is unnumbered on the back.

	MINT	NRMT	EXC
COMPLETE SET (660)	8.00	3.60	1.00
COMPLETE FACT.SET (660)	10.00	4.50	1.25
COMMON CARD (1-647)	.05	.02	.01
COMMON CARD SP (648-660)	.07	.03	.01
SEMISTARS	.10	.05	.01
STARS	.15	.07	.02
COMPLETE MVP SET (26)	3.00	1.35	.35
MVP'S: RANDOM INSERTS IN PACKS			
□ 1 Mark McGwire DK	.30	.14	.04
□ 2 Tim Raines DK	.10	.05	.01
□ 3 Benito Santiago DK	.05	.02	.01
□ 4 Alan Trammell DK	.10	.05	.01
□ 5 Danny Tartabull DK	.05	.02	.01
□ 6 Ron Darling DK	.05	.02	.01
□ 7 Paul Molitor DK	.15	.07	.02
□ 8 Devon White DK	.10	.05	.01
□ 9 Andre Dawson DK	.10	.05	.01
□ 10 Julio Franco DK	.10	.05	.01
□ 11 Scott Fletcher DK	.05	.02	.01
□ 12 Tony Fernandez DK	.05	.02	.01
□ 13 Shane Rawley DK	.05	.02	.01
□ 14 Kal Daniels DK	.05	.02	.01
□ 15 Jack Clark DK	.05	.02	.01
□ 16 Dwight Evans DK	.10	.05	.01
□ 17 Tommy John DK	.10	.05	.01
□ 18 Andy Van Slyke DK	.05	.02	.01
□ 19 Gary Gaetti DK	.05	.02	.01
□ 20 Mark Langston DK	.10	.05	.01
□ 21 Will Clark DK	.15	.07	.02
□ 22 Glenn Hubbard DK	.05	.02	.01
□ 23 Billy Hatcher DK	.05	.02	.01
□ 24 Bob Welch DK	.05	.02	.01
□ 25 Ivan Calderon DK	.05	.02	.01
□ 26 Cal Ripken DK	.40	.18	.05
□ 27 DK Checklist 1-26	.05	.02	.01
□ 28 Mackey Sasser RR	.05	.02	.01
□ 29 Jeff Treadway RR	.05	.02	.01
□ 30 Mike Campbell RR	.05	.02	.01
□ 31 Lance Johnson RR	.40	.18	.05
□ 32 Nelson Liriano RR	.05	.02	.01
□ 33 Shawn Abner RR	.05	.02	.01
□ 34 Roberto Alomar RR	2.00	.90	.25
□ 35 Shawn Hillegas RR	.05	.02	.01

□ 36 Joey Meyer RR	.05	.02	.01
□ 37 Kevin Elster RR	.10	.05	.01
□ 38 Jose Lind RR	.10	.05	.01
□ 39 Kirt Manwaring RR	.10	.05	.01
□ 40 Mark Grace RR	.60	.25	.07
□ 41 Jody Reed RR	.10	.05	.01
□ 42 John Farrell RR	.05	.02	.01
□ 43 Al Leiter RR	.15	.07	.02
□ 44 Gary Thurman RR	.05	.02	.01
□ 45 Vicente Palacios RR	.05	.02	.01
□ 46 Eddie Williams RR	.10	.05	.01
□ 47 Jack McDowell RR	.40	.18	.05
□ 48 Ken Dixon	.05	.02	.01
□ 49 Mike Birkbeck	.05	.02	.01
□ 50 Eric King	.05	.02	.01
□ 51 Roger Clemens	.15	.07	.02
□ 52 Pat Clements	.05	.02	.01
□ 53 Fernando Valenzuela	.10	.05	.01
□ 54 Mark Gubicza	.05	.02	.01
□ 55 Jay Howell	.05	.02	.01
□ 56 Floyd Youmans	.05	.02	.01
□ 57 Ed Correa	.05	.02	.01
□ 58 DeWayne Buice	.05	.02	.01
□ 59 Jose DeLeon	.05	.02	.01
□ 60 Danny Cox	.05	.02	.01
□ 61 Nolan Ryan	.75	.35	.09
□ 62 Steve Bedrosian	.05	.02	.01
□ 63 Tom Browning	.05	.02	.01
□ 64 Mark Davis	.05	.02	.01
□ 65 R.J. Reynolds	.05	.02	.01
□ 66 Kevin Mitchell	.10	.05	.01
□ 67 Ken Oberkfell	.05	.02	.01
□ 68 Rick Sutcliffe	.05	.02	.01
□ 69 Dwight Gooden	.15	.07	.02
□ 70 Scott Bankhead	.05	.02	.01
□ 71 Bert Blyleven	.10	.05	.01
□ 72 Jimmy Key	.10	.05	.01
□ 73 Les Straker	.05	.02	.01
□ 74 Jim Clancy	.05	.02	.01
□ 75 Mike Moore	.05	.02	.01
□ 76 Ron Darling	.05	.02	.01
□ 77 Ed Lynch	.05	.02	.01
□ 78 Dale Murphy	.15	.07	.02
□ 79 Doug Drabek	.10	.05	.01
□ 80 Scott Garrelts	.05	.02	.01
□ 81 Ed Whitson	.05	.02	.01
□ 82 Rob Murphy	.05	.02	.01
□ 83 Shane Rawley	.05	.02	.01
□ 84 Greg Mathews	.05	.02	.01
□ 85 Jim Deshaies	.05	.02	.01
□ 86 Mike Witt	.05	.02	.01
□ 87 Donnie Hill	.05	.02	.01
□ 88 Jeff Reed	.05	.02	.01
□ 89 Mike Boddicker	.05	.02	.01
□ 90 Ted Higuera	.05	.02	.01
□ 91 Walt Terrell	.05	.02	.01
□ 92 Bob Stanley	.05	.02	.01
□ 93 Dave Righetti	.05	.02	.01
□ 94 Orel Hershiser	.10	.05	.01
□ 95 Chris Bando	.05	.02	.01
□ 96 Bret Saberhagen	.10	.05	.01
□ 97 Curt Young	.05	.02	.01
□ 98 Tim Burke	.05	.02	.01
□ 99 Charlie Hough	.10	.05	.01
□ 100A Checklist 28-137	.05	.02	.01
□ 100B Checklist 28-133	.05	.02	.01
□ 101 Bobby Witt	.05	.02	.01
□ 102 George Brett	.40	.18	.05
□ 103 Mickey Tettleton	.10	.05	.01
□ 104 Scott Bailes	.05	.02	.01
□ 105 Mike Pagliarulo	.05	.02	.01
□ 106 Mike Scioscia	.05	.02	.01
□ 107 Tom Brookens	.05	.02	.01
□ 108 Ray Knight	.10	.05	.01
□ 109 Dan Plesac	.05	.02	.01
□ 110 Wally Joyner	.10	.05	.01
□ 111 Bob Forsch	.05	.02	.01
□ 112 Mike Scott	.05	.02	.01
□ 113 Kevin Gross	.05	.02	.01
□ 114 Benito Santiago	.10	.05	.01
□ 115 Bob Kipper	.05	.02	.01
□ 116 Mike Krukow	.05	.02	.01
□ 117 Chris Bosio	.05	.02	.01
□ 118 Sid Fernandez	.05	.02	.01
□ 119 Jody Davis	.05	.02	.01
□ 120 Mike Morgan	.05	.02	.01
□ 121 Mark Eichhorn	.05	.02	.01
□ 122 Jeff Reardon	.10	.05	.01
□ 123 John Franco	.05	.02	.01
□ 124 Richard Dotson	.05	.02	.01
□ 125 Eric Bell	.05	.02	.01
□ 126 Juan Nieves	.05	.02	.01
□ 127 Jack Morris	.15	.07	.02
□ 128 Rick Rhoden	.05	.02	.01
□ 129 Rich Gedman	.05	.02	.01
□ 130 Ken Howell	.05	.02	.01
□ 131 Brook Jacoby	.05	.02	.01
□ 132 Danny Jackson	.05	.02	.01
□ 133 Gene Nelson	.05	.02	.01
□ 134 Neal Heaton	.05	.02	.01
□ 135 Willie Fraser	.05	.02	.01
□ 136 Jose Guzman	.05	.02	.01
□ 137 Ozzie Guillen	.10	.05	.01
□ 138 Bob Knepper	.05	.02	.01
□ 139 Mike Jackson	.10	.05	.01
□ 140 Joe Magrane	.05	.02	.01
□ 141 Jimmy Jones	.05	.02	.01
□ 142 Ted Power	.05	.02	.01
□ 143 Ozzie Virgil	.05	.02	.01
□ 144 Felix Fermin	.05	.02	.01
□ 145 Kelly Downs	.05	.02	.01
□ 146 Shawon Dunston	.05	.02	.01
□ 147 Scott Bradley	.05	.02	.01
□ 148 Dave Stieb	.10	.05	.01
□ 149 Frank Viola	.05	.02	.01
□ 150 Terry Kennedy	.05	.02	.01
□ 151 Bill Wegman	.05	.02	.01
□ 152 Matt Nokes	.05	.02	.01
□ 153 Wade Boggs	.15	.07	.02
□ 154 Wayne Tolleson	.05	.02	.01
□ 155 Mariano Duncan	.05	.02	.01
□ 156 Julio Franco	.10	.05	.01
□ 157 Charlie Leibrandt	.05	.02	.01
□ 158 Terry Steinbach	.10	.05	.01
□ 159 Mike Fitzgerald	.05	.02	.01
□ 160 Jack Lazorko	.05	.02	.01
□ 161 Mitch Williams	.10	.05	.01
□ 162 Greg Walker	.05	.02	.01
□ 163 Alan Ashby	.05	.02	.01
□ 164 Tony Gwynn	.40	.18	.05
□ 165 Bruce Ruffin	.05	.02	.01
□ 166 Ron Robinson	.05	.02	.01
□ 167 Zane Smith	.05	.02	.01
□ 168 Junior Ortiz	.05	.02	.01
□ 169 Jamie Moyer	.05	.02	.01
□ 170 Tony Pena	.05	.02	.01
□ 171 Cal Ripken	.75	.35	.09
□ 172 B.J. Surhoff	.10	.05	.01
□ 173 Lou Whitaker	.15	.07	.02
□ 174 Ellis Burks	.40	.18	.05
□ 175 Ron Guidry	.05	.02	.01
□ 176 Steve Sax	.05	.02	.01
□ 177 Danny Tartabull	.05	.02	.01
□ 178 Carney Lansford	.10	.05	.01
□ 179 Casey Candaele	.05	.02	.01
□ 180 Scott Fletcher	.05	.02	.01
□ 181 Mark McLemore	.05	.02	.01
□ 182 Ivan Calderon	.05	.02	.01
□ 183 Jack Clark	.10	.05	.01
□ 184 Glenn Davis	.05	.02	.01
□ 185 Luis Aguayo	.05	.02	.01
□ 186 Bo Diaz	.05	.02	.01
□ 187 Stan Jefferson	.05	.02	.01
□ 188 Sid Bream	.05	.02	.01
□ 189 Bob Brenly	.05	.02	.01
□ 190 Dion James	.05	.02	.01
□ 191 Leon Durham	.05	.02	.01
□ 192 Jesse Orosco	.05	.02	.01
□ 193 Alvin Davis	.05	.02	.01
□ 194 Gary Gaetti	.05	.02	.01
□ 195 Fred McGriff	.30	.14	.04
□ 196 Steve Lombardozzi	.05	.02	.01
□ 197 Rance Mulliniks	.05	.02	.01
□ 198 Rey Quinones	.05	.02	.01
□ 199 Gary Carter	.15	.07	.02
□ 200A Checklist 138-247	.05	.02	.01
□ 200B Checklist 134-239	.05	.02	.01
□ 201 Keith Moreland	.05	.02	.01
□ 202 Ken Griffey	.05	.02	.01
□ 203 Tommy Gregg	.05	.02	.01
□ 204 Will Clark	.25	.11	.03
□ 205 John Kruk	.15	.07	.02

□ 206 Buddy Bell	.10	.05	.01
□ 207 Von Hayes	.05	.02	.01
□ 208 Tommy Herr	.05	.02	.01
□ 209 Craig Reynolds	.05	.02	.01
□ 210 Gary Pettis	.05	.02	.01
□ 211 Harold Baines	.10	.05	.01
□ 212 Vance Law	.05	.02	.01
□ 213 Ken Gerhart	.05	.02	.01
□ 214 Jim Gantner	.05	.02	.01
□ 215 Chet Lemon	.05	.02	.01
□ 216 Dwight Evans	.10	.05	.01
□ 217 Don Mattingly	.50	.23	.06
□ 218 Franklin Stubbs	.05	.02	.01
□ 219 Pat Tabler	.05	.02	.01
□ 220 Bo Jackson	.15	.07	.02
□ 221 Tony Phillips	.15	.07	.02
□ 222 Tim Wallach	.05	.02	.01
□ 223 Ruben Sierra	.15	.07	.02
□ 224 Steve Buechele	.05	.02	.01
□ 225 Frank White	.10	.05	.01
□ 226 Alfredo Griffin	.05	.02	.01
□ 227 Greg Swindell	.05	.02	.01
□ 228 Willie Randolph	.10	.05	.01
□ 229 Mike Marshall	.05	.02	.01
□ 230 Alan Trammell	.15	.07	.02
□ 231 Eddie Murray	.25	.11	.03
□ 232 Dale Sveum	.05	.02	.01
□ 233 Dick Schofield	.05	.02	.01
□ 234 Jose Oquendo	.05	.02	.01
□ 235 Bill Doran	.05	.02	.01
□ 236 Milt Thompson	.05	.02	.01
□ 237 Marvell Wynne	.05	.02	.01
□ 238 Bobby Bonilla	.10	.05	.01
□ 239 Chris Speier	.05	.02	.01
□ 240 Glenn Braggs	.05	.02	.01
□ 241 Wally Backman	.05	.02	.01
□ 242 Ryne Sandberg	.25	.11	.03
□ 243 Phil Bradley	.05	.02	.01
□ 244 Kelly Gruber	.05	.02	.01
□ 245 Tom Brunansky	.05	.02	.01
□ 246 Ron Oester	.05	.02	.01
□ 247 Bobby Thigpen	.05	.02	.01
□ 248 Fred Lynn	.05	.02	.01
□ 249 Paul Molitor	.20	.09	.03
□ 250 Darrell Evans	.10	.05	.01
□ 251 Gary Ward	.05	.02	.01
□ 252 Bruce Hurst	.05	.02	.01
□ 253 Bob Welch	.05	.02	.01
□ 254 Joe Carter	.15	.07	.02
□ 255 Willie Wilson	.05	.02	.01
□ 256 Mark McGwire	.60	.25	.07
□ 257 Mitch Webster	.05	.02	.01
□ 258 Brian Downing	.05	.02	.01
□ 259 Mike Stanley	.10	.05	.01
□ 260 Carlton Fisk	.15	.07	.02
□ 261 Billy Hatcher	.05	.02	.01
□ 262 Glenn Wilson	.05	.02	.01
□ 263 Ozzie Smith	.20	.09	.03
□ 264 Randy Ready	.05	.02	.01
□ 265 Kurt Stillwell	.05	.02	.01
□ 266 David Palmer	.05	.02	.01
□ 267 Mike Diaz	.05	.02	.01
□ 268 Robby Thompson	.05	.02	.01
□ 269 Andre Dawson	.15	.07	.02
□ 270 Lee Guetterman	.05	.02	.01
□ 271 Willie Upshaw	.05	.02	.01
□ 272 Randy Bush	.05	.02	.01
□ 273 Larry Sheets	.05	.02	.01
□ 274 Rob Deer	.05	.02	.01
□ 275 Kirk Gibson	.10	.05	.01
□ 276 Marty Barrett	.05	.02	.01
□ 277 Rickey Henderson	.15	.07	.02
□ 278 Pedro Guerrero	.10	.05	.01
□ 279 Brett Butler	.10	.05	.01
□ 280 Kevin Seitzer	.10	.05	.01
□ 281 Mike Davis	.05	.02	.01
□ 282 Andres Galarraga	.15	.07	.02
□ 283 Devon White	.15	.07	.02
□ 284 Pete O'Brien	.05	.02	.01
□ 285 Jerry Hairston	.05	.02	.01
□ 286 Kevin Bass	.05	.02	.01
□ 287 Carmelo Martinez	.05	.02	.01
□ 288 Juan Samuel	.05	.02	.01
□ 289 Kal Daniels	.05	.02	.01
□ 290 Albert Hall	.05	.02	.01
□ 291 Andy Van Slyke	.10	.05	.01

□ 292 Lee Smith	.15	.07	.02
□ 293 Vince Coleman	.05	.02	.01
□ 294 Tom Niedenfuer	.05	.02	.01
□ 295 Robin Yount	.15	.07	.02
□ 296 Jeff M. Robinson	.05	.02	.01
□ 297 Todd Benzinger	.10	.05	.01
□ 298 Dave Winfield	.15	.07	.02
□ 299 Mickey Hatcher	.05	.02	.01
□ 300A Checklist 248-357	.05	.02	.01
□ 300B Checklist 240-345	.05	.02	.01
□ 301 Bud Black	.05	.02	.01
□ 302 Jose Canseco	.25	.11	.03
□ 303 Tom Foley	.05	.02	.01
□ 304 Pete Incaviglia	.05	.02	.01
□ 305 Bob Boone	.10	.05	.01
□ 306 Bill Long	.05	.02	.01
□ 307 Willie McGee	.05	.02	.01
□ 308 Ken Caminiti	.75	.35	.09
□ 309 Darren Daulton	.10	.05	.01
□ 310 Tracy Jones	.05	.02	.01
□ 311 Greg Booker	.05	.02	.01
□ 312 Mike LaValliere	.05	.02	.01
□ 313 Chili Davis	.15	.07	.02
□ 314 Glenn Hubbard	.05	.02	.01
□ 315 Paul Noce	.05	.02	.01
□ 316 Keith Hernandez	.10	.05	.01
□ 317 Mark Langston	.10	.05	.01
□ 318 Keith Atherton	.05	.02	.01
□ 319 Tony Fernandez	.05	.02	.01
□ 320 Kent Hrbek	.10	.05	.01
□ 321 John Cerutti	.05	.02	.01
□ 322 Mike Kingery	.05	.02	.01
□ 323 Dave Magadan	.05	.02	.01
□ 324 Rafael Palmeiro	.25	.11	.03
□ 325 Jeff Dedmon	.05	.02	.01
□ 326 Barry Bonds	.60	.25	.07
□ 327 Jeffrey Leonard	.05	.02	.01
□ 328 Tim Flannery	.05	.02	.01
□ 329 Dave Concepcion	.10	.05	.01
□ 330 Mike Schmidt	.20	.09	.03
□ 331 Bill Dawley	.05	.02	.01
□ 332 Larry Andersen	.05	.02	.01
□ 333 Jack Howell	.05	.02	.01
□ 334 Ken Williams	.05	.02	.01
□ 335 Bryn Smith	.05	.02	.01
□ 336 Billy Ripken	.10	.05	.01
□ 337 Greg Brock	.05	.02	.01
□ 338 Mike Heath	.05	.02	.01
□ 339 Mike Greenwell	.15	.07	.02
□ 340 Claudell Washington	.05	.02	.01
□ 341 Jose Gonzalez	.05	.02	.01
□ 342 Mel Hall	.05	.02	.01
□ 343 Jim Eisenreich	.10	.05	.01
□ 344 Tony Bernazard	.05	.02	.01
□ 345 Tim Raines	.15	.07	.02
□ 346 Bob Brower	.05	.02	.01
□ 347 Larry Parrish	.05	.02	.01
□ 348 Thad Bosley	.05	.02	.01
□ 349 Dennis Eckersley	.15	.07	.02
□ 350 Cory Snyder	.05	.02	.01
□ 351 Rick Cerone	.05	.02	.01
□ 352 John Shelby	.05	.02	.01
□ 353 Larry Herndon	.05	.02	.01
□ 354 John Habyan	.05	.02	.01
□ 355 Chuck Crim	.05	.02	.01
□ 356 Gus Polidor	.05	.02	.01
□ 357 Ken Dayley	.05	.02	.01
□ 358 Danny Darwin	.05	.02	.01
□ 359 Lance Parrish	.05	.02	.01
□ 360 James Steels	.05	.02	.01
□ 361 Al Pedrique	.05	.02	.01
□ 362 Mike Aldrete	.05	.02	.01
□ 363 Juan Castillo	.05	.02	.01
□ 364 Len Dykstra	.10	.05	.01
□ 365 Luis Quinones	.05	.02	.01
□ 366 Jim Presley	.05	.02	.01
□ 367 Lloyd Moseby	.05	.02	.01
□ 368 Kirby Puckett	.30	.14	.04
□ 369 Eric Davis	.10	.05	.01
□ 370 Gary Redus	.05	.02	.01
□ 371 Dave Schmidt	.05	.02	.01
□ 372 Mark Clear	.05	.02	.01
□ 373 Dave Bergman	.05	.02	.01
□ 374 Charles Hudson	.05	.02	.01
□ 375 Calvin Schiraldi	.05	.02	.01
□ 376 Alex Trevino	.05	.02	.01

□ 377 Tom Candiotti	.05	.02	.01
□ 378 Steve Farr	.05	.02	.01
□ 379 Mike Gallego	.05	.02	.01
□ 380 Andy McGaffigan	.05	.02	.01
□ 381 Kirk McCaskill	.05	.02	.01
□ 382 Oddibe McDowell	.05	.02	.01
□ 383 Floyd Bannister	.05	.02	.01
□ 384 Denny Walling	.05	.02	.01
□ 385 Don Carman	.05	.02	.01
□ 386 Todd Worrell	.05	.02	.01
□ 387 Eric Show	.05	.02	.01
□ 388 Dave Parker	.15	.07	.02
□ 389 Rick Mahler	.05	.02	.01
□ 390 Mike Dunne	.05	.02	.01
□ 391 Candy Maldonado	.05	.02	.01
□ 392 Bob Dernier	.05	.02	.01
□ 393 Dave Valle	.05	.02	.01
□ 394 Ernie Whitt	.05	.02	.01
□ 395 Juan Berenguer	.05	.02	.01
□ 396 Mike Young	.05	.02	.01
□ 397 Mike Felder	.05	.02	.01
□ 398 Willie Hernandez	.05	.02	.01
□ 399 Jim Rice	.15	.07	.02
□ 400A Checklist 358-467	.05	.02	.01
□ 400B Checklist 346-451	.05	.02	.01
□ 401 Tommy John	.10	.05	.01
□ 402 Brian Holton	.05	.02	.01
□ 403 Carmen Castillo	.05	.02	.01
□ 404 Jamie Quirk	.05	.02	.01
□ 405 Dwayne Murphy	.05	.02	.01
□ 406 Jeff Parrett	.05	.02	.01
□ 407 Don Sutton	.15	.07	.02
□ 408 Jerry Browne	.05	.02	.01
□ 409 Jim Winn	.05	.02	.01
□ 410 Dave Smith	.05	.02	.01
□ 411 Shane Mack	.05	.02	.01
□ 412 Greg Gross	.05	.02	.01
□ 413 Nick Esasky	.05	.02	.01
□ 414 Damaso Garcia	.05	.02	.01
□ 415 Brian Fisher	.05	.02	.01
□ 416 Brian Dayett	.05	.02	.01
□ 417 Curt Ford	.05	.02	.01
□ 418 Mark Williamson	.05	.02	.01
□ 419 Bill Schroeder	.05	.02	.01
□ 420 Mike Henneman	.10	.05	.01
□ 421 John Marzano	.05	.02	.01
□ 422 Ron Kittle	.05	.02	.01
□ 423 Matt Young	.05	.02	.01
□ 424 Steve Balboni	.05	.02	.01
□ 425 Luis Polonia	.15	.07	.02
□ 426 Randy St.Claire	.05	.02	.01
□ 427 Greg Harris	.05	.02	.01
□ 428 Johnny Ray	.05	.02	.01
□ 429 Ray Searage	.05	.02	.01
□ 430 Ricky Horton	.05	.02	.01
□ 431 Gerald Young	.05	.02	.01
□ 432 Rick Schu	.05	.02	.01
□ 433 Paul O'Neill	.15	.07	.02
□ 434 Rich Gossage	.15	.07	.02
□ 435 John Cangelosi	.05	.02	.01
□ 436 Mike LaCoss	.05	.02	.01
□ 437 Gerald Perry	.05	.02	.01
□ 438 Dave Martinez	.05	.02	.01
□ 439 Darryl Strawberry	.15	.07	.02
□ 440 John Moses	.05	.02	.01
□ 441 Greg Gagne	.05	.02	.01
□ 442 Jesse Barfield	.05	.02	.01
□ 443 George Frazier	.05	.02	.01
□ 444 Garth Iorg	.05	.02	.01
□ 445 Ed Nunez	.05	.02	.01
□ 446 Rick Aguilera	.10	.05	.01
□ 447 Jerry Mumphrey	.05	.02	.01
□ 448 Rafael Ramirez	.05	.02	.01
□ 449 John Smiley	.15	.07	.02
□ 450 Atlee Hammaker	.05	.02	.01
□ 451 Lance McCullers	.05	.02	.01
□ 452 Guy Hoffman	.05	.02	.01
□ 453 Chris James	.05	.02	.01
□ 454 Terry Pendleton	.10	.05	.01
□ 455 Dave Meads	.05	.02	.01
□ 456 Bill Buckner	.10	.05	.01
□ 457 John Pawlowski	.05	.02	.01
□ 458 Bob Sebra	.05	.02	.01
□ 459 Jim Dwyer	.05	.02	.01
□ 460 Jay Aldrich	.05	.02	.01
□ 461 Frank Tanana	.05	.02	.01
□ 462 Oil Can Boyd	.05	.02	.01
□ 463 Dan Pasqua	.05	.02	.01
□ 464 Tim Crews	.10	.05	.01
□ 465 Andy Allanson	.05	.02	.01
□ 466 Bill Pecota	.05	.02	.01
□ 467 Steve Ontiveros	.05	.02	.01
□ 468 Hubie Brooks	.05	.02	.01
□ 469 Paul Kilgus	.05	.02	.01
□ 470 Dale Mohorcic	.05	.02	.01
□ 471 Dan Quisenberry	.05	.02	.01
□ 472 Dave Stewart	.10	.05	.01
□ 473 Dave Clark	.05	.02	.01
□ 474 Joel Skinner	.05	.02	.01
□ 475 Dave Anderson	.05	.02	.01
□ 476 Dan Petry	.05	.02	.01
□ 477 Carl Nichols	.05	.02	.01
□ 478 Ernest Riles	.05	.02	.01
□ 479 George Hendrick	.05	.02	.01
□ 480 John Morris	.05	.02	.01
□ 481 Manny Hernandez	.05	.02	.01
□ 482 Jeff Stone	.05	.02	.01
□ 483 Chris Brown	.05	.02	.01
□ 484 Mike Bielecki	.05	.02	.01
□ 485 Dave Dravecky	.10	.05	.01
□ 486 Rick Manning	.05	.02	.01
□ 487 Bill Almon	.05	.02	.01
□ 488 Jim Sundberg	.05	.02	.01
□ 489 Ken Phelps	.05	.02	.01
□ 490 Tom Henke	.05	.02	.01
□ 491 Dan Gladden	.05	.02	.01
□ 492 Barry Larkin	.30	.14	.04
□ 493 Fred Manrique	.05	.02	.01
□ 494 Mike Griffin	.05	.02	.01
□ 495 Mark Knudson	.05	.02	.01
□ 496 Bill Madlock	.05	.02	.01
□ 497 Tim Stoddard	.05	.02	.01
□ 498 Sam Horn	.05	.02	.01
□ 499 Tracy Woodson	.05	.02	.01
□ 500A Checklist 468-577	.05	.02	.01
□ 500B Checklist 452-557	.05	.02	.01
□ 501 Ken Schrom	.05	.02	.01
□ 502 Angel Salazar	.05	.02	.01
□ 503 Eric Plunk	.05	.02	.01
□ 504 Joe Hesketh	.05	.02	.01
□ 505 Greg Minton	.05	.02	.01
□ 506 Geno Petralli	.05	.02	.01
□ 507 Bob James	.05	.02	.01
□ 508 Robbie Wine	.05	.02	.01
□ 509 Jeff Calhoun	.05	.02	.01
□ 510 Steve Lake	.05	.02	.01
□ 511 Mark Grant	.05	.02	.01
□ 512 Frank Williams	.05	.02	.01
□ 513 Jeff Blauser	.15	.07	.02
□ 514 Bob Walk	.05	.02	.01
□ 515 Craig Lefferts	.05	.02	.01
□ 516 Manny Trillo	.05	.02	.01
□ 517 Jerry Reed	.05	.02	.01
□ 518 Rick Leach	.05	.02	.01
□ 519 Mark Davidson	.05	.02	.01
□ 520 Jeff Ballard	.05	.02	.01
□ 521 Dave Stapleton	.05	.02	.01
□ 522 Pat Sheridan	.05	.02	.01
□ 523 Al Nipper	.05	.02	.01
□ 524 Steve Trout	.05	.02	.01
□ 525 Jeff Hamilton	.05	.02	.01
□ 526 Tommy Hinzo	.05	.02	.01
□ 527 Lonnie Smith	.05	.02	.01
□ 528 Greg Cadaret	.05	.02	.01
□ 529 Bob McClure UER (Rob on front)	.05	.02	.01
□ 530 Chuck Finley	.10	.05	.01
□ 531 Jeff Russell	.05	.02	.01
□ 532 Steve Lyons	.05	.02	.01
□ 533 Terry Puhl	.05	.02	.01
□ 534 Eric Nolte	.05	.02	.01
□ 535 Kent Tekulve	.05	.02	.01
□ 536 Pat Pacillo	.05	.02	.01
□ 537 Charlie Puleo	.05	.02	.01
□ 538 Tom Prince	.05	.02	.01
□ 539 Greg Maddux	1.25	.55	.16
□ 540 Jim Lindeman	.05	.02	.01
□ 541 Pete Stanicek	.05	.02	.01
□ 542 Steve Kiefer	.05	.02	.01
□ 543A Jim Morrison ERR (No decimal before lifetime average)	.15	.07	.02

□ 543B Jim Morrison COR	.05	.02	.01
□ 544 Spike Owen	.05	.02	.01
□ 545 Jay Buhner	1.00	.45	.12
□ 546 Mike Devereaux	.15	.07	.02
□ 547 Jerry Don Gleaton	.05	.02	.01
□ 548 Jose Rijo	.05	.02	.01
□ 549 Dennis Martinez	.10	.05	.01
□ 550 Mike Loynd	.05	.02	.01
□ 551 Darrell Miller	.05	.02	.01
□ 552 Dave LaPoint	.05	.02	.01
□ 553 John Tudor	.05	.02	.01
□ 554 Rocky Childress	.05	.02	.01
□ 555 Wally Ritchie	.05	.02	.01
□ 556 Terry McGriff	.05	.02	.01
□ 557 Dave Leiper	.05	.02	.01
□ 558 Jeff D. Robinson	.05	.02	.01
□ 559 Jose Uribe	.05	.02	.01
□ 560 Ted Simmons	.10	.05	.01
□ 561 Les Lancaster	.05	.02	.01
□ 562 Keith A. Miller	.05	.02	.01
□ 563 Harold Reynolds	.05	.02	.01
□ 564 Gene Larkin	.05	.02	.01
□ 565 Cecil Fielder	.15	.07	.02
□ 566 Roy Smalley	.05	.02	.01
□ 567 Duane Ward	.10	.05	.01
□ 568 Bill Wilkinson	.05	.02	.01
□ 569 Howard Johnson	.05	.02	.01
□ 570 Frank DiPino	.05	.02	.01
□ 571 Pete Smith	.05	.02	.01
□ 572 Darnell Coles	.05	.02	.01
□ 573 Don Robinson	.05	.02	.01
□ 574 Rob Nelson UER (Career 0 RBI, but 1 RBI in '87)	.05	.02	.01
□ 575 Dennis Rasmussen	.05	.02	.01
□ 576 Steve Jeltz UER (Photo actually Juan Samuel; Samuel noted for one batting glove and black bat)	.05	.02	.01
□ 577 Tom Pagnozzi	.10	.05	.01
□ 578 Ty Gainey	.05	.02	.01
□ 579 Gary Lucas	.05	.02	.01
□ 580 Ron Hassey	.05	.02	.01
□ 581 Herm Winningham	.05	.02	.01
□ 582 Rene Gonzales	.05	.02	.01
□ 583 Brad Komminsk	.05	.02	.01
□ 584 Doyle Alexander	.05	.02	.01
□ 585 Jeff Sellers	.05	.02	.01
□ 586 Bill Gullickson	.05	.02	.01
□ 587 Tim Belcher	.05	.02	.01
□ 588 Doug Jones	.10	.05	.01
□ 589 Melido Perez	.10	.05	.01
□ 590 Rick Honeycutt	.05	.02	.01
□ 591 Pascual Perez	.05	.02	.01
□ 592 Curt Wilkerson	.05	.02	.01
□ 593 Steve Howe	.05	.02	.01
□ 594 John Davis	.05	.02	.01
□ 595 Storm Davis	.05	.02	.01
□ 596 Sammy Stewart	.05	.02	.01
□ 597 Neil Allen	.05	.02	.01
□ 598 Alejandro Pena	.05	.02	.01
□ 599 Mark Thurmond	.05	.02	.01
□ 600A Checklist 578-660/BC1-BC26	.05	.02	.01
□ 600B Checklist 558-660	.05	.02	.01
□ 601 Jose Mesa	.30	.14	.04
□ 602 Don August	.05	.02	.01
□ 603 Terry Leach SP	.07	.03	.01
□ 604 Tom Newell	.05	.02	.01
□ 605 Randall Byers SP	.07	.03	.01
□ 606 Jim Gott	.05	.02	.01
□ 607 Harry Spilman	.05	.02	.01
□ 608 John Candelaria	.05	.02	.01
□ 609 Mike Brumley	.05	.02	.01
□ 610 Mickey Brantley	.05	.02	.01
□ 611 Jose Nunez SP	.07	.03	.01
□ 612 Tom Nieto	.05	.02	.01
□ 613 Rick Reuschel	.05	.02	.01
□ 614 Lee Mazzilli SP	.07	.03	.01
□ 615 Scott Lusader	.05	.02	.01
□ 616 Bobby Meacham	.05	.02	.01
□ 617 Kevin McReynolds SP	.07	.03	.01
□ 618 Gene Garber	.05	.02	.01
□ 619 Barry Lyons SP	.07	.03	.01
□ 620 Randy Myers	.15	.07	.02
□ 621 Donnie Moore	.05	.02	.01
□ 622 Domingo Ramos	.05	.02	.01
□ 623 Ed Romero	.05	.02	.01
□ 624 Greg Myers	.05	.02	.01
□ 625 Ripken Family (Cal Ripken Sr., Cal Ripken Jr., Billy Ripken)	.40	.18	.05
□ 626 Pat Perry	.05	.02	.01
□ 627 Andres Thomas SP	.07	.03	.01
□ 628 Matt Williams SP	1.50	.70	.19
□ 629 Dave Hengel	.05	.02	.01
□ 630 Jeff Musselman SP	.07	.03	.01
□ 631 Tim Laudner	.05	.02	.01
□ 632 Bob Ojeda SP	.07	.03	.01
□ 633 Rafael Santana	.05	.02	.01
□ 634 Wes Gardner	.05	.02	.01
□ 635 Roberto Kelly SP	.15	.07	.02
□ 636 Mike Flanagan SP	.07	.03	.01
□ 637 Jay Bell	.20	.09	.03
□ 638 Bob Melvin	.05	.02	.01
□ 639 Damon Berryhill UER (Bats: Swithch)	.05	.02	.01
□ 640 David Wells SP	.15	.07	.02
□ 641 Stan Musial PUZ	.15	.07	.02
□ 642 Doug Sisk	.05	.02	.01
□ 643 Keith Hughes	.05	.02	.01
□ 644 Tom Glavine	1.00	.45	.12
□ 645 Al Newman	.05	.02	.01
□ 646 Scott Sanderson	.05	.02	.01
□ 647 Scott Terry	.05	.02	.01
□ 648 Tim Teufel SP	.07	.03	.01
□ 649 Garry Templeton SP	.07	.03	.01
□ 650 Manny Lee SP	.07	.03	.01
□ 651 Roger McDowell SP	.07	.03	.01
□ 652 Mookie Wilson SP	.15	.07	.02
□ 653 David Cone SP	.30	.14	.04
□ 654 Ron Gant SP	.60	.25	.07
□ 655 Joe Price SP	.07	.03	.01
□ 656 George Bell SP	.10	.05	.01
□ 657 Gregg Jefferies SP	.60	.25	.07
□ 658 Todd Stottlemyre SP	.30	.14	.04
□ 659 Geronimo Berroa SP	.40	.18	.05
□ 660 Jerry Royster SP	.07	.03	.01

1988 Donruss Rookies

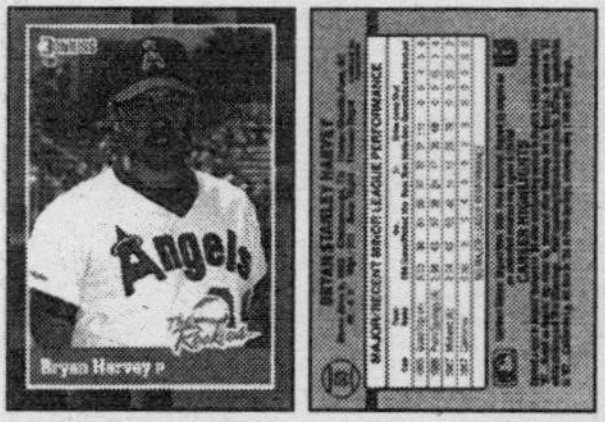

The 1988 Donruss "The Rookies" set features 56 standard-size full-color cards plus a 15-piece puzzle of Stan Musial. This set was distributed exclusively in factory set form in a small, cellophane-wrapped, green and black through hobby dealers. Card fronts are similar in design to the 1988 Donruss regular issue except for the presence of "The Rookies" logo in the lower right corner and a green and black border instead of a blue and black border on the fronts. Extended Rookie Cards in this set include Brady Anderson, Edgar Martinez, and Walt Weiss. Notable second cards were issued of Roberto Alomar and Jay Buhner.

	MINT	NRMT	EXC
COMPLETE FACT.SET (56)	15.00	6.75	1.85
COMMON CARD (1-56)	.07	.03	.01
SEMISTARS	.15	.07	.02
□ 1 Mark Grace	1.50	.70	.19
□ 2 Mike Campbell	.07	.03	.01
□ 3 Todd Frohwirth	.07	.03	.01

□ 4 Dave Stapleton	.07	.03	.01
□ 5 Shawn Abner	.07	.03	.01
□ 6 Jose Cecena	.07	.03	.01
□ 7 Dave Gallagher	.07	.03	.01
□ 8 Mark Parent	.07	.03	.01
□ 9 Cecil Espy	.07	.03	.01
□ 10 Pete Smith	.07	.03	.01
□ 11 Jay Buhner	2.50	1.10	.30
□ 12 Pat Borders	.10	.05	.01
□ 13 Doug Jennings	.07	.03	.01
□ 14 Brady Anderson	2.50	1.10	.30
□ 15 Pete Stanicek	.07	.03	.01
□ 16 Roberto Kelly	.15	.07	.02
□ 17 Jeff Treadway	.07	.03	.01
□ 18 Walt Weiss	.15	.07	.02
□ 19 Paul Gibson	.07	.03	.01
□ 20 Tim Crews	.10	.05	.01
□ 21 Melido Perez	.10	.05	.01
□ 22 Steve Peters	.07	.03	.01
□ 23 Craig Worthington	.07	.03	.01
□ 24 John Trautwein	.07	.03	.01
□ 25 DeWayne Vaughn	.07	.03	.01
□ 26 David Wells	.10	.05	.01
□ 27 Al Leiter	.15	.07	.02
□ 28 Tim Belcher	.10	.05	.01
□ 29 Johnny Paredes	.07	.03	.01
□ 30 Chris Sabo	.10	.05	.01
□ 31 Damon Berryhill	.07	.03	.01
□ 32 Randy Milligan	.07	.03	.01
□ 33 Gary Thurman	.07	.03	.01
□ 34 Kevin Elster	.10	.05	.01
□ 35 Roberto Alomar	5.00	2.20	.60
□ 36 Edgar Martinez UER (Photo actually Edwin Nunez)	2.00	.90	.25
□ 37 Todd Stottlemyre	.50	.23	.06
□ 38 Joey Meyer	.07	.03	.01
□ 39 Carl Nichols	.07	.03	.01
□ 40 Jack McDowell	1.00	.45	.12
□ 41 Jose Bautista	.07	.03	.01
□ 42 Sil Campusano	.07	.03	.01
□ 43 John Dopson	.07	.03	.01
□ 44 Jody Reed	.10	.05	.01
□ 45 Darrin Jackson	.07	.03	.01
□ 46 Mike Capel	.07	.03	.01
□ 47 Ron Gant	1.00	.45	.12
□ 48 John Davis	.07	.03	.01
□ 49 Kevin Coffman	.07	.03	.01
□ 50 Cris Carpenter	.07	.03	.01
□ 51 Mackey Sasser	.07	.03	.01
□ 52 Luis Alicea	.10	.05	.01
□ 53 Bryan Harvey	.10	.05	.01
□ 54 Steve Ellsworth	.07	.03	.01
□ 55 Mike Macfarlane	.15	.07	.02
□ 56 Checklist 1-56	.07	.03	.01

1989 Donruss

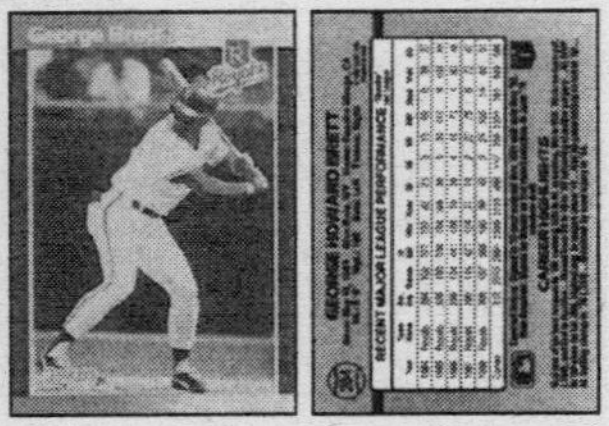

This set consists of 660 standard-size cards. The cards were primarily issued 15-card wax packs, rack packs and hobby and retail factory sets. Each wax pack also contained a puzzle panel (featuring Warren Spahn this year). The cards feature a distinctive black side border with an alternating coating. Subsets include Diamond Kings (1-27) and Rated Rookies (28-47). There are two variations that occur throughout most of the set. On the card backs "Denotes Led League" can be found with one asterisk to the left or with an asterisk on each side. On the card fronts the horizontal lines on the left and right borders can be glossy or non-glossy. Since both of these variation types are relatively minor and seem equally common, there is no premium value for either type. Rather than short-printing 26 cards in order to make room for printing the Bonus MVP's this year, Donruss apparently chose to double print 106 cards. These double prints are listed below by DP. Numbered with the prefix "BC" for bonus card, the 26-card set featuring the most valuable player from each of the 26 teams was randomly inserted in the wax and rack packs. These cards are distinguished by the bold MVP logo in the upper background of the obverse. Rookie Cards in this set include Sandy Alomar Jr., Brady Anderson, Dante Bichette, Craig Biggio, Ken Griffey Jr., Ken Hill, Randy Johnson, Ramon Martinez, Hal Morris, Gary Sheffield, and John Smoltz.

	MINT	NRMT	EXC
COMPLETE SET (660)	10.00	4.50	1.25
COMPLETE FACT.SET (672)	12.00	5.50	1.50
COMMON CARD (1-660)	.05	.02	.01
SEMISTARS	.10	.05	.01
STARS	.15	.07	.02
COMP.GRANDSLAMMERS (12)	2.00	.90	.25
COMPLETE MVP SET (26)	1.50	.70	.19
MVP'S: RANDOM INSERTS IN PACKS			
□ 1 Mike Greenwell DK	.05	.02	.01
□ 2 Bobby Bonilla DK DP	.10	.05	.01
□ 3 Pete Incaviglia DK	.05	.02	.01
□ 4 Chris Sabo DK DP	.05	.02	.01
□ 5 Robin Yount DK	.15	.07	.02
□ 6 Tony Gwynn DK DP	.15	.07	.02
□ 7 Carlton Fisk DK UER (OF on back)	.15	.07	.02
□ 8 Cory Snyder DK	.05	.02	.01
□ 9 David Cone DK UER ("hurdlers")	.10	.05	.01
□ 10 Kevin Seitzer DK	.05	.02	.01
□ 11 Rick Reuschel DK	.05	.02	.01
□ 12 Johnny Ray DK	.05	.02	.01
□ 13 Dave Schmidt DK	.05	.02	.01
□ 14 Andres Galarraga DK	.15	.07	.02
□ 15 Kirk Gibson DK	.10	.05	.01
□ 16 Fred McGriff DK	.15	.07	.02
□ 17 Mark Grace DK	.15	.07	.02
□ 18 Jeff M. Robinson DK	.05	.02	.01
□ 19 Vince Coleman DK DP	.05	.02	.01
□ 20 Dave Henderson DK	.05	.02	.01
□ 21 Harold Reynolds DK	.05	.02	.01
□ 22 Gerald Perry DK	.05	.02	.01
□ 23 Frank Viola DK	.05	.02	.01
□ 24 Steve Bedrosian DK	.05	.02	.01
□ 25 Glenn Davis DK	.05	.02	.01
□ 26 Don Mattingly DK UER (Doesn't mention Don's previous DK in 1985)	.25	.11	.03
□ 27 DK Checklist 1-26 DP	.05	.02	.01
□ 28 Sandy Alomar Jr. RR	.20	.09	.03
□ 29 Steve Searcy RR	.05	.02	.01
□ 30 Cameron Drew RR	.05	.02	.01
□ 31 Gary Sheffield RR	.75	.35	.09
□ 32 Erik Hanson RR	.15	.07	.02
□ 33 Ken Griffey Jr. RR	5.00	2.20	.60
□ 34 Greg W. Harris RR	.05	.02	.01
□ 35 Gregg Jefferies RR	.15	.07	.02
□ 36 Luis Medina RR	.05	.02	.01
□ 37 Carlos Quintana RR	.05	.02	.01
□ 38 Felix Jose RR	.05	.02	.01
□ 39 Cris Carpenter RR	.05	.02	.01
□ 40 Ron Jones RR	.05	.02	.01
□ 41 Dave West RR	.05	.02	.01
□ 42 Randy Johnson RR UER (Card says born in 1964 he was born in 1963)	.75	.35	.09
□ 43 Mike Harkey RR	.05	.02	.01
□ 44 Pete Harnisch RR DP	.10	.05	.01
□ 45 Tom Gordon RR DP	.10	.05	.01

□ 46 Gregg Olson RR DP	.10	.05	.01
□ 47 Alex Sanchez RR DP	.05	.02	.01
□ 48 Ruben Sierra	.10	.05	.01
□ 49 Rafael Palmeiro	.15	.07	.02
□ 50 Ron Gant	.15	.07	.02
□ 51 Cal Ripken	.75	.35	.09
□ 52 Wally Joyner	.10	.05	.01
□ 53 Gary Carter	.15	.07	.02
□ 54 Andy Van Slyke	.10	.05	.01
□ 55 Robin Yount	.15	.07	.02
□ 56 Pete Incaviglia	.10	.05	.01
□ 57 Greg Brock	.05	.02	.01
□ 58 Melido Perez	.05	.02	.01
□ 59 Craig Lefferts	.05	.02	.01
□ 60 Gary Pettis	.05	.02	.01
□ 61 Danny Tartabull	.05	.02	.01
□ 62 Guillermo Hernandez	.05	.02	.01
□ 63 Ozzie Smith	.20	.09	.03
□ 64 Gary Gaetti	.05	.02	.01
□ 65 Mark Davis	.05	.02	.01
□ 66 Lee Smith	.15	.07	.02
□ 67 Dennis Eckersley	.10	.05	.01
□ 68 Wade Boggs	.15	.07	.02
□ 69 Mike Scott	.05	.02	.01
□ 70 Fred McGriff	.20	.09	.03
□ 71 Tom Browning	.05	.02	.01
□ 72 Claudell Washington	.05	.02	.01
□ 73 Mel Hall	.05	.02	.01
□ 74 Don Mattingly	.50	.23	.06
□ 75 Steve Bedrosian	.05	.02	.01
□ 76 Juan Samuel	.05	.02	.01
□ 77 Mike Scioscia	.05	.02	.01
□ 78 Dave Righetti	.05	.02	.01
□ 79 Alfredo Griffin	.05	.02	.01
□ 80 Eric Davis UER (165 games in 1988, should be 135)	.10	.05	.01
□ 81 Juan Berenguer	.05	.02	.01
□ 82 Todd Worrell	.05	.02	.01
□ 83 Joe Carter	.15	.07	.02
□ 84 Steve Sax	.05	.02	.01
□ 85 Frank White	.10	.05	.01
□ 86 John Kruk	.10	.05	.01
□ 87 Rance Mulliniks	.05	.02	.01
□ 88 Alan Ashby	.05	.02	.01
□ 89 Charlie Leibrandt	.05	.02	.01
□ 90 Frank Tanana	.05	.02	.01
□ 91 Jose Canseco	.15	.07	.02
□ 92 Barry Bonds	.40	.18	.05
□ 93 Harold Reynolds	.05	.02	.01
□ 94 Mark McLemore	.05	.02	.01
□ 95 Mark McGwire	.30	.14	.04
□ 96 Eddie Murray	.25	.11	.03
□ 97 Tim Raines	.15	.07	.02
□ 98 Robby Thompson	.05	.02	.01
□ 99 Kevin McReynolds	.05	.02	.01
□ 100 Checklist 28-137	.05	.02	.01
□ 101 Carlton Fisk	.15	.07	.02
□ 102 Dave Martinez	.05	.02	.01
□ 103 Glenn Braggs	.05	.02	.01
□ 104 Dale Murphy	.15	.07	.02
□ 105 Ryne Sandberg	.25	.11	.03
□ 106 Dennis Martinez	.10	.05	.01
□ 107 Pete O'Brien	.05	.02	.01
□ 108 Dick Schofield	.05	.02	.01
□ 109 Henry Cotto	.05	.02	.01
□ 110 Mike Marshall	.05	.02	.01
□ 111 Keith Moreland	.05	.02	.01
□ 112 Tom Brunansky	.05	.02	.01
□ 113 Kelly Gruber UER (Wrong birthdate)	.05	.02	.01
□ 114 Brook Jacoby	.05	.02	.01
□ 115 Keith Brown	.05	.02	.01
□ 116 Matt Nokes	.05	.02	.01
□ 117 Keith Hernandez	.10	.05	.01
□ 118 Bob Forsch	.05	.02	.01
□ 119 Bert Blyleven UER (... 3000 strikeouts in 1987, should be 1986)	.10	.05	.01
□ 120 Willie Wilson	.05	.02	.01
□ 121 Tommy Gregg	.05	.02	.01
□ 122 Jim Rice	.15	.07	.02
□ 123 Bob Knepper	.05	.02	.01
□ 124 Danny Jackson	.05	.02	.01
□ 125 Eric Plunk	.05	.02	.01
□ 126 Brian Fisher	.05	.02	.01
□ 127 Mike Pagliarulo	.05	.02	.01
□ 128 Tony Gwynn	.40	.18	.05
□ 129 Lance McCullers	.05	.02	.01
□ 130 Andres Galarraga	.15	.07	.02
□ 131 Jose Uribe	.05	.02	.01
□ 132 Kirk Gibson UER (Wrong birthdate)	.10	.05	.01
□ 133 David Palmer	.05	.02	.01
□ 134 R.J. Reynolds	.05	.02	.01
□ 135 Greg Walker	.05	.02	.01
□ 136 Kirk McCaskill UER (Wrong birthdate)	.05	.02	.01
□ 137 Shawon Dunston	.05	.02	.01
□ 138 Andy Allanson	.05	.02	.01
□ 139 Rob Murphy	.05	.02	.01
□ 140 Mike Aldrete	.05	.02	.01
□ 141 Terry Kennedy	.05	.02	.01
□ 142 Scott Fletcher	.05	.02	.01
□ 143 Steve Balboni	.05	.02	.01
□ 144 Bret Saberhagen	.10	.05	.01
□ 145 Ozzie Virgil	.05	.02	.01
□ 146 Dale Sveum	.05	.02	.01
□ 147 Darryl Strawberry	.10	.05	.01
□ 148 Harold Baines	.10	.05	.01
□ 149 George Bell	.05	.02	.01
□ 150 Dave Parker	.10	.05	.01
□ 151 Bobby Bonilla	.10	.05	.01
□ 152 Mookie Wilson	.10	.05	.01
□ 153 Ted Power	.05	.02	.01
□ 154 Nolan Ryan	.75	.35	.09
□ 155 Jeff Reardon	.10	.05	.01
□ 156 Tim Wallach	.05	.02	.01
□ 157 Jamie Moyer	.05	.02	.01
□ 158 Rich Gossage	.15	.07	.02
□ 159 Dave Winfield	.15	.07	.02
□ 160 Von Hayes	.05	.02	.01
□ 161 Willie McGee	.05	.02	.01
□ 162 Rich Gedman	.05	.02	.01
□ 163 Tony Pena	.05	.02	.01
□ 164 Mike Morgan	.05	.02	.01
□ 165 Charlie Hough	.10	.05	.01
□ 166 Mike Stanley	.05	.02	.01
□ 167 Andre Dawson	.15	.07	.02
□ 168 Joe Boever	.05	.02	.01
□ 169 Pete Stanicek	.05	.02	.01
□ 170 Bob Boone	.10	.05	.01
□ 171 Ron Darling	.05	.02	.01
□ 172 Bob Walk	.05	.02	.01
□ 173 Rob Deer	.05	.02	.01
□ 174 Steve Buechele	.05	.02	.01
□ 175 Ted Higuera	.05	.02	.01
□ 176 Ozzie Guillen	.05	.02	.01
□ 177 Candy Maldonado	.05	.02	.01
□ 178 Doyle Alexander	.05	.02	.01
□ 179 Mark Gubicza	.05	.02	.01
□ 180 Alan Trammell	.15	.07	.02
□ 181 Vince Coleman	.05	.02	.01
□ 182 Kirby Puckett	.30	.14	.04
□ 183 Chris Brown	.05	.02	.01
□ 184 Marty Barrett	.05	.02	.01
□ 185 Stan Javier	.05	.02	.01
□ 186 Mike Greenwell	.05	.02	.01
□ 187 Billy Hatcher	.05	.02	.01
□ 188 Jimmy Key	.10	.05	.01
□ 189 Nick Esasky	.05	.02	.01
□ 190 Don Slaught	.05	.02	.01
□ 191 Cory Snyder	.05	.02	.01
□ 192 John Candelaria	.05	.02	.01
□ 193 Mike Schmidt	.20	.09	.03
□ 194 Kevin Gross	.05	.02	.01
□ 195 John Tudor	.05	.02	.01
□ 196 Neil Allen	.05	.02	.01
□ 197 Orel Hershiser	.10	.05	.01
□ 198 Kal Daniels	.05	.02	.01
□ 199 Kent Hrbek	.10	.05	.01
□ 200 Checklist 138-247	.05	.02	.01
□ 201 Joe Magrane	.05	.02	.01
□ 202 Scott Bailes	.05	.02	.01
□ 203 Tim Belcher	.05	.02	.01
□ 204 George Brett	.40	.18	.05
□ 205 Benito Santiago	.10	.05	.01
□ 206 Tony Fernandez	.05	.02	.01
□ 207 Gerald Young	.05	.02	.01
□ 208 Bo Jackson	.15	.07	.02
□ 209 Chet Lemon	.05	.02	.01
□ 210 Storm Davis	.05	.02	.01

□ 211	Doug Drabek	.10	.05	.01
□ 212	Mickey Brantley UER (Photo actually Nelson Simmons)	.05	.02	.01
□ 213	Devon White	.10	.05	.01
□ 214	Dave Stewart	.10	.05	.01
□ 215	Dave Schmidt	.05	.02	.01
□ 216	Bryn Smith	.05	.02	.01
□ 217	Brett Butler	.10	.05	.01
□ 218	Bob Ojeda	.05	.02	.01
□ 219	Steve Rosenberg	.05	.02	.01
□ 220	Hubie Brooks	.05	.02	.01
□ 221	B.J. Surhoff	.15	.07	.02
□ 222	Rick Mahler	.05	.02	.01
□ 223	Rick Sutcliffe	.05	.02	.01
□ 224	Neal Heaton	.05	.02	.01
□ 225	Mitch Williams	.05	.02	.01
□ 226	Chuck Finley	.10	.05	.01
□ 227	Mark Langston	.10	.05	.01
□ 228	Jesse Orosco	.05	.02	.01
□ 229	Ed Whitson	.05	.02	.01
□ 230	Terry Pendleton	.10	.05	.01
□ 231	Lloyd Moseby	.05	.02	.01
□ 232	Greg Swindell	.05	.02	.01
□ 233	John Franco	.05	.02	.01
□ 234	Jack Morris	.10	.05	.01
□ 235	Howard Johnson	.05	.02	.01
□ 236	Glenn Davis	.05	.02	.01
□ 237	Frank Viola	.05	.02	.01
□ 238	Kevin Seitzer	.05	.02	.01
□ 239	Gerald Perry	.05	.02	.01
□ 240	Dwight Evans	.10	.05	.01
□ 241	Jim Deshaies	.05	.02	.01
□ 242	Bo Diaz	.05	.02	.01
□ 243	Carney Lansford	.10	.05	.01
□ 244	Mike LaValliere	.05	.02	.01
□ 245	Rickey Henderson	.15	.07	.02
□ 246	Roberto Alomar	.50	.23	.06
□ 247	Jimmy Jones	.05	.02	.01
□ 248	Pascual Perez	.05	.02	.01
□ 249	Will Clark	.20	.09	.03
□ 250	Fernando Valenzuela	.10	.05	.01
□ 251	Shane Rawley	.05	.02	.01
□ 252	Sid Bream	.05	.02	.01
□ 253	Steve Lyons	.05	.02	.01
□ 254	Brian Downing	.05	.02	.01
□ 255	Mark Grace	.20	.09	.03
□ 256	Tom Candiotti	.05	.02	.01
□ 257	Barry Larkin	.20	.09	.03
□ 258	Mike Krukow	.05	.02	.01
□ 259	Billy Ripken	.05	.02	.01
□ 260	Cecilio Guante	.05	.02	.01
□ 261	Scott Bradley	.05	.02	.01
□ 262	Floyd Bannister	.05	.02	.01
□ 263	Pete Smith	.05	.02	.01
□ 264	Jim Gantner UER (Wrong birthdate)	.05	.02	.01
□ 265	Roger McDowell	.05	.02	.01
□ 266	Bobby Thigpen	.05	.02	.01
□ 267	Jim Clancy	.05	.02	.01
□ 268	Terry Steinbach	.10	.05	.01
□ 269	Mike Dunne	.05	.02	.01
□ 270	Dwight Gooden	.10	.05	.01
□ 271	Mike Heath	.05	.02	.01
□ 272	Dave Smith	.05	.02	.01
□ 273	Keith Atherton	.05	.02	.01
□ 274	Tim Burke	.05	.02	.01
□ 275	Damon Berryhill	.05	.02	.01
□ 276	Vance Law	.05	.02	.01
□ 277	Rich Dotson	.05	.02	.01
□ 278	Lance Parrish	.05	.02	.01
□ 279	Denny Walling	.05	.02	.01
□ 280	Roger Clemens	.15	.07	.02
□ 281	Greg Mathews	.05	.02	.01
□ 282	Tom Niedenfuer	.05	.02	.01
□ 283	Paul Kilgus	.05	.02	.01
□ 284	Jose Guzman	.05	.02	.01
□ 285	Calvin Schiraldi	.05	.02	.01
□ 286	Charlie Puleo UER (Career ERA 4.24, should be 4.23)	.05	.02	.01
□ 287	Joe Orsulak	.05	.02	.01
□ 288	Jack Howell	.05	.02	.01
□ 289	Kevin Elster	.10	.05	.01
□ 290	Jose Lind	.05	.02	.01
□ 291	Paul Molitor	.20	.09	.03
□ 292	Cecil Espy	.05	.02	.01
□ 293	Bill Wegman	.05	.02	.01
□ 294	Dan Pasqua	.05	.02	.01
□ 295	Scott Garrelts UER (Wrong birthdate)	.05	.02	.01
□ 296	Walt Terrell	.05	.02	.01
□ 297	Ed Hearn	.05	.02	.01
□ 298	Lou Whitaker	.15	.07	.02
□ 299	Ken Dayley	.05	.02	.01
□ 300	Checklist 248-357	.05	.02	.01
□ 301	Tommy Herr	.05	.02	.01
□ 302	Mike Brumley	.05	.02	.01
□ 303	Ellis Burks	.15	.07	.02
□ 304	Curt Young UER (Wrong birthdate)	.05	.02	.01
□ 305	Jody Reed	.05	.02	.01
□ 306	Bill Doran	.05	.02	.01
□ 307	David Wells	.05	.02	.01
□ 308	Ron Robinson	.05	.02	.01
□ 309	Rafael Santana	.05	.02	.01
□ 310	Julio Franco	.10	.05	.01
□ 311	Jack Clark	.10	.05	.01
□ 312	Chris James	.05	.02	.01
□ 313	Milt Thompson	.05	.02	.01
□ 314	John Shelby	.05	.02	.01
□ 315	Al Leiter	.10	.05	.01
□ 316	Mike Davis	.05	.02	.01
□ 317	Chris Sabo	.05	.02	.01
□ 318	Greg Gagne	.05	.02	.01
□ 319	Jose Oquendo	.05	.02	.01
□ 320	John Farrell	.05	.02	.01
□ 321	Franklin Stubbs	.05	.02	.01
□ 322	Kurt Stillwell	.05	.02	.01
□ 323	Shawn Abner	.05	.02	.01
□ 324	Mike Flanagan	.05	.02	.01
□ 325	Kevin Bass	.05	.02	.01
□ 326	Pat Tabler	.05	.02	.01
□ 327	Mike Henneman	.05	.02	.01
□ 328	Rick Honeycutt	.05	.02	.01
□ 329	John Smiley	.05	.02	.01
□ 330	Rey Quinones	.05	.02	.01
□ 331	Johnny Ray	.05	.02	.01
□ 332	Bob Welch	.05	.02	.01
□ 333	Larry Sheets	.05	.02	.01
□ 334	Jeff Parrett	.05	.02	.01
□ 335	Rick Reuschel UER (For Don Robinson, should be Jeff)	.05	.02	.01
□ 336	Randy Myers	.10	.05	.01
□ 337	Ken Williams	.05	.02	.01
□ 338	Andy McGaffigan	.05	.02	.01
□ 339	Joey Meyer	.05	.02	.01
□ 340	Dion James	.05	.02	.01
□ 341	Les Lancaster	.05	.02	.01
□ 342	Tom Foley	.05	.02	.01
□ 343	Geno Petralli	.05	.02	.01
□ 344	Dan Petry	.05	.02	.01
□ 345	Alvin Davis	.05	.02	.01
□ 346	Mickey Hatcher	.05	.02	.01
□ 347	Marvell Wynne	.05	.02	.01
□ 348	Danny Cox	.05	.02	.01
□ 349	Dave Stieb	.05	.02	.01
□ 350	Jay Bell	.15	.07	.02
□ 351	Jeff Treadway	.05	.02	.01
□ 352	Luis Salazar	.05	.02	.01
□ 353	Len Dykstra	.10	.05	.01
□ 354	Juan Agosto	.05	.02	.01
□ 355	Gene Larkin	.05	.02	.01
□ 356	Steve Farr	.05	.02	.01
□ 357	Paul Assenmacher	.05	.02	.01
□ 358	Todd Benzinger	.05	.02	.01
□ 359	Larry Andersen	.05	.02	.01
□ 360	Paul O'Neill	.15	.07	.02
□ 361	Ron Hassey	.05	.02	.01
□ 362	Jim Gott	.05	.02	.01
□ 363	Ken Phelps	.05	.02	.01
□ 364	Tim Flannery	.05	.02	.01
□ 365	Randy Ready	.05	.02	.01
□ 366	Nelson Santovenia	.05	.02	.01
□ 367	Kelly Downs	.05	.02	.01
□ 368	Danny Heep	.05	.02	.01
□ 369	Phil Bradley	.05	.02	.01
□ 370	Jeff D. Robinson	.05	.02	.01
□ 371	Ivan Calderon	.05	.02	.01
□ 372	Mike Witt	.05	.02	.01
□ 373	Greg Maddux	.75	.35	.09

□ 374 Carmen Castillo	.05	.02	.01
□ 375 Jose Rijo	.05	.02	.01
□ 376 Joe Price	.05	.02	.01
□ 377 Rene Gonzales	.05	.02	.01
□ 378 Oddibe McDowell	.05	.02	.01
□ 379 Jim Presley	.05	.02	.01
□ 380 Brad Wellman	.05	.02	.01
□ 381 Tom Glavine	.25	.11	.03
□ 382 Dan Plesac	.05	.02	.01
□ 383 Wally Backman	.05	.02	.01
□ 384 Dave Gallagher	.05	.02	.01
□ 385 Tom Henke	.05	.02	.01
□ 386 Luis Polonia	.10	.05	.01
□ 387 Junior Ortiz	.05	.02	.01
□ 388 David Cone	.15	.07	.02
□ 389 Dave Bergman	.05	.02	.01
□ 390 Danny Darwin	.05	.02	.01
□ 391 Dan Gladden	.05	.02	.01
□ 392 John Dopson	.05	.02	.01
□ 393 Frank DiPino	.05	.02	.01
□ 394 Al Nipper	.05	.02	.01
□ 395 Willie Randolph	.10	.05	.01
□ 396 Don Carman	.05	.02	.01
□ 397 Scott Terry	.05	.02	.01
□ 398 Rick Cerone	.05	.02	.01
□ 399 Tom Pagnozzi	.05	.02	.01
□ 400 Checklist 358-467	.05	.02	.01
□ 401 Mickey Tettleton	.10	.05	.01
□ 402 Curtis Wilkerson	.05	.02	.01
□ 403 Jeff Russell	.05	.02	.01
□ 404 Pat Perry	.05	.02	.01
□ 405 Jose Alvarez	.05	.02	.01
□ 406 Rick Schu	.05	.02	.01
□ 407 Sherman Corbett	.05	.02	.01
□ 408 Dave Magadan	.05	.02	.01
□ 409 Bob Kipper	.05	.02	.01
□ 410 Don August	.05	.02	.01
□ 411 Bob Brower	.05	.02	.01
□ 412 Chris Bosio	.05	.02	.01
□ 413 Jerry Reuss	.05	.02	.01
□ 414 Atlee Hammaker	.05	.02	.01
□ 415 Jim Walewander	.05	.02	.01
□ 416 Mike Macfarlane	.10	.05	.01
□ 417 Pat Sheridan	.05	.02	.01
□ 418 Pedro Guerrero	.10	.05	.01
□ 419 Allan Anderson	.05	.02	.01
□ 420 Mark Parent	.05	.02	.01
□ 421 Bob Stanley	.05	.02	.01
□ 422 Mike Gallego	.05	.02	.01
□ 423 Bruce Hurst	.05	.02	.01
□ 424 Dave Meads	.05	.02	.01
□ 425 Jesse Barfield	.05	.02	.01
□ 426 Rob Dibble	.10	.05	.01
□ 427 Joel Skinner	.05	.02	.01
□ 428 Ron Kittle	.05	.02	.01
□ 429 Rick Rhoden	.05	.02	.01
□ 430 Bob Dernier	.05	.02	.01
□ 431 Steve Jeltz	.05	.02	.01
□ 432 Rick Dempsey	.05	.02	.01
□ 433 Roberto Kelly	.10	.05	.01
□ 434 Dave Anderson	.05	.02	.01
□ 435 Herm Winningham	.05	.02	.01
□ 436 Al Newman	.05	.02	.01
□ 437 Jose DeLeon	.05	.02	.01
□ 438 Doug Jones	.05	.02	.01
□ 439 Brian Holton	.05	.02	.01
□ 440 Jeff Montgomery	.10	.05	.01
□ 441 Dickie Thon	.05	.02	.01
□ 442 Cecil Fielder	.10	.05	.01
□ 443 John Fishel	.05	.02	.01
□ 444 Jerry Don Gleaton	.05	.02	.01
□ 445 Paul Gibson	.05	.02	.01
□ 446 Walt Weiss	.05	.02	.01
□ 447 Glenn Wilson	.05	.02	.01
□ 448 Mike Moore	.05	.02	.01
□ 449 Chili Davis	.10	.05	.01
□ 450 Dave Henderson	.05	.02	.01
□ 451 Jose Bautista	.05	.02	.01
□ 452 Rex Hudler	.05	.02	.01
□ 453 Bob Brenly	.05	.02	.01
□ 454 Mackey Sasser	.05	.02	.01
□ 455 Daryl Boston	.05	.02	.01
□ 456 Mike R. Fitzgerald	.05	.02	.01
□ 457 Jeffrey Leonard	.05	.02	.01
□ 458 Bruce Sutter	.05	.02	.01
□ 459 Mitch Webster	.05	.02	.01

□ 460 Joe Hesketh	.05	.02	.01
□ 461 Bobby Witt	.05	.02	.01
□ 462 Stew Cliburn	.05	.02	.01
□ 463 Scott Bankhead	.05	.02	.01
□ 464 Ramon Martinez	.25	.11	.03
□ 465 Dave Leiper	.05	.02	.01
□ 466 Luis Alicea	.05	.02	.01
□ 467 John Cerutti	.05	.02	.01
□ 468 Ron Washington	.05	.02	.01
□ 469 Jeff Reed	.05	.02	.01
□ 470 Jeff M. Robinson	.05	.02	.01
□ 471 Sid Fernandez	.05	.02	.01
□ 472 Terry Puhl	.05	.02	.01
□ 473 Charlie Lea	.05	.02	.01
□ 474 Israel Sanchez	.05	.02	.01
□ 475 Bruce Benedict	.05	.02	.01
□ 476 Oil Can Boyd	.05	.02	.01
□ 477 Craig Reynolds	.05	.02	.01
□ 478 Frank Williams	.05	.02	.01
□ 479 Greg Cadaret	.05	.02	.01
□ 480 Randy Kramer	.05	.02	.01
□ 481 Dave Eiland	.05	.02	.01
□ 482 Eric Show	.05	.02	.01
□ 483 Garry Templeton	.05	.02	.01
□ 484 Wallace Johnson	.05	.02	.01
□ 485 Kevin Mitchell	.10	.05	.01
□ 486 Tim Crews	.05	.02	.01
□ 487 Mike Maddux	.05	.02	.01
□ 488 Dave LaPoint	.05	.02	.01
□ 489 Fred Manrique	.05	.02	.01
□ 490 Greg Minton	.05	.02	.01
□ 491 Doug Dascenzo UER (Photo actually Damon Berryhill)	.05	.02	.01
□ 492 Willie Upshaw	.05	.02	.01
□ 493 Jack Armstrong	.05	.02	.01
□ 494 Kirt Manwaring	.05	.02	.01
□ 495 Jeff Ballard	.05	.02	.01
□ 496 Jeff Kunkel	.05	.02	.01
□ 497 Mike Campbell	.05	.02	.01
□ 498 Gary Thurman	.05	.02	.01
□ 499 Zane Smith	.05	.02	.01
□ 500 Checklist 468-577 DP	.05	.02	.01
□ 501 Mike Birkbeck	.05	.02	.01
□ 502 Terry Leach	.05	.02	.01
□ 503 Shawn Hillegas	.05	.02	.01
□ 504 Manny Lee	.05	.02	.01
□ 505 Doug Jennings	.05	.02	.01
□ 506 Ken Oberkfell	.05	.02	.01
□ 507 Tim Teufel	.05	.02	.01
□ 508 Tom Brookens	.05	.02	.01
□ 509 Rafael Ramirez	.05	.02	.01
□ 510 Fred Toliver	.05	.02	.01
□ 511 Brian Holman	.05	.02	.01
□ 512 Mike Bielecki	.05	.02	.01
□ 513 Jeff Pico	.05	.02	.01
□ 514 Charles Hudson	.05	.02	.01
□ 515 Bruce Ruffin	.05	.02	.01
□ 516 Larry McWilliams UER (New Richland, should be North Richland)	.05	.02	.01
□ 517 Jeff Sellers	.05	.02	.01
□ 518 John Costello	.05	.02	.01
□ 519 Brady Anderson	.60	.25	.07
□ 520 Craig McMurtry	.05	.02	.01
□ 521 Ray Hayward DP	.05	.02	.01
□ 522 Drew Hall DP	.05	.02	.01
□ 523 Mark Lemke DP	.10	.05	.01
□ 524 Oswald Peraza DP	.05	.02	.01
□ 525 Bryan Harvey DP	.10	.05	.01
□ 526 Rick Aguilera DP	.15	.07	.02
□ 527 Tom Prince DP	.05	.02	.01
□ 528 Mark Clear DP	.05	.02	.01
□ 529 Jerry Browne DP	.05	.02	.01
□ 530 Juan Castillo DP	.05	.02	.01
□ 531 Jack McDowell DP	.15	.07	.02
□ 532 Chris Speier DP	.05	.02	.01
□ 533 Darrell Evans DP	.10	.05	.01
□ 534 Luis Aquino DP	.05	.02	.01
□ 535 Eric King DP	.05	.02	.01
□ 536 Ken Hill DP	.50	.23	.06
□ 537 Randy Bush DP	.05	.02	.01
□ 538 Shane Mack DP	.05	.02	.01
□ 539 Tom Bolton DP	.05	.02	.01
□ 540 Gene Nelson DP	.05	.02	.01
□ 541 Wes Gardner DP	.05	.02	.01

☐ 542 Ken Caminiti DP	.15	.07	.02
☐ 543 Duane Ward DP	.05	.02	.01
☐ 544 Norm Charlton DP	.10	.05	.01
☐ 545 Hal Morris DP	.15	.07	.02
☐ 546 Rich Yett DP	.05	.02	.01
☐ 547 Hensley Meulens DP	.05	.02	.01
☐ 548 Greg A. Harris DP	.05	.02	.01
☐ 549 Darren Daulton DP	.10	.05	.01
(Posing as right-handed hitter)			
☐ 550 Jeff Hamilton DP	.05	.02	.01
☐ 551 Luis Aguayo DP	.05	.02	.01
☐ 552 Tim Leary DP	.05	.02	.01
(Resembles M.Marshall)			
☐ 553 Ron Oester DP	.05	.02	.01
☐ 554 Steve Lombardozzi DP	.05	.02	.01
☐ 555 Tim Jones DP	.05	.02	.01
☐ 556 Bud Black DP	.05	.02	.01
☐ 557 Alejandro Pena DP	.05	.02	.01
☐ 558 Jose DeJesus DP	.05	.02	.01
☐ 559 Dennis Rasmussen DP	.05	.02	.01
☐ 560 Pat Borders DP	.10	.05	.01
☐ 561 Craig Biggio DP	.40	.18	.05
☐ 562 Luis DeLosSantos DP	.05	.02	.01
☐ 563 Fred Lynn DP	.05	.02	.01
☐ 564 Todd Burns DP	.05	.02	.01
☐ 565 Felix Fermin DP	.05	.02	.01
☐ 566 Darnell Coles DP	.05	.02	.01
☐ 567 Willie Fraser DP	.05	.02	.01
☐ 568 Glenn Hubbard DP	.05	.02	.01
☐ 569 Craig Worthington DP	.05	.02	.01
☐ 570 Johnny Paredes DP	.05	.02	.01
☐ 571 Don Robinson DP	.05	.02	.01
☐ 572 Barry Lyons DP	.05	.02	.01
☐ 573 Bill Long DP	.05	.02	.01
☐ 574 Tracy Jones DP	.05	.02	.01
☐ 575 Juan Nieves DP	.05	.02	.01
☐ 576 Andres Thomas DP	.05	.02	.01
☐ 577 Rolando Roomes DP	.05	.02	.01
☐ 578 Luis Rivera UER DP	.05	.02	.01
(Wrong birthdate)			
☐ 579 Chad Kreuter DP	.05	.02	.01
☐ 580 Tony Armas DP	.05	.02	.01
☐ 581 Jay Buhner	.25	.11	.03
☐ 582 Ricky Horton DP	.05	.02	.01
☐ 583 Andy Hawkins DP	.05	.02	.01
☐ 584 Sil Campusano	.05	.02	.01
☐ 585 Dave Clark	.05	.02	.01
☐ 586 Van Snider DP	.05	.02	.01
☐ 587 Todd Frohwirth DP	.05	.02	.01
☐ 588 Warren Spahn DP PUZ	.15	.07	.02
☐ 589 William Brennan	.05	.02	.01
☐ 590 German Gonzalez	.05	.02	.01
☐ 591 Ernie Whitt DP	.05	.02	.01
☐ 592 Jeff Blauser	.10	.05	.01
☐ 593 Spike Owen DP	.05	.02	.01
☐ 594 Matt Williams	.25	.11	.03
☐ 595 Lloyd McClendon DP	.05	.02	.01
☐ 596 Steve Ontiveros	.05	.02	.01
☐ 597 Scott Medvin	.05	.02	.01
☐ 598 Hipolito Pena DP	.05	.02	.01
☐ 599 Jerald Clark DP	.05	.02	.01
☐ 600A Checklist 578-660 DP	.05	.02	.01
(635 Kurt Schilling)			
☐ 600B Checklist 578-660 DP	.05	.02	.01
(635 Curt Schilling; MVP's not listed on checklist card)			
☐ 600C Checklist 578-660 DP	.05	.02	.01
(635 Curt Schilling; MVP's listed following 660)			
☐ 601 Carmelo Martinez DP	.05	.02	.01
☐ 602 Mike LaCoss	.05	.02	.01
☐ 603 Mike Devereaux	.05	.02	.01
☐ 604 Alex Madrid DP	.05	.02	.01
☐ 605 Gary Redus DP	.05	.02	.01
☐ 606 Lance Johnson	.15	.07	.02
☐ 607 Terry Clark DP	.05	.02	.01
☐ 608 Manny Trillo DP	.05	.02	.01
☐ 609 Scott Jordan	.10	.05	.01
☐ 610 Jay Howell DP	.05	.02	.01
☐ 611 Francisco Melendez	.05	.02	.01
☐ 612 Mike Boddicker	.05	.02	.01
☐ 613 Kevin Brown DP	.10	.05	.01
☐ 614 Dave Valle	.05	.02	.01
☐ 615 Tim Laudner DP	.05	.02	.01
☐ 616 Andy Nezelek UER	.05	.02	.01
(Wrong birthdate)			
☐ 617 Chuck Crim	.05	.02	.01
☐ 618 Jack Savage DP	.05	.02	.01
☐ 619 Adam Peterson	.05	.02	.01
☐ 620 Todd Stottlemyre	.10	.05	.01
☐ 621 Lance Blankenship	.05	.02	.01
☐ 622 Miguel Garcia DP	.05	.02	.01
☐ 623 Keith A. Miller DP	.05	.02	.01
☐ 624 Ricky Jordan DP	.10	.05	.01
☐ 625 Ernest Riles DP	.05	.02	.01
☐ 626 John Moses DP	.05	.02	.01
☐ 627 Nelson Liriano DP	.05	.02	.01
☐ 628 Mike Smithson DP	.05	.02	.01
☐ 629 Scott Sanderson	.05	.02	.01
☐ 630 Dale Mohorcic	.05	.02	.01
☐ 631 Marvin Freeman DP	.05	.02	.01
☐ 632 Mike Young DP	.05	.02	.01
☐ 633 Dennis Lamp	.05	.02	.01
☐ 634 Dante Bichette DP	.60	.25	.07
☐ 635 Curt Schilling DP	.15	.07	.02
☐ 636 Scott May DP	.05	.02	.01
☐ 637 Mike Schooler	.05	.02	.01
☐ 638 Rick Leach	.05	.02	.01
☐ 639 Tom Lampkin UER	.05	.02	.01
(Throws Left, should be Throws Right)			
☐ 640 Brian Meyer	.05	.02	.01
☐ 641 Brian Harper	.05	.02	.01
☐ 642 John Smoltz	.75	.35	.09
☐ 643 Jose Canseco	.15	.07	.02
(40/40 Club)			
☐ 644 Bill Schroeder	.05	.02	.01
☐ 645 Edgar Martinez	.25	.11	.03
☐ 646 Dennis Cook	.05	.02	.01
☐ 647 Barry Jones	.05	.02	.01
☐ 648 Orel Hershiser	.10	.05	.01
(59 and Counting)			
☐ 649 Rod Nichols	.05	.02	.01
☐ 650 Jody Davis	.05	.02	.01
☐ 651 Bob Milacki	.05	.02	.01
☐ 652 Mike Jackson	.05	.02	.01
☐ 653 Derek Lilliquist	.05	.02	.01
☐ 654 Paul Mirabella	.05	.02	.01
☐ 655 Mike Diaz	.05	.02	.01
☐ 656 Jeff Musselman	.05	.02	.01
☐ 657 Jerry Reed	.05	.02	.01
☐ 658 Kevin Blankenship	.05	.02	.01
☐ 659 Wayne Tolleson	.05	.02	.01
☐ 660 Eric Hetzel	.05	.02	.01

1989 Donruss Rookies

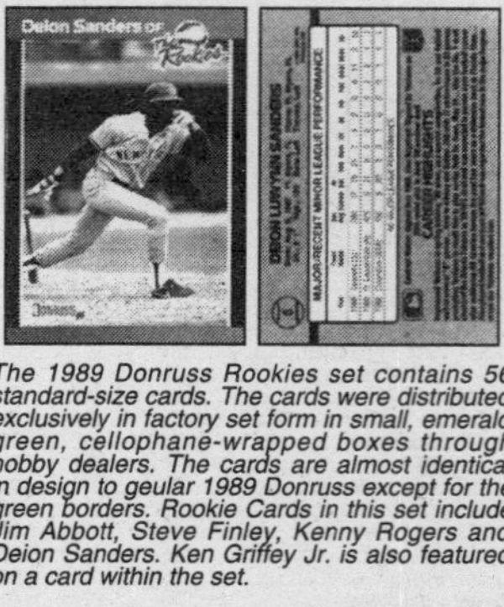

The 1989 Donruss Rookies set contains 56 standard-size cards. The cards were distributed exclusively in factory set form in small, emerald green, cellophane-wrapped boxes through hobby dealers. The cards are almost identical in design to geular 1989 Donruss except for the green borders. Rookie Cards in this set include Jim Abbott, Steve Finley, Kenny Rogers and Deion Sanders. Ken Griffey Jr. is also featured on a card within the set.

	MINT	NRMT	EXC
COMPLETE FACT.SET (56)	8.00	3.60	1.00
COMMON CARD (1-56)	.05	.02	.01
SEMISTARS	.10	.05	.01

□ 1 Gary Sheffield	.75	.35	.09
□ 2 Gregg Jefferies	.15	.07	.02
□ 3 Ken Griffey Jr.	5.00	2.20	.60
□ 4 Tom Gordon	.10	.05	.01
□ 5 Billy Spiers	.05	.02	.01
□ 6 Deion Sanders	.75	.35	.09
□ 7 Donn Pall	.05	.02	.01
□ 8 Steve Carter	.05	.02	.01
□ 9 Francisco Oliveras	.05	.02	.01
□ 10 Steve Wilson	.05	.02	.01
□ 11 Bob Geren	.05	.02	.01
□ 12 Tony Castillo	.05	.02	.01
□ 13 Kenny Rogers	.10	.05	.01
□ 14 Carlos Martinez	.05	.02	.01
□ 15 Edgar Martinez	.25	.11	.03
□ 16 Jim Abbott	.15	.07	.02
□ 17 Torey Lovullo	.05	.02	.01
□ 18 Mark Carreon	.05	.02	.01
□ 19 Geronimo Berroa	.10	.05	.01
□ 20 Luis Medina	.05	.02	.01
□ 21 Sandy Alomar Jr.	.10	.05	.01
□ 22 Bob Milacki	.05	.02	.01
□ 23 Joe Girardi	.15	.07	.02
□ 24 German Gonzalez	.05	.02	.01
□ 25 Craig Worthington	.05	.02	.01
□ 26 Jerome Walton	.10	.05	.01
□ 27 Gary Wayne	.05	.02	.01
□ 28 Tim Jones	.05	.02	.01
□ 29 Dante Bichette	.60	.25	.07
□ 30 Alexis Infante	.05	.02	.01
□ 31 Ken Hill	.50	.23	.06
□ 32 Dwight Smith	.10	.05	.01
□ 33 Luis de los Santos	.05	.02	.01
□ 34 Eric Yelding	.05	.02	.01
□ 35 Gregg Olson	.10	.05	.01
□ 36 Phil Stephenson	.05	.02	.01
□ 37 Ken Patterson	.05	.02	.01
□ 38 Rick Wrona	.05	.02	.01
□ 39 Mike Brumley	.05	.02	.01
□ 40 Cris Carpenter	.05	.02	.01
□ 41 Jeff Brantley	.05	.02	.01
□ 42 Ron Jones	.05	.02	.01
□ 43 Randy Johnson	.75	.35	.09
□ 44 Kevin Brown	.15	.07	.02
□ 45 Ramon Martinez	.25	.11	.03
□ 46 Greg W.Harris	.05	.02	.01
□ 47 Steve Finley	.25	.11	.03
□ 48 Randy Kramer	.05	.02	.01
□ 49 Erik Hanson	.15	.07	.02
□ 50 Matt Merullo	.05	.02	.01
□ 51 Mike Devereaux	.05	.02	.01
□ 52 Clay Parker	.05	.02	.01
□ 53 Omar Vizquel	.40	.18	.05
□ 54 Derek Lilliquist	.05	.02	.01
□ 55 Junior Felix	.05	.02	.01
□ 56 Checklist 1-56	.05	.02	.01

1990 Donruss

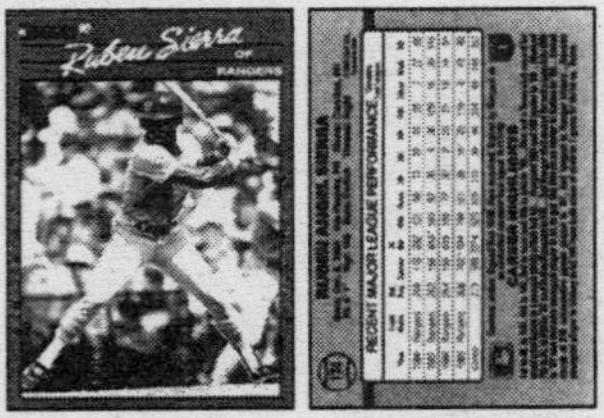

The 1990 Donruss set contains 716 standard-size cards. Cards were issued in wax packs and hobby and retail factory sets. The card fronts feature bright red borders. Subsets include Diamond Kings (1-27) and Rated Rookies (28-47). The set was the largest ever produced by Donruss, unfortunately it also had a large number of errors which were corrected after the cards were released. Most of these feature minor printing flaws and insignificant variations that collectors have found unworthy of price differentials. There are several double-printed cards within the set indicated in the checklists below with a "DP" coding. Rookie Cards of note include Juan Gonzalez, Marquis Grissom, Dave Justice, Ben McDonald, Dean Palmer, Sammy Sosa, Larry Walker and Bernie Williams. Numbered with the prefix "BC", Special Bonus Cards from a set featuring one most valuable player from each of the 26 teams were randomly inserted in all 1990 Donruss unopened pack formats. The factory sets were distributed without the Bonus Cards.

	MINT	NRMT	EXC
COMPLETE SET (716)	8.00	3.60	1.00
COMPLETE FACT.SET (728)	8.00	3.60	1.00
COMMON CARD (1-716)	.05	.02	.01
SEMISTARS	.10	.05	.01
STARS	.15	.07	.02
COMP.BONUS MVP SET (26)	1.50	.70	.19
MVP'S: RANDOM INSERTS IN PACKS			
COMP.GRANDSLAMMERS (12)	1.50	.70	.19
ONE G.SLAM SET PER FACT.SET			
□ 1 Bo Jackson DK	.15	.07	.02
□ 2 Steve Sax DK	.05	.02	.01
□ 3A Ruben Sierra DK ERR (No small line on top border on card back)	.20	.09	.03
□ 3B Ruben Sierra DK COR	.15	.07	.02
□ 4 Ken Griffey Jr. DK	.75	.35	.09
□ 5 Mickey Tettleton DK	.05	.02	.01
□ 6 Dave Stewart DK	.10	.05	.01
□ 7 Jim Deshaies DK DP	.05	.02	.01
□ 8 John Smoltz DK	.15	.07	.02
□ 9 Mike Bielecki DK	.05	.02	.01
□ 10A Brian Downing DK ERR (Reverse negative on card front)	.15	.07	.02
□ 10B Brian Downing DK COR	.05	.02	.01
□ 11 Kevin Mitchell DK	.05	.02	.01
□ 12 Kelly Gruber DK	.05	.02	.01
□ 13 Joe Magrane DK	.05	.02	.01
□ 14 John Franco DK	.05	.02	.01
□ 15 Ozzie Guillen DK	.05	.02	.01
□ 16 Lou Whitaker DK	.10	.05	.01
□ 17 John Smiley DK	.05	.02	.01
□ 18 Howard Johnson DK	.05	.02	.01
□ 19 Willie Randolph DK	.10	.05	.01
□ 20 Chris Bosio DK	.05	.02	.01
□ 21 Tommy Herr DK DP	.05	.02	.01
□ 22 Dan Gladden DK	.05	.02	.01
□ 23 Ellis Burks DK	.15	.07	.02
□ 24 Pete O'Brien DK	.05	.02	.01
□ 25 Bryn Smith DK	.05	.02	.01
□ 26 Ed Whitson DK DP	.05	.02	.01
□ 27 DK Checklist 1-27 DP (Comments on Perez-Steele on back)	.05	.02	.01
□ 28 Robin Ventura RR	.15	.07	.02
□ 29 Todd Zeile RR	.10	.05	.01
□ 30 Sandy Alomar Jr. RR	.10	.05	.01
□ 31 Kent Mercker RR	.10	.05	.01
□ 32 Ben McDonald RR UER (Middle name Benard, not Benjamin)	.15	.07	.02
□ 33A Juan Gonzalez RR ERR (Reverse negative)	5.00	2.20	.60
□ 33B Juan Gonzalez RR COR	2.00	.90	.25
□ 34 Eric Anthony RR	.10	.05	.01
□ 35 Mike Fetters RR	.10	.05	.01
□ 36 Marquis Grissom RR	.60	.25	.07
□ 37 Greg Vaughn RR	.15	.07	.02
□ 38 Brian DuBois RR	.05	.02	.01
□ 39 Steve Avery RR UER (Born in MI, not NJ)	.15	.07	.02
□ 40 Mark Gardner RR	.05	.02	.01
□ 41 Andy Benes RR	.15	.07	.02
□ 42 Delino DeShields RR	.10	.05	.01
□ 43 Scott Coolbaugh RR	.05	.02	.01
□ 44 Pat Combs RR DP	.05	.02	.01
□ 45 Alex Sanchez RR DP	.05	.02	.01

□ 46 Kelly Mann RR DP	.05	.02	.01
□ 47 Julio Machado RR DP	.05	.02	.01
□ 48 Pete Incaviglia	.05	.02	.01
□ 49 Shawon Dunston	.05	.02	.01
□ 50 Jeff Treadway	.05	.02	.01
□ 51 Jeff Ballard	.05	.02	.01
□ 52 Claudell Washington	.05	.02	.01
□ 53 Juan Samuel	.05	.02	.01
□ 54 John Smiley	.10	.05	.01
□ 55 Rob Deer	.05	.02	.01
□ 56 Geno Petralli	.05	.02	.01
□ 57 Chris Bosio	.05	.02	.01
□ 58 Carlton Fisk	.15	.07	.02
□ 59 Kirt Manwaring	.05	.02	.01
□ 60 Chet Lemon	.05	.02	.01
□ 61 Bo Jackson	.15	.07	.02
□ 62 Doyle Alexander	.05	.02	.01
□ 63 Pedro Guerrero	.05	.02	.01
□ 64 Allan Anderson	.05	.02	.01
□ 65 Greg W. Harris	.05	.02	.01
□ 66 Mike Greenwell	.05	.02	.01
□ 67 Walt Weiss	.05	.02	.01
□ 68 Wade Boggs	.15	.07	.02
□ 69 Jim Clancy	.05	.02	.01
□ 70 Junior Felix	.05	.02	.01
□ 71 Barry Larkin	.15	.07	.02
□ 72 Dave LaPoint	.05	.02	.01
□ 73 Joel Skinner	.05	.02	.01
□ 74 Jesse Barfield	.05	.02	.01
□ 75 Tommy Herr	.05	.02	.01
□ 76 Ricky Jordan	.05	.02	.01
□ 77 Eddie Murray	.25	.11	.03
□ 78 Steve Sax	.05	.02	.01
□ 79 Tim Belcher	.05	.02	.01
□ 80 Danny Jackson	.05	.02	.01
□ 81 Kent Hrbek	.10	.05	.01
□ 82 Milt Thompson	.05	.02	.01
□ 83 Brook Jacoby	.05	.02	.01
□ 84 Mike Marshall	.05	.02	.01
□ 85 Kevin Seitzer	.05	.02	.01
□ 86 Tony Gwynn	.40	.18	.05
□ 87 Dave Stieb	.05	.02	.01
□ 88 Dave Smith	.05	.02	.01
□ 89 Bret Saberhagen	.10	.05	.01
□ 90 Alan Trammell	.15	.07	.02
□ 91 Tony Phillips	.15	.07	.02
□ 92 Doug Drabek	.05	.02	.01
□ 93 Jeffrey Leonard	.05	.02	.01
□ 94 Wally Joyner	.10	.05	.01
□ 95 Carney Lansford	.10	.05	.01
□ 96 Cal Ripken	.75	.35	.09
□ 97 Andres Galarraga	.15	.07	.02
□ 98 Kevin Mitchell	.10	.05	.01
□ 99 Howard Johnson	.05	.02	.01
□ 100A Checklist 28-129	.05	.02	.01
□ 100B Checklist 28-125	.05	.02	.01
□ 101 Melido Perez	.05	.02	.01
□ 102 Spike Owen	.05	.02	.01
□ 103 Paul Molitor	.20	.09	.03
□ 104 Geronimo Berroa	.10	.05	.01
□ 105 Ryne Sandberg	.25	.11	.03
□ 106 Bryn Smith	.05	.02	.01
□ 107 Steve Buechele	.05	.02	.01
□ 108 Jim Abbott	.10	.05	.01
□ 109 Alvin Davis	.05	.02	.01
□ 110 Lee Smith	.10	.05	.01
□ 111 Roberto Alomar	.30	.14	.04
□ 112 Rick Reuschel	.05	.02	.01
□ 113A Kelly Gruber ERR (Born 2/22)	.05	.02	.01
□ 113B Kelly Gruber COR (Born 2/26; corrected in factory sets)	.05	.02	.01
□ 114 Joe Carter	.15	.07	.02
□ 115 Jose Rijo	.05	.02	.01
□ 116 Greg Minton	.05	.02	.01
□ 117 Bob Ojeda	.05	.02	.01
□ 118 Glenn Davis	.05	.02	.01
□ 119 Jeff Reardon	.10	.05	.01
□ 120 Kurt Stillwell	.05	.02	.01
□ 121 John Smoltz	.25	.11	.03
□ 122 Dwight Evans	.10	.05	.01
□ 123 Eric Yelding	.05	.02	.01
□ 124 John Franco	.05	.02	.01
□ 125 Jose Canseco	.15	.07	.02
□ 126 Barry Bonds	.25	.11	.03
□ 127 Lee Guetterman	.05	.02	.01
□ 128 Jack Clark	.10	.05	.01
□ 129 Dave Valle	.05	.02	.01
□ 130 Hubie Brooks	.05	.02	.01
□ 131 Ernest Riles	.05	.02	.01
□ 132 Mike Morgan	.05	.02	.01
□ 133 Steve Jeltz	.05	.02	.01
□ 134 Jeff D. Robinson	.05	.02	.01
□ 135 Ozzie Guillen	.05	.02	.01
□ 136 Chili Davis	.10	.05	.01
□ 137 Mitch Webster	.05	.02	.01
□ 138 Jerry Browne	.05	.02	.01
□ 139 Bo Diaz	.05	.02	.01
□ 140 Robby Thompson	.05	.02	.01
□ 141 Craig Worthington	.05	.02	.01
□ 142 Julio Franco	.10	.05	.01
□ 143 Brian Holman	.05	.02	.01
□ 144 George Brett	.40	.18	.05
□ 145 Tom Glavine	.15	.07	.02
□ 146 Robin Yount	.15	.07	.02
□ 147 Gary Carter	.15	.07	.02
□ 148 Ron Kittle	.05	.02	.01
□ 149 Tony Fernandez	.05	.02	.01
□ 150 Dave Stewart	.10	.05	.01
□ 151 Gary Gaetti	.10	.05	.01
□ 152 Kevin Elster	.05	.02	.01
□ 153 Gerald Perry	.05	.02	.01
□ 154 Jesse Orosco	.05	.02	.01
□ 155 Wally Backman	.05	.02	.01
□ 156 Dennis Martinez	.10	.05	.01
□ 157 Rick Sutcliffe	.05	.02	.01
□ 158 Greg Maddux	.60	.25	.07
□ 159 Andy Hawkins	.05	.02	.01
□ 160 John Kruk	.10	.05	.01
□ 161 Jose Oquendo	.05	.02	.01
□ 162 John Dopson	.05	.02	.01
□ 163 Joe Magrane	.05	.02	.01
□ 164 Bill Ripken	.05	.02	.01
□ 165 Fred Manrique	.05	.02	.01
□ 166 Nolan Ryan UER (Did not lead NL in K's in '89 as he was in AL in '89)	.75	.35	.09
□ 167 Damon Berryhill	.05	.02	.01
□ 168 Dale Murphy	.15	.07	.02
□ 169 Mickey Tettleton	.10	.05	.01
□ 170A Kirk McCaskill ERR (Born 4/19)	.05	.02	.01
□ 170B Kirk McCaskill COR (Born 4/9; corrected in factory sets)	.05	.02	.01
□ 171 Dwight Gooden	.10	.05	.01
□ 172 Jose Lind	.05	.02	.01
□ 173 B.J. Surhoff	.10	.05	.01
□ 174 Ruben Sierra	.10	.05	.01
□ 175 Dan Plesac	.05	.02	.01
□ 176 Dan Pasqua	.05	.02	.01
□ 177 Kelly Downs	.05	.02	.01
□ 178 Matt Nokes	.05	.02	.01
□ 179 Luis Aquino	.05	.02	.01
□ 180 Frank Tanana	.05	.02	.01
□ 181 Tony Pena	.05	.02	.01
□ 182 Dan Gladden	.05	.02	.01
□ 183 Bruce Hurst	.05	.02	.01
□ 184 Roger Clemens	.15	.07	.02
□ 185 Mark McGwire	.30	.14	.04
□ 186 Rob Murphy	.05	.02	.01
□ 187 Jim Deshaies	.05	.02	.01
□ 188 Fred McGriff	.15	.07	.02
□ 189 Rob Dibble	.05	.02	.01
□ 190 Don Mattingly	.50	.23	.06
□ 191 Felix Fermin	.05	.02	.01
□ 192 Roberto Kelly	.10	.05	.01
□ 193 Dennis Cook	.05	.02	.01
□ 194 Darren Daulton	.10	.05	.01
□ 195 Alfredo Griffin	.05	.02	.01
□ 196 Eric Plunk	.05	.02	.01
□ 197 Orel Hershiser	.10	.05	.01
□ 198 Paul O'Neill	.10	.05	.01
□ 199 Randy Bush	.05	.02	.01
□ 200A Checklist 130-231	.05	.02	.01
□ 200B Checklist 126-223	.05	.02	.01
□ 201 Ozzie Smith	.20	.09	.03
□ 202 Pete O'Brien	.05	.02	.01
□ 203 Jay Howell	.05	.02	.01
□ 204 Mark Gubicza	.05	.02	.01

□ 205 Ed Whitson	.05	.02	.01
□ 206 George Bell	.05	.02	.01
□ 207 Mike Scott	.05	.02	.01
□ 208 Charlie Leibrandt	.05	.02	.01
□ 209 Mike Heath	.05	.02	.01
□ 210 Dennis Eckersley	.10	.05	.01
□ 211 Mike LaValliere	.05	.02	.01
□ 212 Darnell Coles	.05	.02	.01
□ 213 Lance Parrish	.05	.02	.01
□ 214 Mike Moore	.05	.02	.01
□ 215 Steve Finley	.15	.07	.02
□ 216 Tim Raines	.15	.07	.02
□ 217A Scott Garrelts ERR	.05	.02	.01
(Born 10/20)			
□ 217B Scott Garrelts COR	.05	.02	.01
(Born 10/30; corrected in factory sets)			
□ 218 Kevin McReynolds	.05	.02	.01
□ 219 Dave Gallagher	.05	.02	.01
□ 220 Tim Wallach	.05	.02	.01
□ 221 Chuck Crim	.05	.02	.01
□ 222 Lonnie Smith	.05	.02	.01
□ 223 Andre Dawson	.15	.07	.02
□ 224 Nelson Santovenia	.05	.02	.01
□ 225 Rafael Palmeiro	.15	.07	.02
□ 226 Devon White	.10	.05	.01
□ 227 Harold Reynolds	.05	.02	.01
□ 228 Ellis Burks	.15	.07	.02
□ 229 Mark Parent	.05	.02	.01
□ 230 Will Clark	.15	.07	.02
□ 231 Jimmy Key	.10	.05	.01
□ 232 John Farrell	.05	.02	.01
□ 233 Eric Davis	.10	.05	.01
□ 234 Johnny Ray	.05	.02	.01
□ 235 Darryl Strawberry	.10	.05	.01
□ 236 Bill Doran	.05	.02	.01
□ 237 Greg Gagne	.05	.02	.01
□ 238 Jim Eisenreich	.05	.02	.01
□ 239 Tommy Gregg	.05	.02	.01
□ 240 Marty Barrett	.05	.02	.01
□ 241 Rafael Ramirez	.05	.02	.01
□ 242 Chris Sabo	.05	.02	.01
□ 243 Dave Henderson	.05	.02	.01
□ 244 Andy Van Slyke	.10	.05	.01
□ 245 Alvaro Espinoza	.05	.02	.01
□ 246 Garry Templeton	.05	.02	.01
□ 247 Gene Harris	.05	.02	.01
□ 248 Kevin Gross	.05	.02	.01
□ 249 Brett Butler	.10	.05	.01
□ 250 Willie Randolph	.10	.05	.01
□ 251 Roger McDowell	.05	.02	.01
□ 252 Rafael Belliard	.05	.02	.01
□ 253 Steve Rosenberg	.05	.02	.01
□ 254 Jack Howell	.05	.02	.01
□ 255 Marvell Wynne	.05	.02	.01
□ 256 Tom Candiotti	.05	.02	.01
□ 257 Todd Benzinger	.05	.02	.01
□ 258 Don Robinson	.05	.02	.01
□ 259 Phil Bradley	.05	.02	.01
□ 260 Cecil Espy	.05	.02	.01
□ 261 Scott Bankhead	.05	.02	.01
□ 262 Frank White	.10	.05	.01
□ 263 Andres Thomas	.05	.02	.01
□ 264 Glenn Braggs	.05	.02	.01
□ 265 David Cone	.15	.07	.02
□ 266 Bobby Thigpen	.05	.02	.01
□ 267 Nelson Liriano	.05	.02	.01
□ 268 Terry Steinbach	.10	.05	.01
□ 269 Kirby Puckett UER	.30	.14	.04
(Back doesn't consider Joe Torre's .363 in '71)			
□ 270 Gregg Jefferies	.15	.07	.02
□ 271 Jeff Blauser	.10	.05	.01
□ 272 Cory Snyder	.05	.02	.01
□ 273 Roy Smith	.05	.02	.01
□ 274 Tom Foley	.05	.02	.01
□ 275 Mitch Williams	.05	.02	.01
□ 276 Paul Kilgus	.05	.02	.01
□ 277 Don Slaught	.05	.02	.01
□ 278 Von Hayes	.05	.02	.01
□ 279 Vince Coleman	.05	.02	.01
□ 280 Mike Boddicker	.05	.02	.01
□ 281 Ken Dayley	.05	.02	.01
□ 282 Mike Devereaux	.05	.02	.01
□ 283 Kenny Rogers	.10	.05	.01
□ 284 Jeff Russell	.05	.02	.01
□ 285 Jerome Walton	.05	.02	.01
□ 286 Derek Lilliquist	.05	.02	.01
□ 287 Joe Orsulak	.05	.02	.01
□ 288 Dick Schofield	.05	.02	.01
□ 289 Ron Darling	.05	.02	.01
□ 290 Bobby Bonilla	.10	.05	.01
□ 291 Jim Gantner	.05	.02	.01
□ 292 Bobby Witt	.05	.02	.01
□ 293 Greg Brock	.05	.02	.01
□ 294 Ivan Calderon	.05	.02	.01
□ 295 Steve Bedrosian	.05	.02	.01
□ 296 Mike Henneman	.05	.02	.01
□ 297 Tom Gordon	.05	.02	.01
□ 298 Lou Whitaker	.15	.07	.02
□ 299 Terry Pendleton	.10	.05	.01
□ 300A Checklist 232-333	.05	.02	.01
□ 300B Checklist 224-321	.05	.02	.01
□ 301 Juan Berenguer	.05	.02	.01
□ 302 Mark Davis	.05	.02	.01
□ 303 Nick Esasky	.05	.02	.01
□ 304 Rickey Henderson	.15	.07	.02
□ 305 Rick Cerone	.05	.02	.01
□ 306 Craig Biggio	.15	.07	.02
□ 307 Duane Ward	.05	.02	.01
□ 308 Tom Browning	.05	.02	.01
□ 309 Walt Terrell	.05	.02	.01
□ 310 Greg Swindell	.05	.02	.01
□ 311 Dave Righetti	.05	.02	.01
□ 312 Mike Maddux	.05	.02	.01
□ 313 Len Dykstra	.10	.05	.01
□ 314 Jose Gonzalez	.05	.02	.01
□ 315 Steve Balboni	.05	.02	.01
□ 316 Mike Scioscia	.05	.02	.01
□ 317 Ron Oester	.05	.02	.01
□ 318 Gary Wayne	.05	.02	.01
□ 319 Todd Worrell	.05	.02	.01
□ 320 Doug Jones	.05	.02	.01
□ 321 Jeff Hamilton	.05	.02	.01
□ 322 Danny Tartabull	.05	.02	.01
□ 323 Chris James	.05	.02	.01
□ 324 Mike Flanagan	.05	.02	.01
□ 325 Gerald Young	.05	.02	.01
□ 326 Bob Boone	.10	.05	.01
□ 327 Frank Williams	.05	.02	.01
□ 328 Dave Parker	.10	.05	.01
□ 329 Sid Bream	.05	.02	.01
□ 330 Mike Schooler	.05	.02	.01
□ 331 Bert Blyleven	.10	.05	.01
□ 332 Bob Welch	.05	.02	.01
□ 333 Bob Milacki	.05	.02	.01
□ 334 Tim Burke	.05	.02	.01
□ 335 Jose Uribe	.05	.02	.01
□ 336 Randy Myers	.10	.05	.01
□ 337 Eric King	.05	.02	.01
□ 338 Mark Langston	.10	.05	.01
□ 339 Teddy Higuera	.05	.02	.01
□ 340 Oddibe McDowell	.05	.02	.01
□ 341 Lloyd McClendon	.05	.02	.01
□ 342 Pascual Perez	.05	.02	.01
□ 343 Kevin Brown UER	.10	.05	.01
(Signed is misspelled as signeed on back)			
□ 344 Chuck Finley	.10	.05	.01
□ 345 Erik Hanson	.10	.05	.01
□ 346 Rich Gedman	.05	.02	.01
□ 347 Bip Roberts	.05	.02	.01
□ 348 Matt Williams	.15	.07	.02
□ 349 Tom Henke	.05	.02	.01
□ 350 Brad Komminsk	.05	.02	.01
□ 351 Jeff Reed	.05	.02	.01
□ 352 Brian Downing	.05	.02	.01
□ 353 Frank Viola	.05	.02	.01
□ 354 Terry Puhl	.05	.02	.01
□ 355 Brian Harper	.05	.02	.01
□ 356 Steve Farr	.05	.02	.01
□ 357 Joe Boever	.05	.02	.01
□ 358 Danny Heep	.05	.02	.01
□ 359 Larry Andersen	.05	.02	.01
□ 360 Rolando Roomes	.05	.02	.01
□ 361 Mike Gallego	.05	.02	.01
□ 362 Bob Kipper	.05	.02	.01
□ 363 Clay Parker	.05	.02	.01
□ 364 Mike Pagliarulo	.05	.02	.01
□ 365 Ken Griffey Jr. UER	1.50	.70	.19
(Signed through 1990, should be 1991)			

□ 366 Rex Hudler	.05	.02	.01
□ 367 Pat Sheridan	.05	.02	.01
□ 368 Kirk Gibson	.10	.05	.01
□ 369 Jeff Parrett	.05	.02	.01
□ 370 Bob Walk	.05	.02	.01
□ 371 Ken Patterson	.05	.02	.01
□ 372 Bryan Harvey	.05	.02	.01
□ 373 Mike Bielecki	.05	.02	.01
□ 374 Tom Magrann	.05	.02	.01
□ 375 Rick Mahler	.05	.02	.01
□ 376 Craig Lefferts	.05	.02	.01
□ 377 Gregg Olson	.05	.02	.01
□ 378 Jamie Moyer	.05	.02	.01
□ 379 Randy Johnson	.25	.11	.03
□ 380 Jeff Montgomery	.10	.05	.01
□ 381 Marty Clary	.05	.02	.01
□ 382 Bill Spiers	.05	.02	.01
□ 383 Dave Magadan	.05	.02	.01
□ 384 Greg Hibbard	.05	.02	.01
□ 385 Ernie Whitt	.05	.02	.01
□ 386 Rick Honeycutt	.05	.02	.01
□ 387 Dave West	.05	.02	.01
□ 388 Keith Hernandez	.10	.05	.01
□ 389 Jose Alvarez	.05	.02	.01
□ 390 Joey Belle	1.00	.45	.12
□ 391 Rick Aguilera	.10	.05	.01
□ 392 Mike Fitzgerald	.05	.02	.01
□ 393 Dwight Smith	.05	.02	.01
□ 394 Steve Wilson	.05	.02	.01
□ 395 Bob Geren	.05	.02	.01
□ 396 Randy Ready	.05	.02	.01
□ 397 Ken Hill	.15	.07	.02
□ 398 Jody Reed	.05	.02	.01
□ 399 Tom Brunansky	.05	.02	.01
□ 400A Checklist 334-435	.05	.02	.01
□ 400B Checklist 322-419	.05	.02	.01
□ 401 Rene Gonzales	.05	.02	.01
□ 402 Harold Baines	.10	.05	.01
□ 403 Cecilio Guante	.05	.02	.01
□ 404 Joe Girardi	.10	.05	.01
□ 405A Sergio Valdez ERR (Card front shows black line crossing S in Sergio)	.05	.02	.01
□ 405B Sergio Valdez COR	.05	.02	.01
□ 406 Mark Williamson	.05	.02	.01
□ 407 Glenn Hoffman	.05	.02	.01
□ 408 Jeff Innis	.05	.02	.01
□ 409 Randy Kramer	.05	.02	.01
□ 410 Charlie O'Brien	.05	.02	.01
□ 411 Charlie Hough	.05	.02	.01
□ 412 Gus Polidor	.05	.02	.01
□ 413 Ron Karkovice	.05	.02	.01
□ 414 Trevor Wilson	.05	.02	.01
□ 415 Kevin Ritz	.05	.02	.01
□ 416 Gary Thurman	.05	.02	.01
□ 417 Jeff M. Robinson	.05	.02	.01
□ 418 Scott Terry	.05	.02	.01
□ 419 Tim Laudner	.05	.02	.01
□ 420 Dennis Rasmussen	.05	.02	.01
□ 421 Luis Rivera	.05	.02	.01
□ 422 Jim Corsi	.05	.02	.01
□ 423 Dennis Lamp	.05	.02	.01
□ 424 Ken Caminiti	.15	.07	.02
□ 425 David Wells	.05	.02	.01
□ 426 Norm Charlton	.05	.02	.01
□ 427 Deion Sanders	.20	.09	.03
□ 428 Dion James	.05	.02	.01
□ 429 Chuck Cary	.05	.02	.01
□ 430 Ken Howell	.05	.02	.01
□ 431 Steve Lake	.05	.02	.01
□ 432 Kal Daniels	.05	.02	.01
□ 433 Lance McCullers	.05	.02	.01
□ 434 Lenny Harris	.05	.02	.01
□ 435 Scott Scudder	.05	.02	.01
□ 436 Gene Larkin	.05	.02	.01
□ 437 Dan Quisenberry	.05	.02	.01
□ 438 Steve Olin	.10	.05	.01
□ 439 Mickey Hatcher	.05	.02	.01
□ 440 Willie Wilson	.05	.02	.01
□ 441 Mark Grant	.05	.02	.01
□ 442 Mookie Wilson	.05	.02	.01
□ 443 Alex Trevino	.05	.02	.01
□ 444 Pat Tabler	.05	.02	.01
□ 445 Dave Bergman	.05	.02	.01
□ 446 Todd Burns	.05	.02	.01
□ 447 R.J. Reynolds	.05	.02	.01
□ 448 Jay Buhner	.15	.07	.02
□ 449 Lee Stevens	.05	.02	.01
□ 450 Ron Hassey	.05	.02	.01
□ 451 Bob Melvin	.05	.02	.01
□ 452 Dave Martinez	.05	.02	.01
□ 453 Greg Litton	.05	.02	.01
□ 454 Mark Carreon	.05	.02	.01
□ 455 Scott Fletcher	.05	.02	.01
□ 456 Otis Nixon	.05	.02	.01
□ 457 Tony Fossas	.05	.02	.01
□ 458 John Russell	.05	.02	.01
□ 459 Paul Assenmacher	.05	.02	.01
□ 460 Zane Smith	.05	.02	.01
□ 461 Jack Daugherty	.05	.02	.01
□ 462 Rich Monteleone	.05	.02	.01
□ 463 Greg Briley	.05	.02	.01
□ 464 Mike Smithson	.05	.02	.01
□ 465 Benito Santiago	.05	.02	.01
□ 466 Jeff Brantley	.10	.05	.01
□ 467 Jose Nunez	.05	.02	.01
□ 468 Scott Bailes	.05	.02	.01
□ 469 Ken Griffey Sr.	.05	.02	.01
□ 470 Bob McClure	.05	.02	.01
□ 471 Mackey Sasser	.05	.02	.01
□ 472 Glenn Wilson	.05	.02	.01
□ 473 Kevin Tapani	.10	.05	.01
□ 474 Bill Buckner	.05	.02	.01
□ 475 Ron Gant	.15	.07	.02
□ 476 Kevin Romine	.05	.02	.01
□ 477 Juan Agosto	.05	.02	.01
□ 478 Herm Winningham	.05	.02	.01
□ 479 Storm Davis	.05	.02	.01
□ 480 Jeff King	.10	.05	.01
□ 481 Kevin Mmahat	.05	.02	.01
□ 482 Carmelo Martinez	.05	.02	.01
□ 483 Omar Vizquel	.10	.05	.01
□ 484 Jim Dwyer	.05	.02	.01
□ 485 Bob Knepper	.05	.02	.01
□ 486 Dave Anderson	.05	.02	.01
□ 487 Ron Jones	.05	.02	.01
□ 488 Jay Bell	.10	.05	.01
□ 489 Sammy Sosa	.75	.35	.09
□ 490 Kent Anderson	.05	.02	.01
□ 491 Domingo Ramos	.05	.02	.01
□ 492 Dave Clark	.05	.02	.01
□ 493 Tim Birtsas	.05	.02	.01
□ 494 Ken Oberkfell	.05	.02	.01
□ 495 Larry Sheets	.05	.02	.01
□ 496 Jeff Kunkel	.05	.02	.01
□ 497 Jim Presley	.05	.02	.01
□ 498 Mike Macfarlane	.05	.02	.01
□ 499 Pete Smith	.05	.02	.01
□ 500A Checklist 436-537 DP	.05	.02	.01
□ 500B Checklist 420-517	.05	.02	.01
□ 501 Gary Sheffield	.25	.11	.03
□ 502 Terry Bross	.05	.02	.01
□ 503 Jerry Kutzler	.05	.02	.01
□ 504 Lloyd Moseby	.05	.02	.01
□ 505 Curt Young	.05	.02	.01
□ 506 Al Newman	.05	.02	.01
□ 507 Keith Miller	.05	.02	.01
□ 508 Mike Stanton	.10	.05	.01
□ 509 Rich Yett	.05	.02	.01
□ 510 Tim Drummond	.05	.02	.01
□ 511 Joe Hesketh	.05	.02	.01
□ 512 Rick Wrona	.05	.02	.01
□ 513 Luis Salazar	.05	.02	.01
□ 514 Hal Morris	.10	.05	.01
□ 515 Terry Mulholland	.05	.02	.01
□ 516 John Morris	.05	.02	.01
□ 517 Carlos Quintana	.05	.02	.01
□ 518 Frank DiPino	.05	.02	.01
□ 519 Randy Milligan	.05	.02	.01
□ 520 Chad Kreuter	.05	.02	.01
□ 521 Mike Jeffcoat	.05	.02	.01
□ 522 Mike Harkey	.05	.02	.01
□ 523A Andy Nezelek ERR (Wrong birth year)	.05	.02	.01
□ 523B Andy Nezelek COR (Finally corrected in factory sets)	.15	.07	.02
□ 524 Dave Schmidt	.05	.02	.01
□ 525 Tony Armas	.05	.02	.01
□ 526 Barry Lyons	.05	.02	.01
□ 527 Rick Reed	.05	.02	.01

□ 528	Jerry Reuss	.05	.02	.01
□ 529	Dean Palmer	.40	.18	.05
□ 530	Jeff Peterek	.05	.02	.01
□ 531	Carlos Martinez	.05	.02	.01
□ 532	Atlee Hammaker	.05	.02	.01
□ 533	Mike Brumley	.05	.02	.01
□ 534	Terry Leach	.05	.02	.01
□ 535	Doug Strange	.05	.02	.01
□ 536	Jose DeLeon	.05	.02	.01
□ 537	Shane Rawley	.05	.02	.01
□ 538	Joey Cora	.15	.07	.02
□ 539	Eric Hetzel	.05	.02	.01
□ 540	Gene Nelson	.05	.02	.01
□ 541	Wes Gardner	.05	.02	.01
□ 542	Mark Portugal	.05	.02	.01
□ 543	Al Leiter	.10	.05	.01
□ 544	Jack Armstrong	.05	.02	.01
□ 545	Greg Cadaret	.05	.02	.01
□ 546	Rod Nichols	.05	.02	.01
□ 547	Luis Polonia	.05	.02	.01
□ 548	Charlie Hayes	.10	.05	.01
□ 549	Dickie Thon	.05	.02	.01
□ 550	Tim Crews	.05	.02	.01
□ 551	Dave Winfield	.15	.07	.02
□ 552	Mike Davis	.05	.02	.01
□ 553	Ron Robinson	.05	.02	.01
□ 554	Carmen Castillo	.05	.02	.01
□ 555	John Costello	.05	.02	.01
□ 556	Bud Black	.05	.02	.01
□ 557	Rick Dempsey	.05	.02	.01
□ 558	Jim Acker	.05	.02	.01
□ 559	Eric Show	.05	.02	.01
□ 560	Pat Borders	.05	.02	.01
□ 561	Danny Darwin	.05	.02	.01
□ 562	Rick Luecken	.05	.02	.01
□ 563	Edwin Nunez	.05	.02	.01
□ 564	Felix Jose	.05	.02	.01
□ 565	John Cangelosi	.05	.02	.01
□ 566	Bill Swift	.05	.02	.01
□ 567	Bill Schroeder	.05	.02	.01
□ 568	Stan Javier	.05	.02	.01
□ 569	Jim Traber	.05	.02	.01
□ 570	Wallace Johnson	.05	.02	.01
□ 571	Donell Nixon	.05	.02	.01
□ 572	Sid Fernandez	.05	.02	.01
□ 573	Lance Johnson	.15	.07	.02
□ 574	Andy McGaffigan	.05	.02	.01
□ 575	Mark Knudson	.05	.02	.01
□ 576	Tommy Greene	.05	.02	.01
□ 577	Mark Grace	.15	.07	.02
□ 578	Larry Walker	.50	.23	.06
□ 579	Mike Stanley	.05	.02	.01
□ 580	Mike Witt DP	.05	.02	.01
□ 581	Scott Bradley	.05	.02	.01
□ 582	Greg A. Harris	.05	.02	.01
□ 583A	Kevin Hickey ERR	.15	.07	.02
□ 583B	Kevin Hickey COR	.05	.02	.01
□ 584	Lee Mazzilli	.05	.02	.01
□ 585	Jeff Pico	.05	.02	.01
□ 586	Joe Oliver	.05	.02	.01
□ 587	Willie Fraser DP	.05	.02	.01
□ 588	Carl Yastrzemski Puzzle Card DP	.15	.07	.02
□ 589	Kevin Bass DP	.05	.02	.01
□ 590	John Moses DP	.05	.02	.01
□ 591	Tom Pagnozzi DP	.05	.02	.01
□ 592	Tony Castillo DP	.05	.02	.01
□ 593	Jerald Clark DP	.05	.02	.01
□ 594	Dan Schatzeder	.05	.02	.01
□ 595	Luis Quinones DP	.05	.02	.01
□ 596	Pete Harnisch DP	.05	.02	.01
□ 597	Gary Redus	.05	.02	.01
□ 598	Mel Hall	.05	.02	.01
□ 599	Rick Schu	.05	.02	.01
□ 600A	Checklist 538-639	.05	.02	.01
□ 600B	Checklist 518-617	.05	.02	.01
□ 601	Mike Kingery DP	.05	.02	.01
□ 602	Terry Kennedy DP	.05	.02	.01
□ 603	Mike Sharperson DP	.05	.02	.01
□ 604	Don Carman DP	.05	.02	.01
□ 605	Jim Gott	.05	.02	.01
□ 606	Donn Pall DP	.05	.02	.01
□ 607	Rance Mulliniks	.05	.02	.01
□ 608	Curt Wilkerson DP	.05	.02	.01
□ 609	Mike Felder DP	.05	.02	.01
□ 610	Guillermo Hernandez DP	.05	.02	.01
□ 611	Candy Maldonado DP	.05	.02	.01
□ 612	Mark Thurmond DP	.05	.02	.01
□ 613	Rick Leach DP	.05	.02	.01
□ 614	Jerry Reed DP	.05	.02	.01
□ 615	Franklin Stubbs	.05	.02	.01
□ 616	Billy Hatcher DP	.05	.02	.01
□ 617	Don August DP	.05	.02	.01
□ 618	Tim Teufel	.05	.02	.01
□ 619	Shawn Hillegas DP	.05	.02	.01
□ 620	Manny Lee	.05	.02	.01
□ 621	Gary Ward DP	.05	.02	.01
□ 622	Mark Guthrie DP	.05	.02	.01
□ 623	Jeff Musselman DP	.05	.02	.01
□ 624	Mark Lemke DP	.10	.05	.01
□ 625	Fernando Valenzuela	.10	.05	.01
□ 626	Paul Sorrento DP	.15	.07	.02
□ 627	Glenallen Hill DP	.10	.05	.01
□ 628	Les Lancaster DP	.05	.02	.01
□ 629	Vance Law DP	.05	.02	.01
□ 630	Randy Velarde DP	.05	.02	.01
□ 631	Todd Frohwirth DP	.05	.02	.01
□ 632	Willie McGee	.05	.02	.01
□ 633	Dennis Boyd DP	.05	.02	.01
□ 634	Cris Carpenter DP	.05	.02	.01
□ 635	Brian Holton	.05	.02	.01
□ 636	Tracy Jones DP	.05	.02	.01
□ 637A	Terry Steinbach AS (Recent Major League Performance)	.10	.05	.01
□ 637B	Terry Steinbach AS (All-Star Game Performance)	.10	.05	.01
□ 638	Brady Anderson	.15	.07	.02
□ 639A	Jack Morris ERR (Card front shows black line crossing J in Jack)	.10	.05	.01
□ 639B	Jack Morris COR	.10	.05	.01
□ 640	Jaime Navarro	.05	.02	.01
□ 641	Darrin Jackson	.05	.02	.01
□ 642	Mike Dyer	.05	.02	.01
□ 643	Mike Schmidt	.20	.09	.03
□ 644	Henry Cotto	.05	.02	.01
□ 645	John Cerutti	.05	.02	.01
□ 646	Francisco Cabrera	.05	.02	.01
□ 647	Scott Sanderson	.05	.02	.01
□ 648	Brian Meyer	.05	.02	.01
□ 649	Ray Searage	.05	.02	.01
□ 650A	Bo Jackson AS (Recent Major League Performance)	.15	.07	.02
□ 650B	Bo Jackson AS (All-Star Game Performance)	.15	.07	.02
□ 651	Steve Lyons	.05	.02	.01
□ 652	Mike LaCoss	.05	.02	.01
□ 653	Ted Power	.05	.02	.01
□ 654A	Howard Johnson AS (Recent Major League Performance)	.10	.05	.01
□ 654B	Howard Johnson AS (All-Star Game Performance)	.05	.02	.01
□ 655	Mauro Gozzo	.05	.02	.01
□ 656	Mike Blowers	.15	.07	.02
□ 657	Paul Gibson	.05	.02	.01
□ 658	Neal Heaton	.05	.02	.01
□ 659	Nolan Ryan 5000K COR (Still an error as Ryan did not lead AL in K's in '75)	.40	.18	.05
□ 659A	Nolan Ryan 5000K (665 King of Kings back) ERR	1.50	.70	.19
□ 660A	Harold Baines AS (Black line through star on front; Recent Major League Performance)	.75	.35	.09
□ 660B	Harold Baines AS (Black line through star on front; All-Star Game Performance)	1.00	.45	.12
□ 660C	Harold Baines AS (Black line behind	.15	.07	.02

	star on front; Recent Major League Performance)			
□ 660D	Harold Baines AS (Black line behind star on front; All-Star Game Performance)	.05	.02	.01
□ 661	Gary Pettis	.05	.02	.01
□ 662	Clint Zavaras	.05	.02	.01
□ 663A	Rick Reuschel AS (Recent Major League Performance)	.10	.05	.01
□ 663B	Rick Reuschel AS (All-Star Game Performance)	.05	.02	.01
□ 664	Alejandro Pena	.05	.02	.01
□ 665	Nolan Ryan KING COR	.40	.18	.05
□ 665A	Nolan Ryan KING (659 5000 K back) ERR	1.50	.70	.19
□ 665C	Nolan Ryan KING ERR (No number on back; in factory sets)	.75	.35	.09
□ 666	Ricky Horton	.05	.02	.01
□ 667	Curt Schilling	.05	.02	.01
□ 668	Bill Landrum	.05	.02	.01
□ 669	Todd Stottlemyre	.10	.05	.01
□ 670	Tim Leary	.05	.02	.01
□ 671	John Wetteland	.10	.05	.01
□ 672	Calvin Schiraldi	.05	.02	.01
□ 673A	Ruben Sierra AS (Recent Major League Performance)	.10	.05	.01
□ 673B	Ruben Sierra AS (All-Star Game Performance)	.10	.05	.01
□ 674A	Pedro Guerrero AS (Recent Major League Performance)	.10	.05	.01
□ 674B	Pedro Guerrero AS (All-Star Game Performance)	.05	.02	.01
□ 675	Ken Phelps	.05	.02	.01
□ 676	Cal Ripken AS (All-Star Game Performance)	.40	.18	.05
□ 676A	Cal Ripken AS (Recent Major League Performance)	.75	.35	.09
□ 677	Denny Walling	.05	.02	.01
□ 678	Goose Gossage	.10	.05	.01
□ 679	Gary Mielke	.05	.02	.01
□ 680	Bill Bathe	.05	.02	.01
□ 681	Tom Lawless	.05	.02	.01
□ 682	Xavier Hernandez	.05	.02	.01
□ 683A	Kirby Puckett AS (Recent Major League Performance)	.25	.11	.03
□ 683B	Kirby Puckett AS (All-Star Game Performance)	.25	.11	.03
□ 684	Mariano Duncan	.05	.02	.01
□ 685	Ramon Martinez	.15	.07	.02
□ 686	Tim Jones	.05	.02	.01
□ 687	Tom Filer	.05	.02	.01
□ 688	Steve Lombardozzi	.05	.02	.01
□ 689	Bernie Williams	.75	.35	.09
□ 690	Chip Hale	.05	.02	.01
□ 691	Beau Allred	.05	.02	.01
□ 692A	Ryne Sandberg AS (Recent Major League Performance)	.25	.11	.03
□ 692B	Ryne Sandberg AS (All-Star Game Performance)	.15	.07	.02
□ 693	Jeff Huson	.05	.02	.01
□ 694	Curt Ford	.05	.02	.01
□ 695A	Eric Davis AS (Recent Major League Performance)	.10	.05	.01
□ 695B	Eric Davis AS (All-Star Game Performance)	.10	.05	.01
□ 696	Scott Lusader	.05	.02	.01
□ 697A	Mark McGwire AS (Recent Major League Performance)	.15	.07	.02
□ 697B	Mark McGwire AS (All-Star Game Performance)	.10	.05	.01
□ 698	Steve Cummings	.05	.02	.01
□ 699	George Canale	.05	.02	.01
□ 700A	Checklist 640-715 and BC1-BC26	.15	.07	.02
□ 700B	Checklist 640-716 and BC1-BC26	.10	.05	.01
□ 700C	Checklist 618-716	.05	.02	.01
□ 701A	Julio Franco AS (Recent Major League Performance)	.10	.05	.01
□ 701B	Julio Franco AS (All-Star Game Performance)	.05	.02	.01
□ 702	Dave Johnson (P)	.05	.02	.01
□ 703A	Dave Stewart AS (Recent Major League Performance)	.10	.05	.01
□ 703B	Dave Stewart AS (All-Star Game Performance)	.10	.05	.01
□ 704	Dave Justice	.50	.23	.06
□ 705	Tony Gwynn AS (All-Star Game Performance)	.20	.09	.03
□ 705A	Tony Gwynn AS (Recent Major League Performance)	.25	.11	.03
□ 706	Greg Myers	.05	.02	.01
□ 707A	Will Clark AS (Recent Major League Performance)	.15	.07	.02
□ 707B	Will Clark AS (All-Star Game Performance)	.10	.05	.01
□ 708A	Benito Santiago AS (Recent Major League Performance)	.10	.05	.01
□ 708B	Benito Santiago AS (All-Star Game Performance)	.05	.02	.01
□ 709	Larry McWilliams	.05	.02	.01
□ 710A	Ozzie Smith AS (Recent Major League Performance)	.15	.07	.02
□ 710B	Ozzie Smith AS (All-Star Game Performance)	.10	.05	.01
□ 711	John Olerud	.15	.07	.02
□ 712A	Wade Boggs AS (Recent Major League Performance)	.10	.05	.01
□ 712B	Wade Boggs AS (All-Star Game Performance)	.10	.05	.01
□ 713	Gary Eave	.05	.02	.01
□ 714	Bob Tewksbury	.05	.02	.01
□ 715A	Kevin Mitchell AS (Recent Major League Performance)	.10	.05	.01
□ 715B	Kevin Mitchell AS (All-Star Game Performance)	.05	.02	.01
□ 716	Bart Giamatti COMM (In Memoriam)	.15	.07	.02

1990 Donruss Rookies

The 1990 Donruss Rookies set marked the fifth consecutive year that Donruss issued a boxed set honoring the best rookies of the season. This set, which used the 1990 Donruss design but featured a green border, was issued exclusively through the Donruss dealer network to hobby dealers. This 56-card, standard size set came in its own box and the words "The Rookies" are featured prominently on the front of the cards. The only notable Rookie Card in this set is Carlos Baerga.

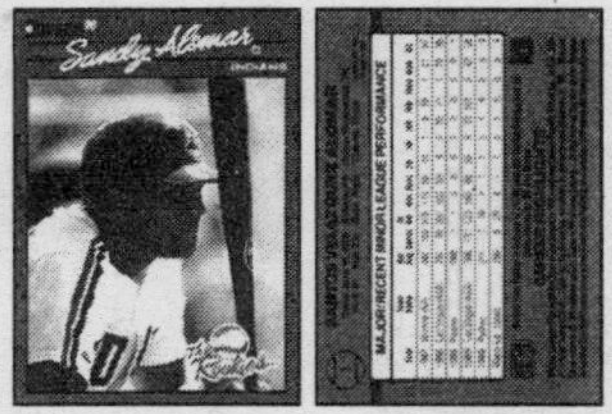

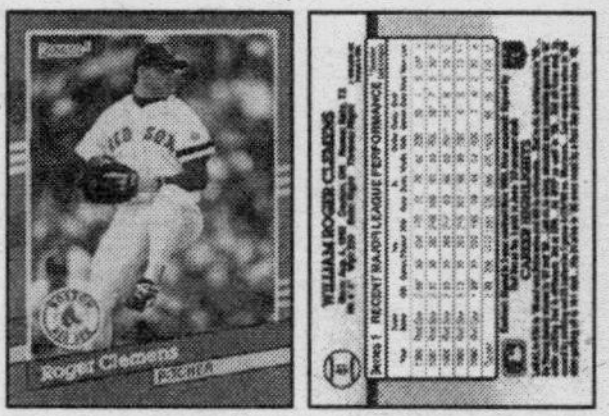

	MINT	NRMT	EXC
COMPLETE FACT.SET (56)	2.00	.90	.25
COMMON CARD (1-56)	.05	.02	.01
SEMISTARS	.10	.05	.01
☐ 1 Sandy Alomar Jr. UER (No stitches on baseball on Donruss logo on card front)	.15	.07	.02
☐ 2 John Olerud	.25	.11	.03
☐ 3 Pat Combs	.05	.02	.01
☐ 4 Brian DuBois	.05	.02	.01
☐ 5 Felix Jose	.05	.02	.01
☐ 6 Delino DeShields	.15	.07	.02
☐ 7 Mike Stanton	.15	.07	.02
☐ 8 Mike Munoz	.05	.02	.01
☐ 9 Craig Grebeck	.05	.02	.01
☐ 10 Joe Kraemer	.05	.02	.01
☐ 11 Jeff Huson	.05	.02	.01
☐ 12 Bill Sampen	.05	.02	.01
☐ 13 Brian Bohanon	.05	.02	.01
☐ 14 Dave Justice	.50	.23	.06
☐ 15 Robin Ventura	.25	.11	.03
☐ 16 Greg Vaughn	.25	.11	.03
☐ 17 Wayne Edwards	.05	.02	.01
☐ 18 Shawn Boskie	.05	.02	.01
☐ 19 Carlos Baerga	.50	.23	.06
☐ 20 Mark Gardner	.05	.02	.01
☐ 21 Kevin Appier	.25	.11	.03
☐ 22 Mike Harkey	.05	.02	.01
☐ 23 Tim Layana	.05	.02	.01
☐ 24 Glenallen Hill	.15	.07	.02
☐ 25 Jerry Kutzler	.05	.02	.01
☐ 26 Mike Blowers	.25	.11	.03
☐ 27 Scott Ruskin	.05	.02	.01
☐ 28 Dana Kiecker	.05	.02	.01
☐ 29 Willie Blair	.05	.02	.01
☐ 30 Ben McDonald	.15	.07	.02
☐ 31 Todd Zeile	.15	.07	.02
☐ 32 Scott Coolbaugh	.05	.02	.01
☐ 33 Xavier Hernandez	.05	.02	.01
☐ 34 Mike Hartley	.05	.02	.01
☐ 35 Kevin Tapani	.15	.07	.02
☐ 36 Kevin Wickander	.05	.02	.01
☐ 37 Carlos Hernandez	.05	.02	.01
☐ 38 Brian Traxler	.05	.02	.01
☐ 39 Marty Brown	.05	.02	.01
☐ 40 Scott Radinsky	.05	.02	.01
☐ 41 Julio Machado	.05	.02	.01
☐ 42 Steve Avery	.15	.07	.02
☐ 43 Mark Lemke	.15	.07	.02
☐ 44 Alan Mills	.05	.02	.01
☐ 45 Marquis Grissom	.60	.25	.07
☐ 46 Greg Olson	.05	.02	.01
☐ 47 Dave Hollins	.15	.07	.02
☐ 48 Jerald Clark	.05	.02	.01
☐ 49 Eric Anthony	.15	.07	.02
☐ 50 Tim Drummond	.05	.02	.01
☐ 51 John Burkett	.15	.07	.02
☐ 52 Brent Knackert	.05	.02	.01
☐ 53 Jeff Shaw	.05	.02	.01
☐ 54 John Orton	.05	.02	.01
☐ 55 Terry Shumpert	.05	.02	.01
☐ 56 Checklist 1-56	.05	.02	.01

1991 Donruss

The 1991 Donruss set was issued in two series of 386 and 384 for a total of 770 standard-size cards. This set marked the first time Donruss issued cards in multiple series. The second series was issued approximately three months after the first series was issued. Cards were issued in wax packs and factory sets. As a separate promotion, wax packs were also given away with six and 12-packs of Coke and Diet Coke. First series cards feature blue borders and second series green borders with some stripes and the players name in white against a red background. Subsets include Diamond Kings (1-27), Rated Rookies (28-47/413-432), AL All-Stars (48-56), MVP's (387-412) and NL All-Stars (433-441). There were also special cards to honor the award winners and the heroes of the World Series. Rookie Cards in the set include Jeff Conine and Brian McRae. On cards 60, 70, 127, 182, 239, 294, 355, 368, and 377, the border stripes are red and yellow.

	MINT	NRMT	EXC
COMPLETE SET (770)	8.00	3.60	1.00
COMP.FACT.w/LEAF PREV	12.00	5.50	1.50
COMP.FACT.w/STUDIO PREV	12.00	5.50	1.50
COMMON CARD (1-770)	.05	.02	.01
SEMISTARS	.10	.05	.01
STARS	.15	.07	.02
COMP.BONUS CARDS (22)	1.50	.70	.19
COMP.GRANDSLAMMERS (14)	2.00	.90	.25
☐ 1 Dave Stieb DK	.05	.02	.01
☐ 2 Craig Biggio DK	.15	.07	.02
☐ 3 Cecil Fielder DK	.10	.05	.01
☐ 4 Barry Bonds DK	.15	.07	.02
☐ 5 Barry Larkin DK	.15	.07	.02
☐ 6 Dave Parker DK	.10	.05	.01
☐ 7 Len Dykstra DK	.10	.05	.01
☐ 8 Bobby Thigpen DK	.05	.02	.01
☐ 9 Roger Clemens DK	.15	.07	.02
☐ 10 Ron Gant DK UER (No trademark on team logo on back)	.15	.07	.02
☐ 11 Delino DeShields DK	.05	.02	.01
☐ 12 Roberto Alomar DK UER (No trademark on team logo on back)	.15	.07	.02
☐ 13 Sandy Alomar Jr. DK	.05	.02	.01
☐ 14 Ryne Sandberg DK UER (Was DK in '85, not '83 as shown)	.15	.07	.02
☐ 15 Ramon Martinez DK	.10	.05	.01
☐ 16 Edgar Martinez DK	.15	.07	.02
☐ 17 Dave Magadan DK	.05	.02	.01
☐ 18 Matt Williams DK	.15	.07	.02
☐ 19 Rafael Palmeiro DK UER (No trademark on team logo on back)	.15	.07	.02
☐ 20 Bob Welch DK	.05	.02	.01
☐ 21 Dave Righetti DK	.05	.02	.01
☐ 22 Brian Harper DK	.05	.02	.01
☐ 23 Gregg Olson DK	.05	.02	.01
☐ 24 Kurt Stillwell DK	.05	.02	.01
☐ 25 Pedro Guerrero DK UER (No trademark on team logo on back)	.05	.02	.01
☐ 26 Chuck Finley DK UER (No trademark on team logo on back)	.05	.02	.01
☐ 27 DK Checklist 1-27	.05	.02	.01
☐ 28 Tino Martinez RR	.15	.07	.02

□ 29 Mark Lewis RR	.05	.02	.01
□ 30 Bernard Gilkey RR	.15	.07	.02
□ 31 Hensley Meulens RR	.05	.02	.01
□ 32 Derek Bell RR	.15	.07	.02
□ 33 Jose Offerman RR	.05	.02	.01
□ 34 Terry Bross RR	.05	.02	.01
□ 35 Leo Gomez RR	.05	.02	.01
□ 36 Derrick May RR	.05	.02	.01
□ 37 Kevin Morton RR	.05	.02	.01
□ 38 Moises Alou RR	.15	.07	.02
□ 39 Julio Valera RR	.05	.02	.01
□ 40 Milt Cuyler RR	.05	.02	.01
□ 41 Phil Plantier RR	.10	.05	.01
□ 42 Scott Chiamparino RR	.05	.02	.01
□ 43 Ray Lankford RR	.15	.07	.02
□ 44 Mickey Morandini RR	.05	.02	.01
□ 45 Dave Hansen RR	.05	.02	.01
□ 46 Kevin Belcher RR	.05	.02	.01
□ 47 Darrin Fletcher RR	.05	.02	.01
□ 48 Steve Sax AS	.05	.02	.01
□ 49 Ken Griffey Jr. AS	.75	.35	.09
□ 50A Jose Canseco AS ERR	.15	.07	.02
(Team in stat box			
should be AL, not A's)			
□ 50B Jose Canseco AS COR	.75	.35	.09
□ 51 Sandy Alomar Jr. AS	.05	.02	.01
□ 52 Cal Ripken AS	.40	.18	.05
□ 53 Rickey Henderson AS	.15	.07	.02
□ 54 Bob Welch AS	.05	.02	.01
□ 55 Wade Boggs AS	.15	.07	.02
□ 56 Mark McGwire AS	.15	.07	.02
□ 57A Jack McDowell ERR	.15	.07	.02
(Career stats do			
not include 1990)			
□ 57B Jack McDowell COR	.25	.11	.03
(Career stats do			
not include 1990)			
□ 58 Jose Lind	.05	.02	.01
□ 59 Alex Fernandez	.15	.07	.02
□ 60 Pat Combs	.05	.02	.01
□ 61 Mike Walker	.05	.02	.01
□ 62 Juan Samuel	.05	.02	.01
□ 63 Mike Blowers UER	.05	.02	.01
(Last line has			
aseball, not baseball)			
□ 64 Mark Guthrie	.05	.02	.01
□ 65 Mark Salas	.05	.02	.01
□ 66 Tim Jones	.05	.02	.01
□ 67 Tim Leary	.05	.02	.01
□ 68 Andres Galarraga	.15	.07	.02
□ 69 Bob Milacki	.05	.02	.01
□ 70 Tim Belcher	.05	.02	.01
□ 71 Todd Zeile	.10	.05	.01
□ 72 Jerome Walton	.05	.02	.01
□ 73 Kevin Seitzer	.05	.02	.01
□ 74 Jerald Clark	.05	.02	.01
□ 75 John Smoltz UER	.15	.07	.02
(Born in Detroit,			
not Warren)			
□ 76 Mike Henneman	.05	.02	.01
□ 77 Ken Griffey Jr.	1.50	.70	.19
□ 78 Jim Abbott	.10	.05	.01
□ 79 Gregg Jefferies	.15	.07	.02
□ 80 Kevin Reimer	.05	.02	.01
□ 81 Roger Clemens	.15	.07	.02
□ 82 Mike Fitzgerald	.05	.02	.01
□ 83 Bruce Hurst UER	.05	.02	.01
(Middle name is			
Lee, not Vee)			
□ 84 Eric Davis	.10	.05	.01
□ 85 Paul Molitor	.20	.09	.03
□ 86 Will Clark	.15	.07	.02
□ 87 Mike Bielecki	.05	.02	.01
□ 88 Bret Saberhagen	.10	.05	.01
□ 89 Nolan Ryan	.75	.35	.09
□ 90 Bobby Thigpen	.05	.02	.01
□ 91 Dickie Thon	.05	.02	.01
□ 92 Duane Ward	.05	.02	.01
□ 93 Luis Polonia	.05	.02	.01
□ 94 Terry Kennedy	.05	.02	.01
□ 95 Kent Hrbek	.10	.05	.01
□ 96 Danny Jackson	.05	.02	.01
□ 97 Sid Fernandez	.05	.02	.01
□ 98 Jimmy Key	.10	.05	.01
□ 99 Franklin Stubbs	.05	.02	.01
□ 100 Checklist 28-103	.05	.02	.01

□ 101 R.J. Reynolds	.05	.02	.01
□ 102 Dave Stewart	.10	.05	.01
□ 103 Dan Pasqua	.05	.02	.01
□ 104 Dan Plesac	.05	.02	.01
□ 105 Mark McGwire	.30	.14	.04
□ 106 John Farrell	.05	.02	.01
□ 107 Don Mattingly	.50	.23	.06
□ 108 Carlton Fisk	.15	.07	.02
□ 109 Ken Oberkfell	.05	.02	.01
□ 110 Darrel Akerfelds	.05	.02	.01
□ 111 Gregg Olson	.05	.02	.01
□ 112 Mike Scioscia	.05	.02	.01
□ 113 Bryn Smith	.05	.02	.01
□ 114 Bob Geren	.05	.02	.01
□ 115 Tom Candiotti	.05	.02	.01
□ 116 Kevin Tapani	.05	.02	.01
□ 117 Jeff Treadway	.05	.02	.01
□ 118 Alan Trammell	.15	.07	.02
□ 119 Pete O'Brien	.05	.02	.01
(Blue shading goes			
through stats)			
□ 120 Joel Skinner	.05	.02	.01
□ 121 Mike LaValliere	.05	.02	.01
□ 122 Dwight Evans	.10	.05	.01
□ 123 Jody Reed	.05	.02	.01
□ 124 Lee Guetterman	.05	.02	.01
□ 125 Tim Burke	.05	.02	.01
□ 126 Dave Johnson	.05	.02	.01
□ 127 Fernando Valenzuela	.10	.05	.01
(Lower large stripe			
in yellow instead			
of blue) UER			
□ 128 Jose DeLeon	.05	.02	.01
□ 129 Andre Dawson	.15	.07	.02
□ 130 Gerald Perry	.05	.02	.01
□ 131 Greg W. Harris	.05	.02	.01
□ 132 Tom Glavine	.15	.07	.02
□ 133 Lance McCullers	.05	.02	.01
□ 134 Randy Johnson	.15	.07	.02
□ 135 Lance Parrish UER	.05	.02	.01
(Born in McKeesport,			
not Clairton)			
□ 136 Mackey Sasser	.05	.02	.01
□ 137 Geno Petralli	.05	.02	.01
□ 138 Dennis Lamp	.05	.02	.01
□ 139 Dennis Martinez	.10	.05	.01
□ 140 Mike Pagliarulo	.05	.02	.01
□ 141 Hal Morris	.05	.02	.01
□ 142 Dave Parker	.10	.05	.01
□ 143 Brett Butler	.10	.05	.01
□ 144 Paul Assenmacher	.05	.02	.01
□ 145 Mark Gubicza	.05	.02	.01
□ 146 Charlie Hough	.05	.02	.01
□ 147 Sammy Sosa	.25	.11	.03
□ 148 Randy Ready	.05	.02	.01
□ 149 Kelly Gruber	.05	.02	.01
□ 150 Devon White	.10	.05	.01
□ 151 Gary Carter	.15	.07	.02
□ 152 Gene Larkin	.05	.02	.01
□ 153 Chris Sabo	.05	.02	.01
□ 154 David Cone	.15	.07	.02
□ 155 Todd Stottlemyre	.05	.02	.01
□ 156 Glenn Wilson	.05	.02	.01
□ 157 Bob Walk	.05	.02	.01
□ 158 Mike Gallego	.05	.02	.01
□ 159 Greg Hibbard	.05	.02	.01
□ 160 Chris Bosio	.05	.02	.01
□ 161 Mike Moore	.05	.02	.01
□ 162 Jerry Browne UER	.05	.02	.01
(Born Christiansted,			
should be St. Croix)			
□ 163 Steve Sax UER	.05	.02	.01
(No asterisk next to			
his 1989 At Bats)			
□ 164 Melido Perez	.05	.02	.01
□ 165 Danny Darwin	.05	.02	.01
□ 166 Roger McDowell	.05	.02	.01
□ 167 Bill Ripken	.05	.02	.01
□ 168 Mike Sharperson	.05	.02	.01
□ 169 Lee Smith	.10	.05	.01
□ 170 Matt Nokes	.05	.02	.01
□ 171 Jesse Orosco	.05	.02	.01
□ 172 Rick Aguilera	.10	.05	.01
□ 173 Jim Presley	.05	.02	.01
□ 174 Lou Whitaker	.15	.07	.02
□ 175 Harold Reynolds	.05	.02	.01

☐ 176 Brook Jacoby	.05	.02	.01
☐ 177 Wally Backman	.05	.02	.01
☐ 178 Wade Boggs	.15	.07	.02
☐ 179 Chuck Cary (Comma after DOB, not on other cards)	.05	.02	.01
☐ 180 Tom Foley	.05	.02	.01
☐ 181 Pete Harnisch	.05	.02	.01
☐ 182 Mike Morgan	.05	.02	.01
☐ 183 Bob Tewksbury	.05	.02	.01
☐ 184 Joe Girardi	.10	.05	.01
☐ 185 Storm Davis	.05	.02	.01
☐ 186 Ed Whitson	.05	.02	.01
☐ 187 Steve Avery UER (Born in New Jersey, should be Michigan)	.15	.07	.02
☐ 188 Lloyd Moseby	.05	.02	.01
☐ 189 Scott Bankhead	.05	.02	.01
☐ 190 Mark Langston	.10	.05	.01
☐ 191 Kevin McReynolds	.05	.02	.01
☐ 192 Julio Franco	.10	.05	.01
☐ 193 John Dopson	.05	.02	.01
☐ 194 Dennis Boyd	.05	.02	.01
☐ 195 Bip Roberts	.05	.02	.01
☐ 196 Billy Hatcher	.05	.02	.01
☐ 197 Edgar Diaz	.05	.02	.01
☐ 198 Greg Litton	.05	.02	.01
☐ 199 Mark Grace	.15	.07	.02
☐ 200 Checklist 104-179	.05	.02	.01
☐ 201 George Brett	.40	.18	.05
☐ 202 Jeff Russell	.05	.02	.01
☐ 203 Ivan Calderon	.05	.02	.01
☐ 204 Ken Howell	.05	.02	.01
☐ 205 Tom Henke	.05	.02	.01
☐ 206 Bryan Harvey	.05	.02	.01
☐ 207 Steve Bedrosian	.05	.02	.01
☐ 208 Al Newman	.05	.02	.01
☐ 209 Randy Myers	.10	.05	.01
☐ 210 Daryl Boston	.05	.02	.01
☐ 211 Manny Lee	.05	.02	.01
☐ 212 Dave Smith	.05	.02	.01
☐ 213 Don Slaught	.05	.02	.01
☐ 214 Walt Weiss	.05	.02	.01
☐ 215 Donn Pall	.05	.02	.01
☐ 216 Jaime Navarro	.05	.02	.01
☐ 217 Willie Randolph	.10	.05	.01
☐ 218 Rudy Seanez	.05	.02	.01
☐ 219 Jim Leyritz	.10	.05	.01
☐ 220 Ron Karkovice	.05	.02	.01
☐ 221 Ken Caminiti	.15	.07	.02
☐ 222 Von Hayes	.05	.02	.01
☐ 223 Cal Ripken	.75	.35	.09
☐ 224 Lenny Harris	.05	.02	.01
☐ 225 Milt Thompson	.05	.02	.01
☐ 226 Alvaro Espinoza	.05	.02	.01
☐ 227 Chris James	.05	.02	.01
☐ 228 Dan Gladden	.05	.02	.01
☐ 229 Jeff Blauser	.05	.02	.01
☐ 230 Mike Heath	.05	.02	.01
☐ 231 Omar Vizquel	.15	.07	.02
☐ 232 Doug Jones	.05	.02	.01
☐ 233 Jeff King	.10	.05	.01
☐ 234 Luis Rivera	.05	.02	.01
☐ 235 Ellis Burks	.15	.07	.02
☐ 236 Greg Cadaret	.05	.02	.01
☐ 237 Dave Martinez	.05	.02	.01
☐ 238 Mark Williamson	.05	.02	.01
☐ 239 Stan Javier	.05	.02	.01
☐ 240 Ozzie Smith	.20	.09	.03
☐ 241 Shawn Boskie	.05	.02	.01
☐ 242 Tom Gordon	.05	.02	.01
☐ 243 Tony Gwynn	.40	.18	.05
☐ 244 Tommy Gregg	.05	.02	.01
☐ 245 Jeff M. Robinson	.05	.02	.01
☐ 246 Keith Comstock	.05	.02	.01
☐ 247 Jack Howell	.05	.02	.01
☐ 248 Keith Miller	.05	.02	.01
☐ 249 Bobby Witt	.05	.02	.01
☐ 250 Rob Murphy UER (Shown as on Reds in '89 in stats, should be Red Sox)	.05	.02	.01
☐ 251 Spike Owen	.05	.02	.01
☐ 252 Garry Templeton	.05	.02	.01
☐ 253 Glenn Braggs	.05	.02	.01
☐ 254 Ron Robinson	.05	.02	.01
☐ 255 Kevin Mitchell	.10	.05	.01
☐ 256 Les Lancaster	.05	.02	.01
☐ 257 Mel Stottlemyre Jr.	.05	.02	.01
☐ 258 Kenny Rogers UER (IP listed as 171, should be 172)	.05	.02	.01
☐ 259 Lance Johnson	.10	.05	.01
☐ 260 John Kruk	.10	.05	.01
☐ 261 Fred McGriff	.15	.07	.02
☐ 262 Dick Schofield	.05	.02	.01
☐ 263 Trevor Wilson	.05	.02	.01
☐ 264 David West	.05	.02	.01
☐ 265 Scott Scudder	.05	.02	.01
☐ 266 Dwight Gooden	.10	.05	.01
☐ 267 Willie Blair	.05	.02	.01
☐ 268 Mark Portugal	.05	.02	.01
☐ 269 Doug Drabek	.05	.02	.01
☐ 270 Dennis Eckersley	.10	.05	.01
☐ 271 Eric King	.05	.02	.01
☐ 272 Robin Yount	.15	.07	.02
☐ 273 Carney Lansford	.10	.05	.01
☐ 274 Carlos Baerga	.15	.07	.02
☐ 275 Dave Righetti	.05	.02	.01
☐ 276 Scott Fletcher	.05	.02	.01
☐ 277 Eric Yelding	.05	.02	.01
☐ 278 Charlie Hayes	.05	.02	.01
☐ 279 Jeff Ballard	.05	.02	.01
☐ 280 Orel Hershiser	.10	.05	.01
☐ 281 Jose Oquendo	.05	.02	.01
☐ 282 Mike Witt	.05	.02	.01
☐ 283 Mitch Webster	.05	.02	.01
☐ 284 Greg Gagne	.05	.02	.01
☐ 285 Greg Olson	.05	.02	.01
☐ 286 Tony Phillips UER (Born 4/15, should be 4/25)	.10	.05	.01
☐ 287 Scott Bradley	.05	.02	.01
☐ 288 Cory Snyder UER (In text, led is repeated and Inglewood is misspelled as Englewood)	.05	.02	.01
☐ 289 Jay Bell UER (Born in Pensacola, not Eglin AFB)	.10	.05	.01
☐ 290 Kevin Romine	.05	.02	.01
☐ 291 Jeff D. Robinson	.05	.02	.01
☐ 292 Steve Frey UER (Bats left, should be right)	.05	.02	.01
☐ 293 Craig Worthington	.05	.02	.01
☐ 294 Tim Crews	.05	.02	.01
☐ 295 Joe Magrane	.05	.02	.01
☐ 296 Hector Villanueva	.05	.02	.01
☐ 297 Terry Shumpert	.05	.02	.01
☐ 298 Joe Carter	.15	.07	.02
☐ 299 Kent Mercker UER (IP listed as 53, should be 52)	.05	.02	.01
☐ 300 Checklist 180-255	.05	.02	.01
☐ 301 Chet Lemon	.05	.02	.01
☐ 302 Mike Schooler	.05	.02	.01
☐ 303 Dante Bichette	.15	.07	.02
☐ 304 Kevin Elster	.05	.02	.01
☐ 305 Jeff Huson	.05	.02	.01
☐ 306 Greg A. Harris	.05	.02	.01
☐ 307 Marquis Grissom UER (Middle name Deon, should be Dean)	.15	.07	.02
☐ 308 Calvin Schiraldi	.05	.02	.01
☐ 309 Mariano Duncan	.05	.02	.01
☐ 310 Bill Spiers	.05	.02	.01
☐ 311 Scott Garrelts	.05	.02	.01
☐ 312 Mitch Williams	.05	.02	.01
☐ 313 Mike Macfarlane	.05	.02	.01
☐ 314 Kevin Brown	.10	.05	.01
☐ 315 Robin Ventura	.15	.07	.02
☐ 316 Darren Daulton	.10	.05	.01
☐ 317 Pat Borders	.05	.02	.01
☐ 318 Mark Eichhorn	.05	.02	.01
☐ 319 Jeff Brantley	.05	.02	.01
☐ 320 Shane Mack	.05	.02	.01
☐ 321 Rob Dibble	.05	.02	.01
☐ 322 John Franco	.05	.02	.01
☐ 323 Junior Felix	.05	.02	.01
☐ 324 Casey Candaele	.05	.02	.01
☐ 325 Bobby Bonilla	.10	.05	.01

□ 326 Dave Henderson	.05	.02	.01
□ 327 Wayne Edwards	.05	.02	.01
□ 328 Mark Knudson	.05	.02	.01
□ 329 Terry Steinbach	.10	.05	.01
□ 330 Colby Ward UER (No comma between city and state)	.05	.02	.01
□ 331 Oscar Azocar	.05	.02	.01
□ 332 Scott Radinsky	.05	.02	.01
□ 333 Eric Anthony	.05	.02	.01
□ 334 Steve Lake	.05	.02	.01
□ 335 Bob Melvin	.05	.02	.01
□ 336 Kal Daniels	.05	.02	.01
□ 337 Tom Pagnozzi	.05	.02	.01
□ 338 Alan Mills	.05	.02	.01
□ 339 Steve Olin	.05	.02	.01
□ 340 Juan Berenguer	.05	.02	.01
□ 341 Francisco Cabrera	.05	.02	.01
□ 342 Dave Bergman	.05	.02	.01
□ 343 Henry Cotto	.05	.02	.01
□ 344 Sergio Valdez	.05	.02	.01
□ 345 Bob Patterson	.05	.02	.01
□ 346 John Marzano	.05	.02	.01
□ 347 Dana Kiecker	.05	.02	.01
□ 348 Dion James	.05	.02	.01
□ 349 Hubie Brooks	.05	.02	.01
□ 350 Bill Landrum	.05	.02	.01
□ 351 Bill Sampen	.05	.02	.01
□ 352 Greg Briley	.05	.02	.01
□ 353 Paul Gibson	.05	.02	.01
□ 354 Dave Eiland	.05	.02	.01
□ 355 Steve Finley	.15	.07	.02
□ 356 Bob Boone	.10	.05	.01
□ 357 Steve Buechele	.05	.02	.01
□ 358 Chris Hoiles	.05	.02	.01
□ 359 Larry Walker	.15	.07	.02
□ 360 Frank DiPino	.05	.02	.01
□ 361 Mark Grant	.05	.02	.01
□ 362 Dave Magadan	.05	.02	.01
□ 363 Robby Thompson	.05	.02	.01
□ 364 Lonnie Smith	.05	.02	.01
□ 365 Steve Farr	.05	.02	.01
□ 366 Dave Valle	.05	.02	.01
□ 367 Tim Naehring	.10	.05	.01
□ 368 Jim Acker	.05	.02	.01
□ 369 Jeff Reardon UER (Born in Pittsfield, not Dalton)	.10	.05	.01
□ 370 Tim Teufel	.05	.02	.01
□ 371 Juan Gonzalez	.75	.35	.09
□ 372 Luis Salazar	.05	.02	.01
□ 373 Rick Honeycutt	.05	.02	.01
□ 374 Greg Maddux	.60	.25	.07
□ 375 Jose Uribe UER (Middle name Elta, should be Alta)	.05	.02	.01
□ 376 Donnie Hill	.05	.02	.01
□ 377 Don Carman	.05	.02	.01
□ 378 Craig Grebeck	.05	.02	.01
□ 379 Willie Fraser	.05	.02	.01
□ 380 Glenallen Hill	.05	.02	.01
□ 381 Joe Oliver	.05	.02	.01
□ 382 Randy Bush	.05	.02	.01
□ 383 Alex Cole	.05	.02	.01
□ 384 Norm Charlton	.05	.02	.01
□ 385 Gene Nelson	.05	.02	.01
□ 386 Checklist 256-331	.05	.02	.01
□ 387 Rickey Henderson MVP	.15	.07	.02
□ 388 Lance Parrish MVP	.05	.02	.01
□ 389 Fred McGriff MVP	.10	.05	.01
□ 390 Dave Parker MVP	.10	.05	.01
□ 391 Candy Maldonado MVP	.05	.02	.01
□ 392 Ken Griffey Jr. MVP	.75	.35	.09
□ 393 Gregg Olson MVP	.05	.02	.01
□ 394 Rafael Palmeiro MVP	.15	.07	.02
□ 395 Roger Clemens MVP	.15	.07	.02
□ 396 George Brett MVP	.20	.09	.03
□ 397 Cecil Fielder MVP	.10	.05	.01
□ 398 Brian Harper MVP UER (Major League Performance, should be Career)	.05	.02	.01
□ 399 Bobby Thigpen MVP	.05	.02	.01
□ 400 Roberto Kelly MVP UER (Second Base on front and OF on back)	.05	.02	.01
□ 401 Danny Darwin MVP	.05	.02	.01
□ 402 Dave Justice MVP	.10	.05	.01
□ 403 Lee Smith MVP	.10	.05	.01
□ 404 Ryne Sandberg MVP	.15	.07	.02
□ 405 Eddie Murray MVP	.15	.07	.02
□ 406 Tim Wallach MVP	.05	.02	.01
□ 407 Kevin Mitchell MVP	.05	.02	.01
□ 408 Darryl Strawberry MVP	.10	.05	.01
□ 409 Joe Carter MVP	.15	.07	.02
□ 410 Len Dykstra MVP	.10	.05	.01
□ 411 Doug Drabek MVP	.05	.02	.01
□ 412 Chris Sabo MVP	.05	.02	.01
□ 413 Paul Marak RR	.05	.02	.01
□ 414 Tim McIntosh RR	.05	.02	.01
□ 415 Brian Barnes RR	.05	.02	.01
□ 416 Eric Gunderson RR	.05	.02	.01
□ 417 Mike Gardiner RR	.05	.02	.01
□ 418 Steve Carter RR	.05	.02	.01
□ 419 Gerald Alexander RR	.05	.02	.01
□ 420 Rich Garces RR	.05	.02	.01
□ 421 Chuck Knoblauch RR	.25	.11	.03
□ 422 Scott Aldred RR	.05	.02	.01
□ 423 Wes Chamberlain RR	.05	.02	.01
□ 424 Lance Dickson RR	.05	.02	.01
□ 425 Greg Colbrunn RR	.10	.05	.01
□ 426 Rich DeLucia RR UER (Misspelled Delucia on card)	.05	.02	.01
□ 427 Jeff Conine RR	.50	.23	.06
□ 428 Steve Decker RR	.05	.02	.01
□ 429 Turner Ward RR	.05	.02	.01
□ 430 Mo Vaughn RR	.50	.23	.06
□ 431 Steve Chitren RR	.05	.02	.01
□ 432 Mike Benjamin RR	.05	.02	.01
□ 433 Ryne Sandberg AS	.15	.07	.02
□ 434 Len Dykstra AS	.10	.05	.01
□ 435 Andre Dawson AS	.15	.07	.02
□ 436A Mike Scioscia AS (White star by name)	.05	.02	.01
□ 436B Mike Scioscia AS (Yellow star by name)	.05	.02	.01
□ 437 Ozzie Smith AS	.15	.07	.02
□ 438 Kevin Mitchell AS	.05	.02	.01
□ 439 Jack Armstrong AS	.05	.02	.01
□ 440 Chris Sabo AS	.05	.02	.01
□ 441 Will Clark AS	.15	.07	.02
□ 442 Mel Hall	.05	.02	.01
□ 443 Mark Gardner	.05	.02	.01
□ 444 Mike Devereaux	.05	.02	.01
□ 445 Kirk Gibson	.10	.05	.01
□ 446 Terry Pendleton	.10	.05	.01
□ 447 Mike Harkey	.05	.02	.01
□ 448 Jim Eisenreich	.10	.05	.01
□ 449 Benito Santiago	.05	.02	.01
□ 450 Oddibe McDowell	.05	.02	.01
□ 451 Cecil Fielder	.10	.05	.01
□ 452 Ken Griffey Sr.	.05	.02	.01
□ 453 Bert Blyleven	.10	.05	.01
□ 454 Howard Johnson	.05	.02	.01
□ 455 Monty Fariss UER (Misspelled Farris on card)	.05	.02	.01
□ 456 Tony Pena	.05	.02	.01
□ 457 Tim Raines	.15	.07	.02
□ 458 Dennis Rasmussen	.05	.02	.01
□ 459 Luis Quinones	.05	.02	.01
□ 460 B.J. Surhoff	.10	.05	.01
□ 461 Ernest Riles	.05	.02	.01
□ 462 Rick Sutcliffe	.05	.02	.01
□ 463 Danny Tartabull	.05	.02	.01
□ 464 Pete Incaviglia	.05	.02	.01
□ 465 Carlos Martinez	.05	.02	.01
□ 466 Ricky Jordan	.05	.02	.01
□ 467 John Cerutti	.05	.02	.01
□ 468 Dave Winfield	.15	.07	.02
□ 469 Francisco Oliveras	.05	.02	.01
□ 470 Roy Smith	.05	.02	.01
□ 471 Barry Larkin	.15	.07	.02
□ 472 Ron Darling	.05	.02	.01
□ 473 David Wells	.05	.02	.01
□ 474 Glenn Davis	.05	.02	.01
□ 475 Neal Heaton	.05	.02	.01
□ 476 Ron Hassey	.05	.02	.01
□ 477 Frank Thomas	2.00	.90	.25
□ 478 Greg Vaughn	.15	.07	.02
□ 479 Todd Burns	.05	.02	.01

☐ 480	Candy Maldonado	.05	.02	.01
☐ 481	Dave LaPoint	.05	.02	.01
☐ 482	Alvin Davis	.05	.02	.01
☐ 483	Mike Scott	.05	.02	.01
☐ 484	Dale Murphy	.15	.07	.02
☐ 485	Ben McDonald	.10	.05	.01
☐ 486	Jay Howell	.05	.02	.01
☐ 487	Vince Coleman	.05	.02	.01
☐ 488	Alfredo Griffin	.05	.02	.01
☐ 489	Sandy Alomar Jr.	.10	.05	.01
☐ 490	Kirby Puckett	.30	.14	.04
☐ 491	Andres Thomas	.05	.02	.01
☐ 492	Jack Morris	.10	.05	.01
☐ 493	Matt Young	.05	.02	.01
☐ 494	Greg Myers	.05	.02	.01
☐ 495	Barry Bonds	.25	.11	.03
☐ 496	Scott Cooper UER (No BA for 1990 and career)	.05	.02	.01
☐ 497	Dan Schatzeder	.05	.02	.01
☐ 498	Jesse Barfield	.05	.02	.01
☐ 499	Jerry Goff	.05	.02	.01
☐ 500	Checklist 332-408	.05	.02	.01
☐ 501	Anthony Telford	.05	.02	.01
☐ 502	Eddie Murray	.25	.11	.03
☐ 503	Omar Olivares	.05	.02	.01
☐ 504	Ryne Sandberg	.25	.11	.03
☐ 505	Jeff Montgomery	.10	.05	.01
☐ 506	Mark Parent	.05	.02	.01
☐ 507	Ron Gant	.15	.07	.02
☐ 508	Frank Tanana	.05	.02	.01
☐ 509	Jay Buhner	.15	.07	.02
☐ 510	Max Venable	.05	.02	.01
☐ 511	Wally Whitehurst	.05	.02	.01
☐ 512	Gary Pettis	.05	.02	.01
☐ 513	Tom Brunansky	.05	.02	.01
☐ 514	Tim Wallach	.05	.02	.01
☐ 515	Craig Lefferts	.05	.02	.01
☐ 516	Tim Layana	.05	.02	.01
☐ 517	Darryl Hamilton	.10	.05	.01
☐ 518	Rick Reuschel	.05	.02	.01
☐ 519	Steve Wilson	.05	.02	.01
☐ 520	Kurt Stillwell	.05	.02	.01
☐ 521	Rafael Palmeiro	.15	.07	.02
☐ 522	Ken Patterson	.05	.02	.01
☐ 523	Len Dykstra	.10	.05	.01
☐ 524	Tony Fernandez	.05	.02	.01
☐ 525	Kent Anderson	.05	.02	.01
☐ 526	Mark Leonard	.05	.02	.01
☐ 527	Allan Anderson	.05	.02	.01
☐ 528	Tom Browning	.05	.02	.01
☐ 529	Frank Viola	.05	.02	.01
☐ 530	John Olerud	.10	.05	.01
☐ 531	Juan Agosto	.05	.02	.01
☐ 532	Zane Smith	.05	.02	.01
☐ 533	Scott Sanderson	.05	.02	.01
☐ 534	Barry Jones	.05	.02	.01
☐ 535	Mike Felder	.05	.02	.01
☐ 536	Jose Canseco	.15	.07	.02
☐ 537	Felix Fermin	.05	.02	.01
☐ 538	Roberto Kelly	.05	.02	.01
☐ 539	Brian Holman	.05	.02	.01
☐ 540	Mark Davidson	.05	.02	.01
☐ 541	Terry Mulholland	.05	.02	.01
☐ 542	Randy Milligan	.05	.02	.01
☐ 543	Jose Gonzalez	.05	.02	.01
☐ 544	Craig Wilson	.05	.02	.01
☐ 545	Mike Hartley	.05	.02	.01
☐ 546	Greg Swindell	.05	.02	.01
☐ 547	Gary Gaetti	.10	.05	.01
☐ 548	Dave Justice	.15	.07	.02
☐ 549	Steve Searcy	.05	.02	.01
☐ 550	Erik Hanson	.05	.02	.01
☐ 551	Dave Stieb	.05	.02	.01
☐ 552	Andy Van Slyke	.10	.05	.01
☐ 553	Mike Greenwell	.05	.02	.01
☐ 554	Kevin Maas	.05	.02	.01
☐ 555	Delino DeShields	.05	.02	.01
☐ 556	Curt Schilling	.05	.02	.01
☐ 557	Ramon Martinez	.10	.05	.01
☐ 558	Pedro Guerrero	.05	.02	.01
☐ 559	Dwight Smith	.05	.02	.01
☐ 560	Mark Davis	.05	.02	.01
☐ 561	Shawn Abner	.05	.02	.01
☐ 562	Charlie Leibrandt	.05	.02	.01
☐ 563	John Shelby	.05	.02	.01
☐ 564	Bill Swift	.05	.02	.01
☐ 565	Mike Fetters	.05	.02	.01
☐ 566	Alejandro Pena	.05	.02	.01
☐ 567	Ruben Sierra	.10	.05	.01
☐ 568	Carlos Quintana	.05	.02	.01
☐ 569	Kevin Gross	.05	.02	.01
☐ 570	Derek Lilliquist	.05	.02	.01
☐ 571	Jack Armstrong	.05	.02	.01
☐ 572	Greg Brock	.05	.02	.01
☐ 573	Mike Kingery	.05	.02	.01
☐ 574	Greg Smith	.05	.02	.01
☐ 575	Brian McRae	.25	.11	.03
☐ 576	Jack Daugherty	.05	.02	.01
☐ 577	Ozzie Guillen	.05	.02	.01
☐ 578	Joe Boever	.05	.02	.01
☐ 579	Luis Sojo	.05	.02	.01
☐ 580	Chili Davis	.10	.05	.01
☐ 581	Don Robinson	.05	.02	.01
☐ 582	Brian Harper	.05	.02	.01
☐ 583	Paul O'Neill	.10	.05	.01
☐ 584	Bob Ojeda	.05	.02	.01
☐ 585	Mookie Wilson	.05	.02	.01
☐ 586	Rafael Ramirez	.05	.02	.01
☐ 587	Gary Redus	.05	.02	.01
☐ 588	Jamie Quirk	.05	.02	.01
☐ 589	Shawn Hillegas	.05	.02	.01
☐ 590	Tom Edens	.05	.02	.01
☐ 591	Joe Klink	.05	.02	.01
☐ 592	Charles Nagy	.10	.05	.01
☐ 593	Eric Plunk	.05	.02	.01
☐ 594	Tracy Jones	.05	.02	.01
☐ 595	Craig Biggio	.15	.07	.02
☐ 596	Jose DeJesus	.05	.02	.01
☐ 597	Mickey Tettleton	.10	.05	.01
☐ 598	Chris Gwynn	.05	.02	.01
☐ 599	Rex Hudler	.05	.02	.01
☐ 600	Checklist 409-506	.05	.02	.01
☐ 601	Jim Gott	.05	.02	.01
☐ 602	Jeff Manto	.05	.02	.01
☐ 603	Nelson Liriano	.05	.02	.01
☐ 604	Mark Lemke	.05	.02	.01
☐ 605	Clay Parker	.05	.02	.01
☐ 606	Edgar Martinez	.15	.07	.02
☐ 607	Mark Whiten	.10	.05	.01
☐ 608	Ted Power	.05	.02	.01
☐ 609	Tom Bolton	.05	.02	.01
☐ 610	Tom Herr	.05	.02	.01
☐ 611	Andy Hawkins UER (Pitched No-Hitter on 7/1, not 7/2)	.05	.02	.01
☐ 612	Scott Ruskin	.05	.02	.01
☐ 613	Ron Kittle	.05	.02	.01
☐ 614	John Wetteland	.10	.05	.01
☐ 615	Mike Perez	.05	.02	.01
☐ 616	Dave Clark	.05	.02	.01
☐ 617	Brent Mayne	.05	.02	.01
☐ 618	Jack Clark	.10	.05	.01
☐ 619	Marvin Freeman	.05	.02	.01
☐ 620	Edwin Nunez	.05	.02	.01
☐ 621	Russ Swan	.05	.02	.01
☐ 622	Johnny Ray	.05	.02	.01
☐ 623	Charlie O'Brien	.05	.02	.01
☐ 624	Joe Bitker	.05	.02	.01
☐ 625	Mike Marshall	.05	.02	.01
☐ 626	Otis Nixon	.05	.02	.01
☐ 627	Andy Benes	.05	.02	.01
☐ 628	Ron Oester	.05	.02	.01
☐ 629	Ted Higuera	.05	.02	.01
☐ 630	Kevin Bass	.05	.02	.01
☐ 631	Damon Berryhill	.05	.02	.01
☐ 632	Bo Jackson	.15	.07	.02
☐ 633	Brad Arnsberg	.05	.02	.01
☐ 634	Jerry Willard	.05	.02	.01
☐ 635	Tommy Greene	.05	.02	.01
☐ 636	Bob MacDonald	.05	.02	.01
☐ 637	Kirk McCaskill	.05	.02	.01
☐ 638	John Burkett	.10	.05	.01
☐ 639	Paul Abbott	.05	.02	.01
☐ 640	Todd Benzinger	.05	.02	.01
☐ 641	Todd Hundley	.15	.07	.02
☐ 642	George Bell	.05	.02	.01
☐ 643	Javier Ortiz	.05	.02	.01
☐ 644	Sid Bream	.05	.02	.01
☐ 645	Bob Welch	.05	.02	.01
☐ 646	Phil Bradley	.05	.02	.01
☐ 647	Bill Krueger	.05	.02	.01

□	648 Rickey Henderson	.15	.07	.02
□	649 Kevin Wickander	.05	.02	.01
□	650 Steve Balboni	.05	.02	.01
□	651 Gene Harris	.05	.02	.01
□	652 Jim Deshaies	.05	.02	.01
□	653 Jason Grimsley	.05	.02	.01
□	654 Joe Orsulak	.05	.02	.01
□	655 Jim Poole	.05	.02	.01
□	656 Felix Jose	.05	.02	.01
□	657 Denis Cook	.05	.02	.01
□	658 Tom Brookens	.05	.02	.01
□	659 Junior Ortiz	.05	.02	.01
□	660 Jeff Parrett	.05	.02	.01
□	661 Jerry Don Gleaton	.05	.02	.01
□	662 Brent Knackert	.05	.02	.01
□	663 Rance Mulliniks	.05	.02	.01
□	664 John Smiley	.05	.02	.01
□	665 Larry Andersen	.05	.02	.01
□	666 Willie McGee	.05	.02	.01
□	667 Chris Nabholz	.05	.02	.01
□	668 Brady Anderson	.15	.07	.02
□	669 Darren Holmes UER	.05	.02	.01
	(19 CG's, should be 0)			
□	670 Ken Hill	.15	.07	.02
□	671 Gary Varsho	.05	.02	.01
□	672 Bill Pecota	.05	.02	.01
□	673 Fred Lynn	.05	.02	.01
□	674 Kevin D. Brown	.05	.02	.01
□	675 Dan Petry	.05	.02	.01
□	676 Mike Jackson	.05	.02	.01
□	677 Wally Joyner	.10	.05	.01
□	678 Danny Jackson	.05	.02	.01
□	679 Bill Haselman	.05	.02	.01
□	680 Mike Boddicker	.05	.02	.01
□	681 Mel Rojas	.10	.05	.01
□	682 Roberto Alomar	.25	.11	.03
□	683 Dave Justice ROY	.10	.05	.01
□	684 Chuck Crim	.05	.02	.01
□	685 Matt Williams	.15	.07	.02
□	686 Shawon Dunston	.05	.02	.01
□	687 Jeff Schulz	.05	.02	.01
□	688 John Barfield	.05	.02	.01
□	689 Gerald Young	.05	.02	.01
□	690 Luis Gonzalez	.15	.07	.02
□	691 Frank Wills	.05	.02	.01
□	692 Chuck Finley	.10	.05	.01
□	693 Sandy Alomar Jr. ROY	.05	.02	.01
□	694 Tim Drummond	.05	.02	.01
□	695 Herm Winningham	.05	.02	.01
□	696 Darryl Strawberry	.10	.05	.01
□	697 Al Leiter	.10	.05	.01
□	698 Karl Rhodes	.05	.02	.01
□	699 Stan Belinda	.05	.02	.01
□	700 Checklist 507-604	.05	.02	.01
□	701 Lance Blankenship	.05	.02	.01
□	702 Willie Stargell PUZ	.15	.07	.02
□	703 Jim Gantner	.05	.02	.01
□	704 Reggie Harris	.05	.02	.01
□	705 Rob Ducey	.05	.02	.01
□	706 Tim Hulett	.05	.02	.01
□	707 Atlee Hammaker	.05	.02	.01
□	708 Xavier Hernandez	.05	.02	.01
□	709 Chuck McElroy	.05	.02	.01
□	710 John Mitchell	.05	.02	.01
□	711 Carlos Hernandez	.05	.02	.01
□	712 Geronimo Pena	.05	.02	.01
□	713 Jim Neidlinger	.05	.02	.01
□	714 John Orton	.05	.02	.01
□	715 Terry Leach	.05	.02	.01
□	716 Mike Stanton	.05	.02	.01
□	717 Walt Terrell	.05	.02	.01
□	718 Luis Aquino	.05	.02	.01
□	719 Bud Black	.05	.02	.01
	(Blue Jays uniform,			
	but Giants logo)			
□	720 Bob Kipper	.05	.02	.01
□	721 Jeff Gray	.05	.02	.01
□	722 Jose Rijo	.05	.02	.01
□	723 Curt Young	.05	.02	.01
□	724 Jose Vizcaino	.05	.02	.01
□	725 Randy Tomlin	.05	.02	.01
□	726 Junior Noboa	.05	.02	.01
□	727 Bob Welch CY	.05	.02	.01
□	728 Gary Ward	.05	.02	.01
□	729 Rob Deer	.05	.02	.01
	(Brewers uniform,			
	but Tigers logo)			
□	730 David Segui	.10	.05	.01
□	731 Mark Carreon	.05	.02	.01
□	732 Vicente Palacios	.05	.02	.01
□	733 Sam Horn	.05	.02	.01
□	734 Howard Farmer	.05	.02	.01
□	735 Ken Dayley	.05	.02	.01
	(Cardinals uniform,			
	but Blue Jays logo)			
□	736 Kelly Mann	.05	.02	.01
□	737 Joe Grahe	.05	.02	.01
□	738 Kelly Downs	.05	.02	.01
□	739 Jimmy Kremers	.05	.02	.01
□	740 Kevin Appier	.10	.05	.01
□	741 Jeff Reed	.05	.02	.01
□	742 Jose Rijo WS	.05	.02	.01
□	743 Dave Rohde	.05	.02	.01
□	744 Dr.Dirt/Mr.Clean	.10	.05	.01
	Len Dykstra			
	Dale Murphy			
	UER (No '91 Donruss			
	logo on card front)			
□	745 Paul Sorrento	.10	.05	.01
□	746 Thomas Howard	.05	.02	.01
□	747 Matt Stark	.05	.02	.01
□	748 Harold Baines	.10	.05	.01
□	749 Doug Dascenzo	.05	.02	.01
□	750 Doug Drabek CY	.05	.02	.01
□	751 Gary Sheffield	.15	.07	.02
□	752 Terry Lee	.05	.02	.01
□	753 Jim Vatcher	.05	.02	.01
□	754 Lee Stevens	.05	.02	.01
□	755 Randy Veres	.05	.02	.01
□	756 Bill Doran	.05	.02	.01
□	757 Gary Wayne	.05	.02	.01
□	758 Pedro Munoz	.10	.05	.01
□	759 Chris Hammond	.05	.02	.01
□	760 Checklist 605-702	.05	.02	.01
□	761 Rickey Henderson MVP	.15	.07	.02
□	762 Barry Bonds MVP	.15	.07	.02
□	763 Billy Hatcher WS	.05	.02	.01
	UER (Line 13, on			
	should be one)			
□	764 Julio Machado	.05	.02	.01
□	765 Jose Mesa	.10	.05	.01
□	766 Willie Randolph WS	.10	.05	.01
□	767 Scott Erickson	.10	.05	.01
□	768 Travis Fryman	.15	.07	.02
□	769 Rich Rodriguez	.05	.02	.01
□	770 Checklist 703-770	.05	.02	.01
	and BC1-BC22			

1991 Donruss Elite

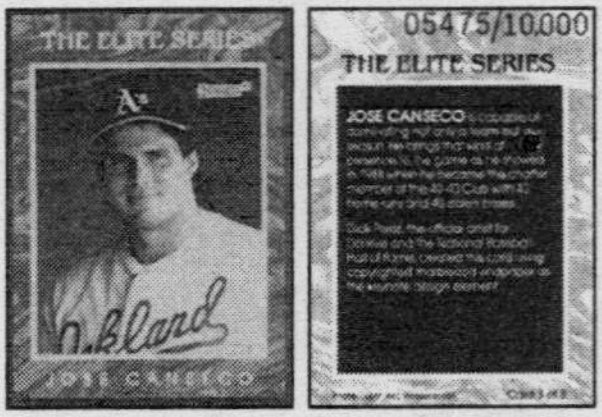

These special cards were inserted in the 1991 Donruss first and second series wax packs. Production was limited to a maximum of 10,000 cards for each card in the Elite series, and lesser production for the Sandberg Signature (5,000) and Ryan Legend (7,500) cards. This was the first time that mainstream insert cards were ever numbered allowing for verifiable proof of print runs. The regular Elite cards are photos enclosed in a bronze marble borders which surround an evenly squared photo of the players. The Sandberg Signature card has a green marble border and is signed in a blue sharpie. The Nolan Ryan Legend card is a Dick

Perez drawing with silver borders. The cards are all numbered on the back, 1 out of 10,000, etc.

	MINT	NRMT	EXC
COMPLETE SET (10)	1000.00	450.00	125.00
COMMON CARD (1-8)	20.00	9.00	2.50
SEMISTARS	40.00	18.00	5.00
RANDOM INSERTS IN PACKS			
□ 1 Barry Bonds	70.00	32.00	8.75
□ 2 George Brett	120.00	55.00	15.00
□ 3 Jose Canseco	60.00	27.00	7.50
□ 4 Andre Dawson	40.00	18.00	5.00
□ 5 Doug Drabek	20.00	9.00	2.50
□ 6 Cecil Fielder	40.00	18.00	5.00
□ 7 Rickey Henderson	40.00	18.00	5.00
□ 8 Matt Williams	60.00	27.00	7.50
□ L1 Nolan Ryan (Legend)	250.00	110.00	31.00
□ S1 Ryne Sandberg (Signature Series)	350.00	160.00	45.00

1991 Donruss Rookies

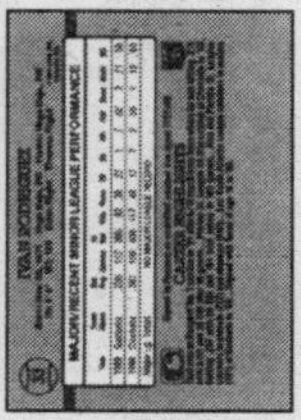

The 1991 Donruss Rookies set was issued exclusively in factory set form through hobby dealers. The cards measure the standard size and a mini puzzle featuring Hall of Famer Willie Stargell was included with the set. The fronts feature color action player photos, with white and red borders. Rookie Cards include Jeff Bagwell and Ivan Rodriguez.

	MINT	NRMT	EXC
COMPLETE FACT.SET (56)	4.00	1.80	.50
COMMON CARD (1-56)	.05	.02	.01
SEMISTARS	.10	.05	.01
□ 1 Pat Kelly	.10	.05	.01
□ 2 Rich DeLucia	.05	.02	.01
□ 3 Wes Chamberlain	.05	.02	.01
□ 4 Scott Leius	.05	.02	.01
□ 5 Darryl Kile	.05	.02	.01
□ 6 Milt Cuyler	.05	.02	.01
□ 7 Todd Van Poppel	.10	.05	.01
□ 8 Ray Lankford	.10	.05	.01
□ 9 Brian R. Hunter	.05	.02	.01
□ 10 Tony Perezchica	.05	.02	.01
□ 11 Ced Landrum	.05	.02	.01
□ 12 Dave Burba	.05	.02	.01
□ 13 Ramon Garcia	.05	.02	.01
□ 14 Ed Sprague	.10	.05	.01
□ 15 Warren Newson	.05	.02	.01
□ 16 Paul Faries	.05	.02	.01
□ 17 Luis Gonzalez	.10	.05	.01
□ 18 Charles Nagy	.10	.05	.01
□ 19 Chris Hammond	.05	.02	.01
□ 20 Frank Castillo	.10	.05	.01
□ 21 Pedro Munoz	.10	.05	.01
□ 22 Orlando Merced	.10	.05	.01
□ 23 Jose Melendez	.05	.02	.01
□ 24 Kirk Dressendorfer	.05	.02	.01
□ 25 Heathcliff Slocumb	.10	.05	.01
□ 26 Doug Simons	.05	.02	.01
□ 27 Mike Timlin	.05	.02	.01
□ 28 Jeff Fassero	.10	.05	.01
□ 29 Mark Leiter	.05	.02	.01
□ 30 Jeff Bagwell	2.50	1.10	.30
□ 31 Brian McRae	.10	.05	.01
□ 32 Mark Whiten	.05	.02	.01
□ 33 Ivan Rodriguez	1.00	.45	.12
□ 34 Wade Taylor	.05	.02	.01
□ 35 Darren Lewis	.10	.05	.01
□ 36 Mo Vaughn	.50	.23	.06
□ 37 Mike Remlinger	.05	.02	.01
□ 38 Rick Wilkins	.05	.02	.01
□ 39 Chuck Knoblauch	.25	.11	.03
□ 40 Kevin Morton	.05	.02	.01
□ 41 Carlos Rodriguez	.05	.02	.01
□ 42 Mark Lewis	.05	.02	.01
□ 43 Brent Mayne	.05	.02	.01
□ 44 Chris Haney	.05	.02	.01
□ 45 Denis Boucher	.05	.02	.01
□ 46 Mike Gardiner	.05	.02	.01
□ 47 Jeff Johnson	.05	.02	.01
□ 48 Dean Palmer	.10	.05	.01
□ 49 Chuck McElroy	.05	.02	.01
□ 50 Chris Jones	.05	.02	.01
□ 51 Scott Kamieniecki	.05	.02	.01
□ 52 Al Osuna	.05	.02	.01
□ 53 Rusty Meacham	.05	.02	.01
□ 54 Chito Martinez	.05	.02	.01
□ 55 Reggie Jefferson	.10	.05	.01
□ 56 Checklist 1-56	.05	.02	.01

1992 Donruss

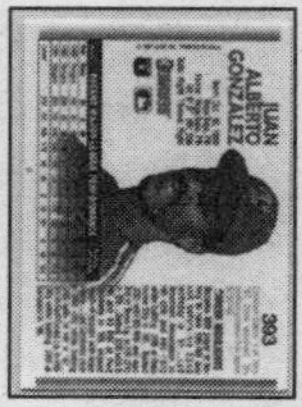

The 1992 Donruss set contains 784 standard-size cards issued in two separate series of 396. Cards were issued in first and second series foil wrapped packs in addition to hobby and retail factory sets. One of 21 different puzzle panels featuring Hall of Famer Rod Carew was inserted into each pack. The basic card design features glossy color player photos with white borders. Two-toned blue stripes overlay the top and bottom of the picture. Subsets include Rated Rookies (1-20, 397-421], All-Stars (21-30/422-431) and Highlights (33, 94, 154, 215, 276, 434, 495, 555, 616, 677). The only notable Rookie Card in the set features John Jaha.

	MINT	NRMT	EXC
COMPLETE SET (784)	12.00	5.50	1.50
COMPLETE HOBBY SET (788)	15.00	6.75	1.85
COMPLETE RETAIL SET (788)	25.00	11.00	3.10
COMPLETE SERIES 1 (396)	6.00	2.70	.75
COMPLETE SERIES 2 (388)	6.00	2.70	.75
COMMON CARD (1-784)	.05	.02	.01
SEMISTARS	.10	.05	.01
STARS	.15	.07	.02
COMP.BONUS CARD SET (8)	2.00	.90	.25
BONUS CARDS: RANDOM INSERTS IN PACKS			
□ 1 Mark Wohlers RR	.15	.07	.02
□ 2 Wil Cordero RR	.10	.05	.01
□ 3 Kyle Abbott RR	.05	.02	.01
□ 4 Dave Nilsson RR	.15	.07	.02
□ 5 Kenny Lofton RR	1.00	.45	.12
□ 6 Luis Mercedes RR	.05	.02	.01
□ 7 Roger Salkeld RR	.05	.02	.01
□ 8 Eddie Zosky RR	.05	.02	.01
□ 9 Todd Van Poppel RR	.05	.02	.01
□ 10 Frank Seminara RR	.05	.02	.01
□ 11 Andy Ashby RR	.10	.05	.01
□ 12 Reggie Jefferson RR	.10	.05	.01
□ 13 Ryan Klesko RR	.75	.35	.09

□ 14 Carlos Garcia RR	.10	.05	.01
□ 15 John Ramos RR	.05	.02	.01
□ 16 Eric Karros RR	.15	.07	.02
□ 17 Patrick Lennon RR	.05	.02	.01
□ 18 Eddie Taubensee RR	.05	.02	.01
□ 19 Roberto Hernandez RR	.15	.07	.02
□ 20 D.J. Dozier RR	.05	.02	.01
□ 21 Dave Henderson AS	.05	.02	.01
□ 22 Cal Ripken AS	.40	.18	.05
□ 23 Wade Boggs AS	.10	.05	.01
□ 24 Ken Griffey Jr. AS	.75	.35	.09
□ 25 Jack Morris AS	.05	.02	.01
□ 26 Danny Tartabull AS	.05	.02	.01
□ 27 Cecil Fielder AS	.05	.02	.01
□ 28 Roberto Alomar AS	.15	.07	.02
□ 29 Sandy Alomar Jr. AS	.05	.02	.01
□ 30 Rickey Henderson AS	.15	.07	.02
□ 31 Ken Hill	.15	.07	.02
□ 32 John Habyan	.05	.02	.01
□ 33 Otis Nixon HL	.05	.02	.01
□ 34 Tim Wallach	.05	.02	.01
□ 35 Cal Ripken	.75	.35	.09
□ 36 Gary Carter	.15	.07	.02
□ 37 Juan Agosto	.05	.02	.01
□ 38 Doug Dascenzo	.05	.02	.01
□ 39 Kirk Gibson	.10	.05	.01
□ 40 Benito Santiago	.05	.02	.01
□ 41 Otis Nixon	.05	.02	.01
□ 42 Andy Allanson	.05	.02	.01
□ 43 Brian Holman	.05	.02	.01
□ 44 Dick Schofield	.05	.02	.01
□ 45 Dave Magadan	.05	.02	.01
□ 46 Rafael Palmeiro	.15	.07	.02
□ 47 Jody Reed	.05	.02	.01
□ 48 Ivan Calderon	.05	.02	.01
□ 49 Greg W. Harris	.05	.02	.01
□ 50 Chris Sabo	.05	.02	.01
□ 51 Paul Molitor	.20	.09	.03
□ 52 Robby Thompson	.05	.02	.01
□ 53 Dave Smith	.05	.02	.01
□ 54 Mark Davis	.05	.02	.01
□ 55 Kevin Brown	.10	.05	.01
□ 56 Donn Pall	.05	.02	.01
□ 57 Len Dykstra	.10	.05	.01
□ 58 Roberto Alomar	.25	.11	.03
□ 59 Jeff D. Robinson	.05	.02	.01
□ 60 Willie McGee	.05	.02	.01
□ 61 Jay Buhner	.15	.07	.02
□ 62 Mike Pagliarulo	.05	.02	.01
□ 63 Paul O'Neill	.10	.05	.01
□ 64 Hubie Brooks	.05	.02	.01
□ 65 Kelly Gruber	.05	.02	.01
□ 66 Ken Caminiti	.15	.07	.02
□ 67 Gary Redus	.05	.02	.01
□ 68 Harold Baines	.10	.05	.01
□ 69 Charlie Hough	.05	.02	.01
□ 70 B.J. Surhoff	.10	.05	.01
□ 71 Walt Weiss	.05	.02	.01
□ 72 Shawn Hillegas	.05	.02	.01
□ 73 Roberto Kelly	.05	.02	.01
□ 74 Jeff Ballard	.05	.02	.01
□ 75 Craig Biggio	.15	.07	.02
□ 76 Pat Combs	.05	.02	.01
□ 77 Jeff M. Robinson	.05	.02	.01
□ 78 Tim Belcher	.05	.02	.01
□ 79 Cris Carpenter	.05	.02	.01
□ 80 Checklist 1-79	.05	.02	.01
□ 81 Steve Avery	.10	.05	.01
□ 82 Chris James	.05	.02	.01
□ 83 Brian Harper	.05	.02	.01
□ 84 Charlie Leibrandt	.05	.02	.01
□ 85 Mickey Tettleton	.05	.02	.01
□ 86 Pete O'Brien	.05	.02	.01
□ 87 Danny Darwin	.05	.02	.01
□ 88 Bob Walk	.05	.02	.01
□ 89 Jeff Reardon	.10	.05	.01
□ 90 Bobby Rose	.05	.02	.01
□ 91 Danny Jackson	.05	.02	.01
□ 92 John Morris	.05	.02	.01
□ 93 Bud Black	.05	.02	.01
□ 94 Tommy Greene HL	.05	.02	.01
□ 95 Rick Aguilera	.05	.02	.01
□ 96 Gary Gaetti	.10	.05	.01
□ 97 David Cone	.15	.07	.02
□ 98 John Olerud	.10	.05	.01
□ 99 Joel Skinner	.05	.02	.01
□ 100 Jay Bell	.10	.05	.01
□ 101 Bob Milacki	.05	.02	.01
□ 102 Norm Charlton	.05	.02	.01
□ 103 Chuck Crim	.05	.02	.01
□ 104 Terry Steinbach	.10	.05	.01
□ 105 Juan Samuel	.05	.02	.01
□ 106 Steve Howe	.05	.02	.01
□ 107 Rafael Belliard	.05	.02	.01
□ 108 Joey Cora	.05	.02	.01
□ 109 Tommy Greene	.05	.02	.01
□ 110 Gregg Olson	.05	.02	.01
□ 111 Frank Tanana	.05	.02	.01
□ 112 Lee Smith	.10	.05	.01
□ 113 Greg A. Harris	.05	.02	.01
□ 114 Dwayne Henry	.05	.02	.01
□ 115 Chili Davis	.10	.05	.01
□ 116 Kent Mercker	.05	.02	.01
□ 117 Brian Barnes	.05	.02	.01
□ 118 Rich DeLucia	.05	.02	.01
□ 119 Andre Dawson	.15	.07	.02
□ 120 Carlos Baerga	.15	.07	.02
□ 121 Mike LaValliere	.05	.02	.01
□ 122 Jeff Gray	.05	.02	.01
□ 123 Bruce Hurst	.05	.02	.01
□ 124 Alvin Davis	.05	.02	.01
□ 125 John Candelaria	.05	.02	.01
□ 126 Matt Nokes	.05	.02	.01
□ 127 George Bell	.05	.02	.01
□ 128 Bret Saberhagen	.10	.05	.01
□ 129 Jeff Russell	.05	.02	.01
□ 130 Jim Abbott	.05	.02	.01
□ 131 Bill Gullickson	.05	.02	.01
□ 132 Todd Zeile	.05	.02	.01
□ 133 Dave Winfield	.15	.07	.02
□ 134 Wally Whitehurst	.05	.02	.01
□ 135 Matt Williams	.15	.07	.02
□ 136 Tom Browning	.05	.02	.01
□ 137 Marquis Grissom	.15	.07	.02
□ 138 Erik Hanson	.05	.02	.01
□ 139 Rob Dibble	.05	.02	.01
□ 140 Don August	.05	.02	.01
□ 141 Tom Henke	.05	.02	.01
□ 142 Dan Pasqua	.05	.02	.01
□ 143 George Brett	.40	.18	.05
□ 144 Jerald Clark	.05	.02	.01
□ 145 Robin Ventura	.15	.07	.02
□ 146 Dale Murphy	.15	.07	.02
□ 147 Dennis Eckersley	.10	.05	.01
□ 148 Eric Yelding	.05	.02	.01
□ 149 Mario Diaz	.05	.02	.01
□ 150 Casey Candaele	.05	.02	.01
□ 151 Steve Olin	.05	.02	.01
□ 152 Luis Salazar	.05	.02	.01
□ 153 Kevin Maas	.05	.02	.01
□ 154 Nolan Ryan HL	.40	.18	.05
□ 155 Barry Jones	.05	.02	.01
□ 156 Chris Hoiles	.05	.02	.01
□ 157 Bobby Ojeda	.05	.02	.01
□ 158 Pedro Guerrero	.05	.02	.01
□ 159 Paul Assenmacher	.05	.02	.01
□ 160 Checklist 80-157	.05	.02	.01
□ 161 Mike Macfarlane	.05	.02	.01
□ 162 Craig Lefferts	.05	.02	.01
□ 163 Brian Hunter	.05	.02	.01
□ 164 Alan Trammell	.15	.07	.02
□ 165 Ken Griffey Jr.	1.50	.70	.19
□ 166 Lance Parrish	.05	.02	.01
□ 167 Brian Downing	.05	.02	.01
□ 168 John Barfield	.05	.02	.01
□ 169 Jack Clark	.10	.05	.01
□ 170 Chris Nabholz	.05	.02	.01
□ 171 Tim Teufel	.05	.02	.01
□ 172 Chris Hammond	.05	.02	.01
□ 173 Robin Yount	.15	.07	.02
□ 174 Dave Righetti	.05	.02	.01
□ 175 Joe Girardi	.05	.02	.01
□ 176 Mike Boddicker	.05	.02	.01
□ 177 Dean Palmer	.10	.05	.01
□ 178 Greg Hibbard	.05	.02	.01
□ 179 Randy Ready	.05	.02	.01
□ 180 Devon White	.10	.05	.01
□ 181 Mark Eichhorn	.05	.02	.01
□ 182 Mike Felder	.05	.02	.01
□ 183 Joe Klink	.05	.02	.01
□ 184 Steve Bedrosian	.05	.02	.01
□ 185 Barry Larkin	.15	.07	.02

☐ 186	John Franco	.05	.02	.01
☐ 187	Ed Sprague	.10	.05	.01
☐ 188	Mark Portugal	.05	.02	.01
☐ 189	Jose Lind	.05	.02	.01
☐ 190	Bob Welch	.05	.02	.01
☐ 191	Alex Fernandez	.15	.07	.02
☐ 192	Gary Sheffield	.15	.07	.02
☐ 193	Rickey Henderson	.15	.07	.02
☐ 194	Rod Nichols	.05	.02	.01
☐ 195	Scott Kamieniecki	.05	.02	.01
☐ 196	Mike Flanagan	.05	.02	.01
☐ 197	Steve Finley	.15	.07	.02
☐ 198	Darren Daulton	.10	.05	.01
☐ 199	Leo Gomez	.05	.02	.01
☐ 200	Mike Morgan	.05	.02	.01
☐ 201	Bob Tewksbury	.05	.02	.01
☐ 202	Sid Bream	.05	.02	.01
☐ 203	Sandy Alomar Jr.	.10	.05	.01
☐ 204	Greg Gagne	.05	.02	.01
☐ 205	Juan Berenguer	.05	.02	.01
☐ 206	Cecil Fielder	.10	.05	.01
☐ 207	Randy Johnson	.15	.07	.02
☐ 208	Tony Pena	.05	.02	.01
☐ 209	Doug Drabek	.05	.02	.01
☐ 210	Wade Boggs	.15	.07	.02
☐ 211	Bryan Harvey	.05	.02	.01
☐ 212	Jose Vizcaino	.05	.02	.01
☐ 213	Alonzo Powell	.05	.02	.01
☐ 214	Will Clark	.15	.07	.02
☐ 215	Rickey Henderson HL	.15	.07	.02
☐ 216	Jack Morris	.10	.05	.01
☐ 217	Junior Felix	.05	.02	.01
☐ 218	Vince Coleman	.05	.02	.01
☐ 219	Jimmy Key	.10	.05	.01
☐ 220	Alex Cole	.05	.02	.01
☐ 221	Bill Landrum	.05	.02	.01
☐ 222	Randy Milligan	.05	.02	.01
☐ 223	Jose Rijo	.05	.02	.01
☐ 224	Greg Vaughn	.15	.07	.02
☐ 225	Dave Stewart	.10	.05	.01
☐ 226	Lenny Harris	.05	.02	.01
☐ 227	Scott Sanderson	.05	.02	.01
☐ 228	Jeff Blauser	.05	.02	.01
☐ 229	Ozzie Guillen	.05	.02	.01
☐ 230	John Kruk	.10	.05	.01
☐ 231	Bob Melvin	.05	.02	.01
☐ 232	Milt Cuyler	.05	.02	.01
☐ 233	Felix Jose	.05	.02	.01
☐ 234	Ellis Burks	.15	.07	.02
☐ 235	Pete Harnisch	.05	.02	.01
☐ 236	Kevin Tapani	.05	.02	.01
☐ 237	Terry Pendleton	.10	.05	.01
☐ 238	Mark Gardner	.05	.02	.01
☐ 239	Harold Reynolds	.05	.02	.01
☐ 240	Checklist 158-237	.05	.02	.01
☐ 241	Mike Harkey	.05	.02	.01
☐ 242	Felix Fermin	.05	.02	.01
☐ 243	Barry Bonds	.25	.11	.03
☐ 244	Roger Clemens	.15	.07	.02
☐ 245	Dennis Rasmussen	.05	.02	.01
☐ 246	Jose DeLeon	.05	.02	.01
☐ 247	Orel Hershiser	.10	.05	.01
☐ 248	Mel Hall	.05	.02	.01
☐ 249	Rick Wilkins	.05	.02	.01
☐ 250	Tom Gordon	.05	.02	.01
☐ 251	Kevin Reimer	.05	.02	.01
☐ 252	Luis Polonia	.05	.02	.01
☐ 253	Mike Henneman	.05	.02	.01
☐ 254	Tom Pagnozzi	.05	.02	.01
☐ 255	Chuck Finley	.05	.02	.01
☐ 256	Mackey Sasser	.05	.02	.01
☐ 257	John Burkett	.10	.05	.01
☐ 258	Hal Morris	.05	.02	.01
☐ 259	Larry Walker	.15	.07	.02
☐ 260	Billy Swift	.05	.02	.01
☐ 261	Joe Oliver	.05	.02	.01
☐ 262	Julio Machado	.05	.02	.01
☐ 263	Todd Stottlemyre	.10	.05	.01
☐ 264	Matt Merullo	.05	.02	.01
☐ 265	Brent Mayne	.05	.02	.01
☐ 266	Thomas Howard	.05	.02	.01
☐ 267	Lance Johnson	.10	.05	.01
☐ 268	Terry Mulholland	.05	.02	.01
☐ 269	Rick Honeycutt	.05	.02	.01
☐ 270	Luis Gonzalez	.10	.05	.01
☐ 271	Jose Guzman	.05	.02	.01
☐ 272	Jimmy Jones	.05	.02	.01
☐ 273	Mark Lewis	.05	.02	.01
☐ 274	Rene Gonzales	.05	.02	.01
☐ 275	Jeff Johnson	.05	.02	.01
☐ 276	Dennis Martinez HL	.05	.02	.01
☐ 277	Delino DeShields	.05	.02	.01
☐ 278	Sam Horn	.05	.02	.01
☐ 279	Kevin Gross	.05	.02	.01
☐ 280	Jose Oquendo	.05	.02	.01
☐ 281	Mark Grace	.15	.07	.02
☐ 282	Mark Gubicza	.05	.02	.01
☐ 283	Fred McGriff	.15	.07	.02
☐ 284	Ron Gant	.15	.07	.02
☐ 285	Lou Whitaker	.15	.07	.02
☐ 286	Edgar Martinez	.15	.07	.02
☐ 287	Ron Tingley	.05	.02	.01
☐ 288	Kevin McReynolds	.05	.02	.01
☐ 289	Ivan Rodriguez	.30	.14	.04
☐ 290	Mike Gardiner	.05	.02	.01
☐ 291	Chris Haney	.05	.02	.01
☐ 292	Darrin Jackson	.05	.02	.01
☐ 293	Bill Doran	.05	.02	.01
☐ 294	Ted Higuera	.05	.02	.01
☐ 295	Jeff Brantley	.10	.05	.01
☐ 296	Les Lancaster	.05	.02	.01
☐ 297	Jim Eisenreich	.05	.02	.01
☐ 298	Ruben Sierra	.10	.05	.01
☐ 299	Scott Radinsky	.05	.02	.01
☐ 300	Jose DeJesus	.05	.02	.01
☐ 301	Mike Timlin	.05	.02	.01
☐ 302	Luis Sojo	.05	.02	.01
☐ 303	Kelly Downs	.05	.02	.01
☐ 304	Scott Bankhead	.05	.02	.01
☐ 305	Pedro Munoz	.05	.02	.01
☐ 306	Scott Scudder	.05	.02	.01
☐ 307	Kevin Elster	.05	.02	.01
☐ 308	Duane Ward	.05	.02	.01
☐ 309	Darryl Kile	.05	.02	.01
☐ 310	Orlando Merced	.05	.02	.01
☐ 311	Dave Henderson	.05	.02	.01
☐ 312	Tim Raines	.15	.07	.02
☐ 313	Mark Lee	.05	.02	.01
☐ 314	Mike Gallego	.05	.02	.01
☐ 315	Charles Nagy	.10	.05	.01
☐ 316	Jesse Barfield	.05	.02	.01
☐ 317	Todd Frohwirth	.05	.02	.01
☐ 318	Al Osuna	.05	.02	.01
☐ 319	Darrin Fletcher	.05	.02	.01
☐ 320	Checklist 238-316	.05	.02	.01
☐ 321	David Segui	.05	.02	.01
☐ 322	Stan Javier	.05	.02	.01
☐ 323	Bryn Smith	.05	.02	.01
☐ 324	Jeff Treadway	.05	.02	.01
☐ 325	Mark Whiten	.10	.05	.01
☐ 326	Kent Hrbek	.10	.05	.01
☐ 327	Dave Justice	.15	.07	.02
☐ 328	Tony Phillips	.10	.05	.01
☐ 329	Rob Murphy	.05	.02	.01
☐ 330	Kevin Morton	.05	.02	.01
☐ 331	John Smiley	.05	.02	.01
☐ 332	Luis Rivera	.05	.02	.01
☐ 333	Wally Joyner	.10	.05	.01
☐ 334	Heathcliff Slocumb	.05	.02	.01
☐ 335	Rick Cerone	.05	.02	.01
☐ 336	Mike Remlinger	.05	.02	.01
☐ 337	Mike Moore	.05	.02	.01
☐ 338	Lloyd McClendon	.05	.02	.01
☐ 339	Al Newman	.05	.02	.01
☐ 340	Kirk McCaskill	.05	.02	.01
☐ 341	Howard Johnson	.05	.02	.01
☐ 342	Greg Myers	.05	.02	.01
☐ 343	Kal Daniels	.05	.02	.01
☐ 344	Bernie Williams	.25	.11	.03
☐ 345	Shane Mack	.05	.02	.01
☐ 346	Gary Thurman	.05	.02	.01
☐ 347	Dante Bichette	.15	.07	.02
☐ 348	Mark McGwire	.30	.14	.04
☐ 349	Travis Fryman	.15	.07	.02
☐ 350	Ray Lankford	.15	.07	.02
☐ 351	Mike Jeffcoat	.05	.02	.01
☐ 352	Jack McDowell	.10	.05	.01
☐ 353	Mitch Williams	.05	.02	.01
☐ 354	Mike Devereaux	.05	.02	.01
☐ 355	Andres Galarraga	.15	.07	.02
☐ 356	Henry Cotto	.05	.02	.01
☐ 357	Scott Bailes	.05	.02	.01

□	358	Jeff Bagwell	.60	.25	.07
□	359	Scott Leius	.05	.02	.01
□	360	Zane Smith	.05	.02	.01
□	361	Bill Pecota	.05	.02	.01
□	362	Tony Fernandez	.05	.02	.01
□	363	Glenn Braggs	.05	.02	.01
□	364	Bill Spiers	.05	.02	.01
□	365	Vicente Palacios	.05	.02	.01
□	366	Tim Burke	.05	.02	.01
□	367	Randy Tomlin	.05	.02	.01
□	368	Kenny Rogers	.05	.02	.01
□	369	Brett Butler	.10	.05	.01
□	370	Pat Kelly	.05	.02	.01
□	371	Bip Roberts	.05	.02	.01
□	372	Gregg Jefferies	.15	.07	.02
□	373	Kevin Bass	.05	.02	.01
□	374	Ron Karkovice	.05	.02	.01
□	375	Paul Gibson	.05	.02	.01
□	376	Bernard Gilkey	.10	.05	.01
□	377	Dave Gallagher	.05	.02	.01
□	378	Bill Wegman	.05	.02	.01
□	379	Pat Borders	.05	.02	.01
□	380	Ed Whitson	.05	.02	.01
□	381	Gilberto Reyes	.05	.02	.01
□	382	Russ Swan	.05	.02	.01
□	383	Andy Van Slyke	.10	.05	.01
□	384	Wes Chamberlain	.05	.02	.01
□	385	Steve Chitren	.05	.02	.01
□	386	Greg Olson	.05	.02	.01
□	387	Brian McRae	.15	.07	.02
□	388	Rich Rodriguez	.05	.02	.01
□	389	Steve Decker	.05	.02	.01
□	390	Chuck Knoblauch	.15	.07	.02
□	391	Bobby Witt	.05	.02	.01
□	392	Eddie Murray	.25	.11	.03
□	393	Juan Gonzalez	.60	.25	.07
□	394	Scott Ruskin	.05	.02	.01
□	395	Jay Howell	.05	.02	.01
□	396	Checklist 317-396	.05	.02	.01
□	397	Royce Clayton RR	.10	.05	.01
□	398	John Jaha RR	.20	.09	.03
□	399	Dan Wilson RR	.15	.07	.02
□	400	Archie Corbin RR	.05	.02	.01
□	401	Barry Manuel RR	.05	.02	.01
□	402	Kim Batiste RR	.05	.02	.01
□	403	Pat Mahomes RR	.05	.02	.01
□	404	Dave Fleming RR	.05	.02	.01
□	405	Jeff Juden RR	.05	.02	.01
□	406	Jim Thome RR	.75	.35	.09
□	407	Sam Militello RR	.05	.02	.01
□	408	Jeff Nelson RR	.05	.02	.01
□	409	Anthony Young RR	.05	.02	.01
□	410	Tino Martinez RR	.15	.07	.02
□	411	Jeff Mutis RR	.05	.02	.01
□	412	Rey Sanchez RR	.05	.02	.01
□	413	Chris Gardner RR	.05	.02	.01
□	414	John Vander Wal RR	.05	.02	.01
□	415	Reggie Sanders RR	.15	.07	.02
□	416	Brian Williams RR	.05	.02	.01
□	417	Mo Sanford RR	.05	.02	.01
□	418	David Weathers RR	.10	.05	.01
□	419	Hector Fajardo RR	.05	.02	.01
□	420	Steve Foster RR	.05	.02	.01
□	421	Lance Dickson RR	.05	.02	.01
□	422	Andre Dawson AS	.15	.07	.02
□	423	Ozzie Smith AS	.15	.07	.02
□	424	Chris Sabo AS	.05	.02	.01
□	425	Tony Gwynn AS	.20	.09	.03
□	426	Tom Glavine AS	.10	.05	.01
□	427	Bobby Bonilla AS	.05	.02	.01
□	428	Will Clark AS	.10	.05	.01
□	429	Ryne Sandberg AS	.15	.07	.02
□	430	Benito Santiago AS	.05	.02	.01
□	431	Ivan Calderon AS	.05	.02	.01
□	432	Ozzie Smith	.20	.09	.03
□	433	Tim Leary	.05	.02	.01
□	434	Bret Saberhagen HL	.05	.02	.01
□	435	Mel Rojas	.10	.05	.01
□	436	Ben McDonald	.05	.02	.01
□	437	Tim Crews	.05	.02	.01
□	438	Rex Hudler	.05	.02	.01
□	439	Chico Walker	.05	.02	.01
□	440	Kurt Stillwell	.05	.02	.01
□	441	Tony Gwynn	.40	.18	.05
□	442	John Smoltz	.15	.07	.02
□	443	Lloyd Moseby	.05	.02	.01
□	444	Mike Schooler	.05	.02	.01
□	445	Joe Grahe	.05	.02	.01
□	446	Dwight Gooden	.10	.05	.01
□	447	Oil Can Boyd	.05	.02	.01
□	448	John Marzano	.05	.02	.01
□	449	Bret Barberie	.05	.02	.01
□	450	Mike Maddux	.05	.02	.01
□	451	Jeff Reed	.05	.02	.01
□	452	Dale Sveum	.05	.02	.01
□	453	Jose Uribe	.05	.02	.01
□	454	Bob Scanlan	.05	.02	.01
□	455	Kevin Appier	.10	.05	.01
□	456	Jeff Huson	.05	.02	.01
□	457	Ken Patterson	.05	.02	.01
□	458	Ricky Jordan	.05	.02	.01
□	459	Tom Candiotti	.05	.02	.01
□	460	Lee Stevens	.05	.02	.01
□	461	Rod Beck	.15	.07	.02
□	462	Dave Valle	.05	.02	.01
□	463	Scott Erickson	.10	.05	.01
□	464	Chris Jones	.05	.02	.01
□	465	Mark Carreon	.05	.02	.01
□	466	Rob Ducey	.05	.02	.01
□	467	Jim Corsi	.05	.02	.01
□	468	Jeff King	.10	.05	.01
□	469	Curt Young	.05	.02	.01
□	470	Bo Jackson	.15	.07	.02
□	471	Chris Bosio	.05	.02	.01
□	472	Jamie Quirk	.05	.02	.01
□	473	Jesse Orosco	.05	.02	.01
□	474	Alvaro Espinoza	.05	.02	.01
□	475	Joe Orsulak	.05	.02	.01
□	476	Checklist 397-477	.05	.02	.01
□	477	Gerald Young	.05	.02	.01
□	478	Wally Backman	.05	.02	.01
□	479	Juan Bell	.05	.02	.01
□	480	Mike Scioscia	.05	.02	.01
□	481	Omar Olivares	.05	.02	.01
□	482	Francisco Cabrera	.05	.02	.01
□	483	Greg Swindell UER (Shown on Indians, but listed on Reds)	.05	.02	.01
□	484	Terry Leach	.05	.02	.01
□	485	Tommy Gregg	.05	.02	.01
□	486	Scott Aldred	.05	.02	.01
□	487	Greg Briley	.05	.02	.01
□	488	Phil Plantier	.10	.05	.01
□	489	Curtis Wilkerson	.05	.02	.01
□	490	Tom Brunansky	.05	.02	.01
□	491	Mike Fetters	.05	.02	.01
□	492	Frank Castillo	.10	.05	.01
□	493	Joe Boever	.05	.02	.01
□	494	Kirt Manwaring	.05	.02	.01
□	495	Wilson Alvarez HL	.10	.05	.01
□	496	Gene Larkin	.05	.02	.01
□	497	Gary DiSarcina	.05	.02	.01
□	498	Frank Viola	.05	.02	.01
□	499	Manuel Lee	.05	.02	.01
□	500	Albert Belle	.60	.25	.07
□	501	Stan Belinda	.05	.02	.01
□	502	Dwight Evans	.10	.05	.01
□	503	Eric Davis	.10	.05	.01
□	504	Darren Holmes	.05	.02	.01
□	505	Mike Bordick	.10	.05	.01
□	506	Dave Hansen	.05	.02	.01
□	507	Lee Guetterman	.05	.02	.01
□	508	Keith Mitchell	.05	.02	.01
□	509	Melido Perez	.05	.02	.01
□	510	Dickie Thon	.05	.02	.01
□	511	Mark Williamson	.05	.02	.01
□	512	Mark Salas	.05	.02	.01
□	513	Milt Thompson	.05	.02	.01
□	514	Mo Vaughn	.40	.18	.05
□	515	Jim Deshaies	.05	.02	.01
□	516	Rich Garces	.05	.02	.01
□	517	Lonnie Smith	.05	.02	.01
□	518	Spike Owen	.05	.02	.01
□	519	Tracy Jones	.05	.02	.01
□	520	Greg Maddux	.75	.35	.09
□	521	Carlos Martinez	.05	.02	.01
□	522	Neal Heaton	.05	.02	.01
□	523	Mike Greenwell	.05	.02	.01
□	524	Andy Benes	.05	.02	.01
□	525	Jeff Schaefer UER (Photo actually Tino Martinez)	.05	.02	.01

□ 526	Mike Sharperson	.05	.02	.01
□ 527	Wade Taylor	.05	.02	.01
□ 528	Jerome Walton	.05	.02	.01
□ 529	Storm Davis	.05	.02	.01
□ 530	Jose Hernandez	.05	.02	.01
□ 531	Mark Langston	.10	.05	.01
□ 532	Rob Deer	.05	.02	.01
□ 533	Geronimo Pena	.05	.02	.01
□ 534	Juan Guzman	.10	.05	.01
□ 535	Pete Schourek	.10	.05	.01
□ 536	Todd Benzinger	.05	.02	.01
□ 537	Billy Hatcher	.05	.02	.01
□ 538	Tom Foley	.05	.02	.01
□ 539	Dave Cochrane	.05	.02	.01
□ 540	Mariano Duncan	.05	.02	.01
□ 541	Edwin Nunez	.05	.02	.01
□ 542	Rance Mulliniks	.05	.02	.01
□ 543	Carlton Fisk	.15	.07	.02
□ 544	Luis Aquino	.05	.02	.01
□ 545	Ricky Bones	.05	.02	.01
□ 546	Craig Grebeck	.05	.02	.01
□ 547	Charlie Hayes	.05	.02	.01
□ 548	Jose Canseco	.15	.07	.02
□ 549	Andujar Cedeno	.05	.02	.01
□ 550	Geno Petralli	.05	.02	.01
□ 551	Javier Ortiz	.05	.02	.01
□ 552	Rudy Seanez	.05	.02	.01
□ 553	Rich Gedman	.05	.02	.01
□ 554	Eric Plunk	.05	.02	.01
□ 555	Nolan Ryan HL (With Rich Gossage)	.25	.11	.03
□ 556	Checklist 478-555	.05	.02	.01
□ 557	Greg Colbrunn	.05	.02	.01
□ 558	Chito Martinez	.05	.02	.01
□ 559	Darryl Strawberry	.10	.05	.01
□ 560	Luis Alicea	.05	.02	.01
□ 561	Dwight Smith	.05	.02	.01
□ 562	Terry Shumpert	.05	.02	.01
□ 563	Jim Vatcher	.05	.02	.01
□ 564	Deion Sanders	.15	.07	.02
□ 565	Walt Terrell	.05	.02	.01
□ 566	Dave Burba	.05	.02	.01
□ 567	Dave Howard	.05	.02	.01
□ 568	Todd Hundley	.15	.07	.02
□ 569	Jack Daugherty	.05	.02	.01
□ 570	Scott Cooper	.05	.02	.01
□ 571	Bill Sampen	.05	.02	.01
□ 572	Jose Melendez	.05	.02	.01
□ 573	Freddie Benavides	.05	.02	.01
□ 574	Jim Gantner	.05	.02	.01
□ 575	Trevor Wilson	.05	.02	.01
□ 576	Ryne Sandberg	.25	.11	.03
□ 577	Kevin Seitzer	.05	.02	.01
□ 578	Gerald Alexander	.05	.02	.01
□ 579	Mike Huff	.05	.02	.01
□ 580	Von Hayes	.05	.02	.01
□ 581	Derek Bell	.10	.05	.01
□ 582	Mike Stanley	.05	.02	.01
□ 583	Kevin Mitchell	.10	.05	.01
□ 584	Mike Jackson	.05	.02	.01
□ 585	Dan Gladden	.05	.02	.01
□ 586	Ted Power UER (Wrong year given for signing with Reds)	.05	.02	.01
□ 587	Jeff Innis	.05	.02	.01
□ 588	Bob MacDonald	.05	.02	.01
□ 589	Jose Tolentino	.05	.02	.01
□ 590	Bob Patterson	.05	.02	.01
□ 591	Scott Brosius	.15	.07	.02
□ 592	Frank Thomas	1.50	.70	.19
□ 593	Darryl Hamilton	.05	.02	.01
□ 594	Kirk Dressendorfer	.05	.02	.01
□ 595	Jeff Shaw	.05	.02	.01
□ 596	Don Mattingly	.50	.23	.06
□ 597	Glenn Davis	.05	.02	.01
□ 598	Andy Mota	.05	.02	.01
□ 599	Jason Grimsley	.05	.02	.01
□ 600	Jimmy Poole	.05	.02	.01
□ 601	Jim Gott	.05	.02	.01
□ 602	Stan Royer	.05	.02	.01
□ 603	Marvin Freeman	.05	.02	.01
□ 604	Denis Boucher	.05	.02	.01
□ 605	Denny Neagle	.10	.05	.01
□ 606	Mark Lemke	.05	.02	.01
□ 607	Jerry Don Gleaton	.05	.02	.01
□ 608	Brent Knackert	.05	.02	.01
□ 609	Carlos Quintana	.05	.02	.01
□ 610	Bobby Bonilla	.10	.05	.01
□ 611	Joe Hesketh	.05	.02	.01
□ 612	Daryl Boston	.05	.02	.01
□ 613	Shawon Dunston	.05	.02	.01
□ 614	Danny Cox	.05	.02	.01
□ 615	Darren Lewis	.05	.02	.01
□ 616	Braves No-Hitter UER Kent Mercker (Misspelled Merker on card front) Alejandro Pena Mark Wohlers	.10	.05	.01
□ 617	Kirby Puckett	.30	.14	.04
□ 618	Franklin Stubbs	.05	.02	.01
□ 619	Chris Donnels	.05	.02	.01
□ 620	David Wells UER (Career Highlights in black not red)	.05	.02	.01
□ 621	Mike Aldrete	.05	.02	.01
□ 622	Bob Kipper	.05	.02	.01
□ 623	Anthony Telford	.05	.02	.01
□ 624	Randy Myers	.10	.05	.01
□ 625	Willie Randolph	.10	.05	.01
□ 626	Joe Slusarski	.05	.02	.01
□ 627	John Wetteland	.10	.05	.01
□ 628	Greg Cadaret	.05	.02	.01
□ 629	Tom Glavine	.15	.07	.02
□ 630	Wilson Alvarez	.15	.07	.02
□ 631	Wally Ritchie	.05	.02	.01
□ 632	Mike Mussina	.30	.14	.04
□ 633	Mark Leiter	.05	.02	.01
□ 634	Gerald Perry	.05	.02	.01
□ 635	Matt Young	.05	.02	.01
□ 636	Checklist 556-635	.05	.02	.01
□ 637	Scott Hemond	.05	.02	.01
□ 638	David West	.05	.02	.01
□ 639	Jim Clancy	.05	.02	.01
□ 640	Doug Piatt UER (Not born in 1955 as on card; incorrect info on How Acquired)	.05	.02	.01
□ 641	Omar Vizquel	.15	.07	.02
□ 642	Rick Sutcliffe	.05	.02	.01
□ 643	Glenallen Hill	.05	.02	.01
□ 644	Gary Varsho	.05	.02	.01
□ 645	Tony Fossas	.05	.02	.01
□ 646	Jack Howell	.05	.02	.01
□ 647	Jim Campanis	.05	.02	.01
□ 648	Chris Gwynn	.05	.02	.01
□ 649	Jim Leyritz	.05	.02	.01
□ 650	Chuck McElroy	.05	.02	.01
□ 651	Sean Berry	.10	.05	.01
□ 652	Donald Harris	.05	.02	.01
□ 653	Don Slaught	.05	.02	.01
□ 654	Rusty Meacham	.05	.02	.01
□ 655	Scott Terry	.05	.02	.01
□ 656	Ramon Martinez	.10	.05	.01
□ 657	Keith Miller	.05	.02	.01
□ 658	Ramon Garcia	.05	.02	.01
□ 659	Milt Hill	.05	.02	.01
□ 660	Steve Frey	.05	.02	.01
□ 661	Bob McClure	.05	.02	.01
□ 662	Ced Landrum	.05	.02	.01
□ 663	Doug Henry	.05	.02	.01
□ 664	Candy Maldonado	.05	.02	.01
□ 665	Carl Willis	.05	.02	.01
□ 666	Jeff Montgomery	.10	.05	.01
□ 667	Craig Shipley	.05	.02	.01
□ 668	Warren Newson	.05	.02	.01
□ 669	Mickey Morandini	.05	.02	.01
□ 670	Brook Jacoby	.05	.02	.01
□ 671	Ryan Bowen	.05	.02	.01
□ 672	Bill Krueger	.05	.02	.01
□ 673	Rob Mallicoat	.05	.02	.01
□ 674	Doug Jones	.05	.02	.01
□ 675	Scott Livingstone	.05	.02	.01
□ 676	Danny Tartabull	.05	.02	.01
□ 677	Joe Carter HL	.15	.07	.02
□ 678	Cecil Espy	.05	.02	.01
□ 679	Randy Velarde	.05	.02	.01
□ 680	Bruce Ruffin	.05	.02	.01
□ 681	Ted Wood	.05	.02	.01
□ 682	Dan Plesac	.05	.02	.01
□ 683	Eric Bullock	.05	.02	.01
□ 684	Junior Ortiz	.05	.02	.01

□ 685 Dave Hollins	.05	.02	.01
□ 686 Dennis Martinez	.10	.05	.01
□ 687 Larry Andersen	.05	.02	.01
□ 688 Doug Simons	.05	.02	.01
□ 689 Tim Spehr	.05	.02	.01
□ 690 Calvin Jones	.05	.02	.01
□ 691 Mark Guthrie	.05	.02	.01
□ 692 Alfredo Griffin	.05	.02	.01
□ 693 Joe Carter	.15	.07	.02
□ 694 Terry Mathews	.05	.02	.01
□ 695 Pascual Perez	.05	.02	.01
□ 696 Gene Nelson	.05	.02	.01
□ 697 Gerald Williams	.05	.02	.01
□ 698 Chris Cron	.05	.02	.01
□ 699 Steve Buechele	.05	.02	.01
□ 700 Paul McClellan	.05	.02	.01
□ 701 Jim Lindeman	.05	.02	.01
□ 702 Francisco Oliveras	.05	.02	.01
□ 703 Rob Maurer	.05	.02	.01
□ 704 Pat Hentgen	.15	.07	.02
□ 705 Jaime Navarro	.05	.02	.01
□ 706 Mike Magnante	.05	.02	.01
□ 707 Nolan Ryan	.75	.35	.09
□ 708 Bobby Thigpen	.05	.02	.01
□ 709 John Cerutti	.05	.02	.01
□ 710 Steve Wilson	.05	.02	.01
□ 711 Hensley Meulens	.05	.02	.01
□ 712 Rheal Cormier	.05	.02	.01
□ 713 Scott Bradley	.05	.02	.01
□ 714 Mitch Webster	.05	.02	.01
□ 715 Roger Mason	.05	.02	.01
□ 716 Checklist 636-716	.05	.02	.01
□ 717 Jeff Fassero	.10	.05	.01
□ 718 Cal Eldred	.05	.02	.01
□ 719 Sid Fernandez	.05	.02	.01
□ 720 Bob Zupcic	.05	.02	.01
□ 721 Jose Offerman	.05	.02	.01
□ 722 Cliff Brantley	.05	.02	.01
□ 723 Ron Darling	.05	.02	.01
□ 724 Dave Stieb	.05	.02	.01
□ 725 Hector Villanueva	.05	.02	.01
□ 726 Mike Hartley	.05	.02	.01
□ 727 Arthur Rhodes	.05	.02	.01
□ 728 Randy Bush	.05	.02	.01
□ 729 Steve Sax	.05	.02	.01
□ 730 Dave Otto	.05	.02	.01
□ 731 John Wehner	.05	.02	.01
□ 732 Dave Martinez	.05	.02	.01
□ 733 Ruben Amaro	.05	.02	.01
□ 734 Billy Ripken	.05	.02	.01
□ 735 Steve Farr	.05	.02	.01
□ 736 Shawn Abner	.05	.02	.01
□ 737 Gil Heredia	.05	.02	.01
□ 738 Ron Jones	.05	.02	.01
□ 739 Tony Castillo	.05	.02	.01
□ 740 Sammy Sosa	.25	.11	.03
□ 741 Julio Franco	.10	.05	.01
□ 742 Tim Naehring	.10	.05	.01
□ 743 Steve Wapnick	.05	.02	.01
□ 744 Craig Wilson	.05	.02	.01
□ 745 Darrin Chapin	.05	.02	.01
□ 746 Chris George	.05	.02	.01
□ 747 Mike Simms	.05	.02	.01
□ 748 Rosario Rodriguez	.05	.02	.01
□ 749 Skeeter Barnes	.05	.02	.01
□ 750 Roger McDowell	.05	.02	.01
□ 751 Dann Howitt	.05	.02	.01
□ 752 Paul Sorrento	.05	.02	.01
□ 753 Braulio Castillo	.05	.02	.01
□ 754 Yorkis Perez	.05	.02	.01
□ 755 Willie Fraser	.05	.02	.01
□ 756 Jeremy Hernandez	.05	.02	.01
□ 757 Curt Schilling	.05	.02	.01
□ 758 Steve Lyons	.05	.02	.01
□ 759 Dave Anderson	.05	.02	.01
□ 760 Willie Banks	.05	.02	.01
□ 761 Mark Leonard	.05	.02	.01
□ 762 Jack Armstrong (Listed on Indians, but shown on Reds)	.05	.02	.01
□ 763 Scott Servais	.05	.02	.01
□ 764 Ray Stephens	.05	.02	.01
□ 765 Junior Noboa	.05	.02	.01
□ 766 Jim Olander	.05	.02	.01
□ 767 Joe Magrane	.05	.02	.01
□ 768 Lance Blankenship	.05	.02	.01
□ 769 Mike Humphreys	.05	.02	.01
□ 770 Jarvis Brown	.05	.02	.01
□ 771 Damon Berryhill	.05	.02	.01
□ 772 Alejandro Pena	.05	.02	.01
□ 773 Jose Mesa	.10	.05	.01
□ 774 Gary Cooper	.05	.02	.01
□ 775 Carney Lansford	.10	.05	.01
□ 776 Mike Bielecki (Shown on Cubs, but listed on Braves)	.05	.02	.01
□ 777 Charlie O'Brien	.05	.02	.01
□ 778 Carlos Hernandez	.05	.02	.01
□ 779 Howard Farmer	.05	.02	.01
□ 780 Mike Stanton	.05	.02	.01
□ 781 Reggie Harris	.05	.02	.01
□ 782 Xavier Hernandez	.05	.02	.01
□ 783 Bryan Hickerson	.05	.02	.01
□ 784 Checklist 717-784 and BC1-BC8	.05	.02	.01

1992 Donruss Diamond Kings

These standard-size cards were randomly inserted in 1992 Donruss I foil packs (cards 1-13 and the checklist only) and in 1992 Donruss II foil packs (cards 14-26). The fronts feature player portraits by noted sports artist Dick Perez. The words "Donruss Diamond Kings" are superimposed at the card top in a gold-trimmed blue and black banner, with the player's name in a similarly designed black stripe at the card bottom. A very limited amount of 5" by 7" cards were produced. These issues were never formally released but these cards were intended to be premiums in retail products. We are not valuing them currently since trading in these cards is very thin.

	MINT	NRMT	EXC
COMPLETE SET (27)	20.00	9.00	2.50
COMPLETE SERIES 1 (14)	16.00	7.25	2.00
COMPLETE SERIES 2 (13)	4.00	1.80	.50
COMMON CARD (DK1-DK27)	.50	.23	.06
SEMISTARS	1.00	.45	.12
RANDOM INSERTS IN PACKS			
□ DK1 Paul Molitor	1.50	.70	.19
□ DK2 Will Clark	1.00	.45	.12
□ DK3 Joe Carter	1.00	.45	.12
□ DK4 Julio Franco	.75	.35	.09
□ DK5 Cal Ripken	8.00	3.60	1.00
□ DK6 Dave Justice	.75	.35	.09
□ DK7 George Bell	.75	.35	.09
□ DK8 Frank Thomas	8.00	3.60	1.00
□ DK9 Wade Boggs	1.00	.45	.12
□ DK10 Scott Sanderson	.50	.23	.06
□ DK11 Jeff Bagwell	5.00	2.20	.60
□ DK12 John Kruk	.75	.35	.09
□ DK13 Felix Jose	.50	.23	.06
□ DK14 Harold Baines	.75	.35	.09
□ DK15 Dwight Gooden	1.00	.45	.12
□ DK16 Brian McRae	.75	.35	.09
□ DK17 Jay Bell	.75	.35	.09
□ DK18 Brett Butler	1.00	.45	.12
□ DK19 Hal Morris	.75	.35	.09
□ DK20 Mark Langston	.75	.35	.09
□ DK21 Scott Erickson	.75	.35	.09

		MINT	NRMT	EXC
□ DK22	Randy Johnson	1.25	.55	.16
□ DK23	Greg Swindell	.50	.23	.06
□ DK24	Dennis Martinez	.75	.35	.09
□ DK25	Tony Phillips	.50	.23	.06
□ DK26	Fred McGriff	1.00	.45	.12
□ DK27	Checklist 1-26 DP (Dick Perez)	.50	.23	.06

1992 Donruss Elite

These cards were random inserts in 1992 Donruss first and second series foil packs. Like the previous year, the cards were indidvidually numbered of 10,000. Card fronts feature dramatic prismatic borders encasing a full color action or posed shot of the player. The numbering of the set is essentially a continuation of the series started the year before. Only 5,000 Ripken Signature Series cards were printed and only 7,500 Henderson Legends cards were printed.

	MINT	NRMT	EXC
COMPLETE SET (12)	800.00	350.00	100.00
COMMON CARD (9-18)	15.00	6.75	1.85
SEMISTARS	25.00	11.00	3.10
RANDOM INSERTS IN PACKS			

		MINT	NRMT	EXC
□ 9	Wade Boggs	25.00	11.00	3.10
□ 10	Joe Carter	25.00	11.00	3.10
□ 11	Will Clark	25.00	11.00	3.10
□ 12	Dwight Gooden	25.00	11.00	3.10
□ 13	Ken Griffey Jr.	150.00	70.00	19.00
□ 14	Tony Gwynn	60.00	27.00	7.50
□ 15	Howard Johnson	15.00	6.75	1.85
□ 16	Terry Pendleton	15.00	6.75	1.85
□ 17	Kirby Puckett	60.00	27.00	7.50
□ 18	Frank Thomas	150.00	70.00	19.00
□ L2	Rickey Henderson (Legend Series)	50.00	22.00	6.25
□ S2	Cal Ripken (Signature Series)	400.00	180.00	50.00

1992 Donruss Update

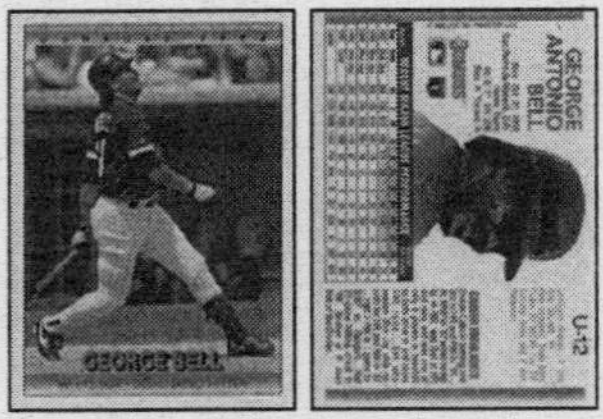

Four cards from this 22-card standard-size set were included in each retail factory set. Card design is identical to regular issue 1992 Donruss cards except for the U-prefixed numbering on back. Card numbers U1-U6 are Rated Rookie cards, while card numbers U7-U9 are Highlights cards. A tough early Kenny Lofton card, his first as a member of the Cleveland Indians, highlights this set.

	MINT	NRMT	EXC
COMPLETE SET (22)	60.00	27.00	7.50
COMMON CARD (U1-U22)	1.00	.45	.12
SEMISTARS	2.00	.90	.25
FOUR PER RETAIL FACTORY SET			

		MINT	NRMT	EXC
□ U1	Pat Listach RR	1.00	.45	.12
□ U2	Andy Stankiewicz RR	1.00	.45	.12
□ U3	Brian Jordan RR	10.00	4.50	1.25
□ U4	Dan Walters RR	1.00	.45	.12
□ U5	Chad Curtis RR	2.00	.90	.25
□ U6	Kenny Lofton RR	30.00	13.50	3.70
□ U7	Mark McGwire HL	10.00	4.50	1.25
□ U8	Eddie Murray HL	8.00	3.60	1.00
□ U9	Jeff Reardon HL	2.00	.90	.25
□ U10	Frank Viola	2.00	.90	.25
□ U11	Gary Sheffield	5.00	2.20	.60
□ U12	George Bell	2.00	.90	.25
□ U13	Rick Sutcliffe	2.00	.90	.25
□ U14	Wally Joyner	2.00	.90	.25
□ U15	Kevin Seitzer	2.00	.90	.25
□ U16	Bill Krueger	1.00	.45	.12
□ U17	Danny Tartabull	2.00	.90	.25
□ U18	Dave Winfield	4.00	1.80	.50
□ U19	Gary Carter	2.00	.90	.25
□ U20	Bobby Bonilla	2.00	.90	.25
□ U21	Cory Snyder	1.00	.45	.12
□ U22	Bill Swift	1.00	.45	.12

1992 Donruss Rookies

After six years of issuing "The Rookies" as a 56-card boxed set, Donruss expanded it to a 132-card standard-size set and distributed the cards exclusively in hobby and retail foil packs. The card design is the same as the 1992 Donruss regular issue except that the two-tone blue color bars have been replaced by green, as in the previous six Donruss Rookies sets. The cards are arranged in alphabetical order and numbered on the back. Rookie Cards in this set include Manny Ramirez, Shane Reynolds and Eric Young.

	MINT	NRMT	EXC
COMPLETE SET (132)	5.00	2.20	.60
COMMON CARD (1-132)	.05	.02	.01
SEMISTARS	.10	.05	.01

		MINT	NRMT	EXC
□ 1	Kyle Abbott	.05	.02	.01
□ 2	Troy Afenir	.05	.02	.01
□ 3	Rich Amaral	.05	.02	.01
□ 4	Ruben Amaro	.05	.02	.01
□ 5	Billy Ashley	.15	.07	.02
□ 6	Pedro Astacio	.10	.05	.01
□ 7	Jim Austin	.05	.02	.01
□ 8	Robert Ayrault	.05	.02	.01
□ 9	Kevin Baez	.05	.02	.01
□ 10	Esteban Beltre	.05	.02	.01
□ 11	Brian Bohanon	.05	.02	.01
□ 12	Kent Bottenfield	.05	.02	.01
□ 13	Jeff Branson	.05	.02	.01
□ 14	Brad Brink	.05	.02	.01
□ 15	John Briscoe	.05	.02	.01

□ 16 Doug Brocail	.05	.02	.01
□ 17 Rico Brogna	.10	.05	.01
□ 18 J.T. Bruett	.05	.02	.01
□ 19 Jacob Brumfield	.05	.02	.01
□ 20 Jim Bullinger	.05	.02	.01
□ 21 Kevin Campbell	.05	.02	.01
□ 22 Pedro Castellano	.05	.02	.01
□ 23 Mike Christopher	.05	.02	.01
□ 24 Archi Cianfrocco	.05	.02	.01
□ 25 Mark Clark	.10	.05	.01
□ 26 Craig Colbert	.05	.02	.01
□ 27 Victor Cole	.05	.02	.01
□ 28 Steve Cooke	.10	.05	.01
□ 29 Tim Costo	.05	.02	.01
□ 30 Chad Curtis	.15	.07	.02
□ 31 Doug Davis	.05	.02	.01
□ 32 Gary DiSarcina	.05	.02	.01
□ 33 John Doherty	.05	.02	.01
□ 34 Mike Draper	.05	.02	.01
□ 35 Monty Fariss	.05	.02	.01
□ 36 Bien Figueroa	.05	.02	.01
□ 37 John Flaherty	.05	.02	.01
□ 38 Tim Fortugno	.05	.02	.01
□ 39 Eric Fox	.05	.02	.01
□ 40 Jeff Frye	.05	.02	.01
□ 41 Ramon Garcia	.05	.02	.01
□ 42 Brent Gates	.10	.05	.01
□ 43 Tom Goodwin	.10	.05	.01
□ 44 Buddy Groom	.05	.02	.01
□ 45 Jeff Grotewold	.05	.02	.01
□ 46 Juan Guerrero	.05	.02	.01
□ 47 Johnny Guzman	.05	.02	.01
□ 48 Shawn Hare	.05	.02	.01
□ 49 Ryan Hawblitzel	.05	.02	.01
□ 50 Bert Hefferman	.05	.02	.01
□ 51 Butch Henry	.05	.02	.01
□ 52 Cesar Hernandez	.05	.02	.01
□ 53 Vince Horsman	.05	.02	.01
□ 54 Steve Hosey	.05	.02	.01
□ 55 Pat Howell	.05	.02	.01
□ 56 Peter Hoy	.05	.02	.01
□ 57 Jonathan Hurst	.05	.02	.01
□ 58 Mark Hutton	.05	.02	.01
□ 59 Shawn Jeter	.05	.02	.01
□ 60 Joel Johnston	.05	.02	.01
□ 61 Jeff Kent	.15	.07	.02
□ 62 Kurt Knudsen	.05	.02	.01
□ 63 Kevin Koslofski	.05	.02	.01
□ 64 Danny Leon	.05	.02	.01
□ 65 Jesse Levis	.05	.02	.01
□ 66 Tom Marsh	.05	.02	.01
□ 67 Ed Martel	.05	.02	.01
□ 68 Al Martin	.15	.07	.02
□ 69 Pedro Martinez	.25	.11	.03
□ 70 Derrick May	.05	.02	.01
□ 71 Matt Maysey	.05	.02	.01
□ 72 Russ McGinnis	.05	.02	.01
□ 73 Tim McIntosh	.05	.02	.01
□ 74 Jim McNamara	.05	.02	.01
□ 75 Jeff McNeely	.05	.02	.01
□ 76 Rusty Meacham	.05	.02	.01
□ 77 Tony Menendez	.05	.02	.01
□ 78 Henry Mercedes	.05	.02	.01
□ 79 Paul Miller	.05	.02	.01
□ 80 Joe Millette	.05	.02	.01
□ 81 Blas Minor	.05	.02	.01
□ 82 Dennis Moeller	.05	.02	.01
□ 83 Raul Mondesi	.60	.25	.07
□ 84 Rob Natal	.05	.02	.01
□ 85 Troy Neel	.05	.02	.01
□ 86 David Nied	.10	.05	.01
□ 87 Jerry Nielson	.05	.02	.01
□ 88 Donovan Osborne	.10	.05	.01
□ 89 John Patterson	.05	.02	.01
□ 90 Roger Pavlik	.25	.11	.03
□ 91 Dan Peltier	.05	.02	.01
□ 92 Jim Pena	.05	.02	.01
□ 93 William Pennyfeather	.05	.02	.01
□ 94 Mike Perez	.05	.02	.01
□ 95 Hipolito Pichardo	.05	.02	.01
□ 96 Greg Pirkl	.05	.02	.01
□ 97 Harvey Pulliam	.05	.02	.01
□ 98 Manny Ramirez	2.00	.90	.25
□ 99 Pat Rapp	.10	.05	.01
□ 100 Jeff Reboulet	.05	.02	.01
□ 101 Darren Reed	.05	.02	.01
□ 102 Shane Reynolds	.30	.14	.04
□ 103 Bill Risley	.05	.02	.01
□ 104 Ben Rivera	.05	.02	.01
□ 105 Henry Rodriguez	.15	.07	.02
□ 106 Rico Rossy	.05	.02	.01
□ 107 Johnny Ruffin	.05	.02	.01
□ 108 Steve Scarsone	.05	.02	.01
□ 109 Tim Scott	.05	.02	.01
□ 110 Steve Shifflett	.05	.02	.01
□ 111 Dave Silvestri	.05	.02	.01
□ 112 Matt Stairs	.05	.02	.01
□ 113 William Suero	.05	.02	.01
□ 114 Jeff Tackett	.05	.02	.01
□ 115 Eddie Taubensee	.05	.02	.01
□ 116 Rick Trlicek	.05	.02	.01
□ 117 Scooter Tucker	.05	.02	.01
□ 118 Shane Turner	.05	.02	.01
□ 119 Julio Valera	.05	.02	.01
□ 120 Paul Wagner	.05	.02	.01
□ 121 Tim Wakefield	.15	.07	.02
□ 122 Mike Walker	.05	.02	.01
□ 123 Bruce Walton	.05	.02	.01
□ 124 Lenny Webster	.05	.02	.01
□ 125 Bob Wickman	.05	.02	.01
□ 126 Mike Williams	.05	.02	.01
□ 127 Kerry Woodson	.05	.02	.01
□ 128 Eric Young	.25	.11	.03
□ 129 Kevin Young	.05	.02	.01
□ 130 Pete Young	.05	.02	.01
□ 131 Checklist 1-66	.05	.02	.01
□ 132 Checklist 67-132	.05	.02	.01

1992 Donruss Rookies Phenoms

This 20-card standard size set features a selection young prospects. The first twelve cards were randomly inserted into 1992 Donruss The Rookies 12-card foil packs. The last eight were inserted one per 1992 Donruss Rookies 30-card jumbo pack. Each glossy card front features a black border surrounding a full color photo and gold foil type.

	MINT	NRMT	EXC
COMPLETE SET (20)	35.00	16.00	4.40
COMPLETE FOIL SET (12)	25.00	11.00	3.10
COMPLETE JUMBO SET (8)	10.00	4.50	1.25
COMMON CARD (BC1-BC12)	.50	.23	.06
RANDOM INSERTS IN PACKS			
COMMON CARD (BC13-BC20)	.50	.23	.06
ONE PER JUMBO PACK			
□ BC1 Moises Alou	1.00	.45	.12
□ BC2 Bret Boone	.75	.35	.09
□ BC3 Jeff Conine	1.50	.70	.19
□ BC4 Dave Fleming	.50	.23	.06
□ BC5 Tyler Green	.50	.23	.06
□ BC6 Eric Karros	1.50	.70	.19
□ BC7 Pat Listach	.50	.23	.06
□ BC8 Kenny Lofton	8.00	3.60	1.00
□ BC9 Mike Piazza	20.00	9.00	2.50
□ BC10 Tim Salmon	5.00	2.20	.60
□ BC11 Andy Stankiewicz	.50	.23	.06
□ BC12 Dan Walters	.50	.23	.06
□ BC13 Ramon Caraballo	.50	.23	.06
□ BC14 Brian Jordan	2.00	.90	.25
□ BC15 Ryan Klesko	6.00	2.70	.75

□ BC16 Sam Militello	.50	.23	.06
□ BC17 Frank Seminara	.50	.23	.06
□ BC18 Salomon Torres	.50	.23	.06
□ BC19 John Valentin	1.50	.70	.19
□ BC20 Wil Cordero	.75	.35	.09

1993 Donruss

The 792-card 1993 Donruss set was issued in two series, each with 396 standard-size cards. Cards were distributed in foil packs. The basic card fronts feature glossy color action photos with white borders. At the bottom of the picture, the team logo appears in a team color-coded diamond with the player's name in a color-coded bar extending to the right. A Rated Rookies (RR) subset , sprinkled throughout the set, spotlights 20 young prospects. There are no key Rookie Cards in this set.

	MINT	NRMT	EXC
COMPLETE SET (792)	30.00	13.50	3.70
COMPLETE SERIES 1 (396)	15.00	6.75	1.85
COMPLETE SERIES 2 (396)	15.00	6.75	1.85
COMMON CARD (1-792)	.05	.02	.01
SEMISTARS	.15	.07	.02
STARS	.30	.14	.04

□ 1 Craig Lefferts	.05	.02	.01
□ 2 Kent Mercker	.05	.02	.01
□ 3 Phil Plantier	.05	.02	.01
□ 4 Alex Arias	.05	.02	.01
□ 5 Julio Valera	.05	.02	.01
□ 6 Dan Wilson	.15	.07	.02
□ 7 Frank Thomas	2.00	.90	.25
□ 8 Eric Anthony	.05	.02	.01
□ 9 Derek Lilliquist	.05	.02	.01
□ 10 Rafael Bournigal	.05	.02	.01
□ 11 Manny Alexander RR	.05	.02	.01
□ 12 Bret Barberie	.05	.02	.01
□ 13 Mickey Tettleton	.05	.02	.01
□ 14 Anthony Young	.05	.02	.01
□ 15 Tim Spehr	.05	.02	.01
□ 16 Bob Ayrault	.05	.02	.01
□ 17 Bill Wegman	.05	.02	.01
□ 18 Jay Bell	.15	.07	.02
□ 19 Rick Aguilera	.05	.02	.01
□ 20 Todd Zeile	.05	.02	.01
□ 21 Steve Farr	.05	.02	.01
□ 22 Andy Benes	.05	.02	.01
□ 23 Lance Blankenship	.05	.02	.01
□ 24 Ted Wood	.05	.02	.01
□ 25 Omar Vizquel	.30	.14	.04
□ 26 Steve Avery	.15	.07	.02
□ 27 Brian Bohanon	.05	.02	.01
□ 28 Rick Wilkins	.05	.02	.01
□ 29 Devon White	.05	.02	.01
□ 30 Bobby Ayala	.15	.07	.02
□ 31 Leo Gomez	.05	.02	.01
□ 32 Mike Simms	.05	.02	.01
□ 33 Ellis Burks	.30	.14	.04
□ 34 Steve Wilson	.05	.02	.01
□ 35 Jim Abbott	.05	.02	.01
□ 36 Tim Wallach	.05	.02	.01
□ 37 Wilson Alvarez	.15	.07	.02
□ 38 Daryl Boston	.05	.02	.01
□ 39 Sandy Alomar Jr.	.15	.07	.02
□ 40 Mitch Williams	.05	.02	.01
□ 41 Rico Brogna	.15	.07	.02
□ 42 Gary Varsho	.05	.02	.01
□ 43 Kevin Appier	.15	.07	.02
□ 44 Eric Wedge RR	.05	.02	.01
□ 45 Dante Bichette	.30	.14	.04
□ 46 Jose Oquendo	.05	.02	.01
□ 47 Mike Trombley	.05	.02	.01
□ 48 Dan Walters	.05	.02	.01
□ 49 Gerald Williams	.05	.02	.01
□ 50 Bud Black	.05	.02	.01
□ 51 Bobby Witt	.05	.02	.01
□ 52 Mark Davis	.05	.02	.01
□ 53 Shawn Barton	.05	.02	.01
□ 54 Paul Assenmacher	.05	.02	.01
□ 55 Kevin Reimer	.05	.02	.01
□ 56 Billy Ashley RR	.05	.02	.01
□ 57 Eddie Zosky	.05	.02	.01
□ 58 Chris Sabo	.05	.02	.01
□ 59 Billy Ripken	.05	.02	.01
□ 60 Scooter Tucker	.05	.02	.01
□ 61 Tim Wakefield RR	.15	.07	.02
□ 62 Mitch Webster	.05	.02	.01
□ 63 Jack Clark	.05	.02	.01
□ 64 Mark Gardner	.05	.02	.01
□ 65 Lee Stevens	.05	.02	.01
□ 66 Todd Hundley	.30	.14	.04
□ 67 Bobby Thigpen	.05	.02	.01
□ 68 Dave Hollins	.05	.02	.01
□ 69 Jack Armstrong	.05	.02	.01
□ 70 Alex Cole	.05	.02	.01
□ 71 Mark Carreon	.05	.02	.01
□ 72 Todd Worrell	.05	.02	.01
□ 73 Steve Shifflett	.05	.02	.01
□ 74 Jerald Clark	.05	.02	.01
□ 75 Paul Molitor	.40	.18	.05
□ 76 Larry Carter	.05	.02	.01
□ 77 Rich Rowland RR	.05	.02	.01
□ 78 Damon Berryhill	.05	.02	.01
□ 79 Willie Banks	.05	.02	.01
□ 80 Hector Villanueva	.05	.02	.01
□ 81 Mike Gallego	.05	.02	.01
□ 82 Tim Belcher	.05	.02	.01
□ 83 Mike Bordick	.05	.02	.01
□ 84 Craig Biggio	.30	.14	.04
□ 85 Lance Parrish	.05	.02	.01
□ 86 Brett Butler	.15	.07	.02
□ 87 Mike Timlin	.05	.02	.01
□ 88 Brian Barnes	.05	.02	.01
□ 89 Brady Anderson	.30	.14	.04
□ 90 D.J. Dozier	.05	.02	.01
□ 91 Frank Viola	.05	.02	.01
□ 92 Darren Daulton	.15	.07	.02
□ 93 Chad Curtis	.15	.07	.02
□ 94 Zane Smith	.05	.02	.01
□ 95 George Bell	.05	.02	.01
□ 96 Rex Hudler	.05	.02	.01
□ 97 Mark Whiten	.05	.02	.01
□ 98 Tim Teufel	.05	.02	.01
□ 99 Kevin Ritz	.05	.02	.01
□ 100 Jeff Brantley	.05	.02	.01
□ 101 Jeff Conine	.30	.14	.04
□ 102 Vinny Castilla	.30	.14	.04
□ 103 Greg Vaughn	.30	.14	.04
□ 104 Steve Buechele	.05	.02	.01
□ 105 Darren Reed	.05	.02	.01
□ 106 Bip Roberts	.05	.02	.01
□ 107 John Habyan	.05	.02	.01
□ 108 Scott Servais	.05	.02	.01
□ 109 Walt Weiss	.05	.02	.01
□ 110 J.T. Snow RR	.30	.14	.04
□ 111 Jay Buhner	.30	.14	.04
□ 112 Darryl Strawberry	.15	.07	.02
□ 113 Roger Pavlik	.15	.07	.02
□ 114 Chris Nabholz	.05	.02	.01
□ 115 Pat Borders	.05	.02	.01
□ 116 Pat Howell	.05	.02	.01
□ 117 Gregg Olson	.05	.02	.01
□ 118 Curt Schilling	.05	.02	.01
□ 119 Roger Clemens	.30	.14	.04
□ 120 Victor Cole	.05	.02	.01
□ 121 Gary DiSarcina	.05	.02	.01
□ 122 Checklist 1-80 (Gary Carter and Kirt Manwaring	.15	.07	.02
□ 123 Steve Sax	.05	.02	.01
□ 124 Chuck Carr	.05	.02	.01
□ 125 Mark Lewis	.05	.02	.01

☐ 126	Tony Gwynn	.75	.35	.09
☐ 127	Travis Fryman	.30	.14	.04
☐ 128	Dave Burba	.05	.02	.01
☐ 129	Wally Joyner	.15	.07	.02
☐ 130	John Smoltz	.30	.14	.04
☐ 131	Cal Eldred	.05	.02	.01
☐ 132	Checklist 81-159 (Roberto Alomar and Devon White)	.30	.14	.04
☐ 133	Arthur Rhodes	.05	.02	.01
☐ 134	Jeff Blauser	.05	.02	.01
☐ 135	Scott Cooper	.05	.02	.01
☐ 136	Doug Strange	.05	.02	.01
☐ 137	Luis Sojo	.05	.02	.01
☐ 138	Jeff Branson	.05	.02	.01
☐ 139	Alex Fernandez	.30	.14	.04
☐ 140	Ken Caminiti	.30	.14	.04
☐ 141	Charles Nagy	.15	.07	.02
☐ 142	Tom Candiotti	.05	.02	.01
☐ 143	Willie Greene RR	.15	.07	.02
☐ 144	John Vander Wal	.05	.02	.01
☐ 145	Kurt Knudsen	.05	.02	.01
☐ 146	John Franco	.05	.02	.01
☐ 147	Eddie Pierce	.05	.02	.01
☐ 148	Kim Batiste	.05	.02	.01
☐ 149	Darren Holmes	.05	.02	.01
☐ 150	Steve Cooke	.05	.02	.01
☐ 151	Terry Jorgensen	.05	.02	.01
☐ 152	Mark Clark	.05	.02	.01
☐ 153	Randy Velarde	.05	.02	.01
☐ 154	Greg W. Harris	.05	.02	.01
☐ 155	Kevin Campbell	.05	.02	.01
☐ 156	John Burkett	.05	.02	.01
☐ 157	Kevin Mitchell	.15	.07	.02
☐ 158	Deion Sanders	.30	.14	.04
☐ 159	Jose Canseco	.30	.14	.04
☐ 160	Jeff Hartsock	.05	.02	.01
☐ 161	Tom Quinlan	.05	.02	.01
☐ 162	Tim Pugh	.05	.02	.01
☐ 163	Glenn Davis	.05	.02	.01
☐ 164	Shane Reynolds	.15	.07	.02
☐ 165	Jody Reed	.05	.02	.01
☐ 166	Mike Sharperson	.05	.02	.01
☐ 167	Scott Lewis	.05	.02	.01
☐ 168	Dennis Martinez	.15	.07	.02
☐ 169	Scott Radinsky	.05	.02	.01
☐ 170	Dave Gallagher	.05	.02	.01
☐ 171	Jim Thome	1.00	.45	.12
☐ 172	Terry Mulholland	.05	.02	.01
☐ 173	Milt Cuyler	.05	.02	.01
☐ 174	Bob Patterson	.05	.02	.01
☐ 175	Jeff Montgomery	.15	.07	.02
☐ 176	Tim Salmon RR	.50	.23	.06
☐ 177	Franklin Stubbs	.05	.02	.01
☐ 178	Donovan Osborne	.05	.02	.01
☐ 179	Jeff Reboulet	.05	.02	.01
☐ 180	Jeremy Hernandez	.05	.02	.01
☐ 181	Charlie Hayes	.05	.02	.01
☐ 182	Matt Williams	.30	.14	.04
☐ 183	Mike Raczka	.05	.02	.01
☐ 184	Francisco Cabrera	.05	.02	.01
☐ 185	Rich DeLucia	.05	.02	.01
☐ 186	Sammy Sosa	.30	.14	.04
☐ 187	Ivan Rodriguez	.40	.18	.05
☐ 188	Bret Boone RR	.15	.07	.02
☐ 189	Juan Guzman	.15	.07	.02
☐ 190	Tom Browning	.05	.02	.01
☐ 191	Randy Milligan	.05	.02	.01
☐ 192	Steve Finley	.30	.14	.04
☐ 193	John Patterson RR	.05	.02	.01
☐ 194	Kip Gross	.05	.02	.01
☐ 195	Tony Fossas	.05	.02	.01
☐ 196	Ivan Calderon	.05	.02	.01
☐ 197	Junior Felix	.05	.02	.01
☐ 198	Pete Schourek	.15	.07	.02
☐ 199	Craig Grebeck	.05	.02	.01
☐ 200	Juan Bell	.05	.02	.01
☐ 201	Glenallen Hill	.05	.02	.01
☐ 202	Danny Jackson	.05	.02	.01
☐ 203	John Kiely	.05	.02	.01
☐ 204	Bob Tewksbury	.05	.02	.01
☐ 205	Kevin Koslofski	.05	.02	.01
☐ 206	Craig Shipley	.05	.02	.01
☐ 207	John Jaha	.15	.07	.02
☐ 208	Royce Clayton	.15	.07	.02
☐ 209	Mike Piazza RR	2.00	.90	.25
☐ 210	Ron Gant	.30	.14	.04
☐ 211	Scott Erickson	.05	.02	.01
☐ 212	Doug Dascenzo	.05	.02	.01
☐ 213	Andy Stankiewicz	.05	.02	.01
☐ 214	Geronimo Berroa	.15	.07	.02
☐ 215	Dennis Eckersley	.15	.07	.02
☐ 216	Al Osuna	.05	.02	.01
☐ 217	Tino Martinez	.15	.07	.02
☐ 218	Henry Rodriguez	.30	.14	.04
☐ 219	Ed Sprague	.15	.07	.02
☐ 220	Ken Hill	.15	.07	.02
☐ 221	Chito Martinez	.05	.02	.01
☐ 222	Bret Saberhagen	.15	.07	.02
☐ 223	Mike Greenwell	.05	.02	.01
☐ 224	Mickey Morandini	.05	.02	.01
☐ 225	Chuck Finley	.05	.02	.01
☐ 226	Denny Neagle	.15	.07	.02
☐ 227	Kirk McCaskill	.05	.02	.01
☐ 228	Rheal Cormier	.05	.02	.01
☐ 229	Paul Sorrento	.05	.02	.01
☐ 230	Darrin Jackson	.05	.02	.01
☐ 231	Rob Deer	.05	.02	.01
☐ 232	Bill Swift	.05	.02	.01
☐ 233	Kevin McReynolds	.05	.02	.01
☐ 234	Terry Pendleton	.15	.07	.02
☐ 235	Dave Nilsson	.15	.07	.02
☐ 236	Chuck McElroy	.05	.02	.01
☐ 237	Derek Parks	.05	.02	.01
☐ 238	Norm Charlton	.05	.02	.01
☐ 239	Matt Nokes	.05	.02	.01
☐ 240	Juan Guerrero	.05	.02	.01
☐ 241	Jeff Parrett	.05	.02	.01
☐ 242	Ryan Thompson RR	.05	.02	.01
☐ 243	Dave Fleming	.05	.02	.01
☐ 244	Dave Hansen	.05	.02	.01
☐ 245	Monty Fariss	.05	.02	.01
☐ 246	Archi Cianfrocco	.05	.02	.01
☐ 247	Pat Hentgen	.30	.14	.04
☐ 248	Bill Pecota	.05	.02	.01
☐ 249	Ben McDonald	.05	.02	.01
☐ 250	Cliff Brantley	.05	.02	.01
☐ 251	John Valentin	.30	.14	.04
☐ 252	Jeff King	.15	.07	.02
☐ 253	Reggie Williams	.05	.02	.01
☐ 254	Checklist 160-238 (Damon Berryhill and Alex Arias)	.05	.02	.01
☐ 255	Ozzie Guillen	.05	.02	.01
☐ 256	Mike Perez	.05	.02	.01
☐ 257	Thomas Howard	.05	.02	.01
☐ 258	Kurt Stillwell	.05	.02	.01
☐ 259	Mike Henneman	.05	.02	.01
☐ 260	Steve Decker	.05	.02	.01
☐ 261	Brent Mayne	.05	.02	.01
☐ 262	Otis Nixon	.05	.02	.01
☐ 263	Mark Kiefer	.05	.02	.01
☐ 264	Checklist 239-317 (Don Mattingly and Mike Bordick)	.30	.14	.04
☐ 265	Richie Lewis	.05	.02	.01
☐ 266	Pat Gomez	.05	.02	.01
☐ 267	Scott Taylor	.05	.02	.01
☐ 268	Shawon Dunston	.05	.02	.01
☐ 269	Greg Myers	.05	.02	.01
☐ 270	Tim Costo	.05	.02	.01
☐ 271	Greg Hibbard	.05	.02	.01
☐ 272	Pete Harnisch	.05	.02	.01
☐ 273	Dave Mlicki	.05	.02	.01
☐ 274	Orel Hershiser	.15	.07	.02
☐ 275	Sean Berry RR	.05	.02	.01
☐ 276	Doug Simons	.05	.02	.01
☐ 277	John Doherty	.05	.02	.01
☐ 278	Eddie Murray	.50	.23	.06
☐ 279	Chris Haney	.05	.02	.01
☐ 280	Stan Javier	.05	.02	.01
☐ 281	Jaime Navarro	.05	.02	.01
☐ 282	Orlando Merced	.15	.07	.02
☐ 283	Kent Hrbek	.15	.07	.02
☐ 284	Bernard Gilkey	.30	.14	.04
☐ 285	Russ Springer	.05	.02	.01
☐ 286	Mike Maddux	.05	.02	.01
☐ 287	Eric Fox	.05	.02	.01
☐ 288	Mark Leonard	.05	.02	.01
☐ 289	Tim Leary	.05	.02	.01
☐ 290	Brian Hunter	.05	.02	.01
☐ 291	Donald Harris	.05	.02	.01

☐	292 Bob Scanlan	.05	.02	.01
☐	293 Turner Ward	.05	.02	.01
☐	294 Hal Morris	.05	.02	.01
☐	295 Jimmy Poole	.05	.02	.01
☐	296 Doug Jones	.05	.02	.01
☐	297 Tony Pena	.05	.02	.01
☐	298 Ramon Martinez	.15	.07	.02
☐	299 Tim Fortugno	.05	.02	.01
☐	300 Marquis Grissom	.30	.14	.04
☐	301 Lance Johnson	.15	.07	.02
☐	302 Jeff Kent	.15	.07	.02
☐	303 Reggie Jefferson	.15	.07	.02
☐	304 Wes Chamberlain	.05	.02	.01
☐	305 Shawn Hare	.05	.02	.01
☐	306 Mike LaValliere	.05	.02	.01
☐	307 Gregg Jefferies	.30	.14	.04
☐	308 Troy Neel RR	.05	.02	.01
☐	309 Pat Listach	.05	.02	.01
☐	310 Geronimo Pena	.05	.02	.01
☐	311 Pedro Munoz	.05	.02	.01
☐	312 Guillermo Velasquez	.05	.02	.01
☐	313 Roberto Kelly	.05	.02	.01
☐	314 Mike Jackson	.05	.02	.01
☐	315 Rickey Henderson	.30	.14	.04
☐	316 Mark Lemke	.05	.02	.01
☐	317 Erik Hanson	.05	.02	.01
☐	318 Derrick May	.05	.02	.01
☐	319 Geno Petralli	.05	.02	.01
☐	320 Melvin Nieves RR	.30	.14	.04
☐	321 Doug Linton	.05	.02	.01
☐	322 Rob Dibble	.05	.02	.01
☐	323 Chris Hoiles	.05	.02	.01
☐	324 Jimmy Jones	.05	.02	.01
☐	325 Dave Staton RR	.05	.02	.01
☐	326 Pedro Martinez	.30	.14	.04
☐	327 Paul Quantrill	.05	.02	.01
☐	328 Greg Colbrunn	.05	.02	.01
☐	329 Hilly Hathaway	.05	.02	.01
☐	330 Jeff Innis	.05	.02	.01
☐	331 Ron Karkovice	.05	.02	.01
☐	332 Keith Shepherd	.05	.02	.01
☐	333 Alan Embree	.05	.02	.01
☐	334 Paul Wagner	.05	.02	.01
☐	335 Dave Haas	.05	.02	.01
☐	336 Ozzie Canseco	.05	.02	.01
☐	337 Bill Sampen	.05	.02	.01
☐	338 Rich Rodriguez	.05	.02	.01
☐	339 Dean Palmer	.15	.07	.02
☐	340 Greg Litton	.05	.02	.01
☐	341 Jim Tatum RR	.05	.02	.01
☐	342 Todd Haney	.05	.02	.01
☐	343 Larry Casian	.05	.02	.01
☐	344 Ryne Sandberg	.50	.23	.06
☐	345 Sterling Hitchcock	.15	.07	.02
☐	346 Chris Hammond	.05	.02	.01
☐	347 Vince Horsman	.05	.02	.01
☐	348 Butch Henry	.05	.02	.01
☐	349 Dann Howitt	.05	.02	.01
☐	350 Roger McDowell	.05	.02	.01
☐	351 Jack Morris	.15	.07	.02
☐	352 Bill Krueger	.05	.02	.01
☐	353 Cris Colon	.05	.02	.01
☐	354 Joe Vitko	.05	.02	.01
☐	355 Willie McGee	.05	.02	.01
☐	356 Jay Baller	.05	.02	.01
☐	357 Pat Mahomes	.05	.02	.01
☐	358 Roger Mason	.05	.02	.01
☐	359 Jerry Nielsen	.05	.02	.01
☐	360 Tom Pagnozzi	.05	.02	.01
☐	361 Kevin Baez	.05	.02	.01
☐	362 Tim Scott	.05	.02	.01
☐	363 Domingo Martinez	.05	.02	.01
☐	364 Kirt Manwaring	.05	.02	.01
☐	365 Rafael Palmeiro	.30	.14	.04
☐	366 Ray Lankford	.30	.14	.04
☐	367 Tim McIntosh	.05	.02	.01
☐	368 Jessie Hollins	.05	.02	.01
☐	369 Scott Leius	.05	.02	.01
☐	370 Bill Doran	.05	.02	.01
☐	371 Sam Militello	.05	.02	.01
☐	372 Ryan Bowen	.05	.02	.01
☐	373 Dave Henderson	.05	.02	.01
☐	374 Dan Smith RR	.05	.02	.01
☐	375 Steve Reed RR	.05	.02	.01
☐	376 Jose Offerman	.05	.02	.01
☐	377 Kevin Brown	.05	.02	.01
☐	378 Darrin Fletcher	.05	.02	.01
☐	379 Duane Ward	.05	.02	.01
☐	380 Wayne Kirby RR	.05	.02	.01
☐	381 Steve Scarsone	.05	.02	.01
☐	382 Mariano Duncan	.05	.02	.01
☐	383 Ken Ryan	.05	.02	.01
☐	384 Lloyd McClendon	.05	.02	.01
☐	385 Brian Holman	.05	.02	.01
☐	386 Braulio Castillo	.05	.02	.01
☐	387 Danny Leon	.05	.02	.01
☐	388 Omar Olivares	.05	.02	.01
☐	389 Kevin Wickander	.05	.02	.01
☐	390 Fred McGriff	.30	.14	.04
☐	391 Phil Clark	.05	.02	.01
☐	392 Darren Lewis	.05	.02	.01
☐	393 Phil Hiatt	.05	.02	.01
☐	394 Mike Morgan	.05	.02	.01
☐	395 Shane Mack	.05	.02	.01
☐	396 Checklist 318-396 (Dennis Eckersley and Art Kusnyer CO)	.15	.07	.02
☐	397 David Segui	.05	.02	.01
☐	398 Rafael Belliard	.05	.02	.01
☐	399 Tim Naehring	.05	.02	.01
☐	400 Frank Castillo	.05	.02	.01
☐	401 Joe Grahe	.05	.02	.01
☐	402 Reggie Sanders	.30	.14	.04
☐	403 Roberto Hernandez	.15	.07	.02
☐	404 Luis Gonzalez	.05	.02	.01
☐	405 Carlos Baerga	.30	.14	.04
☐	406 Carlos Hernandez	.05	.02	.01
☐	407 Pedro Astacio RR	.05	.02	.01
☐	408 Mel Rojas	.15	.07	.02
☐	409 Scott Livingstone	.05	.02	.01
☐	410 Chico Walker	.05	.02	.01
☐	411 Brian McRae	.15	.07	.02
☐	412 Ben Rivera	.05	.02	.01
☐	413 Ricky Bones	.05	.02	.01
☐	414 Andy Van Slyke	.15	.07	.02
☐	415 Chuck Knoblauch	.30	.14	.04
☐	416 Luis Alicea	.05	.02	.01
☐	417 Bob Wickman	.05	.02	.01
☐	418 Doug Brocail	.05	.02	.01
☐	419 Scott Brosius	.05	.02	.01
☐	420 Rod Beck	.15	.07	.02
☐	421 Edgar Martinez	.30	.14	.04
☐	422 Ryan Klesko	1.00	.45	.12
☐	423 Nolan Ryan	1.50	.70	.19
☐	424 Rey Sanchez	.05	.02	.01
☐	425 Roberto Alomar	.50	.23	.06
☐	426 Barry Larkin	.30	.14	.04
☐	427 Mike Mussina	.40	.18	.05
☐	428 Jeff Bagwell	.75	.35	.09
☐	429 Mo Vaughn	.50	.23	.06
☐	430 Eric Karros	.30	.14	.04
☐	431 John Orton	.05	.02	.01
☐	432 Wil Cordero	.15	.07	.02
☐	433 Jack McDowell	.15	.07	.02
☐	434 Howard Johnson	.05	.02	.01
☐	435 Albert Belle	1.00	.45	.12
☐	436 John Kruk	.15	.07	.02
☐	437 Skeeter Barnes	.05	.02	.01
☐	438 Don Slaught	.05	.02	.01
☐	439 Rusty Meacham	.05	.02	.01
☐	440 Tim Laker RR	.05	.02	.01
☐	441 Robin Yount	.30	.14	.04
☐	442 Brian Jordan	.30	.14	.04
☐	443 Kevin Tapani	.05	.02	.01
☐	444 Gary Sheffield	.30	.14	.04
☐	445 Rich Monteleone	.05	.02	.01
☐	446 Will Clark	.30	.14	.04
☐	447 Jerry Browne	.05	.02	.01
☐	448 Jeff Treadway	.05	.02	.01
☐	449 Mike Schooler	.05	.02	.01
☐	450 Mike Harkey	.05	.02	.01
☐	451 Julio Franco	.15	.07	.02
☐	452 Kevin Young RR	.05	.02	.01
☐	453 Kelly Gruber	.05	.02	.01
☐	454 Jose Rijo	.05	.02	.01
☐	455 Mike Devereaux	.05	.02	.01
☐	456 Andujar Cedeno	.05	.02	.01
☐	457 Damion Easley RR	.05	.02	.01
☐	458 Kevin Gross	.05	.02	.01
☐	459 Matt Young	.05	.02	.01
☐	460 Matt Stairs	.05	.02	.01
☐	461 Luis Polonia	.05	.02	.01

□ 462	Dwight Gooden	.15	.07	.02
□ 463	Warren Newson	.05	.02	.01
□ 464	Jose DeLeon	.05	.02	.01
□ 465	Jose Mesa	.15	.07	.02
□ 466	Danny Cox	.05	.02	.01
□ 467	Dan Gladden	.05	.02	.01
□ 468	Gerald Perry	.05	.02	.01
□ 469	Mike Boddicker	.05	.02	.01
□ 470	Jeff Gardner	.05	.02	.01
□ 471	Doug Henry	.05	.02	.01
□ 472	Mike Benjamin	.05	.02	.01
□ 473	Dan Peltier RR	.05	.02	.01
□ 474	Mike Stanton	.05	.02	.01
□ 475	John Smiley	.05	.02	.01
□ 476	Dwight Smith	.05	.02	.01
□ 477	Jim Leyritz	.05	.02	.01
□ 478	Dwayne Henry	.05	.02	.01
□ 479	Mark McGwire	.60	.25	.07
□ 480	Pete Incaviglia	.05	.02	.01
□ 481	Dave Cochrane	.05	.02	.01
□ 482	Eric Davis	.15	.07	.02
□ 483	John Olerud	.05	.02	.01
□ 484	Kent Bottenfield	.05	.02	.01
□ 485	Mark McLemore	.05	.02	.01
□ 486	Dave Magadan	.05	.02	.01
□ 487	John Marzano	.05	.02	.01
□ 488	Ruben Amaro	.05	.02	.01
□ 489	Rob Ducey	.05	.02	.01
□ 490	Stan Belinda	.05	.02	.01
□ 491	Dan Pasqua	.05	.02	.01
□ 492	Joe Magrane	.05	.02	.01
□ 493	Brook Jacoby	.05	.02	.01
□ 494	Gene Harris	.05	.02	.01
□ 495	Mark Leiter	.05	.02	.01
□ 496	Bryan Hickerson	.05	.02	.01
□ 497	Tom Gordon	.05	.02	.01
□ 498	Pete Smith	.05	.02	.01
□ 499	Chris Bosio	.05	.02	.01
□ 500	Shawn Boskie	.05	.02	.01
□ 501	Dave West	.05	.02	.01
□ 502	Milt Hill	.05	.02	.01
□ 503	Pat Kelly	.05	.02	.01
□ 504	Joe Boever	.05	.02	.01
□ 505	Terry Steinbach	.15	.07	.02
□ 506	Butch Huskey RR	.15	.07	.02
□ 507	David Valle	.05	.02	.01
□ 508	Mike Scioscia	.05	.02	.01
□ 509	Kenny Rogers	.05	.02	.01
□ 510	Moises Alou	.30	.14	.04
□ 511	David Wells	.05	.02	.01
□ 512	Mackey Sasser	.05	.02	.01
□ 513	Todd Frohwirth	.05	.02	.01
□ 514	Ricky Jordan	.05	.02	.01
□ 515	Mike Gardiner	.05	.02	.01
□ 516	Gary Redus	.05	.02	.01
□ 517	Gary Gaetti	.15	.07	.02
□ 518	Checklist	.05	.02	.01
□ 519	Carlton Fisk	.30	.14	.04
□ 520	Ozzie Smith	.40	.18	.05
□ 521	Rod Nichols	.05	.02	.01
□ 522	Benito Santiago	.05	.02	.01
□ 523	Bill Gullickson	.05	.02	.01
□ 524	Robby Thompson	.05	.02	.01
□ 525	Mike Macfarlane	.05	.02	.01
□ 526	Sid Bream	.05	.02	.01
□ 527	Darryl Hamilton	.05	.02	.01
□ 528	Checklist	.05	.02	.01
□ 529	Jeff Tackett	.05	.02	.01
□ 530	Greg Olson	.05	.02	.01
□ 531	Bob Zupcic	.05	.02	.01
□ 532	Mark Grace	.30	.14	.04
□ 533	Steve Frey	.05	.02	.01
□ 534	Dave Martinez	.05	.02	.01
□ 535	Robin Ventura	.15	.07	.02
□ 536	Casey Candaele	.05	.02	.01
□ 537	Kenny Lofton	.75	.35	.09
□ 538	Jay Howell	.05	.02	.01
□ 539	Fernando Ramsey RR	.05	.02	.01
□ 540	Larry Walker	.30	.14	.04
□ 541	Cecil Fielder	.15	.07	.02
□ 542	Lee Guetterman	.05	.02	.01
□ 543	Keith Miller	.05	.02	.01
□ 544	Len Dykstra	.15	.07	.02
□ 545	B.J. Surhoff	.15	.07	.02
□ 546	Bob Walk	.05	.02	.01
□ 547	Brian Harper	.05	.02	.01

□ 548	Lee Smith	.15	.07	.02
□ 549	Danny Tartabull	.05	.02	.01
□ 550	Frank Seminara	.05	.02	.01
□ 551	Henry Mercedes	.05	.02	.01
□ 552	Dave Righetti	.05	.02	.01
□ 553	Ken Griffey Jr.	2.00	.90	.25
□ 554	Tom Glavine	.30	.14	.04
□ 555	Juan Gonzalez	1.00	.45	.12
□ 556	Jim Bullinger	.05	.02	.01
□ 557	Derek Bell	.30	.14	.04
□ 558	Cesar Hernandez	.05	.02	.01
□ 559	Cal Ripken	1.50	.70	.19
□ 560	Eddie Taubensee	.05	.02	.01
□ 561	John Flaherty	.05	.02	.01
□ 562	Todd Benzinger	.05	.02	.01
□ 563	Hubie Brooks	.05	.02	.01
□ 564	Delino DeShields	.05	.02	.01
□ 565	Tim Raines	.30	.14	.04
□ 566	Sid Fernandez	.05	.02	.01
□ 567	Steve Olin	.05	.02	.01
□ 568	Tommy Greene	.05	.02	.01
□ 569	Buddy Groom	.05	.02	.01
□ 570	Randy Tomlin	.05	.02	.01
□ 571	Hipolito Pichardo	.05	.02	.01
□ 572	Rene Arocha RR	.05	.02	.01
□ 573	Mike Fetters	.05	.02	.01
□ 574	Felix Jose	.05	.02	.01
□ 575	Gene Larkin	.05	.02	.01
□ 576	Bruce Hurst	.05	.02	.01
□ 577	Bernie Williams	.30	.14	.04
□ 578	Trevor Wilson	.05	.02	.01
□ 579	Bob Welch	.05	.02	.01
□ 580	David Justice	.30	.14	.04
□ 581	Randy Johnson	.30	.14	.04
□ 582	Jose Vizcaino	.05	.02	.01
□ 583	Jeff Huson	.05	.02	.01
□ 584	Rob Maurer RR	.05	.02	.01
□ 585	Todd Stottlemyre	.15	.07	.02
□ 586	Joe Oliver	.05	.02	.01
□ 587	Bob Milacki	.05	.02	.01
□ 588	Rob Murphy	.05	.02	.01
□ 589	Greg Pirkl RR	.05	.02	.01
□ 590	Lenny Harris	.05	.02	.01
□ 591	Luis Rivera	.05	.02	.01
□ 592	John Wetteland	.15	.07	.02
□ 593	Mark Langston	.15	.07	.02
□ 594	Bobby Bonilla	.15	.07	.02
□ 595	Esteban Beltre	.05	.02	.01
□ 596	Mike Hartley	.05	.02	.01
□ 597	Felix Fermin	.05	.02	.01
□ 598	Carlos Garcia	.05	.02	.01
□ 599	Frank Tanana	.05	.02	.01
□ 600	Pedro Guerrero	.05	.02	.01
□ 601	Terry Shumpert	.05	.02	.01
□ 602	Wally Whitehurst	.05	.02	.01
□ 603	Kevin Seitzer	.05	.02	.01
□ 604	Chris James	.05	.02	.01
□ 605	Greg Gohr RR	.05	.02	.01
□ 606	Mark Wohlers	.15	.07	.02
□ 607	Kirby Puckett	.60	.25	.07
□ 608	Greg Maddux	1.25	.55	.16
□ 609	Don Mattingly	1.00	.45	.12
□ 610	Greg Cadaret	.05	.02	.01
□ 611	Dave Stewart	.15	.07	.02
□ 612	Mark Portugal	.05	.02	.01
□ 613	Pete O'Brien	.05	.02	.01
□ 614	Bobby Ojeda	.05	.02	.01
□ 615	Joe Carter	.30	.14	.04
□ 616	Pete Young	.05	.02	.01
□ 617	Sam Horn	.05	.02	.01
□ 618	Vince Coleman	.05	.02	.01
□ 619	Wade Boggs	.30	.14	.04
□ 620	Todd Pratt	.05	.02	.01
□ 621	Ron Tingley	.05	.02	.01
□ 622	Doug Drabek	.05	.02	.01
□ 623	Scott Hemond	.05	.02	.01
□ 624	Tim Jones	.05	.02	.01
□ 625	Dennis Cook	.05	.02	.01
□ 626	Jose Melendez	.05	.02	.01
□ 627	Mike Munoz	.05	.02	.01
□ 628	Jim Pena	.05	.02	.01
□ 629	Gary Thurman	.05	.02	.01
□ 630	Charlie Leibrandt	.05	.02	.01
□ 631	Scott Fletcher	.05	.02	.01
□ 632	Andre Dawson	.30	.14	.04
□ 633	Greg Gagne	.05	.02	.01

□	634 Greg Swindell	.05	.02	.01
□	635 Kevin Maas	.05	.02	.01
□	636 Xavier Hernandez	.05	.02	.01
□	637 Ruben Sierra	.15	.07	.02
□	638 Dmitri Young RR	.50	.23	.06
□	639 Harold Reynolds	.05	.02	.01
□	640 Tom Goodwin	.05	.02	.01
□	641 Todd Burns	.05	.02	.01
□	642 Jeff Fassero	.15	.07	.02
□	643 Dave Winfield	.30	.14	.04
□	644 Willie Randolph	.15	.07	.02
□	645 Luis Mercedes	.05	.02	.01
□	646 Dale Murphy	.30	.14	.04
□	647 Danny Darwin	.05	.02	.01
□	648 Dennis Moeller	.05	.02	.01
□	649 Chuck Crim	.05	.02	.01
□	650 Checklist	.05	.02	.01
□	651 Shawn Abner	.05	.02	.01
□	652 Tracy Woodson	.05	.02	.01
□	653 Scott Scudder	.05	.02	.01
□	654 Tom Lampkin	.05	.02	.01
□	655 Alan Trammell	.30	.14	.04
□	656 Cory Snyder	.05	.02	.01
□	657 Chris Gwynn	.05	.02	.01
□	658 Lonnie Smith	.05	.02	.01
□	659 Jim Austin	.05	.02	.01
□	660 Checklist	.05	.02	.01
□	661 Tim Hulett	.05	.02	.01
□	662 Marvin Freeman	.05	.02	.01
□	663 Greg A. Harris	.05	.02	.01
□	664 Heathcliff Slocumb	.05	.02	.01
□	665 Mike Butcher	.05	.02	.01
□	666 Steve Foster	.05	.02	.01
□	667 Donn Pall	.05	.02	.01
□	668 Darryl Kile	.05	.02	.01
□	669 Jesse Levis	.05	.02	.01
□	670 Jim Gott	.05	.02	.01
□	671 Mark Hutton RR	.05	.02	.01
□	672 Brian Drahman	.05	.02	.01
□	673 Chad Kreuter	.05	.02	.01
□	674 Tony Fernandez	.05	.02	.01
□	675 Jose Lind	.05	.02	.01
□	676 Kyle Abbott	.05	.02	.01
□	677 Dan Plesac	.05	.02	.01
□	678 Barry Bonds	.50	.23	.06
□	679 Chili Davis	.15	.07	.02
□	680 Stan Royer	.05	.02	.01
□	681 Scott Kamieniecki	.05	.02	.01
□	682 Carlos Martinez	.05	.02	.01
□	683 Mike Moore	.05	.02	.01
□	684 Candy Maldonado	.05	.02	.01
□	685 Jeff Nelson	.05	.02	.01
□	686 Lou Whitaker	.30	.14	.04
□	687 Jose Guzman	.05	.02	.01
□	688 Manuel Lee	.05	.02	.01
□	689 Bob MacDonald	.05	.02	.01
□	690 Scott Bankhead	.05	.02	.01
□	691 Alan Mills	.05	.02	.01
□	692 Brian Williams	.05	.02	.01
□	693 Tom Brunansky	.05	.02	.01
□	694 Lenny Webster	.05	.02	.01
□	695 Greg Briley	.05	.02	.01
□	696 Paul O'Neill	.15	.07	.02
□	697 Joey Cora	.05	.02	.01
□	698 Charlie O'Brien	.05	.02	.01
□	699 Junior Ortiz	.05	.02	.01
□	700 Ron Darling	.05	.02	.01
□	701 Tony Phillips	.15	.07	.02
□	702 William Pennyfeather	.05	.02	.01
□	703 Mark Gubicza	.05	.02	.01
□	704 Steve Hosey RR	.05	.02	.01
□	705 Henry Cotto	.05	.02	.01
□	706 David Hulse	.05	.02	.01
□	707 Mike Pagliarulo	.05	.02	.01
□	708 Dave Stieb	.05	.02	.01
□	709 Melido Perez	.05	.02	.01
□	710 Jimmy Key	.15	.07	.02
□	711 Jeff Russell	.05	.02	.01
□	712 David Cone	.30	.14	.04
□	713 Russ Swan	.05	.02	.01
□	714 Mark Guthrie	.05	.02	.01
□	715 Checklist	.05	.02	.01
□	716 Al Martin RR	.15	.07	.02
□	717 Randy Knorr	.05	.02	.01
□	718 Mike Stanley	.05	.02	.01
□	719 Rick Sutcliffe	.05	.02	.01
□	720 Terry Leach	.05	.02	.01
□	721 Chipper Jones RR	2.50	1.10	.30
□	722 Jim Eisenreich	.15	.07	.02
□	723 Tom Henke	.05	.02	.01
□	724 Jeff Frye	.05	.02	.01
□	725 Harold Baines	.15	.07	.02
□	726 Scott Sanderson	.05	.02	.01
□	727 Tom Foley	.05	.02	.01
□	728 Bryan Harvey	.05	.02	.01
□	729 Tom Edens	.05	.02	.01
□	730 Eric Young	.30	.14	.04
□	731 Dave Weathers	.05	.02	.01
□	732 Spike Owen	.05	.02	.01
□	733 Scott Aldred	.05	.02	.01
□	734 Cris Carpenter	.05	.02	.01
□	735 Dion James	.05	.02	.01
□	736 Joe Girardi	.05	.02	.01
□	737 Nigel Wilson RR	.05	.02	.01
□	738 Scott Chiamparino	.05	.02	.01
□	739 Jeff Reardon	.15	.07	.02
□	740 Willie Blair	.05	.02	.01
□	741 Jim Corsi	.05	.02	.01
□	742 Ken Patterson	.05	.02	.01
□	743 Andy Ashby	.15	.07	.02
□	744 Rob Natal	.05	.02	.01
□	745 Kevin Bass	.05	.02	.01
□	746 Freddie Benavides	.05	.02	.01
□	747 Chris Donnels	.05	.02	.01
□	748 Kerry Woodson	.05	.02	.01
□	749 Calvin Jones	.05	.02	.01
□	750 Gary Scott	.05	.02	.01
□	751 Joe Orsulak	.05	.02	.01
□	752 Armando Reynoso	.05	.02	.01
□	753 Monty Fariss	.05	.02	.01
□	754 Billy Hatcher	.05	.02	.01
□	755 Denis Boucher	.05	.02	.01
□	756 Walt Weiss	.05	.02	.01
□	757 Mike Fitzgerald	.05	.02	.01
□	758 Rudy Seanez	.05	.02	.01
□	759 Bret Barberie	.05	.02	.01
□	760 Mo Sanford	.05	.02	.01
□	761 Pedro Castellano	.05	.02	.01
□	762 Chuck Carr	.05	.02	.01
□	763 Steve Howe	.05	.02	.01
□	764 Andres Galarraga	.30	.14	.04
□	765 Jeff Conine	.30	.14	.04
□	766 Ted Power	.05	.02	.01
□	767 Butch Henry	.05	.02	.01
□	768 Steve Decker	.05	.02	.01
□	769 Storm Davis	.05	.02	.01
□	770 Vinny Castilla	.30	.14	.04
□	771 Junior Felix	.05	.02	.01
□	772 Walt Terrell	.05	.02	.01
□	773 Brad Ausmus	.05	.02	.01
□	774 Jamie McAndrew	.05	.02	.01
□	775 Milt Thompson	.05	.02	.01
□	776 Charlie Hayes	.05	.02	.01
□	777 Jack Armstrong	.05	.02	.01
□	778 Dennis Rasmussen	.05	.02	.01
□	779 Darren Holmes	.05	.02	.01
□	780 Alex Arias	.05	.02	.01
□	781 Randy Bush	.05	.02	.01
□	782 Javier Lopez RR	.50	.23	.06
□	783 Dante Bichette	.30	.14	.04
□	784 John Johnstone	.05	.02	.01
□	785 Rene Gonzales	.05	.02	.01
□	786 Alex Cole	.05	.02	.01
□	787 Jeromy Burnitz RR	.05	.02	.01
□	788 Michael Huff	.05	.02	.01
□	789 Anthony Telford	.05	.02	.01
□	790 Jerald Clark	.05	.02	.01
□	791 Joel Johnston	.05	.02	.01
□	792 David Nied RR	.05	.02	.01

1993 Donruss Diamond Kings

These standard-size cards, commemorating Donruss' annual selection of the games top players, were randomly inserted in 1993 Donruss packs. The first 15 cards were available in the first series of the 1993 Donruss and cards 16-31 were inserted with the second series. The cards are gold-foil stamped and

feature player portraits by noted sports artist Dick Perez. Card numbers 27-28 honor the first draft picks of the new Florida Marlins and Colorado Rockies franchises. Collectors 16 years of age and younger could enter Donruss' Diamond King contest by writing an essay of 75 words or less explaining who their favorite Diamond King player was and why. Winners were awarded one of 30 framed watercolors at the National Convention, held in Chicago, July 22-25, 1993.

	MINT	NRMT	EXC
COMPLETE SET (31)	30.00	13.50	3.70
COMPLETE SERIES 1 (15)	20.00	9.00	2.50
COMPLETE SERIES 2 (16)	10.00	4.50	1.25
COMMON CARD (DK1-DK31)	.75	.35	.09
SEMISTARS	1.50	.70	.19
RANDOM INSERTS IN FOIL PACKS			

	MINT	NRMT	EXC
□ DK1 Ken Griffey Jr.	12.00	5.50	1.50
□ DK2 Ryne Sandberg	3.00	1.35	.35
□ DK3 Roger Clemens	1.50	.70	.19
□ DK4 Kirby Puckett	4.00	1.80	.50
□ DK5 Bill Swift	.75	.35	.09
□ DK6 Larry Walker	1.50	.70	.19
□ DK7 Juan Gonzalez	6.00	2.70	.75
□ DK8 Wally Joyner	.75	.35	.09
□ DK9 Andy Van Slyke	.75	.35	.09
□ DK10 Robin Ventura	1.50	.70	.19
□ DK11 Bip Roberts	.75	.35	.09
□ DK12 Roberto Kelly	.75	.35	.09
□ DK13 Carlos Baerga	1.50	.70	.19
□ DK14 Orel Hershiser	1.50	.70	.19
□ DK15 Cecil Fielder	1.50	.70	.19
□ DK16 Robin Yount	1.50	.70	.19
□ DK17 Darren Daulton	.75	.35	.09
□ DK18 Mark McGwire	4.00	1.80	.50
□ DK19 Tom Glavine	1.50	.70	.19
□ DK20 Roberto Alomar	3.00	1.35	.35
□ DK21 Gary Sheffield	2.00	.90	.25
□ DK22 Bob Tewksbury	.75	.35	.09
□ DK23 Brady Anderson	1.50	.70	.19
□ DK24 Craig Biggio	1.50	.70	.19
□ DK25 Eddie Murray	3.00	1.35	.35
□ DK26 Luis Polonia	.75	.35	.09
□ DK27 Nigel Wilson	.75	.35	.09
□ DK28 David Nied	.75	.35	.09
□ DK29 Pat Listach ROY	.75	.35	.09
□ DK30 Eric Karros ROY	1.50	.70	.19
□ DK31 Checklist 1-31	.75	.35	.09

1993 Donruss Elite

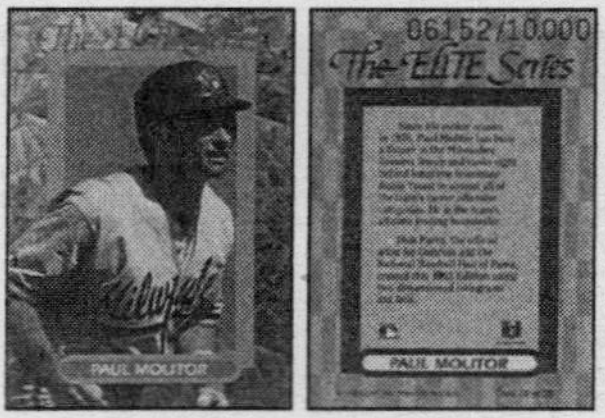

Cards 19-27 were random inserts in 1993 Donruss series I foil packs while cards 28-36 were inserted in series II packs. The numbering on the 1993 Elite cards follows consecutively after that of the 1992 Elite series cards, and each of the 10,000 Elite cards is serially numbered. The backs of the Elite cards also carry the serial number ("X" of 10,000) as well as the card number. The Signature Series Will Clark card was randomly inserted in 1993 Donruss foil packs; he personally autographed 5,000 cards. Featuring a Dick Perez portrait, the ten thousand Legends Series cards honor Robin Yount for his 3,000th hit achievement. The front design of the Elite cards features a cutout color player photo superimposed on a neon-colored panel framed by a gray inner border and a variegated silver metallic outer border.

	MINT	NRMT	EXC
COMPLETE SET (20)	400.00	180.00	50.00
COMMON CARD (19-36)	10.00	4.50	1.25
SEMISTARS	15.00	6.75	1.85
RANDOM INSERTS IN PACKS			

	MINT	NRMT	EXC
□ 19 Fred McGriff	15.00	6.75	1.85
□ 20 Ryne Sandberg	30.00	13.50	3.70
□ 21 Eddie Murray	30.00	13.50	3.70
□ 22 Paul Molitor	30.00	13.50	3.70
□ 23 Barry Larkin	20.00	9.00	2.50
□ 24 Don Mattingly	60.00	27.00	7.50
□ 25 Dennis Eckersley	15.00	6.75	1.85
□ 26 Roberto Alomar	30.00	13.50	3.70
□ 27 Edgar Martinez	15.00	6.75	1.85
□ 28 Gary Sheffield	25.00	11.00	3.10
□ 29 Darren Daulton	10.00	4.50	1.25
□ 30 Larry Walker	15.00	6.75	1.85
□ 31 Barry Bonds	30.00	13.50	3.70
□ 32 Andy Van Slyke	10.00	4.50	1.25
□ 33 Mark McGwire	50.00	22.00	6.25
□ 34 Cecil Fielder	15.00	6.75	1.85
□ 35 Dave Winfield	15.00	6.75	1.85
□ 36 Juan Gonzalez	50.00	22.00	6.25
□ L3 Robin Yount (Legend Series)	20.00	9.00	2.50
□ S3 Will Clark AU (Signature Series)	150.00	70.00	19.00

1993 Donruss Long Ball Leaders

Randomly inserted in 26-card magazine distributor packs (1-9 in series I and 10-18 in series II), these standard-size cards feature some of MLB's outstanding sluggers. The fronts feature full-bleed color action player photos with a red and bright yellow stripe design across the bottom that carries the player's name and team. The Donruss Long Ball Leaders icon rests on the stripe at the lower left. The player's longest home run is printed in gold foil at the upper left.

	MINT	NRMT	EXC
COMPLETE SET (18)	60.00	27.00	7.50
COMPLETE SERIES 1 (9)	30.00	13.50	3.70

COMPLETE SERIES 2 (9)	30.00	13.50	3.70
COMMON CARD (LL1-LL18)	1.50	.70	.19
SEMISTARS	2.50	1.10	.30
RANDOM INSERTS IN 26-CARD JUMBOS...			

☐ LL1 Rob Deer	1.50	.70	.19
☐ LL2 Fred McGriff	2.50	1.10	.30
☐ LL3 Albert Belle	10.00	4.50	1.25
☐ LL4 Mark McGwire	6.00	2.70	.75
☐ LL5 David Justice	1.50	.70	.19
☐ LL6 Jose Canseco	2.50	1.10	.30
☐ LL7 Kent Hrbek	1.50	.70	.19
☐ LL8 Roberto Alomar	5.00	2.20	.60
☐ LL9 Ken Griffey Jr.	20.00	9.00	2.50
☐ LL10 Frank Thomas	20.00	9.00	2.50
☐ LL11 Darryl Strawberry	2.50	1.10	.30
☐ LL12 Felix Jose	1.50	.70	.19
☐ LL13 Cecil Fielder	2.50	1.10	.30
☐ LL14 Juan Gonzalez	10.00	4.50	1.25
☐ LL15 Ryne Sandberg	5.00	2.20	.60
☐ LL16 Gary Sheffield	3.00	1.35	.35
☐ LL17 Jeff Bagwell	8.00	3.60	1.00
☐ LL18 Larry Walker	1.50	.70	.19

1993 Donruss MVPs

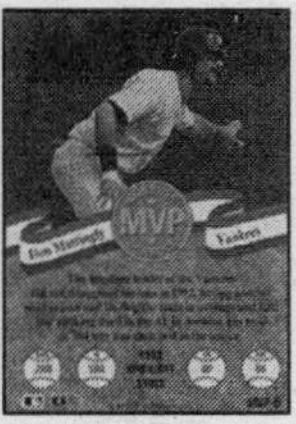

These twenty-six standard size MVP cards were issued 13 cards in each series, and they were inserted one per 23-card jumbo packs. The fronts feature full-bleed color action player photos with a red, white, and blue ribbon design across the bottom that contains the player's name and team. The Donruss MVP icon is gold-foil stamped over the ribbon.

	MINT	NRMT	EXC
COMPLETE SET (26)	30.00	13.50	3.70
COMPLETE SERIES 1 (13)	10.00	4.50	1.25
COMPLETE SERIES 2 (13)	20.00	9.00	2.50
COMMON CARD (1-26)	.50	.23	.06
SEMISTARS	1.00	.45	.12
MVP PREFIX ON CARD NUMBER			
ONE PER 23-CARD JUMBO PACK			

☐ 1 Luis Polonia	.50	.23	.06
☐ 2 Frank Thomas	8.00	3.60	1.00
☐ 3 George Brett	3.00	1.35	.35
☐ 4 Paul Molitor	1.50	.70	.19
☐ 5 Don Mattingly	4.00	1.80	.50
☐ 6 Roberto Alomar	2.00	.90	.25
☐ 7 Terry Pendleton	.50	.23	.06
☐ 8 Eric Karros	1.00	.45	.12
☐ 9 Larry Walker	1.00	.45	.12
☐ 10 Eddie Murray	2.00	.90	.25
☐ 11 Darren Daulton	.50	.23	.06
☐ 12 Ray Lankford	1.00	.45	.12
☐ 13 Will Clark	1.00	.45	.12
☐ 14 Cal Ripken	6.00	2.70	.75
☐ 15 Roger Clemens	1.00	.45	.12
☐ 16 Carlos Baerga	1.00	.45	.12
☐ 17 Cecil Fielder	1.00	.45	.12
☐ 18 Kirby Puckett	2.50	1.10	.30
☐ 19 Mark McGwire	2.50	1.10	.30
☐ 20 Ken Griffey Jr.	8.00	3.60	1.00
☐ 21 Juan Gonzalez	4.00	1.80	.50
☐ 22 Ryne Sandberg	2.00	.90	.25
☐ 23 Bip Roberts	.50	.23	.06
☐ 24 Jeff Bagwell	3.00	1.35	.35
☐ 25 Barry Bonds	2.00	.90	.25
☐ 26 Gary Sheffield	1.25	.55	.16

1993 Donruss Spirit of the Game

These 20 standard-size cards were randomly inserted in 1993 Donruss packs and packed approximately two per box. Cards 1-10 were first-series inserts, and cards 11-20 were second-series inserts. The fronts feature borderless glossy color action player photos. The set title, "Spirit of the Game," is stamped in gold foil script across the top or bottom of the picture.

	MINT	NRMT	EXC
COMPLETE SET (20)	20.00	9.00	2.50
COMPLETE SERIES 1 (10)	8.00	3.60	1.00
COMPLETE SERIES 2 (10)	12.00	5.50	1.50
COMMON CARD (SG1-SG20)	.50	.23	.06
SEMISTARS	1.00	.45	.12
RANDOM INSERTS IN FOIL/JUMBO PACKS			

☐ SG1 Mike Bordick Turning Two	.50	.23	.06
☐ SG2 Dave Justice Play at the Plate	1.00	.45	.12
☐ SG3 Roberto Alomar In There	2.50	1.10	.30
☐ SG4 Dennis Eckersley Pumped	1.00	.45	.12
☐ SG5 Juan Gonzalez and Jose Canseco Dynamic Duo	4.00	1.80	.50
☐ SG6 George Bell and Frank Thomas ... Gone	2.50	1.10	.30
☐ SG7 Wade Boggs and Luis Polonia Safe or Out	1.00	.45	.12
☐ SG8 Will Clark The Thrill	1.00	.45	.12
☐ SG9 Bip Roberts Safe at Home	.50	.23	.06
☐ SG10 Cecil Fielder Rob Deer Mickey Tettleton Thirty 3	1.00	.45	.12
☐ SG11 Kenny Lofton Bag Bandit	4.00	1.80	.50
☐ SG12 Gary Sheffield Fred McGriff Back to Back	1.00	.45	.12
☐ SG13 Greg Gagne Barry Larkin	1.00	.45	.12
☐ SG14 Ryne Sandberg The Ball Stops Here	2.50	1.10	.30
☐ SG15 Carlos Baerga Gary Gaetti Over the Top	1.00	.45	.12
☐ SG16 Danny Tartabull At the Wall	.50	.23	.06
☐ SG17 Brady Anderson Head First	1.25	.55	.16
☐ SG18 Frank Thomas Big Hurt	10.00	4.50	1.25
☐ SG19 Kevin Gross No Hitter	.50	.23	.06
☐ SG20 Robin Yount 3,000 Hits	1.00	.45	.12

1994 Donruss

The 1994 Donruss set was issued in two separate series of 330 standard-size cards for a total of 660. The fronts feature borderless color player action photos on front. The player's name and position appear in gold foil within a team color-coded stripe near the bottom. The team logo appears within a black rectangle framed by a team color near the bottom. The set name and year, stamped in gold foil, also appear in this rectangle. Most of the backs are horizontal, and feature another borderless color player action photo. A black rectangle framed by a team color appears on one side and carries the player's name, team, uniform number, and biography. The player's stats appear within ghosted stripes near the bottom. Rookie Cards include Curtis Pride and Julian Tavarez.

	MINT	NRMT	EXC
COMPLETE SET (660)	50.00	22.00	6.25
COMPLETE SERIES 1 (330)	25.00	11.00	3.10
COMPLETE SERIES 2 (330)	25.00	11.00	3.10
COMMON CARD (1-660)	.10	.05	.01
SEMISTARS	.25	.11	.03
STARS	.50	.23	.06
COMP.SPEC.ED.SET (100)	20.00	9.00	2.50
COMP.SPEC.ED.SER.1 (50)	10.00	4.50	1.25
COMP.SPEC.ED.SER.2 (50)	10.00	4.50	1.25
COMMON SPEC.ED (1-100)	.20	.09	.03
SPEC.EDITION SEMISTARS	.40	.18	.05
*SPEC.ED.STARS: 1X to 2X HI COLUMN			
ONE IN EVERY SER.1 , SER.2 PACK			
SE NUMBERS 51-100 CORRESPOND w/331-380			

		MINT	NRMT	EXC
□ 1	Nolan Ryan	3.00	1.35	.35
□ 2	Mike Piazza	2.00	.90	.25
□ 3	Moises Alou	.25	.11	.03
□ 4	Ken Griffey Jr.	3.00	1.35	.35
□ 5	Gary Sheffield	.50	.23	.06
□ 6	Roberto Alomar	.75	.35	.09
□ 7	John Kruk	.25	.11	.03
□ 8	Gregg Olson	.10	.05	.01
□ 9	Gregg Jefferies	.50	.23	.06
□ 10	Tony Gwynn	1.25	.55	.16
□ 11	Chad Curtis	.10	.05	.01
□ 12	Craig Biggio	.50	.23	.06
□ 13	John Burkett	.10	.05	.01
□ 14	Carlos Baerga	.50	.23	.06
□ 15	Robin Yount	.50	.23	.06
□ 16	Dennis Eckersley	.25	.11	.03
□ 17	Dwight Gooden	.25	.11	.03
□ 18	Ryne Sandberg	.75	.35	.09
□ 19	Rickey Henderson	.50	.23	.06
□ 20	Jack McDowell	.25	.11	.03
□ 21	Jay Bell	.25	.11	.03
□ 22	Kevin Brown	.10	.05	.01
□ 23	Robin Ventura	.25	.11	.03
□ 24	Paul Molitor	.60	.25	.07
□ 25	David Justice	.50	.23	.06
□ 26	Rafael Palmeiro	.50	.23	.06
□ 27	Cecil Fielder	.25	.11	.03
□ 28	Chuck Knoblauch	.50	.23	.06
□ 29	Dave Hollins	.10	.05	.01
□ 30	Jimmy Key	.25	.11	.03
□ 31	Mark Langston	.25	.11	.03
□ 32	Darryl Kile	.10	.05	.01
□ 33	Ruben Sierra	.25	.11	.03
□ 34	Ron Gant	.25	.11	.03
□ 35	Ozzie Smith	.60	.25	.07
□ 36	Wade Boggs	.50	.23	.06
□ 37	Marquis Grissom	.50	.23	.06
□ 38	Will Clark	.50	.23	.06
□ 39	Kenny Lofton	1.00	.45	.12
□ 40	Cal Ripken	2.50	1.10	.30
□ 41	Steve Avery	.25	.11	.03
□ 42	Mo Vaughn	.75	.35	.09
□ 43	Brian McRae	.25	.11	.03
□ 44	Mickey Tettleton	.10	.05	.01
□ 45	Barry Larkin	.50	.23	.06
□ 46	Charlie Hayes	.10	.05	.01
□ 47	Kevin Appier	.25	.11	.03
□ 48	Robby Thompson	.10	.05	.01
□ 49	Juan Gonzalez	1.50	.70	.19
□ 50	Paul O'Neill	.25	.11	.03
□ 51	Marcos Armas	.10	.05	.01
□ 52	Mike Butcher	.10	.05	.01
□ 53	Ken Caminiti	.50	.23	.06
□ 54	Pat Borders	.10	.05	.01
□ 55	Pedro Munoz	.10	.05	.01
□ 56	Tim Belcher	.10	.05	.01
□ 57	Paul Assenmacher	.10	.05	.01
□ 58	Damon Berryhill	.10	.05	.01
□ 59	Ricky Bones	.10	.05	.01
□ 60	Rene Arocha	.10	.05	.01
□ 61	Shawn Boskie	.10	.05	.01
□ 62	Pedro Astacio	.10	.05	.01
□ 63	Frank Bolick	.10	.05	.01
□ 64	Bud Black	.10	.05	.01
□ 65	Sandy Alomar Jr.	.25	.11	.03
□ 66	Rich Amaral	.10	.05	.01
□ 67	Luis Aquino	.10	.05	.01
□ 68	Kevin Baez	.10	.05	.01
□ 69	Mike Devereaux	.10	.05	.01
□ 70	Andy Ashby	.25	.11	.03
□ 71	Larry Andersen	.10	.05	.01
□ 72	Steve Cooke	.10	.05	.01
□ 73	Mario Diaz	.10	.05	.01
□ 74	Rob Deer	.10	.05	.01
□ 75	Bobby Ayala	.10	.05	.01
□ 76	Freddie Benavides	.10	.05	.01
□ 77	Stan Belinda	.10	.05	.01
□ 78	John Doherty	.10	.05	.01
□ 79	Willie Banks	.10	.05	.01
□ 80	Spike Owen	.10	.05	.01
□ 81	Mike Bordick	.10	.05	.01
□ 82	Chili Davis	.25	.11	.03
□ 83	Luis Gonzalez	.10	.05	.01
□ 84	Ed Sprague	.25	.11	.03
□ 85	Jeff Reboulet	.10	.05	.01
□ 86	Jason Bere	.25	.11	.03
□ 87	Mark Hutton	.10	.05	.01
□ 88	Jeff Blauser	.10	.05	.01
□ 89	Cal Eldred	.10	.05	.01
□ 90	Bernard Gilkey	.25	.11	.03
□ 91	Frank Castillo	.10	.05	.01
□ 92	Jim Gott	.10	.05	.01
□ 93	Greg Colbrunn	.10	.05	.01
□ 94	Jeff Brantley	.10	.05	.01
□ 95	Jeremy Hernandez	.10	.05	.01
□ 96	Norm Charlton	.10	.05	.01
□ 97	Alex Arias	.10	.05	.01
□ 98	John Franco	.10	.05	.01
□ 99	Chris Hoiles	.10	.05	.01
□ 100	Brad Ausmus	.10	.05	.01
□ 101	Wes Chamberlain	.10	.05	.01
□ 102	Mark Dewey	.10	.05	.01
□ 103	Benji Gil	.10	.05	.01
□ 104	John Dopson	.10	.05	.01
□ 105	John Smiley	.10	.05	.01
□ 106	David Nied	.10	.05	.01
□ 107	George Brett	1.25	.55	.16
□ 108	Kirk Gibson	.25	.11	.03
□ 109	Larry Casian	.10	.05	.01
□ 110	Checklist 1-82 Ryne Sandberg	.25	.11	.03
□ 111	Brent Gates	.10	.05	.01
□ 112	Damion Easley	.10	.05	.01
□ 113	Pete Harnisch	.10	.05	.01
□ 114	Danny Cox	.10	.05	.01
□ 115	Kevin Tapani	.10	.05	.01
□ 116	Roberto Hernandez	.25	.11	.03
□ 117	Domingo Jean	.10	.05	.01
□ 118	Sid Bream	.10	.05	.01

□ 119	Doug Henry	.10	.05	.01
□ 120	Omar Olivares	.10	.05	.01
□ 121	Mike Harkey	.10	.05	.01
□ 122	Carlos Hernandez	.10	.05	.01
□ 123	Jeff Fassero	.10	.05	.01
□ 124	Dave Burba	.10	.05	.01
□ 125	Wayne Kirby	.10	.05	.01
□ 126	John Cummings	.10	.05	.01
□ 127	Bret Barberie	.10	.05	.01
□ 128	Todd Hundley	.50	.23	.06
□ 129	Tim Hulett	.10	.05	.01
□ 130	Phil Clark	.10	.05	.01
□ 131	Danny Jackson	.10	.05	.01
□ 132	Tom Foley	.10	.05	.01
□ 133	Donald Harris	.10	.05	.01
□ 134	Scott Fletcher	.10	.05	.01
□ 135	Johnny Ruffin	.10	.05	.01
□ 136	Jerald Clark	.10	.05	.01
□ 137	Billy Brewer	.10	.05	.01
□ 138	Dan Gladden	.10	.05	.01
□ 139	Eddie Guardado	.10	.05	.01
□ 140	Checklist 83-164 Cal Ripken	.50	.23	.06
□ 141	Scott Hemond	.10	.05	.01
□ 142	Steve Frey	.10	.05	.01
□ 143	Xavier Hernandez	.10	.05	.01
□ 144	Mark Eichhorn	.10	.05	.01
□ 145	Ellis Burks	.25	.11	.03
□ 146	Jim Leyritz	.10	.05	.01
□ 147	Mark Lemke	.10	.05	.01
□ 148	Pat Listach	.10	.05	.01
□ 149	Donovan Osborne	.10	.05	.01
□ 150	Glenallen Hill	.10	.05	.01
□ 151	Orel Hershiser	.25	.11	.03
□ 152	Darrin Fletcher	.10	.05	.01
□ 153	Royce Clayton	.25	.11	.03
□ 154	Derek Lilliquist	.10	.05	.01
□ 155	Mike Felder	.10	.05	.01
□ 156	Jeff Conine	.50	.23	.06
□ 157	Ryan Thompson	.10	.05	.01
□ 158	Ben McDonald	.10	.05	.01
□ 159	Ricky Gutierrez	.10	.05	.01
□ 160	Terry Mulholland	.10	.05	.01
□ 161	Carlos Garcia	.10	.05	.01
□ 162	Tom Henke	.10	.05	.01
□ 163	Mike Greenwell	.10	.05	.01
□ 164	Thomas Howard	.10	.05	.01
□ 165	Joe Girardi	.10	.05	.01
□ 166	Hubie Brooks	.10	.05	.01
□ 167	Greg Gohr	.10	.05	.01
□ 168	Chip Hale	.10	.05	.01
□ 169	Rick Honeycutt	.10	.05	.01
□ 170	Hilly Hathaway	.10	.05	.01
□ 171	Todd Jones	.10	.05	.01
□ 172	Tony Fernandez	.10	.05	.01
□ 173	Bo Jackson	.50	.23	.06
□ 174	Bobby Munoz	.10	.05	.01
□ 175	Greg McMichael	.10	.05	.01
□ 176	Graeme Lloyd	.10	.05	.01
□ 177	Tom Pagnozzi	.10	.05	.01
□ 178	Derrick May	.10	.05	.01
□ 179	Pedro Martinez	.50	.23	.06
□ 180	Ken Hill	.10	.05	.01
□ 181	Bryan Hickerson	.10	.05	.01
□ 182	Jose Mesa	.25	.11	.03
□ 183	Dave Fleming	.10	.05	.01
□ 184	Henry Cotto	.10	.05	.01
□ 185	Jeff Kent	.10	.05	.01
□ 186	Mark McLemore	.10	.05	.01
□ 187	Trevor Hoffman	.25	.11	.03
□ 188	Todd Pratt	.10	.05	.01
□ 189	Blas Minor	.10	.05	.01
□ 190	Charlie Leibrandt	.10	.05	.01
□ 191	Tony Pena	.10	.05	.01
□ 192	Larry Luebbers	.10	.05	.01
□ 193	Greg W. Harris	.10	.05	.01
□ 194	David Cone	.50	.23	.06
□ 195	Bill Gullickson	.10	.05	.01
□ 196	Brian Harper	.10	.05	.01
□ 197	Steve Karsay	.10	.05	.01
□ 198	Greg Myers	.10	.05	.01
□ 199	Mark Portugal	.10	.05	.01
□ 200	Pat Hentgen	.50	.23	.06
□ 201	Mike LaValliere	.10	.05	.01
□ 202	Mike Stanley	.10	.05	.01
□ 203	Kent Mercker	.10	.05	.01
□ 204	Dave Nilsson	.25	.11	.03
□ 205	Erik Pappas	.10	.05	.01
□ 206	Mike Morgan	.10	.05	.01
□ 207	Roger McDowell	.10	.05	.01
□ 208	Mike Lansing	.25	.11	.03
□ 209	Kirt Manwaring	.10	.05	.01
□ 210	Randy Milligan	.10	.05	.01
□ 211	Erik Hanson	.10	.05	.01
□ 212	Orestes Destrade	.10	.05	.01
□ 213	Mike Maddux	.10	.05	.01
□ 214	Alan Mills	.10	.05	.01
□ 215	Tim Mauser	.10	.05	.01
□ 216	Ben Rivera	.10	.05	.01
□ 217	Don Slaught	.10	.05	.01
□ 218	Bob Patterson	.10	.05	.01
□ 219	Carlos Quintana	.10	.05	.01
□ 220	Checklist 165-247 Tim Raines	.25	.11	.03
□ 221	Hal Morris	.10	.05	.01
□ 222	Darren Holmes	.10	.05	.01
□ 223	Chris Gwynn	.10	.05	.01
□ 224	Chad Kreuter	.10	.05	.01
□ 225	Mike Hartley	.10	.05	.01
□ 226	Scott Lydy	.10	.05	.01
□ 227	Eduardo Perez	.10	.05	.01
□ 228	Greg Swindell	.10	.05	.01
□ 229	Al Leiter	.25	.11	.03
□ 230	Scott Radinsky	.10	.05	.01
□ 231	Bob Wickman	.10	.05	.01
□ 232	Otis Nixon	.10	.05	.01
□ 233	Kevin Reimer	.10	.05	.01
□ 234	Geronimo Pena	.10	.05	.01
□ 235	Kevin Roberson	.10	.05	.01
□ 236	Jody Reed	.10	.05	.01
□ 237	Kirk Rueter	.10	.05	.01
□ 238	Willie McGee	.10	.05	.01
□ 239	Charles Nagy	.25	.11	.03
□ 240	Tim Leary	.10	.05	.01
□ 241	Carl Everett	.10	.05	.01
□ 242	Charlie O'Brien	.10	.05	.01
□ 243	Mike Pagliarulo	.10	.05	.01
□ 244	Kerry Taylor	.10	.05	.01
□ 245	Kevin Stocker	.10	.05	.01
□ 246	Joel Johnston	.10	.05	.01
□ 247	Geno Petralli	.10	.05	.01
□ 248	Jeff Russell	.10	.05	.01
□ 249	Joe Oliver	.10	.05	.01
□ 250	Roberto Mejia	.10	.05	.01
□ 251	Chris Haney	.10	.05	.01
□ 252	Bill Krueger	.10	.05	.01
□ 253	Shane Mack	.10	.05	.01
□ 254	Terry Steinbach	.25	.11	.03
□ 255	Luis Polonia	.10	.05	.01
□ 256	Eddie Taubensee	.10	.05	.01
□ 257	Dave Stewart	.25	.11	.03
□ 258	Tim Raines	.50	.23	.06
□ 259	Bernie Williams	.50	.23	.06
□ 260	John Smoltz	.50	.23	.06
□ 261	Kevin Seitzer	.10	.05	.01
□ 262	Bob Tewksbury	.10	.05	.01
□ 263	Bob Scanlan	.10	.05	.01
□ 264	Henry Rodriguez	.50	.23	.06
□ 265	Tim Scott	.10	.05	.01
□ 266	Scott Sanderson	.10	.05	.01
□ 267	Eric Plunk	.10	.05	.01
□ 268	Edgar Martinez	.50	.23	.06
□ 269	Charlie Hough	.10	.05	.01
□ 270	Joe Orsulak	.10	.05	.01
□ 271	Harold Reynolds	.10	.05	.01
□ 272	Tim Teufel	.10	.05	.01
□ 273	Bobby Thigpen	.10	.05	.01
□ 274	Randy Tomlin	.10	.05	.01
□ 275	Gary Redus	.10	.05	.01
□ 276	Ken Ryan	.10	.05	.01
□ 277	Tim Pugh	.10	.05	.01
□ 278	J. Owens	.10	.05	.01
□ 279	Phil Hiatt	.10	.05	.01
□ 280	Alan Trammell	.50	.23	.06
□ 281	Dave McCarty	.10	.05	.01
□ 282	Bob Welch	.10	.05	.01
□ 283	J.T. Snow	.25	.11	.03
□ 284	Brian Williams	.10	.05	.01
□ 285	Devon White	.10	.05	.01
□ 286	Steve Sax	.10	.05	.01
□ 287	Tony Tarasco	.10	.05	.01
□ 288	Bill Spiers	.10	.05	.01

□	289 Allen Watson	.10	.05	.01
□	290 Checklist 248-330 Rickey Henderson	.25	.11	.03
□	291 Jose Vizcaino	.10	.05	.01
□	292 Darryl Strawberry	.25	.11	.03
□	293 John Wetteland	.25	.11	.03
□	294 Bill Swift	.10	.05	.01
□	295 Jeff Treadway	.10	.05	.01
□	296 Tino Martinez	.25	.11	.03
□	297 Richie Lewis	.10	.05	.01
□	298 Bret Saberhagen	.25	.11	.03
□	299 Arthur Rhodes	.10	.05	.01
□	300 Guillermo Velasquez	.10	.05	.01
□	301 Milt Thompson	.10	.05	.01
□	302 Doug Strange	.10	.05	.01
□	303 Aaron Sele	.25	.11	.03
□	304 Bip Roberts	.10	.05	.01
□	305 Bruce Ruffin	.10	.05	.01
□	306 Jose Lind	.10	.05	.01
□	307 David Wells	.10	.05	.01
□	308 Bobby Witt	.10	.05	.01
□	309 Mark Wohlers	.25	.11	.03
□	310 B.J. Surhoff	.10	.05	.01
□	311 Mark Whiten	.10	.05	.01
□	312 Turk Wendell	.10	.05	.01
□	313 Raul Mondesi	.50	.23	.06
□	314 Brian Turang	.10	.05	.01
□	315 Chris Hammond	.10	.05	.01
□	316 Tim Bogar	.10	.05	.01
□	317 Brad Pennington	.10	.05	.01
□	318 Tim Worrell	.10	.05	.01
□	319 Mitch Williams	.10	.05	.01
□	320 Rondell White	.50	.23	.06
□	321 Frank Viola	.10	.05	.01
□	322 Manny Ramirez	1.00	.45	.12
□	323 Gary Wayne	.10	.05	.01
□	324 Mike Macfarlane	.10	.05	.01
□	325 Russ Springer	.10	.05	.01
□	326 Tim Wallach	.10	.05	.01
□	327 Salomon Torres	.10	.05	.01
□	328 Omar Vizquel	.50	.23	.06
□	329 Andy Tomberlin	.10	.05	.01
□	330 Chris Sabo	.10	.05	.01
□	331 Mike Mussina	.60	.25	.07
□	332 Andy Benes	.25	.11	.03
□	333 Darren Daulton	.25	.11	.03
□	334 Orlando Merced	.25	.11	.03
□	335 Mark McGwire	1.00	.45	.12
□	336 Dave Winfield	.50	.23	.06
□	337 Sammy Sosa	.50	.23	.06
□	338 Eric Karros	.25	.11	.03
□	339 Greg Vaughn	.50	.23	.06
□	340 Don Mattingly	1.50	.70	.19
□	341 Frank Thomas	3.00	1.35	.35
□	342 Fred McGriff	.50	.23	.06
□	343 Kirby Puckett	1.00	.45	.12
□	344 Roberto Kelly	.10	.05	.01
□	345 Wally Joyner	.25	.11	.03
□	346 Andres Galarraga	.50	.23	.06
□	347 Bobby Bonilla	.25	.11	.03
□	348 Benito Santiago	.10	.05	.01
□	349 Barry Bonds	.75	.35	.09
□	350 Delino DeShields	.10	.05	.01
□	351 Albert Belle	1.50	.70	.19
□	352 Randy Johnson	.50	.23	.06
□	353 Tim Salmon	.50	.23	.06
□	354 John Olerud	.10	.05	.01
□	355 Dean Palmer	.25	.11	.03
□	356 Roger Clemens	.50	.23	.06
□	357 Jim Abbott	.10	.05	.01
□	358 Mark Grace	.50	.23	.06
□	359 Ozzie Guillen	.10	.05	.01
□	360 Lou Whitaker	.50	.23	.06
□	361 Jose Rijo	.10	.05	.01
□	362 Jeff Montgomery	.25	.11	.03
□	363 Chuck Finley	.10	.05	.01
□	364 Tom Glavine	.50	.23	.06
□	365 Jeff Bagwell	1.25	.55	.16
□	366 Joe Carter	.50	.23	.06
□	367 Ray Lankford	.50	.23	.06
□	368 Ramon Martinez	.25	.11	.03
□	369 Jay Buhner	.50	.23	.06
□	370 Matt Williams	.50	.23	.06
□	371 Larry Walker	.50	.23	.06
□	372 Jose Canseco	.50	.23	.06
□	373 Lenny Dykstra	.25	.11	.03
□	374 Bryan Harvey	.10	.05	.01
□	375 Andy Van Slyke	.25	.11	.03
□	376 Ivan Rodriguez	.60	.25	.07
□	377 Kevin Mitchell	.25	.11	.03
□	378 Travis Fryman	.50	.23	.06
□	379 Duane Ward	.10	.05	.01
□	380 Greg Maddux	2.00	.90	.25
□	381 Scott Servais	.10	.05	.01
□	382 Greg Olson	.10	.05	.01
□	383 Rey Sanchez	.10	.05	.01
□	384 Tom Kramer	.10	.05	.01
□	385 David Valle	.10	.05	.01
□	386 Eddie Murray	.75	.35	.09
□	387 Kevin Higgins	.10	.05	.01
□	388 Dan Wilson	.25	.11	.03
□	389 Todd Frohwith	.10	.05	.01
□	390 Gerald Williams	.10	.05	.01
□	391 Hipolito Pichardo	.10	.05	.01
□	392 Pat Meares	.10	.05	.01
□	393 Luis Lopez	.10	.05	.01
□	394 Ricky Jordan	.10	.05	.01
□	395 Bob Walk	.10	.05	.01
□	396 Sid Fernandez	.10	.05	.01
□	397 Todd Worrell	.10	.05	.01
□	398 Darryl Hamilton	.10	.05	.01
□	399 Randy Myers	.10	.05	.01
□	400 Rod Brewer	.10	.05	.01
□	401 Lance Blankenship	.10	.05	.01
□	402 Steve Finley	.50	.23	.06
□	403 Phil Leftwich	.10	.05	.01
□	404 Juan Guzman	.25	.11	.03
□	405 Anthony Young	.10	.05	.01
□	406 Jeff Gardner	.10	.05	.01
□	407 Ryan Bowen	.10	.05	.01
□	408 Fernando Valenzuela	.25	.11	.03
□	409 David West	.10	.05	.01
□	410 Kenny Rogers	.10	.05	.01
□	411 Bob Zupcic	.10	.05	.01
□	412 Eric Young	.25	.11	.03
□	413 Bret Boone	.25	.11	.03
□	414 Danny Tartabull	.10	.05	.01
□	415 Bob MacDonald	.10	.05	.01
□	416 Ron Karkovice	.10	.05	.01
□	417 Scott Cooper	.10	.05	.01
□	418 Dante Bichette	.50	.23	.06
□	419 Tripp Cromer	.10	.05	.01
□	420 Billy Ashley	.10	.05	.01
□	421 Roger Smithberg	.10	.05	.01
□	422 Dennis Martinez	.25	.11	.03
□	423 Mike Blowers	.10	.05	.01
□	424 Darren Lewis	.10	.05	.01
□	425 Junior Ortiz	.10	.05	.01
□	426 Butch Huskey	.25	.11	.03
□	427 Jimmy Poole	.10	.05	.01
□	428 Walt Weiss	.10	.05	.01
□	429 Scott Bankhead	.10	.05	.01
□	430 Deion Sanders	.50	.23	.06
□	431 Scott Bullett	.10	.05	.01
□	432 Jeff Huson	.10	.05	.01
□	433 Tyler Green	.10	.05	.01
□	434 Billy Hatcher	.10	.05	.01
□	435 Bob Hamelin	.10	.05	.01
□	436 Reggie Sanders	.50	.23	.06
□	437 Scott Erickson	.10	.05	.01
□	438 Steve Reed	.10	.05	.01
□	439 Randy Velarde	.10	.05	.01
□	440 Checklist 331-412 (Tony Gwynn)	.50	.23	.06
□	441 Terry Leach	.10	.05	.01
□	442 Danny Bautista	.10	.05	.01
□	443 Kent Hrbek	.25	.11	.03
□	444 Rick Wilkins	.10	.05	.01
□	445 Tony Phillips	.25	.11	.03
□	446 Dion James	.10	.05	.01
□	447 Joey Cora	.10	.05	.01
□	448 Andre Dawson	.50	.23	.06
□	449 Pedro Castellano	.10	.05	.01
□	450 Tom Gordon	.10	.05	.01
□	451 Rob Dibble	.10	.05	.01
□	452 Ron Darling	.10	.05	.01
□	453 Chipper Jones	2.50	1.10	.30
□	454 Joe Grahe	.10	.05	.01
□	455 Domingo Cedeno	.10	.05	.01
□	456 Tom Edens	.10	.05	.01
□	457 Mitch Webster	.10	.05	.01
□	458 Jose Bautista	.10	.05	.01

□ 459 Troy O'Leary	.10	.05	.01
□ 460 Todd Zeile	.10	.05	.01
□ 461 Sean Berry	.10	.05	.01
□ 462 Brad Holman	.10	.05	.01
□ 463 Dave Martinez	.10	.05	.01
□ 464 Mark Lewis	.10	.05	.01
□ 465 Paul Carey	.10	.05	.01
□ 466 Jack Armstrong	.10	.05	.01
□ 467 David Telgheder	.10	.05	.01
□ 468 Gene Harris	.10	.05	.01
□ 469 Danny Darwin	.10	.05	.01
□ 470 Kim Batiste	.10	.05	.01
□ 471 Tim Wakefield	.10	.05	.01
□ 472 Craig Lefferts	.10	.05	.01
□ 473 Jacob Brumfield	.10	.05	.01
□ 474 Lance Painter	.10	.05	.01
□ 475 Milt Cuyler	.10	.05	.01
□ 476 Melido Perez	.10	.05	.01
□ 477 Derek Parks	.10	.05	.01
□ 478 Gary DiSarcina	.10	.05	.01
□ 479 Steve Bedrosian	.10	.05	.01
□ 480 Eric Anthony	.10	.05	.01
□ 481 Julio Franco	.25	.11	.03
□ 482 Tommy Greene	.10	.05	.01
□ 483 Pat Kelly	.10	.05	.01
□ 484 Nate Minchey	.10	.05	.01
□ 485 William Pennyfeather	.10	.05	.01
□ 486 Harold Baines	.25	.11	.03
□ 487 Howard Johnson	.10	.05	.01
□ 488 Angel Miranda	.10	.05	.01
□ 489 Scott Sanders	.10	.05	.01
□ 490 Shawon Dunston	.10	.05	.01
□ 491 Mel Rojas	.10	.05	.01
□ 492 Jeff Nelson	.10	.05	.01
□ 493 Archi Cianfrocco	.10	.05	.01
□ 494 Al Martin	.10	.05	.01
□ 495 Mike Gallego	.10	.05	.01
□ 496 Mike Henneman	.10	.05	.01
□ 497 Armando Reynoso	.10	.05	.01
□ 498 Mickey Morandini	.10	.05	.01
□ 499 Rick Renteria	.10	.05	.01
□ 500 Rick Sutcliffe	.10	.05	.01
□ 501 Bobby Jones	.25	.11	.03
□ 502 Gary Gaetti	.25	.11	.03
□ 503 Rick Aguilera	.10	.05	.01
□ 504 Todd Stottlemyre	.10	.05	.01
□ 505 Mike Mohler	.10	.05	.01
□ 506 Mike Stanton	.10	.05	.01
□ 507 Jose Guzman	.10	.05	.01
□ 508 Kevin Rogers	.10	.05	.01
□ 509 Chuck Carr	.10	.05	.01
□ 510 Chris Jones	.10	.05	.01
□ 511 Brent Mayne	.10	.05	.01
□ 512 Greg Harris	.10	.05	.01
□ 513 Dave Henderson	.10	.05	.01
□ 514 Eric Hillman	.10	.05	.01
□ 515 Dan Peltier	.10	.05	.01
□ 516 Craig Shipley	.10	.05	.01
□ 517 John Valentin	.25	.11	.03
□ 518 Wilson Alvarez	.25	.11	.03
□ 519 Andujar Cedeno	.10	.05	.01
□ 520 Troy Neel	.10	.05	.01
□ 521 Tom Candiotti	.10	.05	.01
□ 522 Matt Mieske	.10	.05	.01
□ 523 Jim Thome	.75	.35	.09
□ 524 Lou Frazier	.10	.05	.01
□ 525 Mike Jackson	.10	.05	.01
□ 526 Pedro Martinez	.10	.05	.01
□ 527 Roger Pavlik	.10	.05	.01
□ 528 Kent Bottenfield	.10	.05	.01
□ 529 Felix Jose	.10	.05	.01
□ 530 Mark Guthrie	.10	.05	.01
□ 531 Steve Farr	.10	.05	.01
□ 532 Craig Paquette	.10	.05	.01
□ 533 Doug Jones	.10	.05	.01
□ 534 Luis Alicea	.10	.05	.01
□ 535 Cory Snyder	.10	.05	.01
□ 536 Paul Sorrento	.10	.05	.01
□ 537 Nigel Wilson	.10	.05	.01
□ 538 Jeff King	.25	.11	.03
□ 539 Willie Greene	.25	.11	.03
□ 540 Kirk McCaskill	.10	.05	.01
□ 541 Al Osuna	.10	.05	.01
□ 542 Greg Hibbard	.10	.05	.01
□ 543 Brett Butler	.25	.11	.03
□ 544 Jose Valentin	.25	.11	.03
□ 545 Wil Cordero	.25	.11	.03
□ 546 Chris Bosio	.10	.05	.01
□ 547 Jamie Moyer	.10	.05	.01
□ 548 Jim Eisenreich	.10	.05	.01
□ 549 Vinny Castilla	.50	.23	.06
□ 550 Checklist 413-494 (Dave Winfield)	.50	.23	.06
□ 551 John Roper	.10	.05	.01
□ 552 Lance Johnson	.25	.11	.03
□ 553 Scott Kamieniecki	.10	.05	.01
□ 554 Mike Moore	.10	.05	.01
□ 555 Steve Buechele	.10	.05	.01
□ 556 Terry Pendleton	.25	.11	.03
□ 557 Todd Van Poppel	.10	.05	.01
□ 558 Rob Butler	.10	.05	.01
□ 559 Zane Smith	.10	.05	.01
□ 560 David Hulse	.10	.05	.01
□ 561 Tim Costo	.10	.05	.01
□ 562 John Habyan	.10	.05	.01
□ 563 Terry Jorgensen	.10	.05	.01
□ 564 Matt Nokes	.10	.05	.01
□ 565 Kevin McReynolds	.10	.05	.01
□ 566 Phil Plantier	.10	.05	.01
□ 567 Chris Turner	.10	.05	.01
□ 568 Carlos Delgado	.50	.23	.06
□ 569 John Jaha	.25	.11	.03
□ 570 Dwight Smith	.10	.05	.01
□ 571 John Vander Wal	.10	.05	.01
□ 572 Trevor Wilson	.10	.05	.01
□ 573 Felix Fermin	.10	.05	.01
□ 574 Marc Newfield	.25	.11	.03
□ 575 Jeromy Burnitz	.10	.05	.01
□ 576 Leo Gomez	.10	.05	.01
□ 577 Curt Schilling	.10	.05	.01
□ 578 Kevin Young	.10	.05	.01
□ 579 Jerry Spradlin	.10	.05	.01
□ 580 Curt Leskanic	.10	.05	.01
□ 581 Carl Willis	.10	.05	.01
□ 582 Alex Fernandez	.50	.23	.06
□ 583 Mark Holzemer	.10	.05	.01
□ 584 Domingo Martinez	.10	.05	.01
□ 585 Pete Smith	.10	.05	.01
□ 586 Brian Jordan	.50	.23	.06
□ 587 Kevin Gross	.10	.05	.01
□ 588 J.R. Phillips	.10	.05	.01
□ 589 Chris Nabholz	.10	.05	.01
□ 590 Bill Wertz	.10	.05	.01
□ 591 Derek Bell	.25	.11	.03
□ 592 Brady Anderson	.50	.23	.06
□ 593 Matt Turner	.10	.05	.01
□ 594 Pete Incaviglia	.10	.05	.01
□ 595 Greg Gagne	.10	.05	.01
□ 596 John Flaherty	.10	.05	.01
□ 597 Scott Livingstone	.10	.05	.01
□ 598 Rod Bolton	.10	.05	.01
□ 599 Mike Perez	.10	.05	.01
□ 600 Checklist 495-577 (Roger Clemens)	.50	.23	.06
□ 601 Tony Castillo	.10	.05	.01
□ 602 Henry Mercedes	.10	.05	.01
□ 603 Mike Fetters	.10	.05	.01
□ 604 Rod Beck	.25	.11	.03
□ 605 Damon Buford	.10	.05	.01
□ 606 Matt Whiteside	.10	.05	.01
□ 607 Shawn Green	.25	.11	.03
□ 608 Midre Cummings	.10	.05	.01
□ 609 Jeff McNeely	.10	.05	.01
□ 610 Danny Sheaffer	.10	.05	.01
□ 611 Paul Wagner	.10	.05	.01
□ 612 Torey Lovullo	.10	.05	.01
□ 613 Javier Lopez	.50	.23	.06
□ 614 Mariano Duncan	.10	.05	.01
□ 615 Doug Brocail	.10	.05	.01
□ 616 Dave Hansen	.10	.05	.01
□ 617 Ryan Klesko	.75	.35	.09
□ 618 Eric Davis	.25	.11	.03
□ 619 Scott Ruffcorn	.10	.05	.01
□ 620 Mike Trombley	.10	.05	.01
□ 621 Jaime Navarro	.10	.05	.01
□ 622 Rheal Cormier	.10	.05	.01
□ 623 Jose Offerman	.10	.05	.01
□ 624 David Segui	.10	.05	.01
□ 625 Robb Nen	.25	.11	.03
□ 626 Dave Gallagher	.10	.05	.01
□ 627 Julian Tavarez	.25	.11	.03
□ 628 Chris Gomez	.10	.05	.01

□ 629 Jeffrey Hammonds	.25	.11	.03
□ 630 Scott Brosius	.10	.05	.01
□ 631 Willie Blair	.10	.05	.01
□ 632 Doug Drabek	.10	.05	.01
□ 633 Bill Wegman	.10	.05	.01
□ 634 Jeff McKnight	.10	.05	.01
□ 635 Rich Rodriguez	.10	.05	.01
□ 636 Steve Trachsel	.25	.11	.03
□ 637 Buddy Groom	.10	.05	.01
□ 638 Sterling Hitchcock	.25	.11	.03
□ 639 Chuck McElroy	.10	.05	.01
□ 640 Rene Gonzales	.10	.05	.01
□ 641 Dan Plesac	.10	.05	.01
□ 642 Jeff Branson	.10	.05	.01
□ 643 Darrell Whitmore	.10	.05	.01
□ 644 Paul Quantrill	.10	.05	.01
□ 645 Rich Rowland	.10	.05	.01
□ 646 Curtis Pride	.25	.11	.03
□ 647 Erik Plantenberg	.10	.05	.01
□ 648 Albie Lopez	.25	.11	.03
□ 649 Rich Batchelor	.10	.05	.01
□ 650 Lee Smith	.25	.11	.03
□ 651 Cliff Floyd	.50	.23	.06
□ 652 Pete Schourek	.25	.11	.03
□ 653 Reggie Jefferson	.25	.11	.03
□ 654 Bill Haselman	.10	.05	.01
□ 655 Steve Hosey	.10	.05	.01
□ 656 Mark Clark	.10	.05	.01
□ 657 Mark Davis	.10	.05	.01
□ 658 Dave Magadan	.10	.05	.01
□ 659 Candy Maldonado	.10	.05	.01
□ 660 Checklist 578-660 (Mark Langston)	.10	.05	.01

1994 Donruss Anniversary '84

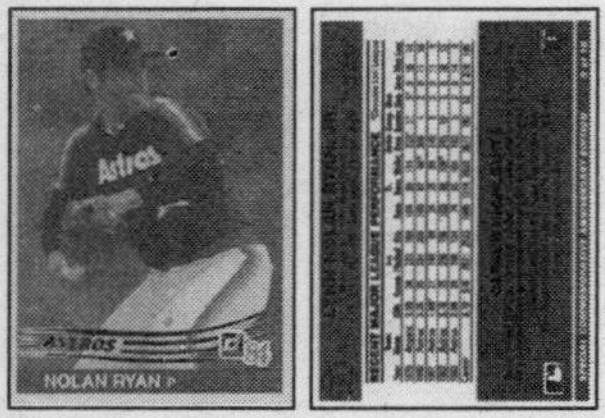

Randomly inserted in hobby foil packs at a rate of one in 12, this ten-card standard-size set reproduces selected cards from the 1984 Donruss baseball set. The cards feature white bordered color player photos on their fronts. The player's name appears in yellow lettering within a colored stripe at the bottom. The player's gold-foil team name is shown within wavy gold-foil lines near the bottom of the photo. The horizontal and white-bordered back carries the player's name and biography within a green-colored stripe across the top. A white area below contains the player's stats and, within a green panel further below, his career highlights. The cards are numbered on the back at the bottom right as "X of 10," and also carry the numbers from the original 1984 set at the upper left.

	MINT	NRMT	EXC
COMPLETE SET (10)	50.00	22.00	6.25
COMMON CARD (1-10)	2.00	.90	.25
RANDOM INSERTS IN SER.1 HOBBY PACKS	4.00	1.80	.50

□ 1 Joe Carter	2.00	.90	.25
□ 2 Robin Yount	3.50	1.55	.45
□ 3 George Brett	6.00	2.70	.75
□ 4 Rickey Henderson	3.50	1.55	.45
□ 5 Nolan Ryan	15.00	6.75	1.85
□ 6 Cal Ripken	15.00	6.75	1.85
□ 7 Wade Boggs UER 1983 runs 10, should be 100	3.50	1.55	.45
□ 8 Don Mattingly	10.00	4.50	1.25
□ 9 Ryne Sandberg	5.00	2.20	.60
□ 10 Tony Gwynn	6.00	2.70	.75

1994 Donruss Award Winner Jumbos

This 10-card set was issued one per jumbo foil and Canadian foil boxes and spotlights players that won various awards in 1993. Cards 1-5 were included in first series boxes and 6-10 with the second series. The cards measure approximately 3 1/2" by 5". Ten-thousand of each card were produced. Card fronts are full-bleed with a color player photo and the Award Winner logo at the top. The backs are individually numbered out of 10,000.

	MINT	NRMT	EXC
COMPLETE SET (10)	90.00	40.00	11.00
COMPLETE SERIES 1 (5)	50.00	22.00	6.25
COMPLETE SERIES 2 (5)	40.00	18.00	5.00
COMMON CARD (1-10)	3.00	1.35	.35
ONE PER JUMBO BOX OR CDN FOIL BOX			

□ 1 Barry Bonds MVP	8.00	3.60	1.00
□ 2 Greg Maddux CY	20.00	9.00	2.50
□ 3 Mike Piazza ROY	20.00	9.00	2.50
□ 4 Barry Bonds HR King	8.00	3.60	1.00
□ 5 Kirby Puckett AS MVP	10.00	4.50	1.25
□ 6 Frank Thomas MVP	30.00	13.50	3.70
□ 7 Jack McDowell CY	3.00	1.35	.35
□ 8 Tim Salmon ROY	5.00	2.20	.60
□ 9 Juan Gonzalez HR King	15.00	6.75	1.85
□ 10 Paul Molitor WS MVP	6.00	2.70	.75

1994 Donruss Diamond Kings

This 30-card standard-size set was split in two series. Cards 1-14 and 29 were randomly inserted in first series packs, while cards 15-28 and 30 were inserted in second series packs. With each series, the insertion rate was one in nine. Jumbo versions of these cards were inserted one per retail box and command up to

twice the values below. The fronts feature full-bleed player portraits by noted sports artist Dick Perez. Red and silver holographic foil lettering across the top provides the set title. The player's name is printed in gold script lettering across the bottom. On a yellow background the backs provide a career summary in red print with a narrow red border. The cards are numbered on the back with the prefix DK.

	MINT	NRMT	EXC
COMPLETE SET (30)	50.00	22.00	6.25
COMPLETE SERIES 1 (15)	25.00	11.00	3.10
COMPLETE SERIES 2 (15)	25.00	11.00	3.10
COMMON CARD (1-30)	.50	.23	.06
SEMISTARS	1.00	.45	.12
DK PREFIX ON CARD NUMBERS			
RANDOM INSERTS IN ALL PACKS			
JUMBO DK's ONE PER RETAIL BOX			
*JUMBO DK's: 1X to 2X BASIC CARDS			

	MINT	NRMT	EXC
□ 1 Barry Bonds	2.50	1.10	.30
□ 2 Mo Vaughn	2.50	1.10	.30
□ 3 Steve Avery	.75	.35	.09
□ 4 Tim Salmon	1.50	.70	.19
□ 5 Rick Wilkins	.50	.23	.06
□ 6 Brian Harper	.50	.23	.06
□ 7 Andres Galarraga	1.00	.45	.12
□ 8 Albert Belle	5.00	2.20	.60
□ 9 John Kruk	.75	.35	.09
□ 10 Ivan Rodriguez	2.00	.90	.25
□ 11 Tony Gwynn	4.00	1.80	.50
□ 12 Brian McRae	.50	.23	.06
□ 13 Bobby Bonilla	1.00	.45	.12
□ 14 Ken Griffey Jr.	10.00	4.50	1.25
□ 15 Mike Piazza	6.00	2.70	.75
□ 16 Don Mattingly	5.00	2.20	.60
□ 17 Barry Larkin	1.00	.45	.12
□ 18 Ruben Sierra	.75	.35	.09
□ 19 Orlando Merced	.50	.23	.06
□ 20 Greg Vaughn	1.00	.45	.12
□ 21 Gregg Jefferies	1.00	.45	.12
□ 22 Cecil Fielder	1.00	.45	.12
□ 23 Moises Alou	.75	.35	.09
□ 24 John Olerud	.75	.35	.09
□ 25 Gary Sheffield	1.50	.70	.19
□ 26 Mike Mussina	2.00	.90	.25
□ 27 Jeff Bagwell	4.00	1.80	.50
□ 28 Frank Thomas	10.00	4.50	1.25
□ 29 Dave Winfield	1.00	.45	.12
□ 30 Checklist	.50	.23	.06

1994 Donruss Dominators

This 20-card, standard-size set was randomly inserted in all packs at a rate of one in 12. The 10 series 1 cards feature the top home run hitters of the '90s, while the 10 series 2 cards depict the decade's batting average leaders. The fronts displayed full-bleed color action shots with the set title printed along the bottom in gold and black lettering. The player's name appears within an oval gold bar. The horizontal backs carry a second player photo on approximately two-thirds of the card back. The remaining section contains the relevant statistics from the 1990s in a box. The player's ranking in the 1990s is also listed. Jumbo Dominators (3 1/2" by 5") were issued one per hobby box and are valued up to twice the prices below.

	MINT	NRMT	EXC
COMPLETE SET (20)	50.00	22.00	6.25
COMPLETE SER.1 SET (10)	20.00	9.00	2.50
COMPLETE SER.2 SET (10)	30.00	13.50	3.70
COMMON SER.1 CARD (A1-A10)	.60	.25	.07
COMMON SER.2 CARD (B1-B10)	.60	.25	.07
SEMISTARS	1.25	.55	.16
RANDOM INSERTS IN ALL PACKS			
JUMBO DOMINATORS ONE PER HOBBY BOX			
*JUMBO DOMINATORS: 1X to 2X BASIC CARDS			

	MINT	NRMT	EXC
□ A1 Cecil Fielder	1.25	.55	.16
□ A2 Barry Bonds	2.50	1.10	.30
□ A3 Fred McGriff	1.25	.55	.16
□ A4 Matt Williams	1.25	.55	.16
□ A5 Joe Carter	1.25	.55	.16
□ A6 Juan Gonzalez	5.00	2.20	.60
□ A7 Jose Canseco	1.25	.55	.16
□ A8 Ron Gant	.60	.25	.07
□ A9 Ken Griffey Jr.	10.00	4.50	1.25
□ A10 Mark McGwire	3.00	1.35	.35
□ B1 Tony Gwynn	4.00	1.80	.50
□ B2 Frank Thomas	10.00	4.50	1.25
□ B3 Paul Molitor	2.00	.90	.25
□ B4 Edgar Martinez	1.25	.55	.16
□ B5 Kirby Puckett	3.00	1.35	.35
□ B6 Ken Griffey Jr.	10.00	4.50	1.25
□ B7 Barry Bonds	2.50	1.10	.30
□ B8 Willie McGee	.60	.25	.07
□ B9 Lenny Dykstra	.60	.25	.07
□ B10 John Kruk	.60	.25	.07

1994 Donruss Elite

This 12-card set was issued in two series of six. Using a continued numbering system from previous years, cards 37-42 were randomly inserted in first series foil packs with cards 43-48 a second series offering. The cards measure the standard size. Only 10,000 of each card were produced. The color player photo inside a diamond design on the front rests on a marbleized panel framed by a red-and-white inner border and a silver foil outer border. Silver foil stripes radiate away from the edges of the picture. The player's name appears across the bottom of the front. The back design is similar, but with a color head shot in a small diamond and a player profile, both resting on a marbleized panel. The bottom carries the card number, the serial number, and the production run figure.

	MINT	NRMT	EXC
COMPLETE SET (12)	200.00	90.00	25.00
COMPLETE SERIES 1 (6)	110.00	50.00	14.00
COMPLETE SERIES 2 (6)	90.00	40.00	11.00
COMMON CARD (37-48)	8.00	3.60	1.00
RANDOM INSERTS IN HOBBY AND RETAIL PACKS			

	MINT	NRMT	EXC
□ 37 Frank Thomas	50.00	22.00	6.25
□ 38 Tony Gwynn	20.00	9.00	2.50
□ 39 Tim Salmon	10.00	4.50	1.25
□ 40 Albert Belle	25.00	11.00	3.10
□ 41 John Kruk	10.00	4.50	1.25
□ 42 Juan Gonzalez	25.00	11.00	3.10
□ 43 John Olerud	8.00	3.60	1.00

□ 44 Barry Bonds	12.00	5.50	1.50
□ 45 Ken Griffey Jr.	50.00	22.00	6.25
□ 46 Mike Piazza	30.00	13.50	3.70
□ 47 Jack McDowell	10.00	4.50	1.25
□ 48 Andres Galarraga	10.00	4.50	1.25

1994 Donruss Long Ball Leaders

Inserted in second series hobby foil packs at a rate of one in 12, this 10-card standard-size set features some of top home run hitters and the distance of their longest home run of 1993. The card fronts have a color photo with a black right-hand border. Within the border is the Long Ball Leaders logo in silver foil. Also in silver foil at bottom, is the player's last name and the distance of the clout. Card backs contain a photo of the park with which the home run occurred as well as information such as the date, the pitcher and other particulars.

	MINT	NRMT	EXC
COMPLETE SET (10)	40.00	18.00	5.00
COMMON CARD (1-10)	1.00	.45	.12
SEMISTARS	1.50	.70	.19
RANDOM INSERTS IN SER.2 HOBBY PACKS			

□ 1 Cecil Fielder	1.50	.70	.19
□ 2 Dean Palmer	1.00	.45	.12
□ 3 Andres Galarraga	1.50	.70	.19
□ 4 Bo Jackson	1.50	.70	.19
□ 5 Ken Griffey Jr.	15.00	6.75	1.85
□ 6 David Justice	1.00	.45	.12
□ 7 Mike Piazza	10.00	4.50	1.25
□ 8 Frank Thomas	15.00	6.75	1.85
□ 9 Barry Bonds	4.00	1.80	.50
□ 10 Juan Gonzalez	8.00	3.60	1.00

1994 Donruss MVPs

Inserted at a rate of one per first and second series jumbo pack, this 28-card standard-size set was split into two series of 14; one player for each team. The first 14 are of National League players with the latter group being American Leaguers. Full-bleed card fronts feature an action photo of the player with "MVP" in large red (American League) or blue (National) letters at the bottom. The player's name and, for Amercian League player cards only, team name are beneath the "MVP". A number of white stars stretches up the left border. The backs, which are horizontal, contain a photo, 1993 statistics, a short write-up and white stars within blue foil along the left border.

	MINT	NRMT	EXC
COMPLETE SET (28)	75.00	34.00	9.50
COMPLETE SERIES 1 (14)	15.00	6.75	1.85
COMPLETE SERIES 2 (14)	60.00	27.00	7.50
COMMON CARD (1-28)	.75	.35	.09
SEMISTARS	1.50	.70	.19
ONE PER JUMBO PACK			

□ 1 David Justice	1.50	.70	.19
□ 2 Mark Grace	1.50	.70	.19
□ 3 Jose Rijo	.75	.35	.09
□ 4 Andres Galarraga	1.50	.70	.19
□ 5 Bryan Harvey	.75	.35	.09
□ 6 Jeff Bagwell	6.00	2.70	.75
□ 7 Mike Piazza	10.00	4.50	1.25
□ 8 Moises Alou	.75	.35	.09
□ 9 Bobby Bonilla	1.50	.70	.19
□ 10 Len Dykstra	.75	.35	.09
□ 11 Jeff King	.75	.35	.09
□ 12 Gregg Jefferies	1.50	.70	.19
□ 13 Tony Gwynn	6.00	2.70	.75
□ 14 Barry Bonds	4.00	1.80	.50
□ 15 Cal Ripken Jr.	15.00	6.75	1.85
□ 16 Mo Vaughn	4.00	1.80	.50
□ 17 Tim Salmon	2.50	1.10	.30
□ 18 Frank Thomas	15.00	6.75	1.85
□ 19 Albert Belle	8.00	3.60	1.00
□ 20 Cecil Fielder	1.50	.70	.19
□ 21 Wally Joyner	.75	.35	.09
□ 22 Greg Vaughn	1.50	.70	.19
□ 23 Kirby Puckett	5.00	2.20	.60
□ 24 Don Mattingly	8.00	3.60	1.00
□ 25 Ruben Sierra	.75	.35	.09
□ 26 Ken Griffey Jr.	15.00	6.75	1.85
□ 27 Juan Gonzalez	8.00	3.60	1.00
□ 28 John Olerud	.75	.35	.09

1994 Donruss Spirit of the Game

Consisting of 10 cards, cards 1-5 were randomly inserted in first-series magazine jumbo packs and cards 6-10 in second series magazine jumbo packs. Measuring the standard-size, the set features horizontal designs on its borderless fronts that have color action player photos superposed upon triple exposure sepia-toned action shots. The set's title appears in dark brown cursive lettering within a prismatic-foil stripe across the bottom. The horizontal back carries a color player close-up that is superposed upon red, white, and blue bunting. An outstanding achievement by the player appears in gold lettering at the upper right, and a ghosted panel immediately below carries black-lettered text providing details. Jumbo sized Spirit of the Game cards, individually numbered out of 10,000, were issued one per magazine jumbo box and carry no additional premium.

	MINT	NRMT	EXC
COMPLETE SET (10)	60.00	27.00	7.50
COMPLETE SERIES 1 (5)	30.00	13.50	3.70

COMPLETE SERIES 2 (5)	30.00	13.50	3.70
COMMON CARD (1-10)	1.00	.45	.12
SEMISTARS	2.00	.90	.25
RANDOM INSERTS IN MAG. JUMBO PACKS			
JUMBO SOG ONE PER MAG. JUMBO BOX...			
*JUMBO SOG: 1.5X VALUE			

□ 1 John Olerud	1.00	.45	.12
□ 2 Barry Bonds	5.00	2.20	.60
□ 3 Ken Griffey Jr.	20.00	9.00	2.50
□ 4 Mike Piazza	12.00	5.50	1.50
□ 5 Juan Gonzalez	10.00	4.50	1.25
□ 6 Frank Thomas	20.00	9.00	2.50
□ 7 Tim Salmon	3.00	1.35	.35
□ 8 David Justice	2.00	.90	.25
□ 9 Don Mattingly	10.00	4.50	1.25
□ 10 Lenny Dykstra	1.00	.45	.12

1995 Donruss

The 1995 Donruss set consists of 550 standard-size cards. The first series had 330 cards while 220 cards comprised the second series. The fronts feature borderless color action player photos. A second, smaller color player photo in a homeplate shape with team color-coded borders appears in the lower left corner. The player's position in silver-foil is above this smaller photo, while his name is printed in a silver-foil bar under the photo. The borderless backs carry a color action player cutout superimposed over the team logo, along with player biography and stats for the last five years. There are no key Rookie Cards in this set.

	MINT	NRMT	EXC
COMPLETE SET (550)	40.00	18.00	5.00
COMPLETE SERIES 1 (330)	25.00	11.00	3.10
COMPLETE SERIES 2 (220)	15.00	6.75	1.85
COMMON CARD (1-550)	.10	.05	.01
SEMISTARS	.25	.11	.03
STARS	.50	.23	.06
COMP.PRESS PROOFS (550)	1600.00	700.00	200.00
COMP.PP SERIES 1 (330)	1000.00	450.00	125.00
COMP.PP SERIES 2 (220)	600.00	275.00	75.00
COMMON PP (1-550)	2.50	1.10	.30
PP SEMISTARS	5.00	2.20	.60
*PP VETERAN STARS: 18X TO 30X HI			
*PP YOUNG STARS: 15X TO 25X HI			
PP: INSERTS IN HOB/RET PACKS			

□ 1 David Justice	.50	.23	.06
□ 2 Rene Arocha	.10	.05	.01
□ 3 Sandy Alomar Jr.	.10	.05	.01
□ 4 Luis Lopez	.10	.05	.01
□ 5 Mike Piazza	2.00	.90	.25
□ 6 Bobby Jones	.25	.11	.03
□ 7 Damion Easley	.10	.05	.01
□ 8 Barry Bonds	.75	.35	.09
□ 9 Mike Mussina	.60	.25	.07
□ 10 Kevin Seitzer	.10	.05	.01
□ 11 John Smiley	.10	.05	.01
□ 12 Wm.VanLandingham	.10	.05	.01
□ 13 Ron Darling	.10	.05	.01
□ 14 Walt Weiss	.10	.05	.01
□ 15 Mike Lansing	.10	.05	.01
□ 16 Allen Watson	.10	.05	.01
□ 17 Aaron Sele	.25	.11	.03
□ 18 Randy Johnson	.50	.23	.06
□ 19 Dean Palmer	.25	.11	.03
□ 20 Jeff Bagwell	1.25	.55	.16
□ 21 Curt Schilling	.10	.05	.01
□ 22 Darrell Whitmore	.10	.05	.01
□ 23 Steve Trachsel	.10	.05	.01
□ 24 Dan Wilson	.25	.11	.03
□ 25 Steve Finley	.25	.11	.03
□ 26 Bret Boone	.25	.11	.03
□ 27 Charles Johnson	.25	.11	.03
□ 28 Mike Stanton	.10	.05	.01
□ 29 Ismael Valdes	.25	.11	.03
□ 30 Salomon Torres	.10	.05	.01
□ 31 Eric Anthony	.10	.05	.01
□ 32 Spike Owen	.10	.05	.01
□ 33 Joey Cora	.10	.05	.01
□ 34 Robert Eenhoorn	.10	.05	.01
□ 35 Rick White	.10	.05	.01
□ 36 Omar Vizquel	.50	.23	.06
□ 37 Carlos Delgado	.50	.23	.06
□ 38 Eddie Williams	.10	.05	.01
□ 39 Shawon Dunston	.10	.05	.01
□ 40 Darrin Fletcher	.10	.05	.01
□ 41 Leo Gomez	.10	.05	.01
□ 42 Juan Gonzalez	1.50	.70	.19
□ 43 Luis Alicea	.10	.05	.01
□ 44 Ken Ryan	.10	.05	.01
□ 45 Lou Whitaker	.50	.23	.06
□ 46 Mike Blowers	.10	.05	.01
□ 47 Willie Blair	.10	.05	.01
□ 48 Todd Van Poppel	.10	.05	.01
□ 49 Roberto Alomar	.75	.35	.09
□ 50 Ozzie Smith	.60	.25	.07
□ 51 Sterling Hitchcock	.25	.11	.03
□ 52 Mo Vaughn	.75	.35	.09
□ 53 Rick Aguilera	.10	.05	.01
□ 54 Kent Mercker	.10	.05	.01
□ 55 Don Mattingly	1.50	.70	.19
□ 56 Bob Scanlan	.10	.05	.01
□ 57 Wilson Alvarez	.25	.11	.03
□ 58 Jose Mesa	.10	.05	.01
□ 59 Scott Kamieniecki	.10	.05	.01
□ 60 Todd Jones	.10	.05	.01
□ 61 John Kruk	.25	.11	.03
□ 62 Mike Stanley	.10	.05	.01
□ 63 Tino Martinez	.25	.11	.03
□ 64 Eddie Zambrano	.10	.05	.01
□ 65 Todd Hundley	.25	.11	.03
□ 66 Jamie Moyer	.10	.05	.01
□ 67 Rich Amaral	.10	.05	.01
□ 68 Jose Valentin	.25	.11	.03
□ 69 Alex Gonzalez	.10	.05	.01
□ 70 Kurt Abbott	.10	.05	.01
□ 71 Delino DeShields	.10	.05	.01
□ 72 Brian Anderson	.10	.05	.01
□ 73 John Vander Wal	.10	.05	.01
□ 74 Turner Ward	.10	.05	.01
□ 75 Tim Raines	.50	.23	.06
□ 76 Mark Acre	.10	.05	.01
□ 77 Jose Offerman	.10	.05	.01
□ 78 Jimmy Key	.25	.11	.03
□ 79 Mark Whiten	.10	.05	.01
□ 80 Mark Gubicza	.10	.05	.01
□ 81 Darren Hall	.10	.05	.01
□ 82 Travis Fryman	.25	.11	.03
□ 83 Cal Ripken	2.50	1.10	.30
□ 84 Geronimo Berroa	.10	.05	.01
□ 85 Bret Barberie	.10	.05	.01
□ 86 Andy Ashby	.25	.11	.03
□ 87 Steve Avery	.25	.11	.03
□ 88 Rich Becker	.10	.05	.01
□ 89 John Valentin	.25	.11	.03
□ 90 Glenallen Hill	.10	.05	.01
□ 91 Carlos Garcia	.10	.05	.01
□ 92 Dennis Martinez	.25	.11	.03
□ 93 Pat Kelly	.10	.05	.01
□ 94 Orlando Miller	.10	.05	.01
□ 95 Felix Jose	.10	.05	.01
□ 96 Mike Kingery	.10	.05	.01
□ 97 Jeff Kent	.10	.05	.01
□ 98 Pete Incaviglia	.10	.05	.01
□ 99 Chad Curtis	.10	.05	.01
□ 100 Thomas Howard	.10	.05	.01
□ 101 Hector Carrasco	.10	.05	.01

☐	102 Tom Pagnozzi	.10	.05	.01
☐	103 Danny Tartabull	.10	.05	.01
☐	104 Donnie Elliott	.10	.05	.01
☐	105 Danny Jackson	.10	.05	.01
☐	106 Steve Dunn	.10	.05	.01
☐	107 Roger Salkeld	.10	.05	.01
☐	108 Jeff King	.25	.11	.03
☐	109 Cecil Fielder	.25	.11	.03
☐	110 Checklist	.10	.05	.01
☐	111 Denny Neagle	.25	.11	.03
☐	112 Troy Neel	.10	.05	.01
☐	113 Rod Beck	.10	.05	.01
☐	114 Alex Rodriguez	4.00	1.80	.50
☐	115 Joey Eischen	.10	.05	.01
☐	116 Tom Candiotti	.10	.05	.01
☐	117 Ray McDavid	.25	.11	.03
☐	118 Vince Coleman	.10	.05	.01
☐	119 Pete Harnisch	.10	.05	.01
☐	120 David Nied	.10	.05	.01
☐	121 Pat Rapp	.10	.05	.01
☐	122 Sammy Sosa	.50	.23	.06
☐	123 Steve Reed	.10	.05	.01
☐	124 Jose Oliva	.10	.05	.01
☐	125 Ricky Bottalico	.25	.11	.03
☐	126 Jose DeLeon	.10	.05	.01
☐	127 Pat Hentgen	.25	.11	.03
☐	128 Will Clark	.50	.23	.06
☐	129 Mark Dewey	.10	.05	.01
☐	130 Greg Vaughn	.25	.11	.03
☐	131 Darren Dreifort	.10	.05	.01
☐	132 Ed Sprague	.25	.11	.03
☐	133 Lee Smith	.25	.11	.03
☐	134 Charles Nagy	.25	.11	.03
☐	135 Phil Plantier	.10	.05	.01
☐	136 Jason Jacome	.10	.05	.01
☐	137 Jose Lima	.10	.05	.01
☐	138 J.R. Phillips	.10	.05	.01
☐	139 J.T. Snow	.25	.11	.03
☐	140 Michael Huff	.10	.05	.01
☐	141 Billy Brewer	.10	.05	.01
☐	142 Jeromy Burnitz	.10	.05	.01
☐	143 Ricky Bones	.10	.05	.01
☐	144 Carlos Rodriguez	.10	.05	.01
☐	145 Luis Gonzalez	.10	.05	.01
☐	146 Mark Lemke	.10	.05	.01
☐	147 Al Martin	.25	.11	.03
☐	148 Mike Bordick	.10	.05	.01
☐	149 Robb Nen	.10	.05	.01
☐	150 Wil Cordero	.10	.05	.01
☐	151 Edgar Martinez	.50	.23	.06
☐	152 Gerald Williams	.10	.05	.01
☐	153 Esteban Beltre	.10	.05	.01
☐	154 Mike Moore	.10	.05	.01
☐	155 Mark Langston	.10	.05	.01
☐	156 Mark Clark	.10	.05	.01
☐	157 Bobby Ayala	.10	.05	.01
☐	158 Rick Wilkins	.10	.05	.01
☐	159 Bobby Munoz	.10	.05	.01
☐	160 Brett Butler CL 2000 Hits	.25	.11	.03
☐	161 Scott Erickson	.10	.05	.01
☐	162 Paul Molitor	.60	.25	.07
☐	163 Jon Lieber	.10	.05	.01
☐	164 Jason Grimsley	.10	.05	.01
☐	165 Norberto Martin	.10	.05	.01
☐	166 Javier Lopez	.50	.23	.06
☐	167 Brian McRae	.25	.11	.03
☐	168 Gary Sheffield	.50	.23	.06
☐	169 Marcus Moore	.10	.05	.01
☐	170 John Hudek	.10	.05	.01
☐	171 Kelly Stinnett	.10	.05	.01
☐	172 Chris Gomez	.10	.05	.01
☐	173 Rey Sanchez	.10	.05	.01
☐	174 Juan Guzman	.25	.11	.03
☐	175 Chan Ho Park	.50	.23	.06
☐	176 Terry Shumpert	.10	.05	.01
☐	177 Steve Ontiveros	.10	.05	.01
☐	178 Brad Ausmus	.10	.05	.01
☐	179 Tim Davis	.10	.05	.01
☐	180 Billy Ashley	.10	.05	.01
☐	181 Vinny Castilla	.25	.11	.03
☐	182 Bill Spiers	.10	.05	.01
☐	183 Randy Knorr	.10	.05	.01
☐	184 Brian Hunter	.50	.23	.06
☐	185 Pat Meares	.10	.05	.01
☐	186 Steve Buechele	.10	.05	.01
☐	187 Kirt Manwaring	.10	.05	.01
☐	188 Tim Naehring	.10	.05	.01
☐	189 Matt Mieske	.25	.11	.03
☐	190 Josias Manzanillo	.10	.05	.01
☐	191 Greg McMichael	.10	.05	.01
☐	192 Chuck Carr	.10	.05	.01
☐	193 Midre Cummings	.10	.05	.01
☐	194 Darryl Strawberry	.25	.11	.03
☐	195 Greg Gagne	.10	.05	.01
☐	196 Steve Cooke	.10	.05	.01
☐	197 Woody Williams	.10	.05	.01
☐	198 Ron Karkovice	.10	.05	.01
☐	199 Phil Leftwich	.10	.05	.01
☐	200 Jim Thome	.60	.25	.07
☐	201 Brady Anderson	.50	.23	.06
☐	202 Pedro Martinez	.10	.05	.01
☐	203 Steve Karsay	.10	.05	.01
☐	204 Reggie Sanders	.25	.11	.03
☐	205 Bill Risley	.10	.05	.01
☐	206 Jay Bell	.25	.11	.03
☐	207 Kevin Brown	.25	.11	.03
☐	208 Tim Scott	.10	.05	.01
☐	209 Lenny Dykstra	.25	.11	.03
☐	210 Willie Greene	.10	.05	.01
☐	211 Jim Eisenreich	.10	.05	.01
☐	212 Cliff Floyd	.25	.11	.03
☐	213 Otis Nixon	.10	.05	.01
☐	214 Eduardo Perez	.10	.05	.01
☐	215 Manuel Lee	.10	.05	.01
☐	216 Armando Benitez	.10	.05	.01
☐	217 Dave McCarty	.10	.05	.01
☐	218 Scott Livingstone	.10	.05	.01
☐	219 Chad Kreuter	.10	.05	.01
☐	220 Don Mattingly CL	.75	.35	.09
☐	221 Brian Jordan	.50	.23	.06
☐	222 Matt Whiteside	.10	.05	.01
☐	223 Jim Edmonds	.50	.23	.06
☐	224 Tony Gwynn	1.25	.55	.16
☐	225 Jose Lind	.10	.05	.01
☐	226 Marvin Freeman	.10	.05	.01
☐	227 Ken Hill	.10	.05	.01
☐	228 David Hulse	.10	.05	.01
☐	229 Joe Hesketh	.10	.05	.01
☐	230 Roberto Petagine	.10	.05	.01
☐	231 Jeffrey Hammonds	.25	.11	.03
☐	232 John Jaha	.25	.11	.03
☐	233 John Burkett	.25	.11	.03
☐	234 Hal Morris	.10	.05	.01
☐	235 Tony Castillo	.10	.05	.01
☐	236 Ryan Bowen	.10	.05	.01
☐	237 Wayne Kirby	.10	.05	.01
☐	238 Brent Mayne	.10	.05	.01
☐	239 Jim Bullinger	.10	.05	.01
☐	240 Mike Lieberthal	.10	.05	.01
☐	241 Barry Larkin	.50	.23	.06
☐	242 David Segui	.10	.05	.01
☐	243 Jose Bautista	.10	.05	.01
☐	244 Hector Fajardo	.10	.05	.01
☐	245 Orel Hershiser	.25	.11	.03
☐	246 James Mouton	.10	.05	.01
☐	247 Scott Leius	.10	.05	.01
☐	248 Tom Glavine	.50	.23	.06
☐	249 Danny Bautista	.10	.05	.01
☐	250 Jose Mercedes	.10	.05	.01
☐	251 Marquis Grissom	.50	.23	.06
☐	252 Charlie Hayes	.10	.05	.01
☐	253 Ryan Klesko	.60	.25	.07
☐	254 Vicente Palacios	.10	.05	.01
☐	255 Matias Carrillo	.10	.05	.01
☐	256 Gary DiSarcina	.10	.05	.01
☐	257 Kirk Gibson	.25	.11	.03
☐	258 Garey Ingram	.10	.05	.01
☐	259 Alex Fernandez	.25	.11	.03
☐	260 John Mabry	.50	.23	.06
☐	261 Chris Howard	.10	.05	.01
☐	262 Miguel Jimenez	.10	.05	.01
☐	263 Heath Slocumb	.10	.05	.01
☐	264 Albert Belle	1.50	.70	.19
☐	265 Dave Clark	.10	.05	.01
☐	266 Joe Orsulak	.10	.05	.01
☐	267 Joey Hamilton	.25	.11	.03
☐	268 Mark Portugal	.10	.05	.01
☐	269 Kevin Tapani	.10	.05	.01
☐	270 Sid Fernandez	.10	.05	.01
☐	271 Steve Dreyer	.10	.05	.01
☐	272 Denny Hocking	.10	.05	.01

☐	273 Troy O'Leary	.10	.05	.01
☐	274 Milt Cuyler	.10	.05	.01
☐	275 Frank Thomas	3.00	1.35	.35
☐	276 Jorge Fabregas	.10	.05	.01
☐	277 Mike Gallego	.10	.05	.01
☐	278 Mickey Morandini	.10	.05	.01
☐	279 Roberto Hernandez	.10	.05	.01
☐	280 Henry Rodriguez	.50	.23	.06
☐	281 Garret Anderson	.50	.23	.06
☐	282 Bob Wickman	.10	.05	.01
☐	283 Gar Finnvold	.10	.05	.01
☐	284 Paul O'Neill	.25	.11	.03
☐	285 Royce Clayton	.10	.05	.01
☐	286 Chuck Knoblauch	.50	.23	.06
☐	287 Johnny Ruffin	.10	.05	.01
☐	288 Dave Nilsson	.25	.11	.03
☐	289 David Cone	.25	.11	.03
☐	290 Chuck McElroy	.10	.05	.01
☐	291 Kevin Stocker	.10	.05	.01
☐	292 Jose Rijo	.10	.05	.01
☐	293 Sean Berry	.10	.05	.01
☐	294 Ozzie Guillen	.10	.05	.01
☐	295 Chris Hoiles	.10	.05	.01
☐	296 Kevin Foster	.10	.05	.01
☐	297 Jeff Frye	.10	.05	.01
☐	298 Lance Johnson	.25	.11	.03
☐	299 Mike Kelly	.10	.05	.01
☐	300 Ellis Burks	.50	.23	.06
☐	301 Roberto Kelly	.10	.05	.01
☐	302 Dante Bichette	.50	.23	.06
☐	303 Alvaro Ezpinoza	.10	.05	.01
☐	304 Alex Cole	.10	.05	.01
☐	305 Rickey Henderson	.50	.23	.06
☐	306 Dave Weathers	.10	.05	.01
☐	307 Shane Reynolds	.10	.05	.01
☐	308 Bobby Bonilla	.25	.11	.03
☐	309 Junior Felix	.10	.05	.01
☐	310 Jeff Fassero	.10	.05	.01
☐	311 Darren Lewis	.10	.05	.01
☐	312 John Doherty	.10	.05	.01
☐	313 Scott Servais	.10	.05	.01
☐	314 Rick Helling	.10	.05	.01
☐	315 Pedro Martinez	.10	.05	.01
☐	316 Wes Chamberlain	.10	.05	.01
☐	317 Bryan Eversgerd	.10	.05	.01
☐	318 Trevor Hoffman	.10	.05	.01
☐	319 John Patterson	.10	.05	.01
☐	320 Matt Walbeck	.10	.05	.01
☐	321 Jeff Montgomery	.25	.11	.03
☐	322 Mel Rojas	.10	.05	.01
☐	323 Eddie Taubensee	.10	.05	.01
☐	324 Ray Lankford	.50	.23	.06
☐	325 Jose Vizcaino	.10	.05	.01
☐	326 Carlos Baerga	.50	.23	.06
☐	327 Jack Voigt	.10	.05	.01
☐	328 Julio Franco	.25	.11	.03
☐	329 Brent Gates	.10	.05	.01
☐	330 Kirby Puckett CL	.50	.23	.06
☐	331 Greg Maddux	2.00	.90	.25
☐	332 Jason Bere	.10	.05	.01
☐	333 Bill Wegman	.10	.05	.01
☐	334 Tuffy Rhodes	.10	.05	.01
☐	335 Kevin Young	.10	.05	.01
☐	336 Andy Benes	.10	.05	.01
☐	337 Pedro Astacio	.10	.05	.01
☐	338 Reggie Jefferson	.25	.11	.03
☐	339 Tim Belcher	.25	.11	.03
☐	340 Ken Griffey Jr.	3.00	1.35	.35
☐	341 Mariano Duncan	.10	.05	.01
☐	342 Andres Galarraga	.50	.23	.06
☐	343 Rondell White	.50	.23	.06
☐	344 Cory Bailey	.10	.05	.01
☐	345 Bryan Harvey	.10	.05	.01
☐	346 John Franco	.10	.05	.01
☐	347 Greg Swindell	.10	.05	.01
☐	348 David West	.10	.05	.01
☐	349 Fred McGriff	.50	.23	.06
☐	350 Jose Canseco	.50	.23	.06
☐	351 Orlando Merced	.10	.05	.01
☐	352 Rheal Cormier	.10	.05	.01
☐	353 Carlos Pulido	.10	.05	.01
☐	354 Terry Steinbach	.25	.11	.03
☐	355 Wade Boggs	.50	.23	.06
☐	356 B.J. Surhoff	.25	.11	.03
☐	357 Rafael Palmeiro	.50	.23	.06
☐	358 Anthony Young	.10	.05	.01
☐	359 Tom Brunansky	.10	.05	.01
☐	360 Todd Stottlemyre	.10	.05	.01
☐	361 Chris Turner	.10	.05	.01
☐	362 Joe Boever	.10	.05	.01
☐	363 Jeff Blauser	.10	.05	.01
☐	364 Derek Bell	.25	.11	.03
☐	365 Matt Williams	.50	.23	.06
☐	366 Jeremy Hernandez	.10	.05	.01
☐	367 Joe Girardi	.10	.05	.01
☐	368 Mike Devereaux	.10	.05	.01
☐	369 Jim Abbott	.10	.05	.01
☐	370 Manny Ramirez	.75	.35	.09
☐	371 Kenny Lofton	.75	.35	.09
☐	372 Mark Smith	.10	.05	.01
☐	373 Dave Fleming	.10	.05	.01
☐	374 Dave Stewart	.25	.11	.03
☐	375 Roger Pavlik	.10	.05	.01
☐	376 Hipolito Pichardo	.10	.05	.01
☐	377 Bill Taylor	.10	.05	.01
☐	378 Robin Ventura	.25	.11	.03
☐	379 Bernard Gilkey	.25	.11	.03
☐	380 Kirby Puckett	1.00	.45	.12
☐	381 Steve Howe	.10	.05	.01
☐	382 Devon White	.25	.11	.03
☐	383 Roberto Mejia	.10	.05	.01
☐	384 Darrin Jackson	.10	.05	.01
☐	385 Mike Morgan	.10	.05	.01
☐	386 Rusty Meacham	.10	.05	.01
☐	387 Bill Swift	.10	.05	.01
☐	388 Lou Frazier	.10	.05	.01
☐	389 Andy Van Slyke	.25	.11	.03
☐	390 Brett Butler	.25	.11	.03
☐	391 Bobby Witt	.10	.05	.01
☐	392 Jeff Conine	.50	.23	.06
☐	393 Tim Hyers	.10	.05	.01
☐	394 Terry Pendleton	.25	.11	.03
☐	395 Ricky Jordan	.10	.05	.01
☐	396 Eric Plunk	.10	.05	.01
☐	397 Melido Perez	.10	.05	.01
☐	398 Darryl Kile	.10	.05	.01
☐	399 Mark McLemore	.10	.05	.01
☐	400 Greg W.Harris	.10	.05	.01
☐	401 Jim Leyritz	.10	.05	.01
☐	402 Doug Strange	.10	.05	.01
☐	403 Tim Salmon	.50	.23	.06
☐	404 Terry Mulholland	.10	.05	.01
☐	405 Robby Thompson	.10	.05	.01
☐	406 Ruben Sierra	.25	.11	.03
☐	407 Tony Phillips	.25	.11	.03
☐	408 Moises Alou	.25	.11	.03
☐	409 Felix Fermin	.10	.05	.01
☐	410 Pat Listach	.10	.05	.01
☐	411 Kevin Bass	.10	.05	.01
☐	412 Ben McDonald	.10	.05	.01
☐	413 Scott Cooper	.10	.05	.01
☐	414 Jody Reed	.10	.05	.01
☐	415 Deion Sanders	.50	.23	.06
☐	416 Ricky Gutierrez	.10	.05	.01
☐	417 Gregg Jefferies	.25	.11	.03
☐	418 Jack McDowell	.25	.11	.03
☐	419 Al Leiter	.25	.11	.03
☐	420 Tony Longmire	.10	.05	.01
☐	421 Paul Wagner	.10	.05	.01
☐	422 Geronimo Pena	.10	.05	.01
☐	423 Ivan Rodriguez	.60	.25	.07
☐	424 Kevin Gross	.10	.05	.01
☐	425 Kirk McCaskill	.10	.05	.01
☐	426 Greg Myers	.10	.05	.01
☐	427 Roger Clemens	.50	.23	.06
☐	428 Chris Hammond	.10	.05	.01
☐	429 Randy Myers	.10	.05	.01
☐	430 Roger Mason	.10	.05	.01
☐	431 Bret Saberhagen	.25	.11	.03
☐	432 Jeff Reboulet	.10	.05	.01
☐	433 John Olerud	.10	.05	.01
☐	434 Bill Gullickson	.10	.05	.01
☐	435 Eddie Murray	.75	.35	.09
☐	436 Pedro Munoz	.10	.05	.01
☐	437 Charlie O'Brien	.10	.05	.01
☐	438 Jeff Nelson	.10	.05	.01
☐	439 Mike Macfarlane	.10	.05	.01
☐	440 Don Mattingly CL 1000 RBI	.75	.35	.09
☐	441 Derrick May	.10	.05	.01
☐	442 John Roper	.10	.05	.01
☐	443 Darryl Hamilton	.10	.05	.01

□ 444 Dan Miceli	.10	.05	.01
□ 445 Tony Eusebio	.10	.05	.01
□ 446 Jerry Browne	.10	.05	.01
□ 447 Wally Joyner	.25	.11	.03
□ 448 Brian Harper	.10	.05	.01
□ 449 Scott Fletcher	.10	.05	.01
□ 450 Bip Roberts	.10	.05	.01
□ 451 Pete Smith	.10	.05	.01
□ 452 Chili Davis	.25	.11	.03
□ 453 Dave Hollins	.10	.05	.01
□ 454 Tony Pena	.10	.05	.01
□ 455 Butch Henry	.10	.05	.01
□ 456 Craig Biggio	.50	.23	.06
□ 457 Zane Smith	.10	.05	.01
□ 458 Ryan Thompson	.10	.05	.01
□ 459 Mike Jackson	.10	.05	.01
□ 460 Mark McGwire	1.00	.45	.12
□ 461 John Smoltz	.50	.23	.06
□ 462 Steve Scarsone	.10	.05	.01
□ 463 Greg Colbrunn	.10	.05	.01
□ 464 Shawn Green	.25	.11	.03
□ 465 David Wells	.10	.05	.01
□ 466 Jose Hernandez	.10	.05	.01
□ 467 Chip Hale	.10	.05	.01
□ 468 Tony Tarasco	.10	.05	.01
□ 469 Kevin Mitchell	.25	.11	.03
□ 470 Billy Hatcher	.10	.05	.01
□ 471 Jay Buhner	.50	.23	.06
□ 472 Ken Caminiti	.50	.23	.06
□ 473 Tom Henke	.10	.05	.01
□ 474 Todd Worrell	.10	.05	.01
□ 475 Mark Eichhorn	.10	.05	.01
□ 476 Bruce Ruffin	.10	.05	.01
□ 477 Chuck Finley	.25	.11	.03
□ 478 Marc Newfield	.25	.11	.03
□ 479 Paul Shuey	.10	.05	.01
□ 480 Bob Tewksbury	.10	.05	.01
□ 481 Ramon J.Martinez	.25	.11	.03
□ 482 Melvin Nieves	.25	.11	.03
□ 483 Todd Zeile	.10	.05	.01
□ 484 Benito Santiago	.10	.05	.01
□ 485 Stan Javier	.10	.05	.01
□ 486 Kirk Rueter	.10	.05	.01
□ 487 Andre Dawson	.50	.23	.06
□ 488 Eric Karros	.25	.11	.03
□ 489 Dave Magadan	.10	.05	.01
□ 490 Joe Carter CL 1000 RBI	.25	.11	.03
□ 491 Randy Velarde	.10	.05	.01
□ 492 Larry Walker	.50	.23	.06
□ 493 Cris Carpenter	.10	.05	.01
□ 494 Tom Gordon	.10	.05	.01
□ 495 Dave Burba	.10	.05	.01
□ 496 Darren Bragg	.25	.11	.03
□ 497 Darren Daulton	.25	.11	.03
□ 498 Don Slaught	.10	.05	.01
□ 499 Pat Borders	.10	.05	.01
□ 500 Lenny Harris	.10	.05	.01
□ 501 Joe Ausanio	.10	.05	.01
□ 502 Alan Trammell	.50	.23	.06
□ 503 Mike Fetters	.10	.05	.01
□ 504 Scott Ruffcorn	.10	.05	.01
□ 505 Rich Rowland	.10	.05	.01
□ 506 Juan Samuel	.10	.05	.01
□ 507 Bo Jackson	.50	.23	.06
□ 508 Jeff Branson	.10	.05	.01
□ 509 Bernie Williams	.50	.23	.06
□ 510 Paul Sorrento	.10	.05	.01
□ 511 Dennis Eckersley	.25	.11	.03
□ 512 Pat Mahomes	.10	.05	.01
□ 513 Rusty Greer	.50	.23	.06
□ 514 Luis Polonia	.10	.05	.01
□ 515 Willie Banks	.10	.05	.01
□ 516 John Wetteland	.25	.11	.03
□ 517 Mike LaValliere	.10	.05	.01
□ 518 Tommy Greene	.10	.05	.01
□ 519 Mark Grace	.50	.23	.06
□ 520 Bob Hamelin	.10	.05	.01
□ 521 Scott Sanderson	.10	.05	.01
□ 522 Joe Carter	.50	.23	.06
□ 523 Jeff Brantley	.10	.05	.01
□ 524 Andrew Lorraine	.25	.11	.03
□ 525 Rico Brogna	.10	.05	.01
□ 526 Shane Mack	.10	.05	.01
□ 527 Mark Wohlers	.25	.11	.03
□ 528 Scott Sanders	.10	.05	.01
□ 529 Chris Bosio	.10	.05	.01
□ 530 Andujar Cedeno	.10	.05	.01
□ 531 Kenny Rogers	.10	.05	.01
□ 532 Doug Drabek	.10	.05	.01
□ 533 Curt Leskanic	.10	.05	.01
□ 534 Craig Shipley	.10	.05	.01
□ 535 Craig Grebeck	.10	.05	.01
□ 536 Cal Eldred	.10	.05	.01
□ 537 Mickey Tettleton	.10	.05	.01
□ 538 Harold Baines	.25	.11	.03
□ 539 Tim Wallach	.10	.05	.01
□ 540 Damon Buford	.10	.05	.01
□ 541 Lenny Webster	.10	.05	.01
□ 542 Kevin Appier	.25	.11	.03
□ 543 Raul Mondesi	.50	.23	.06
□ 544 Eric Young	.25	.11	.03
□ 545 Russ Davis	.10	.05	.01
□ 546 Mike Benjamin	.10	.05	.01
□ 547 Mike Greenwell	.10	.05	.01
□ 548 Scott Brosius	.10	.05	.01
□ 549 Brian Dorsett	.10	.05	.01
□ 550 Chili Davis CL 1000 RBI	.10	.05	.01

1995 Donruss All-Stars

This 18-card standard-size set was randomly inserted into retail packs. The first series has the nine 1994 American League starters while the second series honored the National League starters. The fronts feature the playerís photo against a background of his league's all-star logo. The player and his team are identified on the bottom. His team is noted in the upper left corner. All of this is on a borderless card with a gray background. The horizontal backs have a player photo, a quick blurb about his starting role in the game and his performance in the 1994 All-Star game. The cards are numbered in the upper right with either an "AL-X" or an "NL-X."

	MINT	NRMT	EXC
COMPLETE SET (18)	200.00	90.00	25.00
COMPLETE SERIES 1 (9)	125.00	55.00	15.50
COMPLETE SERIES 2 (9)	75.00	34.00	9.50
COMMON CARD (AL1-AL9)	2.50	1.10	.30
COMMON CARD (NL1-NL9)	2.50	1.10	.30
SEMISTARS	5.00	2.20	.60
RANDOM INSERTS IN JUMBO PACKS			
□ AL1 Jimmy Key	2.50	1.10	.30
□ AL2 Ivan Rodriguez	8.00	3.60	1.00
□ AL3 Frank Thomas	40.00	18.00	5.00
□ AL4 Roberto Alomar	10.00	4.50	1.25
□ AL5 Wade Boggs	5.00	2.20	.60
□ AL6 Cal Ripken	35.00	16.00	4.40
□ AL7 Joe Carter	5.00	2.20	.60
□ AL8 Ken Griffey Jr.	40.00	18.00	5.00
□ AL9 Kirby Puckett	12.00	5.50	1.50
□ NL1 Greg Maddux	25.00	11.00	3.10
□ NL2 Mike Piazza	25.00	11.00	3.10
□ NL3 Gregg Jefferies	5.00	2.20	.60
□ NL4 Mariano Duncan	2.50	1.10	.30
□ NL5 Matt Williams	5.00	2.20	.60
□ NL6 Ozzie Smith	8.00	3.60	1.00
□ NL7 Barry Bonds	10.00	4.50	1.25
□ NL8 Tony Gwynn	15.00	6.75	1.85
□ NL9 David Justice	5.00	2.20	.60

1995 Donruss Bomb Squad

Randomly inserted one in every 24 retail packs and one in every 16 jumbo packs, this set features the top six home run hitters in the National and American League. These cards were only included in first series packs. Each of the six cards shows a different slugger on the either side of the card. Both the fronts and backs are horizontal and feature the player photo with a bomber as background. There are foil bombs to the left indicating how many homers the player hit in 1994. A dog tag indicates the player's position and rank among home run leaders in his league.

	MINT	NRMT	EXC
COMPLETE SET (6)	25.00	11.00	3.10
COMMON CARD (1-6)	1.50	.70	.19
INSERTS IN SER.1 MAG.JUMBO/RETAIL PACKS			

	MINT	NRMT	EXC
□ 1 Ken Griffey / Matt Williams	8.00	3.60	1.00
□ 2 Frank Thomas / Jeff Bagwell	12.00	5.50	1.50
□ 3 Albert Belle / Barry Bonds	5.00	2.20	.60
□ 4 Jose Canseco / Fred McGriff	2.50	1.10	.30
□ 5 Cecil Fielder / Andres Galarraga	1.50	.70	.19
□ 6 Joe Carter / Kevin Mitchell	1.50	.70	.19

1995 Donruss Diamond Kings

The 1995 Donruss Diamond King set consists of 29 standard-size cards that were randomly inserted in packs. The fronts feature water color player portraits by noted sports artist Dick Perez. The player's name and "Diamond Kings" are in gold foil. The backs have a dark blue border with a player photo and text. The cards are numbered on back with a DK prefix.

	MINT	NRMT	EXC
COMPLETE SET (29)	50.00	22.00	6.25
COMPLETE SERIES 1 (14)	20.00	9.00	2.50
COMPLETE SERIES 2 (15)	30.00	13.50	3.70
COMMON CARD (DK1-DK29)	1.00	.45	.12
SEMISTARS	1.50	.70	.19
RANDOM INSERTS IN PACKS			

	MINT	NRMT	EXC
□ DK1 Frank Thomas	12.00	5.50	1.50
□ DK2 Jeff Bagwell	5.00	2.20	.60
□ DK3 Chili Davis	1.50	.70	.19
□ DK4 Dante Bichette	1.50	.70	.19
□ DK5 Ruben Sierra	1.50	.70	.19
□ DK6 Jeff Conine	1.50	.70	.19
□ DK7 Paul O'Neill	1.50	.70	.19
□ DK8 Bobby Bonilla	1.50	.70	.19
□ DK9 Joe Carter	1.50	.70	.19
□ DK10 Moises Alou	1.50	.70	.19
□ DK11 Kenny Lofton	3.00	1.35	.35
□ DK12 Matt Williams	1.50	.70	.19
□ DK13 Kevin Seitzer	1.00	.45	.12
□ DK14 Sammy Sosa	2.00	.90	.25
□ DK15 Scott Cooper	1.00	.45	.12
□ DK16 Raul Mondesi	1.50	.70	.19
□ DK17 Will Clark	1.50	.70	.19
□ DK18 Lenny Dykstra	1.50	.70	.19
□ DK19 Kirby Puckett	4.00	1.80	.50
□ DK20 Hal Morris	1.00	.45	.12
□ DK21 Travis Fryman	1.50	.70	.19
□ DK22 Greg Maddux	8.00	3.60	1.00
□ DK23 Rafael Palmeiro	1.50	.70	.19
□ DK24 Tony Gwynn	5.00	2.20	.60
□ DK25 David Cone	1.50	.70	.19
□ DK26 Al Martin	1.00	.45	.12
□ DK27 Ken Griffey Jr.	12.00	5.50	1.50
□ DK28 Gregg Jefferies	1.50	.70	.19
□ DK29 Checklist	1.00	.45	.12

1995 Donruss Dominators

This nine-card standard-size set was randomly inserted in second series hobby packs. Each of these cards features three of the leading players at each position. The horizontal fronts have photos of all three players and identify only their last name. The words "remove protective film" cover a significant portion of the fronts as well. The backs have small action photos of the three players along with their 1994 stats. The cards are numbered in the upper right corner as "X" of 9.

	MINT	NRMT	EXC
COMPLETE SET (9)	30.00	13.50	3.70
COMMON CARD (1-9)	1.00	.45	.12
RANDOM INSERTS IN SER.2 HOBBY PACKS			

	MINT	NRMT	EXC
□ 1 David Cone / Mike Mussina / Greg Maddux	5.00	2.20	.60
□ 2 Ivan Rodriguez / Mike Piazza / Darren Daulton	3.00	1.35	.35
□ 3 Fred McGriff / Frank Thomas / Jeff Bagwell	10.00	4.50	1.25
□ 4 Roberto Alomar / Carlos Baerga / Craig Biggio	1.50	.70	.19
□ 5 Robin Ventura / Travis Fryman / Matt Williams	1.00	.45	.12
□ 6 Cal Ripken	6.00	2.70	.75

Barry Larkin			
Wil Cordero			
□ 7 Albert Belle	3.00	1.35	.35
Barry Bonds			
Moises Alou			
□ 8 Ken Griffey	8.00	3.60	1.00
Kenny Lofton			
Marquis Grissom			
□ 9 Kirby Puckett	3.00	1.35	.35
Paul O'Neill			
Tony Gwynn			

1995 Donruss Elite

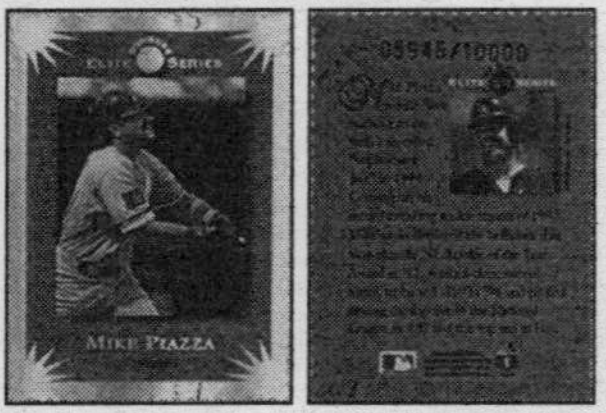

Randomly inserted one in every 210 packs, this set consists of 12 standard-size cards that are numbered (49-60) based on where the previous year's set left off. The fronts contain an action photo surrounded by a marble border. Silver holographic foil borders the card on all four sides. Limited to 10,000, the backs are individually numbered, contain a small photo and write-up.

	MINT	NRMT	EXC
COMPLETE SET (12)	350.00	160.00	45.00
COMPLETE SERIES 1 (6)	200.00	90.00	25.00
COMPLETE SERIES 2 (6)	150.00	70.00	19.00
COMMON CARD (49-60)	8.00	3.60	1.00
RANDOM INSERTS IN PACKS			
□ 49 Jeff Bagwell	25.00	11.00	3.10
□ 50 Paul O'Neill	8.00	3.60	1.00
□ 51 Greg Maddux	50.00	22.00	6.25
□ 52 Mike Piazza	40.00	18.00	5.00
□ 53 Matt Williams	10.00	4.50	1.25
□ 54 Ken Griffey	75.00	34.00	9.50
□ 55 Frank Thomas	75.00	34.00	9.50
□ 56 Barry Bonds	20.00	9.00	2.50
□ 57 Kirby Puckett	25.00	11.00	3.10
□ 58 Fred McGriff	10.00	4.50	1.25
□ 59 Jose Canseco	10.00	4.50	1.25
□ 60 Albert Belle	35.00	16.00	4.40

1995 Donruss Long Ball Leaders

Inserted one in every 24 series one hobby packs, this set features eight top home run hitters. Metallic fronts have much ornamentation including a player photo, the length of the player's home run, the stadium and the date. Horizontal backs have a player photo and photo of the stadium with which the home run occurred. The back also includes all the particulars concerning the home run.

	MINT	NRMT	EXC
COMPLETE SET (8)	20.00	9.00	2.50
COMMON CARD (1-8)	1.00	.45	.12
RANDOM INSERTS IN SER.1 HOBBY PACKS			
□ 1 Frank Thomas	8.00	3.60	1.00
□ 2 Fred McGriff	1.00	.45	.12
□ 3 Ken Griffey	8.00	3.60	1.00
□ 4 Matt Williams	1.00	.45	.12
□ 5 Mike Piazza	5.00	2.20	.60
□ 6 Jose Canseco	1.00	.45	.12
□ 7 Barry Bonds	2.00	.90	.25
□ 8 Jeff Bagwell	3.00	1.35	.35

1995 Donruss Mound Marvels

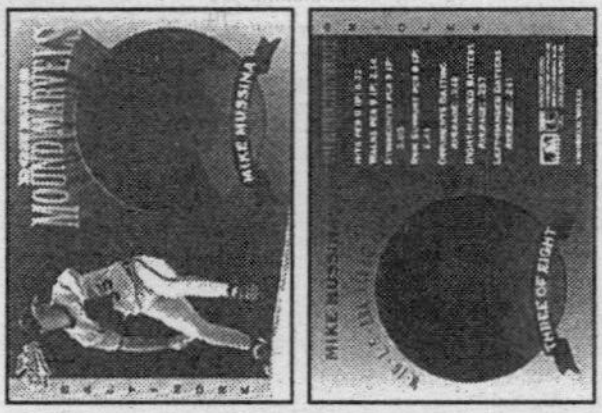

This eight-card standard-size set was randomly inserted into second series magazine jumbo and retail packs. This set features eight of the leading major league starters. The horizontal fronts feature the player's photo on the left with the words "Donruss Mound Marvels" and the player's name on the right. The back features the player's photo within a circular inset along with all his 1994 stats.

	MINT	NRMT	EXC
COMPLETE SET (8)	20.00	9.00	2.50
COMMON CARD (1-8)	1.00	.45	.12
INSERTS IN SER.2 MAG.JUMBO/RETAIL PACKS			
□ 1 Greg Maddux	10.00	4.50	1.25
□ 2 David Cone	1.50	.70	.19
□ 3 Mike Mussina	3.00	1.35	.35
□ 4 Bret Saberhagen	1.00	.45	.12
□ 5 Jimmy Key	1.00	.45	.12
□ 6 Doug Drabek	1.00	.45	.12
□ 7 Randy Johnson	2.50	1.10	.30
□ 8 Jason Bere	1.00	.45	.12

1996 Donruss

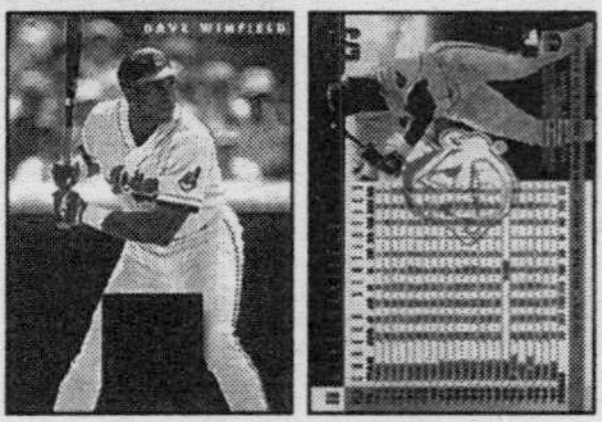

The 1996 Donruss set was issued in two series of 330 and 220 cards respectively, for a total of 550. The 12-card packs had a suggested retail price of $1.79. The full-bleed fronts feature full-

color action photos. The player's name is in white ink in the upper right. The Donruss logo, team name and team logo as well as uniform number and position are located in the bottom middle set against a silver foil background. The horizontal backs feature season and career stats, text, vital stats and another photo. Rookie Cards in this set include Angelo Encarnacion.

	MINT	NRMT	EXC
COMPLETE SET (550)	40.00	18.00	5.00
COMPLETE SERIES 1 (330)	25.00	11.00	3.10
COMPLETE SERIES 2 (220)	15.00	6.75	1.85
COMMON CARD (1-550)	.10	.05	.01
SEMISTARS	.25	.11	.03
STARS	.50	.23	.06

□ 1 Frank Thomas	3.00	1.35	.35
□ 2 Jason Bates	.10	.05	.01
□ 3 Steve Sparks	.10	.05	.01
□ 4 Scott Servais	.10	.05	.01
□ 5 Angelo Encarnacion	.10	.05	.01
□ 6 Scott Sanders	.10	.05	.01
□ 7 Billy Ashley	.10	.05	.01
□ 8 Alex Rodriguez	3.00	1.35	.35
□ 9 Sean Bergman	.10	.05	.01
□ 10 Brad Radke	.10	.05	.01
□ 11 Andy Van Slyke	.25	.11	.03
□ 12 Joe Girardi	.10	.05	.01
□ 13 Mark Grudzielanek	.10	.05	.01
□ 14 Rick Aguilera	.10	.05	.01
□ 15 Randy Veres	.10	.05	.01
□ 16 Tim Bogar	.10	.05	.01
□ 17 Dave Veres	.10	.05	.01
□ 18 Kevin Stocker	.10	.05	.01
□ 19 Marquis Grissom	.50	.23	.06
□ 20 Will Clark	.50	.23	.06
□ 21 Jay Bell	.25	.11	.03
□ 22 Allen Battle	.10	.05	.01
□ 23 Frank Rodriguez	.25	.11	.03
□ 24 Terry Steinbach	.25	.11	.03
□ 25 Gerald Williams	.10	.05	.01
□ 26 Sid Roberson	.10	.05	.01
□ 27 Greg Zaun	.10	.05	.01
□ 28 Ozzie Timmons	.10	.05	.01
□ 29 Vaughn Eshelman	.10	.05	.01
□ 30 Ed Sprague	.25	.11	.03
□ 31 Gary DiSarcina	.10	.05	.01
□ 32 Joe Boever	.10	.05	.01
□ 33 Steve Avery	.25	.11	.03
□ 34 Brad Ausmus	.10	.05	.01
□ 35 Kirt Manwaring	.10	.05	.01
□ 36 Gary Sheffield	.50	.23	.06
□ 37 Jason Bere	.10	.05	.01
□ 38 Jeff Manto	.10	.05	.01
□ 39 David Cone	.50	.23	.06
□ 40 Manny Ramirez	.75	.35	.09
□ 41 Sandy Alomar Jr.	.10	.05	.01
□ 42 Curtis Goodwin	.10	.05	.01
□ 43 Tino Martinez	.50	.23	.06
□ 44 Woody Williams	.10	.05	.01
□ 45 Dean Palmer	.50	.23	.06
□ 46 Hipolito Pichardo	.10	.05	.01
□ 47 Jason Giambi	.50	.23	.06
□ 48 Lance Johnson	.25	.11	.03
□ 49 Bernard Gilkey	.25	.11	.03
□ 50 Kirby Puckett	1.00	.45	.12
□ 51 Tony Fernandez	.10	.05	.01
□ 52 Alex Gonzalez	.10	.05	.01
□ 53 Bret Saberhagen	.10	.05	.01
□ 54 Lyle Mouton	.10	.05	.01
□ 55 Brian McRae	.10	.05	.01
□ 56 Mark Gubicza	.10	.05	.01
□ 57 Sergio Valdez	.10	.05	.01
□ 58 Darrin Fletcher	.10	.05	.01
□ 59 Steve Parris	.10	.05	.01
□ 60 Johnny Damon	.50	.23	.06
□ 61 Rickey Henderson	.50	.23	.06
□ 62 Darrell Whitmore	.10	.05	.01
□ 63 Roberto Petagine	.10	.05	.01
□ 64 Trenidad Hubbard	.10	.05	.01
□ 65 Heathcliff Slocumb	.10	.05	.01
□ 66 Steve Finley	.50	.23	.06
□ 67 Mariano Rivera	.50	.23	.06
□ 68 Brian L.Hunter	.10	.05	.01
□ 69 Jamie Moyer	.10	.05	.01
□ 70 Ellis Burks	.50	.23	.06
□ 71 Pat Kelly	.10	.05	.01
□ 72 Mickey Tettleton	.25	.11	.03
□ 73 Garret Anderson	.50	.23	.06
□ 74 Andy Pettitte	1.00	.45	.12
□ 75 Glenallen Hill	.25	.11	.03
□ 76 Brent Gates	.10	.05	.01
□ 77 Lou Whitaker	.50	.23	.06
□ 78 David Segui	.10	.05	.01
□ 79 Dan Wilson	.10	.05	.01
□ 80 Pat Listach	.10	.05	.01
□ 81 Jeff Bagwell	1.25	.55	.16
□ 82 Ben McDonald	.10	.05	.01
□ 83 John Valentin	.25	.11	.03
□ 84 John Jaha	.10	.05	.01
□ 85 Pete Schourek	.25	.11	.03
□ 86 Bryce Florie	.10	.05	.01
□ 87 Brian Jordan	.50	.23	.06
□ 88 Ron Karkovice	.10	.05	.01
□ 89 Al Leiter	.10	.05	.01
□ 90 Tony Longmire	.10	.05	.01
□ 91 Nelson Liriano	.10	.05	.01
□ 92 David Bell	.10	.05	.01
□ 93 Kevin Gross	.10	.05	.01
□ 94 Tom Candiotti	.10	.05	.01
□ 95 Dave Martinez	.10	.05	.01
□ 96 Greg Myers	.10	.05	.01
□ 97 Rheal Cormier	.10	.05	.01
□ 98 Chris Hammond	.10	.05	.01
□ 99 Randy Myers	.10	.05	.01
□ 100 Bill Pulsipher	.25	.11	.03
□ 101 Jason Isringhausen	.25	.11	.03
□ 102 Dave Stevens	.10	.05	.01
□ 103 Roberto Alomar	.75	.35	.09
□ 104 Bob Higginson	.50	.23	.06
□ 105 Eddie Murray	.75	.35	.09
□ 106 Matt Walbeck	.10	.05	.01
□ 107 Mark Wohlers	.25	.11	.03
□ 108 Jeff Nelson	.10	.05	.01
□ 109 Tom Goodwin	.10	.05	.01
□ 110 Cal Ripken CL	1.25	.55	.16
□ 111 Rey Sanchez	.10	.05	.01
□ 112 Hector Carrasco	.10	.05	.01
□ 113 B.J. Surhoff	.10	.05	.01
□ 114 Dan Miceli	.10	.05	.01
□ 115 Dean Hartgraves	.10	.05	.01
□ 116 John Burkett	.10	.05	.01
□ 117 Gary Gaetti	.25	.11	.03
□ 118 Ricky Bones	.10	.05	.01
□ 119 Mike Macfarlane	.10	.05	.01
□ 120 Bip Roberts	.10	.05	.01
□ 121 Dave Mlicki	.10	.05	.01
□ 122 Chili Davis	.10	.05	.01
□ 123 Mark Whiten	.10	.05	.01
□ 124 Herbert Perry	.10	.05	.01
□ 125 Butch Henry	.10	.05	.01
□ 126 Derek Bell	.50	.23	.06
□ 127 Al Martin	.10	.05	.01
□ 128 John Franco	.10	.05	.01
□ 129 W. VanLandingham	.10	.05	.01
□ 130 Mike Bordick	.25	.11	.03
□ 131 Mike Mordecai	.10	.05	.01
□ 132 Robby Thompson	.10	.05	.01
□ 133 Greg Colbrunn	.10	.05	.01
□ 134 Domingo Cedeno	.10	.05	.01
□ 135 Chad Curtis	.10	.05	.01
□ 136 Jose Hernandez	.10	.05	.01
□ 137 Scott Klingenbeck	.10	.05	.01
□ 138 Ryan Klesko	.60	.25	.07
□ 139 John Smiley	.10	.05	.01
□ 140 Charlie Hayes	.10	.05	.01
□ 141 Jay Buhner	.50	.23	.06
□ 142 Doug Drabek	.10	.05	.01
□ 143 Roger Pavlik	.10	.05	.01
□ 144 Todd Worrell	.25	.11	.03
□ 145 Cal Ripken	2.50	1.10	.30
□ 146 Steve Reed	.10	.05	.01
□ 147 Chuck Finley	.10	.05	.01
□ 148 Mike Blowers	.10	.05	.01
□ 149 Orel Hershiser	.25	.11	.03
□ 150 Allen Watson	.10	.05	.01
□ 151 Ramon Martinez	.50	.23	.06
□ 152 Melvin Nieves	.25	.11	.03
□ 153 Tripp Cromer	.10	.05	.01
□ 154 Yorkis Perez	.10	.05	.01
□ 155 Stan Javier	.10	.05	.01

☐	156 Mel Rojas	.25	.11	.03
☐	157 Aaron Sele	.10	.05	.01
☐	158 Eric Karros	.50	.23	.06
☐	159 Robb Nen	.10	.05	.01
☐	160 Raul Mondesi	.50	.23	.06
☐	161 John Wetteland	.25	.11	.03
☐	162 Tim Scott	.10	.05	.01
☐	163 Kenny Rogers	.10	.05	.01
☐	164 Melvin Bunch	.10	.05	.01
☐	165 Rod Beck	.25	.11	.03
☐	166 Andy Benes	.10	.05	.01
☐	167 Lenny Dykstra	.25	.11	.03
☐	168 Orlando Merced	.25	.11	.03
☐	169 Tomas Perez	.25	.11	.03
☐	170 Xavier Hernandez	.10	.05	.01
☐	171 Ruben Sierra	.10	.05	.01
☐	172 Alan Trammell	.50	.23	.06
☐	173 Mike Fetters	.10	.05	.01
☐	174 Wilson Alvarez	.50	.23	.06
☐	175 Erik Hanson	.10	.05	.01
☐	176 Travis Fryman	.50	.23	.06
☐	177 Jim Abbott	.50	.23	.06
☐	178 Bret Boone	.10	.05	.01
☐	179 Sterling Hitchcock	.10	.05	.01
☐	180 Pat Mahomes	.10	.05	.01
☐	181 Mark Acre	.10	.05	.01
☐	182 Charles Nagy	.25	.11	.03
☐	183 Rusty Greer	.50	.23	.06
☐	184 Mike Stanley	.10	.05	.01
☐	185 Jim Bullinger	.10	.05	.01
☐	186 Shane Andrews	.10	.05	.01
☐	187 Brian Keyser	.10	.05	.01
☐	188 Tyler Green	.10	.05	.01
☐	189 Mark Grace	.50	.23	.06
☐	190 Bob Hamelin	.10	.05	.01
☐	191 Luis Ortiz	.10	.05	.01
☐	192 Joe Carter	.50	.23	.06
☐	193 Eddie Taubensee	.10	.05	.01
☐	194 Brian Anderson	.10	.05	.01
☐	195 Edgardo Alfonzo	.25	.11	.03
☐	196 Pedro Munoz	.10	.05	.01
☐	197 David Justice	.50	.23	.06
☐	198 Trevor Hoffman	.25	.11	.03
☐	199 Bobby Ayala	.10	.05	.01
☐	200 Tony Eusebio	.10	.05	.01
☐	201 Jeff Russell	.10	.05	.01
☐	202 Mike Hampton	.10	.05	.01
☐	203 Walt Weiss	.10	.05	.01
☐	204 Joey Hamilton	.25	.11	.03
☐	205 Roberto Hernandez	.25	.11	.03
☐	206 Greg Vaughn	.50	.23	.06
☐	207 Felipe Lira	.10	.05	.01
☐	208 Harold Baines	.25	.11	.03
☐	209 Tim Wallach	.10	.05	.01
☐	210 Manny Alexander	.10	.05	.01
☐	211 Tim Laker	.10	.05	.01
☐	212 Chris Haney	.10	.05	.01
☐	213 Brian Maxcy	.10	.05	.01
☐	214 Eric Young	.10	.05	.01
☐	215 Darryl Strawberry	.50	.23	.06
☐	216 Barry Bonds	.75	.35	.09
☐	217 Tim Naehring	.25	.11	.03
☐	218 Scott Brosius	.25	.11	.03
☐	219 Reggie Sanders	.50	.23	.06
☐	220 Eddie Murray CL	.50	.23	.06
☐	221 Luis Alicea	.10	.05	.01
☐	222 Albert Belle	1.50	.70	.19
☐	223 Benji Gil	.10	.05	.01
☐	224 Dante Bichette	.50	.23	.06
☐	225 Bobby Bonilla	.50	.23	.06
☐	226 Todd Stottlemyre	.10	.05	.01
☐	227 Jim Edmonds	.50	.23	.06
☐	228 Todd Jones	.10	.05	.01
☐	229 Shawn Green	.50	.23	.06
☐	230 Javier Lopez	.50	.23	.06
☐	231 Ariel Prieto	.10	.05	.01
☐	232 Tony Phillips	.25	.11	.03
☐	233 James Mouton	.10	.05	.01
☐	234 Jose Oquendo	.10	.05	.01
☐	235 Royce Clayton	.10	.05	.01
☐	236 Chuck Carr	.10	.05	.01
☐	237 Doug Jones	.10	.05	.01
☐	238 Mark McLemore	.10	.05	.01
☐	239 Bill Swift	.10	.05	.01
☐	240 Scott Leius	.10	.05	.01
☐	241 Russ Davis	.10	.05	.01
☐	242 Ray Durham	.50	.23	.06
☐	243 Matt Mieske	.10	.05	.01
☐	244 Brent Mayne	.10	.05	.01
☐	245 Thomas Howard	.10	.05	.01
☐	246 Troy O'Leary	.25	.11	.03
☐	247 Jacob Brumfield	.10	.05	.01
☐	248 Mickey Morandini	.10	.05	.01
☐	249 Todd Hundley	.50	.23	.06
☐	250 Chris Bosio	.10	.05	.01
☐	251 Omar Vizquel	.10	.05	.01
☐	252 Mike Lansing	.10	.05	.01
☐	253 John Mabry	.50	.23	.06
☐	254 Mike Perez	.10	.05	.01
☐	255 Delino DeShields	.10	.05	.01
☐	256 Wil Cordero	.10	.05	.01
☐	257 Mike James	.10	.05	.01
☐	258 Todd Van Poppel	.10	.05	.01
☐	259 Joey Cora	.10	.05	.01
☐	260 Andre Dawson	.50	.23	.06
☐	261 Jerry DiPoto	.10	.05	.01
☐	262 Rick Krivda	.10	.05	.01
☐	263 Glenn Dishman	.25	.11	.03
☐	264 Mike Mimbs	.10	.05	.01
☐	265 John Ericks	.10	.05	.01
☐	266 Jose Canseco	.50	.23	.06
☐	267 Jeff Branson	.10	.05	.01
☐	268 Curt Leskanic	.10	.05	.01
☐	269 Jon Nunnally	.10	.05	.01
☐	270 Scott Stahoviak	.10	.05	.01
☐	271 Jeff Montgomery	.10	.05	.01
☐	272 Hal Morris	.10	.05	.01
☐	273 Esteban Loaiza	.10	.05	.01
☐	274 Rico Brogna	.10	.05	.01
☐	275 Dave Winfield	.50	.23	.06
☐	276 J.R. Phillips	.10	.05	.01
☐	277 Todd Zeile	.10	.05	.01
☐	278 Tom Pagnozzi	.10	.05	.01
☐	279 Mark Lemke	.10	.05	.01
☐	280 Dave Magadan	.10	.05	.01
☐	281 Greg McMichael	.10	.05	.01
☐	282 Mike Morgan	.10	.05	.01
☐	283 Moises Alou	.25	.11	.03
☐	284 Dennis Martinez	.25	.11	.03
☐	285 Jeff Kent	.10	.05	.01
☐	286 Mark Johnson	.10	.05	.01
☐	287 Darren Lewis	.10	.05	.01
☐	288 Brad Clontz	.10	.05	.01
☐	289 Chad Fonville	.10	.05	.01
☐	290 Paul Sorrento	.10	.05	.01
☐	291 Lee Smith	.50	.23	.06
☐	292 Tom Glavine	.50	.23	.06
☐	293 Antonio Osuna	.10	.05	.01
☐	294 Kevin Foster	.10	.05	.01
☐	295 Sandy Martinez	.10	.05	.01
☐	296 Mark Leiter	.10	.05	.01
☐	297 Julian Tavarez	.10	.05	.01
☐	298 Mike Kelly	.10	.05	.01
☐	299 Joe Oliver	.10	.05	.01
☐	300 John Flaherty	.10	.05	.01
☐	301 Don Mattingly	1.50	.70	.19
☐	302 Pat Meares	.10	.05	.01
☐	303 John Doherty	.10	.05	.01
☐	304 Joe Vitiello	.10	.05	.01
☐	305 Vinny Castilla	.50	.23	.06
☐	306 Jeff Brantley	.10	.05	.01
☐	307 Mike Greenwell	.10	.05	.01
☐	308 Midre Cummings	.10	.05	.01
☐	309 Curt Schilling	.10	.05	.01
☐	310 Ken Caminiti	.50	.23	.06
☐	311 Scott Erickson	.10	.05	.01
☐	312 Carl Everett	.10	.05	.01
☐	313 Charles Johnson	.50	.23	.06
☐	314 Alex Diaz	.10	.05	.01
☐	315 Jose Mesa	.25	.11	.03
☐	316 Mark Carreon	.10	.05	.01
☐	317 Carlos Perez	.10	.05	.01
☐	318 Ismael Valdes	.25	.11	.03
☐	319 Frank Castillo	.10	.05	.01
☐	320 Tom Henke	.25	.11	.03
☐	321 Spike Owen	.10	.05	.01
☐	322 Joe Orsulak	.10	.05	.01
☐	323 Paul Menhart	.10	.05	.01
☐	324 Pedro Borbon	.10	.05	.01
☐	325 Paul Molitor CL	.50	.23	.06
☐	326 Jeff Cirillo	.10	.05	.01
☐	327 Edwin Hurtado	.10	.05	.01

□	328	Orlando Miller	.10	.05	.01
□	329	Steve Ontiveros	.10	.05	.01
□	330	Kirby Puckett CL	.50	.23	.06
□	331	Scott Bullett	.10	.05	.01
□	332	Andres Galarraga	.50	.23	.06
□	333	Cal Eldred	.10	.05	.01
□	334	Sammy Sosa	.50	.23	.06
□	335	Don Slaught	.10	.05	.01
□	336	Jody Reed	.10	.05	.01
□	337	Roger Cedeno	.25	.11	.03
□	338	Ken Griffey Jr.	3.00	1.35	.35
□	339	Todd Hollandsworth	.50	.23	.06
□	340	Mike Trombley	.10	.05	.01
□	341	Gregg Jefferies	.50	.23	.06
□	342	Larry Walker	.50	.23	.06
□	343	Pedro Martinez	.10	.05	.01
□	344	Dwayne Hosey	.10	.05	.01
□	345	Terry Pendleton	.25	.11	.03
□	346	Pete Harnisch	.10	.05	.01
□	347	Tony Castillo	.10	.05	.01
□	348	Paul Quantrill	.10	.05	.01
□	349	Fred McGriff	.50	.23	.06
□	350	Ivan Rodriguez	.60	.25	.07
□	351	Butch Huskey	.25	.11	.03
□	352	Ozzie Smith	.60	.25	.07
□	353	Marty Cordova	.50	.23	.06
□	354	John Wasdin	.10	.05	.01
□	355	Wade Boggs	.50	.23	.06
□	356	Dave Nilsson	.25	.11	.03
□	357	Rafael Palmeiro	.50	.23	.06
□	358	Luis Gonzalez	.10	.05	.01
□	359	Reggie Jefferson	.10	.05	.01
□	360	Carlos Delgado	.50	.23	.06
□	361	Orlando Palmeiro	.10	.05	.01
□	362	Chris Gomez	.10	.05	.01
□	363	John Smoltz	.50	.23	.06
□	364	Marc Newfield	.25	.11	.03
□	365	Matt Williams	.50	.23	.06
□	366	Jesus Tavarez	.10	.05	.01
□	367	Bruce Ruffin	.10	.05	.01
□	368	Sean Berry	.10	.05	.01
□	369	Randy Velarde	.10	.05	.01
□	370	Tony Pena	.10	.05	.01
□	371	Jim Thome	.60	.25	.07
□	372	Jeffrey Hammonds	.25	.11	.03
□	373	Bob Wolcott	.10	.05	.01
□	374	Juan Guzman	.10	.05	.01
□	375	Juan Gonzalez	1.50	.70	.19
□	376	Michael Tucker	.25	.11	.03
□	377	Doug Johns	.10	.05	.01
□	378	Mike Cameron	1.00	.45	.12
□	379	Ray Lankford	.50	.23	.06
□	380	Jose Parra	.10	.05	.01
□	381	Jimmy Key	.25	.11	.03
□	382	John Olerud	.10	.05	.01
□	383	Kevin Ritz	.10	.05	.01
□	384	Tim Raines	.50	.23	.06
□	385	Rich Amaral	.10	.05	.01
□	386	Keith Lockhart	.10	.05	.01
□	387	Steve Scarsone	.10	.05	.01
□	388	Cliff Floyd	.10	.05	.01
□	389	Rich Aude	.10	.05	.01
□	390	Hideo Nomo	.75	.35	.09
□	391	Geronimo Berroa	.25	.11	.03
□	392	Pat Rapp	.10	.05	.01
□	393	Dustin Hermanson	.25	.11	.03
□	394	Greg Maddux	2.00	.90	.25
□	395	Darren Daulton	.25	.11	.03
□	396	Kenny Lofton	.75	.35	.09
□	397	Ruben Rivera	.60	.25	.07
□	398	Billy Wagner	.10	.05	.01
□	399	Kevin Brown	.25	.11	.03
□	400	Mike Kingery	.10	.05	.01
□	401	Bernie Williams	.50	.23	.06
□	402	Otis Nixon	.10	.05	.01
□	403	Damion Easley	.10	.05	.01
□	404	Paul O'Neill	.10	.05	.01
□	405	Deion Sanders	.50	.23	.06
□	406	Dennis Eckersley	.50	.23	.06
□	407	Tony Clark	.50	.23	.06
□	408	Rondell White	.50	.23	.06
□	409	Luis Sojo	.10	.05	.01
□	410	David Hulse	.10	.05	.01
□	411	Shane Reynolds	.10	.05	.01
□	412	Chris Hoiles	.10	.05	.01
□	413	Lee Tinsley	.10	.05	.01
□	414	Scott Karl	.10	.05	.01
□	415	Ron Gant	.50	.23	.06
□	416	Brian Johnson	.10	.05	.01
□	417	Jose Oliva	.10	.05	.01
□	418	Jack McDowell	.50	.23	.06
□	419	Paul Molitor	.60	.25	.07
□	420	Ricky Bottalico	.10	.05	.01
□	421	Paul Wagner	.10	.05	.01
□	422	Terry Bradshaw	.10	.05	.01
□	423	Bob Tewksbury	.10	.05	.01
□	424	Mike Piazza	2.00	.90	.25
□	425	Luis Andujar	.25	.11	.03
□	426	Mark Langston	.10	.05	.01
□	427	Stan Belinda	.10	.05	.01
□	428	Kurt Abbott	.10	.05	.01
□	429	Shawon Dunston	.10	.05	.01
□	430	Bobby Jones	.10	.05	.01
□	431	Jose Vizcaino	.10	.05	.01
□	432	Matt Lawton	.10	.05	.01
□	433	Pat Hentgen	.50	.23	.06
□	434	Cecil Fielder	.50	.23	.06
□	435	Carlos Baerga	.50	.23	.06
□	436	Rich Becker	.25	.11	.03
□	437	Chipper Jones	2.00	.90	.25
□	438	Bill Risley	.10	.05	.01
□	439	Kevin Appier	.10	.05	.01
□	440	Wade Boggs CL 2500 Career Hits 8/23/95	.25	.11	.03
□	441	Jaime Navarro	.10	.05	.01
□	442	Barry Larkin	.50	.23	.06
□	443	Jose Valentin	.10	.05	.01
□	444	Bryan Rekar	.10	.05	.01
□	445	Rick Wilkins	.10	.05	.01
□	446	Quilvio Veras	.10	.05	.01
□	447	Greg Gagne	.10	.05	.01
□	448	Mark Kiefer	.10	.05	.01
□	449	Bobby Witt	.10	.05	.01
□	450	Andy Ashby	.10	.05	.01
□	451	Alex Ochoa	.25	.11	.03
□	452	Jorge Fabregas	.10	.05	.01
□	453	Gene Schall	.10	.05	.01
□	454	Ken Hill	.10	.05	.01
□	455	Tony Tarasco	.10	.05	.01
□	456	Donnie Wall	.10	.05	.01
□	457	Carlos Garcia	.10	.05	.01
□	458	Ryan Thompson	.10	.05	.01
□	459	Marvin Benard	.10	.05	.01
□	460	Jose Herrera	.10	.05	.01
□	461	Jeff Blauser	.10	.05	.01
□	462	Chris Hook	.10	.05	.01
□	463	Jeff Conine	.50	.23	.06
□	464	Devon White	.10	.05	.01
□	465	Danny Bautista	.10	.05	.01
□	466	Steve Trachsel	.10	.05	.01
□	467	C.J. Nitkowski	.10	.05	.01
□	468	Mike Devereaux	.10	.05	.01
□	469	David Wells	.10	.05	.01
□	470	Jim Eisenreich	.10	.05	.01
□	471	Edgar Martinez	.50	.23	.06
□	472	Craig Biggio	.50	.23	.06
□	473	Jeff Frye	.10	.05	.01
□	474	Karim Garcia	.60	.25	.07
□	475	Jimmy Haynes	.10	.05	.01
□	476	Darren Holmes	.10	.05	.01
□	477	Tim Salmon	.50	.23	.06
□	478	Randy Johnson	.50	.23	.06
□	479	Eric Plunk	.10	.05	.01
□	480	Scott Cooper	.10	.05	.01
□	481	Chan Ho Park	.50	.23	.06
□	482	Ray McDavid	.10	.05	.01
□	483	Mark Petkovsek	.10	.05	.01
□	484	Greg Swindell	.10	.05	.01
□	485	George Williams	.10	.05	.01
□	486	Yamil Benitez	.10	.05	.01
□	487	Tim Wakefield	.10	.05	.01
□	488	Kevin Tapani	.10	.05	.01
□	489	Derrick May	.10	.05	.01
□	490	Ken Griffey Jr. CL 1000 Career Hits 8/16/96	1.50	.70	.19
□	491	Derek Jeter	2.00	.90	.25
□	492	Jeff Fassero	.10	.05	.01
□	493	Benito Santiago	.10	.05	.01
□	494	Tom Gordon	.10	.05	.01
□	495	Jamie Brewington	.10	.05	.01
□	496	Vince Coleman	.10	.05	.01
□	497	Kevin Jordan	.10	.05	.01

□ 498 Jeff King	.25	.11	.03
□ 499 Mike Simms	.10	.05	.01
□ 500 Jose Rijo	.10	.05	.01
□ 501 Denny Neagle	.25	.11	.03
□ 502 Jose Lima	.10	.05	.01
□ 503 Kevin Seitzer	.10	.05	.01
□ 504 Alex Fernandez	.50	.23	.06
□ 505 Mo Vaughn	.75	.35	.09
□ 506 Phil Nevin	.10	.05	.01
□ 507 J.T. Snow	.25	.11	.03
□ 508 Andujar Cedeno	.10	.05	.01
□ 509 Ozzie Guillen	.10	.05	.01
□ 510 Mark Clark	.10	.05	.01
□ 511 Mark McGwire	1.00	.45	.12
□ 512 Jeff Reboulet	.10	.05	.01
□ 513 Armando Benitez	.10	.05	.01
□ 514 LaTroy Hawkins	.10	.05	.01
□ 515 Brett Butler	.10	.05	.01
□ 516 Tavo Alvarez	.10	.05	.01
□ 517 Chris Snopek	.10	.05	.01
□ 518 Mike Mussina	.60	.25	.07
□ 519 Darryl Kile	.10	.05	.01
□ 520 Wally Joyner	.10	.05	.01
□ 521 Willie McGee	.10	.05	.01
□ 522 Kent Mercker	.10	.05	.01
□ 523 Mike Jackson	.10	.05	.01
□ 524 Troy Percival	.10	.05	.01
□ 525 Tony Gwynn	1.25	.55	.16
□ 526 Ron Coomer	.10	.05	.01
□ 527 Darryl Hamilton	.10	.05	.01
□ 528 Phil Plantier	.10	.05	.01
□ 529 Norm Charlton	.10	.05	.01
□ 530 Craig Paquette	.10	.05	.01
□ 531 Dave Burba	.10	.05	.01
□ 532 Mike Henneman	.10	.05	.01
□ 533 Terrell Wade	.50	.23	.06
□ 534 Eddie Williams	.10	.05	.01
□ 535 Robin Ventura	.50	.23	.06
□ 536 Chuck Knoblauch	.50	.23	.06
□ 537 Les Norman	.10	.05	.01
□ 538 Brady Anderson	.50	.23	.06
□ 539 Roger Clemens	.50	.23	.06
□ 540 Mark Portugal	.10	.05	.01
□ 541 Mike Matheny	.10	.05	.01
□ 542 Jeff Parrett	.10	.05	.01
□ 543 Roberto Kelly	.10	.05	.01
□ 544 Damon Buford	.10	.05	.01
□ 545 Chad Ogea	.10	.05	.01
□ 546 Jose Offerman	.10	.05	.01
□ 547 Brian Barber	.10	.05	.01
□ 548 Danny Tartabull	.10	.05	.01
□ 549 Duane Singleton	.10	.05	.01
□ 550 Tony Gwynn CL 1000 Career Runs 5/7/95	.60	.25	.07

1996 Donruss Press Proofs

Randomly inserted at a rate of one in 10 first and second series packs, these cards are parallel to the regular Donruss issue. Even though they are not sequentially numbered, production on these cards were limited to 2,000 cards. Each card is noted as being a Press Proof in gold foil on the front.

	MINT	NRMT	EXC
COMPLETE SET (550)	2000.00	900.00	250.00
COMPLETE SERIES 1 (330)	1200.00	550.00	150.00
COMPLETE SERIES 2 (220)	800.00	350.00	100.00
COMMON CARD (1-550)	2.00	.90	.25
SEMISTARS	5.00	2.20	.60
STARS	12.00	5.50	1.50
*VETERAN STARS: 15X TO 25X BASIC CARDS			
*YOUNG STARS: 9X TO 15X BASIC CARDS			
RANDOM INSERTS IN PACKS			

□ 1 Frank Thomas	75.00	34.00	9.50
□ 8 Alex Rodriguez	75.00	34.00	9.50
□ 145 Cal Ripken	60.00	27.00	7.50
□ 222 Albert Belle	40.00	18.00	5.00
□ 301 Don Mattingly	40.00	18.00	5.00
□ 338 Ken Griffey Jr.	60.00	27.00	7.50
□ 375 Juan Gonzalez	40.00	18.00	5.00
□ 394 Greg Maddux	40.00	18.00	5.00
□ 424 Mike Piazza	40.00	18.00	5.00
□ 437 Chipper Jones	40.00	18.00	5.00
□ 490 Ken Griffey Jr. CL	30.00	13.50	3.70
□ 491 Derek Jeter	40.00	18.00	5.00

1996 Donruss Diamond Kings

These 31 standard-size cards were randomly inserted into packs and issued in two series of 14 and 17 cards. They were inserted at a ratio of approximately one every 60 packs. The cards are sequentially numbered in the back lower right as "X" of 10,000. The fronts feature player portraits by noted sports artist Dick Perez. These cards are gold-foil stamped and the portraits are surrounded by gold-foil borders. The backs feature text about the player as well as a player photo. The cards are numbered on the back with a "DK" prefix.

	MINT	NRMT	EXC
COMPLETE SET (31)	300.00	135.00	38.00
COMPLETE SERIES 1 (14)	150.00	70.00	19.00
COMPLETE SERIES 2 (17)	150.00	70.00	19.00
COMMON CARD (1-31)	4.00	1.80	.50
SEMISTARS	6.00	2.70	.75
RANDOM INSERTS IN BOTH SERIES PACKS			

□ 1 Frank Thomas	50.00	22.00	6.25
□ 2 Mo Vaughn	12.00	5.50	1.50
□ 3 Manny Ramirez	12.00	5.50	1.50
□ 4 Mark McGwire	15.00	6.75	1.85
□ 5 Juan Gonzalez	25.00	11.00	3.10
□ 6 Roberto Alomar	12.00	5.50	1.50
□ 7 Tim Salmon	6.00	2.70	.75
□ 8 Barry Bonds	12.00	5.50	1.50
□ 9 Tony Gwynn	20.00	9.00	2.50
□ 10 Reggie Sanders	6.00	2.70	.75
□ 11 Larry Walker	6.00	2.70	.75
□ 12 Pedro Martinez	4.00	1.80	.50
□ 13 Jeff King	4.00	1.80	.50
□ 14 Mark Grace	6.00	2.70	.75
□ 15 Greg Maddux	25.00	11.00	3.10
□ 16 Don Mattingly	20.00	9.00	2.50
□ 17 Gregg Jefferies	6.00	2.70	.75
□ 18 Chad Curtis	4.00	1.80	.50
□ 19 Jason Isringhausen	4.00	1.80	.50
□ 20 B.J. Surhoff	4.00	1.80	.50
□ 21 Jeff Conine	6.00	2.70	.75
□ 22 Kirby Puckett	15.00	6.75	1.85
□ 23 Derek Bell	4.00	1.80	.50
□ 24 Wally Joyner	4.00	1.80	.50
□ 25 Brian Jordan	6.00	2.70	.75
□ 26 Edgar Martinez	6.00	2.70	.75
□ 27 Hideo Nomo	10.00	4.50	1.25
□ 28 Mike Mussina	8.00	3.60	1.00
□ 29 Eddie Murray	10.00	4.50	1.25
□ 30 Cal Ripken	30.00	13.50	3.70
□ 31 Checklist	4.00	1.80	.50

1996 Donruss Elite

Randomly inserted approximately one in every 75 packs, this 12-card standard-size set is continuously numbered (61-72) from the previous year. The fronts contain an action photo sur-

rounded by a silver border. Limited to 10,000 and sequentially numbered, the backs contain a small photo and write up.

	MINT	NRMT	EXC
COMPLETE SET (12)	300.00	135.00	38.00
COMPLETE SERIES 1 (6)	150.00	70.00	19.00
COMPLETE SERIES 2 (6)	150.00	70.00	19.00
COMMON CARD (61-72)	8.00	3.60	1.00
RANDOM INSERTS IN BOTH SERIES PACKS			

	MINT	NRMT	EXC
□ 61 Cal Ripken	60.00	27.00	7.50
□ 62 Hideo Nomo	25.00	11.00	3.10
□ 63 Reggie Sanders	8.00	3.60	1.00
□ 64 Mo Vaughn	20.00	9.00	2.50
□ 65 Tim Salmon	8.00	3.60	1.00
□ 66 Chipper Jones	50.00	22.00	6.25
□ 67 Manny Ramirez	12.00	5.50	1.50
□ 68 Greg Maddux	30.00	13.50	3.70
□ 69 Frank Thomas	50.00	22.00	6.25
□ 70 Ken Griffey Jr.	50.00	22.00	6.25
□ 71 Dante Bichette	8.00	3.60	1.00
□ 72 Tony Gwynn	20.00	9.00	2.50

1996 Donruss Freeze Frame

Randomly inserted in second series packs at a rate of one in 60, this 8-card standard-size set features the top hitters and pitchers in baseball. Just 5,000 of each card were produced and sequentially numbered. In a horizontal format with round corners, the fronts display a cross-hatched color player photo that is bordered on the left and bottom by thick black borders. A second color player cutout is superposed on the photo. The backs have three small color photos, '95 season highlights, and a brief note.

	MINT	NRMT	EXC
COMPLETE SET (8)	200.00	90.00	25.00
COMMON CARD (1-8)	10.00	4.50	1.25
RANDOM INSERTS IN SER.2 PACKS			

	MINT	NRMT	EXC
□ 1 Frank Thomas	40.00	18.00	5.00
□ 2 Ken Griffey Jr.	40.00	18.00	5.00
□ 3 Cal Ripken	30.00	13.50	3.70
□ 4 Hideo Nomo	10.00	4.50	1.25
□ 5 Greg Maddux	25.00	11.00	3.10
□ 6 Albert Belle	20.00	9.00	2.50
□ 7 Chipper Jones	25.00	11.00	3.10
□ 8 Mike Piazza	25.00	11.00	3.10

1996 Donruss Hit List

This 16-card standard-size set was randomly inserted at a rate of one in every 60 packs and salutes the most consistent hitters in the game. The cards are sequentially numbered out of 10,000. The fronts feature full-color shots set against a silver-foil background that is complemented by a team color duotone and features a gold foil team logo and "Hit List" logo. The backs have a color action photo as well as having year-by-year and career hit and batting average stats.

	MINT	NRMT	EXC
COMPLETE SET (16)	120.00	55.00	15.00
COMPLETE SERIES 1 (8)	60.00	27.00	7.50
COMPLETE SERIES 2 (8)	60.00	27.00	7.50
COMMON CARD (1-16)	3.00	1.35	.35
SEMISTARS	4.00	1.80	.50
RANDOM INSERTS IN BOTH SERIES PACKS			

	MINT	NRMT	EXC
□ 1 Tony Gwynn	12.00	5.50	1.50
□ 2 Ken Griffey Jr.	30.00	13.50	3.70
□ 3 Will Clark	4.00	1.80	.50
□ 4 Mike Piazza	20.00	9.00	2.50
□ 5 Carlos Baerga	3.00	1.35	.35
□ 6 Mo Vaughn	8.00	3.60	1.00
□ 7 Mark Grace	4.00	1.80	.50
□ 8 Kirby Puckett	10.00	4.50	1.25
□ 9 Frank Thomas	30.00	13.50	3.70
□ 10 Barry Bonds	8.00	3.60	1.00
□ 11 Jeff Bagwell	12.00	5.50	1.50
□ 12 Edgar Martinez	4.00	1.80	.50
□ 13 Tim Salmon	4.00	1.80	.50
□ 14 Wade Boggs	4.00	1.80	.50
□ 15 Don Mattingly	15.00	6.75	1.85
□ 16 Eddie Murray	8.00	3.60	1.00

1996 Donruss Long Ball Leaders

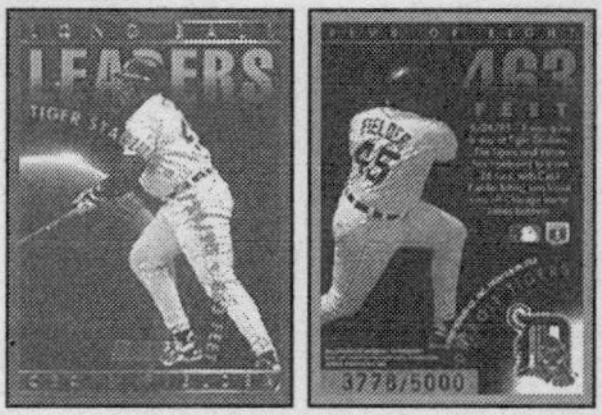

This eight-card standard-size set was randomly inserted into series one retail packs. They were inserted at a rate of approximately one in every 96 packs. The cards are sequentially numbered out of 5,000. The set highlights eight top sluggers and their farthest home run distance of 1995. The fronts feature a player photo set against a silver-foil background. The words "Long Ball Leaders" are on the top of the card while the stadium, date and distance of the *blast are in the middle. The player's name is at the bottom. The back has a player photo and information about the game in which the mighty clout occurred.*

	MINT	NRMT	EXC
COMPLETE SET (8)	200.00	90.00	25.00
COMMON CARD (1-8)	8.00	3.60	1.00
RANDOM INSERTS IN SER.1 RETAIL PACKS			

	MINT	NRMT	EXC
□ 1 Barry Bonds	20.00	9.00	2.50
□ 2 Ryan Klesko	15.00	6.75	1.85
□ 3 Mark McGwire	25.00	11.00	3.10
□ 4 Raul Mondesi	10.00	4.50	1.25
□ 5 Cecil Fielder	8.00	3.60	1.00
□ 6 Ken Griffey Jr.	80.00	36.00	10.00
□ 7 Larry Walker	8.00	3.60	1.00
□ 8 Frank Thomas	80.00	36.00	10.00

1996 Donruss Power Alley

This ten-card standard-size set was randomly inserted into series one hobby packs. They were inserted at a rate of approximately one in every 92 packs. These cards are all sequentially numbered out of 5,000. The first 500 of these cards were issued in a diecut format. These cards feature a player photo set against a diamond design and team holographic background. The horizontal backs feature a player photo, some text and the player's 1995 power statistics.

	MINT	NRMT	EXC
COMPLETE SET (10)	150.00	70.00	19.00
COMMON CARD (1-10)	5.00	2.20	.60
RANDOM INSERTS IN SER.1 HOBBY PACKS			
COMP.DIECUT SET (10)	1200.00		
DIECUTS ARE FIRST 500 NUMBERS OF EACH			
DIECUTS: 5X TO 8X BASIC CARDS			

	MINT	NRMT	EXC
□ 1 Frank Thomas	50.00	22.00	6.25
□ 2 Barry Bonds	12.00	5.50	1.50
□ 3 Reggie Sanders	5.00	2.20	.60
□ 4 Albert Belle	25.00	11.00	3.10
□ 5 Tim Salmon	6.00	2.70	.75
□ 6 Dante Bichette	6.00	2.70	.75
□ 7 Mo Vaughn	12.00	5.50	1.50
□ 8 Jim Edmonds	5.00	2.20	.60
□ 9 Manny Ramirez	12.00	5.50	1.50
□ 10 Ken Griffey Jr.	50.00	22.00	6.25

1996 Donruss Pure Power

Randomly inserted in retail and magazine packs only at a rate of one in eight, this eight-card set features color action player photos of eight of the most powerful players in Major League baseball.

	MINT	NRMT	EXC
COMPLETE SET (8)	175.00	80.00	22.00
COMMON CARD (1-8)	8.00	3.60	1.00
RANDOM INSERTS IN SER.2 RETAIL PACKS			

	MINT	NRMT	EXC
□ 1 Raul Mondesi	8.00	3.60	1.00
□ 2 Barry Bonds	15.00	6.75	1.85
□ 3 Albert Belle	30.00	13.50	3.70
□ 4 Frank Thomas	60.00	27.00	7.50
□ 5 Mike Piazza	40.00	18.00	5.00
□ 6 Dante Bichette	8.00	3.60	1.00
□ 7 Manny Ramirez	15.00	6.75	1.85
□ 8 Mo Vaughn	15.00	6.75	1.85

1996 Donruss Round Trippers

Randomly inserted in second series hobby packs at a rate of one in 55, this 10-card standard-size set honors ten of Baseball's top homerun hitters. Just 5,000 of each card were produced and consecutively numbered. On a sepia-tone background with a home plate icon carrying the 1995 season home run total, the fronts superpose a color player cutout. The player's name and "Round Trippers" are bronze foil stamped at the bottom. The backs have a similar design and present 1995 and career home run statistics by a bar graph.

	MINT	NRMT	EXC
COMPLETE SET (10)	175.00	80.00	22.00
COMMON CARD (1-10)	5.00	2.20	.60
RANDOM INSERTS IN SER.2 HOBBY PACKS			

	MINT	NRMT	EXC
□ 1 Albert Belle	20.00	9.00	2.50
□ 2 Barry Bonds	10.00	4.50	1.25
□ 3 Jeff Bagwell	12.00	5.50	1.50
□ 4 Tim Salmon	5.00	2.20	.60
□ 5 Mo Vaughn	10.00	4.50	1.25
□ 6 Ken Griffey Jr.	40.00	18.00	5.00
□ 7 Mike Piazza	25.00	11.00	3.10
□ 8 Cal Ripken	30.00	13.50	3.70
□ 9 Frank Thomas	40.00	18.00	5.00
□ 10 Dante Bichette	5.00	2.20	.60

1996 Donruss Showdown

This eight-card standard-size set was randomly inserted in series one packs. These cards feature one top hitter and one top pitcher from each league. The cards are sequentially numbered out of 10,000. The horizontal fronts feature gold foil stamping and have the words "Show Down" in the middle. The backs feature color player photos as well as some text about their accomplishments.

	MINT	NRMT	EXC
COMPLETE SET (8)	150.00	70.00	19.00

COMMON CARD (1-8)	4.00	1.80	.50
RANDOM INSERTS IN SER.1 PACKS			
□ 1 Frank Thomas Hideo Nomo	40.00	18.00	5.00
□ 2 Barry Bonds Randy Johnson	12.00	5.50	1.50
□ 3 Greg Maddux Ken Griffey Jr.	50.00	22.00	6.25
□ 4 Roger Clemens Tony Gwynn	15.00	6.75	1.85
□ 5 Mike Piazza Mike Mussina	25.00	11.00	3.10
□ 6 Cal Ripken Pedro J.Martinez	25.00	11.00	3.10
□ 7 Tim Wakefield Matt Williams	4.00	1.80	.50
□ 8 Manny Ramirez Carlos Perez	8.00	3.60	1.00

1997 Donruss

The 1997 Donruss set was issued in one series totalling 270 cards. The 10-card packs have a suggested retail price of $1.99 each. The fronts feature color action player photos while the backs carry another color player photo with player information and career statistics.

	MINT	NRMT	EXC
COMPLETE SERIES 1 (270)	20.00	9.00	2.50
COMMON CARD (1-270)	.10	.05	.01
SEMISTARS	.25	.11	.03
STARS	.50	.23	.06
□ 1 Juan Gonzalez	1.50	.70	.19
□ 2 Jim Edmonds	.25	.11	.03
□ 3 Tony Gwynn	1.25	.55	.16
□ 4 Andres Galarraga	.50	.23	.06
□ 5 Joe Carter	.25	.11	.03
□ 6 Raul Mondesi	.25	.11	.03
□ 7 Greg Maddux	2.00	.90	.25
□ 8 Travis Fryman	.25	.11	.03
□ 9 Brian Jordan	.25	.11	.03
□ 10 Henry Rodriguez	.25	.11	.03
□ 11 Manny Ramirez	.75	.35	.09
□ 12 Mark McGwire	1.00	.45	.12
□ 13 Marc Newfield	.10	.05	.01
□ 14 Craig Biggio	.25	.11	.03
□ 15 Sammy Sosa	.50	.23	.06
□ 16 Brady Anderson	.50	.23	.06
□ 17 Wade Boggs	.50	.23	.06
□ 18 Charles Johnson	.25	.11	.03
□ 19 Matt Williams	.50	.23	.06
□ 20 Denny Neagle	.25	.11	.03
□ 21 Ken Griffey Jr.	3.00	1.35	.35
□ 22 Robin Ventura	.25	.11	.03
□ 23 Barry Larkin	.50	.23	.06
□ 24 Todd Zeile	.10	.05	.01
□ 25 Chuck Knoblauch	.50	.23	.06
□ 26 Todd Hundley	.25	.11	.03
□ 27 Roger Clemens	.50	.23	.06
□ 28 Michael Tucker	.10	.05	.01
□ 29 Rondell White	.25	.11	.03
□ 30 Osvaldo Fernandez	.10	.05	.01
□ 31 Ivan Rodriguez	.60	.25	.07
□ 32 Alex Fernandez	.25	.11	.03
□ 33 Jason Isringhausen	.10	.05	.01
□ 34 Chipper Jones	2.00	.90	.25
□ 35 Paul O'Neill	.25	.11	.03
□ 36 Hideo Nomo	.75	.35	.09
□ 37 Roberto Alomar	.75	.35	.09
□ 38 Derek Bell	.25	.11	.03
□ 39 Paul Molitor	.60	.25	.07
□ 40 Andy Benes	.25	.11	.03
□ 41 Steve Trachsel	.10	.05	.01
□ 42 J.T. Snow	.10	.05	.01
□ 43 Jason Kendall	.25	.11	.03
□ 44 Alex Rodriguez	3.00	1.35	.35
□ 45 Joey Hamilton	.25	.11	.03
□ 46 Carlos Delgado	.25	.11	.03
□ 47 Jason Giambi	.25	.11	.03
□ 48 Larry Walker	.25	.11	.03
□ 49 Derek Jeter	2.00	.90	.25
□ 50 Kenny Lofton	.75	.35	.09
□ 51 Devon White	.10	.05	.01
□ 52 Matt Mieske	.10	.05	.01
□ 53 Melvin Nieves	.10	.05	.01
□ 54 Jose Canseco	.50	.23	.06
□ 55 Tino Martinez	.25	.11	.03
□ 56 Rafael Palmeiro	.50	.23	.06
□ 57 Edgardo Alfonzo	.10	.05	.01
□ 58 Jay Buhner	.50	.23	.06
□ 59 Shane Reynolds	.10	.05	.01
□ 60 Steve Finley	.25	.11	.03
□ 61 Bobby Higginson	.25	.11	.03
□ 62 Dean Palmer	.25	.11	.03
□ 63 Terry Pendleton	.25	.11	.03
□ 64 Marquis Grissom	.25	.11	.03
□ 65 Mike Stanley	.10	.05	.01
□ 66 Moises Alou	.25	.11	.03
□ 67 Ray Lankford	.25	.11	.03
□ 68 Marty Cordova	.25	.11	.03
□ 69 John Olerud	.10	.05	.01
□ 70 David Cone	.25	.11	.03
□ 71 Benito Santiago	.10	.05	.01
□ 72 Ryne Sandberg	.75	.35	.09
□ 73 Rickey Henderson	.25	.11	.03
□ 74 Roger Cedeno	.10	.05	.01
□ 75 Wilson Alvarez	.10	.05	.01
□ 76 Tim Salmon	.50	.23	.06
□ 77 Orlando Merced	.10	.05	.01
□ 78 Vinny Castilla	.25	.11	.03
□ 79 Ismael Valdes	.25	.11	.03
□ 80 Dante Bichette	.50	.23	.06
□ 81 Kevin Brown	.25	.11	.03
□ 82 Andy Pettitte	.75	.35	.09
□ 83 Scott Stahoviak	.10	.05	.01
□ 84 Mickey Tettleton	.10	.05	.01
□ 85 Jack McDowell	.25	.11	.03
□ 86 Tom Glavine	.50	.23	.06
□ 87 Gregg Jefferies	.25	.11	.03
□ 88 Chili Davis	.25	.11	.03
□ 89 Randy Johnson	.50	.23	.06
□ 90 John Mabry	.10	.05	.01
□ 91 Billy Wagner	.25	.11	.03
□ 92 Jeff Cirillo	.10	.05	.01
□ 93 Trevor Hoffman	.10	.05	.01
□ 94 Juan Guzman	.10	.05	.01
□ 95 Geronimo Berroa	.10	.05	.01
□ 96 Bernard Gilkey	.25	.11	.03
□ 97 Danny Tartabull	.10	.05	.01
□ 98 Johnny Damon	.25	.11	.03
□ 99 Charlie Hayes	.10	.05	.01
□ 100 Reggie Sanders	.25	.11	.03
□ 101 Robby Thompson	.10	.05	.01
□ 102 Bobby Bonilla	.25	.11	.03
□ 103 Reggie Jefferson	.10	.05	.01
□ 104 John Smoltz	.50	.23	.06
□ 105 Jim Thome	.50	.23	.06
□ 106 Ruben Rivera	.50	.23	.06
□ 107 Darren Oliver	.10	.05	.01
□ 108 Mo Vaughn	.75	.35	.09
□ 109 Roger Pavlik	.10	.05	.01
□ 110 Terry Steinbach	.25	.11	.03
□ 111 Jermaine Dye	.50	.23	.06
□ 112 Mark Grudzielanek	.10	.05	.01
□ 113 Rick Aguilera	.10	.05	.01
□ 114 Jamey Wright	.10	.05	.01
□ 115 Eddie Murray	.75	.35	.09
□ 116 Brian L. Hunter	.25	.11	.03
□ 117 Hal Morris	.10	.05	.01
□ 118 Tom Pagnozzi	.10	.05	.01
□ 119 Mike Mussina	.60	.25	.07
□ 120 Mark Grace	.50	.23	.06

☐ 121	Cal Ripken	2.50	1.10	.30
☐ 122	Tom Goodwin	.10	.05	.01
☐ 123	Paul Sorrento	.10	.05	.01
☐ 124	Jay Bell	.10	.05	.01
☐ 125	Todd Hollandsworth	.25	.11	.03
☐ 126	Edgar Martinez	.50	.23	.06
☐ 127	George Arias	.10	.05	.01
☐ 128	Greg Vaughn	.25	.11	.03
☐ 129	Roberto Hernandez	.10	.05	.01
☐ 130	Delino DeShields	.10	.05	.01
☐ 131	Bill Pulsipher	.10	.05	.01
☐ 132	Joey Cora	.10	.05	.01
☐ 133	Mariano Rivera	.25	.11	.03
☐ 134	Mike Piazza	2.00	.90	.25
☐ 135	Carlos Baerga	.25	.11	.03
☐ 136	Jose Mesa	.25	.11	.03
☐ 137	Will Clark	.50	.23	.06
☐ 138	Frank Thomas	3.00	1.35	.35
☐ 139	John Wetteland	.25	.11	.03
☐ 140	Shawn Estes	.10	.05	.01
☐ 141	Garret Anderson	.25	.11	.03
☐ 142	Andre Dawson	.25	.11	.03
☐ 143	Eddie Taubensee	.10	.05	.01
☐ 144	Ryan Klesko	.50	.23	.06
☐ 145	Rocky Coppinger	.25	.11	.03
☐ 146	Jeff Bagwell	1.25	.55	.16
☐ 147	Donovan Osborne	.10	.05	.01
☐ 148	Greg Myers	.10	.05	.01
☐ 149	Brant Brown	.10	.05	.01
☐ 150	Kevin Elster	.10	.05	.01
☐ 151	Bob Wells	.10	.05	.01
☐ 152	Wally Joyner	.25	.11	.03
☐ 153	Rico Brogna	.10	.05	.01
☐ 154	Dwight Gooden	.25	.11	.03
☐ 155	Jermaine Allensworth	.10	.05	.01
☐ 156	Ray Durham	.10	.05	.01
☐ 157	Cecil Fielder	.25	.11	.03
☐ 158	John Burkett	.10	.05	.01
☐ 159	Gary Sheffield	.50	.23	.06
☐ 160	Albert Belle	1.50	.70	.19
☐ 161	Tomas Perez	.10	.05	.01
☐ 162	David Doster	.10	.05	.01
☐ 163	John Valentin	.10	.05	.01
☐ 164	Danny Graves	.10	.05	.01
☐ 165	Jose Paniagua	.10	.05	.01
☐ 166	Brian Giles	.10	.05	.01
☐ 167	Barry Bonds	.75	.35	.09
☐ 168	Sterling Hitchcock	.10	.05	.01
☐ 169	Bernie Williams	.50	.23	.06
☐ 170	Fred McGriff	.50	.23	.06
☐ 171	George Williams	.10	.05	.01
☐ 172	Amaury Telemaco	.10	.05	.01
☐ 173	Ken Caminiti	.50	.23	.06
☐ 174	Ron Gant	.25	.11	.03
☐ 175	Dave Justice	.25	.11	.03
☐ 176	James Baldwin	.25	.11	.03
☐ 177	Pat Hentgen	.25	.11	.03
☐ 178	Ben McDonald	.10	.05	.01
☐ 179	Tim Naehring	.10	.05	.01
☐ 180	Jim Eisenreich	.10	.05	.01
☐ 181	Ken Hill	.10	.05	.01
☐ 182	Paul Wilson	.25	.11	.03
☐ 183	Marvin Benard	.10	.05	.01
☐ 184	Alan Benes	.25	.11	.03
☐ 185	Ellis Burks	.25	.11	.03
☐ 186	Scott Servais	.10	.05	.01
☐ 187	David Segui	.10	.05	.01
☐ 188	Scott Brosius	.10	.05	.01
☐ 189	Jose Offerman	.10	.05	.01
☐ 190	Eric Davis	.10	.05	.01
☐ 191	Brett Butler	.25	.11	.03
☐ 192	Curtis Pride	.10	.05	.01
☐ 193	Yamil Benitez	.10	.05	.01
☐ 194	Chan Ho Park	.25	.11	.03
☐ 195	Bret Boone	.10	.05	.01
☐ 196	Omar Vizquel	.25	.11	.03
☐ 197	Orlando Miller	.10	.05	.01
☐ 198	Ramon Martinez	.25	.11	.03
☐ 199	Harold Baines	.25	.11	.03
☐ 200	Eric Young	.25	.11	.03
☐ 201	Fernando Vina	.10	.05	.01
☐ 202	Alex Gonzalez	.10	.05	.01
☐ 203	Fernando Valenzuela	.25	.11	.03
☐ 204	Steve Avery	.10	.05	.01
☐ 205	Ernie Young	.10	.05	.01
☐ 206	Kevin Appier	.25	.11	.03
☐ 207	Randy Myers	.10	.05	.01
☐ 208	Jeff Suppan	.25	.11	.03
☐ 209	James Mouton	.10	.05	.01
☐ 210	Russ Davis	.10	.05	.01
☐ 211	Al Martin	.10	.05	.01
☐ 212	Troy Percival	.25	.11	.03
☐ 213	Al Leiter	.10	.05	.01
☐ 214	Dennis Eckersley	.25	.11	.03
☐ 215	Mark Johnson	.10	.05	.01
☐ 216	Eric Karros	.25	.11	.03
☐ 217	Royce Clayton	.10	.05	.01
☐ 218	Tony Phillips	.25	.11	.03
☐ 219	Tim Wakefield	.10	.05	.01
☐ 220	Alan Trammell	.25	.11	.03
☐ 221	Eduardo Perez	.10	.05	.01
☐ 222	Butch Huskey	.10	.05	.01
☐ 223	Tim Belcher	.10	.05	.01
☐ 224	Jamie Moyer	.10	.05	.01
☐ 225	F.P. Santangelo	.10	.05	.01
☐ 226	Rusty Greer	.25	.11	.03
☐ 227	Jeff Brantley	.10	.05	.01
☐ 228	Mark Langston	.10	.05	.01
☐ 229	Ray Montgomery	.10	.05	.01
☐ 230	Rich Becker	.10	.05	.01
☐ 231	Ozzie Smith	.60	.25	.07
☐ 232	Rey Ordonez	.50	.23	.06
☐ 233	Ricky Otero	.10	.05	.01
☐ 234	Mike Cameron	.25	.11	.03
☐ 235	Mike Sweeney	.10	.05	.01
☐ 236	Mark Lewis	.10	.05	.01
☐ 237	Luis Gonzalez	.10	.05	.01
☐ 238	Marcus Jensen	.10	.05	.01
☐ 239	Ed Sprague	.10	.05	.01
☐ 240	Jose Valentin	.10	.05	.01
☐ 241	Jeff Frye	.10	.05	.01
☐ 242	Charles Nagy	.25	.11	.03
☐ 243	Carlos Garcia	.10	.05	.01
☐ 244	Mike Hampton	.10	.05	.01
☐ 245	B.J. Surhoff	.10	.05	.01
☐ 246	Wilton Guerrero	.25	.11	.03
☐ 247	Frank Rodriguez	.10	.05	.01
☐ 248	Gary Gaetti	.10	.05	.01
☐ 249	Lance Johnson	.25	.11	.03
☐ 250	Darren Bragg	.10	.05	.01
☐ 251	Darryl Hamilton	.10	.05	.01
☐ 252	John Jaha	.10	.05	.01
☐ 253	Craig Paquette	.10	.05	.01
☐ 254	Jaime Navarro	.10	.05	.01
☐ 255	Shawon Dunston	.10	.05	.01
☐ 256	Mark Loretta	.10	.05	.01
☐ 257	Tim Belk	.10	.05	.01
☐ 258	Jeff Darwin	.10	.05	.01
☐ 259	Ruben Sierra	.25	.11	.03
☐ 260	Chuck Finley	.10	.05	.01
☐ 261	Darryl Strawberry	.25	.11	.03
☐ 262	Shannon Stewart	.10	.05	.01
☐ 263	Pedro Martinez	.25	.11	.03
☐ 264	Neifi Perez	.25	.11	.03
☐ 265	Jeff Conine	.25	.11	.03
☐ 266	Orel Hershiser	.25	.11	.03
☐ 267	Eddie Murray CL	.50	.23	.06
☐ 268	Paul Molitor CL	.50	.23	.06
☐ 269	Barry Bonds CL	.50	.23	.06
☐ 270	Mark McGwire CL	.50	.23	.06

1997 Donruss Press Proofs

Randomly inserted in packs, this 270-card set is a parallel set to the regular 1997 Donruss set. The foil stamped words, "Press Proof" down the right distinguishes it from the regular set.

	MINT	NRMT	EXC
COMPLETE SERIES 1 (270)	1200.00	550.00	150.00
COMMON CARD (1-270)	2.00	.90	.25
SEMISTARS	5.00	2.20	.60
STARS	10.00	4.50	1.25
*STARS: 7.5X TO 15X BASIC CARDS			
*GOLD DIECUT: 3X REG.PRESS PROOFS			
RANDOM INSERTS IN PACKS			

☐ 1	Juan Gonzalez	25.00	11.00	3.10
☐ 7	Greg Maddux	30.00	13.50	3.70
☐ 21	Ken Griffey Jr.	50.00	22.00	6.25
☐ 34	Chipper Jones	30.00	13.50	3.70

□ 44 Alex Rodriguez	50.00	22.00	6.25
□ 49 Derek Jeter	30.00	13.50	3.70
□ 121 Cal Ripken	40.00	18.00	5.00
□ 134 Mike Piazza	30.00	13.50	3.70
□ 138 Frank Thomas	50.00	22.00	6.25
□ 160 Albert Belle	25.00	11.00	3.10

1997 Donruss Armed and Dangerous

Randomly inserted in hobby packs only, this 15-card set features the League's hottest arms in the game. The fronts carry color action player photos with foil printing. The backs display player information and a color player head portrait at the end of a ribbon representing a medal. Only 5,000 of this set were produced and are sequentially numbered.

	MINT	NRMT	EXC
COMPLETE SET (15)	160.00	70.00	20.00
COMMON CARD (1-15)	5.00	2.20	.60
RANDOM INSERTS IN HOBBY PACKS			

□ 1 Ken Griffey Jr.	30.00	13.50	3.70
□ 2 Raul Mondesi	5.00	2.20	.60
□ 3 Chipper Jones	20.00	9.00	2.50
□ 4 Ivan Rodriguez	6.00	2.70	.75
□ 5 Randy Johnson	5.00	2.20	.60
□ 6 Alex Rodriguez	30.00	13.50	3.70
□ 7 Larry Walker	5.00	2.20	.60
□ 8 Cal Ripken	25.00	11.00	3.10
□ 9 Kenny Lofton	8.00	3.60	1.00
□ 10 Barry Bonds	8.00	3.60	1.00
□ 11 Derek Jeter	20.00	9.00	2.50
□ 12 Charles Johnson	5.00	2.20	.60
□ 13 Greg Maddux	20.00	9.00	2.50
□ 14 Roberto Alomar	8.00	3.60	1.00
□ 15 Barry Larkin	5.00	2.20	.60

1997 Donruss Diamond Kings

Randomly inserted in packs, this 10-card set commemorates the 15th anniversary of the annual art cards in Donruss Baseball sets. The first 500 of each card were printed on actual canvas stock creating an exclusive parallel set. Ten cards were printed with the number 1,982 representing the year the insert began and could be redeemed for an original artwork by artist Dan Gardiner. Only 10,000 of this set were produced and are sequentially numbered.

	MINT	NRMT	EXC
COMPLETE SET (10)	180.00	80.00	22.00
COMMON CARD (1-10)	6.00	2.70	.75
*CANVAS: 5X VALUE			
CANVAS ARE FIRST 500 NUMBERS			
EACH CARD #1982 WINS ORIGINAL ART			
RANDOM INSERTS IN PACKS			

□ 1 Ken Griffey Jr.	40.00	18.00	5.00
□ 2 Cal Ripken	30.00	13.50	3.70
□ 3 Mo Vaughn	12.00	5.50	1.50
□ 4 Chuck Knoblauch	8.00	3.60	1.00

□ 5 Jeff Bagwell	15.00	6.75	1.85
□ 6 Henry Rodriguez	6.00	2.70	.75
□ 7 Mike Piazza	25.00	11.00	3.10
□ 8 Ivan Rodriguez	10.00	4.50	1.25
□ 9 Frank Thomas	40.00	18.00	5.00
□ 10 Chipper Jones	25.00	11.00	3.10

1997 Donruss Elite

Randomly inserted in packs, this 12-card set honors perennial all-star players of the League. The fronts feature Micro-etched color action player photos, while the backs carry player information. Only 2,500 of this set were produced and are sequentially numbered.

	MINT	NRMT	EXC
COMPLETE SET (12)	600.00	275.00	75.00
COMMON CARD (1-12)	20.00	9.00	2.50
RANDOM INSERTS IN PACKS			

□ 1 Frank Thomas	100.00	45.00	12.50
□ 2 Paul Molitor	25.00	11.00	3.10
□ 3 Sammy Sosa	20.00	9.00	2.50
□ 4 Barry Bonds	30.00	13.50	3.70
□ 5 Chipper Jones	75.00	34.00	9.50
□ 6 Alex Rodriguez	100.00	45.00	12.50
□ 7 Ken Griffey Jr.	100.00	45.00	12.50
□ 8 Jeff Bagwell	40.00	18.00	5.00
□ 9 Cal Ripken	100.00	45.00	12.50
□ 10 Mo Vaughn	30.00	13.50	3.70
□ 11 Mike Piazza	75.00	34.00	9.50
□ 12 Juan Gonzalez	50.00	22.00	6.25

1997 Donruss Rated Rookies

Randomly inserted in packs, this 30-card set honors the top rookie prospects as chosen by Donruss to be the most likely to succeed. The fronts feature color action player photos and silver foil printing. The backs carry a player portrait and player information.

	MINT	NRMT	EXC
COMPLETE SET (30)	60.00	27.00	7.50
COMMON CARD (1-30)	1.00	.45	.12
RANDOM INSERTS IN PACKS			

□ 1 Jason Thompson	1.00	.45	.12
□ 2 LaTroy Hawkins	1.00	.45	.12
□ 3 Scott Rolen	5.00	2.20	.60
□ 4 Trey Beamon	1.00	.45	.12
□ 5 Kimera Bartee	1.00	.45	.12
□ 6 Nerio Rodriguez	1.25	.55	.16
□ 7 Jeff D'Amico	1.00	.45	.12
□ 8 Quinton McCracken	1.00	.45	.12
□ 9 John Wasdin	1.00	.45	.12
□ 10 Robin Jennings	1.00	.45	.12
□ 11 Steve Gibralter	1.00	.45	.12
□ 12 Tyler Houston	1.00	.45	.12
□ 13 Tony Clark	1.00	.45	.12
□ 14 Ugueth Urbina	1.00	.45	.12
□ 15 Karim Garcia	2.00	.90	.25
□ 16 Raul Casanova	1.00	.45	.12
□ 17 Brooks Kieschnick	1.00	.45	.12
□ 18 Luis Castillo	1.25	.55	.16
□ 19 Edgar Renteria	1.25	.55	.16
□ 20 Andruw Jones	20.00	9.00	2.50

□ 21 Chad Mottola	1.00	.45	.12
□ 22 Mac Suzuki	1.00	.45	.12
□ 23 Justin Thompson	1.00	.45	.12
□ 24 Darin Erstad	10.00	4.50	1.25
□ 25 Todd Walker	10.00	4.50	1.25
□ 26 Todd Greene	1.00	.45	.12
□ 27 Vladimir Guerrero	8.00	3.60	1.00
□ 28 Darren Dreifort	1.00	.45	.12
□ 29 John Burke	1.00	.45	.12
□ 30 Damon Mashore	1.00	.45	.12

1995 Emotion

This 200-card standard-size set was produced by Fleer/SkyBox. The first-year brand has double-thick card stock with borderless fronts. Card fronts and backs are either horizontal or vertical. On the front of each player card is a theme such as Class (Cal Ripken) and Confident (Barry Bonds). The backs have two player photos, '94 stats and career numbers. The checklist is arranged as such: Baltimore Orioles (1-8), Boston Red Sox (9-17), California Angels (18-23), Chicago White Sox (24-30), Cleveland Indians (31-40), Detroit Tigers (41-47), Kansas City Royals (48-51), Milwaukee Brewers (52-55), Minnesota Twins (56-58), New York Yankees (59-68), Oakland Athletics (69-75), Seattle Mariners (76-82), Texas Rangers (83-89), Toronto Blue Jays (90-98). National League: Atlanta Braves (99-108), Chicago Cubs (109-114), Cincinnati Reds (115-121), Colorado Rockies (122-126), Florida Marlins (127-133), Houston Astros (134-140), Los Angeles Dodgers (141-147), Montreal Expos (148-156), New York Mets (157-162), Philadelphia Phillies (163-171), Pittsburgh Pirates (172-178), St. Louis Cardinals (179-183), San Diego Padres (184-190) and San Francisco Giants (191-197).

	MINT	NRMT	EXC
COMPLETE SET (200)	40.00	18.00	5.00
COMMON CARD (1-200)	.25	.11	.03
SEMISTARS	.40	.18	.05
STARS	.75	.35	.09
COMP.RIPKEN SET (10)	75.00	34.00	9.50
COMMON RIPKEN (1-10)	8.00	3.60	1.00
RANDOM INSERT IN PACKS			
COMMON MAIL-IN (11-15)	8.00	3.60	1.00

□ 1 Brady Anderson	.75	.35	.09
□ 2 Kevin Brown	.40	.18	.05
□ 3 Curtis Goodwin	.40	.18	.05
□ 4 Jeffrey Hammonds	.40	.18	.05
□ 5 Ben McDonald	.25	.11	.03
□ 6 Mike Mussina	1.00	.45	.12
□ 7 Rafael Palmeiro	.75	.35	.09
□ 8 Cal Ripken Jr.	4.00	1.80	.50
□ 9 Jose Canseco	.75	.35	.09
□ 10 Roger Clemens	.75	.35	.09
□ 11 Vaughn Eshelman	.25	.11	.03
□ 12 Mike Greenwell	.25	.11	.03
□ 13 Erik Hanson	.25	.11	.03
□ 14 Tim Naehring	.25	.11	.03
□ 15 Aaron Sele	.40	.18	.05
□ 16 John Valentin	.40	.18	.05
□ 17 Mo Vaughn	1.25	.55	.16
□ 18 Chili Davis	.40	.18	.05
□ 19 Gary DiSarcina	.25	.11	.03
□ 20 Chuck Finley	.40	.18	.05
□ 21 Tim Salmon	.75	.35	.09
□ 22 Lee Smith	.40	.18	.05
□ 23 J.T. Snow	.40	.18	.05
□ 24 Jim Abbott	.25	.11	.03
□ 25 Jason Bere	.25	.11	.03
□ 26 Ray Durham	.40	.18	.05
□ 27 Ozzie Guillen	.25	.11	.03
□ 28 Tim Raines	.75	.35	.09
□ 29 Frank Thomas	5.00	2.20	.60
□ 30 Robin Ventura	.40	.18	.05
□ 31 Carlos Baerga	.75	.35	.09
□ 32 Albert Belle	2.50	1.10	.30
□ 33 Orel Hershiser	.40	.18	.05
□ 34 Kenny Lofton	1.25	.55	.16
□ 35 Dennis Martinez	.40	.18	.05
□ 36 Eddie Murray	1.25	.55	.16
□ 37 Manny Ramirez	1.25	.55	.16
□ 38 Julian Tavarez	.25	.11	.03
□ 39 Jim Thome	1.00	.45	.12
□ 40 Dave Winfield	.75	.35	.09
□ 41 Chad Curtis	.25	.11	.03
□ 42 Cecil Fielder	.40	.18	.05
□ 43 Travis Fryman	.40	.18	.05
□ 44 Kirk Gibson	.40	.18	.05
□ 45 Bob Higginson	.75	.35	.09
□ 46 Alan Trammell	.75	.35	.09
□ 47 Lou Whitaker	.75	.35	.09
□ 48 Kevin Appier	.40	.18	.05
□ 49 Gary Gaetti	.40	.18	.05
□ 50 Jeff Montgomery	.40	.18	.05
□ 51 Jon Nunnally	.40	.18	.05
□ 52 Ricky Bones	.25	.11	.03
□ 53 Cal Eldred	.25	.11	.03
□ 54 Joe Oliver	.25	.11	.03
□ 55 Kevin Seitzer	.25	.11	.03
□ 56 Marty Cordova	.75	.35	.09
□ 57 Chuck Knoblauch	.75	.35	.09
□ 58 Kirby Puckett	1.50	.70	.19
□ 59 Wade Boggs	.75	.35	.09
□ 60 Derek Jeter	3.00	1.35	.35
□ 61 Jimmy Key	.40	.18	.05
□ 62 Don Mattingly	2.50	1.10	.30
□ 63 Jack McDowell	.40	.18	.05
□ 64 Paul O'Neill	.40	.18	.05
□ 65 Andy Pettitte	2.00	.90	.25
□ 66 Ruben Rivera	2.50	1.10	.30
□ 67 Mike Stanley	.25	.11	.03
□ 68 John Wetteland	.40	.18	.05
□ 69 Geronimo Berroa	.25	.11	.03
□ 70 Dennis Eckersley	.40	.18	.05
□ 71 Rickey Henderson	.75	.35	.09
□ 72 Mark McGwire	1.50	.70	.19
□ 73 Steve Ontiveros	.25	.11	.03
□ 74 Ruben Sierra	.40	.18	.05
□ 75 Terry Steinbach	.40	.18	.05
□ 76 Jay Buhner	.75	.35	.09
□ 77 Ken Griffey Jr.	5.00	2.20	.60
□ 78 Randy Johnson	.75	.35	.09
□ 79 Edgar Martinez	.75	.35	.09
□ 80 Tino Martinez	.40	.18	.05
□ 81 Marc Newfield	.40	.18	.05
□ 82 Alex Rodriguez	6.00	2.70	.75
□ 83 Will Clark	.75	.35	.09
□ 84 Benji Gil	.25	.11	.03
□ 85 Juan Gonzalez	2.50	1.10	.30
□ 86 Rusty Greer	.75	.35	.09
□ 87 Dean Palmer	.40	.18	.05
□ 88 Ivan Rodriguez	1.00	.45	.12
□ 89 Kenny Rogers	.25	.11	.03
□ 90 Roberto Alomar	1.25	.55	.16
□ 91 Joe Carter	.75	.35	.09
□ 92 David Cone	.40	.18	.05
□ 93 Alex Gonzalez	.25	.11	.03
□ 94 Shawn Green	.40	.18	.05
□ 95 Pat Hentgen	.40	.18	.05
□ 96 Paul Molitor	1.00	.45	.12
□ 97 John Olerud	.25	.11	.03
□ 98 Devon White	.40	.18	.05
□ 99 Steve Avery	.40	.18	.05
□ 100 Tom Glavine	.75	.35	.09
□ 101 Marquis Grissom	.75	.35	.09
□ 102 Chipper Jones	3.00	1.35	.35
□ 103 David Justice	.75	.35	.09

□ 104 Ryan Klesko	1.00	.45	.12
□ 105 Javier Lopez	.75	.35	.09
□ 106 Greg Maddux	3.00	1.35	.35
□ 107 Fred McGriff	.75	.35	.09
□ 108 John Smoltz	.75	.35	.09
□ 109 Shawon Dunston	.25	.11	.03
□ 110 Mark Grace	.75	.35	.09
□ 111 Brian McRae	.40	.18	.05
□ 112 Randy Myers	.25	.11	.03
□ 113 Sammy Sosa	.75	.35	.09
□ 114 Steve Trachsel	.25	.11	.03
□ 115 Bret Boone	.40	.18	.05
□ 116 Ron Gant	.40	.18	.05
□ 117 Barry Larkin	.75	.35	.09
□ 118 Deion Sanders	.75	.35	.09
□ 119 Reggie Sanders	.40	.18	.05
□ 120 Pete Schourek	.40	.18	.05
□ 121 John Smiley	.25	.11	.03
□ 122 Jason Bates	.25	.11	.03
□ 123 Dante Bichette	.75	.35	.09
□ 124 Vinny Castilla	.40	.18	.05
□ 125 Andres Galarraga	.75	.35	.09
□ 126 Larry Walker	.75	.35	.09
□ 127 Greg Colbrunn	.25	.11	.03
□ 128 Jeff Conine	.75	.35	.09
□ 129 Andre Dawson	.75	.35	.09
□ 130 Chris Hammond	.25	.11	.03
□ 131 Charles Johnson	.40	.18	.05
□ 132 Gary Sheffield	.75	.35	.09
□ 133 Quilvio Veras	.25	.11	.03
□ 134 Jeff Bagwell	2.00	.90	.25
□ 135 Derek Bell	.40	.18	.05
□ 136 Craig Biggio	.75	.35	.09
□ 137 Jim Dougherty	.25	.11	.03
□ 138 John Hudek	.25	.11	.03
□ 139 Orlando Miller	.25	.11	.03
□ 140 Phil Plantier	.25	.11	.03
□ 141 Eric Karros	.40	.18	.05
□ 142 Ramon Martinez	.40	.18	.05
□ 143 Raul Mondesi	.75	.35	.09
□ 144 Hideo Nomo	5.00	2.20	.60
□ 145 Mike Piazza	3.00	1.35	.35
□ 146 Ismael Valdes	.40	.18	.05
□ 147 Todd Worrell	.25	.11	.03
□ 148 Moises Alou	.40	.18	.05
□ 149 Yamil Benitez	.75	.35	.09
□ 150 Wil Cordero	.25	.11	.03
□ 151 Jeff Fassero	.25	.11	.03
□ 152 Cliff Floyd	.40	.18	.05
□ 153 Pedro Martinez	.40	.18	.05
□ 154 Carlos Perez	.40	.18	.05
□ 155 Tony Tarasco	.25	.11	.03
□ 156 Rondell White	.75	.35	.09
□ 157 Edgardo Alfonzo	.40	.18	.05
□ 158 Bobby Bonilla	.40	.18	.05
□ 159 Rico Brogna	.25	.11	.03
□ 160 Bobby Jones	.40	.18	.05
□ 161 Bill Pulsipher	.40	.18	.05
□ 162 Bret Saberhagen	.40	.18	.05
□ 163 Ricky Bottalico	.40	.18	.05
□ 164 Darren Daulton	.40	.18	.05
□ 165 Lenny Dykstra	.40	.18	.05
□ 166 Charlie Hayes	.25	.11	.03
□ 167 Dave Hollins	.25	.11	.03
□ 168 Gregg Jefferies	.40	.18	.05
□ 169 Michael Mimbs	.40	.18	.05
□ 170 Curt Schilling	.25	.11	.03
□ 171 Heathcliff Slocumb	.25	.11	.03
□ 172 Jay Bell	.40	.18	.05
□ 173 Micah Franklin	.40	.18	.05
□ 174 Mark Johnson	.40	.18	.05
□ 175 Jeff King	.40	.18	.05
□ 176 Al Martin	.40	.18	.05
□ 177 Dan Miceli	.25	.11	.03
□ 178 Denny Neagle	.40	.18	.05
□ 179 Bernard Gilkey	.40	.18	.05
□ 180 Ken Hill	.25	.11	.03
□ 181 Brian Jordan	.75	.35	.09
□ 182 Ray Lankford	.75	.35	.09
□ 183 Ozzie Smith	1.00	.45	.12
□ 184 Andy Benes	.25	.11	.03
□ 185 Ken Caminiti	.75	.35	.09
□ 186 Steve Finley	.40	.18	.05
□ 187 Tony Gwynn	2.00	.90	.25
□ 188 Joey Hamilton	.40	.18	.05
□ 189 Melvin Nieves	.40	.18	.05
□ 190 Scott Sanders	.25	.11	.03
□ 191 Rod Beck	.25	.11	.03
□ 192 Barry Bonds	1.25	.55	.16
□ 193 Royce Clayton	.25	.11	.03
□ 194 Glenallen Hill	.25	.11	.03
□ 195 Darren Lewis	.25	.11	.03
□ 196 Mark Portugal	.25	.11	.03
□ 197 Matt Williams	.75	.35	.09
□ 198 Checklist 1-82	.25	.11	.03
□ 199 Checklist 83-162	.25	.11	.03
□ 200 Checklist 163-200/Inserts	.25	.11	.03
□ P8 Cal Ripken Promo	7.50	3.40	.95

1995 Emotion Masters

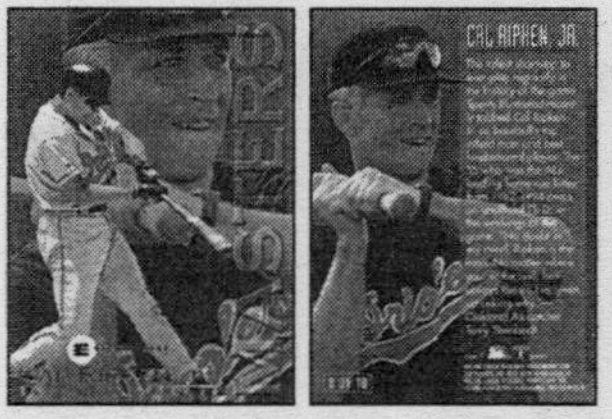

The theme of this 10-card standard-size set is the showcasing of players that come through in the clutch. Randomly inserted at a rate of one in eight packs, a player photo is superimposed over a larger photo that is ghosted in a color emblematic of that team. The player's name and the Emotion logo are at the bottom. The backs have a photo to the left and text to the right. Both sides of the card are shaded in the color scheme of the player's team.

	MINT	NRMT	EXC
COMPLETE SET (10)	75.00	34.00	9.50
COMMON CARD (1-10)	2.50	1.10	.30
RANDOM INSERTS IN PACKS			
□ 1 Barry Bonds	5.00	2.20	.60
□ 2 Juan Gonzalez	10.00	4.50	1.25
□ 3 Ken Griffey Jr.	20.00	9.00	2.50
□ 4 Tony Gwynn	8.00	3.60	1.00
□ 5 Kenny Lofton	5.00	2.20	.60
□ 6 Greg Maddux	12.00	5.50	1.50
□ 7 Raul Mondesi	2.50	1.10	.30
□ 8 Cal Ripken	15.00	6.75	1.85
□ 9 Frank Thomas	20.00	9.00	2.50
□ 10 Matt Williams	4.00	1.80	.50

1995 Emotion N-Tense

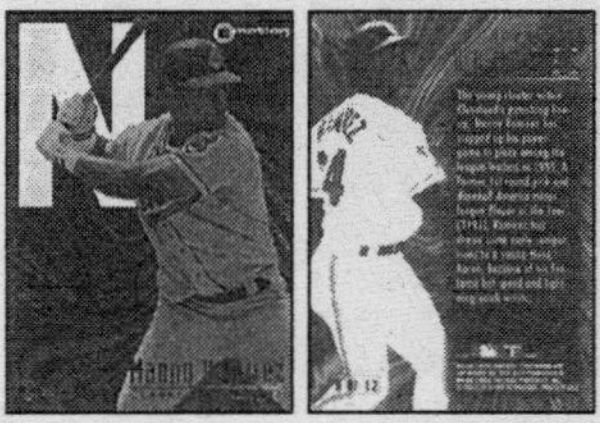

Randomly inserted at a rate of one in 37 packs, this 12-card standard-size set features fronts that have a player photo surrounded by a swirling color scheme and a large holographic "N" in the background. The backs feature a like color scheme with text and player photo.

	MINT	NRMT	EXC
COMPLETE SET (12)	225.00	100.00	28.00
COMMON CARD (1-12)	8.00	3.60	1.00
RANDOM INSERTS IN PACKS			

	MINT	NRMT	EXC
□ 1 Jeff Bagwell	25.00	11.00	3.10
□ 2 Albert Belle	30.00	13.50	3.70
□ 3 Barry Bonds	15.00	6.75	1.85
□ 4 Cecil Fielder	12.00	5.50	1.50
□ 5 Ron Gant	8.00	3.60	1.00
□ 6 Ken Griffey Jr.	60.00	27.00	7.50
□ 7 Mark McGwire	18.00	8.00	2.20
□ 8 Mike Piazza	40.00	18.00	5.00
□ 9 Manny Ramirez	15.00	6.75	1.85
□ 10 Frank Thomas	60.00	27.00	7.50
□ 11 Mo Vaughn	15.00	6.75	1.85
□ 12 Matt Williams	12.00	5.50	1.50

1995 Emotion Rookies

This 10-card standard-size set was inserted at a rate of one in five packs. Card fronts feature an action photo superimposed over background that is in a color consistent with that of the team's. The backs have a player photo and a write-up.

	MINT	NRMT	EXC
COMPLETE SET (10)	25.00	11.00	3.10
COMMON CARD (1-10)	1.00	.45	.12
RANDOM INSERTS IN PACKS			

	MINT	NRMT	EXC
□ 1 Edgardo Alfonzo	1.00	.45	.12
□ 2 Jason Bates	1.00	.45	.12
□ 3 Marty Cordova	2.50	1.10	.30
□ 4 Ray Durham	1.50	.70	.19
□ 5 Alex Gonzalez	1.00	.45	.12
□ 6 Shawn Green	1.00	.45	.12
□ 7 Charles Johnson	1.50	.70	.19
□ 8 Chipper Jones	10.00	4.50	1.25
□ 9 Hideo Nomo	8.00	3.60	1.00
□ 10 Alex Rodriguez	15.00	6.75	1.85

1996 Emotion-XL

The 1996 Emotion-XL set was issued in one series totalling 300 standard-size cards. The 7-card packs retail for $4.99 each. The fronts feature a color action player photo with either a blue, green or maroon frame and the player's name and team printed in a foil-stamped medallion. A descriptive term describing the player completes the front. The backs carry player information and statistics. The cards are grouped alphabetically within teams and checklisted below alphabetically according to teams for each league as follows: Baltimore Orioles (1-10), Boston Red Sox (11-20), California Angels (21-32), Chicago White Sox (33-43), Cleveland Indians (44-57), Detroit Tigers (58-63), Kansas City Royals (64-70), Milwaukee Brewers (71-78), Minnesota Twins (79-86), New York Yankees (87-99), Oakland Athletics (100-108), Seattle Mariners (109-119), Texas Rangers (120-128), Toronto Blue Jays (129-137), Atlanta Braves (138-150), Chicago Cubs (151-160), Cincinnati Reds (161-171), Colorado Rockies (172-181), Florida Marlins (182-193), Houston Astros (194-204), Los Angeles Dodgers (205-217), Montreal Expos (218-227), New York Mets (228-240), Philadelphia Phillies (241-251), Pittsburgh Pirates (252-260), St. Louis Cardinals (261-272), San Diego Padres (273-284), San Francisco Giants (285-297).

	MINT	NRMT	EXC
COMPLETE SET (300)	80.00	36.00	10.00
COMMON CARD (1-300)	.25	.11	.03
SEMISTARS	.50	.23	.06
STARS	1.00	.45	.12
PRODUCED BY FLEER			

	MINT	NRMT	EXC
□ 1 Roberto Alomar	2.00	.90	.25
□ 2 Brady Anderson	1.00	.45	.12
□ 3 Bobby Bonilla	1.00	.45	.12
□ 4 Jeffrey Hammonds	.25	.11	.03
□ 5 Chris Hoiles	.25	.11	.03
□ 6 Mike Mussina	1.50	.70	.19
□ 7 Randy Myers	.25	.11	.03
□ 8 Rafael Palmeiro	1.00	.45	.12
□ 9 Cal Ripken	6.00	2.70	.75
□ 10 B.J. Surhoff	.25	.11	.03
□ 11 Jose Canseco	1.00	.45	.12
□ 12 Roger Clemens	1.00	.45	.12
□ 13 Wil Cordero	.25	.11	.03
□ 14 Mike Greenwell	.25	.11	.03
□ 15 Dwayne Hosey	.25	.11	.03
□ 16 Tim Naehring	.50	.23	.06
□ 17 Troy O'Leary	.25	.11	.03
□ 18 Mike Stanley	.25	.11	.03
□ 19 John Valentin	.50	.23	.06
□ 20 Mo Vaughn	2.00	.90	.25
□ 21 Jim Abbott	.50	.23	.06
□ 22 Garret Anderson	1.00	.45	.12
□ 23 George Arias	.25	.11	.03
□ 24 Chili Davis	.25	.11	.03
□ 25 Jim Edmonds	1.00	.45	.12
□ 26 Chuck Finley	.25	.11	.03
□ 27 Todd Greene	.50	.23	.06
□ 28 Mark Langston	.25	.11	.03
□ 29 Troy Percival	.50	.23	.06
□ 30 Tim Salmon	1.00	.45	.12
□ 31 Lee Smith	1.00	.45	.12
□ 32 J.T. Snow	.50	.23	.06
□ 33 Harold Baines	.50	.23	.06
□ 34 Jason Bere	.25	.11	.03
□ 35 Ray Durham	1.00	.45	.12
□ 36 Alex Fernandez	1.00	.45	.12
□ 37 Ozzie Guillen	.25	.11	.03
□ 38 Darren Lewis	.25	.11	.03
□ 39 Lyle Mouton	.25	.11	.03
□ 40 Tony Phillips	.50	.23	.06
□ 41 Danny Tartabull	.25	.11	.03
□ 42 Frank Thomas	8.00	3.60	1.00
□ 43 Robin Ventura	1.00	.45	.12
□ 44 Sandy Alomar Jr.	.25	.11	.03
□ 45 Carlos Baerga	1.00	.45	.12
□ 46 Albert Belle	4.00	1.80	.50
□ 47 Julio Franco	.50	.23	.06
□ 48 Orel Hershiser	.50	.23	.06
□ 49 Kenny Lofton	2.00	.90	.25
□ 50 Dennis Martinez	.50	.23	.06
□ 51 Jack McDowell	1.00	.45	.12
□ 52 Jose Mesa	.50	.23	.06
□ 53 Eddie Murray	2.00	.90	.25
□ 54 Charles Nagy	.50	.23	.06
□ 55 Manny Ramirez	2.00	.90	.25
□ 56 Jim Thome	1.50	.70	.19
□ 57 Omar Vizquel	.25	.11	.03

☐	58	Chad Curtis	.25	.11	.03
☐	59	Cecil Fielder	1.00	.45	.12
☐	60	Travis Fryman	1.00	.45	.12
☐	61	Chris Gomez	.25	.11	.03
☐	62	Felipe Lira	.25	.11	.03
☐	63	Alan Trammell	1.00	.45	.12
☐	64	Kevin Appier	.50	.23	.06
☐	65	Johnny Damon	1.00	.45	.12
☐	66	Tom Goodwin	.50	.23	.06
☐	67	Mark Gubicza	.25	.11	.03
☐	68	Jeff Montgomery	.25	.11	.03
☐	69	Jon Nunnally	.25	.11	.03
☐	70	Bip Roberts	.25	.11	.03
☐	71	Ricky Bones	.25	.11	.03
☐	72	Chuck Carr	.25	.11	.03
☐	73	John Jaha	.25	.11	.03
☐	74	Ben McDonald	.25	.11	.03
☐	75	Matt Mieske	.25	.11	.03
☐	76	Dave Nilsson	.50	.23	.06
☐	77	Kevin Seitzer	.25	.11	.03
☐	78	Greg Vaughn	1.00	.45	.12
☐	79	Rick Aguilera	.25	.11	.03
☐	80	Marty Cordova	1.00	.45	.12
☐	81	Roberto Kelly	.25	.11	.03
☐	82	Chuck Knoblauch	1.00	.45	.12
☐	83	Pat Meares	.25	.11	.03
☐	84	Paul Molitor	1.50	.70	.19
☐	85	Kirby Puckett	2.50	1.10	.30
☐	86	Brad Radke	.25	.11	.03
☐	87	Wade Boggs	1.00	.45	.12
☐	88	David Cone	1.00	.45	.12
☐	89	Dwight Gooden	1.00	.45	.12
☐	90	Derek Jeter	5.00	2.20	.60
☐	91	Tino Martinez	1.00	.45	.12
☐	92	Paul O'Neill	.25	.11	.03
☐	93	Andy Pettitte	2.50	1.10	.30
☐	94	Tim Raines	1.00	.45	.12
☐	95	Ruben Rivera	1.50	.70	.19
☐	96	Kenny Rogers	.25	.11	.03
☐	97	Ruben Sierra	.25	.11	.03
☐	98	John Wetteland	.50	.23	.06
☐	99	Bernie Williams	1.25	.55	.16
☐	100	Allen Battle	.25	.11	.03
☐	101	Geronimo Berroa	.50	.23	.06
☐	102	Brent Gates	.25	.11	.03
☐	103	Doug Johns	.25	.11	.03
☐	104	Mark McGwire	2.50	1.10	.30
☐	105	Pedro Munoz	.25	.11	.03
☐	106	Ariel Prieto	.25	.11	.03
☐	107	Terry Steinbach	.50	.23	.06
☐	108	Todd Van Poppel	.25	.11	.03
☐	109	Chris Bosio	.25	.11	.03
☐	110	Jay Buhner	1.00	.45	.12
☐	111	Joey Cora	.25	.11	.03
☐	112	Russ Davis	.25	.11	.03
☐	113	Ken Griffey Jr.	8.00	3.60	1.00
☐	114	Sterling Hitchcock	.25	.11	.03
☐	115	Randy Johnson	1.25	.55	.16
☐	116	Edgar Martinez	1.00	.45	.12
☐	117	Alex Rodriguez	8.00	3.60	1.00
☐	118	Paul Sorrento	.25	.11	.03
☐	119	Dan Wilson	.25	.11	.03
☐	120	Will Clark	1.00	.45	.12
☐	121	Juan Gonzalez	4.00	1.80	.50
☐	122	Rusty Greer	1.00	.45	.12
☐	123	Kevin Gross	.25	.11	.03
☐	124	Ken Hill	.25	.11	.03
☐	125	Dean Palmer	1.00	.45	.12
☐	126	Roger Pavlik	.25	.11	.03
☐	127	Ivan Rodriguez	1.50	.70	.19
☐	128	Mickey Tettleton	.50	.23	.06
☐	129	Joe Carter	1.00	.45	.12
☐	130	Carlos Delgado	1.00	.45	.12
☐	131	Alex Gonzalez	.25	.11	.03
☐	132	Shawn Green	.25	.11	.03
☐	133	Erik Hanson	.25	.11	.03
☐	134	Pat Hentgen	1.00	.45	.12
☐	135	Otis Nixon	.25	.11	.03
☐	136	John Olerud	.25	.11	.03
☐	137	Ed Sprague	.50	.23	.06
☐	138	Steve Avery	.50	.23	.06
☐	139	Jermaine Dye	2.00	.90	.25
☐	140	Tom Glavine	1.00	.45	.12
☐	141	Marquis Grissom	1.00	.45	.12
☐	142	Chipper Jones	5.00	2.20	.60
☐	143	David Justice	.50	.23	.06
☐	144	Ryan Klesko	1.50	.70	.19
☐	145	Javier Lopez	1.00	.45	.12
☐	146	Greg Maddux	5.00	2.20	.60
☐	147	Fred McGriff	1.00	.45	.12
☐	148	Jason Schmidt	.25	.11	.03
☐	149	John Smoltz	1.25	.55	.16
☐	150	Mark Wohlers	.50	.23	.06
☐	151	Jim Bullinger	.25	.11	.03
☐	152	Frank Castillo	.25	.11	.03
☐	153	Kevin Foster	.25	.11	.03
☐	154	Luis Gonzalez	.25	.11	.03
☐	155	Mark Grace	1.00	.45	.12
☐	156	Brian McRae	.25	.11	.03
☐	157	Jaime Navarro	.25	.11	.03
☐	158	Rey Sanchez	.25	.11	.03
☐	159	Ryne Sandberg	2.00	.90	.25
☐	160	Sammy Sosa	1.25	.55	.16
☐	161	Bret Boone	.25	.11	.03
☐	162	Jeff Brantley	.25	.11	.03
☐	163	Vince Coleman	.25	.11	.03
☐	164	Steve Gibralter	.25	.11	.03
☐	165	Barry Larkin	1.00	.45	.12
☐	166	Hal Morris	.25	.11	.03
☐	167	Mark Portugal	.25	.11	.03
☐	168	Reggie Sanders	1.00	.45	.12
☐	169	Pete Schourek	.25	.11	.03
☐	170	John Smiley	.25	.11	.03
☐	171	Jason Bates	.25	.11	.03
☐	172	Dante Bichette	1.00	.45	.12
☐	173	Ellis Burks	1.00	.45	.12
☐	174	Vinny Castilla	1.00	.45	.12
☐	175	Andres Galarraga	1.00	.45	.12
☐	176	Kevin Ritz	.25	.11	.03
☐	177	Bill Swift	.25	.11	.03
☐	178	Larry Walker	1.00	.45	.12
☐	179	Walt Weiss	.25	.11	.03
☐	180	Eric Young	.25	.11	.03
☐	181	Kurt Abbott	.25	.11	.03
☐	182	Kevin Brown	.25	.11	.03
☐	183	John Burkett	.25	.11	.03
☐	184	Greg Colbrunn	.25	.11	.03
☐	185	Jeff Conine	.50	.23	.06
☐	186	Chris Hammond	.25	.11	.03
☐	187	Charles Johnson	.50	.23	.06
☐	188	Terry Pendleton	.50	.23	.06
☐	189	Pat Rapp	.25	.11	.03
☐	190	Gary Sheffield	1.25	.55	.16
☐	191	Quilvio Veras	.25	.11	.03
☐	192	Devon White	.25	.11	.03
☐	193	Jeff Bagwell	3.00	1.35	.35
☐	194	Derek Bell	1.00	.45	.12
☐	195	Sean Berry	.25	.11	.03
☐	196	Craig Biggio	1.00	.45	.12
☐	197	Doug Drabek	.25	.11	.03
☐	198	Tony Eusebio	.25	.11	.03
☐	199	Mike Hampton	.25	.11	.03
☐	200	Brian L.Hunter	.25	.11	.03
☐	201	Derrick May	.25	.11	.03
☐	202	Orlando Miller	.25	.11	.03
☐	203	Shane Reynolds	.25	.11	.03
☐	204	Mike Blowers	.25	.11	.03
☐	205	Tom Candiotti	.25	.11	.03
☐	206	Delino DeShields	.25	.11	.03
☐	207	Greg Gagne	.25	.11	.03
☐	208	Karim Garcia	1.50	.70	.19
☐	209	Todd Hollandsworth	1.00	.45	.12
☐	210	Eric Karros	1.00	.45	.12
☐	211	Ramon Martinez	1.00	.45	.12
☐	212	Raul Mondesi	1.00	.45	.12
☐	213	Hideo Nomo	2.00	.90	.25
☐	214	Chan Ho Park	1.00	.45	.12
☐	215	Mike Piazza	5.00	2.20	.60
☐	216	Ismael Valdes	.50	.23	.06
☐	217	Todd Worrell	.50	.23	.06
☐	218	Moises Alou	.50	.23	.06
☐	219	Yamil Benitez	.25	.11	.03
☐	220	Jeff Fassero	.25	.11	.03
☐	221	Darrin Fletcher	.25	.11	.03
☐	222	Cliff Floyd	.25	.11	.03
☐	223	Pedro Martinez	1.00	.45	.12
☐	224	Carlos Perez	.25	.11	.03
☐	225	Mel Rojas	.25	.11	.03
☐	226	David Segui	.25	.11	.03
☐	227	Rondell White	1.00	.45	.12
☐	228	Rico Brogna	.25	.11	.03
☐	229	Carl Everett	.25	.11	.03

□ 230	John Franco	.25	.11	.03
□ 231	Bernard Gilkey	.50	.23	.06
□ 232	Todd Hundley	1.00	.45	.12
□ 233	Jason Isringhausen	.50	.23	.06
□ 234	Lance Johnson	1.00	.45	.12
□ 235	Bobby Jones	.25	.11	.03
□ 236	Jeff Kent	.25	.11	.03
□ 237	Rey Ordonez	1.50	.70	.19
□ 238	Bill Pulsipher	.50	.23	.06
□ 239	Jose Vizcaino	.25	.11	.03
□ 240	Paul Wilson	.50	.23	.06
□ 241	Ricky Bottalico	.25	.11	.03
□ 242	Darren Daulton	.50	.23	.06
□ 243	Lenny Dykstra	.50	.23	.06
□ 244	Jim Eisenreich	.25	.11	.03
□ 245	Sid Fernandez	.25	.11	.03
□ 246	Gregg Jefferies	1.00	.45	.12
□ 247	Mickey Morandini	.25	.11	.03
□ 248	Benito Santiago	.25	.11	.03
□ 249	Curt Schilling	.25	.11	.03
□ 250	Mark Whiten	.25	.11	.03
□ 251	Todd Zeile	.50	.23	.06
□ 252	Jay Bell	.50	.23	.06
□ 253	Carlos Garcia	.25	.11	.03
□ 254	Charlie Hayes	.25	.11	.03
□ 255	Jason Kendall	1.00	.45	.12
□ 256	Jeff King	.50	.23	.06
□ 257	Al Martin	.25	.11	.03
□ 258	Orlando Merced	.50	.23	.06
□ 259	Dan Miceli	.25	.11	.03
□ 260	Denny Neagle	.50	.23	.06
□ 261	Alan Benes	1.00	.45	.12
□ 262	Andy Benes	.25	.11	.03
□ 263	Royce Clayton	.25	.11	.03
□ 264	Dennis Eckersley	1.00	.45	.12
□ 265	Gary Gaetti	.50	.23	.06
□ 266	Ron Gant	1.00	.45	.12
□ 267	Brian Jordan	1.00	.45	.12
□ 268	Ray Lankford	1.00	.45	.12
□ 269	John Mabry	1.00	.45	.12
□ 270	Tom Pagnozzi	.25	.11	.03
□ 271	Ozzie Smith	1.50	.70	.19
□ 272	Todd Stottlemyre	.25	.11	.03
□ 273	Andy Ashby	.25	.11	.03
□ 274	Brad Ausmus	.25	.11	.03
□ 275	Ken Caminiti	1.00	.45	.12
□ 276	Steve Finley	1.00	.45	.12
□ 277	Tony Gwynn	3.00	1.35	.35
□ 278	Joey Hamilton	.50	.23	.06
□ 279	Rickey Henderson	1.00	.45	.12
□ 280	Trevor Hoffman	.50	.23	.06
□ 281	Wally Joyner	.25	.11	.03
□ 282	Jody Reed	.25	.11	.03
□ 283	Bob Tewksbury	.25	.11	.03
□ 284	Fernando Valenzuela	.50	.23	.06
□ 285	Rod Beck	.25	.11	.03
□ 286	Barry Bonds	2.00	.90	.25
□ 287	Mark Carreon	.25	.11	.03
□ 288	Shawon Dunston	.25	.11	.03
□ 289	Osvaldo Fernandez	1.00	.45	.12
□ 290	Glenallen Hill	.25	.11	.03
□ 291	Stan Javier	.25	.11	.03
□ 292	Mark Leiter	.25	.11	.03
□ 293	Kirt Manwaring	.25	.11	.03
□ 294	Robby Thompson	.25	.11	.03
□ 295	William VanLandingham	.25	.11	.03
□ 296	Allen Watson	.25	.11	.03
□ 297	Matt Williams	1.00	.45	.12
□ 298	Checklist	.25	.11	.03
□ 299	Checklist	.25	.11	.03
□ 300	Checklist	.25	.11	.03
□ P55	Manny Ramirez Promo	2.00	.90	.25

1996 Emotion-XL D-Fense

Randomly inserted in packs at a rate of one in four, this 10-card set showcases outstanding defensive players. The fronts feature a color action player cut-out on a sepia portait background with silver foil print and border. The backs carry information about the player on another sepia portrait background.

	MINT	NRMT	EXC
COMPLETE SET (10)	30.00	13.50	3.70
COMMON CARD (1-10)	1.00	.45	.12
SEMISTARS	1.50	.70	.19
RANDOM INSERTS IN PACKS			

□ 1	Roberto Alomar	2.50	1.10	.30
□ 2	Barry Bonds	2.50	1.10	.30
□ 3	Mark Grace	1.50	.70	.19
□ 4	Ken Griffey Jr.	10.00	4.50	1.25
□ 5	Kenny Lofton	2.50	1.10	.30
□ 6	Greg Maddux	6.00	2.70	.75
□ 7	Raul Mondesi	1.00	.45	.12
□ 8	Cal Ripken	8.00	3.60	1.00
□ 9	Ivan Rodriguez	2.00	.90	.25
□ 10	Matt Williams	1.50	.70	.19

1996 Emotion-XL Legion of Boom

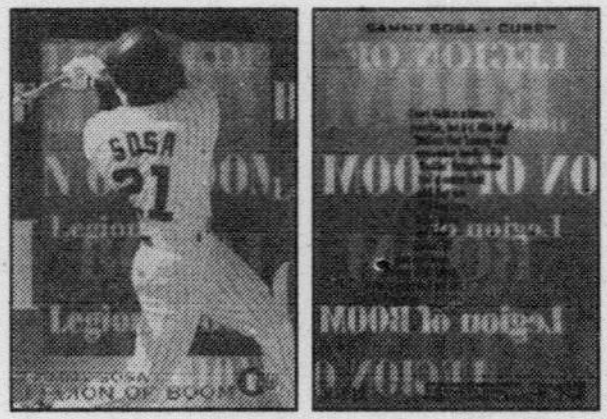

Randomly inserted in packs at a rate of one in 36, this 12-card set features the game's big hitters on cards with translucent card backs. The fronts carry a color action player cut-out with silver foil print.

	MINT	NRMT	EXC
COMPLETE SET (12)	200.00	90.00	25.00
COMMON CARD (1-12)	6.00	2.70	.75
RANDOM INSERTS IN HOBBY PACKS			

□ 1	Albert Belle	25.00	11.00	3.10
□ 2	Barry Bonds	12.00	5.50	1.50
□ 3	Juan Gonzalez	25.00	11.00	3.10
□ 4	Ken Griffey Jr.	50.00	22.00	6.25
□ 5	Mark McGwire	15.00	6.75	1.85
□ 6	Mike Piazza	30.00	13.50	3.70
□ 7	Manny Ramirez	12.00	5.50	1.50
□ 8	Tim Salmon	6.00	2.70	.75
□ 9	Sammy Sosa	8.00	3.60	1.00
□ 10	Frank Thomas	50.00	22.00	6.25
□ 11	Mo Vaughn	12.00	5.50	1.50
□ 12	Matt Williams	6.00	2.70	.75

1996 Emotion-XL N-Tense

Randomly inserted in packs at a rate of one in 12, this 10-card set highlights top-clutch performers on special, front N-shaped die-cut cards. The backs carry information about the player on a player portrait background.

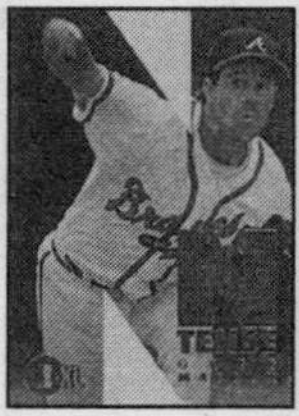

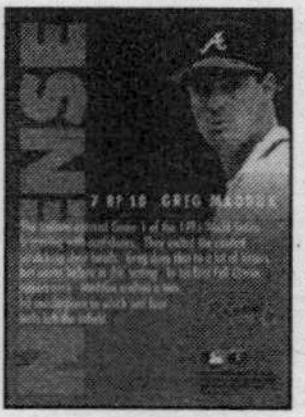

	MINT	NRMT	EXC
COMPLETE SET (10)	100.00	45.00	12.50
COMMON CARD (1-10)	3.00	1.35	.35
RANDOM INSERTS IN PACKS			
□ 1 Albert Belle	12.00	5.50	1.50
□ 2 Barry Bonds	6.00	2.70	.75
□ 3 Jose Canseco	3.00	1.35	.35
□ 4 Ken Griffey Jr.	25.00	11.00	3.10
□ 5 Tony Gwynn	10.00	4.50	1.25
□ 6 Randy Johnson	4.00	1.80	.50
□ 7 Greg Maddux	15.00	6.75	1.85
□ 8 Cal Ripken	20.00	9.00	2.50
□ 9 Frank Thomas	25.00	11.00	3.10
□ 10 Matt Williams	3.00	1.35	.35

1996 Emotion-XL Rare Breed

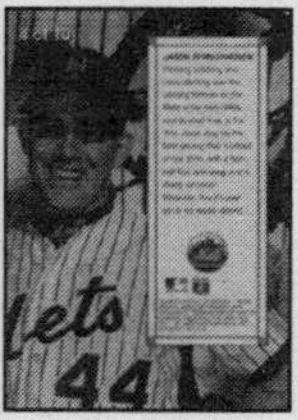

Randomly inserted in packs at a rate of one in 100, this 10-card set showcases young stars on lenticular cards. The fronts feature color action player cut-outs on a baseball graphics background. The backs carry player information over a color player portrait.

	MINT	NRMT	EXC
COMPLETE SET (10)	200.00	90.00	25.00
COMMON CARD (1-10)	6.00	2.70	.75
RANDOM INSERTS IN PACKS			
□ 1 Garret Anderson	6.00	2.70	.75
□ 2 Marty Cordova	15.00	6.75	1.85
□ 3 Brian L.Hunter	12.00	5.50	1.50
□ 4 Jason Isringhausen	15.00	6.75	1.85
□ 5 Charles Johnson	8.00	3.60	1.00
□ 6 Chipper Jones	75.00	34.00	9.50
□ 7 Raul Mondesi	15.00	6.75	1.85
□ 8 Hideo Nomo	30.00	13.50	3.70
□ 9 Manny Ramirez	30.00	13.50	3.70
□ 10 Rondell White	8.00	3.60	1.00

1993 Finest

This 199-card standard-size single series set is widely recognized as one of the most important issues of the 1990's. The Finest brand was Topps first attempt at the super-premium card market. Production was announced at 4,000 cases and cards were distributed exclusively through hobby dealers in the fall of 1993. This was the first time in the history of the hobby that a major manufacturer publicly released production figures. Cards were issued in 7-card foil fin-wrapped packs that carried a suggested retail price of $3.99. The product was a smashing success upon release with pack prices immediately soaring well above suggested retail prices. The popularity of the product has continued to grow throughout the years as it's place in hobby lore is now well soldified. The cards have silver-blue metallic finishes on their fronts and feature color player action photos. The set's title appears at the top, and the player's name is shown at the bottom. There are no key Rookie Cards in this set.

	MINT	NRMT	EXC
COMPLETE SET (199)	250.00	110.00	31.00
COMMON CARD (1-199)	.75	.35	.09
SEMISTARS	1.50	.70	.19
STARS	3.00	1.35	.35
□ 1 David Justice	3.00	1.35	.35
□ 2 Lou Whitaker	3.00	1.35	.35
□ 3 Bryan Harvey	.75	.35	.09
□ 4 Carlos Garcia	.75	.35	.09
□ 5 Sid Fernandez	.75	.35	.09
□ 6 Brett Butler	1.50	.70	.19
□ 7 Scott Cooper	.75	.35	.09
□ 8 B.J. Surhoff	1.50	.70	.19
□ 9 Steve Finley	3.00	1.35	.35
□ 10 Curt Schilling	.75	.35	.09
□ 11 Jeff Bagwell	12.00	5.50	1.50
□ 12 Alex Cole	.75	.35	.09
□ 13 John Olerud	.75	.35	.09
□ 14 John Smiley	.75	.35	.09
□ 15 Bip Roberts	.75	.35	.09
□ 16 Albert Belle	15.00	6.75	1.85
□ 17 Duane Ward	.75	.35	.09
□ 18 Alan Trammell	3.00	1.35	.35
□ 19 Andy Benes	.75	.35	.09
□ 20 Reggie Sanders	3.00	1.35	.35
□ 21 Todd Zeile	.75	.35	.09
□ 22 Rick Aguilera	.75	.35	.09
□ 23 Dave Hollins	.75	.35	.09
□ 24 Jose Rijo	.75	.35	.09
□ 25 Matt Williams	4.00	1.80	.50
□ 26 Sandy Alomar	1.50	.70	.19
□ 27 Alex Fernandez	3.00	1.35	.35
□ 28 Ozzie Smith	6.00	2.70	.75
□ 29 Ramon Martinez	1.50	.70	.19
□ 30 Bernie Williams	5.00	2.20	.60
□ 31 Gary Sheffield	5.00	2.20	.60
□ 32 Eric Karros	3.00	1.35	.35
□ 33 Frank Viola	.75	.35	.09
□ 34 Kevin Young	.75	.35	.09
□ 35 Ken Hill	1.50	.70	.19
□ 36 Tony Fernandez	.75	.35	.09
□ 37 Tim Wakefield	1.50	.70	.19
□ 38 John Kruk	1.50	.70	.19
□ 39 Chris Sabo	.75	.35	.09
□ 40 Marquis Grissom	3.00	1.35	.35
□ 41 Glenn Davis	.75	.35	.09
□ 42 Jeff Montgomery	1.50	.70	.19
□ 43 Kenny Lofton	12.00	5.50	1.50
□ 44 John Burkett	.75	.35	.09
□ 45 Darryl Hamilton	.75	.35	.09
□ 46 Jim Abbott	.75	.35	.09
□ 47 Ivan Rodriguez	6.00	2.70	.75
□ 48 Eric Young	3.00	1.35	.35
□ 49 Mitch Williams	.75	.35	.09
□ 50 Harold Reynolds	.75	.35	.09

□ 51 Brian Harper	.75	.35	.09
□ 52 Rafael Palmeiro	4.00	1.80	.50
□ 53 Bret Saberhagen	1.50	.70	.19
□ 54 Jeff Conine	3.00	1.35	.35
□ 55 Ivan Calderon	.75	.35	.09
□ 56 Juan Guzman	1.50	.70	.19
□ 57 Carlos Baerga	3.00	1.35	.35
□ 58 Charles Nagy	1.50	.70	.19
□ 59 Wally Joyner	1.50	.70	.19
□ 60 Charlie Hayes	.75	.35	.09
□ 61 Shane Mack	.75	.35	.09
□ 62 Pete Harnisch	.75	.35	.09
□ 63 George Brett	12.00	5.50	1.50
□ 64 Lance Johnson	1.50	.70	.19
□ 65 Ben McDonald	.75	.35	.09
□ 66 Bobby Bonilla	1.50	.70	.19
□ 67 Terry Steinbach	1.50	.70	.19
□ 68 Ron Gant	3.00	1.35	.35
□ 69 Doug Jones	.75	.35	.09
□ 70 Paul Molitor	6.00	2.70	.75
□ 71 Brady Anderson	4.00	1.80	.50
□ 72 Chuck Finley	.75	.35	.09
□ 73 Mark Grace	3.00	1.35	.35
□ 74 Mike Devereaux	.75	.35	.09
□ 75 Tony Phillips	1.50	.70	.19
□ 76 Chuck Knoblauch	4.00	1.80	.50
□ 77 Tony Gwynn	12.00	5.50	1.50
□ 78 Kevin Appier	1.50	.70	.19
□ 79 Sammy Sosa	5.00	2.20	.60
□ 80 Mickey Tettleton	.75	.35	.09
□ 81 Felix Jose	.75	.35	.09
□ 82 Mark Langston	1.50	.70	.19
□ 83 Gregg Jefferies	3.00	1.35	.35
□ 84 Andre Dawson AS	3.00	1.35	.35
□ 85 Greg Maddux AS	20.00	9.00	2.50
□ 86 Rickey Henderson AS	3.00	1.35	.35
□ 87 Tom Glavine AS	4.00	1.80	.50
□ 88 Roberto Alomar AS	8.00	3.60	1.00
□ 89 Darryl Strawberry AS	1.50	.70	.19
□ 90 Wade Boggs AS	3.00	1.35	.35
□ 91 Bo Jackson AS	3.00	1.35	.35
□ 92 Mark McGwire AS	10.00	4.50	1.25
□ 93 Robin Ventura AS	1.50	.70	.19
□ 94 Joe Carter AS	3.00	1.35	.35
□ 95 Lee Smith AS	1.50	.70	.19
□ 96 Cal Ripken AS	25.00	11.00	3.10
□ 97 Larry Walker AS	3.00	1.35	.35
□ 98 Don Mattingly AS	15.00	6.75	1.85
□ 99 Jose Canseco AS	4.00	1.80	.50
□ 100 Dennis Eckersley AS	1.50	.70	.19
□ 101 Terry Pendleton AS	1.50	.70	.19
□ 102 Frank Thomas AS	30.00	13.50	3.70
□ 103 Barry Bonds AS	8.00	3.60	1.00
□ 104 Roger Clemens AS	4.00	1.80	.50
□ 105 Ryne Sandberg AS	8.00	3.60	1.00
□ 106 Fred McGriff AS	4.00	1.80	.50
□ 107 Nolan Ryan AS	25.00	11.00	3.10
□ 108 Will Clark AS	4.00	1.80	.50
□ 109 Pat Listach AS	.75	.35	.09
□ 110 Ken Griffey Jr. AS	30.00	13.50	3.70
□ 111 Cecil Fielder AS	1.50	.70	.19
□ 112 Kirby Puckett AS	10.00	4.50	1.25
□ 113 Dwight Gooden AS	1.50	.70	.19
□ 114 Barry Larkin AS	4.00	1.80	.50
□ 115 David Cone AS	3.00	1.35	.35
□ 116 Juan Gonzalez AS	15.00	6.75	1.85
□ 117 Kent Hrbek	1.50	.70	.19
□ 118 Tim Wallach	.75	.35	.09
□ 119 Craig Biggio	3.00	1.35	.35
□ 120 Roberto Kelly	.75	.35	.09
□ 121 Gregg Olson	.75	.35	.09
□ 122 Eddie Murray UER 122 career strikeouts should be 1224	8.00	3.60	1.00
□ 123 Wil Cordero	1.50	.70	.19
□ 124 Jay Buhner	4.00	1.80	.50
□ 125 Carlton Fisk	3.00	1.35	.35
□ 126 Eric Davis	1.50	.70	.19
□ 127 Doug Drabek	.75	.35	.09
□ 128 Ozzie Guillen	.75	.35	.09
□ 129 John Wetteland	1.50	.70	.19
□ 130 Andres Galarraga	4.00	1.80	.50
□ 131 Ken Caminiti	3.00	1.35	.35
□ 132 Tom Candiotti	.75	.35	.09
□ 133 Pat Borders	.75	.35	.09
□ 134 Kevin Brown	.75	.35	.09
□ 135 Travis Fryman	3.00	1.35	.35
□ 136 Kevin Mitchell	1.50	.70	.19
□ 137 Greg Swindell	.75	.35	.09
□ 138 Benito Santiago	.75	.35	.09
□ 139 Reggie Jefferson	1.50	.70	.19
□ 140 Chris Bosio	.75	.35	.09
□ 141 Deion Sanders	4.00	1.80	.50
□ 142 Scott Erickson	.75	.35	.09
□ 143 Howard Johnson	.75	.35	.09
□ 144 Orestes Destrade	.75	.35	.09
□ 145 Jose Guzman	.75	.35	.09
□ 146 Chad Curtis	1.50	.70	.19
□ 147 Cal Eldred	.75	.35	.09
□ 148 Willie Greene	1.50	.70	.19
□ 149 Tommy Greene	.75	.35	.09
□ 150 Erik Hanson	.75	.35	.09
□ 151 Bob Welch	.75	.35	.09
□ 152 John Jaha	1.50	.70	.19
□ 153 Harold Baines	1.50	.70	.19
□ 154 Randy Johnson	5.00	2.20	.60
□ 155 Al Martin	1.50	.70	.19
□ 156 J.T. Snow	3.00	1.35	.35
□ 157 Mike Mussina	6.00	2.70	.75
□ 158 Ruben Sierra	1.50	.70	.19
□ 159 Dean Palmer	1.50	.70	.19
□ 160 Steve Avery	1.50	.70	.19
□ 161 Julio Franco	1.50	.70	.19
□ 162 Dave Winfield	3.00	1.35	.35
□ 163 Tim Salmon	6.00	2.70	.75
□ 164 Tom Henke	.75	.35	.09
□ 165 Mo Vaughn	8.00	3.60	1.00
□ 166 John Smoltz	5.00	2.20	.60
□ 167 Danny Tartabull	.75	.35	.09
□ 168 Delino DeShields	.75	.35	.09
□ 169 Charlie Hough	.75	.35	.09
□ 170 Paul O'Neill	1.50	.70	.19
□ 171 Darren Daulton	1.50	.70	.19
□ 172 Jack McDowell	1.50	.70	.19
□ 173 Junior Felix	.75	.35	.09
□ 174 Jimmy Key	1.50	.70	.19
□ 175 George Bell	.75	.35	.09
□ 176 Mike Stanton	.75	.35	.09
□ 177 Len Dykstra	1.50	.70	.19
□ 178 Norm Charlton	.75	.35	.09
□ 179 Eric Anthony	.75	.35	.09
□ 180 Rob Dibble	.75	.35	.09
□ 181 Otis Nixon	.75	.35	.09
□ 182 Randy Myers	1.50	.70	.19
□ 183 Tim Raines	3.00	1.35	.35
□ 184 Orel Hershiser	1.50	.70	.19
□ 185 Andy Van Slyke	1.50	.70	.19
□ 186 Mike Lansing	1.50	.70	.19
□ 187 Ray Lankford	3.00	1.35	.35
□ 188 Mike Morgan	.75	.35	.09
□ 189 Moises Alou	3.00	1.35	.35
□ 190 Edgar Martinez	4.00	1.80	.50
□ 191 John Franco	.75	.35	.09
□ 192 Robin Yount	4.00	1.80	.50
□ 193 Bob Tewksbury	.75	.35	.09
□ 194 Jay Bell	1.50	.70	.19
□ 195 Luis Gonzalez	.75	.35	.09
□ 196 Dave Fleming	.75	.35	.09
□ 197 Mike Greenwell	.75	.35	.09
□ 198 David Nied	.75	.35	.09
□ 199 Mike Piazza	30.00	13.50	3.70

1993 Finest Refractors

Randomly inserted in packs at a rate of one in 18, these 199 standard-size cards are identical to the regular-issue 1993 Topps Finest except that their fronts have been laminated with a plastic diffraction grating that gives the card a colorful 3-D appearance. Because of the known production numbers, these cards are believed to have a print run of 241 of each card. Several cards are believed to be in short supply and are notated with an asterisk. Topps, however, has never publicly released any verification of short-printed singles, but some of the singles are accepted as being tough to find due to poor regional distribution and hoarding. Due to their high value, these cards are extremely condition sensitive, with much attention paid to centering and minor scratches on the card fronts.

	MINT	NRMT	EXC
COMPLETE SET (199)	40000.00	18000.00	5000.00
COMMON CARD (1-199)	60.00	27.00	7.50
ASTERISK CARDS: PERCEIVED SCARCITY .			
RANDOM INSERTS IN PACKS			

□ 1 David Justice	250.00	110.00	31.00
□ 2 Lou Whitaker	100.00	45.00	12.50
□ 3 Bryan Harvey*	250.00	110.00	31.00
□ 6 Brett Butler	75.00	34.00	9.50
□ 8 B.J. Surhoff	75.00	34.00	9.50
□ 9 Steve Finley	75.00	34.00	9.50
□ 10 Curt Schilling*	300.00	135.00	38.00
□ 11 Jeff Bagwell	1100.00	500.00	140.00
□ 12 Alex Cole	250.00	110.00	31.00
□ 16 Albert Belle	1000.00	450.00	125.00
□ 18 Alan Trammell	100.00	45.00	12.50
□ 20 Reggie Sanders	175.00	80.00	22.00
□ 25 Matt Williams	400.00	180.00	50.00
□ 26 Sandy Alomar	90.00	40.00	11.00
□ 27 Alex Fernandez	125.00	55.00	15.50
□ 28 Ozzie Smith	250.00	110.00	31.00
□ 29 Ramon Martinez	75.00	34.00	9.50
□ 30 Bernie Williams	500.00	220.00	60.00
□ 31 Gary Sheffield	350.00	160.00	45.00
□ 32 Eric Karros	150.00	70.00	19.00
□ 35 Ken Hill	75.00	34.00	9.50
□ 38 John Kruk*	200.00	90.00	25.00
□ 39 Chris Sabo*	200.00	90.00	25.00
□ 40 Marquis Grissom*	400.00	180.00	50.00
□ 41 Glenn Davis*	250.00	110.00	31.00
□ 43 Kenny Lofton	500.00	220.00	60.00
□ 47 Ivan Rodriguez*	700.00	325.00	90.00
□ 48 Eric Young	100.00	45.00	12.50
□ 52 Rafael Palmeiro	225.00	100.00	28.00
□ 54 Jeff Conine	175.00	80.00	22.00
□ 56 Juan Guzman	75.00	34.00	9.50
□ 57 Carlos Baerga	175.00	80.00	22.00
□ 58 Charles Nagy	175.00	80.00	22.00
□ 59 Wally Joyner	100.00	45.00	12.50
□ 63 George Brett	650.00	300.00	80.00
□ 64 Lance Johnson	90.00	40.00	11.00
□ 65 Ben McDonald	75.00	34.00	9.50
□ 66 Bobby Bonilla	90.00	40.00	11.00
□ 67 Terry Steinbach	90.00	40.00	11.00
□ 68 Ron Gant	100.00	45.00	12.50
□ 70 Paul Molitor	600.00	275.00	75.00
□ 71 Brady Anderson	300.00	135.00	38.00
□ 72 Chuck Finley	75.00	34.00	9.50
□ 73 Mark Grace	250.00	110.00	31.00
□ 75 Tony Phillips	75.00	34.00	9.50
□ 76 Chuck Knoblauch	350.00	160.00	45.00
□ 77 Tony Gwynn	650.00	300.00	80.00
□ 78 Kevin Appier	100.00	45.00	12.50
□ 79 Sammy Sosa*	550.00	250.00	70.00
□ 80 Mickey Tettleton	125.00	55.00	15.50
□ 81 Felix Jose*	225.00	100.00	28.00
□ 83 Gregg Jefferies	75.00	34.00	9.50
□ 84 Andre Dawson AS*	225.00	100.00	28.00
□ 85 Greg Maddux AS	1200.00	550.00	150.00
□ 86 Rickey Henderson	225.00	100.00	28.00
□ 87 Tom Glavine AS	250.00	110.00	31.00
□ 88 Roberto Alomar AS	600.00	275.00	75.00
□ 89 Darryl Strawberry AS	125.00	55.00	15.50
□ 90 Wade Boggs AS	225.00	100.00	28.00
□ 91 Bo Jackson AS	100.00	45.00	12.50
□ 92 Mark McGwire AS	600.00	275.00	75.00
□ 93 Robin Ventura AS	125.00	55.00	15.50
□ 94 Joe Carter AS	150.00	70.00	19.00
□ 95 Lee Smith AS	75.00	34.00	9.50
□ 96 Cal Ripken AS	2300.00	1050.00	300.00
□ 97 Larry Walker AS	225.00	100.00	28.00
□ 98 Don Mattingly AS	500.00	220.00	60.00
□ 99 Jose Canseco AS	200.00	90.00	25.00
□ 100 Dennis Eckersley AS	100.00	45.00	12.50
□ 101 Terry Pendleton AS	75.00	34.00	9.50
□ 102 Frank Thomas AS	1500.00	700.00	190.00
□ 103 Barry Bonds AS	700.00	325.00	90.00
□ 104 Roger Clemens AS	250.00	110.00	31.00
□ 105 Ryne Sandberg AS	300.00	135.00	38.00
□ 106 Fred McGriff AS	300.00	135.00	38.00
□ 107 Nolan Ryan AS	1500.00	700.00	190.00
□ 108 Will Clark AS	225.00	100.00	28.00
□ 110 Ken Griffey Jr. AS !	1800.00	800.00	220.00
□ 111 Cecil Fielder AS	200.00	90.00	25.00
□ 112 Kirby Puckett AS	325.00	145.00	40.00
□ 113 Dwight Gooden AS	150.00	70.00	19.00
□ 114 Barry Larkin AS	250.00	110.00	31.00
□ 115 David Cone AS	125.00	55.00	15.50
□ 116 Juan Gonzalez AS	1500.00	700.00	190.00
□ 119 Craig Biggio	150.00	70.00	19.00
□ 122 Eddie Murray UER	650.00	300.00	80.00
122 career strikeouts should be 1224			
□ 124 Jay Buhner	250.00	110.00	31.00
□ 125 Carlton Fisk	150.00	70.00	19.00
□ 126 Eric Davis	75.00	34.00	9.50
□ 129 John Wetteland	100.00	45.00	12.50
□ 130 Andres Galarraga	250.00	110.00	31.00
□ 131 Ken Caminiti	250.00	110.00	31.00
□ 134 Kevin Brown*	200.00	90.00	25.00
□ 135 Travis Fryman	125.00	55.00	15.50
□ 141 Deion Sanders	175.00	80.00	22.00
□ 152 John Jaha	100.00	45.00	12.50
□ 153 Harold Baines	90.00	40.00	11.00
□ 154 Randy Johnson	500.00	220.00	60.00
□ 155 Al Martin *	125.00	55.00	15.50
□ 156 J.T. Snow	125.00	55.00	15.50
□ 157 Mike Mussina	400.00	180.00	50.00
□ 158 Ruben Sierra	75.00	34.00	9.50
□ 159 Dean Palmer	175.00	80.00	22.00
□ 160 Steve Avery	100.00	45.00	12.50
□ 161 Julio Franco	90.00	40.00	11.00
□ 162 Dave Winfield	175.00	80.00	22.00
□ 163 Tim Salmon	400.00	180.00	50.00
□ 165 Mo Vaughn	500.00	220.00	60.00
□ 166 John Smoltz	350.00	160.00	45.00
□ 170 Paul O'Neill	100.00	45.00	12.50
□ 171 Darren Daulton	75.00	34.00	9.50
□ 172 Jack McDowell	100.00	45.00	12.50
□ 173 Junior Felix*	225.00	100.00	28.00
□ 177 Len Dykstra	75.00	34.00	9.50
□ 182 Randy Myers *	75.00	34.00	9.50
□ 183 Tim Raines	75.00	34.00	9.50
□ 184 Orel Hershiser	100.00	45.00	12.50
□ 185 Andy Van Slyke	75.00	34.00	9.50
□ 186 Mike Lansing	75.00	34.00	9.50
□ 187 Ray Lankford	125.00	55.00	15.50
□ 189 Moises Alou*	175.00	80.00	22.00
□ 190 Edgar Martinez	200.00	90.00	25.00
□ 192 Robin Yount	200.00	90.00	25.00
□ 193 Bob Tewksbury*	175.00	80.00	22.00
□ 194 Jay Bell	75.00	34.00	9.50
□ 199 Mike Piazza	1300.00	575.00	160.00

1993 Finest Jumbos

These oversized (approximately 4" by 6") cards were inserted one per sealed box of 1993 Topps Finest packs and feature reproductions of 33 players from that set's All-Star subset (84-116). Some hobby dealers believe because of the known production numbers that slightly less than 1,500 of each of these cards were produced.

	MINT	NRMT	EXC
COMPLETE SET (33)	500.00	220.00	60.00
COMMON CARD (84-116)	4.00	1.80	.50
SEMISTARS	8.00	3.60	1.00
ONE CARD PER SEALED BOX			

□ 84 Andre Dawson	8.00	3.60	1.00
□ 85 Greg Maddux	40.00	18.00	5.00

□ 86 Rickey Henderson	8.00	3.60	1.00
□ 87 Tom Glavine	10.00	4.50	1.25
□ 88 Roberto Alomar	15.00	6.75	1.85
□ 89 Darryl Strawberry	8.00	3.60	1.00
□ 90 Wade Boggs	8.00	3.60	1.00
□ 91 Bo Jackson	8.00	3.60	1.00
□ 92 Mark McGwire	18.00	8.00	2.20
□ 93 Robin Ventura	8.00	3.60	1.00
□ 94 Joe Carter	8.00	3.60	1.00
□ 95 Lee Smith	8.00	3.60	1.00
□ 96 Cal Ripken	50.00	22.00	6.25
□ 97 Larry Walker	6.00	2.70	.75
□ 98 Don Mattingly	30.00	13.50	3.70
□ 99 Jose Canseco	8.00	3.60	1.00
□ 100 Dennis Eckersley	8.00	3.60	1.00
□ 101 Terry Pendleton	4.00	1.80	.50
□ 102 Frank Thomas	60.00	27.00	7.50
□ 103 Barry Bonds	15.00	6.75	1.85
□ 104 Roger Clemens	8.00	3.60	1.00
□ 105 Ryne Sandberg	15.00	6.75	1.85
□ 106 Fred McGriff	8.00	3.60	1.00
□ 107 Nolan Ryan	50.00	22.00	6.25
□ 108 Will Clark	8.00	3.60	1.00
□ 109 Pat Listach	4.00	1.80	.50
□ 110 Ken Griffey Jr.	60.00	27.00	7.50
□ 111 Cecil Fielder	8.00	3.60	1.00
□ 112 Kirby Puckett	18.00	8.00	2.20
□ 113 Dwight Gooden	8.00	3.60	1.00
□ 114 Barry Larkin	10.00	4.50	1.25
□ 115 David Cone	8.00	3.60	1.00
□ 116 Juan Gonzalez	25.00	11.00	3.10

1994 Finest Pre-Production

This 40-card preview standard-size set is identical in design to the basic Finest set. Cards were randomly inserted at a rate of one in 36 in second series Topps packs and three cards were issued with each Topps factory set. The card numbers on back correspond to those of the regular issue. The only way to distinguish between the preview and basic cards is "Pre-Production" in small red letters on back.

	MINT	NRMT	EXC
COMPLETE SET (40)	175.00	80.00	22.00
COMMON CARD	2.50	1.10	.30
SEMISTARS	5.00	2.20	.60
STARS	10.00	4.50	1.25
NUMBERS CORRESPOND TO REGULAR CARDS			
RANDOM INSERTS IN SER.2 TOPPS PACKS			
THREE PER REGULAR TOPPS FACTORY SET			

□ 22P Deion Sanders	5.00	2.20	.60
□ 23P Jose Offerman	2.50	1.10	.30
□ 26P Alex Fernandez	5.00	2.20	.60
□ 31P Steve Finley	5.00	2.20	.60
□ 35P Andres Galarraga	12.00	5.50	1.50
□ 43P Reggie Sanders	5.00	2.20	.60
□ 47P Dave Hollins	2.50	1.10	.30
□ 52P David Cone	5.00	2.20	.60
□ 59P Dante Bichette	12.00	5.50	1.50
□ 61P Orlando Merced	3.50	1.55	.45
□ 62P Brian McRae	3.50	1.55	.45
□ 66P Mike Mussina	20.00	9.00	2.50
□ 76P Mike Stanley	3.50	1.55	.45
□ 78P Mark McGwire	30.00	13.50	3.70
□ 79P Pat Listach	2.50	1.10	.30
□ 82P Dwight Gooden	5.00	2.20	.60
□ 84P Phil Plantier	2.50	1.10	.30
□ 90P Jeff Russell	2.50	1.10	.30
□ 92P Gregg Jefferies	5.00	2.20	.60
□ 93P Jose Guzman	2.50	1.10	.30
□ 100P John Smoltz	15.00	6.75	1.85
□ 102P Jim Thome	25.00	11.00	3.10
□ 121P Moises Alou	5.00	2.20	.60
□ 125P Devon White	3.50	1.55	.45
□ 126P Ivan Rodriguez	20.00	9.00	2.50
□ 130P Dave Magadan	2.50	1.10	.30
□ 136P Ozzie Smith	20.00	9.00	2.50
□ 141P Chris Hoiles	3.50	1.55	.45
□ 149P Jim Abbott	3.50	1.55	.45
□ 151P Bill Swift	2.50	1.10	.30
□ 154P Edgar Martinez	12.00	5.50	1.50
□ 157P J.T. Snow	3.50	1.55	.45
□ 159P Alan Trammell	5.00	2.20	.60
□ 163P Roberto Kelly	2.50	1.10	.30
□ 166P Scott Erickson	3.50	1.55	.45
□ 168P Scott Cooper	2.50	1.10	.30
□ 169P Rod Beck	3.50	1.55	.45
□ 177P Dean Palmer	3.50	1.55	.45
□ 182P Todd Van Poppel	2.50	1.10	.30
□ 185P Paul Sorrento	2.50	1.10	.30

1994 Finest

The 1994 Topps Finest baseball set consists of two series of 220 cards each, for a total of 440 standard-size cards. Each series includes 40 special design Finest cards: 20 top 1993 rookies (1-20), 20 top 1994 rookies (421-440) and 40 top veterans (201-240). These glossy and metallic cards have a color photo on front with green and gold borders. A color photo on back is accompanied by statistics and a "Finest Moment" note. Some series 2 packs contained either one or two series 1 cards. Rookie Cards include Kurt Abbott, Brian Anderson and Chan Ho Park.

	MINT	NRMT	EXC
COMPLETE SET (440)	150.00	70.00	19.00
COMPLETE SERIES 1 (220)	75.00	34.00	9.50
COMPLETE SERIES 2 (220)	75.00	34.00	9.50
COMMON CARD (1-440)	.50	.23	.06
SEMISTARS	1.00	.45	.12
COMP.JUMBO SET (80)	350.00	160.00	45.00
COMP.JUMBO SER.1 (40)	200.00	90.00	25.00
COMP.JUMBO SER.2 (40)	150.00	70.00	19.00
COMMON 1 (1-20/201-220)	1.00	.45	.12
COMMON 2 (221-240/421-440)	1.00	.45	.12
JUMBO SEMISTARS	2.50	1.10	.30
*JUMBO STARS: 1.5X to 3X HI COLUMN			
ONE JUMBO PER SER.1, 2 BOX			

□ 1 Mike Piazza FIN	8.00	3.60	1.00
□ 2 Kevin Stocker FIN	.50	.23	.06
□ 3 Greg McMichael FIN	.50	.23	.06
□ 4 Jeff Conine FIN	1.00	.45	.12
□ 5 Rene Arocha FIN	.50	.23	.06
□ 6 Aaron Sele FIN	.75	.35	.09
□ 7 Brent Gates FIN	.50	.23	.06
□ 8 Chuck Carr FIN	.50	.23	.06
□ 9 Kirk Rueter FIN	.50	.23	.06
□ 10 Mike Lansing FIN	.75	.35	.09
□ 11 Al Martin FIN	.50	.23	.06
□ 12 Jason Bere FIN	.75	.35	.09

☐ 13 Troy Neel FIN	.50	.23	.06
☐ 14 Armando Reynoso FIN	.50	.23	.06
☐ 15 Jeromy Burnitz FIN	.50	.23	.06
☐ 16 Rich Amaral FIN	.50	.23	.06
☐ 17 David McCarty FIN	.50	.23	.06
☐ 18 Tim Salmon FIN	2.00	.90	.25
☐ 19 Steve Cooke FIN	.50	.23	.06
☐ 20 Wil Cordero FIN	.75	.35	.09
☐ 21 Kevin Tapani	.50	.23	.06
☐ 22 Deion Sanders	1.00	.45	.12
☐ 23 Jose Offerman	.50	.23	.06
☐ 24 Mark Langston	.75	.35	.09
☐ 25 Ken Hill	.50	.23	.06
☐ 26 Alex Fernandez	1.00	.45	.12
☐ 27 Jeff Blauser	.50	.23	.06
☐ 28 Royce Clayton	.75	.35	.09
☐ 29 Brad Ausmus	.50	.23	.06
☐ 30 Ryan Bowen	.50	.23	.06
☐ 31 Steve Finley	1.00	.45	.12
☐ 32 Charlie Hayes	.50	.23	.06
☐ 33 Jeff Kent	.50	.23	.06
☐ 34 Mike Henneman	.50	.23	.06
☐ 35 Andres Galarraga	1.00	.45	.12
☐ 36 Wayne Kirby	.50	.23	.06
☐ 37 Joe Oliver	.50	.23	.06
☐ 38 Terry Steinbach	.75	.35	.09
☐ 39 Ryan Thompson	.50	.23	.06
☐ 40 Luis Alicea	.50	.23	.06
☐ 41 Randy Velarde	.50	.23	.06
☐ 42 Bob Tewksbury	.50	.23	.06
☐ 43 Reggie Sanders	1.00	.45	.12
☐ 44 Brian Williams	.50	.23	.06
☐ 45 Joe Orsulak	.50	.23	.06
☐ 46 Jose Lind	.50	.23	.06
☐ 47 Dave Hollins	.50	.23	.06
☐ 48 Graeme Lloyd	.50	.23	.06
☐ 49 Jim Gott	.50	.23	.06
☐ 50 Andre Dawson	1.00	.45	.12
☐ 51 Steve Buechele	.50	.23	.06
☐ 52 David Cone	1.00	.45	.12
☐ 53 Ricky Gutierrez	.50	.23	.06
☐ 54 Lance Johnson	.75	.35	.09
☐ 55 Tino Martinez	.75	.35	.09
☐ 56 Phil Hiatt	.50	.23	.06
☐ 57 Carlos Garcia	.50	.23	.06
☐ 58 Danny Darwin	.50	.23	.06
☐ 59 Dante Bichette	1.50	.70	.19
☐ 60 Scott Kamieniecki	.50	.23	.06
☐ 61 Orlando Merced	.75	.35	.09
☐ 62 Brian McRae	.75	.35	.09
☐ 63 Pat Kelly	.50	.23	.06
☐ 64 Tom Henke	.50	.23	.06
☐ 65 Jeff King	.75	.35	.09
☐ 66 Mike Mussina	2.50	1.10	.30
☐ 67 Tim Pugh	.50	.23	.06
☐ 68 Robby Thompson	.50	.23	.06
☐ 69 Paul O'Neill	.75	.35	.09
☐ 70 Hal Morris	.50	.23	.06
☐ 71 Ron Karkovice	.50	.23	.06
☐ 72 Joe Girardi	.50	.23	.06
☐ 73 Eduardo Perez	.50	.23	.06
☐ 74 Raul Mondesi	2.00	.90	.25
☐ 75 Mike Gallego	.50	.23	.06
☐ 76 Mike Stanley	.50	.23	.06
☐ 77 Kevin Roberson	.50	.23	.06
☐ 78 Mark McGwire	4.00	1.80	.50
☐ 79 Pat Listach	.50	.23	.06
☐ 80 Eric Davis	.75	.35	.09
☐ 81 Mike Bordick	.50	.23	.06
☐ 82 Doc Gooden	.75	.35	.09
☐ 83 Mike Moore	.50	.23	.06
☐ 84 Phil Plantier	.50	.23	.06
☐ 85 Darren Lewis	.50	.23	.06
☐ 86 Rick Wilkins	.50	.23	.06
☐ 87 Darryl Strawberry	.75	.35	.09
☐ 88 Rob Dibble	.50	.23	.06
☐ 89 Greg Vaughn	1.00	.45	.12
☐ 90 Jeff Russell	.50	.23	.06
☐ 91 Mark Lewis	.50	.23	.06
☐ 92 Gregg Jefferies	1.00	.45	.12
☐ 93 Jose Guzman	.50	.23	.06
☐ 94 Kenny Rogers	.50	.23	.06
☐ 95 Mark Lemke	.50	.23	.06
☐ 96 Mike Morgan	.50	.23	.06
☐ 97 Andujar Cedeno	.50	.23	.06
☐ 98 Orel Hershiser	.75	.35	.09

☐ 99 Greg Swindell	.50	.23	.06
☐ 100 John Smoltz	2.00	.90	.25
☐ 101 Pedro Martinez	1.00	.45	.12
☐ 102 Jim Thome	3.00	1.35	.35
☐ 103 David Segui	.50	.23	.06
☐ 104 Charles Nagy	.75	.35	.09
☐ 105 Shane Mack	.50	.23	.06
☐ 106 John Jaha	.75	.35	.09
☐ 107 Tom Candiotti	.50	.23	.06
☐ 108 David Wells	.50	.23	.06
☐ 109 Bobby Jones	.75	.35	.09
☐ 110 Bob Hamelin	.50	.23	.06
☐ 111 Bernard Gilkey	.75	.35	.09
☐ 112 Chili Davis	.75	.35	.09
☐ 113 Todd Stottlemyre	.50	.23	.06
☐ 114 Derek Bell	.75	.35	.09
☐ 115 Mark McLemore	.50	.23	.06
☐ 116 Mark Whiten	.50	.23	.06
☐ 117 Mike Devereaux	.50	.23	.06
☐ 118 Terry Pendleton	.75	.35	.09
☐ 119 Pat Meares	.50	.23	.06
☐ 120 Pete Harnisch	.50	.23	.06
☐ 121 Moises Alou	.75	.35	.09
☐ 122 Jay Buhner	1.00	.45	.12
☐ 123 Wes Chamberlain	.50	.23	.06
☐ 124 Mike Perez	.50	.23	.06
☐ 125 Devon White	.50	.23	.06
☐ 126 Ivan Rodriguez	2.50	1.10	.30
☐ 127 Don Slaught	.50	.23	.06
☐ 128 John Valentin	.75	.35	.09
☐ 129 Jaime Navarro	.50	.23	.06
☐ 130 Dave Magadan	.50	.23	.06
☐ 131 Brady Anderson	1.00	.45	.12
☐ 132 Juan Guzman	.75	.35	.09
☐ 133 John Wetteland	.75	.35	.09
☐ 134 Dave Stewart	.75	.35	.09
☐ 135 Scott Servais	.50	.23	.06
☐ 136 Ozzie Smith	2.50	1.10	.30
☐ 137 Darrin Fletcher	.50	.23	.06
☐ 138 Jose Mesa	.75	.35	.09
☐ 139 Wilson Alvarez	.75	.35	.09
☐ 140 Pete Incaviglia	.50	.23	.06
☐ 141 Chris Hoiles	.50	.23	.06
☐ 142 Darryl Hamilton	.50	.23	.06
☐ 143 Chuck Finley	.50	.23	.06
☐ 144 Archi Cianfrocco	.50	.23	.06
☐ 145 Bill Wegman	.50	.23	.06
☐ 146 Joey Cora	.50	.23	.06
☐ 147 Darrell Whitmore	.50	.23	.06
☐ 148 David Hulse	.50	.23	.06
☐ 149 Jim Abbott	.50	.23	.06
☐ 150 Curt Schilling	.50	.23	.06
☐ 151 Bill Swift	.50	.23	.06
☐ 152 Tommy Greene	.50	.23	.06
☐ 153 Roberto Mejia	.50	.23	.06
☐ 154 Edgar Martinez	1.00	.45	.12
☐ 155 Roger Pavlik	.50	.23	.06
☐ 156 Randy Tomlin	.50	.23	.06
☐ 157 J.T. Snow	.75	.35	.09
☐ 158 Bob Welch	.50	.23	.06
☐ 159 Alan Trammell	1.00	.45	.12
☐ 160 Ed Sprague	.75	.35	.09
☐ 161 Ben McDonald	.50	.23	.06
☐ 162 Derrick May	.50	.23	.06
☐ 163 Roberto Kelly	.50	.23	.06
☐ 164 Bryan Harvey	.50	.23	.06
☐ 165 Ron Gant	.75	.35	.09
☐ 166 Scott Erickson	.50	.23	.06
☐ 167 Anthony Young	.50	.23	.06
☐ 168 Scott Cooper	.50	.23	.06
☐ 169 Rod Beck	.75	.35	.09
☐ 170 John Franco	.50	.23	.06
☐ 171 Gary DiSarcina	.50	.23	.06
☐ 172 Dave Fleming	.50	.23	.06
☐ 173 Wade Boggs	1.00	.45	.12
☐ 174 Kevin Appier	.75	.35	.09
☐ 175 Jose Bautista	.50	.23	.06
☐ 176 Wally Joyner	.75	.35	.09
☐ 177 Dean Palmer	.75	.35	.09
☐ 178 Tony Phillips	.75	.35	.09
☐ 179 John Smiley	.50	.23	.06
☐ 180 Charlie Hough	.50	.23	.06
☐ 181 Scott Fletcher	.50	.23	.06
☐ 182 Todd Van Poppel	.50	.23	.06
☐ 183 Mike Blowers	.50	.23	.06
☐ 184 Willie McGee	.50	.23	.06

□ 185	Paul Sorrento	.50	.23	.06
□ 186	Eric Young	.75	.35	.09
□ 187	Bret Barberie	.50	.23	.06
□ 188	Manuel Lee	.50	.23	.06
□ 189	Jeff Branson	.50	.23	.06
□ 190	Jim Deshaies	.50	.23	.06
□ 191	Ken Caminiti	1.00	.45	.12
□ 192	Tim Raines	1.00	.45	.12
□ 193	Joe Grahe	.50	.23	.06
□ 194	Hipolito Pichardo	.50	.23	.06
□ 195	Denny Neagle	.75	.35	.09
□ 196	Jeff Gardner	.50	.23	.06
□ 197	Mike Benjamin	.50	.23	.06
□ 198	Milt Thompson	.50	.23	.06
□ 199	Bruce Ruffin	.50	.23	.06
□ 200	Chris Hammond UER (Back of card has Mariners; should be Marlins)	.50	.23	.06
□ 201	Tony Gwynn FIN	5.00	2.20	.60
□ 202	Robin Ventura FIN	.75	.35	.09
□ 203	Frank Thomas FIN	12.00	5.50	1.50
□ 204	Kirby Puckett FIN	4.00	1.80	.50
□ 205	Roberto Alomar FIN	3.00	1.35	.35
□ 206	Dennis Eckersley FIN	.75	.35	.09
□ 207	Joe Carter FIN	1.00	.45	.12
□ 208	Albert Belle FIN	6.00	2.70	.75
□ 209	Greg Maddux FIN	8.00	3.60	1.00
□ 210	Ryne Sandberg FIN	3.00	1.35	.35
□ 211	Juan Gonzalez FIN	6.00	2.70	.75
□ 212	Jeff Bagwell FIN	5.00	2.20	.60
□ 213	Randy Johnson FIN	2.00	.90	.25
□ 214	Matt Williams FIN	1.50	.70	.19
□ 215	Dave Winfield FIN	1.00	.45	.12
□ 216	Larry Walker FIN	1.00	.45	.12
□ 217	Roger Clemens FIN	1.00	.45	.12
□ 218	Kenny Lofton FIN	4.00	1.80	.50
□ 219	Cecil Fielder FIN	.75	.35	.09
□ 220	Darren Daulton FIN	.75	.35	.09
□ 221	John Olerud FIN	.50	.23	.06
□ 222	Jose Canseco FIN	1.00	.45	.12
□ 223	Rickey Henderson FIN	1.00	.45	.12
□ 224	Fred McGriff FIN	1.00	.45	.12
□ 225	Gary Sheffield FIN	2.00	.90	.25
□ 226	Jack McDowell FIN	.75	.35	.09
□ 227	Rafael Palmeiro FIN	1.00	.45	.12
□ 228	Travis Fryman FIN	1.00	.45	.12
□ 229	Marquis Grissom FIN	1.00	.45	.12
□ 230	Barry Bonds FIN	3.00	1.35	.35
□ 231	Carlos Baerga FIN	1.00	.45	.12
□ 232	Ken Griffey Jr. FIN	12.00	5.50	1.50
□ 233	David Justice FIN	1.00	.45	.12
□ 234	Bobby Bonilla FIN	.75	.35	.09
□ 235	Cal Ripken FIN	10.00	4.50	1.25
□ 236	Sammy Sosa FIN	2.00	.90	.25
□ 237	Len Dykstra FIN	.75	.35	.09
□ 238	Will Clark FIN	1.00	.45	.12
□ 239	Paul Molitor FIN	2.50	1.10	.30
□ 240	Barry Larkin FIN	1.50	.70	.19
□ 241	Bo Jackson	1.00	.45	.12
□ 242	Mitch Williams	.50	.23	.06
□ 243	Ron Darling	.50	.23	.06
□ 244	Darryl Kile	.50	.23	.06
□ 245	Geronimo Berroa	.75	.35	.09
□ 246	Gregg Olson	.50	.23	.06
□ 247	Brian Harper	.50	.23	.06
□ 248	Rheal Cormier	.50	.23	.06
□ 249	Rey Sanchez	.50	.23	.06
□ 250	Jeff Fassero	.50	.23	.06
□ 251	Sandy Alomar	.75	.35	.09
□ 252	Chris Bosio	.50	.23	.06
□ 253	Andy Stankiewicz	.50	.23	.06
□ 254	Harold Baines	.75	.35	.09
□ 255	Andy Ashby	.75	.35	.09
□ 256	Tyler Green	.50	.23	.06
□ 257	Kevin Brown	.50	.23	.06
□ 258	Mo Vaughn	3.00	1.35	.35
□ 259	Mike Harkey	.50	.23	.06
□ 260	Dave Henderson	.50	.23	.06
□ 261	Kent Hrbek	.75	.35	.09
□ 262	Darrin Jackson	.50	.23	.06
□ 263	Bob Wickman	.50	.23	.06
□ 264	Spike Owen	.50	.23	.06
□ 265	Todd Jones	.50	.23	.06
□ 266	Pat Borders	.50	.23	.06
□ 267	Tom Glavine	1.00	.45	.12
□ 268	Dave Nilsson	.75	.35	.09
□ 269	Rich Batchelor	.50	.23	.06
□ 270	Delino DeShields	.50	.23	.06
□ 271	Felix Fermin	.50	.23	.06
□ 272	Orestes Destrade	.50	.23	.06
□ 273	Mickey Morandini	.50	.23	.06
□ 274	Otis Nixon	.50	.23	.06
□ 275	Ellis Burks	.75	.35	.09
□ 276	Greg Gagne	.50	.23	.06
□ 277	John Doherty	.50	.23	.06
□ 278	Julio Franco	.75	.35	.09
□ 279	Bernie Williams	2.00	.90	.25
□ 280	Rick Aguilera	.50	.23	.06
□ 281	Mickey Tettleton	.50	.23	.06
□ 282	David Nied	.50	.23	.06
□ 283	Johnny Ruffin	.50	.23	.06
□ 284	Dan Wilson	.75	.35	.09
□ 285	Omar Vizquel	1.00	.45	.12
□ 286	Willie Banks	.50	.23	.06
□ 287	Erik Pappas	.50	.23	.06
□ 288	Cal Eldred	.50	.23	.06
□ 289	Bobby Witt	.50	.23	.06
□ 290	Luis Gonzalez	.50	.23	.06
□ 291	Greg Pirkl	.50	.23	.06
□ 292	Alex Cole	.50	.23	.06
□ 293	Ricky Bones	.50	.23	.06
□ 294	Denis Boucher	.50	.23	.06
□ 295	John Burkett	.50	.23	.06
□ 296	Steve Trachsel	.75	.35	.09
□ 297	Ricky Jordan	.50	.23	.06
□ 298	Mark Dewey	.50	.23	.06
□ 299	Jimmy Key	.75	.35	.09
□ 300	Mike Macfarlane	.50	.23	.06
□ 301	Tim Belcher	.50	.23	.06
□ 302	Carlos Reyes	.50	.23	.06
□ 303	Greg A. Harris	.50	.23	.06
□ 304	Brian Anderson	.75	.35	.09
□ 305	Terry Mulholland	.50	.23	.06
□ 306	Felix Jose	.50	.23	.06
□ 307	Darren Holmes	.50	.23	.06
□ 308	Jose Rijo	.50	.23	.06
□ 309	Paul Wagner	.50	.23	.06
□ 310	Bob Scanlan	.50	.23	.06
□ 311	Mike Jackson	.50	.23	.06
□ 312	Jose Vizcaino	.50	.23	.06
□ 313	Rob Butler	.50	.23	.06
□ 314	Kevin Seitzer	.50	.23	.06
□ 315	Geronimo Pena	.50	.23	.06
□ 316	Hector Carrasco	.50	.23	.06
□ 317	Eddie Murray	3.00	1.35	.35
□ 318	Roger Salkeld	.50	.23	.06
□ 319	Todd Hundley	1.00	.45	.12
□ 320	Danny Jackson	.50	.23	.06
□ 321	Kevin Young	.50	.23	.06
□ 322	Mike Greenwell	.50	.23	.06
□ 323	Kevin Mitchell	.75	.35	.09
□ 324	Chuck Knoblauch	1.00	.45	.12
□ 325	Danny Tartabull	.50	.23	.06
□ 326	Vince Coleman	.50	.23	.06
□ 327	Marvin Freeman	.50	.23	.06
□ 328	Andy Benes	.75	.35	.09
□ 329	Mike Kelly	.50	.23	.06
□ 330	Karl Rhodes	.50	.23	.06
□ 331	Allen Watson	.50	.23	.06
□ 332	Damion Easley	.50	.23	.06
□ 333	Reggie Jefferson	.75	.35	.09
□ 334	Kevin McReynolds	.50	.23	.06
□ 335	Arthur Rhodes	.50	.23	.06
□ 336	Brian R. Hunter	.50	.23	.06
□ 337	Tom Browning	.50	.23	.06
□ 338	Pedro Munoz	.50	.23	.06
□ 339	Billy Ripken	.50	.23	.06
□ 340	Gene Harris	.50	.23	.06
□ 341	Fernando Vina	.50	.23	.06
□ 342	Sean Berry	.50	.23	.06
□ 343	Pedro Astacio	.50	.23	.06
□ 344	B.J. Surhoff	.50	.23	.06
□ 345	Doug Drabek	.50	.23	.06
□ 346	Jody Reed	.50	.23	.06
□ 347	Ray Lankford	1.00	.45	.12
□ 348	Steve Farr	.50	.23	.06
□ 349	Eric Anthony	.50	.23	.06
□ 350	Pete Smith	.50	.23	.06
□ 351	Lee Smith	.75	.35	.09
□ 352	Mariano Duncan	.50	.23	.06
□ 353	Doug Strange	.50	.23	.06
□ 354	Tim Bogar	.50	.23	.06

□ 355 Dave Weathers	.50	.23	.06
□ 356 Eric Karros	.75	.35	.09
□ 357 Randy Myers	.50	.23	.06
□ 358 Chad Curtis	.50	.23	.06
□ 359 Steve Avery	.75	.35	.09
□ 360 Brian Jordan	1.00	.45	.12
□ 361 Tim Wallach	.50	.23	.06
□ 362 Pedro Martinez	1.00	.45	.12
□ 363 Bip Roberts	.50	.23	.06
□ 364 Lou Whitaker	1.00	.45	.12
□ 365 Luis Polonia	.50	.23	.06
□ 366 Benny Santiago	.50	.23	.06
□ 367 Brett Butler	.75	.35	.09
□ 368 Shawon Dunston	.50	.23	.06
□ 369 Kelly Stinnett	.50	.23	.06
□ 370 Chris Turner	.50	.23	.06
□ 371 Ruben Sierra	.75	.35	.09
□ 372 Greg A. Harris	.50	.23	.06
□ 373 Xavier Hernandez	.50	.23	.06
□ 374 Howard Johnson	.50	.23	.06
□ 375 Duane Ward	.50	.23	.06
□ 376 Roberto Hernandez	.75	.35	.09
□ 377 Scott Leius	.50	.23	.06
□ 378 Dave Valle	.50	.23	.06
□ 379 Sid Fernandez	.50	.23	.06
□ 380 Doug Jones	.50	.23	.06
□ 381 Zane Smith	.50	.23	.06
□ 382 Craig Biggio	1.00	.45	.12
□ 383 Rick White	.50	.23	.06
□ 384 Tom Pagnozzi	.50	.23	.06
□ 385 Chris James	.50	.23	.06
□ 386 Bret Boone	.75	.35	.09
□ 387 Jeff Montgomery	.75	.35	.09
□ 388 Chad Kreuter	.50	.23	.06
□ 389 Greg Hibbard	.50	.23	.06
□ 390 Mark Grace	1.00	.45	.12
□ 391 Phil Leftwich	.50	.23	.06
□ 392 Don Mattingly	6.00	2.70	.75
□ 393 Ozzie Guillen	.50	.23	.06
□ 394 Gary Gaetti	.75	.35	.09
□ 395 Erik Hanson	.50	.23	.06
□ 396 Scott Brosius	.50	.23	.06
□ 397 Tom Gordon	.50	.23	.06
□ 398 Bill Gullickson	.50	.23	.06
□ 399 Matt Mieske	.50	.23	.06
□ 400 Pat Hentgen	1.00	.45	.12
□ 401 Walt Weiss	.50	.23	.06
□ 402 Greg Blosser	.50	.23	.06
□ 403 Stan Javier	.50	.23	.06
□ 404 Doug Henry	.50	.23	.06
□ 405 Ramon Martinez	.75	.35	.09
□ 406 Frank Viola	.50	.23	.06
□ 407 Mike Hampton	.50	.23	.06
□ 408 Andy Van Slyke	.75	.35	.09
□ 409 Bobby Ayala	.50	.23	.06
□ 410 Todd Zeile	.50	.23	.06
□ 411 Jay Bell	.75	.35	.09
□ 412 Denny Martinez	.75	.35	.09
□ 413 Mark Portugal	.50	.23	.06
□ 414 Bobby Munoz	.50	.23	.06
□ 415 Kirt Manwaring	.50	.23	.06
□ 416 John Kruk	.75	.35	.09
□ 417 Trevor Hoffman	.75	.35	.09
□ 418 Chris Sabo	.50	.23	.06
□ 419 Bret Saberhagen	.75	.35	.09
□ 420 Chris Nabholz	.50	.23	.06
□ 421 James Mouton FIN	.75	.35	.09
□ 422 Tony Tarasco FIN	.50	.23	.06
□ 423 Carlos Delgado FIN	2.00	.90	.25
□ 424 Rondell White FIN	1.00	.45	.12
□ 425 Javier Lopez FIN	1.50	.70	.19
□ 426 Chan Ho Park FIN	3.00	1.35	.35
□ 427 Cliff Floyd FIN	1.00	.45	.12
□ 428 Dave Staton FIN	.50	.23	.06
□ 429 J.R. Phillips FIN	.50	.23	.06
□ 430 Manny Ramirez FIN	4.00	1.80	.50
□ 431 Kurt Abbott FIN	.75	.35	.09
□ 432 Melvin Nieves FIN	.75	.35	.09
□ 433 Alex Gonzalez FIN	.75	.35	.09
□ 434 Rick Helling FIN	.50	.23	.06
□ 435 Danny Bautista FIN	.50	.23	.06
□ 436 Matt Walbeck FIN	.50	.23	.06
□ 437 Ryan Klesko FIN	3.00	1.35	.35
□ 438 Steve Karsay FIN	.50	.23	.06
□ 439 Salomon Torres FIN	.50	.23	.06
□ 440 Scott Ruffcorn FIN	.50	.23	.06

1994 Finest Refractors

The 1994 Topps Finest Refractors baseball set consists of two series of 220 cards each, for a total of 440 cards. These special cards were inserted at a rate of one in every nine packs. They are identical to the basic Finest card except for a more intense luster and 3-D appearance.

	MINT	NRMT	EXC
COMPLETE SET (440)	2800.00	1250.00	350.00
COMPLETE SERIES 1 (220)	1400.00	650.00	180.00
COMPLETE SERIES 2 (220)	1400.00	650.00	180.00
COMMON CARD (1-440)	3.00	1.35	.35
SEMISTARS	6.00	2.70	.75
STARS	12.00	5.50	1.50
*VETERAN STARS: 5X to 10X BASIC CARDS			
*YOUNG STARS: 3X to 6X BASIC CARDS....			
RANDOM INSERTS IN PACKS			

□ 1 Mike Piazza FIN	80.00	36.00	10.00
□ 18 Tim Salmon FIN	20.00	9.00	2.50
□ 35 Andres Galarraga	15.00	6.75	1.85
□ 59 Dante Bichette	15.00	6.75	1.85
□ 66 Mike Mussina	25.00	11.00	3.10
□ 74 Raul Mondesi	20.00	9.00	2.50
□ 78 Mark McGwire	40.00	18.00	5.00
□ 100 John Smoltz	20.00	9.00	2.50
□ 102 Jim Thome	30.00	13.50	3.70
□ 122 Jay Buhner	20.00	9.00	2.50
□ 126 Ivan Rodriguez	25.00	11.00	3.10
□ 131 Brady Anderson	20.00	9.00	2.50
□ 136 Ozzie Smith	25.00	11.00	3.10
□ 154 Edgar Martinez	15.00	6.75	1.85
□ 173 Wade Boggs	15.00	6.75	1.85
□ 201 Tony Gwynn FIN	50.00	22.00	6.25
□ 203 Frank Thomas FIN	125.00	55.00	15.50
□ 204 Kirby Puckett FIN	40.00	18.00	5.00
□ 205 Roberto Alomar FIN	30.00	13.50	3.70
□ 208 Albert Belle FIN	60.00	27.00	7.50
□ 209 Greg Maddux FIN	80.00	36.00	10.00
□ 210 Ryne Sandberg FIN	30.00	13.50	3.70
□ 211 Juan Gonzalez FIN	60.00	27.00	7.50
□ 212 Jeff Bagwell FIN	50.00	22.00	6.25
□ 213 Randy Johnson FIN	20.00	9.00	2.50
□ 214 Matt Williams FIN	15.00	6.75	1.85
□ 215 Dave Winfield FIN	15.00	6.75	1.85
□ 217 Roger Clemens FIN	15.00	6.75	1.85
□ 218 Kenny Lofton FIN	40.00	18.00	5.00
□ 222 Jose Canseco FIN	15.00	6.75	1.85
□ 223 Rickey Henderson FIN	15.00	6.75	1.85
□ 224 Fred McGriff FIN	15.00	6.75	1.85
□ 225 Gary Sheffield FIN	20.00	9.00	2.50
□ 227 Rafael Palmeiro FIN	15.00	6.75	1.85
□ 230 Barry Bonds FIN	40.00	18.00	5.00
□ 232 Ken Griffey Jr. FIN	125.00	55.00	15.50
□ 235 Cal Ripken FIN	100.00	45.00	12.50
□ 236 Sammy Sosa FIN	20.00	9.00	2.50
□ 238 Will Clark FIN	15.00	6.75	1.85
□ 239 Paul Molitor FIN	25.00	11.00	3.10
□ 240 Barry Larkin FIN	15.00	6.75	1.85
□ 258 Mo Vaughn	30.00	13.50	3.70
□ 279 Bernie Williams	25.00	11.00	3.10
□ 317 Eddie Murray	30.00	13.50	3.70
□ 319 Todd Hundley	15.00	6.75	1.85
□ 324 Chuck Knoblauch	20.00	9.00	2.50
□ 392 Don Mattingly	60.00	27.00	7.50
□ 426 Chan Ho Park FIN	15.00	6.75	1.85

□ 430 Manny Ramirez FIN	40.00	18.00	5.00
□ 437 Ryan Klesko FIN	30.00	13.50	3.70

1995 Finest

Consisting of 330 standard-size cards, this set was issued in series of 220 and 110. A protective film, designed to keep the card from scratching and to maintain original gloss, covers the front. With the Finest logo at the top, a silver baseball diamond design surrounded by green (field) form the background to an action photo. Horizontally designed backs have a photo to the right with statistical information to the left. A Finest Moment, or career highlight, is also included. Rookie Cards in this set include Hideo Nomo and Carlos Perez.

	MINT	NRMT	EXC
COMPLETE SET (330)	125.00	55.00	15.50
COMPLETE SERIES 1 (220)	80.00	36.00	10.00
COMPLETE SERIES 2 (110)	45.00	20.00	5.50
COMMON CARD (1-330)	.25	.11	.03
SEMISTARS	.50	.23	.06
STARS	1.25	.55	.16

□ 1 Raul Mondesi	1.25	.55	.16
□ 2 Kurt Abbott	.25	.11	.03
□ 3 Chris Gomez	.25	.11	.03
□ 4 Manny Ramirez	2.50	1.10	.30
□ 5 Rondell White	1.25	.55	.16
□ 6 William VanLandingham	.25	.11	.03
□ 7 Jon Lieber	.25	.11	.03
□ 8 Ryan Klesko	2.00	.90	.25
□ 9 John Hudek	.25	.11	.03
□ 10 Joey Hamilton	1.50	.70	.19
□ 11 Bob Hamelin	.25	.11	.03
□ 12 Brian Anderson	.25	.11	.03
□ 13 Mike Lieberthal	.25	.11	.03
□ 14 Rico Brogna	.25	.11	.03
□ 15 Rusty Greer	1.25	.55	.16
□ 16 Carlos Delgado	1.25	.55	.16
□ 17 Jim Edmonds	1.25	.55	.16
□ 18 Steve Trachsel	.25	.11	.03
□ 19 Matt Walbeck	.25	.11	.03
□ 20 Armando Benitez	.25	.11	.03
□ 21 Steve Karsay	.25	.11	.03
□ 22 Jose Oliva	.25	.11	.03
□ 23 Cliff Floyd	.50	.23	.06
□ 24 Kevin Foster	.25	.11	.03
□ 25 Javier Lopez	1.25	.55	.16
□ 26 Jose Valentin	.50	.23	.06
□ 27 James Mouton	.25	.11	.03
□ 28 Hector Carrasco	.25	.11	.03
□ 29 Orlando Miller	.25	.11	.03
□ 30 Garret Anderson	1.25	.55	.16
□ 31 Marvin Freeman	.25	.11	.03
□ 32 Brett Butler	.50	.23	.06
□ 33 Roberto Kelly	.25	.11	.03
□ 34 Rod Beck	.25	.11	.03
□ 35 Jose Rijo	.25	.11	.03
□ 36 Edgar Martinez	1.25	.55	.16
□ 37 Jim Thome	2.00	.90	.25
□ 38 Rick Wilkins	.25	.11	.03
□ 39 Wally Joyner	.50	.23	.06
□ 40 Wil Cordero	.25	.11	.03
□ 41 Tommy Greene	.25	.11	.03
□ 42 Travis Fryman	.50	.23	.06
□ 43 Don Slaught	.25	.11	.03
□ 44 Brady Anderson	1.25	.55	.16
□ 45 Matt Williams	1.25	.55	.16
□ 46 Rene Arocha	.25	.11	.03
□ 47 Rickey Henderson	1.25	.55	.16
□ 48 Mike Mussina	2.00	.90	.25
□ 49 Greg McMichael	.25	.11	.03
□ 50 Jody Reed	.25	.11	.03
□ 51 Tino Martinez	.50	.23	.06
□ 52 Dave Clark	.25	.11	.03
□ 53 John Valentin	.50	.23	.06
□ 54 Bret Boone	.50	.23	.06
□ 55 Walt Weiss	.25	.11	.03
□ 56 Kenny Lofton	2.50	1.10	.30
□ 57 Scott Leius	.25	.11	.03
□ 58 Eric Karros	.50	.23	.06
□ 59 John Olerud	.25	.11	.03
□ 60 Chris Hoiles	.25	.11	.03
□ 61 Sandy Alomar Jr.	.25	.11	.03
□ 62 Tim Wallach	.25	.11	.03
□ 63 Cal Eldred	.25	.11	.03
□ 64 Tom Glavine	1.25	.55	.16
□ 65 Mark Grace	1.25	.55	.16
□ 66 Rey Sanchez	.25	.11	.03
□ 67 Bobby Ayala	.25	.11	.03
□ 68 Dante Bichette	1.25	.55	.16
□ 69 Andres Galarraga	1.25	.55	.16
□ 70 Chuck Carr	.25	.11	.03
□ 71 Bobby Witt	.25	.11	.03
□ 72 Steve Avery	.50	.23	.06
□ 73 Bobby Jones	.50	.23	.06
□ 74 Delino DeShields	.25	.11	.03
□ 75 Kevin Tapani	.25	.11	.03
□ 76 Randy Johnson	1.50	.70	.19
□ 77 David Nied	.25	.11	.03
□ 78 Pat Hentgen	.50	.23	.06
□ 79 Tim Salmon	1.25	.55	.16
□ 80 Todd Zeile	.25	.11	.03
□ 81 John Wetteland	.50	.23	.06
□ 82 Albert Belle	5.00	2.20	.60
□ 83 Ben McDonald	.25	.11	.03
□ 84 Bobby Munoz	.25	.11	.03
□ 85 Bip Roberts	.25	.11	.03
□ 86 Mo Vaughn	2.50	1.10	.30
□ 87 Chuck Finley	.50	.23	.06
□ 88 Chuck Knoblauch	1.25	.55	.16
□ 89 Frank Thomas	10.00	4.50	1.25
□ 90 Danny Tartabull	.25	.11	.03
□ 91 Dean Palmer	.50	.23	.06
□ 92 Len Dykstra	.50	.23	.06
□ 93 J.R. Phillips	.25	.11	.03
□ 94 Tom Candiotti	.25	.11	.03
□ 95 Marquis Grissom	1.25	.55	.16
□ 96 Barry Larkin	1.25	.55	.16
□ 97 Bryan Harvey	.25	.11	.03
□ 98 David Justice	1.25	.55	.16
□ 99 David Cone	.50	.23	.06
□ 100 Wade Boggs	1.25	.55	.16
□ 101 Jason Bere	.25	.11	.03
□ 102 Hal Morris	.25	.11	.03
□ 103 Fred McGriff	1.25	.55	.16
□ 104 Bobby Bonilla	.50	.23	.06
□ 105 Jay Buhner	1.25	.55	.16
□ 106 Allen Watson	.25	.11	.03
□ 107 Mickey Tettleton	.25	.11	.03
□ 108 Kevin Appier	.50	.23	.06
□ 109 Ivan Rodriguez	2.00	.90	.25
□ 110 Carlos Garcia	.25	.11	.03
□ 111 Andy Benes	.25	.11	.03
□ 112 Eddie Murray	2.50	1.10	.30
□ 113 Mike Piazza	6.00	2.70	.75
□ 114 Greg Vaughn	.50	.23	.06
□ 115 Paul Molitor	2.00	.90	.25
□ 116 Terry Steinbach	.50	.23	.06
□ 117 Jeff Bagwell	4.00	1.80	.50
□ 118 Ken Griffey Jr.	10.00	4.50	1.25
□ 119 Gary Sheffield	1.50	.70	.19
□ 120 Cal Ripken	8.00	3.60	1.00
□ 121 Jeff Kent	.25	.11	.03
□ 122 Jay Bell	.50	.23	.06
□ 123 Will Clark	1.25	.55	.16
□ 124 Cecil Fielder	.50	.23	.06
□ 125 Alex Fernandez	.50	.23	.06
□ 126 Don Mattingly	5.00	2.20	.60
□ 127 Reggie Sanders	.50	.23	.06
□ 128 Moises Alou	.50	.23	.06
□ 129 Craig Biggio	1.25	.55	.16

☐ 130 Eddie Williams	.25	.11	.03
☐ 131 John Franco	.25	.11	.03
☐ 132 John Kruk	.50	.23	.06
☐ 133 Jeff King	.50	.23	.06
☐ 134 Royce Clayton	.25	.11	.03
☐ 135 Doug Drabek	.25	.11	.03
☐ 136 Ray Lankford	1.25	.55	.16
☐ 137 Roberto Alomar	2.50	1.10	.30
☐ 138 Todd Hundley	.50	.23	.06
☐ 139 Alex Cole	.25	.11	.03
☐ 140 Shawon Dunston	.25	.11	.03
☐ 141 John Roper	.25	.11	.03
☐ 142 Mark Langston	.25	.11	.03
☐ 143 Tom Pagnozzi	.25	.11	.03
☐ 144 Wilson Alvarez	.50	.23	.06
☐ 145 Scott Cooper	.25	.11	.03
☐ 146 Kevin Mitchell	.50	.23	.06
☐ 147 Mark Whiten	.25	.11	.03
☐ 148 Jeff Conine	1.25	.55	.16
☐ 149 Chili Davis	.50	.23	.06
☐ 150 Luis Gonzalez	.25	.11	.03
☐ 151 Juan Guzman	.50	.23	.06
☐ 152 Mike Greenwell	.25	.11	.03
☐ 153 Mike Henneman	.25	.11	.03
☐ 154 Rick Aguilera	.25	.11	.03
☐ 155 Dennis Eckersley	.50	.23	.06
☐ 156 Darrin Fletcher	.25	.11	.03
☐ 157 Darren Lewis	.25	.11	.03
☐ 158 Juan Gonzalez	5.00	2.20	.60
☐ 159 Dave Hollins	.25	.11	.03
☐ 160 Jimmy Key	.50	.23	.06
☐ 161 Roberto Hernandez	.25	.11	.03
☐ 162 Randy Myers	.25	.11	.03
☐ 163 Joe Carter	1.25	.55	.16
☐ 164 Darren Daulton	.50	.23	.06
☐ 165 Mike Macfarlane	.25	.11	.03
☐ 166 Bret Saberhagen	.50	.23	.06
☐ 167 Kirby Puckett	3.00	1.35	.35
☐ 168 Lance Johnson	.50	.23	.06
☐ 169 Mark McGwire	3.00	1.35	.35
☐ 170 Jose Canseco	1.25	.55	.16
☐ 171 Mike Stanley	.25	.11	.03
☐ 172 Lee Smith	.50	.23	.06
☐ 173 Robin Ventura	.50	.23	.06
☐ 174 Greg Gagne	.25	.11	.03
☐ 175 Brian McRae	.50	.23	.06
☐ 176 Mike Bordick	.25	.11	.03
☐ 177 Rafael Palmeiro	1.25	.55	.16
☐ 178 Kenny Rogers	.25	.11	.03
☐ 179 Chad Curtis	.25	.11	.03
☐ 180 Devon White	.50	.23	.06
☐ 181 Paul O'Neill	.50	.23	.06
☐ 182 Ken Caminiti	1.25	.55	.16
☐ 183 Dave Nilsson	.50	.23	.06
☐ 184 Tim Naehring	.25	.11	.03
☐ 185 Roger Clemens	1.25	.55	.16
☐ 186 Otis Nixon	.25	.11	.03
☐ 187 Tim Raines	1.25	.55	.16
☐ 188 Denny Martinez	.50	.23	.06
☐ 189 Pedro Martinez	.50	.23	.06
☐ 190 Jim Abbott	.25	.11	.03
☐ 191 Ryan Thompson	.25	.11	.03
☐ 192 Barry Bonds	2.50	1.10	.30
☐ 193 Joe Girardi	.25	.11	.03
☐ 194 Steve Finley	.50	.23	.06
☐ 195 John Jaha	.50	.23	.06
☐ 196 Tony Gwynn	4.00	1.80	.50
☐ 197 Sammy Sosa	1.50	.70	.19
☐ 198 John Burkett	.50	.23	.06
☐ 199 Carlos Baerga	1.25	.55	.16
☐ 200 Ramon Martinez	.50	.23	.06
☐ 201 Aaron Sele	.50	.23	.06
☐ 202 Eduardo Perez	.25	.11	.03
☐ 203 Alan Trammell	1.25	.55	.16
☐ 204 Orlando Merced	.25	.11	.03
☐ 205 Deion Sanders	1.25	.55	.16
☐ 206 Robb Nen	.25	.11	.03
☐ 207 Jack McDowell	.50	.23	.06
☐ 208 Ruben Sierra	.50	.23	.06
☐ 209 Bernie Williams	1.50	.70	.19
☐ 210 Kevin Seitzer	.25	.11	.03
☐ 211 Charles Nagy	.50	.23	.06
☐ 212 Tony Phillips	.50	.23	.06
☐ 213 Greg Maddux	6.00	2.70	.75
☐ 214 Jeff Montgomery	.50	.23	.06
☐ 215 Larry Walker	1.25	.55	.16
☐ 216 Andy Van Slyke	.50	.23	.06
☐ 217 Ozzie Smith	2.00	.90	.25
☐ 218 Geronimo Pena	.25	.11	.03
☐ 219 Gregg Jefferies	.50	.23	.06
☐ 220 Lou Whitaker	1.25	.55	.16
☐ 221 Chipper Jones	6.00	2.70	.75
☐ 222 Benji Gil	.25	.11	.03
☐ 223 Tony Phillips	.50	.23	.06
☐ 224 Trevor Wilson	.25	.11	.03
☐ 225 Tony Tarasco	.25	.11	.03
☐ 226 Roberto Petagine	.25	.11	.03
☐ 227 Mike Macfarlane	.25	.11	.03
☐ 228 Hideo Nomo UER (In 3rd line agianst)	10.00	4.50	1.25
☐ 229 Mark McLemore	.25	.11	.03
☐ 230 Ron Gant	.50	.23	.06
☐ 231 Andujar Cedeno	.25	.11	.03
☐ 232 Mike Mimbs	.50	.23	.06
☐ 233 Jim Abbott	.25	.11	.03
☐ 234 Ricky Bones	.25	.11	.03
☐ 235 Marty Cordova	1.50	.70	.19
☐ 236 Mark Johnson	.50	.23	.06
☐ 237 Marquis Grissom	1.25	.55	.16
☐ 238 Tom Henke	.25	.11	.03
☐ 239 Terry Pendleton	.50	.23	.06
☐ 240 John Wetteland	.50	.23	.06
☐ 241 Lee Smith	.50	.23	.06
☐ 242 Jaime Navarro	.25	.11	.03
☐ 243 Luis Alicea	.25	.11	.03
☐ 244 Scott Cooper	.25	.11	.03
☐ 245 Gary Gaetti	.50	.23	.06
☐ 246 Edgardo Alfonzo UER (Incomplete career BA)	.50	.23	.06
☐ 247 Brad Clontz	.25	.11	.03
☐ 248 Dave Mlicki	.25	.11	.03
☐ 249 Dave Winfield	1.25	.55	.16
☐ 250 Mark Grudzielanek	2.50	1.10	.30
☐ 251 Alex Gonzalez	.25	.11	.03
☐ 252 Kevin Brown	.50	.23	.06
☐ 253 Esteban Loaiza	.25	.11	.03
☐ 254 Vaughn Eshelman	.25	.11	.03
☐ 255 Bill Swift	.25	.11	.03
☐ 256 Brian McRae	.50	.23	.06
☐ 257 Bobby Higginson	1.50	.70	.19
☐ 258 Jack McDowell	.50	.23	.06
☐ 259 Scott Stahoviak	.25	.11	.03
☐ 260 Jon Nunnally	.50	.23	.06
☐ 261 Charlie Hayes	.25	.11	.03
☐ 262 Jacob Brumfield	.25	.11	.03
☐ 263 Chad Curtis	.25	.11	.03
☐ 264 Heathcliff Slocumb	.25	.11	.03
☐ 265 Mark Whiten	.25	.11	.03
☐ 266 Mickey Tettleton	.25	.11	.03
☐ 267 Jose Mesa	.25	.11	.03
☐ 268 Doug Jones	.25	.11	.03
☐ 269 Trevor Hoffman	.25	.11	.03
☐ 270 Paul Sorrento	.25	.11	.03
☐ 271 Shane Andrews	.25	.11	.03
☐ 272 Brett Butler	.50	.23	.06
☐ 273 Curtis Goodwin	.50	.23	.06
☐ 274 Larry Walker	1.25	.55	.16
☐ 275 Phil Plantier	.25	.11	.03
☐ 276 Ken Hill	.25	.11	.03
☐ 277 Vinny Castilla UER Rockies spelled Rockie	.50	.23	.06
☐ 278 Billy Ashley	.25	.11	.03
☐ 279 Derek Jeter	6.00	2.70	.75
☐ 280 Bob Tewksbury	.25	.11	.03
☐ 281 Jose Offerman	.25	.11	.03
☐ 282 Glenallen Hill	.25	.11	.03
☐ 283 Tony Fernandez	.25	.11	.03
☐ 284 Mike Devereaux	.25	.11	.03
☐ 285 John Burkett	.50	.23	.06
☐ 286 Geronimo Berroa	.25	.11	.03
☐ 287 Quilvio Veras	.25	.11	.03
☐ 288 Jason Bates	.25	.11	.03
☐ 289 Lee Tinsley	.25	.11	.03
☐ 290 Derek Bell	.50	.23	.06
☐ 291 Jeff Fassero	.25	.11	.03
☐ 292 Ray Durham	.50	.23	.06
☐ 293 Chad Ogea	.25	.11	.03
☐ 294 Bill Pulsipher	.50	.23	.06
☐ 295 Phil Nevin	.25	.11	.03
☐ 296 Carlos Perez	.50	.23	.06
☐ 297 Roberto Kelly	.25	.11	.03
☐ 298 Tim Wakefield	.25	.11	.03

□ 299 Jeff Manto	.25	.11	.03
□ 300 Brian Hunter	1.25	.55	.16
□ 301 C.J. Nitkowski	.50	.23	.06
□ 302 Dustin Hermanson	.50	.23	.06
□ 303 John Mabry	1.25	.55	.16
□ 304 Orel Hershiser	.50	.23	.06
□ 305 Ron Villone	.25	.11	.03
□ 306 Sean Bergman	.25	.11	.03
□ 307 Tom Goodwin	.25	.11	.03
□ 308 Al Reyes	.25	.11	.03
□ 309 Todd Stottlemyre	.25	.11	.03
□ 310 Rich Becker	.25	.11	.03
□ 311 Joey Cora	.25	.11	.03
□ 312 Ed Sprague	.50	.23	.06
□ 313 John Smoltz UER	1.50	.70	.19
(3rd line; from spelled as form)			
□ 314 Frank Castillo	.25	.11	.03
□ 315 Chris Hammond	.25	.11	.03
□ 316 Ismael Valdes	.50	.23	.06
□ 317 Pete Harnisch	.25	.11	.03
□ 318 Bernard Gilkey	.50	.23	.06
□ 319 John Kruk	.50	.23	.06
□ 320 Marc Newfield	.50	.23	.06
□ 321 Brian Johnson	.25	.11	.03
□ 322 Mark Portugal	.25	.11	.03
□ 323 David Hulse	.25	.11	.03
□ 324 Luis Ortiz UER	.25	.11	.03
(Below spelled beloe)			
□ 325 Mike Benjamin	.25	.11	.03
□ 326 Brian Jordan	1.25	.55	.16
□ 327 Shawn Green	.50	.23	.06
□ 328 Joe Oliver	.25	.11	.03
□ 329 Felipe Lira	.25	.11	.03
□ 330 Andre Dawson	1.25	.55	.16

1995 Finest Refractors

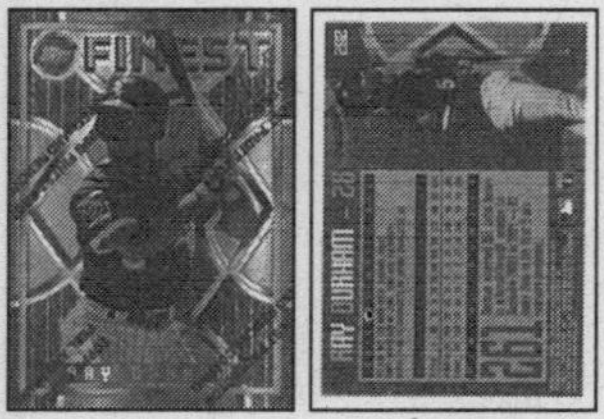

This set is a parallel to the basic Finest set, including the use of protective coating, the difference can be found in the refractive sheen. The cards were inserted at a rate of one in 12 packs.

	MINT	NRMT	EXC
COMPLETE SET (330)	4500.00	2000.00	550.00
COMPLETE SERIES 1 (220)	3500.00	1600.00	450.00
COMPLETE SERIES 2 (110)	1000.00	450.00	125.00
COMMON CARD (1-330)	10.00	4.50	1.25
COMPLETE SET (220)	15.00	6.75	1.85
STARS	30.00	13.50	3.70
*VETERAN STARS: 20X TO 30X BASIC CARDS			
*YOUNG STARS: 15X TO 25X BASIC CARDS			
RANDOM INSERTS IN PACKS			

□ 1 Raul Mondesi	40.00	18.00	5.00
□ 4 Manny Ramirez RT	80.00	36.00	10.00
□ 8 Ryan Klesko	60.00	27.00	7.50
□ 10 Joey Hamilton	40.00	18.00	5.00
□ 17 Jim Edmonds	40.00	18.00	5.00
□ 37 Jim Thome	60.00	27.00	7.50
□ 44 Brady Anderson	40.00	18.00	5.00
□ 45 Matt Williams	40.00	18.00	5.00
□ 48 Mike Mussina	60.00	27.00	7.50
□ 56 Kenny Lofton	80.00	36.00	10.00
□ 64 Tom Glavine	40.00	18.00	5.00
□ 68 Dante Bichette	40.00	18.00	5.00
□ 69 Andres Galarraga	40.00	18.00	5.00
□ 76 Randy Johnson	50.00	22.00	6.25
□ 79 Tim Salmon	40.00	18.00	5.00
□ 82 Albert Belle	150.00	70.00	19.00
□ 86 Mo Vaughn	80.00	36.00	10.00
□ 88 Chuck Knoblauch	50.00	22.00	6.25
□ 89 Frank Thomas	350.00	160.00	45.00
□ 96 Barry Larkin	40.00	18.00	5.00
□ 103 Fred McGriff	40.00	18.00	5.00
□ 105 Jay Buhner	40.00	18.00	5.00
□ 109 Ivan Rodriguez	60.00	27.00	7.50
□ 112 Eddie Murray	75.00	34.00	9.50
□ 113 Mike Piazza	200.00	90.00	25.00
□ 115 Paul Molitor	60.00	27.00	7.50
□ 117 Jeff Bagwell	125.00	55.00	15.50
□ 118 Ken Griffey Jr.	350.00	160.00	45.00
□ 119 Gary Sheffield	50.00	22.00	6.25
□ 120 Cal Ripken Jr.	300.00	135.00	38.00
□ 123 Will Clark	40.00	18.00	5.00
□ 126 Don Mattingly	150.00	70.00	19.00
□ 137 Roberto Alomar	80.00	36.00	10.00
□ 158 Juan Gonzalez	150.00	70.00	19.00
□ 167 Kirby Puckett	100.00	45.00	12.50
□ 169 Mark McGwire	100.00	45.00	12.50
□ 170 Jose Canseco	40.00	18.00	5.00
□ 177 Rafael Palmeiro	40.00	18.00	5.00
□ 185 Roger Clemens	40.00	18.00	5.00
□ 192 Barry Bonds	80.00	36.00	10.00
□ 196 Tony Gwynn	125.00	55.00	15.50
□ 197 Sammy Sosa	50.00	22.00	6.25
□ 209 Bernie Williams	50.00	22.00	6.25
□ 213 Greg Maddux !	300.00	135.00	38.00
□ 217 Ozzie Smith	60.00	27.00	7.50
□ 221 Chipper Jones	200.00	90.00	25.00
□ 228 Hideo Nomo	125.00	55.00	15.50
□ 235 Marty Cordova	40.00	18.00	5.00
□ 250 Mark Grudzielanek	40.00	18.00	5.00
□ 279 Derek Jeter	175.00	80.00	22.00
□ 300 Brian Hunter	40.00	18.00	5.00
□ 313 John Smoltz	50.00	22.00	6.25

1995 Finest Flame Throwers

Randomly inserted in packs, this nine-card set showcases strikeout leaders who bring on the heat. With a protective coating, a player photo is superimposed over a fiery orange background. The backs have a player photo with skills ratings such as velocity.

	MINT	NRMT	EXC
COMPLETE SET (9)	75.00	34.00	9.50
COMMON CARD (1-9)	8.00	3.60	1.00
RANDOM INSERTS IN PACKS			

□ FT1 Jason Bere	8.00	3.60	1.00
□ FT2 Roger Clemens	15.00	6.75	1.85
□ FT3 Juan Guzman	12.00	5.50	1.50
□ FT4 John Hudek	8.00	3.60	1.00
□ FT5 Randy Johnson	20.00	9.00	2.50
□ FT6 Pedro Martinez	12.00	5.50	1.50
□ FT7 Jose Rijo	8.00	3.60	1.00
□ FT8 Bret Saberhagen	8.00	3.60	1.00
□ FT9 John Wetteland	12.00	5.50	1.50

1995 Finest Power Kings

Randomly inserted at a rate of one in 24 packs, Power Kings is an 18-card set highlighting top sluggers. With a protective coating, the fronts feature chromium technology that allows the

player photo to be further enhanced as if to jump out from a blue lightning bolt background. The horizontal backs contain two small photos and power production figures.

	MINT	NRMT	EXC
COMPLETE SET (18)	200.00	90.00	25.00
COMMON CARD (1-18)	5.00	2.20	.60
RANDOM INSERTS IN PACKS			
□ PK1 Bob Hamelin	5.00	2.20	.60
□ PK2 Raul Mondesi	5.00	2.20	.60
□ PK3 Ryan Klesko	10.00	4.50	1.25
□ PK4 Carlos Delgado	6.00	2.70	.75
□ PK5 Manny Ramirez	12.00	5.50	1.50
□ PK6 Mike Piazza	30.00	13.50	3.70
□ PK7 Jeff Bagwell	20.00	9.00	2.50
□ PK8 Mo Vaughn	12.00	5.50	1.50
□ PK9 Frank Thomas	50.00	22.00	6.25
□ PK10 Ken Griffey Jr.	50.00	22.00	6.25
□ PK11 Albert Belle	25.00	11.00	3.10
□ PK12 Sammy Sosa	8.00	3.60	1.00
□ PK13 Dante Bichette	6.00	2.70	.75
□ PK14 Gary Sheffield	8.00	3.60	1.00
□ PK15 Matt Williams	6.00	2.70	.75
□ PK16 Fred McGriff	6.00	2.70	.75
□ PK17 Barry Bonds	12.00	5.50	1.50
□ PK18 Cecil Fielder	5.00	2.20	.60

1996 Finest

The 1996 Finest set was issued in two series of 191 cards and 168 cards respectively, for a total of 359 cards. A protective film, designed to keep the card from scratching and to maintain original gloss, covers the front. The six-card packs retail for $5.00 each and provide collectors with the opportunity to complete a number of sets within sets, each with a different degree of insertion. Each card is numbered twice to indicate the set count and the theme count. Series 1 set covers four distinct themes: Finest Phenoms, Finest Intimidators, Finest Gamers and Finest Sterling. Within the first three themes, some players will be common (bronze trim), some uncommon (silver) and some rare (gold). Finest Sterling consists of star players included within one of the other three themes, but featured with a new design and different photography. The breakdown for the player selection of common, uncommon and rare cards is completely random. There are 110 common, 55 uncommon (1:4 packs) and 25 rare cards (1:24 packs). Series 2 covers four distict themes also with common, uncommon and rare cards seeded at the same ratio. The four themes are: Finest Franchises which features 36 team leaders and bonafide superstars, Finest Additions which features 47 players who have switched teams in '96, Finest Prodigies which features 45 best up-and-coming players, and Finest Sterling with 39 top stars. In addition to the cards' special borders, each card will also have either "common," "uncommon", or "rare" written within the numbering box on the card backs to let collectors know which type of card they hold.

	MINT	NRMT	EXC
COMPLETE SET (359)	1500.00	700.00	190.00
COMPLETE SERIES 1 (191)	1000.00	450.00	125.00
COMPLETE SERIES 2 (168)	550.00	250.00	70.00
COMP.BRONZE SET (220)	70.00	32.00	8.75
COMP.BRONZE SER.1 (110)	30.00	13.50	3.70
COMP.BRONZE SER.2 (110)	40.00	18.00	5.00
COMMON BRONZE	.25	.11	.03
BRONZE SEMISTARS	.75	.35	.09
COMP.GOLD SET (48)	1200.00	550.00	150.00
COMP.GOLD SER.1 (26)	800.00	350.00	100.00
COMP.GOLD SER.2 (22)	400.00	180.00	50.00
COMMON GOLD	12.00	5.50	1.50
COMP.SILVER SET (91)	325.00	145.00	40.00
COMP.SILVER SER.1 (55)	200.00	90.00	25.00
COMP.SILVER SER.2 (36)	125.00	55.00	15.50
COMMON SILVER	2.50	1.10	.30
SILVER SEMISTARS	4.00	1.80	.50
SETS ARE SKIP-NUMBERED BY COLOR			
□ B5 Roberto Hernandez B	.25	.11	.03
□ B8 Terry Pendleton B	.50	.23	.06
□ B12 Ken Caminiti B	.75	.35	.09
□ B15 Dan Miceli B	.25	.11	.03
□ B16 Chipper Jones B	4.00	1.80	.50
□ B17 John Wetteland B	.50	.23	.06
□ B19 Tim Naehring B	.25	.11	.03
□ B21 Eddie Murray B	1.50	.70	.19
□ B23 Kevin Appier B	.50	.23	.06
□ B24 Ken Griffey Jr. B	6.00	2.70	.75
□ B26 Brian McRae B	.50	.23	.06
□ B27 Pedro Martinez B	.50	.23	.06
□ B28 Brian Jordan B	.50	.23	.06
□ B29 Mike Fetters B	.25	.11	.03
□ B30 Carlos Delgado B	.50	.23	.06
□ B31 Shane Reynolds B	.25	.11	.03
□ B32 Terry Steinbach B	.50	.23	.06
□ B34 Mark Leiter B	.25	.11	.03
□ B36 David Segui B	.25	.11	.03
□ B40 Fred McGriff B	.75	.35	.09
□ B44 Glenallen Hill B	.25	.11	.03
□ B45 Brady Anderson B	.75	.35	.09
□ B47 Jim Thome B	1.25	.55	.16
□ B48 Frank Thomas B	6.00	2.70	.75
□ B49 Chuck Knoblauch B	.75	.35	.09
□ B50 Len Dykstra B	.50	.23	.06
□ B53 Tom Pagnozzi B	.25	.11	.03
□ B55 Ricky Bones B	.25	.11	.03
□ B56 David Justice B	.50	.23	.06
□ B57 Steve Avery B	.25	.11	.03
□ B58 Robby Thompson B	.25	.11	.03
□ B61 Tony Gwynn B	2.50	1.10	.30
□ B63 Denny Neagle B	.50	.23	.06
□ B67 Robin Ventura B	.50	.23	.06
□ B70 Kevin Seitzer B	.25	.11	.03
□ B71 Ramon Martinez B	.50	.23	.06
□ B75 Brian L.Hunter B	.50	.23	.06
□ B76 Alan Benes B	.50	.23	.06
□ B80 Ozzie Guillen B	.25	.11	.03
□ B82 Benji Gil B	.25	.11	.03
□ B85 Todd Hundley B	.50	.23	.06
□ B87 Pat Hentgen B	.50	.23	.06
□ B89 Chuck Finley B	.25	.11	.03
□ B92 Derek Jeter B	4.00	1.80	.50
□ B93 Paul O'Neill B	.50	.23	.06
□ B94 Darrin Fletcher B	.25	.11	.03
□ B96 Delino DeShields B	.25	.11	.03
□ B97 Tim Salmon B	.75	.35	.09
□ B98 John Olerud B	.25	.11	.03
□ B101 Tim Wakefield B	.25	.11	.03
□ B103 Dave Stevens B	.25	.11	.03

☐ B104	Orlando Merced B	.25	.11	.03
☐ B106	Jay Bell B	.25	.11	.03
☐ B107	John Burkett B	.25	.11	.03
☐ B108	Chris Hoiles B	.25	.11	.03
☐ B110	Dave Nilsson B	.25	.11	.03
☐ B111	Rod Beck B	.25	.11	.03
☐ B113	Mike Piazza B	4.00	1.80	.50
☐ B114	Mark Langston B	.25	.11	.03
☐ B116	Rico Brogna B	.25	.11	.03
☐ B118	Tom Goodwin B	.25	.11	.03
☐ B119	Bryan Rekar B	.25	.11	.03
☐ B120	David Cone B	.50	.23	.06
☐ B122	Andy Pettitte B	2.00	.90	.25
☐ B123	Chili Davis B	.50	.23	.06
☐ B124	John Smoltz B	1.00	.45	.12
☐ B125	Heathcliff Slocumb B	.25	.11	.03
☐ B126	Dante Bichette B	.75	.35	.09
☐ B128	Alex Gonzalez B	.25	.11	.03
☐ B129	Jeff Montgomery B	.25	.11	.03
☐ B131	Denny Martinez B	.50	.23	.06
☐ B132	Mel Rojas B	.25	.11	.03
☐ B133	Derek Bell B	.50	.23	.06
☐ B134	Trevor Hoffman B	.25	.11	.03
☐ B136	Darren Daulton B	.50	.23	.06
☐ B137	Pete Schourek B	.25	.11	.03
☐ B138	Phil Nevin B	.25	.11	.03
☐ B139	Andres Galarraga B	.75	.35	.09
☐ B140	Chad Fonville B	.25	.11	.03
☐ B144	J.T. Snow B	.25	.11	.03
☐ B146	Barry Bonds B	1.50	.70	.19
☐ B147	Orel Hershiser B	.50	.23	.06
☐ B148	Quilvio Veras B	.25	.11	.03
☐ B149	Will Clark B	.75	.35	.09
☐ B150	Jose Rijo B	.25	.11	.03
☐ B152	Travis Fryman B	.50	.23	.06
☐ B154	Alex Fernandez B	.50	.23	.06
☐ B155	Wade Boggs B	.75	.35	.09
☐ B156	Troy Percival B	.50	.23	.06
☐ B157	Moises Alou B	.50	.23	.06
☐ B158	Javy Lopez B	.50	.23	.06
☐ B159	Jason Giambi B	.50	.23	.06
☐ B162	Mark McGwire B	2.00	.90	.25
☐ B163	Eric Karros B	.50	.23	.06
☐ B166	Mickey Tettleton B	.25	.11	.03
☐ B167	Barry Larkin B	.75	.35	.09
☐ B169	Ruben Sierra B	.50	.23	.06
☐ B170	Bill Swift B	.25	.11	.03
☐ B172	Chad Curtis B	.25	.11	.03
☐ B173	Dean Palmer B	.50	.23	.06
☐ B175	Bobby Bonilla B	.50	.23	.06
☐ B176	Greg Colbrunn B	.25	.11	.03
☐ B177	Jose Mesa B	.50	.23	.06
☐ B178	Mike Greenwell B	.25	.11	.03
☐ B181	Doug Drabek B	.25	.11	.03
☐ B183	Wilson Alvarez B	.25	.11	.03
☐ B184	Marty Cordova B	.75	.35	.09
☐ B185	Hal Morris B	.25	.11	.03
☐ B187	Carlos Garcia B	.25	.11	.03
☐ B190	Marquis Grissom B	.50	.23	.06
☐ B193	Will Clark B	.75	.35	.09
☐ B194	Paul Molitor B	1.25	.55	.16
☐ B195	Kenny Rogers B	.25	.11	.03
☐ B196	Reggie Sanders B	.50	.23	.06
☐ B199	Raul Mondesi B	.75	.35	.09
☐ B200	Lance Johnson B	.50	.23	.06
☐ B201	Alvin Morman B	.25	.11	.03
☐ B203	Jack McDowell B	.50	.23	.06
☐ B204	Randy Myers B	.25	.11	.03
☐ B205	Harold Baines B	.50	.23	.06
☐ B206	Marty Cordova B	.75	.35	.09
☐ B207	Rich Hunter B	.50	.23	.06
☐ B208	Al Leiter B	.25	.11	.03
☐ B209	Greg Gagne B	.25	.11	.03
☐ B210	Ben McDonald B	.25	.11	.03
☐ B212	Terry Adams B	.25	.11	.03
☐ B213	Paul Sorrento B	.25	.11	.03
☐ B214	Albert Belle B	3.00	1.35	.35
☐ B215	Mike Blowers B	.25	.11	.03
☐ B216	Jim Edmonds B	.50	.23	.06
☐ B217	Felipe Crespo B	.25	.11	.03
☐ B219	Shawon Dunston B	.25	.11	.03
☐ B220	Jimmy Haynes B	.25	.11	.03
☐ B221	Jose Canseco B	.75	.35	.09
☐ B222	Eric Davis B	.25	.11	.03
☐ B224	Tim Raines B	.50	.23	.06
☐ B225	Tony Phillips B	.50	.23	.06
☐ B226	Charlie Hayes B	.25	.11	.03
☐ B227	Eric Owens B	.25	.11	.03
☐ B228	Roberto Alomar B	1.50	.70	.19
☐ B233	Kenny Lofton B	1.50	.70	.19
☐ B236	Mark McGwire B	2.00	.90	.25
☐ B237	Jay Buhner B	.75	.35	.09
☐ B238	Craig Biggio B	.50	.23	.06
☐ B240	Barry Bonds B	1.50	.70	.19
☐ B244	Ron Gant B	.50	.23	.06
☐ B245	Paul Wilson B	.50	.23	.06
☐ B246	Todd Hollandsworth B	.75	.35	.09
☐ B247	Todd Zeile B	.25	.11	.03
☐ B248	David Justice B	.50	.23	.06
☐ B250	Moises Alou B	.50	.23	.06
☐ B251	Bob Wolcott B	.25	.11	.03
☐ B252	David Wells B	.25	.11	.03
☐ B253	Juan Gonzalez B	3.00	1.35	.35
☐ B254	Andres Galarraga B	.75	.35	.09
☐ B255	Dave Hollins B	.25	.11	.03
☐ B257	Sammy Sosa B	1.00	.45	.12
☐ B258	Ivan Rodriguez B	1.25	.55	.16
☐ B259	Bip Roberts B	.25	.11	.03
☐ B260	Tino Martinez B	.50	.23	.06
☐ B262	Mike Stanley B	.25	.11	.03
☐ B264	Butch Huskey B	.25	.11	.03
☐ B265	Jeff Conine B	.50	.23	.06
☐ B267	Mark Grace B	.75	.35	.09
☐ B268	Jason Schmidt B	.50	.23	.06
☐ B269	Otis Nixon B	.25	.11	.03
☐ B271	Kirby Puckett B	2.00	.90	.25
☐ B273	Andy Benes B	.50	.23	.06
☐ B275	Mike Piazza B	4.00	1.80	.50
☐ B276	Rey Ordonez B	1.25	.55	.16
☐ B278	Gary Gaetti B	.25	.11	.03
☐ B280	Robin Ventura B	.50	.23	.06
☐ B281	Cal Ripken B	5.00	2.20	.60
☐ B282	Carlos Baerga B	.50	.23	.06
☐ B283	Roger Cedeno B	.25	.11	.03
☐ B285	Terrell Wade B	.25	.11	.03
☐ B286	Kevin Brown B	.50	.23	.06
☐ B287	Rafael Palmeiro B	.75	.35	.09
☐ B288	Mo Vaughn B	1.50	.70	.19
☐ B292	Bob Tewksbury B	.25	.11	.03
☐ B297	T.J. Mathews B	.25	.11	.03
☐ B298	Manny Ramirez B	1.50	.70	.19
☐ B299	Jeff Bagwell B	2.50	1.10	.30
☐ B301	Wade Boggs B	.75	.35	.09
☐ B303	Steve Gibralter B	.25	.11	.03
☐ B304	B.J. Surhoff B	.25	.11	.03
☐ B306	Royce Clayton B	.25	.11	.03
☐ B307	Sal Fasano B	.25	.11	.03
☐ B309	Gary Sheffield B	1.00	.45	.12
☐ B310	Ken Hill B	.25	.11	.03
☐ B311	Joe Girardi B	.25	.11	.03
☐ B312	Matt Lawton B	.25	.11	.03
☐ B314	Julio Franco B	.50	.23	.06
☐ B315	Joe Carter B	.50	.23	.06
☐ B316	Brooks Kieschnick B	.50	.23	.06
☐ B318	Heathcliff Slocumb B	.25	.11	.03
☐ B319	Barry Larkin B	.75	.35	.09
☐ B320	Tony Gwynn B	2.50	1.10	.30
☐ B322	Frank Thomas B	6.00	2.70	.75
☐ B323	Edgar Martinez B	.75	.35	.09
☐ B325	Henry Rodriguez B	.50	.23	.06
☐ B326	Marvin Benard B	.25	.11	.03
☐ B329	Ugueth Urbina B	.25	.11	.03
☐ B331	Roger Salkeld B	.25	.11	.03
☐ B332	Edgar Renteria B	1.00	.45	.12
☐ B333	Ryan Klesko B	1.25	.55	.16
☐ B334	Ray Lankford B	.50	.23	.06
☐ B336	Justin Thompson B	.50	.23	.06
☐ B339	Mark Clark B	.25	.11	.03
☐ B340	Ruben Rivera B	1.25	.55	.16
☐ B342	Matt Williams B	.75	.35	.09
☐ B343	Francisco Cordova B	.25	.11	.03
☐ B344	Cecil Fielder B	.50	.23	.06
☐ B348	Mark Grudzielanek B	.25	.11	.03
☐ B349	Ron Coomer B	.25	.11	.03
☐ B351	Rich Aurilia B	.25	.11	.03
☐ B352	Jose Herrera B	.25	.11	.03
☐ B356	Tony Clark B	.50	.23	.06
☐ B358	Dan Naulty B	.25	.11	.03
☐ B359	Checklist B	.25	.11	.03
☐ G4	Marty Cordova G	20.00	9.00	2.50
☐ G6	Tony Gwynn G	50.00	22.00	6.25
☐ G9	Albert Belle G	60.00	27.00	7.50

□ G18 Kirby Puckett G	40.00	18.00	5.00
□ G20 Karim Garcia G	25.00	11.00	3.10
□ G25 Cal Ripken G	100.00	45.00	12.50
□ G33 Hideo Nomo G	30.00	13.50	3.70
□ G39 Ryne Sandberg G	30.00	13.50	3.70
□ G42 Jeff Bagwell G	50.00	22.00	6.25
□ G51 Jason Isringhausen G	15.00	6.75	1.85
□ G64 Mo Vaughn G	30.00	13.50	3.70
□ G66 Dante Bichette G	20.00	9.00	2.50
□ G74 Mark McGwire G	40.00	18.00	5.00
□ G81 Kenny Lofton G	30.00	13.50	3.70
□ G83 Jim Edmonds G	15.00	6.75	1.85
□ G90 Mike Mussina G	25.00	11.00	3.10
□ G100 Jeff Conine G	15.00	6.75	1.85
□ G102 Johnny Damon G	15.00	6.75	1.85
□ G105 Barry Bonds G	30.00	13.50	3.70
□ G117 Jose Canseco G	20.00	9.00	2.50
□ G135 Ken Griffey Jr. G	120.00	55.00	15.00
□ G141 Chipper Jones G	80.00	36.00	10.00
□ G145 Greg Maddux G	80.00	36.00	10.00
□ G164 Jay Buhner G	15.00	6.75	1.85
□ G186 Frank Thomas G	120.00	55.00	15.00
□ G191 Checklist G	12.00	5.50	1.50
□ G192 Chipper Jones G	80.00	36.00	10.00
□ G197 Roberto Alomar G	30.00	13.50	3.70
□ G198 Dennis Eckersley G	15.00	6.75	1.85
□ G202 George Arias G	15.00	6.75	1.85
□ G232 Hideo Nomo G	30.00	13.50	3.70
□ G243 Chris Snopek G	15.00	6.75	1.85
□ G249 Tim Salmon G	20.00	9.00	2.50
□ G266 Matt Williams G	20.00	9.00	2.50
□ G270 Randy Johnson G	20.00	9.00	2.50
□ G279 Paul Molitor G	25.00	11.00	3.10
□ G290 Cecil Fielder G	15.00	6.75	1.85
□ G294 Livan Hernandez G	20.00	9.00	2.50
□ G300 Marty Janzen G	15.00	6.75	1.85
□ G308 Ron Gant G	15.00	6.75	1.85
□ G321 Ryan Klesko G	25.00	11.00	3.10
□ G324 Jermaine Dye G	30.00	13.50	3.70
□ G330 Jason Giambi G	15.00	6.75	1.85
□ G335 Edgar Martinez G	15.00	6.75	1.85
□ G338 Rey Ordonez G	25.00	11.00	3.10
□ G347 Sammy Sosa G	20.00	9.00	2.50
□ G354 Juan Gonzalez G	60.00	27.00	7.50
□ G355 Craig Biggio G	15.00	6.75	1.85
□ S1 Greg Maddux S UER ('95 stats listed as Mariners)	20.00	9.00	2.50
□ S2 Bernie Williams S	5.00	2.20	.60
□ S3 Ivan Rodriguez S	6.00	2.70	.75
□ S7 Barry Larkin S	4.00	1.80	.50
□ S10 Ray Lankford S	3.00	1.35	.35
□ S11 Mike Piazza S	20.00	9.00	2.50
□ S13 Larry Walker S	3.00	1.35	.35
□ S14 Matt Williams S	4.00	1.80	.50
□ S22 Tim Salmon S	4.00	1.80	.50
□ S35 Edgar Martinez S	4.00	1.80	.50
□ S37 Gregg Jefferies S	3.00	1.35	.35
□ S38 Bill Pulsipher S	2.50	1.10	.30
□ S41 Shawn Green S	2.50	1.10	.30
□ S43 Jim Abbott S	2.50	1.10	.30
□ S46 Roger Clemens S	4.00	1.80	.50
□ S52 Rondell White S	3.00	1.35	.35
□ S54 Dennis Eckersley S	3.00	1.35	.35
□ S59 Hideo Nomo S	8.00	3.60	1.00
□ S60 Gary Sheffield S	5.00	2.20	.60
□ S62 Will Clark S	4.00	1.80	.50
□ S65 Bret Boone S	2.50	1.10	.30
□ S68 Rafael Palmeiro S	4.00	1.80	.50
□ S69 Carlos Baerga S	3.00	1.35	.35
□ S72 Tom Glavine S	4.00	1.80	.50
□ S73 Garret Anderson S	3.00	1.35	.35
□ S77 Randy Johnson S	5.00	2.20	.60
□ S78 Jeff King S	2.50	1.10	.30
□ S79 Kirby Puckett S	10.00	4.50	1.25
□ S84 Cecil Fielder S	3.00	1.35	.35
□ S86 Reggie Sanders S	3.00	1.35	.35
□ S88 Ryan Klesko S	6.00	2.70	.75
□ S91 John Valentin S	2.50	1.10	.30
□ S95 Manny Ramirez S	8.00	3.60	1.00
□ S99 Vinny Castilla S	3.00	1.35	.35
□ S109 Carlos Perez S	2.50	1.10	.30
□ S112 Craig Biggio S	3.00	1.35	.35
□ S115 Juan Gonzalez S	15.00	6.75	1.85
□ S121 Ray Durham S	3.00	1.35	.35
□ S127 C.J. Nitkowski S	2.50	1.10	.30
□ S130 Raul Mondesi S	4.00	1.80	.50
□ S142 Lee Smith S	3.00	1.35	.35
□ S143 Joe Carter S	3.00	1.35	.35
□ S151 Mo Vaughn S	8.00	3.60	1.00
□ S153 Frank Rodriguez S	2.50	1.10	.30
□ S160 Steve Finley S	3.00	1.35	.35
□ S161 Jeff Bagwell S	12.00	5.50	1.50
□ S165 Cal Ripken S	25.00	11.00	3.10
□ S168 Lyle Mouton S	2.50	1.10	.30
□ S171 Sammy Sosa S	5.00	2.20	.60
□ S174 John Franco S	2.50	1.10	.30
□ S179 Greg Vaughn S	3.00	1.35	.35
□ S180 Mark Wohlers S	3.00	1.35	.35
□ S182 Paul O'Neill S	3.00	1.35	.35
□ S188 Albert Belle S	15.00	6.75	1.85
□ S189 Mark Grace S	4.00	1.80	.50
□ S211 Ernie Young S	2.50	1.10	.30
□ S218 Fred McGriff S	4.00	1.80	.50
□ S223 Kimera Bartee S	2.50	1.10	.30
□ S229 Rickey Henderson S	3.00	1.35	.35
□ S230 Sterling Hitchcock S	2.50	1.10	.30
□ S231 Bernard Gilkey S	3.00	1.35	.35
□ S234 Ryne Sandberg S	8.00	3.60	1.00
□ S235 Greg Maddux S	20.00	9.00	2.50
□ S239 Todd Stottlemyre S	2.50	1.10	.30
□ S241 Jason Kendall S	6.00	2.70	.75
□ S242 Paul O'Neill S	3.00	1.35	.35
□ S256 Devon White S	2.50	1.10	.30
□ S261 Chuck Knoblauch S	4.00	1.80	.50
□ S263 Wally Joyner S	3.00	1.35	.35
□ S272 Andy Fox S	2.50	1.10	.30
□ S274 Sean Berry S	2.50	1.10	.30
□ S277 Benito Santiago S	2.50	1.10	.30
□ S284 Chad Mottola S	2.50	1.10	.30
□ S289 Dante Bichette S	4.00	1.80	.50
□ S291 Doc Gooden S	3.00	1.35	.35
□ S293 Kevin Mitchell S	2.50	1.10	.30
□ S295 Russ Davis S	2.50	1.10	.30
□ S296 Chan Ho Park S	3.00	1.35	.35
□ S302 Larry Walker S	3.00	1.35	.35
□ S305 Ken Griffey Jr. S	30.00	13.50	3.70
□ S313 Billy Wagner S	3.00	1.35	.35
□ S317 Mike Grace S	4.00	1.80	.50
□ S327 Kenny Lofton S	8.00	3.60	1.00
□ S328 Derek Bell S	3.00	1.35	.35
□ S337 Gary Sheffield S	5.00	2.20	.60
□ S341 Mark Grace S	4.00	1.80	.50
□ S345 Andres Galarraga S	4.00	1.80	.50
□ S346 Brady Anderson S	4.00	1.80	.50
□ S350 Derek Jeter S	15.00	6.75	1.85
□ S353 Jay Buhner S	4.00	1.80	.50
□ S357 Tino Martinez S	3.00	1.35	.35

1996 Finest Refractors

This 359-card set is parallel to the basic 1996 Finest set. The first 191 cards are parallel to the regular Series 1 with the second 168 cards parallel to regular Series 2. The word "refractor" is printed above the numbers on the card backs. The rate of insertion is one in 12 for a Bronze refractor (common), one in 48 for a Silver refractor (uncommon), and one in 288 for a Gold refractor (rare).

	MINT	NRMT	EXC
COMPLETE SET (359)	15000.00	6800.00	1900.00
COMPLETE SERIES 1 (191)	10000.00	4500.00	1250.00
COMPLETE SERIES 2 (168)	5000.00	2200.00	600.00
COMP.BRONZE SET (220)	1800.00	800.00	220.00
COMP.BRONZE SET (110)	800.00	350.00	100.00
COMP.BRONZE SER.2 (110)	1000.00	450.00	125.00
COMMON BRONZE	4.00	1.80	.50
BRONZE SEMISTARS	12.00	5.50	1.50
COMP.GOLD SET (48)	10000.00	4500.00	1250.00
COMP.GOLD SER.1 (26)	7000.00	3200.00	900.00
COMP.GOLD SER.2 (22)	3000.00	1350.00	375.00
COMMON GOLD	40.00	18.00	5.00
COMP.SILVER SET (91)	3200.00	1450.00	400.00
COMP.SILVER SER.1 (55)	2000.00	900.00	250.00
COMP.SILVER SER.2 (36)	1200.00	550.00	150.00
COMMON SILVER	15.00	6.75	1.85
SILVER SEMISTARS	25.00	11.00	3.10
RANDOM INSERTS IN PACKS			

□ B16	Chipper Jones B	60.00	27.00	7.50
□ B21	Eddie Murray B	25.00	11.00	3.10
□ B24	Ken Griffey Jr. B	100.00	45.00	12.50
□ B47	Jim Thome B	20.00	9.00	2.50
□ B48	Frank Thomas B	100.00	45.00	12.50
□ B61	Tony Gwynn B	40.00	18.00	5.00
□ B92	Derek Jeter B	60.00	27.00	7.50
□ B113	Mike Piazza B	60.00	27.00	7.50
□ B122	Andy Pettitte B	30.00	13.50	3.70
□ B124	John Smoltz B	15.00	6.75	1.85
□ B146	Barry Bonds B	25.00	11.00	3.10
□ B162	Mark McGwire B	30.00	13.50	3.70
□ B194	Paul Molitor B	20.00	9.00	2.50
□ B214	Albert Belle B	50.00	22.00	6.25
□ B228	Roberto Alomar B	25.00	11.00	3.10
□ B233	Kenny Lofton B	25.00	11.00	3.10
□ B236	Mark McGwire B	30.00	13.50	3.70
□ B240	Barry Bonds B	25.00	11.00	3.10
□ B253	Juan Gonzalez B	50.00	22.00	6.25
□ B257	Sammy Sosa B	15.00	6.75	1.85
□ B258	Ivan Rodriguez B	20.00	9.00	2.50
□ B271	Kirby Puckett B	30.00	13.50	3.70
□ B275	Mike Piazza B	60.00	27.00	7.50
□ B276	Rey Ordonez B	20.00	9.00	2.50
□ B281	Cal Ripken B	80.00	36.00	10.00
□ B288	Mo Vaughn B	25.00	11.00	3.10
□ B298	Manny Ramirez B	25.00	11.00	3.10
□ B299	Jeff Bagwell B	40.00	18.00	5.00
□ B309	Gary Sheffield B	15.00	6.75	1.85
□ B320	Tony Gwynn B	40.00	18.00	5.00
□ B322	Frank Thomas B	100.00	45.00	12.50
□ B333	Ryan Klesko B	20.00	9.00	2.50
□ B340	Ruben Rivera B	20.00	9.00	2.50
□ G4	Marty Cordova G	125.00	55.00	15.50
□ G6	Tony Gwynn G	300.00	135.00	38.00
□ G9	Albert Belle G	350.00	160.00	45.00
□ G18	Kirby Puckett G	250.00	110.00	31.00
□ G20	Karim Garcia G	200.00	90.00	25.00
□ G25	Cal Ripken G	600.00	275.00	75.00
□ G33	Hideo Nomo G	200.00	90.00	25.00
□ G39	Ryne Sandberg G	200.00	90.00	25.00
□ G42	Jeff Bagwell G	300.00	135.00	38.00
□ G51	Jason Isringhausen G	100.00	45.00	12.50
□ G64	Mo Vaughn G	250.00	110.00	31.00
□ G66	Dante Bichette G	125.00	55.00	15.50
□ G74	Mark McGwire G	250.00	110.00	31.00
□ G81	Kenny Lofton G	250.00	110.00	31.00
□ G83	Jim Edmonds G	100.00	45.00	12.50
□ G90	Mike Mussina G	150.00	70.00	19.00
□ G100	Jeff Conine G	100.00	45.00	12.50
□ G102	Johnny Damon G	125.00	55.00	15.50
□ G105	Barry Bonds G	250.00	110.00	31.00
□ G117	Jose Canseco G	125.00	55.00	15.50
□ G135	Ken Griffey Jr. G	800.00	350.00	100.00
□ G141	Chipper Jones G	500.00	220.00	60.00
□ G145	Greg Maddux G	500.00	220.00	60.00
□ G164	Jay Buhner G	125.00	55.00	15.50
□ G186	Frank Thomas G	800.00	350.00	100.00
□ G191	Checklist G	40.00	18.00	5.00
□ G192	Chipper Jones G	500.00	220.00	60.00
□ G197	Roberto Alomar G	250.00	110.00	31.00
□ G198	Dennis Eckersley G	100.00	45.00	12.50
□ G202	George Arias G	100.00	45.00	12.50
□ G232	Hideo Nomo G	250.00	110.00	31.00
□ G243	Chris Snopek G	80.00	36.00	10.00
□ G249	Tim Salmon G	125.00	55.00	15.50
□ G266	Matt Williams G	125.00	55.00	15.50
□ G270	Randy Johnson G	125.00	55.00	15.50
□ G279	Paul Molitor G	150.00	70.00	19.00
□ G290	Cecil Fielder G	100.00	45.00	12.50
□ G294	Livan Hernandez G	80.00	36.00	10.00
□ G300	Marty Janzen G	80.00	36.00	10.00
□ G308	Ron Gant G	100.00	45.00	12.50
□ G321	Ryan Klesko G	200.00	90.00	25.00
□ G324	Jermaine Dye G	200.00	90.00	25.00
□ G330	Jason Giambi G	100.00	45.00	12.50
□ G335	Edgar Martinez G	100.00	45.00	12.50
□ G338	Rey Ordonez G	150.00	70.00	19.00
□ G347	Sammy Sosa G	150.00	70.00	19.00
□ G354	Juan Gonzalez G	350.00	160.00	45.00
□ G355	Craig Biggio G	100.00	45.00	12.50
□ S1	Greg Maddux S UER	120.00	55.00	15.00
	('95 stats listed as Mariners)			
□ S2	Bernie Williams S	30.00	13.50	3.70
□ S3	Ivan Rodriguez S	40.00	18.00	5.00
□ S7	Barry Larkin S	25.00	11.00	3.10
□ S11	Mike Piazza S	160.00	70.00	20.00
□ S14	Matt Williams S	25.00	11.00	3.10
□ S22	Tim Salmon S	25.00	11.00	3.10
□ S35	Edgar Martinez S	25.00	11.00	3.10
□ S46	Roger Clemens S	25.00	11.00	3.10
□ S59	Hideo Nomo S	50.00	22.00	6.25
□ S60	Gary Sheffield S	30.00	13.50	3.70
□ S62	Will Clark S	25.00	11.00	3.10
□ S68	Rafael Palmeiro S	25.00	11.00	3.10
□ S72	Tom Glavine S	25.00	11.00	3.10
□ S77	Randy Johnson S	30.00	13.50	3.70
□ S79	Kirby Puckett S	60.00	27.00	7.50
□ S88	Ryan Klesko S	40.00	18.00	5.00
□ S95	Manny Ramirez S	50.00	22.00	6.25
□ S115	Juan Gonzalez S	100.00	45.00	12.50
□ S151	Mo Vaughn S	50.00	22.00	6.25
□ S161	Jeff Bagwell S	80.00	36.00	10.00
□ S165	Cal Ripken S	160.00	70.00	20.00
□ S171	Sammy Sosa S	30.00	13.50	3.70
□ S188	Albert Belle S	100.00	45.00	12.50
□ S218	Fred McGriff S	25.00	11.00	3.10
□ S234	Ryne Sandberg S	50.00	22.00	6.25
□ S235	Greg Maddux S	120.00	55.00	15.00
□ S241	Jason Kendall S	25.00	11.00	3.10
□ S261	Chuck Knoblauch S	25.00	11.00	3.10
□ S289	Dante Bichette S	25.00	11.00	3.10
□ S305	Ken Griffey Jr. S	200.00	90.00	25.00
□ S327	Kenny Lofton S	50.00	22.00	6.25
□ S337	Gary Sheffield S	30.00	13.50	3.70
□ S345	Andres Galarraga S	25.00	11.00	3.10
□ S346	Brady Anderson S	25.00	11.00	3.10
□ S350	Derek Jeter S	120.00	55.00	15.00
□ S353	Jay Buhner S	25.00	11.00	3.10

1993 Flair

This 300-card standard-size set represents Fleer's entrance into the super-premium category of trading cards. Cards were distributed exclusively in specially encased "hardpacks". The cards are made from heavy 24 point board card stock, with an additional three points of high-gloss laminate on each side, and feature full-bleed color fronts that sport two photos of each player, one superposed upon the other. The Flair logo appears at the top and the player's name rests at the bottom, both stamped in gold foil. The cards are numbered alphabetically within teams with National League preceding American league. There are no key Rookie Cards in this set.

	MINT	NRMT	EXC
COMPLETE SET (300)	75.00	34.00	9.50
COMMON CARD (1-300)	.25	.11	.03
SEMISTARS	.50	.23	.06
STARS	1.25	.55	.16

□ 1	Steve Avery	.50	.23	.06
□ 2	Jeff Blauser	.25	.11	.03
□ 3	Ron Gant	1.25	.55	.16
□ 4	Tom Glavine	1.25	.55	.16
□ 5	David Justice	1.25	.55	.16
□ 6	Mark Lemke	.25	.11	.03
□ 7	Greg Maddux	5.00	2.20	.60
□ 8	Fred McGriff	1.25	.55	.16
□ 9	Terry Pendleton	.50	.23	.06
□ 10	Deion Sanders	1.25	.55	.16
□ 11	John Smoltz	1.25	.55	.16

□ 12 Mike Stanton	.25	.11	.03
□ 13 Steve Buechele	.25	.11	.03
□ 14 Mark Grace	1.25	.55	.16
□ 15 Greg Hibbard	.25	.11	.03
□ 16 Derrick May	.25	.11	.03
□ 17 Chuck McElroy	.25	.11	.03
□ 18 Mike Morgan	.25	.11	.03
□ 19 Randy Myers	.50	.23	.06
□ 20 Ryne Sandberg	2.00	.90	.25
□ 21 Dwight Smith	.25	.11	.03
□ 22 Sammy Sosa	1.25	.55	.16
□ 23 Jose Vizcaino	.25	.11	.03
□ 24 Tim Belcher	.25	.11	.03
□ 25 Rob Dibble	.25	.11	.03
□ 26 Roberto Kelly	.25	.11	.03
□ 27 Barry Larkin	1.25	.55	.16
□ 28 Kevin Mitchell	.50	.23	.06
□ 29 Hal Morris	.25	.11	.03
□ 30 Joe Oliver	.25	.11	.03
□ 31 Jose Rijo	.25	.11	.03
□ 32 Bip Roberts	.25	.11	.03
□ 33 Chris Sabo	.25	.11	.03
□ 34 Reggie Sanders	1.25	.55	.16
□ 35 Dante Bichette	1.25	.55	.16
□ 36 Willie Blair	.25	.11	.03
□ 37 Jerald Clark	.25	.11	.03
□ 38 Alex Cole	.25	.11	.03
□ 39 Andres Galarraga	1.25	.55	.16
□ 40 Joe Girardi	.25	.11	.03
□ 41 Charlie Hayes	.25	.11	.03
□ 42 Chris Jones	.25	.11	.03
□ 43 David Nied	.25	.11	.03
□ 44 Eric Young	1.25	.55	.16
□ 45 Alex Arias	.25	.11	.03
□ 46 Jack Armstrong	.25	.11	.03
□ 47 Bret Barberie	.25	.11	.03
□ 48 Chuck Carr	.25	.11	.03
□ 49 Jeff Conine	1.25	.55	.16
□ 50 Orestes Destrade	.25	.11	.03
□ 51 Chris Hammond	.25	.11	.03
□ 52 Bryan Harvey	.25	.11	.03
□ 53 Benito Santiago	.25	.11	.03
□ 54 Gary Sheffield	1.25	.55	.16
□ 55 Walt Weiss	.25	.11	.03
□ 56 Eric Anthony	.25	.11	.03
□ 57 Jeff Bagwell	3.00	1.35	.35
□ 58 Craig Biggio	1.25	.55	.16
□ 59 Ken Caminiti	1.25	.55	.16
□ 60 Andujar Cedeno	.25	.11	.03
□ 61 Doug Drabek	.25	.11	.03
□ 62 Steve Finley	1.25	.55	.16
□ 63 Luis Gonzalez	.25	.11	.03
□ 64 Pete Harnisch	.25	.11	.03
□ 65 Doug Jones	.25	.11	.03
□ 66 Darryl Kile	.25	.11	.03
□ 67 Greg Swindell	.25	.11	.03
□ 68 Brett Butler	.50	.23	.06
□ 69 Jim Gott	.25	.11	.03
□ 70 Orel Hershiser	.50	.23	.06
□ 71 Eric Karros	1.25	.55	.16
□ 72 Pedro Martinez	1.25	.55	.16
□ 73 Ramon Martinez	.50	.23	.06
□ 74 Roger McDowell	.25	.11	.03
□ 75 Mike Piazza	8.00	3.60	1.00
□ 76 Jody Reed	.25	.11	.03
□ 77 Tim Wallach	.25	.11	.03
□ 78 Moises Alou	1.25	.55	.16
□ 79 Greg Colbrunn	.25	.11	.03
□ 80 Wil Cordero	.50	.23	.06
□ 81 Delino DeShields	.25	.11	.03
□ 82 Jeff Fassero	.50	.23	.06
□ 83 Marquis Grissom	1.25	.55	.16
□ 84 Ken Hill	.50	.23	.06
□ 85 Mike Lansing	.50	.23	.06
□ 86 Dennis Martinez	.50	.23	.06
□ 87 Larry Walker	1.25	.55	.16
□ 88 John Wetteland	.50	.23	.06
□ 89 Bobby Bonilla	.50	.23	.06
□ 90 Vince Coleman	.25	.11	.03
□ 91 Dwight Gooden	.50	.23	.06
□ 92 Todd Hundley	1.25	.55	.16
□ 93 Howard Johnson	.25	.11	.03
□ 94 Eddie Murray	2.00	.90	.25
□ 95 Joe Orsulak	.25	.11	.03
□ 96 Bret Saberhagen	.50	.23	.06
□ 97 Darren Daulton	.50	.23	.06
□ 98 Mariano Duncan	.25	.11	.03
□ 99 Len Dykstra	.50	.23	.06
□ 100 Jim Eisenreich	.50	.23	.06
□ 101 Tommy Greene	.25	.11	.03
□ 102 Dave Hollins	.25	.11	.03
□ 103 Pete Incaviglia	.25	.11	.03
□ 104 Danny Jackson	.25	.11	.03
□ 105 John Kruk	.50	.23	.06
□ 106 Terry Mulholland	.25	.11	.03
□ 107 Curt Schilling	.25	.11	.03
□ 108 Mitch Williams	.25	.11	.03
□ 109 Stan Belinda	.25	.11	.03
□ 110 Jay Bell	.50	.23	.06
□ 111 Steve Cooke	.25	.11	.03
□ 112 Carlos Garcia	.25	.11	.03
□ 113 Jeff King	.50	.23	.06
□ 114 Al Martin	.50	.23	.06
□ 115 Orlando Merced	.50	.23	.06
□ 116 Don Slaught	.25	.11	.03
□ 117 Andy Van Slyke	.50	.23	.06
□ 118 Tim Wakefield	.50	.23	.06
□ 119 Rene Arocha	.25	.11	.03
□ 120 Bernard Gilkey	1.25	.55	.16
□ 121 Gregg Jefferies	1.25	.55	.16
□ 122 Ray Lankford	1.25	.55	.16
□ 123 Donovan Osborne	.25	.11	.03
□ 124 Tom Pagnozzi	.25	.11	.03
□ 125 Erik Pappas	.25	.11	.03
□ 126 Geronimo Pena	.25	.11	.03
□ 127 Lee Smith	.50	.23	.06
□ 128 Ozzie Smith	1.50	.70	.19
□ 129 Bob Tewksbury	.25	.11	.03
□ 130 Mark Whiten	.25	.11	.03
□ 131 Derek Bell	1.25	.55	.16
□ 132 Andy Benes	.25	.11	.03
□ 133 Tony Gwynn	3.00	1.35	.35
□ 134 Gene Harris	.25	.11	.03
□ 135 Trevor Hoffman	.50	.23	.06
□ 136 Phil Plantier	.25	.11	.03
□ 137 Rod Beck	.50	.23	.06
□ 138 Barry Bonds	2.00	.90	.25
□ 139 John Burkett	.25	.11	.03
□ 140 Will Clark	1.25	.55	.16
□ 141 Royce Clayton	.50	.23	.06
□ 142 Mike Jackson	.25	.11	.03
□ 143 Darren Lewis	.25	.11	.03
□ 144 Kirt Manwaring	.25	.11	.03
□ 145 Willie McGee	.25	.11	.03
□ 146 Bill Swift	.25	.11	.03
□ 147 Robby Thompson	.25	.11	.03
□ 148 Matt Williams	1.25	.55	.16
□ 149 Brady Anderson	1.25	.55	.16
□ 150 Mike Devereaux	.25	.11	.03
□ 151 Chris Hoiles	.25	.11	.03
□ 152 Ben McDonald	.25	.11	.03
□ 153 Mark McLemore	.25	.11	.03
□ 154 Mike Mussina	1.50	.70	.19
□ 155 Gregg Olson	.25	.11	.03
□ 156 Harold Reynolds	.25	.11	.03
□ 157 Cal Ripken UER (Back refers to his games streak going into 1992; should be 1993) Also streak is spelled steak	6.00	2.70	.75
□ 158 Rick Sutcliffe	.25	.11	.03
□ 159 Fernando Valenzuela	.50	.23	.06
□ 160 Roger Clemens	1.25	.55	.16
□ 161 Scott Cooper	.25	.11	.03
□ 162 Andre Dawson	1.25	.55	.16
□ 163 Scott Fletcher	.25	.11	.03
□ 164 Mike Greenwell	.25	.11	.03
□ 165 Greg A. Harris	.25	.11	.03
□ 166 Billy Hatcher	.25	.11	.03
□ 167 Jeff Russell	.25	.11	.03
□ 168 Mo Vaughn	2.00	.90	.25
□ 169 Frank Viola	.25	.11	.03
□ 170 Chad Curtis	.50	.23	.06
□ 171 Chili Davis	.50	.23	.06
□ 172 Gary DiSarcina	.25	.11	.03
□ 173 Damion Easley	.25	.11	.03
□ 174 Chuck Finley	.25	.11	.03
□ 175 Mark Langston	.50	.23	.06
□ 176 Luis Polonia	.25	.11	.03
□ 177 Tim Salmon	2.00	.90	.25
□ 178 Scott Sanderson	.25	.11	.03
□ 179 J.T.Snow	1.25	.55	.16
□ 180 Wilson Alvarez	.50	.23	.06

□ 181 Ellis Burks	1.25	.55	.16
□ 182 Joey Cora	.25	.11	.03
□ 183 Alex Fernandez	1.25	.55	.16
□ 184 Ozzie Guillen	.25	.11	.03
□ 185 Roberto Hernandez	.50	.23	.06
□ 186 Bo Jackson	1.25	.55	.16
□ 187 Lance Johnson	.50	.23	.06
□ 188 Jack McDowell	.50	.23	.06
□ 189 Frank Thomas	8.00	3.60	1.00
□ 190 Robin Ventura	.50	.23	.06
□ 191 Carlos Baerga	1.25	.55	.16
□ 192 Albert Belle	4.00	1.80	.50
□ 193 Wayne Kirby	.25	.11	.03
□ 194 Derek Lilliquist	.25	.11	.03
□ 195 Kenny Lofton	3.00	1.35	.35
□ 196 Carlos Martinez	.25	.11	.03
□ 197 Jose Mesa	.50	.23	.06
□ 198 Eric Plunk	.25	.11	.03
□ 199 Paul Sorrento	.25	.11	.03
□ 200 John Doherty	.25	.11	.03
□ 201 Cecil Fielder	.50	.23	.06
□ 202 Travis Fryman	1.25	.55	.16
□ 203 Kirk Gibson	.50	.23	.06
□ 204 Mike Henneman	.25	.11	.03
□ 205 Chad Kreuter	.25	.11	.03
□ 206 Scott Livingstone	.25	.11	.03
□ 207 Tony Phillips	.50	.23	.06
□ 208 Mickey Tettleton	.25	.11	.03
□ 209 Alan Trammell	1.25	.55	.16
□ 210 David Wells	.25	.11	.03
□ 211 Lou Whitaker	1.25	.55	.16
□ 212 Kevin Appier	.50	.23	.06
□ 213 George Brett	3.00	1.35	.35
□ 214 David Cone	1.25	.55	.16
□ 215 Tom Gordon	.25	.11	.03
□ 216 Phil Hiatt	.25	.11	.03
□ 217 Felix Jose	.25	.11	.03
□ 218 Wally Joyner	.50	.23	.06
□ 219 Jose Lind	.25	.11	.03
□ 220 Mike Macfarlane	.25	.11	.03
□ 221 Brian McRae	.50	.23	.06
□ 222 Jeff Montgomery	.50	.23	.06
□ 223 Cal Eldred	.25	.11	.03
□ 224 Darryl Hamilton	.25	.11	.03
□ 225 John Jaha	.50	.23	.06
□ 226 Pat Listach	.25	.11	.03
□ 227 Graeme Lloyd	.25	.11	.03
□ 228 Kevin Reimer	.25	.11	.03
□ 229 Bill Spiers	.25	.11	.03
□ 230 B.J.Surhoff	.50	.23	.06
□ 231 Greg Vaughn	1.25	.55	.16
□ 232 Robin Yount	1.25	.55	.16
□ 233 Rick Aguilera	.25	.11	.03
□ 234 Jim Deshaies	.25	.11	.03
□ 235 Brian Harper	.25	.11	.03
□ 236 Kent Hrbek	.50	.23	.06
□ 237 Chuck Knoblauch	1.25	.55	.16
□ 238 Shane Mack	.25	.11	.03
□ 239 David McCarty	.25	.11	.03
□ 240 Pedro Munoz	.25	.11	.03
□ 241 Mike Pagliarulo	.25	.11	.03
□ 242 Kirby Puckett	2.50	1.10	.30
□ 243 Dave Winfield	1.25	.55	.16
□ 244 Jim Abbott	.25	.11	.03
□ 245 Wade Boggs	1.25	.55	.16
□ 246 Pat Kelly	.25	.11	.03
□ 247 Jimmy Key	.50	.23	.06
□ 248 Jim Leyritz	.25	.11	.03
□ 249 Don Mattingly	4.00	1.80	.50
□ 250 Matt Nokes	.25	.11	.03
□ 251 Paul O'Neill	.50	.23	.06
□ 252 Mike Stanley	.25	.11	.03
□ 253 Danny Tartabull	.25	.11	.03
□ 254 Bob Wickman	.25	.11	.03
□ 255 Bernie Williams	1.25	.55	.16
□ 256 Mike Bordick	.25	.11	.03
□ 257 Dennis Eckersley	.50	.23	.06
□ 258 Brent Gates	.50	.23	.06
□ 259 Goose Gossage	.50	.23	.06
□ 260 Rickey Henderson	1.25	.55	.16
□ 261 Mark McGwire	2.50	1.10	.30
□ 262 Ruben Sierra	.50	.23	.06
□ 263 Terry Steinbach	.50	.23	.06
□ 264 Bob Welch	.25	.11	.03
□ 265 Bobby Witt	.25	.11	.03
□ 266 Rich Amaral	.25	.11	.03
□ 267 Chris Bosio	.25	.11	.03
□ 268 Jay Buhner	1.25	.55	.16
□ 269 Norm Charlton	.25	.11	.03
□ 270 Ken Griffey Jr.	8.00	3.60	1.00
□ 271 Erik Hanson	.25	.11	.03
□ 272 Randy Johnson	1.25	.55	.16
□ 273 Edgar Martinez	1.25	.55	.16
□ 274 Tino Martinez	.50	.23	.06
□ 275 Dave Valle	.25	.11	.03
□ 276 Omar Vizquel	1.25	.55	.16
□ 277 Kevin Brown	.25	.11	.03
□ 278 Jose Canseco	1.25	.55	.16
□ 279 Julio Franco	.50	.23	.06
□ 280 Juan Gonzalez	4.00	1.80	.50
□ 281 Tom Henke	.25	.11	.03
□ 282 David Hulse	.25	.11	.03
□ 283 Rafael Palmeiro	1.25	.55	.16
□ 284 Dean Palmer	.50	.23	.06
□ 285 Ivan Rodriguez	1.50	.70	.19
□ 286 Nolan Ryan	6.00	2.70	.75
□ 287 Roberto Alomar	2.00	.90	.25
□ 288 Pat Borders	.25	.11	.03
□ 289 Joe Carter	1.25	.55	.16
□ 290 Juan Guzman	.50	.23	.06
□ 291 Pat Hentgen	1.25	.55	.16
□ 292 Paul Molitor	1.50	.70	.19
□ 293 John Olerud	.25	.11	.03
□ 294 Ed Sprague	.50	.23	.06
□ 295 Dave Stewart	.50	.23	.06
□ 296 Duane Ward	.25	.11	.03
□ 297 Devon White	.25	.11	.03
□ 298 Checklist 1-100	.25	.11	.03
□ 299 Checklist 101-200	.25	.11	.03
□ 300 Checklist 201-300	.25	.11	.03
□ P15 Aaron Sele Promo Card	.25	.11	.03

1993 Flair Wave of the Future

This 20-card standard-size limited edition insert set features a selction of top prospects. Cards were randomly seeded into1993 Flair packs. Each card is made of the same thick card stock as the regular-issue set and features full-bleed color player action photos on the fronts, with the Flair logo, player's name, and the "Wave of the Future" name and logo in gold foil, all superimposed upon an ocean breaker.

	MINT	NRMT	EXC
COMPLETE SET (20)	40.00	18.00	5.00
COMMON CARD (1-20)	1.00	.45	.12
SEMISTARS	1.50	.70	.19
RANDOM INSERTS IN PACKS			
□ 1 Jason Bere	1.50	.70	.19
□ 2 Jeromy Burnitz	1.00	.45	.12
□ 3 Russ Davis	1.50	.70	.19
□ 4 Jim Edmonds	10.00	4.50	1.25
□ 5 Cliff Floyd	1.50	.70	.19
□ 6 Jeffrey Hammonds	1.50	.70	.19
□ 7 Trevor Hoffman	1.50	.70	.19
□ 8 Domingo Jean	1.00	.45	.12
□ 9 David McCarty	1.00	.45	.12
□ 10 Bobby Munoz	1.00	.45	.12
□ 11 Brad Pennington	1.00	.45	.12
□ 12 Mike Piazza	15.00	6.75	1.85

□ 13 Manny Ramirez	10.00	4.50	1.25
□ 14 John Roper	1.00	.45	.12
□ 15 Tim Salmon	5.00	2.20	.60
□ 16 Aaron Sele	1.50	.70	.19
□ 17 Allen Watson	1.00	.45	.12
□ 18 Rondell White	2.00	.90	.25
□ 19 Darrell Whitmore UER (Nigel Wilson back)	1.00	.45	.12
□ 20 Nigel Wilson UER (Darrell Whitmore back)	1.00	.45	.12

1994 Flair

For the second consecutive year Fleer issued a Flair brand. The set consists of 450 full bleed cards in two series of 250 and 200. The card stock is thicker than the traditional standard card. Card fronts feature two photos with the player's name and team name at the bottom in gold foil. The first letter of the player's last name appears within a gold shield to add style to this premium brand product. The backs are horizontal with a player photo and statistics. The team logo and player's name are done in gold foil. The cards are grouped alphabetically by team within each league as follows: Baltimore Orioles (1-9/251-258), Boston Red Sox (10-18/259-266), California Angels (19-27/267-274), Chicago White Sox (28-36/275-281), Cleveland Indians (37-45/282-290), Detroit Tigers (46-53/291-296), Kansas City Royals (54-62/297-302), Milwaukee Brewers (63-71/303-310), Minnesota Twins (72-79/311-317), New York Yankees (80-88/318-326), Oakland Athletics (89-97/327-334), Seattle Mariners (98-106/335-342), Texas Rangers (107-114/343-347), Toronto Blue Jays (115-123/348-351), Atlanta Braves (124-133/352-359), Chicago Cubs (134-142/360-364), Cincinnati Reds (143-150/365-371), Colorado Rockies (151-159/372-377), Florida Marlins (160-167/378-384), Houston Astros (168-176/385-392), Los Angeles Dodgers (177-185/393-399), Montreal Expos (186-194/400-406), New York Mets (195-203/407-410), Philadelphia Phillies (204-213/411-419), Pittsburgh Pirates (214-222/420-426), St. Louis Cardinals (223-230/427-432), San Diego Padres (231-237/433-441), and San Francisco Giants (238-247/442-448). Rookie Cards include Kurt Abbott, Brian Anderson, Chan Ho Park, Alex Rodriguez and Will VanLandingham.

	MINT	NRMT	EXC
COMPLETE SET (450)	60.00	27.00	7.50
COMPLETE SERIES 1 (250)	25.00	11.00	3.10
COMPLETE SERIES 2 (200)	35.00	16.00	4.40
COMMON CARD (1-450)	.15	.07	.02
SEMISTARS	.40	.18	.05
STARS	.75	.35	.09

□ 1 Harold Baines	.40	.18	.05
□ 2 Jeffrey Hammonds	.40	.18	.05
□ 3 Chris Hoiles	.15	.07	.02
□ 4 Ben McDonald	.15	.07	.02
□ 5 Mark McLemore	.15	.07	.02
□ 6 Jamie Moyer	.15	.07	.02
□ 7 Jim Poole	.15	.07	.02
□ 8 Cal Ripken Jr.	4.00	1.80	.50
□ 9 Chris Sabo	.15	.07	.02
□ 10 Scott Bankhead	.15	.07	.02
□ 11 Scott Cooper	.15	.07	.02
□ 12 Danny Darwin	.15	.07	.02
□ 13 Andre Dawson	.75	.35	.09
□ 14 Billy Hatcher	.15	.07	.02
□ 15 Aaron Sele	.40	.18	.05
□ 16 John Valentin	.40	.18	.05
□ 17 Dave Valle	.15	.07	.02
□ 18 Mo Vaughn	1.25	.55	.16
□ 19 Brian Anderson	.40	.18	.05
□ 20 Gary DiSarcina	.15	.07	.02
□ 21 Jim Edmonds	1.00	.45	.12
□ 22 Chuck Finley	.15	.07	.02
□ 23 Bo Jackson	.75	.35	.09
□ 24 Mark Leiter	.15	.07	.02
□ 25 Greg Myers	.15	.07	.02
□ 26 Eduardo Perez	.15	.07	.02
□ 27 Tim Salmon	.75	.35	.09
□ 28 Wilson Alvarez	.40	.18	.05
□ 29 Jason Bere	.40	.18	.05
□ 30 Alex Fernandez	.75	.35	.09
□ 31 Ozzie Guillen	.15	.07	.02
□ 32 Joe Hall	.15	.07	.02
□ 33 Darrin Jackson	.15	.07	.02
□ 34 Kirk McCaskill	.15	.07	.02
□ 35 Tim Raines	.75	.35	.09
□ 36 Frank Thomas	5.00	2.20	.60
□ 37 Carlos Baerga	.75	.35	.09
□ 38 Albert Belle	2.50	1.10	.30
□ 39 Mark Clark	.15	.07	.02
□ 40 Wayne Kirby	.15	.07	.02
□ 41 Dennis Martinez	.40	.18	.05
□ 42 Charles Nagy	.40	.18	.05
□ 43 Manny Ramirez	1.50	.70	.19
□ 44 Paul Sorrento	.15	.07	.02
□ 45 Jim Thome	1.25	.55	.16
□ 46 Eric Davis	.40	.18	.05
□ 47 John Doherty	.15	.07	.02
□ 48 Junior Felix	.15	.07	.02
□ 49 Cecil Fielder	.40	.18	.05
□ 50 Kirk Gibson	.40	.18	.05
□ 51 Mike Moore	.15	.07	.02
□ 52 Tony Phillips	.40	.18	.05
□ 53 Alan Trammell	.75	.35	.09
□ 54 Kevin Appier	.40	.18	.05
□ 55 Stan Belinda	.15	.07	.02
□ 56 Vince Coleman	.15	.07	.02
□ 57 Greg Gagne	.15	.07	.02
□ 58 Bob Hamelin	.15	.07	.02
□ 59 Dave Henderson	.15	.07	.02
□ 60 Wally Joyner	.40	.18	.05
□ 61 Mike Macfarlane	.15	.07	.02
□ 62 Jeff Montgomery	.40	.18	.05
□ 63 Ricky Bones	.15	.07	.02
□ 64 Jeff Bronkey	.15	.07	.02
□ 65 Alex Diaz	.15	.07	.02
□ 66 Cal Eldred	.15	.07	.02
□ 67 Darryl Hamilton	.15	.07	.02
□ 68 John Jaha	.40	.18	.05
□ 69 Mark Kiefer	.15	.07	.02
□ 70 Kevin Seitzer	.15	.07	.02
□ 71 Turner Ward	.15	.07	.02
□ 72 Rich Becker	.40	.18	.05
□ 73 Scott Erickson	.15	.07	.02
□ 74 Keith Garagozzo	.15	.07	.02
□ 75 Kent Hrbek	.40	.18	.05
□ 76 Scott Leius	.15	.07	.02
□ 77 Kirby Puckett	1.50	.70	.19
□ 78 Matt Walbeck	.15	.07	.02
□ 79 Dave Winfield	.75	.35	.09
□ 80 Mike Gallego	.15	.07	.02
□ 81 Xavier Hernandez	.15	.07	.02
□ 82 Jimmy Key	.40	.18	.05
□ 83 Jim Leyritz	.15	.07	.02
□ 84 Don Mattingly	2.50	1.10	.30
□ 85 Matt Nokes	.15	.07	.02
□ 86 Paul O'Neill	.40	.18	.05
□ 87 Melido Perez	.15	.07	.02
□ 88 Danny Tartabull	.15	.07	.02
□ 89 Mike Bordick	.15	.07	.02
□ 90 Ron Darling	.15	.07	.02
□ 91 Dennis Eckersley	.40	.18	.05
□ 92 Stan Javier	.15	.07	.02
□ 93 Steve Karsay	.15	.07	.02
□ 94 Mark McGwire	1.50	.70	.19

□ 95	Troy Neel	.15	.07	.02
□ 96	Terry Steinbach	.40	.18	.05
□ 97	Bill Taylor	.15	.07	.02
□ 98	Eric Anthony	.15	.07	.02
□ 99	Chris Bosio	.15	.07	.02
□ 100	Tim Davis	.15	.07	.02
□ 101	Felix Fermin	.15	.07	.02
□ 102	Dave Fleming	.15	.07	.02
□ 103	Ken Griffey Jr.	5.00	2.20	.60
□ 104	Greg Hibbard	.15	.07	.02
□ 105	Reggie Jefferson	.40	.18	.05
□ 106	Tino Martinez	.40	.18	.05
□ 107	Jack Armstrong	.15	.07	.02
□ 108	Will Clark	.75	.35	.09
□ 109	Juan Gonzalez	2.50	1.10	.30
□ 110	Rick Helling	.15	.07	.02
□ 111	Tom Henke	.15	.07	.02
□ 112	David Hulse	.15	.07	.02
□ 113	Manuel Lee	.15	.07	.02
□ 114	Doug Strange	.15	.07	.02
□ 115	Roberto Alomar	1.25	.55	.16
□ 116	Joe Carter	.75	.35	.09
□ 117	Carlos Delgado	.75	.35	.09
□ 118	Pat Hentgen	.75	.35	.09
□ 119	Paul Molitor	1.00	.45	.12
□ 120	John Olerud	.15	.07	.02
□ 121	Dave Stewart	.40	.18	.05
□ 122	Todd Stottlemyre	.15	.07	.02
□ 123	Mike Timlin	.15	.07	.02
□ 124	Jeff Blauser	.15	.07	.02
□ 125	Tom Glavine	.75	.35	.09
□ 126	David Justice	.75	.35	.09
□ 127	Mike Kelly	.15	.07	.02
□ 128	Ryan Klesko	1.25	.55	.16
□ 129	Javier Lopez	.75	.35	.09
□ 130	Greg Maddux	3.00	1.35	.35
□ 131	Fred McGriff	.75	.35	.09
□ 132	Kent Mercker	.15	.07	.02
□ 133	Mark Wohlers	.40	.18	.05
□ 134	Willie Banks	.15	.07	.02
□ 135	Steve Buechele	.15	.07	.02
□ 136	Shawon Dunston	.15	.07	.02
□ 137	Jose Guzman	.15	.07	.02
□ 138	Glenallen Hill	.15	.07	.02
□ 139	Randy Myers	.15	.07	.02
□ 140	Karl Rhodes	.15	.07	.02
□ 141	Ryne Sandberg	1.25	.55	.16
□ 142	Steve Trachsel	.40	.18	.05
□ 143	Bret Boone	.40	.18	.05
□ 144	Tom Browning	.15	.07	.02
□ 145	Hector Carrasco	.15	.07	.02
□ 146	Barry Larkin	.75	.35	.09
□ 147	Hal Morris	.15	.07	.02
□ 148	Jose Rijo	.15	.07	.02
□ 149	Reggie Sanders	.75	.35	.09
□ 150	John Smiley	.15	.07	.02
□ 151	Dante Bichette	.75	.35	.09
□ 152	Ellis Burks	.40	.18	.05
□ 153	Joe Girardi	.15	.07	.02
□ 154	Mike Harkey	.15	.07	.02
□ 155	Roberto Mejia	.15	.07	.02
□ 156	Marcus Moore	.15	.07	.02
□ 157	Armando Reynoso	.15	.07	.02
□ 158	Bruce Ruffin	.15	.07	.02
□ 159	Eric Young	.40	.18	.05
□ 160	Kurt Abbott	.40	.18	.05
□ 161	Jeff Conine	.75	.35	.09
□ 162	Orestes Destrade	.15	.07	.02
□ 163	Chris Hammond	.15	.07	.02
□ 164	Bryan Harvey	.15	.07	.02
□ 165	Dave Magadan	.15	.07	.02
□ 166	Gary Sheffield	.75	.35	.09
□ 167	David Weathers	.15	.07	.02
□ 168	Andujar Cedeno	.15	.07	.02
□ 169	Tom Edens	.15	.07	.02
□ 170	Luis Gonzalez	.15	.07	.02
□ 171	Pete Harnisch	.15	.07	.02
□ 172	Todd Jones	.15	.07	.02
□ 173	Darryl Kile	.15	.07	.02
□ 174	James Mouton	.40	.18	.05
□ 175	Scott Servais	.15	.07	.02
□ 176	Mitch Williams	.15	.07	.02
□ 177	Pedro Astacio	.15	.07	.02
□ 178	Orel Hershiser	.40	.18	.05
□ 179	Raul Mondesi	.75	.35	.09
□ 180	Jose Offerman	.15	.07	.02
□ 181	Chan Ho Park	1.25	.55	.16
□ 182	Mike Piazza	3.00	1.35	.35
□ 183	Cory Snyder	.15	.07	.02
□ 184	Tim Wallach	.15	.07	.02
□ 185	Todd Worrell	.15	.07	.02
□ 186	Sean Berry	.15	.07	.02
□ 187	Wil Cordero	.40	.18	.05
□ 188	Darrin Fletcher	.15	.07	.02
□ 189	Cliff Floyd	.75	.35	.09
□ 190	Marquis Grissom	.75	.35	.09
□ 191	Rod Henderson	.15	.07	.02
□ 192	Ken Hill	.15	.07	.02
□ 193	Pedro Martinez	.75	.35	.09
□ 194	Kirk Rueter	.15	.07	.02
□ 195	Jeromy Burnitz	.15	.07	.02
□ 196	John Franco	.15	.07	.02
□ 197	Dwight Gooden	.40	.18	.05
□ 198	Todd Hundley	.75	.35	.09
□ 199	Bobby Jones	.40	.18	.05
□ 200	Jeff Kent	.15	.07	.02
□ 201	Mike Maddux	.15	.07	.02
□ 202	Ryan Thompson	.15	.07	.02
□ 203	Jose Vizcaino	.15	.07	.02
□ 204	Darren Daulton	.40	.18	.05
□ 205	Lenny Dykstra	.40	.18	.05
□ 206	Jim Eisenreich	.15	.07	.02
□ 207	Dave Hollins	.15	.07	.02
□ 208	Danny Jackson	.15	.07	.02
□ 209	Doug Jones	.15	.07	.02
□ 210	Jeff Juden	.15	.07	.02
□ 211	Ben Rivera	.15	.07	.02
□ 212	Kevin Stocker	.15	.07	.02
□ 213	Milt Thompson	.15	.07	.02
□ 214	Jay Bell	.40	.18	.05
□ 215	Steve Cooke	.15	.07	.02
□ 216	Mark Dewey	.15	.07	.02
□ 217	Al Martin	.15	.07	.02
□ 218	Orlando Merced	.40	.18	.05
□ 219	Don Slaught	.15	.07	.02
□ 220	Zane Smith	.15	.07	.02
□ 221	Rick White	.15	.07	.02
□ 222	Kevin Young	.15	.07	.02
□ 223	Rene Arocha	.15	.07	.02
□ 224	Rheal Cormier	.15	.07	.02
□ 225	Brian Jordan	.75	.35	.09
□ 226	Ray Lankford	.75	.35	.09
□ 227	Mike Perez	.15	.07	.02
□ 228	Ozzie Smith	1.00	.45	.12
□ 229	Mark Whiten	.15	.07	.02
□ 230	Todd Zeile	.15	.07	.02
□ 231	Derek Bell	.40	.18	.05
□ 232	Archi Cianfrocco	.15	.07	.02
□ 233	Ricky Gutierrez	.15	.07	.02
□ 234	Trevor Hoffman	.40	.18	.05
□ 235	Phil Plantier	.15	.07	.02
□ 236	Dave Staton	.15	.07	.02
□ 237	Wally Whitehurst	.15	.07	.02
□ 238	Todd Benzinger	.15	.07	.02
□ 239	Barry Bonds	1.25	.55	.16
□ 240	John Burkett	.15	.07	.02
□ 241	Royce Clayton	.40	.18	.05
□ 242	Bryan Hickerson	.15	.07	.02
□ 243	Mike Jackson	.15	.07	.02
□ 244	Darren Lewis	.15	.07	.02
□ 245	Kirt Manwaring	.15	.07	.02
□ 246	Mark Portugal	.15	.07	.02
□ 247	Salomon Torres	.15	.07	.02
□ 248	Checklist	.15	.07	.02
□ 249	Checklist	.15	.07	.02
□ 250	Checklist	.15	.07	.02
□ 251	Brady Anderson	.75	.35	.09
□ 252	Mike Devereaux	.15	.07	.02
□ 253	Sid Fernandez	.15	.07	.02
□ 254	Leo Gomez	.15	.07	.02
□ 255	Mike Mussina	1.00	.45	.12
□ 256	Mike Oquist	.15	.07	.02
□ 257	Rafael Palmeiro	.75	.35	.09
□ 258	Lee Smith	.40	.18	.05
□ 259	Damon Berryhill	.15	.07	.02
□ 260	Wes Chamberlain	.15	.07	.02
□ 261	Roger Clemens	.75	.35	.09
□ 262	Gar Finnvold	.15	.07	.02
□ 263	Mike Greenwell	.15	.07	.02
□ 264	Tim Naehring	.15	.07	.02
□ 265	Otis Nixon	.15	.07	.02
□ 266	Ken Ryan	.15	.07	.02

☐	267	Chad Curtis	.15	.07	.02
☐	268	Chili Davis	.40	.18	.05
☐	269	Damion Easley	.15	.07	.02
☐	270	Jorge Fabregas	.15	.07	.02
☐	271	Mark Langston	.40	.18	.05
☐	272	Phil Leftwich	.15	.07	.02
☐	273	Harold Reynolds	.15	.07	.02
☐	274	J.T. Snow	.40	.18	.05
☐	275	Joey Cora	.15	.07	.02
☐	276	Julio Franco	.40	.18	.05
☐	277	Roberto Hernandez	.40	.18	.05
☐	278	Lance Johnson	.40	.18	.05
☐	279	Ron Karkovice	.15	.07	.02
☐	280	Jack McDowell	.40	.18	.05
☐	281	Robin Ventura	.40	.18	.05
☐	282	Sandy Alomar Jr.	.40	.18	.05
☐	283	Kenny Lofton	1.50	.70	.19
☐	284	Jose Mesa	.40	.18	.05
☐	285	Jack Morris	.40	.18	.05
☐	286	Eddie Murray	1.25	.55	.16
☐	287	Chad Ogea	.40	.18	.05
☐	288	Eric Plunk	.15	.07	.02
☐	289	Paul Shuey	.15	.07	.02
☐	290	Omar Vizquel	.75	.35	.09
☐	291	Danny Bautista	.15	.07	.02
☐	292	Travis Fryman	.75	.35	.09
☐	293	Greg Gohr	.15	.07	.02
☐	294	Chris Gomez	.15	.07	.02
☐	295	Mickey Tettleton	.15	.07	.02
☐	296	Lou Whitaker	.75	.35	.09
☐	297	David Cone	.75	.35	.09
☐	298	Gary Gaetti	.40	.18	.05
☐	299	Tom Gordon	.15	.07	.02
☐	300	Felix Jose	.15	.07	.02
☐	301	Jose Lind	.15	.07	.02
☐	302	Brian McRae	.40	.18	.05
☐	303	Mike Fetters	.15	.07	.02
☐	304	Brian Harper	.15	.07	.02
☐	305	Pat Listach	.15	.07	.02
☐	306	Matt Mieske	.15	.07	.02
☐	307	Dave Nilsson	.40	.18	.05
☐	308	Jody Reed	.15	.07	.02
☐	309	Greg Vaughn	.75	.35	.09
☐	310	Bill Wegman	.15	.07	.02
☐	311	Rick Aguilera	.15	.07	.02
☐	312	Alex Cole	.15	.07	.02
☐	313	Denny Hocking	.15	.07	.02
☐	314	Chuck Knoblauch	.75	.35	.09
☐	315	Shane Mack	.15	.07	.02
☐	316	Pat Meares	.15	.07	.02
☐	317	Kevin Tapani	.15	.07	.02
☐	318	Jim Abbott	.15	.07	.02
☐	319	Wade Boggs	.75	.35	.09
☐	320	Sterling Hitchcock	.40	.18	.05
☐	321	Pat Kelly	.15	.07	.02
☐	322	Terry Mulholland	.15	.07	.02
☐	323	Luis Polonia	.15	.07	.02
☐	324	Mike Stanley	.15	.07	.02
☐	325	Bob Wickman	.15	.07	.02
☐	326	Bernie Williams	.75	.35	.09
☐	327	Mark Acre	.15	.07	.02
☐	328	Geronimo Berroa	.40	.18	.05
☐	329	Scott Brosius	.15	.07	.02
☐	330	Brent Gates	.15	.07	.02
☐	331	Rickey Henderson	.75	.35	.09
☐	332	Carlos Reyes	.15	.07	.02
☐	333	Ruben Sierra	.40	.18	.05
☐	334	Bobby Witt	.15	.07	.02
☐	335	Bobby Ayala	.15	.07	.02
☐	336	Jay Buhner	.75	.35	.09
☐	337	Randy Johnson	.75	.35	.09
☐	338	Edgar Martinez	.75	.35	.09
☐	339	Bill Risley	.15	.07	.02
☐	340	Alex Rodriguez	25.00	11.00	3.10
☐	341	Roger Salkeld	.15	.07	.02
☐	342	Dan Wilson	.40	.18	.05
☐	343	Kevin Brown	.15	.07	.02
☐	344	Jose Canseco	.75	.35	.09
☐	345	Dean Palmer	.40	.18	.05
☐	346	Ivan Rodriguez	1.00	.45	.12
☐	347	Kenny Rogers	.15	.07	.02
☐	348	Pat Borders	.15	.07	.02
☐	349	Juan Guzman	.40	.18	.05
☐	350	Ed Sprague	.40	.18	.05
☐	351	Devon White	.15	.07	.02
☐	352	Steve Avery	.40	.18	.05
☐	353	Roberto Kelly	.15	.07	.02
☐	354	Mark Lemke	.15	.07	.02
☐	355	Greg McMichael	.15	.07	.02
☐	356	Terry Pendleton	.40	.18	.05
☐	357	John Smoltz	.75	.35	.09
☐	358	Mike Stanton	.15	.07	.02
☐	359	Tony Tarasco	.15	.07	.02
☐	360	Mark Grace	.75	.35	.09
☐	361	Derrick May	.15	.07	.02
☐	362	Rey Sanchez	.15	.07	.02
☐	363	Sammy Sosa	.75	.35	.09
☐	364	Rick Wilkins	.15	.07	.02
☐	365	Jeff Brantley	.15	.07	.02
☐	366	Tony Fernandez	.15	.07	.02
☐	367	Chuck McElroy	.15	.07	.02
☐	368	Kevin Mitchell	.40	.18	.05
☐	369	John Roper	.15	.07	.02
☐	370	Johnny Ruffin	.15	.07	.02
☐	371	Deion Sanders	.75	.35	.09
☐	372	Marvin Freeman	.15	.07	.02
☐	373	Andres Galarraga	.75	.35	.09
☐	374	Charlie Hayes	.15	.07	.02
☐	375	Nelson Liriano	.15	.07	.02
☐	376	David Nied	.15	.07	.02
☐	377	Walt Weiss	.15	.07	.02
☐	378	Bret Barberie	.15	.07	.02
☐	379	Jerry Browne	.15	.07	.02
☐	380	Chuck Carr	.15	.07	.02
☐	381	Greg Colbrunn	.15	.07	.02
☐	382	Charlie Hough	.15	.07	.02
☐	383	Kurt Miller	.15	.07	.02
☐	384	Benito Santiago	.15	.07	.02
☐	385	Jeff Bagwell	2.00	.90	.25
☐	386	Craig Biggio	.75	.35	.09
☐	387	Ken Caminiti	.75	.35	.09
☐	388	Doug Drabek	.15	.07	.02
☐	389	Steve Finley	.75	.35	.09
☐	390	John Hudek	.15	.07	.02
☐	391	Orlando Miller	.15	.07	.02
☐	392	Shane Reynolds	.40	.18	.05
☐	393	Brett Butler	.40	.18	.05
☐	394	Tom Candiotti	.15	.07	.02
☐	395	Delino DeShields	.15	.07	.02
☐	396	Kevin Gross	.15	.07	.02
☐	397	Eric Karros	.40	.18	.05
☐	398	Ramon Martinez	.40	.18	.05
☐	399	Henry Rodriguez	.75	.35	.09
☐	400	Moises Alou	.40	.18	.05
☐	401	Jeff Fassero	.15	.07	.02
☐	402	Mike Lansing	.40	.18	.05
☐	403	Mel Rojas	.15	.07	.02
☐	404	Larry Walker	.75	.35	.09
☐	405	John Wetteland	.40	.18	.05
☐	406	Gabe White	.15	.07	.02
☐	407	Bobby Bonilla	.40	.18	.05
☐	408	Josias Manzanillo	.15	.07	.02
☐	409	Bret Saberhagen	.40	.18	.05
☐	410	David Segui	.15	.07	.02
☐	411	Mariano Duncan	.15	.07	.02
☐	412	Tommy Greene	.15	.07	.02
☐	413	Billy Hatcher	.15	.07	.02
☐	414	Ricky Jordan	.15	.07	.02
☐	415	John Kruk	.40	.18	.05
☐	416	Bobby Munoz	.15	.07	.02
☐	417	Curt Schilling	.15	.07	.02
☐	418	Fernando Valenzuela	.40	.18	.05
☐	419	David West	.15	.07	.02
☐	420	Carlos Garcia	.15	.07	.02
☐	421	Brian Hunter	.15	.07	.02
☐	422	Jeff King	.40	.18	.05
☐	423	Jon Lieber	.15	.07	.02
☐	424	Ravelo Manzanillo	.15	.07	.02
☐	425	Denny Neagle	.40	.18	.05
☐	426	Andy Van Slyke	.40	.18	.05
☐	427	Bryan Eversgerd	.15	.07	.02
☐	428	Bernard Gilkey	.40	.18	.05
☐	429	Gregg Jefferies	.75	.35	.09
☐	430	Tom Pagnozzi	.15	.07	.02
☐	431	Bob Tewksbury	.15	.07	.02
☐	432	Allen Watson	.15	.07	.02
☐	433	Andy Ashby	.40	.18	.05
☐	434	Andy Benes	.40	.18	.05
☐	435	Donnie Elliott	.15	.07	.02
☐	436	Tony Gwynn	2.00	.90	.25
☐	437	Joey Hamilton	1.00	.45	.12
☐	438	Tim Hyers	.15	.07	.02

		MINT	NRMT	EXC
□ 439	Luis Lopez	.15	.07	.02
□ 440	Bip Roberts	.15	.07	.02
□ 441	Scott Sanders	.15	.07	.02
□ 442	Rod Beck	.40	.18	.05
□ 443	Dave Burba	.15	.07	.02
□ 444	Darryl Strawberry	.40	.18	.05
□ 445	Bill Swift	.15	.07	.02
□ 446	Robby Thompson	.15	.07	.02
□ 447	Bill VanLandingham	.40	.18	.05
□ 448	Matt Williams	.75	.35	.09
□ 449	Checklist	.15	.07	.02
□ 450	Checklist	.15	.07	.02
□ P15	Aaron Sele Promo	1.50	.70	.19

1994 Flair Hot Gloves

Randomly inserted in second series packs at a rate of one in 24, this set highlights 10 of the game's top players that also have outstanding defensive ability. The cards feature a special die-cut "glove" design with the player appearing within the glove. The back has a short write-up and a photo.

	MINT	NRMT	EXC
COMPLETE SET (10)	250.00	110.00	31.00
COMMON CARD (1-10)	10.00	4.50	1.25
RANDOM INSERTS IN SER.2 PACKS			

		MINT	NRMT	EXC
□ 1	Barry Bonds	20.00	9.00	2.50
□ 2	Will Clark	10.00	4.50	1.25
□ 3	Ken Griffey Jr.	80.00	36.00	10.00
□ 4	Kenny Lofton	25.00	11.00	3.10
□ 5	Greg Maddux	50.00	22.00	6.25
□ 6	Don Mattingly	40.00	18.00	5.00
□ 7	Kirby Puckett	25.00	11.00	3.10
□ 8	Cal Ripken Jr.	60.00	27.00	7.50
□ 9	Tim Salmon	15.00	6.75	1.85
□ 10	Matt Williams	10.00	4.50	1.25

1994 Flair Hot Numbers

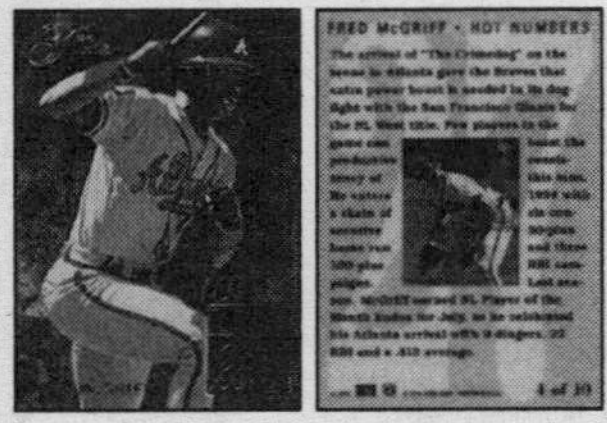

This 10-card set was randomly inserted in first series packs at a rate of one in 24. Metallic fronts feature a player photo with various numbers or statistics serving as background. The player's uniform number is part of the Hot Numbers logo at bottom left or right. The player's name is also at the bottom. The backs have a small photo centered in the middle surrounded by text highlighting achievements.

	MINT	NRMT	EXC
COMPLETE SET (10)	120.00	55.00	15.00
COMMON CARD (1-10)	2.50	1.10	.30
SEMISTARS	5.00	2.20	.60
RANDOM INSERTS IN SER.1 PACKS			

		MINT	NRMT	EXC
□ 1	Roberto Alomar	10.00	4.50	1.25
□ 2	Carlos Baerga	5.00	2.20	.60
□ 3	Will Clark	5.00	2.20	.60
□ 4	Fred McGriff	5.00	2.20	.60
□ 5	Paul Molitor	8.00	3.60	1.00
□ 6	John Olerud	2.50	1.10	.30
□ 7	Mike Piazza	25.00	11.00	3.10
□ 8	Cal Ripken Jr.	35.00	16.00	4.40
□ 9	Ryne Sandberg	10.00	4.50	1.25
□ 10	Frank Thomas	40.00	18.00	5.00

1994 Flair Infield Power

Randomly inserted in second series packs at a rate of one in five, this 10-card standard-size set spotlights major league infielders who are power hitters. Card fronts feature a horizontal format with two photos of the player. The backs contain a short write-up with emphasis on power numbers. The back also has a small photo.

	MINT	NRMT	EXC
COMPLETE SET (10)	20.00	9.00	2.50
COMMON CARD (1-10)	.50	.23	.06
RANDOM INSERTS IN SER.2 PACKS			

		MINT	NRMT	EXC
□ 1	Jeff Bagwell	3.00	1.35	.35
□ 2	Will Clark	1.00	.45	.12
□ 3	Darren Daulton	.50	.23	.06
□ 4	Don Mattingly	4.00	1.80	.50
□ 5	Fred McGriff	1.00	.45	.12
□ 6	Rafael Palmeiro	1.00	.45	.12
□ 7	Mike Piazza	5.00	2.20	.60
□ 8	Cal Ripken Jr.	6.00	2.70	.75
□ 9	Frank Thomas	8.00	3.60	1.00
□ 10	Matt Williams	1.00	.45	.12

1994 Flair Outfield Power

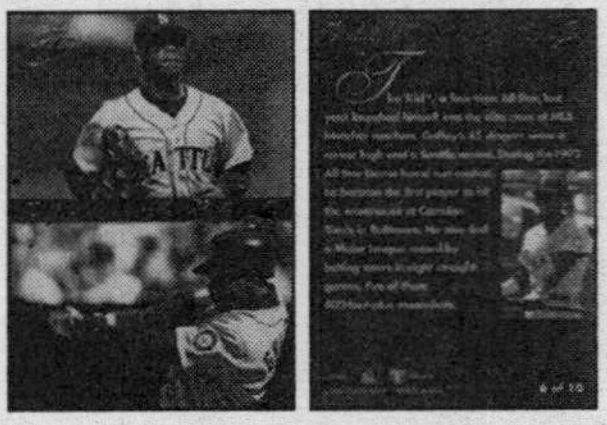

This 10-card standard-size set was randomly inserted in both first and second series packs at a rate of one in five. Two photos on the front feature the player fielding and hitting. The player's name and Outfield Power serve as a divid-

ing point between the photos. The back contains a small photo and text.

	MINT	NRMT	EXC
COMPLETE SET (10)	25.00	11.00	3.10
COMMON CARD (1-10)	.75	.35	.09
SEMISTARS	1.25	.55	.16
RANDOM INSERTS IN SER.1 PACKS			

		MINT	NRMT	EXC
□ 1	Albert Belle	5.00	2.20	.60
□ 2	Barry Bonds	2.50	1.10	.30
□ 3	Joe Carter	1.25	.55	.16
□ 4	Lenny Dykstra	.75	.35	.09
□ 5	Juan Gonzalez	5.00	2.20	.60
□ 6	Ken Griffey Jr.	10.00	4.50	1.25
□ 7	David Justice	.75	.35	.09
□ 8	Kirby Puckett	3.00	1.35	.35
□ 9	Tim Salmon	1.50	.70	.19
□ 10	Dave Winfield	1.25	.55	.16

1994 Flair Wave of the Future

This 20-card standard-size set takes a look at potential big league stars. The cards were randomly inserted in packs at a rate of one in five -- the first 10 in series 1, the second 10 in series 2. The fronts and backs have the player superimposed over a wavy colored background. The front has the Wave of the Future logo and a paragraph or two about the player along with a photo on the back.

	MINT	NRMT	EXC
COMPLETE SET (20)	85.00	38.00	10.50
COMPLETE SER.1 SET (10)	15.00	6.75	1.85
COMPLETE SER.2 SET (10)	70.00	32.00	8.75
COMMON SER.1 CARD (A1-A10)	1.00	.45	.12
COMMON SER.2 CARD (B1-B10)	1.00	.45	.12
RANDOM INSERTS IN PACKS			

		MINT	NRMT	EXC
□ A1	Kurt Abbott	1.50	.70	.19
□ A2	Carlos Delgado	3.00	1.35	.35
□ A3	Steve Karsay	1.00	.45	.12
□ A4	Ryan Klesko	5.00	2.20	.60
□ A5	Javier Lopez	2.50	1.10	.30
□ A6	Raul Mondesi	3.00	1.35	.35
□ A7	James Mouton	1.50	.70	.19
□ A8	Chan Ho Park	4.00	1.80	.50
□ A9	Dave Staton	1.00	.45	.12
□ A10	Rick White	1.00	.45	.12
□ B1	Mark Acre	1.00	.45	.12
□ B2	Chris Gomez	1.00	.45	.12
□ B3	Joey Hamilton	4.00	1.80	.50
□ B4	John Hudek	1.00	.45	.12
□ B5	Jon Lieber	1.00	.45	.12
□ B6	Matt Mieske	1.50	.70	.19
□ B7	Orlando Miller	1.00	.45	.12
□ B8	Alex Rodriguez	65.00	29.00	8.00
□ B9	Tony Tarasco	1.00	.45	.12
□ B10	William VanLandingham	1.00	.45	.12

1995 Flair

This set was issued in two series of 216 cards for a total of 432 standard-size cards. Horizontally designed fronts have a 100 per

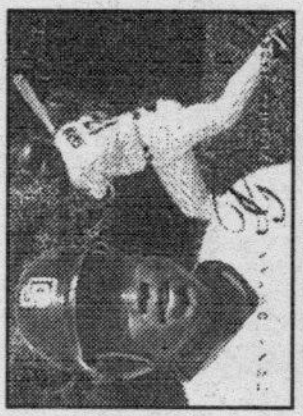

cent etched foil surface containing two player photos. The backs feature a full-bleed photo with yearly statistics superimposed. The check list is arranged alphabetically by league according to series as follows: Baltimore Orioles (1-9/217-225), Boston Red Sox (10-15/226-232), California Angels (16-22/233-239), Chicago White Sox (23-28/240-248), Cleveland Indians (29-36/249-254), Detroit Tigers (37-42/255-261), Kansas City Royals (43-49/262-268), Milwaukee Brewers (50-56/269-276), Minnesota Twins (57-62/277-282), New York Yankees (63-69/283-290), Oakland Athletics (70-77/291-298), Seattle Mariners (78-85/299-304), Texas Rangers (86-93/305-312), Toronto Blue Jays (94-101/313-319), Atlanta Braves (102-110/320-329), Chicago Cubs (111-118/330-336), Cincinnati Reds (119-126/337-341), Colorado Rockies (127-135/342-348), Florida Marlins (136-142/349-356), Houston Astros (143-149/357-364), Los Angeles Dodgers (150-159/365-371), Montreal Expos (160-168/372-379), New York Mets (169-175/380-387), Philadelphia Phillies (176-183/388-396), Pittsburgh Pirates (184-190/397-405), St. Louis Cardinals (191-197/406-413), San Diego Padres (198-205/414-423) and San Francisco Giants (206-213/424-429).

	MINT	NRMT	EXC
COMPLETE SET (432)	90.00	40.00	11.00
COMPLETE SERIES 1 (216)	50.00	22.00	6.25
COMPLETE SERIES (216)	40.00	18.00	5.00
COMMON CARD (1-432)	.25	.11	.03
SEMISTARS	.40	.18	.05
STARS	.75	.35	.09
COMP.RIPKEN SET (10)	120.00	55.00	15.00
COMMON RIPKEN (1-10)	12.00	5.50	1.50
RANDOM INSERTS IN SER.2 PACKS			
COMMON MAIL-IN (11-15)	8.00	3.60	1.00

		MINT	NRMT	EXC
□ 1	Brady Anderson	.75	.35	.09
□ 2	Harold Baines	.40	.18	.05
□ 3	Leo Gomez	.25	.11	.03
□ 4	Alan Mills	.25	.11	.03
□ 5	Jamie Moyer	.25	.11	.03
□ 6	Mike Mussina	1.00	.45	.12
□ 7	Mike Oquist	.25	.11	.03
□ 8	Arthur Rhodes	.25	.11	.03
□ 9	Cal Ripken Jr.	4.00	1.80	.50
□ 10	Roger Clemens	.75	.35	.09
□ 11	Scott Cooper	.25	.11	.03
□ 12	Mike Greenwell	.25	.11	.03
□ 13	Aaron Sele	.40	.18	.05
□ 14	John Valentin	.40	.18	.05
□ 15	Mo Vaughn	1.25	.55	.16
□ 16	Chad Curtis	.25	.11	.03
□ 17	Gary DiSarcina	.25	.11	.03
□ 18	Chuck Finley	.40	.18	.05
□ 19	Andrew Lorraine	.40	.18	.05
□ 20	Spike Owen	.25	.11	.03
□ 21	Tim Salmon	.75	.35	.09
□ 22	J.T. Snow	.40	.18	.05
□ 23	Wilson Alvarez	.40	.18	.05
□ 24	Jason Bere	.25	.11	.03
□ 25	Ozzie Guillen	.25	.11	.03
□ 26	Mike LaValliere	.25	.11	.03
□ 27	Frank Thomas	5.00	2.20	.60
□ 28	Robin Ventura	.40	.18	.05
□ 29	Carlos Baerga	.75	.35	.09

□ 30	Albert Belle	2.50	1.10	.30
□ 31	Jason Grimsley	.25	.11	.03
□ 32	Dennis Martinez	.40	.18	.05
□ 33	Eddie Murray	1.25	.55	.16
□ 34	Charles Nagy	.40	.18	.05
□ 35	Manny Ramirez	1.25	.55	.16
□ 36	Paul Sorrento	.25	.11	.03
□ 37	John Doherty	.25	.11	.03
□ 38	Cecil Fielder	.40	.18	.05
□ 39	Travis Fryman	.40	.18	.05
□ 40	Chris Gomez	.25	.11	.03
□ 41	Tony Phillips	.40	.18	.05
□ 42	Lou Whitaker	.75	.35	.09
□ 43	David Cone	.40	.18	.05
□ 44	Gary Gaetti	.40	.18	.05
□ 45	Mark Gubicza	.25	.11	.03
□ 46	Bob Hamelin	.25	.11	.03
□ 47	Wally Joyner	.40	.18	.05
□ 48	Rusty Meacham	.25	.11	.03
□ 49	Jeff Montgomery	.40	.18	.05
□ 50	Ricky Bones	.25	.11	.03
□ 51	Cal Eldred	.25	.11	.03
□ 52	Pat Listach	.25	.11	.03
□ 53	Matt Mieske	.40	.18	.05
□ 54	Dave Nilsson	.40	.18	.05
□ 55	Greg Vaughn	.40	.18	.05
□ 56	Bill Wegman	.25	.11	.03
□ 57	Chuck Knoblauch	.75	.35	.09
□ 58	Scott Leius	.25	.11	.03
□ 59	Pat Mahomes	.25	.11	.03
□ 60	Pat Meares	.25	.11	.03
□ 61	Pedro Munoz	.25	.11	.03
□ 62	Kirby Puckett	1.50	.70	.19
□ 63	Wade Boggs	.75	.35	.09
□ 64	Jimmy Key	.40	.18	.05
□ 65	Jim Leyritz	.25	.11	.03
□ 66	Don Mattingly	2.50	1.10	.30
□ 67	Paul O'Neill	.40	.18	.05
□ 68	Melido Perez	.25	.11	.03
□ 69	Danny Tartabull	.25	.11	.03
□ 70	John Briscoe	.25	.11	.03
□ 71	Scott Brosius	.25	.11	.03
□ 72	Ron Darling	.25	.11	.03
□ 73	Brent Gates	.25	.11	.03
□ 74	Rickey Henderson	.75	.35	.09
□ 75	Stan Javier	.25	.11	.03
□ 76	Mark McGwire	1.50	.70	.19
□ 77	Todd Van Poppel	.25	.11	.03
□ 78	Bobby Ayala	.25	.11	.03
□ 79	Mike Blowers	.25	.11	.03
□ 80	Jay Buhner	.75	.35	.09
□ 81	Ken Griffey Jr.	5.00	2.20	.60
□ 82	Randy Johnson	.75	.35	.09
□ 83	Tino Martinez	.40	.18	.05
□ 84	Jeff Nelson	.25	.11	.03
□ 85	Alex Rodriguez	6.00	2.70	.75
□ 86	Will Clark	.75	.35	.09
□ 87	Jeff Frye	.25	.11	.03
□ 88	Juan Gonzalez	2.50	1.10	.30
□ 89	Rusty Greer	.75	.35	.09
□ 90	Darren Oliver	.40	.18	.05
□ 91	Dean Palmer	.40	.18	.05
□ 92	Ivan Rodriguez	1.00	.45	.12
□ 93	Matt Whiteside	.25	.11	.03
□ 94	Roberto Alomar	1.25	.55	.16
□ 95	Joe Carter	.75	.35	.09
□ 96	Tony Castillo	.25	.11	.03
□ 97	Juan Guzman	.40	.18	.05
□ 98	Pat Hentgen	.40	.18	.05
□ 99	Mike Huff	.25	.11	.03
□ 100	John Olerud	.25	.11	.03
□ 101	Woody Williams	.25	.11	.03
□ 102	Roberto Kelly	.25	.11	.03
□ 103	Ryan Klesko	1.00	.45	.12
□ 104	Javier Lopez	.75	.35	.09
□ 105	Greg Maddux	3.00	1.35	.35
□ 106	Fred McGriff	.75	.35	.09
□ 107	Jose Oliva	.25	.11	.03
□ 108	John Smoltz	.75	.35	.09
□ 109	Tony Tarasco	.25	.11	.03
□ 110	Mark Wohlers	.40	.18	.05
□ 111	Jim Bullinger	.25	.11	.03
□ 112	Shawon Dunston	.25	.11	.03
□ 113	Derrick May	.25	.11	.03
□ 114	Randy Myers	.25	.11	.03
□ 115	Karl Rhodes	.25	.11	.03
□ 116	Rey Sanchez	.25	.11	.03
□ 117	Steve Trachsel	.25	.11	.03
□ 118	Eddie Zambrano	.25	.11	.03
□ 119	Bret Boone	.40	.18	.05
□ 120	Brian Dorsett	.25	.11	.03
□ 121	Hal Morris	.25	.11	.03
□ 122	Jose Rijo	.25	.11	.03
□ 123	John Roper	.25	.11	.03
□ 124	Reggie Sanders	.40	.18	.05
□ 125	Pete Schourek	.40	.18	.05
□ 126	John Smiley	.25	.11	.03
□ 127	Ellis Burks	.75	.35	.09
□ 128	Vinny Castilla	.40	.18	.05
□ 129	Marvin Freeman	.25	.11	.03
□ 130	Andres Galarraga	.75	.35	.09
□ 131	Mike Munoz	.25	.11	.03
□ 132	David Nied	.25	.11	.03
□ 133	Bruce Ruffin	.25	.11	.03
□ 134	Walt Weiss	.25	.11	.03
□ 135	Eric Young	.40	.18	.05
□ 136	Greg Colbrunn	.25	.11	.03
□ 137	Jeff Conine	.75	.35	.09
□ 138	Jeremy Hernandez	.25	.11	.03
□ 139	Charles Johnson	.40	.18	.05
□ 140	Robb Nen	.25	.11	.03
□ 141	Gary Sheffield	.75	.35	.09
□ 142	Dave Weathers	.25	.11	.03
□ 143	Jeff Bagwell	2.00	.90	.25
□ 144	Craig Biggio	.75	.35	.09
□ 145	Tony Eusebio	.25	.11	.03
□ 146	Luis Gonzalez	.25	.11	.03
□ 147	John Hudek	.25	.11	.03
□ 148	Darryl Kile	.25	.11	.03
□ 149	Dave Veres	.25	.11	.03
□ 150	Billy Ashley	.25	.11	.03
□ 151	Pedro Astacio	.25	.11	.03
□ 152	Rafael Bournigal	.25	.11	.03
□ 153	Delino DeShields	.25	.11	.03
□ 154	Raul Mondesi	.75	.35	.09
□ 155	Mike Piazza	3.00	1.35	.35
□ 156	Rudy Seanez	.25	.11	.03
□ 157	Ismael Valdes	.40	.18	.05
□ 158	Tim Wallach	.25	.11	.03
□ 159	Todd Worrell	.25	.11	.03
□ 160	Moises Alou	.40	.18	.05
□ 161	Cliff Floyd	.40	.18	.05
□ 162	Gil Heredia	.25	.11	.03
□ 163	Mike Lansing	.25	.11	.03
□ 164	Pedro Martinez	.40	.18	.05
□ 165	Kirk Rueter	.25	.11	.03
□ 166	Tim Scott	.25	.11	.03
□ 167	Jeff Shaw	.25	.11	.03
□ 168	Rondell White	.75	.35	.09
□ 169	Bobby Bonilla	.40	.18	.05
□ 170	Rico Brogna	.25	.11	.03
□ 171	Todd Hundley	.40	.18	.05
□ 172	Jeff Kent	.25	.11	.03
□ 173	Jim Lindeman	.25	.11	.03
□ 174	Joe Orsulak	.25	.11	.03
□ 175	Bret Saberhagen	.40	.18	.05
□ 176	Toby Borland	.25	.11	.03
□ 177	Darren Daulton	.40	.18	.05
□ 178	Lenny Dykstra	.40	.18	.05
□ 179	Jim Eisenreich	.25	.11	.03
□ 180	Tommy Greene	.25	.11	.03
□ 181	Tony Longmire	.25	.11	.03
□ 182	Bobby Munoz	.25	.11	.03
□ 183	Kevin Stocker	.25	.11	.03
□ 184	Jay Bell	.40	.18	.05
□ 185	Steve Cooke	.25	.11	.03
□ 186	Ravelo Manzanillo	.25	.11	.03
□ 187	Al Martin	.40	.18	.05
□ 188	Denny Neagle	.40	.18	.05
□ 189	Don Slaught	.25	.11	.03
□ 190	Paul Wagner	.25	.11	.03
□ 191	Rene Arocha	.25	.11	.03
□ 192	Bernard Gilkey	.40	.18	.05
□ 193	Jose Oquendo	.25	.11	.03
□ 194	Tom Pagnozzi	.25	.11	.03
□ 195	Ozzie Smith	1.00	.45	.12
□ 196	Allen Watson	.25	.11	.03
□ 197	Mark Whiten	.25	.11	.03
□ 198	Andy Ashby	.40	.18	.05
□ 199	Donnie Elliott	.25	.11	.03
□ 200	Bryce Florie	.25	.11	.03
□ 201	Tony Gwynn	2.00	.90	.25

☐ 202	Trevor Hoffman	.25	.11	.03
☐ 203	Brian Johnson	.25	.11	.03
☐ 204	Tim Mauser	.25	.11	.03
☐ 205	Bip Roberts	.25	.11	.03
☐ 206	Rod Beck	.25	.11	.03
☐ 207	Barry Bonds	1.25	.55	.16
☐ 208	Royce Clayton	.25	.11	.03
☐ 209	Darren Lewis	.25	.11	.03
☐ 210	Mark Portugal	.25	.11	.03
☐ 211	Kevin Rogers	.25	.11	.03
☐ 212	Wm. VanLandingham	.25	.11	.03
☐ 213	Matt Williams	.75	.35	.09
☐ 214	Checklist	.25	.11	.03
☐ 215	Checklist	.25	.11	.03
☐ 216	Checklist	.25	.11	.03
☐ 217	Bret Barberie	.25	.11	.03
☐ 218	Armando Benitez	.25	.11	.03
☐ 219	Kevin Brown	.40	.18	.05
☐ 220	Sid Fernandez	.25	.11	.03
☐ 221	Chris Hoiles	.25	.11	.03
☐ 222	Doug Jones	.25	.11	.03
☐ 223	Ben McDonald	.25	.11	.03
☐ 224	Rafael Palmeiro	.75	.35	.09
☐ 225	Andy Van Slyke	.40	.18	.05
☐ 226	Jose Canseco	.75	.35	.09
☐ 227	Vaughn Eshelman	.25	.11	.03
☐ 228	Mike Macfarlane	.25	.11	.03
☐ 229	Tim Naehring	.25	.11	.03
☐ 230	Frank Rodriguez	.40	.18	.05
☐ 231	Lee Tinsley	.25	.11	.03
☐ 232	Mark Whiten	.25	.11	.03
☐ 233	Garret Anderson	.75	.35	.09
☐ 234	Chili Davis	.40	.18	.05
☐ 235	Jim Edmonds	.75	.35	.09
☐ 236	Mark Langston	.25	.11	.03
☐ 237	Troy Percival	.25	.11	.03
☐ 238	Tony Phillips	.40	.18	.05
☐ 239	Lee Smith	.40	.18	.05
☐ 240	Jim Abbott	.25	.11	.03
☐ 241	James Baldwin	.75	.35	.09
☐ 242	Mike Devereaux	.25	.11	.03
☐ 243	Ray Durham	.40	.18	.05
☐ 244	Alex Fernandez	.40	.18	.05
☐ 245	Roberto Hernandez	.25	.11	.03
☐ 246	Lance Johnson	.40	.18	.05
☐ 247	Ron Karkovice	.25	.11	.03
☐ 248	Tim Raines	.75	.35	.09
☐ 249	Sandy Alomar Jr.	.25	.11	.03
☐ 250	Orel Hershiser	.40	.18	.05
☐ 251	Julian Tavarez	.25	.11	.03
☐ 252	Jim Thome	1.00	.45	.12
☐ 253	Omar Vizquel	.75	.35	.09
☐ 254	Dave Winfield	.75	.35	.09
☐ 255	Chad Curtis	.25	.11	.03
☐ 256	Kirk Gibson	.40	.18	.05
☐ 257	Mike Henneman	.25	.11	.03
☐ 258	Bob Higginson	.75	.35	.09
☐ 259	Felipe Lira	.25	.11	.03
☐ 260	Rudy Pemberton	.25	.11	.03
☐ 261	Alan Trammell	.75	.35	.09
☐ 262	Kevin Appier	.40	.18	.05
☐ 263	Pat Borders	.25	.11	.03
☐ 264	Tom Gordon	.25	.11	.03
☐ 265	Jose Lind	.25	.11	.03
☐ 266	Jon Nunnally	.40	.18	.05
☐ 267	Dilson Torres	.25	.11	.03
☐ 268	Michael Tucker	.40	.18	.05
☐ 269	Jeff Cirillo	.40	.18	.05
☐ 270	Darryl Hamilton	.25	.11	.03
☐ 271	David Hulse	.25	.11	.03
☐ 272	Mark Kiefer	.25	.11	.03
☐ 273	Graeme Lloyd	.25	.11	.03
☐ 274	Joe Oliver	.25	.11	.03
☐ 275	Al Reyes	.25	.11	.03
☐ 276	Kevin Seitzer	.25	.11	.03
☐ 277	Rick Aguilera	.25	.11	.03
☐ 278	Marty Cordova	.75	.35	.09
☐ 279	Scott Erickson	.25	.11	.03
☐ 280	LaTroy Hawkins	.25	.11	.03
☐ 281	Brad Radke	.40	.18	.05
☐ 282	Kevin Tapani	.25	.11	.03
☐ 283	Tony Fernandez	.25	.11	.03
☐ 284	Sterling Hitchcock	.40	.18	.05
☐ 285	Pat Kelly	.25	.11	.03
☐ 286	Jack McDowell	.40	.18	.05
☐ 287	Andy Pettitte	2.00	.90	.25
☐ 288	Mike Stanley	.25	.11	.03
☐ 289	John Wetteland	.40	.18	.05
☐ 290	Bernie Williams	.75	.35	.09
☐ 291	Mark Acre	.25	.11	.03
☐ 292	Geronimo Berroa	.25	.11	.03
☐ 293	Dennis Eckersley	.40	.18	.05
☐ 294	Steve Ontiveros	.25	.11	.03
☐ 295	Ruben Sierra	.40	.18	.05
☐ 296	Terry Steinbach	.40	.18	.05
☐ 297	Dave Stewart	.40	.18	.05
☐ 298	Todd Stottlemyre	.25	.11	.03
☐ 299	Darren Bragg	.40	.18	.05
☐ 300	Joey Cora	.25	.11	.03
☐ 301	Edgar Martinez	.75	.35	.09
☐ 302	Bill Risley	.25	.11	.03
☐ 303	Ron Villone	.25	.11	.03
☐ 304	Dan Wilson	.40	.18	.05
☐ 305	Benji Gil	.25	.11	.03
☐ 306	Wilson Heredia	.25	.11	.03
☐ 307	Mark McLemore	.25	.11	.03
☐ 308	Otis Nixon	.25	.11	.03
☐ 309	Kenny Rogers	.25	.11	.03
☐ 310	Jeff Russell	.25	.11	.03
☐ 311	Mickey Tettleton	.25	.11	.03
☐ 312	Bob Tewksbury	.25	.11	.03
☐ 313	David Cone	.40	.18	.05
☐ 314	Carlos Delgado	.75	.35	.09
☐ 315	Alex Gonzalez	.25	.11	.03
☐ 316	Shawn Green	.40	.18	.05
☐ 317	Paul Molitor	1.00	.45	.12
☐ 318	Ed Sprague	.40	.18	.05
☐ 319	Devon White	.40	.18	.05
☐ 320	Steve Avery	.40	.18	.05
☐ 321	Jeff Blauser	.25	.11	.03
☐ 322	Brad Clontz	.25	.11	.03
☐ 323	Tom Glavine	.75	.35	.09
☐ 324	Marquis Grissom	.75	.35	.09
☐ 325	Chipper Jones	3.00	1.35	.35
☐ 326	David Justice	.75	.35	.09
☐ 327	Mark Lemke	.25	.11	.03
☐ 328	Kent Mercker	.25	.11	.03
☐ 329	Jason Schmidt	.40	.18	.05
☐ 330	Steve Buechele	.25	.11	.03
☐ 331	Kevin Foster	.25	.11	.03
☐ 332	Mark Grace	.75	.35	.09
☐ 333	Brian McRae	.40	.18	.05
☐ 334	Sammy Sosa	.75	.35	.09
☐ 335	Ozzie Timmons	.25	.11	.03
☐ 336	Rick Wilkins	.25	.11	.03
☐ 337	Hector Carrasco	.25	.11	.03
☐ 338	Ron Gant	.40	.18	.05
☐ 339	Barry Larkin	.75	.35	.09
☐ 340	Deion Sanders	.75	.35	.09
☐ 341	Benito Santiago	.25	.11	.03
☐ 342	Roger Bailey	.25	.11	.03
☐ 343	Jason Bates	.25	.11	.03
☐ 344	Dante Bichette	.75	.35	.09
☐ 345	Joe Girardi	.25	.11	.03
☐ 346	Bill Swift	.25	.11	.03
☐ 347	Mark Thompson	.25	.11	.03
☐ 348	Larry Walker	.75	.35	.09
☐ 349	Kurt Abbott	.25	.11	.03
☐ 350	John Burkett	.40	.18	.05
☐ 351	Chuck Carr	.25	.11	.03
☐ 352	Andre Dawson	.75	.35	.09
☐ 353	Chris Hammond	.25	.11	.03
☐ 354	Charles Johnson	.40	.18	.05
☐ 355	Terry Pendleton	.40	.18	.05
☐ 356	Quilvio Veras	.25	.11	.03
☐ 357	Derek Bell	.40	.18	.05
☐ 358	Jim Dougherty	.25	.11	.03
☐ 359	Doug Drabek	.25	.11	.03
☐ 360	Todd Jones	.25	.11	.03
☐ 361	Orlando Miller	.25	.11	.03
☐ 362	James Mouton	.25	.11	.03
☐ 363	Phil Plantier	.25	.11	.03
☐ 364	Shane Reynolds	.25	.11	.03
☐ 365	Todd Hollandsworth	.75	.35	.09
☐ 366	Eric Karros	.40	.18	.05
☐ 367	Ramon Martinez	.40	.18	.05
☐ 368	Hideo Nomo	5.00	2.20	.60
☐ 369	Jose Offerman	.25	.11	.03
☐ 370	Antonio Osuna	.25	.11	.03
☐ 371	Todd Williams	.25	.11	.03
☐ 372	Shane Andrews	.25	.11	.03
☐ 373	Wil Cordero	.25	.11	.03

□ 374 Jeff Fassero	.25	.11	.03
□ 375 Darrin Fletcher	.25	.11	.03
□ 376 Mark Grudzielanek	1.25	.55	.16
□ 377 Carlos Perez	.40	.18	.05
□ 378 Mel Rojas	.25	.11	.03
□ 379 Tony Tarasco	.25	.11	.03
□ 380 Edgardo Alfonzo	.40	.18	.05
□ 381 Brett Butler	.40	.18	.05
□ 382 Carl Everett	.25	.11	.03
□ 383 John Franco	.25	.11	.03
□ 384 Pete Harnisch	.25	.11	.03
□ 385 Bobby Jones	.40	.18	.05
□ 386 Dave Mlicki	.25	.11	.03
□ 387 Jose Vizcaino	.25	.11	.03
□ 388 Ricky Bottalico	.40	.18	.05
□ 389 Tyler Green	.25	.11	.03
□ 390 Charlie Hayes	.25	.11	.03
□ 391 Dave Hollins	.25	.11	.03
□ 392 Gregg Jefferies	.40	.18	.05
□ 393 Michael Mimbs	.40	.18	.05
□ 394 Mickey Morandini	.25	.11	.03
□ 395 Curt Schilling	.25	.11	.03
□ 396 Heathcliff Slocumb	.25	.11	.03
□ 397 Jason Christiansen	.25	.11	.03
□ 398 Midre Cummings	.25	.11	.03
□ 399 Carlos Garcia	.25	.11	.03
□ 400 Mark Johnson	.40	.18	.05
□ 401 Jeff King	.40	.18	.05
□ 402 Jon Lieber	.25	.11	.03
□ 403 Esteban Loaiza	.25	.11	.03
□ 404 Orlando Merced	.25	.11	.03
□ 405 Gary Wilson	.25	.11	.03
□ 406 Scott Cooper	.25	.11	.03
□ 407 Tom Henke	.25	.11	.03
□ 408 Ken Hill	.25	.11	.03
□ 409 Danny Jackson	.25	.11	.03
□ 410 Brian Jordan	.75	.35	.09
□ 411 Ray Lankford	.75	.35	.09
□ 412 John Mabry	.75	.35	.09
□ 413 Todd Zeile	.25	.11	.03
□ 414 Andy Benes	.25	.11	.03
□ 415 Andres Berumen	.25	.11	.03
□ 416 Ken Caminiti	.75	.35	.09
□ 417 Andujar Cedeno	.25	.11	.03
□ 418 Steve Finley	.40	.18	.05
□ 419 Joey Hamilton	.40	.18	.05
□ 420 Dustin Hermanson	.40	.18	.05
□ 421 Melvin Nieves	.40	.18	.05
□ 422 Roberto Petagine	.25	.11	.03
□ 423 Eddie Williams	.25	.11	.03
□ 424 Glenallen Hill	.25	.11	.03
□ 425 Kirt Manwaring	.25	.11	.03
□ 426 Terry Mulholland	.25	.11	.03
□ 427 J.R. Phillips	.25	.11	.03
□ 428 Joe Rosselli	.25	.11	.03
□ 429 Robby Thompson	.25	.11	.03
□ 430 Checklist	.25	.11	.03
□ 431 Checklist	.25	.11	.03
□ 432 Checklist	.25	.11	.03

1995 Flair Hot Gloves

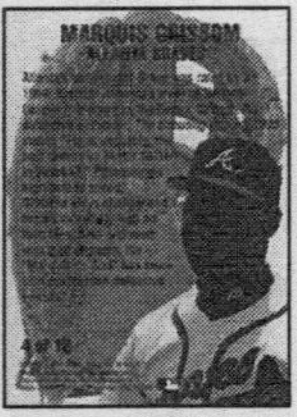

This 12-card standard-size set features players that are known for their defensive prowess. Randomly inserted in series two packs at a rate of one in 25, a player photo is superimposed over an embossed design of a bronze glove. The backs have a photo and write-up with a glove as background.

	MINT	NRMT	EXC
COMPLETE SET (12)	175.00	80.00	22.00
COMMON CARD (1-12)	5.00	2.20	.60
RANDOM INSERTS IN SER.2 PACKS			
□ 1 Roberto Alomar	15.00	6.75	1.85
□ 2 Barry Bonds	15.00	6.75	1.85
□ 3 Ken Griffey Jr.	60.00	27.00	7.50
□ 4 Marquis Grissom	6.00	2.70	.75
□ 5 Barry Larkin	8.00	3.60	1.00
□ 6 Darren Lewis	5.00	2.20	.60
□ 7 Kenny Lofton	15.00	6.75	1.85
□ 8 Don Mattingly	30.00	13.50	3.70
□ 9 Cal Ripken	50.00	22.00	6.25
□ 10 Ivan Rodriguez	12.00	5.50	1.50
□ 11 Devon White	5.00	2.20	.60
□ 12 Matt Williams	8.00	3.60	1.00

1995 Flair Hot Numbers

Randomly inserted in packs at a rate of one in nine, this 10-card standard-size set showcases top players. A player photo on front is superimposed over a gold background that contains player stats from 1994. Horizontal backs have a ghosted player photo to the right with highlights on the left.

	MINT	NRMT	EXC
COMPLETE SET (10)	60.00	27.00	7.50
COMMON CARD (1-10)	2.00	.90	.25
RANDOM INSERTS IN SER.1 PACKS			
□ 1 Jeff Bagwell	6.00	2.70	.75
□ 2 Albert Belle	8.00	3.60	1.00
□ 3 Barry Bonds	4.00	1.80	.50
□ 4 Ken Griffey Jr.	15.00	6.75	1.85
□ 5 Kenny Lofton	4.00	1.80	.50
□ 6 Greg Maddux	10.00	4.50	1.25
□ 7 Mike Piazza	10.00	4.50	1.25
□ 8 Cal Ripken	12.00	5.50	1.50
□ 9 Frank Thomas	15.00	6.75	1.85
□ 10 Matt Williams	2.00	.90	.25

1995 Flair Infield Power

Randomly inserted in second series packs at a rate of one in five, this 10-card standard-size set features sluggers that man the outfield. A player photo on front is surrounded by multiple color schemes with a horizontal back offering a player photo and highlights.

	MINT	NRMT	EXC
COMPLETE SET (10)	15.00	6.75	1.85
COMMON CARD (1-10)	.50	.23	.06
SEMISTARS	1.00	.45	.12
RANDOM INSERTS IN SER.2 PACKS			
□ 1 Jeff Bagwell	3.00	1.35	.35
□ 2 Darren Daulton	.50	.23	.06
□ 3 Cecil Fielder	1.00	.45	.12
□ 4 Andres Galarraga	1.00	.45	.12
□ 5 Fred McGriff	1.00	.45	.12
□ 6 Rafael Palmeiro	1.00	.45	.12
□ 7 Mike Piazza	5.00	2.20	.60
□ 8 Frank Thomas	8.00	3.60	1.00
□ 9 Mo Vaughn	2.00	.90	.25
□ 10 Matt Williams	1.00	.45	.12

1995 Flair Outfield Power

Randomly inserted in first series packs at a rate of one in six, this 10-card standard-size set features sluggers that patrol the outfield. A player photo on front is surrounded by multiple color schemes with a horizontal back offering a player photo and highlights.

	MINT	NRMT	EXC
COMPLETE SET (10)	15.00	6.75	1.85
COMMON CARD (1-10)	.50	.23	.06
SEMISTARS	1.00	.45	.12
RANDOM INSERTS IN SER.1 PACKS			
□ 1 Albert Belle	4.00	1.80	.50
□ 2 Dante Bichette	1.00	.45	.12
□ 3 Barry Bonds	2.00	.90	.25
□ 4 Jose Canseco	1.00	.45	.12
□ 5 Joe Carter	1.00	.45	.12
□ 6 Juan Gonzalez	4.00	1.80	.50
□ 7 Ken Griffey Jr.	8.00	3.60	1.00
□ 8 Kirby Puckett	2.50	1.10	.30
□ 9 Gary Sheffield	1.25	.55	.16
□ 10 Ruben Sierra	.50	.23	.06

1995 Flair Today's Spotlight

This 12-card die-cut set was randomly inserted in first series packs at a rate of one in 25 packs. The upper portion of the player photo on front has the spotlight effect as the remainder of the photo is darkened. Horizontal backs have a circular player photo to the right with text off to the left.

	MINT	NRMT	EXC
COMPLETE SET (12)	150.00	70.00	19.00
COMMON CARD (1-12)	6.00	2.70	.75
RANDOM INSERTS IN SER.1 PACKS			
□ 1 Jeff Bagwell	25.00	11.00	3.10
□ 2 Jason Bere	6.00	2.70	.75
□ 3 Cliff Floyd	6.00	2.70	.75
□ 4 Chuck Knoblauch	10.00	4.50	1.25
□ 5 Kenny Lofton	15.00	6.75	1.85
□ 6 Javier Lopez	6.00	2.70	.75
□ 7 Raul Mondesi	8.00	3.60	1.00
□ 8 Mike Mussina	12.00	5.50	1.50
□ 9 Mike Piazza	40.00	18.00	5.00
□ 10 Manny Ramirez	15.00	6.75	1.85
□ 11 Tim Salmon	8.00	3.60	1.00
□ 12 Frank Thomas	60.00	27.00	7.50

1995 Flair Wave of the Future

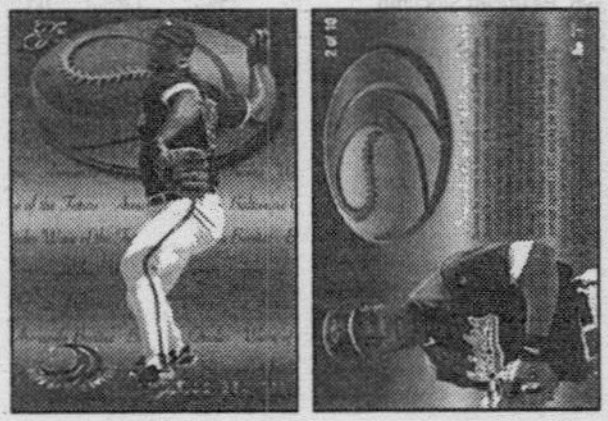

Spotlighting 10 of the game's hottest young stars, cards were randomly inseretd in second series packs at a rate of one in eight. An action photo is superimposed over primarily a solid background save for the player's name, team and same name which appear several times. The backs are horizontal with a photo and write-up.

	MINT	NRMT	EXC
COMPLETE SET (10)	25.00	11.00	3.10
COMMON CARD (1-10)	1.00	.45	.12
RANDOM INSERTS IN SER.2 PACKS			
□ 1 Jason Bates	1.00	.45	.12
□ 2 Armando Benitez	1.00	.45	.12
□ 3 Marty Cordova	3.00	1.35	.35
□ 4 Ray Durham	2.00	.90	.25
□ 5 Vaughn Eshelman	1.00	.45	.12
□ 6 Carl Everett	1.00	.45	.12
□ 7 Shawn Green	1.00	.45	.12
□ 8 Dustin Hermanson	1.00	.45	.12
□ 9 Chipper Jones	12.00	5.50	1.50
□ 10 Hideo Nomo	10.00	4.50	1.25

1996 Flair

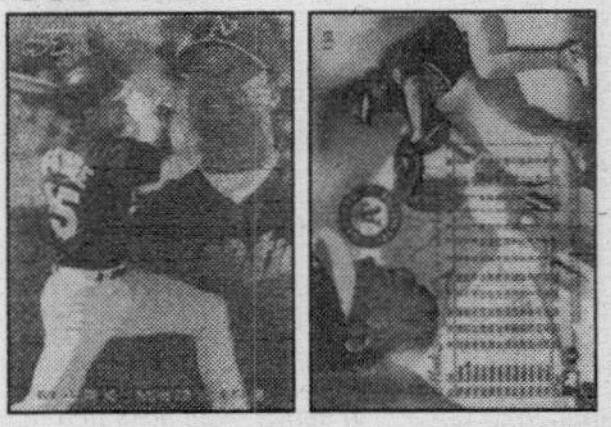

Released in July, 1996, this 400-card set was issued in one series and sold in seven-card packs at a suggested retail price of $4.99. Gold and Silver etched foil front variations exist for

all cards. These color variations were printed in similar quantities and are valued equally. The fronts and backs each carry a color action player cut-out on a player portrait background with player statistics on the backs. The cards are grouped alphabetically within teams and checklisted below alphabetically according to teams for each league.

	MINT	NRMT	EXC
COMPLETE SET (400)	180.00	80.00	22.00
COMMON CARD (1-400)	.50	.23	.06
SEMISTARS	.75	.35	.09
STARS	1.00	.45	.12
GOLD AND SILVER EQUAL VALUE			

□ 1 Roberto Alomar	2.50	1.10	.30
□ 2 Brady Anderson	1.00	.45	.12
□ 3 Bobby Bonilla	1.00	.45	.12
□ 4 Scott Erickson	.50	.23	.06
□ 5 Jeffrey Hammonds	.50	.23	.06
□ 6 Jimmy Haynes	.50	.23	.06
□ 7 Chris Hoiles	.50	.23	.06
□ 8 Kent Mercker	.50	.23	.06
□ 9 Mike Mussina	2.00	.90	.25
□ 10 Randy Myers	.50	.23	.06
□ 11 Rafael Palmeiro	1.00	.45	.12
□ 12 Cal Ripken	8.00	3.60	1.00
□ 13 B.J. Surhoff	.50	.23	.06
□ 14 David Wells	.50	.23	.06
□ 15 Jose Canseco	1.00	.45	.12
□ 16 Roger Clemens	1.00	.45	.12
□ 17 Wil Cordero	.50	.23	.06
□ 18 Tom Gordon	.50	.23	.06
□ 19 Mike Greenwell	.50	.23	.06
□ 20 Dwayne Hosey	.50	.23	.06
□ 21 Jose Malave	.50	.23	.06
□ 22 Tim Naehring	.50	.23	.06
□ 23 Troy O'Leary	.50	.23	.06
□ 24 Aaron Sele	.50	.23	.06
□ 25 Heathcliff Slocumb	.50	.23	.06
□ 26 Mike Stanley	.50	.23	.06
□ 27 Jeff Suppan	.50	.23	.06
□ 28 John Valentin	.75	.35	.09
□ 29 Mo Vaughn	2.50	1.10	.30
□ 30 Tim Wakefield	.50	.23	.06
□ 31 Jim Abbott	1.00	.45	.12
□ 32 Garret Anderson	1.00	.45	.12
□ 33 George Arias	.50	.23	.06
□ 34 Chili Davis	.50	.23	.06
□ 35 Gary DiSarcina	.50	.23	.06
□ 36 Jim Edmonds	1.00	.45	.12
□ 37 Chuck Finley	.50	.23	.06
□ 38 Todd Greene	1.00	.45	.12
□ 39 Mark Langston	.50	.23	.06
□ 40 Troy Percival	.50	.23	.06
□ 41 Tim Salmon	1.25	.55	.16
□ 42 Lee Smith	.75	.35	.09
□ 43 J.T. Snow	.75	.35	.09
□ 44 Randy Velarde	.50	.23	.06
□ 45 Tim Wallach	.50	.23	.06
□ 46 Wilson Alvarez	1.00	.45	.12
□ 47 Harold Baines	1.00	.45	.12
□ 48 Jason Bere	.50	.23	.06
□ 49 Ray Durham	1.00	.45	.12
□ 50 Alex Fernandez	1.00	.45	.12
□ 51 Ozzie Guillen	.50	.23	.06
□ 52 Roberto Hernandez	.75	.35	.09
□ 53 Ron Karkovice	.50	.23	.06
□ 54 Darren Lewis	.50	.23	.06
□ 55 Lyle Mouton	.50	.23	.06
□ 56 Tony Phillips	.75	.35	.09
□ 57 Chris Snopek	.50	.23	.06
□ 58 Kevin Tapani	.50	.23	.06
□ 59 Danny Tartabull	.50	.23	.06
□ 60 Frank Thomas	10.00	4.50	1.25
□ 61 Robin Ventura	1.00	.45	.12
□ 62 Sandy Alomar Jr.	.50	.23	.06
□ 63 Carlos Baerga	1.00	.45	.12
□ 64 Albert Belle	5.00	2.20	.60
□ 65 Julio Franco	.75	.35	.09
□ 66 Orel Hershiser	.75	.35	.09
□ 67 Kenny Lofton	2.50	1.10	.30
□ 68 Dennis Martinez	.75	.35	.09
□ 69 Jack McDowell	1.00	.45	.12
□ 70 Jose Mesa	.75	.35	.09
□ 71 Eddie Murray	2.50	1.10	.30
□ 72 Charles Nagy	.75	.35	.09
□ 73 Tony Pena	.50	.23	.06
□ 74 Manny Ramirez	2.50	1.10	.30
□ 75 Julian Tavarez	.50	.23	.06
□ 76 Jim Thome	2.00	.90	.25
□ 77 Omar Vizquel	.50	.23	.06
□ 78 Chad Curtis	.50	.23	.06
□ 79 Cecil Fielder	1.00	.45	.12
□ 80 Travis Fryman	1.00	.45	.12
□ 81 Chris Gomez	.50	.23	.06
□ 82 Bob Higginson	1.00	.45	.12
□ 83 Mark Lewis	.50	.23	.06
□ 84 Felipe Lira	.50	.23	.06
□ 85 Alan Trammell	1.00	.45	.12
□ 86 Kevin Appier	.75	.35	.09
□ 87 Johnny Damon	1.00	.45	.12
□ 88 Tom Goodwin	.75	.35	.09
□ 89 Mark Gubicza	.50	.23	.06
□ 90 Bob Hamelin	.50	.23	.06
□ 91 Keith Lockhart	.50	.23	.06
□ 92 Jeff Montgomery	.50	.23	.06
□ 93 Jon Nunnally	.50	.23	.06
□ 94 Bip Roberts	.50	.23	.06
□ 95 Michael Tucker	.75	.35	.09
□ 96 Joe Vitiello	.50	.23	.06
□ 97 Ricky Bones	.50	.23	.06
□ 98 Chuck Carr	.50	.23	.06
□ 99 Jeff Cirillo	.50	.23	.06
□ 100 Mike Fetters	.50	.23	.06
□ 101 John Jaha	.75	.35	.09
□ 102 Mike Matheny	.50	.23	.06
□ 103 Ben McDonald	.50	.23	.06
□ 104 Matt Mieske	.50	.23	.06
□ 105 Dave Nilsson	.75	.35	.09
□ 106 Kevin Seitzer	.50	.23	.06
□ 107 Steve Sparks	.50	.23	.06
□ 108 Jose Valentin	.50	.23	.06
□ 109 Greg Vaughn	1.00	.45	.12
□ 110 Rick Aguilera	.50	.23	.06
□ 111 Rich Becker	.75	.35	.09
□ 112 Marty Cordova	1.25	.55	.16
□ 113 LaTroy Hawkins	.50	.23	.06
□ 114 Dave Hollins	.50	.23	.06
□ 115 Roberto Kelly	.50	.23	.06
□ 116 Chuck Knoblauch	1.00	.45	.12
□ 117 Matt Lawton	.50	.23	.06
□ 118 Pat Meares	.50	.23	.06
□ 119 Paul Molitor	2.00	.90	.25
□ 120 Kirby Puckett	3.00	1.35	.35
□ 121 Brad Radke	.50	.23	.06
□ 122 Frank Rodriguez	.75	.35	.09
□ 123 Scott Stahoviak	.50	.23	.06
□ 124 Matt Walbeck	.50	.23	.06
□ 125 Wade Boggs	1.00	.45	.12
□ 126 David Cone	1.00	.45	.12
□ 127 Joe Girardi	.50	.23	.06
□ 128 Dwight Gooden	1.00	.45	.12
□ 129 Derek Jeter	6.00	2.70	.75
□ 130 Jimmy Key	.75	.35	.09
□ 131 Jim Leyritz	.50	.23	.06
□ 132 Tino Martinez	1.00	.45	.12
□ 133 Paul O'Neill	.50	.23	.06
□ 134 Andy Pettitte	3.00	1.35	.35
□ 135 Tim Raines	1.00	.45	.12
□ 136 Ruben Rivera	2.00	.90	.25
□ 137 Kenny Rogers	.50	.23	.06
□ 138 Ruben Sierra	.50	.23	.06
□ 139 John Wetteland	.75	.35	.09
□ 140 Bernie Williams	1.50	.70	.19
□ 141 Tony Batista	.50	.23	.06
□ 142 Allen Battle	.50	.23	.06
□ 143 Geronimo Berroa	.75	.35	.09
□ 144 Mike Bordick	.75	.35	.09
□ 145 Scott Brosius	.75	.35	.09
□ 146 Steve Cox	.50	.23	.06
□ 147 Brent Gates	.50	.23	.06
□ 148 Jason Giambi	1.00	.45	.12
□ 149 Doug Johns	.50	.23	.06
□ 150 Mark McGwire	3.00	1.35	.35
□ 151 Pedro Munoz	.50	.23	.06
□ 152 Ariel Prieto	.50	.23	.06
□ 153 Terry Steinbach	.75	.35	.09
□ 154 Todd Van Poppel	.50	.23	.06
□ 155 Bobby Ayala	.50	.23	.06
□ 156 Chris Bosio	.50	.23	.06

□ 157 Jay Buhner	1.00	.45	.12
□ 158 Joey Cora	.50	.23	.06
□ 159 Russ Davis	.50	.23	.06
□ 160 Ken Griffey Jr.	10.00	4.50	1.25
□ 161 Sterling Hitchcock	.50	.23	.06
□ 162 Randy Johnson	1.50	.70	.19
□ 163 Edgar Martinez	1.00	.45	.12
□ 164 Alex Rodriguez	10.00	4.50	1.25
□ 165 Paul Sorrento	.50	.23	.06
□ 166 Dan Wilson	.50	.23	.06
□ 167 Will Clark	.50	.23	.06
□ 168 Benji Gil	.50	.23	.06
□ 169 Juan Gonzalez	5.00	2.20	.60
□ 170 Rusty Greer	1.00	.45	.12
□ 171 Kevin Gross	.50	.23	.06
□ 172 Darryl Hamilton	.50	.23	.06
□ 173 Mike Henneman	.50	.23	.06
□ 174 Ken Hill	.50	.23	.06
□ 175 Mark McLemore	.50	.23	.06
□ 176 Dean Palmer	1.00	.45	.12
□ 177 Roger Pavlik	.50	.23	.06
□ 178 Ivan Rodriguez	2.00	.90	.25
□ 179 Mickey Tettleton	.75	.35	.09
□ 180 Bobby Witt	.50	.23	.06
□ 181 Joe Carter	.75	.35	.09
□ 182 Felipe Crespo	.50	.23	.06
□ 183 Alex Gonzalez	.50	.23	.06
□ 184 Shawn Green	.50	.23	.06
□ 185 Juan Guzman	.50	.23	.06
□ 186 Erik Hanson	.50	.23	.06
□ 187 Pat Hentgen	1.00	.45	.12
□ 188 Sandy Martinez	.50	.23	.06
□ 189 Otis Nixon	.50	.23	.06
□ 190 John Olerud	.50	.23	.06
□ 191 Paul Quantrill	.50	.23	.06
□ 192 Bill Risley	.50	.23	.06
□ 193 Ed Sprague	.75	.35	.09
□ 194 Steve Avery	.50	.23	.06
□ 195 Jeff Blauser	.50	.23	.06
□ 196 Brad Clontz	.50	.23	.06
□ 197 Jermaine Dye	2.50	1.10	.30
□ 198 Tom Glavine	1.00	.45	.12
□ 199 Marquis Grissom	1.00	.45	.12
□ 200 Chipper Jones	6.00	2.70	.75
□ 201 David Justice	.75	.35	.09
□ 202 Ryan Klesko	2.00	.90	.25
□ 203 Mark Lemke	.50	.23	.06
□ 204 Javier Lopez	1.00	.45	.12
□ 205 Greg Maddux	6.00	2.70	.75
□ 206 Fred McGriff	1.25	.55	.16
□ 207 Greg McMichael	.50	.23	.06
□ 208 Wonderful Monds	.50	.23	.06
□ 209 Jason Schmidt	.75	.35	.09
□ 210 John Smoltz	1.50	.70	.19
□ 211 Mark Wohlers	.75	.35	.09
□ 212 Jim Bullinger	.50	.23	.06
□ 213 Frank Castillo	.50	.23	.06
□ 214 Kevin Foster	.50	.23	.06
□ 215 Luis Gonzalez	.50	.23	.06
□ 216 Mark Grace	1.00	.45	.12
□ 217 Robin Jennings	.50	.23	.06
□ 218 Doug Jones	.50	.23	.06
□ 219 Dave Magadan	.50	.23	.06
□ 220 Brian McRae	.50	.23	.06
□ 221 Jaime Navarro	.50	.23	.06
□ 222 Rey Sanchez	.50	.23	.06
□ 223 Ryne Sandberg	2.50	1.10	.30
□ 224 Scott Servais	.50	.23	.06
□ 225 Sammy Sosa	1.50	.70	.19
□ 226 Ozzie Timmons	.50	.23	.06
□ 227 Bret Boone	.50	.23	.06
□ 228 Jeff Branson	.50	.23	.06
□ 229 Jeff Brantley	.50	.23	.06
□ 230 Dave Burba	.50	.23	.06
□ 231 Vince Coleman	.50	.23	.06
□ 232 Steve Gibralter	.50	.23	.06
□ 233 Mike Kelly	.50	.23	.06
□ 234 Barry Larkin	1.25	.55	.16
□ 235 Hal Morris	.50	.23	.06
□ 236 Mark Portugal	.50	.23	.06
□ 237 Jose Rijo	.50	.23	.06
□ 238 Reggie Sanders	1.00	.45	.12
□ 239 Pete Schourek	.75	.35	.09
□ 240 John Smiley	.50	.23	.06
□ 241 Eddie Taubensee	.50	.23	.06
□ 242 Jason Bates	.50	.23	.06

□ 243 Dante Bichette	1.25	.55	.16
□ 244 Ellis Burks	1.00	.45	.12
□ 245 Vinny Castilla	1.00	.45	.12
□ 246 Andres Galarraga	1.00	.45	.12
□ 247 Darren Holmes	.50	.23	.06
□ 248 Curt Leskanic	.50	.23	.06
□ 249 Steve Reed	.50	.23	.06
□ 250 Kevin Rtiz	.50	.23	.06
□ 251 Bret Saberhagen	.50	.23	.06
□ 252 Bill Swift	.50	.23	.06
□ 253 Larry Walker	1.00	.45	.12
□ 254 Walt Weiss	.50	.23	.06
□ 255 Eric Young	.50	.23	.06
□ 256 Kurt Abbott	.50	.23	.06
□ 257 Kevin Brown	.50	.23	.06
□ 258 John Burkett	.50	.23	.06
□ 259 Greg Colbrunn	.50	.23	.06
□ 260 Jeff Conine	1.00	.45	.12
□ 261 Andre Dawson	1.00	.45	.12
□ 262 Chris Hammond	.50	.23	.06
□ 263 Charles Johnson	.75	.35	.09
□ 264 Al Leiter	.50	.23	.06
□ 265 Robb Nen	.50	.23	.06
□ 266 Terry Pendleton	.75	.35	.09
□ 267 Pat Rapp	.50	.23	.06
□ 268 Gary Sheffield	1.50	.70	.19
□ 269 Quilvio Veras	.50	.23	.06
□ 270 Devon White	.50	.23	.06
□ 271 Bob Abreu	1.00	.45	.12
□ 272 Jeff Bagwell	4.00	1.80	.50
□ 273 Derek Bell	1.00	.45	.12
□ 274 Sean Berry	.50	.23	.06
□ 275 Craig Biggio	1.00	.45	.12
□ 276 Doug Drabek	.50	.23	.06
□ 277 Tony Eusebio	.50	.23	.06
□ 278 Richard Hidalgo	.50	.23	.06
□ 279 Brian L.Hunter	.50	.23	.06
□ 280 Todd Jones	.50	.23	.06
□ 281 Derrick May	.50	.23	.06
□ 282 Orlando Miller	.50	.23	.06
□ 283 James Mouton	.50	.23	.06
□ 284 Shane Reynolds	.50	.23	.06
□ 285 Greg Swindell	.50	.23	.06
□ 286 Mike Blowers	.50	.23	.06
□ 287 Brett Butler	.50	.23	.06
□ 288 Tom Candiotti	.50	.23	.06
□ 289 Roger Cedeno	.75	.35	.09
□ 290 Delino DeShields	.50	.23	.06
□ 291 Greg Gagne	.50	.23	.06
□ 292 Karim Garcia	2.00	.90	.25
□ 293 Todd Hollandsworth	1.25	.55	.16
□ 294 Eric Karros	1.00	.45	.12
□ 295 Ramon Martinez	1.00	.45	.12
□ 296 Raul Mondesi	1.00	.45	.12
□ 297 Hideo Nomo	2.50	1.10	.30
□ 298 Mike Piazza	6.00	2.70	.75
□ 299 Ismael Valdes	.75	.35	.09
□ 300 Todd Worrell	.75	.35	.09
□ 301 Moises Alou	.75	.35	.09
□ 302 Shane Andrews	.50	.23	.06
□ 303 Yamil Benitez	.50	.23	.06
□ 304 Jeff Fassero	.50	.23	.06
□ 305 Darrin Fletcher	.50	.23	.06
□ 306 Cliff Floyd	.50	.23	.06
□ 307 Mark Grudzielanek	.75	.35	.09
□ 308 Mike Lansing	.50	.23	.06
□ 309 Pedro Martinez	1.00	.45	.12
□ 310 Ryan McGuire	.50	.23	.06
□ 311 Carlos Perez	.50	.23	.06
□ 312 Mel Rojas	.75	.35	.09
□ 313 David Segui	.50	.23	.06
□ 314 Rondell White	1.00	.45	.12
□ 315 Edgardo Alfonzo	.75	.35	.09
□ 316 Rico Brogna	.50	.23	.06
□ 317 Carl Everett	.50	.23	.06
□ 318 John Franco	.50	.23	.06
□ 319 Bernard Gilkey	.75	.35	.09
□ 320 Todd Hundley	1.00	.45	.12
□ 321 Jason Isringhausen	1.00	.45	.12
□ 322 Lance Johnson	.75	.35	.09
□ 323 Bobby Jones	.50	.23	.06
□ 324 Jeff Kent	.50	.23	.06
□ 325 Rey Ordonez	2.00	.90	.25
□ 326 Bill Pulsipher	.75	.35	.09
□ 327 Jose Vizcaino	.50	.23	.06
□ 328 Paul Wilson	.75	.35	.09

□ 329	Ricky Bottalico	.50	.23	.06
□ 330	Darren Daulton	.75	.35	.09
□ 331	David Doster	.50	.23	.06
□ 332	Lenny Dykstra	.75	.35	.09
□ 333	Jim Eisenreich	.50	.23	.06
□ 334	Sid Fernandez	.50	.23	.06
□ 335	Gregg Jefferies	1.00	.45	.12
□ 336	Mickey Morandini	.50	.23	.06
□ 337	Benito Santiago	.50	.23	.06
□ 338	Curt Schilling	.50	.23	.06
□ 339	Kevin Stocker	.50	.23	.06
□ 340	David West	.50	.23	.06
□ 341	Mark Whiten	.50	.23	.06
□ 342	Todd Zeile	.75	.35	.09
□ 343	Jay Bell	.75	.35	.09
□ 344	John Ericks	.50	.23	.06
□ 345	Carlos Garcia	.50	.23	.06
□ 346	Charlie Hayes	.50	.23	.06
□ 347	Jason Kendall	1.00	.45	.12
□ 348	Jeff King	.75	.35	.09
□ 349	Mike Kingery	.50	.23	.06
□ 350	Al Martin	.50	.23	.06
□ 351	Orlando Merced	.75	.35	.09
□ 352	Dan Miceli	.50	.23	.06
□ 353	Denny Neagle	.75	.35	.09
□ 354	Alan Benes	1.00	.45	.12
□ 355	Andy Benes	.50	.23	.06
□ 356	Royce Clayton	.50	.23	.06
□ 357	Dennis Eckersley	1.00	.45	.12
□ 358	Gary Gaetti	.75	.35	.09
□ 359	Ron Gant	1.00	.45	.12
□ 360	Brian Jordan	1.00	.45	.12
□ 361	Ray Lankford	1.00	.45	.12
□ 362	John Mabry	1.00	.45	.12
□ 363	T.J. Mathews	.50	.23	.06
□ 364	Mike Morgan	.50	.23	.06
□ 365	Donovan Osborne	.50	.23	.06
□ 366	Tom Pagnozzi	.50	.23	.06
□ 367	Ozzie Smith	2.00	.90	.25
□ 368	Todd Stottlemyre	.50	.23	.06
□ 369	Andy Ashby	.50	.23	.06
□ 370	Brad Ausmus	.50	.23	.06
□ 371	Ken Caminiti	1.00	.45	.12
□ 372	Andujar Cedeno	.50	.23	.06
□ 373	Steve Finley	1.00	.45	.12
□ 374	Tony Gwynn	4.00	1.80	.50
□ 375	Joey Hamilton	.75	.35	.09
□ 376	Rickey Henderson	1.00	.45	.12
□ 377	Trevor Hoffman	.75	.35	.09
□ 378	Wally Joyner	.50	.23	.06
□ 379	Marc Newfield	.75	.35	.09
□ 380	Jody Reed	.50	.23	.06
□ 381	Bob Tewksbury	.50	.23	.06
□ 382	Fernando Valenzuela	.75	.35	.09
□ 383	Rod Beck	.75	.35	.09
□ 384	Barry Bonds	2.50	1.10	.30
□ 385	Mark Carreon	.50	.23	.06
□ 386	Shawon Dunston	.50	.23	.06
□ 387	Osvaldo Fernandez	1.00	.45	.12
□ 388	Glenallen Hill	.50	.23	.06
□ 389	Stan Javier	.50	.23	.06
□ 390	Mark Leiter	.50	.23	.06
□ 391	Kirt Manwaring	.50	.23	.06
□ 392	Robby Thompson	.50	.23	.06
□ 393	William VanLandingham	.50	.23	.06
□ 394	Allen Watson	.50	.23	.06
□ 395	Matt Williams	1.25	.55	.16
□ 396	Checklist (1-92)	.50	.23	.06
□ 397	Checklist (93-180)	.50	.23	.06
□ 398	Checklist (181-272)	.50	.23	.06
□ 399	Checklist (273-365)	.50	.23	.06
□ 400	Checklist (366-400/Inserts)	.50	.23	.06

1996 Flair Diamond Cuts

Randomly inserted in packs at a rate of one in 20, this 12-card set showcases the game's greatest stars with rainbow holofoil and glitter coating on the card.

	MINT	NRMT	EXC
COMPLETE SET (12)	175.00	80.00	22.00
COMMON CARD (1-12)	5.00	2.20	.60
RANDOM INSERTS IN PACKS			

□ 1	Jeff Bagwell	12.00	5.50	1.50
□ 2	Albert Belle	15.00	6.75	1.85
□ 3	Barry Bonds	8.00	3.60	1.00
□ 4	Juan Gonzalez	15.00	6.75	1.85
□ 5	Ken Griffey Jr.	30.00	13.50	3.70
□ 6	Greg Maddux	20.00	9.00	2.50
□ 7	Eddie Murray	8.00	3.60	1.00
□ 8	Mike Piazza	20.00	9.00	2.50
□ 9	Cal Ripken	25.00	11.00	3.10
□ 10	Frank Thomas	30.00	13.50	3.70
□ 11	Mo Vaughn	8.00	3.60	1.00
□ 12	Matt Williams	5.00	2.20	.60

1996 Flair Hot Gloves

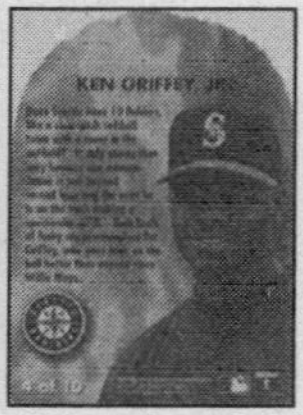

Randomly inserted in hobby packs only at a rate of one in 90, this 10-card set is printed on special, thermo-embossed die-cut cards and spotlights the best defensive players.

	MINT	NRMT	EXC
COMPLETE SET (10)	500.00	220.00	60.00
COMMON CARD (1-10)	20.00	9.00	2.50
RANDOM INSERTS IN HOBBY PACKS			

□ 1	Roberto Alomar	40.00	18.00	5.00
□ 2	Barry Bonds	40.00	18.00	5.00
□ 3	Will Clark	20.00	9.00	2.50
□ 4	Ken Griffey Jr.	150.00	70.00	19.00
□ 5	Kenny Lofton	40.00	18.00	5.00
□ 6	Greg Maddux	100.00	45.00	12.50
□ 7	Mike Piazza	100.00	45.00	12.50
□ 8	Cal Ripken	125.00	55.00	15.50
□ 9	Ivan Rodriguez	30.00	13.50	3.70
□ 10	Matt Williams	20.00	9.00	2.50

1996 Flair Powerline

Randomly inserted in packs at a rate of one in 6, this 10-card set features baseball's leading power hitters. The fronts display a color action close-up player photo with a green overlay indicating his power. The backs carry a player portrait and a statement about the player's hitting power.

	MINT	NRMT	EXC
COMPLETE SET (10)	40.00	18.00	5.00
COMMON CARD (1-10)	1.25	.55	.16
RANDOM INSERTS IN PACKS			

□ 1	Albert Belle	5.00	2.20	.60
□ 2	Barry Bonds	2.50	1.10	.30

□ 3 Juan Gonzalez	5.00	2.20	.60
□ 4 Ken Griffey Jr.	10.00	4.50	1.25
□ 5 Mark McGwire	3.00	1.35	.35
□ 6 Mike Piazza	6.00	2.70	.75
□ 7 Manny Ramirez	2.50	1.10	.30
□ 8 Sammy Sosa	1.50	.70	.19
□ 9 Frank Thomas	10.00	4.50	1.25
□ 10 Matt Williams	1.25	.55	.16

1996 Flair Wave of the Future

Randomly inserted in packs at a rate of one in 72, this 20-card set highlights the top 1996 rookies and prospects on lenticular cards.

	MINT	NRMT	EXC
COMPLETE SET (20)	275.00	125.00	34.00
COMMON CARD (1-20)	10.00	4.50	1.25
□ 1 Bob Abreu	15.00	6.75	1.85
□ 2 George Arias	10.00	4.50	1.25
□ 3 Tony Batista	10.00	4.50	1.25
□ 4 Alan Benes	20.00	9.00	2.50
□ 5 Yamil Benitez	10.00	4.50	1.25
□ 6 Steve Cox	10.00	4.50	1.25
□ 7 David Doster	10.00	4.50	1.25
□ 8 Jermaine Dye	40.00	18.00	5.00
□ 9 Osvaldo Fernandez	10.00	4.50	1.25
□ 10 Karim Garcia	40.00	18.00	5.00
□ 11 Steve Gibralter	10.00	4.50	1.25
□ 12 Todd Greene	15.00	6.75	1.85
□ 13 Richard Hidalgo	20.00	9.00	2.50
□ 14 Robin Jennings	10.00	4.50	1.25
□ 15 Jason Kendall	25.00	11.00	3.10
□ 16 Jose Malave	10.00	4.50	1.25
□ 17 Wonderful Monds	10.00	4.50	1.25
□ 18 Rey Ordonez	40.00	18.00	5.00
□ 19 Ruben Rivera	40.00	18.00	5.00
□ 20 Paul Wilson	25.00	11.00	3.10

1963 Fleer

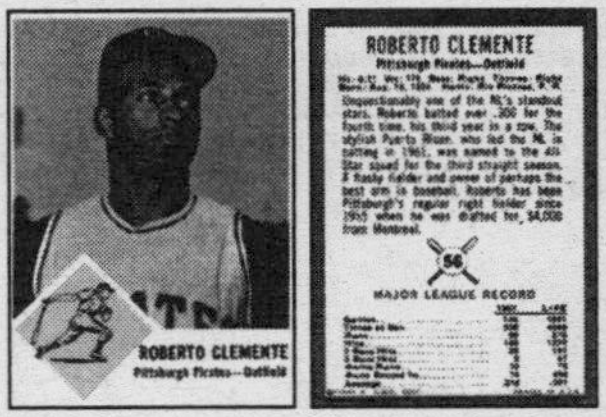

The Fleer set of current baseball players was marketed in 1963 in a gum card-style waxed wrapper package which contained a cherry cookie instead of gum. The cards were printed in sheets of 66 with the scarce card of Joe Adcock (#46) replaced by the unnumbered checklist card for the final press run. The complete set price includes the checklist card. The catalog designation for this set is R418-4. The key Rookie Card in this set is Maury Wills. The set is basically arranged numerically in alphabetical order by teams which are also in alphabetical order.

	NRMT	VG-E	GOOD
COMPLETE SET (67)	2000.00	900.00	250.00
COMMON CARD (1-66)	15.00	6.75	1.85
SEMISTARS	20.00	9.00	2.50
CARDS PRICED IN NM CONDITION !			
□ 1 Steve Barber	25.00	7.50	2.50
□ 4 Brooks Robinson	100.00	45.00	12.50
□ 5 Willie Mays	200.00	90.00	25.00
□ 8 Carl Yastrzemski	100.00	45.00	12.50
□ 22 Jim Kaat	25.00	11.00	3.10
□ 25 Bobby Richardson	30.00	13.50	3.70
□ 32 Ron Santo	25.00	11.00	3.10
□ 41 Don Drysdale	60.00	27.00	7.50
□ 42 Sandy Koufax	200.00	90.00	25.00
□ 43 Maury Wills	100.00	45.00	12.50
□ 45 Warren Spahn	70.00	32.00	8.75
□ 46 Joe Adcock SP	200.00	90.00	25.00
□ 56 Roberto Clemente	250.00	110.00	31.00
□ 59 Bill Mazeroski	30.00	13.50	3.70
□ 60 Ken Boyer	25.00	11.00	3.10
□ 61 Bob Gibson	70.00	32.00	8.75
□ 63 Bill White	25.00	11.00	3.10
□ 64 Orlando Cepeda	30.00	13.50	3.70
□ 66 Billy O'Dell	25.00	7.50	2.50
□ NNO Checklist card	750.00	250.00	100.00

1981 Fleer

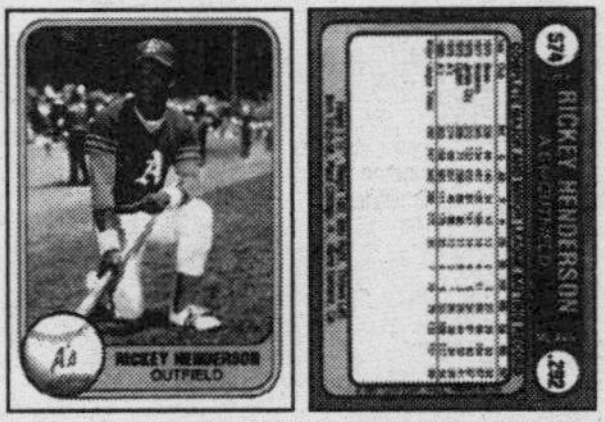

This issue of cards marks Fleer's first entry into the current player baseball card market since 1963. Cards are grouped in team order and teams are ordered based upon their standings from the 1980 season with the World Series champion Philadelphia Phillies starting off the set. Cards 638-660 feature specials and checklists. The cards of pitchers in this set erroneously show a heading (on the card backs) of "Batting Record" over their career pitching statistics. There were three distinct printings: the two following the primary run were designed to correct numerous errors. The variations caused by these multiple printings are noted in the checklist below (P1, P2, or P3). The Craig Nettles variation was corrected before the end of the first printing and thus is not included in the complete set consideration due to scarcity.

Unopened packs contained 17 cards as well as a piece of gum. Unopened boxes contained 38 packs. The key Rookie Cards in this set are Danny Ainge, Harold Baines, Kirk Gibson, Jeff Reardon, and Fernando Valenzuela, whose first name was erroneously spelled Fernand on the card front.

	MINT	NRMT	EXC
COMPLETE SET (660)	40.00	18.00	5.00
COMMON CARD (1-660)	.10	.05	.01
SEMISTARS	.25	.11	.03
STARS	.50	.23	.06
□ 1 Pete Rose UER	2.00	.90	.25
(270 hits in '63,			
should be 170)			
□ 2 Larry Bowa	.25	.11	.03
□ 3 Manny Trillo	.10	.05	.01
□ 4 Bob Boone	.25	.11	.03
□ 5 Mike Schmidt	2.00	.90	.25
(See also 640A)			
□ 6 Steve Carlton P1	1.50	.70	.19
Golden Arm			
(Back "1066 Cardinals";			
Number on back 6)			
□ 6B Steve Carlton P2	1.50	.70	.19
Pitcher of Year			
(Back "1066 Cardinals")			
□ 6C Steve Carlton P3	1.50	.70	.19
(1966 Cardinals)			
□ 7 Tug McGraw	.25	.11	.03
(See 657A)			
□ 8 Larry Christenson	.10	.05	.01
□ 9 Bake McBride	.10	.05	.01
□ 10 Greg Luzinski	.25	.11	.03
□ 11 Ron Reed	.10	.05	.01
□ 12 Dickie Noles	.10	.05	.01
□ 13 Keith Moreland	.25	.11	.03
□ 14 Bob Walk	.25	.11	.03
□ 15 Lonnie Smith	.25	.11	.03
□ 16 Dick Ruthven	.10	.05	.01
□ 17 Sparky Lyle	.25	.11	.03
□ 18 Greg Gross	.10	.05	.01
□ 19 Garry Maddox	.10	.05	.01
□ 20 Nino Espinosa	.10	.05	.01
□ 21 George Vukovich	.10	.05	.01
□ 22 John Vukovich	.10	.05	.01
□ 23 Ramon Aviles	.10	.05	.01
□ 24A Kevin Saucier P1	.10	.05	.01
(Name on back "Ken")			
□ 24B Kevin Saucier P2	.10	.05	.01
(Name on back "Ken")			
□ 24C Kevin Saucier P3	.25	.11	.03
(Name on back "Kevin")			
□ 25 Randy Lerch	.10	.05	.01
□ 26 Del Unser	.10	.05	.01
□ 27 Tim McCarver	.50	.23	.06
□ 28 George Brett	4.00	1.80	.50
(See also 655A)			
□ 29 Willie Wilson	.10	.05	.01
(See also 653A)			
□ 30 Paul Splittorff	.10	.05	.01
□ 31 Dan Quisenberry	.25	.11	.03
□ 32A Amos Otis P1	.25	.11	.03
(Batting Pose;			
"Outfield";			
32 on back)			
□ 32B Amos Otis P2	.25	.11	.03
Series Starter			
483 on back			
□ 33 Steve Busby	.10	.05	.01
□ 34 U.L. Washington	.10	.05	.01
□ 35 Dave Chalk	.10	.05	.01
□ 36 Darrell Porter	.10	.05	.01
□ 37 Marty Pattin	.10	.05	.01
□ 38 Larry Gura	.10	.05	.01
□ 39 Renie Martin	.10	.05	.01
□ 40 Rich Gale	.10	.05	.01
□ 41A Hal McRae P1	.50	.23	.06
("Royals" on front			
in black letters)			
□ 41B Hal McRae P2	.25	.11	.03
("Royals" on front			
in blue letters)			
□ 42 Dennis Leonard	.10	.05	.01
□ 43 Willie Aikens	.10	.05	.01
□ 44 Frank White	.25	.11	.03
□ 45 Clint Hurdle	.10	.05	.01
□ 46 John Wathan	.10	.05	.01
□ 47 Pete LaCock	.10	.05	.01
□ 48 Rance Mulliniks	.10	.05	.01
□ 49 Jeff Twitty	.10	.05	.01
□ 50 Jamie Quirk	.10	.05	.01
□ 51 Art Howe	.10	.05	.01
□ 52 Ken Forsch	.10	.05	.01
□ 53 Vern Ruhle	.10	.05	.01
□ 54 Joe Niekro	.25	.11	.03
□ 55 Frank LaCorte	.10	.05	.01
□ 56 J.R. Richard	.25	.11	.03
□ 57 Nolan Ryan	5.00	2.20	.60
□ 58 Enos Cabell	.10	.05	.01
□ 59 Cesar Cedeno	.25	.11	.03
□ 60 Jose Cruz	.25	.11	.03
□ 61 Bill Virdon MG	.10	.05	.01
□ 62 Terry Puhl	.10	.05	.01
□ 63 Joaquin Andujar	.25	.11	.03
□ 64 Alan Ashby	.10	.05	.01
□ 65 Joe Sambito	.10	.05	.01
□ 66 Denny Walling	.10	.05	.01
□ 67 Jeff Leonard	.25	.11	.03
□ 68 Luis Pujols	.10	.05	.01
□ 69 Bruce Bochy	.10	.05	.01
□ 70 Rafael Landestoy	.10	.05	.01
□ 71 Dave Smith	.25	.11	.03
□ 72 Danny Heep	.10	.05	.01
□ 73 Julio Gonzalez	.10	.05	.01
□ 74 Craig Reynolds	.10	.05	.01
□ 75 Gary Woods	.10	.05	.01
□ 76 Dave Bergman	.10	.05	.01
□ 77 Randy Niemann	.10	.05	.01
□ 78 Joe Morgan	.60	.25	.07
□ 79 Reggie Jackson	1.25	.55	.16
(See also 650A)			
□ 80 Bucky Dent	.25	.11	.03
□ 81 Tommy John	.50	.23	.06
□ 82 Luis Tiant	.25	.11	.03
□ 83 Rick Cerone	.10	.05	.01
□ 84 Dick Howser MG	.25	.11	.03
□ 85 Lou Piniella	.25	.11	.03
□ 86 Ron Davis	.10	.05	.01
□ 87A Graig Nettles P1	10.00	4.50	1.25
ERR (Name on back			
misspelled "Craig")			
□ 87B Graig Nettles P2 COR	.25	.11	.03
("Graig")			
□ 88 Ron Guidry	.25	.11	.03
□ 89 Rich Gossage	.50	.23	.06
□ 90 Rudy May	.10	.05	.01
□ 91 Gaylord Perry	.50	.23	.06
□ 92 Eric Soderholm	.10	.05	.01
□ 93 Bob Watson	.25	.11	.03
□ 94 Bobby Murcer	.25	.11	.03
□ 95 Bobby Brown	.10	.05	.01
□ 96 Jim Spencer	.10	.05	.01
□ 97 Tom Underwood	.10	.05	.01
□ 98 Oscar Gamble	.10	.05	.01
□ 99 Johnny Oates	.25	.11	.03
□ 100 Fred Stanley	.10	.05	.01
□ 101 Ruppert Jones	.10	.05	.01
□ 102 Dennis Werth	.10	.05	.01
□ 103 Joe Lefebvre	.10	.05	.01
□ 104 Brian Doyle	.10	.05	.01
□ 105 Aurelio Rodriguez	.10	.05	.01
□ 106 Doug Bird	.10	.05	.01
□ 107 Mike Griffin	.10	.05	.01
□ 108 Tim Lollar	.10	.05	.01
□ 109 Willie Randolph	.25	.11	.03
□ 110 Steve Garvey	.50	.23	.06
□ 111 Reggie Smith	.25	.11	.03
□ 112 Don Sutton	.50	.23	.06
□ 113 Burt Hooton	.10	.05	.01
□ 114A Dave Lopes P1	.50	.23	.06
(Small hand on back)			
□ 114B Dave Lopes P2	.25	.11	.03
(No hand)			
□ 115 Dusty Baker	.50	.23	.06
□ 116 Tom Lasorda MG	.25	.11	.03
□ 117 Bill Russell	.25	.11	.03
□ 118 Jerry Reuss UER	.25	.11	.03
("Home:" omitted)			
□ 119 Terry Forster	.10	.05	.01

□ 120A Bob Welch P1 (Name on back is "Bob")	.25	.11	.03
□ 120B Bob Welch P2 (Name on back is "Robert")	.50	.23	.06
□ 121 Don Stanhouse	.10	.05	.01
□ 122 Rick Monday	.25	.11	.03
□ 123 Derrel Thomas	.10	.05	.01
□ 124 Joe Ferguson	.10	.05	.01
□ 125 Rick Sutcliffe	.50	.23	.06
□ 126A Ron Cey P1 (Small hand on back)	.50	.23	.06
□ 126B Ron Cey P2 (No hand)	.25	.11	.03
□ 127 Dave Goltz	.10	.05	.01
□ 128 Jay Johnstone	.25	.11	.03
□ 129 Steve Yeager	.10	.05	.01
□ 130 Gary Weiss	.10	.05	.01
□ 131 Mike Scioscia	.50	.23	.06
□ 132 Vic Davalillo	.10	.05	.01
□ 133 Doug Rau	.10	.05	.01
□ 134 Pepe Frias	.10	.05	.01
□ 135 Mickey Hatcher	.25	.11	.03
□ 136 Steve Howe	.25	.11	.03
□ 137 Robert Castillo	.10	.05	.01
□ 138 Gary Thomasson	.10	.05	.01
□ 139 Rudy Law	.10	.05	.01
□ 140 Fernando Valenzuela UER (Misspelled Fernand on card)	2.00	.90	.25
□ 141 Manny Mota	.25	.11	.03
□ 142 Gary Carter	.50	.23	.06
□ 143 Steve Rogers	.10	.05	.01
□ 144 Warren Cromartie	.10	.05	.01
□ 145 Andre Dawson	1.50	.70	.19
□ 146 Larry Parrish	.10	.05	.01
□ 147 Rowland Office	.10	.05	.01
□ 148 Ellis Valentine	.10	.05	.01
□ 149 Dick Williams MG	.10	.05	.01
□ 150 Bill Gullickson	.50	.23	.06
□ 151 Elias Sosa	.10	.05	.01
□ 152 John Tamargo	.10	.05	.01
□ 153 Chris Speier	.10	.05	.01
□ 154 Ron LeFlore	.25	.11	.03
□ 155 Rodney Scott	.10	.05	.01
□ 156 Stan Bahnsen	.10	.05	.01
□ 157 Bill Lee	.25	.11	.03
□ 158 Fred Norman	.10	.05	.01
□ 159 Woodie Fryman	.10	.05	.01
□ 160 David Palmer	.10	.05	.01
□ 161 Jerry White	.10	.05	.01
□ 162 Roberto Ramos	.10	.05	.01
□ 163 John D'Acquisto	.10	.05	.01
□ 164 Tommy Hutton	.10	.05	.01
□ 165 Charlie Lea	.10	.05	.01
□ 166 Scott Sanderson	.10	.05	.01
□ 167 Ken Macha	.10	.05	.01
□ 168 Tony Bernazard	.10	.05	.01
□ 169 Jim Palmer	.75	.35	.09
□ 170 Steve Stone	.25	.11	.03
□ 171 Mike Flanagan	.25	.11	.03
□ 172 Al Bumbry	.25	.11	.03
□ 173 Doug DeCinces	.25	.11	.03
□ 174 Scott McGregor	.10	.05	.01
□ 175 Mark Belanger	.25	.11	.03
□ 176 Tim Stoddard	.10	.05	.01
□ 177A Rick Dempsey P1 (Small hand on front)	.50	.23	.06
□ 177B Rick Dempsey P2 (No hand)	.25	.11	.03
□ 178 Earl Weaver MG	.50	.23	.06
□ 179 Tippy Martinez	.10	.05	.01
□ 180 Dennis Martinez	.25	.11	.03
□ 181 Sammy Stewart	.10	.05	.01
□ 182 Rich Dauer	.10	.05	.01
□ 183 Lee May	.25	.11	.03
□ 184 Eddie Murray	4.00	1.80	.50
□ 185 Benny Ayala	.10	.05	.01
□ 186 John Lowenstein	.10	.05	.01
□ 187 Gary Roenicke	.10	.05	.01
□ 188 Ken Singleton	.25	.11	.03
□ 189 Dan Graham	.10	.05	.01
□ 190 Terry Crowley	.10	.05	.01
□ 191 Kiko Garcia	.10	.05	.01
□ 192 Dave Ford	.10	.05	.01

□ 193 Mark Corey	.10	.05	.01
□ 194 Lenn Sakata	.10	.05	.01
□ 195 Doug DeCinces	.25	.11	.03
□ 196 Johnny Bench	1.25	.55	.16
□ 197 Dave Concepcion	.25	.11	.03
□ 198 Ray Knight	.25	.11	.03
□ 199 Ken Griffey	.25	.11	.03
□ 200 Tom Seaver	1.25	.55	.16
□ 201 Dave Collins	.10	.05	.01
□ 202A George Foster P1 Slugger (Number on back 216)	.25	.11	.03
□ 202B George Foster P2 Slugger (Number on back 202)	.25	.11	.03
□ 203 Junior Kennedy	.10	.05	.01
□ 204 Frank Pastore	.10	.05	.01
□ 205 Dan Driessen	.10	.05	.01
□ 206 Hector Cruz	.10	.05	.01
□ 207 Paul Moskau	.10	.05	.01
□ 208 Charlie Leibrandt	.50	.23	.06
□ 209 Harry Spilman	.10	.05	.01
□ 210 Joe Price	.10	.05	.01
□ 211 Tom Hume	.10	.05	.01
□ 212 Joe Nolan	.10	.05	.01
□ 213 Doug Bair	.10	.05	.01
□ 214 Mario Soto	.10	.05	.01
□ 215A Bill Bonham P1 (Small hand on back)	.50	.23	.06
□ 215B Bill Bonham P2 (No hand)	.10	.05	.01
□ 216 George Foster (See 202)	.25	.11	.03
□ 217 Paul Householder	.10	.05	.01
□ 218 Ron Oester	.10	.05	.01
□ 219 Sam Mejias	.10	.05	.01
□ 220 Sheldon Burnside	.10	.05	.01
□ 221 Carl Yastrzemski	1.00	.45	.12
□ 222 Jim Rice	.50	.23	.06
□ 223 Fred Lynn	.25	.11	.03
□ 224 Carlton Fisk	1.25	.55	.16
□ 225 Rick Burleson	.10	.05	.01
□ 226 Dennis Eckersley	.75	.35	.09
□ 227 Butch Hobson	.10	.05	.01
□ 228 Tom Burgmeier	.10	.05	.01
□ 229 Garry Hancock	.10	.05	.01
□ 230 Don Zimmer MG	.10	.05	.01
□ 231 Steve Renko	.10	.05	.01
□ 232 Dwight Evans	.50	.23	.06
□ 233 Mike Torrez	.10	.05	.01
□ 234 Bob Stanley	.10	.05	.01
□ 235 Jim Dwyer	.10	.05	.01
□ 236 Dave Stapleton	.10	.05	.01
□ 237 Glenn Hoffman	.10	.05	.01
□ 238 Jerry Remy	.10	.05	.01
□ 239 Dick Drago	.10	.05	.01
□ 240 Bill Campbell	.10	.05	.01
□ 241 Tony Perez	.50	.23	.06
□ 242 Phil Niekro	.50	.23	.06
□ 243 Dale Murphy	.75	.35	.09
□ 244 Bob Horner	.25	.11	.03
□ 245 Jeff Burroughs	.10	.05	.01
□ 246 Rick Camp	.10	.05	.01
□ 247 Bobby Cox MG	.25	.11	.03
□ 248 Bruce Benedict	.10	.05	.01
□ 249 Gene Garber	.10	.05	.01
□ 250 Jerry Royster	.10	.05	.01
□ 251A Gary Matthews P1 (Small hand on back)	.50	.23	.06
□ 251B Gary Matthews P2 (No hand)	.25	.11	.03
□ 252 Chris Chambliss	.25	.11	.03
□ 253 Luis Gomez	.10	.05	.01
□ 254 Bill Nahorodny	.10	.05	.01
□ 255 Doyle Alexander	.10	.05	.01
□ 256 Brian Asselstine	.10	.05	.01
□ 257 Biff Pocoroba	.10	.05	.01
□ 258 Mike Lum	.10	.05	.01
□ 259 Charlie Spikes	.10	.05	.01
□ 260 Glenn Hubbard	.10	.05	.01
□ 261 Tommy Boggs	.10	.05	.01
□ 262 Al Hrabosky	.10	.05	.01
□ 263 Rick Matula	.10	.05	.01
□ 264 Preston Hanna	.10	.05	.01
□ 265 Larry Bradford	.10	.05	.01
□ 266 Rafael Ramirez	.10	.05	.01

☐ 267 Larry McWilliams	.10	.05	.01
☐ 268 Rod Carew	.75	.35	.09
☐ 269 Bobby Grich	.25	.11	.03
☐ 270 Carney Lansford	.25	.11	.03
☐ 271 Don Baylor	.50	.23	.06
☐ 272 Joe Rudi	.25	.11	.03
☐ 273 Dan Ford	.10	.05	.01
☐ 274 Jim Fregosi MG	.10	.05	.01
☐ 275 Dave Frost	.10	.05	.01
☐ 276 Frank Tanana	.25	.11	.03
☐ 277 Dickie Thon	.25	.11	.03
☐ 278 Jason Thompson	.10	.05	.01
☐ 279 Rick Miller	.10	.05	.01
☐ 280 Bert Campaneris	.25	.11	.03
☐ 281 Tom Donohue	.10	.05	.01
☐ 282 Brian Downing	.10	.05	.01
☐ 283 Fred Patek	.10	.05	.01
☐ 284 Bruce Kison	.10	.05	.01
☐ 285 Dave LaRoche	.10	.05	.01
☐ 286 Don Aase	.10	.05	.01
☐ 287 Jim Barr	.10	.05	.01
☐ 288 Alfredo Martinez	.10	.05	.01
☐ 289 Larry Harlow	.10	.05	.01
☐ 290 Andy Hassler	.10	.05	.01
☐ 291 Dave Kingman	.25	.11	.03
☐ 292 Bill Buckner	.25	.11	.03
☐ 293 Rick Reuschel	.25	.11	.03
☐ 294 Bruce Sutter	.25	.11	.03
☐ 295 Jerry Martin	.10	.05	.01
☐ 296 Scot Thompson	.10	.05	.01
☐ 297 Ivan DeJesus	.10	.05	.01
☐ 298 Steve Dillard	.10	.05	.01
☐ 299 Dick Tidrow	.10	.05	.01
☐ 300 Randy Martz	.10	.05	.01
☐ 301 Lenny Randle	.10	.05	.01
☐ 302 Lynn McGlothen	.10	.05	.01
☐ 303 Cliff Johnson	.10	.05	.01
☐ 304 Tim Blackwell	.10	.05	.01
☐ 305 Dennis Lamp	.10	.05	.01
☐ 306 Bill Caudill	.10	.05	.01
☐ 307 Carlos Lezcano	.10	.05	.01
☐ 308 Jim Tracy	.10	.05	.01
☐ 309 Doug Capilla UER	.10	.05	.01
(Cubs on front but			
Braves on back)			
☐ 310 Willie Hernandez	.25	.11	.03
☐ 311 Mike Vail	.10	.05	.01
☐ 312 Mike Krukow	.10	.05	.01
☐ 313 Barry Foote	.10	.05	.01
☐ 314 Larry Biittner	.10	.05	.01
☐ 315 Mike Tyson	.10	.05	.01
☐ 316 Lee Mazzilli	.10	.05	.01
☐ 317 John Stearns	.10	.05	.01
☐ 318 Alex Trevino	.10	.05	.01
☐ 319 Craig Swan	.10	.05	.01
☐ 320 Frank Taveras	.10	.05	.01
☐ 321 Steve Henderson	.10	.05	.01
☐ 322 Neil Allen	.10	.05	.01
☐ 323 Mark Bomback	.10	.05	.01
☐ 324 Mike Jorgensen	.10	.05	.01
☐ 325 Joe Torre MG	.25	.11	.03
☐ 326 Elliott Maddox	.10	.05	.01
☐ 327 Pete Falcone	.10	.05	.01
☐ 328 Ray Burris	.10	.05	.01
☐ 329 Claudell Washington	.10	.05	.01
☐ 330 Doug Flynn	.10	.05	.01
☐ 331 Joel Youngblood	.10	.05	.01
☐ 332 Bill Almon	.10	.05	.01
☐ 333 Tom Hausman	.10	.05	.01
☐ 334 Pat Zachry	.10	.05	.01
☐ 335 Jeff Reardon	1.00	.45	.12
☐ 336 Wally Backman	.25	.11	.03
☐ 337 Dan Norman	.10	.05	.01
☐ 338 Jerry Morales	.10	.05	.01
☐ 339 Ed Farmer	.10	.05	.01
☐ 340 Bob Molinaro	.10	.05	.01
☐ 341 Todd Cruz	.10	.05	.01
☐ 342A Britt Burns P1	.50	.23	.06
(Small hand on front)			
☐ 342B Britt Burns P2	.25	.11	.03
(No hand)			
☐ 343 Kevin Bell	.10	.05	.01
☐ 344 Tony LaRussa MG	.25	.11	.03
☐ 345 Steve Trout	.10	.05	.01
☐ 346 Harold Baines	3.00	1.35	.35
☐ 347 Richard Wortham	.10	.05	.01
☐ 348 Wayne Nordhagen	.10	.05	.01
☐ 349 Mike Squires	.10	.05	.01
☐ 350 Lamar Johnson	.10	.05	.01
☐ 351 Rickey Henderson	2.00	.90	.25
(Most Stolen Bases AL)			
☐ 352 Francisco Barrios	.10	.05	.01
☐ 353 Thad Bosley	.10	.05	.01
☐ 354 Chet Lemon	.10	.05	.01
☐ 355 Bruce Kimm	.10	.05	.01
☐ 356 Richard Dotson	.10	.05	.01
☐ 357 Jim Morrison	.10	.05	.01
☐ 358 Mike Proly	.10	.05	.01
☐ 359 Greg Pryor	.10	.05	.01
☐ 360 Dave Parker	.50	.23	.06
☐ 361 Omar Moreno	.10	.05	.01
☐ 362A Kent Tekulve P1	.25	.11	.03
(Back "1071 Waterbury"			
and "1078 Pirates")			
☐ 362B Kent Tekulve P2	.25	.11	.03
("1971 Waterbury" and			
"1978 Pirates")			
☐ 363 Willie Stargell	.75	.35	.09
☐ 364 Phil Garner	.25	.11	.03
☐ 365 Ed Ott	.10	.05	.01
☐ 366 Don Robinson	.10	.05	.01
☐ 367 Chuck Tanner MG	.25	.11	.03
☐ 368 Jim Rooker	.10	.05	.01
☐ 369 Dale Berra	.10	.05	.01
☐ 370 Jim Bibby	.10	.05	.01
☐ 371 Steve Nicosia	.10	.05	.01
☐ 372 Mike Easler	.10	.05	.01
☐ 373 Bill Robinson	.25	.11	.03
☐ 374 Lee Lacy	.10	.05	.01
☐ 375 John Candelaria	.25	.11	.03
☐ 376 Manny Sanguillen	.25	.11	.03
☐ 377 Rick Rhoden	.10	.05	.01
☐ 378 Grant Jackson	.10	.05	.01
☐ 379 Tim Foli	.10	.05	.01
☐ 380 Rod Scurry	.10	.05	.01
☐ 381 Bill Madlock	.25	.11	.03
☐ 382A Kurt Bevacqua	.25	.11	.03
P1 ERR			
(P on cap backwards)			
☐ 382B Kurt Bevacqua P2	.10	.05	.01
COR			
☐ 383 Bert Blyleven	.50	.23	.06
☐ 384 Eddie Solomon	.10	.05	.01
☐ 385 Enrique Romo	.10	.05	.01
☐ 386 John Milner	.10	.05	.01
☐ 387 Mike Hargrove	.25	.11	.03
☐ 388 Jorge Orta	.10	.05	.01
☐ 389 Toby Harrah	.25	.11	.03
☐ 390 Tom Veryzer	.10	.05	.01
☐ 391 Miguel Dilone	.10	.05	.01
☐ 392 Dan Spillner	.10	.05	.01
☐ 393 Jack Brohamer	.10	.05	.01
☐ 394 Wayne Garland	.10	.05	.01
☐ 395 Sid Monge	.10	.05	.01
☐ 396 Rick Waits	.10	.05	.01
☐ 397 Joe Charboneau	.25	.11	.03
☐ 398 Gary Alexander	.10	.05	.01
☐ 399 Jerry Dybzinski	.10	.05	.01
☐ 400 Mike Stanton	.10	.05	.01
☐ 401 Mike Paxton	.10	.05	.01
☐ 402 Gary Gray	.10	.05	.01
☐ 403 Rick Manning	.10	.05	.01
☐ 404 Bo Diaz	.10	.05	.01
☐ 405 Ron Hassey	.10	.05	.01
☐ 406 Ross Grimsley	.10	.05	.01
☐ 407 Victor Cruz	.10	.05	.01
☐ 408 Len Barker	.10	.05	.01
☐ 409 Bob Bailor	.10	.05	.01
☐ 410 Otto Velez	.10	.05	.01
☐ 411 Ernie Whitt	.10	.05	.01
☐ 412 Jim Clancy	.10	.05	.01
☐ 413 Barry Bonnell	.10	.05	.01
☐ 414 Dave Stieb	.25	.11	.03
☐ 415 Damaso Garcia	.10	.05	.01
☐ 416 John Mayberry	.10	.05	.01
☐ 417 Roy Howell	.10	.05	.01
☐ 418 Danny Ainge	3.00	1.35	.35
☐ 419A Jesse Jefferson P1	.10	.05	.01
(Back says Pirates)			
☐ 419B Jesse Jefferson P2	.10	.05	.01
(Back says Pirates)			
☐ 419C Jesse Jefferson P3	.25	.11	.03

	(Back says Blue Jays)			
☐ 420	Joey McLaughlin	.10	.05	.01
☐ 421	Lloyd Moseby	.25	.11	.03
☐ 422	Alvis Woods	.10	.05	.01
☐ 423	Garth Iorg	.10	.05	.01
☐ 424	Doug Ault	.10	.05	.01
☐ 425	Ken Schrom	.10	.05	.01
☐ 426	Mike Willis	.10	.05	.01
☐ 427	Steve Braun	.10	.05	.01
☐ 428	Bob Davis	.10	.05	.01
☐ 429	Jerry Garvin	.10	.05	.01
☐ 430	Alfredo Griffin	.10	.05	.01
☐ 431	Bob Mattick MG	.10	.05	.01
☐ 432	Vida Blue	.25	.11	.03
☐ 433	Jack Clark	.25	.11	.03
☐ 434	Willie McCovey	.75	.35	.09
☐ 435	Mike Ivie	.10	.05	.01
☐ 436A	Darrel Evans P1 ERR	.50	.23	.06
	(Name on front "Darrel")			
☐ 436B	Darrell Evans P2 COR	.50	.23	.06
	(Name on front "Darrell")			
☐ 437	Terry Whitfield	.10	.05	.01
☐ 438	Rennie Stennett	.10	.05	.01
☐ 439	John Montefusco	.10	.05	.01
☐ 440	Jim Wohlford	.10	.05	.01
☐ 441	Bill North	.10	.05	.01
☐ 442	Milt May	.10	.05	.01
☐ 443	Max Venable	.10	.05	.01
☐ 444	Ed Whitson	.10	.05	.01
☐ 445	Al Holland	.10	.05	.01
☐ 446	Randy Moffitt	.10	.05	.01
☐ 447	Bob Knepper	.10	.05	.01
☐ 448	Gary Lavelle	.10	.05	.01
☐ 449	Greg Minton	.10	.05	.01
☐ 450	Johnnie LeMaster	.10	.05	.01
☐ 451	Larry Herndon	.10	.05	.01
☐ 452	Rich Murray	.10	.05	.01
☐ 453	Joe Pettini	.10	.05	.01
☐ 454	Allen Ripley	.10	.05	.01
☐ 455	Dennis Littlejohn	.10	.05	.01
☐ 456	Tom Griffin	.10	.05	.01
☐ 457	Alan Hargesheimer	.10	.05	.01
☐ 458	Joe Strain	.10	.05	.01
☐ 459	Steve Kemp	.10	.05	.01
☐ 460	Sparky Anderson MG	.25	.11	.03
☐ 461	Alan Trammell	1.25	.55	.16
☐ 462	Mark Fidrych	.50	.23	.06
☐ 463	Lou Whitaker	1.00	.45	.12
☐ 464	Dave Rozema	.10	.05	.01
☐ 465	Milt Wilcox	.10	.05	.01
☐ 466	Champ Summers	.10	.05	.01
☐ 467	Lance Parrish	.50	.23	.06
☐ 468	Dan Petry	.25	.11	.03
☐ 469	Pat Underwood	.10	.05	.01
☐ 470	Rick Peters	.10	.05	.01
☐ 471	Al Cowens	.10	.05	.01
☐ 472	John Wockenfuss	.10	.05	.01
☐ 473	Tom Brookens	.10	.05	.01
☐ 474	Richie Hebner	.10	.05	.01
☐ 475	Jack Morris	.50	.23	.06
☐ 476	Jim Lentine	.10	.05	.01
☐ 477	Bruce Robbins	.10	.05	.01
☐ 478	Mark Wagner	.10	.05	.01
☐ 479	Tim Corcoran	.10	.05	.01
☐ 480A	Stan Papi P1	.25	.11	.03
	(Front as Pitcher)			
☐ 480B	Stan Papi P2	.10	.05	.01
	(Front as Shortstop)			
☐ 481	Kirk Gibson	3.00	1.35	.35
☐ 482	Dan Schatzeder	.10	.05	.01
☐ 483A	Amos Otis P1	.25	.11	.03
	(See card 32)			
☐ 483B	Amos Otis P2	.25	.11	.03
	(See card 32)			
☐ 484	Dave Winfield	1.50	.70	.19
☐ 485	Rollie Fingers	.50	.23	.06
☐ 486	Gene Richards	.10	.05	.01
☐ 487	Randy Jones	.10	.05	.01
☐ 488	Ozzie Smith	4.00	1.80	.50
☐ 489	Gene Tenace	.25	.11	.03
☐ 490	Bill Fahey	.10	.05	.01
☐ 491	John Curtis	.10	.05	.01
☐ 492	Dave Cash	.10	.05	.01
☐ 493A	Tim Flannery P1	.25	.11	.03
	(Batting right)			
☐ 493B	Tim Flannery P2	.10	.05	.01
	(Batting left)			
☐ 494	Jerry Mumphrey	.10	.05	.01
☐ 495	Bob Shirley	.10	.05	.01
☐ 496	Steve Mura	.10	.05	.01
☐ 497	Eric Rasmussen	.10	.05	.01
☐ 498	Broderick Perkins	.10	.05	.01
☐ 499	Barry Evans	.10	.05	.01
☐ 500	Chuck Baker	.10	.05	.01
☐ 501	Luis Salazar	.10	.05	.01
☐ 502	Gary Lucas	.10	.05	.01
☐ 503	Mike Armstrong	.10	.05	.01
☐ 504	Jerry Turner	.10	.05	.01
☐ 505	Dennis Kinney	.10	.05	.01
☐ 506	Willie Montanez UER	.10	.05	.01
	(Misspelled Willy on card front)			
☐ 507	Gorman Thomas	.25	.11	.03
☐ 508	Ben Oglivie	.25	.11	.03
☐ 509	Larry Hisle	.10	.05	.01
☐ 510	Sal Bando	.25	.11	.03
☐ 511	Robin Yount	1.50	.70	.19
☐ 512	Mike Caldwell	.10	.05	.01
☐ 513	Sixto Lezcano	.10	.05	.01
☐ 514A	Bill Travers P1 ERR	.25	.11	.03
	("Jerry Augustine" with Augustine back)			
☐ 514B	Bill Travers P2 COR	.10	.05	.01
☐ 515	Paul Molitor	1.50	.70	.19
☐ 516	Moose Haas	.10	.05	.01
☐ 517	Bill Castro	.10	.05	.01
☐ 518	Jim Slaton	.10	.05	.01
☐ 519	Lary Sorensen	.10	.05	.01
☐ 520	Bob McClure	.10	.05	.01
☐ 521	Charlie Moore	.10	.05	.01
☐ 522	Jim Gantner	.25	.11	.03
☐ 523	Reggie Cleveland	.10	.05	.01
☐ 524	Don Money	.10	.05	.01
☐ 525	Bill Travers	.10	.05	.01
☐ 526	Buck Martinez	.10	.05	.01
☐ 527	Dick Davis	.10	.05	.01
☐ 528	Ted Simmons	.25	.11	.03
☐ 529	Garry Templeton	.10	.05	.01
☐ 530	Ken Reitz	.10	.05	.01
☐ 531	Tony Scott	.10	.05	.01
☐ 532	Ken Oberkfell	.10	.05	.01
☐ 533	Bob Sykes	.10	.05	.01
☐ 534	Keith Smith	.10	.05	.01
☐ 535	John Littlefield	.10	.05	.01
☐ 536	Jim Kaat	.25	.11	.03
☐ 537	Bob Forsch	.10	.05	.01
☐ 538	Mike Phillips	.10	.05	.01
☐ 539	Terry Landrum	.10	.05	.01
☐ 540	Leon Durham	.25	.11	.03
☐ 541	Terry Kennedy	.10	.05	.01
☐ 542	George Hendrick	.10	.05	.01
☐ 543	Dane Iorg	.10	.05	.01
☐ 544	Mark Littell	.10	.05	.01
☐ 545	Keith Hernandez	.50	.23	.06
☐ 546	Silvio Martinez	.10	.05	.01
☐ 547A	Don Hood P1 ERR	.25	.11	.03
	("Pete Vuckovich" with Vuckovich back)			
☐ 547B	Don Hood P2 COR	.10	.05	.01
☐ 548	Bobby Bonds	.25	.11	.03
☐ 549	Mike Ramsey	.10	.05	.01
☐ 550	Tom Herr	.25	.11	.03
☐ 551	Roy Smalley	.10	.05	.01
☐ 552	Jerry Koosman	.25	.11	.03
☐ 553	Ken Landreaux	.10	.05	.01
☐ 554	John Castino	.10	.05	.01
☐ 555	Doug Corbett	.10	.05	.01
☐ 556	Bombo Rivera	.10	.05	.01
☐ 557	Ron Jackson	.10	.05	.01
☐ 558	Butch Wynegar	.10	.05	.01
☐ 559	Hosken Powell	.10	.05	.01
☐ 560	Pete Redfern	.10	.05	.01
☐ 561	Roger Erickson	.10	.05	.01
☐ 562	Glenn Adams	.10	.05	.01
☐ 563	Rick Sofield	.10	.05	.01
☐ 564	Geoff Zahn	.10	.05	.01
☐ 565	Pete Mackanin	.10	.05	.01
☐ 566	Mike Cubbage	.10	.05	.01
☐ 567	Darrell Jackson	.10	.05	.01
☐ 568	Dave Edwards	.10	.05	.01

□ 569	Rob Wilfong	.10	.05	.01
□ 570	Sal Butera	.10	.05	.01
□ 571	Jose Morales	.10	.05	.01
□ 572	Rick Langford	.10	.05	.01
□ 573	Mike Norris	.10	.05	.01
□ 574	Rickey Henderson	3.00	1.35	.35
□ 575	Tony Armas	.25	.11	.03
□ 576	Dave Revering	.10	.05	.01
□ 577	Jeff Newman	.10	.05	.01
□ 578	Bob Lacey	.10	.05	.01
□ 579	Brian Kingman	.10	.05	.01
□ 580	Mitchell Page	.10	.05	.01
□ 581	Billy Martin MG	.50	.23	.06
□ 582	Rob Picciolo	.10	.05	.01
□ 583	Mike Heath	.10	.05	.01
□ 584	Mickey Klutts	.10	.05	.01
□ 585	Orlando Gonzalez	.10	.05	.01
□ 586	Mike Davis	.10	.05	.01
□ 587	Wayne Gross	.10	.05	.01
□ 588	Matt Keough	.10	.05	.01
□ 589	Steve McCatty	.10	.05	.01
□ 590	Dwayne Murphy	.10	.05	.01
□ 591	Mario Guerrero	.10	.05	.01
□ 592	Dave McKay	.10	.05	.01
□ 593	Jim Essian	.10	.05	.01
□ 594	Dave Heaverlo	.10	.05	.01
□ 595	Maury Wills MG	.25	.11	.03
□ 596	Juan Beniquez	.10	.05	.01
□ 597	Rodney Craig	.10	.05	.01
□ 598	Jim Anderson	.10	.05	.01
□ 599	Floyd Bannister	.10	.05	.01
□ 600	Bruce Bochte	.10	.05	.01
□ 601	Julio Cruz	.10	.05	.01
□ 602	Ted Cox	.10	.05	.01
□ 603	Dan Meyer	.10	.05	.01
□ 604	Larry Cox	.10	.05	.01
□ 605	Bill Stein	.10	.05	.01
□ 606	Steve Garvey (Most Hits NL)	.50	.23	.06
□ 607	Dave Roberts	.10	.05	.01
□ 608	Leon Roberts	.10	.05	.01
□ 609	Reggie Walton	.10	.05	.01
□ 610	Dave Edler	.10	.05	.01
□ 611	Larry Milbourne	.10	.05	.01
□ 612	Kim Allen	.10	.05	.01
□ 613	Mario Mendoza	.10	.05	.01
□ 614	Tom Paciorek	.10	.05	.01
□ 615	Glenn Abbott	.10	.05	.01
□ 616	Joe Simpson	.10	.05	.01
□ 617	Mickey Rivers	.25	.11	.03
□ 618	Jim Kern	.10	.05	.01
□ 619	Jim Sundberg	.25	.11	.03
□ 620	Richie Zisk	.10	.05	.01
□ 621	Jon Matlack	.10	.05	.01
□ 622	Ferguson Jenkins	.50	.23	.06
□ 623	Pat Corrales MG	.10	.05	.01
□ 624	Ed Figueroa	.10	.05	.01
□ 625	Buddy Bell	.25	.11	.03
□ 626	Al Oliver	.25	.11	.03
□ 627	Doc Medich	.10	.05	.01
□ 628	Bump Wills	.10	.05	.01
□ 629	Rusty Staub	.25	.11	.03
□ 630	Pat Putnam	.10	.05	.01
□ 631	John Grubb	.10	.05	.01
□ 632	Danny Darwin	.25	.11	.03
□ 633	Ken Clay	.10	.05	.01
□ 634	Jim Norris	.10	.05	.01
□ 635	John Butcher	.10	.05	.01
□ 636	Dave Roberts	.10	.05	.01
□ 637	Billy Sample	.10	.05	.01
□ 638	Carl Yastrzemski	1.00	.45	.12
□ 639	Cecil Cooper	.25	.11	.03
□ 640	Mike Schmidt P1 (Portrait; "Third Base"; number on back 5)	2.00	.90	.25
□ 640B	Mike Schmidt P2 ("1980 Home Run King"; 640 on back)	2.00	.90	.25
□ 641A	CL: Phils/Royals P1 41 is Hal McRae	.25	.11	.03
□ 641B	CL: Phils/Royals P2 (41 is Hal McRae, Double Threat)	.25	.11	.03
□ 642	CL: Astros/Yankees	.25	.11	.03
□ 643	CL: Expos/Dodgers	.25	.11	.03
□ 644A	CL: Reds/Orioles P1 (202 is George Foster; Joe Nolan pitcher, should be catcher)	.25	.11	.03
□ 644B	CL: Reds/Orioles P2 (202 is Foster Slugger; Joe Nolan pitcher, should be catcher)	.25	.11	.03
□ 645	Pete Rose Larry Bowa Mike Schmidt Triple Threat P1 (No number on back)	2.50	1.10	.30
□ 645B	Pete Rose Larry Bowa Mike Schmidt Triple Threat P2 (Back numbered 645)	2.50	1.10	.30
□ 646	CL: Braves/Red Sox	.25	.11	.03
□ 647	CL: Cubs/Angels	.25	.11	.03
□ 648	CL: Mets/White Sox	.25	.11	.03
□ 649	CL: Indians/Pirates	.25	.11	.03
□ 650	Reggie Jackson Mr. Baseball P1 (Number on back 79)	1.25	.55	.16
□ 650B	Reggie Jackson Mr. Baseball P2 (Number on back 650)	1.25	.55	.16
□ 651	CL: Giants/Blue Jays	.25	.11	.03
□ 652A	CL: Tigers/Padres P1 (483 is listed)	.25	.11	.03
□ 652B	CL: Tigers/Padres P2 (483 is deleted)	.25	.11	.03
□ 653A	Willie Wilson P1 Most Hits Most Runs (Number on back 29)	.25	.11	.03
□ 653B	Willie Wilson P2 Most Hits Most Runs (Number on back 653)	.25	.11	.03
□ 654A	CL:Brewers/Cards P1 (514 Jerry Augustine; 547 Pete Vuckovich)	.25	.11	.03
□ 654B	CL:Brewers/Cards P2 (514 Billy Travers; 547 Don Hood)	.25	.11	.03
□ 655	George Brett P1 .390 Average (Number on back 28)	4.00	1.80	.50
□ 655B	George Brett P2 .390 Average (Number on back 655)	4.00	1.80	.50
□ 656	CL: Twins/Oakland A's	.25	.11	.03
□ 657A	Tug McGraw P1 Game Saver (Number on back 7)	.25	.11	.03
□ 657B	Tug McGraw P2 Game Saver (Number on back 657)	.25	.11	.03
□ 658	CL: Rangers/Mariners	.25	.11	.03
□ 659A	Checklist P1 of Special Cards (Last lines on front, Wilson Most Hits)	.25	.11	.03
□ 659B	Checklist P2 of Special Cards (Last lines on front, Otis Series Starter)	.25	.11	.03
□ 660	Steve Carlton P1 Golden Arm (Number on back 660; Back "1066 Cardinals")	1.50	.70	.19
□ 660B	Steve Carlton P2 Golden Arm ("1966 Cardinals")	1.50	.70	.19

1982 Fleer

The 1982 Fleer set contains 660-card standard-size cards, of which are grouped in team order based upon standings from the previous season. Cards numbered 628 through 646 are special cards highlighting some of the stars and leaders of the 1981 season. The last 14 cards in the set (647-660) are checklist cards. The backs feature player statistics and a full-color

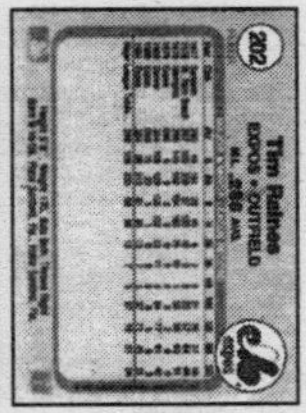

team logo in the upper right-hand corner of each card. The complete set price below does not include any of the more valuable variation cards listed. Fleer was not allowed to insert bubble gum or other confectionary products into these packs; therefore logo stickers were included in these 15-card packs. Notable Rookie Cards in this set include Cal Ripken Jr., Lee Smith, and Dave Stewart.

	MINT	NRMT	EXC
COMPLETE SET (660)	70.00	32.00	8.75
COMMON CARD (1-660)	.10	.05	.01
SEMISTARS	.20	.09	.03
STARS	.40	.18	.05

□ 1 Dusty Baker	.40	.18	.05
□ 2 Robert Castillo	.10	.05	.01
□ 3 Ron Cey	.20	.09	.03
□ 4 Terry Forster	.10	.05	.01
□ 5 Steve Garvey	.40	.18	.05
□ 6 Dave Goltz	.10	.05	.01
□ 7 Pedro Guerrero	.20	.09	.03
□ 8 Burt Hooton	.10	.05	.01
□ 9 Steve Howe	.10	.05	.01
□ 10 Jay Johnstone	.20	.09	.03
□ 11 Ken Landreaux	.10	.05	.01
□ 12 Dave Lopes	.20	.09	.03
□ 13 Mike A. Marshall	.20	.09	.03
□ 14 Bobby Mitchell	.10	.05	.01
□ 15 Rick Monday	.10	.05	.01
□ 16 Tom Niedenfuer	.10	.05	.01
□ 17 Ted Power	.10	.05	.01
□ 18 Jerry Reuss UER ("Home:" omitted)	.20	.09	.03
□ 19 Ron Roenicke	.10	.05	.01
□ 20 Bill Russell	.20	.09	.03
□ 21 Steve Sax	.40	.18	.05
□ 22 Mike Scioscia	.20	.09	.03
□ 23 Reggie Smith	.20	.09	.03
□ 24 Dave Stewart	1.50	.70	.19
□ 25 Rick Sutcliffe	.20	.09	.03
□ 26 Derrel Thomas	.10	.05	.01
□ 27 Fernando Valenzuela	.40	.18	.05
□ 28 Bob Welch	.20	.09	.03
□ 29 Steve Yeager	.10	.05	.01
□ 30 Bobby Brown	.10	.05	.01
□ 31 Rick Cerone	.10	.05	.01
□ 32 Ron Davis	.10	.05	.01
□ 33 Bucky Dent	.20	.09	.03
□ 34 Barry Foote	.10	.05	.01
□ 35 George Frazier	.10	.05	.01
□ 36 Oscar Gamble	.10	.05	.01
□ 37 Rich Gossage	.40	.18	.05
□ 38 Ron Guidry	.20	.09	.03
□ 39 Reggie Jackson	1.00	.45	.12
□ 40 Tommy John	.40	.18	.05
□ 41 Rudy May	.10	.05	.01
□ 42 Larry Milbourne	.10	.05	.01
□ 43 Jerry Mumphrey	.10	.05	.01
□ 44 Bobby Murcer	.20	.09	.03
□ 45 Gene Nelson	.10	.05	.01
□ 46 Graig Nettles	.20	.09	.03
□ 47 Johnny Oates	.20	.09	.03
□ 48 Lou Piniella	.20	.09	.03
□ 49 Willie Randolph	.20	.09	.03
□ 50 Rick Reuschel	.20	.09	.03
□ 51 Dave Revering	.10	.05	.01
□ 52 Dave Righetti	.40	.18	.05
□ 53 Aurelio Rodriguez	.10	.05	.01
□ 54 Bob Watson	.20	.09	.03
□ 55 Dennis Werth	.10	.05	.01
□ 56 Dave Winfield	1.50	.70	.19
□ 57 Johnny Bench	.75	.35	.09
□ 58 Bruce Berenyi	.10	.05	.01
□ 59 Larry Biittner	.10	.05	.01
□ 60 Scott Brown	.10	.05	.01
□ 61 Dave Collins	.10	.05	.01
□ 62 Geoff Combe	.10	.05	.01
□ 63 Dave Concepcion	.20	.09	.03
□ 64 Dan Driessen	.10	.05	.01
□ 65 Joe Edelen	.10	.05	.01
□ 66 George Foster	.20	.09	.03
□ 67 Ken Griffey	.20	.09	.03
□ 68 Paul Householder	.10	.05	.01
□ 69 Tom Hume	.10	.05	.01
□ 70 Junior Kennedy	.10	.05	.01
□ 71 Ray Knight	.20	.09	.03
□ 72 Mike LaCoss	.10	.05	.01
□ 73 Rafael Landestoy	.10	.05	.01
□ 74 Charlie Leibrandt	.10	.05	.01
□ 75 Sam Mejias	.10	.05	.01
□ 76 Paul Moskau	.10	.05	.01
□ 77 Joe Nolan	.10	.05	.01
□ 78 Mike O'Berry	.10	.05	.01
□ 79 Ron Oester	.10	.05	.01
□ 80 Frank Pastore	.10	.05	.01
□ 81 Joe Price	.10	.05	.01
□ 82 Tom Seaver	.75	.35	.09
□ 83 Mario Soto	.10	.05	.01
□ 84 Mike Vail	.10	.05	.01
□ 85 Tony Armas	.10	.05	.01
□ 86 Shooty Babitt	.10	.05	.01
□ 87 Dave Beard	.10	.05	.01
□ 88 Rick Bosetti	.10	.05	.01
□ 89 Keith Drumwright	.10	.05	.01
□ 90 Wayne Gross	.10	.05	.01
□ 91 Mike Heath	.10	.05	.01
□ 92 Rickey Henderson	2.50	1.10	.30
□ 93 Cliff Johnson	.10	.05	.01
□ 94 Jeff Jones	.10	.05	.01
□ 95 Matt Keough	.10	.05	.01
□ 96 Brian Kingman	.10	.05	.01
□ 97 Mickey Klutts	.10	.05	.01
□ 98 Rick Langford	.10	.05	.01
□ 99 Steve McCatty	.10	.05	.01
□ 100 Dave McKay	.10	.05	.01
□ 101 Dwayne Murphy	.10	.05	.01
□ 102 Jeff Newman	.10	.05	.01
□ 103 Mike Norris	.10	.05	.01
□ 104 Bob Owchinko	.10	.05	.01
□ 105 Mitchell Page	.10	.05	.01
□ 106 Rob Picciolo	.10	.05	.01
□ 107 Jim Spencer	.10	.05	.01
□ 108 Fred Stanley	.10	.05	.01
□ 109 Tom Underwood	.10	.05	.01
□ 110 Joaquin Andujar	.20	.09	.03
□ 111 Steve Braun	.10	.05	.01
□ 112 Bob Forsch	.10	.05	.01
□ 113 George Hendrick	.10	.05	.01
□ 114 Keith Hernandez	.40	.18	.05
□ 115 Tom Herr	.20	.09	.03
□ 116 Dane Iorg	.10	.05	.01
□ 117 Jim Kaat	.20	.09	.03
□ 118 Tito Landrum	.10	.05	.01
□ 119 Sixto Lezcano	.10	.05	.01
□ 120 Mark Littell	.10	.05	.01
□ 121 John Martin	.10	.05	.01
□ 122 Silvio Martinez	.10	.05	.01
□ 123 Ken Oberkfell	.10	.05	.01
□ 124 Darrell Porter	.20	.09	.03
□ 125 Mike Ramsey	.10	.05	.01
□ 126 Orlando Sanchez	.10	.05	.01
□ 127 Bob Shirley	.10	.05	.01
□ 128 Lary Sorensen	.10	.05	.01
□ 129 Bruce Sutter	.20	.09	.03
□ 130 Bob Sykes	.10	.05	.01
□ 131 Garry Templeton	.10	.05	.01
□ 132 Gene Tenace	.20	.09	.03
□ 133 Jerry Augustine	.10	.05	.01
□ 134 Sal Bando	.20	.09	.03
□ 135 Mark Brouhard	.10	.05	.01
□ 136 Mike Caldwell	.10	.05	.01
□ 137 Reggie Cleveland	.10	.05	.01
□ 138 Cecil Cooper	.20	.09	.03
□ 139 Jamie Easterly	.10	.05	.01

□ 140 Marshall Edwards	.10	.05	.01
□ 141 Rollie Fingers	.40	.18	.05
□ 142 Jim Gantner	.20	.09	.03
□ 143 Moose Haas	.10	.05	.01
□ 144 Larry Hisle	.10	.05	.01
□ 145 Roy Howell	.10	.05	.01
□ 146 Rickey Keeton	.10	.05	.01
□ 147 Randy Lerch	.10	.05	.01
□ 148 Paul Molitor	1.25	.55	.16
□ 149 Don Money	.10	.05	.01
□ 150 Charlie Moore	.10	.05	.01
□ 151 Ben Oglivie	.20	.09	.03
□ 152 Ted Simmons	.20	.09	.03
□ 153 Jim Slaton	.10	.05	.01
□ 154 Gorman Thomas	.20	.09	.03
□ 155 Robin Yount	1.50	.70	.19
□ 156 Pete Vuckovich	.10	.05	.01
(Should precede Yount in the team order)			
□ 157 Benny Ayala	.10	.05	.01
□ 158 Mark Belanger	.20	.09	.03
□ 159 Al Bumbry	.20	.09	.03
□ 160 Terry Crowley	.10	.05	.01
□ 161 Rich Dauer	.10	.05	.01
□ 162 Doug DeCinces	.20	.09	.03
□ 163 Rick Dempsey	.20	.09	.03
□ 164 Jim Dwyer	.10	.05	.01
□ 165 Mike Flanagan	.20	.09	.03
□ 166 Dave Ford	.10	.05	.01
□ 167 Dan Graham	.10	.05	.01
□ 168 Wayne Krenchicki	.10	.05	.01
□ 169 John Lowenstein	.10	.05	.01
□ 170 Dennis Martinez	.20	.09	.03
□ 171 Tippy Martinez	.10	.05	.01
□ 172 Scott McGregor	.10	.05	.01
□ 173 Jose Morales	.10	.05	.01
□ 174 Eddie Murray	3.50	1.55	.45
□ 175 Jim Palmer	.60	.25	.07
□ 176 Cal Ripken	50.00	22.00	6.25
(Fleer Ripken cards from 1982 through 1993 erroneously have 22 games played in 1981;not 23.)			
□ 177 Gary Roenicke	.10	.05	.01
□ 178 Lenn Sakata	.10	.05	.01
□ 179 Ken Singleton	.20	.09	.03
□ 180 Sammy Stewart	.10	.05	.01
□ 181 Tim Stoddard	.10	.05	.01
□ 182 Steve Stone	.20	.09	.03
□ 183 Stan Bahnsen	.10	.05	.01
□ 184 Ray Burris	.10	.05	.01
□ 185 Gary Carter	.40	.18	.05
□ 186 Warren Cromartie	.10	.05	.01
□ 187 Andre Dawson	1.00	.45	.12
□ 188 Terry Francona	.10	.05	.01
□ 189 Woodie Fryman	.10	.05	.01
□ 190 Bill Gullickson	.10	.05	.01
□ 191 Grant Jackson	.10	.05	.01
□ 192 Wallace Johnson	.10	.05	.01
□ 193 Charlie Lea	.10	.05	.01
□ 194 Bill Lee	.20	.09	.03
□ 195 Jerry Manuel	.10	.05	.01
□ 196 Brad Mills	.10	.05	.01
□ 197 John Milner	.10	.05	.01
□ 198 Rowland Office	.10	.05	.01
□ 199 David Palmer	.10	.05	.01
□ 200 Larry Parrish	.10	.05	.01
□ 201 Mike Phillips	.10	.05	.01
□ 202 Tim Raines	2.00	.90	.25
□ 203 Bobby Ramos	.10	.05	.01
□ 204 Jeff Reardon	.40	.18	.05
□ 205 Steve Rogers	.10	.05	.01
□ 206 Scott Sanderson	.10	.05	.01
□ 207 Rodney Scott UER	.40	.18	.05
(Photo actually Tim Raines)			
□ 208 Elias Sosa	.10	.05	.01
□ 209 Chris Speier	.10	.05	.01
□ 210 Tim Wallach	.50	.23	.06
□ 211 Jerry White	.10	.05	.01
□ 212 Alan Ashby	.10	.05	.01
□ 213 Cesar Cedeno	.20	.09	.03
□ 214 Jose Cruz	.20	.09	.03
□ 215 Kiko Garcia	.10	.05	.01
□ 216 Phil Garner	.20	.09	.03
□ 217 Danny Heep	.10	.05	.01
□ 218 Art Howe	.10	.05	.01
□ 219 Bob Knepper	.10	.05	.01
□ 220 Frank LaCorte	.10	.05	.01
□ 221 Joe Niekro	.20	.09	.03
□ 222 Joe Pittman	.10	.05	.01
□ 223 Terry Puhl	.10	.05	.01
□ 224 Luis Pujols	.10	.05	.01
□ 225 Craig Reynolds	.10	.05	.01
□ 226 J.R. Richard	.20	.09	.03
□ 227 Dave Roberts	.10	.05	.01
□ 228 Vern Ruhle	.10	.05	.01
□ 229 Nolan Ryan	5.00	2.20	.60
□ 230 Joe Sambito	.10	.05	.01
□ 231 Tony Scott	.10	.05	.01
□ 232 Dave Smith	.10	.05	.01
□ 233 Harry Spilman	.10	.05	.01
□ 234 Don Sutton	.40	.18	.05
□ 235 Dickie Thon	.10	.05	.01
□ 236 Denny Walling	.10	.05	.01
□ 237 Gary Woods	.10	.05	.01
□ 238 Luis Aguayo	.10	.05	.01
□ 239 Ramon Aviles	.10	.05	.01
□ 240 Bob Boone	.20	.09	.03
□ 241 Larry Bowa	.20	.09	.03
□ 242 Warren Brusstar	.10	.05	.01
□ 243 Steve Carlton	.75	.35	.09
□ 244 Larry Christenson	.10	.05	.01
□ 245 Dick Davis	.10	.05	.01
□ 246 Greg Gross	.10	.05	.01
□ 247 Sparky Lyle	.20	.09	.03
□ 248 Garry Maddox	.10	.05	.01
□ 249 Gary Matthews	.20	.09	.03
□ 250 Bake McBride	.10	.05	.01
□ 251 Tug McGraw	.20	.09	.03
□ 252 Keith Moreland	.10	.05	.01
□ 253 Dickie Noles	.10	.05	.01
□ 254 Mike Proly	.10	.05	.01
□ 255 Ron Reed	.10	.05	.01
□ 256 Pete Rose	1.50	.70	.19
□ 257 Dick Ruthven	.10	.05	.01
□ 258 Mike Schmidt	2.00	.90	.25
□ 259 Lonnie Smith	.20	.09	.03
□ 260 Manny Trillo	.10	.05	.01
□ 261 Del Unser	.10	.05	.01
□ 262 George Vukovich	.10	.05	.01
□ 263 Tom Brookens	.10	.05	.01
□ 264 George Cappuzzello	.10	.05	.01
□ 265 Marty Castillo	.10	.05	.01
□ 266 Al Cowens	.10	.05	.01
□ 267 Kirk Gibson	.75	.35	.09
□ 268 Richie Hebner	.20	.09	.03
□ 269 Ron Jackson	.10	.05	.01
□ 270 Lynn Jones	.10	.05	.01
□ 271 Steve Kemp	.10	.05	.01
□ 272 Rick Leach	.10	.05	.01
□ 273 Aurelio Lopez	.10	.05	.01
□ 274 Jack Morris	.40	.18	.05
□ 275 Kevin Saucier	.10	.05	.01
□ 276 Lance Parrish	.40	.18	.05
□ 277 Rick Peters	.10	.05	.01
□ 278 Dan Petry	.10	.05	.01
□ 279 Dave Rozema	.10	.05	.01
□ 280 Stan Papi	.10	.05	.01
□ 281 Dan Schatzeder	.10	.05	.01
□ 282 Champ Summers	.10	.05	.01
□ 283 Alan Trammell	1.00	.45	.12
□ 284 Lou Whitaker	.40	.18	.05
□ 285 Milt Wilcox	.10	.05	.01
□ 286 John Wockenfuss	.10	.05	.01
□ 287 Gary Allenson	.10	.05	.01
□ 288 Tom Burgmeier	.10	.05	.01
□ 289 Bill Campbell	.10	.05	.01
□ 290 Mark Clear	.10	.05	.01
□ 291 Steve Crawford	.10	.05	.01
□ 292 Dennis Eckersley	.40	.18	.05
□ 293 Dwight Evans	.40	.18	.05
□ 294 Rich Gedman	.20	.09	.03
□ 295 Garry Hancock	.10	.05	.01
□ 296 Glenn Hoffman	.10	.05	.01
□ 297 Bruce Hurst	.10	.05	.01
□ 298 Carney Lansford	.20	.09	.03
□ 299 Rick Miller	.10	.05	.01
□ 300 Reid Nichols	.10	.05	.01
□ 301 Bob Ojeda	.40	.18	.05
□ 302 Tony Perez	.40	.18	.05
□ 303 Chuck Rainey	.10	.05	.01
□ 304 Jerry Remy	.10	.05	.01

☐ 305 Jim Rice	.40	.18	.05
☐ 306 Joe Rudi	.10	.05	.01
☐ 307 Bob Stanley	.10	.05	.01
☐ 308 Dave Stapleton	.10	.05	.01
☐ 309 Frank Tanana	.20	.09	.03
☐ 310 Mike Torrez	.10	.05	.01
☐ 311 John Tudor	.20	.09	.03
☐ 312 Carl Yastrzemski	.75	.35	.09
☐ 313 Buddy Bell	.20	.09	.03
☐ 314 Steve Comer	.10	.05	.01
☐ 315 Danny Darwin	.10	.05	.01
☐ 316 John Ellis	.10	.05	.01
☐ 317 John Grubb	.10	.05	.01
☐ 318 Rick Honeycutt	.10	.05	.01
☐ 319 Charlie Hough	.20	.09	.03
☐ 320 Ferguson Jenkins	.40	.18	.05
☐ 321 John Henry Johnson	.10	.05	.01
☐ 322 Jim Kern	.10	.05	.01
☐ 323 Jon Matlack	.10	.05	.01
☐ 324 Doc Medich	.10	.05	.01
☐ 325 Mario Mendoza	.10	.05	.01
☐ 326 Al Oliver	.20	.09	.03
☐ 327 Pat Putnam	.10	.05	.01
☐ 328 Mickey Rivers	.10	.05	.01
☐ 329 Leon Roberts	.10	.05	.01
☐ 330 Billy Sample	.10	.05	.01
☐ 331 Bill Stein	.10	.05	.01
☐ 332 Jim Sundberg	.20	.09	.03
☐ 333 Mark Wagner	.10	.05	.01
☐ 334 Bump Wills	.10	.05	.01
☐ 335 Bill Almon	.10	.05	.01
☐ 336 Harold Baines	.40	.18	.05
☐ 337 Ross Baumgarten	.10	.05	.01
☐ 338 Tony Bernazard	.10	.05	.01
☐ 339 Britt Burns	.10	.05	.01
☐ 340 Richard Dotson	.10	.05	.01
☐ 341 Jim Essian	.10	.05	.01
☐ 342 Ed Farmer	.10	.05	.01
☐ 343 Carlton Fisk	.75	.35	.09
☐ 344 Kevin Hickey	.10	.05	.01
☐ 345 LaMarr Hoyt	.10	.05	.01
☐ 346 Lamar Johnson	.10	.05	.01
☐ 347 Jerry Koosman	.20	.09	.03
☐ 348 Rusty Kuntz	.10	.05	.01
☐ 349 Dennis Lamp	.10	.05	.01
☐ 350 Ron LeFlore	.20	.09	.03
☐ 351 Chet Lemon	.10	.05	.01
☐ 352 Greg Luzinski	.20	.09	.03
☐ 353 Bob Molinaro	.10	.05	.01
☐ 354 Jim Morrison	.10	.05	.01
☐ 355 Wayne Nordhagen	.10	.05	.01
☐ 356 Greg Pryor	.10	.05	.01
☐ 357 Mike Squires	.10	.05	.01
☐ 358 Steve Trout	.10	.05	.01
☐ 359 Alan Bannister	.10	.05	.01
☐ 360 Len Barker	.10	.05	.01
☐ 361 Bert Blyleven	.40	.18	.05
☐ 362 Joe Charboneau	.10	.05	.01
☐ 363 John Denny	.10	.05	.01
☐ 364 Bo Diaz	.10	.05	.01
☐ 365 Miguel Dilone	.10	.05	.01
☐ 366 Jerry Dybzinski	.10	.05	.01
☐ 367 Wayne Garland	.10	.05	.01
☐ 368 Mike Hargrove	.20	.09	.03
☐ 369 Toby Harrah	.20	.09	.03
☐ 370 Ron Hassey	.10	.05	.01
☐ 371 Von Hayes	.20	.09	.03
☐ 372 Pat Kelly	.10	.05	.01
☐ 373 Duane Kuiper	.10	.05	.01
☐ 374 Rick Manning	.10	.05	.01
☐ 375 Sid Monge	.10	.05	.01
☐ 376 Jorge Orta	.10	.05	.01
☐ 377 Dave Rosello	.10	.05	.01
☐ 378 Dan Spillner	.10	.05	.01
☐ 379 Mike Stanton	.10	.05	.01
☐ 380 Andre Thornton	.10	.05	.01
☐ 381 Tom Veryzer	.10	.05	.01
☐ 382 Rick Waits	.10	.05	.01
☐ 383 Doyle Alexander	.10	.05	.01
☐ 384 Vida Blue	.20	.09	.03
☐ 385 Fred Breining	.10	.05	.01
☐ 386 Enos Cabell	.10	.05	.01
☐ 387 Jack Clark	.20	.09	.03
☐ 388 Darrell Evans	.20	.09	.03
☐ 389 Tom Griffin	.10	.05	.01
☐ 390 Larry Herndon	.10	.05	.01
☐ 391 Al Holland	.10	.05	.01
☐ 392 Gary Lavelle	.10	.05	.01
☐ 393 Johnnie LeMaster	.10	.05	.01
☐ 394 Jerry Martin	.10	.05	.01
☐ 395 Milt May	.10	.05	.01
☐ 396 Greg Minton	.10	.05	.01
☐ 397 Joe Morgan	.60	.25	.07
☐ 398 Joe Pettini	.10	.05	.01
☐ 399 Allen Ripley	.10	.05	.01
☐ 400 Billy Smith	.10	.05	.01
☐ 401 Rennie Stennett	.10	.05	.01
☐ 402 Ed Whitson	.10	.05	.01
☐ 403 Jim Wohlford	.10	.05	.01
☐ 404 Willie Aikens	.10	.05	.01
☐ 405 George Brett	3.50	1.55	.45
☐ 406 Ken Brett	.10	.05	.01
☐ 407 Dave Chalk	.10	.05	.01
☐ 408 Rich Gale	.10	.05	.01
☐ 409 Cesar Geronimo	.10	.05	.01
☐ 410 Larry Gura	.10	.05	.01
☐ 411 Clint Hurdle	.10	.05	.01
☐ 412 Mike Jones	.10	.05	.01
☐ 413 Dennis Leonard	.10	.05	.01
☐ 414 Renie Martin	.10	.05	.01
☐ 415 Lee May	.20	.09	.03
☐ 416 Hal McRae	.20	.09	.03
☐ 417 Darryl Motley	.10	.05	.01
☐ 418 Rance Mulliniks	.10	.05	.01
☐ 419 Amos Otis	.20	.09	.03
☐ 420 Ken Phelps	.10	.05	.01
☐ 421 Jamie Quirk	.10	.05	.01
☐ 422 Dan Quisenberry	.20	.09	.03
☐ 423 Paul Splittorff	.10	.05	.01
☐ 424 U.L. Washington	.10	.05	.01
☐ 425 John Wathan	.10	.05	.01
☐ 426 Frank White	.20	.09	.03
☐ 427 Willie Wilson	.20	.09	.03
☐ 428 Brian Asselstine	.10	.05	.01
☐ 429 Bruce Benedict	.10	.05	.01
☐ 430 Tommy Boggs	.10	.05	.01
☐ 431 Larry Bradford	.10	.05	.01
☐ 432 Rick Camp	.10	.05	.01
☐ 433 Chris Chambliss	.20	.09	.03
☐ 434 Gene Garber	.10	.05	.01
☐ 435 Preston Hanna	.10	.05	.01
☐ 436 Bob Horner	.20	.09	.03
☐ 437 Glenn Hubbard	.10	.05	.01
☐ 438A All Hrabosky ERR (Height 5'1", All on reverse)	20.00	9.00	2.50
☐ 438B Al Hrabosky ERR (Height 5'1")	.40	.18	.05
☐ 438C Al Hrabosky (Height 5'10")	.20	.09	.03
☐ 439 Rufino Linares	.10	.05	.01
☐ 440 Rick Mahler	.10	.05	.01
☐ 441 Ed Miller	.10	.05	.01
☐ 442 John Montefusco	.10	.05	.01
☐ 443 Dale Murphy	.40	.18	.05
☐ 444 Phil Niekro	.40	.18	.05
☐ 445 Gaylord Perry	.40	.18	.05
☐ 446 Biff Pocoroba	.10	.05	.01
☐ 447 Rafael Ramirez	.10	.05	.01
☐ 448 Jerry Royster	.10	.05	.01
☐ 449 Claudell Washington	.10	.05	.01
☐ 450 Don Aase	.10	.05	.01
☐ 451 Don Baylor	.40	.18	.05
☐ 452 Juan Beniquez	.10	.05	.01
☐ 453 Rick Burleson	.10	.05	.01
☐ 454 Bert Campaneris	.20	.09	.03
☐ 455 Rod Carew	.75	.35	.09
☐ 456 Bob Clark	.10	.05	.01
☐ 457 Brian Downing	.10	.05	.01
☐ 458 Dan Ford	.10	.05	.01
☐ 459 Ken Forsch	.10	.05	.01
☐ 460A Dave Frost (5 mm space before ERA)	.10	.05	.01
☐ 460B Dave Frost (1 mm space)	.10	.05	.01
☐ 461 Bobby Grich	.20	.09	.03
☐ 462 Larry Harlow	.10	.05	.01
☐ 463 John Harris	.10	.05	.01
☐ 464 Andy Hassler	.10	.05	.01
☐ 465 Butch Hobson	.10	.05	.01
☐ 466 Jesse Jefferson	.10	.05	.01
☐ 467 Bruce Kison	.10	.05	.01

□ 468	Fred Lynn	.20	.09	.03
□ 469	Angel Moreno	.10	.05	.01
□ 470	Ed Ott	.10	.05	.01
□ 471	Fred Patek	.10	.05	.01
□ 472	Steve Renko	.10	.05	.01
□ 473	Mike Witt	.20	.09	.03
□ 474	Geoff Zahn	.10	.05	.01
□ 475	Gary Alexander	.10	.05	.01
□ 476	Dale Berra	.10	.05	.01
□ 477	Kurt Bevacqua	.10	.05	.01
□ 478	Jim Bibby	.10	.05	.01
□ 479	John Candelaria	.10	.05	.01
□ 480	Victor Cruz	.10	.05	.01
□ 481	Mike Easler	.10	.05	.01
□ 482	Tim Foli	.10	.05	.01
□ 483	Lee Lacy	.10	.05	.01
□ 484	Vance Law	.10	.05	.01
□ 485	Bill Madlock	.20	.09	.03
□ 486	Willie Montanez	.10	.05	.01
□ 487	Omar Moreno	.10	.05	.01
□ 488	Steve Nicosia	.10	.05	.01
□ 489	Dave Parker	.40	.18	.05
□ 490	Tony Pena	.20	.09	.03
□ 491	Pascual Perez	.10	.05	.01
□ 492	Johnny Ray	.20	.09	.03
□ 493	Rick Rhoden	.10	.05	.01
□ 494	Bill Robinson	.10	.05	.01
□ 495	Don Robinson	.10	.05	.01
□ 496	Enrique Romo	.10	.05	.01
□ 497	Rod Scurry	.10	.05	.01
□ 498	Eddie Solomon	.10	.05	.01
□ 499	Willie Stargell	.40	.18	.05
□ 500	Kent Tekulve	.20	.09	.03
□ 501	Jason Thompson	.10	.05	.01
□ 502	Glenn Abbott	.10	.05	.01
□ 503	Jim Anderson	.10	.05	.01
□ 504	Floyd Bannister	.10	.05	.01
□ 505	Bruce Bochte	.10	.05	.01
□ 506	Jeff Burroughs	.10	.05	.01
□ 507	Bryan Clark	.10	.05	.01
□ 508	Ken Clay	.10	.05	.01
□ 509	Julio Cruz	.10	.05	.01
□ 510	Dick Drago	.10	.05	.01
□ 511	Gary Gray	.10	.05	.01
□ 512	Dan Meyer	.10	.05	.01
□ 513	Jerry Narron	.10	.05	.01
□ 514	Tom Paciorek	.10	.05	.01
□ 515	Casey Parsons	.10	.05	.01
□ 516	Lenny Randle	.10	.05	.01
□ 517	Shane Rawley	.10	.05	.01
□ 518	Joe Simpson	.10	.05	.01
□ 519	Richie Zisk	.10	.05	.01
□ 520	Neil Allen	.10	.05	.01
□ 521	Bob Bailor	.10	.05	.01
□ 522	Hubie Brooks	.20	.09	.03
□ 523	Mike Cubbage	.10	.05	.01
□ 524	Pete Falcone	.10	.05	.01
□ 525	Doug Flynn	.10	.05	.01
□ 526	Tom Hausman	.10	.05	.01
□ 527	Ron Hodges	.10	.05	.01
□ 528	Randy Jones	.10	.05	.01
□ 529	Mike Jorgensen	.10	.05	.01
□ 530	Dave Kingman	.20	.09	.03
□ 531	Ed Lynch	.10	.05	.01
□ 532	Mike G. Marshall	.10	.05	.01
□ 533	Lee Mazzilli	.10	.05	.01
□ 534	Dyar Miller	.10	.05	.01
□ 535	Mike Scott	.20	.09	.03
□ 536	Rusty Staub	.20	.09	.03
□ 537	John Stearns	.10	.05	.01
□ 538	Craig Swan	.10	.05	.01
□ 539	Frank Taveras	.10	.05	.01
□ 540	Alex Trevino	.10	.05	.01
□ 541	Ellis Valentine	.10	.05	.01
□ 542	Mookie Wilson	.20	.09	.03
□ 543	Joel Youngblood	.10	.05	.01
□ 544	Pat Zachry	.10	.05	.01
□ 545	Glenn Adams	.10	.05	.01
□ 546	Fernando Arroyo	.10	.05	.01
□ 547	John Verhoeven	.10	.05	.01
□ 548	Sal Butera	.10	.05	.01
□ 549	John Castino	.10	.05	.01
□ 550	Don Cooper	.10	.05	.01
□ 551	Doug Corbett	.10	.05	.01
□ 552	Dave Engle	.10	.05	.01
□ 553	Roger Erickson	.10	.05	.01
□ 554	Danny Goodwin	.10	.05	.01
□ 555A	Darrell Jackson (Black cap)	.40	.18	.05
□ 555B	Darrell Jackson (Red cap with T)	.20	.09	.03
□ 555C	Darrell Jackson (Red cap, no emblem)	3.00	1.35	.35
□ 556	Pete Mackanin	.10	.05	.01
□ 557	Jack O'Connor	.10	.05	.01
□ 558	Hosken Powell	.10	.05	.01
□ 559	Pete Redfern	.10	.05	.01
□ 560	Roy Smalley	.10	.05	.01
□ 561	Chuck Baker UER (Shortshop on front)	.10	.05	.01
□ 562	Gary Ward	.10	.05	.01
□ 563	Rob Wilfong	.10	.05	.01
□ 564	Al Williams	.10	.05	.01
□ 565	Butch Wynegar	.10	.05	.01
□ 566	Randy Bass	.20	.09	.03
□ 567	Juan Bonilla	.10	.05	.01
□ 568	Danny Boone	.10	.05	.01
□ 569	John Curtis	.10	.05	.01
□ 570	Juan Eichelberger	.10	.05	.01
□ 571	Barry Evans	.10	.05	.01
□ 572	Tim Flannery	.10	.05	.01
□ 573	Ruppert Jones	.10	.05	.01
□ 574	Terry Kennedy	.10	.05	.01
□ 575	Joe Lefebvre	.10	.05	.01
□ 576A	John Littlefield ERR (Left handed; reverse negative)	200.00	90.00	25.00
□ 576B	John Littlefield COR (Right handed)	.20	.09	.03
□ 577	Gary Lucas	.10	.05	.01
□ 578	Steve Mura	.10	.05	.01
□ 579	Broderick Perkins	.10	.05	.01
□ 580	Gene Richards	.10	.05	.01
□ 581	Luis Salazar	.10	.05	.01
□ 582	Ozzie Smith	3.00	1.35	.35
□ 583	John Urrea	.10	.05	.01
□ 584	Chris Welsh	.10	.05	.01
□ 585	Rick Wise	.10	.05	.01
□ 586	Doug Bird	.10	.05	.01
□ 587	Tim Blackwell	.10	.05	.01
□ 588	Bobby Bonds	.20	.09	.03
□ 589	Bill Buckner	.20	.09	.03
□ 590	Bill Caudill	.10	.05	.01
□ 591	Hector Cruz	.10	.05	.01
□ 592	Jody Davis	.10	.05	.01
□ 593	Ivan DeJesus	.10	.05	.01
□ 594	Steve Dillard	.10	.05	.01
□ 595	Leon Durham	.20	.09	.03
□ 596	Rawly Eastwick	.10	.05	.01
□ 597	Steve Henderson	.10	.05	.01
□ 598	Mike Krukow	.10	.05	.01
□ 599	Mike Lum	.10	.05	.01
□ 600	Randy Martz	.10	.05	.01
□ 601	Jerry Morales	.10	.05	.01
□ 602	Ken Reitz	.10	.05	.01
□ 603	Lee Smith ERR (Cubs logo reversed)	6.00	2.70	.75
□ 603B	Lee Smith COR	6.00	2.70	.75
□ 604	Dick Tidrow	.10	.05	.01
□ 605	Jim Tracy	.10	.05	.01
□ 606	Mike Tyson	.10	.05	.01
□ 607	Ty Waller	.10	.05	.01
□ 608	Danny Ainge	1.00	.45	.12
□ 609	Jorge Bell	.75	.35	.09
□ 610	Mark Bomback	.10	.05	.01
□ 611	Barry Bonnell	.10	.05	.01
□ 612	Jim Clancy	.10	.05	.01
□ 613	Damaso Garcia	.10	.05	.01
□ 614	Jerry Garvin	.10	.05	.01
□ 615	Alfredo Griffin	.10	.05	.01
□ 616	Garth Iorg	.10	.05	.01
□ 617	Luis Leal	.10	.05	.01
□ 618	Ken Macha	.10	.05	.01
□ 619	John Mayberry	.10	.05	.01
□ 620	Joey McLaughlin	.10	.05	.01
□ 621	Lloyd Moseby	.10	.05	.01
□ 622	Dave Stieb	.20	.09	.03
□ 623	Jackson Todd	.10	.05	.01
□ 624	Willie Upshaw	.10	.05	.01
□ 625	Otto Velez	.10	.05	.01
□ 626	Ernie Whitt	.10	.05	.01
□ 627	Alvis Woods	.10	.05	.01

□ 628 All Star Game Cleveland, Ohio	.20	.09	.03
□ 629 All Star Infielders Frank White and Bucky Dent	.20	.09	.03
□ 630 Big Red Machine Dan Driessen Dave Concepcion George Foster	.20	.09	.03
□ 631 Bruce Sutter Top NL Relief Pitcher	.20	.09	.03
□ 632 Steve and Carlton Steve Carlton Carlton Fisk	.50	.23	.06
□ 633 Carl Yastrzemski 3000th Game	.60	.25	.07
□ 634 Dynamic Duo Johnny Bench and Tom Seaver	.75	.35	.09
□ 635 West Meets East Fernando Valenzuela and Gary Carter	.20	.09	.03
□ 636A Fernando Valenzuela: NL SO King ("he" NL)	.40	.18	.05
□ 636B Fernando Valenzuela: NL SO King ("the" NL)	.40	.18	.05
□ 637 Mike Schmidt Home Run King	1.00	.45	.12
□ 638 NL All Stars Gary Carter and Dave Parker	.40	.18	.05
□ 639 Perfect Game UER Len Barker and Bo Diaz (Catcher actually Ron Hassey)	.20	.09	.03
□ 640 Pete and Re-Pete Pete Rose and Son	1.00	.45	.12
□ 641 Phillies Finest Lonnie Smith Mike Schmidt Steve Carlton	.50	.23	.06
□ 642 Red Sox Reunion Fred Lynn and Dwight Evans	.20	.09	.03
□ 643 Rickey Henderson Most Hits and Runs	1.00	.45	.12
□ 644 Rollie Fingers Most Saves AL	.20	.09	.03
□ 645 Tom Seaver Most 1981 Wins	.75	.35	.09
□ 646 Yankee Powerhouse Reggie Jackson and Dave Winfield (Comma on back after outfielder)	2.00	.90	.25
□ 646B Yankee Powerhouse Reggie Jackson and Dave Winfield (No comma)	2.00	.90	.25
□ 647 CL: Yankees/Dodgers	.20	.09	.03
□ 648 CL: A's/Reds	.20	.09	.03
□ 649 CL: Cards/Brewers	.20	.09	.03
□ 650 CL: Expos/Orioles	.20	.09	.03
□ 651 CL: Astros/Phillies	.20	.09	.03
□ 652 CL: Tigers/Red Sox	.20	.09	.03
□ 653 CL: Rangers/White Sox	.20	.09	.03
□ 654 CL: Giants/Indians	.20	.09	.03
□ 655 CL: Royals/Braves	.20	.09	.03
□ 656 CL: Angels/Pirates	.20	.09	.03
□ 657 CL: Mariners/Mets	.20	.09	.03
□ 658 CL: Padres/Twins	.20	.09	.03
□ 659 CL: Blue Jays/Cubs	.20	.09	.03
□ 660 Specials Checklist	.20	.09	.03

1983 Fleer

In 1983, for the third straight year, Fleer produced a baseball series of 660 standard-size cards. Of these, 1-628 are player cards, 629-646 are special cards, and 647-660 are checklist cards. The player cards are again ordered alphabetically within team and teams seeded in descending order based upon the previous season's standings. The front of each card has a

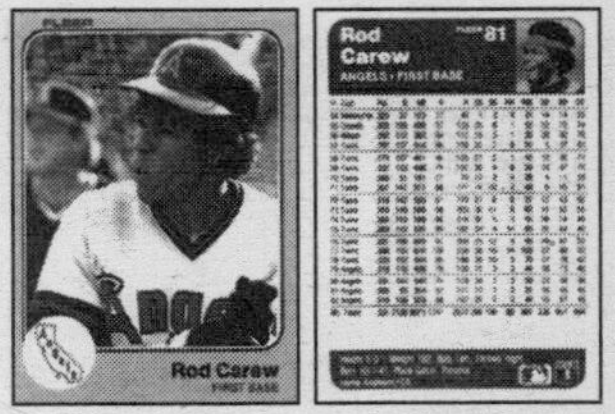

colorful team logo at bottom left and the player's name and position at lower right. The reverses are done in shades of brown on white. Wax packs consisted of 15 cards plus logo stickers in a 38-pack box. Notable Rookie Cards include Wade Boggs, Tony Gwynn and Ryne Sandberg.

	MINT	NRMT	EXC
COMPLETE SET (660)	90.00	40.00	11.00
COMMON CARD (1-660)	.10	.05	.01
SEMISTARS	.20	.09	.03
STARS	.40	.18	.05

□ 1 Joaquin Andujar	.10	.05	.01
□ 2 Doug Bair	.10	.05	.01
□ 3 Steve Braun	.10	.05	.01
□ 4 Glenn Brummer	.10	.05	.01
□ 5 Bob Forsch	.10	.05	.01
□ 6 David Green	.10	.05	.01
□ 7 George Hendrick	.10	.05	.01
□ 8 Keith Hernandez	.40	.18	.05
□ 9 Tom Herr	.20	.09	.03
□ 10 Dane Iorg	.10	.05	.01
□ 11 Jim Kaat	.20	.09	.03
□ 12 Jeff Lahti	.10	.05	.01
□ 13 Tito Landrum	.10	.05	.01
□ 14 Dave LaPoint	.10	.05	.01
□ 15 Willie McGee	.40	.18	.05
□ 16 Steve Mura	.10	.05	.01
□ 17 Ken Oberkfell	.10	.05	.01
□ 18 Darrell Porter	.10	.05	.01
□ 19 Mike Ramsey	.10	.05	.01
□ 20 Gene Roof	.10	.05	.01
□ 21 Lonnie Smith	.10	.05	.01
□ 22 Ozzie Smith	2.00	.90	.25
□ 23 John Stuper	.10	.05	.01
□ 24 Bruce Sutter	.20	.09	.03
□ 25 Gene Tenace	.20	.09	.03
□ 26 Jerry Augustine	.10	.05	.01
□ 27 Dwight Bernard	.10	.05	.01
□ 28 Mark Brouhard	.10	.05	.01
□ 29 Mike Caldwell	.10	.05	.01
□ 30 Cecil Cooper	.20	.09	.03
□ 31 Jamie Easterly	.10	.05	.01
□ 32 Marshall Edwards	.10	.05	.01
□ 33 Rollie Fingers	.40	.18	.05
□ 34 Jim Gantner	.20	.09	.03
□ 35 Moose Haas	.10	.05	.01
□ 36 Roy Howell	.10	.05	.01
□ 37 Pete Ladd	.10	.05	.01
□ 38 Bob McClure	.10	.05	.01
□ 39 Doc Medich	.10	.05	.01
□ 40 Paul Molitor	1.00	.45	.12
□ 41 Don Money	.10	.05	.01
□ 42 Charlie Moore	.10	.05	.01
□ 43 Ben Oglivie	.10	.05	.01
□ 44 Ed Romero	.10	.05	.01
□ 45 Ted Simmons	.20	.09	.03
□ 46 Jim Slaton	.10	.05	.01
□ 47 Don Sutton	.40	.18	.05
□ 48 Gorman Thomas	.10	.05	.01
□ 49 Pete Vuckovich	.10	.05	.01
□ 50 Ned Yost	.10	.05	.01
□ 51 Robin Yount	1.25	.55	.16
□ 52 Benny Ayala	.10	.05	.01
□ 53 Bob Bonner	.10	.05	.01
□ 54 Al Bumbry	.20	.09	.03
□ 55 Terry Crowley	.10	.05	.01
□ 56 Storm Davis	.10	.05	.01

□ 57	Rich Dauer	.10	.05	.01
□ 58	Rick Dempsey UER	.20	.09	.03
	(Posing batting lefty)			
□ 59	Jim Dwyer	.10	.05	.01
□ 60	Mike Flanagan	.20	.09	.03
□ 61	Dan Ford	.10	.05	.01
□ 62	Glenn Gulliver	.10	.05	.01
□ 63	John Lowenstein	.10	.05	.01
□ 64	Dennis Martinez	.20	.09	.03
□ 65	Tippy Martinez	.10	.05	.01
□ 66	Scott McGregor	.10	.05	.01
□ 67	Eddie Murray	2.50	1.10	.30
□ 68	Joe Nolan	.10	.05	.01
□ 69	Jim Palmer	.50	.23	.06
□ 70	Cal Ripken	16.00	7.25	2.00
□ 71	Gary Roenicke	.10	.05	.01
□ 72	Lenn Sakata	.10	.05	.01
□ 73	Ken Singleton	.20	.09	.03
□ 74	Sammy Stewart	.10	.05	.01
□ 75	Tim Stoddard	.10	.05	.01
□ 76	Don Aase	.10	.05	.01
□ 77	Don Baylor	.40	.18	.05
□ 78	Juan Beniquez	.10	.05	.01
□ 79	Bob Boone	.20	.09	.03
□ 80	Rick Burleson	.10	.05	.01
□ 81	Rod Carew	.60	.25	.07
□ 82	Bobby Clark	.10	.05	.01
□ 83	Doug Corbett	.10	.05	.01
□ 84	John Curtis	.10	.05	.01
□ 85	Doug DeCinces	.20	.09	.03
□ 86	Brian Downing	.10	.05	.01
□ 87	Joe Ferguson	.10	.05	.01
□ 88	Tim Foli	.10	.05	.01
□ 89	Ken Forsch	.10	.05	.01
□ 90	Dave Goltz	.10	.05	.01
□ 91	Bobby Grich	.20	.09	.03
□ 92	Andy Hassler	.10	.05	.01
□ 93	Reggie Jackson	1.00	.45	.12
□ 94	Ron Jackson	.10	.05	.01
□ 95	Tommy John	.40	.18	.05
□ 96	Bruce Kison	.10	.05	.01
□ 97	Fred Lynn	.20	.09	.03
□ 98	Ed Ott	.10	.05	.01
□ 99	Steve Renko	.10	.05	.01
□ 100	Luis Sanchez	.10	.05	.01
□ 101	Rob Wilfong	.10	.05	.01
□ 102	Mike Witt	.10	.05	.01
□ 103	Geoff Zahn	.10	.05	.01
□ 104	Willie Aikens	.10	.05	.01
□ 105	Mike Armstrong	.10	.05	.01
□ 106	Vida Blue	.20	.09	.03
□ 107	Bud Black	.20	.09	.03
□ 108	George Brett	3.00	1.35	.35
□ 109	Bill Castro	.10	.05	.01
□ 110	Onix Concepcion	.10	.05	.01
□ 111	Dave Frost	.10	.05	.01
□ 112	Cesar Geronimo	.10	.05	.01
□ 113	Larry Gura	.10	.05	.01
□ 114	Steve Hammond	.10	.05	.01
□ 115	Don Hood	.10	.05	.01
□ 116	Dennis Leonard	.10	.05	.01
□ 117	Jerry Martin	.10	.05	.01
□ 118	Lee May	.20	.09	.03
□ 119	Hal McRae	.20	.09	.03
□ 120	Amos Otis	.20	.09	.03
□ 121	Greg Pryor	.10	.05	.01
□ 122	Dan Quisenberry	.20	.09	.03
□ 123	Don Slaught	.40	.18	.05
□ 124	Paul Splittorff	.10	.05	.01
□ 125	U.L. Washington	.10	.05	.01
□ 126	John Wathan	.10	.05	.01
□ 127	Frank White	.20	.09	.03
□ 128	Willie Wilson	.20	.09	.03
□ 129	Steve Bedrosian UER	.20	.09	.03
	(Height 6'33")			
□ 130	Bruce Benedict	.10	.05	.01
□ 131	Tommy Boggs	.10	.05	.01
□ 132	Brett Butler	.40	.18	.05
□ 133	Rick Camp	.10	.05	.01
□ 134	Chris Chambliss	.20	.09	.03
□ 135	Ken Dayley	.10	.05	.01
□ 136	Gene Garber	.10	.05	.01
□ 137	Terry Harper	.10	.05	.01
□ 138	Bob Horner	.10	.05	.01
□ 139	Glenn Hubbard	.10	.05	.01
□ 140	Rufino Linares	.10	.05	.01
□ 141	Rick Mahler	.10	.05	.01
□ 142	Dale Murphy	.40	.18	.05
□ 143	Phil Niekro	.40	.18	.05
□ 144	Pascual Perez	.10	.05	.01
□ 145	Biff Pocoroba	.10	.05	.01
□ 146	Rafael Ramirez	.10	.05	.01
□ 147	Jerry Royster	.10	.05	.01
□ 148	Ken Smith	.10	.05	.01
□ 149	Bob Walk	.10	.05	.01
□ 150	Claudell Washington	.10	.05	.01
□ 151	Bob Watson	.20	.09	.03
□ 152	Larry Whisenton	.10	.05	.01
□ 153	Porfirio Altamirano	.10	.05	.01
□ 154	Marty Bystrom	.10	.05	.01
□ 155	Steve Carlton	.75	.35	.09
□ 156	Larry Christenson	.10	.05	.01
□ 157	Ivan DeJesus	.10	.05	.01
□ 158	John Denny	.10	.05	.01
□ 159	Bob Dernier	.10	.05	.01
□ 160	Bo Diaz	.10	.05	.01
□ 161	Ed Farmer	.10	.05	.01
□ 162	Greg Gross	.10	.05	.01
□ 163	Mike Krukow	.10	.05	.01
□ 164	Garry Maddox	.10	.05	.01
□ 165	Gary Matthews	.20	.09	.03
□ 166	Tug McGraw	.20	.09	.03
□ 167	Bob Molinaro	.10	.05	.01
□ 168	Sid Monge	.10	.05	.01
□ 169	Ron Reed	.10	.05	.01
□ 170	Bill Robinson	.10	.05	.01
□ 171	Pete Rose	1.25	.55	.16
□ 172	Dick Ruthven	.10	.05	.01
□ 173	Mike Schmidt	1.50	.70	.19
□ 174	Manny Trillo	.10	.05	.01
□ 175	Ozzie Virgil	.10	.05	.01
□ 176	George Vukovich	.10	.05	.01
□ 177	Gary Allenson	.10	.05	.01
□ 178	Luis Aponte	.10	.05	.01
□ 179	Wade Boggs	10.00	4.50	1.25
□ 180	Tom Burgmeier	.10	.05	.01
□ 181	Mark Clear	.10	.05	.01
□ 182	Dennis Eckersley	.40	.18	.05
□ 183	Dwight Evans	.20	.09	.03
□ 184	Rich Gedman	.10	.05	.01
□ 185	Glenn Hoffman	.10	.05	.01
□ 186	Bruce Hurst	.20	.09	.03
□ 187	Carney Lansford	.20	.09	.03
□ 188	Rick Miller	.10	.05	.01
□ 189	Reid Nichols	.10	.05	.01
□ 190	Bob Ojeda	.10	.05	.01
□ 191	Tony Perez	.40	.18	.05
□ 192	Chuck Rainey	.10	.05	.01
□ 193	Jerry Remy	.10	.05	.01
□ 194	Jim Rice	.40	.18	.05
□ 195	Bob Stanley	.10	.05	.01
□ 196	Dave Stapleton	.10	.05	.01
□ 197	Mike Torrez	.10	.05	.01
□ 198	John Tudor	.10	.05	.01
□ 199	Julio Valdez	.10	.05	.01
□ 200	Carl Yastrzemski	.75	.35	.09
□ 201	Dusty Baker	.20	.09	.03
□ 202	Joe Beckwith	.10	.05	.01
□ 203	Greg Brock	.10	.05	.01
□ 204	Ron Cey	.20	.09	.03
□ 205	Terry Forster	.10	.05	.01
□ 206	Steve Garvey	.40	.18	.05
□ 207	Pedro Guerrero	.20	.09	.03
□ 208	Burt Hooton	.10	.05	.01
□ 209	Steve Howe	.10	.05	.01
□ 210	Ken Landreaux	.10	.05	.01
□ 211	Mike Marshall	.10	.05	.01
□ 212	Candy Maldonado	.20	.09	.03
□ 213	Rick Monday	.10	.05	.01
□ 214	Tom Niedenfuer	.10	.05	.01
□ 215	Jorge Orta	.10	.05	.01
□ 216	Jerry Reuss UER	.20	.09	.03
	("Home:" omitted)			
□ 217	Ron Roenicke	.10	.05	.01
□ 218	Vicente Romo	.10	.05	.01
□ 219	Bill Russell	.20	.09	.03
□ 220	Steve Sax	.20	.09	.03
□ 221	Mike Scioscia	.20	.09	.03
□ 222	Dave Stewart	.40	.18	.05
□ 223	Derrel Thomas	.10	.05	.01
□ 224	Fernando Valenzuela	.20	.09	.03
□ 225	Bob Welch	.20	.09	.03

□	226	Ricky Wright	.10	.05	.01
□	227	Steve Yeager	.10	.05	.01
□	228	Bill Almon	.10	.05	.01
□	229	Harold Baines	.40	.18	.05
□	230	Salome Barojas	.10	.05	.01
□	231	Tony Bernazard	.10	.05	.01
□	232	Britt Burns	.10	.05	.01
□	233	Richard Dotson	.10	.05	.01
□	234	Ernesto Escarrega	.10	.05	.01
□	235	Carlton Fisk	.75	.35	.09
□	236	Jerry Hairston	.10	.05	.01
□	237	Kevin Hickey	.10	.05	.01
□	238	LaMarr Hoyt	.20	.09	.03
□	239	Steve Kemp	.10	.05	.01
□	240	Jim Kern	.10	.05	.01
□	241	Ron Kittle	.20	.09	.03
□	242	Jerry Koosman	.20	.09	.03
□	243	Dennis Lamp	.10	.05	.01
□	244	Rudy Law	.10	.05	.01
□	245	Vance Law	.10	.05	.01
□	246	Ron LeFlore	.20	.09	.03
□	247	Greg Luzinski	.20	.09	.03
□	248	Tom Paciorek	.10	.05	.01
□	249	Aurelio Rodriguez	.10	.05	.01
□	250	Mike Squires	.10	.05	.01
□	251	Steve Trout	.10	.05	.01
□	252	Jim Barr	.10	.05	.01
□	253	Dave Bergman	.10	.05	.01
□	254	Fred Breining	.10	.05	.01
□	255	Bob Brenly	.10	.05	.01
□	256	Jack Clark	.20	.09	.03
□	257	Chili Davis	.40	.18	.05
□	258	Darrell Evans	.20	.09	.03
□	259	Alan Fowlkes	.10	.05	.01
□	260	Rich Gale	.10	.05	.01
□	261	Atlee Hammaker	.10	.05	.01
□	262	Al Holland	.10	.05	.01
□	263	Duane Kuiper	.10	.05	.01
□	264	Bill Laskey	.10	.05	.01
□	265	Gary Lavelle	.10	.05	.01
□	266	Johnnie LeMaster	.10	.05	.01
□	267	Renie Martin	.10	.05	.01
□	268	Milt May	.10	.05	.01
□	269	Greg Minton	.10	.05	.01
□	270	Joe Morgan	.40	.18	.05
□	271	Tom O'Malley	.10	.05	.01
□	272	Reggie Smith	.20	.09	.03
□	273	Guy Sularz	.10	.05	.01
□	274	Champ Summers	.10	.05	.01
□	275	Max Venable	.10	.05	.01
□	276	Jim Wohlford	.10	.05	.01
□	277	Ray Burris	.10	.05	.01
□	278	Gary Carter	.40	.18	.05
□	279	Warren Cromartie	.10	.05	.01
□	280	Andre Dawson	.75	.35	.09
□	281	Terry Francona	.10	.05	.01
□	282	Doug Flynn	.10	.05	.01
□	283	Woodie Fryman	.10	.05	.01
□	284	Bill Gullickson	.20	.09	.03
□	285	Wallace Johnson	.10	.05	.01
□	286	Charlie Lea	.10	.05	.01
□	287	Randy Lerch	.10	.05	.01
□	288	Brad Mills	.10	.05	.01
□	289	Dan Norman	.10	.05	.01
□	290	Al Oliver	.20	.09	.03
□	291	David Palmer	.10	.05	.01
□	292	Tim Raines	.50	.23	.06
□	293	Jeff Reardon	.40	.18	.05
□	294	Steve Rogers	.10	.05	.01
□	295	Scott Sanderson	.10	.05	.01
□	296	Dan Schatzeder	.10	.05	.01
□	297	Bryn Smith	.10	.05	.01
□	298	Chris Speier	.10	.05	.01
□	299	Tim Wallach	.20	.09	.03
□	300	Jerry White	.10	.05	.01
□	301	Joel Youngblood	.10	.05	.01
□	302	Ross Baumgarten	.10	.05	.01
□	303	Dale Berra	.10	.05	.01
□	304	John Candelaria	.10	.05	.01
□	305	Dick Davis	.10	.05	.01
□	306	Mike Easler	.10	.05	.01
□	307	Richie Hebner	.20	.09	.03
□	308	Lee Lacy	.10	.05	.01
□	309	Bill Madlock	.20	.09	.03
□	310	Larry McWilliams	.10	.05	.01
□	311	John Milner	.10	.05	.01
□	312	Omar Moreno	.10	.05	.01
□	313	Jim Morrison	.10	.05	.01
□	314	Steve Nicosia	.10	.05	.01
□	315	Dave Parker	.40	.18	.05
□	316	Tony Pena	.20	.09	.03
□	317	Johnny Ray	.10	.05	.01
□	318	Rick Rhoden	.10	.05	.01
□	319	Don Robinson	.10	.05	.01
□	320	Enrique Romo	.10	.05	.01
□	321	Manny Sarmiento	.10	.05	.01
□	322	Rod Scurry	.10	.05	.01
□	323	Jimmy Smith	.10	.05	.01
□	324	Willie Stargell	.40	.18	.05
□	325	Jason Thompson	.10	.05	.01
□	326	Kent Tekulve	.20	.09	.03
□	327A	Tom Brookens (Short .375" brown box shaded in on card back)	.10	.05	.01
□	327B	Tom Brookens (Longer 1.25" brown box shaded in on card back)	.10	.05	.01
□	328	Enos Cabell	.10	.05	.01
□	329	Kirk Gibson	.40	.18	.05
□	330	Larry Herndon	.10	.05	.01
□	331	Mike Ivie	.10	.05	.01
□	332	Howard Johnson	.60	.25	.07
□	333	Lynn Jones	.10	.05	.01
□	334	Rick Leach	.10	.05	.01
□	335	Chet Lemon	.10	.05	.01
□	336	Jack Morris	.40	.18	.05
□	337	Lance Parrish	.20	.09	.03
□	338	Larry Pashnick	.10	.05	.01
□	339	Dan Petry	.10	.05	.01
□	340	Dave Rozema	.10	.05	.01
□	341	Dave Rucker	.10	.05	.01
□	342	Elias Sosa	.10	.05	.01
□	343	Dave Tobik	.10	.05	.01
□	344	Alan Trammell	.40	.18	.05
□	345	Jerry Turner	.10	.05	.01
□	346	Jerry Ujdur	.10	.05	.01
□	347	Pat Underwood	.10	.05	.01
□	348	Lou Whitaker	.40	.18	.05
□	349	Milt Wilcox	.10	.05	.01
□	350	Glenn Wilson	.20	.09	.03
□	351	John Wockenfuss	.10	.05	.01
□	352	Kurt Bevacqua	.10	.05	.01
□	353	Juan Bonilla	.10	.05	.01
□	354	Floyd Chiffer	.10	.05	.01
□	355	Luis DeLeon	.10	.05	.01
□	356	Dave Dravecky	.40	.18	.05
□	357	Dave Edwards	.10	.05	.01
□	358	Juan Eichelberger	.10	.05	.01
□	359	Tim Flannery	.10	.05	.01
□	360	Tony Gwynn	20.00	9.00	2.50
□	361	Ruppert Jones	.10	.05	.01
□	362	Terry Kennedy	.10	.05	.01
□	363	Joe Lefebvre	.10	.05	.01
□	364	Sixto Lezcano	.10	.05	.01
□	365	Tim Lollar	.10	.05	.01
□	366	Gary Lucas	.10	.05	.01
□	367	John Montefusco	.10	.05	.01
□	368	Broderick Perkins	.10	.05	.01
□	369	Joe Pittman	.10	.05	.01
□	370	Gene Richards	.10	.05	.01
□	371	Luis Salazar	.10	.05	.01
□	372	Eric Show	.10	.05	.01
□	373	Garry Templeton	.10	.05	.01
□	374	Chris Welsh	.10	.05	.01
□	375	Alan Wiggins	.10	.05	.01
□	376	Rick Cerone	.10	.05	.01
□	377	Dave Collins	.10	.05	.01
□	378	Roger Erickson	.10	.05	.01
□	379	George Frazier	.10	.05	.01
□	380	Oscar Gamble	.10	.05	.01
□	381	Rich Gossage	.40	.18	.05
□	382	Ken Griffey	.10	.05	.01
□	383	Ron Guidry	.20	.09	.03
□	384	Dave LaRoche	.10	.05	.01
□	385	Rudy May	.10	.05	.01
□	386	John Mayberry	.10	.05	.01
□	387	Lee Mazzilli	.10	.05	.01
□	388	Mike Morgan	.10	.05	.01
□	389	Jerry Mumphrey	.10	.05	.01
□	390	Bobby Murcer	.20	.09	.03
□	391	Graig Nettles	.20	.09	.03
□	392	Lou Piniella	.20	.09	.03

393	Willie Randolph	.20	.09	.03
394	Shane Rawley	.10	.05	.01
395	Dave Righetti	.20	.09	.03
396	Andre Robertson	.10	.05	.01
397	Roy Smalley	.10	.05	.01
398	Dave Winfield	1.25	.55	.16
399	Butch Wynegar	.10	.05	.01
400	Chris Bando	.10	.05	.01
401	Alan Bannister	.10	.05	.01
402	Len Barker	.10	.05	.01
403	Tom Brennan	.10	.05	.01
404	Carmelo Castillo	.10	.05	.01
405	Miguel Dilone	.10	.05	.01
406	Jerry Dybzinski	.10	.05	.01
407	Mike Fischlin	.10	.05	.01
408	Ed Glynn UER (Photo actually Bud Anderson)	.10	.05	.01
409	Mike Hargrove	.20	.09	.03
410	Toby Harrah	.10	.05	.01
411	Ron Hassey	.10	.05	.01
412	Von Hayes	.20	.09	.03
413	Rick Manning	.10	.05	.01
414	Bake McBride	.10	.05	.01
415	Larry Milbourne	.10	.05	.01
416	Bill Nahorodny	.10	.05	.01
417	Jack Perconte	.10	.05	.01
418	Lary Sorensen	.10	.05	.01
419	Dan Spillner	.10	.05	.01
420	Rick Sutcliffe	.20	.09	.03
421	Andre Thornton	.10	.05	.01
422	Rick Waits	.10	.05	.01
423	Eddie Whitson	.10	.05	.01
424	Jesse Barfield	.20	.09	.03
425	Barry Bonnell	.10	.05	.01
426	Jim Clancy	.10	.05	.01
427	Damaso Garcia	.10	.05	.01
428	Jerry Garvin	.10	.05	.01
429	Alfredo Griffin	.10	.05	.01
430	Garth Iorg	.10	.05	.01
431	Roy Lee Jackson	.10	.05	.01
432	Luis Leal	.10	.05	.01
433	Buck Martinez	.10	.05	.01
434	Joey McLaughlin	.10	.05	.01
435	Lloyd Moseby	.10	.05	.01
436	Rance Mulliniks	.10	.05	.01
437	Dale Murray	.10	.05	.01
438	Wayne Nordhagen	.10	.05	.01
439	Geno Petralli	.20	.09	.03
440	Hosken Powell	.10	.05	.01
441	Dave Stieb	.20	.09	.03
442	Willie Upshaw	.10	.05	.01
443	Ernie Whitt	.10	.05	.01
444	Alvis Woods	.10	.05	.01
445	Alan Ashby	.10	.05	.01
446	Jose Cruz	.20	.09	.03
447	Kiko Garcia	.10	.05	.01
448	Phil Garner	.20	.09	.03
449	Danny Heep	.10	.05	.01
450	Art Howe	.10	.05	.01
451	Bob Knepper	.10	.05	.01
452	Alan Knicely	.10	.05	.01
453	Ray Knight	.20	.09	.03
454	Frank LaCorte	.10	.05	.01
455	Mike LaCoss	.10	.05	.01
456	Randy Moffitt	.10	.05	.01
457	Joe Niekro	.20	.09	.03
458	Terry Puhl	.10	.05	.01
459	Luis Pujols	.10	.05	.01
460	Craig Reynolds	.10	.05	.01
461	Bert Roberge	.10	.05	.01
462	Vern Ruhle	.10	.05	.01
463	Nolan Ryan	4.00	1.80	.50
464	Joe Sambito	.10	.05	.01
465	Tony Scott	.10	.05	.01
466	Dave Smith	.10	.05	.01
467	Harry Spilman	.10	.05	.01
468	Dickie Thon	.10	.05	.01
469	Denny Walling	.10	.05	.01
470	Larry Andersen	.10	.05	.01
471	Floyd Bannister	.10	.05	.01
472	Jim Beattie	.10	.05	.01
473	Bruce Bochte	.10	.05	.01
474	Manny Castillo	.10	.05	.01
475	Bill Caudill	.10	.05	.01
476	Bryan Clark	.10	.05	.01
477	Al Cowens	.10	.05	.01
478	Julio Cruz	.10	.05	.01
479	Todd Cruz	.10	.05	.01
480	Gary Gray	.10	.05	.01
481	Dave Henderson	.20	.09	.03
482	Mike Moore	.20	.09	.03
483	Gaylord Perry	.40	.18	.05
484	Dave Revering	.10	.05	.01
485	Joe Simpson	.10	.05	.01
486	Mike Stanton	.10	.05	.01
487	Rick Sweet	.10	.05	.01
488	Ed VandeBerg	.10	.05	.01
489	Richie Zisk	.10	.05	.01
490	Doug Bird	.10	.05	.01
491	Larry Bowa	.20	.09	.03
492	Bill Buckner	.20	.09	.03
493	Bill Campbell	.10	.05	.01
494	Jody Davis	.10	.05	.01
495	Leon Durham	.10	.05	.01
496	Steve Henderson	.10	.05	.01
497	Willie Hernandez	.20	.09	.03
498	Ferguson Jenkins	.40	.18	.05
499	Jay Johnstone	.20	.09	.03
500	Junior Kennedy	.10	.05	.01
501	Randy Martz	.10	.05	.01
502	Jerry Morales	.10	.05	.01
503	Keith Moreland	.10	.05	.01
504	Dickie Noles	.10	.05	.01
505	Mike Proly	.10	.05	.01
506	Allen Ripley	.10	.05	.01
507	Ryne Sandberg UER (Should say High School in Spokane, Washington)	15.00	6.75	1.85
508	Lee Smith	2.00	.90	.25
509	Pat Tabler	.10	.05	.01
510	Dick Tidrow	.10	.05	.01
511	Bump Wills	.10	.05	.01
512	Gary Woods	.10	.05	.01
513	Tony Armas	.10	.05	.01
514	Dave Beard	.10	.05	.01
515	Jeff Burroughs	.10	.05	.01
516	John D'Acquisto	.10	.05	.01
517	Wayne Gross	.10	.05	.01
518	Mike Heath	.10	.05	.01
519	Rickey Henderson UER (Brock record listed as 120 steals)	1.50	.70	.19
520	Cliff Johnson	.10	.05	.01
521	Matt Keough	.10	.05	.01
522	Brian Kingman	.10	.05	.01
523	Rick Langford	.10	.05	.01
524	Dave Lopes	.20	.09	.03
525	Steve McCatty	.10	.05	.01
526	Dave McKay	.10	.05	.01
527	Dan Meyer	.10	.05	.01
528	Dwayne Murphy	.10	.05	.01
529	Jeff Newman	.10	.05	.01
530	Mike Norris	.10	.05	.01
531	Bob Owchinko	.10	.05	.01
532	Joe Rudi	.10	.05	.01
533	Jimmy Sexton	.10	.05	.01
534	Fred Stanley	.10	.05	.01
535	Tom Underwood	.10	.05	.01
536	Neil Allen	.10	.05	.01
537	Wally Backman	.10	.05	.01
538	Bob Bailor	.10	.05	.01
539	Hubie Brooks	.20	.09	.03
540	Carlos Diaz	.10	.05	.01
541	Pete Falcone	.10	.05	.01
542	George Foster	.20	.09	.03
543	Ron Gardenhire	.10	.05	.01
544	Brian Giles	.10	.05	.01
545	Ron Hodges	.10	.05	.01
546	Randy Jones	.10	.05	.01
547	Mike Jorgensen	.10	.05	.01
548	Dave Kingman	.20	.09	.03
549	Ed Lynch	.10	.05	.01
550	Jesse Orosco	.10	.05	.01
551	Rick Ownbey	.10	.05	.01
552	Charlie Puleo	.10	.05	.01
553	Gary Rajsich	.10	.05	.01
554	Mike Scott	.20	.09	.03
555	Rusty Staub	.20	.09	.03
556	John Stearns	.10	.05	.01
557	Craig Swan	.10	.05	.01
558	Ellis Valentine	.10	.05	.01

□ 559	Tom Veryzer	.10	.05	.01
□ 560	Mookie Wilson	.20	.09	.03
□ 561	Pat Zachry	.10	.05	.01
□ 562	Buddy Bell	.20	.09	.03
□ 563	John Butcher	.10	.05	.01
□ 564	Steve Comer	.10	.05	.01
□ 565	Danny Darwin	.10	.05	.01
□ 566	Bucky Dent	.20	.09	.03
□ 567	John Grubb	.10	.05	.01
□ 568	Rick Honeycutt	.10	.05	.01
□ 569	Dave Hostetler	.10	.05	.01
□ 570	Charlie Hough	.20	.09	.03
□ 571	Lamar Johnson	.10	.05	.01
□ 572	Jon Matlack	.10	.05	.01
□ 573	Paul Mirabella	.10	.05	.01
□ 574	Larry Parrish	.10	.05	.01
□ 575	Mike Richardt	.10	.05	.01
□ 576	Mickey Rivers	.10	.05	.01
□ 577	Billy Sample	.10	.05	.01
□ 578	Dave Schmidt	.10	.05	.01
□ 579	Bill Stein	.10	.05	.01
□ 580	Jim Sundberg	.20	.09	.03
□ 581	Frank Tanana	.20	.09	.03
□ 582	Mark Wagner	.10	.05	.01
□ 583	George Wright	.10	.05	.01
□ 584	Johnny Bench	.75	.35	.09
□ 585	Bruce Berenyi	.10	.05	.01
□ 586	Larry Biittner	.10	.05	.01
□ 587	Cesar Cedeno	.20	.09	.03
□ 588	Dave Concepcion	.20	.09	.03
□ 589	Dan Driessen	.10	.05	.01
□ 590	Greg Harris	.10	.05	.01
□ 591	Ben Hayes	.10	.05	.01
□ 592	Paul Householder	.10	.05	.01
□ 593	Tom Hume	.10	.05	.01
□ 594	Wayne Krenchicki	.10	.05	.01
□ 595	Rafael Landestoy	.10	.05	.01
□ 596	Charlie Leibrandt	.10	.05	.01
□ 597	Eddie Milner	.10	.05	.01
□ 598	Ron Oester	.10	.05	.01
□ 599	Frank Pastore	.10	.05	.01
□ 600	Joe Price	.10	.05	.01
□ 601	Tom Seaver	.75	.35	.09
□ 602	Bob Shirley	.10	.05	.01
□ 603	Mario Soto	.10	.05	.01
□ 604	Alex Trevino	.10	.05	.01
□ 605	Mike Vail	.10	.05	.01
□ 606	Duane Walker	.10	.05	.01
□ 607	Tom Brunansky	.20	.09	.03
□ 608	Bobby Castillo	.10	.05	.01
□ 609	John Castino	.10	.05	.01
□ 610	Ron Davis	.10	.05	.01
□ 611	Lenny Faedo	.10	.05	.01
□ 612	Terry Felton	.10	.05	.01
□ 613	Gary Gaetti	.75	.35	.09
□ 614	Mickey Hatcher	.10	.05	.01
□ 615	Brad Havens	.10	.05	.01
□ 616	Kent Hrbek	.40	.18	.05
□ 617	Randy Johnson	.10	.05	.01
□ 618	Tim Laudner	.10	.05	.01
□ 619	Jeff Little	.10	.05	.01
□ 620	Bobby Mitchell	.10	.05	.01
□ 621	Jack O'Connor	.10	.05	.01
□ 622	John Pacella	.10	.05	.01
□ 623	Pete Redfern	.10	.05	.01
□ 624	Jesus Vega	.10	.05	.01
□ 625	Frank Viola	.60	.25	.07
□ 626	Ron Washington	.10	.05	.01
□ 627	Gary Ward	.10	.05	.01
□ 628	Al Williams	.10	.05	.01
□ 629	Red Sox All-Stars Carl Yastrzemski Dennis Eckersley Mark Clear	.40	.18	.05
□ 630	300 Career Wins Gaylord Perry Terry Bulling 5/6/82	.20	.09	.03
□ 631	Pride of Venezuela Dave Concepcion and Manny Trillo	.20	.09	.03
□ 632	All-Star Infielders Robin Yount and Buddy Bell	.40	.18	.05
□ 633	Mr.Vet and Mr.Rookie Dave Winfield and Kent Hrbek	.75	.35	.09
□ 634	Fountain of Youth Willie Stargell and Pete Rose	.60	.25	.07
□ 635	Big Chiefs Toby Harrah and Andre Thornton	.20	.09	.03
□ 636	Smith Brothers Ozzie Smith Lonnie Smith	.75	.35	.09
□ 637	Base Stealers' Threat Bo Diaz and Gary Carter	.20	.09	.03
□ 638	All-Star Catchers Carlton Fisk and Gary Carter	.40	.18	.05
□ 639	The Silver Shoe Rickey Henderson	1.00	.45	.12
□ 640	Home Run Threats Ben Oglivie and Reggie Jackson	.40	.18	.05
□ 641	Two Teams Same Day Joel Youngblood August 4, 1982	.10	.05	.01
□ 642	Last Perfect Game Ron Hassey and Len Barker	.20	.09	.03
□ 643	Black and Blue Vida Blue	.20	.09	.03
□ 644	Black and Blue Bud Black	.10	.05	.01
□ 645	Speed and Power Reggie Jackson	.50	.23	.06
□ 646	Speed and Power Rickey Henderson	1.00	.45	.12
□ 647	CL: Cards/Brewers	.20	.09	.03
□ 648	CL: Orioles/Angels	.20	.09	.03
□ 649	CL: Royals/Braves	.20	.09	.03
□ 650	CL: Phillies/Red Sox	.20	.09	.03
□ 651	CL: Dodgers/White Sox	.20	.09	.03
□ 652	CL: Giants/Expos	.20	.09	.03
□ 653	CL: Pirates/Tigers	.20	.09	.03
□ 654	CL: Padres/Yankees	.20	.09	.03
□ 655	CL: Indians/Blue Jays	.20	.09	.03
□ 656	CL: Astros/Mariners	.20	.09	.03
□ 657	CL: Cubs/A's	.20	.09	.03
□ 658	CL: Mets/Rangers	.20	.09	.03
□ 659	CL: Reds/Twins	.20	.09	.03
□ 660	CL: Specials/Teams	.20	.09	.03

1984 Fleer

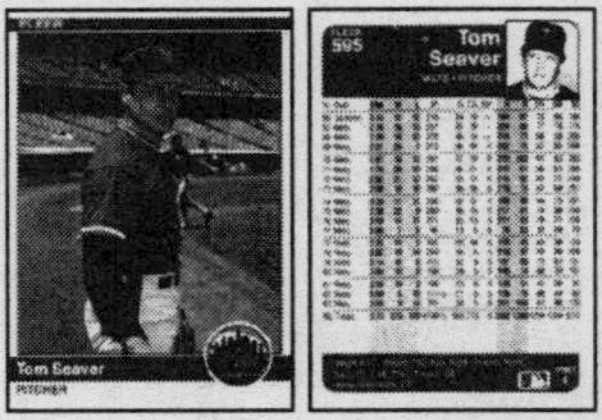

The 1984 Fleer card 660-card standard-size set featured fronts with full-color team logos along with the player's name and position and the Fleer identification. The set features many imaginative photos, several multi-player cards, and many more action shots than the 1983 card set. The backs are quite similar to the 1983 backs except that blue rather than brown ink is used. The player cards are alphabetized within team and the teams are ordered by their 1983 season finish and won-lost record. Specials (626-646) and checklist cards (647-660) make up the end of the set. Wax packs again consisted of 15 cards plus logo stickers. The key Rookie Cards in this set are Don Mattingly, Tony Phillips, Darryl Strawberry, and Andy Van Slyke.

	MINT	NRMT	EXC
COMPLETE SET (660)	90.00	40.00	11.00
COMMON CARD (1-660)	.15	.07	.02
SEMISTARS	.40	.18	.05
STARS	.75	.35	.09

□ 1 Mike Boddicker	.15	.07	.02
□ 2 Al Bumbry	.40	.18	.05
□ 3 Todd Cruz	.15	.07	.02
□ 4 Rich Dauer	.15	.07	.02
□ 5 Storm Davis	.15	.07	.02
□ 6 Rick Dempsey	.15	.07	.02
□ 7 Jim Dwyer	.15	.07	.02
□ 8 Mike Flanagan	.15	.07	.02
□ 9 Dan Ford	.15	.07	.02
□ 10 John Lowenstein	.15	.07	.02
□ 11 Dennis Martinez	.40	.18	.05
□ 12 Tippy Martinez	.15	.07	.02
□ 13 Scott McGregor	.15	.07	.02
□ 14 Eddie Murray	5.00	2.20	.60
□ 15 Joe Nolan	.15	.07	.02
□ 16 Jim Palmer	1.25	.55	.16
□ 17 Cal Ripken	20.00	9.00	2.50
□ 18 Gary Roenicke	.15	.07	.02
□ 19 Lenn Sakata	.15	.07	.02
□ 20 John Shelby	.15	.07	.02
□ 21 Ken Singleton	.15	.07	.02
□ 22 Sammy Stewart	.15	.07	.02
□ 23 Tim Stoddard	.15	.07	.02
□ 24 Marty Bystrom	.15	.07	.02
□ 25 Steve Carlton	2.00	.90	.25
□ 26 Ivan DeJesus	.15	.07	.02
□ 27 John Denny	.15	.07	.02
□ 28 Bob Dernier	.15	.07	.02
□ 29 Bo Diaz	.15	.07	.02
□ 30 Kiko Garcia	.15	.07	.02
□ 31 Greg Gross	.15	.07	.02
□ 32 Kevin Gross	.40	.18	.05
□ 33 Von Hayes	.15	.07	.02
□ 34 Willie Hernandez	.40	.18	.05
□ 35 Al Holland	.15	.07	.02
□ 36 Charles Hudson	.15	.07	.02
□ 37 Joe Lefebvre	.15	.07	.02
□ 38 Sixto Lezcano	.15	.07	.02
□ 39 Garry Maddox	.15	.07	.02
□ 40 Gary Matthews	.15	.07	.02
□ 41 Len Matuszek	.15	.07	.02
□ 42 Tug McGraw	.40	.18	.05
□ 43 Joe Morgan	1.00	.45	.12
□ 44 Tony Perez	.75	.35	.09
□ 45 Ron Reed	.15	.07	.02
□ 46 Pete Rose	3.00	1.35	.35
□ 47 Juan Samuel	.75	.35	.09
□ 48 Mike Schmidt	5.00	2.20	.60
□ 49 Ozzie Virgil	.15	.07	.02
□ 50 Juan Agosto	.15	.07	.02
□ 51 Harold Baines	.75	.35	.09
□ 52 Floyd Bannister	.15	.07	.02
□ 53 Salome Barojas	.15	.07	.02
□ 54 Britt Burns	.15	.07	.02
□ 55 Julio Cruz	.15	.07	.02
□ 56 Richard Dotson	.15	.07	.02
□ 57 Jerry Dybzinski	.15	.07	.02
□ 58 Carlton Fisk	2.00	.90	.25
□ 59 Scott Fletcher	.15	.07	.02
□ 60 Jerry Hairston	.15	.07	.02
□ 61 Kevin Hickey	.15	.07	.02
□ 62 Marc Hill	.15	.07	.02
□ 63 LaMarr Hoyt	.15	.07	.02
□ 64 Ron Kittle	.15	.07	.02
□ 65 Jerry Koosman	.40	.18	.05
□ 66 Dennis Lamp	.15	.07	.02
□ 67 Rudy Law	.15	.07	.02
□ 68 Vance Law	.15	.07	.02
□ 69 Greg Luzinski	.40	.18	.05
□ 70 Tom Paciorek	.15	.07	.02
□ 71 Mike Squires	.15	.07	.02
□ 72 Dick Tidrow	.15	.07	.02
□ 73 Greg Walker	.40	.18	.05
□ 74 Glenn Abbott	.15	.07	.02
□ 75 Howard Bailey	.15	.07	.02
□ 76 Doug Bair	.15	.07	.02
□ 77 Juan Berenguer	.15	.07	.02
□ 78 Tom Brookens	.40	.18	.05
□ 79 Enos Cabell	.15	.07	.02
□ 80 Kirk Gibson	.75	.35	.09
□ 81 John Grubb	.15	.07	.02
□ 82 Larry Herndon	.40	.18	.05
□ 83 Wayne Křenchicki	.15	.07	.02
□ 84 Rick Leach	.15	.07	.02
□ 85 Chet Lemon	.40	.18	.05
□ 86 Aurelio Lopez	.40	.18	.05
□ 87 Jack Morris	.75	.35	.09
□ 88 Lance Parrish	.40	.18	.05
□ 89 Dan Petry	.40	.18	.05
□ 90 Dave Rozema	.15	.07	.02
□ 91 Alan Trammell	.75	.35	.09
□ 92 Lou Whitaker	.75	.35	.09
□ 93 Milt Wilcox	.15	.07	.02
□ 94 Glenn Wilson	.40	.18	.05
□ 95 John Wockenfuss	.15	.07	.02
□ 96 Dusty Baker	.75	.35	.09
□ 97 Joe Beckwith	.15	.07	.02
□ 98 Greg Brock	.15	.07	.02
□ 99 Jack Fimple	.15	.07	.02
□ 100 Pedro Guerrero	.40	.18	.05
□ 101 Rick Honeycutt	.15	.07	.02
□ 102 Burt Hooton	.15	.07	.02
□ 103 Steve Howe	.15	.07	.02
□ 104 Ken Landreaux	.15	.07	.02
□ 105 Mike Marshall	.15	.07	.02
□ 106 Rick Monday	.15	.07	.02
□ 107 Jose Morales	.15	.07	.02
□ 108 Tom Niedenfuer	.15	.07	.02
□ 109 Alejandro Pena	.40	.18	.05
□ 110 Jerry Reuss UER ("Home:" omitted)	.15	.07	.02
□ 111 Bill Russell	.15	.07	.02
□ 112 Steve Sax	.40	.18	.05
□ 113 Mike Scioscia	.15	.07	.02
□ 114 Derrel Thomas	.15	.07	.02
□ 115 Fernando Valenzuela	.40	.18	.05
□ 116 Bob Welch	.15	.07	.02
□ 117 Steve Yeager	.15	.07	.02
□ 118 Pat Zachry	.15	.07	.02
□ 119 Don Baylor	.75	.35	.09
□ 120 Bert Campaneris	.40	.18	.05
□ 121 Rick Cerone	.15	.07	.02
□ 122 Ray Fontenot	.15	.07	.02
□ 123 George Frazier	.15	.07	.02
□ 124 Oscar Gamble	.15	.07	.02
□ 125 Rich Gossage	.75	.35	.09
□ 126 Ken Griffey	.40	.18	.05
□ 127 Ron Guidry	.40	.18	.05
□ 128 Jay Howell	.15	.07	.02
□ 129 Steve Kemp	.15	.07	.02
□ 130 Matt Keough	.15	.07	.02
□ 131 Don Mattingly	25.00	11.00	3.10
□ 132 John Montefusco	.15	.07	.02
□ 133 Omar Moreno	.15	.07	.02
□ 134 Dale Murray	.15	.07	.02
□ 135 Graig Nettles	.40	.18	.05
□ 136 Lou Piniella	.40	.18	.05
□ 137 Willie Randolph	.40	.18	.05
□ 138 Shane Rawley	.15	.07	.02
□ 139 Dave Righetti	.40	.18	.05
□ 140 Andre Robertson	.15	.07	.02
□ 141 Bob Shirley	.15	.07	.02
□ 142 Roy Smalley	.15	.07	.02
□ 143 Dave Winfield	3.00	1.35	.35
□ 144 Butch Wynegar	.15	.07	.02
□ 145 Jim Acker	.15	.07	.02
□ 146 Doyle Alexander	.15	.07	.02
□ 147 Jesse Barfield	.40	.18	.05
□ 148 Jorge Bell	.40	.18	.05
□ 149 Barry Bonnell	.15	.07	.02
□ 150 Jim Clancy	.15	.07	.02
□ 151 Dave Collins	.15	.07	.02
□ 152 Tony Fernandez	.75	.35	.09
□ 153 Damaso Garcia	.15	.07	.02
□ 154 Dave Geisel	.15	.07	.02
□ 155 Jim Gott	.15	.07	.02
□ 156 Alfredo Griffin	.15	.07	.02
□ 157 Garth Iorg	.15	.07	.02
□ 158 Roy Lee Jackson	.15	.07	.02
□ 159 Cliff Johnson	.15	.07	.02
□ 160 Luis Leal	.15	.07	.02
□ 161 Buck Martinez	.15	.07	.02
□ 162 Joey McLaughlin	.15	.07	.02
□ 163 Randy Moffitt	.15	.07	.02
□ 164 Lloyd Moseby	.15	.07	.02
□ 165 Rance Mulliniks	.15	.07	.02

□ 166	Jorge Orta	.15	.07	.02
□ 167	Dave Stieb	.15	.07	.02
□ 168	Willie Upshaw	.15	.07	.02
□ 169	Ernie Whitt	.15	.07	.02
□ 170	Len Barker	.15	.07	.02
□ 171	Steve Bedrosian	.15	.07	.02
□ 172	Bruce Benedict	.15	.07	.02
□ 173	Brett Butler	.75	.35	.09
□ 174	Rick Camp	.15	.07	.02
□ 175	Chris Chambliss	.15	.07	.02
□ 176	Ken Dayley	.15	.07	.02
□ 177	Pete Falcone	.15	.07	.02
□ 178	Terry Forster	.15	.07	.02
□ 179	Gene Garber	.15	.07	.02
□ 180	Terry Harper	.15	.07	.02
□ 181	Bob Horner	.15	.07	.02
□ 182	Glenn Hubbard	.15	.07	.02
□ 183	Randy Johnson	.15	.07	.02
□ 184	Craig McMurtry	.15	.07	.02
□ 185	Donnie Moore	.15	.07	.02
□ 186	Dale Murphy	.75	.35	.09
□ 187	Phil Niekro	.75	.35	.09
□ 188	Pascual Perez	.15	.07	.02
□ 189	Biff Pocoroba	.15	.07	.02
□ 190	Rafael Ramirez	.15	.07	.02
□ 191	Jerry Royster	.15	.07	.02
□ 192	Claudell Washington	.15	.07	.02
□ 193	Bob Watson	.40	.18	.05
□ 194	Jerry Augustine	.15	.07	.02
□ 195	Mark Brouhard	.15	.07	.02
□ 196	Mike Caldwell	.15	.07	.02
□ 197	Tom Candiotti	.75	.35	.09
□ 198	Cecil Cooper	.40	.18	.05
□ 199	Rollie Fingers	.75	.35	.09
□ 200	Jim Gantner	.40	.18	.05
□ 201	Bob L. Gibson	.15	.07	.02
□ 202	Moose Haas	.15	.07	.02
□ 203	Roy Howell	.15	.07	.02
□ 204	Pete Ladd	.15	.07	.02
□ 205	Rick Manning	.15	.07	.02
□ 206	Bob McClure	.15	.07	.02
□ 207	Paul Molitor UER ('83 stats should say .270 BA and 608 AB)	3.00	1.35	.35
□ 208	Don Money	.15	.07	.02
□ 209	Charlie Moore	.15	.07	.02
□ 210	Ben Oglivie	.15	.07	.02
□ 211	Chuck Porter	.15	.07	.02
□ 212	Ed Romero	.15	.07	.02
□ 213	Ted Simmons	.40	.18	.05
□ 214	Jim Slaton	.15	.07	.02
□ 215	Don Sutton	.75	.35	.09
□ 216	Tom Tellmann	.15	.07	.02
□ 217	Pete Vuckovich	.15	.07	.02
□ 218	Ned Yost	.15	.07	.02
□ 219	Robin Yount	3.00	1.35	.35
□ 220	Alan Ashby	.15	.07	.02
□ 221	Kevin Bass	.15	.07	.02
□ 222	Jose Cruz	.40	.18	.05
□ 223	Bill Dawley	.15	.07	.02
□ 224	Frank DiPino	.15	.07	.02
□ 225	Bill Doran	.40	.18	.05
□ 226	Phil Garner	.40	.18	.05
□ 227	Art Howe	.15	.07	.02
□ 228	Bob Knepper	.15	.07	.02
□ 229	Ray Knight	.40	.18	.05
□ 230	Frank LaCorte	.15	.07	.02
□ 231	Mike LaCoss	.15	.07	.02
□ 232	Mike Madden	.15	.07	.02
□ 233	Jerry Mumphrey	.15	.07	.02
□ 234	Joe Niekro	.40	.18	.05
□ 235	Terry Puhl	.15	.07	.02
□ 236	Luis Pujols	.15	.07	.02
□ 237	Craig Reynolds	.15	.07	.02
□ 238	Vern Ruhle	.15	.07	.02
□ 239	Nolan Ryan	12.00	5.50	1.50
□ 240	Mike Scott	.40	.18	.05
□ 241	Tony Scott	.15	.07	.02
□ 242	Dave Smith	.15	.07	.02
□ 243	Dickie Thon	.15	.07	.02
□ 244	Denny Walling	.15	.07	.02
□ 245	Dale Berra	.15	.07	.02
□ 246	Jim Bibby	.15	.07	.02
□ 247	John Candelaria	.15	.07	.02
□ 248	Jose DeLeon	.15	.07	.02
□ 249	Mike Easler	.15	.07	.02

□ 250	Cecilio Guante	.15	.07	.02
□ 251	Richie Hebner	.15	.07	.02
□ 252	Lee Lacy	.15	.07	.02
□ 253	Bill Madlock	.15	.07	.02
□ 254	Milt May	.15	.07	.02
□ 255	Lee Mazzilli	.15	.07	.02
□ 256	Larry McWilliams	.15	.07	.02
□ 257	Jim Morrison	.15	.07	.02
□ 258	Dave Parker	.75	.35	.09
□ 259	Tony Pena	.15	.07	.02
□ 260	Johnny Ray	.15	.07	.02
□ 261	Rick Rhoden	.15	.07	.02
□ 262	Don Robinson	.15	.07	.02
□ 263	Manny Sarmiento	.15	.07	.02
□ 264	Rod Scurry	.15	.07	.02
□ 265	Kent Tekulve	.40	.18	.05
□ 266	Gene Tenace	.40	.18	.05
□ 267	Jason Thompson	.15	.07	.02
□ 268	Lee Tunnell	.15	.07	.02
□ 269	Marvell Wynne	.15	.07	.02
□ 270	Ray Burris	.15	.07	.02
□ 271	Gary Carter	.75	.35	.09
□ 272	Warren Cromartie	.15	.07	.02
□ 273	Andre Dawson	2.50	1.10	.30
□ 274	Doug Flynn	.15	.07	.02
□ 275	Terry Francona	.15	.07	.02
□ 276	Bill Gullickson	.15	.07	.02
□ 277	Bob James	.15	.07	.02
□ 278	Charlie Lea	.15	.07	.02
□ 279	Bryan Little	.15	.07	.02
□ 280	Al Oliver	.40	.18	.05
□ 281	Tim Raines	.75	.35	.09
□ 282	Bobby Ramos	.15	.07	.02
□ 283	Jeff Reardon	.75	.35	.09
□ 284	Steve Rogers	.15	.07	.02
□ 285	Scott Sanderson	.15	.07	.02
□ 286	Dan Schatzeder	.15	.07	.02
□ 287	Bryn Smith	.15	.07	.02
□ 288	Chris Speier	.15	.07	.02
□ 289	Manny Trillo	.15	.07	.02
□ 290	Mike Vail	.15	.07	.02
□ 291	Tim Wallach	.40	.18	.05
□ 292	Chris Welsh	.15	.07	.02
□ 293	Jim Wohlford	.15	.07	.02
□ 294	Kurt Bevacqua	.15	.07	.02
□ 295	Juan Bonilla	.15	.07	.02
□ 296	Bobby Brown	.15	.07	.02
□ 297	Luis DeLeon	.15	.07	.02
□ 298	Dave Dravecky	.40	.18	.05
□ 299	Tim Flannery	.15	.07	.02
□ 300	Steve Garvey	.75	.35	.09
□ 301	Tony Gwynn	10.00	4.50	1.25
□ 302	Andy Hawkins	.15	.07	.02
□ 303	Ruppert Jones	.15	.07	.02
□ 304	Terry Kennedy	.15	.07	.02
□ 305	Tim Lollar	.15	.07	.02
□ 306	Gary Lucas	.15	.07	.02
□ 307	Kevin McReynolds	.75	.35	.09
□ 308	Sid Monge	.15	.07	.02
□ 309	Mario Ramirez	.15	.07	.02
□ 310	Gene Richards	.15	.07	.02
□ 311	Luis Salazar	.15	.07	.02
□ 312	Eric Show	.15	.07	.02
□ 313	Elias Sosa	.15	.07	.02
□ 314	Garry Templeton	.15	.07	.02
□ 315	Mark Thurmond	.15	.07	.02
□ 316	Ed Whitson	.15	.07	.02
□ 317	Alan Wiggins	.15	.07	.02
□ 318	Neil Allen	.15	.07	.02
□ 319	Joaquin Andujar	.15	.07	.02
□ 320	Steve Braun	.15	.07	.02
□ 321	Glenn Brummer	.15	.07	.02
□ 322	Bob Forsch	.15	.07	.02
□ 323	David Green	.15	.07	.02
□ 324	George Hendrick	.15	.07	.02
□ 325	Tom Herr	.40	.18	.05
□ 326	Dane Iorg	.15	.07	.02
□ 327	Jeff Lahti	.15	.07	.02
□ 328	Dave LaPoint	.15	.07	.02
□ 329	Willie McGee	.40	.18	.05
□ 330	Ken Oberkfell	.15	.07	.02
□ 331	Darrell Porter	.15	.07	.02
□ 332	Jamie Quirk	.15	.07	.02
□ 333	Mike Ramsey	.15	.07	.02
□ 334	Floyd Rayford	.15	.07	.02
□ 335	Lonnie Smith	.15	.07	.02

□ 336 Ozzie Smith	4.00	1.80	.50
□ 337 John Stuper	.15	.07	.02
□ 338 Bruce Sutter	.40	.18	.05
□ 339 Andy Van Slyke UER (Batting and throwing both wrong on card back)	1.50	.70	.19
□ 340 Dave Von Ohlen	.15	.07	.02
□ 341 Willie Aikens	.15	.07	.02
□ 342 Mike Armstrong	.15	.07	.02
□ 343 Bud Black	.15	.07	.02
□ 344 George Brett	6.00	2.70	.75
□ 345 Onix Concepcion	.15	.07	.02
□ 346 Keith Creel	.15	.07	.02
□ 347 Larry Gura	.15	.07	.02
□ 348 Don Hood	.15	.07	.02
□ 349 Dennis Leonard	.15	.07	.02
□ 350 Hal McRae	.40	.18	.05
□ 351 Amos Otis	.40	.18	.05
□ 352 Gaylord Perry	.75	.35	.09
□ 353 Greg Pryor	.15	.07	.02
□ 354 Dan Quisenberry	.15	.07	.02
□ 355 Steve Renko	.15	.07	.02
□ 356 Leon Roberts	.15	.07	.02
□ 357 Pat Sheridan	.15	.07	.02
□ 358 Joe Simpson	.15	.07	.02
□ 359 Don Slaught	.40	.18	.05
□ 360 Paul Splittorff	.15	.07	.02
□ 361 U.L. Washington	.15	.07	.02
□ 362 John Wathan	.15	.07	.02
□ 363 Frank White	.40	.18	.05
□ 364 Willie Wilson	.15	.07	.02
□ 365 Jim Barr	.15	.07	.02
□ 366 Dave Bergman	.15	.07	.02
□ 367 Fred Breining	.15	.07	.02
□ 368 Bob Brenly	.15	.07	.02
□ 369 Jack Clark	.40	.18	.05
□ 370 Chili Davis	.75	.35	.09
□ 371 Mark Davis	.15	.07	.02
□ 372 Darrell Evans	.40	.18	.05
□ 373 Atlee Hammaker	.15	.07	.02
□ 374 Mike Krukow	.15	.07	.02
□ 375 Duane Kuiper	.15	.07	.02
□ 376 Bill Laskey	.15	.07	.02
□ 377 Gary Lavelle	.15	.07	.02
□ 378 Johnnie LeMaster	.15	.07	.02
□ 379 Jeff Leonard	.15	.07	.02
□ 380 Randy Lerch	.15	.07	.02
□ 381 Renie Martin	.15	.07	.02
□ 382 Andy McGaffigan	.15	.07	.02
□ 383 Greg Minton	.15	.07	.02
□ 384 Tom O'Malley	.15	.07	.02
□ 385 Max Venable	.15	.07	.02
□ 386 Brad Wellman	.15	.07	.02
□ 387 Joel Youngblood	.15	.07	.02
□ 388 Gary Allenson	.15	.07	.02
□ 389 Luis Aponte	.15	.07	.02
□ 390 Tony Armas	.15	.07	.02
□ 391 Doug Bird	.15	.07	.02
□ 392 Wade Boggs	4.00	1.80	.50
□ 393 Dennis Boyd	.40	.18	.05
□ 394 Mike Brown UER P (shown with record of 31-104)	.15	.07	.02
□ 395 Mark Clear	.15	.07	.02
□ 396 Dennis Eckersley	1.25	.55	.16
□ 397 Dwight Evans	.40	.18	.05
□ 398 Rich Gedman	.15	.07	.02
□ 399 Glenn Hoffman	.15	.07	.02
□ 400 Bruce Hurst	.15	.07	.02
□ 401 John Henry Johnson	.15	.07	.02
□ 402 Ed Jurak	.15	.07	.02
□ 403 Rick Miller	.15	.07	.02
□ 404 Jeff Newman	.15	.07	.02
□ 405 Reid Nichols	.15	.07	.02
□ 406 Bob Ojeda	.15	.07	.02
□ 407 Jerry Remy	.15	.07	.02
□ 408 Jim Rice	.75	.35	.09
□ 409 Bob Stanley	.15	.07	.02
□ 410 Dave Stapleton	.15	.07	.02
□ 411 John Tudor	.15	.07	.02
□ 412 Carl Yastrzemski	1.50	.70	.19
□ 413 Buddy Bell	.40	.18	.05
□ 414 Larry Biittner	.15	.07	.02
□ 415 John Butcher	.15	.07	.02
□ 416 Danny Darwin	.15	.07	.02
□ 417 Bucky Dent	.40	.18	.05
□ 418 Dave Hostetler	.15	.07	.02
□ 419 Charlie Hough	.40	.18	.05
□ 420 Bobby Johnson	.15	.07	.02
□ 421 Odell Jones	.15	.07	.02
□ 422 Jon Matlack	.15	.07	.02
□ 423 Pete O'Brien	.40	.18	.05
□ 424 Larry Parrish	.15	.07	.02
□ 425 Mickey Rivers	.15	.07	.02
□ 426 Billy Sample	.15	.07	.02
□ 427 Dave Schmidt	.15	.07	.02
□ 428 Mike Smithson	.15	.07	.02
□ 429 Bill Stein	.15	.07	.02
□ 430 Dave Stewart	.75	.35	.09
□ 431 Jim Sundberg	.40	.18	.05
□ 432 Frank Tanana	.40	.18	.05
□ 433 Dave Tobik	.15	.07	.02
□ 434 Wayne Tolleson	.15	.07	.02
□ 435 George Wright	.15	.07	.02
□ 436 Bill Almon	.15	.07	.02
□ 437 Keith Atherton	.15	.07	.02
□ 438 Dave Beard	.15	.07	.02
□ 439 Tom Burgmeier	.15	.07	.02
□ 440 Jeff Burroughs	.15	.07	.02
□ 441 Chris Codiroli	.15	.07	.02
□ 442 Tim Conroy	.15	.07	.02
□ 443 Mike Davis	.15	.07	.02
□ 444 Wayne Gross	.15	.07	.02
□ 445 Garry Hancock	.15	.07	.02
□ 446 Mike Heath	.15	.07	.02
□ 447 Rickey Henderson	3.00	1.35	.35
□ 448 Donnie Hill	.15	.07	.02
□ 449 Bob Kearney	.15	.07	.02
□ 450 Bill Krueger	.15	.07	.02
□ 451 Rick Langford	.15	.07	.02
□ 452 Carney Lansford	.40	.18	.05
□ 453 Dave Lopes	.40	.18	.05
□ 454 Steve McCatty	.15	.07	.02
□ 455 Dan Meyer	.15	.07	.02
□ 456 Dwayne Murphy	.15	.07	.02
□ 457 Mike Norris	.15	.07	.02
□ 458 Ricky Peters	.15	.07	.02
□ 459 Tony Phillips	2.00	.90	.25
□ 460 Tom Underwood	.15	.07	.02
□ 461 Mike Warren	.15	.07	.02
□ 462 Johnny Bench	1.50	.70	.19
□ 463 Bruce Berenyi	.15	.07	.02
□ 464 Dann Bilardello	.15	.07	.02
□ 465 Cesar Cedeno	.40	.18	.05
□ 466 Dave Concepcion	.40	.18	.05
□ 467 Dan Driessen	.15	.07	.02
□ 468 Nick Esasky	.15	.07	.02
□ 469 Rich Gale	.15	.07	.02
□ 470 Ben Hayes	.15	.07	.02
□ 471 Paul Householder	.15	.07	.02
□ 472 Tom Hume	.15	.07	.02
□ 473 Alan Knicely	.15	.07	.02
□ 474 Eddie Milner	.15	.07	.02
□ 475 Ron Oester	.15	.07	.02
□ 476 Kelly Paris	.15	.07	.02
□ 477 Frank Pastore	.15	.07	.02
□ 478 Ted Power	.15	.07	.02
□ 479 Joe Price	.15	.07	.02
□ 480 Charlie Puleo	.15	.07	.02
□ 481 Gary Redus	.15	.07	.02
□ 482 Bill Scherrer	.15	.07	.02
□ 483 Mario Soto	.15	.07	.02
□ 484 Alex Trevino	.15	.07	.02
□ 485 Duane Walker	.15	.07	.02
□ 486 Larry Bowa	.40	.18	.05
□ 487 Warren Brusstar	.15	.07	.02
□ 488 Bill Buckner	.40	.18	.05
□ 489 Bill Campbell	.15	.07	.02
□ 490 Ron Cey	.40	.18	.05
□ 491 Jody Davis	.15	.07	.02
□ 492 Leon Durham	.15	.07	.02
□ 493 Mel Hall	.40	.18	.05
□ 494 Ferguson Jenkins	.75	.35	.09
□ 495 Jay Johnstone	.40	.18	.05
□ 496 Craig Lefferts	.15	.07	.02
□ 497 Carmelo Martinez	.15	.07	.02
□ 498 Jerry Morales	.15	.07	.02
□ 499 Keith Moreland	.15	.07	.02
□ 500 Dickie Noles	.15	.07	.02
□ 501 Mike Proly	.15	.07	.02
□ 502 Chuck Rainey	.15	.07	.02
□ 503 Dick Ruthven	.15	.07	.02

□	504	Ryne Sandberg	8.00	3.60	1.00
□	505	Lee Smith	1.50	.70	.19
□	506	Steve Trout	.15	.07	.02
□	507	Gary Woods	.15	.07	.02
□	508	Juan Beniquez	.15	.07	.02
□	509	Bob Boone	.40	.18	.05
□	510	Rick Burleson	.15	.07	.02
□	511	Rod Carew	1.25	.55	.16
□	512	Bobby Clark	.15	.07	.02
□	513	John Curtis	.15	.07	.02
□	514	Doug DeCinces	.15	.07	.02
□	515	Brian Downing	.15	.07	.02
□	516	Tim Foli	.15	.07	.02
□	517	Ken Forsch	.15	.07	.02
□	518	Bobby Grich	.40	.18	.05
□	519	Andy Hassler	.15	.07	.02
□	520	Reggie Jackson	2.50	1.10	.30
□	521	Ron Jackson	.15	.07	.02
□	522	Tommy John	.75	.35	.09
□	523	Bruce Kison	.15	.07	.02
□	524	Steve Lubratich	.15	.07	.02
□	525	Fred Lynn	.40	.18	.05
□	526	Gary Pettis	.15	.07	.02
□	527	Luis Sanchez	.15	.07	.02
□	528	Daryl Sconiers	.15	.07	.02
□	529	Ellis Valentine	.15	.07	.02
□	530	Rob Wilfong	.15	.07	.02
□	531	Mike Witt	.15	.07	.02
□	532	Geoff Zahn	.15	.07	.02
□	533	Bud Anderson	.15	.07	.02
□	534	Chris Bando	.15	.07	.02
□	535	Alan Bannister	.15	.07	.02
□	536	Bert Blyleven	.40	.18	.05
□	537	Tom Brennan	.15	.07	.02
□	538	Jamie Easterly	.15	.07	.02
□	539	Juan Eichelberger	.15	.07	.02
□	540	Jim Essian	.15	.07	.02
□	541	Mike Fischlin	.15	.07	.02
□	542	Julio Franco	.75	.35	.09
□	543	Mike Hargrove	.40	.18	.05
□	544	Toby Harrah	.40	.18	.05
□	545	Ron Hassey	.15	.07	.02
□	546	Neal Heaton	.15	.07	.02
□	547	Bake McBride	.15	.07	.02
□	548	Broderick Perkins	.15	.07	.02
□	549	Lary Sorensen	.15	.07	.02
□	550	Dan Spillner	.15	.07	.02
□	551	Rick Sutcliffe	.40	.18	.05
□	552	Pat Tabler	.15	.07	.02
□	553	Gorman Thomas	.15	.07	.02
□	554	Andre Thornton	.15	.07	.02
□	555	George Vukovich	.15	.07	.02
□	556	Darrell Brown	.15	.07	.02
□	557	Tom Brunansky	.40	.18	.05
□	558	Randy Bush	.15	.07	.02
□	559	Bobby Castillo	.15	.07	.02
□	560	John Castino	.15	.07	.02
□	561	Ron Davis	.15	.07	.02
□	562	Dave Engle	.15	.07	.02
□	563	Lenny Faedo	.15	.07	.02
□	564	Pete Filson	.15	.07	.02
□	565	Gary Gaetti	.40	.18	.05
□	566	Mickey Hatcher	.15	.07	.02
□	567	Kent Hrbek	.75	.35	.09
□	568	Rusty Kuntz	.15	.07	.02
□	569	Tim Laudner	.15	.07	.02
□	570	Rick Lysander	.15	.07	.02
□	571	Bobby Mitchell	.15	.07	.02
□	572	Ken Schrom	.15	.07	.02
□	573	Ray Smith	.15	.07	.02
□	574	Tim Teufel	.15	.07	.02
□	575	Frank Viola	.40	.18	.05
□	576	Gary Ward	.15	.07	.02
□	577	Ron Washington	.15	.07	.02
□	578	Len Whitehouse	.15	.07	.02
□	579	Al Williams	.15	.07	.02
□	580	Bob Bailor	.15	.07	.02
□	581	Mark Bradley	.15	.07	.02
□	582	Hubie Brooks	.15	.07	.02
□	583	Carlos Diaz	.15	.07	.02
□	584	George Foster	.40	.18	.05
□	585	Brian Giles	.15	.07	.02
□	586	Danny Heep	.15	.07	.02
□	587	Keith Hernandez	.75	.35	.09
□	588	Ron Hodges	.15	.07	.02
□	589	Scott Holman	.15	.07	.02
□	590	Dave Kingman	.40	.18	.05
□	591	Ed Lynch	.15	.07	.02
□	592	Jose Oquendo	.40	.18	.05
□	593	Jesse Orosco	.15	.07	.02
□	594	Junior Ortiz	.15	.07	.02
□	595	Tom Seaver	2.00	.90	.25
□	596	Doug Sisk	.15	.07	.02
□	597	Rusty Staub	.40	.18	.05
□	598	John Stearns	.15	.07	.02
□	599	Darryl Strawberry	6.00	2.70	.75
□	600	Craig Swan	.15	.07	.02
□	601	Walt Terrell	.15	.07	.02
□	602	Mike Torrez	.15	.07	.02
□	603	Mookie Wilson	.40	.18	.05
□	604	Jamie Allen	.15	.07	.02
□	605	Jim Beattie	.15	.07	.02
□	606	Tony Bernazard	.15	.07	.02
□	607	Manny Castillo	.15	.07	.02
□	608	Bill Caudill	.15	.07	.02
□	609	Bryan Clark	.15	.07	.02
□	610	Al Cowens	.15	.07	.02
□	611	Dave Henderson	.40	.18	.05
□	612	Steve Henderson	.15	.07	.02
□	613	Orlando Mercado	.15	.07	.02
□	614	Mike Moore	.40	.18	.05
□	615	Ricky Nelson UER (Jamie Nelson's stats on back)	.15	.07	.02
□	616	Spike Owen	.40	.18	.05
□	617	Pat Putnam	.15	.07	.02
□	618	Ron Roenicke	.15	.07	.02
□	619	Mike Stanton	.15	.07	.02
□	620	Bob Stoddard	.15	.07	.02
□	621	Rick Sweet	.15	.07	.02
□	622	Roy Thomas	.15	.07	.02
□	623	Ed VandeBerg	.15	.07	.02
□	624	Matt Young	.15	.07	.02
□	625	Richie Zisk	.15	.07	.02
□	626	Fred Lynn 1982 AS Game RB	.40	.18	.05
□	627	Manny Trillo 1983 AS Game RB	.40	.18	.05
□	628	Steve Garvey NL Iron Man	.75	.35	.09
□	629	Rod Carew AL Batting Runner-Up	.75	.35	.09
□	630	Wade Boggs AL Batting Champion	1.50	.70	.19
□	631	Tim Raines: Letting Go of the Raines	.75	.35	.09
□	632	Al Oliver Double Trouble	.40	.18	.05
□	633	Steve Sax AS Second Base	.40	.18	.05
□	634	Dickie Thon AS Shortstop	.15	.07	.02
□	635	Ace Firemen Dan Quisenberry and Tippy Martinez	.40	.18	.05
□	636	Reds Reunited Joe Morgan Pete Rose Tony Perez	.75	.35	.09
□	637	Backstop Stars Lance Parrish Bob Boone	.40	.18	.05
□	638	George Brett and Gaylord Perry Pine Tar 7/24/83	2.00	.90	.25
□	639	1983 No Hitters Dave Righetti Mike Warren Bob Forsch	.40	.18	.05
□	640	Johnny Bench and Carl Yastrzemski Retiring Superstars	2.00	.90	.25
□	641	Gaylord Perry Going Out In Style	.75	.35	.09
□	642	Steve Carlton 300 Club and Strikeout Record	.75	.35	.09
□	643	Joe Altobelli and Paul Owens World Series Managers	.15	.07	.02
□	644	Rick Dempsey World Series MVP	.40	.18	.05

□ 645 Mike Boddicker WS Rookie Winner	.15	.07	.02
□ 646 Scott McGregor WS Clincher	.15	.07	.02
□ 647 CL: Orioles/Royals Joe Altobelli MG	.40	.18	.05
□ 648 CL: Phillies/Giants Paul Owens MG	.40	.18	.05
□ 649 CL: White Sox/Red Sox Tony LaRussa MG	.40	.18	.05
□ 650 CL: Tigers/Rangers Sparky Anderson MG	.40	.18	.05
□ 651 CL: Dodgers/A's Tommy Lasorda MG	.40	.18	.05
□ 652 CL: Yankees/Reds Billy Martin MG	.40	.18	.05
□ 653 CL: Blue Jays/Cubs Bobby Cox MG	.40	.18	.05
□ 654 CL: Braves/Angels Joe Torre MG	.40	.18	.05
□ 655 CL: Brewers/Indians Rene Lachemann MG	.40	.18	.05
□ 656 CL: Astros/Twins Bob Lillis MG	.40	.18	.05
□ 657 CL: Pirates/Mets Chuck Tanner MG	.40	.18	.05
□ 658 CL: Expos/Mariners Bill Virdon MG	.40	.18	.05
□ 659 CL: Padres/Specials Dick Williams MG	.40	.18	.05
□ 660 CL: Cardinals/Teams Whitey Herzog MG	.40	.18	.05

1984 Fleer Update

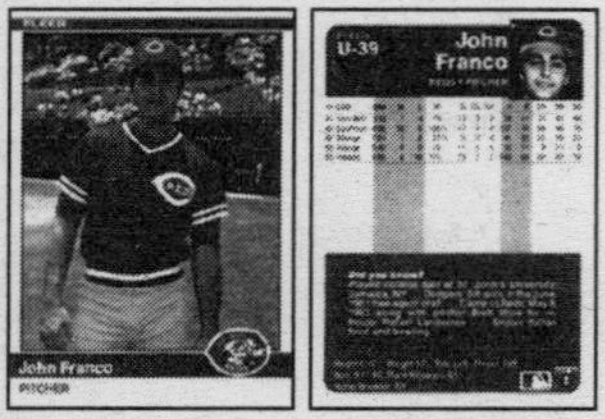

This set was Fleer's first update set and portrayed players with their proper team for the current year and to rookies who were not in their regular issue. Like the Topps Traded sets of the time, the Fleer Update sets were distributed in factory set form through hobby dealers only. The set was quite popular with collectors, and, apparently, the print run was relatively short, as the set was quickly in short supply and exhibited a rapid and dramatic price increase. The cards are numbered on the back with a U prefix and placed in alphabetical order by player name. The key (extended) Rookie Cards in this set are Roger Clemens, John Franco, Dwight Gooden, Jimmy Key, Mark Langston, Kirby Puckett, Jose Rijo, and Bret Saberhagen. Collectors are urged to be careful if purchasing single cards of Clemens, Darling, Gooden, Puckett, Rose, or Saberhagen as these specific cards have been illegally reprinted. These fakes are blurry when compared to the real cards.

	MINT	NRMT	EXC
COMPLETE FACT.SET (132)	500.00	220.00	60.00
COMMON CARD (1-132)	.50	.23	.06
SEMISTARS	1.00	.45	.12
U PREFIX ON CARD NUMBER			
BEWARE OF COUNTERFEITS			

□ 1 Willie Aikens	.50	.23	.06
□ 2 Luis Aponte	.50	.23	.06
□ 3 Mark Bailey	.50	.23	.06
□ 4 Bob Bailor	.50	.23	.06
□ 5 Dusty Baker	1.00	.45	.12
□ 6 Steve Balboni	.50	.23	.06
□ 7 Alan Bannister	.50	.23	.06
□ 8 Marty Barrett	.75	.35	.09
□ 9 Dave Beard	.50	.23	.06
□ 10 Joe Beckwith	.50	.23	.06
□ 11 Dave Bergman	.50	.23	.06
□ 12 Tony Bernazard	.50	.23	.06
□ 13 Bruce Bochte	.50	.23	.06
□ 14 Barry Bonnell	.50	.23	.06
□ 15 Phil Bradley	.75	.35	.09
□ 16 Fred Breining	.50	.23	.06
□ 17 Mike C. Brown	.50	.23	.06
□ 18 Bill Buckner	.75	.35	.09
□ 19 Ray Burris	.50	.23	.06
□ 20 John Butcher	.50	.23	.06
□ 21 Brett Butler	2.00	.90	.25
□ 22 Enos Cabell	.50	.23	.06
□ 23 Bill Campbell	.50	.23	.06
□ 24 Bill Caudill	.50	.23	.06
□ 25 Bobby Clark	.50	.23	.06
□ 26 Bryan Clark	.50	.23	.06
□ 27 Roger Clemens	175.00	80.00	22.00
□ 28 Jaime Cocanower	.50	.23	.06
□ 29 Ron Darling	1.00	.45	.12
□ 30 Alvin Davis	.75	.35	.09
□ 31 Bob Dernier	.50	.23	.06
□ 32 Carlos Diaz	.50	.23	.06
□ 33 Mike Easler	.50	.23	.06
□ 34 Dennis Eckersley	10.00	4.50	1.25
□ 35 Jim Essian	.50	.23	.06
□ 36 Darrell Evans	.75	.35	.09
□ 37 Mike Fitzgerald	.50	.23	.06
□ 38 Tim Foli	.50	.23	.06
□ 39 John Franco	8.00	3.60	1.00
□ 40 George Frazier	.50	.23	.06
□ 41 Rich Gale	.50	.23	.06
□ 42 Barbaro Garbey	.50	.23	.06
□ 43 Dwight Gooden	35.00	16.00	4.40
□ 44 Rich Gossage	1.00	.45	.12
□ 45 Wayne Gross	.50	.23	.06
□ 46 Mark Gubicza	1.00	.45	.12
□ 47 Jackie Gutierrez	.50	.23	.06
□ 48 Toby Harrah	.75	.35	.09
□ 49 Ron Hassey	.50	.23	.06
□ 50 Richie Hebner	.50	.23	.06
□ 51 Willie Hernandez	.75	.35	.09
□ 52 Ed Hodge	.50	.23	.06
□ 53 Ricky Horton	.50	.23	.06
□ 54 Art Howe	.50	.23	.06
□ 55 Dane Iorg	.50	.23	.06
□ 56 Brook Jacoby	.75	.35	.09
□ 57 Dion James	.75	.35	.09
□ 58 Mike Jeffcoat	.50	.23	.06
□ 59 Ruppert Jones	.50	.23	.06
□ 60 Bob Kearney	.50	.23	.06
□ 61 Jimmy Key	8.00	3.60	1.00
□ 62 Dave Kingman	.75	.35	.09
□ 63 Brad Komminsk	.50	.23	.06
□ 64 Jerry Koosman	.75	.35	.09
□ 65 Wayne Krenchicki	.50	.23	.06
□ 66 Rusty Kuntz	.50	.23	.06
□ 67 Frank LaCorte	.50	.23	.06
□ 68 Dennis Lamp	.50	.23	.06
□ 69 Tito Landrum	.50	.23	.06
□ 70 Mark Langston	10.00	4.50	1.25
□ 71 Rick Leach	.50	.23	.06
□ 72 Craig Lefferts	.75	.35	.09
□ 73 Gary Lucas	.50	.23	.06
□ 74 Jerry Martin	.50	.23	.06
□ 75 Carmelo Martinez	.50	.23	.06
□ 76 Mike Mason	.50	.23	.06
□ 77 Gary Matthews	.50	.23	.06
□ 78 Andy McGaffigan	.50	.23	.06
□ 79 Joey McLaughlin	.50	.23	.06
□ 80 Joe Morgan	6.00	2.70	.75
□ 81 Darryl Motley	.50	.23	.06
□ 82 Graig Nettles	.75	.35	.09
□ 83 Phil Niekro	2.00	.90	.25
□ 84 Ken Oberkfell	.50	.23	.06
□ 85 Al Oliver	.75	.35	.09
□ 86 Jorge Orta	.50	.23	.06
□ 87 Amos Otis	.75	.35	.09
□ 88 Bob Owchinko	.50	.23	.06
□ 89 Dave Parker	1.00	.45	.12

□ 90 Jack Perconte	.50	.23	.06
□ 91 Tony Perez	3.00	1.35	.35
□ 92 Gerald Perry	.75	.35	.09
□ 93 Kirby Puckett	250.00	110.00	31.00
□ 94 Shane Rawley	.50	.23	.06
□ 95 Floyd Rayford	.50	.23	.06
□ 96 Ron Reed	.50	.23	.06
□ 97 R.J. Reynolds	.50	.23	.06
□ 98 Gene Richards	.50	.23	.06
□ 99 Jose Rijo	10.00	4.50	1.25
□ 100 Jeff D. Robinson	.50	.23	.06
□ 101 Ron Romanick	.50	.23	.06
□ 102 Pete Rose	25.00	11.00	3.10
□ 103 Bret Saberhagen	10.00	4.50	1.25
□ 104 Scott Sanderson	.50	.23	.06
□ 105 Dick Schofield	.75	.35	.09
□ 106 Tom Seaver	12.00	5.50	1.50
□ 107 Jim Slaton	.50	.23	.06
□ 108 Mike Smithson	.50	.23	.06
□ 109 Lary Sorensen	.50	.23	.06
□ 110 Tim Stoddard	.50	.23	.06
□ 111 Jeff Stone	.50	.23	.06
□ 112 Champ Summers	.50	.23	.06
□ 113 Jim Sundberg	.75	.35	.09
□ 114 Rick Sutcliffe	.75	.35	.09
□ 115 Craig Swan	.50	.23	.06
□ 116 Derrel Thomas	.50	.23	.06
□ 117 Gorman Thomas	.50	.23	.06
□ 118 Alex Trevino	.50	.23	.06
□ 119 Manny Trillo	.50	.23	.06
□ 120 John Tudor	.50	.23	.06
□ 121 Tom Underwood	.50	.23	.06
□ 122 Mike Vail	.50	.23	.06
□ 123 Tom Waddell	.50	.23	.06
□ 124 Gary Ward	.50	.23	.06
□ 125 Terry Whitfield	.50	.23	.06
□ 126 Curtis Wilkerson	.50	.23	.06
□ 127 Frank Williams	.50	.23	.06
□ 128 Glenn Wilson	.75	.35	.09
□ 129 John Wockenfuss	.50	.23	.06
□ 130 Ned Yost	.50	.23	.06
□ 131 Mike Young	.50	.23	.06
□ 132 Checklist 1-132	.50	.23	.06

1985 Fleer

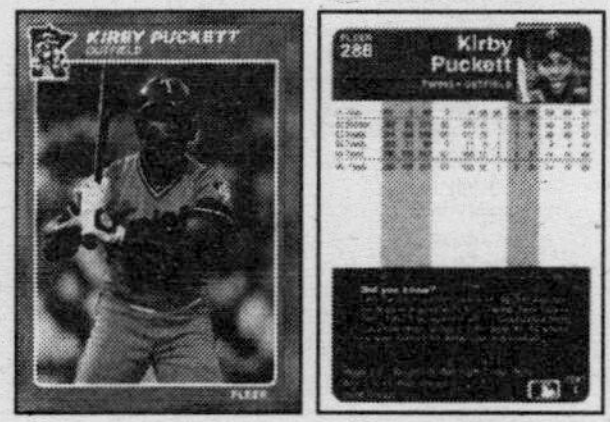

The 1985 Fleer set consists of 660 standard-size cards. Wax packs contained 15 cards plus logo stickers. Card fronts feature a full color photo, team logo along with the player's name and position. The borders enclosing the photo are color-coded to correspond to the player's team. The cards are ordered alphabetically within team. The teams are ordered based on their respective performance during the prior year. Subsets include Specials (626-643) and Major League Prospects (644-653). The black and white photo on the reverse is included for the third straight year. Notable Rookie Cards include Roger Clemens, Eric Davis, Shawon Dunston, John Franco, Dwight Gooden, Orel Hershiser, Jimmy Key, Mark Langston, Terry Pendleton, Kirby Puckett, Jose Rijo, Bret Saberhagen, and Danny Tartabull.

	MINT	NRMT	EXC
COMPLETE SET (660)	120.00	55.00	15.00
COMMON CARD (1-660)	.10	.05	.01
SEMISTARS	.20	.09	.03
STARS	.40	.18	.05
CONDITION SENSITIVE SET			

□ 1 Doug Bair	.10	.05	.01
□ 2 Juan Berenguer	.10	.05	.01
□ 3 Dave Bergman	.10	.05	.01
□ 4 Tom Brookens	.10	.05	.01
□ 5 Marty Castillo	.10	.05	.01
□ 6 Darrell Evans	.20	.09	.03
□ 7 Barbaro Garbey	.10	.05	.01
□ 8 Kirk Gibson	.40	.18	.05
□ 9 John Grubb	.10	.05	.01
□ 10 Willie Hernandez	.10	.05	.01
□ 11 Larry Herndon	.10	.05	.01
□ 12 Howard Johnson	.20	.09	.03
□ 13 Ruppert Jones	.10	.05	.01
□ 14 Rusty Kuntz	.10	.05	.01
□ 15 Chet Lemon	.10	.05	.01
□ 16 Aurelio Lopez	.10	.05	.01
□ 17 Sid Monge	.10	.05	.01
□ 18 Jack Morris	.40	.18	.05
□ 19 Lance Parrish	.20	.09	.03
□ 20 Dan Petry	.10	.05	.01
□ 21 Dave Rozema	.10	.05	.01
□ 22 Bill Scherrer	.10	.05	.01
□ 23 Alan Trammell	.40	.18	.05
□ 24 Lou Whitaker	.40	.18	.05
□ 25 Milt Wilcox	.10	.05	.01
□ 26 Kurt Bevacqua	.10	.05	.01
□ 27 Greg Booker	.10	.05	.01
□ 28 Bobby Brown	.10	.05	.01
□ 29 Luis DeLeon	.10	.05	.01
□ 30 Dave Dravecky	.20	.09	.03
□ 31 Tim Flannery	.10	.05	.01
□ 32 Steve Garvey	.40	.18	.05
□ 33 Rich Gossage	.40	.18	.05
□ 34 Tony Gwynn	6.00	2.70	.75
□ 35 Greg Harris	.10	.05	.01
□ 36 Andy Hawkins	.10	.05	.01
□ 37 Terry Kennedy	.10	.05	.01
□ 38 Craig Lefferts	.10	.05	.01
□ 39 Tim Lollar	.10	.05	.01
□ 40 Carmelo Martinez	.10	.05	.01
□ 41 Kevin McReynolds	.20	.09	.03
□ 42 Graig Nettles	.20	.09	.03
□ 43 Luis Salazar	.10	.05	.01
□ 44 Eric Show	.10	.05	.01
□ 45 Garry Templeton	.10	.05	.01
□ 46 Mark Thurmond	.10	.05	.01
□ 47 Ed Whitson	.10	.05	.01
□ 48 Alan Wiggins	.10	.05	.01
□ 49 Rich Bordi	.10	.05	.01
□ 50 Larry Bowa	.20	.09	.03
□ 51 Warren Brusstar	.10	.05	.01
□ 52 Ron Cey	.20	.09	.03
□ 53 Henry Cotto	.10	.05	.01
□ 54 Jody Davis	.10	.05	.01
□ 55 Bob Dernier	.10	.05	.01
□ 56 Leon Durham	.10	.05	.01
□ 57 Dennis Eckersley	.40	.18	.05
□ 58 George Frazier	.10	.05	.01
□ 59 Richie Hebner	.10	.05	.01
□ 60 Dave Lopes	.20	.09	.03
□ 61 Gary Matthews	.10	.05	.01
□ 62 Keith Moreland	.10	.05	.01
□ 63 Rick Reuschel	.10	.05	.01
□ 64 Dick Ruthven	.10	.05	.01
□ 65 Ryne Sandberg	5.00	2.20	.60
□ 66 Scott Sanderson	.10	.05	.01
□ 67 Lee Smith	1.00	.45	.12
□ 68 Tim Stoddard	.10	.05	.01
□ 69 Rick Sutcliffe	.10	.05	.01
□ 70 Steve Trout	.10	.05	.01
□ 71 Gary Woods	.10	.05	.01
□ 72 Wally Backman	.10	.05	.01
□ 73 Bruce Berenyi	.10	.05	.01
□ 74 Hubie Brooks UER (Kelvin Chapman's stats on card back)	.10	.05	.01
□ 75 Kelvin Chapman	.10	.05	.01
□ 76 Ron Darling	.20	.09	.03
□ 77 Sid Fernandez	.40	.18	.05
□ 78 Mike Fitzgerald	.10	.05	.01
□ 79 George Foster	.20	.09	.03
□ 80 Brent Gaff	.10	.05	.01

□ 81 Ron Gardenhire	.10	.05	.01
□ 82 Dwight Gooden	4.00	1.80	.50
□ 83 Tom Gorman	.10	.05	.01
□ 84 Danny Heep	.10	.05	.01
□ 85 Keith Hernandez	.20	.09	.03
□ 86 Ray Knight	.20	.09	.03
□ 87 Ed Lynch	.10	.05	.01
□ 88 Jose Oquendo	.10	.05	.01
□ 89 Jesse Orosco	.10	.05	.01
□ 90 Rafael Santana	.10	.05	.01
□ 91 Doug Sisk	.10	.05	.01
□ 92 Rusty Staub	.20	.09	.03
□ 93 Darryl Strawberry	1.00	.45	.12
□ 94 Walt Terrell	.10	.05	.01
□ 95 Mookie Wilson	.20	.09	.03
□ 96 Jim Acker	.10	.05	.01
□ 97 Willie Aikens	.10	.05	.01
□ 98 Doyle Alexander	.10	.05	.01
□ 99 Jesse Barfield	.10	.05	.01
□ 100 George Bell	.20	.09	.03
□ 101 Jim Clancy	.10	.05	.01
□ 102 Dave Collins	.10	.05	.01
□ 103 Tony Fernandez	.20	.09	.03
□ 104 Damaso Garcia	.10	.05	.01
□ 105 Jim Gott	.10	.05	.01
□ 106 Alfredo Griffin	.10	.05	.01
□ 107 Garth Iorg	.10	.05	.01
□ 108 Roy Lee Jackson	.10	.05	.01
□ 109 Cliff Johnson	.10	.05	.01
□ 110 Jimmy Key	1.00	.45	.12
□ 111 Dennis Lamp	.10	.05	.01
□ 112 Rick Leach	.10	.05	.01
□ 113 Luis Leal	.10	.05	.01
□ 114 Buck Martinez	.10	.05	.01
□ 115 Lloyd Moseby	.10	.05	.01
□ 116 Rance Mulliniks	.10	.05	.01
□ 117 Dave Stieb	.20	.09	.03
□ 118 Willie Upshaw	.10	.05	.01
□ 119 Ernie Whitt	.10	.05	.01
□ 120 Mike Armstrong	.10	.05	.01
□ 121 Don Baylor	.40	.18	.05
□ 122 Marty Bystrom	.10	.05	.01
□ 123 Rick Cerone	.10	.05	.01
□ 124 Joe Cowley	.10	.05	.01
□ 125 Brian Dayett	.10	.05	.01
□ 126 Tim Foli	.10	.05	.01
□ 127 Ray Fontenot	.10	.05	.01
□ 128 Ken Griffey	.20	.09	.03
□ 129 Ron Guidry	.20	.09	.03
□ 130 Toby Harrah	.10	.05	.01
□ 131 Jay Howell	.10	.05	.01
□ 132 Steve Kemp	.10	.05	.01
□ 133 Don Mattingly	8.00	3.60	1.00
□ 134 Bobby Meacham	.10	.05	.01
□ 135 John Montefusco	.10	.05	.01
□ 136 Omar Moreno	.10	.05	.01
□ 137 Dale Murray	.10	.05	.01
□ 138 Phil Niekro	.40	.18	.05
□ 139 Mike Pagliarulo	.10	.05	.01
□ 140 Willie Randolph	.20	.09	.03
□ 141 Dennis Rasmussen	.10	.05	.01
□ 142 Dave Righetti	.20	.09	.03
□ 143 Jose Rijo	1.00	.45	.12
□ 144 Andre Robertson	.10	.05	.01
□ 145 Bob Shirley	.10	.05	.01
□ 146 Dave Winfield	1.50	.70	.19
□ 147 Butch Wynegar	.10	.05	.01
□ 148 Gary Allenson	.10	.05	.01
□ 149 Tony Armas	.10	.05	.01
□ 150 Marty Barrett	.10	.05	.01
□ 151 Wade Boggs	2.50	1.10	.30
□ 152 Dennis Boyd	.10	.05	.01
□ 153 Bill Buckner	.20	.09	.03
□ 154 Mark Clear	.10	.05	.01
□ 155 Roger Clemens	18.00	8.00	2.20
□ 156 Steve Crawford	.10	.05	.01
□ 157 Mike Easler	.10	.05	.01
□ 158 Dwight Evans	.20	.09	.03
□ 159 Rich Gedman	.10	.05	.01
□ 160 Jackie Gutierrez (Wade Boggs shown on deck)	.20	.09	.03
□ 161 Bruce Hurst	.10	.05	.01
□ 162 John Henry Johnson	.10	.05	.01
□ 163 Rick Miller	.10	.05	.01
□ 164 Reid Nichols	.10	.05	.01
□ 165 Al Nipper	.10	.05	.01
□ 166 Bob Ojeda	.10	.05	.01
□ 167 Jerry Remy	.10	.05	.01
□ 168 Jim Rice	.20	.09	.03
□ 169 Bob Stanley	.10	.05	.01
□ 170 Mike Boddicker	.10	.05	.01
□ 171 Al Bumbry	.10	.05	.01
□ 172 Todd Cruz	.10	.05	.01
□ 173 Rich Dauer	.10	.05	.01
□ 174 Storm Davis	.10	.05	.01
□ 175 Rick Dempsey	.10	.05	.01
□ 176 Jim Dwyer	.10	.05	.01
□ 177 Mike Flanagan	.10	.05	.01
□ 178 Dan Ford	.10	.05	.01
□ 179 Wayne Gross	.10	.05	.01
□ 180 John Lowenstein	.10	.05	.01
□ 181 Dennis Martinez	.20	.09	.03
□ 182 Tippy Martinez	.10	.05	.01
□ 183 Scott McGregor	.10	.05	.01
□ 184 Eddie Murray	3.00	1.35	.35
□ 185 Joe Nolan	.10	.05	.01
□ 186 Floyd Rayford	.10	.05	.01
□ 187 Cal Ripken	8.00	3.60	1.00
□ 188 Gary Roenicke	.10	.05	.01
□ 189 Lenn Sakata	.10	.05	.01
□ 190 John Shelby	.10	.05	.01
□ 191 Ken Singleton	.10	.05	.01
□ 192 Sammy Stewart	.10	.05	.01
□ 193 Bill Swaggerty	.10	.05	.01
□ 194 Tom Underwood	.10	.05	.01
□ 195 Mike Young	.10	.05	.01
□ 196 Steve Balboni	.10	.05	.01
□ 197 Joe Beckwith	.10	.05	.01
□ 198 Bud Black	.10	.05	.01
□ 199 George Brett	4.00	1.80	.50
□ 200 Onix Concepcion	.10	.05	.01
□ 201 Mark Gubicza	.40	.18	.05
□ 202 Larry Gura	.10	.05	.01
□ 203 Mark Huismann	.10	.05	.01
□ 204 Dane Iorg	.10	.05	.01
□ 205 Danny Jackson	.10	.05	.01
□ 206 Charlie Leibrandt	.10	.05	.01
□ 207 Hal McRae	.20	.09	.03
□ 208 Darryl Motley	.10	.05	.01
□ 209 Jorge Orta	.10	.05	.01
□ 210 Greg Pryor	.10	.05	.01
□ 211 Dan Quisenberry	.20	.09	.03
□ 212 Bret Saberhagen	1.50	.70	.19
□ 213 Pat Sheridan	.10	.05	.01
□ 214 Don Slaught	.10	.05	.01
□ 215 U.L. Washington	.10	.05	.01
□ 216 John Wathan	.10	.05	.01
□ 217 Frank White	.20	.09	.03
□ 218 Willie Wilson	.10	.05	.01
□ 219 Neil Allen	.10	.05	.01
□ 220 Joaquin Andujar	.10	.05	.01
□ 221 Steve Braun	.10	.05	.01
□ 222 Danny Cox	.10	.05	.01
□ 223 Bob Forsch	.10	.05	.01
□ 224 David Green	.10	.05	.01
□ 225 George Hendrick	.10	.05	.01
□ 226 Tom Herr	.20	.09	.03
□ 227 Ricky Horton	.10	.05	.01
□ 228 Art Howe	.10	.05	.01
□ 229 Mike Jorgensen	.10	.05	.01
□ 230 Kurt Kepshire	.10	.05	.01
□ 231 Jeff Lahti	.10	.05	.01
□ 232 Tito Landrum	.10	.05	.01
□ 233 Dave LaPoint	.10	.05	.01
□ 234 Willie McGee	.20	.09	.03
□ 235 Tom Nieto	.10	.05	.01
□ 236 Terry Pendleton	1.50	.70	.19
□ 237 Darrell Porter	.10	.05	.01
□ 238 Dave Rucker	.10	.05	.01
□ 239 Lonnie Smith	.10	.05	.01
□ 240 Ozzie Smith	2.50	1.10	.30
□ 241 Bruce Sutter	.20	.09	.03
□ 242 Andy Van Slyke UER (Bats Right, Throws Left)	.40	.18	.05
□ 243 Dave Von Ohlen	.10	.05	.01
□ 244 Larry Andersen	.10	.05	.01
□ 245 Bill Campbell	.10	.05	.01
□ 246 Steve Carlton	.75	.35	.09
□ 247 Tim Corcoran	.10	.05	.01
□ 248 Ivan DeJesus	.10	.05	.01

□ 249	John Denny	.10	.05	.01
□ 250	Bo Diaz	.10	.05	.01
□ 251	Greg Gross	.10	.05	.01
□ 252	Kevin Gross	.10	.05	.01
□ 253	Von Hayes	.10	.05	.01
□ 254	Al Holland	.10	.05	.01
□ 255	Charles Hudson	.10	.05	.01
□ 256	Jerry Koosman	.10	.05	.01
□ 257	Joe Lefebvre	.10	.05	.01
□ 258	Sixto Lezcano	.10	.05	.01
□ 259	Garry Maddox	.10	.05	.01
□ 260	Len Matuszek	.10	.05	.01
□ 261	Tug McGraw	.20	.09	.03
□ 262	Al Oliver	.20	.09	.03
□ 263	Shane Rawley	.10	.05	.01
□ 264	Juan Samuel	.10	.05	.01
□ 265	Mike Schmidt	2.50	1.10	.30
□ 266	Jeff Stone	.10	.05	.01
□ 267	Ozzie Virgil	.10	.05	.01
□ 268	Glenn Wilson	.10	.05	.01
□ 269	John Wockenfuss	.10	.05	.01
□ 270	Darrell Brown	.10	.05	.01
□ 271	Tom Brunansky	.20	.09	.03
□ 272	Randy Bush	.10	.05	.01
□ 273	John Butcher	.10	.05	.01
□ 274	Bobby Castillo	.10	.05	.01
□ 275	Ron Davis	.10	.05	.01
□ 276	Dave Engle	.10	.05	.01
□ 277	Pete Filson	.10	.05	.01
□ 278	Gary Gaetti	.20	.09	.03
□ 279	Mickey Hatcher	.10	.05	.01
□ 280	Ed Hodge	.10	.05	.01
□ 281	Kent Hrbek	.20	.09	.03
□ 282	Houston Jimenez	.10	.05	.01
□ 283	Tim Laudner	.10	.05	.01
□ 284	Rick Lysander	.10	.05	.01
□ 285	Dave Meier	.10	.05	.01
□ 286	Kirby Puckett	30.00	13.50	3.70
□ 287	Pat Putnam	.10	.05	.01
□ 288	Ken Schrom	.10	.05	.01
□ 289	Mike Smithson	.10	.05	.01
□ 290	Tim Teufel	.10	.05	.01
□ 291	Frank Viola	.20	.09	.03
□ 292	Ron Washington	.10	.05	.01
□ 293	Don Aase	.10	.05	.01
□ 294	Juan Beniquez	.10	.05	.01
□ 295	Bob Boone	.20	.09	.03
□ 296	Mike C. Brown	.10	.05	.01
□ 297	Rod Carew	.60	.25	.07
□ 298	Doug Corbett	.10	.05	.01
□ 299	Doug DeCinces	.10	.05	.01
□ 300	Brian Downing	.10	.05	.01
□ 301	Ken Forsch	.10	.05	.01
□ 302	Bobby Grich	.20	.09	.03
□ 303	Reggie Jackson	1.50	.70	.19
□ 304	Tommy John	.40	.18	.05
□ 305	Curt Kaufman	.10	.05	.01
□ 306	Bruce Kison	.10	.05	.01
□ 307	Fred Lynn	.20	.09	.03
□ 308	Gary Pettis	.10	.05	.01
□ 309	Ron Romanick	.10	.05	.01
□ 310	Luis Sanchez	.10	.05	.01
□ 311	Dick Schofield	.10	.05	.01
□ 312	Daryl Sconiers	.10	.05	.01
□ 313	Jim Slaton	.10	.05	.01
□ 314	Derrel Thomas	.10	.05	.01
□ 315	Rob Wilfong	.10	.05	.01
□ 316	Mike Witt	.10	.05	.01
□ 317	Geoff Zahn	.10	.05	.01
□ 318	Len Barker	.10	.05	.01
□ 319	Steve Bedrosian	.10	.05	.01
□ 320	Bruce Benedict	.10	.05	.01
□ 321	Rick Camp	.10	.05	.01
□ 322	Chris Chambliss	.10	.05	.01
□ 323	Jeff Dedmon	.10	.05	.01
□ 324	Terry Forster	.10	.05	.01
□ 325	Gene Garber	.10	.05	.01
□ 326	Albert Hall	.10	.05	.01
□ 327	Terry Harper	.10	.05	.01
□ 328	Bob Horner	.10	.05	.01
□ 329	Glenn Hubbard	.10	.05	.01
□ 330	Randy Johnson	.10	.05	.01
□ 331	Brad Komminsk	.10	.05	.01
□ 332	Rick Mahler	.10	.05	.01
□ 333	Craig McMurtry	.10	.05	.01
□ 334	Donnie Moore	.10	.05	.01
□ 335	Dale Murphy	.40	.18	.05
□ 336	Ken Oberkfell	.10	.05	.01
□ 337	Pascual Perez	.10	.05	.01
□ 338	Gerald Perry	.10	.05	.01
□ 339	Rafael Ramirez	.10	.05	.01
□ 340	Jerry Royster	.10	.05	.01
□ 341	Alex Trevino	.10	.05	.01
□ 342	Claudell Washington	.10	.05	.01
□ 343	Alan Ashby	.10	.05	.01
□ 344	Mark Bailey	.10	.05	.01
□ 345	Kevin Bass	.10	.05	.01
□ 346	Enos Cabell	.10	.05	.01
□ 347	Jose Cruz	.20	.09	.03
□ 348	Bill Dawley	.10	.05	.01
□ 349	Frank DiPino	.10	.05	.01
□ 350	Bill Doran	.10	.05	.01
□ 351	Phil Garner	.10	.05	.01
□ 352	Bob Knepper	.10	.05	.01
□ 353	Mike LaCoss	.10	.05	.01
□ 354	Jerry Mumphrey	.10	.05	.01
□ 355	Joe Niekro	.10	.05	.01
□ 356	Terry Puhl	.10	.05	.01
□ 357	Craig Reynolds	.10	.05	.01
□ 358	Vern Ruhle	.10	.05	.01
□ 359	Nolan Ryan	8.00	3.60	1.00
□ 360	Joe Sambito	.10	.05	.01
□ 361	Mike Scott	.10	.05	.01
□ 362	Dave Smith	.10	.05	.01
□ 363	Julio Solano	.10	.05	.01
□ 364	Dickie Thon	.10	.05	.01
□ 365	Denny Walling	.10	.05	.01
□ 366	Dave Anderson	.10	.05	.01
□ 367	Bob Bailor	.10	.05	.01
□ 368	Greg Brock	.10	.05	.01
□ 369	Carlos Diaz	.10	.05	.01
□ 370	Pedro Guerrero	.20	.09	.03
□ 371	Orel Hershiser	2.50	1.10	.30
□ 372	Rick Honeycutt	.10	.05	.01
□ 373	Burt Hooton	.10	.05	.01
□ 374	Ken Howell	.10	.05	.01
□ 375	Ken Landreaux	.10	.05	.01
□ 376	Candy Maldonado	.10	.05	.01
□ 377	Mike Marshall	.10	.05	.01
□ 378	Tom Niedenfuer	.10	.05	.01
□ 379	Alejandro Pena	.10	.05	.01
□ 380	Jerry Reuss UER ("Home:" omitted)	.10	.05	.01
□ 381	R.J. Reynolds	.10	.05	.01
□ 382	German Rivera	.10	.05	.01
□ 383	Bill Russell	.10	.05	.01
□ 384	Steve Sax	.20	.09	.03
□ 385	Mike Scioscia	.10	.05	.01
□ 386	Franklin Stubbs	.10	.05	.01
□ 387	Fernando Valenzuela	.20	.09	.03
□ 388	Bob Welch	.10	.05	.01
□ 389	Terry Whitfield	.10	.05	.01
□ 390	Steve Yeager	.10	.05	.01
□ 391	Pat Zachry	.10	.05	.01
□ 392	Fred Breining	.10	.05	.01
□ 393	Gary Carter	.40	.18	.05
□ 394	Andre Dawson	1.25	.55	.16
□ 395	Miguel Dilone	.10	.05	.01
□ 396	Dan Driessen	.10	.05	.01
□ 397	Doug Flynn	.10	.05	.01
□ 398	Terry Francona	.10	.05	.01
□ 399	Bill Gullickson	.10	.05	.01
□ 400	Bob James	.10	.05	.01
□ 401	Charlie Lea	.10	.05	.01
□ 402	Bryan Little	.10	.05	.01
□ 403	Gary Lucas	.10	.05	.01
□ 404	David Palmer	.10	.05	.01
□ 405	Tim Raines	.40	.18	.05
□ 406	Mike Ramsey	.10	.05	.01
□ 407	Jeff Reardon	.20	.09	.03
□ 408	Steve Rogers	.10	.05	.01
□ 409	Dan Schatzeder	.10	.05	.01
□ 410	Bryn Smith	.10	.05	.01
□ 411	Mike Stenhouse	.10	.05	.01
□ 412	Tim Wallach	.20	.09	.03
□ 413	Jim Wohlford	.10	.05	.01
□ 414	Bill Almon	.10	.05	.01
□ 415	Keith Atherton	.10	.05	.01
□ 416	Bruce Bochte	.10	.05	.01
□ 417	Tom Burgmeier	.10	.05	.01
□ 418	Ray Burris	.10	.05	.01
□ 419	Bill Caudill	.10	.05	.01

□ 420	Chris Codiroli	.10	.05	.01
□ 421	Tim Conroy	.10	.05	.01
□ 422	Mike Davis	.10	.05	.01
□ 423	Jim Essian	.10	.05	.01
□ 424	Mike Heath	.10	.05	.01
□ 425	Rickey Henderson	1.50	.70	.19
□ 426	Donnie Hill	.10	.05	.01
□ 427	Dave Kingman	.20	.09	.03
□ 428	Bill Krueger	.10	.05	.01
□ 429	Carney Lansford	.20	.09	.03
□ 430	Steve McCatty	.10	.05	.01
□ 431	Joe Morgan	.50	.23	.06
□ 432	Dwayne Murphy	.10	.05	.01
□ 433	Tony Phillips	.40	.18	.05
□ 434	Lary Sorensen	.10	.05	.01
□ 435	Mike Warren	.10	.05	.01
□ 436	Curt Young	.10	.05	.01
□ 437	Luis Aponte	.10	.05	.01
□ 438	Chris Bando	.10	.05	.01
□ 439	Tony Bernazard	.10	.05	.01
□ 440	Bert Blyleven	.40	.18	.05
□ 441	Brett Butler	.40	.18	.05
□ 442	Ernie Camacho	.10	.05	.01
□ 443	Joe Carter	6.00	2.70	.75
□ 444	Carmelo Castillo	.10	.05	.01
□ 445	Jamie Easterly	.10	.05	.01
□ 446	Steve Farr	.20	.09	.03
□ 447	Mike Fischlin	.10	.05	.01
□ 448	Julio Franco	.40	.18	.05
□ 449	Mel Hall	.10	.05	.01
□ 450	Mike Hargrove	.20	.09	.03
□ 451	Neal Heaton	.10	.05	.01
□ 452	Brook Jacoby	.10	.05	.01
□ 453	Mike Jeffcoat	.10	.05	.01
□ 454	Don Schulze	.10	.05	.01
□ 455	Roy Smith	.10	.05	.01
□ 456	Pat Tabler	.10	.05	.01
□ 457	Andre Thornton	.10	.05	.01
□ 458	George Vukovich	.10	.05	.01
□ 459	Tom Waddell	.10	.05	.01
□ 460	Jerry Willard	.10	.05	.01
□ 461	Dale Berra	.10	.05	.01
□ 462	John Candelaria	.10	.05	.01
□ 463	Jose DeLeon	.10	.05	.01
□ 464	Doug Frobel	.10	.05	.01
□ 465	Cecilio Guante	.10	.05	.01
□ 466	Brian Harper	.20	.09	.03
□ 467	Lee Lacy	.10	.05	.01
□ 468	Bill Madlock	.10	.05	.01
□ 469	Lee Mazzilli	.10	.05	.01
□ 470	Larry McWilliams	.10	.05	.01
□ 471	Jim Morrison	.10	.05	.01
□ 472	Tony Pena	.10	.05	.01
□ 473	Johnny Ray	.10	.05	.01
□ 474	Rick Rhoden	.10	.05	.01
□ 475	Don Robinson	.10	.05	.01
□ 476	Rod Scurry	.10	.05	.01
□ 477	Kent Tekulve	.10	.05	.01
□ 478	Jason Thompson	.10	.05	.01
□ 479	John Tudor	.10	.05	.01
□ 480	Lee Tunnell	.10	.05	.01
□ 481	Marvell Wynne	.10	.05	.01
□ 482	Salome Barojas	.10	.05	.01
□ 483	Dave Beard	.10	.05	.01
□ 484	Jim Beattie	.10	.05	.01
□ 485	Barry Bonnell	.10	.05	.01
□ 486	Phil Bradley	.20	.09	.03
□ 487	Al Cowens	.10	.05	.01
□ 488	Alvin Davis	.20	.09	.03
□ 489	Dave Henderson	.20	.09	.03
□ 490	Steve Henderson	.10	.05	.01
□ 491	Bob Kearney	.10	.05	.01
□ 492	Mark Langston	1.25	.55	.16
□ 493	Larry Milbourne	.10	.05	.01
□ 494	Paul Mirabella	.10	.05	.01
□ 495	Mike Moore	.10	.05	.01
□ 496	Edwin Nunez	.10	.05	.01
□ 497	Spike Owen	.10	.05	.01
□ 498	Jack Perconte	.10	.05	.01
□ 499	Ken Phelps	.10	.05	.01
□ 500	Jim Presley	.20	.09	.03
□ 501	Mike Stanton	.10	.05	.01
□ 502	Bob Stoddard	.10	.05	.01
□ 503	Gorman Thomas	.10	.05	.01
□ 504	Ed VandeBerg	.10	.05	.01
□ 505	Matt Young	.10	.05	.01
□ 506	Juan Agosto	.10	.05	.01
□ 507	Harold Baines	.20	.09	.03
□ 508	Floyd Bannister	.10	.05	.01
□ 509	Britt Burns	.10	.05	.01
□ 510	Julio Cruz	.10	.05	.01
□ 511	Richard Dotson	.10	.05	.01
□ 512	Jerry Dybzinski	.10	.05	.01
□ 513	Carlton Fisk	.75	.35	.09
□ 514	Scott Fletcher	.10	.05	.01
□ 515	Jerry Hairston	.10	.05	.01
□ 516	Marc Hill	.10	.05	.01
□ 517	LaMarr Hoyt	.10	.05	.01
□ 518	Ron Kittle	.10	.05	.01
□ 519	Rudy Law	.10	.05	.01
□ 520	Vance Law	.10	.05	.01
□ 521	Greg Luzinski	.20	.09	.03
□ 522	Gene Nelson	.10	.05	.01
□ 523	Tom Paciorek	.10	.05	.01
□ 524	Ron Reed	.10	.05	.01
□ 525	Bert Roberge	.10	.05	.01
□ 526	Tom Seaver	.75	.35	.09
□ 527	Roy Smalley	.10	.05	.01
□ 528	Dan Spillner	.10	.05	.01
□ 529	Mike Squires	.10	.05	.01
□ 530	Greg Walker	.10	.05	.01
□ 531	Cesar Cedeno	.20	.09	.03
□ 532	Dave Concepcion	.20	.09	.03
□ 533	Eric Davis	1.50	.70	.19
□ 534	Nick Esasky	.10	.05	.01
□ 535	Tom Foley	.10	.05	.01
□ 536	John Franco UER (Koufax misspelled as Kofax on back)	1.00	.45	.12
□ 537	Brad Gulden	.10	.05	.01
□ 538	Tom Hume	.10	.05	.01
□ 539	Wayne Krenchicki	.10	.05	.01
□ 540	Andy McGaffigan	.10	.05	.01
□ 541	Eddie Milner	.10	.05	.01
□ 542	Ron Oester	.10	.05	.01
□ 543	Bob Owchinko	.10	.05	.01
□ 544	Dave Parker	.40	.18	.05
□ 545	Frank Pastore	.10	.05	.01
□ 546	Tony Perez	.40	.18	.05
□ 547	Ted Power	.10	.05	.01
□ 548	Joe Price	.10	.05	.01
□ 549	Gary Redus	.10	.05	.01
□ 550	Pete Rose	2.00	.90	.25
□ 551	Jeff Russell	.20	.09	.03
□ 552	Mario Soto	.10	.05	.01
□ 553	Jay Tibbs	.10	.05	.01
□ 554	Duane Walker	.10	.05	.01
□ 555	Alan Bannister	.10	.05	.01
□ 556	Buddy Bell	.20	.09	.03
□ 557	Danny Darwin	.10	.05	.01
□ 558	Charlie Hough	.20	.09	.03
□ 559	Bobby Jones	.10	.05	.01
□ 560	Odell Jones	.10	.05	.01
□ 561	Jeff Kunkel	.10	.05	.01
□ 562	Mike Mason	.10	.05	.01
□ 563	Pete O'Brien	.10	.05	.01
□ 564	Larry Parrish	.10	.05	.01
□ 565	Mickey Rivers	.10	.05	.01
□ 566	Billy Sample	.10	.05	.01
□ 567	Dave Schmidt	.10	.05	.01
□ 568	Donnie Scott	.10	.05	.01
□ 569	Dave Stewart	.20	.09	.03
□ 570	Frank Tanana	.10	.05	.01
□ 571	Wayne Tolleson	.10	.05	.01
□ 572	Gary Ward	.10	.05	.01
□ 573	Curtis Wilkerson	.10	.05	.01
□ 574	George Wright	.10	.05	.01
□ 575	Ned Yost	.10	.05	.01
□ 576	Mark Brouhard	.10	.05	.01
□ 577	Mike Caldwell	.10	.05	.01
□ 578	Bobby Clark	.10	.05	.01
□ 579	Jaime Cocanower	.10	.05	.01
□ 580	Cecil Cooper	.20	.09	.03
□ 581	Rollie Fingers	.40	.18	.05
□ 582	Jim Gantner	.10	.05	.01
□ 583	Moose Haas	.10	.05	.01
□ 584	Dion James	.10	.05	.01
□ 585	Pete Ladd	.10	.05	.01
□ 586	Rick Manning	.10	.05	.01
□ 587	Bob McClure	.10	.05	.01
□ 588	Paul Molitor	2.00	.90	.25
□ 589	Charlie Moore	.10	.05	.01

□ 590 Ben Oglivie	.10	.05	.01
□ 591 Chuck Porter	.10	.05	.01
□ 592 Randy Ready	.10	.05	.01
□ 593 Ed Romero	.10	.05	.01
□ 594 Bill Schroeder	.10	.05	.01
□ 595 Ray Searage	.10	.05	.01
□ 596 Ted Simmons	.20	.09	.03
□ 597 Jim Sundberg	.10	.05	.01
□ 598 Don Sutton	.40	.18	.05
□ 599 Tom Tellmann	.10	.05	.01
□ 600 Rick Waits	.10	.05	.01
□ 601 Robin Yount	2.00	.90	.25
□ 602 Dusty Baker	.20	.09	.03
□ 603 Bob Brenly	.10	.05	.01
□ 604 Jack Clark	.20	.09	.03
□ 605 Chili Davis	.20	.09	.03
□ 606 Mark Davis	.10	.05	.01
□ 607 Dan Gladden	.20	.09	.03
□ 608 Atlee Hammaker	.10	.05	.01
□ 609 Mike Krukow	.10	.05	.01
□ 610 Duane Kuiper	.10	.05	.01
□ 611 Bob Lacey	.10	.05	.01
□ 612 Bill Laskey	.10	.05	.01
□ 613 Gary Lavelle	.10	.05	.01
□ 614 Johnnie LeMaster	.10	.05	.01
□ 615 Jeff Leonard	.10	.05	.01
□ 616 Randy Lerch	.10	.05	.01
□ 617 Greg Minton	.10	.05	.01
□ 618 Steve Nicosia	.10	.05	.01
□ 619 Gene Richards	.10	.05	.01
□ 620 Jeff D. Robinson	.10	.05	.01
□ 621 Scot Thompson	.10	.05	.01
□ 622 Manny Trillo	.10	.05	.01
□ 623 Brad Wellman	.10	.05	.01
□ 624 Frank Williams	.10	.05	.01
□ 625 Joel Youngblood	.10	.05	.01
□ 626 Cal Ripken IA	5.00	2.20	.60
□ 627 Mike Schmidt IA	1.50	.70	.19
□ 628 Giving The Signs	.20	.09	.03
Sparky Anderson			
□ 629 AL Pitcher's Nightmare	1.50	.70	.19
Dave Winfield			
Rickey Henderson			
□ 630 NL Pitcher's Nightmare	1.50	.70	.19
Mike Schmidt			
Ryne Sandberg			
□ 631 NL All-Stars	.60	.25	.07
Darryl Strawberry			
Gary Carter			
Steve Garvey			
Ozzie Smith			
□ 632 A-S Winning Battery	.40	.18	.05
Gary Carter			
Charlie Lea			
□ 633 NL Pennant Clinchers	.40	.18	.05
Steve Garvey			
Rich Gossage			
□ 634 NL Rookie Phenoms	.75	.35	.09
Dwight Gooden			
Juan Samuel			
□ 635 Toronto's Big Guns	.10	.05	.01
Willie Upshaw			
□ 636 Toronto's Big Guns	.10	.05	.01
Lloyd Moseby			
□ 637 HOLLAND: Al Holland	.10	.05	.01
□ 638 TUNNELL: Lee Tunnell	.10	.05	.01
□ 639 500th Homer	1.00	.45	.12
Reggie Jackson			
□ 640 4000th Hit	1.25	.55	.16
Pete Rose			
□ 641 Father and Son	5.00	2.20	.60
Cal Ripken Jr.			
Cal Ripken Sr.			
□ 642 Cubs: Division Champs	.20	.09	.03
□ 643 Two Perfect Games	.20	.09	.03
and One No-Hitter:			
Mike Witt			
David Palmer			
Jack Morris			
□ 644 Willie Lozado and	.10	.05	.01
Vic Mata			
□ 645 Kelly Gruber and	.20	.09	.03
Randy O'Neal			
□ 646 Jose Roman and	.10	.05	.01
Joel Skinner			
□ 647 Steve Kiefer and	1.00	.45	.12
Danny Tartabull			
□ 648 Rob Deer and	.20	.09	.03
Alejandro Sanchez			
□ 649 Billy Hatcher and	1.00	.45	.12
Shawon Dunston			
□ 650 Ron Robinson and	.10	.05	.01
Mike Bielecki			
□ 651 Zane Smith and	.20	.09	.03
Paul Zuvella			
□ 652 Joe Hesketh and	.20	.09	.03
Glenn Davis			
□ 653 John Russell and	.10	.05	.01
Steve Jeltz			
□ 654 CL: Tigers/Padres	.20	.09	.03
and Cubs/Mets			
□ 655 CL: Blue Jays/Yankees	.20	.09	.03
and Red Sox/Orioles			
□ 656 CL: Royals/Cardinals	.20	.09	.03
and Phillies/Twins			
□ 657 CL: Angels/Braves	.20	.09	.03
and Astros/Dodgers			
□ 658 CL: Expos/A's	.20	.09	.03
and Indians/Pirates			
□ 659 CL: Mariners/White Sox	.20	.09	.03
and Reds/Rangers			
□ 660 CL: Brewers/Giants	.20	.09	.03
and Special Cards			

1985 Fleer Update

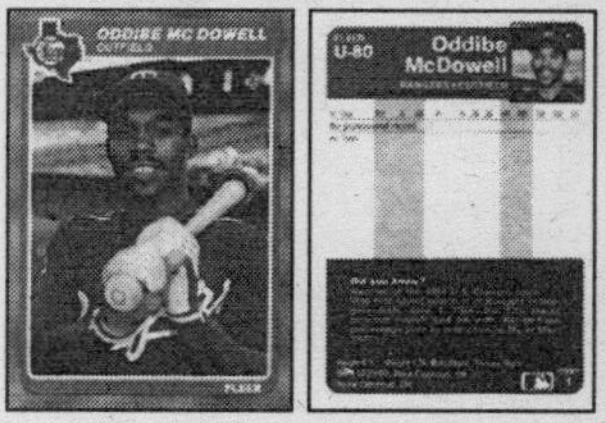

This 132-card standard-size update set was issued in factory set form exclusively through hobby dealers. Design is identical to the regular-issue 1985 Fleer cards except for the U prefixed card numbers on back. Cards are ordered alphabetically by the player's name. This set features the extended Rookie Cards of Vince Coleman, Darren Daulton, Mariano Duncan, Ozzie Guillen and Mickey Tettleton.

	MINT	NRMT	EXC
COMPLETE FACT.SET (132)	20.00	9.00	2.50
COMMON CARD (1-132)	.15	.07	.02
SEMISTARS	.40	.18	.05
STARS	.75	.35	.09
U PREFIX ON CARD NUMBER			

□ 1 Don Aase	.15	.07	.02
□ 2 Bill Almon	.15	.07	.02
□ 3 Dusty Baker	.40	.18	.05
□ 4 Dale Berra	.15	.07	.02
□ 5 Karl Best	.15	.07	.02
□ 6 Tim Birtsas	.15	.07	.02
□ 7 Vida Blue	.40	.18	.05
□ 8 Rich Bordi	.15	.07	.02
□ 9 Daryl Boston	.15	.07	.02
□ 10 Hubie Brooks	.15	.07	.02
□ 11 Chris Brown	.15	.07	.02
□ 12 Tom Browning	.40	.18	.05
□ 13 Al Bumbry	.15	.07	.02
□ 14 Tim Burke	.15	.07	.02
□ 15 Ray Burris	.15	.07	.02
□ 16 Jeff Burroughs	.15	.07	.02
□ 17 Ivan Calderon	.15	.07	.02
□ 18 Jeff Calhoun	.15	.07	.02
□ 19 Bill Campbell	.15	.07	.02
□ 20 Don Carman	.15	.07	.02
□ 21 Gary Carter	.75	.35	.09
□ 22 Bobby Castillo	.15	.07	.02

□ 23 Bill Caudill	.15	.07	.02
□ 24 Rick Cerone	.15	.07	.02
□ 25 Jack Clark	.40	.18	.05
□ 26 Pat Clements	.15	.07	.02
□ 27 Stewart Cliburn	.15	.07	.02
□ 28 Vince Coleman	1.00	.45	.12
□ 29 Dave Collins	.15	.07	.02
□ 30 Fritz Connally	.15	.07	.02
□ 31 Henry Cotto	.15	.07	.02
□ 32 Danny Darwin	.15	.07	.02
□ 33 Darren Daulton	8.00	3.60	1.00
□ 34 Jerry Davis	.15	.07	.02
□ 35 Brian Dayett	.15	.07	.02
□ 36 Ken Dixon	.15	.07	.02
□ 37 Tommy Dunbar	.15	.07	.02
□ 38 Mariano Duncan	.75	.35	.09
□ 39 Bob Fallon	.15	.07	.02
□ 40 Brian Fisher	.15	.07	.02
□ 41 Mike Fitzgerald	.15	.07	.02
□ 42 Ray Fontenot	.15	.07	.02
□ 43 Greg Gagne	.40	.18	.05
□ 44 Oscar Gamble	.15	.07	.02
□ 45 Jim Gott	.15	.07	.02
□ 46 David Green	.15	.07	.02
□ 47 Alfredo Griffin	.15	.07	.02
□ 48 Ozzie Guillen	1.50	.70	.19
□ 49 Toby Harrah	.15	.07	.02
□ 50 Ron Hassey	.15	.07	.02
□ 51 Rickey Henderson	1.50	.70	.19
□ 52 Steve Henderson	.15	.07	.02
□ 53 George Hendrick	.15	.07	.02
□ 54 Teddy Higuera	.40	.18	.05
□ 55 Al Holland	.15	.07	.02
□ 56 Burt Hooton	.15	.07	.02
□ 57 Jay Howell	.15	.07	.02
□ 58 LaMarr Hoyt	.15	.07	.02
□ 59 Tim Hulett	.15	.07	.02
□ 60 Bob James	.15	.07	.02
□ 61 Cliff Johnson	.15	.07	.02
□ 62 Howard Johnson	.40	.18	.05
□ 63 Ruppert Jones	.15	.07	.02
□ 64 Steve Kemp	.15	.07	.02
□ 65 Bruce Kison	.15	.07	.02
□ 66 Mike LaCoss	.15	.07	.02
□ 67 Lee Lacy	.15	.07	.02
□ 68 Dave LaPoint	.15	.07	.02
□ 69 Gary Lavelle	.15	.07	.02
□ 70 Vance Law	.15	.07	.02
□ 71 Manny Lee	.15	.07	.02
□ 72 Sixto Lezcano	.15	.07	.02
□ 73 Tim Lollar	.15	.07	.02
□ 74 Urbano Lugo	.15	.07	.02
□ 75 Fred Lynn	.40	.18	.05
□ 76 Steve Lyons	.40	.18	.05
□ 77 Mickey Mahler	.15	.07	.02
□ 78 Ron Mathis	.15	.07	.02
□ 79 Len Matuszek	.15	.07	.02
□ 80 Oddibe McDowell UER (Part of bio actually Roger's)	.40	.18	.05
□ 81 Roger McDowell UER (Part of bio actually Oddibe's)	.40	.18	.05
□ 82 Donnie Moore	.15	.07	.02
□ 83 Ron Musselman	.15	.07	.02
□ 84 Al Oliver	.40	.18	.05
□ 85 Joe Orsulak	.40	.18	.05
□ 86 Dan Pasqua	.40	.18	.05
□ 87 Chris Pittaro	.15	.07	.02
□ 88 Rick Reuschel	.15	.07	.02
□ 89 Earnie Riles	.15	.07	.02
□ 90 Jerry Royster	.15	.07	.02
□ 91 Dave Rozema	.15	.07	.02
□ 92 Dave Rucker	.15	.07	.02
□ 93 Vern Ruhle	.15	.07	.02
□ 94 Mark Salas	.15	.07	.02
□ 95 Luis Salazar	.15	.07	.02
□ 96 Joe Sambito	.15	.07	.02
□ 97 Billy Sample	.15	.07	.02
□ 98 Alejandro Sanchez	.15	.07	.02
□ 99 Calvin Schiraldi	.15	.07	.02
□ 100 Rick Schu	.15	.07	.02
□ 101 Larry Sheets	.15	.07	.02
□ 102 Ron Shephard	.15	.07	.02
□ 103 Nelson Simmons	.15	.07	.02
□ 104 Don Slaught	.15	.07	.02
□ 105 Roy Smalley	.15	.07	.02
□ 106 Lonnie Smith	.15	.07	.02
□ 107 Nate Snell	.15	.07	.02
□ 108 Lary Sorensen	.15	.07	.02
□ 109 Chris Speier	.15	.07	.02
□ 110 Mike Stenhouse	.15	.07	.02
□ 111 Tim Stoddard	.15	.07	.02
□ 112 John Stuper	.15	.07	.02
□ 113 Jim Sundberg	.15	.07	.02
□ 114 Bruce Sutter	.40	.18	.05
□ 115 Don Sutton	.75	.35	.09
□ 116 Bruce Tanner	.15	.07	.02
□ 117 Kent Tekulve	.15	.07	.02
□ 118 Walt Terrell	.15	.07	.02
□ 119 Mickey Tettleton	4.00	1.80	.50
□ 120 Rich Thompson	.15	.07	.02
□ 121 Louis Thornton	.15	.07	.02
□ 122 Alex Trevino	.15	.07	.02
□ 123 John Tudor	.15	.07	.02
□ 124 Jose Uribe	.15	.07	.02
□ 125 Dave Valle	.15	.07	.02
□ 126 Dave Von Ohlen	.15	.07	.02
□ 127 Curt Wardle	.15	.07	.02
□ 128 U.L. Washington	.15	.07	.02
□ 129 Ed Whitson	.15	.07	.02
□ 130 Herm Winningham	.15	.07	.02
□ 131 Rich Yett	.15	.07	.02
□ 132 Checklist U1-U132	.15	.07	.02

1986 Fleer

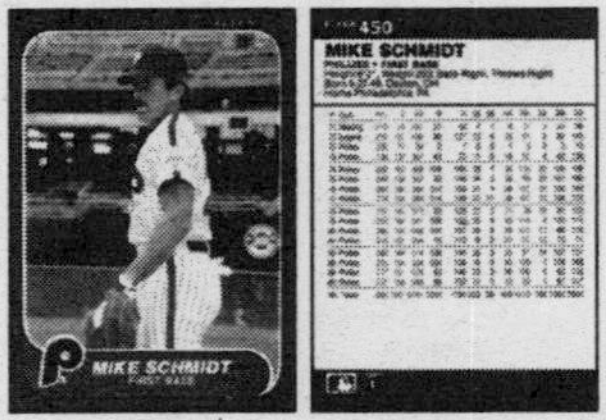

The 1986 Fleer set consists of 660-card standard-size cards. Wax packs included 15 cards plus logo stickers. Card fronts feature dark blue borders, a team logo along with the player's name and position. The player cards are alphabetized within team and the teams are ordered by their 1985 season finish and won-lost record. Subsets include Specials (626-643) and Major League Prospects (644-653). The Dennis and Tippy Martinez cards were apparently switched in the set numbering, as their adjacent numbers (279 and 280) were reversed on the Orioles checklist card. The set includes the Rookie Cards of Rick Aguilera, Jose Canseco, Darren Daulton, Len Dykstra, Cecil Fielder, Andres Galarraga, Paul O'Neill,and Mickey Tettleton.

	MINT	NRMT	EXC
COMPLETE SET (660)	60.00	27.00	7.50
COMPLETE FACT.SET (660)	70.00	32.00	8.75
COMMON CARD (1-660)	.10	.05	.01
SEMISTARS	.20	.09	.03
STARS	.40	.18	.05

□ 1 Steve Balboni	.10	.05	.01
□ 2 Joe Beckwith	.10	.05	.01
□ 3 Buddy Biancalana	.10	.05	.01
□ 4 Bud Black	.10	.05	.01
□ 5 George Brett	2.00	.90	.25
□ 6 Onix Concepcion	.10	.05	.01
□ 7 Steve Farr	.20	.09	.03
□ 8 Mark Gubicza	.20	.09	.03
□ 9 Dane Iorg	.10	.05	.01
□ 10 Danny Jackson	.10	.05	.01
□ 11 Lynn Jones	.10	.05	.01
□ 12 Mike Jones	.10	.05	.01
□ 13 Charlie Leibrandt	.10	.05	.01
□ 14 Hal McRae	.20	.09	.03

☐ 15	Omar Moreno	.10	.05	.01
☐ 16	Darryl Motley	.10	.05	.01
☐ 17	Jorge Orta	.10	.05	.01
☐ 18	Dan Quisenberry	.10	.05	.01
☐ 19	Bret Saberhagen	.30	.14	.04
☐ 20	Pat Sheridan	.10	.05	.01
☐ 21	Lonnie Smith	.10	.05	.01
☐ 22	Jim Sundberg	.10	.05	.01
☐ 23	John Wathan	.10	.05	.01
☐ 24	Frank White	.20	.09	.03
☐ 25	Willie Wilson	.10	.05	.01
☐ 26	Joaquin Andujar	.10	.05	.01
☐ 27	Steve Braun	.10	.05	.01
☐ 28	Bill Campbell	.10	.05	.01
☐ 29	Cesar Cedeno	.20	.09	.03
☐ 30	Jack Clark	.20	.09	.03
☐ 31	Vince Coleman	.30	.14	.04
☐ 32	Danny Cox	.10	.05	.01
☐ 33	Ken Dayley	.10	.05	.01
☐ 34	Ivan DeJesus	.10	.05	.01
☐ 35	Bob Forsch	.10	.05	.01
☐ 36	Brian Harper	.10	.05	.01
☐ 37	Tom Herr	.10	.05	.01
☐ 38	Ricky Horton	.10	.05	.01
☐ 39	Kurt Kepshire	.10	.05	.01
☐ 40	Jeff Lahti	.10	.05	.01
☐ 41	Tito Landrum	.10	.05	.01
☐ 42	Willie McGee	.10	.05	.01
☐ 43	Tom Nieto	.10	.05	.01
☐ 44	Terry Pendleton	.30	.14	.04
☐ 45	Darrell Porter	.20	.09	.03
☐ 46	Ozzie Smith	1.00	.45	.12
☐ 47	John Tudor	.10	.05	.01
☐ 48	Andy Van Slyke	.20	.09	.03
☐ 49	Todd Worrell	.20	.09	.03
☐ 50	Jim Acker	.10	.05	.01
☐ 51	Doyle Alexander	.10	.05	.01
☐ 52	Jesse Barfield	.10	.05	.01
☐ 53	George Bell	.20	.09	.03
☐ 54	Jeff Burroughs	.10	.05	.01
☐ 55	Bill Caudill	.10	.05	.01
☐ 56	Jim Clancy	.10	.05	.01
☐ 57	Tony Fernandez	.10	.05	.01
☐ 58	Tom Filer	.10	.05	.01
☐ 59	Damaso Garcia	.10	.05	.01
☐ 60	Tom Henke	.20	.09	.03
☐ 61	Garth Iorg	.10	.05	.01
☐ 62	Cliff Johnson	.10	.05	.01
☐ 63	Jimmy Key	.30	.14	.04
☐ 64	Dennis Lamp	.10	.05	.01
☐ 65	Gary Lavelle	.10	.05	.01
☐ 66	Buck Martinez	.10	.05	.01
☐ 67	Lloyd Moseby	.10	.05	.01
☐ 68	Rance Mulliniks	.10	.05	.01
☐ 69	Al Oliver	.20	.09	.03
☐ 70	Dave Stieb	.10	.05	.01
☐ 71	Louis Thornton	.10	.05	.01
☐ 72	Willie Upshaw	.10	.05	.01
☐ 73	Ernie Whitt	.10	.05	.01
☐ 74	Rick Aguilera	.50	.23	.06
☐ 75	Wally Backman	.10	.05	.01
☐ 76	Gary Carter	.30	.14	.04
☐ 77	Ron Darling	.10	.05	.01
☐ 78	Len Dykstra	2.00	.90	.25
☐ 79	Sid Fernandez	.20	.09	.03
☐ 80	George Foster	.20	.09	.03
☐ 81	Dwight Gooden	.60	.25	.07
☐ 82	Tom Gorman	.10	.05	.01
☐ 83	Danny Heep	.10	.05	.01
☐ 84	Keith Hernandez	.30	.14	.04
☐ 85	Howard Johnson	.20	.09	.03
☐ 86	Ray Knight	.20	.09	.03
☐ 87	Terry Leach	.10	.05	.01
☐ 88	Ed Lynch	.10	.05	.01
☐ 89	Roger McDowell	.20	.09	.03
☐ 90	Jesse Orosco	.10	.05	.01
☐ 91	Tom Paciorek	.10	.05	.01
☐ 92	Ronn Reynolds	.10	.05	.01
☐ 93	Rafael Santana	.10	.05	.01
☐ 94	Doug Sisk	.10	.05	.01
☐ 95	Rusty Staub	.20	.09	.03
☐ 96	Darryl Strawberry	.30	.14	.04
☐ 97	Mookie Wilson	.20	.09	.03
☐ 98	Neil Allen	.10	.05	.01
☐ 99	Don Baylor	.30	.14	.04
☐ 100	Dale Berra	.10	.05	.01
☐ 101	Rich Bordi	.10	.05	.01
☐ 102	Marty Bystrom	.10	.05	.01
☐ 103	Joe Cowley	.10	.05	.01
☐ 104	Brian Fisher	.10	.05	.01
☐ 105	Ken Griffey	.10	.05	.01
☐ 106	Ron Guidry	.10	.05	.01
☐ 107	Ron Hassey	.10	.05	.01
☐ 108	Rickey Henderson UER (SB Record of 120, sic)	.75	.35	.09
☐ 109	Don Mattingly	3.00	1.35	.35
☐ 110	Bobby Meacham	.10	.05	.01
☐ 111	John Montefusco	.10	.05	.01
☐ 112	Phil Niekro	.30	.14	.04
☐ 113	Mike Pagliarulo	.10	.05	.01
☐ 114	Dan Pasqua	.10	.05	.01
☐ 115	Willie Randolph	.20	.09	.03
☐ 116	Dave Righetti	.10	.05	.01
☐ 117	Andre Robertson	.10	.05	.01
☐ 118	Billy Sample	.10	.05	.01
☐ 119	Bob Shirley	.10	.05	.01
☐ 120	Ed Whitson	.10	.05	.01
☐ 121	Dave Winfield	.60	.25	.07
☐ 122	Butch Wynegar	.10	.05	.01
☐ 123	Dave Anderson	.10	.05	.01
☐ 124	Bob Bailor	.10	.05	.01
☐ 125	Greg Brock	.10	.05	.01
☐ 126	Enos Cabell	.10	.05	.01
☐ 127	Bobby Castillo	.10	.05	.01
☐ 128	Carlos Diaz	.10	.05	.01
☐ 129	Mariano Duncan	.30	.14	.04
☐ 130	Pedro Guerrero	.20	.09	.03
☐ 131	Orel Hershiser	.30	.14	.04
☐ 132	Rick Honeycutt	.10	.05	.01
☐ 133	Ken Howell	.10	.05	.01
☐ 134	Ken Landreaux	.10	.05	.01
☐ 135	Bill Madlock	.10	.05	.01
☐ 136	Candy Maldonado	.10	.05	.01
☐ 137	Mike Marshall	.10	.05	.01
☐ 138	Len Matuszek	.10	.05	.01
☐ 139	Tom Niedenfuer	.10	.05	.01
☐ 140	Alejandro Pena	.10	.05	.01
☐ 141	Jerry Reuss	.10	.05	.01
☐ 142	Bill Russell	.10	.05	.01
☐ 143	Steve Sax	.10	.05	.01
☐ 144	Mike Scioscia	.10	.05	.01
☐ 145	Fernando Valenzuela	.20	.09	.03
☐ 146	Bob Welch	.10	.05	.01
☐ 147	Terry Whitfield	.10	.05	.01
☐ 148	Juan Beniquez	.10	.05	.01
☐ 149	Bob Boone	.20	.09	.03
☐ 150	John Candelaria	.10	.05	.01
☐ 151	Rod Carew	.50	.23	.06
☐ 152	Stewart Cliburn	.10	.05	.01
☐ 153	Doug DeCinces	.10	.05	.01
☐ 154	Brian Downing	.10	.05	.01
☐ 155	Ken Forsch	.10	.05	.01
☐ 156	Craig Gerber	.10	.05	.01
☐ 157	Bobby Grich	.20	.09	.03
☐ 158	George Hendrick	.10	.05	.01
☐ 159	Al Holland	.10	.05	.01
☐ 160	Reggie Jackson	.75	.35	.09
☐ 161	Ruppert Jones	.10	.05	.01
☐ 162	Urbano Lugo	.10	.05	.01
☐ 163	Kirk McCaskill	.20	.09	.03
☐ 164	Donnie Moore	.10	.05	.01
☐ 165	Gary Pettis	.10	.05	.01
☐ 166	Ron Romanick	.10	.05	.01
☐ 167	Dick Schofield	.10	.05	.01
☐ 168	Daryl Sconiers	.10	.05	.01
☐ 169	Jim Slaton	.10	.05	.01
☐ 170	Don Sutton	.30	.14	.04
☐ 171	Mike Witt	.10	.05	.01
☐ 172	Buddy Bell	.20	.09	.03
☐ 173	Tom Browning	.10	.05	.01
☐ 174	Dave Concepcion	.20	.09	.03
☐ 175	Eric Davis	.30	.14	.04
☐ 176	Bo Diaz	.10	.05	.01
☐ 177	Nick Esasky	.10	.05	.01
☐ 178	John Franco	.20	.09	.03
☐ 179	Tom Hume	.10	.05	.01
☐ 180	Wayne Krenchicki	.10	.05	.01
☐ 181	Andy McGaffigan	.10	.05	.01
☐ 182	Eddie Milner	.10	.05	.01
☐ 183	Ron Oester	.10	.05	.01
☐ 184	Dave Parker	.30	.14	.04
☐ 185	Frank Pastore	.10	.05	.01

□ 186	Tony Perez	.30	.14	.04
□ 187	Ted Power	.10	.05	.01
□ 188	Joe Price	.10	.05	.01
□ 189	Gary Redus	.10	.05	.01
□ 190	Ron Robinson	.10	.05	.01
□ 191	Pete Rose	.75	.35	.09
□ 192	Mario Soto	.10	.05	.01
□ 193	John Stuper	.10	.05	.01
□ 194	Jay Tibbs	.10	.05	.01
□ 195	Dave Van Gorder	.10	.05	.01
□ 196	Max Venable	.10	.05	.01
□ 197	Juan Agosto	.10	.05	.01
□ 198	Harold Baines	.20	.09	.03
□ 199	Floyd Bannister	.10	.05	.01
□ 200	Britt Burns	.10	.05	.01
□ 201	Julio Cruz	.10	.05	.01
□ 202	Joel Davis	.10	.05	.01
□ 203	Richard Dotson	.10	.05	.01
□ 204	Carlton Fisk	.30	.14	.04
□ 205	Scott Fletcher	.10	.05	.01
□ 206	Ozzie Guillen	.30	.14	.04
□ 207	Jerry Hairston	.10	.05	.01
□ 208	Tim Hulett	.10	.05	.01
□ 209	Bob James	.10	.05	.01
□ 210	Ron Kittle	.10	.05	.01
□ 211	Rudy Law	.10	.05	.01
□ 212	Bryan Little	.10	.05	.01
□ 213	Gene Nelson	.10	.05	.01
□ 214	Reid Nichols	.10	.05	.01
□ 215	Luis Salazar	.10	.05	.01
□ 216	Tom Seaver	.50	.23	.06
□ 217	Dan Spillner	.10	.05	.01
□ 218	Bruce Tanner	.10	.05	.01
□ 219	Greg Walker	.10	.05	.01
□ 220	Dave Wehrmeister	.10	.05	.01
□ 221	Juan Berenguer	.10	.05	.01
□ 222	Dave Bergman	.10	.05	.01
□ 223	Tom Brookens	.10	.05	.01
□ 224	Darrell Evans	.20	.09	.03
□ 225	Barbaro Garbey	.10	.05	.01
□ 226	Kirk Gibson	.20	.09	.03
□ 227	John Grubb	.10	.05	.01
□ 228	Willie Hernandez	.10	.05	.01
□ 229	Larry Herndon	.10	.05	.01
□ 230	Chet Lemon	.10	.05	.01
□ 231	Aurelio Lopez	.10	.05	.01
□ 232	Jack Morris	.20	.09	.03
□ 233	Randy O'Neal	.10	.05	.01
□ 234	Lance Parrish	.20	.09	.03
□ 235	Dan Petry	.10	.05	.01
□ 236	Alejandro Sanchez	.10	.05	.01
□ 237	Bill Scherrer	.10	.05	.01
□ 238	Nelson Simmons	.10	.05	.01
□ 239	Frank Tanana	.10	.05	.01
□ 240	Walt Terrell	.10	.05	.01
□ 241	Alan Trammell	.30	.14	.04
□ 242	Lou Whitaker	.30	.14	.04
□ 243	Milt Wilcox	.10	.05	.01
□ 244	Hubie Brooks	.10	.05	.01
□ 245	Tim Burke	.10	.05	.01
□ 246	Andre Dawson	.30	.14	.04
□ 247	Mike Fitzgerald	.10	.05	.01
□ 248	Terry Francona	.10	.05	.01
□ 249	Bill Gullickson	.10	.05	.01
□ 250	Joe Hesketh	.10	.05	.01
□ 251	Bill Laskey	.10	.05	.01
□ 252	Vance Law	.10	.05	.01
□ 253	Charlie Lea	.10	.05	.01
□ 254	Gary Lucas	.10	.05	.01
□ 255	David Palmer	.10	.05	.01
□ 256	Tim Raines	.30	.14	.04
□ 257	Jeff Reardon	.20	.09	.03
□ 258	Bert Roberge	.10	.05	.01
□ 259	Dan Schatzeder	.10	.05	.01
□ 260	Bryn Smith	.10	.05	.01
□ 261	Randy St.Claire	.10	.05	.01
□ 262	Scot Thompson	.10	.05	.01
□ 263	Tim Wallach	.10	.05	.01
□ 264	U.L. Washington	.10	.05	.01
□ 265	Mitch Webster	.10	.05	.01
□ 266	Herm Winningham	.10	.05	.01
□ 267	Floyd Youmans	.10	.05	.01
□ 268	Don Aase	.10	.05	.01
□ 269	Mike Boddicker	.10	.05	.01
□ 270	Rich Dauer	.10	.05	.01
□ 271	Storm Davis	.10	.05	.01
□ 272	Rick Dempsey	.10	.05	.01
□ 273	Ken Dixon	.10	.05	.01
□ 274	Jim Dwyer	.10	.05	.01
□ 275	Mike Flanagan	.10	.05	.01
□ 276	Wayne Gross	.10	.05	.01
□ 277	Lee Lacy	.10	.05	.01
□ 278	Fred Lynn	.20	.09	.03
□ 279	Tippy Martinez	.10	.05	.01
□ 280	Dennis Martinez	.20	.09	.03
□ 281	Scott McGregor	.10	.05	.01
□ 282	Eddie Murray	1.25	.55	.16
□ 283	Floyd Rayford	.10	.05	.01
□ 284	Cal Ripken	5.00	2.20	.60
□ 285	Gary Roenicke	.10	.05	.01
□ 286	Larry Sheets	.10	.05	.01
□ 287	John Shelby	.10	.05	.01
□ 288	Nate Snell	.10	.05	.01
□ 289	Sammy Stewart	.10	.05	.01
□ 290	Alan Wiggins	.10	.05	.01
□ 291	Mike Young	.10	.05	.01
□ 292	Alan Ashby	.10	.05	.01
□ 293	Mark Bailey	.10	.05	.01
□ 294	Kevin Bass	.10	.05	.01
□ 295	Jeff Calhoun	.10	.05	.01
□ 296	Jose Cruz	.10	.05	.01
□ 297	Glenn Davis	.20	.09	.03
□ 298	Bill Dawley	.10	.05	.01
□ 299	Frank DiPino	.10	.05	.01
□ 300	Bill Doran	.10	.05	.01
□ 301	Phil Garner	.10	.05	.01
□ 302	Jeff Heathcock	.10	.05	.01
□ 303	Charlie Kerfeld	.10	.05	.01
□ 304	Bob Knepper	.10	.05	.01
□ 305	Ron Mathis	.10	.05	.01
□ 306	Jerry Mumphrey	.10	.05	.01
□ 307	Jim Pankovits	.10	.05	.01
□ 308	Terry Puhl	.10	.05	.01
□ 309	Craig Reynolds	.10	.05	.01
□ 310	Nolan Ryan	5.00	2.20	.60
□ 311	Mike Scott	.10	.05	.01
□ 312	Dave Smith	.10	.05	.01
□ 313	Dickie Thon	.10	.05	.01
□ 314	Denny Walling	.10	.05	.01
□ 315	Kurt Bevacqua	.10	.05	.01
□ 316	Al Bumbry	.10	.05	.01
□ 317	Jerry Davis	.10	.05	.01
□ 318	Luis DeLeon	.10	.05	.01
□ 319	Dave Dravecky	.20	.09	.03
□ 320	Tim Flannery	.10	.05	.01
□ 321	Steve Garvey	.30	.14	.04
□ 322	Rich Gossage	.30	.14	.04
□ 323	Tony Gwynn	2.50	1.10	.30
□ 324	Andy Hawkins	.10	.05	.01
□ 325	LaMarr Hoyt	.10	.05	.01
□ 326	Roy Lee Jackson	.10	.05	.01
□ 327	Terry Kennedy	.10	.05	.01
□ 328	Craig Lefferts	.10	.05	.01
□ 329	Carmelo Martinez	.10	.05	.01
□ 330	Lance McCullers	.10	.05	.01
□ 331	Kevin McReynolds	.20	.09	.03
□ 332	Graig Nettles	.20	.09	.03
□ 333	Jerry Royster	.10	.05	.01
□ 334	Eric Show	.10	.05	.01
□ 335	Tim Stoddard	.10	.05	.01
□ 336	Garry Templeton	.10	.05	.01
□ 337	Mark Thurmond	.10	.05	.01
□ 338	Ed Wojna	.10	.05	.01
□ 339	Tony Armas	.10	.05	.01
□ 340	Marty Barrett	.10	.05	.01
□ 341	Wade Boggs	1.00	.45	.12
□ 342	Dennis Boyd	.10	.05	.01
□ 343	Bill Buckner	.20	.09	.03
□ 344	Mark Clear	.10	.05	.01
□ 345	Roger Clemens	2.50	1.10	.30
□ 346	Steve Crawford	.10	.05	.01
□ 347	Mike Easler	.10	.05	.01
□ 348	Dwight Evans	.20	.09	.03
□ 349	Rich Gedman	.10	.05	.01
□ 350	Jackie Gutierrez	.10	.05	.01
□ 351	Glenn Hoffman	.10	.05	.01
□ 352	Bruce Hurst	.10	.05	.01
□ 353	Bruce Kison	.10	.05	.01
□ 354	Tim Lollar	.10	.05	.01
□ 355	Steve Lyons	.10	.05	.01
□ 356	Al Nipper	.10	.05	.01
□ 357	Bob Ojeda	.10	.05	.01

□ 358	Jim Rice	.30	.14	.04
□ 359	Bob Stanley	.10	.05	.01
□ 360	Mike Trujillo	.10	.05	.01
□ 361	Thad Bosley	.10	.05	.01
□ 362	Warren Brusstar	.10	.05	.01
□ 363	Ron Cey	.20	.09	.03
□ 364	Jody Davis	.10	.05	.01
□ 365	Bob Dernier	.10	.05	.01
□ 366	Shawon Dunston	.20	.09	.03
□ 367	Leon Durham	.10	.05	.01
□ 368	Dennis Eckersley	.20	.09	.03
□ 369	Ray Fontenot	.10	.05	.01
□ 370	George Frazier	.10	.05	.01
□ 371	Billy Hatcher	.20	.09	.03
□ 372	Dave Lopes	.20	.09	.03
□ 373	Gary Matthews	.10	.05	.01
□ 374	Ron Meridith	.10	.05	.01
□ 375	Keith Moreland	.10	.05	.01
□ 376	Reggie Patterson	.10	.05	.01
□ 377	Dick Ruthven	.10	.05	.01
□ 378	Ryne Sandberg	2.00	.90	.25
□ 379	Scott Sanderson	.10	.05	.01
□ 380	Lee Smith	.30	.14	.04
□ 381	Lary Sorensen	.10	.05	.01
□ 382	Chris Speier	.10	.05	.01
□ 383	Rick Sutcliffe	.10	.05	.01
□ 384	Steve Trout	.10	.05	.01
□ 385	Gary Woods	.10	.05	.01
□ 386	Bert Blyleven	.30	.14	.04
□ 387	Tom Brunansky	.10	.05	.01
□ 388	Randy Bush	.10	.05	.01
□ 389	John Butcher	.10	.05	.01
□ 390	Ron Davis	.10	.05	.01
□ 391	Dave Engle	.10	.05	.01
□ 392	Frank Eufemia	.10	.05	.01
□ 393	Pete Filson	.10	.05	.01
□ 394	Gary Gaetti	.20	.09	.03
□ 395	Greg Gagne	.20	.09	.03
□ 396	Mickey Hatcher	.10	.05	.01
□ 397	Kent Hrbek	.30	.14	.04
□ 398	Tim Laudner	.10	.05	.01
□ 399	Rick Lysander	.10	.05	.01
□ 400	Dave Meier	.10	.05	.01
□ 401	Kirby Puckett UER (Card has him in NL, should be AL)	5.00	2.20	.60
□ 402	Mark Salas	.10	.05	.01
□ 403	Ken Schrom	.10	.05	.01
□ 404	Roy Smalley	.10	.05	.01
□ 405	Mike Smithson	.10	.05	.01
□ 406	Mike Stenhouse	.10	.05	.01
□ 407	Tim Teufel	.10	.05	.01
□ 408	Frank Viola	.10	.05	.01
□ 409	Ron Washington	.10	.05	.01
□ 410	Keith Atherton	.10	.05	.01
□ 411	Dusty Baker	.20	.09	.03
□ 412	Tim Birtsas	.10	.05	.01
□ 413	Bruce Bochte	.10	.05	.01
□ 414	Chris Codiroli	.10	.05	.01
□ 415	Dave Collins	.10	.05	.01
□ 416	Mike Davis	.10	.05	.01
□ 417	Alfredo Griffin	.10	.05	.01
□ 418	Mike Heath	.10	.05	.01
□ 419	Steve Henderson	.10	.05	.01
□ 420	Donnie Hill	.10	.05	.01
□ 421	Jay Howell	.10	.05	.01
□ 422	Tommy John	.30	.14	.04
□ 423	Dave Kingman	.20	.09	.03
□ 424	Bill Krueger	.10	.05	.01
□ 425	Rick Langford	.10	.05	.01
□ 426	Carney Lansford	.20	.09	.03
□ 427	Steve McCatty	.10	.05	.01
□ 428	Dwayne Murphy	.10	.05	.01
□ 429	Steve Ontiveros	.20	.09	.03
□ 430	Tony Phillips	.30	.14	.04
□ 431	Jose Rijo	.30	.14	.04
□ 432	Mickey Tettleton	2.00	.90	.25
□ 433	Luis Aguayo	.10	.05	.01
□ 434	Larry Andersen	.10	.05	.01
□ 435	Steve Carlton	.50	.23	.06
□ 436	Don Carman	.10	.05	.01
□ 437	Tim Corcoran	.10	.05	.01
□ 438	Darren Daulton	2.50	1.10	.30
□ 439	John Denny	.10	.05	.01
□ 440	Tom Foley	.10	.05	.01
□ 441	Greg Gross	.10	.05	.01
□ 442	Kevin Gross	.10	.05	.01
□ 443	Von Hayes	.10	.05	.01
□ 444	Charles Hudson	.10	.05	.01
□ 445	Garry Maddox	.10	.05	.01
□ 446	Shane Rawley	.10	.05	.01
□ 447	Dave Rucker	.10	.05	.01
□ 448	John Russell	.10	.05	.01
□ 449	Juan Samuel	.10	.05	.01
□ 450	Mike Schmidt	1.00	.45	.12
□ 451	Rick Schu	.10	.05	.01
□ 452	Dave Shipanoff	.10	.05	.01
□ 453	Dave Stewart	.20	.09	.03
□ 454	Jeff Stone	.10	.05	.01
□ 455	Kent Tekulve	.10	.05	.01
□ 456	Ozzie Virgil	.10	.05	.01
□ 457	Glenn Wilson	.10	.05	.01
□ 458	Jim Beattie	.10	.05	.01
□ 459	Karl Best	.10	.05	.01
□ 460	Barry Bonnell	.10	.05	.01
□ 461	Phil Bradley	.10	.05	.01
□ 462	Ivan Calderon	.20	.09	.03
□ 463	Al Cowens	.10	.05	.01
□ 464	Alvin Davis	.10	.05	.01
□ 465	Dave Henderson	.10	.05	.01
□ 466	Bob Kearney	.10	.05	.01
□ 467	Mark Langston	.30	.14	.04
□ 468	Bob Long	.10	.05	.01
□ 469	Mike Moore	.10	.05	.01
□ 470	Edwin Nunez	.10	.05	.01
□ 471	Spike Owen	.10	.05	.01
□ 472	Jack Perconte	.10	.05	.01
□ 473	Jim Presley	.10	.05	.01
□ 474	Donnie Scott	.10	.05	.01
□ 475	Bill Swift	.20	.09	.03
□ 476	Danny Tartabull	.20	.09	.03
□ 477	Gorman Thomas	.10	.05	.01
□ 478	Roy Thomas	.10	.05	.01
□ 479	Ed VandeBerg	.10	.05	.01
□ 480	Frank Wills	.10	.05	.01
□ 481	Matt Young	.10	.05	.01
□ 482	Ray Burris	.10	.05	.01
□ 483	Jaime Cocanower	.10	.05	.01
□ 484	Cecil Cooper	.20	.09	.03
□ 485	Danny Darwin	.10	.05	.01
□ 486	Rollie Fingers	.30	.14	.04
□ 487	Jim Gantner	.10	.05	.01
□ 488	Bob L. Gibson	.10	.05	.01
□ 489	Moose Haas	.10	.05	.01
□ 490	Teddy Higuera	.20	.09	.03
□ 491	Paul Householder	.10	.05	.01
□ 492	Pete Ladd	.10	.05	.01
□ 493	Rick Manning	.10	.05	.01
□ 494	Bob McClure	.10	.05	.01
□ 495	Paul Molitor	1.00	.45	.12
□ 496	Charlie Moore	.10	.05	.01
□ 497	Ben Oglivie	.10	.05	.01
□ 498	Randy Ready	.10	.05	.01
□ 499	Earnie Riles	.10	.05	.01
□ 500	Ed Romero	.10	.05	.01
□ 501	Bill Schroeder	.10	.05	.01
□ 502	Ray Searage	.10	.05	.01
□ 503	Ted Simmons	.20	.09	.03
□ 504	Pete Vuckovich	.10	.05	.01
□ 505	Rick Waits	.10	.05	.01
□ 506	Robin Yount	.75	.35	.09
□ 507	Len Barker	.10	.05	.01
□ 508	Steve Bedrosian	.10	.05	.01
□ 509	Bruce Benedict	.10	.05	.01
□ 510	Rick Camp	.10	.05	.01
□ 511	Rick Cerone	.10	.05	.01
□ 512	Chris Chambliss	.20	.09	.03
□ 513	Jeff Dedmon	.10	.05	.01
□ 514	Terry Forster	.10	.05	.01
□ 515	Gene Garber	.10	.05	.01
□ 516	Terry Harper	.10	.05	.01
□ 517	Bob Horner	.10	.05	.01
□ 518	Glenn Hubbard	.10	.05	.01
□ 519	Joe Johnson	.10	.05	.01
□ 520	Brad Komminsk	.10	.05	.01
□ 521	Rick Mahler	.10	.05	.01
□ 522	Dale Murphy	.30	.14	.04
□ 523	Ken Oberkfell	.10	.05	.01
□ 524	Pascual Perez	.10	.05	.01
□ 525	Gerald Perry	.10	.05	.01
□ 526	Rafael Ramirez	.10	.05	.01
□ 527	Steve Shields	.10	.05	.01

□ 528	Zane Smith	.10	.05	.01
□ 529	Bruce Sutter	.20	.09	.03
□ 530	Milt Thompson	.20	.09	.03
□ 531	Claudell Washington	.10	.05	.01
□ 532	Paul Zuvella	.10	.05	.01
□ 533	Vida Blue	.20	.09	.03
□ 534	Bob Brenly	.10	.05	.01
□ 535	Chris Brown	.10	.05	.01
□ 536	Chili Davis	.30	.14	.04
□ 537	Mark Davis	.10	.05	.01
□ 538	Rob Deer	.20	.09	.03
□ 539	Dan Driessen	.10	.05	.01
□ 540	Scott Garrelts	.10	.05	.01
□ 541	Dan Gladden	.10	.05	.01
□ 542	Jim Gott	.10	.05	.01
□ 543	David Green	.10	.05	.01
□ 544	Atlee Hammaker	.10	.05	.01
□ 545	Mike Jeffcoat	.10	.05	.01
□ 546	Mike Krukow	.10	.05	.01
□ 547	Dave LaPoint	.10	.05	.01
□ 548	Jeff Leonard	.10	.05	.01
□ 549	Greg Minton	.10	.05	.01
□ 550	Alex Trevino	.10	.05	.01
□ 551	Manny Trillo	.10	.05	.01
□ 552	Jose Uribe	.10	.05	.01
□ 553	Brad Wellman	.10	.05	.01
□ 554	Frank Williams	.10	.05	.01
□ 555	Joel Youngblood	.10	.05	.01
□ 556	Alan Bannister	.10	.05	.01
□ 557	Glenn Brummer	.10	.05	.01
□ 558	Steve Buechele	.20	.09	.03
□ 559	Jose Guzman	.10	.05	.01
□ 560	Toby Harrah	.10	.05	.01
□ 561	Greg Harris	.10	.05	.01
□ 562	Dwayne Henry	.10	.05	.01
□ 563	Burt Hooton	.10	.05	.01
□ 564	Charlie Hough	.20	.09	.03
□ 565	Mike Mason	.10	.05	.01
□ 566	Oddibe McDowell	.10	.05	.01
□ 567	Dickie Noles	.10	.05	.01
□ 568	Pete O'Brien	.10	.05	.01
□ 569	Larry Parrish	.10	.05	.01
□ 570	Dave Rozema	.10	.05	.01
□ 571	Dave Schmidt	.10	.05	.01
□ 572	Don Slaught	.10	.05	.01
□ 573	Wayne Tolleson	.10	.05	.01
□ 574	Duane Walker	.10	.05	.01
□ 575	Gary Ward	.10	.05	.01
□ 576	Chris Welsh	.10	.05	.01
□ 577	Curtis Wilkerson	.10	.05	.01
□ 578	George Wright	.10	.05	.01
□ 579	Chris Bando	.10	.05	.01
□ 580	Tony Bernazard	.10	.05	.01
□ 581	Brett Butler	.30	.14	.04
□ 582	Ernie Camacho	.10	.05	.01
□ 583	Joe Carter	2.50	1.10	.30
□ 584	Carmen Castillo	.10	.05	.01
□ 585	Jamie Easterly	.10	.05	.01
□ 586	Julio Franco	.30	.14	.04
□ 587	Mel Hall	.10	.05	.01
□ 588	Mike Hargrove	.20	.09	.03
□ 589	Neal Heaton	.10	.05	.01
□ 590	Brook Jacoby	.10	.05	.01
□ 591	Otis Nixon	.30	.14	.04
□ 592	Jerry Reed	.10	.05	.01
□ 593	Vern Ruhle	.10	.05	.01
□ 594	Pat Tabler	.10	.05	.01
□ 595	Rich Thompson	.10	.05	.01
□ 596	Andre Thornton	.10	.05	.01
□ 597	Dave Von Ohlen	.10	.05	.01
□ 598	George Vukovich	.10	.05	.01
□ 599	Tom Waddell	.10	.05	.01
□ 600	Curt Wardle	.10	.05	.01
□ 601	Jerry Willard	.10	.05	.01
□ 602	Bill Almon	.10	.05	.01
□ 603	Mike Bielecki	.10	.05	.01
□ 604	Sid Bream	.10	.05	.01
□ 605	Mike C. Brown	.10	.05	.01
□ 606	Pat Clements	.10	.05	.01
□ 607	Jose DeLeon	.10	.05	.01
□ 608	Denny Gonzalez	.10	.05	.01
□ 609	Cecilio Guante	.10	.05	.01
□ 610	Steve Kemp	.10	.05	.01
□ 611	Sammy Khalifa	.10	.05	.01
□ 612	Lee Mazzilli	.10	.05	.01
□ 613	Larry McWilliams	.10	.05	.01
□ 614	Jim Morrison	.10	.05	.01
□ 615	Joe Orsulak	.10	.05	.01
□ 616	Tony Pena	.10	.05	.01
□ 617	Johnny Ray	.10	.05	.01
□ 618	Rick Reuschel	.10	.05	.01
□ 619	R.J. Reynolds	.10	.05	.01
□ 620	Rick Rhoden	.10	.05	.01
□ 621	Don Robinson	.10	.05	.01
□ 622	Jason Thompson	.10	.05	.01
□ 623	Lee Tunnell	.10	.05	.01
□ 624	Jim Winn	.10	.05	.01
□ 625	Marvell Wynne	.10	.05	.01
□ 626	Dwight Gooden IA	.30	.14	.04
□ 627	Don Mattingly IA	1.25	.55	.16
□ 628	4192 (Pete Rose)	.50	.23	.06
□ 629	3000 Career Hits	.30	.14	.04
	Rod Carew			
□ 630	300 Career Wins	.30	.14	.04
	Tom Seaver			
	Phil Niekro			
□ 631	Ouch (Don Baylor)	.20	.09	.03
□ 632	Instant Offense	.30	.14	.04
	Darryl Strawberry			
	Tim Raines			
□ 633	Shortstops Supreme	2.00	.90	.25
	Cal Ripken			
	Alan Trammell			
□ 634	Boggs and "Hero"	1.25	.55	.16
	Wade Boggs			
	George Brett			
□ 635	Braves Dynamic Duo	.20	.09	.03
	Bob Horner			
	Dale Murphy			
□ 636	Cardinal Ignitors	.20	.09	.03
	Willie McGee			
	Vince Coleman			
□ 637	Terror on Basepaths	.20	.09	.03
	Vince Coleman			
□ 638	Charlie Hustle / Dr.K	.50	.23	.06
	Pete Rose			
	Dwight Gooden			
□ 639	1984 and 1985 AL	1.00	.45	.12
	Batting Champs			
	Wade Boggs			
	Don Mattingly			
□ 640	NL West Sluggers	.20	.09	.03
	Dale Murphy			
	Steve Garvey			
	Dave Parker			
□ 641	Staff Aces	.20	.09	.03
	Fernando Valenzuela			
	Dwight Gooden			
□ 642	Blue Jay Stoppers	.30	.14	.04
	Jimmy Key			
	Dave Stieb			
□ 643	AL All-Star Backstops	.20	.09	.03
	Carlton Fisk			
	Rich Gedman			
□ 644	Gene Walter and	.50	.23	.06
	Benito Santiago			
□ 645	Mike Woodard and	.10	.05	.01
	Colin Ward			
□ 646	Kal Daniels and	2.00	.90	.25
	Paul O'Neill			
□ 647	Andres Galarraga and	5.00	2.20	.60
	Fred Toliver			
□ 648	Bob Kipper and	.10	.05	.01
	Curt Ford			
□ 649	Jose Canseco and	10.00	4.50	1.25
	Eric Plunk			
□ 650	Mark McLemore and	.50	.23	.06
	Gus Polidor			
□ 651	Rob Woodward and	.10	.05	.01
	Mickey Brantley			
□ 652	Billy Joe Robidoux and	.10	.05	.01
	Mark Funderburk			
□ 653	Cecil Fielder and	5.00	2.20	.60
	Cory Snyder			
□ 654	CL: Royals/Cardinals	.20	.09	.03
	Blue Jays/Mets			
□ 655	CL: Yankees/Dodgers	.20	.09	.03
	Angels/Reds UER			
	(168 Darly Sconiers)			
□ 656	CL: White Sox/Tigers	.20	.09	.03
	Expos/Orioles			
	(279 Dennis,			

	280 Tippy)			
□ 657	CL: Astros/Padres	.20	.09	.03
	Red Sox/Cubs			
□ 658	CL: Twins/A's	.20	.09	.03
	Phillies/Mariners			
□ 659	CL: Brewers/Braves	.20	.09	.03
	Giants/Rangers			
□ 660	CL: Indians/Pirates	.20	.09	.03
	Special Cards			

1986 Fleer All-Stars

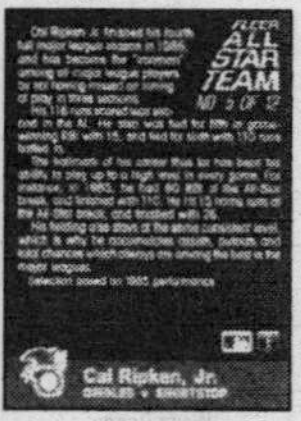

Randomly inserted in wax and cello packs, this 12-card standard-size set features top stars. The cards feature red backgrounds (American Leaguers) and blue backgrounds (National Leaguers). The 12 selections cover each position, left and right-handed starting pitchers, a reliever, and a designated hitter.

	MINT	NRMT	EXC
COMPLETE SET (12)	30.00	13.50	3.70
COMMON CARD (1-12)	.25	.11	.03
SEMISTARS	.50	.23	.06
RANDOM INSERTS IN PACKS			

□ 1	Don Mattingly	6.00	2.70	.75
□ 2	Tom Herr	.25	.11	.03
□ 3	George Brett	6.00	2.70	.75
□ 4	Gary Carter	.50	.23	.06
□ 5	Cal Ripken	15.00	6.75	1.85
□ 6	Dave Parker	.35	.16	.04
□ 7	Rickey Henderson UER (Misspelled Ricky on card back)	2.50	1.10	.30
□ 8	Pedro Guerrero	.35	.16	.04
□ 9	Dan Quisenberry	.25	.11	.03
□ 10	Dwight Gooden	1.50	.70	.19
□ 11	Gorman Thomas	.25	.11	.03
□ 12	John Tudor	.25	.11	.03

1986 Fleer Future Hall of Famers

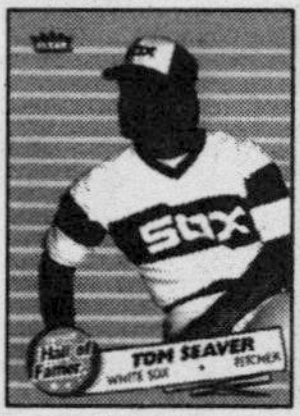

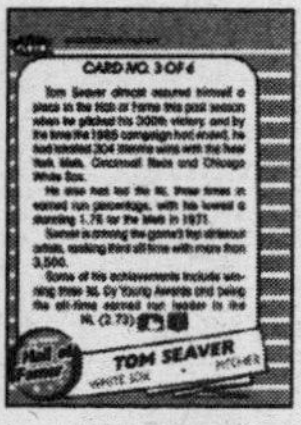

These six standard-size cards were issued one per Fleer three-packs. This set features players that Fleer predicts will be "Future Hall of Famers." The card backs describe career highlights, records, and honors won by the player.

	MINT	NRMT	EXC
COMPLETE SET (6)	18.00	8.00	2.20
COMMON CARD (1-6)	2.00	.90	.25
ONE PER RACK PACK			

□ 1	Pete Rose	3.00	1.35	.35
□ 2	Steve Carlton	2.00	.90	.25
□ 3	Tom Seaver	2.00	.90	.25
□ 4	Rod Carew	2.00	.90	.25
□ 5	Nolan Ryan	10.00	4.50	1.25
□ 6	Reggie Jackson	2.50	1.10	.30

1986 Fleer Update

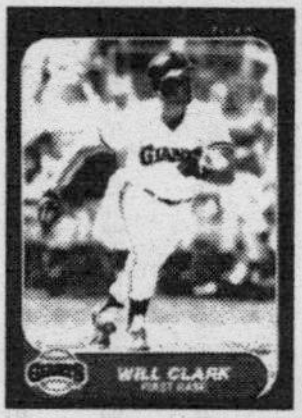

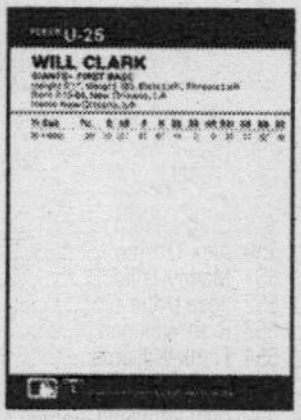

This 132-card standard-size set was distributed in factory set form through hobby dealers. In addition to the complete set of 132 cards, the box also contains 25 Team Logo Stickers. The card fronts look very similar to the 1986 Fleer regular issue. The cards are numbered (with a U prefix) alphabetically according to player's last name. The extended Rookie Cards in this set include Barry Bonds, Bobby Bonilla, Will Clark, Wally Joyner, John Kruk, Kevin Mitchell, and Ruben Sierra.

	MINT	NRMT	EXC
COMPLETE FACT.SET (132)	15.00	6.75	1.85
COMMON CARD (1-132)	.07	.03	.01
SEMISTARS	.15	.07	.02
U PREFIX ON CARD NUMBER			

□ 1	Mike Aldrete	.07	.03	.01
□ 2	Andy Allanson	.07	.03	.01
□ 3	Neil Allen	.07	.03	.01
□ 4	Joaquin Andujar	.07	.03	.01
□ 5	Paul Assenmacher	.07	.03	.01
□ 6	Scott Bailes	.07	.03	.01
□ 7	Jay Baller	.07	.03	.01
□ 8	Scott Bankhead	.07	.03	.01
□ 9	Bill Bathe	.07	.03	.01
□ 10	Don Baylor	.40	.18	.05
□ 11	Billy Beane	.07	.03	.01
□ 12	Steve Bedrosian	.07	.03	.01
□ 13	Juan Beniquez	.07	.03	.01
□ 14	Barry Bonds	5.00	2.20	.60
□ 15	Bobby Bonilla UER (Wrong birthday)	1.00	.45	.12
□ 16	Rich Bordi	.07	.03	.01
□ 17	Bill Campbell	.07	.03	.01
□ 18	Tom Candiotti	.07	.03	.01
□ 19	John Cangelosi	.07	.03	.01
□ 20	Jose Canseco UER (Headings on back for a pitcher)	3.00	1.35	.35
□ 21	Chuck Cary	.07	.03	.01
□ 22	Juan Castillo	.07	.03	.01
□ 23	Rick Cerone	.07	.03	.01
□ 24	John Cerutti	.07	.03	.01
□ 25	Will Clark	2.50	1.10	.30
□ 26	Mark Clear	.07	.03	.01
□ 27	Darnell Coles	.07	.03	.01
□ 28	Dave Collins	.07	.03	.01
□ 29	Tim Conroy	.07	.03	.01
□ 30	Ed Correa	.07	.03	.01
□ 31	Joe Cowley	.07	.03	.01
□ 32	Bill Dawley	.07	.03	.01
□ 33	Rob Deer	.20	.09	.03
□ 34	John Denny	.07	.03	.01
□ 35	Jim Deshaies	.07	.03	.01
□ 36	Doug Drabek	.60	.25	.07

□ 37 Mike Easler	.07	.03	.01
□ 38 Mark Eichhorn	.07	.03	.01
□ 39 Dave Engle	.07	.03	.01
□ 40 Mike Fischlin	.07	.03	.01
□ 41 Scott Fletcher	.07	.03	.01
□ 42 Terry Forster	.07	.03	.01
□ 43 Terry Francona	.07	.03	.01
□ 44 Andres Galarraga	1.50	.70	.19
□ 45 Lee Guetterman	.07	.03	.01
□ 46 Bill Gullickson	.07	.03	.01
□ 47 Jackie Gutierrez	.07	.03	.01
□ 48 Moose Haas	.07	.03	.01
□ 49 Billy Hatcher	.20	.09	.03
□ 50 Mike Heath	.07	.03	.01
□ 51 Guy Hoffman	.07	.03	.01
□ 52 Tom Hume	.07	.03	.01
□ 53 Pete Incaviglia	.40	.18	.05
□ 54 Dane Iorg	.07	.03	.01
□ 55 Chris James	.07	.03	.01
□ 56 Stan Javier	.20	.09	.03
□ 57 Tommy John	.40	.18	.05
□ 58 Tracy Jones	.07	.03	.01
□ 59 Wally Joyner	1.00	.45	.12
□ 60 Wayne Krenchicki	.07	.03	.01
□ 61 John Kruk	.75	.35	.09
□ 62 Mike LaCoss	.07	.03	.01
□ 63 Pete Ladd	.07	.03	.01
□ 64 Dave LaPoint	.07	.03	.01
□ 65 Mike LaValliere	.07	.03	.01
□ 66 Rudy Law	.07	.03	.01
□ 67 Dennis Leonard	.07	.03	.01
□ 68 Steve Lombardozzi	.07	.03	.01
□ 69 Aurelio Lopez	.07	.03	.01
□ 70 Mickey Mahler	.07	.03	.01
□ 71 Candy Maldonado	.07	.03	.01
□ 72 Roger Mason	.07	.03	.01
□ 73 Greg Mathews	.07	.03	.01
□ 74 Andy McGaffigan	.07	.03	.01
□ 75 Joel McKeon	.07	.03	.01
□ 76 Kevin Mitchell	.40	.18	.05
□ 77 Bill Mooneyham	.07	.03	.01
□ 78 Omar Moreno	.07	.03	.01
□ 79 Jerry Mumphrey	.07	.03	.01
□ 80 Al Newman	.20	.09	.03
□ 81 Phil Niekro	.40	.18	.05
□ 82 Randy Niemann	.07	.03	.01
□ 83 Juan Nieves	.07	.03	.01
□ 84 Bob Ojeda	.07	.03	.01
□ 85 Rick Ownbey	.07	.03	.01
□ 86 Tom Paciorek	.07	.03	.01
□ 87 David Palmer	.07	.03	.01
□ 88 Jeff Parrett	.07	.03	.01
□ 89 Pat Perry	.07	.03	.01
□ 90 Dan Plesac	.07	.03	.01
□ 91 Darrell Porter	.07	.03	.01
□ 92 Luis Quinones	.07	.03	.01
□ 93 Rey Quinones UER (Misspelled Quinonez)	.07	.03	.01
□ 94 Gary Redus	.07	.03	.01
□ 95 Jeff Reed	.07	.03	.01
□ 96 Bip Roberts	.40	.18	.05
□ 97 Billy Joe Robidoux	.07	.03	.01
□ 98 Gary Roenicke	.07	.03	.01
□ 99 Ron Roenicke	.07	.03	.01
□ 100 Angel Salazar	.07	.03	.01
□ 101 Joe Sambito	.07	.03	.01
□ 102 Billy Sample	.07	.03	.01
□ 103 Dave Schmidt	.07	.03	.01
□ 104 Ken Schrom	.07	.03	.01
□ 105 Ruben Sierra	1.50	.70	.19
□ 106 Ted Simmons	.20	.09	.03
□ 107 Sammy Stewart	.07	.03	.01
□ 108 Kurt Stillwell	.07	.03	.01
□ 109 Dale Sveum	.07	.03	.01
□ 110 Tim Teufel	.07	.03	.01
□ 111 Bob Tewksbury	.20	.09	.03
□ 112 Andres Thomas	.07	.03	.01
□ 113 Jason Thompson	.07	.03	.01
□ 114 Milt Thompson	.20	.09	.03
□ 115 Robby Thompson	.20	.09	.03
□ 116 Jay Tibbs	.07	.03	.01
□ 117 Fred Toliver	.07	.03	.01
□ 118 Wayne Tolleson	.07	.03	.01
□ 119 Alex Trevino	.07	.03	.01
□ 120 Manny Trillo	.07	.03	.01
□ 121 Ed VandeBerg	.07	.03	.01
□ 122 Ozzie Virgil	.07	.03	.01
□ 123 Tony Walker	.07	.03	.01
□ 124 Gene Walter	.07	.03	.01
□ 125 Duane Ward	.20	.09	.03
□ 126 Jerry Willard	.07	.03	.01
□ 127 Mitch Williams	.20	.09	.03
□ 128 Reggie Williams	.07	.03	.01
□ 129 Bobby Witt	.20	.09	.03
□ 130 Marvell Wynne	.07	.03	.01
□ 131 Steve Yeager	.07	.03	.01
□ 132 Checklist 1-132	.07	.03	.01

1987 Fleer

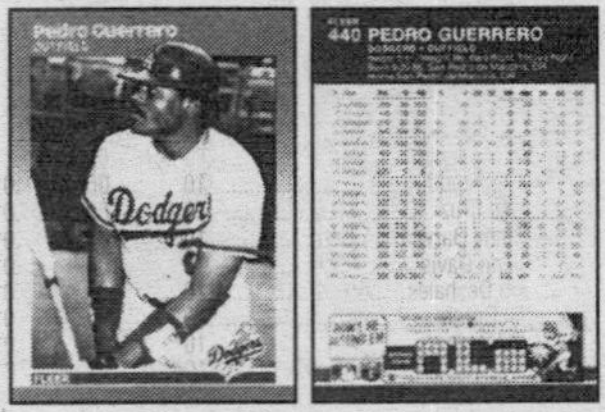

This set consists of 660 standard-size cards. Cards were primarily issued in 17-card wax packs, rack packs and hobby and retail factory sets. Card fronts feature a distinctive light blue and white blended border encasing a color photo. Cards are again organized numerically by teams with team ordering based on the previous seasons record. The last 36 cards in the set consist of Specials (625-643), Rookie Pairs (644-653), and checklists (654-660). The key Rookie Cards in this set are Barry Bonds, Bobby Bonilla, Will Clark, Chuck Finley, Bo Jackson, Wally Joyner, John Kruk, Barry Larkin, Kevin Mitchell, Kevin Seitzer, Ruben Sierra and Devon White.

	MINT	NRMT	EXC
COMPLETE SET (660)	50.00	22.00	6.25
COMPLETE FACT.SET (672)	50.00	22.00	6.25
COMMON CARD (1-660)	.10	.05	.01
SEMISTARS	.25	.11	.03
STARS	.60	.25	.07
COMP.WORLD SERIES SET (12)	2.00	.90	.25
ONE WORLD SERIES SET PER FACTORY SET			

□ 1 Rick Aguilera	.25	.11	.03
□ 2 Richard Anderson	.10	.05	.01
□ 3 Wally Backman	.10	.05	.01
□ 4 Gary Carter	.60	.25	.07
□ 5 Ron Darling	.10	.05	.01
□ 6 Len Dykstra	.25	.11	.03
□ 7 Kevin Elster	.60	.25	.07
□ 8 Sid Fernandez	.10	.05	.01
□ 9 Dwight Gooden	.60	.25	.07
□ 10 Ed Hearn	.10	.05	.01
□ 11 Danny Heep	.10	.05	.01
□ 12 Keith Hernandez	.25	.11	.03
□ 13 Howard Johnson	.10	.05	.01
□ 14 Ray Knight	.25	.11	.03
□ 15 Lee Mazzilli	.10	.05	.01
□ 16 Roger McDowell	.10	.05	.01
□ 17 Kevin Mitchell	.60	.25	.07
□ 18 Randy Niemann	.10	.05	.01
□ 19 Bob Ojeda	.10	.05	.01
□ 20 Jesse Orosco	.10	.05	.01
□ 21 Rafael Santana	.10	.05	.01
□ 22 Doug Sisk	.10	.05	.01
□ 23 Darryl Strawberry	.60	.25	.07
□ 24 Tim Teufel	.10	.05	.01
□ 25 Mookie Wilson	.25	.11	.03
□ 26 Tony Armas	.10	.05	.01
□ 27 Marty Barrett	.10	.05	.01
□ 28 Don Baylor	.60	.25	.07
□ 29 Wade Boggs	.60	.25	.07
□ 30 Oil Can Boyd	.10	.05	.01

□ 31	Bill Buckner	.25	.11	.03
□ 32	Roger Clemens	1.50	.70	.19
□ 33	Steve Crawford	.10	.05	.01
□ 34	Dwight Evans	.25	.11	.03
□ 35	Rich Gedman	.10	.05	.01
□ 36	Dave Henderson	.10	.05	.01
□ 37	Bruce Hurst	.10	.05	.01
□ 38	Tim Lollar	.10	.05	.01
□ 39	Al Nipper	.10	.05	.01
□ 40	Spike Owen	.10	.05	.01
□ 41	Jim Rice	.60	.25	.07
□ 42	Ed Romero	.10	.05	.01
□ 43	Joe Sambito	.10	.05	.01
□ 44	Calvin Schiraldi	.10	.05	.01
□ 45	Tom Seaver UER Lifetime saves total 0, should be 1	.60	.25	.07
□ 46	Jeff Sellers	.10	.05	.01
□ 47	Bob Stanley	.10	.05	.01
□ 48	Sammy Stewart	.10	.05	.01
□ 49	Larry Andersen	.10	.05	.01
□ 50	Alan Ashby	.10	.05	.01
□ 51	Kevin Bass	.10	.05	.01
□ 52	Jeff Calhoun	.10	.05	.01
□ 53	Jose Cruz	.10	.05	.01
□ 54	Danny Darwin	.10	.05	.01
□ 55	Glenn Davis	.10	.05	.01
□ 56	Jim Deshaies	.10	.05	.01
□ 57	Bill Doran	.10	.05	.01
□ 58	Phil Garner	.10	.05	.01
□ 59	Billy Hatcher	.10	.05	.01
□ 60	Charlie Kerfeld	.10	.05	.01
□ 61	Bob Knepper	.10	.05	.01
□ 62	Dave Lopes	.25	.11	.03
□ 63	Aurelio Lopez	.10	.05	.01
□ 64	Jim Pankovits	.10	.05	.01
□ 65	Terry Puhl	.10	.05	.01
□ 66	Craig Reynolds	.10	.05	.01
□ 67	Nolan Ryan	3.00	1.35	.35
□ 68	Mike Scott	.10	.05	.01
□ 69	Dave Smith	.10	.05	.01
□ 70	Dickie Thon	.10	.05	.01
□ 71	Tony Walker	.10	.05	.01
□ 72	Denny Walling	.10	.05	.01
□ 73	Bob Boone	.25	.11	.03
□ 74	Rick Burleson	.10	.05	.01
□ 75	John Candelaria	.10	.05	.01
□ 76	Doug Corbett	.10	.05	.01
□ 77	Doug DeCinces	.10	.05	.01
□ 78	Brian Downing	.10	.05	.01
□ 79	Chuck Finley	.75	.35	.09
□ 80	Terry Forster	.10	.05	.01
□ 81	Bob Grich	.25	.11	.03
□ 82	George Hendrick	.10	.05	.01
□ 83	Jack Howell	.10	.05	.01
□ 84	Reggie Jackson	.60	.25	.07
□ 85	Ruppert Jones	.10	.05	.01
□ 86	Wally Joyner	1.00	.45	.12
□ 87	Gary Lucas	.10	.05	.01
□ 88	Kirk McCaskill	.10	.05	.01
□ 89	Donnie Moore	.10	.05	.01
□ 90	Gary Pettis	.10	.05	.01
□ 91	Vern Ruhle	.10	.05	.01
□ 92	Dick Schofield	.10	.05	.01
□ 93	Don Sutton	.60	.25	.07
□ 94	Rob Wilfong	.10	.05	.01
□ 95	Mike Witt	.10	.05	.01
□ 96	Doug Drabek	.75	.35	.09
□ 97	Mike Easler	.10	.05	.01
□ 98	Mike Fischlin	.10	.05	.01
□ 99	Brian Fisher	.10	.05	.01
□ 100	Ron Guidry	.10	.05	.01
□ 101	Rickey Henderson	.60	.25	.07
□ 102	Tommy John	.25	.11	.03
□ 103	Ron Kittle	.10	.05	.01
□ 104	Don Mattingly	2.00	.90	.25
□ 105	Bobby Meacham	.10	.05	.01
□ 106	Joe Niekro	.10	.05	.01
□ 107	Mike Pagliarulo	.10	.05	.01
□ 108	Dan Pasqua	.10	.05	.01
□ 109	Willie Randolph	.25	.11	.03
□ 110	Dennis Rasmussen	.10	.05	.01
□ 111	Dave Righetti	.10	.05	.01
□ 112	Gary Roenicke	.10	.05	.01
□ 113	Rod Scurry	.10	.05	.01
□ 114	Bob Shirley	.10	.05	.01
□ 115	Joel Skinner	.10	.05	.01
□ 116	Tim Stoddard	.10	.05	.01
□ 117	Bob Tewksbury	.25	.11	.03
□ 118	Wayne Tolleson	.10	.05	.01
□ 119	Claudell Washington	.10	.05	.01
□ 120	Dave Winfield	.60	.25	.07
□ 121	Steve Buechele	.10	.05	.01
□ 122	Ed Correa	.10	.05	.01
□ 123	Scott Fletcher	.10	.05	.01
□ 124	Jose Guzman	.10	.05	.01
□ 125	Toby Harrah	.10	.05	.01
□ 126	Greg Harris	.10	.05	.01
□ 127	Charlie Hough	.10	.05	.01
□ 128	Pete Incaviglia	.25	.11	.03
□ 129	Mike Mason	.10	.05	.01
□ 130	Oddibe McDowell	.10	.05	.01
□ 131	Dale Mohorcic	.10	.05	.01
□ 132	Pete O'Brien	.10	.05	.01
□ 133	Tom Paciorek	.10	.05	.01
□ 134	Larry Parrish	.10	.05	.01
□ 135	Geno Petralli	.10	.05	.01
□ 136	Darrell Porter	.10	.05	.01
□ 137	Jeff Russell	.10	.05	.01
□ 138	Ruben Sierra	2.50	1.10	.30
□ 139	Don Slaught	.10	.05	.01
□ 140	Gary Ward	.10	.05	.01
□ 141	Curtis Wilkerson	.10	.05	.01
□ 142	Mitch Williams	.25	.11	.03
□ 143	Bobby Witt UER (Tulsa misspelled as Tusla; ERA should be 6.43, not .643)	.25	.11	.03
□ 144	Dave Bergman	.10	.05	.01
□ 145	Tom Brookens	.10	.05	.01
□ 146	Bill Campbell	.10	.05	.01
□ 147	Chuck Cary	.10	.05	.01
□ 148	Darnell Coles	.10	.05	.01
□ 149	Dave Collins	.10	.05	.01
□ 150	Darrell Evans	.25	.11	.03
□ 151	Kirk Gibson	.25	.11	.03
□ 152	John Grubb	.10	.05	.01
□ 153	Willie Hernandez	.10	.05	.01
□ 154	Larry Herndon	.10	.05	.01
□ 155	Eric King	.10	.05	.01
□ 156	Chet Lemon	.10	.05	.01
□ 157	Dwight Lowry	.10	.05	.01
□ 158	Jack Morris	.25	.11	.03
□ 159	Randy O'Neal	.10	.05	.01
□ 160	Lance Parrish	.25	.11	.03
□ 161	Dan Petry	.10	.05	.01
□ 162	Pat Sheridan	.10	.05	.01
□ 163	Jim Slaton	.10	.05	.01
□ 164	Frank Tanana	.10	.05	.01
□ 165	Walt Terrell	.10	.05	.01
□ 166	Mark Thurmond	.10	.05	.01
□ 167	Alan Trammell	.60	.25	.07
□ 168	Lou Whitaker	.60	.25	.07
□ 169	Luis Aguayo	.10	.05	.01
□ 170	Steve Bedrosian	.10	.05	.01
□ 171	Don Carman	.10	.05	.01
□ 172	Darren Daulton	.25	.11	.03
□ 173	Greg Gross	.10	.05	.01
□ 174	Kevin Gross	.10	.05	.01
□ 175	Von Hayes	.10	.05	.01
□ 176	Charles Hudson	.10	.05	.01
□ 177	Tom Hume	.10	.05	.01
□ 178	Steve Jeltz	.10	.05	.01
□ 179	Mike Maddux	.10	.05	.01
□ 180	Shane Rawley	.10	.05	.01
□ 181	Gary Redus	.10	.05	.01
□ 182	Ron Roenicke	.10	.05	.01
□ 183	Bruce Ruffin	.10	.05	.01
□ 184	John Russell	.10	.05	.01
□ 185	Juan Samuel	.10	.05	.01
□ 186	Dan Schatzeder	.10	.05	.01
□ 187	Mike Schmidt	.75	.35	.09
□ 188	Rick Schu	.10	.05	.01
□ 189	Jeff Stone	.10	.05	.01
□ 190	Kent Tekulve	.10	.05	.01
□ 191	Milt Thompson	.10	.05	.01
□ 192	Glenn Wilson	.10	.05	.01
□ 193	Buddy Bell	.25	.11	.03
□ 194	Tom Browning	.10	.05	.01
□ 195	Sal Butera	.10	.05	.01
□ 196	Dave Concepcion	.25	.11	.03
□ 197	Kal Daniels	.10	.05	.01
□ 198	Eric Davis	.60	.25	.07

□ 199 John Denny	.10	.05	.01
□ 200 Bo Diaz	.10	.05	.01
□ 201 Nick Esasky	.10	.05	.01
□ 202 John Franco	.10	.05	.01
□ 203 Bill Gullickson	.10	.05	.01
□ 204 Barry Larkin	6.00	2.70	.75
□ 205 Eddie Milner	.10	.05	.01
□ 206 Rob Murphy	.10	.05	.01
□ 207 Ron Oester	.10	.05	.01
□ 208 Dave Parker	.60	.25	.07
□ 209 Tony Perez	.60	.25	.07
□ 210 Ted Power	.10	.05	.01
□ 211 Joe Price	.10	.05	.01
□ 212 Ron Robinson	.10	.05	.01
□ 213 Pete Rose	.75	.35	.09
□ 214 Mario Soto	.10	.05	.01
□ 215 Kurt Stillwell	.10	.05	.01
□ 216 Max Venable	.10	.05	.01
□ 217 Chris Welsh	.10	.05	.01
□ 218 Carl Willis	.10	.05	.01
□ 219 Jesse Barfield	.10	.05	.01
□ 220 George Bell	.10	.05	.01
□ 221 Bill Caudill	.10	.05	.01
□ 222 John Cerutti	.10	.05	.01
□ 223 Jim Clancy	.10	.05	.01
□ 224 Mark Eichhorn	.10	.05	.01
□ 225 Tony Fernandez	.10	.05	.01
□ 226 Damaso Garcia	.10	.05	.01
□ 227 Kelly Gruber ERR (Wrong birth year)	.10	.05	.01
□ 228 Tom Henke	.10	.05	.01
□ 229 Garth Iorg	.10	.05	.01
□ 230 Joe Johnson	.10	.05	.01
□ 231 Cliff Johnson	.10	.05	.01
□ 232 Jimmy Key	.25	.11	.03
□ 233 Dennis Lamp	.10	.05	.01
□ 234 Rick Leach	.10	.05	.01
□ 235 Buck Martinez	.10	.05	.01
□ 236 Lloyd Moseby	.10	.05	.01
□ 237 Rance Mulliniks	.10	.05	.01
□ 238 Dave Stieb	.10	.05	.01
□ 239 Willie Upshaw	.10	.05	.01
□ 240 Ernie Whitt	.10	.05	.01
□ 241 Andy Allanson	.10	.05	.01
□ 242 Scott Bailes	.10	.05	.01
□ 243 Chris Bando	.10	.05	.01
□ 244 Tony Bernazard	.10	.05	.01
□ 245 John Butcher	.10	.05	.01
□ 246 Brett Butler	.25	.11	.03
□ 247 Ernie Camacho	.10	.05	.01
□ 248 Tom Candiotti	.10	.05	.01
□ 249 Joe Carter	.75	.35	.09
□ 250 Carmen Castillo	.10	.05	.01
□ 251 Julio Franco	.25	.11	.03
□ 252 Mel Hall	.10	.05	.01
□ 253 Brook Jacoby	.10	.05	.01
□ 254 Phil Niekro	.60	.25	.07
□ 255 Otis Nixon	.25	.11	.03
□ 256 Dickie Noles	.10	.05	.01
□ 257 Bryan Oelkers	.10	.05	.01
□ 258 Ken Schrom	.10	.05	.01
□ 259 Don Schulze	.10	.05	.01
□ 260 Cory Snyder	.10	.05	.01
□ 261 Pat Tabler	.10	.05	.01
□ 262 Andre Thornton	.10	.05	.01
□ 263 Rich Yett	.10	.05	.01
□ 264 Mike Aldrete	.25	.11	.03
□ 265 Juan Berenguer	.10	.05	.01
□ 266 Vida Blue	.25	.11	.03
□ 267 Bob Brenly	.10	.05	.01
□ 268 Chris Brown	.10	.05	.01
□ 269 Will Clark	5.00	2.20	.60
□ 270 Chili Davis	.25	.11	.03
□ 271 Mark Davis	.10	.05	.01
□ 272 Kelly Downs	.10	.05	.01
□ 273 Scott Garrelts	.10	.05	.01
□ 274 Dan Gladden	.10	.05	.01
□ 275 Mike Krukow	.10	.05	.01
□ 276 Randy Kutcher	.10	.05	.01
□ 277 Mike LaCoss	.10	.05	.01
□ 278 Jeff Leonard	.10	.05	.01
□ 279 Candy Maldonado	.10	.05	.01
□ 280 Roger Mason	.10	.05	.01
□ 281 Bob Melvin	.10	.05	.01
□ 282 Greg Minton	.10	.05	.01
□ 283 Jeff D. Robinson	.10	.05	.01
□ 284 Harry Spilman	.10	.05	.01
□ 285 Robby Thompson	.25	.11	.03
□ 286 Jose Uribe	.10	.05	.01
□ 287 Frank Williams	.10	.05	.01
□ 288 Joel Youngblood	.10	.05	.01
□ 289 Jack Clark	.25	.11	.03
□ 290 Vince Coleman	.10	.05	.01
□ 291 Tim Conroy	.10	.05	.01
□ 292 Danny Cox	.10	.05	.01
□ 293 Ken Dayley	.10	.05	.01
□ 294 Curt Ford	.10	.05	.01
□ 295 Bob Forsch	.10	.05	.01
□ 296 Tom Herr	.10	.05	.01
□ 297 Ricky Horton	.10	.05	.01
□ 298 Clint Hurdle	.10	.05	.01
□ 299 Jeff Lahti	.10	.05	.01
□ 300 Steve Lake	.10	.05	.01
□ 301 Tito Landrum	.10	.05	.01
□ 302 Mike LaValliere	.10	.05	.01
□ 303 Greg Mathews	.10	.05	.01
□ 304 Willie McGee	.10	.05	.01
□ 305 Jose Oquendo	.10	.05	.01
□ 306 Terry Pendleton	.25	.11	.03
□ 307 Pat Perry	.10	.05	.01
□ 308 Ozzie Smith	.75	.35	.09
□ 309 Ray Soff	.10	.05	.01
□ 310 John Tudor	.10	.05	.01
□ 311 Andy Van Slyke UER (Bats R, Throws L)	.25	.11	.03
□ 312 Todd Worrell	.25	.11	.03
□ 313 Dann Bilardello	.10	.05	.01
□ 314 Hubie Brooks	.10	.05	.01
□ 315 Tim Burke	.10	.05	.01
□ 316 Andre Dawson	.60	.25	.07
□ 317 Mike Fitzgerald	.10	.05	.01
□ 318 Tom Foley	.10	.05	.01
□ 319 Andres Galarraga	1.00	.45	.12
□ 320 Joe Hesketh	.10	.05	.01
□ 321 Wallace Johnson	.10	.05	.01
□ 322 Wayne Krenchicki	.10	.05	.01
□ 323 Vance Law	.10	.05	.01
□ 324 Dennis Martinez	.25	.11	.03
□ 325 Bob McClure	.10	.05	.01
□ 326 Andy McGaffigan	.10	.05	.01
□ 327 Al Newman	.10	.05	.01
□ 328 Tim Raines	.25	.11	.03
□ 329 Jeff Reardon	.25	.11	.03
□ 330 Luis Rivera	.10	.05	.01
□ 331 Bob Sebra	.10	.05	.01
□ 332 Bryn Smith	.10	.05	.01
□ 333 Jay Tibbs	.10	.05	.01
□ 334 Tim Wallach	.10	.05	.01
□ 335 Mitch Webster	.10	.05	.01
□ 336 Jim Wohlford	.10	.05	.01
□ 337 Floyd Youmans	.10	.05	.01
□ 338 Chris Bosio	.25	.11	.03
□ 339 Glenn Braggs	.10	.05	.01
□ 340 Rick Cerone	.10	.05	.01
□ 341 Mark Clear	.10	.05	.01
□ 342 Bryan Clutterbuck	.10	.05	.01
□ 343 Cecil Cooper	.25	.11	.03
□ 344 Rob Deer	.10	.05	.01
□ 345 Jim Gantner	.10	.05	.01
□ 346 Ted Higuera	.10	.05	.01
□ 347 John Henry Johnson	.10	.05	.01
□ 348 Tim Leary	.10	.05	.01
□ 349 Rick Manning	.10	.05	.01
□ 350 Paul Molitor	.75	.35	.09
□ 351 Charlie Moore	.10	.05	.01
□ 352 Juan Nieves	.10	.05	.01
□ 353 Ben Oglivie	.10	.05	.01
□ 354 Dan Plesac	.10	.05	.01
□ 355 Ernest Riles	.10	.05	.01
□ 356 Billy Joe Robidoux	.10	.05	.01
□ 357 Bill Schroeder	.10	.05	.01
□ 358 Dale Sveum	.10	.05	.01
□ 359 Gorman Thomas	.10	.05	.01
□ 360 Bill Wegman	.10	.05	.01
□ 361 Robin Yount	.60	.25	.07
□ 362 Steve Balboni	.10	.05	.01
□ 363 Scott Bankhead	.10	.05	.01
□ 364 Buddy Biancalana	.10	.05	.01
□ 365 Bud Black	.10	.05	.01
□ 366 George Brett	1.50	.70	.19
□ 367 Steve Farr	.10	.05	.01
□ 368 Mark Gubicza	.10	.05	.01

□ 369	Bo Jackson	3.00	1.35	.35
□ 370	Danny Jackson	.10	.05	.01
□ 371	Mike Kingery	.25	.11	.03
□ 372	Rudy Law	.10	.05	.01
□ 373	Charlie Leibrandt	.10	.05	.01
□ 374	Dennis Leonard	.10	.05	.01
□ 375	Hal McRae	.25	.11	.03
□ 376	Jorge Orta	.10	.05	.01
□ 377	Jamie Quirk	.10	.05	.01
□ 378	Dan Quisenberry	.10	.05	.01
□ 379	Bret Saberhagen	.25	.11	.03
□ 380	Angel Salazar	.10	.05	.01
□ 381	Lonnie Smith	.10	.05	.01
□ 382	Jim Sundberg	.10	.05	.01
□ 383	Frank White	.25	.11	.03
□ 384	Willie Wilson	.10	.05	.01
□ 385	Joaquin Andujar	.10	.05	.01
□ 386	Doug Bair	.10	.05	.01
□ 387	Dusty Baker	.25	.11	.03
□ 388	Bruce Bochte	.10	.05	.01
□ 389	Jose Canseco	2.00	.90	.25
□ 390	Chris Codiroli	.10	.05	.01
□ 391	Mike Davis	.10	.05	.01
□ 392	Alfredo Griffin	.10	.05	.01
□ 393	Moose Haas	.10	.05	.01
□ 394	Donnie Hill	.10	.05	.01
□ 395	Jay Howell	.10	.05	.01
□ 396	Dave Kingman	.25	.11	.03
□ 397	Carney Lansford	.25	.11	.03
□ 398	Dave Leiper	.10	.05	.01
□ 399	Bill Mooneyham	.10	.05	.01
□ 400	Dwayne Murphy	.10	.05	.01
□ 401	Steve Ontiveros	.10	.05	.01
□ 402	Tony Phillips	.60	.25	.07
□ 403	Eric Plunk	.10	.05	.01
□ 404	Jose Rijo	.10	.05	.01
□ 405	Terry Steinbach	1.00	.45	.12
□ 406	Dave Stewart	.25	.11	.03
□ 407	Mickey Tettleton	.25	.11	.03
□ 408	Dave Von Ohlen	.10	.05	.01
□ 409	Jerry Willard	.10	.05	.01
□ 410	Curt Young	.10	.05	.01
□ 411	Bruce Bochy	.10	.05	.01
□ 412	Dave Dravecky	.25	.11	.03
□ 413	Tim Flannery	.10	.05	.01
□ 414	Steve Garvey	.60	.25	.07
□ 415	Rich Gossage	.25	.11	.03
□ 416	Tony Gwynn	1.50	.70	.19
□ 417	Andy Hawkins	.10	.05	.01
□ 418	LaMarr Hoyt	.10	.05	.01
□ 419	Terry Kennedy	.10	.05	.01
□ 420	John Kruk	1.00	.45	.12
□ 421	Dave LaPoint	.10	.05	.01
□ 422	Craig Lefferts	.10	.05	.01
□ 423	Carmelo Martinez	.10	.05	.01
□ 424	Lance McCullers	.10	.05	.01
□ 425	Kevin McReynolds	.10	.05	.01
□ 426	Graig Nettles	.25	.11	.03
□ 427	Bip Roberts	.75	.35	.09
□ 428	Jerry Royster	.10	.05	.01
□ 429	Benito Santiago	.25	.11	.03
□ 430	Eric Show	.10	.05	.01
□ 431	Bob Stoddard	.10	.05	.01
□ 432	Garry Templeton	.10	.05	.01
□ 433	Gene Walter	.10	.05	.01
□ 434	Ed Whitson	.10	.05	.01
□ 435	Marvell Wynne	.10	.05	.01
□ 436	Dave Anderson	.10	.05	.01
□ 437	Greg Brock	.10	.05	.01
□ 438	Enos Cabell	.10	.05	.01
□ 439	Mariano Duncan	.10	.05	.01
□ 440	Pedro Guerrero	.25	.11	.03
□ 441	Orel Hershiser	.60	.25	.07
□ 442	Rick Honeycutt	.10	.05	.01
□ 443	Ken Howell	.10	.05	.01
□ 444	Ken Landreaux	.10	.05	.01
□ 445	Bill Madlock	.10	.05	.01
□ 446	Mike Marshall	.10	.05	.01
□ 447	Len Matuszek	.10	.05	.01
□ 448	Tom Niedenfuer	.10	.05	.01
□ 449	Alejandro Pena	.10	.05	.01
□ 450	Dennis Powell	.10	.05	.01
□ 451	Jerry Reuss	.10	.05	.01
□ 452	Bill Russell	.10	.05	.01
□ 453	Steve Sax	.10	.05	.01
□ 454	Mike Scioscia	.10	.05	.01
□ 455	Franklin Stubbs	.10	.05	.01
□ 456	Alex Trevino	.10	.05	.01
□ 457	Fernando Valenzuela	.25	.11	.03
□ 458	Ed VandeBerg	.10	.05	.01
□ 459	Bob Welch	.10	.05	.01
□ 460	Reggie Williams	.10	.05	.01
□ 461	Don Aase	.10	.05	.01
□ 462	Juan Beniquez	.10	.05	.01
□ 463	Mike Boddicker	.10	.05	.01
□ 464	Juan Bonilla	.10	.05	.01
□ 465	Rich Bordi	.10	.05	.01
□ 466	Storm Davis	.10	.05	.01
□ 467	Rick Dempsey	.25	.11	.03
□ 468	Ken Dixon	.10	.05	.01
□ 469	Jim Dwyer	.10	.05	.01
□ 470	Mike Flanagan	.10	.05	.01
□ 471	Jackie Gutierrez	.10	.05	.01
□ 472	Brad Havens	.10	.05	.01
□ 473	Lee Lacy	.10	.05	.01
□ 474	Fred Lynn	.10	.05	.01
□ 475	Scott McGregor	.10	.05	.01
□ 476	Eddie Murray	1.00	.45	.12
□ 477	Tom O'Malley	.10	.05	.01
□ 478	Cal Ripken Jr.	3.00	1.35	.35
□ 479	Larry Sheets	.10	.05	.01
□ 480	John Shelby	.10	.05	.01
□ 481	Nate Snell	.10	.05	.01
□ 482	Jim Traber	.10	.05	.01
□ 483	Mike Young	.10	.05	.01
□ 484	Neil Allen	.10	.05	.01
□ 485	Harold Baines	.25	.11	.03
□ 486	Floyd Bannister	.10	.05	.01
□ 487	Daryl Boston	.10	.05	.01
□ 488	Ivan Calderon	.10	.05	.01
□ 489	John Cangelosi	.10	.05	.01
□ 490	Steve Carlton	.60	.25	.07
□ 491	Joe Cowley	.10	.05	.01
□ 492	Julio Cruz	.10	.05	.01
□ 493	Bill Dawley	.10	.05	.01
□ 494	Jose DeLeon	.10	.05	.01
□ 495	Richard Dotson	.10	.05	.01
□ 496	Carlton Fisk	.60	.25	.07
□ 497	Ozzie Guillen	.25	.11	.03
□ 498	Jerry Hairston	.10	.05	.01
□ 499	Ron Hassey	.10	.05	.01
□ 500	Tim Hulett	.10	.05	.01
□ 501	Bob James	.10	.05	.01
□ 502	Steve Lyons	.10	.05	.01
□ 503	Joel McKeon	.10	.05	.01
□ 504	Gene Nelson	.10	.05	.01
□ 505	Dave Schmidt	.10	.05	.01
□ 506	Ray Searage	.10	.05	.01
□ 507	Bobby Thigpen	.25	.11	.03
□ 508	Greg Walker	.10	.05	.01
□ 509	Jim Acker	.10	.05	.01
□ 510	Doyle Alexander	.10	.05	.01
□ 511	Paul Assenmacher	.10	.05	.01
□ 512	Bruce Benedict	.10	.05	.01
□ 513	Chris Chambliss	.10	.05	.01
□ 514	Jeff Dedmon	.10	.05	.01
□ 515	Gene Garber	.10	.05	.01
□ 516	Ken Griffey	.10	.05	.01
□ 517	Terry Harper	.10	.05	.01
□ 518	Bob Horner	.10	.05	.01
□ 519	Glenn Hubbard	.10	.05	.01
□ 520	Rick Mahler	.10	.05	.01
□ 521	Omar Moreno	.10	.05	.01
□ 522	Dale Murphy	.60	.25	.07
□ 523	Ken Oberkfell	.10	.05	.01
□ 524	Ed Olwine	.10	.05	.01
□ 525	David Palmer	.10	.05	.01
□ 526	Rafael Ramirez	.10	.05	.01
□ 527	Billy Sample	.10	.05	.01
□ 528	Ted Simmons	.25	.11	.03
□ 529	Zane Smith	.10	.05	.01
□ 530	Bruce Sutter	.10	.05	.01
□ 531	Andres Thomas	.10	.05	.01
□ 532	Ozzie Virgil	.10	.05	.01
□ 533	Allan Anderson	.10	.05	.01
□ 534	Keith Atherton	.10	.05	.01
□ 535	Billy Beane	.10	.05	.01
□ 536	Bert Blyleven	.25	.11	.03
□ 537	Tom Brunansky	.10	.05	.01
□ 538	Randy Bush	.10	.05	.01
□ 539	George Frazier	.10	.05	.01
□ 540	Gary Gaetti	.10	.05	.01

☐ 541 Greg Gagne	.10	.05	.01
☐ 542 Mickey Hatcher	.10	.05	.01
☐ 543 Neal Heaton	.10	.05	.01
☐ 544 Kent Hrbek	.60	.25	.07
☐ 545 Roy Lee Jackson	.10	.05	.01
☐ 546 Tim Laudner	.10	.05	.01
☐ 547 Steve Lombardozzi	.10	.05	.01
☐ 548 Mark Portugal	.25	.11	.03
☐ 549 Kirby Puckett	3.00	1.35	.35
☐ 550 Jeff Reed	.10	.05	.01
☐ 551 Mark Salas	.10	.05	.01
☐ 552 Roy Smalley	.10	.05	.01
☐ 553 Mike Smithson	.10	.05	.01
☐ 554 Frank Viola	.10	.05	.01
☐ 555 Thad Bosley	.10	.05	.01
☐ 556 Ron Cey	.25	.11	.03
☐ 557 Jody Davis	.10	.05	.01
☐ 558 Ron Davis	.10	.05	.01
☐ 559 Bob Dernier	.10	.05	.01
☐ 560 Frank DiPino	.10	.05	.01
☐ 561 Shawon Dunston UER	.25	.11	.03
(Wrong birth year			
listed on card back)			
☐ 562 Leon Durham	.10	.05	.01
☐ 563 Dennis Eckersley	.25	.11	.03
☐ 564 Terry Francona	.10	.05	.01
☐ 565 Dave Gumpert	.10	.05	.01
☐ 566 Guy Hoffman	.10	.05	.01
☐ 567 Ed Lynch	.10	.05	.01
☐ 568 Gary Matthews	.10	.05	.01
☐ 569 Keith Moreland	.10	.05	.01
☐ 570 Jamie Moyer	.25	.11	.03
☐ 571 Jerry Mumphrey	.10	.05	.01
☐ 572 Ryne Sandberg	1.00	.45	.12
☐ 573 Scott Sanderson	.10	.05	.01
☐ 574 Lee Smith	.60	.25	.07
☐ 575 Chris Speier	.10	.05	.01
☐ 576 Rick Sutcliffe	.10	.05	.01
☐ 577 Manny Trillo	.10	.05	.01
☐ 578 Steve Trout	.10	.05	.01
☐ 579 Karl Best	.10	.05	.01
☐ 580 Scott Bradley	.10	.05	.01
☐ 581 Phil Bradley	.10	.05	.01
☐ 582 Mickey Brantley	.10	.05	.01
☐ 583 Mike G. Brown P	.10	.05	.01
☐ 584 Alvin Davis	.10	.05	.01
☐ 585 Lee Guetterman	.10	.05	.01
☐ 586 Mark Huismann	.10	.05	.01
☐ 587 Bob Kearney	.10	.05	.01
☐ 588 Pete Ladd	.10	.05	.01
☐ 589 Mark Langston	.25	.11	.03
☐ 590 Mike Moore	.10	.05	.01
☐ 591 Mike Morgan	.10	.05	.01
☐ 592 John Moses	.10	.05	.01
☐ 593 Ken Phelps	.10	.05	.01
☐ 594 Jim Presley	.10	.05	.01
☐ 595 Rey Quinones UER	.10	.05	.01
(Quinonez on front)			
☐ 596 Harold Reynolds	.10	.05	.01
☐ 597 Billy Swift	.10	.05	.01
☐ 598 Danny Tartabull	.25	.11	.03
☐ 599 Steve Yeager	.10	.05	.01
☐ 600 Matt Young	.10	.05	.01
☐ 601 Bill Almon	.10	.05	.01
☐ 602 Rafael Belliard	.10	.05	.01
☐ 603 Mike Bielecki	.10	.05	.01
☐ 604 Barry Bonds	20.00	9.00	2.50
☐ 605 Bobby Bonilla	2.00	.90	.25
☐ 606 Sid Bream	.10	.05	.01
☐ 607 Mike C. Brown	.10	.05	.01
☐ 608 Pat Clements	.10	.05	.01
☐ 609 Mike Diaz	.10	.05	.01
☐ 610 Cecilio Guante	.10	.05	.01
☐ 611 Barry Jones	.10	.05	.01
☐ 612 Bob Kipper	.10	.05	.01
☐ 613 Larry McWilliams	.10	.05	.01
☐ 614 Jim Morrison	.10	.05	.01
☐ 615 Joe Orsulak	.10	.05	.01
☐ 616 Junior Ortiz	.10	.05	.01
☐ 617 Tony Pena	.10	.05	.01
☐ 618 Johnny Ray	.10	.05	.01
☐ 619 Rick Reuschel	.10	.05	.01
☐ 620 R.J. Reynolds	.10	.05	.01
☐ 621 Rick Rhoden	.10	.05	.01
☐ 622 Don Robinson	.10	.05	.01
☐ 623 Bob Walk	.10	.05	.01
☐ 624 Jim Winn	.10	.05	.01
☐ 625 Youthful Power	.60	.25	.07
Pete Incaviglia			
Jose Canseco			
☐ 626 300 Game Winners	.25	.11	.03
Don Sutton			
Phil Niekro			
☐ 627 AL Firemen	.10	.05	.01
Dave Righetti			
Don Aase			
☐ 628 Rookie All-Stars	.60	.25	.07
Wally Joyner			
Jose Canseco			
☐ 629 Magic Mets	.25	.11	.03
Gary Carter			
Sid Fernandez			
Dwight Gooden			
Keith Hernandez			
Darryl Strawberry			
☐ 630 NL Best Righties	.10	.05	.01
Mike Scott			
Mike Krukow			
☐ 631 Sensational Southpaws	.10	.05	.01
Fernando Valenzuela			
John Franco			
☐ 632 Count'Em	.10	.05	.01
Bob Horner			
☐ 633 AL Pitcher's Nightmare	1.00	.45	.12
Jose Canseco			
Jim Rice			
Kirby Puckett			
☐ 634 All-Star Battery	.60	.25	.07
Gary Carter			
Roger Clemens			
☐ 635 4000 Strikeouts	.60	.25	.07
Steve Carlton			
☐ 636 Big Bats at First	.60	.25	.07
Glenn Davis			
Eddie Murray			
☐ 637 On Base	.60	.25	.07
Wade Boggs			
Keith Hernandez			
☐ 638 Sluggers Left Side	.60	.25	.07
Don Mattingly			
Darryl Strawberry			
☐ 639 Former MVP's	.25	.11	.03
Dave Parker			
Ryne Sandberg			
☐ 640 Dr. K and Super K	.60	.25	.07
Dwight Gooden			
Roger Clemens			
☐ 641 AL West Stoppers	.10	.05	.01
Mike Witt			
Charlie Hough			
☐ 642 Doubles and Triples	.25	.11	.03
Juan Samuel			
Tim Raines			
☐ 643 Outfielders with Punch	.25	.11	.03
Harold Baines			
Jesse Barfield			
☐ 644 Dave Clark and	.60	.25	.07
Greg Swindell			
☐ 645 Ron Karkovice and	.25	.11	.03
Russ Morman			
☐ 646 Devon White and	.75	.35	.09
Willie Fraser			
☐ 647 Mike Stanley and	.60	.25	.07
Jerry Browne			
☐ 648 Dave Magadan and	.25	.11	.03
Phil Lombardi			
☐ 649 Jose Gonzalez and	.10	.05	.01
Ralph Bryant			
☐ 650 Jimmy Jones and	.10	.05	.01
Randy Asadoor			
☐ 651 Tracy Jones and	.25	.11	.03
Marvin Freeman			
☐ 652 John Stefero and	.75	.35	.09
Kevin Seitzer			
☐ 653 Rob Nelson and	.10	.05	.01
Steve Fireovid			
☐ 654 CL: Mets/Red Sox	.25	.11	.03
Astros/Angels			
☐ 655 CL: Yankees/Rangers	.25	.11	.03
Tigers/Phillies			
☐ 656 CL: Reds/Blue Jays	.25	.11	.03
Indians/Giants			

		MINT	NRMT	EXC
	ERR (230/231 wrong)			
□ 657	CL: Cardinals/Expos Brewers/Royals	.25	.11	.03
□ 658	CL: A's/Padres Dodgers/Orioles	.25	.11	.03
□ 659	CL: White Sox/Braves Twins/Cubs	.25	.11	.03
□ 660	CL: Mariners/Pirates Special Cards ER (580/581 wrong)	.25	.11	.03

1987 Fleer All-Stars

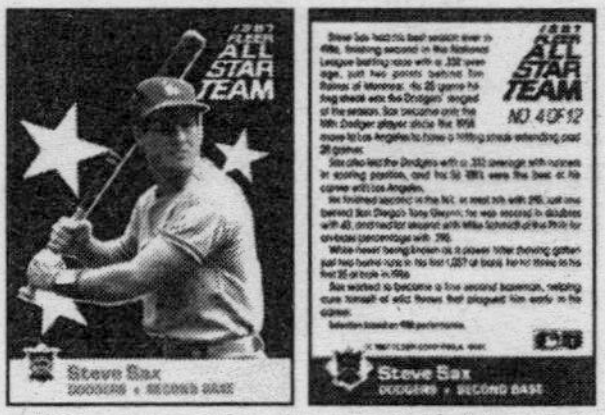

This 12-card standard-size set was distributed as an insert in packs of the Fleer regular issue. The cards are designed with a color player photo superimposed on a gray or black background with yellow stars. The player's name, team, and position are printed in orange on black or gray at the bottom of the obverse. The card backs are done predominantly in gray, red, and black and are numbered on the back in the upper right hand corner.

	MINT	NRMT	EXC
COMPLETE SET (12)	22.00	10.00	2.70
COMMON CARD (1-12)	.30	.14	.04
SEMISTARS	.50	.23	.06
RANDOM INSERTS IN PACKS			
□ 1 Don Mattingly	6.00	2.70	.75
□ 2 Gary Carter	.50	.23	.06
□ 3 Tony Fernandez	.30	.14	.04
□ 4 Steve Sax	.30	.14	.04
□ 5 Kirby Puckett	10.00	4.50	1.25
□ 6 Mike Schmidt	2.50	1.10	.30
□ 7 Mike Easler	.30	.14	.04
□ 8 Todd Worrell	.30	.14	.04
□ 9 George Bell	.30	.14	.04
□ 10 Fernando Valenzuela	.50	.23	.06
□ 11 Roger Clemens	5.00	2.20	.60
□ 12 Tim Raines	.50	.23	.06

1987 Fleer Headliners

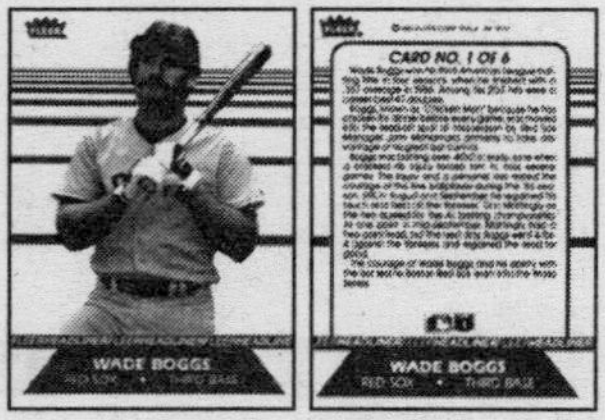

This six-card standard-size set was distributed one per rack pack as well as with three-pack wax pack rack packs. The obverse features the player photo against a beige background with irregular red stripes. The checklist below also lists each player's team affiliation. The set is sequenced in alphabetical order.

	MINT	NRMT	EXC
COMPLETE SET (6)	6.00	2.70	.75
COMMON CARD (1-6)	.50	.23	.06
ONE PER RACK PACK			
□ 1 Wade Boggs	1.00	.45	.12
□ 2 Jose Canseco	3.00	1.35	.35
□ 3 Dwight Gooden	.50	.23	.06
□ 4 Rickey Henderson	1.00	.45	.12
□ 5 Keith Hernandez	.50	.23	.06
□ 6 Jim Rice	.50	.23	.06

1987 Fleer Update

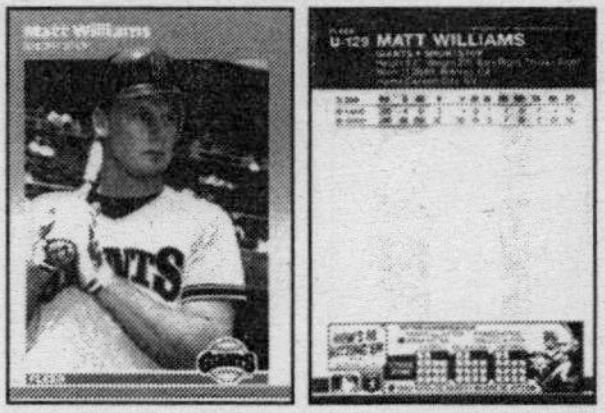

This 132-card standard-size set was distributed exclusively in factory set form by hobby dealers. In addition to the complete set of 132 cards, the box also contained 25 Team Logo stickers. The cards look very similar to the 1987 Fleer regular issue except for the U-prefixed numbering on back. Cards are ordered alphabetically according to player's last name. The key extended Rookie Cards in this set are Ellis Burks, Mike Greenwell, Greg Maddux, Fred McGriff, Mark McGwire and Matt Williams.

	MINT	NRMT	EXC
COMPLETE FACT.SET (132)	15.00	6.75	1.85
COMMON CARD (1-132)	.05	.02	.01
SEMISTARS	.10	.05	.01
U PREFIX ON CARD NUMBER			
□ 1 Scott Bankhead	.05	.02	.01
□ 2 Eric Bell	.05	.02	.01
□ 3 Juan Beniquez	.05	.02	.01
□ 4 Juan Berenguer	.05	.02	.01
□ 5 Mike Birkbeck	.05	.02	.01
□ 6 Randy Bockus	.05	.02	.01
□ 7 Rod Booker	.05	.02	.01
□ 8 Thad Bosley	.05	.02	.01
□ 9 Greg Brock	.05	.02	.01
□ 10 Bob Brower	.05	.02	.01
□ 11 Chris Brown	.05	.02	.01
□ 12 Jerry Browne	.05	.02	.01
□ 13 Ralph Bryant	.05	.02	.01
□ 14 DeWayne Buice	.05	.02	.01
□ 15 Ellis Burks	1.00	.45	.12
□ 16 Casey Candaele	.05	.02	.01
□ 17 Steve Carlton	.20	.09	.03
□ 18 Juan Castillo	.05	.02	.01
□ 19 Chuck Crim	.05	.02	.01
□ 20 Mark Davidson	.05	.02	.01
□ 21 Mark Davis	.05	.02	.01
□ 22 Storm Davis	.05	.02	.01
□ 23 Bill Dawley	.05	.02	.01
□ 24 Andre Dawson	.20	.09	.03
□ 25 Brian Dayett	.05	.02	.01
□ 26 Rick Dempsey	.10	.05	.01
□ 27 Ken Dowell	.05	.02	.01
□ 28 Dave Dravecky	.10	.05	.01
□ 29 Mike Dunne	.05	.02	.01
□ 30 Dennis Eckersley	.10	.05	.01
□ 31 Cecil Fielder	.75	.35	.09
□ 32 Brian Fisher	.05	.02	.01
□ 33 Willie Fraser	.05	.02	.01
□ 34 Ken Gerhart	.05	.02	.01
□ 35 Jim Gott	.05	.02	.01
□ 36 Dan Gladden	.05	.02	.01
□ 37 Mike Greenwell	.20	.09	.03

□ 38 Cecilio Guante	.05	.02	.01
□ 39 Albert Hall	.05	.02	.01
□ 40 Atlee Hammaker	.05	.02	.01
□ 41 Mickey Hatcher	.05	.02	.01
□ 42 Mike Heath	.05	.02	.01
□ 43 Neal Heaton	.05	.02	.01
□ 44 Mike Henneman	.20	.09	.03
□ 45 Guy Hoffman	.05	.02	.01
□ 46 Charles Hudson	.05	.02	.01
□ 47 Chuck Jackson	.05	.02	.01
□ 48 Mike Jackson	.10	.05	.01
□ 49 Reggie Jackson	.50	.23	.06
□ 50 Chris James	.05	.02	.01
□ 51 Dion James	.05	.02	.01
□ 52 Stan Javier	.05	.02	.01
□ 53 Stan Jefferson	.05	.02	.01
□ 54 Jimmy Jones	.05	.02	.01
□ 55 Tracy Jones	.05	.02	.01
□ 56 Terry Kennedy	.05	.02	.01
□ 57 Mike Kingery	.10	.05	.01
□ 58 Ray Knight	.10	.05	.01
□ 59 Gene Larkin	.05	.02	.01
□ 60 Mike LaValliere	.05	.02	.01
□ 61 Jack Lazorko	.05	.02	.01
□ 62 Terry Leach	.05	.02	.01
□ 63 Rick Leach	.05	.02	.01
□ 64 Craig Lefferts	.05	.02	.01
□ 65 Jim Lindeman	.05	.02	.01
□ 66 Bill Long	.05	.02	.01
□ 67 Mike Loynd	.05	.02	.01
□ 68 Greg Maddux	10.00	4.50	1.25
□ 69 Bill Madlock	.05	.02	.01
□ 70 Dave Magadan	.10	.05	.01
□ 71 Joe Magrane	.05	.02	.01
□ 72 Fred Manrique	.05	.02	.01
□ 73 Mike Mason	.05	.02	.01
□ 74 Lloyd McClendon	.05	.02	.01
□ 75 Fred McGriff	2.00	.90	.25
□ 76 Mark McGwire	2.00	.90	.25
□ 77 Mark McLemore	.05	.02	.01
□ 78 Kevin McReynolds	.05	.02	.01
□ 79 Dave Meads	.05	.02	.01
□ 80 Greg Minton	.05	.02	.01
□ 81 John Mitchell	.05	.02	.01
□ 82 Kevin Mitchell	.20	.09	.03
□ 83 John Morris	.05	.02	.01
□ 84 Jeff Musselman	.05	.02	.01
□ 85 Randy Myers	.40	.18	.05
□ 86 Gene Nelson	.05	.02	.01
□ 87 Joe Niekro	.05	.02	.01
□ 88 Tom Nieto	.05	.02	.01
□ 89 Reid Nichols	.05	.02	.01
□ 90 Matt Nokes	.10	.05	.01
□ 91 Dickie Noles	.05	.02	.01
□ 92 Edwin Nunez	.05	.02	.01
□ 93 Jose Nunez	.05	.02	.01
□ 94 Paul O'Neill	.50	.23	.06
□ 95 Jim Paciorek	.05	.02	.01
□ 96 Lance Parrish	.10	.05	.01
□ 97 Bill Pecota	.05	.02	.01
□ 98 Tony Pena	.05	.02	.01
□ 99 Luis Polonia	.20	.09	.03
□ 100 Randy Ready	.05	.02	.01
□ 101 Jeff Reardon	.10	.05	.01
□ 102 Gary Redus	.05	.02	.01
□ 103 Rick Rhoden	.05	.02	.01
□ 104 Wally Ritchie	.05	.02	.01
□ 105 Jeff M. Robinson UER (Wrong Jeff's stats on back)	.05	.02	.01
□ 106 Mark Salas	.05	.02	.01
□ 107 Dave Schmidt	.05	.02	.01
□ 108 Kevin Seitzer UER (Wrong birth year)	.10	.05	.01
□ 109 John Shelby	.05	.02	.01
□ 110 John Smiley	.10	.05	.01
□ 111 Lary Sorensen	.05	.02	.01
□ 112 Chris Speier	.05	.02	.01
□ 113 Randy St.Claire	.05	.02	.01
□ 114 Jim Sundberg	.05	.02	.01
□ 115 B.J. Surhoff	.30	.14	.04
□ 116 Greg Swindell	.20	.09	.03
□ 117 Danny Tartabull	.10	.05	.01
□ 118 Dorn Taylor	.05	.02	.01
□ 119 Lee Tunnell	.05	.02	.01
□ 120 Ed VandeBerg	.05	.02	.01
□ 121 Andy Van Slyke	.10	.05	.01
□ 122 Gary Ward	.05	.02	.01
□ 123 Devon White	.20	.09	.03
□ 124 Alan Wiggins	.05	.02	.01
□ 125 Bill Wilkinson	.05	.02	.01
□ 126 Jim Winn	.05	.02	.01
□ 127 Frank Williams	.05	.02	.01
□ 128 Ken Williams	.05	.02	.01
□ 129 Matt Williams	4.00	1.80	.50
□ 130 Herm Willingham	.05	.02	.01
□ 131 Matt Young	.05	.02	.01
□ 132 Checklist 1-132	.05	.02	.01

1988 Fleer

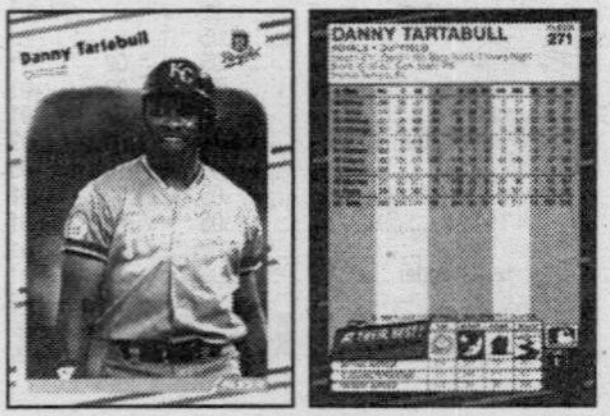

This set consists of 660 standard-size cards. Cards were primarily issued in 15-card wax packs and hobby and retail factory sets. Each wax pack contained one of 26 different "Stadium Card" stickers. Card fronts feature a distinctive white background with red and blue diagonal stripes across the card. Cards are again organized numerically by teams and team order is based upon the previous season's record. Subsets include Specials (622-640), Rookie Pairs (641-653), and checklists (654-660). Rookie Cards in this set include Jay Bell, John Burkett, Ellis Burks, Ken Caminiti, Ron Gant, Tom Glavine, Mark Grace, Gregg Jefferies, Edgar Martinez, Jack McDowell, Jeff Montgomery, and Matt Williams.

	MINT	NRMT	EXC
COMPLETE SET (660)	20.00	9.00	2.50
COMPLETE RETAIL SET (660)	20.00	9.00	2.50
COMPLETE HOBBY SET (672)	25.00	11.00	3.10
COMMON CARD (1-660)	.05	.02	.01
SEMISTARS	.15	.07	.02
STARS	.30	.14	.04
COMP.WORLD SERIES SET (12)	2.00	.90	.25

□ 1 Keith Atherton	.05	.02	.01
□ 2 Don Baylor	.30	.14	.04
□ 3 Juan Berenguer	.05	.02	.01
□ 4 Bert Blyleven	.15	.07	.02
□ 5 Tom Brunansky	.05	.02	.01
□ 6 Randy Bush	.05	.02	.01
□ 7 Steve Carlton	.30	.14	.04
□ 8 Mark Davidson	.05	.02	.01
□ 9 George Frazier	.05	.02	.01
□ 10 Gary Gaetti	.05	.02	.01
□ 11 Greg Gagne	.05	.02	.01
□ 12 Dan Gladden	.05	.02	.01
□ 13 Kent Hrbek	.15	.07	.02
□ 14 Gene Larkin	.05	.02	.01
□ 15 Tim Laudner	.05	.02	.01
□ 16 Steve Lombardozzi	.05	.02	.01
□ 17 Al Newman	.05	.02	.01
□ 18 Joe Niekro	.05	.02	.01
□ 19 Kirby Puckett	.60	.25	.07
□ 20 Jeff Reardon	.15	.07	.02
□ 21A Dan Schatzeder ERR (Misspelled Schatzader on card front)	.15	.07	.02
□ 21B Dan Schatzeder COR	.05	.02	.01
□ 22 Roy Smalley	.05	.02	.01
□ 23 Mike Smithson	.05	.02	.01
□ 24 Les Straker	.05	.02	.01
□ 25 Frank Viola	.05	.02	.01

□ 26 Jack Clark	.15	.07	.02
□ 27 Vince Coleman	.05	.02	.01
□ 28 Danny Cox	.05	.02	.01
□ 29 Bill Dawley	.05	.02	.01
□ 30 Ken Dayley	.05	.02	.01
□ 31 Doug DeCinces	.05	.02	.01
□ 32 Curt Ford	.05	.02	.01
□ 33 Bob Forsch	.05	.02	.01
□ 34 David Green	.05	.02	.01
□ 35 Tom Herr	.05	.02	.01
□ 36 Ricky Horton	.05	.02	.01
□ 37 Lance Johnson	.75	.35	.09
□ 38 Steve Lake	.05	.02	.01
□ 39 Jim Lindeman	.05	.02	.01
□ 40 Joe Magrane	.05	.02	.01
□ 41 Greg Mathews	.05	.02	.01
□ 42 Willie McGee	.05	.02	.01
□ 43 John Morris	.05	.02	.01
□ 44 Jose Oquendo	.05	.02	.01
□ 45 Tony Pena	.05	.02	.01
□ 46 Terry Pendleton	.15	.07	.02
□ 47 Ozzie Smith	.40	.18	.05
□ 48 John Tudor	.05	.02	.01
□ 49 Lee Tunnell	.05	.02	.01
□ 50 Todd Worrell	.05	.02	.01
□ 51 Doyle Alexander	.05	.02	.01
□ 52 Dave Bergman	.05	.02	.01
□ 53 Tom Brookens	.05	.02	.01
□ 54 Darrell Evans	.15	.07	.02
□ 55 Kirk Gibson	.15	.07	.02
□ 56 Mike Heath	.05	.02	.01
□ 57 Mike Henneman	.15	.07	.02
□ 58 Willie Hernandez	.05	.02	.01
□ 59 Larry Herndon	.05	.02	.01
□ 60 Eric King	.05	.02	.01
□ 61 Chet Lemon	.05	.02	.01
□ 62 Scott Lusader	.05	.02	.01
□ 63 Bill Madlock	.05	.02	.01
□ 64 Jack Morris	.30	.14	.04
□ 65 Jim Morrison	.05	.02	.01
□ 66 Matt Nokes	.05	.02	.01
□ 67 Dan Petry	.05	.02	.01
□ 68A Jeff M. Robinson ERR (Stats for Jeff D. Robinson on card back, Born 12-13-60)	.30	.14	.04
□ 68B Jeff M. Robinson COR (Born 12-14-61)	.05	.02	.01
□ 69 Pat Sheridan	.05	.02	.01
□ 70 Nate Snell	.05	.02	.01
□ 71 Frank Tanana	.05	.02	.01
□ 72 Walt Terrell	.05	.02	.01
□ 73 Mark Thurmond	.05	.02	.01
□ 74 Alan Trammell	.30	.14	.04
□ 75 Lou Whitaker	.30	.14	.04
□ 76 Mike Aldrete	.05	.02	.01
□ 77 Bob Brenly	.05	.02	.01
□ 78 Will Clark	.50	.23	.06
□ 79 Chili Davis	.30	.14	.04
□ 80 Kelly Downs	.05	.02	.01
□ 81 Dave Dravecky	.15	.07	.02
□ 82 Scott Garrelts	.05	.02	.01
□ 83 Atlee Hammaker	.05	.02	.01
□ 84 Dave Henderson	.05	.02	.01
□ 85 Mike Krukow	.05	.02	.01
□ 86 Mike LaCoss	.05	.02	.01
□ 87 Craig Lefferts	.05	.02	.01
□ 88 Jeff Leonard	.05	.02	.01
□ 89 Candy Maldonado	.05	.02	.01
□ 90 Eddie Milner	.05	.02	.01
□ 91 Bob Melvin	.05	.02	.01
□ 92 Kevin Mitchell	.15	.07	.02
□ 93 Jon Perlman	.05	.02	.01
□ 94 Rick Reuschel	.05	.02	.01
□ 95 Don Robinson	.05	.02	.01
□ 96 Chris Speier	.05	.02	.01
□ 97 Harry Spilman	.05	.02	.01
□ 98 Robby Thompson	.05	.02	.01
□ 99 Jose Uribe	.05	.02	.01
□ 100 Mark Wasinger	.05	.02	.01
□ 101 Matt Williams	2.50	1.10	.30
□ 102 Jesse Barfield	.05	.02	.01
□ 103 George Bell	.05	.02	.01
□ 104 Juan Beniquez	.05	.02	.01
□ 105 John Cerutti	.05	.02	.01
□ 106 Jim Clancy	.05	.02	.01
□ 107 Rob Ducey	.05	.02	.01
□ 108 Mark Eichhorn	.05	.02	.01
□ 109 Tony Fernandez	.05	.02	.01
□ 110 Cecil Fielder	.30	.14	.04
□ 111 Kelly Gruber	.05	.02	.01
□ 112 Tom Henke	.05	.02	.01
□ 113A Garth Iorg ERR (Misspelled Iorq on card front)	.30	.14	.04
□ 113B Garth Iorg COR	.05	.02	.01
□ 114 Jimmy Key	.15	.07	.02
□ 115 Rick Leach	.05	.02	.01
□ 116 Manny Lee	.05	.02	.01
□ 117 Nelson Liriano	.05	.02	.01
□ 118 Fred McGriff	1.00	.45	.12
□ 119 Lloyd Moseby	.05	.02	.01
□ 120 Rance Mulliniks	.05	.02	.01
□ 121 Jeff Musselman	.05	.02	.01
□ 122 Jose Nunez	.05	.02	.01
□ 123 Dave Stieb	.15	.07	.02
□ 124 Willie Upshaw	.05	.02	.01
□ 125 Duane Ward	.15	.07	.02
□ 126 Ernie Whitt	.05	.02	.01
□ 127 Rick Aguilera	.30	.14	.04
□ 128 Wally Backman	.05	.02	.01
□ 129 Mark Carreon	.30	.14	.04
□ 130 Gary Carter	.30	.14	.04
□ 131 David Cone	.50	.23	.06
□ 132 Ron Darling	.05	.02	.01
□ 133 Len Dykstra	.15	.07	.02
□ 134 Sid Fernandez	.05	.02	.01
□ 135 Dwight Gooden	.30	.14	.04
□ 136 Keith Hernandez	.15	.07	.02
□ 137 Gregg Jefferies	1.00	.45	.12
□ 138 Howard Johnson	.05	.02	.01
□ 139 Terry Leach	.05	.02	.01
□ 140 Barry Lyons	.05	.02	.01
□ 141 Dave Magadan	.05	.02	.01
□ 142 Roger McDowell	.05	.02	.01
□ 143 Kevin McReynolds	.05	.02	.01
□ 144 Keith A. Miller	.05	.02	.01
□ 145 John Mitchell	.05	.02	.01
□ 146 Randy Myers	.30	.14	.04
□ 147 Bob Ojeda	.05	.02	.01
□ 148 Jesse Orosco	.05	.02	.01
□ 149 Rafael Santana	.05	.02	.01
□ 150 Doug Sisk	.05	.02	.01
□ 151 Darryl Strawberry	.30	.14	.04
□ 152 Tim Teufel	.05	.02	.01
□ 153 Gene Walter	.05	.02	.01
□ 154 Mookie Wilson	.15	.07	.02
□ 155 Jay Aldrich	.05	.02	.01
□ 156 Chris Bosio	.05	.02	.01
□ 157 Glenn Braggs	.05	.02	.01
□ 158 Greg Brock	.05	.02	.01
□ 159 Juan Castillo	.05	.02	.01
□ 160 Mark Clear	.05	.02	.01
□ 161 Cecil Cooper	.15	.07	.02
□ 162 Chuck Crim	.05	.02	.01
□ 163 Rob Deer	.05	.02	.01
□ 164 Mike Felder	.05	.02	.01
□ 165 Jim Gantner	.05	.02	.01
□ 166 Ted Higuera	.05	.02	.01
□ 167 Steve Kiefer	.05	.02	.01
□ 168 Rick Manning	.05	.02	.01
□ 169 Paul Molitor	.40	.18	.05
□ 170 Juan Nieves	.05	.02	.01
□ 171 Dan Plesac	.05	.02	.01
□ 172 Earnest Riles	.05	.02	.01
□ 173 Bill Schroeder	.05	.02	.01
□ 174 Steve Stanicek	.05	.02	.01
□ 175 B.J. Surhoff	.15	.07	.02
□ 176 Dale Sveum	.05	.02	.01
□ 177 Bill Wegman	.05	.02	.01
□ 178 Robin Yount	.30	.14	.04
□ 179 Hubie Brooks	.05	.02	.01
□ 180 Tim Burke	.05	.02	.01
□ 181 Casey Candaele	.05	.02	.01
□ 182 Mike Fitzgerald	.05	.02	.01
□ 183 Tom Foley	.05	.02	.01
□ 184 Andres Galarraga	.30	.14	.04
□ 185 Neal Heaton	.05	.02	.01
□ 186 Wallace Johnson	.05	.02	.01
□ 187 Vance Law	.05	.02	.01
□ 188 Dennis Martinez	.15	.07	.02
□ 189 Bob McClure	.05	.02	.01

□	190	Andy McGaffigan	.05	.02	.01
□	191	Reid Nichols	.05	.02	.01
□	192	Pascual Perez	.05	.02	.01
□	193	Tim Raines	.30	.14	.04
□	194	Jeff Reed	.05	.02	.01
□	195	Bob Sebra	.05	.02	.01
□	196	Bryn Smith	.05	.02	.01
□	197	Randy St.Claire	.05	.02	.01
□	198	Tim Wallach	.05	.02	.01
□	199	Mitch Webster	.05	.02	.01
□	200	Herm Winningham	.05	.02	.01
□	201	Floyd Youmans	.05	.02	.01
□	202	Brad Arnsberg	.05	.02	.01
□	203	Rick Cerone	.05	.02	.01
□	204	Pat Clements	.05	.02	.01
□	205	Henry Cotto	.05	.02	.01
□	206	Mike Easler	.05	.02	.01
□	207	Ron Guidry	.05	.02	.01
□	208	Bill Gullickson	.05	.02	.01
□	209	Rickey Henderson	.30	.14	.04
□	210	Charles Hudson	.05	.02	.01
□	211	Tommy John	.15	.07	.02
□	212	Roberto Kelly	.30	.14	.04
□	213	Ron Kittle	.05	.02	.01
□	214	Don Mattingly	1.00	.45	.12
□	215	Bobby Meacham	.05	.02	.01
□	216	Mike Pagliarulo	.05	.02	.01
□	217	Dan Pasqua	.05	.02	.01
□	218	Willie Randolph	.15	.07	.02
□	219	Rick Rhoden	.05	.02	.01
□	220	Dave Righetti	.15	.07	.02
□	221	Jerry Royster	.05	.02	.01
□	222	Tim Stoddard	.05	.02	.01
□	223	Wayne Tolleson	.05	.02	.01
□	224	Gary Ward	.05	.02	.01
□	225	Claudell Washington	.05	.02	.01
□	226	Dave Winfield	.30	.14	.04
□	227	Buddy Bell	.15	.07	.02
□	228	Tom Browning	.05	.02	.01
□	229	Dave Concepcion	.15	.07	.02
□	230	Kal Daniels	.05	.02	.01
□	231	Eric Davis	.15	.07	.02
□	232	Bo Diaz	.05	.02	.01
□	233	Nick Esasky (Has a dollar sign before '87 SB totals)	.05	.02	.01
□	234	John Franco	.05	.02	.01
□	235	Guy Hoffman	.05	.02	.01
□	236	Tom Hume	.05	.02	.01
□	237	Tracy Jones	.05	.02	.01
□	2[illegible]	Bill Landrum	.05	.02	.01
□	2[illegible]	Barry Larkin	.75	.35	.09
□	2[illegible]	Terry McGriff	.05	.02	.01
□	241	Rob Murphy	.05	.02	.01
□	242	Ron Oester	.05	.02	.01
□	243	Dave Parker	.30	.14	.04
□	244	Pat Perry	.05	.02	.01
□	245	Ted Power	.05	.02	.01
□	246	Dennis Rasmussen	.05	.02	.01
□	247	Ron Robinson	.05	.02	.01
□	248	Kurt Stillwell	.05	.02	.01
□	249	Jeff Treadway	.05	.02	.01
□	250	Frank Williams	.05	.02	.01
□	251	Steve Balboni	.05	.02	.01
□	252	Bud Black	.05	.02	.01
□	253	Thad Bosley	.05	.02	.01
□	2[illegible]	George Brett	.75	.35	.09
□	2[illegible]	John Davis	.05	.02	.01
□	2[illegible]	Steve Farr	.05	.02	.01
□	2[illegible]	Gene Garber	.05	.02	.01
□	258	Jerry Don Gleaton	.05	.02	.01
□	259	Mark Gubicza	.05	.02	.01
□	260	Bo Jackson	.30	.14	.04
□	261	Danny Jackson	.05	.02	.01
□	262	Ross Jones	.05	.02	.01
□	263	Charlie Leibrandt	.05	.02	.01
□	264	Bill Pecota	.05	.02	.01
□	265	Melido Perez	.15	.07	.02
□	266	Jamie Quirk	.05	.02	.01
□	267	Dan Quisenberry	.05	.02	.01
□	268	Bret Saberhagen	.15	.07	.02
□	269	Angel Salazar	.05	.02	.01
□	270	Kevin Seitzer UER (Wrong birth year)	.15	.07	.02
□	271	Danny Tartabull	.05	.02	.01
□	272	Gary Thurman	.05	.02	.01
□	273	Frank White	.15	.07	.02
□	274	Willie Wilson	.05	.02	.01
□	275	Tony Bernazard	.05	.02	.01
□	276	Jose Canseco	.60	.25	.07
□	277	Mike Davis	.05	.02	.01
□	278	Storm Davis	.05	.02	.01
□	279	Dennis Eckersley	.30	.14	.04
□	280	Alfredo Griffin	.05	.02	.01
□	281	Rick Honeycutt	.05	.02	.01
□	282	Jay Howell	.05	.02	.01
□	283	Reggie Jackson	.50	.23	.06
□	284	Dennis Lamp	.05	.02	.01
□	285	Carney Lansford	.15	.07	.02
□	286	Mark McGwire	1.25	.55	.16
□	287	Dwayne Murphy	.05	.02	.01
□	288	Gene Nelson	.05	.02	.01
□	289	Steve Ontiveros	.05	.02	.01
□	290	Tony Phillips	.30	.14	.04
□	291	Eric Plunk	.05	.02	.01
□	292	Luis Polonia	.30	.14	.04
□	293	Rick Rodriguez	.05	.02	.01
□	294	Terry Steinbach	.15	.07	.02
□	295	Dave Stewart	.30	.14	.04
□	296	Curt Young	.05	.02	.01
□	297	Luis Aguayo	.05	.02	.01
□	298	Steve Bedrosian	.05	.02	.01
□	299	Jeff Calhoun	.05	.02	.01
□	300	Don Carman	.05	.02	.01
□	301	Todd Frohwirth	.05	.02	.01
□	302	Greg Gross	.05	.02	.01
□	303	Kevin Gross	.05	.02	.01
□	304	Von Hayes	.05	.02	.01
□	305	Keith Hughes	.05	.02	.01
□	306	Mike Jackson	.15	.07	.02
□	307	Chris James	.05	.02	.01
□	308	Steve Jeltz	.05	.02	.01
□	309	Mike Maddux	.05	.02	.01
□	310	Lance Parrish	.05	.02	.01
□	311	Shane Rawley	.05	.02	.01
□	312	Wally Ritchie	.05	.02	.01
□	313	Bruce Ruffin	.05	.02	.01
□	314	Juan Samuel	.05	.02	.01
□	315	Mike Schmidt	.40	.18	.05
□	316	Rick Schu	.05	.02	.01
□	317	Jeff Stone	.05	.02	.01
□	318	Kent Tekulve	.05	.02	.01
□	319	Milt Thompson	.05	.02	.01
□	320	Glenn Wilson	.05	.02	.01
□	321	Rafael Belliard	.05	.02	.01
□	322	Barry Bonds	1.25	.55	.16
□	323	Bobby Bonilla UER (Wrong birth year)	.15	.07	.02
□	324	Sid Bream	.05	.02	.01
□	325	John Cangelosi	.05	.02	.01
□	326	Mike Diaz	.05	.02	.01
□	327	Doug Drabek	.15	.07	.02
□	328	Mike Dunne	.05	.02	.01
□	329	Brian Fisher	.05	.02	.01
□	330	Brett Gideon	.05	.02	.01
□	331	Terry Harper	.05	.02	.01
□	332	Bob Kipper	.05	.02	.01
□	333	Mike LaValliere	.05	.02	.01
□	334	Jose Lind	.15	.07	.02
□	335	Junior Ortiz	.05	.02	.01
□	336	Vicente Palacios	.05	.02	.01
□	337	Bob Patterson	.05	.02	.01
□	338	Al Pedrique	.05	.02	.01
□	339	R.J. Reynolds	.05	.02	.01
□	340	John Smiley	.30	.14	.04
□	341	Andy Van Slyke UER (Wrong batting and throwing listed)	.15	.07	.02
□	342	Bob Walk	.05	.02	.01
□	343	Marty Barrett	.05	.02	.01
□	344	Todd Benzinger	.15	.07	.02
□	345	Wade Boggs	.30	.14	.04
□	346	Tom Bolton	.05	.02	.01
□	347	Oil Can Boyd	.05	.02	.01
□	348	Ellis Burks	1.00	.45	.12
□	349	Roger Clemens	.30	.14	.04
□	350	Steve Crawford	.05	.02	.01
□	351	Dwight Evans	.15	.07	.02
□	352	Wes Gardner	.05	.02	.01
□	353	Rich Gedman	.05	.02	.01
□	354	Mike Greenwell	.30	.14	.04
□	355	Sam Horn	.05	.02	.01

□	356	Bruce Hurst	.05	.02	.01
□	357	John Marzano	.05	.02	.01
□	358	Al Nipper	.05	.02	.01
□	359	Spike Owen	.05	.02	.01
□	360	Jody Reed	.15	.07	.02
□	361	Jim Rice	.30	.14	.04
□	362	Ed Romero	.05	.02	.01
□	363	Kevin Romine	.05	.02	.01
□	364	Joe Sambito	.05	.02	.01
□	365	Calvin Schiraldi	.05	.02	.01
□	366	Jeff Sellers	.05	.02	.01
□	367	Bob Stanley	.05	.02	.01
□	368	Scott Bankhead	.05	.02	.01
□	369	Phil Bradley	.05	.02	.01
□	370	Scott Bradley	.05	.02	.01
□	371	Mickey Brantley	.05	.02	.01
□	372	Mike Campbell	.05	.02	.01
□	373	Alvin Davis	.05	.02	.01
□	374	Lee Guetterman	.05	.02	.01
□	375	Dave Hengel	.05	.02	.01
□	376	Mike Kingery	.05	.02	.01
□	377	Mark Langston	.15	.07	.02
□	378	Edgar Martinez	2.50	1.10	.30
□	379	Mike Moore	.05	.02	.01
□	380	Mike Morgan	.05	.02	.01
□	381	John Moses	.05	.02	.01
□	382	Donell Nixon	.05	.02	.01
□	383	Edwin Nunez	.05	.02	.01
□	384	Ken Phelps	.05	.02	.01
□	385	Jim Presley	.05	.02	.01
□	386	Rey Quinones	.05	.02	.01
□	387	Jerry Reed	.05	.02	.01
□	388	Harold Reynolds	.05	.02	.01
□	389	Dave Valle	.05	.02	.01
□	390	Bill Wilkinson	.05	.02	.01
□	391	Harold Baines	.15	.07	.02
□	392	Floyd Bannister	.05	.02	.01
□	393	Daryl Boston	.05	.02	.01
□	394	Ivan Calderon	.05	.02	.01
□	395	Jose DeLeon	.05	.02	.01
□	396	Richard Dotson	.05	.02	.01
□	397	Carlton Fisk	.30	.14	.04
□	398	Ozzie Guillen	.15	.07	.02
□	399	Ron Hassey	.05	.02	.01
□	400	Donnie Hill	.05	.02	.01
□	401	Bob James	.05	.02	.01
□	402	Dave LaPoint	.05	.02	.01
□	403	Bill Lindsey	.05	.02	.01
□	404	Bill Long	.05	.02	.01
□	405	Steve Lyons	.05	.02	.01
□	406	Fred Manrique	.05	.02	.01
□	407	Jack McDowell	1.00	.45	.12
□	408	Gary Redus	.05	.02	.01
□	409	Ray Searage	.05	.02	.01
□	410	Bobby Thigpen	.05	.02	.01
□	411	Greg Walker	.05	.02	.01
□	412	Ken Williams	.05	.02	.01
□	413	Jim Winn	.05	.02	.01
□	414	Jody Davis	.05	.02	.01
□	415	Andre Dawson	.30	.14	.04
□	416	Brian Dayett	.05	.02	.01
□	417	Bob Dernier	.05	.02	.01
□	418	Frank DiPino	.05	.02	.01
□	419	Shawon Dunston	.05	.02	.01
□	420	Leon Durham	.05	.02	.01
□	421	Les Lancaster	.05	.02	.01
□	422	Ed Lynch	.05	.02	.01
□	423	Greg Maddux	3.00	1.35	.35
□	424	Dave Martinez	.05	.02	.01
□	425A	Keith Moreland ERR (Photo actually Jody Davis)	1.50	.70	.19
□	425B	Keith Moreland COR (Bat on shoulder)	.15	.07	.02
□	426	Jamie Moyer	.05	.02	.01
□	427	Jerry Mumphrey	.05	.02	.01
□	428	Paul Noce	.05	.02	.01
□	429	Rafael Palmeiro	.60	.25	.07
□	430	Wade Rowdon	.05	.02	.01
□	431	Ryne Sandberg	.50	.23	.06
□	432	Scott Sanderson	.05	.02	.01
□	433	Lee Smith	.30	.14	.04
□	434	Jim Sundberg	.05	.02	.01
□	435	Rick Sutcliffe	.05	.02	.01
□	436	Manny Trillo	.05	.02	.01
□	437	Juan Agosto	.05	.02	.01
□	438	Larry Andersen	.05	.02	.01
□	439	Alan Ashby	.05	.02	.01
□	440	Kevin Bass	.05	.02	.01
□	441	Ken Caminiti	2.00	.90	.25
□	442	Rocky Childress	.05	.02	.01
□	443	Jose Cruz	.05	.02	.01
□	444	Danny Darwin	.05	.02	.01
□	445	Glenn Davis	.05	.02	.01
□	446	Jim Deshaies	.05	.02	.01
□	447	Bill Doran	.05	.02	.01
□	448	Ty Gainey	.05	.02	.01
□	449	Billy Hatcher	.05	.02	.01
□	450	Jeff Heathcock	.05	.02	.01
□	451	Bob Knepper	.05	.02	.01
□	452	Rob Mallicoat	.05	.02	.01
□	453	Dave Meads	.05	.02	.01
□	454	Craig Reynolds	.05	.02	.01
□	455	Nolan Ryan	1.50	.70	.19
□	456	Mike Scott	.05	.02	.01
□	457	Dave Smith	.05	.02	.01
□	458	Denny Walling	.05	.02	.01
□	459	Robbie Wine	.05	.02	.01
□	460	Gerald Young	.05	.02	.01
□	461	Bob Brower	.05	.02	.01
□	462A	Jerry Browne ERR (Photo actually Bob Brower, white player)	1.50	.70	.19
□	462B	Jerry Browne COR (Black player)	.15	.07	.02
□	463	Steve Buechele	.05	.02	.01
□	464	Edwin Correa	.05	.02	.01
□	465	Cecil Espy	.05	.02	.01
□	466	Scott Fletcher	.05	.02	.01
□	467	Jose Guzman	.05	.02	.01
□	468	Greg Harris	.05	.02	.01
□	469	Charlie Hough	.15	.07	.02
□	470	Pete Incaviglia	.05	.02	.01
□	471	Paul Kilgus	.05	.02	.01
□	472	Mike Loynd	.05	.02	.01
□	473	Oddibe McDowell	.05	.02	.01
□	474	Dale Mohorcic	.05	.02	.01
□	475	Pete O'Brien	.05	.02	.01
□	476	Larry Parrish	.05	.02	.01
□	477	Geno Petralli	.05	.02	.01
□	478	Jeff Russell	.05	.02	.01
□	479	Ruben Sierra	.30	.14	.04
□	480	Mike Stanley	.15	.07	.02
□	481	Curtis Wilkerson	.05	.02	.01
□	482	Mitch Williams	.15	.07	.02
□	483	Bobby Witt	.05	.02	.01
□	484	Tony Armas	.05	.02	.01
□	485	Bob Boone	.15	.07	.02
□	486	Bill Buckner	.15	.07	.02
□	487	DeWayne Buice	.05	.02	.01
□	488	Brian Downing	.05	.02	.01
□	489	Chuck Finley	.15	.07	.02
□	490	Willie Fraser UER (Wrong bio stats, for George Hendrick)	.05	.02	.01
□	491	Jack Howell	.05	.02	.01
□	492	Ruppert Jones	.05	.02	.01
□	493	Wally Joyner	.15	.07	.02
□	494	Jack Lazorko	.05	.02	.01
□	495	Gary Lucas	.05	.02	.01
□	496	Kirk McCaskill	.05	.02	.01
□	497	Mark McLemore	.05	.02	.01
□	498	Darrell Miller	.05	.02	.01
□	499	Greg Minton	.05	.02	.01
□	500	Donnie Moore	.05	.02	.01
□	501	Gus Polidor	.05	.02	.01
□	502	Johnny Ray	.05	.02	.01
□	503	Mark Ryal	.05	.02	.01
□	504	Dick Schofield	.05	.02	.01
□	505	Don Sutton	.30	.14	.04
□	506	Devon White	.30	.14	.04
□	507	Mike Witt	.05	.02	.01
□	508	Dave Anderson	.05	.02	.01
□	509	Tim Belcher	.15	.07	.02
□	510	Ralph Bryant	.05	.02	.01
□	511	Tim Crews	.15	.07	.02
□	512	Mike Devereaux	.30	.14	.04
□	513	Mariano Duncan	.05	.02	.01
□	514	Pedro Guerrero	.15	.07	.02
□	515	Jeff Hamilton	.05	.02	.01
□	516	Mickey Hatcher	.05	.02	.01

□ 517	Brad Havens	.05	.02	.01
□ 518	Orel Hershiser	.30	.14	.04
□ 519	Shawn Hillegas	.05	.02	.01
□ 520	Ken Howell	.05	.02	.01
□ 521	Tim Leary	.05	.02	.01
□ 522	Mike Marshall	.05	.02	.01
□ 523	Steve Sax	.05	.02	.01
□ 524	Mike Scioscia	.05	.02	.01
□ 525	Mike Sharperson	.05	.02	.01
□ 526	John Shelby	.05	.02	.01
□ 527	Franklin Stubbs	.05	.02	.01
□ 528	Fernando Valenzuela	.15	.07	.02
□ 529	Bob Welch	.05	.02	.01
□ 530	Matt Young	.05	.02	.01
□ 531	Jim Acker	.05	.02	.01
□ 532	Paul Assenmacher	.05	.02	.01
□ 533	Jeff Blauser	.30	.14	.04
□ 534	Joe Boever	.05	.02	.01
□ 535	Martin Clary	.05	.02	.01
□ 536	Kevin Coffman	.05	.02	.01
□ 537	Jeff Dedmon	.05	.02	.01
□ 538	Ron Gant	1.00	.45	.12
□ 539	Tom Glavine	2.50	1.10	.30
□ 540	Ken Griffey	.05	.02	.01
□ 541	Albert Hall	.05	.02	.01
□ 542	Glenn Hubbard	.05	.02	.01
□ 543	Dion James	.05	.02	.01
□ 544	Dale Murphy	.30	.14	.04
□ 545	Ken Oberkfell	.05	.02	.01
□ 546	David Palmer	.05	.02	.01
□ 547	Gerald Perry	.05	.02	.01
□ 548	Charlie Puleo	.05	.02	.01
□ 549	Ted Simmons	.15	.07	.02
□ 550	Zane Smith	.05	.02	.01
□ 551	Andres Thomas	.05	.02	.01
□ 552	Ozzie Virgil	.05	.02	.01
□ 553	Don Aase	.05	.02	.01
□ 554	Jeff Ballard	.05	.02	.01
□ 555	Eric Bell	.05	.02	.01
□ 556	Mike Boddicker	.05	.02	.01
□ 557	Ken Dixon	.05	.02	.01
□ 558	Jim Dwyer	.05	.02	.01
□ 559	Ken Gerhart	.05	.02	.01
□ 560	Rene Gonzales	.05	.02	.01
□ 561	Mike Griffin	.05	.02	.01
□ 562	John Habyan UER (Misspelled Hayban on both sides of card)	.05	.02	.01
□ 563	Terry Kennedy	.05	.02	.01
□ 564	Ray Knight	.15	.07	.02
□ 565	Lee Lacy	.05	.02	.01
□ 566	Fred Lynn	.05	.02	.01
□ 567	Eddie Murray	.50	.23	.06
□ 568	Tom Niedenfuer	.05	.02	.01
□ 569	Bill Ripken	.15	.07	.02
□ 570	Cal Ripken	1.50	.70	.19
□ 571	Dave Schmidt	.05	.02	.01
□ 572	Larry Sheets	.05	.02	.01
□ 573	Pete Stanicek	.05	.02	.01
□ 574	Mark Williamson	.05	.02	.01
□ 575	Mike Young	.05	.02	.01
□ 576	Shawn Abner	.05	.02	.01
□ 577	Greg Booker	.05	.02	.01
□ 578	Chris Brown	.05	.02	.01
□ 579	Keith Comstock	.05	.02	.01
□ 580	Joey Cora	.25	.11	.03
□ 581	Mark Davis	.05	.02	.01
□ 582	Tim Flannery (With surfboard)	.30	.14	.04
□ 583	Goose Gossage	.30	.14	.04
□ 584	Mark Grant	.05	.02	.01
□ 585	Tony Gwynn	.75	.35	.09
□ 586	Andy Hawkins	.05	.02	.01
□ 587	Stan Jefferson	.05	.02	.01
□ 588	Jimmy Jones	.05	.02	.01
□ 589	John Kruk	.30	.14	.04
□ 590	Shane Mack	.05	.02	.01
□ 591	Carmelo Martinez	.05	.02	.01
□ 592	Lance McCullers UER (6'11" tall)	.05	.02	.01
□ 593	Eric Nolte	.05	.02	.01
□ 594	Randy Ready	.05	.02	.01
□ 595	Luis Salazar	.05	.02	.01
□ 596	Benito Santiago	.15	.07	.02
□ 597	Eric Show	.05	.02	.01
□ 598	Garry Templeton	.05	.02	.01
□ 599	Ed Whitson	.05	.02	.01
□ 600	Scott Bailes	.05	.02	.01
□ 601	Chris Bando	.05	.02	.01
□ 602	Jay Bell	.40	.18	.05
□ 603	Brett Butler	.15	.07	.02
□ 604	Tom Candiotti	.05	.02	.01
□ 605	Joe Carter	.30	.14	.04
□ 606	Carmen Castillo	.05	.02	.01
□ 607	Brian Dorsett	.05	.02	.01
□ 608	John Farrell	.05	.02	.01
□ 609	Julio Franco	.15	.07	.02
□ 610	Mel Hall	.05	.02	.01
□ 611	Tommy Hinzo	.05	.02	.01
□ 612	Brook Jacoby	.05	.02	.01
□ 613	Doug Jones	.15	.07	.02
□ 614	Ken Schrom	.05	.02	.01
□ 615	Cory Snyder	.05	.02	.01
□ 616	Sammy Stewart	.05	.02	.01
□ 617	Greg Swindell	.05	.02	.01
□ 618	Pat Tabler	.05	.02	.01
□ 619	Ed VandeBerg	.05	.02	.01
□ 620	Eddie Williams	.15	.07	.02
□ 621	Rich Yett	.05	.02	.01
□ 622	Slugging Sophomores Wally Joyner Cory Snyder	.15	.07	.02
□ 623	Dominican Dynamite George Bell Pedro Guerrero	.05	.02	.01
□ 624	Oakland's Power Team Mark McGwire Jose Canseco	.60	.25	.07
□ 625	Classic Relief Dave Righetti Dan Plesac	.05	.02	.01
□ 626	All Star Righties Bret Saberhagen Mike Witt Jack Morris	.15	.07	.02
□ 627	Game Closers John Franco Steve Bedrosian	.05	.02	.01
□ 628	Masters/Double Play Ozzie Smith Ryne Sandberg	.40	.18	.05
□ 629	Rookie Record Setter Mark McGwire	.60	.25	.07
□ 630	Changing the Guard Mike Greenwell Ellis Burks Todd Benzinger	.30	.14	.04
□ 631	NL Batting Champs Tony Gwynn Tim Raines	.30	.14	.04
□ 632	Pitching Magic Mike Scott Orel Hershiser	.15	.07	.02
□ 633	Big Bats at First Pat Tabler Mark McGwire	.40	.18	.05
□ 634	Hitting King/Thief Tony Gwynn Vince Coleman	.05	.02	.01
□ 635	Slugging Shortstops Tony Fernandez Cal Ripken Alan Trammell	.50	.23	.06
□ 636	Tried/True Sluggers Mike Schmidt Gary Carter	.05	.02	.01
□ 637	Crunch Time Darryl Strawberry Eric Davis	.15	.07	.02
□ 638	AL All-Stars Matt Nokes Kirby Puckett	.30	.14	.04
□ 639	NL All-Stars Keith Hernandez Dale Murphy	.15	.07	.02
□ 640	The O's Brothers Billy Ripken Cal Ripken	.75	.35	.09
□ 641	Mark Grace and Darrin Jackson	1.50	.70	.19
□ 642	Damon Berryhill and Jeff Montgomery	.40	.18	.05

□ 643 Felix Fermin and Jesse Reid	.05	.02	.01
□ 644 Greg Myers and Greg Tabor	.05	.02	.01
□ 645 Joey Meyer and Jim Eppard	.05	.02	.01
□ 646 Adam Peterson and Randy Velarde	.15	.07	.02
□ 647 Pete Smith and Chris Gwynn	.15	.07	.02
□ 648 Tom Newell and Greg Jelks	.05	.02	.01
□ 649 Mario Diaz and Clay Parker	.05	.02	.01
□ 650 Jack Savage and Todd Simmons	.05	.02	.01
□ 651 John Burkett and Kirt Manwaring	.30	.14	.04
□ 652 Dave Otto and Walt Weiss	.15	.07	.02
□ 653 Jeff King and Randell Byers	.50	.23	.06
□ 654 CL: Twins/Cards Tigers/Giants UER (90 Bob Melvin, 91 Eddie Milner)	.15	.07	.02
□ 655 CL: Blue Jays/Mets Brewers/Expos UER (Mets listed before Blue Jays on card)	.15	.07	.02
□ 656 CL: Yankees/Reds Royals/A's	.15	.07	.02
□ 657 CL: Phillies/Pirates Red Sox/Mariners	.15	.07	.02
□ 658 CL: White Sox/Cubs Astros/Rangers	.15	.07	.02
□ 659 CL: Angels/Dodgers Braves/Orioles	.15	.07	.02
□ 660 CL: Padres/Indians Rookies/Specials	.15	.07	.02

1988 Fleer All-Stars

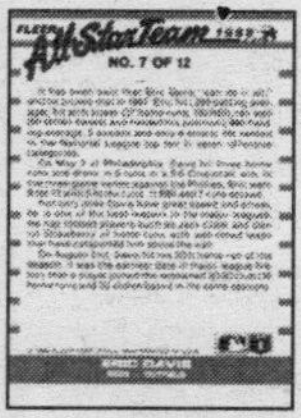

These 12 standard-size cards were inserted randomly in wax and cello packs of the 1988 Fleer set. The cards show the player silhouetted against a light green background with dark green stripes. The player's name, team, and position are printed in yellow at the bottom of the obverse. The card backs are done predominantly in green, white, and black. The players are the "best" at each position, three pitchers, eight position players, and a designated hitter.

	MINT	NRMT	EXC
COMPLETE SET (12)	6.00	2.70	.75
COMMON CARD (1-12)	.30	.14	.04
SEMISTARS	.50	.23	.06
RANDOM INSERTS IN PACKS			

□ 1 Matt Nokes	.30	.14	.04
□ 2 Tom Henke	.30	.14	.04
□ 3 Ted Higuera	.30	.14	.04
□ 4 Roger Clemens	1.50	.70	.19
□ 5 George Bell	.30	.14	.04
□ 6 Andre Dawson	1.00	.45	.12
□ 7 Eric Davis	.50	.23	.06
□ 8 Wade Boggs	1.00	.45	.12
□ 9 Alan Trammell	.50	.23	.06
□ 10 Juan Samuel	.30	.14	.04
□ 11 Jack Clark	.30	.14	.04
□ 12 Paul Molitor	1.50	.70	.19

1988 Fleer Headliners

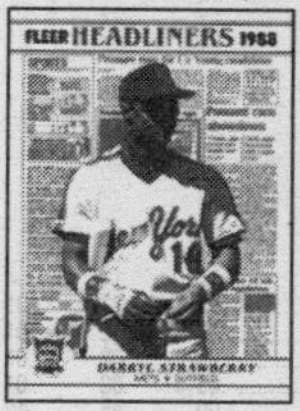

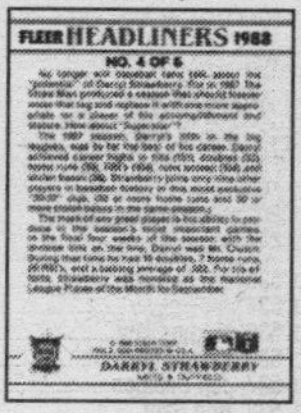

This six-card standard-size set was distributed one per rack pack. The obverse features the player photo superimposed on a gray newsprint background. The cards are printed in red, black, and white on the back describing why that particular player made headlines the previous season. The set is sequenced in alphabetical order.

	MINT	NRMT	EXC
COMPLETE SET (6)	5.00	2.20	.60
COMMON CARD (1-6)	.75	.35	.09
ONE PER RACK PACK			

□ 1 Don Mattingly	2.50	1.10	.30
□ 2 Mark McGwire	2.50	1.10	.30
□ 3 Jack Morris	.75	.35	.09
□ 4 Darryl Strawberry	1.25	.55	.16
□ 5 Dwight Gooden	1.50	.70	.19
□ 6 Tim Raines	1.00	.45	.12

1988 Fleer Update

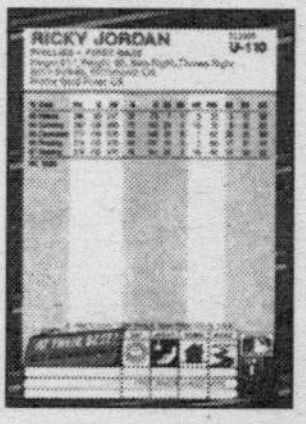

This 132-card standard-size set was distributed exclusively in factory set form in a red, white and blue, cellophane-wrapped box through hobby dealers. In addition to the complete set of 132 cards, the box also contained 25 Team Logo stickers. The cards look very similar to the 1988 Fleer regular issue except for the U-prefixed numbering on back. Cards are ordered alphabetically by player's last name. This was the first Fleer Update set to adopt the Fleer "alphabetical within team" numbering system. The key extended Rookie Cards in this set are Roberto Alomar, Craig Biggio and John Smoltz.

	MINT	NRMT	EXC
COMPLETE FACT.SET (132)	12.00	5.50	1.50
COMMON CARD (1-132)	.05	.02	.01
SEMISTARS	.10	.05	.01
U PREFIX ON CARD NUMBER			

□ 1 Jose Bautista	.05	.02	.01
□ 2 Joe Orsulak	.05	.02	.01
□ 3 Doug Sisk	.05	.02	.01
□ 4 Craig Worthington	.05	.02	.01
□ 5 Mike Boddicker	.05	.02	.01

□ 6 Rick Cerone	.05	.02	.01
□ 7 Larry Parrish	.05	.02	.01
□ 8 Lee Smith	.15	.07	.02
□ 9 Mike Smithson	.05	.02	.01
□ 10 John Trautwein	.05	.02	.01
□ 11 Sherman Corbett	.05	.02	.01
□ 12 Chili Davis	.15	.07	.02
□ 13 Jim Eppard	.05	.02	.01
□ 14 Bryan Harvey	.10	.05	.01
□ 15 John Davis	.05	.02	.01
□ 16 Dave Gallagher	.05	.02	.01
□ 17 Ricky Horton	.05	.02	.01
□ 18 Dan Pasqua	.05	.02	.01
□ 19 Melido Perez	.10	.05	.01
□ 20 Jose Segura	.05	.02	.01
□ 21 Andy Allanson	.05	.02	.01
□ 22 Jon Perlman	.05	.02	.01
□ 23 Domingo Ramos	.05	.02	.01
□ 24 Rick Rodriguez	.05	.02	.01
□ 25 Willie Upshaw	.05	.02	.01
□ 26 Paul Gibson	.05	.02	.01
□ 27 Don Heinkel	.05	.02	.01
□ 28 Ray Knight	.10	.05	.01
□ 29 Gary Pettis	.05	.02	.01
□ 30 Luis Salazar	.05	.02	.01
□ 31 Mike Macfarlane	.15	.07	.02
□ 32 Jeff Montgomery	.15	.07	.02
□ 33 Ted Power	.05	.02	.01
□ 34 Israel Sanchez	.05	.02	.01
□ 35 Kurt Stillwell	.05	.02	.01
□ 36 Pat Tabler	.05	.02	.01
□ 37 Don August	.05	.02	.01
□ 38 Darryl Hamilton	.10	.05	.01
□ 39 Jeff Leonard	.05	.02	.01
□ 40 Joey Meyer	.05	.02	.01
□ 41 Allan Anderson	.05	.02	.01
□ 42 Brian Harper	.05	.02	.01
□ 43 Tom Herr	.05	.02	.01
□ 44 Charlie Lea	.05	.02	.01
□ 45 John Moses (Listed as Hohn on checklist card)	.05	.02	.01
□ 46 John Candelaria	.05	.02	.01
□ 47 Jack Clark	.10	.05	.01
□ 48 Richard Dotson	.05	.02	.01
□ 49 Al Leiter	.15	.07	.02
□ 50 Rafael Santana	.05	.02	.01
□ 51 Don Slaught	.05	.02	.01
□ 52 Todd Burns	.05	.02	.01
□ 53 Dave Henderson	.05	.02	.01
□ 54 Doug Jennings	.05	.02	.01
□ 55 Dave Parker	.15	.07	.02
□ 56 Walt Weiss	.15	.07	.02
□ 57 Bob Welch	.05	.02	.01
□ 58 Henry Cotto	.05	.02	.01
□ 59 Mario Diaz UER (Listed as Marion on card front)	.05	.02	.01
□ 60 Mike Jackson	.05	.02	.01
□ 61 Bill Swift	.05	.02	.01
□ 62 Jose Cecena	.05	.02	.01
□ 63 Ray Hayward	.05	.02	.01
□ 64 Jim Steels UER (Listed as Jim Steele on card back)	.05	.02	.01
□ 65 Pat Borders	.10	.05	.01
□ 66 Sil Campusano	.05	.02	.01
□ 67 Mike Flanagan	.05	.02	.01
□ 68 Todd Stottlemyre	.50	.23	.06
□ 69 David Wells	.15	.07	.02
□ 70 Jose Alvarez	.05	.02	.01
□ 71 Paul Runge	.05	.02	.01
□ 72 Cesar Jimenez (Card was intended for German Jiminez, it's his photo)	.05	.02	.01
□ 73 Pete Smith	.05	.02	.01
□ 74 John Smoltz	4.00	1.80	.50
□ 75 Damon Berryhill	.05	.02	.01
□ 76 Goose Gossage	.15	.07	.02
□ 77 Mark Grace	1.50	.70	.19
□ 78 Darrin Jackson	.05	.02	.01
□ 79 Vance Law	.05	.02	.01
□ 80 Jeff Pico	.05	.02	.01
□ 81 Gary Varsho	.05	.02	.01
□ 82 Tim Birtsas	.05	.02	.01
□ 83 Rob Dibble	.10	.05	.01
□ 84 Danny Jackson	.05	.02	.01
□ 85 Paul O'Neill	.15	.07	.02
□ 86 Jose Rijo	.05	.02	.01
□ 87 Chris Sabo	.10	.05	.01
□ 88 John Fishel	.05	.02	.01
□ 89 Craig Biggio	2.00	.90	.25
□ 90 Terry Puhl	.05	.02	.01
□ 91 Rafael Ramirez	.05	.02	.01
□ 92 Louie Meadows	.05	.02	.01
□ 93 Kirk Gibson	.10	.05	.01
□ 94 Alfredo Griffin	.05	.02	.01
□ 95 Jay Howell	.05	.02	.01
□ 96 Jesse Orosco	.05	.02	.01
□ 97 Alejandro Pena	.05	.02	.01
□ 98 Tracy Woodson	.05	.02	.01
□ 99 John Dopson	.05	.02	.01
□ 100 Brian Holman	.05	.02	.01
□ 101 Rex Hudler	.05	.02	.01
□ 102 Jeff Parrett	.05	.02	.01
□ 103 Nelson Santovenia	.05	.02	.01
□ 104 Kevin Elster	.15	.07	.02
□ 105 Jeff Innis	.05	.02	.01
□ 106 Mackey Sasser	.05	.02	.01
□ 107 Phil Bradley	.05	.02	.01
□ 108 Danny Clay	.05	.02	.01
□ 109 Greg A.Harris	.05	.02	.01
□ 110 Ricky Jordan	.10	.05	.01
□ 111 David Palmer	.05	.02	.01
□ 112 Jim Gott	.05	.02	.01
□ 113 Tommy Gregg UER (Photo actually Randy Milligan)	.05	.02	.01
□ 114 Barry Jones	.05	.02	.01
□ 115 Randy Milligan	.05	.02	.01
□ 116 Luis Alicea	.10	.05	.01
□ 117 Tom Brunansky	.05	.02	.01
□ 118 John Costello	.05	.02	.01
□ 119 Jose DeLeon	.05	.02	.01
□ 120 Bob Horner	.05	.02	.01
□ 121 Scott Terry	.05	.02	.01
□ 122 Roberto Alomar	5.00	2.20	.60
□ 123 Dave Leiper	.05	.02	.01
□ 124 Keith Moreland	.05	.02	.01
□ 125 Mark Parent	.05	.02	.01
□ 126 Dennis Rasmussen	.05	.02	.01
□ 127 Randy Bockus	.05	.02	.01
□ 128 Brett Butler	.10	.05	.01
□ 129 Donell Nixon	.05	.02	.01
□ 130 Earnest Riles	.05	.02	.01
□ 131 Roger Samuels	.05	.02	.01
□ 132 Checklist U1-U132	.05	.02	.01

1989 Fleer

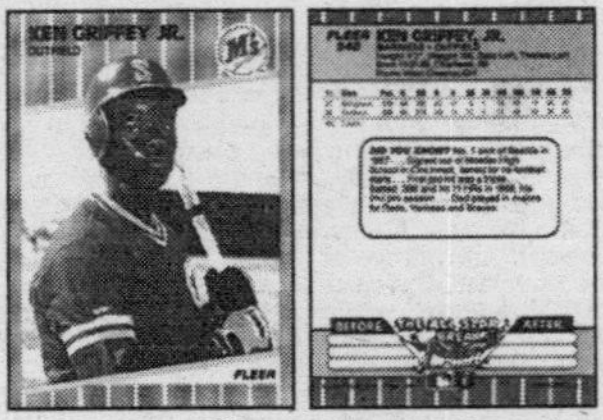

This set consists of 660 standard-size cards. Cards were primarily issued in 15-card wax packs, rack packs and hobby and retail factory sets. Card fronts feature a distinctive gray border background with white and yellow trim. Cards are again organized alphabetically within teams and teams ordered by previous season record. The last 33 cards in the set consist of Specials (628-639), Rookie Pairs (640-653), and checklists (654-660). Approximately half of the California Angels players have white rather than yellow halos. Certain Oakland A's player cards have red instead of green lines for front photo borders. Checklist cards are available

either with or without positions listed for each player. Rookie Cards in this set include Sandy Alomar Jr., Brady Anderson, Dante Bichette, Craig Biggio, Ken Griffey Jr., Charlie Hayes, Ken Hill, Randy Johnson, Ramon Martinez, Hal Morris, Gary Sheffield, and John Smoltz.

	MINT	NRMT	EXC
COMPLETE SET (660)	12.00	5.50	1.50
COMPLETE RETAIL SET (660)	12.00	5.50	1.50
COMPLETE HOBBY SET (672)	12.00	5.50	1.50
COMMON CARD (1-660)	.05	.02	.01
SEMISTARS	.10	.05	.01
STARS	.15	.07	.02
COMP. WORLD SERIES (12)	2.00	.90	.25

□ 1 Don Baylor	.15	.07	.02
□ 2 Lance Blankenship	.05	.02	.01
□ 3 Todd Burns UER (Wrong birthdate; before/after All-Star stats missing)	.05	.02	.01
□ 4 Greg Cadaret UER (All-Star Break stats show 3 losses, should be 2)	.05	.02	.01
□ 5 Jose Canseco	.15	.07	.02
□ 6 Storm Davis	.05	.02	.01
□ 7 Dennis Eckersley	.10	.05	.01
□ 8 Mike Gallego	.05	.02	.01
□ 9 Ron Hassey	.05	.02	.01
□ 10 Dave Henderson	.05	.02	.01
□ 11 Rick Honeycutt	.05	.02	.01
□ 12 Glenn Hubbard	.05	.02	.01
□ 13 Stan Javier	.05	.02	.01
□ 14 Doug Jennings	.05	.02	.01
□ 15 Felix Jose	.05	.02	.01
□ 16 Carney Lansford	.10	.05	.01
□ 17 Mark McGwire	.30	.14	.04
□ 18 Gene Nelson	.05	.02	.01
□ 19 Dave Parker	.10	.05	.01
□ 20 Eric Plunk	.05	.02	.01
□ 21 Luis Polonia	.10	.05	.01
□ 22 Terry Steinbach	.10	.05	.01
□ 23 Dave Stewart	.10	.05	.01
□ 24 Walt Weiss	.05	.02	.01
□ 25 Bob Welch	.05	.02	.01
□ 26 Curt Young	.05	.02	.01
□ 27 Rick Aguilera	.15	.07	.02
□ 28 Wally Backman	.05	.02	.01
□ 29 Mark Carreon UER (After All-Star Break batting 7.14)	.05	.02	.01
□ 30 Gary Carter	.15	.07	.02
□ 31 David Cone	.15	.07	.02
□ 32 Ron Darling	.05	.02	.01
□ 33 Len Dykstra	.10	.05	.01
□ 34 Kevin Elster	.10	.05	.01
□ 35 Sid Fernandez	.05	.02	.01
□ 36 Dwight Gooden	.10	.05	.01
□ 37 Keith Hernandez	.10	.05	.01
□ 38 Gregg Jefferies	.15	.07	.02
□ 39 Howard Johnson	.05	.02	.01
□ 40 Terry Leach	.05	.02	.01
□ 41 Dave Magadan UER (Bio says 15 doubles, should be 13)	.05	.02	.01
□ 42 Bob McClure	.05	.02	.01
□ 43 Roger McDowell UER (Led Mets with 58, should be 62)	.05	.02	.01
□ 44 Kevin McReynolds	.05	.02	.01
□ 45 Keith A. Miller	.05	.02	.01
□ 46 Randy Myers	.10	.05	.01
□ 47 Bob Ojeda	.05	.02	.01
□ 48 Mackey Sasser	.05	.02	.01
□ 49 Darryl Strawberry	.10	.05	.01
□ 50 Tim Teufel	.05	.02	.01
□ 51 Dave West	.05	.02	.01
□ 52 Mookie Wilson	.10	.05	.01
□ 53 Dave Anderson	.05	.02	.01
□ 54 Tim Belcher	.05	.02	.01
□ 55 Mike Davis	.05	.02	.01
□ 56 Mike Devereaux	.05	.02	.01
□ 57 Kirk Gibson	.10	.05	.01
□ 58 Alfredo Griffin	.05	.02	.01
□ 59 Chris Gwynn	.05	.02	.01
□ 60 Jeff Hamilton	.05	.02	.01
□ 61A Danny Heep (Home: Lake Hills)	.15	.07	.02
□ 61B Danny Heep (Home: San Antonio)	.05	.02	.01
□ 62 Orel Hershiser	.10	.05	.01
□ 63 Brian Holton	.05	.02	.01
□ 64 Jay Howell	.05	.02	.01
□ 65 Tim Leary	.05	.02	.01
□ 66 Mike Marshall	.05	.02	.01
□ 67 Ramon Martinez	.25	.11	.03
□ 68 Jesse Orosco	.05	.02	.01
□ 69 Alejandro Pena	.05	.02	.01
□ 70 Steve Sax	.05	.02	.01
□ 71 Mike Scioscia	.05	.02	.01
□ 72 Mike Sharperson	.05	.02	.01
□ 73 John Shelby	.05	.02	.01
□ 74 Franklin Stubbs	.05	.02	.01
□ 75 John Tudor	.05	.02	.01
□ 76 Fernando Valenzuela	.10	.05	.01
□ 77 Tracy Woodson	.05	.02	.01
□ 78 Marty Barrett	.05	.02	.01
□ 79 Todd Benzinger	.05	.02	.01
□ 80 Mike Boddicker UER (Rochester in '76, should be '78)	.05	.02	.01
□ 81 Wade Boggs	.15	.07	.02
□ 82 Oil Can Boyd	.05	.02	.01
□ 83 Ellis Burks	.15	.07	.02
□ 84 Rick Cerone	.05	.02	.01
□ 85 Roger Clemens	.15	.07	.02
□ 86 Steve Curry	.05	.02	.01
□ 87 Dwight Evans	.10	.05	.01
□ 88 Wes Gardner	.05	.02	.01
□ 89 Rich Gedman	.05	.02	.01
□ 90 Mike Greenwell	.05	.02	.01
□ 91 Bruce Hurst	.05	.02	.01
□ 92 Dennis Lamp	.05	.02	.01
□ 93 Spike Owen	.05	.02	.01
□ 94 Larry Parrish UER (Before All-Star Break batting 1.90)	.05	.02	.01
□ 95 Carlos Quintana	.05	.02	.01
□ 96 Jody Reed	.05	.02	.01
□ 97 Jim Rice	.15	.07	.02
□ 98A Kevin Romine ERR (Photo actually Randy Kutcher batting)	.15	.07	.02
□ 98B Kevin Romine COR (Arms folded)	.05	.02	.01
□ 99 Lee Smith	.15	.07	.02
□ 100 Mike Smithson	.05	.02	.01
□ 101 Bob Stanley	.05	.02	.01
□ 102 Allan Anderson	.05	.02	.01
□ 103 Keith Atherton	.05	.02	.01
□ 104 Juan Berenguer	.05	.02	.01
□ 105 Bert Blyleven	.10	.05	.01
□ 106 Eric Bullock UER (Bats/Throws Right, should be Left)	.05	.02	.01
□ 107 Randy Bush	.05	.02	.01
□ 108 John Christensen	.05	.02	.01
□ 109 Mark Davidson	.05	.02	.01
□ 110 Gary Gaetti	.05	.02	.01
□ 111 Greg Gagne	.05	.02	.01
□ 112 Dan Gladden	.05	.02	.01
□ 113 German Gonzalez	.05	.02	.01
□ 114 Brian Harper	.05	.02	.01
□ 115 Tom Herr	.05	.02	.01
□ 116 Kent Hrbek	.10	.05	.01
□ 117 Gene Larkin	.05	.02	.01
□ 118 Tim Laudner	.05	.02	.01
□ 119 Charlie Lea	.05	.02	.01
□ 120 Steve Lombardozzi	.05	.02	.01
□ 121A John Moses (Home: Tempe)	.15	.07	.02
□ 121B John Moses (Home: Phoenix)	.05	.02	.01
□ 122 Al Newman	.05	.02	.01
□ 123 Mark Portugal	.05	.02	.01
□ 124 Kirby Puckett	.30	.14	.04
□ 125 Jeff Reardon	.10	.05	.01
□ 126 Fred Toliver	.05	.02	.01
□ 127 Frank Viola	.05	.02	.01
□ 128 Doyle Alexander	.05	.02	.01

□ 129	Dave Bergman	.05	.02	.01
□ 130A	Tom Brookens ERR (Mike Heath back)	.75	.35	.09
□ 130B	Tom Brookens COR	.05	.02	.01
□ 131	Paul Gibson	.05	.02	.01
□ 132A	Mike Heath ERR (Tom Brookens back)	.75	.35	.09
□ 132B	Mike Heath COR	.05	.02	.01
□ 133	Don Heinkel	.05	.02	.01
□ 134	Mike Henneman	.05	.02	.01
□ 135	Guillermo Hernandez	.05	.02	.01
□ 136	Eric King	.05	.02	.01
□ 137	Chet Lemon	.05	.02	.01
□ 138	Fred Lynn UER ('74, '75 stats missing)	.05	.02	.01
□ 139	Jack Morris	.10	.05	.01
□ 140	Matt Nokes	.05	.02	.01
□ 141	Gary Pettis	.05	.02	.01
□ 142	Ted Power	.05	.02	.01
□ 143	Jeff M. Robinson	.05	.02	.01
□ 144	Luis Salazar	.05	.02	.01
□ 145	Steve Searcy	.05	.02	.01
□ 146	Pat Sheridan	.05	.02	.01
□ 147	Frank Tanana	.05	.02	.01
□ 148	Alan Trammell	.15	.07	.02
□ 149	Walt Terrell	.05	.02	.01
□ 150	Jim Walewander	.05	.02	.01
□ 151	Lou Whitaker	.15	.07	.02
□ 152	Tim Birtsas	.05	.02	.01
□ 153	Tom Browning	.05	.02	.01
□ 154	Keith Brown	.05	.02	.01
□ 155	Norm Charlton	.10	.05	.01
□ 156	Dave Concepcion	.10	.05	.01
□ 157	Kal Daniels	.05	.02	.01
□ 158	Eric Davis	.10	.05	.01
□ 159	Bo Diaz	.05	.02	.01
□ 160	Rob Dibble	.10	.05	.01
□ 161	Nick Esasky	.05	.02	.01
□ 162	John Franco	.05	.02	.01
□ 163	Danny Jackson	.05	.02	.01
□ 164	Barry Larkin	.20	.09	.03
□ 165	Rob Murphy	.05	.02	.01
□ 166	Paul O'Neill	.15	.07	.02
□ 167	Jeff Reed	.05	.02	.01
□ 168	Jose Rijo	.05	.02	.01
□ 169	Ron Robinson	.05	.02	.01
□ 170	Chris Sabo	.05	.02	.01
□ 171	Candy Sierra	.05	.02	.01
□ 172	Van Snider	.05	.02	.01
□ 173A	Jeff Treadway (Target registration mark above head on front in light blue)	5.00	2.20	.60
□ 173B	Jeff Treadway (No target on front)	.05	.02	.01
□ 174	Frank Williams (After All-Star Break stats are jumbled)	.05	.02	.01
□ 175	Herm Winningham	.05	.02	.01
□ 176	Jim Adduci	.05	.02	.01
□ 177	Don August	.05	.02	.01
□ 178	Mike Birkbeck	.05	.02	.01
□ 179	Chris Bosio	.05	.02	.01
□ 180	Glenn Braggs	.05	.02	.01
□ 181	Greg Brock	.05	.02	.01
□ 182	Mark Clear	.05	.02	.01
□ 183	Chuck Crim	.05	.02	.01
□ 184	Rob Deer	.05	.02	.01
□ 185	Tom Filer	.05	.02	.01
□ 186	Jim Gantner	.05	.02	.01
□ 187	Darryl Hamilton	.10	.05	.01
□ 188	Ted Higuera	.05	.02	.01
□ 189	Odell Jones	.05	.02	.01
□ 190	Jeffrey Leonard	.05	.02	.01
□ 191	Joey Meyer	.05	.02	.01
□ 192	Paul Mirabella	.05	.02	.01
□ 193	Paul Molitor	.20	.09	.03
□ 194	Charlie O'Brien	.05	.02	.01
□ 195	Dan Plesac	.05	.02	.01
□ 196	Gary Sheffield	.75	.35	.09
□ 197	B.J. Surhoff	.15	.07	.02
□ 198	Dale Sveum	.05	.02	.01
□ 199	Bill Wegman	.05	.02	.01
□ 200	Robin Yount	.15	.07	.02
□ 201	Rafael Belliard	.05	.02	.01
□ 202	Barry Bonds	.40	.18	.05
□ 203	Bobby Bonilla	.10	.05	.01
□ 204	Sid Bream	.05	.02	.01
□ 205	Benny Distefano	.05	.02	.01
□ 206	Doug Drabek	.10	.05	.01
□ 207	Mike Dunne	.05	.02	.01
□ 208	Felix Fermin	.05	.02	.01
□ 209	Brian Fisher	.05	.02	.01
□ 210	Jim Gott	.05	.02	.01
□ 211	Bob Kipper	.05	.02	.01
□ 212	Dave LaPoint	.05	.02	.01
□ 213	Mike LaValliere	.05	.02	.01
□ 214	Jose Lind	.05	.02	.01
□ 215	Junior Ortiz	.05	.02	.01
□ 216	Vicente Palacios	.05	.02	.01
□ 217	Tom Prince	.05	.02	.01
□ 218	Gary Redus	.05	.02	.01
□ 219	R.J. Reynolds	.05	.02	.01
□ 220	Jeff D. Robinson	.05	.02	.01
□ 221	John Smiley	.05	.02	.01
□ 222	Andy Van Slyke	.10	.05	.01
□ 223	Bob Walk	.05	.02	.01
□ 224	Glenn Wilson	.05	.02	.01
□ 225	Jesse Barfield	.05	.02	.01
□ 226	George Bell	.05	.02	.01
□ 227	Pat Borders	.10	.05	.01
□ 228	John Cerutti	.05	.02	.01
□ 229	Jim Clancy	.05	.02	.01
□ 230	Mark Eichhorn	.05	.02	.01
□ 231	Tony Fernandez	.05	.02	.01
□ 232	Cecil Fielder	.10	.05	.01
□ 233	Mike Flanagan	.05	.02	.01
□ 234	Kelly Gruber	.05	.02	.01
□ 235	Tom Henke	.05	.02	.01
□ 236	Jimmy Key	.10	.05	.01
□ 237	Rick Leach	.05	.02	.01
□ 238	Manny Lee UER (Bio says regular shortstop, sic, Tony Fernandez)	.05	.02	.01
□ 239	Nelson Liriano	.05	.02	.01
□ 240	Fred McGriff	.20	.09	.03
□ 241	Lloyd Moseby	.05	.02	.01
□ 242	Rance Mulliniks	.05	.02	.01
□ 243	Jeff Musselman	.05	.02	.01
□ 244	Dave Stieb	.05	.02	.01
□ 245	Todd Stottlemyre	.10	.05	.01
□ 246	Duane Ward	.05	.02	.01
□ 247	David Wells	.05	.02	.01
□ 248	Ernie Whitt UER (HR total 21, should be 121)	.05	.02	.01
□ 249	Luis Aguayo	.05	.02	.01
□ 250A	Neil Allen (Home: Sarasota, FL)	.75	.35	.09
□ 250B	Neil Allen (Home: Syosset, NY)	.05	.02	.01
□ 251	John Candelaria	.05	.02	.01
□ 252	Jack Clark	.10	.05	.01
□ 253	Richard Dotson	.05	.02	.01
□ 254	Rickey Henderson	.15	.07	.02
□ 255	Tommy John	.10	.05	.01
□ 256	Roberto Kelly	.10	.05	.01
□ 257	Al Leiter	.10	.05	.01
□ 258	Don Mattingly	.50	.23	.06
□ 259	Dale Mohorcic	.05	.02	.01
□ 260	Hal Morris	.15	.07	.02
□ 261	Scott Nielsen	.05	.02	.01
□ 262	Mike Pagliarulo UER (Wrong birthdate)	.05	.02	.01
□ 263	Hipolito Pena	.05	.02	.01
□ 264	Ken Phelps	.05	.02	.01
□ 265	Willie Randolph	.10	.05	.01
□ 266	Rick Rhoden	.05	.02	.01
□ 267	Dave Righetti	.05	.02	.01
□ 268	Rafael Santana	.05	.02	.01
□ 269	Steve Shields	.05	.02	.01
□ 270	Joel Skinner	.05	.02	.01
□ 271	Don Slaught	.05	.02	.01
□ 272	Claudell Washington	.05	.02	.01
□ 273	Gary Ward	.05	.02	.01
□ 274	Dave Winfield	.15	.07	.02
□ 275	Luis Aquino	.05	.02	.01
□ 276	Floyd Bannister	.05	.02	.01
□ 277	George Brett	.40	.18	.05

□ 278	Bill Buckner	.10	.05	.01
□ 279	Nick Capra	.05	.02	.01
□ 280	Jose DeJesus	.05	.02	.01
□ 281	Steve Farr	.05	.02	.01
□ 282	Jerry Don Gleaton	.05	.02	.01
□ 283	Mark Gubicza	.05	.02	.01
□ 284	Tom Gordon UER	.10	.05	.01
	(16.2 innings in '88, should be 15.2)			
□ 285	Bo Jackson	.15	.07	.02
□ 286	Charlie Leibrandt	.05	.02	.01
□ 287	Mike Macfarlane	.10	.05	.01
□ 288	Jeff Montgomery	.10	.05	.01
□ 289	Bill Pecota UER	.05	.02	.01
	(Photo actually Brad Wellman)			
□ 290	Jamie Quirk	.05	.02	.01
□ 291	Bret Saberhagen	.10	.05	.01
□ 292	Kevin Seitzer	.05	.02	.01
□ 293	Kurt Stillwell	.05	.02	.01
□ 294	Pat Tabler	.05	.02	.01
□ 295	Danny Tartabull	.05	.02	.01
□ 296	Gary Thurman	.05	.02	.01
□ 297	Frank White	.10	.05	.01
□ 298	Willie Wilson	.05	.02	.01
□ 299	Roberto Alomar	.50	.23	.06
□ 300	Sandy Alomar Jr. UER	.20	.09	.03
	(Wrong birthdate, says 6/16/66, should say 6/18/66)			
□ 301	Chris Brown	.05	.02	.01
□ 302	Mike Brumley UER	.05	.02	.01
	(133 hits in '88, should be 134)			
□ 303	Mark Davis	.05	.02	.01
□ 304	Mark Grant	.05	.02	.01
□ 305	Tony Gwynn	.40	.18	.05
□ 306	Greg W. Harris	.05	.02	.01
□ 307	Andy Hawkins	.05	.02	.01
□ 308	Jimmy Jones	.05	.02	.01
□ 309	John Kruk	.10	.05	.01
□ 310	Dave Leiper	.05	.02	.01
□ 311	Carmelo Martinez	.05	.02	.01
□ 312	Lance McCullers	.05	.02	.01
□ 313	Keith Moreland	.05	.02	.01
□ 314	Dennis Rasmussen	.05	.02	.01
□ 315	Randy Ready UER	.05	.02	.01
	(1214 games in '88, should be 114)			
□ 316	Benito Santiago	.10	.05	.01
□ 317	Eric Show	.05	.02	.01
□ 318	Todd Simmons	.05	.02	.01
□ 319	Garry Templeton	.05	.02	.01
□ 320	Dickie Thon	.05	.02	.01
□ 321	Ed Whitson	.05	.02	.01
□ 322	Marvell Wynne	.05	.02	.01
□ 323	Mike Aldrete	.05	.02	.01
□ 324	Brett Butler	.10	.05	.01
□ 325	Will Clark UER	.20	.09	.03
	(Three consecutive 100 RBI seasons)			
□ 326	Kelly Downs UER	.05	.02	.01
	('88 stats missing)			
□ 327	Dave Dravecky	.10	.05	.01
□ 328	Scott Garrelts	.05	.02	.01
□ 329	Atlee Hammaker	.05	.02	.01
□ 330	Charlie Hayes	.15	.07	.02
□ 331	Mike Krukow	.05	.02	.01
□ 332	Craig Lefferts	.05	.02	.01
□ 333	Candy Maldonado	.05	.02	.01
□ 334	Kirt Manwaring UER	.05	.02	.01
	(Bats Rights)			
□ 335	Bob Melvin	.05	.02	.01
□ 336	Kevin Mitchell	.10	.05	.01
□ 337	Donell Nixon	.05	.02	.01
□ 338	Tony Perezchica	.05	.02	.01
□ 339	Joe Price	.05	.02	.01
□ 340	Rick Reuschel	.05	.02	.01
□ 341	Earnest Riles	.05	.02	.01
□ 342	Don Robinson	.05	.02	.01
□ 343	Chris Speier	.05	.02	.01
□ 344	Robby Thompson UER	.05	.02	.01
	(West Plam Beach)			
□ 345	Jose Uribe	.05	.02	.01
□ 346	Matt Williams	.25	.11	.03
□ 347	Trevor Wilson	.05	.02	.01
□ 348	Juan Agosto	.05	.02	.01
□ 349	Larry Andersen	.05	.02	.01
□ 350A	Alan Ashby ERR	2.00	.90	.25
	(Throws Rig)			
□ 350B	Alan Ashby COR	.05	.02	.01
□ 351	Kevin Bass	.05	.02	.01
□ 352	Buddy Bell	.10	.05	.01
□ 353	Craig Biggio	.40	.18	.05
□ 354	Danny Darwin	.05	.02	.01
□ 355	Glenn Davis	.05	.02	.01
□ 356	Jim Deshaies	.05	.02	.01
□ 357	Bill Doran	.05	.02	.01
□ 358	John Fishel	.05	.02	.01
□ 359	Billy Hatcher	.05	.02	.01
□ 360	Bob Knepper	.05	.02	.01
□ 361	Louie Meadows UER	.05	.02	.01
	(Bio says 10 EBH's and 6 SB's in '88, should be 3 and 4)			
□ 362	Dave Meads	.05	.02	.01
□ 363	Jim Pankovits	.05	.02	.01
□ 364	Terry Puhl	.05	.02	.01
□ 365	Rafael Ramirez	.05	.02	.01
□ 366	Craig Reynolds	.05	.02	.01
□ 367	Mike Scott	.05	.02	.01
	(Card number listed as 368 on Astros CL)			
□ 368	Nolan Ryan	.75	.35	.09
	(Card number listed as 367 on Astros CL)			
□ 369	Dave Smith	.05	.02	.01
□ 370	Gerald Young	.05	.02	.01
□ 371	Hubie Brooks	.05	.02	.01
□ 372	Tim Burke	.05	.02	.01
□ 373	John Dopson	.05	.02	.01
□ 374	Mike R. Fitzgerald	.05	.02	.01
□ 375	Tom Foley	.05	.02	.01
□ 376	Andres Galarraga UER	.15	.07	.02
	(Home: Caracus)			
□ 377	Neal Heaton	.05	.02	.01
□ 378	Joe Hesketh	.05	.02	.01
□ 379	Brian Holman	.05	.02	.01
□ 380	Rex Hudler	.05	.02	.01
□ 381	Randy Johnson UER	.75	.35	.09
	(Innings for '85 and '86 shown as 27 and 120, should be 27.1 and 119.2)			
□ 382	Wallace Johnson	.05	.02	.01
□ 383	Tracy Jones	.05	.02	.01
□ 384	Dave Martinez	.05	.02	.01
□ 385	Dennis Martinez	.10	.05	.01
□ 386	Andy McGaffigan	.05	.02	.01
□ 387	Otis Nixon	.05	.02	.01
□ 388	Johnny Paredes	.05	.02	.01
□ 389	Jeff Parrett	.05	.02	.01
□ 390	Pascual Perez	.05	.02	.01
□ 391	Tim Raines	.15	.07	.02
□ 392	Luis Rivera	.05	.02	.01
□ 393	Nelson Santovenia	.05	.02	.01
□ 394	Bryn Smith	.05	.02	.01
□ 395	Tim Wallach	.05	.02	.01
□ 396	Andy Allanson UER	.05	.02	.01
	(1214 hits in '88, should be 114)			
□ 397	Rod Allen	.05	.02	.01
□ 398	Scott Bailes	.05	.02	.01
□ 399	Tom Candiotti	.05	.02	.01
□ 400	Joe Carter	.15	.07	.02
□ 401	Carmen Castillo UER	.05	.02	.01
	(After All-Star Break batting 2.50)			
□ 402	Dave Clark UER	.05	.02	.01
	(Card front shows position as Rookie; after All-Star Break batting 3.14)			
□ 403	John Farrell UER	.05	.02	.01
	(Typo in runs allowed in '88)			
□ 404	Julio Franco	.10	.05	.01
□ 405	Don Gordon	.05	.02	.01
□ 406	Mel Hall	.05	.02	.01
□ 407	Brad Havens	.05	.02	.01
□ 408	Brook Jacoby	.05	.02	.01
□ 409	Doug Jones	.05	.02	.01

□ 410 Jeff Kaiser	.05	.02	.01
□ 411 Luis Medina	.05	.02	.01
□ 412 Cory Snyder	.05	.02	.01
□ 413 Greg Swindell	.05	.02	.01
□ 414 Ron Tingley UER (Hit HR in first ML at-bat, should be first AL at-bat)	.05	.02	.01
□ 415 Willie Upshaw	.05	.02	.01
□ 416 Ron Washington	.05	.02	.01
□ 417 Rich Yett	.05	.02	.01
□ 418 Damon Berryhill	.05	.02	.01
□ 419 Mike Bielecki	.05	.02	.01
□ 420 Doug Dascenzo	.05	.02	.01
□ 421 Jody Davis UER (Braves stats for '88 missing)	.05	.02	.01
□ 422 Andre Dawson	.15	.07	.02
□ 423 Frank DiPino	.05	.02	.01
□ 424 Shawon Dunston	.05	.02	.01
□ 425 Rich Gossage	.15	.07	.02
□ 426 Mark Grace UER (Minor League stats for '88 missing)	.20	.09	.03
□ 427 Mike Harkey	.05	.02	.01
□ 428 Darrin Jackson	.05	.02	.01
□ 429 Les Lancaster	.05	.02	.01
□ 430 Vance Law	.05	.02	.01
□ 431 Greg Maddux	.75	.35	.09
□ 432 Jamie Moyer	.05	.02	.01
□ 433 Al Nipper	.05	.02	.01
□ 434 Rafael Palmeiro UER (170 hits in '88, should be 178)	.15	.07	.02
□ 435 Pat Perry	.05	.02	.01
□ 436 Jeff Pico	.05	.02	.01
□ 437 Ryne Sandberg	.25	.11	.03
□ 438 Calvin Schiraldi	.05	.02	.01
□ 439 Rick Sutcliffe	.05	.02	.01
□ 440A Manny Trillo ERR (Throws Rig)	2.00	.90	.25
□ 440B Manny Trillo COR	.05	.02	.01
□ 441 Gary Varsho UER (Wrong birthdate; .303 should be .302; 11/28 should be 9/19)	.05	.02	.01
□ 442 Mitch Webster	.05	.02	.01
□ 443 Luis Alicea	.05	.02	.01
□ 444 Tom Brunansky	.05	.02	.01
□ 445 Vince Coleman UER (Third straight with 83, should be fourth straight with 81)	.05	.02	.01
□ 446 John Costello UER (Home California, should be New York)	.05	.02	.01
□ 447 Danny Cox	.05	.02	.01
□ 448 Ken Dayley	.05	.02	.01
□ 449 Jose DeLeon	.05	.02	.01
□ 450 Curt Ford	.05	.02	.01
□ 451 Pedro Guerrero	.10	.05	.01
□ 452 Bob Horner	.05	.02	.01
□ 453 Tim Jones	.05	.02	.01
□ 454 Steve Lake	.05	.02	.01
□ 455 Joe Magrane UER (Des Moines, IO)	.05	.02	.01
□ 456 Greg Mathews	.05	.02	.01
□ 457 Willie McGee	.05	.02	.01
□ 458 Larry McWilliams	.05	.02	.01
□ 459 Jose Oquendo	.05	.02	.01
□ 460 Tony Pena	.05	.02	.01
□ 461 Terry Pendleton	.10	.05	.01
□ 462 Steve Peters UER (Lives in Harrah, not Harah)	.05	.02	.01
□ 463 Ozzie Smith	.20	.09	.03
□ 464 Scott Terry	.05	.02	.01
□ 465 Denny Walling	.05	.02	.01
□ 466 Todd Worrell	.05	.02	.01
□ 467 Tony Armas UER (Before All-Star Break batting 2.39)	.05	.02	.01
□ 468 Dante Bichette	.60	.25	.07
□ 469 Bob Boone	.10	.05	.01
□ 470 Terry Clark	.05	.02	.01
□ 471 Stew Cliburn	.05	.02	.01
□ 472 Mike Cook UER (TM near Angels logo missing from front)	.05	.02	.01
□ 473 Sherman Corbett	.05	.02	.01
□ 474 Chili Davis	.10	.05	.01
□ 475 Brian Downing	.05	.02	.01
□ 476 Jim Eppard	.05	.02	.01
□ 477 Chuck Finley	.10	.05	.01
□ 478 Willie Fraser	.05	.02	.01
□ 479 Bryan Harvey UER (ML record shows 0-0, should be 7-5)	.10	.05	.01
□ 480 Jack Howell	.05	.02	.01
□ 481 Wally Joyner UER (Yorba Linda, GA)	.10	.05	.01
□ 482 Jack Lazorko	.05	.02	.01
□ 483 Kirk McCaskill	.05	.02	.01
□ 484 Mark McLemore	.05	.02	.01
□ 485 Greg Minton	.05	.02	.01
□ 486 Dan Petry	.05	.02	.01
□ 487 Johnny Ray	.05	.02	.01
□ 488 Dick Schofield	.05	.02	.01
□ 489 Devon White	.10	.05	.01
□ 490 Mike Witt	.05	.02	.01
□ 491 Harold Baines	.10	.05	.01
□ 492 Daryl Boston	.05	.02	.01
□ 493 Ivan Calderon UER ('80 stats shifted)	.05	.02	.01
□ 494 Mike Diaz	.05	.02	.01
□ 495 Carlton Fisk	.15	.07	.02
□ 496 Dave Gallagher	.05	.02	.01
□ 497 Ozzie Guillen	.05	.02	.01
□ 498 Shawn Hillegas	.05	.02	.01
□ 499 Lance Johnson	.15	.07	.02
□ 500 Barry Jones	.05	.02	.01
□ 501 Bill Long	.05	.02	.01
□ 502 Steve Lyons	.05	.02	.01
□ 503 Fred Manrique	.05	.02	.01
□ 504 Jack McDowell	.15	.07	.02
□ 505 Donn Pall	.05	.02	.01
□ 506 Kelly Paris	.05	.02	.01
□ 507 Dan Pasqua	.05	.02	.01
□ 508 Ken Patterson	.05	.02	.01
□ 509 Melido Perez	.05	.02	.01
□ 510 Jerry Reuss	.05	.02	.01
□ 511 Mark Salas	.05	.02	.01
□ 512 Bobby Thigpen UER ('86 ERA 4.69, should be 4.68)	.05	.02	.01
□ 513 Mike Woodard	.05	.02	.01
□ 514 Bob Brower	.05	.02	.01
□ 515 Steve Buechele	.05	.02	.01
□ 516 Jose Cecena	.05	.02	.01
□ 517 Cecil Espy	.05	.02	.01
□ 518 Scott Fletcher	.05	.02	.01
□ 519 Cecilio Guante ('87 Yankee stats are off-centered)	.05	.02	.01
□ 520 Jose Guzman	.05	.02	.01
□ 521 Ray Hayward	.05	.02	.01
□ 522 Charlie Hough	.10	.05	.01
□ 523 Pete Incaviglia	.10	.05	.01
□ 524 Mike Jeffcoat	.05	.02	.01
□ 525 Paul Kilgus	.05	.02	.01
□ 526 Chad Kreuter	.05	.02	.01
□ 527 Jeff Kunkel	.05	.02	.01
□ 528 Oddibe McDowell	.05	.02	.01
□ 529 Pete O'Brien	.05	.02	.01
□ 530 Geno Petralli	.05	.02	.01
□ 531 Jeff Russell	.05	.02	.01
□ 532 Ruben Sierra	.10	.05	.01
□ 533 Mike Stanley	.05	.02	.01
□ 534A Ed VandeBerg ERR (Throws Lef)	2.00	.90	.25
□ 534B Ed VandeBerg COR	.05	.02	.01
□ 535 Curtis Wilkerson ERR (Pitcher headings at bottom)	.05	.02	.01
□ 536 Mitch Williams	.05	.02	.01
□ 537 Bobby Witt UER ('85 ERA .643, should be 6.43)	.05	.02	.01
□ 538 Steve Balboni	.05	.02	.01
□ 539 Scott Bankhead	.05	.02	.01
□ 540 Scott Bradley	.05	.02	.01
□ 541 Mickey Brantley	.05	.02	.01

□ 542	Jay Buhner	.25	.11	.03
□ 543	Mike Campbell	.05	.02	.01
□ 544	Darnell Coles	.05	.02	.01
□ 545	Henry Cotto	.05	.02	.01
□ 546	Alvin Davis	.05	.02	.01
□ 547	Mario Diaz	.05	.02	.01
□ 548	Ken Griffey Jr.	5.00	2.20	.60
□ 549	Erik Hanson	.15	.07	.02
□ 550	Mike Jackson UER (Lifetime ERA 3.345, should be 3.45)	.05	.02	.01
□ 551	Mark Langston	.10	.05	.01
□ 552	Edgar Martinez	.25	.11	.03
□ 553	Bill McGuire	.05	.02	.01
□ 554	Mike Moore	.05	.02	.01
□ 555	Jim Presley	.05	.02	.01
□ 556	Rey Quinones	.05	.02	.01
□ 557	Jerry Reed	.05	.02	.01
□ 558	Harold Reynolds	.05	.02	.01
□ 559	Mike Schooler	.05	.02	.01
□ 560	Bill Swift	.05	.02	.01
□ 561	Dave Valle	.05	.02	.01
□ 562	Steve Bedrosian	.05	.02	.01
□ 563	Phil Bradley	.05	.02	.01
□ 564	Don Carman	.05	.02	.01
□ 565	Bob Dernier	.05	.02	.01
□ 566	Marvin Freeman	.05	.02	.01
□ 567	Todd Frohwirth	.05	.02	.01
□ 568	Greg Gross	.05	.02	.01
□ 569	Kevin Gross	.05	.02	.01
□ 570	Greg A. Harris	.05	.02	.01
□ 571	Von Hayes	.05	.02	.01
□ 572	Chris James	.05	.02	.01
□ 573	Steve Jeltz	.05	.02	.01
□ 574	Ron Jones UER (Led IL in '88 with 85, should be 75)	.05	.02	.01
□ 575	Ricky Jordan	.10	.05	.01
□ 576	Mike Maddux	.05	.02	.01
□ 577	David Palmer	.05	.02	.01
□ 578	Lance Parrish	.05	.02	.01
□ 579	Shane Rawley	.05	.02	.01
□ 580	Bruce Ruffin	.05	.02	.01
□ 581	Juan Samuel	.05	.02	.01
□ 582	Mike Schmidt	.20	.09	.03
□ 583	Kent Tekulve	.05	.02	.01
□ 584	Milt Thompson UER (19 hits in '88, should be 109)	.05	.02	.01
□ 585	Jose Alvarez	.05	.02	.01
□ 586	Paul Assenmacher	.05	.02	.01
□ 587	Bruce Benedict	.05	.02	.01
□ 588	Jeff Blauser	.10	.05	.01
□ 589	Terry Blocker	.05	.02	.01
□ 590	Ron Gant	.15	.07	.02
□ 591	Tom Glavine	.25	.11	.03
□ 592	Tommy Gregg	.05	.02	.01
□ 593	Albert Hall	.05	.02	.01
□ 594	Dion James	.05	.02	.01
□ 595	Rick Mahler	.05	.02	.01
□ 596	Dale Murphy	.15	.07	.02
□ 597	Gerald Perry	.05	.02	.01
□ 598	Charlie Puleo	.05	.02	.01
□ 599	Ted Simmons	.10	.05	.01
□ 600	Pete Smith	.05	.02	.01
□ 601	Zane Smith	.05	.02	.01
□ 602	John Smoltz	.75	.35	.09
□ 603	Bruce Sutter	.05	.02	.01
□ 604	Andres Thomas	.05	.02	.01
□ 605	Ozzie Virgil	.05	.02	.01
□ 606	Brady Anderson	.60	.25	.07
□ 607	Jeff Ballard	.05	.02	.01
□ 608	Jose Bautista	.05	.02	.01
□ 609	Ken Gerhart	.05	.02	.01
□ 610	Terry Kennedy	.05	.02	.01
□ 611	Eddie Murray	.25	.11	.03
□ 612	Carl Nichols UER (Before All-Star Break batting 1.88)	.05	.02	.01
□ 613	Tom Niedenfuer	.05	.02	.01
□ 614	Joe Orsulak	.05	.02	.01
□ 615	Oswald Peraza UER (Shown as Oswaldo)	.05	.02	.01
□ 616A	Bill Ripken ERR (Rick Face written on knob of bat)	5.00	2.20	.60
□ 616B	Bill Ripken (Bat knob whited out)	40.00	18.00	5.00
□ 616C	Bill Ripken (Words on bat knob scribbled out)	5.00	2.20	.60
□ 616D	Bill Ripken DP (Black box covering bat knob)	.15	.07	.02
□ 617	Cal Ripken	.75	.35	.09
□ 618	Dave Schmidt	.05	.02	.01
□ 619	Rick Schu	.05	.02	.01
□ 620	Larry Sheets	.05	.02	.01
□ 621	Doug Sisk	.05	.02	.01
□ 622	Pete Stanicek	.05	.02	.01
□ 623	Mickey Tettleton	.10	.05	.01
□ 624	Jay Tibbs	.05	.02	.01
□ 625	Jim Traber	.05	.02	.01
□ 626	Mark Williamson	.05	.02	.01
□ 627	Craig Worthington	.05	.02	.01
□ 628	Speed/Power Jose Canseco	.15	.07	.02
□ 629	Pitcher Perfect Tom Browning	.05	.02	.01
□ 630	Like Father/Like Sons Roberto Alomar Sandy Alomar Jr. (Names on card listed in wrong order) UER	.30	.14	.04
□ 631	NL All Stars UER Will Clark Rafael Palmeiro (Gallaraga, sic; Clark 3 consecutive 100 RBI seasons; third with 102 RBI's)	.15	.07	.02
□ 632	Homeruns - Coast to Coast UER Darryl Strawberry Will Clark (Homeruns should be two words)	.10	.05	.01
□ 633	Hot Corners - Hot Hitters UER Wade Boggs Carney Lansford (Boggs hit .366 in '86, should be '88)	.10	.05	.01
□ 634	Triple A's Jose Canseco Terry Steinbach Mark McGwire	.10	.05	.01
□ 635	Dual Heat Mark Davis Dwight Gooden	.15	.07	.02
□ 636	NL Pitching Power UER Danny Jackson David Cone (Hersheiser, sic)	.10	.05	.01
□ 637	Cannon Arms UER Chris Sabo Bobby Bonilla (Bobby Bonds, sic)	.10	.05	.01
□ 638	Double Trouble UER Andres Galarraga (Misspelled Gallaraga on card back) Gerald Perry	.10	.05	.01
□ 639	Power Center Kirby Puckett Eric Davis	.15	.07	.02
□ 640	Steve Wilson and Cameron Drew	.05	.02	.01
□ 641	Kevin Brown and Kevin Reimer	.15	.07	.02
□ 642	Brad Pounders and Jerald Clark	.05	.02	.01
□ 643	Mike Capel and Drew Hall	.05	.02	.01
□ 644	Joe Girardi and Rolando Roomes	.15	.07	.02
□ 645	Lenny Harris and Marty Brown	.10	.05	.01
□ 646	Luis DeLosSantos and Jim Campbell	.05	.02	.01
□ 647	Randy Kramer and Miguel Garcia	.05	.02	.01

□ 648 Torey Lovullo and Robert Palacios	.05	.02	.01
□ 649 Jim Corsi and Bob Milacki	.05	.02	.01
□ 650 Grady Hall and Mike Rochford	.05	.02	.01
□ 651 Terry Taylor and Vance Lovelace	.05	.02	.01
□ 652 Ken Hill and Dennis Cook	.50	.23	.06
□ 653 Scott Service and Shane Turner	.05	.02	.01
□ 654 CL: Oakland/Mets Dodgers/Red Sox (10 Henderson; 68 Jess Orosco)	.05	.02	.01
□ 655A CL: Twins/Tigers ERR Reds/Brewers (179 Boslo and Twins/Tigers positions listed)	.05	.02	.01
□ 655B CL: Twins/Tigers COR Reds/Brewers (179 Boslo but Twins/Tigers positions not listed)	.05	.02	.01
□ 656 CL: Pirates/Blue Jays Yankees/Royals (225 Jess Barfield)	.05	.02	.01
□ 657 CL: Padres/Giants Astros/Expos (367/368 wrong)	.05	.02	.01
□ 658 CL: Indians/Cubs Cardinals/Angels (449 Deleon)	.05	.02	.01
□ 659 CL: White Sox/Rangers Mariners/Phillies	.05	.02	.01
□ 660 CL: Braves/Orioles Specials/Checklists (632 hyphenated differently and 650 Hali; 595 Rich Mahler; 619 Rich Schu)	.05	.02	.01

1989 Fleer All-Stars

This twelve-card standard-size subset was randomly inserted in Fleer wax and cello packs. The players selected are the 1989 Fleer Major League All-Star team. One player has been selected for each position along with a DH and three pitchers. The cards feature a distinctive green background on the card fronts. The set is sequenced in alphabetical order.

	MINT	NRMT	EXC
COMPLETE SET (12)	5.00	2.20	.60
COMMON CARD (1-12)	.25	.11	.03
SEMISTARS	.40	.18	.05
RANDOM INSERTS IN PACKS			

□ 1 Bobby Bonilla	.40	.18	.05
□ 2 Jose Canseco	1.00	.45	.12
□ 3 Will Clark	1.25	.55	.16
□ 4 Dennis Eckersley	.40	.18	.05
□ 5 Julio Franco	.40	.18	.05
□ 6 Mike Greenwell	.25	.11	.03
□ 7 Orel Hershiser	.40	.18	.05
□ 8 Paul Molitor	1.25	.55	.16
□ 9 Mike Scioscia	.25	.11	.03
□ 10 Darryl Strawberry	.40	.18	.05
□ 11 Alan Trammell	.40	.18	.05
□ 12 Frank Viola	.25	.11	.03

1989 Fleer For The Record

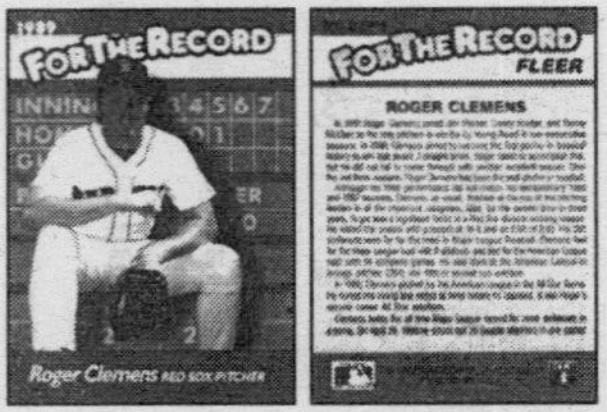

This six-card standard-size insert set was distributed one per rack pack. The set is subtitled "For The Record" and commemorates record-breaking events for those players from the previous season. The card backs are printed in red, black, and gray on white card stock. The set is sequenced in alphabetical order.

	MINT	NRMT	EXC
COMPLETE SET (6)	8.00	3.60	1.00
COMMON CARD (1-6)	.30	.14	.04
ONE PER RACK PACK			

□ 1 Wade Boggs	.75	.35	.09
□ 2 Roger Clemens	1.00	.45	.12
□ 3 Andres Galarraga	1.00	.45	.12
□ 4 Kirk Gibson	.30	.14	.04
□ 5 Greg Maddux	5.00	2.20	.60
□ 6 Don Mattingly UER (Won batting title '83, should say '84)	3.00	1.35	.35

1989 Fleer Update

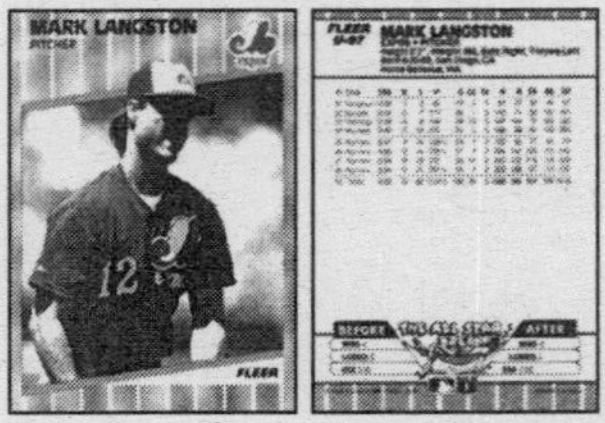

The 1989 Fleer Update set contains 132 standard-size cards. The cards were distributed exclusively in factory set form in grey and white, cellophane wrapped boxes through hobby dealers. The cards are identical in design to regular issue 1989 Fleer cards except for the U-prefixed numbering on back. The set numbering is in team order with players within teams ordered alphabetically. The set includes special cards for Nolan Ryan's 5,000th strikeout and Mike Schmidt's retirement. Rookie Cards include Kevin Appier, Joey (Albert) Belle, Deion Sanders, Greg Vaughn, Robin Ventura and Todd Zeile.

	MINT	NRMT	EXC
COMPLETE FACT.SET (132)	5.00	2.20	.60
COMMON CARD (1-132)	.05	.02	.01
SEMISTARS	.10	.05	.01
U PREFIX ON CARD NUMBER			
□ 1 Phil Bradley	.05	.02	.01
□ 2 Mike Devereaux	.05	.02	.01
□ 3 Steve Finley	.25	.11	.03
□ 4 Kevin Hickey	.05	.02	.01
□ 5 Brian Holton	.05	.02	.01
□ 6 Bob Milacki	.05	.02	.01
□ 7 Randy Milligan	.05	.02	.01
□ 8 John Dopson	.05	.02	.01
□ 9 Nick Esasky	.05	.02	.01
□ 10 Rob Murphy	.05	.02	.01
□ 11 Jim Abbott	.15	.07	.02
□ 12 Bert Blyleven	.10	.05	.01
□ 13 Jeff Manto	.05	.02	.01
□ 14 Bob McClure	.05	.02	.01
□ 15 Lance Parrish	.05	.02	.01
□ 16 Lee Stevens	.10	.05	.01
□ 17 Claudell Washington	.05	.02	.01
□ 18 Mark Davis	.05	.02	.01
□ 19 Eric King	.05	.02	.01
□ 20 Ron Kittle	.05	.02	.01
□ 21 Matt Merullo	.05	.02	.01
□ 22 Steve Rosenberg	.05	.02	.01
□ 23 Robin Ventura	.40	.18	.05
□ 24 Keith Atherton	.05	.02	.01
□ 25 Joey Belle	3.00	1.35	.35
□ 26 Jerry Browne	.05	.02	.01
□ 27 Felix Fermin	.05	.02	.01
□ 28 Brad Komminsk	.05	.02	.01
□ 29 Pete O'Brien	.05	.02	.01
□ 30 Mike Brumley	.05	.02	.01
□ 31 Tracy Jones	.05	.02	.01
□ 32 Mike Schwabe	.05	.02	.01
□ 33 Gary Ward	.05	.02	.01
□ 34 Frank Williams	.05	.02	.01
□ 35 Kevin Appier	.40	.18	.05
□ 36 Bob Boone	.10	.05	.01
□ 37 Luis DeLosSantos	.05	.02	.01
□ 38 Jim Eisenreich	.10	.05	.01
□ 39 Jaime Navarro	.15	.07	.02
□ 40 Bill Spiers	.05	.02	.01
□ 41 Greg Vaughn	.50	.23	.06
□ 42 Randy Veres	.05	.02	.01
□ 43 Wally Backman	.05	.02	.01
□ 44 Shane Rawley	.05	.02	.01
□ 45 Steve Balboni	.05	.02	.01
□ 46 Jesse Barfield	.05	.02	.01
□ 47 Alvaro Espinoza	.05	.02	.01
□ 48 Bob Geren	.05	.02	.01
□ 49 Mel Hall	.05	.02	.01
□ 50 Andy Hawkins	.05	.02	.01
□ 51 Hensley Meulens	.05	.02	.01
□ 52 Steve Sax	.05	.02	.01
□ 53 Deion Sanders	.75	.35	.09
□ 54 Rickey Henderson	.15	.07	.02
□ 55 Mike Moore	.05	.02	.01
□ 56 Tony Phillips	.15	.07	.02
□ 57 Greg Briley	.05	.02	.01
□ 58 Gene Harris	.05	.02	.01
□ 59 Randy Johnson	.75	.35	.09
□ 60 Jeffrey Leonard	.05	.02	.01
□ 61 Dennis Powell	.05	.02	.01
□ 62 Omar Vizquel	.40	.18	.05
□ 63 Kevin Brown	.15	.07	.02
□ 64 Julio Franco	.10	.05	.01
□ 65 Jamie Moyer	.05	.02	.01
□ 66 Rafael Palmeiro	.15	.07	.02
□ 67 Nolan Ryan	1.50	.70	.19
□ 68 Francisco Cabrera	.15	.07	.02
□ 69 Junior Felix	.05	.02	.01
□ 70 Al Leiter	.10	.05	.01
□ 71 Alex Sanchez	.05	.02	.01
□ 72 Geronimo Berroa	.10	.05	.01
□ 73 Derek Lilliquist	.05	.02	.01
□ 74 Lonnie Smith	.05	.02	.01
□ 75 Jeff Treadway	.05	.02	.01
□ 76 Paul Kilgus	.05	.02	.01
□ 77 Lloyd McClendon	.05	.02	.01
□ 78 Scott Sanderson	.05	.02	.01
□ 79 Dwight Smith	.10	.05	.01
□ 80 Jerome Walton	.10	.05	.01
□ 81 Mitch Williams	.05	.02	.01
□ 82 Steve Wilson	.05	.02	.01
□ 83 Todd Benzinger	.05	.02	.01
□ 84 Ken Griffey Sr.	.05	.02	.01
□ 85 Rick Mahler	.05	.02	.01
□ 86 Rolando Roomes	.05	.02	.01
□ 87 Scott Scudder	.05	.02	.01
□ 88 Jim Clancy	.05	.02	.01
□ 89 Rick Rhoden	.05	.02	.01
□ 90 Dan Schatzeder	.05	.02	.01
□ 91 Mike Morgan	.05	.02	.01
□ 92 Eddie Murray	.25	.11	.03
□ 93 Willie Randolph	.10	.05	.01
□ 94 Ray Searage	.05	.02	.01
□ 95 Mike Aldrete	.05	.02	.01
□ 96 Kevin Gross	.05	.02	.01
□ 97 Mark Langston	.10	.05	.01
□ 98 Spike Owen	.05	.02	.01
□ 99 Zane Smith	.05	.02	.01
□ 100 Don Aase	.05	.02	.01
□ 101 Barry Lyons	.05	.02	.01
□ 102 Juan Samuel	.05	.02	.01
□ 103 Wally Whitehurst	.05	.02	.01
□ 104 Dennis Cook	.05	.02	.01
□ 105 Len Dykstra	.10	.05	.01
□ 106 Charlie Hayes	.15	.07	.02
□ 107 Tommy Herr	.05	.02	.01
□ 108 Ken Howell	.05	.02	.01
□ 109 John Kruk	.10	.05	.01
□ 110 Roger McDowell	.05	.02	.01
□ 111 Terry Mulholland	.05	.02	.01
□ 112 Jeff Parrett	.05	.02	.01
□ 113 Neal Heaton	.05	.02	.01
□ 114 Jeff King	.10	.05	.01
□ 115 Randy Kramer	.05	.02	.01
□ 116 Bill Landrum	.05	.02	.01
□ 117 Cris Carpenter	.05	.02	.01
□ 118 Frank DiPino	.05	.02	.01
□ 119 Ken Hill	.50	.23	.06
□ 120 Dan Quisenberry	.05	.02	.01
□ 121 Milt Thompson	.05	.02	.01
□ 122 Todd Zeile	.15	.07	.02
□ 123 Jack Clark	.10	.05	.01
□ 124 Bruce Hurst	.05	.02	.01
□ 125 Mark Parent	.05	.02	.01
□ 126 Bip Roberts	.10	.05	.01
□ 127 Jeff Brantley UER (Photo actually Joe Kmak)	.05	.02	.01
□ 128 Terry Kennedy	.05	.02	.01
□ 129 Mike LaCoss	.05	.02	.01
□ 130 Greg Litton	.05	.02	.01
□ 131 Mike Schmidt	.50	.23	.06
□ 132 Checklist 1-132	.05	.02	.01

1990 Fleer

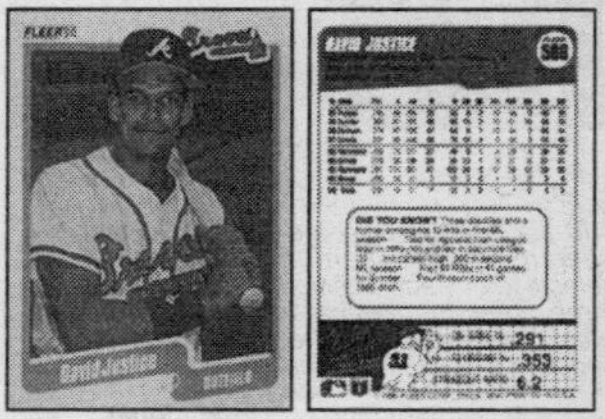

The 1990 Fleer set contains 660 standard-size cards. Cards were primarily issued in wax packs, rack packs and hobby and retail factory sets. Card fronts feature white outer borders with ribbon-like, colored inner borders. The set is again ordered numerically by teams based upon the previous season's record. Subsets include Decade Greats (621-630), Superstar Combinations (631-639), Rookie Prospects (640-653) and checklists (654-660). Rookie

Cards of note include Moises Alou, Juan Gonzalez, Marquis Grissom, Dave Justice, Ben McDonald, Sammy Sosa, and Larry Walker.

	MINT	NRMT	EXC
COMPLETE SET (660)	8.00	3.60	1.00
COMPLETE RETAIL SET (660)	8.00	3.60	1.00
COMPLETE HOBBY SET (672)	10.00	4.50	1.25
COMMON CARD (1-660)	.05	.02	.01
SEMISTARS	.10	.05	.01
STARS	.15	.07	.02
COMP. WORLD SERIES (12)	1.00	.45	.12
□ 1 Lance Blankenship	.05	.02	.01
□ 2 Todd Burns	.05	.02	.01
□ 3 Jose Canseco	.15	.07	.02
□ 4 Jim Corsi	.05	.02	.01
□ 5 Storm Davis	.05	.02	.01
□ 6 Dennis Eckersley	.10	.05	.01
□ 7 Mike Gallego	.05	.02	.01
□ 8 Ron Hassey	.05	.02	.01
□ 9 Dave Henderson	.05	.02	.01
□ 10 Rickey Henderson	.15	.07	.02
□ 11 Rick Honeycutt	.05	.02	.01
□ 12 Stan Javier	.05	.02	.01
□ 13 Felix Jose	.05	.02	.01
□ 14 Carney Lansford	.10	.05	.01
□ 15 Mark McGwire UER (1989 runs listed as 4, should be 74)	.30	.14	.04
□ 16 Mike Moore	.05	.02	.01
□ 17 Gene Nelson	.05	.02	.01
□ 18 Dave Parker	.10	.05	.01
□ 19 Tony Phillips	.15	.07	.02
□ 20 Terry Steinbach	.10	.05	.01
□ 21 Dave Stewart	.10	.05	.01
□ 22 Walt Weiss	.05	.02	.01
□ 23 Bob Welch	.05	.02	.01
□ 24 Curt Young	.05	.02	.01
□ 25 Paul Assenmacher	.05	.02	.01
□ 26 Damon Berryhill	.05	.02	.01
□ 27 Mike Bielecki	.05	.02	.01
□ 28 Kevin Blankenship	.05	.02	.01
□ 29 Andre Dawson	.15	.07	.02
□ 30 Shawon Dunston	.05	.02	.01
□ 31 Joe Girardi	.10	.05	.01
□ 32 Mark Grace	.15	.07	.02
□ 33 Mike Harkey	.05	.02	.01
□ 34 Paul Kilgus	.05	.02	.01
□ 35 Les Lancaster	.05	.02	.01
□ 36 Vance Law	.05	.02	.01
□ 37 Greg Maddux	.60	.25	.07
□ 38 Lloyd McClendon	.05	.02	.01
□ 39 Jeff Pico	.05	.02	.01
□ 40 Ryne Sandberg	.25	.11	.03
□ 41 Scott Sanderson	.05	.02	.01
□ 42 Dwight Smith	.05	.02	.01
□ 43 Rick Sutcliffe	.05	.02	.01
□ 44 Jerome Walton	.05	.02	.01
□ 45 Mitch Webster	.05	.02	.01
□ 46 Curt Wilkerson	.05	.02	.01
□ 47 Dean Wilkins	.05	.02	.01
□ 48 Mitch Williams	.05	.02	.01
□ 49 Steve Wilson	.05	.02	.01
□ 50 Steve Bedrosian	.05	.02	.01
□ 51 Mike Benjamin	.05	.02	.01
□ 52 Jeff Brantley	.10	.05	.01
□ 53 Brett Butler	.10	.05	.01
□ 54 Will Clark UER (Did You Know says first in runs, should say tied for first)	.15	.07	.02
□ 55 Kelly Downs	.05	.02	.01
□ 56 Scott Garrelts	.05	.02	.01
□ 57 Atlee Hammaker	.05	.02	.01
□ 58 Terry Kennedy	.05	.02	.01
□ 59 Mike LaCoss	.05	.02	.01
□ 60 Craig Lefferts	.05	.02	.01
□ 61 Greg Litton	.05	.02	.01
□ 62 Candy Maldonado	.05	.02	.01
□ 63 Kirt Manwaring UER (No '88 Phoenix stats as noted in box)	.05	.02	.01
□ 64 Randy McCament	.05	.02	.01
□ 65 Kevin Mitchell	.10	.05	.01
□ 66 Donell Nixon	.05	.02	.01
□ 67 Ken Oberkfell	.05	.02	.01
□ 68 Rick Reuschel	.05	.02	.01
□ 69 Ernest Riles	.05	.02	.01
□ 70 Don Robinson	.05	.02	.01
□ 71 Pat Sheridan	.05	.02	.01
□ 72 Chris Speier	.05	.02	.01
□ 73 Robby Thompson	.05	.02	.01
□ 74 Jose Uribe	.05	.02	.01
□ 75 Matt Williams	.15	.07	.02
□ 76 George Bell	.05	.02	.01
□ 77 Pat Borders	.05	.02	.01
□ 78 John Cerutti	.05	.02	.01
□ 79 Junior Felix	.05	.02	.01
□ 80 Tony Fernandez	.05	.02	.01
□ 81 Mike Flanagan	.05	.02	.01
□ 82 Mauro Gozzo	.05	.02	.01
□ 83 Kelly Gruber	.05	.02	.01
□ 84 Tom Henke	.05	.02	.01
□ 85 Jimmy Key	.10	.05	.01
□ 86 Manny Lee	.05	.02	.01
□ 87 Nelson Liriano UER (Should say "led the IL" instead of "led the TL")	.05	.02	.01
□ 88 Lee Mazzilli	.05	.02	.01
□ 89 Fred McGriff	.15	.07	.02
□ 90 Lloyd Moseby	.05	.02	.01
□ 91 Rance Mulliniks	.05	.02	.01
□ 92 Alex Sanchez	.05	.02	.01
□ 93 Dave Stieb	.05	.02	.01
□ 94 Todd Stottlemyre	.10	.05	.01
□ 95 Duane Ward UER (Double line of '87 Syracuse stats)	.05	.02	.01
□ 96 David Wells	.05	.02	.01
□ 97 Ernie Whitt	.05	.02	.01
□ 98 Frank Wills	.05	.02	.01
□ 99 Mookie Wilson	.05	.02	.01
□ 100 Kevin Appier	.15	.07	.02
□ 101 Luis Aquino	.05	.02	.01
□ 102 Bob Boone	.10	.05	.01
□ 103 George Brett	.40	.18	.05
□ 104 Jose DeJesus	.05	.02	.01
□ 105 Luis De Los Santos	.05	.02	.01
□ 106 Jim Eisenreich	.05	.02	.01
□ 107 Steve Farr	.05	.02	.01
□ 108 Tom Gordon	.05	.02	.01
□ 109 Mark Gubicza	.05	.02	.01
□ 110 Bo Jackson	.15	.07	.02
□ 111 Terry Leach	.05	.02	.01
□ 112 Charlie Leibrandt	.05	.02	.01
□ 113 Rick Luecken	.05	.02	.01
□ 114 Mike Macfarlane	.05	.02	.01
□ 115 Jeff Montgomery	.10	.05	.01
□ 116 Bret Saberhagen	.10	.05	.01
□ 117 Kevin Seitzer	.05	.02	.01
□ 118 Kurt Stillwell	.05	.02	.01
□ 119 Pat Tabler	.05	.02	.01
□ 120 Danny Tartabull	.05	.02	.01
□ 121 Gary Thurman	.05	.02	.01
□ 122 Frank White	.10	.05	.01
□ 123 Willie Wilson	.05	.02	.01
□ 124 Matt Winters	.05	.02	.01
□ 125 Jim Abbott	.10	.05	.01
□ 126 Tony Armas	.05	.02	.01
□ 127 Dante Bichette	.15	.07	.02
□ 128 Bert Blyleven	.10	.05	.01
□ 129 Chili Davis	.10	.05	.01
□ 130 Brian Downing	.05	.02	.01
□ 131 Mike Fetters	.10	.05	.01
□ 132 Chuck Finley	.10	.05	.01
□ 133 Willie Fraser	.05	.02	.01
□ 134 Bryan Harvey	.05	.02	.01
□ 135 Jack Howell	.05	.02	.01
□ 136 Wally Joyner	.10	.05	.01
□ 137 Jeff Manto	.05	.02	.01
□ 138 Kirk McCaskill	.05	.02	.01
□ 139 Bob McClure	.05	.02	.01
□ 140 Greg Minton	.05	.02	.01
□ 141 Lance Parrish	.05	.02	.01
□ 142 Dan Petry	.05	.02	.01
□ 143 Johnny Ray	.05	.02	.01
□ 144 Dick Schofield	.05	.02	.01
□ 145 Lee Stevens	.05	.02	.01
□ 146 Claudell Washington	.05	.02	.01
□ 147 Devon White	.10	.05	.01

148	Mike Witt	.05	.02	.01
149	Roberto Alomar	.30	.14	.04
150	Sandy Alomar Jr.	.10	.05	.01
151	Andy Benes	.15	.07	.02
152	Jack Clark	.10	.05	.01
153	Pat Clements	.05	.02	.01
154	Joey Cora	.15	.07	.02
155	Mark Davis	.05	.02	.01
156	Mark Grant	.05	.02	.01
157	Tony Gwynn	.40	.18	.05
158	Greg W. Harris	.05	.02	.01
159	Bruce Hurst	.05	.02	.01
160	Darrin Jackson	.05	.02	.01
161	Chris James	.05	.02	.01
162	Carmelo Martinez	.05	.02	.01
163	Mike Pagliarulo	.05	.02	.01
164	Mark Parent	.05	.02	.01
165	Dennis Rasmussen	.05	.02	.01
166	Bip Roberts	.05	.02	.01
167	Benito Santiago	.05	.02	.01
168	Calvin Schiraldi	.05	.02	.01
169	Eric Show	.05	.02	.01
170	Garry Templeton	.05	.02	.01
171	Ed Whitson	.05	.02	.01
172	Brady Anderson	.15	.07	.02
173	Jeff Ballard	.05	.02	.01
174	Phil Bradley	.05	.02	.01
175	Mike Devereaux	.05	.02	.01
176	Steve Finley	.15	.07	.02
177	Pete Harnisch	.05	.02	.01
178	Kevin Hickey	.05	.02	.01
179	Brian Holton	.05	.02	.01
180	Ben McDonald	.15	.07	.02
181	Bob Melvin	.05	.02	.01
182	Bob Milacki	.05	.02	.01
183	Randy Milligan UER (Double line of '87 stats)	.05	.02	.01
184	Gregg Olson	.05	.02	.01
185	Joe Orsulak	.05	.02	.01
186	Bill Ripken	.05	.02	.01
187	Cal Ripken	.75	.35	.09
188	Dave Schmidt	.05	.02	.01
189	Larry Sheets	.05	.02	.01
190	Mickey Tettleton	.10	.05	.01
191	Mark Thurmond	.05	.02	.01
192	Jay Tibbs	.05	.02	.01
193	Jim Traber	.05	.02	.01
194	Mark Williamson	.05	.02	.01
195	Craig Worthington	.05	.02	.01
196	Don Aase	.05	.02	.01
197	Blaine Beatty	.05	.02	.01
198	Mark Carreon	.05	.02	.01
199	Gary Carter	.15	.07	.02
200	David Cone	.15	.07	.02
201	Ron Darling	.05	.02	.01
202	Kevin Elster	.05	.02	.01
203	Sid Fernandez	.05	.02	.01
204	Dwight Gooden	.10	.05	.01
205	Keith Hernandez	.10	.05	.01
206	Jeff Innis	.05	.02	.01
207	Gregg Jefferies	.15	.07	.02
208	Howard Johnson	.05	.02	.01
209	Barry Lyons UER (Double line of '87 stats)	.05	.02	.01
210	Dave Magadan	.05	.02	.01
211	Kevin McReynolds	.05	.02	.01
212	Jeff Musselman	.05	.02	.01
213	Randy Myers	.10	.05	.01
214	Bob Ojeda	.05	.02	.01
215	Juan Samuel	.05	.02	.01
216	Mackey Sasser	.05	.02	.01
217	Darryl Strawberry	.10	.05	.01
218	Tim Teufel	.05	.02	.01
219	Frank Viola	.05	.02	.01
220	Juan Agosto	.05	.02	.01
221	Larry Andersen	.05	.02	.01
222	Eric Anthony	.10	.05	.01
223	Kevin Bass	.05	.02	.01
224	Craig Biggio	.15	.07	.02
225	Ken Caminiti	.15	.07	.02
226	Jim Clancy	.05	.02	.01
227	Danny Darwin	.05	.02	.01
228	Glenn Davis	.05	.02	.01
229	Jim Deshaies	.05	.02	.01
230	Bill Doran	.05	.02	.01
231	Bob Forsch	.05	.02	.01
232	Brian Meyer	.05	.02	.01
233	Terry Puhl	.05	.02	.01
234	Rafael Ramirez	.05	.02	.01
235	Rick Rhoden	.05	.02	.01
236	Dan Schatzeder	.05	.02	.01
237	Mike Scott	.05	.02	.01
238	Dave Smith	.05	.02	.01
239	Alex Trevino	.05	.02	.01
240	Glenn Wilson	.05	.02	.01
241	Gerald Young	.05	.02	.01
242	Tom Brunansky	.05	.02	.01
243	Cris Carpenter	.05	.02	.01
244	Alex Cole	.10	.05	.01
245	Vince Coleman	.05	.02	.01
246	John Costello	.05	.02	.01
247	Ken Dayley	.05	.02	.01
248	Jose DeLeon	.05	.02	.01
249	Frank DiPino	.05	.02	.01
250	Pedro Guerrero	.05	.02	.01
251	Ken Hill	.15	.07	.02
252	Joe Magrane	.05	.02	.01
253	Willie McGee UER (No decimal point before 353)	.05	.02	.01
254	John Morris	.05	.02	.01
255	Jose Oquendo	.05	.02	.01
256	Tony Pena	.05	.02	.01
257	Terry Pendleton	.10	.05	.01
258	Ted Power	.05	.02	.01
259	Dan Quisenberry	.05	.02	.01
260	Ozzie Smith	.20	.09	.03
261	Scott Terry	.05	.02	.01
262	Milt Thompson	.05	.02	.01
263	Denny Walling	.05	.02	.01
264	Todd Worrell	.05	.02	.01
265	Todd Zeile	.10	.05	.01
266	Marty Barrett	.05	.02	.01
267	Mike Boddicker	.05	.02	.01
268	Wade Boggs	.15	.07	.02
269	Ellis Burks	.15	.07	.02
270	Rick Cerone	.05	.02	.01
271	Roger Clemens	.15	.07	.02
272	John Dopson	.05	.02	.01
273	Nick Esasky	.05	.02	.01
274	Dwight Evans	.10	.05	.01
275	Wes Gardner	.05	.02	.01
276	Rich Gedman	.05	.02	.01
277	Mike Greenwell	.05	.02	.01
278	Danny Heep	.05	.02	.01
279	Eric Hetzel	.05	.02	.01
280	Dennis Lamp	.05	.02	.01
281	Rob Murphy UER ('89 stats say Reds, should say Red Sox)	.05	.02	.01
282	Joe Price	.05	.02	.01
283	Carlos Quintana	.05	.02	.01
284	Jody Reed	.05	.02	.01
285	Luis Rivera	.05	.02	.01
286	Kevin Romine	.05	.02	.01
287	Lee Smith	.10	.05	.01
288	Mike Smithson	.05	.02	.01
289	Bob Stanley	.05	.02	.01
290	Harold Baines	.10	.05	.01
291	Kevin Brown	.10	.05	.01
292	Steve Buechele	.05	.02	.01
293	Scott Coolbaugh	.05	.02	.01
294	Jack Daugherty	.05	.02	.01
295	Cecil Espy	.05	.02	.01
296	Julio Franco	.10	.05	.01
297	Juan Gonzalez	2.00	.90	.25
298	Cecilio Guante	.05	.02	.01
299	Drew Hall	.05	.02	.01
300	Charlie Hough	.05	.02	.01
301	Pete Incaviglia	.05	.02	.01
302	Mike Jeffcoat	.05	.02	.01
303	Chad Kreuter	.05	.02	.01
304	Jeff Kunkel	.05	.02	.01
305	Rick Leach	.05	.02	.01
306	Fred Manrique	.05	.02	.01
307	Jamie Moyer	.05	.02	.01
308	Rafael Palmeiro	.15	.07	.02
309	Geno Petralli	.05	.02	.01
310	Kevin Reimer	.05	.02	.01
311	Kenny Rogers	.10	.05	.01

□ 312 Jeff Russell .05 .02 .01
□ 313 Nolan Ryan .75 .35 .09
□ 314 Ruben Sierra .10 .05 .01
□ 315 Bobby Witt .05 .02 .01
□ 316 Chris Bosio .05 .02 .01
□ 317 Glenn Braggs UER .05 .02 .01
(Stats say 111 K's, but bio says 117 K's)
□ 318 Greg Brock .05 .02 .01
□ 319 Chuck Crim .05 .02 .01
□ 320 Rob Deer .05 .02 .01
□ 321 Mike Felder .05 .02 .01
□ 322 Tom Filer .05 .02 .01
□ 323 Tony Fossas .05 .02 .01
□ 324 Jim Gantner .05 .02 .01
□ 325 Darryl Hamilton .10 .05 .01
□ 326 Teddy Higuera .05 .02 .01
□ 327 Mark Knudson .05 .02 .01
□ 328 Bill Krueger UER .05 .02 .01
('86 stats missing)
□ 329 Tim McIntosh .05 .02 .01
□ 330 Paul Molitor .20 .09 .03
□ 331 Jaime Navarro .05 .02 .01
□ 332 Charlie O'Brien .05 .02 .01
□ 333 Jeff Peterek .05 .02 .01
□ 334 Dan Plesac .05 .02 .01
□ 335 Jerry Reuss .05 .02 .01
□ 336 Gary Sheffield UER .25 .11 .03
(Bio says played for 3 teams in '87, but stats say in '88)
□ 337 Bill Spiers .05 .02 .01
□ 338 B.J. Surhoff .10 .05 .01
□ 339 Greg Vaughn .15 .07 .02
□ 340 Robin Yount .15 .07 .02
□ 341 Hubie Brooks .05 .02 .01
□ 342 Tim Burke .05 .02 .01
□ 343 Mike Fitzgerald .05 .02 .01
□ 344 Tom Foley .05 .02 .01
□ 345 Andres Galarraga .15 .07 .02
□ 346 Damaso Garcia .05 .02 .01
□ 347 Marquis Grissom .60 .25 .07
□ 348 Kevin Gross .05 .02 .01
□ 349 Joe Hesketh .05 .02 .01
□ 350 Jeff Huson .05 .02 .01
□ 351 Wallace Johnson .05 .02 .01
□ 352 Mark Langston .10 .05 .01
□ 353A Dave Martinez 2.00 .90 .25
(Yellow on front)
□ 353B Dave Martinez .05 .02 .01
(Red on front)
□ 354 Dennis Martinez UER .10 .05 .01
('87 ERA is 616, should be 6.16)
□ 355 Andy McGaffigan .05 .02 .01
□ 356 Otis Nixon .05 .02 .01
□ 357 Spike Owen .05 .02 .01
□ 358 Pascual Perez .05 .02 .01
□ 359 Tim Raines .15 .07 .02
□ 360 Nelson Santovenia .05 .02 .01
□ 361 Bryn Smith .05 .02 .01
□ 362 Zane Smith .05 .02 .01
□ 363 Larry Walker .50 .23 .06
□ 364 Tim Wallach .05 .02 .01
□ 365 Rick Aguilera .10 .05 .01
□ 366 Allan Anderson .05 .02 .01
□ 367 Wally Backman .05 .02 .01
□ 368 Doug Baker .05 .02 .01
□ 369 Juan Berenguer .05 .02 .01
□ 370 Randy Bush .05 .02 .01
□ 371 Carmen Castillo .05 .02 .01
□ 372 Mike Dyer .05 .02 .01
□ 373 Gary Gaetti .10 .05 .01
□ 374 Greg Gagne .05 .02 .01
□ 375 Dan Gladden .05 .02 .01
□ 376 German Gonzalez UER .05 .02 .01
(Bio says 31 saves in '88, but stats say 30)
□ 377 Brian Harper .05 .02 .01
□ 378 Kent Hrbek .10 .05 .01
□ 379 Gene Larkin .05 .02 .01
□ 380 Tim Laudner UER .05 .02 .01
(No decimal point before '85 BA of 238)
□ 381 John Moses .05 .02 .01
□ 382 Al Newman .05 .02 .01
□ 383 Kirby Puckett .30 .14 .04
□ 384 Shane Rawley .05 .02 .01
□ 385 Jeff Reardon .10 .05 .01
□ 386 Roy Smith .05 .02 .01
□ 387 Gary Wayne .05 .02 .01
□ 388 Dave West .05 .02 .01
□ 389 Tim Belcher .05 .02 .01
□ 390 Tim Crews UER .05 .02 .01
(Stats say 163 IP for '83, but bio says 136)
□ 391 Mike Davis .05 .02 .01
□ 392 Rick Dempsey .05 .02 .01
□ 393 Kirk Gibson .10 .05 .01
□ 394 Jose Gonzalez .05 .02 .01
□ 395 Alfredo Griffin .05 .02 .01
□ 396 Jeff Hamilton .05 .02 .01
□ 397 Lenny Harris .05 .02 .01
□ 398 Mickey Hatcher .05 .02 .01
□ 399 Orel Hershiser .10 .05 .01
□ 400 Jay Howell .05 .02 .01
□ 401 Mike Marshall .05 .02 .01
□ 402 Ramon Martinez .15 .07 .02
□ 403 Mike Morgan .05 .02 .01
□ 404 Eddie Murray .25 .11 .03
□ 405 Alejandro Pena .05 .02 .01
□ 406 Willie Randolph .10 .05 .01
□ 407 Mike Scioscia .05 .02 .01
□ 408 Ray Searage .05 .02 .01
□ 409 Fernando Valenzuela .10 .05 .01
□ 410 Jose Vizcaino .15 .07 .02
□ 411 John Wetteland .10 .05 .01
□ 412 Jack Armstrong .05 .02 .01
□ 413 Todd Benzinger UER .05 .02 .01
(Bio says .323 at Pawtucket, but stats say .321)
□ 414 Tim Birtsas .05 .02 .01
□ 415 Tom Browning .05 .02 .01
□ 416 Norm Charlton .05 .02 .01
□ 417 Eric Davis .10 .05 .01
□ 418 Rob Dibble .05 .02 .01
□ 419 John Franco .05 .02 .01
□ 420 Ken Griffey Sr. .05 .02 .01
□ 421 Chris Hammond .05 .02 .01
(No 1989 used for "Did Not Play" stat, actually did play for Nashville in 1989)
□ 422 Danny Jackson .05 .02 .01
□ 423 Barry Larkin .15 .07 .02
□ 424 Tim Leary .05 .02 .01
□ 425 Rick Mahler .05 .02 .01
□ 426 Joe Oliver .05 .02 .01
□ 427 Paul O'Neill .10 .05 .01
□ 428 Luis Quinones UER .05 .02 .01
('86-'88 stats are omitted from card but included in totals)
□ 429 Jeff Reed .05 .02 .01
□ 430 Jose Rijo .05 .02 .01
□ 431 Ron Robinson .05 .02 .01
□ 432 Rolando Roomes .05 .02 .01
□ 433 Chris Sabo .05 .02 .01
□ 434 Scott Scudder .05 .02 .01
□ 435 Herm Winningham .05 .02 .01
□ 436 Steve Balboni .05 .02 .01
□ 437 Jesse Barfield .05 .02 .01
□ 438 Mike Blowers .15 .07 .02
□ 439 Tom Brookens .05 .02 .01
□ 440 Greg Cadaret .05 .02 .01
□ 441 Alvaro Espinoza UER .05 .02 .01
(Career games say 218, should be 219)
□ 442 Bob Geren .05 .02 .01
□ 443 Lee Guetterman .05 .02 .01
□ 444 Mel Hall .05 .02 .01
□ 445 Andy Hawkins .05 .02 .01
□ 446 Roberto Kelly .10 .05 .01
□ 447 Don Mattingly .50 .23 .06
□ 448 Lance McCullers .05 .02 .01
□ 449 Hensley Meulens .05 .02 .01
□ 450 Dale Mohorcic .05 .02 .01
□ 451 Clay Parker .05 .02 .01
□ 452 Eric Plunk .05 .02 .01
□ 453 Dave Righetti .05 .02 .01
□ 454 Deion Sanders .20 .09 .03

☐ 455	Steve Sax	.05	.02	.01
☐ 456	Don Slaught	.05	.02	.01
☐ 457	Walt Terrell	.05	.02	.01
☐ 458	Dave Winfield	.15	.07	.02
☐ 459	Jay Bell	.10	.05	.01
☐ 460	Rafael Belliard	.05	.02	.01
☐ 461	Barry Bonds	.25	.11	.03
☐ 462	Bobby Bonilla	.10	.05	.01
☐ 463	Sid Bream	.05	.02	.01
☐ 464	Benny Distefano	.05	.02	.01
☐ 465	Doug Drabek	.05	.02	.01
☐ 466	Jim Gott	.05	.02	.01
☐ 467	Billy Hatcher UER (.1 hits for Cubs in 1984)	.05	.02	.01
☐ 468	Neal Heaton	.05	.02	.01
☐ 469	Jeff King	.10	.05	.01
☐ 470	Bob Kipper	.05	.02	.01
☐ 471	Randy Kramer	.05	.02	.01
☐ 472	Bill Landrum	.05	.02	.01
☐ 473	Mike LaValliere	.05	.02	.01
☐ 474	Jose Lind	.05	.02	.01
☐ 475	Junior Ortiz	.05	.02	.01
☐ 476	Gary Redus	.05	.02	.01
☐ 477	Rick Reed	.05	.02	.01
☐ 478	R.J. Reynolds	.05	.02	.01
☐ 479	Jeff D. Robinson	.05	.02	.01
☐ 480	John Smiley	.10	.05	.01
☐ 481	Andy Van Slyke	.10	.05	.01
☐ 482	Bob Walk	.05	.02	.01
☐ 483	Andy Allanson	.05	.02	.01
☐ 484	Scott Bailes	.05	.02	.01
☐ 485	Joey Belle UER (Has Jay Bell "Did You Know")	1.00	.45	.12
☐ 486	Bud Black	.05	.02	.01
☐ 487	Jerry Browne	.05	.02	.01
☐ 488	Tom Candiotti	.05	.02	.01
☐ 489	Joe Carter	.15	.07	.02
☐ 490	Dave Clark (No '84 stats)	.05	.02	.01
☐ 491	John Farrell	.05	.02	.01
☐ 492	Felix Fermin	.05	.02	.01
☐ 493	Brook Jacoby	.05	.02	.01
☐ 494	Dion James	.05	.02	.01
☐ 495	Doug Jones	.05	.02	.01
☐ 496	Brad Komminsk	.05	.02	.01
☐ 497	Rod Nichols	.05	.02	.01
☐ 498	Pete O'Brien	.05	.02	.01
☐ 499	Steve Olin	.10	.05	.01
☐ 500	Jesse Orosco	.05	.02	.01
☐ 501	Joel Skinner	.05	.02	.01
☐ 502	Cory Snyder	.05	.02	.01
☐ 503	Greg Swindell	.05	.02	.01
☐ 504	Rich Yett	.05	.02	.01
☐ 505	Scott Bankhead	.05	.02	.01
☐ 506	Scott Bradley	.05	.02	.01
☐ 507	Greg Briley UER (28 SB's in bio, but 27 in stats)	.05	.02	.01
☐ 508	Jay Buhner	.15	.07	.02
☐ 509	Darnell Coles	.05	.02	.01
☐ 510	Keith Comstock	.05	.02	.01
☐ 511	Henry Cotto	.05	.02	.01
☐ 512	Alvin Davis	.05	.02	.01
☐ 513	Ken Griffey Jr.	1.50	.70	.19
☐ 514	Erik Hanson	.10	.05	.01
☐ 515	Gene Harris	.05	.02	.01
☐ 516	Brian Holman	.05	.02	.01
☐ 517	Mike Jackson	.05	.02	.01
☐ 518	Randy Johnson	.25	.11	.03
☐ 519	Jeffrey Leonard	.05	.02	.01
☐ 520	Edgar Martinez	.15	.07	.02
☐ 521	Dennis Powell	.05	.02	.01
☐ 522	Jim Presley	.05	.02	.01
☐ 523	Jerry Reed	.05	.02	.01
☐ 524	Harold Reynolds	.05	.02	.01
☐ 525	Mike Schooler	.05	.02	.01
☐ 526	Bill Swift	.05	.02	.01
☐ 527	Dave Valle	.05	.02	.01
☐ 528	Omar Vizquel	.10	.05	.01
☐ 529	Ivan Calderon	.05	.02	.01
☐ 530	Carlton Fisk UER (Bellow Falls, should be Bellows Falls)	.15	.07	.02
☐ 531	Scott Fletcher	.05	.02	.01
☐ 532	Dave Gallagher	.05	.02	.01
☐ 533	Ozzie Guillen	.05	.02	.01
☐ 534	Greg Hibbard	.05	.02	.01
☐ 535	Shawn Hillegas	.05	.02	.01
☐ 536	Lance Johnson	.15	.07	.02
☐ 537	Eric King	.05	.02	.01
☐ 538	Ron Kittle	.05	.02	.01
☐ 539	Steve Lyons	.05	.02	.01
☐ 540	Carlos Martinez	.05	.02	.01
☐ 541	Tom McCarthy	.05	.02	.01
☐ 542	Matt Merullo (Had 5 ML runs scored entering '90, not 6)	.05	.02	.01
☐ 543	Donn Pall UER (Stats say pro career began in '85, bio says '88)	.05	.02	.01
☐ 544	Dan Pasqua	.05	.02	.01
☐ 545	Ken Patterson	.05	.02	.01
☐ 546	Melido Perez	.05	.02	.01
☐ 547	Steve Rosenberg	.05	.02	.01
☐ 548	Sammy Sosa	.75	.35	.09
☐ 549	Bobby Thigpen	.05	.02	.01
☐ 550	Robin Ventura	.15	.07	.02
☐ 551	Greg Walker	.05	.02	.01
☐ 552	Don Carman	.05	.02	.01
☐ 553	Pat Combs (6 walks for Phillies in '89 in stats, brief bio says 4)	.05	.02	.01
☐ 554	Dennis Cook	.05	.02	.01
☐ 555	Darren Daulton	.10	.05	.01
☐ 556	Len Dykstra	.10	.05	.01
☐ 557	Curt Ford	.05	.02	.01
☐ 558	Charlie Hayes	.10	.05	.01
☐ 559	Von Hayes	.05	.02	.01
☐ 560	Tommy Herr	.05	.02	.01
☐ 561	Ken Howell	.05	.02	.01
☐ 562	Steve Jeltz	.05	.02	.01
☐ 563	Ron Jones	.05	.02	.01
☐ 564	Ricky Jordan UER (Duplicate line of statistics on back)	.05	.02	.01
☐ 565	John Kruk	.10	.05	.01
☐ 566	Steve Lake	.05	.02	.01
☐ 567	Roger McDowell	.05	.02	.01
☐ 568	Terry Mulholland UER (Did You Know refers to Dave Magadan)	.05	.02	.01
☐ 569	Dwayne Murphy	.05	.02	.01
☐ 570	Jeff Parrett	.05	.02	.01
☐ 571	Randy Ready	.05	.02	.01
☐ 572	Bruce Ruffin	.05	.02	.01
☐ 573	Dickie Thon	.05	.02	.01
☐ 574	Jose Alvarez UER ('78 and '79 stats are reversed)	.05	.02	.01
☐ 575	Geronimo Berroa	.10	.05	.01
☐ 576	Jeff Blauser	.10	.05	.01
☐ 577	Joe Boever	.05	.02	.01
☐ 578	Marty Clary UER (No comma between city and state)	.05	.02	.01
☐ 579	Jody Davis	.05	.02	.01
☐ 580	Mark Eichhorn	.05	.02	.01
☐ 581	Darrell Evans	.10	.05	.01
☐ 582	Ron Gant	.15	.07	.02
☐ 583	Tom Glavine	.15	.07	.02
☐ 584	Tommy Greene	.05	.02	.01
☐ 585	Tommy Gregg	.05	.02	.01
☐ 586	Dave Justice UER (Actually had 16 2B in Sumter in '86)	.50	.23	.06
☐ 587	Mark Lemke	.10	.05	.01
☐ 588	Derek Lilliquist	.05	.02	.01
☐ 589	Oddibe McDowell	.05	.02	.01
☐ 590	Kent Mercker ERA (Bio says 2.75 ERA, stats say 2.68 ERA)	.10	.05	.01
☐ 591	Dale Murphy	.15	.07	.02
☐ 592	Gerald Perry	.05	.02	.01
☐ 593	Lonnie Smith	.05	.02	.01
☐ 594	Pete Smith	.05	.02	.01
☐ 595	John Smoltz	.25	.11	.03
☐ 596	Mike Stanton UER (No comma between	.10	.05	.01

city and state)			
□ 597 Andres Thomas	.05	.02	.01
□ 598 Jeff Treadway	.05	.02	.01
□ 599 Doyle Alexander	.05	.02	.01
□ 600 Dave Bergman	.05	.02	.01
□ 601 Brian DuBois	.05	.02	.01
□ 602 Paul Gibson	.05	.02	.01
□ 603 Mike Heath	.05	.02	.01
□ 604 Mike Henneman	.05	.02	.01
□ 605 Guillermo Hernandez	.05	.02	.01
□ 606 Shawn Holman	.05	.02	.01
□ 607 Tracy Jones	.05	.02	.01
□ 608 Chet Lemon	.05	.02	.01
□ 609 Fred Lynn	.05	.02	.01
□ 610 Jack Morris	.10	.05	.01
□ 611 Matt Nokes	.05	.02	.01
□ 612 Gary Pettis	.05	.02	.01
□ 613 Kevin Ritz	.05	.02	.01
□ 614 Jeff M. Robinson ('88 stats are not in line)	.05	.02	.01
□ 615 Steve Searcy	.05	.02	.01
□ 616 Frank Tanana	.05	.02	.01
□ 617 Alan Trammell	.15	.07	.02
□ 618 Gary Ward	.05	.02	.01
□ 619 Lou Whitaker	.15	.07	.02
□ 620 Frank Williams	.05	.02	.01
□ 621 George Brett '80 COR	.20	.09	.03
□ 621A George Brett '80 ERR (Had 10 .390 hitting seasons)	1.50	.70	.19
□ 622 Fern.Valenzuela '81	.10	.05	.01
□ 623 Dale Murphy '82	.15	.07	.02
□ 624A Cal Ripken '83 ERR (Misspelled Ripkin on card back)	5.00	2.20	.60
□ 624B Cal Ripken '83 COR	.40	.18	.05
□ 625 Ryne Sandberg '84	.15	.07	.02
□ 626 Don Mattingly '85	.25	.11	.03
□ 627 Roger Clemens '86	.15	.07	.02
□ 628 George Bell '87	.05	.02	.01
□ 629 Jose Canseco '88 UER (Reggie won MVP in '83, should say '73)	.15	.07	.02
□ 630A Will Clark '89 ERR (32 total bases on card back)	1.00	.45	.12
□ 630B Will Clark '89 COR (321 total bases; technically still an error, listing only 24 runs)	.15	.07	.02
□ 631 Game Savers Mark Davis Mitch Williams	.05	.02	.01
□ 632 Boston Igniters Wade Boggs Mike Greenwell	.15	.07	.02
□ 633 Starter and Stopper Mark Gubicza Jeff Russell	.05	.02	.01
□ 634 League's Best Shortstops Tony Fernandez Cal Ripken	.25	.11	.03
□ 635 Human Dynamos Kirby Puckett Bo Jackson	.15	.07	.02
□ 636 300 Strikeout Club Nolan Ryan Mike Scott	.25	.11	.03
□ 637 The Dynamic Duo Will Clark Kevin Mitchell	.10	.05	.01
□ 638 AL All-Stars Don Mattingly Mark McGwire	.30	.14	.04
□ 639 NL East Rivals Howard Johnson Ryne Sandberg	.15	.07	.02
□ 640 Rudy Seanez Colin Charland	.05	.02	.01
□ 641 George Canale Kevin Maas UER (Canale listed as INF on front, 1B on back)	.15	.07	.02
□ 642 Kelly Mann and Dave Hansen	.05	.02	.01
□ 643 Greg Smith and Stu Tate	.05	.02	.01
□ 644 Tom Drees and Dann Howitt	.05	.02	.01
□ 645 Mike Roesler and Derrick May	.15	.07	.02
□ 646 Scott Hemond and Mark Gardner	.05	.02	.01
□ 647 John Orton and Scott Leius	.05	.02	.01
□ 648 Rich Monteleone and Dana Williams	.05	.02	.01
□ 649 Mike Huff and Steve Frey	.05	.02	.01
□ 650 Chuck McElroy and Moises Alou	.20	.09	.03
□ 651 Bobby Rose and Mike Hartley	.05	.02	.01
□ 652 Matt Kinzer and Wayne Edwards	.05	.02	.01
□ 653 Delino DeShields and Jason Grimsley	.10	.05	.01
□ 654 CL: A's/Cubs Giants/Blue Jays	.05	.02	.01
□ 655 CL: Royals/Angels Padres/Orioles	.05	.02	.01
□ 656 CL: Mets/Astros Cards/Red Sox	.05	.02	.01
□ 657 CL: Rangers/Brewers Expos/Twins	.05	.02	.01
□ 658 CL: Dodgers/Reds Yankees/Pirates	.05	.02	.01
□ 659 CL: Indians/Mariners White Sox/Phillies	.05	.02	.01
□ 660A CL: Braves/Tigers Specials/Checklists (Checklist-660 in smaller print on card front)	.05	.02	.01
□ 660B CL: Braves/Tigers Specials/Checklists (Checklist-660 in normal print on card front)	.05	.02	.01

1990 Fleer All-Stars

The 1990 Fleer All-Star insert set includes 12 standard-size cards. The set was randomly inserted in 33-card cellos and wax packs. The set is sequenced in alphabetical order. The fronts are white with a light gray screen and bright red stripes. The player selection for the set is Fleer's opinion of the best Major League at each position.

	MINT	NRMT	EXC
COMPLETE SET (12)	3.00	1.35	.35
COMMON CARD (1-12)	.15	.07	.02
SEMISTARS	.30	.14	.04
RANDOM INSERTS IN PACKS			
□ 1 Harold Baines	.30	.14	.04
□ 2 Will Clark	.40	.18	.05
□ 3 Mark Davis	.15	.07	.02
□ 4 Howard Johnson UER (In middle of 5th line, the is	.15	.07	.02

misspelled th)			
□ 5 Joe Magrane	.15	.07	.02
□ 6 Kevin Mitchell	.30	.14	.04
□ 7 Kirby Puckett	.75	.35	.09
□ 8 Cal Ripken	2.00	.90	.25
□ 9 Ryne Sandberg	.60	.25	.07
□ 10 Mike Scott UER Astros spelled Asatros on back	.15	.07	.02
□ 11 Ruben Sierra	.30	.14	.04
□ 12 Mickey Tettleton	.30	.14	.04

1990 Fleer League Standouts

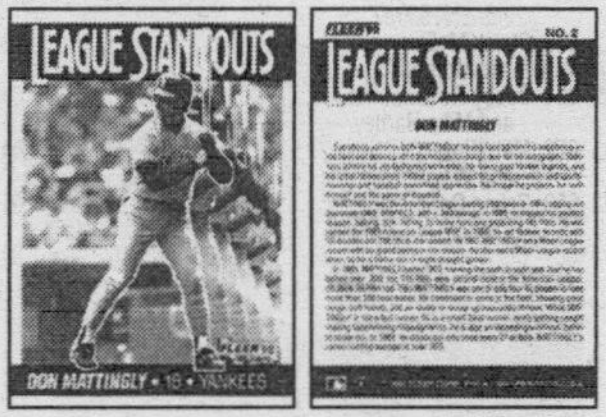

This six-card standard-size insert set was distributed one per 45-card rack pack. The set is subtitled "Standouts" and commemorates outstanding events for those players from the previous season.

	MINT	NRMT	EXC
COMPLETE SET (6)	6.00	2.70	.75
COMMON CARD (1-6)	.50	.23	.06
SEMISTARS	.75	.35	.09
ONE PER RACK PACK			

□ 1 Barry Larkin	1.00	.45	.12
□ 2 Don Mattingly	3.00	1.35	.35
□ 3 Darryl Strawberry	.75	.35	.09
□ 4 Jose Canseco	1.00	.45	.12
□ 5 Wade Boggs	.75	.35	.09
□ 6 Mark Grace UER (Chris Sabo misspelled as Cris)	.75	.35	.09

1990 Fleer Soaring Stars

The 1990 Fleer Soaring Stars set was issued exclusively in jumbo cello packs. This 12-card, standard-size set features some of the most popular young players entering the 1990 season. The set gives the visual impression of rockets exploding in the air to honor these young players.

	MINT	NRMT	EXC
COMPLETE SET (12)	25.00	11.00	3.10
COMMON CARD (1-12)	.50	.23	.06
RANDOM INSERTS IN JUMBO PACKS			

□ 1 Todd Zeile	.75	.35	.09
□ 2 Mike Stanton	.50	.23	.06
□ 3 Larry Walker	4.00	1.80	.50
□ 4 Robin Ventura	1.50	.70	.19
□ 5 Scott Coolbaugh	.50	.23	.06
□ 6 Ken Griffey Jr.	20.00	9.00	2.50
□ 7 Tom Gordon	.50	.23	.06
□ 8 Jerome Walton	.50	.23	.06
□ 9 Junior Felix	.50	.23	.06
□ 10 Jim Abbott	.75	.35	.09
□ 11 Ricky Jordan	.50	.23	.06
□ 12 Dwight Smith	.50	.23	.06

1990 Fleer Update

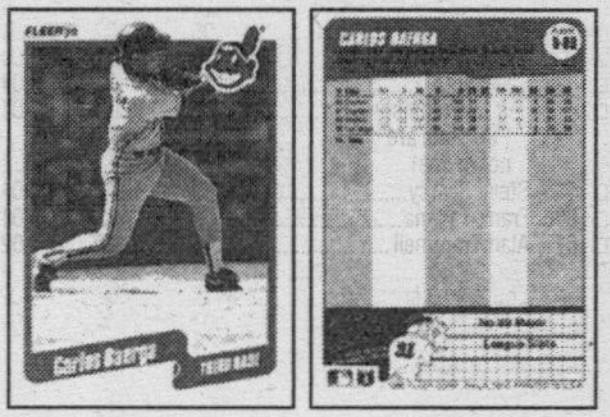

The 1990 Fleer Update set contains 132 standard-size cards. This set marked the seventh consecutive year Fleer issued an end of season Update set. The set was issued exclusively as a boxed set through hobby dealers. The set is checklisted alphabetically by team for each league and then alphabetically within each team. The fronts are styled the same as the 1990 Fleer regular issue set. The backs are numbered with the prefix "U" for Update. Rookie Cards in this set include Carlos Baerga, Alex Fernandez, Travis Fryman, Todd Hundley and Frank Thomas.

	MINT	NRMT	EXC
COMPLETE FACT.SET (132)	5.00	2.20	.60
COMMON CARD (1-132)	.05	.02	.01
SEMISTARS	.10	.05	.01
U PREFIX ON CARD NUMBERS			

□ 1 Steve Avery	.15	.07	.02
□ 2 Francisco Cabrera	.05	.02	.01
□ 3 Nick Esasky	.05	.02	.01
□ 4 Jim Kremers	.05	.02	.01
□ 5 Greg Olson	.05	.02	.01
□ 6 Jim Presley	.05	.02	.01
□ 7 Shawn Boskie	.05	.02	.01
□ 8 Joe Kraemer	.05	.02	.01
□ 9 Luis Salazar	.05	.02	.01
□ 10 Hector Villanueva	.05	.02	.01
□ 11 Glenn Braggs	.05	.02	.01
□ 12 Mariano Duncan	.05	.02	.01
□ 13 Billy Hatcher	.05	.02	.01
□ 14 Tim Layana	.05	.02	.01
□ 15 Hal Morris	.10	.05	.01
□ 16 Javier Ortiz	.05	.02	.01
□ 17 Dave Rohde	.05	.02	.01
□ 18 Eric Yelding	.05	.02	.01
□ 19 Hubie Brooks	.05	.02	.01
□ 20 Kal Daniels	.05	.02	.01
□ 21 Dave Hansen	.05	.02	.01
□ 22 Mike Hartley	.05	.02	.01
□ 23 Stan Javier	.05	.02	.01
□ 24 Jose Offerman	.10	.05	.01
□ 25 Juan Samuel	.05	.02	.01
□ 26 Dennis Boyd	.05	.02	.01
□ 27 Delino DeShields	.10	.05	.01
□ 28 Steve Frey	.05	.02	.01
□ 29 Mark Gardner	.05	.02	.01
□ 30 Chris Nabholz	.05	.02	.01
□ 31 Bill Sampen	.05	.02	.01
□ 32 Dave Schmidt	.05	.02	.01
□ 33 Daryl Boston	.05	.02	.01
□ 34 Chuck Carr	.15	.07	.02
□ 35 John Franco	.05	.02	.01
□ 36 Todd Hundley	.60	.25	.07

□ 37 Julio Machado	.05	.02	.01
□ 38 Alejandro Pena	.05	.02	.01
□ 39 Darren Reed	.05	.02	.01
□ 40 Kelvin Torve	.05	.02	.01
□ 41 Darrel Akerfelds	.05	.02	.01
□ 42 Jose DeJesus	.05	.02	.01
□ 43 Dave Hollins UER (Misspelled Dane on card back)	.15	.07	.02
□ 44 Carmelo Martinez	.05	.02	.01
□ 45 Brad Moore	.05	.02	.01
□ 46 Dale Murphy	.15	.07	.02
□ 47 Wally Backman	.05	.02	.01
□ 48 Stan Belinda	.05	.02	.01
□ 49 Bob Patterson	.05	.02	.01
□ 50 Ted Power	.05	.02	.01
□ 51 Don Slaught	.05	.02	.01
□ 52 Geronimo Pena	.05	.02	.01
□ 53 Lee Smith	.10	.05	.01
□ 54 John Tudor	.05	.02	.01
□ 55 Joe Carter	.15	.07	.02
□ 56 Thomas Howard	.05	.02	.01
□ 57 Craig Lefferts	.05	.02	.01
□ 58 Rafael Valdez	.05	.02	.01
□ 59 Dave Anderson	.05	.02	.01
□ 60 Kevin Bass	.05	.02	.01
□ 61 John Burkett	.10	.05	.01
□ 62 Gary Carter	.15	.07	.02
□ 63 Rick Parker	.05	.02	.01
□ 64 Trevor Wilson	.05	.02	.01
□ 65 Chris Hoiles	.15	.07	.02
□ 66 Tim Hulett	.05	.02	.01
□ 67 Dave Johnson	.05	.02	.01
□ 68 Curt Schilling	.05	.02	.01
□ 69 David Segui	.15	.07	.02
□ 70 Tom Brunansky	.05	.02	.01
□ 71 Greg A. Harris	.05	.02	.01
□ 72 Dana Kiecker	.05	.02	.01
□ 73 Tim Naehring	.15	.07	.02
□ 74 Tony Pena	.05	.02	.01
□ 75 Jeff Reardon	.10	.05	.01
□ 76 Jerry Reed	.05	.02	.01
□ 77 Mark Eichhorn	.05	.02	.01
□ 78 Mark Langston	.10	.05	.01
□ 79 John Orton	.05	.02	.01
□ 80 Luis Polonia	.05	.02	.01
□ 81 Dave Winfield	.15	.07	.02
□ 82 Cliff Young	.05	.02	.01
□ 83 Wayne Edwards	.05	.02	.01
□ 84 Alex Fernandez	.60	.25	.07
□ 85 Craig Grebeck	.05	.02	.01
□ 86 Scott Radinsky	.05	.02	.01
□ 87 Frank Thomas	4.00	1.80	.50
□ 88 Beau Allred	.05	.02	.01
□ 89 Sandy Alomar Jr.	.10	.05	.01
□ 90 Carlos Baerga	.50	.23	.06
□ 91 Kevin Bearse	.05	.02	.01
□ 92 Chris James	.05	.02	.01
□ 93 Candy Maldonado	.05	.02	.01
□ 94 Jeff Manto	.05	.02	.01
□ 95 Cecil Fielder	.10	.05	.01
□ 96 Travis Fryman	.50	.23	.06
□ 97 Lloyd Moseby	.05	.02	.01
□ 98 Edwin Nunez	.05	.02	.01
□ 99 Tony Phillips	.15	.07	.02
□ 100 Larry Sheets	.05	.02	.01
□ 101 Mark Davis	.05	.02	.01
□ 102 Storm Davis	.05	.02	.01
□ 103 Gerald Perry	.05	.02	.01
□ 104 Terry Shumpert	.05	.02	.01
□ 105 Edgar Diaz	.05	.02	.01
□ 106 Dave Parker	.10	.05	.01
□ 107 Tim Drummond	.05	.02	.01
□ 108 Junior Ortiz	.05	.02	.01
□ 109 Park Pittman	.05	.02	.01
□ 110 Kevin Tapani	.10	.05	.01
□ 111 Oscar Azocar	.05	.02	.01
□ 112 Jim Leyritz	.15	.07	.02
□ 113 Kevin Maas	.05	.02	.01
□ 114 Alan Mills	.05	.02	.01
□ 115 Matt Nokes	.05	.02	.01
□ 116 Pascual Perez	.05	.02	.01
□ 117 Ozzie Canseco	.05	.02	.01
□ 118 Scott Sanderson	.05	.02	.01
□ 119 Tino Martinez	.15	.07	.02
□ 120 Jeff Schaefer	.05	.02	.01
□ 121 Matt Young	.05	.02	.01
□ 122 Brian Bohanon	.05	.02	.01
□ 123 Jeff Huson	.05	.02	.01
□ 124 Ramon Manon	.05	.02	.01
□ 125 Gary Mielke UER (Shown as Blue Jay on front)	.05	.02	.01
□ 126 Willie Blair	.05	.02	.01
□ 127 Glenallen Hill	.10	.05	.01
□ 128 John Olerud UER (Listed as throwing right, should be left)	.15	.07	.02
□ 129 Luis Sojo	.05	.02	.01
□ 130 Mark Whiten	.15	.07	.02
□ 131 Nolan Ryan	.75	.35	.09
□ 132 Checklist U1-U132	.05	.02	.01

1991 Fleer

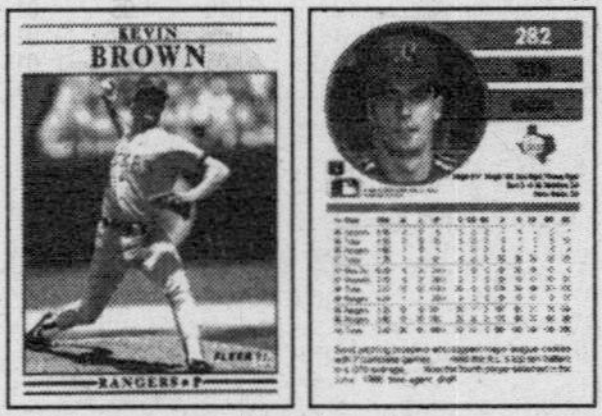

The 1991 Fleer set consists of 720 standard-size cards. Cards were primarily issued in wax packs, cello packs and factory sets. This set does not have what has been a Fleer tradition in recent years, the two-player rookie cards and there are less two-player special cards than in prior years. The design features solid yellow borders with the information in black indicating name, position, and team. The set is again ordered numerically by teams, followed by combination cards, rookie prospect pairs, and checklists. Rookie Cards in this set include Jeff Conine and Brian McRae. A number of the cards in the set can be found with photos cropped (very slightly) differently as Fleer used two separate printers in their attempt to maximize production.

	MINT	NRMT	EXC
COMPLETE SET (720)	8.00	3.60	1.00
COMPLETE RETAIL SET (732)	10.00	4.50	1.25
COMPLETE HOBBY SET (732)	10.00	4.50	1.25
COMMON CARD (1-720)	.05	.02	.01
SEMISTARS	.10	.05	.01
STARS	.15	.07	.02
COMP. WORLD SERIES (8)	2.00	.90	.25

□ 1 Troy Afenir	.05	.02	.01
□ 2 Harold Baines	.10	.05	.01
□ 3 Lance Blankenship	.05	.02	.01
□ 4 Todd Burns	.05	.02	.01
□ 5 Jose Canseco	.15	.07	.02
□ 6 Dennis Eckersley	.10	.05	.01
□ 7 Mike Gallego	.05	.02	.01
□ 8 Ron Hassey	.05	.02	.01
□ 9 Dave Henderson	.05	.02	.01
□ 10 Rickey Henderson	.15	.07	.02
□ 11 Rick Honeycutt	.05	.02	.01
□ 12 Doug Jennings	.05	.02	.01
□ 13 Joe Klink	.05	.02	.01
□ 14 Carney Lansford	.10	.05	.01
□ 15 Darren Lewis	.10	.05	.01
□ 16 Willie McGee UER (Height 6'11")	.05	.02	.01
□ 17 Mark McGwire UER (183 extra base hits in 1987)	.30	.14	.04
□ 18 Mike Moore	.05	.02	.01
□ 19 Gene Nelson	.05	.02	.01
□ 20 Dave Otto	.05	.02	.01

□ 21	Jamie Quirk	.05	.02	.01
□ 22	Willie Randolph	.10	.05	.01
□ 23	Scott Sanderson	.05	.02	.01
□ 24	Terry Steinbach	.10	.05	.01
□ 25	Dave Stewart	.10	.05	.01
□ 26	Walt Weiss	.05	.02	.01
□ 27	Bob Welch	.05	.02	.01
□ 28	Curt Young	.05	.02	.01
□ 29	Wally Backman	.05	.02	.01
□ 30	Stan Belinda UER (Born in Huntington, should be State College)	.05	.02	.01
□ 31	Jay Bell	.10	.05	.01
□ 32	Rafael Belliard	.05	.02	.01
□ 33	Barry Bonds	.25	.11	.03
□ 34	Bobby Bonilla	.10	.05	.01
□ 35	Sid Bream	.05	.02	.01
□ 36	Doug Drabek	.05	.02	.01
□ 37	Carlos Garcia	.15	.07	.02
□ 38	Neal Heaton	.05	.02	.01
□ 39	Jeff King	.10	.05	.01
□ 40	Bob Kipper	.05	.02	.01
□ 41	Bill Landrum	.05	.02	.01
□ 42	Mike LaValliere	.05	.02	.01
□ 43	Jose Lind	.05	.02	.01
□ 44	Carmelo Martinez	.05	.02	.01
□ 45	Bob Patterson	.05	.02	.01
□ 46	Ted Power	.05	.02	.01
□ 47	Gary Redus	.05	.02	.01
□ 48	R.J. Reynolds	.05	.02	.01
□ 49	Don Slaught	.05	.02	.01
□ 50	John Smiley	.05	.02	.01
□ 51	Zane Smith	.05	.02	.01
□ 52	Randy Tomlin	.05	.02	.01
□ 53	Andy Van Slyke	.10	.05	.01
□ 54	Bob Walk	.05	.02	.01
□ 55	Jack Armstrong	.05	.02	.01
□ 56	Todd Benzinger	.05	.02	.01
□ 57	Glenn Braggs	.05	.02	.01
□ 58	Keith Brown	.05	.02	.01
□ 59	Tom Browning	.05	.02	.01
□ 60	Norm Charlton	.05	.02	.01
□ 61	Eric Davis	.10	.05	.01
□ 62	Rob Dibble	.05	.02	.01
□ 63	Bill Doran	.05	.02	.01
□ 64	Mariano Duncan	.05	.02	.01
□ 65	Chris Hammond	.05	.02	.01
□ 66	Billy Hatcher	.05	.02	.01
□ 67	Danny Jackson	.05	.02	.01
□ 68	Barry Larkin	.15	.07	.02
□ 69	Tim Layana (Black line over made in first text line)	.05	.02	.01
□ 70	Terry Lee	.05	.02	.01
□ 71	Rick Mahler	.05	.02	.01
□ 72	Hal Morris	.05	.02	.01
□ 73	Randy Myers	.10	.05	.01
□ 74	Ron Oester	.05	.02	.01
□ 75	Joe Oliver	.05	.02	.01
□ 76	Paul O'Neill	.10	.05	.01
□ 77	Luis Quinones	.05	.02	.01
□ 78	Jeff Reed	.05	.02	.01
□ 79	Jose Rijo	.05	.02	.01
□ 80	Chris Sabo	.05	.02	.01
□ 81	Scott Scudder	.05	.02	.01
□ 82	Herm Winningham	.05	.02	.01
□ 83	Larry Andersen	.05	.02	.01
□ 84	Marty Barrett	.05	.02	.01
□ 85	Mike Boddicker	.05	.02	.01
□ 86	Wade Boggs	.15	.07	.02
□ 87	Tom Bolton	.05	.02	.01
□ 88	Tom Brunansky	.05	.02	.01
□ 89	Ellis Burks	.15	.07	.02
□ 90	Roger Clemens	.15	.07	.02
□ 91	Scott Cooper	.05	.02	.01
□ 92	John Dopson	.05	.02	.01
□ 93	Dwight Evans	.10	.05	.01
□ 94	Wes Gardner	.05	.02	.01
□ 95	Jeff Gray	.05	.02	.01
□ 96	Mike Greenwell	.05	.02	.01
□ 97	Greg A. Harris	.05	.02	.01
□ 98	Daryl Irvine	.05	.02	.01
□ 99	Dana Kiecker	.05	.02	.01
□ 100	Randy Kutcher	.05	.02	.01
□ 101	Dennis Lamp	.05	.02	.01
□ 102	Mike Marshall	.05	.02	.01

□ 103	John Marzano	.05	.02	.01
□ 104	Rob Murphy	.05	.02	.01
□ 105	Tim Naehring	.10	.05	.01
□ 106	Tony Pena	.05	.02	.01
□ 107	Phil Plantier	.10	.05	.01
□ 108	Carlos Quintana	.05	.02	.01
□ 109	Jeff Reardon	.10	.05	.01
□ 110	Jerry Reed	.05	.02	.01
□ 111	Jody Reed	.05	.02	.01
□ 112	Luis Rivera UER (Born 1/3/84)	.05	.02	.01
□ 113	Kevin Romine	.05	.02	.01
□ 114	Phil Bradley	.05	.02	.01
□ 115	Ivan Calderon	.05	.02	.01
□ 116	Wayne Edwards	.05	.02	.01
□ 117	Alex Fernandez	.15	.07	.02
□ 118	Carlton Fisk	.15	.07	.02
□ 119	Scott Fletcher	.05	.02	.01
□ 120	Craig Grebeck	.05	.02	.01
□ 121	Ozzie Guillen	.05	.02	.01
□ 122	Greg Hibbard	.05	.02	.01
□ 123	Lance Johnson UER (Born Cincinnati, should be Lincoln Heights)	.10	.05	.01
□ 124	Barry Jones	.05	.02	.01
□ 125	Ron Karkovice	.05	.02	.01
□ 126	Eric King	.05	.02	.01
□ 127	Steve Lyons	.05	.02	.01
□ 128	Carlos Martinez	.05	.02	.01
□ 129	Jack McDowell UER (Stanford misspelled as Standford on back)	.10	.05	.01
□ 130	Donn Pall (No dots over any i's in text)	.05	.02	.01
□ 131	Dan Pasqua	.05	.02	.01
□ 132	Ken Patterson	.05	.02	.01
□ 133	Melido Perez	.05	.02	.01
□ 134	Adam Peterson	.05	.02	.01
□ 135	Scott Radinsky	.05	.02	.01
□ 136	Sammy Sosa	.25	.11	.03
□ 137	Bobby Thigpen	.05	.02	.01
□ 138	Frank Thomas	2.00	.90	.25
□ 139	Robin Ventura	.15	.07	.02
□ 140	Daryl Boston	.05	.02	.01
□ 141	Chuck Carr	.05	.02	.01
□ 142	Mark Carreon	.05	.02	.01
□ 143	David Cone	.15	.07	.02
□ 144	Ron Darling	.05	.02	.01
□ 145	Kevin Elster	.05	.02	.01
□ 146	Sid Fernandez	.05	.02	.01
□ 147	John Franco	.05	.02	.01
□ 148	Dwight Gooden	.10	.05	.01
□ 149	Tom Herr	.05	.02	.01
□ 150	Todd Hundley	.15	.07	.02
□ 151	Gregg Jefferies	.15	.07	.02
□ 152	Howard Johnson	.05	.02	.01
□ 153	Dave Magadan	.05	.02	.01
□ 154	Kevin McReynolds	.05	.02	.01
□ 155	Keith Miller UER (Text says Rochester in '87, stats say Tidewater, mixed up with other Keith Miller)	.05	.02	.01
□ 156	Bob Ojeda	.05	.02	.01
□ 157	Tom O'Malley	.05	.02	.01
□ 158	Alejandro Pena	.05	.02	.01
□ 159	Darren Reed	.05	.02	.01
□ 160	Mackey Sasser	.05	.02	.01
□ 161	Darryl Strawberry	.10	.05	.01
□ 162	Tim Teufel	.05	.02	.01
□ 163	Kelvin Torve	.05	.02	.01
□ 164	Julio Valera	.05	.02	.01
□ 165	Frank Viola	.05	.02	.01
□ 166	Wally Whitehurst	.05	.02	.01
□ 167	Jim Acker	.05	.02	.01
□ 168	Derek Bell	.15	.07	.02
□ 169	George Bell	.05	.02	.01
□ 170	Willie Blair	.05	.02	.01
□ 171	Pat Borders	.05	.02	.01
□ 172	John Cerutti	.05	.02	.01
□ 173	Junior Felix	.05	.02	.01
□ 174	Tony Fernandez	.05	.02	.01
□ 175	Kelly Gruber UER (Born in Houston, should be Bellaire)	.05	.02	.01

☐ 176	Tom Henke	.05	.02	.01
☐ 177	Glenallen Hill	.05	.02	.01
☐ 178	Jimmy Key	.10	.05	.01
☐ 179	Manny Lee	.05	.02	.01
☐ 180	Fred McGriff	.15	.07	.02
☐ 181	Rance Mulliniks	.05	.02	.01
☐ 182	Greg Myers	.05	.02	.01
☐ 183	John Olerud UER	.10	.05	.01
	(Listed as throwing right, should be left)			
☐ 184	Luis Sojo	.05	.02	.01
☐ 185	Dave Stieb	.05	.02	.01
☐ 186	Todd Stottlemyre	.05	.02	.01
☐ 187	Duane Ward	.05	.02	.01
☐ 188	David Wells	.05	.02	.01
☐ 189	Mark Whiten	.10	.05	.01
☐ 190	Ken Williams	.05	.02	.01
☐ 191	Frank Wills	.05	.02	.01
☐ 192	Mookie Wilson	.05	.02	.01
☐ 193	Don Aase	.05	.02	.01
☐ 194	Tim Belcher UER	.05	.02	.01
	(Born Sparta, Ohio, should say Mt. Gilead)			
☐ 195	Hubie Brooks	.05	.02	.01
☐ 196	Dennis Cook	.05	.02	.01
☐ 197	Tim Crews	.05	.02	.01
☐ 198	Kal Daniels	.05	.02	.01
☐ 199	Kirk Gibson	.10	.05	.01
☐ 200	Jim Gott	.05	.02	.01
☐ 201	Alfredo Griffin	.05	.02	.01
☐ 202	Chris Gwynn	.05	.02	.01
☐ 203	Dave Hansen	.05	.02	.01
☐ 204	Lenny Harris	.05	.02	.01
☐ 205	Mike Hartley	.05	.02	.01
☐ 206	Mickey Hatcher	.05	.02	.01
☐ 207	Carlos Hernandez	.05	.02	.01
☐ 208	Orel Hershiser	.10	.05	.01
☐ 209	Jay Howell UER	.05	.02	.01
	(No 1982 Yankee stats)			
☐ 210	Mike Huff	.05	.02	.01
☐ 211	Stan Javier	.05	.02	.01
☐ 212	Ramon Martinez	.10	.05	.01
☐ 213	Mike Morgan	.05	.02	.01
☐ 214	Eddie Murray	.25	.11	.03
☐ 215	Jim Neidlinger	.05	.02	.01
☐ 216	Jose Offerman	.05	.02	.01
☐ 217	Jim Poole	.05	.02	.01
☐ 218	Juan Samuel	.05	.02	.01
☐ 219	Mike Scioscia	.05	.02	.01
☐ 220	Ray Searage	.05	.02	.01
☐ 221	Mike Sharperson	.05	.02	.01
☐ 222	Fernando Valenzuela	.10	.05	.01
☐ 223	Jose Vizcaino	.05	.02	.01
☐ 224	Mike Aldrete	.05	.02	.01
☐ 225	Scott Anderson	.05	.02	.01
☐ 226	Dennis Boyd	.05	.02	.01
☐ 227	Tim Burke	.05	.02	.01
☐ 228	Delino DeShields	.05	.02	.01
☐ 229	Mike Fitzgerald	.05	.02	.01
☐ 230	Tom Foley	.05	.02	.01
☐ 231	Steve Frey	.05	.02	.01
☐ 232	Andres Galarraga	.15	.07	.02
☐ 233	Mark Gardner	.05	.02	.01
☐ 234	Marquis Grissom	.15	.07	.02
☐ 235	Kevin Gross	.05	.02	.01
	(No date given for first Expos win)			
☐ 236	Drew Hall	.05	.02	.01
☐ 237	Dave Martinez	.05	.02	.01
☐ 238	Dennis Martinez	.10	.05	.01
☐ 239	Dale Mohorcic	.05	.02	.01
☐ 240	Chris Nabholz	.05	.02	.01
☐ 241	Otis Nixon	.05	.02	.01
☐ 242	Junior Noboa	.05	.02	.01
☐ 243	Spike Owen	.05	.02	.01
☐ 244	Tim Raines	.15	.07	.02
☐ 245	Mel Rojas UER	.10	.05	.01
	(Stats show 3.60 ERA, bio says 3.19 ERA)			
☐ 246	Scott Ruskin	.05	.02	.01
☐ 247	Bill Sampen	.05	.02	.01
☐ 248	Nelson Santovenia	.05	.02	.01
☐ 249	Dave Schmidt	.05	.02	.01
☐ 250	Larry Walker	.15	.07	.02
☐ 251	Tim Wallach	.05	.02	.01
☐ 252	Dave Anderson	.05	.02	.01
☐ 253	Kevin Bass	.05	.02	.01
☐ 254	Steve Bedrosian	.05	.02	.01
☐ 255	Jeff Brantley	.05	.02	.01
☐ 256	John Burkett	.10	.05	.01
☐ 257	Brett Butler	.10	.05	.01
☐ 258	Gary Carter	.15	.07	.02
☐ 259	Will Clark	.15	.07	.02
☐ 260	Steve Decker	.05	.02	.01
☐ 261	Kelly Downs	.05	.02	.01
☐ 262	Scott Garrelts	.05	.02	.01
☐ 263	Terry Kennedy	.05	.02	.01
☐ 264	Mike LaCoss	.05	.02	.01
☐ 265	Mark Leonard	.05	.02	.01
☐ 266	Greg Litton	.05	.02	.01
☐ 267	Kevin Mitchell	.10	.05	.01
☐ 268	Randy O'Neal	.05	.02	.01
☐ 269	Rick Parker	.05	.02	.01
☐ 270	Rick Reuschel	.05	.02	.01
☐ 271	Ernest Riles	.05	.02	.01
☐ 272	Don Robinson	.05	.02	.01
☐ 273	Robby Thompson	.05	.02	.01
☐ 274	Mark Thurmond	.05	.02	.01
☐ 275	Jose Uribe	.05	.02	.01
☐ 276	Matt Williams	.15	.07	.02
☐ 277	Trevor Wilson	.05	.02	.01
☐ 278	Gerald Alexander	.05	.02	.01
☐ 279	Brad Arnsberg	.05	.02	.01
☐ 280	Kevin Belcher	.05	.02	.01
☐ 281	Joe Bitker	.05	.02	.01
☐ 282	Kevin Brown	.10	.05	.01
☐ 283	Steve Buechele	.05	.02	.01
☐ 284	Jack Daugherty	.05	.02	.01
☐ 285	Julio Franco	.10	.05	.01
☐ 286	Juan Gonzalez	.75	.35	.09
☐ 287	Bill Haselman	.05	.02	.01
☐ 288	Charlie Hough	.05	.02	.01
☐ 289	Jeff Huson	.05	.02	.01
☐ 290	Pete Incaviglia	.05	.02	.01
☐ 291	Mike Jeffcoat	.05	.02	.01
☐ 292	Jeff Kunkel	.05	.02	.01
☐ 293	Gary Mielke	.05	.02	.01
☐ 294	Jamie Moyer	.05	.02	.01
☐ 295	Rafael Palmeiro	.15	.07	.02
☐ 296	Geno Petralli	.05	.02	.01
☐ 297	Gary Pettis	.05	.02	.01
☐ 298	Kevin Reimer	.05	.02	.01
☐ 299	Kenny Rogers	.05	.02	.01
☐ 300	Jeff Russell	.05	.02	.01
☐ 301	John Russell	.05	.02	.01
☐ 302	Nolan Ryan	.75	.35	.09
☐ 303	Ruben Sierra	.10	.05	.01
☐ 304	Bobby Witt	.05	.02	.01
☐ 305	Jim Abbott UER	.10	.05	.01
	(Text on back states he won Sullivan Award (outstanding amateur athlete) in 1989;should be '88)			
☐ 306	Kent Anderson	.05	.02	.01
☐ 307	Dante Bichette	.15	.07	.02
☐ 308	Bert Blyleven	.10	.05	.01
☐ 309	Chili Davis	.10	.05	.01
☐ 310	Brian Downing	.05	.02	.01
☐ 311	Mark Eichhorn	.05	.02	.01
☐ 312	Mike Fetters	.05	.02	.01
☐ 313	Chuck Finley	.10	.05	.01
☐ 314	Willie Fraser	.05	.02	.01
☐ 315	Bryan Harvey	.05	.02	.01
☐ 316	Donnie Hill	.05	.02	.01
☐ 317	Wally Joyner	.10	.05	.01
☐ 318	Mark Langston	.10	.05	.01
☐ 319	Kirk McCaskill	.05	.02	.01
☐ 320	John Orton	.05	.02	.01
☐ 321	Lance Parrish	.05	.02	.01
☐ 322	Luis Polonia UER	.05	.02	.01
	(1984 Madfison, should be Madison)			
☐ 323	Johnny Ray	.05	.02	.01
☐ 324	Bobby Rose	.05	.02	.01
☐ 325	Dick Schofield	.05	.02	.01
☐ 326	Rick Schu	.05	.02	.01
☐ 327	Lee Stevens	.05	.02	.01
☐ 328	Devon White	.10	.05	.01
☐ 329	Dave Winfield	.15	.07	.02
☐ 330	Cliff Young	.05	.02	.01
☐ 331	Dave Bergman	.05	.02	.01
☐ 332	Phil Clark	.05	.02	.01
☐ 333	Darnell Coles	.05	.02	.01

□ 334 Milt Cuyler	.05	.02	.01
□ 335 Cecil Fielder	.10	.05	.01
□ 336 Travis Fryman	.15	.07	.02
□ 337 Paul Gibson	.05	.02	.01
□ 338 Jerry Don Gleaton	.05	.02	.01
□ 339 Mike Heath	.05	.02	.01
□ 340 Mike Henneman	.05	.02	.01
□ 341 Chet Lemon	.05	.02	.01
□ 342 Lance McCullers	.05	.02	.01
□ 343 Jack Morris	.10	.05	.01
□ 344 Lloyd Moseby	.05	.02	.01
□ 345 Edwin Nunez	.05	.02	.01
□ 346 Clay Parker	.05	.02	.01
□ 347 Dan Petry	.05	.02	.01
□ 348 Tony Phillips	.10	.05	.01
□ 349 Jeff M. Robinson	.05	.02	.01
□ 350 Mark Salas	.05	.02	.01
□ 351 Mike Schwabe	.05	.02	.01
□ 352 Larry Sheets	.05	.02	.01
□ 353 John Shelby	.05	.02	.01
□ 354 Frank Tanana	.05	.02	.01
□ 355 Alan Trammell	.15	.07	.02
□ 356 Gary Ward	.05	.02	.01
□ 357 Lou Whitaker	.15	.07	.02
□ 358 Beau Allred	.05	.02	.01
□ 359 Sandy Alomar Jr.	.10	.05	.01
□ 360 Carlos Baerga	.15	.07	.02
□ 361 Kevin Bearse	.05	.02	.01
□ 362 Tom Brookens	.05	.02	.01
□ 363 Jerry Browne UER (No dot over i in first text line)	.05	.02	.01
□ 364 Tom Candiotti	.05	.02	.01
□ 365 Alex Cole	.05	.02	.01
□ 366 John Farrell UER (Born in Neptune, should be Monmouth)	.05	.02	.01
□ 367 Felix Fermin	.05	.02	.01
□ 368 Keith Hernandez	.10	.05	.01
□ 369 Brook Jacoby	.05	.02	.01
□ 370 Chris James	.05	.02	.01
□ 371 Dion James	.05	.02	.01
□ 372 Doug Jones	.05	.02	.01
□ 373 Candy Maldonado	.05	.02	.01
□ 374 Steve Olin	.05	.02	.01
□ 375 Jesse Orosco	.05	.02	.01
□ 376 Rudy Seanez	.05	.02	.01
□ 377 Joel Skinner	.05	.02	.01
□ 378 Cory Snyder	.05	.02	.01
□ 379 Greg Swindell	.05	.02	.01
□ 380 Sergio Valdez	.05	.02	.01
□ 381 Mike Walker	.05	.02	.01
□ 382 Colby Ward	.05	.02	.01
□ 383 Turner Ward	.05	.02	.01
□ 384 Mitch Webster	.05	.02	.01
□ 385 Kevin Wickander	.05	.02	.01
□ 386 Darrel Akerfelds	.05	.02	.01
□ 387 Joe Boever	.05	.02	.01
□ 388 Rod Booker	.05	.02	.01
□ 389 Sil Campusano	.05	.02	.01
□ 390 Don Carman	.05	.02	.01
□ 391 Wes Chamberlain	.05	.02	.01
□ 392 Pat Combs	.05	.02	.01
□ 393 Darren Daulton	.10	.05	.01
□ 394 Jose DeJesus	.05	.02	.01
□ 395A Len Dykstra Name spelled Lenny on back	.15	.07	.02
□ 395B Len Dykstra Name spelled Len on back	.10	.05	.01
□ 396 Jason Grimsley	.05	.02	.01
□ 397 Charlie Hayes	.05	.02	.01
□ 398 Von Hayes	.05	.02	.01
□ 399 David Hollins UER (Atl-bats, should say at-bats)	.05	.02	.01
□ 400 Ken Howell	.05	.02	.01
□ 401 Ricky Jordan	.05	.02	.01
□ 402 John Kruk	.10	.05	.01
□ 403 Steve Lake	.05	.02	.01
□ 404 Chuck Malone	.05	.02	.01
□ 405 Roger McDowell UER (Says Phillies is saves, should say in)	.05	.02	.01
□ 406 Chuck McElroy	.05	.02	.01
□ 407 Mickey Morandini	.05	.02	.01
□ 408 Terry Mulholland	.05	.02	.01
□ 409 Dale Murphy	.15	.07	.02
□ 410A Randy Ready ERR (No Brewers stats listed for 1983)	.05	.02	.01
□ 410B Randy Ready COR	.05	.02	.01
□ 411 Bruce Ruffin	.05	.02	.01
□ 412 Dickie Thon	.05	.02	.01
□ 413 Paul Assenmacher	.05	.02	.01
□ 414 Damon Berryhill	.05	.02	.01
□ 415 Mike Bielecki	.05	.02	.01
□ 416 Shawn Boskie	.05	.02	.01
□ 417 Dave Clark	.05	.02	.01
□ 418 Doug Dascenzo	.05	.02	.01
□ 419A Andre Dawson ERR (No stats for 1976)	.15	.07	.02
□ 419B Andre Dawson COR	.15	.07	.02
□ 420 Shawon Dunston	.05	.02	.01
□ 421 Joe Girardi	.10	.05	.01
□ 422 Mark Grace	.15	.07	.02
□ 423 Mike Harkey	.05	.02	.01
□ 424 Les Lancaster	.05	.02	.01
□ 425 Bill Long	.05	.02	.01
□ 426 Greg Maddux	.60	.25	.07
□ 427 Derrick May	.05	.02	.01
□ 428 Jeff Pico	.05	.02	.01
□ 429 Domingo Ramos	.05	.02	.01
□ 430 Luis Salazar	.05	.02	.01
□ 431 Ryne Sandberg	.25	.11	.03
□ 432 Dwight Smith	.05	.02	.01
□ 433 Greg Smith	.05	.02	.01
□ 434 Rick Sutcliffe	.05	.02	.01
□ 435 Gary Varsho	.05	.02	.01
□ 436 Hector Villanueva	.05	.02	.01
□ 437 Jerome Walton	.05	.02	.01
□ 438 Curtis Wilkerson	.05	.02	.01
□ 439 Mitch Williams	.05	.02	.01
□ 440 Steve Wilson	.05	.02	.01
□ 441 Marvell Wynne	.05	.02	.01
□ 442 Scott Bankhead	.05	.02	.01
□ 443 Scott Bradley	.05	.02	.01
□ 444 Greg Briley	.05	.02	.01
□ 445 Mike Brumley UER (Text 40 SB's in 1988, stats say 41)	.05	.02	.01
□ 446 Jay Buhner	.15	.07	.02
□ 447 Dave Burba	.05	.02	.01
□ 448 Henry Cotto	.05	.02	.01
□ 449 Alvin Davis	.05	.02	.01
□ 450 Ken Griffey Jr. (Bat around .300)	1.50	.70	.19
□ 450A Ken Griffey Jr. (Bat .300)	1.50	.70	.19
□ 451 Erik Hanson	.05	.02	.01
□ 452 Gene Harris UER (63 career runs, should be 73)	.05	.02	.01
□ 453 Brian Holman	.05	.02	.01
□ 454 Mike Jackson	.05	.02	.01
□ 455 Randy Johnson	.15	.07	.02
□ 456 Jeffrey Leonard	.05	.02	.01
□ 457 Edgar Martinez	.15	.07	.02
□ 458 Tino Martinez	.15	.07	.02
□ 459 Pete O'Brien UER (1987 BA .266, should be .286)	.05	.02	.01
□ 460 Harold Reynolds	.05	.02	.01
□ 461 Mike Schooler	.05	.02	.01
□ 462 Bill Swift	.05	.02	.01
□ 463 David Valle	.05	.02	.01
□ 464 Omar Vizquel	.15	.07	.02
□ 465 Matt Young	.05	.02	.01
□ 466 Brady Anderson	.15	.07	.02
□ 467 Jeff Ballard UER (Missing top of right parenthesis after Saberhagen in last text line)	.05	.02	.01
□ 468 Juan Bell	.05	.02	.01
□ 469A Mike Devereaux (First line of text ends with six)	.10	.05	.01
□ 469B Mike Devereaux (First line of text ends with runs)	.10	.05	.01
□ 470 Steve Finley	.15	.07	.02
□ 471 Dave Gallagher	.05	.02	.01

□	472 Leo Gomez	.05	.02	.01
□	473 Rene Gonzales	.05	.02	.01
□	474 Pete Harnisch	.05	.02	.01
□	475 Kevin Hickey	.05	.02	.01
□	476 Chris Hoiles	.05	.02	.01
□	477 Sam Horn	.05	.02	.01
□	478 Tim Hulett	.05	.02	.01
	(Photo shows National Leaguer sliding into second base)			
□	479 Dave Johnson	.05	.02	.01
□	480 Ron Kittle UER	.05	.02	.01
	(Edmonton misspelled as Edmundton)			
□	481 Ben McDonald	.10	.05	.01
□	482 Bob Melvin	.05	.02	.01
□	483 Bob Milacki	.05	.02	.01
□	484 Randy Milligan	.05	.02	.01
□	485 John Mitchell	.05	.02	.01
□	486 Gregg Olson	.05	.02	.01
□	487 Joe Orsulak	.05	.02	.01
□	488 Joe Price	.05	.02	.01
□	489 Bill Ripken	.05	.02	.01
□	490 Cal Ripken	.75	.35	.09
□	491 Curt Schilling	.05	.02	.01
□	492 David Segui	.10	.05	.01
□	493 Anthony Telford	.05	.02	.01
□	494 Mickey Tettleton	.10	.05	.01
□	495 Mark Williamson	.05	.02	.01
□	496 Craig Worthington	.05	.02	.01
□	497 Juan Agosto	.05	.02	.01
□	498 Eric Anthony	.05	.02	.01
□	499 Craig Biggio	.15	.07	.02
□	500 Ken Caminiti UER	.15	.07	.02
	(Born 4/4, should be 4/21)			
□	501 Casey Candaele	.05	.02	.01
□	502 Andujar Cedeno	.05	.02	.01
□	503 Danny Darwin	.05	.02	.01
□	504 Mark Davidson	.05	.02	.01
□	505 Glenn Davis	.05	.02	.01
□	506 Jim Deshaies	.05	.02	.01
□	507 Luis Gonzalez	.15	.07	.02
□	508 Bill Gullickson	.05	.02	.01
□	509 Xavier Hernandez	.05	.02	.01
□	510 Brian Meyer	.05	.02	.01
□	511 Ken Oberkfell	.05	.02	.01
□	512 Mark Portugal	.05	.02	.01
□	513 Rafael Ramirez	.05	.02	.01
□	514 Karl Rhodes	.05	.02	.01
□	515 Mike Scott	.05	.02	.01
□	516 Mike Simms	.05	.02	.01
□	517 Dave Smith	.05	.02	.01
□	518 Franklin Stubbs	.05	.02	.01
□	519 Glenn Wilson	.05	.02	.01
□	520 Eric Yelding UER	.05	.02	.01
	(Text has 63 steals, stats have 64, which is correct)			
□	521 Gerald Young	.05	.02	.01
□	522 Shawn Abner	.05	.02	.01
□	523 Roberto Alomar	.25	.11	.03
□	524 Andy Benes	.05	.02	.01
□	525 Joe Carter	.15	.07	.02
□	526 Jack Clark	.10	.05	.01
□	527 Joey Cora	.10	.05	.01
□	528 Paul Faries	.05	.02	.01
□	529 Tony Gwynn	.40	.18	.05
□	530 Atlee Hammaker	.05	.02	.01
□	531 Greg W. Harris	.05	.02	.01
□	532 Thomas Howard	.05	.02	.01
□	533 Bruce Hurst	.05	.02	.01
□	534 Craig Lefferts	.05	.02	.01
□	535 Derek Lilliquist	.05	.02	.01
□	536 Fred Lynn	.05	.02	.01
□	537 Mike Pagliarulo	.05	.02	.01
□	538 Mark Parent	.05	.02	.01
□	539 Dennis Rasmussen	.05	.02	.01
□	540 Bip Roberts	.05	.02	.01
□	541 Richard Rodriguez	.05	.02	.01
□	542 Benito Santiago	.05	.02	.01
□	543 Calvin Schiraldi	.05	.02	.01
□	544 Eric Show	.05	.02	.01
□	545 Phil Stephenson	.05	.02	.01
□	546 Garry Templeton UER	.05	.02	.01
	(Born 3/24/57, should be 3/24/56)			
□	547 Ed Whitson	.05	.02	.01
□	548 Eddie Williams	.05	.02	.01
□	549 Kevin Appier	.10	.05	.01
□	550 Luis Aquino	.05	.02	.01
□	551 Bob Boone	.10	.05	.01
□	552 George Brett	.40	.18	.05
□	553 Jeff Conine	.50	.23	.06
□	554 Steve Crawford	.05	.02	.01
□	555 Mark Davis	.05	.02	.01
□	556 Storm Davis	.05	.02	.01
□	557 Jim Eisenreich	.10	.05	.01
□	558 Steve Farr	.05	.02	.01
□	559 Tom Gordon	.05	.02	.01
□	560 Mark Gubicza	.05	.02	.01
□	561 Bo Jackson	.15	.07	.02
□	562 Mike Macfarlane	.05	.02	.01
□	563 Brian McRae	.25	.11	.03
□	564 Jeff Montgomery	.10	.05	.01
□	565 Bill Pecota	.05	.02	.01
□	566 Gerald Perry	.05	.02	.01
□	567 Bret Saberhagen	.10	.05	.01
□	568 Jeff Schulz	.05	.02	.01
□	569 Kevin Seitzer	.05	.02	.01
□	570 Terry Shumpert	.05	.02	.01
□	571 Kurt Stillwell	.05	.02	.01
□	572 Danny Tartabull	.05	.02	.01
□	573 Gary Thurman	.05	.02	.01
□	574 Frank White	.10	.05	.01
□	575 Willie Wilson	.05	.02	.01
□	576 Chris Bosio	.05	.02	.01
□	577 Greg Brock	.05	.02	.01
□	578 George Canale	.05	.02	.01
□	579 Chuck Crim	.05	.02	.01
□	580 Rob Deer	.05	.02	.01
□	581 Edgar Diaz	.05	.02	.01
□	582 Tom Edens	.05	.02	.01
□	583 Mike Felder	.05	.02	.01
□	584 Jim Gantner	.05	.02	.01
□	585 Darryl Hamilton	.10	.05	.01
□	586 Ted Higuera	.05	.02	.01
□	587 Mark Knudson	.05	.02	.01
□	588 Bill Krueger	.05	.02	.01
□	589 Tim McIntosh	.05	.02	.01
□	590 Paul Mirabella	.05	.02	.01
□	591 Paul Molitor	.20	.09	.03
□	592 Jaime Navarro	.05	.02	.01
□	593 Dave Parker	.10	.05	.01
□	594 Dan Plesac	.05	.02	.01
□	595 Ron Robinson	.05	.02	.01
□	596 Gary Sheffield	.15	.07	.02
□	597 Bill Spiers	.05	.02	.01
□	598 B.J. Surhoff	.10	.05	.01
□	599 Greg Vaughn	.15	.07	.02
□	600 Randy Veres	.05	.02	.01
□	601 Robin Yount	.15	.07	.02
□	602 Rick Aguilera	.10	.05	.01
□	603 Allan Anderson	.05	.02	.01
□	604 Juan Berenguer	.05	.02	.01
□	605 Randy Bush	.05	.02	.01
□	606 Carmen Castillo	.05	.02	.01
□	607 Tim Drummond	.05	.02	.01
□	608 Scott Erickson	.10	.05	.01
□	609 Gary Gaetti	.10	.05	.01
□	610 Greg Gagne	.05	.02	.01
□	611 Dan Gladden	.05	.02	.01
□	612 Mark Guthrie	.05	.02	.01
□	613 Brian Harper	.05	.02	.01
□	614 Kent Hrbek	.10	.05	.01
□	615 Gene Larkin	.05	.02	.01
□	616 Terry Leach	.05	.02	.01
□	617 Nelson Liriano	.05	.02	.01
□	618 Shane Mack	.05	.02	.01
□	619 John Moses	.05	.02	.01
□	620 Pedro Munoz	.10	.05	.01
□	621 Al Newman	.05	.02	.01
□	622 Junior Ortiz	.05	.02	.01
□	623 Kirby Puckett	.30	.14	.04
□	624 Roy Smith	.05	.02	.01
□	625 Kevin Tapani	.05	.02	.01
□	626 Gary Wayne	.05	.02	.01
□	627 David West	.05	.02	.01
□	628 Cris Carpenter	.05	.02	.01
□	629 Vince Coleman	.05	.02	.01
□	630 Ken Dayley	.05	.02	.01
□	631A Jose DeLeon ERR	.05	.02	.01

(missing '79 Bradenton stats)			
□ 631B Jose DeLeon COR	.05	.02	.01
(with '79 Bradenton stats)			
□ 632 Frank DiPino	.05	.02	.01
□ 633 Bernard Gilkey	.15	.07	.02
□ 634A Pedro Guerrero ERR	.10	.05	.01
(career SB shown as "$91")			
□ 634B Pedro Guerrero COR	.05	.02	.01
□ 635 Ken Hill	.15	.07	.02
□ 636 Felix Jose	.05	.02	.01
□ 637 Ray Lankford	.15	.07	.02
□ 638 Joe Magrane	.05	.02	.01
□ 639 Tom Niedenfuer	.05	.02	.01
□ 640 Jose Oquendo	.05	.02	.01
□ 641 Tom Pagnozzi	.05	.02	.01
□ 642 Terry Pendleton	.10	.05	.01
□ 643 Mike Perez	.05	.02	.01
□ 644 Bryn Smith	.05	.02	.01
□ 645 Lee Smith	.10	.05	.01
□ 646 Ozzie Smith	.20	.09	.03
□ 647 Scott Terry	.05	.02	.01
□ 648 Bob Tewksbury	.05	.02	.01
□ 649 Milt Thompson	.05	.02	.01
□ 650 John Tudor	.05	.02	.01
□ 651 Denny Walling	.05	.02	.01
□ 652 Craig Wilson	.05	.02	.01
□ 653 Todd Worrell	.05	.02	.01
□ 654 Todd Zeile	.10	.05	.01
□ 655 Oscar Azocar	.05	.02	.01
□ 656 Steve Balboni UER	.05	.02	.01
(Born 1/5/57, should be 1/16)			
□ 657 Jesse Barfield	.05	.02	.01
□ 658 Greg Cadaret	.05	.02	.01
□ 659 Chuck Cary	.05	.02	.01
□ 660 Rick Cerone	.05	.02	.01
□ 661 Dave Eiland	.05	.02	.01
□ 662 Alvaro Espinoza	.05	.02	.01
□ 663 Bob Geren	.05	.02	.01
□ 664 Lee Guetterman	.05	.02	.01
□ 665 Mel Hall	.05	.02	.01
□ 666 Andy Hawkins	.05	.02	.01
□ 667 Jimmy Jones	.05	.02	.01
□ 668 Roberto Kelly	.05	.02	.01
□ 669 Dave LaPoint UER	.05	.02	.01
(No '81 Brewers stats, totals also are wrong)			
□ 670 Tim Leary	.05	.02	.01
□ 671 Jim Leyritz	.10	.05	.01
□ 672 Kevin Maas	.05	.02	.01
□ 673 Don Mattingly	.50	.23	.06
□ 674 Matt Nokes	.05	.02	.01
□ 675 Pascual Perez	.05	.02	.01
□ 676 Eric Plunk	.05	.02	.01
□ 677 Dave Righetti	.05	.02	.01
□ 678 Jeff D. Robinson	.05	.02	.01
□ 679 Steve Sax	.05	.02	.01
□ 680 Mike Witt	.05	.02	.01
□ 681 Steve Avery UER	.15	.07	.02
(Born in New Jersey, should say Michigan)			
□ 682 Mike Bell	.05	.02	.01
□ 683 Jeff Blauser	.05	.02	.01
□ 684 Francisco Cabrera UER	.05	.02	.01
(Born 10/16, should say 10/10)			
□ 685 Tony Castillo	.05	.02	.01
□ 686 Marty Clary UER	.05	.02	.01
(Shown pitching righty, but bio has left)			
□ 687 Nick Esasky	.05	.02	.01
□ 688 Ron Gant	.15	.07	.02
□ 689 Tom Glavine	.15	.07	.02
□ 690 Mark Grant	.05	.02	.01
□ 691 Tommy Gregg	.05	.02	.01
□ 692 Dwayne Henry	.05	.02	.01
□ 693 Dave Justice	.15	.07	.02
□ 694 Jimmy Kremers	.05	.02	.01
□ 695 Charlie Leibrandt	.05	.02	.01
□ 696 Mark Lemke	.05	.02	.01
□ 697 Oddibe McDowell	.05	.02	.01
□ 698 Greg Olson	.05	.02	.01
□ 699 Jeff Parrett	.05	.02	.01
□ 700 Jim Presley	.05	.02	.01
□ 701 Victor Rosario	.05	.02	.01
□ 702 Lonnie Smith	.05	.02	.01
□ 703 Pete Smith	.05	.02	.01
□ 704 John Smoltz	.15	.07	.02
□ 705 Mike Stanton	.05	.02	.01
□ 706 Andres Thomas	.05	.02	.01
□ 707 Jeff Treadway	.05	.02	.01
□ 708 Jim Vatcher	.05	.02	.01
□ 709 Home Run Kings	.15	.07	.02
Ryne Sandberg			
Cecil Fielder			
□ 710 2nd Generation Stars	.50	.23	.06
Barry Bonds			
Ken Griffey Jr.			
□ 711 NLCS Team Leaders	.15	.07	.02
Bobby Bonilla			
Barry Larkin			
□ 712 Top Game Savers	.05	.02	.01
Bobby Thigpen			
John Franco			
□ 713 Chicago's 100 Club	.10	.05	.01
Andre Dawson			
Ryne Sandberg UER			
(Ryno misspelled Rhino)			
□ 714 CL:A's/Pirates	.05	.02	.01
Reds/Red Sox			
□ 715 CL:White Sox/Mets	.05	.02	.01
Blue Jays/Dodgers			
□ 716 CL:Expos/Giants	.05	.02	.01
Rangers/Angels			
□ 717 CL:Tigers/Indians	.05	.02	.01
Phillies/Cubs			
□ 718 CL:Mariners/Orioles	.05	.02	.01
Astros/Padres			
□ 719 CL:Royals/Brewers	.05	.02	.01
Twins/Cardinals			
□ 720 CL:Yankees/Braves	.05	.02	.01
Superstars/Specials			

1991 Fleer All-Stars

For the sixth consecutive year Fleer issued an All-Star insert set. This year the cards were only available as random inserts in Fleer cello packs. This ten-card standard-size set is reminiscent of the 1971 Topps Greatest Moments set with two pictures on the (black-bordered) front as well as a photo on the back.

	MINT	NRMT	EXC
COMPLETE SET (10)	15.00	6.75	1.85
COMMON CARD (1-10)	.50	.23	.06
SEMISTARS	1.00	.45	.12
RANDOM INSERTS IN CELLO PACKS			
□ 1 Ryne Sandberg	2.00	.90	.25
□ 2 Barry Larkin	1.25	.55	.16
□ 3 Matt Williams	1.00	.45	.12
□ 4 Cecil Fielder	1.00	.45	.12
□ 5 Barry Bonds	2.00	.90	.25
□ 6 Rickey Henderson	1.00	.45	.12
□ 7 Ken Griffey Jr.	10.00	4.50	1.25
□ 8 Jose Canseco	1.00	.45	.12
□ 9 Benito Santiago	.50	.23	.06
□ 10 Roger Clemens	1.00	.45	.12

1991 Fleer Pro-Visions

This 12-card standard-size insert set features paintings by artist Terry Smith framed by dis-

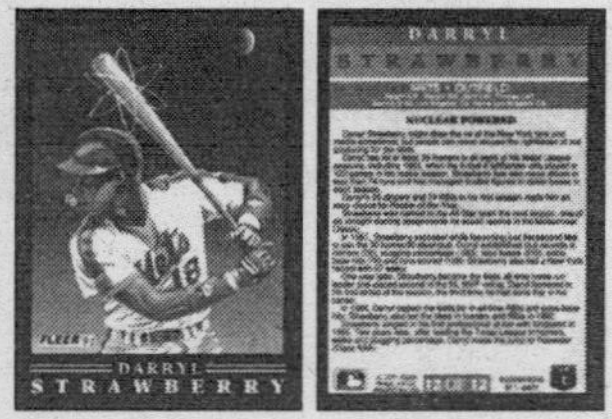

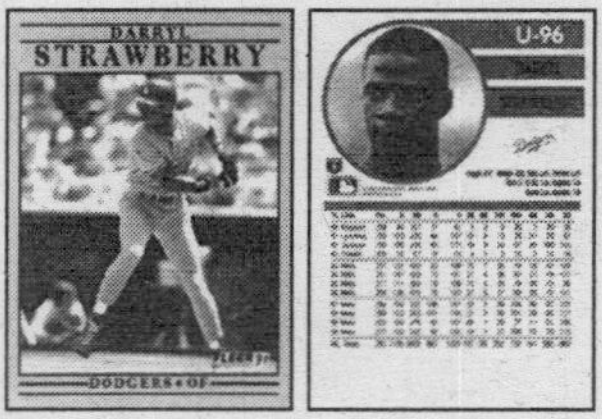

tinctive black borders on each card front. The cards were randomly inserted in wax and rack packs. An additional four-card set was issued only in 1991 Fleer factory sets. Those cards are numbered F1-F4. Unlike the 12 cards inserted in packs, these factory set cards feature white borders on front.

	MINT	NRMT	EXC
COMPLETE REG.SET (12)	4.00	1.80	.50
COMMON REG.CARD (R1-R12)	.20	.09	.03
SEMISTARS	.40	.18	.05
RANDOM INSERTS IN PACKS			
COMPLETE FACT.SET (4)	2.00	.90	.25
COMMON FACT.CARD (F1-F4)	.25	.11	.03
F1-F4 IN FACTORY SETS			

□ 1 Kirby Puckett UER (.326 average, should be .328)	1.00	.45	.12
□ 2 Will Clark UER (On tenth line, pennant misspelled pennent)	.40	.18	.05
□ 3 Ruben Sierra UER (No apostrophe in hasn't)	.40	.18	.05
□ 4 Mark McGwire UER (Fisk won ROY in '72, not '82)	1.00	.45	.12
□ 5 Bo Jackson (Bio says 6', others have him at 6'1")	.40	.18	.05
□ 6 Jose Canseco UER (Bio 6'3", 230, text has 6'4", 240)	.40	.18	.05
□ 7 Dwight Gooden UER (2.80 ERA in Lynchburg, should be 2.50)	.40	.18	.05
□ 8 Mike Greenwell UER (.328 BA and 87 RBI, should be .325 and 95)	.20	.09	.03
□ 9 Roger Clemens	.40	.18	.05
□ 10 Eric Davis	.40	.18	.05
□ 11 Don Mattingly	1.00	.45	.12
□ 12 Darryl Strawberry	.40	.18	.05
□ F1 Barry Bonds	.75	.35	.09
□ F2 Rickey Henderson	.40	.18	.05
□ F3 Ryne Sandberg	.75	.35	.09
□ F4 Dave Stewart	.40	.18	.05

1991 Fleer Update

The 1991 Fleer Update set contains 132 standard-size cards. The cards were distributed exclusively in factory set form through hobby dealers. Card design is identical to regular issue 1991 Fleer cards except for the U-prefixed numbering on back. The cards are ordered alphabetically by team. The key Rookie Cards in this set are Jeff Bagwell and Ivan Rodriguez.

	MINT	NRMT	EXC
COMPLETE FACT.SET (132)	4.00	1.80	.50
COMMON CARD (1-132)	.05	.02	.01
SEMISTARS	.10	.05	.01
U PREFIX ON CARD NUMBER			

□ 1 Glenn Davis	.05	.02	.01
□ 2 Dwight Evans	.10	.05	.01
□ 3 Jose Mesa	.10	.05	.01
□ 4 Jack Clark	.10	.05	.01
□ 5 Danny Darwin	.05	.02	.01
□ 6 Steve Lyons	.05	.02	.01
□ 7 Mo Vaughn	.50	.23	.06
□ 8 Floyd Bannister	.05	.02	.01
□ 9 Gary Gaetti	.10	.05	.01
□ 10 Dave Parker	.10	.05	.01
□ 11 Joey Cora	.10	.05	.01
□ 12 Charlie Hough	.05	.02	.01
□ 13 Matt Merullo	.05	.02	.01
□ 14 Warren Newson	.05	.02	.01
□ 15 Tim Raines	.15	.07	.02
□ 16 Albert Belle	.60	.25	.07
□ 17 Glenallen Hill	.05	.02	.01
□ 18 Shawn Hillegas	.05	.02	.01
□ 19 Mark Lewis	.05	.02	.01
□ 20 Charles Nagy	.10	.05	.01
□ 21 Mark Whiten	.10	.05	.01
□ 22 John Cerutti	.05	.02	.01
□ 23 Rob Deer	.05	.02	.01
□ 24 Mickey Tettleton	.10	.05	.01
□ 25 Warren Cromartie	.05	.02	.01
□ 26 Kirk Gibson	.10	.05	.01
□ 27 David Howard	.05	.02	.01
□ 28 Brent Mayne	.05	.02	.01
□ 29 Dante Bichette	.15	.07	.02
□ 30 Mark Lee	.05	.02	.01
□ 31 Julio Machado	.05	.02	.01
□ 32 Edwin Nunez	.05	.02	.01
□ 33 Willie Randolph	.10	.05	.01
□ 34 Franklin Stubbs	.05	.02	.01
□ 35 Bill Wegman	.05	.02	.01
□ 36 Chili Davis	.10	.05	.01
□ 37 Chuck Knoblauch	.25	.11	.03
□ 38 Scott Leius	.05	.02	.01
□ 39 Jack Morris	.10	.05	.01
□ 40 Mike Pagliarulo	.05	.02	.01
□ 41 Lenny Webster	.05	.02	.01
□ 42 John Habyan	.05	.02	.01
□ 43 Steve Howe	.05	.02	.01
□ 44 Jeff Johnson	.05	.02	.01
□ 45 Scott Kamieniecki	.05	.02	.01
□ 46 Pat Kelly	.10	.05	.01
□ 47 Hensley Meulens	.05	.02	.01
□ 48 Wade Taylor	.05	.02	.01
□ 49 Bernie Williams	.25	.11	.03
□ 50 Kirk Dressendorfer	.05	.02	.01
□ 51 Ernest Riles	.05	.02	.01
□ 52 Rich DeLucia	.05	.02	.01
□ 53 Tracy Jones	.05	.02	.01
□ 54 Bill Krueger	.05	.02	.01
□ 55 Alonzo Powell	.05	.02	.01
□ 56 Jeff Schaefer	.05	.02	.01
□ 57 Russ Swan	.05	.02	.01
□ 58 John Barfield	.05	.02	.01
□ 59 Rich Gossage	.10	.05	.01
□ 60 Jose Guzman	.05	.02	.01
□ 61 Dean Palmer	.10	.05	.01
□ 62 Ivan Rodriguez	1.00	.45	.12
□ 63 Roberto Alomar	.25	.11	.03
□ 64 Tom Candiotti	.05	.02	.01
□ 65 Joe Carter	.15	.07	.02
□ 66 Ed Sprague	.10	.05	.01
□ 67 Pat Tabler	.05	.02	.01
□ 68 Mike Timlin	.05	.02	.01
□ 69 Devon White	.10	.05	.01
□ 70 Rafael Belliard	.05	.02	.01
□ 71 Juan Berenguer	.05	.02	.01
□ 72 Sid Bream	.05	.02	.01

□ 73 Marvin Freeman	.05	.02	.01
□ 74 Kent Mercker	.05	.02	.01
□ 75 Otis Nixon	.05	.02	.01
□ 76 Terry Pendleton	.10	.05	.01
□ 77 George Bell	.05	.02	.01
□ 78 Danny Jackson	.05	.02	.01
□ 79 Chuck McElroy	.05	.02	.01
□ 80 Gary Scott	.05	.02	.01
□ 81 Heathcliff Slocumb	.15	.07	.02
□ 82 Dave Smith	.05	.02	.01
□ 83 Rick Wilkins	.05	.02	.01
□ 84 Freddie Benavides	.05	.02	.01
□ 85 Ted Power	.05	.02	.01
□ 86 Mo Sanford	.05	.02	.01
□ 87 Jeff Bagwell	2.50	1.10	.30
□ 88 Steve Finley	.15	.07	.02
□ 89 Pete Harnisch	.05	.02	.01
□ 90 Darryl Kile	.05	.02	.01
□ 91 Brett Butler	.10	.05	.01
□ 92 John Candelaria	.05	.02	.01
□ 93 Gary Carter	.15	.07	.02
□ 94 Kevin Gross	.05	.02	.01
□ 95 Bob Ojeda	.05	.02	.01
□ 96 Darryl Strawberry	.10	.05	.01
□ 97 Ivan Calderon	.05	.02	.01
□ 98 Ron Hassey	.05	.02	.01
□ 99 Gilberto Reyes	.05	.02	.01
□ 100 Hubie Brooks	.05	.02	.01
□ 101 Rick Cerone	.05	.02	.01
□ 102 Vince Coleman	.05	.02	.01
□ 103 Jeff Innis	.05	.02	.01
□ 104 Pete Schourek	.15	.07	.02
□ 105 Andy Ashby	.15	.07	.02
□ 106 Wally Backman	.05	.02	.01
□ 107 Darrin Fletcher	.05	.02	.01
□ 108 Tommy Greene	.05	.02	.01
□ 109 John Morris	.05	.02	.01
□ 110 Mitch Williams	.05	.02	.01
□ 111 Lloyd McClendon	.05	.02	.01
□ 112 Orlando Merced	.15	.07	.02
□ 113 Vicente Palacios	.05	.02	.01
□ 114 Gary Varsho	.05	.02	.01
□ 115 John Wehner	.05	.02	.01
□ 116 Rex Hudler	.05	.02	.01
□ 117 Tim Jones	.05	.02	.01
□ 118 Geronimo Pena	.05	.02	.01
□ 119 Gerald Perry	.05	.02	.01
□ 120 Larry Andersen	.05	.02	.01
□ 121 Jerald Clark	.05	.02	.01
□ 122 Scott Coolbaugh	.05	.02	.01
□ 123 Tony Fernandez	.05	.02	.01
□ 124 Darrin Jackson	.05	.02	.01
□ 125 Fred McGriff	.15	.07	.02
□ 126 Jose Mota	.05	.02	.01
□ 127 Tim Teufel	.05	.02	.01
□ 128 Bud Black	.05	.02	.01
□ 129 Mike Felder	.05	.02	.01
□ 130 Willie McGee	.05	.02	.01
□ 131 Dave Righetti	.05	.02	.01
□ 132 Checklist U1-U132	.05	.02	.01

1992 Fleer

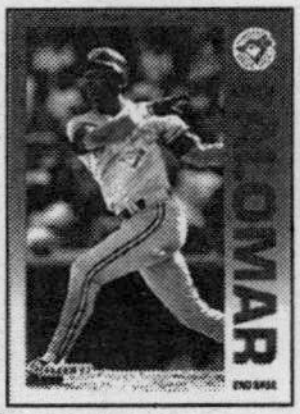

The 1992 Fleer set contains 720 standard-size cards issued in one comprehensive series. The cards were distributed in plastic wrapped packs, 35-card cello packs, 42-card rack packs and factory sets. The card fronts shade from metallic pale green to white as one moves down the face. The team logo and player's name appear to the right of the picture, running the length of the card. The cards are ordered alphabetically within and according to teams for each league with AL preceding NL. Topical subsets feature Major League Prospects (652-680), Record Setters (681-687), League Leaders (688-697), Super Star Specials (698-707) and Pro Visions (708-713). The only notable Rookie Card features Vinny Castilla.

	MINT	NRMT	EXC
COMPLETE SET (720)	15.00	6.75	1.85
COMPLETE HOBBY SET (732)	25.00	11.00	3.10
COMPLETE RETAIL SET (732)	25.00	11.00	3.10
COMMON CARD (1-720)	.05	.02	.01
SEMISTARS	.10	.05	.01
STARS	.15	.07	.02
COMPLETE CLEMENS (12)	10.00	4.50	1.25
COMMON CLEMENS (1-12)	1.00	.45	.12
CLEMENS: RANDOM INSERTS IN PACKS....			
CLEMENS MAIL-IN (13-15)	1.00	.45	.12
MAIL-IN DISTRIB.VIA WRAPPER EXCH......			

□ 1 Brady Anderson	.15	.07	.02
□ 2 Jose Bautista	.05	.02	.01
□ 3 Juan Bell	.05	.02	.01
□ 4 Glenn Davis	.05	.02	.01
□ 5 Mike Devereaux	.05	.02	.01
□ 6 Dwight Evans	.10	.05	.01
□ 7 Mike Flanagan	.05	.02	.01
□ 8 Leo Gomez	.05	.02	.01
□ 9 Chris Hoiles	.05	.02	.01
□ 10 Sam Horn	.05	.02	.01
□ 11 Tim Hulett	.05	.02	.01
□ 12 Dave Johnson	.05	.02	.01
□ 13 Chito Martinez	.05	.02	.01
□ 14 Ben McDonald	.05	.02	.01
□ 15 Bob Melvin	.05	.02	.01
□ 16 Luis Mercedes	.05	.02	.01
□ 17 Jose Mesa	.10	.05	.01
□ 18 Bob Milacki	.05	.02	.01
□ 19 Randy Milligan	.05	.02	.01
□ 20 Mike Mussina UER (Card back refers to him as Jeff)	.30	.14	.04
□ 21 Gregg Olson	.05	.02	.01
□ 22 Joe Orsulak	.05	.02	.01
□ 23 Jim Poole	.05	.02	.01
□ 24 Arthur Rhodes	.05	.02	.01
□ 25 Billy Ripken	.05	.02	.01
□ 26 Cal Ripken	.75	.35	.09
□ 27 David Segui	.05	.02	.01
□ 28 Roy Smith	.05	.02	.01
□ 29 Anthony Telford	.05	.02	.01
□ 30 Mark Williamson	.05	.02	.01
□ 31 Craig Worthington	.05	.02	.01
□ 32 Wade Boggs	.15	.07	.02
□ 33 Tom Bolton	.05	.02	.01
□ 34 Tom Brunansky	.05	.02	.01
□ 35 Ellis Burks	.15	.07	.02
□ 36 Jack Clark	.10	.05	.01
□ 37 Roger Clemens	.15	.07	.02
□ 38 Danny Darwin	.05	.02	.01
□ 39 Mike Greenwell	.05	.02	.01
□ 40 Joe Hesketh	.05	.02	.01
□ 41 Daryl Irvine	.05	.02	.01
□ 42 Dennis Lamp	.05	.02	.01
□ 43 Tony Pena	.05	.02	.01
□ 44 Phil Plantier	.10	.05	.01
□ 45 Carlos Quintana	.05	.02	.01
□ 46 Jeff Reardon	.10	.05	.01
□ 47 Jody Reed	.05	.02	.01
□ 48 Luis Rivera	.05	.02	.01
□ 49 Mo Vaughn	.40	.18	.05
□ 50 Jim Abbott	.05	.02	.01
□ 51 Kyle Abbott	.05	.02	.01
□ 52 Ruben Amaro Jr.	.05	.02	.01
□ 53 Scott Bailes	.05	.02	.01
□ 54 Chris Beasley	.05	.02	.01
□ 55 Mark Eichhorn	.05	.02	.01
□ 56 Mike Fetters	.05	.02	.01
□ 57 Chuck Finley	.05	.02	.01
□ 58 Gary Gaetti	.10	.05	.01
□ 59 Dave Gallagher	.05	.02	.01
□ 60 Donnie Hill	.05	.02	.01

□ 61 Bryan Harvey UER (Lee Smith led the Majors with 47 saves)	.05	.02	.01
□ 62 Wally Joyner	.10	.05	.01
□ 63 Mark Langston	.10	.05	.01
□ 64 Kirk McCaskill	.05	.02	.01
□ 65 John Orton	.05	.02	.01
□ 66 Lance Parrish	.05	.02	.01
□ 67 Luis Polonia	.05	.02	.01
□ 68 Bobby Rose	.05	.02	.01
□ 69 Dick Schofield	.05	.02	.01
□ 70 Luis Sojo	.05	.02	.01
□ 71 Lee Stevens	.05	.02	.01
□ 72 Dave Winfield	.15	.07	.02
□ 73 Cliff Young	.05	.02	.01
□ 74 Wilson Alvarez	.15	.07	.02
□ 75 Esteban Beltre	.05	.02	.01
□ 76 Joey Cora	.05	.02	.01
□ 77 Brian Drahman	.05	.02	.01
□ 78 Alex Fernandez	.15	.07	.02
□ 79 Carlton Fisk	.15	.07	.02
□ 80 Scott Fletcher	.05	.02	.01
□ 81 Craig Grebeck	.05	.02	.01
□ 82 Ozzie Guillen	.05	.02	.01
□ 83 Greg Hibbard	.05	.02	.01
□ 84 Charlie Hough	.05	.02	.01
□ 85 Mike Huff	.05	.02	.01
□ 86 Bo Jackson	.15	.07	.02
□ 87 Lance Johnson	.10	.05	.01
□ 88 Ron Karkovice	.05	.02	.01
□ 89 Jack McDowell	.10	.05	.01
□ 90 Matt Merullo	.05	.02	.01
□ 91 Warren Newson	.05	.02	.01
□ 92 Donn Pall UER (Called Dunn on card back)	.05	.02	.01
□ 93 Dan Pasqua	.05	.02	.01
□ 94 Ken Patterson	.05	.02	.01
□ 95 Melido Perez	.05	.02	.01
□ 96 Scott Radinsky	.05	.02	.01
□ 97 Tim Raines	.15	.07	.02
□ 98 Sammy Sosa	.25	.11	.03
□ 99 Bobby Thigpen	.05	.02	.01
□ 100 Frank Thomas	1.50	.70	.19
□ 101 Robin Ventura	.15	.07	.02
□ 102 Mike Aldrete	.05	.02	.01
□ 103 Sandy Alomar Jr.	.10	.05	.01
□ 104 Carlos Baerga	.15	.07	.02
□ 105 Albert Belle	.60	.25	.07
□ 106 Willie Blair	.05	.02	.01
□ 107 Jerry Browne	.05	.02	.01
□ 108 Alex Cole	.05	.02	.01
□ 109 Felix Fermin	.05	.02	.01
□ 110 Glenallen Hill	.05	.02	.01
□ 111 Shawn Hillegas	.05	.02	.01
□ 112 Chris James	.05	.02	.01
□ 113 Reggie Jefferson	.10	.05	.01
□ 114 Doug Jones	.05	.02	.01
□ 115 Eric King	.05	.02	.01
□ 116 Mark Lewis	.05	.02	.01
□ 117 Carlos Martinez	.05	.02	.01
□ 118 Charles Nagy UER (Throws right, but card says left)	.10	.05	.01
□ 119 Rod Nichols	.05	.02	.01
□ 120 Steve Olin	.05	.02	.01
□ 121 Jesse Orosco	.05	.02	.01
□ 122 Rudy Seanez	.05	.02	.01
□ 123 Joel Skinner	.05	.02	.01
□ 124 Greg Swindell	.05	.02	.01
□ 125 Jim Thome	.75	.35	.09
□ 126 Mark Whiten	.10	.05	.01
□ 127 Scott Aldred	.05	.02	.01
□ 128 Andy Allanson	.05	.02	.01
□ 129 John Cerutti	.05	.02	.01
□ 130 Milt Cuyler	.05	.02	.01
□ 131 Mike Dalton	.05	.02	.01
□ 132 Rob Deer	.05	.02	.01
□ 133 Cecil Fielder	.10	.05	.01
□ 134 Travis Fryman	.15	.07	.02
□ 135 Dan Gakeler	.05	.02	.01
□ 136 Paul Gibson	.05	.02	.01
□ 137 Bill Gullickson	.05	.02	.01
□ 138 Mike Henneman	.05	.02	.01
□ 139 Pete Incaviglia	.05	.02	.01
□ 140 Mark Leiter	.05	.02	.01
□ 141 Scott Livingstone	.05	.02	.01
□ 142 Lloyd Moseby	.05	.02	.01
□ 143 Tony Phillips	.10	.05	.01
□ 144 Mark Salas	.05	.02	.01
□ 145 Frank Tanana	.05	.02	.01
□ 146 Walt Terrell	.05	.02	.01
□ 147 Mickey Tettleton	.05	.02	.01
□ 148 Alan Trammell	.15	.07	.02
□ 149 Lou Whitaker	.15	.07	.02
□ 150 Kevin Appier	.10	.05	.01
□ 151 Luis Aquino	.05	.02	.01
□ 152 Todd Benzinger	.05	.02	.01
□ 153 Mike Boddicker	.05	.02	.01
□ 154 George Brett	.40	.18	.05
□ 155 Storm Davis	.05	.02	.01
□ 156 Jim Eisenreich	.05	.02	.01
□ 157 Kirk Gibson	.10	.05	.01
□ 158 Tom Gordon	.05	.02	.01
□ 159 Mark Gubicza	.05	.02	.01
□ 160 David Howard	.05	.02	.01
□ 161 Mike Macfarlane	.05	.02	.01
□ 162 Brent Mayne	.05	.02	.01
□ 163 Brian McRae	.15	.07	.02
□ 164 Jeff Montgomery	.10	.05	.01
□ 165 Bill Pecota	.05	.02	.01
□ 166 Harvey Pulliam	.05	.02	.01
□ 167 Bret Saberhagen	.10	.05	.01
□ 168 Kevin Seitzer	.05	.02	.01
□ 169 Terry Shumpert	.05	.02	.01
□ 170 Kurt Stillwell	.05	.02	.01
□ 171 Danny Tartabull	.05	.02	.01
□ 172 Gary Thurman	.05	.02	.01
□ 173 Dante Bichette	.15	.07	.02
□ 174 Kevin D. Brown	.05	.02	.01
□ 175 Chuck Crim	.05	.02	.01
□ 176 Jim Gantner	.05	.02	.01
□ 177 Darryl Hamilton	.05	.02	.01
□ 178 Ted Higuera	.05	.02	.01
□ 179 Darren Holmes	.05	.02	.01
□ 180 Mark Lee	.05	.02	.01
□ 181 Julio Machado	.05	.02	.01
□ 182 Paul Molitor	.20	.09	.03
□ 183 Jaime Navarro	.05	.02	.01
□ 184 Edwin Nunez	.05	.02	.01
□ 185 Dan Plesac	.05	.02	.01
□ 186 Willie Randolph	.10	.05	.01
□ 187 Ron Robinson	.05	.02	.01
□ 188 Gary Sheffield	.15	.07	.02
□ 189 Bill Spiers	.05	.02	.01
□ 190 B.J. Surhoff	.10	.05	.01
□ 191 Dale Sveum	.05	.02	.01
□ 192 Greg Vaughn	.15	.07	.02
□ 193 Bill Wegman	.05	.02	.01
□ 194 Robin Yount	.15	.07	.02
□ 195 Rick Aguilera	.05	.02	.01
□ 196 Allan Anderson	.05	.02	.01
□ 197 Steve Bedrosian	.05	.02	.01
□ 198 Randy Bush	.05	.02	.01
□ 199 Larry Casian	.05	.02	.01
□ 200 Chili Davis	.10	.05	.01
□ 201 Scott Erickson	.10	.05	.01
□ 202 Greg Gagne	.05	.02	.01
□ 203 Dan Gladden	.05	.02	.01
□ 204 Brian Harper	.05	.02	.01
□ 205 Kent Hrbek	.10	.05	.01
□ 206 Chuck Knoblauch UER (Career hit total of 59 is wrong)	.15	.07	.02
□ 207 Gene Larkin	.05	.02	.01
□ 208 Terry Leach	.05	.02	.01
□ 209 Scott Leius	.05	.02	.01
□ 210 Shane Mack	.05	.02	.01
□ 211 Jack Morris	.10	.05	.01
□ 212 Pedro Munoz	.05	.02	.01
□ 213 Denny Neagle	.10	.05	.01
□ 214 Al Newman	.05	.02	.01
□ 215 Junior Ortiz	.05	.02	.01
□ 216 Mike Pagliarulo	.05	.02	.01
□ 217 Kirby Puckett	.30	.14	.04
□ 218 Paul Sorrento	.05	.02	.01
□ 219 Kevin Tapani	.05	.02	.01
□ 220 Lenny Webster	.05	.02	.01
□ 221 Jesse Barfield	.05	.02	.01
□ 222 Greg Cadaret	.05	.02	.01
□ 223 Dave Eiland	.05	.02	.01
□ 224 Alvaro Espinoza	.05	.02	.01

□ 225	Steve Farr	.05	.02	.01
□ 226	Bob Geren	.05	.02	.01
□ 227	Lee Guetterman	.05	.02	.01
□ 228	John Habyan	.05	.02	.01
□ 229	Mel Hall	.05	.02	.01
□ 230	Steve Howe	.05	.02	.01
□ 231	Mike Humphreys	.05	.02	.01
□ 232	Scott Kamieniecki	.05	.02	.01
□ 233	Pat Kelly	.05	.02	.01
□ 234	Roberto Kelly	.05	.02	.01
□ 235	Tim Leary	.05	.02	.01
□ 236	Kevin Maas	.05	.02	.01
□ 237	Don Mattingly	.50	.23	.06
□ 238	Hensley Meulens	.05	.02	.01
□ 239	Matt Nokes	.05	.02	.01
□ 240	Pascual Perez	.05	.02	.01
□ 241	Eric Plunk	.05	.02	.01
□ 242	John Ramos	.05	.02	.01
□ 243	Scott Sanderson	.05	.02	.01
□ 244	Steve Sax	.05	.02	.01
□ 245	Wade Taylor	.05	.02	.01
□ 246	Randy Velarde	.05	.02	.01
□ 247	Bernie Williams	.25	.11	.03
□ 248	Troy Afenir	.05	.02	.01
□ 249	Harold Baines	.10	.05	.01
□ 250	Lance Blankenship	.05	.02	.01
□ 251	Mike Bordick	.10	.05	.01
□ 252	Jose Canseco	.15	.07	.02
□ 253	Steve Chitren	.05	.02	.01
□ 254	Ron Darling	.05	.02	.01
□ 255	Dennis Eckersley	.10	.05	.01
□ 256	Mike Gallego	.05	.02	.01
□ 257	Dave Henderson	.05	.02	.01
□ 258	Rickey Henderson UER (Wearing 24 on front and 22 on back)	.15	.07	.02
□ 259	Rick Honeycutt	.05	.02	.01
□ 260	Brook Jacoby	.05	.02	.01
□ 261	Carney Lansford	.10	.05	.01
□ 262	Mark McGwire	.30	.14	.04
□ 263	Mike Moore	.05	.02	.01
□ 264	Gene Nelson	.05	.02	.01
□ 265	Jamie Quirk	.05	.02	.01
□ 266	Joe Slusarski	.05	.02	.01
□ 267	Terry Steinbach	.10	.05	.01
□ 268	Dave Stewart	.10	.05	.01
□ 269	Todd Van Poppel	.05	.02	.01
□ 270	Walt Weiss	.05	.02	.01
□ 271	Bob Welch	.05	.02	.01
□ 272	Curt Young	.05	.02	.01
□ 273	Scott Bradley	.05	.02	.01
□ 274	Greg Briley	.05	.02	.01
□ 275	Jay Buhner	.15	.07	.02
□ 276	Henry Cotto	.05	.02	.01
□ 277	Alvin Davis	.05	.02	.01
□ 278	Rich DeLucia	.05	.02	.01
□ 279	Ken Griffey Jr.	1.50	.70	.19
□ 280	Erik Hanson	.05	.02	.01
□ 281	Brian Holman	.05	.02	.01
□ 282	Mike Jackson	.05	.02	.01
□ 283	Randy Johnson	.15	.07	.02
□ 284	Tracy Jones	.05	.02	.01
□ 285	Bill Krueger	.05	.02	.01
□ 286	Edgar Martinez	.15	.07	.02
□ 287	Tino Martinez	.15	.07	.02
□ 288	Rob Murphy	.05	.02	.01
□ 289	Pete O'Brien	.05	.02	.01
□ 290	Alonzo Powell	.05	.02	.01
□ 291	Harold Reynolds	.05	.02	.01
□ 292	Mike Schooler	.05	.02	.01
□ 293	Russ Swan	.05	.02	.01
□ 294	Bill Swift	.05	.02	.01
□ 295	Dave Valle	.05	.02	.01
□ 296	Omar Vizquel	.15	.07	.02
□ 297	Gerald Alexander	.05	.02	.01
□ 298	Brad Arnsberg	.05	.02	.01
□ 299	Kevin Brown	.10	.05	.01
□ 300	Jack Daugherty	.05	.02	.01
□ 301	Mario Diaz	.05	.02	.01
□ 302	Brian Downing	.05	.02	.01
□ 303	Julio Franco	.10	.05	.01
□ 304	Juan Gonzalez	.60	.25	.07
□ 305	Rich Gossage	.10	.05	.01
□ 306	Jose Guzman	.05	.02	.01
□ 307	Jose Hernandez	.05	.02	.01
□ 308	Jeff Huson	.05	.02	.01
□ 309	Mike Jeffcoat	.05	.02	.01
□ 310	Terry Mathews	.05	.02	.01
□ 311	Rafael Palmeiro	.15	.07	.02
□ 312	Dean Palmer	.10	.05	.01
□ 313	Geno Petralli	.05	.02	.01
□ 314	Gary Pettis	.05	.02	.01
□ 315	Kevin Reimer	.05	.02	.01
□ 316	Ivan Rodriguez	.30	.14	.04
□ 317	Kenny Rogers	.05	.02	.01
□ 318	Wayne Rosenthal	.05	.02	.01
□ 319	Jeff Russell	.05	.02	.01
□ 320	Nolan Ryan	.75	.35	.09
□ 321	Ruben Sierra	.10	.05	.01
□ 322	Jim Acker	.05	.02	.01
□ 323	Roberto Alomar	.25	.11	.03
□ 324	Derek Bell	.10	.05	.01
□ 325	Pat Borders	.05	.02	.01
□ 326	Tom Candiotti	.05	.02	.01
□ 327	Joe Carter	.15	.07	.02
□ 328	Rob Ducey	.05	.02	.01
□ 329	Kelly Gruber	.05	.02	.01
□ 330	Juan Guzman	.10	.05	.01
□ 331	Tom Henke	.05	.02	.01
□ 332	Jimmy Key	.10	.05	.01
□ 333	Manny Lee	.05	.02	.01
□ 334	Al Leiter	.10	.05	.01
□ 335	Bob MacDonald	.05	.02	.01
□ 336	Candy Maldonado	.05	.02	.01
□ 337	Rance Mulliniks	.05	.02	.01
□ 338	Greg Myers	.05	.02	.01
□ 339	John Olerud UER (1991 BA has .256, but text says .258)	.10	.05	.01
□ 340	Ed Sprague	.10	.05	.01
□ 341	Dave Stieb	.05	.02	.01
□ 342	Todd Stottlemyre	.10	.05	.01
□ 343	Mike Timlin	.05	.02	.01
□ 344	Duane Ward	.05	.02	.01
□ 345	David Wells	.05	.02	.01
□ 346	Devon White	.10	.05	.01
□ 347	Mookie Wilson	.05	.02	.01
□ 348	Eddie Zosky	.05	.02	.01
□ 349	Steve Avery	.10	.05	.01
□ 350	Mike Bell	.05	.02	.01
□ 351	Rafael Belliard	.05	.02	.01
□ 352	Juan Berenguer	.05	.02	.01
□ 353	Jeff Blauser	.05	.02	.01
□ 354	Sid Bream	.05	.02	.01
□ 355	Francisco Cabrera	.05	.02	.01
□ 356	Marvin Freeman	.05	.02	.01
□ 357	Ron Gant	.15	.07	.02
□ 358	Tom Glavine	.15	.07	.02
□ 359	Brian Hunter	.05	.02	.01
□ 360	Dave Justice	.15	.07	.02
□ 361	Charlie Leibrandt	.05	.02	.01
□ 362	Mark Lemke	.05	.02	.01
□ 363	Kent Mercker	.05	.02	.01
□ 364	Keith Mitchell	.05	.02	.01
□ 365	Greg Olson	.05	.02	.01
□ 366	Terry Pendleton	.10	.05	.01
□ 367	Armando Reynoso	.05	.02	.01
□ 368	Deion Sanders	.15	.07	.02
□ 369	Lonnie Smith	.05	.02	.01
□ 370	Pete Smith	.05	.02	.01
□ 371	John Smoltz	.15	.07	.02
□ 372	Mike Stanton	.05	.02	.01
□ 373	Jeff Treadway	.05	.02	.01
□ 374	Mark Wohlers	.15	.07	.02
□ 375	Paul Assenmacher	.05	.02	.01
□ 376	George Bell	.05	.02	.01
□ 377	Shawn Boskie	.05	.02	.01
□ 378	Frank Castillo	.10	.05	.01
□ 379	Andre Dawson	.15	.07	.02
□ 380	Shawon Dunston	.05	.02	.01
□ 381	Mark Grace	.15	.07	.02
□ 382	Mike Harkey	.05	.02	.01
□ 383	Danny Jackson	.05	.02	.01
□ 384	Les Lancaster	.05	.02	.01
□ 385	Ced Landrum	.05	.02	.01
□ 386	Greg Maddux	.75	.35	.09
□ 387	Derrick May	.05	.02	.01
□ 388	Chuck McElroy	.05	.02	.01
□ 389	Ryne Sandberg	.25	.11	.03
□ 390	Heathcliff Slocumb	.05	.02	.01
□ 391	Dave Smith	.05	.02	.01
□ 392	Dwight Smith	.05	.02	.01

□ 393 Rick Sutcliffe	.05	.02	.01
□ 394 Hector Villanueva	.05	.02	.01
□ 395 Chico Walker	.05	.02	.01
□ 396 Jerome Walton	.05	.02	.01
□ 397 Rick Wilkins	.05	.02	.01
□ 398 Jack Armstrong	.05	.02	.01
□ 399 Freddie Benavides	.05	.02	.01
□ 400 Glenn Braggs	.05	.02	.01
□ 401 Tom Browning	.05	.02	.01
□ 402 Norm Charlton	.05	.02	.01
□ 403 Eric Davis	.10	.05	.01
□ 404 Rob Dibble	.05	.02	.01
□ 405 Bill Doran	.05	.02	.01
□ 406 Mariano Duncan	.05	.02	.01
□ 407 Kip Gross	.05	.02	.01
□ 408 Chris Hammond	.05	.02	.01
□ 409 Billy Hatcher	.05	.02	.01
□ 410 Chris Jones	.05	.02	.01
□ 411 Barry Larkin	.15	.07	.02
□ 412 Hal Morris	.05	.02	.01
□ 413 Randy Myers	.10	.05	.01
□ 414 Joe Oliver	.05	.02	.01
□ 415 Paul O'Neill	.10	.05	.01
□ 416 Ted Power	.05	.02	.01
□ 417 Luis Quinones	.05	.02	.01
□ 418 Jeff Reed	.05	.02	.01
□ 419 Jose Rijo	.05	.02	.01
□ 420 Chris Sabo	.05	.02	.01
□ 421 Reggie Sanders	.15	.07	.02
□ 422 Scott Scudder	.05	.02	.01
□ 423 Glenn Sutko	.05	.02	.01
□ 424 Eric Anthony	.05	.02	.01
□ 425 Jeff Bagwell	.60	.25	.07
□ 426 Craig Biggio	.15	.07	.02
□ 427 Ken Caminiti	.15	.07	.02
□ 428 Casey Candaele	.05	.02	.01
□ 429 Mike Capel	.05	.02	.01
□ 430 Andujar Cedeno	.05	.02	.01
□ 431 Jim Corsi	.05	.02	.01
□ 432 Mark Davidson	.05	.02	.01
□ 433 Steve Finley	.15	.07	.02
□ 434 Luis Gonzalez	.10	.05	.01
□ 435 Pete Harnisch	.05	.02	.01
□ 436 Dwayne Henry	.05	.02	.01
□ 437 Xavier Hernandez	.05	.02	.01
□ 438 Jimmy Jones	.05	.02	.01
□ 439 Darryl Kile	.05	.02	.01
□ 440 Rob Mallicoat	.05	.02	.01
□ 441 Andy Mota	.05	.02	.01
□ 442 Al Osuna	.05	.02	.01
□ 443 Mark Portugal	.05	.02	.01
□ 444 Scott Servais	.05	.02	.01
□ 445 Mike Simms	.05	.02	.01
□ 446 Gerald Young	.05	.02	.01
□ 447 Tim Belcher	.05	.02	.01
□ 448 Brett Butler	.10	.05	.01
□ 449 John Candelaria	.05	.02	.01
□ 450 Gary Carter	.15	.07	.02
□ 451 Dennis Cook	.05	.02	.01
□ 452 Tim Crews	.05	.02	.01
□ 453 Kal Daniels	.05	.02	.01
□ 454 Jim Gott	.05	.02	.01
□ 455 Alfredo Griffin	.05	.02	.01
□ 456 Kevin Gross	.05	.02	.01
□ 457 Chris Gwynn	.05	.02	.01
□ 458 Lenny Harris	.05	.02	.01
□ 459 Orel Hershiser	.10	.05	.01
□ 460 Jay Howell	.05	.02	.01
□ 461 Stan Javier	.05	.02	.01
□ 462 Eric Karros	.15	.07	.02
□ 463 Ramon Martinez UER (Card says bats right, should be left)	.10	.05	.01
□ 464 Roger McDowell UER (Wins add up to 54, totals have 51)	.05	.02	.01
□ 465 Mike Morgan	.05	.02	.01
□ 466 Eddie Murray	.25	.11	.03
□ 467 Jose Offerman	.05	.02	.01
□ 468 Bob Ojeda	.05	.02	.01
□ 469 Juan Samuel	.05	.02	.01
□ 470 Mike Scioscia	.05	.02	.01
□ 471 Darryl Strawberry	.10	.05	.01
□ 472 Bret Barberie	.05	.02	.01
□ 473 Brian Barnes	.05	.02	.01
□ 474 Eric Bullock	.05	.02	.01

□ 475 Ivan Calderon	.05	.02	.01
□ 476 Delino DeShields	.05	.02	.01
□ 477 Jeff Fassero	.10	.05	.01
□ 478 Mike Fitzgerald	.05	.02	.01
□ 479 Steve Frey	.05	.02	.01
□ 480 Andres Galarraga	.15	.07	.02
□ 481 Mark Gardner	.05	.02	.01
□ 482 Marquis Grissom	.15	.07	.02
□ 483 Chris Haney	.05	.02	.01
□ 484 Barry Jones	.05	.02	.01
□ 485 Dave Martinez	.05	.02	.01
□ 486 Dennis Martinez	.10	.05	.01
□ 487 Chris Nabholz	.05	.02	.01
□ 488 Spike Owen	.05	.02	.01
□ 489 Gilberto Reyes	.05	.02	.01
□ 490 Mel Rojas	.10	.05	.01
□ 491 Scott Ruskin	.05	.02	.01
□ 492 Bill Sampen	.05	.02	.01
□ 493 Larry Walker	.15	.07	.02
□ 494 Tim Wallach	.05	.02	.01
□ 495 Daryl Boston	.05	.02	.01
□ 496 Hubie Brooks	.05	.02	.01
□ 497 Tim Burke	.05	.02	.01
□ 498 Mark Carreon	.05	.02	.01
□ 499 Tony Castillo	.05	.02	.01
□ 500 Vince Coleman	.05	.02	.01
□ 501 David Cone	.15	.07	.02
□ 502 Kevin Elster	.05	.02	.01
□ 503 Sid Fernandez	.05	.02	.01
□ 504 John Franco	.05	.02	.01
□ 505 Dwight Gooden	.10	.05	.01
□ 506 Todd Hundley	.15	.07	.02
□ 507 Jeff Innis	.05	.02	.01
□ 508 Gregg Jefferies	.15	.07	.02
□ 509 Howard Johnson	.05	.02	.01
□ 510 Dave Magadan	.05	.02	.01
□ 511 Terry McDaniel	.05	.02	.01
□ 512 Kevin McReynolds	.05	.02	.01
□ 513 Keith Miller	.05	.02	.01
□ 514 Charlie O'Brien	.05	.02	.01
□ 515 Mackey Sasser	.05	.02	.01
□ 516 Pete Schourek	.10	.05	.01
□ 517 Julio Valera	.05	.02	.01
□ 518 Frank Viola	.05	.02	.01
□ 519 Wally Whitehurst	.05	.02	.01
□ 520 Anthony Young	.05	.02	.01
□ 521 Andy Ashby	.10	.05	.01
□ 522 Kim Batiste	.05	.02	.01
□ 523 Joe Boever	.05	.02	.01
□ 524 Wes Chamberlain	.05	.02	.01
□ 525 Pat Combs	.05	.02	.01
□ 526 Danny Cox	.05	.02	.01
□ 527 Darren Daulton	.10	.05	.01
□ 528 Jose DeJesus	.05	.02	.01
□ 529 Len Dykstra	.10	.05	.01
□ 530 Darrin Fletcher	.05	.02	.01
□ 531 Tommy Greene	.05	.02	.01
□ 532 Jason Grimsley	.05	.02	.01
□ 533 Charlie Hayes	.05	.02	.01
□ 534 Von Hayes	.05	.02	.01
□ 535 Dave Hollins	.05	.02	.01
□ 536 Ricky Jordan	.05	.02	.01
□ 537 John Kruk	.10	.05	.01
□ 538 Jim Lindeman	.05	.02	.01
□ 539 Mickey Morandini	.05	.02	.01
□ 540 Terry Mulholland	.05	.02	.01
□ 541 Dale Murphy	.15	.07	.02
□ 542 Randy Ready	.05	.02	.01
□ 543 Wally Ritchie UER (Letters in data are cut off on card)	.05	.02	.01
□ 544 Bruce Ruffin	.05	.02	.01
□ 545 Steve Searcy	.05	.02	.01
□ 546 Dickie Thon	.05	.02	.01
□ 547 Mitch Williams	.05	.02	.01
□ 548 Stan Belinda	.05	.02	.01
□ 549 Jay Bell	.10	.05	.01
□ 550 Barry Bonds	.25	.11	.03
□ 551 Bobby Bonilla	.10	.05	.01
□ 552 Steve Buechele	.05	.02	.01
□ 553 Doug Drabek	.05	.02	.01
□ 554 Neal Heaton	.05	.02	.01
□ 555 Jeff King	.10	.05	.01
□ 556 Bob Kipper	.05	.02	.01
□ 557 Bill Landrum	.05	.02	.01
□ 558 Mike LaValliere	.05	.02	.01

□ 559 Jose Lind	.05	.02	.01
□ 560 Lloyd McClendon	.05	.02	.01
□ 561 Orlando Merced	.05	.02	.01
□ 562 Bob Patterson	.05	.02	.01
□ 563 Joe Redfield	.05	.02	.01
□ 564 Gary Redus	.05	.02	.01
□ 565 Rosario Rodriguez	.05	.02	.01
□ 566 Don Slaught	.05	.02	.01
□ 567 John Smiley	.05	.02	.01
□ 568 Zane Smith	.05	.02	.01
□ 569 Randy Tomlin	.05	.02	.01
□ 570 Andy Van Slyke	.10	.05	.01
□ 571 Gary Varsho	.05	.02	.01
□ 572 Bob Walk	.05	.02	.01
□ 573 John Wehner UER	.05	.02	.01
(Actually played for Carolina in 1991, not Cards)			
□ 574 Juan Agosto	.05	.02	.01
□ 575 Cris Carpenter	.05	.02	.01
□ 576 Jose DeLeon	.05	.02	.01
□ 577 Rich Gedman	.05	.02	.01
□ 578 Bernard Gilkey	.10	.05	.01
□ 579 Pedro Guerrero	.05	.02	.01
□ 580 Ken Hill	.15	.07	.02
□ 581 Rex Hudler	.05	.02	.01
□ 582 Felix Jose	.05	.02	.01
□ 583 Ray Lankford	.15	.07	.02
□ 584 Omar Olivares	.05	.02	.01
□ 585 Jose Oquendo	.05	.02	.01
□ 586 Tom Pagnozzi	.05	.02	.01
□ 587 Geronimo Pena	.05	.02	.01
□ 588 Mike Perez	.05	.02	.01
□ 589 Gerald Perry	.05	.02	.01
□ 590 Bryn Smith	.05	.02	.01
□ 591 Lee Smith	.10	.05	.01
□ 592 Ozzie Smith	.20	.09	.03
□ 593 Scott Terry	.05	.02	.01
□ 594 Bob Tewksbury	.05	.02	.01
□ 595 Milt Thompson	.05	.02	.01
□ 596 Todd Zeile	.05	.02	.01
□ 597 Larry Andersen	.05	.02	.01
□ 598 Oscar Azocar	.05	.02	.01
□ 599 Andy Benes	.05	.02	.01
□ 600 Ricky Bones	.05	.02	.01
□ 601 Jerald Clark	.05	.02	.01
□ 602 Pat Clements	.05	.02	.01
□ 603 Paul Faries	.05	.02	.01
□ 604 Tony Fernandez	.05	.02	.01
□ 605 Tony Gwynn	.40	.18	.05
□ 606 Greg W. Harris	.05	.02	.01
□ 607 Thomas Howard	.05	.02	.01
□ 608 Bruce Hurst	.05	.02	.01
□ 609 Darrin Jackson	.05	.02	.01
□ 610 Tom Lampkin	.05	.02	.01
□ 611 Craig Lefferts	.05	.02	.01
□ 612 Jim Lewis	.05	.02	.01
□ 613 Mike Maddux	.05	.02	.01
□ 614 Fred McGriff	.15	.07	.02
□ 615 Jose Melendez	.05	.02	.01
□ 616 Jose Mota	.05	.02	.01
□ 617 Dennis Rasmussen	.05	.02	.01
□ 618 Bip Roberts	.05	.02	.01
□ 619 Rich Rodriguez	.05	.02	.01
□ 620 Benito Santiago	.05	.02	.01
□ 621 Craig Shipley	.05	.02	.01
□ 622 Tim Teufel	.05	.02	.01
□ 623 Kevin Ward	.05	.02	.01
□ 624 Ed Whitson	.05	.02	.01
□ 625 Dave Anderson	.05	.02	.01
□ 626 Kevin Bass	.05	.02	.01
□ 627 Rod Beck	.15	.07	.02
□ 628 Bud Black	.05	.02	.01
□ 629 Jeff Brantley	.10	.05	.01
□ 630 John Burkett	.10	.05	.01
□ 631 Will Clark	.15	.07	.02
□ 632 Royce Clayton	.10	.05	.01
□ 633 Steve Decker	.05	.02	.01
□ 634 Kelly Downs	.05	.02	.01
□ 635 Mike Felder	.05	.02	.01
□ 636 Scott Garrelts	.05	.02	.01
□ 637 Eric Gunderson	.05	.02	.01
□ 638 Bryan Hickerson	.05	.02	.01
□ 639 Darren Lewis	.05	.02	.01
□ 640 Greg Litton	.05	.02	.01
□ 641 Kirt Manwaring	.05	.02	.01
□ 642 Paul McClellan	.05	.02	.01
□ 643 Willie McGee	.05	.02	.01
□ 644 Kevin Mitchell	.10	.05	.01
□ 645 Francisco Oliveras	.05	.02	.01
□ 646 Mike Remlinger	.05	.02	.01
□ 647 Dave Righetti	.05	.02	.01
□ 648 Robby Thompson	.05	.02	.01
□ 649 Jose Uribe	.05	.02	.01
□ 650 Matt Williams	.15	.07	.02
□ 651 Trevor Wilson	.05	.02	.01
□ 652 Tom Goodwin MLP UER	.10	.05	.01
(Timed in 3.5, should be be timed)			
□ 653 Terry Bross MLP	.05	.02	.01
□ 654 Mike Christopher MLP	.05	.02	.01
□ 655 Kenny Lofton MLP	1.00	.45	.12
□ 656 Chris Cron MLP	.05	.02	.01
□ 657 Willie Banks MLP	.05	.02	.01
□ 658 Pat Rice MLP	.05	.02	.01
□ 659A Rob Maurer MLP ERR	.75	.35	.09
(Name misspelled as Mauer on card front)			
□ 659B Rob Maurer MLP COR	.10	.05	.01
□ 660 Don Harris MLP	.05	.02	.01
□ 661 Henry Rodriguez MLP	.15	.07	.02
□ 662 Cliff Brantley MLP	.05	.02	.01
□ 663 Mike Linskey MLP UER	.05	.02	.01
(220 pounds in data, 200 in text)			
□ 664 Gary DiSarcina MLP	.05	.02	.01
□ 665 Gil Heredia MLP	.05	.02	.01
□ 666 Vinny Castilla MLP	.50	.23	.06
□ 667 Paul Abbott MLP	.05	.02	.01
□ 668 Monty Fariss MLP UER	.05	.02	.01
(Called Paul on back)			
□ 669 Jarvis Brown MLP	.05	.02	.01
□ 670 Wayne Kirby MLP	.05	.02	.01
□ 671 Scott Brosius MLP	.15	.07	.02
□ 672 Bob Hamelin MLP	.05	.02	.01
□ 673 Joel Johnston MLP	.05	.02	.01
□ 674 Tim Spehr MLP	.05	.02	.01
□ 675A Jeff Gardner MLP ERR	.75	.35	.09
(P on front, should be SS)			
□ 675B Jeff Gardner MLP COR	.25	.11	.03
□ 676 Rico Rossy MLP	.05	.02	.01
□ 677 Roberto Hernandez MLP	.15	.07	.02
□ 678 Ted Wood MLP	.05	.02	.01
□ 679 Cal Eldred MLP	.05	.02	.01
□ 680 Sean Berry MLP	.10	.05	.01
□ 681 Rickey Henderson RS	.15	.07	.02
□ 682 Nolan Ryan RS	.40	.18	.05
□ 683 Dennis Martinez RS	.05	.02	.01
□ 684 Wilson Alvarez RS	.10	.05	.01
□ 685 Joe Carter RS	.15	.07	.02
□ 686 Dave Winfield RS	.10	.05	.01
□ 687 David Cone RS	.10	.05	.01
□ 688 Jose Canseco LL UER	.10	.05	.01
(Text on back has 42 stolen bases in '88; should be 40)			
□ 689 Howard Johnson LL	.05	.02	.01
□ 690 Julio Franco LL	.05	.02	.01
□ 691 Terry Pendleton LL	.05	.02	.01
□ 692 Cecil Fielder LL	.05	.02	.01
□ 693 Scott Erickson LL	.05	.02	.01
□ 694 Tom Glavine LL	.10	.05	.01
□ 695 Dennis Martinez LL	.05	.02	.01
□ 696 Bryan Harvey LL	.05	.02	.01
□ 697 Lee Smith LL	.05	.02	.01
□ 698 Super Siblings	.10	.05	.01
Roberto Alomar			
Sandy Alomar Jr.			
□ 699 The Indispensables	.10	.05	.01
Bobby Bonilla			
Will Clark			
□ 700 Teamwork	.05	.02	.01
Mark Wohlers			
Kent Mercker			
Alejandro Pena			
□ 701 Tiger Tandems	.50	.23	.06
Stacy Jones			
Bo Jackson			
Gregg Olson			
Frank Thomas			
□ 702 The Ignitors	.15	.07	.02
Paul Molitor			

Brett Butler			
□ 703 Indispensables II	.50	.23	.06
Cal Ripken			
Joe Carter			
□ 704 Power Packs	.25	.11	.03
Barry Larkin			
Kirby Puckett			
□ 705 Today and Tomorrow	.15	.07	.02
Mo Vaughn			
Cecil Fielder			
□ 706 Teenage Sensations	.10	.05	.01
Ramon Martinez			
Ozzie Guillen			
□ 707 Designated Hitters	.15	.07	.02
Harold Baines			
Wade Boggs			
□ 708 Robin Yount PV	.15	.07	.02
□ 709 Ken Griffey Jr. PV UER	.75	.35	.09
(Missing quotations on back; BA has .322, but was actually .327)			
□ 710 Nolan Ryan PV	.40	.18	.05
□ 711 Cal Ripken PV	.40	.18	.05
□ 712 Frank Thomas PV	.75	.35	.09
□ 713 Dave Justice PV	.10	.05	.01
□ 714 Checklist 1-101	.05	.02	.01
□ 715 Checklist 102-194	.05	.02	.01
□ 716 Checklist 195-296	.05	.02	.01
□ 717 Checklist 297-397	.05	.02	.01
□ 718 Checklist 398-494	.05	.02	.01
□ 719 Checklist 495-596	.05	.02	.01
□ 720A Checklist 597-720 ERR	.05	.02	.01
(659 Rob Mauer)			
□ 720B Checklist 597-720 COR	.05	.02	.01
(659 Rob Maurer)			

1992 Fleer All-Stars

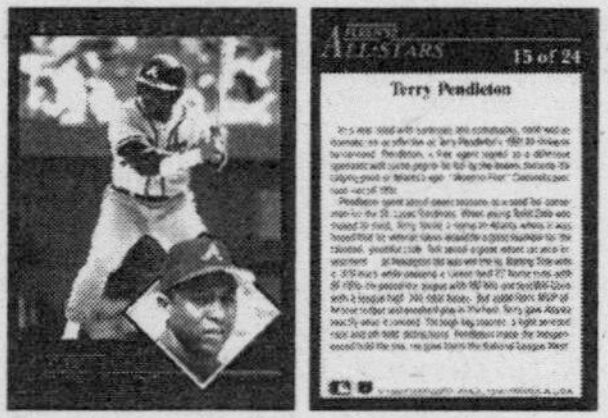

Cards from this 24-card standard-size set were randomly inserted in plastic wrap packs. Selected members of the American and National League 1991 All-Star squads comprise this set. The glossy color photos on the fronts are bordered in black and accented above and below with gold stripes and lettering. A diamond with a color head shot of the player is superimposed at the lower right corner of the picture.

	MINT	NRMT	EXC
COMPLETE SET (24)	35.00	16.00	4.40
COMMON CARD (1-24)	.50	.23	.06
SEMISTARS	1.00	.45	.12
RANDOM INSERTS IN WAX PACKS			
□ 1 Felix Jose	.50	.23	.06
□ 2 Tony Gwynn	2.50	1.10	.30
□ 3 Barry Bonds	2.00	.90	.25
□ 4 Bobby Bonilla	1.00	.45	.12
□ 5 Mike LaValliere	.50	.23	.06
□ 6 Tom Glavine	1.00	.45	.12
□ 7 Ramon Martinez	1.00	.45	.12
□ 8 Lee Smith	1.00	.45	.12
□ 9 Mickey Tettleton	.50	.23	.06
□ 10 Scott Erickson	1.00	.45	.12
□ 11 Frank Thomas	10.00	4.50	1.25
□ 12 Danny Tartabull	.50	.23	.06
□ 13 Will Clark	1.00	.45	.12
□ 14 Ryne Sandberg	1.50	.70	.19
□ 15 Terry Pendleton	.50	.23	.06
□ 16 Barry Larkin	1.00	.45	.12
□ 17 Rafael Palmeiro	1.00	.45	.12
□ 18 Julio Franco	.50	.23	.06
□ 19 Robin Ventura	1.00	.45	.12
□ 20 Cal Ripken UER	8.00	3.60	1.00
(Candidte; total bases misspelled as based)			
□ 21 Joe Carter	1.00	.45	.12
□ 22 Kirby Puckett	2.00	.90	.25
□ 23 Ken Griffey Jr.	10.00	4.50	1.25
□ 24 Jose Canseco	1.00	.45	.12

1992 Fleer Lumber Company

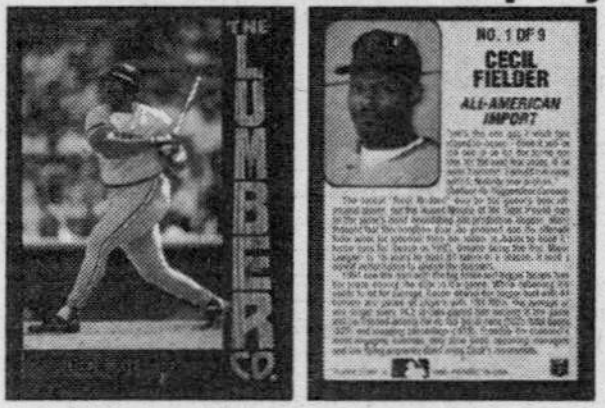

The 1992 Fleer Lumber Company standard-size set features nine outstanding hitters in Major League Baseball. This set was only available as a bonus in Fleer hobby factory sets. Inside a black glossy frame, the fronts display color action player photos, with the player's name printed in black in a gold foil bar beneath the picture. The wider right border contains the catch phrase "The Lumber Co." in the shape of a baseball bat, complete with woodgrain streaks.

	MINT	NRMT	EXC
COMPLETE SET (9)	10.00	4.50	1.25
COMMON CARD (L1-L9)	.75	.35	.09
ONE SET PER HOBBY FACTORY SET			
□ L1 Cecil Fielder	1.00	.45	.12
□ L2 Mickey Tettleton	.75	.35	.09
□ L3 Darryl Strawberry	1.00	.45	.12
□ L4 Ryne Sandberg	1.50	.70	.19
□ L5 Jose Canseco	1.00	.45	.12
□ L6 Matt Williams UER	1.00	.45	.12
In 17th line, cycle is spelled cyle			
□ L7 Cal Ripken	8.00	3.60	1.00
□ L8 Barry Bonds	1.50	.70	.19
□ L9 Ron Gant	.75	.35	.09

1992 Fleer Rookie Sensations

Cards from the 20-card Fleer Rookie Sensations set were randomly inserted in 1992 Fleer 35-card cello packs. The cards were extremely popular upon release resulting in packs selling for levels far above suggested retail levels. The glossy color photos on the

fronts have a white border on a royal blue card face. The words "Rookie Sensations" appear above the picture in gold foil lettering, while the player's name appears on a gold foil plaque beneath the picture. Through a mail-in offer for ten Fleer baseball card wrappers and 1.00 for postage and handling, Fleer offered an uncut 8 1/2" by 11" numbered promo sheet picturing ten of the 20-card set on each side in a reduced-size front-only format. The offer indicated an expiration date of July 31, 1992, or whenever the production quantity of 250,000 sheets was exhausted.

	MINT	NRMT	EXC
COMPLETE SET (20)	50.00	22.00	6.25
COMMON CARD (1-20)	1.00	.45	.12
SEMISTARS	1.50	.70	.19
RANDOM INSERTS IN CELLO PACKS			

□ 1 Frank Thomas	30.00	13.50	3.70
□ 2 Todd Van Poppel	1.00	.45	.12
□ 3 Orlando Merced	1.50	.70	.19
□ 4 Jeff Bagwell	12.00	5.50	1.50
□ 5 Jeff Fassero	1.50	.70	.19
□ 6 Darren Lewis	1.00	.45	.12
□ 7 Milt Cuyler	1.00	.45	.12
□ 8 Mike Timlin	1.00	.45	.12
□ 9 Brian McRae	1.50	.70	.19
□ 10 Chuck Knoblauch	4.00	1.80	.50
□ 11 Rich DeLucia	1.00	.45	.12
□ 12 Ivan Rodriguez	5.00	2.20	.60
□ 13 Juan Guzman	1.50	.70	.19
□ 14 Steve Chitren	1.00	.45	.12
□ 15 Mark Wohlers	2.50	1.10	.30
□ 16 Wes Chamberlain	1.00	.45	.12
□ 17 Ray Lankford	3.00	1.35	.35
□ 18 Chito Martinez	1.00	.45	.12
□ 19 Phil Plantier	1.00	.45	.12
□ 20 Scott Leius UER (Misspelled Lieus on card front)	1.00	.45	.12

1992 Fleer Smoke 'n Heat

This 12-card standard-size set features outstanding major league pitchers, especially the premier fastball pitchers in both leagues. These cards were only available in Fleer's 1992 Christmas factory set. The front design features color action player photos bordered in black. The player's name appears in a gold foil bar beneath the picture, and the words "Smoke 'n Heat" are printed vertically in the wider right border.

	MINT	NRMT	EXC
COMPLETE SET (12)	10.00	4.50	1.25
COMMON CARD (S1-S12)	.50	.23	.06
SEMISTARS	1.00	.45	.12
ONE SET PER RETAIL FACTORY SET			

□ S1 Lee Smith	1.00	.45	.12
□ S2 Jack McDowell	1.00	.45	.12
□ S3 David Cone	1.00	.45	.12
□ S4 Roger Clemens	1.00	.45	.12
□ S5 Nolan Ryan	6.00	2.70	.75
□ S6 Scott Erickson	.50	.23	.06
□ S7 Tom Glavine	1.00	.45	.12
□ S8 Dwight Gooden	1.00	.45	.12
□ S9 Andy Benes	1.00	.45	.12
□ S10 Steve Avery	.50	.23	.06
□ S11 Randy Johnson	1.00	.45	.12
□ S12 Jim Abbott	1.00	.45	.12

1992 Fleer Team Leaders

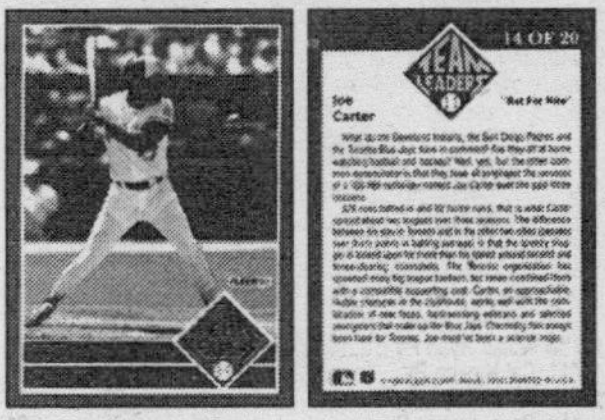

Cards from the 20-card Fleer Team Leaders set were randomly inserted in 1992 Fleer 42-card rack packs. The glossy color photos on the fronts are bordered in white and green. Two gold foil stripes below the picture intersect a diamond-shaped "Team Leaders" emblem.

	MINT	NRMT	EXC
COMPLETE SET (20)	45.00	20.00	5.50
COMMON CARD (1-20)	1.00	.45	.12
SEMISTARS	2.00	.90	.25
ONE TL OR CLEMENS PER RACK PACK			

□ 1 Don Mattingly	8.00	3.60	1.00
□ 2 Howard Johnson	1.00	.45	.12
□ 3 Chris Sabo UER (Where he it, should be Where he hit)	1.00	.45	.12
□ 4 Carlton Fisk	2.00	.90	.25
□ 5 Kirby Puckett	5.00	2.20	.60
□ 6 Cecil Fielder	2.00	.90	.25
□ 7 Tony Gwynn	6.00	2.70	.75
□ 8 Will Clark	2.00	.90	.25
□ 9 Bobby Bonilla	2.00	.90	.25
□ 10 Len Dykstra	2.00	.90	.25
□ 11 Tom Glavine	2.00	.90	.25
□ 12 Rafael Palmeiro	2.00	.90	.25
□ 13 Wade Boggs	2.00	.90	.25
□ 14 Joe Carter	2.00	.90	.25
□ 15 Ken Griffey Jr.	20.00	9.00	2.50
□ 16 Darryl Strawberry	2.00	.90	.25
□ 17 Cal Ripken	15.00	6.75	1.85
□ 18 Danny Tartabull	1.00	.45	.12
□ 19 Jose Canseco	2.00	.90	.25
□ 20 Andre Dawson	2.00	.90	.25

1992 Fleer Update

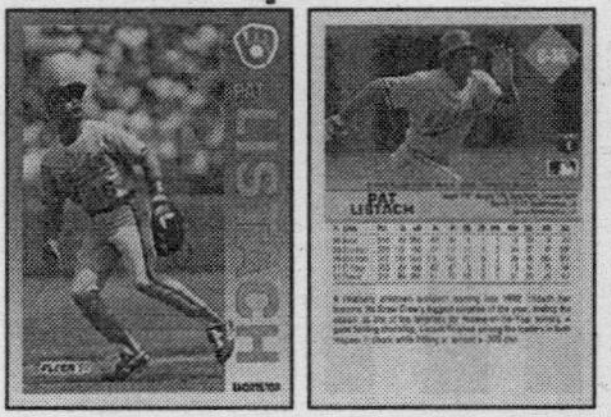

The 1992 Fleer Update set contains 132 standard-size cards. Cards were distributed exclusively in factory sets through hobby dealers. Factory sets included a four-card, black-bordered "92 Headliners" insert set for a total of 136 cards. Due to lackluster retail response for previous Fleer Update sets, wholesale orders

for this product were low, resulting in a short print run. As word got out that the cards were in short supply, the secondary market prices soared not soon after release. The basic card design is identical to the regular issue 1992 Fleer cards except for the U-prefixed numbering on back. The cards are checklisted alphabetically within and according to teams for each league with AL preceding NL. Rookie Cards in this set include John Jaha, Mike Piazza, John Valentin and Eric Young. The Piazza card is widely recognized as one of the more desirable singles issued in the 1990's.

	MINT	NRMT	EXC
COMPLETE FACT.SET (136)	160.00	70.00	20.00
COMPLETE HEADLINERS (4)	20.00	9.00	2.50
COMPLETE SET (132)	140.00	65.00	17.50
COMMON CARD (1-132)	.25	.11	.03
SEMISTARS	.50	.23	.06
STARS	1.00	.45	.12
U PREFIX ON REG.CARD NUMBERS			

□ 1 Todd Frohwirth	.25	.11	.03
□ 2 Alan Mills	.25	.11	.03
□ 3 Rick Sutcliffe	.25	.11	.03
□ 4 John Valentin	3.00	1.35	.35
□ 5 Frank Viola	.25	.11	.03
□ 6 Bob Zupcic	.25	.11	.03
□ 7 Mike Butcher	.25	.11	.03
□ 8 Chad Curtis	1.00	.45	.12
□ 9 Damion Easley	.50	.23	.06
□ 10 Tim Salmon	18.00	8.00	2.20
□ 11 Julio Valera	.25	.11	.03
□ 12 George Bell	.25	.11	.03
□ 13 Roberto Hernandez	1.50	.70	.19
□ 14 Shawn Jeter	.25	.11	.03
□ 15 Thomas Howard	.25	.11	.03
□ 16 Jesse Levis	.25	.11	.03
□ 17 Kenny Lofton	35.00	16.00	4.40
□ 18 Paul Sorrento	.25	.11	.03
□ 19 Rico Brogna	.50	.23	.06
□ 20 John Doherty	.25	.11	.03
□ 21 Dan Gladden	.25	.11	.03
□ 22 Buddy Groom	.25	.11	.03
□ 23 Shawn Hare	.25	.11	.03
□ 24 John Kiely	.25	.11	.03
□ 25 Kurt Knudsen	.25	.11	.03
□ 26 Gregg Jefferies	1.00	.45	.12
□ 27 Wally Joyner	.50	.23	.06
□ 28 Kevin Koslofski	.25	.11	.03
□ 29 Kevin McReynolds	.25	.11	.03
□ 30 Rusty Meacham	.25	.11	.03
□ 31 Keith Miller	.25	.11	.03
□ 32 Hipolito Pichardo	.25	.11	.03
□ 33 James Austin	.25	.11	.03
□ 34 Scott Fletcher	.25	.11	.03
□ 35 John Jaha	3.00	1.35	.35
□ 36 Pat Listach	.50	.23	.06
□ 37 Dave Nilsson	2.00	.90	.25
□ 38 Kevin Seitzer	.25	.11	.03
□ 39 Tom Edens	.25	.11	.03
□ 40 Pat Mahomes	.25	.11	.03
□ 41 John Smiley	.25	.11	.03
□ 42 Charlie Hayes	.25	.11	.03
□ 43 Sam Militello	.25	.11	.03
□ 44 Andy Stankiewicz	.25	.11	.03
□ 45 Danny Tartabull	.25	.11	.03
□ 46 Bob Wickman	.25	.11	.03
□ 47 Jerry Browne	.25	.11	.03
□ 48 Kevin Campbell	.25	.11	.03
□ 49 Vince Horsman	.25	.11	.03
□ 50 Troy Neel	.25	.11	.03
□ 51 Ruben Sierra	.50	.23	.06
□ 52 Bruce Walton	.25	.11	.03
□ 53 Willie Wilson	.25	.11	.03
□ 54 Bret Boone	1.00	.45	.12
□ 55 Dave Fleming	.25	.11	.03
□ 56 Kevin Mitchell	.50	.23	.06
□ 57 Jeff Nelson	.25	.11	.03
□ 58 Shane Turner	.25	.11	.03
□ 59 Jose Canseco	2.50	1.10	.30
□ 60 Jeff Frye	.25	.11	.03
□ 61 Danny Leon	.25	.11	.03
□ 62 Roger Pavlik	2.00	.90	.25
□ 63 David Cone	1.00	.45	.12
□ 64 Pat Hentgen	5.00	2.20	.60
□ 65 Randy Knorr	.25	.11	.03
□ 66 Jack Morris	.50	.23	.06
□ 67 Dave Winfield	1.50	.70	.19
□ 68 David Nied	.50	.23	.06
□ 69 Otis Nixon	.25	.11	.03
□ 70 Alejandro Pena	.25	.11	.03
□ 71 Jeff Reardon	.50	.23	.06
□ 72 Alex Arias	.25	.11	.03
□ 73 Jim Bullinger	.25	.11	.03
□ 74 Mike Morgan	.25	.11	.03
□ 75 Rey Sanchez	.25	.11	.03
□ 76 Bob Scanlan	.25	.11	.03
□ 77 Sammy Sosa	4.00	1.80	.50
□ 78 Scott Bankhead	.25	.11	.03
□ 79 Tim Belcher	.25	.11	.03
□ 80 Steve Foster	.25	.11	.03
□ 81 Willie Greene	.50	.23	.06
□ 82 Bip Roberts	.25	.11	.03
□ 83 Scott Ruskin	.25	.11	.03
□ 84 Greg Swindell	.25	.11	.03
□ 85 Juan Guerrero	.25	.11	.03
□ 86 Butch Henry	.25	.11	.03
□ 87 Doug Jones	.25	.11	.03
□ 88 Brian Williams	.25	.11	.03
□ 89 Tom Candiotti	.25	.11	.03
□ 90 Eric Davis	.50	.23	.06
□ 91 Carlos Hernandez	.25	.11	.03
□ 92 Mike Piazza	100.00	45.00	12.50
□ 93 Mike Sharperson	.25	.11	.03
□ 94 Eric Young	3.00	1.35	.35
□ 95 Moises Alou	2.00	.90	.25
□ 96 Greg Colbrunn	.25	.11	.03
□ 97 Wil Cordero	.50	.23	.06
□ 98 Ken Hill	1.00	.45	.12
□ 99 John Vander Wal	.25	.11	.03
□ 100 John Wetteland	.50	.23	.06
□ 101 Bobby Bonilla	.50	.23	.06
□ 102 Eric Hillman	.25	.11	.03
□ 103 Pat Howell	.25	.11	.03
□ 104 Jeff Kent	1.50	.70	.19
□ 105 Dick Schofield	.25	.11	.03
□ 106 Ryan Thompson	.25	.11	.03
□ 107 Chico Walker	.25	.11	.03
□ 108 Juan Bell	.25	.11	.03
□ 109 Mariano Duncan	.25	.11	.03
□ 110 Jeff Grotewold	.25	.11	.03
□ 111 Ben Rivera	.25	.11	.03
□ 112 Curt Schilling	.25	.11	.03
□ 113 Victor Cole	.25	.11	.03
□ 114 Albert Martin	1.00	.45	.12
□ 115 Roger Mason	.25	.11	.03
□ 116 Blas Minor	.25	.11	.03
□ 117 Tim Wakefield	1.00	.45	.12
□ 118 Mark Clark	.50	.23	.06
□ 119 Rheal Cormier	.25	.11	.03
□ 120 Donovan Osborne	.50	.23	.06
□ 121 Todd Worrell	.25	.11	.03
□ 122 Jeremy Hernandez	.25	.11	.03
□ 123 Randy Myers	.50	.23	.06
□ 124 Frank Seminara	.25	.11	.03
□ 125 Gary Sheffield	3.00	1.35	.35
□ 126 Dan Walters	.25	.11	.03
□ 127 Steve Hosey	.25	.11	.03
□ 128 Mike Jackson	.25	.11	.03
□ 129 Jim Pena	.25	.11	.03
□ 130 Cory Snyder	.25	.11	.03
□ 131 Bill Swift	.25	.11	.03
□ 132 Checklist U1-U132	.25	.11	.03
□ H1 Ken Griffey Jr.	15.00	6.75	1.85
□ H2 Robin Yount	2.00	.90	.25
□ H3 Jeff Reardon	.25	.11	.03
□ H4 Cecil Fielder	1.50	.70	.19

1993 Fleer

The 720-card 1993 Fleer baseball set contains two series of 360 standard-size cards. Cards were distributed in plastic wrapped packs, cello packs, jumbo packs and rack packs. For the first time in years, Fleer did not issue a factory set. In fact, Fleer discontinued issuing factory sets from 1993-on. The card fronts show glossy color action player photos bordered in silver. A team color-coded stripe edges the left side of

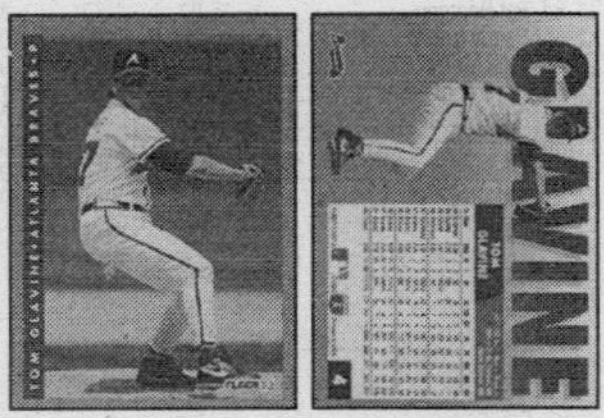

the picture and carries the player's name and team name. The cards are checklisted below alphabetically within and according to teams for each league with NL preceding AL. Topical subsets include League Leaders (344-348/704-708), Round Trippers (349-353/709-713), and Super Star Specials (354-357/714-717). Each series concludes with checklists (358-360/718-720). There are no key Rookie Cards in this set.

	MINT	NRMT	EXC
COMPLETE SET (720)	45.00	20.00	5.50
COMPLETE SERIES 1 (360)	22.50	10.00	2.80
COMPLETE SERIES 2 (360)	22.50	10.00	2.80
COMMON CARD (1-720)	.05	.02	.01
SEMISTARS	.15	.07	.02
STARS	.30	.14	.04
COMP.GLAVINE SET (12)	4.00	1.80	.50
COMMON GLAVINE (1-12)	.50	.23	.06
CERTIFIED GLAVINE AUTO	80.00	36.00	10.00
GLAVINE: RANDOM INSERTS IN ALL PACKS			
COMMON GLAV.MAIL (13-15)	2.00	.90	.25
GLAVINE MAIL-IN DIST.VIA WRAPPER EXCH.			

□ 1 Steve Avery	.15	.07	.02
□ 2 Sid Bream	.05	.02	.01
□ 3 Ron Gant	.30	.14	.04
□ 4 Tom Glavine	.30	.14	.04
□ 5 Brian Hunter	.05	.02	.01
□ 6 Ryan Klesko	1.00	.45	.12
□ 7 Charlie Leibrandt	.05	.02	.01
□ 8 Kent Mercker	.05	.02	.01
□ 9 David Nied	.05	.02	.01
□ 10 Otis Nixon	.05	.02	.01
□ 11 Greg Olson	.05	.02	.01
□ 12 Terry Pendleton	.15	.07	.02
□ 13 Deion Sanders	.30	.14	.04
□ 14 John Smoltz	.30	.14	.04
□ 15 Mike Stanton	.05	.02	.01
□ 16 Mark Wohlers	.15	.07	.02
□ 17 Paul Assenmacher	.05	.02	.01
□ 18 Steve Buechele	.05	.02	.01
□ 19 Shawon Dunston	.05	.02	.01
□ 20 Mark Grace	.30	.14	.04
□ 21 Derrick May	.05	.02	.01
□ 22 Chuck McElroy	.05	.02	.01
□ 23 Mike Morgan	.05	.02	.01
□ 24 Rey Sanchez	.05	.02	.01
□ 25 Ryne Sandberg	.50	.23	.06
□ 26 Bob Scanlan	.05	.02	.01
□ 27 Sammy Sosa	.30	.14	.04
□ 28 Rick Wilkins	.05	.02	.01
□ 29 Bobby Ayala	.15	.07	.02
□ 30 Tim Belcher	.05	.02	.01
□ 31 Jeff Branson	.05	.02	.01
□ 32 Norm Charlton	.05	.02	.01
□ 33 Steve Foster	.05	.02	.01
□ 34 Willie Greene	.15	.07	.02
□ 35 Chris Hammond	.05	.02	.01
□ 36 Milt Hill	.05	.02	.01
□ 37 Hal Morris	.05	.02	.01
□ 38 Joe Oliver	.05	.02	.01
□ 39 Paul O'Neill	.15	.07	.02
□ 40 Tim Pugh	.05	.02	.01
□ 41 Jose Rijo	.05	.02	.01
□ 42 Bip Roberts	.05	.02	.01
□ 43 Chris Sabo	.05	.02	.01
□ 44 Reggie Sanders	.30	.14	.04
□ 45 Eric Anthony	.05	.02	.01
□ 46 Jeff Bagwell	.75	.35	.09
□ 47 Craig Biggio	.30	.14	.04
□ 48 Joe Boever	.05	.02	.01
□ 49 Casey Candaele	.05	.02	.01
□ 50 Steve Finley	.30	.14	.04
□ 51 Luis Gonzalez	.05	.02	.01
□ 52 Pete Harnisch	.05	.02	.01
□ 53 Xavier Hernandez	.05	.02	.01
□ 54 Doug Jones	.05	.02	.01
□ 55 Eddie Taubensee	.05	.02	.01
□ 56 Brian Williams	.05	.02	.01
□ 57 Pedro Astacio	.05	.02	.01
□ 58 Todd Benzinger	.05	.02	.01
□ 59 Brett Butler	.15	.07	.02
□ 60 Tom Candiotti	.05	.02	.01
□ 61 Lenny Harris	.05	.02	.01
□ 62 Carlos Hernandez	.05	.02	.01
□ 63 Orel Hershiser	.15	.07	.02
□ 64 Eric Karros	.30	.14	.04
□ 65 Ramon Martinez	.15	.07	.02
□ 66 Jose Offerman	.05	.02	.01
□ 67 Mike Scioscia	.05	.02	.01
□ 68 Mike Sharperson	.05	.02	.01
□ 69 Eric Young	.30	.14	.04
□ 70 Moises Alou	.30	.14	.04
□ 71 Ivan Calderon	.05	.02	.01
□ 72 Archi Cianfrocco	.05	.02	.01
□ 73 Wil Cordero	.15	.07	.02
□ 74 Delino DeShields	.05	.02	.01
□ 75 Mark Gardner	.05	.02	.01
□ 76 Ken Hill	.15	.07	.02
□ 77 Tim Laker	.05	.02	.01
□ 78 Chris Nabholz	.05	.02	.01
□ 79 Mel Rojas	.15	.07	.02
□ 80 John Vander Wal UER (Misspelled Vander Wall in letters on back)	.05	.02	.01
□ 81 Larry Walker	.30	.14	.04
□ 82 Tim Wallach	.05	.02	.01
□ 83 John Wetteland	.15	.07	.02
□ 84 Bobby Bonilla	.15	.07	.02
□ 85 Daryl Boston	.05	.02	.01
□ 86 Sid Fernandez	.05	.02	.01
□ 87 Eric Hillman	.05	.02	.01
□ 88 Todd Hundley	.30	.14	.04
□ 89 Howard Johnson	.05	.02	.01
□ 90 Jeff Kent	.15	.07	.02
□ 91 Eddie Murray	.50	.23	.06
□ 92 Bill Pecota	.05	.02	.01
□ 93 Bret Saberhagen	.15	.07	.02
□ 94 Dick Schofield	.05	.02	.01
□ 95 Pete Schourek	.15	.07	.02
□ 96 Anthony Young	.05	.02	.01
□ 97 Ruben Amaro Jr.	.05	.02	.01
□ 98 Juan Bell	.05	.02	.01
□ 99 Wes Chamberlain	.05	.02	.01
□ 100 Darren Daulton	.15	.07	.02
□ 101 Mariano Duncan	.05	.02	.01
□ 102 Mike Hartley	.05	.02	.01
□ 103 Ricky Jordan	.05	.02	.01
□ 104 John Kruk	.15	.07	.02
□ 105 Mickey Morandini	.05	.02	.01
□ 106 Terry Mulholland	.05	.02	.01
□ 107 Ben Rivera	.05	.02	.01
□ 108 Curt Schilling	.05	.02	.01
□ 109 Keith Shepherd	.05	.02	.01
□ 110 Stan Belinda	.05	.02	.01
□ 111 Jay Bell	.15	.07	.02
□ 112 Barry Bonds	.50	.23	.06
□ 113 Jeff King	.15	.07	.02
□ 114 Mike LaValliere	.05	.02	.01
□ 115 Jose Lind	.05	.02	.01
□ 116 Roger Mason	.05	.02	.01
□ 117 Orlando Merced	.15	.07	.02
□ 118 Bob Patterson	.05	.02	.01
□ 119 Don Slaught	.05	.02	.01
□ 120 Zane Smith	.05	.02	.01
□ 121 Randy Tomlin	.05	.02	.01
□ 122 Andy Van Slyke	.15	.07	.02
□ 123 Tim Wakefield	.15	.07	.02
□ 124 Rheal Cormier	.05	.02	.01
□ 125 Bernard Gilkey	.30	.14	.04
□ 126 Felix Jose	.05	.02	.01
□ 127 Ray Lankford	.30	.14	.04
□ 128 Bob McClure	.05	.02	.01
□ 129 Donovan Osborne	.05	.02	.01
□ 130 Tom Pagnozzi	.05	.02	.01

□ 131	Geronimo Pena	.05	.02	.01
□ 132	Mike Perez	.05	.02	.01
□ 133	Lee Smith	.15	.07	.02
□ 134	Bob Tewksbury	.05	.02	.01
□ 135	Todd Worrell	.05	.02	.01
□ 136	Todd Zeile	.05	.02	.01
□ 137	Jerald Clark	.05	.02	.01
□ 138	Tony Gwynn	.75	.35	.09
□ 139	Greg W. Harris	.05	.02	.01
□ 140	Jeremy Hernandez	.05	.02	.01
□ 141	Darrin Jackson	.05	.02	.01
□ 142	Mike Maddux	.05	.02	.01
□ 143	Fred McGriff	.30	.14	.04
□ 144	Jose Melendez	.05	.02	.01
□ 145	Rich Rodriguez	.05	.02	.01
□ 146	Frank Seminara	.05	.02	.01
□ 147	Gary Sheffield	.30	.14	.04
□ 148	Kurt Stillwell	.05	.02	.01
□ 149	Dan Walters	.05	.02	.01
□ 150	Rod Beck	.15	.07	.02
□ 151	Bud Black	.05	.02	.01
□ 152	Jeff Brantley	.05	.02	.01
□ 153	John Burkett	.05	.02	.01
□ 154	Will Clark	.30	.14	.04
□ 155	Royce Clayton	.15	.07	.02
□ 156	Mike Jackson	.05	.02	.01
□ 157	Darren Lewis	.05	.02	.01
□ 158	Kirt Manwaring	.05	.02	.01
□ 159	Willie McGee	.05	.02	.01
□ 160	Cory Snyder	.05	.02	.01
□ 161	Bill Swift	.05	.02	.01
□ 162	Trevor Wilson	.05	.02	.01
□ 163	Brady Anderson	.30	.14	.04
□ 164	Glenn Davis	.05	.02	.01
□ 165	Mike Devereaux	.05	.02	.01
□ 166	Todd Frohwirth	.05	.02	.01
□ 167	Leo Gomez	.05	.02	.01
□ 168	Chris Hoiles	.05	.02	.01
□ 169	Ben McDonald	.05	.02	.01
□ 170	Randy Milligan	.05	.02	.01
□ 171	Alan Mills	.05	.02	.01
□ 172	Mike Mussina	.40	.18	.05
□ 173	Gregg Olson	.05	.02	.01
□ 174	Arthur Rhodes	.05	.02	.01
□ 175	David Segui	.05	.02	.01
□ 176	Ellis Burks	.30	.14	.04
□ 177	Roger Clemens	.30	.14	.04
□ 178	Scott Cooper	.05	.02	.01
□ 179	Danny Darwin	.05	.02	.01
□ 180	Tony Fossas	.05	.02	.01
□ 181	Paul Quantrill	.05	.02	.01
□ 182	Jody Reed	.05	.02	.01
□ 183	John Valentin	.30	.14	.04
□ 184	Mo Vaughn	.50	.23	.06
□ 185	Frank Viola	.05	.02	.01
□ 186	Bob Zupcic	.05	.02	.01
□ 187	Jim Abbott	.05	.02	.01
□ 188	Gary DiSarcina	.05	.02	.01
□ 189	Damion Easley	.05	.02	.01
□ 190	Junior Felix	.05	.02	.01
□ 191	Chuck Finley	.05	.02	.01
□ 192	Joe Grahe	.05	.02	.01
□ 193	Bryan Harvey	.05	.02	.01
□ 194	Mark Langston	.15	.07	.02
□ 195	John Orton	.05	.02	.01
□ 196	Luis Polonia	.05	.02	.01
□ 197	Tim Salmon	.50	.23	.06
□ 198	Luis Sojo	.05	.02	.01
□ 199	Wilson Alvarez	.15	.07	.02
□ 200	George Bell	.05	.02	.01
□ 201	Alex Fernandez	.30	.14	.04
□ 202	Craig Grebeck	.05	.02	.01
□ 203	Ozzie Guillen	.05	.02	.01
□ 204	Lance Johnson	.15	.07	.02
□ 205	Ron Karkovice	.05	.02	.01
□ 206	Kirk McCaskill	.05	.02	.01
□ 207	Jack McDowell	.15	.07	.02
□ 208	Scott Radinsky	.05	.02	.01
□ 209	Tim Raines	.30	.14	.04
□ 210	Frank Thomas	2.00	.90	.25
□ 211	Robin Ventura	.15	.07	.02
□ 212	Sandy Alomar Jr.	.15	.07	.02
□ 213	Carlos Baerga	.30	.14	.04
□ 214	Dennis Cook	.05	.02	.01
□ 215	Thomas Howard	.05	.02	.01
□ 216	Mark Lewis	.05	.02	.01
□ 217	Derek Lilliquist	.05	.02	.01
□ 218	Kenny Lofton	.75	.35	.09
□ 219	Charles Nagy	.15	.07	.02
□ 220	Steve Olin	.05	.02	.01
□ 221	Paul Sorrento	.05	.02	.01
□ 222	Jim Thome	1.00	.45	.12
□ 223	Mark Whiten	.05	.02	.01
□ 224	Milt Cuyler	.05	.02	.01
□ 225	Rob Deer	.05	.02	.01
□ 226	John Doherty	.05	.02	.01
□ 227	Cecil Fielder	.15	.07	.02
□ 228	Travis Fryman	.30	.14	.04
□ 229	Mike Henneman	.05	.02	.01
□ 230	John Kiely UER (Card has batting stats of Pat Kelly)	.05	.02	.01
□ 231	Kurt Knudsen	.05	.02	.01
□ 232	Scott Livingstone	.05	.02	.01
□ 233	Tony Phillips	.15	.07	.02
□ 234	Mickey Tettleton	.05	.02	.01
□ 235	Kevin Appier	.15	.07	.02
□ 236	George Brett	.75	.35	.09
□ 237	Tom Gordon	.05	.02	.01
□ 238	Gregg Jefferies	.30	.14	.04
□ 239	Wally Joyner	.15	.07	.02
□ 240	Kevin Koslofski	.05	.02	.01
□ 241	Mike Macfarlane	.05	.02	.01
□ 242	Brian McRae	.15	.07	.02
□ 243	Rusty Meacham	.05	.02	.01
□ 244	Keith Miller	.05	.02	.01
□ 245	Jeff Montgomery	.15	.07	.02
□ 246	Hipolito Pichardo	.05	.02	.01
□ 247	Ricky Bones	.05	.02	.01
□ 248	Cal Eldred	.05	.02	.01
□ 249	Mike Fetters	.05	.02	.01
□ 250	Darryl Hamilton	.05	.02	.01
□ 251	Doug Henry	.05	.02	.01
□ 252	John Jaha	.15	.07	.02
□ 253	Pat Listach	.05	.02	.01
□ 254	Paul Molitor	.40	.18	.05
□ 255	Jaime Navarro	.05	.02	.01
□ 256	Kevin Seitzer	.05	.02	.01
□ 257	B.J. Surhoff	.15	.07	.02
□ 258	Greg Vaughn	.30	.14	.04
□ 259	Bill Wegman	.05	.02	.01
□ 260	Robin Yount	.30	.14	.04
□ 261	Rick Aguilera	.05	.02	.01
□ 262	Chili Davis	.15	.07	.02
□ 263	Scott Erickson	.05	.02	.01
□ 264	Greg Gagne	.05	.02	.01
□ 265	Mark Guthrie	.05	.02	.01
□ 266	Brian Harper	.05	.02	.01
□ 267	Kent Hrbek	.15	.07	.02
□ 268	Terry Jorgensen	.05	.02	.01
□ 269	Gene Larkin	.05	.02	.01
□ 270	Scott Leius	.05	.02	.01
□ 271	Pat Mahomes	.05	.02	.01
□ 272	Pedro Munoz	.05	.02	.01
□ 273	Kirby Puckett	.60	.25	.07
□ 274	Kevin Tapani	.05	.02	.01
□ 275	Carl Willis	.05	.02	.01
□ 276	Steve Farr	.05	.02	.01
□ 277	John Habyan	.05	.02	.01
□ 278	Mel Hall	.05	.02	.01
□ 279	Charlie Hayes	.05	.02	.01
□ 280	Pat Kelly	.05	.02	.01
□ 281	Don Mattingly	1.00	.45	.12
□ 282	Sam Militello	.05	.02	.01
□ 283	Matt Nokes	.05	.02	.01
□ 284	Melido Perez	.05	.02	.01
□ 285	Andy Stankiewicz	.05	.02	.01
□ 286	Danny Tartabull	.05	.02	.01
□ 287	Randy Velarde	.05	.02	.01
□ 288	Bob Wickman	.05	.02	.01
□ 289	Bernie Williams	.30	.14	.04
□ 290	Lance Blankenship	.05	.02	.01
□ 291	Mike Bordick	.05	.02	.01
□ 292	Jerry Browne	.05	.02	.01
□ 293	Dennis Eckersley	.15	.07	.02
□ 294	Rickey Henderson	.30	.14	.04
□ 295	Vince Horsman	.05	.02	.01
□ 296	Mark McGwire	.60	.25	.07
□ 297	Jeff Parrett	.05	.02	.01
□ 298	Ruben Sierra	.15	.07	.02
□ 299	Terry Steinbach	.15	.07	.02
□ 300	Walt Weiss	.05	.02	.01

□ 301 Bob Welch	.05	.02	.01
□ 302 Willie Wilson	.05	.02	.01
□ 303 Bobby Witt	.05	.02	.01
□ 304 Bret Boone	.15	.07	.02
□ 305 Jay Buhner	.30	.14	.04
□ 306 Dave Fleming	.05	.02	.01
□ 307 Ken Griffey Jr.	2.00	.90	.25
□ 308 Erik Hanson	.05	.02	.01
□ 309 Edgar Martinez	.30	.14	.04
□ 310 Tino Martinez	.15	.07	.02
□ 311 Jeff Nelson	.05	.02	.01
□ 312 Dennis Powell	.05	.02	.01
□ 313 Mike Schooler	.05	.02	.01
□ 314 Russ Swan	.05	.02	.01
□ 315 Dave Valle	.05	.02	.01
□ 316 Omar Vizquel	.30	.14	.04
□ 317 Kevin Brown	.05	.02	.01
□ 318 Todd Burns	.05	.02	.01
□ 319 Jose Canseco	.30	.14	.04
□ 320 Julio Franco	.15	.07	.02
□ 321 Jeff Frye	.05	.02	.01
□ 322 Juan Gonzalez	1.00	.45	.12
□ 323 Jose Guzman	.05	.02	.01
□ 324 Jeff Huson	.05	.02	.01
□ 325 Dean Palmer	.15	.07	.02
□ 326 Kevin Reimer	.05	.02	.01
□ 327 Ivan Rodriguez	.40	.18	.05
□ 328 Kenny Rogers	.05	.02	.01
□ 329 Dan Smith	.05	.02	.01
□ 330 Roberto Alomar	.50	.23	.06
□ 331 Derek Bell	.30	.14	.04
□ 332 Pat Borders	.05	.02	.01
□ 333 Joe Carter	.30	.14	.04
□ 334 Kelly Gruber	.05	.02	.01
□ 335 Tom Henke	.05	.02	.01
□ 336 Jimmy Key	.15	.07	.02
□ 337 Manuel Lee	.05	.02	.01
□ 338 Candy Maldonado	.05	.02	.01
□ 339 John Olerud	.05	.02	.01
□ 340 Todd Stottlemyre	.15	.07	.02
□ 341 Duane Ward	.05	.02	.01
□ 342 Devon White	.05	.02	.01
□ 343 Dave Winfield	.30	.14	.04
□ 344 Edgar Martinez LL	.15	.07	.02
□ 345 Cecil Fielder LL	.05	.02	.01
□ 346 Kenny Lofton LL	.30	.14	.04
□ 347 Jack Morris LL	.05	.02	.01
□ 348 Roger Clemens LL	.30	.14	.04
□ 349 Fred McGriff RT	.30	.14	.04
□ 350 Barry Bonds RT	.30	.14	.04
□ 351 Gary Sheffield RT	.30	.14	.04
□ 352 Darren Daulton RT	.05	.02	.01
□ 353 Dave Hollins RT	.05	.02	.01
□ 354 Brothers in Blue	.05	.02	.01
Pedro Martinez			
Ramon Martinez			
□ 355 Power Packs	.60	.25	.07
Ivan Rodriguez			
Kirby Puckett			
□ 356 Triple Threats	.30	.14	.04
Ryne Sandberg			
Gary Sheffield			
□ 357 Infield Trifecta	.30	.14	.04
Roberto Alomar			
Chuck Knoblauch			
Carlos Baerga			
□ 358 Checklist 1-120	.05	.02	.01
□ 359 Checklist 121-240	.05	.02	.01
□ 360 Checklist 241-360	.05	.02	.01
□ 361 Rafael Belliard	.05	.02	.01
□ 362 Damon Berryhill	.05	.02	.01
□ 363 Mike Bielecki	.05	.02	.01
□ 364 Jeff Blauser	.05	.02	.01
□ 365 Francisco Cabrera	.05	.02	.01
□ 366 Marvin Freeman	.05	.02	.01
□ 367 David Justice	.30	.14	.04
□ 368 Mark Lemke	.05	.02	.01
□ 369 Alejandro Pena	.05	.02	.01
□ 370 Jeff Reardon	.15	.07	.02
□ 371 Lonnie Smith	.05	.02	.01
□ 372 Pete Smith	.05	.02	.01
□ 373 Shawn Boskie	.05	.02	.01
□ 374 Jim Bullinger	.05	.02	.01
□ 375 Frank Castillo	.05	.02	.01
□ 376 Doug Dascenzo	.05	.02	.01
□ 377 Andre Dawson	.30	.14	.04
□ 378 Mike Harkey	.05	.02	.01
□ 379 Greg Hibbard	.05	.02	.01
□ 380 Greg Maddux	1.25	.55	.16
□ 381 Ken Patterson	.05	.02	.01
□ 382 Jeff D. Robinson	.05	.02	.01
□ 383 Luis Salazar	.05	.02	.01
□ 384 Dwight Smith	.05	.02	.01
□ 385 Jose Vizcaino	.05	.02	.01
□ 386 Scott Bankhead	.05	.02	.01
□ 387 Tom Browning	.05	.02	.01
□ 388 Darnell Coles	.05	.02	.01
□ 389 Rob Dibble	.05	.02	.01
□ 390 Bill Doran	.05	.02	.01
□ 391 Dwayne Henry	.05	.02	.01
□ 392 Cesar Hernandez	.05	.02	.01
□ 393 Roberto Kelly	.05	.02	.01
□ 394 Barry Larkin	.30	.14	.04
□ 395 Dave Martinez	.05	.02	.01
□ 396 Kevin Mitchell	.15	.07	.02
□ 397 Jeff Reed	.05	.02	.01
□ 398 Scott Ruskin	.05	.02	.01
□ 399 Greg Swindell	.05	.02	.01
□ 400 Dan Wilson	.15	.07	.02
□ 401 Andy Ashby	.15	.07	.02
□ 402 Freddie Benavides	.05	.02	.01
□ 403 Dante Bichette	.30	.14	.04
□ 404 Willie Blair	.05	.02	.01
□ 405 Denis Boucher	.05	.02	.01
□ 406 Vinny Castilla	.30	.14	.04
□ 407 Braulio Castillo	.05	.02	.01
□ 408 Alex Cole	.05	.02	.01
□ 409 Andres Galarraga	.30	.14	.04
□ 410 Joe Girardi	.05	.02	.01
□ 411 Butch Henry	.05	.02	.01
□ 412 Darren Holmes	.05	.02	.01
□ 413 Calvin Jones	.05	.02	.01
□ 414 Steve Reed	.05	.02	.01
□ 415 Kevin Ritz	.05	.02	.01
□ 416 Jim Tatum	.05	.02	.01
□ 417 Jack Armstrong	.05	.02	.01
□ 418 Bret Barberie	.05	.02	.01
□ 419 Ryan Bowen	.05	.02	.01
□ 420 Cris Carpenter	.05	.02	.01
□ 421 Chuck Carr	.05	.02	.01
□ 422 Scott Chiamparino	.05	.02	.01
□ 423 Jeff Conine	.30	.14	.04
□ 424 Jim Corsi	.05	.02	.01
□ 425 Steve Decker	.05	.02	.01
□ 426 Chris Donnels	.05	.02	.01
□ 427 Monty Fariss	.05	.02	.01
□ 428 Bob Natal	.05	.02	.01
□ 429 Pat Rapp	.15	.07	.02
□ 430 Dave Weathers	.05	.02	.01
□ 431 Nigel Wilson	.05	.02	.01
□ 432 Ken Caminiti	.30	.14	.04
□ 433 Andujar Cedeno	.05	.02	.01
□ 434 Tom Edens	.05	.02	.01
□ 435 Juan Guerrero	.05	.02	.01
□ 436 Pete Incaviglia	.05	.02	.01
□ 437 Jimmy Jones	.05	.02	.01
□ 438 Darryl Kile	.05	.02	.01
□ 439 Rob Murphy	.05	.02	.01
□ 440 Al Osuna	.05	.02	.01
□ 441 Mark Portugal	.05	.02	.01
□ 442 Scott Servais	.05	.02	.01
□ 443 John Candelaria	.05	.02	.01
□ 444 Tim Crews	.05	.02	.01
□ 445 Eric Davis	.15	.07	.02
□ 446 Tom Goodwin	.05	.02	.01
□ 447 Jim Gott	.05	.02	.01
□ 448 Kevin Gross	.05	.02	.01
□ 449 Dave Hansen	.05	.02	.01
□ 450 Jay Howell	.05	.02	.01
□ 451 Roger McDowell	.05	.02	.01
□ 452 Bob Ojeda	.05	.02	.01
□ 453 Henry Rodriguez	.30	.14	.04
□ 454 Darryl Strawberry	.15	.07	.02
□ 455 Mitch Webster	.05	.02	.01
□ 456 Steve Wilson	.05	.02	.01
□ 457 Brian Barnes	.05	.02	.01
□ 458 Sean Berry	.05	.02	.01
□ 459 Jeff Fassero	.15	.07	.02
□ 460 Darrin Fletcher	.05	.02	.01
□ 461 Marquis Grissom	.30	.14	.04
□ 462 Dennis Martinez	.15	.07	.02
□ 463 Spike Owen	.05	.02	.01

□	464 Matt Stairs	.05	.02	.01
□	465 Sergio Valdez	.05	.02	.01
□	466 Kevin Bass	.05	.02	.01
□	467 Vince Coleman	.05	.02	.01
□	468 Mark Dewey	.05	.02	.01
□	469 Kevin Elster	.05	.02	.01
□	470 Tony Fernandez	.05	.02	.01
□	471 John Franco	.05	.02	.01
□	472 Dave Gallagher	.05	.02	.01
□	473 Paul Gibson	.05	.02	.01
□	474 Dwight Gooden	.15	.07	.02
□	475 Lee Guetterman	.05	.02	.01
□	476 Jeff Innis	.05	.02	.01
□	477 Dave Magadan	.05	.02	.01
□	478 Charlie O'Brien	.05	.02	.01
□	479 Willie Randolph	.15	.07	.02
□	480 Mackey Sasser	.05	.02	.01
□	481 Ryan Thompson	.05	.02	.01
□	482 Chico Walker	.05	.02	.01
□	483 Kyle Abbott	.05	.02	.01
□	484 Bob Ayrault	.05	.02	.01
□	485 Kim Batiste	.05	.02	.01
□	486 Cliff Brantley	.05	.02	.01
□	487 Jose DeLeon	.05	.02	.01
□	488 Len Dykstra	.15	.07	.02
□	489 Tommy Greene	.05	.02	.01
□	490 Jeff Grotewold	.05	.02	.01
□	491 Dave Hollins	.05	.02	.01
□	492 Danny Jackson	.05	.02	.01
□	493 Stan Javier	.05	.02	.01
□	494 Tom Marsh	.05	.02	.01
□	495 Greg Mathews	.05	.02	.01
□	496 Dale Murphy	.30	.14	.04
□	497 Todd Pratt	.05	.02	.01
□	498 Mitch Williams	.05	.02	.01
□	499 Danny Cox	.05	.02	.01
□	500 Doug Drabek	.05	.02	.01
□	501 Carlos Garcia	.05	.02	.01
□	502 Lloyd McClendon	.05	.02	.01
□	503 Denny Neagle	.15	.07	.02
□	504 Gary Redus	.05	.02	.01
□	505 Bob Walk	.05	.02	.01
□	506 John Wehner	.05	.02	.01
□	507 Luis Alicea	.05	.02	.01
□	508 Mark Clark	.05	.02	.01
□	509 Pedro Guerrero	.05	.02	.01
□	510 Rex Hudler	.05	.02	.01
□	511 Brian Jordan	.30	.14	.04
□	512 Omar Olivares	.05	.02	.01
□	513 Jose Oquendo	.05	.02	.01
□	514 Gerald Perry	.05	.02	.01
□	515 Bryn Smith	.05	.02	.01
□	516 Craig Wilson	.05	.02	.01
□	517 Tracy Woodson	.05	.02	.01
□	518 Larry Andersen	.05	.02	.01
□	519 Andy Benes	.05	.02	.01
□	520 Jim Deshaies	.05	.02	.01
□	521 Bruce Hurst	.05	.02	.01
□	522 Randy Myers	.15	.07	.02
□	523 Benito Santiago	.05	.02	.01
□	524 Tim Scott	.05	.02	.01
□	525 Tim Teufel	.05	.02	.01
□	526 Mike Benjamin	.05	.02	.01
□	527 Dave Burba	.05	.02	.01
□	528 Craig Colbert	.05	.02	.01
□	529 Mike Felder	.05	.02	.01
□	530 Bryan Hickerson	.05	.02	.01
□	531 Chris James	.05	.02	.01
□	532 Mark Leonard	.05	.02	.01
□	533 Greg Litton	.05	.02	.01
□	534 Francisco Oliveras	.05	.02	.01
□	535 John Patterson	.05	.02	.01
□	536 Jim Pena	.05	.02	.01
□	537 Dave Righetti	.05	.02	.01
□	538 Robby Thompson	.05	.02	.01
□	539 Jose Uribe	.05	.02	.01
□	540 Matt Williams	.30	.14	.04
□	541 Storm Davis	.05	.02	.01
□	542 Sam Horn	.05	.02	.01
□	543 Tim Hulett	.05	.02	.01
□	544 Craig Lefferts	.05	.02	.01
□	545 Chito Martinez	.05	.02	.01
□	546 Mark McLemore	.05	.02	.01
□	547 Luis Mercedes	.05	.02	.01
□	548 Bob Milacki	.05	.02	.01
□	549 Joe Orsulak	.05	.02	.01
□	550 Billy Ripken	.05	.02	.01
□	551 Cal Ripken Jr.	1.50	.70	.19
□	552 Rick Sutcliffe	.05	.02	.01
□	553 Jeff Tackett	.05	.02	.01
□	554 Wade Boggs	.30	.14	.04
□	555 Tom Brunansky	.05	.02	.01
□	556 Jack Clark	.05	.02	.01
□	557 John Dopson	.05	.02	.01
□	558 Mike Gardiner	.05	.02	.01
□	559 Mike Greenwell	.05	.02	.01
□	560 Greg A. Harris	.05	.02	.01
□	561 Billy Hatcher	.05	.02	.01
□	562 Joe Hesketh	.05	.02	.01
□	563 Tony Pena	.05	.02	.01
□	564 Phil Plantier	.05	.02	.01
□	565 Luis Rivera	.05	.02	.01
□	566 Herm Winningham	.05	.02	.01
□	567 Matt Young	.05	.02	.01
□	568 Bert Blyleven	.15	.07	.02
□	569 Mike Butcher	.05	.02	.01
□	570 Chuck Crim	.05	.02	.01
□	571 Chad Curtis	.15	.07	.02
□	572 Tim Fortugno	.05	.02	.01
□	573 Steve Frey	.05	.02	.01
□	574 Gary Gaetti	.15	.07	.02
□	575 Scott Lewis	.05	.02	.01
□	576 Lee Stevens	.05	.02	.01
□	577 Ron Tingley	.05	.02	.01
□	578 Julio Valera	.05	.02	.01
□	579 Shawn Abner	.05	.02	.01
□	580 Joey Cora	.05	.02	.01
□	581 Chris Cron	.05	.02	.01
□	582 Carlton Fisk	.30	.14	.04
□	583 Roberto Hernandez	.15	.07	.02
□	584 Charlie Hough	.05	.02	.01
□	585 Terry Leach	.05	.02	.01
□	586 Donn Pall	.05	.02	.01
□	587 Dan Pasqua	.05	.02	.01
□	588 Steve Sax	.05	.02	.01
□	589 Bobby Thigpen	.05	.02	.01
□	590 Albert Belle	1.00	.45	.12
□	591 Felix Fermin	.05	.02	.01
□	592 Glenallen Hill	.05	.02	.01
□	593 Brook Jacoby	.05	.02	.01
□	594 Reggie Jefferson	.15	.07	.02
□	595 Carlos Martinez	.05	.02	.01
□	596 Jose Mesa	.15	.07	.02
□	597 Rod Nichols	.05	.02	.01
□	598 Junior Ortiz	.05	.02	.01
□	599 Eric Plunk	.05	.02	.01
□	600 Ted Power	.05	.02	.01
□	601 Scott Scudder	.05	.02	.01
□	602 Kevin Wickander	.05	.02	.01
□	603 Skeeter Barnes	.05	.02	.01
□	604 Mark Carreon	.05	.02	.01
□	605 Dan Gladden	.05	.02	.01
□	606 Bill Gullickson	.05	.02	.01
□	607 Chad Kreuter	.05	.02	.01
□	608 Mark Leiter	.05	.02	.01
□	609 Mike Munoz	.05	.02	.01
□	610 Rich Rowland	.05	.02	.01
□	611 Frank Tanana	.05	.02	.01
□	612 Walt Terrell	.05	.02	.01
□	613 Alan Trammell	.30	.14	.04
□	614 Lou Whitaker	.30	.14	.04
□	615 Luis Aquino	.05	.02	.01
□	616 Mike Boddicker	.05	.02	.01
□	617 Jim Eisenreich	.15	.07	.02
□	618 Mark Gubicza	.05	.02	.01
□	619 David Howard	.05	.02	.01
□	620 Mike Magnante	.05	.02	.01
□	621 Brent Mayne	.05	.02	.01
□	622 Kevin McReynolds	.05	.02	.01
□	623 Ed Pierce	.05	.02	.01
□	624 Bill Sampen	.05	.02	.01
□	625 Steve Shifflett	.05	.02	.01
□	626 Gary Thurman	.05	.02	.01
□	627 Curtis Wilkerson	.05	.02	.01
□	628 Chris Bosio	.05	.02	.01
□	629 Scott Fletcher	.05	.02	.01
□	630 Jim Gantner	.05	.02	.01
□	631 Dave Nilsson	.15	.07	.02
□	632 Jesse Orosco	.05	.02	.01
□	633 Dan Plesac	.05	.02	.01
□	634 Ron Robinson	.05	.02	.01
□	635 Bill Spiers	.05	.02	.01

□	636 Franklin Stubbs	.05	.02	.01
□	637 Willie Banks	.05	.02	.01
□	638 Randy Bush	.05	.02	.01
□	639 Chuck Knoblauch	.30	.14	.04
□	640 Shane Mack	.05	.02	.01
□	641 Mike Pagliarulo	.05	.02	.01
□	642 Jeff Reboulet	.05	.02	.01
□	643 John Smiley	.05	.02	.01
□	644 Mike Trombley	.05	.02	.01
□	645 Gary Wayne	.05	.02	.01
□	646 Lenny Webster	.05	.02	.01
□	647 Tim Burke	.05	.02	.01
□	648 Mike Gallego	.05	.02	.01
□	649 Dion James	.05	.02	.01
□	650 Jeff Johnson	.05	.02	.01
□	651 Scott Kamieniecki	.05	.02	.01
□	652 Kevin Maas	.05	.02	.01
□	653 Rich Monteleone	.05	.02	.01
□	654 Jerry Nielsen	.05	.02	.01
□	655 Scott Sanderson	.05	.02	.01
□	656 Mike Stanley	.05	.02	.01
□	657 Gerald Williams	.05	.02	.01
□	658 Curt Young	.05	.02	.01
□	659 Harold Baines	.15	.07	.02
□	660 Kevin Campbell	.05	.02	.01
□	661 Ron Darling	.05	.02	.01
□	662 Kelly Downs	.05	.02	.01
□	663 Eric Fox	.05	.02	.01
□	664 Dave Henderson	.05	.02	.01
□	665 Rick Honeycutt	.05	.02	.01
□	666 Mike Moore	.05	.02	.01
□	667 Jamie Quirk	.05	.02	.01
□	668 Jeff Russell	.05	.02	.01
□	669 Dave Stewart	.15	.07	.02
□	670 Greg Briley	.05	.02	.01
□	671 Dave Cochrane	.05	.02	.01
□	672 Henry Cotto	.05	.02	.01
□	673 Rich DeLucia	.05	.02	.01
□	674 Brian Fisher	.05	.02	.01
□	675 Mark Grant	.05	.02	.01
□	676 Randy Johnson	.30	.14	.04
□	677 Tim Leary	.05	.02	.01
□	678 Pete O'Brien	.05	.02	.01
□	679 Lance Parrish	.05	.02	.01
□	680 Harold Reynolds	.05	.02	.01
□	681 Shane Turner	.05	.02	.01
□	682 Jack Daugherty	.05	.02	.01
□	683 David Hulse	.05	.02	.01
□	684 Terry Mathews	.05	.02	.01
□	685 Al Newman	.05	.02	.01
□	686 Edwin Nunez	.05	.02	.01
□	687 Rafael Palmeiro	.30	.14	.04
□	688 Roger Pavlik	.15	.07	.02
□	689 Geno Petralli	.05	.02	.01
□	690 Nolan Ryan	1.50	.70	.19
□	691 David Cone	.30	.14	.04
□	692 Alfredo Griffin	.05	.02	.01
□	693 Juan Guzman	.15	.07	.02
□	694 Pat Hentgen	.30	.14	.04
□	695 Randy Knorr	.05	.02	.01
□	696 Bob MacDonald	.05	.02	.01
□	697 Jack Morris	.15	.07	.02
□	698 Ed Sprague	.15	.07	.02
□	699 Dave Stieb	.05	.02	.01
□	700 Pat Tabler	.05	.02	.01
□	701 Mike Timlin	.05	.02	.01
□	702 David Wells	.05	.02	.01
□	703 Eddie Zosky	.05	.02	.01
□	704 Gary Sheffield LL	.30	.14	.04
□	705 Darren Daulton LL	.05	.02	.01
□	706 Marquis Grissom LL	.15	.07	.02
□	707 Greg Maddux LL	.60	.25	.07
□	708 Bill Swift LL	.05	.02	.01
□	709 Juan Gonzalez RT	.30	.14	.04
□	710 Mark McGwire RT	.30	.14	.04
□	711 Cecil Fielder RT	.05	.02	.01
□	712 Albert Belle RT	.50	.23	.06
□	713 Joe Carter RT	.15	.07	.02
□	714 Cecil Fielder SS Frank Thomas Power Brokers	.50	.23	.06
□	715 Larry Walker SS Darren Daulton Unsung Heroes	.15	.07	.02
□	716 Edgar Martinez SS Robin Ventura Hot Corner Hammers	.30	.14	.04
□	717 Roger Clemens SS Dennis Eckersley Start to Finish	.30	.14	.04
□	718 Checklist 361-480	.05	.02	.01
□	719 Checklist 481-600	.05	.02	.01
□	720 Checklist 601-720	.05	.02	.01

1993 Fleer All-Stars

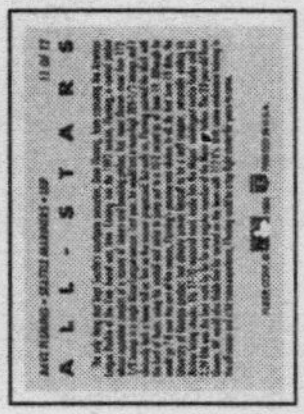

This 24-card standard-size set featuring members of the American and National league All-Star squads, was randomly inserted in wax packs. 12 American League players were seeded in series 1 packs and 12 National League players in series 2. The horizontal fronts feature a color close-up photo cut out and superposed upon a black-and-white action scene framed by white borders. The player's name and the word "All-Stars" are printed in gold foil lettering across the bottom of the picture.

	MINT	NRMT	EXC
COMPLETE SET (24)	40.00	18.00	5.00
COMPLETE SER.1 (12)	25.00	11.00	3.10
COMPLETE SER.2 (12)	15.00	6.75	1.85
COMMON CARD (AL1-AL12)	.75	.35	.09
COMMON CARD (NL1-NL12)	.75	.35	.09
SEMISTARS	1.50	.70	.19
AL: RANDOM INSERTS IN SER.1 PACKS.....			
NL: RANDOM INSERTS IN SER.2 PACKS			

□	AL1 Frank Thomas	12.00	5.50	1.50
□	AL2 Roberto Alomar	3.00	1.35	.35
□	AL3 Edgar Martinez	1.50	.70	.19
□	AL4 Pat Listach	.75	.35	.09
□	AL5 Cecil Fielder	1.50	.70	.19
□	AL6 Juan Gonzalez	6.00	2.70	.75
□	AL7 Ken Griffey Jr.	12.00	5.50	1.50
□	AL8 Joe Carter	1.50	.70	.19
□	AL9 Kirby Puckett	4.00	1.80	.50
□	AL10 Brian Harper	.75	.35	.09
□	AL11 Dave Fleming	.75	.35	.09
□	AL12 Jack McDowell	1.50	.70	.19
□	NL1 Fred McGriff	1.50	.70	.19
□	NL2 Delino DeShields	1.50	.70	.19
□	NL3 Gary Sheffield	2.00	.90	.25
□	NL4 Barry Larkin	1.50	.70	.19
□	NL5 Felix Jose	.75	.35	.09
□	NL6 Larry Walker	1.50	.70	.19
□	NL7 Barry Bonds	3.00	1.35	.35
□	NL8 Andy Van Slyke	1.50	.70	.19
□	NL9 Darren Daulton	1.50	.70	.19
□	NL10 Greg Maddux	8.00	3.60	1.00
□	NL11 Tom Glavine	1.50	.70	.19
□	NL12 Lee Smith	1.50	.70	.19

1993 Fleer Golden Moments

Cards from this six-card standard-size set, featuring memorable moments from the previous season, were randomly inserted in 1993 Fleer wax packs, three each in series 1 and 2. The fronts feature glossy color action photos framed by thin aqua and white lines and a black outer border. A gold foil baseball icon appears at each corner of the picture, and the player's name and the set title "Golden Moments"

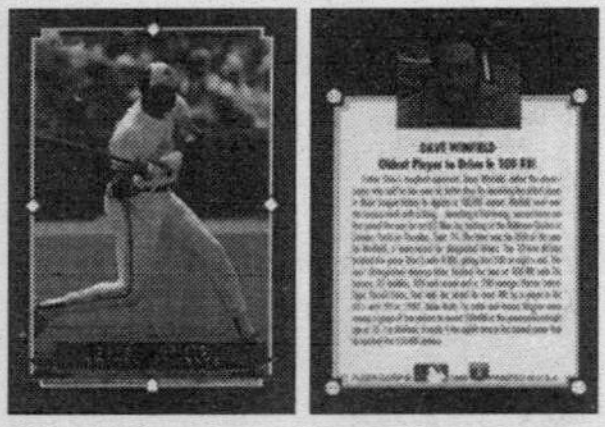

appears in a gold foil bar toward the bottom of the picture. The cards are unnumbered and checklisted below in alphabetical order.

	MINT	NRMT	EXC
COMPLETE SET (6)	16.00	7.25	2.00
COMPLETE SER.1 (3)	6.00	2.70	.75
COMPLETE SER.2 (3)	10.00	4.50	1.25
COMMON SERIES 1 (A1-A3)	.50	.23	.06
COMMON SERIES 2 (B1-B3)	.50	.23	.06
RANDOM INSERTS IN WAX PACKS			

□ A1 George Brett	5.00	2.20	.60
□ A2 Mickey Morandini	.50	.23	.06
□ A3 Dave Winfield	1.00	.45	.12
□ B1 Dennis Eckersley	1.00	.45	.12
□ B2 Bip Roberts	.50	.23	.06
□ B3 Frank Thomas and Juan Gonzalez	8.00	3.60	1.00

1993 Fleer Major League Prospects

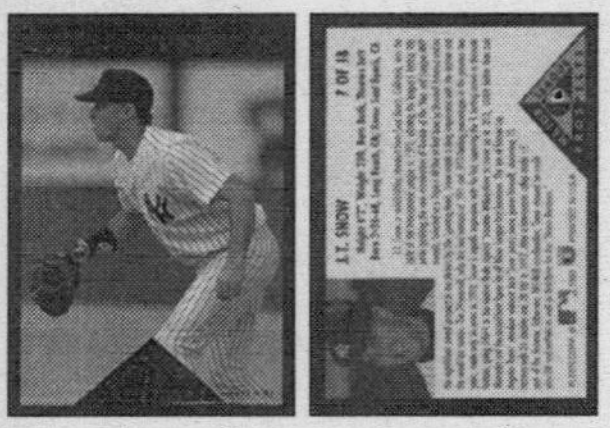

Cards from this 36-card standard-size set, featuring a selection of prospects, were randomly inserted in wax packs, 18 each in series 1 and 2. These cards feature black-bordered color player action photos on their fronts. The player's name appears in gold foil at the top, and the set's name and logo appear in gold foil and black at the bottom. The key card in this set is Mike Piazza.

	MINT	NRMT	EXC
COMPLETE SET (36)	30.00	13.50	3.70
COMPLETE SERIES 1 (18)	20.00	9.00	2.50
COMPLETE SERIES 2 (18)	10.00	4.50	1.25
COMMON SERIES 1 (A1-A18)	.50	.23	.06
COMMON SERIES 2 (B1-B18)	.50	.23	.06
SEMISTARS	1.00	.45	.12
RANDOM INSERTS IN WAX PACKS			

□ A1 Melvin Nieves	1.00	.45	.12
□ A2 Sterling Hitchcock	.50	.23	.06
□ A3 Tim Costo	.50	.23	.06
□ A4 Manny Alexander	.50	.23	.06
□ A5 Alan Embree	.50	.23	.06
□ A6 Kevin Young	.50	.23	.06
□ A7 J.T. Snow	1.00	.45	.12
□ A8 Russ Springer	.50	.23	.06
□ A9 Billy Ashley	.50	.23	.06
□ A10 Kevin Rogers	.50	.23	.06
□ A11 Steve Hosey	.50	.23	.06
□ A12 Eric Wedge	.50	.23	.06
□ A13 Mike Piazza	20.00	9.00	2.50
□ A14 Jesse Levis	.50	.23	.06
□ A15 Rico Brogna	1.00	.45	.12
□ A16 Alex Arias	.50	.23	.06
□ A17 Rod Brewer	.50	.23	.06
□ A18 Troy Neel	.50	.23	.06
□ B1 Scooter Tucker	.50	.23	.06
□ B2 Kerry Woodson	.50	.23	.06
□ B3 Greg Colbrunn	1.00	.45	.12
□ B4 Pedro Martinez	2.00	.90	.25
□ B5 Dave Silvestri	.50	.23	.06
□ B6 Kent Bottenfield	.50	.23	.06
□ B7 Rafael Bournigal	.50	.23	.06
□ B8 J.T. Bruett	.50	.23	.06
□ B9 Dave Mlicki	.50	.23	.06
□ B10 Paul Wagner	.50	.23	.06
□ B11 Mike Williams	.50	.23	.06
□ B12 Henry Mercedes	.50	.23	.06
□ B13 Scott Taylor	.50	.23	.06
□ B14 Dennis Moeller	.50	.23	.06
□ B15 Javier Lopez	5.00	2.20	.60
□ B16 Steve Cooke	.50	.23	.06
□ B17 Pete Young	.50	.23	.06
□ B18 Ken Ryan	.50	.23	.06

1993 Fleer Pro-Visions

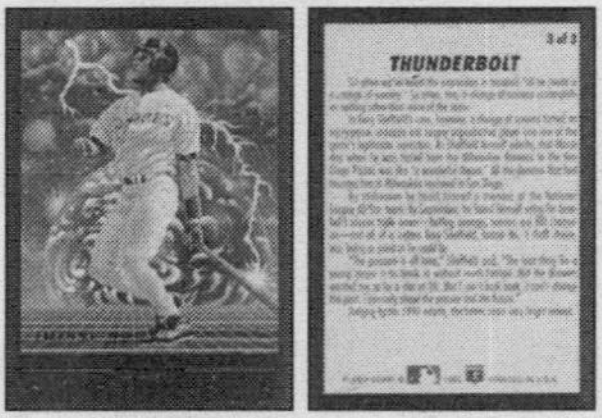

Cards from this six-card standard-size set, featuring a selection of superstars in fantasy paintings, were randomly inserted in poly packs, three each in series 1 and 2. These cards feature black-bordered fanciful color artwork of the players in action. The player's name appears in gold foil within the bottom black margin of each.

	MINT	NRMT	EXC
COMPLETE SET (6)	6.00	2.70	.75
COMPLETE SERIES 1 (3)	4.00	1.80	.50
COMPLETE SERIES 2 (3)	2.00	.90	.25
COMMON SERIES 1 (A1-A3)	.75	.35	.09
COMMON SERIES 2 (B1-B3)	.75	.35	.09
RANDOM INSERTS IN WAX PACKS			

□ A1 Roberto Alomar	3.00	1.35	.35
□ A2 Dennis Eckersley	.75	.35	.09
□ A3 Gary Sheffield	2.00	.90	.25
□ B1 Andy Van Slyke	.75	.35	.09
□ B2 Tom Glavine	1.50	.70	.19
□ B3 Cecil Fielder	.75	.35	.09

1993 Fleer Rookie Sensations

Cards from this 20-card standard-size set, featuring a selection of 1993's top rookies, were randomly inserted in cello packs, 10 each in series 1 and 2. The cards feature blue-bordered fronts with cutout color player photos, each superposed upon a silver-colored background. The set's title and the player's name appear in gold foil in an upper corner. The key card in this set is Kenny Lofton.

	MINT	NRMT	EXC
COMPLETE SET (20)	30.00	13.50	3.70

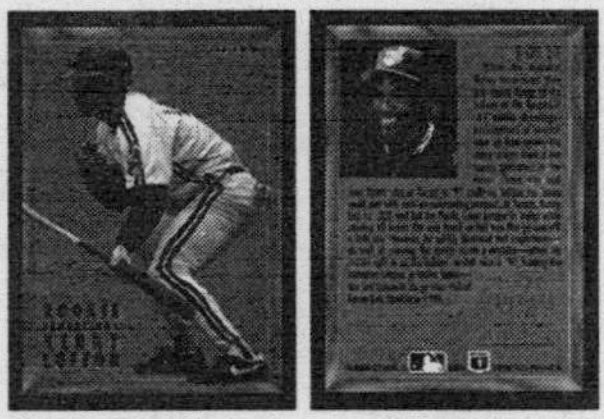

COMPLETE SERIES 1 (10)	20.00	9.00	2.50
COMPLETE SERIES 2 (10)	10.00	4.50	1.25
COMMON CARD (RSA1-RSA10)	1.00	.45	.12
COMMON CARD (RSB1-RSB10)	1.00	.45	.12
SEMISTARS	1.50	.70	.19
RANDOM INSERTS IN CELLO PACKS			

□ RSA1 Kenny Lofton	15.00	6.75	1.85
□ RSA2 Cal Eldred	1.00	.45	.12
□ RSA3 Pat Listach	1.00	.45	.12
□ RSA4 Roberto Hernandez	1.50	.70	.19
□ RSA5 Dave Fleming	1.00	.45	.12
□ RSA6 Eric Karros	3.00	1.35	.35
□ RSA7 Reggie Sanders	3.00	1.35	.35
□ RSA8 Derrick May	1.00	.45	.12
□ RSA9 Mike Perez	1.00	.45	.12
□ RSA10 Donovan Osborne	1.00	.45	.12
□ RSB1 Moises Alou	1.50	.70	.19
□ RSB2 Pedro Astacio	1.00	.45	.12
□ RSB3 Jim Austin	1.00	.45	.12
□ RSB4 Chad Curtis	1.50	.70	.19
□ RSB5 Gary DiSarcina	1.00	.45	.12
□ RSB6 Scott Livingstone	1.00	.45	.12
□ RSB7 Sam Militello	1.00	.45	.12
□ RSB8 Arthur Rhodes	1.00	.45	.12
□ RSB9 Tim Wakefield	1.50	.70	.19
□ RSB10 Bob Zupcic	1.00	.45	.12

1993 Fleer Team Leaders

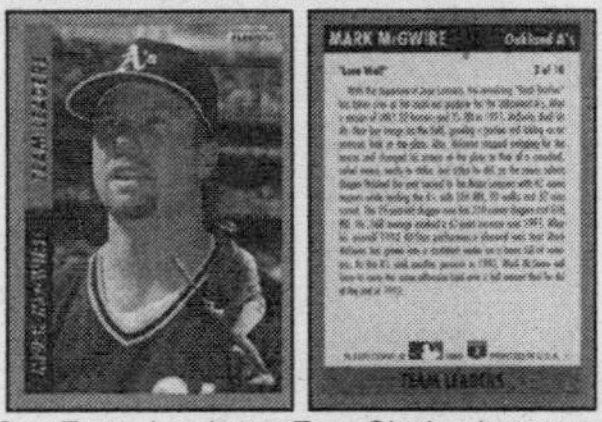

One Team Leader or Tom Glavine insert was seeded into each Fleer rack pack. Series 1 racks included 10 American League players, while series 2 racks included 10 National League players. Each of the tan-bordered standard-size cards comprising this set feature a posed color player photo on its front with a smaller cutout color action photo superposed in a lower corner. The player's name and the set's title appear vertically in gold foil along the left side within team color-coded bars.

	MINT	NRMT	EXC
COMPLETE SET (20)	70.00	32.00	8.75
COMPLETE SERIES 1 (10)	50.00	22.00	6.25
COMPLETE SERIES 2 (10)	20.00	9.00	2.50
COMMON CARD (AL1-AL10)	1.00	.45	.12
COMMON CARD (NL1-NL10)	1.00	.45	.12
SEMISTARS	2.50	1.10	.30
AL IN SERIES 1 NL IN SEARIES 2			
NL: RANDOM INSERTS IN SER.2 PACKS			
ONE TL OR GLAVINE PER RACK PACK			

□ AL1 Kirby Puckett	6.00	2.70	.75
□ AL2 Mark McGwire	6.00	2.70	.75
□ AL3 Pat Listach	1.00	.45	.12
□ AL4 Roger Clemens	2.00	.90	.25
□ AL5 Frank Thomas	20.00	9.00	2.50
□ AL6 Carlos Baerga	2.00	.90	.25
□ AL7 Brady Anderson	2.00	.90	.25
□ AL8 Juan Gonzalez	10.00	4.50	1.25
□ AL9 Roberto Alomar	5.00	2.20	.60
□ AL10 Ken Griffey Jr.	20.00	9.00	2.50
□ NL1 Will Clark	2.00	.90	.25
□ NL2 Terry Pendleton	1.00	.45	.12
□ NL3 Ray Lankford	2.00	.90	.25
□ NL4 Eric Karros	2.00	.90	.25
□ NL5 Gary Sheffield	3.00	1.35	.35
□ NL6 Ryne Sandberg	5.00	2.20	.60
□ NL7 Marquis Grissom	2.00	.90	.25
□ NL8 John Kruk	2.00	.90	.25
□ NL9 Jeff Bagwell	8.00	3.60	1.00
□ NL10 Andy Van Slyke	2.00	.90	.25

1993 Fleer Final Edition

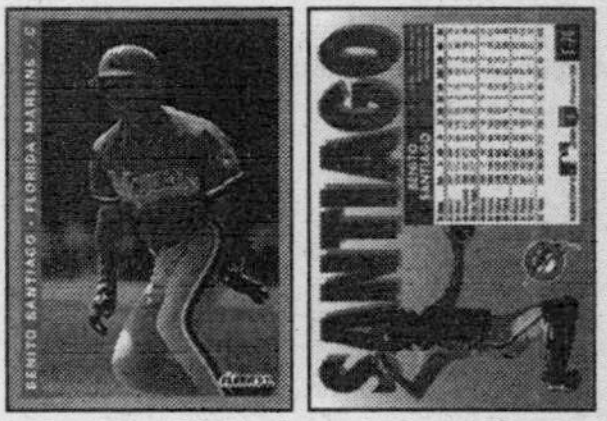

This 300-card standard-size set was issued exclusively in factory set form (along with ten Diamond Tribute inserts) to update and feature rookies not in the regular 1993 Fleer set. The cards are identical in design to regular issue 1993 Fleer cards excpt for the F-prefixed numbering. Cards are ordered alphabetically within teams with NL preceding AL. The set closes with checklist cards (298-300). The only key Rookie Card in this set features Jim Edmonds.

	MINT	NRMT	EXC
COMPLETE FACT.SET (310)	10.00	4.50	1.25
COMPLETE SET (300)	6.00	2.70	.75
COMMON CARD (1-300)	.05	.02	.01
SEMISTARS	.15	.07	.02
STARS	.30	.14	.04
F PREFIX ON REG.CARD NUMBERS			
COMP.DIAM.TRIB.SET (10)	4.00	1.80	.50
COMMON DIA.TRIB (DT1-DT10)	.30	.14	.04
ONE DIAM.TRIB SET PER FACTORY SET			

□ 1 Steve Bedrosian	.05	.02	.01
□ 2 Jay Howell	.05	.02	.01
□ 3 Greg Maddux	1.25	.55	.16
□ 4 Greg McMichael	.15	.07	.02
□ 5 Tony Tarasco	.15	.07	.02
□ 6 Jose Bautista	.05	.02	.01
□ 7 Jose Guzman	.05	.02	.01
□ 8 Greg Hibbard	.05	.02	.01
□ 9 Candy Maldonado	.05	.02	.01
□ 10 Randy Myers	.15	.07	.02
□ 11 Matt Walbeck	.05	.02	.01
□ 12 Turk Wendell	.05	.02	.01
□ 13 Willie Wilson	.05	.02	.01
□ 14 Greg Cadaret	.05	.02	.01
□ 15 Roberto Kelly	.05	.02	.01
□ 16 Randy Milligan	.05	.02	.01
□ 17 Kevin Mitchell	.15	.07	.02
□ 18 Jeff Reardon	.15	.07	.02
□ 19 John Roper	.05	.02	.01
□ 20 John Smiley	.05	.02	.01
□ 21 Andy Ashby	.15	.07	.02
□ 22 Dante Bichette	.30	.14	.04
□ 23 Willie Blair	.05	.02	.01
□ 24 Pedro Castellano	.05	.02	.01

□ 25 Vinny Castilla	.30	.14	.04
□ 26 Jerald Clark	.05	.02	.01
□ 27 Alex Cole	.05	.02	.01
□ 28 Scott Fredrickson	.05	.02	.01
□ 29 Jay Gainer	.05	.02	.01
□ 30 Andres Galarraga	.30	.14	.04
□ 31 Joe Girardi	.05	.02	.01
□ 32 Ryan Hawblitzel	.05	.02	.01
□ 33 Charlie Hayes	.05	.02	.01
□ 34 Darren Holmes	.05	.02	.01
□ 35 Chris Jones	.05	.02	.01
□ 36 David Nied	.05	.02	.01
□ 37 J.Owens	.15	.07	.02
□ 38 Lance Painter	.05	.02	.01
□ 39 Jeff Parrett	.05	.02	.01
□ 40 Steve Reed	.05	.02	.01
□ 41 Armando Reynoso	.05	.02	.01
□ 42 Bruce Ruffin	.05	.02	.01
□ 43 Danny Sheaffer	.05	.02	.01
□ 44 Keith Shepherd	.05	.02	.01
□ 45 Jim Tatum	.05	.02	.01
□ 46 Gary Wayne	.05	.02	.01
□ 47 Eric Young	.30	.14	.04
□ 48 Luis Aquino	.05	.02	.01
□ 49 Alex Arias	.05	.02	.01
□ 50 Jack Armstrong	.05	.02	.01
□ 51 Bret Barberie	.05	.02	.01
□ 52 Geronimo Berroa	.15	.07	.02
□ 53 Ryan Bowen	.05	.02	.01
□ 54 Greg Briley	.05	.02	.01
□ 55 Cris Carpenter	.05	.02	.01
□ 56 Chuck Carr	.05	.02	.01
□ 57 Jeff Conine	.30	.14	.04
□ 58 Jim Corsi	.05	.02	.01
□ 59 Orestes Destrade	.05	.02	.01
□ 60 Junior Felix	.05	.02	.01
□ 61 Chris Hammond	.05	.02	.01
□ 62 Bryan Harvey	.05	.02	.01
□ 63 Charlie Hough	.05	.02	.01
□ 64 Joe Klink	.05	.02	.01
□ 65 Richie Lewis UER (Refers to place of birth and residence as Illinois instead of Indiana)	.05	.02	.01
□ 66 Mitch Lyden	.05	.02	.01
□ 67 Bob Natal	.05	.02	.01
□ 68 Scott Pose	.05	.02	.01
□ 69 Rich Renteria	.05	.02	.01
□ 70 Benito Santiago	.05	.02	.01
□ 71 Gary Sheffield	.30	.14	.04
□ 72 Matt Turner	.05	.02	.01
□ 73 Walt Weiss	.05	.02	.01
□ 74 Darrell Whitmore	.05	.02	.01
□ 75 Nigel Wilson	.05	.02	.01
□ 76 Kevin Bass	.05	.02	.01
□ 77 Doug Drabek	.05	.02	.01
□ 78 Tom Edens	.05	.02	.01
□ 79 Chris James	.05	.02	.01
□ 80 Greg Swindell	.05	.02	.01
□ 81 Omar Daal	.15	.07	.02
□ 82 Raul Mondesi	.60	.25	.07
□ 83 Jody Reed	.05	.02	.01
□ 84 Cory Snyder	.05	.02	.01
□ 85 Rick Trlicek	.05	.02	.01
□ 86 Tim Wallach	.05	.02	.01
□ 87 Todd Worrell	.05	.02	.01
□ 88 Tavo Alvarez	.05	.02	.01
□ 89 Frank Bolick	.05	.02	.01
□ 90 Kent Bottenfield	.05	.02	.01
□ 91 Greg Colbrunn	.05	.02	.01
□ 92 Cliff Floyd	.30	.14	.04
□ 93 Lou Frazier	.05	.02	.01
□ 94 Mike Gardiner	.05	.02	.01
□ 95 Mike Lansing	.15	.07	.02
□ 96 Bill Risley	.05	.02	.01
□ 97 Jeff Shaw	.05	.02	.01
□ 98 Kevin Baez	.05	.02	.01
□ 99 Tim Bogar	.05	.02	.01
□ 100 Jeromy Burnitz	.05	.02	.01
□ 101 Mike Draper	.05	.02	.01
□ 102 Darrin Jackson	.05	.02	.01
□ 103 Mike Maddux	.05	.02	.01
□ 104 Joe Orsulak	.05	.02	.01
□ 105 Doug Saunders	.05	.02	.01
□ 106 Frank Tanana	.05	.02	.01
□ 107 Dave Telgheder	.05	.02	.01
□ 108 Larry Andersen	.05	.02	.01
□ 109 Jim Eisenreich	.15	.07	.02
□ 110 Pete Incaviglia	.05	.02	.01
□ 111 Danny Jackson	.05	.02	.01
□ 112 David West	.05	.02	.01
□ 113 Al Martin	.15	.07	.02
□ 114 Blas Minor	.05	.02	.01
□ 115 Dennis Moeller	.05	.02	.01
□ 116 William Pennyfeather	.05	.02	.01
□ 117 Rich Robertson	.05	.02	.01
□ 118 Ben Shelton	.05	.02	.01
□ 119 Lonnie Smith	.05	.02	.01
□ 120 Freddie Toliver	.05	.02	.01
□ 121 Paul Wagner	.05	.02	.01
□ 122 Kevin Young	.05	.02	.01
□ 123 Rene Arocha	.05	.02	.01
□ 124 Gregg Jefferies	.30	.14	.04
□ 125 Paul Kilgus	.05	.02	.01
□ 126 Les Lancaster	.05	.02	.01
□ 127 Joe Magrane	.05	.02	.01
□ 128 Rob Murphy	.05	.02	.01
□ 129 Erik Pappas	.05	.02	.01
□ 130 Stan Royer	.05	.02	.01
□ 131 Ozzie Smith	.40	.18	.05
□ 132 Tom Urbani	.05	.02	.01
□ 133 Mark Whiten	.05	.02	.01
□ 134 Derek Bell	.30	.14	.04
□ 135 Doug Brocail	.05	.02	.01
□ 136 Phil Clark	.05	.02	.01
□ 137 Mark Ettles	.05	.02	.01
□ 138 Jeff Gardner	.05	.02	.01
□ 139 Pat Gomez	.05	.02	.01
□ 140 Ricky Gutierrez	.05	.02	.01
□ 141 Gene Harris	.05	.02	.01
□ 142 Kevin Higgins	.05	.02	.01
□ 143 Trevor Hoffman	.15	.07	.02
□ 144 Phil Plantier	.05	.02	.01
□ 145 Kerry Taylor	.05	.02	.01
□ 146 Guillermo Velasquez	.05	.02	.01
□ 147 Wally Whitehurst	.05	.02	.01
□ 148 Tim Worrell	.05	.02	.01
□ 149 Todd Benzinger	.05	.02	.01
□ 150 Barry Bonds	.50	.23	.06
□ 151 Greg Brummett	.05	.02	.01
□ 152 Mark Carreon	.05	.02	.01
□ 153 Dave Martinez	.05	.02	.01
□ 154 Jeff Reed	.05	.02	.01
□ 155 Kevin Rogers	.05	.02	.01
□ 156 Harold Baines	.15	.07	.02
□ 157 Damon Buford	.05	.02	.01
□ 158 Paul Carey	.05	.02	.01
□ 159 Jeffrey Hammonds	.15	.07	.02
□ 160 Jamie Moyer	.05	.02	.01
□ 161 Sherman Obando	.05	.02	.01
□ 162 John O'Donoghue	.05	.02	.01
□ 163 Brad Pennington	.05	.02	.01
□ 164 Jim Poole	.05	.02	.01
□ 165 Harold Reynolds	.05	.02	.01
□ 166 Fernando Valenzuela	.15	.07	.02
□ 167 Jack Voigt	.05	.02	.01
□ 168 Mark Williamson	.05	.02	.01
□ 169 Scott Bankhead	.05	.02	.01
□ 170 Greg Blosser	.05	.02	.01
□ 171 Jim Byrd	.05	.02	.01
□ 172 Ivan Calderon	.05	.02	.01
□ 173 Andre Dawson	.30	.14	.04
□ 174 Scott Fletcher	.05	.02	.01
□ 175 Jose Melendez	.05	.02	.01
□ 176 Carlos Quintana	.05	.02	.01
□ 177 Jeff Russell	.05	.02	.01
□ 178 Aaron Sele	.15	.07	.02
□ 179 Rod Correia	.05	.02	.01
□ 180 Chili Davis	.15	.07	.02
□ 181 Jim Edmonds	1.50	.70	.19
□ 182 Rene Gonzales	.05	.02	.01
□ 183 Hilly Hathaway	.05	.02	.01
□ 184 Torey Lovullo	.05	.02	.01
□ 185 Greg Myers	.05	.02	.01
□ 186 Gene Nelson	.05	.02	.01
□ 187 Troy Percival	.15	.07	.02
□ 188 Scott Sanderson	.05	.02	.01
□ 189 Darryl Scott	.05	.02	.01
□ 190 J.T. Snow	.30	.14	.04
□ 191 Russ Springer	.05	.02	.01
□ 192 Jason Bere	.15	.07	.02
□ 193 Rodney Bolton	.05	.02	.01
□ 194 Ellis Burks	.30	.14	.04

□ 195 Bo Jackson	.30	.14	.04
□ 196 Mike LaValliere	.05	.02	.01
□ 197 Scott Ruffcorn	.05	.02	.01
□ 198 Jeff Schwartz	.05	.02	.01
□ 199 Jerry DiPoto	.05	.02	.01
□ 200 Alvaro Espinoza	.05	.02	.01
□ 201 Wayne Kirby	.05	.02	.01
□ 202 Tom Kramer	.05	.02	.01
□ 203 Jesse Levis	.05	.02	.01
□ 204 Manny Ramirez	1.25	.55	.16
□ 205 Jeff Treadway	.05	.02	.01
□ 206 Bill Wertz	.05	.02	.01
□ 207 Cliff Young	.05	.02	.01
□ 208 Matt Young	.05	.02	.01
□ 209 Kirk Gibson	.15	.07	.02
□ 210 Greg Gohr	.05	.02	.01
□ 211 Bill Krueger	.05	.02	.01
□ 212 Bob MacDonald	.05	.02	.01
□ 213 Mike Moore	.05	.02	.01
□ 214 David Wells	.05	.02	.01
□ 215 Billy Brewer	.05	.02	.01
□ 216 David Cone	.30	.14	.04
□ 217 Greg Gagne	.05	.02	.01
□ 218 Mark Gardner	.05	.02	.01
□ 219 Chris Haney	.05	.02	.01
□ 220 Phil Hiatt	.05	.02	.01
□ 221 Jose Lind	.05	.02	.01
□ 222 Juan Bell	.05	.02	.01
□ 223 Tom Brunansky	.05	.02	.01
□ 224 Mike Ignasiak	.05	.02	.01
□ 225 Joe Kmak	.05	.02	.01
□ 226 Tom Lampkin	.05	.02	.01
□ 227 Graeme Lloyd	.05	.02	.01
□ 228 Carlos Maldonado	.05	.02	.01
□ 229 Matt Mieske	.15	.07	.02
□ 230 Angel Miranda	.05	.02	.01
□ 231 Troy O'Leary	.30	.14	.04
□ 232 Kevin Reimer	.05	.02	.01
□ 233 Larry Casian	.05	.02	.01
□ 234 Jim Deshaies	.05	.02	.01
□ 235 Eddie Guardado	.05	.02	.01
□ 236 Chip Hale	.05	.02	.01
□ 237 Mike Maksudian	.05	.02	.01
□ 238 David McCarty	.05	.02	.01
□ 239 Pat Meares	.15	.07	.02
□ 240 George Tsamis	.05	.02	.01
□ 241 Dave Winfield	.30	.14	.04
□ 242 Jim Abbott	.05	.02	.01
□ 243 Wade Boggs	.30	.14	.04
□ 244 Andy Cook	.05	.02	.01
□ 245 Russ Davis	.15	.07	.02
□ 246 Mike Humphreys	.05	.02	.01
□ 247 Jimmy Key	.15	.07	.02
□ 248 Jim Leyritz	.05	.02	.01
□ 249 Bobby Munoz	.05	.02	.01
□ 250 Paul O'Neill	.15	.07	.02
□ 251 Spike Owen	.05	.02	.01
□ 252 Dave Silvestri	.05	.02	.01
□ 253 Marcos Armas	.05	.02	.01
□ 254 Brent Gates	.15	.07	.02
□ 255 Goose Gossage	.15	.07	.02
□ 256 Scott Lydy	.05	.02	.01
□ 257 Henry Mercedes	.05	.02	.01
□ 258 Mike Mohler	.05	.02	.01
□ 259 Troy Neel	.05	.02	.01
□ 260 Edwin Nunez	.05	.02	.01
□ 261 Craig Paquette	.05	.02	.01
□ 262 Kevin Seitzer	.05	.02	.01
□ 263 Rich Amaral	.05	.02	.01
□ 264 Mike Blowers	.05	.02	.01
□ 265 Chris Bosio	.05	.02	.01
□ 266 Norm Charlton	.05	.02	.01
□ 267 Jim Converse	.05	.02	.01
□ 268 John Cummings	.05	.02	.01
□ 269 Mike Felder	.05	.02	.01
□ 270 Mike Hampton	.05	.02	.01
□ 271 Bill Haselman	.05	.02	.01
□ 272 Dwayne Henry	.05	.02	.01
□ 273 Greg Litton	.05	.02	.01
□ 274 Mackey Sasser	.05	.02	.01
□ 275 Lee Tinsley	.15	.07	.02
□ 276 David Wainhouse	.05	.02	.01
□ 277 Jeff Bronkey	.05	.02	.01
□ 278 Benji Gil	.15	.07	.02
□ 279 Tom Henke	.05	.02	.01
□ 280 Charlie Leibrandt	.05	.02	.01
□ 281 Robb Nen	.15	.07	.02
□ 282 Bill Ripken	.05	.02	.01
□ 283 Jon Shave	.05	.02	.01
□ 284 Doug Strange	.05	.02	.01
□ 285 Matt Whiteside	.05	.02	.01
□ 286 Scott Brow	.05	.02	.01
□ 287 Willie Canate	.05	.02	.01
□ 288 Tony Castillo	.05	.02	.01
□ 289 Domingo Cedeno	.05	.02	.01
□ 290 Darnell Coles	.05	.02	.01
□ 291 Danny Cox	.05	.02	.01
□ 292 Mark Eichhorn	.05	.02	.01
□ 293 Tony Fernandez	.05	.02	.01
□ 294 Al Leiter	.15	.07	.02
□ 295 Paul Molitor	.40	.18	.05
□ 296 Dave Stewart	.15	.07	.02
□ 297 Woody Williams	.05	.02	.01
□ 298 Checklist F1-F100	.05	.02	.01
□ 299 Checklist F101-F200	.05	.02	.01
□ 300 Checklist F201-F300	.05	.02	.01
□ DT1 Wade Boggs	.50	.23	.06
□ DT2 George Brett	1.25	.55	.16
□ DT3 Andre Dawson	.50	.23	.06
□ DT4 Carlton Fisk	.50	.23	.06
□ DT5 Paul Molitor	.60	.25	.07
□ DT6 Nolan Ryan	3.00	1.35	.35
□ DT7 Lee Smith	.15	.07	.02
□ DT8 Ozzie Smith	.60	.25	.07
□ DT9 Dave Winfield	.50	.23	.06
□ DT10 Robin Yount	.50	.23	.06

1994 Fleer

The 1994 Fleer baseball set consists of 720 standard-size cards. The white-bordered fronts feature color player action photos. In one corner, the player's name and position appear in a gold foil lettered arc; his team logo appears within. The backs are also white-bordered and feature a color player photo, some action, others posed. One side of the picture is ghosted and color-screened, and carries the player's name, biography, and career highlights. The bottom of the photo is also color-screened and ghosted, and carries the player's statistics. The cards are numbered on the back, grouped alphabetically within teams, and checklisted below alphabetically according to teams for each league as follows: Baltimore Orioles (1-24), Boston Red Sox (25-47), California Angels (48-72), Chicago White Sox (73-97), Cleveland Indians (98-123), Detroit Tigers (124-146), Kansas City Royals (147-172), Milwaukee Brewers (173-197), Minnesota Twins (198-223), New York Yankees (224-251), Oakland Athletics (252-277), Seattle Mariners (278-301), Texas Rangers (302-323), Toronto Blue Jays (324-349), Atlanta Braves (350-378), Chicago Cubs (379-403), Cincinnati Reds (404-431), Colorado Rockies (432-457), Florida Marlins (458-481), Houston Astros (482-503), Los Angeles Dodgers (504-530), Montreal Expos (531-556), New York Mets (557-580), Philadelphia Phillies (581-604), Pittsburgh Pirates (605-626), St. Louis Cardinals (627-651), San Diego Padres (652-679), and San Francisco Giants (680-705). The set closes with a Superstar Specials (706-713) subset. There are no key Rookie Cards in this set.

	MINT	NRMT	EXC
COMPLETE SET (720)	60.00	27.00	7.50
COMMON CARD (1-720)	.10	.05	.01
SEMISTARS	.25	.11	.03
STARS	.50	.23	.06
COMP.SALMON SET (12)	25.00	11.00	3.10
COMMON SALMON (1-12)	2.50	1.10	.30
CERTIFIED SALMON AU			
SALMON: RANDOM INSERTS IN ALL PACKS			
COMMON SALM.EXCH. (13-15)	2.50	1.10	.30
SALMON EXCH. AVAIL VIA WRAPPER EXCH.			

	MINT	NRMT	EXC
□ 1 Brady Anderson	.50	.23	.06
□ 2 Harold Baines	.25	.11	.03
□ 3 Mike Devereaux	.10	.05	.01
□ 4 Todd Frohwirth	.10	.05	.01
□ 5 Jeffrey Hammonds	.25	.11	.03
□ 6 Chris Hoiles	.10	.05	.01
□ 7 Tim Hulett	.10	.05	.01
□ 8 Ben McDonald	.10	.05	.01
□ 9 Mark McLemore	.10	.05	.01
□ 10 Alan Mills	.10	.05	.01
□ 11 Jamie Moyer	.10	.05	.01
□ 12 Mike Mussina	.60	.25	.07
□ 13 Gregg Olson	.10	.05	.01
□ 14 Mike Pagliarulo	.10	.05	.01
□ 15 Brad Pennington	.10	.05	.01
□ 16 Jim Poole	.10	.05	.01
□ 17 Harold Reynolds	.10	.05	.01
□ 18 Arthur Rhodes	.10	.05	.01
□ 19 Cal Ripken Jr.	2.50	1.10	.30
□ 20 David Segui	.10	.05	.01
□ 21 Rick Sutcliffe	.10	.05	.01
□ 22 Fernando Valenzuela	.25	.11	.03
□ 23 Jack Voigt	.10	.05	.01
□ 24 Mark Williamson	.10	.05	.01
□ 25 Scott Bankhead	.10	.05	.01
□ 26 Roger Clemens	.50	.23	.06
□ 27 Scott Cooper	.10	.05	.01
□ 28 Danny Darwin	.10	.05	.01
□ 29 Andre Dawson	.50	.23	.06
□ 30 Rob Deer	.10	.05	.01
□ 31 John Dopson	.10	.05	.01
□ 32 Scott Fletcher	.10	.05	.01
□ 33 Mike Greenwell	.10	.05	.01
□ 34 Greg A. Harris	.10	.05	.01
□ 35 Billy Hatcher	.10	.05	.01
□ 36 Bob Melvin	.10	.05	.01
□ 37 Tony Pena	.10	.05	.01
□ 38 Paul Quantrill	.10	.05	.01
□ 39 Carlos Quintana	.10	.05	.01
□ 40 Ernest Riles	.10	.05	.01
□ 41 Jeff Russell	.10	.05	.01
□ 42 Ken Ryan	.10	.05	.01
□ 43 Aaron Sele	.25	.11	.03
□ 44 John Valentin	.25	.11	.03
□ 45 Mo Vaughn	.75	.35	.09
□ 46 Frank Viola	.10	.05	.01
□ 47 Bob Zupcic	.10	.05	.01
□ 48 Mike Butcher	.10	.05	.01
□ 49 Rod Correia	.10	.05	.01
□ 50 Chad Curtis	.10	.05	.01
□ 51 Chili Davis	.25	.11	.03
□ 52 Gary DiSarcina	.10	.05	.01
□ 53 Damion Easley	.10	.05	.01
□ 54 Jim Edmonds	.60	.25	.07
□ 55 Chuck Finley	.10	.05	.01
□ 56 Steve Frey	.10	.05	.01
□ 57 Rene Gonzales	.10	.05	.01
□ 58 Joe Grahe	.10	.05	.01
□ 59 Hilly Hathaway	.10	.05	.01
□ 60 Stan Javier	.10	.05	.01
□ 61 Mark Langston	.25	.11	.03
□ 62 Phil Leftwich	.10	.05	.01
□ 63 Torey Lovullo	.10	.05	.01
□ 64 Joe Magrane	.10	.05	.01
□ 65 Greg Myers	.10	.05	.01
□ 66 Ken Patterson	.10	.05	.01
□ 67 Eduardo Perez	.10	.05	.01
□ 68 Luis Polonia	.10	.05	.01
□ 69 Tim Salmon	.50	.23	.06
□ 70 J.T. Snow	.25	.11	.03
□ 71 Ron Tingley	.10	.05	.01
□ 72 Julio Valera	.10	.05	.01
□ 73 Wilson Alvarez	.25	.11	.03
□ 74 Tim Belcher	.10	.05	.01
□ 75 George Bell	.10	.05	.01
□ 76 Jason Bere	.25	.11	.03
□ 77 Rod Bolton	.10	.05	.01
□ 78 Ellis Burks	.25	.11	.03
□ 79 Joey Cora	.10	.05	.01
□ 80 Alex Fernandez	.50	.23	.06
□ 81 Craig Grebeck	.10	.05	.01
□ 82 Ozzie Guillen	.10	.05	.01
□ 83 Roberto Hernandez	.25	.11	.03
□ 84 Bo Jackson	.50	.23	.06
□ 85 Lance Johnson	.25	.11	.03
□ 86 Ron Karkovice	.10	.05	.01
□ 87 Mike LaValliere	.10	.05	.01
□ 88 Kirk McCaskill	.10	.05	.01
□ 89 Jack McDowell	.25	.11	.03
□ 90 Warren Newson	.10	.05	.01
□ 91 Dan Pasqua	.10	.05	.01
□ 92 Scott Radinsky	.10	.05	.01
□ 93 Tim Raines	.50	.23	.06
□ 94 Steve Sax	.10	.05	.01
□ 95 Jeff Schwarz	.10	.05	.01
□ 96 Frank Thomas	3.00	1.35	.35
□ 97 Robin Ventura	.25	.11	.03
□ 98 Sandy Alomar Jr.	.25	.11	.03
□ 99 Carlos Baerga	.50	.23	.06
□ 100 Albert Belle	1.50	.70	.19
□ 101 Mark Clark	.10	.05	.01
□ 102 Jerry DiPoto	.10	.05	.01
□ 103 Alvaro Espinoza	.10	.05	.01
□ 104 Felix Fermin	.10	.05	.01
□ 105 Jeremy Hernandez	.10	.05	.01
□ 106 Reggie Jefferson	.25	.11	.03
□ 107 Wayne Kirby	.10	.05	.01
□ 108 Tom Kramer	.10	.05	.01
□ 109 Mark Lewis	.10	.05	.01
□ 110 Derek Lilliquist	.10	.05	.01
□ 111 Kenny Lofton	1.00	.45	.12
□ 112 Candy Maldonado	.10	.05	.01
□ 113 Jose Mesa	.25	.11	.03
□ 114 Jeff Mutis	.10	.05	.01
□ 115 Charles Nagy	.25	.11	.03
□ 116 Bob Ojeda	.10	.05	.01
□ 117 Junior Ortiz	.10	.05	.01
□ 118 Eric Plunk	.10	.05	.01
□ 119 Manny Ramirez	1.00	.45	.12
□ 120 Paul Sorrento	.10	.05	.01
□ 121 Jim Thome	.75	.35	.09
□ 122 Jeff Treadway	.10	.05	.01
□ 123 Bill Wertz	.10	.05	.01
□ 124 Skeeter Barnes	.10	.05	.01
□ 125 Milt Cuyler	.10	.05	.01
□ 126 Eric Davis	.25	.11	.03
□ 127 John Doherty	.10	.05	.01
□ 128 Cecil Fielder	.25	.11	.03
□ 129 Travis Fryman	.50	.23	.06
□ 130 Kirk Gibson	.25	.11	.03
□ 131 Dan Gladden	.10	.05	.01
□ 132 Greg Gohr	.10	.05	.01
□ 133 Chris Gomez	.10	.05	.01
□ 134 Bill Gullickson	.10	.05	.01
□ 135 Mike Henneman	.10	.05	.01
□ 136 Kurt Knudsen	.10	.05	.01
□ 137 Chad Kreuter	.10	.05	.01
□ 138 Bill Krueger	.10	.05	.01
□ 139 Scott Livingstone	.10	.05	.01
□ 140 Bob MacDonald	.10	.05	.01
□ 141 Mike Moore	.10	.05	.01
□ 142 Tony Phillips	.25	.11	.03
□ 143 Mickey Tettleton	.10	.05	.01
□ 144 Alan Trammell	.50	.23	.06
□ 145 David Wells	.10	.05	.01
□ 146 Lou Whitaker	.50	.23	.06
□ 147 Kevin Appier	.25	.11	.03
□ 148 Stan Belinda	.10	.05	.01
□ 149 George Brett	1.25	.55	.16
□ 150 Billy Brewer	.10	.05	.01
□ 151 Hubie Brooks	.10	.05	.01
□ 152 David Cone	.50	.23	.06
□ 153 Gary Gaetti	.25	.11	.03
□ 154 Greg Gagne	.10	.05	.01
□ 155 Tom Gordon	.10	.05	.01
□ 156 Mark Gubicza	.10	.05	.01
□ 157 Chris Gwynn	.10	.05	.01
□ 158 John Habyan	.10	.05	.01
□ 159 Chris Haney	.10	.05	.01
□ 160 Phil Hiatt	.10	.05	.01

□ 161	Felix Jose	.10	.05	.01
□ 162	Wally Joyner	.25	.11	.03
□ 163	Jose Lind	.10	.05	.01
□ 164	Mike Macfarlane	.10	.05	.01
□ 165	Mike Magnante	.10	.05	.01
□ 166	Brent Mayne	.10	.05	.01
□ 167	Brian McRae	.25	.11	.03
□ 168	Kevin McReynolds	.10	.05	.01
□ 169	Keith Miller	.10	.05	.01
□ 170	Jeff Montgomery	.25	.11	.03
□ 171	Hipolito Pichardo	.10	.05	.01
□ 172	Rico Rossy	.10	.05	.01
□ 173	Juan Bell	.10	.05	.01
□ 174	Ricky Bones	.10	.05	.01
□ 175	Cal Eldred	.10	.05	.01
□ 176	Mike Fetters	.10	.05	.01
□ 177	Darryl Hamilton	.10	.05	.01
□ 178	Doug Henry	.10	.05	.01
□ 179	Mike Ignasiak	.10	.05	.01
□ 180	John Jaha	.25	.11	.03
□ 181	Pat Listach	.10	.05	.01
□ 182	Graeme Lloyd	.10	.05	.01
□ 183	Matt Mieske	.10	.05	.01
□ 184	Angel Miranda	.10	.05	.01
□ 185	Jaime Navarro	.10	.05	.01
□ 186	Dave Nilsson	.25	.11	.03
□ 187	Troy O'Leary	.10	.05	.01
□ 188	Jesse Orosco	.10	.05	.01
□ 189	Kevin Reimer	.10	.05	.01
□ 190	Kevin Seitzer	.10	.05	.01
□ 191	Bill Spiers	.10	.05	.01
□ 192	B.J. Surhoff	.10	.05	.01
□ 193	Dickie Thon	.10	.05	.01
□ 194	Jose Valentin	.25	.11	.03
□ 195	Greg Vaughn	.50	.23	.06
□ 196	Bill Wegman	.10	.05	.01
□ 197	Robin Yount	.50	.23	.06
□ 198	Rick Aguilera	.10	.05	.01
□ 199	Willie Banks	.10	.05	.01
□ 200	Bernardo Brito	.10	.05	.01
□ 201	Larry Casian	.10	.05	.01
□ 202	Scott Erickson	.10	.05	.01
□ 203	Eddie Guardado	.10	.05	.01
□ 204	Mark Guthrie	.10	.05	.01
□ 205	Chip Hale	.10	.05	.01
□ 206	Brian Harper	.10	.05	.01
□ 207	Mike Hartley	.10	.05	.01
□ 208	Kent Hrbek	.25	.11	.03
□ 209	Terry Jorgensen	.10	.05	.01
□ 210	Chuck Knoblauch	.50	.23	.06
□ 211	Gene Larkin	.10	.05	.01
□ 212	Shane Mack	.10	.05	.01
□ 213	David McCarty	.10	.05	.01
□ 214	Pat Meares	.10	.05	.01
□ 215	Pedro Munoz	.10	.05	.01
□ 216	Derek Parks	.10	.05	.01
□ 217	Kirby Puckett	1.00	.45	.12
□ 218	Jeff Reboulet	.10	.05	.01
□ 219	Kevin Tapani	.10	.05	.01
□ 220	Mike Trombley	.10	.05	.01
□ 221	George Tsamis	.10	.05	.01
□ 222	Carl Willis	.10	.05	.01
□ 223	Dave Winfield	.50	.23	.06
□ 224	Jim Abbott	.10	.05	.01
□ 225	Paul Assenmacher	.10	.05	.01
□ 226	Wade Boggs	.50	.23	.06
□ 227	Russ Davis	.25	.11	.03
□ 228	Steve Farr	.10	.05	.01
□ 229	Mike Gallego	.10	.05	.01
□ 230	Paul Gibson	.10	.05	.01
□ 231	Steve Howe	.10	.05	.01
□ 232	Dion James	.10	.05	.01
□ 233	Domingo Jean	.10	.05	.01
□ 234	Scott Kamieniecki	.10	.05	.01
□ 235	Pat Kelly	.10	.05	.01
□ 236	Jimmy Key	.25	.11	.03
□ 237	Jim Leyritz	.10	.05	.01
□ 238	Kevin Maas	.10	.05	.01
□ 239	Don Mattingly	1.50	.70	.19
□ 240	Rich Monteleone	.10	.05	.01
□ 241	Bobby Munoz	.10	.05	.01
□ 242	Matt Nokes	.10	.05	.01
□ 243	Paul O'Neill	.25	.11	.03
□ 244	Spike Owen	.10	.05	.01
□ 245	Melido Perez	.10	.05	.01
□ 246	Lee Smith	.25	.11	.03

□ 247	Mike Stanley	.10	.05	.01
□ 248	Danny Tartabull	.10	.05	.01
□ 249	Randy Velarde	.10	.05	.01
□ 250	Bob Wickman	.10	.05	.01
□ 251	Bernie Williams	.50	.23	.06
□ 252	Mike Aldrete	.10	.05	.01
□ 253	Marcos Armas	.10	.05	.01
□ 254	Lance Blankenship	.10	.05	.01
□ 255	Mike Bordick	.10	.05	.01
□ 256	Scott Brosius	.10	.05	.01
□ 257	Jerry Browne	.10	.05	.01
□ 258	Ron Darling	.10	.05	.01
□ 259	Kelly Downs	.10	.05	.01
□ 260	Dennis Eckersley	.25	.11	.03
□ 261	Brent Gates	.10	.05	.01
□ 262	Goose Gossage	.25	.11	.03
□ 263	Scott Hemond	.10	.05	.01
□ 264	Dave Henderson	.10	.05	.01
□ 265	Rick Honeycutt	.10	.05	.01
□ 266	Vince Horsman	.10	.05	.01
□ 267	Scott Lydy	.10	.05	.01
□ 268	Mark McGwire	1.00	.45	.12
□ 269	Mike Mohler	.10	.05	.01
□ 270	Troy Neel	.10	.05	.01
□ 271	Edwin Nunez	.10	.05	.01
□ 272	Craig Paquette	.10	.05	.01
□ 273	Ruben Sierra	.25	.11	.03
□ 274	Terry Steinbach	.25	.11	.03
□ 275	Todd Van Poppel	.10	.05	.01
□ 276	Bob Welch	.10	.05	.01
□ 277	Bobby Witt	.10	.05	.01
□ 278	Rich Amaral	.10	.05	.01
□ 279	Mike Blowers	.10	.05	.01
□ 280	Bret Boone UER (Name spelled Brett on front)	.25	.11	.03
□ 281	Chris Bosio	.10	.05	.01
□ 282	Jay Buhner	.50	.23	.06
□ 283	Norm Charlton	.10	.05	.01
□ 284	Mike Felder	.10	.05	.01
□ 285	Dave Fleming	.10	.05	.01
□ 286	Ken Griffey Jr.	3.00	1.35	.35
□ 287	Erik Hanson	.10	.05	.01
□ 288	Bill Haselman	.10	.05	.01
□ 289	Brad Holman	.10	.05	.01
□ 290	Randy Johnson	.50	.23	.06
□ 291	Tim Leary	.10	.05	.01
□ 292	Greg Litton	.10	.05	.01
□ 293	Dave Magadan	.10	.05	.01
□ 294	Edgar Martinez	.50	.23	.06
□ 295	Tino Martinez	.25	.11	.03
□ 296	Jeff Nelson	.10	.05	.01
□ 297	Erik Plantenberg	.10	.05	.01
□ 298	Mackey Sasser	.10	.05	.01
□ 299	Brian Turang	.10	.05	.01
□ 300	Dave Valle	.10	.05	.01
□ 301	Omar Vizquel	.50	.23	.06
□ 302	Brian Bohanon	.10	.05	.01
□ 303	Kevin Brown	.10	.05	.01
□ 304	Jose Canseco UER (Back mentions 1991 as his 40/40 MVP season; should be '88)	.50	.23	.06
□ 305	Mario Diaz	.10	.05	.01
□ 306	Julio Franco	.25	.11	.03
□ 307	Juan Gonzalez	1.50	.70	.19
□ 308	Tom Henke	.10	.05	.01
□ 309	David Hulse	.10	.05	.01
□ 310	Manuel Lee	.10	.05	.01
□ 311	Craig Lefferts	.10	.05	.01
□ 312	Charlie Leibrandt	.10	.05	.01
□ 313	Rafael Palmeiro	.50	.23	.06
□ 314	Dean Palmer	.25	.11	.03
□ 315	Roger Pavlik	.10	.05	.01
□ 316	Dan Peltier	.10	.05	.01
□ 317	Gene Petralli	.10	.05	.01
□ 318	Gary Redus	.10	.05	.01
□ 319	Ivan Rodriguez	.60	.25	.07
□ 320	Kenny Rogers	.10	.05	.01
□ 321	Nolan Ryan	2.50	1.10	.30
□ 322	Doug Strange	.10	.05	.01
□ 323	Matt Whiteside	.10	.05	.01
□ 324	Roberto Alomar	.75	.35	.09
□ 325	Pat Borders	.10	.05	.01
□ 326	Joe Carter	.50	.23	.06
□ 327	Tony Castillo	.10	.05	.01
□ 328	Darnell Coles	.10	.05	.01
□ 329	Danny Cox	.10	.05	.01

□	330 Mark Eichhorn	.10	.05	.01
□	331 Tony Fernandez	.10	.05	.01
□	332 Alfredo Griffin	.10	.05	.01
□	333 Juan Guzman	.25	.11	.03
□	334 Rickey Henderson	.50	.23	.06
□	335 Pat Hentgen	.50	.23	.06
□	336 Randy Knorr	.10	.05	.01
□	337 Al Leiter	.25	.11	.03
□	338 Paul Molitor	.60	.25	.07
□	339 Jack Morris	.25	.11	.03
□	340 John Olerud	.10	.05	.01
□	341 Dick Schofield	.10	.05	.01
□	342 Ed Sprague	.25	.11	.03
□	343 Dave Stewart	.25	.11	.03
□	344 Todd Stottlemyre	.10	.05	.01
□	345 Mike Timlin	.10	.05	.01
□	346 Duane Ward	.10	.05	.01
□	347 Turner Ward	.10	.05	.01
□	348 Devon White	.10	.05	.01
□	349 Woody Williams	.10	.05	.01
□	350 Steve Avery	.25	.11	.03
□	351 Steve Bedrosian	.10	.05	.01
□	352 Rafael Belliard	.10	.05	.01
□	353 Damon Berryhill	.10	.05	.01
□	354 Jeff Blauser	.10	.05	.01
□	355 Sid Bream	.10	.05	.01
□	356 Francisco Cabrera	.10	.05	.01
□	357 Marvin Freeman	.10	.05	.01
□	358 Ron Gant	.25	.11	.03
□	359 Tom Glavine	.50	.23	.06
□	360 Jay Howell	.10	.05	.01
□	361 David Justice	.50	.23	.06
□	362 Ryan Klesko	.75	.35	.09
□	363 Mark Lemke	.10	.05	.01
□	364 Javier Lopez	.50	.23	.06
□	365 Greg Maddux	2.00	.90	.25
□	366 Fred McGriff	.50	.23	.06
□	367 Greg McMichael	.10	.05	.01
□	368 Kent Mercker	.10	.05	.01
□	369 Otis Nixon	.10	.05	.01
□	370 Greg Olson	.10	.05	.01
□	371 Bill Pecota	.10	.05	.01
□	372 Terry Pendleton	.25	.11	.03
□	373 Deion Sanders	.50	.23	.06
□	374 Pete Smith	.10	.05	.01
□	375 John Smoltz	.50	.23	.06
□	376 Mike Stanton	.10	.05	.01
□	377 Tony Tarasco	.10	.05	.01
□	378 Mark Wohlers	.25	.11	.03
□	379 Jose Bautista	.10	.05	.01
□	380 Shawn Boskie	.10	.05	.01
□	381 Steve Buechele	.10	.05	.01
□	382 Frank Castillo	.10	.05	.01
□	383 Mark Grace	.50	.23	.06
□	384 Jose Guzman	.10	.05	.01
□	385 Mike Harkey	.10	.05	.01
□	386 Greg Hibbard	.10	.05	.01
□	387 Glenallen Hill	.10	.05	.01
□	388 Steve Lake	.10	.05	.01
□	389 Derrick May	.10	.05	.01
□	390 Chuck McElroy	.10	.05	.01
□	391 Mike Morgan	.10	.05	.01
□	392 Randy Myers	.10	.05	.01
□	393 Dan Plesac	.10	.05	.01
□	394 Kevin Roberson	.10	.05	.01
□	395 Rey Sanchez	.10	.05	.01
□	396 Ryne Sandberg	.75	.35	.09
□	397 Bob Scanlan	.10	.05	.01
□	398 Dwight Smith	.10	.05	.01
□	399 Sammy Sosa	.50	.23	.06
□	400 Jose Vizcaino	.10	.05	.01
□	401 Rick Wilkins	.10	.05	.01
□	402 Willie Wilson	.10	.05	.01
□	403 Eric Yelding	.10	.05	.01
□	404 Bobby Ayala	.10	.05	.01
□	405 Jeff Branson	.10	.05	.01
□	406 Tom Browning	.10	.05	.01
□	407 Jacob Brumfield	.10	.05	.01
□	408 Tim Costo	.10	.05	.01
□	409 Rob Dibble	.10	.05	.01
□	410 Willie Greene	.25	.11	.03
□	411 Thomas Howard	.10	.05	.01
□	412 Roberto Kelly	.10	.05	.01
□	413 Bill Landrum	.10	.05	.01
□	414 Barry Larkin	.50	.23	.06
□	415 Larry Luebbers	.10	.05	.01
□	416 Kevin Mitchell	.25	.11	.03
□	417 Hal Morris	.10	.05	.01
□	418 Joe Oliver	.10	.05	.01
□	419 Tim Pugh	.10	.05	.01
□	420 Jeff Reardon	.25	.11	.03
□	421 Jose Rijo	.10	.05	.01
□	422 Bip Roberts	.10	.05	.01
□	423 John Roper	.10	.05	.01
□	424 Johnny Ruffin	.10	.05	.01
□	425 Chris Sabo	.10	.05	.01
□	426 Juan Samuel	.10	.05	.01
□	427 Reggie Sanders	.50	.23	.06
□	428 Scott Service	.10	.05	.01
□	429 John Smiley	.10	.05	.01
□	430 Jerry Spradlin	.10	.05	.01
□	431 Kevin Wickander	.10	.05	.01
□	432 Freddie Benavides	.10	.05	.01
□	433 Dante Bichette	.50	.23	.06
□	434 Willie Blair	.10	.05	.01
□	435 Daryl Boston	.10	.05	.01
□	436 Kent Bottenfield	.10	.05	.01
□	437 Vinny Castilla	.50	.23	.06
□	438 Jerald Clark	.10	.05	.01
□	439 Alex Cole	.10	.05	.01
□	440 Andres Galarraga	.50	.23	.06
□	441 Joe Girardi	.10	.05	.01
□	442 Greg W. Harris	.10	.05	.01
□	443 Charlie Hayes	.10	.05	.01
□	444 Darren Holmes	.10	.05	.01
□	445 Chris Jones	.10	.05	.01
□	446 Roberto Mejia	.10	.05	.01
□	447 David Nied	.10	.05	.01
□	448 J. Owens	.10	.05	.01
□	449 Jeff Parrett	.10	.05	.01
□	450 Steve Reed	.10	.05	.01
□	451 Armando Reynoso	.10	.05	.01
□	452 Bruce Ruffin	.10	.05	.01
□	453 Mo Sanford	.10	.05	.01
□	454 Danny Sheaffer	.10	.05	.01
□	455 Jim Tatum	.10	.05	.01
□	456 Gary Wayne	.10	.05	.01
□	457 Eric Young	.25	.11	.03
□	458 Luis Aquino	.10	.05	.01
□	459 Alex Arias	.10	.05	.01
□	460 Jack Armstrong	.10	.05	.01
□	461 Bret Barberie	.10	.05	.01
□	462 Ryan Bowen	.10	.05	.01
□	463 Chuck Carr	.10	.05	.01
□	464 Jeff Conine	.50	.23	.06
□	465 Henry Cotto	.10	.05	.01
□	466 Orestes Destrade	.10	.05	.01
□	467 Chris Hammond	.10	.05	.01
□	468 Bryan Harvey	.10	.05	.01
□	469 Charlie Hough	.10	.05	.01
□	470 Joe Klink	.10	.05	.01
□	471 Richie Lewis	.10	.05	.01
□	472 Bob Natal	.10	.05	.01
□	473 Pat Rapp	.10	.05	.01
□	474 Rich Renteria	.10	.05	.01
□	475 Rich Rodriguez	.10	.05	.01
□	476 Benito Santiago	.10	.05	.01
□	477 Gary Sheffield	.50	.23	.06
□	478 Matt Turner	.10	.05	.01
□	479 David Weathers	.10	.05	.01
□	480 Walt Weiss	.10	.05	.01
□	481 Darrell Whitmore	.10	.05	.01
□	482 Eric Anthony	.10	.05	.01
□	483 Jeff Bagwell	1.25	.55	.16
□	484 Kevin Bass	.10	.05	.01
□	485 Craig Biggio	.50	.23	.06
□	486 Ken Caminiti	.50	.23	.06
□	487 Andujar Cedeno	.10	.05	.01
□	488 Chris Donnels	.10	.05	.01
□	489 Doug Drabek	.10	.05	.01
□	490 Steve Finley	.50	.23	.06
□	491 Luis Gonzalez	.10	.05	.01
□	492 Pete Harnisch	.10	.05	.01
□	493 Xavier Hernandez	.10	.05	.01
□	494 Doug Jones	.10	.05	.01
□	495 Todd Jones	.10	.05	.01
□	496 Darryl Kile	.10	.05	.01
□	497 Al Osuna	.10	.05	.01
□	498 Mark Portugal	.10	.05	.01
□	499 Scott Servais	.10	.05	.01
□	500 Greg Swindell	.10	.05	.01
□	501 Eddie Taubensee	.10	.05	.01

□ 502	Jose Uribe	.10	.05	.01
□ 503	Brian Williams	.10	.05	.01
□ 504	Billy Ashley	.10	.05	.01
□ 505	Pedro Astacio	.10	.05	.01
□ 506	Brett Butler	.25	.11	.03
□ 507	Tom Candiotti	.10	.05	.01
□ 508	Omar Daal	.10	.05	.01
□ 509	Jim Gott	.10	.05	.01
□ 510	Kevin Gross	.10	.05	.01
□ 511	Dave Hansen	.10	.05	.01
□ 512	Carlos Hernandez	.10	.05	.01
□ 513	Orel Hershiser	.25	.11	.03
□ 514	Eric Karros	.25	.11	.03
□ 515	Pedro Martinez	.50	.23	.06
□ 516	Ramon Martinez	.25	.11	.03
□ 517	Roger McDowell	.10	.05	.01
□ 518	Raul Mondesi	.50	.23	.06
□ 519	Jose Offerman	.10	.05	.01
□ 520	Mike Piazza	2.00	.90	.25
□ 521	Jody Reed	.10	.05	.01
□ 522	Henry Rodriguez	.50	.23	.06
□ 523	Mike Sharperson	.10	.05	.01
□ 524	Cory Snyder	.10	.05	.01
□ 525	Darryl Strawberry	.25	.11	.03
□ 526	Rick Trlicek	.10	.05	.01
□ 527	Tim Wallach	.10	.05	.01
□ 528	Mitch Webster	.10	.05	.01
□ 529	Steve Wilson	.10	.05	.01
□ 530	Todd Worrell	.10	.05	.01
□ 531	Moises Alou	.25	.11	.03
□ 532	Brian Barnes	.10	.05	.01
□ 533	Sean Berry	.10	.05	.01
□ 534	Greg Colbrunn	.10	.05	.01
□ 535	Delino DeShields	.10	.05	.01
□ 536	Jeff Fassero	.10	.05	.01
□ 537	Darrin Fletcher	.10	.05	.01
□ 538	Cliff Floyd	.50	.23	.06
□ 539	Lou Frazier	.10	.05	.01
□ 540	Marquis Grissom	.50	.23	.06
□ 541	Butch Henry	.10	.05	.01
□ 542	Ken Hill	.10	.05	.01
□ 543	Mike Lansing	.25	.11	.03
□ 544	Brian Looney	.10	.05	.01
□ 545	Dennis Martinez	.25	.11	.03
□ 546	Chris Nabholz	.10	.05	.01
□ 547	Randy Ready	.10	.05	.01
□ 548	Mel Rojas	.10	.05	.01
□ 549	Kirk Rueter	.10	.05	.01
□ 550	Tim Scott	.10	.05	.01
□ 551	Jeff Shaw	.10	.05	.01
□ 552	Tim Spehr	.10	.05	.01
□ 553	John VanderWal	.10	.05	.01
□ 554	Larry Walker	.50	.23	.06
□ 555	John Wetteland	.25	.11	.03
□ 556	Rondell White	.50	.23	.06
□ 557	Tim Bogar	.10	.05	.01
□ 558	Bobby Bonilla	.25	.11	.03
□ 559	Jeromy Burnitz	.10	.05	.01
□ 560	Sid Fernandez	.10	.05	.01
□ 561	John Franco	.10	.05	.01
□ 562	Dave Gallagher	.10	.05	.01
□ 563	Dwight Gooden	.25	.11	.03
□ 564	Eric Hillman	.10	.05	.01
□ 565	Todd Hundley	.50	.23	.06
□ 566	Jeff Innis	.10	.05	.01
□ 567	Darrin Jackson	.10	.05	.01
□ 568	Howard Johnson	.10	.05	.01
□ 569	Bobby Jones	.25	.11	.03
□ 570	Jeff Kent	.10	.05	.01
□ 571	Mike Maddux	.10	.05	.01
□ 572	Jeff McKnight	.10	.05	.01
□ 573	Eddie Murray	.75	.35	.09
□ 574	Charlie O'Brien	.10	.05	.01
□ 575	Joe Orsulak	.10	.05	.01
□ 576	Bret Saberhagen	.25	.11	.03
□ 577	Pete Schourek	.25	.11	.03
□ 578	Dave Telgheder	.10	.05	.01
□ 579	Ryan Thompson	.10	.05	.01
□ 580	Anthony Young	.10	.05	.01
□ 581	Ruben Amaro	.10	.05	.01
□ 582	Larry Andersen	.10	.05	.01
□ 583	Kim Batiste	.10	.05	.01
□ 584	Wes Chamberlain	.10	.05	.01
□ 585	Darren Daulton	.25	.11	.03
□ 586	Mariano Duncan	.10	.05	.01
□ 587	Lenny Dykstra	.25	.11	.03
□ 588	Jim Eisenreich	.10	.05	.01
□ 589	Tommy Greene	.10	.05	.01
□ 590	Dave Hollins	.10	.05	.01
□ 591	Pete Incaviglia	.10	.05	.01
□ 592	Danny Jackson	.10	.05	.01
□ 593	Ricky Jordan	.10	.05	.01
□ 594	John Kruk	.25	.11	.03
□ 595	Roger Mason	.10	.05	.01
□ 596	Mickey Morandini	.10	.05	.01
□ 597	Terry Mulholland	.10	.05	.01
□ 598	Todd Pratt	.10	.05	.01
□ 599	Ben Rivera	.10	.05	.01
□ 600	Curt Schilling	.10	.05	.01
□ 601	Kevin Stocker	.10	.05	.01
□ 602	Milt Thompson	.10	.05	.01
□ 603	David West	.10	.05	.01
□ 604	Mitch Williams	.10	.05	.01
□ 605	Jay Bell	.25	.11	.03
□ 606	Dave Clark	.10	.05	.01
□ 607	Steve Cooke	.10	.05	.01
□ 608	Tom Foley	.10	.05	.01
□ 609	Carlos Garcia	.10	.05	.01
□ 610	Joel Johnston	.10	.05	.01
□ 611	Jeff King	.25	.11	.03
□ 612	Al Martin	.10	.05	.01
□ 613	Lloyd McClendon	.10	.05	.01
□ 614	Orlando Merced	.25	.11	.03
□ 615	Blas Minor	.10	.05	.01
□ 616	Denny Neagle	.25	.11	.03
□ 617	Mark Petkovsek	.10	.05	.01
□ 618	Tom Prince	.10	.05	.01
□ 619	Don Slaught	.10	.05	.01
□ 620	Zane Smith	.10	.05	.01
□ 621	Randy Tomlin	.10	.05	.01
□ 622	Andy Van Slyke	.25	.11	.03
□ 623	Paul Wagner	.10	.05	.01
□ 624	Tim Wakefield	.10	.05	.01
□ 625	Bob Walk	.10	.05	.01
□ 626	Kevin Young	.10	.05	.01
□ 627	Luis Alicea	.10	.05	.01
□ 628	Rene Arocha	.10	.05	.01
□ 629	Rod Brewer	.10	.05	.01
□ 630	Rheal Cormier	.10	.05	.01
□ 631	Bernard Gilkey	.25	.11	.03
□ 632	Lee Guetterman	.10	.05	.01
□ 633	Gregg Jefferies	.50	.23	.06
□ 634	Brian Jordan	.50	.23	.06
□ 635	Les Lancaster	.10	.05	.01
□ 636	Ray Lankford	.50	.23	.06
□ 637	Rob Murphy	.10	.05	.01
□ 638	Omar Olivares	.10	.05	.01
□ 639	Jose Oquendo	.10	.05	.01
□ 640	Donovan Osborne	.10	.05	.01
□ 641	Tom Pagnozzi	.10	.05	.01
□ 642	Erik Pappas	.10	.05	.01
□ 643	Geronimo Pena	.10	.05	.01
□ 644	Mike Perez	.10	.05	.01
□ 645	Gerald Perry	.10	.05	.01
□ 646	Ozzie Smith	.60	.25	.07
□ 647	Bob Tewksbury	.10	.05	.01
□ 648	Allen Watson	.10	.05	.01
□ 649	Mark Whiten	.10	.05	.01
□ 650	Tracy Woodson	.10	.05	.01
□ 651	Todd Zeile	.10	.05	.01
□ 652	Andy Ashby	.25	.11	.03
□ 653	Brad Ausmus	.10	.05	.01
□ 654	Billy Bean	.10	.05	.01
□ 655	Derek Bell	.25	.11	.03
□ 656	Andy Benes	.25	.11	.03
□ 657	Doug Brocail	.10	.05	.01
□ 658	Jarvis Brown	.10	.05	.01
□ 659	Archi Cianfrocco	.10	.05	.01
□ 660	Phil Clark	.10	.05	.01
□ 661	Mark Davis	.10	.05	.01
□ 662	Jeff Gardner	.10	.05	.01
□ 663	Pat Gomez	.10	.05	.01
□ 664	Ricky Gutierrez	.10	.05	.01
□ 665	Tony Gwynn	1.25	.55	.16
□ 666	Gene Harris	.10	.05	.01
□ 667	Kevin Higgins	.10	.05	.01
□ 668	Trevor Hoffman	.25	.11	.03
□ 669	Pedro Martinez	.10	.05	.01
□ 670	Tim Mauser	.10	.05	.01
□ 671	Melvin Nieves	.25	.11	.03
□ 672	Phil Plantier	.10	.05	.01
□ 673	Frank Seminara	.10	.05	.01

□ 674	Craig Shipley	.10	.05	.01
□ 675	Kerry Taylor	.10	.05	.01
□ 676	Tim Teufel	.10	.05	.01
□ 677	Guillermo Velasquez	.10	.05	.01
□ 678	Wally Whitehurst	.10	.05	.01
□ 679	Tim Worrell	.10	.05	.01
□ 680	Rod Beck	.25	.11	.03
□ 681	Mike Benjamin	.10	.05	.01
□ 682	Todd Benzinger	.10	.05	.01
□ 683	Bud Black	.10	.05	.01
□ 684	Barry Bonds	.75	.35	.09
□ 685	Jeff Brantley	.10	.05	.01
□ 686	Dave Burba	.10	.05	.01
□ 687	John Burkett	.10	.05	.01
□ 688	Mark Carreon	.10	.05	.01
□ 689	Will Clark	.50	.23	.06
□ 690	Royce Clayton	.25	.11	.03
□ 691	Bryan Hickerson	.10	.05	.01
□ 692	Mike Jackson	.10	.05	.01
□ 693	Darren Lewis	.10	.05	.01
□ 694	Kirt Manwaring	.10	.05	.01
□ 695	Dave Martinez	.10	.05	.01
□ 696	Willie McGee	.10	.05	.01
□ 697	John Patterson	.10	.05	.01
□ 698	Jeff Reed	.10	.05	.01
□ 699	Kevin Rogers	.10	.05	.01
□ 700	Scott Sanderson	.10	.05	.01
□ 701	Steve Scarsone	.10	.05	.01
□ 702	Billy Swift	.10	.05	.01
□ 703	Robby Thompson	.10	.05	.01
□ 704	Matt Williams	.50	.23	.06
□ 705	Trevor Wilson	.10	.05	.01
□ 706	Brave New World Fred McGriff Ron Gant David Justice	.50	.23	.06
□ 707	1-2 Punch John Olerud Paul Molitor	.25	.11	.03
□ 708	American Heat Mike Mussina Jack McDowell	.25	.11	.03
□ 709	Together Again Lou Whitaker Alan Trammell	.50	.23	.06
□ 710	Lone Star Lumber Rafael Palmeiro Juan Gonzalez	.50	.23	.06
□ 711	Batmen Brett Butler Tony Gwynn	.50	.23	.06
□ 712	Twin Peaks Kirby Puckett Chuck Knoblauch	.50	.23	.06
□ 713	Back to Back Mike Piazza Eric Karros	.60	.25	.07
□ 714	Checklist 1	.10	.05	.01
□ 715	Checklist 2	.10	.05	.01
□ 716	Checklist 3	.10	.05	.01
□ 717	Checklist 4	.10	.05	.01
□ 718	Checklist 5	.10	.05	.01
□ 719	Checklist 6	.10	.05	.01
□ 720	Checklist 7	.10	.05	.01
□ P69	Tim Salmon Promo	1.50	.70	.19

1994 Fleer All-Rookies

Collectors could redeem an All-Rookie Team Exchange card by mail for this nine-card set of top 1994 rookies at each position as chosen by Fleer. The expiration date to remeem this set was September 30, 1994. None of these players were in the basic 1994 Fleer set. The exchange card was randomly inserted into all pack types.

	MINT	NRMT	EXC
COMPLETE SET (9)	8.00	3.60	1.00
COMMON CARD (M1-M9)	.50	.23	.06
SEMISTARS	.75	.35	.09
ONE SET PER EXCHANGE CARD VIA MAIL			

□ M1	Kurt Abbott	.75	.35	.09
□ M2	Rich Becker	.75	.35	.09

□ M3	Carlos Delgado	4.00	1.80	.50
□ M4	Jorge Fabregas	.50	.23	.06
□ M5	Bob Hamelin	.50	.23	.06
□ M6	John Hudek	.50	.23	.06
□ M7	Tim Hyers	.50	.23	.06
□ M8	Luis S.Lopez	.50	.23	.06
□ M9	James Mouton	.50	.23	.06
□ NNO	Expired All-Rookie Exch.	1.50	.70	.19

1994 Fleer All-Stars

Fleer issued this 50-card standard-size set in 1994, to commemorate the All-Stars of the 1993 season. The cards were exclusively available in the Fleer wax packs at a rate of one in two. The set features 25 American League (1-25) and 25 National League (26-50) All-Stars. The full-bleed fronts feature color action player cut-out photos with an American flag background. The player's name is stamped in gold foil along the bottom edge adjacent to a 1993 All-Stars Game logo. The borderless backs carry a similar flag background with a player head shot near the bottom. The player's name and career highlights round out the back. Each league's all-stars are sequenced in alphabetical order.

	MINT	NRMT	EXC
COMPLETE SET (50)	25.00	11.00	3.10
COMMON CARD (1-50)	.25	.11	.03
SEMISTARS	.50	.23	.06
RANDOM INSERTS IN FOIL PACKS			

□ 1	Roberto Alomar	1.00	.45	.12
□ 2	Carlos Baerga	.50	.23	.06
□ 3	Albert Belle	2.00	.90	.25
□ 4	Wade Boggs	.50	.23	.06
□ 5	Joe Carter	.50	.23	.06
□ 6	Scott Cooper	.25	.11	.03
□ 7	Cecil Fielder	.50	.23	.06
□ 8	Travis Fryman	.50	.23	.06
□ 9	Juan Gonzalez	2.00	.90	.25
□ 10	Ken Griffey Jr.	4.00	1.80	.50
□ 11	Pat Hentgen	.50	.23	.06
□ 12	Randy Johnson	.60	.25	.07
□ 13	Jimmy Key	.25	.11	.03
□ 14	Mark Langston	.25	.11	.03
□ 15	Jack McDowell	.25	.11	.03
□ 16	Paul Molitor	.75	.35	.09
□ 17	Jeff Montgomery	.25	.11	.03
□ 18	Mike Mussina	.75	.35	.09
□ 19	John Olerud	.25	.11	.03

□ 20	Kirby Puckett	1.25	.55	.16
□ 21	Cal Ripken	3.00	1.35	.35
□ 22	Ivan Rodriguez	.75	.35	.09
□ 23	Frank Thomas	4.00	1.80	.50
□ 24	Greg Vaughn	.25	.11	.03
□ 25	Duane Ward	.25	.11	.03
□ 26	Steve Avery	.25	.11	.03
□ 27	Rod Beck	.25	.11	.03
□ 28	Jay Bell	.25	.11	.03
□ 29	Andy Benes	.25	.11	.03
□ 30	Jeff Blauser	.25	.11	.03
□ 31	Barry Bonds	1.00	.45	.12
□ 32	Bobby Bonilla	.50	.23	.06
□ 33	John Burkett	.25	.11	.03
□ 34	Darren Daulton	.50	.23	.06
□ 35	Andres Galarraga	.50	.23	.06
□ 36	Tom Glavine	.50	.23	.06
□ 37	Mark Grace	.50	.23	.06
□ 38	Marquis Grissom	.50	.23	.06
□ 39	Tony Gwynn	1.50	.70	.19
□ 40	Bryan Harvey	.25	.11	.03
□ 41	Dave Hollins	.25	.11	.03
□ 42	David Justice	.50	.23	.06
□ 43	Darryl Kile	.25	.11	.03
□ 44	John Kruk	.25	.11	.03
□ 45	Barry Larkin	.50	.23	.06
□ 46	Terry Mulholland	.25	.11	.03
□ 47	Mike Piazza	2.50	1.10	.30
□ 48	Ryne Sandberg	1.00	.45	.12
□ 49	Gary Sheffield	.60	.25	.07
□ 50	John Smoltz	.60	.25	.07

1994 Fleer Award Winners

Randomly inserted in foil packs at a rate of one in 37, this six-card standard-size set spotlights six outstanding players who received awards. Inside beige borders, the horizontal fronts feature three views of the same color player photo. The words "Fleer Award Winners" and the player's name are printed in gold foil toward the bottom. The backs have a similar design to the fronts, only with one color player cutout and a season summary.

	MINT	NRMT	EXC
COMPLETE SET (6)	12.00	5.50	1.50
COMMON CARD (1-6)	.50	.23	.06
RANDOM INSERTS IN ALL PACKS			

□ 1	Frank Thomas	5.00	2.20	.60
□ 2	Barry Bonds	1.25	.55	.16
□ 3	Jack McDowell	.50	.23	.06
□ 4	Greg Maddux	3.00	1.35	.35
□ 5	Tim Salmon	.75	.35	.09
□ 6	Mike Piazza	3.00	1.35	.35

1994 Fleer Golden Moments

Standard-size and jumbo-size (3 1/2" by 5") Golden Moments were distributed in various forms. The standard-size cards were issued one per blue retail jumbo pack. A shrink-wrapped package containing a jumbo set was issued one per Fleer hobby case. Jumbos were later issued for retail purposes. The front feature borderless color player action photos. The player's name, along with his golden moment accomplishment, appear in gold foil at the bottom. The set's title appears in gold foil at the top. The back carries another borderless color player photo, which fades on one side into a color background for the white-lettered narrative of the player's golden moment. The production number out of a total of 10,000 appears near the bottom of the jumbos. The standard-size cards are not individually numbered.

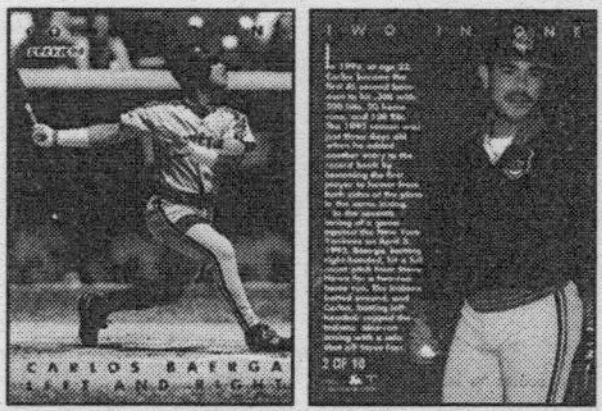

	MINT	NRMT	EXC
COMPLETE SET (10)	40.00	18.00	5.00
COMMON CARD (1-10)	.75	.35	.09
SEMISTARS	1.50	.70	.19
ONE PER BLUE RETAIL JUMBO PACK			
*JUMBO GM's: SAME VALUE			
ONE JUMBO SET PER HOBBY CASE			
JUMBOS ALSO REPACKAGED FOR RETAIL.			

□ 1	Mark Whiten	.75	.35	.09
□ 2	Carlos Baerga	1.50	.70	.19
□ 3	Dave Winfield	1.00	.45	.12
□ 4	Ken Griffey Jr.	12.00	5.50	1.50
□ 5	Bo Jackson	1.50	.70	.19
□ 6	George Brett	5.00	2.20	.60
□ 7	Nolan Ryan	12.00	5.50	1.50
□ 8	Fred McGriff	1.50	.70	.19
□ 9	Frank Thomas	12.00	5.50	1.50
□ 10	Chris Bosio Jim Abbott Darryl Kile	.75	.35	.09

1994 Fleer League Leaders

Randomly inserted in all pack types at arate of one in 17, this 28-card set features six statistical leaders each for the American (1-6) and the National (7-12) Leagues. Inside a beige border, the fronts feature a color action player cutout superimposed on a black-and-white player photo. The player's name and the set title are gold foil stamped in the bottom border, while the player's achievement is printed vertically along the right edge of the picture. The horizontal backs have a color close-up shot on the left portion and a player summary on the right.

	MINT	NRMT	EXC
COMPLETE SET (12)	6.00	2.70	.75
COMMON CARD (1-12)	.25	.11	.03
SEMISTARS	.50	.23	.06
RANDOM INSERTS IN ALL PACKS			

□ 1	John Olerud	.25	.11	.03
□ 2	Albert Belle	2.50	1.10	.30

□ 3 Rafael Palmeiro	.50	.23	.06
□ 4 Kenny Lofton	1.50	.70	.19
□ 5 Jack McDowell	.50	.23	.06
□ 6 Kevin Appier	.50	.23	.06
□ 7 Andres Galarraga	.50	.23	.06
□ 8 Barry Bonds	1.25	.55	.16
□ 9 Lenny Dykstra	.50	.23	.06
□ 10 Chuck Carr	.25	.11	.03
□ 11 Tom Glavine UER No number on back of card	.50	.23	.06
□ 12 Greg Maddux	3.00	1.35	.35

1994 Fleer Lumber Company

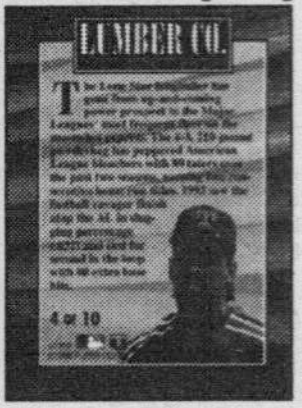

Randomly inserted in jumbo packs at a rate of one in five, this ten-card standard-size set features the best hitters in the game. The full-bleed fronts have a color action player cutout on a wood background. The player's name, team name, and the set title "Lumber Company" appear in an oval-shaped seal burned in the wood, just as one would find on a bat. On a background consisting of wooden bats laying on infield sand, the backs present a color headshot and a player profile on a ghosted panel. The cards are numbered alphabetically.

	MINT	NRMT	EXC
COMPLETE SET (10)	12.00	5.50	1.50
COMMON CARD (1-10)	.40	.18	.05
SEMISTARS	.60	.25	.07
RANDOM INSERTS IN JUMBO PACKS			

□ 1 Albert Belle	2.50	1.10	.30
□ 2 Barry Bonds	1.25	.55	.16
□ 3 Ron Gant	.60	.25	.07
□ 4 Juan Gonzalez	2.50	1.10	.30
□ 5 Ken Griffey Jr.	5.00	2.20	.60
□ 6 David Justice	.40	.18	.05
□ 7 Fred McGriff	.60	.25	.07
□ 8 Rafael Palmeiro	.60	.25	.07
□ 9 Frank Thomas	5.00	2.20	.60
□ 10 Matt Williams	.60	.25	.07

1994 Fleer Major League Prospects

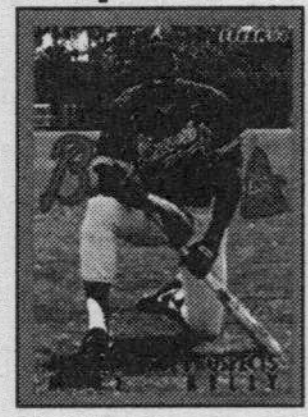

Randomly inserted in all pack types at a rate of one in six, this 35-card standard-size set showcases some of the outstanding young players in Major League Baseball. Inside beige borders, the fronts display color action photos superimposed over ghosted versions of the team logos. The set title and the player's name are gold foil stamped across the bottom of the card. On a beige background with thin blue pinstripes, the backs show a color player cutout and, on a powder blue panel, a player profile. The cards are numbered on the back "X of 35" and are sequenced in alphabetical order.

	MINT	NRMT	EXC
COMPLETE SET (35)	15.00	6.75	1.85
COMMON CARD (1-35)	.25	.11	.03
SEMISTARS	.50	.23	.06
RANDOM INSERTS IN ALL PACKS			

□ 1 Kurt Abbott	.50	.23	.06
□ 2 Brian Anderson	.25	.11	.03
□ 3 Rich Aude	.25	.11	.03
□ 4 Cory Bailey	.25	.11	.03
□ 5 Danny Bautista	.25	.11	.03
□ 6 Marty Cordova	2.00	.90	.25
□ 7 Tripp Cromer	.25	.11	.03
□ 8 Midre Cummings	.25	.11	.03
□ 9 Carlos Delgado	2.50	1.10	.30
□ 10 Steve Dreyer	.25	.11	.03
□ 11 Steve Dunn	.25	.11	.03
□ 12 Jeff Granger	.50	.23	.06
□ 13 Tyrone Hill	.25	.11	.03
□ 14 Denny Hocking	.25	.11	.03
□ 15 John Hope	.25	.11	.03
□ 16 Butch Huskey	.50	.23	.06
□ 17 Miguel Jimenez	.25	.11	.03
□ 18 Chipper Jones	10.00	4.50	1.25
□ 19 Steve Karsay	.50	.23	.06
□ 20 Mike Kelly	.25	.11	.03
□ 21 Mike Lieberthal	.25	.11	.03
□ 22 Albie Lopez	.50	.23	.06
□ 23 Jeff McNeely	.25	.11	.03
□ 24 Dan Miceli	.25	.11	.03
□ 25 Nate Minchey	.25	.11	.03
□ 26 Marc Newfield	.50	.23	.06
□ 27 Darren Oliver	1.50	.70	.19
□ 28 Luis Ortiz	.25	.11	.03
□ 29 Curtis Pride	.50	.23	.06
□ 30 Roger Salkeld	.25	.11	.03
□ 31 Scott Sanders	.25	.11	.03
□ 32 Dave Staton	.25	.11	.03
□ 33 Salomon Torres	.25	.11	.03
□ 34 Steve Trachsel	.50	.23	.06
□ 35 Chris Turner	.25	.11	.03

1994 Fleer Pro-Visions

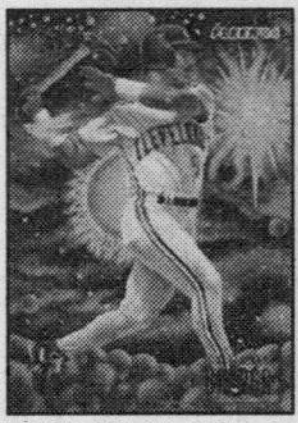

Randomly inserted in all pack types at a rate of one in 12, this nine-card standard-size set features on its fronts colorful artistic player caricatures with surrealistic backgrounds drawn by illustrator Wayne Still. The player's name is gold foil stamped at the lower right corner. When all nine cards are placed in order in a collector sheet, the backgrounds fit together to form a composite. The backs shade from one bright color to another and present career summaries. The cards are numbered on the back "X of 9."

	MINT	NRMT	EXC
COMPLETE SET (9)	5.00	2.20	.60

COMMON CARD (1-9)	.25	.11	.03
SEMISTARS	.50	.23	.06
RANDOM INSERTS IN ALL PACKS			
□ 1 Darren Daulton	.25	.11	.03
□ 2 John Olerud	.25	.11	.03
□ 3 Matt Williams	.50	.23	.06
□ 4 Carlos Baerga	.50	.23	.06
□ 5 Ozzie Smith	.75	.35	.09
□ 6 Juan Gonzalez	2.00	.90	.25
□ 7 Jack McDowell	.50	.23	.06
□ 8 Mike Piazza	2.50	1.10	.30
□ 9 Tony Gwynn	1.50	.70	.19

1994 Fleer Rookie Sensations

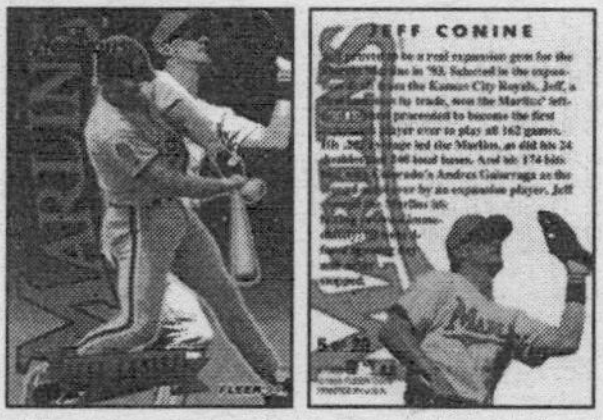

Randomly inserted in jumbo packs at a rate of one in four, this 20-card standard-size set features outstanding rookies. The fronts are "double exposed," with a player action cutout superimposed over a second photo. The team logo also appears in the team color-coded background. The set title is gold foil stamped toward the top, and the player's name is gold foil stamped on a team color-coded ribbon toward the bottom. On a white background featuring a ghosted version of the team logo, the backs have a player cutout photo and a season summary. The cards are numbered on the back "X of 20" and are sequenced in alphabetical order.

	MINT	NRMT	EXC
COMPLETE SET (20)	18.00	8.00	2.20
COMMON CARD (1-20)	.75	.35	.09
SEMISTARS	1.50	.70	.19
RANDOM INSERTS IN JUMBO PACKS			
□ 1 Rene Arocha	.75	.35	.09
□ 2 Jason Bere	1.50	.70	.19
□ 3 Jeromy Burnitz	1.50	.70	.19
□ 4 Chuck Carr	.75	.35	.09
□ 5 Jeff Conine	1.50	.70	.19
□ 6 Steve Cooke	.75	.35	.09
□ 7 Cliff Floyd	1.50	.70	.19
□ 8 Jeffrey Hammonds	1.50	.70	.19
□ 9 Wayne Kirby	.75	.35	.09
□ 10 Mike Lansing	.75	.35	.09
□ 11 Al Martin	1.50	.70	.19
□ 12 Greg McMichael	.75	.35	.09
□ 13 Troy Neel	.75	.35	.09
□ 14 Mike Piazza	12.00	5.50	1.50
□ 15 Armando Reynoso	.75	.35	.09
□ 16 Kirk Rueter	.75	.35	.09
□ 17 Tim Salmon	3.00	1.35	.35
□ 18 Aaron Sele	1.50	.70	.19
□ 19 J.T. Snow	1.50	.70	.19
□ 20 Kevin Stocker	.75	.35	.09

1994 Fleer Smoke 'n Heat

Randomly inserted in wax packs at a rate of one in 36, this 12-card standard-size set showcases the best pitchers in the game. On the fronts, color action player cutouts are superimposed on a red-and-gold fiery background that has a metallic sheen to it. The set title "Smoke 'n Heat" is printed in large block lettering. On a reddish marbleized background, the backs have another player cutout and season summary. The cards are numbered on the back "X of 12." and are sequenced in alphabetical order.

	MINT	NRMT	EXC
COMPLETE SET (12)	70.00	32.00	8.75
COMMON CARD (1-12)	2.00	.90	.25
SEMISTARS	3.00	1.35	.35
RANDOM INSERTS IN ALL PACKS			
□ 1 Roger Clemens	4.00	1.80	.50
□ 2 David Cone	3.00	1.35	.35
□ 3 Juan Guzman	3.00	1.35	.35
□ 4 Pete Harnisch	2.00	.90	.25
□ 5 Randy Johnson	5.00	2.20	.60
□ 6 Mark Langston	2.00	.90	.25
□ 7 Greg Maddux	20.00	9.00	2.50
□ 8 Mike Mussina	6.00	2.70	.75
□ 9 Jose Rijo	2.00	.90	.25
□ 10 Nolan Ryan	30.00	13.50	3.70
□ 11 Curt Schilling	2.00	.90	.25
□ 12 John Smoltz	5.00	2.20	.60

1994 Fleer Team Leaders

Randomly inserted in all pack types, this 28-card standard-size set features Fleer's selected top player from each of the 28 major league teams. The fronts feature an action player cutout superposed on a larger close-up photo with a team color-coded background, all inside beige borders. The set title, player's name, team name, and position are printed in gold foil across the bottom. On a white background with a ghosted version of the team logo, the horizontal backs carry a second color player cutout and a summary of the player's performance. The card numbering is arranged alphabetically by city according to the American (1-14) and the National (15-28) Leagues.

	MINT	NRMT	EXC
COMPLETE SET (28)	25.00	11.00	3.10
COMMON CARD (1-28)	.25	.11	.03
SEMISTARS	.60	.25	.07
RANDOM INSERTS IN ALL PACKS			
□ 1 Cal Ripken	4.00	1.80	.50
□ 2 Mo Vaughn	1.25	.55	.16
□ 3 Tim Salmon	.75	.35	.09
□ 4 Frank Thomas	5.00	2.20	.60
□ 5 Carlos Baerga	.60	.25	.07
□ 6 Cecil Fielder	.60	.25	.07
□ 7 Brian McRae	.25	.11	.03
□ 8 Greg Vaughn	.60	.25	.07
□ 9 Kirby Puckett	1.50	.70	.19
□ 10 Don Mattingly	2.50	1.10	.30
□ 11 Mark McGwire	1.50	.70	.19
□ 12 Ken Griffey Jr.	5.00	2.20	.60
□ 13 Juan Gonzalez	2.50	1.10	.30
□ 14 Paul Molitor	1.00	.45	.12
□ 15 David Justice	.60	.25	.07
□ 16 Ryne Sandberg	1.25	.55	.16
□ 17 Barry Larkin	.60	.25	.07
□ 18 Andres Galarraga	.60	.25	.07
□ 19 Gary Sheffield	.75	.35	.09
□ 20 Jeff Bagwell	2.00	.90	.25

□ 21 Mike Piazza	3.00	1.35	.35
□ 22 Marquis Grissom	.60	.25	.07
□ 23 Bobby Bonilla	.60	.25	.07
□ 24 Lenny Dykstra	.60	.25	.07
□ 25 Jay Bell	.25	.11	.03
□ 26 Gregg Jefferies	.60	.25	.07
□ 27 Tony Gwynn	2.00	.90	.25
□ 28 Will Clark	.60	.25	.07

1994 Fleer Update

This 200-card standard-size set highlights traded players in their new uniforms and promising young rookies. A ten card Diamond Tribute set was included in each factory set for a total of 210 cards. The cards are numbered on the back, grouped alphabetically by team by league as follows: Baltimore Orioles (1-8), Boston Red Sox (9-14), California Angels (15-22), Chicago White Sox (23-30), Cleveland Indians (31-38), Detroit Tigers (39-46), Kansas City Royals (47-51), Milwaukee Brewers (52-58), Minnesota Twins (59-66), New York Yankees (67-71), Oakland Athletics (72-78), Seattle Mariners (79-88), Texas Rangers (89-95), Toronto Blue Jays (96-100), Atlanta Braves (101-105), Chicago Cubs (106-113), Cincinnati Reds (114-121), Colorado Rockies (122-131), Florida Marlins (132-139), Houston Astros (140-147), Los Angeles Dodgers (148-151), Montreal Expos (152-155), New York Mets (156-163), Philadelphia Phillies (164-171), Pittsburgh Pirates (172-177), St. Louis Cardinals (178-183), San Diego Padres (184-191), and San Francisco Giants (192-198). Rookie Cards include Kurt Abbott, Brian Anderson, Chan Ho Park, Alex Rodriguez and Will VanLandingham.

	MINT	NRMT	EXC
COMPLETE FACT.SET (210)	20.00	9.00	2.50
COMPLETE SET (200)	18.00	8.00	2.20
COMMON CARD (U1-U200)	.10	.05	.01
SEMISTARS	.30	.14	.04
STARS	.60	.25	.07
U PREFIX ON REG.CARD NUMBERS			
COMP.DIAMOND TRIBUTE (10)	3.00	1.35	.35
COMMON DIA.TRIB (DT1-DT10)	.15	.07	.02
ONE DIAM.TRIB.SET PER FACTORY SET			

□ 1 Mark Eichhorn	.10	.05	.01
□ 2 Sid Fernandez	.10	.05	.01
□ 3 Leo Gomez	.10	.05	.01
□ 4 Mike Oquist	.10	.05	.01
□ 5 Rafael Palmeiro	.40	.18	.05
□ 6 Chris Sabo	.10	.05	.01
□ 7 Dwight Smith	.10	.05	.01
□ 8 Lee Smith	.25	.11	.03
□ 9 Damon Berryhill	.10	.05	.01
□ 10 Wes Chamberlain	.10	.05	.01
□ 11 Gar Finnvold	.10	.05	.01
□ 12 Chris Howard	.10	.05	.01
□ 13 Tim Naehring	.10	.05	.01
□ 14 Otis Nixon	.10	.05	.01
□ 15 Brian Anderson	.25	.11	.03
□ 16 Jorge Fabregas	.10	.05	.01
□ 17 Rex Hudler	.10	.05	.01
□ 18 Bo Jackson	.40	.18	.05
□ 19 Mark Leiter	.10	.05	.01
□ 20 Spike Owen	.10	.05	.01
□ 21 Harold Reynolds	.10	.05	.01
□ 22 Chris Turner	.10	.05	.01
□ 23 Dennis Cook	.10	.05	.01
□ 24 Jose DeLeon	.10	.05	.01
□ 25 Julio Franco	.25	.11	.03
□ 26 Joe Hall	.10	.05	.01
□ 27 Darrin Jackson	.10	.05	.01
□ 28 Dane Johnson	.10	.05	.01
□ 29 Norberto Martin	.10	.05	.01
□ 30 Scott Sanderson	.10	.05	.01
□ 31 Jason Grimsley	.10	.05	.01
□ 32 Dennis Martinez	.25	.11	.03
□ 33 Jack Morris	.25	.11	.03
□ 34 Eddie Murray	1.25	.55	.16
□ 35 Chad Ogea	.25	.11	.03
□ 36 Tony Pena	.10	.05	.01
□ 37 Paul Shuey	.10	.05	.01
□ 38 Omar Vizquel	.40	.18	.05
□ 39 Danny Bautista	.10	.05	.01
□ 40 Tim Belcher	.10	.05	.01
□ 41 Joe Boever	.10	.05	.01
□ 42 Storm Davis	.10	.05	.01
□ 43 Junior Felix	.10	.05	.01
□ 44 Mike Gardiner	.10	.05	.01
□ 45 Buddy Groom	.10	.05	.01
□ 46 Juan Samuel	.10	.05	.01
□ 47 Vince Coleman	.10	.05	.01
□ 48 Bob Hamelin	.10	.05	.01
□ 49 Dave Henderson	.10	.05	.01
□ 50 Rusty Meacham	.10	.05	.01
□ 51 Terry Shumpert	.10	.05	.01
□ 52 Jeff Bronkey	.10	.05	.01
□ 53 Alex Diaz	.10	.05	.01
□ 54 Brian Harper	.10	.05	.01
□ 55 Jose Mercedes	.10	.05	.01
□ 56 Jody Reed	.10	.05	.01
□ 57 Bob Scanlan	.10	.05	.01
□ 58 Turner Ward	.10	.05	.01
□ 59 Rich Becker	.25	.11	.03
□ 60 Alex Cole	.10	.05	.01
□ 61 Denny Hocking	.10	.05	.01
□ 62 Scott Leius	.10	.05	.01
□ 63 Pat Mahomes	.10	.05	.01
□ 64 Carlos Pulido	.10	.05	.01
□ 65 Dave Stevens	.10	.05	.01
□ 66 Matt Walbeck	.10	.05	.01
□ 67 Xavier Hernandez	.10	.05	.01
□ 68 Sterling Hitchcock	.25	.11	.03
□ 69 Terry Mulholland	.10	.05	.01
□ 70 Luis Polonia	.10	.05	.01
□ 71 Gerald Williams	.10	.05	.01
□ 72 Mark Acre	.10	.05	.01
□ 73 Geronimo Berroa	.25	.11	.03
□ 74 Rickey Henderson	.40	.18	.05
□ 75 Stan Javier	.10	.05	.01
□ 76 Steve Karsay	.10	.05	.01
□ 77 Carlos Reyes	.10	.05	.01
□ 78 Bill Taylor	.10	.05	.01
□ 79 Eric Anthony	.10	.05	.01
□ 80 Bobby Ayala	.10	.05	.01
□ 81 Tim Davis	.10	.05	.01
□ 82 Felix Fermin	.10	.05	.01
□ 83 Reggie Jefferson	.25	.11	.03
□ 84 Keith Mitchell	.10	.05	.01
□ 85 Bill Risley	.10	.05	.01
□ 86 Alex Rodriguez	15.00	6.75	1.85
□ 87 Roger Salkeld	.10	.05	.01
□ 88 Dan Wilson	.25	.11	.03
□ 89 Cris Carpenter	.10	.05	.01
□ 90 Will Clark	.40	.18	.05
□ 91 Jeff Frye	.10	.05	.01
□ 92 Rick Helling	.10	.05	.01
□ 93 Chris James	.10	.05	.01
□ 94 Oddibe McDowell	.10	.05	.01
□ 95 Billy Ripken	.10	.05	.01
□ 96 Carlos Delgado	1.00	.45	.12
□ 97 Alex Gonzalez	.25	.11	.03
□ 98 Shawn Green	.25	.11	.03
□ 99 Darren Hall	.10	.05	.01
□ 100 Mike Huff	.10	.05	.01
□ 101 Mike Kelly	.10	.05	.01
□ 102 Roberto Kelly	.10	.05	.01
□ 103 Charlie O'Brien	.10	.05	.01
□ 104 Jose Oliva	.25	.11	.03

□ 105 Gregg Olson	.10	.05	.01
□ 106 Willie Banks	.10	.05	.01
□ 107 Jim Bullinger	.10	.05	.01
□ 108 Chuck Crim	.10	.05	.01
□ 109 Shawon Dunston	.10	.05	.01
□ 110 Karl Rhodes	.10	.05	.01
□ 111 Steve Trachsel	.25	.11	.03
□ 112 Anthony Young	.10	.05	.01
□ 113 Eddie Zambrano	.10	.05	.01
□ 114 Bret Boone	.25	.11	.03
□ 115 Jeff Brantley	.10	.05	.01
□ 116 Hector Carrasco	.10	.05	.01
□ 117 Tony Fernandez	.10	.05	.01
□ 118 Tim Fortugno	.10	.05	.01
□ 119 Erik Hanson	.10	.05	.01
□ 120 Chuck McElroy	.10	.05	.01
□ 121 Deion Sanders	.40	.18	.05
□ 122 Ellis Burks	.25	.11	.03
□ 123 Marvin Freeman	.10	.05	.01
□ 124 Mike Harkey	.10	.05	.01
□ 125 Howard Johnson	.10	.05	.01
□ 126 Mike Kingery	.10	.05	.01
□ 127 Nelson Liriano	.10	.05	.01
□ 128 Marcus Moore	.10	.05	.01
□ 129 Mike Munoz	.10	.05	.01
□ 130 Kevin Ritz	.10	.05	.01
□ 131 Walt Weiss	.10	.05	.01
□ 132 Kurt Abbott	.25	.11	.03
□ 133 Jerry Browne	.10	.05	.01
□ 134 Greg Colbrunn	.10	.05	.01
□ 135 Jeremy Hernandez	.10	.05	.01
□ 136 Dave Magadan	.10	.05	.01
□ 137 Kurt Miller	.10	.05	.01
□ 138 Robb Nen	.25	.11	.03
□ 139 Jesus Tavarez	.10	.05	.01
□ 140 Sid Bream	.10	.05	.01
□ 141 Tom Edens	.10	.05	.01
□ 142 Tony Eusebio	.10	.05	.01
□ 143 John Hudek	.10	.05	.01
□ 144 Brian L. Hunter	1.25	.55	.16
□ 145 Orlando Miller	.10	.05	.01
□ 146 James Mouton	.25	.11	.03
□ 147 Shane Reynolds	.25	.11	.03
□ 148 Rafael Bournigal	.10	.05	.01
□ 149 Delino DeShields	.10	.05	.01
□ 150 Garey Ingram	.10	.05	.01
□ 151 Chan Ho Park	1.25	.55	.16
□ 152 Wil Cordero	.25	.11	.03
□ 153 Pedro Martinez	.40	.18	.05
□ 154 Randy Milligan	.10	.05	.01
□ 155 Lenny Webster	.10	.05	.01
□ 156 Rico Brogna	.10	.05	.01
□ 157 Josias Manzanillo	.10	.05	.01
□ 158 Kevin McReynolds	.10	.05	.01
□ 159 Mike Remlinger	.10	.05	.01
□ 160 David Segui	.10	.05	.01
□ 161 Pete Smith	.10	.05	.01
□ 162 Kelly Stinnett	.10	.05	.01
□ 163 Jose Vizcaino	.10	.05	.01
□ 164 Billy Hatcher	.10	.05	.01
□ 165 Doug Jones	.10	.05	.01
□ 166 Mike Lieberthal	.10	.05	.01
□ 167 Tony Longmire	.10	.05	.01
□ 168 Bobby Munoz	.10	.05	.01
□ 169 Paul Quantrill	.10	.05	.01
□ 170 Heathcliff Slocumb	.25	.11	.03
□ 171 Fernando Valenzuela	.25	.11	.03
□ 172 Mark Dewey	.10	.05	.01
□ 173 Brian R. Hunter	.10	.05	.01
□ 174 Jon Lieber	.10	.05	.01
□ 175 Ravelo Manzanillo	.10	.05	.01
□ 176 Dan Miceli	.10	.05	.01
□ 177 Rick White	.10	.05	.01
□ 178 Bryan Eversgerd	.10	.05	.01
□ 179 John Habyan	.10	.05	.01
□ 180 Terry McGriff	.10	.05	.01
□ 181 Vicente Palacios	.10	.05	.01
□ 182 Rich Rodriguez	.10	.05	.01
□ 183 Rick Sutcliffe	.10	.05	.01
□ 184 Donnie Elliott	.10	.05	.01
□ 185 Joey Hamilton	1.00	.45	.12
□ 186 Tim Hyers	.10	.05	.01
□ 187 Luis Lopez	.10	.05	.01
□ 188 Ray McDavid	.25	.11	.03
□ 189 Bip Roberts	.10	.05	.01
□ 190 Scott Sanders	.10	.05	.01
□ 191 Eddie Williams	.10	.05	.01
□ 192 Steve Frey	.10	.05	.01
□ 193 Pat Gomez	.10	.05	.01
□ 194 Rich Monteleone	.10	.05	.01
□ 195 Mark Portugal	.10	.05	.01
□ 196 Darryl Strawberry	.25	.11	.03
□ 197 Salomon Torres	.10	.05	.01
□ 198 W.VanLandingham	.25	.11	.03
□ 199 Checklist	.10	.05	.01
□ 200 Checklist	.10	.05	.01
□ DT1 Barry Bonds	.50	.23	.06
□ DT2 Joe Carter	.15	.07	.02
□ DT3 Will Clark	.25	.11	.03
□ DT4 Roger Clemens	.25	.11	.03
□ DT5 Tony Gwynn	.75	.35	.09
□ DT6 Don Mattingly	1.00	.45	.12
□ DT7 Fred McGriff	.40	.18	.05
□ DT8 Eddie Murray	.50	.23	.06
□ DT9 Kirby Puckett	.60	.25	.07
□ DT10 Cal Ripken Jr.	2.00	.90	.25

1995 Fleer

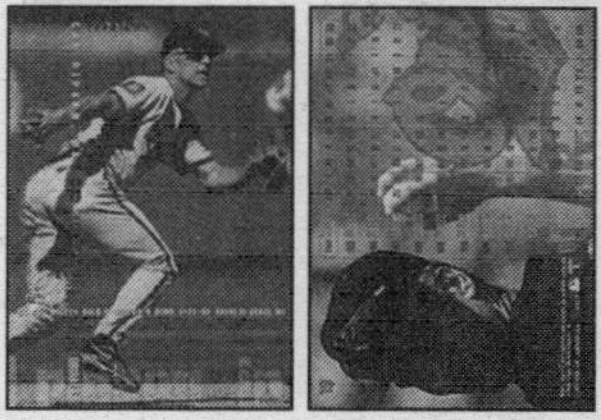

The 1995 Fleer set consists of 600 standard-size cards issued as one series. Each pack contained at least one insert card with some 'Hot Packs" containing nothing but insert cards. Full-bleed fronts have two player photos and, atypical of baseball cards fronts, biographical information such as height, weight, etc. The backgrounds are multi-colored. The backs are horizontal and contain year-by-year statistics along with a photo. There was a different design for each of baseball's six divisions. The checklist is arranged alphabetically by teams within each league as follows: Baltimore Orioles (1-22), Boston Red Sox (23-43), Detroit Tigers (44-64), New York Yankees (65-86), Toronto Blue Jays (87-108), Chicago White Sox (109-129), Cleveland Indians (130-151), Kansas City Royals (152-173), Milwaukee Brewers (174-195), Minnesota Twins (196-217), California Angels (218-237), Oakland Athletics (238-257), Seattle Mariners (258-279), Texas Rangers (280-298), Atlanta Braves (299-322), Florida Marlins (323-343), Montreal Expos (344-364), New York Mets (365-385), Philadelphia Phillies (386-407), Chicago Cubs (408-428), Cincinnati Reds (429-450), Houston Astros (451-471), Pittsburgh Pirates (472-492), St. Louis Cardinals (493-513), Colorado Rockies (514-531), Los Angeles Dodgers (532-552), San Diego Padres (553-571), and San Francisco Giants (572-593). Eight card promo sets were issued which included the following players: These cards are extremely difficult to tell apart from the regular cards are have the same value as the regular cards. The players in this set are Marquis Grissom, David Cone, Ozzie Smith, Roger Clemens, Tim Salmon, Paul O'Neill, Juan Gonzalez and Dante Bichette.

	MINT	NRMT	EXC
COMPLETE SET (600)	50.00	22.00	6.25
COMMON CARD (1-600)	.10	.05	.01
SEMISTARS	.25	.11	.03
STARS	.50	.23	.06

□ 1 Brady Anderson	.50	.23	.06
□ 2 Harold Baines	.25	.11	.03
□ 3 Damon Buford	.10	.05	.01
□ 4 Mike Devereaux	.10	.05	.01
□ 5 Mark Eichhorn	.10	.05	.01
□ 6 Sid Fernandez	.10	.05	.01
□ 7 Leo Gomez	.10	.05	.01
□ 8 Jeffrey Hammonds	.25	.11	.03
□ 9 Chris Hoiles	.10	.05	.01
□ 10 Rick Krivda	.10	.05	.01
□ 11 Ben McDonald	.10	.05	.01
□ 12 Mark McLemore	.10	.05	.01
□ 13 Alan Mills	.10	.05	.01
□ 14 Jamie Moyer	.10	.05	.01
□ 15 Mike Mussina	.60	.25	.07
□ 16 Mike Oquist	.10	.05	.01
□ 17 Rafael Palmeiro	.50	.23	.06
□ 18 Arthur Rhodes	.10	.05	.01
□ 19 Cal Ripken Jr.	2.50	1.10	.30
□ 20 Chris Sabo	.10	.05	.01
□ 21 Lee Smith	.25	.11	.03
□ 22 Jack Voigt	.10	.05	.01
□ 23 Damon Berryhill	.10	.05	.01
□ 24 Tom Brunansky	.10	.05	.01
□ 25 Wes Chamberlain	.10	.05	.01
□ 26 Roger Clemens	.50	.23	.06
□ 27 Scott Cooper	.10	.05	.01
□ 28 Andre Dawson	.50	.23	.06
□ 29 Gar Finnvold	.10	.05	.01
□ 30 Tony Fossas	.10	.05	.01
□ 31 Mike Greenwell	.10	.05	.01
□ 32 Joe Hesketh	.10	.05	.01
□ 33 Chris Howard	.10	.05	.01
□ 34 Chris Nabholz	.10	.05	.01
□ 35 Tim Naehring	.10	.05	.01
□ 36 Otis Nixon	.10	.05	.01
□ 37 Carlos Rodriguez	.10	.05	.01
□ 38 Rich Rowland	.10	.05	.01
□ 39 Ken Ryan	.10	.05	.01
□ 40 Aaron Sele	.25	.11	.03
□ 41 John Valentin	.25	.11	.03
□ 42 Mo Vaughn	.75	.35	.09
□ 43 Frank Viola	.10	.05	.01
□ 44 Danny Bautista	.10	.05	.01
□ 45 Joe Boever	.10	.05	.01
□ 46 Milt Cuyler	.10	.05	.01
□ 47 Storm Davis	.10	.05	.01
□ 48 John Doherty	.10	.05	.01
□ 49 Junior Felix	.10	.05	.01
□ 50 Cecil Fielder	.25	.11	.03
□ 51 Travis Fryman	.25	.11	.03
□ 52 Mike Gardiner	.10	.05	.01
□ 53 Kirk Gibson	.25	.11	.03
□ 54 Chris Gomez	.10	.05	.01
□ 55 Buddy Groom	.10	.05	.01
□ 56 Mike Henneman	.10	.05	.01
□ 57 Chad Kreuter	.10	.05	.01
□ 58 Mike Moore	.10	.05	.01
□ 59 Tony Phillips	.25	.11	.03
□ 60 Juan Samuel	.10	.05	.01
□ 61 Mickey Tettleton	.10	.05	.01
□ 62 Alan Trammell	.50	.23	.06
□ 63 David Wells	.10	.05	.01
□ 64 Lou Whitaker	.50	.23	.06
□ 65 Jim Abbott	.10	.05	.01
□ 66 Joe Ausanio	.10	.05	.01
□ 67 Wade Boggs	.50	.23	.06
□ 68 Mike Gallego	.10	.05	.01
□ 69 Xavier Hernandez	.10	.05	.01
□ 70 Sterling Hitchcock	.25	.11	.03
□ 71 Steve Howe	.10	.05	.01
□ 72 Scott Kamieniecki	.10	.05	.01
□ 73 Pat Kelly	.10	.05	.01
□ 74 Jimmy Key	.25	.11	.03
□ 75 Jim Leyritz	.10	.05	.01
□ 76 Don Mattingly UER	1.50	.70	.19
Photo is a reversed negative			
□ 77 Terry Mulholland	.10	.05	.01
□ 78 Paul O'Neill	.25	.11	.03
□ 79 Melido Perez	.10	.05	.01
□ 80 Luis Polonia	.10	.05	.01
□ 81 Mike Stanley	.10	.05	.01
□ 82 Danny Tartabull	.10	.05	.01
□ 83 Randy Velarde	.10	.05	.01
□ 84 Bob Wickman	.10	.05	.01
□ 85 Bernie Williams	.50	.23	.06
□ 86 Gerald Williams	.10	.05	.01
□ 87 Roberto Alomar	.75	.35	.09
□ 88 Pat Borders	.10	.05	.01
□ 89 Joe Carter	.50	.23	.06
□ 90 Tony Castillo	.10	.05	.01
□ 91 Brad Cornett	.10	.05	.01
□ 92 Carlos Delgado	.50	.23	.06
□ 93 Alex Gonzalez	.10	.05	.01
□ 94 Shawn Green	.25	.11	.03
□ 95 Juan Guzman	.25	.11	.03
□ 96 Darren Hall	.10	.05	.01
□ 97 Pat Hentgen	.25	.11	.03
□ 98 Mike Huff	.10	.05	.01
□ 99 Randy Knorr	.10	.05	.01
□ 100 Al Leiter	.25	.11	.03
□ 101 Paul Molitor	.60	.25	.07
□ 102 John Olerud	.10	.05	.01
□ 103 Dick Schofield	.10	.05	.01
□ 104 Ed Sprague	.25	.11	.03
□ 105 Dave Stewart	.25	.11	.03
□ 106 Todd Stottlemyre	.10	.05	.01
□ 107 Devon White	.25	.11	.03
□ 108 Woody Williams	.10	.05	.01
□ 109 Wilson Alvarez	.25	.11	.03
□ 110 Paul Assenmacher	.10	.05	.01
□ 111 Jason Bere	.10	.05	.01
□ 112 Dennis Cook	.10	.05	.01
□ 113 Joey Cora	.10	.05	.01
□ 114 Jose DeLeon	.10	.05	.01
□ 115 Alex Fernandez	.25	.11	.03
□ 116 Julio Franco	.25	.11	.03
□ 117 Craig Grebeck	.10	.05	.01
□ 118 Ozzie Guillen	.10	.05	.01
□ 119 Roberto Hernandez	.10	.05	.01
□ 120 Darrin Jackson	.10	.05	.01
□ 121 Lance Johnson	.25	.11	.03
□ 122 Ron Karkovice	.10	.05	.01
□ 123 Mike LaValliere	.10	.05	.01
□ 124 Norberto Martin	.10	.05	.01
□ 125 Kirk McCaskill	.10	.05	.01
□ 126 Jack McDowell	.25	.11	.03
□ 127 Tim Raines	.50	.23	.06
□ 128 Frank Thomas	3.00	1.35	.35
□ 129 Robin Ventura	.25	.11	.03
□ 130 Sandy Alomar Jr.	.10	.05	.01
□ 131 Carlos Baerga	.50	.23	.06
□ 132 Albert Belle	1.50	.70	.19
□ 133 Mark Clark	.10	.05	.01
□ 134 Alvaro Espinoza	.10	.05	.01
□ 135 Jason Grimsley	.10	.05	.01
□ 136 Wayne Kirby	.10	.05	.01
□ 137 Kenny Lofton	.75	.35	.09
□ 138 Albie Lopez	.10	.05	.01
□ 139 Dennis Martinez	.25	.11	.03
□ 140 Jose Mesa	.10	.05	.01
□ 141 Eddie Murray	.75	.35	.09
□ 142 Charles Nagy	.25	.11	.03
□ 143 Tony Pena	.10	.05	.01
□ 144 Eric Plunk	.10	.05	.01
□ 145 Manny Ramirez	.75	.35	.09
□ 146 Jeff Russell	.10	.05	.01
□ 147 Paul Shuey	.10	.05	.01
□ 148 Paul Sorrento	.10	.05	.01
□ 149 Jim Thome	.60	.25	.07
□ 150 Omar Vizquel	.50	.23	.06
□ 151 Dave Winfield	.50	.23	.06
□ 152 Kevin Appier	.25	.11	.03
□ 153 Billy Brewer	.10	.05	.01
□ 154 Vince Coleman	.10	.05	.01
□ 155 David Cone	.25	.11	.03
□ 156 Gary Gaetti	.25	.11	.03
□ 157 Greg Gagne	.10	.05	.01
□ 158 Tom Gordon	.10	.05	.01
□ 159 Mark Gubicza	.10	.05	.01
□ 160 Bob Hamelin	.10	.05	.01
□ 161 Dave Henderson	.10	.05	.01
□ 162 Felix Jose	.10	.05	.01
□ 163 Wally Joyner	.25	.11	.03
□ 164 Jose Lind	.10	.05	.01
□ 165 Mike Macfarlane	.10	.05	.01
□ 166 Mike Magnante	.10	.05	.01
□ 167 Brent Mayne	.10	.05	.01
□ 168 Brian McRae	.25	.11	.03
□ 169 Rusty Meacham	.10	.05	.01
□ 170 Jeff Montgomery	.25	.11	.03
□ 171 Hipolito Pichardo	.10	.05	.01

☐ 172 Terry Shumpert	.10	.05	.01
☐ 173 Michael Tucker	.25	.11	.03
☐ 174 Ricky Bones	.10	.05	.01
☐ 175 Jeff Cirillo	.25	.11	.03
☐ 176 Alex Diaz	.10	.05	.01
☐ 177 Cal Eldred	.10	.05	.01
☐ 178 Mike Fetters	.10	.05	.01
☐ 179 Darryl Hamilton	.10	.05	.01
☐ 180 Brian Harper	.10	.05	.01
☐ 181 John Jaha	.25	.11	.03
☐ 182 Pat Listach	.10	.05	.01
☐ 183 Graeme Lloyd	.10	.05	.01
☐ 184 Jose Mercedes	.10	.05	.01
☐ 185 Matt Mieske	.25	.11	.03
☐ 186 Dave Nilsson	.25	.11	.03
☐ 187 Jody Reed	.10	.05	.01
☐ 188 Bob Scanlan	.10	.05	.01
☐ 189 Kevin Seitzer	.10	.05	.01
☐ 190 Bill Spiers	.10	.05	.01
☐ 191 B.J. Surhoff	.25	.11	.03
☐ 192 Jose Valentin	.25	.11	.03
☐ 193 Greg Vaughn	.25	.11	.03
☐ 194 Turner Ward	.10	.05	.01
☐ 195 Bill Wegman	.10	.05	.01
☐ 196 Rick Aguilera	.10	.05	.01
☐ 197 Rich Becker	.10	.05	.01
☐ 198 Alex Cole	.10	.05	.01
☐ 199 Marty Cordova	.50	.23	.06
☐ 200 Steve Dunn	.10	.05	.01
☐ 201 Scott Erickson	.10	.05	.01
☐ 202 Mark Guthrie	.10	.05	.01
☐ 203 Chip Hale	.10	.05	.01
☐ 204 LaTroy Hawkins	.10	.05	.01
☐ 205 Denny Hocking	.10	.05	.01
☐ 206 Chuck Knoblauch	.50	.23	.06
☐ 207 Scott Leius	.10	.05	.01
☐ 208 Shane Mack	.10	.05	.01
☐ 209 Pat Mahomes	.10	.05	.01
☐ 210 Pat Meares	.10	.05	.01
☐ 211 Pedro Munoz	.10	.05	.01
☐ 212 Kirby Puckett	1.00	.45	.12
☐ 213 Jeff Reboulet	.10	.05	.01
☐ 214 Dave Stevens	.10	.05	.01
☐ 215 Kevin Tapani	.10	.05	.01
☐ 216 Matt Walbeck	.10	.05	.01
☐ 217 Carl Willis	.10	.05	.01
☐ 218 Brian Anderson	.10	.05	.01
☐ 219 Chad Curtis	.10	.05	.01
☐ 220 Chili Davis	.25	.11	.03
☐ 221 Gary DiSarcina	.10	.05	.01
☐ 222 Damion Easley	.10	.05	.01
☐ 223 Jim Edmonds	.50	.23	.06
☐ 224 Chuck Finley	.25	.11	.03
☐ 225 Joe Grahe	.10	.05	.01
☐ 226 Rex Hudler	.10	.05	.01
☐ 227 Bo Jackson	.50	.23	.06
☐ 228 Mark Langston	.10	.05	.01
☐ 229 Phil Leftwich	.10	.05	.01
☐ 230 Mark Leiter	.10	.05	.01
☐ 231 Spike Owen	.10	.05	.01
☐ 232 Bob Patterson	.10	.05	.01
☐ 233 Troy Percival	.10	.05	.01
☐ 234 Eduardo Perez	.10	.05	.01
☐ 235 Tim Salmon	.50	.23	.06
☐ 236 J.T. Snow	.25	.11	.03
☐ 237 Chris Turner	.10	.05	.01
☐ 238 Mark Acre	.10	.05	.01
☐ 239 Geronimo Berroa	.10	.05	.01
☐ 240 Mike Bordick	.10	.05	.01
☐ 241 John Briscoe	.10	.05	.01
☐ 242 Scott Brosius	.10	.05	.01
☐ 243 Ron Darling	.10	.05	.01
☐ 244 Dennis Eckersley	.25	.11	.03
☐ 245 Brent Gates	.10	.05	.01
☐ 246 Rickey Henderson	.50	.23	.06
☐ 247 Stan Javier	.10	.05	.01
☐ 248 Steve Karsay	.10	.05	.01
☐ 249 Mark McGwire	1.00	.45	.12
☐ 250 Troy Neel	.10	.05	.01
☐ 251 Steve Ontiveros	.10	.05	.01
☐ 252 Carlos Reyes	.10	.05	.01
☐ 253 Ruben Sierra	.25	.11	.03
☐ 254 Terry Steinbach	.25	.11	.03
☐ 255 Bill Taylor	.10	.05	.01
☐ 256 Todd Van Poppel	.10	.05	.01
☐ 257 Bobby Witt	.10	.05	.01

☐ 258 Rich Amaral	.10	.05	.01
☐ 259 Eric Anthony	.10	.05	.01
☐ 260 Bobby Ayala	.10	.05	.01
☐ 261 Mike Blowers	.10	.05	.01
☐ 262 Chris Bosio	.10	.05	.01
☐ 263 Jay Buhner	.50	.23	.06
☐ 264 John Cummings	.10	.05	.01
☐ 265 Tim Davis	.10	.05	.01
☐ 266 Felix Fermin	.10	.05	.01
☐ 267 Dave Fleming	.10	.05	.01
☐ 268 Goose Gossage	.25	.11	.03
☐ 269 Ken Griffey Jr.	3.00	1.35	.35
☐ 270 Reggie Jefferson	.25	.11	.03
☐ 271 Randy Johnson	.50	.23	.06
☐ 272 Edgar Martinez	.50	.23	.06
☐ 273 Tino Martinez	.25	.11	.03
☐ 274 Greg Pirkl	.10	.05	.01
☐ 275 Bill Risley	.10	.05	.01
☐ 276 Roger Salkeld	.10	.05	.01
☐ 277 Luis Sojo	.10	.05	.01
☐ 278 Mac Suzuki	.25	.11	.03
☐ 279 Dan Wilson	.25	.11	.03
☐ 280 Kevin Brown	.25	.11	.03
☐ 281 Jose Canseco	.50	.23	.06
☐ 282 Cris Carpenter	.10	.05	.01
☐ 283 Will Clark	.50	.23	.06
☐ 284 Jeff Frye	.10	.05	.01
☐ 285 Juan Gonzalez	1.50	.70	.19
☐ 286 Rick Helling	.10	.05	.01
☐ 287 Tom Henke	.10	.05	.01
☐ 288 David Hulse	.10	.05	.01
☐ 289 Chris James	.10	.05	.01
☐ 290 Manuel Lee	.10	.05	.01
☐ 291 Oddibe McDowell	.10	.05	.01
☐ 292 Dean Palmer	.25	.11	.03
☐ 293 Roger Pavlik	.10	.05	.01
☐ 294 Bill Ripken	.10	.05	.01
☐ 295 Ivan Rodriguez	.60	.25	.07
☐ 296 Kenny Rogers	.10	.05	.01
☐ 297 Doug Strange	.10	.05	.01
☐ 298 Matt Whiteside	.10	.05	.01
☐ 299 Steve Avery	.25	.11	.03
☐ 300 Steve Bedrosian	.10	.05	.01
☐ 301 Rafael Belliard	.10	.05	.01
☐ 302 Jeff Blauser	.10	.05	.01
☐ 303 Dave Gallagher	.10	.05	.01
☐ 304 Tom Glavine	.50	.23	.06
☐ 305 David Justice	.50	.23	.06
☐ 306 Mike Kelly	.10	.05	.01
☐ 307 Roberto Kelly	.10	.05	.01
☐ 308 Ryan Klesko	.60	.25	.07
☐ 309 Mark Lemke	.10	.05	.01
☐ 310 Javier Lopez	.50	.23	.06
☐ 311 Greg Maddux	2.00	.90	.25
☐ 312 Fred McGriff	.50	.23	.06
☐ 313 Greg McMichael	.10	.05	.01
☐ 314 Kent Mercker	.10	.05	.01
☐ 315 Charlie O'Brien	.10	.05	.01
☐ 316 Jose Oliva	.10	.05	.01
☐ 317 Terry Pendleton	.25	.11	.03
☐ 318 John Smoltz	.50	.23	.06
☐ 319 Mike Stanton	.10	.05	.01
☐ 320 Tony Tarasco	.10	.05	.01
☐ 321 Terrell Wade	.25	.11	.03
☐ 322 Mark Wohlers	.25	.11	.03
☐ 323 Kurt Abbott	.10	.05	.01
☐ 324 Luis Aquino	.10	.05	.01
☐ 325 Bret Barberie	.10	.05	.01
☐ 326 Ryan Bowen	.10	.05	.01
☐ 327 Jerry Browne	.10	.05	.01
☐ 328 Chuck Carr	.10	.05	.01
☐ 329 Matias Carrillo	.10	.05	.01
☐ 330 Greg Colbrunn	.10	.05	.01
☐ 331 Jeff Conine	.50	.23	.06
☐ 332 Mark Gardner	.10	.05	.01
☐ 333 Chris Hammond	.10	.05	.01
☐ 334 Bryan Harvey	.10	.05	.01
☐ 335 Richie Lewis	.10	.05	.01
☐ 336 Dave Magadan	.10	.05	.01
☐ 337 Terry Mathews	.10	.05	.01
☐ 338 Robb Nen	.10	.05	.01
☐ 339 Yorkis Perez	.10	.05	.01
☐ 340 Pat Rapp	.10	.05	.01
☐ 341 Benito Santiago	.10	.05	.01
☐ 342 Gary Sheffield	.50	.23	.06
☐ 343 Dave Weathers	.10	.05	.01

□	344 Moises Alou	.25	.11	.03
□	345 Sean Berry	.10	.05	.01
□	346 Wil Cordero	.10	.05	.01
□	347 Joey Eischen	.10	.05	.01
□	348 Jeff Fassero	.10	.05	.01
□	349 Darrin Fletcher	.10	.05	.01
□	350 Cliff Floyd	.25	.11	.03
□	351 Marquis Grissom	.50	.23	.06
□	352 Butch Henry	.10	.05	.01
□	353 Gil Heredia	.10	.05	.01
□	354 Ken Hill	.10	.05	.01
□	355 Mike Lansing	.10	.05	.01
□	356 Pedro Martinez	.25	.11	.03
□	357 Mel Rojas	.10	.05	.01
□	358 Kirk Rueter	.10	.05	.01
□	359 Tim Scott	.10	.05	.01
□	360 Jeff Shaw	.10	.05	.01
□	361 Larry Walker	.50	.23	.06
□	362 Lenny Webster	.10	.05	.01
□	363 John Wetteland	.25	.11	.03
□	364 Rondell White	.50	.23	.06
□	365 Bobby Bonilla	.25	.11	.03
□	366 Rico Brogna	.10	.05	.01
□	367 Jeromy Burnitz	.10	.05	.01
□	368 John Franco	.10	.05	.01
□	369 Dwight Gooden	.25	.11	.03
□	370 Todd Hundley	.25	.11	.03
□	371 Jason Jacome	.10	.05	.01
□	372 Bobby Jones	.25	.11	.03
□	373 Jeff Kent	.10	.05	.01
□	374 Jim Lindeman	.10	.05	.01
□	375 Josias Manzanillo	.10	.05	.01
□	376 Roger Mason	.10	.05	.01
□	377 Kevin McReynolds	.10	.05	.01
□	378 Joe Orsulak	.10	.05	.01
□	379 Bill Pulsipher	.25	.11	.03
□	380 Bret Saberhagen	.25	.11	.03
□	381 David Segui	.10	.05	.01
□	382 Pete Smith	.10	.05	.01
□	383 Kelly Stinnett	.10	.05	.01
□	384 Ryan Thompson	.10	.05	.01
□	385 Jose Vizcaino	.10	.05	.01
□	386 Toby Borland	.10	.05	.01
□	387 Ricky Bottalico	.25	.11	.03
□	388 Darren Daulton	.25	.11	.03
□	389 Mariano Duncan	.10	.05	.01
□	390 Lenny Dykstra	.25	.11	.03
□	391 Jim Eisenreich	.10	.05	.01
□	392 Tommy Greene	.10	.05	.01
□	393 Dave Hollins	.10	.05	.01
□	394 Pete Incaviglia	.10	.05	.01
□	395 Danny Jackson	.10	.05	.01
□	396 Doug Jones	.10	.05	.01
□	397 Ricky Jordan	.10	.05	.01
□	398 John Kruk	.25	.11	.03
□	399 Mike Lieberthal	.10	.05	.01
□	400 Tony Longmire	.10	.05	.01
□	401 Mickey Morandini	.10	.05	.01
□	402 Bobby Munoz	.10	.05	.01
□	403 Curt Schilling	.10	.05	.01
□	404 Heathcliff Slocumb	.10	.05	.01
□	405 Kevin Stocker	.10	.05	.01
□	406 Fernando Valenzuela	.25	.11	.03
□	407 David West	.10	.05	.01
□	408 Willie Banks	.10	.05	.01
□	409 Jose Bautista	.10	.05	.01
□	410 Steve Buechele	.10	.05	.01
□	411 Jim Bullinger	.10	.05	.01
□	412 Chuck Crim	.10	.05	.01
□	413 Shawon Dunston	.10	.05	.01
□	414 Kevin Foster	.10	.05	.01
□	415 Mark Grace	.50	.23	.06
□	416 Jose Hernandez	.10	.05	.01
□	417 Glenallen Hill	.10	.05	.01
□	418 Brooks Kieschnick	.25	.11	.03
□	419 Derrick May	.10	.05	.01
□	420 Randy Myers	.10	.05	.01
□	421 Dan Plesac	.10	.05	.01
□	422 Karl Rhodes	.10	.05	.01
□	423 Rey Sanchez	.10	.05	.01
□	424 Sammy Sosa	.50	.23	.06
□	425 Steve Trachsel	.10	.05	.01
□	426 Rick Wilkins	.10	.05	.01
□	427 Anthony Young	.10	.05	.01
□	428 Eddie Zambrano	.10	.05	.01
□	429 Bret Boone	.25	.11	.03
□	430 Jeff Branson	.10	.05	.01
□	431 Jeff Brantley	.10	.05	.01
□	432 Hector Carrasco	.10	.05	.01
□	433 Brian Dorsett	.10	.05	.01
□	434 Tony Fernandez	.10	.05	.01
□	435 Tim Fortugno	.10	.05	.01
□	436 Erik Hanson	.10	.05	.01
□	437 Thomas Howard	.10	.05	.01
□	438 Kevin Jarvis	.10	.05	.01
□	439 Barry Larkin	.50	.23	.06
□	440 Chuck McElroy	.10	.05	.01
□	441 Kevin Mitchell	.25	.11	.03
□	442 Hal Morris	.10	.05	.01
□	443 Jose Rijo	.10	.05	.01
□	444 John Roper	.10	.05	.01
□	445 Johnny Ruffin	.10	.05	.01
□	446 Deion Sanders	.50	.23	.06
□	447 Reggie Sanders	.25	.11	.03
□	448 Pete Schourek	.25	.11	.03
□	449 John Smiley	.10	.05	.01
□	450 Eddie Taubensee	.10	.05	.01
□	451 Jeff Bagwell	1.25	.55	.16
□	452 Kevin Bass	.10	.05	.01
□	453 Craig Biggio	.50	.23	.06
□	454 Ken Caminiti	.50	.23	.06
□	455 Andujar Cedeno	.10	.05	.01
□	456 Doug Drabek	.10	.05	.01
□	457 Tony Eusebio	.10	.05	.01
□	458 Mike Felder	.10	.05	.01
□	459 Steve Finley	.25	.11	.03
□	460 Luis Gonzalez	.10	.05	.01
□	461 Mike Hampton	.10	.05	.01
□	462 Pete Harnisch	.10	.05	.01
□	463 John Hudek	.10	.05	.01
□	464 Todd Jones	.10	.05	.01
□	465 Darryl Kile	.10	.05	.01
□	466 James Mouton	.10	.05	.01
□	467 Shane Reynolds	.10	.05	.01
□	468 Scott Servais	.10	.05	.01
□	469 Greg Swindell	.10	.05	.01
□	470 Dave Veres	.10	.05	.01
□	471 Brian Williams	.10	.05	.01
□	472 Jay Bell	.25	.11	.03
□	473 Jacob Brumfield	.10	.05	.01
□	474 Dave Clark	.10	.05	.01
□	475 Steve Cooke	.10	.05	.01
□	476 Midre Cummings	.10	.05	.01
□	477 Mark Dewey	.10	.05	.01
□	478 Tom Foley	.10	.05	.01
□	479 Carlos Garcia	.10	.05	.01
□	480 Jeff King	.25	.11	.03
□	481 Jon Lieber	.10	.05	.01
□	482 Ravelo Manzanillo	.10	.05	.01
□	483 Al Martin	.25	.11	.03
□	484 Orlando Merced	.10	.05	.01
□	485 Danny Miceli	.10	.05	.01
□	486 Denny Neagle	.25	.11	.03
□	487 Lance Parrish	.10	.05	.01
□	488 Don Slaught	.10	.05	.01
□	489 Zane Smith	.10	.05	.01
□	490 Andy Van Slyke	.25	.11	.03
□	491 Paul Wagner	.10	.05	.01
□	492 Rick White	.10	.05	.01
□	493 Luis Alicea	.10	.05	.01
□	494 Rene Arocha	.10	.05	.01
□	495 Rheal Cormier	.10	.05	.01
□	496 Bryan Eversgerd	.10	.05	.01
□	497 Bernard Gilkey	.25	.11	.03
□	498 John Habyan	.10	.05	.01
□	499 Gregg Jefferies	.25	.11	.03
□	500 Brian Jordan	.50	.23	.06
□	501 Ray Lankford	.50	.23	.06
□	502 John Mabry	.50	.23	.06
□	503 Terry McGriff	.10	.05	.01
□	504 Tom Pagnozzi	.10	.05	.01
□	505 Vicente Palacios	.10	.05	.01
□	506 Geronimo Pena	.10	.05	.01
□	507 Gerald Perry	.10	.05	.01
□	508 Rich Rodriguez	.10	.05	.01
□	509 Ozzie Smith	.60	.25	.07
□	510 Bob Tewksbury	.10	.05	.01
□	511 Allen Watson	.10	.05	.01
□	512 Mark Whiten	.10	.05	.01
□	513 Todd Zeile	.10	.05	.01
□	514 Dante Bichette	.50	.23	.06
□	515 Willie Blair	.10	.05	.01

□ 516 Ellis Burks	.50	.23	.06
□ 517 Marvin Freeman	.10	.05	.01
□ 518 Andres Galarraga	.50	.23	.06
□ 519 Joe Girardi	.10	.05	.01
□ 520 Greg W. Harris	.10	.05	.01
□ 521 Charlie Hayes	.10	.05	.01
□ 522 Mike Kingery	.10	.05	.01
□ 523 Nelson Liriano	.10	.05	.01
□ 524 Mike Munoz	.10	.05	.01
□ 525 David Nied	.10	.05	.01
□ 526 Steve Reed	.10	.05	.01
□ 527 Kevin Ritz	.10	.05	.01
□ 528 Bruce Ruffin	.10	.05	.01
□ 529 John Vander Wal	.10	.05	.01
□ 530 Walt Weiss	.10	.05	.01
□ 531 Eric Young	.25	.11	.03
□ 532 Billy Ashley	.10	.05	.01
□ 533 Pedro Astacio	.10	.05	.01
□ 534 Rafael Bournigal	.10	.05	.01
□ 535 Brett Butler	.25	.11	.03
□ 536 Tom Candiotti	.10	.05	.01
□ 537 Omar Daal	.10	.05	.01
□ 538 Delino DeShields	.10	.05	.01
□ 539 Darren Dreifort	.10	.05	.01
□ 540 Kevin Gross	.10	.05	.01
□ 541 Orel Hershiser	.25	.11	.03
□ 542 Garey Ingram	.10	.05	.01
□ 543 Eric Karros	.25	.11	.03
□ 544 Ramon Martinez	.25	.11	.03
□ 545 Raul Mondesi	.50	.23	.06
□ 546 Chan Ho Park	.50	.23	.06
□ 547 Mike Piazza	2.00	.90	.25
□ 548 Henry Rodriguez	.50	.23	.06
□ 549 Rudy Seanez	.10	.05	.01
□ 550 Ismael Valdes	.25	.11	.03
□ 551 Tim Wallach	.10	.05	.01
□ 552 Todd Worrell	.10	.05	.01
□ 553 Andy Ashby	.25	.11	.03
□ 554 Brad Ausmus	.10	.05	.01
□ 555 Derek Bell	.25	.11	.03
□ 556 Andy Benes	.10	.05	.01
□ 557 Phil Clark	.10	.05	.01
□ 558 Donnie Elliott	.10	.05	.01
□ 559 Ricky Gutierrez	.10	.05	.01
□ 560 Tony Gwynn	1.25	.55	.16
□ 561 Joey Hamilton	.25	.11	.03
□ 562 Trevor Hoffman	.10	.05	.01
□ 563 Luis Lopez	.10	.05	.01
□ 564 Pedro A. Martinez	.10	.05	.01
□ 565 Tim Mauser	.10	.05	.01
□ 566 Phil Plantier	.10	.05	.01
□ 567 Bip Roberts	.10	.05	.01
□ 568 Scott Sanders	.10	.05	.01
□ 569 Craig Shipley	.10	.05	.01
□ 570 Jeff Tabaka	.10	.05	.01
□ 571 Eddie Williams	.10	.05	.01
□ 572 Rod Beck	.10	.05	.01
□ 573 Mike Benjamin	.10	.05	.01
□ 574 Barry Bonds	.75	.35	.09
□ 575 Dave Burba	.10	.05	.01
□ 576 John Burkett	.25	.11	.03
□ 577 Mark Carreon	.10	.05	.01
□ 578 Royce Clayton	.10	.05	.01
□ 579 Steve Frey	.10	.05	.01
□ 580 Bryan Hickerson	.10	.05	.01
□ 581 Mike Jackson	.10	.05	.01
□ 582 Darren Lewis	.10	.05	.01
□ 583 Kirt Manwaring	.10	.05	.01
□ 584 Rich Monteleone	.10	.05	.01
□ 585 John Patterson	.10	.05	.01
□ 586 J.R. Phillips	.10	.05	.01
□ 587 Mark Portugal	.10	.05	.01
□ 588 Joe Rosselli	.10	.05	.01
□ 589 Darryl Strawberry	.25	.11	.03
□ 590 Bill Swift	.10	.05	.01
□ 591 Robby Thompson	.10	.05	.01
□ 592 William VanLandingham	.10	.05	.01
□ 593 Matt Williams	.50	.23	.06
□ 594 Checklist	.10	.05	.01
□ 595 Checklist	.10	.05	.01
□ 596 Checklist	.10	.05	.01
□ 597 Checklist	.10	.05	.01
□ 598 Checklist	.10	.05	.01
□ 599 Checklist	.10	.05	.01
□ 600 Checklist	.10	.05	.01

1995 Fleer All-Fleer

This nine-card standard-size set was available through '95 Fleer wrapper offer. Nine of the leading players for each position are featured in this set. The wrapper redemption offer expired on September 30, 1995. The fronts feature the player's photo covering most of the card with a small section on the right set off for the words "All Fleer 9" along with the playerís name. The backs feature player information as to why they are among the best in the game.

	MINT	NRMT	EXC
COMPLETE SET (9)	10.00	4.50	1.25
COMMON CARD (1-9)	.50	.23	.06
SETS WERE AVAILABLE VIA WRAPPER OFFER			
□ 1 Mike Piazza	2.00	.90	.25
□ 2 Frank Thomas	3.00	1.35	.35
□ 3 Roberto Alomar	.75	.35	.09
□ 4 Cal Ripken	2.50	1.10	.30
□ 5 Matt Williams	.50	.23	.06
□ 6 Barry Bonds	.75	.35	.09
□ 7 Ken Griffey Jr.	3.00	1.35	.35
□ 8 Tony Gwynn	1.00	.45	.12
□ 9 Greg Maddux	2.00	.90	.25

1995 Fleer All-Rookies

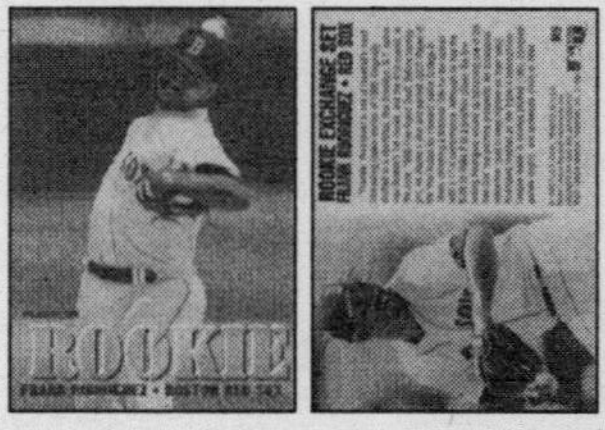

This nine-card standard-size set was available through a Rookie Exchange redemption card randomly inserted in packs. The redemption deadline was 9/30/95. This set features players who made their major league debut in 1995. The fronts have an action photo with a grainy background. The player's name and team are in gold foil at the bottom. Horizontal backs have a player photo the left and minor league highlights to the right. The set is sequenced in alphabetical order.

	MINT	NRMT	EXC
COMPLETE SET (9)	6.00	2.70	.75
COMMON CARD (M1-M9)	.75	.35	.09
ONE SET PER EXCHANGE CARD VIA MAIL..			
□ M1 Edgardo Alfonzo	1.50	.70	.19
□ M2 Jason Bates	.75	.35	.09
□ M3 Brian Boehringer	.75	.35	.09
□ M4 Darren Bragg	1.50	.70	.19
□ M5 Brad Clontz	.75	.35	.09
□ M6 Jim Dougherty	.75	.35	.09

□ M7 Todd Hollandsworth	4.00	1.80	.50
□ M8 Rudy Pemberton	.75	.35	.09
□ M9 Frank Rodriguez	1.50	.70	.19
□ NNO Expired All-Rookie Exch.	1.50	.70	.19

1995 Fleer All-Stars

Randomly inserted in all pack types at a rate of one in three, this 25-card standard-size set showcases those that participated in the 1994 mid-season classic held in Pittsburgh. Horizontally designed, the fronts contain photos of American League stars with the back protraying the National League player from the same position. On each side, the 1994 All-Star Game logo appears in gold foil as does either the A.L. or N.L. logo in silver foil.

	MINT	NRMT	EXC
COMPLETE SET (25)	12.00	5.50	1.50
COMMON CARD (1-25)	.25	.11	.03
SEMISTARS	.50	.23	.06
RANDOM INSERTS IN PACKS			
□ 1 Ivan Rodriguez Mike Piazza	2.00	.90	.25
□ 2 Frank Thomas Gregg Jefferies	3.00	1.35	.35
□ 3 Robert Alomar Mariano Duncan	.75	.35	.09
□ 4 Wade Boggs Matt Williams	.50	.23	.06
□ 5 Cal Ripken Jr. Ozzie Smith	2.50	1.10	.30
□ 6 Joe Carter Barry Bonds	.75	.35	.09
□ 7 Ken Griffey Jr. Tony Gwynn	4.00	1.80	.50
□ 8 Kirby Puckett David Justice	1.25	.55	.16
□ 9 Jimmy Key Greg Maddux	2.00	.90	.25
□ 10 Chuck Knoblauch Wil Cordero	.50	.23	.06
□ 11 Scott Cooper Ken Caminiti	.25	.11	.03
□ 12 Will Clark Carlos Garcia	.50	.23	.06
□ 13 Paul Molitor Jeff Bagwell	1.00	.45	.12
□ 14 Travis Fryman Craig Biggio	.50	.23	.06
□ 15 Mickey Tettleton Fred McGriff	.50	.23	.06
□ 16 Kenny Lofton Moises Alou	.50	.23	.06
□ 17 Albert Belle Marquis Grissom	1.50	.70	.19
□ 18 Paul O'Neill Dante Bichette	.50	.23	.06
□ 19 David Cone Ken Hill	.50	.23	.06
□ 20 Mike Mussina Doug Drabek	.50	.23	.06
□ 21 Randy Johnson John Hudek	.50	.23	.06
□ 22 Pat Hentgen Danny Jackson	.50	.23	.06
□ 23 Wilson Alvarez Rod Beck	.25	.11	.03
□ 24 Lee Smith Randy Myers	.50	.23	.06
□ 25 Jason Bere Doug Jones	.25	.11	.03

1995 Fleer Award Winners

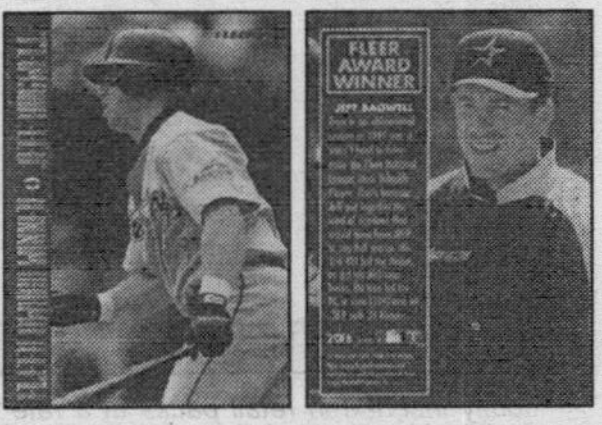

Randomly inserted in all pack types at a rate of one in 24, this six card standard-size set highlights the major award winners of 1994. Card fronts feature action photos that are full-bleed on the right border and have gold border on the left. Within the gold border are the player's name and Fleer Award Winner. The backs contain a photo with text that references 1994 accomplishments.

	MINT	NRMT	EXC
COMPLETE SET (6)	10.00	4.50	1.25
COMMON CARD (1-6)	.50	.23	.06
RANDOM INSERTS IN PACKS			
□ 1 Frank Thomas	5.00	2.20	.60
□ 2 Jeff Bagwell	2.00	.90	.25
□ 3 David Cone	.75	.35	.09
□ 4 Greg Maddux	3.00	1.35	.35
□ 5 Bob Hamelin	.50	.23	.06
□ 6 Raul Mondesi	.75	.35	.09

1995 Fleer League Leaders

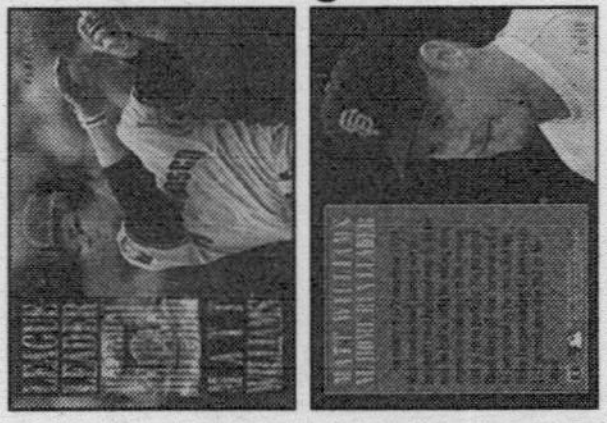

Randomly inserted in all pack types at a rate of one in 12, this 10-card standard-size set features 1994 American and National League leaders in various categories. The horizontal cards have player photos on front and back. The back also has a brief write-up concerning the accomplishment.

	MINT	NRMT	EXC
COMPLETE SET (10)	10.00	4.50	1.25
COMMON CARD (1-10)	.50	.23	.06
RANDOM INSERTS IN PACKS			
□ 1 Paul O'Neill	.50	.23	.06
□ 2 Ken Griffey Jr.	5.00	2.20	.60
□ 3 Kirby Puckett	1.50	.70	.19
□ 4 Jimmy Key	.50	.23	.06
□ 5 Randy Johnson	.75	.35	.09
□ 6 Tony Gwynn	2.00	.90	.25
□ 7 Matt Williams	.50	.23	.06
□ 8 Jeff Bagwell	2.00	.90	.25

□ 9 Greg Maddux Ken Hill	1.50	.70	.19
□ 10 Andy Benes	.50	.23	.06

1995 Fleer Lumber Company

Randomly inserted in retail packs at a rate of one in 24, this standard-size set highlights 10 of the game's top sluggers. Full-bleed card fronts feature an action photo with the Lumber Company logo, which includes the player's name, toward the bottom of the photo. Card backs have a player photo and woodgrain background with a write-up that highlights individual achievements. The set is sequenced in alphabetical order.

	MINT	NRMT	EXC
COMPLETE SET (10)	40.00	18.00	5.00
COMMON CARD (1-10)	1.00	.45	.12
SEMISTARS	2.00	.90	.25
RANDOM INSERTS IN RETAIL PACKS			

□ 1 Jeff Bagwell	6.00	2.70	.75
□ 2 Albert Belle	8.00	3.60	1.00
□ 3 Barry Bonds	4.00	1.80	.50
□ 4 Jose Canseco	2.00	.90	.25
□ 5 Joe Carter	2.00	.90	.25
□ 6 Ken Griffey Jr.	15.00	6.75	1.85
□ 7 Fred McGriff	2.00	.90	.25
□ 8 Kevin Mitchell	1.00	.45	.12
□ 9 Frank Thomas	15.00	6.75	1.85
□ 10 Matt Williams	2.00	.90	.25

1995 Fleer Major League Prospects

Randomly inserted in all pack types at a rate of one in six, this 10-card standard-size set spotlights major league hopefuls. Card fronts feature a player photo with the words "Major League Prospects" serving as part of the background. The player's name and team appear in silver foil at the bottom. The backs have a photo and a write-up on his minor league career. The cards are sequenced in alphabetical order.

	MINT	NRMT	EXC
COMPLETE SET (10)	12.00	5.50	1.50
COMMON CARD (1-10)	.50	.23	.06
SEMISTARS	.75	.35	.09
RANDOM INSERTS IN PACKS			

□ 1 Garret Anderson	.75	.35	.09
□ 2 James Baldwin	1.25	.55	.16
□ 3 Alan Benes	1.00	.45	.12
□ 4 Armando Benitez	.50	.23	.06
□ 5 Ray Durham	.75	.35	.09
□ 6 Brian L. Hunter	1.00	.45	.12
□ 7 Derek Jeter	5.00	2.20	.60
□ 8 Charles Johnson	.75	.35	.09
□ 9 Orlando Miller	.75	.35	.09
□ 10 Alex Rodriguez	8.00	3.60	1.00

1995 Fleer Pro-Visions

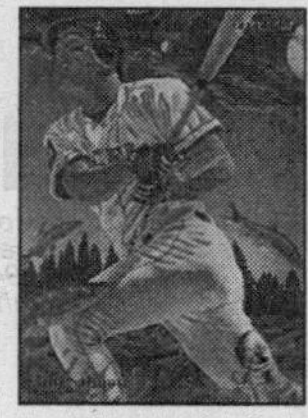
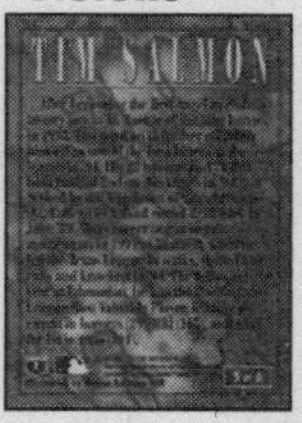

Randomly inserted in all pack types at a rate of one in nine, this six card standard-size set features top players illustrated by Wayne Anthony Still. The colorful artwork on front features the player in a surrealistic setting. The backs offer write-up on the player's previous season.

	MINT	NRMT	EXC
COMPLETE SET (6)	4.00	1.80	.50
COMMON CARD (1-6)	.25	.11	.03
RANDOM INSERTS IN PACKS			

□ 1 Mike Mussina	.25	.11	.03
□ 2 Raul Mondesi	.25	.11	.03
□ 3 Jeff Bagwell	1.25	.55	.16
□ 4 Greg Maddux	2.00	.90	.25
□ 5 Tim Salmon	.25	.11	.03
□ 6 Manny Ramirez	.75	.35	.09

1995 Fleer Rookie Sensations

Randomly inserted in 18-card packs, this 20-card standard-size set features top rookies from the 1994 season. The fronts have full-bleed color photos with the team and player's name in gold foil along the right edge. The backs also have full-bleed color photos along with player information. The set is sequenced in alphabetical order.

	MINT	NRMT	EXC
COMPLETE SET (20)	50.00	22.00	6.25
COMMON CARD (1-20)	1.00	.45	.12
SEMISTARS	2.00	.90	.25
RANDOM INSERTS IN JUMBO PACKS			

□	1 Kurt Abbott	1.50	.70	.19
□	2 Rico Brogna	1.50	.70	.19
□	3 Hector Carrasco	1.00	.45	.12
□	4 Kevin Foster	1.00	.45	.12
□	5 Chris Gomez	1.00	.45	.12
□	6 Darren Hall	1.00	.45	.12
□	7 Bob Hamelin	1.00	.45	.12
□	8 Joey Hamilton	5.00	2.20	.60
□	9 John Hudek	1.00	.45	.12
□	10 Ryan Klesko	10.00	4.50	1.25
□	11 Javier Lopez	5.00	2.20	.60
□	12 Matt Mieske	1.50	.70	.19
□	13 Raul Mondesi	6.00	2.70	.75
□	14 Manny Ramirez	12.00	5.50	1.50
□	15 Shane Reynolds	1.50	.70	.19
□	16 Bill Risley	1.00	.45	.12
□	17 Johnny Ruffin	1.00	.45	.12
□	18 Steve Trachsel	1.00	.45	.12
□	19 William VanLandingham	1.00	.45	.12
□	20 Rondell White	5.00	2.20	.60

1995 Fleer Team Leaders

Randomly inserted in 12-card hobby packs at a rate of one in 24, this 28-card standard-size set features top players from each team. Each team is represented with card the has the team's leading hitter on one side with the leading pitcher on the other side. The team logo, "Team Leaders" and the player's name are gold foil stamped on front and back.

	MINT	NRMT	EXC
COMPLETE SET (28)	225.00	100.00	28.00
COMMON CARD (1-28)	3.00	1.35	.35
SEMISTARS	4.00	1.80	.50
RANDOM INSERTS IN HOBBY PACKS			

□	1 Cal Ripken Jr. Mike Mussina	40.00	18.00	5.00
□	2 Mo Vaughn Roger Clemens	12.00	5.50	1.50
□	3 Tim Salmon Chuck Finley	3.00	1.35	.35
□	4 Frank Thomas Jack McDowell	40.00	18.00	5.00
□	5 Albert Belle Dennis Martinez	20.00	9.00	2.50
□	6 Cecil Fielder Mike Moore	3.00	1.35	.35
□	7 Bob Hamelin David Cone	3.00	1.35	.35
□	8 Greg Vaughn Ricky Bones	3.00	1.35	.35
□	9 Kirby Puckett Rick Aguilera	12.00	5.50	1.50
□	10 Don Mattingly Jimmy Key	20.00	9.00	2.50
□	11 Ruben Sierra Dennis Eckersley	3.00	1.35	.35
□	12 Ken Griffey Jr. Randy Johnson	40.00	18.00	5.00
□	13 Jose Canseco Kenny Rogers	3.00	1.35	.35
□	14 Joe Carter Pat Hentgen	4.00	1.80	.50
□	15 David Justice Greg Maddux	25.00	11.00	3.10
□	16 Sammy Sosa Steve Trachsel	5.00	2.20	.60
□	17 Kevin Mitchell Jose Rijo	3.00	1.35	.35
□	18 Dante Bichette Bruce Ruffin	3.00	1.35	.35
□	19 Jeff Conine Robb Nen	3.00	1.35	.35
□	20 Jeff Bagwell Doug Drabek	15.00	6.75	1.85
□	21 Mike Piazza Ramon Martinez	20.00	9.00	2.50
□	22 Moises Alou Ken Hill	3.00	1.35	.35
□	23 Bobby Bonilla Bret Saberhagen	3.00	1.35	.35
□	24 Darren Daulton Danny Jackson	3.00	1.35	.35
□	25 Jay Bell Zane Smith	3.00	1.35	.35
□	26 Gregg Jefferies Bob Tewksbury	3.00	1.35	.35
□	27 Tony Gwynn Andy Benes	15.00	6.75	1.85
□	28 Matt Williams Rod Beck	3.00	1.35	.35

1995 Fleer Update

This 200-card standard-size set features many players who were either rookies in 1995 or played for new teams. These cards were issued in either 12-card packs with a suggested retail price of $1.49 or 18-card packs that had a suggested retail price of $2.29. Each Fleer Update pack included one card from several insert sets produced with this product. Hot packs featuring only these insert cards were included one every 72 packs. The full-bleed fronts have two player photos and, atypical of baseball card fronts, biographical information such as height, weight, etc. The backgrounds are multi-colored. The backs are horizontal, have yearly statistics, a photo, and are numbered with the prefix "U". The checklist is arranged alphabetically by team within each leagueís divisions: Baltimore Orioles (1-7), Boston Red Sox (8-16), Detroit Tigers (17-24), New York Yankees (25-28), Toronto Blue Jays (29-31), Chicago White Sox (32-38), Cleveland Indians (39-43), Kansas City Royals (44-50), Milwaukee Brewers (51-57), Minnesota Twins (58-63), California Angels (64-69), Oakland Athletics (70-73), Seattle Mariners (74-79), Texas Rangers (80-88), Atlanta Braves (89-93), Florida Marlins (94-102), Montreal Expos (103-109), New York Mets (110-117), Philadelphia Phillies (118-124), Chicago Cubs (125-130), Cincinnati Reds (131-137), Houston Astros (138-144), Pittsburgh Pirates (145-152), St. Louis Cardinals (153-163), Colorado Rockies (164-171), Los Angeles Dodgers (172-179), San Diego Padres (180-191) and San Francisco Giants (192-197). Rookie Cards in this set include Hideo Nomo and Carlos Perez.

	MINT	NRMT	EXC
COMPLETE SET (200)	20.00	9.00	2.50
COMMON CARD (1-200)	.05	.02	.01
SEMISTARS	.15	.07	.02
STARS	.30	.14	.04

ONE INSERT PER PACK
U PREFIX ON CARD NUMBERS

□ 1 Manny Alexander	.05	.02	.01
□ 2 Bret Barberie	.05	.02	.01
□ 3 Armando Benitez	.05	.02	.01
□ 4 Kevin Brown	.15	.07	.02
□ 5 Doug Jones	.05	.02	.01
□ 6 Sherman Obando	.05	.02	.01
□ 7 Andy Van Slyke	.15	.07	.02
□ 8 Stan Belinda	.05	.02	.01
□ 9 Jose Canseco	.30	.14	.04
□ 10 Vaughn Eshelman	.05	.02	.01
□ 11 Mike Macfarlane	.05	.02	.01
□ 12 Troy O'Leary	.05	.02	.01
□ 13 Steve Rodriguez	.05	.02	.01
□ 14 Lee Tinsley	.05	.02	.01
□ 15 Tim Vanegmond	.05	.02	.01
□ 16 Mark Whiten	.05	.02	.01
□ 17 Sean Bergman	.05	.02	.01
□ 18 Chad Curtis	.05	.02	.01
□ 19 John Flaherty	.05	.02	.01
□ 20 Bob Higginson	.30	.14	.04
□ 21 Felipe Lira	.05	.02	.01
□ 22 Shannon Penn	.05	.02	.01
□ 23 Todd Steverson	.05	.02	.01
□ 24 Sean Whiteside	.05	.02	.01
□ 25 Tony Fernandez	.05	.02	.01
□ 26 Jack McDowell	.15	.07	.02
□ 27 Andy Pettitte	.75	.35	.09
□ 28 John Wetteland	.15	.07	.02
□ 29 David Cone	.15	.07	.02
□ 30 Mike Timlin	.05	.02	.01
□ 31 Duane Ward	.05	.02	.01
□ 32 Jim Abbott	.05	.02	.01
□ 33 James Baldwin	.30	.14	.04
□ 34 Mike Devereaux	.05	.02	.01
□ 35 Ray Durham	.15	.07	.02
□ 36 Tim Fortugno	.05	.02	.01
□ 37 Scott Ruffcorn	.05	.02	.01
□ 38 Chris Sabo	.05	.02	.01
□ 39 Paul Assenmacher	.05	.02	.01
□ 40 Bud Black	.05	.02	.01
□ 41 Orel Hershiser	.15	.07	.02
□ 42 Julian Tavarez	.05	.02	.01
□ 43 Dave Winfield	.30	.14	.04
□ 44 Pat Borders	.05	.02	.01
□ 45 Melvin Bunch	.05	.02	.01
□ 46 Tom Goodwin	.05	.02	.01
□ 47 Jon Nunnally	.15	.07	.02
□ 48 Joe Randa	.05	.02	.01
□ 49 Dilson Torres	.05	.02	.01
□ 50 Joe Vitiello	.05	.02	.01
□ 51 David Hulse	.05	.02	.01
□ 52 Scott Karl	.05	.02	.01
□ 53 Mark Kiefer	.05	.02	.01
□ 54 Derrick May	.05	.02	.01
□ 55 Joe Oliver	.05	.02	.01
□ 56 Al Reyes	.05	.02	.01
□ 57 Steve Sparks	.05	.02	.01
□ 58 Jerald Clark	.05	.02	.01
□ 59 Eddie Guardado	.05	.02	.01
□ 60 Kevin Maas	.05	.02	.01
□ 61 David McCarty	.05	.02	.01
□ 62 Brad Radke	.15	.07	.02
□ 63 Scott Stahoviak	.05	.02	.01
□ 64 Garret Anderson	.30	.14	.04
□ 65 Shawn Boskie	.05	.02	.01
□ 66 Mike James	.05	.02	.01
□ 67 Tony Phillips	.15	.07	.02
□ 68 Lee Smith	.15	.07	.02
□ 69 Mitch Williams	.05	.02	.01
□ 70 Jim Corsi	.05	.02	.01
□ 71 Mark Harkey	.05	.02	.01
□ 72 Dave Stewart	.15	.07	.02
□ 73 Todd Stottlemyre	.05	.02	.01
□ 74 Joey Cora	.05	.02	.01
□ 75 Chad Kreuter	.05	.02	.01
□ 76 Jeff Nelson	.05	.02	.01
□ 77 Alex Rodriguez	2.50	1.10	.30
□ 78 Ron Villone	.05	.02	.01
□ 79 Bob Wells	.05	.02	.01
□ 80 Jose Alberro	.05	.02	.01
□ 81 Terry Burrows	.05	.02	.01
□ 82 Kevin Gross	.05	.02	.01
□ 83 Wilson Heredia	.05	.02	.01
□ 84 Mark McLemore	.05	.02	.01
□ 85 Otis Nixon	.05	.02	.01
□ 86 Jeff Russell	.05	.02	.01
□ 87 Mickey Tettleton	.05	.02	.01
□ 88 Bob Tewksbury	.05	.02	.01
□ 89 Pedro Borbon	.05	.02	.01
□ 90 Marquis Grissom	.30	.14	.04
□ 91 Chipper Jones	1.25	.55	.16
□ 92 Mike Mordecai	.05	.02	.01
□ 93 Jason Schmidt	.15	.07	.02
□ 94 John Burkett	.15	.07	.02
□ 95 Andre Dawson	.30	.14	.04
□ 96 Matt Dunbar	.05	.02	.01
□ 97 Charles Johnson	.15	.07	.02
□ 98 Terry Pendleton	.15	.07	.02
□ 99 Rich Scheid	.05	.02	.01
□ 100 Quilvio Veras	.05	.02	.01
□ 101 Bobby Witt	.05	.02	.01
□ 102 Eddie Zosky	.05	.02	.01
□ 103 Shane Andrews	.05	.02	.01
□ 104 Reid Cornelius	.05	.02	.01
□ 105 Chad Fonville	.15	.07	.02
□ 106 Mark Grudzielanek	.50	.23	.06
□ 107 Roberto Kelly	.05	.02	.01
□ 108 Carlos Perez	.15	.07	.02
□ 109 Tony Tarasco	.05	.02	.01
□ 110 Brett Butler	.15	.07	.02
□ 111 Carl Everett	.05	.02	.01
□ 112 Pete Harnisch	.05	.02	.01
□ 113 Doug Henry	.05	.02	.01
□ 114 Kevin Lomon	.05	.02	.01
□ 115 Blas Minor	.05	.02	.01
□ 116 Dave Mlicki	.05	.02	.01
□ 117 Ricky Otero	.05	.02	.01
□ 118 Norm Charlton	.05	.02	.01
□ 119 Tyler Green	.05	.02	.01
□ 120 Gene Harris	.05	.02	.01
□ 121 Charlie Hayes	.05	.02	.01
□ 122 Gregg Jefferies	.15	.07	.02
□ 123 Michael Mimbs	.15	.07	.02
□ 124 Paul Quantrill	.05	.02	.01
□ 125 Frank Castillo	.05	.02	.01
□ 126 Brian McRae	.15	.07	.02
□ 127 Jaime Navarro	.05	.02	.01
□ 128 Mike Perez	.05	.02	.01
□ 129 Tanyon Sturtze	.05	.02	.01
□ 130 Ozzie Timmons	.05	.02	.01
□ 131 John Courtright	.05	.02	.01
□ 132 Ron Gant	.15	.07	.02
□ 133 Xavier Hernandez	.05	.02	.01
□ 134 Brian Hunter	.05	.02	.01
□ 135 Benito Santiago	.05	.02	.01
□ 136 Pete Smith	.05	.02	.01
□ 137 Scott Sullivan	.05	.02	.01
□ 138 Derek Bell	.15	.07	.02
□ 139 Doug Brocail	.05	.02	.01
□ 140 Ricky Gutierrez	.05	.02	.01
□ 141 Pedro Martinez	.15	.07	.02
□ 142 Orlando Miller	.05	.02	.01
□ 143 Phil Plantier	.05	.02	.01
□ 144 Craig Shipley	.05	.02	.01
□ 145 Rich Aude	.05	.02	.01
□ 146 Jason Christiansen	.05	.02	.01
□ 147 Freddy Garcia	.15	.07	.02
□ 148 Jim Gott	.05	.02	.01
□ 149 Mark Johnson	.15	.07	.02
□ 150 Esteban Loaiza	.05	.02	.01
□ 151 Dan Plesac	.05	.02	.01
□ 152 Gary Wilson	.05	.02	.01
□ 153 Allen Battle	.05	.02	.01
□ 154 Terry Bradshaw	.05	.02	.01
□ 155 Scott Cooper	.05	.02	.01
□ 156 Tripp Cromer	.05	.02	.01
□ 157 John Frascatore	.05	.02	.01
□ 158 John Habyan	.05	.02	.01
□ 159 Tom Henke	.05	.02	.01
□ 160 Ken Hill	.05	.02	.01
□ 161 Danny Jackson	.05	.02	.01
□ 162 Donovan Osborne	.05	.02	.01
□ 163 Tom Urbani	.05	.02	.01
□ 164 Roger Bailey	.05	.02	.01
□ 165 Jorge Brito	.05	.02	.01
□ 166 Vinny Castilla	.15	.07	.02
□ 167 Darren Holmes	.05	.02	.01
□ 168 Roberto Mejia	.05	.02	.01
□ 169 Bill Swift	.05	.02	.01

□ 170 Mark Thompson	.05	.02	.01
□ 171 Larry Walker	.30	.14	.04
□ 172 Greg Hansell	.05	.02	.01
□ 173 Dave Hansen	.05	.02	.01
□ 174 Carlos Hernandez	.05	.02	.01
□ 175 Hideo Nomo	2.00	.90	.25
□ 176 Jose Offerman	.05	.02	.01
□ 177 Antonio Osuna	.05	.02	.01
□ 178 Reggie Williams	.05	.02	.01
□ 179 Todd Williams	.05	.02	.01
□ 180 Andres Berumen	.05	.02	.01
□ 181 Ken Caminiti	.30	.14	.04
□ 182 Andujar Cedeno	.05	.02	.01
□ 183 Steve Finley	.15	.07	.02
□ 184 Bryce Florie	.05	.02	.01
□ 185 Dustin Hermanson	.15	.07	.02
□ 186 Ray Holbert	.05	.02	.01
□ 187 Melvin Nieves	.15	.07	.02
□ 188 Roberto Petagine	.05	.02	.01
□ 189 Jody Reed	.05	.02	.01
□ 190 Fernando Valenzuela	.15	.07	.02
□ 191 Brian Williams	.05	.02	.01
□ 192 Mark Dewey	.05	.02	.01
□ 193 Glenallen Hill	.05	.02	.01
□ 194 Chris Hook	.05	.02	.01
□ 195 Terry Mulholland	.05	.02	.01
□ 196 Steve Scarsone	.05	.02	.01
□ 197 Trevor Wilson	.05	.02	.01
□ 198 Checklist	.05	.02	.01
□ 199 Checklist	.05	.02	.01
□ 200 Checklist	.05	.02	.01

1995 Fleer Update Diamond Tribute

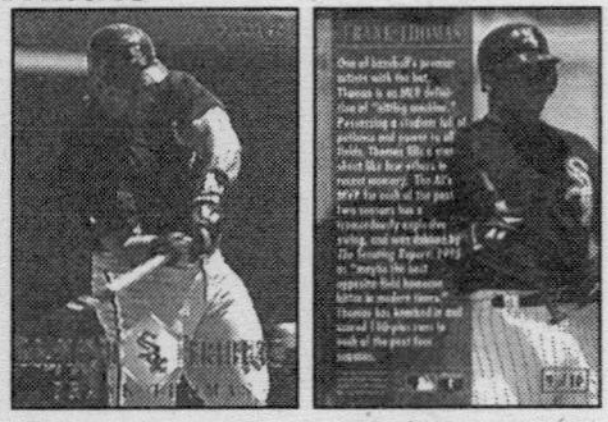

This 10-card standard-size set was inserted at a rate of one in five packs. This set features ten top players. The full-bleed fronts feature a player photo, the "Fleer 95" logo in the upper left corner, the words "Diamond Tribute" surrounding the player's team logo and the player's name on the bottom. All the words in front are in gold foil. The back is split between player information and a player photo. The cards are numbered in the lower right with an "X" of 10. The cards are sequenced in alphabetical order.

	MINT	NRMT	EXC
COMPLETE SET (10)	8.00	3.60	1.00
COMMON CARD (1-10)	.30	.14	.04
RANDOM INSERTS IN HOBBY AND RETAIL PACKS			

□ 1 Jeff Bagwell	1.25	.55	.16
□ 2 Albert Belle	1.50	.70	.19
□ 3 Barry Bonds	.75	.35	.09
□ 4 David Cone	.30	.14	.04
□ 5 Dennis Eckersley	.30	.14	.04
□ 6 Ken Griffey Jr.	3.00	1.35	.35
□ 7 Rickey Henderson	.30	.14	.04
□ 8 Greg Maddux	2.00	.90	.25
□ 9 Frank Thomas	3.00	1.35	.35
□ 10 Matt Williams	.30	.14	.04

1995 Fleer Update Headliners

Inserted one every three packs, this 20-card standard-size set features various major league

stars. The fronts feature the playerís photo set against a newspaper headline. The word "Headliner" as well as the playerís name is printed on the bottom on the card in gold foil. The backs have some player information as well as another player photo. The cards are numbered in the lower left as "X" of 20. The cards are sequenced in alphabetical order.

	MINT	NRMT	EXC
COMPLETE SET (20)	14.00	6.25	1.75
COMMON CARD (1-20)	.25	.11	.03
RANDOM INSERTS IN PACKS			

□ 1 Jeff Bagwell	1.25	.55	.16
□ 2 Albert Belle	1.50	.70	.19
□ 3 Barry Bonds	.75	.35	.09
□ 4 Jose Canseco	.50	.23	.06
□ 5 Joe Carter	.50	.23	.06
□ 6 Will Clark	.50	.23	.06
□ 7 Roger Clemens	.50	.23	.06
□ 8 Lenny Dykstra	.25	.11	.03
□ 9 Cecil Fielder	.50	.23	.06
□ 10 Juan Gonzalez	1.50	.70	.19
□ 11 Ken Griffey Jr.	3.00	1.35	.35
□ 12 Kenny Lofton	.75	.35	.09
□ 13 Greg Maddux	2.00	.90	.25
□ 14 Fred McGriff	.50	.23	.06
□ 15 Mike Piazza	2.00	.90	.25
□ 16 Kirby Puckett	1.00	.45	.12
□ 17 Tim Salmon	.50	.23	.06
□ 18 Frank Thomas	3.00	1.35	.35
□ 19 Mo Vaughn	.75	.35	.09
□ 20 Matt Williams	.50	.23	.06

1995 Fleer Update Rookie Update

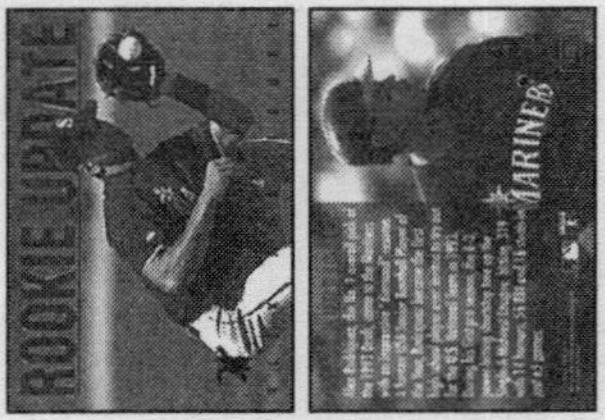

Inserted one in every four packs, this 10-card standard-size set features some of 1995's best rookies. The horizontal fronts feature the words "Rookie Update" in large letters at the top, and the "Fleer 95" logo as well as the player's name at the bottom. The rest of the card has the player's photo. To the left, the back has background information as well as a photo on the right. The cards are numbered as "X of 10". Chipper Jones and Hideo Nomo are among the players included in this set. The set is sequenced in alphabetical order.

	MINT	NRMT	EXC
COMPLETE SET (10)	15.00	6.75	1.85
COMMON CARD (1-10)	.25	.11	.03
SEMISTARS	.75	.35	.09
RANDOM INSERTS IN PACKS			

□ 1 Shane Andrews	.25	.11	.03
□ 2 Ray Durham	.75	.35	.09
□ 3 Shawn Green	.25	.11	.03
□ 4 Charles Johnson	.75	.35	.09
□ 5 Chipper Jones	5.00	2.20	.60
□ 6 Esteban Loaiza	.25	.11	.03
□ 7 Hideo Nomo	4.00	1.80	.50
□ 8 Jon Nunnally	.25	.11	.03
□ 9 Alex Rodriguez	8.00	3.60	1.00
□ 10 Julian Tavarez	.25	.11	.03

1995 Fleer Update Smooth Leather

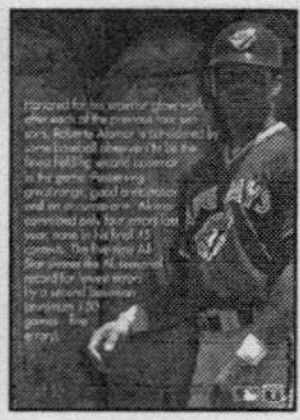

Inserted one every five packs, this 10-card standard-size set features many leading defensive wizards. The card fronts feature a player photo. Underneath the player photo, is his name along with the words "smooth leather" on the bottom. The right corner features a glove. All of this information as well as the "Fleer 95" logo is in gold print. All of this is on a card with a special leather-like coating. The back features a photo as well as fielding information. The cards are numbered in the lower left as "X of 10" and are sequenced in alphabetical order.

	MINT	NRMT	EXC
COMPLETE SET (10)	25.00	11.00	3.10
COMMON CARD (1-10)	.75	.35	.09
SEMISTARS	1.25	.55	.16
RANDOM INSERTS IN JUMBOS			

□ 1 Roberto Alomar	2.50	1.10	.30
□ 2 Barry Bonds	2.50	1.10	.30
□ 3 Ken Griffey Jr.	10.00	4.50	1.25
□ 4 Marquis Grissom	1.25	.55	.16
□ 5 Darren Lewis	.75	.35	.09
□ 6 Kenny Lofton	2.50	1.10	.30
□ 7 Don Mattingly	5.00	2.20	.60
□ 8 Cal Ripken	8.00	3.60	1.00
□ 9 Ivan Rodriguez	2.00	.90	.25
□ 10 Matt Williams	1.25	.55	.16

1995 Fleer Update Soaring Stars

This nine-card standard-size set was inserted one every 36 packs. The fronts feature the player's photo set against a prismatic background of baseballs. The player's name, the "Soaring Stars" logo as well as a star are all printed in gold foil at the bottom. The back has a player photo, his name as well as some career information. The cards are numbered in the upper right "X of 9" and are sequenced in alphabetical order.

	MINT	NRMT	EXC
COMPLETE SET (9)	60.00	27.00	7.50

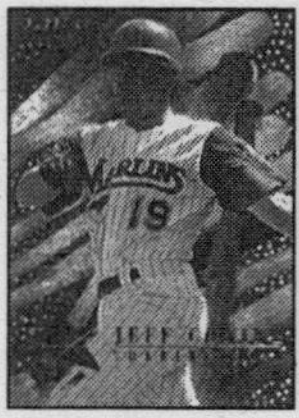

COMMON CARD (1-9)	2.50	1.10	.30
RANDOM INSERTS IN PACKS			

□ 1 Moises Alou UER (says .399 BA in 1994)	4.00	1.80	.50
□ 2 Jason Bere	2.50	1.10	.30
□ 3 Jeff Conine	4.00	1.80	.50
□ 4 Cliff Floyd	2.50	1.10	.30
□ 5 Pat Hentgen	4.00	1.80	.50
□ 6 Kenny Lofton	12.00	5.50	1.50
□ 7 Raul Mondesi	6.00	2.70	.75
□ 8 Mike Piazza	30.00	13.50	3.70
□ 9 Tim Salmon	6.00	2.70	.75

1996 Fleer

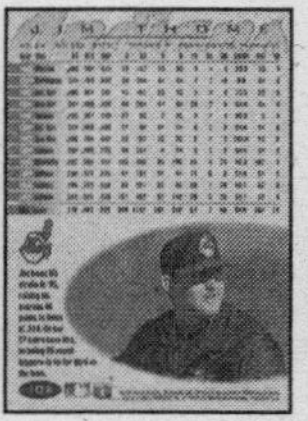

The 1996 Fleer baseball set consists of 600 standard-size cards. Cards were issued in 11-card packs with a suggested retail price of $1.49. Borderless fronts are matte-finished and have full-color action shots with the player's name, team and position stamped in gold foil. Backs contain a biography and career stats on the top and a full-color head shot with a 1995 synopsis on the bottom. The matte finish on the cards was designed so collectors could have an easier surface for cards to be autographed. Fleer included in each pack a "Thanks a Million" scratch-off game card redeemable for instant-win prizes and a chance to play for a million-dollar prize in a Major League park. Rookie Cards in this set include Matt Lawton and Mike Sweeney.

	MINT	NRMT	EXC
COMPLETE SET (600)	70.00	32.00	8.75
COMMON CARD (1-600)	.10	.05	.01
SEMISTARS	.25	.11	.03
STARS	.50	.23	.06
COMP.TIFFANY SET (600)	250.00	110.00	31.00
COMMON TIFFANY (1-600)	.40	.18	.05
TIFFANY SEMISTARS	1.50	.70	.19
TIFFANY STARS	3.00	1.35	.35
*TIFFANY STARS: 2.5X to 5X HI COLUMN			
*TIFFANY YOUNG STARS: 2X to 4X HI			
ONE TIFFANY PER PACK			

□ 1 Manny Alexander	.10	.05	.01
□ 2 Brady Anderson	.50	.23	.06
□ 3 Harold Baines	.25	.11	.03
□ 4 Armando Benitez	.10	.05	.01
□ 5 Bobby Bonilla	.50	.23	.06
□ 6 Kevin Brown	.25	.11	.03

□	7	Scott Erickson	.10	.05	.01
□	8	Curtis Goodwin	.10	.05	.01
□	9	Jeffrey Hammonds	.10	.05	.01
□	10	Jimmy Haynes	.10	.05	.01
□	11	Chris Hoiles	.10	.05	.01
□	12	Doug Jones	.10	.05	.01
□	13	Rick Krivda	.10	.05	.01
□	14	Jeff Manto	.10	.05	.01
□	15	Ben McDonald	.10	.05	.01
□	16	Jamie Moyer	.10	.05	.01
□	17	Mike Mussina	.60	.25	.07
□	18	Jesse Orosco	.10	.05	.01
□	19	Rafael Palmeiro	.50	.23	.06
□	20	Cal Ripken	2.50	1.10	.30
□	21	Rick Aguilera	.10	.05	.01
□	22	Luis Alicea	.10	.05	.01
□	23	Stan Belinda	.10	.05	.01
□	24	Jose Canseco	.50	.23	.06
□	25	Roger Clemens	.50	.23	.06
□	26	Vaughn Eshelman	.10	.05	.01
□	27	Mike Greenwell	.10	.05	.01
□	28	Erik Hanson	.10	.05	.01
□	29	Dwayne Hosey	.10	.05	.01
□	30	Mike Macfarlane UER	.10	.05	.01
□	31	Tim Naehring	.10	.05	.01
□	32	Troy O'Leary	.10	.05	.01
□	33	Aaron Sele	.10	.05	.01
□	34	Zane Smith	.10	.05	.01
□	35	Jeff Suppan	.25	.11	.03
□	36	Lee Tinsley	.10	.05	.01
□	37	John Valentin	.25	.11	.03
□	38	Mo Vaughn	.75	.35	.09
□	39	Tim Wakefield	.10	.05	.01
□	40	Jim Abbott	.50	.23	.06
□	41	Brian Anderson	.10	.05	.01
□	42	Garret Anderson	.50	.23	.06
□	43	Chili Davis	.10	.05	.01
□	44	Gary DiSarcina	.10	.05	.01
□	45	Damion Easley	.10	.05	.01
□	46	Jim Edmonds	.50	.23	.06
□	47	Chuck Finley	.10	.05	.01
□	48	Todd Greene	.50	.23	.06
□	49	Mike Harkey	.10	.05	.01
□	50	Mike James	.10	.05	.01
□	51	Mark Langston	.10	.05	.01
□	52	Greg Myers	.10	.05	.01
□	53	Orlando Palmeiro	.10	.05	.01
□	54	Bob Patterson	.10	.05	.01
□	55	Troy Percival	.25	.11	.03
□	56	Tony Phillips	.25	.11	.03
□	57	Tim Salmon	.50	.23	.06
□	58	Lee Smith	.50	.23	.06
□	59	J.T. Snow	.25	.11	.03
□	60	Randy Velarde	.10	.05	.01
□	61	Wilson Alvarez	.50	.23	.06
□	62	Luis Andujar	.10	.05	.01
□	63	Jason Bere	.10	.05	.01
□	64	Ray Durham	.50	.23	.06
□	65	Alex Fernandez	.50	.23	.06
□	66	Ozzie Guillen	.10	.05	.01
□	67	Roberto Hernandez	.25	.11	.03
□	68	Lance Johnson	.25	.11	.03
□	69	Matt Karchner	.10	.05	.01
□	70	Ron Karkovice	.10	.05	.01
□	71	Norberto Martin	.10	.05	.01
□	72	Dave Martinez	.10	.05	.01
□	73	Kirk McCaskill	.10	.05	.01
□	74	Lyle Mouton	.10	.05	.01
□	75	Tim Raines	.50	.23	.06
□	76	Mike Sirotka	.10	.05	.01
□	77	Frank Thomas	3.00	1.35	.35
□	78	Larry Thomas	.10	.05	.01
□	79	Robin Ventura	.50	.23	.06
□	80	Sandy Alomar, Jr.	.10	.05	.01
□	81	Paul Assenmacher	.10	.05	.01
□	82	Carlos Baerga	.50	.23	.06
□	83	Albert Belle	1.50	.70	.19
□	84	Mark Clark	.10	.05	.01
□	85	Alan Embree	.10	.05	.01
□	86	Alvaro Espinoza	.10	.05	.01
□	87	Orel Hershiser	.25	.11	.03
□	88	Ken Hill	.10	.05	.01
□	89	Kenny Lofton	.75	.35	.09
□	90	Dennis Martinez	.25	.11	.03
□	91	Jose Mesa	.25	.11	.03
□	92	Eddie Murray	.75	.35	.09
□	93	Charles Nagy	.25	.11	.03
□	94	Chad Ogea	.10	.05	.01
□	95	Tony Pena	.10	.05	.01
□	96	Herb Perry	.10	.05	.01
□	97	Eric Plunk	.10	.05	.01
□	98	Jim Poole	.10	.05	.01
□	99	Manny Ramirez	.75	.35	.09
□	100	Paul Sorrento	.10	.05	.01
□	101	Julian Tavarez	.10	.05	.01
□	102	Jim Thome	.60	.25	.07
□	103	Omar Vizquel	.10	.05	.01
□	104	Dave Winfield	.50	.23	.06
□	105	Danny Bautista	.10	.05	.01
□	106	Joe Boever	.10	.05	.01
□	107	Chad Curtis	.10	.05	.01
□	108	John Doherty	.10	.05	.01
□	109	Cecil Fielder	.50	.23	.06
□	110	John Flaherty	.10	.05	.01
□	111	Travis Fryman	.50	.23	.06
□	112	Chris Gomez	.10	.05	.01
□	113	Bob Higginson	.50	.23	.06
□	114	Mark Lewis	.10	.05	.01
□	115	Jose Lima	.10	.05	.01
□	116	Felipe Lira	.10	.05	.01
□	117	Brian Maxcy	.10	.05	.01
□	118	C.J. Nitkowski	.10	.05	.01
□	119	Phil Plantier	.10	.05	.01
□	120	Clint Sodowsky	.10	.05	.01
□	121	Alan Trammell	.50	.23	.06
□	122	Lou Whitaker	.50	.23	.06
□	123	Kevin Appier	.25	.11	.03
□	124	Johnny Damon	.50	.23	.06
□	125	Gary Gaetti	.25	.11	.03
□	126	Tom Goodwin	.25	.11	.03
□	127	Tom Gordon	.10	.05	.01
□	128	Mark Gubicza	.10	.05	.01
□	129	Bob Hamelin	.10	.05	.01
□	130	David Howard	.10	.05	.01
□	131	Jason Jacome	.10	.05	.01
□	132	Wally Joyner	.10	.05	.01
□	133	Keith Lockhart	.10	.05	.01
□	134	Brent Mayne	.10	.05	.01
□	135	Jeff Montgomery	.10	.05	.01
□	136	Jon Nunnally	.10	.05	.01
□	137	Juan Samuel	.10	.05	.01
□	138	Mike Sweeney	.60	.25	.07
□	139	Michael Tucker	.25	.11	.03
□	140	Joe Vitiello	.10	.05	.01
□	141	Ricky Bones	.10	.05	.01
□	142	Chuck Carr	.10	.05	.01
□	143	Jeff Cirillo	.10	.05	.01
□	144	Mike Fetters	.10	.05	.01
□	145	Darryl Hamilton	.10	.05	.01
□	146	David Hulse	.10	.05	.01
□	147	John Jaha	.25	.11	.03
□	148	Scott Karl	.10	.05	.01
□	149	Mark Kiefer	.10	.05	.01
□	150	Pat Listach	.10	.05	.01
□	151	Mark Loretta	.10	.05	.01
□	152	Mike Matheny	.10	.05	.01
□	153	Matt Mieske	.10	.05	.01
□	154	Dave Nilsson	.25	.11	.03
□	155	Joe Oliver	.10	.05	.01
□	156	Al Reyes	.10	.05	.01
□	157	Kevin Seitzer	.10	.05	.01
□	158	Steve Sparks	.10	.05	.01
□	159	B.J. Surhoff	.10	.05	.01
□	160	Jose Valentin	.10	.05	.01
□	161	Greg Vaughn	.50	.23	.06
□	162	Fernando Vina	.10	.05	.01
□	163	Rich Becker	.25	.11	.03
□	164	Ron Coomer	.10	.05	.01
□	165	Marty Cordova	.25	.11	.03
□	166	Chuck Knoblauch	.50	.23	.06
□	167	Matt Lawton	.10	.05	.01
□	168	Pat Meares	.10	.05	.01
□	169	Paul Molitor	.60	.25	.07
□	170	Pedro Munoz	.10	.05	.01
□	171	Jose Parra	.10	.05	.01
□	172	Kirby Puckett	1.00	.45	.12
□	173	Brad Radke	.10	.05	.01
□	174	Jeff Reboulet	.10	.05	.01
□	175	Rich Robertson	.10	.05	.01
□	176	Frank Rodriguez	.25	.11	.03
□	177	Scott Stahoviak	.10	.05	.01
□	178	Dave Stevens	.10	.05	.01

□ 179 Matt Walbeck	.10	.05	.01
□ 180 Wade Boggs	.50	.23	.06
□ 181 David Cone	.50	.23	.06
□ 182 Tony Fernandez	.10	.05	.01
□ 183 Joe Girardi	.10	.05	.01
□ 184 Derek Jeter	2.00	.90	.25
□ 185 Scott Kamieniecki	.10	.05	.01
□ 186 Pat Kelly	.10	.05	.01
□ 187 Jim Leyritz	.10	.05	.01
□ 188 Tino Martinez	.50	.23	.06
□ 189 Don Mattingly	1.50	.70	.19
□ 190 Jack McDowell	.50	.23	.06
□ 191 Jeff Nelson	.10	.05	.01
□ 192 Paul O'Neill	.10	.05	.01
□ 193 Melido Perez	.10	.05	.01
□ 194 Andy Pettitte	.50	.23	.06
□ 195 Mariano Rivera	.50	.23	.06
□ 196 Ruben Sierra	.10	.05	.01
□ 197 Mike Stanley	.10	.05	.01
□ 198 Darryl Strawberry	.50	.23	.06
□ 199 John Wetteland	.25	.11	.03
□ 200 Bob Wickman	.10	.05	.01
□ 201 Bernie Williams	.50	.23	.06
□ 202 Mark Acre	.10	.05	.01
□ 203 Geronimo Berroa	.25	.11	.03
□ 204 Mike Bordick	.25	.11	.03
□ 205 Scott Brosius	.25	.11	.03
□ 206 Dennis Eckersley	.50	.23	.06
□ 207 Brent Gates	.10	.05	.01
□ 208 Jason Giambi	.50	.23	.06
□ 209 Rickey Henderson	.50	.23	.06
□ 210 Jose Herrera	.10	.05	.01
□ 211 Stan Javier	.10	.05	.01
□ 212 Doug Johns	.10	.05	.01
□ 213 Mark McGwire	.50	.23	.06
□ 214 Steve Ontiveros	.10	.05	.01
□ 215 Craig Paquette	.10	.05	.01
□ 216 Ariel Prieto	.10	.05	.01
□ 217 Carlos Reyes	.10	.05	.01
□ 218 Terry Steinbach	.25	.11	.03
□ 219 Todd Stottlemyre	.10	.05	.01
□ 220 Danny Tartabull	.10	.05	.01
□ 221 Todd Van Poppel	.10	.05	.01
□ 222 John Wasdin	.10	.05	.01
□ 223 George Williams	.10	.05	.01
□ 224 Steve Wojciechowski	.10	.05	.01
□ 225 Rich Amaral	.10	.05	.01
□ 226 Bobby Ayala	.10	.05	.01
□ 227 Tim Belcher	.10	.05	.01
□ 228 Andy Benes	.10	.05	.01
□ 229 Chris Bosio	.10	.05	.01
□ 230 Darren Bragg	.10	.05	.01
□ 231 Jay Buhner	.50	.23	.06
□ 232 Norm Charlton	.10	.05	.01
□ 233 Vince Coleman	.10	.05	.01
□ 234 Joey Cora	.10	.05	.01
□ 235 Russ Davis	.10	.05	.01
□ 236 Alex Diaz	.10	.05	.01
□ 237 Felix Fermin	.10	.05	.01
□ 238 Ken Griffey Jr.	3.00	1.35	.35
□ 239 Sterling Hitchcock	.10	.05	.01
□ 240 Randy Johnson	.50	.23	.06
□ 241 Edgar Martinez	.50	.23	.06
□ 242 Bill Risley	.10	.05	.01
□ 243 Alex Rodriguez	3.00	1.35	.35
□ 244 Luis Sojo	.10	.05	.01
□ 245 Dan Wilson	.10	.05	.01
□ 246 Bob Wolcott	.10	.05	.01
□ 247 Will Clark	.50	.23	.06
□ 248 Jeff Frye	.10	.05	.01
□ 249 Benji Gil	.10	.05	.01
□ 250 Juan Gonzalez	1.50	.70	.19
□ 251 Rusty Greer	.50	.23	.06
□ 252 Kevin Gross	.10	.05	.01
□ 253 Roger McDowell	.10	.05	.01
□ 254 Mark McLemore	.10	.05	.01
□ 255 Otis Nixon	.10	.05	.01
□ 256 Luis Ortiz	.10	.05	.01
□ 257 Mike Pagliarulo	.10	.05	.01
□ 258 Dean Palmer	.50	.23	.06
□ 259 Roger Pavlik	.10	.05	.01
□ 260 Ivan Rodriguez	.60	.25	.07
□ 261 Kenny Rogers	.10	.05	.01
□ 262 Jeff Russell	.10	.05	.01
□ 263 Mickey Tettleton	.25	.11	.03
□ 264 Bob Tewksbury	.10	.05	.01

□ 265 Dave Valle	.10	.05	.01
□ 266 Matt Whiteside	.10	.05	.01
□ 267 Roberto Alomar	.75	.35	.09
□ 268 Joe Carter	.50	.23	.06
□ 269 Tony Castillo	.10	.05	.01
□ 270 Domingo Cedeno	.10	.05	.01
□ 271 Tim Crabtree UER	.10	.05	.01
□ 272 Carlos Delgado	.50	.23	.06
□ 273 Alex Gonzalez	.10	.05	.01
□ 274 Shawn Green	.25	.11	.03
□ 275 Juan Guzman	.10	.05	.01
□ 276 Pat Hentgen	.50	.23	.06
□ 277 Al Leiter	.10	.05	.01
□ 278 Sandy Martinez	.10	.05	.01
□ 279 Paul Menhart	.10	.05	.01
□ 280 John Olerud	.10	.05	.01
□ 281 Paul Quantrill	.10	.05	.01
□ 282 Ken Robinson	.10	.05	.01
□ 283 Ed Sprague	.25	.11	.03
□ 284 Mike Timlin	.10	.05	.01
□ 285 Steve Avery	.25	.11	.03
□ 286 Rafael Belliard	.10	.05	.01
□ 287 Jeff Blauser	.10	.05	.01
□ 288 Pedro Borbon	.10	.05	.01
□ 289 Brad Clontz	.10	.05	.01
□ 290 Mike Devereaux	.10	.05	.01
□ 291 Tom Glavine	.50	.23	.06
□ 292 Marquis Grissom	.50	.23	.06
□ 293 Chipper Jones	2.00	.90	.25
□ 294 David Justice	.25	.11	.03
□ 295 Mike Kelly	.10	.05	.01
□ 296 Ryan Klesko	.60	.25	.07
□ 297 Mark Lemke	.10	.05	.01
□ 298 Javier Lopez	.50	.23	.06
□ 299 Greg Maddux	2.00	.90	.25
□ 300 Fred McGriff	.50	.23	.06
□ 301 Greg McMichael	.10	.05	.01
□ 302 Kent Mercker	.10	.05	.01
□ 303 Mike Mordecai	.10	.05	.01
□ 304 Charlie O'Brien	.10	.05	.01
□ 305 Eduardo Perez	.10	.05	.01
□ 306 Luis Polonia	.10	.05	.01
□ 307 Jason Schmidt	.25	.11	.03
□ 308 John Smoltz	.50	.23	.06
□ 309 Terrell Wade	.50	.23	.06
□ 310 Mark Wohlers	.25	.11	.03
□ 311 Scott Bullett	.10	.05	.01
□ 312 Jim Bullinger	.10	.05	.01
□ 313 Larry Casian	.10	.05	.01
□ 314 Frank Castillo	.10	.05	.01
□ 315 Shawon Dunston	.10	.05	.01
□ 316 Kevin Foster	.10	.05	.01
□ 317 Matt Franco	.10	.05	.01
□ 318 Luis Gonzalez	.10	.05	.01
□ 319 Mark Grace	.50	.23	.06
□ 320 Jose Hernandez	.10	.05	.01
□ 321 Mike Hubbard	.10	.05	.01
□ 322 Brian McRae	.10	.05	.01
□ 323 Randy Myers	.10	.05	.01
□ 324 Jaime Navarro	.10	.05	.01
□ 325 Mark Parent	.10	.05	.01
□ 326 Mike Perez	.10	.05	.01
□ 327 Rey Sanchez	.10	.05	.01
□ 328 Ryne Sandberg	.75	.35	.09
□ 329 Scott Servais	.10	.05	.01
□ 330 Sammy Sosa	.50	.23	.06
□ 331 Ozzie Timmons	.10	.05	.01
□ 332 Steve Trachsel	.10	.05	.01
□ 333 Todd Zeile	.25	.11	.03
□ 334 Bret Boone	.10	.05	.01
□ 335 Jeff Branson	.10	.05	.01
□ 336 Jeff Brantley	.10	.05	.01
□ 337 Dave Burba	.10	.05	.01
□ 338 Hector Carrasco	.10	.05	.01
□ 339 Mariano Duncan	.10	.05	.01
□ 340 Ron Gant	.50	.23	.06
□ 341 Lenny Harris	.10	.05	.01
□ 342 Xavier Hernandez	.10	.05	.01
□ 343 Thomas Howard	.10	.05	.01
□ 344 Mike Jackson	.10	.05	.01
□ 345 Barry Larkin	.50	.23	.06
□ 346 Darren Lewis	.10	.05	.01
□ 347 Hal Morris	.10	.05	.01
□ 348 Eric Owens	.10	.05	.01
□ 349 Mark Portugal	.10	.05	.01
□ 350 Jose Rijo	.10	.05	.01

□	351	Reggie Sanders	.50	.23	.06
□	352	Benito Santiago	.10	.05	.01
□	353	Pete Schourek	.25	.11	.03
□	354	John Smiley	.10	.05	.01
□	355	Eddie Taubensee	.10	.05	.01
□	356	Jerome Walton	.10	.05	.01
□	357	David Wells	.10	.05	.01
□	358	Roger Bailey	.10	.05	.01
□	359	Jason Bates	.10	.05	.01
□	360	Dante Bichette	.50	.23	.06
□	361	Ellis Burks	.50	.23	.06
□	362	Vinny Castilla	.50	.23	.06
□	363	Andres Galarraga	.50	.23	.06
□	364	Darren Holmes	.10	.05	.01
□	365	Mike Kingery	.10	.05	.01
□	366	Curt Leskanic	.10	.05	.01
□	367	Quinton McCracken	.10	.05	.01
□	368	Mike Munoz	.10	.05	.01
□	369	David Nied	.10	.05	.01
□	370	Steve Reed	.10	.05	.01
□	371	Bryan Rekar	.10	.05	.01
□	372	Kevin Ritz	.10	.05	.01
□	373	Bruce Ruffin	.10	.05	.01
□	374	Bret Saberhagen	.10	.05	.01
□	375	Bill Swift	.10	.05	.01
□	376	John Vander Wal	.10	.05	.01
□	377	Larry Walker	.50	.23	.06
□	378	Walt Weiss	.10	.05	.01
□	379	Eric Young	.10	.05	.01
□	380	Kurt Abbott	.10	.05	.01
□	381	Alex Arias	.10	.05	.01
□	382	Jerry Browne	.10	.05	.01
□	383	John Burkett	.10	.05	.01
□	384	Greg Colbrunn	.10	.05	.01
□	385	Jeff Conine	.50	.23	.06
□	386	Andre Dawson	.50	.23	.06
□	387	Chris Hammond	.10	.05	.01
□	388	Charles Johnson	.25	.11	.03
□	389	Terry Mathews	.10	.05	.01
□	390	Robb Nen	.10	.05	.01
□	391	Joe Orsulak	.10	.05	.01
□	392	Terry Pendleton	.25	.11	.03
□	393	Pat Rapp	.10	.05	.01
□	394	Gary Sheffield	.50	.23	.06
□	395	Jesus Tavarez	.10	.05	.01
□	396	Marc Valdes	.10	.05	.01
□	397	Quilvio Veras	.10	.05	.01
□	398	Randy Veres	.10	.05	.01
□	399	Devon White	.10	.05	.01
□	400	Jeff Bagwell	1.25	.55	.16
□	401	Derek Bell	.25	.11	.03
□	402	Craig Biggio	.50	.23	.06
□	403	John Cangelosi	.10	.05	.01
□	404	Jim Dougherty	.10	.05	.01
□	405	Doug Drabek	.10	.05	.01
□	406	Tony Eusebio	.10	.05	.01
□	407	Ricky Gutierrez	.10	.05	.01
□	408	Mike Hampton	.10	.05	.01
□	409	Dean Hartgraves	.10	.05	.01
□	410	John Hudek	.10	.05	.01
□	411	Brian L. Hunter	.10	.05	.01
□	412	Todd Jones	.10	.05	.01
□	413	Darryl Kile	.10	.05	.01
□	414	Dave Magadan	.10	.05	.01
□	415	Derrick May	.10	.05	.01
□	416	Orlando Miller	.10	.05	.01
□	417	James Mouton	.10	.05	.01
□	418	Shane Reynolds	.10	.05	.01
□	419	Greg Swindell	.10	.05	.01
□	420	Jeff Tabaka	.10	.05	.01
□	421	Dave Veres	.10	.05	.01
□	422	Billy Wagner	.10	.05	.01
□	423	Donne Wall	.10	.05	.01
□	424	Rick Wilkins	.10	.05	.01
□	425	Billy Ashley	.10	.05	.01
□	426	Mike Blowers	.10	.05	.01
□	427	Brett Butler	.10	.05	.01
□	428	Tom Candiotti	.10	.05	.01
□	429	Juan Castro	.10	.05	.01
□	430	John Cummings	.10	.05	.01
□	431	Delino DeShields	.10	.05	.01
□	432	Joey Eischen	.10	.05	.01
□	433	Chad Fonville	.10	.05	.01
□	434	Greg Gagne	.10	.05	.01
□	435	Dave Hansen	.10	.05	.01
□	436	Carlos Hernandez	.10	.05	.01

□	437	Todd Hollandsworth	.50	.23	.06
□	438	Eric Karros	.50	.23	.06
□	439	Roberto Kelly	.10	.05	.01
□	440	Ramon Martinez	.25	.11	.03
□	441	Raul Mondesi	.50	.23	.06
□	442	Hideo Nomo	.75	.35	.09
□	443	Antonio Osuna	.10	.05	.01
□	444	Chan Ho Park	.50	.23	.06
□	445	Mike Piazza	2.00	.90	.25
□	446	Felix Rodriguez	.10	.05	.01
□	447	Kevin Tapani	.10	.05	.01
□	448	Ismael Valdes	.10	.05	.01
□	449	Todd Worrell	.25	.11	.03
□	450	Moises Alou	.25	.11	.03
□	451	Shane Andrews	.10	.05	.01
□	452	Yamil Benitez	.10	.05	.01
□	453	Sean Berry	.10	.05	.01
□	454	Wil Cordero	.10	.05	.01
□	455	Jeff Fassero	.10	.05	.01
□	456	Darrin Fletcher	.10	.05	.01
□	457	Cliff Floyd	.10	.05	.01
□	458	Mark Grudzielanek	.25	.11	.03
□	459	Gil Heredia	.10	.05	.01
□	460	Tim Laker	.10	.05	.01
□	461	Mike Lansing	.10	.05	.01
□	462	Pedro J.Martinez	.50	.23	.06
□	463	Carlos Perez	.10	.05	.01
□	464	Curtis Pride	.10	.05	.01
□	465	Mel Rojas	.25	.11	.03
□	466	Kirk Rueter	.10	.05	.01
□	467	F.P. Santangelo	.10	.05	.01
□	468	Tim Scott	.10	.05	.01
□	469	David Segui	.10	.05	.01
□	470	Tony Tarasco	.10	.05	.01
□	471	Rondell White	.50	.23	.06
□	472	Edgardo Alfonzo	.25	.11	.03
□	473	Tim Bogar	.10	.05	.01
□	474	Rico Brogna	.10	.05	.01
□	475	Damon Buford	.10	.05	.01
□	476	Paul Byrd	.10	.05	.01
□	477	Carl Everett	.10	.05	.01
□	478	John Franco	.10	.05	.01
□	479	Todd Hundley	.50	.23	.06
□	480	Butch Huskey	.25	.11	.03
□	481	Jason Isringhausen	.25	.11	.03
□	482	Bobby Jones	.10	.05	.01
□	483	Chris Jones	.10	.05	.01
□	484	Jeff Kent	.10	.05	.01
□	485	Dave Mlicki	.10	.05	.01
□	486	Robert Person	.10	.05	.01
□	487	Bill Pulsipher	.25	.11	.03
□	488	Kelly Stinnett	.10	.05	.01
□	489	Ryan Thompson	.10	.05	.01
□	490	Jose Vizcaino	.10	.05	.01
□	491	Howard Battle	.10	.05	.01
□	492	Toby Borland	.10	.05	.01
□	493	Ricky Bottalico	.10	.05	.01
□	494	Darren Daulton	.25	.11	.03
□	495	Lenny Dykstra	.25	.11	.03
□	496	Jim Eisenreich	.10	.05	.01
□	497	Sid Fernandez	.10	.05	.01
□	498	Tyler Green	.10	.05	.01
□	499	Charlie Hayes	.10	.05	.01
□	500	Gregg Jefferies	.50	.23	.06
□	501	Kevin Jordan	.10	.05	.01
□	502	Tony Longmire	.10	.05	.01
□	503	Tom Marsh	.10	.05	.01
□	504	Michael Mimbs	.10	.05	.01
□	505	Mickey Morandini	.10	.05	.01
□	506	Gene Schall	.10	.05	.01
□	507	Curt Schilling	.10	.05	.01
□	508	Heathcliff Slocumb	.10	.05	.01
□	509	Kevin Stocker	.10	.05	.01
□	510	Andy Van Slyke	.25	.11	.03
□	511	Lenny Webster	.10	.05	.01
□	512	Mark Whiten	.10	.05	.01
□	513	Mike Williams	.10	.05	.01
□	514	Jay Bell	.25	.11	.03
□	515	Jacob Brumfield	.10	.05	.01
□	516	Jason Christiansen	.10	.05	.01
□	517	Dave Clark	.10	.05	.01
□	518	Midre Cummings	.10	.05	.01
□	519	Angelo Encarnacion	.10	.05	.01
□	520	John Ericks	.10	.05	.01
□	521	Carlos Garcia	.10	.05	.01
□	522	Mark Johnson	.10	.05	.01

☐ 523 Jeff King	.25	.11	.03
☐ 524 Nelson Liriano	.10	.05	.01
☐ 525 Esteban Loaiza	.10	.05	.01
☐ 526 Al Martin	.10	.05	.01
☐ 527 Orlando Merced	.25	.11	.03
☐ 528 Dan Miceli	.10	.05	.01
☐ 529 Ramon Morel	.10	.05	.01
☐ 530 Denny Neagle	.25	.11	.03
☐ 531 Steve Parris	.10	.05	.01
☐ 532 Dan Plesac	.10	.05	.01
☐ 533 Don Slaught	.10	.05	.01
☐ 534 Paul Wagner	.10	.05	.01
☐ 535 John Wehner	.10	.05	.01
☐ 536 Kevin Young	.10	.05	.01
☐ 537 Allen Battle	.10	.05	.01
☐ 538 David Bell	.10	.05	.01
☐ 539 Alan Benes	.50	.23	.06
☐ 540 Scott Cooper	.10	.05	.01
☐ 541 Tripp Cromer	.10	.05	.01
☐ 542 Tony Fossas	.10	.05	.01
☐ 543 Bernard Gilkey	.25	.11	.03
☐ 544 Tom Henke	.25	.11	.03
☐ 545 Brian Jordan	.50	.23	.06
☐ 546 Ray Lankford	.50	.23	.06
☐ 547 John Mabry	.50	.23	.06
☐ 548 T.J. Mathews	.10	.05	.01
☐ 549 Mike Morgan	.10	.05	.01
☐ 550 Jose Oliva	.10	.05	.01
☐ 551 Jose Oquendo	.10	.05	.01
☐ 552 Donovan Osborne	.10	.05	.01
☐ 553 Tom Pagnozzi	.10	.05	.01
☐ 554 Mark Petkovsek	.10	.05	.01
☐ 555 Danny Sheaffer	.10	.05	.01
☐ 556 Ozzie Smith	.60	.25	.07
☐ 557 Mark Sweeney	.10	.05	.01
☐ 558 Allen Watson	.10	.05	.01
☐ 559 Andy Ashby	.10	.05	.01
☐ 560 Brad Ausmus	.10	.05	.01
☐ 561 Willie Blair	.10	.05	.01
☐ 562 Ken Caminiti	.50	.23	.06
☐ 563 Andujar Cedeno	.10	.05	.01
☐ 564 Glenn Dishman	.10	.05	.01
☐ 565 Steve Finley	.50	.23	.06
☐ 566 Bryce Florie	.10	.05	.01
☐ 567 Tony Gwynn	1.25	.55	.16
☐ 568 Joey Hamilton	.10	.05	.01
☐ 569 Dustin Hermanson UER	.10	.05	.01
☐ 570 Trevor Hoffman	.25	.11	.03
☐ 571 Brian Johnson	.10	.05	.01
☐ 572 Marc Kroon	.10	.05	.01
☐ 573 Scott Livingstone	.10	.05	.01
☐ 574 Marc Newfield	.10	.05	.01
☐ 575 Melvin Nieves	.25	.11	.03
☐ 576 Jody Reed	.10	.05	.01
☐ 577 Bip Roberts	.10	.05	.01
☐ 578 Scott Sanders	.10	.05	.01
☐ 579 Fernando Valenzuela	.25	.11	.03
☐ 580 Eddie Williams	.10	.05	.01
☐ 581 Rod Beck	.25	.11	.03
☐ 582 Marvin Benard	.10	.05	.01
☐ 583 Barry Bonds	.75	.35	.09
☐ 584 Jamie Brewington	.10	.05	.01
☐ 585 Mark Carreon	.10	.05	.01
☐ 586 Royce Clayton	.10	.05	.01
☐ 587 Shawn Estes	.10	.05	.01
☐ 588 Glenallen Hill	.25	.11	.03
☐ 589 Mark Leiter	.10	.05	.01
☐ 590 Kirt Manwaring	.10	.05	.01
☐ 591 David McCarty	.10	.05	.01
☐ 592 Terry Mulholland	.10	.05	.01
☐ 593 John Patterson	.10	.05	.01
☐ 594 J.R. Phillips	.10	.05	.01
☐ 595 Deion Sanders	.50	.23	.06
☐ 596 Steve Scarsone	.10	.05	.01
☐ 597 Robby Thompson	.10	.05	.01
☐ 598 Sergio Valdez	.10	.05	.01
☐ 599 William Van Landingham	.10	.05	.01
☐ 600 Matt Williams	.50	.23	.06
☐ P20 Cal Ripken Promo	2.00	.90	.25

1996 Fleer Checklists

Checklist cards were seeded one per six regular packs and have glossy, borderless fronts

with full-color shots of the Major League's best. "Checklist" and the player's name are stamped in gold foil. Backs list the entire rundown of '96 Fleer cards printed in black type on a white background.

	MINT	NRMT	EXC
COMPLETE SET (10)	5.00	2.20	.60
COMMON CARD (1-10)	.25	.11	.03
RANDOM INSERTS IN PACKS			

☐ 1 Barry Bonds	.40	.18	.05
☐ 2 Ken Griffey Jr.	1.50	.70	.19
☐ 3 Chipper Jones	1.00	.45	.12
☐ 4 Greg Maddux	1.00	.45	.12
☐ 5 Mike Piazza	1.00	.45	.12
☐ 6 Manny Ramirez	.40	.18	.05
☐ 7 Cal Ripken	1.25	.55	.16
☐ 8 Frank Thomas	1.50	.70	.19
☐ 9 Mo Vaughn	.40	.18	.05
☐ 10 Matt Williams	.25	.11	.03

1996 Fleer Golden Memories

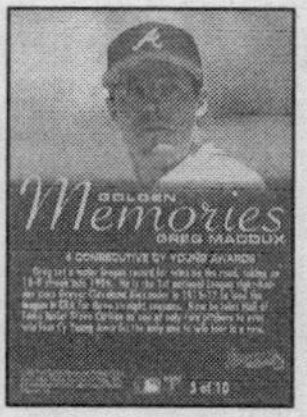

Randomly inserted at a rate of one in 10 regular packs, this 10-card standard-size set features important highlights of the 1995 season. Fronts have two action shots, one serving as a background, the other a full-color cutout. "Golden Memories" and player's name are printed vertically in white type. Backs contain a biography, player close-up and career statistics.

	MINT	NRMT	EXC
COMPLETE SET (10)	12.00	5.50	1.50
COMMON CARD (1-10)	.25	.11	.03
SEMISTARS	.40	.18	.05
RANDOM INSERTS IN PACKS			

☐ 1 Albert Belle	2.50	1.10	.30
☐ 2 Barry Bonds Sammy Sosa	1.25	.55	.16
☐ 3 Greg Maddux	3.00	1.35	.35
☐ 4 Edgar Martinez	.40	.18	.05
☐ 5 Ramon Martinez	.25	.11	.03
☐ 6 Mark McGwire	1.50	.70	.19
☐ 7 Eddie Murray	1.25	.55	.16
☐ 8 Cal Ripken	4.00	1.80	.50
☐ 9 Frank Thomas	5.00	2.20	.60
☐ 10 Alan Trammell Lou Whitaker	.40	.18	.05

1996 Fleer Lumber Company

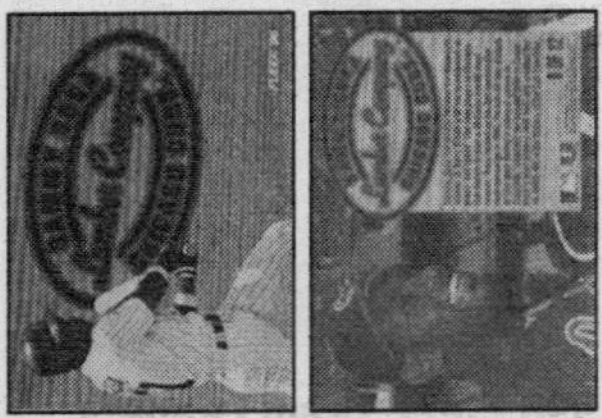

This retail-exclusive 12-card set was inserted one in every nine packs and features RBI and HR power hitters. The fronts display a color action player cut-out on a wood background with embossed printing. The backs carry a player photo and information about the player.

	MINT	NRMT	EXC
COMPLETE SET (12)	30.00	13.50	3.70
COMMON CARD (1-12)	1.00	.45	.12
RANDOM INSERTS IN RETAIL PACKS			

	MINT	NRMT	EXC
□ 1 Albert Belle	5.00	2.20	.60
□ 2 Dante Bichette	1.00	.45	.12
□ 3 Barry Bonds	2.50	1.10	.30
□ 4 Ken Griffey Jr.	10.00	4.50	1.25
□ 5 Mark McGwire	3.00	1.35	.35
□ 6 Mike Piazza	6.00	2.70	.75
□ 7 Manny Ramirez	2.50	1.10	.30
□ 8 Tim Salmon	1.00	.45	.12
□ 9 Sammy Sosa	1.50	.70	.19
□ 10 Frank Thomas	10.00	4.50	1.25
□ 11 Mo Vaughn	2.50	1.10	.30
□ 12 Matt Williams	1.00	.45	.12

1996 Fleer Postseason Glory

Randomly inserted in regular packs at a rate of one in five, this five-card standard-size set highlights great moments of the 1996 Divisional, League Championship and World Series games. Horizontal, white-bordered fronts feature a player in three full-color action cutouts with black strips on top and bottom. "Post-Season Glory" appears on top and the player's name is printed in silver hologram foil. White-bordered backs are split between a full-color player close-up and a description of his post-season play printed in white type on a black background.

	MINT	NRMT	EXC
COMPLETE SET (5)	2.00	.90	.25
COMMON CARD (1-5)	.10	.05	.01
SEMISTARS	.25	.11	.03
RANDOM INSERTS IN PACKS			

	MINT	NRMT	EXC
□ 1 Tom Glavine	.25	.11	.03
□ 2 Ken Griffey Jr.	1.50	.70	.19
□ 3 Orel Hershiser	.10	.05	.01
□ 4 Randy Johnson	.25	.11	.03
□ 5 Jim Thome	.25	.11	.03

1996 Fleer Prospects

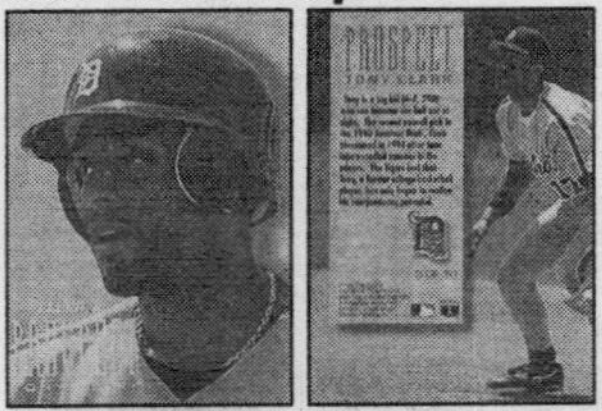

Randomly inserted at a rate of one in six regular packs, this ten-card standard-size set focuses on players moving up through the farm system. Borderless fronts have full-color head shots on one-color backgrounds. "Prospect" and the player's name are stamped in silver hologram foil. Backs feature a full-color action shot with a synopsis of talent printed in a green box.

	MINT	NRMT	EXC
COMPLETE SET (10)	5.00	2.20	.60
COMMON CARD (1-10)	.25	.11	.03
SEMISTARS	.50	.23	.06
RANDOM INSERTS IN PACKS			

	MINT	NRMT	EXC
□ 1 Yamil Benitez	.50	.23	.06
□ 2 Roger Cedeno	.50	.23	.06
□ 3 Tony Clark	.50	.23	.06
□ 4 Micah Franklin	.25	.11	.03
□ 5 Karim Garcia	2.00	.90	.25
□ 6 Todd Greene	.50	.23	.06
□ 7 Alex Ochoa	1.00	.45	.12
□ 8 Ruben Rivera	2.00	.90	.25
□ 9 Chris Snopek	.25	.11	.03
□ 10 Shannon Stewart	.25	.11	.03

1996 Fleer Road Warriors

Randomly inserted in regular packs at a rate of one in 13, this 10-card standard-size set focuses on players who thrive on the road. Fronts feature a full-color player cutout set against a winding rural highway background. "Road Warriors" is printed in reverse type with a hazy white border and the player's name is printed in white type underneath. Backs include the player's road stats, biography and a close-up shot.

	MINT	NRMT	EXC
COMPLETE SET (10)	12.00	5.50	1.50
COMMON CARD (1-10)	.75	.35	.09
RANDOM INSERTS IN PACKS			

	MINT	NRMT	EXC
□ 1 Derek Bell	.75	.35	.09
□ 2 Tony Gwynn	2.00	.90	.25
□ 3 Greg Maddux	3.00	1.35	.35
□ 4 Mark McGwire	1.50	.70	.19

□ 5 Mike Piazza	3.00	1.35	.35
□ 6 Manny Ramirez	1.25	.55	.16
□ 7 Tim Salmon	.75	.35	.09
□ 8 Frank Thomas	5.00	2.20	.60
□ 9 Mo Vaughn	1.25	.55	.16
□ 10 Matt Williams	1.00	.45	.12

1996 Fleer Rookie Sensations

Randomly inserted at a rate of one in 11 regular packs, this 15-card standard-size set highlights 1995's best rookies. Borderless, horizontal fronts have a full-color action shot and a silver hologram strip containing the player's name and team logo. Horizontal backs have full-color head shots with a player profile all printed on a white background.

	MINT	NRMT	EXC
COMPLETE SET (15)	20.00	9.00	2.50
COMMON CARD (1-15)	1.00	.45	.12
SEMISTARS	1.50	.70	.19
RANDOM INSERTS IN PACKS			

□ 1 Garret Anderson	1.50	.70	.19
□ 2 Marty Cordova	2.00	.90	.25
□ 3 Johnny Damon	1.50	.70	.19
□ 4 Ray Durham	1.50	.70	.19
□ 5 Carl Everett	1.50	.70	.19
□ 6 Shawn Green	1.00	.45	.12
□ 7 Brian L.Hunter	1.50	.70	.19
□ 8 Jason Isringhausen	1.00	.45	.12
□ 9 Charles Johnson	1.50	.70	.19
□ 10 Chipper Jones	10.00	4.50	1.25
□ 11 John Mabry	1.50	.70	.19
□ 12 Hideo Nomo	4.00	1.80	.50
□ 13 Troy Percival	1.50	.70	.19
□ 14 Andy Pettitte	5.00	2.20	.60
□ 15 Quilvio Veras	1.00	.45	.12

1996 Fleer Smoke 'n Heat

Randomly inserted at a rate of one in nine regular packs, this 10-card standard-size set celebrates the pitchers with rifle arms and a high strikeout count. Fronts feature a full-color player cutout set against a red flame background. "Smoke 'n Heat" and the player's name are printed in gold type. Backs feature the pitcher's 1995 numbers, a biography and career stats along with a full-color close-up.

	MINT	NRMT	EXC
COMPLETE SET (10)	8.00	3.60	1.00
COMMON CARD (1-10)	.30	.14	.04
SEMISTARS	.60	.25	.07
RANDOM INSERTS IN PACKS			

□ 1 Kevin Appier	.30	.14	.04
□ 2 Roger Clemens	.60	.25	.07
□ 3 David Cone	.60	.25	.07
□ 4 Chuck Finley	.30	.14	.04
□ 5 Randy Johnson	.75	.35	.09
□ 6 Greg Maddux	3.00	1.35	.35
□ 7 Pedro Martinez	.30	.14	.04
□ 8 Hideo Nomo	1.25	.55	.16
□ 9 John Smoltz	.75	.35	.09
□ 10 Todd Stottlemyre	.30	.14	.04

1996 Fleer Team Leaders

This hobby-exclusive 28-card set was randomly inserted one in every nine packs and features statistical and inspirational leaders. The fronts display color action player cut-out on a foil background of the team name and logo. The backs carry a player portrait and player information.

	MINT	NRMT	EXC
COMPLETE SET (28)	80.00	36.00	10.00
COMMON CARD (1-28)	1.00	.45	.12
SEMISTARS	2.00	.90	.25
RANDOM INSERTS IN HOBBY PACKS			

□ 1 Cal Ripken	12.00	5.50	1.50
□ 2 Mo Vaughn	4.00	1.80	.50
□ 3 Jim Edmonds	2.00	.90	.25
□ 4 Frank Thomas	15.00	6.75	1.85
□ 5 Kenny Lofton	4.00	1.80	.50
□ 6 Travis Fryman	2.00	.90	.25
□ 7 Gary Gaetti	1.00	.45	.12
□ 8 B.J. Surhoff	1.00	.45	.12
□ 9 Kirby Puckett	5.00	2.20	.60
□ 10 Don Mattingly	8.00	3.60	1.00
□ 11 Mark McGwire	5.00	2.20	.60
□ 12 Ken Griffey Jr.	15.00	6.75	1.85
□ 13 Juan Gonzalez	8.00	3.60	1.00
□ 14 Joe Carter	2.00	.90	.25
□ 15 Greg Maddux	10.00	4.50	1.25
□ 16 Sammy Sosa	2.50	1.10	.30
□ 17 Barry Larkin	2.00	.90	.25
□ 18 Dante Bichette	2.00	.90	.25
□ 19 Jeff Conine	1.00	.45	.12
□ 20 Jeff Bagwell	6.00	2.70	.75
□ 21 Mike Piazza	10.00	4.50	1.25
□ 22 Rondell White	1.00	.45	.12
□ 23 Rico Brogna	1.00	.45	.12
□ 24 Darren Daulton	1.00	.45	.12
□ 25 Jeff King	1.00	.45	.12
□ 26 Ray Lankford	2.00	.90	.25
□ 27 Tony Gwynn	6.00	2.70	.75
□ 28 Barry Bonds	4.00	1.80	.50

1996 Fleer Tomorrow's Legends

Randomly inserted in regular packs at a rate of one in 13, this 10-card set focuses on young

talent with bright futures. Multicolored fronts have four panels of art that serve as a background and a full-color player cutout. "Tomorrow's Legends" and player's name are printed in white type at the bottom. Backs include the player's '95 stats, biography and a full-color close-up shot.

	MINT	NRMT	EXC
COMPLETE SET (10)	15.00	6.75	1.85
COMMON CARD (1-10)	1.00	.45	.12
SEMISTARS	1.50	.70	.19
RANDOM INSERTS IN PACKS			

	MINT	NRMT	EXC
☐ 1 Garret Anderson	1.00	.45	.12
☐ 2 Jim Edmonds	1.50	.70	.19
☐ 3 Brian L.Hunter	1.00	.45	.12
☐ 4 Jason Isringhausen	1.00	.45	.12
☐ 5 Charles Johnson	1.00	.45	.12
☐ 6 Chipper Jones	8.00	3.60	1.00
☐ 7 Ryan Klesko	2.50	1.10	.30
☐ 8 Hideo Nomo	3.00	1.35	.35
☐ 9 Manny Ramirez	3.00	1.35	.35
☐ 10 Rondell White	1.50	.70	.19

1996 Fleer Zone

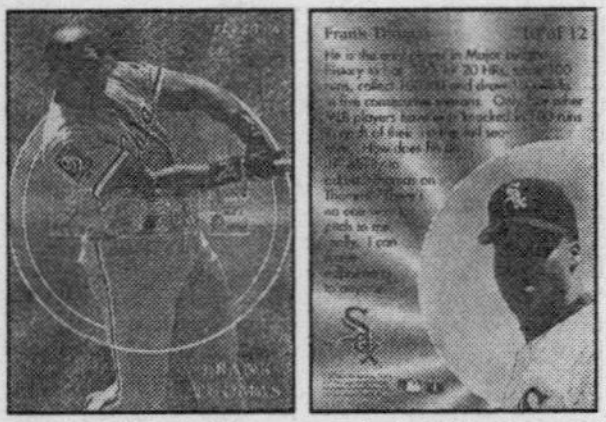

This 12-card set was randomly inserted one in every 90 packs and features "unstoppable" hitters and "unhittable" pitchers. The fronts display a color action player cut-out printed on holographic foil. The backs carry a player portrait with information as to why they were selected for this set.

	MINT	NRMT	EXC
COMPLETE SET (12)	225.00	100.00	28.00
COMMON CARD (1-12)	6.00	2.70	.75
RANDOM INSERTS IN PACKS			

	MINT	NRMT	EXC
☐ 1 Albert Belle	25.00	11.00	3.10
☐ 2 Barry Bonds	12.00	5.50	1.50
☐ 3 Ken Griffey Jr.	50.00	22.00	6.25
☐ 4 Tony Gwynn	20.00	9.00	2.50
☐ 5 Randy Johnson	8.00	3.60	1.00
☐ 6 Kenny Lofton	12.00	5.50	1.50
☐ 7 Greg Maddux	30.00	13.50	3.70
☐ 8 Edgar Martinez	6.00	2.70	.75
☐ 9 Mike Piazza	30.00	13.50	3.70
☐ 10 Frank Thomas	50.00	22.00	6.25
☐ 11 Mo Vaughn	12.00	5.50	1.50
☐ 12 Matt Williams	6.00	2.70	.75

1996 Fleer Update

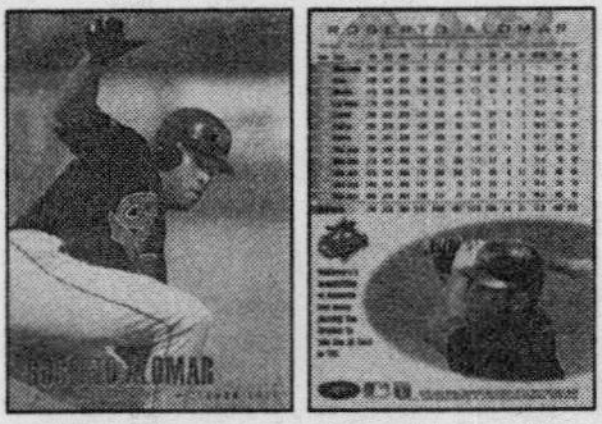

The 1996 Fleer Update set was issued in one series totalling 250 cards. The 11-card packs retail for $1.49 each. The fronts feature color action player photos. The backs carry complete player stats and a "Did you know?" fact. The cards are grouped alphabetically within teams and checklisted below alphabetically according to teams for each league as follows: Baltimore Orioles (U1-U10), Boston Red Sox (U11-U18), California Angels (U19-U22), Chicago White Sox (U23-U30), Cleveland Indians (U31-U32), Detroit Tigers (U33-U37), Kansas City Royals (U38-U44), Milwaukee Brewers (U45-U49), Minnesota Twins (U50-U57), New York Yankees (U58-U69), Oakland Athletics (U70-U77), Seattle Mariners (U78-U85), Texas Rangers (U86-U92), Toronto Blue Jays (U93-U103), Atlanta Braves (U104-U107), Chicago Cubs (U108-U115), Cincinnati Reds (U116-U126), Colorado Rockies (U127-U130), Florida Marlins (U131-U135), Houston Astros (U136-U140), Los Angeles Dodgers (U141-U145), Montreal Expos (U146-U153), New York Mets (U154-U162), Philadelphia Phillis (U163-U173), Pittsburgh Pirates (U174-U180), St. Louis Cardinals (U181-U194), San Diego Padres (U195-U201) and San Francisco Giants (U202-U210). The set contains the subset: Encore (U211-U245).

	MINT	NRMT	EXC
COMPLETE SET (250)	20.00	9.00	2.50
COMMON CARD (U1-U250)	.10	.05	.01
SEMISTARS	.25	.11	.03
STARS	.50	.23	.06
COMP.TIFFANY SET (250)	100.00	45.00	12.50
COMMON TIFFANY (1-250)	.25	.11	.03
TIFFANY SEMISTARS	1.00	.45	.12
*TIFFANY STARS: 3X to 6X HI COLUMN			
*TIFFANY YOUNG STARS: 2.5X to 5X HI			
ONE TIFFANY PER PACK			

	MINT	NRMT	EXC
☐ U1 Roberto Alomar	.75	.35	.09
☐ U2 Mike Devereaux	.10	.05	.01
☐ U3 Scott McClain	.10	.05	.01
☐ U4 Roger McDowell	.10	.05	.01
☐ U5 Kent Mercker	.10	.05	.01
☐ U6 Jimmy Myers	.10	.05	.01
☐ U7 Randy Myers	.10	.05	.01
☐ U8 B.J. Surhoff	.10	.05	.01
☐ U9 Tony Tarasco	.10	.05	.01
☐ U10 David Wells	.10	.05	.01
☐ U11 Wil Cordero	.10	.05	.01
☐ U12 Tom Gordon	.10	.05	.01
☐ U13 Reggie Jefferson	.10	.05	.01
☐ U14 Jose Malave	.10	.05	.01
☐ U15 Kevin Mitchell	.10	.05	.01
☐ U16 Jamie Moyer	.10	.05	.01
☐ U17 Heathcliff Slocumb	.10	.05	.01
☐ U18 Mike Stanley	.10	.05	.01
☐ U19 George Arias	.10	.05	.01
☐ U20 Jorge Fabregas	.10	.05	.01
☐ U21 Don Slaught	.10	.05	.01
☐ U22 Randy Velarde	.10	.05	.01
☐ U23 Harold Baines	.25	.11	.03
☐ U24 Mike Cameron	1.00	.45	.12
☐ U25 Darren Lewis	.10	.05	.01

☐ U26 Tony Phillips	.25	.11	.03
☐ U27 Bill Simas	.10	.05	.01
☐ U28 Chris Snopek	.10	.05	.01
☐ U29 Kevin Tapani	.10	.05	.01
☐ U30 Danny Tartabull	.10	.05	.01
☐ U31 Julio Franco	.25	.11	.03
☐ U32 Jack McDowell	.50	.23	.06
☐ U33 Kimera Bartee	.10	.05	.01
☐ U34 Mark Lewis	.10	.05	.01
☐ U35 Melvin Nieves	.25	.11	.03
☐ U36 Mark Parent	.10	.05	.01
☐ U37 Eddie Williams	.10	.05	.01
☐ U38 Tim Belcher	.10	.05	.01
☐ U39 Sal Fasano	.10	.05	.01
☐ U40 Chris Haney	.10	.05	.01
☐ U41 Mike Macfarlane	.10	.05	.01
☐ U42 Jose Offerman	.10	.05	.01
☐ U43 Joe Randa	.10	.05	.01
☐ U44 Bip Roberts	.10	.05	.01
☐ U45 Chuck Carr	.10	.05	.01
☐ U46 Bobby Hughes	.10	.05	.01
☐ U47 Graeme Lloyd	.10	.05	.01
☐ U48 Ben McDonald	.10	.05	.01
☐ U49 Kevin Wickander	.10	.05	.01
☐ U50 Rick Aguilera	.10	.05	.01
☐ U51 Mike Durant	.10	.05	.01
☐ U52 Chip Hale	.10	.05	.01
☐ U53 LaTroy Hawkins	.10	.05	.01
☐ U54 Dave Hollins	.10	.05	.01
☐ U55 Roberto Kelly	.10	.05	.01
☐ U56 Paul Molitor	.60	.25	.07
☐ U57 Dan Naulty	.10	.05	.01
☐ U58 Mariano Duncan	.10	.05	.01
☐ U59 Andy Fox	.10	.05	.01
☐ U60 Joe Girardi	.10	.05	.01
☐ U61 Dwight Gooden	.50	.23	.06
☐ U62 Jimmy Key	.25	.11	.03
☐ U63 Matt Luke	.10	.05	.01
☐ U64 Tino Martinez	.50	.23	.06
☐ U65 Jeff Nelson	.10	.05	.01
☐ U66 Tim Raines	.50	.23	.06
☐ U67 Ruben Rivera	.60	.25	.07
☐ U68 Kenny Rogers	.10	.05	.01
☐ U69 Gerald Williams	.10	.05	.01
☐ U70 Tony Batista	.25	.11	.03
☐ U71 Allen Battle	.10	.05	.01
☐ U72 Jim Corsi	.10	.05	.01
☐ U73 Steve Cox	.10	.05	.01
☐ U74 Pedro Munoz	.10	.05	.01
☐ U75 Phil Plantier	.10	.05	.01
☐ U76 Scott Spiezio	.10	.05	.01
☐ U77 Ernie Young	.10	.05	.01
☐ U78 Russ Davis	.10	.05	.01
☐ U79 Sterling Hitchcock	.10	.05	.01
☐ U80 Edwin Hurtado	.10	.05	.01
☐ U81 Raul Ibanez	.10	.05	.01
☐ U82 Mike Jackson	.10	.05	.01
☐ U83 Ricky Jordan	.10	.05	.01
☐ U84 Paul Sorrento	.10	.05	.01
☐ U85 Doug Strange	.10	.05	.01
☐ U86 Mark Brandenberg	.10	.05	.01
☐ U87 Damon Buford	.10	.05	.01
☐ U88 Kevin Elster	.25	.11	.03
☐ U89 Darryl Hamilton	.10	.05	.01
☐ U90 Ken Hill	.25	.11	.03
☐ U91 Ed Vosberg	.10	.05	.01
☐ U92 Craig Worthington	.10	.05	.01
☐ U93 Tilson Brito	.10	.05	.01
☐ U94 Giovanni Carrara	.10	.05	.01
☐ U95 Felipe Crespo	.10	.05	.01
☐ U96 Erik Hanson	.10	.05	.01
☐ U97 Marty Janzen	.10	.05	.01
☐ U98 Otis Nixon	.10	.05	.01
☐ U99 Charlie O'Brien	.10	.05	.01
☐ U100 Robert Perez	.10	.05	.01
☐ U101 Paul Quantrill	.10	.05	.01
☐ U102 Bill Risley	.10	.05	.01
☐ U103 Juan Samuel	.10	.05	.01
☐ U104 Jermaine Dye	.75	.35	.09
☐ U105 Wonderful Monds	.10	.05	.01
☐ U106 Dwight Smith	.10	.05	.01
☐ U107 Jerome Walton	.10	.05	.01
☐ U108 Terry Adams	.10	.05	.01
☐ U109 Leo Gomez	.10	.05	.01
☐ U110 Robin Jennings	.10	.05	.01
☐ U111 Doug Jones	.10	.05	.01
☐ U112 Brooks Kieschnick	.10	.05	.01
☐ U113 Dave Magadan	.10	.05	.01
☐ U114 Jason Maxwell	.10	.05	.01
☐ U115 Rodney Myers	.10	.05	.01
☐ U116 Eric Anthony	.10	.05	.01
☐ U117 Vince Coleman	.10	.05	.01
☐ U118 Eric Davis	.25	.11	.03
☐ U119 Steve Gibralter	.10	.05	.01
☐ U120 Curtis Goodwin	.10	.05	.01
☐ U121 Willie Greene	.10	.05	.01
☐ U122 Mike Kelly	.10	.05	.01
☐ U123 Marcus Moore	.10	.05	.01
☐ U124 Chad Mottola	.10	.05	.01
☐ U125 Chris Sabo	.10	.05	.01
☐ U126 Roger Salkeld	.10	.05	.01
☐ U127 Pedro Castellano	.10	.05	.01
☐ U128 Trenidad Hubbard	.10	.05	.01
☐ U129 Jayhawk Owens	.10	.05	.01
☐ U130 Jeff Reed	.10	.05	.01
☐ U131 Kevin Brown	.25	.11	.03
☐ U132 Al Leiter	.10	.05	.01
☐ U133 Matt Mantei	.10	.05	.01
☐ U134 Dave Weathers	.10	.05	.01
☐ U135 Devon White	.10	.05	.01
☐ U136 Bob Abreu	.50	.23	.06
☐ U137 Sean Berry	.10	.05	.01
☐ U138 Doug Brocail	.10	.05	.01
☐ U139 Richard Hidalgo	.10	.05	.01
☐ U140 Alvin Morman	.10	.05	.01
☐ U141 Mike Blowers	.10	.05	.01
☐ U142 Roger Cedeno	.25	.11	.03
☐ U143 Greg Gagne	.10	.05	.01
☐ U144 Karim Garcia	.60	.25	.07
☐ U145 Wilton Guerrero	.60	.25	.07
☐ U146 Israel Alcantara	.10	.05	.01
☐ U147 Omar Daal	.10	.05	.01
☐ U148 Ryan McGuire	.10	.05	.01
☐ U149 Sherman Obando	.10	.05	.01
☐ U150 Jose Paniagua	.10	.05	.01
☐ U151 Henry Rodriguez	.50	.23	.06
☐ U152 Andy Stankiewicz	.10	.05	.01
☐ U153 Dave Veres	.10	.05	.01
☐ U154 Juan Acevedo	.10	.05	.01
☐ U155 Mark Clark	.10	.05	.01
☐ U156 Bernard Gilkey	.25	.11	.03
☐ U157 Pete Harnisch	.10	.05	.01
☐ U158 Lance Johnson	.25	.11	.03
☐ U159 Brent Mayne	.10	.05	.01
☐ U160 Rey Ordonez	.60	.25	.07
☐ U161 Kevin Roberson	.10	.05	.01
☐ U162 Paul Wilson	.25	.11	.03
☐ U163 David Doster	.10	.05	.01
☐ U164 Mike Grace	.10	.05	.01
☐ U165 Rich Hunter	.10	.05	.01
☐ U166 Pete Incaviglia	.10	.05	.01
☐ U167 Mike Lieberthal	.10	.05	.01
☐ U168 Terry Mulholland	.10	.05	.01
☐ U169 Ken Ryan	.10	.05	.01
☐ U170 Benito Santiago	.10	.05	.01
☐ U171 Kevin Sefcik	.10	.05	.01
☐ U172 Lee Tinsley	.10	.05	.01
☐ U173 Todd Zeile	.25	.11	.03
☐ U174 Francisco Cordova	.10	.05	.01
☐ U175 Danny Darwin	.10	.05	.01
☐ U176 Charlie Hayes	.10	.05	.01
☐ U177 Jason Kendall	.50	.23	.06
☐ U178 Mike Kingery	.10	.05	.01
☐ U179 Jon Lieber	.10	.05	.01
☐ U180 Zane Smith	.10	.05	.01
☐ U181 Luis Alicea	.10	.05	.01
☐ U182 Cory Bailey	.10	.05	.01
☐ U183 Andy Benes	.10	.05	.01
☐ U184 Pat Borders	.10	.05	.01
☐ U185 Mike Busby	.10	.05	.01
☐ U186 Royce Clayton	.10	.05	.01
☐ U187 Dennis Eckersley	.50	.23	.06
☐ U188 Gary Gaetti	.25	.11	.03
☐ U189 Ron Gant	.50	.23	.06
☐ U190 Aaron Holbert	.10	.05	.01
☐ U191 Willie McGee	.10	.05	.01
☐ U192 Miguel Mejia	.10	.05	.01
☐ U193 Jeff Parrett	.10	.05	.01
☐ U194 Todd Stottlemyre	.10	.05	.01
☐ U195 Sean Bergman	.10	.05	.01
☐ U196 Archi Cianfrocco	.10	.05	.01
☐ U197 Rickey Henderson	.50	.23	.06

□ U198 Wally Joyner	.10	.05	.01
□ U199 Craig Shipley	.10	.05	.01
□ U200 Bob Tewksbury	.10	.05	.01
□ U201 Tim Worrell	.10	.05	.01
□ U202 Rich Aurilia	.10	.05	.01
□ U203 Doug Creek	.10	.05	.01
□ U204 Shawon Dunston	.10	.05	.01
□ U205 Osvaldo Fernandez	.50	.23	.06
□ U206 Mark Gardner	.10	.05	.01
□ U207 Stan Javier	.10	.05	.01
□ U208 Marcus Jensen	.10	.05	.01
□ U209 Chris Singleton	.10	.05	.01
□ U210 Allen Watson	.10	.05	.01
□ U211 Jeff Bagwell ENC	.60	.25	.07
□ U212 Derek Bell ENC	.25	.11	.03
□ U213 Albert Belle ENC	.75	.35	.09
□ U214 Wade Boggs ENC	.50	.23	.06
□ U215 Barry Bonds ENC	.50	.23	.06
□ U216 Jose Canseco ENC	.50	.23	.06
□ U217 Marty Cordova ENC	.25	.11	.03
□ U218 Jim Edmonds ENC	.25	.11	.03
□ U219 Cecil Fielder ENC	.50	.23	.06
□ U220 Andres Galarraga ENC	.50	.23	.06
□ U221 Juan Gonzalez ENC	.75	.35	.09
□ U222 Mark Grace ENC	.50	.23	.06
□ U223 Ken Griffey Jr. ENC	1.50	.70	.19
□ U224 Tony Gwynn ENC	.60	.25	.07
□ U225 Jason Isringhausen ENC	.10	.05	.01
□ U226 Derek Jeter ENC	1.00	.45	.12
□ U227 Randy Johnson ENC	.25	.11	.03
□ U228 Chipper Jones ENC	1.00	.45	.12
□ U229 Ryan Klesko ENC	.25	.11	.03
□ U230 Barry Larkin ENC	.50	.23	.06
□ U231 Kenny Lofton ENC	.50	.23	.06
□ U232 Greg Maddux ENC	1.00	.45	.12
□ U233 Raul Mondesi ENC	.25	.11	.03
□ U234 Hideo Nomo ENC	.50	.23	.06
□ U235 Mike Piazza ENC	1.00	.45	.12
□ U236 Manny Ramirez ENC	.25	.11	.03
□ U237 Cal Ripken ENC	1.25	.55	.16
□ U238 Tim Salmon ENC	.25	.11	.03
□ U239 Ryne Sandberg ENC	.50	.23	.06
□ U240 Reggie Sanders ENC	.25	.11	.03
□ U241 Gary Sheffield ENC	.50	.23	.06
□ U242 Sammy Sosa ENC	.50	.23	.06
□ U243 Frank Thomas ENC	1.50	.70	.19
□ U244 Mo Vaughn ENC	.50	.23	.06
□ U245 Matt Williams ENC	.50	.23	.06
□ U246 Barry Bonds CL	.50	.23	.06
□ U247 Ken Griffey Jr. CL	1.50	.70	.19
□ U248 Rey Ordonez CL	.25	.11	.03
□ U249 Ryne Sandberg CL	.50	.23	.06
□ U250 Frank Thomas CL	1.50	.70	.19

1996 Fleer Update Diamond Tribute

Randomly inserted in packs at a rate of one in 100, this 10-card set spotlights ten future Hall of Famers with holographic foils in a diamond design.

	MINT	NRMT	EXC
COMPLETE SET (10)	250.00	110.00	31.00
COMMON CARD (1-10)	6.00	2.70	.75
RANDOM INSERTS IN PACKS			

□ 1 Wade Boggs	6.00	2.70	.75
□ 2 Barry Bonds	15.00	6.75	1.85
□ 3 Ken Griffey Jr.	60.00	27.00	7.50
□ 4 Tony Gwynn	25.00	11.00	3.10
□ 5 Rickey Henderson	6.00	2.70	.75
□ 6 Greg Maddux	40.00	18.00	5.00
□ 7 Eddie Murray	15.00	6.75	1.85
□ 8 Cal Ripken	50.00	22.00	6.25
□ 9 Ozzie Smith	12.00	5.50	1.50
□ 10 Frank Thomas	60.00	27.00	7.50

1996 Fleer Update Headliners

Randomly inserted exclusively in retail packs at a rate of one in 20, cards from this 20-card set feature raised textured printing. The fronts carry color action player photos with the word "headliner" running continuously across the background.

	MINT	NRMT	EXC
COMPLETE SET (20)	50.00	22.00	6.25
COMMON CARD (1-20)	1.00	.45	.12
RANDOM INSERTS IN PACKS			

□ 1 Roberto Alomar	2.00	.90	.25
□ 2 Jeff Bagwell	3.00	1.35	.35
□ 3 Albert Belle	4.00	1.80	.50
□ 4 Barry Bonds	2.00	.90	.25
□ 5 Cecil Fielder	1.00	.45	.12
□ 6 Juan Gonzalez	4.00	1.80	.50
□ 7 Ken Griffey Jr.	8.00	3.60	1.00
□ 8 Tony Gwynn	3.00	1.35	.35
□ 9 Randy Johnson	1.00	.45	.12
□ 10 Chipper Jones	5.00	2.20	.60
□ 11 Ryan Klesko	1.50	.70	.19
□ 12 Kenny Lofton	2.00	.90	.25
□ 13 Greg Maddux	5.00	2.20	.60
□ 14 Hideo Nomo	2.00	.90	.25
□ 15 Mike Piazza	5.00	2.20	.60
□ 16 Manny Ramirez	2.00	.90	.25
□ 17 Cal Ripken	6.00	2.70	.75
□ 18 Tim Salmon	1.00	.45	.12
□ 19 Frank Thomas	8.00	3.60	1.00
□ 20 Matt Williams	1.00	.45	.12

1996 Fleer Update New Horizons

Randomly inserted in hobby packs only at a rate of one in five, this 20-card set features 1996 rookies and prospects. The fronts carry

player action color photos printed on foil cards. The backs display a player portrait and information about the player.

	MINT	NRMT	EXC
COMPLETE SET (20)	15.00	6.75	1.85
COMMON CARD (1-20)	.50	.23	.06
SEMISTARS	1.00	.45	.12
RANDOM INSERTS IN HOBBY PACKS			

	MINT	NRMT	EXC
□ 1 Bob Abreu	1.00	.45	.12
□ 2 George Arias	.50	.23	.06
□ 3 Tony Batista	1.00	.45	.12
□ 4 Steve Cox	.50	.23	.06
□ 5 Jermaine Dye	3.00	1.35	.35
□ 6 Andy Fox	.50	.23	.06
□ 7 Mike Grace	.50	.23	.06
□ 8 Todd Greene	1.00	.45	.12
□ 9 Wilton Guerrero	1.50	.70	.19
□ 10 Richard Hidalgo	1.50	.70	.19
□ 11 Raul Ibanez	.50	.23	.06
□ 12 Robin Jennings	.50	.23	.06
□ 13 Marcus Jensen	.50	.23	.06
□ 14 Jason Kendall	2.00	.90	.25
□ 15 Jason Maxwell	.50	.23	.06
□ 16 Ryan McGuire	.50	.23	.06
□ 17 Miguel Mejia	.50	.23	.06
□ 18 Wonderful Monds	.50	.23	.06
□ 19 Rey Ordonez	2.50	1.10	.30
□ 20 Paul Wilson	1.50	.70	.19

1996 Fleer Update Smooth Leather

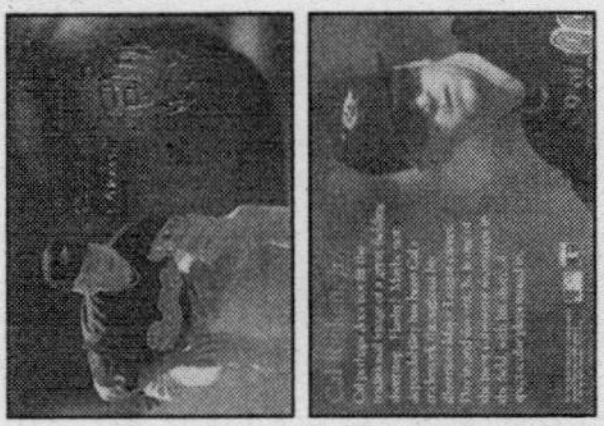

Randomly inserted in packs at a rate of one in 5, this 10-card set features ten defensive stars. The fronts display color player photos and gold foil printing. The backs carry a player portrait and information about why the player was selected for this set.

	MINT	NRMT	EXC
COMPLETE SET (10)	12.00	5.50	1.50
COMMON CARD (1-10)	.50	.23	.06
RANDOM INSERTS IN PACKS			

	MINT	NRMT	EXC
□ 1 Roberto Alomar	1.00	.45	.12
□ 2 Barry Bonds	1.00	.45	.12
□ 3 Will Clark	.50	.23	.06
□ 4 Ken Griffey Jr.	4.00	1.80	.50
□ 5 Kenny Lofton	1.00	.45	.12
□ 6 Greg Maddux	2.50	1.10	.30
□ 7 Raul Mondesi	.50	.23	.06
□ 8 Rey Ordonez	.60	.25	.07
□ 9 Cal Ripken	3.00	1.35	.35
□ 10 Matt Williams	.50	.23	.06

1996 Fleer Update Soaring Stars

Randomly inserted in packs at a rate of one in 11, this 10-card set features 10 of the hottest young players. The fronts carry color player cutouts on a background of soaring baseballs in

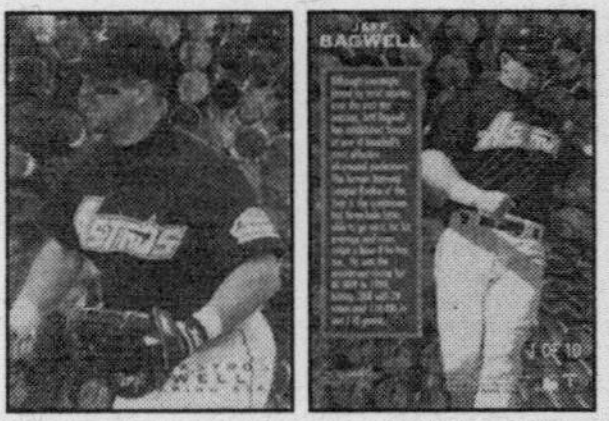

etched foil. The backs display another player photo on the same background with player information.

	MINT	NRMT	EXC
COMPLETE SET (10)	30.00	13.50	3.70
COMMON CARD (1-10)	1.00	.45	.12
RANDOM INSERTS IN PACKS			

	MINT	NRMT	EXC
□ 1 Jeff Bagwell	3.00	1.35	.35
□ 2 Barry Bonds	2.00	.90	.25
□ 3 Juan Gonzalez	4.00	1.80	.50
□ 4 Ken Griffey Jr.	8.00	3.60	1.00
□ 5 Chipper Jones	5.00	2.20	.60
□ 6 Greg Maddux	5.00	2.20	.60
□ 7 Mike Piazza	5.00	2.20	.60
□ 8 Manny Ramirez	2.00	.90	.25
□ 9 Frank Thomas	8.00	3.60	1.00
□ 10 Matt Williams	1.00	.45	.12

1996 Fleer Circa

The 1996 Circa set was issued in one series totalling 200 cards. The eight-card packs retail for $1.99 each. The cards feature color action player photos on one of 28 different background designs and colors indicating the player's major league team. The backs carry player information and statistics.

	MINT	NRMT	EXC
COMPLETE SET (200)	30.00	13.50	3.70
COMMON CARD (1-200)	.10	.05	.01
SEMISTARS	.25	.11	.03
STARS	.50	.23	.06

	MINT	NRMT	EXC
□ 1 Roberto Alomar	.75	.35	.09
□ 2 Brady Anderson	.50	.23	.06
□ 3 Rocky Coppinger	.60	.25	.07
□ 4 Eddie Murray	.75	.35	.09
□ 5 Mike Mussina	.60	.25	.07
□ 6 Randy Myers	.10	.05	.01
□ 7 Rafael Palmeiro	.50	.23	.06
□ 8 Cal Ripken	2.50	1.10	.30
□ 9 Jose Canseco	.50	.23	.06
□ 10 Roger Clemens	.50	.23	.06
□ 11 Mike Greenwell	.10	.05	.01
□ 12 Tim Naehring	.10	.05	.01
□ 13 John Valentin	.25	.11	.03
□ 14 Mo Vaughn	.75	.35	.09
□ 15 Tim Wakefield	.10	.05	.01
□ 16 Jim Abbott	.50	.23	.06
□ 17 Garret Anderson	.50	.23	.06

□ 18	Jim Edmonds	.50	.23	.06
□ 19	Darin Erstad	4.00	1.80	.50
□ 20	Chuck Finley	.10	.05	.01
□ 21	Troy Percival	.25	.11	.03
□ 22	Tim Salmon	.50	.23	.06
□ 23	J.T. Snow	.25	.11	.03
□ 24	Wilson Alvarez	.50	.23	.06
□ 25	Harold Baines	.25	.11	.03
□ 26	Ray Durham	.50	.23	.06
□ 27	Alex Fernandez	.50	.23	.06
□ 28	Tony Phillips	.25	.11	.03
□ 29	Frank Thomas	3.00	1.35	.35
□ 30	Robin Ventura	.50	.23	.06
□ 31	Sandy Alomar Jr.	.10	.05	.01
□ 32	Albert Belle	1.50	.70	.19
□ 33	Kenny Lofton	.75	.35	.09
□ 34	Dennis Martinez	.25	.11	.03
□ 35	Jose Mesa	.25	.11	.03
□ 36	Charles Nagy	.10	.05	.01
□ 37	Manny Ramirez	.75	.35	.09
□ 38	Jim Thome	.60	.25	.07
□ 39	Travis Fryman	.50	.23	.06
□ 40	Bob Higginson	.50	.23	.06
□ 41	Melvin Nieves	.25	.11	.03
□ 42	Alan Trammell	.50	.23	.06
□ 43	Kevin Appier	.25	.11	.03
□ 44	Johnny Damon	.50	.23	.06
□ 45	Keith Lockhart	.10	.05	.01
□ 46	Jeff Montgomery	.10	.05	.01
□ 47	Joe Randa	.10	.05	.01
□ 48	Bip Roberts	.10	.05	.01
□ 49	Ricky Bones	.10	.05	.01
□ 50	Jeff Cirillo	.10	.05	.01
□ 51	Marc Newfield	.25	.11	.03
□ 52	Dave Nilsson	.25	.11	.03
□ 53	Kevin Seitzer	.10	.05	.01
□ 54	Ron Coomer	.10	.05	.01
□ 55	Marty Cordova	.50	.23	.06
□ 56	Roberto Kelly	.10	.05	.01
□ 57	Chuck Knoblauch	.50	.23	.06
□ 58	Paul Molitor	.60	.25	.07
□ 59	Kirby Puckett	1.00	.45	.12
□ 60	Scott Stahoviak	.10	.05	.01
□ 61	Wade Boggs	.50	.23	.06
□ 62	David Cone	.50	.23	.06
□ 63	Cecil Fielder	.50	.23	.06
□ 64	Dwight Gooden	.50	.23	.06
□ 65	Derek Jeter	2.00	.90	.25
□ 66	Tino Martinez	.25	.11	.03
□ 67	Paul O'Neill	.10	.05	.01
□ 68	Andy Pettitte	1.00	.45	.12
□ 69	Ruben Rivera	.60	.25	.07
□ 70	Bernie Williams	.50	.23	.06
□ 71	Geronimo Berroa	.25	.11	.03
□ 72	Jason Giambi	.50	.23	.06
□ 73	Mark McGwire	1.00	.45	.12
□ 74	Terry Steinbach	.25	.11	.03
□ 75	Todd Van Poppel	.10	.05	.01
□ 76	Jay Buhner	.50	.23	.06
□ 77	Norm Charlton	.10	.05	.01
□ 78	Ken Griffey Jr.	3.00	1.35	.35
□ 79	Randy Johnson	.50	.23	.06
□ 80	Edgar Martinez	.50	.23	.06
□ 81	Alex Rodriguez	3.00	1.35	.35
□ 82	Paul Sorrento	.10	.05	.01
□ 83	Dan Wilson	.10	.05	.01
□ 84	Will Clark	.50	.23	.06
□ 85	Kevin Elster	.25	.11	.03
□ 86	Juan Gonzalez	1.50	.70	.19
□ 87	Rusty Greer	.50	.23	.06
□ 88	Ken Hill	.25	.11	.03
□ 89	Mark McLemore	.10	.05	.01
□ 90	Dean Palmer	.50	.23	.06
□ 91	Roger Pavlik	.10	.05	.01
□ 92	Ivan Rodriguez	.60	.25	.07
□ 93	Joe Carter	.50	.23	.06
□ 94	Carlos Delgado	.50	.23	.06
□ 95	Juan Guzman	.10	.05	.01
□ 96	John Olerud	.10	.05	.01
□ 97	Ed Sprague	.25	.11	.03
□ 98	Jermaine Dye	.60	.25	.07
□ 99	Tom Glavine	.50	.23	.06
□ 100	Marquis Grissom	.50	.23	.06
□ 101	Andruw Jones	5.00	2.20	.60
□ 102	Chipper Jones	2.00	.90	.25
□ 103	David Justice	.25	.11	.03
□ 104	Ryan Klesko	.60	.25	.07
□ 105	Greg Maddux	2.00	.90	.25
□ 106	Fred McGriff	.50	.23	.06
□ 107	John Smoltz	.50	.23	.06
□ 108	Brant Brown	.10	.05	.01
□ 109	Mark Grace	.50	.23	.06
□ 110	Brian McRae	.10	.05	.01
□ 111	Ryne Sandberg	.75	.35	.09
□ 112	Sammy Sosa	.50	.23	.06
□ 113	Steve Trachsel	.10	.05	.01
□ 114	Bret Boone	.10	.05	.01
□ 115	Eric Davis	.25	.11	.03
□ 116	Steve Gibralter	.10	.05	.01
□ 117	Barry Larkin	.10	.05	.01
□ 118	Reggie Sanders	.50	.23	.06
□ 119	John Smiley	.10	.05	.01
□ 120	Dante Bichette	.50	.23	.06
□ 121	Ellis Burks	.50	.23	.06
□ 122	Vinny Castilla	.50	.23	.06
□ 123	Andres Galarraga	.50	.23	.06
□ 124	Larry Walker	.50	.23	.06
□ 125	Eric Young	.10	.05	.01
□ 126	Kevin Brown	.25	.11	.03
□ 127	Greg Colbrunn	.10	.05	.01
□ 128	Jeff Conine	.50	.23	.06
□ 129	Charles Johnson	.10	.05	.01
□ 130	Al Leiter	.10	.05	.01
□ 131	Gary Sheffield	.50	.23	.06
□ 132	Devon White	.10	.05	.01
□ 133	Jeff Bagwell	1.25	.55	.16
□ 134	Derek Bell	.25	.11	.03
□ 135	Craig Biggio	.50	.23	.06
□ 136	Doug Drabek	.10	.05	.01
□ 137	Brian L.Hunter	.10	.05	.01
□ 138	Darryl Kile	.10	.05	.01
□ 139	Shane Reynolds	.10	.05	.01
□ 140	Brett Butler	.10	.05	.01
□ 141	Eric Karros	.50	.23	.06
□ 142	Ramon Martinez	.50	.23	.06
□ 143	Raul Mondesi	.50	.23	.06
□ 144	Hideo Nomo	.75	.35	.09
□ 145	Chan Ho Park	.50	.23	.06
□ 146	Mike Piazza	2.00	.90	.25
□ 147	Moises Alou	.25	.11	.03
□ 148	Yamil Benitez	.10	.05	.01
□ 149	Mark Grudzielanek	.25	.11	.03
□ 150	Pedro Martinez	.25	.11	.03
□ 151	Henry Rodriguez	.50	.23	.06
□ 152	David Segui	.10	.05	.01
□ 153	Rondell White	.50	.23	.06
□ 154	Carlos Baerga	.50	.23	.06
□ 155	John Franco	.10	.05	.01
□ 156	Bernard Gilkey	.25	.11	.03
□ 157	Todd Hundley	.50	.23	.06
□ 158	Jason Isringhausen	.25	.11	.03
□ 159	Lance Johnson	.25	.11	.03
□ 160	Alex Ochoa	.25	.11	.03
□ 161	Rey Ordonez	.60	.25	.07
□ 162	Paul Wilson	.25	.11	.03
□ 163	Ron Blazier	.10	.05	.01
□ 164	Ricky Bottalico	.10	.05	.01
□ 165	Jim Eisenreich	.10	.05	.01
□ 166	Pete Incaviglia	.10	.05	.01
□ 167	Mickey Morandini	.10	.05	.01
□ 168	Ricky Otero	.10	.05	.01
□ 169	Curt Schilling	.10	.05	.01
□ 170	Jay Bell	.25	.11	.03
□ 171	Charlie Hayes	.10	.05	.01
□ 172	Jason Kendall	.50	.23	.06
□ 173	Jeff King	.25	.11	.03
□ 174	Al Martin	.10	.05	.01
□ 175	Alan Benes	.50	.23	.06
□ 176	Royce Clayton	.10	.05	.01
□ 177	Brian Jordan	.50	.23	.06
□ 178	Ray Lankford	.50	.23	.06
□ 179	John Mabry	.50	.23	.06
□ 180	Willie McGee	.10	.05	.01
□ 181	Ozzie Smith	.60	.25	.07
□ 182	Todd Stottlemyre	.10	.05	.01
□ 183	Andy Ashby	.10	.05	.01
□ 184	Ken Caminiti	.50	.23	.06
□ 185	Steve Finley	.50	.23	.06
□ 186	Tony Gwynn	1.25	.55	.16
□ 187	Rickey Henderson	.50	.23	.06
□ 188	Wally Joyner	.10	.05	.01
□ 189	Fernando Valenzuela	.25	.11	.03

□ 190 Greg Vaughn	.50	.23	.06
□ 191 Rod Beck	.10	.05	.01
□ 192 Barry Bonds	.75	.35	.09
□ 193 Shawon Dunston	.10	.05	.01
□ 194 Chris Singleton	.10	.05	.01
□ 195 Robby Thompson	.10	.05	.01
□ 196 Matt Williams	.50	.23	.06
□ 197 Barry Bonds CL	.50	.23	.06
□ 198 Ken Griffey Jr. CL	1.50	.70	.19
□ 199 Cal Ripken CL	1.25	.55	.16
□ 200 Frank Thomas CL	1.50	.70	.19

1996 Fleer Circa Rave

Randomly inserted in packs at a rate of one in 60, this 200-card set is parallel and similar in design to the regular set. Each card is individually numbered with less than 150 of each card produced.

	MINT	NRMT	EXC
COMMON CARD (1-200)	20.00	9.00	2.50
SEMISTARS	30.00	13.50	3.70
□ 1 Roberto Alomar	80.00	36.00	10.00
□ 4 Eddie Murray	80.00	36.00	10.00
□ 5 Mike Mussina	60.00	27.00	7.50
□ 8 Cal Ripken	250.00	110.00	31.00
□ 14 Mo Vaughn	80.00	36.00	10.00
□ 19 Darin Erstad	150.00	70.00	19.00
□ 29 Frank Thomas	300.00	135.00	38.00
□ 32 Albert Belle	150.00	70.00	19.00
□ 33 Kenny Lofton	80.00	36.00	10.00
□ 37 Manny Ramirez	80.00	36.00	10.00
□ 38 Jim Thome	60.00	27.00	7.50
□ 58 Paul Molitor	60.00	27.00	7.50
□ 59 Kirby Puckett	100.00	45.00	12.50
□ 65 Derek Jeter	175.00	80.00	22.00
□ 68 Andy Pettitte	100.00	45.00	12.50
□ 70 Bernie Williams	50.00	22.00	6.25
□ 73 Mark McGwire	100.00	45.00	12.50
□ 78 Ken Griffey Jr.	300.00	135.00	38.00
□ 79 Randy Johnson	50.00	22.00	6.25
□ 81 Alex Rodriguez	300.00	135.00	38.00
□ 86 Juan Gonzalez	150.00	70.00	19.00
□ 92 Ivan Rodriguez	60.00	27.00	7.50
□ 101 Andruw Jones	400.00	180.00	50.00
□ 102 Chipper Jones	200.00	90.00	25.00
□ 104 Ryan Klesko	60.00	27.00	7.50
□ 105 Greg Maddux	200.00	90.00	25.00
□ 107 John Smoltz	50.00	22.00	6.25
□ 111 Ryne Sandberg	80.00	36.00	10.00
□ 112 Sammy Sosa	50.00	22.00	6.25
□ 131 Gary Sheffield	50.00	22.00	6.25
□ 133 Jeff Bagwell	125.00	55.00	15.50
□ 144 Hideo Nomo	80.00	36.00	10.00
□ 146 Mike Piazza	200.00	90.00	25.00
□ 161 Rey Ordonez	60.00	27.00	7.50
□ 181 Ozzie Smith	60.00	27.00	7.50
□ 186 Tony Gwynn	125.00	55.00	15.50
□ 192 Barry Bonds	80.00	36.00	10.00
□ 198 Ken Griffey Jr. CL	150.00	70.00	19.00
□ 199 Cal Ripken CL	125.00	55.00	15.50
□ 200 Frank Thomas CL	150.00	70.00	19.00

1996 Fleer Circa Access

Randomly inserted in packs at a rate of one in 12, this 30-card limited edition set features a fold-out, three-panel card showcasing some of the hottest superstars of the game. The panels display color player photos, player statistics and personal information on team-colored backgrounds.

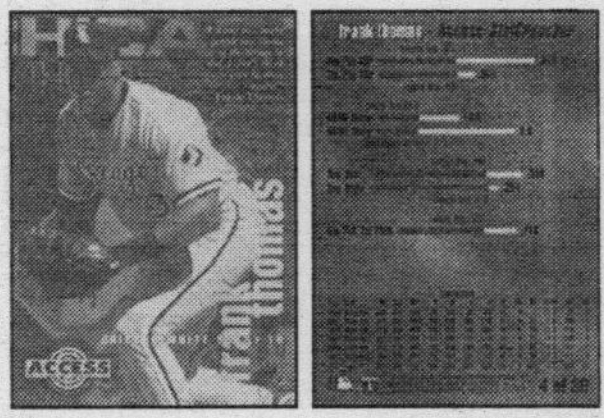

	MINT	NRMT	EXC
COMPLETE SET (30)	125.00	55.00	15.50
COMMON CARD (1-30)	2.00	.90	.25
RANDOM INSERTS IN PACKS			
□ 1 Cal Ripken	15.00	6.75	1.85
□ 2 Mo Vaughn	5.00	2.20	.60
□ 3 Tim Salmon	2.50	1.10	.30
□ 4 Frank Thomas	20.00	9.00	2.50
□ 5 Albert Belle	10.00	4.50	1.25
□ 6 Kenny Lofton	5.00	2.20	.60
□ 7 Manny Ramirez	5.00	2.20	.60
□ 8 Paul Molitor	4.00	1.80	.50
□ 9 Kirby Puckett	6.00	2.70	.75
□ 10 Paul O'Neill	2.00	.90	.25
□ 11 Mark McGwire	6.00	2.70	.75
□ 12 Ken Griffey Jr.	20.00	9.00	2.50
□ 13 Randy Johnson	3.00	1.35	.35
□ 14 Greg Maddux	12.00	5.50	1.50
□ 15 John Smoltz	3.00	1.35	.35
□ 16 Sammy Sosa	3.00	1.35	.35
□ 17 Barry Larkin	2.50	1.10	.30
□ 18 Gary Sheffield	3.00	1.35	.35
□ 19 Jeff Bagwell	8.00	3.60	1.00
□ 20 Hideo Nomo	5.00	2.20	.60
□ 21 Mike Piazza	12.00	5.50	1.50
□ 22 Moises Alou	2.00	.90	.25
□ 23 Henry Rodriguez	2.00	.90	.25
□ 24 Rey Ordonez	4.00	1.80	.50
□ 25 Jay Bell	2.00	.90	.25
□ 26 Ozzie Smith	4.00	1.80	.50
□ 27 Tony Gwynn	8.00	3.60	1.00
□ 28 Rickey Henderson	2.50	1.10	.30
□ 29 Barry Bonds	5.00	2.20	.60
□ 30 Matt Williams	2.50	1.10	.30

1996 Fleer Circa Boss

Randomly inserted in packs at a rate of one in six, this 50-card set features a sculpted embossed player image on a team-colored background containing the team logo. The backs carry information about the player's career.

	MINT	NRMT	EXC
COMPLETE SET (50)	120.00	55.00	15.00
COMMON CARD (1-50)	1.50	.70	.19
SEMISTARS	2.00	.90	.25
RANDOM INSERTS IN PACKS			
□ 1 Roberto Alomar	4.00	1.80	.50
□ 2 Cal Ripken	12.00	5.50	1.50
□ 3 Jose Canseco	2.00	.90	.25
□ 4 Mo Vaughn	4.00	1.80	.50
□ 5 Tim Salmon	2.00	.90	.25
□ 6 Frank Thomas	15.00	6.75	1.85
□ 7 Robin Ventura	2.00	.90	.25
□ 8 Albert Belle	8.00	3.60	1.00
□ 9 Kenny Lofton	4.00	1.80	.50
□ 10 Manny Ramirez	4.00	1.80	.50
□ 11 Dave Nilsson	1.50	.70	.19

□ 12 Chuck Knoblauch	2.00	.90	.25
□ 13 Paul Molitor	3.00	1.35	.35
□ 14 Kirby Puckett	5.00	2.20	.60
□ 15 Wade Boggs	2.00	.90	.25
□ 16 Dwight Gooden	2.00	.90	.25
□ 17 Paul O'Neill	1.50	.70	.19
□ 18 Mark McGwire	5.00	2.20	.60
□ 19 Jay Buhner	2.00	.90	.25
□ 20 Ken Griffey Jr.	15.00	6.75	1.85
□ 21 Randy Johnson	2.00	.90	.25
□ 22 Will Clark	2.00	.90	.25
□ 23 Juan Gonzalez	8.00	3.60	1.00
□ 24 Joe Carter	2.00	.90	.25
□ 25 Tom Glavine	2.00	.90	.25
□ 26 Ryan Klesko	3.00	1.35	.35
□ 27 Greg Maddux	10.00	4.50	1.25
□ 28 John Smoltz	2.00	.90	.25
□ 29 Ryne Sandberg	4.00	1.80	.50
□ 30 Sammy Sosa	2.00	.90	.25
□ 31 Barry Larkin	2.00	.90	.25
□ 32 Reggie Sanders	2.00	.90	.25
□ 33 Dante Bichette	2.00	.90	.25
□ 34 Andres Galarraga	2.00	.90	.25
□ 35 Charles Johnson	1.50	.70	.19
□ 36 Gary Sheffield	2.00	.90	.25
□ 37 Jeff Bagwell	6.00	2.70	.75
□ 38 Hideo Nomo	4.00	1.80	.50
□ 39 Mike Piazza	10.00	4.50	1.25
□ 40 Moises Alou	1.50	.70	.19
□ 41 Henry Rodriguez	1.50	.70	.19
□ 42 Rey Ordonez	3.00	1.35	.35
□ 43 Ricky Otero	1.50	.70	.19
□ 44 Jay Bell	1.50	.70	.19
□ 45 Royce Clayton	1.50	.70	.19
□ 46 Ozzie Smith	3.00	1.35	.35
□ 47 Tony Gwynn	6.00	2.70	.75
□ 48 Rickey Henderson	2.00	.90	.25
□ 49 Barry Bonds	4.00	1.80	.50
□ 50 Matt Williams	2.00	.90	.25

1993 Fun Pack

This 225-card standard-size single series set was issued by Upper Deck and targeted primarily at youngsters. Cards were distributed exclusively in hobby and retail foil fin-wrapped packs. Each card has a front that display action player photos on a bright multicolored background. The team name is printed in yellow at the top right and the player's name appears below the photo within the irregular green border. Topical subsets featured are Stars of Tomorrow (1-9), Hot Shots (10-21), Kid Stars (22-27), Upper Deck Heroes (28-36), All-Star Advice (210-215), All-Star Fold Outs (216-220), and Checklists (221-225) and randomly numbered Glow Stars. Card numbers 37-209 are arranged alphabetically according to team names, with each team subset beginning with a Glow Star card. There are no key Rookie Cards in this set.The Hot Shot subset cards were only available in retail packs or through a as a mail-in redemption promotion available in hobby packs.

	MINT	NRMT	EXC
COMPLETE SET (225)	40.00	18.00	5.00
COMMON CARD (1-225)	.05	.02	.01
HOT SHOTS (10-21)	.30	.14	.04
SEMISTARS	.15	.07	.02
STARS	.30	.14	.04
MASCOT FIVE-CARD SET	4.00	1.80	.50
MASCOTS: RANDOM INSERTS IN PACKS			

□ 1 Wil Cordero SOT	.05	.02	.01
□ 2 Brent Gates SOT	.15	.07	.02
□ 3 Benji Gil SOT	.15	.07	.02
□ 4 Phil Hiatt SOT	.05	.02	.01
□ 5 David McCarty SOT	.05	.02	.01
□ 6 Mike Piazza SOT	2.00	.90	.25
□ 7 Tim Salmon SOT	.50	.23	.06
□ 8 J.T. Snow SOT	.30	.14	.04
□ 9 Kevin Young SOT	.05	.02	.01
□ 10 Roberto Alomar HS	1.00	.45	.12
□ 11 Barry Bonds HS	1.00	.45	.12
□ 12 Jose Canseco HS	.30	.14	.04
□ 13 Will Clark HS	.30	.14	.04
□ 14 Roger Clemens HS	.30	.14	.04
□ 15 Juan Gonzalez HS	2.00	.90	.25
□ 16 Ken Griffey Jr. HS	4.00	1.80	.50
□ 17 Mark McGwire HS	1.25	.55	.16
□ 18 Nolan Ryan HS	4.00	1.80	.50
□ 19 Ryne Sandberg HS	1.00	.45	.12
□ 20 Gary Sheffield HS	.30	.14	.04
□ 21 Frank Thomas HS	4.00	1.80	.50
□ 22 Roberto Alomar KS	.30	.14	.04
□ 23 Roger Clemens KS	.30	.14	.04
□ 24 Ken Griffey Jr. KS	1.00	.45	.12
□ 25 Gary Sheffield KS	.30	.14	.04
□ 26 Nolan Ryan KS	.75	.35	.09
□ 27 Frank Thomas KS	1.00	.45	.12
□ 28 Reggie Jackson HERO	.30	.14	.04
□ 29 Roger Clemens HERO	.30	.14	.04
□ 30 Ken Griffey Jr. HERO	1.00	.45	.12
□ 31 Bo Jackson HERO	.30	.14	.04
□ 32 Cal Ripken Jr. HERO	.75	.35	.09
□ 33 Nolan Ryan HERO	.75	.35	.09
□ 34 Deion Sanders HERO	.30	.14	.04
□ 35 Ozzie Smith HERO	.30	.14	.04
□ 36 Frank Thomas HERO	1.00	.45	.12
□ 37 Tim Salmon GS	.15	.07	.02
□ 38 Chili Davis	.15	.07	.02
□ 39 Chuck Finley	.05	.02	.01
□ 40 Mark Langston	.15	.07	.02
□ 41 Luis Polonia	.05	.02	.01
□ 42 Jeff Bagwell GS	.40	.18	.05
□ 43 Jeff Bagwell	.75	.35	.09
□ 44 Craig Biggio	.30	.14	.04
□ 45 Ken Caminiti	.30	.14	.04
□ 46 Doug Drabek	.05	.02	.01
□ 47 Steve Finley	.30	.14	.04
□ 48 Mark McGwire GS	.30	.14	.04
□ 49 Dennis Eckersley	.15	.07	.02
□ 50 Rickey Henderson	.30	.14	.04
□ 51 Mark McGwire	.60	.25	.07
□ 52 Ruben Sierra	.15	.07	.02
□ 53 Terry Steinbach	.15	.07	.02
□ 54 Roberto Alomar GS	.30	.14	.04
□ 55 Roberto Alomar	.50	.23	.06
□ 56 Joe Carter	.30	.14	.04
□ 57 Juan Guzman	.15	.07	.02
□ 58 Paul Molitor	.40	.18	.05
□ 59 Jack Morris	.15	.07	.02
□ 60 John Olerud	.05	.02	.01
□ 61 Tom Glavine GS	.15	.07	.02
□ 62 Steve Avery	.15	.07	.02
□ 63 Tom Glavine	.30	.14	.04
□ 64 David Justice	.30	.14	.04
□ 65 Greg Maddux	1.25	.55	.16
□ 66 Terry Pendleton	.15	.07	.02
□ 67 Deion Sanders	.30	.14	.04
□ 68 John Smoltz	.30	.14	.04
□ 69 Robin Yount GS	.15	.07	.02
□ 70 Cal Eldred	.05	.02	.01
□ 71 Pat Listach	.05	.02	.01
□ 72 Greg Vaughn	.30	.14	.04
□ 73 Robin Yount	.30	.14	.04
□ 74 Ozzie Smith GS	.30	.14	.04
□ 75 Gregg Jefferies	.30	.14	.04
□ 76 Ray Lankford	.30	.14	.04
□ 77 Lee Smith	.15	.07	.02
□ 78 Ozzie Smith	.40	.18	.05
□ 79 Bob Tewksbury	.05	.02	.01
□ 80 Ryne Sandberg GS	.30	.14	.04
□ 81 Mark Grace	.30	.14	.04

□	82 Mike Morgan	.05	.02	.01
□	83 Randy Myers	.15	.07	.02
□	84 Ryne Sandberg	.50	.23	.06
□	85 Sammy Sosa	.30	.14	.04
□	86 Eric Karros GS	.15	.07	.02
□	87 Brett Butler	.15	.07	.02
□	88 Orel Hershiser	.15	.07	.02
□	89 Eric Karros	.30	.14	.04
□	90 Ramon Martinez	.15	.07	.02
□	91 Jose Offerman	.05	.02	.01
□	92 Darryl Strawberry	.15	.07	.02
□	93 Marquis Grissom GS	.15	.07	.02
□	94 Delino DeShields	.05	.02	.01
□	95 Marquis Grissom	.30	.14	.04
□	96 Ken Hill	.15	.07	.02
□	97 Dennis Martinez	.15	.07	.02
□	98 Larry Walker	.30	.14	.04
□	99 Barry Bonds GS	.30	.14	.04
□	100 Barry Bonds	.50	.23	.06
□	101 Will Clark	.30	.14	.04
□	102 Bill Swift	.05	.02	.01
□	103 Robby Thompson	.05	.02	.01
□	104 Matt Williams	.30	.14	.04
□	105 Carlos Baerga GS	.15	.07	.02
□	106 Sandy Alomar Jr.	.15	.07	.02
□	107 Carlos Baerga	.30	.14	.04
□	108 Albert Belle	1.00	.45	.12
□	109 Kenny Lofton	.75	.35	.09
□	110 Charles Nagy	.15	.07	.02
□	111 Ken Griffey Jr. GS	1.00	.45	.12
□	112 Jay Buhner	.30	.14	.04
□	113 Dave Fleming	.05	.02	.01
□	114 Ken Griffey Jr.	2.00	.90	.25
□	115 Randy Johnson	.30	.14	.04
□	116 Edgar Martinez	.30	.14	.04
□	117 Benito Santiago GS	.05	.02	.01
□	118 Bret Barberie	.05	.02	.01
□	119 Jeff Conine	.30	.14	.04
□	120 Brian Harvey	.05	.02	.01
□	121 Benito Santiago	.05	.02	.01
□	122 Walt Weiss	.05	.02	.01
□	123 Dwight Gooden GS	.05	.02	.01
□	124 Bobby Bonilla	.15	.07	.02
□	125 Tony Fernandez	.05	.02	.01
□	126 Dwight Gooden	.15	.07	.02
□	127 Howard Johnson	.05	.02	.01
□	128 Eddie Murray	.50	.23	.06
□	129 Bret Saberhagen	.15	.07	.02
□	130 Cal Ripken Jr. GS	.75	.35	.09
□	131 Brady Anderson	.30	.14	.04
□	132 Mike Devereaux	.05	.02	.01
□	133 Ben McDonald	.05	.02	.01
□	134 Mike Mussina	.40	.18	.05
□	135 Cal Ripken Jr.	1.50	.70	.19
□	136 Fred McGriff GS	.30	.14	.04
□	137 Andy Benes	.05	.02	.01
□	138 Tony Gwynn	.75	.35	.09
□	139 Fred McGriff	.30	.14	.04
□	140 Phil Plantier	.05	.02	.01
□	141 Gary Sheffield	.30	.14	.04
□	142 Darren Daulton GS	.05	.02	.01
□	143 Darren Daulton	.15	.07	.02
□	144 Len Dykstra	.15	.07	.02
□	145 Dave Hollins	.05	.02	.01
□	146 John Kruk	.15	.07	.02
□	147 Mitch Williams	.05	.02	.01
□	148 Andy Van Slyke GS	.05	.02	.01
□	149 Jay Bell	.15	.07	.02
□	150 Zane Smith	.05	.02	.01
□	151 Andy Van Slyke	.15	.07	.02
□	152 Tim Wakefield	.15	.07	.02
□	153 Juan Gonzalez GS	.30	.14	.04
□	154 Kevin Brown	.05	.02	.01
□	155 Jose Canseco	.30	.14	.04
□	156 Juan Gonzalez	1.00	.45	.12
□	157 Rafael Palmeiro	.30	.14	.04
□	158 Dean Palmer	.15	.07	.02
□	159 Ivan Rodriguez	.40	.18	.05
□	160 Nolan Ryan	1.50	.70	.19
□	161 Roger Clemens GS	.30	.14	.04
□	162 Roger Clemens	.30	.14	.04
□	163 Andre Dawson	.30	.14	.04
□	164 Mike Greenwell	.05	.02	.01
□	165 Tony Pena	.05	.02	.01
□	166 Frank Viola	.05	.02	.01
□	167 Barry Larkin GS	.15	.07	.02

□	168 Rob Dibble	.05	.02	.01
□	169 Roberto Kelly	.05	.02	.01
□	170 Barry Larkin	.30	.14	.04
□	171 Kevin Mitchell	.15	.07	.02
□	172 Bip Roberts	.05	.02	.01
□	173 Andres Galarraga GS	.30	.14	.04
□	174 Dante Bichette	.30	.14	.04
□	175 Jerald Clark	.05	.02	.01
□	176 Andres Galarraga	.30	.14	.04
□	177 Charlie Hayes	.05	.02	.01
□	178 David Nied	.05	.02	.01
□	179 David Cone GS	.15	.07	.02
□	180 Kevin Appier	.15	.07	.02
□	181 George Brett	.75	.35	.09
□	182 David Cone	.30	.14	.04
□	183 Felix Jose	.05	.02	.01
□	184 Wally Joyner	.15	.07	.02
□	185 Cecil Fielder GS	.05	.02	.01
□	186 Cecil Fielder	.15	.07	.02
□	187 Travis Fryman	.30	.14	.04
□	188 Tony Phillips	.15	.07	.02
□	189 Mickey Tettleton	.05	.02	.01
□	190 Lou Whitaker	.30	.14	.04
□	191 Kirby Puckett GS	.30	.14	.04
□	192 Scott Erickson	.05	.02	.01
□	193 Chuck Knoblauch	.30	.14	.04
□	194 Shane Mack	.05	.02	.01
□	195 Kirby Puckett	.60	.25	.07
□	196 Dave Winfield	.30	.14	.04
□	197 Frank Thomas GS	1.00	.45	.12
□	198 George Bell	.05	.02	.01
□	199 Bo Jackson	.30	.14	.04
□	200 Jack McDowell	.15	.07	.02
□	201 Tim Raines	.30	.14	.04
□	202 Frank Thomas	2.00	.90	.25
□	203 Robin Ventura	.15	.07	.02
□	204 Jim Abbott GS	.05	.02	.01
□	205 Jim Abbott	.05	.02	.01
□	206 Wade Boggs	.30	.14	.04
□	207 Jimmy Key	.15	.07	.02
□	208 Don Mattingly	1.00	.45	.12
□	209 Danny Tartabull	.05	.02	.01
□	210 Brett Butler ASA	.05	.02	.01
□	211 Tony Gwynn ASA	.40	.18	.05
□	212 Rickey Henderson ASA	.15	.07	.02
□	213 Ramon Martinez ASA	.05	.02	.01
□	214 Nolan Ryan ASA	.75	.35	.09
□	215 Ozzie Smith ASA	.30	.14	.04
□	216 Marquis Grissom FOLD	.15	.07	.02
□	217 Dean Palmer FOLD	.05	.02	.01
□	218 Cal Ripken Jr. FOLD	.75	.35	.09
□	219 Deion Sanders FOLD	.30	.14	.04
□	220 Darryl Strawberry FOLD	.05	.02	.01
□	221 David McCarty CL	.05	.02	.01
□	222 Barry Bonds CL	.30	.14	.04
□	223 Juan Gonzalez CL	.30	.14	.04
□	224 Ken Griffey Jr. CL	1.00	.45	.12
□	225 Frank Thomas CL	1.00	.45	.12
□	NNO Hot Shots Card Expired	.30	.14	.04
□	NNO Hot Shots Card Punched	.15	.07	.02

1993 Fun Pack All-Stars

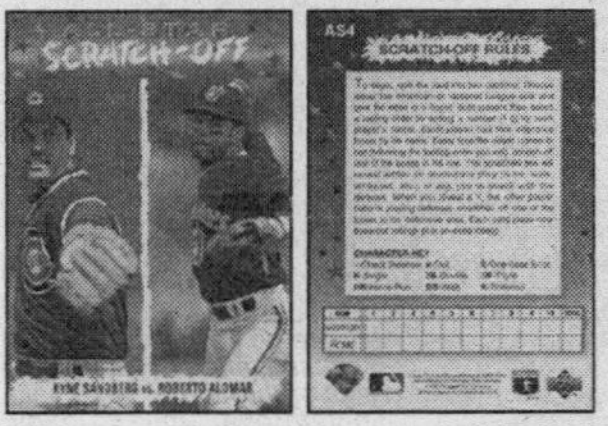

Randomly inserted in 1993 Upper Deck Fun Packs, these nine foldouts feature combinations by position for American and National leaue All-Stars. The cards measure the standard size when closed and 2 1/2" by 7" when opened. The front of each features side-by-side color

action photos of an American League and a National League player. The set's title appears above the photos within a blue stripe. The players' names appear within an irregular white stripe near the bottom. The blue-and-white back carries the rules for playing the scratch-off game and a section to keep score. The actual scratch-off lineups appear when the card is opened. The American League players and their scratch-off circles are displayed within the reddish left side of the foldout, and their National League counterparts appear within the bluish right side.

	MINT	NRMT	EXC
COMPLETE SET (9)	15.00	6.75	1.85
COMMON PAIR (AS1-AS9)	.50	.23	.06
RANDOM INSERTS IN PACKS			

	MINT	NRMT	EXC
□ AS1 Frank Thomas / Fred McGriff	5.00	2.20	.60
□ AS2 Ivan Rodriguez / Darren Daulton	.75	.35	.09
□ AS3 Mark McGwire / Will Clark	1.00	.45	.12
□ AS4 Roberto Alomar / Ryne Sandberg	2.00	.90	.25
□ AS5 Robin Ventura / Terry Pendleton	.50	.23	.06
□ AS6 Cal Ripken / Ozzie Smith	4.00	1.80	.50
□ AS7 Juan Gonzalez / Barry Bonds	2.50	1.10	.30
□ AS8 Ken Griffey Jr. / Marquis Grissom	4.00	1.80	.50
□ AS9 Kirby Puckett / Tony Gwynn	4.00	1.80	.50

1994 Fun Pack

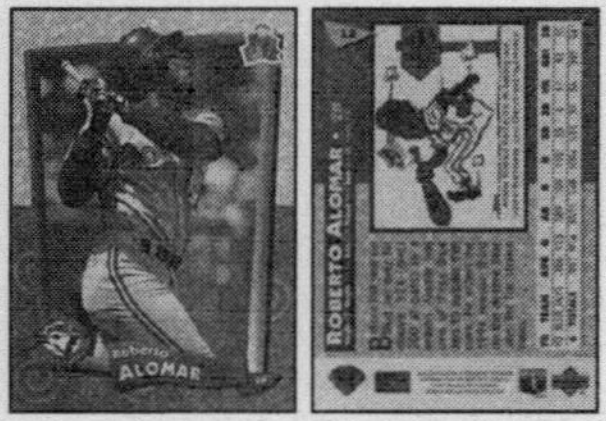

Issued by Upper Deck for the second straight year, the Fun Pack set consists of 240 cards. Bright yellow and green borders surround a color player photo on the front. The backs, with much the same color scheme, are horizontal and contain a cartoon relating to the player and statistics. The following subsets are included in this set: Stars of Tomorrow (1-9), Standouts (175-192), Pro-Files (193-198), Headline Stars (199-207), What's the Call (208-216), Foldouts (217-225) and Fun Cards (226-234). Michael Jordan's Rookie Card is in this set.

	MINT	NRMT	EXC
COMPLETE SET (240)	65.00	29.00	8.00
COMMON CARD (1-240)	.10	.05	.01
HEADLINE STARS (199-207)	.30	.14	.04
SEMISTARS	.25	.11	.03
STARS	.50	.23	.06
PRODUCED BY UPPER DECK			

	MINT	NRMT	EXC
□ 1 Manny Ramirez	1.00	.45	.12
□ 2 Cliff Floyd	.50	.23	.06
□ 3 Rondell White	.50	.23	.06
□ 4 Carlos Delgado	.50	.23	.06
□ 5 Chipper Jones	2.50	1.10	.30
□ 6 Javier Lopez	.50	.23	.06
□ 7 Ryan Klesko	.75	.35	.09
□ 8 Steve Karsay	.10	.05	.01
□ 9 Rich Becker	.25	.11	.03
□ 10 Gary Sheffield	.50	.23	.06
□ 11 Jeffrey Hammonds	.25	.11	.03
□ 12 Roberto Alomar	.75	.35	.09
□ 13 Brent Gates	.10	.05	.01
□ 14 Andres Galarraga	.50	.23	.06
□ 15 Tim Salmon	.50	.23	.06
□ 16 Dwight Gooden	.25	.11	.03
□ 17 Mark Grace	.50	.23	.06
□ 18 Andy Van Slyke	.25	.11	.03
□ 19 Juan Gonzalez	1.50	.70	.19
□ 20 Mickey Tettleton	.10	.05	.01
□ 21 Roger Clemens	.50	.23	.06
□ 22 Will Clark	.50	.23	.06
□ 23 David Justice	.50	.23	.06
□ 24 Ken Griffey Jr.	3.00	1.35	.35
□ 25 Barry Bonds	.75	.35	.09
□ 26 Bill Swift	.10	.05	.01
□ 27 Fred McGriff	.50	.23	.06
□ 28 Randy Myers	.10	.05	.01
□ 29 Joe Carter	.50	.23	.06
□ 30 Nigel Wilson	.10	.05	.01
□ 31 Mike Piazza	2.00	.90	.25
□ 32 Dave Winfield	.50	.23	.06
□ 33 Steve Avery	.25	.11	.03
□ 34 Kirby Puckett	1.00	.45	.12
□ 35 Frank Thomas	3.00	1.35	.35
□ 36 Aaron Sele	.25	.11	.03
□ 37 Ricky Gutierrez	.10	.05	.01
□ 38 Curt Schilling	.10	.05	.01
□ 39 Mike Greenwell	.10	.05	.01
□ 40 Andy Benes	.25	.11	.03
□ 41 Kevin Brown	.10	.05	.01
□ 42 Mo Vaughn	.75	.35	.09
□ 43 Dennis Eckersley	.25	.11	.03
□ 44 Ken Hill	.10	.05	.01
□ 45 Cecil Fielder	.25	.11	.03
□ 46 Bobby Jones	.25	.11	.03
□ 47 Tom Glavine	.50	.23	.06
□ 48 Wally Joyner	.25	.11	.03
□ 49 Ellis Burks	.25	.11	.03
□ 50 Jason Bere	.25	.11	.03
□ 51 Randy Johnson	.50	.23	.06
□ 52 Darryl Kile	.10	.05	.01
□ 53 Jeff Montgomery	.25	.11	.03
□ 54 Alex Fernandez	.50	.23	.06
□ 55 Kevin Appier	.25	.11	.03
□ 56 Brian McRae	.25	.11	.03
□ 57 John Wetteland	.25	.11	.03
□ 58 Bob Tewksbury	.10	.05	.01
□ 59 Todd Van Poppel	.10	.05	.01
□ 60 Ryne Sandberg	.75	.35	.09
□ 61 Bret Barberie	.10	.05	.01
□ 62 Phil Plantier	.10	.05	.01
□ 63 Chris Hoiles	.10	.05	.01
□ 64 Tony Phillips	.25	.11	.03
□ 65 Salomon Torres	.10	.05	.01
□ 66 Juan Guzman	.25	.11	.03
□ 67 Paul O'Neill	.25	.11	.03
□ 68 Dante Bichette	.50	.23	.06
□ 69 Lenny Dykstra	.25	.11	.03
□ 70 Ivan Rodriguez	.60	.25	.07
□ 71 Dean Palmer	.25	.11	.03
□ 72 Brett Butler	.25	.11	.03
□ 73 Rick Aguilera	.10	.05	.01
□ 74 Robby Thompson	.10	.05	.01
□ 75 Jim Abbott	.10	.05	.01
□ 76 Al Martin	.10	.05	.01
□ 77 Roberto Hernandez	.25	.11	.03
□ 78 Jay Buhner	.50	.23	.06
□ 79 Devon White	.10	.05	.01
□ 80 Travis Fryman	.50	.23	.06
□ 81 Jeromy Burnitz	.10	.05	.01
□ 82 John Burkett	.10	.05	.01
□ 83 Orlando Merced	.25	.11	.03
□ 84 Jose Rijo	.10	.05	.01
□ 85 Eddie Murray	.75	.35	.09
□ 86 Howard Johnson	.10	.05	.01
□ 87 Chuck Carr	.10	.05	.01
□ 88 Pedro J. Martinez	.50	.23	.06
□ 89 Charlie Hayes	.10	.05	.01
□ 90 Matt Williams	.50	.23	.06
□ 91 Steve Finley	.50	.23	.06
□ 92 Pat Listach	.10	.05	.01
□ 93 Sandy Alomar Jr.	.25	.11	.03
□ 94 Delino DeShields	.10	.05	.01

□ 95 Rod Beck	.25	.11	.03
□ 96 Todd Zeile UER	.10	.05	.01
(Card misnumbered 97)			
□ 97 Duane Ward UER	.10	.05	.01
(Card misnumbered 98)			
□ 98 Darryl Hamilton	.10	.05	.01
□ 99 John Olerud	.10	.05	.01
□ 100 Andre Dawson	.50	.23	.06
□ 101 Ozzie Smith	.60	.25	.07
□ 102 Rick Wilkins	.10	.05	.01
□ 103 Alan Trammell	.50	.23	.06
□ 104 Jeff Blauser	.10	.05	.01
□ 105 Bret Boone	.25	.11	.03
□ 106 J.T. Snow	.25	.11	.03
□ 107 Kenny Lofton	1.00	.45	.12
□ 108 Cal Ripken Jr.	2.50	1.10	.30
□ 109 Carlos Baerga	.50	.23	.06
□ 110 Bip Roberts	.10	.05	.01
□ 111 Barry Larkin	.50	.23	.06
□ 112 Mark Langston	.25	.11	.03
□ 113 Ozzie Guillen	.10	.05	.01
□ 114 Chad Curtis	.10	.05	.01
□ 115 Dave Hollins	.10	.05	.01
□ 116 Reggie Sanders	.50	.23	.06
□ 117 Jeff Conine	.50	.23	.06
□ 118 Mark Whiten	.10	.05	.01
□ 119 Tony Gwynn	1.25	.55	.16
□ 120 John Kruk	.25	.11	.03
□ 121 Eduardo Perez	.10	.05	.01
□ 122 Walt Weiss	.10	.05	.01
□ 123 Don Mattingly	1.50	.70	.19
□ 124 Rickey Henderson	.50	.23	.06
□ 125 Mark McGwire	1.00	.45	.12
□ 126 Wade Boggs	.50	.23	.06
□ 127 Bobby Bonilla	.25	.11	.03
□ 128 Jeff King	.25	.11	.03
□ 129 Jack McDowell	.25	.11	.03
□ 130 Albert Belle	1.50	.70	.19
□ 131 Greg Maddux	2.00	.90	.25
□ 132 Dennis Martinez	.25	.11	.03
□ 133 Jose Canseco	.50	.23	.06
□ 134 Bryan Harvey	.10	.05	.01
□ 135 Dave Fleming	.10	.05	.01
□ 136 Larry Walker	.50	.23	.06
□ 137 Ken Caminiti	.50	.23	.06
□ 138 Doug Drabek	.10	.05	.01
□ 139 Alex Gonzalez	.25	.11	.03
□ 140 Darren Daulton	.25	.11	.03
□ 141 Ruben Sierra	.25	.11	.03
□ 142 Kirk Rueter	.10	.05	.01
□ 143 Raul Mondesi	.50	.23	.06
□ 144 Greg Vaughn	.50	.23	.06
□ 145 Danny Tartabull	.10	.05	.01
□ 146 Eric Karros	.25	.11	.03
□ 147 Chuck Knoblauch	.50	.23	.06
□ 148 Mike Mussina	.60	.25	.07
□ 149 Brady Anderson	.50	.23	.06
□ 150 Paul Molitor	.60	.25	.07
□ 151 Bo Jackson	.50	.23	.06
□ 152 Jeff Bagwell	1.25	.55	.16
□ 153 Gregg Jefferies UER	.50	.23	.06
Name spelled Greg on front			
□ 154 Rafael Palmeiro	.50	.23	.06
□ 155 Orel Hershiser	.25	.11	.03
□ 156 Derek Bell	.25	.11	.03
□ 157 Jeff Kent	.10	.05	.01
□ 158 Craig Biggio	.50	.23	.06
□ 159 Marquis Grissom	.50	.23	.06
□ 160 Matt Mieske	.10	.05	.01
□ 161 Jay Bell	.25	.11	.03
□ 162 Sammy Sosa	.50	.23	.06
□ 163 Robin Ventura	.25	.11	.03
□ 164 Deion Sanders	.50	.23	.06
□ 165 Jimmy Key	.25	.11	.03
□ 166 Cal Eldred	.10	.05	.01
□ 167 David McCarty	.10	.05	.01
□ 168 Carlos Garcia	.10	.05	.01
□ 169 Willie Greene	.25	.11	.03
□ 170 Michael Jordan	10.00	4.50	1.25
□ 171 Roberto Mejia	.10	.05	.01
□ 172 Phil Hiatt UER	.10	.05	.01
(Card misnumbered 72)			
□ 173 Marc Newfield	.25	.11	.03
□ 174 Kevin Stocker	.10	.05	.01
□ 175 Randy Johnson STA	.25	.11	.03
□ 176 Ivan Rodriguez STA	.50	.23	.06
□ 177 Frank Thomas STA	1.50	.70	.19
□ 178 Roberto Alomar STA	.50	.23	.06
□ 179 Travis Fryman STA	.25	.11	.03
□ 180 Cal Ripken Jr. STA	1.25	.55	.16
□ 181 Juan Gonzalez STA	.75	.35	.09
□ 182 Ken Griffey Jr. STA	1.50	.70	.19
□ 183 Albert Belle STA	.75	.35	.09
□ 184 Greg Maddux STA	1.00	.45	.12
□ 185 Mike Piazza STA	1.00	.45	.12
□ 186 Fred McGriff STA	.50	.23	.06
□ 187 Robby Thompson STA	.10	.05	.01
□ 188 Matt Williams STA	.50	.23	.06
□ 189 Jeff Blauser STA	.10	.05	.01
□ 190 Barry Bonds STA	.50	.23	.06
□ 191 Lenny Dykstra STA	.10	.05	.01
□ 192 David Justice STA	.25	.11	.03
□ 193 Ken Griffey Jr. PF	1.50	.70	.19
□ 194 Barry Bonds PF	.50	.23	.06
□ 195 Frank Thomas PF	1.50	.70	.19
□ 196 Juan Gonzalez PF	.50	.23	.06
□ 197 Randy Johnson PF	.25	.11	.03
□ 198 Chuck Carr PF	.10	.05	.01
□ 199 Barry Bonds HES	1.25	.55	.16
Juan Gonzalez			
□ 200 Ken Griffey Jr. HES	2.50	1.10	.30
Don Mattingly			
□ 201 Roberto Alomar HES	.30	.14	.04
Carlos Baerga			
□ 202 Dave Winfield HES	.50	.23	.06
Robin Yount			
□ 203 Mike Piazza HES	.75	.35	.09
Tim Salmon			
□ 204 Albert Belle HES	2.50	1.10	.30
Frank Thomas			
□ 205 Cliff Floyd HES	.30	.14	.04
Rondell White			
□ 206 Kirby Puckett HES	1.25	.55	.16
Tony Gwynn			
□ 207 Roger Clemens HES	1.25	.55	.16
Greg Maddux			
□ 208 Mike Piazza WC	1.00	.45	.12
□ 209 Jose Canseco WC	.50	.23	.06
□ 210 Frank Thomas WC	1.50	.70	.19
□ 211 Roberto Alomar WC	.50	.23	.06
□ 212 Barry Bonds WC	.50	.23	.06
□ 213 Rickey Henderson WC	.50	.23	.06
□ 214 John Kruk WC	.10	.05	.01
□ 215 Juan Gonzalez WC	.50	.23	.06
□ 216 Ken Griffey Jr. WC	1.50	.70	.19
□ 217 Roberto Alomar FOLD	.50	.23	.06
□ 218 Craig Biggio FOLD	.25	.11	.03
□ 219 Cal Ripken Jr. FOLD	1.25	.55	.16
□ 220 Mike Piazza FOLD	1.00	.45	.12
□ 221 Brent Gates FOLD	.10	.05	.01
□ 222 Walt Weiss FOLD	.10	.05	.01
□ 223 Bobby Bonilla FOLD	.10	.05	.01
□ 224 Ken Griffey Jr. FOLD	1.50	.70	.19
□ 225 Barry Bonds FOLD	.50	.23	.06
□ 226 Barry Bonds FUN	.50	.23	.06
□ 227 Joe Carter FUN	.50	.23	.06
□ 228 Mike Greenwell FUN	.10	.05	.01
□ 229 Ken Griffey Jr. FUN	1.50	.70	.19
□ 230 John Kruk FUN	.10	.05	.01
□ 231 Mike Piazza FUN	1.00	.45	.12
□ 232 Kirby Puckett FUN	.50	.23	.06
□ 233 John Smoltz FUN	.50	.23	.06
□ 234 Rick Wilkins FUN	.10	.05	.01
□ 235 Ken Griffey Jr.	1.50	.70	.19
Checklist 1-40			
□ 236 Frank Thomas	1.50	.70	.19
Checklist 41-80			
□ 237 Barry Bonds	.50	.23	.06
Checklist 81-120			
□ 238 Mike Piazza	1.00	.45	.12
Checklist 121-160			
□ 239 Tim Salmon	.50	.23	.06
Checklist 161-200			
□ 240 Juan Gonzalez	.50	.23	.06
Checklist 201-240			

1948-49 Leaf

The cards in this 98-card set measure 2 3/8" by 2 7/8". The 1948-49 Leaf set was the first post-war baseball series issued in color. In hobby

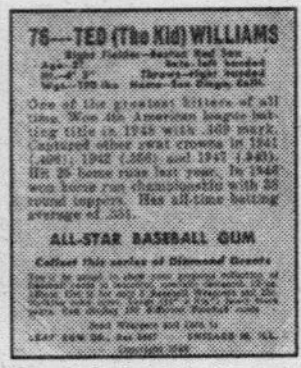

circles, it has been speculated that the set was issued in the spring of 1949. This effort was not entirely successful due to a lack of refinement which resulted in many color variations and cards out of register. In addition, the set was skip numbered from 1-168, with 49 of the 98 cards printed in limited quantities (marked with SP in the checklist). Cards 102 and 136 have variations, and cards are sometimes found with overprinted or incorrect backs. The notable rookie cards in this set include Stan Musial, Satchel Paige, and Jackie Robinson.

	NRMT	VG-E	GOOD
COMPLETE SET (98)	25000.00	11200.00	3100.00
COMMON CARD (1-168)	25.00	11.00	3.10
SP (13/19/33/36)	225.00	100.00	28.00
SP (43/45/48/54/62/63)	225.00	100.00	28.00
SP (66/68/78/81/88)	225.00	100.00	28.00
SP (104/108/113)	225.00	100.00	28.00
SP (123/129/131/137)	225.00	100.00	28.00
SP (143/144/149/153/160)	225.00	100.00	28.00
VAR (102A/136B)	225.00	100.00	28.00
COMMON DODGERS: 1.5X COM. VALUE			
COMMON YANKEES: 1.5X COM. VALUE			
SET IS SKIP NUMBERED			
CARDS PRICED IN NM CONDITION !			

	NRMT	VG-E	GOOD
□ 1 Joe DiMaggio	2100.00	850.00	210.00
□ 3 Babe Ruth	2500.00	1100.00	300.00
□ 4 Stan Musial	850.00	375.00	105.00
□ 5 Virgil Trucks SP	325.00	145.00	40.00
□ 8 Satchel Paige SP	2100.00	950.00	250.00
□ 11 Phil Rizzuto	250.00	110.00	31.00
□ 20 Hank Sauer SP	325.00	145.00	40.00
□ 30 Billy Goodman SP	275.00	125.00	34.00
□ 32 Warren Spahn	275.00	125.00	34.00
□ 38 Ted Kluszewski	150.00	70.00	19.00
□ 39 Ewell Blackwell	55.00	25.00	7.00
□ 46 Johnny Mize	100.00	45.00	12.50
□ 49 Del Ennis	50.00	22.00	6.25
□ 51 Al Dark SP	400.00	180.00	50.00
□ 53 Johnny VanderMeer	40.00	18.00	5.00
□ 55 Tommy Henrich SP	400.00	180.00	50.00
□ 59 Luke Appling	100.00	45.00	12.50
□ 65 Robert Elliott UER (Misspelled Elliot on card front)	40.00	18.00	5.00
□ 70 Honus Wagner CO	275.00	125.00	34.00
□ 75 Dom DiMaggio SP	500.00	220.00	60.00
□ 76 Ted Williams	800.00	350.00	100.00
□ 79 Jackie Robinson	1000.00	450.00	125.00
□ 83 Bobby Doerr	100.00	45.00	12.50
□ 85 Dave Philley SP	275.00	125.00	34.00
□ 91 Ralph Kiner	200.00	90.00	25.00
□ 93 Bob Feller SP	1250.00	550.00	160.00
□ 97 Marty Marion	55.00	25.00	7.00
□ 98 Hal Newhouser SP	500.00	220.00	60.00
□ 106 Lou Boudreau	100.00	45.00	12.50
□ 120 George Kell SP	500.00	220.00	60.00
□ 121 Johnny Pesky SP	325.00	145.00	40.00
□ 127 Enos Slaughter SP	600.00	275.00	75.00
□ 133 Tommy Holmes SP	400.00	180.00	50.00
□ 138 Larry Doby SP	500.00	220.00	60.00
□ 142 Danny Murtaugh SP	325.00	145.00	40.00
□ 146 Pete Reiser SP	400.00	180.00	50.00
□ 158 Harry Brecheen SP	325.00	145.00	40.00
□ 161 Vern Stephens SP	325.00	145.00	40.00
□ 163 Fred Hutchinson SP	325.00	145.00	40.00
□ 165 Dale Mitchell SP	325.00	145.00	40.00
□ 168 Phil Cavarretta SP	400.00	160.00	40.00

1990 Leaf

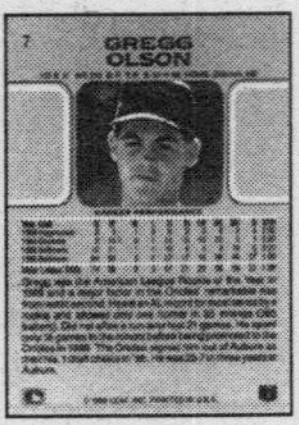

The 1990 Leaf set was the first premium set introduced by Donruss.The cards were issued in 15-card foil wrapped packs and were not available in factory sets. Each pack also contained one three-piece puzzle panel of a 63-piece Yogi Berra "Donruss Hall of Fame Diamond King" puzzle. This set, which was produced on high quality paper stock, was issued in two separate series of 264 standard-size cards each. The second series was issued approximately six weeks after the release of the first series. The cards feature full-color photos on both the front and back. Rookie Cards in the set include Carlos Baerga, Bernard Gilkey, Marquis Grissom, David Justice, Ben McDonald, Sammy Sosa, Frank Thomas and Larry Walker.

	MINT	NRMT	EXC
COMPLETE SET (528)	200.00	90.00	25.00
COMPLETE SERIES 1 (264)	80.00	36.00	10.00
COMPLETE SERIES 2 (264)	120.00	55.00	15.00
COMMON CARD (1-528)	.25	.11	.03
SEMISTARS	.50	.23	.06
STARS	.75	.35	.09
BEWARE THOMAS COUNTERFEIT			

	MINT	NRMT	EXC
□ 1 Introductory Card	.25	.11	.03
□ 2 Mike Henneman	.25	.11	.03
□ 3 Steve Bedrosian	.25	.11	.03
□ 4 Mike Scott	.25	.11	.03
□ 5 Allan Anderson	.25	.11	.03
□ 6 Rick Sutcliffe	.25	.11	.03
□ 7 Gregg Olson	.25	.11	.03
□ 8 Kevin Elster	.25	.11	.03
□ 9 Pete O'Brien	.25	.11	.03
□ 10 Carlton Fisk	.75	.35	.09
□ 11 Joe Magrane	.25	.11	.03
□ 12 Roger Clemens	1.00	.45	.12
□ 13 Tom Glavine	2.50	1.10	.30
□ 14 Tom Gordon	.25	.11	.03
□ 15 Todd Benzinger	.25	.11	.03
□ 16 Hubie Brooks	.25	.11	.03
□ 17 Roberto Kelly	.50	.23	.06
□ 18 Barry Larkin	1.25	.55	.16
□ 19 Mike Boddicker	.25	.11	.03
□ 20 Roger McDowell	.25	.11	.03
□ 21 Nolan Ryan	6.00	2.70	.75
□ 22 John Farrell	.25	.11	.03
□ 23 Bruce Hurst	.25	.11	.03
□ 24 Wally Joyner	.50	.23	.06
□ 25 Greg Maddux	18.00	8.00	2.20
□ 26 Chris Bosio	.25	.11	.03
□ 27 John Cerutti	.25	.11	.03
□ 28 Tim Burke	.25	.11	.03
□ 29 Dennis Eckersley	.50	.23	.06
□ 30 Glenn Davis	.25	.11	.03
□ 31 Jim Abbott	.50	.23	.06
□ 32 Mike LaValliere	.25	.11	.03
□ 33 Andres Thomas	.25	.11	.03
□ 34 Lou Whitaker	.75	.35	.09
□ 35 Alvin Davis	.25	.11	.03
□ 36 Melido Perez	.25	.11	.03
□ 37 Craig Biggio	1.00	.45	.12
□ 38 Rick Aguilera	.50	.23	.06
□ 39 Pete Harnisch	.25	.11	.03
□ 40 David Cone	1.50	.70	.19

□ 41 Scott Garrelts	.25	.11	.03
□ 42 Jay Howell	.25	.11	.03
□ 43 Eric King	.25	.11	.03
□ 44 Pedro Guerrero	.25	.11	.03
□ 45 Mike Bielecki	.25	.11	.03
□ 46 Bob Boone	.50	.23	.06
□ 47 Kevin Brown	.50	.23	.06
□ 48 Jerry Browne	.25	.11	.03
□ 49 Mike Scioscia	.25	.11	.03
□ 50 Chuck Cary	.25	.11	.03
□ 51 Wade Boggs	.75	.35	.09
□ 52 Von Hayes	.25	.11	.03
□ 53 Tony Fernandez	.25	.11	.03
□ 54 Dennis Martinez	.50	.23	.06
□ 55 Tom Candiotti	.25	.11	.03
□ 56 Andy Benes	.75	.35	.09
□ 57 Rob Dibble	.25	.11	.03
□ 58 Chuck Crim	.25	.11	.03
□ 59 John Smoltz	4.00	1.80	.50
□ 60 Mike Heath	.25	.11	.03
□ 61 Kevin Gross	.25	.11	.03
□ 62 Mark McGwire	2.50	1.10	.30
□ 63 Bert Blyleven	.50	.23	.06
□ 64 Bob Walk	.25	.11	.03
□ 65 Mickey Tettleton	.50	.23	.06
□ 66 Sid Fernandez	.25	.11	.03
□ 67 Terry Kennedy	.25	.11	.03
□ 68 Fernando Valenzuela	.50	.23	.06
□ 69 Don Mattingly	4.00	1.80	.50
□ 70 Paul O'Neill	.50	.23	.06
□ 71 Robin Yount	1.00	.45	.12
□ 72 Bret Saberhagen	.50	.23	.06
□ 73 Geno Petralli	.25	.11	.03
□ 74 Brook Jacoby	.25	.11	.03
□ 75 Roberto Alomar	3.00	1.35	.35
□ 76 Devon White	.50	.23	.06
□ 77 Jose Lind	.25	.11	.03
□ 78 Pat Combs	.25	.11	.03
□ 79 Dave Stieb	.25	.11	.03
□ 80 Tim Wallach	.25	.11	.03
□ 81 Dave Stewart	.50	.23	.06
□ 82 Eric Anthony	.50	.23	.06
□ 83 Randy Bush	.25	.11	.03
□ 84 Checklist 1-88 (Rickey Henderson)	.50	.23	.06
□ 85 Jaime Navarro	.25	.11	.03
□ 86 Tommy Gregg	.25	.11	.03
□ 87 Frank Tanana	.25	.11	.03
□ 88 Omar Vizquel	2.00	.90	.25
□ 89 Ivan Calderon	.25	.11	.03
□ 90 Vince Coleman	.25	.11	.03
□ 91 Barry Bonds	2.00	.90	.25
□ 92 Randy Milligan	.25	.11	.03
□ 93 Frank Viola	.25	.11	.03
□ 94 Matt Williams	2.50	1.10	.30
□ 95 Alfredo Griffin	.25	.11	.03
□ 96 Steve Sax	.25	.11	.03
□ 97 Gary Gaetti	.50	.23	.06
□ 98 Ryne Sandberg	2.00	.90	.25
□ 99 Danny Tartabull	.25	.11	.03
□ 100 Rafael Palmeiro	2.50	1.10	.30
□ 101 Jesse Orosco	.25	.11	.03
□ 102 Garry Templeton	.25	.11	.03
□ 103 Frank DiPino	.25	.11	.03
□ 104 Tony Pena	.25	.11	.03
□ 105 Dickie Thon	.25	.11	.03
□ 106 Kelly Gruber	.25	.11	.03
□ 107 Marquis Grissom	6.00	2.70	.75
□ 108 Jose Canseco	1.00	.45	.12
□ 109 Mike Blowers	.75	.35	.09
□ 110 Tom Browning	.25	.11	.03
□ 111 Greg Vaughn	1.50	.70	.19
□ 112 Oddibe McDowell	.25	.11	.03
□ 113 Gary Ward	.25	.11	.03
□ 114 Jay Buhner	2.00	.90	.25
□ 115 Eric Show	.25	.11	.03
□ 116 Bryan Harvey	.25	.11	.03
□ 117 Andy Van Slyke	.50	.23	.06
□ 118 Jeff Ballard	.25	.11	.03
□ 119 Barry Lyons	.25	.11	.03
□ 120 Kevin Mitchell	.50	.23	.06
□ 121 Mike Gallego	.25	.11	.03
□ 122 Dave Smith	.25	.11	.03
□ 123 Kirby Puckett	2.50	1.10	.30
□ 124 Jerome Walton	.25	.11	.03
□ 125 Bo Jackson	.75	.35	.09
□ 126 Harold Baines	.50	.23	.06
□ 127 Scott Bankhead	.25	.11	.03
□ 128 Ozzie Guillen	.25	.11	.03
□ 129 Jose Oquendo UER (League misspelled as Legue)	.25	.11	.03
□ 130 John Dopson	.25	.11	.03
□ 131 Charlie Hayes	.50	.23	.06
□ 132 Fred McGriff	1.25	.55	.16
□ 133 Chet Lemon	.25	.11	.03
□ 134 Gary Carter	.75	.35	.09
□ 135 Rafael Ramirez	.25	.11	.03
□ 136 Shane Mack	.25	.11	.03
□ 137 Mark Grace UER (Card back has OB:L, should be B:L)	1.00	.45	.12
□ 138 Phil Bradley	.25	.11	.03
□ 139 Dwight Gooden	.50	.23	.06
□ 140 Harold Reynolds	.25	.11	.03
□ 141 Scott Fletcher	.25	.11	.03
□ 142 Ozzie Smith	1.50	.70	.19
□ 143 Mike Greenwell	.25	.11	.03
□ 144 Pete Smith	.25	.11	.03
□ 145 Mark Gubicza	.25	.11	.03
□ 146 Chris Sabo	.25	.11	.03
□ 147 Ramon Martinez	.75	.35	.09
□ 148 Tim Leary	.25	.11	.03
□ 149 Randy Myers	.50	.23	.06
□ 150 Jody Reed	.25	.11	.03
□ 151 Bruce Ruffin	.25	.11	.03
□ 152 Jeff Russell	.25	.11	.03
□ 153 Doug Jones	.25	.11	.03
□ 154 Tony Gwynn	3.00	1.35	.35
□ 155 Mark Langston	.50	.23	.06
□ 156 Mitch Williams	.25	.11	.03
□ 157 Gary Sheffield	4.00	1.80	.50
□ 158 Tom Henke	.25	.11	.03
□ 159 Oil Can Boyd	.25	.11	.03
□ 160 Rickey Henderson	.75	.35	.09
□ 161 Bill Doran	.25	.11	.03
□ 162 Chuck Finley	.50	.23	.06
□ 163 Jeff King	.50	.23	.06
□ 164 Nick Esasky	.25	.11	.03
□ 165 Cecil Fielder	.50	.23	.06
□ 166 Dave Valle	.25	.11	.03
□ 167 Robin Ventura	2.00	.90	.25
□ 168 Jim Deshaies	.25	.11	.03
□ 169 Juan Berenguer	.25	.11	.03
□ 170 Craig Worthington	.25	.11	.03
□ 171 Gregg Jeffries	.75	.35	.09
□ 172 Will Clark	1.00	.45	.12
□ 173 Kirk Gibson	.50	.23	.06
□ 174 Checklist 89-176 (Carlton Fisk)	.75	.35	.09
□ 175 Bobby Thigpen	.25	.11	.03
□ 176 John Tudor	.25	.11	.03
□ 177 Andre Dawson	.75	.35	.09
□ 178 George Brett	3.00	1.35	.35
□ 179 Steve Buechele	.25	.11	.03
□ 180 Joey Belle	20.00	9.00	2.50
□ 181 Eddie Murray	2.00	.90	.25
□ 182 Bob Geren	.25	.11	.03
□ 183 Rob Murphy	.25	.11	.03
□ 184 Tom Herr	.25	.11	.03
□ 185 George Bell	.25	.11	.03
□ 186 Spike Owen	.25	.11	.03
□ 187 Cory Snyder	.25	.11	.03
□ 188 Fred Lynn	.25	.11	.03
□ 189 Eric Davis	.50	.23	.06
□ 190 Dave Parker	.50	.23	.06
□ 191 Jeff Blauser	.50	.23	.06
□ 192 Matt Nokes	.25	.11	.03
□ 193 Delino DeShields	1.00	.45	.12
□ 194 Scott Sanderson	.25	.11	.03
□ 195 Lance Parrish	.25	.11	.03
□ 196 Bobby Bonilla	.50	.23	.06
□ 197 Cal Ripken UER (Reistertown, should be Reisterstown)	6.00	2.70	.75
□ 198 Kevin McReynolds	.25	.11	.03
□ 199 Robby Thompson	.25	.11	.03
□ 200 Tim Belcher	.25	.11	.03
□ 201 Jesse Barfield	.25	.11	.03
□ 202 Mariano Duncan	.25	.11	.03
□ 203 Bill Spiers	.25	.11	.03
□ 204 Frank White	.50	.23	.06

□ 205	Julio Franco	.50	.23	.06
□ 206	Greg Swindell	.25	.11	.03
□ 207	Benito Santiago	.25	.11	.03
□ 208	Johnny Ray	.25	.11	.03
□ 209	Gary Redus	.25	.11	.03
□ 210	Jeff Parrett	.25	.11	.03
□ 211	Jimmy Key	.50	.23	.06
□ 212	Tim Raines	.50	.23	.06
□ 213	Carney Lansford	.50	.23	.06
□ 214	Gerald Young	.25	.11	.03
□ 215	Gene Larkin	.25	.11	.03
□ 216	Dan Plesac	.25	.11	.03
□ 217	Lonnie Smith	.25	.11	.03
□ 218	Alan Trammell	.75	.35	.09
□ 219	Jeffrey Leonard	.25	.11	.03
□ 220	Sammy Sosa	8.00	3.60	1.00
□ 221	Todd Zeile	.50	.23	.06
□ 222	Bill Landrum	.25	.11	.03
□ 223	Mike Devereaux	.25	.11	.03
□ 224	Mike Marshall	.25	.11	.03
□ 225	Jose Uribe	.25	.11	.03
□ 226	Juan Samuel	.25	.11	.03
□ 227	Mel Hall	.25	.11	.03
□ 228	Kent Hrbek	.50	.23	.06
□ 229	Shawon Dunston	.25	.11	.03
□ 230	Kevin Seitzer	.25	.11	.03
□ 231	Pete Incaviglia	.25	.11	.03
□ 232	Sandy Alomar Jr.	.50	.23	.06
□ 233	Bip Roberts	.25	.11	.03
□ 234	Scott Terry	.25	.11	.03
□ 235	Dwight Evans	.50	.23	.06
□ 236	Ricky Jordan	.25	.11	.03
□ 237	John Olerud	1.00	.45	.12
□ 238	Zane Smith	.25	.11	.03
□ 239	Walt Weiss	.25	.11	.03
□ 240	Alvaro Espinoza	.25	.11	.03
□ 241	Billy Hatcher	.25	.11	.03
□ 242	Paul Molitor	1.50	.70	.19
□ 243	Dale Murphy	.75	.35	.09
□ 244	Dave Bergman	.25	.11	.03
□ 245	Ken Griffey Jr.	25.00	11.00	3.10
□ 246	Ed Whitson	.25	.11	.03
□ 247	Kirk McCaskill	.25	.11	.03
□ 248	Jay Bell	.50	.23	.06
□ 249	Ben McDonald	1.50	.70	.19
□ 250	Darryl Strawberry	.50	.23	.06
□ 251	Brett Butler	.50	.23	.06
□ 252	Terry Steinbach	.50	.23	.06
□ 253	Ken Caminiti	2.00	.90	.25
□ 254	Dan Gladden	.25	.11	.03
□ 255	Dwight Smith	.25	.11	.03
□ 256	Kurt Stillwell	.25	.11	.03
□ 257	Ruben Sierra	.50	.23	.06
□ 258	Mike Schooler	.25	.11	.03
□ 259	Lance Johnson	.75	.35	.09
□ 260	Terry Pendleton	.50	.23	.06
□ 261	Ellis Burks	.75	.35	.09
□ 262	Len Dykstra	.50	.23	.06
□ 263	Mookie Wilson	.25	.11	.03
□ 264	Checklist 177-264 (Nolan Ryan) UER (No TM after Ranger logo)	.75	.35	.09
□ 265	No Hit King (Nolan Ryan)	3.00	1.35	.35
□ 266	Brian DuBois	.25	.11	.03
□ 267	Don Robinson	.25	.11	.03
□ 268	Glenn Wilson	.25	.11	.03
□ 269	Kevin Tapani	.50	.23	.06
□ 270	Marvell Wynne	.25	.11	.03
□ 271	Billy Ripken	.25	.11	.03
□ 272	Howard Johnson	.25	.11	.03
□ 273	Brian Holman	.25	.11	.03
□ 274	Dan Pasqua	.25	.11	.03
□ 275	Ken Dayley	.25	.11	.03
□ 276	Jeff Reardon	.50	.23	.06
□ 277	Jim Presley	.25	.11	.03
□ 278	Jim Eisenreich	.25	.11	.03
□ 279	Danny Jackson	.25	.11	.03
□ 280	Orel Hershiser	.50	.23	.06
□ 281	Andy Hawkins	.25	.11	.03
□ 282	Jose Rijo	.25	.11	.03
□ 283	Luis Rivera	.25	.11	.03
□ 284	John Kruk	.50	.23	.06
□ 285	Jeff Huson	.25	.11	.03
□ 286	Joel Skinner	.25	.11	.03
□ 287	Jack Clark	.50	.23	.06
□ 288	Chili Davis	.50	.23	.06
□ 289	Joe Girardi	.50	.23	.06
□ 290	B.J. Surhoff	.50	.23	.06
□ 291	Luis Sojo	.25	.11	.03
□ 292	Tom Foley	.25	.11	.03
□ 293	Mike Moore	.25	.11	.03
□ 294	Ken Oberkfell	.25	.11	.03
□ 295	Luis Polonia	.25	.11	.03
□ 296	Doug Drabek	.25	.11	.03
□ 297	Dave Justice	5.00	2.20	.60
□ 298	Paul Gibson	.25	.11	.03
□ 299	Edgar Martinez	2.50	1.10	.30
□ 300	Frank Thomas UER (No B in front of birthdate)	85.00	38.00	10.50
□ 301	Eric Yelding	.25	.11	.03
□ 302	Greg Gagne	.25	.11	.03
□ 303	Brad Komminsk	.25	.11	.03
□ 304	Ron Darling	.25	.11	.03
□ 305	Kevin Bass	.25	.11	.03
□ 306	Jeff Hamilton	.25	.11	.03
□ 307	Ron Karkovice	.25	.11	.03
□ 308	Milt Thompson UER (Ray Lankford pictured on card back)	.75	.35	.09
□ 309	Mike Harkey	.25	.11	.03
□ 310	Mel Stottlemyre Jr.	.25	.11	.03
□ 311	Kenny Rogers	.50	.23	.06
□ 312	Mitch Webster	.25	.11	.03
□ 313	Kal Daniels	.25	.11	.03
□ 314	Matt Nokes	.25	.11	.03
□ 315	Dennis Lamp	.25	.11	.03
□ 316	Ken Howell	.25	.11	.03
□ 317	Glenallen Hill	.50	.23	.06
□ 318	Dave Martinez	.25	.11	.03
□ 319	Chris James	.25	.11	.03
□ 320	Mike Pagliarulo	.25	.11	.03
□ 321	Hal Morris	.50	.23	.06
□ 322	Rob Deer	.25	.11	.03
□ 323	Greg Olson	.25	.11	.03
□ 324	Tony Phillips	.75	.35	.09
□ 325	Larry Walker	5.00	2.20	.60
□ 326	Ron Hassey	.25	.11	.03
□ 327	Jack Howell	.25	.11	.03
□ 328	John Smiley	.50	.23	.06
□ 329	Steve Finley	1.00	.45	.12
□ 330	Dave Magadan	.25	.11	.03
□ 331	Greg Litton	.25	.11	.03
□ 332	Mickey Hatcher	.25	.11	.03
□ 333	Lee Guetterman	.25	.11	.03
□ 334	Norm Charlton	.25	.11	.03
□ 335	Edgar Diaz	.25	.11	.03
□ 336	Willie Wilson	.25	.11	.03
□ 337	Bobby Witt	.25	.11	.03
□ 338	Candy Maldonado	.25	.11	.03
□ 339	Craig Lefferts	.25	.11	.03
□ 340	Dante Bichette	3.00	1.35	.35
□ 341	Wally Backman	.25	.11	.03
□ 342	Dennis Cook	.25	.11	.03
□ 343	Pat Borders	.25	.11	.03
□ 344	Wallace Johnson	.25	.11	.03
□ 345	Willie Randolph	.50	.23	.06
□ 346	Danny Darwin	.25	.11	.03
□ 347	Al Newman	.25	.11	.03
□ 348	Mark Knudson	.25	.11	.03
□ 349	Joe Boever	.25	.11	.03
□ 350	Larry Sheets	.25	.11	.03
□ 351	Mike Jackson	.25	.11	.03
□ 352	Wayne Edwards	.25	.11	.03
□ 353	Bernard Gilkey	4.00	1.80	.50
□ 354	Don Slaught	.25	.11	.03
□ 355	Joe Orsulak	.25	.11	.03
□ 356	John Franco	.25	.11	.03
□ 357	Jeff Brantley	.50	.23	.06
□ 358	Mike Morgan	.25	.11	.03
□ 359	Deion Sanders	3.00	1.35	.35
□ 360	Terry Leach	.25	.11	.03
□ 361	Les Lancaster	.25	.11	.03
□ 362	Storm Davis	.25	.11	.03
□ 363	Scott Coolbaugh	.25	.11	.03
□ 364	Checklist 265-352 (Ozzie Smith)	.75	.35	.09
□ 365	Cecilio Guante	.25	.11	.03
□ 366	Joey Cora	.75	.35	.09
□ 367	Willie McGee	.25	.11	.03

□ 368	Jerry Reed	.25	.11	.03
□ 369	Darren Daulton	.50	.23	.06
□ 370	Manny Lee	.25	.11	.03
□ 371	Mark Gardner	.25	.11	.03
□ 372	Rick Honeycutt	.25	.11	.03
□ 373	Steve Balboni	.25	.11	.03
□ 374	Jack Armstrong	.25	.11	.03
□ 375	Charlie O'Brien	.25	.11	.03
□ 376	Ron Gant	1.00	.45	.12
□ 377	Lloyd Moseby	.25	.11	.03
□ 378	Gene Harris	.25	.11	.03
□ 379	Joe Carter	.75	.35	.09
□ 380	Scott Bailes	.25	.11	.03
□ 381	R.J. Reynolds	.25	.11	.03
□ 382	Bob Melvin	.25	.11	.03
□ 383	Tim Teufel	.25	.11	.03
□ 384	John Burkett	.50	.23	.06
□ 385	Felix Jose	.25	.11	.03
□ 386	Larry Andersen	.25	.11	.03
□ 387	David West	.25	.11	.03
□ 388	Luis Salazar	.25	.11	.03
□ 389	Mike Macfarlane	.25	.11	.03
□ 390	Charlie Hough	.25	.11	.03
□ 391	Greg Briley	.25	.11	.03
□ 392	Donn Pall	.25	.11	.03
□ 393	Bryn Smith	.25	.11	.03
□ 394	Carlos Quintana	.25	.11	.03
□ 395	Steve Lake	.25	.11	.03
□ 396	Mark Whiten	.75	.35	.09
□ 397	Edwin Nunez	.25	.11	.03
□ 398	Rick Parker	.25	.11	.03
□ 399	Mark Portugal	.25	.11	.03
□ 400	Roy Smith	.25	.11	.03
□ 401	Hector Villanueva	.25	.11	.03
□ 402	Bob Milacki	.25	.11	.03
□ 403	Alejandro Pena	.25	.11	.03
□ 404	Scott Bradley	.25	.11	.03
□ 405	Ron Kittle	.25	.11	.03
□ 406	Bob Tewksbury	.25	.11	.03
□ 407	Wes Gardner	.25	.11	.03
□ 408	Ernie Whitt	.25	.11	.03
□ 409	Terry Shumpert	.25	.11	.03
□ 410	Tim Layana	.25	.11	.03
□ 411	Chris Gwynn	.25	.11	.03
□ 412	Jeff D. Robinson	.25	.11	.03
□ 413	Scott Scudder	.25	.11	.03
□ 414	Kevin Romine	.25	.11	.03
□ 415	Jose DeJesus	.25	.11	.03
□ 416	Mike Jeffcoat	.25	.11	.03
□ 417	Rudy Seanez	.25	.11	.03
□ 418	Mike Dunne	.25	.11	.03
□ 419	Dick Schofield	.25	.11	.03
□ 420	Steve Wilson	.25	.11	.03
□ 421	Bill Krueger	.25	.11	.03
□ 422	Junior Felix	.25	.11	.03
□ 423	Drew Hall	.25	.11	.03
□ 424	Curt Young	.25	.11	.03
□ 425	Franklin Stubbs	.25	.11	.03
□ 426	Dave Winfield	.75	.35	.09
□ 427	Rick Reed	.25	.11	.03
□ 428	Charlie Leibrandt	.25	.11	.03
□ 429	Jeff M. Robinson	.25	.11	.03
□ 430	Erik Hanson	.50	.23	.06
□ 431	Barry Jones	.25	.11	.03
□ 432	Alex Trevino	.25	.11	.03
□ 433	John Moses	.25	.11	.03
□ 434	Dave Johnson	.25	.11	.03
□ 435	Mackey Sasser	.25	.11	.03
□ 436	Rick Leach	.25	.11	.03
□ 437	Lenny Harris	.25	.11	.03
□ 438	Carlos Martinez	.25	.11	.03
□ 439	Rex Hudler	.25	.11	.03
□ 440	Domingo Ramos	.25	.11	.03
□ 441	Gerald Perry	.25	.11	.03
□ 442	Jeff Russell	.25	.11	.03
□ 443	Carlos Baerga	5.00	2.20	.60
□ 444	Checklist 353-440 (Will Clark)	.75	.35	.09
□ 445	Stan Javier	.25	.11	.03
□ 446	Kevin Maas	.50	.23	.06
□ 447	Tom Brunansky	.25	.11	.03
□ 448	Carmelo Martinez	.25	.11	.03
□ 449	Willie Blair	.25	.11	.03
□ 450	Andres Galarraga	1.00	.45	.12
□ 451	Bud Black	.25	.11	.03
□ 452	Greg W. Harris	.25	.11	.03
□ 453	Joe Oliver	.25	.11	.03
□ 454	Greg Brock	.25	.11	.03
□ 455	Jeff Treadway	.25	.11	.03
□ 456	Lance McCullers	.25	.11	.03
□ 457	Dave Schmidt	.25	.11	.03
□ 458	Todd Burns	.25	.11	.03
□ 459	Max Venable	.25	.11	.03
□ 460	Neal Heaton	.25	.11	.03
□ 461	Mark Williamson	.25	.11	.03
□ 462	Keith Miller	.25	.11	.03
□ 463	Mike LaCoss	.25	.11	.03
□ 464	Jose Offerman	.50	.23	.06
□ 465	Jim Leyritz	.75	.35	.09
□ 466	Glenn Braggs	.25	.11	.03
□ 467	Ron Robinson	.25	.11	.03
□ 468	Mark Davis	.25	.11	.03
□ 469	Gary Pettis	.25	.11	.03
□ 470	Keith Hernandez	.50	.23	.06
□ 471	Dennis Rasmussen	.25	.11	.03
□ 472	Mark Eichhorn	.25	.11	.03
□ 473	Ted Power	.25	.11	.03
□ 474	Terry Mulholland	.25	.11	.03
□ 475	Todd Stottlemyre	.50	.23	.06
□ 476	Jerry Goff	.25	.11	.03
□ 477	Gene Nelson	.25	.11	.03
□ 478	Rich Gedman	.25	.11	.03
□ 479	Brian Harper	.25	.11	.03
□ 480	Mike Felder	.25	.11	.03
□ 481	Steve Avery	1.50	.70	.19
□ 482	Jack Morris	.50	.23	.06
□ 483	Randy Johnson	4.00	1.80	.50
□ 484	Scott Radinsky	.25	.11	.03
□ 485	Jose DeLeon	.25	.11	.03
□ 486	Stan Belinda	.25	.11	.03
□ 487	Brian Holton	.25	.11	.03
□ 488	Mark Carreon	.25	.11	.03
□ 489	Trevor Wilson	.25	.11	.03
□ 490	Mike Sharperson	.25	.11	.03
□ 491	Alan Mills	.25	.11	.03
□ 492	John Candelaria	.25	.11	.03
□ 493	Paul Assenmacher	.25	.11	.03
□ 494	Steve Crawford	.25	.11	.03
□ 495	Brad Arnsberg	.25	.11	.03
□ 496	Sergio Valdez	.25	.11	.03
□ 497	Mark Parent	.25	.11	.03
□ 498	Tom Pagnozzi	.25	.11	.03
□ 499	Greg A. Harris	.25	.11	.03
□ 500	Randy Ready	.25	.11	.03
□ 501	Duane Ward	.25	.11	.03
□ 502	Nelson Santovenia	.25	.11	.03
□ 503	Joe Klink	.25	.11	.03
□ 504	Eric Plunk	.25	.11	.03
□ 505	Jeff Reed	.25	.11	.03
□ 506	Ted Higuera	.25	.11	.03
□ 507	Joe Hesketh	.25	.11	.03
□ 508	Dan Petry	.25	.11	.03
□ 509	Matt Young	.25	.11	.03
□ 510	Jerald Clark	.25	.11	.03
□ 511	John Orton	.25	.11	.03
□ 512	Scott Ruskin	.25	.11	.03
□ 513	Chris Hoiles	1.00	.45	.12
□ 514	Daryl Boston	.25	.11	.03
□ 515	Francisco Oliveras	.25	.11	.03
□ 516	Ozzie Canseco	.25	.11	.03
□ 517	Xavier Hernandez	.25	.11	.03
□ 518	Fred Manrique	.25	.11	.03
□ 519	Shawn Boskie	.25	.11	.03
□ 520	Jeff Montgomery	.50	.23	.06
□ 521	Jack Daugherty	.25	.11	.03
□ 522	Keith Comstock	.25	.11	.03
□ 523	Greg Hibbard	.25	.11	.03
□ 524	Lee Smith	.50	.23	.06
□ 525	Dana Kiecker	.25	.11	.03
□ 526	Darrel Akerfelds	.25	.11	.03
□ 527	Greg Myers	.25	.11	.03
□ 528	Checklist 441-528 (Ryne Sandberg)	.75	.35	.09

1991 Leaf Previews

The 1991 Leaf Previews set consists of 26 standard-size cards. Cards from this set were issued as inserts (four at a time) inside specially marked 1991 Donruss hobby factory sets.

The front design has color action player photos, with white and silver borders.

	MINT	NRMT	EXC
COMPLETE SET (26)	35.00	16.00	4.40
COMMON CARD (1-26)	1.00	.45	.12
SEMISTARS	2.00	.90	.25
FOUR PER DONRUSS HOBBY FACTORY SET			
□ 1 Dave Justice	2.50	1.10	.30
□ 2 Ryne Sandberg	5.00	2.20	.60
□ 3 Barry Larkin	3.00	1.35	.35
□ 4 Craig Biggio	2.00	.90	.25
□ 5 Ramon Martinez	2.00	.90	.25
□ 6 Tim Wallach	1.00	.45	.12
□ 7 Dwight Gooden	2.00	.90	.25
□ 8 Len Dykstra	2.00	.90	.25
□ 9 Barry Bonds	5.00	2.20	.60
□ 10 Ray Lankford	3.00	1.35	.35
□ 11 Tony Gwynn	6.00	2.70	.75
□ 12 Will Clark	2.00	.90	.25
□ 13 Leo Gomez	1.00	.45	.12
□ 14 Wade Boggs	2.00	.90	.25
□ 15 Chuck Finley UER (Position on card back is First Base)	1.00	.45	.12
□ 16 Carlton Fisk	2.00	.90	.25
□ 17 Sandy Alomar Jr.	2.00	.90	.25
□ 18 Cecil Fielder	2.00	.90	.25
□ 19 Bo Jackson	2.00	.90	.25
□ 20 Paul Molitor	2.50	1.10	.30
□ 21 Kirby Puckett	6.00	2.70	.75
□ 22 Don Mattingly	8.00	3.60	1.00
□ 23 Rickey Henderson	2.00	.90	.25
□ 24 Tino Martinez	2.00	.90	.25
□ 25 Nolan Ryan	15.00	6.75	1.85
□ 26 Dave Stieb	1.00	.45	.12

1991 Leaf

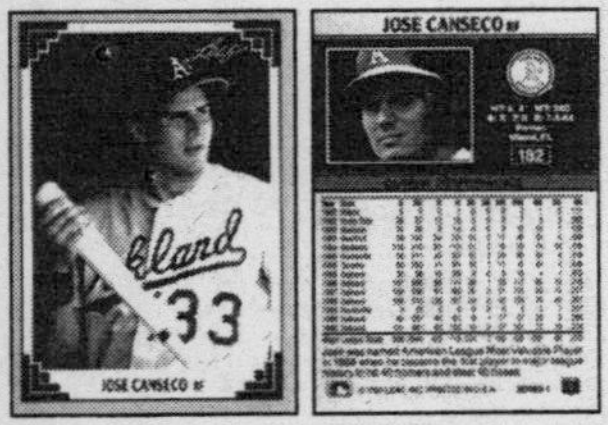

This 528-card standard size set was issued by Donruss in two separate series of 264 cards. Cards were exclusively issued in foil packs. The front design has color action player photos, with white and silver borders. A thicker stock was used for these (then) premium level cards. Rookie Cards in the set include Brian McRae and Denny Neagle.

	MINT	NRMT	EXC
COMPLETE SET (528)	16.00	7.25	2.00
COMPLETE SERIES 1 (264)	6.00	2.70	.75
COMPLETE SERIES 2 (264)	10.00	4.50	1.25
COMMON CARD (1-528)	.05	.02	.01
SEMISTARS	.15	.07	.02
STARS	.30	.14	.04
□ 1 The Leaf Card	.05	.02	.01
□ 2 Kurt Stillwell	.05	.02	.01
□ 3 Bobby Witt	.05	.02	.01
□ 4 Tony Phillips	.15	.07	.02
□ 5 Scott Garrelts	.05	.02	.01
□ 6 Greg Swindell	.05	.02	.01
□ 7 Billy Ripken	.05	.02	.01
□ 8 Dave Martinez	.05	.02	.01
□ 9 Kelly Gruber	.05	.02	.01
□ 10 Juan Samuel	.05	.02	.01
□ 11 Brian Holman	.05	.02	.01
□ 12 Craig Biggio	.30	.14	.04
□ 13 Lonnie Smith	.05	.02	.01
□ 14 Ron Robinson	.05	.02	.01
□ 15 Mike LaValliere	.05	.02	.01
□ 16 Mark Davis	.05	.02	.01
□ 17 Jack Daugherty	.05	.02	.01
□ 18 Mike Henneman	.05	.02	.01
□ 19 Mike Greenwell	.05	.02	.01
□ 20 Dave Magadan	.05	.02	.01
□ 21 Mark Williamson	.05	.02	.01
□ 22 Marquis Grissom	.30	.14	.04
□ 23 Pat Borders	.05	.02	.01
□ 24 Mike Scioscia	.05	.02	.01
□ 25 Shawon Dunston	.05	.02	.01
□ 26 Randy Bush	.05	.02	.01
□ 27 John Smoltz	.30	.14	.04
□ 28 Chuck Crim	.05	.02	.01
□ 29 Don Slaught	.05	.02	.01
□ 30 Mike Macfarlane	.05	.02	.01
□ 31 Wally Joyner	.15	.07	.02
□ 32 Pat Combs	.05	.02	.01
□ 33 Tony Pena	.05	.02	.01
□ 34 Howard Johnson	.05	.02	.01
□ 35 Leo Gomez	.05	.02	.01
□ 36 Spike Owen	.05	.02	.01
□ 37 Eric Davis	.15	.07	.02
□ 38 Roberto Kelly	.05	.02	.01
□ 39 Jerome Walton	.05	.02	.01
□ 40 Shane Mack	.05	.02	.01
□ 41 Kent Mercker	.05	.02	.01
□ 42 B.J. Surhoff	.15	.07	.02
□ 43 Jerry Browne	.05	.02	.01
□ 44 Lee Smith	.15	.07	.02
□ 45 Chuck Finley	.15	.07	.02
□ 46 Terry Mulholland	.05	.02	.01
□ 47 Tom Bolton	.05	.02	.01
□ 48 Tom Herr	.05	.02	.01
□ 49 Jim Deshaies	.05	.02	.01
□ 50 Walt Weiss	.05	.02	.01
□ 51 Hal Morris	.05	.02	.01
□ 52 Lee Guetterman	.05	.02	.01
□ 53 Paul Assenmacher	.05	.02	.01
□ 54 Brian Harper	.05	.02	.01
□ 55 Paul Gibson	.05	.02	.01
□ 56 John Burkett	.15	.07	.02
□ 57 Doug Jones	.05	.02	.01
□ 58 Jose Oquendo	.05	.02	.01
□ 59 Dick Schofield	.05	.02	.01
□ 60 Dickie Thon	.05	.02	.01
□ 61 Ramon Martinez	.15	.07	.02
□ 62 Jay Buhner	.30	.14	.04
□ 63 Mark Portugal	.05	.02	.01
□ 64 Bob Welch	.05	.02	.01
□ 65 Chris Sabo	.05	.02	.01
□ 66 Chuck Cary	.05	.02	.01
□ 67 Mark Langston	.15	.07	.02
□ 68 Joe Boever	.05	.02	.01
□ 69 Jody Reed	.05	.02	.01
□ 70 Alejandro Pena	.05	.02	.01
□ 71 Jeff King	.15	.07	.02
□ 72 Tom Pagnozzi	.05	.02	.01
□ 73 Joe Oliver	.05	.02	.01
□ 74 Mike Witt	.05	.02	.01
□ 75 Hector Villanueva	.05	.02	.01
□ 76 Dan Gladden	.05	.02	.01
□ 77 Dave Justice	.30	.14	.04
□ 78 Mike Gallego	.05	.02	.01
□ 79 Tom Candiotti	.05	.02	.01
□ 80 Ozzie Smith	.40	.18	.05
□ 81 Luis Polonia	.05	.02	.01
□ 82 Randy Ready	.05	.02	.01

□ 83	Greg A. Harris	.05	.02	.01
□ 84	Checklist 1-92 Dave Justice	.15	.07	.02
□ 85	Kevin Mitchell	.15	.07	.02
□ 86	Mark McLemore	.05	.02	.01
□ 87	Terry Steinbach	.15	.07	.02
□ 88	Tom Browning	.05	.02	.01
□ 89	Matt Nokes	.05	.02	.01
□ 90	Mike Harkey	.05	.02	.01
□ 91	Omar Vizquel	.30	.14	.04
□ 92	Dave Bergman	.05	.02	.01
□ 93	Matt Williams	.30	.14	.04
□ 94	Steve Olin	.05	.02	.01
□ 95	Craig Wilson	.05	.02	.01
□ 96	Dave Stieb	.05	.02	.01
□ 97	Ruben Sierra	.15	.07	.02
□ 98	Jay Howell	.05	.02	.01
□ 99	Scott Bradley	.05	.02	.01
□ 100	Eric Yelding	.05	.02	.01
□ 101	Rickey Henderson	.30	.14	.04
□ 102	Jeff Reed	.05	.02	.01
□ 103	Jimmy Key	.15	.07	.02
□ 104	Terry Shumpert	.05	.02	.01
□ 105	Kenny Rogers	.05	.02	.01
□ 106	Cecil Fielder	.15	.07	.02
□ 107	Robby Thompson	.05	.02	.01
□ 108	Alex Cole	.05	.02	.01
□ 109	Randy Milligan	.05	.02	.01
□ 110	Andres Galarraga	.30	.14	.04
□ 111	Bill Spiers	.05	.02	.01
□ 112	Kal Daniels	.05	.02	.01
□ 113	Henry Cotto	.05	.02	.01
□ 114	Casey Candaele	.05	.02	.01
□ 115	Jeff Blauser	.05	.02	.01
□ 116	Robin Yount	.30	.14	.04
□ 117	Ben McDonald	.15	.07	.02
□ 118	Bret Saberhagen	.15	.07	.02
□ 119	Juan Gonzalez	1.50	.70	.19
□ 120	Lou Whitaker	.30	.14	.04
□ 121	Ellis Burks	.30	.14	.04
□ 122	Charlie O'Brien	.05	.02	.01
□ 123	John Smiley	.05	.02	.01
□ 124	Tim Burke	.05	.02	.01
□ 125	John Olerud	.15	.07	.02
□ 126	Eddie Murray	.50	.23	.06
□ 127	Greg Maddux	1.25	.55	.16
□ 128	Kevin Tapani	.05	.02	.01
□ 129	Ron Gant	.30	.14	.04
□ 130	Jay Bell	.15	.07	.02
□ 131	Chris Hoiles	.05	.02	.01
□ 132	Tom Gordon	.05	.02	.01
□ 133	Kevin Seitzer	.05	.02	.01
□ 134	Jeff Huson	.05	.02	.01
□ 135	Jerry Don Gleaton	.05	.02	.01
□ 136	Jeff Brantley UER (Photo actually Rick Leach on back)	.05	.02	.01
□ 137	Felix Fermin	.05	.02	.01
□ 138	Mike Devereaux	.05	.02	.01
□ 139	Delino DeShields	.05	.02	.01
□ 140	David Wells	.05	.02	.01
□ 141	Tim Crews	.05	.02	.01
□ 142	Erik Hanson	.05	.02	.01
□ 143	Mark Davidson	.05	.02	.01
□ 144	Tommy Gregg	.05	.02	.01
□ 145	Jim Gantner	.05	.02	.01
□ 146	Jose Lind	.05	.02	.01
□ 147	Danny Tartabull	.05	.02	.01
□ 148	Geno Petralli	.05	.02	.01
□ 149	Travis Fryman	.30	.14	.04
□ 150	Tim Naehring	.15	.07	.02
□ 151	Kevin McReynolds	.05	.02	.01
□ 152	Joe Orsulak	.05	.02	.01
□ 153	Steve Frey	.05	.02	.01
□ 154	Duane Ward	.05	.02	.01
□ 155	Stan Javier	.05	.02	.01
□ 156	Damon Berryhill	.05	.02	.01
□ 157	Gene Larkin	.05	.02	.01
□ 158	Greg Olson	.05	.02	.01
□ 159	Mark Knudson	.05	.02	.01
□ 160	Carmelo Martinez	.05	.02	.01
□ 161	Storm Davis	.05	.02	.01
□ 162	Jim Abbott	.15	.07	.02
□ 163	Len Dykstra	.15	.07	.02
□ 164	Tom Brunansky	.05	.02	.01
□ 165	Dwight Gooden	.15	.07	.02
□ 166	Jose Mesa	.15	.07	.02
□ 167	Oil Can Boyd	.05	.02	.01
□ 168	Barry Larkin	.30	.14	.04
□ 169	Scott Sanderson	.05	.02	.01
□ 170	Mark Grace	.30	.14	.04
□ 171	Mark Guthrie	.05	.02	.01
□ 172	Tom Glavine	.30	.14	.04
□ 173	Gary Sheffield	.30	.14	.04
□ 174	Checklist 93-184 Roger Clemens	.30	.14	.04
□ 175	Chris James	.05	.02	.01
□ 176	Milt Thompson	.05	.02	.01
□ 177	Donnie Hill	.05	.02	.01
□ 178	Wes Chamberlain	.05	.02	.01
□ 179	John Marzano	.05	.02	.01
□ 180	Frank Viola	.05	.02	.01
□ 181	Eric Anthony	.05	.02	.01
□ 182	Jose Canseco	.30	.14	.04
□ 183	Scott Scudder	.05	.02	.01
□ 184	Dave Eiland	.05	.02	.01
□ 185	Luis Salazar	.05	.02	.01
□ 186	Pedro Munoz	.15	.07	.02
□ 187	Steve Searcy	.05	.02	.01
□ 188	Don Robinson	.05	.02	.01
□ 189	Sandy Alomar Jr.	.15	.07	.02
□ 190	Jose DeLeon	.05	.02	.01
□ 191	John Orton	.05	.02	.01
□ 192	Darren Daulton	.15	.07	.02
□ 193	Mike Morgan	.05	.02	.01
□ 194	Greg Briley	.05	.02	.01
□ 195	Karl Rhodes	.05	.02	.01
□ 196	Harold Baines	.15	.07	.02
□ 197	Bill Doran	.05	.02	.01
□ 198	Alvaro Espinoza	.05	.02	.01
□ 199	Kirk McCaskill	.05	.02	.01
□ 200	Jose DeJesus	.05	.02	.01
□ 201	Jack Clark	.15	.07	.02
□ 202	Daryl Boston	.05	.02	.01
□ 203	Randy Tomlin	.05	.02	.01
□ 204	Pedro Guerrero	.05	.02	.01
□ 205	Billy Hatcher	.05	.02	.01
□ 206	Tim Leary	.05	.02	.01
□ 207	Ryne Sandberg	.50	.23	.06
□ 208	Kirby Puckett	.60	.25	.07
□ 209	Charlie Leibrandt	.05	.02	.01
□ 210	Rick Honeycutt	.05	.02	.01
□ 211	Joel Skinner	.05	.02	.01
□ 212	Rex Hudler	.05	.02	.01
□ 213	Bryan Harvey	.05	.02	.01
□ 214	Charlie Hayes	.05	.02	.01
□ 215	Matt Young	.05	.02	.01
□ 216	Terry Kennedy	.05	.02	.01
□ 217	Carl Nichols	.05	.02	.01
□ 218	Mike Moore	.05	.02	.01
□ 219	Paul O'Neill	.15	.07	.02
□ 220	Steve Sax	.05	.02	.01
□ 221	Shawn Boskie	.05	.02	.01
□ 222	Rich DeLucia	.05	.02	.01
□ 223	Lloyd Moseby	.05	.02	.01
□ 224	Mike Kingery	.05	.02	.01
□ 225	Carlos Baerga	.30	.14	.04
□ 226	Bryn Smith	.05	.02	.01
□ 227	Todd Stottlemyre	.05	.02	.01
□ 228	Julio Franco	.15	.07	.02
□ 229	Jim Gott	.05	.02	.01
□ 230	Mike Schooler	.05	.02	.01
□ 231	Steve Finley	.30	.14	.04
□ 232	Dave Henderson	.05	.02	.01
□ 233	Luis Quinones	.05	.02	.01
□ 234	Mark Whiten	.15	.07	.02
□ 235	Brian McRae	.40	.18	.05
□ 236	Rich Gossage	.15	.07	.02
□ 237	Rob Deer	.05	.02	.01
□ 238	Will Clark	.30	.14	.04
□ 239	Albert Belle	1.25	.55	.16
□ 240	Bob Melvin	.05	.02	.01
□ 241	Larry Walker	.30	.14	.04
□ 242	Dante Bichette	.30	.14	.04
□ 243	Orel Hershiser	.15	.07	.02
□ 244	Pete O'Brien	.05	.02	.01
□ 245	Pete Harnisch	.05	.02	.01
□ 246	Jeff Treadway	.05	.02	.01
□ 247	Julio Machado	.05	.02	.01
□ 248	Dave Johnson	.05	.02	.01
□ 249	Kirk Gibson	.15	.07	.02
□ 250	Kevin Brown	.15	.07	.02

□ 251	Milt Cuyler	.05	.02	.01
□ 252	Jeff Reardon	.15	.07	.02
□ 253	David Cone	.30	.14	.04
□ 254	Gary Redus	.05	.02	.01
□ 255	Junior Noboa	.05	.02	.01
□ 256	Greg Myers	.05	.02	.01
□ 257	Dennis Cook	.05	.02	.01
□ 258	Joe Girardi	.15	.07	.02
□ 259	Allan Anderson	.05	.02	.01
□ 260	Paul Marak	.05	.02	.01
□ 261	Barry Bonds	.50	.23	.06
□ 262	Juan Bell	.05	.02	.01
□ 263	Russ Morman	.05	.02	.01
□ 264	Checklist 185-264	.30	.14	.04
	and BC1-BC12			
	George Brett			
□ 265	Jerald Clark	.05	.02	.01
□ 266	Dwight Evans	.15	.07	.02
□ 267	Roberto Alomar	.50	.23	.06
□ 268	Danny Jackson	.05	.02	.01
□ 269	Brian Downing	.05	.02	.01
□ 270	John Cerutti	.05	.02	.01
□ 271	Robin Ventura	.30	.14	.04
□ 272	Gerald Perry	.05	.02	.01
□ 273	Wade Boggs	.30	.14	.04
□ 274	Dennis Martinez	.15	.07	.02
□ 275	Andy Benes	.05	.02	.01
□ 276	Tony Fossas	.05	.02	.01
□ 277	Franklin Stubbs	.05	.02	.01
□ 278	John Kruk	.15	.07	.02
□ 279	Kevin Gross	.05	.02	.01
□ 280	Von Hayes	.05	.02	.01
□ 281	Frank Thomas	4.00	1.80	.50
□ 282	Rob Dibble	.05	.02	.01
□ 283	Mel Hall	.05	.02	.01
□ 284	Rick Mahler	.05	.02	.01
□ 285	Dennis Eckersley	.15	.07	.02
□ 286	Bernard Gilkey	.30	.14	.04
□ 287	Dan Plesac	.05	.02	.01
□ 288	Jason Grimsley	.05	.02	.01
□ 289	Mark Lewis	.05	.02	.01
□ 290	Tony Gwynn	.75	.35	.09
□ 291	Jeff Russell	.05	.02	.01
□ 292	Curt Schilling	.05	.02	.01
□ 293	Pascual Perez	.05	.02	.01
□ 294	Jack Morris	.15	.07	.02
□ 295	Hubie Brooks	.05	.02	.01
□ 296	Alex Fernandez	.30	.14	.04
□ 297	Harold Reynolds	.05	.02	.01
□ 298	Craig Worthington	.05	.02	.01
□ 299	Willie Wilson	.05	.02	.01
□ 300	Mike Maddux	.05	.02	.01
□ 301	Dave Righetti	.05	.02	.01
□ 302	Paul Molitor	.40	.18	.05
□ 303	Gary Gaetti	.15	.07	.02
□ 304	Terry Pendleton	.15	.07	.02
□ 305	Kevin Elster	.05	.02	.01
□ 306	Scott Fletcher	.05	.02	.01
□ 307	Jeff Robinson	.05	.02	.01
□ 308	Jesse Barfield	.05	.02	.01
□ 309	Mike LaCoss	.05	.02	.01
□ 310	Andy Van Slyke	.15	.07	.02
□ 311	Glenallen Hill	.05	.02	.01
□ 312	Bud Black	.05	.02	.01
□ 313	Kent Hrbek	.15	.07	.02
□ 314	Tim Teufel	.05	.02	.01
□ 315	Tony Fernandez	.05	.02	.01
□ 316	Beau Allred	.05	.02	.01
□ 317	Curtis Wilkerson	.05	.02	.01
□ 318	Bill Sampen	.05	.02	.01
□ 319	Randy Johnson	.30	.14	.04
□ 320	Mike Heath	.05	.02	.01
□ 321	Sammy Sosa	.60	.25	.07
□ 322	Mickey Tettleton	.15	.07	.02
□ 323	Jose Vizcaino	.05	.02	.01
□ 324	John Candelaria	.05	.02	.01
□ 325	Dave Howard	.05	.02	.01
□ 326	Jose Rijo	.05	.02	.01
□ 327	Todd Zeile	.15	.07	.02
□ 328	Gene Nelson	.05	.02	.01
□ 329	Dwayne Henry	.05	.02	.01
□ 330	Mike Boddicker	.05	.02	.01
□ 331	Ozzie Guillen	.05	.02	.01
□ 332	Sam Horn	.05	.02	.01
□ 333	Wally Whitehurst	.05	.02	.01
□ 334	Dave Parker	.15	.07	.02
□ 335	George Brett	.75	.35	.09
□ 336	Bobby Thigpen	.05	.02	.01
□ 337	Ed Whitson	.05	.02	.01
□ 338	Ivan Calderon	.05	.02	.01
□ 339	Mike Pagliarulo	.05	.02	.01
□ 340	Jack McDowell	.15	.07	.02
□ 341	Dana Kiecker	.05	.02	.01
□ 342	Fred McGriff	.30	.14	.04
□ 343	Mark Lee	.05	.02	.01
□ 344	Alfredo Griffin	.05	.02	.01
□ 345	Scott Bankhead	.05	.02	.01
□ 346	Darrin Jackson	.05	.02	.01
□ 347	Rafael Palmeiro	.30	.14	.04
□ 348	Steve Farr	.05	.02	.01
□ 349	Hensley Meulens	.05	.02	.01
□ 350	Danny Cox	.05	.02	.01
□ 351	Alan Trammell	.30	.14	.04
□ 352	Edwin Nunez	.05	.02	.01
□ 353	Joe Carter	.30	.14	.04
□ 354	Eric Show	.05	.02	.01
□ 355	Vance Law	.05	.02	.01
□ 356	Jeff Gray	.05	.02	.01
□ 357	Bobby Bonilla	.15	.07	.02
□ 358	Ernest Riles	.05	.02	.01
□ 359	Ron Hassey	.05	.02	.01
□ 360	Willie McGee	.05	.02	.01
□ 361	Mackey Sasser	.05	.02	.01
□ 362	Glenn Braggs	.05	.02	.01
□ 363	Mario Diaz	.05	.02	.01
□ 364	Checklist 265-356	.30	.14	.04
	Barry Bonds			
□ 365	Kevin Bass	.05	.02	.01
□ 366	Pete Incaviglia	.05	.02	.01
□ 367	Luis Sojo UER	.05	.02	.01
	(1989 stats inter-			
	spersed with 1990's)			
□ 368	Lance Parrish	.05	.02	.01
□ 369	Mark Leonard	.05	.02	.01
□ 370	Heathcliff Slocumb	.30	.14	.04
□ 371	Jimmy Jones	.05	.02	.01
□ 372	Ken Griffey Jr.	3.00	1.35	.35
□ 373	Chris Hammond	.05	.02	.01
□ 374	Chili Davis	.15	.07	.02
□ 375	Joey Cora	.15	.07	.02
□ 376	Ken Hill	.30	.14	.04
□ 377	Darryl Strawberry	.15	.07	.02
□ 378	Ron Darling	.05	.02	.01
□ 379	Sid Bream	.05	.02	.01
□ 380	Bill Swift	.05	.02	.01
□ 381	Shawn Abner	.05	.02	.01
□ 382	Eric King	.05	.02	.01
□ 383	Mickey Morandini	.05	.02	.01
□ 384	Carlton Fisk	.30	.14	.04
□ 385	Steve Lake	.05	.02	.01
□ 386	Mike Jeffcoat	.05	.02	.01
□ 387	Darren Holmes	.05	.02	.01
□ 388	Tim Wallach	.05	.02	.01
□ 389	George Bell	.05	.02	.01
□ 390	Craig Lefferts	.05	.02	.01
□ 391	Ernie Whitt	.05	.02	.01
□ 392	Felix Jose	.05	.02	.01
□ 393	Kevin Maas	.05	.02	.01
□ 394	Devon White	.15	.07	.02
□ 395	Otis Nixon	.05	.02	.01
□ 396	Chuck Knoblauch	.50	.23	.06
□ 397	Scott Coolbaugh	.05	.02	.01
□ 398	Glenn Davis	.05	.02	.01
□ 399	Manny Lee	.05	.02	.01
□ 400	Andre Dawson	.30	.14	.04
□ 401	Scott Chiamparino	.05	.02	.01
□ 402	Bill Gullickson	.05	.02	.01
□ 403	Lance Johnson	.15	.07	.02
□ 404	Juan Agosto	.05	.02	.01
□ 405	Danny Darwin	.05	.02	.01
□ 406	Barry Jones	.05	.02	.01
□ 407	Larry Andersen	.05	.02	.01
□ 408	Luis Rivera	.05	.02	.01
□ 409	Jaime Navarro	.05	.02	.01
□ 410	Roger McDowell	.05	.02	.01
□ 411	Brett Butler	.15	.07	.02
□ 412	Dale Murphy	.30	.14	.04
□ 413	Tim Raines UER	.30	.14	.04
	(Listed as hitting .500			
	in 1980, should be .050)			
□ 414	Norm Charlton	.05	.02	.01
□ 415	Greg Cadaret	.05	.02	.01

□ 416 Chris Nabholz	.05	.02	.01
□ 417 Dave Stewart	.15	.07	.02
□ 418 Rich Gedman	.05	.02	.01
□ 419 Willie Randolph	.15	.07	.02
□ 420 Mitch Williams	.05	.02	.01
□ 421 Brook Jacoby	.05	.02	.01
□ 422 Greg W. Harris	.05	.02	.01
□ 423 Nolan Ryan	1.50	.70	.19
□ 424 Dave Rohde	.05	.02	.01
□ 425 Don Mattingly	1.00	.45	.12
□ 426 Greg Gagne	.05	.02	.01
□ 427 Vince Coleman	.05	.02	.01
□ 428 Dan Pasqua	.05	.02	.01
□ 429 Alvin Davis	.05	.02	.01
□ 430 Cal Ripken	1.50	.70	.19
□ 431 Jamie Quirk	.05	.02	.01
□ 432 Benito Santiago	.05	.02	.01
□ 433 Jose Uribe	.05	.02	.01
□ 434 Candy Maldonado	.05	.02	.01
□ 435 Junior Felix	.05	.02	.01
□ 436 Deion Sanders	.30	.14	.04
□ 437 John Franco	.05	.02	.01
□ 438 Greg Hibbard	.05	.02	.01
□ 439 Floyd Bannister	.05	.02	.01
□ 440 Steve Howe	.05	.02	.01
□ 441 Steve Decker	.05	.02	.01
□ 442 Vicente Palacios	.05	.02	.01
□ 443 Pat Tabler	.05	.02	.01
□ 444 Checklist 357-448 Darryl Strawberry	.30	.14	.04
□ 445 Mike Felder	.05	.02	.01
□ 446 Al Newman	.05	.02	.01
□ 447 Chris Donnels	.05	.02	.01
□ 448 Rich Rodriguez	.05	.02	.01
□ 449 Turner Ward	.05	.02	.01
□ 450 Bob Walk	.05	.02	.01
□ 451 Gilberto Reyes	.05	.02	.01
□ 452 Mike Jackson	.05	.02	.01
□ 453 Rafael Belliard	.05	.02	.01
□ 454 Wayne Edwards	.05	.02	.01
□ 455 Andy Allanson	.05	.02	.01
□ 456 Dave Smith	.05	.02	.01
□ 457 Gary Carter	.30	.14	.04
□ 458 Warren Cromartie	.05	.02	.01
□ 459 Jack Armstrong	.05	.02	.01
□ 460 Bob Tewksbury	.05	.02	.01
□ 461 Joe Klink	.05	.02	.01
□ 462 Xavier Hernandez	.05	.02	.01
□ 463 Scott Radinsky	.05	.02	.01
□ 464 Jeff Robinson	.05	.02	.01
□ 465 Gregg Jefferies	.30	.14	.04
□ 466 Denny Neagle	.60	.25	.07
□ 467 Carmelo Martinez	.05	.02	.01
□ 468 Donn Pall	.05	.02	.01
□ 469 Bruce Hurst	.05	.02	.01
□ 470 Eric Bullock	.05	.02	.01
□ 471 Rick Aguilera	.15	.07	.02
□ 472 Charlie Hough	.05	.02	.01
□ 473 Carlos Quintana	.05	.02	.01
□ 474 Marty Barrett	.05	.02	.01
□ 475 Kevin D. Brown	.05	.02	.01
□ 476 Bobby Ojeda	.05	.02	.01
□ 477 Edgar Martinez	.30	.14	.04
□ 478 Bip Roberts	.05	.02	.01
□ 479 Mike Flanagan	.05	.02	.01
□ 480 John Habyan	.05	.02	.01
□ 481 Larry Casian	.05	.02	.01
□ 482 Wally Backman	.05	.02	.01
□ 483 Doug Dascenzo	.05	.02	.01
□ 484 Rick Dempsey	.05	.02	.01
□ 485 Ed Sprague	.15	.07	.02
□ 486 Steve Chitren	.05	.02	.01
□ 487 Mark McGwire	.60	.25	.07
□ 488 Roger Clemens	.30	.14	.04
□ 489 Orlando Merced	.30	.14	.04
□ 490 Rene Gonzales	.05	.02	.01
□ 491 Mike Stanton	.05	.02	.01
□ 492 Al Osuna	.05	.02	.01
□ 493 Rick Cerone	.05	.02	.01
□ 494 Mariano Duncan	.05	.02	.01
□ 495 Zane Smith	.05	.02	.01
□ 496 John Morris	.05	.02	.01
□ 497 Frank Tanana	.05	.02	.01
□ 498 Junior Ortiz	.05	.02	.01
□ 499 Dave Winfield	.30	.14	.04
□ 500 Gary Varsho	.05	.02	.01
□ 501 Chico Walker	.05	.02	.01
□ 502 Ken Caminiti	.30	.14	.04
□ 503 Ken Griffey Sr.	.05	.02	.01
□ 504 Randy Myers	.15	.07	.02
□ 505 Steve Bedrosian	.05	.02	.01
□ 506 Cory Snyder	.05	.02	.01
□ 507 Cris Carpenter	.05	.02	.01
□ 508 Tim Belcher	.05	.02	.01
□ 509 Jeff Hamilton	.05	.02	.01
□ 510 Steve Avery	.30	.14	.04
□ 511 Dave Valle	.05	.02	.01
□ 512 Tom Lampkin	.05	.02	.01
□ 513 Shawn Hillegas	.05	.02	.01
□ 514 Reggie Jefferson	.15	.07	.02
□ 515 Ron Karkovice	.05	.02	.01
□ 516 Doug Drabek	.05	.02	.01
□ 517 Tom Henke	.05	.02	.01
□ 518 Chris Bosio	.05	.02	.01
□ 519 Gregg Olson	.05	.02	.01
□ 520 Bob Scanlan	.05	.02	.01
□ 521 Alonzo Powell	.05	.02	.01
□ 522 Jeff Ballard	.05	.02	.01
□ 523 Ray Lankford	.30	.14	.04
□ 524 Tommy Greene	.05	.02	.01
□ 525 Mike Timlin	.05	.02	.01
□ 526 Juan Berenguer	.05	.02	.01
□ 527 Scott Erickson	.15	.07	.02
□ 528 Checklist 449-528 and BC13-BC26 Sandy Alomar Jr.	.05	.02	.01

1991 Leaf Gold Rookies

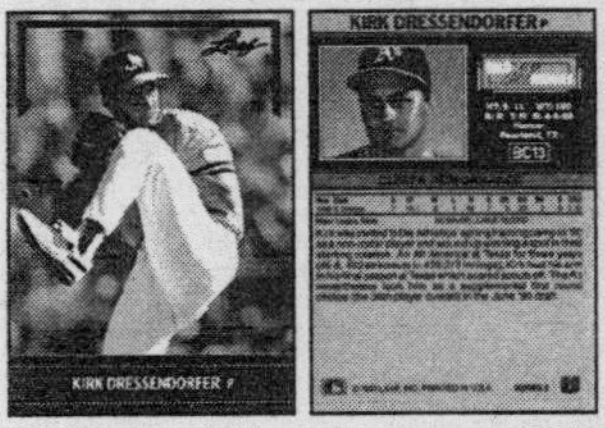

This 26-card standard size set was issued by Leaf as an insert to their 1991 Leaf regular issue. The first twelve cards were issued as random inserts in with the first series of 1991 Leaf foil packs. The rest were issued as random inserts in with the second series. The set features a selection of rookie prospects. The earliest Leaf Gold Rookie cards issued with the first series can sometimes be found with erroneous regular numbered backs 265 through 276 instead of the correct BC1 through BC12. These numbered variations are very tough to find and are valued at ten times the values listed below.

	MINT	NRMT	EXC
COMPLETE SET (26)	25.00	11.00	3.10
COMMON CARD (BC1-BC26)	.50	.23	.06
SEMISTARS	1.00	.45	.12
RANDOM INSERTS IN BOTH SERIES			
□ BC1 Scott Leius	.50	.23	.06
□ BC2 Luis Gonzalez	1.00	.45	.12
□ BC3 Wil Cordero	1.00	.45	.12
□ BC4 Gary Scott	.50	.23	.06
□ BC5 Willie Banks	.50	.23	.06
□ BC6 Arthur Rhodes	1.00	.45	.12
□ BC7 Mo Vaughn	6.00	2.70	.75
□ BC8 Henry Rodriguez	2.00	.90	.25
□ BC9 Todd Van Poppel	1.00	.45	.12
□ BC10 Reggie Sanders	1.25	.55	.16
□ BC11 Rico Brogna	1.00	.45	.12
□ BC12 Mike Mussina	4.00	1.80	.50
□ BC13 Kirk Dressendorfer	.50	.23	.06
□ BC14 Jeff Bagwell	6.00	2.70	.75
□ BC15 Pete Schourek	1.00	.45	.12

□ BC16 Wade Taylor	.50	.23	.06
□ BC17 Pat Kelly	.50	.23	.06
□ BC18 Tim Costo	.50	.23	.06
□ BC19 Roger Salkeld	.50	.23	.06
□ BC20 Andujar Cedeno	.50	.23	.06
□ BC21 Ryan Klesko UER (1990 Sumter BA .289; should be .368)	5.00	2.20	.60
□ BC22 Mike Huff	.50	.23	.06
□ BC23 Anthony Young	.50	.23	.06
□ BC24 Eddie Zosky	.50	.23	.06
□ BC25 Nolan Ryan DP UER No Hitter 7 (Word other repeated in 7th line)	1.50	.70	.19
□ BC26 Rickey Henderson DP Record Steal	1.00	.45	.12

1992 Leaf Previews

Four Leaf Preview standard-size cards were included in each 1992 Donruss hobby factory set. The cards were intended to show collectors and dealers the style of the 1992 Leaf set. The fronts carry glossy color player photos framed by silver borders. The player's name, position, and the team logo appear in a black stripe beneath the picture. The horizontal backs have a second color photo, with biography, statistics (on a white panel), and player profile filling out the rest of the card.

	MINT	NRMT	EXC
COMPLETE SET (26)	60.00	27.00	7.50
COMMON CARD (1-26)	1.00	.45	.12
SEMISTARS	1.50	.70	.19
FOUR PER DONRUSS HOBBY FACTORY SET			

□ 1 Steve Avery	1.50	.70	.19
□ 2 Ryne Sandberg	4.00	1.80	.50
□ 3 Chris Sabo	1.00	.45	.12
□ 4 Jeff Bagwell	8.00	3.60	1.00
□ 5 Darryl Strawberry	1.50	.70	.19
□ 6 Bret Barberie	1.00	.45	.12
□ 7 Howard Johnson	1.00	.45	.12
□ 8 John Kruk	1.50	.70	.19
□ 9 Andy Van Slyke	1.50	.70	.19
□ 10 Felix Jose	1.00	.45	.12
□ 11 Fred McGriff	1.50	.70	.19
□ 12 Will Clark	1.50	.70	.19
□ 13 Cal Ripken	10.00	4.50	1.25
□ 14 Phil Plantier	1.00	.45	.12
□ 15 Lee Stevens	1.00	.45	.12
□ 16 Frank Thomas	18.00	8.00	2.20
□ 17 Mark Whiten	1.00	.45	.12
□ 18 Cecil Fielder	1.50	.70	.19
□ 19 George Brett	5.00	2.20	.60
□ 20 Robin Yount	1.50	.70	.19
□ 21 Scott Erickson	1.00	.45	.12
□ 22 Don Mattingly	6.00	2.70	.75
□ 23 Jose Canseco	1.50	.70	.19
□ 24 Ken Griffey Jr.	18.00	8.00	2.20
□ 25 Nolan Ryan	10.00	4.50	1.25
□ 26 Joe Carter	1.50	.70	.19

1992 Leaf

The 1992 Leaf set consists of 528 cards, issued in two separate 264-card series. Cards

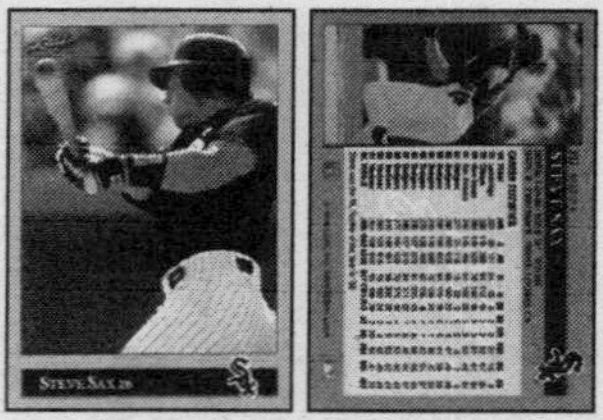

were distributed in first and second series 15-card foil packs. Each pack contained a selection of basic cards and one black gold parallel card. The basic card fronts feature color action player photos on a silver card face. The player's name appears in a black bar edged at the bottom by a thin red stripe. The team logo overlaps the bar at the right corner. There are no significant Rookie Cards in this set.

	MINT	NRMT	EXC
COMPLETE SET (528)	16.00	7.25	2.00
COMPLETE SERIES 1 (264)	6.00	2.70	.75
COMPLETE SERIES 2 (264)	10.00	4.50	1.25
COMMON CARD (1-528)	.05	.02	.01
SEMISTARS	.10	.05	.01
STARS	.25	.11	.03
COMP.BLACK GOLD (528)	80.00	36.00	10.00
COMP.B.GOLD SER.1 (264)	40.00	18.00	5.00
COMP.B.GOLD SER.2 (264)	40.00	18.00	5.00
COMMON BLACK GOLD (1-528)	.10	.05	.01
BLACK GOLD SEMISTARS	.25	.11	.03
*BLACK GOLD STARS: 3X to 5X HI COLUMN			
*BLACK GOLD YOUNG STARS: 1.5X to 3X HI			
ONE B.GOLD PER SER.1 , SER.2 PACK			

□ 1 Jim Abbott	.05	.02	.01
□ 2 Cal Eldred	.05	.02	.01
□ 3 Bud Black	.05	.02	.01
□ 4 Dave Howard	.05	.02	.01
□ 5 Luis Sojo	.05	.02	.01
□ 6 Gary Scott	.05	.02	.01
□ 7 Joe Oliver	.05	.02	.01
□ 8 Chris Gardner	.05	.02	.01
□ 9 Sandy Alomar Jr.	.10	.05	.01
□ 10 Greg W. Harris	.05	.02	.01
□ 11 Doug Drabek	.05	.02	.01
□ 12 Darryl Hamilton	.05	.02	.01
□ 13 Mike Mussina	.50	.23	.06
□ 14 Kevin Tapani	.05	.02	.01
□ 15 Ron Gant	.25	.11	.03
□ 16 Mark McGwire	.50	.23	.06
□ 17 Robin Ventura	.25	.11	.03
□ 18 Pedro Guerrero	.05	.02	.01
□ 19 Roger Clemens	.25	.11	.03
□ 20 Steve Farr	.05	.02	.01
□ 21 Frank Tanana	.05	.02	.01
□ 22 Joe Hesketh	.05	.02	.01
□ 23 Erik Hanson	.05	.02	.01
□ 24 Greg Cadaret	.05	.02	.01
□ 25 Rex Hudler	.05	.02	.01
□ 26 Mark Grace	.25	.11	.03
□ 27 Kelly Gruber	.05	.02	.01
□ 28 Jeff Bagwell	1.00	.45	.12
□ 29 Darryl Strawberry	.10	.05	.01
□ 30 Dave Smith	.05	.02	.01
□ 31 Kevin Appier	.10	.05	.01
□ 32 Steve Chitren	.05	.02	.01
□ 33 Kevin Gross	.05	.02	.01
□ 34 Rick Aguilera	.05	.02	.01
□ 35 Juan Guzman	.10	.05	.01
□ 36 Joe Orsulak	.05	.02	.01
□ 37 Tim Raines	.25	.11	.03
□ 38 Harold Reynolds	.05	.02	.01
□ 39 Charlie Hough	.05	.02	.01
□ 40 Tony Phillips	.10	.05	.01
□ 41 Nolan Ryan	1.25	.55	.16
□ 42 Vince Coleman	.05	.02	.01
□ 43 Andy Van Slyke	.10	.05	.01
□ 44 Tim Burke	.05	.02	.01

☐ 45	Luis Polonia	.05	.02	.01
☐ 46	Tom Browning	.05	.02	.01
☐ 47	Willie McGee	.05	.02	.01
☐ 48	Gary DiSarcina	.05	.02	.01
☐ 49	Mark Lewis	.05	.02	.01
☐ 50	Phil Plantier	.10	.05	.01
☐ 51	Doug Dascenzo	.05	.02	.01
☐ 52	Cal Ripken	1.25	.55	.16
☐ 53	Pedro Munoz	.05	.02	.01
☐ 54	Carlos Hernandez	.05	.02	.01
☐ 55	Jerald Clark	.05	.02	.01
☐ 56	Jeff Brantley	.10	.05	.01
☐ 57	Don Mattingly	.75	.35	.09
☐ 58	Roger McDowell	.05	.02	.01
☐ 59	Steve Avery	.10	.05	.01
☐ 60	John Olerud	.10	.05	.01
☐ 61	Bill Gullickson	.05	.02	.01
☐ 62	Juan Gonzalez	1.00	.45	.12
☐ 63	Felix Jose	.05	.02	.01
☐ 64	Robin Yount	.25	.11	.03
☐ 65	Greg Briley	.05	.02	.01
☐ 66	Steve Finley	.25	.11	.03
☐ 67	Checklist 1-88	.25	.11	.03
	Frank Thomas			
☐ 68	Tom Gordon	.05	.02	.01
☐ 69	Rob Dibble	.05	.02	.01
☐ 70	Glenallen Hill	.05	.02	.01
☐ 71	Calvin Jones	.05	.02	.01
☐ 72	Joe Girardi	.05	.02	.01
☐ 73	Barry Larkin	.25	.11	.03
☐ 74	Andy Benes	.05	.02	.01
☐ 75	Milt Cuyler	.05	.02	.01
☐ 76	Kevin Bass	.05	.02	.01
☐ 77	Pete Harnisch	.05	.02	.01
☐ 78	Wilson Alvarez	.25	.11	.03
☐ 79	Mike Devereaux	.05	.02	.01
☐ 80	Doug Henry	.05	.02	.01
☐ 81	Orel Hershiser	.10	.05	.01
☐ 82	Shane Mack	.05	.02	.01
☐ 83	Mike Macfarlane	.05	.02	.01
☐ 84	Thomas Howard	.05	.02	.01
☐ 85	Alex Fernandez	.25	.11	.03
☐ 86	Reggie Jefferson	.10	.05	.01
☐ 87	Leo Gomez	.05	.02	.01
☐ 88	Mel Hall	.05	.02	.01
☐ 89	Mike Greenwell	.05	.02	.01
☐ 90	Jeff Russell	.05	.02	.01
☐ 91	Steve Buechele	.05	.02	.01
☐ 92	David Cone	.25	.11	.03
☐ 93	Kevin Reimer	.05	.02	.01
☐ 94	Mark Lemke	.05	.02	.01
☐ 95	Bob Tewksbury	.05	.02	.01
☐ 96	Zane Smith	.05	.02	.01
☐ 97	Mark Eichhorn	.05	.02	.01
☐ 98	Kirby Puckett	.50	.23	.06
☐ 99	Paul O'Neill	.10	.05	.01
☐ 100	Dennis Eckersley	.10	.05	.01
☐ 101	Duane Ward	.05	.02	.01
☐ 102	Matt Nokes	.05	.02	.01
☐ 103	Mo Vaughn	.60	.25	.07
☐ 104	Pat Kelly	.05	.02	.01
☐ 105	Ron Karkovice	.05	.02	.01
☐ 106	Bill Spiers	.05	.02	.01
☐ 107	Gary Gaetti	.10	.05	.01
☐ 108	Mackey Sasser	.05	.02	.01
☐ 109	Robby Thompson	.05	.02	.01
☐ 110	Marvin Freeman	.05	.02	.01
☐ 111	Jimmy Key	.10	.05	.01
☐ 112	Dwight Gooden	.10	.05	.01
☐ 113	Charlie Leibrandt	.05	.02	.01
☐ 114	Devon White	.10	.05	.01
☐ 115	Charles Nagy	.10	.05	.01
☐ 116	Rickey Henderson	.25	.11	.03
☐ 117	Paul Assenmacher	.05	.02	.01
☐ 118	Junior Felix	.05	.02	.01
☐ 119	Julio Franco	.10	.05	.01
☐ 120	Norm Charlton	.05	.02	.01
☐ 121	Scott Servais	.05	.02	.01
☐ 122	Gerald Perry	.05	.02	.01
☐ 123	Brian McRae	.25	.11	.03
☐ 124	Don Slaught	.05	.02	.01
☐ 125	Juan Samuel	.05	.02	.01
☐ 126	Harold Baines	.10	.05	.01
☐ 127	Scott Livingstone	.05	.02	.01
☐ 128	Jay Buhner	.25	.11	.03
☐ 129	Darrin Jackson	.05	.02	.01
☐ 130	Luis Mercedes	.05	.02	.01
☐ 131	Brian Harper	.05	.02	.01
☐ 132	Howard Johnson	.05	.02	.01
☐ 133	Checklist 89-176	.25	.11	.03
	Nolan Ryan			
☐ 134	Dante Bichette	.25	.11	.03
☐ 135	Dave Righetti	.05	.02	.01
☐ 136	Jeff Montgomery	.10	.05	.01
☐ 137	Joe Grahe	.05	.02	.01
☐ 138	Delino DeShields	.05	.02	.01
☐ 139	Jose Rijo	.05	.02	.01
☐ 140	Ken Caminiti	.25	.11	.03
☐ 141	Steve Olin	.05	.02	.01
☐ 142	Kurt Stillwell	.05	.02	.01
☐ 143	Jay Bell	.10	.05	.01
☐ 144	Jaime Navarro	.05	.02	.01
☐ 145	Ben McDonald	.05	.02	.01
☐ 146	Greg Gagne	.05	.02	.01
☐ 147	Jeff Blauser	.05	.02	.01
☐ 148	Carney Lansford	.10	.05	.01
☐ 149	Ozzie Guillen	.05	.02	.01
☐ 150	Milt Thompson	.05	.02	.01
☐ 151	Jeff Reardon	.10	.05	.01
☐ 152	Scott Sanderson	.05	.02	.01
☐ 153	Cecil Fielder	.10	.05	.01
☐ 154	Greg A. Harris	.05	.02	.01
☐ 155	Rich DeLucia	.05	.02	.01
☐ 156	Roberto Kelly	.05	.02	.01
☐ 157	Bryn Smith	.05	.02	.01
☐ 158	Chuck McElroy	.05	.02	.01
☐ 159	Tom Henke	.05	.02	.01
☐ 160	Luis Gonzalez	.10	.05	.01
☐ 161	Steve Wilson	.05	.02	.01
☐ 162	Shawn Boskie	.05	.02	.01
☐ 163	Mark Davis	.05	.02	.01
☐ 164	Mike Moore	.05	.02	.01
☐ 165	Mike Scioscia	.05	.02	.01
☐ 166	Scott Erickson	.10	.05	.01
☐ 167	Todd Stottlemyre	.10	.05	.01
☐ 168	Alvin Davis	.05	.02	.01
☐ 169	Greg Hibbard	.05	.02	.01
☐ 170	David Valle	.05	.02	.01
☐ 171	Dave Winfield	.25	.11	.03
☐ 172	Alan Trammell	.25	.11	.03
☐ 173	Kenny Rogers	.05	.02	.01
☐ 174	John Franco	.05	.02	.01
☐ 175	Jose Lind	.05	.02	.01
☐ 176	Pete Schourek	.10	.05	.01
☐ 177	Von Hayes	.05	.02	.01
☐ 178	Chris Hammond	.05	.02	.01
☐ 179	John Burkett	.10	.05	.01
☐ 180	Dickie Thon	.05	.02	.01
☐ 181	Joel Skinner	.05	.02	.01
☐ 182	Scott Cooper	.05	.02	.01
☐ 183	Andre Dawson	.25	.11	.03
☐ 184	Billy Ripken	.05	.02	.01
☐ 185	Kevin Mitchell	.10	.05	.01
☐ 186	Brett Butler	.10	.05	.01
☐ 187	Tony Fernandez	.05	.02	.01
☐ 188	Cory Snyder	.05	.02	.01
☐ 189	John Habyan	.05	.02	.01
☐ 190	Dennis Martinez	.10	.05	.01
☐ 191	John Smoltz	.25	.11	.03
☐ 192	Greg Myers	.05	.02	.01
☐ 193	Rob Deer	.05	.02	.01
☐ 194	Ivan Rodriguez	.50	.23	.06
☐ 195	Ray Lankford	.25	.11	.03
☐ 196	Bill Wegman	.05	.02	.01
☐ 197	Edgar Martinez	.25	.11	.03
☐ 198	Darryl Kile	.05	.02	.01
☐ 199	Checklist 177-264	.25	.11	.03
	Cal Ripken			
☐ 200	Brent Mayne	.05	.02	.01
☐ 201	Larry Walker	.25	.11	.03
☐ 202	Carlos Baerga	.25	.11	.03
☐ 203	Russ Swan	.05	.02	.01
☐ 204	Mike Morgan	.05	.02	.01
☐ 205	Hal Morris	.05	.02	.01
☐ 206	Tony Gwynn	.60	.25	.07
☐ 207	Mark Leiter	.05	.02	.01
☐ 208	Kirt Manwaring	.05	.02	.01
☐ 209	Al Osuna	.05	.02	.01
☐ 210	Bobby Thigpen	.05	.02	.01
☐ 211	Chris Hoiles	.05	.02	.01
☐ 212	B.J. Surhoff	.10	.05	.01
☐ 213	Lenny Harris	.05	.02	.01

□	214	Scott Leius	.05	.02	.01
□	215	Gregg Jefferies	.25	.11	.03
□	216	Bruce Hurst	.05	.02	.01
□	217	Steve Sax	.05	.02	.01
□	218	Dave Otto	.05	.02	.01
□	219	Sam Horn	.05	.02	.01
□	220	Charlie Hayes	.05	.02	.01
□	221	Frank Viola	.05	.02	.01
□	222	Jose Guzman	.10	.05	.01
□	223	Gary Redus	.05	.02	.01
□	224	Dave Gallagher	.05	.02	.01
□	225	Dean Palmer	.10	.05	.01
□	226	Greg Olson	.05	.02	.01
□	227	Jose DeLeon	.05	.02	.01
□	228	Mike LaValliere	.05	.02	.01
□	229	Mark Langston	.10	.05	.01
□	230	Chuck Knoblauch	.25	.11	.03
□	231	Bill Doran	.05	.02	.01
□	232	Dave Henderson	.05	.02	.01
□	233	Roberto Alomar	.40	.18	.05
□	234	Scott Fletcher	.05	.02	.01
□	235	Tim Naehring	.10	.05	.01
□	236	Mike Gallego	.05	.02	.01
□	237	Lance Johnson	.10	.05	.01
□	238	Paul Molitor	.30	.14	.04
□	239	Dan Gladden	.05	.02	.01
□	240	Willie Randolph	.10	.05	.01
□	241	Will Clark	.25	.11	.03
□	242	Sid Bream	.05	.02	.01
□	243	Derek Bell	.10	.05	.01
□	244	Bill Pecota	.05	.02	.01
□	245	Terry Pendleton	.10	.05	.01
□	246	Randy Ready	.05	.02	.01
□	247	Jack Armstrong	.05	.02	.01
□	248	Todd Van Poppel	.05	.02	.01
□	249	Shawon Dunston	.05	.02	.01
□	250	Bobby Rose	.05	.02	.01
□	251	Jeff Huson	.05	.02	.01
□	252	Bip Roberts	.05	.02	.01
□	253	Doug Jones	.05	.02	.01
□	254	Lee Smith	.10	.05	.01
□	255	George Brett	.60	.25	.07
□	256	Randy Tomlin	.05	.02	.01
□	257	Todd Benzinger	.05	.02	.01
□	258	Dave Stewart	.10	.05	.01
□	259	Mark Carreon	.05	.02	.01
□	260	Pete O'Brien	.05	.02	.01
□	261	Tim Teufel	.05	.02	.01
□	262	Bob Milacki	.05	.02	.01
□	263	Mark Guthrie	.05	.02	.01
□	264	Darrin Fletcher	.05	.02	.01
□	265	Omar Vizquel	.25	.11	.03
□	266	Chris Bosio	.05	.02	.01
□	267	Jose Canseco	.25	.11	.03
□	268	Mike Boddicker	.05	.02	.01
□	269	Lance Parrish	.05	.02	.01
□	270	Jose Vizcaino	.05	.02	.01
□	271	Chris Sabo	.05	.02	.01
□	272	Royce Clayton	.10	.05	.01
□	273	Marquis Grissom	.25	.11	.03
□	274	Fred McGriff	.25	.11	.03
□	275	Barry Bonds	.40	.18	.05
□	276	Greg Vaughn	.25	.11	.03
□	277	Gregg Olson	.05	.02	.01
□	278	Dave Hollins	.05	.02	.01
□	279	Tom Glavine	.25	.11	.03
□	280	Bryan Hickerson UER	.05	.02	.01
		Name spelled Brian on front			
□	281	Scott Radinsky	.05	.02	.01
□	282	Omar Olivares	.05	.02	.01
□	283	Ivan Calderon	.05	.02	.01
□	284	Kevin Maas	.05	.02	.01
□	285	Mickey Tettleton	.05	.02	.01
□	286	Wade Boggs	.25	.11	.03
□	287	Stan Belinda	.05	.02	.01
□	288	Bret Barberie	.05	.02	.01
□	289	Jose Oquendo	.05	.02	.01
□	290	Frank Castillo	.10	.05	.01
□	291	Dave Stieb	.05	.02	.01
□	292	Tommy Greene	.05	.02	.01
□	293	Eric Karros	.25	.11	.03
□	294	Greg Maddux	1.25	.55	.16
□	295	Jim Eisenreich	.05	.02	.01
□	296	Rafael Palmeiro	.25	.11	.03
□	297	Ramon Martinez	.10	.05	.01
□	298	Tim Wallach	.05	.02	.01
□	299	Jim Thome	1.25	.55	.16
□	300	Chito Martinez	.05	.02	.01
□	301	Mitch Williams	.05	.02	.01
□	302	Randy Johnson	.25	.11	.03
□	303	Carlton Fisk	.25	.11	.03
□	304	Travis Fryman	.25	.11	.03
□	305	Bobby Witt	.05	.02	.01
□	306	Dave Magadan	.05	.02	.01
□	307	Alex Cole	.05	.02	.01
□	308	Bobby Bonilla	.10	.05	.01
□	309	Bryan Harvey	.05	.02	.01
□	310	Rafael Belliard	.05	.02	.01
□	311	Mariano Duncan	.05	.02	.01
□	312	Chuck Crim	.05	.02	.01
□	313	John Kruk	.10	.05	.01
□	314	Ellis Burks	.25	.11	.03
□	315	Craig Biggio	.25	.11	.03
□	316	Glenn Davis	.05	.02	.01
□	317	Ryne Sandberg	.40	.18	.05
□	318	Mike Sharperson	.05	.02	.01
□	319	Rich Rodriguez	.05	.02	.01
□	320	Lee Guetterman	.05	.02	.01
□	321	Benito Santiago	.05	.02	.01
□	322	Jose Offerman	.05	.02	.01
□	323	Tony Pena	.05	.02	.01
□	324	Pat Borders	.05	.02	.01
□	325	Mike Henneman	.05	.02	.01
□	326	Kevin Brown	.10	.05	.01
□	327	Chris Nabholz	.05	.02	.01
□	328	Franklin Stubbs	.05	.02	.01
□	329	Tino Martinez	.25	.11	.03
□	330	Mickey Morandini	.05	.02	.01
□	331	Checklist 265-352	.25	.11	.03
		Ryne Sandberg			
□	332	Mark Gubicza	.05	.02	.01
□	333	Bill Landrum	.05	.02	.01
□	334	Mark Whiten	.10	.05	.01
□	335	Darren Daulton	.10	.05	.01
□	336	Rick Wilkins	.05	.02	.01
□	337	Brian Jordan	.50	.23	.06
□	338	Kevin Ward	.05	.02	.01
□	339	Ruben Amaro	.05	.02	.01
□	340	Trevor Wilson	.05	.02	.01
□	341	Andujar Cedeno	.05	.02	.01
□	342	Michael Huff	.05	.02	.01
□	343	Brady Anderson	.25	.11	.03
□	344	Craig Grebeck	.05	.02	.01
□	345	Bobby Ojeda	.05	.02	.01
□	346	Mike Pagliarulo	.05	.02	.01
□	347	Terry Shumpert	.05	.02	.01
□	348	Dann Bilardello	.05	.02	.01
□	349	Frank Thomas	2.50	1.10	.30
□	350	Albert Belle	1.00	.45	.12
□	351	Jose Mesa	.10	.05	.01
□	352	Rich Monteleone	.05	.02	.01
□	353	Bob Walk	.05	.02	.01
□	354	Monty Fariss	.05	.02	.01
□	355	Luis Rivera	.05	.02	.01
□	356	Anthony Young	.05	.02	.01
□	357	Geno Petralli	.05	.02	.01
□	358	Otis Nixon	.05	.02	.01
□	359	Tom Pagnozzi	.05	.02	.01
□	360	Reggie Sanders	.25	.11	.03
□	361	Lee Stevens	.05	.02	.01
□	362	Kent Hrbek	.10	.05	.01
□	363	Orlando Merced	.05	.02	.01
□	364	Mike Bordick	.10	.05	.01
□	365	Dion James UER	.05	.02	.01
		(Blue Jays logo on card back)			
□	366	Jack Clark	.10	.05	.01
□	367	Mike Stanley	.05	.02	.01
□	368	Randy Velarde	.05	.02	.01
□	369	Dan Pasqua	.05	.02	.01
□	370	Pat Listach	.10	.05	.01
□	371	Mike Fitzgerald	.05	.02	.01
□	372	Tom Foley	.05	.02	.01
□	373	Matt Williams	.25	.11	.03
□	374	Brian Hunter	.05	.02	.01
□	375	Joe Carter	.25	.11	.03
□	376	Bret Saberhagen	.10	.05	.01
□	377	Mike Stanton	.05	.02	.01
□	378	Hubie Brooks	.05	.02	.01
□	379	Eric Bell	.05	.02	.01
□	380	Walt Weiss	.05	.02	.01
□	381	Danny Jackson	.05	.02	.01

□ 382 Manuel Lee	.05	.02	.01
□ 383 Ruben Sierra	.10	.05	.01
□ 384 Greg Swindell	.05	.02	.01
□ 385 Ryan Bowen	.05	.02	.01
□ 386 Kevin Ritz	.05	.02	.01
□ 387 Curtis Wilkerson	.05	.02	.01
□ 388 Gary Varsho	.05	.02	.01
□ 389 Dave Hansen	.05	.02	.01
□ 390 Bob Welch	.05	.02	.01
□ 391 Lou Whitaker	.25	.11	.03
□ 392 Ken Griffey Jr.	2.50	1.10	.30
□ 393 Mike Maddux	.05	.02	.01
□ 394 Arthur Rhodes	.05	.02	.01
□ 395 Chili Davis	.10	.05	.01
□ 396 Eddie Murray	.25	.11	.03
□ 397 Checklist 353-440 Robin Yount	.10	.05	.01
□ 398 Dave Cochrane	.05	.02	.01
□ 399 Kevin Seitzer	.05	.02	.01
□ 400 Ozzie Smith	.30	.14	.04
□ 401 Paul Sorrento	.05	.02	.01
□ 402 Les Lancaster	.05	.02	.01
□ 403 Junior Noboa	.05	.02	.01
□ 404 David Justice	.25	.11	.03
□ 405 Andy Ashby	.10	.05	.01
□ 406 Danny Tartabull	.05	.02	.01
□ 407 Bill Swift	.05	.02	.01
□ 408 Craig Lefferts	.05	.02	.01
□ 409 Tom Candiotti	.05	.02	.01
□ 410 Lance Blankenship	.05	.02	.01
□ 411 Jeff Tackett	.05	.02	.01
□ 412 Sammy Sosa	.40	.18	.05
□ 413 Jody Reed	.05	.02	.01
□ 414 Bruce Ruffin	.05	.02	.01
□ 415 Gene Larkin	.05	.02	.01
□ 416 John Vander Wal	.05	.02	.01
□ 417 Tim Belcher	.05	.02	.01
□ 418 Steve Frey	.05	.02	.01
□ 419 Dick Schofield	.05	.02	.01
□ 420 Jeff King	.10	.05	.01
□ 421 Kim Batiste	.05	.02	.01
□ 422 Jack McDowell	.10	.05	.01
□ 423 Damon Berryhill	.05	.02	.01
□ 424 Gary Wayne	.05	.02	.01
□ 425 Jack Morris	.10	.05	.01
□ 426 Moises Alou	.25	.11	.03
□ 427 Mark McLemore	.05	.02	.01
□ 428 Juan Guerrero	.05	.02	.01
□ 429 Scott Scudder	.05	.02	.01
□ 430 Eric Davis	.10	.05	.01
□ 431 Joe Slusarski	.05	.02	.01
□ 432 Todd Zeile	.05	.02	.01
□ 433 Dwayne Henry	.05	.02	.01
□ 434 Cliff Brantley	.05	.02	.01
□ 435 Butch Henry	.05	.02	.01
□ 436 Todd Worrell	.05	.02	.01
□ 437 Bob Scanlan	.05	.02	.01
□ 438 Wally Joyner	.10	.05	.01
□ 439 John Flaherty	.05	.02	.01
□ 440 Brian Downing	.05	.02	.01
□ 441 Darren Lewis	.05	.02	.01
□ 442 Gary Carter	.25	.11	.03
□ 443 Wally Ritchie	.05	.02	.01
□ 444 Chris Jones	.05	.02	.01
□ 445 Jeff Kent	.25	.11	.03
□ 446 Gary Sheffield	.25	.11	.03
□ 447 Ron Darling	.05	.02	.01
□ 448 Deion Sanders	.25	.11	.03
□ 449 Andres Galarraga	.25	.11	.03
□ 450 Chuck Finley	.05	.02	.01
□ 451 Derek Lilliquist	.05	.02	.01
□ 452 Carl Willis	.05	.02	.01
□ 453 Wes Chamberlain	.05	.02	.01
□ 454 Roger Mason	.05	.02	.01
□ 455 Spike Owen	.05	.02	.01
□ 456 Thomas Howard	.05	.02	.01
□ 457 Dave Martinez	.05	.02	.01
□ 458 Pete Incaviglia	.05	.02	.01
□ 459 Keith A. Miller	.05	.02	.01
□ 460 Mike Fetters	.05	.02	.01
□ 461 Paul Gibson	.05	.02	.01
□ 462 George Bell	.05	.02	.01
□ 463 Checklist 441-528 Bobby Bonilla	.10	.05	.01
□ 464 Terry Mulholland	.05	.02	.01
□ 465 Storm Davis	.05	.02	.01

□ 466 Gary Pettis	.05	.02	.01
□ 467 Randy Bush	.05	.02	.01
□ 468 Ken Hill	.25	.11	.03
□ 469 Rheal Cormier	.05	.02	.01
□ 470 Andy Stankiewicz	.05	.02	.01
□ 471 Dave Burba	.05	.02	.01
□ 472 Henry Cotto	.05	.02	.01
□ 473 Dale Sveum	.05	.02	.01
□ 474 Rich Gossage	.10	.05	.01
□ 475 William Suero	.05	.02	.01
□ 476 Doug Strange	.05	.02	.01
□ 477 Bill Krueger	.05	.02	.01
□ 478 John Wetteland	.10	.05	.01
□ 479 Melido Perez	.05	.02	.01
□ 480 Lonnie Smith	.05	.02	.01
□ 481 Mike Jackson	.05	.02	.01
□ 482 Mike Gardiner	.05	.02	.01
□ 483 David Wells	.05	.02	.01
□ 484 Barry Jones	.05	.02	.01
□ 485 Scott Bankhead	.05	.02	.01
□ 486 Terry Leach	.05	.02	.01
□ 487 Vince Horsman	.05	.02	.01
□ 488 Dave Eiland	.05	.02	.01
□ 489 Alejandro Pena	.05	.02	.01
□ 490 Julio Valera	.05	.02	.01
□ 491 Joe Boever	.05	.02	.01
□ 492 Paul Miller	.05	.02	.01
□ 493 Archi Cianfrocco	.05	.02	.01
□ 494 Dave Fleming	.05	.02	.01
□ 495 Kyle Abbott	.05	.02	.01
□ 496 Chad Kreuter	.05	.02	.01
□ 497 Chris James	.05	.02	.01
□ 498 Donnie Hill	.05	.02	.01
□ 499 Jacob Brumfield	.05	.02	.01
□ 500 Ricky Bones	.05	.02	.01
□ 501 Terry Steinbach	.10	.05	.01
□ 502 Bernard Gilkey	.10	.05	.01
□ 503 Dennis Cook	.05	.02	.01
□ 504 Len Dykstra	.10	.05	.01
□ 505 Mike Bielecki	.05	.02	.01
□ 506 Bob Kipper	.05	.02	.01
□ 507 Jose Melendez	.05	.02	.01
□ 508 Rick Sutcliffe	.05	.02	.01
□ 509 Ken Patterson	.05	.02	.01
□ 510 Andy Allanson	.05	.02	.01
□ 511 Al Newman	.05	.02	.01
□ 512 Mark Gardner	.05	.02	.01
□ 513 Jeff Schaefer	.05	.02	.01
□ 514 Jim McNamara	.05	.02	.01
□ 515 Peter Hoy	.05	.02	.01
□ 516 Curt Schilling	.05	.02	.01
□ 517 Kirk McCaskill	.05	.02	.01
□ 518 Chris Gwynn	.05	.02	.01
□ 519 Sid Fernandez	.05	.02	.01
□ 520 Jeff Parrett	.05	.02	.01
□ 521 Scott Ruskin	.05	.02	.01
□ 522 Kevin McReynolds	.05	.02	.01
□ 523 Rick Cerone	.05	.02	.01
□ 524 Jesse Orosco	.05	.02	.01
□ 525 Troy Afenir	.05	.02	.01
□ 526 John Smiley	.05	.02	.01
□ 527 Dale Murphy	.25	.11	.03
□ 528 Leaf Set Card	.05	.02	.01

1992 Leaf Gold Rookies

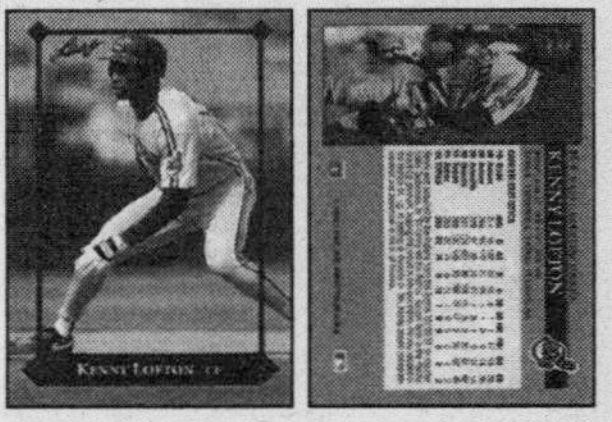

This 24-card standard-size set honors 1992's most promising newcomers. The first 12 cards were randomly inserted in Leaf series I foil

packs, while the second 12 cards were featured only in series II packs. The fronts display full-bleed color action photos highlighted by gold foil border stripes. A gold foil diamond appears at the corners of the picture frame, and the player's name appears in a black bar that extends between the bottom two diamonds. The key cards in this set are Kenny Lofton and Raul Mondesi.

	MINT	NRMT	EXC
COMPLETE SET (24)	20.00	9.00	2.50
COMPLETE SERIES 1 (12)	8.00	3.60	1.00
COMPLETE SERIES 2 (12)	12.00	5.50	1.50
COMMON CARD (BC1-BC24)	.25	.11	.03
SEMISTARS	.50	.23	.06
RANDOM INSERTS IN BOTH SERIES			
□ BC1 Chad Curtis	.50	.23	.06
□ BC2 Brent Gates	.50	.23	.06
□ BC3 Pedro Martinez	1.50	.70	.19
□ BC4 Kenny Lofton	6.00	2.70	.75
□ BC5 Turk Wendell	.25	.11	.03
□ BC6 Mark Hutton	.25	.11	.03
□ BC7 Todd Hundley	1.00	.45	.12
□ BC8 Matt Stairs	.25	.11	.03
□ BC9 Eddie Taubensee	.50	.23	.06
□ BC10 David Nied	.50	.23	.06
□ BC11 Salomon Torres	.25	.11	.03
□ BC12 Bret Boone	.50	.23	.06
□ BC13 Johnny Ruffin	.25	.11	.03
□ BC14 Ed Martel	.25	.11	.03
□ BC15 Rick Trlicek	.25	.11	.03
□ BC16 Raul Mondesi	5.00	2.20	.60
□ BC17 Pat Mahomes	.25	.11	.03
□ BC18 Dan Wilson	1.00	.45	.12
□ BC19 Donovan Osborne	.50	.23	.06
□ BC20 Dave Silvestri	.25	.11	.03
□ BC21 Gary DiSarcina	.25	.11	.03
□ BC22 Denny Neagle	1.50	.70	.19
□ BC23 Steve Hosey	.25	.11	.03
□ BC24 John Doherty	.25	.11	.03

1993 Leaf

The 1993 Leaf baseball set consists of three series of 220, 220, and 110 standard-size cards, respectively. Cards were distributed in 14-card foil packs, jumbo packs and magazine packs. The card fronts feature color action photos that are full-bleed except at the bottom where a diagonal black stripe (gold-foil stamped with the player's name) separates the picture from a team color-coded slate triangle. The Leaf seal embossed with gold foil is superimposed at the lower right corner. There are no key Rookie Cards in this set.

	MINT	NRMT	EXC
COMPLETE SET (550)	40.00	18.00	5.00
COMPLETE SERIES 1 (220)	18.00	8.00	2.20
COMPLETE SERIES 2 (220)	18.00	8.00	2.20
COMPLETE UPDATE (110)	5.00	2.20	.60
COMMON CARD (1-550)	.10	.05	.01
SEMISTARS	.25	.11	.03
STARS	.50	.23	.06
COMP.F.THOMAS SET (10)	40.00	18.00	5.00
COMMON F.THOMAS (1-10)	5.00	2.20	.60
THOMAS: RANDOM INSERTS IN SER.1, 2 PACKS			
COMP.JUMBO THOM.SET (10)	60.00	27.00	7.50
COMMON JUMBO THOM. (1-10)	7.00	3.10	.85
ONE JUMBO THOMAS PER UPDATE BOX			
□ 1 Ben McDonald	.10	.05	.01
□ 2 Sid Fernandez	.10	.05	.01
□ 3 Juan Guzman	.20	.09	.03
□ 4 Curt Schilling	.10	.05	.01
□ 5 Ivan Rodriguez	.60	.25	.07
□ 6 Don Slaught	.10	.05	.01
□ 7 Terry Steinbach	.20	.09	.03
□ 8 Todd Zeile	.10	.05	.01
□ 9 Andy Stankiewicz	.10	.05	.01
□ 10 Tim Teufel	.10	.05	.01
□ 11 Marvin Freeman	.10	.05	.01
□ 12 Jim Austin	.10	.05	.01
□ 13 Bob Scanlan	.10	.05	.01
□ 14 Rusty Meacham	.10	.05	.01
□ 15 Casey Candaele	.10	.05	.01
□ 16 Travis Fryman	.30	.14	.04
□ 17 Jose Offerman	.10	.05	.01
□ 18 Albert Belle	1.50	.70	.19
□ 19 John Vander Wal	.10	.05	.01
□ 20 Dan Pasqua	.10	.05	.01
□ 21 Frank Viola	.10	.05	.01
□ 22 Terry Mulholland	.10	.05	.01
□ 23 Gregg Olson	.10	.05	.01
□ 24 Randy Tomlin	.10	.05	.01
□ 25 Todd Stottlemyre	.20	.09	.03
□ 26 Jose Oquendo	.10	.05	.01
□ 27 Julio Franco	.20	.09	.03
□ 28 Tony Gwynn	1.25	.55	.16
□ 29 Ruben Sierra	.20	.09	.03
□ 30 Robby Thompson	.10	.05	.01
□ 31 Jim Bullinger	.10	.05	.01
□ 32 Rick Aguilera	.10	.05	.01
□ 33 Scott Servais	.10	.05	.01
□ 34 Cal Eldred	.10	.05	.01
□ 35 Mike Piazza	3.00	1.35	.35
□ 36 Brent Mayne	.10	.05	.01
□ 37 Wil Cordero	.20	.09	.03
□ 38 Milt Cuyler	.10	.05	.01
□ 39 Howard Johnson	.10	.05	.01
□ 40 Kenny Lofton	1.25	.55	.16
□ 41 Alex Fernandez	.30	.14	.04
□ 42 Denny Neagle	.20	.09	.03
□ 43 Tony Pena	.10	.05	.01
□ 44 Bob Tewksbury	.10	.05	.01
□ 45 Glenn Davis	.10	.05	.01
□ 46 Fred McGriff	.30	.14	.04
□ 47 John Olerud	.10	.05	.01
□ 48 Steve Hosey	.10	.05	.01
□ 49 Rafael Palmeiro	.30	.14	.04
□ 50 David Justice	.30	.14	.04
□ 51 Pete Harnisch	.10	.05	.01
□ 52 Sam Militello	.10	.05	.01
□ 53 Orel Hershiser	.20	.09	.03
□ 54 Pat Mahomes	.10	.05	.01
□ 55 Greg Colbrunn	.10	.05	.01
□ 56 Greg Vaughn	.30	.14	.04
□ 57 Vince Coleman	.10	.05	.01
□ 58 Brian McRae	.20	.09	.03
□ 59 Len Dykstra	.20	.09	.03
□ 60 Dan Gladden	.10	.05	.01
□ 61 Ted Power	.10	.05	.01
□ 62 Donovan Osborne	.10	.05	.01
□ 63 Ron Karkovice	.10	.05	.01
□ 64 Frank Seminara	.10	.05	.01
□ 65 Bob Zupcic	.10	.05	.01
□ 66 Kirt Manwaring	.10	.05	.01
□ 67 Mike Devereaux	.10	.05	.01
□ 68 Mark Lemke	.10	.05	.01
□ 69 Devon White	.10	.05	.01
□ 70 Sammy Sosa	.30	.14	.04
□ 71 Pedro Astacio	.10	.05	.01
□ 72 Dennis Eckersley	.20	.09	.03
□ 73 Chris Nabholz	.10	.05	.01
□ 74 Melido Perez	.10	.05	.01
□ 75 Todd Hundley	.30	.14	.04
□ 76 Kent Hrbek	.20	.09	.03
□ 77 Mickey Morandini	.10	.05	.01
□ 78 Tim McIntosh	.10	.05	.01
□ 79 Andy Van Slyke	.20	.09	.03
□ 80 Kevin McReynolds	.10	.05	.01
□ 81 Mike Henneman	.10	.05	.01
□ 82 Greg W. Harris	.10	.05	.01

□	83	Sandy Alomar Jr.	.20	.09	.03
□	84	Mike Jackson	.10	.05	.01
□	85	Ozzie Guillen	.10	.05	.01
□	86	Jeff Blauser	.10	.05	.01
□	87	John Valentin	.30	.14	.04
□	88	Rey Sanchez	.10	.05	.01
□	89	Rick Sutcliffe	.10	.05	.01
□	90	Luis Gonzalez	.10	.05	.01
□	91	Jeff Fassero	.20	.09	.03
□	92	Kenny Rogers	.10	.05	.01
□	93	Bret Saberhagen	.20	.09	.03
□	94	Bob Welch	.10	.05	.01
□	95	Darren Daulton	.20	.09	.03
□	96	Mike Gallego	.10	.05	.01
□	97	Orlando Merced	.20	.09	.03
□	98	Chuck Knoblauch	.30	.14	.04
□	99	Bernard Gilkey	.30	.14	.04
□	100	Billy Ashley	.10	.05	.01
□	101	Kevin Appier	.20	.09	.03
□	102	Jeff Brantley	.10	.05	.01
□	103	Bill Gullickson	.10	.05	.01
□	104	John Smoltz	.30	.14	.04
□	105	Paul Sorrento	.10	.05	.01
□	106	Steve Buechele	.10	.05	.01
□	107	Steve Sax	.10	.05	.01
□	108	Andujar Cedeno	.10	.05	.01
□	109	Billy Hatcher	.10	.05	.01
□	110	Checklist	.10	.05	.01
□	111	Alan Mills	.10	.05	.01
□	112	John Franco	.10	.05	.01
□	113	Jack Morris	.20	.09	.03
□	114	Mitch Williams	.10	.05	.01
□	115	Nolan Ryan	2.50	1.10	.30
□	116	Jay Bell	.20	.09	.03
□	117	Mike Bordick	.10	.05	.01
□	118	Geronimo Pena	.10	.05	.01
□	119	Danny Tartabull	.10	.05	.01
□	120	Checklist	.10	.05	.01
□	121	Steve Avery	.20	.09	.03
□	122	Ricky Bones	.10	.05	.01
□	123	Mike Morgan	.10	.05	.01
□	124	Jeff Montgomery	.20	.09	.03
□	125	Jeff Bagwell	1.25	.55	.16
□	126	Tony Phillips	.20	.09	.03
□	127	Lenny Harris	.10	.05	.01
□	128	Glenallen Hill	.10	.05	.01
□	129	Marquis Grissom	.30	.14	.04
□	130	Gerald Williams UER (Bernie Williams picture and stats)	.10	.05	.01
□	131	Greg A. Harris	.10	.05	.01
□	132	Tommy Greene	.10	.05	.01
□	133	Chris Hoiles	.10	.05	.01
□	134	Bob Walk	.10	.05	.01
□	135	Duane Ward	.10	.05	.01
□	136	Tom Pagnozzi	.10	.05	.01
□	137	Jeff Huson	.10	.05	.01
□	138	Kurt Stillwell	.10	.05	.01
□	139	Dave Henderson	.10	.05	.01
□	140	Darrin Jackson	.10	.05	.01
□	141	Frank Castillo	.10	.05	.01
□	142	Scott Erickson	.10	.05	.01
□	143	Darryl Kile	.10	.05	.01
□	144	Bill Wegman	.10	.05	.01
□	145	Steve Wilson	.10	.05	.01
□	146	George Brett	1.25	.55	.16
□	147	Moises Alou	.30	.14	.04
□	148	Lou Whitaker	.30	.14	.04
□	149	Chico Walker	.10	.05	.01
□	150	Jerry Browne	.10	.05	.01
□	151	Kirk McCaskill	.10	.05	.01
□	152	Zane Smith	.10	.05	.01
□	153	Matt Young	.10	.05	.01
□	154	Lee Smith	.20	.09	.03
□	155	Leo Gomez	.10	.05	.01
□	156	Dan Walters	.10	.05	.01
□	157	Pat Borders	.10	.05	.01
□	158	Matt Williams	.30	.14	.04
□	159	Dean Palmer	.20	.09	.03
□	160	John Patterson	.10	.05	.01
□	161	Doug Jones	.10	.05	.01
□	162	John Habyan	.10	.05	.01
□	163	Pedro Martinez	.30	.14	.04
□	164	Carl Willis	.10	.05	.01
□	165	Darrin Fletcher	.10	.05	.01
□	166	B.J. Surhoff	.20	.09	.03
□	167	Eddie Murray	.75	.35	.09
□	168	Keith Miller	.10	.05	.01
□	169	Ricky Jordan	.10	.05	.01
□	170	Juan Gonzalez	1.50	.70	.19
□	171	Charles Nagy	.20	.09	.03
□	172	Mark Clark	.10	.05	.01
□	173	Bobby Thigpen	.10	.05	.01
□	174	Tim Scott	.10	.05	.01
□	175	Scott Cooper	.10	.05	.01
□	176	Royce Clayton	.20	.09	.03
□	177	Brady Anderson	.30	.14	.04
□	178	Sid Bream	.10	.05	.01
□	179	Derek Bell	.30	.14	.04
□	180	Otis Nixon	.10	.05	.01
□	181	Kevin Gross	.10	.05	.01
□	182	Ron Darling	.10	.05	.01
□	183	John Wetteland	.20	.09	.03
□	184	Mike Stanley	.10	.05	.01
□	185	Jeff Kent	.20	.09	.03
□	186	Brian Harper	.10	.05	.01
□	187	Mariano Duncan	.10	.05	.01
□	188	Robin Yount	.30	.14	.04
□	189	Al Martin	.20	.09	.03
□	190	Eddie Zosky	.10	.05	.01
□	191	Mike Munoz	.10	.05	.01
□	192	Andy Benes	.10	.05	.01
□	193	Dennis Cook	.10	.05	.01
□	194	Bill Swift	.10	.05	.01
□	195	Frank Thomas	3.00	1.35	.35
□	196	Damon Berryhill	.10	.05	.01
□	197	Mike Greenwell	.10	.05	.01
□	198	Mark Grace	.30	.14	.04
□	199	Darryl Hamilton	.10	.05	.01
□	200	Derrick May	.10	.05	.01
□	201	Ken Hill	.20	.09	.03
□	202	Kevin Brown	.10	.05	.01
□	203	Dwight Gooden	.20	.09	.03
□	204	Bobby Witt	.10	.05	.01
□	205	Juan Bell	.10	.05	.01
□	206	Kevin Maas	.10	.05	.01
□	207	Jeff King	.20	.09	.03
□	208	Scott Leius	.10	.05	.01
□	209	Rheal Cormier	.10	.05	.01
□	210	Darryl Strawberry	.20	.09	.03
□	211	Tom Gordon	.10	.05	.01
□	212	Bud Black	.10	.05	.01
□	213	Mickey Tettleton	.10	.05	.01
□	214	Pete Smith	.10	.05	.01
□	215	Felix Fermin	.10	.05	.01
□	216	Rick Wilkins	.10	.05	.01
□	217	George Bell	.10	.05	.01
□	218	Eric Anthony	.10	.05	.01
□	219	Pedro Munoz	.10	.05	.01
□	220	Checklist	.10	.05	.01
□	221	Lance Blankenship	.10	.05	.01
□	222	Deion Sanders	.30	.14	.04
□	223	Craig Biggio	.30	.14	.04
□	224	Ryne Sandberg	.75	.35	.09
□	225	Ron Gant	.30	.14	.04
□	226	Tom Brunansky	.10	.05	.01
□	227	Chad Curtis	.20	.09	.03
□	228	Joe Carter	.30	.14	.04
□	229	Brian Jordan	.30	.14	.04
□	230	Brett Butler	.20	.09	.03
□	231	Frank Bolick	.10	.05	.01
□	232	Rod Beck	.20	.09	.03
□	233	Carlos Baerga	.30	.14	.04
□	234	Eric Karros	.30	.14	.04
□	235	Jack Armstrong	.10	.05	.01
□	236	Bobby Bonilla	.20	.09	.03
□	237	Don Mattingly	1.50	.70	.19
□	238	Jeff Gardner	.10	.05	.01
□	239	Dave Hollins	.10	.05	.01
□	240	Steve Cooke	.10	.05	.01
□	241	Jose Canseco	.30	.14	.04
□	242	Ivan Calderon	.10	.05	.01
□	243	Tim Belcher	.10	.05	.01
□	244	Freddie Benavides	.10	.05	.01
□	245	Roberto Alomar	.75	.35	.09
□	246	Rob Deer	.10	.05	.01
□	247	Will Clark	.30	.14	.04
□	248	Mike Felder	.10	.05	.01
□	249	Harold Baines	.20	.09	.03
□	250	David Cone	.30	.14	.04
□	251	Mark Guthrie	.10	.05	.01
□	252	Ellis Burks	.30	.14	.04

□ 253	Jim Abbott	.10	.05	.01
□ 254	Chili Davis	.20	.09	.03
□ 255	Chris Bosio	.10	.05	.01
□ 256	Bret Barberie	.10	.05	.01
□ 257	Hal Morris	.10	.05	.01
□ 258	Dante Bichette	.30	.14	.04
□ 259	Storm Davis	.10	.05	.01
□ 260	Gary DiSarcina	.10	.05	.01
□ 261	Ken Caminiti	.30	.14	.04
□ 262	Paul Molitor	.60	.25	.07
□ 263	Joe Oliver	.10	.05	.01
□ 264	Pat Listach	.10	.05	.01
□ 265	Gregg Jefferies	.30	.14	.04
□ 266	Jose Guzman	.10	.05	.01
□ 267	Eric Davis	.20	.09	.03
□ 268	Delino DeShields	.10	.05	.01
□ 269	Barry Bonds	.75	.35	.09
□ 270	Mike Bielecki	.10	.05	.01
□ 271	Jay Buhner	.30	.14	.04
□ 272	Scott Pose	.10	.05	.01
□ 273	Tony Fernandez	.10	.05	.01
□ 274	Chito Martinez	.10	.05	.01
□ 275	Phil Plantier	.10	.05	.01
□ 276	Pete Incaviglia	.10	.05	.01
□ 277	Carlos Garcia	.10	.05	.01
□ 278	Tom Henke	.10	.05	.01
□ 279	Roger Clemens	.30	.14	.04
□ 280	Rob Dibble	.10	.05	.01
□ 281	Daryl Boston	.10	.05	.01
□ 282	Greg Gagne	.10	.05	.01
□ 283	Cecil Fielder	.20	.09	.03
□ 284	Carlton Fisk	.30	.14	.04
□ 285	Wade Boggs	.30	.14	.04
□ 286	Damion Easley	.10	.05	.01
□ 287	Norm Charlton	.10	.05	.01
□ 288	Jeff Conine	.30	.14	.04
□ 289	Roberto Kelly	.10	.05	.01
□ 290	Jerald Clark	.10	.05	.01
□ 291	Rickey Henderson	.30	.14	.04
□ 292	Chuck Finley	.10	.05	.01
□ 293	Doug Drabek	.10	.05	.01
□ 294	Dave Stewart	.20	.09	.03
□ 295	Tom Glavine	.30	.14	.04
□ 296	Jaime Navarro	.10	.05	.01
□ 297	Ray Lankford	.30	.14	.04
□ 298	Greg Hibbard	.10	.05	.01
□ 299	Jody Reed	.10	.05	.01
□ 300	Dennis Martinez	.20	.09	.03
□ 301	Dave Martinez	.10	.05	.01
□ 302	Reggie Jefferson	.20	.09	.03
□ 303	John Cummings	.10	.05	.01
□ 304	Orestes Destrade	.10	.05	.01
□ 305	Mike Maddux	.10	.05	.01
□ 306	David Segui	.10	.05	.01
□ 307	Gary Sheffield	.30	.14	.04
□ 308	Danny Jackson	.10	.05	.01
□ 309	Craig Lefferts	.10	.05	.01
□ 310	Andre Dawson	.30	.14	.04
□ 311	Barry Larkin	.30	.14	.04
□ 312	Alex Cole	.10	.05	.01
□ 313	Mark Gardner	.10	.05	.01
□ 314	Kirk Gibson	.20	.09	.03
□ 315	Shane Mack	.10	.05	.01
□ 316	Bo Jackson	.30	.14	.04
□ 317	Jimmy Key	.20	.09	.03
□ 318	Greg Myers	.10	.05	.01
□ 319	Ken Griffey Jr.	3.00	1.35	.35
□ 320	Monty Fariss	.10	.05	.01
□ 321	Kevin Mitchell	.20	.09	.03
□ 322	Andres Galarraga	.30	.14	.04
□ 323	Mark McGwire	1.00	.45	.12
□ 324	Mark Langston	.20	.09	.03
□ 325	Steve Finley	.30	.14	.04
□ 326	Greg Maddux	2.00	.90	.25
□ 327	Dave Nilsson	.20	.09	.03
□ 328	Ozzie Smith	.60	.25	.07
□ 329	Candy Maldonado	.10	.05	.01
□ 330	Checklist	.10	.05	.01
□ 331	Tim Pugh	.10	.05	.01
□ 332	Joe Girardi	.10	.05	.01
□ 333	Junior Felix	.10	.05	.01
□ 334	Greg Swindell	.10	.05	.01
□ 335	Ramon Martinez	.20	.09	.03
□ 336	Sean Berry	.10	.05	.01
□ 337	Joe Orsulak	.10	.05	.01
□ 338	Wes Chamberlain	.10	.05	.01
□ 339	Stan Belinda	.10	.05	.01
□ 340	Checklist UER (306 Luis Mercedes)	.10	.05	.01
□ 341	Bruce Hurst	.10	.05	.01
□ 342	John Burkett	.10	.05	.01
□ 343	Mike Mussina	.60	.25	.07
□ 344	Scott Fletcher	.10	.05	.01
□ 345	Rene Gonzales	.10	.05	.01
□ 346	Roberto Hernandez	.20	.09	.03
□ 347	Carlos Martinez	.10	.05	.01
□ 348	Bill Krueger	.10	.05	.01
□ 349	Felix Jose	.10	.05	.01
□ 350	John Jaha	.20	.09	.03
□ 351	Willie Banks	.10	.05	.01
□ 352	Matt Nokes	.10	.05	.01
□ 353	Kevin Seitzer	.10	.05	.01
□ 354	Erik Hanson	.10	.05	.01
□ 355	David Hulse	.10	.05	.01
□ 356	Domingo Martinez	.10	.05	.01
□ 357	Greg Olson	.10	.05	.01
□ 358	Randy Myers	.20	.09	.03
□ 359	Tom Browning	.10	.05	.01
□ 360	Charlie Hayes	.10	.05	.01
□ 361	Bryan Harvey	.10	.05	.01
□ 362	Eddie Taubensee	.10	.05	.01
□ 363	Tim Wallach	.10	.05	.01
□ 364	Mel Rojas	.20	.09	.03
□ 365	Frank Tanana	.10	.05	.01
□ 366	John Kruk	.20	.09	.03
□ 367	Tim Laker	.10	.05	.01
□ 368	Rich Rodriguez	.10	.05	.01
□ 369	Darren Lewis	.10	.05	.01
□ 370	Harold Reynolds	.10	.05	.01
□ 371	Jose Melendez	.10	.05	.01
□ 372	Joe Grahe	.10	.05	.01
□ 373	Lance Johnson	.20	.09	.03
□ 374	Jose Mesa	.20	.09	.03
□ 375	Scott Livingstone	.10	.05	.01
□ 376	Wally Joyner	.20	.09	.03
□ 377	Kevin Reimer	.10	.05	.01
□ 378	Kirby Puckett	1.00	.45	.12
□ 379	Paul O'Neill	.20	.09	.03
□ 380	Randy Johnson	.30	.14	.04
□ 381	Manuel Lee	.10	.05	.01
□ 382	Dick Schofield	.10	.05	.01
□ 383	Darren Holmes	.10	.05	.01
□ 384	Charlie Hough	.10	.05	.01
□ 385	John Orton	.10	.05	.01
□ 386	Edgar Martinez	.30	.14	.04
□ 387	Terry Pendleton	.20	.09	.03
□ 388	Dan Plesac	.10	.05	.01
□ 389	Jeff Reardon	.20	.09	.03
□ 390	David Nied	.10	.05	.01
□ 391	Dave Magadan	.10	.05	.01
□ 392	Larry Walker	.30	.14	.04
□ 393	Ben Rivera	.10	.05	.01
□ 394	Lonnie Smith	.10	.05	.01
□ 395	Craig Shipley	.10	.05	.01
□ 396	Willie McGee	.10	.05	.01
□ 397	Arthur Rhodes	.10	.05	.01
□ 398	Mike Stanton	.10	.05	.01
□ 399	Luis Polonia	.10	.05	.01
□ 400	Jack McDowell	.20	.09	.03
□ 401	Mike Moore	.10	.05	.01
□ 402	Jose Lind	.10	.05	.01
□ 403	Bill Spiers	.10	.05	.01
□ 404	Kevin Tapani	.10	.05	.01
□ 405	Spike Owen	.10	.05	.01
□ 406	Tino Martinez	.20	.09	.03
□ 407	Charlie Leibrandt	.10	.05	.01
□ 408	Ed Sprague	.20	.09	.03
□ 409	Bryn Smith	.10	.05	.01
□ 410	Benito Santiago	.10	.05	.01
□ 411	Jose Rijo	.10	.05	.01
□ 412	Pete O'Brien	.10	.05	.01
□ 413	Willie Wilson	.10	.05	.01
□ 414	Bip Roberts	.10	.05	.01
□ 415	Eric Young	.30	.14	.04
□ 416	Walt Weiss	.10	.05	.01
□ 417	Milt Thompson	.10	.05	.01
□ 418	Chris Sabo	.10	.05	.01
□ 419	Scott Sanderson	.10	.05	.01
□ 420	Tim Raines	.30	.14	.04
□ 421	Alan Trammell	.30	.14	.04
□ 422	Mike Macfarlane	.10	.05	.01
□ 423	Dave Winfield	.30	.14	.04

□ 424 Bob Wickman	.10	.05	.01
□ 425 David Valle	.10	.05	.01
□ 426 Gary Redus	.10	.05	.01
□ 427 Turner Ward	.10	.05	.01
□ 428 Reggie Sanders	.30	.14	.04
□ 429 Todd Worrell	.10	.05	.01
□ 430 Julio Valera	.10	.05	.01
□ 431 Cal Ripken Jr.	2.50	1.10	.30
□ 432 Mo Vaughn	.75	.35	.09
□ 433 John Smiley	.10	.05	.01
□ 434 Omar Vizquel	.30	.14	.04
□ 435 Billy Ripken	.10	.05	.01
□ 436 Cory Snyder	.10	.05	.01
□ 437 Carlos Quintana	.10	.05	.01
□ 438 Omar Olivares	.10	.05	.01
□ 439 Robin Ventura	.20	.09	.03
□ 440 Checklist	.10	.05	.01
□ 441 Kevin Higgins	.10	.05	.01
□ 442 Carlos Hernandez	.10	.05	.01
□ 443 Dan Peltier	.10	.05	.01
□ 444 Derek Lilliquist	.10	.05	.01
□ 445 Tim Salmon	.75	.35	.09
□ 446 Sherman Obando	.10	.05	.01
□ 447 Pat Kelly	.10	.05	.01
□ 448 Todd Van Poppel	.10	.05	.01
□ 449 Mark Whiten	.10	.05	.01
□ 450 Checklist	.10	.05	.01
□ 451 Pat Meares	.20	.09	.03
□ 452 Tony Tarasco	.20	.09	.03
□ 453 Chris Gwynn	.10	.05	.01
□ 454 Armando Reynoso	.10	.05	.01
□ 455 Danny Darwin	.10	.05	.01
□ 456 Willie Greene	.20	.09	.03
□ 457 Mike Blowers	.10	.05	.01
□ 458 Kevin Roberson	.10	.05	.01
□ 459 Graeme Lloyd	.10	.05	.01
□ 460 David West	.10	.05	.01
□ 461 Joey Cora	.10	.05	.01
□ 462 Alex Arias	.10	.05	.01
□ 463 Chad Kreuter	.10	.05	.01
□ 464 Mike Lansing	.20	.09	.03
□ 465 Mike Timlin	.10	.05	.01
□ 466 Paul Wagner	.10	.05	.01
□ 467 Mark Portugal	.10	.05	.01
□ 468 Jim Leyritz	.10	.05	.01
□ 469 Ryan Klesko	1.50	.70	.19
□ 470 Mario Diaz	.10	.05	.01
□ 471 Guillermo Velasquez	.10	.05	.01
□ 472 Fernando Valenzuela	.20	.09	.03
□ 473 Raul Mondesi	1.00	.45	.12
□ 474 Mike Pagliarulo	.10	.05	.01
□ 475 Chris Hammond	.10	.05	.01
□ 476 Torey Lovullo	.10	.05	.01
□ 477 Trevor Wilson	.10	.05	.01
□ 478 Marcos Armas	.10	.05	.01
□ 479 Dave Gallagher	.10	.05	.01
□ 480 Jeff Treadway	.10	.05	.01
□ 481 Jeff Branson	.10	.05	.01
□ 482 Dickie Thon	.10	.05	.01
□ 483 Eduardo Perez	.10	.05	.01
□ 484 David Wells	.10	.05	.01
□ 485 Brian Williams	.10	.05	.01
□ 486 Domingo Cedeno	.10	.05	.01
□ 487 Tom Candiotti	.10	.05	.01
□ 488 Steve Frey	.10	.05	.01
□ 489 Greg McMichael	.20	.09	.03
□ 490 Marc Newfield	.20	.09	.03
□ 491 Larry Andersen	.10	.05	.01
□ 492 Damon Buford	.10	.05	.01
□ 493 Ricky Gutierrez	.10	.05	.01
□ 494 Jeff Russell	.10	.05	.01
□ 495 Vinny Castilla	.30	.14	.04
□ 496 Wilson Alvarez	.20	.09	.03
□ 497 Scott Bullett	.10	.05	.01
□ 498 Larry Casian	.10	.05	.01
□ 499 Jose Vizcaino	.10	.05	.01
□ 500 J.T. Snow	.30	.14	.04
□ 501 Bryan Hickerson	.10	.05	.01
□ 502 Jeremy Hernandez	.10	.05	.01
□ 503 Jeromy Burnitz	.10	.05	.01
□ 504 Steve Farr	.10	.05	.01
□ 505 J. Owens	.20	.09	.03
□ 506 Craig Paquette	.10	.05	.01
□ 507 Jim Eisenreich	.20	.09	.03
□ 508 Matt Whiteside	.10	.05	.01
□ 509 Luis Aquino	.10	.05	.01
□ 510 Mike LaValliere	.10	.05	.01
□ 511 Jim Gott	.10	.05	.01
□ 512 Mark McLemore	.10	.05	.01
□ 513 Randy Milligan	.10	.05	.01
□ 514 Gary Gaetti	.20	.09	.03
□ 515 Lou Frazier	.10	.05	.01
□ 516 Rich Amaral	.10	.05	.01
□ 517 Gene Harris	.10	.05	.01
□ 518 Aaron Sele	.20	.09	.03
□ 519 Mark Wohlers	.20	.09	.03
□ 520 Scott Kamieniecki	.10	.05	.01
□ 521 Kent Mercker	.10	.05	.01
□ 522 Jim Deshaies	.10	.05	.01
□ 523 Kevin Stocker	.20	.09	.03
□ 524 Jason Bere	.20	.09	.03
□ 525 Tim Bogar	.10	.05	.01
□ 526 Brad Pennington	.10	.05	.01
□ 527 Curt Leskanic	.10	.05	.01
□ 528 Wayne Kirby	.10	.05	.01
□ 529 Tim Costo	.10	.05	.01
□ 530 Doug Henry	.10	.05	.01
□ 531 Trevor Hoffman	.20	.09	.03
□ 532 Kelly Gruber	.10	.05	.01
□ 533 Mike Harkey	.10	.05	.01
□ 534 John Doherty	.10	.05	.01
□ 535 Erik Pappas	.10	.05	.01
□ 536 Brent Gates	.20	.09	.03
□ 537 Roger McDowell	.10	.05	.01
□ 538 Chris Haney	.10	.05	.01
□ 539 Blas Minor	.10	.05	.01
□ 540 Pat Hentgen	.30	.14	.04
□ 541 Chuck Carr	.10	.05	.01
□ 542 Doug Strange	.10	.05	.01
□ 543 Xavier Hernandez	.10	.05	.01
□ 544 Paul Quantrill	.10	.05	.01
□ 545 Anthony Young	.10	.05	.01
□ 546 Bret Boone	.20	.09	.03
□ 547 Dwight Smith	.10	.05	.01
□ 548 Bobby Munoz	.10	.05	.01
□ 549 Russ Springer	.10	.05	.01
□ 550 Roger Pavlik	.20	.09	.03
□ DW Dave Winfield 3000 Hits	1.00	.45	.12
□ FT Frank Thomas AU/3500 (Certified autograph)	250.00	110.00	31.00

1993 Leaf Fasttrack

These 20 standard-size cards, featuring a selection of talented young stars, were randomly inserted into 1993 Leaf retail packs; the first ten were series I inserts, the second ten were series II inserts. The fronts feature borderless color player action photos, except in the lower right corner, where an oblique white stripe carries the motion-streaked set title.

	MINT	NRMT	EXC
COMPLETE SET (20)	100.00	45.00	12.50
COMPLETE SERIES 1 (10)	60.00	27.00	7.50
COMPLETE SERIES 2 (10)	40.00	18.00	5.00
COMMON CARD (1-20)	2.00	.90	.25
SEMISTARS	5.00	2.20	.60
RANDOM INSERTS IN RETAIL PACKS			
□ 1 Frank Thomas	40.00	18.00	5.00
□ 2 Tim Wakefield	2.00	.90	.25
□ 3 Kenny Lofton	15.00	6.75	1.85
□ 4 Mike Mussina	8.00	3.60	1.00

□ 5 Juan Gonzalez	20.00	9.00	2.50
□ 6 Chuck Knoblauch	6.00	2.70	.75
□ 7 Eric Karros	4.00	1.80	.50
□ 8 Ray Lankford	4.00	1.80	.50
□ 9 Juan Guzman	2.00	.90	.25
□ 10 Pat Listach	2.00	.90	.25
□ 11 Carlos Baerga	4.00	1.80	.50
□ 12 Felix Jose	2.00	.90	.25
□ 13 Steve Avery	4.00	1.80	.50
□ 14 Robin Ventura	4.00	1.80	.50
□ 15 Ivan Rodriguez	8.00	3.60	1.00
□ 16 Cal Eldred	2.00	.90	.25
□ 17 Jeff Bagwell	15.00	6.75	1.85
□ 18 David Justice	4.00	1.80	.50
□ 19 Travis Fryman	4.00	1.80	.50
□ 20 Marquis Grissom	4.00	1.80	.50

1993 Leaf Gold All-Stars

These 30 standard-size dual-sided cards feature members of the American and National league All-Star squads. The first 20 were inserted one per 1993 Leaf jumbo packs; the first ten were series I inserts, the second ten were series II inserts. The final ten cards were randomly inserted in 1993 Leaf Update packs. The card design features full color action photos with a diagonal stripe at the base.

	MINT	NRMT	EXC
COMPLETE REG.SET (20)	40.00	18.00	5.00
COMPLETE UPDATE SET (10)	12.00	5.50	1.50
COMMON REG.CARD (R1-R20)	.50	.23	.06
COMMON UPDATE CARD (U1-U10)	.50	.23	.06
SEMISTARS	1.00	.45	.12
REG.CARDS ONE PER JUMBO PACK			
UPDATES INSERTS IN UPDATE PACKS			

□ R1 Ivan Rodriguez	1.00	.45	.12
Darren Daulton			
□ R2 Don Mattingly	3.00	1.35	.35
Fred McGriff			
□ R3 Cecil Fielder	3.00	1.35	.35
Jeff Bagwell			
□ R4 Carlos Baerga	2.50	1.10	.30
Ryne Sandberg			
□ R5 Chuck Knoblauch	1.00	.45	.12
Delino DeShields			
□ R6 Robin Ventura	.50	.23	.06
Terry Pendleton			
□ R7 Ken Griffey Jr.	5.00	2.20	.60
Andy Van Slyke			
□ R8 Joe Carter	1.00	.45	.12
Dave Justice			
□ R9 Jose Canseco	3.00	1.35	.35
Tony Gwynn			
□ R10 Dennis Eckersley	.50	.23	.06
Rob Dibble			
□ R11 Mark McGwire	2.00	.90	.25
Will Clark			
□ R12 Frank Thomas	5.00	2.20	.60
Mark Grace			
□ R13 Roberto Alomar	1.25	.55	.16
Craig Biggio			
□ R14 Cal Ripken	5.00	2.20	.60
Barry Larkin			
□ R15 Edgar Martinez	1.00	.45	.12
Gary Sheffield			
□ R16 Juan Gonzalez	4.00	1.80	.50
Barry Bonds			
□ R17 Kirby Puckett	2.50	1.10	.30
Marquis Grissom			
□ R18 Jim Abbott	1.00	.45	.12
Tom Glavine			
□ R19 Nolan Ryan	10.00	4.50	1.25
Greg Maddux			
□ R20 Roger Clemens	1.00	.45	.12
Doug Drabek			
□ U1 Mark Langston	.50	.23	.06
Terry Mulholland			
□ U2 Ivan Rodriguez	1.00	.45	.12
Darren Daulton			
□ U3 John Olerud	.50	.23	.06
John Kruk			
□ U4 Roberto Alomar	2.50	1.10	.30
Ryne Sandberg			
□ U5 Wade Boggs	1.00	.45	.12
Gary Sheffield			
□ U6 Cal Ripken	5.00	2.20	.60
Barry Larkin			
□ U7 Kirby Puckett	2.50	1.10	.30
Bobby Bonds			
□ U8 Ken Griffey Jr.	5.00	2.20	.60
Marquis Grissom			
□ U9 Joe Carter	1.00	.45	.12
David Justice			
□ U10 Paul Molitor	1.00	.45	.12
Mark Grace			

1993 Leaf Gold Rookies

These cards of promising newcomers were randomly inserted into 1993 Leaf packs; the first ten in series I, the last ten in series II, and five in the Update product. The front of each standard-size card features a borderless color player action shot. The player's name appears in white cursive lettering within a wide gray lithic stripe near the bottom, which is set off by gold-foil lines and carries the set's title in simulated bas-relief. Leaf produced jumbo (3 1/2 by 5 inch) versions for retail repacks; they are valued at approximately double the prices below.

	MINT	NRMT	EXC
COMPLETE REG.SET (20)	40.00	18.00	5.00
COMPLETE UPDATE SET (5)	20.00	9.00	2.50
COMMON REG.CARD (R1-R20)	1.00	.45	.12
COMMON UPDATE CARD (U1-U5)	.75	.35	.09
SEMISTARS	1.50	.70	.19
REG.CARDS INSERTS IN HOBBY PACKS			
UPDATE CARDS INSERTS IN UPDATE PACKS		25.00	11.00
3.10			

□ R1 Kevin Young	1.00	.45	.12
□ R2 Wil Cordero	1.50	.70	.19
□ R3 Mark Kiefer	1.00	.45	.12
□ R4 Gerald Williams	1.00	.45	.12
□ R5 Brandon Wilson	1.00	.45	.12
□ R6 Greg Gohr	1.00	.45	.12
□ R7 Ryan Thompson	1.00	.45	.12
□ R8 Tim Wakefield	1.50	.70	.19
□ R9 Troy Neel	1.00	.45	.12
□ R10 Tim Salmon	8.00	3.60	1.00
□ R11 Kevin Rogers	1.00	.45	.12
□ R12 Rod Bolton	1.00	.45	.12
□ R13 Ken Ryan	1.00	.45	.12
□ R14 Phil Hiatt	1.00	.45	.12

□ R15 Rene Arocha	1.00	.45	.12
□ R16 Nigel Wilson	1.00	.45	.12
□ R17 J.T. Snow	1.50	.70	.19
□ R18 Benji Gil	1.00	.45	.12
□ R19 Chipper Jones	30.00	13.50	3.70
□ R20 Darrell Sherman	1.00	.45	.12
□ U1 Allen Watson	1.50	.70	.19
□ U2 Jeffrey Hammonds	1.50	.70	.19
□ U3 Dave McCarty	.75	.35	.09
□ U4 Mike Piazza	20.00	9.00	2.50
□ U5 Roberto Mejia	.75	.35	.09

1993 Leaf Heading for the Hall

Randomly inserted into 1993 Leaf series 1 and 2 packs, this ten-card standard-size set features potential Hall of Famers. Cards 1-5 were series I inserts and cards 6-10 were series II inserts. The fronts feature borderless color player action shots, with the player's name appearing within a lithic banner near the bottom, below the set's logo.

	MINT	NRMT	EXC
COMPLETE SET (10)	30.00	13.50	3.70
COMPLETE SERIES 1 (5)	20.00	9.00	2.50
COMPLETE SERIES 2 (5)	10.00	4.50	1.25
COMMON CARD (1-10)	1.50	.70	.19
RANDOM INSERTS IN PACKS	3.00	1.35	.35

□ 1 Nolan Ryan	12.00	5.50	1.50
□ 2 Tony Gwynn	5.00	2.20	.60
□ 3 Robin Yount	1.50	.70	.19
□ 4 Eddie Murray	3.00	1.35	.35
□ 5 Cal Ripken	12.00	5.50	1.50
□ 6 Roger Clemens	1.50	.70	.19
□ 7 George Brett	5.00	2.20	.60
□ 8 Ryne Sandberg	3.00	1.35	.35
□ 9 Kirby Puckett	4.00	1.80	.50
□ 10 Ozzie Smith	2.50	1.10	.30

1994 Leaf

The 1994 Leaf baseball set consists of two series of 220 standard-size cards for a total of 440. Certain "Super Packs" contained complete insert sets. The fronts feature color action player photos, with team color-coded designs on the bottom. The player's name and the Leaf logo are foil stamped, the team name appears under the player's name. The backs carry a photo of the player's home stadium in the background with a silhouetted photo of the player in the foreground. Additionally, a headshot appears in a ticket stub-like design with biographical information, while player statistics appear on the bottom. Cards featuring players from the Texas Rangers, Cleveland Indians, Milwaukee Brewers and Houston Astros were held out of the first series in order to have up-to-date photography in each team's new uniforms. A limited number of players from the San Francisco Giants are featured in the first series because of minor modifications to the team's uniforms. Randomly inserted in hobby packs at a rate of one in 36 was a stamped version of Frank Thomas' 1990 Leaf rookie card. Rookie Cards in this set include Kurt Abbott.

	MINT	NRMT	EXC
COMPLETE SET (440)	30.00	13.50	3.70
COMPLETE SERIES 1 (220)	15.00	6.75	1.85
COMPLETE SERIES 2 (220)	15.00	6.75	1.85
COMMON CARD (1-440)	.10	.05	.01
SEMISTARS	.25	.11	.03
STARS	.50	.23	.06
SUPER PACKS CONTAIN INSERT SETS			

□ 1 Cal Ripken Jr.	2.50	1.10	.30
□ 2 Tony Tarasco	.10	.05	.01
□ 3 Joe Girardi	.10	.05	.01
□ 4 Bernie Williams	.50	.23	.06
□ 5 Chad Kreuter	.10	.05	.01
□ 6 Troy Neel	.10	.05	.01
□ 7 Tom Pagnozzi	.10	.05	.01
□ 8 Kirk Rueter	.10	.05	.01
□ 9 Chris Bosio	.10	.05	.01
□ 10 Dwight Gooden	.25	.11	.03
□ 11 Mariano Duncan	.10	.05	.01
□ 12 Jay Bell	.25	.11	.03
□ 13 Lance Johnson	.25	.11	.03
□ 14 Richie Lewis	.10	.05	.01
□ 15 Dave Martinez	.10	.05	.01
□ 16 Orel Hershiser	.25	.11	.03
□ 17 Rob Butler	.10	.05	.01
□ 18 Glenallen Hill	.10	.05	.01
□ 19 Chad Curtis	.10	.05	.01
□ 20 Mike Stanton	.10	.05	.01
□ 21 Tim Wallach	.10	.05	.01
□ 22 Milt Thompson	.10	.05	.01
□ 23 Kevin Young	.10	.05	.01
□ 24 John Smiley	.10	.05	.01
□ 25 Jeff Montgomery	.25	.11	.03
□ 26 Robin Ventura	.25	.11	.03
□ 27 Scott Lydy	.10	.05	.01
□ 28 Todd Stottlemyre	.10	.05	.01
□ 29 Mark Whiten	.10	.05	.01
□ 30 Robby Thompson	.10	.05	.01
□ 31 Bobby Bonilla	.25	.11	.03
□ 32 Andy Ashby	.25	.11	.03
□ 33 Greg Myers	.10	.05	.01
□ 34 Billy Hatcher	.10	.05	.01
□ 35 Brad Holman	.10	.05	.01
□ 36 Mark McLemore	.10	.05	.01
□ 37 Scott Sanders	.10	.05	.01
□ 38 Jim Abbott	.10	.05	.01
□ 39 David Wells	.10	.05	.01
□ 40 Roberto Kelly	.10	.05	.01
□ 41 Jeff Conine	.50	.23	.06
□ 42 Sean Berry	.10	.05	.01
□ 43 Mark Grace	.50	.23	.06
□ 44 Eric Young	.25	.11	.03
□ 45 Rick Aguilera	.10	.05	.01
□ 46 Chipper Jones	2.50	1.10	.30
□ 47 Mel Rojas	.10	.05	.01
□ 48 Ryan Thompson	.10	.05	.01
□ 49 Al Martin	.10	.05	.01
□ 50 Cecil Fielder	.25	.11	.03
□ 51 Pat Kelly	.10	.05	.01
□ 52 Kevin Tapani	.10	.05	.01
□ 53 Tim Costo	.10	.05	.01
□ 54 Dave Hollins	.10	.05	.01
□ 55 Kirt Manwaring	.10	.05	.01
□ 56 Gregg Jefferies	.50	.23	.06
□ 57 Ron Darling	.10	.05	.01
□ 58 Bill Haselman	.10	.05	.01
□ 59 Phil Plantier	.10	.05	.01

□ 60 Frank Viola	.10	.05	.01
□ 61 Todd Zeile	.10	.05	.01
□ 62 Bret Barberie	.10	.05	.01
□ 63 Roberto Mejia	.10	.05	.01
□ 64 Chuck Knoblauch	.50	.23	.06
□ 65 Jose Lind	.10	.05	.01
□ 66 Brady Anderson	.50	.23	.06
□ 67 Ruben Sierra	.25	.11	.03
□ 68 Jose Vizcaino	.10	.05	.01
□ 69 Joe Grahe	.10	.05	.01
□ 70 Kevin Appier	.25	.11	.03
□ 71 Wilson Alvarez	.25	.11	.03
□ 72 Tom Candiotti	.10	.05	.01
□ 73 John Burkett	.10	.05	.01
□ 74 Anthony Young	.10	.05	.01
□ 75 Scott Cooper	.10	.05	.01
□ 76 Nigel Wilson	.10	.05	.01
□ 77 John Valentin	.25	.11	.03
□ 78 Dave McCarty	.10	.05	.01
□ 79 Archi Cianfrocco	.10	.05	.01
□ 80 Lou Whitaker	.50	.23	.06
□ 81 Dante Bichette	.50	.23	.06
□ 82 Mark Dewey	.10	.05	.01
□ 83 Danny Jackson	.10	.05	.01
□ 84 Harold Baines	.25	.11	.03
□ 85 Todd Benzinger	.10	.05	.01
□ 86 Damion Easley	.10	.05	.01
□ 87 Danny Cox	.10	.05	.01
□ 88 Jose Bautista	.10	.05	.01
□ 89 Mike Lansing	.25	.11	.03
□ 90 Phil Hiatt	.10	.05	.01
□ 91 Tim Pugh	.10	.05	.01
□ 92 Tino Martinez	.25	.11	.03
□ 93 Raul Mondesi	.50	.23	.06
□ 94 Greg Maddux	2.00	.90	.25
□ 95 Al Leiter	.25	.11	.03
□ 96 Benito Santiago	.10	.05	.01
□ 97 Lenny Dykstra	.25	.11	.03
□ 98 Sammy Sosa	.50	.23	.06
□ 99 Tim Bogar	.10	.05	.01
□ 100 Checklist	.10	.05	.01
□ 101 Deion Sanders	.50	.23	.06
□ 102 Bobby Witt	.10	.05	.01
□ 103 Wil Cordero	.25	.11	.03
□ 104 Rich Amaral	.10	.05	.01
□ 105 Mike Mussina	.60	.25	.07
□ 106 Reggie Sanders	.50	.23	.06
□ 107 Ozzie Guillen	.10	.05	.01
□ 108 Paul O'Neill	.25	.11	.03
□ 109 Tim Salmon	.50	.23	.06
□ 110 Rheal Cormier	.10	.05	.01
□ 111 Billy Ashley	.10	.05	.01
□ 112 Jeff Kent	.10	.05	.01
□ 113 Derek Bell	.25	.11	.03
□ 114 Danny Darwin	.10	.05	.01
□ 115 Chip Hale	.10	.05	.01
□ 116 Tim Raines	.50	.23	.06
□ 117 Ed Sprague	.25	.11	.03
□ 118 Darrin Fletcher	.10	.05	.01
□ 119 Darren Holmes	.10	.05	.01
□ 120 Alan Trammell	.50	.23	.06
□ 121 Don Mattingly	1.50	.70	.19
□ 122 Greg Gagne	.10	.05	.01
□ 123 Jose Offerman	.10	.05	.01
□ 124 Joe Orsulak	.10	.05	.01
□ 125 Jack McDowell	.25	.11	.03
□ 126 Barry Larkin	.50	.23	.06
□ 127 Ben McDonald	.10	.05	.01
□ 128 Mike Bordick	.10	.05	.01
□ 129 Devon White	.10	.05	.01
□ 130 Mike Perez	.10	.05	.01
□ 131 Jay Buhner	.50	.23	.06
□ 132 Phil Leftwich	.10	.05	.01
□ 133 Tommy Greene	.10	.05	.01
□ 134 Charlie Hayes	.10	.05	.01
□ 135 Don Slaught	.10	.05	.01
□ 136 Mike Gallego	.10	.05	.01
□ 137 Dave Winfield	.50	.23	.06
□ 138 Steve Avery	.25	.11	.03
□ 139 Derrick May	.10	.05	.01
□ 140 Bryan Harvey	.10	.05	.01
□ 141 Wally Joyner	.25	.11	.03
□ 142 Andre Dawson	.50	.23	.06
□ 143 Andy Benes	.25	.11	.03
□ 144 John Franco	.10	.05	.01
□ 145 Jeff King	.25	.11	.03
□ 146 Joe Oliver	.10	.05	.01
□ 147 Bill Gullickson	.10	.05	.01
□ 148 Armando Reynoso	.10	.05	.01
□ 149 Dave Fleming	.10	.05	.01
□ 150 Checklist	.10	.05	.01
□ 151 Todd Van Poppel	.10	.05	.01
□ 152 Bernard Gilkey	.25	.11	.03
□ 153 Kevin Gross	.10	.05	.01
□ 154 Mike Devereaux	.10	.05	.01
□ 155 Tim Wakefield	.10	.05	.01
□ 156 Andres Galarraga	.50	.23	.06
□ 157 Pat Meares	.10	.05	.01
□ 158 Jim Leyritz	.10	.05	.01
□ 159 Mike Macfarlane	.10	.05	.01
□ 160 Tony Phillips	.25	.11	.03
□ 161 Brent Gates	.10	.05	.01
□ 162 Mark Langston	.25	.11	.03
□ 163 Allen Watson	.10	.05	.01
□ 164 Randy Johnson	.50	.23	.06
□ 165 Doug Brocail	.10	.05	.01
□ 166 Rob Dibble	.10	.05	.01
□ 167 Roberto Hernandez	.25	.11	.03
□ 168 Felix Jose	.10	.05	.01
□ 169 Steve Cooke	.10	.05	.01
□ 170 Darren Daulton	.25	.11	.03
□ 171 Eric Karros	.25	.11	.03
□ 172 Geronimo Pena	.10	.05	.01
□ 173 Gary DiSarcina	.10	.05	.01
□ 174 Marquis Grissom	.50	.23	.06
□ 175 Joey Cora	.10	.05	.01
□ 176 Jim Eisenreich	.10	.05	.01
□ 177 Brad Pennington	.10	.05	.01
□ 178 Terry Steinbach	.25	.11	.03
□ 179 Pat Borders	.10	.05	.01
□ 180 Steve Buechele	.10	.05	.01
□ 181 Jeff Fassero	.10	.05	.01
□ 182 Mike Greenwell	.10	.05	.01
□ 183 Mike Henneman	.10	.05	.01
□ 184 Ron Karkovice	.10	.05	.01
□ 185 Pat Hentgen	.50	.23	.06
□ 186 Jose Guzman	.10	.05	.01
□ 187 Brett Butler	.25	.11	.03
□ 188 Charlie Hough	.10	.05	.01
□ 189 Terry Pendleton	.25	.11	.03
□ 190 Melido Perez	.10	.05	.01
□ 191 Orestes Destrade	.10	.05	.01
□ 192 Mike Morgan	.10	.05	.01
□ 193 Joe Carter	.50	.23	.06
□ 194 Jeff Blauser	.10	.05	.01
□ 195 Chris Hoiles	.10	.05	.01
□ 196 Ricky Gutierrez	.10	.05	.01
□ 197 Mike Moore	.10	.05	.01
□ 198 Carl Willis	.10	.05	.01
□ 199 Aaron Sele	.25	.11	.03
□ 200 Checklist	.10	.05	.01
□ 201 Tim Naehring	.10	.05	.01
□ 202 Scott Livingstone	.10	.05	.01
□ 203 Luis Alicea	.10	.05	.01
□ 204 Torey Lovullo	.10	.05	.01
□ 205 Jim Gott	.10	.05	.01
□ 206 Bob Wickman	.10	.05	.01
□ 207 Greg McMichael	.10	.05	.01
□ 208 Scott Brosius	.10	.05	.01
□ 209 Chris Gwynn	.10	.05	.01
□ 210 Steve Sax	.10	.05	.01
□ 211 Dick Schofield	.10	.05	.01
□ 212 Robb Nen	.25	.11	.03
□ 213 Ben Rivera	.10	.05	.01
□ 214 Vinny Castilla	.50	.23	.06
□ 215 Jamie Moyer	.10	.05	.01
□ 216 Wally Whitehurst	.10	.05	.01
□ 217 Frank Castillo	.10	.05	.01
□ 218 Mike Blowers	.10	.05	.01
□ 219 Tim Scott	.10	.05	.01
□ 220 Paul Wagner	.10	.05	.01
□ 221 Jeff Bagwell	1.25	.55	.16
□ 222 Ricky Bones	.10	.05	.01
□ 223 Sandy Alomar Jr.	.25	.11	.03
□ 224 Rod Beck	.25	.11	.03
□ 225 Roberto Alomar	.75	.35	.09
□ 226 Jack Armstrong	.10	.05	.01
□ 227 Scott Erickson	.10	.05	.01
□ 228 Rene Arocha	.10	.05	.01
□ 229 Eric Anthony	.10	.05	.01
□ 230 Jeromy Burnitz	.10	.05	.01
□ 231 Kevin Brown	.10	.05	.01

□ 232	Tim Belcher	.10	.05	.01
□ 233	Bret Boone	.25	.11	.03
□ 234	Dennis Eckersley	.25	.11	.03
□ 235	Tom Glavine	.50	.23	.06
□ 236	Craig Biggio	.50	.23	.06
□ 237	Pedro Astacio	.10	.05	.01
□ 238	Ryan Bowen	.10	.05	.01
□ 239	Brad Ausmus	.10	.05	.01
□ 240	Vince Coleman	.10	.05	.01
□ 241	Jason Bere	.25	.11	.03
□ 242	Ellis Burks	.25	.11	.03
□ 243	Wes Chamberlain	.10	.05	.01
□ 244	Ken Caminiti	.50	.23	.06
□ 245	Willie Banks	.10	.05	.01
□ 246	Sid Fernandez	.10	.05	.01
□ 247	Carlos Baerga	.50	.23	.06
□ 248	Carlos Garcia	.10	.05	.01
□ 249	Jose Canseco	.50	.23	.06
□ 250	Alex Diaz	.10	.05	.01
□ 251	Albert Belle	1.50	.70	.19
□ 252	Moises Alou	.25	.11	.03
□ 253	Bobby Ayala	.10	.05	.01
□ 254	Tony Gwynn	1.25	.55	.16
□ 255	Roger Clemens	.50	.23	.06
□ 256	Eric Davis	.25	.11	.03
□ 257	Wade Boggs	.50	.23	.06
□ 258	Chili Davis	.25	.11	.03
□ 259	Rickey Henderson	.50	.23	.06
□ 260	Andujar Cedeno	.10	.05	.01
□ 261	Cris Carpenter	.10	.05	.01
□ 262	Juan Guzman	.25	.11	.03
□ 263	David Justice	.50	.23	.06
□ 264	Barry Bonds	.75	.35	.09
□ 265	Pete Incaviglia	.10	.05	.01
□ 266	Tony Fernandez	.10	.05	.01
□ 267	Cal Eldred	.10	.05	.01
□ 268	Alex Fernandez	.50	.23	.06
□ 269	Kent Hrbek	.25	.11	.03
□ 270	Steve Farr	.10	.05	.01
□ 271	Doug Drabek	.10	.05	.01
□ 272	Brian Jordan	.50	.23	.06
□ 273	Xavier Hernandez	.10	.05	.01
□ 274	David Cone	.50	.23	.06
□ 275	Brian Hunter	.10	.05	.01
□ 276	Mike Harkey	.10	.05	.01
□ 277	Delino DeShields	.10	.05	.01
□ 278	David Hulse	.10	.05	.01
□ 279	Mickey Tettleton	.10	.05	.01
□ 280	Kevin McReynolds	.10	.05	.01
□ 281	Darryl Hamilton	.10	.05	.01
□ 282	Ken Hill	.10	.05	.01
□ 283	Wayne Kirby	.10	.05	.01
□ 284	Chris Hammond	.10	.05	.01
□ 285	Mo Vaughn	.75	.35	.09
□ 286	Ryan Klesko	.75	.35	.09
□ 287	Rick Wilkins	.10	.05	.01
□ 288	Bill Swift	.10	.05	.01
□ 289	Rafael Palmeiro	.50	.23	.06
□ 290	Brian Harper	.10	.05	.01
□ 291	Chris Turner	.10	.05	.01
□ 292	Luis Gonzalez	.10	.05	.01
□ 293	Kenny Rogers	.10	.05	.01
□ 294	Kirby Puckett	1.00	.45	.12
□ 295	Mike Stanley	.10	.05	.01
□ 296	Carlos Reyes	.10	.05	.01
□ 297	Charles Nagy	.25	.11	.03
□ 298	Reggie Jefferson	.25	.11	.03
□ 299	Bip Roberts	.10	.05	.01
□ 300	Darrin Jackson	.10	.05	.01
□ 301	Mike Jackson	.10	.05	.01
□ 302	Dave Nilsson	.25	.11	.03
□ 303	Ramon Martinez	.25	.11	.03
□ 304	Bobby Jones	.25	.11	.03
□ 305	Johnny Ruffin	.10	.05	.01
□ 306	Brian McRae	.25	.11	.03
□ 307	Bo Jackson	.50	.23	.06
□ 308	Dave Stewart	.25	.11	.03
□ 309	John Smoltz	.50	.23	.06
□ 310	Dennis Martinez	.25	.11	.03
□ 311	Dean Palmer	.25	.11	.03
□ 312	David Nied	.10	.05	.01
□ 313	Eddie Murray	.75	.35	.09
□ 314	Darryl Kile	.10	.05	.01
□ 315	Rick Sutcliffe	.10	.05	.01
□ 316	Shawon Dunston	.10	.05	.01
□ 317	John Jaha	.25	.11	.03
□ 318	Salomon Torres	.10	.05	.01
□ 319	Gary Sheffield	.50	.23	.06
□ 320	Curt Schilling	.10	.05	.01
□ 321	Greg Vaughn	.50	.23	.06
□ 322	Jay Howell	.10	.05	.01
□ 323	Todd Hundley	.50	.23	.06
□ 324	Chris Sabo	.10	.05	.01
□ 325	Stan Javier	.10	.05	.01
□ 326	Willie Greene	.25	.11	.03
□ 327	Hipolito Pichardo	.10	.05	.01
□ 328	Doug Strange	.10	.05	.01
□ 329	Dan Wilson	.25	.11	.03
□ 330	Checklist	.10	.05	.01
□ 331	Omar Vizquel	.50	.23	.06
□ 332	Scott Servais	.10	.05	.01
□ 333	Bob Tewksbury	.10	.05	.01
□ 334	Matt Williams	.50	.23	.06
□ 335	Tom Foley	.10	.05	.01
□ 336	Jeff Russell	.10	.05	.01
□ 337	Scott Leius	.10	.05	.01
□ 338	Ivan Rodriguez	.60	.25	.07
□ 339	Kevin Seitzer	.10	.05	.01
□ 340	Jose Rijo	.10	.05	.01
□ 341	Eduardo Perez	.10	.05	.01
□ 342	Kirk Gibson	.25	.11	.03
□ 343	Randy Milligan	.10	.05	.01
□ 344	Edgar Martinez	.50	.23	.06
□ 345	Fred McGriff	.50	.23	.06
□ 346	Kurt Abbott	.25	.11	.03
□ 347	John Kruk	.25	.11	.03
□ 348	Mike Felder	.10	.05	.01
□ 349	Dave Staton	.10	.05	.01
□ 350	Kenny Lofton	1.00	.45	.12
□ 351	Graeme Lloyd	.10	.05	.01
□ 352	David Segui	.10	.05	.01
□ 353	Danny Tartabull	.10	.05	.01
□ 354	Bob Welch	.10	.05	.01
□ 355	Duane Ward	.10	.05	.01
□ 356	Karl Rhodes	.10	.05	.01
□ 357	Lee Smith	.25	.11	.03
□ 358	Chris James	.10	.05	.01
□ 359	Walt Weiss	.10	.05	.01
□ 360	Pedro Munoz	.10	.05	.01
□ 361	Paul Sorrento	.10	.05	.01
□ 362	Todd Worrell	.10	.05	.01
□ 363	Bob Hamelin	.10	.05	.01
□ 364	Julio Franco	.25	.11	.03
□ 365	Roberto Petagine	.25	.11	.03
□ 366	Willie McGee	.10	.05	.01
□ 367	Pedro Martinez	.50	.23	.06
□ 368	Ken Griffey Jr.	3.00	1.35	.35
□ 369	B.J. Surhoff	.10	.05	.01
□ 370	Kevin Mitchell	.25	.11	.03
□ 371	John Doherty	.10	.05	.01
□ 372	Manuel Lee	.10	.05	.01
□ 373	Terry Mulholland	.10	.05	.01
□ 374	Zane Smith	.10	.05	.01
□ 375	Otis Nixon	.10	.05	.01
□ 376	Jody Reed	.10	.05	.01
□ 377	Doug Jones	.10	.05	.01
□ 378	John Olerud	.10	.05	.01
□ 379	Greg Swindell	.10	.05	.01
□ 380	Checklist	.10	.05	.01
□ 381	Royce Clayton	.25	.11	.03
□ 382	Jim Thome	.75	.35	.09
□ 383	Steve Finley	.50	.23	.06
□ 384	Ray Lankford	.50	.23	.06
□ 385	Henry Rodriguez	.50	.23	.06
□ 386	Dave Magadan	.10	.05	.01
□ 387	Gary Redus	.10	.05	.01
□ 388	Orlando Merced	.25	.11	.03
□ 389	Tom Gordon	.10	.05	.01
□ 390	Luis Polonia	.10	.05	.01
□ 391	Mark McGwire	1.00	.45	.12
□ 392	Mark Lemke	.10	.05	.01
□ 393	Doug Henry	.10	.05	.01
□ 394	Chuck Finley	.10	.05	.01
□ 395	Paul Molitor	.60	.25	.07
□ 396	Randy Myers	.10	.05	.01
□ 397	Larry Walker	.50	.23	.06
□ 398	Pete Harnisch	.10	.05	.01
□ 399	Darren Lewis	.10	.05	.01
□ 400	Frank Thomas	3.00	1.35	.35
□ 401	Jack Morris	.25	.11	.03
□ 402	Greg Hibbard	.10	.05	.01
□ 403	Jeffrey Hammonds	.25	.11	.03

□ 404 Will Clark	.50	.23	.06
□ 405 Travis Fryman	.50	.23	.06
□ 406 Scott Sanderson	.10	.05	.01
□ 407 Gene Harris	.10	.05	.01
□ 408 Chuck Carr	.10	.05	.01
□ 409 Ozzie Smith	.60	.25	.07
□ 410 Kent Mercker	.10	.05	.01
□ 411 Andy Van Slyke	.25	.11	.03
□ 412 Jimmy Key	.25	.11	.03
□ 413 Pat Mahomes	.10	.05	.01
□ 414 John Wetteland	.25	.11	.03
□ 415 Todd Jones	.10	.05	.01
□ 416 Greg Harris	.10	.05	.01
□ 417 Kevin Stocker	.10	.05	.01
□ 418 Juan Gonzalez	1.50	.70	.19
□ 419 Pete Smith	.10	.05	.01
□ 420 Pat Listach	.10	.05	.01
□ 421 Trevor Hoffman	.25	.11	.03
□ 422 Scott Fletcher	.10	.05	.01
□ 423 Mark Lewis	.10	.05	.01
□ 424 Mickey Morandini	.10	.05	.01
□ 425 Ryne Sandberg	.75	.35	.09
□ 426 Erik Hanson	.10	.05	.01
□ 427 Gary Gaetti	.25	.11	.03
□ 428 Harold Reynolds	.10	.05	.01
□ 429 Mark Portugal	.10	.05	.01
□ 430 David Valle	.10	.05	.01
□ 431 Mitch Williams	.10	.05	.01
□ 432 Howard Johnson	.10	.05	.01
□ 433 Hal Morris	.10	.05	.01
□ 434 Tom Henke	.10	.05	.01
□ 435 Shane Mack	.10	.05	.01
□ 436 Mike Piazza	2.00	.90	.25
□ 437 Bret Saberhagen	.25	.11	.03
□ 438 Jose Mesa	.25	.11	.03
□ 439 Jaime Navarro	.10	.05	.01
□ 440 Checklist	.10	.05	.01
□ A300 Frank Thomas Leaf 5th Anniversary	4.00	1.80	.50

1994 Leaf Clean-Up Crew

Inserted in magazine jumbo packs at a rate of one in 12, this 12-card set was issued in two series of six. Full-bleed fronts contain an action photo with the Clean-Up Crew logo at bottom right and the player's name in a colored band toward bottom left. The backs contain a photo and 1993 statistics when batting fourth. The home plate area serves as background.

	MINT	NRMT	EXC
COMPLETE SET (12)	60.00	27.00	7.50
COMPLETE SERIES 1 (6)	10.00	4.50	1.25
COMPLETE SERIES 2 (6)	50.00	22.00	6.25
COMMON CARD (1-12)	3.00	1.35	.35
SEMISTARS	6.00	2.70	.75
RANDOM INSERTS IN MAGAZINE JUMBO PACKS			

□ 1 Larry Walker	5.00	2.20	.60
□ 2 Andres Galarraga	5.00	2.20	.60
□ 3 Dave Hollins	3.00	1.35	.35
□ 4 Bobby Bonilla	3.00	1.35	.35
□ 5 Cecil Fielder	5.00	2.20	.60
□ 6 Danny Tartabull	3.00	1.35	.35
□ 7 Juan Gonzalez	25.00	11.00	3.10
□ 8 Joe Carter	5.00	2.20	.60
□ 9 Fred McGriff	5.00	2.20	.60
□ 10 Matt Williams	5.00	2.20	.60
□ 11 Albert Belle	25.00	11.00	3.10
□ 12 Harold Baines	3.00	1.35	.35

1994 Leaf Gamers

A close-up photo of the player highlights this 12-card standard-size set that was issued in two series of six. They were randomly inserted in jumbo packs at a rate of one in eight. The player's name appears at the top of the photo with the Leaf Gamers hologram logo at the bottom. The backs feature a variety of color photos including a frame by frame series resembling a film strip. There is also a small write-up.

	MINT	NRMT	EXC
COMPLETE SET (12)	150.00	70.00	19.00
COMPLETE SERIES 1 (6)	70.00	32.00	8.75
COMPLETE SERIES 2 (6)	80.00	36.00	10.00
COMMON CARD (1-12)	3.00	1.35	.35
SEMISTARS	5.00	2.20	.60
RANDOM INSERTS IN JUMBO PACKS			

□ 1 Ken Griffey Jr.	40.00	18.00	5.00
□ 2 Lenny Dykstra	3.00	1.35	.35
□ 3 Juan Gonzalez	20.00	9.00	2.50
□ 4 Don Mattingly	20.00	9.00	2.50
□ 5 David Justice	3.00	1.35	.35
□ 6 Mark Grace	5.00	2.20	.60
□ 7 Frank Thomas	40.00	18.00	5.00
□ 8 Barry Bonds	10.00	4.50	1.25
□ 9 Kirby Puckett	12.00	5.50	1.50
□ 10 Will Clark	5.00	2.20	.60
□ 11 John Kruk	3.00	1.35	.35
□ 12 Mike Piazza	25.00	11.00	3.10

1994 Leaf Gold Rookies

This set, which was randomly inserted in all packs at a rate of one in 18, features 20 of the hottest young stars in the majors. A color player cutout is layed over a dark brownish background that contains "94 Gold Leaf Rookie". The player's name and team appear at the bottom in silver. Horizontal backs include career highlights and two photos.

	MINT	NRMT	EXC
COMPLETE SET (20)	16.00	7.25	2.00
COMPLETE SERIES 1 (10)	12.00	5.50	1.50
COMPLETE SERIES 2 (10)	4.00	1.80	.50
COMMON CARD (1-20)	.50	.23	.06

SEMISTARS	1.00	.45	.12
RANDOM INSERTS IN ALL PACKS			

☐ 1 Javier Lopez	2.00	.90	.25
☐ 2 Rondell White	1.25	.55	.16
☐ 3 Butch Huskey	1.00	.45	.12
☐ 4 Midre Cummings	.50	.23	.06
☐ 5 Scott Ruffcorn	.50	.23	.06
☐ 6 Manny Ramirez	5.00	2.20	.60
☐ 7 Danny Bautista	.50	.23	.06
☐ 8 Russ Davis	.50	.23	.06
☐ 9 Steve Karsay	.50	.23	.06
☐ 10 Carlos Delgado	2.50	1.10	.30
☐ 11 Bob Hamelin	.50	.23	.06
☐ 12 Marcus Moore	.50	.23	.06
☐ 13 Miguel Jimenez	.50	.23	.06
☐ 14 Matt Walbeck	.50	.23	.06
☐ 15 James Mouton	1.00	.45	.12
☐ 16 Rich Becker	1.00	.45	.12
☐ 17 Brian Anderson	.50	.23	.06
☐ 18 Cliff Floyd	1.00	.45	.12
☐ 19 Steve Trachsel	1.00	.45	.12
☐ 20 Hector Carrasco	.50	.23	.06

1994 Leaf Gold Stars

Randomly inserted in all packs at a rate of one in 90, the 15 standard-size cards in this set are individually numbered and limited to 10,000 per player. The cards were issued in two series with eight cards in series one and seven in series two. The fronts are bordered by gold and have a green marble appearance with the player appearing within a diamond (outlined in gold) in the card's upper half. The player's name, gold facsimile autograph and team name appear below the photo. The backs are similar to the fronts except for 1993 highlights and the individual numbering. They are numbered "X/10,000".

	MINT	NRMT	EXC
COMPLETE SET (15)	200.00	90.00	25.00
COMPLETE SERIES 1 (8)	125.00	55.00	15.50
COMPLETE SERIES 2 (7)	75.00	34.00	9.50
COMMON CARD (1-15)	5.00	2.20	.60
RANDOM INSERTS IN ALL PACKS			

☐ 1 Roberto Alomar	12.00	5.50	1.50
☐ 2 Barry Bonds	12.00	5.50	1.50
☐ 3 David Justice	5.00	2.20	.60
☐ 4 Ken Griffey Jr.	50.00	22.00	6.25
☐ 5 Lenny Dykstra	5.00	2.20	.60
☐ 6 Don Mattingly	25.00	11.00	3.10
☐ 7 Andres Galarraga	5.00	2.20	.60
☐ 8 Greg Maddux	30.00	13.50	3.70
☐ 9 Carlos Baerga	5.00	2.20	.60
☐ 10 Paul Molitor	10.00	4.50	1.25
☐ 11 Frank Thomas	50.00	22.00	6.25
☐ 12 John Olerud	5.00	2.20	.60
☐ 13 Juan Gonzalez	25.00	11.00	3.10
☐ 14 Fred McGriff	6.00	2.70	.75
☐ 15 Jack McDowell	5.00	2.20	.60

1994 Leaf MVP Contenders

This 30-card standard-size set contains 15 players from each league who were projected

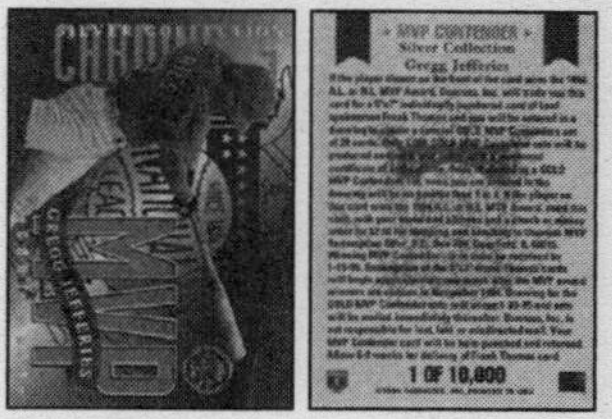

to be 1994 MVP hopefuls. These unnumbered cards were randomly inserted in all second series packs at a rate of one in 36. If the player appearing on the card was named his league's MVP (Frank Thomas American League and Jeff Bagwell National League), the card could be redeemed for a 5" x 7" Frank Thomas card individually numbered out of 20,000. Also, the collector was entered in a drawing to win one of 5,000 special Gold MVP Contenders sets. The fronts contain a color player photo with a black and white National or American League logo serving as a background. The backs contain all the rules and read "1 of 10,000". The expiration for redeeming Thomas and Bagwell cards was Jan. 19, 1995.

	MINT	NRMT	EXC
COMPLETE SET (30)	150.00	70.00	19.00
COMMON CARD	2.00	.90	.25
SEMISTARS	4.00	1.80	.50
MVPs WERE REDEEMABLE FOR THOMAS J400			
GOLD VERSIONS: SAME VALUE			
UNNUMBERED INSERTS IN ALL SER.2 PACKS			

☐ A1 Carlos Baerga	4.00	1.80	.50
☐ A2 Albert Belle	15.00	6.75	1.85
☐ A3 Jose Canseco	4.00	1.80	.50
☐ A4 Joe Carter	4.00	1.80	.50
☐ A5 Will Clark	4.00	1.80	.50
☐ A6 Cecil Fielder	4.00	1.80	.50
☐ A7 Juan Gonzalez	15.00	6.75	1.85
☐ A8 Ken Griffey Jr.	30.00	13.50	3.70
☐ A9 Paul Molitor	6.00	2.70	.75
☐ A10 Rafael Palmeiro	4.00	1.80	.50
☐ A11 Kirby Puckett	10.00	4.50	1.25
☐ A12 Cal Ripken Jr.	25.00	11.00	3.10
☐ A13 Frank Thomas	30.00	13.50	3.70
☐ A14 Mo Vaughn	8.00	3.60	1.00
☐ A15 AL Bonus Card	2.00	.90	.25
☐ N1 Jeff Bagwell	12.00	5.50	1.50
☐ N2 Dante Bichette	4.00	1.80	.50
☐ N3 Barry Bonds	8.00	3.60	1.00
☐ N4 Darren Daulton	2.00	.90	.25
☐ N5 Andres Galarraga	4.00	1.80	.50
☐ N6 Gregg Jefferies	4.00	1.80	.50
☐ N7 David Justice	2.00	.90	.25
☐ N8 Ray Lankford	4.00	1.80	.50
☐ N9 Barry Larkin	4.00	1.80	.50
☐ N10 Fred McGriff	4.00	1.80	.50
☐ N11 Mike Piazza	20.00	9.00	2.50
☐ N12 Deion Sanders	4.00	1.80	.50
☐ N13 Gary Sheffield	5.00	2.20	.60
☐ N14 Matt Williams	4.00	1.80	.50
☐ N15 NL Bonus Card	2.00	.90	.25
☐ J400 Frank Thomas Jumbo	20.00	9.00	2.50

1994 Leaf Power Brokers

Inserted in second series retail and hobby foil packs at a rate of one in 12, this 10-card standard-size set spotlights top sluggers. Both fronts and backs are horizontal. The fronts have a small player cutout with a black background and "Power Brokers" dominating the card. Fireworks appear within "Power". The backs contain various pie charts that document the player's home run tendencies as far as home vs. away etc. There is also a small photo.

	MINT	NRMT	EXC
COMPLETE SET (10)	20.00	9.00	2.50
COMMON CARD (1-10)	.50	.23	.06
SEMISTARS	1.00	.45	.12
INSERTS IN SER.2 HOBBY AND RETAIL			

	MINT	NRMT	EXC
□ 1 Frank Thomas	8.00	3.60	1.00
□ 2 David Justice	.50	.23	.06
□ 3 Barry Bonds	2.00	.90	.25
□ 4 Juan Gonzalez	4.00	1.80	.50
□ 5 Ken Griffey Jr.	8.00	3.60	1.00
□ 6 Mike Piazza	5.00	2.20	.60
□ 7 Cecil Fielder	1.00	.45	.12
□ 8 Fred McGriff	1.00	.45	.12
□ 9 Joe Carter	1.00	.45	.12
□ 10 Albert Belle	4.00	1.80	.50

1994 Leaf Slideshow

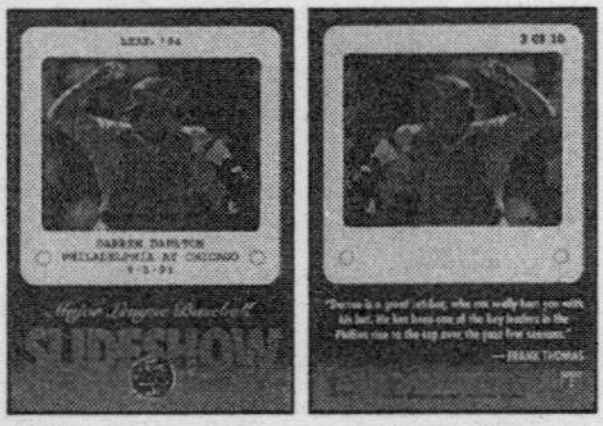

Randomly inserted in first and second series packs at a rate of one in 54, these ten standard-size cards simulate mounted photographic slides, but the images of the players are actually printed on acetate. The color transparencies can be seen best when they are held up to the light. The front of each transparency is framed by a simulated white slide holder, which at its bottom bears the player's name and the game from which the photo was shot. The insert set-s's title is shown in blue and merges with the blue-edged bottom. The remaining edges are black. The back, in addition to the appearance of the slide's reverse image, carries comments about the player from Frank Thomas.

	MINT	NRMT	EXC
COMPLETE SET (10)	60.00	27.00	7.50
COMPLETE SERIES 1 (5)	30.00	13.50	3.70
COMPLETE SERIES 2 (5)	30.00	13.50	3.70
COMMON CARD (1-10)	1.50	.70	.19
RANDOM INSERTS IN ALL PACKS			

	MINT	NRMT	EXC
□ 1 Frank Thomas	20.00	9.00	2.50
□ 2 Mike Piazza	12.00	5.50	1.50
□ 3 Darren Daulton	1.50	.70	.19
□ 4 Ryne Sandberg	5.00	2.20	.60
□ 5 Roberto Alomar	5.00	2.20	.60
□ 6 Barry Bonds	5.00	2.20	.60
□ 7 Juan Gonzalez	10.00	4.50	1.25
□ 8 Tim Salmon	3.00	1.35	.35
□ 9 Ken Griffey Jr.	20.00	9.00	2.50
□ 10 David Justice	1.50	.70	.19

1994 Leaf Statistical Standouts

Inserted in retail and hobby foil packs at a rate of one in 12, this 10-card standard-size set features players that had significant statistical achievements in 1993. For example: Cal Ripken's home run record for a shortstop. Card fronts contain a player photo that stands out from a background that is the colors of that player's team. The back contains a photo and statistical information.

	MINT	NRMT	EXC
COMPLETE SET (10)	20.00	9.00	2.50
COMMON CARD (1-10)	.50	.23	.06
INSERTS IN SER.1 HOBBY AND RETAIL	1.50	.70	.19

	MINT	NRMT	EXC
□ 1 Frank Thomas	5.00	2.20	.60
□ 2 Barry Bonds	1.25	.55	.16
□ 3 Juan Gonzalez	2.50	1.10	.30
□ 4 Mike Piazza	3.00	1.35	.35
□ 5 Greg Maddux	3.00	1.35	.35
□ 6 Ken Griffey Jr.	5.00	2.20	.60
□ 7 Joe Carter	.50	.23	.06
□ 8 Dave Winfield	.50	.23	.06
□ 9 Tony Gwynn	2.00	.90	.25
□ 10 Cal Ripken	4.00	1.80	.50

1995 Leaf

The 1995 Leaf set was issued in two series of 200 standard-size cards for a total of 400. Full-bleed fronts contain diamond-shaped player hologram in the upper left. The team name is done in silver foil up the left side. Peculiar backs contain two photos, the card number within a stamp or seal like emblem in the upper right and '94 and career stats graph toward bottom left. There are no key Rookie Cards in this set.

	MINT	NRMT	EXC
COMPLETE SET (400)	40.00	18.00	5.00
COMPLETE SERIES 1 (200)	15.00	6.75	1.85
COMPLETE SERIES 2 (200)	25.00	11.00	3.10
COMMON CARD (1-400)	.10	.05	.01
SEMISTARS	.25	.11	.03
STARS	.50	.23	.06
COMP.F.THOMAS SET (6)	25.00	11.00	3.10

COMMON F.THOMAS (1-6)	5.00	2.20	.60
RANDOM INSERTS IN SER.2 PACKS			
□ 1 Frank Thomas	3.00	1.35	.35
□ 2 Carlos Garcia	.10	.05	.01
□ 3 Todd Hundley	.25	.11	.03
□ 4 Damion Easley	.10	.05	.01
□ 5 Roberto Mejia	.10	.05	.01
□ 6 John Mabry	.50	.23	.06
□ 7 Aaron Sele	.25	.11	.03
□ 8 Kenny Lofton	.75	.35	.09
□ 9 John Doherty	.10	.05	.01
□ 10 Joe Carter	.50	.23	.06
□ 11 Mike Lansing	.10	.05	.01
□ 12 John Valentin	.25	.11	.03
□ 13 Ismael Valdes	.25	.11	.03
□ 14 Dave McCarty	.10	.05	.01
□ 15 Melvin Nieves	.25	.11	.03
□ 16 Bobby Jones	.25	.11	.03
□ 17 Trevor Hoffman	.10	.05	.01
□ 18 John Smoltz	.50	.23	.06
□ 19 Leo Gomez	.10	.05	.01
□ 20 Roger Pavlik	.10	.05	.01
□ 21 Dean Palmer	.25	.11	.03
□ 22 Rickey Henderson	.50	.23	.06
□ 23 Eddie Taubensee	.10	.05	.01
□ 24 Damon Buford	.10	.05	.01
□ 25 Mark Wohlers	.25	.11	.03
□ 26 Jim Edmonds	.50	.23	.06
□ 27 Wilson Alvarez	.25	.11	.03
□ 28 Matt Williams	.50	.23	.06
□ 29 Jeff Montgomery	.25	.11	.03
□ 30 Shawon Dunston	.10	.05	.01
□ 31 Tom Pagnozzi	.10	.05	.01
□ 32 Jose Lind	.10	.05	.01
□ 33 Royce Clayton	.10	.05	.01
□ 34 Cal Eldred	.10	.05	.01
□ 35 Chris Gomez	.10	.05	.01
□ 36 Henry Rodriguez	.50	.23	.06
□ 37 Dave Fleming	.10	.05	.01
□ 38 Jon Lieber	.10	.05	.01
□ 39 Scott Servais	.10	.05	.01
□ 40 Wade Boggs	.50	.23	.06
□ 41 John Olerud	.10	.05	.01
□ 42 Eddie Williams	.10	.05	.01
□ 43 Paul Sorrento	.10	.05	.01
□ 44 Ron Karkovice	.10	.05	.01
□ 45 Kevin Foster	.10	.05	.01
□ 46 Miguel Jimenez	.10	.05	.01
□ 47 Reggie Sanders	.25	.11	.03
□ 48 Rondell White	.50	.23	.06
□ 49 Scott Leius	.10	.05	.01
□ 50 Jose Valentin	.25	.11	.03
□ 51 Wm. VanLandingham	.10	.05	.01
□ 52 Denny Hocking	.10	.05	.01
□ 53 Jeff Fassero	.10	.05	.01
□ 54 Chris Hoiles	.10	.05	.01
□ 55 Walt Weiss	.10	.05	.01
□ 56 Geronimo Berroa	.10	.05	.01
□ 57 Rich Rowland	.10	.05	.01
□ 58 Dave Weathers	.10	.05	.01
□ 59 Sterling Hitchcock	.25	.11	.03
□ 60 Raul Mondesi	.50	.23	.06
□ 61 Rusty Greer	.50	.23	.06
□ 62 David Justice	.50	.23	.06
□ 63 Cecil Fielder	.25	.11	.03
□ 64 Brian Jordan	.50	.23	.06
□ 65 Mike Lieberthal	.10	.05	.01
□ 66 Rick Aguilera	.10	.05	.01
□ 67 Chuck Finley	.25	.11	.03
□ 68 Andy Ashby	.25	.11	.03
□ 69 Alex Fernandez	.25	.11	.03
□ 70 Ed Sprague	.25	.11	.03
□ 71 Steve Buechele	.10	.05	.01
□ 72 Willie Greene	.10	.05	.01
□ 73 Dave Nilsson	.25	.11	.03
□ 74 Bret Saberhagen	.25	.11	.03
□ 75 Jimmy Key	.25	.11	.03
□ 76 Darren Lewis	.10	.05	.01
□ 77 Steve Cooke	.10	.05	.01
□ 78 Kirk Gibson	.25	.11	.03
□ 79 Ray Lankford	.50	.23	.06
□ 80 Paul O'Neill	.25	.11	.03
□ 81 Mike Bordick	.10	.05	.01
□ 82 Wes Chamberlain	.10	.05	.01
□ 83 Rico Brogna	.10	.05	.01
□ 84 Kevin Appier	.25	.11	.03
□ 85 Juan Guzman	.25	.11	.03
□ 86 Kevin Seitzer	.10	.05	.01
□ 87 Mickey Morandini	.10	.05	.01
□ 88 Pedro Martinez	.25	.11	.03
□ 89 Matt Mieske	.25	.11	.03
□ 90 Tino Martinez	.25	.11	.03
□ 91 Paul Shuey	.10	.05	.01
□ 92 Bip Roberts	.10	.05	.01
□ 93 Chili Davis	.25	.11	.03
□ 94 Deion Sanders	.50	.23	.06
□ 95 Darrell Whitmore	.10	.05	.01
□ 96 Joe Orsulak	.10	.05	.01
□ 97 Bret Boone	.25	.11	.03
□ 98 Kent Mercker	.10	.05	.01
□ 99 Scott Livingstone	.10	.05	.01
□ 100 Brady Anderson	.50	.23	.06
□ 101 James Mouton	.10	.05	.01
□ 102 Jose Rijo	.10	.05	.01
□ 103 Bobby Munoz	.10	.05	.01
□ 104 Ramon Martinez	.25	.11	.03
□ 105 Bernie Williams	.50	.23	.06
□ 106 Troy Neel	.10	.05	.01
□ 107 Ivan Rodriguez	.60	.25	.07
□ 108 Salomon Torres	.10	.05	.01
□ 109 Johnny Ruffin	.10	.05	.01
□ 110 Darryl Kile	.10	.05	.01
□ 111 Bobby Ayala	.10	.05	.01
□ 112 Ron Darling	.10	.05	.01
□ 113 Jose Lima	.10	.05	.01
□ 114 Joey Hamilton	.25	.11	.03
□ 115 Greg Maddux	2.00	.90	.25
□ 116 Greg Colbrunn	.10	.05	.01
□ 117 Ozzie Guillen	.10	.05	.01
□ 118 Brian Anderson	.10	.05	.01
□ 119 Jeff Bagwell	1.25	.55	.16
□ 120 Pat Listach	.10	.05	.01
□ 121 Sandy Alomar Jr.	.10	.05	.01
□ 122 Jose Vizcaino	.10	.05	.01
□ 123 Rick Helling	.10	.05	.01
□ 124 Allen Watson	.10	.05	.01
□ 125 Pedro Munoz	.10	.05	.01
□ 126 Craig Biggio	.50	.23	.06
□ 127 Kevin Stocker	.10	.05	.01
□ 128 Wil Cordero	.10	.05	.01
□ 129 Rafael Palmeiro	.50	.23	.06
□ 130 Gar Finnvold	.10	.05	.01
□ 131 Darren Hall	.10	.05	.01
□ 132 Heath Slocumb	.10	.05	.01
□ 133 Darrin Fletcher	.10	.05	.01
□ 134 Cal Ripken	2.50	1.10	.30
□ 135 Dante Bichette	.50	.23	.06
□ 136 Don Slaught	.10	.05	.01
□ 137 Pedro Astacio	.10	.05	.01
□ 138 Ryan Thompson	.10	.05	.01
□ 139 Greg Gohr	.10	.05	.01
□ 140 Javier Lopez	.50	.23	.06
□ 141 Lenny Dykstra	.25	.11	.03
□ 142 Pat Rapp	.10	.05	.01
□ 143 Mark Kiefer	.10	.05	.01
□ 144 Greg Gagne	.10	.05	.01
□ 145 Eduardo Perez	.10	.05	.01
□ 146 Felix Fermin	.10	.05	.01
□ 147 Jeff Frye	.10	.05	.01
□ 148 Terry Steinbach	.25	.11	.03
□ 149 Jim Eisenreich	.10	.05	.01
□ 150 Brad Ausmus	.10	.05	.01
□ 151 Randy Myers	.10	.05	.01
□ 152 Rick White	.10	.05	.01
□ 153 Mark Portugal	.10	.05	.01
□ 154 Delino DeShields	.10	.05	.01
□ 155 Scott Cooper	.10	.05	.01
□ 156 Pat Hentgen	.25	.11	.03
□ 157 Mark Gubicza	.10	.05	.01
□ 158 Carlos Baerga	.50	.23	.06
□ 159 Joe Girardi	.10	.05	.01
□ 160 Rey Sanchez	.10	.05	.01
□ 161 Todd Jones	.10	.05	.01
□ 162 Luis Polonia	.10	.05	.01
□ 163 Steve Trachsel	.10	.05	.01
□ 164 Roberto Hernandez	.10	.05	.01
□ 165 John Patterson	.10	.05	.01
□ 166 Rene Arocha	.10	.05	.01
□ 167 Will Clark	.50	.23	.06
□ 168 Jim Leyritz	.10	.05	.01
□ 169 Todd Van Poppel	.10	.05	.01

☐ 170	Robb Nen	.10	.05	.01
☐ 171	Midre Cummings	.10	.05	.01
☐ 172	Jay Buhner	.50	.23	.06
☐ 173	Kevin Tapani	.10	.05	.01
☐ 174	Mark Lemke	.10	.05	.01
☐ 175	Marcus Moore	.10	.05	.01
☐ 176	Wayne Kirby	.10	.05	.01
☐ 177	Rich Amaral	.10	.05	.01
☐ 178	Lou Whitaker	.50	.23	.06
☐ 179	Jay Bell	.25	.11	.03
☐ 180	Rick Wilkins	.10	.05	.01
☐ 181	Paul Molitor	.60	.25	.07
☐ 182	Gary Sheffield	.50	.23	.06
☐ 183	Kirby Puckett	1.00	.45	.12
☐ 184	Cliff Floyd	.25	.11	.03
☐ 185	Darren Oliver	.25	.11	.03
☐ 186	Tim Naehring	.10	.05	.01
☐ 187	John Hudek	.10	.05	.01
☐ 188	Eric Young	.25	.11	.03
☐ 189	Roger Salkeld	.10	.05	.01
☐ 190	Kirt Manwaring	.10	.05	.01
☐ 191	Kurt Abbott	.10	.05	.01
☐ 192	David Nied	.10	.05	.01
☐ 193	Todd Zeile	.10	.05	.01
☐ 194	Wally Joyner	.25	.11	.03
☐ 195	Dennis Martinez	.25	.11	.03
☐ 196	Billy Ashley	.10	.05	.01
☐ 197	Ben McDonald	.10	.05	.01
☐ 198	Bob Hamelin	.10	.05	.01
☐ 199	Chris Turner	.10	.05	.01
☐ 200	Lance Johnson	.25	.11	.03
☐ 201	Willie Banks	.10	.05	.01
☐ 202	Juan Gonzalez	1.50	.70	.19
☐ 203	Scott Sanders	.10	.05	.01
☐ 204	Scott Brosius	.10	.05	.01
☐ 205	Curt Schilling	.10	.05	.01
☐ 206	Alex Gonzalez	.10	.05	.01
☐ 207	Travis Fryman	.25	.11	.03
☐ 208	Tim Raines	.50	.23	.06
☐ 209	Steve Avery	.25	.11	.03
☐ 210	Hal Morris	.10	.05	.01
☐ 211	Ken Griffey Jr.	3.00	1.35	.35
☐ 212	Ozzie Smith	.60	.25	.07
☐ 213	Chuck Carr	.10	.05	.01
☐ 214	Ryan Klesko	.60	.25	.07
☐ 215	Robin Ventura	.25	.11	.03
☐ 216	Luis Gonzalez	.10	.05	.01
☐ 217	Ken Ryan	.10	.05	.01
☐ 218	Mike Piazza	2.00	.90	.25
☐ 219	Matt Walbeck	.10	.05	.01
☐ 220	Jeff Kent	.10	.05	.01
☐ 221	Orlando Miller	.10	.05	.01
☐ 222	Kenny Rogers	.10	.05	.01
☐ 223	J.T. Snow	.25	.11	.03
☐ 224	Alan Trammell	.50	.23	.06
☐ 225	John Franco	.10	.05	.01
☐ 226	Gerald Williams	.10	.05	.01
☐ 227	Andy Benes	.10	.05	.01
☐ 228	Dan Wilson	.25	.11	.03
☐ 229	Dave Hollins	.10	.05	.01
☐ 230	Vinny Castilla	.25	.11	.03
☐ 231	Devon White	.25	.11	.03
☐ 232	Fred McGriff	.50	.23	.06
☐ 233	Quilvio Veras	.10	.05	.01
☐ 234	Tom Candiotti	.10	.05	.01
☐ 235	Jason Bere	.10	.05	.01
☐ 236	Mark Langston	.10	.05	.01
☐ 237	Mel Rojas	.10	.05	.01
☐ 238	Chuck Knoblauch	.50	.23	.06
☐ 239	Bernard Gilkey	.25	.11	.03
☐ 240	Mark McGwire	1.00	.45	.12
☐ 241	Kirk Rueter	.10	.05	.01
☐ 242	Pat Kelly	.10	.05	.01
☐ 243	Ruben Sierra	.25	.11	.03
☐ 244	Randy Johnson	.50	.23	.06
☐ 245	Shane Reynolds	.10	.05	.01
☐ 246	Danny Tartabull	.10	.05	.01
☐ 247	Darryl Hamilton	.10	.05	.01
☐ 248	Danny Bautista	.10	.05	.01
☐ 249	Tom Gordon	.10	.05	.01
☐ 250	Tom Glavine	.50	.23	.06
☐ 251	Orlando Merced	.10	.05	.01
☐ 252	Eric Karros	.25	.11	.03
☐ 253	Benji Gil	.10	.05	.01
☐ 254	Sean Bergman	.10	.05	.01
☐ 255	Roger Clemens	.50	.23	.06

☐ 256	Roberto Alomar	.75	.35	.09
☐ 257	Benito Santiago	.10	.05	.01
☐ 258	Robby Thompson	.10	.05	.01
☐ 259	Marvin Freeman	.10	.05	.01
☐ 260	Jose Offerman	.10	.05	.01
☐ 261	Greg Vaughn	.25	.11	.03
☐ 262	David Segui	.10	.05	.01
☐ 263	Geronimo Pena	.10	.05	.01
☐ 264	Tim Salmon	.50	.23	.06
☐ 265	Eddie Murray	.75	.35	.09
☐ 266	Mariano Duncan	.10	.05	.01
☐ 267	Hideo Nomo	3.00	1.35	.35
☐ 268	Derek Bell	.25	.11	.03
☐ 269	Mo Vaughn	.75	.35	.09
☐ 270	Jeff King	.25	.11	.03
☐ 271	Edgar Martinez	.50	.23	.06
☐ 272	Sammy Sosa	.50	.23	.06
☐ 273	Scott Ruffcorn	.10	.05	.01
☐ 274	Darren Daulton	.25	.11	.03
☐ 275	John Jaha	.25	.11	.03
☐ 276	Andres Galarraga	.50	.23	.06
☐ 277	Mark Grace	.50	.23	.06
☐ 278	Mike Moore	.10	.05	.01
☐ 279	Barry Bonds	.75	.35	.09
☐ 280	Manny Ramirez	.75	.35	.09
☐ 281	Ellis Burks	.50	.23	.06
☐ 282	Greg Swindell	.10	.05	.01
☐ 283	Barry Larkin	.50	.23	.06
☐ 284	Albert Belle	1.50	.70	.19
☐ 285	Shawn Green	.25	.11	.03
☐ 286	John Roper	.10	.05	.01
☐ 287	Scott Erickson	.10	.05	.01
☐ 288	Moises Alou	.25	.11	.03
☐ 289	Mike Blowers	.10	.05	.01
☐ 290	Brent Gates	.10	.05	.01
☐ 291	Sean Berry	.10	.05	.01
☐ 292	Mike Stanley	.10	.05	.01
☐ 293	Jeff Conine	.50	.23	.06
☐ 294	Tim Wallach	.10	.05	.01
☐ 295	Bobby Bonilla	.25	.11	.03
☐ 296	Bruce Ruffin	.10	.05	.01
☐ 297	Chad Curtis	.10	.05	.01
☐ 298	Mike Greenwell	.10	.05	.01
☐ 299	Tony Gwynn	1.25	.55	.16
☐ 300	Russ Davis	.10	.05	.01
☐ 301	Danny Jackson	.10	.05	.01
☐ 302	Pete Harnisch	.10	.05	.01
☐ 303	Don Mattingly	1.50	.70	.19
☐ 304	Rheal Cormier	.10	.05	.01
☐ 305	Larry Walker	.50	.23	.06
☐ 306	Hector Carrasco	.10	.05	.01
☐ 307	Jason Jacome	.10	.05	.01
☐ 308	Phil Plantier	.10	.05	.01
☐ 309	Harold Baines	.25	.11	.03
☐ 310	Mitch Williams	.10	.05	.01
☐ 311	Charles Nagy	.25	.11	.03
☐ 312	Ken Caminiti	.50	.23	.06
☐ 313	Alex Rodriguez	4.00	1.80	.50
☐ 314	Chris Sabo	.10	.05	.01
☐ 315	Gary Gaetti	.25	.11	.03
☐ 316	Andre Dawson	.50	.23	.06
☐ 317	Mark Clark	.10	.05	.01
☐ 318	Vince Coleman	.10	.05	.01
☐ 319	Brad Clontz	.10	.05	.01
☐ 320	Steve Finley	.25	.11	.03
☐ 321	Doug Drabek	.10	.05	.01
☐ 322	Mark McLemore	.10	.05	.01
☐ 323	Stan Javier	.10	.05	.01
☐ 324	Ron Gant	.25	.11	.03
☐ 325	Charlie Hayes	.10	.05	.01
☐ 326	Carlos Delgado	.50	.23	.06
☐ 327	Ricky Bottalico	.25	.11	.03
☐ 328	Rod Beck	.10	.05	.01
☐ 329	Mark Acre	.10	.05	.01
☐ 330	Chris Bosio	.10	.05	.01
☐ 331	Tony Phillips	.25	.11	.03
☐ 332	Garret Anderson	.50	.23	.06
☐ 333	Pat Meares	.10	.05	.01
☐ 334	Todd Worrell	.10	.05	.01
☐ 335	Marquis Grissom	.50	.23	.06
☐ 336	Brent Mayne	.10	.05	.01
☐ 337	Lee Tinsley	.10	.05	.01
☐ 338	Terry Pendleton	.25	.11	.03
☐ 339	David Cone	.25	.11	.03
☐ 340	Tony Fernandez	.10	.05	.01
☐ 341	Jim Bullinger	.10	.05	.01

□ 342 Armando Benitez	.10	.05	.01
□ 343 John Smiley	.10	.05	.01
□ 344 Dan Miceli	.10	.05	.01
□ 345 Charles Johnson	.25	.11	.03
□ 346 Lee Smith	.25	.11	.03
□ 347 Brian McRae	.25	.11	.03
□ 348 Jim Thome	.60	.25	.07
□ 349 Jose Oliva	.10	.05	.01
□ 350 Terry Mulholland	.10	.05	.01
□ 351 Tom Henke	.10	.05	.01
□ 352 Dennis Eckersley	.25	.11	.03
□ 353 Sid Fernandez	.10	.05	.01
□ 354 Paul Wagner	.10	.05	.01
□ 355 John Dettmer	.10	.05	.01
□ 356 John Wetteland	.25	.11	.03
□ 357 John Burkett	.25	.11	.03
□ 358 Marty Cordova	.50	.23	.06
□ 359 Norm Charlton	.10	.05	.01
□ 360 Mike Devereaux	.10	.05	.01
□ 361 Alex Cole	.10	.05	.01
□ 362 Brett Butler	.25	.11	.03
□ 363 Mickey Tettleton	.10	.05	.01
□ 364 Al Martin	.25	.11	.03
□ 365 Tony Tarasco	.10	.05	.01
□ 366 Pat Mahomes	.10	.05	.01
□ 367 Gary DiSarcina	.10	.05	.01
□ 368 Bill Swift	.10	.05	.01
□ 369 Chipper Jones	2.00	.90	.25
□ 370 Orel Hershiser	.25	.11	.03
□ 371 Kevin Gross	.10	.05	.01
□ 372 Dave Winfield	.50	.23	.06
□ 373 Andujar Cedeno	.10	.05	.01
□ 374 Jim Abbott	.10	.05	.01
□ 375 Glenallen Hill	.10	.05	.01
□ 376 Otis Nixon	.10	.05	.01
□ 377 Roberto Kelly	.10	.05	.01
□ 378 Chris Hammond	.10	.05	.01
□ 379 Mike Macfarlane	.10	.05	.01
□ 380 J.R. Phillips	.10	.05	.01
□ 381 Luis Alicea	.10	.05	.01
□ 382 Bret Barberie	.10	.05	.01
□ 383 Tom Goodwin	.10	.05	.01
□ 384 Mark Whiten	.10	.05	.01
□ 385 Jeffrey Hammonds	.25	.11	.03
□ 386 Omar Vizquel	.50	.23	.06
□ 387 Mike Mussina	.60	.25	.07
□ 388 Ricky Bones	.10	.05	.01
□ 389 Steve Ontiveros	.10	.05	.01
□ 390 Jeff Blauser	.10	.05	.01
□ 391 Jose Canseco	.50	.23	.06
□ 392 Bob Tewksbury	.10	.05	.01
□ 393 Jacob Brumfield	.10	.05	.01
□ 394 Doug Jones	.10	.05	.01
□ 395 Ken Hill	.10	.05	.01
□ 396 Pat Borders	.10	.05	.01
□ 397 Carl Everett	.10	.05	.01
□ 398 Gregg Jefferies	.25	.11	.03
□ 399 Jack McDowell	.25	.11	.03
□ 400 Denny Neagle	.25	.11	.03

1995 Leaf 300 Club

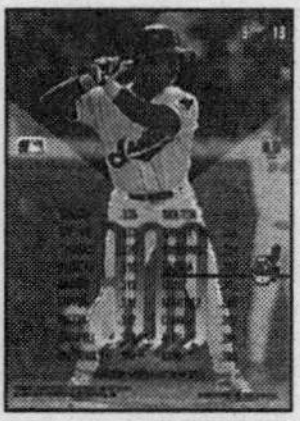

Randomly inserted in first and second series mini and retail packs on a three per box basis, this set depicts all 18 players who had a career average of .300 or better entering the 1995 campaign. A large ghosted 300 serves as background to a player photo. Gold foil is at the bottom in either corner including career average in the right corner. Full-bleed backs list the 18 players and their averages to that point.

	MINT	NRMT	EXC
COMPLETE SET (18)	125.00	55.00	15.50
COMPLETE SERIES 1 (9)	50.00	22.00	6.25
COMPLETE SERIES 2 (9)	75.00	34.00	9.50
COMMON CARD (1-18)	2.00	.90	.25
SEMISTARS	4.00	1.80	.50
RANDOM INSERTS IN MAG.JUMBO AND RETAIL PACKS			

□ 1 Frank Thomas	30.00	13.50	3.70
□ 2 Paul Molitor	6.00	2.70	.75
□ 3 Mike Piazza	20.00	9.00	2.50
□ 4 Moises Alou	2.00	.90	.25
□ 5 Mike Greenwell	2.00	.90	.25
□ 6 Will Clark	4.00	1.80	.50
□ 7 Hal Morris	2.00	.90	.25
□ 8 Edgar Martinez	4.00	1.80	.50
□ 9 Carlos Baerga	4.00	1.80	.50
□ 10 Ken Griffey Jr.	30.00	13.50	3.70
□ 11 Wade Boggs	4.00	1.80	.50
□ 12 Jeff Bagwell	12.00	5.50	1.50
□ 13 Tony Gwynn	12.00	5.50	1.50
□ 14 John Kruk	2.00	.90	.25
□ 15 Don Mattingly	15.00	6.75	1.85
□ 16 Mark Grace	4.00	1.80	.50
□ 17 Kirby Puckett	10.00	4.50	1.25
□ 18 Kenny Lofton	8.00	3.60	1.00

1995 Leaf Checklists

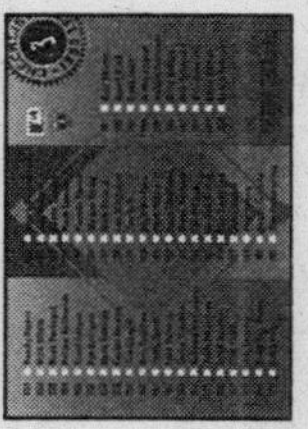

Four checklist cards were randomly inserted in either series for a total of eight standard-size cards. Horizontal fronts feature a player photo from left to center with the start of the checklist to the right which continues on the back.

	MINT	NRMT	EXC
COMPLETE SET (8)	8.00	3.60	1.00
COMPLETE SERIES 1 (4)	4.00	1.80	.50
COMPLETE SERIES 2 (4)	4.00	1.80	.50
COMMON CARD (1-8)	.50	.23	.06
RANDOM INSERTS IN PACKS			

□ 1 Bob Hamelin UER (Name spelled Hamlin)	.50	.23	.06
□ 2 David Cone	.75	.35	.09
□ 3 Frank Thomas	3.00	1.35	.35
□ 4 Paul O'Neill	.75	.35	.09
□ 5 Raul Mondesi	.75	.35	.09
□ 6 Greg Maddux	2.00	.90	.25
□ 7 Tony Gwynn	1.25	.55	.16
□ 8 Jeff Bagwell	1.25	.55	.16

1995 Leaf Cornerstones

Cards from this six-card standard-size set were randomly inserted in first series packs. Horizontally designed, leading first and thrid basemen from the same team are featured. The fronts have silver foil borders and team names with the team logo serving as background to the photos.The backs have a photo of either player with offensive and defensive stats.

	MINT	NRMT	EXC
COMPLETE SET (6)	10.00	4.50	1.25
COMMON CARD (1-6)	1.00	.45	.12
RANDOM INSERTS IN SERIES 1 PACKS			

	MINT	NRMT	EXC
□ 1 Frank Thomas / Robin Ventura	6.00	2.70	.75
□ 2 Cecil Fielder / Travis Fryman	1.50	.70	.19
□ 3 Don Mattingly / Wade Boggs	3.00	1.35	.35
□ 4 Jeff Bagwell / Ken Caminiti	2.50	1.10	.30
□ 5 Will Clark / Dean Palmer	1.50	.70	.19
□ 6 J.R. Phillips / Matt Williams	1.00	.45	.12

1995 Leaf Gold Rookies

Inserted in every other first series pack, this 16-card standard-size set showcases those that were expected to have an impact in 1995. Card fronts offer two photos with various gold foil ornamentation. The backs have a large black and white photo with a smaller color photo inset at top left. The backs also contain career minor league stats.

	MINT	NRMT	EXC
COMPLETE SET (16)	6.00	2.70	.75
COMMON CARD (1-16)	.25	.11	.03
SEMISTARS	.75	.35	.09
RANDOM INSERTS IN SER.1 PACKS			

	MINT	NRMT	EXC
□ 1 Alex Rodriguez	5.00	2.20	.60
□ 2 Garret Anderson	.75	.35	.09
□ 3 Shawn Green	.75	.35	.09
□ 4 Armando Benitez	.25	.11	.03
□ 5 Darren Dreifort	.25	.11	.03
□ 6 Orlando Miller	.75	.35	.09
□ 7 Jose Oliva	.25	.11	.03
□ 8 Ricky Bottalico	.75	.35	.09
□ 9 Charles Johnson	.75	.35	.09
□ 10 Brian L.Hunter	.75	.35	.09
□ 11 Ray McDavid	.25	.11	.03
□ 12 Chan Ho Park	.75	.35	.09
□ 13 Mike Kelly	.25	.11	.03
□ 14 Cory Bailey	.25	.11	.03
□ 15 Alex Gonzalez	.75	.35	.09
□ 16 Andrew Lorraine	.25	.11	.03

1995 Leaf Gold Stars

Randomly inserted in first and second series packs at a rate of one in 110, this 14-card standard-size set (eight first series, six second series) showcases some of the game's superstars.Individually numbered on back out of 10,000, the cards feature fronts that have a player photo superimposed metallic, refractive background. A die-cut star is in the lower left corner. The backs have a small player photo and brief write-up in addition to the numbering.

	MINT	NRMT	EXC
COMPLETE SET (14)	300.00	135.00	38.00
COMPLETE SERIES 1 (8)	150.00	70.00	19.00
COMPLETE SERIES 2 (6)	150.00	70.00	19.00
COMMON CARD (1-14)	8.00	3.60	1.00
RANDOM INSERTS IN PACKS			

	MINT	NRMT	EXC
□ 1 Jeff Bagwell	20.00	9.00	2.50
□ 2 Albert Belle	25.00	11.00	3.10
□ 3 Tony Gwynn	20.00	9.00	2.50
□ 4 Ken Griffey Jr.	50.00	22.00	6.25
□ 5 Barry Bonds	12.00	5.50	1.50
□ 6 Don Mattingly	25.00	11.00	3.10
□ 7 Raul Mondesi	8.00	3.60	1.00
□ 8 Joe Carter	8.00	3.60	1.00
□ 9 Greg Maddux	35.00	16.00	4.40
□ 10 Frank Thomas	50.00	22.00	6.25
□ 11 Mike Piazza	30.00	13.50	3.70
□ 12 Jose Canseco	8.00	3.60	1.00
□ 13 Kirby Puckett	15.00	6.75	1.85
□ 14 Matt Williams	8.00	3.60	1.00

1995 Leaf Great Gloves

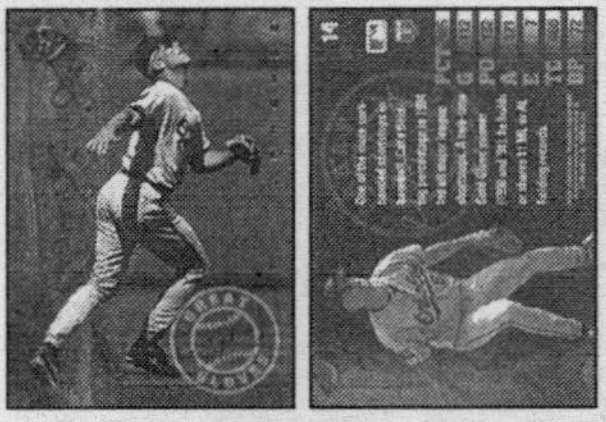

This 16-card standard-size set was randomly inserted in series two packs at a rate of approximately two cards every three packs. The players featured are leading defensive players. Action photos are set against a background that includes part of a glove. The player's name and team are stamped in gold foil. The horizontal backs feature a photo set against a glove, information about the player and their 1994 defensive statistics. The cards are numbered "X" of 16 in the upper right.

	MINT	NRMT	EXC
COMPLETE SET (16)	10.00	4.50	1.25
COMMON CARD (1-16)	.25	.11	.03
RANDOM INSERTS IN PACKS			
□ 1 Jeff Bagwell	1.25	.55	.16
□ 2 Roberto Alomar	.75	.35	.09
□ 3 Barry Bonds	.75	.35	.09
□ 4 Wade Boggs	.25	.11	.03
□ 5 Andres Galarraga	.25	.11	.03
□ 6 Ken Griffey Jr.	3.00	1.35	.35
□ 7 Marquis Grissom	.25	.11	.03
□ 8 Kenny Lofton	.75	.35	.09
□ 9 Barry Larkin	.25	.11	.03
□ 10 Don Mattingly	1.50	.70	.19
□ 11 Greg Maddux	2.00	.90	.25
□ 12 Kirby Puckett	1.00	.45	.12
□ 13 Ozzie Smith	.60	.25	.07
□ 14 Cal Ripken Jr.	2.50	1.10	.30
□ 15 Matt Williams	.25	.11	.03
□ 16 Ivan Rodriguez	.60	.25	.07

1995 Leaf Heading for the Hall

This eight-card standard-size set was randomly inserted into series two hobby packs. The cards are cut in the shape of a Hall of Fame plaque and are designed as if this were the actual information on the playerís plaque in Cooperstown. The backs feature a black and white photo along with career statistics. The cards are individually numbered out of 5,000 as well.

	MINT	NRMT	EXC
COMPLETE SET (8)	300.00	135.00	38.00
COMMON CARD (1-8)	15.00	6.75	1.85
RANDOM INSERTS IN SER.2 HOBBY PACKS			
□ 1 Frank Thomas	80.00	36.00	10.00
□ 2 Ken Griffey Jr.	80.00	36.00	10.00
□ 3 Jeff Bagwell	30.00	13.50	3.70
□ 4 Barry Bonds	20.00	9.00	2.50
□ 5 Kirby Puckett	25.00	11.00	3.10
□ 6 Cal Ripken	60.00	27.00	7.50
□ 7 Tony Gwynn	30.00	13.50	3.70
□ 8 Paul Molitor	15.00	6.75	1.85

1995 Leaf Slideshow

This 16-card standard-size set was issued eight per series and randomly inserted at a rate of per box. The eight cards in the first series are numbered 1A-8A and repeated with different photos in the second series as 1B-8B. Both version carry the same value. The left side of the card front is semi-circular featuring three player translucent "slides".

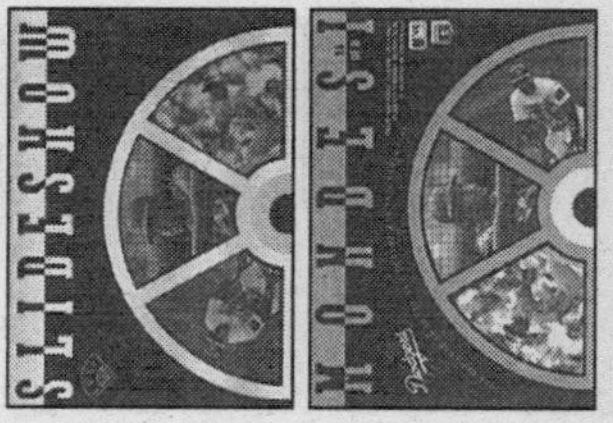

	MINT	NRMT	EXC
COMPLETE SET (16)	80.00	36.00	10.00
COMPLETE SERIES 1 (8)	40.00	18.00	5.00
COMPLETE SERIES 2 (8)	40.00	18.00	5.00
COMMON CARD (1-8)	2.00	.90	.25
SERIES 1 AND 2 CARDS SAME VALUE			
SER.1 HAVE SUFFIX A/SER.2 HAVE SUFFIX B			
RANDOM INSERTS IN PACKS			
□ 1 Raul Mondesi	2.00	.90	.25
□ 2 Frank Thomas	15.00	6.75	1.85
□ 3 Fred McGriff	4.00	1.80	.50
□ 4 Cal Ripken	12.00	5.50	1.50
□ 5 Jeff Bagwell	6.00	2.70	.75
□ 6 Will Clark	4.00	1.80	.50
□ 7 Matt Williams	4.00	1.80	.50
□ 8 Ken Griffey Jr.	15.00	6.75	1.85

1995 Leaf Statistical Standouts

Randomly inserted in first series hobby packs at a rate of one in 70, this set features nine players who stood out from the rest statistically. The fronts contain a player photo between embossed seams or stitches of a baseball. The backs have a small circular player photo with 1994 highlights.

	MINT	NRMT	EXC
COMPLETE SET (9)	450.00	200.00	55.00
COMMON CARD (1-9)	15.00	6.75	1.85
RANDOM INSERTS IN SER.1 HOBBY PACKS			
□ 1 Joe Carter	15.00	6.75	1.85
□ 2 Ken Griffey Jr.	125.00	55.00	15.50
□ 3 Don Mattingly	60.00	27.00	7.50
□ 4 Fred McGriff	15.00	6.75	1.85
□ 5 Paul Molitor	25.00	11.00	3.10
□ 6 Kirby Puckett	40.00	18.00	5.00
□ 7 Cal Ripken	100.00	45.00	12.50
□ 8 Frank Thomas	125.00	55.00	15.50
□ 9 Matt Williams	15.00	6.75	1.85

1996 Leaf

The 1996 Leaf set was issued in one series totalling 220 cards. The fronts feature color action player photos with silver foil printing and lines forming a border on the left and bottom. The backs display another player photo with 1995 season and career statistics. Card num-

ber 210 is a checklist for the insert sets and cards number 211-220 feature rookies. The fronts of these 10 cards are different in design from the first 200 with a color action player cut-out over a green-shadow background of the same picture and gold lettering. The horizontal backs carry another player cut-out on a purple-and-black background with 1995 season statistics and personal information.

	MINT	NRMT	EXC
COMPLETE SET (220)	15.00	6.75	1.85
COMMON CARD (1-220)	.10	.05	.01
SEMISTARS	.25	.11	.03
STARS	.50	.23	.06
COMP.F.THOMAS SET (8)	150.00	70.00	19.00
COMMON F.THOMAS (1-7)	25.00	11.00	3.10
COMMON THOMAS EXCH. (8)	30.00	13.50	3.70

THOMAS: 1-4 RANDOM INSERTS IN HOBBY PACKS
THOMAS: 5-7 RANDOM INSERTS IN RETAIL PACKS
THOMAS: CARD 8 AVAILABLE VIA MAIL OFFER

□ 1 John Smoltz	.50	.23	.06
□ 2 Dennis Eckersley	.50	.23	.06
□ 3 Delino DeShields	.10	.05	.01
□ 4 Cliff Floyd	.10	.05	.01
□ 5 Chuck Finley	.10	.05	.01
□ 6 Cecil Fielder	.50	.23	.06
□ 7 Tim Naehring	.10	.05	.01
□ 8 Carlos Perez	.10	.05	.01
□ 9 Brad Ausmus	.10	.05	.01
□ 10 Matt Lawton	.10	.05	.01
□ 11 Alan Trammell	.50	.23	.06
□ 12 Steve Finley	.50	.23	.06
□ 13 Paul O'Neill	.10	.05	.01
□ 14 Gary Sheffield	.50	.23	.06
□ 15 Mark McGwire	1.00	.45	.12
□ 16 Bernie Williams	.50	.23	.06
□ 17 Jeff Montgomery	.10	.05	.01
□ 18 Chan Ho Park	.50	.23	.06
□ 19 Greg Vaughn	.50	.23	.06
□ 20 Jeff Kent	.10	.05	.01
□ 21 Cal Ripken	2.50	1.10	.30
□ 22 Charles Johnson	.25	.11	.03
□ 23 Eric Karros	.50	.23	.06
□ 24 Alex Rodriguez	3.00	1.35	.35
□ 25 Chris Snopek	.10	.05	.01
□ 26 Jason Isringhausen	.25	.11	.03
□ 27 Chili Davis	.10	.05	.01
□ 28 Chipper Jones	2.00	.90	.25
□ 29 Bret Saberhagen	.10	.05	.01
□ 30 Tony Clark	.50	.23	.06
□ 31 Marty Cordova	.50	.23	.06
□ 32 Dwayne Hosey	.10	.05	.01
□ 33 Fred McGriff	.50	.23	.06
□ 34 Deion Sanders	.50	.23	.06
□ 35 Orlando Merced	.10	.05	.01
□ 36 Brady Anderson	.50	.23	.06
□ 37 Ray Lankford	.50	.23	.06
□ 38 Manny Ramirez	.75	.35	.09
□ 39 Alex Fernandez	.50	.23	.06
□ 40 Greg Colbrunn	.10	.05	.01
□ 41 Ken Griffey, Jr.	3.00	1.35	.35
□ 42 Mickey Moradini	.10	.05	.01
□ 43 Chuck Knoblauch	.50	.23	.06
□ 44 Quinton McCracken	.10	.05	.01
□ 45 Tim Salmon	.50	.23	.06
□ 46 Jose Mesa	.25	.11	.03
□ 47 Marquis Grissom	.50	.23	.06
□ 48 Checklist	.10	.05	.01
□ 49 Raul Mondesi	.50	.23	.06
□ 50 Mark Grudzielanek	.25	.11	.03
□ 51 Ray Durham	.50	.23	.06
□ 52 Matt Williams	.50	.23	.06
□ 53 Bob Hamelin	.10	.05	.01
□ 54 Lenny Dykstra	.25	.11	.03
□ 55 Jeff King	.25	.11	.03
□ 56 LaTroy Hawkins	.10	.05	.01
□ 57 Terry Pendleton	.10	.05	.01
□ 58 Kevin Stocker	.10	.05	.01
□ 59 Ozzie Timmons	.10	.05	.01
□ 60 David Justice	.25	.11	.03
□ 61 Ricky Bottalico	.10	.05	.01
□ 62 Andy Ashby	.10	.05	.01
□ 63 Larry Walker	.50	.23	.06
□ 64 Jose Canseco	.50	.23	.06
□ 65 Bret Boone	.10	.05	.01
□ 66 Shawn Green	.10	.05	.01
□ 67 Chad Curtis	.10	.05	.01
□ 68 Travis Fryman	.50	.23	.06
□ 69 Roger Clemens	.50	.23	.06
□ 70 David Bell	.10	.05	.01
□ 71 Rusty Greer	.50	.23	.06
□ 72 Bob Higginson	.50	.23	.06
□ 73 Joey Hamilton	.25	.11	.03
□ 74 Kevin Seitzer	.10	.05	.01
□ 75 Julian Tavarez	.10	.05	.01
□ 76 Troy Percival	.10	.05	.01
□ 77 Kirby Puckett	1.00	.45	.12
□ 78 Barry Bonds	.75	.35	.09
□ 79 Michael Tucker	.25	.11	.03
□ 80 Paul Molitor	.60	.25	.07
□ 81 Carlos Garcia	.10	.05	.01
□ 82 Johnny Damon	.50	.23	.06
□ 83 Mike Hampton	.10	.05	.01
□ 84 Ariel Prieto	.10	.05	.01
□ 85 Tony Tarasco	.10	.05	.01
□ 86 Pete Schourek	.25	.11	.03
□ 87 Tom Glavine	.50	.23	.06
□ 88 Rondell White	.50	.23	.06
□ 89 Jim Edmonds	.50	.23	.06
□ 90 Robby Thompson	.10	.05	.01
□ 91 Wade Boggs	.50	.23	.06
□ 92 Pedro Martinez	.10	.05	.01
□ 93 Gregg Jefferies	.50	.23	.06
□ 94 Albert Belle	1.50	.70	.19
□ 95 Benji Gil	.10	.05	.01
□ 96 Denny Neagle	.25	.11	.03
□ 97 Mark Langston	.10	.05	.01
□ 98 Sandy Alomar, Jr.	.10	.05	.01
□ 99 Tony Gwynn	1.25	.55	.16
□ 100 Todd Hundley	.50	.23	.06
□ 101 Dante Bichette	.50	.23	.06
□ 102 Eddie Murray	.75	.35	.09
□ 103 Lyle Mouton	.10	.05	.01
□ 104 John Jaha	.10	.05	.01
□ 105 Checklist	.10	.05	.01
□ 106 Jon Nunnally	.10	.05	.01
□ 107 Juan Gonzalez	1.50	.70	.19
□ 108 Kevin Appier	.25	.11	.03
□ 109 Brian McRae	.10	.05	.01
□ 110 Lee Smith	.50	.23	.06
□ 111 Tim Wakefield	.10	.05	.01
□ 112 Sammy Sosa	.50	.23	.06
□ 113 Jay Buhner	.50	.23	.06
□ 114 Garret Anderson	.50	.23	.06
□ 115 Edgar Martinez	.50	.23	.06
□ 116 Edgardo Alfonzo	.25	.11	.03
□ 117 Billy Ashley	.10	.05	.01
□ 118 Joe Carter	.50	.23	.06
□ 119 Javy Lopez	.50	.23	.06
□ 120 Bobby Bonilla	.50	.23	.06
□ 121 Ken Caminiti	.50	.23	.06
□ 122 Barry Larkin	.50	.23	.06
□ 123 Shannon Stewart	.10	.05	.01
□ 124 Orel Hershiser	.25	.11	.03
□ 125 Jeff Conine	.50	.23	.06
□ 126 Mark Grace	.50	.23	.06
□ 127 Kenny Lofton	.75	.35	.09
□ 128 Luis Gonzalez	.10	.05	.01
□ 129 Rico Brogna	.10	.05	.01
□ 130 Mo Vaughn	.75	.35	.09
□ 131 Brad Radke	.10	.05	.01
□ 132 Jose Herrera	.10	.05	.01
□ 133 Rick Aguilera	.10	.05	.01
□ 134 Gary DiSarcina	.10	.05	.01

□ 135 Andres Galarraga	.50	.23	.06
□ 136 Carl Everett	.10	.05	.01
□ 137 Steve Avery	.25	.11	.03
□ 138 Vinny Castilla	.50	.23	.06
□ 139 Dennis Martinez	.25	.11	.03
□ 140 John Wetteland	.25	.11	.03
□ 141 Alex Gonzalez	.10	.05	.01
□ 142 Brian Jordan	.50	.23	.06
□ 143 Todd Hollandsworth	.50	.23	.06
□ 144 Terrell Wade	.50	.23	.06
□ 145 Wilson Alvarez	.50	.23	.06
□ 146 Reggie Sanders	.50	.23	.06
□ 147 Will Clark	.50	.23	.06
□ 148 Hideo Nomo	.75	.35	.09
□ 149 J.T.Snow	.25	.11	.03
□ 150 Frank Thomas	3.00	1.35	.35
□ 151 Ivan Rodriguez	.60	.25	.07
□ 152 Jay Bell	.25	.11	.03
□ 153 Checklist	.10	.05	.01
□ 154 David Cone	.50	.23	.06
□ 155 Roberto Alomar	.75	.35	.09
□ 156 Carlos Delgado	.50	.23	.06
□ 157 Carlos Baerga	.50	.23	.06
□ 158 Geronimo Berroa	.25	.11	.03
□ 159 Joe Vitiello	.10	.05	.01
□ 160 Terry Steinbach	.25	.11	.03
□ 161 Doug Drabek	.10	.05	.01
□ 162 David Segui	.10	.05	.01
□ 163 Ozzie Smith	.60	.25	.07
□ 164 Kurt Abbott	.10	.05	.01
□ 165 Randy Johnson	.50	.23	.06
□ 166 John Valentin	.25	.11	.03
□ 167 Mickey Tettleton	.25	.11	.03
□ 168 Ruben Sierra	.10	.05	.01
□ 169 Jim Thome	.60	.25	.07
□ 170 Mike Greenwell	.10	.05	.01
□ 171 Quilvio Veras	.10	.05	.01
□ 172 Robin Ventura	.25	.11	.03
□ 173 Bill Pulsipher	.25	.11	.03
□ 174 Rafael Palmeiro	.50	.23	.06
□ 175 Hal Morris	.10	.05	.01
□ 176 Ryan Klesko	.60	.25	.07
□ 177 Eric Young	.10	.05	.01
□ 178 Shane Andrews	.10	.05	.01
□ 179 Brian L.Hunter	.10	.05	.01
□ 180 Brett Butler	.10	.05	.01
□ 181 John Olerud	.10	.05	.01
□ 182 Moises Alou	.25	.11	.03
□ 183 Glenallen Hill	.10	.05	.01
□ 184 Ismael Valdes	.25	.11	.03
□ 185 Andy Pettitte	1.00	.45	.12
□ 186 Yamil Benitez	.10	.05	.01
□ 187 Jason Bere	.10	.05	.01
□ 188 Dean Palmer	.25	.11	.03
□ 189 Jimmy Haynes	.10	.05	.01
□ 190 Trevor Hoffman	.25	.11	.03
□ 191 Mike Mussina	.60	.25	.07
□ 192 Greg Maddux	2.00	.90	.25
□ 193 Ozzie Guillen	.10	.05	.01
□ 194 Pat Listach	.10	.05	.01
□ 195 Derek Bell	.25	.11	.03
□ 196 Darren Daulton	.25	.11	.03
□ 197 John Mabry	.50	.23	.06
□ 198 Ramon Martinez	.50	.23	.06
□ 199 Jeff Bagwell	1.25	.55	.16
□ 200 Mike Piazza	2.00	.90	.25
□ 201 Al Martin	.10	.05	.01
□ 202 Aaron Sele	.10	.05	.01
□ 203 Ed Sprague	.25	.11	.03
□ 204 Rod Beck	.25	.11	.03
□ 205 Checklist	.10	.05	.01
□ 206 Mike Lansing	.10	.05	.01
□ 207 Craig Biggio	.50	.23	.06
□ 208 Jeffrey Hammonds	.10	.05	.01
□ 209 Dave Nilsson	.25	.11	.03
□ 210 Checklist	.10	.05	.01
□ 211 Derek Jeter	2.00	.90	.25
□ 212 Alan Benes	.50	.23	.06
□ 213 Jason Schmidt	.25	.11	.03
□ 214 Alex Ochoa	.25	.11	.03
□ 215 Ruben Rivera	.60	.25	.07
□ 216 Roger Cedeno	.25	.11	.03
□ 217 Jeff Suppan	.25	.11	.03
□ 218 Billy Wagner	.10	.05	.01
□ 219 Mark Loretta	.10	.05	.01
□ 220 Karim Garcia	.60	.25	.07

1996 Leaf Press Proofs

This 220-card set is parallel to the regular Leaf set and between the three types of press proofs were inserted at a rate of one in 10 packs. Similar in design to the regular set, 2,000 bronze cards were produced and feature a special holographic foil.

	MINT	NRMT	EXC
COMP.BRONZE SET (220)	750.00	350.00	95.00
COMMON BRONZE (1-220)	1.00	.45	.12
BRONZE SEMISTARS	2.50	1.10	.30
BRONZE STARS	5.00	2.20	.60
*SILVER: 2X BRONZE			
*GOLD: 5X BRONZE			
RANDOM INSERTS IN PACKS			
BRONZE CARDS LISTED BELOW			
□ 1 John Smoltz	6.00	2.70	.75
□ 14 Gary Sheffield	6.00	2.70	.75
□ 15 Mark McGwire	12.00	5.50	1.50
□ 16 Bernie Williams	6.00	2.70	.75
□ 21 Cal Ripken	30.00	13.50	3.70
□ 24 Alex Rodriguez	40.00	18.00	5.00
□ 28 Chipper Jones	25.00	11.00	3.10
□ 38 Manny Ramirez	10.00	4.50	1.25
□ 41 Ken Griffey Jr.	40.00	18.00	5.00
□ 77 Kirby Puckett	12.00	5.50	1.50
□ 78 Barry Bonds	10.00	4.50	1.25
□ 80 Paul Molitor	8.00	3.60	1.00
□ 94 Albert Belle	20.00	9.00	2.50
□ 99 Tony Gwynn	15.00	6.75	1.85
□ 102 Eddie Murray	10.00	4.50	1.25
□ 107 Juan Gonzalez	20.00	9.00	2.50
□ 112 Sammy Sosa	6.00	2.70	.75
□ 127 Kenny Lofton	10.00	4.50	1.25
□ 130 Mo Vaughn	10.00	4.50	1.25
□ 148 Hideo Nomo	10.00	4.50	1.25
□ 150 Frank Thomas	40.00	18.00	5.00
□ 151 Ivan Rodriguez	8.00	3.60	1.00
□ 155 Roberto Alomar	10.00	4.50	1.25
□ 163 Ozzie Smith	8.00	3.60	1.00
□ 165 Randy Johnson	6.00	2.70	.75
□ 169 Jim Thome	8.00	3.60	1.00
□ 176 Ryan Klesko	8.00	3.60	1.00
□ 185 Andy Pettitte	12.00	5.50	1.50
□ 191 Mike Mussina	8.00	3.60	1.00
□ 192 Greg Maddux	25.00	11.00	3.10
□ 199 Jeff Bagwell	15.00	6.75	1.85
□ 200 Mike Piazza	25.00	11.00	3.10
□ 211 Derek Jeter	25.00	11.00	3.10
□ 215 Ruben Rivera	8.00	3.60	1.00
□ 220 Karim Garcia	8.00	3.60	1.00

1996 Leaf All-Star Game MVP Contenders

This 20 card set features possible contenders for the MVP at the 1996 All-Star Game held in Philadelphia. If the player on the front of the card won the MVP Award, the holder could send it in for a special Gold MVP Contenders set of which only 5,000 were produced. The fronts display a color action player photo. The backs carry the instructions on how to redeem the card.

	MINT	NRMT	EXC
COMPLETE SET (20	40.00	18.00	5.00
COMMON CARD (1-20)	.75	.35	.09
RANDOM INSERTS IN PACKS			
COMPLETE GOLD SET (20)	40.00	18.00	5.00
*GOLD CARDS: 1X BASIC CARDS			
ONE GOLD SET PER PIAZZA W VIA MAIL			

	MINT	NRMT	EXC
☐ 1 Frank Thomas	6.00	2.70	.75
☐ 2 Mike Piazza	6.00	2.70	.75
☐ 3 Sammy Sosa	1.25	.55	.16
☐ 4 Cal Ripken	5.00	2.20	.60
☐ 5 Jeff Bagwell	2.50	1.10	.30
☐ 6 Reggie Sanders	.75	.35	.09
☐ 7 Mo Vaughn	1.50	.70	.19
☐ 8 Tony Gwynn	2.50	1.10	.30
☐ 9 Dante Bichette	.75	.35	.09
☐ 10 Tim Salmon	.75	.35	.09
☐ 11 Chipper Jones	4.00	1.80	.50
☐ 12 Kenny Lofton	1.50	.70	.19
☐ 13 Manny Ramirez	1.50	.70	.19
☐ 14 Barry Bonds	1.50	.70	.19
☐ 15 Raul Mondesi	.75	.35	.09
☐ 16 Kirby Puckett	2.00	.90	.25
☐ 17 Albert Belle	3.00	1.35	.35
☐ 18 Ken Griffey Jr.	6.00	2.70	.75
☐ 19 Greg Maddux	4.00	1.80	.50
☐ 20 Bonus Card	.75	.35	.09

1996 Leaf Gold Stars

Randomly inserted in hobby and retail packs at a rate of one in 200, this 15-card set honors some of the games great players on 22 karat gold trim cards. Only 2,500 cards of each player were printed and are individually numbered.

	MINT	NRMT	EXC
COMPLETE SET (15)	650.00	300.00	80.00
COMMON CARD (1-15)	12.00	5.50	1.50
RANDOM INSERTS IN PACKS			

	MINT	NRMT	EXC
☐ 1 Frank Thomas	100.00	45.00	12.50
☐ 2 Dante Bichette	12.00	5.50	1.50
☐ 3 Sammy Sosa	15.00	6.75	1.85
☐ 4 Ken Griffey Jr.	100.00	45.00	12.50
☐ 5 Mike Piazza	60.00	27.00	7.50
☐ 6 Tim Salmon	12.00	5.50	1.50
☐ 7 Hideo Nomo	25.00	11.00	3.10
☐ 8 Cal Ripken	80.00	36.00	10.00
☐ 9 Chipper Jones	60.00	27.00	7.50
☐ 10 Albert Belle	50.00	22.00	6.25
☐ 11 Tony Gwynn	40.00	18.00	5.00
☐ 12 Mo Vaughn	25.00	11.00	3.10
☐ 13 Barry Larkin	12.00	5.50	1.50
☐ 14 Manny Ramirez	25.00	11.00	3.10
☐ 15 Greg Maddux	60.00	27.00	7.50

1996 Leaf Hats Off

Randomly inserted in retail packs only at a rate of one in 72, this 8-card set was printed and embossed on a wool-like material with the feel of a Major League ball cap. Only 5,000 of each player was produced and is individually numbered.

	MINT	NRMT	EXC
COMPLETE SET (8)	200.00	90.00	25.00
COMMON CARD (1-8)	6.00	2.70	.75
RANDOM INSERTS IN RETAIL PACKS			

	MINT	NRMT	EXC
☐ 1 Cal Ripken	40.00	18.00	5.00
☐ 2 Barry Larkin	6.00	2.70	.75
☐ 3 Frank Thomas	50.00	22.00	6.25
☐ 4 Mo Vaughn	12.00	5.50	1.50
☐ 5 Ken Griffey Jr.	50.00	22.00	6.25
☐ 6 Hideo Nomo	12.00	5.50	1.50
☐ 7 Albert Belle	25.00	11.00	3.10
☐ 8 Greg Maddux	30.00	13.50	3.70

1996 Leaf Picture Perfect

Randomly inserted in hobby (1-6) and retail (7-12) packs at a rate of one in 140, this 12-card set is printed on real wood with gold foil trim. The fronts feature a color player action framed photo. The backs carry another player photo with player information. Only 5,000 of each card were printed and are individually numbered.

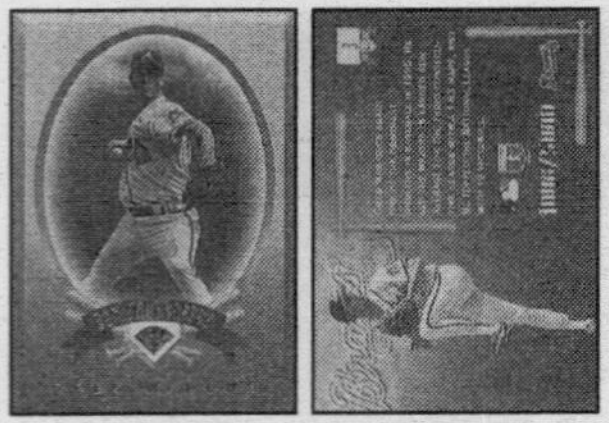

	MINT	NRMT	EXC
COMPLETE SET (12)	250.00	110.00	31.00
COMMON CARD (1-12)	10.00	4.50	1.25
CARDS 1-6 RANDOM INSERTS IN HOBBY PACKS			
CARDS 7-12 RANDOM INSERTS IN RETAIL PACKS			

	MINT	NRMT	EXC
☐ 1 Frank Thomas	40.00	18.00	5.00
☐ 2 Cal Ripken	30.00	13.50	3.70
☐ 3 Greg Maddux	25.00	11.00	3.10
☐ 4 Manny Ramirez	10.00	4.50	1.25
☐ 5 Chipper Jones	25.00	11.00	3.10
☐ 6 Tony Gwynn	15.00	6.75	1.85
☐ 7 Ken Griffey Jr.	40.00	18.00	5.00
☐ 8 Albert Belle	20.00	9.00	2.50
☐ 9 Jeff Bagwell	15.00	6.75	1.85
☐ 10 Mike Piazza	25.00	11.00	3.10
☐ 11 Mo Vaughn	10.00	4.50	1.25
☐ 12 Barry Bonds	10.00	4.50	1.25

1996 Leaf Statistical Standouts

Randomly inserted in hobby packs only at a rate of one in 210, this 8-card set features eight players who stood out from the rest statistically. The cards were printed on a material with the feel of the leather that's between the seams or stitches of a baseball. Only 2,500 of each card was printed and is numbered individually.

	MINT	NRMT	EXC
COMPLETE SET (8)	450.00	200.00	55.00
COMMON CARD (1-8)	30.00	13.50	3.70
RANDOM INSERTS IN HOBBY PACKS			

	MINT	NRMT	EXC
☐ 1 Cal Ripken	100.00	45.00	12.50
☐ 2 Tony Gwynn	50.00	22.00	6.25
☐ 3 Frank Thomas	120.00	55.00	15.00
☐ 4 Ken Griffey Jr.	120.00	55.00	15.00
☐ 5 Hideo Nomo	30.00	13.50	3.70
☐ 6 Greg Maddux	75.00	34.00	9.50
☐ 7 Albert Belle	60.00	27.00	7.50
☐ 8 Chipper Jones	75.00	34.00	9.50

1996 Leaf Total Bases

Randomly inserted in hobby packs only at a rate of one in 72, this 12-card set is printed on canvas and features the top offensive stars. Only 5,000 of each card was printed and are individually numbered. The fronts carry a color action player cut-out over a base background. The backs display another player photo and 1995 stats.

	MINT	NRMT	EXC
COMPLETE SET (12)	150.00	70.00	19.00
COMMON CARD (1-12)	3.00	1.35	.35
SEMISTARS	5.00	2.20	.60
RANDOM INSERTS IN HOBBY PACKS			

□ 1 Frank Thomas	30.00	13.50	3.70
□ 2 Albert Belle	15.00	6.75	1.85
□ 3 Rafael Palmeiro	5.00	2.20	.60
□ 4 Barry Bonds	8.00	3.60	1.00
□ 5 Kirby Puckett	10.00	4.50	1.25
□ 6 Joe Carter	5.00	2.20	.60
□ 7 Paul Molitor	6.00	2.70	.75
□ 8 Fred McGriff	5.00	2.20	.60
□ 9 Ken Griffey Jr.	30.00	13.50	3.70
□ 10 Carlos Baerga	3.00	1.35	.35
□ 11 Juan Gonzalez	15.00	6.75	1.85
□ 12 Cal Ripken	25.00	11.00	3.10

1994 Leaf Limited

This 160-card standard-size set was issued exclusively to hobby dealers. The fronts display silver holographic Spectra Tech foiling and a silhouetted player action photo over full silver foil. The backs contain silver holographic Spectra Tech foil, two photos, and a quote about the player by well-known baseball personalities. The cards are numbered on the back, grouped alphabetically within teams, and checklisted below alphabetically according to teams for each league as follows: Baltimore Orioles (1-6), Boston Red Sox (7-12), California Angels (13-18), Chicago White Sox (19-25), Cleveland Indians (26-30), Detroit Tigers (31-35), Kansas City Royals (36-41), Milwaukee Brewers (42-47), Minnesota Twins (48-52), New York Yankees (53-58), Oakland Athletics (59-63), Seattle Mariners (64-69), Texas Rangers (70-74), Toronto Blue Jays (75-80), Atlanta Braves (81-88), Chicago Cubs (89-93), Cincinnati Reds (94-99), Colorado Rockies (100-104), Florida Marlins (105-109), Houston Astros (110-115), Los Angeles Dodgers (116-122), Montreal Expos (123-128), New York Mets (129-133), Philadelphia Phillies (134-138), Pittsburgh Pirates (139-143), St. Louis Cardinals (144-149), San Diego Padres (150-154), and San Francisco Giants (155-160). The only Rookie Card is Brian Anderson.

	MINT	NRMT	EXC
COMPLETE SET (160)	80.00	36.00	10.00
COMMON CARD (1-160)	.25	.11	.03
SEMISTARS	.50	.23	.06
STARS	1.25	.55	.16

□ 1 Jeffrey Hammonds	.50	.23	.06
□ 2 Ben McDonald	.25	.11	.03
□ 3 Mike Mussina	2.00	.90	.25
□ 4 Rafael Palmeiro	1.25	.55	.16
□ 5 Cal Ripken Jr.	8.00	3.60	1.00
□ 6 Lee Smith	.50	.23	.06
□ 7 Roger Clemens	1.25	.55	.16
□ 8 Scott Cooper	.25	.11	.03
□ 9 Andre Dawson	1.25	.55	.16
□ 10 Mike Greenwell	.25	.11	.03
□ 11 Aaron Sele	.50	.23	.06
□ 12 Mo Vaughn	2.50	1.10	.30
□ 13 Brian Anderson	.50	.23	.06
□ 14 Chad Curtis	.25	.11	.03
□ 15 Chili Davis	.50	.23	.06
□ 16 Gary DiSarcina	.25	.11	.03
□ 17 Mark Langston	.50	.23	.06
□ 18 Tim Salmon	1.50	.70	.19
□ 19 Wilson Alvarez	.50	.23	.06
□ 20 Jason Bere	.50	.23	.06
□ 21 Julio Franco	.50	.23	.06
□ 22 Jack McDowell	.50	.23	.06
□ 23 Tim Raines	1.25	.55	.16
□ 24 Frank Thomas	10.00	4.50	1.25
□ 25 Robin Ventura	.50	.23	.06
□ 26 Carlos Baerga	1.25	.55	.16
□ 27 Albert Belle	5.00	2.20	.60
□ 28 Kenny Lofton	3.00	1.35	.35
□ 29 Eddie Murray	2.50	1.10	.30
□ 30 Manny Ramirez	3.00	1.35	.35
□ 31 Cecil Fielder	.50	.23	.06
□ 32 Travis Fryman	1.25	.55	.16
□ 33 Mickey Tettleton	.25	.11	.03
□ 34 Alan Trammell	1.25	.55	.16
□ 35 Lou Whitaker	1.25	.55	.16
□ 36 David Cone	1.25	.55	.16
□ 37 Gary Gaetti	.50	.23	.06
□ 38 Greg Gagne	.25	.11	.03
□ 39 Bob Hamelin	.25	.11	.03
□ 40 Wally Joyner	.50	.23	.06
□ 41 Brian McRae	.50	.23	.06
□ 42 Ricky Bones	.25	.11	.03
□ 43 Brian Harper	.25	.11	.03
□ 44 John Jaha	.50	.23	.06
□ 45 Pat Listach	.25	.11	.03
□ 46 Dave Nilsson	.50	.23	.06
□ 47 Greg Vaughn	1.25	.55	.16
□ 48 Kent Hrbek	.50	.23	.06
□ 49 Chuck Knoblauch	1.25	.55	.16
□ 50 Shane Mack	.25	.11	.03
□ 51 Kirby Puckett	3.00	1.35	.35
□ 52 Dave Winfield	1.25	.55	.16
□ 53 Jim Abbott	.25	.11	.03
□ 54 Wade Boggs	1.25	.55	.16
□ 55 Jimmy Key	.50	.23	.06
□ 56 Don Mattingly	5.00	2.20	.60
□ 57 Paul O'Neill	.50	.23	.06
□ 58 Danny Tartabull	.25	.11	.03
□ 59 Dennis Eckersley	.50	.23	.06
□ 60 Rickey Henderson	1.25	.55	.16
□ 61 Mark McGwire	3.00	1.35	.35
□ 62 Troy Neel	.25	.11	.03
□ 63 Ruben Sierra	.50	.23	.06
□ 64 Eric Anthony	.25	.11	.03
□ 65 Jay Buhner	1.25	.55	.16
□ 66 Ken Griffey Jr.	10.00	4.50	1.25
□ 67 Randy Johnson	1.50	.70	.19
□ 68 Edgar Martinez	1.25	.55	.16
□ 69 Tino Martinez	.50	.23	.06
□ 70 Jose Canseco	1.25	.55	.16
□ 71 Will Clark	1.25	.55	.16
□ 72 Juan Gonzalez	5.00	2.20	.60
□ 73 Dean Palmer	.50	.23	.06
□ 74 Ivan Rodriguez	2.00	.90	.25
□ 75 Roberto Alomar	2.50	1.10	.30
□ 76 Joe Carter	1.25	.55	.16
□ 77 Carlos Delgado	1.50	.70	.19
□ 78 Paul Molitor	2.00	.90	.25
□ 79 John Olerud	.25	.11	.03
□ 80 Devon White	.25	.11	.03
□ 81 Steve Avery	.50	.23	.06
□ 82 Tom Glavine	1.25	.55	.16
□ 83 David Justice	1.25	.55	.16
□ 84 Roberto Kelly	.25	.11	.03
□ 85 Ryan Klesko	2.50	1.10	.30
□ 86 Javier Lopez	1.25	.55	.16
□ 87 Greg Maddux	6.00	2.70	.75
□ 88 Fred McGriff	1.25	.55	.16

□ 89 Shawon Dunston	.25	.11	.03
□ 90 Mark Grace	1.25	.55	.16
□ 91 Derrick May	.25	.11	.03
□ 92 Sammy Sosa	1.50	.70	.19
□ 93 Rick Wilkins	.25	.11	.03
□ 94 Bret Boone	.50	.23	.06
□ 95 Barry Larkin	1.25	.55	.16
□ 96 Kevin Mitchell	.50	.23	.06
□ 97 Hal Morris	.25	.11	.03
□ 98 Deion Sanders	1.25	.55	.16
□ 99 Reggie Sanders	1.25	.55	.16
□ 100 Dante Bichette	1.25	.55	.16
□ 101 Ellis Burks	.50	.23	.06
□ 102 Andres Galarraga	1.25	.55	.16
□ 103 Joe Girardi	.25	.11	.03
□ 104 Charlie Hayes	.25	.11	.03
□ 105 Chuck Carr	.25	.11	.03
□ 106 Jeff Conine	1.25	.55	.16
□ 107 Bryan Harvey	.25	.11	.03
□ 108 Benito Santiago	.25	.11	.03
□ 109 Gary Sheffield	1.50	.70	.19
□ 110 Jeff Bagwell	4.00	1.80	.50
□ 111 Craig Biggio	1.25	.55	.16
□ 112 Ken Caminiti	1.25	.55	.16
□ 113 Andujar Cedeno	.25	.11	.03
□ 114 Doug Drabek	.25	.11	.03
□ 115 Luis Gonzalez	.25	.11	.03
□ 116 Brett Butler	.50	.23	.06
□ 117 Delino DeShields	.25	.11	.03
□ 118 Eric Karros	.50	.23	.06
□ 119 Raul Mondesi	1.50	.70	.19
□ 120 Mike Piazza	6.00	2.70	.75
□ 121 Henry Rodriguez	1.25	.55	.16
□ 122 Tim Wallach	.25	.11	.03
□ 123 Moises Alou	.50	.23	.06
□ 124 Cliff Floyd	1.25	.55	.16
□ 125 Marquis Grissom	1.25	.55	.16
□ 126 Ken Hill	.25	.11	.03
□ 127 Larry Walker	1.25	.55	.16
□ 128 John Wetteland	.50	.23	.06
□ 129 Bobby Bonilla	.50	.23	.06
□ 130 John Franco	.25	.11	.03
□ 131 Jeff Kent	.25	.11	.03
□ 132 Bret Saberhagen	.50	.23	.06
□ 133 Ryan Thompson	.25	.11	.03
□ 134 Darren Daulton	.50	.23	.06
□ 135 Mariano Duncan	.25	.11	.03
□ 136 Lenny Dykstra	.50	.23	.06
□ 137 Danny Jackson	.25	.11	.03
□ 138 John Kruk	.50	.23	.06
□ 139 Jay Bell	.50	.23	.06
□ 140 Jeff King	.50	.23	.06
□ 141 Al Martin	.25	.11	.03
□ 142 Orlando Merced	.50	.23	.06
□ 143 Andy Van Slyke	.50	.23	.06
□ 144 Bernard Gilkey	.50	.23	.06
□ 145 Gregg Jefferies	1.25	.55	.16
□ 146 Ray Lankford	1.25	.55	.16
□ 147 Ozzie Smith	2.00	.90	.25
□ 148 Mark Whiten	.25	.11	.03
□ 149 Todd Zeile	.25	.11	.03
□ 150 Derek Bell	.50	.23	.06
□ 151 Andy Benes	.50	.23	.06
□ 152 Tony Gwynn	4.00	1.80	.50
□ 153 Phil Plantier	.25	.11	.03
□ 154 Bip Roberts	.25	.11	.03
□ 155 Rod Beck	.50	.23	.06
□ 156 Barry Bonds	2.50	1.10	.30
□ 157 John Burkett	.25	.11	.03
□ 158 Royce Clayton	.50	.23	.06
□ 159 Bill Swift	.25	.11	.03
□ 160 Matt Williams	1.25	.55	.16

1994 Leaf Limited Gold All-Stars

Randomly inserted in packs at a rate of one in eight, this 18-card standard-size set features the starting players at each position in both the National and American leagues for the 1994 All-Star Game. They are identical in design to the basic Limited product except for being gold and individually numbered out of 10,000.

	MINT	NRMT	EXC
COMPLETE SET (18)	200.00	90.00	25.00
COMMON CARD (1-18)	3.00	1.35	.35
SEMISTARS	5.00	2.20	.60
RANDOM INSERTS IN PACKS			

□ 1 Frank Thomas	40.00	18.00	5.00
□ 2 Gregg Jefferies	5.00	2.20	.60
□ 3 Roberto Alomar	10.00	4.50	1.25
□ 4 Mariano Duncan	3.00	1.35	.35
□ 5 Wade Boggs	5.00	2.20	.60
□ 6 Matt Williams	5.00	2.20	.60
□ 7 Cal Ripken Jr.	30.00	13.50	3.70
□ 8 Ozzie Smith	8.00	3.60	1.00
□ 9 Kirby Puckett	12.00	5.50	1.50
□ 10 Barry Bonds	10.00	4.50	1.25
□ 11 Ken Griffey Jr.	40.00	18.00	5.00
□ 12 Tony Gwynn	15.00	6.75	1.85
□ 13 Joe Carter	5.00	2.20	.60
□ 14 David Justice	5.00	2.20	.60
□ 15 Ivan Rodriguez	8.00	3.60	1.00
□ 16 Mike Piazza	25.00	11.00	3.10
□ 17 Jimmy Key	3.00	1.35	.35
□ 18 Greg Maddux	25.00	11.00	3.10

1994 Leaf Limited Rookies

This 80-card standard-size set was issued exclusively to hobby dealers. The set showcases top rookies and prospects of 1994. The fronts display silver holographic Spectra Tech foiling and a silhouetted player action photo over full silver foil. The word "Rookies" appears in black letters above the Leaf Limited logo at top. The backs contain silver holographic Spectra Tech foil, two photos, and a quote about the player by well-known baseball personalities. Rookie Cards in this set include Kurt Abbott, Rusty Greer, Bill VanLandingham and Ismael Valdes.

	MINT	NRMT	EXC
COMPLETE SET (80)	35.00	16.00	4.40
COMMON CARD (1-80)	.25	.11	.03
SEMISTARS	.50	.23	.06
STARS	1.00	.45	.12

□ 1 Charles Johnson	1.00	.45	.12
□ 2 Rico Brogna	.25	.11	.03
□ 3 Melvin Nieves	.50	.23	.06
□ 4 Rich Becker	.50	.23	.06
□ 5 Russ Davis	.50	.23	.06
□ 6 Matt Mieske	.25	.11	.03

☐ 7 Paul Shuey	.25	.11	.03
☐ 8 Hector Carrasco	.25	.11	.03
☐ 9 J.R. Phillips	.25	.11	.03
☐ 10 Scott Ruffcorn	.25	.11	.03
☐ 11 Kurt Abbott	.50	.23	.06
☐ 12 Danny Bautista	.25	.11	.03
☐ 13 Rick White	.25	.11	.03
☐ 14 Steve Dunn	.25	.11	.03
☐ 15 Joe Ausanio	.25	.11	.03
☐ 16 Salomon Torres	.25	.11	.03
☐ 17 Ricky Bottalico	1.50	.70	.19
☐ 18 Johnny Ruffin	.25	.11	.03
☐ 19 Kevin Foster	.25	.11	.03
☐ 20 W.VanLandingham	.50	.23	.06
☐ 21 Troy O'Leary	.25	.11	.03
☐ 22 Mark Acre	.25	.11	.03
☐ 23 Norberto Martin	.25	.11	.03
☐ 24 Jason Jacome	.50	.23	.06
☐ 25 Steve Trachsel	.50	.23	.06
☐ 26 Denny Hocking	.25	.11	.03
☐ 27 Mike Lieberthal	.25	.11	.03
☐ 28 Gerald Williams	.25	.11	.03
☐ 29 John Mabry	2.00	.90	.25
☐ 30 Greg Blosser	.25	.11	.03
☐ 31 Carl Everett	.25	.11	.03
☐ 32 Steve Karsay	.25	.11	.03
☐ 33 Jose Valentin	1.25	.55	.16
☐ 34 Jon Lieber	.25	.11	.03
☐ 35 Chris Gomez	.25	.11	.03
☐ 36 Jesus Tavarez	.25	.11	.03
☐ 37 Tony Longmire	.25	.11	.03
☐ 38 Luis Lopez	.25	.11	.03
☐ 39 Matt Walbeck	.25	.11	.03
☐ 40 Rikkert Faneyte	.25	.11	.03
☐ 41 Shane Reynolds	.50	.23	.06
☐ 42 Joey Hamilton	2.00	.90	.25
☐ 43 Ismael Valdes	4.00	1.80	.50
☐ 44 Danny Miceli	.25	.11	.03
☐ 45 Darren Bragg	.50	.23	.06
☐ 46 Alex Gonzalez	.50	.23	.06
☐ 47 Rick Helling	.25	.11	.03
☐ 48 Jose Oliva	.50	.23	.06
☐ 49 Jim Edmonds	2.00	.90	.25
☐ 50 Miguel Jimenez	.25	.11	.03
☐ 51 Tony Eusebio	.25	.11	.03
☐ 52 Shawn Green	.50	.23	.06
☐ 53 Billy Ashley	.25	.11	.03
☐ 54 Rondell White	1.00	.45	.12
☐ 55 Cory Bailey	.25	.11	.03
☐ 56 Tim Davis	.25	.11	.03
☐ 57 John Hudek	.25	.11	.03
☐ 58 Darren Hall	.25	.11	.03
☐ 59 Darren Dreifort	.50	.23	.06
☐ 60 Mike Kelly	.25	.11	.03
☐ 61 Marcus Moore	.25	.11	.03
☐ 62 Garret Anderson	1.00	.45	.12
☐ 63 Brian L.Hunter	1.50	.70	.19
☐ 64 Mark Smith	.25	.11	.03
☐ 65 Garey Ingram	.25	.11	.03
☐ 66 Rusty Greer	4.00	1.80	.50
☐ 67 Marc Newfield	.50	.23	.06
☐ 68 Gar Finnvold	.25	.11	.03
☐ 69 Paul Spoljaric	.25	.11	.03
☐ 70 Ray McDavid	.50	.23	.06
☐ 71 Orlando Miller	.25	.11	.03
☐ 72 Jorge Fabregas	.25	.11	.03
☐ 73 Ray Holbert	.25	.11	.03
☐ 74 Armando Benitez	.25	.11	.03
☐ 75 Ernie Young	1.00	.45	.12
☐ 76 James Mouton	.50	.23	.06
☐ 77 Robert Perez	.25	.11	.03
☐ 78 Chan Ho Park	2.50	1.10	.30
☐ 79 Roger Salkeld	.25	.11	.03
☐ 80 Tony Tarasco	.25	.11	.03

1994 Leaf Limited Rookies Phenoms

This 10-card standard-size set was randomly inserted in Leaf Limited Rookies packs at a rate of approximately of one in eight. Limited to 5,000, the set showcases top 1994 rookies. The fronts are designed much like the Limited Rookies except the card is comprised of gold foil instead of silver. Gold backs are also virtually identical to the Limited Rookies in terms of content and layout. The cards are individually numbered on back out of 5,000.

	MINT	NRMT	EXC
COMPLETE SET (10)	200.00	90.00	25.00
COMMON CARD (1-10)	8.00	3.60	1.00
RANDOM INSERTS IN PACKS			
☐ 1 Raul Mondesi	20.00	9.00	2.50
☐ 2 Bob Hamelin	8.00	3.60	1.00
☐ 3 Midre Cummings	8.00	3.60	1.00
☐ 4 Carlos Delgado	15.00	6.75	1.85
☐ 5 Cliff Floyd	10.00	4.50	1.25
☐ 6 Jeffrey Hammonds	8.00	3.60	1.00
☐ 7 Ryan Klesko	25.00	11.00	3.10
☐ 8 Javier Lopez	15.00	6.75	1.85
☐ 9 Manny Ramirez	30.00	13.50	3.70
☐ 10 Alex Rodriguez	100.00	45.00	12.50

1995 Leaf Limited

This 192 standard-size card set was issued in two series. Each series contained 96 cards. These cards were issued in six-box cases with 20 packs per box and five cards per pack. Dealer initial cost was $60 per box. Forty-five thousand boxes of each series was produced. The fronts feature a player photo shot against a silver holographic foil background. The player is identified on the top with his team name on the right. The "Leaf Limited" logo is on the bottom of the card. The horizontal backs contain two player photos along with career stats broken down on a monthly basis. The cards are numbered in the upper right corner. Rookie Cards in this set include Bob Higginson, Ariel Prieto and Carlos Perez.

	MINT	NRMT	EXC
COMPLETE SET (192)	80.00	36.00	10.00
COMPLETE SERIES 1 (96)	40.00	18.00	5.00
COMPLETE SERIES 2 (96)	40.00	18.00	5.00
COMMON CARD (1-192)	.25	.11	.03
COMMON CARD (97-192)	.50	.23	.06
STARS	1.00	.45	.12
COMP.GOLD SET (24)	50.00	22.00	6.25
*GOLD: EQUAL VALUE TO LISTED CARDS..			
GOLD: ONE PER SER.1 PACK			
☐ 1 Frank Thomas	8.00	3.60	1.00
☐ 2 Geronimo Berroa	.25	.11	.03

☐ 3 Tony Phillips	.50	.23	.06
☐ 4 Roberto Alomar	2.50	1.10	.30
☐ 5 Steve Avery	.50	.23	.06
☐ 6 Darryl Hamilton	.25	.11	.03
☐ 7 Scott Cooper	.25	.11	.03
☐ 8 Mark Grace	1.00	.45	.12
☐ 9 Billy Ashley	.25	.11	.03
☐ 10 Wil Cordero	.25	.11	.03
☐ 11 Barry Bonds	2.00	.90	.25
☐ 12 Kenny Lofton	2.00	.90	.25
☐ 13 Jay Buhner	1.00	.45	.12
☐ 14 Alex Rodriguez	10.00	4.50	1.25
☐ 15 Bobby Bonilla	.50	.23	.06
☐ 16 Brady Anderson	1.00	.45	.12
☐ 17 Ken Caminiti	1.00	.45	.12
☐ 18 Charlie Hayes	.25	.11	.03
☐ 19 Jay Bell	.50	.23	.06
☐ 20 Will Clark	1.00	.45	.12
☐ 21 Jose Canseco	1.00	.45	.12
☐ 22 Bret Boone	.50	.23	.06
☐ 23 Dante Bichette	1.00	.45	.12
☐ 24 Kevin Appier	.50	.23	.06
☐ 25 Chad Curtis	.25	.11	.03
☐ 26 Marty Cordova	1.00	.45	.12
☐ 27 Jason Bere	.25	.11	.03
☐ 28 Jimmy Key	.50	.23	.06
☐ 29 Rickey Henderson	1.00	.45	.12
☐ 30 Tim Salmon	1.00	.45	.12
☐ 31 Joe Carter	1.00	.45	.12
☐ 32 Tom Glavine	1.00	.45	.12
☐ 33 Pat Listach	.25	.11	.03
☐ 34 Brian Jordan	1.00	.45	.12
☐ 35 Brian McRae	.50	.23	.06
☐ 36 Eric Karros	.50	.23	.06
☐ 37 Pedro Martinez	.50	.23	.06
☐ 38 Royce Clayton	.25	.11	.03
☐ 39 Eddie Murray	2.00	.90	.25
☐ 40 Randy Johnson	1.00	.45	.12
☐ 41 Jeff Conine	1.00	.45	.12
☐ 42 Brett Butler	.50	.23	.06
☐ 43 Jeffrey Hammonds	.50	.23	.06
☐ 44 Andujar Cedeno	.25	.11	.03
☐ 45 Dave Hollins	.25	.11	.03
☐ 46 Jeff King	.50	.23	.06
☐ 47 Benji Gil	.25	.11	.03
☐ 48 Roger Clemens	1.00	.45	.12
☐ 49 Barry Larkin	1.00	.45	.12
☐ 50 Joe Girardi	.25	.11	.03
☐ 51 Bob Hamelin	.25	.11	.03
☐ 52 Travis Fryman	.50	.23	.06
☐ 53 Chuck Knoblauch	1.00	.45	.12
☐ 54 Ray Durham	.50	.23	.06
☐ 55 Don Mattingly	4.00	1.80	.50
☐ 56 Ruben Sierra	.50	.23	.06
☐ 57 J.T. Snow	.50	.23	.06
☐ 58 Derek Bell	.50	.23	.06
☐ 59 David Cone	.50	.23	.06
☐ 60 Marquis Grissom	1.00	.45	.12
☐ 61 Kevin Seitzer	.25	.11	.03
☐ 62 Ozzie Smith	1.50	.70	.19
☐ 63 Rick Wilkins	.25	.11	.03
☐ 64 Hideo Nomo	8.00	3.60	1.00
☐ 65 Tony Tarasco	.25	.11	.03
☐ 66 Manny Ramirez	2.00	.90	.25
☐ 67 Charles Johnson	.50	.23	.06
☐ 68 Craig Biggio	1.00	.45	.12
☐ 69 Bobby Jones	.50	.23	.06
☐ 70 Mike Mussina	1.50	.70	.19
☐ 71 Alex Gonzalez	.25	.11	.03
☐ 72 Gregg Jefferies	.50	.23	.06
☐ 73 Rusty Greer	1.00	.45	.12
☐ 74 Mike Greenwell	.25	.11	.03
☐ 75 Hal Morris	.25	.11	.03
☐ 76 Paul O'Neill	.50	.23	.06
☐ 77 Luis Gonzalez	.25	.11	.03
☐ 78 Chipper Jones	5.00	2.20	.60
☐ 79 Mike Piazza	5.00	2.20	.60
☐ 80 Rondell White	1.00	.45	.12
☐ 81 Glenallen Hill	.25	.11	.03
☐ 82 Shawn Green	.50	.23	.06
☐ 83 Bernie Williams	1.00	.45	.12
☐ 84 Jim Thome	1.50	.70	.19
☐ 85 Terry Pendleton	.50	.23	.06
☐ 86 Rafael Palmeiro	1.00	.45	.12
☐ 87 Tony Gwynn	3.00	1.35	.35
☐ 88 Mickey Tettleton	.25	.11	.03
☐ 89 John Valentin	.50	.23	.06
☐ 90 Deion Sanders	1.00	.45	.12
☐ 91 Larry Walker	1.00	.45	.12
☐ 92 Michael Tucker	.50	.23	.06
☐ 93 Alan Trammell	1.00	.45	.12
☐ 94 Tim Raines	1.00	.45	.12
☐ 95 David Justice	1.00	.45	.12
☐ 96 Tino Martinez	.50	.23	.06
☐ 97 Cal Ripken, Jr.	6.00	2.70	.75
☐ 98 Deion Sanders	1.00	.45	.12
☐ 99 Darren Daulton	.50	.23	.06
☐ 100 Paul Molitor	1.50	.70	.19
☐ 101 Randy Myers	.25	.11	.03
☐ 102 Wally Joyner	.50	.23	.06
☐ 103 Carlos Perez	.50	.23	.06
☐ 104 Brian Hunter	1.00	.45	.12
☐ 105 Wade Boggs	1.00	.45	.12
☐ 106 Bob Higginson	1.25	.55	.16
☐ 107 Jeff Kent	.25	.11	.03
☐ 108 Jose Offerman	.25	.11	.03
☐ 109 Dennis Eckersley	.50	.23	.06
☐ 110 Dave Nilsson	.50	.23	.06
☐ 111 Chuck Finley	.50	.23	.06
☐ 112 Devon White	.50	.23	.06
☐ 113 Bip Roberts	.25	.11	.03
☐ 114 Ramon Martinez	.50	.23	.06
☐ 115 Greg Maddux	5.00	2.20	.60
☐ 116 Curtis Goodwin	.50	.23	.06
☐ 117 John Jaha	.50	.23	.06
☐ 118 Ken Griffey Jr.	8.00	3.60	1.00
☐ 119 Geronimo Pena	.25	.11	.03
☐ 120 Shawon Dunston	.25	.11	.03
☐ 121 Ariel Prieto	.50	.23	.06
☐ 122 Kirby Puckett	2.50	1.10	.30
☐ 123 Carlos Baerga	1.00	.45	.12
☐ 124 Todd Hundley	.50	.23	.06
☐ 125 Tim Naehring	.25	.11	.03
☐ 126 Gary Sheffield	1.00	.45	.12
☐ 127 Dean Palmer	.50	.23	.06
☐ 128 Rondell White	1.00	.45	.12
☐ 129 Greg Gagne	.25	.11	.03
☐ 130 Jose Rijo	.25	.11	.03
☐ 131 Ivan Rodriguez	1.50	.70	.19
☐ 132 Jeff Bagwell	3.00	1.35	.35
☐ 133 Greg Vaughn	.50	.23	.06
☐ 134 Chili Davis	.50	.23	.06
☐ 135 Al Martin	.50	.23	.06
☐ 136 Kenny Rogers	.25	.11	.03
☐ 137 Aaron Sele	.50	.23	.06
☐ 138 Raul Mondesi	1.00	.45	.12
☐ 139 Cecil Fielder	.50	.23	.06
☐ 140 Tim Wallach	.25	.11	.03
☐ 141 Andres Galarraga	1.00	.45	.12
☐ 142 Lou Whitaker	1.00	.45	.12
☐ 143 Jack McDowell	.50	.23	.06
☐ 144 Matt Williams	1.00	.45	.12
☐ 145 Ryan Klesko	1.50	.70	.19
☐ 146 Carlos Garcia	.25	.11	.03
☐ 147 Albert Belle	4.00	1.80	.50
☐ 148 Ryan Thompson	.25	.11	.03
☐ 149 Roberto Kelly	.25	.11	.03
☐ 150 Edgar Martinez	1.00	.45	.12
☐ 151 Robby Thompson	.25	.11	.03
☐ 152 Mo Vaughn	2.00	.90	.25
☐ 153 Todd Zeile	.25	.11	.03
☐ 154 Harold Baines	.50	.23	.06
☐ 155 Phil Plantier	.25	.11	.03
☐ 156 Mike Stanley	.25	.11	.03
☐ 157 Ed Sprague	.50	.23	.06
☐ 158 Moises Alou	.50	.23	.06
☐ 159 Quilvio Veras	.25	.11	.03
☐ 160 Reggie Sanders	.50	.23	.06
☐ 161 Delino DeShields	.25	.11	.03
☐ 162 Rico Brogna	.25	.11	.03
☐ 163 Greg Colbrunn	.25	.11	.03
☐ 164 Steve Finley	.50	.23	.06
☐ 165 Orlando Merced	.25	.11	.03
☐ 166 Mark McGwire	2.50	1.10	.30
☐ 167 Garret Anderson	1.00	.45	.12
☐ 168 Paul Sorrento	.25	.11	.03
☐ 169 Mark Langston	.25	.11	.03
☐ 170 Danny Tartabull	.25	.11	.03
☐ 171 Vinny Castilla	.50	.23	.06
☐ 172 Javier Lopez	1.00	.45	.12
☐ 173 Bret Saberhagen	.50	.23	.06
☐ 174 Eddie Williams	.25	.11	.03

□ 175 Scott Leius	.25	.11	.03
□ 176 Juan Gonzalez	4.00	1.80	.50
□ 177 Gary Gaetti	.50	.23	.06
□ 178 Jim Edmonds	1.00	.45	.12
□ 179 John Olerud	.25	.11	.03
□ 180 Lenny Dykstra	.50	.23	.06
□ 181 Ray Lankford	1.00	.45	.12
□ 182 Ron Gant	.50	.23	.06
□ 183 Doug Drabek	.25	.11	.03
□ 184 Fred McGriff	1.00	.45	.12
□ 185 Andy Benes	.25	.11	.03
□ 186 Kurt Abbott	.25	.11	.03
□ 187 Bernard Gilkey	.50	.23	.06
□ 188 Sammy Sosa	1.00	.45	.12
□ 189 Lee Smith	.50	.23	.06
□ 190 Dennis Martinez	.50	.23	.06
□ 191 Ozzie Guillen	.25	.11	.03
□ 192 Robin Ventura	.50	.23	.06

1995 Leaf Limited Bat Patrol

These 24 standard-size cards were inserted one per series two pack. The fronts feature a full-bleed player photo with the player being identified on the top and the words "Bat Patrol" covering most of the middle. The horizontal backs feature another player photo as well as a year by year breakdown. The cards are numbered in the upper right corner as "X" of 24.

	MINT	NRMT	EXC
COMPLETE SET (24)	30.00	13.50	3.70
COMMON CARD (1-24)	.75	.35	.09
ONE PER SER.2 PACK			

□ 1 Frank Thomas	8.00	3.60	1.00
□ 2 Tony Gwynn	3.00	1.35	.35
□ 3 Wade Boggs	1.50	.70	.19
□ 4 Larry Walker	.75	.35	.09
□ 5 Ken Griffey, Jr.	8.00	3.60	1.00
□ 6 Jeff Bagwell	3.00	1.35	.35
□ 7 Manny Ramirez	2.00	.90	.25
□ 8 Mark Grace	1.50	.70	.19
□ 9 Kenny Lofton	2.00	.90	.25
□ 10 Mike Piazza	5.00	2.20	.60
□ 11 Will Clark	1.50	.70	.19
□ 12 Mo Vaughn	2.00	.90	.25
□ 13 Carlos Baerga	.75	.35	.09
□ 14 Rafael Palmeiro	1.50	.70	.19
□ 15 Barry Bonds	2.00	.90	.25
□ 16 Kirby Puckett	2.50	1.10	.30
□ 17 Roberto Alomar	2.00	.90	.25
□ 18 Barry Larkin	1.50	.70	.19
□ 19 Eddie Murray	2.00	.90	.25
□ 20 Tim Salmon	.75	.35	.09
□ 21 Don Mattingly	4.00	1.80	.50
□ 22 Fred McGriff	1.50	.70	.19
□ 23 Albert Belle	4.00	1.80	.50
□ 24 Dante Bichette	.75	.35	.09

1995 Leaf Limited Lumberjacks

These eight standard-size cards were randomly inserted into second series packs. The cards are individually numbered out of 5,000. The fronts feature a player photo surrounded by his name, the word "Lumberjacks" and "Handcrafted" in an semi-circular pattern. The team logo is in the background. The UV-coated horizontal backs feature a player photo against a forest background on the right along with some information on the left side. The player's career statistics are directly above the individual numbering (out of 5,000) of the card. The cards are numbered in the upper right corner.

	MINT	NRMT	EXC
COMPLETE SET (16)	600.00	275.00	75.00
COMPLETE SERIES 1 (8)	275.00	125.00	34.00
COMPLETE SERIES 2 (8)	325.00	145.00	40.00
COMMON CARD (1-16)	10.00	4.50	1.25

□ 1 Albert Belle	50.00	22.00	6.25
□ 2 Barry Bonds	25.00	11.00	3.10
□ 3 Juan Gonzalez	50.00	22.00	6.25
□ 4 Ken Griffey Jr.	100.00	45.00	12.50
□ 5 Fred McGriff	12.00	5.50	1.50
□ 6 Mike Piazza	50.00	22.00	6.25
□ 7 Kirby Puckett	30.00	13.50	3.70
□ 8 Mo Vaughn	25.00	11.00	3.10
□ 9 Frank Thomas	100.00	45.00	12.50
□ 10 Jeff Bagwell	40.00	18.00	5.00
□ 11 Matt Williams	12.00	5.50	1.50
□ 12 Jose Canseco	12.00	5.50	1.50
□ 13 Raul Mondesi	12.00	5.50	1.50
□ 14 Manny Ramirez	25.00	11.00	3.10
□ 15 Cecil Fielder	10.00	4.50	1.25
□ 16 Cal Ripken, Jr.	80.00	36.00	10.00

1996 Leaf Limited

The 1996 Leaf Limited set was issued in hobby series only totalling 90 cards with a maximun production run of 45,000 boxes. Each box contained two smaller mini-boxes, enabling the dealer to use his imagination in the marketing of this product. The five-card packs retailed for $3.24. Each Master Box was sequentially- numbered via a box topper. If this number matched the 1996 year-ending stats, the collector and the dealer both had a chance to win prizes such as a Frank Thomas game-used bat, autographed batting glove, or a "Two Biggest Weapons" poster. The collector would return the winning box number to the hobby shop, and the dealer would mail it to Donruss with both receiving the same prize. The card fronts dis-

played color player photos with another photo and player information on the backs.

	MINT	NRMT	EXC
COMPLETE SET (90)	50.00	22.00	6.25
COMMON CARD (1-90)	.25	.11	.03
SEMISTARS	.50	.23	.06
STARS	1.00	.45	.12
*GOLD: 10X VALUE			
GOLD CARDS RANDOM INSERTS IN PACKS			

	MINT	NRMT	EXC
□ 1 Ivan Rodriguez	1.50	.70	.19
□ 2 Roger Clemens	1.00	.45	.12
□ 3 Gary Sheffield	1.00	.45	.12
□ 4 Tino Martinez	.50	.23	.06
□ 5 Sammy Sosa	1.00	.45	.12
□ 6 Reggie Sanders	1.00	.45	.12
□ 7 Ray Lankford	1.00	.45	.12
□ 8 Manny Ramirez	2.00	.90	.25
□ 9 Jeff Bagwell	3.00	1.35	.35
□ 10 Greg Maddux	5.00	2.20	.60
□ 11 Ken Griffey Jr.	8.00	3.60	1.00
□ 12 Rondell White	1.00	.45	.12
□ 13 Mike Piazza	5.00	2.20	.60
□ 14 Marc Newfield	.50	.23	.06
□ 15 Cal Ripken	6.00	2.70	.75
□ 16 Carlos Delgado	1.00	.45	.12
□ 17 Tim Salmon	1.00	.45	.12
□ 18 Andres Galarraga	1.00	.45	.12
□ 19 Chuck Knoblauch	1.00	.45	.12
□ 20 Matt Williams	1.00	.45	.12
□ 21 Mark McGwire	2.50	1.10	.30
□ 22 Ben McDonald	.25	.11	.03
□ 23 Frank Thomas	8.00	3.60	1.00
□ 24 Johnny Damon	.50	.23	.06
□ 25 Gregg Jefferies	.50	.23	.06
□ 26 Travis Fryman	1.00	.45	.12
□ 27 Chipper Jones	5.00	2.20	.60
□ 28 David Cone	1.00	.45	.12
□ 29 Kenny Lofton	2.00	.90	.25
□ 30 Mike Mussina	1.50	.70	.19
□ 31 Alex Rodriguez	8.00	3.60	1.00
□ 32 Carlos Baerga	1.00	.45	.12
□ 33 Brian Hunter	.25	.11	.03
□ 34 Juan Gonzalez	4.00	1.80	.50
□ 35 Bernie Williams	1.00	.45	.12
□ 36 Wally Joyner	.25	.11	.03
□ 37 Fred McGriff	1.00	.45	.12
□ 38 Randy Johnson	1.00	.45	.12
□ 39 Marty Cordova	1.00	.45	.12
□ 40 Garret Anderson	.50	.23	.06
□ 41 Albert Belle	4.00	1.80	.50
□ 42 Edgar Martinez	1.00	.45	.12
□ 43 Barry Larkin	1.00	.45	.12
□ 44 Paul O'Neill	.25	.11	.03
□ 45 Cecil Fielder	1.00	.45	.12
□ 46 Rusty Greer	1.00	.45	.12
□ 47 Mo Vaughn	2.00	.90	.25
□ 48 Dante Bichette	1.00	.45	.12
□ 49 Ryan Klesko	1.50	.70	.19
□ 50 Roberto Alomar	2.00	.90	.25
□ 51 Raul Mondesi	1.00	.45	.12
□ 52 Robin Ventura	1.00	.45	.12
□ 53 Tony Gwynn	3.00	1.35	.35
□ 54 Mark Grace	1.00	.45	.12
□ 55 Jim Thome	1.50	.70	.19
□ 56 Jason Giambi	.50	.23	.06
□ 57 Tom Glavine	1.00	.45	.12
□ 58 Jim Edmonds	1.00	.45	.12
□ 59 Pedro Martinez	.50	.23	.06
□ 60 Charles Johnson	.50	.23	.06
□ 61 Wade Boggs	1.00	.45	.12
□ 62 Orlando Merced	.50	.23	.06
□ 63 Craig Biggio	1.00	.45	.12
□ 64 Brady Anderson	1.00	.45	.12
□ 65 Hideo Nomo	2.00	.90	.25
□ 66 Ozzie Smith	1.50	.70	.19
□ 67 Eddie Murray	2.00	.90	.25
□ 68 Will Clark	1.00	.45	.12
□ 69 Jay Buhner	1.00	.45	.12
□ 70 Kirby Puckett	2.50	1.10	.30
□ 71 Barry Bonds	2.00	.90	.25
□ 72 Ray Durham	1.00	.45	.12
□ 73 Sterling Hitchcock	.25	.11	.03
□ 74 John Smoltz	1.00	.45	.12
□ 75 Andre Dawson	1.00	.45	.12
□ 76 Joe Carter	1.00	.45	.12
□ 77 Ryne Sandberg	2.00	.90	.25
□ 78 Rickey Henderson	1.00	.45	.12
□ 79 Brian Jordan	1.00	.45	.12
□ 80 Greg Vaughn	1.00	.45	.12
□ 81 Andy Pettitte	2.50	1.10	.30
□ 82 Dean Palmer	1.00	.45	.12
□ 83 Paul Molitor	1.50	.70	.19
□ 84 Rafael Palmeiro	1.00	.45	.12
□ 85 Henry Rodriguez	.25	.11	.03
□ 86 Larry Walker	1.00	.45	.12
□ 87 Ismael Valdes	.50	.23	.06
□ 88 Derek Bell	.50	.23	.06
□ 89 J.T. Snow	.50	.23	.06
□ 90 Jack McDowell	1.00	.45	.12

1996 Leaf Limited Lumberjacks

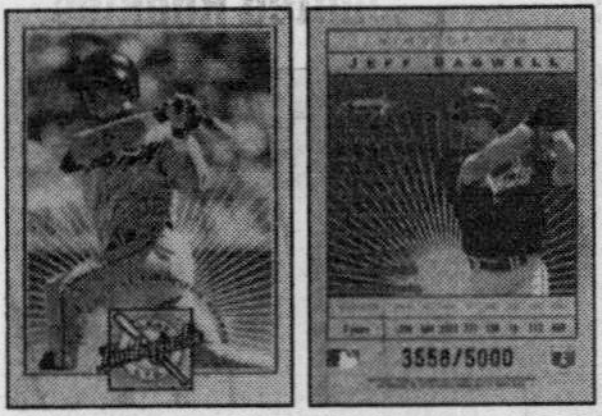

Printed with maple stock that puts wood grains on both sides, this 10-card insert set features the league's top sluggers. The fronts carry color player photos with player information and statistics on the backs. Only 5,000 sets were produced and each card is individually numbered.

	MINT	NRMT	EXC
COMPLETE SET (10)	250.00	110.00	31.00
COMMON CARD (1-10)	10.00	4.50	1.25
*BLACK: 5X VALUE			
RANDOM INSERTS IN PACKS			

	MINT	NRMT	EXC
□ 1 Ken Griffey Jr.	50.00	22.00	6.25
□ 2 Sammy Sosa	10.00	4.50	1.25
□ 3 Cal Ripken	40.00	18.00	5.00
□ 4 Frank Thomas	50.00	22.00	6.25
□ 5 Alex Rodriguez	50.00	22.00	6.25
□ 6 Mo Vaughn	12.00	5.50	1.50
□ 7 Chipper Jones	30.00	13.50	3.70
□ 8 Mike Piazza	30.00	13.50	3.70
□ 9 Jeff Bagwell	20.00	9.00	2.50
□ 10 Mark McGwire	15.00	6.75	1.85

1996 Leaf Limited Pennant Craze

This 10-card insert set features 10 superstars who have a thirst for the pennant. A special

flocking technique puts the felt feel of a pennant on a die cut card. Only 2,500 sets were produced and are individually numbered.

	MINT	NRMT	EXC
COMPLETE SET (10)	550.00	250.00	70.00
COMMON CARD (1-10)	20.00	9.00	2.50
RANDOM INSERTS IN PACKS			
□ 1 Juan Gonzalez	50.00	22.00	6.25
□ 2 Cal Ripken	80.00	36.00	10.00
□ 3 Frank Thomas	100.00	45.00	12.50
□ 4 Ken Griffey Jr.	100.00	45.00	12.50
□ 5 Albert Belle	50.00	22.00	6.25
□ 6 Greg Maddux	60.00	27.00	7.50
□ 7 Paul Molitor	20.00	9.00	2.50
□ 8 Alex Rodriguez	100.00	45.00	12.50
□ 9 Barry Bonds	25.00	11.00	3.10
□ 10 Chipper Jones	60.00	27.00	7.50

1996 Leaf Limited Rookies

Randomly inserted in packs at a rate of one in seven, this 10-card set printed in silver holographic foil features some of the hottest rookies of the year.

	MINT	NRMT	EXC
COMPLETE SET (10)	75.00	34.00	9.50
COMMON CARD (1-10)	2.50	1.10	.30
*GOLD: 3X VALUE			
RANDOM INSERTS IN PACKS			
□ 1 Alex Ochoa	3.00	1.35	.35
□ 2 Darin Erstad	15.00	6.75	1.85
□ 3 Ruben Rivera	6.00	2.70	.75
□ 4 Derek Jeter	15.00	6.75	1.85
□ 5 Jermaine Dye	6.00	2.70	.75
□ 6 Jason Kendall	4.00	1.80	.50
□ 7 Mike Grace	2.50	1.10	.30
□ 8 Andruw Jones	30.00	13.50	3.70
□ 9 Rey Ordonez	6.00	2.70	.75
□ 10 George Arias	2.50	1.10	.30

1996 Leaf Preferred

The 1996 Leaf Preferred set was issued in one series totalling 150 cards. The 6-card packs retail for $3.49 each. Each card was printed on 20-point card stock for extra thickness and durability. The fronts feature a color action player photo and silver foil printing. The backs carry another player photo, player information and statistics. One in every ten packs contains an insert card.

	MINT	NRMT	EXC
COMPLETE SET (150)	25.00	11.00	3.10
COMMON CARD (1-150)	.10	.05	.01
SEMISTARS	.25	.11	.03
STARS	.50	.23	.06
□ 1 Ken Griffey Jr.	3.00	1.35	.35
□ 2 Rico Brogna	.10	.05	.01
□ 3 Gregg Jefferies	.50	.23	.06
□ 4 Reggie Sanders	.50	.23	.06
□ 5 Manny Ramirez	.75	.35	.09
□ 6 Shawn Green	.10	.05	.01
□ 7 Tino Martinez	.50	.23	.06
□ 8 Jeff Bagwell	1.25	.55	.16
□ 9 Marc Newfield	.25	.11	.03
□ 10 Ray Lankford	.50	.23	.06
□ 11 Jay Bell	.10	.05	.01
□ 12 Greg Maddux	2.00	.90	.25
□ 13 Frank Thomas	3.00	1.35	.35
□ 14 Travis Fryman	.50	.23	.06
□ 15 Mark McGwire	1.00	.45	.12
□ 16 Chuck Knoblauch	.50	.23	.06
□ 17 Sammy Sosa	.50	.23	.06
□ 18 Matt Williams	.50	.23	.06
□ 19 Roger Clemens	.50	.23	.06
□ 20 Rondell White	.50	.23	.06
□ 21 Ivan Rodriguez	.60	.25	.07
□ 22 Cal Ripken	2.50	1.10	.30
□ 23 Ben McDonald	.10	.05	.01
□ 24 Kenny Lofton	.75	.35	.09
□ 25 Mike Piazza	2.00	.90	.25
□ 26 David Cone	.50	.23	.06
□ 27 Gary Sheffield	.50	.23	.06
□ 28 Tim Salmon	.25	.11	.03
□ 29 Andres Galarraga	.50	.23	.06
□ 30 Johnny Damon	.10	.05	.01
□ 31 Ozzie Smith	.60	.25	.07
□ 32 Carlos Baerga	.50	.23	.06
□ 33 Raul Mondesi	.50	.23	.06
□ 34 Moises Alou	.10	.05	.01
□ 35 Alex Rodriguez	3.00	1.35	.35
□ 36 Mike Mussina	.60	.25	.07
□ 37 Jason Isringhausen	.10	.05	.01
□ 38 Barry Larkin	.50	.23	.06
□ 39 Bernie Williams	.50	.23	.06
□ 40 Chipper Jones	2.00	.90	.25
□ 41 Joey Hamilton	.25	.11	.03
□ 42 Charles Johnson	.10	.05	.01
□ 43 Juan Gonzalez	1.50	.70	.19
□ 44 Greg Vaughn	.50	.23	.06
□ 45 Robin Ventura	.25	.11	.03
□ 46 Albert Belle	1.50	.70	.19
□ 47 Rafael Palmeiro	.50	.23	.06
□ 48 Brian L.Hunter	.10	.05	.01
□ 49 Mo Vaughn	.75	.35	.09
□ 50 Paul O'Neill	.10	.05	.01
□ 51 Mark Grace	.50	.23	.06
□ 52 Randy Johnson	.50	.23	.06
□ 53 Pedro Martinez	.25	.11	.03
□ 54 Marty Cordova	.50	.23	.06
□ 55 Garret Anderson	.50	.23	.06
□ 56 Joe Carter	.50	.23	.06
□ 57 Jim Thome	.60	.25	.07
□ 58 Edgardo Alfonzo	.10	.05	.01
□ 59 Dante Bichette	.50	.23	.06
□ 60 Darryl Hamilton	.10	.05	.01
□ 61 Roberto Alomar	.75	.35	.09
□ 62 Fred McGriff	.50	.23	.06
□ 63 Kirby Puckett	1.00	.45	.12
□ 64 Hideo Nomo	.75	.35	.09
□ 65 Alex Fernandez	.50	.23	.06
□ 66 Ryan Klesko	.60	.25	.07
□ 67 Wade Boggs	.50	.23	.06
□ 68 Eddie Murray	.75	.35	.09
□ 69 Eric Karros	.50	.23	.06
□ 70 Jim Edmonds	.50	.23	.06
□ 71 Edgar Martinez	.50	.23	.06
□ 72 Andy Pettitte	1.00	.45	.12
□ 73 Mark Grudzielanek	.25	.11	.03
□ 74 Tom Glavine	.50	.23	.06

□ 75 Ken Caminiti	.50	.23	.06
□ 76 Will Clark	.50	.23	.06
□ 77 Craig Biggio	.50	.23	.06
□ 78 Brady Anderson	.50	.23	.06
□ 79 Tony Gwynn	1.25	.55	.16
□ 80 Larry Walker	.50	.23	.06
□ 81 Brian Jordan	.50	.23	.06
□ 82 Lenny Dykstra	.25	.11	.03
□ 83 Butch Huskey	.25	.11	.03
□ 84 Jack McDowell	.50	.23	.06
□ 85 Cecil Fielder	.50	.23	.06
□ 86 Jose Canseco	.50	.23	.06
□ 87 Jason Giambi	.25	.11	.03
□ 88 Rickey Henderson	.50	.23	.06
□ 89 Kevin Seitzer	.10	.05	.01
□ 90 Carlos Delgado	.50	.23	.06
□ 91 Ryne Sandberg	.75	.35	.09
□ 92 Dwight Gooden	.50	.23	.06
□ 93 Michael Tucker	.10	.05	.01
□ 94 Barry Bonds	.75	.35	.09
□ 95 Eric Young	.10	.05	.01
□ 96 Dean Palmer	.50	.23	.06
□ 97 Henry Rodriguez	.10	.05	.01
□ 98 John Mabry	.50	.23	.06
□ 99 J.T. Snow	.25	.11	.03
□ 100 Andre Dawson	.50	.23	.06
□ 101 Ismael Valdes	.25	.11	.03
□ 102 Charles Nagy	.10	.05	.01
□ 103 Jay Buhner	.50	.23	.06
□ 104 Derek Bell	.25	.11	.03
□ 105 Paul Molitor	.60	.25	.07
□ 106 Hal Morris	.10	.05	.01
□ 107 Ray Durham	.50	.23	.06
□ 108 Bernard Gilkey	.25	.11	.03
□ 109 John Valentin	.25	.11	.03
□ 110 Melvin Nieves	.25	.11	.03
□ 111 John Smoltz	.50	.23	.06
□ 112 Terrell Wade	.25	.11	.03
□ 113 Chad Mottola	.10	.05	.01
□ 114 Tony Clark	.50	.23	.06
□ 115 John Wasdin	.10	.05	.01
□ 116 Derek Jeter	2.00	.90	.25
□ 117 Rey Ordonez	.60	.25	.07
□ 118 Jason Thompson	.10	.05	.01
□ 119 Robin Jennings	.10	.05	.01
□ 120 Rocky Coppinger	.60	.25	.07
□ 121 Billy Wagner	.10	.05	.01
□ 122 Steve Gibralter	.10	.05	.01
□ 123 Jermaine Dye	.75	.35	.09
□ 124 Jason Kendall	.50	.23	.06
□ 125 Mike Grace	.10	.05	.01
□ 126 Jason Schmidt	.25	.11	.03
□ 127 Paul Wilson	.25	.11	.03
□ 128 Alan Benes	.50	.23	.06
□ 129 Justin Thompson	.10	.05	.01
□ 130 Brooks Kieschnick	.10	.05	.01
□ 131 George Arias	.10	.05	.01
□ 132 Osvaldo Fernandez	.25	.11	.03
□ 133 Todd Hollandsworth	.50	.23	.06
□ 134 Eric Owens	.10	.05	.01
□ 135 Chan Ho Park	.50	.23	.06
□ 136 Mark Loretta	.10	.05	.01
□ 137 Ruben Rivera	.60	.25	.07
□ 138 Jeff Suppan	.25	.11	.03
□ 139 Ugueth Urbina	.10	.05	.01
□ 140 LaTroy Hawkins	.10	.05	.01
□ 141 Chris Snopek	.10	.05	.01
□ 142 Edgar Renteria	.50	.23	.06
□ 143 Raul Casanova	.25	.11	.03
□ 144 Jose Herrera	.10	.05	.01
□ 145 Matt Lawton	.10	.05	.01
□ 146 Ralph Milliard	.10	.05	.01
□ 147 Frank Thomas CL (1-64)	1.50	.70	.19
□ 148 Jeff Bagwell CL (65-128)	.60	.25	.07
□ 149 Ken Griffey Jr. CL (129-150/inserts)	1.50	.70	.19
□ 150 Mike Piazza CL (inserts)	1.00	.45	.12

1996 Leaf Preferred Press Proofs

Parallel to the regular set, these 150 cards are each individually numbered to 500. The cards were seeded at an approximate rate of one in every 48 packs.

	MINT	NRMT	EXC
COMPLETE SET (150)	2000.00	900.00	250.00
COMMON CARD (1-150)	4.00	1.80	.50
SEMISTARS	12.00	5.50	1.50
STARS	25.00	11.00	3.10
*STARS: 30X to 50X BASIC CARDS			
*YOUNG STARS: 25X to 40X BASIC CARDS			
RANDOM INSERTS IN PACKS			

□ 1 Ken Griffey Jr.	150.00	70.00	19.00
□ 12 Greg Maddux	100.00	45.00	12.50
□ 13 Frank Thomas	150.00	70.00	19.00
□ 22 Cal Ripken	125.00	55.00	15.50
□ 25 Mike Piazza	100.00	45.00	12.50
□ 35 Alex Rodriguez	150.00	70.00	19.00
□ 40 Chipper Jones	100.00	45.00	12.50
□ 43 Juan Gonzalez	75.00	34.00	9.50
□ 46 Albert Belle	75.00	34.00	9.50
□ 116 Derek Jeter	80.00	36.00	10.00
□ 147 Frank Thomas CL	80.00	36.00	10.00
□ 149 Ken Griffey Jr. CL	80.00	36.00	10.00

1996 Leaf Preferred Staremaster

Randomly inserted at an approximate rate of one in every 144 packs, these twelve cards feature mug shots of the games most intense stares. Each card is printed on silver holographic card stock. Only 2,500 of each card was produced and are individually numbered.

	MINT	NRMT	EXC
COMPLETE SET (12)	650.00	300.00	80.00
COMMON CARD (1-12)	25.00	11.00	3.10
RANDOM INSERTS IN PACKS			

□ 1 Chipper Jones	60.00	27.00	7.50
□ 2 Alex Rodriguez	100.00	45.00	12.50
□ 3 Derek Jeter	60.00	27.00	7.50
□ 4 Tony Gwynn	40.00	18.00	5.00
□ 5 Frank Thomas	100.00	45.00	12.50
□ 6 Ken Griffey Jr.	100.00	45.00	12.50
□ 7 Cal Ripken	80.00	36.00	10.00
□ 8 Greg Maddux	60.00	27.00	7.50
□ 9 Albert Belle	50.00	22.00	6.25
□ 10 Barry Bonds	25.00	11.00	3.10
□ 11 Jeff Bagwell	40.00	18.00	5.00
□ 12 Mike Piazza	60.00	27.00	7.50

1996 Leaf Preferred Steel

Seeded one per pack, this all-steel, metalized set features silver framed color action player photos of the leagues most dominant players on a silver tinted background with a scriptive letter "S". The backs carry another player photo with the card logo as background and player statistics.

	MINT	NRMT	EXC
COMPLETE SET (77)	125.00	55.00	15.50
COMMON CARD (1-77)	1.00	.45	.12
SEMISTARS	1.50	.70	.19
ONE STEEL PER PACK			
*GOLD STARS: 10X BASIC CARDS			
GOLD: RANDOM INSERTS IN PACKS			

□	1 Frank Thomas	10.00	4.50	1.25
□	2 Paul Molitor	2.00	.90	.25
□	3 Kenny Lofton	2.50	1.10	.30
□	4 Travis Fryman	1.50	.70	.19
□	5 Jeff Conine	1.50	.70	.19
□	6 Barry Bonds	2.50	1.10	.30
□	7 Gregg Jefferies	1.50	.70	.19
□	8 Alex Rodriguez	10.00	4.50	1.25
□	9 Wade Boggs	1.50	.70	.19
□	10 David Justice	1.00	.45	.12
□	11 Hideo Nomo	2.50	1.10	.30
□	12 Roberto Alomar	2.50	1.10	.30
□	13 Todd Hollandsworth	1.50	.70	.19
□	14 Mark McGwire	3.00	1.35	.35
□	15 Rafael Palmeiro	1.50	.70	.19
□	16 Will Clark	1.50	.70	.19
□	17 Cal Ripken	8.00	3.60	1.00
□	18 Derek Bell	1.00	.45	.12
□	19 Gary Sheffield	1.50	.70	.19
□	20 Juan Gonzalez	5.00	2.20	.60
□	21 Garret Anderson	1.00	.45	.12
□	22 Mo Vaughn	2.50	1.10	.30
□	23 Robin Ventura	1.50	.70	.19
□	24 Carlos Baerga	1.50	.70	.19
□	25 Tim Salmon	1.50	.70	.19
□	26 Matt Williams	1.50	.70	.19
□	27 Fred McGriff	1.50	.70	.19
□	28 Rondell White	1.50	.70	.19
□	29 Ray Lankford	1.50	.70	.19
□	30 Lenny Dykstra	1.00	.45	.12
□	31 J.T. Snow	1.00	.45	.12
□	32 Sammy Sosa	1.50	.70	.19
□	33 Chipper Jones	6.00	2.70	.75
□	34 Bobby Bonilla	1.50	.70	.19
□	35 Paul Wilson	1.00	.45	.12
□	36 Darren Daulton	1.00	.45	.12
□	37 Larry Walker	1.50	.70	.19
□	38 Raul Mondesi	1.00	.45	.12
□	39 Jeff Bagwell	4.00	1.80	.50
□	40 Derek Jeter	6.00	2.70	.75
□	41 Kirby Puckett	3.00	1.35	.35
□	42 Jason Isringhausen	1.00	.45	.12
□	43 Vinny Castilla	1.50	.70	.19
□	44 Jim Edmonds	1.50	.70	.19
□	45 Ron Gant	1.50	.70	.19
□	46 Carlos Delgado	1.50	.70	.19
□	47 Jose Canseco	1.50	.70	.19
□	48 Tony Gwynn	4.00	1.80	.50
□	49 Mike Mussina	2.00	.90	.25
□	50 Charles Johnson	1.00	.45	.12
□	51 Mike Piazza	6.00	2.70	.75
□	52 Ken Griffey Jr.	10.00	4.50	1.25
□	53 Greg Maddux	6.00	2.70	.75
□	54 Mark Grace	1.50	.70	.19
□	55 Ryan Klesko	2.00	.90	.25
□	56 Dennis Eckersley	1.50	.70	.19
□	57 Rickey Henderson	1.50	.70	.19
□	58 Michael Tucker	1.00	.45	.12
□	59 Joe Carter	1.50	.70	.19
□	60 Randy Johnson	1.50	.70	.19
□	61 Brian Jordan	1.50	.70	.19
□	62 Shawn Green	1.00	.45	.12
□	63 Roger Clemens	1.50	.70	.19
□	64 Andres Galarraga	1.50	.70	.19
□	65 Johnny Damon	1.00	.45	.12
□	66 Ryne Sandberg	2.50	1.10	.30
□	67 Alan Benes	1.50	.70	.19
□	68 Albert Belle	5.00	2.20	.60
□	69 Barry Larkin	1.50	.70	.19
□	70 Marty Cordova	1.50	.70	.19
□	71 Dante Bichette	1.50	.70	.19
□	72 Craig Biggio	1.50	.70	.19
□	73 Reggie Sanders	1.50	.70	.19
□	74 Moises Alou	1.00	.45	.12
□	75 Chuck Knoblauch	1.50	.70	.19
□	76 Cecil Fielder	1.50	.70	.19
□	77 Manny Ramirez	2.50	1.10	.30

1996 Leaf Preferred Steel Power

This eight-card set combines a micro-etched foil card with corner interior lightening-symbol diecutting and honors eight of the top power hitters. The fronts carry a color player photo while the backs display a statement explaining why the player is included in the set along with his 1995 season hitting statistics. Only 5,000 sets were produced, and each card carries a serial number.

	MINT	NRMT	EXC
COMPLETE SET (8)	200.00	90.00	25.00
COMMON CARD (1-8)	12.00	5.50	1.50
RANDOM INSERTS IN PACKS			

□	1 Albert Belle	25.00	11.00	3.10
□	2 Mo Vaughn	12.00	5.50	1.50
□	3 Ken Griffey Jr.	50.00	22.00	6.25
□	4 Cal Ripken	40.00	18.00	5.00
□	5 Mike Piazza	30.00	13.50	3.70
□	6 Barry Bonds	12.00	5.50	1.50
□	7 Jeff Bagwell	20.00	9.00	2.50
□	8 Frank Thomas	50.00	22.00	6.25

1996 Leaf Signature

The 1996 Leaf Signature Set was issued in two series totalling 150 cards. The four-card packs have a suggested retail price of $9.99 each. It's interesting to note that the Extended Series was the last of the 1996 releases. In fact, it was released in January, 1997 - so late in the year that it's categorization as a 1996 issues is in question by some hobbyists. Production for the Extended Series was only 40% that of the regular issue. Card fronts feature borderless color action player photos with the card name printed in a silver foil emblem. The backs carry player information. The only notable Rookie Card is of Darin Erstad.

	MINT	NRMT	EXC
COMPLETE SERIES 1 (100)	50.00	22.00	6.25
COMMON CARD (1-100)	.15	.07	.02
SEMISTARS SER.1	.40	.18	.05
STARS SER.1	.75	.35	.09

□ 1 Mike Piazza	3.00	1.35	.35
□ 2 Juan Gonzalez	2.50	1.10	.30
□ 3 Greg Maddux	3.00	1.35	.35
□ 4 Marc Newfield	.15	.07	.02
□ 5 Wade Boggs	.75	.35	.09
□ 6 Ray Lankford	.40	.18	.05
□ 7 Frank Thomas	5.00	2.20	.60
□ 8 Rico Brogna	.15	.07	.02
□ 9 Tim Salmon	.75	.35	.09
□ 10 Ken Griffey Jr.	5.00	2.20	.60
□ 11 Manny Ramirez	1.25	.55	.16
□ 12 Cecil Fielder	.40	.18	.05
□ 13 Gregg Jefferies	.40	.18	.05
□ 14 Rondell White	.40	.18	.05
□ 15 Cal Ripken	4.00	1.80	.50
□ 16 Alex Rodriguez	5.00	2.20	.60
□ 17 Bernie Williams	.75	.35	.09
□ 18 Andres Galarraga	.75	.35	.09
□ 19 Mike Mussina	1.00	.45	.12
□ 20 Chuck Knoblauch	.75	.35	.09
□ 21 Joe Carter	.40	.18	.05
□ 22 Jeff Bagwell	2.00	.90	.25
□ 23 Mark McGwire	1.50	.70	.19
□ 24 Sammy Sosa	.75	.35	.09
□ 25 Reggie Sanders	.40	.18	.05
□ 26 Chipper Jones	3.00	1.35	.35
□ 27 Jeff Cirillo	.15	.07	.02
□ 28 Roger Clemens	.75	.35	.09
□ 29 Craig Biggio	.40	.18	.05
□ 30 Gary Sheffield	.75	.35	.09
□ 31 Paul O'Neill	.40	.18	.05
□ 32 Johnny Damon	.40	.18	.05
□ 33 Jason Isringhausen	.40	.18	.05
□ 34 Jay Bell	.15	.07	.02
□ 35 Henry Rodriguez	.40	.18	.05
□ 36 Matt Williams	.75	.35	.09
□ 37 Randy Johnson	.75	.35	.09
□ 38 Fred McGriff	.75	.35	.09
□ 39 Jason Giambi	.40	.18	.05
□ 40 Ivan Rodriguez	1.00	.45	.12
□ 41 Raul Mondesi	.40	.18	.05
□ 42 Barry Larkin	.75	.35	.09
□ 43 Ryan Klesko	1.00	.45	.12
□ 44 Joey Hamilton	.40	.18	.05
□ 45 Todd Hundley	.40	.18	.05
□ 46 Jim Edmonds	.40	.18	.05
□ 47 Dante Bichette	.75	.35	.09
□ 48 Roberto Alomar	1.25	.55	.16
□ 49 Mark Grace	.75	.35	.09
□ 50 Brady Anderson	.75	.35	.09
□ 51 Hideo Nomo	1.25	.55	.16
□ 52 Ozzie Smith	1.00	.45	.12
□ 53 Robin Ventura	.40	.18	.05
□ 54 Andy Pettitte	1.50	.70	.19
□ 55 Kenny Lofton	1.25	.55	.16
□ 56 John Mabry	.15	.07	.02
□ 57 Paul Molitor	1.00	.45	.12
□ 58 Rey Ordonez	1.00	.45	.12
□ 59 Albert Belle	2.50	1.10	.30
□ 60 Charles Johnson	.15	.07	.02
□ 61 Edgar Martinez	.75	.35	.09
□ 62 Derek Bell	.40	.18	.05
□ 63 Carlos Delgado	.40	.18	.05
□ 64 Raul Casanova	.15	.07	.02
□ 65 Ismael Valdes	.40	.18	.05
□ 66 J.T. Snow	.15	.07	.02
□ 67 Derek Jeter	3.00	1.35	.35
□ 68 Jason Kendall	.75	.35	.09
□ 69 John Smoltz	.75	.35	.09
□ 70 Chad Mottola	.15	.07	.02
□ 71 Jim Thome	1.00	.45	.12
□ 72 Will Clark	.75	.35	.09
□ 73 Mo Vaughn	1.25	.55	.16
□ 74 John Wasdin	.15	.07	.02
□ 75 Rafael Palmeiro	.75	.35	.09
□ 76 Mark Grudzielanek	.15	.07	.02
□ 77 Larry Walker	.40	.18	.05
□ 78 Alan Benes	.75	.35	.09
□ 79 Michael Tucker	.15	.07	.02
□ 80 Billy Wagner	.15	.07	.02
□ 81 Paul Wilson	.40	.18	.05
□ 82 Greg Vaughn	.40	.18	.05
□ 83 Dean Palmer	.40	.18	.05
□ 84 Ryne Sandberg	1.25	.55	.16
□ 85 Eric Young	.40	.18	.05
□ 86 Jay Buhner	.75	.35	.09
□ 87 Tony Clark	.40	.18	.05
□ 88 Jermaine Dye	1.50	.70	.19
□ 89 Barry Bonds	1.25	.55	.16
□ 90 Ugueth Urbina	.15	.07	.02
□ 91 Charles Nagy	.40	.18	.05
□ 92 Ruben Rivera	1.25	.55	.16
□ 93 Todd Hollandsworth	.75	.35	.09
□ 94 Darin Erstad	5.00	2.20	.60
□ 95 Brooks Kieschnick	.40	.18	.05
□ 96 Edgar Renteria	.75	.35	.09
□ 97 Lenny Dykstra	.40	.18	.05
□ 98 Tony Gwynn	2.00	.90	.25
□ 99 Kirby Puckett	1.50	.70	.19
□ 100 Checklist	.15	.07	.02

1996 Leaf Signature Gold Press Proofs

Randomly inserted in packs at an approximate rate of one in 12, this 100-card set is parallel to the regular version. The first 100 cards were seeded into regular packs and the last fifty cards in Extended series packs. The design is similar to the regular card with the exception of the card name being printed in a gold foil emblem and the words "Press Proof" printed in gold foil vertically down the side. Please refer to the multipliers provided below to ascertain value for singles.

	MINT	NRMT	EXC
COMPLETE SERIES 1 (100)	800.00	350.00	100.00
COMMON CARD (1-100)	3.00	1.35	.35
SEMISTARS	6.00	2.70	.75
STARS	12.00	5.50	1.50
*STARS: 12X to 20X BASIC CARDS			
*YOUNG STARS: 9X to 15X BASIC CARDS			
RANDOM INSERTS IN PACKS			

□ 1 Mike Piazza	50.00	22.00	6.25
□ 2 Juan Gonzalez	40.00	18.00	5.00
□ 3 Greg Maddux	50.00	22.00	6.25
□ 7 Frank Thomas	80.00	36.00	10.00
□ 10 Ken Griffey Jr.	80.00	36.00	10.00
□ 15 Cal Ripken	60.00	27.00	7.50
□ 16 Alex Rodriguez	80.00	36.00	10.00
□ 59 Albert Belle	40.00	18.00	5.00
□ 67 Derek Jeter	40.00	18.00	5.00
□ 94 Darin Erstad	30.00	13.50	3.70

1996 Leaf Signature Autographs

Inserted exclusively into basic 1996 Leaf Signature Series packs, these 246 unnumbered cards were one of the first major autograph issues featured in a trading card set. Packs contained at least one autograph, with the chance of getting more. Donruss reports that all but 10 players in the Leaf Signature

Series signed close to 5,000 total autographs (3,500 bronze, 1,000 silver, 500 gold). The 10 players who signed 1,000 (700 bronze, 200 silver, 100 gold) are: Roberto Alomar, Wade Boggs, Derek Jeter, Kenny Lofton, Paul Molitor, Raul Mondesi, Manny Ramirez, Alex Rodriguez, Frank Thomas and Mo Vaughn. Six players returned their cards too late for inclusion in the regular packs, and were inserted in the Extended packs instead: Carlos Delgado, Brian L.Hunter, Terrell Wade, Phil Plantier, Ernie Young and Jim Thome. These six cards technically could be considered part of either (or neither) set since the design matches the original autographs, but the distribution was exclusively in Extended packs.

	MINT	NRMT	EXC
COMP.BRONZE SET (246)	2000.00	900.00	250.00
COMMON BRONZE (1-252)	4.00	1.80	.50
BRONZE SEMISTARS	8.00	3.60	1.00
*SILVER: 2X BASIC CARDS			
*GOLD: 3X BASIC CARDS			
CARDS ARE UNNUMBERED			
NON-SP: 3500 BRONZE/1000 SILVER/500 GOLD			
SP: 700 BRONZE/200 SILVER/100 GOLD			
ONE OR MORE AUTOGRAPHS PER PACK			

□ 1 Kurt Abbott	4.00	1.80	.50
□ 2 Juan Acevedo	4.00	1.80	.50
□ 3 Terry Adams	4.00	1.80	.50
□ 4 Manny Alexander	4.00	1.80	.50
□ 5 Roberto Alomar SP	75.00	34.00	9.50
□ 6 Moises Alou	6.00	2.70	.75
□ 7 Wilson Alvarez	8.00	3.60	1.00
□ 8 Garret Anderson	8.00	3.60	1.00
□ 9 Shane Andrews	4.00	1.80	.50
□ 10 Andy Ashby	4.00	1.80	.50
□ 11 Pedro Astacio	4.00	1.80	.50
□ 12 Brad Ausmus	4.00	1.80	.50
□ 13 Bobby Ayala	4.00	1.80	.50
□ 14 Carlos Baerga	10.00	4.50	1.25
□ 15 Harold Baines	8.00	3.60	1.00
□ 16 Jason Bates	4.00	1.80	.50
□ 17 Allen Battle	4.00	1.80	.50
□ 18 Rich Becker	4.00	1.80	.50
□ 19 David Bell	4.00	1.80	.50
□ 20 Rafael Belliard	4.00	1.80	.50
□ 21 Andy Benes	4.00	1.80	.50
□ 22 Armando Benitez	4.00	1.80	.50
□ 23 Jason Bere	4.00	1.80	.50
□ 24 Geronimo Berroa	4.00	1.80	.50
□ 25 Willie Blair	4.00	1.80	.50
□ 26 Mike Blowers	4.00	1.80	.50
□ 27 Wade Boggs SP	75.00	34.00	9.50
□ 28 Ricky Bones	4.00	1.80	.50
□ 29 Mike Bordick	4.00	1.80	.50
□ 30 Toby Borland	4.00	1.80	.50
□ 31 Ricky Bottalico	4.00	1.80	.50
□ 32 Darren Bragg	4.00	1.80	.50
□ 33 Jeff Branson	4.00	1.80	.50
□ 34 Tilson Brito	4.00	1.80	.50
□ 35 Rico Brogna	4.00	1.80	.50
□ 36 Scott Brosius	4.00	1.80	.50
□ 37 Damon Buford	4.00	1.80	.50
□ 38 Mike Busby	4.00	1.80	.50
□ 39 Tom Candiotti	4.00	1.80	.50
□ 40 Frank Castillo	4.00	1.80	.50
□ 41 Andujar Cedeno	4.00	1.80	.50
□ 42 Domingo Cedeno	4.00	1.80	.50
□ 43 Roger Cedeno	6.00	2.70	.75
□ 44 Norm Charlton	4.00	1.80	.50
□ 45 Jeff Cirillo	4.00	1.80	.50
□ 46 Will Clark	15.00	6.75	1.85
□ 47 Jeff Conine	10.00	4.50	1.25
□ 48 Steve Cooke	4.00	1.80	.50
□ 49 Joey Cora	4.00	1.80	.50
□ 50 Marty Cordova	15.00	6.75	1.85
□ 51 Rheal Cormier	4.00	1.80	.50
□ 52 Felipe Crespo	4.00	1.80	.50
□ 53 Chad Curtis	4.00	1.80	.50
□ 54 Johnny Damon	12.00	5.50	1.50
□ 55 Russ Davis	4.00	1.80	.50
□ 56 Andre Dawson	12.00	5.50	1.50
□ 58 Doug Drabek	4.00	1.80	.50
□ 59 Darren Dreifort	4.00	1.80	.50
□ 60 Shawon Dunston	4.00	1.80	.50
□ 61 Ray Durham	6.00	2.70	.75
□ 62 Jim Edmonds	12.00	5.50	1.50
□ 63 Joey Eischen	4.00	1.80	.50
□ 64 Jim Eisenreich	4.00	1.80	.50
□ 65 Sal Fasano	4.00	1.80	.50
□ 66 Jeff Fassero	4.00	1.80	.50
□ 67 Alex Fernandez	10.00	4.50	1.25
□ 68 Darrin Fletcher	4.00	1.80	.50
□ 69 Chad Fonville	4.00	1.80	.50
□ 70 Kevin Foster	4.00	1.80	.50
□ 71 John Franco	4.00	1.80	.50
□ 72 Julio Franco	6.00	2.70	.75
□ 73 Marvin Freeman	4.00	1.80	.50
□ 74 Travis Fryman	10.00	4.50	1.25
□ 75 Gary Gaetti	6.00	2.70	.75
□ 76 Carlos Garcia	4.00	1.80	.50
□ 77 Jason Giambi	12.00	5.50	1.50
□ 78 Benji Gil	4.00	1.80	.50
□ 79 Greg Gohr	4.00	1.80	.50
□ 80 Chris Gomez	4.00	1.80	.50
□ 81 Leo Gomez	4.00	1.80	.50
□ 82 Tom Goodwin	4.00	1.80	.50
□ 83 Mike Grace	4.00	1.80	.50
□ 84 Mike Greenwell	4.00	1.80	.50
□ 85 Rusty Greer	10.00	4.50	1.25
□ 86 Mark Grudzielanek	6.00	2.70	.75
□ 87 Mark Gubicza	4.00	1.80	.50
□ 88 Juan Guzman	4.00	1.80	.50
□ 89 Darryl Hamilton	4.00	1.80	.50
□ 90 Joey Hamilton	4.00	1.80	.50
□ 91 Chris Hammond	4.00	1.80	.50
□ 92 Mike Hampton	4.00	1.80	.50
□ 93 Chris Haney	4.00	1.80	.50
□ 94 Todd Haney	4.00	1.80	.50
□ 95 Erik Hanson	4.00	1.80	.50
□ 96 Pete Harnisch	4.00	1.80	.50
□ 97 LaTroy Hawkins	4.00	1.80	.50
□ 98 Charlie Hayes	4.00	1.80	.50
□ 99 Jimmy Haynes	4.00	1.80	.50
□ 100 Roberto Hernandez	6.00	2.70	.75
□ 101 Bobby Higginson	8.00	3.60	1.00
□ 102 Glenallen Hill	4.00	1.80	.50
□ 103 Ken Hill	6.00	2.70	.75
□ 104 Sterling Hitchcock	4.00	1.80	.50
□ 105 Trevor Hoffman	6.00	2.70	.75
□ 106 Dave Hollins	4.00	1.80	.50
□ 107 Dwayne Hosey	4.00	1.80	.50
□ 108 Thomas Howard	4.00	1.80	.50
□ 109 Steve Howe	4.00	1.80	.50
□ 110 John Hudek	4.00	1.80	.50
□ 111 Rex Hudler	4.00	1.80	.50
□ 113 Butch Huskey	6.00	2.70	.75
□ 114 Mark Hutton	4.00	1.80	.50
□ 115 Jason Jacome	4.00	1.80	.50
□ 116 John Jaha	4.00	1.80	.50
□ 117 Reggie Jefferson	4.00	1.80	.50
□ 118 Derek Jeter SP	125.00	55.00	15.50
□ 119 Bobby Jones	4.00	1.80	.50
□ 120 Todd Jones	4.00	1.80	.50
□ 121 Brian Jordan	6.00	2.70	.75
□ 122 Kevin Jordan	4.00	1.80	.50
□ 123 Jeff Juden	4.00	1.80	.50
□ 124 Ron Karkovice	4.00	1.80	.50
□ 125 Roberto Kelly	4.00	1.80	.50
□ 126 Mark Kiefer	4.00	1.80	.50
□ 127 Brooks Kieschnick	4.00	1.80	.50
□ 128 Jeff King	6.00	2.70	.75
□ 129 Mike Lansing	4.00	1.80	.50
□ 130 Matt Lawton	4.00	1.80	.50
□ 131 Al Leiter	4.00	1.80	.50
□ 132 Mark Leiter	4.00	1.80	.50
□ 133 Curtis Leskanic	4.00	1.80	.50
□ 134 Darren Lewis	4.00	1.80	.50
□ 135 Mark Lewis	4.00	1.80	.50
□ 136 Felipe Lira	4.00	1.80	.50
□ 137 Pat Listach	4.00	1.80	.50
□ 138 Keith Lockhart	4.00	1.80	.50
□ 139 Kenny Lofton SP	75.00	34.00	9.50
□ 140 John Mabry	8.00	3.60	1.00
□ 141 Mike Macfarlane	4.00	1.80	.50
□ 142 Kirt Manwaring	4.00	1.80	.50
□ 143 Al Martin	4.00	1.80	.50
□ 144 Norberto Martin	4.00	1.80	.50
□ 145 Dennis Martinez	6.00	2.70	.75
□ 146 Pedro Martinez	4.00	1.80	.50

□ 147	Sandy Martinez	4.00	1.80	.50
□ 148	Mike Matheny	4.00	1.80	.50
□ 149	T.J. Mathews	4.00	1.80	.50
□ 150	David McCarty	4.00	1.80	.50
□ 151	Ben McDonald	4.00	1.80	.50
□ 152	Pat Meares	4.00	1.80	.50
□ 153	Orlando Merced	4.00	1.80	.50
□ 154	Jose Mesa	6.00	2.70	.75
□ 155	Matt Mieske	4.00	1.80	.50
□ 156	Orlando Miller	4.00	1.80	.50
□ 157	Mike Mimbs	4.00	1.80	.50
□ 158	Paul Molitor SP	75.00	34.00	9.50
□ 159	Raul Mondesi SP	50.00	22.00	6.25
□ 160	Jeff Montgomery	4.00	1.80	.50
□ 161	Mickey Morandini	4.00	1.80	.50
□ 162	Lyle Mouton	4.00	1.80	.50
□ 163	James Mouton	4.00	1.80	.50
□ 164	Jamie Moyer	4.00	1.80	.50
□ 165	Rodney Myers	4.00	1.80	.50
□ 166	Denny Neagle	6.00	2.70	.75
□ 167	Robb Nen	4.00	1.80	.50
□ 168	Marc Newfield	6.00	2.70	.75
□ 169	Dave Nilsson	6.00	2.70	.75
□ 170	Jon Nunnally	4.00	1.80	.50
□ 171	Chad Ogea	4.00	1.80	.50
□ 172	Troy O'Leary	4.00	1.80	.50
□ 173	Rey Ordonez	15.00	6.75	1.85
□ 174	Jayhawk Owens	4.00	1.80	.50
□ 175	Tom Pagnozzi	4.00	1.80	.50
□ 176	Dean Palmer	8.00	3.60	1.00
□ 177	Roger Pavlik	4.00	1.80	.50
□ 178	Troy Percival	4.00	1.80	.50
□ 179	Carlos Perez	4.00	1.80	.50
□ 180	Robert Perez	4.00	1.80	.50
□ 181	Andy Pettitte	30.00	13.50	3.70
□ 183	Mike Potts	4.00	1.80	.50
□ 184	Curtis Pride	4.00	1.80	.50
□ 185	Ariel Prieto	4.00	1.80	.50
□ 186	Bill Pulsipher	6.00	2.70	.75
□ 187	Brad Radke	4.00	1.80	.50
□ 188	Manny Ramirez SP	50.00	22.00	6.25
□ 189	Joe Randa	4.00	1.80	.50
□ 190	Pat Rapp	4.00	1.80	.50
□ 191	Bryan Rekar	4.00	1.80	.50
□ 192	Shane Reynolds	4.00	1.80	.50
□ 193	Arthur Rhodes	4.00	1.80	.50
□ 194	Mariano Rivera	15.00	6.75	1.85
□ 195	Alex Rodriguez SP	250.00	110.00	31.00
□ 196	Frank Rodriguez	4.00	1.80	.50
□ 197	Mel Rojas	4.00	1.80	.50
□ 198	Ken Ryan	4.00	1.80	.50
□ 199	Bret Saberhagen	4.00	1.80	.50
□ 200	Tim Salmon	15.00	6.75	1.85
□ 201	Rey Sanchez	4.00	1.80	.50
□ 202	Scott Sanders	4.00	1.80	.50
□ 203	Steve Scarsone	4.00	1.80	.50
□ 204	Curt Schilling	4.00	1.80	.50
□ 205	Jason Schmidt	4.00	1.80	.50
□ 206	David Segui	4.00	1.80	.50
□ 207	Kevin Seitzer	4.00	1.80	.50
□ 208	Scott Servais	4.00	1.80	.50
□ 209	Don Slaught	4.00	1.80	.50
□ 210	Zane Smith	4.00	1.80	.50
□ 211	Paul Sorrento	4.00	1.80	.50
□ 212	Scott Stahoviak	4.00	1.80	.50
□ 213	Mike Stanley	4.00	1.80	.50
□ 214	Terry Steinbach	4.00	1.80	.50
□ 215	Kevin Stocker	4.00	1.80	.50
□ 216	Jeff Suppan	10.00	4.50	1.25
□ 217	Bill Swift	4.00	1.80	.50
□ 218	Greg Swindell	4.00	1.80	.50
□ 219	Kevin Tapani	4.00	1.80	.50
□ 220	Danny Tartabull	4.00	1.80	.50
□ 221	Julian Tavarez	4.00	1.80	.50
□ 222	Frank Thomas SP	250.00	110.00	31.00
□ 224	Ozzie Timmons	4.00	1.80	.50
□ 225	Michael Tucker	6.00	2.70	.75
□ 226	Ismael Valdes	4.00	1.80	.50
□ 227	Jose Valentin	4.00	1.80	.50
□ 228	Todd Van Poppel	4.00	1.80	.50
□ 229	Mo Vaughn SP	75.00	34.00	9.50
□ 230	Quilvio Veras	4.00	1.80	.50
□ 231	Fernando Vina	4.00	1.80	.50
□ 232	Joe Vitiello	4.00	1.80	.50
□ 233	Jose Vizcaino	4.00	1.80	.50
□ 234	Omar Vizquel	10.00	4.50	1.25
□ 236	Paul Wagner	4.00	1.80	.50
□ 237	Matt Walbeck	4.00	1.80	.50
□ 238	Jerome Walton	4.00	1.80	.50
□ 239	Turner Ward	4.00	1.80	.50
□ 240	Allen Watson	4.00	1.80	.50
□ 241	David Weathers	4.00	1.80	.50
□ 242	Walt Weiss	4.00	1.80	.50
□ 243	Turk Wendell	4.00	1.80	.50
□ 244	Rondell White	10.00	4.50	1.25
□ 245	Brian Williams	4.00	1.80	.50
□ 246	George Williams	4.00	1.80	.50
□ 247	Paul Wilson	12.00	5.50	1.50
□ 248	Bobby Witt	4.00	1.80	.50
□ 249	Bob Wolcott	4.00	1.80	.50
□ 250	Eric Young	4.00	1.80	.50
□ 252	Greg Zaun	4.00	1.80	.50

1996 Metal Universe

The Fleer Metal Universe set was issued in one series totalling 250 standard-size cards. All sorts of interesting details are in the original artwork background of the cards. The cards are grouped alphabetically within teams and checklisted below alphabetically according to teams for each league as follows: Baltimore Orioles (1-10), Boston Red Sox (11-22), California Angels (23-34), Chicago White Sox (35-41), Cleveland Indians (42-55), Detroit Tigers (56-61), Kansas City Royals (62-67), Milwaukee Brewers (68-74), Minnesota Twins (75-83), New York Yankees (84-97), Oakland Athletics (98-103), Seattle Mariners (104-111), Texas Rangers (112-117), Toronto Blue Jays (118-125), Atlanta Braves (126-137), Chicago Cubs (138-146), Cincinnati Reds (147-153), Colorado Rockies (154-160), Florida Marlins (161-171), Houston Astros (172-180), Los Angeles Dodgers (181-187), Montreal Expos (188-196), New York Mets (197-206), Philadelphia Phillies (207-213), Pittsburgh Pirates (214-220), St. Louis Cardinals (221-230), San Diego Padres (231-239), San Francisco Giants (240-247).

	MINT	NRMT	EXC
COMPLETE SET (250)	40.00	18.00	5.00
COMMON CARD (1-250)	.15	.07	.02
SEMISTARS	.30	.14	.04
STARS	.60	.25	.07
COMP.PLATINUM SET (250)	150.00	70.00	19.00
COMMON PLATINUM (1-250)	.25	.11	.03
PLATINUM SEMISTARS	1.00	.45	.12
PLATINUM STARS	2.00	.90	.25
*PLATINUM STARS: 1.5X to 3X HI COLUMN			
*PLATINUM YOUNG STARS: 1.25X to 2.5X HI			
ONE PLATINUM PER PACK			

□ 1	Roberto Alomar	1.00	.45	.12
□ 2	Brady Anderson	.60	.25	.07
□ 3	Bobby Bonilla	.60	.25	.07
□ 4	Chris Hoiles	.15	.07	.02
□ 5	Ben McDonald	.15	.07	.02
□ 6	Mike Mussina	.75	.35	.09
□ 7	Randy Myers	.15	.07	.02
□ 8	Rafael Palmeiro	.60	.25	.07
□ 9	Cal Ripken	3.00	1.35	.35
□ 10	B.J. Surhoff	.15	.07	.02
□ 11	Luis Alicea	.15	.07	.02
□ 12	Jose Canseco	.60	.25	.07

□	13 Roger Clemens	.60	.25	.07
□	14 Will Cordero	.15	.07	.02
□	15 Tom Gordon	.15	.07	.02
□	16 Mike Greenwall	.15	.07	.02
□	17 Tim Naehring	.15	.07	.02
□	18 Troy O'Leary	.15	.07	.02
□	19 Mike Stanley	.15	.07	.02
□	20 John Valentin	.30	.14	.04
□	21 Mo Vaughn	1.00	.45	.12
□	22 Tim Wakefield	.15	.07	.02
□	23 Garret Anderson	.60	.25	.07
□	24 Chili Davis	.15	.07	.02
□	25 Gary DiSarcina	.15	.07	.02
□	26 Jim Edmonds	.60	.25	.07
□	27 Chuck Finley	.15	.07	.02
□	28 Todd Greene	.60	.25	.07
□	29 Mark Langston	.15	.07	.02
□	30 Troy Percival	.30	.14	.04
□	31 Tony Phillips	.30	.14	.04
□	32 Tim Salmon	.60	.25	.07
□	33 Lee Smith	.60	.25	.07
□	34 J.T. Snow	.30	.14	.04
□	35 Ray Durham	.60	.25	.07
□	36 Alex Fernandez	.60	.25	.07
□	37 Ozzie Guillen	.15	.07	.02
□	38 Roberto Hernandez	.30	.14	.04
□	39 Lyle Mouton	.15	.07	.02
□	40 Frank Thomas	4.00	1.80	.50
□	41 Robin Ventura	.60	.25	.07
□	42 Sandy Alomar, Jr.	.15	.07	.02
□	43 Carlos Baerga	.60	.25	.07
□	44 Albert Belle	2.00	.90	.25
□	45 Orel Hershiser	.30	.14	.04
□	46 Kenny Lofton	1.00	.45	.12
□	47 Dennis Martinez	.30	.14	.04
□	48 Jack McDowell	.60	.25	.07
□	49 Jose Mesa	.30	.14	.04
□	50 Eddie Murray	1.00	.45	.12
□	51 Charles Nagy	.30	.14	.04
□	52 Manny Ramirez	1.00	.45	.12
□	53 Julian Tavarez	.15	.07	.02
□	54 Jim Thome	.75	.35	.09
□	55 Omar Vizquel	.15	.07	.02
□	56 Chad Curtis	.15	.07	.02
□	57 Cecil Fielder	.60	.25	.07
□	58 John Flaherty	.15	.07	.02
□	59 Travis Fryman	.60	.25	.07
□	60 Chris Gomez	.15	.07	.02
□	61 Felipe Lira	.15	.07	.02
□	62 Kevin Appier	.30	.14	.04
□	63 Johnny Damon	.60	.25	.07
□	64 Tom Goodwin	.30	.14	.04
□	65 Mark Gubicza	.15	.07	.02
□	66 Jeff Montgomery	.15	.07	.02
□	67 Jon Nunnally	.15	.07	.02
□	68 Ricky Bones	.15	.07	.02
□	69 Jeff Cirillo	.15	.07	.02
□	70 John Jaha	.30	.14	.04
□	71 Dave Nilsson	.30	.14	.04
□	72 Joe Oliver	.15	.07	.02
□	73 Kevin Seitzer	.15	.07	.02
□	74 Greg Vaughn	.60	.25	.07
□	75 Marty Cordova	.60	.25	.07
□	76 Chuck Knoblauch	.60	.25	.07
□	77 Pat Meares	.15	.07	.02
□	78 Paul Molitor	.75	.35	.09
□	79 Pedro Munoz	.15	.07	.02
□	80 Kirby Puckett	1.25	.55	.16
□	81 Brad Radke	.15	.07	.02
□	82 Scott Stahoviak	.15	.07	.02
□	83 Matt Walbeck	.15	.07	.02
□	84 Wade Boggs	.60	.25	.07
□	85 David Cone	.60	.25	.07
□	86 Joe Girardi	.15	.07	.02
□	87 Derek Jeter	2.50	1.10	.30
□	88 Jim Leyritz	.15	.07	.02
□	89 Tino Martinez	.60	.25	.07
□	90 Don Mattingly	2.00	.90	.25
□	91 Paul O'Neill	.15	.07	.02
□	92 Andy Pettitte	1.25	.55	.16
□	93 Tim Raines	.60	.25	.07
□	94 Kenny Rogers	.15	.07	.02
□	95 Ruben Sierra	.15	.07	.02
□	96 John Wetteland	.30	.14	.04
□	97 Bernie Williams	.60	.25	.07
□	98 Geronimo Berroa	.30	.14	.04
□	99 Dennis Eckersley	.60	.25	.07
□	100 Brent Gates	.15	.07	.02
□	101 Mark McGwire	1.25	.55	.16
□	102 Steve Ontiveros	.15	.07	.02
□	103 Terry Steinbach	.30	.14	.04
□	104 Jay Buhner	.60	.25	.07
□	105 Vince Coleman	.15	.07	.02
□	106 Joey Cora	.15	.07	.02
□	107 Ken Griffey, Jr.	4.00	1.80	.50
□	108 Randy Johnson	.60	.25	.07
□	109 Edgar Martinez	.60	.25	.07
□	110 Alex Rodriguez	4.00	1.80	.50
□	111 Paul Sorrento	.15	.07	.02
□	112 Will Clark	.60	.25	.07
□	113 Juan Gonzalez	2.00	.90	.25
□	114 Rusty Greer	.60	.25	.07
□	115 Dean Palmer	.60	.25	.07
□	116 Ivan Rodriguez	.75	.35	.09
□	117 Mickey Tettleton	.30	.14	.04
□	118 Joe Carter	.60	.25	.07
□	119 Alex Gonzalez	.15	.07	.02
□	120 Shawn Green	.15	.07	.02
□	121 Erik Hanson	.15	.07	.02
□	122 Pat Hentgen	.60	.25	.07
□	123 Sandy Martinez	.15	.07	.02
□	124 Otis Nixon	.15	.07	.02
□	125 John Olerud	.15	.07	.02
□	126 Steve Avery	.30	.14	.04
□	127 Tom Glavine	.60	.25	.07
□	128 Marquis Grissom	.60	.25	.07
□	129 Chipper Jones	2.50	1.10	.30
□	130 David Justice	.60	.25	.07
□	131 Ryan Klesko	.75	.35	.09
□	132 Mark Lemke	.15	.07	.02
□	133 Javier Lopez	.60	.25	.07
□	134 Greg Maddux	2.50	1.10	.30
□	135 Fred McGriff	.60	.25	.07
□	136 John Smoltz	.60	.25	.07
□	137 Mark Wohlers	.30	.14	.04
□	138 Frank Castillo	.15	.07	.02
□	139 Shawon Dunston	.15	.07	.02
□	140 Luis Gonzalez	.15	.07	.02
□	141 Mark Grace	.60	.25	.07
□	142 Brian McRae	.15	.07	.02
□	143 Jaime Navarro	.15	.07	.02
□	144 Rey Sanchez	.15	.07	.02
□	145 Ryne Sandberg	1.00	.45	.12
□	146 Sammy Sosa	.60	.25	.07
□	147 Bret Boone	.15	.07	.02
□	148 Curtis Goodwin	.15	.07	.02
□	149 Barry Larkin	.60	.25	.07
□	150 Hal Morris	.15	.07	.02
□	151 Reggie Sanders	.60	.25	.07
□	152 Pete Schourek	.30	.14	.04
□	153 John Smiley	.15	.07	.02
□	154 Dante Bichette	.60	.25	.07
□	155 Vinny Castilla	.60	.25	.07
□	156 Andres Galarraga	.60	.25	.07
□	157 Bret Saberhagen	.15	.07	.02
□	158 Bill Swift	.15	.07	.02
□	159 Larry Walker	.60	.25	.07
□	160 Walt Weiss	.15	.07	.02
□	161 Kurt Abbott	.15	.07	.02
□	162 John Burkett	.15	.07	.02
□	163 Greg Colbrunn	.15	.07	.02
□	164 Jeff Conine	.60	.25	.07
□	165 Chris Hammond	.15	.07	.02
□	166 Charles Johnson	.15	.07	.02
□	167 Al Leiter	.15	.07	.02
□	168 Pat Rapp	.15	.07	.02
□	169 Gary Sheffield	.60	.25	.07
□	170 Quilvio Veras	.15	.07	.02
□	171 Devon White	.15	.07	.02
□	172 Jeff Bagwell	1.50	.70	.19
□	173 Derek Bell	.30	.14	.04
□	174 Sean Berry	.15	.07	.02
□	175 Craig Biggio	.60	.25	.07
□	176 Doug Drabek	.15	.07	.02
□	177 Tony Eusebio	.15	.07	.02
□	178 Brian L.Hunter	.15	.07	.02
□	179 Orlando Miller	.15	.07	.02
□	180 Shane Reynolds	.15	.07	.02
□	181 Mike Blowers	.15	.07	.02
□	182 Roger Cedeno	.30	.14	.04
□	183 Eric Karros	.60	.25	.07
□	184 Ramon Martinez	.60	.25	.07

□ 185 Raul Mondesi	.60	.25	.07
□ 186 Hideo Nomo	1.00	.45	.12
□ 187 Mike Piazza	2.50	1.10	.30
□ 188 Moises Alou	.30	.14	.04
□ 189 Yamil Benitez	.15	.07	.02
□ 190 Darrin Fletcher	.15	.07	.02
□ 191 Cliff Floyd	.15	.07	.02
□ 192 Pedro Martinez	.30	.14	.04
□ 193 Carlos Perez	.15	.07	.02
□ 194 David Segui	.15	.07	.02
□ 195 Tony Tarasco	.15	.07	.02
□ 196 Rondell White	.60	.25	.07
□ 197 Edgardo Alfonzo	.30	.14	.04
□ 198 Rico Brogna	.15	.07	.02
□ 199 Carl Everett	.15	.07	.02
□ 200 Todd Hundley	.60	.25	.07
□ 201 Jason Isringhausen	.30	.14	.04
□ 202 Lance Johnson	.30	.14	.04
□ 203 Bobby Jones	.15	.07	.02
□ 204 Jeff Kent	.15	.07	.02
□ 205 Bill Pulsipher	.30	.14	.04
□ 206 Jose Vizcaino	.15	.07	.02
□ 207 Ricky Bottalico	.15	.07	.02
□ 208 Darren Daulton	.30	.14	.04
□ 209 Lenny Dykstra	.30	.14	.04
□ 210 Jim Eisenreich	.15	.07	.02
□ 211 Gregg Jefferies	.60	.25	.07
□ 212 Mickey Morandini	.15	.07	.02
□ 213 Heathcliff Slocumb	.15	.07	.02
□ 214 Jay Bell	.30	.14	.04
□ 215 Carlos Garcia	.15	.07	.02
□ 216 Jeff King	.30	.14	.04
□ 217 Al Martin	.15	.07	.02
□ 218 Orlando Merced	.30	.14	.04
□ 219 Dan Miceli	.15	.07	.02
□ 220 Denny Neagle	.30	.14	.04
□ 221 Andy Benes	.15	.07	.02
□ 222 Royce Clayton	.15	.07	.02
□ 223 Gary Gaetti	.30	.14	.04
□ 224 Ron Gant	.60	.25	.07
□ 225 Bernard Gilkey	.30	.14	.04
□ 226 Brian Jordan	.60	.25	.07
□ 227 Ray Lankford	.60	.25	.07
□ 228 John Mabry	.60	.25	.07
□ 229 Ozzie Smith	.75	.35	.09
□ 230 Todd Stottlemyre	.15	.07	.02
□ 231 Andy Ashby	.15	.07	.02
□ 232 Brad Ausmus	.15	.07	.02
□ 233 Ken Caminiti	.60	.25	.07
□ 234 Steve Finley	.60	.25	.07
□ 235 Tony Gwynn	1.50	.70	.19
□ 236 Joey Hamilton	.30	.14	.04
□ 237 Rickey Henderson	.60	.25	.07
□ 238 Trevor Hoffman	.30	.14	.04
□ 239 Wally Joyner	.15	.07	.02
□ 240 Rod Beck	.30	.14	.04
□ 241 Barry Bonds	1.00	.45	.12
□ 242 Glenallen Hill	.15	.07	.02
□ 243 Stan Javier	.15	.07	.02
□ 244 Mark Leiter	.15	.07	.02
□ 245 Deion Sanders	.60	.25	.07
□ 246 William Van Landingham	.15	.07	.02
□ 247 Matt Williams	.60	.25	.07
□ 248 Checklist	.15	.07	.02
□ 249 Checklist	.15	.07	.02
□ 250 Checklist	.15	.07	.02

1996 Metal Universe Heavy Metal

Randomly inserted in packs at a rate of one in 8 this 10-card set features the Power Hitters of Baseball. The fronts feature a color action player cut-out over a silver foil background. The backs carry a player portrait and information about the player.

	MINT	NRMT	EXC
COMPLETE SET (10)	25.00	11.00	3.10
COMMON CARD (1-10)	1.50	.70	.19
RANDOM INSERTS IN PACKS			

□ 1 Albert Belle	5.00	2.20	.60
□ 2 Barry Bonds	2.50	1.10	.30

□ 3 Juan Gonzalez	5.00	2.20	.60
□ 4 Ken Griffey Jr.	10.00	4.50	1.25
□ 5 Mark McGwire	3.00	1.35	.35
□ 6 Mike Piazza	6.00	2.70	.75
□ 7 Sammy Sosa	1.50	.70	.19
□ 8 Frank Thomas	10.00	4.50	1.25
□ 9 Mo Vaughn	2.50	1.10	.30
□ 10 Matt Williams	1.50	.70	.19

1996 Metal Universe Mining For Gold

Randomly inserted in retail packs only at a rate of one in 12, this 12-card set highlights major prospects and rookies.

	MINT	NRMT	EXC
COMPLETE SET (12)	60.00	27.00	7.50
COMMON CARD (1-12)	1.50	.70	.19
SEMISTARS	4.00	1.80	.50
RANDOM INSERTS IN RETAIL PACKS			

□ 1 Yamil Benitez	1.50	.70	.19
□ 2 Marty Cordova	5.00	2.20	.60
□ 3 Shawn Green	1.50	.70	.19
□ 4 Todd Greene	4.00	1.80	.50
□ 5 Brian Hunter	4.00	1.80	.50
□ 6 Derek Jeter	20.00	9.00	2.50
□ 7 Charles Johnson	4.00	1.80	.50
□ 8 Chipper Jones	20.00	9.00	2.50
□ 9 Hideo Nomo	10.00	4.50	1.25
□ 10 Alex Ochoa	4.00	1.80	.50
□ 11 Andy Pettitte	12.00	5.50	1.50
□ 12 Quilvio Veras	1.50	.70	.19

1996 Metal Universe Mother Lode

Randomly inserted in hobby packs only at a rate of one in 12, this 12-card set features multi-tool players. The fronts carry a color action player cut-out over a silver-foil, scroll-design background. The backs display another player photo and information about the player.

	MINT	NRMT	EXC
COMPLETE SET (12)	60.00	27.00	7.50
COMMON CARD (1-12)	2.00	.90	.25
RANDOM INSERTS IN HOBBY PACKS			

□ 1 Barry Bonds	4.00	1.80	.50
□ 2 Jim Edmonds	2.00	.90	.25

□ 3 Ken Griffey Jr.	15.00	6.75	1.85
□ 4 Kenny Lofton	4.00	1.80	.50
□ 5 Raul Mondesi	2.00	.90	.25
□ 6 Rafael Palmeiro	2.00	.90	.25
□ 7 Manny Ramirez	4.00	1.80	.50
□ 8 Cal Ripken	12.00	5.50	1.50
□ 9 Tim Salmon	2.00	.90	.25
□ 10 Ryne Sandberg	4.00	1.80	.50
□ 11 Frank Thomas	15.00	6.75	1.85
□ 12 Matt Williams	2.00	.90	.25

1996 Metal Universe Platinum Portraits

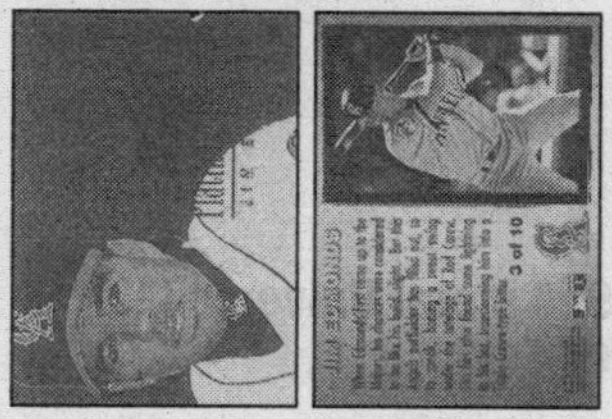

Randomly inserted in packs at a rate of one in four, this 10-card set features ten of the hottest young stars. The fronts display a player portrait on a platinum foil background. The backs carry a color action player photo and why the player is hot.

	MINT	NRMT	EXC
COMPLETE SET (10)	12.00	5.50	1.50
COMMON CARD (1-10)	.50	.23	.06
SEMISTARS	1.00	.45	.12
RANDOM INSERTS IN PACKS			

□ 1 Garret Anderson	1.00	.45	.12
□ 2 Marty Cordova	1.00	.45	.12
□ 3 Jim Edmonds	1.00	.45	.12
□ 4 Jason Isringhausen	.50	.23	.06
□ 5 Chipper Jones	5.00	2.20	.60
□ 6 Ryan Klesko	1.50	.70	.19
□ 7 Hideo Nomo	2.00	.90	.25
□ 8 Carlos Perez	.50	.23	.06
□ 9 Manny Ramirez	2.00	.90	.25
□ 10 Rondell White	1.00	.45	.12

1996 Metal Universe Titanium

Randomly inserted in packs at a rate of one in 24, this 10-card set features ten of the fans' favorite players. The fronts feature an action color player cut-out on a foil baseball background. The backs display a player portrait and why the player is liked by the fans.

	MINT	NRMT	EXC
COMPLETE SET (10)	125.00	55.00	15.50
COMMON CARD (1-10)	3.00	1.35	.35
RANDOM INSERTS IN PACKS			

□ 1 Albert Belle	12.00	5.50	1.50
□ 2 Barry Bonds	6.00	2.70	.75
□ 3 Ken Griffey Jr.	25.00	11.00	3.10
□ 4 Tony Gwynn	10.00	4.50	1.25
□ 5 Greg Maddux	15.00	6.75	1.85
□ 6 Mike Piazza	15.00	6.75	1.85
□ 7 Cal Ripken	20.00	9.00	2.50
□ 8 Frank Thomas	25.00	11.00	3.10
□ 9 Mo Vaughn	6.00	2.70	.75
□ 10 Matt Williams	3.00	1.35	.35

1994 Pacific

The 660 standard-size cards comprising this set feature color player action shots on their fronts that are borderless, except at the bottom, where a team color-coded marbleized border set off by a gold-foil line carries the team color-coded player's name. The set's gold-foil-stamped crown logo rests at the lower left. The back carries another color player action photo that is bordered only at the bottom, where the photo appears "torn away," revealing the gray marbleized area that carries the player's name, biography in both English and Spanish, statistics, and a ghosted team logo. The cards are numbered on the back, grouped alphabetically within teams, and checklisted below alphabetically according to teams as follows: Atlanta Braves (1-23), Baltimore Orioles (24-47), Boston Red Sox (48-70), California Angels (71-93), Chicago Cubs (94-117), Chicago White Sox (118-140), Cincinnati Reds (141-163), Cleveland Indians (164-186), Colorado Rockies (187-209), Detroit Tigers (210-232), Florida Marlins (233-255), Houston Astros (256-278), Kansas City Royals (279-301), Los Angeles Dodgers (302-324), Milwaukee Brewers (325-348), Minnesota Twins (349-371), Montreal Expos (372-394), New York Mets (395-419), New York Yankees (420-443), Oakland Athletics (444-466), Philadelphia Phillies (467-490), Pittsburgh Pirates (491-514), San Diego Padres (515-537), San Francisco Giants (538-560), Seattle Mariners (561-584), St. Louis Cardinals (585-608), Texas Rangers (609-631), and Toronto Blue Jays (632-654). The set closes with an Award Winners subset (655-660). There are no key Rookie Cards in this set.

	MINT	NRMT	EXC
COMPLETE SET (660)	30.00	13.50	3.70
COMMON CARD (1-660)	.05	.02	.01
SEMISTARS	.15	.07	.02
STARS	.30	.14	.04
CL SIX-CARD SET	2.00	.90	.25

□ 1 Steve Avery	.15	.07	.02
□ 2 Steve Bedrosian	.05	.02	.01
□ 3 Damon Berryhill	.05	.02	.01
□ 4 Jeff Blauser	.05	.02	.01
□ 5 Sid Bream	.05	.02	.01
□ 6 Francisco Cabrera	.05	.02	.01
□ 7 Ramon Caraballo	.05	.02	.01
□ 8 Ron Gant	.15	.07	.02
□ 9 Tom Glavine	.30	.14	.04
□ 10 Chipper Jones	1.50	.70	.19
□ 11 Dave Justice	.30	.14	.04
□ 12 Ryan Klesko	.50	.23	.06

□	13	Mark Lemke	.05	.02	.01
□	14	Javier Lopez	.30	.14	.04
□	15	Greg Maddux	1.25	.55	.16
□	16	Fred McGriff	.30	.14	.04
□	17	Greg McMichael	.05	.02	.01
□	18	Kent Mercker	.05	.02	.01
□	19	Otis Nixon	.05	.02	.01
□	20	Terry Pendleton	.15	.07	.02
□	21	Deion Sanders	.30	.14	.04
□	22	John Smoltz	.30	.14	.04
□	23	Tony Tarasco	.05	.02	.01
□	24	Manny Alexander	.05	.02	.01
□	25	Brady Anderson	.30	.14	.04
□	26	Harold Baines	.15	.07	.02
□	27	Damon Buford	.05	.02	.01
□	28	Paul Carey	.05	.02	.01
□	29	Mike Devereaux	.05	.02	.01
□	30	Todd Frohwirth	.05	.02	.01
□	31	Leo Gomez	.05	.02	.01
□	32	Jeffrey Hammonds	.15	.07	.02
□	33	Chris Hoiles	.05	.02	.01
□	34	Tim Hulett	.05	.02	.01
□	35	Ben McDonald	.05	.02	.01
□	36	Mark McLemore	.05	.02	.01
□	37	Alan Mills	.05	.02	.01
□	38	Mike Mussina	.40	.18	.05
□	39	Sherman Obando	.05	.02	.01
□	40	Gregg Olson	.05	.02	.01
□	41	Mike Pagliarulo	.05	.02	.01
□	42	Jim Poole	.05	.02	.01
□	43	Harold Reynolds	.05	.02	.01
□	44	Cal Ripken	1.50	.70	.19
□	45	David Segui	.05	.02	.01
□	46	Fernando Valenzuela	.15	.07	.02
□	47	Jack Voigt	.05	.02	.01
□	48	Scott Bankhead	.05	.02	.01
□	49	Roger Clemens	.30	.14	.04
□	50	Scott Cooper	.05	.02	.01
□	51	Danny Darwin	.05	.02	.01
□	52	Andre Dawson	.30	.14	.04
□	53	John Dopson	.05	.02	.01
□	54	Scott Fletcher	.05	.02	.01
□	55	Tony Fossas	.05	.02	.01
□	56	Mike Greenwell	.05	.02	.01
□	57	Billy Hatcher	.05	.02	.01
□	58	Jeff McNeely	.05	.02	.01
□	59	Jose Melendez	.05	.02	.01
□	60	Tim Naehring	.05	.02	.01
□	61	Tony Pena	.05	.02	.01
□	62	Carlos Quintana	.05	.02	.01
□	63	Paul Quantrill	.05	.02	.01
□	64	Luis Rivera	.05	.02	.01
□	65	Jeff Russell	.05	.02	.01
□	66	Aaron Sele	.15	.07	.02
□	67	John Valentin	.15	.07	.02
□	68	Mo Vaughn	.50	.23	.06
□	69	Frank Viola	.05	.02	.01
□	70	Bob Zupcic	.05	.02	.01
□	71	Mike Butcher	.05	.02	.01
□	72	Rod Correia	.05	.02	.01
□	73	Chad Curtis	.05	.02	.01
□	74	Chili Davis	.15	.07	.02
□	75	Gary DiSarcina	.05	.02	.01
□	76	Damion Easley	.05	.02	.01
□	77	John Farrell	.05	.02	.01
□	78	Chuck Finley	.05	.02	.01
□	79	Joe Grahe	.05	.02	.01
□	80	Stan Javier	.05	.02	.01
□	81	Mark Langston	.15	.07	.02
□	82	Phil Leftwich	.05	.02	.01
□	83	Torey Lovullo	.05	.02	.01
□	84	Joe Magrane	.05	.02	.01
□	85	Greg Myers	.05	.02	.01
□	86	Eduardo Perez	.05	.02	.01
□	87	Luis Polonia	.05	.02	.01
□	88	Tim Salmon	.30	.14	.04
□	89	J.T. Snow	.15	.07	.02
□	90	Kurt Stillwell	.05	.02	.01
□	91	Ron Tingley	.05	.02	.01
□	92	Chris Turner	.05	.02	.01
□	93	Julio Valera	.05	.02	.01
□	94	Jose Bautista	.05	.02	.01
□	95	Shawn Boskie	.05	.02	.01
□	96	Steve Buechele	.05	.02	.01
□	97	Frank Castillo	.05	.02	.01
□	98	Mark Grace UER (stats have 98 home runs in 1993; should be 14)	.30	.14	.04

□	99	Jose Guzman	.05	.02	.01
□	100	Mike Harkey	.05	.02	.01
□	101	Greg Hibbard	.05	.02	.01
□	102	Doug Jennings	.05	.02	.01
□	103	Derrick May	.05	.02	.01
□	104	Mike Morgan	.05	.02	.01
□	105	Randy Myers	.05	.02	.01
□	106	Karl Rhodes	.05	.02	.01
□	107	Kevin Roberson	.05	.02	.01
□	108	Rey Sanchez	.05	.02	.01
□	109	Ryne Sandberg	.50	.23	.06
□	110	Tommy Shields	.05	.02	.01
□	111	Dwight Smith	.05	.02	.01
□	112	Sammy Sosa	.30	.14	.04
□	113	Jose Vizcaino	.05	.02	.01
□	114	Turk Wendell	.05	.02	.01
□	115	Rick Wilkins	.05	.02	.01
□	116	Willie Wilson	.05	.02	.01
□	117	Eduardo Zambrano	.05	.02	.01
□	118	Wilson Alvarez	.15	.07	.02
□	119	Tim Belcher	.05	.02	.01
□	120	Jason Bere	.15	.07	.02
□	121	Rodney Bolton	.05	.02	.01
□	122	Ellis Burks	.15	.07	.02
□	123	Joey Cora	.05	.02	.01
□	124	Alex Fernandez	.30	.14	.04
□	125	Ozzie Guillen	.05	.02	.01
□	126	Craig Grebeck	.05	.02	.01
□	127	Roberto Hernandez	.15	.07	.02
□	128	Bo Jackson	.30	.14	.04
□	129	Lance Johnson	.15	.07	.02
□	130	Ron Karkovice	.05	.02	.01
□	131	Mike LaValliere	.05	.02	.01
□	132	Norberto Martin	.05	.02	.01
□	133	Kirk McCaskill	.05	.02	.01
□	134	Jack McDowell	.15	.07	.02
□	135	Scott Radinsky	.05	.02	.01
□	136	Tim Raines	.30	.14	.04
□	137	Steve Sax	.05	.02	.01
□	138	Frank Thomas	2.00	.90	.25
□	139	Dan Pasqua	.05	.02	.01
□	140	Robin Ventura	.15	.07	.02
□	141	Jeff Branson	.05	.02	.01
□	142	Tom Browning	.05	.02	.01
□	143	Jacob Brumfield	.05	.02	.01
□	144	Tim Costo	.05	.02	.01
□	145	Rob Dibble	.05	.02	.01
□	146	Brian Dorsett	.05	.02	.01
□	147	Steve Foster	.05	.02	.01
□	148	Cesar Hernandez	.05	.02	.01
□	149	Roberto Kelly	.05	.02	.01
□	150	Barry Larkin	.30	.14	.04
□	151	Larry Luebbers	.05	.02	.01
□	152	Kevin Mitchell	.15	.07	.02
□	153	Joe Oliver	.05	.02	.01
□	154	Tim Pugh	.05	.02	.01
□	155	Jeff Reardon	.15	.07	.02
□	156	Jose Rijo	.05	.02	.01
□	157	Bip Roberts	.05	.02	.01
□	158	Chris Sabo	.05	.02	.01
□	159	Juan Samuel	.05	.02	.01
□	160	Reggie Sanders	.30	.14	.04
□	161	John Smiley	.05	.02	.01
□	162	Jerry Spradlin	.05	.02	.01
□	163	Gary Varsho	.05	.02	.01
□	164	Sandy Alomar Jr.	.15	.07	.02
□	165	Albert Belle	1.00	.45	.12
□	166	Carlos Baerga	.30	.14	.04
□	167	Mark Clark	.05	.02	.01
□	168	Alvaro Espinoza	.05	.02	.01
□	169	Felix Fermin	.05	.02	.01
□	170	Reggie Jefferson	.15	.07	.02
□	171	Wayne Kirby	.05	.02	.01
□	172	Tom Kramer	.05	.02	.01
□	173	Kenny Lofton	.60	.25	.07
□	174	Jesse Levis	.05	.02	.01
□	175	Candy Maldonado	.05	.02	.01
□	176	Carlos Martinez	.05	.02	.01
□	177	Jose Mesa	.15	.07	.02
□	178	Jeff Mutis	.05	.02	.01
□	179	Charles Nagy	.15	.07	.02
□	180	Bob Ojeda	.05	.02	.01
□	181	Junior Ortiz	.05	.02	.01
□	182	Eric Plunk	.05	.02	.01

☐	183 Manny Ramirez	.60	.25	.07
☐	184 Paul Sorrento	.05	.02	.01
☐	185 Jeff Treadway	.05	.02	.01
☐	186 Bill Wertz	.05	.02	.01
☐	187 Freddie Benavides	.05	.02	.01
☐	188 Dante Bichette	.30	.14	.04
☐	189 Willie Blair	.05	.02	.01
☐	190 Daryl Boston	.05	.02	.01
☐	191 Pedro Castellano	.05	.02	.01
☐	192 Vinny Castilla	.30	.14	.04
☐	193 Jerald Clark	.05	.02	.01
☐	194 Alex Cole	.05	.02	.01
☐	195 Andres Galarraga	.30	.14	.04
☐	196 Joe Girardi	.05	.02	.01
☐	197 Charlie Hayes	.05	.02	.01
☐	198 Darren Holmes	.05	.02	.01
☐	199 Chris Jones	.05	.02	.01
☐	200 Curt Leskanic	.05	.02	.01
☐	201 Roberto Mejia	.05	.02	.01
☐	202 David Nied	.05	.02	.01
☐	203 J. Owens	.05	.02	.01
☐	204 Steve Reed	.05	.02	.01
☐	205 Armando Reynoso	.05	.02	.01
☐	206 Bruce Ruffin	.05	.02	.01
☐	207 Keith Shepherd	.05	.02	.01
☐	208 Jim Tatum	.05	.02	.01
☐	209 Eric Young	.15	.07	.02
☐	210 Skeeter Barnes	.05	.02	.01
☐	211 Danny Bautista	.05	.02	.01
☐	212 Tom Bolton	.05	.02	.01
☐	213 Eric Davis	.15	.07	.02
☐	214 Storm Davis	.05	.02	.01
☐	215 Cecil Fielder	.15	.07	.02
☐	216 Travis Fryman	.30	.14	.04
☐	217 Kirk Gibson	.15	.07	.02
☐	218 Dan Gladden	.05	.02	.01
☐	219 John Doherty	.05	.02	.01
☐	220 Chris Gomez	.05	.02	.01
☐	221 David Haas	.05	.02	.01
☐	222 Bill Krueger	.05	.02	.01
☐	223 Chad Kreuter	.05	.02	.01
☐	224 Mark Leiter	.05	.02	.01
☐	225 Bob MacDonald	.05	.02	.01
☐	226 Mike Moore	.05	.02	.01
☐	227 Tony Phillips	.15	.07	.02
☐	228 Rich Rowland	.05	.02	.01
☐	229 Mickey Tettleton	.05	.02	.01
☐	230 Alan Trammell	.30	.14	.04
☐	231 David Wells	.05	.02	.01
☐	232 Lou Whitaker	.30	.14	.04
☐	233 Luis Aquino	.05	.02	.01
☐	234 Alex Arias	.05	.02	.01
☐	235 Jack Armstrong	.05	.02	.01
☐	236 Ryan Bowen	.05	.02	.01
☐	237 Chuck Carr	.05	.02	.01
☐	238 Matias Carrillo	.05	.02	.01
☐	239 Jeff Conine	.30	.14	.04
☐	240 Henry Cotto	.05	.02	.01
☐	241 Orestes Destrade	.05	.02	.01
☐	242 Chris Hammond	.05	.02	.01
☐	243 Bryan Harvey	.05	.02	.01
☐	244 Charlie Hough	.05	.02	.01
☐	245 Richie Lewis	.05	.02	.01
☐	246 Mitch Lyden	.05	.02	.01
☐	247 Dave Magadan	.05	.02	.01
☐	248 Bob Natal	.05	.02	.01
☐	249 Benito Santiago	.05	.02	.01
☐	250 Gary Sheffield	.30	.14	.04
☐	251 Matt Turner	.05	.02	.01
☐	252 David Weathers	.05	.02	.01
☐	253 Walt Weiss	.05	.02	.01
☐	254 Darrell Whitmore	.05	.02	.01
☐	255 Nigel Wilson	.05	.02	.01
☐	256 Eric Anthony	.05	.02	.01
☐	257 Jeff Bagwell	.75	.35	.09
☐	258 Kevin Bass	.05	.02	.01
☐	259 Craig Biggio	.30	.14	.04
☐	260 Ken Caminiti	.30	.14	.04
☐	261 Andujar Cedeno	.05	.02	.01
☐	262 Chris Donnels	.05	.02	.01
☐	263 Doug Drabek	.05	.02	.01
☐	264 Tom Edens	.05	.02	.01
☐	265 Steve Finley	.30	.14	.04
☐	266 Luis Gonzalez	.05	.02	.01
☐	267 Pete Harnisch	.05	.02	.01
☐	268 Xavier Hernandez	.05	.02	.01
☐	269 Todd Jones	.05	.02	.01
☐	270 Darryl Kile	.05	.02	.01
☐	271 Al Osuna	.05	.02	.01
☐	272 Rick Parker	.05	.02	.01
☐	273 Mark Portugal	.05	.02	.01
☐	274 Scott Servais	.05	.02	.01
☐	275 Greg Swindell	.05	.02	.01
☐	276 Eddie Taubensee	.05	.02	.01
☐	277 Jose Uribe	.05	.02	.01
☐	278 Brian Williams	.05	.02	.01
☐	279 Kevin Appier	.15	.07	.02
☐	280 Billy Brewer	.05	.02	.01
☐	281 David Cone	.30	.14	.04
☐	282 Greg Gagne	.05	.02	.01
☐	283 Tom Gordon	.05	.02	.01
☐	284 Chris Gwynn	.05	.02	.01
☐	285 John Habyan	.05	.02	.01
☐	286 Chris Haney	.05	.02	.01
☐	287 Phil Hiatt	.05	.02	.01
☐	288 David Howard	.05	.02	.01
☐	289 Felix Jose	.05	.02	.01
☐	290 Wally Joyner	.15	.07	.02
☐	291 Kevin Koslofski	.05	.02	.01
☐	292 Jose Lind	.05	.02	.01
☐	293 Brent Mayne	.05	.02	.01
☐	294 Mike Macfarlane	.05	.02	.01
☐	295 Brian McRae	.15	.07	.02
☐	296 Kevin McReynolds	.05	.02	.01
☐	297 Keith Miller	.05	.02	.01
☐	298 Jeff Montgomery	.15	.07	.02
☐	299 Hipolito Pichardo	.05	.02	.01
☐	300 Rico Rossy	.05	.02	.01
☐	301 Curtis Wilkerson	.05	.02	.01
☐	302 Pedro Astacio	.05	.02	.01
☐	303 Rafael Bournigal	.05	.02	.01
☐	304 Brett Butler	.15	.07	.02
☐	305 Tom Candiotti	.05	.02	.01
☐	306 Omar Daal	.05	.02	.01
☐	307 Jim Gott	.05	.02	.01
☐	308 Kevin Gross	.05	.02	.01
☐	309 Dave Hansen	.05	.02	.01
☐	310 Carlos Hernandez	.05	.02	.01
☐	311 Orel Hershiser	.15	.07	.02
☐	312 Eric Karros	.15	.07	.02
☐	313 Pedro Martinez	.30	.14	.04
☐	314 Ramon Martinez	.15	.07	.02
☐	315 Roger McDowell	.05	.02	.01
☐	316 Raul Mondesi	.30	.14	.04
☐	317 Jose Offerman	.05	.02	.01
☐	318 Mike Piazza	1.25	.55	.16
☐	319 Jody Reed	.05	.02	.01
☐	320 Henry Rodriguez	.30	.14	.04
☐	321 Cory Snyder	.05	.02	.01
☐	322 Darryl Strawberry	.15	.07	.02
☐	323 Tim Wallach	.05	.02	.01
☐	324 Steve Wilson	.05	.02	.01
☐	325 Juan Bell	.05	.02	.01
☐	326 Ricky Bones	.05	.02	.01
☐	327 Alex Diaz	.05	.02	.01
☐	328 Cal Eldred	.05	.02	.01
☐	329 Darryl Hamilton	.05	.02	.01
☐	330 Doug Henry	.05	.02	.01
☐	331 John Jaha	.15	.07	.02
☐	332 Pat Listach	.05	.02	.01
☐	333 Graeme Lloyd	.05	.02	.01
☐	334 Carlos Maldonado	.05	.02	.01
☐	335 Angel Miranda	.05	.02	.01
☐	336 Jaime Navarro	.05	.02	.01
☐	337 Dave Nilsson	.15	.07	.02
☐	338 Rafael Novoa	.05	.02	.01
☐	339 Troy O'Leary	.05	.02	.01
☐	340 Jesse Orosco	.05	.02	.01
☐	341 Kevin Seitzer	.05	.02	.01
☐	342 Bill Spiers	.05	.02	.01
☐	343 William Suero	.05	.02	.01
☐	344 B.J. Surhoff	.05	.02	.01
☐	345 Dickie Thon	.05	.02	.01
☐	346 Jose Valentin	.15	.07	.02
☐	347 Greg Vaughn	.30	.14	.04
☐	348 Robin Yount	.30	.14	.04
☐	349 Willie Banks	.05	.02	.01
☐	350 Bernardo Brito	.05	.02	.01
☐	351 Scott Erickson	.05	.02	.01
☐	352 Mark Guthrie	.05	.02	.01
☐	353 Chip Hale	.05	.02	.01
☐	354 Brian Harper	.05	.02	.01

☐ 355	Kent Hrbek	.15	.07	.02
☐ 356	Terry Jorgensen	.05	.02	.01
☐ 357	Chuck Knoblauch	.30	.14	.04
☐ 358	Gene Larkin	.05	.02	.01
☐ 359	Scott Leius	.05	.02	.01
☐ 360	Shane Mack	.05	.02	.01
☐ 361	David McCarty	.05	.02	.01
☐ 362	Pat Meares	.05	.02	.01
☐ 363	Pedro Munoz	.05	.02	.01
☐ 364	Derek Parks	.05	.02	.01
☐ 365	Kirby Puckett	.60	.25	.07
☐ 366	Jeff Reboulet	.05	.02	.01
☐ 367	Kevin Tapani	.05	.02	.01
☐ 368	Mike Trombley	.05	.02	.01
☐ 369	George Tsamis	.05	.02	.01
☐ 370	Carl Willis	.05	.02	.01
☐ 371	Dave Winfield	.30	.14	.04
☐ 372	Moises Alou	.15	.07	.02
☐ 373	Brian Barnes	.05	.02	.01
☐ 374	Sean Berry	.05	.02	.01
☐ 375	Frank Bolick	.05	.02	.01
☐ 376	Wil Cordero	.15	.07	.02
☐ 377	Delino DeShields	.05	.02	.01
☐ 378	Jeff Fassero	.05	.02	.01
☐ 379	Darrin Fletcher	.05	.02	.01
☐ 380	Cliff Floyd	.30	.14	.04
☐ 381	Lou Frazier	.05	.02	.01
☐ 382	Marquis Grissom	.30	.14	.04
☐ 383	Gil Heredia	.05	.02	.01
☐ 384	Mike Lansing	.15	.07	.02
☐ 385	Oreste Marrero	.05	.02	.01
☐ 386	Dennis Martinez	.15	.07	.02
☐ 387	Curtis Pride	.15	.07	.02
☐ 388	Mel Rojas	.05	.02	.01
☐ 389	Kirk Rueter	.05	.02	.01
☐ 390	Joe Siddall	.05	.02	.01
☐ 391	John Vander Wal	.05	.02	.01
☐ 392	Larry Walker	.30	.14	.04
☐ 393	John Wetteland	.15	.07	.02
☐ 394	Rondell White	.30	.14	.04
☐ 395	Tim Bogar	.05	.02	.01
☐ 396	Bobby Bonilla	.15	.07	.02
☐ 397	Jeromy Burnitz	.05	.02	.01
☐ 398	Mike Draper	.05	.02	.01
☐ 399	Sid Fernandez	.05	.02	.01
☐ 400	John Franco	.05	.02	.01
☐ 401	Dave Gallagher	.05	.02	.01
☐ 402	Dwight Gooden	.15	.07	.02
☐ 403	Eric Hillman	.05	.02	.01
☐ 404	Todd Hundley	.30	.14	.04
☐ 405	Butch Huskey	.15	.07	.02
☐ 406	Jeff Innis	.05	.02	.01
☐ 407	Howard Johnson	.05	.02	.01
☐ 408	Jeff Kent	.05	.02	.01
☐ 409	Ced Landrum	.05	.02	.01
☐ 410	Mike Maddux	.05	.02	.01
☐ 411	Josias Manzanillo	.05	.02	.01
☐ 412	Jeff McKnight	.05	.02	.01
☐ 413	Eddie Murray	.50	.23	.06
☐ 414	Tito Navarro	.05	.02	.01
☐ 415	Joe Orsulak	.05	.02	.01
☐ 416	Bret Saberhagen	.15	.07	.02
☐ 417	Dave Telgheder	.05	.02	.01
☐ 418	Ryan Thompson	.05	.02	.01
☐ 419	Chico Walker	.05	.02	.01
☐ 420	Jim Abbott	.05	.02	.01
☐ 421	Wade Boggs	.30	.14	.04
☐ 422	Mike Gallego	.05	.02	.01
☐ 423	Mark Hutton	.05	.02	.01
☐ 424	Dion James	.05	.02	.01
☐ 425	Domingo Jean	.05	.02	.01
☐ 426	Pat Kelly	.05	.02	.01
☐ 427	Jimmy Key	.15	.07	.02
☐ 428	Jim Leyritz	.05	.02	.01
☐ 429	Kevin Maas	.05	.02	.01
☐ 430	Don Mattingly	1.00	.45	.12
☐ 431	Bobby Munoz	.05	.02	.01
☐ 432	Matt Nokes	.05	.02	.01
☐ 433	Paul O'Neill	.15	.07	.02
☐ 434	Spike Owen	.05	.02	.01
☐ 435	Melido Perez	.05	.02	.01
☐ 436	Lee Smith	.15	.07	.02
☐ 437	Andy Stankiewicz	.05	.02	.01
☐ 438	Mike Stanley	.05	.02	.01
☐ 439	Danny Tartabull	.05	.02	.01
☐ 440	Randy Velarde	.05	.02	.01
☐ 441	Bernie Williams	.30	.14	.04
☐ 442	Gerald Williams	.05	.02	.01
☐ 443	Mike Witt	.05	.02	.01
☐ 444	Marcos Armas	.05	.02	.01
☐ 445	Lance Blankenship	.05	.02	.01
☐ 446	Mike Bordick	.05	.02	.01
☐ 447	Ron Darling UER	.05	.02	.01
	Reversed negative on front			
☐ 448	Dennis Eckersley	.15	.07	.02
☐ 449	Brent Gates	.05	.02	.01
☐ 450	Goose Gossage	.15	.07	.02
☐ 451	Scott Hemond	.05	.02	.01
☐ 452	Dave Henderson	.05	.02	.01
☐ 453	Shawn Hillegas	.05	.02	.01
☐ 454	Rick Honeycutt	.05	.02	.01
☐ 455	Scott Lydy	.05	.02	.01
☐ 456	Mark McGwire	.60	.25	.07
☐ 457	Henry Mercedes	.05	.02	.01
☐ 458	Mike Mohler	.05	.02	.01
☐ 459	Troy Neel	.05	.02	.01
☐ 460	Edwin Nunez	.05	.02	.01
☐ 461	Craig Paquette	.05	.02	.01
☐ 462	Ruben Sierra	.15	.07	.02
☐ 463	Terry Steinbach	.15	.07	.02
☐ 464	Todd Van Poppel	.05	.02	.01
☐ 465	Bob Welch	.05	.02	.01
☐ 466	Bobby Witt	.05	.02	.01
☐ 467	Ruben Amaro	.05	.02	.01
☐ 468	Larry Andersen	.05	.02	.01
☐ 469	Kim Batiste	.05	.02	.01
☐ 470	Wes Chamberlain	.05	.02	.01
☐ 471	Darren Daulton	.15	.07	.02
☐ 472	Mariano Duncan	.05	.02	.01
☐ 473	Len Dykstra	.15	.07	.02
☐ 474	Jim Eisenreich	.05	.02	.01
☐ 475	Tommy Greene	.05	.02	.01
☐ 476	Dave Hollins	.05	.02	.01
☐ 477	Pete Incaviglia	.05	.02	.01
☐ 478	Danny Jackson	.05	.02	.01
☐ 479	John Kruk	.15	.07	.02
☐ 480	Tony Longmire	.05	.02	.01
☐ 481	Jeff Manto	.05	.02	.01
☐ 482	Mickey Morandini	.05	.02	.01
☐ 483	Terry Mulholland	.05	.02	.01
☐ 484	Todd Pratt	.05	.02	.01
☐ 485	Ben Rivera	.05	.02	.01
☐ 486	Curt Schilling	.05	.02	.01
☐ 487	Kevin Stocker	.05	.02	.01
☐ 488	Milt Thompson	.05	.02	.01
☐ 489	David West	.05	.02	.01
☐ 490	Mitch Williams	.05	.02	.01
☐ 491	Jeff Ballard	.05	.02	.01
☐ 492	Jay Bell	.15	.07	.02
☐ 493	Scott Bullett	.05	.02	.01
☐ 494	Dave Clark	.05	.02	.01
☐ 495	Steve Cooke	.05	.02	.01
☐ 496	Midre Cummings	.05	.02	.01
☐ 497	Mark Dewey	.05	.02	.01
☐ 498	Carlos Garcia	.05	.02	.01
☐ 499	Jeff King	.15	.07	.02
☐ 500	Al Martin	.05	.02	.01
☐ 501	Lloyd McClendon	.05	.02	.01
☐ 502	Orlando Merced	.15	.07	.02
☐ 503	Blas Minor	.05	.02	.01
☐ 504	Denny Neagle	.15	.07	.02
☐ 505	Tom Prince	.05	.02	.01
☐ 506	Don Slaught	.05	.02	.01
☐ 507	Zane Smith	.05	.02	.01
☐ 508	Randy Tomlin	.05	.02	.01
☐ 509	Andy Van Slyke	.15	.07	.02
☐ 510	Paul Wagner	.05	.02	.01
☐ 511	Tim Wakefield	.05	.02	.01
☐ 512	Bob Walk	.05	.02	.01
☐ 513	John Wehner	.05	.02	.01
☐ 514	Kevin Young	.05	.02	.01
☐ 515	Billy Bean	.05	.02	.01
☐ 516	Andy Benes	.15	.07	.02
☐ 517	Derek Bell	.15	.07	.02
☐ 518	Doug Brocail	.05	.02	.01
☐ 519	Jarvis Brown	.05	.02	.01
☐ 520	Phil Clark	.05	.02	.01
☐ 521	Mark Davis	.05	.02	.01
☐ 522	Jeff Gardner	.05	.02	.01
☐ 523	Pat Gomez	.05	.02	.01
☐ 524	Ricky Gutierrez	.05	.02	.01
☐ 525	Tony Gwynn	.75	.35	.09

□ 526 Gene Harris	.05	.02	.01
□ 527 Kevin Higgins	.05	.02	.01
□ 528 Trevor Hoffman	.15	.07	.02
□ 529 Luis Lopez	.05	.02	.01
□ 530 Pedro Martinez	.30	.14	.04
□ 531 Melvin Nieves	.15	.07	.02
□ 532 Phil Plantier	.05	.02	.01
□ 533 Frank Seminara	.05	.02	.01
□ 534 Craig Shipley	.05	.02	.01
□ 535 Tim Teufel	.05	.02	.01
□ 536 Guillermo Velasquez	.05	.02	.01
□ 537 Wally Whitehurst	.05	.02	.01
□ 538 Rod Beck	.15	.07	.02
□ 539 Todd Benzinger	.05	.02	.01
□ 540 Barry Bonds	.50	.23	.06
□ 541 Jeff Brantley	.05	.02	.01
□ 542 Dave Burba	.05	.02	.01
□ 543 John Burkett	.05	.02	.01
□ 544 Will Clark	.30	.14	.04
□ 545 Royce Clayton	.15	.07	.02
□ 546 Bryan Hickerson	.05	.02	.01
□ 547 Mike Jackson	.05	.02	.01
□ 548 Darren Lewis	.05	.02	.01
□ 549 Kirt Manwaring	.05	.02	.01
□ 550 Dave Martinez	.05	.02	.01
□ 551 Willie McGee	.05	.02	.01
□ 552 Jeff Reed	.05	.02	.01
□ 553 Dave Righetti	.05	.02	.01
□ 554 Kevin Rogers	.05	.02	.01
□ 555 Steve Scarsone	.05	.02	.01
□ 556 Bill Swift	.05	.02	.01
□ 557 Robby Thompson	.05	.02	.01
□ 558 Salomon Torres	.05	.02	.01
□ 559 Matt Williams	.30	.14	.04
□ 560 Trevor Wilson	.05	.02	.01
□ 561 Rich Amaral	.05	.02	.01
□ 562 Mike Blowers	.05	.02	.01
□ 563 Chris Bosio	.05	.02	.01
□ 564 Jay Buhner	.30	.14	.04
□ 565 Norm Charlton	.05	.02	.01
□ 566 Jim Converse	.05	.02	.01
□ 567 Rich DeLucia	.05	.02	.01
□ 568 Mike Felder	.05	.02	.01
□ 569 Dave Fleming	.05	.02	.01
□ 570 Ken Griffey Jr.	2.00	.90	.25
□ 571 Bill Haselman	.05	.02	.01
□ 572 Dwayne Henry	.05	.02	.01
□ 573 Brad Holman	.05	.02	.01
□ 574 Randy Johnson	.30	.14	.04
□ 575 Greg Litton	.05	.02	.01
□ 576 Edgar Martinez	.30	.14	.04
□ 577 Tino Martinez	.15	.07	.02
□ 578 Jeff Nelson	.05	.02	.01
□ 579 Marc Newfield	.15	.07	.02
□ 580 Roger Salkeld	.05	.02	.01
□ 581 Mackey Sasser	.05	.02	.01
□ 582 Brian Turang	.05	.02	.01
□ 583 Omar Vizquel	.30	.14	.04
□ 584 Dave Valle	.05	.02	.01
□ 585 Luis Alicea	.05	.02	.01
□ 586 Rene Arocha	.05	.02	.01
□ 587 Rheal Cormier	.05	.02	.01
□ 588 Tripp Cromer	.05	.02	.01
□ 589 Bernard Gilkey	.15	.07	.02
□ 590 Lee Guetterman	.05	.02	.01
□ 591 Gregg Jefferies	.30	.14	.04
□ 592 Tim Jones	.05	.02	.01
□ 593 Paul Kilgus	.05	.02	.01
□ 594 Les Lancaster	.05	.02	.01
□ 595 Omar Olivares	.05	.02	.01
□ 596 Jose Oquendo	.05	.02	.01
□ 597 Donovan Osborne	.05	.02	.01
□ 598 Tom Pagnozzi	.05	.02	.01
□ 599 Erik Pappas	.05	.02	.01
□ 600 Geronimo Pena	.05	.02	.01
□ 601 Mike Perez	.05	.02	.01
□ 602 Gerald Perry	.05	.02	.01
□ 603 Stan Royer	.05	.02	.01
□ 604 Ozzie Smith	.40	.18	.05
□ 605 Bob Tewksbury	.05	.02	.01
□ 606 Allen Watson	.05	.02	.01
□ 607 Mark Whiten	.05	.02	.01
□ 608 Todd Zeile	.05	.02	.01
□ 609 Jeff Bronkey	.05	.02	.01
□ 610 Kevin Brown	.05	.02	.01
□ 611 Jose Canseco	.30	.14	.04
□ 612 Doug Dascenzo	.05	.02	.01
□ 613 Butch Davis	.05	.02	.01
□ 614 Mario Diaz	.05	.02	.01
□ 615 Julio Franco	.15	.07	.02
□ 616 Benji Gil	.05	.02	.01
□ 617 Juan Gonzalez	1.00	.45	.12
□ 618 Tom Henke	.05	.02	.01
□ 619 Jeff Huson	.05	.02	.01
□ 620 David Hulse	.05	.02	.01
□ 621 Craig Lefferts	.05	.02	.01
□ 622 Rafael Palmeiro	.30	.14	.04
□ 623 Dean Palmer	.15	.07	.02
□ 624 Bob Patterson	.05	.02	.01
□ 625 Roger Pavlik	.05	.02	.01
□ 626 Gary Redus	.05	.02	.01
□ 627 Ivan Rodriguez	.40	.18	.05
□ 628 Kenny Rogers	.05	.02	.01
□ 629 Jon Shave	.05	.02	.01
□ 630 Doug Strange	.05	.02	.01
□ 631 Matt Whiteside	.05	.02	.01
□ 632 Roberto Alomar	.50	.23	.06
□ 633 Pat Borders	.05	.02	.01
□ 634 Scott Brow	.05	.02	.01
□ 635 Rob Butler	.05	.02	.01
□ 636 Joe Carter	.30	.14	.04
□ 637 Tony Castillo	.05	.02	.01
□ 638 Mark Eichhorn	.05	.02	.01
□ 639 Tony Fernandez	.05	.02	.01
□ 640 Huck Flener	.05	.02	.01
□ 641 Alfredo Griffin	.05	.02	.01
□ 642 Juan Guzman	.15	.07	.02
□ 643 Rickey Henderson	.30	.14	.04
□ 644 Pat Hentgen	.30	.14	.04
□ 645 Randy Knorr	.05	.02	.01
□ 646 Al Leiter	.15	.07	.02
□ 647 Domingo Martinez	.05	.02	.01
□ 648 Paul Molitor	.40	.18	.05
□ 649 Jack Morris	.15	.07	.02
□ 650 John Olerud	.05	.02	.01
□ 651 Ed Sprague	.15	.07	.02
□ 652 Dave Stewart	.15	.07	.02
□ 653 Devon White	.05	.02	.01
□ 654 Woody Williams	.05	.02	.01
□ 655 Barry Bonds MVP	.30	.14	.04
□ 656 Greg Maddux CY	.60	.25	.07
□ 657 Jack McDowell CY	.05	.02	.01
□ 658 Mike Piazza ROY	.60	.25	.07
□ 659 Tim Salmon ROY	.30	.14	.04
□ 660 Frank Thomas MVP	1.00	.45	.12

1994 Pacific All-Latino

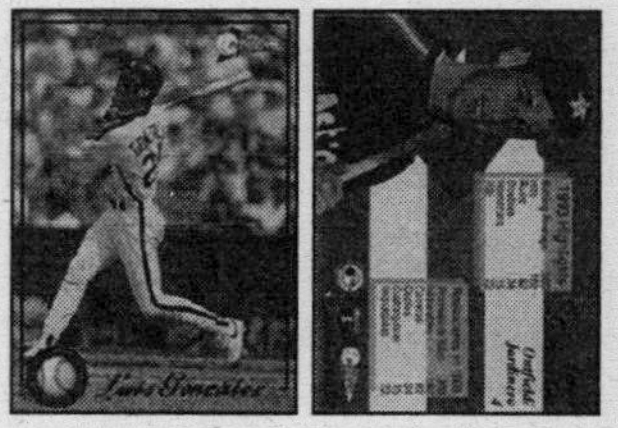

Randomly inserted in Pacific purple foil packs at a rate of one in 25, this 20-card standard-size set spotlights the greatest Latin players chosen by the Pacific staff. Print run was limited to 8,000 sets. The fronts feature a full-bleed color player photo with gold foil stamping. The player's name in gold foil appears on the bottom of the photo. Superimposed on the player's native country's flag, the horizontal backs show a close-up color player photo on the left, while 1993 highlights, printed in English and Spanish, appear on the right. The set subdivides into National League (1-10) and American League (11-20) players.

	MINT	NRMT	EXC
COMPLETE SET (20)	25.00	11.00	3.10
COMMON CARD (1-20)	1.00	.45	.12
SEMISTARS	3.00	1.35	.35
RANDOM INSERTS IN PURPLE REGULAR PACKS			

		MINT	NRMT	EXC
□ 1	Benito Santiago	1.00	.45	.12
□ 2	Dave Magadan	1.00	.45	.12
□ 3	Andres Galarraga	3.00	1.35	.35
□ 4	Luis Gonzalez	1.00	.45	.12
□ 5	Jose Offerman	1.00	.45	.12
□ 6	Bobby Bonilla	3.00	1.35	.35
□ 7	Dennis Martinez	1.00	.45	.12
□ 8	Mariano Duncan	1.00	.45	.12
□ 9	Orlando Merced	1.00	.45	.12
□ 10	Jose Rijo	1.00	.45	.12
□ 11	Danny Tartabull	1.00	.45	.12
□ 12	Ruben Sierra	3.00	1.35	.35
□ 13	Ivan Rodriguez	5.00	2.20	.60
□ 14	Juan Gonzalez	12.00	5.50	1.50
□ 15	Jose Canseco	3.00	1.35	.35
□ 16	Rafael Palmeiro	3.00	1.35	.35
□ 17	Roberto Alomar	6.00	2.70	.75
□ 18	Eduardo Perez	1.00	.45	.12
□ 19	Alex Fernandez	3.00	1.35	.35
□ 20	Omar Vizquel	1.00	.45	.12

1994 Pacific Gold Prisms

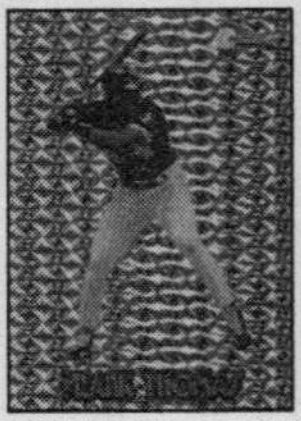

Randomly inserted in Pacific purple foil packs at a rate of one in 25, this 20-card standard-size prismatic "Home Run Leaders" set honors the top 1993 home run leaders. Print run was reportedly limited to 8,000 sets. The fronts feature a cut-out color player photo against a gold prism background. The player's name appears at the bottom, highlighted in team colors. Superimposed on a baseball field, the horizontal backs show a close-up color player photo on the left, while the number of home runs the player hit in 1993 is highlighted on a large baseball icon on the right. The set subdivides into American League (1-10) and National League (11-20) players.

	MINT	NRMT	EXC
COMPLETE SET (20)	90.00	40.00	11.00
COMMON CARD (1-20)	1.50	.70	.19
SEMISTARS	3.00	1.35	.35
RANDOM INSERTS IN PURPLE REGULAR PACKS			

		MINT	NRMT	EXC
□ 1	Juan Gonzalez	12.00	5.50	1.50
□ 2	Ken Griffey Jr.	25.00	11.00	3.10
□ 3	Frank Thomas	25.00	11.00	3.10
□ 4	Albert Belle	12.00	5.50	1.50
□ 5	Rafael Palmeiro	3.00	1.35	.35
□ 6	Joe Carter	3.00	1.35	.35
□ 7	Dean Palmer	3.00	1.35	.35
□ 8	Mickey Tettleton	1.50	.70	.19
□ 9	Tim Salmon	4.00	1.80	.50
□ 10	Danny Tartabull	1.50	.70	.19
□ 11	Barry Bonds	6.00	2.70	.75
□ 12	Dave Justice	3.00	1.35	.35
□ 13	Matt Williams	3.00	1.35	.35
□ 14	Fred McGriff	3.00	1.35	.35
□ 15	Ron Gant	3.00	1.35	.35
□ 16	Mike Piazza	15.00	6.75	1.85
□ 17	Bobby Bonilla	3.00	1.35	.35
□ 18	Phil Plantier	1.50	.70	.19
□ 19	Sammy Sosa	4.00	1.80	.50
□ 20	Rick Wilkins	1.50	.70	.19

1994 Pacific Silver Prisms

Randomly inserted in Pacific foil packs, this 36-card standard-size set is also known as "Jewels of the Crown". The print run was reportedly limited to 8,000 sets. The cards measure the standard size. The fronts feature a cut-out color player photo against a prism background that is either circular or triangular. The triangular versions were randomly inserted in purple packs and the circular one per black retail pack. The circular versions are valued 25 to percent the triangular. The player's name appears at the bottom, highlighted in team colors. On a red velvet background, the horizontal backs show a close-up color player photo on the left, while highlights of the 1993 season in English and Spanish are printed over a unique jewel design on the right. The set divides into American League (1-18) and National League (19-36) players.

	MINT	NRMT	EXC
COMPLETE SET (36)	125.00	55.00	15.50
COMMON CARD (1-36)	1.00	.45	.12
SEMISTARS	2.50	1.10	.30
TRIANGULAR INSERTS IN PURPLE PACKS.			
CIRCULAR ONE PER BLACK RETAIL PACK..			
*CIRCULAR: .25X TO .50X BASIC CARDS ...			

		MINT	NRMT	EXC
□ 1	Robin Yount	2.50	1.10	.30
□ 2	Juan Gonzalez	10.00	4.50	1.25
□ 3	Rafael Palmeiro	2.50	1.10	.30
□ 4	Paul Molitor	4.00	1.80	.50
□ 5	Roberto Alomar	5.00	2.20	.60
□ 6	John Olerud	1.00	.45	.12
□ 7	Randy Johnson	3.00	1.35	.35
□ 8	Ken Griffey Jr.	20.00	9.00	2.50
□ 9	Wade Boggs	2.50	1.10	.30
□ 10	Don Mattingly	10.00	4.50	1.25
□ 11	Kirby Puckett	6.00	2.70	.75
□ 12	Tim Salmon	3.00	1.35	.35
□ 13	Frank Thomas	20.00	9.00	2.50
□ 14	Fernando Valenzuela	2.50	1.10	.30
□ 15	Cal Ripken	15.00	6.75	1.85
□ 16	Carlos Baerga	2.50	1.10	.30
□ 17	Kenny Lofton	6.00	2.70	.75
□ 18	Cecil Fielder	2.50	1.10	.30
□ 19	John Burkett	1.00	.45	.12
□ 20	Andres Galarraga	2.50	1.10	.30
□ 21	Charlie Hayes	1.00	.45	.12
□ 22	Orestes Destrade	1.00	.45	.12
□ 23	Jeff Conine	2.50	1.10	.30
□ 24	Jeff Bagwell	8.00	3.60	1.00
□ 25	Mark Grace	2.50	1.10	.30
□ 26	Ryne Sandberg	5.00	2.20	.60
□ 27	Gregg Jefferies	2.50	1.10	.30
□ 28	Barry Bonds	5.00	2.20	.60
□ 29	Mike Piazza	12.00	5.50	1.50
□ 30	Greg Maddux	12.00	5.50	1.50
□ 31	Darren Dalton	2.50	1.10	.30
□ 32	John Kruk	2.50	1.10	.30
□ 33	Lenny Dykstra	2.50	1.10	.30
□ 34	Orlando Merced	1.00	.45	.12
□ 35	Tony Gwynn	8.00	3.60	1.00
□ 36	Robby Thompson	1.00	.45	.12

1995 Pacific

This 450-card standard-size set was issued in one series. The full-bleed fronts have action photos; the "Pacific Collection" logo is on the upper left and the player's name is at the bottom. The horizontal backs have a player photo on the left with 1994 stats and some career highlights on the right. The career highlights are in both English and Spanish. The cards are numbered in the lower right corner. The cards are grouped alphabetically within teams and checklisted below alphabetically according to teams for each league as follows: Atlanta Braves (1-16), Baltimore Orioles (17-32), Boston Red Sox (33-49), California Angels (50-65), Chicago Cubs (66-81), Chicago White Sox (82-98), Cincinnati Reds (99-114), Cleveland Indians (115-131), Colorado Rockies (132-147), Detroit Tigers (148-163), Florida Marlins (164-179), Houston Astros (180-195), Kansas City Royals (196-211), Los Angeles Dodgers (212-227), Milwaukee Brewers (228-243), Minnesota Twins (244-259), Montreal Expos (260-275), New York Mets (276-291), New York Yankees (292-307), Oakland Athletics (308-323), Philadelphia Phillies (324-339), Pittsburgh Pirates (340-355), San Diego Padres (356-371), San Francisco Giants (372-387), Seattle Mariners (388-403), St. Louis Cardinals (404-419), Texas Rangers (420-434) and Toronto Blue Jays (435-450). There are no key Rookie Cards in this set.

	MINT	NRMT	EXC
COMPLETE SET (450)	30.00	13.50	3.70
COMMON CARD (1-450)	.05	.02	.01
SEMISTARS	.15	.07	.02
STARS	.30	.14	.04

□ 1 Steve Avery	.15	.07	.02
□ 2 Rafael Belliard	.05	.02	.01
□ 3 Jeff Blauser	.05	.02	.01
□ 4 Tom Glavine	.30	.14	.04
□ 5 David Justice	.30	.14	.04
□ 6 Mike Kelly	.05	.02	.01
□ 7 Roberto Kelly	.05	.02	.01
□ 8 Ryan Klesko	.40	.18	.05
□ 9 Mark Lemke	.05	.02	.01
□ 10 Javier Lopez	.30	.14	.04
□ 11 Greg Maddux	1.25	.55	.16
□ 12 Fred McGriff	.30	.14	.04
□ 13 Greg McMichael	.05	.02	.01
□ 14 Jose Oliva	.05	.02	.01
□ 15 John Smoltz	.30	.14	.04
□ 16 Tony Tarasco	.05	.02	.01
□ 17 Brady Anderson	.30	.14	.04
□ 18 Harold Baines	.15	.07	.02
□ 19 Armando Benitez	.05	.02	.01
□ 20 Mike Devereaux	.05	.02	.01
□ 21 Leo Gomez	.05	.02	.01
□ 22 Jeffrey Hammonds	.15	.07	.02
□ 23 Chris Hoiles	.05	.02	.01
□ 24 Ben McDonald	.05	.02	.01
□ 25 Mark McLemore	.05	.02	.01
□ 26 Jamie Moyer	.05	.02	.01
□ 27 Mike Mussina	.40	.18	.05
□ 28 Rafael Palmeiro	.30	.14	.04
□ 29 Jim Poole	.05	.02	.01
□ 30 Cal Ripken Jr.	1.50	.70	.19
□ 31 Lee Smith	.15	.07	.02
□ 32 Mark Smith	.05	.02	.01
□ 33 Jose Canseco	.30	.14	.04
□ 34 Roger Clemens	.30	.14	.04
□ 35 Scott Cooper	.05	.02	.01
□ 36 Andre Dawson	.30	.14	.04
□ 37 Tony Fossas	.05	.02	.01
□ 38 Mike Greenwell	.05	.02	.01
□ 39 Chris Howard	.05	.02	.01
□ 40 Jose Melendez	.05	.02	.01
□ 41 Nate Minchey	.05	.02	.01
□ 42 Tim Naehring	.05	.02	.01
□ 43 Otis Nixon	.05	.02	.01
□ 44 Carlos Rodriguez	.05	.02	.01
□ 45 Aaron Sele	.15	.07	.02
□ 46 Lee Tinsley	.05	.02	.01
□ 47 Sergio Valdez	.05	.02	.01
□ 48 John Valentin	.15	.07	.02
□ 49 Mo Vaughn	.50	.23	.06
□ 50 Brian Anderson	.05	.02	.01
□ 51 Garret Anderson	.30	.14	.04
□ 52 Rod Correia	.05	.02	.01
□ 53 Chad Curtis	.05	.02	.01
□ 54 Mark Dalesandro	.05	.02	.01
□ 55 Chili Davis	.15	.07	.02
□ 56 Gary DiSarcina	.05	.02	.01
□ 57 Damion Easley	.05	.02	.01
□ 58 Jim Edmonds	.30	.14	.04
□ 59 Jorge Fabregas	.05	.02	.01
□ 60 Chuck Finley	.15	.07	.02
□ 61 Bo Jackson	.30	.14	.04
□ 62 Mark Langston	.05	.02	.01
□ 63 Eduardo Perez	.05	.02	.01
□ 64 Tim Salmon	.30	.14	.04
□ 65 J.T. Snow	.15	.07	.02
□ 66 Willie Banks	.05	.02	.01
□ 67 Jose Bautista	.05	.02	.01
□ 68 Shawon Dunston	.05	.02	.01
□ 69 Kevin Foster	.05	.02	.01
□ 70 Mark Grace	.30	.14	.04
□ 71 Jose Guzman	.05	.02	.01
□ 72 Jose Hernandez	.05	.02	.01
□ 73 Blaise Ilsley	.05	.02	.01
□ 74 Derrick May	.05	.02	.01
□ 75 Randy Myers	.05	.02	.01
□ 76 Karl Rhodes	.05	.02	.01
□ 77 Kevin Roberson	.05	.02	.01
□ 78 Rey Sanchez	.05	.02	.01
□ 79 Sammy Sosa	.30	.14	.04
□ 80 Steve Trachsel	.05	.02	.01
□ 81 Eddie Zambrano	.05	.02	.01
□ 82 Wilson Alvarez	.15	.07	.02
□ 83 Jason Bere	.05	.02	.01
□ 84 Joey Cora	.05	.02	.01
□ 85 Jose DeLeon	.05	.02	.01
□ 86 Alex Fernandez	.15	.07	.02
□ 87 Julio Franco	.15	.07	.02
□ 88 Ozzie Guillen	.05	.02	.01
□ 89 Joe Hall	.05	.02	.01
□ 90 Roberto Hernandez	.05	.02	.01
□ 91 Darrin Jackson	.05	.02	.01
□ 92 Lance Johnson	.15	.07	.02
□ 93 Norberto Martin	.05	.02	.01
□ 94 Jack McDowell	.15	.07	.02
□ 95 Tim Raines	.30	.14	.04
□ 96 Olmedo Saenz	.05	.02	.01
□ 97 Frank Thomas	2.00	.90	.25
□ 98 Robin Ventura	.15	.07	.02
□ 99 Bret Boone	.15	.07	.02
□ 100 Jeff Brantley	.05	.02	.01
□ 101 Jacob Brumfield	.05	.02	.01
□ 102 Hector Carrasco	.05	.02	.01
□ 103 Brian Dorsett	.05	.02	.01
□ 104 Tony Fernandez	.05	.02	.01
□ 105 Willie Greene	.05	.02	.01
□ 106 Erik Hanson	.05	.02	.01
□ 107 Kevin Jarvis	.05	.02	.01
□ 108 Barry Larkin	.30	.14	.04
□ 109 Kevin Mitchell	.15	.07	.02
□ 110 Hal Morris	.05	.02	.01
□ 111 Jose Rijo	.05	.02	.01
□ 112 Johnny Ruffin	.05	.02	.01
□ 113 Deion Sanders	.30	.14	.04
□ 114 Reggie Sanders	.15	.07	.02
□ 115 Sandy Alomar Jr.	.05	.02	.01

□ 116	Ruben Amaro	.05	.02	.01
□ 117	Carlos Baerga	.30	.14	.04
□ 118	Albert Belle	1.00	.45	.12
□ 119	Alvaro Espinoza	.05	.02	.01
□ 120	Rene Gonzales	.05	.02	.01
□ 121	Wayne Kirby	.05	.02	.01
□ 122	Kenny Lofton	.50	.23	.06
□ 123	Candy Maldonado	.05	.02	.01
□ 124	Dennis Martinez	.15	.07	.02
□ 125	Eddie Murray	.50	.23	.06
□ 126	Charles Nagy	.15	.07	.02
□ 127	Tony Pena	.05	.02	.01
□ 128	Manny Ramirez	.50	.23	.06
□ 129	Paul Sorrento	.05	.02	.01
□ 130	Jim Thome	.40	.18	.05
□ 131	Omar Vizquel	.30	.14	.04
□ 132	Dante Bichette	.30	.14	.04
□ 133	Ellis Burks	.30	.14	.04
□ 134	Vinny Castilla	.15	.07	.02
□ 135	Marvin Freeman	.05	.02	.01
□ 136	Andres Galarraga	.30	.14	.04
□ 137	Joe Girardi	.05	.02	.01
□ 138	Charlie Hayes	.05	.02	.01
□ 139	Mike Kingery	.05	.02	.01
□ 140	Nelson Liriano	.05	.02	.01
□ 141	Roberto Mejia	.05	.02	.01
□ 142	David Nied	.05	.02	.01
□ 143	Steve Reed	.05	.02	.01
□ 144	Armando Reynoso	.05	.02	.01
□ 145	Bruce Ruffin	.05	.02	.01
□ 146	John VanderWal	.05	.02	.01
□ 147	Walt Weiss	.05	.02	.01
□ 148	Skeeter Barnes	.05	.02	.01
□ 149	Tim Belcher	.15	.07	.02
□ 150	Junior Felix	.05	.02	.01
□ 151	Cecil Fielder	.15	.07	.02
□ 152	Travis Fryman	.15	.07	.02
□ 153	Kirk Gibson	.15	.07	.02
□ 154	Chris Gomez	.05	.02	.01
□ 155	Buddy Groom	.05	.02	.01
□ 156	Chad Kreuter	.05	.02	.01
□ 157	Mike Moore	.05	.02	.01
□ 158	Tony Phillips	.15	.07	.02
□ 159	Juan Samuel	.05	.02	.01
□ 160	Mickey Tettleton	.05	.02	.01
□ 161	Alan Trammell	.30	.14	.04
□ 162	David Wells	.05	.02	.01
□ 163	Lou Whitaker	.30	.14	.04
□ 164	Kurt Abbott	.05	.02	.01
□ 165	Luis Aquino	.05	.02	.01
□ 166	Alex Arias	.05	.02	.01
□ 167	Bret Barberie	.05	.02	.01
□ 168	Jerry Browne	.05	.02	.01
□ 169	Chuck Carr	.05	.02	.01
□ 170	Matias Carrillo	.05	.02	.01
□ 171	Greg Colbrunn	.05	.02	.01
□ 172	Jeff Conine	.30	.14	.04
□ 173	Carl Everett	.05	.02	.01
□ 174	Robb Nen	.05	.02	.01
□ 175	Yorkis Perez	.05	.02	.01
□ 176	Pat Rapp	.05	.02	.01
□ 177	Benito Santiago	.05	.02	.01
□ 178	Gary Sheffield	.30	.14	.04
□ 179	Darrell Whitmore	.05	.02	.01
□ 180	Jeff Bagwell	.75	.35	.09
□ 181	Kevin Bass	.05	.02	.01
□ 182	Craig Biggio	.30	.14	.04
□ 183	Andujar Cedeno	.05	.02	.01
□ 184	Doug Drabek	.05	.02	.01
□ 185	Tony Eusebio	.05	.02	.01
□ 186	Steve Finley	.15	.07	.02
□ 187	Luis Gonzalez	.05	.02	.01
□ 188	Pete Harnisch	.05	.02	.01
□ 189	John Hudek	.05	.02	.01
□ 190	Orlando Miller	.05	.02	.01
□ 191	James Mouton	.05	.02	.01
□ 192	Roberto Petagine	.05	.02	.01
□ 193	Shane Reynolds	.05	.02	.01
□ 194	Greg Swindell	.05	.02	.01
□ 195	Dave Veres	.05	.02	.01
□ 196	Kevin Appier	.15	.07	.02
□ 197	Stan Belinda	.05	.02	.01
□ 198	Vince Coleman	.05	.02	.01
□ 199	David Cone	.15	.07	.02
□ 200	Gary Gaetti	.15	.07	.02
□ 201	Greg Gagne	.05	.02	.01
□ 202	Mark Gubicza	.05	.02	.01
□ 203	Bob Hamelin	.05	.02	.01
□ 204	Dave Henderson	.05	.02	.01
□ 205	Felix Jose	.05	.02	.01
□ 206	Wally Joyner	.15	.07	.02
□ 207	Jose Lind	.05	.02	.01
□ 208	Mike Macfarlane	.05	.02	.01
□ 209	Brian McRae	.15	.07	.02
□ 210	Jeff Montgomery	.15	.07	.02
□ 211	Hipolito Pichardo	.05	.02	.01
□ 212	Pedro Astacio	.05	.02	.01
□ 213	Brett Butler	.15	.07	.02
□ 214	Omar Daal	.05	.02	.01
□ 215	Delino DeShields	.05	.02	.01
□ 216	Darren Dreifort	.05	.02	.01
□ 217	Carlos Hernandez	.05	.02	.01
□ 218	Orel Hershiser	.15	.07	.02
□ 219	Garey Ingram	.05	.02	.01
□ 220	Eric Karros	.15	.07	.02
□ 221	Ramon Martinez	.15	.07	.02
□ 222	Raul Mondesi	.30	.14	.04
□ 223	Jose Offerman	.05	.02	.01
□ 224	Mike Piazza	1.25	.55	.16
□ 225	Henry Rodriguez	.30	.14	.04
□ 226	Ismael Valdes	.15	.07	.02
□ 227	Tim Wallach	.05	.02	.01
□ 228	Jeff Cirillo	.15	.07	.02
□ 229	Alex Diaz	.05	.02	.01
□ 230	Cal Eldred	.05	.02	.01
□ 231	Mike Fetters	.05	.02	.01
□ 232	Brian Harper	.05	.02	.01
□ 233	Ted Higuera	.05	.02	.01
□ 234	John Jaha	.15	.07	.02
□ 235	Graeme Lloyd	.05	.02	.01
□ 236	Jose Mercedes	.05	.02	.01
□ 237	Jaime Navarro	.05	.02	.01
□ 238	Dave Nilsson	.15	.07	.02
□ 239	Jesse Orosco	.05	.02	.01
□ 240	Jody Reed	.05	.02	.01
□ 241	Jose Valentin	.15	.07	.02
□ 242	Greg Vaughn	.15	.07	.02
□ 243	Turner Ward	.05	.02	.01
□ 244	Rick Aguilera	.05	.02	.01
□ 245	Rich Becker	.05	.02	.01
□ 246	Jim Deshaies	.05	.02	.01
□ 247	Steve Dunn	.05	.02	.01
□ 248	Scott Erickson	.05	.02	.01
□ 249	Kent Hrbek	.15	.07	.02
□ 250	Chuck Knoblauch	.30	.14	.04
□ 251	Scott Leius	.05	.02	.01
□ 252	David McCarty	.05	.02	.01
□ 253	Pat Meares	.05	.02	.01
□ 254	Pedro Munoz	.05	.02	.01
□ 255	Kirby Puckett	.60	.25	.07
□ 256	Carlos Pulido	.05	.02	.01
□ 257	Kevin Tapani	.05	.02	.01
□ 258	Matt Walbeck	.05	.02	.01
□ 259	Dave Winfield	.30	.14	.04
□ 260	Moises Alou	.15	.07	.02
□ 261	Juan Bell	.05	.02	.01
□ 262	Freddie Benavides	.05	.02	.01
□ 263	Sean Berry	.05	.02	.01
□ 264	Wil Cordero	.05	.02	.01
□ 265	Jeff Fassero	.05	.02	.01
□ 266	Darrin Fletcher	.05	.02	.01
□ 267	Cliff Floyd	.15	.07	.02
□ 268	Marquis Grissom	.30	.14	.04
□ 269	Gil Heredia	.05	.02	.01
□ 270	Ken Hill	.05	.02	.01
□ 271	Pedro J. Martinez	.15	.07	.02
□ 272	Mel Rojas	.05	.02	.01
□ 273	Larry Walker	.30	.14	.04
□ 274	John Wetteland	.15	.07	.02
□ 275	Rondell White	.30	.14	.04
□ 276	Tim Bogar	.05	.02	.01
□ 277	Bobby Bonilla	.15	.07	.02
□ 278	Rico Brogna	.05	.02	.01
□ 279	Jeromy Burnitz	.05	.02	.01
□ 280	John Franco	.05	.02	.01
□ 281	Eric Hillman	.05	.02	.01
□ 282	Todd Hundley	.15	.07	.02
□ 283	Jeff Kent	.05	.02	.01
□ 284	Mike Maddux	.05	.02	.01
□ 285	Joe Orsulak	.05	.02	.01
□ 286	Luis Rivera	.05	.02	.01
□ 287	Bret Saberhagen	.15	.07	.02

□ 288	David Segui	.05	.02	.01
□ 289	Ryan Thompson	.05	.02	.01
□ 290	Fernando Vina	.05	.02	.01
□ 291	Jose Vizcaino	.05	.02	.01
□ 292	Jim Abbott	.05	.02	.01
□ 293	Wade Boggs	.30	.14	.04
□ 294	Russ Davis	.05	.02	.01
□ 295	Mike Gallego	.05	.02	.01
□ 296	Xavier Hernandez	.05	.02	.01
□ 297	Steve Howe	.05	.02	.01
□ 298	Jimmy Key	.15	.07	.02
□ 299	Don Mattingly	1.00	.45	.12
□ 300	Terry Mulholland	.05	.02	.01
□ 301	Paul O'Neill	.15	.07	.02
□ 302	Luis Polonia	.05	.02	.01
□ 303	Mike Stanley	.05	.02	.01
□ 304	Danny Tartabull	.05	.02	.01
□ 305	Randy Velarde	.05	.02	.01
□ 306	Bob Wickman	.05	.02	.01
□ 307	Bernie Williams	.30	.14	.04
□ 308	Mark Acre	.05	.02	.01
□ 309	Geronimo Berroa	.05	.02	.01
□ 310	Mike Bordick	.05	.02	.01
□ 311	Dennis Eckersley	.15	.07	.02
□ 312	Rickey Henderson	.30	.14	.04
□ 313	Stan Javier	.05	.02	.01
□ 314	Miguel Jimenez	.05	.02	.01
□ 315	Francisco Matos	.05	.02	.01
□ 316	Mark McGwire	.60	.25	.07
□ 317	Troy Neel	.05	.02	.01
□ 318	Steve Ontiveros	.05	.02	.01
□ 319	Carlos Reyes	.05	.02	.01
□ 320	Ruben Sierra	.15	.07	.02
□ 321	Terry Steinbach	.15	.07	.02
□ 322	Bob Welch	.05	.02	.01
□ 323	Bobby Witt	.05	.02	.01
□ 324	Larry Andersen	.05	.02	.01
□ 325	Kim Batiste	.05	.02	.01
□ 326	Darren Daulton	.15	.07	.02
□ 327	Mariano Duncan	.05	.02	.01
□ 328	Lenny Dykstra	.15	.07	.02
□ 329	Jim Eisenreich	.05	.02	.01
□ 330	Danny Jackson	.05	.02	.01
□ 331	John Kruk	.15	.07	.02
□ 332	Tony Longmire	.05	.02	.01
□ 333	Tom Marsh	.05	.02	.01
□ 334	Mickey Morandini	.05	.02	.01
□ 335	Bobby Munoz	.05	.02	.01
□ 336	Todd Pratt	.05	.02	.01
□ 337	Tom Quinlan	.05	.02	.01
□ 338	Kevin Stocker	.05	.02	.01
□ 339	Fernando Valenzuela	.15	.07	.02
□ 340	Jay Bell	.15	.07	.02
□ 341	Dave Clark	.05	.02	.01
□ 342	Steve Cooke	.05	.02	.01
□ 343	Carlos Garcia	.05	.02	.01
□ 344	Jeff King	.15	.07	.02
□ 345	Jon Lieber	.05	.02	.01
□ 346	Ravelo Manzanillo	.05	.02	.01
□ 347	Al Martin	.15	.07	.02
□ 348	Orlando Merced	.05	.02	.01
□ 349	Denny Neagle	.15	.07	.02
□ 350	Alejandro Pena	.05	.02	.01
□ 351	Don Slaught	.05	.02	.01
□ 352	Zane Smith	.05	.02	.01
□ 353	Andy Van Slyke	.15	.07	.02
□ 354	Rick White	.05	.02	.01
□ 355	Kevin Young	.05	.02	.01
□ 356	Andy Ashby	.15	.07	.02
□ 357	Derek Bell	.15	.07	.02
□ 358	Andy Benes	.05	.02	.01
□ 359	Phil Clark	.05	.02	.01
□ 360	Donnie Elliott	.05	.02	.01
□ 361	Ricky Gutierrez	.05	.02	.01
□ 362	Tony Gwynn	.75	.35	.09
□ 363	Trevor Hoffman	.05	.02	.01
□ 364	Tim Hyers	.05	.02	.01
□ 365	Luis Lopez	.05	.02	.01
□ 366	Jose Martinez	.05	.02	.01
□ 367	Pedro A. Martinez	.05	.02	.01
□ 368	Phil Plantier	.05	.02	.01
□ 369	Bip Roberts	.05	.02	.01
□ 370	A.J. Sager	.05	.02	.01
□ 371	Jeff Tabaka	.05	.02	.01
□ 372	Todd Benzinger	.05	.02	.01
□ 373	Barry Bonds	.50	.23	.06
□ 374	John Burkett	.15	.07	.02
□ 375	Mark Carreon	.05	.02	.01
□ 376	Royce Clayton	.05	.02	.01
□ 377	Pat Gomez	.05	.02	.01
□ 378	Erik Johnson	.05	.02	.01
□ 379	Darren Lewis	.05	.02	.01
□ 380	Kirt Manwaring	.05	.02	.01
□ 381	Dave Martinez	.05	.02	.01
□ 382	John Patterson	.05	.02	.01
□ 383	Mark Portugal	.05	.02	.01
□ 384	Darryl Strawberry	.15	.07	.02
□ 385	Salomon Torres	.05	.02	.01
□ 386	Wm. VanLandingham	.05	.02	.01
□ 387	Matt Williams	.30	.14	.04
□ 388	Rich Amaral	.05	.02	.01
□ 389	Bobby Ayala	.05	.02	.01
□ 390	Mike Blowers	.05	.02	.01
□ 391	Chris Bosio	.05	.02	.01
□ 392	Jay Buhner	.30	.14	.04
□ 393	Jim Converse	.05	.02	.01
□ 394	Tim Davis	.05	.02	.01
□ 395	Felix Fermin	.05	.02	.01
□ 396	Dave Fleming	.05	.02	.01
□ 397	Goose Gossage	.15	.07	.02
□ 398	Ken Griffey Jr.	2.00	.90	.25
□ 399	Randy Johnson	.30	.14	.04
□ 400	Edgar Martinez	.30	.14	.04
□ 401	Tino Martinez	.15	.07	.02
□ 402	Alex Rodriguez	2.50	1.10	.30
□ 403	Dan Wilson	.15	.07	.02
□ 404	Luis Alicea	.05	.02	.01
□ 405	Rene Arocha	.05	.02	.01
□ 406	Bernard Gilkey	.15	.07	.02
□ 407	Gregg Jefferies	.15	.07	.02
□ 408	Ray Lankford	.30	.14	.04
□ 409	Terry McGriff	.05	.02	.01
□ 410	Omar Olivares	.05	.02	.01
□ 411	Jose Oquendo	.05	.02	.01
□ 412	Vicente Palacios	.05	.02	.01
□ 413	Geronimo Pena	.05	.02	.01
□ 414	Mike Perez	.05	.02	.01
□ 415	Gerald Perry	.05	.02	.01
□ 416	Ozzie Smith	.40	.18	.05
□ 417	Bob Tewksbury	.05	.02	.01
□ 418	Mark Whiten	.05	.02	.01
□ 419	Todd Zeile	.05	.02	.01
□ 420	Esteban Beltre	.05	.02	.01
□ 421	Kevin Brown	.15	.07	.02
□ 422	Cris Carpenter	.05	.02	.01
□ 423	Will Clark	.30	.14	.04
□ 424	Hector Fajardo	.05	.02	.01
□ 425	Jeff Frye	.05	.02	.01
□ 426	Juan Gonzalez	1.00	.45	.12
□ 427	Rusty Greer	.30	.14	.04
□ 428	Rick Honeycutt	.05	.02	.01
□ 429	David Hulse	.05	.02	.01
□ 430	Manny Lee	.05	.02	.01
□ 431	Junior Ortiz	.05	.02	.01
□ 432	Dean Palmer	.15	.07	.02
□ 433	Ivan Rodriguez	.40	.18	.05
□ 434	Dan Smith	.05	.02	.01
□ 435	Roberto Alomar	.50	.23	.06
□ 436	Pat Borders	.05	.02	.01
□ 437	Scott Brow	.05	.02	.01
□ 438	Rob Butler	.05	.02	.01
□ 439	Joe Carter	.30	.14	.04
□ 440	Tony Castillo	.05	.02	.01
□ 441	Domingo Cedeno	.05	.02	.01
□ 442	Brad Cornett	.05	.02	.01
□ 443	Carlos Delgado	.30	.14	.04
□ 444	Alex Gonzalez	.05	.02	.01
□ 445	Juan Guzman	.15	.07	.02
□ 446	Darren Hall	.05	.02	.01
□ 447	Paul Molitor	.40	.18	.05
□ 448	John Olerud	.05	.02	.01
□ 449	Robert Perez	.05	.02	.01
□ 450	Devon White	.15	.07	.02

1995 Pacific Gold Crown Diecuts

Inserted approximately one in every 18 packs, these cards are in a diecut design. The player photo goes to the full-bleed bottom borders

while the top has a gold crown. The player is identified on the bottom. The back of the card features a gold crown, player information in both English and Spanish, and a player photo against a blue background. The cards are sequenced in alphabetical order according to team name.

	MINT	NRMT	EXC
COMPLETE SET (20)	250.00	110.00	31.00
COMMON CARD (1-20)	3.00	1.35	.35
SEMISTARS	5.00	2.20	.60
RANDOM INSERTS IN PACKS			
□ 1 Greg Maddux	25.00	11.00	3.10
□ 2 Fred McGriff	5.00	2.20	.60
□ 3 Rafael Palmeiro	5.00	2.20	.60
□ 4 Cal Ripken Jr.	30.00	13.50	3.70
□ 5 Jose Canseco	5.00	2.20	.60
□ 6 Frank Thomas	40.00	18.00	5.00
□ 7 Albert Belle	20.00	9.00	2.50
□ 8 Manny Ramirez	10.00	4.50	1.25
□ 9 Andres Galarraga	5.00	2.20	.60
□ 10 Jeff Bagwell	15.00	6.75	1.85
□ 11 Chan Ho Park	5.00	2.20	.60
□ 12 Raul Mondesi	3.00	1.35	.35
□ 13 Mike Piazza	25.00	11.00	3.10
□ 14 Kirby Puckett	12.00	5.50	1.50
□ 15 Barry Bonds	10.00	4.50	1.25
□ 16 Ken Griffey Jr.	40.00	18.00	5.00
□ 17 Alex Rodriguez	40.00	18.00	5.00
□ 18 Juan Gonzalez	20.00	9.00	2.50
□ 19 Roberto Alomar	10.00	4.50	1.25
□ 20 Carlos Delgado	3.00	1.35	.35

1995 Pacific Gold Prisms

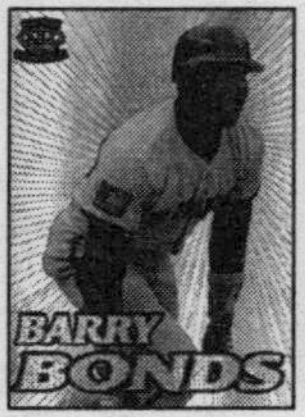

This 36-card standard-size set was inserted approximately one in every 12 packs. The fronts feature a player photo set against a gold metallic background. The player is identified on the bottom of the card. The horizontal backs feature a player photo set against a group of baseballs on the left side. Another photo is on the right along with the player's name, his career totals and some brief information in English and Spanish.

	MINT	NRMT	EXC
COMPLETE SET (36)	150.00	70.00	19.00
COMMON CARD (1-36)	1.50	.70	.19
SEMISTARS	3.00	1.35	.35
RANDOM INSERTS IN PACKS			
□ 1 Jose Canseco	3.00	1.35	.35
□ 2 Gregg Jefferies	3.00	1.35	.35
□ 3 Fred McGriff	3.00	1.35	.35
□ 4 Joe Carter	3.00	1.35	.35
□ 5 Tim Salmon	3.00	1.35	.35
□ 6 Wade Boggs	3.00	1.35	.35
□ 7 Dave Winfield	3.00	1.35	.35
□ 8 Bob Hamelin	1.50	.70	.19
□ 9 Cal Ripken Jr.	20.00	9.00	2.50
□ 10 Don Mattingly	12.00	5.50	1.50
□ 11 Juan Gonzalez	12.00	5.50	1.50
□ 12 Carlos Delgado	3.00	1.35	.35
□ 13 Barry Bonds	6.00	2.70	.75
□ 14 Albert Belle	12.00	5.50	1.50
□ 15 Raul Mondesi	3.00	1.35	.35
□ 16 Jeff Bagwell	10.00	4.50	1.25
□ 17 Mike Piazza	15.00	6.75	1.85
□ 18 Rafael Palmeiro	3.00	1.35	.35
□ 19 Frank Thomas	25.00	11.00	3.10
□ 20 Matt Williams	3.00	1.35	.35
□ 21 Ken Griffey Jr.	25.00	11.00	3.10
□ 22 Will Clark	3.00	1.35	.35
□ 23 Bobby Bonilla	3.00	1.35	.35
□ 24 Kenny Lofton	6.00	2.70	.75
□ 25 Paul Molitor	5.00	2.20	.60
□ 26 Kirby Puckett	8.00	3.60	1.00
□ 27 David Justice	3.00	1.35	.35
□ 28 Jeff Conine	3.00	1.35	.35
□ 29 Bret Boone	1.50	.70	.19
□ 30 Larry Walker	3.00	1.35	.35
□ 31 Cecil Fielder	3.00	1.35	.35
□ 32 Manny Ramirez	6.00	2.70	.75
□ 33 Javier Lopez	3.00	1.35	.35
□ 34 Jimmy Key	1.50	.70	.19
□ 35 Andres Galarraga	3.00	1.35	.35
□ 36 Tony Gwynn	10.00	4.50	1.25

1995 Pacific Latinos Destacados

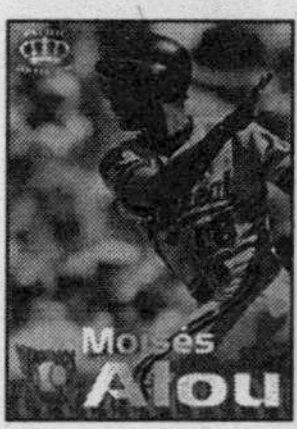

This 36-card standard size set was inserted approximately one in every nine packs. A literal translation for this set is Hot Hispanics and features only Spanish players. The full-bleed fronts feature color photos with the playerís name at the bottom along with a fire design. The backs have the player's name spelled vertically in the upper left with a sentence in both English and Spanish. The bottom left has the team logo while the right side had a player photo. The cards are numbered and arranged in alphabetical order.

	MINT	NRMT	EXC
COMPLETE SET (36)	50.00	22.00	6.25
COMMON CARD (1-36)	1.00	.45	.12
SEMISTARS	2.50	1.10	.30
RANDOM INSERTS IN PACKS			
□ 1 Roberto Alomar	5.00	2.20	.60
□ 2 Moises Alou	1.50	.70	.19
□ 3 Wilson Alvarez	1.50	.70	.19
□ 4 Carlos Baerga	2.50	1.10	.30
□ 5 Geronimo Berroa	1.00	.45	.12
□ 6 Jose Canseco	2.50	1.10	.30

□ 7 Hector Carrasco	1.00	.45	.12
□ 8 Wil Cordero	1.50	.70	.19
□ 9 Carlos Delgado	1.50	.70	.19
□ 10 Damion Easley	1.00	.45	.12
□ 11 Tony Eusebio	1.00	.45	.12
□ 12 Hector Fajardo	1.00	.45	.12
□ 13 Andres Galarraga	2.50	1.10	.30
□ 14 Carlos Garcia	1.00	.45	.12
□ 15 Chris Gomez	1.00	.45	.12
□ 16 Alex Gonzalez	1.50	.70	.19
□ 17 Juan Gonzalez	10.00	4.50	1.25
□ 18 Luis Gonzalez	1.00	.45	.12
□ 19 Felix Jose	1.00	.45	.12
□ 20 Javier Lopez	2.50	1.10	.30
□ 21 Luis Lopez	1.00	.45	.12
□ 22 Dennis Martinez	1.50	.70	.19
□ 23 Orlando Miller	1.00	.45	.12
□ 24 Raul Mondesi	2.50	1.10	.30
□ 25 Jose Oliva	1.00	.45	.12
□ 26 Rafael Palmeiro	2.50	1.10	.30
□ 27 Yorkis Perez	1.00	.45	.12
□ 28 Manny Ramirez	5.00	2.20	.60
□ 29 Jose Rijo	1.00	.45	.12
□ 30 Alex Rodriguez	18.00	8.00	2.20
□ 31 Ivan Rodriguez	4.00	1.80	.50
□ 32 Carlos Rodriguez	1.00	.45	.12
□ 33 Sammy Sosa	3.00	1.35	.35
□ 34 Tony Tarasco	1.00	.45	.12
□ 35 Ismael Valdes	1.00	.45	.12
□ 36 Bernie Williams	2.50	1.10	.30

1996 Pacific

This 450-card set was issued in 12-card packs. The fronts feature borderless color action player photos with double-etched gold foil printing. The horizontal backs carry a color player portrait with player information in both English and Spanish and 1995 season player statistics.

	MINT	NRMT	EXC
COMPLETE SET (450)	30.00	13.50	3.70
COMMON CARD (1-450)	.05	.02	.01
SEMISTARS	.15	.07	.02
STARS	.30	.14	.04

□ 1 Steve Avery	.15	.07	.02
□ 2 Ryan Klesko	.40	.18	.05
□ 3 Pedro Borbon	.05	.02	.01
□ 4 Chipper Jones	1.25	.55	.16
□ 5 Kent Mercker	.05	.02	.01
□ 6 Greg Maddux	1.25	.55	.16
□ 7 Greg McMichael	.05	.02	.01
□ 8 Mark Wohlers	.15	.07	.02
□ 9 Fred McGriff	.30	.14	.04
□ 10 John Smoltz	.30	.14	.04
□ 11 Rafael Belliard	.05	.02	.01
□ 12 Mark Lemke	.05	.02	.01
□ 13 Tom Glavine	.30	.14	.04
□ 14 Javier Lopez	.30	.14	.04
□ 15 Jeff Blauser	.05	.02	.01
□ 16 David Justice	.15	.07	.02
□ 17 Marquis Grissom	.30	.14	.04
□ 18 Greg Maddux CY	.60	.25	.07
□ 19 Randy Myers	.05	.02	.01
□ 20 Scott Servais	.05	.02	.01
□ 21 Sammy Sosa	.30	.14	.04
□ 22 Kevin Foster	.05	.02	.01
□ 23 Jose Hernandez	.05	.02	.01
□ 24 Jim Bullinger	.05	.02	.01
□ 25 Mike Perez	.05	.02	.01
□ 26 Shawon Dunston	.05	.02	.01
□ 27 Rey Sanchez	.05	.02	.01
□ 28 Frank Castillo	.05	.02	.01
□ 29 Jaime Navarro	.05	.02	.01
□ 30 Brian McRae	.05	.02	.01
□ 31 Mark Grace	.30	.14	.04
□ 32 Roberto Rivera	.05	.02	.01
□ 33 Luis Gonzalez	.05	.02	.01
□ 34 Hector Carrasco	.05	.02	.01
□ 35 Bret Boone	.05	.02	.01
□ 36 Thomas Howard	.05	.02	.01
□ 37 Hal Morris	.05	.02	.01
□ 38 John Smiley	.05	.02	.01
□ 39 Jeff Brantley	.05	.02	.01
□ 40 Barry Larkin	.30	.14	.04
□ 41 Mariano Duncan	.05	.02	.01
□ 42 Xavier Hernandez	.05	.02	.01
□ 43 Pete Schourek	.15	.07	.02
□ 44 Reggie Sanders	.30	.14	.04
□ 45 Dave Burba	.05	.02	.01
□ 46 Jeff Branson	.05	.02	.01
□ 47 Mark Portugal	.05	.02	.01
□ 48 Ron Gant	.15	.07	.02
□ 49 Benito Santiago	.05	.02	.01
□ 50 Barry Larkin MVP	.30	.14	.04
□ 51 Steve Reed	.05	.02	.01
□ 52 Kevin Ritz	.05	.02	.01
□ 53 Dante Bichette	.30	.14	.04
□ 54 Darren Holmes	.05	.02	.01
□ 55 Ellis Burks	.30	.14	.04
□ 56 Walt Weiss	.05	.02	.01
□ 57 Armando Reynoso	.05	.02	.01
□ 58 Vinny Castilla	.30	.14	.04
□ 59 Jason Bates	.05	.02	.01
□ 60 Mike Kingery	.05	.02	.01
□ 61 Bryan Rekar	.05	.02	.01
□ 62 Curtis Leskanic	.05	.02	.01
□ 63 Bret Saberhagen	.05	.02	.01
□ 64 Andres Galarraga	.30	.14	.04
□ 65 Larry Walker	.30	.14	.04
□ 66 Joe Girardi	.05	.02	.01
□ 67 Quilvio Veras	.05	.02	.01
□ 68 Robb Nen	.05	.02	.01
□ 69 Mario Diaz	.05	.02	.01
□ 70 Chuck Carr	.05	.02	.01
□ 71 Alex Arias	.05	.02	.01
□ 72 Pat Rapp	.05	.02	.01
□ 73 Rich Garces	.05	.02	.01
□ 74 Kurt Abbott	.05	.02	.01
□ 75 Andre Dawson	.30	.14	.04
□ 76 Greg Colbrunn	.05	.02	.01
□ 77 John Burkett	.05	.02	.01
□ 78 Terry Pendleton	.15	.07	.02
□ 79 Jesus Tavarez	.05	.02	.01
□ 80 Charles Johnson	.15	.07	.02
□ 81 Yorkis Perez	.05	.02	.01
□ 82 Jeff Conine	.30	.14	.04
□ 83 Gary Sheffield	.30	.14	.04
□ 84 Brian L. Hunter	.05	.02	.01
□ 85 Derrick May	.05	.02	.01
□ 86 Greg Swindell	.05	.02	.01
□ 87 Derek Bell	.15	.07	.02
□ 88 Dave Veres	.05	.02	.01
□ 89 Jeff Bagwell	.75	.35	.09
□ 90 Todd Jones	.05	.02	.01
□ 91 Orlando Miller	.05	.02	.01
□ 92 Pedro A. Martinez	.05	.02	.01
□ 93 Tony Eusebio	.05	.02	.01
□ 94 Craig Biggio	.30	.14	.04
□ 95 Shane Reynolds	.05	.02	.01
□ 96 James Mouton	.05	.02	.01
□ 97 Doug Drabek	.05	.02	.01
□ 98 Dave Magadan	.05	.02	.01
□ 99 Ricky Gutierrez	.05	.02	.01
□ 100 Hideo Nomo	.50	.23	.06
□ 101 Delino DeShields	.05	.02	.01
□ 102 Tom Candiotti	.05	.02	.01
□ 103 Mike Piazza	1.25	.55	.16
□ 104 Ramon Martinez	.30	.14	.04
□ 105 Pedro Astacio	.05	.02	.01
□ 106 Chad Fonville	.05	.02	.01
□ 107 Raul Mondesi	.30	.14	.04
□ 108 Ismael Valdes	.15	.07	.02
□ 109 Jose Offerman	.05	.02	.01

□ 110	Todd Worrell	.15	.07	.02
□ 111	Eric Karros	.30	.14	.04
□ 112	Brett Butler	.05	.02	.01
□ 113	Juan Castro	.05	.02	.01
□ 114	Roberto Kelly	.05	.02	.01
□ 115	Omar Daal	.05	.02	.01
□ 116	Antonio Osuna	.05	.02	.01
□ 117	Hideo Nomo ROY	.30	.14	.04
□ 118	Mike Lansing	.05	.02	.01
□ 119	Mel Rojas	.15	.07	.02
□ 120	Sean Berry	.05	.02	.01
□ 121	David Segui	.05	.02	.01
□ 122	Tavo Alvarez	.05	.02	.01
□ 123	Pedro Martinez	.30	.14	.04
□ 124	F.P. Santangelo	.05	.02	.01
□ 125	Rondell White	.30	.14	.04
□ 126	Cliff Floyd	.05	.02	.01
□ 127	Henry Rodriguez	.30	.14	.04
□ 128	Tony Tarasco	.05	.02	.01
□ 129	Yamil Benitez	.05	.02	.01
□ 130	Carlos Perez	.05	.02	.01
□ 131	Wil Cordero	.05	.02	.01
□ 132	Jeff Fassero	.05	.02	.01
□ 133	Moises Alou	.15	.07	.02
□ 134	John Franco	.05	.02	.01
□ 135	Rico Brogna	.05	.02	.01
□ 136	Dave Mlicki	.05	.02	.01
□ 137	Bill Pulsipher	.15	.07	.02
□ 138	Jose Vizcaino	.05	.02	.01
□ 139	Carl Everett	.05	.02	.01
□ 140	Edgardo Alfonzo	.15	.07	.02
□ 141	Bobby Jones	.05	.02	.01
□ 142	Alberto Castillo	.05	.02	.01
□ 143	Joe Orsulak	.05	.02	.01
□ 144	Jeff Kent	.05	.02	.01
□ 145	Ryan Thompson	.05	.02	.01
□ 146	Jason Isringhausen	.15	.07	.02
□ 147	Todd Hundley	.30	.14	.04
□ 148	Alex Ochoa	.15	.07	.02
□ 149	Charlie Hayes	.05	.02	.01
□ 150	Michael Mimbs	.05	.02	.01
□ 151	Darren Daulton	.15	.07	.02
□ 152	Toby Borland	.05	.02	.01
□ 153	Andy Van Slyke	.15	.07	.02
□ 154	Mickey Morandini	.05	.02	.01
□ 155	Sid Fernandez	.05	.02	.01
□ 156	Tom Marsh	.05	.02	.01
□ 157	Kevin Stocker	.05	.02	.01
□ 158	Paul Quantrill	.05	.02	.01
□ 159	Gregg Jefferies	.30	.14	.04
□ 160	Ricky Bottalico	.05	.02	.01
□ 161	Lenny Dykstra	.15	.07	.02
□ 162	Mark Whiten	.05	.02	.01
□ 163	Tyler Green	.05	.02	.01
□ 164	Jim Eisenreich	.05	.02	.01
□ 165	Heathcliff Slocumb	.05	.02	.01
□ 166	Esteban Loaiza	.05	.02	.01
□ 167	Rich Aude	.05	.02	.01
□ 168	Jason Christiansen	.05	.02	.01
□ 169	Ramon Morel	.05	.02	.01
□ 170	Orlando Merced	.15	.07	.02
□ 171	Paul Wagner	.05	.02	.01
□ 172	Jeff King	.15	.07	.02
□ 173	Jay Bell	.15	.07	.02
□ 174	Jacob Brumfield	.05	.02	.01
□ 175	Nelson Liriano	.05	.02	.01
□ 176	Dan Miceli	.05	.02	.01
□ 177	Carlos Garcia	.05	.02	.01
□ 178	Denny Neagle	.15	.07	.02
□ 179	Angelo Encarnacion	.05	.02	.01
□ 180	Al Martin	.05	.02	.01
□ 181	Midre Cummings	.05	.02	.01
□ 182	Eddie Williams	.05	.02	.01
□ 183	Roberto Petagine	.05	.02	.01
□ 184	Tony Gwynn	.75	.35	.09
□ 185	Andy Ashby	.05	.02	.01
□ 186	Melvin Nieves	.15	.07	.02
□ 187	Phil Clark	.05	.02	.01
□ 188	Brad Ausmus	.05	.02	.01
□ 189	Bip Roberts	.05	.02	.01
□ 190	Fernando Valenzuela	.15	.07	.02
□ 191	Marc Newfield	.15	.07	.02
□ 192	Steve Finley	.30	.14	.04
□ 193	Trevor Hoffman	.15	.07	.02
□ 194	Andujar Cedeno	.05	.02	.01
□ 195	Jody Reed	.05	.02	.01
□ 196	Ken Caminiti	.30	.14	.04
□ 197	Joey Hamilton	.15	.07	.02
□ 198	Tony Gwynn BAC	.40	.18	.05
□ 199	Shawn Barton	.05	.02	.01
□ 200	Deion Sanders	.30	.14	.04
□ 201	Rikkert Faneyte	.05	.02	.01
□ 202	Barry Bonds	.50	.23	.06
□ 203	Matt Williams	.30	.14	.04
□ 204	Jose Bautista	.05	.02	.01
□ 205	Mark Leiter	.05	.02	.01
□ 206	Mark Carreon	.05	.02	.01
□ 207	Robby Thompson	.05	.02	.01
□ 208	Terry Mulholland	.05	.02	.01
□ 209	Rod Beck	.05	.02	.01
□ 210	Royce Clayton	.05	.02	.01
□ 211	J.R. Phillips	.05	.02	.01
□ 212	Kirt Manwaring	.05	.02	.01
□ 213	Glenallen Hill	.05	.02	.01
□ 214	William VanLandingham	.05	.02	.01
□ 215	Scott Cooper	.05	.02	.01
□ 216	Bernard Gilkey	.15	.07	.02
□ 217	Allen Watson	.05	.02	.01
□ 218	Donovan Osborne	.05	.02	.01
□ 219	Ray Lankford	.30	.14	.04
□ 220	Tony Fossas	.05	.02	.01
□ 221	Tom Pagnozzi	.05	.02	.01
□ 222	John Mabry	.30	.14	.04
□ 223	Tripp Cromer	.05	.02	.01
□ 224	Mark Petkovsek	.05	.02	.01
□ 225	Mike Morgan	.05	.02	.01
□ 226	Ozzie Smith	.40	.18	.05
□ 227	Tom Henke	.15	.07	.02
□ 228	Jose Oquendo	.05	.02	.01
□ 229	Brian Jordan	.30	.14	.04
□ 230	Cal Ripken	1.50	.70	.19
□ 231	Scott Erickson	.05	.02	.01
□ 232	Harold Baines	.15	.07	.02
□ 233	Jeff Manto	.05	.02	.01
□ 234	Jesse Orosco	.05	.02	.01
□ 235	Jeffrey Hammonds	.05	.02	.01
□ 236	Brady Anderson	.30	.14	.04
□ 237	Manny Alexander	.05	.02	.01
□ 238	Chris Hoiles	.05	.02	.01
□ 239	Rafael Palmeiro	.30	.14	.04
□ 240	Ben McDonald	.05	.02	.01
□ 241	Curtis Goodwin	.05	.02	.01
□ 242	Bobby Bonilla	.15	.07	.02
□ 243	Mike Mussina	.40	.18	.05
□ 244	Kevin Brown	.05	.02	.01
□ 245	Armando Benitez	.05	.02	.01
□ 246	Jose Canseco	.30	.14	.04
□ 247	Erik Hanson	.05	.02	.01
□ 248	Mo Vaughn	.50	.23	.06
□ 249	Tim Naehring	.05	.02	.01
□ 250	Vaughn Eshelman	.05	.02	.01
□ 251	Mike Greenwell	.05	.02	.01
□ 252	Troy O'Leary	.05	.02	.01
□ 253	Tim Wakefield	.05	.02	.01
□ 254	Dwayne Hosey	.05	.02	.01
□ 255	John Valentin	.15	.07	.02
□ 256	Rick Aguilera	.05	.02	.01
□ 257	Mike Macfarlane	.05	.02	.01
□ 258	Roger Clemens	.30	.14	.04
□ 259	Luis Alicea	.05	.02	.01
□ 260	Mo Vaughn MVP	.30	.14	.04
□ 261	Mark Langston	.05	.02	.01
□ 262	Jim Edmonds	.30	.14	.04
□ 263	Rod Correia	.05	.02	.01
□ 264	Tim Salmon	.30	.14	.04
□ 265	J.T. Snow	.15	.07	.02
□ 266	Orlando Palmeiro	.05	.02	.01
□ 267	Jorge Fabregas	.05	.02	.01
□ 268	Jim Abbott	.30	.14	.04
□ 269	Eduardo Perez	.05	.02	.01
□ 270	Lee Smith	.30	.14	.04
□ 271	Gary DiSarcina	.05	.02	.01
□ 272	Damion Easley	.05	.02	.01
□ 273	Tony Phillips	.05	.02	.01
□ 274	Garret Anderson	.30	.14	.04
□ 275	Chuck Finley	.05	.02	.01
□ 276	Chili Davis	.05	.02	.01
□ 277	Lance Johnson	.15	.07	.02
□ 278	Alex Fernandez	.30	.14	.04
□ 279	Robin Ventura	.15	.07	.02
□ 280	Chris Snopek	.05	.02	.01
□ 281	Brian Keyser	.05	.02	.01

□ 282	Lyle Mouton	.05	.02	.01
□ 283	Luis Andujar	.05	.02	.01
□ 284	Tim Raines	.30	.14	.04
□ 285	Larry Thomas	.05	.02	.01
□ 286	Ozzie Guillen	.05	.02	.01
□ 287	Frank Thomas	2.00	.90	.25
□ 288	Roberto Hernandez	.15	.07	.02
□ 289	Dave Martinez	.05	.02	.01
□ 290	Ray Durham	.30	.14	.04
□ 291	Ron Karkovice	.05	.02	.01
□ 292	Wilson Alvarez	.30	.14	.04
□ 293	Omar Vizquel	.05	.02	.01
□ 294	Eddie Murray	.50	.23	.06
□ 295	Sandy Alomar, Jr.	.05	.02	.01
□ 296	Orel Hershiser	.15	.07	.02
□ 297	Jose Mesa	.15	.07	.02
□ 298	Julian Tavarez	.05	.02	.01
□ 299	Dennis Martinez	.15	.07	.02
□ 300	Carlos Baerga	.30	.14	.04
□ 301	Manny Ramirez	.50	.23	.06
□ 302	Jim Thome	.40	.18	.05
□ 303	Kenny Lofton	.50	.23	.06
□ 304	Tony Pena	.05	.02	.01
□ 305	Alvaro Espinoza	.05	.02	.01
□ 306	Paul Sorrento	.05	.02	.01
□ 307	Albert Belle	1.00	.45	.12
□ 308	Danny Bautista	.05	.02	.01
□ 309	Chris Gomez	.05	.02	.01
□ 310	Jose Lima	.05	.02	.01
□ 311	Phil Nevin	.05	.02	.01
□ 312	Alan Trammell	.30	.14	.04
□ 313	Chad Curtis	.05	.02	.01
□ 314	John Flaherty	.05	.02	.01
□ 315	Travis Fryman	.30	.14	.04
□ 316	Todd Steverson	.05	.02	.01
□ 317	Brian Bohanon	.05	.02	.01
□ 318	Lou Whitaker	.30	.14	.04
□ 319	Bobby Higginson	.30	.14	.04
□ 320	Steve Rodriguez	.05	.02	.01
□ 321	Cecil Fielder	.30	.14	.04
□ 322	Felipe Lira	.05	.02	.01
□ 323	Juan Samuel	.05	.02	.01
□ 324	Bob Hamelin	.05	.02	.01
□ 325	Tom Goodwin	.15	.07	.02
□ 326	Johnny Damon	.30	.14	.04
□ 327	Hipolito Pichardo	.05	.02	.01
□ 328	Dilson Torres	.05	.02	.01
□ 329	Kevin Appier	.05	.02	.01
□ 330	Mark Gubicza	.05	.02	.01
□ 331	Jon Nunnally	.05	.02	.01
□ 332	Gary Gaetti	.15	.07	.02
□ 333	Brent Mayne	.05	.02	.01
□ 334	Brent Cookson	.05	.02	.01
□ 335	Tom Gordon	.05	.02	.01
□ 336	Wally Joyner	.05	.02	.01
□ 337	Greg Gagne	.05	.02	.01
□ 338	Fernando Vina	.05	.02	.01
□ 339	Joe Oliver	.05	.02	.01
□ 340	John Jaha	.15	.07	.02
□ 341	Jeff Cirillo	.05	.02	.01
□ 342	Pat Listach	.05	.02	.01
□ 343	Dave Nilsson	.15	.07	.02
□ 344	Steve Sparks	.05	.02	.01
□ 345	Ricky Bones	.05	.02	.01
□ 346	David Hulse	.05	.02	.01
□ 347	Scott Karl	.05	.02	.01
□ 348	Darryl Hamilton	.05	.02	.01
□ 349	B.J. Surhoff	.05	.02	.01
□ 350	Angel Miranda	.05	.02	.01
□ 351	Sid Roberson	.05	.02	.01
□ 352	Matt Mieske	.05	.02	.01
□ 353	Jose Valentin	.05	.02	.01
□ 354	Matt Lawton	.05	.02	.01
□ 355	Eddie Guardado	.05	.02	.01
□ 356	Brad Radke	.05	.02	.01
□ 357	Pedro Munoz	.05	.02	.01
□ 358	Scott Stahoviak	.05	.02	.01
□ 359	Erik Schullstrom	.05	.02	.01
□ 360	Pat Meares	.05	.02	.01
□ 361	Marty Cordova	.30	.14	.04
□ 362	Scott Leius	.05	.02	.01
□ 363	Matt Walbeck	.05	.02	.01
□ 364	Rich Becker	.15	.07	.02
□ 365	Kirby Puckett	.60	.25	.07
□ 366	Oscar Munoz	.05	.02	.01
□ 367	Chuck Knoblauch	.30	.14	.04
□ 368	Marty Cordova ROY	.15	.07	.02
□ 369	Bernie Williams	.30	.14	.04
□ 370	Mike Stanley	.05	.02	.01
□ 371	Andy Pettitte	.60	.25	.07
□ 372	Jack McDowell	.30	.14	.04
□ 373	Sterling Hitchcock	.05	.02	.01
□ 374	David Cone	.30	.14	.04
□ 375	Randy Velarde	.05	.02	.01
□ 376	Don Mattingly	1.00	.45	.12
□ 377	Melido Perez	.05	.02	.01
□ 378	Wade Boggs	.30	.14	.04
□ 379	Ruben Sierra	.05	.02	.01
□ 380	Tony Fernandez	.05	.02	.01
□ 381	John Wetteland	.15	.07	.02
□ 382	Mariano Rivera	.30	.14	.04
□ 383	Derek Jeter	1.25	.55	.16
□ 384	Paul O'Neill	.05	.02	.01
□ 385	Mark McGwire	.60	.25	.07
□ 386	Scott Brosius	.15	.07	.02
□ 387	Don Wengert	.05	.02	.01
□ 388	Terry Steinbach	.15	.07	.02
□ 389	Brent Gates	.05	.02	.01
□ 390	Craig Paquette	.05	.02	.01
□ 391	Mike Bordick	.15	.07	.02
□ 392	Ariel Prieto	.05	.02	.01
□ 393	Dennis Eckersley	.30	.14	.04
□ 394	Carlos Reyes	.05	.02	.01
□ 395	Todd Stottleymyre	.05	.02	.01
□ 396	Rickey Henderson	.30	.14	.04
□ 397	Geronimo Berroa	.15	.07	.02
□ 398	Steve Ontiveros	.05	.02	.01
□ 399	Mike Gallego	.05	.02	.01
□ 400	Stan Javier	.05	.02	.01
□ 401	Randy Johnson	.30	.14	.04
□ 402	Norm Charlton	.05	.02	.01
□ 403	Mike Blowers	.05	.02	.01
□ 404	Tino Martinez	.30	.14	.04
□ 405	Dan Wilson	.05	.02	.01
□ 406	Andy Benes	.05	.02	.01
□ 407	Alex Diaz	.05	.02	.01
□ 408	Edgar Martinez	.30	.14	.04
□ 409	Chris Bosio	.05	.02	.01
□ 410	Ken Griffey, Jr.	2.00	.90	.25
□ 411	Luis Sojo	.05	.02	.01
□ 412	Bob Wolcott	.05	.02	.01
□ 413	Vince Coleman	.05	.02	.01
□ 414	Rich Amaral	.05	.02	.01
□ 415	Jay Buhner	.30	.14	.04
□ 416	Alex Rodriguez	2.00	.90	.25
□ 417	Joey Cora	.05	.02	.01
□ 418	Randy Johnson CY	.30	.14	.04
□ 419	Edgar Martinez BAC	.30	.14	.04
□ 420	Ivan Rodriguez	.40	.18	.05
□ 421	Mark McLemore	.05	.02	.01
□ 422	Mickey Tettleton	.15	.07	.02
□ 423	Juan Gonzalez	1.00	.45	.12
□ 424	Will Clark	.30	.14	.04
□ 425	Kevin Gross	.05	.02	.01
□ 426	Dean Palmer	.30	.14	.04
□ 427	Kenny Rogers	.05	.02	.01
□ 428	Bob Tewksbury	.05	.02	.01
□ 429	Benji Gil	.05	.02	.01
□ 430	Jeff Russell	.05	.02	.01
□ 431	Rusty Greer	.30	.14	.04
□ 432	Roger Pavlik	.05	.02	.01
□ 433	Esteban Beltre	.05	.02	.01
□ 434	Otis Nixon	.05	.02	.01
□ 435	Paul Molitor	.40	.18	.05
□ 436	Carlos Delgado	.30	.14	.04
□ 437	Ed Sprague	.15	.07	.02
□ 438	Juan Guzman	.05	.02	.01
□ 439	Domingo Cedeno	.05	.02	.01
□ 440	Pat Hentgen	.30	.14	.04
□ 441	Tomas Perez	.05	.02	.01
□ 442	John Olerud	.05	.02	.01
□ 443	Shawn Green	.15	.07	.02
□ 444	Al Leiter	.05	.02	.01
□ 445	Joe Carter	.30	.14	.04
□ 446	Robert Perez	.05	.02	.01
□ 447	Devon White	.05	.02	.01
□ 448	Tony Castillo	.05	.02	.01
□ 449	Alex Gonzalez	.05	.02	.01
□ 450	Roberto Alomar	.50	.23	.06

1996 Pacific Cramer's Choice

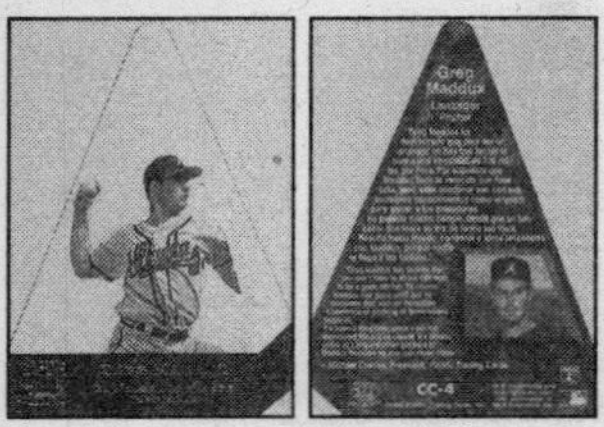

Randomly inserted in packs at a rate of one in 721, this 10-card set features the top Major League Baseball players as chosen by Pacific President and CEO, Michael Cramer. The fronts display a color player cut-out on a pyramid diecut shaped background. The backs carry information about why the player was selected for this set in both English and Spanish.

	MINT	NRMT	EXC
COMPLETE SET (10)	1400.00	650.00	180.00
COMMON CARD (CC1-CC10)	40.00	18.00	5.00
RANDOM INSERTS IN PACKS			

	MINT	NRMT	EXC
□ CC1 Roberto Alomar	75.00	34.00	9.50
□ CC2 Wade Boggs	40.00	18.00	5.00
□ CC3 Cal Ripken	225.00	100.00	28.00
□ CC4 Greg Maddux	200.00	90.00	25.00
□ CC5 Frank Thomas	275.00	125.00	34.00
□ CC6 Tony Gwynn	120.00	55.00	15.00
□ CC7 Mike Piazza	200.00	90.00	25.00
□ CC8 Ken Griffey Jr.	275.00	125.00	34.00
□ CC9 Manny Ramirez	75.00	34.00	9.50
□ CC10 Edgar Martinez	50.00	22.00	6.25

1996 Pacific Estrellas Latinas

Randomly inserted in packs at a rate of four in 37, this 36-card set salutes the great Latino players in the major leagues today. The fronts feature color player action cut-outs on a black and gold foil background. The horizontal backs carry a player portrait with information about the player in both English and Spanish.

	MINT	NRMT	EXC
COMPLETE SET (36)	50.00	22.00	6.25
COMMON CARD (EL1-EL36)	1.00	.45	.12
SEMISTARS	2.00	.90	.25
RANDOM INSERTS IN PACKS			

	MINT	NRMT	EXC
□ EL1 Roberto Alomar	4.00	1.80	.50
□ EL2 Moises Alou	1.00	.45	.12
□ EL3 Carlos Baerga	2.00	.90	.25
□ EL4 Geronimo Berroa	1.00	.45	.12
□ EL5 Ricky Bones	1.00	.45	.12
□ EL6 Bobby Bonilla	2.00	.90	.25
□ EL7 Jose Canseco	2.00	.90	.25
□ EL8 Vinny Castilla	2.00	.90	.25
□ EL9 Pedro Martinez	1.00	.45	.12
□ EL10 John Valentin	1.00	.45	.12
□ EL11 Andres Galarraga	2.00	.90	.25
□ EL12 Juan Gonzalez	8.00	3.60	1.00
□ EL13 Ozzie Guillen	1.00	.45	.12
□ EL14 Esteban Loaiza	1.00	.45	.12
□ EL15 Javier Lopez	2.00	.90	.25
□ EL16 Dennis Martinez	1.00	.45	.12
□ EL17 Edgar Martinez	2.00	.90	.25
□ EL18 Tino Martinez	1.00	.45	.12
□ EL19 Orlando Merced	1.00	.45	.12
□ EL20 Jose Mesa	1.00	.45	.12
□ EL21 Raul Mondesi	2.00	.90	.25
□ EL22 Jaime Navarro	1.00	.45	.12
□ EL23 Rafael Palmeiro	2.00	.90	.25
□ EL24 Carlos Perez	1.00	.45	.12
□ EL25 Manny Ramirez	4.00	1.80	.50
□ EL26 Alex Rodriguez	15.00	6.75	1.85
□ EL27 Ivan Rodriguez	3.00	1.35	.35
□ EL28 David Segui	1.00	.45	.12
□ EL29 Ruben Sierra	2.00	.90	.25
□ EL30 Sammy Sosa	2.50	1.10	.30
□ EL31 Julian Tavarez	1.00	.45	.12
□ EL32 Ismael Valdes	1.00	.45	.12
□ EL33 Fernando Valenzuela	2.00	.90	.25
□ EL34 Quilvio Veras	1.00	.45	.12
□ EL35 Omar Vizquel	1.00	.45	.12
□ EL36 Bernie Williams	2.00	.90	.25

1996 Pacific Gold Crown Diecuts

Randomly inserted in packs at a rate of one in 37, this 36-card set features 1996 Major League Baseball Super Stars. The fronts display color action player photos with a diecut gold crown at the top and gold foil printing. The backs carry a color player portrait and information about the player in English and Spanish.

	MINT	NRMT	EXC
COMPLETE SET (36)	450.00	200.00	55.00
COMMON CARD (DC1-DC36)	4.00	1.80	.50
SEMISTARS	6.00	2.70	.75
RANDOM INSERTS IN PACKS			

	MINT	NRMT	EXC
□ DC1 Roberto Alomar	12.00	5.50	1.50
□ DC2 Will Clark	6.00	2.70	.75
□ DC3 Johnny Damon	4.00	1.80	.50
□ DC4 Don Mattingly	25.00	11.00	3.10
□ DC5 Edgar Martinez	6.00	2.70	.75
□ DC6 Manny Ramirez	12.00	5.50	1.50
□ DC7 Mike Piazza	30.00	13.50	3.70
□ DC8 Quilvio Veras	4.00	1.80	.50
□ DC9 Rickey Henderson	6.00	2.70	.75
□ DC10 Jeff Bagwell	20.00	9.00	2.50
□ DC11 Andres Galarraga	6.00	2.70	.75
□ DC12 Tim Salmon	6.00	2.70	.75
□ DC13 Ken Griffey Jr.	50.00	22.00	6.25
□ DC14 Sammy Sosa	8.00	3.60	1.00
□ DC15 Cal Ripken	40.00	18.00	5.00
□ DC16 Raul Mondesi	6.00	2.70	.75
□ DC17 Jose Canseco	6.00	2.70	.75
□ DC18 Frank Thomas	50.00	22.00	6.25
□ DC19 Hideo Nomo	12.00	5.50	1.50

□ DC20 Wade Boggs	6.00	2.70	.75
□ DC21 Reggie Sanders	6.00	2.70	.75
□ DC22 Carlos Baerga	6.00	2.70	.75
□ DC23 Mo Vaughn	12.00	5.50	1.50
□ DC24 Ivan Rodriguez	10.00	4.50	1.25
□ DC25 Kirby Puckett	15.00	6.75	1.85
□ DC26 Albert Belle	25.00	11.00	3.10
□ DC27 Vinny Castilla	4.00	1.80	.50
□ DC28 Greg Maddux	30.00	13.50	3.70
□ DC29 Dante Bichette	6.00	2.70	.75
□ DC30 Deion Sanders	6.00	2.70	.75
□ DC31 Chipper Jones	30.00	13.50	3.70
□ DC32 Cecil Fielder	6.00	2.70	.75
□ DC33 Randy Johnson	8.00	3.60	1.00
□ DC34 Mark McGwire	15.00	6.75	1.85
□ DC35 Tony Gwynn	20.00	9.00	2.50
□ DC36 Barry Bonds	12.00	5.50	1.50

1996 Pacific Hometowns

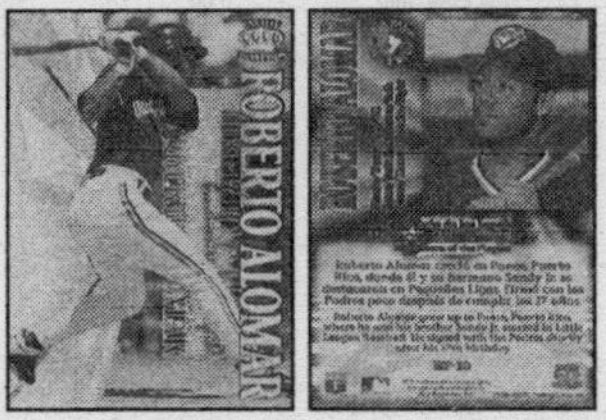

Randomly inserted in packs at a rate of two in 37, this 20-card set features color action player photos with a gold foil border on the left and gold foil printing. The backs carry a player portrait with the player's hometown or city and country and player information printed in both English and Spanish.

	MINT	NRMT	EXC
COMPLETE SET (20)	120.00	55.00	15.00
COMMON CARD (HP1-HP20)	1.50	.70	.19
SEMISTARS	2.50	1.10	.30
RANDOM INSERTS IN PACKS			

□ HP1 Mike Piazza	12.00	5.50	1.50
□ HP2 Greg Maddux	12.00	5.50	1.50
□ HP3 Tony Gwynn	8.00	3.60	1.00
□ HP4 Carlos Baerga	2.50	1.10	.30
□ HP5 Don Mattingly	10.00	4.50	1.25
□ HP6 Cal Ripken	15.00	6.75	1.85
□ HP7 Chipper Jones	12.00	5.50	1.50
□ HP8 Andres Galarraga	2.50	1.10	.30
□ HP9 Manny Ramirez	5.00	2.20	.60
□ HP10 Roberto Alomar	5.00	2.20	.60
□ HP11 Ken Griffey Jr.	20.00	9.00	2.50
□ HP12 Jose Canseco	2.50	1.10	.30
□ HP13 Frank Thomas	20.00	9.00	2.50
□ HP14 Vinny Castilla	1.50	.70	.19
□ HP15 Roberto Kelly	1.50	.70	.19
□ HP16 Dennis Martinez	1.50	.70	.19
□ HP17 Kirby Puckett	6.00	2.70	.75
□ HP18 Raul Mondesi	2.50	1.10	.30
□ HP19 Hideo Nomo	5.00	2.20	.60
□ HP20 Edgar Martinez	2.50	1.10	.30

1996 Pacific Milestones

Randomly inserted in packs at a rate of one in 37, this 10-card set denotes the outstanding milestone and record-breaking achievements of baseball's superstars in 1995. The fronts feature a color action player cut-out on a blue foil background with embossed symbols represting the team logo, baseball, and the milestone or achievement. The backs carry a player portrait with the milestone or achievement printed in both English and Spanish.

	MINT	NRMT	EXC
COMPLETE SET (10)	75.00	34.00	9.50
COMMON CARD (M1-M10)	2.50	1.10	.30
RANDOM INSERTS IN PACKS			

□ M1 Albert Belle	10.00	4.50	1.25
□ M2 Don Mattingly	10.00	4.50	1.25
□ M3 Tony Gwynn	8.00	3.60	1.00
□ M4 Jose Canseco	4.00	1.80	.50
□ M5 Marty Cordova	2.50	1.10	.30
□ M6 Wade Boggs	4.00	1.80	.50
□ M7 Greg Maddux	12.00	5.50	1.50
□ M8 Eddie Murray	5.00	2.20	.60
□ M9 Ken Griffey Jr.	20.00	9.00	2.50
□ M10 Cal Ripken	15.00	6.75	1.85

1996 Pacific October Moments

Randomly inserted in packs at a rate of one in 37, this 20-card set highlights 1995 postseason heroics and the players involved. The fronts feature borderless color player action photos with a bronze foil background and printing. The backs carry a player portrait with the heroic action printed in both English and Spanish.

	MINT	NRMT	EXC
COMPLETE SET (20)	150.00	70.00	19.00
COMMON CARD (OM1-OM20)	2.50	1.10	.30
SEMISTARS	4.00	1.80	.50
RANDOM INSERTS IN PACKS			

□ OM1 Carlos Baerga	2.50	1.10	.30
□ OM2 Albert Belle	15.00	6.75	1.85
□ OM3 Dante Bichette	2.50	1.10	.30
□ OM4 Jose Canseco	4.00	1.80	.50
□ OM5 Tom Glavine	4.00	1.80	.50
□ OM6 Ken Griffey Jr.	30.00	13.50	3.70
□ OM7 Randy Johnson	5.00	2.20	.60
□ OM8 Chipper Jones	20.00	9.00	2.50
□ OM9 David Justice	4.00	1.80	.50
□ OM10 Ryan Klesko	6.00	2.70	.75
□ OM11 Kenny Lofton	8.00	3.60	1.00
□ OM12 Javier Lopez	4.00	1.80	.50
□ OM13 Greg Maddux	20.00	9.00	2.50
□ OM14 Edgar Martinez	4.00	1.80	.50
□ OM15 Don Mattingly	15.00	6.75	1.85
□ OM16 Hideo Nomo	8.00	3.60	1.00
□ OM17 Mike Piazza	20.00	9.00	2.50
□ OM18 Manny Ramirez	8.00	3.60	1.00
□ OM19 Reggie Sanders	2.50	1.10	.30
□ OM20 Jim Thome	6.00	2.70	.75

1995 Pacific Prisms

This 144-card standard-size set was issued for the first time as a stand alone set instead as an insert set. Total production of this product was 2,999 individually numbered cases that contained 20 boxes of 36 packs. The full-bleed fronts feature a player photo against a silver prismatic background with the playerís name on the bottom. The backs have a full-color photo with some biographical information. The cards are grouped alphabetically according to teams for each league as follows: Atlanta Braves (1-6), Baltimore Orioles (7-11), Boston Red Sox (12-16), California Angels (17-21), Chicago Cubs (22-26), Chicago White Sox (27-31), Cincinnati Reds (32-36), Cleveland Indians (37-42), Colorado Rockies (43-46), Detroit Tigers (47-52), Florida Marlins (53-57), Houston Astros (58-62), Kansas City Royals (63-67), Los Angeles Dodgers (68-73), Milwaukee Brewers (74-77), Minnesota Twins (78-83), Montreal Expos (84-89), New York Mets (90-94), New York Yankees (95-100), Oakland Aís (101-104), Philadelphia Phillies (105-110), Pittsburgh Pirates (111-114), San Diego Padres (115-118), San Francisco Giants (119-123), Seattle Mariners (124-129), St. Louis Cardinals (130-133), Texas Rangers (134-137), and Toronto Blue Jays (138-144). There are no key Rookie Cards in this set.

	MINT	NRMT	EXC
COMPLETE SET (144)	150.00	70.00	19.00
COMMON CARD (1-144)	1.00	.45	.12
CL (CL1/CL2)	.25	.11	.03
SEMISTARS	1.50	.70	.19
STARS	2.00	.90	.25
COMP.TEAM LOGO SET (28)	5.00	2.20	.60
ONE CL OR LOGO OR TEAM LOGO PER PACK			

□ 1 David Justice	2.00	.90	.25
□ 2 Ryan Klesko	3.00	1.35	.35
□ 3 Javier Lopez	2.00	.90	.25
□ 4 Greg Maddux	10.00	4.50	1.25
□ 5 Fred McGriff	2.00	.90	.25
□ 6 Tony Tarasco	1.00	.45	.12
□ 7 Jeffrey Hammonds	1.50	.70	.19
□ 8 Mike Mussina	3.00	1.35	.35
□ 9 Rafael Palmeiro	2.00	.90	.25
□ 10 Cal Ripken	12.00	5.50	1.50
□ 11 Lee Smith	1.50	.70	.19
□ 12 Roger Clemens	2.00	.90	.25
□ 13 Scott Cooper	1.00	.45	.12
□ 14 Mike Greenwell	1.00	.45	.12
□ 15 Carlos Rodriguez	1.00	.45	.12
□ 16 Mo Vaughn	4.00	1.80	.50
□ 17 Chili Davis	1.50	.70	.19
□ 18 Jim Edmonds	2.00	.90	.25
□ 19 Jorge Fabregas	1.00	.45	.12
□ 20 Bo Jackson	2.00	.90	.25
□ 21 Tim Salmon	2.00	.90	.25
□ 22 Mark Grace	2.00	.90	.25
□ 23 Jose Guzman	1.00	.45	.12
□ 24 Randy Myers	1.00	.45	.12
□ 25 Rey Sanchez	1.00	.45	.12
□ 26 Sammy Sosa	2.50	1.10	.30
□ 27 Wilson Alvarez	1.50	.70	.19
□ 28 Julio Franco	1.50	.70	.19
□ 29 Ozzie Guillen	1.00	.45	.12
□ 30 Jack McDowell	1.50	.70	.19
□ 31 Frank Thomas	15.00	6.75	1.85
□ 32 Bret Boone	1.50	.70	.19
□ 33 Barry Larkin	2.00	.90	.25
□ 34 Hal Morris	1.00	.45	.12
□ 35 Jose Rijo	1.00	.45	.12
□ 36 Deion Sanders	2.00	.90	.25
□ 37 Carlos Baerga	2.00	.90	.25
□ 38 Albert Belle	8.00	3.60	1.00
□ 39 Kenny Lofton	4.00	1.80	.50
□ 40 Dennis Martinez	1.50	.70	.19
□ 41 Manny Ramirez	4.00	1.80	.50
□ 42 Omar Vizquel	2.00	.90	.25
□ 43 Dante Bichette	2.00	.90	.25
□ 44 Marvin Freeman	1.00	.45	.12
□ 45 Andres Galarraga	2.00	.90	.25
□ 46 Mike Kingery	1.00	.45	.12
□ 47 Danny Bautista	1.00	.45	.12
□ 48 Cecil Fielder	1.50	.70	.19
□ 49 Travis Fryman	1.50	.70	.19
□ 50 Tony Phillips	1.50	.70	.19
□ 51 Alan Trammell	2.00	.90	.25
□ 52 Lou Whitaker	2.00	.90	.25
□ 53 Alex Arias	1.00	.45	.12
□ 54 Bret Barberie	1.00	.45	.12
□ 55 Jeff Conine	2.00	.90	.25
□ 56 Charles Johnson	1.50	.70	.19
□ 57 Gary Sheffield	2.50	1.10	.30
□ 58 Jeff Bagwell	6.00	2.70	.75
□ 59 Craig Biggio	2.00	.90	.25
□ 60 Doug Drabek	1.00	.45	.12
□ 61 Tony Eusebio	1.00	.45	.12
□ 62 Luis Gonzalez	1.00	.45	.12
□ 63 David Cone	1.50	.70	.19
□ 64 Bob Hamelin	1.00	.45	.12
□ 65 Felix Jose	1.00	.45	.12
□ 66 Wally Joyner	1.50	.70	.19
□ 67 Brian McRae	1.50	.70	.19
□ 68 Brett Butler	1.50	.70	.19
□ 69 Garey Ingram	1.00	.45	.12
□ 70 Ramon Martinez	1.50	.70	.19
□ 71 Raul Mondesi	2.00	.90	.25
□ 72 Mike Piazza	10.00	4.50	1.25
□ 73 Henry Rodriguez	2.00	.90	.25
□ 74 Ricky Bones	1.00	.45	.12
□ 75 Pat Listach	1.00	.45	.12
□ 76 Dave Nilsson	1.50	.70	.19
□ 77 Jose Valentin	1.50	.70	.19
□ 78 Rick Aguilera	1.00	.45	.12
□ 79 Denny Hocking	1.00	.45	.12
□ 80 Shane Mack	1.00	.45	.12
□ 81 Pedro Munoz	1.00	.45	.12
□ 82 Kirby Puckett	5.00	2.20	.60
□ 83 Dave Winfield	2.00	.90	.25
□ 84 Moises Alou	1.50	.70	.19
□ 85 Wil Cordero	1.00	.45	.12
□ 86 Cliff Floyd	1.50	.70	.19
□ 87 Marquis Grissom	2.00	.90	.25
□ 88 Pedro J. Martinez	1.50	.70	.19
□ 89 Larry Walker	2.00	.90	.25
□ 90 Bobby Bonilla	1.50	.70	.19
□ 91 Jeromy Burnitz	1.00	.45	.12
□ 92 John Franco	1.00	.45	.12
□ 93 Jeff Kent	1.00	.45	.12
□ 94 Jose Vizcaino	1.00	.45	.12
□ 95 Wade Boggs	2.00	.90	.25
□ 96 Jimmy Key	1.50	.70	.19
□ 97 Don Mattingly	8.00	3.60	1.00
□ 98 Paul O'Neill	1.50	.70	.19
□ 99 Luis Polonia	1.00	.45	.12
□ 100 Danny Tartabull	1.00	.45	.12
□ 101 Geronimo Berroa	1.00	.45	.12
□ 102 Rickey Henderson	2.00	.90	.25
□ 103 Ruben Sierra	1.50	.70	.19
□ 104 Terry Steinbach	1.50	.70	.19
□ 105 Darren Daulton	1.50	.70	.19
□ 106 Mariano Duncan	1.00	.45	.12
□ 107 Lenny Dykstra	1.50	.70	.19
□ 108 Mike Lieberthal	1.00	.45	.12
□ 109 Tony Longmire	1.00	.45	.12
□ 110 Tom Marsh	1.00	.45	.12
□ 111 Jay Bell	1.50	.70	.19
□ 112 Carlos Garcia	1.00	.45	.12
□ 113 Orlando Merced	1.00	.45	.12
□ 114 Andy Van Slyke	1.50	.70	.19

□ 115	Derek Bell	1.50	.70	.19
□ 116	Tony Gwynn	6.00	2.70	.75
□ 117	Luis Lopez	1.00	.45	.12
□ 118	Bip Roberts	1.00	.45	.12
□ 119	Rod Beck	1.00	.45	.12
□ 120	Barry Bonds	4.00	1.80	.50
□ 121	Darryl Strawberry	1.50	.70	.19
□ 122	Wm. Van Landingham	1.00	.45	.12
□ 123	Matt Williams	2.00	.90	.25
□ 124	Jay Buhner	2.00	.90	.25
□ 125	Felix Fermin	1.00	.45	.12
□ 126	Ken Griffey Jr.	15.00	6.75	1.85
□ 127	Randy Johnson	2.00	.90	.25
□ 128	Edgar Martinez	2.00	.90	.25
□ 129	Alex Rodriguez	20.00	9.00	2.50
□ 130	Rene Arocha	1.00	.45	.12
□ 131	Gregg Jefferies	1.50	.70	.19
□ 132	Mike Perez	1.00	.45	.12
□ 133	Ozzie Smith	3.00	1.35	.35
□ 134	Jose Canseco	2.00	.90	.25
□ 135	Will Clark	2.00	.90	.25
□ 136	Juan Gonzalez	8.00	3.60	1.00
□ 137	Ivan Rodriguez	3.00	1.35	.35
□ 138	Roberto Alomar	4.00	1.80	.50
□ 139	Joe Carter	2.00	.90	.25
□ 140	Carlos Delgado	2.00	.90	.25
□ 141	Alex Gonzalez	1.00	.45	.12
□ 142	Juan Guzman	1.50	.70	.19
□ 143	Paul Molitor	3.00	1.35	.35
□ 144	John Olerud	1.00	.45	.12
□ NNO	Pacific Logo	.25	.11	.03

1996 Pacific Prisms

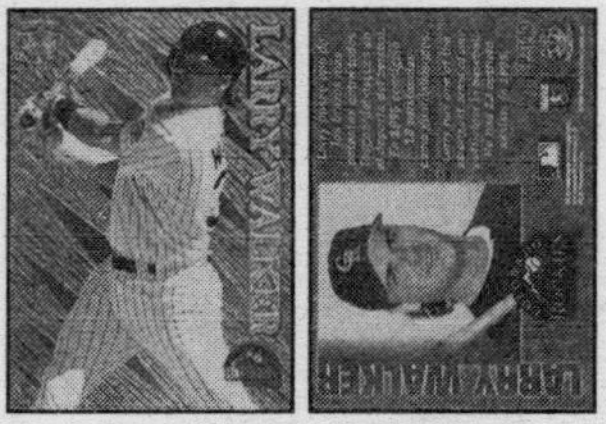

This 144-card set features a color action player cut-out over a double-etched silver foil prismatic background. The backs carry a color player portrait with information about the player in both English and Spanish.

	MINT	NRMT	EXC
COMPLETE SET (144)	150.00	70.00	19.00
COMMON CARD (1-144)	1.00	.45	.12
SEMISTARS	1.50	.70	.19
STARS	2.00	.90	.25
*GOLD STARS: 4X BASIC CARDS			
GOLD: RANDOM INSERTS IN PACKS			

□ P1	Tom Glavine	2.00	.90	.25
□ P2	Chipper Jones	10.00	4.50	1.25
□ P3	David Justice	1.50	.70	.19
□ P4	Ryan Klesko	3.00	1.35	.35
□ P5	Javy Lopez	2.00	.90	.25
□ P6	Greg Maddux	10.00	4.50	1.25
□ P7	Fred McGriff	2.00	.90	.25
□ P8	Frank Castillo	1.00	.45	.12
□ P9	Luis Gonzalez	1.00	.45	.12
□ P10	Mark Grace	2.00	.90	.25
□ P11	Brian McRae	1.00	.45	.12
□ P12	Jaime Navarro	1.00	.45	.12
□ P13	Sammy Sosa	2.50	1.10	.30
□ P14	Bret Boone	1.00	.45	.12
□ P15	Ron Gant	2.00	.90	.25
□ P16	Barry Larkin	2.00	.90	.25
□ P17	Reggie Sanders	2.00	.90	.25
□ P18	Benito Santiago	1.00	.45	.12
□ P19	Dante Bichette	2.00	.90	.25
□ P20	Vinny Castilla	2.00	.90	.25
□ P21	Andres Galarraga	2.00	.90	.25
□ P22	Bryan Rekar	1.00	.45	.12
□ P23	Roberto Alomar	4.00	1.80	.50
□ P24	Jeff Conine	2.00	.90	.25
□ P25	Andre Dawson	2.00	.90	.25
□ P26	Charles Johnson	1.50	.70	.19
□ P27	Gary Sheffield	2.50	1.10	.30
□ P28	Quilvio Veras	1.00	.45	.12
□ P29	Jeff Bagwell	6.00	2.70	.75
□ P30	Derek Bell	1.50	.70	.19
□ P31	Craig Biggio	2.00	.90	.25
□ P32	Tony Eusebio	1.00	.45	.12
□ P33	Karim Garcia	3.00	1.35	.35
□ P34	Eric Karros	2.00	.90	.25
□ P35	Ramon Martinez	2.00	.90	.25
□ P36	Raul Mondesi	2.00	.90	.25
□ P37	Hideo Nomo	4.00	1.80	.50
□ P38	Mike Piazza	10.00	4.50	1.25
□ P39	Ismael Valdes	1.50	.70	.19
□ P40	Moises Alou	1.50	.70	.19
□ P41	Wil Cordero	1.00	.45	.12
□ P42	Pedro Martinez	1.50	.70	.19
□ P43	Mel Rojas	1.50	.70	.19
□ P44	David Segui	1.00	.45	.12
□ P45	Edfardo Alfonzo	1.50	.70	.19
□ P46	Rico Brogna	1.00	.45	.12
□ P47	John Franco	1.00	.45	.12
□ P48	Jason Isringhausen	1.50	.70	.19
□ P49	Jose Vizcaino	1.00	.45	.12
□ P50	Ricky Bottalico	1.00	.45	.12
□ P51	Darren Daulton	1.50	.70	.19
□ P52	Lenny Dykstra	1.50	.70	.19
□ P53	Tyler Green	1.00	.45	.12
□ P54	Gregg Jefferies	2.00	.90	.25
□ P55	Jay Bell	1.50	.70	.19
□ P56	Jason Christiansen	1.00	.45	.12
□ P57	Carlos Garcia	1.00	.45	.12
□ P58	Esteban Loaiza	1.00	.45	.12
□ P59	Orlando Merced	1.50	.70	.19
□ P60	Andujar Cedeno	1.00	.45	.12
□ P61	Tony Gwynn	6.00	2.70	.75
□ P62	Melvin Nieves	1.50	.70	.19
□ P63	Phil Plantier	1.00	.45	.12
□ P64	Fernando Valenzuela	1.50	.70	.19
□ P65	Barry Bonds	4.00	1.80	.50
□ P66	J.R. Phillips	1.00	.45	.12
□ P67	Deion Sanders	2.00	.90	.25
□ P68	Matt Williams	2.00	.90	.25
□ P69	Bernard Gilkey	1.50	.70	.19
□ P70	Tom Henke	1.50	.70	.19
□ P71	Brian Jordan	2.00	.90	.25
□ P72	Ozzie Smith	3.00	1.35	.35
□ P73	Manny Alexander	1.00	.45	.12
□ P74	Bobby Bonilla	2.00	.90	.25
□ P75	Mike Mussina	3.00	1.35	.35
□ P76	Rafael Palmeiro	2.00	.90	.25
□ P77	Cal Ripken	12.00	5.50	1.50
□ P78	Jose Canseco	2.00	.90	.25
□ P79	Roger Clemens	2.00	.90	.25
□ P80	John Valentin	1.50	.70	.19
□ P81	Mo Vaughn	4.00	1.80	.50
□ P82	Tim Wakefield	1.00	.45	.12
□ P83	Garret Anderson	2.00	.90	.25
□ P84	Damion Easley	1.00	.45	.12
□ P85	Jim Edmonds	2.00	.90	.25
□ P86	Tim Salmon	2.00	.90	.25
□ P87	Wilson Alvarez	2.00	.90	.25
□ P88	Alex Fernandez	2.00	.90	.25
□ P89	Ozzie Guillen	1.00	.45	.12
□ P90	Roberto Hernandez	1.50	.70	.19
□ P91	Frank Thomas	15.00	6.75	1.85
□ P92	Robin Ventura	2.00	.90	.25
□ P93	Carlos Baerga	2.00	.90	.25
□ P94	Albert Belle	8.00	3.60	1.00
□ P95	Kenny Lofton	4.00	1.80	.50
□ P96	Dennis Martinez	1.50	.70	.19
□ P97	Eddie Murray	4.00	1.80	.50
□ P98	Manny Ramirez	4.00	1.80	.50
□ P99	Omar Vizquel	1.00	.45	.12
□ P100	Chad Curtis	1.00	.45	.12
□ P101	Cecil Fielder	2.00	.90	.25
□ P102	Felipe Lira	1.00	.45	.12
□ P103	Alan Trammell	2.00	.90	.25
□ P104	Kevin Appier	1.50	.70	.19
□ P105	Johnny Damon	2.00	.90	.25
□ P106	Gary Gaetti	1.50	.70	.19
□ P107	Wally Joyner	1.00	.45	.12

P108	Ricky Bones	1.00	.45	.12
P109	John Jaha	1.50	.70	.19
P110	B.J. Surhoff	1.00	.45	.12
P111	Jose Valentin	1.00	.45	.12
P112	Fernando Vina	1.00	.45	.12
P113	Marty Cordova	2.00	.90	.25
P114	Chuck Knoblauch	2.00	.90	.25
P115	Scott Leius	1.00	.45	.12
P116	Pedro Munoz	1.00	.45	.12
P117	Kirby Puckett	5.00	2.20	.60
P118	Wade Boggs	2.00	.90	.25
P119	Don Mattingly	8.00	3.60	1.00
P120	Jack McDowell	2.00	.90	.25
P121	Paul O'Neill	1.00	.45	.12
P122	Ruben Rivera	3.00	1.35	.35
P123	Bernie Williams	2.50	1.10	.30
P124	Geronimo Berroa	1.50	.70	.19
P125	Rickey Henderson	2.00	.90	.25
P126	Mark McGwire	5.00	2.20	.60
P127	Terry Steinbach	1.50	.70	.19
P128	Danny Tartabull	1.00	.45	.12
P129	Jay Buhner	2.00	.90	.25
P130	Joey Cora	1.00	.45	.12
P131	Ken Griffey, Jr.	15.00	6.75	1.85
P132	Randy Johnson	2.50	1.10	.30
P133	Edgar Martinez	2.00	.90	.25
P134	Tino Martinez	2.00	.90	.25
P135	Will Clark	2.00	.90	.25
P136	Juan Gonzalez	8.00	3.60	1.00
P137	Dean Palmer	2.00	.90	.25
P138	Ivan Rodriguez	3.00	1.35	.35
P139	Mickey Tettleton	1.50	.70	.19
P140	Larry Walker	2.00	.90	.25
P141	Joe Carter	2.00	.90	.25
P142	Carlos Delgado	2.00	.90	.25
P143	Alex Gonzalez	1.00	.45	.12
P144	Paul Molitor	3.00	1.35	.35

1996 Pacific Prisms Fence Busters

Randomly inserted in packs at a rate of one in 37, this 20-card set highlights 20 of baseball's hardest hitters. The fronts feature an embossed color player action cut-out with a borderless foil baseball field as background. The backs carry a player photo with information as to why the player was selected for this set in both English and Spanish.

	MINT	NRMT	EXC
COMPLETE SET (20)	180.00	80.00	22.00
COMMON CARD (1-20)	3.00	1.35	.35
SEMISTARS	5.00	2.20	.60
RANDOM INSERTS IN PACKS			

FB1	Albert Belle	20.00	9.00	2.50
FB2	Dante Bichette	5.00	2.20	.60
FB3	Barry Bonds	10.00	4.50	1.25
FB4	Jay Buhner	5.00	2.20	.60
FB5	Jose Canseco	5.00	2.20	.60
FB6	Ken Griffey Jr.	40.00	18.00	5.00
FB7	Chipper Jones	25.00	11.00	3.10
FB8	Dave Justice	3.00	1.35	.35
FB9	Eric Karros	5.00	2.20	.60
FB10	Edgar Martinez	5.00	2.20	.60
FB11	Mark McGwire	12.00	5.50	1.50
FB12	Eddie Murray	10.00	4.50	1.25
FB13	Mike Piazza	25.00	11.00	3.10
FB14	Kirby Puckett	12.00	5.50	1.50
FB15	Cal Ripken	30.00	13.50	3.70
FB16	Tim Salmon	5.00	2.20	.60
FB17	Sammy Sosa	6.00	2.70	.75
FB18	Frank Thomas	40.00	18.00	5.00
FB19	Mo Vaughn	10.00	4.50	1.25
FB20	Larry Walker	3.00	1.35	.35

1996 Pacific Prisms Flame Throwers

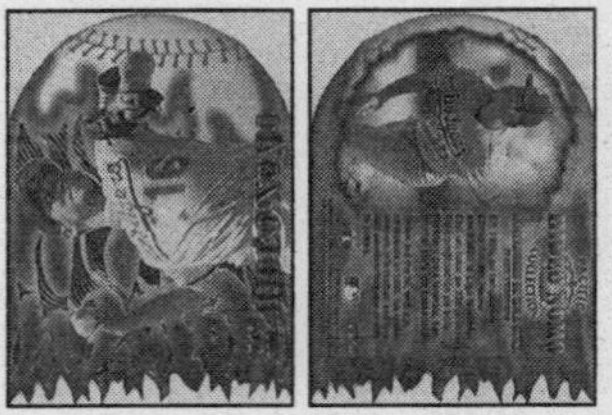

Randomly inserted in packs at a rate of one in 73, this 10-card set features 10 of Major League Baseball's hardest throwing pitchers. The fronts display a color action player photo printed on a diecut baseball-shaped card with gold foil flames indicating the force of the thrown ball. The backs carry another player photo with information of why the player was selected for this set printed in both English and Spanish.

	MINT	NRMT	EXC
COMPLETE SET (10)	150.00	70.00	19.00
COMMON CARD (1-10)	8.00	3.60	1.00
RANDOM INSERTS IN PACKS			

FT1	Randy Johnson	15.00	6.75	1.85
FT2	Mike Mussina	20.00	9.00	2.50
FT3	Roger Clemens	12.00	5.50	1.50
FT4	Tom Glavine	12.00	5.50	1.50
FT5	Hideo Nomo	25.00	11.00	3.10
FT6	Jose Rijo	8.00	3.60	1.00
FT7	Greg Maddux	60.00	27.00	7.50
FT8	David Cone	10.00	4.50	1.25
FT9	Ramon Martinez	10.00	4.50	1.25
FT10	Jose Mesa	8.00	3.60	1.00

1996 Pacific Prisms Red Hot Stars

Randomly inserted in packs at a rate of one in 37, this 20-card set features 20 of Major League Baseball's hottest stars. The fronts display a color action player cut-out on a red foil background. The backs carry a color player photo with information about the player printed in both English and Spanish.

	MINT	NRMT	EXC
COMPLETE SET (20)	250.00	110.00	31.00
COMMON CARD (1-20)	3.00	1.35	.35
SEMISTARS	5.00	2.20	.60
RANDOM INSERTS IN PACKS			

		MINT	NRMT	EXC
□ RH1	Roberto Alomar	10.00	4.50	1.25
□ RH2	Jose Canseco	5.00	2.20	.60
□ RH3	Chipper Jones	25.00	11.00	3.10
□ RH4	Mike Piazza	25.00	11.00	3.10
□ RH5	Tim Salmon	3.00	1.35	.35
□ RH6	Jeff Bagwell	15.00	6.75	1.85
□ RH7	Ken Griffey Jr.	40.00	18.00	5.00
□ RH8	Greg Maddux	25.00	11.00	3.10
□ RH9	Kirby Puckett	12.00	5.50	1.50
□ RH10	Frank Thomas	40.00	18.00	5.00
□ RH11	Albert Belle	20.00	9.00	2.50
□ RH12	Tony Gwynn	15.00	6.75	1.85
□ RH13	Edgar Martinez	3.00	1.35	.35
□ RH14	Manny Ramirez	10.00	4.50	1.25
□ RH15	Barry Bonds	10.00	4.50	1.25
□ RH16	Wade Boggs	5.00	2.20	.60
□ RH17	Randy Johnson	6.00	2.70	.75
□ RH18	Don Mattingly	20.00	9.00	2.50
□ RH19	Cal Ripken	40.00	18.00	5.00
□ RH20	Mo Vaughn	10.00	4.50	1.25

1992 Pinnacle

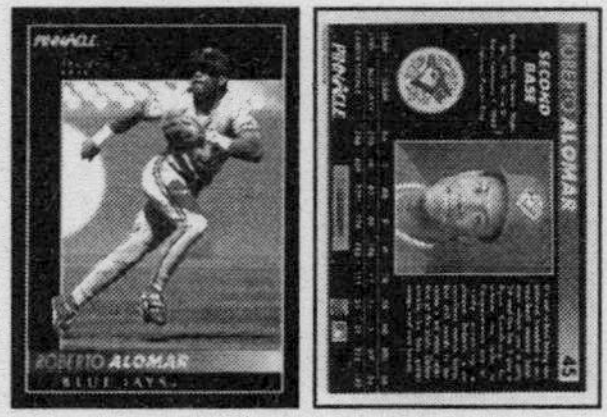

The 1992 Pinnacle set (issued by Score) consists of two series each with 310 standard-size cards. Cards were distributed in first and second series 16-card foil packs and 27-card cello packs. The card fronts feature glossy color player photos, on a black background accented by thin white borders. An anti-counterfeit device appears in the bottom border of each card back. A special ribbed plastic lenticular detector card was made available that allowed the user to view the anti-counterfeit device and unscramble the coding with the word "Pinnacle" appearing. Special subsets featured include '92 Rookie Prospects (52, 55, 168, 247-261, 263-280), Idols (281-286/584-591), Sidelines (287-294/592-596), Draft Picks (295-304), Shades (305-310/601-605), Grips (606-612), and Technicians (614-620). Rookie Cards in the set include Brian Jordan and Manny Ramirez.

	MINT	NRMT	EXC
COMPLETE SET (620)	40.00	18.00	5.00
COMPLETE SERIES 1 (310)	25.00	11.00	3.10
COMPLETE SERIES 2 (310)	15.00	6.75	1.85
COMMON CARD (1-620)	.10	.05	.01
SEMISTARS	.15	.07	.02
STARS	.30	.14	.04

		MINT	NRMT	EXC
□ 1	Frank Thomas	3.00	1.35	.35
□ 2	Benito Santiago	.10	.05	.01
□ 3	Carlos Baerga	.30	.14	.04
□ 4	Cecil Fielder	.15	.07	.02
□ 5	Barry Larkin	.30	.14	.04
□ 6	Ozzie Smith	.40	.18	.05
□ 7	Willie McGee	.10	.05	.01
□ 8	Paul Molitor	.40	.18	.05
□ 9	Andy Van Slyke	.15	.07	.02
□ 10	Ryne Sandberg	.50	.23	.06
□ 11	Kevin Seitzer	.10	.05	.01
□ 12	Len Dykstra	.15	.07	.02
□ 13	Edgar Martinez	.30	.14	.04
□ 14	Ruben Sierra	.15	.07	.02
□ 15	Howard Johnson	.10	.05	.01
□ 16	Dave Henderson	.10	.05	.01
□ 17	Devon White	.15	.07	.02
□ 18	Terry Pendleton	.15	.07	.02
□ 19	Steve Finley	.30	.14	.04
□ 20	Kirby Puckett	.60	.25	.07
□ 21	Orel Hershiser	.15	.07	.02
□ 22	Hal Morris	.10	.05	.01
□ 23	Don Mattingly	1.00	.45	.12
□ 24	Delino DeShields	.10	.05	.01
□ 25	Dennis Eckersley	.15	.07	.02
□ 26	Ellis Burks	.30	.14	.04
□ 27	Jay Buhner	.30	.14	.04
□ 28	Matt Williams	.30	.14	.04
□ 29	Lou Whitaker	.30	.14	.04
□ 30	Alex Fernandez	.30	.14	.04
□ 31	Albert Belle	1.25	.55	.16
□ 32	Todd Zeile	.10	.05	.01
□ 33	Tony Pena	.10	.05	.01
□ 34	Jay Bell	.15	.07	.02
□ 35	Rafael Palmeiro	.30	.14	.04
□ 36	Wes Chamberlain	.10	.05	.01
□ 37	George Bell	.10	.05	.01
□ 38	Robin Yount	.30	.14	.04
□ 39	Vince Coleman	.10	.05	.01
□ 40	Bruce Hurst	.10	.05	.01
□ 41	Harold Baines	.15	.07	.02
□ 42	Chuck Finley	.10	.05	.01
□ 43	Ken Caminiti	.30	.14	.04
□ 44	Ben McDonald	.10	.05	.01
□ 45	Roberto Alomar	.50	.23	.06
□ 46	Chili Davis	.15	.07	.02
□ 47	Bill Doran	.10	.05	.01
□ 48	Jerald Clark	.10	.05	.01
□ 49	Jose Lind	.10	.05	.01
□ 50	Nolan Ryan	1.50	.70	.19
□ 51	Phil Plantier	.15	.07	.02
□ 52	Gary DiSarcina	.10	.05	.01
□ 53	Kevin Bass	.10	.05	.01
□ 54	Pat Kelly	.10	.05	.01
□ 55	Mark Wohlers	.30	.14	.04
□ 56	Walt Weiss	.10	.05	.01
□ 57	Lenny Harris	.10	.05	.01
□ 58	Ivan Calderon	.10	.05	.01
□ 59	Harold Reynolds	.10	.05	.01
□ 60	George Brett	.75	.35	.09
□ 61	Gregg Olson	.10	.05	.01
□ 62	Orlando Merced	.15	.07	.02
□ 63	Steve Decker	.10	.05	.01
□ 64	John Franco	.10	.05	.01
□ 65	Greg Maddux	1.50	.70	.19
□ 66	Alex Cole	.10	.05	.01
□ 67	Dave Hollins	.10	.05	.01
□ 68	Kent Hrbek	.15	.07	.02
□ 69	Tom Pagnozzi	.10	.05	.01
□ 70	Jeff Bagwell	1.25	.55	.16
□ 71	Jim Gantner	.10	.05	.01
□ 72	Matt Nokes	.10	.05	.01
□ 73	Brian Harper	.10	.05	.01
□ 74	Andy Benes	.10	.05	.01
□ 75	Tom Glavine	.30	.14	.04
□ 76	Terry Steinbach	.15	.07	.02
□ 77	Dennis Martinez	.15	.07	.02
□ 78	John Olerud	.15	.07	.02
□ 79	Ozzie Guillen	.10	.05	.01
□ 80	Darryl Strawberry	.15	.07	.02
□ 81	Gary Gaetti	.15	.07	.02
□ 82	Dave Righetti	.10	.05	.01
□ 83	Chris Hoiles	.10	.05	.01
□ 84	Andujar Cedeno	.10	.05	.01
□ 85	Jack Clark	.15	.07	.02
□ 86	David Howard	.10	.05	.01
□ 87	Bill Gullickson	.10	.05	.01
□ 88	Bernard Gilkey	.15	.07	.02
□ 89	Kevin Elster	.10	.05	.01
□ 90	Kevin Maas	.10	.05	.01
□ 91	Mark Lewis	.10	.05	.01
□ 92	Greg Vaughn	.30	.14	.04
□ 93	Bret Barberie	.10	.05	.01
□ 94	Dave Smith	.10	.05	.01
□ 95	Roger Clemens	.30	.14	.04
□ 96	Doug Drabek	.10	.05	.01
□ 97	Omar Vizquel	.30	.14	.04
□ 98	Jose Guzman	.10	.05	.01

□ 99 Juan Samuel	.10	.05	.01
□ 100 Dave Justice	.30	.14	.04
□ 101 Tom Browning	.10	.05	.01
□ 102 Mark Gubicza	.10	.05	.01
□ 103 Mickey Morandini	.10	.05	.01
□ 104 Ed Whitson	.10	.05	.01
□ 105 Lance Parrish	.10	.05	.01
□ 106 Scott Erickson	.15	.07	.02
□ 107 Jack McDowell	.15	.07	.02
□ 108 Dave Stieb	.10	.05	.01
□ 109 Mike Moore	.10	.05	.01
□ 110 Travis Fryman	.30	.14	.04
□ 111 Dwight Gooden	.15	.07	.02
□ 112 Fred McGriff	.30	.14	.04
□ 113 Alan Trammell	.30	.14	.04
□ 114 Roberto Kelly	.10	.05	.01
□ 115 Andre Dawson	.30	.14	.04
□ 116 Bill Landrum	.10	.05	.01
□ 117 Brian McRae	.30	.14	.04
□ 118 B.J. Surhoff	.15	.07	.02
□ 119 Chuck Knoblauch	.30	.14	.04
□ 120 Steve Olin	.10	.05	.01
□ 121 Robin Ventura	.30	.14	.04
□ 122 Will Clark	.30	.14	.04
□ 123 Tino Martinez	.30	.14	.04
□ 124 Dale Murphy	.30	.14	.04
□ 125 Pete O'Brien	.10	.05	.01
□ 126 Ray Lankford	.30	.14	.04
□ 127 Juan Gonzalez	1.25	.55	.16
□ 128 Ron Gant	.30	.14	.04
□ 129 Marquis Grissom	.30	.14	.04
□ 130 Jose Canseco	.30	.14	.04
□ 131 Mike Greenwell	.10	.05	.01
□ 132 Mark Langston	.15	.07	.02
□ 133 Brett Butler	.15	.07	.02
□ 134 Kelly Gruber	.10	.05	.01
□ 135 Chris Sabo	.10	.05	.01
□ 136 Mark Grace	.30	.14	.04
□ 137 Tony Fernandez	.10	.05	.01
□ 138 Glenn Davis	.10	.05	.01
□ 139 Pedro Munoz	.10	.05	.01
□ 140 Craig Biggio	.30	.14	.04
□ 141 Pete Schourek	.15	.07	.02
□ 142 Mike Boddicker	.10	.05	.01
□ 143 Robby Thompson	.10	.05	.01
□ 144 Mel Hall	.10	.05	.01
□ 145 Bryan Harvey	.10	.05	.01
□ 146 Mike LaValliere	.10	.05	.01
□ 147 John Kruk	.15	.07	.02
□ 148 Joe Carter	.30	.14	.04
□ 149 Greg Olson	.10	.05	.01
□ 150 Julio Franco	.15	.07	.02
□ 151 Darryl Hamilton	.10	.05	.01
□ 152 Felix Fermin	.10	.05	.01
□ 153 Jose Offerman	.10	.05	.01
□ 154 Paul O'Neill	.15	.07	.02
□ 155 Tommy Greene	.10	.05	.01
□ 156 Ivan Rodriguez	.60	.25	.07
□ 157 Dave Stewart	.15	.07	.02
□ 158 Jeff Reardon	.15	.07	.02
□ 159 Felix Jose	.10	.05	.01
□ 160 Doug Dascenzo	.10	.05	.01
□ 161 Tim Wallach	.10	.05	.01
□ 162 Dan Plesac	.10	.05	.01
□ 163 Luis Gonzalez	.15	.07	.02
□ 164 Mike Henneman	.10	.05	.01
□ 165 Mike Devereaux	.10	.05	.01
□ 166 Luis Polonia	.10	.05	.01
□ 167 Mike Sharperson	.10	.05	.01
□ 168 Chris Donnels	.10	.05	.01
□ 169 Greg W. Harris	.10	.05	.01
□ 170 Deion Sanders	.30	.14	.04
□ 171 Mike Schooler	.10	.05	.01
□ 172 Jose DeJesus	.10	.05	.01
□ 173 Jeff Montgomery	.15	.07	.02
□ 174 Milt Cuyler	.10	.05	.01
□ 175 Wade Boggs	.30	.14	.04
□ 176 Kevin Tapani	.10	.05	.01
□ 177 Bill Spiers	.10	.05	.01
□ 178 Tim Raines	.30	.14	.04
□ 179 Randy Milligan	.10	.05	.01
□ 180 Rob Dibble	.10	.05	.01
□ 181 Kirt Manwaring	.10	.05	.01
□ 182 Pascual Perez	.10	.05	.01
□ 183 Juan Guzman	.15	.07	.02
□ 184 John Smiley	.10	.05	.01
□ 185 David Segui	.10	.05	.01
□ 186 Omar Olivares	.10	.05	.01
□ 187 Joe Slusarski	.10	.05	.01
□ 188 Erik Hanson	.10	.05	.01
□ 189 Mark Portugal	.10	.05	.01
□ 190 Walt Terrell	.10	.05	.01
□ 191 John Smoltz	.30	.14	.04
□ 192 Wilson Alvarez	.30	.14	.04
□ 193 Jimmy Key	.15	.07	.02
□ 194 Larry Walker	.30	.14	.04
□ 195 Lee Smith	.15	.07	.02
□ 196 Pete Harnisch	.10	.05	.01
□ 197 Mike Harkey	.10	.05	.01
□ 198 Frank Tanana	.10	.05	.01
□ 199 Terry Mulholland	.10	.05	.01
□ 200 Cal Ripken	1.50	.70	.19
□ 201 Dave Magadan	.10	.05	.01
□ 202 Bud Black	.10	.05	.01
□ 203 Terry Shumpert	.10	.05	.01
□ 204 Mike Mussina	.60	.25	.07
□ 205 Mo Vaughn	.75	.35	.09
□ 206 Steve Farr	.10	.05	.01
□ 207 Darrin Jackson	.10	.05	.01
□ 208 Jerry Browne	.10	.05	.01
□ 209 Jeff Russell	.10	.05	.01
□ 210 Mike Scioscia	.10	.05	.01
□ 211 Rick Aguilera	.10	.05	.01
□ 212 Jaime Navarro	.10	.05	.01
□ 213 Randy Tomlin	.10	.05	.01
□ 214 Bobby Thigpen	.10	.05	.01
□ 215 Mark Gardner	.10	.05	.01
□ 216 Norm Charlton	.10	.05	.01
□ 217 Mark McGwire	.60	.25	.07
□ 218 Skeeter Barnes	.10	.05	.01
□ 219 Bob Tewksbury	.10	.05	.01
□ 220 Junior Felix	.10	.05	.01
□ 221 Sam Horn	.10	.05	.01
□ 222 Jody Reed	.10	.05	.01
□ 223 Luis Sojo	.10	.05	.01
□ 224 Jerome Walton	.10	.05	.01
□ 225 Darryl Kile	.10	.05	.01
□ 226 Mickey Tettleton	.10	.05	.01
□ 227 Dan Pasqua	.10	.05	.01
□ 228 Jim Gott	.10	.05	.01
□ 229 Bernie Williams	.50	.23	.06
□ 230 Shane Mack	.10	.05	.01
□ 231 Steve Avery	.15	.07	.02
□ 232 Dave Valle	.10	.05	.01
□ 233 Mark Leonard	.10	.05	.01
□ 234 Spike Owen	.10	.05	.01
□ 235 Gary Sheffield	.30	.14	.04
□ 236 Steve Chitren	.10	.05	.01
□ 237 Zane Smith	.10	.05	.01
□ 238 Tom Gordon	.10	.05	.01
□ 239 Jose Oquendo	.10	.05	.01
□ 240 Todd Stottlemyre	.15	.07	.02
□ 241 Darren Daulton	.15	.07	.02
□ 242 Tim Naehring	.15	.07	.02
□ 243 Tony Phillips	.15	.07	.02
□ 244 Shawon Dunston	.10	.05	.01
□ 245 Manuel Lee	.10	.05	.01
□ 246 Mike Pagliarulo	.10	.05	.01
□ 247 Jim Thome	1.50	.70	.19
□ 248 Luis Mercedes	.10	.05	.01
□ 249 Cal Eldred	.10	.05	.01
□ 250 Derek Bell	.15	.07	.02
□ 251 Arthur Rhodes	.10	.05	.01
□ 252 Scott Cooper	.10	.05	.01
□ 253 Roberto Hernandez	.30	.14	.04
□ 254 Mo Sanford	.10	.05	.01
□ 255 Scott Servais	.10	.05	.01
□ 256 Eric Karros	.30	.14	.04
□ 257 Andy Mota	.10	.05	.01
□ 258 Keith Mitchell	.10	.05	.01
□ 259 Joel Johnston	.10	.05	.01
□ 260 John Wehner	.10	.05	.01
□ 261 Gino Minutelli	.10	.05	.01
□ 262 Greg Gagne	.10	.05	.01
□ 263 Stan Royer	.10	.05	.01
□ 264 Carlos Garcia	.15	.07	.02
□ 265 Andy Ashby	.15	.07	.02
□ 266 Kim Batiste	.10	.05	.01
□ 267 Julio Valera	.10	.05	.01
□ 268 Royce Clayton	.15	.07	.02
□ 269 Gary Scott	.10	.05	.01
□ 270 Kirk Dressendorfer	.10	.05	.01

□	271	Sean Berry	.15	.07	.02
□	272	Lance Dickson	.10	.05	.01
□	273	Rob Maurer	.10	.05	.01
□	274	Scott Brosius	.30	.14	.04
□	275	Dave Fleming	.10	.05	.01
□	276	Lenny Webster	.10	.05	.01
□	277	Mike Humphreys	.10	.05	.01
□	278	Freddie Benavides	.10	.05	.01
□	279	Harvey Pulliam	.10	.05	.01
□	280	Jeff Carter	.10	.05	.01
□	281	Jim Abbott I Nolan Ryan	.30	.14	.04
□	282	Wade Boggs I George Brett	.40	.18	.05
□	283	Ken Griffey Jr. I Rickey Henderson	.75	.35	.09
□	284	Wally Joyner I Dale Murphy	.15	.07	.02
□	285	Chuck Knoblauch I Ozzie Smith	.30	.14	.04
□	286	Robin Ventura I Lou Gehrig	.50	.23	.06
□	287	Robin Yount SIDE	.30	.14	.04
□	288	Bob Tewksbury SIDE	.10	.05	.01
□	289	Kirby Puckett SIDE	.30	.14	.04
□	290	Kenny Lofton SIDE	1.25	.55	.16
□	291	Jack McDowell SIDE	.10	.05	.01
□	292	John Burkett SIDE	.10	.05	.01
□	293	Dwight Smith SIDE	.10	.05	.01
□	294	Nolan Ryan SIDE	.75	.35	.09
□	295	Manny Ramirez DP	4.00	1.80	.50
□	296	Cliff Floyd DP UER (Throws right, not left as indicated on back)	.40	.18	.05
□	297	Al Shirley DP	.15	.07	.02
□	298	Brian Barber DP	.15	.07	.02
□	299	Jon Farrell DP	.10	.05	.01
□	300	Scott Ruffcorn DP	.15	.07	.02
□	301	Tyrone Hill DP	.10	.05	.01
□	302	Benji Gil DP	.30	.14	.04
□	303	Tyler Green DP	.15	.07	.02
□	304	Allen Watson DP	.15	.07	.02
□	305	Jay Buhner SH	.30	.14	.04
□	306	Roberto Alomar SH	.30	.14	.04
□	307	Chuck Knoblauch SH	.30	.14	.04
□	308	Darryl Strawberry SH	.10	.05	.01
□	309	Danny Tartabull SH	.10	.05	.01
□	310	Bobby Bonilla SH	.10	.05	.01
□	311	Mike Felder	.10	.05	.01
□	312	Storm Davis	.10	.05	.01
□	313	Tim Teufel	.10	.05	.01
□	314	Tom Brunansky	.10	.05	.01
□	315	Rex Hudler	.10	.05	.01
□	316	Dave Otto	.10	.05	.01
□	317	Jeff King	.15	.07	.02
□	318	Dan Gladden	.10	.05	.01
□	319	Bill Pecota	.10	.05	.01
□	320	Franklin Stubbs	.10	.05	.01
□	321	Gary Carter	.30	.14	.04
□	322	Melido Perez	.10	.05	.01
□	323	Eric Davis	.15	.07	.02
□	324	Greg Myers	.10	.05	.01
□	325	Pete Incaviglia	.10	.05	.01
□	326	Von Hayes	.10	.05	.01
□	327	Greg Swindell	.10	.05	.01
□	328	Steve Sax	.10	.05	.01
□	329	Chuck McElroy	.10	.05	.01
□	330	Gregg Jefferies	.30	.14	.04
□	331	Joe Oliver	.10	.05	.01
□	332	Paul Faries	.10	.05	.01
□	333	David West	.10	.05	.01
□	334	Craig Grebeck	.10	.05	.01
□	335	Chris Hammond	.10	.05	.01
□	336	Billy Ripken	.10	.05	.01
□	337	Scott Sanderson	.10	.05	.01
□	338	Dick Schofield	.10	.05	.01
□	339	Bob Milacki	.10	.05	.01
□	340	Kevin Reimer	.10	.05	.01
□	341	Jose DeLeon	.10	.05	.01
□	342	Henry Cotto	.10	.05	.01
□	343	Daryl Boston	.10	.05	.01
□	344	Kevin Gross	.10	.05	.01
□	345	Milt Thompson	.10	.05	.01
□	346	Luis Rivera	.10	.05	.01
□	347	Al Osuna	.10	.05	.01
□	348	Rob Deer	.10	.05	.01
□	349	Tim Leary	.10	.05	.01
□	350	Mike Stanton	.10	.05	.01
□	351	Dean Palmer	.15	.07	.02
□	352	Trevor Wilson	.10	.05	.01
□	353	Mark Eichhorn	.10	.05	.01
□	354	Scott Aldred	.10	.05	.01
□	355	Mark Whiten	.15	.07	.02
□	356	Leo Gomez	.10	.05	.01
□	357	Rafael Belliard	.10	.05	.01
□	358	Carlos Quintana	.10	.05	.01
□	359	Mark Davis	.10	.05	.01
□	360	Chris Nabholz	.10	.05	.01
□	361	Carlton Fisk	.30	.14	.04
□	362	Joe Orsulak	.10	.05	.01
□	363	Eric Anthony	.10	.05	.01
□	364	Greg Hibbard	.10	.05	.01
□	365	Scott Leius	.10	.05	.01
□	366	Hensley Meulens	.10	.05	.01
□	367	Chris Bosio	.10	.05	.01
□	368	Brian Downing	.10	.05	.01
□	369	Sammy Sosa	.50	.23	.06
□	370	Stan Belinda	.10	.05	.01
□	371	Joe Grahe	.10	.05	.01
□	372	Luis Salazar	.10	.05	.01
□	373	Lance Johnson	.15	.07	.02
□	374	Kal Daniels	.10	.05	.01
□	375	Dave Winfield	.30	.14	.04
□	376	Brook Jacoby	.10	.05	.01
□	377	Mariano Duncan	.10	.05	.01
□	378	Ron Darling	.10	.05	.01
□	379	Randy Johnson	.30	.14	.04
□	380	Chito Martinez	.10	.05	.01
□	381	Andres Galarraga	.30	.14	.04
□	382	Willie Randolph	.15	.07	.02
□	383	Charles Nagy	.15	.07	.02
□	384	Tim Belcher	.10	.05	.01
□	385	Duane Ward	.10	.05	.01
□	386	Vicente Palacios	.10	.05	.01
□	387	Mike Gallego	.10	.05	.01
□	388	Rich DeLucia	.10	.05	.01
□	389	Scott Radinsky	.10	.05	.01
□	390	Damon Berryhill	.10	.05	.01
□	391	Kirk McCaskill	.10	.05	.01
□	392	Pedro Guerrero	.10	.05	.01
□	393	Kevin Mitchell	.15	.07	.02
□	394	Dickie Thon	.10	.05	.01
□	395	Bobby Bonilla	.15	.07	.02
□	396	Bill Wegman	.10	.05	.01
□	397	Dave Martinez	.10	.05	.01
□	398	Rick Sutcliffe	.10	.05	.01
□	399	Larry Andersen	.10	.05	.01
□	400	Tony Gwynn	.75	.35	.09
□	401	Rickey Henderson	.30	.14	.04
□	402	Greg Cadaret	.10	.05	.01
□	403	Keith Miller	.10	.05	.01
□	404	Bip Roberts	.10	.05	.01
□	405	Kevin Brown	.15	.07	.02
□	406	Mitch Williams	.10	.05	.01
□	407	Frank Viola	.10	.05	.01
□	408	Darren Lewis	.10	.05	.01
□	409	Bob Welch	.10	.05	.01
□	410	Bob Walk	.10	.05	.01
□	411	Todd Frohwirth	.10	.05	.01
□	412	Brian Hunter	.10	.05	.01
□	413	Ron Karkovice	.10	.05	.01
□	414	Mike Morgan	.10	.05	.01
□	415	Joe Hesketh	.10	.05	.01
□	416	Don Slaught	.10	.05	.01
□	417	Tom Henke	.10	.05	.01
□	418	Kurt Stillwell	.10	.05	.01
□	419	Hector Villanueva	.10	.05	.01
□	420	Glenallen Hill	.10	.05	.01
□	421	Pat Borders	.10	.05	.01
□	422	Charlie Hough	.10	.05	.01
□	423	Charlie Leibrandt	.10	.05	.01
□	424	Eddie Murray	.50	.23	.06
□	425	Jesse Barfield	.10	.05	.01
□	426	Mark Lemke	.10	.05	.01
□	427	Kevin McReynolds	.10	.05	.01
□	428	Gilberto Reyes	.10	.05	.01
□	429	Ramon Martinez	.15	.07	.02
□	430	Steve Buechele	.10	.05	.01
□	431	David Wells	.10	.05	.01
□	432	Kyle Abbott	.10	.05	.01
□	433	John Habyan	.10	.05	.01
□	434	Kevin Appier	.15	.07	.02

☐ 435	Gene Larkin	.10	.05	.01
☐ 436	Sandy Alomar Jr.	.15	.07	.02
☐ 437	Mike Jackson	.10	.05	.01
☐ 438	Todd Benzinger	.10	.05	.01
☐ 439	Teddy Higuera	.10	.05	.01
☐ 440	Reggie Sanders	.30	.14	.04
☐ 441	Mark Carreon	.10	.05	.01
☐ 442	Bret Saberhagen	.15	.07	.02
☐ 443	Gene Nelson	.10	.05	.01
☐ 444	Jay Howell	.10	.05	.01
☐ 445	Roger McDowell	.10	.05	.01
☐ 446	Sid Bream	.10	.05	.01
☐ 447	Mackey Sasser	.10	.05	.01
☐ 448	Bill Swift	.10	.05	.01
☐ 449	Hubie Brooks	.10	.05	.01
☐ 450	David Cone	.30	.14	.04
☐ 451	Bobby Witt	.10	.05	.01
☐ 452	Brady Anderson	.30	.14	.04
☐ 453	Lee Stevens	.10	.05	.01
☐ 454	Luis Aquino	.10	.05	.01
☐ 455	Carney Lansford	.15	.07	.02
☐ 456	Carlos Hernandez	.10	.05	.01
☐ 457	Danny Jackson	.10	.05	.01
☐ 458	Gerald Young	.10	.05	.01
☐ 459	Tom Candiotti	.10	.05	.01
☐ 460	Billy Hatcher	.10	.05	.01
☐ 461	John Wetteland	.15	.07	.02
☐ 462	Mike Bordick	.15	.07	.02
☐ 463	Don Robinson	.10	.05	.01
☐ 464	Jeff Johnson	.10	.05	.01
☐ 465	Lonnie Smith	.10	.05	.01
☐ 466	Paul Assenmacher	.10	.05	.01
☐ 467	Alvin Davis	.10	.05	.01
☐ 468	Jim Eisenreich	.10	.05	.01
☐ 469	Brent Mayne	.10	.05	.01
☐ 470	Jeff Brantley	.15	.07	.02
☐ 471	Tim Burke	.10	.05	.01
☐ 472	Pat Mahomes	.10	.05	.01
☐ 473	Ryan Bowen	.10	.05	.01
☐ 474	Bryn Smith	.10	.05	.01
☐ 475	Mike Flanagan	.10	.05	.01
☐ 476	Reggie Jefferson	.15	.07	.02
☐ 477	Jeff Blauser	.10	.05	.01
☐ 478	Craig Lefferts	.10	.05	.01
☐ 479	Todd Worrell	.10	.05	.01
☐ 480	Scott Scudder	.10	.05	.01
☐ 481	Kirk Gibson	.15	.07	.02
☐ 482	Kenny Rogers	.10	.05	.01
☐ 483	Jack Morris	.15	.07	.02
☐ 484	Russ Swan	.10	.05	.01
☐ 485	Mike Huff	.10	.05	.01
☐ 486	Ken Hill	.30	.14	.04
☐ 487	Geronimo Pena	.10	.05	.01
☐ 488	Charlie O'Brien	.10	.05	.01
☐ 489	Mike Maddux	.10	.05	.01
☐ 490	Scott Livingstone	.10	.05	.01
☐ 491	Carl Willis	.10	.05	.01
☐ 492	Kelly Downs	.10	.05	.01
☐ 493	Dennis Cook	.10	.05	.01
☐ 494	Joe Magrane	.10	.05	.01
☐ 495	Bob Kipper	.10	.05	.01
☐ 496	Jose Mesa	.15	.07	.02
☐ 497	Charlie Hayes	.10	.05	.01
☐ 498	Joe Girardi	.10	.05	.01
☐ 499	Doug Jones	.10	.05	.01
☐ 500	Barry Bonds	.50	.23	.06
☐ 501	Bill Krueger	.10	.05	.01
☐ 502	Glenn Braggs	.10	.05	.01
☐ 503	Eric King	.10	.05	.01
☐ 504	Frank Castillo	.15	.07	.02
☐ 505	Mike Gardiner	.10	.05	.01
☐ 506	Cory Snyder	.10	.05	.01
☐ 507	Steve Howe	.10	.05	.01
☐ 508	Jose Rijo	.10	.05	.01
☐ 509	Sid Fernandez	.10	.05	.01
☐ 510	Archi Cianfrocco	.10	.05	.01
☐ 511	Mark Guthrie	.10	.05	.01
☐ 512	Bob Ojeda	.10	.05	.01
☐ 513	John Doherty	.10	.05	.01
☐ 514	Dante Bichette	.30	.14	.04
☐ 515	Juan Berenguer	.10	.05	.01
☐ 516	Jeff M. Robinson	.10	.05	.01
☐ 517	Mike Macfarlane	.10	.05	.01
☐ 518	Matt Young	.10	.05	.01
☐ 519	Otis Nixon	.10	.05	.01
☐ 520	Brian Holman	.10	.05	.01

☐ 521	Chris Haney	.10	.05	.01
☐ 522	Jeff Kent	.30	.14	.04
☐ 523	Chad Curtis	.30	.14	.04
☐ 524	Vince Horsman	.10	.05	.01
☐ 525	Rod Nichols	.10	.05	.01
☐ 526	Peter Hoy	.10	.05	.01
☐ 527	Shawn Boskie	.10	.05	.01
☐ 528	Alejandro Pena	.10	.05	.01
☐ 529	Dave Burba	.10	.05	.01
☐ 530	Ricky Jordan	.10	.05	.01
☐ 531	Dave Silvestri	.10	.05	.01
☐ 532	John Patterson UER (Listed as being born in 1960; should be 1967)	.10	.05	.01
☐ 533	Jeff Branson	.10	.05	.01
☐ 534	Derrick May	.10	.05	.01
☐ 535	Esteban Beltre	.10	.05	.01
☐ 536	Jose Melendez	.10	.05	.01
☐ 537	Wally Joyner	.15	.07	.02
☐ 538	Eddie Taubensee	.10	.05	.01
☐ 539	Jim Abbott	.10	.05	.01
☐ 540	Brian Williams	.10	.05	.01
☐ 541	Donovan Osborne	.15	.07	.02
☐ 542	Patrick Lennon	.10	.05	.01
☐ 543	Mike Groppuso	.10	.05	.01
☐ 544	Jarvis Brown	.10	.05	.01
☐ 545	Shawn Livsey	.10	.05	.01
☐ 546	Jeff Ware	.10	.05	.01
☐ 547	Danny Tartabull	.10	.05	.01
☐ 548	Bobby Jones	.40	.18	.05
☐ 549	Ken Griffey Jr.	3.00	1.35	.35
☐ 550	Rey Sanchez	.10	.05	.01
☐ 551	Pedro Astacio	.15	.07	.02
☐ 552	Juan Guerrero	.10	.05	.01
☐ 553	Jacob Brumfield	.10	.05	.01
☐ 554	Ben Rivera	.10	.05	.01
☐ 555	Brian Jordan	.75	.35	.09
☐ 556	Denny Neagle	.15	.07	.02
☐ 557	Cliff Brantley	.10	.05	.01
☐ 558	Anthony Young	.10	.05	.01
☐ 559	John Vander Wal	.10	.05	.01
☐ 560	Monty Fariss	.10	.05	.01
☐ 561	Russ Springer	.10	.05	.01
☐ 562	Pat Listach	.15	.07	.02
☐ 563	Pat Hentgen	.30	.14	.04
☐ 564	Andy Stankiewicz	.10	.05	.01
☐ 565	Mike Perez	.10	.05	.01
☐ 566	Mike Bielecki	.10	.05	.01
☐ 567	Butch Henry	.10	.05	.01
☐ 568	Dave Nilsson	.30	.14	.04
☐ 569	Scott Hatteberg	.10	.05	.01
☐ 570	Ruben Amaro Jr.	.10	.05	.01
☐ 571	Todd Hundley	.30	.14	.04
☐ 572	Moises Alou	.30	.14	.04
☐ 573	Hector Fajardo	.10	.05	.01
☐ 574	Todd Van Poppel	.10	.05	.01
☐ 575	Willie Banks	.10	.05	.01
☐ 576	Bob Zupcic	.10	.05	.01
☐ 577	J.J. Johnson	.15	.07	.02
☐ 578	John Burkett	.15	.07	.02
☐ 579	Trever Miller	.10	.05	.01
☐ 580	Scott Bankhead	.10	.05	.01
☐ 581	Rich Amaral	.10	.05	.01
☐ 582	Kenny Lofton	2.50	1.10	.30
☐ 583	Matt Stairs	.10	.05	.01
☐ 584	Don Mattingly Rod Carew IDOLS	.40	.18	.05
☐ 585	Steve Avery Jack Morris IDOLS	.15	.07	.02
☐ 586	Roberto Alomar Sandy Alomar SR. IDOLS	.30	.14	.04
☐ 587	Scott Sanderson Catfish Hunter IDOLS	.15	.07	.02
☐ 588	Dave Justice Willie Stargell IDOLS	.30	.14	.04
☐ 589	Rex Hudler Roger Staubach IDOLS	.30	.14	.04
☐ 590	David Cone Jackie Gleason IDOLS	.30	.14	.04
☐ 591	Tony Gwynn Willie Davis IDOLS	.30	.14	.04
☐ 592	Orel Hershiser SIDE	.15	.07	.02
☐ 593	John Wetteland SIDE	.10	.05	.01
☐ 594	Tom Glavine SIDE	.15	.07	.02
☐ 595	Randy Johnson SIDE	.15	.07	.02
☐ 596	Jim Gott SIDE	.10	.05	.01

□ 597 Donald Harris	.10	.05	.01
□ 598 Shawn Hare	.10	.05	.01
□ 599 Chris Gardner	.10	.05	.01
□ 600 Rusty Meacham	.10	.05	.01
□ 601 Benito Santiago	.10	.05	.01
□ 602 Eric Davis SHADE	.10	.05	.01
□ 603 Jose Lind SHADE	.10	.05	.01
□ 604 Dave Justice SHADE	.15	.07	.02
□ 605 Tim Raines SHADE	.15	.07	.02
□ 606 Randy Tomlin GRIP	.10	.05	.01
□ 607 Jack McDowell GRIP	.10	.05	.01
□ 608 Greg Maddux GRIP	.60	.25	.07
□ 609 Charles Nagy GRIP	.10	.05	.01
□ 610 Tom Candiotti GRIP	.10	.05	.01
□ 611 David Cone GRIP	.15	.07	.02
□ 612 Steve Avery GRIP	.15	.07	.02
□ 613 Rod Beck GRIP	.40	.18	.05
□ 614 Rickey Henderson TECH	.30	.14	.04
□ 615 Benito Santiago TECH	.10	.05	.01
□ 616 Ruben Sierra TECH	.10	.05	.01
□ 617 Ryne Sandberg TECH	.30	.14	.04
□ 618 Nolan Ryan TECH	.75	.35	.09
□ 619 Brett Butler TECH	.10	.05	.01
□ 620 Dave Justice TECH	.15	.07	.02

1992 Pinnacle Rookie Idols

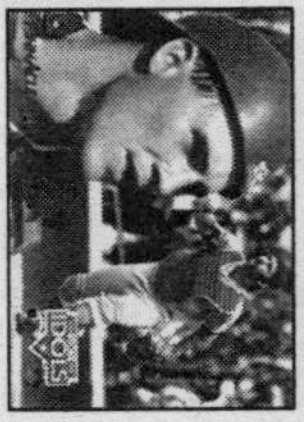

This 18-card insert set is a spin-off on the Idols subset featured in the regular series. The cards were randomly inserted in Series II wax packs. The set features full-bleed color photos of 18 rookies along with their pick of sports figures or other individuals who had the greatest impact on their careers. Both sides of the cards are horizontally oriented. The fronts carry a close-up photo of the rookie superimposed on an action game shot of his idol.

	MINT	NRMT	EXC
COMPLETE SET (18)	140.00	65.00	17.50
COMMON PAIR (1-18)	3.00	1.35	.35
RANDOM INSERTS IN SER.2 FOIL PACKS...			

□ 1 Reggie Sanders and Eric Davis	8.00	3.60	1.00
□ 2 Hector Fajardo and Jim Abbott	3.00	1.35	.35
□ 3 Gary Cooper and George Brett	15.00	6.75	1.85
□ 4 Mark Wohlers and Roger Clemens	10.00	4.50	1.25
□ 5 Luis Mercedes and Julio Franco	3.00	1.35	.35
□ 6 Willie Banks and Doc Gooden	3.00	1.35	.35
□ 7 Kenny Lofton and Rickey Henderson	30.00	13.50	3.70
□ 8 Keith Mitchell and Dave Henderson	3.00	1.35	.35
□ 9 Kim Batiste and Barry Larkin	6.00	2.70	.75
□ 10 Todd Hundley and Thurman Munson	10.00	4.50	1.25
□ 11 Eddie Zosky and Cal Ripken	25.00	11.00	3.10
□ 12 Todd Van Poppel and Nolan Ryan	25.00	11.00	3.10
□ 13 Jim Thome and Ryne Sandberg	25.00	11.00	3.10
□ 14 Dave Fleming and Bobby Murcer	3.00	1.35	.35
□ 15 Royce Clayton and Ozzie Smith	8.00	3.60	1.00
□ 16 Donald Harris and Darryl Strawberry	3.00	1.35	.35
□ 17 Chad Curtis and Alan Trammell	4.00	1.80	.50
□ 18 Derek Bell and Dave Winfield	8.00	3.60	1.00

1992 Pinnacle Slugfest

This 15-card set highlights the games top sluggers.The cards were issued exclusively as an insert with specially marked cello packs. The horizontally oriented fronts feature glossy photos of players at bat. The player's name is printed in gold and the word "Slugfest" is printed in red in a black border across the bottom of the picture.

	MINT	NRMT	EXC
COMPLETE SET (15)	40.00	18.00	5.00
COMMON CARD (1-15)	.75	.35	.09
SEMISTARS	1.25	.55	.16
ONE PER SLUGFEST JUMBO PACK			

□ 1 Cecil Fielder	.75	.35	.09
□ 2 Mark McGwire	2.50	1.10	.30
□ 3 Jose Canseco	.75	.35	.09
□ 4 Barry Bonds	2.00	.90	.25
□ 5 David Justice	.75	.35	.09
□ 6 Bobby Bonilla	.75	.35	.09
□ 7 Ken Griffey Jr.	10.00	4.50	1.25
□ 8 Ron Gant	.75	.35	.09
□ 9 Ryne Sandberg	2.00	.90	.25
□ 10 Ruben Sierra	.75	.35	.09
□ 11 Frank Thomas	10.00	4.50	1.25
□ 12 Will Clark	.75	.35	.09
□ 13 Kirby Puckett	2.50	1.10	.30
□ 14 Cal Ripken	8.00	3.60	1.00
□ 15 Jeff Bagwell	5.00	2.20	.60

1992 Pinnacle Team 2000

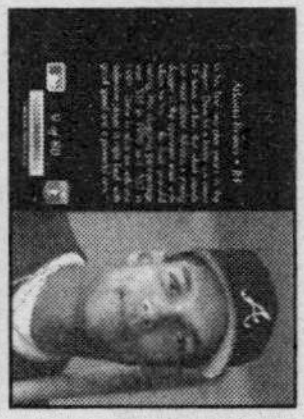

This 80-card standard-size set focuses on young players who were projected to be stars in the year 2000. Cards 1-40 were inserted in Series 1 jumbo packs while cards 41-80 were featured in Series 2 jumbo packs. The fronts features action color player photos. The cards are bordered by a 1/2" black stripe that runs

along the left edge and bottom forming a right angle. The two ends of the black stripe are sloped. The words "Team 2000" and the player's name appear in gold foil in the stripe. The team logo is displayed in the lower left corner.

	MINT	NRMT	EXC
COMPLETE SET (80)	30.00	13.50	3.70
COMPLETE SERIES 1 (40)	20.00	9.00	2.50
COMPLETE SERIES 2 (40)	10.00	4.50	1.25
COMMON CARD (1-80)	.15	.07	.02
SEMISTARS	.30	.14	.04
THREE PER JUMBO PACK			

□ 1 Mike Mussina	1.00	.45	.12
□ 2 Phil Plantier	.15	.07	.02
□ 3 Frank Thomas	5.00	2.20	.60
□ 4 Travis Fryman	.25	.11	.03
□ 5 Kevin Appier	.25	.11	.03
□ 6 Chuck Knoblauch	.60	.25	.07
□ 7 Pat Kelly	.15	.07	.02
□ 8 Ivan Rodriguez	1.00	.45	.12
□ 9 Dave Justice	.25	.11	.03
□ 10 Jeff Bagwell	2.00	.90	.25
□ 11 Marquis Grissom	.25	.11	.03
□ 12 Andy Benes	.15	.07	.02
□ 13 Gregg Olson	.15	.07	.02
□ 14 Kevin Morton	.15	.07	.02
□ 15 Tim Naehring	.25	.11	.03
□ 16 Dave Hollins	.15	.07	.02
□ 17 Sandy Alomar Jr.	.25	.11	.03
□ 18 Albert Belle	2.00	.90	.25
□ 19 Charles Nagy	.25	.11	.03
□ 20 Brian McRae	.25	.11	.03
□ 21 Larry Walker	.25	.11	.03
□ 22 Delino DeShields	.15	.07	.02
□ 23 Jeff Johnson	.15	.07	.02
□ 24 Bernie Williams	.75	.35	.09
□ 25 Jose Offerman	.15	.07	.02
□ 26 Juan Gonzalez	2.00	.90	.25
□ 27A Juan Guzman (Pinnacle logo at top)	.25	.11	.03
□ 27B Juan Guzman (Pinnacle logo at bottom)	.25	.11	.03
□ 28 Eric Anthony	.15	.07	.02
□ 29 Brian Hunter	.15	.07	.02
□ 30 John Smoltz	.60	.25	.07
□ 31 Deion Sanders	.25	.11	.03
□ 32 Greg Maddux	3.00	1.35	.35
□ 33 Andujar Cedeno	.15	.07	.02
□ 34 Royce Clayton	.25	.11	.03
□ 35 Kenny Lofton	2.50	1.10	.30
□ 36 Cal Eldred	.15	.07	.02
□ 37 Jim Thome	3.00	1.35	.35
□ 38 Gary DiSarcina	.15	.07	.02
□ 39 Brian Jordan	1.50	.70	.19
□ 40 Chad Curtis	.25	.11	.03
□ 41 Ben McDonald	.15	.07	.02
□ 42 Jim Abbott	.15	.07	.02
□ 43 Robin Ventura	.25	.11	.03
□ 44 Milt Cuyler	.15	.07	.02
□ 45 Gregg Jefferies	.25	.11	.03
□ 46 Scott Radinsky	.15	.07	.02
□ 47 Ken Griffey Jr.	5.00	2.20	.60
□ 48 Roberto Alomar	.75	.35	.09
□ 49 Ramon Martinez	.25	.11	.03
□ 50 Bret Barberie	.15	.07	.02
□ 51 Ray Lankford	.25	.11	.03
□ 52 Leo Gomez	.15	.07	.02
□ 53 Tommy Greene	.15	.07	.02
□ 54 Mo Vaughn	1.25	.55	.16
□ 55 Sammy Sosa	.75	.35	.09
□ 56 Carlos Baerga	.60	.25	.07
□ 57 Mark Lewis	.15	.07	.02
□ 58 Tom Gordon	.15	.07	.02
□ 59 Gary Sheffield	.60	.25	.07
□ 60 Scott Erickson	.25	.11	.03
□ 61 Pedro Munoz	.15	.07	.02
□ 62 Tino Martinez	.25	.11	.03
□ 63 Darren Lewis	.15	.07	.02
□ 64 Dean Palmer	.25	.11	.03
□ 65 John Olerud	.25	.11	.03
□ 66 Steve Avery	.25	.11	.03
□ 67 Pete Harnisch	.15	.07	.02
□ 68 Luis Gonzalez	.25	.11	.03
□ 69 Kim Batiste	.15	.07	.02
□ 70 Reggie Sanders	.25	.11	.03
□ 71 Luis Mercedes	.15	.07	.02
□ 72 Todd Van Poppel	.15	.07	.02
□ 73 Gary Scott	.15	.07	.02
□ 74 Monty Fariss	.15	.07	.02
□ 75 Kyle Abbott	.15	.07	.02
□ 76 Eric Karros	.25	.11	.03
□ 77 Mo Sanford	.15	.07	.02
□ 78 Todd Hundley	.60	.25	.07
□ 79 Reggie Jefferson	.15	.07	.02
□ 80 Pat Mahomes	.15	.07	.02

1992 Pinnacle Team Pinnacle

This 12-card, double-sided insert set features the National League and American League All-Star team as selected by Pinnacle. The standard-size cards were randomly inserted in Series I wax packs. The cards feature illustrations by sports artist Chris Greco with the National League All-Star on one side and the corresponding American League All-Star by position on the other. The words "Team Pinnacle" are printed vertically down the left side of the card in red for American League on one side and blue for National League on the other.

	MINT	NRMT	EXC
COMPLETE SET (12)	100.00	45.00	12.50
COMMON PAIR (1-12)	5.00	2.20	.60
RANDOM INSERTS IN SER.1 FOIL PACKS...			

□ 1 Roger Clemens and Ramon Martinez	6.00	2.70	.75
□ 2 Jim Abbott and Steve Avery	5.00	2.20	.60
□ 3 Ivan Rodriguez and Benito Santiago	8.00	3.60	1.00
□ 4 Frank Thomas and Will Clark	30.00	13.50	3.70
□ 5 Roberto Alomar and Ryne Sandberg	18.00	8.00	2.20
□ 6 Robin Ventura and Matt Williams	6.00	2.70	.75
□ 7 Cal Ripken and Barry Larkin	30.00	13.50	3.70
□ 8 Danny Tartabull and Barry Bonds	8.00	3.60	1.00
□ 9 Ken Griffey Jr. and Brett Butler	20.00	9.00	2.50
□ 10 Ruben Sierra and Dave Justice	5.00	2.20	.60
□ 11 Dennis Eckersley and Rob Dibble	5.00	2.20	.60
□ 12 Scott Radinsky and John Franco	5.00	2.20	.60

1992 Pinnacle Rookies

This 30-card boxed set features top rookies of the 1992 season, with at least one player from each team. A total of 180,000 sets were produced. The fronts feature full-bleed color action player photos except at the bottom where a team-color coded bar carries the player's name

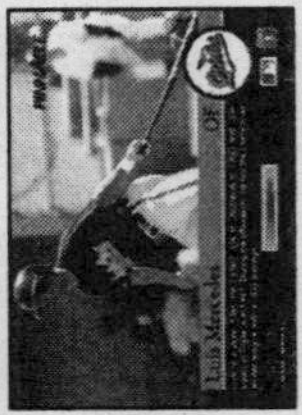

(in gold foil lettering) and a black bar has the words "1992 Rookie." The team logo appears in a gold foil circle at the lower right corner.

	MINT	NRMT	EXC
COMPLETE FACT.SET (30)	6.00	2.70	.75
COMMON CARD (1-30)	.10	.05	.01
□ 1 Luis Mercedes	.10	.05	.01
□ 2 Scott Cooper	.10	.05	.01
□ 3 Kenny Lofton	4.00	1.80	.50
□ 4 John Doherty	.10	.05	.01
□ 5 Pat Listach	.20	.09	.03
□ 6 Andy Stankiewicz	.10	.05	.01
□ 7 Derek Bell	.40	.18	.05
□ 8 Gary DiSarcina	.10	.05	.01
□ 9 Roberto Hernandez	.40	.18	.05
□ 10 Joel Johnston	.10	.05	.01
□ 11 Pat Mahomes	.10	.05	.01
□ 12 Todd Van Poppel	.10	.05	.01
□ 13 Dave Fleming	.20	.09	.03
□ 14 Monty Fariss	.10	.05	.01
□ 15 Gary Scott	.10	.05	.01
□ 16 Moises Alou	.40	.18	.05
□ 17 Todd Hundley	.40	.18	.05
□ 18 Kim Batiste	.10	.05	.01
□ 19 Denny Neagle	.20	.09	.03
□ 20 Donovan Osborne	.20	.09	.03
□ 21 Mark Wohlers	.20	.09	.03
□ 22 Reggie Sanders	.75	.35	.09
□ 23 Brian Williams	.10	.05	.01
□ 24 Eric Karros	.75	.35	.09
□ 25 Frank Seminara	.10	.05	.01
□ 26 Royce Clayton	.20	.09	.03
□ 27 Dave Nilsson	.20	.09	.03
□ 28 Matt Stairs	.10	.05	.01
□ 29 Chad Curtis	.20	.09	.03
□ 30 Carlos Hernandez	.10	.05	.01

1993 Pinnacle

The 1993 Pinnacle set (by Score) contains 620 standard-size cards issued in two series of 310 cards each. Cards were distributed in hobby and retail foil packs and 27-card jumbo super-packs. The fronts feature color action player photos bordered in white and set on a black card face. The player's name appears below the photo, the player's team is above. The set includes the following topical subsets: Rookies (238-288, 575-620), Now and Then (289-296, 470-476), Idols (297-303, 477-483), Hometown Heroes (304-310, 484-490), and Draft Picks (455-469). Rookie Cards in this set include Derek Jeter and Jason Kendall.

	MINT	NRMT	EXC
COMPLETE SET (620)	50.00	22.00	6.25
COMPLETE SERIES 1 (310)	25.00	11.00	3.10
COMPLETE SERIES 2 (310)	25.00	11.00	3.10
COMMON CARD (1-620)	.10	.05	.01
SEMISTARS	.25	.11	.03
STARS	.50	.23	.06
COMP.TRIBUTE SET (10)	75.00	34.00	9.50
COMMON BRETT TRIB (1-5)	6.00	2.70	.75
COMMON RYAN TRIB (6-10)	10.00	4.50	1.25
TRIBUTE: RANDOM INSERTS IN SER.2 PACKS			
□ 1 Gary Sheffield	.50	.23	.06
□ 2 Cal Eldred	.10	.05	.01
□ 3 Larry Walker	.50	.23	.06
□ 4 Deion Sanders	.50	.23	.06
□ 5 Dave Fleming	.10	.05	.01
□ 6 Carlos Baerga	.50	.23	.06
□ 7 Bernie Williams	.50	.23	.06
□ 8 John Kruk	.25	.11	.03
□ 9 Jimmy Key	.25	.11	.03
□ 10 Jeff Bagwell	1.25	.55	.16
□ 11 Jim Abbott	.10	.05	.01
□ 12 Terry Steinbach	.25	.11	.03
□ 13 Bob Tewksbury	.10	.05	.01
□ 14 Eric Karros	.50	.23	.06
□ 15 Ryne Sandberg	.75	.35	.09
□ 16 Will Clark	.50	.23	.06
□ 17 Edgar Martinez	.50	.23	.06
□ 18 Eddie Murray	.75	.35	.09
□ 19 Andy Van Slyke	.25	.11	.03
□ 20 Cal Ripken Jr.	2.50	1.10	.30
□ 21 Ivan Rodriguez	.60	.25	.07
□ 22 Barry Larkin	.50	.23	.06
□ 23 Don Mattingly	1.50	.70	.19
□ 24 Gregg Jefferies	.50	.23	.06
□ 25 Roger Clemens	.50	.23	.06
□ 26 Cecil Fielder	.25	.11	.03
□ 27 Kent Hrbek	.25	.11	.03
□ 28 Robin Ventura	.25	.11	.03
□ 29 Rickey Henderson	.50	.23	.06
□ 30 Roberto Alomar	.75	.35	.09
□ 31 Luis Polonia	.10	.05	.01
□ 32 Andujar Cedeno	.10	.05	.01
□ 33 Pat Listach	.10	.05	.01
□ 34 Mark Grace	.50	.23	.06
□ 35 Otis Nixon	.10	.05	.01
□ 36 Felix Jose	.10	.05	.01
□ 37 Mike Sharperson	.10	.05	.01
□ 38 Dennis Martinez	.25	.11	.03
□ 39 Willie McGee	.10	.05	.01
□ 40 Kenny Lofton	1.25	.55	.16
□ 41 Randy Johnson	.50	.23	.06
□ 42 Andy Benes	.10	.05	.01
□ 43 Bobby Bonilla	.25	.11	.03
□ 44 Mike Mussina	.60	.25	.07
□ 45 Len Dykstra	.25	.11	.03
□ 46 Ellis Burks	.50	.23	.06
□ 47 Chris Sabo	.10	.05	.01
□ 48 Jay Bell	.25	.11	.03
□ 49 Jose Canseco	.50	.23	.06
□ 50 Craig Biggio	.50	.23	.06
□ 51 Wally Joyner	.25	.11	.03
□ 52 Mickey Tettleton	.10	.05	.01
□ 53 Tim Raines	.50	.23	.06
□ 54 Brian Harper	.10	.05	.01
□ 55 Rene Gonzales	.10	.05	.01
□ 56 Mark Langston	.25	.11	.03
□ 57 Jack Morris	.25	.11	.03
□ 58 Mark McGwire	1.00	.45	.12
□ 59 Ken Caminiti	.50	.23	.06
□ 60 Terry Pendleton	.25	.11	.03
□ 61 Dave Nilsson	.25	.11	.03
□ 62 Tom Pagnozzi	.10	.05	.01
□ 63 Mike Morgan	.10	.05	.01
□ 64 Darryl Strawberry	.25	.11	.03
□ 65 Charles Nagy	.25	.11	.03
□ 66 Ken Hill	.25	.11	.03
□ 67 Matt Williams	.50	.23	.06
□ 68 Jay Buhner	.50	.23	.06
□ 69 Vince Coleman	.10	.05	.01
□ 70 Brady Anderson	.50	.23	.06
□ 71 Fred McGriff	.50	.23	.06

□	72 Ben McDonald	.10	.05	.01
□	73 Terry Mulholland	.10	.05	.01
□	74 Randy Tomlin	.10	.05	.01
□	75 Nolan Ryan	2.50	1.10	.30
□	76 Frank Viola UER (Card incorrectly states he has a surgically repaired elbow)	.10	.05	.01
□	77 Jose Rijo	.10	.05	.01
□	78 Shane Mack	.10	.05	.01
□	79 Travis Fryman	.50	.23	.06
□	80 Jack McDowell	.25	.11	.03
□	81 Mark Gubicza	.10	.05	.01
□	82 Matt Nokes	.10	.05	.01
□	83 Bert Blyleven	.25	.11	.03
□	84 Eric Anthony	.10	.05	.01
□	85 Mike Bordick	.10	.05	.01
□	86 John Olerud	.10	.05	.01
□	87 B.J.Surhoff	.25	.11	.03
□	88 Bernard Gilkey	.50	.23	.06
□	89 Shawon Dunston	.10	.05	.01
□	90 Tom Glavine	.50	.23	.06
□	91 Brett Butler	.25	.11	.03
□	92 Moises Alou	.50	.23	.06
□	93 Albert Belle	1.50	.70	.19
□	94 Darren Lewis	.10	.05	.01
□	95 Omar Vizquel	.50	.23	.06
□	96 Dwight Gooden	.25	.11	.03
□	97 Gregg Olson	.10	.05	.01
□	98 Tony Gwynn	1.25	.55	.16
□	99 Darren Daulton	.25	.11	.03
□	100 Dennis Eckersley	.25	.11	.03
□	101 Rob Dibble	.10	.05	.01
□	102 Mike Greenwell	.10	.05	.01
□	103 Jose Lind	.10	.05	.01
□	104 Julio Franco	.25	.11	.03
□	105 Tom Gordon	.10	.05	.01
□	106 Scott Livingstone	.10	.05	.01
□	107 Chuck Knoblauch	.50	.23	.06
□	108 Frank Thomas	3.00	1.35	.35
□	109 Melido Perez	.10	.05	.01
□	110 Ken Griffey Jr.	3.00	1.35	.35
□	111 Harold Baines	.25	.11	.03
□	112 Gary Gaetti	.25	.11	.03
□	113 Pete Harnisch	.10	.05	.01
□	114 David Wells	.10	.05	.01
□	115 Charlie Leibrandt	.10	.05	.01
□	116 Ray Lankford	.50	.23	.06
□	117 Kevin Seitzer	.10	.05	.01
□	118 Robin Yount	.50	.23	.06
□	119 Lenny Harris	.10	.05	.01
□	120 Chris James	.10	.05	.01
□	121 Delino DeShields	.10	.05	.01
□	122 Kirt Manwaring	.10	.05	.01
□	123 Glenallen Hill	.10	.05	.01
□	124 Hensley Meulens	.10	.05	.01
□	125 Darrin Jackson	.10	.05	.01
□	126 Todd Hundley	.50	.23	.06
□	127 Dave Hollins	.10	.05	.01
□	128 Sam Horn	.10	.05	.01
□	129 Roberto Hernandez	.25	.11	.03
□	130 Vicente Palacios	.10	.05	.01
□	131 George Brett	1.25	.55	.16
□	132 Dave Martinez	.10	.05	.01
□	133 Kevin Appier	.25	.11	.03
□	134 Pat Kelly	.10	.05	.01
□	135 Pedro Munoz	.10	.05	.01
□	136 Mark Carreon	.10	.05	.01
□	137 Lance Johnson	.25	.11	.03
□	138 Devon White	.10	.05	.01
□	139 Julio Valera	.10	.05	.01
□	140 Eddie Taubensee	.10	.05	.01
□	141 Willie Wilson	.10	.05	.01
□	142 Stan Belinda	.10	.05	.01
□	143 John Smoltz	.50	.23	.06
□	144 Darryl Hamilton	.10	.05	.01
□	145 Sammy Sosa	.50	.23	.06
□	146 Carlos Hernandez	.10	.05	.01
□	147 Tom Candiotti	.10	.05	.01
□	148 Mike Felder	.10	.05	.01
□	149 Rusty Meacham	.10	.05	.01
□	150 Ivan Calderon	.10	.05	.01
□	151 Pete O'Brien	.10	.05	.01
□	152 Erik Hanson	.10	.05	.01
□	153 Billy Ripken	.10	.05	.01
□	154 Kurt Stillwell	.10	.05	.01
□	155 Jeff Kent	.25	.11	.03
□	156 Mickey Morandini	.10	.05	.01
□	157 Randy Milligan	.10	.05	.01
□	158 Reggie Sanders	.50	.23	.06
□	159 Luis Rivera	.10	.05	.01
□	160 Orlando Merced	.25	.11	.03
□	161 Dean Palmer	.25	.11	.03
□	162 Mike Perez	.10	.05	.01
□	163 Scott Erickson	.10	.05	.01
□	164 Kevin McReynolds	.10	.05	.01
□	165 Kevin Maas	.10	.05	.01
□	166 Ozzie Guillen	.10	.05	.01
□	167 Rob Deer	.10	.05	.01
□	168 Danny Tartabull	.10	.05	.01
□	169 Lee Stevens	.10	.05	.01
□	170 Dave Henderson	.10	.05	.01
□	171 Derek Bell	.50	.23	.06
□	172 Steve Finley	.50	.23	.06
□	173 Greg Olson	.10	.05	.01
□	174 Geronimo Pena	.10	.05	.01
□	175 Paul Quantrill	.10	.05	.01
□	176 Steve Buechele	.10	.05	.01
□	177 Kevin Gross	.10	.05	.01
□	178 Tim Wallach	.10	.05	.01
□	179 Dave Valle	.10	.05	.01
□	180 Dave Silvestri	.10	.05	.01
□	181 Bud Black	.10	.05	.01
□	182 Henry Rodriguez	.50	.23	.06
□	183 Tim Teufel	.10	.05	.01
□	184 Mark McLemore	.10	.05	.01
□	185 Bret Saberhagen	.25	.11	.03
□	186 Chris Hoiles	.10	.05	.01
□	187 Ricky Jordan	.10	.05	.01
□	188 Don Slaught	.10	.05	.01
□	189 Mo Vaughn	.75	.35	.09
□	190 Joe Oliver	.10	.05	.01
□	191 Juan Gonzalez	1.50	.70	.19
□	192 Scott Leius	.10	.05	.01
□	193 Milt Cuyler	.10	.05	.01
□	194 Chris Haney	.10	.05	.01
□	195 Ron Karkovice	.10	.05	.01
□	196 Steve Farr	.10	.05	.01
□	197 John Orton	.10	.05	.01
□	198 Kelly Gruber	.10	.05	.01
□	199 Ron Darling	.10	.05	.01
□	200 Ruben Sierra	.25	.11	.03
□	201 Chuck Finley	.10	.05	.01
□	202 Mike Moore	.10	.05	.01
□	203 Pat Borders	.10	.05	.01
□	204 Sid Bream	.10	.05	.01
□	205 Todd Zeile	.10	.05	.01
□	206 Rick Wilkins	.10	.05	.01
□	207 Jim Gantner	.10	.05	.01
□	208 Frank Castillo	.10	.05	.01
□	209 Dave Hansen	.10	.05	.01
□	210 Trevor Wilson	.10	.05	.01
□	211 Sandy Alomar Jr.	.25	.11	.03
□	212 Sean Berry	.10	.05	.01
□	213 Tino Martinez	.25	.11	.03
□	214 Chito Martinez	.10	.05	.01
□	215 Dan Walters	.10	.05	.01
□	216 John Franco	.10	.05	.01
□	217 Glenn Davis	.10	.05	.01
□	218 Mariano Duncan	.10	.05	.01
□	219 Mike LaValliere	.10	.05	.01
□	220 Rafael Palmeiro	.50	.23	.06
□	221 Jack Clark	.10	.05	.01
□	222 Hal Morris	.10	.05	.01
□	223 Ed Sprague	.25	.11	.03
□	224 John Valentin	.50	.23	.06
□	225 Sam Militello	.10	.05	.01
□	226 Bob Wickman	.10	.05	.01
□	227 Damion Easley	.10	.05	.01
□	228 John Jaha	.25	.11	.03
□	229 Bob Ayrault	.10	.05	.01
□	230 Mo Sanford	.10	.05	.01
□	231 Walt Weiss	.10	.05	.01
□	232 Dante Bichette	.50	.23	.06
□	233 Steve Decker	.10	.05	.01
□	234 Jerald Clark	.10	.05	.01
□	235 Bryan Harvey	.10	.05	.01
□	236 Joe Girardi	.10	.05	.01
□	237 Dave Magadan	.10	.05	.01
□	238 David Nied	.10	.05	.01
□	239 Eric Wedge	.10	.05	.01
□	240 Rico Brogna	.25	.11	.03

□ 241	J.T.Bruett	.10	.05	.01
□ 242	Jonathan Hurst	.10	.05	.01
□ 243	Bret Boone	.25	.11	.03
□ 244	Manny Alexander	.10	.05	.01
□ 245	Scooter Tucker	.10	.05	.01
□ 246	Troy Neel	.10	.05	.01
□ 247	Eddie Zosky	.10	.05	.01
□ 248	Melvin Nieves	.50	.23	.06
□ 249	Ryan Thompson	.10	.05	.01
□ 250	Shawn Barton	.10	.05	.01
□ 251	Ryan Klesko	1.50	.70	.19
□ 252	Mike Piazza	3.00	1.35	.35
□ 253	Steve Hosey	.10	.05	.01
□ 254	Shane Reynolds	.25	.11	.03
□ 255	Dan Wilson	.25	.11	.03
□ 256	Tom Marsh	.10	.05	.01
□ 257	Barry Manuel	.10	.05	.01
□ 258	Paul Miller	.10	.05	.01
□ 259	Pedro Martinez	.50	.23	.06
□ 260	Steve Cooke	.10	.05	.01
□ 261	Johnny Guzman	.10	.05	.01
□ 262	Mike Butcher	.10	.05	.01
□ 263	Bien Figueroa	.10	.05	.01
□ 264	Rich Rowland	.10	.05	.01
□ 265	Shawn Jeter	.10	.05	.01
□ 266	Gerald Williams	.10	.05	.01
□ 267	Derek Parks	.10	.05	.01
□ 268	Henry Mercedes	.10	.05	.01
□ 269	David Hulse	.10	.05	.01
□ 270	Tim Pugh	.10	.05	.01
□ 271	William Suero	.10	.05	.01
□ 272	Ozzie Canseco	.10	.05	.01
□ 273	Fernando Ramsey	.10	.05	.01
□ 274	Bernardo Brito	.10	.05	.01
□ 275	Dave Mlicki	.10	.05	.01
□ 276	Tim Salmon	.75	.35	.09
□ 277	Mike Raczka	.10	.05	.01
□ 278	Ken Ryan	.10	.05	.01
□ 279	Rafael Bournigal	.10	.05	.01
□ 280	Wil Cordero	.25	.11	.03
□ 281	Billy Ashley	.10	.05	.01
□ 282	Paul Wagner	.10	.05	.01
□ 283	Blas Minor	.10	.05	.01
□ 284	Rick Trlicek	.10	.05	.01
□ 285	Willie Greene	.25	.11	.03
□ 286	Ted Wood	.10	.05	.01
□ 287	Phil Clark	.10	.05	.01
□ 288	Jesse Levis	.10	.05	.01
□ 289	Tony Gwynn NT	.60	.25	.07
□ 290	Nolan Ryan NT	1.25	.55	.16
□ 291	Dennis Martinez NT	.10	.05	.01
□ 292	Eddie Murray NT	.50	.23	.06
□ 293	Robin Yount NT	.25	.11	.03
□ 294	George Brett NT	.60	.25	.07
□ 295	Dave Winfield NT	.50	.23	.06
□ 296	Bert Blyleven NT	.25	.11	.03
□ 297	Jeff Bagwell	.50	.23	.06
	Carl Yastrzemski			
□ 298	John Smoltz	.50	.23	.06
	Jack Morris			
□ 299	Larry Walker	.50	.23	.06
	Mike Bossy			
□ 300	Gary Sheffield	.50	.23	.06
	Barry Larkin			
□ 301	Ivan Rodriguez	.50	.23	.06
	Carlton Fisk			
□ 302	Delino DeShields	.50	.23	.06
	Malcolm X			
□ 303	Tim Salmon	.25	.11	.03
	Dwight Evans			
□ 304	Bernard Gilkey HH	.25	.11	.03
□ 305	Cal Ripken Jr. HH	1.25	.55	.16
□ 306	Barry Larkin HH	.25	.11	.03
□ 307	Kent Hrbek HH	.10	.05	.01
□ 308	Rickey Henderson HH	.25	.11	.03
□ 309	Darryl Strawberry HH	.10	.05	.01
□ 310	John Franco HH	.10	.05	.01
□ 311	Todd Stottlemyre	.25	.11	.03
□ 312	Luis Gonzalez	.10	.05	.01
□ 313	Tommy Greene	.10	.05	.01
□ 314	Randy Velarde	.10	.05	.01
□ 315	Steve Avery	.25	.11	.03
□ 316	Jose Oquendo	.10	.05	.01
□ 317	Rey Sanchez	.10	.05	.01
□ 318	Greg Vaughn	.50	.23	.06
□ 319	Orel Hershiser	.25	.11	.03
□ 320	Paul Sorrento	.10	.05	.01
□ 321	Royce Clayton	.25	.11	.03
□ 322	John Vander Wal	.10	.05	.01
□ 323	Henry Cotto	.10	.05	.01
□ 324	Pete Schourek	.25	.11	.03
□ 325	David Segui	.10	.05	.01
□ 326	Arthur Rhodes	.10	.05	.01
□ 327	Bruce Hurst	.10	.05	.01
□ 328	Wes Chamberlain	.10	.05	.01
□ 329	Ozzie Smith	.60	.25	.07
□ 330	Scott Cooper	.10	.05	.01
□ 331	Felix Fermin	.10	.05	.01
□ 332	Mike Macfarlane	.10	.05	.01
□ 333	Dan Gladden	.10	.05	.01
□ 334	Kevin Tapani	.10	.05	.01
□ 335	Steve Sax	.10	.05	.01
□ 336	Jeff Montgomery	.25	.11	.03
□ 337	Gary DiSarcina	.10	.05	.01
□ 338	Lance Blankenship	.10	.05	.01
□ 339	Brian Williams	.10	.05	.01
□ 340	Duane Ward	.10	.05	.01
□ 341	Chuck McElroy	.10	.05	.01
□ 342	Joe Magrane	.10	.05	.01
□ 343	Jaime Navarro	.10	.05	.01
□ 344	Dave Justice	.50	.23	.06
□ 345	Jose Offerman	.10	.05	.01
□ 346	Marquis Grissom	.50	.23	.06
□ 347	Bill Swift	.10	.05	.01
□ 348	Jim Thome	1.50	.70	.19
□ 349	Archi Cianfrocco	.10	.05	.01
□ 350	Anthony Young	.10	.05	.01
□ 351	Leo Gomez	.10	.05	.01
□ 352	Bill Gullickson	.10	.05	.01
□ 353	Alan Trammell	.50	.23	.06
□ 354	Dan Pasqua	.10	.05	.01
□ 355	Jeff King	.25	.11	.03
□ 356	Kevin Brown	.10	.05	.01
□ 357	Tim Belcher	.10	.05	.01
□ 358	Bip Roberts	.10	.05	.01
□ 359	Brent Mayne	.10	.05	.01
□ 360	Rheal Cormier	.10	.05	.01
□ 361	Mark Guthrie	.10	.05	.01
□ 362	Craig Grebeck	.10	.05	.01
□ 363	Andy Stankiewicz	.10	.05	.01
□ 364	Juan Guzman	.25	.11	.03
□ 365	Bobby Witt	.10	.05	.01
□ 366	Mark Portugal	.10	.05	.01
□ 367	Brian McRae	.25	.11	.03
□ 368	Mark Lemke	.10	.05	.01
□ 369	Bill Wegman	.10	.05	.01
□ 370	Donovan Osborne	.10	.05	.01
□ 371	Derrick May	.10	.05	.01
□ 372	Carl Willis	.10	.05	.01
□ 373	Chris Nabholz	.10	.05	.01
□ 374	Mark Lewis	.10	.05	.01
□ 375	John Burkett	.10	.05	.01
□ 376	Luis Mercedes	.10	.05	.01
□ 377	Ramon Martinez	.25	.11	.03
□ 378	Kyle Abbott	.10	.05	.01
□ 379	Mark Wohlers	.25	.11	.03
□ 380	Bob Walk	.10	.05	.01
□ 381	Kenny Rogers	.10	.05	.01
□ 382	Tim Naehring	.10	.05	.01
□ 383	Alex Fernandez	.50	.23	.06
□ 384	Keith Miller	.10	.05	.01
□ 385	Mike Henneman	.10	.05	.01
□ 386	Rick Aguilera	.10	.05	.01
□ 387	George Bell	.10	.05	.01
□ 388	Mike Gallego	.10	.05	.01
□ 389	Howard Johnson	.10	.05	.01
□ 390	Kim Batiste	.10	.05	.01
□ 391	Jerry Browne	.10	.05	.01
□ 392	Damon Berryhill	.10	.05	.01
□ 393	Ricky Bones	.10	.05	.01
□ 394	Omar Olivares	.10	.05	.01
□ 395	Mike Harkey	.10	.05	.01
□ 396	Pedro Astacio	.10	.05	.01
□ 397	John Wetteland	.25	.11	.03
□ 398	Rod Beck	.25	.11	.03
□ 399	Thomas Howard	.10	.05	.01
□ 400	Mike Devereaux	.10	.05	.01
□ 401	Tim Wakefield	.25	.11	.03
□ 402	Curt Schilling	.10	.05	.01
□ 403	Zane Smith	.10	.05	.01
□ 404	Bob Zupcic	.10	.05	.01
□ 405	Tom Browning	.10	.05	.01

☐	406	Tony Phillips	.25	.11	.03
☐	407	John Doherty	.10	.05	.01
☐	408	Pat Mahomes	.10	.05	.01
☐	409	John Habyan	.10	.05	.01
☐	410	Steve Olin	.10	.05	.01
☐	411	Chad Curtis	.25	.11	.03
☐	412	Joe Grahe	.10	.05	.01
☐	413	John Patterson	.10	.05	.01
☐	414	Brian Hunter	.10	.05	.01
☐	415	Doug Henry	.10	.05	.01
☐	416	Lee Smith	.25	.11	.03
☐	417	Bob Scanlan	.10	.05	.01
☐	418	Kent Mercker	.10	.05	.01
☐	419	Mel Rojas	.25	.11	.03
☐	420	Mark Whiten	.10	.05	.01
☐	421	Carlton Fisk	.50	.23	.06
☐	422	Candy Maldonado	.10	.05	.01
☐	423	Doug Drabek	.10	.05	.01
☐	424	Wade Boggs	.50	.23	.06
☐	425	Mark Davis	.10	.05	.01
☐	426	Kirby Puckett	1.00	.45	.12
☐	427	Joe Carter	.50	.23	.06
☐	428	Paul Molitor	.60	.25	.07
☐	429	Eric Davis	.25	.11	.03
☐	430	Darryl Kile	.10	.05	.01
☐	431	Jeff Parrett	.10	.05	.01
☐	432	Jeff Blauser	.10	.05	.01
☐	433	Dan Plesac	.10	.05	.01
☐	434	Andres Galarraga	.50	.23	.06
☐	435	Jim Gott	.10	.05	.01
☐	436	Jose Mesa	.25	.11	.03
☐	437	Ben Rivera	.10	.05	.01
☐	438	Dave Winfield	.50	.23	.06
☐	439	Norm Charlton	.10	.05	.01
☐	440	Chris Bosio	.10	.05	.01
☐	441	Wilson Alvarez	.25	.11	.03
☐	442	Dave Stewart	.25	.11	.03
☐	443	Doug Jones	.10	.05	.01
☐	444	Jeff Russell	.10	.05	.01
☐	445	Ron Gant	.50	.23	.06
☐	446	Paul O'Neill	.25	.11	.03
☐	447	Charlie Hayes	.10	.05	.01
☐	448	Joe Hesketh	.10	.05	.01
☐	449	Chris Hammond	.10	.05	.01
☐	450	Hipolito Pichardo	.10	.05	.01
☐	451	Scott Radinsky	.10	.05	.01
☐	452	Bobby Thigpen	.10	.05	.01
☐	453	Xavier Hernandez	.10	.05	.01
☐	454	Lonnie Smith	.10	.05	.01
☐	455	Jamie Arnold DP	.25	.11	.03
☐	456	B.J. Wallace DP	.10	.05	.01
☐	457	Derek Jeter DP	6.00	2.70	.75
☐	458	Jason Kendall DP	2.00	.90	.25
☐	459	Rick Helling DP	.25	.11	.03
☐	460	Derek Wallace DP	.10	.05	.01
☐	461	Sean Lowe DP	.25	.11	.03
☐	462	Shannon Stewart DP	.50	.23	.06
☐	463	Benji Grigsby DP	.10	.05	.01
☐	464	Todd Steverson DP	.25	.11	.03
☐	465	Dan Serafini DP	.50	.23	.06
☐	466	Michael Tucker DP	.50	.23	.06
☐	467	Chris Roberts DP	.25	.11	.03
☐	468	Pete Janicki DP	.10	.05	.01
☐	469	Jeff Schmidt DP	.10	.05	.01
☐	470	Don Mattingly NT	.75	.35	.09
☐	471	Cal Ripken Jr. NT	1.25	.55	.16
☐	472	Jack Morris NT	.10	.05	.01
☐	473	Terry Pendleton NT	.10	.05	.01
☐	474	Dennis Eckersley NT	.10	.05	.01
☐	475	Carlton Fisk NT	.25	.11	.03
☐	476	Wade Boggs NT	.50	.23	.06
☐	477	Len Dykstra	.25	.11	.03
		Ken Stabler			
☐	478	Danny Tartabull	.10	.05	.01
		Jose Tartabull			
☐	479	Jeff Conine	.50	.23	.06
		Dale Murphy			
☐	480	Gregg Jefferies	.25	.11	.03
		Ron Cey			
☐	481	Paul Molitor	.30	.14	.04
		Harmon Killebrew			
☐	482	John Valentin	.25	.11	.03
		Dave Concepcion			
☐	483	Alex Arias	.25	.11	.03
		Dave Winfield			
☐	484	Barry Bonds HH	.50	.23	.06
☐	485	Doug Drabek HH	.10	.05	.01
☐	486	Dave Winfield HH	.50	.23	.06
☐	487	Brett Butler HH	.10	.05	.01
☐	488	Harold Baines HH	.10	.05	.01
☐	489	David Cone HH	.25	.11	.03
☐	490	Willie McGee HH	.10	.05	.01
☐	491	Robby Thompson	.10	.05	.01
☐	492	Pete Incaviglia	.10	.05	.01
☐	493	Manuel Lee	.10	.05	.01
☐	494	Rafael Belliard	.10	.05	.01
☐	495	Scott Fletcher	.10	.05	.01
☐	496	Jeff Frye	.10	.05	.01
☐	497	Andre Dawson	.50	.23	.06
☐	498	Mike Scioscia	.10	.05	.01
☐	499	Spike Owen	.10	.05	.01
☐	500	Sid Fernandez	.10	.05	.01
☐	501	Joe Orsulak	.10	.05	.01
☐	502	Benito Santiago	.10	.05	.01
☐	503	Dale Murphy	.50	.23	.06
☐	504	Barry Bonds	.75	.35	.09
☐	505	Jose Guzman	.10	.05	.01
☐	506	Tony Pena	.10	.05	.01
☐	507	Greg Swindell	.10	.05	.01
☐	508	Mike Pagliarulo	.10	.05	.01
☐	509	Lou Whitaker	.50	.23	.06
☐	510	Greg Gagne	.10	.05	.01
☐	511	Butch Henry	.10	.05	.01
☐	512	Jeff Brantley	.10	.05	.01
☐	513	Jack Armstrong	.10	.05	.01
☐	514	Danny Jackson	.10	.05	.01
☐	515	Junior Felix	.10	.05	.01
☐	516	Milt Thompson	.10	.05	.01
☐	517	Greg Maddux	2.00	.90	.25
☐	518	Eric Young	.50	.23	.06
☐	519	Jody Reed	.10	.05	.01
☐	520	Roberto Kelly	.10	.05	.01
☐	521	Darren Holmes	.10	.05	.01
☐	522	Craig Lefferts	.10	.05	.01
☐	523	Charlie Hough	.10	.05	.01
☐	524	Bo Jackson	.50	.23	.06
☐	525	Bill Spiers	.10	.05	.01
☐	526	Orestes Destrade	.10	.05	.01
☐	527	Greg Hibbard	.10	.05	.01
☐	528	Roger McDowell	.10	.05	.01
☐	529	Cory Snyder	.10	.05	.01
☐	530	Harold Reynolds	.10	.05	.01
☐	531	Kevin Reimer	.10	.05	.01
☐	532	Rick Sutcliffe	.10	.05	.01
☐	533	Tony Fernandez	.10	.05	.01
☐	534	Tom Brunansky	.10	.05	.01
☐	535	Jeff Reardon	.25	.11	.03
☐	536	Chili Davis	.25	.11	.03
☐	537	Bob Ojeda	.10	.05	.01
☐	538	Greg Colbrunn	.10	.05	.01
☐	539	Phil Plantier	.10	.05	.01
☐	540	Brian Jordan	.50	.23	.06
☐	541	Pete Smith	.10	.05	.01
☐	542	Frank Tanana	.10	.05	.01
☐	543	John Smiley	.10	.05	.01
☐	544	David Cone	.50	.23	.06
☐	545	Daryl Boston	.10	.05	.01
☐	546	Tom Henke	.10	.05	.01
☐	547	Bill Krueger	.10	.05	.01
☐	548	Freddie Benavides	.10	.05	.01
☐	549	Randy Myers	.25	.11	.03
☐	550	Reggie Jefferson	.25	.11	.03
☐	551	Kevin Mitchell	.25	.11	.03
☐	552	Dave Stieb	.10	.05	.01
☐	553	Bret Barberie	.10	.05	.01
☐	554	Tim Crews	.10	.05	.01
☐	555	Doug Dascenzo	.10	.05	.01
☐	556	Alex Cole	.10	.05	.01
☐	557	Jeff Innis	.10	.05	.01
☐	558	Carlos Garcia	.10	.05	.01
☐	559	Steve Howe	.10	.05	.01
☐	560	Kirk McCaskill	.10	.05	.01
☐	561	Frank Seminara	.10	.05	.01
☐	562	Cris Carpenter	.10	.05	.01
☐	563	Mike Stanley	.10	.05	.01
☐	564	Carlos Quintana	.10	.05	.01
☐	565	Mitch Williams	.10	.05	.01
☐	566	Juan Bell	.10	.05	.01
☐	567	Eric Fox	.10	.05	.01
☐	568	Al Leiter	.25	.11	.03
☐	569	Mike Stanton	.10	.05	.01
☐	570	Scott Kamieniecki	.10	.05	.01

□ 571 Ryan Bowen	.10	.05	.01
□ 572 Andy Ashby	.25	.11	.03
□ 573 Bob Welch	.10	.05	.01
□ 574 Scott Sanderson	.10	.05	.01
□ 575 Joe Kmak	.10	.05	.01
□ 576 Scott Pose	.10	.05	.01
□ 577 Ricky Gutierrez	.10	.05	.01
□ 578 Mike Trombley	.10	.05	.01
□ 579 Sterling Hitchcock	.25	.11	.03
□ 580 Rodney Bolton	.10	.05	.01
□ 581 Tyler Green	.10	.05	.01
□ 582 Tim Costo	.10	.05	.01
□ 583 Tim Laker	.10	.05	.01
□ 584 Steve Reed	.10	.05	.01
□ 585 Tom Kramer	.10	.05	.01
□ 586 Robb Nen	.25	.11	.03
□ 587 Jim Tatum	.10	.05	.01
□ 588 Frank Bolick	.10	.05	.01
□ 589 Kevin Young	.10	.05	.01
□ 590 Matt Whiteside	.10	.05	.01
□ 591 Cesar Hernandez	.10	.05	.01
□ 592 Mike Mohler	.10	.05	.01
□ 593 Alan Embree	.10	.05	.01
□ 594 Terry Jorgensen	.10	.05	.01
□ 595 John Cummings	.10	.05	.01
□ 596 Domingo Martinez	.10	.05	.01
□ 597 Benji Gil	.25	.11	.03
□ 598 Todd Pratt	.10	.05	.01
□ 599 Rene Arocha	.10	.05	.01
□ 600 Dennis Moeller	.10	.05	.01
□ 601 Jeff Conine	.50	.23	.06
□ 602 Trevor Hoffman	.25	.11	.03
□ 603 Daniel Smith	.10	.05	.01
□ 604 Lee Tinsley	.25	.11	.03
□ 605 Dan Peltier	.10	.05	.01
□ 606 Billy Brewer	.10	.05	.01
□ 607 Matt Walbeck	.10	.05	.01
□ 608 Richie Lewis	.10	.05	.01
□ 609 J.T. Snow	.50	.23	.06
□ 610 Pat Gomez	.10	.05	.01
□ 611 Phil Hiatt	.10	.05	.01
□ 612 Alex Arias	.10	.05	.01
□ 613 Kevin Rogers	.10	.05	.01
□ 614 Al Martin	.25	.11	.03
□ 615 Greg Gohr	.10	.05	.01
□ 616 Graeme Lloyd	.10	.05	.01
□ 617 Kent Bottenfield	.10	.05	.01
□ 618 Chuck Carr	.10	.05	.01
□ 619 Darrell Sherman	.10	.05	.01
□ 620 Mike Lansing	.25	.11	.03

1993 Pinnacle Expansion Opening Day

This nine-card standard-size dual-sided set was issued to commemorate openning day for the two 1993 expansion teams, the Colorado Rockies and the Florida Marlins. The cards were inserted on top of sealed series two hobby boxes. These cards were also available through a mail-in offer. The full-bleed fronts feature glossy color action player photos. Across the bottom is a team color-coded bar containing the player's name, position, and opening day date. A logo for the Expansion Draft is printed in the lower right corner. An anti-counterfeit device is printed in the bottom black border. The backs carry the same design as the fronts with a player from the Rockies appearing on one side and a Marlin's player on the flip side. The cards are numbered on both sides.

	MINT	NRMT	EXC
COMPLETE SET (9)	25.00	11.00	3.10
COMMON PAIR (1-9)	1.50	.70	.19
ONE CARD PER SEALED SER.2 HOBBY BOX			
SETS DISTRIBUTED VIA MAIL-IN OFFER.....			
□ 1 Charlie Hough David Nied	2.50	1.10	.30
□ 2 Benito Santiago Joe Girardi	2.50	1.10	.30
□ 3 Orestes Destrade Andres Galarraga	6.00	2.70	.75
□ 4 Bret Barberie Eric Young	2.50	1.10	.30
□ 5 Dave Magadan Charlie Hayes	2.50	1.10	.30
□ 6 Walt Weiss Freddie Benavides	2.50	1.10	.30
□ 7 Jeff Conine Jerald Clark	5.00	2.20	.60
□ 8 Scott Pose Alex Cole	1.50	.70	.19
□ 9 Junior Felix Dante Bichette	8.00	3.60	1.00

1993 Pinnacle Rookie Team Pinnacle

Cards from this 10-card standard-size set were randomly inserted into one in every 90 series 2 foil packs and each features an American League rookie on one side and a National League rookie on the other. Each double-sided card displays paintings by artist Christopher Greco encased by a bold black border. The cards are numbered on the front and back.

	MINT	NRMT	EXC
COMPLETE SET (10)	135.00	60.00	17.00
COMMON PAIR (1-10)	5.00	2.20	.60
SEMISTARS	8.00	3.60	1.00
RANDOM INSERTS IN SER.2 PACKS			
□ 1 Pedro Martinez Mike Trombley	8.00	3.60	1.00
□ 2 Kevin Rogers Sterling Hitchcock	5.00	2.20	.60
□ 3 Mike Piazza Jesse Levis	60.00	27.00	7.50
□ 4 Ryan Klesko J.T. Snow	30.00	13.50	3.70
□ 5 John Patterson Bret Boone	8.00	3.60	1.00
□ 6 Kevin Young Domingo Martinez	5.00	2.20	.60
□ 7 Wil Cordero Manny Alexander	8.00	3.60	1.00
□ 8 Steve Hosey Tim Salmon	20.00	9.00	2.50
□ 9 Ryan Thompson Gerald Williams	5.00	2.20	.60
□ 10 Melvin Nieves David Hulse	8.00	3.60	1.00

1993 Pinnacle Slugfest

These 30 standard-size cards salute baseball's top hitters and were randomly inserted in series 2 jumbo superpacks. The fronts feature color player action shots that are borderless, except at the bottom, where a black stripe carries the player's name in white lettering. The set's title appears below in black lettering within a gold foil stripe.

	MINT	NRMT	EXC
COMPLETE SET (30)	60.00	27.00	7.50
COMMON CARD (1-30)	1.00	.45	.12
SEMISTARS	2.00	.90	.25
ONE PER SER.2 JUMBO PACK			

	MINT	NRMT	EXC
□ 1 Juan Gonzalez	8.00	3.60	1.00
□ 2 Mark McGwire	5.00	2.20	.60
□ 3 Cecil Fielder	2.00	.90	.25
□ 4 Joe Carter	2.00	.90	.25
□ 5 Fred McGriff	2.00	.90	.25
□ 6 Barry Bonds	4.00	1.80	.50
□ 7 Gary Sheffield	2.50	1.10	.30
□ 8 Dave Hollins	1.00	.45	.12
□ 9 Frank Thomas	15.00	6.75	1.85
□ 10 Danny Tartabull	1.00	.45	.12
□ 11 Albert Belle	8.00	3.60	1.00
□ 12 Ruben Sierra	1.00	.45	.12
□ 13 Larry Walker	2.00	.90	.25
□ 14 Jeff Bagwell	6.00	2.70	.75
□ 15 David Justice	2.00	.90	.25
□ 16 Kirby Puckett	5.00	2.20	.60
□ 17 John Kruk	1.00	.45	.12
□ 18 Howard Johnson	1.00	.45	.12
□ 19 Darryl Strawberry	2.00	.90	.25
□ 20 Will Clark	2.00	.90	.25
□ 21 Kevin Mitchell	1.00	.45	.12
□ 22 Mickey Tettleton	1.00	.45	.12
□ 23 Don Mattingly	6.00	2.70	.75
□ 24 Jose Canseco	2.00	.90	.25
□ 25 George Bell	1.00	.45	.12
□ 26 Andre Dawson	2.00	.90	.25
□ 27 Ryne Sandberg	4.00	1.80	.50
□ 28 Ken Griffey Jr.	15.00	6.75	1.85
□ 29 Carlos Baerga	2.00	.90	.25
□ 30 Travis Fryman	2.00	.90	.25

1993 Pinnacle Team 2001

This 30-card standard-size set salutes players expected to be stars in the year 2001. The cards were inserted one per pack in first series jumbo superpacks and feature color player action shots on their fronts. These photos are borderless at the top and right, and black-bordered on the bottom and left. The player's name appears in gold-foil in the bottom margin, and his gold-foil-encircled team logo rests in the bottom left.

	MINT	NRMT	EXC
COMPLETE SET (30)	40.00	18.00	5.00
COMMON CARD (1-30)	.75	.35	.09
SEMISTARS	1.50	.70	.19
ONE PER SER.1 JUMBO PACK			

	MINT	NRMT	EXC
□ 1 Wil Cordero	.75	.35	.09
□ 2 Cal Eldred	.75	.35	.09
□ 3 Mike Mussina	3.00	1.35	.35
□ 4 Chuck Knoblauch	2.50	1.10	.30
□ 5 Melvin Nieves	1.50	.70	.19
□ 6 Tim Wakefield	.75	.35	.09
□ 7 Carlos Baerga	1.50	.70	.19
□ 8 Bret Boone	1.50	.70	.19
□ 9 Jeff Bagwell	6.00	2.70	.75
□ 10 Travis Fryman	1.50	.70	.19
□ 11 Royce Clayton	.75	.35	.09
□ 12 Delino DeShields	.75	.35	.09
□ 13 Juan Gonzalez	8.00	3.60	1.00
□ 14 Pedro Martinez	.75	.35	.09
□ 15 Bernie Williams	3.00	1.35	.35
□ 16 Billy Ashley	.75	.35	.09
□ 17 Marquis Grissom	1.50	.70	.19
□ 18 Kenny Lofton	6.00	2.70	.75
□ 19 Ray Lankford	1.50	.70	.19
□ 20 Tim Salmon	3.00	1.35	.35
□ 21 Steve Hosey	.75	.35	.09
□ 22 Charles Nagy	.75	.35	.09
□ 23 Dave Fleming	.75	.35	.09
□ 24 Reggie Sanders	1.50	.70	.19
□ 25 Sam Militello	.75	.35	.09
□ 26 Eric Karros	1.50	.70	.19
□ 27 Ryan Klesko	5.00	2.20	.60
□ 28 Dean Palmer	1.50	.70	.19
□ 29 Ivan Rodriguez	3.00	1.35	.35
□ 30 Sterling Hitchcock	.75	.35	.09

1993 Pinnacle Team Pinnacle

Cards from this ten-card dual-sided set, featuring a selection of top stars paired of by position, were randomly inserted into one in every 24 first series foil packs. Each double-sided card displays paintings by artist Christopher Greco. A special bonus Team Pinnacle card (11) was available to collectors only through a mail-in offer for ten 1993 Pinnacle baseball wrappers plus 1.50 for shipping and handling. Moreover, hobby dealers who ordered Pinnacle received two bonus cards and an advertisement display promoting the offer.

	MINT	NRMT	EXC
COMPLETE SET (10)	90.00	40.00	11.00
COMMON PAIR (1-10/B11)	3.00	1.35	.35
RANDOM INSERTS IN SER.1 PACKS			
B11 DISTRIBUTED ONLY BY MAIL			

	MINT	NRMT	EXC
□ 1 Greg Maddux Mike Mussina	25.00	11.00	3.10
□ 2 Tom Glavine	5.00	2.20	.60

John Smiley			
□ 3 Darren Daulton	8.00	3.60	1.00
Ivan Rodriguez			
□ 4 Fred McGriff	30.00	13.50	3.70
Frank Thomas			
□ 5 Delino DeShields	6.00	2.70	.75
Carlos Baerga			
□ 6 Gary Sheffield	8.00	3.60	1.00
Edgar Martinez			
□ 7 Ozzie Smith	8.00	3.60	1.00
Pat Listach			
□ 8 Barry Bonds	20.00	9.00	2.50
Juan Gonzalez			
□ 9 Andy Van Slyke	12.00	5.50	1.50
Kirby Puckett			
□ 10 Larry Walker	8.00	3.60	1.00
Joe Carter			
□ B11 Rob Dibble	3.00	1.35	.35
Rick Aguilera			

1994 Pinnacle

The 540-card 1994 Pinnacle standard-size set was issued in two series of 270. The fronts feature full-bleed color action player photos. In one of the upper corners, the new Pinnacle logo appears with the brand name immediately below in small white lettering. Toward the bottom, the player's last name in gold foil on a black bar overlays a two-color emblem carrying his first name and his team name. On most of the backs, a ghosted version of the front picture forms the background for a player cutout, biography, and statistics. Subsets include Rookie Prospects subset (224-261) and a Draft Picks subset (262-270/430-438). Rookie Cards include Brian Anderson, Matt Drews, Brooks Kieschnick, Derrek Lee, Trot Nixon, Kirk Presley and Billy Wagner.

	MINT	NRMT	EXC
COMPLETE SET (540)	30.00	13.50	3.70
COMPLETE SERIES 1 (270)	15.00	6.75	1.85
COMPLETE SERIES 2 (270)	15.00	6.75	1.85
COMMON CARD (1-540)	.10	.05	.01
SEMISTARS	.25	.11	.03
STARS	.50	.23	.06
COMP.MUSEUM SET (540)	800.00	350.00	100.00
COMP.MUSEUM SER.1 (270)	500.00	220.00	60.00
COMP.MUSEUM SER.2 (270)	300.00	135.00	38.00
COMMON MUSEUM (1-540)	1.00	.45	.12
MUSEUM TRADE (279/313/328)	3.00	1.35	.35
MUSEUM TRADE (382/387)	3.00	1.35	.35
MUSEUM SEMISTARS	2.50	1.10	.30
MUSEUM STARS	4.00	1.80	.50
MUSEUM STARS: 6X to 12X HI COLUMN			
MUSEUM YOUNG STARS: 5X to 10X HI			
COMPLETE AP SET (540)	3500.00	1600.00	450.00
COMP.AP SERIES 1 (270)	2250.00	1000.00	275.00
COMP.AP SERIES 2 (270)	1250.00	550.00	160.00
COMMON AP (1-540)	3.00	1.35	.35
AP SEMISTARS	6.00	2.70	.75
AP STARS	10.00	4.50	1.25
*AP VETERAN STARS: 15X TO 30X HI			
*AP YOUNG STARS: 10X TO 20X HI			
AP/MUSEUM: INSERTS IN PACKS			

□ 1 Frank Thomas	3.00	1.35	.35
□ 2 Carlos Baerga	.50	.23	.06
□ 3 Sammy Sosa	.50	.23	.06
□ 4 Tony Gwynn	1.25	.55	.16
□ 5 John Olerud	.10	.05	.01
□ 6 Ryne Sandberg	.75	.35	.09
□ 7 Moises Alou	.25	.11	.03
□ 8 Steve Avery	.25	.11	.03
□ 9 Tim Salmon	.50	.23	.06
□ 10 Cecil Fielder	.25	.11	.03
□ 11 Greg Maddux	2.00	.90	.25
□ 12 Barry Larkin	.50	.23	.06
□ 13 Mike Devereaux	.10	.05	.01
□ 14 Charlie Hayes	.10	.05	.01
□ 15 Albert Belle	1.50	.70	.19
□ 16 Andy Van Slyke	.25	.11	.03
□ 17 Mo Vaughn	.75	.35	.09
□ 18 Brian McRae	.25	.11	.03
□ 19 Cal Eldred	.10	.05	.01
□ 20 Craig Biggio	.50	.23	.06
□ 21 Kirby Puckett	1.00	.45	.12
□ 22 Derek Bell	.25	.11	.03
□ 23 Don Mattingly	1.50	.70	.19
□ 24 John Burkett	.10	.05	.01
□ 25 Roger Clemens	.50	.23	.06
□ 26 Barry Bonds	.75	.35	.09
□ 27 Paul Molitor	.60	.25	.07
□ 28 Mike Piazza	2.00	.90	.25
□ 29 Robin Ventura	.25	.11	.03
□ 30 Jeff Conine	.50	.23	.06
□ 31 Wade Boggs	.50	.23	.06
□ 32 Dennis Eckersley	.25	.11	.03
□ 33 Bobby Bonilla	.25	.11	.03
□ 34 Lenny Dykstra	.25	.11	.03
□ 35 Manny Alexander	.10	.05	.01
□ 36 Ray Lankford	.50	.23	.06
□ 37 Greg Vaughn	.50	.23	.06
□ 38 Chuck Finley	.10	.05	.01
□ 39 Todd Benzinger	.10	.05	.01
□ 40 Dave Justice	.50	.23	.06
□ 41 Rob Dibble	.10	.05	.01
□ 42 Tom Henke	.10	.05	.01
□ 43 David Nied	.10	.05	.01
□ 44 Sandy Alomar Jr.	.25	.11	.03
□ 45 Pete Harnisch	.10	.05	.01
□ 46 Jeff Russell	.10	.05	.01
□ 47 Terry Mulholland	.10	.05	.01
□ 48 Kevin Appier	.25	.11	.03
□ 49 Randy Tomlin	.10	.05	.01
□ 50 Cal Ripken Jr.	2.50	1.10	.30
□ 51 Andy Benes	.25	.11	.03
□ 52 Jimmy Key	.25	.11	.03
□ 53 Kirt Manwaring	.10	.05	.01
□ 54 Kevin Tapani	.10	.05	.01
□ 55 Jose Guzman	.10	.05	.01
□ 56 Todd Stottlemyre	.10	.05	.01
□ 57 Jack McDowell	.25	.11	.03
□ 58 Orel Hershiser	.25	.11	.03
□ 59 Chris Hammond	.10	.05	.01
□ 60 Chris Nabholz	.10	.05	.01
□ 61 Ruben Sierra	.25	.11	.03
□ 62 Dwight Gooden	.25	.11	.03
□ 63 John Kruk	.25	.11	.03
□ 64 Omar Vizquel	.50	.23	.06
□ 65 Tim Naehring	.10	.05	.01
□ 66 Dwight Smith	.10	.05	.01
□ 67 Mickey Tettleton	.10	.05	.01
□ 68 J.T. Snow	.25	.11	.03
□ 69 Greg McMichael	.10	.05	.01
□ 70 Kevin Mitchell	.25	.11	.03
□ 71 Kevin Brown	.10	.05	.01
□ 72 Scott Cooper	.10	.05	.01
□ 73 Jim Thome	.75	.35	.09
□ 74 Joe Girardi	.10	.05	.01
□ 75 Eric Anthony	.10	.05	.01
□ 76 Orlando Merced	.25	.11	.03
□ 77 Felix Jose	.10	.05	.01
□ 78 Tommy Greene	.10	.05	.01
□ 79 Bernard Gilkey	.25	.11	.03
□ 80 Phil Plantier	.10	.05	.01
□ 81 Danny Tartabull	.10	.05	.01
□ 82 Trevor Wilson	.10	.05	.01
□ 83 Chuck Knoblauch	.50	.23	.06
□ 84 Rick Wilkins	.10	.05	.01
□ 85 Devon White	.10	.05	.01
□ 86 Lance Johnson	.25	.11	.03
□ 87 Eric Karros	.25	.11	.03
□ 88 Gary Sheffield	.50	.23	.06

☐ 89 Wil Cordero	.25	.11	.03
☐ 90 Ron Darling	.10	.05	.01
☐ 91 Darren Daulton	.25	.11	.03
☐ 92 Joe Orsulak	.10	.05	.01
☐ 93 Steve Cooke	.10	.05	.01
☐ 94 Darryl Hamilton	.10	.05	.01
☐ 95 Aaron Sele	.25	.11	.03
☐ 96 John Doherty	.10	.05	.01
☐ 97 Gary DiSarcina	.10	.05	.01
☐ 98 Jeff Blauser	.10	.05	.01
☐ 99 John Smiley	.10	.05	.01
☐ 100 Ken Griffey Jr.	3.00	1.35	.35
☐ 101 Dean Palmer	.25	.11	.03
☐ 102 Felix Fermin	.10	.05	.01
☐ 103 Jerald Clark	.10	.05	.01
☐ 104 Doug Drabek	.10	.05	.01
☐ 105 Curt Schilling	.10	.05	.01
☐ 106 Jeff Montgomery	.25	.11	.03
☐ 107 Rene Arocha	.10	.05	.01
☐ 108 Carlos Garcia	.10	.05	.01
☐ 109 Wally Whitehurst	.10	.05	.01
☐ 110 Jim Abbott	.10	.05	.01
☐ 111 Royce Clayton	.25	.11	.03
☐ 112 Chris Hoiles	.10	.05	.01
☐ 113 Mike Morgan	.10	.05	.01
☐ 114 Joe Magrane	.10	.05	.01
☐ 115 Tom Candiotti	.10	.05	.01
☐ 116 Ron Karkovice	.10	.05	.01
☐ 117 Ryan Bowen	.10	.05	.01
☐ 118 Rod Beck	.25	.11	.03
☐ 119 John Wetteland	.25	.11	.03
☐ 120 Terry Steinbach	.25	.11	.03
☐ 121 Dave Hollins	.10	.05	.01
☐ 122 Jeff Kent	.10	.05	.01
☐ 123 Ricky Bones	.10	.05	.01
☐ 124 Brian Jordan	.50	.23	.06
☐ 125 Chad Kreuter	.10	.05	.01
☐ 126 John Valentin	.25	.11	.03
☐ 127 Hilly Hathaway	.10	.05	.01
☐ 128 Wilson Alvarez	.25	.11	.03
☐ 129 Tino Martinez	.25	.11	.03
☐ 130 Rodney Bolton	.10	.05	.01
☐ 131 David Segui	.10	.05	.01
☐ 132 Wayne Kirby	.10	.05	.01
☐ 133 Eric Young	.25	.11	.03
☐ 134 Scott Servais	.10	.05	.01
☐ 135 Scott Radinsky	.10	.05	.01
☐ 136 Bret Barberie	.10	.05	.01
☐ 137 John Roper	.10	.05	.01
☐ 138 Ricky Gutierrez	.10	.05	.01
☐ 139 Bernie Williams	.50	.23	.06
☐ 140 Bud Black	.10	.05	.01
☐ 141 Jose Vizcaino	.10	.05	.01
☐ 142 Gerald Williams	.10	.05	.01
☐ 143 Duane Ward	.10	.05	.01
☐ 144 Danny Jackson	.10	.05	.01
☐ 145 Allen Watson	.10	.05	.01
☐ 146 Scott Fletcher	.10	.05	.01
☐ 147 Delino DeShields	.10	.05	.01
☐ 148 Shane Mack	.10	.05	.01
☐ 149 Jim Eisenreich	.10	.05	.01
☐ 150 Troy Neel	.10	.05	.01
☐ 151 Jay Bell	.25	.11	.03
☐ 152 B.J. Surhoff	.10	.05	.01
☐ 153 Mark Whiten	.10	.05	.01
☐ 154 Mike Henneman	.10	.05	.01
☐ 155 Todd Hundley	.50	.23	.06
☐ 156 Greg Myers	.10	.05	.01
☐ 157 Ryan Klesko	.75	.35	.09
☐ 158 Dave Fleming	.10	.05	.01
☐ 159 Mickey Morandini	.10	.05	.01
☐ 160 Blas Minor	.10	.05	.01
☐ 161 Reggie Jefferson	.25	.11	.03
☐ 162 David Hulse	.10	.05	.01
☐ 163 Greg Swindell	.10	.05	.01
☐ 164 Roberto Hernandez	.25	.11	.03
☐ 165 Brady Anderson	.50	.23	.06
☐ 166 Jack Armstrong	.10	.05	.01
☐ 167 Phil Clark	.10	.05	.01
☐ 168 Melido Perez	.10	.05	.01
☐ 169 Darren Lewis	.10	.05	.01
☐ 170 Sam Horn	.10	.05	.01
☐ 171 Mike Harkey	.10	.05	.01
☐ 172 Juan Guzman	.25	.11	.03
☐ 173 Bob Natal	.10	.05	.01
☐ 174 Deion Sanders	.50	.23	.06
☐ 175 Carlos Quintana	.10	.05	.01
☐ 176 Mel Rojas	.10	.05	.01
☐ 177 Willie Banks	.10	.05	.01
☐ 178 Ben Rivera	.10	.05	.01
☐ 179 Kenny Lofton	1.00	.45	.12
☐ 180 Leo Gomez	.10	.05	.01
☐ 181 Roberto Mejia	.10	.05	.01
☐ 182 Mike Perez	.10	.05	.01
☐ 183 Travis Fryman	.50	.23	.06
☐ 184 Ben McDonald	.10	.05	.01
☐ 185 Steve Frey	.10	.05	.01
☐ 186 Kevin Young	.10	.05	.01
☐ 187 Dave Magadan	.10	.05	.01
☐ 188 Bobby Munoz	.10	.05	.01
☐ 189 Pat Rapp	.10	.05	.01
☐ 190 Jose Offerman	.10	.05	.01
☐ 191 Vinny Castilla	.50	.23	.06
☐ 192 Ivan Calderon	.10	.05	.01
☐ 193 Ken Caminiti	.50	.23	.06
☐ 194 Benji Gil	.10	.05	.01
☐ 195 Chuck Carr	.10	.05	.01
☐ 196 Derrick May	.10	.05	.01
☐ 197 Pat Kelly	.10	.05	.01
☐ 198 Jeff Brantley	.10	.05	.01
☐ 199 Jose Lind	.10	.05	.01
☐ 200 Steve Buechele	.10	.05	.01
☐ 201 Wes Chamberlain	.10	.05	.01
☐ 202 Eduardo Perez	.10	.05	.01
☐ 203 Bret Saberhagen	.25	.11	.03
☐ 204 Gregg Jefferies	.50	.23	.06
☐ 205 Darrin Fletcher	.10	.05	.01
☐ 206 Kent Hrbek	.25	.11	.03
☐ 207 Kim Batiste	.10	.05	.01
☐ 208 Jeff King	.25	.11	.03
☐ 209 Donovan Osborne	.10	.05	.01
☐ 210 Dave Nilsson	.25	.11	.03
☐ 211 Al Martin	.10	.05	.01
☐ 212 Mike Moore	.10	.05	.01
☐ 213 Sterling Hitchcock	.25	.11	.03
☐ 214 Geronimo Pena	.10	.05	.01
☐ 215 Kevin Higgins	.10	.05	.01
☐ 216 Norm Charlton	.10	.05	.01
☐ 217 Don Slaught	.10	.05	.01
☐ 218 Mitch Williams	.10	.05	.01
☐ 219 Derek Lilliquist	.10	.05	.01
☐ 220 Armando Reynoso	.10	.05	.01
☐ 221 Kenny Rogers	.10	.05	.01
☐ 222 Doug Jones	.10	.05	.01
☐ 223 Luis Aquino	.10	.05	.01
☐ 224 Mike Oquist	.10	.05	.01
☐ 225 Darryl Scott	.10	.05	.01
☐ 226 Kurt Abbott	.25	.11	.03
☐ 227 Andy Tomberlin	.10	.05	.01
☐ 228 Norberto Martin	.10	.05	.01
☐ 229 Pedro Castellano	.10	.05	.01
☐ 230 Curtis Pride	.25	.11	.03
☐ 231 Jeff McNeely	.10	.05	.01
☐ 232 Scott Lydy	.10	.05	.01
☐ 233 Darren Oliver	.40	.18	.05
☐ 234 Danny Bautista	.10	.05	.01
☐ 235 Butch Huskey	.25	.11	.03
☐ 236 Chipper Jones	2.50	1.10	.30
☐ 237 Eddie Zambrano	.10	.05	.01
☐ 238 Domingo Jean	.10	.05	.01
☐ 239 Javier Lopez	.50	.23	.06
☐ 240 Nigel Wilson	.10	.05	.01
☐ 241 Drew Denson	.10	.05	.01
☐ 242 Raul Mondesi	.50	.23	.06
☐ 243 Luis Ortiz	.10	.05	.01
☐ 244 Manny Ramirez	1.00	.45	.12
☐ 245 Greg Blosser	.10	.05	.01
☐ 246 Rondell White	.50	.23	.06
☐ 247 Steve Karsay	.10	.05	.01
☐ 248 Scott Stahoviak	.10	.05	.01
☐ 249 Jose Valentin	.25	.11	.03
☐ 250 Marc Newfield	.25	.11	.03
☐ 251 Keith Kessinger	.10	.05	.01
☐ 252 Carl Everett	.10	.05	.01
☐ 253 John O'Donoghue	.10	.05	.01
☐ 254 Turk Wendell	.10	.05	.01
☐ 255 Scott Ruffcorn	.10	.05	.01
☐ 256 Tony Tarasco	.10	.05	.01
☐ 257 Andy Cook	.10	.05	.01
☐ 258 Matt Mieske	.10	.05	.01
☐ 259 Luis Lopez	.10	.05	.01
☐ 260 Ramon Caraballo	.10	.05	.01

□	261 Salomon Torres	.10	.05	.01
□	262 Brooks Kieschnick	.60	.25	.07
□	263 Daron Kirkreit	.25	.11	.03
□	264 Bill Wagner	.75	.35	.09
□	265 Matt Drews	.40	.18	.05
□	266 Scott Christman	.25	.11	.03
□	267 Torii Hunter	.25	.11	.03
□	268 Jamey Wright	.75	.35	.09
□	269 Jeff Granger	.25	.11	.03
□	270 Trot Nixon	.50	.23	.06
□	271 Randy Myers	.10	.05	.01
□	272 Trevor Hoffman	.25	.11	.03
□	273 Bob Wickman	.10	.05	.01
□	274 Willie McGee	.10	.05	.01
□	275 Hipolito Pichardo	.10	.05	.01
□	276 Bobby Witt	.10	.05	.01
□	277 Gregg Olson	.10	.05	.01
□	278 Randy Johnson	.50	.23	.06
□	279 Robb Nen	.25	.11	.03
□	280 Paul O'Neill	.25	.11	.03
□	281 Lou Whitaker	.50	.23	.06
□	282 Chad Curtis	.10	.05	.01
□	283 Doug Henry	.10	.05	.01
□	284 Tom Glavine	.50	.23	.06
□	285 Mike Greenwell	.10	.05	.01
□	286 Roberto Kelly	.10	.05	.01
□	287 Roberto Alomar	.75	.35	.09
□	288 Charlie Hough	.10	.05	.01
□	289 Alex Fernandez	.50	.23	.06
□	290 Jeff Bagwell	1.25	.55	.16
□	291 Wally Joyner	.25	.11	.03
□	292 Andujar Cedeno	.10	.05	.01
□	293 Rick Aguilera	.10	.05	.01
□	294 Darryl Strawberry	.25	.11	.03
□	295 Mike Mussina	.60	.25	.07
□	296 Jeff Gardner	.10	.05	.01
□	297 Chris Gwynn	.10	.05	.01
□	298 Matt Williams	.50	.23	.06
□	299 Brent Gates	.10	.05	.01
□	300 Mark McGwire	1.00	.45	.12
□	301 Jim Deshaies	.10	.05	.01
□	302 Edgar Martinez	.50	.23	.06
□	303 Danny Darwin	.10	.05	.01
□	304 Pat Meares	.10	.05	.01
□	305 Benito Santiago	.10	.05	.01
□	306 Jose Canseco	.50	.23	.06
□	307 Jim Gott	.10	.05	.01
□	308 Paul Sorrento	.10	.05	.01
□	309 Scott Kamieniecki	.10	.05	.01
□	310 Larry Walker	.50	.23	.06
□	311 Mark Langston	.25	.11	.03
□	312 John Jaha	.25	.11	.03
□	313 Stan Javier	.10	.05	.01
□	314 Hal Morris	.10	.05	.01
□	315 Robby Thompson	.10	.05	.01
□	316 Pat Hentgen	.50	.23	.06
□	317 Tom Gordon	.10	.05	.01
□	318 Joey Cora	.10	.05	.01
□	319 Luis Alicea	.10	.05	.01
□	320 Andre Dawson	.50	.23	.06
□	321 Darryl Kile	.10	.05	.01
□	322 Jose Rijo	.10	.05	.01
□	323 Luis Gonzalez	.10	.05	.01
□	324 Billy Ashley	.10	.05	.01
□	325 David Cone	.50	.23	.06
□	326 Bill Swift	.10	.05	.01
□	327 Phil Hiatt	.10	.05	.01
□	328 Craig Paquette	.10	.05	.01
□	329 Bob Welch	.10	.05	.01
□	330 Tony Phillips	.25	.11	.03
□	331 Archi Cianfrocco	.10	.05	.01
□	332 Dave Winfield	.50	.23	.06
□	333 David McCarty	.10	.05	.01
□	334 Al Leiter	.25	.11	.03
□	335 Tom Browning	.10	.05	.01
□	336 Mark Grace	.50	.23	.06
□	337 Jose Mesa	.25	.11	.03
□	338 Mike Stanley	.10	.05	.01
□	339 Roger McDowell	.10	.05	.01
□	340 Damion Easley	.10	.05	.01
□	341 Angel Miranda	.10	.05	.01
□	342 John Smoltz	.50	.23	.06
□	343 Jay Buhner	.50	.23	.06
□	344 Bryan Harvey	.10	.05	.01
□	345 Joe Carter	.50	.23	.06
□	346 Dante Bichette	.50	.23	.06
□	347 Jason Bere	.25	.11	.03
□	348 Frank Viola	.10	.05	.01
□	349 Ivan Rodriguez	.60	.25	.07
□	350 Juan Gonzalez	1.50	.70	.19
□	351 Steve Finley	.50	.23	.06
□	352 Mike Felder	.10	.05	.01
□	353 Ramon Martinez	.25	.11	.03
□	354 Greg Gagne	.10	.05	.01
□	355 Ken Hill	.10	.05	.01
□	356 Pedro Munoz	.10	.05	.01
□	357 Todd Van Poppel	.10	.05	.01
□	358 Marquis Grissom	.50	.23	.06
□	359 Milt Cuyler	.10	.05	.01
□	360 Reggie Sanders	.50	.23	.06
□	361 Scott Erickson	.10	.05	.01
□	362 Billy Hatcher	.10	.05	.01
□	363 Gene Harris	.10	.05	.01
□	364 Rene Gonzales	.10	.05	.01
□	365 Kevin Rogers	.10	.05	.01
□	366 Eric Plunk	.10	.05	.01
□	367 Todd Zeile	.10	.05	.01
□	368 John Franco	.10	.05	.01
□	369 Brett Butler	.25	.11	.03
□	370 Bill Spiers	.10	.05	.01
□	371 Terry Pendleton	.25	.11	.03
□	372 Chris Bosio	.10	.05	.01
□	373 Orestes Destrade	.10	.05	.01
□	374 Dave Stewart	.25	.11	.03
□	375 Darren Holmes	.10	.05	.01
□	376 Doug Strange	.10	.05	.01
□	377 Brian Turang	.10	.05	.01
□	378 Carl Wills	.10	.05	.01
□	379 Mark McLemore	.10	.05	.01
□	380 Bobby Jones	.25	.11	.03
□	381 Scott Sanders	.10	.05	.01
□	382 Kirk Rueter	.10	.05	.01
□	383 Randy Velarde	.10	.05	.01
□	384 Fred McGriff	.50	.23	.06
□	385 Charles Nagy	.25	.11	.03
□	386 Rich Amaral	.10	.05	.01
□	387 Geronimo Berroa	.25	.11	.03
□	388 Eric Davis	.25	.11	.03
□	389 Ozzie Smith	.60	.25	.07
□	390 Alex Arias	.10	.05	.01
□	391 Brad Ausmus	.10	.05	.01
□	392 Cliff Floyd	.50	.23	.06
□	393 Roger Salkeld	.10	.05	.01
□	394 Jim Edmonds	.60	.25	.07
□	395 Jeromy Burnitz	.10	.05	.01
□	396 Dave Staton	.10	.05	.01
□	397 Rob Butler	.10	.05	.01
□	398 Marcos Armas	.10	.05	.01
□	399 Darrell Whitmore	.10	.05	.01
□	400 Ryan Thompson	.10	.05	.01
□	401 Ross Powell	.10	.05	.01
□	402 Joe Oliver	.10	.05	.01
□	403 Paul Carey	.10	.05	.01
□	404 Bob Hamelin	.10	.05	.01
□	405 Chris Turner	.10	.05	.01
□	406 Nate Minchey	.10	.05	.01
□	407 Lonnie Maclin	.10	.05	.01
□	408 Harold Baines	.25	.11	.03
□	409 Brian Williams	.10	.05	.01
□	410 Johnny Ruffin	.10	.05	.01
□	411 Julian Tavarez	.25	.11	.03
□	412 Mark Hutton	.10	.05	.01
□	413 Carlos Delgado	.50	.23	.06
□	414 Chris Gomez	.10	.05	.01
□	415 Mike Hampton	.10	.05	.01
□	416 Alex Diaz	.10	.05	.01
□	417 Jeffrey Hammonds	.25	.11	.03
□	418 Jayhawk Owens	.10	.05	.01
□	419 J.R. Phillips	.10	.05	.01
□	420 Cory Bailey	.10	.05	.01
□	421 Denny Hocking	.10	.05	.01
□	422 Jon Shave	.10	.05	.01
□	423 Damon Buford	.10	.05	.01
□	424 Troy O'Leary	.10	.05	.01
□	425 Tripp Cromer	.10	.05	.01
□	426 Albie Lopez	.25	.11	.03
□	427 Tony Fernandez	.10	.05	.01
□	428 Ozzie Guillen	.10	.05	.01
□	429 Alan Trammell	.50	.23	.06
□	430 John Wasdin	.40	.18	.05
□	431 Marc Valdes	.25	.11	.03
□	432 Brian Anderson	.25	.11	.03

□ 433 Matt Brunson	.25	.11	.03
□ 434 Wayne Gomes	.25	.11	.03
□ 435 Jay Powell	.25	.11	.03
□ 436 Kirk Presley	.50	.23	.06
□ 437 Jon Ratliff	.25	.11	.03
□ 438 Derrek Lee	2.00	.90	.25
□ 439 Tom Pagnozzi	.10	.05	.01
□ 440 Kent Mercker	.10	.05	.01
□ 441 Phil Leftwich	.10	.05	.01
□ 442 Jamie Moyer	.10	.05	.01
□ 443 John Flaherty	.10	.05	.01
□ 444 Mark Wohlers	.25	.11	.03
□ 445 Jose Bautista	.10	.05	.01
□ 446 Andres Galarraga	.50	.23	.06
□ 447 Mark Lemke	.10	.05	.01
□ 448 Tim Wakefield	.10	.05	.01
□ 449 Pat Listach	.10	.05	.01
□ 450 Rickey Henderson	.50	.23	.06
□ 451 Mike Gallego	.10	.05	.01
□ 452 Bob Tewksbury	.10	.05	.01
□ 453 Kirk Gibson	.25	.11	.03
□ 454 Pedro Astacio	.10	.05	.01
□ 455 Mike Lansing	.25	.11	.03
□ 456 Sean Berry	.10	.05	.01
□ 457 Bob Walk	.10	.05	.01
□ 458 Chili Davis	.25	.11	.03
□ 459 Ed Sprague	.25	.11	.03
□ 460 Kevin Stocker	.10	.05	.01
□ 461 Mike Stanton	.10	.05	.01
□ 462 Tim Raines	.50	.23	.06
□ 463 Mike Bordick	.10	.05	.01
□ 464 David Wells	.10	.05	.01
□ 465 Tim Laker	.10	.05	.01
□ 466 Cory Snyder	.10	.05	.01
□ 467 Alex Cole	.10	.05	.01
□ 468 Pete Incaviglia	.10	.05	.01
□ 469 Roger Pavlik	.10	.05	.01
□ 470 Greg W. Harris	.10	.05	.01
□ 471 Xavier Hernandez	.10	.05	.01
□ 472 Erik Hanson	.10	.05	.01
□ 473 Jesse Orosco	.10	.05	.01
□ 474 Greg Colbrunn	.10	.05	.01
□ 475 Harold Reynolds	.10	.05	.01
□ 476 Greg A. Harris	.10	.05	.01
□ 477 Pat Borders	.10	.05	.01
□ 478 Melvin Nieves	.25	.11	.03
□ 479 Mariano Duncan	.10	.05	.01
□ 480 Greg Hibbard	.10	.05	.01
□ 481 Tim Pugh	.10	.05	.01
□ 482 Bobby Ayala	.10	.05	.01
□ 483 Sid Fernandez	.10	.05	.01
□ 484 Tim Wallach	.10	.05	.01
□ 485 Randy Milligan	.10	.05	.01
□ 486 Walt Weiss	.10	.05	.01
□ 487 Matt Walbeck	.10	.05	.01
□ 488 Mike Macfarlane	.10	.05	.01
□ 489 Jerry Browne	.10	.05	.01
□ 490 Chris Sabo	.10	.05	.01
□ 491 Tim Belcher	.10	.05	.01
□ 492 Spike Owen	.10	.05	.01
□ 493 Rafael Palmeiro	.50	.23	.06
□ 494 Brian Harper	.10	.05	.01
□ 495 Eddie Murray	.75	.35	.09
□ 496 Ellis Burks	.25	.11	.03
□ 497 Karl Rhodes	.10	.05	.01
□ 498 Otis Nixon	.10	.05	.01
□ 499 Lee Smith	.25	.11	.03
□ 500 Bip Roberts	.10	.05	.01
□ 501 Pedro Martinez	.50	.23	.06
□ 502 Brian Hunter	.10	.05	.01
□ 503 Tyler Green	.10	.05	.01
□ 504 Bruce Hurst	.10	.05	.01
□ 505 Alex Gonzalez	.25	.11	.03
□ 506 Mark Portugal	.10	.05	.01
□ 507 Bob Ojeda	.10	.05	.01
□ 508 Dave Henderson	.10	.05	.01
□ 509 Bo Jackson	.50	.23	.06
□ 510 Bret Boone	.25	.11	.03
□ 511 Mark Eichhorn	.10	.05	.01
□ 512 Luis Polonia	.10	.05	.01
□ 513 Will Clark	.50	.23	.06
□ 514 Dave Valle	.10	.05	.01
□ 515 Dan Wilson	.25	.11	.03
□ 516 Dennis Martinez	.25	.11	.03
□ 517 Jim Leyritz	.10	.05	.01
□ 518 Howard Johnson	.10	.05	.01
□ 519 Jody Reed	.10	.05	.01
□ 520 Julio Franco	.25	.11	.03
□ 521 Jeff Reardon	.25	.11	.03
□ 522 Willie Greene	.25	.11	.03
□ 523 Shawon Dunston	.10	.05	.01
□ 524 Keith Mitchell	.10	.05	.01
□ 525 Rick Helling	.10	.05	.01
□ 526 Mark Kiefer	.10	.05	.01
□ 527 Chan Ho Park	.75	.35	.09
□ 528 Tony Longmire	.10	.05	.01
□ 529 Rich Becker	.25	.11	.03
□ 530 Tim Hyers	.10	.05	.01
□ 531 Darrin Jackson	.10	.05	.01
□ 532 Jack Morris	.25	.11	.03
□ 533 Rick White	.10	.05	.01
□ 534 Mike Kelly	.10	.05	.01
□ 535 James Mouton	.25	.11	.03
□ 536 Steve Trachsel	.25	.11	.03
□ 537 Tony Eusebio	.10	.05	.01
□ 538 Kelly Stinnett	.10	.05	.01
□ 539 Paul Spoljaric	.10	.05	.01
□ 540 Darren Dreifort	.25	.11	.03
□ SR1 C.Delgado Super Rook	10.00	4.50	1.25

1994 Pinnacle Rookie Team Pinnacle

These nine double-front standard-size cards of the "Rookie Team Pinnacle" set feature a top AL and a top NL rookie prospect by position. The insertion rate for these is one per 48 packs. These special portrait cards were painted by artists Christopher Greco and Ron DeFelice. The front features the National League player and card number. Both sides contain a gold Rookie Team Pinnacle logo.

	MINT	NRMT	EXC
COMPLETE SET (9)	100.00	45.00	12.50
COMMON PAIR (1-9)	5.00	2.20	.60
SEMISTARS	10.00	4.50	1.25
INSERTS IN SER.1 HOBBY AND RETAIL PACKS			

□ 1 Carlos Delgado Javier Lopez	12.00	5.50	1.50
□ 2 Bob Hamelin J.R. Phillips	5.00	2.20	.60
□ 3 Jon Shave Keith Kessinger	5.00	2.20	.60
□ 4 Luis Ortiz Butch Huskey	10.00	4.50	1.25
□ 5 Kurt Abbott Chipper Jones	40.00	18.00	5.00
□ 6 Manny Ramirez Rondell White	20.00	9.00	2.50
□ 7 Jeffrey Hammonds Cliff Floyd	10.00	4.50	1.25
□ 8 Marc Newfield Nigel Wilson	10.00	4.50	1.25
□ 9 Mark Hutton Salomon Torres	5.00	2.20	.60

1994 Pinnacle Run Creators

Randomly inserted at an approximate rate of one in four jumbo packs, this 22-card standard-size set spotlights top run producers. The play-

er stands out from a solid background on front. His last name and the Pinnacle logo run up the right border in gold foil. The Run Creators logo is at bottom center. A solid colored back contains the team logo as background to statistical highlights including runs created.

	MINT	NRMT	EXC
COMPLETE SET (44)	150.00	70.00	19.00
COMPLETE SERIES 1 (22)	90.00	40.00	11.00
COMPLETE SERIES 2 (22)	60.00	27.00	7.50
COMMON CARD (RC1-RC44)	1.00	.45	.12
SEMISTARS	2.50	1.10	.30
RANDOM INSERTS IN JUMBO PACKS			

	MINT	NRMT	EXC
□ RC1 John Olerud	1.50	.70	.19
□ RC2 Frank Thomas	20.00	9.00	2.50
□ RC3 Ken Griffey Jr.	20.00	9.00	2.50
□ RC4 Paul Molitor	4.00	1.80	.50
□ RC5 Rafael Palmeiro	2.00	.90	.25
□ RC6 Roberto Alomar	5.00	2.20	.60
□ RC7 Juan Gonzalez	10.00	4.50	1.25
□ RC8 Albert Belle	10.00	4.50	1.25
□ RC9 Travis Fryman	2.00	.90	.25
□ RC10 Rickey Henderson	2.00	.90	.25
□ RC11 Tony Phillips	1.00	.45	.12
□ RC12 Mo Vaughn	5.00	2.20	.60
□ RC13 Tim Salmon	3.00	1.35	.35
□ RC14 Kenny Lofton	6.00	2.70	.75
□ RC15 Carlos Baerga	2.00	.90	.25
□ RC16 Greg Vaughn	2.00	.90	.25
□ RC17 Jay Buhner	2.00	.90	.25
□ RC18 Chris Hoiles	1.00	.45	.12
□ RC19 Mickey Tettleton	1.50	.70	.19
□ RC20 Kirby Puckett	6.00	2.70	.75
□ RC21 Danny Tartabull	1.50	.70	.19
□ RC22 Devon White	1.50	.70	.19
□ RC23 Barry Bonds	5.00	2.20	.60
□ RC24 Lenny Dykstra	1.50	.70	.19
□ RC25 John Kruk	1.50	.70	.19
□ RC26 Fred McGriff	2.00	.90	.25
□ RC27 Gregg Jefferies	2.00	.90	.25
□ RC28 Mike Piazza	12.00	5.50	1.50
□ RC29 Jeff Blauser	1.00	.45	.12
□ RC30 Andres Galarraga	2.00	.90	.25
□ RC31 Darren Daulton	1.50	.70	.19
□ RC32 Dave Justice	1.50	.70	.19
□ RC33 Craig Biggio	2.00	.90	.25
□ RC34 Mark Grace	2.00	.90	.25
□ RC35 Tony Gwynn	8.00	3.60	1.00
□ RC36 Jeff Bagwell	8.00	3.60	1.00
□ RC37 Jay Bell	1.00	.45	.12
□ RC38 Marquis Grissom	2.00	.90	.25
□ RC39 Matt Williams	2.00	.90	.25
□ RC40 Charlie Hayes	1.00	.45	.12
□ RC41 Dante Bichette	2.00	.90	.25
□ RC42 Bernard Gilkey	2.00	.90	.25
□ RC43 Brett Butler	1.50	.70	.19
□ RC44 Rick Wilkins	1.00	.45	.12

1994 Pinnacle Team Pinnacle

Identical in design to the Rookie Team Pinnacle set, these double-front cards feature top players from each of the nine positions. Randomly inserted in second series hobby and retail packs at a rate of one in 48, these special portrait cards were painted by artists Christopher Greco and Ron DeFelice. The front features the National League player and card number. Both sides contain a gold Team Pinnacle logo.

	MINT	NRMT	EXC
COMPLETE SET (9)	200.00	90.00	25.00
COMMON PAIR (1-9)	8.00	3.60	1.00
INSERTS IN SER.2 HOBBY AND RETAIL PACKS			

	MINT	NRMT	EXC
□ 1 Jeff Bagwell Frank Thomas	70.00	32.00	8.75
□ 2 Carlos Baerga Robby Thompson	12.00	5.50	1.50
□ 3 Matt Williams Dean Palmer	8.00	3.60	1.00
□ 4 Cal Ripken Jr. Jay Bell	35.00	16.00	4.40
□ 5 Ivan Rodriguez Mike Piazza	30.00	13.50	3.70
□ 6 Lenny Dykstra Ken Griffey Jr.	40.00	18.00	5.00
□ 7 Juan Gonzalez Barry Bonds	30.00	13.50	3.70
□ 8 Tim Salmon Dave Justice	8.00	3.60	1.00
□ 9 Greg Maddux Jack McDowell	30.00	13.50	3.70

1994 Pinnacle Tribute

Randomly inserted in hobby packs at a rate of one in 18, this 18-card set was issued in two series of nine. Showcasing some of the top superstar veterans, the fronts have a color player photo with "Tribute" up the left border in a black stripe. The player's name appears at the bottom with a notation given to describe the player. The backs are primarily black with a close-up photo of the player. The cards are numbered with a TR prefix.

	MINT	NRMT	EXC
COMPLETE SET (18)	100.00	45.00	12.50
COMPLETE SERIES 1 (9)	30.00	13.50	3.70
COMPLETE SERIES 2 (9)	70.00	32.00	8.75
COMMON CARD (TR1-TR18)	1.00	.45	.12
SEMISTARS	2.50	1.10	.30
RANDOM INSERTS IN HOBBY PACKS			

	MINT	NRMT	EXC
□ TR1 Paul Molitor	4.00	1.80	.50
□ TR2 Jim Abbott	2.50	1.10	.30
□ TR3 Dave Winfield	2.50	1.10	.30
□ TR4 Bo Jackson	2.50	1.10	.30
□ TR5 David Justice	2.50	1.10	.30
□ TR6 Len Dykstra	2.50	1.10	.30
□ TR7 Mike Piazza	12.00	5.50	1.50
□ TR8 Barry Bonds	5.00	2.20	.60
□ TR9 Randy Johnson	3.00	1.35	.35
□ TR10 Ozzie Smith	4.00	1.80	.50
□ TR11 Mark Whiten	1.00	.45	.12
□ TR12 Greg Maddux	12.00	5.50	1.50
□ TR13 Cal Ripken Jr.	15.00	6.75	1.85
□ TR14 Frank Thomas	20.00	9.00	2.50
□ TR15 Juan Gonzalez	10.00	4.50	1.25
□ TR16 Roberto Alomar	5.00	2.20	.60

□ TR17 Ken Griffey Jr.	20.00	9.00	2.50
□ TR18 Lee Smith	2.50	1.10	.30

1995 Pinnacle

This 450-card standard-size set was issued in two series of 225 cards. They were released in 12-card packs, 24 packs to a box and 18 boxes in a case. The full-bleed fronts feature action photos. The player's last name is printed in black ink against a gold foil background. The horizontal backs feature a portrait, an action shot and brief text about the player's career. Seasonal and career stats are on the bottom. Rookie Cards in this set include Scott Elarton and Antone Williamson.

	MINT	NRMT	EXC
COMPLETE SET (450)	40.00	18.00	5.00
COMPLETE SERIES 1 (225)	20.00	9.00	2.50
COMPLETE SERIES 2 (225)	20.00	9.00	2.50
COMMON CARD (1-450)	.10	.05	.01
SEMISTARS	.25	.11	.03
STARS	.50	.23	.06
COMP.MUSEUM SET (450)	600.00	275.00	75.00
COMP.MUSEUM SER.1 (225)	300.00	135.00	38.00
COMP.MUSEUM SER.2 (225)	300.00	135.00	38.00
COMMON MUSEUM (1-450)	1.00	.45	.12
TRADE (410/413/416/420)	3.00	1.35	.35
TRADE (423/426/444)	3.00	1.35	.35
MUSEUM SEMISTARS	2.50	1.10	.30
MUSEUM STARS	6.00	2.70	.75
*MUSEUM STARS: 5X to 10X BASIC CARDS			
*MUSEUM YOUNG STARS: 4X to 8X BASIC CARDS			
MUSEUM: RANDOM INS.IN BOTH SERIES PACKS 1600.00			
700.00	200.00		
COMP.AP SERIES 1 (225)	800.00	350.00	100.00
COMP.AP SERIES 2 (225)	800.00	350.00	100.00
COMMON AP (1-450)	2.50	1.10	.30
AP SEMISTARS	5.00	2.20	.60
AP STARS	10.00	4.50	1.25
*AP VETERAN STARS: 18X TO 30X HI			
*AP YOUNG STARS: 15X TO 25X HI			
AP/MUSEUM: INSERTS IN HOB/RET PACKS			

□ 1 Jeff Bagwell	1.25	.55	.16
□ 2 Roger Clemens	.50	.23	.06
□ 3 Mark Whiten	.10	.05	.01
□ 4 Shawon Dunston	.10	.05	.01
□ 5 Bobby Bonilla	.25	.11	.03
□ 6 Kevin Tapani	.10	.05	.01
□ 7 Eric Karros	.25	.11	.03
□ 8 Cliff Floyd	.25	.11	.03
□ 9 Pat Kelly	.10	.05	.01
□ 10 Jeffrey Hammonds	.25	.11	.03
□ 11 Jeff Conine	.50	.23	.06
□ 12 Fred McGriff	.50	.23	.06
□ 13 Chris Bosio	.10	.05	.01
□ 14 Mike Mussina	.60	.25	.07
□ 15 Danny Bautista	.10	.05	.01
□ 16 Mickey Morandini	.10	.05	.01
□ 17 Chuck Finley	.25	.11	.03
□ 18 Jim Thome	.60	.25	.07
□ 19 Luis Ortiz	.10	.05	.01
□ 20 Walt Weiss	.10	.05	.01
□ 21 Don Mattingly	1.50	.70	.19
□ 22 Bob Hamelin	.10	.05	.01
□ 23 Melido Perez	.10	.05	.01
□ 24 Keith Mitchell	.10	.05	.01
□ 25 John Smoltz	.50	.23	.06
□ 26 Hector Carrasco	.10	.05	.01
□ 27 Pat Hentgen	.25	.11	.03
□ 28 Derrick May	.10	.05	.01
□ 29 Mike Kingery	.10	.05	.01
□ 30 Chuck Carr	.10	.05	.01
□ 31 Billy Ashley	.10	.05	.01
□ 32 Todd Hundley	.25	.11	.03
□ 33 Luis Gonzalez	.10	.05	.01
□ 34 Marquis Grissom	.50	.23	.06
□ 35 Jeff King	.25	.11	.03
□ 36 Eddie Williams	.10	.05	.01
□ 37 Tom Pagnozzi	.10	.05	.01
□ 38 Chris Hoiles	.10	.05	.01
□ 39 Sandy Alomar Jr.	.10	.05	.01
□ 40 Mike Greenwell	.10	.05	.01
□ 41 Lance Johnson	.25	.11	.03
□ 42 Junior Felix	.10	.05	.01
□ 43 Felix Jose	.10	.05	.01
□ 44 Scott Leius	.10	.05	.01
□ 45 Ruben Sierra	.25	.11	.03
□ 46 Kevin Seitzer	.10	.05	.01
□ 47 Wade Boggs	.50	.23	.06
□ 48 Reggie Jefferson	.25	.11	.03
□ 49 Jose Canseco	.50	.23	.06
□ 50 David Justice	.50	.23	.06
□ 51 John Smiley	.10	.05	.01
□ 52 Joe Carter	.50	.23	.06
□ 53 Rick Wilkins	.10	.05	.01
□ 54 Ellis Burks	.50	.23	.06
□ 55 Dave Weathers	.10	.05	.01
□ 56 Pedro Astacio	.10	.05	.01
□ 57 Ryan Thompson	.10	.05	.01
□ 58 James Mouton	.10	.05	.01
□ 59 Mel Rojas	.10	.05	.01
□ 60 Orlando Merced	.10	.05	.01
□ 61 Matt Williams	.50	.23	.06
□ 62 Bernard Gilkey	.25	.11	.03
□ 63 J.R. Phillips	.10	.05	.01
□ 64 Lee Smith	.25	.11	.03
□ 65 Jim Edmonds	.50	.23	.06
□ 66 Darrin Jackson	.10	.05	.01
□ 67 Scott Cooper	.10	.05	.01
□ 68 Ron Karkovice	.10	.05	.01
□ 69 Chris Gomez	.10	.05	.01
□ 70 Kevin Appier	.25	.11	.03
□ 71 Bobby Jones	.25	.11	.03
□ 72 Doug Drabek	.10	.05	.01
□ 73 Matt Mieske	.25	.11	.03
□ 74 Sterling Hitchcock	.25	.11	.03
□ 75 John Valentin	.25	.11	.03
□ 76 Reggie Sanders	.25	.11	.03
□ 77 Wally Joyner	.25	.11	.03
□ 78 Turk Wendell	.10	.05	.01
□ 79 Charlie Hayes	.10	.05	.01
□ 80 Bret Barberie	.10	.05	.01
□ 81 Troy Neel	.10	.05	.01
□ 82 Ken Caminiti	.50	.23	.06
□ 83 Milt Thompson	.10	.05	.01
□ 84 Paul Sorrento	.10	.05	.01
□ 85 Trevor Hoffman	.10	.05	.01
□ 86 Jay Bell	.25	.11	.03
□ 87 Mark Portugal	.10	.05	.01
□ 88 Sid Fernandez	.10	.05	.01
□ 89 Charles Nagy	.25	.11	.03
□ 90 Jeff Montgomery	.25	.11	.03
□ 91 Chuck Knoblauch	.50	.23	.06
□ 92 Jeff Frye	.10	.05	.01
□ 93 Tony Gwynn	1.25	.55	.16
□ 94 John Olerud	.10	.05	.01
□ 95 David Nied	.10	.05	.01
□ 96 Chris Hammond	.10	.05	.01
□ 97 Edgar Martinez	.50	.23	.06
□ 98 Kevin Stocker	.10	.05	.01
□ 99 Jeff Fassero	.10	.05	.01
□ 100 Curt Schilling	.10	.05	.01
□ 101 Dave Clark	.10	.05	.01
□ 102 Delino DeShields	.10	.05	.01
□ 103 Leo Gomez	.10	.05	.01
□ 104 Dave Hollins	.10	.05	.01
□ 105 Tim Naehring	.10	.05	.01
□ 106 Otis Nixon	.10	.05	.01
□ 107 Ozzie Guillen	.10	.05	.01
□ 108 Jose Lind	.10	.05	.01
□ 109 Stan Javier	.10	.05	.01
□ 110 Greg Vaughn	.25	.11	.03

□ 111	Chipper Jones	2.00	.90	.25
□ 112	Ed Sprague	.25	.11	.03
□ 113	Mike Macfarlane	.10	.05	.01
□ 114	Steve Finley	.25	.11	.03
□ 115	Ken Hill	.10	.05	.01
□ 116	Carlos Garcia	.10	.05	.01
□ 117	Lou Whitaker	.50	.23	.06
□ 118	Todd Zeile	.10	.05	.01
□ 119	Gary Sheffield	.50	.23	.06
□ 120	Ben McDonald	.10	.05	.01
□ 121	Pete Harnisch	.10	.05	.01
□ 122	Ivan Rodriguez	.60	.25	.07
□ 123	Wilson Alvarez	.25	.11	.03
□ 124	Travis Fryman	.25	.11	.03
□ 125	Pedro Munoz	.10	.05	.01
□ 126	Mark Lemke	.10	.05	.01
□ 127	Jose Valentin	.25	.11	.03
□ 128	Ken Griffey Jr.	3.00	1.35	.35
□ 129	Omar Vizquel	.50	.23	.06
□ 130	Milt Cuyler	.10	.05	.01
□ 131	Steve Trachsel	.10	.05	.01
□ 132	Alex Rodriguez	4.00	1.80	.50
□ 133	Garret Anderson	.50	.23	.06
□ 134	Armando Benitez	.10	.05	.01
□ 135	Shawn Green	.25	.11	.03
□ 136	Jorge Fabregas	.10	.05	.01
□ 137	Orlando Miller	.10	.05	.01
□ 138	Rikkert Faneyte	.10	.05	.01
□ 139	Ismael Valdes	.25	.11	.03
□ 140	Jose Oliva	.10	.05	.01
□ 141	Aaron Small	.10	.05	.01
□ 142	Tim Davis	.10	.05	.01
□ 143	Ricky Bottalico	.25	.11	.03
□ 144	Mike Matheny	.10	.05	.01
□ 145	Roberto Petagine	.10	.05	.01
□ 146	Fausto Cruz	.10	.05	.01
□ 147	Bryce Florie	.10	.05	.01
□ 148	Jose Lima	.10	.05	.01
□ 149	John Hudek	.10	.05	.01
□ 150	Duane Singleton	.10	.05	.01
□ 151	John Mabry	.50	.23	.06
□ 152	Robert Eenhoorn	.10	.05	.01
□ 153	Jon Lieber	.10	.05	.01
□ 154	Garey Ingram	.10	.05	.01
□ 155	Paul Shuey	.10	.05	.01
□ 156	Mike Lieberthal	.10	.05	.01
□ 157	Steve Dunn	.10	.05	.01
□ 158	Charles Johnson	.25	.11	.03
□ 159	Ernie Young	.25	.11	.03
□ 160	Jose Martinez	.10	.05	.01
□ 161	Kurt Miller	.10	.05	.01
□ 162	Joey Eischen	.10	.05	.01
□ 163	Dave Stevens	.10	.05	.01
□ 164	Brian L.Hunter	.50	.23	.06
□ 165	Jeff Cirillo	.25	.11	.03
□ 166	Mark Smith	.10	.05	.01
□ 167	McKay Christensen	.25	.11	.03
□ 168	C.J. Nitkowski	.25	.11	.03
□ 169	Antone Williamson	.50	.23	.06
□ 170	Paul Konerko	2.50	1.10	.30
□ 171	Scott Elarton	.50	.23	.06
□ 172	Jacob Shumate	.25	.11	.03
□ 173	Terrence Long	.25	.11	.03
□ 174	Mark Johnson	.25	.11	.03
□ 175	Ben Grieve	1.25	.55	.16
□ 176	Jayson Peterson	.25	.11	.03
□ 177	Checklist	.10	.05	.01
□ 178	Checklist	.10	.05	.01
□ 179	Checklist	.10	.05	.01
□ 180	Checklist	.10	.05	.01
□ 181	Brian Anderson	.10	.05	.01
□ 182	Steve Buechele	.10	.05	.01
□ 183	Mark Clark	.10	.05	.01
□ 184	Cecil Fielder	.25	.11	.03
□ 185	Steve Avery	.25	.11	.03
□ 186	Devon White	.25	.11	.03
□ 187	Craig Shipley	.10	.05	.01
□ 188	Brady Anderson	.50	.23	.06
□ 189	Kenny Lofton	.75	.35	.09
□ 190	Alex Cole	.10	.05	.01
□ 191	Brent Gates	.10	.05	.01
□ 192	Dean Palmer	.25	.11	.03
□ 193	Alex Gonzalez	.10	.05	.01
□ 194	Steve Cooke	.10	.05	.01
□ 195	Ray Lankford	.50	.23	.06
□ 196	Mark McGwire	1.00	.45	.12
□ 197	Marc Newfield	.25	.11	.03
□ 198	Pat Rapp	.10	.05	.01
□ 199	Darren Lewis	.10	.05	.01
□ 200	Carlos Baerga	.50	.23	.06
□ 201	Rickey Henderson	.50	.23	.06
□ 202	Kurt Abbott	.10	.05	.01
□ 203	Kirt Manwaring	.10	.05	.01
□ 204	Cal Ripken	2.50	1.10	.30
□ 205	Darren Daulton	.25	.11	.03
□ 206	Greg Colbrunn	.10	.05	.01
□ 207	Darryl Hamilton	.10	.05	.01
□ 208	Bo Jackson	.50	.23	.06
□ 209	Tony Phillips	.25	.11	.03
□ 210	Geronimo Berroa	.10	.05	.01
□ 211	Rich Becker	.10	.05	.01
□ 212	Tony Tarasco	.10	.05	.01
□ 213	Karl Rhodes	.10	.05	.01
□ 214	Phil Plantier	.10	.05	.01
□ 215	J.T. Snow	.25	.11	.03
□ 216	Mo Vaughn	.75	.35	.09
□ 217	Greg Gagne	.10	.05	.01
□ 218	Ricky Bones	.10	.05	.01
□ 219	Mike Bordick	.10	.05	.01
□ 220	Chad Curtis	.10	.05	.01
□ 221	Royce Clayton	.10	.05	.01
□ 222	Roberto Alomar	.75	.35	.09
□ 223	Jose Rijo	.10	.05	.01
□ 224	Ryan Klesko	.60	.25	.07
□ 225	Mark Langston	.10	.05	.01
□ 226	Frank Thomas	3.00	1.35	.35
□ 227	Juan Gonzalez	1.50	.70	.19
□ 228	Ron Gant	.25	.11	.03
□ 229	Javier Lopez	.50	.23	.06
□ 230	Sammy Sosa	.50	.23	.06
□ 231	Kevin Brown	.25	.11	.03
□ 232	Gary DiSarcina	.10	.05	.01
□ 233	Albert Belle	1.50	.70	.19
□ 234	Jay Buhner	.50	.23	.06
□ 235	Pedro J.Martinez	.25	.11	.03
□ 236	Bob Tewksbury	.10	.05	.01
□ 237	Mike Piazza	2.00	.90	.25
□ 238	Darryl Kile	.10	.05	.01
□ 239	Bryan Harvey	.10	.05	.01
□ 240	Andres Galarraga	.50	.23	.06
□ 241	Jeff Blauser	.10	.05	.01
□ 242	Jeff Kent	.10	.05	.01
□ 243	Bobby Munoz	.10	.05	.01
□ 244	Greg Maddux	2.00	.90	.25
□ 245	Paul O'Neill	.25	.11	.03
□ 246	Lenny Dykstra	.25	.11	.03
□ 247	Todd Van Poppel	.10	.05	.01
□ 248	Bernie Williams	.50	.23	.06
□ 249	Glenallen Hill	.10	.05	.01
□ 250	Duane Ward	.10	.05	.01
□ 251	Dennis Eckersley	.25	.11	.03
□ 252	Pat Mahomes	.10	.05	.01
□ 253	Rusty Greer	.50	.23	.06
□ 254	Roberto Kelly	.10	.05	.01
□ 255	Randy Myers	.10	.05	.01
□ 256	Scott Ruffcorn	.10	.05	.01
□ 257	Robin Ventura	.25	.11	.03
□ 258	Eduardo Perez	.10	.05	.01
□ 259	Aaron Sele	.25	.11	.03
□ 260	Paul Molitor	.60	.25	.07
□ 261	Juan Guzman	.25	.11	.03
□ 262	Darren Oliver	.25	.11	.03
□ 263	Mike Stanley	.10	.05	.01
□ 264	Tom Glavine	.50	.23	.06
□ 265	Rico Brogna	.10	.05	.01
□ 266	Craig Biggio	.50	.23	.06
□ 267	Darrell Whitmore	.10	.05	.01
□ 268	Jimmy Key	.25	.11	.03
□ 269	Will Clark	.50	.23	.06
□ 270	David Cone	.25	.11	.03
□ 271	Brian Jordan	.50	.23	.06
□ 272	Barry Bonds	.75	.35	.09
□ 273	Danny Tartabull	.10	.05	.01
□ 274	Ramon J.Martinez	.25	.11	.03
□ 275	Al Martin	.25	.11	.03
□ 276	Fred McGriff SM	.25	.11	.03
□ 277	Carlos Delgado SM	.25	.11	.03
□ 278	Juan Gonzalez SM	.75	.35	.09
□ 279	Shawn Green SM	.10	.05	.01
□ 280	Carlos Baerga SM	.25	.11	.03
□ 281	Cliff Floyd SM	.10	.05	.01
□ 282	Ozzie Smith SM	.50	.23	.06

□ 283 Alex Rodriguez SM	2.00	.90	.25
□ 284 Kenny Lofton SM	.50	.23	.06
□ 285 Dave Justice SM	.25	.11	.03
□ 286 Tim Salmon SM	.25	.11	.03
□ 287 Manny Ramirez SM	.50	.23	.06
□ 288 Will Clark SM	.25	.11	.03
□ 289 Garret Anderson SM	.25	.11	.03
□ 290 Billy Ashley SM	.10	.05	.01
□ 291 Tony Gwynn SM	.60	.25	.07
□ 292 Raul Mondesi SM	.25	.11	.03
□ 293 Rafael Palmeiro SM	.25	.11	.03
□ 294 Matt Williams SM	.25	.11	.03
□ 295 Don Mattingly SM	.75	.35	.09
□ 296 Kirby Puckett SM	.50	.23	.06
□ 297 Paul Molitor SM	.50	.23	.06
□ 298 Albert Belle SM	.75	.35	.09
□ 299 Barry Bonds SM	.50	.23	.06
□ 300 Mike Piazza SM	1.00	.45	.12
□ 301 Jeff Bagwell SM	.60	.25	.07
□ 302 Frank Thomas SM	1.50	.70	.19
□ 303 Chipper Jones SM	1.00	.45	.12
□ 304 Ken Griffey Jr. SM	1.50	.70	.19
□ 305 Cal Ripken Jr. SM	1.25	.55	.16
□ 306 Eric Anthony	.10	.05	.01
□ 307 Todd Benzinger	.10	.05	.01
□ 308 Jacob Brumfield	.10	.05	.01
□ 309 Wes Chamberlain	.10	.05	.01
□ 310 Tino Martinez	.25	.11	.03
□ 311 Roberto Mejia	.10	.05	.01
□ 312 Jose Offerman	.10	.05	.01
□ 313 David Segui	.10	.05	.01
□ 314 Eric Young	.25	.11	.03
□ 315 Rey Sanchez	.10	.05	.01
□ 316 Raul Mondesi	.50	.23	.06
□ 317 Bret Boone	.25	.11	.03
□ 318 Andre Dawson	.50	.23	.06
□ 319 Brian McRae	.25	.11	.03
□ 320 Dave Nilsson	.25	.11	.03
□ 321 Moises Alou	.25	.11	.03
□ 322 Don Slaught	.10	.05	.01
□ 323 Dave McCarty	.10	.05	.01
□ 324 Mike Huff	.10	.05	.01
□ 325 Rick Aguilera	.10	.05	.01
□ 326 Rod Beck	.10	.05	.01
□ 327 Kenny Rogers	.10	.05	.01
□ 328 Andy Benes	.10	.05	.01
□ 329 Allen Watson	.10	.05	.01
□ 330 Randy Johnson	.50	.23	.06
□ 331 Willie Greene	.10	.05	.01
□ 332 Hal Morris	.10	.05	.01
□ 333 Ozzie Smith	.60	.25	.07
□ 334 Jason Bere	.10	.05	.01
□ 335 Scott Erickson	.10	.05	.01
□ 336 Dante Bichette	.50	.23	.06
□ 337 Willie Banks	.10	.05	.01
□ 338 Eric Davis	.25	.11	.03
□ 339 Rondell White	.50	.23	.06
□ 340 Kirby Puckett	1.00	.45	.12
□ 341 Deion Sanders	.50	.23	.06
□ 342 Eddie Murray	.75	.35	.09
□ 343 Mike Harkey	.10	.05	.01
□ 344 Joey Hamilton	.25	.11	.03
□ 345 Roger Salkeld	.10	.05	.01
□ 346 Wil Cordero	.10	.05	.01
□ 347 John Wetteland	.25	.11	.03
□ 348 Geronimo Pena	.10	.05	.01
□ 349 Kirk Gibson	.25	.11	.03
□ 350 Manny Ramirez	.75	.35	.09
□ 351 Wm.VanLandingham	.10	.05	.01
□ 352 B.J. Surhoff	.25	.11	.03
□ 353 Ken Ryan	.10	.05	.01
□ 354 Terry Steinbach	.25	.11	.03
□ 355 Bret Saberhagen	.25	.11	.03
□ 356 John Jaha	.25	.11	.03
□ 357 Joe Girardi	.10	.05	.01
□ 358 Steve Karsay	.10	.05	.01
□ 359 Alex Fernandez	.25	.11	.03
□ 360 Salomon Torres	.10	.05	.01
□ 361 John Burkett	.25	.11	.03
□ 362 Derek Bell	.25	.11	.03
□ 363 Tom Henke	.10	.05	.01
□ 364 Gregg Jefferies	.25	.11	.03
□ 365 Jack McDowell	.25	.11	.03
□ 366 Andujar Cedeno	.10	.05	.01
□ 367 Dave Winfield	.50	.23	.06
□ 368 Carl Everett	.10	.05	.01

□ 369 Danny Jackson	.10	.05	.01
□ 370 Jeromy Burnitz	.10	.05	.01
□ 371 Mark Grace	.50	.23	.06
□ 372 Larry Walker	.50	.23	.06
□ 373 Bill Swift	.10	.05	.01
□ 374 Dennis Martinez	.25	.11	.03
□ 375 Mickey Tettleton	.10	.05	.01
□ 376 Mel Nieves	.25	.11	.03
□ 377 Cal Eldred	.10	.05	.01
□ 378 Orel Hershiser	.25	.11	.03
□ 379 David Wells	.10	.05	.01
□ 380 Gary Gaetti	.25	.11	.03
□ 381 Jeromy Burnitz	.10	.05	.01
□ 382 Barry Larkin	.50	.23	.06
□ 383 Jason Jacome	.10	.05	.01
□ 384 Tim Wallach	.10	.05	.01
□ 385 Robby Thompson	.10	.05	.01
□ 386 Frank Viola	.10	.05	.01
□ 387 Dave Stewart	.25	.11	.03
□ 388 Bip Roberts	.10	.05	.01
□ 389 Ron Darling	.10	.05	.01
□ 390 Carlos Delgado	.50	.23	.06
□ 391 Tim Salmon	.50	.23	.06
□ 392 Alan Trammell	.50	.23	.06
□ 393 Kevin Foster	.10	.05	.01
□ 394 Jim Abbott	.10	.05	.01
□ 395 John Kruk	.25	.11	.03
□ 396 Andy Van Slyke	.25	.11	.03
□ 397 Dave Magadan	.10	.05	.01
□ 398 Rafael Palmeiro	.50	.23	.06
□ 399 Mike Devereaux	.10	.05	.01
□ 400 Benito Santiago	.10	.05	.01
□ 401 Brett Butler	.25	.11	.03
□ 402 John Franco	.10	.05	.01
□ 403 Matt Walbeck	.10	.05	.01
□ 404 Terry Pendleton	.25	.11	.03
□ 405 Chris Sabo	.10	.05	.01
□ 406 Andrew Lorraine	.25	.11	.03
□ 407 Dan Wilson	.25	.11	.03
□ 408 Mike Lansing	.10	.05	.01
□ 409 Ray McDavid	.25	.11	.03
□ 410 Shane Andrews	.10	.05	.01
□ 411 Tom Gordon	.10	.05	.01
□ 412 Chad Ogea	.10	.05	.01
□ 413 James Baldwin	.50	.23	.06
□ 414 Russ Davis	.10	.05	.01
□ 415 Ray Holbert	.10	.05	.01
□ 416 Ray Durham	.25	.11	.03
□ 417 Matt Nokes	.10	.05	.01
□ 418 Rod Henderson	.10	.05	.01
□ 419 Gabe White	.10	.05	.01
□ 420 Todd Hollandsworth	.50	.23	.06
□ 421 Midre Cummings	.10	.05	.01
□ 422 Harold Baines	.25	.11	.03
□ 423 Troy Percival	.10	.05	.01
□ 424 Joe Vitiello	.10	.05	.01
□ 425 Andy Ashby	.25	.11	.03
□ 426 Michael Tucker	.25	.11	.03
□ 427 Mark Gubicza	.10	.05	.01
□ 428 Jim Bullinger	.10	.05	.01
□ 429 Jose Malave	.10	.05	.01
□ 430 Pete Schourek	.25	.11	.03
□ 431 Bobby Ayala	.10	.05	.01
□ 432 Marvin Freeman	.10	.05	.01
□ 433 Pat Listach	.10	.05	.01
□ 434 Eddie Taubensee	.10	.05	.01
□ 435 Steve Howe	.10	.05	.01
□ 436 Kent Mercker	.10	.05	.01
□ 437 Hector Fajardo	.10	.05	.01
□ 438 Scott Kamieniecki	.10	.05	.01
□ 439 Robb Nen	.10	.05	.01
□ 440 Mike Kelly	.10	.05	.01
□ 441 Tom Candiotti	.10	.05	.01
□ 442 Albie Lopez	.10	.05	.01
□ 443 Jeff Granger	.10	.05	.01
□ 444 Rich Aude	.10	.05	.01
□ 445 Luis Polonia	.10	.05	.01
□ 446 Frank Thomas CL	1.50	.70	.19
□ 447 Ken Griffey Jr. CL	1.50	.70	.19
□ 448 Mike Piazza CL	1.00	.45	.12
□ 449 Jeff Bagwell CL	.60	.25	.07
□ 450 Checklist Jeff Bagwell Frank Thomas Ken Griffey Jr. Mike Piazza	2.00	.90	.25

1995 Pinnacle ETA

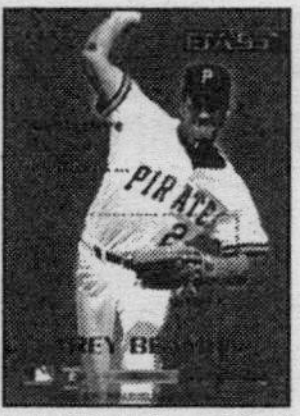

This six-card standard-sized set was randomly inserted approximately one in every 24 first series hobby packs. This set features players who were among the leading prospects for major league stardom. The fronts feature a player photo as well as a quick information bit. The player's name is located on the top. The busy full-bleed backs feature a player photo and some quick comments. On the bottom is the player's name and the card is numbered with an "ETA" prefix in the upper left corner.

	MINT	NRMT	EXC
COMPLETE SET (6)	25.00	11.00	3.10
COMMON CARD (1-6)	2.50	1.10	.30
RANDOM INSERTS IN HOBBY PACKS			

	MINT	NRMT	EXC
□ 1 Ben Grieve	15.00	6.75	1.85
□ 2 Alex Ochoa	4.00	1.80	.50
□ 3 Joe Vitiello	2.50	1.10	.30
□ 4 Johnny Damon	8.00	3.60	1.00
□ 5 Trey Beamon	4.00	1.80	.50
□ 6 Brooks Kieschnick	4.00	1.80	.50

1995 Pinnacle Gate Attractions

This 18-card standard-size set was inserted approximately one every 12 second series jumbo packs. The fronts feature two photos, with the words "Gate Attraction" at the bottom left. The player is identified on the top. The horizontal full-bleed backs have the player's name on the left, a player photo in the middle and some career information in the lower right. The cards are numbered with a "GA" prefix in the upper right corner.

	MINT	NRMT	EXC
COMPLETE SET (18)	125.00	55.00	15.50
COMMON CARD (GA1-GA18)	2.00	.90	.25
SEMISTARS	3.00	1.35	.35
RANDOM INSERTS IN SER.2 JUMBOS			

	MINT	NRMT	EXC
□ GA1 Ken Griffey Jr.	25.00	11.00	3.10
□ GA2 Frank Thomas	25.00	11.00	3.10
□ GA3 Cal Ripken	20.00	9.00	2.50
□ GA4 Jeff Bagwell	10.00	4.50	1.25
□ GA5 Mike Piazza	15.00	6.75	1.85
□ GA6 Barry Bonds	6.00	2.70	.75
□ GA7 Kirby Puckett	8.00	3.60	1.00
□ GA8 Albert Belle	12.00	5.50	1.50
□ GA9 Tony Gwynn	10.00	4.50	1.25
□ GA10 Raul Mondesi	2.00	.90	.25
□ GA11 Will Clark	3.00	1.35	.35
□ GA12 Don Mattingly	12.00	5.50	1.50
□ GA13 Roger Clemens	3.00	1.35	.35
□ GA14 Paul Molitor	5.00	2.20	.60
□ GA15 Matt Williams	3.00	1.35	.35
□ GA16 Greg Maddux	15.00	6.75	1.85
□ GA17 Kenny Lofton	6.00	2.70	.75
□ GA18 Cliff Floyd	2.00	.90	.25

1995 Pinnacle New Blood

This nine-card standard-size set was inserted approximately one in every 90 second series hobby and retail packs. This set features nine players who were leading prospects entering the 1995 season. The Dufex enhanced fronts feature two player photos. One photo is a color shot while the other one is a black and white background photo. The words "New Blood" and player's name are on the bottom. The full-bleed backs feature two more photos. Player information is set against these photos. The card is numbered with an "NB" prefix in the upper left corner.

	MINT	NRMT	EXC
COMPLETE SET (9)	120.00	55.00	15.00
COMMON CARD (NB1-NB9)	4.00	1.80	.50
RANDOM INSERTS IN PACKS			

	MINT	NRMT	EXC
□ NB1 Alex Rodriguez	75.00	34.00	9.50
□ NB2 Shawn Green	4.00	1.80	.50
□ NB3 Brian Hunter	10.00	4.50	1.25
□ NB4 Garret Anderson	5.00	2.20	.60
□ NB5 Charles Johnson	5.00	2.20	.60
□ NB6 Chipper Jones	50.00	22.00	6.25
□ NB7 Carlos Delgado	10.00	4.50	1.25
□ NB8 Billy Ashley	4.00	1.80	.50
□ NB9 J.R. Phillips UER Dodgers logo on back Phillips plays for the Giants	4.00	1.80	.50

1995 Pinnacle Performers

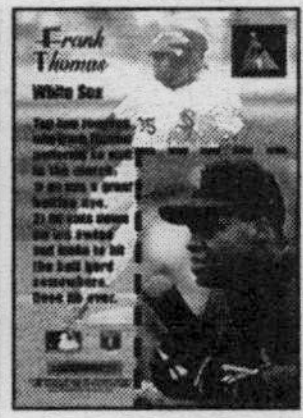

These 18 standard-size cards were randomly inserted approximately one in every 12 first series jumbo packs. The full-bleed fronts feature a player photo against a shiny background. The player's name is in white lettering in the

upper right corner. The backs have two photos: one a color portrait with the other one being a shaded black and white. There is also some text pertaining to that player. The cards are numbered in the upper right corner with a "PP" prefix.

	MINT	NRMT	EXC
COMPLETE SERIES 1 (18)	100.00	45.00	12.50
COMMON CARD (1-18)	2.00	.90	.25
SEMISTARS	4.00	1.80	.50
RANDOM INSERTS IN JUMBO PACKS			

□ PP1 Frank Thomas	30.00	13.50	3.70
□ PP2 Albert Belle	15.00	6.75	1.85
□ PP3 Barry Bonds	8.00	3.60	1.00
□ PP4 Juan Gonzalez	15.00	6.75	1.85
□ PP5 Andres Galarraga	4.00	1.80	.50
□ PP6 Raul Mondesi	4.00	1.80	.50
□ PP7 Paul Molitor	6.00	2.70	.75
□ PP8 Tim Salmon	4.00	1.80	.50
□ PP9 Mike Piazza	20.00	9.00	2.50
□ PP10 Gregg Jefferies	4.00	1.80	.50
□ PP11 Will Clark	4.00	1.80	.50
□ PP12 Greg Maddux	20.00	9.00	2.50
□ PP13 Manny Ramirez	8.00	3.60	1.00
□ PP14 Kirby Puckett	10.00	4.50	1.25
□ PP15 Shawn Green	2.00	.90	.25
□ PP16 Rafael Palmeiro	4.00	1.80	.50
□ PP17 Paul O'Neill	4.00	1.80	.50
□ PP18 Jason Bere	2.00	.90	.25

1995 Pinnacle Pin Redemption

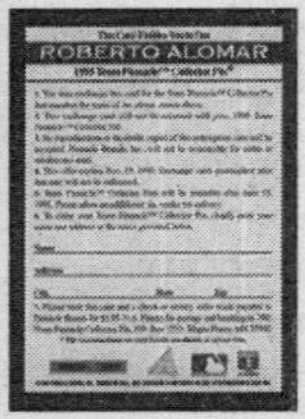

This 18-card standard-size set was randomly inserted in all second series packs. Printed odds indicate that these cards were inserted approximately one every in 48 hobby and retail packs and one in every 36 jumbo packs. The horizontal full-bleed fronts feature an action photo, a team logo and another small player photo. The backs explain the rules for ordering the "Team Pinnacle" Collector Pin. The offer expired on November 15, 1995.

	MINT	NRMT	EXC
COMPLETE SET (18)	80.00	36.00	10.00
COMMON CARD (1-18)	1.00	.45	.12
SEMISTARS	2.00	.90	.25
UNNUMBERED INSERTS IN SER.2 PACKS			

□ 1 Greg Maddux	10.00	4.50	1.25
□ 2 Mike Mussina	3.00	1.35	.35
□ 3 Mike Piazza	10.00	4.50	1.25
□ 4 Carlos Delgado	1.00	.45	.12
□ 5 Jeff Bagwell	6.00	2.70	.75
□ 6 Frank Thomas	15.00	6.75	1.85
□ 7 Craig Biggio	2.00	.90	.25
□ 8 Roberto Alomar	4.00	1.80	.50
□ 9 Ozzie Smith	3.00	1.35	.35
□ 10 Cal Ripken Jr.	12.00	5.50	1.50
□ 11 Matt Williams	2.00	.90	.25
□ 12 Travis Fryman	2.00	.90	.25
□ 13 Barry Bonds	4.00	1.80	.50
□ 14 Ken Griffey Jr.	15.00	6.75	1.85
□ 15 Dave Justice	1.00	.45	.12
□ 16 Albert Belle	8.00	3.60	1.00
□ 17 Tony Gwynn	6.00	2.70	.75
□ 18 Kirby Puckett	5.00	2.20	.60

1995 Pinnacle Red Hot/White Hot

This 25-card standard-size set was randomly inserted into second series packs. The Red Hots were inserted in both hobby and retail packs while the White Hots were only in hobby packs. The fronts feature a player photo on the right, with his name, an inset portrait and either the words "Red Hot" or "White Hot" on the left. The upper right corner has either an "r" or a "w" in a circle. The background is either white or red depending on the card. The backs have the words "Red Hot" or "White Hot" in the background with a player photo and some information set against it. The cards are numbered in the upper right corner with either a "WH" or a "RH" prefix.

	MINT	NRMT	EXC
COMPLETE SET (25)	80.00	36.00	10.00
COMMON CARD (1-25)	1.00	.45	.12
SEMISTARS	2.00	.90	.25
WHITE HOT: 2X TO 4X BASIC CARDS			
RED HOTS INSERTS IN SER.2 PACKS			
WHITE HOTS INSERTS IN SER.2 HOBBY PACKS			

□ 1 Cal Ripken Jr.	12.00	5.50	1.50
□ 2 Ken Griffey Jr.	15.00	6.75	1.85
□ 3 Frank Thomas	15.00	6.75	1.85
□ 4 Jeff Bagwell	6.00	2.70	.75
□ 5 Mike Piazza	10.00	4.50	1.25
□ 6 Barry Bonds	4.00	1.80	.50
□ 7 Albert Belle	8.00	3.60	1.00
□ 8 Tony Gwynn	6.00	2.70	.75
□ 9 Kirby Puckett	5.00	2.20	.60
□ 10 Don Mattingly	8.00	3.60	1.00
□ 11 Matt Williams	2.00	.90	.25
□ 12 Greg Maddux	10.00	4.50	1.25
□ 13 Raul Mondesi	1.00	.45	.12
□ 14 Paul Molitor	3.00	1.35	.35
□ 15 Manny Ramirez	4.00	1.80	.50
□ 16 Joe Carter	2.00	.90	.25
□ 17 Will Clark	2.00	.90	.25
□ 18 Roger Clemens	2.00	.90	.25
□ 19 Tim Salmon	2.00	.90	.25
□ 20 Dave Justice	1.00	.45	.12
□ 21 Kenny Lofton	4.00	1.80	.50
□ 22 Deion Sanders	2.00	.90	.25
□ 23 Roberto Alomar	4.00	1.80	.50
□ 24 Cliff Floyd	1.00	.45	.12
□ 25 Carlos Baerga	2.00	.90	.25

1995 Pinnacle Team Pinnacle

Randomly inserted in series one hobby and retail packs at a rate of one in 90, this nine-card standard-size set showcases the game's top players in an etched-foil design. A player photo is superimposed over the player's team logo. The Team Pinnacle logo, player's name and position are printed in silver foil on a black strip at the bottom left of the card. Cards are numbered with the prefix "TP".

	MINT	NRMT	EXC
COMPLETE SET (9)	250.00	110.00	31.00
COMMON CARD (1-9)	8.00	3.60	1.00
KEY SIDE DUFEX: 1.25X VALUE			
RANDOM INSERTS IN HOBBY AND RETAIL PACKS			

	MINT	NRMT	EXC
□ TP1 Mike Mussina / Greg Maddux	40.00	18.00	5.00
□ TP2 Carlos Delgado / Mike Piazza	30.00	13.50	3.70
□ TP3 Frank Thomas / Jeff Bagwell	60.00	27.00	7.50
□ TP4 Roberto Alomar / Craig Biggio	15.00	6.75	1.85
□ TP5 Cal Ripken / Ozzie Smith	50.00	22.00	6.25
□ TP6 Travis Fryman / Matt Williams	8.00	3.60	1.00
□ TP7 Ken Griffey Jr. / Barry Bonds	50.00	22.00	6.25
□ TP8 Albert Belle / David Justice	25.00	11.00	3.10
□ TP9 Kirby Puckett / Tony Gwynn	30.00	13.50	3.70

1995 Pinnacle Upstarts

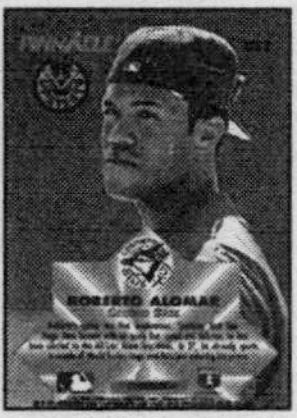

Top young players are featured in this 30-card standard-size set. The cards were randomly inserted in series one hobby and retail packs at a rate of one in eight. Multi-colored foil fronts feature the player in a action cutout set against a star background. The player's name is wrapped around the "Upstarts" logo which is printed on the lower left of the front. The player's team logo is printed at the top right of the front. Backs are full-bleed color action photos of the player and are numbered at the top right with the prefix "US". A gold polygonal box encloses the player's name and '94 stats along with the team logo. The Pinnacle and '95 Upstarts logo are printed on the top left of the back.

	MINT	NRMT	EXC
COMPLETE SET (30)	60.00	27.00	7.50
COMMON CARD (US1-US30)	1.00	.45	.12
SEMISTARS	2.50	1.10	.30
RANDOM INSERTS IN HOBBY AND RETAIL PACKS			

	MINT	NRMT	EXC
□ US1 Frank Thomas	20.00	9.00	2.50
□ US2 Roberto Alomar	5.00	2.20	.60
□ US3 Mike Piazza	12.00	5.50	1.50
□ US4 Javier Lopez	2.50	1.10	.30
□ US5 Albert Belle	10.00	4.50	1.25
□ US6 Carlos Delgado	2.50	1.10	.30
□ US7 Brent Gates	1.00	.45	.12
□ US8 Tim Salmon	2.50	1.10	.30
□ US9 Raul Mondesi	2.50	1.10	.30
□ US10 Juan Gonzalez	10.00	4.50	1.25
□ US11 Manny Ramirez	5.00	2.20	.60
□ US12 Sammy Sosa	3.00	1.35	.35
□ US13 Jeff Kent	1.00	.45	.12
□ US14 Melvin Nieves	1.00	.45	.12
□ US15 Rondell White	1.50	.70	.19
□ US16 Shawn Green	1.00	.45	.12
□ US17 Bernie Williams	2.50	1.10	.30
□ US18 Aaron Sele	1.00	.45	.12
□ US19 Jason Bere	1.50	.70	.19
□ US20 Joey Hamilton	1.50	.70	.19
□ US21 Mike Kelly	1.00	.45	.12
□ US22 Wil Cordero	1.00	.45	.12
□ US23 Moises Alou	1.50	.70	.19
□ US24 Roberto Kelly	1.00	.45	.12
□ US25 Deion Sanders	2.50	1.10	.30
□ US26 Steve Karsay	1.00	.45	.12
□ US27 Bret Boone	1.50	.70	.19
□ US28 Willie Greene	2.50	1.10	.30
□ US29 Billy Ashley	1.00	.45	.12
□ US30 Brian Anderson	1.00	.45	.12

1996 Pinnacle

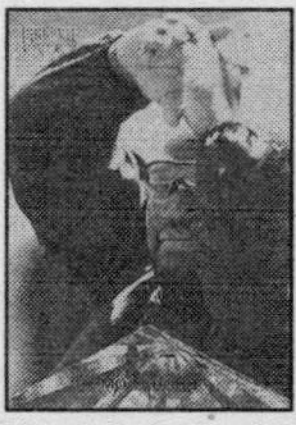

The 1996 Pinnacle set was issued in two separate series of 200 cards each. The 10-card packs retailed for $2.49. On 20-point card stock, the fronts feature full-bleed color action photos, bordered at the bottom by a gold foil triangle. The backs carry a color closeup photo, biography, and statistics. The Series I set features the following topical subsets: The Naturals (134-163), '95 Rookies (164-193) and Checklists (194-200). Series II set features these subsets: Hardball Heroes (30 cards), 300 Series (17 cards), Rookies (25 cards), and Checklists (7 cards). Numbering for the 300 Series subset was based on player's career batting average. At that time, both Paul Molitor and Jeff Bagwell had identical career batting averages of .305, thus Pinnacle numbered both of their 300 Series subset cards as 305. Do to this quirky numbering, the set only runs through card 399, but actually contains 400 cards. A special Cal Ripken Jr. Tribute card was inserted in Series I packs at the rate of one in 150.

	MINT	NRMT	EXC
COMPLETE SET (400)	30.00	13.50	3.70
COMPLETE SERIES 1 (200)	15.00	6.75	1.85
COMPLETE SERIES 2 (200)	15.00	6.75	1.85
COMMON CARD (1-399)	.10	.05	.01
SEMISTARS	.25	.11	.03
STARS	.50	.23	.06
COMPLETE FOIL SET (200)	25.00	11.00	3.10
*FOIL: 1.5X BASIC CARDS			
FOIL AVAIL.IN SER.2 RETAIL SUPER PACKS			

	MINT	NRMT	EXC
□ 1 Greg Maddux	2.00	.90	.25
□ 2 Bill Pulsipher	.25	.11	.03
□ 3 Dante Bichette	.50	.23	.06
□ 4 Mike Piazza	2.00	.90	.25
□ 5 Garret Anderson	.25	.11	.03
□ 6 Steve Finley	.25	.11	.03
□ 7 Andy Benes	.10	.05	.01
□ 8 Chuck Knoblauch	.50	.23	.06
□ 9 Tom Gordon	.10	.05	.01
□ 10 Jeff Bagwell	1.25	.55	.16
□ 11 Wil Cordero	.10	.05	.01
□ 12 John Mabry	.50	.23	.06
□ 13 Jeff Frye	.10	.05	.01
□ 14 Travis Fryman	.25	.11	.03
□ 15 John Wetteland	.25	.11	.03
□ 16 Jason Bates	.10	.05	.01
□ 17 Danny Tartabull	.10	.05	.01

□ 18 Charles Nagy	.10	.05	.01
□ 19 Robin Ventura	.25	.11	.03
□ 20 Reggie Sanders	.25	.11	.03
□ 21 Dave Clark	.10	.05	.01
□ 22 Jaime Navarro	.10	.05	.01
□ 23 Joey Hamilton	.10	.05	.01
□ 24 Al Leiter	.10	.05	.01
□ 25 Deion Sanders	.50	.23	.06
□ 26 Tim Salmon	.50	.23	.06
□ 27 Tino Martinez	.10	.05	.01
□ 28 Mike Greenwell	.10	.05	.01
□ 29 Phil Plantier	.10	.05	.01
□ 30 Bobby Bonilla	.25	.11	.03
□ 31 Kenny Rogers	.10	.05	.01
□ 32 Chili Davis	.10	.05	.01
□ 33 Joe Carter	.50	.23	.06
□ 34 Mike Mussina	.60	.25	.07
□ 35 Matt Mieske	.10	.05	.01
□ 36 Jose Canseco	.50	.23	.06
□ 37 Brad Radke	.10	.05	.01
□ 38 Juan Gonzalez	1.50	.70	.19
□ 39 David Segui	.10	.05	.01
□ 40 Alex Fernandez	.25	.11	.03
□ 41 Jeff Kent	.10	.05	.01
□ 42 Todd Zeile	.10	.05	.01
□ 43 Darryl Strawberry	.25	.11	.03
□ 44 Jose Rijo	.10	.05	.01
□ 45 Ramon Martinez	.10	.05	.01
□ 46 Manny Ramirez	.75	.35	.09
□ 47 Gregg Jefferies	.25	.11	.03
□ 48 Bryan Rekar	.10	.05	.01
□ 49 Jeff King	.10	.05	.01
□ 50 John Olerud	.10	.05	.01
□ 51 Marc Newfield	.25	.11	.03
□ 52 Charles Johnson	.25	.11	.03
□ 53 Robby Thompson	.10	.05	.01
□ 54 Brian L. Hunter	.10	.05	.01
□ 55 Mike Blowers	.10	.05	.01
□ 56 Keith Lockhart	.10	.05	.01
□ 57 Ray Lankford	.25	.11	.03
□ 58 Tim Wallach	.10	.05	.01
□ 59 Ivan Rodriguez	.60	.25	.07
□ 60 Ed Sprague	.25	.11	.03
□ 61 Paul Molitor	.60	.25	.07
□ 62 Eric Karros	.25	.11	.03
□ 63 Glenallen Hill	.10	.05	.01
□ 64 Jay Bell	.25	.11	.03
□ 65 Tom Pagnozzi	.10	.05	.01
□ 66 Greg Colbrunn	.10	.05	.01
□ 67 Edgar Martinez	.50	.23	.06
□ 68 Paul Sorrento	.10	.05	.01
□ 69 Kirt Manwaring	.10	.05	.01
□ 70 Pete Schourek	.25	.11	.03
□ 71 Orlando Merced	.10	.05	.01
□ 72 Shawon Dunston	.10	.05	.01
□ 73 Ricky Bottalico	.10	.05	.01
□ 74 Brady Anderson	.50	.23	.06
□ 75 Steve Ontiveros	.10	.05	.01
□ 76 Jim Abbott	.10	.05	.01
□ 77 Carl Everett	.10	.05	.01
□ 78 Mo Vaughn	.75	.35	.09
□ 79 Pedro Martinez	.25	.11	.03
□ 80 Harold Baines	.25	.11	.03
□ 81 Alan Trammell	.50	.23	.06
□ 82 Steve Avery	.10	.05	.01
□ 83 Jeff Cirillo	.10	.05	.01
□ 84 John Valentin	.10	.05	.01
□ 85 Bernie Williams	.50	.23	.06
□ 86 Andre Dawson	.50	.23	.06
□ 87 Dave Winfield	.50	.23	.06
□ 88 B.J. Surhoff	.10	.05	.01
□ 89 Jeff Blauser	.10	.05	.01
□ 90 Barry Larkin	.50	.23	.06
□ 91 Cliff Floyd	.10	.05	.01
□ 92 Sammy Sosa	.50	.23	.06
□ 93 Andres Galarraga	.50	.23	.06
□ 94 Dave Nilsson	.25	.11	.03
□ 95 James Mouton	.10	.05	.01
□ 96 Marquis Grissom	.25	.11	.03
□ 97 Matt Williams	.50	.23	.06
□ 98 John Jaha	.25	.11	.03
□ 99 Don Mattingly	1.50	.70	.19
□ 100 Tim Naehring	.10	.05	.01
□ 101 Kevin Appier	.10	.05	.01
□ 102 Bobby Higginson	.25	.11	.03
□ 103 Andy Pettitte	1.00	.45	.12
□ 104 Ozzie Smith	.60	.25	.07
□ 105 Kenny Lofton	.75	.35	.09
□ 106 Ken Caminiti	.50	.23	.06
□ 107 Walt Weiss	.10	.05	.01
□ 108 Jack McDowell	.25	.11	.03
□ 109 Brian McRae	.10	.05	.01
□ 110 Gary Gaetti	.25	.11	.03
□ 111 Curtis Goodwin	.10	.05	.01
□ 112 Dennis Martinez	.25	.11	.03
□ 113 Omar Vizquel	.10	.05	.01
□ 114 Chipper Jones	2.00	.90	.25
□ 115 Mark Gubicza	.10	.05	.01
□ 116 Ruben Sierra	.10	.05	.01
□ 117 Eddie Murray	.75	.35	.09
□ 118 Chad Curtis	.10	.05	.01
□ 119 Hal Morris	.10	.05	.01
□ 120 Ben McDonald	.10	.05	.01
□ 121 Marty Cordova	.50	.23	.06
□ 122 Ken Griffey Jr. UER Card says Ken homered from both sides He is only a left hitter	3.00	1.35	.35
□ 123 Gary Sheffield	.50	.23	.06
□ 124 Charlie Hayes	.10	.05	.01
□ 125 Shawn Green	.25	.11	.03
□ 126 Jason Giambi	.50	.23	.06
□ 127 Mark Langston	.10	.05	.01
□ 128 Mark Whiten	.10	.05	.01
□ 129 Greg Vaughn	.25	.11	.03
□ 130 Mark McGwire	1.00	.45	.12
□ 131 Hideo Nomo	.75	.35	.09
□ 132 Eric Karros Mike Piazza Raul Mondesi Hideo Nomo	.75	.35	.09
□ 133 Jason Bere	.10	.05	.01
□ 134 Ken Griffey Jr. NAT	1.50	.70	.19
□ 135 Frank Thomas NAT	1.50	.70	.19
□ 136 Cal Ripken NAT	1.25	.55	.16
□ 137 Albert Belle NAT	.75	.35	.09
□ 138 Mike Piazza NAT	1.00	.45	.12
□ 139 Dante Bichette NAT	.25	.11	.03
□ 140 Sammy Sosa NAT	.25	.11	.03
□ 141 Mo Vaughn NAT	.50	.23	.06
□ 142 Tim Salmon NAT	.25	.11	.03
□ 143 Reggie Sanders NAT	.10	.05	.01
□ 144 Cecil Fielder NAT	.10	.05	.01
□ 145 Jim Edmonds NAT	.25	.11	.03
□ 146 Rafael Palmeiro NAT	.25	.11	.03
□ 147 Edgar Martinez NAT	.25	.11	.03
□ 148 Barry Bonds NAT	.50	.23	.06
□ 149 Manny Ramirez NAT	.50	.23	.06
□ 150 Larry Walker NAT	.25	.11	.03
□ 151 Jeff Bagwell NAT	.60	.25	.07
□ 152 Ron Gant NAT	.10	.05	.01
□ 153 Andres Galarraga NAT	.25	.11	.03
□ 154 Eddie Murray NAT	.50	.23	.06
□ 155 Kirby Puckett NAT	.50	.23	.06
□ 156 Will Clark NAT	.25	.11	.03
□ 157 Don Mattingly NAT	.75	.35	.09
□ 158 Mark McGwire NAT	.50	.23	.06
□ 159 Dean Palmer NAT	.10	.05	.01
□ 160 Matt Williams NAT	.25	.11	.03
□ 161 Fred McGriff NAT	.25	.11	.03
□ 162 Joe Carter NAT	.25	.11	.03
□ 163 Juan Gonzalez NAT	.75	.35	.09
□ 164 Alex Ochoa	.25	.11	.03
□ 165 Ruben Rivera	.60	.25	.07
□ 166 Tony Clark	.50	.23	.06
□ 167 Brian Barber	.10	.05	.01
□ 168 Matt Lawton	.10	.05	.01
□ 169 Terrell Wade	.25	.11	.03
□ 170 Johnny Damon	.25	.11	.03
□ 171 Derek Jeter	2.00	.90	.25
□ 172 Phil Nevin	.10	.05	.01
□ 173 Robert Perez	.10	.05	.01
□ 174 C.J. Nitkowski	.10	.05	.01
□ 175 Joe Vitiello	.10	.05	.01
□ 176 Roger Cedeno	.25	.11	.03
□ 177 Ron Coomer	.10	.05	.01
□ 178 Chris Widger	.10	.05	.01
□ 179 Jimmy Haynes	.10	.05	.01
□ 180 Mike Sweeney	.60	.25	.07
□ 181 Howard Battle	.10	.05	.01
□ 182 John Wasdin	.10	.05	.01
□ 183 Jim Pittsley	.10	.05	.01
□ 184 Bob Wolcott	.10	.05	.01

☐	185 LaTroy Hawkins	.10	.05	.01
☐	186 Nigel Wilson	.10	.05	.01
☐	187 Dustin Hermanson	.10	.05	.01
☐	188 Chris Snopek	.10	.05	.01
☐	189 Mariano Rivera	.50	.23	.06
☐	190 Jose Herrera	.10	.05	.01
☐	191 Chris Stynes	.10	.05	.01
☐	192 Larry Thomas	.10	.05	.01
☐	193 David Bell	.10	.05	.01
☐	194 Frank Thomas CL	1.50	.70	.19
☐	195 Ken Griffey Jr. CL	1.50	.70	.19
☐	196 Cal Ripken CL	1.25	.55	.16
☐	197 Jeff Bagwell CL	.60	.25	.07
☐	198 Mike Piazza CL	1.00	.45	.12
☐	199 Barry Bonds CL	.50	.23	.06
☐	200 Garret Anderson CL Chipper Jones	.75	.35	.09
☐	201 Frank Thomas	3.00	1.35	.35
☐	202 Michael Tucker	.10	.05	.01
☐	203 Kirby Puckett	1.00	.45	.12
☐	204 Alex Gonzalez	.10	.05	.01
☐	205 Tony Gwynn	1.25	.55	.16
☐	206 Moises Alou	.10	.05	.01
☐	207 Albert Belle	1.50	.70	.19
☐	208 Barry Bonds	.75	.35	.09
☐	209 Fred McGriff	.50	.23	.06
☐	210 Dennis Eckersley	.25	.11	.03
☐	211 Craig Biggio	.50	.23	.06
☐	212 David Cone	.25	.11	.03
☐	213 Will Clark	.50	.23	.06
☐	214 Cal Ripken	2.50	1.10	.30
☐	215 Wade Boggs	.50	.23	.06
☐	216 Pete Schourek	.25	.11	.03
☐	217 Darren Daulton	.25	.11	.03
☐	218 Carlos Baerga	.50	.23	.06
☐	219 Larry Walker	.50	.23	.06
☐	220 Denny Neagle	.10	.05	.01
☐	221 Jim Edmonds	.50	.23	.06
☐	222 Lee Smith	.25	.11	.03
☐	223 Jason Isringhausen	.25	.11	.03
☐	224 Jay Buhner	.50	.23	.06
☐	225 John Olerud	.10	.05	.01
☐	226 Jeff Conine	.25	.11	.03
☐	227 Dean Palmer	.25	.11	.03
☐	228 Jim Abbott	.10	.05	.01
☐	229 Raul Mondesi	.50	.23	.06
☐	230 Tom Glavine	.50	.23	.06
☐	231 Kevin Seitzer	.10	.05	.01
☐	232 Lenny Dykstra	.25	.11	.03
☐	233 Brian Jordan	.25	.11	.03
☐	234 Rondell White	.50	.23	.06
☐	235 Bret Boone	.10	.05	.01
☐	236 Randy Johnson	.50	.23	.06
☐	237 Paul O'Neill	.10	.05	.01
☐	238 Jim Thome	.60	.25	.07
☐	239 Edgardo Alfonzo	.25	.11	.03
☐	240 Terry Pendleton	.25	.11	.03
☐	241 Harold Baines	.25	.11	.03
☐	242 Roberto Alomar	.75	.35	.09
☐	243 Mark Grace	.50	.23	.06
☐	244 Derek Bell	.25	.11	.03
☐	245 Vinny Castilla	.10	.05	.01
☐	246 Cecil Fielder	.25	.11	.03
☐	247 Roger Clemens	.50	.23	.06
☐	248 Orel Hershiser	.25	.11	.03
☐	249 J.T. Snow	.10	.05	.01
☐	250 Rafael Palmeiro	.50	.23	.06
☐	251 Bret Saberhagen	.10	.05	.01
☐	252 Todd Hollandsworth	.50	.23	.06
☐	253 Ryan Klesko	.60	.25	.07
☐	254 Greg Maddux HH	1.00	.45	.12
☐	255 Ken Griffey Jr. HH	1.50	.70	.19
☐	256 Hideo Nomo HH	.50	.23	.06
☐	257 Frank Thomas HH	1.50	.70	.19
☐	258 Cal Ripken HH	1.25	.55	.16
☐	259 Jeff Bagwell HH	.60	.25	.07
☐	260 Barry Bonds HH	.50	.23	.06
☐	261 Mo Vaughn HH	.50	.23	.06
☐	262 Albert Belle HH	.75	.35	.09
☐	263 Sammy Sosa HH	.25	.11	.03
☐	264 Reggie Sanders HH	.10	.05	.01
☐	265 Mike Piazza HH	1.00	.45	.12
☐	266 Chipper Jones HH	1.00	.45	.12
☐	267 Tony Gwynn HH	.60	.25	.07
☐	268 Kirby Puckett HH	.50	.23	.06
☐	269 Wade Boggs HH	.25	.11	.03
☐	270 Will Clark HH	.25	.11	.03
☐	271 Gary Sheffield HH	.25	.11	.03
☐	272 Dante Bichette HH	.25	.11	.03
☐	273 Randy Johnson HH	.25	.11	.03
☐	274 Matt Williams HH	.25	.11	.03
☐	275 Alex Rodriguez HH	1.50	.70	.19
☐	276 Tim Salmon HH	.25	.11	.03
☐	277 Johnny Damon HH	.10	.05	.01
☐	278 Manny Ramirez HH	.50	.23	.06
☐	279 Derek Jeter HH	1.00	.45	.12
☐	280 Eddie Murray HH	.50	.23	.06
☐	281 Ozzie Smith HH	.50	.23	.06
☐	282 Garret Anderson HH	.10	.05	.01
☐	283 Raul Mondesi HH	.25	.11	.03
☐	284 Terry Steinbach	.10	.05	.01
☐	285 Carlos Garcia	.10	.05	.01
☐	286 Dave Justice	.25	.11	.03
☐	287 Eric Anthony	.10	.05	.01
☐	288 Benji Gil	.10	.05	.01
☐	289 Bob Hamelin	.10	.05	.01
☐	290 Dwayne Hosey	.10	.05	.01
☐	291 Andy Pettitte	1.00	.45	.12
☐	292 Rod Beck	.10	.05	.01
☐	293 Shane Andrews	.10	.05	.01
☐	294 Julian Tavarez	.10	.05	.01
☐	295 Willie Greene	.10	.05	.01
☐	296 Ismael Valdes	.25	.11	.03
☐	297 Glenallen Hill	.10	.05	.01
☐	298 Troy Percival	.10	.05	.01
☐	299 Ray Durham	.25	.11	.03
☐	300 Jeff Conine 300	.10	.05	.01
☐	301 Ken Griffey Jr. 300	1.50	.70	.19
☐	302 Will Clark 300	.25	.11	.03
☐	303 Mike Greenwell 300	.10	.05	.01
☐	304 Carlos Baerga 300	.25	.11	.03
☐	305A Paul Molitor 300	.50	.23	.06
☐	305B Jeff Bagwell 300	.60	.25	.07
☐	306 Mark Grace 300	.25	.11	.03
☐	307 Don Mattingly 300	.75	.35	.09
☐	308 Hal Morris 300	.10	.05	.01
☐	309 Butch Huskey	.10	.05	.01
☐	310 Ozzie Guillen	.10	.05	.01
☐	311 Erik Hanson	.10	.05	.01
☐	312 Kenny Lofton 300	.50	.23	.06
☐	313 Edgar Martinez 300	.25	.11	.03
☐	314 Kurt Abbott	.10	.05	.01
☐	315 John Smoltz	.50	.23	.06
☐	316 Ariel Prieto	.10	.05	.01
☐	317 Mark Carreon	.10	.05	.01
☐	318 Kirby Puckett 300	.50	.23	.06
☐	319 Carlos Perez	.10	.05	.01
☐	320 Gary DiSarcina	.10	.05	.01
☐	321 Trevor Hoffman	.25	.11	.03
☐	322 Mike Piazza 300	1.00	.45	.12
☐	323 Frank Thomas 300	1.50	.70	.19
☐	324 Juan Acevedo	.10	.05	.01
☐	325 Bip Roberts	.10	.05	.01
☐	326 Javier Lopez	.50	.23	.06
☐	327 Benito Santiago	.10	.05	.01
☐	328 Mark Lewis	.10	.05	.01
☐	329 Royce Clayton	.10	.05	.01
☐	330 Tom Gordon	.10	.05	.01
☐	331 Ben McDonald	.10	.05	.01
☐	332 Dan Wilson	.10	.05	.01
☐	333 Ron Gant	.25	.11	.03
☐	334 Wade Boggs 300	.25	.11	.03
☐	335 Paul Molitor	.60	.25	.07
☐	336 Tony Gwynn 300	.60	.25	.07
☐	337 Sean Berry	.10	.05	.01
☐	338 Rickey Henderson	.50	.23	.06
☐	339 Wil Cordero	.10	.05	.01
☐	340 Kent Mercker	.10	.05	.01
☐	341 Kenny Rogers	.10	.05	.01
☐	342 Ryne Sandberg	.75	.35	.09
☐	343 Charlie Hayes	.10	.05	.01
☐	344 Andy Benes	.10	.05	.01
☐	345 Sterling Hitchcock	.10	.05	.01
☐	346 Bernard Gilkey	.25	.11	.03
☐	347 Julio Franco	.25	.11	.03
☐	348 Ken Hill	.10	.05	.01
☐	349 Russ Davis	.10	.05	.01
☐	350 Mike Blowers	.10	.05	.01
☐	351 B.J. Surhoff	.10	.05	.01
☐	352 Lance Johnson	.25	.11	.03
☐	353 Darryl Hamilton	.10	.05	.01
☐	354 Shawon Dunston	.10	.05	.01

□ 355 Rick Aguilera	.10	.05	.01
□ 356 Danny Tartabull	.10	.05	.01
□ 357 Todd Stottlemyre	.10	.05	.01
□ 358 Mike Bordick	.10	.05	.01
□ 359 Jack McDowell	.25	.11	.03
□ 360 Todd Zeile	.10	.05	.01
□ 361 Tino Martinez	.10	.05	.01
□ 362 Greg Gagne	.10	.05	.01
□ 363 Mike Kelly	.10	.05	.01
□ 364 Tim Raines	.25	.11	.03
□ 365 Ernie Young	.10	.05	.01
□ 366 Mike Stanley	.10	.05	.01
□ 367 Wally Joyner	.10	.05	.01
□ 368 Karim Garcia	.60	.25	.07
□ 369 Paul Wilson	.25	.11	.03
□ 370 Sal Fasano	.10	.05	.01
□ 371 Jason Schmidt	.25	.11	.03
□ 372 Livan Hernandez	.50	.23	.06
□ 373 George Arias	.10	.05	.01
□ 374 Steve Gibralter	.10	.05	.01
□ 375 Jermaine Dye	.75	.35	.09
□ 376 Jason Kendall	.25	.11	.03
□ 377 Brooks Kieschnick	.10	.05	.01
□ 378 Jeff Ware	.10	.05	.01
□ 379 Alan Benes	.50	.23	.06
□ 380 Rey Ordonez	.60	.25	.07
□ 381 Jay Powell	.10	.05	.01
□ 382 Osvaldo Fernandez	.25	.11	.03
□ 383 Wilton Guerrero	.60	.25	.07
□ 384 Eric Owens	.10	.05	.01
□ 385 George Williams	.10	.05	.01
□ 386 Chan Ho Park	.25	.11	.03
□ 387 Jeff Suppan	.25	.11	.03
□ 388 F.P. Santangelo	.10	.05	.01
□ 389 Terry Adams	.10	.05	.01
□ 390 Bob Abreu	.50	.23	.06
□ 391 Quinton McCracken	.10	.05	.01
□ 392 Mike Busby	.10	.05	.01
□ 393 Cal Ripken CL	1.25	.55	.16
□ 394 Ken Griffey Jr. CL	1.50	.70	.19
□ 395 Frank Thomas CL	1.50	.70	.19
□ 396 Chipper Jones CL	1.00	.45	.12
□ 397 Greg Maddux CL	1.00	.45	.12
□ 398 Mike Piazza CL	1.00	.45	.12
□ 399 Superstar CL	1.50	.70	.19
□ CR1 Cal Ripken Tribute	25.00	11.00	3.10

1996 Pinnacle Christie Brinkley Collection

Randomly inserted at the rate of one in 23 packs, this 16-card set features the 1995 World Series participants captured by the lens of supermodel and photographer Christie Brinkley. The fronts feature color player photos in various poses with different backgrounds. The backs carry a color portrait of the player and Ms. Brinkley with an explanation as to why she posed them as she did.

	MINT	NRMT	EXC
COMPLETE SET (16)	75.00	34.00	9.50
COMMON CARD (1-16)	2.00	.90	.25
SEMISTARS	3.00	1.35	.35
RANDOM INSERTS IN SER.2 PACKS			

□ 1 Greg Maddux	15.00	6.75	1.85
□ 2 Ryan Klesko	5.00	2.20	.60
□ 3 Dave Justice	2.00	.90	.25
□ 4 Tom Glavine	3.00	1.35	.35
□ 5 Chipper Jones	15.00	6.75	1.85
□ 6 Fred McGriff	3.00	1.35	.35
□ 7 Javier Lopez	3.00	1.35	.35
□ 8 Marquis Grissom	3.00	1.35	.35
□ 9 Jason Schmidt	2.00	.90	.25
□ 10 Albert Belle	12.00	5.50	1.50
□ 11 Manny Ramirez	6.00	2.70	.75
□ 12 Carlos Baerga	3.00	1.35	.35
□ 13 Sandy Alomar	2.00	.90	.25
□ 14 Jim Thome	5.00	2.20	.60
□ 15 Julio Franco	2.00	.90	.25
□ 16 Kenny Lofton	6.00	2.70	.75

1996 Pinnacle Essence of the Game

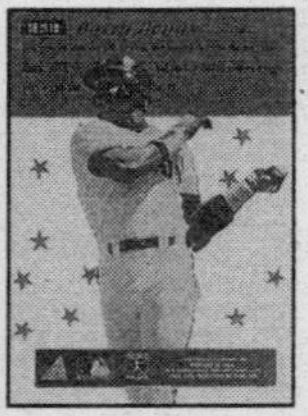

Randomly inserted in hobby packs only at a rate of one in 23, this 18-card standard-size set takes a unique perspective, photographically capturing the persona of 18 of the game's most popular icons. Using a micro-etched print technology, the fronts display a color player cutout on an acetate card studded with stars, with "Essence of the Game" appearing on a holographic design across the top. On the back, this holographic design carries a highlight.

	MINT	NRMT	EXC
COMPLETE SET (18)	150.00	70.00	19.00
COMMON CARD (1-18)	2.00	.90	.25
SEMISTARS	3.00	1.35	.35
RANDOM INSERTS IN SER.1 HOBBY PACKS			

□ 1 Cal Ripken	20.00	9.00	2.50
□ 2 Greg Maddux	15.00	6.75	1.85
□ 3 Frank Thomas	25.00	11.00	3.10
□ 4 Matt Williams	3.00	1.35	.35
□ 5 Chipper Jones	15.00	6.75	1.85
□ 6 Reggie Sanders	2.00	.90	.25
□ 7 Ken Griffey Jr.	25.00	11.00	3.10
□ 8 Kirby Puckett	8.00	3.60	1.00
□ 9 Hideo Nomo	6.00	2.70	.75
□ 10 Mike Piazza	15.00	6.75	1.85
□ 11 Jeff Bagwell	10.00	4.50	1.25
□ 12 Mo Vaughn	6.00	2.70	.75
□ 13 Albert Belle	12.00	5.50	1.50
□ 14 Tim Salmon	3.00	1.35	.35
□ 15 Don Mattingly	12.00	5.50	1.50
□ 16 Will Clark	3.00	1.35	.35
□ 17 Eddie Murray	6.00	2.70	.75
□ 18 Barry Bonds	6.00	2.70	.75

1996 Pinnacle First Rate

Randomly inserted in retail packs only at a rate of one in 23, this 18-card set features former first-round draft picks who have become major league superstars done in Dufex print.

	MINT	NRMT	EXC
COMPLETE SET (18)	125.00	55.00	15.50
COMMON CARD (1-18)	2.50	1.10	.30
SEMISTARS	4.00	1.80	.50
RANDOM INSERTS IN SER.1 RETAIL PACKS			

□ 1 Ken Griffey Jr.	30.00	13.50	3.70
□ 2 Frank Thomas	30.00	13.50	3.70
□ 3 Mo Vaughn	8.00	3.60	1.00
□ 4 Chipper Jones	20.00	9.00	2.50
□ 5 Alex Rodriguez	30.00	13.50	3.70
□ 6 Kirby Puckett	10.00	4.50	1.25
□ 7 Gary Sheffield	5.00	2.20	.60
□ 8 Matt Williams	4.00	1.80	.50
□ 9 Barry Bonds	8.00	3.60	1.00
□ 10 Craig Biggio	2.50	1.10	.30
□ 11 Robin Ventura	4.00	1.80	.50
□ 12 Michael Tucker	2.50	1.10	.30
□ 13 Derek Jeter	20.00	9.00	2.50
□ 14 Manny Ramirez	8.00	3.60	1.00
□ 15 Barry Larkin	4.00	1.80	.50
□ 16 Shawn Green	2.50	1.10	.30
□ 17 Will Clark	4.00	1.80	.50
□ 18 Mark McGwire	10.00	4.50	1.25

1996 Pinnacle Power

Randomly inserted in packs at a rate of one in 35 retail and hobby packs, or one in 29 jumbo packs, this 20-card set highlights the league's top long-ball hitters in die-cut holographic foil technology. On a black card face, the fronts have a color player cutout superposed over a holographic homeplate. All printing on the front, including the player's name, is stamped in gold foil. The horizontal backs present a color close-up on the left and a player profile on the right.

	MINT	NRMT	EXC
COMPLETE SET (20)	125.00	55.00	15.50
COMMON CARD (1-20)	2.50	1.10	.30
SEMISTARS	4.00	1.80	.50
RANDOM INSERTS IN SER.1 PACKS			

□ 1 Frank Thomas	30.00	13.50	3.70
□ 2 Mo Vaughn	8.00	3.60	1.00
□ 3 Ken Griffey Jr.	30.00	13.50	3.70
□ 4 Matt Williams	4.00	1.80	.50
□ 5 Barry Bonds	8.00	3.60	1.00
□ 6 Reggie Sanders	2.50	1.10	.30
□ 7 Mike Piazza	20.00	9.00	2.50
□ 8 Jim Edmonds	2.50	1.10	.30
□ 9 Dante Bichette	4.00	1.80	.50
□ 10 Sammy Sosa	5.00	2.20	.60
□ 11 Jeff Bagwell	12.00	5.50	1.50
□ 12 Fred McGriff	4.00	1.80	.50
□ 13 Albert Belle	15.00	6.75	1.85
□ 14 Tim Salmon	4.00	1.80	.50
□ 15 Joe Carter	4.00	1.80	.50
□ 16 Manny Ramirez	8.00	3.60	1.00
□ 17 Eddie Murray	8.00	3.60	1.00
□ 18 Cecil Fielder	4.00	1.80	.50
□ 19 Larry Walker	4.00	1.80	.50
□ 20 Juan Gonzalez	15.00	6.75	1.85

1996 Pinnacle Project Stardom

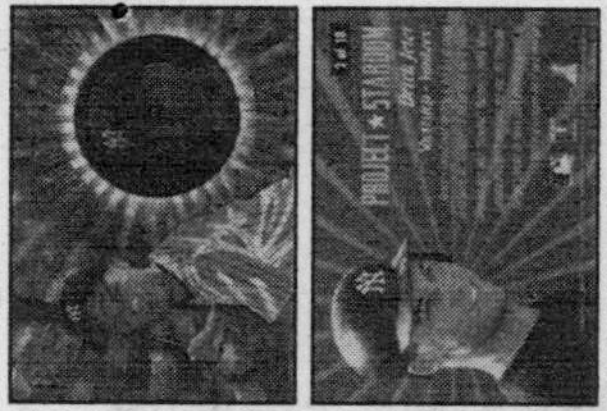

This 18-card set was randomly inserted in hobby packs at the rate of one in 35. The fronts feature a color action player photo on a blue foil background with a player portrait framed by silver foil rays depicting a star shining. The backs carry another player portrait with rays coming from behind his head to give the impression of a shining star, and information about the player is printed on the side.

	MINT	NRMT	EXC
COMPLETE SET (18)	150.00	70.00	19.00
COMMON CARD (1-18)	3.00	1.35	.35
SEMISTARS	5.00	2.20	.60
RANDOM INSERTS IN SER.2 HOBBY PACKS			

□ 1 Paul Wilson	6.00	2.70	.75
□ 2 Derek Jeter	25.00	11.00	3.10
□ 3 Karim Garcia	10.00	4.50	1.25
□ 4 Johnny Damon	5.00	2.20	.60
□ 5 Alex Rodriguez	50.00	22.00	6.25
□ 6 Chipper Jones	25.00	11.00	3.10
□ 7 Charles Johnson	5.00	2.20	.60
□ 8 Bob Abreu	3.00	1.35	.35
□ 9 Alan Benes	3.00	1.35	.35
□ 10 Richard Hidalgo	3.00	1.35	.35
□ 11 Brooks Kieschnick	3.00	1.35	.35
□ 12 Garret Anderson	5.00	2.20	.60
□ 13 Livan Hernandez	5.00	2.20	.60
□ 14 Manny Ramirez	12.00	5.50	1.50
□ 15 Jermaine Dye	12.00	5.50	1.50
□ 16 Todd Hollandsworth	6.00	2.70	.75
□ 17 Raul Mondesi	6.00	2.70	.75
□ 18 Ryan Klesko	10.00	4.50	1.25

1996 Pinnacle Skylines

Randomly inserted in magazine packs at the rate of one in 29, this 18-card set features baseball's best players pictured against their city's skyline and printed on clear plastic stock. The backs carry the same player portrait with information about the player and the city printed below.

	MINT	NRMT	EXC
COMPLETE SET (18)	225.00	100.00	28.00
COMMON CARD (1-18)	5.00	2.20	.60
RANDOM INSERTS IN SER.2 MAGAZINE PACKS			

	MINT	NRMT	EXC
□ 1 Ken Griffey Jr.	40.00	18.00	5.00
□ 2 Frank Thomas	40.00	18.00	5.00
□ 3 Greg Maddux	25.00	11.00	3.10
□ 4 Cal Ripken	30.00	13.50	3.70
□ 5 Albert Belle	20.00	9.00	2.50
□ 6 Mo Vaughn	10.00	4.50	1.25
□ 7 Mike Piazza	25.00	11.00	3.10
□ 8 Wade Boggs	5.00	2.20	.60
□ 9 Will Clark	5.00	2.20	.60
□ 10 Barry Bonds	10.00	4.50	1.25
□ 11 Gary Sheffield	6.00	2.70	.75
□ 12 Hideo Nomo	10.00	4.50	1.25
□ 13 Tony Gwynn	15.00	6.75	1.85
□ 14 Kirby Puckett	12.00	5.50	1.50
□ 15 Chipper Jones	25.00	11.00	3.10
□ 16 Jeff Bagwell	15.00	6.75	1.85
□ 17 Manny Ramirez	10.00	4.50	1.25
□ 18 Raul Mondesi	5.00	2.20	.60

1996 Pinnacle Slugfest

Randomly inserted exclusively into one in every 35 series 2 retail packs, cards from this 18 cards set feature a selection of baseball's top slugging stars. The fronts carry a color action player photo on a silver foil starburst background. The backs display a color player photo in a wooden bat with player information on the side.

	MINT	NRMT	EXC
COMPLETE SET (18)	200.00	90.00	25.00
COMMON CARD (1-18)	3.00	1.35	.35
SEMISTARS	5.00	2.20	.60
RANDOM INSERTS IN SER.2 RETAIL PACKS			

	MINT	NRMT	EXC
□ 1 Frank Thomas	40.00	18.00	5.00
□ 2 Ken Griffey Jr.	40.00	18.00	5.00
□ 3 Jeff Bagwell	15.00	6.75	1.85
□ 4 Barry Bonds	10.00	4.50	1.25
□ 5 Mo Vaughn	10.00	4.50	1.25
□ 6 Albert Belle	20.00	9.00	2.50
□ 7 Mike Piazza	25.00	11.00	3.10
□ 8 Matt Williams	5.00	2.20	.60
□ 9 Dante Bichette	5.00	2.20	.60
□ 10 Sammy Sosa	6.00	2.70	.75
□ 11 Gary Sheffield	6.00	2.70	.75
□ 12 Reggie Sanders	3.00	1.35	.35
□ 13 Manny Ramirez	10.00	4.50	1.25
□ 14 Eddie Murray	10.00	4.50	1.25
□ 15 Juan Gonzalez	20.00	9.00	2.50
□ 16 Dean Palmer	3.00	1.35	.35
□ 17 Rafael Palmeiro	5.00	2.20	.60
□ 18 Cecil Fielder	5.00	2.20	.60

1996 Pinnacle Starburst

Randomly inserted in packs at a rate of one in seven, this 200-card quasi-parallel standard-size insert set features a select group of major league baseball's hottest superstars from the 399-card regular set printed on all-foil Dufex card stock. The front design is used but the cards numbers are changed from the regular issue.

	MINT	NRMT	EXC
COMPLETE SET (200)	600.00	275.00	75.00
COMPLETE SERIES 1 (100)	300.00	135.00	38.00
COMPLETE SERIES 2 (100)	300.00	135.00	38.00
COMMON CARD (1-200)	.75	.35	.09
SEMISTARS	1.50	.70	.19
STARS	4.00	1.80	.50
*ART.PROOF STARS: 3X BASIC CARDS			
*ART.PROOF YOUNG STARS: 2.5X BASIC CARDS			
RANDOM INSERTS IN BOTH SERIES PACKS			

	MINT	NRMT	EXC
□ 1 Greg Maddux	20.00	9.00	2.50
□ 2 Bill Pulsipher	.75	.35	.09
□ 3 Dante Bichette	4.00	1.80	.50
□ 4 Mike Piazza	20.00	9.00	2.50
□ 5 Garret Anderson	.75	.35	.09
□ 6 Chuck Knoblauch	4.00	1.80	.50
□ 7 Jeff Bagwell	12.00	5.50	1.50
□ 8 Wil Cordero	.75	.35	.09
□ 9 Travis Fryman	2.00	.90	.25
□ 10 Reggie Sanders	2.00	.90	.25
□ 11 Deion Sanders	2.00	.90	.25
□ 12 Tim Salmon	4.00	1.80	.50
□ 13 Tino Martinez	2.00	.90	.25
□ 14 Bobby Bonilla	2.00	.90	.25
□ 15 Joe Carter	2.00	.90	.25
□ 16 Mike Mussina	6.00	2.70	.75
□ 17 Jose Canseco	4.00	1.80	.50
□ 18 Manny Ramirez	8.00	3.60	1.00
□ 19 Gregg Jefferies	2.00	.90	.25
□ 20 Charles Johnson	.75	.35	.09
□ 21 Brian L. Hunter	.75	.35	.09
□ 22 Ray Lankford	2.00	.90	.25
□ 23 Ivan Rodriguez	6.00	2.70	.75
□ 24 Paul Molitor	6.00	2.70	.75
□ 25 Eric Karros	2.00	.90	.25
□ 26 Edgar Martinez	4.00	1.80	.50
□ 27 Shawon Dunston	.75	.35	.09
□ 28 Mo Vaughn	8.00	3.60	1.00
□ 29 Pedro J. Martinez	2.00	.90	.25
□ 30 Marty Cordova	2.00	.90	.25
□ 31 Ken Caminiti	4.00	1.80	.50
□ 32 Gary Sheffield	5.00	2.20	.60
□ 33 Shawn Green	.75	.35	.09
□ 34 Cliff Floyd	.75	.35	.09
□ 35 Andres Galarraga	4.00	1.80	.50
□ 36 Matt Williams	4.00	1.80	.50
□ 37 Don Mattingly	15.00	6.75	1.85
□ 38 Kevin Appier	2.00	.90	.25
□ 39 Ozzie Smith	6.00	2.70	.75
□ 40 Kenny Lofton	8.00	3.60	1.00
□ 41 Ken Griffey Jr. UER card mentions him as a swtich-hitter Griffey only bats left	30.00	13.50	3.70
□ 42 Jack McDowell	2.00	.90	.25
□ 43 Gary Gaetti	.75	.35	.09
□ 44 Dennis Martinez	2.00	.90	.25
□ 45 Chipper Jones	20.00	9.00	2.50
□ 46 Eddie Murray	8.00	3.60	1.00
□ 47 Bernie Williams	5.00	2.20	.60
□ 48 Andre Dawson	4.00	1.80	.50
□ 49 Dave Winfield	2.00	.90	.25
□ 50 B.J. Surhoff	.75	.35	.09
□ 51 Barry Larkin	4.00	1.80	.50
□ 52 Alan Trammell	4.00	1.80	.50
□ 53 Sammy Sosa	5.00	2.20	.60
□ 54 Hideo Nomo	8.00	3.60	1.00
□ 55 Mark McGwire	10.00	4.50	1.25
□ 56 Jay Bell	.75	.35	.09
□ 57 Juan Gonzalez	15.00	6.75	1.85
□ 58 Chili Davis	.75	.35	.09
□ 59 Robin Ventura	2.00	.90	.25
□ 60 John Mabry	.75	.35	.09
□ 61 Ken Griffey Jr. NAT	15.00	6.75	1.85
□ 62 Frank Thomas NAT	15.00	6.75	1.85
□ 63 Cal Ripken NAT	12.00	5.50	1.50
□ 64 Albert Belle NAT	8.00	3.60	1.00
□ 65 Mike Piazza NAT	10.00	4.50	1.25
□ 66 Dante Bichette NAT	2.00	.90	.25
□ 67 Sammy Sosa NAT	2.00	.90	.25
□ 68 Mo Vaughn NAT	4.00	1.80	.50
□ 69 Tim Salmon NAT	2.00	.90	.25
□ 70 Reggie Sanders NAT	2.00	.90	.25

□ 71 Cecil Fielder NAT	2.00	.90	.25
□ 72 Jim Edmonds NAT	2.00	.90	.25
□ 73 Rafael Palmeiro NAT	2.00	.90	.25
□ 74 Edgar Martinez NAT	2.00	.90	.25
□ 75 Barry Bonds NAT	4.00	1.80	.50
□ 76 Manny Ramirez NAT	4.00	1.80	.50
□ 77 Larry Walker NAT	2.00	.90	.25
□ 78 Jeff Bagwell NAT	6.00	2.70	.75
□ 79 Ron Gant NAT	2.00	.90	.25
□ 80 Andres Galarraga NAT	2.00	.90	.25
□ 81 Eddie Murray NAT	4.00	1.80	.50
□ 82 Kirby Puckett NAT	5.00	2.20	.60
□ 83 Will Clark NAT	2.00	.90	.25
□ 84 Don Mattingly NAT	8.00	3.60	1.00
□ 85 Mark McGwire NAT	5.00	2.20	.60
□ 86 Dean Palmer NAT	2.00	.90	.25
□ 87 Matt Williams NAT	2.00	.90	.25
□ 88 Fred McGriff NAT	2.00	.90	.25
□ 89 Joe Carter NAT	2.00	.90	.25
□ 90 Juan Gonzalez NAT	8.00	3.60	1.00
□ 91 Alex Ochoa	2.00	.90	.25
□ 92 Ruben Rivera	6.00	2.70	.75
□ 93 Tony Clark	2.00	.90	.25
□ 94 Pete Schourek	.75	.35	.09
□ 95 Terrell Wade	.75	.35	.09
□ 96 Johnny Damon	2.00	.90	.25
□ 97 Derek Jeter	20.00	9.00	2.50
□ 98 Phil Nevin	.75	.35	.09
□ 99 Robert Perez	.75	.35	.09
□ 100 Dustin Hermanson	.75	.35	.09
□ 101 Frank Thomas	30.00	13.50	3.70
□ 102 Michael Tucker	.75	.35	.09
□ 103 Kirby Puckett	10.00	4.50	1.25
□ 104 Alex Gonzalez	.75	.35	.09
□ 105 Tony Gwynn	12.00	5.50	1.50
□ 106 Moises Alou	2.00	.90	.25
□ 107 Albert Belle	15.00	6.75	1.85
□ 108 Barry Bonds	8.00	3.60	1.00
□ 109 Fred McGriff	4.00	1.80	.50
□ 110 Dennis Eckersley	2.00	.90	.25
□ 111 Craig Biggio	2.00	.90	.25
□ 112 David Cone	2.00	.90	.25
□ 113 Will Clark	4.00	1.80	.50
□ 114 Cal Ripken	25.00	11.00	3.10
□ 115 Wade Boggs	4.00	1.80	.50
□ 116 Pete Schourek	.75	.35	.09
□ 117 Darren Daulton	2.00	.90	.25
□ 118 Carlos Baerga	2.00	.90	.25
□ 119 Larry Walker	2.00	.90	.25
□ 120 Denny Neagle	2.00	.90	.25
□ 121 Jim Edmonds	2.00	.90	.25
□ 122 Lee Smith	2.00	.90	.25
□ 123 Jason Isringhausen	2.00	.90	.25
□ 124 Jay Buhner	4.00	1.80	.50
□ 125 John Olerud	.75	.35	.09
□ 126 Jeff Conine	2.00	.90	.25
□ 127 Dean Palmer	2.00	.90	.25
□ 128 Jim Abbott	.75	.35	.09
□ 129 Raul Mondesi	2.00	.90	.25
□ 130 Tom Glavine	4.00	1.80	.50
□ 131 Kevin Seitzer	.75	.35	.09
□ 132 Lenny Dykstra	2.00	.90	.25
□ 133 Brian Jordan	2.00	.90	.25
□ 134 Rondell White	2.00	.90	.25
□ 135 Bret Boone	.75	.35	.09
□ 136 Randy Johnson	5.00	2.20	.60
□ 137 Paul O'Neill	.75	.35	.09
□ 138 Jim Thome	6.00	2.70	.75
□ 139 Edgardo Alfonzo	.75	.35	.09
□ 140 Terry Pendleton	2.00	.90	.25
□ 141 Harold Baines	2.00	.90	.25
□ 142 Roberto Alomar	8.00	3.60	1.00
□ 143 Mark Grace	4.00	1.80	.50
□ 144 Derek Bell	2.00	.90	.25
□ 145 Vinny Castilla	2.00	.90	.25
□ 146 Cecil Fielder	2.00	.90	.25
□ 147 Roger Clemens	4.00	1.80	.50
□ 148 Orel Hershiser	2.00	.90	.25
□ 149 J.T. Snow	.75	.35	.09
□ 150 Rafael Palmeiro	4.00	1.80	.50
□ 151 Bret Saberhagen	.75	.35	.09
□ 152 Todd Hollandsworth	4.00	1.80	.50
□ 153 Ryan Klesko	6.00	2.70	.75
□ 154 Greg Maddux HH	10.00	4.50	1.25
□ 155 Ken Griffey Jr. HH	15.00	6.75	1.85
□ 156 Hideo Nomo HH	4.00	1.80	.50
□ 157 Frank Thomas HH	15.00	6.75	1.85
□ 158 Cal Ripken HH	12.00	5.50	1.50
□ 159 Jeff Bagwell HH	6.00	2.70	.75
□ 160 Barry Bonds HH	4.00	1.80	.50
□ 161 Mo Vaughn HH	4.00	1.80	.50
□ 162 Albert Belle HH	8.00	3.60	1.00
□ 163 Sammy Sosa HH	2.00	.90	.25
□ 164 Reggie Sanders HH	2.00	.90	.25
□ 165 Mike Piazza HH	10.00	4.50	1.25
□ 166 Chipper Jones HH	10.00	4.50	1.25
□ 167 Tony Gwynn HH	6.00	2.70	.75
□ 168 Kirby Puckett HH	5.00	2.20	.60
□ 169 Wade Boggs HH	2.00	.90	.25
□ 170 Will Clark HH	2.00	.90	.25
□ 171 Gary Sheffield HH	2.00	.90	.25
□ 172 Dante Bichette HH	2.00	.90	.25
□ 173 Randy Johnson HH	2.00	.90	.25
□ 174 Matt Williams HH	2.00	.90	.25
□ 175 Alex Rodriguez HH	15.00	6.75	1.85
□ 176 Tim Salmon HH	2.00	.90	.25
□ 177 Johnny Damon HH	2.00	.90	.25
□ 178 Manny Ramirez HH	4.00	1.80	.50
□ 179 Derek Jeter HH	10.00	4.50	1.25
□ 180 Eddie Murray HH	4.00	1.80	.50
□ 181 Ozzie Smith HH	4.00	1.80	.50
□ 182 Garret Anderson HH	.75	.35	.09
□ 183 Raul Mondesi HH	2.00	.90	.25
□ 184 Jeff Conine 300	2.00	.90	.25
□ 185 Ken Griffey Jr. 300	15.00	6.75	1.85
□ 186 Will Clark 300	2.00	.90	.25
□ 187 Mike Greenwell 300	.75	.35	.09
□ 188 Carlos Baerga 300	2.00	.90	.25
□ 189 Paul Molitor 300	4.00	1.80	.50
□ 190 Jeff Bagwell 300	6.00	2.70	.75
□ 191 Mark Grace 300	2.00	.90	.25
□ 192 Don Mattingly 300	8.00	3.60	1.00
□ 193 Hal Morris 300	.75	.35	.09
□ 194 Kenny Lofton 300	4.00	1.80	.50
□ 195 Edgar Martinez 300	2.00	.90	.25
□ 196 Kirby Puckett 300	5.00	2.20	.60
□ 197 Mike Piazza 300	10.00	4.50	1.25
□ 198 Frank Thomas 300	15.00	6.75	1.85
□ 199 Wade Boggs 300	2.00	.90	.25
□ 200 Tony Gwynn 300	6.00	2.70	.75

1996 Pinnacle Team Pinnacle

Randomly inserted in packs at a rate of one in 72, this 9-card set spotlights double-front all-foil Dufex card designs featuring nine top AL and NL players, by position, back-to-back. On a gold foil background displaying a baseball, the fronts present a color player cutout extending beyond the picture frame. "Team Pinnacle," the player's name, and an abbreviation for his position are printed in the bottom border. Only one side of each card is Dufexed.

	MINT	NRMT	EXC
COMPLETE SET (9)	200.00	90.00	25.00
COMMON CARD (1-9)	8.00	3.60	1.00
RANDOM INSERTS IN SER.1 PACKS			
□ 1 Frank Thomas Jeff Bagwell	50.00	22.00	6.25
□ 2 Chuck Knoblauch Craig Biggio	8.00	3.60	1.00

□ 3 Jim Thome / Matt Williams	12.00	5.50	1.50
□ 4 Barrry Larkin / Cal Ripken	40.00	18.00	5.00
□ 5 Barry Bonds / Tim Salmon	15.00	6.75	1.85
□ 6 Ken Griffey Jr. / Reggie Sanders	40.00	18.00	5.00
□ 7 Albert Belle / Sammy Sosa	25.00	11.00	3.10
□ 8 Ivan Rodriguez / Mike Piazza	30.00	13.50	3.70
□ 9 Greg Maddux / Randy Johnson	30.00	13.50	3.70

1996 Pinnacle Team Spirit

Randomly inserted at the rate of one in 72 packs, this 12-card set features color action player images in holographic foil stamping over a silver foil ball outlined in baseball stitching. The backs carry two player photos and player information.

	MINT	NRMT	EXC
COMPLETE SET (12)	300.00	135.00	38.00
COMMON CARD (1-12)	6.00	2.70	.75
RANDOM INSERTS IN SER.2 PACKS			

□ 1 Greg Maddux	30.00	13.50	3.70
□ 2 Ken Griffey Jr.	50.00	22.00	6.25
□ 3 Derek Jeter	25.00	11.00	3.10
□ 4 Mike Piazza	30.00	13.50	3.70
□ 5 Cal Ripken	40.00	18.00	5.00
□ 6 Frank Thomas	50.00	22.00	6.25
□ 7 Jeff Bagwell	20.00	9.00	2.50
□ 8 Mo Vaughn	12.00	5.50	1.50
□ 9 Albert Belle	25.00	11.00	3.10
□ 10 Chipper Jones	30.00	13.50	3.70
□ 11 Johnny Damon	6.00	2.70	.75
□ 12 Barry Bonds	12.00	5.50	1.50

1996 Pinnacle Team Tomorrow

Randomly inserted in jumbo packs at a rate of one in 19, this 10-card set is a jumbo exclusive and features the next crop of superstars. The fronts are printed in an all-foil Dufex design with two of the same color player action cutouts--one close up and the other full-length. The backs carry a color player portrait and information about the player.

	MINT	NRMT	EXC
COMPLETE SET (10)	125.00	55.00	15.50
COMMON CARD (1-10)	3.00	1.35	.35
RANDOM INSERTS IN SER.1 JUMBO PACKS			

□ 1 Ruben Rivera	10.00	4.50	1.25
□ 2 Johnny Damon	5.00	2.20	.60
□ 3 Raul Mondesi	6.00	2.70	.75
□ 4 Manny Ramirez	12.00	5.50	1.50
□ 5 Hideo Nomo	12.00	5.50	1.50
□ 6 Chipper Jones	30.00	13.50	3.70
□ 7 Garret Anderson	3.00	1.35	.35
□ 8 Alex Rodriguez	50.00	22.00	6.25
□ 9 Derek Jeter	25.00	11.00	3.10
□ 10 Karim Garcia	10.00	4.50	1.25

1996 Pinnacle Aficionado

The 1996 Aficionado set was issued in one series totalling 200 cards. The five-card packs retail for $3.99 and have a special bubble gum scent which is released when the packs are opened. The fronts feature action player photos in sepia tone for players who have played in the Major League for over five years and in color for those who have played less than five years. A heliographic player head print and the player's name printed in gold foil on a wood-look bar round out the front. The backs carry positional comparison statistics between the player and the league average at that position in different eras. The nicknames of some players also appear on the back. Cards numbered 151-160 are a subset titled "Global Reach" and feature color action player cut-outs of international players on a background of a map, a global baseball, and their country's flag. The backs of these cards display the player's name, team name, country, and a short player summary.

	MINT	NRMT	EXC
COMPLETE SET (200)	65.00	29.00	8.00
COMMON CARD (1-200)	.25	.11	.03
SEMISTARS	.50	.23	.06
STARS	1.00	.45	.12

□ 1 Jack McDowell	1.00	.45	.12
□ 2 Jay Bell	.25	.11	.03
□ 3 Rafael Palmeiro	1.00	.45	.12
□ 4 Wally Joyner	.25	.11	.03
□ 5 Ozzie Smith	1.25	.55	.16
□ 6 Mark McGwire	2.00	.90	.25
□ 7 Kevin Seitzer	.25	.11	.03
□ 8 Fred McGriff	1.00	.45	.12
□ 9 Roger Clemens	1.00	.45	.12
□ 10 Randy Johnson	1.00	.45	.12
□ 11 Cecil Fielder	1.00	.45	.12
□ 12 David Cone	1.00	.45	.12
□ 13 Chili Davis	.25	.11	.03
□ 14 Andres Galarraga	1.00	.45	.12
□ 15 Joe Carter	1.00	.45	.12
□ 16 Ryne Sandberg	1.50	.70	.19
□ 17 Paul O'Neill	.25	.11	.03

□	18 Cal Ripken	5.00	2.20	.60
□	19 Wade Boggs	1.00	.45	.12
□	20 Greg Gagne	.25	.11	.03
□	21 Edgar Martinez	1.00	.45	.12
□	22 Greg Maddux	4.00	1.80	.50
□	23 Ken Caminiti	1.00	.45	.12
□	24 Kirby Puckett	2.00	.90	.25
□	25 Craig Biggio	1.00	.45	.12
□	26 Will Clark	1.00	.45	.12
□	27 Ron Gant	1.00	.45	.12
□	28 Eddie Murray	1.50	.70	.19
□	29 Lance Johnson	.50	.23	.06
□	30 Tony Gwynn	2.50	1.10	.30
□	31 Dante Bichette	1.00	.45	.12
□	32 Darren Daulton	.50	.23	.06
□	33 Danny Tartabull	.25	.11	.03
□	34 Jeff King	.25	.11	.03
□	35 Tom Glavine	1.00	.45	.12
□	36 Rickey Henderson	1.00	.45	.12
□	37 Jose Canseco	1.00	.45	.12
□	38 Barry Larkin	1.00	.45	.12
□	39 Dennis Martinez	.50	.23	.06
□	40 Ruben Sierra	.25	.11	.03
□	41 Bobby Bonilla	1.00	.45	.12
□	42 Jeff Conine	.50	.23	.06
□	43 Lee Smith	1.00	.45	.12
□	44 Charlie Hayes	.25	.11	.03
□	45 Walt Weiss	.25	.11	.03
□	46 Jay Buhner	1.00	.45	.12
□	47 Kenny Rogers	.25	.11	.03
□	48 Paul Molitor	1.25	.55	.16
□	49 Hal Morris	.25	.11	.03
□	50 Todd Stottlemyre	.25	.11	.03
□	51 Mike Stanley	.25	.11	.03
□	52 Mark Grace	1.00	.45	.12
□	53 Lenny Dykstra	.50	.23	.06
□	54 Andre Dawson	1.00	.45	.12
□	55 Dennis Eckersley	1.00	.45	.12
□	56 Ben McDonald	.25	.11	.03
□	57 Ray Lankford	1.00	.45	.12
□	58 Mo Vaughn	1.50	.70	.19
□	59 Frank Thomas	6.00	2.70	.75
□	60 Julio Franco	.25	.11	.03
□	61 Jim Abbott	1.00	.45	.12
□	62 Greg Vaughn	1.00	.45	.12
□	63 Marquis Grissom	1.00	.45	.12
□	64 Tino Martinez	.50	.23	.06
□	65 Kevin Appier	.50	.23	.06
□	66 Matt Williams	1.00	.45	.12
□	67 Sammy Sosa	1.00	.45	.12
□	68 Larry Walker	1.00	.45	.12
□	69 Ivan Rodriguez	1.25	.55	.16
□	70 Eric Karros	1.00	.45	.12
□	71 Bernie Williams	1.00	.45	.12
□	72 Carlos Baerga	1.00	.45	.12
□	73 Jeff Bagwell	2.50	1.10	.30
□	74 Pete Schourek	.25	.11	.03
□	75 Ken Griffey Jr.	6.00	2.70	.75
□	76 Bernard Gilkey	.50	.23	.06
□	77 Albert Belle	3.00	1.35	.35
□	78 Chuck Knoblauch	1.00	.45	.12
□	79 John Smoltz	1.00	.45	.12
□	80 Barry Bonds	1.50	.70	.19
□	81 Vinny Castilla	1.00	.45	.12
□	82 John Olerud	.25	.11	.03
□	83 Mike Mussina	1.25	.55	.16
□	84 Alex Fernandez	1.00	.45	.12
□	85 Shawon Dunston	.25	.11	.03
□	86 Travis Fryman	1.00	.45	.12
□	87 Moises Alou	.25	.11	.03
□	88 Dean Palmer	.50	.23	.06
□	89 Gregg Jefferies	1.00	.45	.12
□	90 Jim Thome	1.25	.55	.16
□	91 Dave Justice	.50	.23	.06
□	92 B.J. Surhoff	.25	.11	.03
□	93 Ramon Martinez	1.00	.45	.12
□	94 Gary Sheffield	1.00	.45	.12
□	95 Andy Benes	.25	.11	.03
□	96 Reggie Sanders	1.00	.45	.12
□	97 Roberto Alomar	1.50	.70	.19
□	98 Omar Vizquel	.25	.11	.03
□	99 Juan Gonzalez	3.00	1.35	.35
□	100 Robin Ventura	1.00	.45	.12
□	101 Jason Isringhausen	.50	.23	.06
□	102 Greg Colbrunn	.25	.11	.03
□	103 Brian Jordan	1.00	.45	.12
□	104 Shawn Green	.25	.11	.03
□	105 Brian Hunter	.25	.11	.03
□	106 Rondell White	1.00	.45	.12
□	107 Ryan Klesko	1.25	.55	.16
□	108 Sterling Hitchcock	.25	.11	.03
□	109 Manny Ramirez	1.50	.70	.19
□	110 Bret Boone	.25	.11	.03
□	111 Michael Tucker	.50	.23	.06
□	112 Julian Tavarez	.25	.11	.03
□	113 Benji Gil	.25	.11	.03
□	114 Kenny Lofton	1.50	.70	.19
□	115 Mike Kelly	.25	.11	.03
□	116 Ray Durham	1.00	.45	.12
□	117 Trevor Hoffman	.50	.23	.06
□	118 Butch Huskey	.50	.23	.06
□	119 Phil Nevin	.25	.11	.03
□	120 Pedro Martinez	.25	.11	.03
□	121 Wil Cordero	.25	.11	.03
□	122 Tim Salmon	1.00	.45	.12
□	123 Jim Edmonds	1.00	.45	.12
□	124 Mike Piazza	4.00	1.80	.50
□	125 Rico Brogna	.25	.11	.03
□	126 John Mabry	1.00	.45	.12
□	127 Chipper Jones	4.00	1.80	.50
□	128 Johnny Damon	.25	.11	.03
□	129 Raul Mondesi	1.00	.45	.12
□	130 Denny Neagle	.50	.23	.06
□	131 Marc Newfield	.50	.23	.06
□	132 Hideo Nomo	1.50	.70	.19
□	133 Joe Vitiello	.25	.11	.03
□	134 Garret Anderson	1.00	.45	.12
□	135 Dave Nilsson	.50	.23	.06
□	136 Alex Rodriguez	6.00	2.70	.75
□	137 Russ Davis	.25	.11	.03
□	138 Frank Rodriguez	.25	.11	.03
□	139 Royce Clayton	.25	.11	.03
□	140 John Valentin	.50	.23	.06
□	141 Marty Cordova	1.00	.45	.12
□	142 Alex Gonzalez	.25	.11	.03
□	143 Carlos Delgado	1.00	.45	.12
□	144 Willie Greene	.25	.11	.03
□	145 Cliff Floyd	.25	.11	.03
□	146 Bobby Higginson	1.00	.45	.12
□	147 J.T. Snow	.50	.23	.06
□	148 Derek Bell	.50	.23	.06
□	149 Edgardo Alfonzo	.50	.23	.06
□	150 Charles Johnson	.50	.23	.06
□	151 Hideo Nomo GR	1.00	.45	.12
□	152 Larry Walker GR	.50	.23	.06
□	153 Bob Abreu GR	1.00	.45	.12
□	154 Karim Garcia GR	.50	.23	.06
□	155 Dave Nilsson GR	.25	.11	.03
□	156 Chan Ho Park GR	1.00	.45	.12
□	157 Dennis Martinez GR	.25	.11	.03
□	158 Sammy Sosa GR	1.00	.45	.12
□	159 Rey Ordonez GR	1.00	.45	.12
□	160 Roberto Alomar GR	1.00	.45	.12
□	161 George Arias	.25	.11	.03
□	162 Jason Schmidt	.25	.11	.03
□	163 Derek Jeter	4.00	1.80	.50
□	164 Chris Snopek	.25	.11	.03
□	165 Todd Hollandsworth	1.00	.45	.12
□	166 Sal Fasano	.25	.11	.03
□	167 Jay Powell	.25	.11	.03
□	168 Paul Wilson	.50	.23	.06
□	169 Jim Pittsley	.25	.11	.03
□	170 LaTroy Hawkins	.25	.11	.03
□	171 Bob Abreu	1.00	.45	.12
□	172 Mike Grace	.25	.11	.03
□	173 Karim Garcia	1.25	.55	.16
□	174 Richard Hidalgo	.25	.11	.03
□	175 Felipe Crespo	.25	.11	.03
□	176 Terrell Wade	1.00	.45	.12
□	177 Steve Gibralter	.25	.11	.03
□	178 Jermaine Dye	1.50	.70	.19
□	179 Alan Benes	1.00	.45	.12
□	180 Wilton Guerrero	1.25	.55	.16
□	181 Brooks Kieschnick	.25	.11	.03
□	182 Roger Cedeno	.50	.23	.06
□	183 Osvaldo Fernandez	.50	.23	.06
□	184 Matt Lawton	.25	.11	.03
□	185 George Williams	.25	.11	.03
□	186 Jimmy Haynes	.25	.11	.03
□	187 Mike Busby	.50	.23	.06
□	188 Chan Ho Park	1.00	.45	.12
□	189 Marc Barcelo	.25	.11	.03

□ 190 Jason Kendall	1.00	.45	.12
□ 191 Rey Ordonez	1.25	.55	.16
□ 192 Tyler Houston	.25	.11	.03
□ 193 John Wasdin	.25	.11	.03
□ 194 Jeff Suppan	.50	.23	.06
□ 195 Jeff Ware	.25	.11	.03
□ 196 Ken Griffey Jr. CL	3.00	1.35	.35
□ 197 Albert Belle CL	1.50	.70	.19
□ 198 Mike Piazza CL	2.00	.90	.25
□ 199 Greg Maddux CL	2.00	.90	.25
□ 200 Frank Thomas CL	3.00	1.35	.35

1996 Pinnacle Aficionado Artist's Proofs

Randomly inserted in packs at a rate of one in 35, this 200-card set is a parallel set to the regular Pinnacle Aficionado set. A gold foil stamp in the shape of an artist's pen with the words, "Artist's Proof," printed above the wood-grain look bar containing the player's name distinguishes it from the regular set.

	MINT	NRMT	EXC
COMPLETE SET (200)	2000.00	900.00	250.00
COMMON CARD (1-200)	5.00	2.20	.60
SEMISTARS	12.00	5.50	1.50
STARS	30.00	13.50	3.70
*VETERAN STARS:15X to 30X BASIC CARDS			
*YOUNG STARS:12.5X to 25X BASIC CARDS			
RANDOM INSERTS IN PACKS			

□ 18 Cal Ripken	150.00	70.00	19.00
□ 22 Greg Maddux	125.00	55.00	15.50
□ 59 Frank Thomas	200.00	90.00	25.00
□ 75 Ken Griffey Jr.	200.00	90.00	25.00
□ 77 Albert Belle	100.00	45.00	12.50
□ 99 Juan Gonzalez	100.00	45.00	12.50
□ 124 Mike Piazza	125.00	55.00	15.50
□ 127 Chipper Jones	125.00	55.00	15.50
□ 136 Alex Rodriguez	200.00	90.00	25.00
□ 163 Derek Jeter	125.00	55.00	15.50
□ 196 Ken Griffey Jr. CL	100.00	45.00	12.50
□ 200 Frank Thomas CL	100.00	45.00	12.50

1996 Pinnacle Aficionado Magic Numbers

Randomly inserted in packs at a rate of one in 72, this 10-card set is printed on actual maple wood and features ten of of today's top superstars. The fronts feature an embossed color action player cut-out on a wood background. The backs carry trivia regarding the player's jersey number and those players from the past and present who share this same jersey number.

	MINT	NRMT	EXC
COMPLETE SET (10)	250.00	110.00	31.00
COMMON CARD (1-10)	6.00	2.70	.75
RANDOM INSERTS IN PACKS			

□ 1 Ken Griffey Jr.	50.00	22.00	6.25
□ 2 Greg Maddux	30.00	13.50	3.70
□ 3 Frank Thomas	50.00	22.00	6.25
□ 4 Mo Vaughn	12.00	5.50	1.50
□ 5 Jeff Bagwell	20.00	9.00	2.50
□ 6 Chipper Jones	30.00	13.50	3.70
□ 7 Albert Belle	25.00	11.00	3.10
□ 8 Cal Ripken	40.00	18.00	5.00
□ 9 Matt Williams	6.00	2.70	.75
□ 10 Sammy Sosa	8.00	3.60	1.00

1996 Pinnacle Aficionado Rivals

Randomly inserted in packs at a rate of one in 24, this 24-card set features two spot embossed color player photos of rival players. The backs carry a head photo of each and candid player comments on each other.

	MINT	NRMT	EXC
COMPLETE SET (24)	300.00	135.00	38.00
COMMON CARD (1-24)	10.00	4.50	1.25
SEMISTARS	15.00	6.75	1.85
RANDOM INSERTS IN PACKS			

□ 1 Ken Griffey Frank Thomas	25.00	11.00	3.10
□ 2 Frank Thomas Cal Ripken	25.00	11.00	3.10
□ 3 Cal Ripken Mo Vaughn	15.00	6.75	1.85
□ 4 Mo Vaughn Ken Griffey Jr.	18.00	8.00	2.20
□ 5 Ken Griffey Jr. Cal Ripken	25.00	11.00	3.10
□ 6 Frank Thomas Mo Vaughn	18.00	8.00	2.20
□ 7 Cal Ripken Ken Griffey Jr.	25.00	11.00	3.10
□ 8 Mo Vaughn Frank Thomas	18.00	8.00	2.20
□ 9 Ken Griffey Jr. Mo Vaughn	18.00	8.00	2.20
□ 10 Frank Thomas Ken Griffey Jr.	25.00	11.00	3.10
□ 11 Cal Ripken Frank Thomas	25.00	11.00	3.10
□ 12 Mo Vaughn Cal Ripken	15.00	6.75	1.85
□ 13 Mike Piazza Jeff Bagwell	10.00	4.50	1.25
□ 14 Jeff Bagwell Barry Bonds	10.00	4.50	1.25
□ 15 Jeff Bagwell Mike Piazza	10.00	4.50	1.25
□ 16 Tony Gwynn Mike Piazza	10.00	4.50	1.25
□ 17 Mike Piazza Barry Bonds	10.00	4.50	1.25
□ 18 Jeff Bagwell Tony Gwynn	10.00	4.50	1.25
□ 19 Barry Bonds Mike Piazza	10.00	4.50	1.25
□ 20 Tony Gwynn Jeff Bagwell	10.00	4.50	1.25
□ 21 Mike Piazza Tony Gwynn	10.00	4.50	1.25
□ 22 Barry Bonds Jeff Bagwell	10.00	4.50	1.25

	MINT	NRMT	EXC
□ 23 Tony Gwynn Barry Bonds	10.00	4.50	1.25
□ 24 Barry Bonds Tony Gwynn	10.00	4.50	1.25

1996 Pinnacle Aficionado Slick Picks

Randomly inserted in packs at a rate of one in 10, this 32-card set honors 32 draft picks for their future all-star abilities. Printed using a spectroetch print technology, the fronts feature a color action player photo on a black background on one side with a black-and-white player portrait on the other. A small simulated autograph and team name are printed below the portrait. The backs carry another color player portrait on a white background with a three-sided black border and information about when the player was drafted printed over a gray number indicating the round the player was selected in.

	MINT	NRMT	EXC
COMPLETE SET (32)	200.00	90.00	25.00
COMMON CARD (1-32)	2.00	.90	.25
SEMISTARS	3.00	1.35	.35
RANDOM INSERTS IN PACKS			

□ 1 Mike Piazza	15.00	6.75	1.85
□ 2 Cal Ripken	20.00	9.00	2.50
□ 3 Ken Griffey Jr.	25.00	11.00	3.10
□ 4 Paul Wilson	2.00	.90	.25
□ 5 Frank Thomas	25.00	11.00	3.10
□ 6 Mo Vaughn	6.00	2.70	.75
□ 7 Barry Bonds	6.00	2.70	.75
□ 8 Albert Belle	12.00	5.50	1.50
□ 9 Jeff Bagwell	10.00	4.50	1.25
□ 10 Dante Bichette	3.00	1.35	.35
□ 11 Hideo Nomo	6.00	2.70	.75
□ 12 Raul Mondesi	3.00	1.35	.35
□ 13 Manny Ramirez	6.00	2.70	.75
□ 14 Greg Maddux	15.00	6.75	1.85
□ 15 Tony Gwynn	10.00	4.50	1.25
□ 16 Ryne Sandberg	6.00	2.70	.75
□ 17 Reggie Sanders	2.00	.90	.25
□ 18 Derek Jeter	15.00	6.75	1.85
□ 19 Johnny Damon	2.00	.90	.25
□ 20 Alex Rodriguez	25.00	11.00	3.10
□ 21 Ryan Klesko	5.00	2.20	.60
□ 22 Jim Thome	5.00	2.20	.60
□ 23 Kenny Lofton	6.00	2.70	.75
□ 24 Tino Martinez	2.00	.90	.25
□ 25 Randy Johnson	4.00	1.80	.50
□ 26 Wade Boggs	3.00	1.35	.35
□ 27 Juan Gonzalez	12.00	5.50	1.50
□ 28 Kirby Puckett	8.00	3.60	1.00
□ 29 Tim Salmon	3.00	1.35	.35
□ 30 Chipper Jones	15.00	6.75	1.85
□ 31 Garret Anderson	2.00	.90	.25
□ 32 Eddie Murray	6.00	2.70	.75

1988 Score

This set consists of 660 standard-size cards. The set was distributed by Major League Marketing and features six distinctive border

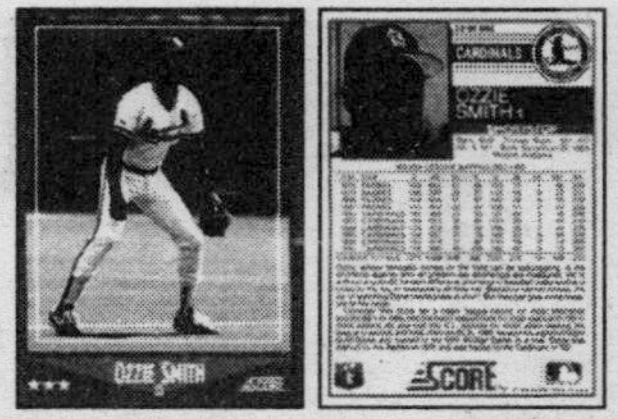

colors on the front. Subsets include Reggie Jackson Tribute (500-504), Highlights (652-660) and Rookie Prospects (623-647). Card number 501, showing Reggie as a member of the Baltimore Orioles, is one of the few opportunities collectors have to visually remember Reggie's one-year stay with the Orioles. The set is distinguished by the fact that each card back shows a full-color picture of the player. Rookie Cards in this set include Ellis Burks, Ken Caminiti, Ron Gant, Tom Glavine, Gregg Jefferies, Jeff Montgomery, and Matt Williams.

	MINT	NRMT	EXC
COMPLETE SET (660)	10.00	4.50	1.25
COMPLETE FACT.SET (660)	12.00	5.50	1.50
COMMON CARD (1-660)	.05	.02	.01
SEMISTARS	.10	.05	.01
STARS	.15	.07	.02

□ 1 Don Mattingly	.50	.23	.06
□ 2 Wade Boggs	.15	.07	.02
□ 3 Tim Raines	.15	.07	.02
□ 4 Andre Dawson	.15	.07	.02
□ 5 Mark McGwire	.60	.25	.07
□ 6 Kevin Seitzer	.10	.05	.01
□ 7 Wally Joyner	.10	.05	.01
□ 8 Jesse Barfield	.05	.02	.01
□ 9 Pedro Guerrero	.10	.05	.01
□ 10 Eric Davis	.10	.05	.01
□ 11 George Brett	.40	.18	.05
□ 12 Ozzie Smith	.20	.09	.03
□ 13 Rickey Henderson	.15	.07	.02
□ 14 Jim Rice	.15	.07	.02
□ 15 Matt Nokes	.05	.02	.01
□ 16 Mike Schmidt	.20	.09	.03
□ 17 Dave Parker	.15	.07	.02
□ 18 Eddie Murray	.25	.11	.03
□ 19 Andres Galarraga	.15	.07	.02
□ 20 Tony Fernandez	.05	.02	.01
□ 21 Kevin McReynolds	.05	.02	.01
□ 22 B.J. Surhoff	.10	.05	.01
□ 23 Pat Tabler	.05	.02	.01
□ 24 Kirby Puckett	.30	.14	.04
□ 25 Benny Santiago	.10	.05	.01
□ 26 Ryne Sandberg	.25	.11	.03
□ 27 Kelly Downs (Will Clark in background, out of focus)	.05	.02	.01
□ 28 Jose Cruz	.05	.02	.01
□ 29 Pete O'Brien	.05	.02	.01
□ 30 Mark Langston	.15	.07	.02
□ 31 Lee Smith	.15	.07	.02
□ 32 Juan Samuel	.05	.02	.01
□ 33 Kevin Bass	.05	.02	.01
□ 34 R.J. Reynolds	.05	.02	.01
□ 35 Steve Sax	.05	.02	.01
□ 36 John Kruk	.15	.07	.02
□ 37 Alan Trammell	.15	.07	.02
□ 38 Chris Bosio	.05	.02	.01
□ 39 Brook Jacoby	.05	.02	.01
□ 40 Willie McGee UER (Excited misspelled as excitd)	.05	.02	.01
□ 41 Dave Magadan	.05	.02	.01
□ 42 Fred Lynn	.05	.02	.01
□ 43 Kent Hrbek	.10	.05	.01
□ 44 Brian Downing	.05	.02	.01
□ 45 Jose Canseco	.25	.11	.03
□ 46 Jim Presley	.05	.02	.01

□ 47 Mike Stanley	.10	.05	.01
□ 48 Tony Pena	.05	.02	.01
□ 49 David Cone	.15	.07	.02
□ 50 Rick Sutcliffe	.05	.02	.01
□ 51 Doug Drabek	.10	.05	.01
□ 52 Bill Doran	.05	.02	.01
□ 53 Mike Scioscia	.05	.02	.01
□ 54 Candy Maldonado	.05	.02	.01
□ 55 Dave Winfield	.15	.07	.02
□ 56 Lou Whitaker	.15	.07	.02
□ 57 Tom Henke	.05	.02	.01
□ 58 Ken Gerhart	.05	.02	.01
□ 59 Glenn Braggs	.05	.02	.01
□ 60 Julio Franco	.10	.05	.01
□ 61 Charlie Leibrandt	.05	.02	.01
□ 62 Gary Gaetti	.05	.02	.01
□ 63 Bob Boone	.10	.05	.01
□ 64 Luis Polonia	.15	.07	.02
□ 65 Dwight Evans	.10	.05	.01
□ 66 Phil Bradley	.05	.02	.01
□ 67 Mike Boddicker	.05	.02	.01
□ 68 Vince Coleman	.05	.02	.01
□ 69 Howard Johnson	.05	.02	.01
□ 70 Tim Wallach	.05	.02	.01
□ 71 Keith Moreland	.05	.02	.01
□ 72 Barry Larkin	.30	.14	.04
□ 73 Alan Ashby	.05	.02	.01
□ 74 Rick Rhoden	.05	.02	.01
□ 75 Darrell Evans	.10	.05	.01
□ 76 Dave Stieb	.10	.05	.01
□ 77 Dan Plesac	.05	.02	.01
□ 78 Will Clark UER	.25	.11	.03
(Born 3/17/64, should be 3/13/64)			
□ 79 Frank White	.10	.05	.01
□ 80 Joe Carter	.15	.07	.02
□ 81 Mike Witt	.05	.02	.01
□ 82 Terry Steinbach	.10	.05	.01
□ 83 Alvin Davis	.05	.02	.01
□ 84 Tommy Herr	.10	.05	.01
(Will Clark shown sliding into second)			
□ 85 Vance Law	.05	.02	.01
□ 86 Kal Daniels	.05	.02	.01
□ 87 Rick Honeycutt UER	.05	.02	.01
(Wrong years for stats on back)			
□ 88 Alfredo Griffin	.05	.02	.01
□ 89 Bret Saberhagen	.10	.05	.01
□ 90 Bert Blyleven	.10	.05	.01
□ 91 Jeff Reardon	.10	.05	.01
□ 92 Cory Snyder	.05	.02	.01
□ 93A Greg Walker ERR	2.00	.90	.25
(93 of 66)			
□ 93B Greg Walker COR	.05	.02	.01
(93 of 660)			
□ 94 Joe Magrane	.05	.02	.01
□ 95 Rob Deer	.05	.02	.01
□ 96 Ray Knight	.10	.05	.01
□ 97 Casey Candaele	.05	.02	.01
□ 98 John Cerutti	.05	.02	.01
□ 99 Buddy Bell	.10	.05	.01
□ 100 Jack Clark	.10	.05	.01
□ 101 Eric Bell	.05	.02	.01
□ 102 Willie Wilson	.05	.02	.01
□ 103 Dave Schmidt	.05	.02	.01
□ 104 Dennis Eckersley UER	.15	.07	.02
(Complete games stats are wrong)			
□ 105 Don Sutton	.15	.07	.02
□ 106 Danny Tartabull	.05	.02	.01
□ 107 Fred McGriff	.30	.14	.04
□ 108 Les Straker	.05	.02	.01
□ 109 Lloyd Moseby	.05	.02	.01
□ 110 Roger Clemens	.15	.07	.02
□ 111 Glenn Hubbard	.05	.02	.01
□ 112 Ken Williams	.05	.02	.01
□ 113 Ruben Sierra	.15	.07	.02
□ 114 Stan Jefferson	.05	.02	.01
□ 115 Milt Thompson	.05	.02	.01
□ 116 Bobby Bonilla	.10	.05	.01
□ 117 Wayne Tolleson	.05	.02	.01
□ 118 Matt Williams	1.00	.45	.12
□ 119 Chet Lemon	.05	.02	.01
□ 120 Dale Sveum	.05	.02	.01
□ 121 Dennis Boyd	.05	.02	.01
□ 122 Brett Butler	.10	.05	.01
□ 123 Terry Kennedy	.05	.02	.01
□ 124 Jack Howell	.05	.02	.01
□ 125 Curt Young	.05	.02	.01
□ 126A Dave Valle ERR	.10	.05	.01
(Misspelled Dale on card front)			
□ 126B Dave Valle COR	.05	.02	.01
□ 127 Curt Wilkerson	.05	.02	.01
□ 128 Tim Teufel	.05	.02	.01
□ 129 Ozzie Virgil	.05	.02	.01
□ 130 Brian Fisher	.05	.02	.01
□ 131 Lance Parrish	.05	.02	.01
□ 132 Tom Browning	.05	.02	.01
□ 133A Larry Andersen ERR	.10	.05	.01
(Misspelled Anderson on card front)			
□ 133B Larry Andersen COR	.05	.02	.01
□ 134A Bob Brenly ERR	.10	.05	.01
(Misspelled Brenley on card front)			
□ 134B Bob Brenly COR	.05	.02	.01
□ 135 Mike Marshall	.05	.02	.01
□ 136 Gerald Perry	.05	.02	.01
□ 137 Bobby Meacham	.05	.02	.01
□ 138 Larry Herndon	.05	.02	.01
□ 139 Fred Manrique	.05	.02	.01
□ 140 Charlie Hough	.10	.05	.01
□ 141 Ron Darling	.05	.02	.01
□ 142 Herm Winningham	.05	.02	.01
□ 143 Mike Diaz	.05	.02	.01
□ 144 Mike Jackson	.10	.05	.01
□ 145 Denny Walling	.05	.02	.01
□ 146 Robby Thompson	.05	.02	.01
□ 147 Franklin Stubbs	.05	.02	.01
□ 148 Albert Hall	.05	.02	.01
□ 149 Bobby Witt	.05	.02	.01
□ 150 Lance McCullers	.05	.02	.01
□ 151 Scott Bradley	.05	.02	.01
□ 152 Mark McLemore	.05	.02	.01
□ 153 Tim Laudner	.05	.02	.01
□ 154 Greg Swindell	.05	.02	.01
□ 155 Marty Barrett	.05	.02	.01
□ 156 Mike Heath	.05	.02	.01
□ 157 Gary Ward	.05	.02	.01
□ 158A Lee Mazzilli ERR	.10	.05	.01
(Misspelled Mazilli on card front)			
□ 158B Lee Mazzilli COR	.05	.02	.01
□ 159 Tom Foley	.05	.02	.01
□ 160 Robin Yount	.15	.07	.02
□ 161 Steve Bedrosian	.05	.02	.01
□ 162 Bob Walk	.05	.02	.01
□ 163 Nick Esasky	.05	.02	.01
□ 164 Ken Caminiti	.75	.35	.09
□ 165 Jose Uribe	.05	.02	.01
□ 166 Dave Anderson	.05	.02	.01
□ 167 Ed Whitson	.05	.02	.01
□ 168 Ernie Whitt	.05	.02	.01
□ 169 Cecil Cooper	.10	.05	.01
□ 170 Mike Pagliarulo	.05	.02	.01
□ 171 Pat Sheridan	.05	.02	.01
□ 172 Chris Bando	.05	.02	.01
□ 173 Lee Lacy	.05	.02	.01
□ 174 Steve Lombardozzi	.05	.02	.01
□ 175 Mike Greenwell	.15	.07	.02
□ 176 Greg Minton	.05	.02	.01
□ 177 Moose Haas	.05	.02	.01
□ 178 Mike Kingery	.05	.02	.01
□ 179 Greg A. Harris	.05	.02	.01
□ 180 Bo Jackson	.15	.07	.02
□ 181 Carmelo Martinez	.05	.02	.01
□ 182 Alex Trevino	.05	.02	.01
□ 183 Ron Oester	.05	.02	.01
□ 184 Danny Darwin	.05	.02	.01
□ 185 Mike Krukow	.05	.02	.01
□ 186 Rafael Palmeiro	.25	.11	.03
□ 187 Tim Burke	.05	.02	.01
□ 188 Roger McDowell	.05	.02	.01
□ 189 Garry Templeton	.05	.02	.01
□ 190 Terry Pendleton	.10	.05	.01
□ 191 Larry Parrish	.05	.02	.01
□ 192 Rey Quinones	.05	.02	.01
□ 193 Joaquin Andujar	.05	.02	.01
□ 194 Tom Brunansky	.05	.02	.01
□ 195 Donnie Moore	.05	.02	.01

□ 196 Dan Pasqua	.05	.02	.01
□ 197 Jim Gantner	.05	.02	.01
□ 198 Mark Eichhorn	.05	.02	.01
□ 199 John Grubb	.05	.02	.01
□ 200 Bill Ripken	.10	.05	.01
□ 201 Sam Horn	.05	.02	.01
□ 202 Todd Worrell	.05	.02	.01
□ 203 Terry Leach	.05	.02	.01
□ 204 Garth Iorg	.05	.02	.01
□ 205 Brian Dayett	.05	.02	.01
□ 206 Bo Diaz	.05	.02	.01
□ 207 Craig Reynolds	.05	.02	.01
□ 208 Brian Holton	.05	.02	.01
□ 209 Marvell Wynne UER (Misspelled Marvelle on card front)	.05	.02	.01
□ 210 Dave Concepcion	.10	.05	.01
□ 211 Mike Davis	.05	.02	.01
□ 212 Devon White	.15	.07	.02
□ 213 Mickey Brantley	.05	.02	.01
□ 214 Greg Gagne	.05	.02	.01
□ 215 Oddibe McDowell	.05	.02	.01
□ 216 Jimmy Key	.10	.05	.01
□ 217 Dave Bergman	.05	.02	.01
□ 218 Calvin Schiraldi	.05	.02	.01
□ 219 Larry Sheets	.05	.02	.01
□ 220 Mike Easler	.05	.02	.01
□ 221 Kurt Stillwell	.05	.02	.01
□ 222 Chuck Jackson	.05	.02	.01
□ 223 Dave Martinez	.05	.02	.01
□ 224 Tim Leary	.05	.02	.01
□ 225 Steve Garvey	.15	.07	.02
□ 226 Greg Mathews	.05	.02	.01
□ 227 Doug Sisk	.05	.02	.01
□ 228 Dave Henderson (Wearing Red Sox uniform; Red Sox logo on back)	.05	.02	.01
□ 229 Jimmy Dwyer	.05	.02	.01
□ 230 Larry Owen	.05	.02	.01
□ 231 Andre Thornton	.10	.05	.01
□ 232 Mark Salas	.05	.02	.01
□ 233 Tom Brookens	.05	.02	.01
□ 234 Greg Brock	.05	.02	.01
□ 235 Rance Mulliniks	.05	.02	.01
□ 236 Bob Brower	.05	.02	.01
□ 237 Joe Niekro	.05	.02	.01
□ 238 Scott Bankhead	.05	.02	.01
□ 239 Doug DeCinces	.05	.02	.01
□ 240 Tommy John	.10	.05	.01
□ 241 Rich Gedman	.05	.02	.01
□ 242 Ted Power	.05	.02	.01
□ 243 Dave Meads	.05	.02	.01
□ 244 Jim Sundberg	.05	.02	.01
□ 245 Ken Oberkfell	.05	.02	.01
□ 246 Jimmy Jones	.05	.02	.01
□ 247 Ken Landreaux	.05	.02	.01
□ 248 Jose Oquendo	.05	.02	.01
□ 249 John Mitchell	.05	.02	.01
□ 250 Don Baylor	.15	.07	.02
□ 251 Scott Fletcher	.05	.02	.01
□ 252 Al Newman	.05	.02	.01
□ 253 Carney Lansford	.10	.05	.01
□ 254 Johnny Ray	.05	.02	.01
□ 255 Gary Pettis	.05	.02	.01
□ 256 Ken Phelps	.05	.02	.01
□ 257 Rick Leach	.05	.02	.01
□ 258 Tim Stoddard	.05	.02	.01
□ 259 Ed Romero	.05	.02	.01
□ 260 Sid Bream	.05	.02	.01
□ 261A Tom Niedenfuer ERR (Misspelled Neidenfuer on card front)	.10	.05	.01
□ 261B Tom Niedenfuer COR	.05	.02	.01
□ 262 Rick Dempsey	.05	.02	.01
□ 263 Lonnie Smith	.05	.02	.01
□ 264 Bob Forsch	.05	.02	.01
□ 265 Barry Bonds	.60	.25	.07
□ 266 Willie Randolph	.10	.05	.01
□ 267 Mike Ramsey	.05	.02	.01
□ 268 Don Slaught	.05	.02	.01
□ 269 Mickey Tettleton	.10	.05	.01
□ 270 Jerry Reuss	.05	.02	.01
□ 271 Marc Sullivan	.05	.02	.01
□ 272 Jim Morrison	.05	.02	.01
□ 273 Steve Balboni	.05	.02	.01
□ 274 Dick Schofield	.05	.02	.01
□ 275 John Tudor	.05	.02	.01
□ 276 Gene Larkin	.05	.02	.01
□ 277 Harold Reynolds	.05	.02	.01
□ 278 Jerry Browne	.05	.02	.01
□ 279 Willie Upshaw	.05	.02	.01
□ 280 Ted Higuera	.05	.02	.01
□ 281 Terry McGriff	.05	.02	.01
□ 282 Terry Puhl	.05	.02	.01
□ 283 Mark Wasinger	.05	.02	.01
□ 284 Luis Salazar	.05	.02	.01
□ 285 Ted Simmons	.10	.05	.01
□ 286 John Shelby	.05	.02	.01
□ 287 John Smiley	.15	.07	.02
□ 288 Curt Ford	.05	.02	.01
□ 289 Steve Crawford	.05	.02	.01
□ 290 Dan Quisenberry	.05	.02	.01
□ 291 Alan Wiggins	.05	.02	.01
□ 292 Randy Bush	.05	.02	.01
□ 293 John Candelaria	.05	.02	.01
□ 294 Tony Phillips	.15	.07	.02
□ 295 Mike Morgan	.05	.02	.01
□ 296 Bill Wegman	.05	.02	.01
□ 297A Terry Francona ERR (Misspelled Franconia on card front)	.10	.05	.01
□ 297B Terry Francona COR	.05	.02	.01
□ 298 Mickey Hatcher	.05	.02	.01
□ 299 Andres Thomas	.05	.02	.01
□ 300 Bob Stanley	.05	.02	.01
□ 301 Al Pedrique	.05	.02	.01
□ 302 Jim Lindeman	.05	.02	.01
□ 303 Wally Backman	.05	.02	.01
□ 304 Paul O'Neill	.15	.07	.02
□ 305 Hubie Brooks	.05	.02	.01
□ 306 Steve Buechele	.05	.02	.01
□ 307 Bobby Thigpen	.05	.02	.01
□ 308 George Hendrick	.05	.02	.01
□ 309 John Moses	.05	.02	.01
□ 310 Ron Guidry	.05	.02	.01
□ 311 Bill Schroeder	.05	.02	.01
□ 312 Jose Nunez	.05	.02	.01
□ 313 Bud Black	.05	.02	.01
□ 314 Joe Sambito	.05	.02	.01
□ 315 Scott McGregor	.05	.02	.01
□ 316 Rafael Santana	.05	.02	.01
□ 317 Frank Williams	.05	.02	.01
□ 318 Mike Fitzgerald	.05	.02	.01
□ 319 Rick Mahler	.05	.02	.01
□ 320 Jim Gott	.05	.02	.01
□ 321 Mariano Duncan	.05	.02	.01
□ 322 Jose Guzman	.05	.02	.01
□ 323 Lee Guetterman	.05	.02	.01
□ 324 Dan Gladden	.05	.02	.01
□ 325 Gary Carter	.15	.07	.02
□ 326 Tracy Jones	.05	.02	.01
□ 327 Floyd Youmans	.05	.02	.01
□ 328 Bill Dawley	.05	.02	.01
□ 329 Paul Noce	.05	.02	.01
□ 330 Angel Salazar	.05	.02	.01
□ 331 Goose Gossage	.15	.07	.02
□ 332 George Frazier	.05	.02	.01
□ 333 Ruppert Jones	.05	.02	.01
□ 334 Billy Joe Robidoux	.05	.02	.01
□ 335 Mike Scott	.05	.02	.01
□ 336 Randy Myers	.10	.05	.01
□ 337 Bob Sebra	.05	.02	.01
□ 338 Eric Show	.05	.02	.01
□ 339 Mitch Williams	.10	.05	.01
□ 340 Paul Molitor	.20	.09	.03
□ 341 Gus Polidor	.05	.02	.01
□ 342 Steve Trout	.05	.02	.01
□ 343 Jerry Don Gleaton	.05	.02	.01
□ 344 Bob Knepper	.05	.02	.01
□ 345 Mitch Webster	.05	.02	.01
□ 346 John Morris	.05	.02	.01
□ 347 Andy Hawkins	.05	.02	.01
□ 348 Dave Leiper	.05	.02	.01
□ 349 Ernest Riles	.05	.02	.01
□ 350 Dwight Gooden	.15	.07	.02
□ 351 Dave Righetti	.10	.05	.01
□ 352 Pat Dodson	.05	.02	.01
□ 353 John Habyan	.05	.02	.01
□ 354 Jim Deshaies	.05	.02	.01
□ 355 Butch Wynegar	.05	.02	.01
□ 356 Bryn Smith	.05	.02	.01
□ 357 Matt Young	.05	.02	.01

□ 358	Tom Pagnozzi	.10	.05	.01
□ 359	Floyd Rayford	.05	.02	.01
□ 360	Darryl Strawberry	.15	.07	.02
□ 361	Sal Butera	.05	.02	.01
□ 362	Domingo Ramos	.05	.02	.01
□ 363	Chris Brown	.05	.02	.01
□ 364	Jose Gonzalez	.05	.02	.01
□ 365	Dave Smith	.05	.02	.01
□ 366	Andy McGaffigan	.05	.02	.01
□ 367	Stan Javier	.05	.02	.01
□ 368	Henry Cotto	.05	.02	.01
□ 369	Mike Birkbeck	.05	.02	.01
□ 370	Len Dykstra	.10	.05	.01
□ 371	Dave Collins	.05	.02	.01
□ 372	Spike Owen	.05	.02	.01
□ 373	Geno Petralli	.05	.02	.01
□ 374	Ron Karkovice	.05	.02	.01
□ 375	Shane Rawley	.05	.02	.01
□ 376	DeWayne Buice	.05	.02	.01
□ 377	Bill Pecota	.05	.02	.01
□ 378	Leon Durham	.05	.02	.01
□ 379	Ed Olwine	.05	.02	.01
□ 380	Bruce Hurst	.05	.02	.01
□ 381	Bob McClure	.05	.02	.01
□ 382	Mark Thurmond	.05	.02	.01
□ 383	Buddy Biancalana	.05	.02	.01
□ 384	Tim Conroy	.05	.02	.01
□ 385	Tony Gwynn	.40	.18	.05
□ 386	Greg Gross	.05	.02	.01
□ 387	Barry Lyons	.05	.02	.01
□ 388	Mike Felder	.05	.02	.01
□ 389	Pat Clements	.05	.02	.01
□ 390	Ken Griffey	.05	.02	.01
□ 391	Mark Davis	.05	.02	.01
□ 392	Jose Rijo	.05	.02	.01
□ 393	Mike Young	.05	.02	.01
□ 394	Willie Fraser	.05	.02	.01
□ 395	Dion James	.05	.02	.01
□ 396	Steve Shields	.05	.02	.01
□ 397	Randy St.Claire	.05	.02	.01
□ 398	Danny Jackson	.05	.02	.01
□ 399	Cecil Fielder	.15	.07	.02
□ 400	Keith Hernandez	.10	.05	.01
□ 401	Don Carman	.05	.02	.01
□ 402	Chuck Crim	.05	.02	.01
□ 403	Rob Woodward	.05	.02	.01
□ 404	Junior Ortiz	.05	.02	.01
□ 405	Glenn Wilson	.05	.02	.01
□ 406	Ken Howell	.05	.02	.01
□ 407	Jeff Kunkel	.05	.02	.01
□ 408	Jeff Reed	.05	.02	.01
□ 409	Chris James	.05	.02	.01
□ 410	Zane Smith	.05	.02	.01
□ 411	Ken Dixon	.05	.02	.01
□ 412	Ricky Horton	.05	.02	.01
□ 413	Frank DiPino	.05	.02	.01
□ 414	Shane Mack	.05	.02	.01
□ 415	Danny Cox	.05	.02	.01
□ 416	Andy Van Slyke	.10	.05	.01
□ 417	Danny Heep	.05	.02	.01
□ 418	John Cangelosi	.05	.02	.01
□ 419A	John Christensen ERR (Christiansen on card front)	.10	.05	.01
□ 419B	John Christensen COR	.05	.02	.01
□ 420	Joey Cora	.15	.07	.02
□ 421	Mike LaValliere	.05	.02	.01
□ 422	Kelly Gruber	.05	.02	.01
□ 423	Bruce Benedict	.05	.02	.01
□ 424	Len Matuszek	.05	.02	.01
□ 425	Kent Tekulve	.05	.02	.01
□ 426	Rafael Ramirez	.05	.02	.01
□ 427	Mike Flanagan	.05	.02	.01
□ 428	Mike Gallego	.05	.02	.01
□ 429	Juan Castillo	.05	.02	.01
□ 430	Neal Heaton	.05	.02	.01
□ 431	Phil Garner	.05	.02	.01
□ 432	Mike Dunne	.05	.02	.01
□ 433	Wallace Johnson	.05	.02	.01
□ 434	Jack O'Connor	.05	.02	.01
□ 435	Steve Jeltz	.05	.02	.01
□ 436	Donell Nixon	.05	.02	.01
□ 437	Jack Lazorko	.05	.02	.01
□ 438	Keith Comstock	.05	.02	.01
□ 439	Jeff D. Robinson	.05	.02	.01
□ 440	Graig Nettles	.10	.05	.01
□ 441	Mel Hall	.05	.02	.01
□ 442	Gerald Young	.05	.02	.01
□ 443	Gary Redus	.05	.02	.01
□ 444	Charlie Moore	.05	.02	.01
□ 445	Bill Madlock	.05	.02	.01
□ 446	Mark Clear	.05	.02	.01
□ 447	Greg Booker	.05	.02	.01
□ 448	Rick Schu	.05	.02	.01
□ 449	Ron Kittle	.05	.02	.01
□ 450	Dale Murphy	.15	.07	.02
□ 451	Bob Dernier	.05	.02	.01
□ 452	Dale Mohorcic	.05	.02	.01
□ 453	Rafael Belliard	.05	.02	.01
□ 454	Charlie Puleo	.05	.02	.01
□ 455	Dwayne Murphy	.05	.02	.01
□ 456	Jim Eisenreich	.10	.05	.01
□ 457	David Palmer	.05	.02	.01
□ 458	Dave Stewart	.15	.07	.02
□ 459	Pascual Perez	.05	.02	.01
□ 460	Glenn Davis	.05	.02	.01
□ 461	Dan Petry	.05	.02	.01
□ 462	Jim Winn	.05	.02	.01
□ 463	Darrell Miller	.05	.02	.01
□ 464	Mike Moore	.05	.02	.01
□ 465	Mike LaCoss	.05	.02	.01
□ 466	Steve Farr	.05	.02	.01
□ 467	Jerry Mumphrey	.05	.02	.01
□ 468	Kevin Gross	.05	.02	.01
□ 469	Bruce Bochy	.05	.02	.01
□ 470	Orel Hershiser	.15	.07	.02
□ 471	Eric King	.05	.02	.01
□ 472	Ellis Burks	.40	.18	.05
□ 473	Darren Daulton	.10	.05	.01
□ 474	Mookie Wilson	.10	.05	.01
□ 475	Frank Viola	.05	.02	.01
□ 476	Ron Robinson	.05	.02	.01
□ 477	Bob Melvin	.05	.02	.01
□ 478	Jeff Musselman	.05	.02	.01
□ 479	Charlie Kerfeld	.05	.02	.01
□ 480	Richard Dotson	.05	.02	.01
□ 481	Kevin Mitchell	.10	.05	.01
□ 482	Gary Roenicke	.05	.02	.01
□ 483	Tim Flannery	.05	.02	.01
□ 484	Rich Yett	.05	.02	.01
□ 485	Pete Incaviglia	.05	.02	.01
□ 486	Rick Cerone	.05	.02	.01
□ 487	Tony Armas	.05	.02	.01
□ 488	Jerry Reed	.05	.02	.01
□ 489	Dave Lopes	.10	.05	.01
□ 490	Frank Tanana	.05	.02	.01
□ 491	Mike Loynd	.05	.02	.01
□ 492	Bruce Ruffin	.05	.02	.01
□ 493	Chris Speier	.05	.02	.01
□ 494	Tom Hume	.05	.02	.01
□ 495	Jesse Orosco	.05	.02	.01
□ 496	Robbie Wine UER (Misspelled Robby on card front)	.05	.02	.01
□ 497	Jeff Montgomery	.20	.09	.03
□ 498	Jeff Dedmon	.05	.02	.01
□ 499	Luis Aguayo	.05	.02	.01
□ 500	Reggie Jackson (Oakland A's)	.15	.07	.02
□ 501	Reggie Jackson (Baltimore Orioles)	.15	.07	.02
□ 502	Reggie Jackson (New York Yankees)	.15	.07	.02
□ 503	Reggie Jackson (California Angels)	.15	.07	.02
□ 504	Reggie Jackson (Oakland A's)	.15	.07	.02
□ 505	Billy Hatcher	.05	.02	.01
□ 506	Ed Lynch	.05	.02	.01
□ 507	Willie Hernandez	.05	.02	.01
□ 508	Jose DeLeon	.05	.02	.01
□ 509	Joel Youngblood	.05	.02	.01
□ 510	Bob Welch	.05	.02	.01
□ 511	Steve Ontiveros	.05	.02	.01
□ 512	Randy Ready	.05	.02	.01
□ 513	Juan Nieves	.05	.02	.01
□ 514	Jeff Russell	.05	.02	.01
□ 515	Von Hayes	.05	.02	.01
□ 516	Mark Gubicza	.05	.02	.01
□ 517	Ken Dayley	.05	.02	.01
□ 518	Don Aase	.05	.02	.01
□ 519	Rick Reuschel	.05	.02	.01

□ 520	Mike Henneman	.10	.05	.01
□ 521	Rick Aguilera	.10	.05	.01
□ 522	Jay Howell	.05	.02	.01
□ 523	Ed Correa	.05	.02	.01
□ 524	Manny Trillo	.05	.02	.01
□ 525	Kirk Gibson	.10	.05	.01
□ 526	Wally Ritchie	.05	.02	.01
□ 527	Al Nipper	.05	.02	.01
□ 528	Atlee Hammaker	.05	.02	.01
□ 529	Shawon Dunston	.05	.02	.01
□ 530	Jim Clancy	.05	.02	.01
□ 531	Tom Paciorek	.05	.02	.01
□ 532	Joel Skinner	.05	.02	.01
□ 533	Scott Garrelts	.05	.02	.01
□ 534	Tom O'Malley	.05	.02	.01
□ 535	John Franco	.05	.02	.01
□ 536	Paul Kilgus	.05	.02	.01
□ 537	Darrell Porter	.05	.02	.01
□ 538	Walt Terrell	.05	.02	.01
□ 539	Bill Long	.05	.02	.01
□ 540	George Bell	.05	.02	.01
□ 541	Jeff Sellers	.05	.02	.01
□ 542	Joe Boever	.05	.02	.01
□ 543	Steve Howe	.05	.02	.01
□ 544	Scott Sanderson	.05	.02	.01
□ 545	Jack Morris	.15	.07	.02
□ 546	Todd Benzinger	.10	.05	.01
□ 547	Steve Henderson	.05	.02	.01
□ 548	Eddie Milner	.05	.02	.01
□ 549	Jeff M. Robinson	.05	.02	.01
□ 550	Cal Ripken	.75	.35	.09
□ 551	Jody Davis	.05	.02	.01
□ 552	Kirk McCaskill	.05	.02	.01
□ 553	Craig Lefferts	.05	.02	.01
□ 554	Darnell Coles	.05	.02	.01
□ 555	Phil Niekro	.15	.07	.02
□ 556	Mike Aldrete	.05	.02	.01
□ 557	Pat Perry	.05	.02	.01
□ 558	Juan Agosto	.05	.02	.01
□ 559	Rob Murphy	.05	.02	.01
□ 560	Dennis Rasmussen	.05	.02	.01
□ 561	Manny Lee	.05	.02	.01
□ 562	Jeff Blauser	.15	.07	.02
□ 563	Bob Ojeda	.05	.02	.01
□ 564	Dave Dravecky	.10	.05	.01
□ 565	Gene Garber	.05	.02	.01
□ 566	Ron Roenicke	.05	.02	.01
□ 567	Tommy Hinzo	.05	.02	.01
□ 568	Eric Nolte	.05	.02	.01
□ 569	Ed Hearn	.05	.02	.01
□ 570	Mark Davidson	.05	.02	.01
□ 571	Jim Walewander	.05	.02	.01
□ 572	Donnie Hill UER (84 Stolen Base total listed as 7)	.05	.02	.01
□ 573	Jamie Moyer	.05	.02	.01
□ 574	Ken Schrom	.05	.02	.01
□ 575	Nolan Ryan	.75	.35	.09
□ 576	Jim Acker	.05	.02	.01
□ 577	Jamie Quirk	.05	.02	.01
□ 578	Jay Aldrich	.05	.02	.01
□ 579	Claudell Washington	.05	.02	.01
□ 580	Jeff Leonard	.05	.02	.01
□ 581	Carmen Castillo	.05	.02	.01
□ 582	Daryl Boston	.05	.02	.01
□ 583	Jeff DeWillis	.05	.02	.01
□ 584	John Marzano	.05	.02	.01
□ 585	Bill Gullickson	.05	.02	.01
□ 586	Andy Allanson	.05	.02	.01
□ 587	Lee Tunnell UER (1987 stat line reads .4.84 ERA)	.05	.02	.01
□ 588	Gene Nelson	.05	.02	.01
□ 589	Dave LaPoint	.05	.02	.01
□ 590	Harold Baines	.10	.05	.01
□ 591	Bill Buckner	.10	.05	.01
□ 592	Carlton Fisk	.15	.07	.02
□ 593	Rick Manning	.05	.02	.01
□ 594	Doug Jones	.10	.05	.01
□ 595	Tom Candiotti	.05	.02	.01
□ 596	Steve Lake	.05	.02	.01
□ 597	Jose Lind	.10	.05	.01
□ 598	Ross Jones	.05	.02	.01
□ 599	Gary Matthews	.05	.02	.01
□ 600	Fernando Valenzuela	.10	.05	.01
□ 601	Dennis Martinez	.10	.05	.01
□ 602	Les Lancaster	.05	.02	.01
□ 603	Ozzie Guillen	.10	.05	.01
□ 604	Tony Bernazard	.05	.02	.01
□ 605	Chili Davis	.15	.07	.02
□ 606	Roy Smalley	.05	.02	.01
□ 607	Ivan Calderon	.05	.02	.01
□ 608	Jay Tibbs	.05	.02	.01
□ 609	Guy Hoffman	.05	.02	.01
□ 610	Doyle Alexander	.05	.02	.01
□ 611	Mike Bielecki	.05	.02	.01
□ 612	Shawn Hillegas	.05	.02	.01
□ 613	Keith Atherton	.05	.02	.01
□ 614	Eric Plunk	.05	.02	.01
□ 615	Sid Fernandez	.05	.02	.01
□ 616	Dennis Lamp	.05	.02	.01
□ 617	Dave Engle	.05	.02	.01
□ 618	Harry Spilman	.05	.02	.01
□ 619	Don Robinson	.05	.02	.01
□ 620	John Farrell	.05	.02	.01
□ 621	Nelson Liriano	.05	.02	.01
□ 622	Floyd Bannister	.05	.02	.01
□ 623	Randy Milligan	.05	.02	.01
□ 624	Kevin Elster	.15	.07	.02
□ 625	Jody Reed	.10	.05	.01
□ 626	Shawn Abner	.05	.02	.01
□ 627	Kirt Manwaring	.10	.05	.01
□ 628	Pete Stanicek	.05	.02	.01
□ 629	Rob Ducey	.05	.02	.01
□ 630	Steve Kiefer	.05	.02	.01
□ 631	Gary Thurman	.05	.02	.01
□ 632	Darrel Akerfelds	.05	.02	.01
□ 633	Dave Clark	.05	.02	.01
□ 634	Roberto Kelly	.15	.07	.02
□ 635	Keith Hughes	.05	.02	.01
□ 636	John Davis	.05	.02	.01
□ 637	Mike Devereaux	.15	.07	.02
□ 638	Tom Glavine	1.00	.45	.12
□ 639	Keith A. Miller	.05	.02	.01
□ 640	Chris Gwynn UER (Wrong batting and throwing on back)	.10	.05	.01
□ 641	Tim Crews	.10	.05	.01
□ 642	Mackey Sasser	.05	.02	.01
□ 643	Vicente Palacios	.05	.02	.01
□ 644	Kevin Romine	.05	.02	.01
□ 645	Gregg Jefferies	.40	.18	.05
□ 646	Jeff Treadway	.05	.02	.01
□ 647	Ron Gant	.40	.18	.05
□ 648	Mark McGwire and Matt Nokes (Rookie Sluggers)	.15	.07	.02
□ 649	Eric Davis and Tim Raines (Speed and Power)	.10	.05	.01
□ 650	Don Mattingly and Jack Clark	.20	.09	.03
□ 651	Tony Fernandez, Alan Trammell, and Cal Ripken	.30	.14	.04
□ 652	Vince Coleman HL 100 Stolen Bases	.05	.02	.01
□ 653	Kirby Puckett HL 10 Hits in a Row	.15	.07	.02
□ 654	Benito Santiago HL Hitting Streak	.05	.02	.01
□ 655	Juan Nieves HL No Hitter	.05	.02	.01
□ 656	Steve Bedrosian HL Saves Record	.05	.02	.01
□ 657	Mike Schmidt HL 500 Homers	.15	.07	.02
□ 658	Don Mattingly HL Home Run Streak	.25	.11	.03
□ 659	Mark McGwire HL Rookie HR Record	.30	.14	.04
□ 660	Paul Molitor HL Hitting Streak	.15	.07	.02

1988 Score Rookie/Traded

This 110-card standard-size set features traded players (1-65) and rookies (66-110) for the 1988 season. The cards are distinguishable from the regular Score set by the orange borders and by the fact that the numbering on the

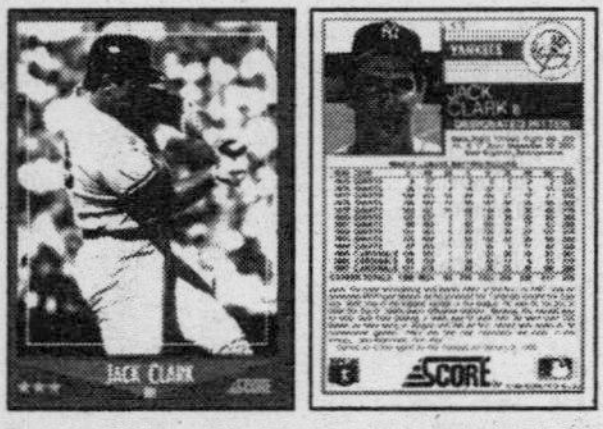

back has a T suffix. The cards were distributed exclusively in factory set form along with some trivia cards. Apparently Score's first attempt at a Rookie/Traded set was produced very conservatively, resulting in a set which is now recognized as being much tougher to find than the other Rookie/Traded sets from the other major companies of that year. Extended Rookie Cards in this set include Roberto Alomar, Brady Anderson, Craig Biggio, Jay Buhner, Mark Grace, Darryl Hamilton, Jack McDowell, Todd Stottlemyre and Walt Weiss.

	MINT	NRMT	EXC
COMPLETE FACT.SET (110)	50.00	22.00	6.25
COMMON CARD (1T-110T)	.15	.07	.02
SEMISTARS	.40	.18	.05
STARS	.75	.35	.09
□ 1T Jack Clark	.40	.18	.05
□ 2T Danny Jackson	.15	.07	.02
□ 3T Brett Butler	.40	.18	.05
□ 4T Kurt Stillwell	.15	.07	.02
□ 5T Tom Brunansky	.15	.07	.02
□ 6T Dennis Lamp	.15	.07	.02
□ 7T Jose DeLeon	.15	.07	.02
□ 8T Tom Herr	.15	.07	.02
□ 9T Keith Moreland	.15	.07	.02
□ 10T Kirk Gibson	.40	.18	.05
□ 11T Bud Black	.15	.07	.02
□ 12T Rafael Ramirez	.15	.07	.02
□ 13T Luis Salazar	.15	.07	.02
□ 14T Goose Gossage	.75	.35	.09
□ 15T Bob Welch	.15	.07	.02
□ 16T Vance Law	.15	.07	.02
□ 17T Ray Knight	.40	.18	.05
□ 18T Dan Quisenberry	.15	.07	.02
□ 19T Don Slaught	.15	.07	.02
□ 20T Lee Smith	.75	.35	.09
□ 21T Rick Cerone	.15	.07	.02
□ 22T Pat Tabler	.15	.07	.02
□ 23T Larry McWilliams	.15	.07	.02
□ 24T Ricky Horton	.15	.07	.02
□ 25T Graig Nettles	.40	.18	.05
□ 26T Dan Petry	.15	.07	.02
□ 27T Jose Rijo	.15	.07	.02
□ 28T Chili Davis	.75	.35	.09
□ 29T Dickie Thon	.15	.07	.02
□ 30T Mackey Sasser	.15	.07	.02
□ 31T Mickey Tettleton	.40	.18	.05
□ 32T Rick Dempsey	.15	.07	.02
□ 33T Ron Hassey	.15	.07	.02
□ 34T Phil Bradley	.15	.07	.02
□ 35T Jay Howell	.15	.07	.02
□ 36T Bill Buckner	.40	.18	.05
□ 37T Alfredo Griffin	.15	.07	.02
□ 38T Gary Pettis	.15	.07	.02
□ 39T Calvin Schiraldi	.15	.07	.02
□ 40T John Candelaria	.15	.07	.02
□ 41T Joe Orsulak	.15	.07	.02
□ 42T Willie Upshaw	.15	.07	.02
□ 43T Herm Winningham	.15	.07	.02
□ 44T Ron Kittle	.15	.07	.02
□ 45T Bob Dernier	.15	.07	.02
□ 46T Steve Balboni	.15	.07	.02
□ 47T Steve Shields	.15	.07	.02
□ 48T Henry Cotto	.15	.07	.02
□ 49T Dave Henderson	.15	.07	.02
□ 50T Dave Parker	.75	.35	.09
□ 51T Mike Young	.15	.07	.02
□ 52T Mark Salas	.15	.07	.02
□ 53T Mike Davis	.15	.07	.02
□ 54T Rafael Santana	.15	.07	.02
□ 55T Don Baylor	.75	.35	.09
□ 56T Dan Pasqua	.15	.07	.02
□ 57T Ernest Riles	.15	.07	.02
□ 58T Glenn Hubbard	.15	.07	.02
□ 59T Mike Smithson	.15	.07	.02
□ 60T Richard Dotson	.15	.07	.02
□ 61T Jerry Reuss	.15	.07	.02
□ 62T Mike Jackson	.40	.18	.05
□ 63T Floyd Bannister	.15	.07	.02
□ 64T Jesse Orosco	.15	.07	.02
□ 65T Larry Parrish	.15	.07	.02
□ 66T Jeff Bittiger	.15	.07	.02
□ 67T Ray Hayward	.15	.07	.02
□ 68T Ricky Jordan	.40	.18	.05
□ 69T Tommy Gregg	.15	.07	.02
□ 70T Brady Anderson	12.00	5.50	1.50
□ 71T Jeff Montgomery	.75	.35	.09
□ 72T Darryl Hamilton	.40	.18	.05
□ 73T Cecil Espy	.15	.07	.02
□ 74T Greg Briley	.15	.07	.02
□ 75T Joey Meyer	.15	.07	.02
□ 76T Mike Macfarlane	.75	.35	.09
□ 77T Oswald Peraza	.15	.07	.02
□ 78T Jack Armstrong	.15	.07	.02
□ 79T Don Heinkel	.15	.07	.02
□ 80T Mark Grace	8.00	3.60	1.00
□ 81T Steve Curry	.15	.07	.02
□ 82T Damon Berryhill	.15	.07	.02
□ 83T Steve Ellsworth	.15	.07	.02
□ 84T Pete Smith	.15	.07	.02
□ 85T Jack McDowell	5.00	2.20	.60
□ 86T Rob Dibble	.40	.18	.05
□ 87T Bryan Harvey UER (Games Pitched 47, Innings 5)	.40	.18	.05
□ 88T John Dopson	.15	.07	.02
□ 89T Dave Gallagher	.15	.07	.02
□ 90T Todd Stottlemyre	1.50	.70	.19
□ 91T Mike Schooler	.15	.07	.02
□ 92T Don Gordon	.15	.07	.02
□ 93T Sil Campusano	.15	.07	.02
□ 94T Jeff Pico	.15	.07	.02
□ 95T Jay Buhner	12.00	5.50	1.50
□ 96T Nelson Santovenia	.15	.07	.02
□ 97T Al Leiter	.75	.35	.09
□ 98T Luis Alicea	.40	.18	.05
□ 99T Pat Borders	.40	.18	.05
□ 100T Chris Sabo	.40	.18	.05
□ 101T Tim Belcher	.15	.07	.02
□ 102T Walt Weiss	.40	.18	.05
□ 103T Craig Biggio	8.00	3.60	1.00
□ 104T Don August	.15	.07	.02
□ 105T Roberto Alomar	25.00	11.00	3.10
□ 106T Todd Burns	.15	.07	.02
□ 107T John Costello	.15	.07	.02
□ 108T Melido Perez	.40	.18	.05
□ 109T Darrin Jackson	.40	.18	.05
□ 110T Orestes Destrade	.75	.35	.09

1989 Score

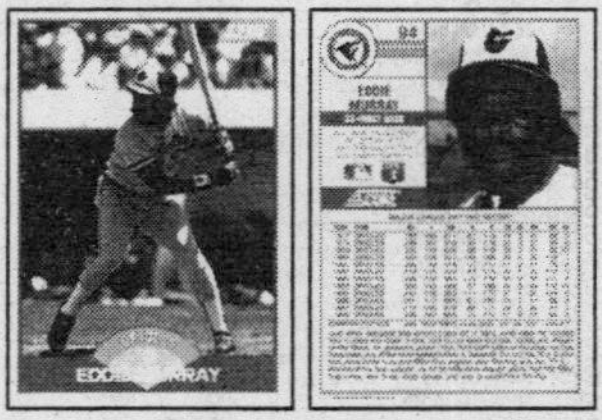

This 660-card standard-size set was distributed by Major League Marketing. Cards were issued primarily in fin-wrapped plastic packs and factory sets. Cards feature six distinctive inner border (inside a white outer border) colors on the

front. Subsets include Highlights (652-660) and Rookie Prospects (621-651). Rookie Cards in this set include Sandy Alomar Jr., Brady Anderson, Craig Biggio, Charlie Hayes, Randy Johnson, Ramon Martinez, Gary Sheffield, and John Smoltz.

	MINT	NRMT	EXC
COMPLETE SET (660)	8.00	3.60	1.00
COMPLETE FACT.SET (660)	8.00	3.60	1.00
COMMON CARD (1-660)	.05	.02	.01
SEMISTARS	.10	.05	.01
STARS	.15	.07	.02
□ 1 Jose Canseco	.15	.07	.02
□ 2 Andre Dawson	.15	.07	.02
□ 3 Mark McGwire UER	.30	.14	.04
□ 4 Benito Santiago	.10	.05	.01
□ 5 Rick Reuschel	.05	.02	.01
□ 6 Fred McGriff	.20	.09	.03
□ 7 Kal Daniels	.05	.02	.01
□ 8 Gary Gaetti	.05	.02	.01
□ 9 Ellis Burks	.15	.07	.02
□ 10 Darryl Strawberry	.10	.05	.01
□ 11 Julio Franco	.10	.05	.01
□ 12 Lloyd Moseby	.05	.02	.01
□ 13 Jeff Pico	.05	.02	.01
□ 14 Johnny Ray	.05	.02	.01
□ 15 Cal Ripken	.75	.35	.09
□ 16 Dick Schofield	.05	.02	.01
□ 17 Mel Hall	.05	.02	.01
□ 18 Bill Ripken	.05	.02	.01
□ 19 Brook Jacoby	.05	.02	.01
□ 20 Kirby Puckett	.30	.14	.04
□ 21 Bill Doran	.05	.02	.01
□ 22 Pete O'Brien	.05	.02	.01
□ 23 Matt Nokes	.05	.02	.01
□ 24 Brian Fisher	.05	.02	.01
□ 25 Jack Clark	.10	.05	.01
□ 26 Gary Pettis	.05	.02	.01
□ 27 Dave Valle	.05	.02	.01
□ 28 Willie Wilson	.05	.02	.01
□ 29 Curt Young	.05	.02	.01
□ 30 Dale Murphy	.15	.07	.02
□ 31 Barry Larkin	.20	.09	.03
□ 32 Dave Stewart	.10	.05	.01
□ 33 Mike LaValliere	.05	.02	.01
□ 34 Glenn Hubbard	.05	.02	.01
□ 35 Ryne Sandberg	.25	.11	.03
□ 36 Tony Pena	.05	.02	.01
□ 37 Greg Walker	.05	.02	.01
□ 38 Von Hayes	.05	.02	.01
□ 39 Kevin Mitchell	.10	.05	.01
□ 40 Tim Raines	.15	.07	.02
□ 41 Keith Hernandez	.10	.05	.01
□ 42 Keith Moreland	.05	.02	.01
□ 43 Ruben Sierra	.10	.05	.01
□ 44 Chet Lemon	.05	.02	.01
□ 45 Willie Randolph	.10	.05	.01
□ 46 Andy Allanson	.05	.02	.01
□ 47 Candy Maldonado	.05	.02	.01
□ 48 Sid Bream	.05	.02	.01
□ 49 Denny Walling	.05	.02	.01
□ 50 Dave Winfield	.15	.07	.02
□ 51 Alvin Davis	.05	.02	.01
□ 52 Cory Snyder	.05	.02	.01
□ 53 Hubie Brooks	.05	.02	.01
□ 54 Chili Davis	.10	.05	.01
□ 55 Kevin Seitzer	.05	.02	.01
□ 56 Jose Uribe	.05	.02	.01
□ 57 Tony Fernandez	.05	.02	.01
□ 58 Tim Teufel	.05	.02	.01
□ 59 Oddibe McDowell	.05	.02	.01
□ 60 Les Lancaster	.05	.02	.01
□ 61 Billy Hatcher	.05	.02	.01
□ 62 Dan Gladden	.05	.02	.01
□ 63 Marty Barrett	.05	.02	.01
□ 64 Nick Esasky	.05	.02	.01
□ 65 Wally Joyner	.10	.05	.01
□ 66 Mike Greenwell	.05	.02	.01
□ 67 Ken Williams	.05	.02	.01
□ 68 Bob Horner	.05	.02	.01
□ 69 Steve Sax	.05	.02	.01
□ 70 Rickey Henderson	.15	.07	.02
□ 71 Mitch Webster	.05	.02	.01
□ 72 Rob Deer	.05	.02	.01
□ 73 Jim Presley	.05	.02	.01
□ 74 Albert Hall	.05	.02	.01
□ 75 George Brett COR (At age 35)	.40	.18	.05
□ 75A George Brett ERR (At age 33)	.75	.35	.09
□ 76 Brian Downing	.05	.02	.01
□ 77 Dave Martinez	.05	.02	.01
□ 78 Scott Fletcher	.05	.02	.01
□ 79 Phil Bradley	.05	.02	.01
□ 80 Ozzie Smith	.20	.09	.03
□ 81 Larry Sheets	.05	.02	.01
□ 82 Mike Aldrete	.05	.02	.01
□ 83 Darnell Coles	.05	.02	.01
□ 84 Len Dykstra	.10	.05	.01
□ 85 Jim Rice	.15	.07	.02
□ 86 Jeff Treadway	.05	.02	.01
□ 87 Jose Lind	.05	.02	.01
□ 88 Willie McGee	.05	.02	.01
□ 89 Mickey Brantley	.05	.02	.01
□ 90 Tony Gwynn	.40	.18	.05
□ 91 R.J. Reynolds	.05	.02	.01
□ 92 Milt Thompson	.05	.02	.01
□ 93 Kevin McReynolds	.05	.02	.01
□ 94 Eddie Murray UER ('86 batting .205, should be .305)	.25	.11	.03
□ 95 Lance Parrish	.05	.02	.01
□ 96 Ron Kittle	.05	.02	.01
□ 97 Gerald Young	.05	.02	.01
□ 98 Ernie Whitt	.05	.02	.01
□ 99 Jeff Reed	.05	.02	.01
□ 100 Don Mattingly	.50	.23	.06
□ 101 Gerald Perry	.05	.02	.01
□ 102 Vance Law	.05	.02	.01
□ 103 John Shelby	.05	.02	.01
□ 104 Chris Sabo	.05	.02	.01
□ 105 Danny Tartabull	.05	.02	.01
□ 106 Glenn Wilson	.05	.02	.01
□ 107 Mark Davidson	.05	.02	.01
□ 108 Dave Parker	.10	.05	.01
□ 109 Eric Davis	.10	.05	.01
□ 110 Alan Trammell	.15	.07	.02
□ 111 Ozzie Virgil	.05	.02	.01
□ 112 Frank Tanana	.05	.02	.01
□ 113 Rafael Ramirez	.05	.02	.01
□ 114 Dennis Martinez	.10	.05	.01
□ 115 Jose DeLeon	.05	.02	.01
□ 116 Bob Ojeda	.05	.02	.01
□ 117 Doug Drabek	.10	.05	.01
□ 118 Andy Hawkins	.05	.02	.01
□ 119 Greg Maddux	.75	.35	.09
□ 120 Cecil Fielder UER (Photo on back reversed)	.10	.05	.01
□ 121 Mike Scioscia	.05	.02	.01
□ 122 Dan Petry	.05	.02	.01
□ 123 Terry Kennedy	.05	.02	.01
□ 124 Kelly Downs	.05	.02	.01
□ 125 Greg Gross UER (Gregg on back)	.05	.02	.01
□ 126 Fred Lynn	.05	.02	.01
□ 127 Barry Bonds	.40	.18	.05
□ 128 Harold Baines	.10	.05	.01
□ 129 Doyle Alexander	.05	.02	.01
□ 130 Kevin Elster	.10	.05	.01
□ 131 Mike Heath	.05	.02	.01
□ 132 Teddy Higuera	.05	.02	.01
□ 133 Charlie Leibrandt	.05	.02	.01
□ 134 Tim Laudner	.05	.02	.01
□ 135A Ray Knight ERR (Reverse negative)	.15	.07	.02
□ 135B Ray Knight COR	.05	.02	.01
□ 136 Howard Johnson	.05	.02	.01
□ 137 Terry Pendleton	.10	.05	.01
□ 138 Andy McGaffigan	.05	.02	.01
□ 139 Ken Oberkfell	.05	.02	.01
□ 140 Butch Wynegar	.05	.02	.01
□ 141 Rob Murphy	.05	.02	.01
□ 142 Rich Renteria	.05	.02	.01
□ 143 Jose Guzman	.05	.02	.01
□ 144 Andres Galarraga	.15	.07	.02
□ 145 Ricky Horton	.05	.02	.01
□ 146 Frank DiPino	.05	.02	.01
□ 147 Glenn Braggs	.05	.02	.01
□ 148 John Kruk	.10	.05	.01

☐ 149	Mike Schmidt	.20	.09	.03
☐ 150	Lee Smith	.15	.07	.02
☐ 151	Robin Yount	.15	.07	.02
☐ 152	Mark Eichhorn	.05	.02	.01
☐ 153	DeWayne Buice	.05	.02	.01
☐ 154	B.J. Surhoff	.15	.07	.02
☐ 155	Vince Coleman	.05	.02	.01
☐ 156	Tony Phillips	.15	.07	.02
☐ 157	Willie Fraser	.05	.02	.01
☐ 158	Lance McCullers	.05	.02	.01
☐ 159	Greg Gagne	.05	.02	.01
☐ 160	Jesse Barfield	.05	.02	.01
☐ 161	Mark Langston	.10	.05	.01
☐ 162	Kurt Stillwell	.05	.02	.01
☐ 163	Dion James	.05	.02	.01
☐ 164	Glenn Davis	.05	.02	.01
☐ 165	Walt Weiss	.05	.02	.01
☐ 166	Dave Concepcion	.10	.05	.01
☐ 167	Alfredo Griffin	.05	.02	.01
☐ 168	Don Heinkel	.05	.02	.01
☐ 169	Luis Rivera	.05	.02	.01
☐ 170	Shane Rawley	.05	.02	.01
☐ 171	Darrell Evans	.10	.05	.01
☐ 172	Robby Thompson	.05	.02	.01
☐ 173	Jody Davis	.05	.02	.01
☐ 174	Andy Van Slyke	.10	.05	.01
☐ 175	Wade Boggs UER (Bio says .364, should be .356)	.15	.07	.02
☐ 176	Garry Templeton ('85 stats off-centered)	.05	.02	.01
☐ 177	Gary Redus	.05	.02	.01
☐ 178	Craig Lefferts	.05	.02	.01
☐ 179	Carney Lansford	.10	.05	.01
☐ 180	Ron Darling	.05	.02	.01
☐ 181	Kirk McCaskill	.05	.02	.01
☐ 182	Tony Armas	.05	.02	.01
☐ 183	Steve Farr	.05	.02	.01
☐ 184	Tom Brunansky	.05	.02	.01
☐ 185	Bryan Harvey UER ('87 games 47, should be 3)	.10	.05	.01
☐ 186	Mike Marshall	.05	.02	.01
☐ 187	Bo Diaz	.05	.02	.01
☐ 188	Willie Upshaw	.05	.02	.01
☐ 189	Mike Pagliarulo	.05	.02	.01
☐ 190	Mike Krukow	.05	.02	.01
☐ 191	Tommy Herr	.05	.02	.01
☐ 192	Jim Pankovits	.05	.02	.01
☐ 193	Dwight Evans	.10	.05	.01
☐ 194	Kelly Gruber	.05	.02	.01
☐ 195	Bobby Bonilla	.10	.05	.01
☐ 196	Wallace Johnson	.05	.02	.01
☐ 197	Dave Stieb	.05	.02	.01
☐ 198	Pat Borders	.10	.05	.01
☐ 199	Rafael Palmeiro	.15	.07	.02
☐ 200	Dwight Gooden	.10	.05	.01
☐ 201	Pete Incaviglia	.10	.05	.01
☐ 202	Chris James	.05	.02	.01
☐ 203	Marvell Wynne	.05	.02	.01
☐ 204	Pat Sheridan	.05	.02	.01
☐ 205	Don Baylor	.15	.07	.02
☐ 206	Paul O'Neill	.15	.07	.02
☐ 207	Pete Smith	.05	.02	.01
☐ 208	Mark McLemore	.05	.02	.01
☐ 209	Henry Cotto	.05	.02	.01
☐ 210	Kirk Gibson	.10	.05	.01
☐ 211	Claudell Washington	.05	.02	.01
☐ 212	Randy Bush	.05	.02	.01
☐ 213	Joe Carter	.15	.07	.02
☐ 214	Bill Buckner	.10	.05	.01
☐ 215	Bert Blyleven UER (Wrong birth year)	.10	.05	.01
☐ 216	Brett Butler	.10	.05	.01
☐ 217	Lee Mazzilli	.05	.02	.01
☐ 218	Spike Owen	.05	.02	.01
☐ 219	Bill Swift	.05	.02	.01
☐ 220	Tim Wallach	.05	.02	.01
☐ 221	David Cone	.15	.07	.02
☐ 222	Don Carman	.05	.02	.01
☐ 223	Rich Gossage	.15	.07	.02
☐ 224	Bob Walk	.05	.02	.01
☐ 225	Dave Righetti	.05	.02	.01
☐ 226	Kevin Bass	.05	.02	.01
☐ 227	Kevin Gross	.05	.02	.01
☐ 228	Tim Burke	.05	.02	.01
☐ 229	Rick Mahler	.05	.02	.01
☐ 230	Lou Whitaker UER (252 games in '85, should be 152)	.15	.07	.02
☐ 231	Luis Alicea	.05	.02	.01
☐ 232	Roberto Alomar	.50	.23	.06
☐ 233	Bob Boone	.10	.05	.01
☐ 234	Dickie Thon	.05	.02	.01
☐ 235	Shawon Dunston	.05	.02	.01
☐ 236	Pete Stanicek	.05	.02	.01
☐ 237	Craig Biggio (Inconsistent design, portrait on front)	.40	.18	.05
☐ 238	Dennis Boyd	.05	.02	.01
☐ 239	Tom Candiotti	.05	.02	.01
☐ 240	Gary Carter	.15	.07	.02
☐ 241	Mike Stanley	.05	.02	.01
☐ 242	Ken Phelps	.05	.02	.01
☐ 243	Chris Bosio	.05	.02	.01
☐ 244	Les Straker	.05	.02	.01
☐ 245	Dave Smith	.05	.02	.01
☐ 246	John Candelaria	.05	.02	.01
☐ 247	Joe Orsulak	.05	.02	.01
☐ 248	Storm Davis	.05	.02	.01
☐ 249	Floyd Bannister UER (ML Batting Record)	.05	.02	.01
☐ 250	Jack Morris	.10	.05	.01
☐ 251	Bret Saberhagen	.10	.05	.01
☐ 252	Tom Niedenfuer	.05	.02	.01
☐ 253	Neal Heaton	.05	.02	.01
☐ 254	Eric Show	.05	.02	.01
☐ 255	Juan Samuel	.05	.02	.01
☐ 256	Dale Sveum	.05	.02	.01
☐ 257	Jim Gott	.05	.02	.01
☐ 258	Scott Garrelts	.05	.02	.01
☐ 259	Larry McWilliams	.05	.02	.01
☐ 260	Steve Bedrosian	.05	.02	.01
☐ 261	Jack Howell	.05	.02	.01
☐ 262	Jay Tibbs	.05	.02	.01
☐ 263	Jamie Moyer	.05	.02	.01
☐ 264	Doug Sisk	.05	.02	.01
☐ 265	Todd Worrell	.05	.02	.01
☐ 266	John Farrell	.05	.02	.01
☐ 267	Dave Collins	.05	.02	.01
☐ 268	Sid Fernandez	.05	.02	.01
☐ 269	Tom Brookens	.05	.02	.01
☐ 270	Shane Mack	.05	.02	.01
☐ 271	Paul Kilgus	.05	.02	.01
☐ 272	Chuck Crim	.05	.02	.01
☐ 273	Bob Knepper	.05	.02	.01
☐ 274	Mike Moore	.05	.02	.01
☐ 275	Guillermo Hernandez	.05	.02	.01
☐ 276	Dennis Eckersley	.10	.05	.01
☐ 277	Graig Nettles	.10	.05	.01
☐ 278	Rich Dotson	.05	.02	.01
☐ 279	Larry Herndon	.05	.02	.01
☐ 280	Gene Larkin	.05	.02	.01
☐ 281	Roger McDowell	.05	.02	.01
☐ 282	Greg Swindell	.05	.02	.01
☐ 283	Juan Agosto	.05	.02	.01
☐ 284	Jeff M. Robinson	.05	.02	.01
☐ 285	Mike Dunne	.05	.02	.01
☐ 286	Greg Mathews	.05	.02	.01
☐ 287	Kent Tekulve	.05	.02	.01
☐ 288	Jerry Mumphrey	.05	.02	.01
☐ 289	Jack McDowell	.15	.07	.02
☐ 290	Frank Viola	.05	.02	.01
☐ 291	Mark Gubicza	.05	.02	.01
☐ 292	Dave Schmidt	.05	.02	.01
☐ 293	Mike Henneman	.05	.02	.01
☐ 294	Jimmy Jones	.05	.02	.01
☐ 295	Charlie Hough	.10	.05	.01
☐ 296	Rafael Santana	.05	.02	.01
☐ 297	Chris Speier	.05	.02	.01
☐ 298	Mike Witt	.05	.02	.01
☐ 299	Pascual Perez	.05	.02	.01
☐ 300	Nolan Ryan	.75	.35	.09
☐ 301	Mitch Williams	.05	.02	.01
☐ 302	Mookie Wilson	.10	.05	.01
☐ 303	Mackey Sasser	.05	.02	.01
☐ 304	John Cerutti	.05	.02	.01
☐ 305	Jeff Reardon	.10	.05	.01
☐ 306	Randy Myers UER (6 hits in '87, should be 61)	.10	.05	.01

□ 307	Greg Brock	.05	.02	.01
□ 308	Bob Welch	.05	.02	.01
□ 309	Jeff D. Robinson	.05	.02	.01
□ 310	Harold Reynolds	.05	.02	.01
□ 311	Jim Walewander	.05	.02	.01
□ 312	Dave Magadan	.05	.02	.01
□ 313	Jim Gantner	.05	.02	.01
□ 314	Walt Terrell	.05	.02	.01
□ 315	Wally Backman	.05	.02	.01
□ 316	Luis Salazar	.05	.02	.01
□ 317	Rick Rhoden	.05	.02	.01
□ 318	Tom Henke	.05	.02	.01
□ 319	Mike Macfarlane	.10	.05	.01
□ 320	Dan Plesac	.05	.02	.01
□ 321	Calvin Schiraldi	.05	.02	.01
□ 322	Stan Javier	.05	.02	.01
□ 323	Devon White	.10	.05	.01
□ 324	Scott Bradley	.05	.02	.01
□ 325	Bruce Hurst	.05	.02	.01
□ 326	Manny Lee	.05	.02	.01
□ 327	Rick Aguilera	.15	.07	.02
□ 328	Bruce Ruffin	.05	.02	.01
□ 329	Ed Whitson	.05	.02	.01
□ 330	Bo Jackson	.15	.07	.02
□ 331	Ivan Calderon	.05	.02	.01
□ 332	Mickey Hatcher	.05	.02	.01
□ 333	Barry Jones	.05	.02	.01
□ 334	Ron Hassey	.05	.02	.01
□ 335	Bill Wegman	.05	.02	.01
□ 336	Damon Berryhill	.05	.02	.01
□ 337	Steve Ontiveros	.05	.02	.01
□ 338	Dan Pasqua	.05	.02	.01
□ 339	Bill Pecota	.05	.02	.01
□ 340	Greg Cadaret	.05	.02	.01
□ 341	Scott Bankhead	.05	.02	.01
□ 342	Ron Guidry	.05	.02	.01
□ 343	Danny Heep	.05	.02	.01
□ 344	Bob Brower	.05	.02	.01
□ 345	Rich Gedman	.05	.02	.01
□ 346	Nelson Santovenia	.05	.02	.01
□ 347	George Bell	.05	.02	.01
□ 348	Ted Power	.05	.02	.01
□ 349	Mark Grant	.05	.02	.01
□ 350A	Roger Clemens ERR (778 career wins)	2.00	.90	.25
□ 350B	Roger Clemens COR (78 career wins)	.15	.07	.02
□ 351	Bill Long	.05	.02	.01
□ 352	Jay Bell	.15	.07	.02
□ 353	Steve Balboni	.05	.02	.01
□ 354	Bob Kipper	.05	.02	.01
□ 355	Steve Jeltz	.05	.02	.01
□ 356	Jesse Orosco	.05	.02	.01
□ 357	Bob Dernier	.05	.02	.01
□ 358	Mickey Tettleton	.10	.05	.01
□ 359	Duane Ward	.05	.02	.01
□ 360	Darrin Jackson	.05	.02	.01
□ 361	Rey Quinones	.05	.02	.01
□ 362	Mark Grace	.20	.09	.03
□ 363	Steve Lake	.05	.02	.01
□ 364	Pat Perry	.05	.02	.01
□ 365	Terry Steinbach	.10	.05	.01
□ 366	Alan Ashby	.05	.02	.01
□ 367	Jeff Montgomery	.10	.05	.01
□ 368	Steve Buechele	.05	.02	.01
□ 369	Chris Brown	.05	.02	.01
□ 370	Orel Hershiser	.15	.07	.02
□ 371	Todd Benzinger	.05	.02	.01
□ 372	Ron Gant	.15	.07	.02
□ 373	Paul Assenmacher	.05	.02	.01
□ 374	Joey Meyer	.05	.02	.01
□ 375	Neil Allen	.05	.02	.01
□ 376	Mike Davis	.05	.02	.01
□ 377	Jeff Parrett	.05	.02	.01
□ 378	Jay Howell	.05	.02	.01
□ 379	Rafael Belliard	.05	.02	.01
□ 380	Luis Polonia UER (2 triples in '87, should be 10)	.10	.05	.01
□ 381	Keith Atherton	.05	.02	.01
□ 382	Kent Hrbek	.10	.05	.01
□ 383	Bob Stanley	.05	.02	.01
□ 384	Dave LaPoint	.05	.02	.01
□ 385	Rance Mulliniks	.05	.02	.01
□ 386	Melido Perez	.05	.02	.01
□ 387	Doug Jones	.05	.02	.01
□ 388	Steve Lyons	.05	.02	.01
□ 389	Alejandro Pena	.05	.02	.01
□ 390	Frank White	.10	.05	.01
□ 391	Pat Tabler	.05	.02	.01
□ 392	Eric Plunk	.05	.02	.01
□ 393	Mike Maddux	.05	.02	.01
□ 394	Allan Anderson	.05	.02	.01
□ 395	Bob Brenly	.05	.02	.01
□ 396	Rick Cerone	.05	.02	.01
□ 397	Scott Terry	.05	.02	.01
□ 398	Mike Jackson	.05	.02	.01
□ 399	Bobby Thigpen UER (Bio says 37 saves in '88, should be 34)	.05	.02	.01
□ 400	Don Sutton	.15	.07	.02
□ 401	Cecil Espy	.05	.02	.01
□ 402	Junior Ortiz	.05	.02	.01
□ 403	Mike Smithson	.05	.02	.01
□ 404	Bud Black	.05	.02	.01
□ 405	Tom Foley	.05	.02	.01
□ 406	Andres Thomas	.05	.02	.01
□ 407	Rick Sutcliffe	.05	.02	.01
□ 408	Brian Harper	.05	.02	.01
□ 409	John Smiley	.05	.02	.01
□ 410	Juan Nieves	.05	.02	.01
□ 411	Shawn Abner	.05	.02	.01
□ 412	Wes Gardner	.05	.02	.01
□ 413	Darren Daulton	.10	.05	.01
□ 414	Juan Berenguer	.05	.02	.01
□ 415	Charles Hudson	.05	.02	.01
□ 416	Rick Honeycutt	.05	.02	.01
□ 417	Greg Booker	.05	.02	.01
□ 418	Tim Belcher	.05	.02	.01
□ 419	Don August	.05	.02	.01
□ 420	Dale Mohorcic	.05	.02	.01
□ 421	Steve Lombardozzi	.05	.02	.01
□ 422	Atlee Hammaker	.05	.02	.01
□ 423	Jerry Don Gleaton	.05	.02	.01
□ 424	Scott Bailes	.05	.02	.01
□ 425	Bruce Sutter	.05	.02	.01
□ 426	Randy Ready	.05	.02	.01
□ 427	Jerry Reed	.05	.02	.01
□ 428	Bryn Smith	.05	.02	.01
□ 429	Tim Leary	.05	.02	.01
□ 430	Mark Clear	.05	.02	.01
□ 431	Terry Leach	.05	.02	.01
□ 432	John Moses	.05	.02	.01
□ 433	Ozzie Guillen	.05	.02	.01
□ 434	Gene Nelson	.05	.02	.01
□ 435	Gary Ward	.05	.02	.01
□ 436	Luis Aguayo	.05	.02	.01
□ 437	Fernando Valenzuela	.10	.05	.01
□ 438	Jeff Russell UER (Saves total does not add up correctly)	.05	.02	.01
□ 439	Cecilio Guante	.05	.02	.01
□ 440	Don Robinson	.05	.02	.01
□ 441	Rick Anderson	.05	.02	.01
□ 442	Tom Glavine	.25	.11	.03
□ 443	Daryl Boston	.05	.02	.01
□ 444	Joe Price	.05	.02	.01
□ 445	Stewart Cliburn	.05	.02	.01
□ 446	Manny Trillo	.05	.02	.01
□ 447	Joel Skinner	.05	.02	.01
□ 448	Charlie Puleo	.05	.02	.01
□ 449	Carlton Fisk	.15	.07	.02
□ 450	Will Clark	.20	.09	.03
□ 451	Otis Nixon	.05	.02	.01
□ 452	Rick Schu	.05	.02	.01
□ 453	Todd Stottlemyre UER (ML Batting Record)	.10	.05	.01
□ 454	Tim Birtsas	.05	.02	.01
□ 455	Dave Gallagher	.05	.02	.01
□ 456	Barry Lyons	.05	.02	.01
□ 457	Fred Manrique	.05	.02	.01
□ 458	Ernest Riles	.05	.02	.01
□ 459	Doug Jennings	.05	.02	.01
□ 460	Joe Magrane	.05	.02	.01
□ 461	Jamie Quirk	.05	.02	.01
□ 462	Jack Armstrong	.05	.02	.01
□ 463	Bobby Witt	.05	.02	.01
□ 464	Keith A. Miller	.05	.02	.01
□ 465	Todd Burns	.05	.02	.01
□ 466	John Dopson	.05	.02	.01
□ 467	Rich Yett	.05	.02	.01
□ 468	Craig Reynolds	.05	.02	.01

□ 469 Dave Bergman	.05	.02	.01
□ 470 Rex Hudler	.05	.02	.01
□ 471 Eric King	.05	.02	.01
□ 472 Joaquin Andujar	.05	.02	.01
□ 473 Sil Campusano	.05	.02	.01
□ 474 Terry Mulholland	.05	.02	.01
□ 475 Mike Flanagan	.05	.02	.01
□ 476 Greg A. Harris	.05	.02	.01
□ 477 Tommy John	.10	.05	.01
□ 478 Dave Anderson	.05	.02	.01
□ 479 Fred Toliver	.05	.02	.01
□ 480 Jimmy Key	.10	.05	.01
□ 481 Donell Nixon	.05	.02	.01
□ 482 Mark Portugal	.05	.02	.01
□ 483 Tom Pagnozzi	.05	.02	.01
□ 484 Jeff Kunkel	.05	.02	.01
□ 485 Frank Williams	.05	.02	.01
□ 486 Jody Reed	.05	.02	.01
□ 487 Roberto Kelly	.10	.05	.01
□ 488 Shawn Hillegas UER (165 innings in '87, should be 165.2)	.05	.02	.01
□ 489 Jerry Reuss	.05	.02	.01
□ 490 Mark Davis	.05	.02	.01
□ 491 Jeff Sellers	.05	.02	.01
□ 492 Zane Smith	.05	.02	.01
□ 493 Al Newman	.05	.02	.01
□ 494 Mike Young	.05	.02	.01
□ 495 Larry Parrish	.05	.02	.01
□ 496 Herm Winningham	.05	.02	.01
□ 497 Carmen Castillo	.05	.02	.01
□ 498 Joe Hesketh	.05	.02	.01
□ 499 Darrell Miller	.05	.02	.01
□ 500 Mike LaCoss	.05	.02	.01
□ 501 Charlie Lea	.05	.02	.01
□ 502 Bruce Benedict	.05	.02	.01
□ 503 Chuck Finley	.10	.05	.01
□ 504 Brad Wellman	.05	.02	.01
□ 505 Tim Crews	.05	.02	.01
□ 506 Ken Gerhart	.05	.02	.01
□ 507A Brian Holton ERR (Born 1/25/65 Denver, should be 11/29/59 in McKeesport)	.05	.02	.01
□ 507B Brian Holton COR	2.00	.90	.25
□ 508 Dennis Lamp	.05	.02	.01
□ 509 Bobby Meacham UER ('84 games 099)	.05	.02	.01
□ 510 Tracy Jones	.05	.02	.01
□ 511 Mike R. Fitzgerald	.05	.02	.01
□ 512 Jeff Bittiger	.05	.02	.01
□ 513 Tim Flannery	.05	.02	.01
□ 514 Ray Hayward	.05	.02	.01
□ 515 Dave Leiper	.05	.02	.01
□ 516 Rod Scurry	.05	.02	.01
□ 517 Carmelo Martinez	.05	.02	.01
□ 518 Curtis Wilkerson	.05	.02	.01
□ 519 Stan Jefferson	.05	.02	.01
□ 520 Dan Quisenberry	.05	.02	.01
□ 521 Lloyd McClendon	.05	.02	.01
□ 522 Steve Trout	.05	.02	.01
□ 523 Larry Andersen	.05	.02	.01
□ 524 Don Aase	.05	.02	.01
□ 525 Bob Forsch	.05	.02	.01
□ 526 Geno Petralli	.05	.02	.01
□ 527 Angel Salazar	.05	.02	.01
□ 528 Mike Schooler	.05	.02	.01
□ 529 Jose Oquendo	.05	.02	.01
□ 530 Jay Buhner UER (Wearing 43 on front, listed as 34 on back)	.25	.11	.03
□ 531 Tom Bolton	.05	.02	.01
□ 532 Al Nipper	.05	.02	.01
□ 533 Dave Henderson	.05	.02	.01
□ 534 John Costello	.05	.02	.01
□ 535 Donnie Moore	.05	.02	.01
□ 536 Mike Laga	.05	.02	.01
□ 537 Mike Gallego	.05	.02	.01
□ 538 Jim Clancy	.05	.02	.01
□ 539 Joel Youngblood	.05	.02	.01
□ 540 Rick Leach	.05	.02	.01
□ 541 Kevin Romine	.05	.02	.01
□ 542 Mark Salas	.05	.02	.01
□ 543 Greg Minton	.05	.02	.01
□ 544 Dave Palmer	.05	.02	.01
□ 545 Dwayne Murphy UER (Game-sinning)	.05	.02	.01
□ 546 Jim Deshaies	.05	.02	.01
□ 547 Don Gordon	.05	.02	.01
□ 548 Ricky Jordan	.10	.05	.01
□ 549 Mike Boddicker	.05	.02	.01
□ 550 Mike Scott	.05	.02	.01
□ 551 Jeff Ballard	.05	.02	.01
□ 552A Jose Rijo ERR (Uniform listed as 27 on back)	.15	.07	.02
□ 552B Jose Rijo COR (Uniform listed as 24 on back)	.15	.07	.02
□ 553 Danny Darwin	.05	.02	.01
□ 554 Tom Browning	.05	.02	.01
□ 555 Danny Jackson	.05	.02	.01
□ 556 Rick Dempsey	.05	.02	.01
□ 557 Jeffrey Leonard	.05	.02	.01
□ 558 Jeff Musselman	.05	.02	.01
□ 559 Ron Robinson	.05	.02	.01
□ 560 John Tudor	.05	.02	.01
□ 561 Don Slaught UER (237 games in 1987)	.05	.02	.01
□ 562 Dennis Rasmussen	.05	.02	.01
□ 563 Brady Anderson	.60	.25	.07
□ 564 Pedro Guerrero	.10	.05	.01
□ 565 Paul Molitor	.20	.09	.03
□ 566 Terry Clark	.05	.02	.01
□ 567 Terry Puhl	.05	.02	.01
□ 568 Mike Campbell	.05	.02	.01
□ 569 Paul Mirabella	.05	.02	.01
□ 570 Jeff Hamilton	.05	.02	.01
□ 571 Oswald Peraza	.05	.02	.01
□ 572 Bob McClure	.05	.02	.01
□ 573 Jose Bautista	.05	.02	.01
□ 574 Alex Trevino	.05	.02	.01
□ 575 John Franco	.05	.02	.01
□ 576 Mark Parent	.05	.02	.01
□ 577 Nelson Liriano	.05	.02	.01
□ 578 Steve Shields	.05	.02	.01
□ 579 Odell Jones	.05	.02	.01
□ 580 Al Leiter	.10	.05	.01
□ 581 Dave Stapleton	.05	.02	.01
□ 582 World Series '88 Orel Hershiser Jose Canseco Kirk Gibson Dave Stewart	.10	.05	.01
□ 583 Donnie Hill	.05	.02	.01
□ 584 Chuck Jackson	.05	.02	.01
□ 585 Rene Gonzales	.05	.02	.01
□ 586 Tracy Woodson	.05	.02	.01
□ 587 Jim Adduci	.05	.02	.01
□ 588 Mario Soto	.05	.02	.01
□ 589 Jeff Blauser	.10	.05	.01
□ 590 Jim Traber	.05	.02	.01
□ 591 Jon Perlman	.05	.02	.01
□ 592 Mark Williamson	.05	.02	.01
□ 593 Dave Meads	.05	.02	.01
□ 594 Jim Eisenreich	.10	.05	.01
□ 595A Paul Gibson P1	1.00	.45	.12
□ 595B Paul Gibson P2 (Airbrushed leg on player in background)	.05	.02	.01
□ 596 Mike Birkbeck	.05	.02	.01
□ 597 Terry Francona	.05	.02	.01
□ 598 Paul Zuvella	.05	.02	.01
□ 599 Franklin Stubbs	.05	.02	.01
□ 600 Gregg Jefferies	.15	.07	.02
□ 601 John Cangelosi	.05	.02	.01
□ 602 Mike Sharperson	.05	.02	.01
□ 603 Mike Diaz	.05	.02	.01
□ 604 Gary Varsho	.05	.02	.01
□ 605 Terry Blocker	.05	.02	.01
□ 606 Charlie O'Brien	.05	.02	.01
□ 607 Jim Eppard	.05	.02	.01
□ 608 John Davis	.05	.02	.01
□ 609 Ken Griffey Sr.	.05	.02	.01
□ 610 Buddy Bell	.10	.05	.01
□ 611 Ted Simmons UER ('78 stats Cardinal)	.10	.05	.01
□ 612 Matt Williams	.25	.11	.03
□ 613 Danny Cox	.05	.02	.01
□ 614 Al Pedrique	.05	.02	.01
□ 615 Ron Oester	.05	.02	.01
□ 616 John Smoltz	.75	.35	.09

□ 617 Bob Melvin	.05	.02	.01
□ 618 Rob Dibble	.10	.05	.01
□ 619 Kirt Manwaring	.05	.02	.01
□ 620 Felix Fermin	.05	.02	.01
□ 621 Doug Dascenzo	.05	.02	.01
□ 622 Bill Brennan	.05	.02	.01
□ 623 Carlos Quintana	.05	.02	.01
□ 624 Mike Harkey UER (13 and 31 walks in '88, should be 35 and 33)	.05	.02	.01
□ 625 Gary Sheffield	.75	.35	.09
□ 626 Tom Prince	.05	.02	.01
□ 627 Steve Searcy	.05	.02	.01
□ 628 Charlie Hayes (Listed as outfielder)	.15	.07	.02
□ 629 Felix Jose UER (Modesto misspelled as Modesta)	.05	.02	.01
□ 630 Sandy Alomar Jr. (Inconsistent design, portrait on front)	.20	.09	.03
□ 631 Derek Lilliquist	.05	.02	.01
□ 632 Geronimo Berroa	.10	.05	.01
□ 633 Luis Medina	.05	.02	.01
□ 634 Tom Gordon UER (Height 6'0")	.10	.05	.01
□ 635 Ramon Martinez	.25	.11	.03
□ 636 Craig Worthington	.05	.02	.01
□ 637 Edgar Martinez	.25	.11	.03
□ 638 Chad Kreuter	.05	.02	.01
□ 639 Ron Jones	.05	.02	.01
□ 640 Van Snider	.05	.02	.01
□ 641 Lance Blankenship	.05	.02	.01
□ 642 Dwight Smith UER (10 HR's in '87, should be 18)	.10	.05	.01
□ 643 Cameron Drew	.05	.02	.01
□ 644 Jerald Clark	.05	.02	.01
□ 645 Randy Johnson	.75	.35	.09
□ 646 Norm Charlton	.10	.05	.01
□ 647 Todd Frohwirth UER (Southpaw on back)	.05	.02	.01
□ 648 Luis De Los Santos	.05	.02	.01
□ 649 Tim Jones	.05	.02	.01
□ 650 Dave West UER (ML hits 3, should be 6)	.05	.02	.01
□ 651 Bob Milacki	.05	.02	.01
□ 652 Wrigley Field HL (Let There Be Lights)	.10	.05	.01
□ 653 Orel Hershiser HL (The Streak)	.10	.05	.01
□ 654A Wade Boggs HL ERR (Wade Whacks 'Em) ("seaason" on back)	1.50	.70	.19
□ 654B Wade Boggs HL COR (Wade Whacks 'Em)	.15	.07	.02
□ 655 Jose Canseco HL (One of a Kind)	.15	.07	.02
□ 656 Doug Jones HL (Doug Sets Saves)	.05	.02	.01
□ 657 Rickey Henderson HL (Rickey Rocks 'Em)	.15	.07	.02
□ 658 Tom Browning HL (Tom Perfect Pitches)	.05	.02	.01
□ 659 Mike Greenwell HL (Greenwell Gamers)	.05	.02	.01
□ 660 Boston Red Sox HL (Joe Morgan MG, Sox Sock 'Em)	.05	.02	.01

1989 Score Rookie/Traded

The 1989 Score Rookie and Traded set contains 110 standard-size cards. The set was issued exclusively in factory set form through hobby dealers. The set was distributed in a blue box with 10 Magic Motion trivia cards. The fronts have coral green borders with pink diamonds at the bottom. Cards 1-80 feature traded players; cards 81-110 feature 1989 rookies. Rookie Cards in this set include Jim Abbott, Joey (Albert) Belle, Ken Griffey Jr., Ken Hill and John Wetteland.

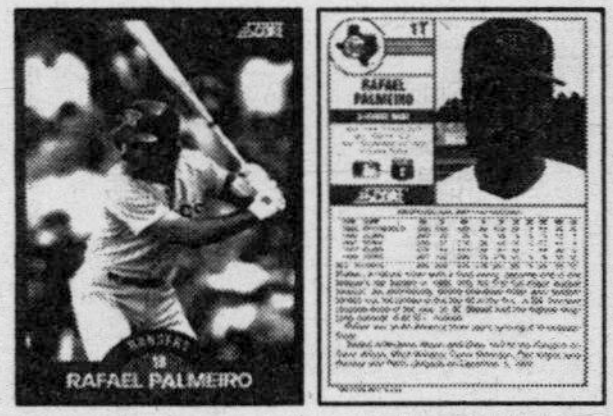

	MINT	NRMT	EXC
COMPLETE FACT.SET (110)	8.00	3.60	1.00
COMMON CARD (1T-110T)	.05	.02	.01
SEMISTARS	.10	.05	.01
□ 1T Rafael Palmeiro	.15	.07	.02
□ 2T Nolan Ryan	1.50	.70	.19
□ 3T Jack Clark	.10	.05	.01
□ 4T Dave LaPoint	.05	.02	.01
□ 5T Mike Moore	.05	.02	.01
□ 6T Pete O'Brien	.05	.02	.01
□ 7T Jeffrey Leonard	.05	.02	.01
□ 8T Rob Murphy	.05	.02	.01
□ 9T Tom Herr	.05	.02	.01
□ 10T Claudell Washington	.05	.02	.01
□ 11T Mike Pagliarulo	.05	.02	.01
□ 12T Steve Lake	.05	.02	.01
□ 13T Spike Owen	.05	.02	.01
□ 14T Andy Hawkins	.05	.02	.01
□ 15T Todd Benzinger	.05	.02	.01
□ 16T Mookie Wilson	.10	.05	.01
□ 17T Bert Blyleven	.10	.05	.01
□ 18T Jeff Treadway	.05	.02	.01
□ 19T Bruce Hurst	.05	.02	.01
□ 20T Steve Sax	.05	.02	.01
□ 21T Juan Samuel	.05	.02	.01
□ 22T Jesse Barfield	.05	.02	.01
□ 23T Carmen Castillo	.05	.02	.01
□ 24T Terry Leach	.05	.02	.01
□ 25T Mark Langston	.10	.05	.01
□ 26T Eric King	.05	.02	.01
□ 27T Steve Balboni	.05	.02	.01
□ 28T Len Dykstra	.10	.05	.01
□ 29T Keith Moreland	.05	.02	.01
□ 30T Terry Kennedy	.05	.02	.01
□ 31T Eddie Murray	.25	.11	.03
□ 32T Mitch Williams	.05	.02	.01
□ 33T Jeff Parrett	.05	.02	.01
□ 34T Wally Backman	.05	.02	.01
□ 35T Julio Franco	.10	.05	.01
□ 36T Lance Parrish	.05	.02	.01
□ 37T Nick Esasky	.05	.02	.01
□ 38T Luis Polonia	.10	.05	.01
□ 39T Kevin Gross	.05	.02	.01
□ 40T John Dopson	.05	.02	.01
□ 41T Willie Randolph	.10	.05	.01
□ 42T Jim Clancy	.05	.02	.01
□ 43T Tracy Jones	.05	.02	.01
□ 44T Phil Bradley	.05	.02	.01
□ 45T Milt Thompson	.05	.02	.01
□ 46T Chris James	.05	.02	.01
□ 47T Scott Fletcher	.05	.02	.01
□ 48T Kal Daniels	.05	.02	.01
□ 49T Steve Bedrosian	.05	.02	.01
□ 50T Rickey Henderson	.15	.07	.02
□ 51T Dion James	.05	.02	.01
□ 52T Tim Leary	.05	.02	.01
□ 53T Roger McDowell	.05	.02	.01
□ 54T Mel Hall	.05	.02	.01
□ 55T Dickie Thon	.05	.02	.01
□ 56T Zane Smith	.05	.02	.01
□ 57T Danny Heep	.05	.02	.01
□ 58T Bob McClure	.05	.02	.01
□ 59T Brian Holton	.05	.02	.01
□ 60T Randy Ready	.05	.02	.01
□ 61T Bob Melvin	.05	.02	.01
□ 62T Harold Baines	.10	.05	.01
□ 63T Lance McCullers	.05	.02	.01
□ 64T Jody Davis	.05	.02	.01

□ 65T Darrell Evans	.10	.05	.01
□ 66T Joel Youngblood	.05	.02	.01
□ 67T Frank Viola	.05	.02	.01
□ 68T Mike Aldrete	.05	.02	.01
□ 69T Greg Cadaret	.05	.02	.01
□ 70T John Kruk	.10	.05	.01
□ 71T Pat Sheridan	.05	.02	.01
□ 72T Oddibe McDowell	.05	.02	.01
□ 73T Tom Brookens	.05	.02	.01
□ 74T Bob Boone	.10	.05	.01
□ 75T Walt Terrell	.05	.02	.01
□ 76T Joel Skinner	.05	.02	.01
□ 77T Randy Johnson	.75	.35	.09
□ 78T Felix Fermin	.05	.02	.01
□ 79T Rick Mahler	.05	.02	.01
□ 80T Richard Dotson	.05	.02	.01
□ 81T Cris Carpenter	.05	.02	.01
□ 82T Bill Spiers	.05	.02	.01
□ 83T Junior Felix	.05	.02	.01
□ 84T Joe Girardi	.15	.07	.02
□ 85T Jerome Walton	.10	.05	.01
□ 86T Greg Litton	.05	.02	.01
□ 87T Greg W.Harris	.05	.02	.01
□ 88T Jim Abbott	.15	.07	.02
□ 89T Kevin Brown	.15	.07	.02
□ 90T John Wetteland	.40	.18	.05
□ 91T Gary Wayne	.05	.02	.01
□ 92T Rich Monteleone	.05	.02	.01
□ 93T Bob Geren	.05	.02	.01
□ 94T Clay Parker	.05	.02	.01
□ 95T Steve Finley	.25	.11	.03
□ 96T Gregg Olson	.10	.05	.01
□ 97T Ken Patterson	.05	.02	.01
□ 98T Ken Hill	.50	.23	.06
□ 99T Scott Scudder	.05	.02	.01
□ 100T Ken Griffey Jr.	5.00	2.20	.60
□ 101T Jeff Brantley	.05	.02	.01
□ 102T Donn Pall	.05	.02	.01
□ 103T Carlos Martinez	.05	.02	.01
□ 104T Joe Oliver	.15	.07	.02
□ 105T Omar Vizquel	.40	.18	.05
□ 106T Joey Belle	3.00	1.35	.35
□ 107T Kenny Rogers	.10	.05	.01
□ 108T Mark Carreon	.05	.02	.01
□ 109T Rolando Roomes	.05	.02	.01
□ 110T Pete Harnisch	.10	.05	.01

1990 Score

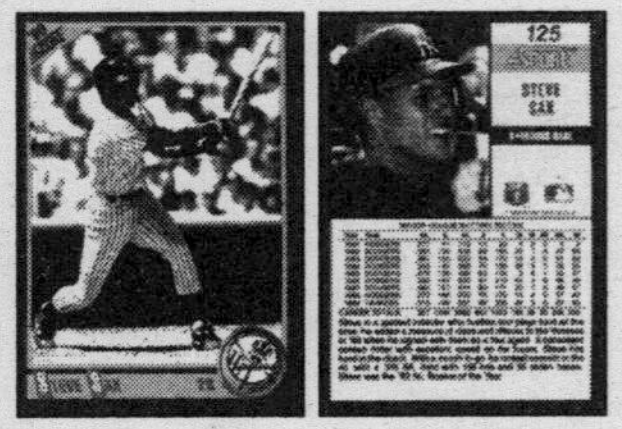

The 1990 Score set contains 704 standard-size cards. The front borders are red, blue, green or white. The vertically oriented backs are white with borders that match the fronts, and feature color mugshots. Subsets include Draft Picks (661-682) and Dream Team (683-695). Rookie Cards of note include Juan Gonzalez, Marquis Grissom, Dave Justice, Chuck Knoblauch, Ben McDonald, Dean Palmer, Sammy Sosa, Frank Thomas, Mo Vaughn, Larry Walker and Bernie Williams. A ten-card set of Dream Team Rookies was inserted into each hobby factory set, but was not included in retail factory sets.

	MINT	NRMT	EXC
COMPLETE SET (704)	10.00	4.50	1.25
COMPLETE RETAIL SET (704)	10.00	4.50	1.25
COMPLETE HOBBY SET (714)	15.00	6.75	1.85
COMMON CARD (1-704)	.05	.02	.01
SEMISTARS	.10	.05	.01
STARS	.15	.07	.02
□ 1 Don Mattingly	.50	.23	.06
□ 2 Cal Ripken	.75	.35	.09
□ 3 Dwight Evans	.10	.05	.01
□ 4 Barry Bonds	.25	.11	.03
□ 5 Kevin McReynolds	.05	.02	.01
□ 6 Ozzie Guillen	.05	.02	.01
□ 7 Terry Kennedy	.05	.02	.01
□ 8 Bryan Harvey	.05	.02	.01
□ 9 Alan Trammell	.15	.07	.02
□ 10 Cory Snyder	.05	.02	.01
□ 11 Jody Reed	.05	.02	.01
□ 12 Roberto Alomar	.30	.14	.04
□ 13 Pedro Guerrero	.05	.02	.01
□ 14 Gary Redus	.05	.02	.01
□ 15 Marty Barrett	.05	.02	.01
□ 16 Ricky Jordan	.05	.02	.01
□ 17 Joe Magrane	.05	.02	.01
□ 18 Sid Fernandez	.05	.02	.01
□ 19 Richard Dotson	.05	.02	.01
□ 20 Jack Clark	.10	.05	.01
□ 21 Bob Walk	.05	.02	.01
□ 22 Ron Karkovice	.05	.02	.01
□ 23 Lenny Harris	.05	.02	.01
□ 24 Phil Bradley	.05	.02	.01
□ 25 Andres Galarraga	.15	.07	.02
□ 26 Brian Downing	.05	.02	.01
□ 27 Dave Martinez	.05	.02	.01
□ 28 Eric King	.05	.02	.01
□ 29 Barry Lyons	.05	.02	.01
□ 30 Dave Schmidt	.05	.02	.01
□ 31 Mike Boddicker	.05	.02	.01
□ 32 Tom Foley	.05	.02	.01
□ 33 Brady Anderson	.15	.07	.02
□ 34 Jim Presley	.05	.02	.01
□ 35 Lance Parrish	.05	.02	.01
□ 36 Von Hayes	.05	.02	.01
□ 37 Lee Smith	.10	.05	.01
□ 38 Herm Winningham	.05	.02	.01
□ 39 Alejandro Pena	.05	.02	.01
□ 40 Mike Scott	.05	.02	.01
□ 41 Joe Orsulak	.05	.02	.01
□ 42 Rafael Ramirez	.05	.02	.01
□ 43 Gerald Young	.05	.02	.01
□ 44 Dick Schofield	.05	.02	.01
□ 45 Dave Smith	.05	.02	.01
□ 46 Dave Magadan	.05	.02	.01
□ 47 Dennis Martinez	.10	.05	.01
□ 48 Greg Minton	.05	.02	.01
□ 49 Milt Thompson	.05	.02	.01
□ 50 Orel Hershiser	.10	.05	.01
□ 51 Bip Roberts	.05	.02	.01
□ 52 Jerry Browne	.05	.02	.01
□ 53 Bob Ojeda	.05	.02	.01
□ 54 Fernando Valenzuela	.10	.05	.01
□ 55 Matt Nokes	.05	.02	.01
□ 56 Brook Jacoby	.05	.02	.01
□ 57 Frank Tanana	.05	.02	.01
□ 58 Scott Fletcher	.05	.02	.01
□ 59 Ron Oester	.05	.02	.01
□ 60 Bob Boone	.10	.05	.01
□ 61 Dan Gladden	.05	.02	.01
□ 62 Darnell Coles	.05	.02	.01
□ 63 Gregg Olson	.05	.02	.01
□ 64 Todd Burns	.05	.02	.01
□ 65 Todd Benzinger	.05	.02	.01
□ 66 Dale Murphy	.15	.07	.02
□ 67 Mike Flanagan	.05	.02	.01
□ 68 Jose Oquendo	.05	.02	.01
□ 69 Cecil Espy	.05	.02	.01
□ 70 Chris Sabo	.05	.02	.01
□ 71 Shane Rawley	.05	.02	.01
□ 72 Tom Brunansky	.05	.02	.01
□ 73 Vance Law	.05	.02	.01
□ 74 B.J. Surhoff	.10	.05	.01
□ 75 Lou Whitaker	.15	.07	.02
□ 76 Ken Caminiti UER (Euclid, Ohio should be Hanford, California)	.15	.07	.02
□ 77 Nelson Liriano	.05	.02	.01
□ 78 Tommy Gregg	.05	.02	.01
□ 79 Don Slaught	.05	.02	.01
□ 80 Eddie Murray	.25	.11	.03

☐ 81	Joe Boever	.05	.02	.01
☐ 82	Charlie Leibrandt	.05	.02	.01
☐ 83	Jose Lind	.05	.02	.01
☐ 84	Tony Phillips	.15	.07	.02
☐ 85	Mitch Webster	.05	.02	.01
☐ 86	Dan Plesac	.05	.02	.01
☐ 87	Rick Mahler	.05	.02	.01
☐ 88	Steve Lyons	.05	.02	.01
☐ 89	Tony Fernandez	.05	.02	.01
☐ 90	Ryne Sandberg	.25	.11	.03
☐ 91	Nick Esasky	.05	.02	.01
☐ 92	Luis Salazar	.05	.02	.01
☐ 93	Pete Incaviglia	.05	.02	.01
☐ 94	Ivan Calderon	.05	.02	.01
☐ 95	Jeff Treadway	.05	.02	.01
☐ 96	Kurt Stillwell	.05	.02	.01
☐ 97	Gary Sheffield	.25	.11	.03
☐ 98	Jeffrey Leonard	.05	.02	.01
☐ 99	Andres Thomas	.05	.02	.01
☐ 100	Roberto Kelly	.10	.05	.01
☐ 101	Alvaro Espinoza	.05	.02	.01
☐ 102	Greg Gagne	.05	.02	.01
☐ 103	John Farrell	.05	.02	.01
☐ 104	Willie Wilson	.05	.02	.01
☐ 105	Glenn Braggs	.05	.02	.01
☐ 106	Chet Lemon	.05	.02	.01
☐ 107A	Jamie Moyer ERR	.05	.02	.01
	(Scintilating)			
☐ 107B	Jamie Moyer COR	.10	.05	.01
	(Scintillating)			
☐ 108	Chuck Crim	.05	.02	.01
☐ 109	Dave Valle	.05	.02	.01
☐ 110	Walt Weiss	.05	.02	.01
☐ 111	Larry Sheets	.05	.02	.01
☐ 112	Don Robinson	.05	.02	.01
☐ 113	Danny Heep	.05	.02	.01
☐ 114	Carmelo Martinez	.05	.02	.01
☐ 115	Dave Gallagher	.05	.02	.01
☐ 116	Mike LaValliere	.05	.02	.01
☐ 117	Bob McClure	.05	.02	.01
☐ 118	Rene Gonzales	.05	.02	.01
☐ 119	Mark Parent	.05	.02	.01
☐ 120	Wally Joyner	.10	.05	.01
☐ 121	Mark Gubicza	.05	.02	.01
☐ 122	Tony Pena	.05	.02	.01
☐ 123	Carmen Castillo	.05	.02	.01
☐ 124	Howard Johnson	.05	.02	.01
☐ 125	Steve Sax	.05	.02	.01
☐ 126	Tim Belcher	.05	.02	.01
☐ 127	Tim Burke	.05	.02	.01
☐ 128	Al Newman	.05	.02	.01
☐ 129	Dennis Rasmussen	.05	.02	.01
☐ 130	Doug Jones	.05	.02	.01
☐ 131	Fred Lynn	.05	.02	.01
☐ 132	Jeff Hamilton	.05	.02	.01
☐ 133	German Gonzalez	.05	.02	.01
☐ 134	John Morris	.05	.02	.01
☐ 135	Dave Parker	.10	.05	.01
☐ 136	Gary Pettis	.05	.02	.01
☐ 137	Dennis Boyd	.05	.02	.01
☐ 138	Candy Maldonado	.05	.02	.01
☐ 139	Rick Cerone	.05	.02	.01
☐ 140	George Brett	.40	.18	.05
☐ 141	Dave Clark	.05	.02	.01
☐ 142	Dickie Thon	.05	.02	.01
☐ 143	Junior Ortiz	.05	.02	.01
☐ 144	Don August	.05	.02	.01
☐ 145	Gary Gaetti	.10	.05	.01
☐ 146	Kirt Manwaring	.05	.02	.01
☐ 147	Jeff Reed	.05	.02	.01
☐ 148	Jose Alvarez	.05	.02	.01
☐ 149	Mike Schooler	.05	.02	.01
☐ 150	Mark Grace	.15	.07	.02
☐ 151	Geronimo Berroa	.10	.05	.01
☐ 152	Barry Jones	.05	.02	.01
☐ 153	Geno Petralli	.05	.02	.01
☐ 154	Jim Deshaies	.05	.02	.01
☐ 155	Barry Larkin	.15	.07	.02
☐ 156	Alfredo Griffin	.05	.02	.01
☐ 157	Tom Henke	.05	.02	.01
☐ 158	Mike Jeffcoat	.05	.02	.01
☐ 159	Bob Welch	.05	.02	.01
☐ 160	Julio Franco	.10	.05	.01
☐ 161	Henry Cotto	.05	.02	.01
☐ 162	Terry Steinbach	.10	.05	.01
☐ 163	Damon Berryhill	.05	.02	.01
☐ 164	Tim Crews	.05	.02	.01
☐ 165	Tom Browning	.05	.02	.01
☐ 166	Fred Manrique	.05	.02	.01
☐ 167	Harold Reynolds	.05	.02	.01
☐ 168A	Ron Hassey ERR	.05	.02	.01
	(27 on back)			
☐ 168B	Ron Hassey COR	.50	.23	.06
	(24 on back)			
☐ 169	Shawon Dunston	.05	.02	.01
☐ 170	Bobby Bonilla	.10	.05	.01
☐ 171	Tommy Herr	.05	.02	.01
☐ 172	Mike Heath	.05	.02	.01
☐ 173	Rich Gedman	.05	.02	.01
☐ 174	Bill Ripken	.05	.02	.01
☐ 175	Pete O'Brien	.05	.02	.01
☐ 176A	Lloyd McClendon ERR	.50	.23	.06
	(Uniform number on back listed as 1)			
☐ 176B	Lloyd McClendon COR	.05	.02	.01
	(Uniform number on back listed as 10)			
☐ 177	Brian Holton	.05	.02	.01
☐ 178	Jeff Blauser	.10	.05	.01
☐ 179	Jim Eisenreich	.05	.02	.01
☐ 180	Bert Blyleven	.10	.05	.01
☐ 181	Rob Murphy	.05	.02	.01
☐ 182	Bill Doran	.05	.02	.01
☐ 183	Curt Ford	.05	.02	.01
☐ 184	Mike Henneman	.05	.02	.01
☐ 185	Eric Davis	.10	.05	.01
☐ 186	Lance McCullers	.05	.02	.01
☐ 187	Steve Davis	.05	.02	.01
☐ 188	Bill Wegman	.05	.02	.01
☐ 189	Brian Harper	.05	.02	.01
☐ 190	Mike Moore	.05	.02	.01
☐ 191	Dale Mohorcic	.05	.02	.01
☐ 192	Tim Wallach	.05	.02	.01
☐ 193	Keith Hernandez	.10	.05	.01
☐ 194	Dave Righetti	.05	.02	.01
☐ 195A	Bret Saberhagen ERR	.10	.05	.01
	(Joke)			
☐ 195B	Bret Saberhagen COR	.10	.05	.01
	(Joker)			
☐ 196	Paul Kilgus	.05	.02	.01
☐ 197	Bud Black	.05	.02	.01
☐ 198	Juan Samuel	.05	.02	.01
☐ 199	Kevin Seitzer	.05	.02	.01
☐ 200	Darryl Strawberry	.10	.05	.01
☐ 201	Dave Stieb	.05	.02	.01
☐ 202	Charlie Hough	.05	.02	.01
☐ 203	Jack Morris	.10	.05	.01
☐ 204	Rance Mulliniks	.05	.02	.01
☐ 205	Alvin Davis	.05	.02	.01
☐ 206	Jack Howell	.05	.02	.01
☐ 207	Ken Patterson	.05	.02	.01
☐ 208	Terry Pendleton	.10	.05	.01
☐ 209	Craig Lefferts	.05	.02	.01
☐ 210	Kevin Brown UER	.10	.05	.01
	(First mention of '89 Rangers should be '88)			
☐ 211	Dan Petry	.05	.02	.01
☐ 212	Dave Leiper	.05	.02	.01
☐ 213	Daryl Boston	.05	.02	.01
☐ 214	Kevin Hickey	.05	.02	.01
☐ 215	Mike Krukow	.05	.02	.01
☐ 216	Terry Francona	.05	.02	.01
☐ 217	Kirk McCaskill	.05	.02	.01
☐ 218	Scott Bailes	.05	.02	.01
☐ 219	Bob Forsch	.05	.02	.01
☐ 220A	Mike Aldrete ERR	.05	.02	.01
	(25 on back)			
☐ 220B	Mike Aldrete COR	.10	.05	.01
	(24 on back)			
☐ 221	Steve Buechele	.05	.02	.01
☐ 222	Jesse Barfield	.05	.02	.01
☐ 223	Juan Berenguer	.05	.02	.01
☐ 224	Andy McGaffigan	.05	.02	.01
☐ 225	Pete Smith	.05	.02	.01
☐ 226	Mike Witt	.05	.02	.01
☐ 227	Jay Howell	.05	.02	.01
☐ 228	Scott Bradley	.05	.02	.01
☐ 229	Jerome Walton	.05	.02	.01
☐ 230	Greg Swindell	.05	.02	.01
☐ 231	Atlee Hammaker	.05	.02	.01
☐ 232A	Mike Devereaux ERR	.05	.02	.01
	(RF on front)			

☐ 232B Mike Devereaux COR	.50	.23	.06
(CF on front)			
☐ 233 Ken Hill	.15	.07	.02
☐ 234 Craig Worthington	.05	.02	.01
☐ 235 Scott Terry	.05	.02	.01
☐ 236 Brett Butler	.10	.05	.01
☐ 237 Doyle Alexander	.05	.02	.01
☐ 238 Dave Anderson	.05	.02	.01
☐ 239 Bob Milacki	.05	.02	.01
☐ 240 Dwight Smith	.05	.02	.01
☐ 241 Otis Nixon	.05	.02	.01
☐ 242 Pat Tabler	.05	.02	.01
☐ 243 Derek Lilliquist	.05	.02	.01
☐ 244 Danny Tartabull	.05	.02	.01
☐ 245 Wade Boggs	.15	.07	.02
☐ 246 Scott Garrelts	.05	.02	.01
(Should say Relief Pitcher on front)			
☐ 247 Spike Owen	.05	.02	.01
☐ 248 Norm Charlton	.05	.02	.01
☐ 249 Gerald Perry	.05	.02	.01
☐ 250 Nolan Ryan	.75	.35	.09
☐ 251 Kevin Gross	.05	.02	.01
☐ 252 Randy Milligan	.05	.02	.01
☐ 253 Mike LaCoss	.05	.02	.01
☐ 254 Dave Bergman	.05	.02	.01
☐ 255 Tony Gwynn	.40	.18	.05
☐ 256 Felix Fermin	.05	.02	.01
☐ 257 Greg W. Harris	.05	.02	.01
☐ 258 Junior Felix	.05	.02	.01
☐ 259 Mark Davis	.05	.02	.01
☐ 260 Vince Coleman	.05	.02	.01
☐ 261 Paul Gibson	.05	.02	.01
☐ 262 Mitch Williams	.05	.02	.01
☐ 263 Jeff Russell	.05	.02	.01
☐ 264 Omar Vizquel	.10	.05	.01
☐ 265 Andre Dawson	.15	.07	.02
☐ 266 Storm Davis	.05	.02	.01
☐ 267 Guillermo Hernandez	.05	.02	.01
☐ 268 Mike Felder	.05	.02	.01
☐ 269 Tom Candiotti	.05	.02	.01
☐ 270 Bruce Hurst	.05	.02	.01
☐ 271 Fred McGriff	.15	.07	.02
☐ 272 Glenn Davis	.05	.02	.01
☐ 273 John Franco	.05	.02	.01
☐ 274 Rich Yett	.05	.02	.01
☐ 275 Craig Biggio	.15	.07	.02
☐ 276 Gene Larkin	.05	.02	.01
☐ 277 Rob Dibble	.05	.02	.01
☐ 278 Randy Bush	.05	.02	.01
☐ 279 Kevin Bass	.05	.02	.01
☐ 280A Bo Jackson ERR	.15	.07	.02
(Watham)			
☐ 280B Bo Jackson COR	.15	.07	.02
(Wathan)			
☐ 281 Wally Backman	.05	.02	.01
☐ 282 Larry Andersen	.05	.02	.01
☐ 283 Chris Bosio	.05	.02	.01
☐ 284 Juan Agosto	.05	.02	.01
☐ 285 Ozzie Smith	.20	.09	.03
☐ 286 George Bell	.05	.02	.01
☐ 287 Rex Hudler	.05	.02	.01
☐ 288 Pat Borders	.05	.02	.01
☐ 289 Danny Jackson	.05	.02	.01
☐ 290 Carlton Fisk	.15	.07	.02
☐ 291 Tracy Jones	.05	.02	.01
☐ 292 Allan Anderson	.05	.02	.01
☐ 293 Johnny Ray	.05	.02	.01
☐ 294 Lee Guetterman	.05	.02	.01
☐ 295 Paul O'Neill	.10	.05	.01
☐ 296 Carney Lansford	.10	.05	.01
☐ 297 Tom Brookens	.05	.02	.01
☐ 298 Claudell Washington	.05	.02	.01
☐ 299 Hubie Brooks	.05	.02	.01
☐ 300 Will Clark	.15	.07	.02
☐ 301 Kenny Rogers	.10	.05	.01
☐ 302 Darrell Evans	.10	.05	.01
☐ 303 Greg Briley	.05	.02	.01
☐ 304 Donn Pall	.05	.02	.01
☐ 305 Teddy Higuera	.05	.02	.01
☐ 306 Dan Pasqua	.05	.02	.01
☐ 307 Dave Winfield	.15	.07	.02
☐ 308 Dennis Powell	.05	.02	.01
☐ 309 Jose DeLeon	.05	.02	.01
☐ 310 Roger Clemens UER	.15	.07	.02
(Dominate, should say dominant)			
☐ 311 Melido Perez	.05	.02	.01
☐ 312 Devon White	.10	.05	.01
☐ 313 Dwight Gooden	.10	.05	.01
☐ 314 Carlos Martinez	.05	.02	.01
☐ 315 Dennis Eckersley	.10	.05	.01
☐ 316 Clay Parker UER	.05	.02	.01
(Height 6'11")			
☐ 317 Rick Honeycutt	.05	.02	.01
☐ 318 Tim Laudner	.05	.02	.01
☐ 319 Joe Carter	.15	.07	.02
☐ 320 Robin Yount	.15	.07	.02
☐ 321 Felix Jose	.05	.02	.01
☐ 322 Mickey Tettleton	.10	.05	.01
☐ 323 Mike Gallego	.05	.02	.01
☐ 324 Edgar Martinez	.15	.07	.02
☐ 325 Dave Henderson	.05	.02	.01
☐ 326 Chili Davis	.10	.05	.01
☐ 327 Steve Balboni	.05	.02	.01
☐ 328 Jody Davis	.05	.02	.01
☐ 329 Shawn Hillegas	.05	.02	.01
☐ 330 Jim Abbott	.10	.05	.01
☐ 331 John Dopson	.05	.02	.01
☐ 332 Mark Williamson	.05	.02	.01
☐ 333 Jeff D. Robinson	.05	.02	.01
☐ 334 John Smiley	.10	.05	.01
☐ 335 Bobby Thigpen	.05	.02	.01
☐ 336 Garry Templeton	.05	.02	.01
☐ 337 Marvell Wynne	.05	.02	.01
☐ 338A Ken Griffey Sr. ERR	.05	.02	.01
(Uniform number on back listed as 25)			
☐ 338B Ken Griffey Sr. COR	.50	.23	.06
(Uniform number on back listed as 30)			
☐ 339 Steve Finley	.15	.07	.02
☐ 340 Ellis Burks	.15	.07	.02
☐ 341 Frank Williams	.05	.02	.01
☐ 342 Mike Morgan	.05	.02	.01
☐ 343 Kevin Mitchell	.10	.05	.01
☐ 344 Joel Youngblood	.05	.02	.01
☐ 345 Mike Greenwell	.05	.02	.01
☐ 346 Glenn Wilson	.05	.02	.01
☐ 347 John Costello	.05	.02	.01
☐ 348 Wes Gardner	.05	.02	.01
☐ 349 Jeff Ballard	.05	.02	.01
☐ 350 Mark Thurmond UER	.05	.02	.01
(ERA is 192, should be 1.92)			
☐ 351 Randy Myers	.10	.05	.01
☐ 352 Shawn Abner	.05	.02	.01
☐ 353 Jesse Orosco	.05	.02	.01
☐ 354 Greg Walker	.05	.02	.01
☐ 355 Pete Harnisch	.05	.02	.01
☐ 356 Steve Farr	.05	.02	.01
☐ 357 Dave LaPoint	.05	.02	.01
☐ 358 Willie Fraser	.05	.02	.01
☐ 359 Mickey Hatcher	.05	.02	.01
☐ 360 Rickey Henderson	.15	.07	.02
☐ 361 Mike Fitzgerald	.05	.02	.01
☐ 362 Bill Schroeder	.05	.02	.01
☐ 363 Mark Carreon	.05	.02	.01
☐ 364 Ron Jones	.05	.02	.01
☐ 365 Jeff Montgomery	.10	.05	.01
☐ 366 Bill Krueger	.05	.02	.01
☐ 367 John Cangelosi	.05	.02	.01
☐ 368 Jose Gonzalez	.05	.02	.01
☐ 369 Greg Hibbard	.05	.02	.01
☐ 370 John Smoltz	.25	.11	.03
☐ 371 Jeff Brantley	.10	.05	.01
☐ 372 Frank White	.10	.05	.01
☐ 373 Ed Whitson	.05	.02	.01
☐ 374 Willie McGee	.05	.02	.01
☐ 375 Jose Canseco	.15	.07	.02
☐ 376 Randy Ready	.05	.02	.01
☐ 377 Don Aase	.05	.02	.01
☐ 378 Tony Armas	.05	.02	.01
☐ 379 Steve Bedrosian	.05	.02	.01
☐ 380 Chuck Finley	.10	.05	.01
☐ 381 Kent Hrbek	.10	.05	.01
☐ 382 Jim Gantner	.05	.02	.01
☐ 383 Mel Hall	.05	.02	.01
☐ 384 Mike Marshall	.05	.02	.01
☐ 385 Mark McGwire	.30	.14	.04
☐ 386 Wayne Tolleson	.05	.02	.01
☐ 387 Brian Holman	.05	.02	.01

□ 388 John Wetteland	.10	.05	.01
□ 389 Darren Daulton	.10	.05	.01
□ 390 Rob Deer	.05	.02	.01
□ 391 John Moses	.05	.02	.01
□ 392 Todd Worrell	.05	.02	.01
□ 393 Chuck Cary	.05	.02	.01
□ 394 Stan Javier	.05	.02	.01
□ 395 Willie Randolph	.10	.05	.01
□ 396 Bill Buckner	.05	.02	.01
□ 397 Robby Thompson	.05	.02	.01
□ 398 Mike Scioscia	.05	.02	.01
□ 399 Lonnie Smith	.05	.02	.01
□ 400 Kirby Puckett	.30	.14	.04
□ 401 Mark Langston	.10	.05	.01
□ 402 Danny Darwin	.05	.02	.01
□ 403 Greg Maddux	.60	.25	.07
□ 404 Lloyd Moseby	.05	.02	.01
□ 405 Rafael Palmeiro	.15	.07	.02
□ 406 Chad Kreuter	.05	.02	.01
□ 407 Jimmy Key	.10	.05	.01
□ 408 Tim Birtsas	.05	.02	.01
□ 409 Tim Raines	.15	.07	.02
□ 410 Dave Stewart	.10	.05	.01
□ 411 Eric Yelding	.05	.02	.01
□ 412 Kent Anderson	.05	.02	.01
□ 413 Les Lancaster	.05	.02	.01
□ 414 Rick Dempsey	.05	.02	.01
□ 415 Randy Johnson	.25	.11	.03
□ 416 Gary Carter	.15	.07	.02
□ 417 Rolando Roomes	.05	.02	.01
□ 418 Dan Schatzeder	.05	.02	.01
□ 419 Bryn Smith	.05	.02	.01
□ 420 Ruben Sierra	.10	.05	.01
□ 421 Steve Jeltz	.05	.02	.01
□ 422 Ken Oberkfell	.05	.02	.01
□ 423 Sid Bream	.05	.02	.01
□ 424 Jim Clancy	.05	.02	.01
□ 425 Kelly Gruber	.05	.02	.01
□ 426 Rick Leach	.05	.02	.01
□ 427 Len Dykstra	.10	.05	.01
□ 428 Jeff Pico	.05	.02	.01
□ 429 John Cerutti	.05	.02	.01
□ 430 David Cone	.15	.07	.02
□ 431 Jeff Kunkel	.05	.02	.01
□ 432 Luis Aquino	.05	.02	.01
□ 433 Ernie Whitt	.05	.02	.01
□ 434 Bo Diaz	.05	.02	.01
□ 435 Steve Lake	.05	.02	.01
□ 436 Pat Perry	.05	.02	.01
□ 437 Mike Davis	.05	.02	.01
□ 438 Cecilio Guante	.05	.02	.01
□ 439 Duane Ward	.05	.02	.01
□ 440 Andy Van Slyke	.10	.05	.01
□ 441 Gene Nelson	.05	.02	.01
□ 442 Luis Polonia	.05	.02	.01
□ 443 Kevin Elster	.05	.02	.01
□ 444 Keith Moreland	.05	.02	.01
□ 445 Roger McDowell	.05	.02	.01
□ 446 Ron Darling	.05	.02	.01
□ 447 Ernest Riles	.05	.02	.01
□ 448 Mookie Wilson	.05	.02	.01
□ 449A Billy Spiers ERR (No birth year)	.15	.07	.02
□ 449B Billy Spiers COR (Born in 1966)	.05	.02	.01
□ 450 Rick Sutcliffe	.05	.02	.01
□ 451 Nelson Santovenia	.05	.02	.01
□ 452 Andy Allanson	.05	.02	.01
□ 453 Bob Melvin	.05	.02	.01
□ 454 Benito Santiago	.05	.02	.01
□ 455 Jose Uribe	.05	.02	.01
□ 456 Bill Landrum	.05	.02	.01
□ 457 Bobby Witt	.05	.02	.01
□ 458 Kevin Romine	.05	.02	.01
□ 459 Lee Mazzilli	.05	.02	.01
□ 460 Paul Molitor	.20	.09	.03
□ 461 Ramon Martinez	.15	.07	.02
□ 462 Frank DiPino	.05	.02	.01
□ 463 Walt Terrell	.05	.02	.01
□ 464 Bob Geren	.05	.02	.01
□ 465 Rick Reuschel	.05	.02	.01
□ 466 Mark Grant	.05	.02	.01
□ 467 John Kruk	.10	.05	.01
□ 468 Gregg Jefferies	.15	.07	.02
□ 469 R.J. Reynolds	.05	.02	.01
□ 470 Harold Baines	.10	.05	.01
□ 471 Dennis Lamp	.05	.02	.01
□ 472 Tom Gordon	.05	.02	.01
□ 473 Terry Puhl	.05	.02	.01
□ 474 Curt Wilkerson	.05	.02	.01
□ 475 Dan Quisenberry	.05	.02	.01
□ 476 Oddibe McDowell	.05	.02	.01
□ 477A Zane Smith ERR (Career ERA .393)	.05	.02	.01
□ 477B Zane Smith COR (career ERA 3.93)	.05	.02	.01
□ 478 Franklin Stubbs	.05	.02	.01
□ 479 Wallace Johnson	.05	.02	.01
□ 480 Jay Tibbs	.05	.02	.01
□ 481 Tom Glavine	.15	.07	.02
□ 482 Manny Lee	.05	.02	.01
□ 483 Joe Hesketh UER (Says Rookiess on back, should say Rookies)	.05	.02	.01
□ 484 Mike Bielecki	.05	.02	.01
□ 485 Greg Brock	.05	.02	.01
□ 486 Pascual Perez	.05	.02	.01
□ 487 Kirk Gibson	.10	.05	.01
□ 488 Scott Sanderson	.05	.02	.01
□ 489 Domingo Ramos	.05	.02	.01
□ 490 Kal Daniels	.05	.02	.01
□ 491A David Wells ERR (Reverse negative photo on card back)	.50	.23	.06
□ 491B David Wells COR	.05	.02	.01
□ 492 Jerry Reed	.05	.02	.01
□ 493 Eric Show	.05	.02	.01
□ 494 Mike Pagliarulo	.05	.02	.01
□ 495 Ron Robinson	.05	.02	.01
□ 496 Brad Komminsk	.05	.02	.01
□ 497 Greg Litton	.05	.02	.01
□ 498 Chris James	.05	.02	.01
□ 499 Luis Quinones	.05	.02	.01
□ 500 Frank Viola	.05	.02	.01
□ 501 Tim Teufel UER (Twins '85, the s is lower case, should be upper case)	.05	.02	.01
□ 502 Terry Leach	.05	.02	.01
□ 503 Matt Williams UER (Wearing 10 on front, listed as 9 on back)	.15	.07	.02
□ 504 Tim Leary	.05	.02	.01
□ 505 Doug Drabek	.05	.02	.01
□ 506 Mariano Duncan	.05	.02	.01
□ 507 Charlie Hayes	.10	.05	.01
□ 508 Joey Belle	1.00	.45	.12
□ 509 Pat Sheridan	.05	.02	.01
□ 510 Mackey Sasser	.05	.02	.01
□ 511 Jose Rijo	.05	.02	.01
□ 512 Mike Smithson	.05	.02	.01
□ 513 Gary Ward	.05	.02	.01
□ 514 Dion James	.05	.02	.01
□ 515 Jim Gott	.05	.02	.01
□ 516 Drew Hall	.05	.02	.01
□ 517 Doug Bair	.05	.02	.01
□ 518 Scott Scudder	.05	.02	.01
□ 519 Rick Aguilera	.10	.05	.01
□ 520 Rafael Belliard	.05	.02	.01
□ 521 Jay Buhner	.15	.07	.02
□ 522 Jeff Reardon	.10	.05	.01
□ 523 Steve Rosenberg	.05	.02	.01
□ 524 Randy Velarde	.05	.02	.01
□ 525 Jeff Musselman	.05	.02	.01
□ 526 Bill Long	.05	.02	.01
□ 527 Gary Wayne	.05	.02	.01
□ 528 Dave Johnson (P)	.05	.02	.01
□ 529 Ron Kittle	.05	.02	.01
□ 530 Erik Hanson UER (5th line on back says seson, should say season)	.10	.05	.01
□ 531 Steve Wilson	.05	.02	.01
□ 532 Joey Meyer	.05	.02	.01
□ 533 Curt Young	.05	.02	.01
□ 534 Kelly Downs	.05	.02	.01
□ 535 Joe Girardi	.10	.05	.01
□ 536 Lance Blankenship	.05	.02	.01
□ 537 Greg Mathews	.05	.02	.01
□ 538 Donell Nixon	.05	.02	.01
□ 539 Mark Knudson	.05	.02	.01
□ 540 Jeff Wetherby	.05	.02	.01

☐ 541 Darrin Jackson	.05	.02	.01
☐ 542 Terry Mulholland	.05	.02	.01
☐ 543 Eric Hetzel	.05	.02	.01
☐ 544 Rick Reed	.05	.02	.01
☐ 545 Dennis Cook	.05	.02	.01
☐ 546 Mike Jackson	.05	.02	.01
☐ 547 Brian Fisher	.05	.02	.01
☐ 548 Gene Harris	.05	.02	.01
☐ 549 Jeff King	.10	.05	.01
☐ 550 Dave Dravecky	.15	.07	.02
☐ 551 Randy Kutcher	.05	.02	.01
☐ 552 Mark Portugal	.05	.02	.01
☐ 553 Jim Corsi	.05	.02	.01
☐ 554 Todd Stottlemyre	.10	.05	.01
☐ 555 Scott Bankhead	.05	.02	.01
☐ 556 Ken Dayley	.05	.02	.01
☐ 557 Rick Wrona	.05	.02	.01
☐ 558 Sammy Sosa	.75	.35	.09
☐ 559 Keith Miller	.05	.02	.01
☐ 560 Ken Griffey Jr.	1.50	.70	.19
☐ 561A Ryne Sandberg HL ERR (Position on front listed as 3B)	8.00	3.60	1.00
☐ 561B Ryne Sandberg HL COR	.15	.07	.02
☐ 562 Billy Hatcher	.05	.02	.01
☐ 563 Jay Bell	.10	.05	.01
☐ 564 Jack Daugherty	.05	.02	.01
☐ 565 Rich Monteleone	.05	.02	.01
☐ 566 Bo Jackson AS-MVP	.15	.07	.02
☐ 567 Tony Fossas	.05	.02	.01
☐ 568 Roy Smith	.05	.02	.01
☐ 569 Jaime Navarro	.05	.02	.01
☐ 570 Lance Johnson	.15	.07	.02
☐ 571 Mike Dyer	.05	.02	.01
☐ 572 Kevin Ritz	.05	.02	.01
☐ 573 Dave West	.05	.02	.01
☐ 574 Gary Mielke	.05	.02	.01
☐ 575 Scott Lusader	.05	.02	.01
☐ 576 Joe Oliver	.05	.02	.01
☐ 577 Sandy Alomar Jr.	.10	.05	.01
☐ 578 Andy Benes UER (Extra comma between day and year)	.15	.07	.02
☐ 579 Tim Jones	.05	.02	.01
☐ 580 Randy McCament	.05	.02	.01
☐ 581 Curt Schilling	.05	.02	.01
☐ 582 John Orton	.05	.02	.01
☐ 583A Milt Cuyler ERR (998 games)	.50	.23	.06
☐ 583B Milt Cuyler COR (98 games; the extra 9 was ghosted out and may still be visible)	.05	.02	.01
☐ 584 Eric Anthony	.10	.05	.01
☐ 585 Greg Vaughn	.15	.07	.02
☐ 586 Deion Sanders	.20	.09	.03
☐ 587 Jose DeJesus	.05	.02	.01
☐ 588 Chip Hale	.05	.02	.01
☐ 589 John Olerud	.15	.07	.02
☐ 590 Steve Olin	.10	.05	.01
☐ 591 Marquis Grissom	.60	.25	.07
☐ 592 Moises Alou	.20	.09	.03
☐ 593 Mark Lemke	.10	.05	.01
☐ 594 Dean Palmer	.40	.18	.05
☐ 595 Robin Ventura	.15	.07	.02
☐ 596 Tino Martinez	.15	.07	.02
☐ 597 Mike Huff	.05	.02	.01
☐ 598 Scott Hemond	.05	.02	.01
☐ 599 Wally Whitehurst	.05	.02	.01
☐ 600 Todd Zeile	.10	.05	.01
☐ 601 Glenallen Hill	.10	.05	.01
☐ 602 Hal Morris	.10	.05	.01
☐ 603 Juan Bell	.05	.02	.01
☐ 604 Bobby Rose	.05	.02	.01
☐ 605 Matt Merullo	.05	.02	.01
☐ 606 Kevin Maas	.10	.05	.01
☐ 607 Randy Nosek	.05	.02	.01
☐ 608A Billy Bates (Text mentions 12 triples in tenth line)	.10	.05	.01
☐ 608B Billy Bates (Text has no mention of triples)	.10	.05	.01
☐ 609 Mike Stanton	.10	.05	.01
☐ 610 Mauro Gozzo	.05	.02	.01
☐ 611 Charles Nagy	.20	.09	.03
☐ 612 Scott Coolbaugh	.05	.02	.01
☐ 613 Jose Vizcaino	.15	.07	.02
☐ 614 Greg Smith	.05	.02	.01
☐ 615 Jeff Huson	.05	.02	.01
☐ 616 Mickey Weston	.05	.02	.01
☐ 617 John Pawlowski	.05	.02	.01
☐ 618A Joe Skalski ERR (27 on back)	.05	.02	.01
☐ 618B Joe Skalski COR (67 on back)	.50	.23	.06
☐ 619 Bernie Williams	.75	.35	.09
☐ 620 Shawn Holman	.05	.02	.01
☐ 621 Gary Eave	.05	.02	.01
☐ 622 Darrin Fletcher UER (Elmherst, should be Elmhurst)	.10	.05	.01
☐ 623 Pat Combs	.05	.02	.01
☐ 624 Mike Blowers	.15	.07	.02
☐ 625 Kevin Appier	.15	.07	.02
☐ 626 Pat Austin	.05	.02	.01
☐ 627 Kelly Mann	.05	.02	.01
☐ 628 Matt Kinzer	.05	.02	.01
☐ 629 Chris Hammond	.05	.02	.01
☐ 630 Dean Wilkins	.05	.02	.01
☐ 631 Larry Walker UER (Uniform number 55 on front and 33 on back; Home is Maple Ridge, not Maple River)	.50	.23	.06
☐ 632 Blaine Beatty	.05	.02	.01
☐ 633A Tommy Barrett ERR (29 on back)	.05	.02	.01
☐ 633B Tommy Barrett COR (14 on back)	.50	.23	.06
☐ 634 Stan Belinda	.05	.02	.01
☐ 635 Mike (Tex) Smith	.05	.02	.01
☐ 636 Hensley Meulens	.05	.02	.01
☐ 637 Juan Gonzalez UER (Sarasots on back, should be Sarasota)	2.00	.90	.25
☐ 638 Lenny Webster	.05	.02	.01
☐ 639 Mark Gardner	.05	.02	.01
☐ 640 Tommy Greene	.05	.02	.01
☐ 641 Mike Hartley	.05	.02	.01
☐ 642 Phil Stephenson	.05	.02	.01
☐ 643 Kevin Mmahat	.05	.02	.01
☐ 644 Ed Whited	.05	.02	.01
☐ 645 Delino DeShields	.10	.05	.01
☐ 646 Kevin Blankenship	.05	.02	.01
☐ 647 Paul Sorrento	.15	.07	.02
☐ 648 Mike Roesler	.05	.02	.01
☐ 649 Jason Grimsley	.05	.02	.01
☐ 650 Dave Justice	.50	.23	.06
☐ 651 Scott Cooper	.05	.02	.01
☐ 652 Dave Eiland	.05	.02	.01
☐ 653 Mike Munoz	.05	.02	.01
☐ 654 Jeff Fischer	.05	.02	.01
☐ 655 Terry Jorgensen	.05	.02	.01
☐ 656 George Canale	.05	.02	.01
☐ 657 Brian DuBois UER (Misspelled Dubois on card)	.05	.02	.01
☐ 658 Carlos Quintana	.05	.02	.01
☐ 659 Luis de los Santos	.05	.02	.01
☐ 660 Jerald Clark	.05	.02	.01
☐ 661 Donald Harris DC	.05	.02	.01
☐ 662 Paul Coleman DC	.05	.02	.01
☐ 663 Frank Thomas DC	4.00	1.80	.50
☐ 664 Brent Mayne DC	.05	.02	.01
☐ 665 Eddie Zosky DC	.05	.02	.01
☐ 666 Steve Hosey DC	.05	.02	.01
☐ 667 Scott Bryant DC	.05	.02	.01
☐ 668 Tom Goodwin DC	.20	.09	.03
☐ 669 Cal Eldred DC	.10	.05	.01
☐ 670 Earl Cunningham DC	.05	.02	.01
☐ 671 Alan Zinter DC	.05	.02	.01
☐ 672 Chuck Knoblauch DC	.75	.35	.09
☐ 673 Kyle Abbott DC	.05	.02	.01
☐ 674 Roger Salkeld DC	.05	.02	.01
☐ 675 Maurice Vaughn DC	1.50	.70	.19
☐ 676 Keith(Kiki) Jones DC	.05	.02	.01
☐ 677 Tyler Houston DC	.15	.07	.02
☐ 678 Jeff Jackson DC	.05	.02	.01
☐ 679 Greg Gohr DC	.05	.02	.01
☐ 680 Ben McDonald DC	.15	.07	.02
☐ 681 Greg Blosser DC	.05	.02	.01

□ 682 Willie Green DC UER (Name misspelled on card, should be Greene)	.15	.07	.02
□ 683A Wade Boggs DT ERR (Text says 215 hits in '89, should be 205)	.15	.07	.02
□ 683B Wade Boggs DT COR (Text says 205 hits in '89)	.05	.02	.01
□ 684 Will Clark DT	.15	.07	.02
□ 685 Tony Gwynn DT UER (Text reads battling instead of batting)	.20	.09	.03
□ 686 Rickey Henderson DT	.15	.07	.02
□ 687 Bo Jackson DT	.15	.07	.02
□ 688 Mark Langston DT	.10	.05	.01
□ 689 Barry Larkin DT	.15	.07	.02
□ 690 Kirby Puckett DT	.15	.07	.02
□ 691 Ryne Sandberg DT	.15	.07	.02
□ 692 Mike Scott DT	.05	.02	.01
□ 693A Terry Steinbach DT ERR (cathers)	.05	.02	.01
□ 693B Terry Steinbach DT COR (catchers)	.05	.02	.01
□ 694 Bobby Thigpen DT	.05	.02	.01
□ 695 Mitch Williams DT	.05	.02	.01
□ 696 Nolan Ryan HL	.40	.18	.05
□ 697 Bo Jackson FB/BB	.50	.23	.06
□ 698 Rickey Henderson ALCS-MVP	.15	.07	.02
□ 699 Will Clark NLCS-MVP	.15	.07	.02
□ 700 WS Games 1/2 (Dave Stewart and Mike Moore)	.10	.05	.01
□ 701 Lights Out: Candlestick 5:04pm (10/17/89)	.15	.07	.02
□ 702 WS Game 3 Bashers Blast Giants (Carney Lansford, Ricky Henderson, Jose Canseco, Dave Henderson)	.15	.07	.02
□ 703 WS Game 4/Wrap-up A's Sweep Battle of of the Bay (A's Celebrate)	.05	.02	.01
□ 704 Wade Boggs HL Wade Raps 200	.15	.07	.02

1990 Score Rookie Dream Team

A ten-card set of Dream Team Rookies was inserted only into hobby factory sets. These standard size cards carry a B prefix on the card number and include a player at each position plus a commemorative card honoring the late Baseball Commissioner A. Bartlett Giamatti.

	MINT	NRMT	EXC
COMPLETE SET (10)	5.00	2.20	.60
COMMON CARD (B1-B10)	.25	.11	.03
SEMISTARS	.40	.18	.05
ONE SET PER HOBBY FACTORY SET			
□ B1 A.Bartlett Giamatti COMM MEM	.40	.18	.05
□ B2 Pat Combs	.25	.11	.03
□ B3 Todd Zeile	.40	.18	.05
□ B4 Luis de los Santos	.25	.11	.03
□ B5 Mark Lemke	.40	.18	.05
□ B6 Robin Ventura	.75	.35	.09
□ B7 Jeff Huson	.25	.11	.03
□ B8 Greg Vaughn	.60	.25	.07
□ B9 Marquis Grissom	2.50	1.10	.30
□ B10 Eric Anthony	.40	.18	.05

1990 Score Rookie/Traded

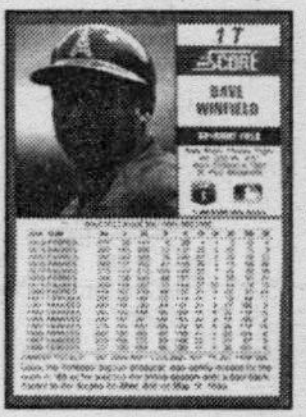

The standard-size 110-card1990 Score Rookie and Traded set marked the third consecutive year Score had issued an end of the year set to note trades and give rookies early cards. The set was issued through hobby accounts and only in factory set form. The first 66 cards are traded players while the last 44 cards are rookie cards. Hockey star Eric Lindros is included in this set. Rookie Cards in the set include Carlos Baerga, Derek Bell, Todd Hundley and Ray Lankford.

	MINT	NRMT	EXC
COMPLETE FACT.SET (110)	6.00	2.70	.75
COMMON CARD (1T-110T)	.05	.02	.01
SEMISTARS	.10	.05	.01
□ 1T Dave Winfield	.15	.07	.02
□ 2T Kevin Bass	.05	.02	.01
□ 3T Nick Esasky	.05	.02	.01
□ 4T Mitch Webster	.05	.02	.01
□ 5T Pascual Perez	.05	.02	.01
□ 6T Gary Pettis	.05	.02	.01
□ 7T Tony Pena	.05	.02	.01
□ 8T Candy Maldonado	.05	.02	.01
□ 9T Cecil Fielder	.10	.05	.01
□ 10T Carmelo Martinez	.05	.02	.01
□ 11T Mark Langston	.10	.05	.01
□ 12T Dave Parker	.10	.05	.01
□ 13T Don Slaught	.05	.02	.01
□ 14T Tony Phillips	.15	.07	.02
□ 15T John Franco	.05	.02	.01
□ 16T Randy Myers	.10	.05	.01
□ 17T Jeff Reardon	.10	.05	.01
□ 18T Sandy Alomar Jr.	.10	.05	.01
□ 19T Joe Carter	.15	.07	.02
□ 20T Fred Lynn	.05	.02	.01
□ 21T Storm Davis	.05	.02	.01
□ 22T Craig Lefferts	.05	.02	.01
□ 23T Pete O'Brien	.05	.02	.01
□ 24T Dennis Boyd	.05	.02	.01
□ 25T Lloyd Moseby	.05	.02	.01
□ 26T Mark Davis	.05	.02	.01
□ 27T Tim Leary	.05	.02	.01
□ 28T Gerald Perry	.05	.02	.01
□ 29T Don Aase	.05	.02	.01
□ 30T Ernie Whitt	.05	.02	.01
□ 31T Dale Murphy	.15	.07	.02
□ 32T Alejandro Pena	.05	.02	.01
□ 33T Juan Samuel	.05	.02	.01
□ 34T Hubie Brooks	.05	.02	.01
□ 35T Gary Carter	.15	.07	.02
□ 36T Jim Presley	.05	.02	.01
□ 37T Wally Backman	.05	.02	.01
□ 38T Matt Nokes	.05	.02	.01
□ 39T Dan Petry	.05	.02	.01
□ 40T Franklin Stubbs	.05	.02	.01

□ 41T Jeff Huson	.05	.02	.01
□ 42T Billy Hatcher	.05	.02	.01
□ 43T Terry Leach	.05	.02	.01
□ 44T Phil Bradley	.05	.02	.01
□ 45T Claudell Washington	.05	.02	.01
□ 46T Luis Polonia	.05	.02	.01
□ 47T Daryl Boston	.05	.02	.01
□ 48T Lee Smith	.10	.05	.01
□ 49T Tom Brunansky	.05	.02	.01
□ 50T Mike Witt	.05	.02	.01
□ 51T Willie Randolph	.10	.05	.01
□ 52T Stan Javier	.05	.02	.01
□ 53T Brad Komminsk	.05	.02	.01
□ 54T John Candelaria	.05	.02	.01
□ 55T Bryn Smith	.05	.02	.01
□ 56T Glenn Braggs	.05	.02	.01
□ 57T Keith Hernandez	.10	.05	.01
□ 58T Ken Oberkfell	.05	.02	.01
□ 59T Steve Jeltz	.05	.02	.01
□ 60T Chris James	.05	.02	.01
□ 61T Scott Sanderson	.05	.02	.01
□ 62T Bill Long	.05	.02	.01
□ 63T Rick Cerone	.05	.02	.01
□ 64T Scott Bailes	.05	.02	.01
□ 65T Larry Sheets	.05	.02	.01
□ 66T Junior Ortiz	.05	.02	.01
□ 67T Francisco Cabrera	.05	.02	.01
□ 68T Gary DiSarcina	.15	.07	.02
□ 69T Greg Olson	.05	.02	.01
□ 70T Beau Allred	.05	.02	.01
□ 71T Oscar Azocar	.05	.02	.01
□ 72T Kent Mercker	.10	.05	.01
□ 73T John Burkett	.10	.05	.01
□ 74T Carlos Baerga	.50	.23	.06
□ 75T Dave Hollins	.15	.07	.02
□ 76T Todd Hundley	.60	.25	.07
□ 77T Rick Parker	.05	.02	.01
□ 78T Steve Cummings	.05	.02	.01
□ 79T Bill Sampen	.05	.02	.01
□ 80T Jerry Kutzler	.05	.02	.01
□ 81T Derek Bell	.75	.35	.09
□ 82T Kevin Tapani	.10	.05	.01
□ 83T Jim Leyritz	.15	.07	.02
□ 84T Ray Lankford	.50	.23	.06
□ 85T Wayne Edwards	.05	.02	.01
□ 86T Frank Thomas	4.00	1.80	.50
□ 87T Tim Naehring	.15	.07	.02
□ 88T Willie Blair	.05	.02	.01
□ 89T Alan Mills	.05	.02	.01
□ 90T Scott Radinsky	.05	.02	.01
□ 91T Howard Farmer	.05	.02	.01
□ 92T Julio Machado	.05	.02	.01
□ 93T Rafael Valdez	.05	.02	.01
□ 94T Shawn Boskie	.05	.02	.01
□ 95T David Segui	.15	.07	.02
□ 96T Chris Hoiles	.15	.07	.02
□ 97T D.J. Dozier	.10	.05	.01
□ 98T Hector Villanueva	.05	.02	.01
□ 99T Eric Gunderson	.05	.02	.01
□ 100T Eric Lindros	2.00	.90	.25
□ 101T Dave Otto	.05	.02	.01
□ 102T Dana Kiecker	.05	.02	.01
□ 103T Tim Drummond	.05	.02	.01
□ 104T Mickey Pina	.05	.02	.01
□ 105T Craig Grebeck	.05	.02	.01
□ 106T Bernard Gilkey	.40	.18	.05
□ 107T Tim Layana	.05	.02	.01
□ 108T Scott Chiamparino	.05	.02	.01
□ 109T Steve Avery	.15	.07	.02
□ 110T Terry Shumpert	.05	.02	.01

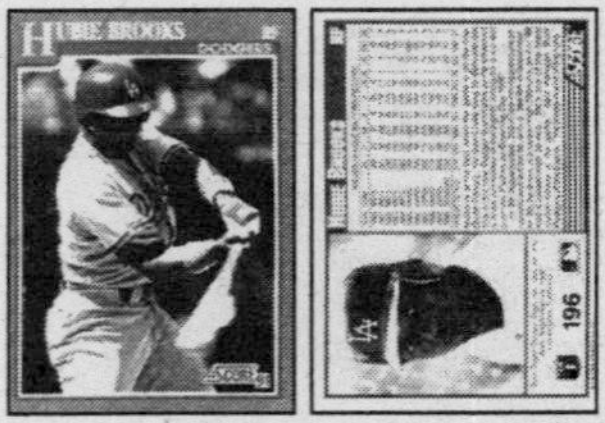

1991 Score

The 1991 Score set contains 893 standard-size cards issued in two separate series of 441 and 452 cards each. This set marks the fourth consecutive year that Score has issued a major set but the first time Score issued the set in two series. Cards were distributed in plastic-wrap packs, blister packs and factory sets. The card fronts feature one of four different solid color borders (black, blue, teal and white) framing the full-color photo of the cards. Subsets include Rookie Prospects (331-379), First Draft Picks (380-391, 671-682), AL All-Stars (392-401), Master Blasters (402-406, 689-693), K-Men (407-411, 684-688), Rifleman (412-416, 694-698), NL All-Stars (661-670), No-Hitters (699-707), Franchise (849-874), Award Winners (875-881) and Dream Team (882-893). An American Flag card (737) was issued to honor the American soldiers involved in Desert Storm. Rookie Cards in the set include Jeff Conine, Chipper Jones, Brian McRae, Mike Mussina and Rondell White. There are a number of pitchers whose card backs show Innings Pitched totals which do not equal the added year-by-year total; the following card numbers were affected, 4, 24, 29, 30, 51, 81, 109, 111, 118, 141, 150, 156, 177, 204, 218, 232, 235, 255, 287, 289, 311, and 328.

	MINT	NRMT	EXC
COMPLETE SET (893)	12.00	5.50	1.50
COMPLETE FACT.SET (900)	20.00	9.00	2.50
COMMON CARD (1-893)	.05	.02	.01
SEMISTARS	.10	.05	.01
STARS	.15	.07	.02
COMP.MANTLE SET (7)	250.00	110.00	31.00
COMMON MANTLE (1-7)	40.00	18.00	5.00
MANTLE AUTO (AU)	500.00	220.00	60.00
RANDOM INSERTS IN SER.2 PACKS			

□ 1 Jose Canseco	.15	.07	.02
□ 2 Ken Griffey Jr.	1.50	.70	.19
□ 3 Ryne Sandberg	.25	.11	.03
□ 4 Nolan Ryan	.75	.35	.09
□ 5 Bo Jackson	.15	.07	.02
□ 6 Bret Saberhagen UER (In bio, missed misspelled as mised)	.10	.05	.01
□ 7 Will Clark	.15	.07	.02
□ 8 Ellis Burks	.15	.07	.02
□ 9 Joe Carter	.15	.07	.02
□ 10 Rickey Henderson	.15	.07	.02
□ 11 Ozzie Guillen	.05	.02	.01
□ 12 Wade Boggs	.15	.07	.02
□ 13 Jerome Walton	.05	.02	.01
□ 14 John Franco	.05	.02	.01
□ 15 Ricky Jordan UER (League misspelled as legue)	.05	.02	.01
□ 16 Wally Backman	.05	.02	.01
□ 17 Rob Dibble	.05	.02	.01
□ 18 Glenn Braggs	.05	.02	.01
□ 19 Cory Snyder	.05	.02	.01
□ 20 Kal Daniels	.05	.02	.01
□ 21 Mark Langston	.10	.05	.01
□ 22 Kevin Gross	.05	.02	.01
□ 23 Don Mattingly UER (First line, ' is missing from Yankee)	.50	.23	.06
□ 24 Dave Righetti	.05	.02	.01
□ 25 Roberto Alomar	.25	.11	.03
□ 26 Robby Thompson	.05	.02	.01
□ 27 Jack McDowell	.10	.05	.01
□ 28 Bip Roberts UER (Bio reads playd)	.05	.02	.01
□ 29 Jay Howell	.05	.02	.01
□ 30 Dave Stieb UER (17 wins in bio, 18 in stats)	.05	.02	.01
□ 31 Johnny Ray	.05	.02	.01
□ 32 Steve Sax	.05	.02	.01
□ 33 Terry Mulholland	.05	.02	.01

☐	34 Lee Guetterman	.05	.02	.01
☐	35 Tim Raines	.15	.07	.02
☐	36 Scott Fletcher	.05	.02	.01
☐	37 Lance Parrish	.05	.02	.01
☐	38 Tony Phillips UER (Born 4/15, should be 4/25)	.10	.05	.01
☐	39 Todd Stottlemyre	.05	.02	.01
☐	40 Alan Trammell	.15	.07	.02
☐	41 Todd Burns	.05	.02	.01
☐	42 Mookie Wilson	.05	.02	.01
☐	43 Chris Bosio	.05	.02	.01
☐	44 Jeffrey Leonard	.05	.02	.01
☐	45 Doug Jones	.05	.02	.01
☐	46 Mike Scott UER (In first line, dominate should read dominating)	.05	.02	.01
☐	47 Andy Hawkins	.05	.02	.01
☐	48 Harold Reynolds	.05	.02	.01
☐	49 Paul Molitor	.20	.09	.03
☐	50 John Farrell	.05	.02	.01
☐	51 Danny Darwin	.05	.02	.01
☐	52 Jeff Blauser	.05	.02	.01
☐	53 John Tudor UER (41 wins in '81)	.05	.02	.01
☐	54 Milt Thompson	.05	.02	.01
☐	55 Dave Justice	.15	.07	.02
☐	56 Greg Olson	.05	.02	.01
☐	57 Willie Blair	.05	.02	.01
☐	58 Rick Parker	.05	.02	.01
☐	59 Shawn Boskie	.05	.02	.01
☐	60 Kevin Tapani	.05	.02	.01
☐	61 Dave Hollins	.05	.02	.01
☐	62 Scott Radinsky	.05	.02	.01
☐	63 Francisco Cabrera	.05	.02	.01
☐	64 Tim Layana	.05	.02	.01
☐	65 Jim Leyritz	.10	.05	.01
☐	66 Wayne Edwards	.05	.02	.01
☐	67 Lee Stevens	.05	.02	.01
☐	68 Bill Sampen UER (Fourth line, long is spelled along)	.05	.02	.01
☐	69 Craig Grebeck UER (Born in Cerritos, not Johnstown)	.05	.02	.01
☐	70 John Burkett	.10	.05	.01
☐	71 Hector Villanueva	.05	.02	.01
☐	72 Oscar Azocar	.05	.02	.01
☐	73 Alan Mills	.05	.02	.01
☐	74 Carlos Baerga	.15	.07	.02
☐	75 Charles Nagy	.10	.05	.01
☐	76 Tim Drummond	.05	.02	.01
☐	77 Dana Kiecker	.05	.02	.01
☐	78 Tom Edens	.05	.02	.01
☐	79 Kent Mercker	.05	.02	.01
☐	80 Steve Avery	.15	.07	.02
☐	81 Lee Smith	.10	.05	.01
☐	82 Dave Martinez	.05	.02	.01
☐	83 Dave Winfield	.15	.07	.02
☐	84 Bill Spiers	.05	.02	.01
☐	85 Dan Pasqua	.05	.02	.01
☐	86 Randy Milligan	.05	.02	.01
☐	87 Tracy Jones	.05	.02	.01
☐	88 Greg Myers	.05	.02	.01
☐	89 Keith Hernandez	.10	.05	.01
☐	90 Todd Benzinger	.05	.02	.01
☐	91 Mike Jackson	.05	.02	.01
☐	92 Mike Stanley	.05	.02	.01
☐	93 Candy Maldonado	.05	.02	.01
☐	94 John Kruk UER (No decimal point before 1990 BA)	.10	.05	.01
☐	95 Cal Ripken UER (Genius spelled genuis)	.75	.35	.09
☐	96 Willie Fraser	.05	.02	.01
☐	97 Mike Felder	.05	.02	.01
☐	98 Bill Landrum	.05	.02	.01
☐	99 Chuck Crim	.05	.02	.01
☐	100 Chuck Finley	.10	.05	.01
☐	101 Kirt Manwaring	.05	.02	.01
☐	102 Jaime Navarro	.05	.02	.01
☐	103 Dickie Thon	.05	.02	.01
☐	104 Brian Downing	.05	.02	.01
☐	105 Jim Abbott	.10	.05	.01
☐	106 Tom Brookens	.05	.02	.01
☐	107 Darryl Hamilton UER (Bio info is for Jeff Hamilton)	.10	.05	.01
☐	108 Bryan Harvey	.05	.02	.01
☐	109 Greg A. Harris UER (Shown pitching lefty, bio says righty)	.05	.02	.01
☐	110 Greg Swindell	.05	.02	.01
☐	111 Juan Berenguer	.05	.02	.01
☐	112 Mike Heath	.05	.02	.01
☐	113 Scott Bradley	.05	.02	.01
☐	114 Jack Morris	.10	.05	.01
☐	115 Barry Jones	.05	.02	.01
☐	116 Kevin Romine	.05	.02	.01
☐	117 Garry Templeton	.05	.02	.01
☐	118 Scott Sanderson	.05	.02	.01
☐	119 Roberto Kelly	.05	.02	.01
☐	120 George Brett	.40	.18	.05
☐	121 Oddibe McDowell	.05	.02	.01
☐	122 Jim Acker	.05	.02	.01
☐	123 Bill Swift UER (Born 12/27/61, should be 10/27)	.05	.02	.01
☐	124 Eric King	.05	.02	.01
☐	125 Jay Buhner	.15	.07	.02
☐	126 Matt Young	.05	.02	.01
☐	127 Alvaro Espinoza	.05	.02	.01
☐	128 Greg Hibbard	.05	.02	.01
☐	129 Jeff M. Robinson	.05	.02	.01
☐	130 Mike Greenwell	.05	.02	.01
☐	131 Dion James	.05	.02	.01
☐	132 Donn Pall UER (1988 ERA in stats 0.00)	.05	.02	.01
☐	133 Lloyd Moseby	.05	.02	.01
☐	134 Randy Velarde	.05	.02	.01
☐	135 Allan Anderson	.05	.02	.01
☐	136 Mark Davis	.05	.02	.01
☐	137 Eric Davis	.10	.05	.01
☐	138 Phil Stephenson	.05	.02	.01
☐	139 Felix Fermin	.05	.02	.01
☐	140 Pedro Guerrero	.05	.02	.01
☐	141 Charlie Hough	.05	.02	.01
☐	142 Mike Henneman	.05	.02	.01
☐	143 Jeff Montgomery	.10	.05	.01
☐	144 Lenny Harris	.05	.02	.01
☐	145 Bruce Hurst	.05	.02	.01
☐	146 Eric Anthony	.05	.02	.01
☐	147 Paul Assenmacher	.05	.02	.01
☐	148 Jesse Barfield	.05	.02	.01
☐	149 Carlos Quintana	.05	.02	.01
☐	150 Dave Stewart	.10	.05	.01
☐	151 Roy Smith	.05	.02	.01
☐	152 Paul Gibson	.05	.02	.01
☐	153 Mickey Hatcher	.05	.02	.01
☐	154 Jim Eisenreich	.10	.05	.01
☐	155 Kenny Rogers	.05	.02	.01
☐	156 Dave Schmidt	.05	.02	.01
☐	157 Lance Johnson	.10	.05	.01
☐	158 Dave West	.05	.02	.01
☐	159 Steve Balboni	.05	.02	.01
☐	160 Jeff Brantley	.05	.02	.01
☐	161 Craig Biggio	.15	.07	.02
☐	162 Brook Jacoby	.05	.02	.01
☐	163 Dan Gladden	.05	.02	.01
☐	164 Jeff Reardon UER (Total IP shown as 943.2, should be 943.1)	.10	.05	.01
☐	165 Mark Carreon	.05	.02	.01
☐	166 Mel Hall	.05	.02	.01
☐	167 Gary Mielke	.05	.02	.01
☐	168 Cecil Fielder	.10	.05	.01
☐	169 Darrin Jackson	.05	.02	.01
☐	170 Rick Aguilera	.10	.05	.01
☐	171 Walt Weiss	.05	.02	.01
☐	172 Steve Farr	.05	.02	.01
☐	173 Jody Reed	.05	.02	.01
☐	174 Mike Jeffcoat	.05	.02	.01
☐	175 Mark Grace	.15	.07	.02
☐	176 Larry Sheets	.05	.02	.01
☐	177 Bill Gullickson	.05	.02	.01
☐	178 Chris Gwynn	.05	.02	.01
☐	179 Melido Perez	.05	.02	.01
☐	180 Sid Fernandez UER (779 runs in 1990)	.05	.02	.01
☐	181 Tim Burke	.05	.02	.01
☐	182 Gary Pettis	.05	.02	.01

□ 183 Rob Murphy	.05	.02	.01
□ 184 Craig Lefferts	.05	.02	.01
□ 185 Howard Johnson	.05	.02	.01
□ 186 Ken Caminiti	.15	.07	.02
□ 187 Tim Belcher	.05	.02	.01
□ 188 Greg Cadaret	.05	.02	.01
□ 189 Matt Williams	.15	.07	.02
□ 190 Dave Magadan	.05	.02	.01
□ 191 Geno Petralli	.05	.02	.01
□ 192 Jeff D. Robinson	.05	.02	.01
□ 193 Jim Deshaies	.05	.02	.01
□ 194 Willie Randolph	.10	.05	.01
□ 195 George Bell	.05	.02	.01
□ 196 Hubie Brooks	.05	.02	.01
□ 197 Tom Gordon	.05	.02	.01
□ 198 Mike Fitzgerald	.05	.02	.01
□ 199 Mike Pagliarulo	.05	.02	.01
□ 200 Kirby Puckett	.30	.14	.04
□ 201 Shawon Dunston	.05	.02	.01
□ 202 Dennis Boyd	.05	.02	.01
□ 203 Junior Felix UER (Text has him in NL)	.05	.02	.01
□ 204 Alejandro Pena	.05	.02	.01
□ 205 Pete Smith	.05	.02	.01
□ 206 Tom Glavine UER (Lefty spelled leftie)	.15	.07	.02
□ 207 Luis Salazar	.05	.02	.01
□ 208 John Smoltz	.15	.07	.02
□ 209 Doug Dascenzo	.05	.02	.01
□ 210 Tim Wallach	.05	.02	.01
□ 211 Greg Gagne	.05	.02	.01
□ 212 Mark Gubicza	.05	.02	.01
□ 213 Mark Parent	.05	.02	.01
□ 214 Ken Oberkfell	.05	.02	.01
□ 215 Gary Carter	.15	.07	.02
□ 216 Rafael Palmeiro	.15	.07	.02
□ 217 Tom Niedenfuer	.05	.02	.01
□ 218 Dave LaPoint	.05	.02	.01
□ 219 Jeff Treadway	.05	.02	.01
□ 220 Mitch Williams UER ('89 ERA shown as 2.76, should be 2.64)	.05	.02	.01
□ 221 Jose DeLeon	.05	.02	.01
□ 222 Mike LaValliere	.05	.02	.01
□ 223 Darrel Akerfelds	.05	.02	.01
□ 224A Kent Anderson ERR (First line, flachy should read flashy)	.10	.05	.01
□ 224B Kent Anderson COR (Corrected in factory sets)	.10	.05	.01
□ 225 Dwight Evans	.10	.05	.01
□ 226 Gary Redus	.05	.02	.01
□ 227 Paul O'Neill	.10	.05	.01
□ 228 Marty Barrett	.05	.02	.01
□ 229 Tom Browning	.05	.02	.01
□ 230 Terry Pendleton	.10	.05	.01
□ 231 Jack Armstrong	.05	.02	.01
□ 232 Mike Boddicker	.05	.02	.01
□ 233 Neal Heaton	.05	.02	.01
□ 234 Marquis Grissom	.15	.07	.02
□ 235 Bert Blyleven	.10	.05	.01
□ 236 Curt Young	.05	.02	.01
□ 237 Don Carman	.05	.02	.01
□ 238 Charlie Hayes	.05	.02	.01
□ 239 Mark Knudson	.05	.02	.01
□ 240 Todd Zeile	.10	.05	.01
□ 241 Larry Walker UER (Maple River, should be Maple Ridge)	.15	.07	.02
□ 242 Jerald Clark	.05	.02	.01
□ 243 Jeff Ballard	.05	.02	.01
□ 244 Jeff King	.10	.05	.01
□ 245 Tom Brunansky	.05	.02	.01
□ 246 Darren Daulton	.10	.05	.01
□ 247 Scott Terry	.05	.02	.01
□ 248 Rob Deer	.05	.02	.01
□ 249 Brady Anderson UER (1990 Hagerstown 1 hit, should say 13 hits)	.15	.07	.02
□ 250 Len Dykstra	.10	.05	.01
□ 251 Greg W. Harris	.05	.02	.01
□ 252 Mike Hartley	.05	.02	.01
□ 253 Joey Cora	.10	.05	.01
□ 254 Ivan Calderon	.05	.02	.01
□ 255 Ted Power	.05	.02	.01
□ 256 Sammy Sosa	.25	.11	.03
□ 257 Steve Buechele	.05	.02	.01
□ 258 Mike Devereaux UER (No comma between city and state)	.05	.02	.01
□ 259 Brad Komminsk UER (Last text line, Ba should be BA)	.05	.02	.01
□ 260 Teddy Higuera	.05	.02	.01
□ 261 Shawn Abner	.05	.02	.01
□ 262 Dave Valle	.05	.02	.01
□ 263 Jeff Huson	.05	.02	.01
□ 264 Edgar Martinez	.15	.07	.02
□ 265 Carlton Fisk	.15	.07	.02
□ 266 Steve Finley	.15	.07	.02
□ 267 John Wetteland	.10	.05	.01
□ 268 Kevin Appier	.10	.05	.01
□ 269 Steve Lyons	.05	.02	.01
□ 270 Mickey Tettleton	.10	.05	.01
□ 271 Luis Rivera	.05	.02	.01
□ 272 Steve Jeltz	.05	.02	.01
□ 273 R.J. Reynolds	.05	.02	.01
□ 274 Carlos Martinez	.05	.02	.01
□ 275 Dan Plesac	.05	.02	.01
□ 276 Mike Morgan UER (Total IP shown as 1149.1, should be 1149)	.05	.02	.01
□ 277 Jeff Russell	.05	.02	.01
□ 278 Pete Incaviglia	.05	.02	.01
□ 279 Kevin Seitzer UER (Bio has 200 hits twice and .300 four times, should be once and three times)	.05	.02	.01
□ 280 Bobby Thigpen	.05	.02	.01
□ 281 Stan Javier UER (Born 1/9, should say 9/1)	.05	.02	.01
□ 282 Henry Cotto	.05	.02	.01
□ 283 Gary Wayne	.05	.02	.01
□ 284 Shane Mack	.05	.02	.01
□ 285 Brian Holman	.05	.02	.01
□ 286 Gerald Perry	.05	.02	.01
□ 287 Steve Crawford	.05	.02	.01
□ 288 Nelson Liriano	.05	.02	.01
□ 289 Don Aase	.05	.02	.01
□ 290 Randy Johnson	.15	.07	.02
□ 291 Harold Baines	.10	.05	.01
□ 292 Kent Hrbek	.10	.05	.01
□ 293A Les Lancaster ERR (No comma between Dallas and Texas)	.05	.02	.01
□ 293B Les Lancaster COR (Corrected in factory sets)	.05	.02	.01
□ 294 Jeff Musselman	.05	.02	.01
□ 295 Kurt Stillwell	.05	.02	.01
□ 296 Stan Belinda	.05	.02	.01
□ 297 Lou Whitaker	.15	.07	.02
□ 298 Glenn Wilson	.05	.02	.01
□ 299 Omar Vizquel UER (Born 5/15, should be 4/24, there is a decimal before GP total for '90)	.15	.07	.02
□ 300 Ramon Martinez	.10	.05	.01
□ 301 Dwight Smith	.05	.02	.01
□ 302 Tim Crews	.05	.02	.01
□ 303 Lance Blankenship	.05	.02	.01
□ 304 Sid Bream	.05	.02	.01
□ 305 Rafael Ramirez	.05	.02	.01
□ 306 Steve Wilson	.05	.02	.01
□ 307 Mackey Sasser	.05	.02	.01
□ 308 Franklin Stubbs	.05	.02	.01
□ 309 Jack Daugherty UER (Born 6/3/60, should say July)	.05	.02	.01
□ 310 Eddie Murray	.25	.11	.03
□ 311 Bob Welch	.05	.02	.01
□ 312 Brian Harper	.05	.02	.01
□ 313 Lance McCullers	.05	.02	.01
□ 314 Dave Smith	.05	.02	.01
□ 315 Bobby Bonilla	.10	.05	.01
□ 316 Jerry Don Gleaton	.05	.02	.01
□ 317 Greg Maddux	.60	.25	.07
□ 318 Keith Miller	.05	.02	.01
□ 319 Mark Portugal	.05	.02	.01

□ 320 Robin Ventura	.15	.07	.02
□ 321 Bob Ojeda	.05	.02	.01
□ 322 Mike Harkey	.05	.02	.01
□ 323 Jay Bell	.10	.05	.01
□ 324 Mark McGwire	.30	.14	.04
□ 325 Gary Gaetti	.10	.05	.01
□ 326 Jeff Pico	.05	.02	.01
□ 327 Kevin McReynolds	.05	.02	.01
□ 328 Frank Tanana	.05	.02	.01
□ 329 Eric Yelding UER (Listed as 6'3", should be 5'11")	.05	.02	.01
□ 330 Barry Bonds	.25	.11	.03
□ 331 Brian McRae UER (No comma between city and state)	.25	.11	.03
□ 332 Pedro Munoz	.10	.05	.01
□ 333 Daryl Irvine	.05	.02	.01
□ 334 Chris Hoiles	.05	.02	.01
□ 335 Thomas Howard	.05	.02	.01
□ 336 Jeff Schulz	.05	.02	.01
□ 337 Jeff Manto	.05	.02	.01
□ 338 Beau Allred	.05	.02	.01
□ 339 Mike Bordick	.15	.07	.02
□ 340 Todd Hundley	.15	.07	.02
□ 341 Jim Vatcher UER (Height 6'9", should be 5'9")	.05	.02	.01
□ 342 Luis Sojo	.05	.02	.01
□ 343 Jose Offerman UER (Born 1969, should say 1968)	.05	.02	.01
□ 344 Pete Coachman	.05	.02	.01
□ 345 Mike Benjamin	.05	.02	.01
□ 346 Ozzie Canseco	.05	.02	.01
□ 347 Tim McIntosh	.05	.02	.01
□ 348 Phil Plantier	.10	.05	.01
□ 349 Terry Shumpert	.05	.02	.01
□ 350 Darren Lewis	.10	.05	.01
□ 351 David Walsh	.05	.02	.01
□ 352A Scott Chiamparino ERR (Bats left, should be right)	.10	.05	.01
□ 352B Scott Chiamparino COR (corrected in factory sets)	.10	.05	.01
□ 353 Julio Valera UER (Progressed misspelled as progessed)	.05	.02	.01
□ 354 Anthony Telford	.05	.02	.01
□ 355 Kevin Wickander	.05	.02	.01
□ 356 Tim Naehring	.10	.05	.01
□ 357 Jim Poole	.05	.02	.01
□ 358 Mark Whiten UER (Shown hitting lefty, bio says righty)	.10	.05	.01
□ 359 Terry Wells	.05	.02	.01
□ 360 Rafael Valdez	.05	.02	.01
□ 361 Mel Stottlemyre Jr.	.05	.02	.01
□ 362 David Segui	.10	.05	.01
□ 363 Paul Abbott	.05	.02	.01
□ 364 Steve Howard	.05	.02	.01
□ 365 Karl Rhodes	.05	.02	.01
□ 366 Rafael Novoa	.05	.02	.01
□ 367 Joe Grahe	.05	.02	.01
□ 368 Darren Reed	.05	.02	.01
□ 369 Jeff McKnight	.05	.02	.01
□ 370 Scott Leius	.05	.02	.01
□ 371 Mark Dewey	.05	.02	.01
□ 372 Mark Lee UER (Shown hitting lefty, bio says righty, born in Dakota, should say North Dakota)	.05	.02	.01
□ 373 Rosario Rodriguez (Shown hitting lefty, bio says righty) UER	.05	.02	.01
□ 374 Chuck McElroy	.05	.02	.01
□ 375 Mike Bell	.05	.02	.01
□ 376 Mickey Morandini	.05	.02	.01
□ 377 Bill Haselman	.05	.02	.01
□ 378 Dave Pavlas	.05	.02	.01
□ 379 Derrick May	.05	.02	.01
□ 380 Jeromy Burnitz FDP	.10	.05	.01
□ 381 Donald Peters FDP	.05	.02	.01
□ 382 Alex Fernandez FDP	.15	.07	.02

□ 383 Mike Mussina FDP	1.00	.45	.12
□ 384 Dan Smith FDP	.05	.02	.01
□ 385 Lance Dickson FDP	.05	.02	.01
□ 386 Carl Everett FDP	.15	.07	.02
□ 387 Thomas Nevers FDP	.05	.02	.01
□ 388 Adam Hyzdu FDP	.05	.02	.01
□ 389 Todd Van Poppel FDP	.10	.05	.01
□ 390 Rondell White FDP	.40	.18	.05
□ 391 Marc Newfield FDP	.15	.07	.02
□ 392 Julio Franco AS	.05	.02	.01
□ 393 Wade Boggs AS	.15	.07	.02
□ 394 Ozzie Guillen AS	.05	.02	.01
□ 395 Cecil Fielder AS	.10	.05	.01
□ 396 Ken Griffey Jr. AS	.75	.35	.09
□ 397 Rickey Henderson AS	.15	.07	.02
□ 398 Jose Canseco AS	.15	.07	.02
□ 399 Roger Clemens AS	.15	.07	.02
□ 400 Sandy Alomar Jr. AS	.05	.02	.01
□ 401 Bobby Thigpen AS	.05	.02	.01
□ 402 Bobby Bonilla MB	.10	.05	.01
□ 403 Eric Davis MB	.10	.05	.01
□ 404 Fred McGriff MB	.15	.07	.02
□ 405 Glenn Davis MB	.05	.02	.01
□ 406 Kevin Mitchell MB	.05	.02	.01
□ 407 Rob Dibble KM	.05	.02	.01
□ 408 Ramon Martinez KM	.10	.05	.01
□ 409 David Cone KM	.15	.07	.02
□ 410 Bobby Witt KM	.05	.02	.01
□ 411 Mark Langston KM	.05	.02	.01
□ 412 Bo Jackson RIF	.15	.07	.02
□ 413 Shawon Dunston RIF UER (In the baseball, should say in baseball)	.05	.02	.01
□ 414 Jesse Barfield RIF	.05	.02	.01
□ 415 Ken Caminiti RIF	.15	.07	.02
□ 416 Benito Santiago RIF	.05	.02	.01
□ 417 Nolan Ryan HL	.40	.18	.05
□ 418 Bobby Thigpen HL UER (Back refers to Hal McRae Jr., should say Brian McRae)	.05	.02	.01
□ 419 Ramon Martinez HL	.10	.05	.01
□ 420 Bo Jackson HL	.15	.07	.02
□ 421 Carlton Fisk HL	.15	.07	.02
□ 422 Jimmy Key	.10	.05	.01
□ 423 Junior Noboa	.05	.02	.01
□ 424 Al Newman	.05	.02	.01
□ 425 Pat Borders	.05	.02	.01
□ 426 Von Hayes	.05	.02	.01
□ 427 Tim Teufel	.05	.02	.01
□ 428 Eric Plunk UER (Text says Eric's had, no apostrophe needed)	.05	.02	.01
□ 429 John Moses	.05	.02	.01
□ 430 Mike Witt	.05	.02	.01
□ 431 Otis Nixon	.05	.02	.01
□ 432 Tony Fernandez	.05	.02	.01
□ 433 Rance Mulliniks	.05	.02	.01
□ 434 Dan Petry	.05	.02	.01
□ 435 Bob Geren	.05	.02	.01
□ 436 Steve Frey	.05	.02	.01
□ 437 Jamie Moyer	.05	.02	.01
□ 438 Junior Ortiz	.05	.02	.01
□ 439 Tom O'Malley	.05	.02	.01
□ 440 Pat Combs	.05	.02	.01
□ 441 Jose Canseco DT	.15	.07	.02
□ 442 Alfredo Griffin	.05	.02	.01
□ 443 Andres Galarraga	.15	.07	.02
□ 444 Bryn Smith	.05	.02	.01
□ 445 Andre Dawson	.15	.07	.02
□ 446 Juan Samuel	.05	.02	.01
□ 447 Mike Aldrete	.05	.02	.01
□ 448 Ron Gant	.15	.07	.02
□ 449 Fernando Valenzuela	.10	.05	.01
□ 450 Vince Coleman UER (Should say topped majors in steals four times, not three times)	.05	.02	.01
□ 451 Kevin Mitchell	.10	.05	.01
□ 452 Spike Owen	.05	.02	.01
□ 453 Mike Bielecki	.05	.02	.01
□ 454 Dennis Martinez	.10	.05	.01
□ 455 Brett Butler	.10	.05	.01
□ 456 Ron Darling	.05	.02	.01
□ 457 Dennis Rasmussen	.05	.02	.01
□ 458 Ken Howell	.05	.02	.01

459	Steve Bedrosian	.05	.02	.01
460	Frank Viola	.05	.02	.01
461	Jose Lind	.05	.02	.01
462	Chris Sabo	.05	.02	.01
463	Dante Bichette	.15	.07	.02
464	Rick Mahler	.05	.02	.01
465	John Smiley	.05	.02	.01
466	Devon White	.10	.05	.01
467	John Orton	.05	.02	.01
468	Mike Stanton	.05	.02	.01
469	Billy Hatcher	.05	.02	.01
470	Wally Joyner	.10	.05	.01
471	Gene Larkin	.05	.02	.01
472	Doug Drabek	.05	.02	.01
473	Gary Sheffield	.15	.07	.02
474	David Wells	.05	.02	.01
475	Andy Van Slyke	.10	.05	.01
476	Mike Gallego	.05	.02	.01
477	B.J. Surhoff	.10	.05	.01
478	Gene Nelson	.05	.02	.01
479	Mariano Duncan	.05	.02	.01
480	Fred McGriff	.15	.07	.02
481	Jerry Browne	.05	.02	.01
482	Alvin Davis	.05	.02	.01
483	Bill Wegman	.05	.02	.01
484	Dave Parker	.10	.05	.01
485	Dennis Eckersley	.10	.05	.01
486	Erik Hanson UER (Basketball misspelled as baseketball)	.05	.02	.01
487	Bill Ripken	.05	.02	.01
488	Tom Candiotti	.05	.02	.01
489	Mike Schooler	.05	.02	.01
490	Gregg Olson	.05	.02	.01
491	Chris James	.05	.02	.01
492	Pete Harnisch	.05	.02	.01
493	Julio Franco	.10	.05	.01
494	Greg Briley	.05	.02	.01
495	Ruben Sierra	.10	.05	.01
496	Steve Olin	.05	.02	.01
497	Mike Fetters	.05	.02	.01
498	Mark Williamson	.05	.02	.01
499	Bob Tewksbury	.05	.02	.01
500	Tony Gwynn	.40	.18	.05
501	Randy Myers	.10	.05	.01
502	Keith Comstock	.05	.02	.01
503	Craig Worthington UER (DeCinces misspelled DiCinces on back)	.05	.02	.01
504	Mark Eichhorn UER (Stats incomplete, doesn't have '89 Braves stint)	.05	.02	.01
505	Barry Larkin	.15	.07	.02
506	Dave Johnson	.05	.02	.01
507	Bobby Witt	.05	.02	.01
508	Joe Orsulak	.05	.02	.01
509	Pete O'Brien	.05	.02	.01
510	Brad Arnsberg	.05	.02	.01
511	Storm Davis	.05	.02	.01
512	Bob Milacki	.05	.02	.01
513	Bill Pecota	.05	.02	.01
514	Glenallen Hill	.05	.02	.01
515	Danny Tartabull	.05	.02	.01
516	Mike Moore	.05	.02	.01
517	Ron Robinson UER (577 K's in 1990)	.05	.02	.01
518	Mark Gardner	.05	.02	.01
519	Rick Wrona	.05	.02	.01
520	Mike Scioscia	.05	.02	.01
521	Frank Wills	.05	.02	.01
522	Greg Brock	.05	.02	.01
523	Jack Clark	.10	.05	.01
524	Bruce Ruffin	.05	.02	.01
525	Robin Yount	.15	.07	.02
526	Tom Foley	.05	.02	.01
527	Pat Perry	.05	.02	.01
528	Greg Vaughn	.15	.07	.02
529	Wally Whitehurst	.05	.02	.01
530	Norm Charlton	.05	.02	.01
531	Marvell Wynne	.05	.02	.01
532	Jim Gantner	.05	.02	.01
533	Greg Litton	.05	.02	.01
534	Manny Lee	.05	.02	.01
535	Scott Bailes	.05	.02	.01
536	Charlie Leibrandt	.05	.02	.01
537	Roger McDowell	.05	.02	.01
538	Andy Benes	.05	.02	.01
539	Rick Honeycutt	.05	.02	.01
540	Dwight Gooden	.10	.05	.01
541	Scott Garrelts	.05	.02	.01
542	Dave Clark	.05	.02	.01
543	Lonnie Smith	.05	.02	.01
544	Rick Reuschel	.05	.02	.01
545	Delino DeShields UER (Rockford misspelled as Rock Ford in '88)	.05	.02	.01
546	Mike Sharperson	.05	.02	.01
547	Mike Kingery	.05	.02	.01
548	Terry Kennedy	.05	.02	.01
549	David Cone	.15	.07	.02
550	Orel Hershiser	.10	.05	.01
551	Matt Nokes	.05	.02	.01
552	Eddie Williams	.05	.02	.01
553	Frank DiPino	.05	.02	.01
554	Fred Lynn	.05	.02	.01
555	Alex Cole	.05	.02	.01
556	Terry Leach	.05	.02	.01
557	Chet Lemon	.05	.02	.01
558	Paul Mirabella	.05	.02	.01
559	Bill Long	.05	.02	.01
560	Phil Bradley	.05	.02	.01
561	Duane Ward	.05	.02	.01
562	Dave Bergman	.05	.02	.01
563	Eric Show	.05	.02	.01
564	Xavier Hernandez	.05	.02	.01
565	Jeff Parrett	.05	.02	.01
566	Chuck Cary	.05	.02	.01
567	Ken Hill	.15	.07	.02
568	Bob Welch Hand (Complement should be compliment) UER	.05	.02	.01
569	John Mitchell	.05	.02	.01
570	Travis Fryman	.15	.07	.02
571	Derek Lilliquist	.05	.02	.01
572	Steve Lake	.05	.02	.01
573	John Barfield	.05	.02	.01
574	Randy Bush	.05	.02	.01
575	Joe Magrane	.05	.02	.01
576	Eddie Diaz	.05	.02	.01
577	Casey Candaele	.05	.02	.01
578	Jesse Orosco	.05	.02	.01
579	Tom Henke	.05	.02	.01
580	Rick Cerone UER (Actually his third go-round with Yankees)	.05	.02	.01
581	Drew Hall	.05	.02	.01
582	Tony Castillo	.05	.02	.01
583	Jimmy Jones	.05	.02	.01
584	Rick Reed	.05	.02	.01
585	Joe Girardi	.10	.05	.01
586	Jeff Gray	.05	.02	.01
587	Luis Polonia	.05	.02	.01
588	Joe Klink	.05	.02	.01
589	Rex Hudler	.05	.02	.01
590	Kirk McCaskill	.05	.02	.01
591	Juan Agosto	.05	.02	.01
592	Wes Gardner	.05	.02	.01
593	Rich Rodriguez	.05	.02	.01
594	Mitch Webster	.05	.02	.01
595	Kelly Gruber	.05	.02	.01
596	Dale Mohorcic	.05	.02	.01
597	Willie McGee	.05	.02	.01
598	Bill Krueger	.05	.02	.01
599	Bob Walk UER (Cards says he's 33, but actually he's 34)	.05	.02	.01
600	Kevin Maas	.05	.02	.01
601	Danny Jackson	.05	.02	.01
602	Craig McMurtry UER (Anonymously misspelled anonimously)	.05	.02	.01
603	Curtis Wilkerson	.05	.02	.01
604	Adam Peterson	.05	.02	.01
605	Sam Horn	.05	.02	.01
606	Tommy Gregg	.05	.02	.01
607	Ken Dayley	.05	.02	.01
608	Carmelo Castillo	.05	.02	.01
609	John Shelby	.05	.02	.01
610	Don Slaught	.05	.02	.01
611	Calvin Schiraldi	.05	.02	.01
612	Dennis Lamp	.05	.02	.01

□	613	Andres Thomas	.05	.02	.01
□	614	Jose Gonzalez	.05	.02	.01
□	615	Randy Ready	.05	.02	.01
□	616	Kevin Bass	.05	.02	.01
□	617	Mike Marshall	.05	.02	.01
□	618	Daryl Boston	.05	.02	.01
□	619	Andy McGaffigan	.05	.02	.01
□	620	Joe Oliver	.05	.02	.01
□	621	Jim Gott	.05	.02	.01
□	622	Jose Oquendo	.05	.02	.01
□	623	Jose DeJesus	.05	.02	.01
□	624	Mike Brumley	.05	.02	.01
□	625	John Olerud	.10	.05	.01
□	626	Ernest Riles	.05	.02	.01
□	627	Gene Harris	.05	.02	.01
□	628	Jose Uribe	.05	.02	.01
□	629	Darnell Coles	.05	.02	.01
□	630	Carney Lansford	.10	.05	.01
□	631	Tim Leary	.05	.02	.01
□	632	Tim Hulett	.05	.02	.01
□	633	Kevin Elster	.05	.02	.01
□	634	Tony Fossas	.05	.02	.01
□	635	Francisco Oliveras	.05	.02	.01
□	636	Bob Patterson	.05	.02	.01
□	637	Gary Ward	.05	.02	.01
□	638	Rene Gonzales	.05	.02	.01
□	639	Don Robinson	.05	.02	.01
□	640	Darryl Strawberry	.10	.05	.01
□	641	Dave Anderson	.05	.02	.01
□	642	Scott Scudder	.05	.02	.01
□	643	Reggie Harris UER (Hepatitis misspelled as hepititis)	.05	.02	.01
□	644	Dave Henderson	.05	.02	.01
□	645	Ben McDonald	.10	.05	.01
□	646	Bob Kipper	.05	.02	.01
□	647	Hal Morris UER (It's should be its)	.05	.02	.01
□	648	Tim Birtsas	.05	.02	.01
□	649	Steve Searcy	.05	.02	.01
□	650	Dale Murphy	.15	.07	.02
□	651	Ron Oester	.05	.02	.01
□	652	Mike LaCoss	.05	.02	.01
□	653	Ron Jones	.05	.02	.01
□	654	Kelly Downs	.05	.02	.01
□	655	Roger Clemens	.15	.07	.02
□	656	Herm Winningham	.05	.02	.01
□	657	Trevor Wilson	.05	.02	.01
□	658	Jose Rijo	.05	.02	.01
□	659	Dann Bilardello UER (Bio has 13 games, 1 hit, and 32 AB, stats show 19, 2, and 37)	.05	.02	.01
□	660	Gregg Jefferies	.15	.07	.02
□	661	Doug Drabek AS UER (Through is mis-spelled though)	.05	.02	.01
□	662	Randy Myers AS	.05	.02	.01
□	663	Benny Santiago AS	.05	.02	.01
□	664	Will Clark AS	.15	.07	.02
□	665	Ryne Sandberg AS	.15	.07	.02
□	666	Barry Larkin AS UER (Line 13, coolly misspelled cooly)	.15	.07	.02
□	667	Matt Williams AS	.15	.07	.02
□	668	Barry Bonds AS	.15	.07	.02
□	669	Eric Davis AS	.10	.05	.01
□	670	Bobby Bonilla AS	.10	.05	.01
□	671	Chipper Jones FDP	3.00	1.35	.35
□	672	Eric Christopherson FDP	.05	.02	.01
□	673	Robbie Beckett FDP	.05	.02	.01
□	674	Shane Andrews FDP	.10	.05	.01
□	675	Steve Karsay FDP	.10	.05	.01
□	676	Aaron Holbert FDP	.05	.02	.01
□	677	Donovan Osborne FDP	.15	.07	.02
□	678	Todd Ritchie FDP	.05	.02	.01
□	679	Ron Walden FDP	.05	.02	.01
□	680	Tim Costo FDP	.05	.02	.01
□	681	Dan Wilson FDP	.25	.11	.03
□	682	Kurt Miller FDP	.05	.02	.01
□	683	Mike Lieberthal FDP	.10	.05	.01
□	684	Roger Clemens KM	.15	.07	.02
□	685	Doc Gooden KM	.10	.05	.01
□	686	Nolan Ryan KM	.40	.18	.05
□	687	Frank Viola KM	.05	.02	.01
□	688	Erik Hanson KM	.05	.02	.01
□	689	Matt Williams MB	.15	.07	.02
□	690	Jose Canseco MB UER (Mammoth misspelled as monmouth)	.15	.07	.02
□	691	Darryl Strawberry MB	.10	.05	.01
□	692	Bo Jackson MB	.15	.07	.02
□	693	Cecil Fielder MB	.10	.05	.01
□	694	Sandy Alomar Jr. RF	.05	.02	.01
□	695	Cory Snyder RF	.05	.02	.01
□	696	Eric Davis RF	.10	.05	.01
□	697	Ken Griffey Jr. RF	.75	.35	.09
□	698	Andy Van Slyke RF UER (Line 2, outfielders does not need)	.05	.02	.01
□	699	Langston/Witt NH Mark Langston Mike Witt	.05	.02	.01
□	700	Randy Johnson NH	.15	.07	.02
□	701	Nolan Ryan NH	.40	.18	.05
□	702	Dave Stewart NH	.05	.02	.01
□	703	Fernando Valenzuela NH	.10	.05	.01
□	704	Andy Hawkins NH	.05	.02	.01
□	705	Melido Perez NH	.05	.02	.01
□	706	Terry Mulholland NH	.05	.02	.01
□	707	Dave Stieb NH	.05	.02	.01
□	708	Brian Barnes	.05	.02	.01
□	709	Bernard Gilkey	.15	.07	.02
□	710	Steve Decker	.05	.02	.01
□	711	Paul Faries	.05	.02	.01
□	712	Paul Marak	.05	.02	.01
□	713	Wes Chamberlain	.05	.02	.01
□	714	Kevin Belcher	.05	.02	.01
□	715	Dan Boone UER (IP adds up to 101, but card has 101.2)	.05	.02	.01
□	716	Steve Adkins	.05	.02	.01
□	717	Geronimo Pena	.05	.02	.01
□	718	Howard Farmer	.05	.02	.01
□	719	Mark Leonard	.05	.02	.01
□	720	Tom Lampkin	.05	.02	.01
□	721	Mike Gardiner	.05	.02	.01
□	722	Jeff Conine	.50	.23	.06
□	723	Efrain Valdez	.05	.02	.01
□	724	Chuck Malone	.05	.02	.01
□	725	Leo Gomez	.05	.02	.01
□	726	Paul McClellan	.05	.02	.01
□	727	Mark Leiter	.05	.02	.01
□	728	Rich DeLucia UER (Line 2, all told is written alltold)	.05	.02	.01
□	729	Mel Rojas	.10	.05	.01
□	730	Hector Wagner	.05	.02	.01
□	731	Ray Lankford	.15	.07	.02
□	732	Turner Ward	.05	.02	.01
□	733	Gerald Alexander	.05	.02	.01
□	734	Scott Anderson	.05	.02	.01
□	735	Tony Perezchica	.05	.02	.01
□	736	Jimmy Kremers	.05	.02	.01
□	737	American Flag (Pray for Peace)	.15	.07	.02
□	738	Mike York	.05	.02	.01
□	739	Mike Rochford	.05	.02	.01
□	740	Scott Aldred	.05	.02	.01
□	741	Rico Brogna	.10	.05	.01
□	742	Dave Burba	.05	.02	.01
□	743	Ray Stephens	.05	.02	.01
□	744	Eric Gunderson	.05	.02	.01
□	745	Troy Afenir	.05	.02	.01
□	746	Jeff Shaw	.05	.02	.01
□	747	Orlando Merced	.15	.07	.02
□	748	Omar Olivares UER (Line 9, league is misspelled legaue)	.05	.02	.01
□	749	Jerry Kutzler	.05	.02	.01
□	750	Mo Vaughn UER (44 SB's in 1990)	.50	.23	.06
□	751	Matt Stark	.05	.02	.01
□	752	Randy Hennis	.05	.02	.01
□	753	Andujar Cedeno	.05	.02	.01
□	754	Kelvin Torve	.05	.02	.01
□	755	Joe Kraemer	.05	.02	.01
□	756	Phil Clark	.05	.02	.01
□	757	Ed Vosberg	.05	.02	.01
□	758	Mike Perez	.05	.02	.01
□	759	Scott Lewis	.05	.02	.01

□ 760 Steve Chitren	.05	.02	.01
□ 761 Ray Young	.05	.02	.01
□ 762 Andres Santana	.05	.02	.01
□ 763 Rodney McCray	.05	.02	.01
□ 764 Sean Berry UER (Name misspelled Barry on card front)	.10	.05	.01
□ 765 Brent Mayne	.05	.02	.01
□ 766 Mike Simms	.05	.02	.01
□ 767 Glenn Sutko	.05	.02	.01
□ 768 Gary DiSarcina	.05	.02	.01
□ 769 George Brett HL	.20	.09	.03
□ 770 Cecil Fielder HL	.10	.05	.01
□ 771 Jim Presley	.05	.02	.01
□ 772 John Dopson	.05	.02	.01
□ 773 Bo Jackson Breaker	.15	.07	.02
□ 774 Brent Knackert UER (Born in 1954, shown throwing righty, but bio says lefty)	.05	.02	.01
□ 775 Bill Doran UER (Reds in NL East)	.05	.02	.01
□ 776 Dick Schofield	.05	.02	.01
□ 777 Nelson Santovenia	.05	.02	.01
□ 778 Mark Guthrie	.05	.02	.01
□ 779 Mark Lemke	.05	.02	.01
□ 780 Terry Steinbach	.10	.05	.01
□ 781 Tom Bolton	.05	.02	.01
□ 782 Randy Tomlin	.05	.02	.01
□ 783 Jeff Kunkel	.05	.02	.01
□ 784 Felix Jose	.05	.02	.01
□ 785 Rick Sutcliffe	.05	.02	.01
□ 786 John Cerutti	.05	.02	.01
□ 787 Jose Vizcaino UER (Offerman, not Opperman)	.05	.02	.01
□ 788 Curt Schilling	.05	.02	.01
□ 789 Ed Whitson	.05	.02	.01
□ 790 Tony Pena	.05	.02	.01
□ 791 John Candelaria	.05	.02	.01
□ 792 Carmelo Martinez	.05	.02	.01
□ 793 Sandy Alomar Jr. UER (Indian's should say Indians')	.10	.05	.01
□ 794 Jim Neidlinger	.05	.02	.01
□ 795 Barry Larkin WS and Chris Sabo	.15	.07	.02
□ 796 Paul Sorrento	.10	.05	.01
□ 797 Tom Pagnozzi	.05	.02	.01
□ 798 Tino Martinez	.15	.07	.02
□ 799 Scott Ruskin UER (Text says first three seasons but lists averages for four)	.05	.02	.01
□ 800 Kirk Gibson	.10	.05	.01
□ 801 Walt Terrell	.05	.02	.01
□ 802 John Russell	.05	.02	.01
□ 803 Chili Davis	.10	.05	.01
□ 804 Chris Nabholz	.05	.02	.01
□ 805 Juan Gonzalez	.75	.35	.09
□ 806 Ron Hassey	.05	.02	.01
□ 807 Todd Worrell	.05	.02	.01
□ 808 Tommy Greene	.05	.02	.01
□ 809 Joel Skinner UER (Joel, not Bob, was drafted in 1979)	.05	.02	.01
□ 810 Benito Santiago	.05	.02	.01
□ 811 Pat Tabler UER (Line 3, always misspelled alway)	.05	.02	.01
□ 812 Scott Erickson UER (Record spelled rcord)	.10	.05	.01
□ 813 Moises Alou	.15	.07	.02
□ 814 Dale Sveum	.05	.02	.01
□ 815 Ryne Sandberg MANYR	.15	.07	.02
□ 816 Rick Dempsey	.05	.02	.01
□ 817 Scott Bankhead	.05	.02	.01
□ 818 Jason Grimsley	.05	.02	.01
□ 819 Doug Jennings	.05	.02	.01
□ 820 Tom Herr	.05	.02	.01
□ 821 Rob Ducey	.05	.02	.01
□ 822 Luis Quinones	.05	.02	.01
□ 823 Greg Minton	.05	.02	.01
□ 824 Mark Grant	.05	.02	.01
□ 825 Ozzie Smith UER (Shortstop misspelled shortsop)	.20	.09	.03
□ 826 Dave Eiland	.05	.02	.01
□ 827 Danny Heep	.05	.02	.01
□ 828 Hensley Meulens	.05	.02	.01
□ 829 Charlie O'Brien	.05	.02	.01
□ 830 Glenn Davis	.05	.02	.01
□ 831 John Marzano UER (International mis-spelled Internaional)	.05	.02	.01
□ 832 Steve Ontiveros	.05	.02	.01
□ 833 Ron Karkovice	.05	.02	.01
□ 834 Jerry Goff	.05	.02	.01
□ 835 Ken Griffey Sr.	.05	.02	.01
□ 836 Kevin Reimer	.05	.02	.01
□ 837 Randy Kutcher UER (Infectious mis-spelled infectous)	.05	.02	.01
□ 838 Mike Blowers	.05	.02	.01
□ 839 Mike Macfarlane	.05	.02	.01
□ 840 Frank Thomas UER (1989 Sarasota stats, 15 games but 188 AB)	2.00	.90	.25
□ 841 The Griffeys Ken Griffey Jr. Ken Griffey Sr.	.75	.35	.09
□ 842 Jack Howell	.05	.02	.01
□ 843 Goose Gozzo	.05	.02	.01
□ 844 Gerald Young	.05	.02	.01
□ 845 Zane Smith	.05	.02	.01
□ 846 Kevin Brown	.10	.05	.01
□ 847 Sil Campusano	.05	.02	.01
□ 848 Larry Andersen	.05	.02	.01
□ 849 Cal Ripken FRAN	.40	.18	.05
□ 850 Roger Clemens FRAN	.15	.07	.02
□ 851 Sandy Alomar Jr. FRAN	.05	.02	.01
□ 852 Alan Trammell FRAN	.15	.07	.02
□ 853 George Brett FRAN	.20	.09	.03
□ 854 Robin Yount FRAN	.15	.07	.02
□ 855 Kirby Puckett FRAN	.15	.07	.02
□ 856 Don Mattingly FRAN	.25	.11	.03
□ 857 Rickey Henderson FRAN	.15	.07	.02
□ 858 Ken Griffey Jr. FRAN	.75	.35	.09
□ 859 Ruben Sierra FRAN	.10	.05	.01
□ 860 John Olerud FRAN	.05	.02	.01
□ 861 Dave Justice FRAN	.10	.05	.01
□ 862 Ryne Sandberg FRAN	.15	.07	.02
□ 863 Eric Davis FRAN	.10	.05	.01
□ 864 Darryl Strawberry FRAN	.10	.05	.01
□ 865 Tim Wallach FRAN	.05	.02	.01
□ 866 Doc Gooden FRAN	.10	.05	.01
□ 867 Len Dykstra FRAN	.10	.05	.01
□ 868 Barry Bonds FRAN	.15	.07	.02
□ 869 Todd Zeile FRAN UER (Powerful misspelled as poweful)	.05	.02	.01
□ 870 Benito Santiago FRAN	.05	.02	.01
□ 871 Will Clark FRAN	.15	.07	.02
□ 872 Craig Biggio FRAN	.10	.05	.01
□ 873 Wally Joyner FRAN	.05	.02	.01
□ 874 Frank Thomas FRAN	1.00	.45	.12
□ 875 Rickey Henderson MVP	.15	.07	.02
□ 876 Barry Bonds MVP	.15	.07	.02
□ 877 Bob Welch CY	.05	.02	.01
□ 878 Doug Drabek CY	.05	.02	.01
□ 879 Sandy Alomar Jr ROY	.05	.02	.01
□ 880 Dave Justice ROY	.10	.05	.01
□ 881 Damon Berryhill	.05	.02	.01
□ 882 Frank Viola DT	.05	.02	.01
□ 883 Dave Stewart DT	.05	.02	.01
□ 884 Doug Jones DT	.05	.02	.01
□ 885 Randy Myers DT	.05	.02	.01
□ 886 Will Clark DT	.15	.07	.02
□ 887 Roberto Alomar DT	.25	.11	.03
□ 888 Barry Larkin DT	.15	.07	.02
□ 889 Wade Boggs DT	.15	.07	.02
□ 890 Rickey Henderson DT	.15	.07	.02
□ 891 Kirby Puckett DT	.30	.14	.04
□ 892 Ken Griffey Jr DT	1.50	.70	.19
□ 893 Benny Santiago DT	.05	.02	.01

1991 Score Cooperstown

This seven-card standard-size set was available only in complete set form as an insert with 1991 Score factory sets. The card design is not like the regular 1991 Score cards. The card

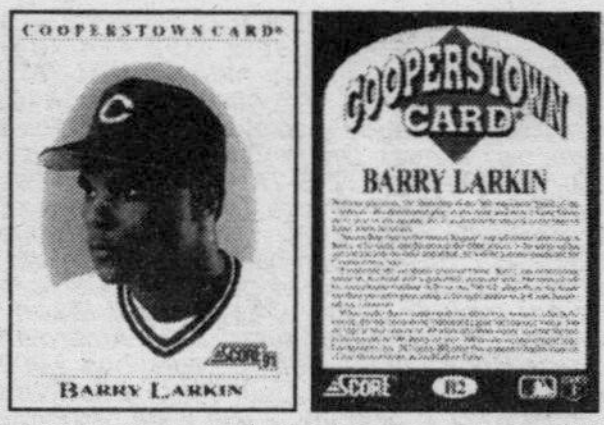

front features a portrait of the player in an oval on a white background. The words "Cooperstown Card" are prominently displayed on the front. The cards are numbered on the back with a B prefix.

	MINT	NRMT	EXC
COMPLETE SET (7)	8.00	3.60	1.00
COMMON CARD (B1-B7)	.50	.23	.06
SEMISTARS	.75	.35	.09
ONE SET PER FACTORY SET			

	MINT	NRMT	EXC
□ B1 Wade Boggs	.50	.23	.06
□ B2 Barry Larkin	1.00	.45	.12
□ B3 Ken Griffey Jr.	5.00	2.20	.60
□ B4 Rickey Henderson	.50	.23	.06
□ B5 George Brett	1.50	.70	.19
□ B6 Will Clark	.50	.23	.06
□ B7 Nolan Ryan	3.00	1.35	.35

1991 Score Hot Rookies

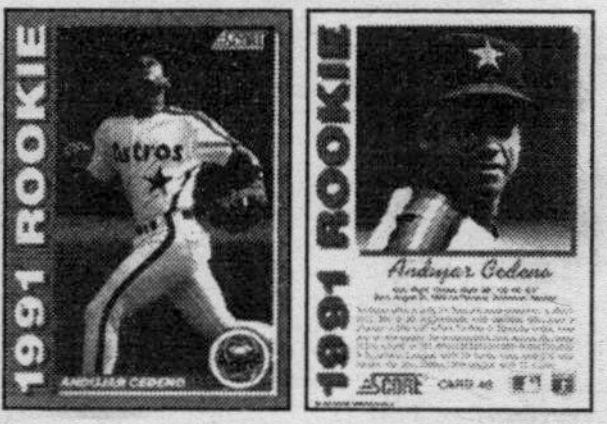

This ten-card standard-size set was inserted in the one per 1991 Score 100-card blister pack. The front features a color action player photo, with white borders and the words "Hot Rookie" in yellow above the picture. The card background shades from orange to yellow to orange as one moves down the card face. In a horizontal format, the left half of the back has a color head shot, while the right half has career summary.

	MINT	NRMT	EXC
COMPLETE SET (10)	15.00	6.75	1.85
COMMON CARD (1-10)	.50	.23	.06
SEMISTARS	.75	.35	.09
ONE PER BLISTER PACK			

	MINT	NRMT	EXC
□ 1 Dave Justice	.75	.35	.09
□ 2 Kevin Maas	.50	.23	.06
□ 3 Hal Morris	.50	.23	.06
□ 4 Frank Thomas	10.00	4.50	1.25
□ 5 Jeff Conine	1.25	.55	.16
□ 6 Sandy Alomar Jr.	.75	.35	.09
□ 7 Ray Lankford	1.25	.55	.16
□ 8 Steve Decker	.50	.23	.06
□ 9 Juan Gonzalez	5.00	2.20	.60
□ 10 Jose Offerman	.50	.23	.06

1991 Score Rookie/Traded

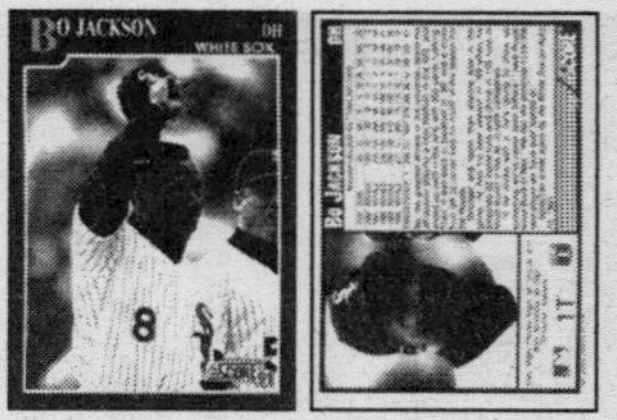

The 1991 Score Rookie and Traded contains 110 standard-size player cards and was issued exclusively in factory set form along with 10 "World Series II" magic motion trivia cards through hobby dealers. The front design is identical to the regular issue 1991 Score set except for the distinctive mauve borders and T-suffixed numbering. Cards 1T-80T feature traded players, while cards 81T-110T focus on rookies. Rookie Cards in the set inlcude Jeff Bagwell and Ivan Rodriguez.

	MINT	NRMT	EXC
COMPLETE FACT.SET (110)	4.00	1.80	.50
COMMON CARD (1T-110T)	.05	.02	.01
SEMISTARS	.10	.05	.01

	MINT	NRMT	EXC
□ 1T Bo Jackson	.15	.07	.02
□ 2T Mike Flanagan	.05	.02	.01
□ 3T Pete Incaviglia	.05	.02	.01
□ 4T Jack Clark	.10	.05	.01
□ 5T Hubie Brooks	.05	.02	.01
□ 6T Ivan Calderon	.05	.02	.01
□ 7T Glenn Davis	.05	.02	.01
□ 8T Wally Backman	.05	.02	.01
□ 9T Dave Smith	.05	.02	.01
□ 10T Tim Raines	.15	.07	.02
□ 11T Joe Carter	.15	.07	.02
□ 12T Sid Bream	.05	.02	.01
□ 13T George Bell	.05	.02	.01
□ 14T Steve Bedrosian	.05	.02	.01
□ 15T Willie Wilson	.05	.02	.01
□ 16T Darryl Strawberry	.10	.05	.01
□ 17T Danny Jackson	.05	.02	.01
□ 18T Kirk Gibson	.10	.05	.01
□ 19T Willie McGee	.05	.02	.01
□ 20T Junior Felix	.05	.02	.01
□ 21T Steve Farr	.05	.02	.01
□ 22T Pat Tabler	.05	.02	.01
□ 23T Brett Butler	.10	.05	.01
□ 24T Danny Darwin	.05	.02	.01
□ 25T Mickey Tettleton	.10	.05	.01
□ 26T Gary Carter	.15	.07	.02
□ 27T Mitch Williams	.05	.02	.01
□ 28T Candy Maldonado	.05	.02	.01
□ 29T Otis Nixon	.05	.02	.01
□ 30T Brian Downing	.05	.02	.01
□ 31T Tom Candiotti	.05	.02	.01
□ 32T John Candelaria	.05	.02	.01
□ 33T Rob Murphy	.05	.02	.01
□ 34T Deion Sanders	.15	.07	.02
□ 35T Willie Randolph	.10	.05	.01
□ 36T Pete Harnisch	.05	.02	.01
□ 37T Dante Bichette	.15	.07	.02
□ 38T Garry Templeton	.05	.02	.01
□ 39T Gary Gaetti	.10	.05	.01
□ 40T John Cerutti	.05	.02	.01
□ 41T Rick Cerone	.05	.02	.01
□ 42T Mike Pagliarulo	.05	.02	.01
□ 43T Ron Hassey	.05	.02	.01
□ 44T Roberto Alomar	.25	.11	.03
□ 45T Mike Boddicker	.05	.02	.01
□ 46T Bud Black	.05	.02	.01
□ 47T Rob Deer	.05	.02	.01
□ 48T Devon White	.10	.05	.01
□ 49T Luis Sojo	.05	.02	.01
□ 50T Terry Pendleton	.10	.05	.01
□ 51T Kevin Gross	.05	.02	.01
□ 52T Mike Huff	.05	.02	.01
□ 53T Dave Righetti	.05	.02	.01
□ 54T Matt Young	.05	.02	.01
□ 55T Earnest Riles	.05	.02	.01

□ 56T	Bill Gullickson	.05	.02	.01
□ 57T	Vince Coleman	.05	.02	.01
□ 58T	Fred McGriff	.15	.07	.02
□ 59T	Franklin Stubbs	.05	.02	.01
□ 60T	Eric King	.05	.02	.01
□ 61T	Cory Snyder	.05	.02	.01
□ 62T	Dwight Evans	.10	.05	.01
□ 63T	Gerald Perry	.05	.02	.01
□ 64T	Eric Show	.05	.02	.01
□ 65T	Shawn Hillegas	.05	.02	.01
□ 66T	Tony Fernandez	.05	.02	.01
□ 67T	Tim Teufel	.05	.02	.01
□ 68T	Mitch Webster	.05	.02	.01
□ 69T	Mike Heath	.05	.02	.01
□ 70T	Chili Davis	.10	.05	.01
□ 71T	Larry Andersen	.05	.02	.01
□ 72T	Gary Varsho	.05	.02	.01
□ 73T	Juan Berenguer	.05	.02	.01
□ 74T	Jack Morris	.10	.05	.01
□ 75T	Barry Jones	.05	.02	.01
□ 76T	Rafael Belliard	.05	.02	.01
□ 77T	Steve Buechele	.05	.02	.01
□ 78T	Scott Sanderson	.05	.02	.01
□ 79T	Bob Ojeda	.05	.02	.01
□ 80T	Curt Schilling	.05	.02	.01
□ 81T	Brian Drahman	.05	.02	.01
□ 82T	Ivan Rodriguez	1.00	.45	.12
□ 83T	David Howard	.05	.02	.01
□ 84T	Heathcliff Slocumb	.15	.07	.02
□ 85T	Mike Timlin	.05	.02	.01
□ 86T	Darryl Kile	.05	.02	.01
□ 87T	Pete Schourek	.15	.07	.02
□ 88T	Bruce Walton	.05	.02	.01
□ 89T	Al Osuna	.05	.02	.01
□ 90T	Gary Scott	.05	.02	.01
□ 91T	Doug Simons	.05	.02	.01
□ 92T	Chris Jones	.05	.02	.01
□ 93T	Chuck Knoblauch	.25	.11	.03
□ 94T	Dana Allison	.05	.02	.01
□ 95T	Erik Pappas	.05	.02	.01
□ 96T	Jeff Bagwell	2.50	1.10	.30
□ 97T	Kirk Dressendorfer	.05	.02	.01
□ 98T	Freddie Benavides	.05	.02	.01
□ 99T	Luis Gonzalez	.15	.07	.02
□ 100T	Wade Taylor	.05	.02	.01
□ 101T	Ed Sprague	.10	.05	.01
□ 102T	Bob Scanlan	.05	.02	.01
□ 103T	Rick Wilkins	.05	.02	.01
□ 104T	Chris Donnels	.05	.02	.01
□ 105T	Joe Slusarski	.05	.02	.01
□ 106T	Mark Lewis	.05	.02	.01
□ 107T	Pat Kelly	.10	.05	.01
□ 108T	John Briscoe	.05	.02	.01
□ 109T	Luis Lopez	.05	.02	.01
□ 110T	Jeff Johnson	.05	.02	.01

1992 Score

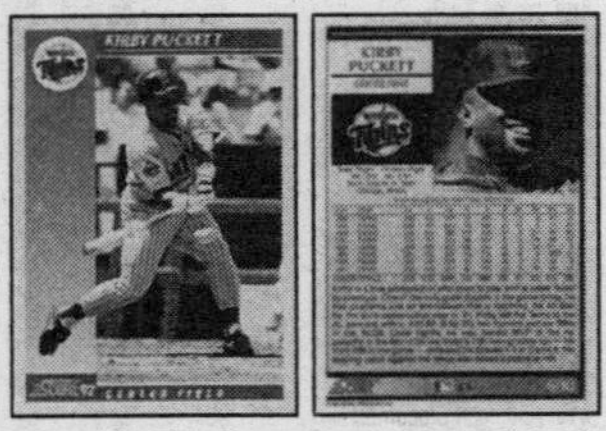

The 1992 Score set marked the second year that Score released their set in two different series. The first series contains 442 cards while the second series contains 451 cards. Cards were distributed in plastic wrapped packs, blister packs, jumbo packs and factory sets. Each pack included a special "World Series II" trivia card. The glossy color action photos on the basic card fronts are bordered above and below by stripes of the same color, and a thicker, different color stripe runs the length of the card to one side of the picture. Topical subsets include Rookie Prospects (395-424/736-772/814-877), No-Hit Club (425-428/784-787), Highlights (429-430), AL All-Stars (431-440; with color montages displaying Chris Greco's player caricatures), Dream Team (441-442/883-893), NL All-Stars (773-782), Highlights (783, 795-797), Draft Picks (799-810), and Memorabilia (878-882). All of the Rookie Prospects (736-772) can be found with or without the Rookie Prospect stripe. Rookie Cards in the set include Vinny Castilla and Manny Ramirez. Chuck Knoblauch, 1991 American League Rookie of the Year, autographed 3,000 of his own 1990 Score Draft Pick cards (card number 672) in gold ink, 2,989 were randomly inserted in Series 2 poly packs, while the other 11 were given away in a sweepstakes. The backs of these Knoblauch autograph cards have special holograms to differentiate them.

	MINT	NRMT	EXC
COMPLETE SET (893)	16.00	7.25	2.00
COMPLETE FACT.SET (910)	20.00	9.00	2.50
COMPLETE SERIES 1 (442)	8.00	3.60	1.00
COMPLETE SERIES 2 (451)	8.00	3.60	1.00
COMMON CARD (1-893)	.05	.02	.01
SEMISTARS	.10	.05	.01
STARS	.15	.07	.02
COMP.DIMAGGIO SET (5)	150.00	70.00	19.00
COMMON DIMAGGIO (1-5)	30.00	13.50	3.70
CERTIFIED DIMAGGIO AUTO	550.00	250.00	70.00

DIMAGGIO: RANDOM INSERTS IN SER.1 PACKS

□ 1	Ken Griffey Jr.	1.50	.70	.19
□ 2	Nolan Ryan	.75	.35	.09
□ 3	Will Clark	.15	.07	.02
□ 4	Dave Justice	.15	.07	.02
□ 5	Dave Henderson	.05	.02	.01
□ 6	Bret Saberhagen	.10	.05	.01
□ 7	Fred McGriff	.15	.07	.02
□ 8	Erik Hanson	.05	.02	.01
□ 9	Darryl Strawberry	.10	.05	.01
□ 10	Dwight Gooden	.10	.05	.01
□ 11	Juan Gonzalez	.60	.25	.07
□ 12	Mark Langston	.10	.05	.01
□ 13	Lonnie Smith	.05	.02	.01
□ 14	Jeff Montgomery	.10	.05	.01
□ 15	Roberto Alomar	.25	.11	.03
□ 16	Delino DeShields	.05	.02	.01
□ 17	Steve Bedrosian	.05	.02	.01
□ 18	Terry Pendleton	.10	.05	.01
□ 19	Mark Carreon	.05	.02	.01
□ 20	Mark McGwire	.30	.14	.04
□ 21	Roger Clemens	.15	.07	.02
□ 22	Chuck Crim	.05	.02	.01
□ 23	Don Mattingly	.50	.23	.06
□ 24	Dickie Thon	.05	.02	.01
□ 25	Ron Gant	.15	.07	.02
□ 26	Milt Cuyler	.05	.02	.01
□ 27	Mike Macfarlane	.05	.02	.01
□ 28	Dan Gladden	.05	.02	.01
□ 29	Melido Perez	.05	.02	.01
□ 30	Willie Randolph	.10	.05	.01
□ 31	Albert Belle	.60	.25	.07
□ 32	Dave Winfield	.15	.07	.02
□ 33	Jimmy Jones	.05	.02	.01
□ 34	Kevin Gross	.05	.02	.01
□ 35	Andres Galarraga	.15	.07	.02
□ 36	Mike Devereaux	.05	.02	.01
□ 37	Chris Bosio	.05	.02	.01
□ 38	Mike LaValliere	.05	.02	.01
□ 39	Gary Gaetti	.10	.05	.01
□ 40	Felix Jose	.05	.02	.01
□ 41	Alvaro Espinoza	.05	.02	.01
□ 42	Rick Aguilera	.05	.02	.01
□ 43	Mike Gallego	.05	.02	.01
□ 44	Eric Davis	.10	.05	.01
□ 45	George Bell	.05	.02	.01
□ 46	Tom Brunansky	.05	.02	.01
□ 47	Steve Farr	.05	.02	.01
□ 48	Duane Ward	.05	.02	.01
□ 49	David Wells	.05	.02	.01
□ 50	Cecil Fielder	.10	.05	.01
□ 51	Walt Weiss	.05	.02	.01
□ 52	Todd Zeile	.05	.02	.01

□ 53 Doug Jones	.05	.02	.01
□ 54 Bob Walk	.05	.02	.01
□ 55 Rafael Palmeiro	.15	.07	.02
□ 56 Rob Deer	.05	.02	.01
□ 57 Paul O'Neill	.10	.05	.01
□ 58 Jeff Reardon	.10	.05	.01
□ 59 Randy Ready	.05	.02	.01
□ 60 Scott Erickson	.10	.05	.01
□ 61 Paul Molitor	.20	.09	.03
□ 62 Jack McDowell	.10	.05	.01
□ 63 Jim Acker	.05	.02	.01
□ 64 Jay Buhner	.15	.07	.02
□ 65 Travis Fryman	.15	.07	.02
□ 66 Marquis Grissom	.15	.07	.02
□ 67 Mike Harkey	.05	.02	.01
□ 68 Luis Polonia	.05	.02	.01
□ 69 Ken Caminiti	.15	.07	.02
□ 70 Chris Sabo	.05	.02	.01
□ 71 Gregg Olson	.05	.02	.01
□ 72 Carlton Fisk	.15	.07	.02
□ 73 Juan Samuel	.05	.02	.01
□ 74 Todd Stottlemyre	.10	.05	.01
□ 75 Andre Dawson	.15	.07	.02
□ 76 Alvin Davis	.05	.02	.01
□ 77 Bill Doran	.05	.02	.01
□ 78 B.J. Surhoff	.10	.05	.01
□ 79 Kirk McCaskill	.05	.02	.01
□ 80 Dale Murphy	.15	.07	.02
□ 81 Jose DeLeon	.05	.02	.01
□ 82 Alex Fernandez	.15	.07	.02
□ 83 Ivan Calderon	.05	.02	.01
□ 84 Brent Mayne	.05	.02	.01
□ 85 Jody Reed	.05	.02	.01
□ 86 Randy Tomlin	.05	.02	.01
□ 87 Randy Milligan	.05	.02	.01
□ 88 Pascual Perez	.05	.02	.01
□ 89 Hensley Meulens	.05	.02	.01
□ 90 Joe Carter	.15	.07	.02
□ 91 Mike Moore	.05	.02	.01
□ 92 Ozzie Guillen	.05	.02	.01
□ 93 Shawn Hillegas	.05	.02	.01
□ 94 Chili Davis	.10	.05	.01
□ 95 Vince Coleman	.05	.02	.01
□ 96 Jimmy Key	.10	.05	.01
□ 97 Billy Ripken	.05	.02	.01
□ 98 Dave Smith	.05	.02	.01
□ 99 Tom Bolton	.05	.02	.01
□ 100 Barry Larkin	.15	.07	.02
□ 101 Kenny Rogers	.05	.02	.01
□ 102 Mike Boddicker	.05	.02	.01
□ 103 Kevin Elster	.05	.02	.01
□ 104 Ken Hill	.15	.07	.02
□ 105 Charlie Leibrandt	.05	.02	.01
□ 106 Pat Combs	.05	.02	.01
□ 107 Hubie Brooks	.05	.02	.01
□ 108 Julio Franco	.10	.05	.01
□ 109 Vicente Palacios	.05	.02	.01
□ 110 Kal Daniels	.05	.02	.01
□ 111 Bruce Hurst	.05	.02	.01
□ 112 Willie McGee	.05	.02	.01
□ 113 Ted Power	.05	.02	.01
□ 114 Milt Thompson	.05	.02	.01
□ 115 Doug Drabek	.05	.02	.01
□ 116 Rafael Belliard	.05	.02	.01
□ 117 Scott Garrelts	.05	.02	.01
□ 118 Terry Mulholland	.05	.02	.01
□ 119 Jay Howell	.05	.02	.01
□ 120 Danny Jackson	.05	.02	.01
□ 121 Scott Ruskin	.05	.02	.01
□ 122 Robin Ventura	.15	.07	.02
□ 123 Bip Roberts	.05	.02	.01
□ 124 Jeff Russell	.05	.02	.01
□ 125 Hal Morris	.05	.02	.01
□ 126 Teddy Higuera	.05	.02	.01
□ 127 Luis Sojo	.05	.02	.01
□ 128 Carlos Baerga	.15	.07	.02
□ 129 Jeff Ballard	.05	.02	.01
□ 130 Tom Gordon	.05	.02	.01
□ 131 Sid Bream	.05	.02	.01
□ 132 Rance Mulliniks	.05	.02	.01
□ 133 Andy Benes	.05	.02	.01
□ 134 Mickey Tettleton	.05	.02	.01
□ 135 Rich DeLucia	.05	.02	.01
□ 136 Tom Pagnozzi	.05	.02	.01
□ 137 Harold Baines	.10	.05	.01
□ 138 Danny Darwin	.05	.02	.01
□ 139 Kevin Bass	.05	.02	.01
□ 140 Chris Nabholz	.05	.02	.01
□ 141 Pete O'Brien	.05	.02	.01
□ 142 Jeff Treadway	.05	.02	.01
□ 143 Mickey Morandini	.05	.02	.01
□ 144 Eric King	.05	.02	.01
□ 145 Danny Tartabull	.05	.02	.01
□ 146 Lance Johnson	.10	.05	.01
□ 147 Casey Candaele	.05	.02	.01
□ 148 Felix Fermin	.05	.02	.01
□ 149 Rich Rodriguez	.05	.02	.01
□ 150 Dwight Evans	.10	.05	.01
□ 151 Joe Klink	.05	.02	.01
□ 152 Kevin Reimer	.05	.02	.01
□ 153 Orlando Merced	.05	.02	.01
□ 154 Mel Hall	.05	.02	.01
□ 155 Randy Myers	.10	.05	.01
□ 156 Greg A. Harris	.05	.02	.01
□ 157 Jeff Brantley	.10	.05	.01
□ 158 Jim Eisenreich	.05	.02	.01
□ 159 Luis Rivera	.05	.02	.01
□ 160 Cris Carpenter	.05	.02	.01
□ 161 Bruce Ruffin	.05	.02	.01
□ 162 Omar Vizquel	.15	.07	.02
□ 163 Gerald Alexander	.05	.02	.01
□ 164 Mark Guthrie	.05	.02	.01
□ 165 Scott Lewis	.05	.02	.01
□ 166 Bill Sampen	.05	.02	.01
□ 167 Dave Anderson	.05	.02	.01
□ 168 Kevin McReynolds	.05	.02	.01
□ 169 Jose Vizcaino	.05	.02	.01
□ 170 Bob Geren	.05	.02	.01
□ 171 Mike Morgan	.05	.02	.01
□ 172 Jim Gott	.05	.02	.01
□ 173 Mike Pagliarulo	.05	.02	.01
□ 174 Mike Jeffcoat	.05	.02	.01
□ 175 Craig Lefferts	.05	.02	.01
□ 176 Steve Finley	.15	.07	.02
□ 177 Wally Backman	.05	.02	.01
□ 178 Kent Mercker	.05	.02	.01
□ 179 John Cerutti	.05	.02	.01
□ 180 Jay Bell	.10	.05	.01
□ 181 Dale Sveum	.05	.02	.01
□ 182 Greg Gagne	.05	.02	.01
□ 183 Donnie Hill	.05	.02	.01
□ 184 Rex Hudler	.05	.02	.01
□ 185 Pat Kelly	.05	.02	.01
□ 186 Jeff D. Robinson	.05	.02	.01
□ 187 Jeff Gray	.05	.02	.01
□ 188 Jerry Willard	.05	.02	.01
□ 189 Carlos Quintana	.05	.02	.01
□ 190 Dennis Eckersley	.10	.05	.01
□ 191 Kelly Downs	.05	.02	.01
□ 192 Gregg Jefferies	.15	.07	.02
□ 193 Darrin Fletcher	.05	.02	.01
□ 194 Mike Jackson	.05	.02	.01
□ 195 Eddie Murray	.25	.11	.03
□ 196 Bill Landrum	.05	.02	.01
□ 197 Eric Yelding	.05	.02	.01
□ 198 Devon White	.10	.05	.01
□ 199 Larry Walker	.15	.07	.02
□ 200 Ryne Sandberg	.25	.11	.03
□ 201 Dave Magadan	.05	.02	.01
□ 202 Steve Chitren	.05	.02	.01
□ 203 Scott Fletcher	.05	.02	.01
□ 204 Dwayne Henry	.05	.02	.01
□ 205 Scott Coolbaugh	.05	.02	.01
□ 206 Tracy Jones	.05	.02	.01
□ 207 Von Hayes	.05	.02	.01
□ 208 Bob Melvin	.05	.02	.01
□ 209 Scott Scudder	.05	.02	.01
□ 210 Luis Gonzalez	.10	.05	.01
□ 211 Scott Sanderson	.05	.02	.01
□ 212 Chris Donnels	.05	.02	.01
□ 213 Heathcliff Slocumb	.05	.02	.01
□ 214 Mike Timlin	.05	.02	.01
□ 215 Brian Harper	.05	.02	.01
□ 216 Juan Berenguer UER (Decimal point missing in IP total)	.05	.02	.01
□ 217 Mike Henneman	.05	.02	.01
□ 218 Bill Spiers	.05	.02	.01
□ 219 Scott Terry	.05	.02	.01
□ 220 Frank Viola	.05	.02	.01
□ 221 Mark Eichhorn	.05	.02	.01
□ 222 Ernest Riles	.05	.02	.01

□ 223 Ray Lankford	.15	.07	.02
□ 224 Pete Harnisch	.05	.02	.01
□ 225 Bobby Bonilla	.10	.05	.01
□ 226 Mike Scioscia	.05	.02	.01
□ 227 Joel Skinner	.05	.02	.01
□ 228 Brian Holman	.05	.02	.01
□ 229 Gilberto Reyes	.05	.02	.01
□ 230 Matt Williams	.15	.07	.02
□ 231 Jaime Navarro	.05	.02	.01
□ 232 Jose Rijo	.05	.02	.01
□ 233 Atlee Hammaker	.05	.02	.01
□ 234 Tim Teufel	.05	.02	.01
□ 235 John Kruk	.10	.05	.01
□ 236 Kurt Stillwell	.05	.02	.01
□ 237 Dan Pasqua	.05	.02	.01
□ 238 Tim Crews	.05	.02	.01
□ 239 Dave Gallagher	.05	.02	.01
□ 240 Leo Gomez	.05	.02	.01
□ 241 Steve Avery	.10	.05	.01
□ 242 Bill Gullickson	.05	.02	.01
□ 243 Mark Portugal	.05	.02	.01
□ 244 Lee Guetterman	.05	.02	.01
□ 245 Benito Santiago	.05	.02	.01
□ 246 Jim Gantner	.05	.02	.01
□ 247 Robby Thompson	.05	.02	.01
□ 248 Terry Shumpert	.05	.02	.01
□ 249 Mike Bell	.05	.02	.01
□ 250 Harold Reynolds	.05	.02	.01
□ 251 Mike Felder	.05	.02	.01
□ 252 Bill Pecota	.05	.02	.01
□ 253 Bill Krueger	.05	.02	.01
□ 254 Alfredo Griffin	.05	.02	.01
□ 255 Lou Whitaker	.15	.07	.02
□ 256 Roy Smith	.05	.02	.01
□ 257 Jerald Clark	.05	.02	.01
□ 258 Sammy Sosa	.25	.11	.03
□ 259 Tim Naehring	.10	.05	.01
□ 260 Dave Righetti	.05	.02	.01
□ 261 Paul Gibson	.05	.02	.01
□ 262 Chris James	.05	.02	.01
□ 263 Larry Andersen	.05	.02	.01
□ 264 Storm Davis	.05	.02	.01
□ 265 Jose Lind	.05	.02	.01
□ 266 Greg Hibbard	.05	.02	.01
□ 267 Norm Charlton	.05	.02	.01
□ 268 Paul Kilgus	.05	.02	.01
□ 269 Greg Maddux	.75	.35	.09
□ 270 Ellis Burks	.15	.07	.02
□ 271 Frank Tanana	.05	.02	.01
□ 272 Gene Larkin	.05	.02	.01
□ 273 Ron Hassey	.05	.02	.01
□ 274 Jeff M. Robinson	.05	.02	.01
□ 275 Steve Howe	.05	.02	.01
□ 276 Daryl Boston	.05	.02	.01
□ 277 Mark Lee	.05	.02	.01
□ 278 Jose Segura	.05	.02	.01
□ 279 Lance Blankenship	.05	.02	.01
□ 280 Don Slaught	.05	.02	.01
□ 281 Russ Swan	.05	.02	.01
□ 282 Bob Tewksbury	.05	.02	.01
□ 283 Geno Petralli	.05	.02	.01
□ 284 Shane Mack	.05	.02	.01
□ 285 Bob Scanlan	.05	.02	.01
□ 286 Tim Leary	.05	.02	.01
□ 287 John Smoltz	.15	.07	.02
□ 288 Pat Borders	.05	.02	.01
□ 289 Mark Davidson	.05	.02	.01
□ 290 Sam Horn	.05	.02	.01
□ 291 Lenny Harris	.05	.02	.01
□ 292 Franklin Stubbs	.05	.02	.01
□ 293 Thomas Howard	.05	.02	.01
□ 294 Steve Lyons	.05	.02	.01
□ 295 Francisco Oliveras	.05	.02	.01
□ 296 Terry Leach	.05	.02	.01
□ 297 Barry Jones	.05	.02	.01
□ 298 Lance Parrish	.05	.02	.01
□ 299 Wally Whitehurst	.05	.02	.01
□ 300 Bob Welch	.05	.02	.01
□ 301 Charlie Hayes	.05	.02	.01
□ 302 Charlie Hough	.05	.02	.01
□ 303 Gary Redus	.05	.02	.01
□ 304 Scott Bradley	.05	.02	.01
□ 305 Jose Oquendo	.05	.02	.01
□ 306 Pete Incaviglia	.05	.02	.01
□ 307 Marvin Freeman	.05	.02	.01
□ 308 Gary Pettis	.05	.02	.01
□ 309 Joe Slusarski	.05	.02	.01
□ 310 Kevin Seitzer	.05	.02	.01
□ 311 Jeff Reed	.05	.02	.01
□ 312 Pat Tabler	.05	.02	.01
□ 313 Mike Maddux	.05	.02	.01
□ 314 Bob Milacki	.05	.02	.01
□ 315 Eric Anthony	.05	.02	.01
□ 316 Dante Bichette	.15	.07	.02
□ 317 Steve Decker	.05	.02	.01
□ 318 Jack Clark	.10	.05	.01
□ 319 Doug Dascenzo	.05	.02	.01
□ 320 Scott Leius	.05	.02	.01
□ 321 Jim Lindeman	.05	.02	.01
□ 322 Bryan Harvey	.05	.02	.01
□ 323 Spike Owen	.05	.02	.01
□ 324 Roberto Kelly	.05	.02	.01
□ 325 Stan Belinda	.05	.02	.01
□ 326 Joey Cora	.05	.02	.01
□ 327 Jeff Innis	.05	.02	.01
□ 328 Willie Wilson	.05	.02	.01
□ 329 Juan Agosto	.05	.02	.01
□ 330 Charles Nagy	.10	.05	.01
□ 331 Scott Bailes	.05	.02	.01
□ 332 Pete Schourek	.10	.05	.01
□ 333 Mike Flanagan	.05	.02	.01
□ 334 Omar Olivares	.05	.02	.01
□ 335 Dennis Lamp	.05	.02	.01
□ 336 Tommy Greene	.05	.02	.01
□ 337 Randy Velarde	.05	.02	.01
□ 338 Tom Lampkin	.05	.02	.01
□ 339 John Russell	.05	.02	.01
□ 340 Bob Kipper	.05	.02	.01
□ 341 Todd Burns	.05	.02	.01
□ 342 Ron Jones	.05	.02	.01
□ 343 Dave Valle	.05	.02	.01
□ 344 Mike Heath	.05	.02	.01
□ 345 John Olerud	.10	.05	.01
□ 346 Gerald Young	.05	.02	.01
□ 347 Ken Patterson	.05	.02	.01
□ 348 Les Lancaster	.05	.02	.01
□ 349 Steve Crawford	.05	.02	.01
□ 350 John Candelaria	.05	.02	.01
□ 351 Mike Aldrete	.05	.02	.01
□ 352 Mariano Duncan	.05	.02	.01
□ 353 Julio Machado	.05	.02	.01
□ 354 Ken Williams	.05	.02	.01
□ 355 Walt Terrell	.05	.02	.01
□ 356 Mitch Williams	.05	.02	.01
□ 357 Al Newman	.05	.02	.01
□ 358 Bud Black	.05	.02	.01
□ 359 Joe Hesketh	.05	.02	.01
□ 360 Paul Assenmacher	.05	.02	.01
□ 361 Bo Jackson	.15	.07	.02
□ 362 Jeff Blauser	.05	.02	.01
□ 363 Mike Brumley	.05	.02	.01
□ 364 Jim Deshaies	.05	.02	.01
□ 365 Brady Anderson	.15	.07	.02
□ 366 Chuck McElroy	.05	.02	.01
□ 367 Matt Merullo	.05	.02	.01
□ 368 Tim Belcher	.05	.02	.01
□ 369 Luis Aquino	.05	.02	.01
□ 370 Joe Oliver	.05	.02	.01
□ 371 Greg Swindell	.05	.02	.01
□ 372 Lee Stevens	.05	.02	.01
□ 373 Mark Knudson	.05	.02	.01
□ 374 Bill Wegman	.05	.02	.01
□ 375 Jerry Don Gleaton	.05	.02	.01
□ 376 Pedro Guerrero	.05	.02	.01
□ 377 Randy Bush	.05	.02	.01
□ 378 Greg W. Harris	.05	.02	.01
□ 379 Eric Plunk	.05	.02	.01
□ 380 Jose DeJesus	.05	.02	.01
□ 381 Bobby Witt	.05	.02	.01
□ 382 Curtis Wilkerson	.05	.02	.01
□ 383 Gene Nelson	.05	.02	.01
□ 384 Wes Chamberlain	.05	.02	.01
□ 385 Tom Henke	.05	.02	.01
□ 386 Mark Lemke	.05	.02	.01
□ 387 Greg Briley	.05	.02	.01
□ 388 Rafael Ramirez	.05	.02	.01
□ 389 Tony Fossas	.05	.02	.01
□ 390 Henry Cotto	.05	.02	.01
□ 391 Tim Hulett	.05	.02	.01
□ 392 Dean Palmer	.10	.05	.01
□ 393 Glenn Braggs	.05	.02	.01
□ 394 Mark Salas	.05	.02	.01

□ 395	Rusty Meacham	.05	.02	.01
□ 396	Andy Ashby	.10	.05	.01
□ 397	Jose Melendez	.05	.02	.01
□ 398	Warren Newson	.05	.02	.01
□ 399	Frank Castillo	.10	.05	.01
□ 400	Chito Martinez	.05	.02	.01
□ 401	Bernie Williams	.25	.11	.03
□ 402	Derek Bell	.10	.05	.01
□ 403	Javier Ortiz	.05	.02	.01
□ 404	Tim Sherrill	.05	.02	.01
□ 405	Rob MacDonald	.05	.02	.01
□ 406	Phil Plantier	.10	.05	.01
□ 407	Troy Afenir	.05	.02	.01
□ 408	Gino Minutelli	.05	.02	.01
□ 409	Reggie Jefferson	.10	.05	.01
□ 410	Mike Remlinger	.05	.02	.01
□ 411	Carlos Rodriguez	.05	.02	.01
□ 412	Joe Redfield	.05	.02	.01
□ 413	Alonzo Powell	.05	.02	.01
□ 414	Scott Livingstone UER (Travis Fryman, not Woody, should be referenced on back)	.05	.02	.01
□ 415	Scott Kamieniecki	.05	.02	.01
□ 416	Tim Spehr	.05	.02	.01
□ 417	Brian Hunter	.05	.02	.01
□ 418	Ced Landrum	.05	.02	.01
□ 419	Bret Barberie	.05	.02	.01
□ 420	Kevin Morton	.05	.02	.01
□ 421	Doug Henry	.05	.02	.01
□ 422	Doug Piatt	.05	.02	.01
□ 423	Pat Rice	.05	.02	.01
□ 424	Juan Guzman	.10	.05	.01
□ 425	Nolan Ryan NH	.40	.18	.05
□ 426	Tommy Greene NH	.05	.02	.01
□ 427	Bob Milacki and Mike Flanagan NH (Mark Williamson and Gregg Olson)	.05	.02	.01
□ 428	Wilson Alvarez NH	.10	.05	.01
□ 429	Otis Nixon HL	.05	.02	.01
□ 430	Rickey Henderson HL	.15	.07	.02
□ 431	Cecil Fielder AS	.05	.02	.01
□ 432	Julio Franco AS	.05	.02	.01
□ 433	Cal Ripken AS	.40	.18	.05
□ 434	Wade Boggs AS	.10	.05	.01
□ 435	Joe Carter AS	.15	.07	.02
□ 436	Ken Griffey Jr. AS	.75	.35	.09
□ 437	Ruben Sierra AS	.05	.02	.01
□ 438	Scott Erickson AS	.05	.02	.01
□ 439	Tom Henke AS	.05	.02	.01
□ 440	Terry Steinbach AS	.05	.02	.01
□ 441	Rickey Henderson DT	.15	.07	.02
□ 442	Ryne Sandberg DT	.25	.11	.03
□ 443	Otis Nixon	.05	.02	.01
□ 444	Scott Radinsky	.05	.02	.01
□ 445	Mark Grace	.15	.07	.02
□ 446	Tony Pena	.05	.02	.01
□ 447	Billy Hatcher	.05	.02	.01
□ 448	Glenallen Hill	.05	.02	.01
□ 449	Chris Gwynn	.05	.02	.01
□ 450	Tom Glavine	.15	.07	.02
□ 451	John Habyan	.05	.02	.01
□ 452	Al Osuna	.05	.02	.01
□ 453	Tony Phillips	.10	.05	.01
□ 454	Greg Cadaret	.05	.02	.01
□ 455	Rob Dibble	.05	.02	.01
□ 456	Rick Honeycutt	.05	.02	.01
□ 457	Jerome Walton	.05	.02	.01
□ 458	Mookie Wilson	.05	.02	.01
□ 459	Mark Gubicza	.05	.02	.01
□ 460	Craig Biggio	.15	.07	.02
□ 461	Dave Cochrane	.05	.02	.01
□ 462	Keith Miller	.05	.02	.01
□ 463	Alex Cole	.05	.02	.01
□ 464	Pete Smith	.05	.02	.01
□ 465	Brett Butler	.10	.05	.01
□ 466	Jeff Huson	.05	.02	.01
□ 467	Steve Lake	.05	.02	.01
□ 468	Lloyd Moseby	.05	.02	.01
□ 469	Tim McIntosh	.05	.02	.01
□ 470	Dennis Martinez	.10	.05	.01
□ 471	Greg Myers	.05	.02	.01
□ 472	Mackey Sasser	.05	.02	.01
□ 473	Junior Ortiz	.05	.02	.01
□ 474	Greg Olson	.05	.02	.01
□ 475	Steve Sax	.05	.02	.01
□ 476	Ricky Jordan	.05	.02	.01
□ 477	Max Venable	.05	.02	.01
□ 478	Brian McRae	.15	.07	.02
□ 479	Doug Simons	.05	.02	.01
□ 480	Rickey Henderson	.15	.07	.02
□ 481	Gary Varsho	.05	.02	.01
□ 482	Carl Willis	.05	.02	.01
□ 483	Rick Wilkins	.05	.02	.01
□ 484	Donn Pall	.05	.02	.01
□ 485	Edgar Martinez	.15	.07	.02
□ 486	Tom Foley	.05	.02	.01
□ 487	Mark Williamson	.05	.02	.01
□ 488	Jack Armstrong	.05	.02	.01
□ 489	Gary Carter	.15	.07	.02
□ 490	Ruben Sierra	.10	.05	.01
□ 491	Gerald Perry	.05	.02	.01
□ 492	Rob Murphy	.05	.02	.01
□ 493	Zane Smith	.05	.02	.01
□ 494	Darryl Kile	.05	.02	.01
□ 495	Kelly Gruber	.05	.02	.01
□ 496	Jerry Browne	.05	.02	.01
□ 497	Darryl Hamilton	.05	.02	.01
□ 498	Mike Stanton	.05	.02	.01
□ 499	Mark Leonard	.05	.02	.01
□ 500	Jose Canseco	.15	.07	.02
□ 501	Dave Martinez	.05	.02	.01
□ 502	Jose Guzman	.05	.02	.01
□ 503	Terry Kennedy	.05	.02	.01
□ 504	Ed Sprague	.10	.05	.01
□ 505	Frank Thomas UER (His Gulf Coast League stats are wrong)	1.50	.70	.19
□ 506	Darren Daulton	.10	.05	.01
□ 507	Kevin Tapani	.05	.02	.01
□ 508	Luis Salazar	.05	.02	.01
□ 509	Paul Faries	.05	.02	.01
□ 510	Sandy Alomar Jr.	.10	.05	.01
□ 511	Jeff King	.10	.05	.01
□ 512	Gary Thurman	.05	.02	.01
□ 513	Chris Hammond	.05	.02	.01
□ 514	Pedro Munoz	.05	.02	.01
□ 515	Alan Trammell	.15	.07	.02
□ 516	Geronimo Pena	.05	.02	.01
□ 517	Rodney McCray UER (Stole 6 bases in 1990, not 5; career totals are correct at 7)	.05	.02	.01
□ 518	Manny Lee	.05	.02	.01
□ 519	Junior Felix	.05	.02	.01
□ 520	Kirk Gibson	.10	.05	.01
□ 521	Darrin Jackson	.05	.02	.01
□ 522	John Burkett	.10	.05	.01
□ 523	Jeff Johnson	.05	.02	.01
□ 524	Jim Corsi	.05	.02	.01
□ 525	Robin Yount	.15	.07	.02
□ 526	Jamie Quirk	.05	.02	.01
□ 527	Bob Ojeda	.05	.02	.01
□ 528	Mark Lewis	.05	.02	.01
□ 529	Bryn Smith	.05	.02	.01
□ 530	Kent Hrbek	.10	.05	.01
□ 531	Dennis Boyd	.05	.02	.01
□ 532	Ron Karkovice	.05	.02	.01
□ 533	Don August	.05	.02	.01
□ 534	Todd Frohwirth	.05	.02	.01
□ 535	Wally Joyner	.10	.05	.01
□ 536	Dennis Rasmussen	.05	.02	.01
□ 537	Andy Allanson	.05	.02	.01
□ 538	Goose Gossage	.10	.05	.01
□ 539	John Marzano	.05	.02	.01
□ 540	Cal Ripken	.75	.35	.09
□ 541	Bill Swift UER (Brewers logo on front)	.05	.02	.01
□ 542	Kevin Appier	.10	.05	.01
□ 543	Dave Bergman	.05	.02	.01
□ 544	Bernard Gilkey	.10	.05	.01
□ 545	Mike Greenwell	.05	.02	.01
□ 546	Jose Uribe	.05	.02	.01
□ 547	Jesse Orosco	.05	.02	.01
□ 548	Bob Patterson	.05	.02	.01
□ 549	Mike Stanley	.05	.02	.01
□ 550	Howard Johnson	.05	.02	.01
□ 551	Joe Orsulak	.05	.02	.01
□ 552	Dick Schofield	.05	.02	.01
□ 553	Dave Hollins	.05	.02	.01
□ 554	David Segui	.05	.02	.01

□ 555 Barry Bonds	.25	.11	.03
□ 556 Mo Vaughn	.40	.18	.05
□ 557 Craig Wilson	.05	.02	.01
□ 558 Bobby Rose	.05	.02	.01
□ 559 Rod Nichols	.05	.02	.01
□ 560 Len Dykstra	.10	.05	.01
□ 561 Craig Grebeck	.05	.02	.01
□ 562 Darren Lewis	.05	.02	.01
□ 563 Todd Benzinger	.05	.02	.01
□ 564 Ed Whitson	.05	.02	.01
□ 565 Jesse Barfield	.05	.02	.01
□ 566 Lloyd McClendon	.05	.02	.01
□ 567 Dan Plesac	.05	.02	.01
□ 568 Danny Cox	.05	.02	.01
□ 569 Skeeter Barnes	.05	.02	.01
□ 570 Bobby Thigpen	.05	.02	.01
□ 571 Deion Sanders	.15	.07	.02
□ 572 Chuck Knoblauch	.15	.07	.02
□ 573 Matt Nokes	.05	.02	.01
□ 574 Herm Winningham	.05	.02	.01
□ 575 Tom Candiotti	.05	.02	.01
□ 576 Jeff Bagwell	.60	.25	.07
□ 577 Brook Jacoby	.05	.02	.01
□ 578 Chico Walker	.05	.02	.01
□ 579 Brian Downing	.05	.02	.01
□ 580 Dave Stewart	.10	.05	.01
□ 581 Francisco Cabrera	.05	.02	.01
□ 582 Rene Gonzales	.05	.02	.01
□ 583 Stan Javier	.05	.02	.01
□ 584 Randy Johnson	.15	.07	.02
□ 585 Chuck Finley	.05	.02	.01
□ 586 Mark Gardner	.05	.02	.01
□ 587 Mark Whiten	.10	.05	.01
□ 588 Garry Templeton	.05	.02	.01
□ 589 Gary Sheffield	.15	.07	.02
□ 590 Ozzie Smith	.20	.09	.03
□ 591 Candy Maldonado	.05	.02	.01
□ 592 Mike Sharperson	.05	.02	.01
□ 593 Carlos Martinez	.05	.02	.01
□ 594 Scott Bankhead	.05	.02	.01
□ 595 Tim Wallach	.05	.02	.01
□ 596 Tino Martinez	.15	.07	.02
□ 597 Roger McDowell	.05	.02	.01
□ 598 Cory Snyder	.05	.02	.01
□ 599 Andujar Cedeno	.05	.02	.01
□ 600 Kirby Puckett	.30	.14	.04
□ 601 Rick Parker	.05	.02	.01
□ 602 Todd Hundley	.15	.07	.02
□ 603 Greg Litton	.05	.02	.01
□ 604 Dave Johnson	.05	.02	.01
□ 605 John Franco	.05	.02	.01
□ 606 Mike Fetters	.05	.02	.01
□ 607 Luis Alicea	.05	.02	.01
□ 608 Trevor Wilson	.05	.02	.01
□ 609 Rob Ducey	.05	.02	.01
□ 610 Ramon Martinez	.10	.05	.01
□ 611 Dave Burba	.05	.02	.01
□ 612 Dwight Smith	.05	.02	.01
□ 613 Kevin Maas	.05	.02	.01
□ 614 John Costello	.05	.02	.01
□ 615 Glenn Davis	.05	.02	.01
□ 616 Shawn Abner	.05	.02	.01
□ 617 Scott Hemond	.05	.02	.01
□ 618 Tom Prince	.05	.02	.01
□ 619 Wally Ritchie	.05	.02	.01
□ 620 Jim Abbott	.05	.02	.01
□ 621 Charlie O'Brien	.05	.02	.01
□ 622 Jack Daugherty	.05	.02	.01
□ 623 Tommy Gregg	.05	.02	.01
□ 624 Jeff Shaw	.05	.02	.01
□ 625 Tony Gwynn	.40	.18	.05
□ 626 Mark Leiter	.05	.02	.01
□ 627 Jim Clancy	.05	.02	.01
□ 628 Tim Layana	.05	.02	.01
□ 629 Jeff Schaefer	.05	.02	.01
□ 630 Lee Smith	.10	.05	.01
□ 631 Wade Taylor	.05	.02	.01
□ 632 Mike Simms	.05	.02	.01
□ 633 Terry Steinbach	.10	.05	.01
□ 634 Shawon Dunston	.05	.02	.01
□ 635 Tim Raines	.15	.07	.02
□ 636 Kirt Manwaring	.05	.02	.01
□ 637 Warren Cromartie	.05	.02	.01
□ 638 Luis Quinones	.05	.02	.01
□ 639 Greg Vaughn	.15	.07	.02
□ 640 Kevin Mitchell	.10	.05	.01
□ 641 Chris Hoiles	.05	.02	.01
□ 642 Tom Browning	.05	.02	.01
□ 643 Mitch Webster	.05	.02	.01
□ 644 Steve Olin	.05	.02	.01
□ 645 Tony Fernandez	.05	.02	.01
□ 646 Juan Bell	.05	.02	.01
□ 647 Joe Boever	.05	.02	.01
□ 648 Carney Lansford	.10	.05	.01
□ 649 Mike Benjamin	.05	.02	.01
□ 650 George Brett	.40	.18	.05
□ 651 Tim Burke	.05	.02	.01
□ 652 Jack Morris	.10	.05	.01
□ 653 Orel Hershiser	.10	.05	.01
□ 654 Mike Schooler	.05	.02	.01
□ 655 Andy Van Slyke	.10	.05	.01
□ 656 Dave Stieb	.05	.02	.01
□ 657 Dave Clark	.05	.02	.01
□ 658 Ben McDonald	.05	.02	.01
□ 659 John Smiley	.05	.02	.01
□ 660 Wade Boggs	.15	.07	.02
□ 661 Eric Bullock	.05	.02	.01
□ 662 Eric Show	.05	.02	.01
□ 663 Lenny Webster	.05	.02	.01
□ 664 Mike Huff	.05	.02	.01
□ 665 Rick Sutcliffe	.05	.02	.01
□ 666 Jeff Manto	.05	.02	.01
□ 667 Mike Fitzgerald	.05	.02	.01
□ 668 Matt Young	.05	.02	.01
□ 669 Dave West	.05	.02	.01
□ 670 Mike Hartley	.05	.02	.01
□ 671 Curt Schilling	.05	.02	.01
□ 672 Brian Bohanon	.05	.02	.01
□ 673 Cecil Espy	.05	.02	.01
□ 674 Joe Grahe	.05	.02	.01
□ 675 Sid Fernandez	.05	.02	.01
□ 676 Edwin Nunez	.05	.02	.01
□ 677 Hector Villanueva	.05	.02	.01
□ 678 Sean Berry	.10	.05	.01
□ 679 Dave Eiland	.05	.02	.01
□ 680 Dave Cone	.15	.07	.02
□ 681 Mike Bordick	.10	.05	.01
□ 682 Tony Castillo	.05	.02	.01
□ 683 John Barfield	.05	.02	.01
□ 684 Jeff Hamilton	.05	.02	.01
□ 685 Ken Dayley	.05	.02	.01
□ 686 Carmelo Martinez	.05	.02	.01
□ 687 Mike Capel	.05	.02	.01
□ 688 Scott Chiamparino	.05	.02	.01
□ 689 Rich Gedman	.05	.02	.01
□ 690 Rich Monteleone	.05	.02	.01
□ 691 Alejandro Pena	.05	.02	.01
□ 692 Oscar Azocar	.05	.02	.01
□ 693 Jim Poole	.05	.02	.01
□ 694 Mike Gardiner	.05	.02	.01
□ 695 Steve Buechele	.05	.02	.01
□ 696 Rudy Seanez	.05	.02	.01
□ 697 Paul Abbott	.05	.02	.01
□ 698 Steve Searcy	.05	.02	.01
□ 699 Jose Offerman	.05	.02	.01
□ 700 Ivan Rodriguez	.25	.11	.03
□ 701 Joe Girardi	.05	.02	.01
□ 702 Tony Perezchica	.05	.02	.01
□ 703 Paul McClellan	.05	.02	.01
□ 704 David Howard	.05	.02	.01
□ 705 Dan Petry	.05	.02	.01
□ 706 Jack Howell	.05	.02	.01
□ 707 Jose Mesa	.10	.05	.01
□ 708 Randy St. Claire	.05	.02	.01
□ 709 Kevin Brown	.10	.05	.01
□ 710 Ron Darling	.05	.02	.01
□ 711 Jason Grimsley	.05	.02	.01
□ 712 John Orton	.05	.02	.01
□ 713 Shawn Boskie	.05	.02	.01
□ 714 Pat Clements	.05	.02	.01
□ 715 Brian Barnes	.05	.02	.01
□ 716 Luis Lopez	.05	.02	.01
□ 717 Bob McClure	.05	.02	.01
□ 718 Mark Davis	.05	.02	.01
□ 719 Dann Bilardello	.05	.02	.01
□ 720 Tom Edens	.05	.02	.01
□ 721 Willie Fraser	.05	.02	.01
□ 722 Curt Young	.05	.02	.01
□ 723 Neal Heaton	.05	.02	.01
□ 724 Craig Worthington	.05	.02	.01
□ 725 Mel Rojas	.10	.05	.01
□ 726 Daryl Irvine	.05	.02	.01

□	727 Roger Mason	.05	.02	.01
□	728 Kirk Dressendorfer	.05	.02	.01
□	729 Scott Aldred	.05	.02	.01
□	730 Willie Blair	.05	.02	.01
□	731 Allan Anderson	.05	.02	.01
□	732 Dana Kiecker	.05	.02	.01
□	733 Jose Gonzalez	.05	.02	.01
□	734 Brian Drahman	.05	.02	.01
□	735 Brad Komminsk	.05	.02	.01
□	736 Arthur Rhodes	.05	.02	.01
□	737 Terry Mathews	.05	.02	.01
□	738 Jeff Fassero	.10	.05	.01
□	739 Mike Magnante	.05	.02	.01
□	740 Kip Gross	.05	.02	.01
□	741 Jim Hunter	.05	.02	.01
□	742 Jose Mota	.05	.02	.01
□	743 Joe Bitker	.05	.02	.01
□	744 Tim Mauser	.05	.02	.01
□	745 Ramon Garcia	.05	.02	.01
□	746 Rod Beck	.15	.07	.02
□	747 Jim Austin	.05	.02	.01
□	748 Keith Mitchell	.05	.02	.01
□	749 Wayne Rosenthal	.05	.02	.01
□	750 Bryan Hickerson	.05	.02	.01
□	751 Bruce Egloff	.05	.02	.01
□	752 John Wehner	.05	.02	.01
□	753 Darren Holmes	.05	.02	.01
□	754 Dave Hansen	.05	.02	.01
□	755 Mike Mussina	.30	.14	.04
□	756 Anthony Young	.05	.02	.01
□	757 Ron Tingley	.05	.02	.01
□	758 Ricky Bones	.05	.02	.01
□	759 Mark Wohlers	.15	.07	.02
□	760 Wilson Alvarez	.15	.07	.02
□	761 Harvey Pulliam	.05	.02	.01
□	762 Ryan Bowen	.05	.02	.01
□	763 Terry Bross	.05	.02	.01
□	764 Joel Johnston	.05	.02	.01
□	765 Terry McDaniel	.05	.02	.01
□	766 Esteban Beltre	.05	.02	.01
□	767 Rob Maurer	.05	.02	.01
□	768 Ted Wood	.05	.02	.01
□	769 Mo Sanford	.05	.02	.01
□	770 Jeff Carter	.05	.02	.01
□	771 Gil Heredia	.05	.02	.01
□	772 Monty Fariss	.05	.02	.01
□	773 Will Clark AS	.10	.05	.01
□	774 Ryne Sandberg AS	.15	.07	.02
□	775 Barry Larkin AS	.10	.05	.01
□	776 Howard Johnson AS	.05	.02	.01
□	777 Barry Bonds AS	.15	.07	.02
□	778 Brett Butler AS	.05	.02	.01
□	779 Tony Gwynn AS	.20	.09	.03
□	780 Ramon Martinez AS	.05	.02	.01
□	781 Lee Smith AS	.05	.02	.01
□	782 Mike Scioscia AS	.05	.02	.01
□	783 Dennis Martinez HL UER (Card has both 13th and 15th perfect game in Major League history)	.05	.02	.01
□	784 Dennis Martinez NH	.05	.02	.01
□	785 Mark Gardner NH	.05	.02	.01
□	786 Bret Saberhagen NH	.05	.02	.01
□	787 Kent Mercker NH Mark Wohlers Alejandro Pena	.05	.02	.01
□	788 Cal Ripken MVP	.40	.18	.05
□	789 Terry Pendleton MVP	.05	.02	.01
□	790 Roger Clemens CY	.15	.07	.02
□	791 Tom Glavine CY	.10	.05	.01
□	792 Chuck Knoblauch ROY	.15	.07	.02
□	793 Jeff Bagwell ROY	.30	.14	.04
□	794 Cal Ripken MANYR	.40	.18	.05
□	795 David Cone HL	.10	.05	.01
□	796 Kirby Puckett HL	.15	.07	.02
□	797 Steve Avery HL	.10	.05	.01
□	798 Jack Morris HL	.05	.02	.01
□	799 Allen Watson DC	.10	.05	.01
□	800 Manny Ramirez DC	2.00	.90	.25
□	801 Cliff Floyd DC	.20	.09	.03
□	802 Al Shirley DC	.10	.05	.01
□	803 Brian Barber DC	.10	.05	.01
□	804 Jon Farrell DC	.05	.02	.01
□	805 Brent Gates DC	.10	.05	.01
□	806 Scott Ruffcorn DC	.10	.05	.01
□	807 Tyrone Hill DC	.05	.02	.01
□	808 Benji Gil DC	.15	.07	.02
□	809 Aaron Sele DC	.15	.07	.02
□	810 Tyler Green DC	.10	.05	.01
□	811 Chris Jones	.05	.02	.01
□	812 Steve Wilson	.05	.02	.01
□	813 Freddie Benavides	.05	.02	.01
□	814 Don Wakamatsu	.05	.02	.01
□	815 Mike Humphreys	.05	.02	.01
□	816 Scott Servais	.05	.02	.01
□	817 Rico Rossy	.05	.02	.01
□	818 John Ramos	.05	.02	.01
□	819 Rob Mallicoat	.05	.02	.01
□	820 Milt Hill	.05	.02	.01
□	821 Carlos Garcia	.10	.05	.01
□	822 Stan Royer	.05	.02	.01
□	823 Jeff Plympton	.05	.02	.01
□	824 Braulio Castillo	.05	.02	.01
□	825 David Haas	.05	.02	.01
□	826 Luis Mercedes	.05	.02	.01
□	827 Eric Karros	.15	.07	.02
□	828 Shawn Hare	.05	.02	.01
□	829 Reggie Sanders	.15	.07	.02
□	830 Tom Goodwin	.10	.05	.01
□	831 Dan Gakeler	.05	.02	.01
□	832 Stacy Jones	.05	.02	.01
□	833 Kim Batiste	.05	.02	.01
□	834 Cal Eldred	.05	.02	.01
□	835 Chris George	.05	.02	.01
□	836 Wayne Housie	.05	.02	.01
□	837 Mike Ignasiak	.05	.02	.01
□	838 Josias Manzanillo	.05	.02	.01
□	839 Jim Olander	.05	.02	.01
□	840 Gary Cooper	.05	.02	.01
□	841 Royce Clayton	.10	.05	.01
□	842 Hector Fajardo	.05	.02	.01
□	843 Blaine Beatty	.05	.02	.01
□	844 Jorge Pedre	.05	.02	.01
□	845 Kenny Lofton	1.00	.45	.12
□	846 Scott Brosius	.15	.07	.02
□	847 Chris Cron	.05	.02	.01
□	848 Denis Boucher	.05	.02	.01
□	849 Kyle Abbott	.05	.02	.01
□	850 Robert Zupcic	.05	.02	.01
□	851 Rheal Cormier	.05	.02	.01
□	852 Jim Lewis	.05	.02	.01
□	853 Anthony Telford	.05	.02	.01
□	854 Cliff Brantley	.05	.02	.01
□	855 Kevin Campbell	.05	.02	.01
□	856 Craig Shipley	.05	.02	.01
□	857 Chuck Carr	.05	.02	.01
□	858 Tony Eusebio	.05	.02	.01
□	859 Jim Thome	.75	.35	.09
□	860 Vinny Castilla	.50	.23	.06
□	861 Dann Howitt	.05	.02	.01
□	862 Kevin Ward	.05	.02	.01
□	863 Steve Wapnick	.05	.02	.01
□	864 Rod Brewer	.05	.02	.01
□	865 Todd Van Poppel	.05	.02	.01
□	866 Jose Hernandez	.05	.02	.01
□	867 Amalio Carreno	.05	.02	.01
□	868 Calvin Jones	.05	.02	.01
□	869 Jeff Gardner	.05	.02	.01
□	870 Jarvis Brown	.05	.02	.01
□	871 Eddie Taubensee	.05	.02	.01
□	872 Andy Mota	.05	.02	.01
□	873 Chris Haney	.05	.02	.01
□	874 Roberto Hernandez	.15	.07	.02
□	875 Laddie Renfroe	.05	.02	.01
□	876 Scott Cooper	.05	.02	.01
□	877 Armando Reynoso	.05	.02	.01
□	878 Ty Cobb MEMO	.25	.11	.03
□	879 Babe Ruth MEMO	.30	.14	.04
□	880 Honus Wagner MEMO	.20	.09	.03
□	881 Lou Gehrig MEMO	.25	.11	.03
□	882 Satchel Paige MEMO	.20	.09	.03
□	883 Will Clark DT	.10	.05	.01
□	884 Cal Ripken DT	2.00	.90	.25
□	885 Wade Boggs DT	.10	.05	.01
□	886 Kirby Puckett DT	.30	.14	.04
□	887 Tony Gwynn DT	.30	.14	.04
□	888 Craig Biggio DT	.10	.05	.01
□	889 Scott Erickson DT	.05	.02	.01
□	890 Tom Glavine DT	.10	.05	.01
□	891 Rob Dibble DT	.05	.02	.01
□	892 Mitch Williams DT	.05	.02	.01
□	893 Frank Thomas DT	1.50	.70	.19

		MINT	NRMT	EXC
☐ X672	Chuck Knoblauch AU (1990 Score card, autographed with special hologram on back)	60.00	27.00	7.50

1992 Score Factory Inserts

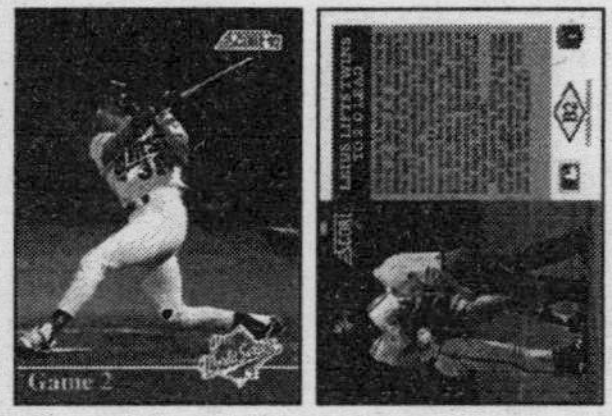

This 17-card insert standard-size set was distributed only in 1992 Score factory sets and consists of four topical subsets. Cards B1-B7 capture a moment from each game of the 1991 World Series. Cards B8-B11 are Cooperstown cards, honoring future Hall of Famers. Cards B12-B14 form a "Joe D" subset paying tribute to Joe DiMaggio. Cards B15-B17, subtitled "Yaz", conclude the set by commemorating Carl Yastrzemski's heroic feats twenty-five years ago in winning the Triple Crown and lifting the Red Sox to their first American League pennant in 21 years. Each subset displayed a different front design. The World Series cards carry full-bleed color action photos except for a blue stripe at the bottom, while the Cooperstown cards have a color portrait on a white card face. Both the DiMaggio and Yastrzemski subsets have action photos with silver borders; they differ in that the DiMaggio photos are black and white, the Yastrzemski photos color. The DiMaggio and Yastrzemski subsets are numbered on the back within each subset (e.g., "1 of 3") and as a part of the 17-card insert set (e.g., "B1"). In the DiMaggio and Yastrzemski subsets, Score varied the insert set slightly in retail versus hobby factory sets. In the hobby set, the DiMaggio cards display different black-and-white photos that are bordered beneath by a dark blue stripe (the stripe is green in the retail factory insert). On the backs, these hobby inserts have a red stripe at the bottom; the same stripe is dark blue on the retail inserts. The Yastrzemski cards in the hobby set have different color photos on their fronts than the retail inserts.

	MINT	NRMT	EXC
COMPLETE SET (17)	6.00	2.70	.75
COMMON WS (B1-B7)	.25	.11	.03
COM.COOPERSTWN (B8-B11)	.75	.35	.09
COMMON DIMAGGIO (B12-B14)	1.50	.70	.19
COMMON YAZ (B15-B17)	.30	.14	.04
ONE SET PER FACTORY SET			

		MINT	NRMT	EXC
☐ B1	Greg Gagne WS	.25	.11	.03
☐ B2	Scott Leius WS	.25	.11	.03
☐ B3	Mark Lemke WS David Justice	.25	.11	.03
☐ B4	Lonnie Smith WS Brian Harper	.25	.11	.03
☐ B5	David Justice WS	.75	.35	.09
☐ B6	Kirby Puckett WS	2.50	1.10	.30
☐ B7	Gene Larkin WS	.25	.11	.03
☐ B8	Carlton Fisk	.75	.35	.09
☐ B9	Ozzie Smith	1.50	.70	.19
☐ B10	Dave Winfield	.75	.35	.09
☐ B11	Robin Yount	1.00	.45	.12
☐ B12	Joe DiMaggio	1.50	.70	.19
☐ B13	Joe DiMaggio	1.50	.70	.19
☐ B14	Joe DiMaggio	1.50	.70	.19
☐ B15	Carl Yastrzemski	.30	.14	.04
☐ B16	Carl Yastrzemski	.30	.14	.04
☐ B17	Carl Yastrzemski	.30	.14	.04

1992 Score Franchise

This four-card standard-size set features three all-time greats, Stan Musial, Mickey Mantle, and Carl Yastrzemski. Each former player autographed 2,000 of his 1992 Score cards, and 500 of the combo cards were signed by all three. In addition to these signed cards, Score produced 150,000 of each Franchise card, and both signed and unsigned cards were randomly inserted in 1992 Score Series II poly packs, blister packs, and cello packs. The first three cards feature color action photos of each player. The fourth is horizontally oriented and pictures each player in a batting stance. A forest green stripe borders the top and bottom. The words "The Franchise" and the Score logo appear at the top, and the player's name is printed on the green stripe at the bottom. The backs of the first three cards have a close-up photo and a career summary. The fourth card is a combo card, summarizing the career of all three players.

	MINT	NRMT	EXC
COMPLETE SET (4)	30.00	13.50	3.70
COMMON CARD (1-4)	6.00	2.70	.75
RANDOM INSERTS IN SER.2 PACKS			

		MINT	NRMT	EXC
☐ 1	Stan Musial	6.00	2.70	.75
☐ 2	Mickey Mantle	15.00	6.75	1.85
☐ 3	Carl Yastrzemski	6.00	2.70	.75
☐ 4	The Franchise Players Stan Musial Mickey Mantle Carl Yastrzemski	12.00	5.50	1.50
☐ AU1	Stan Musial (Autographed with certified signature)	225.00	100.00	28.00
☐ AU2	Mickey Mantle (Autographed with certified signature)	550.00	250.00	70.00
☐ AU3	Carl Yastrzemski (Autographed with certified signature)	175.00	80.00	22.00
☐ AU4	Franchise Players Stan Musial Mickey Mantle Carl Yastrzemski (Autographed with certified signatures of all three)	1600.00	700.00	200.00

1992 Score Hot Rookies

This ten-card standard-size set features color action player photos on a white face. These cards were inserted one per blister pack. The words "Hot Rookie" appear in orange and yellow vertically along the left edge of the photo, and the team logo is in the lower left corner. The player's name is printed in yellow on a red box accented with a shadow detail.

	MINT	NRMT	EXC
COMPLETE SET (10)	15.00	6.75	1.85
COMMON CARD (1-10)	.50	.23	.06

SEMISTARS	1.00	.45	.12
ONE PER BLISTER PACK			
□ 1 Cal Eldred	.50	.23	.06
□ 2 Royce Clayton	.75	.35	.09
□ 3 Kenny Lofton	10.00	4.50	1.25
□ 4 Todd Van Poppel	.50	.23	.06
□ 5 Scott Cooper	.50	.23	.06
□ 6 Todd Hundley	2.00	.90	.25
□ 7 Tino Martinez	1.50	.70	.19
□ 8 Anthony Telford	.50	.23	.06
□ 9 Derek Bell	2.00	.90	.25
□ 10 Reggie Jefferson	.75	.35	.09

1992 Score Impact Players

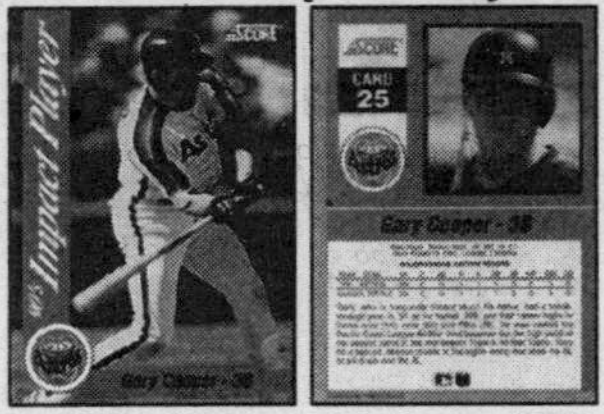

The 1992 Score Impact Players insert set was issued in two series each with 45 standard-size cards with the respective series of the 1992 regular issue Score cards. Five of these cards were inserted in each 1992 Score jumbo pack. The fronts feature full-bleed color action player photos. The pictures are enhanced by a wide vertical stripe running near the left edge containing the words "90's Impact Player" and a narrower stripe at the bottom printed with the player's name.

	MINT	NRMT	EXC
COMPLETE SET (90)	20.00	9.00	2.50
COMPLETE SERIES 1 (45)	14.00	6.25	1.75
COMPLETE SERIES 2 (45)	6.00	2.70	.75
COMMON CARD (1-90)	.15	.07	.02
SEMISTARS	.40	.18	.05
FIVE PER JUMBO PACK			
□ 1 Chuck Knoblauch	.50	.23	.06
□ 2 Jeff Bagwell	1.50	.70	.19
□ 3 Juan Guzman	.25	.11	.03
□ 4 Milt Cuyler	.15	.07	.02
□ 5 Ivan Rodriguez	.75	.35	.09
□ 6 Rich DeLucia	.15	.07	.02
□ 7 Orlando Merced	.25	.11	.03
□ 8 Ray Lankford	.40	.18	.05
□ 9 Brian Hunter	.15	.07	.02
□ 10 Roberto Alomar	.60	.25	.07
□ 11 Wes Chamberlain	.15	.07	.02
□ 12 Steve Avery	.25	.11	.03
□ 13 Scott Erickson	.25	.11	.03
□ 14 Jim Abbott	.15	.07	.02
□ 15 Mark Whiten	.25	.11	.03
□ 16 Leo Gomez	.15	.07	.02
□ 17 Doug Henry	.15	.07	.02
□ 18 Brent Mayne	.15	.07	.02
□ 19 Charles Nagy	.25	.11	.03
□ 20 Phil Plantier	.15	.07	.02
□ 21 Mo Vaughn	1.00	.45	.12
□ 22 Craig Biggio	.40	.18	.05
□ 23 Derek Bell	.25	.11	.03
□ 24 Royce Clayton	.25	.11	.03
□ 25 Gary Cooper	.15	.07	.02
□ 26 Scott Cooper	.15	.07	.02
□ 27 Juan Gonzalez	1.50	.70	.19
□ 28 Ken Griffey Jr.	4.00	1.80	.50
□ 29 Larry Walker	.40	.18	.05
□ 30 John Smoltz	.50	.23	.06
□ 31 Todd Hundley	.50	.23	.06
□ 32 Kenny Lofton	2.00	.90	.25
□ 33 Andy Mota	.15	.07	.02
□ 34 Todd Zeile	.15	.07	.02
□ 35 Arthur Rhodes	.15	.07	.02
□ 36 Jim Thome	2.50	1.10	.30
□ 37 Todd Van Poppel	.15	.07	.02
□ 38 Mark Wohlers	.40	.18	.05
□ 39 Anthony Young	.15	.07	.02
□ 40 Sandy Alomar Jr.	.25	.11	.03
□ 41 John Olerud	.25	.11	.03
□ 42 Robin Ventura	.40	.18	.05
□ 43 Frank Thomas	4.00	1.80	.50
□ 44 Dave Justice	.40	.18	.05
□ 45 Hal Morris	.15	.07	.02
□ 46 Ruben Sierra	.25	.11	.03
□ 47 Travis Fryman	.40	.18	.05
□ 48 Mike Mussina	.75	.35	.09
□ 49 Tom Glavine	.40	.18	.05
□ 50 Barry Larkin	.40	.18	.05
□ 51 Will Clark UER	.40	.18	.05
Career Totals spelled To als			
□ 52 Jose Canseco	.40	.18	.05
□ 53 Bo Jackson	.40	.18	.05
□ 54 Dwight Gooden	.25	.11	.03
□ 55 Barry Bonds	.60	.25	.07
□ 56 Fred McGriff	.40	.18	.05
□ 57 Roger Clemens	.40	.18	.05
□ 58 Benito Santiago	.15	.07	.02
□ 59 Darryl Strawberry	.25	.11	.03
□ 60 Cecil Fielder	.25	.11	.03
□ 61 John Franco	.15	.07	.02
□ 62 Matt Williams	.40	.18	.05
□ 63 Marquis Grissom	.40	.18	.05
□ 64 Danny Tartabull	.15	.07	.02
□ 65 Ron Gant	.40	.18	.05
□ 66 Paul O'Neill	.25	.11	.03
□ 67 Devon White	.25	.11	.03
□ 68 Rafael Palmeiro	.40	.18	.05
□ 69 Tom Gordon	.15	.07	.02
□ 70 Shawon Dunston	.15	.07	.02
□ 71 Rob Dibble	.15	.07	.02
□ 72 Eddie Zosky	.15	.07	.02
□ 73 Jack McDowell	.25	.11	.03
□ 74 Len Dykstra	.25	.11	.03
□ 75 Ramon Martinez	.25	.11	.03
□ 76 Reggie Sanders	.40	.18	.05
□ 77 Greg Maddux	2.50	1.10	.30
□ 78 Ellis Burks	.40	.18	.05
□ 79 John Smiley	.15	.07	.02
□ 80 Roberto Kelly	.15	.07	.02
□ 81 Ben McDonald	.15	.07	.02
□ 82 Mark Lewis	.15	.07	.02
□ 83 Jose Rijo	.15	.07	.02
□ 84 Ozzie Guillen	.15	.07	.02
□ 85 Lance Dickson	.15	.07	.02
□ 86 Kim Batiste	.15	.07	.02
□ 87 Gregg Olson	.15	.07	.02
□ 88 Andy Benes	.15	.07	.02
□ 89 Cal Eldred	.15	.07	.02
□ 90 David Cone	.40	.18	.05

1992 Score Rookie/Traded

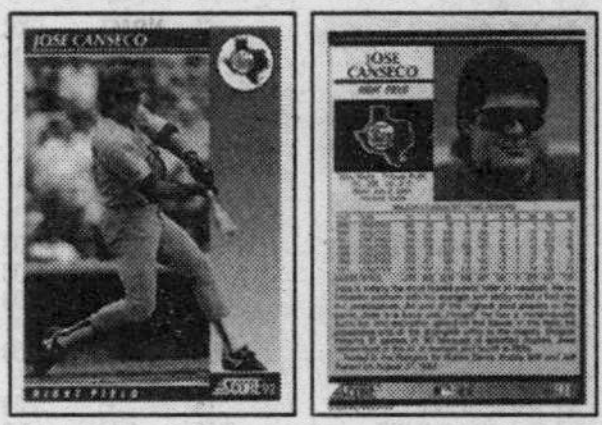

The 1992 Score Rookie and Traded set contains 110 standard-size cards featuring traded veterans and rookies. This set was issued in complete set form and was released through hobby dealers. The fronts display color action player photos edged on one side by an orange stripe that fades to white as one moves down the card face. The player's name appears in a purple bar above the picture, while his position

is printed in a purple bar below the picture. The set is arranged numerically such that cards 1T-79T are traded players and cards 80T-110T feature rookies. The only notable Rookie Card in this set features Brian Jordan.

	MINT	NRMT	EXC
COMPLETE FACT.SET (110)	25.00	11.00	3.10
COMMON CARD (1T-110T)	.10	.05	.01
SEMISTARS	.20	.09	.03
STARS	.40	.18	.05

□ 1T Gary Sheffield	.75	.35	.09
□ 2T Kevin Seitzer	.10	.05	.01
□ 3T Danny Tartabull	.10	.05	.01
□ 4T Steve Sax	.10	.05	.01
□ 5T Bobby Bonilla	.20	.09	.03
□ 6T Frank Viola	.10	.05	.01
□ 7T Dave Winfield	.60	.25	.07
□ 8T Rick Sutcliffe	.10	.05	.01
□ 9T Jose Canseco	.75	.35	.09
□ 10T Greg Swindell	.10	.05	.01
□ 11T Eddie Murray	.75	.35	.09
□ 12T Randy Myers	.20	.09	.03
□ 13T Wally Joyner	.20	.09	.03
□ 14T Kenny Lofton	8.00	3.60	1.00
□ 15T Jack Morris	.20	.09	.03
□ 16T Charlie Hayes	.10	.05	.01
□ 17T Pete Incaviglia	.10	.05	.01
□ 18T Kevin Mitchell	.20	.09	.03
□ 19T Kurt Stillwell	.10	.05	.01
□ 20T Bret Saberhagen	.20	.09	.03
□ 21T Steve Buechele	.10	.05	.01
□ 22T John Smiley	.10	.05	.01
□ 23T Sammy Sosa	1.25	.55	.16
□ 24T George Bell	.10	.05	.01
□ 25T Curt Schilling	.10	.05	.01
□ 26T Dick Schofield	.10	.05	.01
□ 27T David Cone	.35	.16	.04
□ 28T Dan Gladden	.10	.05	.01
□ 29T Kirk McCaskill	.10	.05	.01
□ 30T Mike Gallego	.10	.05	.01
□ 31T Kevin McReynolds	.10	.05	.01
□ 32T Bill Swift	.10	.05	.01
□ 33T Dave Martinez	.10	.05	.01
□ 34T Storm Davis	.10	.05	.01
□ 35T Willie Randolph	.20	.09	.03
□ 36T Melido Perez	.10	.05	.01
□ 37T Mark Carreon	.10	.05	.01
□ 38T Doug Jones	.10	.05	.01
□ 39T Gregg Jefferies	.35	.16	.04
□ 40T Mike Jackson	.10	.05	.01
□ 41T Dickie Thon	.10	.05	.01
□ 42T Eric King	.10	.05	.01
□ 43T Herm Winningham	.10	.05	.01
□ 44T Derek Lilliquist	.10	.05	.01
□ 45T Dave Anderson	.10	.05	.01
□ 46T Jeff Reardon	.20	.09	.03
□ 47T Scott Bankhead	.10	.05	.01
□ 48T Cory Snyder	.10	.05	.01
□ 49T Al Newman	.10	.05	.01
□ 50T Keith Miller	.10	.05	.01
□ 51T Dave Burba	.10	.05	.01
□ 52T Bill Pecota	.10	.05	.01
□ 53T Chuck Crim	.10	.05	.01
□ 54T Mariano Duncan	.10	.05	.01
□ 55T Dave Gallagher	.10	.05	.01
□ 56T Chris Gwynn	.10	.05	.01
□ 57T Scott Ruskin	.10	.05	.01
□ 58T Jack Armstrong	.10	.05	.01
□ 59T Gary Carter	.35	.16	.04
□ 60T Andres Galarraga	.35	.16	.04
□ 61T Ken Hill	.35	.16	.04
□ 62T Eric Davis	.20	.09	.03
□ 63T Ruben Sierra	.20	.09	.03
□ 64T Darrin Fletcher	.10	.05	.01
□ 65T Tim Belcher	.10	.05	.01
□ 66T Mike Morgan	.10	.05	.01
□ 67T Scott Scudder	.10	.05	.01
□ 68T Tom Candiotti	.10	.05	.01
□ 69T Hubie Brooks	.10	.05	.01
□ 70T Kal Daniels	.10	.05	.01
□ 71T Bruce Ruffin	.10	.05	.01
□ 72T Billy Hatcher	.10	.05	.01
□ 73T Bob Melvin	.10	.05	.01
□ 74T Lee Guetterman	.10	.05	.01
□ 75T Rene Gonzales	.10	.05	.01
□ 76T Kevin Bass	.10	.05	.01
□ 77T Tom Bolton	.10	.05	.01
□ 78T John Wetteland	.20	.09	.03
□ 79T Bip Roberts	.10	.05	.01
□ 80T Pat Listach	.20	.09	.03
□ 81T John Doherty	.10	.05	.01
□ 82T Sam Militello	.10	.05	.01
□ 83T Brian Jordan	2.00	.90	.25
□ 84T Jeff Kent	.35	.16	.04
□ 85T Dave Fleming	.10	.05	.01
□ 86T Jeff Tackett	.10	.05	.01
□ 87T Chad Curtis	.35	.16	.04
□ 88T Eric Fox	.10	.05	.01
□ 89T Denny Neagle	1.00	.45	.12
□ 90T Donovan Osborne	.20	.09	.03
□ 91T Carlos Hernandez	.10	.05	.01
□ 92T Tim Wakefield	.35	.16	.04
□ 93T Tim Salmon	5.00	2.20	.60
□ 94T Dave Nilsson	.35	.16	.04
□ 95T Mike Perez	.10	.05	.01
□ 96T Pat Hentgen	.35	.16	.04
□ 97T Frank Seminara	.10	.05	.01
□ 98T Ruben Amaro Jr.	.10	.05	.01
□ 99T Archi Cianfrocco	.10	.05	.01
□ 100T Andy Stankiewicz	.10	.05	.01
□ 101T Jim Bullinger	.10	.05	.01
□ 102T Pat Mahomes	.10	.05	.01
□ 103T Hipolito Pichardo	.10	.05	.01
□ 104T Bret Boone	.35	.16	.04
□ 105T John Vander Wal	.10	.05	.01
□ 106T Vince Horsman	.10	.05	.01
□ 107T James Austin	.10	.05	.01
□ 108T Brian Williams	.10	.05	.01
□ 109T Dan Walters	.10	.05	.01
□ 110T Wil Cordero	.20	.09	.03

1993 Score

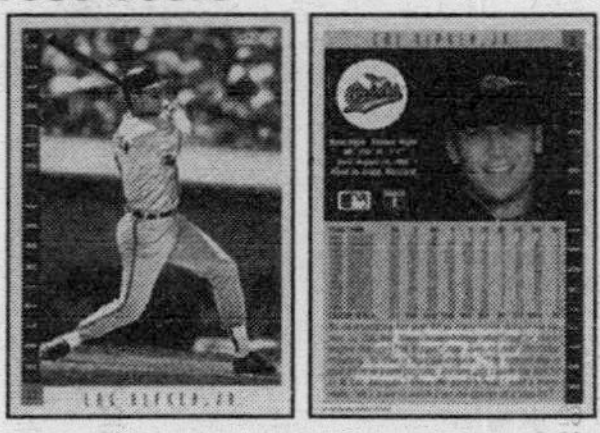

The 1993 Score baseball set consists of 660 standard-size cards issued in one sinle series. The cards were distributed in 16-card poly packs and 35-card jumbo superpacks. The fronts feature color action player photos surrounded by white borders. The player's name appears in the bottom white border, while the team name and position appear in a team color-coded stripe that edges the left side of the picture. Topical subsets featured are Award Winners (481-486), Draft Picks (487-501), All-Star Caricature (502-512 [AL], 522-531 [NL]), Highlights (513-519), World Series Highlights (520-521), Dream Team (532-542) and Rookies (sprinkled throughout the set). Rookie Cards in this set include Derek Jeter and Jason Kendall.

	MINT	NRMT	EXC
COMPLETE SET (660)	40.00	18.00	5.00
COMMON CARD (1-660)	.05	.02	.01
SEMISTARS	.15	.07	.02
STARS	.30	.14	.04

□ 1 Ken Griffey Jr.	2.00	.90	.25
□ 2 Gary Sheffield	.15	.07	.02
□ 3 Frank Thomas	2.00	.90	.25
□ 4 Ryne Sandberg	.50	.23	.06
□ 5 Larry Walker	.15	.07	.02
□ 6 Cal Ripken Jr.	1.50	.70	.19
□ 7 Roger Clemens	.15	.07	.02
□ 8 Bobby Bonilla	.10	.05	.01

□ 9 Carlos Baerga	.15	.07	.02
□ 10 Darren Daulton	.10	.05	.01
□ 11 Travis Fryman	.15	.07	.02
□ 12 Andy Van Slyke	.10	.05	.01
□ 13 Jose Canseco	.15	.07	.02
□ 14 Roberto Alomar	.50	.23	.06
□ 15 Tom Glavine	.15	.07	.02
□ 16 Barry Larkin	.15	.07	.02
□ 17 Gregg Jefferies	.15	.07	.02
□ 18 Craig Biggio	.15	.07	.02
□ 19 Shane Mack	.05	.02	.01
□ 20 Brett Butler	.10	.05	.01
□ 21 Dennis Eckersley	.10	.05	.01
□ 22 Will Clark	.15	.07	.02
□ 23 Don Mattingly	1.00	.45	.12
□ 24 Tony Gwynn	.75	.35	.09
□ 25 Ivan Rodriguez	.40	.18	.05
□ 26 Shawon Dunston	.05	.02	.01
□ 27 Mike Mussina	.40	.18	.05
□ 28 Marquis Grissom	.15	.07	.02
□ 29 Charles Nagy	.10	.05	.01
□ 30 Len Dykstra	.10	.05	.01
□ 31 Cecil Fielder	.10	.05	.01
□ 32 Jay Bell	.10	.05	.01
□ 33 B.J. Surhoff	.10	.05	.01
□ 34 Bob Tewksbury	.05	.02	.01
□ 35 Danny Tartabull	.05	.02	.01
□ 36 Terry Pendleton	.10	.05	.01
□ 37 Jack Morris	.10	.05	.01
□ 38 Hal Morris	.05	.02	.01
□ 39 Luis Polonia	.05	.02	.01
□ 40 Ken Caminiti	.15	.07	.02
□ 41 Robin Ventura	.10	.05	.01
□ 42 Darryl Strawberry	.10	.05	.01
□ 43 Wally Joyner	.10	.05	.01
□ 44 Fred McGriff	.15	.07	.02
□ 45 Kevin Tapani	.05	.02	.01
□ 46 Matt Williams	.15	.07	.02
□ 47 Robin Yount	.15	.07	.02
□ 48 Ken Hill	.10	.05	.01
□ 49 Edgar Martinez	.15	.07	.02
□ 50 Mark Grace	.15	.07	.02
□ 51 Juan Gonzalez	1.00	.45	.12
□ 52 Curt Schilling	.05	.02	.01
□ 53 Dwight Gooden	.10	.05	.01
□ 54 Chris Hoiles	.05	.02	.01
□ 55 Frank Viola	.05	.02	.01
□ 56 Ray Lankford	.15	.07	.02
□ 57 George Brett	.75	.35	.09
□ 58 Kenny Lofton	.75	.35	.09
□ 59 Nolan Ryan	1.50	.70	.19
□ 60 Mickey Tettleton	.05	.02	.01
□ 61 John Smoltz	.15	.07	.02
□ 62 Howard Johnson	.05	.02	.01
□ 63 Eric Karros	.15	.07	.02
□ 64 Rick Aguilera	.05	.02	.01
□ 65 Steve Finley	.15	.07	.02
□ 66 Mark Langston	.10	.05	.01
□ 67 Bill Swift	.05	.02	.01
□ 68 John Olerud	.05	.02	.01
□ 69 Kevin McReynolds	.05	.02	.01
□ 70 Jack McDowell	.10	.05	.01
□ 71 Rickey Henderson	.15	.07	.02
□ 72 Brian Harper	.05	.02	.01
□ 73 Mike Morgan	.05	.02	.01
□ 74 Rafael Palmeiro	.15	.07	.02
□ 75 Dennis Martinez	.10	.05	.01
□ 76 Tino Martinez	.10	.05	.01
□ 77 Eddie Murray	.50	.23	.06
□ 78 Ellis Burks	.15	.07	.02
□ 79 John Kruk	.10	.05	.01
□ 80 Gregg Olson	.05	.02	.01
□ 81 Bernard Gilkey	.15	.07	.02
□ 82 Milt Cuyler	.05	.02	.01
□ 83 Mike LaValliere	.05	.02	.01
□ 84 Albert Belle	1.00	.45	.12
□ 85 Bip Roberts	.05	.02	.01
□ 86 Melido Perez	.05	.02	.01
□ 87 Otis Nixon	.05	.02	.01
□ 88 Bill Spiers	.05	.02	.01
□ 89 Jeff Bagwell	.75	.35	.09
□ 90 Orel Hershiser	.10	.05	.01
□ 91 Andy Benes	.05	.02	.01
□ 92 Devon White	.05	.02	.01
□ 93 Willie McGee	.05	.02	.01
□ 94 Ozzie Guillen	.05	.02	.01
□ 95 Ivan Calderon	.05	.02	.01
□ 96 Keith Miller	.05	.02	.01
□ 97 Steve Buechele	.05	.02	.01
□ 98 Kent Hrbek	.10	.05	.01
□ 99 Dave Hollins	.05	.02	.01
□ 100 Mike Bordick	.05	.02	.01
□ 101 Randy Tomlin	.05	.02	.01
□ 102 Omar Vizquel	.15	.07	.02
□ 103 Lee Smith	.10	.05	.01
□ 104 Leo Gomez	.05	.02	.01
□ 105 Jose Rijo	.05	.02	.01
□ 106 Mark Whiten	.05	.02	.01
□ 107 Dave Justice	.15	.07	.02
□ 108 Eddie Taubensee	.05	.02	.01
□ 109 Lance Johnson	.10	.05	.01
□ 110 Felix Jose	.05	.02	.01
□ 111 Mike Harkey	.05	.02	.01
□ 112 Randy Milligan	.05	.02	.01
□ 113 Anthony Young	.05	.02	.01
□ 114 Rico Brogna	.10	.05	.01
□ 115 Bret Saberhagen	.10	.05	.01
□ 116 Sandy Alomar	.10	.05	.01
□ 117 Terry Mulholland	.05	.02	.01
□ 118 Darryl Hamilton	.05	.02	.01
□ 119 Todd Zeile	.05	.02	.01
□ 120 Bernie Williams	.15	.07	.02
□ 121 Zane Smith	.05	.02	.01
□ 122 Derek Bell	.15	.07	.02
□ 123 Deion Sanders	.15	.07	.02
□ 124 Luis Sojo	.05	.02	.01
□ 125 Joe Oliver	.05	.02	.01
□ 126 Craig Grebeck	.05	.02	.01
□ 127 Andujar Cedeno	.05	.02	.01
□ 128 Brian McRae	.10	.05	.01
□ 129 Jose Offerman	.05	.02	.01
□ 130 Pedro Munoz	.05	.02	.01
□ 131 Bud Black	.05	.02	.01
□ 132 Mo Vaughn	.50	.23	.06
□ 133 Bruce Hurst	.05	.02	.01
□ 134 Dave Henderson	.05	.02	.01
□ 135 Tom Pagnozzi	.05	.02	.01
□ 136 Erik Hanson	.05	.02	.01
□ 137 Orlando Merced	.10	.05	.01
□ 138 Dean Palmer	.10	.05	.01
□ 139 John Franco	.05	.02	.01
□ 140 Brady Anderson	.15	.07	.02
□ 141 Ricky Jordan	.05	.02	.01
□ 142 Jeff Blauser	.05	.02	.01
□ 143 Sammy Sosa	.15	.07	.02
□ 144 Bob Walk	.05	.02	.01
□ 145 Delino DeShields	.05	.02	.01
□ 146 Kevin Brown	.05	.02	.01
□ 147 Mark Lemke	.05	.02	.01
□ 148 Chuck Knoblauch	.15	.07	.02
□ 149 Chris Sabo	.05	.02	.01
□ 150 Bobby Witt	.05	.02	.01
□ 151 Luis Gonzalez	.05	.02	.01
□ 152 Ron Karkovice	.05	.02	.01
□ 153 Jeff Brantley	.05	.02	.01
□ 154 Kevin Appier	.10	.05	.01
□ 155 Darrin Jackson	.05	.02	.01
□ 156 Kelly Gruber	.05	.02	.01
□ 157 Royce Clayton	.10	.05	.01
□ 158 Chuck Finley	.05	.02	.01
□ 159 Jeff King	.10	.05	.01
□ 160 Greg Vaughn	.15	.07	.02
□ 161 Geronimo Pena	.05	.02	.01
□ 162 Steve Farr	.05	.02	.01
□ 163 Jose Oquendo	.05	.02	.01
□ 164 Mark Lewis	.05	.02	.01
□ 165 John Wetteland	.10	.05	.01
□ 166 Mike Henneman	.05	.02	.01
□ 167 Todd Hundley	.15	.07	.02
□ 168 Wes Chamberlain	.05	.02	.01
□ 169 Steve Avery	.10	.05	.01
□ 170 Mike Devereaux	.05	.02	.01
□ 171 Reggie Sanders	.15	.07	.02
□ 172 Jay Buhner	.15	.07	.02
□ 173 Eric Anthony	.05	.02	.01
□ 174 John Burkett	.05	.02	.01
□ 175 Tom Candiotti	.05	.02	.01
□ 176 Phil Plantier	.05	.02	.01
□ 177 Doug Henry	.05	.02	.01
□ 178 Scott Leius	.05	.02	.01
□ 179 Kirt Manwaring	.05	.02	.01
□ 180 Jeff Parrett	.05	.02	.01

□ 181	Don Slaught	.05	.02	.01
□ 182	Scott Radinsky	.05	.02	.01
□ 183	Luis Alicea	.05	.02	.01
□ 184	Tom Gordon	.05	.02	.01
□ 185	Rick Wilkins	.05	.02	.01
□ 186	Todd Stottlemyre	.10	.05	.01
□ 187	Moises Alou	.15	.07	.02
□ 188	Joe Grahe	.05	.02	.01
□ 189	Jeff Kent	.10	.05	.01
□ 190	Bill Wegman	.05	.02	.01
□ 191	Kim Batiste	.05	.02	.01
□ 192	Matt Nokes	.05	.02	.01
□ 193	Mark Wohlers	.10	.05	.01
□ 194	Paul Sorrento	.05	.02	.01
□ 195	Chris Hammond	.05	.02	.01
□ 196	Scott Livingstone	.05	.02	.01
□ 197	Doug Jones	.05	.02	.01
□ 198	Scott Cooper	.05	.02	.01
□ 199	Ramon Martinez	.10	.05	.01
□ 200	Dave Valle	.05	.02	.01
□ 201	Mariano Duncan	.05	.02	.01
□ 202	Ben McDonald	.05	.02	.01
□ 203	Darren Lewis	.05	.02	.01
□ 204	Kenny Rogers	.05	.02	.01
□ 205	Manuel Lee	.05	.02	.01
□ 206	Scott Erickson	.05	.02	.01
□ 207	Dan Gladden	.05	.02	.01
□ 208	Bob Welch	.05	.02	.01
□ 209	Greg Olson	.05	.02	.01
□ 210	Dan Pasqua	.05	.02	.01
□ 211	Tim Wallach	.05	.02	.01
□ 212	Jeff Montgomery	.10	.05	.01
□ 213	Derrick May	.05	.02	.01
□ 214	Ed Sprague	.10	.05	.01
□ 215	David Haas	.05	.02	.01
□ 216	Darrin Fletcher	.05	.02	.01
□ 217	Brian Jordan	.15	.07	.02
□ 218	Jaime Navarro	.05	.02	.01
□ 219	Randy Velarde	.05	.02	.01
□ 220	Ron Gant	.15	.07	.02
□ 221	Paul Quantrill	.05	.02	.01
□ 222	Damion Easley	.05	.02	.01
□ 223	Charlie Hough	.05	.02	.01
□ 224	Brad Brink	.05	.02	.01
□ 225	Barry Manuel	.05	.02	.01
□ 226	Kevin Koslofski	.05	.02	.01
□ 227	Ryan Thompson	.05	.02	.01
□ 228	Mike Munoz	.05	.02	.01
□ 229	Dan Wilson	.10	.05	.01
□ 230	Peter Hoy	.05	.02	.01
□ 231	Pedro Astacio	.05	.02	.01
□ 232	Matt Stairs	.05	.02	.01
□ 233	Jeff Reboulet	.05	.02	.01
□ 234	Manny Alexander	.05	.02	.01
□ 235	Willie Banks	.05	.02	.01
□ 236	John Jaha	.10	.05	.01
□ 237	Scooter Tucker	.05	.02	.01
□ 238	Russ Springer	.05	.02	.01
□ 239	Paul Miller	.05	.02	.01
□ 240	Dan Peltier	.05	.02	.01
□ 241	Ozzie Canseco	.05	.02	.01
□ 242	Ben Rivera	.05	.02	.01
□ 243	John Valentin	.15	.07	.02
□ 244	Henry Rodriguez	.15	.07	.02
□ 245	Derek Parks	.05	.02	.01
□ 246	Carlos Garcia	.05	.02	.01
□ 247	Tim Pugh	.05	.02	.01
□ 248	Melvin Nieves	.15	.07	.02
□ 249	Rich Amaral	.05	.02	.01
□ 250	Willie Greene	.10	.05	.01
□ 251	Tim Scott	.05	.02	.01
□ 252	Dave Silvestri	.05	.02	.01
□ 253	Rob Mallicoat	.05	.02	.01
□ 254	Donald Harris	.05	.02	.01
□ 255	Craig Colbert	.05	.02	.01
□ 256	Jose Guzman	.05	.02	.01
□ 257	Domingo Martinez	.05	.02	.01
□ 258	William Suero	.05	.02	.01
□ 259	Juan Guerrero	.05	.02	.01
□ 260	J.T. Snow	.15	.07	.02
□ 261	Tony Pena	.05	.02	.01
□ 262	Tim Fortugno	.05	.02	.01
□ 263	Tom Marsh	.05	.02	.01
□ 264	Kurt Knudsen	.05	.02	.01
□ 265	Tim Costo	.05	.02	.01
□ 266	Steve Shifflett	.05	.02	.01
□ 267	Billy Ashley	.05	.02	.01
□ 268	Jerry Nielsen	.05	.02	.01
□ 269	Pete Young	.05	.02	.01
□ 270	Johnny Guzman	.05	.02	.01
□ 271	Greg Colbrunn	.05	.02	.01
□ 272	Jeff Nelson	.05	.02	.01
□ 273	Kevin Young	.05	.02	.01
□ 274	Jeff Frye	.05	.02	.01
□ 275	J.T. Bruett	.05	.02	.01
□ 276	Todd Pratt	.05	.02	.01
□ 277	Mike Butcher	.05	.02	.01
□ 278	John Flaherty	.05	.02	.01
□ 279	John Patterson	.05	.02	.01
□ 280	Eric Hillman	.05	.02	.01
□ 281	Bien Figueroa	.05	.02	.01
□ 282	Shane Reynolds	.10	.05	.01
□ 283	Rich Rowland	.05	.02	.01
□ 284	Steve Foster	.05	.02	.01
□ 285	Dave Mlicki	.05	.02	.01
□ 286	Mike Piazza	2.00	.90	.25
□ 287	Mike Trombley	.05	.02	.01
□ 288	Jim Pena	.05	.02	.01
□ 289	Bob Ayrault	.05	.02	.01
□ 290	Henry Mercedes	.05	.02	.01
□ 291	Bob Wickman	.05	.02	.01
□ 292	Jacob Brumfield	.05	.02	.01
□ 293	David Hulse	.05	.02	.01
□ 294	Ryan Klesko	1.00	.45	.12
□ 295	Doug Linton	.05	.02	.01
□ 296	Steve Cooke	.05	.02	.01
□ 297	Eddie Zosky	.05	.02	.01
□ 298	Gerald Williams	.05	.02	.01
□ 299	Jonathan Hurst	.05	.02	.01
□ 300	Larry Carter	.05	.02	.01
□ 301	William Pennyfeather	.05	.02	.01
□ 302	Cesar Hernandez	.05	.02	.01
□ 303	Steve Hosey	.05	.02	.01
□ 304	Blas Minor	.05	.02	.01
□ 305	Jeff Grotewald	.05	.02	.01
□ 306	Bernardo Brito	.05	.02	.01
□ 307	Rafael Bournigal	.05	.02	.01
□ 308	Jeff Branson	.05	.02	.01
□ 309	Tom Quinlan	.05	.02	.01
□ 310	Pat Gomez	.05	.02	.01
□ 311	Sterling Hitchcock	.10	.05	.01
□ 312	Kent Bottenfield	.05	.02	.01
□ 313	Alan Trammell	.15	.07	.02
□ 314	Cris Colon	.05	.02	.01
□ 315	Paul Wagner	.05	.02	.01
□ 316	Matt Maysey	.05	.02	.01
□ 317	Mike Stanton	.05	.02	.01
□ 318	Rick Trlicek	.05	.02	.01
□ 319	Kevin Rogers	.05	.02	.01
□ 320	Mark Clark	.05	.02	.01
□ 321	Pedro Martinez	.15	.07	.02
□ 322	Al Martin	.10	.05	.01
□ 323	Mike Macfarlane	.05	.02	.01
□ 324	Rey Sanchez	.05	.02	.01
□ 325	Roger Pavlik	.10	.05	.01
□ 326	Troy Neel	.05	.02	.01
□ 327	Kerry Woodson	.05	.02	.01
□ 328	Wayne Kirby	.05	.02	.01
□ 329	Ken Ryan	.05	.02	.01
□ 330	Jesse Levis	.05	.02	.01
□ 331	James Austin	.05	.02	.01
□ 332	Dan Walters	.05	.02	.01
□ 333	Brian Williams	.05	.02	.01
□ 334	Wil Cordero	.10	.05	.01
□ 335	Bret Boone	.10	.05	.01
□ 336	Hipolito Pichardo	.05	.02	.01
□ 337	Pat Mahomes	.05	.02	.01
□ 338	Andy Stankiewicz	.05	.02	.01
□ 339	Jim Bullinger	.05	.02	.01
□ 340	Archi Cianfrocco	.05	.02	.01
□ 341	Ruben Amaro Jr.	.05	.02	.01
□ 342	Frank Seminara	.05	.02	.01
□ 343	Pat Hentgen	.15	.07	.02
□ 344	Dave Nilsson	.10	.05	.01
□ 345	Mike Perez	.05	.02	.01
□ 346	Tim Salmon	.50	.23	.06
□ 347	Tim Wakefield	.10	.05	.01
□ 348	Carlos Hernandez	.05	.02	.01
□ 349	Donovan Osborne	.05	.02	.01
□ 350	Denny Neagle	.10	.05	.01
□ 351	Sam Militello	.05	.02	.01
□ 352	Eric Fox	.05	.02	.01

□ 353	John Doherty	.05	.02	.01
□ 354	Chad Curtis	.10	.05	.01
□ 355	Jeff Tackett	.05	.02	.01
□ 356	Dave Fleming	.05	.02	.01
□ 357	Pat Listach	.05	.02	.01
□ 358	Kevin Wickander	.05	.02	.01
□ 359	John Vander Wal	.05	.02	.01
□ 360	Arthur Rhodes	.05	.02	.01
□ 361	Bob Scanlan	.05	.02	.01
□ 362	Bob Zupcic	.05	.02	.01
□ 363	Mel Rojas	.10	.05	.01
□ 364	Jim Thome	1.00	.45	.12
□ 365	Bill Pecota	.05	.02	.01
□ 366	Mark Carreon	.05	.02	.01
□ 367	Mitch Williams	.05	.02	.01
□ 368	Cal Eldred	.05	.02	.01
□ 369	Stan Belinda	.05	.02	.01
□ 370	Pat Kelly	.05	.02	.01
□ 371	Rheal Cormier	.05	.02	.01
□ 372	Juan Guzman	.10	.05	.01
□ 373	Damon Berryhill	.05	.02	.01
□ 374	Gary DiSarcina	.05	.02	.01
□ 375	Norm Charlton	.05	.02	.01
□ 376	Roberto Hernandez	.10	.05	.01
□ 377	Scott Kamieniecki	.05	.02	.01
□ 378	Rusty Meacham	.05	.02	.01
□ 379	Kurt Stillwell	.05	.02	.01
□ 380	Lloyd McClendon	.05	.02	.01
□ 381	Mark Leonard	.05	.02	.01
□ 382	Jerry Browne	.05	.02	.01
□ 383	Glenn Davis	.05	.02	.01
□ 384	Randy Johnson	.15	.07	.02
□ 385	Mike Greenwell	.05	.02	.01
□ 386	Scott Chiamparino	.05	.02	.01
□ 387	George Bell	.05	.02	.01
□ 388	Steve Olin	.05	.02	.01
□ 389	Chuck McElroy	.05	.02	.01
□ 390	Mark Gardner	.05	.02	.01
□ 391	Rod Beck	.10	.05	.01
□ 392	Dennis Rasmussen	.05	.02	.01
□ 393	Charlie Leibrandt	.05	.02	.01
□ 394	Julio Franco	.10	.05	.01
□ 395	Pete Harnisch	.05	.02	.01
□ 396	Sid Bream	.05	.02	.01
□ 397	Milt Thompson	.05	.02	.01
□ 398	Glenallen Hill	.05	.02	.01
□ 399	Chico Walker	.05	.02	.01
□ 400	Alex Cole	.05	.02	.01
□ 401	Trevor Wilson	.05	.02	.01
□ 402	Jeff Conine	.15	.07	.02
□ 403	Kyle Abbott	.05	.02	.01
□ 404	Tom Browning	.05	.02	.01
□ 405	Jerald Clark	.05	.02	.01
□ 406	Vince Horsman	.05	.02	.01
□ 407	Kevin Mitchell	.10	.05	.01
□ 408	Pete Smith	.05	.02	.01
□ 409	Jeff Innis	.05	.02	.01
□ 410	Mike Timlin	.05	.02	.01
□ 411	Charlie Hayes	.05	.02	.01
□ 412	Alex Fernandez	.15	.07	.02
□ 413	Jeff Russell	.05	.02	.01
□ 414	Jody Reed	.05	.02	.01
□ 415	Mickey Morandini	.05	.02	.01
□ 416	Darnell Coles	.05	.02	.01
□ 417	Xavier Hernandez	.05	.02	.01
□ 418	Steve Sax	.05	.02	.01
□ 419	Joe Girardi	.05	.02	.01
□ 420	Mike Fetters	.05	.02	.01
□ 421	Danny Jackson	.05	.02	.01
□ 422	Jim Gott	.05	.02	.01
□ 423	Tim Belcher	.05	.02	.01
□ 424	Jose Mesa	.10	.05	.01
□ 425	Junior Felix	.05	.02	.01
□ 426	Thomas Howard	.05	.02	.01
□ 427	Julio Valera	.05	.02	.01
□ 428	Dante Bichette	.15	.07	.02
□ 429	Mike Sharperson	.05	.02	.01
□ 430	Darryl Kile	.05	.02	.01
□ 431	Lonnie Smith	.05	.02	.01
□ 432	Monty Fariss	.05	.02	.01
□ 433	Reggie Jefferson	.10	.05	.01
□ 434	Bob McClure	.05	.02	.01
□ 435	Craig Lefferts	.05	.02	.01
□ 436	Duane Ward	.05	.02	.01
□ 437	Shawn Abner	.05	.02	.01
□ 438	Roberto Kelly	.05	.02	.01
□ 439	Paul O'Neill	.10	.05	.01
□ 440	Alan Mills	.05	.02	.01
□ 441	Roger Mason	.05	.02	.01
□ 442	Gary Pettis	.05	.02	.01
□ 443	Steve Lake	.05	.02	.01
□ 444	Gene Larkin	.05	.02	.01
□ 445	Larry Andersen	.05	.02	.01
□ 446	Doug Dascenzo	.05	.02	.01
□ 447	Daryl Boston	.05	.02	.01
□ 448	John Candelaria	.05	.02	.01
□ 449	Storm Davis	.05	.02	.01
□ 450	Tom Edens	.05	.02	.01
□ 451	Mike Maddux	.05	.02	.01
□ 452	Tim Naehring	.05	.02	.01
□ 453	John Orton	.05	.02	.01
□ 454	Joey Cora	.05	.02	.01
□ 455	Chuck Crim	.05	.02	.01
□ 456	Dan Plesac	.05	.02	.01
□ 457	Mike Bielecki	.05	.02	.01
□ 458	Terry Jorgensen	.05	.02	.01
□ 459	John Habyan	.05	.02	.01
□ 460	Pete O'Brien	.05	.02	.01
□ 461	Jeff Treadway	.05	.02	.01
□ 462	Frank Castillo	.05	.02	.01
□ 463	Jimmy Jones	.05	.02	.01
□ 464	Tommy Greene	.05	.02	.01
□ 465	Tracy Woodson	.05	.02	.01
□ 466	Rich Rodriguez	.05	.02	.01
□ 467	Joe Hesketh	.05	.02	.01
□ 468	Greg Myers	.05	.02	.01
□ 469	Kirk McCaskill	.05	.02	.01
□ 470	Ricky Bones	.05	.02	.01
□ 471	Lenny Webster	.05	.02	.01
□ 472	Francisco Cabrera	.05	.02	.01
□ 473	Turner Ward	.05	.02	.01
□ 474	Dwayne Henry	.05	.02	.01
□ 475	Al Osuna	.05	.02	.01
□ 476	Craig Wilson	.05	.02	.01
□ 477	Chris Nabholz	.05	.02	.01
□ 478	Rafael Belliard	.05	.02	.01
□ 479	Terry Leach	.05	.02	.01
□ 480	Tim Teufel	.05	.02	.01
□ 481	Dennis Eckersley AW	.05	.02	.01
□ 482	Barry Bonds AW	.15	.07	.02
□ 483	Dennis Eckersley AW	.05	.02	.01
□ 484	Greg Maddux AW	.60	.25	.07
□ 485	Pat Listach AW	.05	.02	.01
□ 486	Eric Karros AW	.10	.05	.01
□ 487	Jamie Arnold DP	.10	.05	.01
□ 488	B.J. Wallace DP	.05	.02	.01
□ 489	Derek Jeter DP	4.00	1.80	.50
□ 490	Jason Kendall DP	1.25	.55	.16
□ 491	Rick Helling DP	.10	.05	.01
□ 492	Derek Wallace DP	.05	.02	.01
□ 493	Sean Lowe DP	.10	.05	.01
□ 494	Shannon Stewart DP	.30	.14	.04
□ 495	Benji Grigsby DP	.05	.02	.01
□ 496	Todd Steverson DP	.10	.05	.01
□ 497	Dan Serafini DP	.30	.14	.04
□ 498	Michael Tucker DP	.15	.07	.02
□ 499	Chris Roberts DP	.10	.05	.01
□ 500	Pete Janicki DP	.05	.02	.01
□ 501	Jeff Schmidt DP	.05	.02	.01
□ 502	Edgar Martinez AS	.10	.05	.01
□ 503	Omar Vizquel AS	.10	.05	.01
□ 504	Ken Griffey Jr. AS	1.00	.45	.12
□ 505	Kirby Puckett AS	.15	.07	.02
□ 506	Joe Carter AS	.10	.05	.01
□ 507	Ivan Rodriguez AS	.15	.07	.02
□ 508	Jack Morris AS	.05	.02	.01
□ 509	Dennis Eckersley AS	.05	.02	.01
□ 510	Frank Thomas AS	1.00	.45	.12
□ 511	Roberto Alomar AS	.15	.07	.02
□ 512	Mickey Morandini AS	.05	.02	.01
□ 513	Dennis Eckersley HL	.05	.02	.01
□ 514	Jeff Reardon HL	.05	.02	.01
□ 515	Danny Tartabull HL	.05	.02	.01
□ 516	Bip Roberts HL	.05	.02	.01
□ 517	George Brett HL	.40	.18	.05
□ 518	Robin Yount HL	.10	.05	.01
□ 519	Kevin Gross HL	.05	.02	.01
□ 520	Ed Sprague WS	.10	.05	.01
□ 521	Dave Winfield WS	.15	.07	.02
□ 522	Ozzie Smith AS	.15	.07	.02
□ 523	Barry Bonds AS	.15	.07	.02
□ 524	Andy Van Slyke AS	.05	.02	.01

□ 525 Tony Gwynn AS	.40	.18	.05
□ 526 Darren Daulton AS	.05	.02	.01
□ 527 Greg Maddux AS	.60	.25	.07
□ 528 Fred McGriff AS	.15	.07	.02
□ 529 Lee Smith AS	.05	.02	.01
□ 530 Ryne Sandberg AS	.15	.07	.02
□ 531 Gary Sheffield AS	.15	.07	.02
□ 532 Ozzie Smith DT	.15	.07	.02
□ 533 Kirby Puckett DT	.15	.07	.02
□ 534 Gary Sheffield DT	.15	.07	.02
□ 535 Andy Van Slyke DT	.05	.02	.01
□ 536 Ken Griffey Jr. DT	1.00	.45	.12
□ 537 Ivan Rodriguez DT	.15	.07	.02
□ 538 Charles Nagy DT	.05	.02	.01
□ 539 Tom Glavine DT	.10	.05	.01
□ 540 Dennis Eckersley DT	.05	.02	.01
□ 541 Frank Thomas DT	1.00	.45	.12
□ 542 Roberto Alomar DT	.15	.07	.02
□ 543 Sean Berry	.05	.02	.01
□ 544 Mike Schooler	.05	.02	.01
□ 545 Chuck Carr	.05	.02	.01
□ 546 Lenny Harris	.05	.02	.01
□ 547 Gary Scott	.05	.02	.01
□ 548 Derek Lilliquist	.05	.02	.01
□ 549 Brian Hunter	.05	.02	.01
□ 550 Kirby Puckett MOY	.15	.07	.02
□ 551 Jim Eisenreich	.10	.05	.01
□ 552 Andre Dawson	.15	.07	.02
□ 553 David Nied	.05	.02	.01
□ 554 Spike Owen	.05	.02	.01
□ 555 Greg Gagne	.05	.02	.01
□ 556 Sid Fernandez	.05	.02	.01
□ 557 Mark McGwire	.60	.25	.07
□ 558 Bryan Harvey	.05	.02	.01
□ 559 Harold Reynolds	.05	.02	.01
□ 560 Barry Bonds	.50	.23	.06
□ 561 Eric Wedge	.05	.02	.01
□ 562 Ozzie Smith	.40	.18	.05
□ 563 Rick Sutcliffe	.05	.02	.01
□ 564 Jeff Reardon	.10	.05	.01
□ 565 Alex Arias	.05	.02	.01
□ 566 Greg Swindell	.05	.02	.01
□ 567 Brook Jacoby	.05	.02	.01
□ 568 Pete Incaviglia	.05	.02	.01
□ 569 Butch Henry	.05	.02	.01
□ 570 Eric Davis	.10	.05	.01
□ 571 Kevin Seitzer	.05	.02	.01
□ 572 Tony Fernandez	.05	.02	.01
□ 573 Steve Reed	.05	.02	.01
□ 574 Cory Snyder	.05	.02	.01
□ 575 Joe Carter	.15	.07	.02
□ 576 Greg Maddux	1.25	.55	.16
□ 577 Bert Blyleven UER (Should say 3701 career strikeouts)	.10	.05	.01
□ 578 Kevin Bass	.05	.02	.01
□ 579 Carlton Fisk	.15	.07	.02
□ 580 Doug Drabek	.05	.02	.01
□ 581 Mark Gubicza	.05	.02	.01
□ 582 Bobby Thigpen	.05	.02	.01
□ 583 Chili Davis	.10	.05	.01
□ 584 Scott Bankhead	.05	.02	.01
□ 585 Harold Baines	.10	.05	.01
□ 586 Eric Young	.15	.07	.02
□ 587 Lance Parrish	.05	.02	.01
□ 588 Juan Bell	.05	.02	.01
□ 589 Bob Ojeda	.05	.02	.01
□ 590 Joe Orsulak	.05	.02	.01
□ 591 Benito Santiago	.05	.02	.01
□ 592 Wade Boggs	.15	.07	.02
□ 593 Robby Thompson	.05	.02	.01
□ 594 Eric Plunk	.05	.02	.01
□ 595 Hensley Meulens	.05	.02	.01
□ 596 Lou Whitaker	.15	.07	.02
□ 597 Dale Murphy	.15	.07	.02
□ 598 Paul Molitor	.40	.18	.05
□ 599 Greg W. Harris	.05	.02	.01
□ 600 Darren Holmes	.05	.02	.01
□ 601 Dave Martinez	.05	.02	.01
□ 602 Tom Henke	.05	.02	.01
□ 603 Mike Benjamin	.05	.02	.01
□ 604 Rene Gonzales	.05	.02	.01
□ 605 Roger McDowell	.05	.02	.01
□ 606 Kirby Puckett	.60	.25	.07
□ 607 Randy Myers	.10	.05	.01
□ 608 Ruben Sierra	.10	.05	.01
□ 609 Wilson Alvarez	.10	.05	.01
□ 610 David Segui	.05	.02	.01
□ 611 Juan Samuel	.05	.02	.01
□ 612 Tom Brunansky	.05	.02	.01
□ 613 Willie Randolph	.10	.05	.01
□ 614 Tony Phillips	.10	.05	.01
□ 615 Candy Maldonado	.05	.02	.01
□ 616 Chris Bosio	.05	.02	.01
□ 617 Bret Barberie	.05	.02	.01
□ 618 Scott Sanderson	.05	.02	.01
□ 619 Ron Darling	.05	.02	.01
□ 620 Dave Winfield	.15	.07	.02
□ 621 Mike Felder	.05	.02	.01
□ 622 Greg Hibbard	.05	.02	.01
□ 623 Mike Scioscia	.05	.02	.01
□ 624 John Smiley	.05	.02	.01
□ 625 Alejandro Pena	.05	.02	.01
□ 626 Terry Steinbach	.10	.05	.01
□ 627 Freddie Benavides	.05	.02	.01
□ 628 Kevin Reimer	.05	.02	.01
□ 629 Braulio Castillo	.05	.02	.01
□ 630 Dave Stieb	.05	.02	.01
□ 631 Dave Magadan	.05	.02	.01
□ 632 Scott Fletcher	.05	.02	.01
□ 633 Cris Carpenter	.05	.02	.01
□ 634 Kevin Maas	.05	.02	.01
□ 635 Todd Worrell	.05	.02	.01
□ 636 Rob Deer	.05	.02	.01
□ 637 Dwight Smith	.05	.02	.01
□ 638 Chito Martinez	.05	.02	.01
□ 639 Jimmy Key	.10	.05	.01
□ 640 Greg A. Harris	.05	.02	.01
□ 641 Mike Moore	.05	.02	.01
□ 642 Pat Borders	.05	.02	.01
□ 643 Bill Gullickson	.05	.02	.01
□ 644 Gary Gaetti	.10	.05	.01
□ 645 David Howard	.05	.02	.01
□ 646 Jim Abbott	.05	.02	.01
□ 647 Willie Wilson	.05	.02	.01
□ 648 David Wells	.05	.02	.01
□ 649 Andres Galarraga	.15	.07	.02
□ 650 Vince Coleman	.05	.02	.01
□ 651 Rob Dibble	.05	.02	.01
□ 652 Frank Tanana	.05	.02	.01
□ 653 Steve Decker	.05	.02	.01
□ 654 David Cone	.15	.07	.02
□ 655 Jack Armstrong	.05	.02	.01
□ 656 Dave Stewart	.10	.05	.01
□ 657 Billy Hatcher	.05	.02	.01
□ 658 Tim Raines	.15	.07	.02
□ 659 Walt Weiss	.05	.02	.01
□ 660 Jose Lind	.05	.02	.01

1993 Score Boys of Summer

Randomly inserted exclusively into one in every four 1993 Score 35-card super packs, cards from this standard-size set feature 30 rookies expected to be the best in their class. The fronts are borderless with a color action player photo superimposed over an illustration of the sun. The player's name appears in cursive lettering within a greenish stripe across the bottom. An early Mike Piazza card highlights this set.

	MINT	NRMT	EXC
COMPLETE SET (30)	60.00	27.00	7.50
COMMON CARD (1-30)	1.00	.45	.12

SEMISTARS	2.00	.90	.25
RANDOM INSERTS IN JUMBO PACKS			

□ 1 Billy Ashley	1.00	.45	.12
□ 2 Tim Salmon	10.00	4.50	1.25
□ 3 Pedro Martinez	3.00	1.35	.35
□ 4 Luis Mercedes	1.00	.45	.12
□ 5 Mike Piazza	30.00	13.50	3.70
□ 6 Troy Neel	1.00	.45	.12
□ 7 Melvin Nieves	2.00	.90	.25
□ 8 Ryan Klesko	15.00	6.75	1.85
□ 9 Ryan Thompson	1.00	.45	.12
□ 10 Kevin Young	1.00	.45	.12
□ 11 Gerald Williams	1.00	.45	.12
□ 12 Willie Greene	2.00	.90	.25
□ 13 John Patterson	1.00	.45	.12
□ 14 Carlos Garcia	2.00	.90	.25
□ 15 Ed Zosky	1.00	.45	.12
□ 16 Sean Berry	1.00	.45	.12
□ 17 Rico Brogna	2.00	.90	.25
□ 18 Larry Carter	1.00	.45	.12
□ 19 Bobby Ayala	1.00	.45	.12
□ 20 Alan Embree	1.00	.45	.12
□ 21 Donald Harris	1.00	.45	.12
□ 22 Sterling Hitchcock	1.00	.45	.12
□ 23 David Nied	1.00	.45	.12
□ 24 Henry Mercedes	1.00	.45	.12
□ 25 Ozzie Canseco	1.00	.45	.12
□ 26 David Hulse	1.00	.45	.12
□ 27 Al Martin	2.00	.90	.25
□ 28 Dan Wilson	2.00	.90	.25
□ 29 Paul Miller	1.00	.45	.12
□ 30 Rich Rowland	1.00	.45	.12

1993 Score Franchise

This 28-card set honors the top player on each of the 28 teams. These cards were randomly inserted into one in every 24 16-card packs. The full-bleed, color action photos on the fronts have the background darkened so that the player stands out. His name appears in white lettering within a team color-coded bar near the bottom, which conjoins with the set logo in the lower left.

	MINT	NRMT	EXC
COMPLETE SET (28)	125.00	55.00	15.50
COMMON CARD (1-28)	1.50	.70	.19
SEMISTARS	4.00	1.80	.50
RANDOM INSERTS IN FOIL PACKS			

□ 1 Cal Ripken	25.00	11.00	3.10
□ 2 Roger Clemens	4.00	1.80	.50
□ 3 Mark Langston	1.50	.70	.19
□ 4 Frank Thomas	30.00	13.50	3.70
□ 5 Carlos Baerga	4.00	1.80	.50
□ 6 Cecil Fielder	4.00	1.80	.50
□ 7 Gregg Jefferies	4.00	1.80	.50
□ 8 Robin Yount	4.00	1.80	.50
□ 9 Kirby Puckett	10.00	4.50	1.25
□ 10 Don Mattingly	15.00	6.75	1.85
□ 11 Dennis Eckersley	4.00	1.80	.50
□ 12 Ken Griffey Jr.	30.00	13.50	3.70
□ 13 Juan Gonzalez	15.00	6.75	1.85
□ 14 Roberto Alomar	8.00	3.60	1.00
□ 15 Terry Pendleton	1.50	.70	.19
□ 16 Ryne Sandberg	8.00	3.60	1.00
□ 17 Barry Larkin	5.00	2.20	.60
□ 18 Jeff Bagwell	12.00	5.50	1.50
□ 19 Brett Butler	1.50	.70	.19
□ 20 Larry Walker	4.00	1.80	.50
□ 21 Bobby Bonilla	4.00	1.80	.50
□ 22 Darren Daulton	1.50	.70	.19
□ 23 Andy Van Slyke	1.50	.70	.19
□ 24 Ray Lankford	1.50	.70	.19
□ 25 Gary Sheffield	5.00	2.20	.60
□ 26 Will Clark	4.00	1.80	.50
□ 27 Bryan Harvey	1.50	.70	.19
□ 28 David Nied	4.00	1.80	.50

1993 Score Gold Dream Team

Cards from this 12-card standard-size set feature Score's selection of the best players in baseball at each position. The cards were available only through a mail-in offer. Each card front features sepia tone photos of the players out of uniform, with the exception of Griffey's card (of whom is pictured in his Mariners togs). The photo edges are rounded with an airbrush effect. The words "Dream Team" are printed in gold lettering at the top. The player's name is printed in sepia tones on the bottom edge.

	MINT	NRMT	EXC
COMPLETE SET (12)	6.00	2.70	.75
COMMON CARD (1-11)	.25	.11	.03
SEMISTARS	.40	.18	.05
HEADER CARD (NNO)	.50	.23	.06
SETS DISTRIBUTED VIA MAIL-IN OFFER			

□ 1 Ozzie Smith	.40	.18	.05
□ 2 Kirby Puckett	.60	.25	.07
□ 3 Gary Sheffield	.40	.18	.05
□ 4 Andy Van Slyke	.25	.11	.03
□ 5 Ken Griffey Jr.	2.00	.90	.25
□ 6 Ivan Rodriguez	.40	.18	.05
□ 7 Charles Nagy	.25	.11	.03
□ 8 Tom Glavine	.40	.18	.05
□ 9 Dennis Eckersley	.40	.18	.05
□ 10 Frank Thomas	2.00	.90	.25
□ 11 Roberto Alomar	.50	.23	.06
□ NNO Header Card	.50	.23	.06

1994 Score

The 1994 Score set of 660 standard-size cards was issued in two series of 330. The navy blue bordered fronts feature color action photos with

the player's name and team name appearing on two team color-coded stripes across the bottom. The horizontal back features a narrow-cropped color player close-up shot on the left side. On a team color-coded stripe at the top are the player's name and position, and below are the team logo, biography, player profile, and career statistics. Among the subsets are American League stadiums (317-330) and National League stadiums (647-660). Rookie Cards include Brian Anderson, Matt Drews, Brooks Kieschnick, Derrek Lee, Trot Nixon and Kirk Presley.

	MINT	NRMT	EXC
COMPLETE SET (660)	30.00	13.50	3.70
COMPLETE SERIES 1 (330)	15.00	6.75	1.85
COMPLETE SERIES 2 (330)	15.00	6.75	1.85
COMMON CARD (1-660)	.05	.02	.01
SEMISTARS	.15	.07	.02
STARS	.30	.14	.04
COMP.G.RUSH SET (660)	160.00	70.00	20.00
COMP.G.RUSH SER.1 (330)	80.00	36.00	10.00
COMP.G.RUSH SER.2 (330)	80.00	36.00	10.00
COMMON GOLD RUSH (1-660)	.25	.11	.03
GOLD RUSH SEMISTARS	.50	.23	.06
*GOLD RUSH STARS: 2.5X to 5X BASIC CARDS			
*GOLD RUSH YOUNG STARS 2X TO 4X BASIC CARDS			
ONE GOLD RUSH PER PACK			

□ 1 Barry Bonds	.50	.23	.06
□ 2 John Olerud	.05	.02	.01
□ 3 Ken Griffey Jr.	2.00	.90	.25
□ 4 Jeff Bagwell	.75	.35	.09
□ 5 John Burkett	.05	.02	.01
□ 6 Jack McDowell	.10	.05	.01
□ 7 Albert Belle	1.00	.45	.12
□ 8 Andres Galarraga	.15	.07	.02
□ 9 Mike Mussina	.40	.18	.05
□ 10 Will Clark	.15	.07	.02
□ 11 Travis Fryman	.15	.07	.02
□ 12 Tony Gwynn	.75	.35	.09
□ 13 Robin Yount	.15	.07	.02
□ 14 Dave Magadan	.05	.02	.01
□ 15 Paul O'Neill	.10	.05	.01
□ 16 Ray Lankford	.15	.07	.02
□ 17 Damion Easley	.05	.02	.01
□ 18 Andy Van Slyke	.10	.05	.01
□ 19 Brian McRae	.10	.05	.01
□ 20 Ryne Sandberg	.50	.23	.06
□ 21 Kirby Puckett	.60	.25	.07
□ 22 Dwight Gooden	.10	.05	.01
□ 23 Don Mattingly	1.00	.45	.12
□ 24 Kevin Mitchell	.10	.05	.01
□ 25 Roger Clemens	.15	.07	.02
□ 26 Eric Karros	.10	.05	.01
□ 27 Juan Gonzalez	1.00	.45	.12
□ 28 John Kruk	.10	.05	.01
□ 29 Gregg Jefferies	.15	.07	.02
□ 30 Tom Glavine	.15	.07	.02
□ 31 Ivan Rodriguez	.40	.18	.05
□ 32 Jay Bell	.10	.05	.01
□ 33 Randy Johnson	.15	.07	.02
□ 34 Darren Daulton	.10	.05	.01
□ 35 Rickey Henderson	.15	.07	.02
□ 36 Eddie Murray	.50	.23	.06
□ 37 Brian Harper	.05	.02	.01
□ 38 Delino DeShields	.05	.02	.01
□ 39 Jose Lind	.05	.02	.01
□ 40 Benito Santiago	.05	.02	.01
□ 41 Frank Thomas	2.00	.90	.25
□ 42 Mark Grace	.15	.07	.02
□ 43 Roberto Alomar	.50	.23	.06
□ 44 Andy Benes	.10	.05	.01
□ 45 Luis Polonia	.05	.02	.01
□ 46 Brett Butler	.10	.05	.01
□ 47 Terry Steinbach	.10	.05	.01
□ 48 Craig Biggio	.15	.07	.02
□ 49 Greg Vaughn	.15	.07	.02
□ 50 Charlie Hayes	.05	.02	.01
□ 51 Mickey Tettleton	.05	.02	.01
□ 52 Jose Rijo	.05	.02	.01
□ 53 Carlos Baerga	.15	.07	.02
□ 54 Jeff Blauser	.05	.02	.01
□ 55 Leo Gomez	.05	.02	.01
□ 56 Bob Tewksbury	.05	.02	.01
□ 57 Mo Vaughn	.50	.23	.06
□ 58 Orlando Merced	.10	.05	.01
□ 59 Tino Martinez	.10	.05	.01
□ 60 Lenny Dykstra	.10	.05	.01
□ 61 Jose Canseco	.15	.07	.02
□ 62 Tony Fernandez	.05	.02	.01
□ 63 Donovan Osborne	.05	.02	.01
□ 64 Ken Hill	.05	.02	.01
□ 65 Kent Hrbek	.10	.05	.01
□ 66 Bryan Harvey	.05	.02	.01
□ 67 Wally Joyner	.10	.05	.01
□ 68 Derrick May	.05	.02	.01
□ 69 Lance Johnson	.10	.05	.01
□ 70 Willie McGee	.05	.02	.01
□ 71 Mark Langston	.10	.05	.01
□ 72 Terry Pendleton	.10	.05	.01
□ 73 Joe Carter	.15	.07	.02
□ 74 Barry Larkin	.15	.07	.02
□ 75 Jimmy Key	.10	.05	.01
□ 76 Joe Girardi	.05	.02	.01
□ 77 B.J. Surhoff	.05	.02	.01
□ 78 Pete Harnisch	.05	.02	.01
□ 79 Lou Whitaker UER (Milt Cuyler pictured on front)	.15	.07	.02
□ 80 Cory Snyder	.05	.02	.01
□ 81 Kenny Lofton	.60	.25	.07
□ 82 Fred McGriff	.15	.07	.02
□ 83 Mike Greenwell	.05	.02	.01
□ 84 Mike Perez	.05	.02	.01
□ 85 Cal Ripken	1.50	.70	.19
□ 86 Don Slaught	.05	.02	.01
□ 87 Omar Vizquel	.15	.07	.02
□ 88 Curt Schilling	.05	.02	.01
□ 89 Chuck Knoblauch	.15	.07	.02
□ 90 Moises Alou	.10	.05	.01
□ 91 Greg Gagne	.05	.02	.01
□ 92 Bret Saberhagen	.10	.05	.01
□ 93 Ozzie Guillen	.05	.02	.01
□ 94 Matt Williams	.15	.07	.02
□ 95 Chad Curtis	.05	.02	.01
□ 96 Mike Harkey	.05	.02	.01
□ 97 Devon White	.05	.02	.01
□ 98 Walt Weiss	.05	.02	.01
□ 99 Kevin Brown	.05	.02	.01
□ 100 Gary Sheffield	.15	.07	.02
□ 101 Wade Boggs	.15	.07	.02
□ 102 Orel Hershiser	.10	.05	.01
□ 103 Tony Phillips	.10	.05	.01
□ 104 Andujar Cedeno	.05	.02	.01
□ 105 Bill Spiers	.05	.02	.01
□ 106 Otis Nixon	.05	.02	.01
□ 107 Felix Fermin	.05	.02	.01
□ 108 Bip Roberts	.05	.02	.01
□ 109 Dennis Eckersley	.10	.05	.01
□ 110 Dante Bichette	.15	.07	.02
□ 111 Ben McDonald	.05	.02	.01
□ 112 Jim Poole	.05	.02	.01
□ 113 John Dopson	.05	.02	.01
□ 114 Rob Dibble	.05	.02	.01
□ 115 Jeff Treadway	.05	.02	.01
□ 116 Ricky Jordan	.05	.02	.01
□ 117 Mike Henneman	.05	.02	.01
□ 118 Willie Blair	.05	.02	.01
□ 119 Doug Henry	.05	.02	.01
□ 120 Gerald Perry	.05	.02	.01
□ 121 Greg Myers	.05	.02	.01
□ 122 John Franco	.05	.02	.01
□ 123 Roger Mason	.05	.02	.01
□ 124 Chris Hammond	.05	.02	.01
□ 125 Hubie Brooks	.05	.02	.01
□ 126 Kent Mercker	.05	.02	.01
□ 127 Jim Abbott	.05	.02	.01
□ 128 Kevin Bass	.05	.02	.01
□ 129 Rick Aguilera	.05	.02	.01
□ 130 Mitch Webster	.05	.02	.01
□ 131 Eric Plunk	.05	.02	.01
□ 132 Mark Carreon	.05	.02	.01
□ 133 Dave Stewart	.10	.05	.01
□ 134 Willie Wilson	.05	.02	.01
□ 135 Dave Fleming	.05	.02	.01
□ 136 Jeff Tackett	.05	.02	.01
□ 137 Geno Petralli	.05	.02	.01
□ 138 Gene Harris	.05	.02	.01
□ 139 Scott Bankhead	.05	.02	.01
□ 140 Trevor Wilson	.05	.02	.01

□	141	Alvaro Espinoza	.05	.02	.01
□	142	Ryan Bowen	.05	.02	.01
□	143	Mike Moore	.05	.02	.01
□	144	Bill Pecota	.05	.02	.01
□	145	Jaime Navarro	.05	.02	.01
□	146	Jack Daugherty	.05	.02	.01
□	147	Bob Wickman	.05	.02	.01
□	148	Chris Jones	.05	.02	.01
□	149	Todd Stottlemyre	.05	.02	.01
□	150	Brian Williams	.05	.02	.01
□	151	Chuck Finley	.05	.02	.01
□	152	Lenny Harris	.05	.02	.01
□	153	Alex Fernandez	.15	.07	.02
□	154	Candy Maldonado	.05	.02	.01
□	155	Jeff Montgomery	.10	.05	.01
□	156	David West	.05	.02	.01
□	157	Mark Williamson	.05	.02	.01
□	158	Milt Thompson	.05	.02	.01
□	159	Ron Darling	.05	.02	.01
□	160	Stan Belinda	.05	.02	.01
□	161	Henry Cotto	.05	.02	.01
□	162	Mel Rojas	.05	.02	.01
□	163	Doug Strange	.05	.02	.01
□	164	Rene Arocha	.05	.02	.01
□	165	Tim Hulett	.05	.02	.01
□	166	Steve Avery	.10	.05	.01
□	167	Jim Thome	.50	.23	.06
□	168	Tom Browning	.05	.02	.01
□	169	Mario Diaz	.05	.02	.01
□	170	Steve Reed	.05	.02	.01
□	171	Scott Livingstone	.05	.02	.01
□	172	Chris Donnels	.05	.02	.01
□	173	John Jaha	.10	.05	.01
□	174	Carlos Hernandez	.05	.02	.01
□	175	Dion James	.05	.02	.01
□	176	Bud Black	.05	.02	.01
□	177	Tony Castillo	.05	.02	.01
□	178	Jose Guzman	.05	.02	.01
□	179	Torey Lovullo	.05	.02	.01
□	180	John Vander Wal	.05	.02	.01
□	181	Mike LaValliere	.05	.02	.01
□	182	Sid Fernandez	.05	.02	.01
□	183	Brent Mayne	.05	.02	.01
□	184	Terry Mulholland	.05	.02	.01
□	185	Willie Banks	.05	.02	.01
□	186	Steve Cooke	.05	.02	.01
□	187	Brent Gates	.05	.02	.01
□	188	Erik Pappas	.05	.02	.01
□	189	Bill Haselman	.05	.02	.01
□	190	Fernando Valenzuela	.10	.05	.01
□	191	Gary Redus	.05	.02	.01
□	192	Danny Darwin	.05	.02	.01
□	193	Mark Portugal	.05	.02	.01
□	194	Derek Lilliquist	.05	.02	.01
□	195	Charlie O'Brien	.05	.02	.01
□	196	Matt Nokes	.05	.02	.01
□	197	Danny Sheaffer	.05	.02	.01
□	198	Bill Gullickson	.05	.02	.01
□	199	Alex Arias	.05	.02	.01
□	200	Mike Fetters	.05	.02	.01
□	201	Brian Jordan	.15	.07	.02
□	202	Joe Grahe	.05	.02	.01
□	203	Tom Candiotti	.05	.02	.01
□	204	Jeremy Hernandez	.05	.02	.01
□	205	Mike Stanton	.05	.02	.01
□	206	David Howard	.05	.02	.01
□	207	Darren Holmes	.05	.02	.01
□	208	Rick Honeycutt	.05	.02	.01
□	209	Danny Jackson	.05	.02	.01
□	210	Rich Amaral	.05	.02	.01
□	211	Blas Minor	.05	.02	.01
□	212	Kenny Rogers	.05	.02	.01
□	213	Jim Leyritz	.05	.02	.01
□	214	Mike Morgan	.05	.02	.01
□	215	Dan Gladden	.05	.02	.01
□	216	Randy Velarde	.05	.02	.01
□	217	Mitch Williams	.05	.02	.01
□	218	Hipolito Pichardo	.05	.02	.01
□	219	Dave Burba	.05	.02	.01
□	220	Wilson Alvarez	.10	.05	.01
□	221	Bob Zupcic	.05	.02	.01
□	222	Francisco Cabrera	.05	.02	.01
□	223	Julio Valera	.05	.02	.01
□	224	Paul Assenmacher	.05	.02	.01
□	225	Jeff Branson	.05	.02	.01
□	226	Todd Frohwirth	.05	.02	.01
□	227	Armando Reynoso	.05	.02	.01
□	228	Rich Rowland	.05	.02	.01
□	229	Freddie Benavides	.05	.02	.01
□	230	Wayne Kirby	.05	.02	.01
□	231	Darryl Kile	.05	.02	.01
□	232	Skeeter Barnes	.05	.02	.01
□	233	Ramon Martinez	.10	.05	.01
□	234	Tom Gordon	.05	.02	.01
□	235	Dave Gallagher	.05	.02	.01
□	236	Ricky Bones	.05	.02	.01
□	237	Larry Andersen	.05	.02	.01
□	238	Pat Meares	.05	.02	.01
□	239	Zane Smith	.05	.02	.01
□	240	Tim Leary	.05	.02	.01
□	241	Phil Clark	.05	.02	.01
□	242	Danny Cox	.05	.02	.01
□	243	Mike Jackson	.05	.02	.01
□	244	Mike Gallego	.05	.02	.01
□	245	Lee Smith	.10	.05	.01
□	246	Todd Jones	.05	.02	.01
□	247	Steve Bedrosian	.05	.02	.01
□	248	Troy Neel	.05	.02	.01
□	249	Jose Bautista	.05	.02	.01
□	250	Steve Frey	.05	.02	.01
□	251	Jeff Reardon	.10	.05	.01
□	252	Stan Javier	.05	.02	.01
□	253	Mo Sanford	.05	.02	.01
□	254	Steve Sax	.05	.02	.01
□	255	Luis Aquino	.05	.02	.01
□	256	Domingo Jean	.05	.02	.01
□	257	Scott Servais	.05	.02	.01
□	258	Brad Pennington	.05	.02	.01
□	259	Dave Hansen	.05	.02	.01
□	260	Goose Gossage	.10	.05	.01
□	261	Jeff Fassero	.05	.02	.01
□	262	Junior Ortiz	.05	.02	.01
□	263	Anthony Young	.05	.02	.01
□	264	Chris Bosio	.05	.02	.01
□	265	Ruben Amaro Jr.	.05	.02	.01
□	266	Mark Eichhorn	.05	.02	.01
□	267	Dave Clark	.05	.02	.01
□	268	Gary Thurman	.05	.02	.01
□	269	Les Lancaster	.05	.02	.01
□	270	Jamie Moyer	.05	.02	.01
□	271	Ricky Gutierrez	.05	.02	.01
□	272	Greg A.Harris	.05	.02	.01
□	273	Mike Benjamin	.05	.02	.01
□	274	Gene Nelson	.05	.02	.01
□	275	Damon Berryhill	.05	.02	.01
□	276	Scott Radinsky	.05	.02	.01
□	277	Mike Aldrete	.05	.02	.01
□	278	Jerry DiPoto	.05	.02	.01
□	279	Chris Haney	.05	.02	.01
□	280	Richie Lewis	.05	.02	.01
□	281	Jarvis Brown	.05	.02	.01
□	282	Juan Bell	.05	.02	.01
□	283	Joe Klink	.05	.02	.01
□	284	Graeme Lloyd	.05	.02	.01
□	285	Casey Candaele	.05	.02	.01
□	286	Bob MacDonald	.05	.02	.01
□	287	Mike Sharperson	.05	.02	.01
□	288	Gene Larkin	.05	.02	.01
□	289	Brian Barnes	.05	.02	.01
□	290	David McCarty	.05	.02	.01
□	291	Jeff Innis	.05	.02	.01
□	292	Bob Patterson	.05	.02	.01
□	293	Ben Rivera	.05	.02	.01
□	294	John Habyan	.05	.02	.01
□	295	Rich Rodriguez	.05	.02	.01
□	296	Edwin Nunez	.05	.02	.01
□	297	Rod Brewer	.05	.02	.01
□	298	Mike Timlin	.05	.02	.01
□	299	Jesse Orosco	.05	.02	.01
□	300	Gary Gaetti	.10	.05	.01
□	301	Todd Benzinger	.05	.02	.01
□	302	Jeff Nelson	.05	.02	.01
□	303	Rafael Belliard	.05	.02	.01
□	304	Matt Whiteside	.05	.02	.01
□	305	Vinny Castilla	.15	.07	.02
□	306	Matt Turner	.05	.02	.01
□	307	Eduardo Perez	.05	.02	.01
□	308	Joel Johnston	.05	.02	.01
□	309	Chris Gomez	.05	.02	.01
□	310	Pat Rapp	.05	.02	.01
□	311	Jim Tatum	.05	.02	.01
□	312	Kirk Rueter	.05	.02	.01

□ 313 John Flaherty	.05	.02	.01
□ 314 Tom Kramer	.05	.02	.01
□ 315 Mark Whiten	.05	.02	.01
□ 316 Chris Bosio	.05	.02	.01
□ 317 Baltimore Orioles CL	.05	.02	.01
□ 318 Boston Red Sox CL UER (Viola listed as 316; should be 331)	.05	.02	.01
□ 319 California Angels CL	.05	.02	.01
□ 320 Chicago White Sox CL	.05	.02	.01
□ 321 Cleveland Indians CL	.05	.02	.01
□ 322 Detroit Tigers CL	.05	.02	.01
□ 323 Kansas City Royals CL	.05	.02	.01
□ 324 Milwaukee Brewers CL	.05	.02	.01
□ 325 Minnesota Twins CL	.05	.02	.01
□ 326 New York Yankees CL	.05	.02	.01
□ 327 Oakland Athletics CL	.05	.02	.01
□ 328 Seattle Mariners CL	.05	.02	.01
□ 329 Texas Rangers CL	.05	.02	.01
□ 330 Toronto Blue Jays CL	.05	.02	.01
□ 331 Frank Viola	.05	.02	.01
□ 332 Ron Gant	.10	.05	.01
□ 333 Charles Nagy	.10	.05	.01
□ 334 Roberto Kelly	.05	.02	.01
□ 335 Brady Anderson	.15	.07	.02
□ 336 Alex Cole	.05	.02	.01
□ 337 Alan Trammell	.15	.07	.02
□ 338 Derek Bell	.10	.05	.01
□ 339 Bernie Williams	.15	.07	.02
□ 340 Jose Offerman	.05	.02	.01
□ 341 Bill Wegman	.05	.02	.01
□ 342 Ken Caminiti	.15	.07	.02
□ 343 Pat Borders	.05	.02	.01
□ 344 Kirt Manwaring	.05	.02	.01
□ 345 Chili Davis	.10	.05	.01
□ 346 Steve Buechele	.05	.02	.01
□ 347 Robin Ventura	.10	.05	.01
□ 348 Teddy Higuera	.05	.02	.01
□ 349 Jerry Browne	.05	.02	.01
□ 350 Scott Kamieniecki	.05	.02	.01
□ 351 Kevin Tapani	.05	.02	.01
□ 352 Marquis Grissom	.15	.07	.02
□ 353 Jay Buhner	.15	.07	.02
□ 354 Dave Hollins	.05	.02	.01
□ 355 Dan Wilson	.10	.05	.01
□ 356 Bob Walk	.05	.02	.01
□ 357 Chris Hoiles	.05	.02	.01
□ 358 Todd Zeile	.05	.02	.01
□ 359 Kevin Appier	.10	.05	.01
□ 360 Chris Sabo	.05	.02	.01
□ 361 David Segui	.05	.02	.01
□ 362 Jerald Clark	.05	.02	.01
□ 363 Tony Pena	.05	.02	.01
□ 364 Steve Finley	.15	.07	.02
□ 365 Roger Pavlik	.05	.02	.01
□ 366 John Smoltz	.15	.07	.02
□ 367 Scott Fletcher	.05	.02	.01
□ 368 Jody Reed	.05	.02	.01
□ 369 David Wells	.05	.02	.01
□ 370 Jose Vizcaino	.05	.02	.01
□ 371 Pat Listach	.05	.02	.01
□ 372 Orestes Destrade	.05	.02	.01
□ 373 Danny Tartabull	.05	.02	.01
□ 374 Greg W. Harris	.05	.02	.01
□ 375 Juan Guzman	.10	.05	.01
□ 376 Larry Walker	.15	.07	.02
□ 377 Gary DiSarcina	.05	.02	.01
□ 378 Bobby Bonilla	.10	.05	.01
□ 379 Tim Raines	.15	.07	.02
□ 380 Tommy Greene	.05	.02	.01
□ 381 Chris Gwynn	.05	.02	.01
□ 382 Jeff King	.10	.05	.01
□ 383 Shane Mack	.05	.02	.01
□ 384 Ozzie Smith	.40	.18	.05
□ 385 Eddie Zambrano	.05	.02	.01
□ 386 Mike Devereaux	.05	.02	.01
□ 387 Erik Hanson	.05	.02	.01
□ 388 Scott Cooper	.05	.02	.01
□ 389 Dean Palmer	.10	.05	.01
□ 390 John Wetteland	.10	.05	.01
□ 391 Reggie Jefferson	.10	.05	.01
□ 392 Mark Lemke	.05	.02	.01
□ 393 Cecil Fielder	.10	.05	.01
□ 394 Reggie Sanders	.15	.07	.02
□ 395 Darryl Hamilton	.05	.02	.01
□ 396 Daryl Boston	.05	.02	.01
□ 397 Pat Kelly	.05	.02	.01
□ 398 Joe Orsulak	.05	.02	.01
□ 399 Ed Sprague	.10	.05	.01
□ 400 Eric Anthony	.05	.02	.01
□ 401 Scott Sanderson	.05	.02	.01
□ 402 Jim Gott	.05	.02	.01
□ 403 Ron Karkovice	.05	.02	.01
□ 404 Phil Plantier	.05	.02	.01
□ 405 David Cone	.15	.07	.02
□ 406 Robby Thompson	.05	.02	.01
□ 407 Dave Winfield	.15	.07	.02
□ 408 Dwight Smith	.05	.02	.01
□ 409 Ruben Sierra	.10	.05	.01
□ 410 Jack Armstrong	.05	.02	.01
□ 411 Mike Felder	.05	.02	.01
□ 412 Wil Cordero	.10	.05	.01
□ 413 Julio Franco	.10	.05	.01
□ 414 Howard Johnson	.05	.02	.01
□ 415 Mark McLemore	.05	.02	.01
□ 416 Pete Incaviglia	.05	.02	.01
□ 417 John Valentin	.10	.05	.01
□ 418 Tim Wakefield	.05	.02	.01
□ 419 Jose Mesa	.10	.05	.01
□ 420 Bernard Gilkey	.10	.05	.01
□ 421 Kirk Gibson	.10	.05	.01
□ 422 Dave Justice	.15	.07	.02
□ 423 Tom Brunansky	.05	.02	.01
□ 424 John Smiley	.05	.02	.01
□ 425 Kevin Maas	.05	.02	.01
□ 426 Doug Drabek	.05	.02	.01
□ 427 Paul Molitor	.40	.18	.05
□ 428 Darryl Strawberry	.10	.05	.01
□ 429 Tim Naehring	.05	.02	.01
□ 430 Bill Swift	.05	.02	.01
□ 431 Ellis Burks	.10	.05	.01
□ 432 Greg Hibbard	.05	.02	.01
□ 433 Felix Jose	.05	.02	.01
□ 434 Bret Barberie	.05	.02	.01
□ 435 Pedro Munoz	.05	.02	.01
□ 436 Darrin Fletcher	.05	.02	.01
□ 437 Bobby Witt	.05	.02	.01
□ 438 Wes Chamberlain	.05	.02	.01
□ 439 Mackey Sasser	.05	.02	.01
□ 440 Mark Whiten	.05	.02	.01
□ 441 Harold Reynolds	.05	.02	.01
□ 442 Greg Olson	.05	.02	.01
□ 443 Billy Hatcher	.05	.02	.01
□ 444 Joe Oliver	.05	.02	.01
□ 445 Sandy Alomar Jr.	.10	.05	.01
□ 446 Tim Wallach	.05	.02	.01
□ 447 Karl Rhodes	.05	.02	.01
□ 448 Royce Clayton	.10	.05	.01
□ 449 Cal Eldred	.05	.02	.01
□ 450 Rick Wilkins	.05	.02	.01
□ 451 Mike Stanley	.05	.02	.01
□ 452 Charlie Hough	.05	.02	.01
□ 453 Jack Morris	.10	.05	.01
□ 454 Jon Ratliff	.10	.05	.01
□ 455 Rene Gonzales	.05	.02	.01
□ 456 Eddie Taubensee	.05	.02	.01
□ 457 Roberto Hernandez	.10	.05	.01
□ 458 Todd Hundley	.15	.07	.02
□ 459 Mike Macfarlane	.05	.02	.01
□ 460 Mickey Morandini	.05	.02	.01
□ 461 Scott Erickson	.05	.02	.01
□ 462 Lonnie Smith	.05	.02	.01
□ 463 Dave Henderson	.05	.02	.01
□ 464 Ryan Klesko	.50	.23	.06
□ 465 Edgar Martinez	.15	.07	.02
□ 466 Tom Pagnozzi	.05	.02	.01
□ 467 Charlie Leibrandt	.05	.02	.01
□ 468 Brian Anderson	.10	.05	.01
□ 469 Harold Baines	.10	.05	.01
□ 470 Tim Belcher	.05	.02	.01
□ 471 Andre Dawson	.15	.07	.02
□ 472 Eric Young	.10	.05	.01
□ 473 Paul Sorrento	.05	.02	.01
□ 474 Luis Gonzalez	.05	.02	.01
□ 475 Rob Deer	.05	.02	.01
□ 476 Mike Piazza	1.25	.55	.16
□ 477 Kevin Reimer	.05	.02	.01
□ 478 Jeff Gardner	.05	.02	.01
□ 479 Melido Perez	.05	.02	.01
□ 480 Darren Lewis	.05	.02	.01
□ 481 Duane Ward	.05	.02	.01
□ 482 Rey Sanchez	.05	.02	.01

□ 483	Mark Lewis	.05	.02	.01
□ 484	Jeff Conine	.15	.07	.02
□ 485	Joey Cora	.05	.02	.01
□ 486	Trot Nixon	.15	.07	.02
□ 487	Kevin McReynolds	.05	.02	.01
□ 488	Mike Lansing	.10	.05	.01
□ 489	Mike Pagliarulo	.05	.02	.01
□ 490	Mariano Duncan	.05	.02	.01
□ 491	Mike Bordick	.05	.02	.01
□ 492	Kevin Young	.05	.02	.01
□ 493	Dave Valle	.05	.02	.01
□ 494	Wayne Gomes	.10	.05	.01
□ 495	Rafael Palmeiro	.15	.07	.02
□ 496	Deion Sanders	.15	.07	.02
□ 497	Rick Sutcliffe	.05	.02	.01
□ 498	Randy Milligan	.05	.02	.01
□ 499	Carlos Quintana	.05	.02	.01
□ 500	Chris Turner	.05	.02	.01
□ 501	Thomas Howard	.05	.02	.01
□ 502	Greg Swindell	.05	.02	.01
□ 503	Chad Kreuter	.05	.02	.01
□ 504	Eric Davis	.10	.05	.01
□ 505	Dickie Thon	.05	.02	.01
□ 506	Matt Drews	.25	.11	.03
□ 507	Spike Owen	.05	.02	.01
□ 508	Rod Beck	.10	.05	.01
□ 509	Pat Hentgen	.15	.07	.02
□ 510	Sammy Sosa	.15	.07	.02
□ 511	J.T. Snow	.10	.05	.01
□ 512	Chuck Carr	.05	.02	.01
□ 513	Bo Jackson	.15	.07	.02
□ 514	Dennis Martinez	.10	.05	.01
□ 515	Phil Hiatt	.05	.02	.01
□ 516	Jeff Kent	.05	.02	.01
□ 517	Brooks Kieschnick	.40	.18	.05
□ 518	Kirk Presley	.15	.07	.02
□ 519	Kevin Seitzer	.05	.02	.01
□ 520	Carlos Garcia	.05	.02	.01
□ 521	Mike Blowers	.05	.02	.01
□ 522	Luis Alicea	.05	.02	.01
□ 523	David Hulse	.05	.02	.01
□ 524	Greg Maddux UER (career strikeout totals listed as 113; should be 1134)	1.25	.55	.16
□ 525	Gregg Olson	.05	.02	.01
□ 526	Hal Morris	.05	.02	.01
□ 527	Daron Kirkreit	.10	.05	.01
□ 528	David Nied	.05	.02	.01
□ 529	Jeff Russell	.05	.02	.01
□ 530	Kevin Gross	.05	.02	.01
□ 531	John Doherty	.05	.02	.01
□ 532	Matt Brunson	.10	.05	.01
□ 533	Dave Nilsson	.10	.05	.01
□ 534	Randy Myers	.05	.02	.01
□ 535	Steve Farr	.05	.02	.01
□ 536	Billy Wagner	.50	.23	.06
□ 537	Darnell Coles	.05	.02	.01
□ 538	Frank Tanana	.05	.02	.01
□ 539	Tim Salmon	.15	.07	.02
□ 540	Kim Batiste	.05	.02	.01
□ 541	George Bell	.05	.02	.01
□ 542	Tom Henke	.05	.02	.01
□ 543	Sam Horn	.05	.02	.01
□ 544	Doug Jones	.05	.02	.01
□ 545	Scott Leius	.05	.02	.01
□ 546	Al Martin	.05	.02	.01
□ 547	Bob Welch	.05	.02	.01
□ 548	Scott Christman	.10	.05	.01
□ 549	Norm Charlton	.05	.02	.01
□ 550	Mark McGwire	.60	.25	.07
□ 551	Greg McMichael	.05	.02	.01
□ 552	Tim Costo	.05	.02	.01
□ 553	Rodney Bolton	.05	.02	.01
□ 554	Pedro Martinez	.15	.07	.02
□ 555	Marc Valdes	.10	.05	.01
□ 556	Darrell Whitmore	.05	.02	.01
□ 557	Tim Bogar	.05	.02	.01
□ 558	Steve Karsay	.05	.02	.01
□ 559	Danny Bautista	.05	.02	.01
□ 560	Jeffrey Hammonds	.10	.05	.01
□ 561	Aaron Sele	.10	.05	.01
□ 562	Russ Springer	.05	.02	.01
□ 563	Jason Bere	.10	.05	.01
□ 564	Billy Brewer	.05	.02	.01
□ 565	Sterling Hitchcock	.10	.05	.01
□ 566	Bobby Munoz	.05	.02	.01
□ 567	Craig Paquette	.05	.02	.01
□ 568	Bret Boone	.10	.05	.01
□ 569	Dan Peltier	.05	.02	.01
□ 570	Jeromy Burnitz	.05	.02	.01
□ 571	John Wasdin	.25	.11	.03
□ 572	Chipper Jones	1.50	.70	.19
□ 573	Jamey Wright	.50	.23	.06
□ 574	Jeff Granger	.10	.05	.01
□ 575	Jay Powell	.10	.05	.01
□ 576	Ryan Thompson	.05	.02	.01
□ 577	Lou Frazier	.05	.02	.01
□ 578	Paul Wagner	.05	.02	.01
□ 579	Brad Ausmus	.05	.02	.01
□ 580	Jack Voigt	.05	.02	.01
□ 581	Kevin Rogers	.05	.02	.01
□ 582	Damon Buford	.05	.02	.01
□ 583	Paul Quantrill	.05	.02	.01
□ 584	Marc Newfield	.10	.05	.01
□ 585	Derrek Lee	1.25	.55	.16
□ 586	Shane Reynolds	.10	.05	.01
□ 587	Cliff Floyd	.15	.07	.02
□ 588	Jeff Schwarz	.05	.02	.01
□ 589	Ross Powell	.05	.02	.01
□ 590	Gerald Williams	.05	.02	.01
□ 591	Mike Trombley	.05	.02	.01
□ 592	Ken Ryan	.05	.02	.01
□ 593	John O'Donoghue	.05	.02	.01
□ 594	Rod Correia	.05	.02	.01
□ 595	Darrell Sherman	.05	.02	.01
□ 596	Steve Scarsone	.05	.02	.01
□ 597	Sherman Obando	.05	.02	.01
□ 598	Kurt Abbott	.10	.05	.01
□ 599	Dave Telgheder	.05	.02	.01
□ 600	Rick Trlicek	.05	.02	.01
□ 601	Carl Everett	.05	.02	.01
□ 602	Luis Ortiz	.05	.02	.01
□ 603	Larry Luebbers	.05	.02	.01
□ 604	Kevin Roberson	.05	.02	.01
□ 605	Butch Huskey	.10	.05	.01
□ 606	Benji Gil	.05	.02	.01
□ 607	Todd Van Poppel	.05	.02	.01
□ 608	Mark Hutton	.05	.02	.01
□ 609	Chip Hale	.05	.02	.01
□ 610	Matt Maysey	.05	.02	.01
□ 611	Scott Ruffcorn	.05	.02	.01
□ 612	Hilly Hathaway	.05	.02	.01
□ 613	Allen Watson	.05	.02	.01
□ 614	Carlos Delgado	.15	.07	.02
□ 615	Roberto Mejia	.05	.02	.01
□ 616	Turk Wendell	.05	.02	.01
□ 617	Tony Tarasco	.05	.02	.01
□ 618	Raul Mondesi	.15	.07	.02
□ 619	Kevin Stocker	.05	.02	.01
□ 620	Javier Lopez	.15	.07	.02
□ 621	Keith Kessinger	.05	.02	.01
□ 622	Bob Hamelin	.05	.02	.01
□ 623	John Roper	.05	.02	.01
□ 624	Lenny Dykstra WS	.05	.02	.01
□ 625	Joe Carter WS	.15	.07	.02
□ 626	Jim Abbott HL	.05	.02	.01
□ 627	Lee Smith HL	.05	.02	.01
□ 628	Ken Griffey Jr. HL	1.00	.45	.12
□ 629	Dave Winfield HL	.15	.07	.02
□ 630	Darryl Kile HL	.05	.02	.01
□ 631	Frank Thomas AL MVP	1.00	.45	.12
□ 632	Barry Bonds NL MVP	.15	.07	.02
□ 633	Jack McDowell AL CY	.05	.02	.01
□ 634	Greg Maddux NL CY	.60	.25	.07
□ 635	Tim Salmon AL ROY	.15	.07	.02
□ 636	Mike Piazza NL ROY	.60	.25	.07
□ 637	Brian Turang	.05	.02	.01
□ 638	Rondell White	.15	.07	.02
□ 639	Nigel Wilson	.05	.02	.01
□ 640	Torii Hunter	.10	.05	.01
□ 641	Salomon Torres	.05	.02	.01
□ 642	Kevin Higgins	.05	.02	.01
□ 643	Eric Wedge	.05	.02	.01
□ 644	Roger Salkeld	.05	.02	.01
□ 645	Manny Ramirez	.60	.25	.07
□ 646	Jeff McNeely	.05	.02	.01
□ 647	Atlanta Braves CL	.05	.02	.01
□ 648	Chicago Cubs CL	.05	.02	.01
□ 649	Cincinnati Reds CL	.05	.02	.01
□ 650	Colorado Rockies CL	.05	.02	.01
□ 651	Florida Marlins CL	.05	.02	.01
□ 652	Houston Astros CL	.05	.02	.01

□ 653 Los Angeles Dodgers CL	.05	.02	.01
□ 654 Montreal Expos CL	.05	.02	.01
□ 655 New York Mets CL	.05	.02	.01
□ 656 Philadelphia Phillies CL	.05	.02	.01
□ 657 Pittsburgh Pirates CL	.05	.02	.01
□ 658 St. Louis Cardinals CL	.05	.02	.01
□ 659 San Diego Padres CL	.05	.02	.01
□ 660 San Francisco Giants CL	.05	.02	.01

1994 Score Boys of Summer

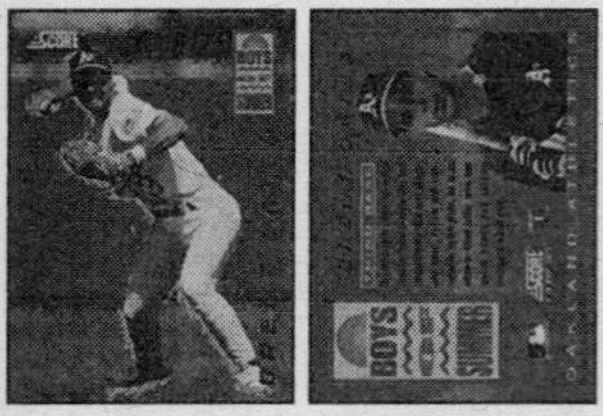

Randomly inserted in super packs at a rate of one in four, this 60-card set features top young stars and hopefuls. The set was issued in two series of 30 cards. The fronts have a color player photo that is outlined by what resembles static electricity. The backgrounds are blurred and the player's name and Boys of Summer logo appear up the right-hand side. An orange back contains a player photo and text.

	MINT	NRMT	EXC
COMPLETE SET (60)	120.00	55.00	15.00
COMPLETE SERIES 1 (30)	50.00	22.00	6.25
COMPLETE SERIES 2 (30)	70.00	32.00	8.75
COMMON CARD (1-60)	1.50	.70	.19
SEMISTARS	3.00	1.35	.35
RANDOM INSERTS IN SUPER PACKS			

□ 1 Jeff Conine	3.00	1.35	.35
□ 2 Aaron Sele	1.50	.70	.19
□ 3 Kevin Stocker	1.50	.70	.19
□ 4 Pat Meares	1.50	.70	.19
□ 5 Jeromy Burnitz	1.50	.70	.19
□ 6 Mike Piazza	25.00	11.00	3.10
□ 7 Allen Watson	1.50	.70	.19
□ 8 Jeffrey Hammonds	1.50	.70	.19
□ 9 Kevin Roberson	1.50	.70	.19
□ 10 Hilly Hathaway	1.50	.70	.19
□ 11 Kirk Rueter	1.50	.70	.19
□ 12 Eduardo Perez	1.50	.70	.19
□ 13 Ricky Gutierrez	1.50	.70	.19
□ 14 Domingo Jean	1.50	.70	.19
□ 15 David Nied	1.50	.70	.19
□ 16 Wayne Kirby	1.50	.70	.19
□ 17 Mike Lansing	1.50	.70	.19
□ 18 Jason Bere	1.50	.70	.19
□ 19 Brent Gates	1.50	.70	.19
□ 20 Javier Lopez	5.00	2.20	.60
□ 21 Greg McMichael	1.50	.70	.19
□ 22 David Hulse	1.50	.70	.19
□ 23 Roberto Mejia	1.50	.70	.19
□ 24 Tim Salmon	6.00	2.70	.75
□ 25 Rene Arocha	1.50	.70	.19
□ 26 Bret Boone	3.00	1.35	.35
□ 27 David McCarty	1.50	.70	.19
□ 28 Todd Van Poppel	1.50	.70	.19
□ 29 Lance Painter	1.50	.70	.19
□ 30 Erik Pappas	1.50	.70	.19
□ 31 Chuck Carr	1.50	.70	.19
□ 32 Mark Hutton	1.50	.70	.19
□ 33 Jeff McNeely	1.50	.70	.19
□ 34 Willie Greene	3.00	1.35	.35
□ 35 Nigel Wilson	1.50	.70	.19
□ 36 Rondell White	4.00	1.80	.50
□ 37 Brian Turang	1.50	.70	.19
□ 38 Manny Ramirez	12.00	5.50	1.50
□ 39 Salomon Torres	1.50	.70	.19
□ 40 Melvin Nieves	3.00	1.35	.35
□ 41 Ryan Klesko	10.00	4.50	1.25
□ 42 Keith Kessinger	1.50	.70	.19
□ 43 Brad Ausmus	1.50	.70	.19
□ 44 Bob Hamelin	1.50	.70	.19
□ 45 Carlos Delgado	5.00	2.20	.60
□ 46 Marc Newfield	3.00	1.35	.35
□ 47 Raul Mondesi	6.00	2.70	.75
□ 48 Tim Costo	1.50	.70	.19
□ 49 Pedro Martinez	3.00	1.35	.35
□ 50 Steve Karsay	1.50	.70	.19
□ 51 Danny Bautista	1.50	.70	.19
□ 52 Butch Huskey	3.00	1.35	.35
□ 53 Kurt Abbott	3.00	1.35	.35
□ 54 Darrell Sherman	1.50	.70	.19
□ 55 Damon Buford	1.50	.70	.19
□ 56 Ross Powell	1.50	.70	.19
□ 57 Darrell Whitmore	1.50	.70	.19
□ 58 Chipper Jones	30.00	13.50	3.70
□ 59 Jeff Granger	1.50	.70	.19
□ 60 Cliff Floyd	3.00	1.35	.35

1994 Score Cycle

This 20-card set was randomly inserted in second series foil and jumbo packs at a rate of one in 90. The set is arranged according to players with the most singles (1-5), doubles (6-10), triples (11-15) and home runs (16-20). The front contains an oval player photo with "The Cycle" at top and the players name at the bottom. Also at the bottom, is the number of of that particular base hit the player accumulated in 1993. A small baseball diamond appears beneath the oval photo. The back lists the top five of the given base hit category. A dark blue border surrounds both sides. The cards are number with a TC prefix.

	MINT	NRMT	EXC
COMPLETE SET (20)	150.00	70.00	19.00
COMMON CARD (TC1-TC20)	2.50	1.10	.30
SEMISTARS	5.00	2.20	.60
INSERTS IN SER.2 FOIL AND JUMBO PACKS			

□ TC1 Brett Butler	5.00	2.20	.60
□ TC2 Kenny Lofton	15.00	6.75	1.85
□ TC3 Paul Molitor	10.00	4.50	1.25
□ TC4 Carlos Baerga	5.00	2.20	.60
□ TC5 Gregg Jefferies Tony Phillips	5.00	2.20	.60
□ TC6 John Olerud	2.50	1.10	.30
□ TC7 Charlie Hayes	2.50	1.10	.30
□ TC8 Lenny Dykstra	5.00	2.20	.60
□ TC9 Dante Bichette	6.00	2.70	.75
□ TC10 Devon White	5.00	2.20	.60
□ TC11 Lance Johnson	5.00	2.20	.60
□ TC12 Joey Cora Steve Finley	2.50	1.10	.30
□ TC13 Tony Fernandez	2.50	1.10	.30
□ TC14 David Hulse Brett Butler	2.50	1.10	.30
□ TC15 Jay Bell Brian McRae Mickey Morandini	2.50	1.10	.30
□ TC16 Juan Gonzalez Barry Bonds	20.00	9.00	2.50
□ TC17 Ken Griffey Jr.	50.00	22.00	6.25
□ TC18 Frank Thomas	50.00	22.00	6.25

□ TC19	Dave Justice	5.00	2.20	.60
□ TC20	Matt Williams Albert Belle	15.00	6.75	1.85

1994 Score Dream Team

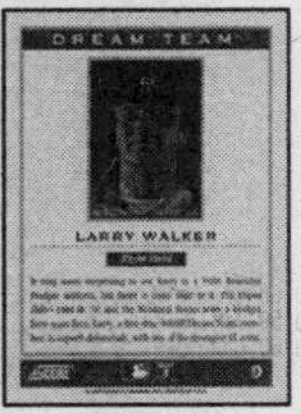

Randomly inserted in first series foil and jumbo packs at a rate of one in 72, this ten-card set feature's baseball's Dream Team as selected by Pinnacle Brands. Banded by forest green stripes above and below, the player photos on the fronts feature ten of baseball's best players sporting historical team uniforms from the 1930's. The set title and player's name appear in gold foil lettering on black bars above and below the picture. The backs carry a color head shot and brief player profile.

	MINT	NRMT	EXC
COMPLETE SET (10)	60.00	27.00	7.50
COMMON CARD (1-10)	2.50	1.10	.30
SEMISTARS	6.00	2.70	.75
INSERTS IN SER.1 FOIL AND JUMBO PACKS			

□ 1	Mike Mussina	10.00	4.50	1.25
□ 2	Tom Glavine	6.00	2.70	.75
□ 3	Don Mattingly	25.00	11.00	3.10
□ 4	Carlos Baerga	6.00	2.70	.75
□ 5	Barry Larkin	6.00	2.70	.75
□ 6	Matt Williams	6.00	2.70	.75
□ 7	Juan Gonzalez	25.00	11.00	3.10
□ 8	Andy Van Slyke	2.50	1.10	.30
□ 9	Larry Walker	6.00	2.70	.75
□ 10	Mike Stanley	2.50	1.10	.30

1994 Score Gold Stars

Randomly inserted at a rate of one in every 18 hobby packs, this 60-card set features National and American stars. Split into two series of 30 cards, the first series (1-30) comprises of National League players and the second series (31-60) American Leaguers. The fronts feature a color action player photo cut out and superimposed on a foil background. At the bottom, a navy blue triangle carries the set title and the player's name appears in a white bar. The backs have a color close-up shot and a player profile.

	MINT	NRMT	EXC
COMPLETE SET (60)	250.00	110.00	31.00
COMPLETE NL SERIES (30)	100.00	45.00	12.50
COMPLETE AL SERIES (30)	150.00	70.00	19.00
COMMON CARD (1-60)	2.00	.90	.25
SEMISTARS	4.00	1.80	.50
RANDOM INSERTS IN HOBBY FOIL PACKS.			

□ 1	Barry Bonds	8.00	3.60	1.00
□ 2	Orlando Merced	2.00	.90	.25
□ 3	Mark Grace	4.00	1.80	.50
□ 4	Darren Daulton	3.00	1.35	.35
□ 5	Jeff Blauser	2.00	.90	.25
□ 6	Deion Sanders	4.00	1.80	.50
□ 7	John Kruk	3.00	1.35	.35
□ 8	Jeff Bagwell	12.00	5.50	1.50
□ 9	Gregg Jefferies	4.00	1.80	.50
□ 10	Matt Williams	4.00	1.80	.50
□ 11	Andres Galarraga	4.00	1.80	.50
□ 12	Jay Bell	2.00	.90	.25
□ 13	Mike Piazza	20.00	9.00	2.50
□ 14	Ron Gant	4.00	1.80	.50
□ 15	Barry Larkin	4.00	1.80	.50
□ 16	Tom Glavine	4.00	1.80	.50
□ 17	Lenny Dykstra	3.00	1.35	.35
□ 18	Fred McGriff	4.00	1.80	.50
□ 19	Andy Van Slyke	3.00	1.35	.35
□ 20	Gary Sheffield	5.00	2.20	.60
□ 21	John Burkett	2.00	.90	.25
□ 22	Dante Bichette	4.00	1.80	.50
□ 23	Tony Gwynn	12.00	5.50	1.50
□ 24	Dave Justice	4.00	1.80	.50
□ 25	Marquis Grissom	4.00	1.80	.50
□ 26	Bobby Bonilla	4.00	1.80	.50
□ 27	Larry Walker	3.00	1.35	.35
□ 28	Brett Butler	3.00	1.35	.35
□ 29	Robby Thompson	2.00	.90	.25
□ 30	Jeff Conine	4.00	1.80	.50
□ 31	Joe Carter	4.00	1.80	.50
□ 32	Ken Griffey Jr.	30.00	13.50	3.70
□ 33	Juan Gonzalez	15.00	6.75	1.85
□ 34	Rickey Henderson	4.00	1.80	.50
□ 35	Bo Jackson	4.00	1.80	.50
□ 36	Cal Ripken	25.00	11.00	3.10
□ 37	John Olerud	3.00	1.35	.35
□ 38	Carlos Baerga	4.00	1.80	.50
□ 39	Jack McDowell	4.00	1.80	.50
□ 40	Cecil Fielder	4.00	1.80	.50
□ 41	Kenny Lofton	10.00	4.50	1.25
□ 42	Roberto Alomar	8.00	3.60	1.00
□ 43	Randy Johnson	5.00	2.20	.60
□ 44	Tim Salmon	5.00	2.20	.60
□ 45	Frank Thomas	30.00	13.50	3.70
□ 46	Albert Belle	15.00	6.75	1.85
□ 47	Greg Vaughn	4.00	1.80	.50
□ 48	Travis Fryman	4.00	1.80	.50
□ 49	Don Mattingly	15.00	6.75	1.85
□ 50	Wade Boggs	4.00	1.80	.50
□ 51	Mo Vaughn	8.00	3.60	1.00
□ 52	Kirby Puckett	10.00	4.50	1.25
□ 53	Devon White	3.00	1.35	.35
□ 54	Tony Phillips	2.00	.90	.25
□ 55	Brian Harper	2.00	.90	.25
□ 56	Chad Curtis	2.00	.90	.25
□ 57	Paul Molitor	6.00	2.70	.75
□ 58	Ivan Rodriguez	6.00	2.70	.75
□ 59	Rafael Palmeiro	4.00	1.80	.50
□ 60	Brian McRae	3.00	1.35	.35

1994 Score Rookie/Traded

The 1994 Score Rookie and Traded set consists of 165 standard-size cards featuring rookie standouts, traded players, and new young prospects. The set is delineated by traded players (RT1-RT70) and rookies/young prospects (RT71-RT163). The set closes with checklists (RT164-RT165). Each foil pack contained one Gold Rush card. The cards are numbered on the back with an "RT" prefix. A special unnumbered September Call-Up Redemption card could be exchanged for an Alex Rodriguez card. The expiration date was January 31, 1995. Odds of finding a redemption card are approximately one in 240 retail and hobby packs. Rookie Cards include Jose Lima and Chan Ho Park.

	MINT	NRMT	EXC
COMPLETE SET (165)	10.00	4.50	1.25
COMMON CARD (RT1-RT165)	.05	.02	.01
SEMISTARS	.15	.07	.02
STARS	.30	.14	.04
COMP.GOLD RUSH SET (165)	50.00	22.00	6.25
COMMON GOLD RUSH (1-165)	.25	.11	.03
GOLD RUSH SEMISTARS	.50	.23	.06
*GOLD RUSH STARS: 3X to 5X BASIC CARDS			
*GOLD RUSH YOUNG STARS: 2X to 4X BASIC CARDS			
ONE GOLD RUSH PER PACK			

□ RT1 Will Clark	.30	.14	.04
□ RT2 Lee Smith	.15	.07	.02
□ RT3 Bo Jackson	.30	.14	.04
□ RT4 Ellis Burks	.15	.07	.02
□ RT5 Eddie Murray	.50	.23	.06
□ RT6 Delino DeShields	.05	.02	.01
□ RT7 Erik Hanson	.05	.02	.01
□ RT8 Rafael Palmeiro	.30	.14	.04
□ RT9 Luis Polonia	.05	.02	.01
□ RT10 Omar Vizquel	.30	.14	.04
□ RT11 Kurt Abbott	.15	.07	.02
□ RT12 Vince Coleman	.05	.02	.01
□ RT13 Rickey Henderson	.30	.14	.04
□ RT14 Terry Mulholland	.05	.02	.01
□ RT15 Greg Hibbard	.05	.02	.01
□ RT16 Walt Weiss	.05	.02	.01
□ RT17 Chris Sabo	.05	.02	.01
□ RT18 Dave Henderson	.05	.02	.01
□ RT19 Rick Sutcliffe	.05	.02	.01
□ RT20 Harold Reynolds	.05	.02	.01
□ RT21 Jack Morris	.15	.07	.02
□ RT22 Dan Wilson	.15	.07	.02
□ RT23 Dave Magadan	.05	.02	.01
□ RT24 Dennis Martinez	.15	.07	.02
□ RT25 Wes Chamberlain	.05	.02	.01
□ RT26 Otis Nixon	.05	.02	.01
□ RT27 Eric Anthony	.05	.02	.01
□ RT28 Randy Milligan	.05	.02	.01
□ RT29 Julio Franco	.15	.07	.02
□ RT30 Kevin McReynolds	.05	.02	.01
□ RT31 Anthony Young	.05	.02	.01
□ RT32 Brian Harper	.05	.02	.01
□ RT33 Gene Harris	.05	.02	.01
□ RT34 Eddie Taubensee	.05	.02	.01
□ RT35 David Segui	.05	.02	.01
□ RT36 Stan Javier	.05	.02	.01
□ RT37 Felix Fermin	.05	.02	.01
□ RT38 Darrin Jackson	.05	.02	.01
□ RT39 Tony Fernandez	.05	.02	.01
□ RT40 Jose Vizcaino	.05	.02	.01
□ RT41 Willie Banks	.05	.02	.01
□ RT42 Brian Hunter	.05	.02	.01
□ RT43 Reggie Jefferson	.15	.07	.02
□ RT44 Junior Felix	.05	.02	.01
□ RT45 Jack Armstrong	.05	.02	.01
□ RT46 Bip Roberts	.05	.02	.01
□ RT47 Jerry Browne	.05	.02	.01
□ RT48 Marvin Freeman	.05	.02	.01
□ RT49 Jody Reed	.05	.02	.01
□ RT50 Alex Cole	.05	.02	.01
□ RT51 Sid Fernandez	.05	.02	.01
□ RT52 Pete Smith	.05	.02	.01
□ RT53 Xavier Hernandez	.05	.02	.01
□ RT54 Scott Sanderson	.05	.02	.01
□ RT55 Turner Ward	.05	.02	.01
□ RT56 Rex Hudler	.05	.02	.01
□ RT57 Deion Sanders	.30	.14	.04
□ RT58 Sid Bream	.05	.02	.01
□ RT59 Tony Pena	.05	.02	.01
□ RT60 Bret Boone	.15	.07	.02
□ RT61 Bobby Ayala	.05	.02	.01
□ RT62 Pedro Martinez	.30	.14	.04
□ RT63 Howard Johnson	.05	.02	.01
□ RT64 Mark Portugal	.05	.02	.01
□ RT65 Roberto Kelly	.05	.02	.01
□ RT66 Spike Owen	.05	.02	.01
□ RT67 Jeff Treadway	.05	.02	.01
□ RT68 Mike Harkey	.05	.02	.01
□ RT69 Doug Jones	.05	.02	.01
□ RT70 Steve Farr	.05	.02	.01
□ RT71 Billy Taylor	.05	.02	.01
□ RT72 Manny Ramirez	.60	.25	.07
□ RT73 Bob Hamelin	.05	.02	.01
□ RT74 Steve Karsay	.05	.02	.01
□ RT75 Ryan Klesko	.50	.23	.06
□ RT76 Cliff Floyd	.30	.14	.04
□ RT77 Jeffrey Hammonds	.15	.07	.02
□ RT78 Javier Lopez	.30	.14	.04
□ RT79 Roger Salkeld	.05	.02	.01
□ RT80 Hector Carrasco	.05	.02	.01
□ RT81 Gerald Williams	.05	.02	.01
□ RT82 Raul Mondesi	.30	.14	.04
□ RT83 Sterling Hitchcock	.15	.07	.02
□ RT84 Danny Bautista	.05	.02	.01
□ RT85 Chris Turner	.05	.02	.01
□ RT86 Shane Reynolds	.15	.07	.02
□ RT87 Rondell White	.30	.14	.04
□ RT88 Salomon Torres	.05	.02	.01
□ RT89 Turk Wendell	.05	.02	.01
□ RT90 Tony Tarasco	.05	.02	.01
□ RT91 Shawn Green	.15	.07	.02
□ RT92 Greg Colbrunn	.05	.02	.01
□ RT93 Eddie Zambrano	.05	.02	.01
□ RT94 Rich Becker	.15	.07	.02
□ RT95 Chris Gomez	.05	.02	.01
□ RT96 John Patterson	.05	.02	.01
□ RT97 Derek Parks	.05	.02	.01
□ RT98 Rich Rowland	.05	.02	.01
□ RT99 James Mouton	.15	.07	.02
□ RT100 Tim Hyers	.05	.02	.01
□ RT101 Jose Valentin	.15	.07	.02
□ RT102 Carlos Delgado	.30	.14	.04
□ RT103 Robert Eenhoorn	.05	.02	.01
□ RT104 John Hudek	.05	.02	.01
□ RT105 Domingo Cedeno	.05	.02	.01
□ RT106 Denny Hocking	.05	.02	.01
□ RT107 Greg Pirkl	.05	.02	.01
□ RT108 Mark Smith	.05	.02	.01
□ RT109 Paul Shuey	.05	.02	.01
□ RT110 Jorge Fabregas	.05	.02	.01
□ RT111 Rikkert Faneyte	.05	.02	.01
□ RT112 Rob Butler	.05	.02	.01
□ RT113 Darren Oliver	.30	.14	.04
□ RT114 Troy O'Leary	.05	.02	.01
□ RT115 Scott Brow	.05	.02	.01
□ RT116 Tony Eusebio	.05	.02	.01
□ RT117 Carlos Reyes	.05	.02	.01
□ RT118 J.R. Phillips	.05	.02	.01
□ RT119 Alex Diaz	.05	.02	.01
□ RT120 Charles Johnson	.30	.14	.04
□ RT121 Nate Minchey	.05	.02	.01
□ RT122 Scott Sanders	.05	.02	.01
□ RT123 Daryl Boston	.05	.02	.01
□ RT124 Joey Hamilton	.40	.18	.05
□ RT125 Brian Anderson	.15	.07	.02
□ RT126 Dan Miceli	.05	.02	.01
□ RT127 Tom Brunansky	.05	.02	.01
□ RT128 Dave Staton	.05	.02	.01
□ RT129 Mike Oquist	.05	.02	.01
□ RT130 John Mabry	.40	.18	.05
□ RT131 Norberto Martin	.05	.02	.01
□ RT132 Hector Fajardo	.05	.02	.01
□ RT133 Mark Hutton	.05	.02	.01
□ RT134 Fernando Vina	.05	.02	.01
□ RT135 Lee Tinsley	.15	.07	.02
□ RT136 Chan Ho Park	.50	.23	.06
□ RT137 Paul Spoljaric	.05	.02	.01
□ RT138 Matias Carrillo	.05	.02	.01
□ RT139 Mark Kiefer	.05	.02	.01
□ RT140 Stan Royer	.05	.02	.01
□ RT141 Bryan Eversgerd	.05	.02	.01
□ RT142 Brian L.Hunter	.30	.14	.04
□ RT143 Joe Hall	.05	.02	.01

□ RT144	Johnny Ruffin	.05	.02	.01
□ RT145	Alex Gonzalez	.15	.07	.02
□ RT146	Keith Lockhart	.05	.02	.01
□ RT147	Tom Marsh	.05	.02	.01
□ RT148	Tony Longmire	.05	.02	.01
□ RT149	Keith Mitchell	.05	.02	.01
□ RT150	Melvin Nieves	.15	.07	.02
□ RT151	Kelly Stinnett	.05	.02	.01
□ RT152	Miguel Jimenez	.05	.02	.01
□ RT153	Jeff Juden	.05	.02	.01
□ RT154	Matt Walbeck	.05	.02	.01
□ RT155	Marc Newfield	.15	.07	.02
□ RT156	Matt Mieske	.05	.02	.01
□ RT157	Marcus Moore	.05	.02	.01
□ RT158	Jose Lima SP	1.00	.45	.12
□ RT159	Mike Kelly	.05	.02	.01
□ RT160	Jim Edmonds	.40	.18	.05
□ RT161	Steve Trachsel	.15	.07	.02
□ RT162	Greg Blosser	.05	.02	.01
□ RT163	Marc Acre	.05	.02	.01
□ RT164	AL Checklist	.05	.02	.01
□ RT165	NL Checklist	.05	.02	.01
□ HC1	Alex Rodriguez Call-Up Redemption	60.00	27.00	7.50

1994 Score R/T Changing Places

Randomly inserted in both retail and hobby packs at a rate of one in 36 Rookie/Traded packs, this 10-card standard-size set focuses on ten veteran superstar players who were traded prior to or during the 1994 season. Cards fronts feature a color photo with a slanted design. The backs have a short write-up and a distorted photo.

	MINT	NRMT	EXC
COMPLETE SET (10)	30.00	13.50	3.70
COMMON CARD (CP1-CP10)	2.50	1.10	.30
SEMISTARS	5.00	2.20	.60
RANDOM INSERTS IN HOBBY AND RETAIL PACKS			

□ CP1	Will Clark	8.00	3.60	1.00
□ CP2	Rafael Palmeiro	8.00	3.60	1.00
□ CP3	Roberto Kelly	2.50	1.10	.30
□ CP4	Bo Jackson	5.00	2.20	.60
□ CP5	Otis Nixon	2.50	1.10	.30
□ CP6	Rickey Henderson	5.00	2.20	.60
□ CP7	Ellis Burks	5.00	2.20	.60
□ CP8	Lee Smith	5.00	2.20	.60
□ CP9	Delino DeShields	2.50	1.10	.30
□ CP10	Deion Sanders	5.00	2.20	.60

1994 Score R/T Super Rookies

Randomly inserted in hobby packs at a rate of one in 36, this 18-card standard-size set focuses on top rookies of 1994. Odds of finding one of these cards is approximately one in 36 hobby packs. Designed much like the Gold Rush, the cards have an all-foil design. The fronts have a player photo and the backs have a photo that serves as background to the Super Rookies logo and text.

	MINT	NRMT	EXC
COMPLETE SET (18)	80.00	36.00	10.00
COMMON CARD (SU1-SU18)	2.50	1.10	.30
SEMISTARS	4.00	1.80	.50
RANDOM INSERTS IN HOBBY PACKS			

□ SU1	Carlos Delgado	6.00	2.70	.75
□ SU2	Manny Ramirez	15.00	6.75	1.85
□ SU3	Ryan Klesko	12.00	5.50	1.50
□ SU4	Raul Mondesi	8.00	3.60	1.00
□ SU5	Bob Hamelin	2.50	1.10	.30
□ SU6	Steve Karsay	2.50	1.10	.30
□ SU7	Jeffrey Hammonds	4.00	1.80	.50
□ SU8	Cliff Floyd	4.00	1.80	.50
□ SU9	Kurt Abbott	2.50	1.10	.30
□ SU10	Marc Newfield	4.00	1.80	.50
□ SU11	Javier Lopez	6.00	2.70	.75
□ SU12	Rich Becker	2.50	1.10	.30
□ SU13	Greg Pirkl	2.50	1.10	.30
□ SU14	Rondell White	5.00	2.20	.60
□ SU15	James Mouton	2.50	1.10	.30
□ SU16	Tony Tarasco	2.50	1.10	.30
□ SU17	Brian Anderson	2.50	1.10	.30
□ SU18	Jim Edmonds	8.00	3.60	1.00

1995 Score

The 1995 Score set consists of 605 standard-size cards. The horizontal and vertical fronts feature color action player shots with irregular dark green and sand brown borders. The player's name, position and the team logo appear in a blue bar under the photo. The horizontal backs have the same design as the fronts. They carry another small color headshot on the left, with the player's name, short biography, career highlights and statistics on the right. Hobby packs featured a special signed Ryan Klesko (RG1)card. Retail packs also had a Klesko card (SG1) but these were not signed. There are no key Rookie Cards in this set.

	MINT	NRMT	EXC
COMPLETE SERIES 1 (330)	24.00	11.00	3.00
COMPLETE SET (605)	12.00	5.50	1.50
COMPLETE SERIES 2 (275)	12.00	5.50	1.50
COMMON CARD (1-605)	.05	.02	.01
SEMISTARS	.15	.07	.02
STARS	.30	.14	.04
COMP.G.RUSH SET (605)	120.00	55.00	15.00
COMP.G.RUSH SER.1 (330)	60.00	27.00	7.50
COMP.G.RUSH SER.2 (275)	60.00	27.00	7.50
GOLD RUSH COMMON (1-605)	.15	.07	.02

GOLD RUSH SEMISTARS	.40	.18	.05
*GOLD RUSH STARS: 3X to 6X BASIC CARDS			
*GOLD RUSH YOUNG STARS: 2.5X to 5X BASIC CARDS			
ONE GOLD RUSH PER PACK			
COMP.PLATINUM SET (587)	300.00	135.00	38.00
COMP.PLATINUM SER.1 (316)	200.00	90.00	25.00
COMP.PLATINUM SER.2 (271)	100.00	45.00	12.50
*PLATINUM STARS: 5X to 10X BASIC CARD			
*PLATINUM YOUNG STARS: 4X to 8X BASIC CARD			
ONE PLAT.TEAM PER G.RUSH TEAM VIA MAIL			
COMP.YOU TRADE EM SET (11)	1.50	.70	.19
KLESKO RG1 INSERT IN SER.1 RETAIL PACKS			
KLESKO SG1 INSERT IN SER.1 HOBBY PACKS			

□ 1 Frank Thomas	2.00	.90	.25
□ 2 Roberto Alomar	.50	.23	.06
□ 3 Cal Ripken	1.50	.70	.19
□ 4 Jose Canseco	.30	.14	.04
□ 5 Matt Williams	.30	.14	.04
□ 6 Esteban Beltre	.05	.02	.01
□ 7 Domingo Cedeno	.05	.02	.01
□ 8 John Valentin	.15	.07	.02
□ 9 Glenallen Hill	.05	.02	.01
□ 10 Rafael Belliard	.05	.02	.01
□ 11 Randy Myers	.05	.02	.01
□ 12 Mo Vaughn	.50	.23	.06
□ 13 Hector Carrasco	.05	.02	.01
□ 14 Chili Davis	.15	.07	.02
□ 15 Dante Bichette	.30	.14	.04
□ 16 Darrin Jackson	.05	.02	.01
□ 17 Mike Piazza	1.25	.55	.16
□ 18 Junior Felix	.05	.02	.01
□ 19 Moises Alou	.15	.07	.02
□ 20 Mark Gubicza	.05	.02	.01
□ 21 Bret Saberhagen	.15	.07	.02
□ 22 Lenny Dykstra	.15	.07	.02
□ 23 Steve Howe	.05	.02	.01
□ 24 Mark Dewey	.05	.02	.01
□ 25 Brian Harper	.05	.02	.01
□ 26 Ozzie Smith	.40	.18	.05
□ 27 Scott Erickson	.05	.02	.01
□ 28 Tony Gwynn	.75	.35	.09
□ 29 Bob Welch	.05	.02	.01
□ 30 Barry Bonds	.50	.23	.06
□ 31 Leo Gomez	.05	.02	.01
□ 32 Greg Maddux	1.25	.55	.16
□ 33 Mike Greenwell	.05	.02	.01
□ 34 Sammy Sosa	.30	.14	.04
□ 35 Darnell Coles	.05	.02	.01
□ 36 Tommy Greene	.05	.02	.01
□ 37 Will Clark	.30	.14	.04
□ 38 Steve Ontiveros	.05	.02	.01
□ 39 Stan Javier	.05	.02	.01
□ 40 Bip Roberts	.05	.02	.01
□ 41 Paul O'Neill	.15	.07	.02
□ 42 Bill Haselman	.05	.02	.01
□ 43 Shane Mack	.05	.02	.01
□ 44 Orlando Merced	.05	.02	.01
□ 45 Kevin Seitzer	.05	.02	.01
□ 46 Trevor Hoffman	.05	.02	.01
□ 47 Greg Gagne	.05	.02	.01
□ 48 Jeff Kent	.05	.02	.01
□ 49 Tony Phillips	.15	.07	.02
□ 50 Ken Hill	.05	.02	.01
□ 51 Carlos Baerga	.30	.14	.04
□ 52 Henry Rodriguez	.30	.14	.04
□ 53 Scott Sanderson	.05	.02	.01
□ 54 Jeff Conine	.30	.14	.04
□ 55 Chris Turner	.05	.02	.01
□ 56 Ken Caminiti	.30	.14	.04
□ 57 Harold Baines	.15	.07	.02
□ 58 Charlie Hayes	.05	.02	.01
□ 59 Roberto Kelly	.05	.02	.01
□ 60 John Olerud	.05	.02	.01
□ 61 Tim Davis	.05	.02	.01
□ 62 Rich Rowland	.05	.02	.01
□ 63 Rey Sanchez	.05	.02	.01
□ 64 Junior Ortiz	.05	.02	.01
□ 65 Ricky Gutierrez	.05	.02	.01
□ 66 Rex Hudler	.05	.02	.01
□ 67 Johnny Ruffin	.05	.02	.01
□ 68 Jay Buhner	.30	.14	.04
□ 69 Tom Pagnozzi	.05	.02	.01
□ 70 Julio Franco	.15	.07	.02
□ 71 Eric Young	.15	.07	.02
□ 72 Mike Bordick	.05	.02	.01
□ 73 Don Slaught	.05	.02	.01
□ 74 Goose Gossage	.15	.07	.02
□ 75 Lonnie Smith	.05	.02	.01
□ 76 Jimmy Key	.15	.07	.02
□ 77 Dave Hollins	.05	.02	.01
□ 78 Mickey Tettleton	.05	.02	.01
□ 79 Luis Gonzalez	.05	.02	.01
□ 80 Dave Winfield	.30	.14	.04
□ 81 Ryan Thompson	.05	.02	.01
□ 82 Felix Jose	.05	.02	.01
□ 83 Rusty Meacham	.05	.02	.01
□ 84 Darryl Hamilton	.05	.02	.01
□ 85 John Wetteland	.15	.07	.02
□ 86 Tom Brunansky	.05	.02	.01
□ 87 Mark Lemke	.05	.02	.01
□ 88 Spike Owen	.05	.02	.01
□ 89 Shawon Dunston	.05	.02	.01
□ 90 Wilson Alvarez	.15	.07	.02
□ 91 Lee Smith	.15	.07	.02
□ 92 Scott Kamieniecki	.05	.02	.01
□ 93 Jacob Brumfield	.05	.02	.01
□ 94 Kirk Gibson	.15	.07	.02
□ 95 Joe Girardi	.05	.02	.01
□ 96 Mike Macfarlane	.05	.02	.01
□ 97 Greg Colbrunn	.05	.02	.01
□ 98 Ricky Bones	.05	.02	.01
□ 99 Delino DeShields	.05	.02	.01
□ 100 Pat Meares	.05	.02	.01
□ 101 Jeff Fassero	.05	.02	.01
□ 102 Jim Leyritz	.05	.02	.01
□ 103 Gary Redus	.05	.02	.01
□ 104 Terry Steinbach	.15	.07	.02
□ 105 Kevin McReynolds	.05	.02	.01
□ 106 Felix Fermin	.05	.02	.01
□ 107 Danny Jackson	.05	.02	.01
□ 108 Chris James	.05	.02	.01
□ 109 Jeff King	.15	.07	.02
□ 110 Pat Hentgen	.15	.07	.02
□ 111 Gerald Perry	.05	.02	.01
□ 112 Tim Raines	.30	.14	.04
□ 113 Eddie Williams	.05	.02	.01
□ 114 Jamie Moyer	.05	.02	.01
□ 115 Bud Black	.05	.02	.01
□ 116 Chris Gomez	.05	.02	.01
□ 117 Luis Lopez	.05	.02	.01
□ 118 Roger Clemens	.30	.14	.04
□ 119 Javier Lopez	.30	.14	.04
□ 120 Dave Nilsson	.15	.07	.02
□ 121 Karl Rhodes	.05	.02	.01
□ 122 Rick Aguilera	.05	.02	.01
□ 123 Tony Fernandez	.05	.02	.01
□ 124 Bernie Williams	.30	.14	.04
□ 125 James Mouton	.05	.02	.01
□ 126 Mark Langston	.05	.02	.01
□ 127 Mike Lansing	.05	.02	.01
□ 128 Tino Martinez	.15	.07	.02
□ 129 Joe Orsulak	.05	.02	.01
□ 130 David Hulse	.05	.02	.01
□ 131 Pete Incaviglia	.05	.02	.01
□ 132 Mark Clark	.05	.02	.01
□ 133 Tony Eusebio	.05	.02	.01
□ 134 Chuck Finley	.15	.07	.02
□ 135 Lou Frazier	.05	.02	.01
□ 136 Craig Grebeck	.05	.02	.01
□ 137 Kelly Stinnett	.05	.02	.01
□ 138 Paul Shuey	.05	.02	.01
□ 139 David Nied	.05	.02	.01
□ 140 Billy Brewer	.05	.02	.01
□ 141 Dave Weathers	.05	.02	.01
□ 142 Scott Leius	.05	.02	.01
□ 143 Brian Jordan	.30	.14	.04
□ 144 Melido Perez	.05	.02	.01
□ 145 Tony Tarasco	.05	.02	.01
□ 146 Dan Wilson	.15	.07	.02
□ 147 Rondell White	.30	.14	.04
□ 148 Mike Henneman	.05	.02	.01
□ 149 Brian Johnson	.05	.02	.01
□ 150 Tom Henke	.05	.02	.01
□ 151 John Patterson	.05	.02	.01
□ 152 Bobby Witt	.05	.02	.01
□ 153 Eddie Taubensee	.05	.02	.01
□ 154 Pat Borders	.05	.02	.01
□ 155 Ramon Martinez	.15	.07	.02
□ 156 Mike Kingery	.05	.02	.01
□ 157 Zane Smith	.05	.02	.01
□ 158 Benito Santiago	.05	.02	.01

☐	159 Matias Carrillo	.05	.02	.01
☐	160 Scott Brosius	.05	.02	.01
☐	161 Dave Clark	.05	.02	.01
☐	162 Mark McLemore	.05	.02	.01
☐	163 Curt Schilling	.05	.02	.01
☐	164 J.T. Snow	.15	.07	.02
☐	165 Rod Beck	.05	.02	.01
☐	166 Scott Fletcher	.05	.02	.01
☐	167 Bob Tewksbury	.05	.02	.01
☐	168 Mike LaValliere	.05	.02	.01
☐	169 Dave Hansen	.05	.02	.01
☐	170 Pedro Martinez	.15	.07	.02
☐	171 Kirk Rueter	.05	.02	.01
☐	172 Jose Lind	.05	.02	.01
☐	173 Luis Alicea	.05	.02	.01
☐	174 Mike Moore	.05	.02	.01
☐	175 Andy Ashby	.15	.07	.02
☐	176 Jody Reed	.05	.02	.01
☐	177 Darryl Kile	.05	.02	.01
☐	178 Carl Willis	.05	.02	.01
☐	179 Jeromy Burnitz	.05	.02	.01
☐	180 Mike Gallego	.05	.02	.01
☐	181 Bill VanLandingham	.05	.02	.01
☐	182 Sid Fernandez	.05	.02	.01
☐	183 Kim Batiste	.05	.02	.01
☐	184 Greg Myers	.05	.02	.01
☐	185 Steve Avery	.15	.07	.02
☐	186 Steve Farr	.05	.02	.01
☐	187 Robb Nen	.05	.02	.01
☐	188 Dan Pasqua	.05	.02	.01
☐	189 Bruce Ruffin	.05	.02	.01
☐	190 Jose Valentin	.15	.07	.02
☐	191 Willie Banks	.05	.02	.01
☐	192 Mike Aldrete	.05	.02	.01
☐	193 Randy Milligan	.05	.02	.01
☐	194 Steve Karsay	.05	.02	.01
☐	195 Mike Stanley	.05	.02	.01
☐	196 Jose Mesa	.05	.02	.01
☐	197 Tom Browning	.05	.02	.01
☐	198 John Vander Wal	.05	.02	.01
☐	199 Kevin Brown	.15	.07	.02
☐	200 Mike Oquist	.05	.02	.01
☐	201 Greg Swindell	.05	.02	.01
☐	202 Eddie Zambrano	.05	.02	.01
☐	203 Joe Boever	.05	.02	.01
☐	204 Gary Varsho	.05	.02	.01
☐	205 Chris Gwynn	.05	.02	.01
☐	206 David Howard	.05	.02	.01
☐	207 Jerome Walton	.05	.02	.01
☐	208 Danny Darwin	.05	.02	.01
☐	209 Darryl Strawberry	.15	.07	.02
☐	210 Todd Van Poppel	.05	.02	.01
☐	211 Scott Livingstone	.05	.02	.01
☐	212 Dave Fleming	.05	.02	.01
☐	213 Todd Worrell	.05	.02	.01
☐	214 Carlos Delgado	.30	.14	.04
☐	215 Bill Pecota	.05	.02	.01
☐	216 Jim Lindeman	.05	.02	.01
☐	217 Rick White	.05	.02	.01
☐	218 Jose Oquendo	.05	.02	.01
☐	219 Tony Castillo	.05	.02	.01
☐	220 Fernando Vina	.05	.02	.01
☐	221 Jeff Bagwell	.75	.35	.09
☐	222 Randy Johnson	.30	.14	.04
☐	223 Albert Belle	1.00	.45	.12
☐	224 Chuck Carr	.05	.02	.01
☐	225 Mark Leiter	.05	.02	.01
☐	226 Hal Morris	.05	.02	.01
☐	227 Robin Ventura	.15	.07	.02
☐	228 Mike Munoz	.05	.02	.01
☐	229 Jim Thome	.40	.18	.05
☐	230 Mario Diaz	.05	.02	.01
☐	231 John Doherty	.05	.02	.01
☐	232 Bobby Jones	.15	.07	.02
☐	233 Raul Mondesi	.30	.14	.04
☐	234 Ricky Jordan	.05	.02	.01
☐	235 John Jaha	.15	.07	.02
☐	236 Carlos Garcia	.05	.02	.01
☐	237 Kirby Puckett	.60	.25	.07
☐	238 Orel Hershiser	.15	.07	.02
☐	239 Don Mattingly	1.00	.45	.12
☐	240 Sid Bream	.05	.02	.01
☐	241 Brent Gates	.05	.02	.01
☐	242 Tony Longmire	.05	.02	.01
☐	243 Robby Thompson	.05	.02	.01
☐	244 Rick Sutcliffe	.05	.02	.01
☐	245 Dean Palmer	.15	.07	.02
☐	246 Marquis Grissom	.30	.14	.04
☐	247 Paul Molitor	.40	.18	.05
☐	248 Mark Carreon	.05	.02	.01
☐	249 Jack Voigt	.05	.02	.01
☐	250 Greg McMichael UER (photo on front is Mike Stanton)	.05	.02	.01
☐	251 Damon Berryhill	.05	.02	.01
☐	252 Brian Dorsett	.05	.02	.01
☐	253 Jim Edmonds	.30	.14	.04
☐	254 Barry Larkin	.30	.14	.04
☐	255 Jack McDowell	.15	.07	.02
☐	256 Wally Joyner	.15	.07	.02
☐	257 Eddie Murray	.50	.23	.06
☐	258 Lenny Webster	.05	.02	.01
☐	259 Milt Cuyler	.05	.02	.01
☐	260 Todd Benzinger	.05	.02	.01
☐	261 Vince Coleman	.05	.02	.01
☐	262 Todd Stottlemyre	.05	.02	.01
☐	263 Turner Ward	.05	.02	.01
☐	264 Ray Lankford	.30	.14	.04
☐	265 Matt Walbeck	.05	.02	.01
☐	266 Deion Sanders	.30	.14	.04
☐	267 Gerald Williams	.05	.02	.01
☐	268 Jim Gott	.05	.02	.01
☐	269 Jeff Frye	.05	.02	.01
☐	270 Jose Rijo	.05	.02	.01
☐	271 Dave Justice	.30	.14	.04
☐	272 Ismael Valdes	.15	.07	.02
☐	273 Ben McDonald	.05	.02	.01
☐	274 Darren Lewis	.05	.02	.01
☐	275 Graeme Lloyd	.05	.02	.01
☐	276 Luis Ortiz	.05	.02	.01
☐	277 Julian Tavarez	.05	.02	.01
☐	278 Mark Dalesandro	.05	.02	.01
☐	279 Brett Merriman	.05	.02	.01
☐	280 Ricky Bottalico	.15	.07	.02
☐	281 Robert Eenhoorn	.05	.02	.01
☐	282 Rikkert Faneyte	.05	.02	.01
☐	283 Mike Kelly	.05	.02	.01
☐	284 Mark Smith	.05	.02	.01
☐	285 Turk Wendell	.05	.02	.01
☐	286 Greg Blosser	.05	.02	.01
☐	287 Garey Ingram	.05	.02	.01
☐	288 Jorge Fabregas	.05	.02	.01
☐	289 Blaise Ilsley	.05	.02	.01
☐	290 Joe Hall	.05	.02	.01
☐	291 Orlando Miller	.05	.02	.01
☐	292 Jose Lima	.05	.02	.01
☐	293 Greg O'Halloran	.05	.02	.01
☐	294 Mark Kiefer	.05	.02	.01
☐	295 Jose Oliva	.05	.02	.01
☐	296 Rich Becker	.05	.02	.01
☐	297 Brian L. Hunter	.30	.14	.04
☐	298 Dave Silvestri	.05	.02	.01
☐	299 Armando Benitez	.05	.02	.01
☐	300 Darren Dreifort	.05	.02	.01
☐	301 John Mabry	.30	.14	.04
☐	302 Greg Pirkl	.05	.02	.01
☐	303 J.R. Phillips	.05	.02	.01
☐	304 Shawn Green	.15	.07	.02
☐	305 Roberto Petagine	.05	.02	.01
☐	306 Keith Lockhart	.05	.02	.01
☐	307 Jonathan Hurst	.05	.02	.01
☐	308 Paul Spoljaric	.05	.02	.01
☐	309 Mike Lieberthal	.05	.02	.01
☐	310 Garret Anderson	.30	.14	.04
☐	311 John Johnstone	.05	.02	.01
☐	312 Alex Rodriguez	2.50	1.10	.30
☐	313 Kent Mercker HL	.05	.02	.01
☐	314 John Valentin HL	.05	.02	.01
☐	315 Kenny Rogers HL	.05	.02	.01
☐	316 Fred McGriff HL	.15	.07	.02
☐	317 Team Checklists	.05	.02	.01
☐	318 Team Checklists	.05	.02	.01
☐	319 Team Checklists	.05	.02	.01
☐	320 Team Checklists	.05	.02	.01
☐	321 Team Checklists	.05	.02	.01
☐	322 Team Checklists	.05	.02	.01
☐	323 Team Checklists	.05	.02	.01
☐	324 Team Checklists	.05	.02	.01
☐	325 Team Checklists	.05	.02	.01
☐	326 Team Checklists	.05	.02	.01
☐	327 Team Checklists	.05	.02	.01
☐	328 Team Checklists	.05	.02	.01
☐	329 Team Checklists	.05	.02	.01

□ 330 Team Checklists	.05	.02	.01
□ 331 Pedro Munoz	.05	.02	.01
□ 332 Ryan Klesko	.40	.18	.05
□ 333 Andre Dawson	.30	.14	.04
□ 333T Andre Dawson Marlins UER (position listed as DH)	.30	.14	.04
□ 334 Derrick May	.05	.02	.01
□ 335 Aaron Sele	.15	.07	.02
□ 336 Kevin Mitchell	.15	.07	.02
□ 337 Steve Trachsel	.05	.02	.01
□ 338 Andres Galarraga	.30	.14	.04
□ 339 Terry Pendleton	.15	.07	.02
□ 339T Terry Pendleton Marlins	.15	.07	.02
□ 340 Gary Sheffield	.30	.14	.04
□ 341 Travis Fryman	.15	.07	.02
□ 342 Bo Jackson	.30	.14	.04
□ 343 Gary Gaetti	.15	.07	.02
□ 344 Brett Butler	.15	.07	.02
□ 344T Brett Butler Mets	.15	.07	.02
□ 345 B.J. Surhoff	.15	.07	.02
□ 346 Larry Walker	.30	.14	.04
□ 346T Larry Walker Rockies	.50	.23	.06
□ 347 Kevin Tapani	.05	.02	.01
□ 348 Rick Wilkins	.05	.02	.01
□ 349 Wade Boggs	.30	.14	.04
□ 350 Mariano Duncan	.05	.02	.01
□ 351 Ruben Sierra	.15	.07	.02
□ 352 Andy Van Slyke	.15	.07	.02
□ 352T Andy Van Slyke Orioles	.30	.14	.04
□ 353 Reggie Jefferson	.15	.07	.02
□ 354 Gregg Jefferies	.15	.07	.02
□ 355 Tim Naehring	.05	.02	.01
□ 356 John Roper	.05	.02	.01
□ 357 Joe Carter	.30	.14	.04
□ 358 Kurt Abbott	.05	.02	.01
□ 359 Lenny Harris	.05	.02	.01
□ 360 Lance Johnson	.15	.07	.02
□ 361 Brian Anderson	.05	.02	.01
□ 362 Jim Eisenreich	.05	.02	.01
□ 363 Jerry Browne	.05	.02	.01
□ 364 Mark Grace	.30	.14	.04
□ 365 Devon White	.15	.07	.02
□ 366 Reggie Sanders	.15	.07	.02
□ 367 Ivan Rodriguez	.40	.18	.05
□ 368 Kirt Manwaring	.05	.02	.01
□ 369 Pat Kelly	.05	.02	.01
□ 370 Ellis Burks	.30	.14	.04
□ 371 Charles Nagy	.15	.07	.02
□ 372 Kevin Bass	.05	.02	.01
□ 373 Lou Whitaker	.30	.14	.04
□ 374 Rene Arocha	.05	.02	.01
□ 375 Derek Parks	.05	.02	.01
□ 376 Mark Whiten	.05	.02	.01
□ 377 Mark McGwire	.60	.25	.07
□ 378 Doug Drabek	.05	.02	.01
□ 379 Greg Vaughn	.15	.07	.02
□ 380 Al Martin	.15	.07	.02
□ 381 Ron Darling	.05	.02	.01
□ 382 Tim Wallach	.05	.02	.01
□ 383 Alan Trammell	.30	.14	.04
□ 384 Randy Velarde	.05	.02	.01
□ 385 Chris Sabo	.05	.02	.01
□ 386 Wil Cordero	.05	.02	.01
□ 387 Darrin Fletcher	.05	.02	.01
□ 388 David Segui	.05	.02	.01
□ 389 Steve Buechele	.05	.02	.01
□ 390 Dave Gallagher	.05	.02	.01
□ 391 Thomas Howard	.05	.02	.01
□ 392 Chad Curtis	.05	.02	.01
□ 392T Chad Curtis Tigers	.30	.14	.04
□ 393 Cal Eldred	.05	.02	.01
□ 394 Jason Bere	.05	.02	.01
□ 395 Bret Barberie	.05	.02	.01
□ 396 Paul Sorrento	.05	.02	.01
□ 397 Steve Finley	.15	.07	.02
□ 398 Cecil Fielder	.15	.07	.02
□ 399 Eric Karros	.15	.07	.02
□ 400 Jeff Montgomery	.15	.07	.02
□ 401 Cliff Floyd	.15	.07	.02
□ 402 Matt Mieske	.15	.07	.02
□ 403 Brian Hunter	.05	.02	.01
□ 404 Alex Cole	.05	.02	.01
□ 405 Kevin Stocker	.05	.02	.01
□ 406 Eric Davis	.15	.07	.02
□ 407 Marvin Freeman	.05	.02	.01
□ 408 Dennis Eckersley	.15	.07	.02
□ 409 Todd Zeile	.05	.02	.01
□ 410 Keith Mitchell	.05	.02	.01
□ 411 Andy Benes	.05	.02	.01
□ 412 Juan Bell	.05	.02	.01
□ 413 Royce Clayton	.05	.02	.01
□ 414 Ed Sprague	.15	.07	.02
□ 415 Mike Mussina	.40	.18	.05
□ 416 Todd Hundley	.15	.07	.02
□ 417 Pat Listach	.05	.02	.01
□ 418 Joe Oliver	.05	.02	.01
□ 419 Rafael Palmeiro	.30	.14	.04
□ 420 Tim Salmon	.30	.14	.04
□ 421 Brady Anderson	.30	.14	.04
□ 422 Kenny Lofton	.50	.23	.06
□ 423 Craig Biggio	.30	.14	.04
□ 424 Bobby Bonilla	.15	.07	.02
□ 425 Kenny Rogers	.05	.02	.01
□ 426 Derek Bell	.15	.07	.02
□ 427 Scott Cooper	.05	.02	.01
□ 427T Scott Cooper Cardinals	.15	.07	.02
□ 428 Ozzie Guillen	.05	.02	.01
□ 429 Omar Vizquel	.30	.14	.04
□ 430 Phil Plantier	.05	.02	.01
□ 431 Chuck Knoblauch	.30	.14	.04
□ 432 Darren Daulton	.15	.07	.02
□ 433 Bob Hamelin	.05	.02	.01
□ 434 Tom Glavine	.30	.14	.04
□ 435 Walt Weiss	.05	.02	.01
□ 436 Jose Vizcaino	.05	.02	.01
□ 437 Ken Griffey Jr.	2.00	.90	.25
□ 438 Jay Bell	.15	.07	.02
□ 439 Juan Gonzalez	1.00	.45	.12
□ 440 Jeff Blauser	.05	.02	.01
□ 441 Rickey Henderson	.30	.14	.04
□ 442 Bobby Ayala	.05	.02	.01
□ 443 David Cone	.15	.07	.02
□ 443T David Cone Blue Jays	.25	.11	.03
□ 444 Pedro J. Martinez	.15	.07	.02
□ 445 Manny Ramirez	.50	.23	.06
□ 446 Mark Portugal	.05	.02	.01
□ 447 Damion Easley	.05	.02	.01
□ 448 Gary DiSarcina	.05	.02	.01
□ 449 Roberto Hernandez	.05	.02	.01
□ 450 Jeffrey Hammonds	.15	.07	.02
□ 451 Jeff Treadway	.05	.02	.01
□ 452 Jim Abbott	.05	.02	.01
□ 452T Jim Abbott White Sox	.30	.14	.04
□ 453 Carlos Rodriguez	.05	.02	.01
□ 454 Joey Cora	.05	.02	.01
□ 455 Bret Boone	.15	.07	.02
□ 456 Danny Tartabull	.05	.02	.01
□ 457 John Franco	.05	.02	.01
□ 458 Roger Salkeld	.05	.02	.01
□ 459 Fred McGriff	.30	.14	.04
□ 460 Pedro Astacio	.05	.02	.01
□ 461 Jon Lieber	.05	.02	.01
□ 462 Luis Polonia	.05	.02	.01
□ 463 Geronimo Pena	.05	.02	.01
□ 464 Tom Gordon	.05	.02	.01
□ 465 Brad Ausmus	.05	.02	.01
□ 466 Willie McGee	.05	.02	.01
□ 467 Doug Jones	.05	.02	.01
□ 468 John Smoltz	.30	.14	.04
□ 469 Troy Neel	.05	.02	.01
□ 470 Luis Sojo	.05	.02	.01
□ 471 John Smiley	.05	.02	.01
□ 472 Rafael Bournigal	.05	.02	.01
□ 473 Bill Taylor	.05	.02	.01
□ 474 Juan Guzman	.15	.07	.02
□ 475 Dave Magadan	.05	.02	.01
□ 476 Mike Devereaux	.05	.02	.01
□ 477 Andujar Cedeno	.05	.02	.01
□ 478 Edgar Martinez	.30	.14	.04
□ 479 Milt Thompson	.05	.02	.01
□ 480 Allen Watson	.05	.02	.01
□ 481 Ron Karkovice	.05	.02	.01
□ 482 Joey Hamilton	.15	.07	.02
□ 483 Vinny Castilla	.15	.07	.02
□ 484 Tim Belcher	.15	.07	.02
□ 485 Bernard Gilkey	.15	.07	.02
□ 486 Scott Servais	.05	.02	.01
□ 487 Cory Snyder	.05	.02	.01
□ 488 Mel Rojas	.05	.02	.01
□ 489 Carlos Reyes	.05	.02	.01
□ 490 Chip Hale	.05	.02	.01
□ 491 Bill Swift	.05	.02	.01

☐ 492 Pat Rapp	.05	.02	.01
☐ 493 Brian McRae	.15	.07	.02
☐ 493T Brian McRae Cubs	.30	.14	.04
☐ 494 Mickey Morandini	.05	.02	.01
☐ 495 Tony Pena	.05	.02	.01
☐ 496 Danny Bautista	.05	.02	.01
☐ 497 Armando Reynoso	.05	.02	.01
☐ 498 Ken Ryan	.05	.02	.01
☐ 499 Billy Ripken	.05	.02	.01
☐ 500 Pat Mahomes	.05	.02	.01
☐ 501 Mark Acre	.05	.02	.01
☐ 502 Geronimo Berroa	.05	.02	.01
☐ 503 Norberto Martin	.05	.02	.01
☐ 504 Chad Kreuter	.05	.02	.01
☐ 505 Howard Johnson	.05	.02	.01
☐ 506 Eric Anthony	.05	.02	.01
☐ 507 Mark Wohlers	.15	.07	.02
☐ 508 Scott Sanders	.05	.02	.01
☐ 509 Pete Harnisch	.05	.02	.01
☐ 510 Wes Chamberlain	.05	.02	.01
☐ 511 Tom Candiotti	.05	.02	.01
☐ 512 Albie Lopez	.05	.02	.01
☐ 513 Denny Neagle	.15	.07	.02
☐ 514 Sean Berry	.05	.02	.01
☐ 515 Billy Hatcher	.05	.02	.01
☐ 516 Todd Jones	.05	.02	.01
☐ 517 Wayne Kirby	.05	.02	.01
☐ 518 Butch Henry	.05	.02	.01
☐ 519 Sandy Alomar Jr.	.05	.02	.01
☐ 520 Kevin Appier	.15	.07	.02
☐ 521 Roberto Mejia	.05	.02	.01
☐ 522 Steve Cooke	.05	.02	.01
☐ 523 Terry Shumpert	.05	.02	.01
☐ 524 Mike Jackson	.05	.02	.01
☐ 525 Kent Mercker	.05	.02	.01
☐ 526 David Wells	.05	.02	.01
☐ 527 Juan Samuel	.05	.02	.01
☐ 528 Salomon Torres	.05	.02	.01
☐ 529 Duane Ward	.05	.02	.01
☐ 530 Rob Dibble	.05	.02	.01
☐ 530T Rob Dibble White Sox	.15	.07	.02
☐ 531 Mike Blowers	.05	.02	.01
☐ 532 Mark Eichhorn	.05	.02	.01
☐ 533 Alex Diaz	.05	.02	.01
☐ 534 Dan Miceli	.05	.02	.01
☐ 535 Jeff Branson	.05	.02	.01
☐ 536 Dave Stevens	.05	.02	.01
☐ 537 Charlie O'Brien	.05	.02	.01
☐ 538 Shane Reynolds	.05	.02	.01
☐ 539 Rich Amaral	.05	.02	.01
☐ 540 Rusty Greer	.30	.14	.04
☐ 541 Alex Arias	.05	.02	.01
☐ 542 Eric Plunk	.05	.02	.01
☐ 543 John Hudek	.05	.02	.01
☐ 544 Kirk McCaskill	.05	.02	.01
☐ 545 Jeff Reboulet	.05	.02	.01
☐ 546 Sterling Hitchcock	.15	.07	.02
☐ 547 Warren Newson	.05	.02	.01
☐ 548 Bryan Harvey	.05	.02	.01
☐ 549 Mike Huff	.05	.02	.01
☐ 550 Lance Parrish	.05	.02	.01
☐ 551 Ken Griffey Jr. HIT	1.00	.45	.12
☐ 552 Matt Williams HIT	.15	.07	.02
☐ 553 Roberto Alomar HIT UER (Card says he's a NL All-Star He plays in the AL)	.30	.14	.04
☐ 554 Jeff Bagwell HIT	.40	.18	.05
☐ 555 Dave Justice HIT	.15	.07	.02
☐ 556 Cal Ripken Jr. HIT	.75	.35	.09
☐ 557 Albert Belle HIT	.50	.23	.06
☐ 558 Mike Piazza HIT	.60	.25	.07
☐ 559 Kirby Puckett HIT	.30	.14	.04
☐ 560 Wade Boggs HIT	.30	.14	.04
☐ 561 Tony Gwynn HIT UER card has him winning AL batting titles he's played whole career in the NL	.40	.18	.05
☐ 562 Barry Bonds HIT	.30	.14	.04
☐ 563 Mo Vaughn HIT	.30	.14	.04
☐ 564 Don Mattingly HIT	.50	.23	.06
☐ 565 Carlos Baerga HIT	.15	.07	.02
☐ 566 Paul Molitor HIT	.30	.14	.04
☐ 567 Raul Mondesi HIT	.15	.07	.02
☐ 568 Manny Ramirez HIT	.30	.14	.04
☐ 569 Alex Rodriguez HIT	1.25	.55	.16
☐ 570 Will Clark HIT	.15	.07	.02
☐ 571 Frank Thomas HIT	1.00	.45	.12
☐ 572 Moises Alou HIT	.05	.02	.01
☐ 573 Jeff Conine HIT	.15	.07	.02
☐ 574 Joe Ausanio	.05	.02	.01
☐ 575 Charles Johnson	.15	.07	.02
☐ 576 Ernie Young	.15	.07	.02
☐ 577 Jeff Granger	.05	.02	.01
☐ 578 Robert Perez	.05	.02	.01
☐ 579 Melvin Nieves	.15	.07	.02
☐ 580 Gar Finnvold	.05	.02	.01
☐ 581 Duane Singleton	.05	.02	.01
☐ 582 Chan Ho Park	.30	.14	.04
☐ 583 Fausto Cruz	.05	.02	.01
☐ 584 Dave Staton	.05	.02	.01
☐ 585 Denny Hocking	.05	.02	.01
☐ 586 Nate Minchey	.05	.02	.01
☐ 587 Marc Newfield	.15	.07	.02
☐ 588 Jayhawk Owens UER Front Photo is Jim Tatum	.05	.02	.01
☐ 589 Darren Bragg	.15	.07	.02
☐ 590 Kevin King	.05	.02	.01
☐ 591 Kurt Miller	.05	.02	.01
☐ 592 Aaron Small	.05	.02	.01
☐ 593 Troy O'Leary	.05	.02	.01
☐ 594 Phil Stidham	.05	.02	.01
☐ 595 Steve Dunn	.05	.02	.01
☐ 596 Cory Bailey	.05	.02	.01
☐ 597 Alex Gonzalez	.05	.02	.01
☐ 598 Jim Bowie	.05	.02	.01
☐ 599 Jeff Cirillo	.15	.07	.02
☐ 600 Mark Hutton	.05	.02	.01
☐ 601 Russ Davis	.05	.02	.01
☐ 602 Checklist	.05	.02	.01
☐ 603 Checklist	.05	.02	.01
☐ 604 Checklist	.05	.02	.01
☐ 605 Checklist	.05	.02	.01
☐ RG1 R.Klesko Rook.Greatness	20.00	9.00	2.50
☐ SG1 Ryan Klesko AU/6100	40.00	18.00	5.00
☐ NNO Trade Hall of Gold	1.00	.45	.12

1995 Score Airmail

This 18-card set was randomly inserted in series two jumbo packs at a rate of one in eight. The fronts have a color photo of the player in a home run swing with the sky in the background. Broken red and blue inner borders frame the player. A gold stamp with the words "Air Mail" is prominent in upper left. The backs have a color photo with player information including how many home runs per at-bats he averaged. A sunset serves as background.

	MINT	NRMT	EXC
COMPLETE SET (18)	50.00	22.00	6.25
COMMON CARD (1-18)	2.00	.90	.25
RANDOM INSERTS IN SER.2 JUMBOS			

☐ AM1 Bob Hamelin	2.00	.90	.25
☐ AM2 John Mabry	2.50	1.10	.30
☐ AM3 Marc Newfield	2.50	1.10	.30
☐ AM4 Jose Oliva	2.00	.90	.25
☐ AM5 Charles Johnson	2.50	1.10	.30
☐ AM6 Russ Davis	2.00	.90	.25
☐ AM7 Ernie Young	2.50	1.10	.30
☐ AM8 Billy Ashley	2.00	.90	.25
☐ AM9 Ryan Klesko	6.00	2.70	.75
☐ AM10 J.R. Phillips	2.00	.90	.25
☐ AM11 Cliff Floyd	2.50	1.10	.30
☐ AM12 Carlos Delgado	4.00	1.80	.50

□ AM13	Melvin Nieves	2.50	1.10	.30
□ AM14	Raul Mondesi	4.00	1.80	.50
□ AM15	Manny Ramirez	8.00	3.60	1.00
□ AM16	Mike Kelly	2.00	.90	.25
□ AM17	Alex Rodriguez	30.00	13.50	3.70
□ AM18	Rusty Greer	3.00	1.35	.35

1995 Score Double Gold Champs

This 12-card set was randomly inserted in second series hobby packs at a rate of one in 36. Horizontally-designed fronts have a color action photo with the words "Double Gold Champs" in gold-foil at the bottom above the player's name. The backs have a color photo and a list of the player's accomplishments.

	MINT	NRMT	EXC
COMPLETE SET (12)	100.00	45.00	12.50
COMMON CARD (1-12)	2.50	1.10	.30
RANDOM INSERTS IN SER.2 HOBBY PACKS			

□ GC1	Frank Thomas	20.00	9.00	2.50
□ GC2	Ken Griffey Jr.	20.00	9.00	2.50
□ GC3	Barry Bonds	5.00	2.20	.60
□ GC4	Tony Gwynn	8.00	3.60	1.00
□ GC5	Don Mattingly	10.00	4.50	1.25
□ GC6	Greg Maddux	12.00	5.50	1.50
□ GC7	Roger Clemens	2.50	1.10	.30
□ GC8	Kenny Lofton	5.00	2.20	.60
□ GC9	Jeff Bagwell	8.00	3.60	1.00
□ GC10	Matt Williams	2.50	1.10	.30
□ GC11	Kirby Puckett	6.00	2.70	.75
□ GC12	Cal Ripken	15.00	6.75	1.85

1995 Score Draft Picks

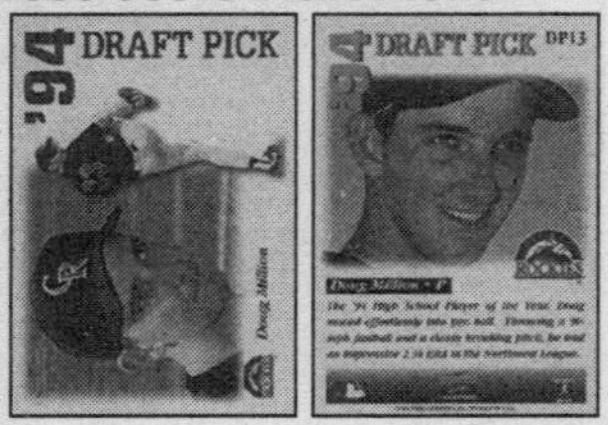

Randomly inserted in first series hobby packs at a rate of one in 36, this 18-card set takes a look at top picks selected in June of 1994. Horizontal fronts have two player photos on a white background. Vertical backs have a player photo and 1994 season's highlights. The cards are numbered with a DP prefix.

	MINT	NRMT	EXC
COMPLETE SET (18)	75.00	34.00	9.50
COMMON CARD (DP1-DP18)	3.00	1.35	.35
RANDOM INSERTS IN SERIES 1 HOBBY PACKS			

□ DP1	McKay Christensen	3.00	1.35	.35
□ DP2	Brett Wagner	3.00	1.35	.35
□ DP3	Paul Wilson	8.00	3.60	1.00
□ DP4	C.J. Nitkowski	3.00	1.35	.35
□ DP5	Josh Booty	6.00	2.70	.75
□ DP6	Antone Williamson	7.00	3.10	.85
□ DP7	Paul Konerko	15.00	6.75	1.85
□ DP8	Scott Elarton	5.00	2.20	.60
□ DP9	Jacob Shumate	3.00	1.35	.35
□ DP10	Terrance Long	5.00	2.20	.60
□ DP11	Mark Johnson	3.00	1.35	.35
□ DP12	Ben Grieve	12.00	5.50	1.50
□ DP13	Doug Million	5.00	2.20	.60
□ DP14	Jayson Peterson	3.00	1.35	.35
□ DP15	Dustin Hermanson	3.00	1.35	.35
□ DP16	Matt Smith	3.00	1.35	.35
□ DP17	Kevin Witt	4.00	1.80	.50
□ DP18	Brian Buchanan	3.00	1.35	.35

1995 Score Dream Team

Randomly inserted in first series hobby and retail packs at a rate of one in 72 packs, this 12-card hologram set showcases top performers from the 1994 season. The holographic fronts have two player images. The horizontal backs are not holographic. They are multi-colored with a small player close-up and a brief write-up. The cards are numbered with a DG prefix.

	MINT	NRMT	EXC
COMPLETE SET (12)	150.00	70.00	19.00
COMMON CARD (DG1-DG12)	2.50	1.10	.30
SEMISTARS	5.00	2.20	.60
RANDOM INSERTS IN SER.1 PACKS			

□ DG1	Frank Thomas	40.00	18.00	5.00
□ DG2	Roberto Alomar	10.00	4.50	1.25
□ DG3	Cal Ripken	30.00	13.50	3.70
□ DG4	Matt Williams	5.00	2.20	.60
□ DG5	Mike Piazza	25.00	11.00	3.10
□ DG6	Albert Belle	20.00	9.00	2.50
□ DG7	Ken Griffey Jr.	40.00	18.00	5.00
□ DG8	Tony Gwynn	15.00	6.75	1.85
□ DG9	Paul Molitor	8.00	3.60	1.00
□ DG10	Jimmy Key	2.50	1.10	.30
□ DG11	Greg Maddux	25.00	11.00	3.10
□ DG12	Lee Smith	5.00	2.20	.60

1995 Score Hall of Gold

Randomly inserted in packs at a rate one in six, this 110-card set is a collection of top stars and young hopefuls. Metallic fronts are presented in

shades of silver and gold that overlay a player photo. The Hall of Gold logo appears in the upper right-hand corner. Black backs contain a brief write-up and a player photo. The cards are numbered with an HG prefix. Five players who switched teams were issued later in the year. This five-card set, which was redeemed by mail with each Trade Hall of Gold card sent in, is not considered part of the complete set.

	MINT	NRMT	EXC
COMPLETE SET (110)	80.00	36.00	10.00
COMPLETE SERIES 1 (55)	50.00	22.00	6.25
COMPLETE SERIES 2 (55)	30.00	13.50	3.70
COMPLETE TRADE SET (5)	4.00	1.80	.50
COMMON CARD (HG1-HG110)	.50	.23	.06
SEMISTARS	1.00	.45	.12
STARS	1.50	.70	.19
RANDOM INSERTS IN PACKS			

□ HG1 Ken Griffey Jr.	12.00	5.50	1.50
□ HG2 Matt Williams	1.50	.70	.19
□ HG3 Roberto Alomar	3.00	1.35	.35
□ HG4 Jeff Bagwell	5.00	2.20	.60
□ HG5 Dave Justice	1.00	.45	.12
□ HG6 Cal Ripken	10.00	4.50	1.25
□ HG7 Randy Johnson	2.00	.90	.25
□ HG8 Barry Larkin	1.50	.70	.19
□ HG9 Albert Belle	6.00	2.70	.75
□ HG10 Mike Piazza	8.00	3.60	1.00
□ HG11 Kirby Puckett	4.00	1.80	.50
□ HG12 Moises Alou	.50	.23	.06
□ HG13 Jose Canseco	1.50	.70	.19
□ HG14 Tony Gwynn	5.00	2.20	.60
□ HG15 Roger Clemens	1.50	.70	.19
□ HG16 Barry Bonds	3.00	1.35	.35
□ HG17 Mo Vaughn	3.00	1.35	.35
□ HG18 Greg Maddux	8.00	3.60	1.00
□ HG19 Dante Bichette	1.50	.70	.19
□ HG20 Will Clark	1.50	.70	.19
□ HG21 Lenny Dykstra	1.00	.45	.12
□ HG22 Don Mattingly	6.00	2.70	.75
□ HG23 Carlos Baerga	1.50	.70	.19
□ HG24 Ozzie Smith	2.50	1.10	.30
□ HG25 Paul Molitor	2.50	1.10	.30
□ HG26 Paul O'Neill	1.00	.45	.12
□ HG27 Deion Sanders	1.50	.70	.19
□ HG28 Jeff Conine	1.50	.70	.19
□ HG29 John Olerud	.50	.23	.06
□ HG30 Jose Rijo	.50	.23	.06
□ HG31 Sammy Sosa	2.00	.90	.25
□ HG32 Robin Ventura	1.50	.70	.19
□ HG33 Raul Mondesi	1.50	.70	.19
□ HG34 Eddie Murray	3.00	1.35	.35
□ HG35 Marquis Grissom	1.50	.70	.19
□ HG36 Darryl Strawberry	1.50	.70	.19
□ HG37 Dave Nilsson	1.00	.45	.12
□ HG38 Manny Ramirez	3.00	1.35	.35
□ HG39 Delino DeShields	.50	.23	.06
□ HG40 Lee Smith	1.00	.45	.12
□ HG41 Alex Rodriguez	10.00	4.50	1.25
□ HG42 Julio Franco	.50	.23	.06
□ HG43 Bret Saberhagen	.50	.23	.06
□ HG44 Ken Hill	.50	.23	.06
□ HG45 Roberto Kelly	.50	.23	.06
□ HG46 Hal Morris	.50	.23	.06
□ HG47 Jimmy Key	.50	.23	.06
□ HG48 Terry Steinbach	.50	.23	.06
□ HG49 Mickey Tettleton	.50	.23	.06
□ HG50 Tony Phillips	.50	.23	.06
□ HG51 Carlos Garcia	.50	.23	.06
□ HG52 Jim Edmonds	1.50	.70	.19
□ HG53 Rod Beck	.50	.23	.06
□ HG54 Shane Mack	.50	.23	.06
□ HG55 Ken Caminiti	1.50	.70	.19
□ HG56 Frank Thomas	12.00	5.50	1.50
□ HG57 Kenny Lofton	3.00	1.35	.35
□ HG58 Juan Gonzalez	6.00	2.70	.75
□ HG59 Jason Bere	.50	.23	.06
□ HG60 Joe Carter	1.50	.70	.19
□ HG61 Gary Sheffield	2.00	.90	.25
□ HG62 Andres Galarraga	1.50	.70	.19
□ HG63 Ellis Burks	1.50	.70	.19
□ HG64 Bobby Bonilla	1.50	.70	.19
□ HG65 Tom Glavine	1.50	.70	.19
□ HG66 John Smoltz	2.00	.90	.25
□ HG67 Fred McGriff	1.50	.70	.19
□ HG68 Craig Biggio	1.50	.70	.19
□ HG69 Reggie Sanders	1.00	.45	.12
□ HG70 Kevin Mitchell	.50	.23	.06
□ HG71 Larry Walker	1.50	.70	.19
□ HG71T Larry Walker Rockies	2.00	.90	.25
□ HG72 Carlos Delgado	1.50	.70	.19
□ HG73 Alex Gonzalez	1.00	.45	.12
□ HG74 Ivan Rodriguez	2.50	1.10	.30
□ HG75 Ryan Klesko	2.50	1.10	.30
□ HG76 John Kruk	.50	.23	.06
□ HG76T John Kruk White Sox	1.00	.45	.12
□ HG77 Brian McRae	.50	.23	.06
□ HG77T Brian McRae Cubs	1.00	.45	.12
□ HG78 Tim Salmon	1.50	.70	.19
□ HG79 Travis Fryman	1.50	.70	.19
□ HG80 Chuck Knoblauch	1.00	.45	.12
□ HG81 Jay Bell	.50	.23	.06
□ HG82 Cecil Fielder	1.50	.70	.19
□ HG83 Cliff Floyd	1.00	.45	.12
□ HG84 Ruben Sierra	1.00	.45	.12
□ HG85 Mike Mussina	2.50	1.10	.30
□ HG86 Mark Grace	1.50	.70	.19
□ HG87 Dennis Eckersley	1.50	.70	.19
□ HG88 Dennis Martinez	1.00	.45	.12
□ HG89 Rafael Palmeiro	1.50	.70	.19
□ HG90 Ben McDonald	1.00	.45	.12
□ HG91 Dave Hollins	.50	.23	.06
□ HG92 Steve Avery	1.00	.45	.12
□ HG93 David Cone	1.00	.45	.12
□ HG93T David Cone Blue Jays	1.50	.70	.19
□ HG94 Darren Daulton	1.00	.45	.12
□ HG95 Bret Boone	.50	.23	.06
□ HG96 Wade Boggs	1.50	.70	.19
□ HG97 Doug Drabek	.50	.23	.06
□ HG98 Andy Benes	.50	.23	.06
□ HG99 Jim Thome	2.50	1.10	.30
□ HG100 Chili Davis	.50	.23	.06
□ HG101 Jeffrey Hammonds	.50	.23	.06
□ HG102 Rickey Henderson	1.50	.70	.19
□ HG103 Brett Butler	1.00	.45	.12
□ HG104 Tim Wallach	.50	.23	.06
□ HG105 Wil Cordero	.50	.23	.06
□ HG106 Mark Whiten	.50	.23	.06
□ HG107 Bob Hamelin	.50	.23	.06
□ HG108 Rondell White	1.00	.45	.12
□ HG109 Devon White	.50	.23	.06
□ HG110 Tony Tarasco	.50	.23	.06
□ HG110T Tony Tarasco Expos	1.00	.45	.12
□ NNO Trade Hall of Gold	2.00	.90	.25

1995 Score Rookie Dream Team

This 12-card set was randomly inserted in second series retail and hobby packs at a rate of one in 12. The fronts contain a color photo with a metallic background. The "Rookie Dream Team" title occupy two of the borders. The playerís name is at the bottom in gold-foil. The backs are horizontally designed, have a head shot and player information with the sky serving as a background. The cards are numbered with a RDT prefix.

	MINT	NRMT	EXC
COMPLETE SET (12)	60.00	27.00	7.50
COMMON CARD (1-12)	3.00	1.35	.35
SEMISTARS			

☐ RDT1 J.R. Phillips	3.00	1.35	.35
☐ RDT2 Alex Gonzalez	3.00	1.35	.35
☐ RDT3 Alex Rodriguez	40.00	18.00	5.00
☐ RDT4 Jose Oliva	3.00	1.35	.35
☐ RDT5 Charles Johnson	4.00	1.80	.50
☐ RDT6 Shawn Green	3.00	1.35	.35
☐ RDT7 Brian Hunter	6.00	2.70	.75
☐ RDT8 Garret Anderson	3.00	1.35	.35
☐ RDT9 Julian Tavarez	3.00	1.35	.35
☐ RDT10 Jose Lima	3.00	1.35	.35
☐ RDT11 Armando Benitez	3.00	1.35	.35
☐ RDT12 Ricky Bottalico	3.00	1.35	.35

1995 Score Rules

Randomly inserted in first series jumbo packs, this 30-card standard-size set features top big league players. Card fronts offer a player photo to the left. At right, the player's name is spelled vertically within a green vapor trail left by a baseball that is at the top. A horizontally designed back features three images of the player and a brief write-up. The cards are numbered with an "SR" prefix. A jumbo version of each card was produced as well. These 7 1/2" by 10 1/2" cards were issued in special Score collector kits. These cards were issued one per collector kit and were individually numbered out of 3,333. The value of these cards are currently the same as the standard-size cards.

	MINT	NRMT	EXC
COMPLETE SET (30)	125.00	55.00	15.50
COMMON CARD (SR1-SR30)	1.50	.70	.19
SEMISTARS	2.50	1.10	.30
RANDOM INSERTS IN SER.1 JUMBO PACKS			

☐ SR1 Ken Griffey Jr.	20.00	9.00	2.50
☐ SR2 Frank Thomas	20.00	9.00	2.50
☐ SR3 Mike Piazza	12.00	5.50	1.50
☐ SR4 Jeff Bagwell	8.00	3.60	1.00
☐ SR5 Alex Rodriguez	20.00	9.00	2.50
☐ SR6 Albert Belle	10.00	4.50	1.25
☐ SR7 Matt Williams	2.50	1.10	.30
☐ SR8 Roberto Alomar	5.00	2.20	.60
☐ SR9 Barry Bonds	5.00	2.20	.60
☐ SR10 Raul Mondesi	1.50	.70	.19
☐ SR11 Jose Canseco	2.50	1.10	.30
☐ SR12 Kirby Puckett	6.00	2.70	.75
☐ SR13 Fred McGriff	2.50	1.10	.30
☐ SR14 Kenny Lofton	5.00	2.20	.60
☐ SR15 Greg Maddux	12.00	5.50	1.50
☐ SR16 Juan Gonzalez	10.00	4.50	1.25
☐ SR17 Cliff Floyd	1.50	.70	.19
☐ SR18 Cal Ripken Jr.	15.00	6.75	1.85
☐ SR19 Will Clark	2.50	1.10	.30
☐ SR20 Tim Salmon	2.50	1.10	.30
☐ SR21 Paul O'Neill	1.50	.70	.19
☐ SR22 Jason Bere	1.50	.70	.19
☐ SR23 Tony Gwynn	8.00	3.60	1.00
☐ SR24 Manny Ramirez	5.00	2.20	.60
☐ SR25 Don Mattingly	10.00	4.50	1.25
☐ SR26 Dave Justice	2.50	1.10	.30
☐ SR27 Javier Lopez	2.50	1.10	.30
☐ SR28 Ryan Klesko	4.00	1.80	.50
☐ SR29 Carlos Delgado	2.50	1.10	.30
☐ SR30 Mike Mussina	4.00	1.80	.50

1996 Score

This set consists of 517 standard-size cards. These cards were issued in packs of 10 that retailed for 99 cents per pack. A Cal Ripken tribute card was issued at a rate of 1 every 300 packs. The fronts feature an action photo surrounded by white borders. The "Score 96" logo is in the upper left, while the player is identified on the bottom. The backs have season and career stats as well as a player photo and some text.

	MINT	NRMT	EXC
COMPLETE SET (517)	24.00	11.00	3.00
COMPLETE SERIES 1 (275)	12.00	5.50	1.50
COMPLETE SERIES 2 (242)	12.00	5.50	1.50
COMMON CARD (1-517)	.05	.02	.01
SEMISTARS	.15	.07	.02
STARS	.30	.14	.04
PRODUCED BY PINNACLE			

☐ 1 Will Clark	.30	.14	.04
☐ 2 Rich Becker	.15	.07	.02
☐ 3 Ryan Klesko	.40	.18	.05
☐ 4 Jim Edmonds	.30	.14	.04
☐ 5 Barry Larkin	.30	.14	.04
☐ 6 Jim Thome	.40	.18	.05
☐ 7 Raul Mondesi	.30	.14	.04
☐ 8 Don Mattingly	1.00	.45	.12
☐ 9 Jeff Conine	.30	.14	.04
☐ 10 Rickey Henderson	.30	.14	.04
☐ 11 Chad Curtis	.05	.02	.01
☐ 12 Darren Daulton	.15	.07	.02
☐ 13 Larry Walker	.30	.14	.04
☐ 14 Carlos Garcia	.05	.02	.01
☐ 15 Carlos Baerga	.30	.14	.04
☐ 16 Tony Gwynn	.75	.35	.09
☐ 17 Jon Nunnally	.05	.02	.01
☐ 18 Deion Sanders	.30	.14	.04
☐ 19 Mark Grace	.30	.14	.04
☐ 20 Alex Rodriguez	2.00	.90	.25
☐ 21 Frank Thomas	2.00	.90	.25
☐ 22 Brian Jordan	.30	.14	.04
☐ 23 J.T. Snow	.15	.07	.02
☐ 24 Shawn Green	.15	.07	.02
☐ 25 Tim Wakefield	.05	.02	.01
☐ 26 Curtis Goodwin	.05	.02	.01
☐ 27 John Smoltz	.30	.14	.04
☐ 28 Devon White	.05	.02	.01
☐ 29 Johnny Damon	.15	.07	.02
☐ 30 Tim Salmon	.30	.14	.04
☐ 31 Rafael Palmeiro	.30	.14	.04
☐ 32 Bernard Gilkey	.15	.07	.02
☐ 33 John Valentin	.15	.07	.02
☐ 34 Randy Johnson	.30	.14	.04
☐ 35 Garret Anderson	.30	.14	.04
☐ 36 Rikkert Faneyte	.05	.02	.01
☐ 37 Ray Durham	.30	.14	.04
☐ 38 Bip Roberts	.05	.02	.01
☐ 39 Jaime Navarro	.05	.02	.01
☐ 40 Mark Johnson	.05	.02	.01
☐ 41 Darren Lewis	.05	.02	.01
☐ 42 Tyler Green	.05	.02	.01
☐ 43 Bill Pulsipher	.15	.07	.02
☐ 44 Jason Giambi	.30	.14	.04
☐ 45 Kevin Ritz	.05	.02	.01
☐ 46 Jack McDowell	.30	.14	.04
☐ 47 Felipe Lira	.05	.02	.01

□ 48 Rico Brogna	.05	.02	.01
□ 49 Terry Pendleton	.15	.07	.02
□ 50 Rondell White	.30	.14	.04
□ 51 Andre Dawson	.30	.14	.04
□ 52 Kirby Puckett	.60	.25	.07
□ 53 Wally Joyner	.05	.02	.01
□ 54 B.J. Surhoff	.05	.02	.01
□ 55 Randy Velarde	.05	.02	.01
□ 56 Greg Vaughn	.30	.14	.04
□ 57 Roberto Alomar	.50	.23	.06
□ 58 David Justice	.15	.07	.02
□ 59 Kevin Seitzer	.05	.02	.01
□ 60 Cal Ripken	1.50	.70	.19
□ 61 Ozzie Smith	.40	.18	.05
□ 62 Mo Vaughn	.50	.23	.06
□ 63 Ricky Bones	.05	.02	.01
□ 64 Gary DiSarcina	.05	.02	.01
□ 65 Matt Williams	.30	.14	.04
□ 66 Wilson Alvarez	.30	.14	.04
□ 67 Lenny Dykstra	.15	.07	.02
□ 68 Brian McRae	.05	.02	.01
□ 69 Todd Stottlemyre	.05	.02	.01
□ 70 Bret Boone	.05	.02	.01
□ 71 Sterling Hitchcock	.05	.02	.01
□ 72 Albert Belle	1.00	.45	.12
□ 73 Todd Hundley	.30	.14	.04
□ 74 Vinny Castilla	.30	.14	.04
□ 75 Moises Alou	.15	.07	.02
□ 76 Cecil Fielder	.30	.14	.04
□ 77 Brad Radke	.05	.02	.01
□ 78 Quilvio Veras	.05	.02	.01
□ 79 Eddie Murray	.50	.23	.06
□ 80 James Mouton	.05	.02	.01
□ 81 Pat Listach	.05	.02	.01
□ 82 Mark Gubicza	.05	.02	.01
□ 83 Dave Winfield	.30	.14	.04
□ 84 Fred McGriff	.30	.14	.04
□ 85 Darryl Hamilton	.05	.02	.01
□ 86 Jeffrey Hammonds	.05	.02	.01
□ 87 Pedro Munoz	.05	.02	.01
□ 88 Craig Biggio	.30	.14	.04
□ 89 Cliff Floyd	.05	.02	.01
□ 90 Tim Naehring	.15	.07	.02
□ 91 Brett Butler	.05	.02	.01
□ 92 Kevin Foster	.05	.02	.01
□ 93 Pat Kelly	.05	.02	.01
□ 94 John Smiley	.05	.02	.01
□ 95 Terry Steinbach	.15	.07	.02
□ 96 Orel Hershiser	.15	.07	.02
□ 97 Darrin Fletcher	.05	.02	.01
□ 98 Walt Weiss	.05	.02	.01
□ 99 John Wetteland	.15	.07	.02
□ 100 Alan Trammell	.30	.14	.04
□ 101 Steve Avery	.15	.07	.02
□ 102 Tony Eusebio	.05	.02	.01
□ 103 Sandy Alomar Jr.	.05	.02	.01
□ 104 Joe Girardi	.05	.02	.01
□ 105 Rick Aguilera	.05	.02	.01
□ 106 Tony Tarasco	.05	.02	.01
□ 107 Chris Hammond	.05	.02	.01
□ 108 Mike Macfarlane	.05	.02	.01
□ 109 Doug Drabek	.05	.02	.01
□ 110 Derek Bell	.15	.07	.02
□ 111 Ed Sprague	.15	.07	.02
□ 112 Todd Hollandsworth	.30	.14	.04
□ 113 Otis Nixon	.05	.02	.01
□ 114 Keith Lockhart	.05	.02	.01
□ 115 Donovan Osborne	.05	.02	.01
□ 116 Dave Magadan	.05	.02	.01
□ 117 Edgar Martinez	.30	.14	.04
□ 118 Chuck Carr	.05	.02	.01
□ 119 J.R. Phillips	.05	.02	.01
□ 120 Sean Bergman	.05	.02	.01
□ 121 Andujar Cedeno	.05	.02	.01
□ 122 Eric Young	.05	.02	.01
□ 123 Al Martin	.05	.02	.01
□ 124 Mark Lemke	.05	.02	.01
□ 125 Jim Eisenreich	.05	.02	.01
□ 126 Benito Santiago	.05	.02	.01
□ 127 Ariel Prieto	.05	.02	.01
□ 128 Jim Bullinger	.05	.02	.01
□ 129 Russ Davis	.05	.02	.01
□ 130 Jim Abbott	.30	.14	.04
□ 131 Jason Isringhausen	.15	.07	.02
□ 132 Carlos Perez	.05	.02	.01
□ 133 David Segui	.05	.02	.01
□ 134 Troy O'Leary	.15	.07	.02
□ 135 Pat Meares	.05	.02	.01
□ 136 Chris Hoiles	.05	.02	.01
□ 137 Ismael Valdes	.15	.07	.02
□ 138 Jose Oliva	.05	.02	.01
□ 139 Carlos Delgado	.15	.07	.02
□ 140 Tom Goodwin	.15	.07	.02
□ 141 Bob Tewksbury	.05	.02	.01
□ 142 Chris Gomez	.05	.02	.01
□ 143 Jose Oquendo	.05	.02	.01
□ 144 Mark Lewis	.05	.02	.01
□ 145 Salomon Torres	.05	.02	.01
□ 146 Luis Gonzalez	.05	.02	.01
□ 147 Mark Carreon	.05	.02	.01
□ 148 Lance Johnson	.15	.07	.02
□ 149 Melvin Nieves	.15	.07	.02
□ 150 Lee Smith	.30	.14	.04
□ 151 Jacob Brumfield	.05	.02	.01
□ 152 Armando Benitez	.05	.02	.01
□ 153 Curt Schilling	.05	.02	.01
□ 154 Javier Lopez	.30	.14	.04
□ 155 Frank Rodriguez	.15	.07	.02
□ 156 Alex Gonzalez	.05	.02	.01
□ 157 Todd Worrell	.15	.07	.02
□ 158 Benji Gil	.05	.02	.01
□ 159 Greg Gagne	.05	.02	.01
□ 160 Tom Henke	.15	.07	.02
□ 161 Randy Myers	.05	.02	.01
□ 162 Joey Cora	.05	.02	.01
□ 163 Scott Ruffcorn	.05	.02	.01
□ 164 W. VanLandingham	.05	.02	.01
□ 165 Tony Phillips	.15	.07	.02
□ 166 Eddie Williams	.05	.02	.01
□ 167 Bobby Bonilla	.30	.14	.04
□ 168 Denny Neagle	.15	.07	.02
□ 169 Troy Percival	.15	.07	.02
□ 170 Billy Ashley	.05	.02	.01
□ 171 Andy Van Slyke	.15	.07	.02
□ 172 Jose Offerman	.05	.02	.01
□ 173 Mark Parent	.05	.02	.01
□ 174 Edgardo Alfonzo	.15	.07	.02
□ 175 Trevor Hoffman	.15	.07	.02
□ 176 David Cone	.30	.14	.04
□ 177 Dan Wilson	.05	.02	.01
□ 178 Steve Ontiveros	.05	.02	.01
□ 179 Dean Palmer	.30	.14	.04
□ 180 Mike Kelly	.05	.02	.01
□ 181 Jim Leyritz	.05	.02	.01
□ 182 Ron Karkovice	.05	.02	.01
□ 183 Kevin Brown	.15	.07	.02
□ 184 Jose Valentin	.05	.02	.01
□ 185 Jorge Fabregas	.05	.02	.01
□ 186 Jose Mesa	.15	.07	.02
□ 187 Brent Mayne	.05	.02	.01
□ 188 Carl Everett	.05	.02	.01
□ 189 Paul Sorrento	.05	.02	.01
□ 190 Pete Schourek	.30	.14	.04
□ 191 Scott Kamieniecki	.05	.02	.01
□ 192 Roberto Hernandez	.15	.07	.02
□ 193 Randy Johnson RR	.30	.14	.04
□ 194 Greg Maddux RR	.60	.25	.07
□ 195 Hideo Nomo RR	.30	.14	.04
□ 196 David Cone RR	.30	.14	.04
□ 197 Mike Mussina RR	.30	.14	.04
□ 198 Andy Benes RR	.05	.02	.01
□ 199 Kevin Appier RR	.05	.02	.01
□ 200 John Smoltz RR	.30	.14	.04
□ 201 John Wetteland RR	.15	.07	.02
□ 202 Mark Wohlers RR	.15	.07	.02
□ 203 Stan Belinda	.05	.02	.01
□ 204 Brian Anderson	.05	.02	.01
□ 205 Mike Devereaux	.05	.02	.01
□ 206 Mark Wohlers	.15	.07	.02
□ 207 Omar Vizquel	.05	.02	.01
□ 208 Jose Rijo	.05	.02	.01
□ 209 Willie Blair	.05	.02	.01
□ 210 Jamie Moyer	.05	.02	.01
□ 211 Craig Shipley	.05	.02	.01
□ 212 Shane Reynolds	.15	.07	.02
□ 213 Chad Fonville	.05	.02	.01
□ 214 Jose Vizcaino	.05	.02	.01
□ 215 Sid Fernandez	.05	.02	.01
□ 216 Andy Ashby	.05	.02	.01
□ 217 Frank Castillo	.05	.02	.01
□ 218 Kevin Tapani	.05	.02	.01
□ 219 Kent Mercker	.05	.02	.01

□	220	Karim Garcia	.40	.18	.05
□	221	Antonio Osuna	.05	.02	.01
□	222	Tim Unroe	.05	.02	.01
□	223	Johnny Damon	.30	.14	.04
□	224	LaTroy Hawkins	.05	.02	.01
□	225	Mariano Rivera	.30	.14	.04
□	226	Jose Alberro	.05	.02	.01
□	227	Angel Martinez	.05	.02	.01
□	228	Jason Schmidt	.15	.07	.02
□	229	Tony Clark	.30	.14	.04
□	230	Kevin Jordan UER	.05	.02	.01
		Ricky Jordan pictured on both sides			
□	231	Mark Thompson	.05	.02	.01
□	232	Jim Dougherty	.05	.02	.01
□	233	Roger Cedeno	.15	.07	.02
□	234	Ugueth Urbina	.05	.02	.01
□	235	Ricky Otero	.05	.02	.01
□	236	Mark Smith	.05	.02	.01
□	237	Brian Barber	.05	.02	.01
□	238	Kevin Flora	.05	.02	.01
□	239	Joe Rosselli	.05	.02	.01
□	240	Derek Jeter	1.25	.55	.16
□	241	Michael Tucker	.15	.07	.02
□	242	Ben Blomdahl	.05	.02	.01
□	243	Joe Vitiello	.05	.02	.01
□	244	Todd Steverson	.05	.02	.01
□	245	James Baldwin	.30	.14	.04
□	246	Alan Embree	.05	.02	.01
□	247	Shannon Penn	.05	.02	.01
□	248	Chris Stynes	.05	.02	.01
□	249	Oscar Munoz	.05	.02	.01
□	250	Jose Herrera	.05	.02	.01
□	251	Scott Sullivan	.05	.02	.01
□	252	Reggie Williams	.05	.02	.01
□	253	Mark Grudzielanek	.05	.02	.01
□	254	Steve Rodriguez	.05	.02	.01
□	255	Terry Bradshaw	.05	.02	.01
□	256	F.P. Santangelo	.05	.02	.01
□	257	Lyle Mouton	.05	.02	.01
□	258	George Williams	.05	.02	.01
□	259	Larry Thomas	.05	.02	.01
□	260	Rudy Pemberton	.05	.02	.01
□	261	Jim Pittsley	.15	.07	.02
□	262	Les Norman	.05	.02	.01
□	263	Ruben Rivera	.40	.18	.05
□	264	Cesar Devarez	.05	.02	.01
□	265	Greg Zaun	.05	.02	.01
□	266	Dustin Hermanson	.15	.07	.02
□	267	John Frascatore	.05	.02	.01
□	268	Joe Randa	.05	.02	.01
□	269	Jeff Bagwell CL	.40	.18	.05
□	270	Mike Piazza CL	.60	.25	.07
□	271	Dante Bichette CL	.15	.07	.02
□	272	Frank Thomas CL	1.00	.45	.12
□	273	Ken Griffey Jr. CL	1.00	.45	.12
□	274	Cal Ripken CL	.75	.35	.09
□	275	Greg Maddux CL	.60	.25	.07
		Albert Belle			
□	276	Greg Maddux	1.25	.55	.16
□	277	Pedro Martinez	.15	.07	.02
□	278	Bobby Higginson	.30	.14	.04
□	279	Ray Lankford	.30	.14	.04
□	280	Shawon Dunston	.05	.02	.01
□	281	Gary Sheffield	.30	.14	.04
□	282	Ken Griffey, Jr.	2.00	.90	.25
□	283	Paul Molitor	.40	.18	.05
□	284	Kevin Appier	.15	.07	.02
□	285	Chuck Knoblauch	.30	.14	.04
□	286	Alex Fernandez	.30	.14	.04
□	287	Steve Finley	.30	.14	.04
□	288	Jeff Blauser	.05	.02	.01
□	289	Charles Johnson	.15	.07	.02
□	290	John Franco	.05	.02	.01
□	291	Mark Langston	.05	.02	.01
□	292	Bret Saberhagen	.05	.02	.01
□	293	John Mabry	.30	.14	.04
□	294	Ramon Martinez	.30	.14	.04
□	295	Mike Blowers	.05	.02	.01
□	296	Paul O'Neill	.05	.02	.01
□	297	Dave Nilsson	.15	.07	.02
□	298	Dante Bichette	.15	.07	.02
□	299	Marty Cordova	.30	.14	.04
□	300	Jay Bell	.15	.07	.02
□	301	Mike Mussina	.40	.18	.05
□	302	Ivan Rodriguez	.40	.18	.05
□	303	Jose Canseco	.30	.14	.04

□	304	Jeff Bagwell	.75	.35	.09
□	305	Manny Ramirez	.50	.23	.06
□	306	Dennis Martinez	.15	.07	.02
□	307	Charlie Hayes	.05	.02	.01
□	308	Joe Carter	.30	.14	.04
□	309	Travis Fryman	.30	.14	.04
□	310	Mark McGwire	.60	.25	.07
□	311	Reggie Sanders UER	.15	.07	.02
		Photo on front is John Roper			
□	312	Julian Tavarez	.05	.02	.01
□	313	Jeff Montgomery	.05	.02	.01
□	314	Andy Benes	.05	.02	.01
□	315	John Jaha	.15	.07	.02
□	316	Jeff Kent	.05	.02	.01
□	317	Mike Piazza	1.25	.55	.16
□	318	Erik Hanson	.05	.02	.01
□	319	Kenny Rogers	.05	.02	.01
□	320	Hideo Nomo	.50	.23	.06
□	321	Gregg Jefferies	.30	.14	.04
□	322	Chipper Jones	1.25	.55	.16
□	323	Jay Buhner	.30	.14	.04
□	324	Dennis Eckersley	.30	.14	.04
□	325	Kenny Lofton	.50	.23	.06
□	326	Robin Ventura	.30	.14	.04
□	327	Tom Glavine	.30	.14	.04
□	328	Tim Salmon	.30	.14	.04
□	329	Andres Galarraga	.30	.14	.04
□	330	Hal Morris	.05	.02	.01
□	331	Brady Anderson	.30	.14	.04
□	332	Chili Davis	.05	.02	.01
□	333	Roger Clemens	.30	.14	.04
□	334	Marquis Grissom	.30	.14	.04
□	335	Mike Greenwell UER	.05	.02	.01
		Name spelled Jeff on Front			
□	336	Sammy Sosa	.30	.14	.04
□	337	Ron Gant	.30	.14	.04
□	338	Ken Caminiti	.30	.14	.04
□	339	Danny Tartabull	.05	.02	.01
□	340	Barry Bonds	.50	.23	.06
□	341	Ben McDonald	.05	.02	.01
□	342	Ruben Sierra	.05	.02	.01
□	343	Bernie Williams	.30	.14	.04
□	344	Wil Cordero	.05	.02	.01
□	345	Wade Boggs	.30	.14	.04
□	346	Gary Gaetti	.15	.07	.02
□	347	Greg Colbrunn	.05	.02	.01
□	348	Juan Gonzalez	1.00	.45	.12
□	349	Marc Newfield	.05	.02	.01
□	350	Charles Nagy	.05	.02	.01
□	351	Robby Thompson	.05	.02	.01
□	352	Roberto Petagine	.05	.02	.01
□	353	Darryl Strawberry	.30	.14	.04
□	354	Tino Martinez	.05	.02	.01
□	355	Eric Karros	.05	.02	.01
□	356	Cal Ripken SS	.75	.35	.09
□	357	Cecil Fielder SS	.30	.14	.04
□	358	Kirby Puckett SS	.30	.14	.04
□	359	Jim Edmonds SS	.15	.07	.02
□	360	Matt Williams SS	.30	.14	.04
□	361	Alex Rodriguez SS	1.00	.45	.12
□	362	Barry Larkin SS	.30	.14	.04
□	363	Rafael Palmeiro SS	.30	.14	.04
□	364	David Cone SS	.30	.14	.04
□	365	Roberto Alomar SS	.30	.14	.04
□	366	Eddie Murray SS	.30	.14	.04
□	367	Randy Johnson SS	.30	.14	.04
□	368	Ryan Klesko SS	.15	.07	.02
□	369	Raul Mondesi SS	.15	.07	.02
□	370	Mo Vaughn SS	.30	.14	.04
□	371	Will Clark SS	.30	.14	.04
□	372	Carlos Baerga SS	.15	.07	.02
□	373	Frank Thomas SS	1.00	.45	.12
□	374	Larry Walker SS	.05	.02	.01
□	375	Garret Anderson SS	.05	.02	.01
□	376	Edgar Martinez SS	.30	.14	.04
□	377	Don Mattingly SS	.50	.23	.06
□	378	Tony Gwynn SS	.40	.18	.05
□	379	Albert Belle SS	.50	.23	.06
□	380	Jason Isringhausen SS	.05	.02	.01
□	381	Ruben Rivera SS	.15	.07	.02
□	382	Johnny Damon SS	.05	.02	.01
□	383	Karim Garcia SS	.05	.02	.01
□	384	Derek Jeter SS	.50	.23	.06
□	385	David Justice SS	.05	.02	.01
□	386	Royce Clayton	.05	.02	.01
□	387	Mark Whiten	.05	.02	.01

☐ 388 Mickey Tettleton	.15	.07	.02
☐ 389 Steve Trachsel	.05	.02	.01
☐ 390 Danny Bautista	.05	.02	.01
☐ 391 Midre Cummings	.05	.02	.01
☐ 392 Scott Leius	.05	.02	.01
☐ 393 Manny Alexander	.05	.02	.01
☐ 394 Brent Gates	.05	.02	.01
☐ 395 Rey Sanchez	.05	.02	.01
☐ 396 Andy Pettitte	.60	.25	.07
☐ 397 Jeff Cirillo	.05	.02	.01
☐ 398 Kurt Abbott	.05	.02	.01
☐ 399 Lee Tinsley	.05	.02	.01
☐ 400 Paul Assenmacher	.05	.02	.01
☐ 401 Scott Erickson	.05	.02	.01
☐ 402 Todd Zeile	.05	.02	.01
☐ 403 Tom Pagnozzi	.05	.02	.01
☐ 404 Ozzie Guillen	.05	.02	.01
☐ 405 Jeff Frye	.05	.02	.01
☐ 406 Kirt Manwaring	.05	.02	.01
☐ 407 Chad Ogea	.05	.02	.01
☐ 408 Harold Baines	.15	.07	.02
☐ 409 Jason Bere	.05	.02	.01
☐ 410 Chuck Finley	.05	.02	.01
☐ 411 Jeff Fassero	.05	.02	.01
☐ 412 Joey Hamilton	.15	.07	.02
☐ 413 John Olerud	.05	.02	.01
☐ 414 Kevin Stocker	.05	.02	.01
☐ 415 Eric Anthony	.05	.02	.01
☐ 416 Aaron Sele	.05	.02	.01
☐ 417 Chris Bosio	.05	.02	.01
☐ 418 Michael Mimbs	.05	.02	.01
☐ 419 Orlando Miller	.05	.02	.01
☐ 420 Stan Javier	.05	.02	.01
☐ 421 Matt Mieske	.05	.02	.01
☐ 422 Jason Bates	.05	.02	.01
☐ 423 Orlando Merced	.15	.07	.02
☐ 424 John Flaherty	.05	.02	.01
☐ 425 Reggie Jefferson	.05	.02	.01
☐ 426 Scott Stahoviak	.05	.02	.01
☐ 427 John Burkett	.05	.02	.01
☐ 428 Rod Beck	.05	.02	.01
☐ 429 Bill Swift	.05	.02	.01
☐ 430 Scott Cooper	.05	.02	.01
☐ 431 Mel Rojas	.05	.02	.01
☐ 432 Todd Van Poppel	.05	.02	.01
☐ 433 Bobby Jones	.05	.02	.01
☐ 434 Mike Harkey	.05	.02	.01
☐ 435 Sean Berry	.05	.02	.01
☐ 436 Glenallen Hill	.05	.02	.01
☐ 437 Ryan Thompson	.05	.02	.01
☐ 438 Luis Alicea	.05	.02	.01
☐ 439 Esteban Loaiza	.05	.02	.01
☐ 440 Jeff Reboulet	.05	.02	.01
☐ 441 Vince Coleman	.05	.02	.01
☐ 442 Ellis Burks	.30	.14	.04
☐ 443 Allen Battle	.05	.02	.01
☐ 444 Jimmy Key	.15	.07	.02
☐ 445 Ricky Bottalico	.05	.02	.01
☐ 446 Delino DeShields	.05	.02	.01
☐ 447 Albie Lopez	.05	.02	.01
☐ 448 Mark Petkovsek	.05	.02	.01
☐ 449 Tim Raines	.30	.14	.04
☐ 450 Bryan Harvey	.05	.02	.01
☐ 451 Pat Hentgen	.30	.14	.04
☐ 452 Tim Laker	.05	.02	.01
☐ 453 Tom Gordon	.05	.02	.01
☐ 454 Phil Plantier	.05	.02	.01
☐ 455 Ernie Young	.05	.02	.01
☐ 456 Pete Harnisch	.05	.02	.01
☐ 457 Roberto Kelly	.05	.02	.01
☐ 458 Mark Portugal	.05	.02	.01
☐ 459 Mark Leiter	.05	.02	.01
☐ 460 Tony Pena	.05	.02	.01
☐ 461 Roger Pavlik	.05	.02	.01
☐ 462 Jeff King	.15	.07	.02
☐ 463 Bryan Rekar	.05	.02	.01
☐ 464 Al Leiter	.05	.02	.01
☐ 465 Phil Nevin	.05	.02	.01
☐ 466 Jose Lima	.05	.02	.01
☐ 467 Mike Stanley	.05	.02	.01
☐ 468 David McCarty	.05	.02	.01
☐ 469 Herb Perry	.05	.02	.01
☐ 470 Geronimo Berroa	.15	.07	.02
☐ 471 David Wells	.05	.02	.01
☐ 472 Vaughn Eshelman	.05	.02	.01
☐ 473 Greg Swindell	.05	.02	.01
☐ 474 Steve Sparks	.05	.02	.01
☐ 475 Luis Sojo	.05	.02	.01
☐ 476 Derrick May	.05	.02	.01
☐ 477 Joe Oliver	.05	.02	.01
☐ 478 Alex Arias	.05	.02	.01
☐ 479 Brad Ausmus	.05	.02	.01
☐ 480 Gabe White	.05	.02	.01
☐ 481 Pat Rapp	.05	.02	.01
☐ 482 Damon Buford	.05	.02	.01
☐ 483 Turk Wendell	.05	.02	.01
☐ 484 Jeff Brantley	.05	.02	.01
☐ 485 Curtis Leskanic	.05	.02	.01
☐ 486 Robb Nen	.05	.02	.01
☐ 487 Lou Whitaker	.15	.07	.02
☐ 488 Melido Perez	.05	.02	.01
☐ 489 Luis Polonia	.05	.02	.01
☐ 490 Scott Brosius	.15	.07	.02
☐ 491 Robert Perez	.05	.02	.01
☐ 492 Mike Sweeney	.40	.18	.05
☐ 493 Mark Loretta	.05	.02	.01
☐ 494 Alex Ochoa	.15	.07	.02
☐ 495 Matt Lawton	.05	.02	.01
☐ 496 Shawn Estes	.15	.07	.02
☐ 497 John Wasdin	.05	.02	.01
☐ 498 Marc Kroon	.05	.02	.01
☐ 499 Chris Snopek	.05	.02	.01
☐ 500 Jeff Suppan	.05	.02	.01
☐ 501 Terrell Wade	.30	.14	.04
☐ 502 Marvin Benard	.05	.02	.01
☐ 503 Chris Widger	.05	.02	.01
☐ 504 Quinton McCracken	.05	.02	.01
☐ 505 Bob Wolcott	.05	.02	.01
☐ 506 C.J. Nitkowski	.05	.02	.01
☐ 507 Aaron Ledesma	.05	.02	.01
☐ 508 Scott Hatteberg	.05	.02	.01
☐ 509 Jimmy Haynes	.05	.02	.01
☐ 510 Howard Battle	.05	.02	.01
☐ 511 Marty Cordova CL	.15	.07	.02
☐ 512 Randy Johnson CL	.30	.14	.04
☐ 513 Mo Vaughn CL	.30	.14	.04
☐ 514 Chan Ho Park CL	.30	.14	.04
☐ 515 Greg Maddux CL	.60	.25	.07
☐ 516 Barry Larkin CL	.30	.14	.04
☐ 517 Tom Glavine CL	.30	.14	.04
☐ NNO Cal Ripken 2131	30.00	13.50	3.70

1996 Score All-Stars

Randomly inserted in jumbo packs at a rate of one in nine, this 20-card set was printed in rainbow holographic prismatic foil.

	MINT	NRMT	EXC
COMPLETE SET (20)	100.00	45.00	12.50
COMMON CARD (1-20)	2.00	.90	.25
SEMISTARS	3.00	1.35	.35
RANDOM INSERTS IN SER.2 JUMBO PACKS			

☐ 1 Frank Thomas	20.00	9.00	2.50
☐ 2 Albert Belle	10.00	4.50	1.25
☐ 3 Ken Griffey Jr.	20.00	9.00	2.50
☐ 4 Cal Ripken	15.00	6.75	1.85
☐ 5 Mo Vaughn	5.00	2.20	.60
☐ 6 Matt Williams	3.00	1.35	.35
☐ 7 Barry Bonds	5.00	2.20	.60
☐ 8 Dante Bichette	2.00	.90	.25
☐ 9 Tony Gwynn	8.00	3.60	1.00
☐ 10 Greg Maddux	12.00	5.50	1.50
☐ 11 Randy Johnson	3.00	1.35	.35
☐ 12 Hideo Nomo	5.00	2.20	.60
☐ 13 Tim Salmon	2.00	.90	.25
☐ 14 Jeff Bagwell	8.00	3.60	1.00
☐ 15 Edgar Martinez	3.00	1.35	.35
☐ 16 Reggie Sanders	2.00	.90	.25
☐ 17 Larry Walker	2.00	.90	.25
☐ 18 Chipper Jones	12.00	5.50	1.50
☐ 19 Manny Ramirez	5.00	2.20	.60
☐ 20 Eddie Murray	5.00	2.20	.60

1996 Score Big Bats

This 20-card set was randomly inserted in retail packs at a rate of approximately one in 31. The fronts feature a player photo set against a gold-

foil background. The words "Big Bats" as well as the player's name is printed in white at the bottom. The backs feature a photo against a multi-colored background. The cards are numbered "X" of 20 in the upper left corner.

	MINT	NRMT	EXC
COMPLETE SET (20)	125.00	55.00	15.50
COMMON CARD (1-20)	2.00	.90	.25
SEMISTARS	3.00	1.35	.35
RANDOM INSERTS IN SER.1 RETAIL PACKS			

□ 1 Cal Ripken	20.00	9.00	2.50
□ 2 Ken Griffey Jr.	25.00	11.00	3.10
□ 3 Frank Thomas	25.00	11.00	3.10
□ 4 Jeff Bagwell	10.00	4.50	1.25
□ 5 Mike Piazza	15.00	6.75	1.85
□ 6 Barry Bonds	6.00	2.70	.75
□ 7 Matt Williams	3.00	1.35	.35
□ 8 Raul Mondesi	2.00	.90	.25
□ 9 Tony Gwynn	10.00	4.50	1.25
□ 10 Albert Belle	12.00	5.50	1.50
□ 11 Manny Ramirez	6.00	2.70	.75
□ 12 Carlos Baerga	2.00	.90	.25
□ 13 Mo Vaughn	6.00	2.70	.75
□ 14 Derek Bell	2.00	.90	.25
□ 15 Larry Walker	3.00	1.35	.35
□ 16 Kenny Lofton	6.00	2.70	.75
□ 17 Edgar Martinez	3.00	1.35	.35
□ 18 Reggie Sanders	2.00	.90	.25
□ 19 Eddie Murray	6.00	2.70	.75
□ 20 Chipper Jones	15.00	6.75	1.85

1996 Score Diamond Aces

This 30-card set features some of baseball's best players. These cards were inserted approximately one every eight jumbo packs. The fronts display a color player cutout on a computer-generated background with gold foil accenting. On a similar background, the backs carry a color closeup.

	MINT	NRMT	EXC
COMPLETE SET (30)	175.00	80.00	22.00
COMMON CARD (1-30)	2.50	1.10	.30
SEMISTARS	4.00	1.80	.50
RANDOM INSERTS IN SER.1 JUMBO PACKS			

□ 1 Hideo Nomo	6.00	2.70	.75
□ 2 Brian L.Hunter	2.50	1.10	.30
□ 3 Ray Durham	4.00	1.80	.50
□ 4 Frank Thomas	25.00	11.00	3.10
□ 5 Cal Ripken	20.00	9.00	2.50
□ 6 Barry Bonds	6.00	2.70	.75
□ 7 Greg Maddux	15.00	6.75	1.85
□ 8 Chipper Jones	15.00	6.75	1.85
□ 9 Raul Mondesi	2.50	1.10	.30
□ 10 Mike Piazza	15.00	6.75	1.85
□ 11 Derek Jeter	15.00	6.75	1.85
□ 12 Bill Pulsipher	2.50	1.10	.30
□ 13 Larry Walker	4.00	1.80	.50
□ 14 Ken Griffey Jr.	25.00	11.00	3.10
□ 15 Alex Rodriguez	25.00	11.00	3.10
□ 16 Manny Ramirez	6.00	2.70	.75
□ 17 Mo Vaughn	6.00	2.70	.75
□ 18 Reggie Sanders	2.50	1.10	.30
□ 19 Derek Bell	2.50	1.10	.30
□ 20 Jim Edmonds	2.50	1.10	.30
□ 21 Albert Belle	12.00	5.50	1.50
□ 22 Eddie Murray	6.00	2.70	.75
□ 23 Tony Gwynn	10.00	4.50	1.25
□ 24 Jeff Bagwell	10.00	4.50	1.25
□ 25 Carlos Baerga	4.00	1.80	.50
□ 26 Matt Williams	4.00	1.80	.50
□ 27 Garret Anderson	2.50	1.10	.30
□ 28 Todd Hollandsworth	4.00	1.80	.50
□ 29 Johnny Damon	2.50	1.10	.30
□ 30 Tim Salmon	4.00	1.80	.50

1996 Score Dream Team

This nine-card set was randomly inserted in approximately one in 72 packs. This set features a leading player at each position. The fronts feature a player photo set against a holographic foil background. The words "1995 Dream Team" as well as his name and team are printed on the bottom of the card. The horizontal backs feature a player photo and some text. The cards are numbered in the upper right as "X" of nine.

	MINT	NRMT	EXC
COMPLETE SET (9)	100.00	45.00	12.50
COMMON CARD (1-9)	2.00	.90	.25
SEMISTARS	3.00	1.35	.35
RANDOM INSERTS IN SER.1 PACKS			

□ 1 Cal Ripken	20.00	9.00	2.50
□ 2 Frank Thomas	25.00	11.00	3.10
□ 3 Carlos Baerga	2.00	.90	.25
□ 4 Matt Williams	3.00	1.35	.35
□ 5 Mike Piazza	15.00	6.75	1.85
□ 6 Barry Bonds	6.00	2.70	.75
□ 7 Ken Griffey Jr.	25.00	11.00	3.10
□ 8 Manny Ramirez	6.00	2.70	.75
□ 9 Greg Maddux	15.00	6.75	1.85

1996 Score Dugout Collection

This set is a mini-parallel to the regular issue. Only 110 cards of each Series I and Series II were selected. Randomly inserted approximately one in every three packs, these cards have all gold foil printing that gives them a shiny copper cast. The words "Dugout Collection" are printed on the back.

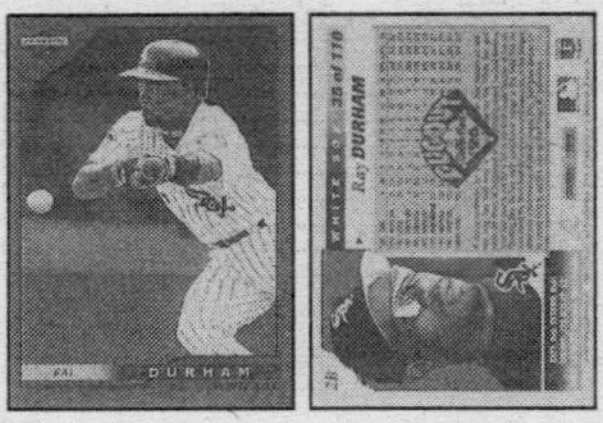

	MINT	NRMT	EXC
COMPLETE SER.1 SET (110)	50.00	22.00	6.25
COMPLETE SER.2 SET (110)	50.00	22.00	6.25
COMMON SERIES 1 (A1-A110)	.30	.14	.04
COMMON SERIES 2 (B1-B110)	.30	.14	.04
SEMISTARS	.60	.25	.07
STARS	1.25	.55	.16
COMP.ART.PRF.SER.1 (110)	350.00	160.00	45.00
COMP.ART.PRF.SER.2 (110)	350.00	160.00	45.00
COMMON AP SER.1 (A1-A110)	2.00	.90	.25
COMMON AP SER.2 (B1-B110)	2.00	.90	.25
ARTIST'S PROOFS SEMISTARS	4.00	1.80	.50
ARTIST'S PROOFS STARS	10.00	4.50	1.25
*ART.PRF.STARS: 4X to 8X HI COLUMN			
*ART.PRF.YOUNG STARS: 2.5X to 5X HI			
RANDOM INSERTS IN BOTH SERIES PACKS			

□ A3 Ryan Klesko	1.50	.70	.19
□ A6 Jim Thome	1.50	.70	.19
□ A8 Don Mattingly	4.00	1.80	.50
□ A15 Tony Gwynn	3.00	1.35	.35
□ A19 Alex Rodriguez	8.00	3.60	1.00
□ A20 Frank Thomas	8.00	3.60	1.00
□ A45 Kirby Puckett	2.50	1.10	.30
□ A50 Roberto Alomar	2.00	.90	.25
□ A52 Cal Ripken	6.00	2.70	.75
□ A53 Ozzie Smith	1.50	.70	.19
□ A54 Mo Vaughn	2.00	.90	.25
□ A59 Albert Belle	4.00	1.80	.50
□ A65 Eddie Murray	2.00	.90	.25
□ A102 Karim Garcia	1.50	.70	.19
□ A106 Derek Jeter	5.00	2.20	.60
□ A109 Ruben Rivera	1.50	.70	.19
□ B1 Greg Maddux	5.00	2.20	.60
□ B7 Ken Griffey Jr.	8.00	3.60	1.00
□ B26 Mike Mussina	1.50	.70	.19
□ B29 Jeff Bagwell	3.00	1.35	.35
□ B30 Manny Ramirez	2.00	.90	.25
□ B35 Mark McGwire	2.50	1.10	.30
□ B42 Mike Piazza	5.00	2.20	.60
□ B45 Hideo Nomo	2.00	.90	.25
□ B47 Chipper Jones	5.00	2.20	.60
□ B50 Kenny Lofton	2.00	.90	.25
□ B65 Barry Bonds	2.00	.90	.25
□ B73 Juan Gonzalez	4.00	1.80	.50
□ B81 Cal Ripken SS	3.00	1.35	.35
□ B86 Alex Rodriguez SS	4.00	1.80	.50
□ B98 Frank Thomas SS	4.00	1.80	.50
□ B102 Don Mattingly SS	2.00	.90	.25
□ B103 Tony Gwynn SS	1.50	.70	.19
□ B104 Albert Belle SS	2.00	.90	.25
□ B109 Derek Jeter SS	5.00	2.20	.60

1996 Score Future Franchise

Randomly inserted in retail packs at a rate of one in 72, this 16-card set honors young stars of the game. The fronts feature a color action player cutout on a special holographic foil printed background. The backs carry another player color photo with player information.

	MINT	NRMT	EXC
COMPLETE SET (16)	135.00	60.00	17.00
COMMON CARD (1-16)	4.00	1.80	.50
RANDOM INSERTS IN SER.2 PACKS			

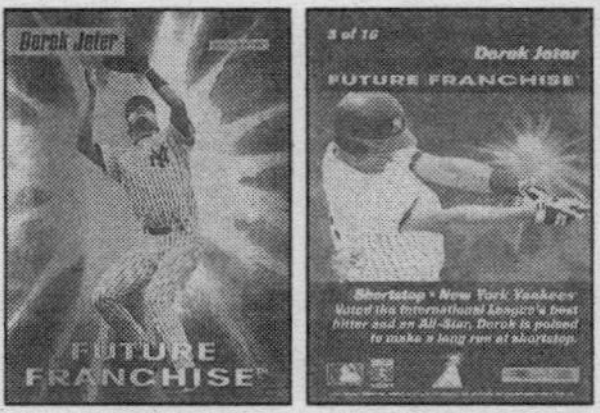

□ 1 Jason Isringhausen	5.00	2.20	.60
□ 2 Chipper Jones	25.00	11.00	3.10
□ 3 Derek Jeter	25.00	11.00	3.10
□ 4 Alex Rodriguez	50.00	22.00	6.25
□ 5 Alex Ochoa	5.00	2.20	.60
□ 6 Manny Ramirez	12.00	5.50	1.50
□ 7 Johnny Damon	5.00	2.20	.60
□ 8 Ruben Rivera	10.00	4.50	1.25
□ 9 Karim Garcia	10.00	4.50	1.25
□ 10 Garret Anderson	4.00	1.80	.50
□ 11 Marty Cordova	6.00	2.70	.75
□ 12 Bill Pulsipher	4.00	1.80	.50
□ 13 Hideo Nomo	12.00	5.50	1.50
□ 14 Marc Newfield	4.00	1.80	.50
□ 15 Charles Johnson	4.00	1.80	.50
□ 16 Raul Mondesi	6.00	2.70	.75

1996 Score Gold Stars

Randomly inserted in packs at a rate of one in 15, this 30-card set features borderless color action player photos with a special sepia player cutout inserted behind a gold foil stamp designating the star player. The backs display another player photo with player information.

	MINT	NRMT	EXC
COMPLETE SET (30)	60.00	27.00	7.50
COMMON CARD (1-30)	.75	.35	.09
SEMISTARS	1.25	.55	.16
RANDOM INSERTS IN SER.2 PACKS			

□ 1 Ken Griffey Jr.	10.00	4.50	1.25
□ 2 Frank Thomas	10.00	4.50	1.25
□ 3 Reggie Sanders	.75	.35	.09
□ 4 Tim Salmon	.75	.35	.09
□ 5 Mike Piazza	6.00	2.70	.75
□ 6 Tony Gwynn	4.00	1.80	.50
□ 7 Gary Sheffield	1.50	.70	.19
□ 8 Matt Williams	1.25	.55	.16
□ 9 Bernie Williams	1.50	.70	.19
□ 10 Jason Isringhausen	.75	.35	.09
□ 11 Albert Belle	5.00	2.20	.60
□ 12 Chipper Jones	6.00	2.70	.75
□ 13 Edgar Martinez	1.25	.55	.16
□ 14 Barry Larkin	1.25	.55	.16
□ 15 Barry Bonds	2.50	1.10	.30
□ 16 Jeff Bagwell	4.00	1.80	.50
□ 17 Greg Maddux	6.00	2.70	.75
□ 18 Mo Vaughn	2.50	1.10	.30
□ 19 Ryan Klesko	2.00	.90	.25
□ 20 Sammy Sosa	1.50	.70	.19
□ 21 Darren Daulton	.75	.35	.09

□ 22 Ivan Rodriguez	2.00	.90	.25
□ 23 Dante Bichette	1.25	.55	.16
□ 24 Hideo Nomo	2.50	1.10	.30
□ 25 Cal Ripken	8.00	3.60	1.00
□ 26 Rafael Palmeiro	1.25	.55	.16
□ 27 Larry Walker	1.25	.55	.16
□ 28 Carlos Baerga	1.25	.55	.16
□ 29 Randy Johnson	1.50	.70	.19
□ 30 Manny Ramirez	2.50	1.10	.30

1996 Score Numbers Game

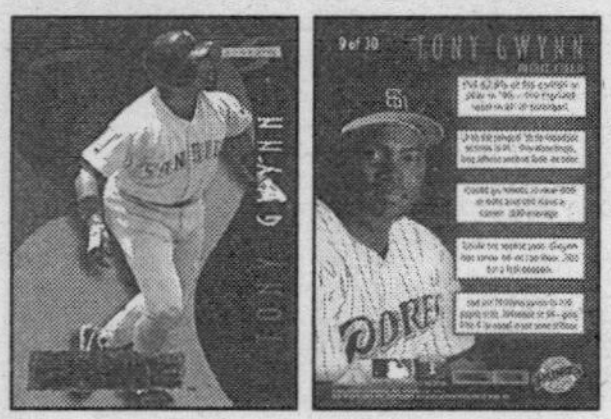

This 30-card set was inserted approximately one in every 15 packs. The fronts feature two player photos. The player's name is spelled vertically on the right while the words "Numbers Game" are printed against a gold-foil background. The backs contain five quick information bytes that feature that player's accomplishments. The cards are numbered as "X" of 30 in the upper left corner.

	MINT	NRMT	EXC
COMPLETE SET (30)	60.00	27.00	7.50
COMMON CARD (1-30)	.75	.35	.09
SEMISTARS	1.25	.55	.16
RANDOM INSERTS IN SER.1 PACKS			

□ 1 Cal Ripken	8.00	3.60	1.00
□ 2 Frank Thomas	10.00	4.50	1.25
□ 3 Ken Griffey Jr.	10.00	4.50	1.25
□ 4 Mike Piazza	6.00	2.70	.75
□ 5 Barry Bonds	2.50	1.10	.30
□ 6 Greg Maddux	6.00	2.70	.75
□ 7 Jeff Bagwell	4.00	1.80	.50
□ 8 Derek Bell	.75	.35	.09
□ 9 Tony Gwynn	4.00	1.80	.50
□ 10 Hideo Nomo	2.50	1.10	.30
□ 11 Raul Mondesi	2.00	.90	.25
□ 12 Manny Ramirez	2.50	1.10	.30
□ 13 Albert Belle	5.00	2.20	.60
□ 14 Matt Williams	1.25	.55	.16
□ 15 Jim Edmonds	.75	.35	.09
□ 16 Edgar Martinez	1.25	.55	.16
□ 17 Mo Vaughn	2.50	1.10	.30
□ 18 Reggie Sanders	.75	.35	.09
□ 19 Chipper Jones	6.00	2.70	.75
□ 20 Larry Walker	1.25	.55	.16
□ 21 Juan Gonzalez	5.00	2.20	.60
□ 22 Kenny Lofton	2.50	1.10	.30
□ 23 Don Mattingly	5.00	2.20	.60
□ 24 Ivan Rodriguez	2.00	.90	.25
□ 25 Randy Johnson	1.50	.70	.19
□ 26 Derek Jeter	6.00	2.70	.75
□ 27 J.T. Snow	.75	.35	.09
□ 28 Will Clark	1.25	.55	.16
□ 29 Rafael Palmeiro	1.25	.55	.16
□ 30 Alex Rodriguez	10.00	4.50	1.25

1996 Score Power Pace

Randomly inserted in retail packs at a rate of one in 31, this 18-card set features homerun hitters. The fronts display color action player cutouts on a gold foil background. The backs carry another player photo with player information including how frequently he can be expected to hit a homerun based on his career at-bats.

	MINT	NRMT	EXC
COMPLETE SET (18)	90.00	40.00	11.00
COMMON CARD (1-18)	2.00	.90	.25
SEMISTARS	3.00	1.35	.35
RANDOM INSERTS IN SER.2 RETAIL PACKS			

□ 1 Mark McGwire	8.00	3.60	1.00
□ 2 Albert Belle	12.00	5.50	1.50
□ 3 Jay Buhner	3.00	1.35	.35
□ 4 Frank Thomas	25.00	11.00	3.10
□ 5 Matt Williams	3.00	1.35	.35
□ 6 Gary Sheffield	4.00	1.80	.50
□ 7 Mike Piazza	15.00	6.75	1.85
□ 8 Larry Walker	2.00	.90	.25
□ 9 Mo Vaughn	6.00	2.70	.75
□ 10 Rafael Palmeiro	3.00	1.35	.35
□ 11 Dante Bichette	3.00	1.35	.35
□ 12 Ken Griffey, Jr.	25.00	11.00	3.10
□ 13 Barry Bonds	6.00	2.70	.75
□ 14 Manny Ramirez	6.00	2.70	.75
□ 15 Sammy Sosa	4.00	1.80	.50
□ 16 Tim Salmon	2.00	.90	.25
□ 17 Dave Justice	2.00	.90	.25
□ 18 Eric Karros	2.00	.90	.25

1996 Score Reflextions

This 20-card set was randomly inserted approximately one in every 31 hobby packs. Two players per card are featured, a veteran player and a younger star playing the same position. These cards feature a mirror effect on the front.

	MINT	NRMT	EXC
COMPLETE SET (20)	125.00	55.00	15.50
COMMON CARD (1-20)	2.00	.90	.25
RANDOM INSERTS IN SER.1 HOBBY PACKS			

□ 1 Cal Ripken Chipper Jones	30.00	13.50	3.70
□ 2 Ken Griffey Jr. Alex Rodriguez	40.00	18.00	5.00
□ 3 Frank Thomas Mo Vaughn	25.00	11.00	3.10
□ 4 Kenny Lofton Brian L.Hunter	6.00	2.70	.75
□ 5 Don Mattingly J.T.Snow	10.00	4.50	1.25
□ 6 Manny Ramirez	6.00	2.70	.75

Raul Mondesi			
□ 7 Tony Gwynn	8.00	3.60	1.00
Garret Anderson			
□ 8 Roberto Alomar	6.00	2.70	.75
Carlos Baerga			
□ 9 Andre Dawson	2.00	.90	.25
Larry Walker			
□ 10 Barry Larkin	15.00	6.75	1.85
Derek Jeter			
□ 11 Barry Bonds	6.00	2.70	.75
Reggie Sanders			
□ 12 Mike Piazza	20.00	9.00	2.50
Albert Belle			
□ 13 Wade Boggs	2.00	.90	.25
Edgar Martinez			
□ 14 David Cone	2.00	.90	.25
John Smoltz			
□ 15 Will Clark	10.00	4.50	1.25
Jeff Bagwell			
□ 16 Mark McGwire	8.00	3.60	1.00
Cecil Fielder			
□ 17 Greg Maddux	15.00	6.75	1.85
Mike Mussina			
□ 18 Randy Johnson	8.00	3.60	1.00
Hideo Nomo			
□ 19 Jim Thome	5.00	2.20	.60
Dean Palmer			
□ 20 Chuck Knoblauch	2.00	.90	.25
Craig Biggio			

1996 Score Titanic Taters

Randomly inserted in hobby packs at a rate of one in 31, this 18-card set features long home run hitters. The fronts display a color action player cutout on a gold foil background of a baseball park. The backs carry another player photo with information about the player's longest home run and the park where it was hit.

	MINT	NRMT	EXC
COMPLETE SET (18)	100.00	45.00	12.50
COMMON CARD (1-18)	2.00	.90	.25
SEMISTARS	3.00	1.35	.35
RANDOM INSERTS IN SER.2 HOBBY PACKS			

□ 1 Albert Belle	12.00	5.50	1.50
□ 2 Frank Thomas	25.00	11.00	3.10
□ 3 Mo Vaughn	6.00	2.70	.75
□ 4 Ken Griffey Jr.	25.00	11.00	3.10
□ 5 Matt Williams	3.00	1.35	.35
□ 6 Mark McGwire	8.00	3.60	1.00
□ 7 Dante Bichette	3.00	1.35	.35
□ 8 Tim Salmon	3.00	1.35	.35
□ 9 Jeff Bagwell	10.00	4.50	1.25
□ 10 Rafael Palmeiro	3.00	1.35	.35
□ 11 Mike Piazza	15.00	6.75	1.85
□ 12 Cecil Fielder	3.00	1.35	.35
□ 13 Larry Walker	2.00	.90	.25
□ 14 Sammy Sosa	4.00	1.80	.50
□ 15 Manny Ramirez	6.00	2.70	.75
□ 16 Gary Sheffield	4.00	1.80	.50
□ 17 Barry Bonds	6.00	2.70	.75
□ 18 Jay Buhner	3.00	1.35	.35

1997 Score

The 1997 Score Series 1 has a total of 330 cards. The 10-card packs retail for $.99 each.

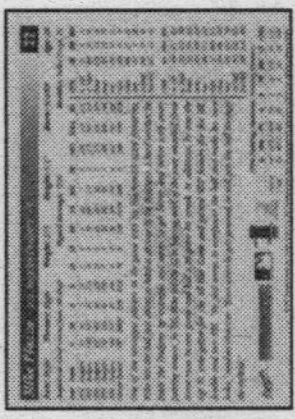

The fronts feature color player action photos in a white border. The backs carry player information and career statistics. Prices below refer to the retail-only regular cards, NOT the hobby-only Premium Stock version.

	MINT	NRMT	EXC
COMPLETE SET (330)	15.00	6.75	1.85
COMMON CARD (1-330)	.05	.02	.01
SEMISTARS	.10	.05	.01
STARS	.15	.07	.02
COMP.SHOWCASE SET (330)	250.00	110.00	31.00
COMMON SHOWCASE (1-330)	.50	.23	.06
*SHOWCASE VETS: 4X TO 8X BASIC CARDS			
*SHOWCASE YOUNG STARS: 3X TO 6X BASIC CARDS			
COMP.ARTIST'S PROOFS (330)	1000.00	450.00	125.00
COMMON ARTIST'S PROOF (1-330)	1.50	.70	.19
*ARTIST'S PROOF VETS: 15X TO 30X BASIC CARDS			
*ARTIST'S PROOF YOUNG STARS: 10X TO 20X BASIC CARDS			

□ 1 Jeff Bagwell	.75	.35	.09
□ 2 Mickey Tettleton	.05	.02	.01
□ 3 Johnny Damon	.10	.05	.01
□ 4 Jeff Conine	.10	.05	.01
□ 5 Bernie Williams	.15	.07	.02
□ 6 Will Clark	.15	.07	.02
□ 7 Ryan Klesko	.15	.07	.02
□ 8 Cecil Fielder	.10	.05	.01
□ 9 Paul Wilson	.10	.05	.01
□ 10 Gregg Jefferies	.10	.05	.01
□ 11 Chili Davis	.10	.05	.01
□ 12 Albert Belle	1.00	.45	.12
□ 13 Ken Hill	.05	.02	.01
□ 14 Cliff Floyd	.05	.02	.01
□ 15 Jaime Navarro	.05	.02	.01
□ 16 Ismael Valdes	.10	.05	.01
□ 17 Jeff King	.05	.02	.01
□ 18 Chris Bosio	.05	.02	.01
□ 19 Reggie Sanders	.10	.05	.01
□ 20 Darren Daulton	.10	.05	.01
□ 21 Ken Caminiti	.15	.07	.02
□ 22 Mike Piazza	1.25	.55	.16
□ 23 Chad Mottola	.05	.02	.01
□ 24 Darin Erstad	1.00	.45	.12
□ 25 Dante Bichette	.15	.07	.02
□ 26 Frank Thomas	2.00	.90	.25
□ 27 Ben McDonald	.05	.02	.01
□ 28 Raul Casanova	.05	.02	.01
□ 29 Kevin Ritz	.05	.02	.01
□ 30 Garret Anderson	.10	.05	.01
□ 31 Jason Kendall	.10	.05	.01
□ 32 Billy Wagner	.10	.05	.01
□ 33 Dave Justice	.10	.05	.01
□ 34 Marty Cordova	.10	.05	.01
□ 35 Derek Jeter	1.25	.55	.16
□ 36 Trevor Hoffman	.05	.02	.01
□ 37 Geronimo Berroa	.05	.02	.01
□ 38 Walt Weiss	.05	.02	.01
□ 39 Kirt Manwaring	.05	.02	.01
□ 40 Alex Gonzalez	.05	.02	.01
□ 41 Sean Berry	.05	.02	.01
□ 42 Kevin Appier	.10	.05	.01
□ 43 Rusty Greer	.10	.05	.01
□ 44 Pete Incaviglia	.05	.02	.01
□ 45 Rafael Palmeiro	.15	.07	.02
□ 46 Eddie Murray	.50	.23	.06
□ 47 Moises Alou	.10	.05	.01
□ 48 Mark Lewis	.05	.02	.01
□ 49 Hal Morris	.05	.02	.01
□ 50 Edgar Renteria	.15	.07	.02

□ 51	Rickey Henderson	.10	.05	.01
□ 52	Pat Listach	.05	.02	.01
□ 53	John Wasdin	.05	.02	.01
□ 54	James Baldwin	.10	.05	.01
□ 55	Brian Jordan	.10	.05	.01
□ 56	Edgar Martinez	.15	.07	.02
□ 57	Wil Cordero	.05	.02	.01
□ 58	Danny Tartabull	.05	.02	.01
□ 59	Keith Lockhart	.05	.02	.01
□ 60	Rico Brogna	.05	.02	.01
□ 61	Ricky Bottalico	.05	.02	.01
□ 62	Terry Pendleton	.10	.05	.01
□ 63	Bret Boone	.05	.02	.01
□ 64	Charlie Hayes	.05	.02	.01
□ 65	Marc Newfield	.05	.02	.01
□ 66	Sterling Hitchcock	.05	.02	.01
□ 67	Roberto Alomar	.50	.23	.06
□ 68	John Jaha	.05	.02	.01
□ 69	Greg Colbrunn	.05	.02	.01
□ 70	Sal Fasano	.05	.02	.01
□ 71	Brooks Kieschnick	.10	.05	.01
□ 72	Pedro Martinez	.10	.05	.01
□ 73	Kevin Elster	.05	.02	.01
□ 74	Ellis Burks	.10	.05	.01
□ 75	Chuck Finley	.05	.02	.01
□ 76	John Olerud	.05	.02	.01
□ 77	Jay Bell	.05	.02	.01
□ 78	Allen Watson	.05	.02	.01
□ 79	Darryl Strawberry	.10	.05	.01
□ 80	Orlando Miller	.05	.02	.01
□ 81	Jose Herrera	.05	.02	.01
□ 82	Andy Pettitte	.50	.23	.06
□ 83	Juan Guzman	.05	.02	.01
□ 84	Alan Benes	.10	.05	.01
□ 85	Jack McDowell	.10	.05	.01
□ 86	Ugueth Urbina	.05	.02	.01
□ 87	Rocky Coppinger	.10	.05	.01
□ 88	Jeff Cirillo	.05	.02	.01
□ 89	Tom Glavine	.15	.07	.02
□ 90	Robby Thompson	.05	.02	.01
□ 91	Barry Bonds	.50	.23	.06
□ 92	Carlos Delgado	.10	.05	.01
□ 93	Mo Vaughn	.50	.23	.06
□ 94	Ryne Sandberg	.50	.23	.06
□ 95	Alex Rodriguez	2.00	.90	.25
□ 96	Brady Anderson	.15	.07	.02
□ 97	Scott Brosius	.05	.02	.01
□ 98	Dennis Eckersley	.10	.05	.01
□ 99	Brian McRae	.10	.05	.01
□ 100	Rey Ordonez	.15	.07	.02
□ 101	John Valentin	.05	.02	.01
□ 102	Brett Butler	.10	.05	.01
□ 103	Eric Karros	.10	.05	.01
□ 104	Harold Baines	.10	.05	.01
□ 105	Javier Lopez	.10	.05	.01
□ 106	Alan Trammell	.10	.05	.01
□ 107	Jim Thome	.15	.07	.02
□ 108	Frank Rodriguez	.05	.02	.01
□ 109	Bernard Gilkey	.10	.05	.01
□ 110	Reggie Jefferson	.05	.02	.01
□ 111	Scott Stahoviak	.05	.02	.01
□ 112	Steve Gibralter	.05	.02	.01
□ 113	Todd Hollandsworth	.10	.05	.01
□ 114	Ruben Rivera	.15	.07	.02
□ 115	Dennis Martinez	.10	.05	.01
□ 116	Mariano Rivera	.10	.05	.01
□ 117	John Smoltz	.15	.07	.02
□ 118	John Mabry	.05	.02	.01
□ 119	Tom Gordon	.05	.02	.01
□ 120	Alex Ochoa	.10	.05	.01
□ 121	Jamey Wright	.05	.02	.01
□ 122	Dave Nilsson	.05	.02	.01
□ 123	Bobby Bonilla	.10	.05	.01
□ 124	Al Leiter	.05	.02	.01
□ 125	Rick Aguilera	.05	.02	.01
□ 126	Jeff Brantley	.05	.02	.01
□ 127	Kevin Brown	.10	.05	.01
□ 128	George Arias	.05	.02	.01
□ 129	Darren Oliver	.05	.02	.01
□ 130	Bill Pulsipher	.05	.02	.01
□ 131	Roberto Hernandez	.05	.02	.01
□ 132	Delino DeShields	.05	.02	.01
□ 133	Mark Grudzielanek	.05	.02	.01
□ 134	John Wetteland	.10	.05	.01
□ 135	Carlos Baerga	.10	.05	.01
□ 136	Paul Sorrento	.05	.02	.01
□ 137	Leo Gomez	.05	.02	.01
□ 138	Andy Ashby	.05	.02	.01
□ 139	Julio Franco	.10	.05	.01
□ 140	Brian Hunter	.10	.05	.01
□ 141	Jermaine Dye	.15	.07	.02
□ 142	Tony Clark	.10	.05	.01
□ 143	Ruben Sierra	.10	.05	.01
□ 144	Donovan Osborne	.05	.02	.01
□ 145	Mark McLemore	.05	.02	.01
□ 146	Terry Steinbach	.10	.05	.01
□ 147	Bob Wells	.05	.02	.01
□ 148	Chan Ho Park	.10	.05	.01
□ 149	Tim Salmon	.15	.07	.02
□ 150	Paul O'Neill	.10	.05	.01
□ 151	Cal Ripken	1.50	.70	.19
□ 152	Wally Joyner	.10	.05	.01
□ 153	Omar Vizquel	.10	.05	.01
□ 154	Mike Mussina	.40	.18	.05
□ 155	Andres Galarraga	.15	.07	.02
□ 156	Ken Griffey Jr.	2.00	.90	.25
□ 157	Kenny Lofton	.50	.23	.06
□ 158	Ray Durham	.05	.02	.01
□ 159	Hideo Nomo	.50	.23	.06
□ 160	Ozzie Guillen	.05	.02	.01
□ 161	Roger Pavlik	.05	.02	.01
□ 162	Manny Ramirez	.50	.23	.06
□ 163	Mark Lemke	.05	.02	.01
□ 164	Mike Stanley	.05	.02	.01
□ 165	Chuck Knoblauch	.15	.07	.02
□ 166	Kimera Bartee	.05	.02	.01
□ 167	Wade Boggs	.15	.07	.02
□ 168	Jay Buhner	.15	.07	.02
□ 169	Eric Young	.10	.05	.01
□ 170	Jose Canseco	.15	.07	.02
□ 171	Dwight Gooden	.10	.05	.01
□ 172	Fred McGriff	.15	.07	.02
□ 173	Sandy Alomar Jr.	.05	.02	.01
□ 174	Andy Benes	.10	.05	.01
□ 175	Dean Palmer	.10	.05	.01
□ 176	Larry Walker	.10	.05	.01
□ 177	Charles Nagy	.10	.05	.01
□ 178	David Cone	.10	.05	.01
□ 179	Mark Grace	.15	.07	.02
□ 180	Robin Ventura	.10	.05	.01
□ 181	Roger Clemens	.15	.07	.02
□ 182	Bobby Witt	.05	.02	.01
□ 183	Vinny Castilla	.10	.05	.01
□ 184	Gary Sheffield	.15	.07	.02
□ 185	Dan Wilson	.05	.02	.01
□ 186	Roger Cedeno	.05	.02	.01
□ 187	Mark McGwire	.60	.25	.07
□ 188	Darren Bragg	.05	.02	.01
□ 189	Quinton McCracken	.05	.02	.01
□ 190	Randy Myers	.05	.02	.01
□ 191	Jeromy Burnitz	.05	.02	.01
□ 192	Randy Johnson	.15	.07	.02
□ 193	Chipper Jones	1.25	.55	.16
□ 194	Greg Vaughn	.10	.05	.01
□ 195	Travis Fryman	.10	.05	.01
□ 196	Tim Naehring	.05	.02	.01
□ 197	B.J. Surhoff	.05	.02	.01
□ 198	Juan Gonzalez	1.00	.45	.12
□ 199	Terrell Wade	.05	.02	.01
□ 200	Jeff Frye	.05	.02	.01
□ 201	Joey Cora	.05	.02	.01
□ 202	Raul Mondesi	.10	.05	.01
□ 203	Ivan Rodriguez	.40	.18	.05
□ 204	Armando Reynoso	.05	.02	.01
□ 205	Jeffrey Hammonds	.05	.02	.01
□ 206	Darren Dreifort	.05	.02	.01
□ 207	Kevin Seitzer	.05	.02	.01
□ 208	Tino Martinez	.10	.05	.01
□ 209	Jim Bruske	.05	.02	.01
□ 210	Jeff Suppan	.10	.05	.01
□ 211	Mark Carreon	.05	.02	.01
□ 212	Wilson Alvarez	.05	.02	.01
□ 213	John Burkett	.05	.02	.01
□ 214	Tony Phillips	.10	.05	.01
□ 215	Greg Maddux	1.25	.55	.16
□ 216	Mark Whiten	.05	.02	.01
□ 217	Curtis Pride	.05	.02	.01
□ 218	Lyle Mouton	.05	.02	.01
□ 219	Todd Hundley	.10	.05	.01
□ 220	Greg Gagne	.05	.02	.01
□ 221	Rich Amaral	.05	.02	.01
□ 222	Tom Goodwin	.05	.02	.01

☐ 223	Chris Hoiles	.05	.02	.01
☐ 224	Jayhawk Owens	.05	.02	.01
☐ 225	Kenny Rogers	.05	.02	.01
☐ 226	Mike Greenwell	.05	.02	.01
☐ 227	Mark Wohlers	.10	.05	.01
☐ 228	Henry Rodriguez	.10	.05	.01
☐ 229	Robert Perez	.05	.02	.01
☐ 230	Jeff Kent	.05	.02	.01
☐ 231	Darryl Hamilton	.05	.02	.01
☐ 232	Alex Fernandez	.10	.05	.01
☐ 233	Ron Karkovice	.05	.02	.01
☐ 234	Jimmy Haynes	.05	.02	.01
☐ 235	Craig Biggio	.10	.05	.01
☐ 236	Ray Lankford	.10	.05	.01
☐ 237	Lance Johnson	.10	.05	.01
☐ 238	Matt Williams	.15	.07	.02
☐ 239	Chad Curtis	.05	.02	.01
☐ 240	Mark Thompson	.05	.02	.01
☐ 241	Jason Giambi	.10	.05	.01
☐ 242	Barry Larkin	.15	.07	.02
☐ 243	Paul Molitor	.40	.18	.05
☐ 244	Sammy Sosa	.15	.07	.02
☐ 245	Kevin Tapani	.05	.02	.01
☐ 246	Marquis Grissom	.10	.05	.01
☐ 247	Joe Carter	.10	.05	.01
☐ 248	Ramon Martinez	.10	.05	.01
☐ 249	Tony Gwynn	.75	.35	.09
☐ 250	Andy Fox	.05	.02	.01
☐ 251	Troy O'Leary	.05	.02	.01
☐ 252	Warren Newson	.05	.02	.01
☐ 253	Troy Percival	.10	.05	.01
☐ 254	Jamie Moyer	.05	.02	.01
☐ 255	Danny Graves	.05	.02	.01
☐ 256	David Wells	.05	.02	.01
☐ 257	Todd Zeile	.05	.02	.01
☐ 258	Raul Ibanez	.05	.02	.01
☐ 259	Tyler Houston	.05	.02	.01
☐ 260	LaTroy Hawkins	.05	.02	.01
☐ 261	Joey Hamilton	.10	.05	.01
☐ 262	Mike Sweeney	.05	.02	.01
☐ 263	Brant Brown	.05	.02	.01
☐ 264	Pat Hentgen	.10	.05	.01
☐ 265	Mark Johnson	.05	.02	.01
☐ 266	Robb Nen	.05	.02	.01
☐ 267	Justin Thompson	.05	.02	.01
☐ 268	Ron Gant	.10	.05	.01
☐ 269	Jeff D'Amico	.10	.05	.01
☐ 270	Shawn Estes	.05	.02	.01
☐ 271	Derek Bell	.10	.05	.01
☐ 272	Fernando Valenzuela	.10	.05	.01
☐ 273	Tom Pagnozzi	.05	.02	.01
☐ 274	John Burke	.05	.02	.01
☐ 275	Ed Sprague	.05	.02	.01
☐ 276	F.P. Santangelo	.05	.02	.01
☐ 277	Todd Greene	.10	.05	.01
☐ 278	Butch Huskey	.05	.02	.01
☐ 279	Steve Finley	.10	.05	.01
☐ 280	Eric Davis	.05	.02	.01
☐ 281	Shawn Green	.05	.02	.01
☐ 282	Al Martin	.05	.02	.01
☐ 283	Michael Tucker	.05	.02	.01
☐ 284	Shane Reynolds	.05	.02	.01
☐ 285	Matt Mieske	.05	.02	.01
☐ 286	Jose Rosado	.05	.02	.01
☐ 287	Mark Langston	.05	.02	.01
☐ 288	Ralph Milliard	.05	.02	.01
☐ 289	Mike Lansing	.05	.02	.01
☐ 290	Scott Servais	.05	.02	.01
☐ 291	Royce Clayton	.05	.02	.01
☐ 292	Mike Grace	.05	.02	.01
☐ 293	James Mouton	.05	.02	.01
☐ 294	Charles Johnson	.10	.05	.01
☐ 295	Gary Gaetti	.05	.02	.01
☐ 296	Kevin Mitchell	.05	.02	.01
☐ 297	Carlos Garcia	.05	.02	.01
☐ 298	Desi Relaford	.05	.02	.01
☐ 299	Jason Thompson	.05	.02	.01
☐ 300	Osvaldo Fernandez	.05	.02	.01
☐ 301	Fernando Vina	.05	.02	.01
☐ 302	Jose Offerman	.05	.02	.01
☐ 303	Yamil Benitez	.05	.02	.01
☐ 304	J.T. Snow	.05	.02	.01
☐ 305	Rafael Bournigal	.05	.02	.01
☐ 306	Jason Isringhausen	.05	.02	.01
☐ 307	Bobby Higginson	.10	.05	.01
☐ 308	Nerio Rodriguez	.25	.11	.03
☐ 309	Brian Giles	.05	.02	.01
☐ 310	Andruw Jones	2.00	.90	.25
☐ 311	Tony Graffanino	.05	.02	.01
☐ 312	Arquimedez Pozo	.05	.02	.01
☐ 313	Jermaine Allensworth	.05	.02	.01
☐ 314	Jeff Darwin	.05	.02	.01
☐ 315	George Williams	.05	.02	.01
☐ 316	Karim Garcia	.40	.18	.05
☐ 317	Trey Beamon	.05	.02	.01
☐ 318	Makato Suzuki	.05	.02	.01
☐ 319	Robin Jennings	.05	.02	.01
☐ 320	Danny Patterson	.05	.02	.01
☐ 321	Damon Mashore	.05	.02	.01
☐ 322	Wendell Magee	.05	.02	.01
☐ 323	Dax Jones	.05	.02	.01
☐ 324	Kevin Brown	.10	.05	.01
☐ 325	Marvin Benard	.05	.02	.01
☐ 326	Mike Cameron	.10	.05	.01
☐ 327	Marcus Jensen	.05	.02	.01
☐ 328	Eddie Murray CL (1-168)	.15	.07	.02
☐ 329	Paul Molitor CL (169-330)	.15	.07	.02
☐ 330	Checklist (inserts)	.05	.02	.01

1997 Score Franchise

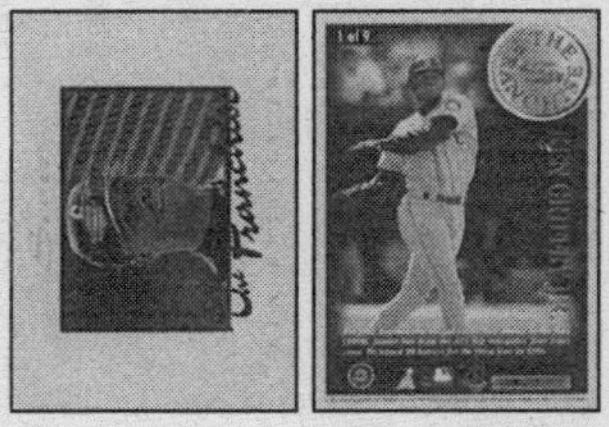

Randomly inserted in hobby packs only at a rate of one in 72, this nine-card set honors superstar players for their irreplaceable contribution to their team. The fronts display sepia player portraits on a white baseball replica background. The backs carry an action player photo with a sentence about the player which explains why he was selected for this set.

	MINT	NRMT	EXC
COMPLETE SET (9)	125.00	55.00	15.50
COMMON CARD (1-9)	5.00	2.20	.60
*GLOWING: 2.5X VALUE			
RANDOM INSERTS IN HOBBY PACKS			

☐ 1	Ken Griffey Jr.	30.00	13.50	3.70
☐ 2	John Smoltz	5.00	2.20	.60
☐ 3	Cal Ripken	25.00	11.00	3.10
☐ 4	Chipper Jones	20.00	9.00	2.50
☐ 5	Mike Piazza	20.00	9.00	2.50
☐ 6	Albert Belle	15.00	6.75	1.85
☐ 7	Frank Thomas	30.00	13.50	3.70
☐ 8	Sammy Sosa	5.00	2.20	.60
☐ 9	Roberto Alomar	8.00	3.60	1.00

1997 Score Pitcher Perfect

Randomly inserted in packs at a rate of one in 23, this 15-card set features players photographed by Randy Johnson in unique poses and foil stamping. The backs carry player information.

	MINT	NRMT	EXC
COMPLETE SET (15)	80.00	36.00	10.00
COMMON CARD (1-15)	1.50	.70	.19
SEMISTARS	2.50	1.10	.30
RANDOM INSERTS IN PACKS			

☐ 1	Cal Ripken	12.00	5.50	1.50
☐ 2	Alex Rodriguez	15.00	6.75	1.85
☐ 3	Alex Rodriguez Cal Ripken	15.00	6.75	1.85

□ 4 Edgar Martinez	2.50	1.10	.30
□ 5 Ivan Rodriguez	3.00	1.35	.35
□ 6 Mark McGwire	5.00	2.20	.60
□ 7 Tim Salmon	2.50	1.10	.30
□ 8 Chili Davis	1.50	.70	.19
□ 9 Joe Carter	2.50	1.10	.30
□ 10 Frank Thomas	15.00	6.75	1.85
□ 11 Will Clark	2.50	1.10	.30
□ 12 Mo Vaughn	4.00	1.80	.50
□ 13 Wade Boggs	2.50	1.10	.30
□ 14 Ken Griffey Jr.	15.00	6.75	1.85
□ 15 Randy Johnson	2.50	1.10	.30

1997 Score Titanic Taters

Randomly inserted in retail packs only at a rate of one in 35, this 18-card set honors the long-ball ability of some of the league's top sluggers and uses dot matrix holographic printing.

	MINT	NRMT	EXC
COMPLETE SET (18)	125.00	55.00	15.50
COMMON CARD (1-18)	2.50	1.10	.30
SEMISTARS	4.00	1.80	.50
RANDOM INSERTS IN RETAIL PACKS			
□ 1 Mark McGwire	8.00	3.60	1.00
□ 2 Mike Piazza	15.00	6.75	1.85
□ 3 Ken Griffey Jr.	25.00	11.00	3.10
□ 4 Juan Gonzalez	12.00	5.50	1.50
□ 5 Frank Thomas	25.00	11.00	3.10
□ 6 Albert Belle	12.00	5.50	1.50
□ 7 Sammy Sosa	4.00	1.80	.50
□ 8 Jeff Bagwell	10.00	4.50	1.25
□ 9 Todd Hundley	2.50	1.10	.30
□ 10 Ryan Klesko	5.00	2.20	.60
□ 11 Brady Anderson	4.00	1.80	.50
□ 12 Mo Vaughn	6.00	2.70	.75
□ 13 Jay Buhner	4.00	1.80	.50
□ 14 Chipper Jones	15.00	6.75	1.85
□ 15 Barry Bonds	6.00	2.70	.75
□ 16 Gary Sheffield	4.00	1.80	.50
□ 17 Alex Rodriguez	25.00	11.00	3.10
□ 18 Cecil Fielder	2.50	1.10	.30

1993 Select

Seeking a niche in the premium, mid-price market, Score produced a new 405-card standard-size set entitled Select in 1993. The set includes regular players, rookies, and draft picks, and was sold in 15-card hobby and retail packs and 28-card super packs. The front photos, composed either horizontally or vertically, are ultra-violet coated while the two-toned green borders received a matte finish. The player's name appears in mustard-colored lettering in the bottom border. Subset cards include Draft Picks and Rookies, both sprinkled throughout the latter part of the set. Rookie Cards in this set include Derek Jeter and Jason Kendall.

	MINT	NRMT	EXC
COMPLETE SET (405)	30.00	13.50	3.70
COMMON CARD (1-405)	.10	.05	.01
SEMISTARS	.25	.11	.03
STARS	.50	.23	.06
□ 1 Barry Bonds	.75	.35	.09
□ 2 Ken Griffey Jr.	3.00	1.35	.35
□ 3 Will Clark	.40	.18	.05
□ 4 Kirby Puckett	1.00	.45	.12
□ 5 Tony Gwynn	1.25	.55	.16
□ 6 Frank Thomas	3.00	1.35	.35
□ 7 Tom Glavine	.40	.18	.05
□ 8 Roberto Alomar	.75	.35	.09
□ 9 Andre Dawson	.40	.18	.05
□ 10 Ron Darling	.10	.05	.01
□ 11 Bobby Bonilla	.25	.11	.03
□ 12 Danny Tartabull	.10	.05	.01
□ 13 Darren Daulton	.25	.11	.03
□ 14 Roger Clemens	.40	.18	.05
□ 15 Ozzie Smith	.60	.25	.07
□ 16 Mark McGwire	1.00	.45	.12
□ 17 Terry Pendleton	.25	.11	.03
□ 18 Cal Ripken	2.50	1.10	.30
□ 19 Fred McGriff	.40	.18	.05
□ 20 Cecil Fielder	.25	.11	.03
□ 21 Darryl Strawberry	.25	.11	.03
□ 22 Robin Yount	.40	.18	.05
□ 23 Barry Larkin	.40	.18	.05
□ 24 Don Mattingly	1.50	.70	.19
□ 25 Craig Biggio	.40	.18	.05
□ 26 Sandy Alomar Jr.	.25	.11	.03
□ 27 Larry Walker	.40	.18	.05
□ 28 Junior Felix	.10	.05	.01
□ 29 Eddie Murray	.75	.35	.09
□ 30 Robin Ventura	.25	.11	.03
□ 31 Greg Maddux	2.00	.90	.25
□ 32 Dave Winfield	.40	.18	.05
□ 33 John Kruk	.25	.11	.03
□ 34 Wally Joyner	.25	.11	.03
□ 35 Andy Van Slyke	.25	.11	.03
□ 36 Chuck Knoblauch	.50	.23	.06
□ 37 Tom Pagnozzi	.10	.05	.01
□ 38 Dennis Eckersley	.25	.11	.03
□ 39 Dave Justice	.40	.18	.05
□ 40 Juan Gonzalez	1.50	.70	.19
□ 41 Gary Sheffield	.50	.23	.06
□ 42 Paul Molitor	.60	.25	.07
□ 43 Delino DeShields	.10	.05	.01
□ 44 Travis Fryman	.40	.18	.05
□ 45 Hal Morris	.10	.05	.01
□ 46 Greg Olson	.10	.05	.01
□ 47 Ken Caminiti	.40	.18	.05
□ 48 Wade Boggs	.40	.18	.05
□ 49 Orel Hershiser	.25	.11	.03
□ 50 Albert Belle	1.50	.70	.19
□ 51 Bill Swift	.10	.05	.01
□ 52 Mark Langston	.25	.11	.03
□ 53 Joe Girardi	.10	.05	.01

□ 54	Keith Miller	.10	.05	.01
□ 55	Gary Carter	.40	.18	.05
□ 56	Brady Anderson	.40	.18	.05
□ 57	Dwight Gooden	.25	.11	.03
□ 58	Julio Franco	.25	.11	.03
□ 59	Lenny Dykstra	.25	.11	.03
□ 60	Mickey Tettleton	.10	.05	.01
□ 61	Randy Tomlin	.10	.05	.01
□ 62	B.J. Surhoff	.25	.11	.03
□ 63	Todd Zeile	.10	.05	.01
□ 64	Roberto Kelly	.10	.05	.01
□ 65	Rob Dibble	.10	.05	.01
□ 66	Leo Gomez	.10	.05	.01
□ 67	Doug Jones	.10	.05	.01
□ 68	Ellis Burks	.40	.18	.05
□ 69	Mike Scioscia	.10	.05	.01
□ 70	Charles Nagy	.25	.11	.03
□ 71	Cory Snyder	.10	.05	.01
□ 72	Devon White	.10	.05	.01
□ 73	Mark Grace	.40	.18	.05
□ 74	Luis Polonia	.10	.05	.01
□ 75	John Smiley 2X	.10	.05	.01
□ 76	Carlton Fisk	.40	.18	.05
□ 77	Luis Sojo	.10	.05	.01
□ 78	George Brett	1.25	.55	.16
□ 79	Mitch Williams	.10	.05	.01
□ 80	Kent Hrbek	.25	.11	.03
□ 81	Jay Bell	.25	.11	.03
□ 82	Edgar Martinez	.40	.18	.05
□ 83	Lee Smith	.25	.11	.03
□ 84	Deion Sanders	.40	.18	.05
□ 85	Bill Gullickson	.10	.05	.01
□ 86	Paul O'Neill	.25	.11	.03
□ 87	Kevin Seitzer	.10	.05	.01
□ 88	Steve Finley	.40	.18	.05
□ 89	Mel Hall	.10	.05	.01
□ 90	Nolan Ryan	2.50	1.10	.30
□ 91	Eric Davis	.25	.11	.03
□ 92	Mike Mussina	.60	.25	.07
□ 93	Tony Fernandez	.10	.05	.01
□ 94	Frank Viola	.10	.05	.01
□ 95	Matt Williams	.40	.18	.05
□ 96	Joe Carter	.40	.18	.05
□ 97	Ryne Sandberg	.75	.35	.09
□ 98	Jim Abbott	.10	.05	.01
□ 99	Marquis Grissom	.40	.18	.05
□ 100	George Bell	.10	.05	.01
□ 101	Howard Johnson	.10	.05	.01
□ 102	Kevin Appier	.25	.11	.03
□ 103	Dale Murphy	.40	.18	.05
□ 104	Shane Mack	.10	.05	.01
□ 105	Jose Lind	.10	.05	.01
□ 106	Rickey Henderson	.40	.18	.05
□ 107	Bob Tewksbury	.10	.05	.01
□ 108	Kevin Mitchell	.25	.11	.03
□ 109	Steve Avery	.25	.11	.03
□ 110	Candy Maldonado	.10	.05	.01
□ 111	Bip Roberts	.10	.05	.01
□ 112	Lou Whitaker	.40	.18	.05
□ 113	Jeff Bagwell	1.25	.55	.16
□ 114	Dante Bichette	.40	.18	.05
□ 115	Brett Butler	.25	.11	.03
□ 116	Melido Perez	.10	.05	.01
□ 117	Andy Benes	.10	.05	.01
□ 118	Randy Johnson	.50	.23	.06
□ 119	Willie McGee	.10	.05	.01
□ 120	Jody Reed	.10	.05	.01
□ 121	Shawon Dunston	.10	.05	.01
□ 122	Carlos Baerga	.40	.18	.05
□ 123	Bret Saberhagen	.25	.11	.03
□ 124	John Olerud	.10	.05	.01
□ 125	Ivan Calderon	.10	.05	.01
□ 126	Bryan Harvey	.10	.05	.01
□ 127	Terry Mulholland	.10	.05	.01
□ 128	Ozzie Guillen	.10	.05	.01
□ 129	Steve Buechele	.10	.05	.01
□ 130	Kevin Tapani	.10	.05	.01
□ 131	Felix Jose	.10	.05	.01
□ 132	Terry Steinbach	.25	.11	.03
□ 133	Ron Gant	.40	.18	.05
□ 134	Harold Reynolds	.10	.05	.01
□ 135	Chris Sabo	.10	.05	.01
□ 136	Ivan Rodriguez	.60	.25	.07
□ 137	Eric Anthony	.10	.05	.01
□ 138	Mike Henneman	.10	.05	.01
□ 139	Robby Thompson	.10	.05	.01
□ 140	Scott Fletcher	.10	.05	.01
□ 141	Bruce Hurst	.10	.05	.01
□ 142	Kevin Maas	.10	.05	.01
□ 143	Tom Candiotti	.10	.05	.01
□ 144	Chris Hoiles	.10	.05	.01
□ 145	Mike Morgan	.10	.05	.01
□ 146	Mark Whiten	.10	.05	.01
□ 147	Dennis Martinez	.25	.11	.03
□ 148	Tony Pena	.10	.05	.01
□ 149	Dave Magadan	.10	.05	.01
□ 150	Mark Lewis	.10	.05	.01
□ 151	Mariano Duncan	.10	.05	.01
□ 152	Gregg Jefferies	.40	.18	.05
□ 153	Doug Drabek	.10	.05	.01
□ 154	Brian Harper	.10	.05	.01
□ 155	Ray Lankford	.40	.18	.05
□ 156	Carney Lansford	.25	.11	.03
□ 157	Mike Sharperson	.10	.05	.01
□ 158	Jack Morris	.25	.11	.03
□ 159	Otis Nixon	.10	.05	.01
□ 160	Steve Sax	.10	.05	.01
□ 161	Mark Lemke	.10	.05	.01
□ 162	Rafael Palmeiro	.40	.18	.05
□ 163	Jose Rijo	.10	.05	.01
□ 164	Omar Vizquel	.40	.18	.05
□ 165	Sammy Sosa	.50	.23	.06
□ 166	Milt Cuyler	.10	.05	.01
□ 167	John Franco	.10	.05	.01
□ 168	Darryl Hamilton	.10	.05	.01
□ 169	Ken Hill	.25	.11	.03
□ 170	Mike Devereaux	.10	.05	.01
□ 171	Don Slaught	.10	.05	.01
□ 172	Steve Farr	.10	.05	.01
□ 173	Bernard Gilkey	.40	.18	.05
□ 174	Mike Fetters	.10	.05	.01
□ 175	Vince Coleman	.10	.05	.01
□ 176	Kevin McReynolds	.10	.05	.01
□ 177	John Smoltz	.50	.23	.06
□ 178	Greg Gagne	.10	.05	.01
□ 179	Greg Swindell	.10	.05	.01
□ 180	Juan Guzman	.25	.11	.03
□ 181	Kal Daniels	.10	.05	.01
□ 182	Rick Sutcliffe	.10	.05	.01
□ 183	Orlando Merced	.25	.11	.03
□ 184	Bill Wegman	.10	.05	.01
□ 185	Mark Gardner	.10	.05	.01
□ 186	Rob Deer	.10	.05	.01
□ 187	Dave Hollins	.10	.05	.01
□ 188	Jack Clark	.10	.05	.01
□ 189	Brian Hunter	.10	.05	.01
□ 190	Tim Wallach	.10	.05	.01
□ 191	Tim Belcher	.10	.05	.01
□ 192	Walt Weiss	.10	.05	.01
□ 193	Kurt Stillwell	.10	.05	.01
□ 194	Charlie Hayes	.10	.05	.01
□ 195	Willie Randolph	.25	.11	.03
□ 196	Jack McDowell	.25	.11	.03
□ 197	Jose Offerman	.10	.05	.01
□ 198	Chuck Finley	.10	.05	.01
□ 199	Darrin Jackson	.10	.05	.01
□ 200	Kelly Gruber	.10	.05	.01
□ 201	John Wetteland	.25	.11	.03
□ 202	Jay Buhner	.40	.18	.05
□ 203	Mike LaValliere	.10	.05	.01
□ 204	Kevin Brown	.10	.05	.01
□ 205	Luis Gonzalez	.10	.05	.01
□ 206	Rick Aguilera	.10	.05	.01
□ 207	Norm Charlton	.10	.05	.01
□ 208	Mike Bordick	.10	.05	.01
□ 209	Charlie Leibrandt	.10	.05	.01
□ 210	Tom Brunansky	.10	.05	.01
□ 211	Tom Henke	.10	.05	.01
□ 212	Randy Milligan	.10	.05	.01
□ 213	Ramon Martinez	.25	.11	.03
□ 214	Mo Vaughn	.75	.35	.09
□ 215	Randy Myers	.25	.11	.03
□ 216	Greg Hibbard	.10	.05	.01
□ 217	Wes Chamberlain	.10	.05	.01
□ 218	Tony Phillips	.25	.11	.03
□ 219	Pete Harnisch	.10	.05	.01
□ 220	Mike Gallego	.10	.05	.01
□ 221	Bud Black	.10	.05	.01
□ 222	Greg Vaughn	.40	.18	.05
□ 223	Milt Thompson	.10	.05	.01
□ 224	Ben McDonald	.10	.05	.01
□ 225	Billy Hatcher	.10	.05	.01

□ 226 Paul Sorrento	.10	.05	.01
□ 227 Mark Gubicza	.10	.05	.01
□ 228 Mike Greenwell	.10	.05	.01
□ 229 Curt Schilling	.10	.05	.01
□ 230 Alan Trammell	.40	.18	.05
□ 231 Zane Smith	.10	.05	.01
□ 232 Bobby Thigpen	.10	.05	.01
□ 233 Greg Olson	.10	.05	.01
□ 234 Joe Orsulak	.10	.05	.01
□ 235 Joe Oliver	.10	.05	.01
□ 236 Tim Raines	.40	.18	.05
□ 237 Juan Samuel	.10	.05	.01
□ 238 Chili Davis	.25	.11	.03
□ 239 Spike Owen	.10	.05	.01
□ 240 Dave Stewart	.25	.11	.03
□ 241 Jim Eisenreich	.25	.11	.03
□ 242 Phil Plantier	.10	.05	.01
□ 243 Sid Fernandez	.10	.05	.01
□ 244 Dan Gladden	.10	.05	.01
□ 245 Mickey Morandini	.10	.05	.01
□ 246 Tino Martinez	.25	.11	.03
□ 247 Kirt Manwaring	.10	.05	.01
□ 248 Dean Palmer	.25	.11	.03
□ 249 Tom Browning	.10	.05	.01
□ 250 Brian McRae	.25	.11	.03
□ 251 Scott Leius	.10	.05	.01
□ 252 Bert Blyleven	.25	.11	.03
□ 253 Scott Erickson	.10	.05	.01
□ 254 Bob Welch	.10	.05	.01
□ 255 Pat Kelly	.10	.05	.01
□ 256 Felix Fermin	.10	.05	.01
□ 257 Harold Baines	.25	.11	.03
□ 258 Duane Ward	.10	.05	.01
□ 259 Bill Spiers	.10	.05	.01
□ 260 Jaime Navarro	.10	.05	.01
□ 261 Scott Sanderson	.10	.05	.01
□ 262 Gary Gaetti	.25	.11	.03
□ 263 Bob Ojeda	.10	.05	.01
□ 264 Jeff Montgomery	.25	.11	.03
□ 265 Scott Bankhead	.10	.05	.01
□ 266 Lance Johnson	.25	.11	.03
□ 267 Rafael Belliard	.10	.05	.01
□ 268 Kevin Reimer	.10	.05	.01
□ 269 Benito Santiago	.10	.05	.01
□ 270 Mike Moore	.10	.05	.01
□ 271 Dave Fleming	.10	.05	.01
□ 272 Moises Alou	.40	.18	.05
□ 273 Pat Listach	.10	.05	.01
□ 274 Reggie Sanders	.40	.18	.05
□ 275 Kenny Lofton	1.25	.55	.16
□ 276 Donovan Osborne	.10	.05	.01
□ 277 Rusty Meacham	.10	.05	.01
□ 278 Eric Karros	.40	.18	.05
□ 279 Andy Stankiewicz	.10	.05	.01
□ 280 Brian Jordan	.40	.18	.05
□ 281 Gary DiSarcina	.10	.05	.01
□ 282 Mark Wohlers	.25	.11	.03
□ 283 Dave Nilsson	.25	.11	.03
□ 284 Anthony Young	.10	.05	.01
□ 285 Jim Bullinger	.10	.05	.01
□ 286 Derek Bell	.40	.18	.05
□ 287 Brian Williams	.10	.05	.01
□ 288 Julio Valera	.10	.05	.01
□ 289 Dan Walters	.10	.05	.01
□ 290 Chad Curtis	.25	.11	.03
□ 291 Michael Tucker DP	.40	.18	.05
□ 292 Bob Zupcic	.10	.05	.01
□ 293 Todd Hundley	.40	.18	.05
□ 294 Jeff Tackett	.10	.05	.01
□ 295 Greg Colbrunn	.10	.05	.01
□ 296 Cal Eldred	.10	.05	.01
□ 297 Chris Roberts DP	.25	.11	.03
□ 298 John Doherty	.10	.05	.01
□ 299 Denny Neagle	.25	.11	.03
□ 300 Arthur Rhodes	.10	.05	.01
□ 301 Mark Clark	.10	.05	.01
□ 302 Scott Cooper	.10	.05	.01
□ 303 Jamie Arnold DP	.25	.11	.03
□ 304 Jim Thome	1.50	.70	.19
□ 305 Frank Seminara	.10	.05	.01
□ 306 Kurt Knudsen	.10	.05	.01
□ 307 Tim Wakefield	.25	.11	.03
□ 308 John Jaha	.25	.11	.03
□ 309 Pat Hentgen	.40	.18	.05
□ 310 B.J. Wallace DP	.10	.05	.01
□ 311 Roberto Hernandez	.25	.11	.03
□ 312 Hipolito Pichardo	.10	.05	.01
□ 313 Eric Fox	.10	.05	.01
□ 314 Willie Banks	.10	.05	.01
□ 315 Sam Militello	.10	.05	.01
□ 316 Vince Horsman	.10	.05	.01
□ 317 Carlos Hernandez	.10	.05	.01
□ 318 Jeff Kent	.25	.11	.03
□ 319 Mike Perez	.10	.05	.01
□ 320 Scott Livingstone	.10	.05	.01
□ 321 Jeff Conine	.40	.18	.05
□ 322 James Austin	.10	.05	.01
□ 323 John Vander Wal	.10	.05	.01
□ 324 Pat Mahomes	.10	.05	.01
□ 325 Pedro Astacio	.10	.05	.01
□ 326 Bret Boone UER (Misspelled Brett)	.25	.11	.03
□ 327 Matt Stairs	.10	.05	.01
□ 328 Damion Easley	.10	.05	.01
□ 329 Ben Rivera	.10	.05	.01
□ 330 Reggie Jefferson	.25	.11	.03
□ 331 Luis Mercedes	.10	.05	.01
□ 332 Kyle Abbott	.10	.05	.01
□ 333 Eddie Taubensee	.10	.05	.01
□ 334 Tim McIntosh	.10	.05	.01
□ 335 Phil Clark	.10	.05	.01
□ 336 Wil Cordero	.25	.11	.03
□ 337 Russ Springer	.10	.05	.01
□ 338 Craig Colbert	.10	.05	.01
□ 339 Tim Salmon	.75	.35	.09
□ 340 Braulio Castillo	.10	.05	.01
□ 341 Donald Harris	.10	.05	.01
□ 342 Eric Young	.40	.18	.05
□ 343 Bob Wickman	.10	.05	.01
□ 344 John Valentin	.40	.18	.05
□ 345 Dan Wilson	.25	.11	.03
□ 346 Steve Hosey	.10	.05	.01
□ 347 Mike Piazza	3.00	1.35	.35
□ 348 Willie Greene	.25	.11	.03
□ 349 Tom Goodwin	.10	.05	.01
□ 350 Eric Hillman	.10	.05	.01
□ 351 Steve Reed	.10	.05	.01
□ 352 Dan Serafini DP	.50	.23	.06
□ 353 Todd Steverson DP	.25	.11	.03
□ 354 Benji Grigsby DP	.10	.05	.01
□ 355 Shannon Stewart DP	.50	.23	.06
□ 356 Sean Lowe DP	.25	.11	.03
□ 357 Derek Wallace DP	.10	.05	.01
□ 358 Rick Helling DP	.25	.11	.03
□ 359 Jason Kendall DP	2.00	.90	.25
□ 360 Derek Jeter DP	6.00	2.70	.75
□ 361 David Cone	.40	.18	.05
□ 362 Jeff Reardon	.25	.11	.03
□ 363 Bobby Witt	.10	.05	.01
□ 364 Jose Canseco	.40	.18	.05
□ 365 Jeff Russell	.10	.05	.01
□ 366 Ruben Sierra	.25	.11	.03
□ 367 Alan Mills	.10	.05	.01
□ 368 Matt Nokes	.10	.05	.01
□ 369 Pat Borders	.10	.05	.01
□ 370 Pedro Munoz	.10	.05	.01
□ 371 Danny Jackson	.10	.05	.01
□ 372 Geronimo Pena	.10	.05	.01
□ 373 Craig Lefferts	.10	.05	.01
□ 374 Joe Grahe	.10	.05	.01
□ 375 Roger McDowell	.10	.05	.01
□ 376 Jimmy Key	.25	.11	.03
□ 377 Steve Olin	.10	.05	.01
□ 378 Glenn Davis	.10	.05	.01
□ 379 Rene Gonzales	.10	.05	.01
□ 380 Manuel Lee	.10	.05	.01
□ 381 Ron Karkovice	.10	.05	.01
□ 382 Sid Bream	.10	.05	.01
□ 383 Gerald Williams	.10	.05	.01
□ 384 Lenny Harris	.10	.05	.01
□ 385 J.T. Snow	.40	.18	.05
□ 386 Dave Stieb	.10	.05	.01
□ 387 Kirk McCaskill	.10	.05	.01
□ 388 Lance Parrish	.10	.05	.01
□ 389 Craig Grebeck	.10	.05	.01
□ 390 Rick Wilkins	.10	.05	.01
□ 391 Manny Alexander	.10	.05	.01
□ 392 Mike Schooler	.10	.05	.01
□ 393 Bernie Williams	.50	.23	.06
□ 394 Kevin Koslofski	.10	.05	.01
□ 395 Willie Wilson	.10	.05	.01
□ 396 Jeff Parrett	.10	.05	.01

□ 397 Mike Harkey	.10	.05	.01
□ 398 Frank Tanana	.10	.05	.01
□ 399 Doug Henry	.10	.05	.01
□ 400 Royce Clayton	.25	.11	.03
□ 401 Eric Wedge	.10	.05	.01
□ 402 Derrick May	.10	.05	.01
□ 403 Carlos Garcia	.10	.05	.01
□ 404 Henry Rodriguez	.40	.18	.05
□ 405 Ryan Klesko	1.50	.70	.19

1993 Select Aces

This 24-card standard-size set features some of the top starting pitchers in both leagues. The cards were randomly inserted into one in every eight 28-card super packs. The fronts display an action player pose cut out and superimposed on a metallic variegated red and silver diamond design. The diamond itself rests on a background consisting of silver metallic streaks that emanate from the center of the card. In imitation of playing card design, the fronts have a large "A" for Ace in upper left and lower right corners. The player's name in the upper right corner rounds out the card face.

	MINT	NRMT	EXC
COMPLETE SET (24)	80.00	36.00	10.00
COMMON CARD (1-24)	2.50	1.10	.30
SEMISTARS	5.00	2.20	.60
RANDOM INSERTS IN JUMBO PACKS			
□ 1 Roger Clemens	8.00	3.60	1.00
□ 2 Tom Glavine	8.00	3.60	1.00
□ 3 Jack McDowell	5.00	2.20	.60
□ 4 Greg Maddux	30.00	13.50	3.70
□ 5 Jack Morris	5.00	2.20	.60
□ 6 Dennis Martinez	5.00	2.20	.60
□ 7 Kevin Brown	2.50	1.10	.30
□ 8 Dwight Gooden	5.00	2.20	.60
□ 9 Kevin Appier	5.00	2.20	.60
□ 10 Mike Morgan	2.50	1.10	.30
□ 11 Juan Guzman	5.00	2.20	.60
□ 12 Charles Nagy	5.00	2.20	.60
□ 13 John Smiley	2.50	1.10	.30
□ 14 Ken Hill	5.00	2.20	.60
□ 15 Bob Tewksbury	2.50	1.10	.30
□ 16 Doug Drabek	5.00	2.20	.60
□ 17 John Smoltz	8.00	3.60	1.00
□ 18 Greg Swindell	2.50	1.10	.30
□ 19 Bruce Hurst	2.50	1.10	.30
□ 20 Mike Mussina	10.00	4.50	1.25
□ 21 Cal Eldred	2.50	1.10	.30
□ 22 Melido Perez	2.50	1.10	.30
□ 23 Dave Fleming	2.50	1.10	.30
□ 24 Kevin Tapani	2.50	1.10	.30

1993 Select Chase Rookies

This 21-card standard-size set showcases 1992's best rookies. The cards were randomly inserted into one in every eighteen 15-card hobby packs. The fronts exhibit Score's "dufex" printing process, in which a color photo is printed on a metallic base creating an unusual, three-dimensional look. The pictures are tilted slightly to the left and edged on the left and bottom by red metallic borders.

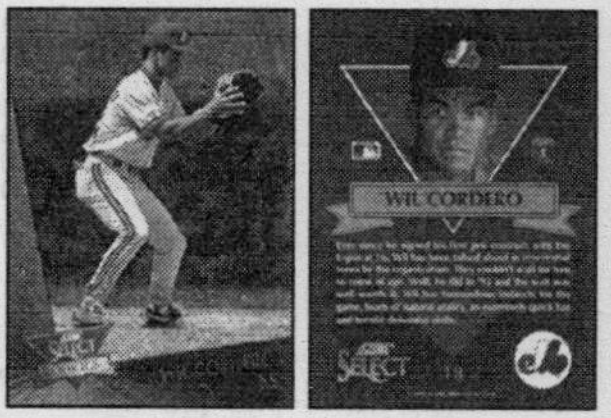

	MINT	NRMT	EXC
COMPLETE SET (21)	150.00	70.00	19.00
COMMON CARD (1-21)	2.50	1.10	.30
SEMISTARS	5.00	2.20	.60
RANDOM INSERTS IN HOBBY PACKS			
□ 1 Pat Listach	2.50	1.10	.30
□ 2 Moises Alou	5.00	2.20	.60
□ 3 Reggie Sanders	10.00	4.50	1.25
□ 4 Kenny Lofton	50.00	22.00	6.25
□ 5 Eric Karros	10.00	4.50	1.25
□ 6 Brian Williams	2.50	1.10	.30
□ 7 Donovan Osborne	5.00	2.20	.60
□ 8 Sam Militello	2.50	1.10	.30
□ 9 Chad Curtis	5.00	2.20	.60
□ 10 Bob Zupcic	2.50	1.10	.30
□ 11 Tim Salmon	30.00	13.50	3.70
□ 12 Jeff Conine	10.00	4.50	1.25
□ 13 Pedro Astacio	5.00	2.20	.60
□ 14 Arthur Rhodes	2.50	1.10	.30
□ 15 Cal Eldred	2.50	1.10	.30
□ 16 Tim Wakefield	5.00	2.20	.60
□ 17 Andy Stankiewicz	2.50	1.10	.30
□ 18 Wil Cordero	5.00	2.20	.60
□ 19 Todd Hundley	15.00	6.75	1.85
□ 20 Dave Fleming	2.50	1.10	.30
□ 21 Bret Boone	5.00	2.20	.60

1993 Select Chase Stars

This 24-card standard-size set showcases the top players in Major League Baseball. The cards were randomly inserted into one in every eighteen retail 15-card packs. The fronts exhibit Score's "dufex" printing process, in which a color photo is printed on a metallic base creating an unusual, three-dimensional look. The pictures are tilted slightly to the left and edged on the left and bottom by green metallic borders.

	MINT	NRMT	EXC
COMPLETE SET (24)	150.00	70.00	19.00
COMMON CARD (1-24)	2.00	.90	.25
SEMISTARS	4.00	1.80	.50
RANDOM INSERTS IN RETAIL PACKS			
□ 1 Fred McGriff	5.00	2.20	.60
□ 2 Ryne Sandberg	10.00	4.50	1.25
□ 3 Ozzie Smith	8.00	3.60	1.00
□ 4 Gary Sheffield	6.00	2.70	.75
□ 5 Darren Daulton	2.00	.90	.25
□ 6 Andy Van Slyke	2.00	.90	.25

□ 7 Barry Bonds	10.00	4.50	1.25
□ 8 Tony Gwynn	15.00	6.75	1.85
□ 9 Greg Maddux	25.00	11.00	3.10
□ 10 Tom Glavine	5.00	2.20	.60
□ 11 John Franco	2.00	.90	.25
□ 12 Lee Smith	4.00	1.80	.50
□ 13 Cecil Fielder	4.00	1.80	.50
□ 14 Roberto Alomar	10.00	4.50	1.25
□ 15 Cal Ripken	30.00	13.50	3.70
□ 16 Edgar Martinez	5.00	2.20	.60
□ 17 Ivan Rodriguez	8.00	3.60	1.00
□ 18 Kirby Puckett	12.00	5.50	1.50
□ 19 Ken Griffey Jr.	40.00	18.00	5.00
□ 20 Joe Carter	4.00	1.80	.50
□ 21 Roger Clemens	5.00	2.20	.60
□ 22 Dave Fleming	2.00	.90	.25
□ 23 Paul Molitor	8.00	3.60	1.00
□ 24 Dennis Eckersley	4.00	1.80	.50

1993 Select Stat Leaders

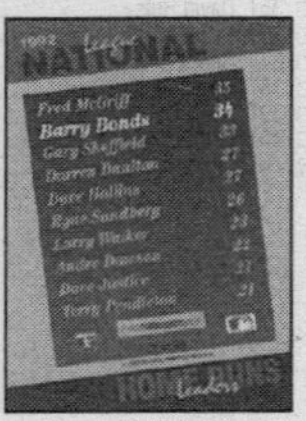

Featuring 45 cards from each league, these 90 Stat Leaders were inserted one per 1993 Score pack in every regular pack and super pack. The fronts feature color player action photos that are borderless on the sides and have oblique green borders at the top and bottom. The player's name appears within an oblique orange stripe across the bottom of the photo. The player's league appears within the top border, and the set's title appears within the bottom border.

	MINT	NRMT	EXC
COMPLETE SET (90)	12.00	5.50	1.50
COMMON CARD (1-90)	.15	.07	.02
SEMISTARS	.30	.14	.04
ONE PER SCORE PACK			
□ 1 Edgar Martinez	.30	.14	.04
□ 2 Kirby Puckett	.60	.25	.07
□ 3 Frank Thomas	2.00	.90	.25
□ 4 Gary Sheffield	.30	.14	.04
□ 5 Andy Van Slyke	.30	.14	.04
□ 6 John Kruk	.30	.14	.04
□ 7 Kirby Puckett	.60	.25	.07
□ 8 Carlos Baerga	.30	.14	.04
□ 9 Paul Molitor	.40	.18	.05
□ 10 Terry Pendleton	.15	.07	.02
Andy Van Slyke			
□ 11 Ryne Sandberg	.50	.23	.06
□ 12 Mark Grace	.30	.14	.04
□ 13 Frank Thomas	1.00	.45	.12
Edgar Martinez			
□ 14 Don Mattingly	.50	.23	.06
Robin Yount			
□ 15 Ken Griffey	2.00	.90	.25
□ 16 Andy Van Slyke	.30	.14	.04
□ 17 Mariano Duncan	.30	.14	.04
Will Clark			
Ray Lankford			
□ 18 Marquis Grissom	.30	.14	.04
Terry Pendleton			
□ 19 Lance Johnson	.30	.14	.04
□ 20 Mike Devereaux	.15	.07	.02
□ 21 Brady Anderson	.30	.14	.04
□ 22 Deion Sanders	.30	.14	.04
□ 23 Steve Finley	.30	.14	.04
□ 24 Andy Van Slyke	.30	.14	.04
□ 25 Juan Gonzalez	1.00	.45	.12
□ 26 Mark McGwire	.60	.25	.07
□ 27 Cecil Fielder	.30	.14	.04
□ 28 Fred McGriff	.30	.14	.04
□ 29 Barry Bonds	.50	.23	.06
□ 30 Gary Sheffield	.30	.14	.04
□ 31 Cecil Fielder	.30	.14	.04
□ 32 Joe Carter	.30	.14	.04
□ 33 Frank Thomas	2.00	.90	.25
□ 34 Darren Daulton	.30	.14	.04
□ 35 Terry Pendleton	.30	.14	.04
□ 36 Fred McGriff	.30	.14	.04
□ 37 Tony Phillips	.30	.14	.04
□ 38 Frank Thomas	2.00	.90	.25
□ 39 Roberto Alomar	.50	.23	.06
□ 40 Barry Bonds	.50	.23	.06
□ 41 Dave Hollins	.15	.07	.02
□ 42 Andy Van Slyke	.30	.14	.04
□ 43 Mark McGwire	.60	.25	.07
□ 44 Edgar Martinez	.30	.14	.04
□ 45 Frank Thomas	2.00	.90	.25
□ 46 Barry Bonds	.50	.23	.06
□ 47 Gary Sheffield	.30	.14	.04
□ 48 Fred McGriff	.30	.14	.04
□ 49 Frank Thomas	2.00	.90	.25
□ 50 Danny Tartabull	.15	.07	.02
□ 51 Roberto Alomar	.50	.23	.06
□ 52 Barry Bonds	.50	.23	.06
□ 53 John Kruk	.30	.14	.04
□ 54 Brett Butler	.30	.14	.04
□ 55 Kenny Lofton	.75	.35	.09
□ 56 Pat Listach	.15	.07	.02
□ 57 Brady Anderson	.30	.14	.04
□ 58 Marquis Grissom	.30	.14	.04
□ 59 Delino DeShields	.15	.07	.02
□ 60 Bip Roberts	.30	.14	.04
Steve Finley			
□ 61 Jack McDowell	.30	.14	.04
□ 62 Kevin Brown	.30	.14	.04
Roger Clemens			
□ 63 Charles Nagy	.15	.07	.02
Melido Perez			
□ 64 Terry Mulholland	.15	.07	.02
□ 65 Curt Schilling	.15	.07	.02
Doug Drabek			
□ 66 Greg Maddux	1.00	.45	.12
John Smoltz			
□ 67 Dennis Eckersley	.30	.14	.04
□ 68 Rick Aguilera	.15	.07	.02
□ 69 Jeff Montgomery	.30	.14	.04
□ 70 Lee Smith	.30	.14	.04
□ 71 Randy Myers	.30	.14	.04
□ 72 John Wetteland	.30	.14	.04
□ 73 Randy Johnson	.30	.14	.04
□ 74 Melido Perez	.15	.07	.02
□ 75 Roger Clemens	.30	.14	.04
□ 76 John Smoltz	.30	.14	.04
□ 77 David Cone	.30	.14	.04
□ 78 Greg Maddux	1.25	.55	.16
□ 79 Roger Clemens	.30	.14	.04
□ 80 Kevin Appier	.30	.14	.04
□ 81 Mike Mussina	.40	.18	.05
□ 82 Bill Swift	.15	.07	.02
□ 83 Bob Tewksbury	.15	.07	.02
□ 84 Greg Maddux	1.25	.55	.16
□ 85 Jack Morris	.30	.14	.04
Kevin Brown			
□ 86 Jack McDowell	.30	.14	.04
□ 87 Roger Clemens	.40	.18	.05
Mike Mussina			
□ 88 Tom Glavine	1.00	.45	.12
Greg Maddux			
□ 89 Ken Hill	.15	.07	.02
Bob Tewksbury			
□ 90 Mike Morgan	.15	.07	.02
Dennis Martinez			

1993 Select Triple Crown

Honoring the three most recent Triple Crown winners since 1993, cards from this 3-card standard-size set were randomly inserted in 15-card hobby packs. The fronts exhibit Score's "dufex" printing process, in which a color photo is printed on a metallic base creating an unusual, three-dimensional look. The color player

photos on the fronts have a forest green metallic border. The player's name and the year he won the Triple Crown appear above the picture, while the words "Triple Crown" are written in script beneath it.

	MINT	NRMT	EXC
COMPLETE SET (3)	110.00	50.00	14.00
COMMON CARD (1-3)	20.00	9.00	2.50
RANDOM INSERTS IN HOBBY PACKS			
□ 1 Mickey Mantle	80.00	36.00	10.00
□ 2 Carl Yastrzemski	20.00	9.00	2.50
□ 3 Frank Robinson	20.00	9.00	2.50

1993 Select Rookie/Traded

These 150 standard-size cards feature rookies and traded veteran players. The production run comprised 1,950 individually numbered cases. Cards were distributed in foil packs. Card design is similar to the regular 1993 Select cards excpt for the dramatic royal blue borders (instead of emerald green for the regular cards) and T-suffixed numbering. There are no key Rookie Cards in this set. Two Rookie of the Year insert cards and a Nolan Ryan Tribute card were randomly inserted in the foil packs. The chances of finding a Nolan Ryan card was listed at not less than one per 288 packs. The two ROY cards, featuring American League Rookie of the Year, Tim Salmon and National League Rookie of the Year, Mike Piazza were randomly inserted into one in every 576 packs.

	MINT	NRMT	EXC
COMPLETE SET (150)	20.00	9.00	2.50
COMMON CARD (1T-150T)	.10	.05	.01
SEMISTARS	.25	.11	.03
STARS	.50	.23	.06
□ 1T Rickey Henderson	.50	.23	.06
□ 2T Rob Deer	.10	.05	.01
□ 3T Tim Belcher	.10	.05	.01
□ 4T Gary Sheffield	1.00	.45	.12
□ 5T Fred McGriff	.75	.35	.09
□ 6T Mark Whiten	.10	.05	.01
□ 7T Jeff Russell	.10	.05	.01
□ 8T Harold Baines	.25	.11	.03
□ 9T Dave Winfield	.50	.23	.06
□ 10T Ellis Burks	.50	.23	.06
□ 11T Andre Dawson	.50	.23	.06
□ 12T Gregg Jefferies	.50	.23	.06
□ 13T Jimmy Key	.25	.11	.03
□ 14T Harold Reynolds	.10	.05	.01
□ 15T Tom Henke	.10	.05	.01
□ 16T Paul Molitor	1.25	.55	.16
□ 17T Wade Boggs	.50	.23	.06
□ 18T David Cone	.50	.23	.06
□ 19T Tony Fernandez	.10	.05	.01
□ 20T Roberto Kelly	.10	.05	.01
□ 21T Paul O'Neill	.25	.11	.03
□ 22T Jose Lind	.10	.05	.01
□ 23T Barry Bonds	1.50	.70	.19
□ 24T Dave Stewart	.25	.11	.03
□ 25T Randy Myers	.25	.11	.03
□ 26T Benito Santiago	.10	.05	.01
□ 27T Tim Wallach	.10	.05	.01
□ 28T Greg Gagne	.10	.05	.01
□ 29T Kevin Mitchell	.25	.11	.03
□ 30T Jim Abbott	.10	.05	.01
□ 31T Lee Smith	.25	.11	.03
□ 32T Bobby Munoz	.10	.05	.01
□ 33T Mo Sanford	.10	.05	.01
□ 34T John Roper	.10	.05	.01
□ 35T David Hulse	.10	.05	.01
□ 36T Pedro Martinez	.50	.23	.06
□ 37T Chuck Carr	.10	.05	.01
□ 38T Armando Reynoso	.10	.05	.01
□ 39T Ryan Thompson	.10	.05	.01
□ 40T Carlos Garcia	.10	.05	.01
□ 41T Matt Whiteside	.10	.05	.01
□ 42T Benji Gil	.25	.11	.03
□ 43T Rodney Bolton	.10	.05	.01
□ 44T J.T. Snow	.50	.23	.06
□ 45T David McCarty	.10	.05	.01
□ 46T Paul Quantrill	.10	.05	.01
□ 47T Al Martin	.25	.11	.03
□ 48T Lance Painter	.10	.05	.01
□ 49T Lou Frazier	.10	.05	.01
□ 50T Eduardo Perez	.10	.05	.01
□ 51T Kevin Young	.10	.05	.01
□ 52T Mike Trombley	.10	.05	.01
□ 53T Sterling Hitchcock	1.00	.45	.12
□ 54T Tim Bogar	.10	.05	.01
□ 55T Hilly Hathaway	.10	.05	.01
□ 56T Wayne Kirby	.10	.05	.01
□ 57T Craig Paquette	.10	.05	.01
□ 58T Bret Boone	.25	.11	.03
□ 59T Greg McMichael	.25	.11	.03
□ 60T Mike Lansing	.25	.11	.03
□ 61T Brent Gates	.25	.11	.03
□ 62T Rene Arocha	.10	.05	.01
□ 63T Ricky Gutierrez	.10	.05	.01
□ 64T Kevin Rogers	.10	.05	.01
□ 65T Ken Ryan	.10	.05	.01
□ 66T Phil Hiatt	.10	.05	.01
□ 67T Pat Meares	.25	.11	.03
□ 68T Troy Neel	.10	.05	.01
□ 69T Steve Cooke	.10	.05	.01
□ 70T Sherman Obando	.10	.05	.01
□ 71T Blas Minor	.10	.05	.01
□ 72T Angel Miranda	.10	.05	.01
□ 73T Tom Kramer	.10	.05	.01
□ 74T Chip Hale	.10	.05	.01
□ 75T Brad Pennington	.10	.05	.01
□ 76T Graeme Lloyd	.10	.05	.01
□ 77T Darrell Whitmore	.10	.05	.01
□ 78T David Nied	.10	.05	.01
□ 79T Todd Van Poppel	.10	.05	.01
□ 80T Chris Gomez	.25	.11	.03
□ 81T Jason Bere	.25	.11	.03
□ 82T Jeffrey Hammonds	.25	.11	.03
□ 83T Brad Ausmus	.10	.05	.01
□ 84T Kevin Stocker	.25	.11	.03
□ 85T Jeromy Burnitz	.10	.05	.01
□ 86T Aaron Sele	.25	.11	.03
□ 87T Roberto Mejia	.10	.05	.01
□ 88T Kirk Rueter	.10	.05	.01
□ 89T Kevin Roberson	.10	.05	.01
□ 90T Allen Watson	.10	.05	.01
□ 91T Charlie Leibrandt	.10	.05	.01
□ 92T Eric Davis	.25	.11	.03
□ 93T Jody Reed	.10	.05	.01
□ 94T Danny Jackson	.10	.05	.01
□ 95T Gary Gaetti	.25	.11	.03
□ 96T Norm Charlton	.10	.05	.01
□ 97T Doug Drabek	.10	.05	.01
□ 98T Scott Fletcher	.10	.05	.01

□ 99T Greg Swindell	.10	.05	.01
□ 100T John Smiley	.10	.05	.01
□ 101T Kevin Reimer	.10	.05	.01
□ 102T Andres Galarraga	.50	.23	.06
□ 103T Greg Hibbard	.10	.05	.01
□ 104T Chris Hammond	.10	.05	.01
□ 105T Darnell Coles	.10	.05	.01
□ 106T Mike Felder	.10	.05	.01
□ 107T Jose Guzman	.10	.05	.01
□ 108T Chris Bosio	.10	.05	.01
□ 109T Spike Owen	.10	.05	.01
□ 110T Felix Jose	.10	.05	.01
□ 111T Cory Snyder	.10	.05	.01
□ 112T Craig Lefferts	.10	.05	.01
□ 113T David Wells	.10	.05	.01
□ 114T Pete Incaviglia	.10	.05	.01
□ 115T Mike Pagliarulo	.10	.05	.01
□ 116T Dave Magadan	.10	.05	.01
□ 117T Charlie Hough	.10	.05	.01
□ 118T Ivan Calderon	.10	.05	.01
□ 119T Manuel Lee	.10	.05	.01
□ 120T Bob Patterson	.10	.05	.01
□ 121T Bob Ojeda	.10	.05	.01
□ 122T Scott Bankhead	.10	.05	.01
□ 123T Greg Maddux	4.00	1.80	.50
□ 124T Chili Davis	.25	.11	.03
□ 125T Milt Thompson	.10	.05	.01
□ 126T Dave Martinez	.10	.05	.01
□ 127T Frank Tanana	.10	.05	.01
□ 128T Phil Plantier	.10	.05	.01
□ 129T Juan Samuel	.10	.05	.01
□ 130T Eric Young	.50	.23	.06
□ 131T Joe Orsulak	.10	.05	.01
□ 132T Derek Bell	.50	.23	.06
□ 133T Darrin Jackson	.10	.05	.01
□ 134T Tom Brunansky	.10	.05	.01
□ 135T Jeff Reardon	.25	.11	.03
□ 136T Kevin Higgins	.10	.05	.01
□ 137T Joel Johnston	.10	.05	.01
□ 138T Rick Trlicek	.10	.05	.01
□ 139T Richie Lewis	.10	.05	.01
□ 140T Jeff Gardner	.10	.05	.01
□ 141T Jack Voigt	.10	.05	.01
□ 142T Rod Correia	.10	.05	.01
□ 143T Billy Brewer	.10	.05	.01
□ 144T Terry Jorgensen	.10	.05	.01
□ 145T Rich Amaral	.10	.05	.01
□ 146T Sean Berry	.10	.05	.01
□ 147T Dan Peltier	.10	.05	.01
□ 148T Paul Wagner	.10	.05	.01
□ 149T Damon Buford	.10	.05	.01
□ 150T Wil Cordero	.25	.11	.03
□ NR1 Nolan Ryan Tribute	125.00	55.00	15.50
□ ROY1 Tim Salmon AL ROY	30.00	13.50	3.70
□ ROY2 Mike Piazza NL ROY	80.00	36.00	10.00

1993 Select R/T All-Star Rookies

This ten-card standard-size set was randomly inserted in foil packs of 1993 Select Rookie and Traded. The insertion rate was reportedly not less than one in 36 packs. The cards feature on their fronts color player action shots that have a grainy metallic appearance. These photos are borderless, except at the top, where the silver-colored player's name is displayed upon red and blue metallic stripes. The set's title appears within a metallic silver-colored stripe near the bottom, which has a star-and-baseball icon emblazoned over its center. This combination of the set's title, stripe, and star-and-baseball icon reappears at the top of the non-metallic back, but in a red, white, and blue design. The player's name, position, and team logo are shown on the red-colored right half of the card. His career highlights appear in white lettering on the blue-colored left half.

	MINT	NRMT	EXC
COMPLETE SET (10)	150.00	70.00	19.00
COMMON CARD (1-10)	5.00	2.20	.60
SEMISTARS	8.00	3.60	1.00
RANDOM INSERTS IN PACKS			

□ 1 Jeff Conine	12.00	5.50	1.50
□ 2 Brent Gates	8.00	3.60	1.00
□ 3 Mike Lansing	8.00	3.60	1.00
□ 4 Kevin Stocker	8.00	3.60	1.00
□ 5 Mike Piazza	80.00	36.00	10.00
□ 6 Jeffrey Hammonds	8.00	3.60	1.00
□ 7 David Hulse	5.00	2.20	.60
□ 8 Tim Salmon	30.00	13.50	3.70
□ 9 Rene Arocha	5.00	2.20	.60
□ 10 Greg McMichael	5.00	2.20	.60

1994 Select

Measuring the standard size, the 1994 Select set consists of 420 cards that were issued in two series of 210. The horizontal fronts feature a color player action photo and a duo-tone player shot. The backs are vertical and contain a photo, 1993 and career statistics and highlights. Special Dave Winfield and Cal Ripken cards were inserted in first series packs. A Paul Molitor MVP card and a Carlos Delgado Rookie of the Year card were inserted in second series packs. The insertion rate for ech card was one in 360 packs. Rookie Cards include Kurt Abbott, Brian Anderson and Chan Ho Park.

	MINT	NRMT	EXC
COMPLETE SET (420)	30.00	13.50	3.70
COMPLETE SERIES 1 (210)	18.00	8.00	2.20
COMPLETE SERIES 2 (210)	12.00	5.50	1.50
COMMON CARD (1-420)	.10	.05	.01
SEMISTARS	.25	.11	.03
STARS	.50	.23	.06

□ 1 Ken Griffey Jr.	3.00	1.35	.35
□ 2 Greg Maddux	2.00	.90	.25
□ 3 Paul Molitor	.60	.25	.07
□ 4 Mike Piazza	2.00	.90	.25
□ 5 Jay Bell	.25	.11	.03
□ 6 Frank Thomas	3.00	1.35	.35
□ 7 Barry Larkin	.50	.23	.06
□ 8 Paul O'Neill	.25	.11	.03
□ 9 Darren Daulton	.25	.11	.03
□ 10 Mike Greenwell	.10	.05	.01
□ 11 Chuck Carr	.10	.05	.01
□ 12 Joe Carter	.50	.23	.06
□ 13 Lance Johnson	.25	.11	.03
□ 14 Jeff Blauser	.10	.05	.01
□ 15 Chris Hoiles	.10	.05	.01
□ 16 Rick Wilkins	.10	.05	.01
□ 17 Kirby Puckett	1.00	.45	.12

□ 18	Larry Walker	.50	.23	.06
□ 19	Randy Johnson	.50	.23	.06
□ 20	Bernard Gilkey	.25	.11	.03
□ 21	Devon White	.10	.05	.01
□ 22	Randy Myers	.10	.05	.01
□ 23	Don Mattingly	1.50	.70	.19
□ 24	John Kruk	.25	.11	.03
□ 25	Ozzie Guillen	.10	.05	.01
□ 26	Jeff Conine	.50	.23	.06
□ 27	Mike Macfarlane	.10	.05	.01
□ 28	Dave Hollins	.10	.05	.01
□ 29	Chuck Knoblauch	.50	.23	.06
□ 30	Ozzie Smith	.60	.25	.07
□ 31	Harold Baines	.25	.11	.03
□ 32	Ryne Sandberg	.75	.35	.09
□ 33	Ron Karkovice	.10	.05	.01
□ 34	Terry Pendleton	.25	.11	.03
□ 35	Wally Joyner	.25	.11	.03
□ 36	Mike Mussina	.60	.25	.07
□ 37	Felix Jose	.10	.05	.01
□ 38	Derrick May	.10	.05	.01
□ 39	Scott Cooper	.10	.05	.01
□ 40	Jose Rijo	.10	.05	.01
□ 41	Robin Ventura	.25	.11	.03
□ 42	Charlie Hayes	.10	.05	.01
□ 43	Jimmy Key	.25	.11	.03
□ 44	Eric Karros	.25	.11	.03
□ 45	Ruben Sierra	.25	.11	.03
□ 46	Ryan Thompson	.10	.05	.01
□ 47	Brian McRae	.25	.11	.03
□ 48	Pat Hentgen	.50	.23	.06
□ 49	John Valentin	.25	.11	.03
□ 50	Al Martin	.10	.05	.01
□ 51	Jose Lind	.10	.05	.01
□ 52	Kevin Stocker	.10	.05	.01
□ 53	Mike Gallego	.10	.05	.01
□ 54	Dwight Gooden	.25	.11	.03
□ 55	Brady Anderson	.50	.23	.06
□ 56	Jeff King	.25	.11	.03
□ 57	Mark McGwire	1.00	.45	.12
□ 58	Sammy Sosa	.50	.23	.06
□ 59	Ryan Bowen	.10	.05	.01
□ 60	Mark Lemke	.10	.05	.01
□ 61	Roger Clemens	.50	.23	.06
□ 62	Brian Jordan	.50	.23	.06
□ 63	Andres Galarraga	.50	.23	.06
□ 64	Kevin Appier	.25	.11	.03
□ 65	Don Slaught	.10	.05	.01
□ 66	Mike Blowers	.10	.05	.01
□ 67	Wes Chamberlain	.10	.05	.01
□ 68	Troy Neel	.10	.05	.01
□ 69	John Wetteland	.25	.11	.03
□ 70	Joe Girardi	.10	.05	.01
□ 71	Reggie Sanders	.50	.23	.06
□ 72	Edgar Martinez	.50	.23	.06
□ 73	Todd Hundley	.50	.23	.06
□ 74	Pat Borders	.10	.05	.01
□ 75	Roberto Mejia	.10	.05	.01
□ 76	David Cone	.50	.23	.06
□ 77	Tony Gwynn	1.25	.55	.16
□ 78	Jim Abbott	.10	.05	.01
□ 79	Jay Buhner	.50	.23	.06
□ 80	Mark McLemore	.10	.05	.01
□ 81	Wil Cordero	.25	.11	.03
□ 82	Pedro Astacio	.10	.05	.01
□ 83	Bob Tewksbury	.10	.05	.01
□ 84	Dave Winfield	.50	.23	.06
□ 85	Jeff Kent	.10	.05	.01
□ 86	Todd Van Poppel	.10	.05	.01
□ 87	Steve Avery	.25	.11	.03
□ 88	Mike Lansing	.25	.11	.03
□ 89	Lenny Dykstra	.25	.11	.03
□ 90	Jose Guzman	.10	.05	.01
□ 91	Brian R. Hunter	.10	.05	.01
□ 92	Tim Raines	.50	.23	.06
□ 93	Andre Dawson	.50	.23	.06
□ 94	Joe Orsulak	.10	.05	.01
□ 95	Ricky Jordan	.10	.05	.01
□ 96	Billy Hatcher	.10	.05	.01
□ 97	Jack McDowell	.25	.11	.03
□ 98	Tom Pagnozzi	.10	.05	.01
□ 99	Darryl Strawberry	.25	.11	.03
□ 100	Mike Stanley	.10	.05	.01
□ 101	Bret Saberhagen	.25	.11	.03
□ 102	Willie Greene	.25	.11	.03
□ 103	Bryan Harvey	.10	.05	.01
□ 104	Tim Bogar	.10	.05	.01
□ 105	Jack Voigt	.10	.05	.01
□ 106	Brad Ausmus	.10	.05	.01
□ 107	Ramon Martinez	.25	.11	.03
□ 108	Mike Perez	.10	.05	.01
□ 109	Jeff Montgomery	.25	.11	.03
□ 110	Danny Darwin	.10	.05	.01
□ 111	Wilson Alvarez	.25	.11	.03
□ 112	Kevin Mitchell	.25	.11	.03
□ 113	David Nied	.10	.05	.01
□ 114	Rich Amaral	.10	.05	.01
□ 115	Stan Javier	.10	.05	.01
□ 116	Mo Vaughn	.75	.35	.09
□ 117	Ben McDonald	.10	.05	.01
□ 118	Tom Gordon	.10	.05	.01
□ 119	Carlos Garcia	.10	.05	.01
□ 120	Phil Plantier	.10	.05	.01
□ 121	Mike Morgan	.10	.05	.01
□ 122	Pat Meares	.10	.05	.01
□ 123	Kevin Young	.10	.05	.01
□ 124	Jeff Fassero	.10	.05	.01
□ 125	Gene Harris	.10	.05	.01
□ 126	Bob Welch	.10	.05	.01
□ 127	Walt Weiss	.10	.05	.01
□ 128	Bobby Witt	.10	.05	.01
□ 129	Andy Van Slyke	.25	.11	.03
□ 130	Steve Cooke	.10	.05	.01
□ 131	Mike Devereaux	.10	.05	.01
□ 132	Joey Cora	.10	.05	.01
□ 133	Bret Barberie	.10	.05	.01
□ 134	Orel Hershiser	.25	.11	.03
□ 135	Ed Sprague	.25	.11	.03
□ 136	Shawon Dunston	.10	.05	.01
□ 137	Alex Arias	.10	.05	.01
□ 138	Archi Cianfrocco	.10	.05	.01
□ 139	Tim Wallach	.10	.05	.01
□ 140	Bernie Williams	.50	.23	.06
□ 141	Karl Rhodes	.10	.05	.01
□ 142	Pat Kelly	.10	.05	.01
□ 143	Dave Magadan	.10	.05	.01
□ 144	Kevin Tapani	.10	.05	.01
□ 145	Eric Young	.25	.11	.03
□ 146	Derek Bell	.25	.11	.03
□ 147	Dante Bichette	.50	.23	.06
□ 148	Geronimo Pena	.10	.05	.01
□ 149	Joe Oliver	.10	.05	.01
□ 150	Orestes Destrade	.10	.05	.01
□ 151	Tim Naehring	.10	.05	.01
□ 152	Ray Lankford	.50	.23	.06
□ 153	Phil Clark	.10	.05	.01
□ 154	David McCarty	.10	.05	.01
□ 155	Tommy Greene	.10	.05	.01
□ 156	Wade Boggs	.50	.23	.06
□ 157	Kevin Gross	.10	.05	.01
□ 158	Hal Morris	.10	.05	.01
□ 159	Moises Alou	.25	.11	.03
□ 160	Rick Aguilera	.10	.05	.01
□ 161	Curt Schilling	.10	.05	.01
□ 162	Chip Hale	.10	.05	.01
□ 163	Tino Martinez	.25	.11	.03
□ 164	Mark Whiten	.10	.05	.01
□ 165	Dave Stewart	.25	.11	.03
□ 166	Steve Buechele	.10	.05	.01
□ 167	Bobby Jones	.25	.11	.03
□ 168	Darrin Fletcher	.10	.05	.01
□ 169	John Smiley	.10	.05	.01
□ 170	Cory Snyder	.10	.05	.01
□ 171	Scott Erickson	.10	.05	.01
□ 172	Kirk Rueter	.10	.05	.01
□ 173	Dave Fleming	.10	.05	.01
□ 174	John Smoltz	.50	.23	.06
□ 175	Ricky Gutierrez	.10	.05	.01
□ 176	Mike Bordick	.10	.05	.01
□ 177	Chan Ho Park	.75	.35	.09
□ 178	Alex Gonzalez	.25	.11	.03
□ 179	Steve Karsay	.10	.05	.01
□ 180	Jeffrey Hammonds	.25	.11	.03
□ 181	Manny Ramirez	1.00	.45	.12
□ 182	Salomon Torres	.10	.05	.01
□ 183	Raul Mondesi	.50	.23	.06
□ 184	James Mouton	.25	.11	.03
□ 185	Cliff Floyd	.50	.23	.06
□ 186	Danny Bautista	.10	.05	.01
□ 187	Kurt Abbott	.25	.11	.03
□ 188	Javier Lopez	.50	.23	.06
□ 189	John Patterson	.10	.05	.01

□ 190 Greg Blosser	.10	.05	.01
□ 191 Bob Hamelin	.10	.05	.01
□ 192 Tony Eusebio	.10	.05	.01
□ 193 Carlos Delgado	.50	.23	.06
□ 194 Chris Gomez	.10	.05	.01
□ 195 Kelly Stinnett	.10	.05	.01
□ 196 Shane Reynolds	.25	.11	.03
□ 197 Ryan Klesko	.75	.35	.09
□ 198 Jim Edmonds UER	.60	.25	.07
Mark Dalesandro pictured on front			
□ 199 James Hurst	.10	.05	.01
□ 200 Dave Staton	.10	.05	.01
□ 201 Rondell White	.50	.23	.06
□ 202 Keith Mitchell	.10	.05	.01
□ 203 Darren Oliver	.40	.18	.05
□ 204 Mike Matheny	.10	.05	.01
□ 205 Chris Turner	.10	.05	.01
□ 206 Matt Mieske	.10	.05	.01
□ 207 NL Team Checklist	.10	.05	.01
□ 208 NL Team Checklist	.10	.05	.01
□ 209 AL Team Checklist	.10	.05	.01
□ 210 AL Team Checklist	.10	.05	.01
□ 211 Barry Bonds	.75	.35	.09
□ 212 Juan Gonzalez	1.50	.70	.19
□ 213 Jim Eisenreich	.10	.05	.01
□ 214 Ivan Rodriguez	.60	.25	.07
□ 215 Tony Phillips	.25	.11	.03
□ 216 John Jaha	.25	.11	.03
□ 217 Lee Smith	.25	.11	.03
□ 218 Bip Roberts	.10	.05	.01
□ 219 Dave Hansen	.10	.05	.01
□ 220 Pat Listach	.10	.05	.01
□ 221 Willie McGee	.10	.05	.01
□ 222 Damion Easley	.10	.05	.01
□ 223 Dean Palmer	.25	.11	.03
□ 224 Mike Moore	.10	.05	.01
□ 225 Brian Harper	.10	.05	.01
□ 226 Gary DiSarcina	.10	.05	.01
□ 227 Delino DeShields	.10	.05	.01
□ 228 Otis Nixon	.10	.05	.01
□ 229 Roberto Alomar	.75	.35	.09
□ 230 Mark Grace	.50	.23	.06
□ 231 Kenny Lofton	1.00	.45	.12
□ 232 Gregg Jefferies	.50	.23	.06
□ 233 Cecil Fielder	.25	.11	.03
□ 234 Jeff Bagwell	1.25	.55	.16
□ 235 Albert Belle	1.50	.70	.19
□ 236 Dave Justice	.50	.23	.06
□ 237 Tom Henke	.10	.05	.01
□ 238 Bobby Bonilla	.25	.11	.03
□ 239 John Olerud	.10	.05	.01
□ 240 Robby Thompson	.10	.05	.01
□ 241 Dave Valle	.10	.05	.01
□ 242 Marquis Grissom	.50	.23	.06
□ 243 Greg Swindell	.10	.05	.01
□ 244 Todd Zeile	.10	.05	.01
□ 245 Dennis Eckersley	.25	.11	.03
□ 246 Jose Offerman	.10	.05	.01
□ 247 Greg McMichael	.10	.05	.01
□ 248 Tim Belcher	.10	.05	.01
□ 249 Cal Ripken Jr.	2.50	1.10	.30
□ 250 Tom Glavine	.50	.23	.06
□ 251 Luis Polonia	.10	.05	.01
□ 252 Bill Swift	.10	.05	.01
□ 253 Juan Guzman	.25	.11	.03
□ 254 Rickey Henderson	.50	.23	.06
□ 255 Terry Mulholland	.10	.05	.01
□ 256 Gary Sheffield	.50	.23	.06
□ 257 Terry Steinbach	.25	.11	.03
□ 258 Brett Butler	.25	.11	.03
□ 259 Jason Bere	.25	.11	.03
□ 260 Doug Strange	.10	.05	.01
□ 261 Kent Hrbek	.25	.11	.03
□ 262 Graeme Lloyd	.10	.05	.01
□ 263 Lou Frazier	.10	.05	.01
□ 264 Charles Nagy	.25	.11	.03
□ 265 Bret Boone	.25	.11	.03
□ 266 Kirk Gibson	.25	.11	.03
□ 267 Kevin Brown	.10	.05	.01
□ 268 Fred McGriff	.50	.23	.06
□ 269 Matt Williams	.50	.23	.06
□ 270 Greg Gagne	.10	.05	.01
□ 271 Mariano Duncan	.10	.05	.01
□ 272 Jeff Russell	.10	.05	.01
□ 273 Eric Davis	.25	.11	.03
□ 274 Shane Mack	.10	.05	.01
□ 275 Jose Vizcaino	.10	.05	.01
□ 276 Jose Canseco	.50	.23	.06
□ 277 Roberto Hernandez	.25	.11	.03
□ 278 Royce Clayton	.25	.11	.03
□ 279 Carlos Baerga	.50	.23	.06
□ 280 Pete Incaviglia	.10	.05	.01
□ 281 Brent Gates	.10	.05	.01
□ 282 Jeromy Burnitz	.10	.05	.01
□ 283 Chili Davis	.25	.11	.03
□ 284 Pete Harnisch	.10	.05	.01
□ 285 Alan Trammell	.50	.23	.06
□ 286 Eric Anthony	.10	.05	.01
□ 287 Ellis Burks	.25	.11	.03
□ 288 Julio Franco	.25	.11	.03
□ 289 Jack Morris	.25	.11	.03
□ 290 Erik Hanson	.10	.05	.01
□ 291 Chuck Finley	.10	.05	.01
□ 292 Reggie Jefferson	.25	.11	.03
□ 293 Kevin McReynolds	.10	.05	.01
□ 294 Greg Hibbard	.10	.05	.01
□ 295 Travis Fryman	.50	.23	.06
□ 296 Craig Biggio	.50	.23	.06
□ 297 Kenny Rogers	.10	.05	.01
□ 298 Dave Henderson	.10	.05	.01
□ 299 Jim Thome	.75	.35	.09
□ 300 Rene Arocha	.10	.05	.01
□ 301 Pedro Munoz	.10	.05	.01
□ 302 David Hulse	.10	.05	.01
□ 303 Greg Vaughn	.50	.23	.06
□ 304 Darren Lewis	.10	.05	.01
□ 305 Deion Sanders	.50	.23	.06
□ 306 Danny Tartabull	.10	.05	.01
□ 307 Darryl Hamilton	.10	.05	.01
□ 308 Andujar Cedeno	.10	.05	.01
□ 309 Tim Salmon	.50	.23	.06
□ 310 Tony Fernandez	.10	.05	.01
□ 311 Alex Fernandez	.50	.23	.06
□ 312 Roberto Kelly	.10	.05	.01
□ 313 Harold Reynolds	.10	.05	.01
□ 314 Chris Sabo	.10	.05	.01
□ 315 Howard Johnson	.10	.05	.01
□ 316 Mark Portugal	.10	.05	.01
□ 317 Rafael Palmeiro	.50	.23	.06
□ 318 Pete Smith	.10	.05	.01
□ 319 Will Clark	.50	.23	.06
□ 320 Henry Rodriguez	.50	.23	.06
□ 321 Omar Vizquel	.50	.23	.06
□ 322 David Segui	.10	.05	.01
□ 323 Lou Whitaker	.50	.23	.06
□ 324 Felix Fermin	.10	.05	.01
□ 325 Spike Owen	.10	.05	.01
□ 326 Darryl Kile	.10	.05	.01
□ 327 Chad Kreuter	.10	.05	.01
□ 328 Rod Beck	.25	.11	.03
□ 329 Eddie Murray	.75	.35	.09
□ 330 B.J. Surhoff	.10	.05	.01
□ 331 Mickey Tettleton	.10	.05	.01
□ 332 Pedro Martinez	.50	.23	.06
□ 333 Roger Pavlik	.10	.05	.01
□ 334 Eddie Taubensee	.10	.05	.01
□ 335 John Doherty	.10	.05	.01
□ 336 Jody Reed	.10	.05	.01
□ 337 Aaron Sele	.25	.11	.03
□ 338 Leo Gomez	.10	.05	.01
□ 339 Dave Nilsson	.25	.11	.03
□ 340 Rob Dibble	.10	.05	.01
□ 341 John Burkett	.10	.05	.01
□ 342 Wayne Kirby	.10	.05	.01
□ 343 Dan Wilson	.25	.11	.03
□ 344 Armando Reynoso	.10	.05	.01
□ 345 Chad Curtis	.10	.05	.01
□ 346 Dennis Martinez	.25	.11	.03
□ 347 Cal Eldred	.10	.05	.01
□ 348 Luis Gonzalez	.10	.05	.01
□ 349 Doug Drabek	.10	.05	.01
□ 350 Jim Leyritz	.10	.05	.01
□ 351 Mark Langston	.25	.11	.03
□ 352 Darrin Jackson	.10	.05	.01
□ 353 Sid Fernandez	.10	.05	.01
□ 354 Benito Santiago	.10	.05	.01
□ 355 Kevin Seitzer	.10	.05	.01
□ 356 Bo Jackson	.50	.23	.06
□ 357 David Wells	.10	.05	.01
□ 358 Paul Sorrento	.10	.05	.01
□ 359 Ken Caminiti	.50	.23	.06
□ 360 Eduardo Perez	.10	.05	.01

□ 361	Orlando Merced	.25	.11	.03
□ 362	Steve Finley	.50	.23	.06
□ 363	Andy Benes	.25	.11	.03
□ 364	Manuel Lee	.10	.05	.01
□ 365	Todd Benzinger	.10	.05	.01
□ 366	Sandy Alomar Jr.	.25	.11	.03
□ 367	Rex Hudler	.10	.05	.01
□ 368	Mike Henneman	.10	.05	.01
□ 369	Vince Coleman	.10	.05	.01
□ 370	Kirt Manwaring	.10	.05	.01
□ 371	Ken Hill	.10	.05	.01
□ 372	Glenallen Hill	.10	.05	.01
□ 373	Sean Berry	.10	.05	.01
□ 374	Geronimo Berroa	.25	.11	.03
□ 375	Duane Ward	.10	.05	.01
□ 376	Allen Watson	.10	.05	.01
□ 377	Marc Newfield	.25	.11	.03
□ 378	Dan Miceli	.10	.05	.01
□ 379	Denny Hocking	.10	.05	.01
□ 380	Mark Kiefer	.10	.05	.01
□ 381	Tony Tarasco	.10	.05	.01
□ 382	Tony Longmire	.10	.05	.01
□ 383	Brian Anderson	.25	.11	.03
□ 384	Fernando Vina	.10	.05	.01
□ 385	Hector Carrasco	.10	.05	.01
□ 386	Mike Kelly	.10	.05	.01
□ 387	Greg Colbrunn	.10	.05	.01
□ 388	Roger Salkeld	.10	.05	.01
□ 389	Steve Trachsel	.25	.11	.03
□ 390	Rich Becker	.25	.11	.03
□ 391	Billy Taylor	.10	.05	.01
□ 392	Rich Rowland	.10	.05	.01
□ 393	Carl Everett	.10	.05	.01
□ 394	Johnny Ruffin	.10	.05	.01
□ 395	Keith Lockhart	.10	.05	.01
□ 396	J.R. Phillips	.10	.05	.01
□ 397	Sterling Hitchcock	.25	.11	.03
□ 398	Jorge Fabregas	.10	.05	.01
□ 399	Jeff Granger	.25	.11	.03
□ 400	Eddie Zambrano	.10	.05	.01
□ 401	Rikkert Faneyte	.10	.05	.01
□ 402	Gerald Williams	.10	.05	.01
□ 403	Joey Hamilton	.60	.25	.07
□ 404	Joe Hall	.10	.05	.01
□ 405	John Hudek	.10	.05	.01
□ 406	Roberto Petagine	.25	.11	.03
□ 407	Charles Johnson	.50	.23	.06
□ 408	Mark Smith	.10	.05	.01
□ 409	Jeff Juden	.10	.05	.01
□ 410	Carlos Pulido	.10	.05	.01
□ 411	Paul Shuey	.10	.05	.01
□ 412	Rob Butler	.10	.05	.01
□ 413	Mark Acre	.10	.05	.01
□ 414	Greg Pirkl	.10	.05	.01
□ 415	Melvin Nieves	.25	.11	.03
□ 416	Tim Hyers	.10	.05	.01
□ 417	NL Checklist	.10	.05	.01
□ 418	NL Checklist	.10	.05	.01
□ 419	AL Checklist	.10	.05	.01
□ 420	AL Checklist	.10	.05	.01
□ RY1	Carlos Delgado	10.00	4.50	1.25
□ SS1	Cal Ripken Jr. Salute	60.00	27.00	7.50
□ SS2	Dave Winfield Salute	10.00	4.50	1.25
□ MVP1	Paul Molitor	15.00	6.75	1.85

1994 Select Crown Contenders

This ten-card set showcases top contenders for various awards such as batting champion, Cy Young Award winner and Most Valuable Player. The cards were inserted in first series packs at a rate of one in 24 and measure the standard size. The horizontal fronts feature color action player shots on a holographic gold foil background. The backs carry a color player close-up photo and highlights. The cards are numbered on the back with a CC prefix.

	MINT	NRMT	EXC
COMPLETE SET (10)	100.00	45.00	12.50
COMMON CARD (CC1-CC10)	3.00	1.35	.35
RANDOM INSERTS IN SER.1 PACKS			

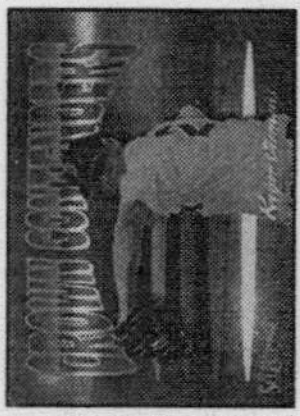

□ CC1	Lenny Dykstra	3.00	1.35	.35
□ CC2	Greg Maddux	15.00	6.75	1.85
□ CC3	Roger Clemens	3.00	1.35	.35
□ CC4	Randy Johnson	4.00	1.80	.50
□ CC5	Frank Thomas	25.00	11.00	3.10
□ CC6	Barry Bonds	6.00	2.70	.75
□ CC7	Juan Gonzalez	12.00	5.50	1.50
□ CC8	John Olerud	3.00	1.35	.35
□ CC9	Mike Piazza	15.00	6.75	1.85
□ CC10	Ken Griffey Jr.	25.00	11.00	3.10

1994 Select Rookie Surge

This 18-card standard-size set showcased potential top rookies for 1994. The set was divided into two series of nine cards. The cards were randomly inserted in packs at a rate of one in 48. The fronts exhibit Score's "dufex" printing process, in which a color photo is printed on a metallic base creating an unusual, three-dimensional look. On a multi-colored background, the horizontal backs present a color player headshot. The cards are numbered on the back with an RS prefix.

	MINT	NRMT	EXC
COMPLETE SET (18)	90.00	40.00	11.00
COMPLETE SERIES 1 (9)	40.00	18.00	5.00
COMPLETE SERIES 2 (9)	50.00	22.00	6.25
COMMON CARD (RS1-RS18)	2.50	1.10	.30
SEMISTARS	5.00	2.20	.60
RANDOM INSERTS IN PACKS			

□ RS1	Cliff Floyd	5.00	2.20	.60
□ RS2	Bob Hamelin	2.50	1.10	.30
□ RS3	Ryan Klesko	15.00	6.75	1.85
□ RS4	Carlos Delgado	10.00	4.50	1.25
□ RS5	Jeffrey Hammonds	5.00	2.20	.60
□ RS6	Rondell White	8.00	3.60	1.00
□ RS7	Salomon Torres	2.50	1.10	.30
□ RS8	Steve Karsay	2.50	1.10	.30
□ RS9	Javier Lopez	10.00	4.50	1.25
□ RS10	Manny Ramirez	25.00	11.00	3.10
□ RS11	Tony Tarasco	2.50	1.10	.30
□ RS12	Kurt Abbott	2.50	1.10	.30
□ RS13	Chan Ho Park	12.00	5.50	1.50
□ RS14	Rich Becker	5.00	2.20	.60
□ RS15	James Mouton	5.00	2.20	.60
□ RS16	Alex Gonzalez	5.00	2.20	.60
□ RS17	Raul Mondesi	12.00	5.50	1.50
□ RS18	Steve Trachsel	2.50	1.10	.30

1994 Select Skills

This 10-card standard-size set takes an up close look at the leagues top statistical leaders. The cards were randomly inserted in second series packs at a rate of approximately one in 24. A foil front has a holographic appearance that allows the player to stand out. The bottom of the front notes the player as being the best at something. For example, the front of Barry Bonds' card notes, "Select's Best Run Producer". The back has a small photo with text. The cards are numbered with an "SK" prefix.

	MINT	NRMT	EXC
COMPLETE SET (10)	60.00	27.00	7.50
COMMON CARD (SK1-SK10)	4.00	1.80	.50
RANDOM INSERTS IN SER.2 PACKS			
□ SK1 Randy Johnson	8.00	3.60	1.00
□ SK2 Barry Larkin	6.00	2.70	.75
□ SK3 Lenny Dykstra	4.00	1.80	.50
□ SK4 Kenny Lofton	15.00	6.75	1.85
□ SK5 Juan Gonzalez	25.00	11.00	3.10
□ SK6 Barry Bonds	12.00	5.50	1.50
□ SK7 Marquis Grissom	5.00	2.20	.60
□ SK8 Ivan Rodriguez	10.00	4.50	1.25
□ SK9 Larry Walker	5.00	2.20	.60
□ SK10 Travis Fryman	5.00	2.20	.60

1995 Select

This 250-card set was issued in 12-card packs with 24 packs per box and 24 boxes per case. There was an announced production run of 4,950 cases. These horizontal cards feature an action photo over most of the card with the playerís profile and name on the right side. The "Select 95" logo is in the upper left corner. The vertical backs have a black and white photo on the top. The middle of the card is dedicated to a brief biography as well as seasonal and career stats. A specific important stat is included at the bottom of the card. A special card of Hideo Nomo (#251) was issued to hobby dealers who had bought cases of the Select product.

	MINT	NRMT	EXC
COMPLETE SET (250)	15.00	6.75	1.85
COMMON CARD (1-250)	.05	.02	.01
SEMISTARS	.15	.07	.02
STARS	.30	.14	.04
NOMO CARD ISSUED DIRECT TO DEALERS			
□ 1 Cal Ripken Jr.	1.50	.70	.19
□ 2 Robin Ventura	.15	.07	.02
□ 3 Al Martin	.15	.07	.02
□ 4 Jeff Frye	.05	.02	.01
□ 5 Darryl Strawberry	.15	.07	.02
□ 6 Chan Ho Park	.30	.14	.04
□ 7 Steve Avery	.15	.07	.02
□ 8 Bret Boone	.15	.07	.02
□ 9 Danny Tartabull	.05	.02	.01
□ 10 Dante Bichette	.30	.14	.04
□ 11 Rondell White	.30	.14	.04
□ 12 Dave McCarty	.05	.02	.01
□ 13 Bernard Gilkey	.15	.07	.02
□ 14 Mark McGwire	.60	.25	.07
□ 15 Ruben Sierra	.15	.07	.02
□ 16 Wade Boggs	.30	.14	.04
□ 17 Mike Piazza	1.25	.55	.16
□ 18 Jeffrey Hammonds	.15	.07	.02
□ 19 Mike Mussina	.40	.18	.05
□ 20 Darryl Kile	.05	.02	.01
□ 21 Greg Maddux	1.25	.55	.16
□ 22 Frank Thomas	2.00	.90	.25
□ 23 Kevin Appier	.15	.07	.02
□ 24 Jay Bell	.15	.07	.02
□ 25 Kirk Gibson	.15	.07	.02
□ 26 Pat Hentgen	.15	.07	.02
□ 27 Joey Hamilton	.15	.07	.02
□ 28 Bernie Williams	.30	.14	.04
□ 29 Aaron Sele	.15	.07	.02
□ 30 Delino DeShields	.05	.02	.01
□ 31 Danny Bautista	.05	.02	.01
□ 32 Jim Thome	.40	.18	.05
□ 33 Rikkert Faneyte	.05	.02	.01
□ 34 Roberto Alomar	.50	.23	.06
□ 35 Paul Molitor	.40	.18	.05
□ 36 Allen Watson	.05	.02	.01
□ 37 Jeff Bagwell	.75	.35	.09
□ 38 Jay Buhner	.30	.14	.04
□ 39 Marquis Grissom	.30	.14	.04
□ 40 Jim Edmonds	.30	.14	.04
□ 41 Ryan Klesko	.40	.18	.05
□ 42 Fred McGriff	.30	.14	.04
□ 43 Tony Tarasco	.05	.02	.01
□ 44 Darren Daulton	.15	.07	.02
□ 45 Marc Newfield	.15	.07	.02
□ 46 Barry Bonds	.50	.23	.06
□ 47 Bobby Bonilla	.15	.07	.02
□ 48 Greg Pirkl	.05	.02	.01
□ 49 Steve Karsay	.05	.02	.01
□ 50 Bob Hamelin	.05	.02	.01
□ 51 Javier Lopez	.30	.14	.04
□ 52 Barry Larkin	.30	.14	.04
□ 53 Kevin Young	.05	.02	.01
□ 54 Sterling Hitchcock	.15	.07	.02
□ 55 Tom Glavine	.30	.14	.04
□ 56 Carlos Delgado	.30	.14	.04
□ 57 Darren Oliver	.15	.07	.02
□ 58 Cliff Floyd	.15	.07	.02
□ 59 Tim Salmon	.30	.14	.04
□ 60 Albert Belle	1.00	.45	.12
□ 61 Salomon Torres	.05	.02	.01
□ 62 Gary Sheffield	.30	.14	.04
□ 63 Ivan Rodriguez	.40	.18	.05
□ 64 Charles Nagy	.15	.07	.02
□ 65 Eduardo Perez	.05	.02	.01
□ 66 Terry Steinbach	.15	.07	.02
□ 67 Dave Justice	.30	.14	.04
□ 68 Jason Bere	.05	.02	.01
□ 69 Dave Nilsson	.15	.07	.02
□ 70 Brian Anderson	.05	.02	.01
□ 71 Billy Ashley	.05	.02	.01
□ 72 Roger Clemens	.30	.14	.04
□ 73 Jimmy Key	.15	.07	.02
□ 74 Wally Joyner	.15	.07	.02
□ 75 Andy Benes	.05	.02	.01
□ 76 Ray Lankford	.30	.14	.04
□ 77 Jeff Kent	.05	.02	.01
□ 78 Moises Alou	.15	.07	.02
□ 79 Kirby Puckett	.60	.25	.07
□ 80 Joe Carter	.30	.14	.04
□ 81 Manny Ramirez	.50	.23	.06
□ 82 J.R. Phillips	.05	.02	.01
□ 83 Matt Mieske	.15	.07	.02

□ 84	John Olerud	.05	.02	.01
□ 85	Andres Galarraga	.30	.14	.04
□ 86	Juan Gonzalez	1.00	.45	.12
□ 87	Pedro Martinez	.15	.07	.02
□ 88	Dean Palmer	.15	.07	.02
□ 89	Ken Griffey Jr.	2.00	.90	.25
□ 90	Brian Jordan	.30	.14	.04
□ 91	Hal Morris	.05	.02	.01
□ 92	Lenny Dykstra	.15	.07	.02
□ 93	Wil Cordero	.05	.02	.01
□ 94	Tony Gwynn	.75	.35	.09
□ 95	Alex Gonzalez	.05	.02	.01
□ 96	Cecil Fielder	.15	.07	.02
□ 97	Mo Vaughn	.50	.23	.06
□ 98	John Valentin	.15	.07	.02
□ 99	Will Clark	.30	.14	.04
□ 100	Geronimo Pena	.05	.02	.01
□ 101	Don Mattingly	1.00	.45	.12
□ 102	Charles Johnson	.15	.07	.02
□ 103	Raul Mondesi	.30	.14	.04
□ 104	Reggie Sanders	.15	.07	.02
□ 105	Royce Clayton	.05	.02	.01
□ 106	Reggie Jefferson	.15	.07	.02
□ 107	Craig Biggio	.30	.14	.04
□ 108	Jack McDowell	.15	.07	.02
□ 109	James Mouton	.05	.02	.01
□ 110	Mike Greenwell	.05	.02	.01
□ 111	David Cone	.15	.07	.02
□ 112	Matt Williams	.30	.14	.04
□ 113	Garret Anderson	.30	.14	.04
□ 114	Carlos Garcia	.05	.02	.01
□ 115	Alex Fernandez	.15	.07	.02
□ 116	Deion Sanders	.30	.14	.04
□ 117	Chili Davis	.15	.07	.02
□ 118	Mike Kelly	.05	.02	.01
□ 119	Jeff Conine	.30	.14	.04
□ 120	Kenny Lofton	.50	.23	.06
□ 121	Rafael Palmeiro	.30	.14	.04
□ 122	Chuck Knoblauch	.30	.14	.04
□ 123	Ozzie Smith	.40	.18	.05
□ 124	Carlos Baerga	.30	.14	.04
□ 125	Brett Butler	.15	.07	.02
□ 126	Sammy Sosa	.30	.14	.04
□ 127	Ellis Burks	.30	.14	.04
□ 128	Bret Saberhagen	.15	.07	.02
□ 129	Doug Drabek	.05	.02	.01
□ 130	Dennis Martinez	.15	.07	.02
□ 131	Paul O'Neill	.15	.07	.02
□ 132	Travis Fryman	.15	.07	.02
□ 133	Brent Gates	.05	.02	.01
□ 134	Rickey Henderson	.30	.14	.04
□ 135	Randy Johnson	.30	.14	.04
□ 136	Mark Langston	.05	.02	.01
□ 137	Greg Colbrunn	.05	.02	.01
□ 138	Jose Rijo	.05	.02	.01
□ 139	Bryan Harvey	.05	.02	.01
□ 140	Dennis Eckersley	.15	.07	.02
□ 141	Ron Gant	.15	.07	.02
□ 142	Carl Everett	.05	.02	.01
□ 143	Jeff Granger	.05	.02	.01
□ 144	Ben McDonald	.05	.02	.01
□ 145	Kurt Abbott UER (Mariners logo on front	.05	.02	.01
□ 146	Jim Abbott	.05	.02	.01
□ 147	Jason Jacome	.05	.02	.01
□ 148	Rico Brogna	.05	.02	.01
□ 149	Cal Eldred	.05	.02	.01
□ 150	Rich Becker	.05	.02	.01
□ 151	Pete Harnisch	.05	.02	.01
□ 152	Roberto Petagine	.05	.02	.01
□ 153	Jacob Brumfield	.05	.02	.01
□ 154	Todd Hundley	.15	.07	.02
□ 155	Roger Cedeno	.15	.07	.02
□ 156	Harold Baines	.15	.07	.02
□ 157	Steve Dunn	.05	.02	.01
□ 158	Tim Belk	.05	.02	.01
□ 159	Marty Cordova	.30	.14	.04
□ 160	Russ Davis	.05	.02	.01
□ 161	Jose Malave	.05	.02	.01
□ 162	Brian Hunter	.30	.14	.04
□ 163	Andy Pettitte	.75	.35	.09
□ 164	Brooks Kieschnick	.15	.07	.02
□ 165	Midre Cummings	.05	.02	.01
□ 166	Frank Rodriguez	.15	.07	.02
□ 167	Chad Mottola	.15	.07	.02
□ 168	Brian Barber	.05	.02	.01
□ 169	Tim Unroe	.15	.07	.02
□ 170	Shane Andrews	.05	.02	.01
□ 171	Kevin Flora	.05	.02	.01
□ 172	Ray Durham	.15	.07	.02
□ 173	Chipper Jones	1.25	.55	.16
□ 174	Butch Huskey	.15	.07	.02
□ 175	Ray McDavid	.15	.07	.02
□ 176	Jeff Cirillo	.15	.07	.02
□ 177	Terry Pendleton	.15	.07	.02
□ 178	Scott Ruffcorn	.05	.02	.01
□ 179	Ray Holbert	.05	.02	.01
□ 180	Joe Randa	.05	.02	.01
□ 181	Jose Oliva	.05	.02	.01
□ 182	Andy Van Slyke	.15	.07	.02
□ 183	Albie Lopez	.05	.02	.01
□ 184	Chad Curtis	.05	.02	.01
□ 185	Ozzie Guillen	.05	.02	.01
□ 186	Chad Ogea	.05	.02	.01
□ 187	Dan Wilson	.15	.07	.02
□ 188	Tony Fernandez	.05	.02	.01
□ 189	John Smoltz	.30	.14	.04
□ 190	Willie Greene	.05	.02	.01
□ 191	Darren Lewis	.05	.02	.01
□ 192	Orlando Miller	.05	.02	.01
□ 193	Kurt Miller	.05	.02	.01
□ 194	Andrew Lorraine	.15	.07	.02
□ 195	Ernie Young	.15	.07	.02
□ 196	Jimmy Haynes	.15	.07	.02
□ 197	Raul Casanova	.50	.23	.06
□ 198	Joe Vitiello	.05	.02	.01
□ 199	Brad Woodall	.05	.02	.01
□ 200	Juan Acevedo	.05	.02	.01
□ 201	Michael Tucker	.15	.07	.02
□ 202	Shawn Green	.15	.07	.02
□ 203	Alex Rodriguez	2.50	1.10	.30
□ 204	Julian Tavarez	.05	.02	.01
□ 205	Jose Lima	.05	.02	.01
□ 206	Wilson Alvarez	.15	.07	.02
□ 207	Rich Aude	.05	.02	.01
□ 208	Armando Benitez	.05	.02	.01
□ 209	Dwayne Hosey	.05	.02	.01
□ 210	Gabe White	.05	.02	.01
□ 211	Joey Eischen	.05	.02	.01
□ 212	Bill Pulsipher	.15	.07	.02
□ 213	Robby Thompson	.05	.02	.01
□ 214	Toby Borland	.05	.02	.01
□ 215	Rusty Greer	.30	.14	.04
□ 216	Fausto Cruz	.05	.02	.01
□ 217	Luis Ortiz	.05	.02	.01
□ 218	Duane Singleton	.05	.02	.01
□ 219	Troy Percival	.05	.02	.01
□ 220	Gregg Jefferies	.15	.07	.02
□ 221	Mark Grace	.30	.14	.04
□ 222	Mickey Tettleton	.05	.02	.01
□ 223	Phil Plantier	.05	.02	.01
□ 224	Larry Walker	.30	.14	.04
□ 225	Ken Caminiti	.30	.14	.04
□ 226	Dave Winfield	.30	.14	.04
□ 227	Brady Anderson	.30	.14	.04
□ 228	Kevin Brown	.15	.07	.02
□ 229	Andujar Cedeno	.05	.02	.01
□ 230	Roberto Kelly	.05	.02	.01
□ 231	Jose Canseco	.30	.14	.04
□ 232	Scott Ruffcorn ST	.05	.02	.01
□ 233	Billy Ashley ST	.05	.02	.01
□ 234	J.R. Phillips ST	.05	.02	.01
□ 235	Chipper Jones ST	.60	.25	.07
□ 236	Charles Johnson ST	.15	.07	.02
□ 237	Midre Cummings ST	.05	.02	.01
□ 238	Brian L.Hunter SH	.15	.07	.02
□ 239	Garret Anderson ST	.15	.07	.02
□ 240	Shawn Green SH	.05	.02	.01
□ 241	Alex Rodriguez ST	1.25	.55	.16
□ 242	Frank Thomas CL	1.00	.45	.12
□ 243	Ken Griffey Jr. CL	1.00	.45	.12
□ 244	Albert Belle CL	.50	.23	.06
□ 245	Cal Ripken Jr. CL	.75	.35	.09
□ 246	Barry Bonds CL	.25	.11	.03
□ 247	Raul Mondesi CL	.15	.07	.02
□ 248	Mike Piazza CL	.60	.25	.07
□ 249	Jeff Bagwell CL	.40	.18	.05
□ 250	Jeff Bagwell Ken Griffey Jr. Frank Thomas Mike Piazza CL	1.50	.70	.19
□ 251S	Hideo Nomo	2.50	1.10	.30

1995 Select Artist's Proofs

This 250-card set is parallel to the regular Select set. These cards were inserted at a rate of one per 24 packs. The only difference between these cards and the regular issue cards are the words "Artist's Proof" printed in the lower left corner.

	MINT	NRMT	EXC
COMPLETE SET (250)	3000.00	1350.00	375.00
COMMON CARD (1-250)	5.00	2.20	.60
SEMISTARS	10.00	4.50	1.25
STARS	20.00	9.00	2.50

*VETERAN STARS: 40X TO 80X BASIC CARDS
*YOUNG STARS: 30X TO 60X BASIC CARDS
RANDOM INSERTS IN PACKS
NOMO RANDOMLY DISTRIBUTED TO DEALERS

	MINT	NRMT	EXC
□ 1 Cal Ripken	120.00	55.00	15.00
□ 17 Mike Piazza	100.00	45.00	12.50
□ 21 Greg Maddux	100.00	45.00	12.50
□ 22 Frank Thomas	150.00	70.00	19.00
□ 37 Jeff Bagwell	60.00	27.00	7.50
□ 60 Albert Belle	80.00	36.00	10.00
□ 86 Juan Gonzalez	80.00	36.00	10.00
□ 89 Ken Griffey Jr.	150.00	70.00	19.00
□ 94 Tony Gwynn	60.00	27.00	7.50
□ 101 Don Mattingly	80.00	36.00	10.00
□ 163 Andy Pettitte	60.00	27.00	7.50
□ 173 Chipper Jones	100.00	45.00	12.50
□ 203 Alex Rodriguez	150.00	70.00	19.00
□ 241 Alex Rodriguez SH	80.00	36.00	10.00
□ 242 Frank Thomas CL	80.00	36.00	10.00
□ 243 Ken Griffey Jr. CL	80.00	36.00	10.00
□ 245 Cal Ripken CL	60.00	27.00	7.50
□ 250 Jeff Bagwell CL Frank Thomas Ken Griffey Jr. Mike Piazza	150.00	70.00	19.00
□ 251S Hideo Nomo	60.00	27.00	7.50

1995 Select Big Sticks

Randomly inserted in packs, these 12 cards feature leading hitters. The fronts picture the playerís photo against a metallic background. The words "Big Sticks 95" as well as the player's name is on the bottom. The player's team is noted in the middle of the background. The backs contain a player photo, personal information as well as some notes about his career. The cards are numbered in the upper right corner with a "BS" prefix.

	MINT	NRMT	EXC
COMPLETE SET (12)	150.00	70.00	19.00
COMMON CARD (1-12)	4.00	1.80	.50
RANDOM INSERTS IN PACKS			

	MINT	NRMT	EXC
□ BS1 Frank Thomas	30.00	13.50	3.70
□ BS2 Ken Griffey Jr.	30.00	13.50	3.70
□ BS3 Cal Ripken Jr.	25.00	11.00	3.10
□ BS4 Mike Piazza	20.00	9.00	2.50
□ BS5 Don Mattingly	15.00	6.75	1.85
□ BS6 Will Clark	4.00	1.80	.50
□ BS7 Tony Gwynn	12.00	5.50	1.50
□ BS8 Jeff Bagwell	12.00	5.50	1.50
□ BS9 Barry Bonds	8.00	3.60	1.00
□ BS10 Paul Molitor	6.00	2.70	.75
□ BS11 Matt Williams	4.00	1.80	.50
□ BS12 Albert Belle	15.00	6.75	1.85

1995 Select Can't Miss

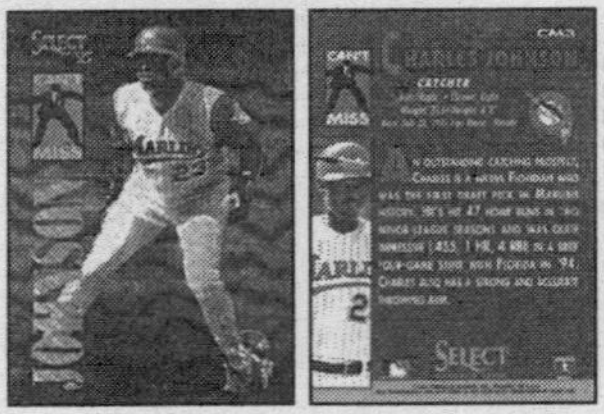

These 12 cards featuring promising young players were inserted one per 24 packs. The player is pictured against a wavy red background. His last name is identified on the bottom left with the "Can't Miss" logo directly above the name. In the middle of the "Can't Miss" logo is a drawing of an umpire signaling safe. The backs have a blue background and include an inset photo, some professional information and biographical data. The cards are numbered with a "CM" prefix in the upper right corner.

	MINT	NRMT	EXC
COMPLETE SET (12)	60.00	27.00	7.50
COMMON CARD (1-12)	2.00	.90	.25
RANDOM INSERTS IN PACKS			

	MINT	NRMT	EXC
□ CM1 Cliff Floyd	2.00	.90	.25
□ CM2 Ryan Klesko	6.00	2.70	.75
□ CM3 Charles Johnson	2.00	.90	.25
□ CM4 Raul Mondesi	4.00	1.80	.50
□ CM5 Manny Ramirez	8.00	3.60	1.00
□ CM6 Billy Ashley	2.00	.90	.25
□ CM7 Alex Gonzalez	2.00	.90	.25
□ CM8 Carlos Delgado	4.00	1.80	.50
□ CM9 Garret Anderson	2.50	1.10	.30
□ CM10 Alex Rodriguez	30.00	13.50	3.70
□ CM11 Chipper Jones	20.00	9.00	2.50
□ CM12 Shawn Green	2.00	.90	.25

1995 Select Sure Shots

These 10 cards were randomly inserted into packs. This set features some of the top 1994 draft picks. The fronts feature the player's photo against a gold metallic background. The phrase "Sure Shots" is printed on gold ink against a blue background on the left. The player is identified in white ink on the bottom. The backs contain some information about the player as well as an inset photo. All this information is set against a blue background with a white light effect. The cards are numbered with an "SS" prefix in the upper right corner.

	MINT	NRMT	EXC
COMPLETE SET (10)	100.00	45.00	12.50
COMMON CARD (1-10)	6.00	2.70	.75
RANDOM INSERTS IN PACKS			

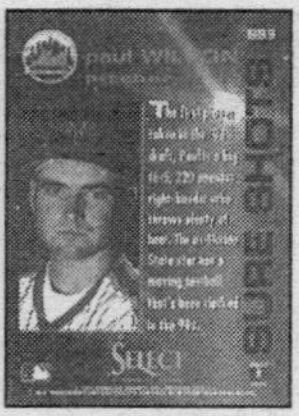

☐ SS1 Ben Grieve	25.00	11.00	3.10
☐ SS2 Kevin Witt	8.00	3.60	1.00
☐ SS3 Mark Farris	6.00	2.70	.75
☐ SS4 Paul Konerko	30.00	13.50	3.70
☐ SS5 Dustin Hermanson	6.00	2.70	.75
☐ SS6 Ramon Castro	6.00	2.70	.75
☐ SS7 McKay Christensen	6.00	2.70	.75
☐ SS8 Brian Buchanan	6.00	2.70	.75
☐ SS9 Paul Wilson	15.00	6.75	1.85
☐ SS10 Terrence Long	10.00	4.50	1.25

1996 Select

The 1996 Select set was issued in one series totalling 200 cards. The 10-card packs retail for $1.99 each. The fronts feature a color action player photo over most of the card with a small player photo framed and name in gold foil printing. The backs carry another player photo, player information and statistics. The set contains the topical subsets: Lineup Leaders (151-160) and Rookies (161-195).

	MINT	NRMT	EXC
COMPLETE SET (200)	20.00	9.00	2.50
COMMON CARD (1-200)	.10	.05	.01
SEMISTARS	.25	.11	.03
STARS	.50	.23	.06

☐ 1 Wade Boggs	.50	.23	.06
☐ 2 Shawn Green	.25	.11	.03
☐ 3 Andres Galarraga	.50	.23	.06
☐ 4 Bill Pulsipher	.25	.11	.03
☐ 5 Chuck Knoblauch	.50	.23	.06
☐ 6 Ken Griffey Jr.	3.00	1.35	.35
☐ 7 Greg Maddux	2.00	.90	.25
☐ 8 Manny Ramirez	.75	.35	.09
☐ 9 Ivan Rodriguez	.60	.25	.07
☐ 10 Tim Salmon	.50	.23	.06
☐ 11 Frank Thomas	3.00	1.35	.35
☐ 12 Jeff Bagwell	1.25	.55	.16
☐ 13 Travis Fryman	.50	.23	.06
☐ 14 Kenny Lofton	.75	.35	.09
☐ 15 Matt Williams	.50	.23	.06
☐ 16 Jay Bell	.25	.11	.03
☐ 17 Ken Caminiti	.50	.23	.06
☐ 18 Ray Lankford	.50	.23	.06
☐ 19 Cal Ripken	2.50	1.10	.30
☐ 20 Roger Clemens	.50	.23	.06
☐ 21 Carlos Baerga	.50	.23	.06
☐ 22 Mike Piazza	2.00	.90	.25
☐ 23 Gregg Jefferies	.50	.23	.06
☐ 24 Reggie Sanders	.50	.23	.06
☐ 25 Rondell White	.50	.23	.06
☐ 26 Sammy Sosa	.50	.23	.06
☐ 27 Kevin Appier	.25	.11	.03
☐ 28 Kevin Seitzer	.10	.05	.01
☐ 29 Gary Sheffield	.50	.23	.06
☐ 30 Mike Mussina	.60	.25	.07
☐ 31 Mark McGwire	1.00	.45	.12
☐ 32 Barry Larkin	.50	.23	.06
☐ 33 Marc Newfield	.25	.11	.03
☐ 34 Ismael Valdes	.25	.11	.03
☐ 35 Marty Cordova	.50	.23	.06
☐ 36 Albert Belle	1.50	.70	.19
☐ 37 Johnny Damon	.25	.11	.03
☐ 38 Garret Anderson	.50	.23	.06
☐ 39 Cecil Fielder	.50	.23	.06
☐ 40 John Mabry	.50	.23	.06
☐ 41 Chipper Jones	2.00	.90	.25
☐ 42 Omar Vizquel	.10	.05	.01
☐ 43 Jose Rijo	.10	.05	.01
☐ 44 Charles Johnson	.25	.11	.03
☐ 45 Alex Rodriguez	3.00	1.35	.35
☐ 46 Rico Brogna	.10	.05	.01
☐ 47 Joe Carter	.50	.23	.06
☐ 48 Mo Vaughn	.75	.35	.09
☐ 49 Moises Alou	.25	.11	.03
☐ 50 Raul Mondesi	.50	.23	.06
☐ 51 Robin Ventura	.50	.23	.06
☐ 52 Jim Thome	.60	.25	.07
☐ 53 David Justice	.25	.11	.03
☐ 54 Jeff King	.25	.11	.03
☐ 55 Brian L.Hunter	.10	.05	.01
☐ 56 Juan Gonzalez	1.50	.70	.19
☐ 57 John Olerud	.10	.05	.01
☐ 58 Rafael Palmeiro	.50	.23	.06
☐ 59 Tony Gwynn	1.25	.55	.16
☐ 60 Eddie Murray	.75	.35	.09
☐ 61 Jason Isringhausen	.10	.05	.01
☐ 62 Dante Bichette	.50	.23	.06
☐ 63 Randy Johnson	.50	.23	.06
☐ 64 Kirby Puckett	1.00	.45	.12
☐ 65 Jim Edmonds	.50	.23	.06
☐ 66 David Cone	.50	.23	.06
☐ 67 Ozzie Smith	.60	.25	.07
☐ 68 Fred McGriff	.50	.23	.06
☐ 69 Darren Daulton	.25	.11	.03
☐ 70 Edgar Martinez	.50	.23	.06
☐ 71 J.T. Snow	.25	.11	.03
☐ 72 Butch Huskey	.25	.11	.03
☐ 73 Hideo Nomo	.75	.35	.09
☐ 74 Pedro Martinez	.50	.23	.06
☐ 75 Bobby Bonilla	.50	.23	.06
☐ 76 Jeff Conine	.25	.11	.03
☐ 77 Ryan Klesko	.60	.25	.07
☐ 78 Bernie Williams	.50	.23	.06
☐ 79 Andre Dawson	.50	.23	.06
☐ 80 Trevor Hoffman	.25	.11	.03
☐ 81 Mark Grace	.50	.23	.06
☐ 82 Benji Gil	.10	.05	.01
☐ 83 Eric Karros	.50	.23	.06
☐ 84 Pete Schourek	.10	.05	.01
☐ 85 Edgardo Alfonzo	.25	.11	.03
☐ 86 Jay Buhner	.50	.23	.06
☐ 87 Vinny Castilla	.50	.23	.06
☐ 88 Bret Boone	.10	.05	.01
☐ 89 Ray Durham	.50	.23	.06
☐ 90 Brian Jordan	.50	.23	.06
☐ 91 Jose Canseco	.50	.23	.06
☐ 92 Paul O'Neill	.10	.05	.01
☐ 93 Chili Davis	.10	.05	.01
☐ 94 Tom Glavine	.50	.23	.06
☐ 95 Julian Tavarez	.10	.05	.01
☐ 96 Derek Bell	.10	.05	.01
☐ 97 Will Clark	.50	.23	.06
☐ 98 Larry Walker	.25	.11	.03
☐ 99 Denny Neagle	.25	.11	.03
☐ 100 Alex Fernandez	.50	.23	.06
☐ 101 Barry Bonds	.75	.35	.09
☐ 102 Ben McDonald	.10	.05	.01
☐ 103 Andy Pettitte	1.00	.45	.12
☐ 104 Tino Martinez	.25	.11	.03
☐ 105 Sterling Hitchcock	.10	.05	.01
☐ 106 Royce Clayton	.10	.05	.01
☐ 107 Jim Abbott	.50	.23	.06
☐ 108 Rickey Henderson	.50	.23	.06
☐ 109 Ramon Martinez	.25	.11	.03
☐ 110 Paul Molitor	.60	.25	.07
☐ 111 Dennis Eckersley	.50	.23	.06
☐ 112 Alex Gonzalez	.10	.05	.01

□ 113 Marquis Grissom	.50	.23	.06
□ 114 Greg Vaughn	.50	.23	.06
□ 115 Lance Johnson	.25	.11	.03
□ 116 Todd Stottlemyre	.10	.05	.01
□ 117 Jack McDowell	.25	.11	.03
□ 118 Ruben Sierra	.10	.05	.01
□ 119 Brady Anderson	.50	.23	.06
□ 120 Julio Franco	.25	.11	.03
□ 121 Brooks Kieschnick	.10	.05	.01
□ 122 Roberto Alomar	.75	.35	.09
□ 123 Greg Gagne	.10	.05	.01
□ 124 Wally Joyner	.10	.05	.01
□ 125 John Smoltz	.50	.23	.06
□ 126 John Valentin	.25	.11	.03
□ 127 Russ Davis	.10	.05	.01
□ 128 Joe Vitiello	.10	.05	.01
□ 129 Shawon Dunston	.10	.05	.01
□ 130 Frank Rodriguez	.10	.05	.01
□ 131 Charlie Hayes	.10	.05	.01
□ 132 Andy Benes	.10	.05	.01
□ 133 B.J. Surhoff	.10	.05	.01
□ 134 Dave Nilsson	.25	.11	.03
□ 135 Carlos Delgado	.50	.23	.06
□ 136 Walt Weiss	.10	.05	.01
□ 137 Mike Stanley	.10	.05	.01
□ 138 Greg Colbrunn	.10	.05	.01
□ 139 Mike Kelly	.10	.05	.01
□ 140 Ryne Sandberg	.75	.35	.09
□ 141 Lee Smith	.50	.23	.06
□ 142 Dennis Martinez	.25	.11	.03
□ 143 Bernard Gilkey	.25	.11	.03
□ 144 Lenny Dykstra	.10	.05	.01
□ 145 Danny Tartabull	.10	.05	.01
□ 146 Dean Palmer	.50	.23	.06
□ 147 Craig Biggio	.50	.23	.06
□ 148 Juan Acevedo	.10	.05	.01
□ 149 Michael Tucker	.10	.05	.01
□ 150 Bobby Higginson	.50	.23	.06
□ 151 Ken Griffey Jr. LUL	1.50	.70	.19
□ 152 Frank Thomas LUL	1.50	.70	.19
□ 153 Cal Ripken LUL	1.25	.55	.16
□ 154 Albert Belle LUL	.75	.35	.09
□ 155 Mike Piazza LUL	1.00	.45	.12
□ 156 Barry Bonds LUL	.50	.23	.06
□ 157 Sammy Sosa LUL	.50	.23	.06
□ 158 Mo Vaughn LUL	.50	.23	.06
□ 159 Greg Maddux LUL	1.00	.45	.12
□ 160 Jeff Bagwell LUL	.60	.25	.07
□ 161 Derek Jeter	2.00	.90	.25
□ 162 Paul Wilson	.10	.05	.01
□ 163 Chris Snopek	.10	.05	.01
□ 164 Jason Schmidt	.10	.05	.01
□ 165 Jimmy Haynes	.10	.05	.01
□ 166 George Arias	.10	.05	.01
□ 167 Steve Gibralter	.10	.05	.01
□ 168 Bob Wolcott	.10	.05	.01
□ 169 Jason Kendall	.50	.23	.06
□ 170 Greg Zaun	.10	.05	.01
□ 171 Quinton McCracken	.10	.05	.01
□ 172 Alan Benes	.50	.23	.06
□ 173 Rey Ordonez	.60	.25	.07
□ 174 Livan Hernandez	.50	.23	.06
□ 175 Osvaldo Fernandez	.25	.11	.03
□ 176 Marc Barcelo	.10	.05	.01
□ 177 Sal Fasano	.10	.05	.01
□ 178 Mike Grace	.10	.05	.01
□ 179 Chan Ho Park	.50	.23	.06
□ 180 Robert Perez	.10	.05	.01
□ 181 Todd Hollandsworth	.50	.23	.06
□ 182 Wilton Guerrero	.60	.25	.07
□ 183 John Wasdin	.10	.05	.01
□ 184 Jim Pittsley	.10	.05	.01
□ 185 LaTroy Hawkins	.10	.05	.01
□ 186 Jay Powell	.10	.05	.01
□ 187 Felipe Crespo	.10	.05	.01
□ 188 Jermaine Dye	.75	.35	.09
□ 189 Bob Abreu	.50	.23	.06
□ 190 Matt Luke	.10	.05	.01
□ 191 Richard Hidalgo	.10	.05	.01
□ 192 Karim Garcia	.60	.25	.07
□ 193 Marvin Benard	.10	.05	.01
□ 194 Andy Fox	.10	.05	.01
□ 195 Terrell Wade	.50	.23	.06
□ 196 Frank Thomas CL	1.25	.55	.16
□ 197 Ken Griffey Jr. CL	1.25	.55	.16
□ 198 Greg Maddux CL	.75	.35	.09
□ 199 Mike Piazza CL	.75	.35	.09
□ 200 Cal Ripken CL	1.00	.45	.12

1996 Select Artist's Proofs

Randomly inserted one in 35 packs, this 200-card set is parallel and similar in design to the regular set. The difference is the holographic foil-stamped Artist's Proof logo on the card front.

	MINT	NRMT	EXC
COMPLETE SET (200)	2500.00	1100.00	300.00
COMMON CARD (1-200)	4.00	1.80	.50
SEMISTARS	12.00	5.50	1.50
STARS	25.00	11.00	3.10
*STARS: 25X TO 50X BASIC CARDS			
*YOUNG STARS: 20X TO 40X BASIC CARDS			
RANDOM INSERTS IN PACKS			

□ 6 Ken Griffey Jr.	125.00	55.00	15.50
□ 7 Greg Maddux	80.00	36.00	10.00
□ 11 Frank Thomas	125.00	55.00	15.50
□ 19 Cal Ripken	100.00	45.00	12.50
□ 22 Mike Piazza	80.00	36.00	10.00
□ 36 Albert Belle	60.00	27.00	7.50
□ 41 Chipper Jones	80.00	36.00	10.00
□ 45 Alex Rodriguez	125.00	55.00	15.50
□ 56 Juan Gonzalez	60.00	27.00	7.50
□ 151 Ken Griffey Jr. LUL	60.00	27.00	7.50
□ 152 Frank Thomas LUL	60.00	27.00	7.50
□ 161 Derek Jeter	80.00	36.00	10.00
□ 196 Frank Thomas CL	60.00	27.00	7.50
□ 197 Ken Griffey Jr. CL	60.00	27.00	7.50

1996 Select Claim To Fame

Randomly inserted in packs at a rate of one in 72, this 20-card set features potential Hall of Famers. The fronts display a color player portrait on a diecut plaque similar to the ones that enshrine Hall of Famers. The backs carry information about the player's claim to fame. Only 2100 of these sets were produced.

	MINT	NRMT	EXC
COMPLETE SET (20)	325.00	145.00	40.00
COMMON CARD (1-20)	4.00	1.80	.50
SEMISTARS	6.00	2.70	.75
RANDOM INSERTS IN PACKS			

□ 1 Cal Ripken	40.00	18.00	5.00
□ 2 Greg Maddux	30.00	13.50	3.70
□ 3 Ken Griffey Jr.	50.00	22.00	6.25
□ 4 Frank Thomas	50.00	22.00	6.25
□ 5 Mo Vaughn	12.00	5.50	1.50
□ 6 Albert Belle	25.00	11.00	3.10
□ 7 Jeff Bagwell	20.00	9.00	2.50
□ 8 Sammy Sosa	8.00	3.60	1.00
□ 9 Reggie Sanders	4.00	1.80	.50
□ 10 Hideo Nomo	12.00	5.50	1.50
□ 11 Chipper Jones	30.00	13.50	3.70
□ 12 Mike Piazza	30.00	13.50	3.70
□ 13 Matt Williams	6.00	2.70	.75
□ 14 Tony Gwynn	20.00	9.00	2.50
□ 15 Johnny Damon	4.00	1.80	.50
□ 16 Dante Bichette	6.00	2.70	.75
□ 17 Kirby Puckett	15.00	6.75	1.85
□ 18 Barry Bonds	12.00	5.50	1.50
□ 19 Randy Johnson	8.00	3.60	1.00
□ 20 Eddie Murray	12.00	5.50	1.50

1996 Select En Fuego

Randomly inserted in packs at a rate of one in 48, this 25-card set is printed with all-foil Dufex technology, etched highlights and transparent inks that make each card shine. Spanish for "on fire," En Fuego is an expression popularized by ESPN sportscaster Dan Patrick, who provides the commentary for each player on the card back. The fronts feature color action player photos while the backs display more player photos and the commentary.

	MINT	NRMT	EXC
COMPLETE SET (25)	300.00	135.00	38.00
COMMON CARD (1-25)	3.00	1.35	.35
SEMISTARS	5.00	2.20	.60
RANDOM INSERTS IN PACKS			
□ 1 Ken Griffey Jr.	40.00	18.00	5.00
□ 2 Frank Thomas	40.00	18.00	5.00
□ 3 Cal Ripken	30.00	13.50	3.70
□ 4 Greg Maddux	25.00	11.00	3.10
□ 5 Jeff Bagwell	15.00	6.75	1.85
□ 6 Barry Bonds	10.00	4.50	1.25
□ 7 Mo Vaughn	10.00	4.50	1.25
□ 8 Albert Belle	20.00	9.00	2.50
□ 9 Sammy Sosa	6.00	2.70	.75
□ 10 Reggie Sanders	3.00	1.35	.35
□ 11 Mike Piazza	25.00	11.00	3.10
□ 12 Chipper Jones	25.00	11.00	3.10
□ 13 Tony Gwynn	15.00	6.75	1.85
□ 14 Kirby Puckett	12.00	5.50	1.50
□ 15 Wade Boggs	5.00	2.20	.60
□ 16 Dan Patrick	8.00	3.60	1.00
□ 17 Gary Sheffield	6.00	2.70	.75
□ 18 Dante Bichette	5.00	2.20	.60
□ 19 Randy Johnson	6.00	2.70	.75
□ 20 Matt Williams	5.00	2.20	.60
□ 21 Alex Rodriguez	40.00	18.00	5.00
□ 22 Tim Salmon	5.00	2.20	.60
□ 23 Johnny Damon	3.00	1.35	.35
□ 24 Manny Ramirez	10.00	4.50	1.25
□ 25 Hideo Nomo	10.00	4.50	1.25

1996 Select Team Nucleus

Randomly inserted in packs at a rate of one in 18, this 28-card set is printed on clear plastic with holographic and micro-etched highlights and gold foil stamping. The fronts feature color pictures of three team players with the backs displaying the same photos, the players' names, and a sentence stating why these players are special.

	MINT	NRMT	EXC
COMPLETE SET (28)	100.00	45.00	12.50
COMMON CARD (1-28)	2.00	.90	.25
SEMISTARS	4.00	1.80	.50
RANDOM INSERTS IN PACKS			
□ 1 Albert Belle Manny Ramirez Carlos Baerga	12.00	5.50	1.50
□ 2 Ray Lankford Brian Jordan Ozzie Smith	4.00	1.80	.50
□ 3 Jay Bell Jeff King Denny Neagle	2.00	.90	.25
□ 4 Dante Bichette Andres Galarraga Larry Walker	4.00	1.80	.50
□ 5 Mark McGwire Mike Bordick Terry Steinbach	4.00	1.80	.50
□ 6 Bernie Williams Wade Boggs David Cone	4.00	1.80	.50
□ 7 Joe Carter Alex Gonzalez Shawn Green	2.00	.90	.25
□ 8 Roger Clemens Mo Vaughn Jose Canseco	6.00	2.70	.75
□ 9 Ken Griffey Jr. Edgar Martinez Randy Johnson	15.00	6.75	1.85
□ 10 Gregg Jefferies Darren Daulton Len Dykstra	2.00	.90	.25
□ 11 Mike Piazza Raul Mondesi Hideo Nomo	12.00	5.50	1.50
□ 12 Greg Maddux Chipper Jones Ryan Klesko	20.00	9.00	2.50
□ 13 Cecil Fielder Travis Fryman Phil Nevin	2.00	.90	.25
□ 14 Ivan Rodriguez Will Clark Juan Gonzalez	10.00	4.50	1.25
□ 15 Ryne Sandberg Sammy Sosa Mark Grace	6.00	2.70	.75
□ 16 Gary Sheffield Charles Johnson Andre Dawson	2.00	.90	.25
□ 17 Johnny Damon Michael Tucker Kevin Appier	2.00	.90	.25
□ 18 Barry Bonds Matt Williams Rod Beck	4.00	1.80	.50
□ 19 Kirby Puckett Chuck Knoblauch Marty Cordova	6.00	2.70	.75
□ 20 Cal Ripken Barry Bonilla Mike Mussina	12.00	5.50	1.50
□ 21 Jason Isringhausen Bill Pulsipher Rico Brogna	2.00	.90	.25
□ 22 Tony Gwynn Ken Caminiti Mark Newfield	6.00	2.70	.75
□ 23 Tim Salmon Garret Anderson Jim Edmonds	2.00	.90	.25
□ 24 Moises Alou Rondell White Cliff Floyd	2.00	.90	.25
□ 25 Barry Larkin Reggie Sanders Bret Boone	2.00	.90	.25
□ 26 Jeff Bagwell Craig Biggio Derek Bell	6.00	2.70	.75
□ 27 Frank Thomas Robin Ventura Alex Fernandez	12.00	5.50	1.50
□ 28 John Jaha Greg Vaughn Kevin Seitzer	2.00	.90	.25

1995 Select Certified

This 135-card standard-size set was issued through hobby outlets only. This product was issued in six-card packs. There are also tribute cards to Eddie Murray and Cal Ripken in this

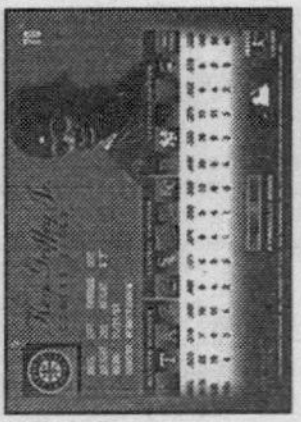

set. The cards are made with 24-point stock and are all metallic and double laminated. The fronts feature a player photo, his name in the lower right and the "Select '95 Certified" logo in the upper right. The horizontal backs feature a team by team seasonal summary and a player photo. The cards are numbered in the upper right corner. Rookie Cards in this set include Hideo Nomo and Carlos Perez.

	MINT	NRMT	EXC
COMPLETE SET (135)	50.00	22.00	6.25
COMMON CARD (1-135)	.25	.11	.03
SEMISTARS	.40	.18	.05
STARS	.75	.35	.09
COMP. CHECKLIST SET (7)	4.00	1.80	.50

SET INCLUDES CARD 2131 -- NO CARD 18 EXISTS

□ 1	Barry Bonds	1.25	.55	.16
□ 2	Reggie Sanders	.40	.18	.05
□ 3	Terry Steinbach	.40	.18	.05
□ 4	Eduardo Perez	.25	.11	.03
□ 5	Frank Thomas	5.00	2.20	.60
□ 6	Wil Cordero	.25	.11	.03
□ 7	John Olerud	.25	.11	.03
□ 8	Deion Sanders	.75	.35	.09
□ 9	Mike Mussina	1.00	.45	.12
□ 10	Mo Vaughn	1.25	.55	.16
□ 11	Will Clark	.75	.35	.09
□ 12	Chili Davis	.40	.18	.05
□ 13	Jimmy Key	.40	.18	.05
□ 14	Eddie Murray	1.25	.55	.16
□ 15	Bernard Gilkey	.40	.18	.05
□ 16	David Cone	.40	.18	.05
□ 17	Tim Salmon	.75	.35	.09
□ 19	Steve Ontiveros	.25	.11	.03
□ 20	Andres Galarraga	.75	.35	.09
□ 21	Don Mattingly	2.50	1.10	.30
□ 22	Kevin Appier	.40	.18	.05
□ 23	Paul Molitor	1.00	.45	.12
□ 24	Edgar Martinez	.75	.35	.09
□ 25	Andy Benes	.25	.11	.03
□ 26	Rafael Palmeiro	.75	.35	.09
□ 27	Barry Larkin	.75	.35	.09
□ 28	Gary Sheffield	.75	.35	.09
□ 29	Wally Joyner	.40	.18	.05
□ 30	Wade Boggs	.75	.35	.09
□ 31	Rico Brogna	.25	.11	.03
□ 32	Eddie Murray 3000th Hit	1.25	.55	.16
□ 33	Kirby Puckett	1.50	.70	.19
□ 34	Bobby Bonilla	.40	.18	.05
□ 35	Hal Morris	.25	.11	.03
□ 36	Moises Alou	.40	.18	.05
□ 37	Javier Lopez	.75	.35	.09
□ 38	Chuck Knoblauch	.75	.35	.09
□ 39	Mike Piazza	3.00	1.35	.35
□ 40	Travis Fryman	.40	.18	.05
□ 41	Rickey Henderson	.75	.35	.09
□ 42	Jim Thome	1.00	.45	.12
□ 43	Carlos Baerga	.75	.35	.09
□ 44	Dean Palmer	.40	.18	.05
□ 45	Kirk Gibson	.40	.18	.05
□ 46	Bret Saberhagen	.40	.18	.05
□ 47	Cecil Fielder	.40	.18	.05
□ 48	Manny Ramirez	1.25	.55	.16
□ 49	Derek Bell	.40	.18	.05
□ 50	Mark McGwire	1.50	.70	.19
□ 51	Jim Edmonds	.75	.35	.09
□ 52	Robin Ventura	.40	.18	.05
□ 53	Ryan Klesko	1.00	.45	.12
□ 54	Jeff Bagwell	2.00	.90	.25
□ 55	Ozzie Smith	1.00	.45	.12
□ 56	Albert Belle	2.50	1.10	.30
□ 57	Darren Daulton	.40	.18	.05
□ 58	Jeff Conine	.75	.35	.09
□ 59	Greg Maddux	3.00	1.35	.35
□ 60	Lenny Dykstra	.40	.18	.05
□ 61	Randy Johnson	.75	.35	.09
□ 62	Fred McGriff	.75	.35	.09
□ 63	Ray Lankford	.75	.35	.09
□ 64	David Justice	.75	.35	.09
□ 65	Paul O'Neill	.40	.18	.05
□ 66	Tony Gwynn	2.00	.90	.25
□ 67	Matt Williams	.75	.35	.09
□ 68	Dante Bichette	.75	.35	.09
□ 69	Craig Biggio	.75	.35	.09
□ 70	Ken Griffey Jr.	5.00	2.20	.60
□ 71	J.T. Snow	.40	.18	.05
□ 72	Cal Ripken	4.00	1.80	.50
□ 73	Jay Bell	.40	.18	.05
□ 74	Joe Carter	.75	.35	.09
□ 75	Roberto Alomar	1.25	.55	.16
□ 76	Benji Gil	.25	.11	.03
□ 77	Ivan Rodriguez	1.00	.45	.12
□ 78	Raul Mondesi	.75	.35	.09
□ 79	Cliff Floyd	.40	.18	.05
□ 80	Eric Karros Mike Piazza Raul Mondesi	1.00	.45	.12
□ 81	Royce Clayton	.25	.11	.03
□ 82	Billy Ashley	.25	.11	.03
□ 83	Joey Hamilton	.40	.18	.05
□ 84	Sammy Sosa	.75	.35	.09
□ 85	Jason Bere	.25	.11	.03
□ 86	Dennis Martinez	.40	.18	.05
□ 87	Greg Vaughn	.40	.18	.05
□ 88	Roger Clemens	.75	.35	.09
□ 89	Larry Walker	.75	.35	.09
□ 90	Mark Grace	.75	.35	.09
□ 91	Kenny Lofton	1.25	.55	.16
□ 92	Carlos Perez	.40	.18	.05
□ 93	Roger Cedeno	.40	.18	.05
□ 94	Scott Ruffcorn	.25	.11	.03
□ 95	Jim Pittsley	.40	.18	.05
□ 96	Andy Pettitte	2.00	.90	.25
□ 97	James Baldwin	.75	.35	.09
□ 98	Hideo Nomo	5.00	2.20	.60
□ 99	Ismael Valdes	.40	.18	.05
□ 100	Armando Benitez	.25	.11	.03
□ 101	Jose Malave	.25	.11	.03
□ 102	Bob Higginson	.75	.35	.09
□ 103	LaTroy Hawkins	.25	.11	.03
□ 104	Russ Davis	.25	.11	.03
□ 105	Shawn Green	.40	.18	.05
□ 106	Joe Vitiello	.25	.11	.03
□ 107	Chipper Jones	3.00	1.35	.35
□ 108	Shane Andrews	.25	.11	.03
□ 109	Jose Oliva	.25	.11	.03
□ 110	Ray Durham	.40	.18	.05
□ 111	Jon Nunnally	.40	.18	.05
□ 112	Alex Gonzalez	.25	.11	.03
□ 113	Vaughn Eshelman	.25	.11	.03
□ 114	Marty Cordova	.75	.35	.09
□ 115	Mark Grudzielanek	1.25	.55	.16
□ 116	Brian L.Hunter	.75	.35	.09
□ 117	Charles Johnson	.40	.18	.05
□ 118	Alex Rodriguez	6.00	2.70	.75
□ 119	David Bell	.25	.11	.03
□ 120	Todd Hollandsworth	.75	.35	.09
□ 121	Joe Randa	.25	.11	.03
□ 122	Derek Jeter	3.00	1.35	.35
□ 123	Frank Rodriguez	.40	.18	.05
□ 124	Curtis Goodwin	.40	.18	.05
□ 125	Bill Pulsipher	.40	.18	.05
□ 126	John Mabry	.75	.35	.09
□ 127	Julian Tavarez	.25	.11	.03
□ 128	Edgardo Alfonzo	.40	.18	.05
□ 129	Orlando Miller	.25	.11	.03
□ 130	Juan Acevedo	.25	.11	.03
□ 131	Jeff Cirillo	.40	.18	.05
□ 132	Roberto Petagine	.25	.11	.03
□ 133	Antonio Osuna	.25	.11	.03
□ 134	Michael Tucker	.40	.18	.05
□ 135	Garret Anderson	.75	.35	.09
□ 2131	Cal Ripken TRIB	5.00	2.20	.60

1995 Select Certified Mirror Gold

This 135-card set is a parallel to the regular issue. Pinnacle used their all-holographic foil technology on the fronts. The backs are identical to the regular issue but the words "Mirror Gold" are in the middle. These cards were inserted approximately one every five packs.

	MINT	NRMT	EXC
COMPLETE SET (135)	900.00	400.00	110.00
COMMON CARD (1-135)	2.00	.90	.25
SEMISTARS	5.00	2.20	.60
*VETERAN STARS: 7.5X to 15X BASIC CARDS			
*YOUNG STARS: 6X to 12X BASIC CARDS..			
RANDOM INSERTS IN PACKS			

□ 1 Barry Bonds	20.00	9.00	2.50
□ 5 Frank Thomas	75.00	34.00	9.50
□ 10 Mo Vaughn	20.00	9.00	2.50
□ 14 Eddie Murray	20.00	9.00	2.50
□ 21 Don Mattingly	40.00	18.00	5.00
□ 32 Eddie Murray 3000 TRIB	20.00	9.00	2.50
□ 33 Kirby Puckett	25.00	11.00	3.10
□ 39 Mike Piazza	50.00	22.00	6.25
□ 48 Manny Ramirez	20.00	9.00	2.50
□ 50 Mark McGwire	25.00	11.00	3.10
□ 54 Jeff Bagwell	30.00	13.50	3.70
□ 56 Albert Belle	40.00	18.00	5.00
□ 59 Greg Maddux	50.00	22.00	6.25
□ 66 Tony Gwynn	30.00	13.50	3.70
□ 70 Ken Griffey Jr.	75.00	34.00	9.50
□ 72 Cal Ripken	60.00	27.00	7.50
□ 75 Roberto Alomar	20.00	9.00	2.50
□ 91 Kenny Lofton	20.00	9.00	2.50
□ 96 Andy Pettitte	30.00	13.50	3.70
□ 98 Hideo Nomo	40.00	18.00	5.00
□ 107 Chipper Jones	50.00	22.00	6.25
□ 118 Alex Rodriguez	75.00	34.00	9.50
□ 122 Derek Jeter	50.00	22.00	6.25
□ 2131 Cal Ripken TRIB	75.00	34.00	9.50

1995 Select Certified Future

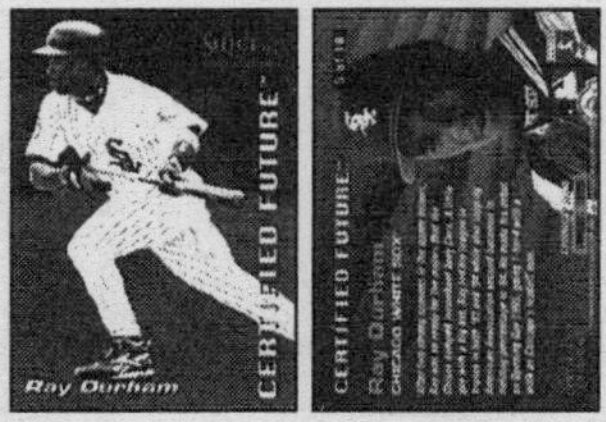

This ten-card set was inserted approximately one in every 19 packs. Ten leading 1995 rookie players are included in this set. These cards were produced using Pinnacle's Dufex technology. The fronts feature a player photo with his name on the bottom. The words "Certified Future" are spelled vertically on the right. The horizontal backs feature some textual information and a player photo.

	MINT	NRMT	EXC
COMPLETE SET (10)	75.00	34.00	9.50
COMMON CARD (1-10)	2.50	1.10	.30
RANDOM INSERTS IN PACKS			

□ 1 Chipper Jones	20.00	9.00	2.50
□ 2 Curtis Goodwin	2.50	1.10	.30
□ 3 Hideo Nomo	12.00	5.50	1.50
□ 4 Shawn Green	8.00	3.60	1.00
□ 5 Ray Durham	5.00	2.20	.60
□ 6 Todd Hollandsworth	4.00	1.80	.50
□ 7 Brian L.Hunter	4.00	1.80	.50
□ 8 Carlos Delgado	6.00	2.70	.75
□ 9 Michael Tucker UER (front photo is Jon Nunnally)	8.00	3.60	1.00
□ 10 Alex Rodriguez	30.00	13.50	3.70

1995 Select Certified Gold Team

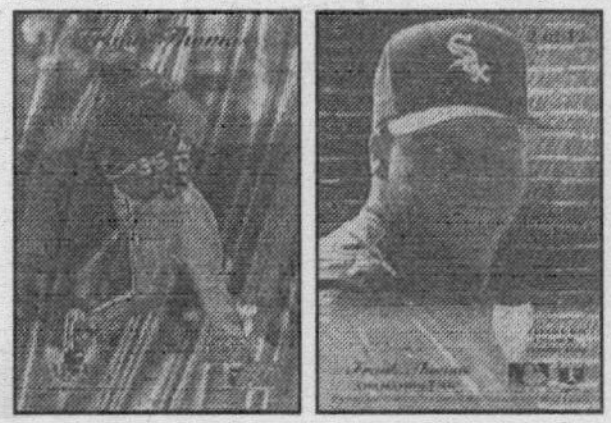

This 12-card was inserted approximately one in every 41 packs. This set features some of the leading players in baseball. These cards feature double-sided all-gold-foil Dufex technology.

	MINT	NRMT	EXC
COMPLETE SET (12)	300.00	135.00	38.00
COMMON CARD (1-12)	8.00	3.60	1.00
RANDOM INSERTS IN PACKS			

□ 1 Ken Griffey Jr.	60.00	27.00	7.50
□ 2 Frank Thomas	60.00	27.00	7.50
□ 3 Cal Ripken	50.00	22.00	6.25
□ 4 Jeff Bagwell	25.00	11.00	3.10
□ 5 Mike Piazza	40.00	18.00	5.00
□ 6 Barry Bonds	15.00	6.75	1.85
□ 7 Matt Williams	8.00	3.60	1.00
□ 8 Don Mattingly	30.00	13.50	3.70
□ 9 Will Clark	8.00	3.60	1.00
□ 10 Tony Gwynn	25.00	11.00	3.10
□ 11 Kirby Puckett	20.00	9.00	2.50
□ 12 Jose Canseco	8.00	3.60	1.00

1995 Select Certified Potential Unlimited

These 20 were randomly inserted into packs. Two varieties of each card were produced. Cards numbered out of 1,975 were randomly inserted into packs while cards numbered out of 903 were randomly inserted on top of boxes. These cards feature Pinnacle's all-foil Dufex printing technology. The fronts feature a player photo in the middle. The words "Potential Unlimited" appear in the upper left and the player's name in the bottom left. The horizontal back has a player photo and some text set against a background of a baseball. The cards are numbered 1 of either 1,975 or 903 at bottom right. The cards are also numbered as part of the set as "X" of 20 in the upper right. According to Pinnacle, across the production

run these cards were inserted one every 29 packs. Prices below reflect cards numbered out of 1975.

	MINT	NRMT	EXC
COMP. 1975 SET (20)	250.00	110.00	31.00
COMMON 1975 CARD (1-20)	5.00	2.20	.60
SEMISTARS	8.00	3.60	1.00

903 NUMBERED CARDS: 1.25X BASIC CARDS
1975 VERSIONS RANDOM INSERTS IN PACKS
903 VERSIONS RANDOM INSERTS IN BOXES
CARDS W/1975 NUMBERS PRICED BELOW

□ 1 Cliff Floyd	8.00	3.60	1.00
□ 2 Manny Ramirez	25.00	11.00	3.10
□ 3 Raul Mondesi	12.00	5.50	1.50
□ 4 Scott Ruffcorn	5.00	2.20	.60
□ 5 Billy Ashley	5.00	2.20	.60
□ 6 Alex Gonzalez	5.00	2.20	.60
□ 7 Midre Cummings	5.00	2.20	.60
□ 8 Charles Johnson	8.00	3.60	1.00
□ 9 Garret Anderson	8.00	3.60	1.00
□ 10 Hideo Nomo	40.00	18.00	5.00
□ 11 Chipper Jones	60.00	27.00	7.50
□ 12 Curtis Goodwin	5.00	2.20	.60
□ 13 Frank Rodriguez	5.00	2.20	.60
□ 14 Shawn Green	5.00	2.20	.60
□ 15 Ray Durham	8.00	3.60	1.00
□ 16 Todd Hollandsworth	12.00	5.50	1.50
□ 17 Brian L.Hunter	12.00	5.50	1.50
□ 18 Carlos Delgado	12.00	5.50	1.50
□ 19 Michael Tucker	8.00	3.60	1.00
□ 20 Alex Rodriguez	100.00	45.00	12.50

1996 Select Certified

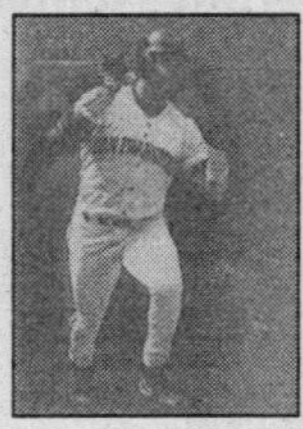

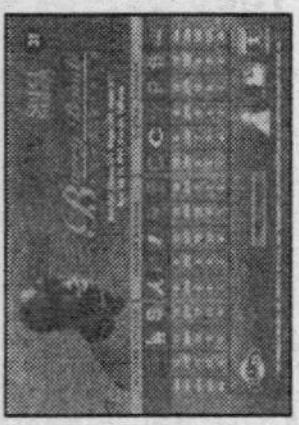

The 1996 Select Certified hobby only set was issued in one series totalling 144 cards. Each six-card pack sells for $4.99. Printed on special 24-point silver mirror mylar card stock, the fronts feature a color player photo on a gray and black background. The backs carry another color player photo with information about his playing abilities.

	MINT	NRMT	EXC
COMPLETE SET (144)	40.00	18.00	5.00
COMMON CARD (1-144)	.15	.07	.02
SEMISTARS	.40	.18	.05
STARS	.60	.25	.07
COMP.CERT.BLUE SET (144)	5000.00	2200.00	600.00
*CERTIFIED BLUE:25X to 50X BASIC CARDS			
COMP.ARTIST'S PROOF SET (144)	2000.00	900.00	250.00
*ARTIST'S PROOFS: 10X to 20X BASIC CARDS			
COMP.CERT.RED SET (144)	750.00	350.00	95.00
*CERTIFIED RED: 4X to 8X BASIC CARDS...			
RANDOM INSERTS IN PACKS			

□ 1 Frank Thomas	5.00	2.20	.60
□ 2 Tino Martinez	.15	.07	.02
□ 3 Gary Sheffield	.75	.35	.09
□ 4 Kenny Lofton	1.25	.55	.16
□ 5 Joe Carter	.60	.25	.07
□ 6 Alex Rodriguez	5.00	2.20	.60
□ 7 Chipper Jones	3.00	1.35	.35
□ 8 Roger Clemens	.60	.25	.07
□ 9 Jay Bell	.15	.07	.02
□ 10 Eddie Murray	1.25	.55	.16
□ 11 Will Clark	.60	.25	.07
□ 12 Mike Mussina	1.00	.45	.12
□ 13 Hideo Nomo	1.25	.55	.16
□ 14 Andres Galarraga	.60	.25	.07
□ 15 Marc Newfield	.40	.18	.05
□ 16 Jason Isringhausen	.40	.18	.05
□ 17 Randy Johnson	1.00	.45	.12
□ 18 Chuck Knoblauch	.60	.25	.07
□ 19 J.T. Snow	.40	.18	.05
□ 20 Mark McGwire	1.50	.70	.19
□ 21 Tony Gwynn	2.00	.90	.25
□ 22 Albert Belle	2.50	1.10	.30
□ 23 Gregg Jefferies	.40	.18	.05
□ 24 Reggie Sanders	.40	.18	.05
□ 25 Bernie Williams	.75	.35	.09
□ 26 Ray Lankford	.40	.18	.05
□ 27 Johnny Damon	.40	.18	.05
□ 28 Ryne Sandberg	1.25	.55	.16
□ 29 Rondell White	.60	.25	.07
□ 30 Mike Piazza	3.00	1.35	.35
□ 31 Barry Bonds	1.25	.55	.16
□ 32 Greg Maddux	3.00	1.35	.35
□ 33 Craig Biggio	.60	.25	.07
□ 34 John Valentin	.15	.07	.02
□ 35 Ivan Rodriguez	1.00	.45	.12
□ 36 Rico Brogna	.15	.07	.02
□ 37 Tim Salmon	.60	.25	.07
□ 38 Sterling Hitchcock	.15	.07	.02
□ 39 Charles Johnson	.40	.18	.05
□ 40 Travis Fryman	.40	.18	.05
□ 41 Barry Larkin	.60	.25	.07
□ 42 Tom Glavine	.60	.25	.07
□ 43 Marty Cordova	.60	.25	.07
□ 44 Shawn Green	.40	.18	.05
□ 45 Ben McDonald	.15	.07	.02
□ 46 Robin Ventura	.40	.18	.05
□ 47 Ken Griffey Jr.	5.00	2.20	.60
□ 48 Orlando Merced	.15	.07	.02
□ 49 Paul O'Neill	.15	.07	.02
□ 50 Ozzie Smith	1.00	.45	.12
□ 51 Manny Ramirez	1.25	.55	.16
□ 52 Ismael Valdes	.40	.18	.05
□ 53 Cal Ripken	4.00	1.80	.50
□ 54 Jeff Bagwell	2.00	.90	.25
□ 55 Greg Vaughn	.40	.18	.05
□ 56 Juan Gonzalez	2.50	1.10	.30
□ 57 Raul Mondesi	.60	.25	.07
□ 58 Carlos Baerga	.60	.25	.07
□ 59 Sammy Sosa	.75	.35	.09
□ 60 Mike Kelly	.15	.07	.02
□ 61 Edgar Martinez	.60	.25	.07
□ 62 Kirby Puckett	1.50	.70	.19
□ 63 Cecil Fielder	.40	.18	.05
□ 64 David Cone	.40	.18	.05
□ 65 Moises Alou	.15	.07	.02
□ 66 Fred McGriff	.60	.25	.07
□ 67 Mo Vaughn	1.25	.55	.16
□ 68 Edgardo Alfonzo	.40	.18	.05
□ 69 Jim Thome	1.00	.45	.12
□ 70 Rickey Henderson	.60	.25	.07
□ 71 Dante Bichette	.60	.25	.07
□ 72 Lenny Dykstra	.40	.18	.05
□ 73 Benji Gil	.15	.07	.02
□ 74 Wade Boggs	.60	.25	.07
□ 75 Jim Edmonds	.60	.25	.07
□ 76 Michael Tucker	.15	.07	.02
□ 77 Carlos Delgado	.40	.18	.05
□ 78 Butch Huskey	.15	.07	.02
□ 79 Billy Ashley	.15	.07	.02
□ 80 Dean Palmer	.40	.18	.05
□ 81 Paul Molitor	1.00	.45	.12

□ 82 Ryan Klesko	1.00	.45	.12
□ 83 Brian L.Hunter	.15	.07	.02
□ 84 Jay Buhner	.60	.25	.07
□ 85 Larry Walker	.60	.25	.07
□ 86 Mike Bordick	.15	.07	.02
□ 87 Matt Williams	.60	.25	.07
□ 88 Jack McDowell	.40	.18	.05
□ 89 Hal Morris	.15	.07	.02
□ 90 Brian Jordan	.40	.18	.05
□ 91 Andy Pettitte	1.50	.70	.19
□ 92 Melvin Nieves	.40	.18	.05
□ 93 Pedro Martinez	.40	.18	.05
□ 94 Mark Grace	.60	.25	.07
□ 95 Garret Anderson	.40	.18	.05
□ 96 Andre Dawson	.60	.25	.07
□ 97 Ray Durham	.40	.18	.05
□ 98 Jose Canseco	.60	.25	.07
□ 99 Roberto Alomar	1.25	.55	.16
□ 100 Derek Jeter	3.00	1.35	.35
□ 101 Alan Benes	.60	.25	.07
□ 102 Karim Garcia	1.00	.45	.12
□ 103 Robin Jennings	.15	.07	.02
□ 104 Bob Abreu	.60	.25	.07
□ 105 Sal Fasano UER (name on front is Livan Hernandez)	.15	.07	.02
□ 106 Steve Gibralter	.15	.07	.02
□ 107 Jermaine Dye	1.25	.55	.16
□ 108 Jason Kendall	.40	.18	.05
□ 109 Mike Grace	.40	.18	.05
□ 110 Jason Schmidt	.40	.18	.05
□ 111 Paul Wilson	.40	.18	.05
□ 112 Rey Ordonez	1.00	.45	.12
□ 113 Wilton Guerrero	1.00	.45	.12
□ 114 Brooks Kieschnick	.15	.07	.02
□ 115 George Arias	.15	.07	.02
□ 116 Osvaldo Fernandez	.40	.18	.05
□ 117 Todd Hollandsworth	.60	.25	.07
□ 118 John Wasdin	.15	.07	.02
□ 119 Eric Owens	.15	.07	.02
□ 120 Chan Ho Park	.40	.18	.05
□ 121 Mark Loretta	.15	.07	.02
□ 122 Richard Hidalgo	.40	.18	.05
□ 123 Jeff Suppan	.40	.18	.05
□ 124 Jim Pittsley	.15	.07	.02
□ 125 LaTroy Hawkins	.15	.07	.02
□ 126 Chris Snopek	.15	.07	.02
□ 127 Justin Thompson	.15	.07	.02
□ 128 Jay Powell	.15	.07	.02
□ 129 Alex Ochoa	.40	.18	.05
□ 130 Felipe Crespo	.15	.07	.02
□ 131 Matt Lawton	.15	.07	.02
□ 132 Jimmy Haynes	.15	.07	.02
□ 133 Terrell Wade	.40	.18	.05
□ 134 Ruben Rivera	1.00	.45	.12
□ 135 Frank Thomas PP	2.50	1.10	.30
□ 136 Ken Griffey Jr. PP	2.50	1.10	.30
□ 137 Greg Maddux PP	1.50	.70	.19
□ 138 Mike Piazza PP	1.50	.70	.19
□ 139 Cal Ripken PP	2.00	.90	.25
□ 140 Albert Belle PP	1.25	.55	.16
□ 141 Mo Vaughn PP	.60	.25	.07
□ 142 Chipper Jones PP	1.50	.70	.19
□ 143 Hideo Nomo PP	.60	.25	.07
□ 144 Ryan Klesko PP			

1996 Select Certified Mirror Blue

Randomly inserted in packs at a rate of one in 200, this 144-card set is parallel to the base set with only 45 sets being produced. This set is a blue holographic foil rendition of the base set.

	MINT	NRMT	EXC
COMMON CARD (1-144)	40.00	18.00	5.00
SEMISTARS	80.00	36.00	10.00
STARS	120.00	55.00	15.00
*STARS: 125X to 200X BASIC CARDS			
*YOUNG STARS: 90X to 150X BASIC CARDS			
RANDOM INSERTS IN PACKS			

□ 1 Frank Thomas	1000.00	450.00	125.00
□ 6 Alex Rodriguez	1000.00	450.00	125.00
□ 7 Chipper Jones	600.00	275.00	75.00
□ 21 Tony Gwynn	400.00	180.00	50.00
□ 22 Albert Belle	500.00	220.00	60.00
□ 30 Mike Piazza	600.00	275.00	75.00
□ 32 Greg Maddux	600.00	275.00	75.00
□ 47 Ken Griffey Jr.	1000.00	450.00	125.00
□ 53 Cal Ripken	750.00	350.00	95.00
□ 54 Jeff Bagwell	400.00	180.00	50.00
□ 56 Juan Gonzalez	500.00	220.00	60.00
□ 100 Derek Jeter	600.00	275.00	75.00
□ 135 Frank Thomas PP	500.00	220.00	60.00
□ 136 Ken Griffey Jr. PP	500.00	220.00	60.00
□ 139 Cal Ripken PP	400.00	180.00	50.00

1996 Select Certified Mirror Gold

Randomly inserted in packs at a rate of one in 300, this 144-card set is parallel to the base set with only 30 sets being produced. This set is a gold holographic foil rendition of the base set.

	MINT	NRMT	EXC
COMMON CARD (1-144)	100.00	45.00	12.50
SEMISTARS	200.00	90.00	25.00
STARS	300.00	135.00	38.00
*STARS: 300X to 500X BASIC CARDS			
*YOUNG STARS: 250X to 400X BASIC CARDS			
RANDOM INSERTS IN PACKS			

□ 1 Frank Thomas	2500.00	1100.00	300.00
□ 6 Alex Rodriguez	2500.00	1100.00	300.00
□ 7 Chipper Jones	1500.00	700.00	190.00
□ 20 Mark McGwire	800.00	350.00	100.00
□ 21 Tony Gwynn	1000.00	450.00	125.00
□ 22 Albert Belle	1200.00	550.00	150.00
□ 30 Mike Piazza	1500.00	700.00	190.00
□ 32 Greg Maddux	1500.00	700.00	190.00
□ 47 Ken Griffey Jr.	2500.00	1100.00	300.00
□ 53 Cal Ripken	2000.00	900.00	250.00
□ 54 Jeff Bagwell	1000.00	450.00	125.00
□ 56 Juan Gonzalez	1200.00	550.00	150.00
□ 62 Kirby Puckett	800.00	350.00	100.00
□ 100 Derek Jeter	1200.00	550.00	150.00
□ 135 Frank Thomas PP	1200.00	550.00	150.00
□ 136 Ken Griffey Jr. PP	1200.00	550.00	150.00
□ 139 Cal Ripken PP	1000.00	450.00	125.00

1996 Select Certified Mirror Red

Randomly inserted in packs at a rate of one in 100, this 144-card set is parallel to the base set with only 90 sets being produced. This set is a red holographic foil rendition of the base set.

	MINT	NRMT	EXC
COMMON CARD (1-144)	20.00	9.00	2.50
SEMISTARS	40.00	18.00	5.00
STARS	60.00	27.00	7.50
*STARS: 60X to 100X BASIC CARDS			
*YOUNG STARS: 50X to 80X BASIC CARDS			
RANDOM INSERTS IN PACKS			

□ 1 Frank Thomas	500.00	220.00	60.00
□ 6 Alex Rodriguez	500.00	220.00	60.00
□ 7 Chipper Jones	300.00	135.00	38.00
□ 20 Mark McGwire	175.00	80.00	22.00
□ 21 Tony Gwynn	200.00	90.00	25.00
□ 22 Albert Belle	250.00	110.00	31.00
□ 30 Mike Piazza	300.00	135.00	38.00
□ 32 Greg Maddux	300.00	135.00	38.00
□ 47 Ken Griffey Jr.	500.00	220.00	60.00
□ 53 Cal Ripken	400.00	180.00	50.00
□ 54 Jeff Bagwell	200.00	90.00	25.00
□ 56 Juan Gonzalez	250.00	110.00	31.00
□ 62 Kirby Puckett	175.00	80.00	22.00
□ 100 Derek Jeter	300.00	135.00	38.00
□ 135 Frank Thomas PP	250.00	110.00	31.00
□ 136 Ken Griffey Jr. PP	250.00	110.00	31.00
□ 139 Cal Ripken PP	200.00	90.00	25.00

1996 Select Certified Interleague Preview

Randomly inserted in packs at a rate of one in 42, this 25-card set gets ready for the start of interleague play in the 1997 season. Printed on Silver Prime Frost foil stock with gold lettering, the fronts feature color player cutouts of two opposing players. The backs carry another color cutout of the two players with information as to why they are a great matchup.

	MINT	NRMT	EXC
COMPLETE SET (25)	400.00	180.00	50.00
COMMON CARD (1-25)	6.00	2.70	.75
RANDOM INSERTS IN PACKS			

	MINT	NRMT	EXC
□ 1 Ken Griffey Jr.	60.00	27.00	7.50
Hideo Nomo			
□ 2 Greg Maddux	40.00	18.00	5.00
Mo Vaughn			
□ 3 Frank Thomas	40.00	18.00	5.00
Sammy Sosa			
□ 4 Mike Piazza	30.00	13.50	3.70
Jim Edmonds			
□ 5 Ryan Klesko	12.00	5.50	1.50
Roger Clemens			
□ 6 Derek Jeter	30.00	13.50	3.70
Rey Ordonez			
□ 7 Johnny Damon	6.00	2.70	.75
Ray Lankford			
□ 8 Manny Ramirez	12.00	5.50	1.50
Reggie Sanders			
□ 9 Barry Bonds	15.00	6.75	1.85
Jay Buhner			
□ 10 Jason Isringhausen	8.00	3.60	1.00
Wade Boggs			
□ 11 David Cone	30.00	13.50	3.70
Chipper Jones			
□ 12 Jeff Bagwell	20.00	9.00	2.50
Will Clark			
□ 13 Tony Gwynn	25.00	11.00	3.10
Randy Johnson			
□ 14 Cal Ripken	40.00	18.00	5.00
Tom Glavine			
□ 15 Kirby Puckett	12.00	5.50	1.50
Andy Benes			
□ 16 Gary Sheffield	15.00	6.75	1.85
Mike Mussina			
□ 17 Raul Mondesi	10.00	4.50	1.25
Tim Salmon			
□ 18 Rondell White	6.00	2.70	.75
Carlos Delgado			
□ 19 Cecil Fielder	12.00	5.50	1.50
Ryne Sandberg			
□ 20 Kenny Lofton	12.00	5.50	1.50
Brian L.Hunter			
□ 21 Paul Wilson	6.00	2.70	.75
Paul O'Neill			
□ 22 Ismael Valdes	6.00	2.70	.75
Edgar Martinez			
□ 23 Matt Williams	15.00	6.75	1.85
Mark McGwire			
□ 24 Albert Belle	25.00	11.00	3.10
Barry Larkin			
□ 25 Brady Anderson	8.00	3.60	1.00
Marquis Grissom			

1996 Select Certified Select Few

Randomly inserted in packs at a rate of one in 60, this 18-card set honors superstar athletes with unmatched playing field talents. Utilizing the all-new Dot Matrix hologram technology, the fronts feature color action player cutouts. The backs carry player information.

	MINT	NRMT	EXC
COMPLETE SET (18)	400.00	180.00	50.00
COMMON CARD (1-18)	8.00	3.60	1.00
RANDOM INSERTS IN PACKS			

	MINT	NRMT	EXC
□ 1 Sammy Sosa	10.00	4.50	1.25
□ 2 Derek Jeter	40.00	18.00	5.00
□ 3 Ken Griffey Jr.	60.00	27.00	7.50
□ 4 Albert Belle	30.00	13.50	3.70
□ 5 Cal Ripken	50.00	22.00	6.25
□ 6 Greg Maddux	40.00	18.00	5.00
□ 7 Frank Thomas	60.00	27.00	7.50
□ 8 Mo Vaughn	15.00	6.75	1.85
□ 9 Chipper Jones	40.00	18.00	5.00
□ 10 Mike Piazza	40.00	18.00	5.00
□ 11 Ryan Klesko	12.00	5.50	1.50
□ 12 Hideo Nomo	15.00	6.75	1.85
□ 13 Alan Benes	8.00	3.60	1.00
□ 14 Manny Ramirez	15.00	6.75	1.85
□ 15 Gary Sheffield	10.00	4.50	1.25
□ 16 Barry Bonds	15.00	6.75	1.85
□ 17 Matt Williams	8.00	3.60	1.00
□ 18 Johnny Damon	8.00	3.60	1.00

1993 SP

This 290-card standard-size set features fronts with action color player photos. The player's name and position appear within a team-colored stripe at the bottom edge that shades from dark to light, left to right. A team color-checkered stripe is in the upper left and the team name in a gold-lettered arc appears at the top with a gold underline that extends down the right side. The copper foil-stamped SP logo appears at the bottom right. The back displays an action shot of the player in the top half with a team color-checkered stripe in the upper right. The bottom half carries the player's biography, statistics, and career highlights. Special subsets include All Star players (1-18) and Foil Prospects (271-290). Cards 19-270 are in

alphabetical order by team nickname. The foil Rookie Cards are: Roger Cedeno, Johnny Damon, Russ Davis, Derek Jeter, Chad Mottola and Todd Steverson. Other Rookie Cards in the set include J.T. Snow.

	MINT	NRMT	EXC
COMPLETE SET (290)	75.00	34.00	9.50
COMMON CARD (1-290)	.15	.07	.02
FOIL PROSPECTS (271-290)	.50	.23	.06
SEMISTARS	.50	.23	.06
STARS	1.00	.45	.12

		MINT	NRMT	EXC
□ 1	Roberto Alomar AS	2.00	.90	.25
□ 2	Wade Boggs AS	1.00	.45	.12
□ 3	Joe Carter AS	1.00	.45	.12
□ 4	Ken Griffey Jr. AS	8.00	3.60	1.00
□ 5	Mark Langston AS	.50	.23	.06
□ 6	John Olerud AS	.15	.07	.02
□ 7	Kirby Puckett AS	2.50	1.10	.30
□ 8	Cal Ripken Jr. AS	6.00	2.70	.75
□ 9	Ivan Rodriguez AS	1.50	.70	.19
□ 10	Barry Bonds AS	2.00	.90	.25
□ 11	Darren Daulton AS	.50	.23	.06
□ 12	Marquis Grissom AS	1.00	.45	.12
□ 13	David Justice AS	1.00	.45	.12
□ 14	John Kruk AS	.50	.23	.06
□ 15	Barry Larkin AS	1.00	.45	.12
□ 16	Terry Mulholland AS	.15	.07	.02
□ 17	Ryne Sandberg AS	2.00	.90	.25
□ 18	Gary Sheffield AS	1.00	.45	.12
□ 19	Chad Curtis	.50	.23	.06
□ 20	Chili Davis	.50	.23	.06
□ 21	Gary DiSarcina	.15	.07	.02
□ 22	Damion Easley	.15	.07	.02
□ 23	Chuck Finley	.15	.07	.02
□ 24	Luis Polonia	.15	.07	.02
□ 25	Tim Salmon	2.00	.90	.25
□ 26	J.T. Snow	1.00	.45	.12
□ 27	Russ Springer	.15	.07	.02
□ 28	Jeff Bagwell	3.00	1.35	.35
□ 29	Craig Biggio	1.00	.45	.12
□ 30	Ken Caminiti	1.00	.45	.12
□ 31	Andujar Cedeno	.15	.07	.02
□ 32	Doug Drabek	.15	.07	.02
□ 33	Steve Finley	1.00	.45	.12
□ 34	Luis Gonzalez	.15	.07	.02
□ 35	Pete Harnisch	.15	.07	.02
□ 36	Darryl Kile	.15	.07	.02
□ 37	Mike Bordick	.15	.07	.02
□ 38	Dennis Eckersley	.50	.23	.06
□ 39	Brent Gates	.50	.23	.06
□ 40	Rickey Henderson	1.00	.45	.12
□ 41	Mark McGwire	2.50	1.10	.30
□ 42	Craig Paquette	.15	.07	.02
□ 43	Ruben Sierra	.50	.23	.06
□ 44	Terry Steinbach	.50	.23	.06
□ 45	Todd Van Poppel	.15	.07	.02
□ 46	Pat Borders	.15	.07	.02
□ 47	Tony Fernandez	.15	.07	.02
□ 48	Juan Guzman	.50	.23	.06
□ 49	Pat Hentgen	1.00	.45	.12
□ 50	Paul Molitor	1.50	.70	.19
□ 51	Jack Morris	.50	.23	.06
□ 52	Ed Sprague	.50	.23	.06
□ 53	Duane Ward	.15	.07	.02
□ 54	Devon White	.15	.07	.02
□ 55	Steve Avery	.50	.23	.06
□ 56	Jeff Blauser	.15	.07	.02
□ 57	Ron Gant	1.00	.45	.12
□ 58	Tom Glavine	1.00	.45	.12
□ 59	Greg Maddux	5.00	2.20	.60
□ 60	Fred McGriff	1.00	.45	.12
□ 61	Terry Pendleton	.50	.23	.06
□ 62	Deion Sanders	1.00	.45	.12
□ 63	John Smoltz	1.00	.45	.12
□ 64	Cal Eldred	.15	.07	.02
□ 65	Darryl Hamilton	.15	.07	.02
□ 66	John Jaha	.50	.23	.06
□ 67	Pat Listach	.15	.07	.02
□ 68	Jaime Navarro	.15	.07	.02
□ 69	Kevin Reimer	.15	.07	.02
□ 70	B.J. Surhoff	.50	.23	.06
□ 71	Greg Vaughn	1.00	.45	.12
□ 72	Robin Yount	1.00	.45	.12
□ 73	Rene Arocha	.15	.07	.02
□ 74	Bernard Gilkey	1.00	.45	.12
□ 75	Gregg Jefferies	1.00	.45	.12
□ 76	Ray Lankford	1.00	.45	.12
□ 77	Tom Pagnozzi	.15	.07	.02
□ 78	Lee Smith	.50	.23	.06
□ 79	Ozzie Smith	1.50	.70	.19
□ 80	Bob Tewksbury	.15	.07	.02
□ 81	Mark Whiten	.15	.07	.02
□ 82	Steve Buechele	.15	.07	.02
□ 83	Mark Grace	1.00	.45	.12
□ 84	Jose Guzman	.15	.07	.02
□ 85	Derrick May	.15	.07	.02
□ 86	Mike Morgan	.15	.07	.02
□ 87	Randy Myers	.50	.23	.06
□ 88	Kevin Roberson	.15	.07	.02
□ 89	Sammy Sosa	1.00	.45	.12
□ 90	Rick Wilkins	.15	.07	.02
□ 91	Brett Butler	.50	.23	.06
□ 92	Eric Davis	.50	.23	.06
□ 93	Orel Hershiser	.50	.23	.06
□ 94	Eric Karros	1.00	.45	.12
□ 95	Ramon Martinez	.50	.23	.06
□ 96	Raul Mondesi	2.50	1.10	.30
□ 97	Jose Offerman	.15	.07	.02
□ 98	Mike Piazza	8.00	3.60	1.00
□ 99	Darryl Strawberry	.50	.23	.06
□ 100	Moises Alou	1.00	.45	.12
□ 101	Wil Cordero	.50	.23	.06
□ 102	Delino DeShields	.15	.07	.02
□ 103	Darrin Fletcher	.15	.07	.02
□ 104	Ken Hill	.50	.23	.06
□ 105	Mike Lansing	.50	.23	.06
□ 106	Dennis Martinez	.50	.23	.06
□ 107	Larry Walker	1.00	.45	.12
□ 108	John Wetteland	.50	.23	.06
□ 109	Rod Beck	.50	.23	.06
□ 110	John Burkett	.15	.07	.02
□ 111	Will Clark	1.00	.45	.12
□ 112	Royce Clayton	.50	.23	.06
□ 113	Darren Lewis	.15	.07	.02
□ 114	Willie McGee	.15	.07	.02
□ 115	Bill Swift	.15	.07	.02
□ 116	Robby Thompson	.15	.07	.02
□ 117	Matt Williams	1.00	.45	.12
□ 118	Sandy Alomar Jr.	.50	.23	.06
□ 119	Carlos Baerga	1.00	.45	.12
□ 120	Albert Belle	4.00	1.80	.50
□ 121	Reggie Jefferson	.50	.23	.06
□ 122	Wayne Kirby	.15	.07	.02
□ 123	Kenny Lofton	2.50	1.10	.30
□ 124	Carlos Martinez	.15	.07	.02
□ 125	Charles Nagy	.50	.23	.06
□ 126	Paul Sorrento	.15	.07	.02
□ 127	Rich Amaral	.15	.07	.02
□ 128	Jay Buhner	1.00	.45	.12
□ 129	Norm Charlton	.15	.07	.02
□ 130	Dave Fleming	.15	.07	.02
□ 131	Erik Hanson	.15	.07	.02
□ 132	Randy Johnson	1.00	.45	.12
□ 133	Edgar Martinez	1.00	.45	.12
□ 134	Tino Martinez	.50	.23	.06
□ 135	Omar Vizquel	1.00	.45	.12
□ 136	Bret Barberie	.15	.07	.02
□ 137	Chuck Carr	.15	.07	.02
□ 138	Jeff Conine	1.00	.45	.12
□ 139	Orestes Destrade	.15	.07	.02
□ 140	Chris Hammond	.15	.07	.02
□ 141	Bryan Harvey	.15	.07	.02
□ 142	Benito Santiago	.15	.07	.02
□ 143	Walt Weiss	.15	.07	.02
□ 144	Darrell Whitmore	.15	.07	.02
□ 145	Tim Bogar	.15	.07	.02
□ 146	Bobby Bonilla	.50	.23	.06
□ 147	Jeromy Burnitz	.15	.07	.02
□ 148	Vince Coleman	.15	.07	.02
□ 149	Dwight Gooden	.50	.23	.06
□ 150	Todd Hundley	1.00	.45	.12
□ 151	Howard Johnson	.15	.07	.02
□ 152	Eddie Murray	2.00	.90	.25
□ 153	Bret Saberhagen	.50	.23	.06
□ 154	Brady Anderson	1.00	.45	.12
□ 155	Mike Devereaux	.15	.07	.02
□ 156	Jeffrey Hammonds	.50	.23	.06
□ 157	Chris Hoiles	.15	.07	.02
□ 158	Ben McDonald	.15	.07	.02
□ 159	Mark McLemore	.15	.07	.02

□	160 Mike Mussina	1.50	.70	.19
□	161 Gregg Olson	.15	.07	.02
□	162 David Segui	.15	.07	.02
□	163 Derek Bell	1.00	.45	.12
□	164 Andy Benes	.15	.07	.02
□	165 Archi Cianfrocco	.15	.07	.02
□	166 Ricky Gutierrez	.15	.07	.02
□	167 Tony Gwynn	3.00	1.35	.35
□	168 Gene Harris	.15	.07	.02
□	169 Trevor Hoffman	.50	.23	.06
□	170 Ray McDavid	.50	.23	.06
□	171 Phil Plantier	.15	.07	.02
□	172 Mariano Duncan	.15	.07	.02
□	173 Len Dykstra	.50	.23	.06
□	174 Tommy Greene	.15	.07	.02
□	175 Dave Hollins	.15	.07	.02
□	176 Pete Incaviglia	.15	.07	.02
□	177 Mickey Morandini	.15	.07	.02
□	178 Curt Schilling	.15	.07	.02
□	179 Kevin Stocker	.50	.23	.06
□	180 Mitch Williams	.15	.07	.02
□	181 Stan Belinda	.15	.07	.02
□	182 Jay Bell	.50	.23	.06
□	183 Steve Cooke	.15	.07	.02
□	184 Carlos Garcia	.15	.07	.02
□	185 Jeff King	.50	.23	.06
□	186 Orlando Merced	.50	.23	.06
□	187 Don Slaught	.15	.07	.02
□	188 Andy Van Slyke	.50	.23	.06
□	189 Kevin Young	.15	.07	.02
□	190 Kevin Brown	.15	.07	.02
□	191 Jose Canseco	1.00	.45	.12
□	192 Julio Franco	.50	.23	.06
□	193 Benji Gil	.50	.23	.06
□	194 Juan Gonzalez	4.00	1.80	.50
□	195 Tom Henke	.15	.07	.02
□	196 Rafael Palmeiro	1.00	.45	.12
□	197 Dean Palmer	.50	.23	.06
□	198 Nolan Ryan	6.00	2.70	.75
□	199 Roger Clemens	1.00	.45	.12
□	200 Scott Cooper	.15	.07	.02
□	201 Andre Dawson	1.00	.45	.12
□	202 Mike Greenwell	.15	.07	.02
□	203 Carlos Quintana	.15	.07	.02
□	204 Jeff Russell	.15	.07	.02
□	205 Aaron Sele	.50	.23	.06
□	206 Mo Vaughn	2.00	.90	.25
□	207 Frank Viola	.15	.07	.02
□	208 Rob Dibble	.15	.07	.02
□	209 Roberto Kelly	.15	.07	.02
□	210 Kevin Mitchell	.50	.23	.06
□	211 Hal Morris	.15	.07	.02
□	212 Joe Oliver	.15	.07	.02
□	213 Jose Rijo	.15	.07	.02
□	214 Bip Roberts	.15	.07	.02
□	215 Chris Sabo	.15	.07	.02
□	216 Reggie Sanders	1.00	.45	.12
□	217 Dante Bichette	1.00	.45	.12
□	218 Jerald Clark	.15	.07	.02
□	219 Alex Cole	.15	.07	.02
□	220 Andres Galarraga	1.00	.45	.12
□	221 Joe Girardi	.15	.07	.02
□	222 Charlie Hayes	.15	.07	.02
□	223 Roberto Mejia	.15	.07	.02
□	224 Armando Reynoso	.15	.07	.02
□	225 Eric Young	1.00	.45	.12
□	226 Kevin Appier	.50	.23	.06
□	227 George Brett	3.00	1.35	.35
□	228 David Cone	1.00	.45	.12
□	229 Phil Hiatt	.15	.07	.02
□	230 Felix Jose	.15	.07	.02
□	231 Wally Joyner	.50	.23	.06
□	232 Mike Macfarlane	.15	.07	.02
□	233 Brian McRae	.50	.23	.06
□	234 Jeff Montgomery	.50	.23	.06
□	235 Rob Deer	.15	.07	.02
□	236 Cecil Fielder	.50	.23	.06
□	237 Travis Fryman	1.00	.45	.12
□	238 Mike Henneman	.15	.07	.02
□	239 Tony Phillips	.50	.23	.06
□	240 Mickey Tettleton	.15	.07	.02
□	241 Alan Trammell	1.00	.45	.12
□	242 David Wells	.15	.07	.02
□	243 Lou Whitaker	1.00	.45	.12
□	244 Rick Aguilera	.15	.07	.02
□	245 Scott Erickson	.15	.07	.02
□	246 Brian Harper	.15	.07	.02
□	247 Kent Hrbek	.50	.23	.06
□	248 Chuck Knoblauch	1.00	.45	.12
□	249 Shane Mack	.15	.07	.02
□	250 David McCarty	.15	.07	.02
□	251 Pedro Munoz	.15	.07	.02
□	252 Dave Winfield	1.00	.45	.12
□	253 Alex Fernandez	1.00	.45	.12
□	254 Ozzie Guillen	.15	.07	.02
□	255 Bo Jackson	1.00	.45	.12
□	256 Lance Johnson	.50	.23	.06
□	257 Ron Karkovice	.15	.07	.02
□	258 Jack McDowell	.50	.23	.06
□	259 Tim Raines	1.00	.45	.12
□	260 Frank Thomas	8.00	3.60	1.00
□	261 Robin Ventura	.50	.23	.06
□	262 Jim Abbott	.15	.07	.02
□	263 Steve Farr	.15	.07	.02
□	264 Jimmy Key	.50	.23	.06
□	265 Don Mattingly	4.00	1.80	.50
□	266 Paul O'Neill	.50	.23	.06
□	267 Mike Stanley	.15	.07	.02
□	268 Danny Tartabull	.15	.07	.02
□	269 Bob Wickman	.15	.07	.02
□	270 Bernie Williams	1.00	.45	.12
□	271 Jason Bere FOIL	.50	.23	.06
□	272 Roger Cedeno FOIL	4.00	1.80	.50
□	273 Johnny Damon FOIL	8.00	3.60	1.00
□	274 Russ Davis FOIL	1.00	.45	.12
□	275 Carlos Delgado FOIL	3.00	1.35	.35
□	276 Carl Everett FOIL	.50	.23	.06
□	277 Cliff Floyd FOIL	1.00	.45	.12
□	278 Alex Gonzalez FOIL	1.00	.45	.12
□	279 Derek Jeter FOIL	20.00	9.00	2.50
□	280 Chipper Jones FOIL	12.00	5.50	1.50
□	281 Javier Lopez FOIL	2.50	1.10	.30
□	282 Chad Mottola FOIL	1.00	.45	.12
□	283 Marc Newfield FOIL	1.00	.45	.12
□	284 Eduardo Perez FOIL	.50	.23	.06
□	285 Manny Ramirez FOIL	8.00	3.60	1.00
□	286 Todd Steverson FOIL	.50	.23	.06
□	287 Michael Tucker FOIL	1.00	.45	.12
□	288 Allen Watson FOIL	.50	.23	.06
□	289 Rondell White FOIL	2.00	.90	.25
□	290 Dmitri Young FOIL	2.00	.90	.25

1993 SP Platinum Power

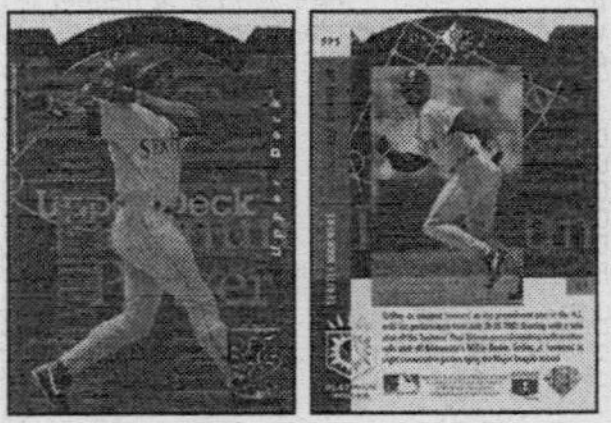

Cards from this 20-card standard-size set were randomly inserted in packs and feature power hitters from the American and National Leagues. The color action cut-out shot is superimposed on a royal blue background that contains lettering for Upper Deck Platinum Power and about the player. The top edge of the front is cut out in an arc with a copper foil stripe containing the player's name. The copper foil-stamped Platinum Power logo appears in the lower right. The back displays a color action player photo over the same royal blue background as depicted on the front. On a white background below the player photo is a career summary. The cards are numbered on the back with a "PP" prefix alphabetically by player's name.

	MINT	NRMT	EXC
COMPLETE SET (20)	140.00	65.00	17.50
COMMON CARD (PP1-PP20)	4.00	1.80	.50

SEMISTARS	5.00	2.20	.60
RANDOM INSERTS IN PACKS			
□ PP1 Albert Belle	20.00	9.00	2.50
□ PP2 Barry Bonds	10.00	4.50	1.25
□ PP3 Joe Carter	5.00	2.20	.60
□ PP4 Will Clark	5.00	2.20	.60
□ PP5 Darren Daulton	4.00	1.80	.50
□ PP6 Cecil Fielder	5.00	2.20	.60
□ PP7 Ron Gant	5.00	2.20	.60
□ PP8 Juan Gonzalez	20.00	9.00	2.50
□ PP9 Ken Griffey Jr.	40.00	18.00	5.00
□ PP10 Dave Hollins	4.00	1.80	.50
□ PP11 David Justice	5.00	2.20	.60
□ PP12 Fred McGriff	5.00	2.20	.60
□ PP13 Mark McGwire	12.00	5.50	1.50
□ PP14 Dean Palmer	5.00	2.20	.60
□ PP15 Mike Piazza	25.00	11.00	3.10
□ PP16 Tim Salmon	8.00	3.60	1.00
□ PP17 Ryne Sandberg	10.00	4.50	1.25
□ PP18 Gary Sheffield	6.00	2.70	.75
□ PP19 Frank Thomas	40.00	18.00	5.00
□ PP20 Matt Williams	5.00	2.20	.60

1994 SP Previews

These 15 cards were distributed regionally as inserts in second series Upper Deck hobby packs. They were inserted at a rate of one in 35. The manner of distribution was five cards per Central, East and West region. The cards are nearly identical to the basic SP issue. Card fronts differ in that the region is at bottom right where the team name is located on the SP cards.

	MINT	NRMT	EXC
COMPLETE SET (15)	180.00	80.00	22.00
COMPLETE CENTRAL (5)	85.00	38.00	10.50
COMPLETE EAST (5)	40.00	18.00	5.00
COMPLETE WEST (5)	55.00	25.00	7.00
COMMON CARD	2.50	1.10	.30
REGIONAL INSERTS IN SER.2 UD HOBBY PACKS			
□ CR1 Jeff Bagwell	12.00	5.50	1.50
□ CR2 Michael Jordan	30.00	13.50	3.70
□ CR3 Kirby Puckett	10.00	4.50	1.25
□ CR4 Manny Ramirez	10.00	4.50	1.25
□ CR5 Frank Thomas	30.00	13.50	3.70
□ ER1 Roberto Alomar	6.00	2.70	.75
□ ER2 Cliff Floyd	2.50	1.10	.30
□ ER3 Javier Lopez	3.00	1.35	.35
□ ER4 Don Mattingly	12.00	5.50	1.50
□ ER5 Cal Ripken	25.00	11.00	3.10
□ WR1 Barry Bonds	8.00	3.60	1.00
□ WR2 Juan Gonzalez	15.00	6.75	1.85
□ WR3 Ken Griffey Jr.	30.00	13.50	3.70
□ WR4 Mike Piazza	20.00	9.00	2.50
□ WR5 Tim Salmon	5.00	2.20	.60

1994 SP

This 200-card standard-size set primarily contains the game's top players and prospects. The first 20 cards in the set are Foil Prospects which are brighter and more metallic than the rest of the set. Cards 21-200 are in alphabetical order by team nickname. In either case, card fronts have a metallic finish with color player photos and a gold right-hand border. The backs contain a color player photo, 1993, career and best season statistics. The left side has a black border. The Upper Deck hologram on back is gold. Rookie Cards include Brooks Kieschnick, Derrek Lee, Trot Nixon, Chan Ho Park, Alex Rodriguez and Glenn Williams.

	MINT	NRMT	EXC
COMPLETE SET (200)	60.00	27.00	7.50
COMMON CARD (1-200)	.15	.07	.02
SEMISTARS	.30	.14	.04
STARS	.60	.25	.07
COMP.DIE CUT SET (200)	150.00	70.00	19.00
COMMON DIE CUT (1-200)	.25	.11	.03
DIE CUT SEMISTARS	.50	.23	.06
*DIE CUT STARS: 1.5X to 3X HI COLUMN			
*DIE CUT YOUNG STARS: 1X to 2X HI			
ONE DIE CUT PER PACK			
DIE CUTS HAVE SILVER HOLOGRAMS			
FOIL CARDS CONDITION SENSITIVE			
□ 1 Mike Bell FOIL	1.50	.70	.19
□ 2 D.J. Boston FOIL	.30	.14	.04
□ 3 Johnny Damon FOIL	1.50	.70	.19
□ 4 Brad Fullmer FOIL	1.50	.70	.19
□ 5 Joey Hamilton FOIL	1.50	.70	.19
□ 6 Todd Hollandsworth FOIL	2.00	.90	.25
□ 7 Brian L. Hunter FOIL	1.25	.55	.16
□ 8 LaTroy Hawkins FOIL	.30	.14	.04
□ 9 Brooks Kieschnick FOIL	1.50	.70	.19
□ 10 Derrek Lee FOIL	5.00	2.20	.60
□ 11 Trot Nixon FOIL	.60	.25	.07
□ 12 Alex Ochoa FOIL	.30	.14	.04
□ 13 Chan Ho Park FOIL	2.00	.90	.25
□ 14 Kirk Presley FOIL	.60	.25	.07
□ 15 Alex Rodriguez FOIL	45.00	20.00	5.50
□ 16 Jose Silva FOIL	.60	.25	.07
□ 17 Terrell Wade FOIL	1.50	.70	.19
□ 18 Billy Wagner FOIL	2.00	.90	.25
□ 19 Glenn Williams FOIL	1.25	.55	.16
□ 20 Preston Wilson FOIL	.60	.25	.07
□ 21 Brian Anderson	.30	.14	.04
□ 22 Chad Curtis	.15	.07	.02
□ 23 Chili Davis	.30	.14	.04
□ 24 Bo Jackson	.60	.25	.07
□ 25 Mark Langston	.30	.14	.04
□ 26 Tim Salmon	.60	.25	.07
□ 27 Jeff Bagwell	1.50	.70	.19
□ 28 Craig Biggio	.60	.25	.07
□ 29 Ken Caminiti	.60	.25	.07
□ 30 Doug Drabek	.15	.07	.02
□ 31 John Hudek	.15	.07	.02
□ 32 Greg Swindell	.15	.07	.02
□ 33 Brent Gates	.15	.07	.02
□ 34 Rickey Henderson	.60	.25	.07
□ 35 Steve Karsay	.15	.07	.02
□ 36 Mark McGwire	1.25	.55	.16
□ 37 Ruben Sierra	.30	.14	.04
□ 38 Terry Steinbach	.30	.14	.04
□ 39 Roberto Alomar	1.00	.45	.12
□ 40 Joe Carter	.60	.25	.07
□ 41 Carlos Delgado	.60	.25	.07
□ 42 Alex Gonzalez	.30	.14	.04
□ 43 Juan Guzman	.30	.14	.04
□ 44 Paul Molitor	.75	.35	.09
□ 45 John Olerud	.15	.07	.02
□ 46 Devon White	.15	.07	.02
□ 47 Steve Avery	.30	.14	.04
□ 48 Jeff Blauser	.15	.07	.02
□ 49 Tom Glavine	.60	.25	.07
□ 50 David Justice	.60	.25	.07
□ 51 Roberto Kelly	.15	.07	.02
□ 52 Ryan Klesko	1.00	.45	.12
□ 53 Javier Lopez	.60	.25	.07
□ 54 Greg Maddux	2.50	1.10	.30
□ 55 Fred McGriff	.60	.25	.07
□ 56 Ricky Bones	.15	.07	.02
□ 57 Cal Eldred	.15	.07	.02
□ 58 Brian Harper	.15	.07	.02
□ 59 Pat Listach	.15	.07	.02
□ 60 B.J. Surhoff	.15	.07	.02
□ 61 Greg Vaughn	.60	.25	.07
□ 62 Bernard Gilkey	.30	.14	.04
□ 63 Gregg Jefferies	.60	.25	.07
□ 64 Ray Lankford	.60	.25	.07
□ 65 Ozzie Smith	.75	.35	.09

□ 66 Bob Tewksbury	.15	.07	.02
□ 67 Mark Whiten	.15	.07	.02
□ 68 Todd Zeile	.15	.07	.02
□ 69 Mark Grace	.60	.25	.07
□ 70 Randy Myers	.15	.07	.02
□ 71 Ryne Sandberg	1.00	.45	.12
□ 72 Sammy Sosa	.60	.25	.07
□ 73 Steve Trachsel	.30	.14	.04
□ 74 Rick Wilkins	.15	.07	.02
□ 75 Brett Butler	.30	.14	.04
□ 76 Delino DeShields	.15	.07	.02
□ 77 Orel Hershiser	.30	.14	.04
□ 78 Eric Karros	.30	.14	.04
□ 79 Raul Mondesi	.60	.25	.07
□ 80 Mike Piazza	2.50	1.10	.30
□ 81 Tim Wallach	.15	.07	.02
□ 82 Moises Alou	.30	.14	.04
□ 83 Cliff Floyd	.60	.25	.07
□ 84 Marquis Grissom	.60	.25	.07
□ 85 Pedro J. Martinez	.60	.25	.07
□ 86 Larry Walker	.60	.25	.07
□ 87 John Wetteland	.30	.14	.04
□ 88 Rondell White	.60	.25	.07
□ 89 Rod Beck	.30	.14	.04
□ 90 Barry Bonds	1.00	.45	.12
□ 91 John Burkett	.15	.07	.02
□ 92 Royce Clayton	.30	.14	.04
□ 93 Billy Swift	.15	.07	.02
□ 94 Robby Thompson	.15	.07	.02
□ 95 Matt Williams	.60	.25	.07
□ 96 Carlos Baerga	.60	.25	.07
□ 97 Albert Belle	2.00	.90	.25
□ 98 Kenny Lofton	1.25	.55	.16
□ 99 Dennis Martinez	.30	.14	.04
□ 100 Eddie Murray	1.00	.45	.12
□ 101 Manny Ramirez	1.25	.55	.16
□ 102 Eric Anthony	.15	.07	.02
□ 103 Chris Bosio	.15	.07	.02
□ 104 Jay Buhner	.60	.25	.07
□ 105 Ken Griffey Jr.	4.00	1.80	.50
□ 106 Randy Johnson	.60	.25	.07
□ 107 Edgar Martinez	.60	.25	.07
□ 108 Chuck Carr	.15	.07	.02
□ 109 Jeff Conine	.60	.25	.07
□ 110 Carl Everett	.15	.07	.02
□ 111 Chris Hammond	.15	.07	.02
□ 112 Bryan Harvey	.15	.07	.02
□ 113 Charles Johnson	.60	.25	.07
□ 114 Gary Sheffield	.60	.25	.07
□ 115 Bobby Bonilla	.30	.14	.04
□ 116 Dwight Gooden	.30	.14	.04
□ 117 Todd Hundley	.60	.25	.07
□ 118 Bobby Jones	.30	.14	.04
□ 119 Jeff Kent	.15	.07	.02
□ 120 Bret Saberhagen	.30	.14	.04
□ 121 Jeffrey Hammonds	.30	.14	.04
□ 122 Chris Hoiles	.15	.07	.02
□ 123 Ben McDonald	.15	.07	.02
□ 124 Mike Mussina	.75	.35	.09
□ 125 Rafael Palmeiro	.60	.25	.07
□ 126 Cal Ripken Jr.	3.00	1.35	.35
□ 127 Lee Smith	.30	.14	.04
□ 128 Derek Bell	.30	.14	.04
□ 129 Andy Benes	.30	.14	.04
□ 130 Tony Gwynn	1.50	.70	.19
□ 131 Trevor Hoffman	.30	.14	.04
□ 132 Phil Plantier	.15	.07	.02
□ 133 Bip Roberts	.15	.07	.02
□ 134 Darren Daulton	.30	.14	.04
□ 135 Lenny Dykstra	.30	.14	.04
□ 136 Dave Hollins	.15	.07	.02
□ 137 Danny Jackson	.15	.07	.02
□ 138 John Kruk	.30	.14	.04
□ 139 Kevin Stocker	.15	.07	.02
□ 140 Jay Bell	.30	.14	.04
□ 141 Carlos Garcia	.15	.07	.02
□ 142 Jeff King	.30	.14	.04
□ 143 Orlando Merced	.30	.14	.04
□ 144 Andy Van Slyke	.30	.14	.04
□ 145 Rick White	.15	.07	.02
□ 146 Jose Canseco	.60	.25	.07
□ 147 Will Clark	.60	.25	.07
□ 148 Juan Gonzalez	2.00	.90	.25
□ 149 Rick Helling	.15	.07	.02
□ 150 Dean Palmer	.30	.14	.04
□ 151 Ivan Rodriguez	.75	.35	.09
□ 152 Roger Clemens	.60	.25	.07
□ 153 Scott Cooper	.15	.07	.02
□ 154 Andre Dawson	.60	.25	.07
□ 155 Mike Greenwell	.15	.07	.02
□ 156 Aaron Sele	.30	.14	.04
□ 157 Mo Vaughn	1.00	.45	.12
□ 158 Bret Boone	.30	.14	.04
□ 159 Barry Larkin	.60	.25	.07
□ 160 Kevin Mitchell	.30	.14	.04
□ 161 Jose Rijo	.15	.07	.02
□ 162 Deion Sanders	.60	.25	.07
□ 163 Reggie Sanders	.60	.25	.07
□ 164 Dante Bichette	.60	.25	.07
□ 165 Ellis Burks	.30	.14	.04
□ 166 Andres Galarraga	.60	.25	.07
□ 167 Charlie Hayes	.15	.07	.02
□ 168 David Nied	.15	.07	.02
□ 169 Walt Weiss	.15	.07	.02
□ 170 Kevin Appier	.30	.14	.04
□ 171 David Cone	.60	.25	.07
□ 172 Jeff Granger	.30	.14	.04
□ 173 Felix Jose	.15	.07	.02
□ 174 Wally Joyner	.30	.14	.04
□ 175 Brian McRae	.30	.14	.04
□ 176 Cecil Fielder	.30	.14	.04
□ 177 Travis Fryman	.60	.25	.07
□ 178 Mike Henneman	.15	.07	.02
□ 179 Tony Phillips	.30	.14	.04
□ 180 Mickey Tettleton	.15	.07	.02
□ 181 Alan Trammell	.60	.25	.07
□ 182 Rick Aguilera	.15	.07	.02
□ 183 Rich Becker	.30	.14	.04
□ 184 Scott Erickson	.15	.07	.02
□ 185 Chuck Knoblauch	.60	.25	.07
□ 186 Kirby Puckett	1.25	.55	.16
□ 187 Dave Winfield	.60	.25	.07
□ 188 Wilson Alvarez	.30	.14	.04
□ 189 Jason Bere	.30	.14	.04
□ 190 Alex Fernandez	.60	.25	.07
□ 191 Julio Franco	.30	.14	.04
□ 192 Jack McDowell	.30	.14	.04
□ 193 Frank Thomas	4.00	1.80	.50
□ 194 Robin Ventura	.30	.14	.04
□ 195 Jim Abbott	.15	.07	.02
□ 196 Wade Boggs	.60	.25	.07
□ 197 Jimmy Key	.30	.14	.04
□ 198 Don Mattingly	2.00	.90	.25
□ 199 Paul O'Neill	.30	.14	.04
□ 200 Danny Tartabull	.15	.07	.02

1994 SP Holoview Blue

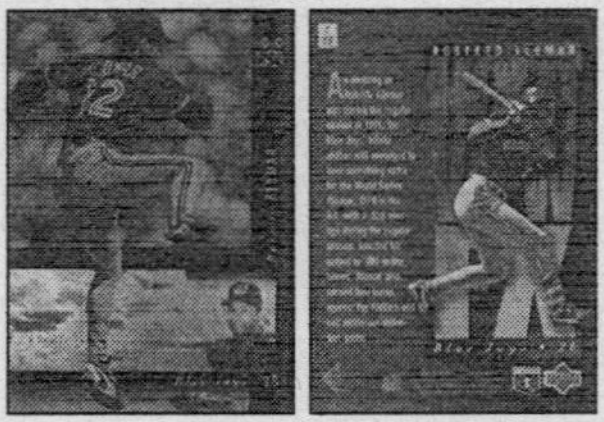

Randomly inserted in SP foil packs at a rate of one in five, this 38-card set contains top stars and prospects. Card fronts have a color player photo with a black and blue border to the right with which the player's name appears. A player hologram that runs the width of the card is at the bottom. The backs are primarily blue with a player photo and text.

	MINT	NRMT	EXC
COMPLETE SET (38)	150.00	70.00	19.00
COMMON CARD (1-38)	2.00	.90	.25
SEMISTARS	4.00	1.80	.50
RANDOM INSERTS IN PACKS			
□ 1 Roberto Alomar	8.00	3.60	1.00
□ 2 Kevin Appier	2.00	.90	.25

□ 3 Jeff Bagwell	12.00	5.50	1.50
□ 4 Barry Bonds	4.00	1.80	.50
□ 5 Roger Clemens	4.00	1.80	.50
□ 6 Carlos Delgado	4.00	1.80	.50
□ 7 Cecil Fielder	4.00	1.80	.50
□ 8 Cliff Floyd	2.00	.90	.25
□ 9 Travis Fryman	4.00	1.80	.50
□ 10 Andres Galarraga	4.00	1.80	.50
□ 11 Juan Gonzalez	15.00	6.75	1.85
□ 12 Ken Griffey Jr.	30.00	13.50	3.70
□ 13 Tony Gwynn	12.00	5.50	1.50
□ 14 Jeffrey Hammonds	2.00	.90	.25
□ 15 Bo Jackson	4.00	1.80	.50
□ 16 Michael Jordan	35.00	16.00	4.40
□ 17 David Justice	4.00	1.80	.50
□ 18 Steve Karsay	2.00	.90	.25
□ 19 Jeff Kent	2.00	.90	.25
□ 20 Brooks Kieschnick	4.00	1.80	.50
□ 21 Ryan Klesko	8.00	3.60	1.00
□ 22 John Kruk	2.00	.90	.25
□ 23 Barry Larkin	4.00	1.80	.50
□ 24 Pat Listach	2.00	.90	.25
□ 25 Don Mattingly	15.00	6.75	1.85
□ 26 Mark McGwire	10.00	4.50	1.25
□ 27 Raul Mondesi	5.00	2.20	.60
□ 28 Trot Nixon	4.00	1.80	.50
□ 29 Mike Piazza	20.00	9.00	2.50
□ 30 Kirby Puckett	10.00	4.50	1.25
□ 31 Manny Ramirez	10.00	4.50	1.25
□ 32 Cal Ripken	25.00	11.00	3.10
□ 33 Alex Rodriguez	45.00	20.00	5.50
□ 34 Tim Salmon	5.00	2.20	.60
□ 35 Gary Sheffield	5.00	2.20	.60
□ 36 Ozzie Smith	6.00	2.70	.75
□ 37 Sammy Sosa	5.00	2.20	.60
□ 38 Andy Van Slyke	2.00	.90	.25

1994 SP Holoview Red

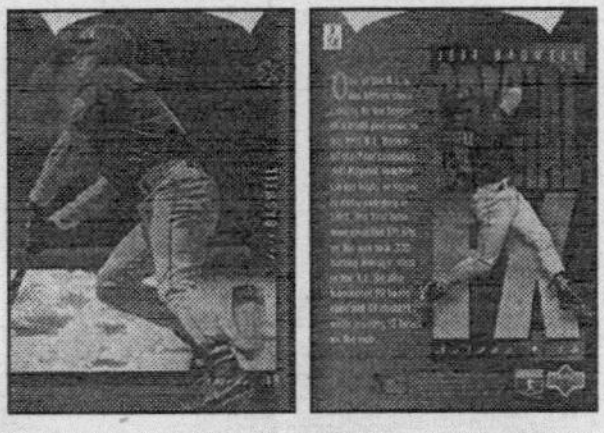

Parallel to the Holoview Blue set, this 38-card issue was also randomly inserted in SP packs. They are much more difficult to pull than the Blue version with an insertion rate of one in 75. Card fronts have a color player photo with a black and red border to the right with which the player's name appears. A player hologram that runs the width of the card is at the bottom. The backs are primarily red with a player photo and text.

	MINT	NRMT	EXC
COMPLETE SET (38)	2000.00	900.00	250.00
COMMON CARD (1-38)	12.00	5.50	1.50
SEMISTARS	25.00	11.00	3.10
RED HOLOVIEWS ARE DIECUT			
RANDOM INSERTS IN PACKS			

□ 1 Roberto Alomar	60.00	27.00	7.50
□ 3 Jeff Bagwell	100.00	45.00	12.50
□ 4 Barry Bonds	30.00	13.50	3.70
□ 5 Roger Clemens	30.00	13.50	3.70
□ 6 Carlos Delgado	30.00	13.50	3.70
□ 10 Andres Galarraga	30.00	13.50	3.70
□ 11 Juan Gonzalez	125.00	55.00	15.50
□ 12 Ken Griffey Jr.	250.00	110.00	31.00
□ 13 Tony Gwynn	100.00	45.00	12.50
□ 16 Michael Jordan	300.00	135.00	38.00
□ 20 Brooks Kieschnick	30.00	13.50	3.70
□ 21 Ryan Klesko	60.00	27.00	7.50
□ 23 Barry Larkin	30.00	13.50	3.70
□ 25 Don Mattingly	120.00	55.00	15.00
□ 26 Mark McGwire	75.00	34.00	9.50
□ 27 Raul Mondesi	40.00	18.00	5.00
□ 29 Mike Piazza	150.00	70.00	19.00
□ 30 Kirby Puckett	75.00	34.00	9.50
□ 31 manny Ramirez	75.00	34.00	9.50
□ 32 Cal Ripken	200.00	90.00	25.00
□ 33 Alex Rodriguez	325.00	145.00	40.00
□ 34 Tim Salmon	50.00	22.00	6.25
□ 35 Gary Sheffield	40.00	18.00	5.00
□ 36 Ozzie Smith	50.00	22.00	6.25
□ 37 Sammy Sosa	40.00	18.00	5.00

1995 SP

This set consists of 207 cards being sold in eight-card, hobby-only packs with a suggested retail price of $3.99. The fronts have full-bleed photos and a large chevron on the left. The chevron consists of red and gold foil for American League players and blue and gold for National Leaguers. The backs have a photo with player information and statistics at the bottom. The backs also have a gold hologram to prevent counterfeiting. Subsets featured are Salute (1-4) and Premier Prospects (5-24). Rookie Cards in this set include Raul Casanova, Hideo Nomo and Carlos Perez.

	MINT	NRMT	EXC
COMPLETE SET (207)	40.00	18.00	5.00
COMMON CARD (1-207)	.15	.07	.02
FOIL PROSPECTS (5-24)	.25	.11	.03
SEMISTARS	.30	.14	.04
STARS	.60	.25	.07
COMPLETE SILVER SET (207)	100.00	45.00	12.50
COMMON SILVER (1-207)	.25	.11	.03
SILVER SEMISTARS	.50	.23	.06
*SILVER STARS: 1.5X to 3X HI COLUMN			
*SILVER YOUNG STARS: 1.25X to 2.5X HI			
ONE SILVER PER PACK			

□ 1 Cal Ripken Salute	3.00	1.35	.35
□ 2 Nolan Ryan Salute	2.50	1.10	.30
□ 3 George Brett Salute	1.00	.45	.12
□ 4 Mike Schmidt Salute	.75	.35	.09
□ 5 Dustin Hermanson FOIL	.30	.14	.04
□ 6 Antonio Osuna FOIL	.30	.14	.04
□ 7 Mark Grudzielanek FOIL	1.00	.45	.12
□ 8 Ray Durham FOIL	.60	.25	.07
□ 9 Ugueth Urbina FOIL	.30	.14	.04
□ 10 Ruben Rivera FOIL	2.00	.90	.25
□ 11 Curtis Goodwin FOIL	.30	.14	.04
□ 12 Jimmy Hurst FOIL	.30	.14	.04
□ 13 Jose Malave FOIL	.30	.14	.04
□ 14 Hideo Nomo FOIL	4.00	1.80	.50
□ 15 Juan Acevedo FOIL	.30	.14	.04
□ 16 Tony Clark FOIL	1.00	.45	.12
□ 17 Jim Pittsley FOIL	.30	.14	.04
□ 18 Freddy Garcia FOIL	.30	.14	.04
□ 19 Carlos Perez FOIL	.30	.14	.04
□ 20 Raul Casanova FOIL	.60	.25	.07
□ 21 Quilvio Veras FOIL	.30	.14	.04
□ 22 Edgardo Alfonzo FOIL	.30	.14	.04
□ 23 Marty Cordova FOIL	.60	.25	.07
□ 24 C.J. Nitkowski FOIL	.30	.14	.04
□ 25 Wade Boggs CL	.60	.25	.07
□ 26 Dave Winfield CL	.60	.25	.07

□ 27	Eddie Murray CL	1.00	.45	.12
□ 28	David Justice	.60	.25	.07
□ 29	Marquis Grissom	.60	.25	.07
□ 30	Fred McGriff	.60	.25	.07
□ 31	Greg Maddux	2.50	1.10	.30
□ 32	Tom Glavine	.60	.25	.07
□ 33	Steve Avery	.30	.14	.04
□ 34	Chipper Jones	2.50	1.10	.30
□ 35	Sammy Sosa	.60	.25	.07
□ 36	Jaime Navarro	.15	.07	.02
□ 37	Randy Myers	.15	.07	.02
□ 38	Mark Grace	.60	.25	.07
□ 39	Todd Zeile	.15	.07	.02
□ 40	Brian McRae	.30	.14	.04
□ 41	Reggie Sanders	.30	.14	.04
□ 42	Ron Gant	.30	.14	.04
□ 43	Deion Sanders	.60	.25	.07
□ 44	Bret Boone	.30	.14	.04
□ 45	Barry Larkin	.60	.25	.07
□ 46	Jose Rijo	.15	.07	.02
□ 47	Jason Bates	.15	.07	.02
□ 48	Andres Galarraga	.60	.25	.07
□ 49	Bill Swift	.15	.07	.02
□ 50	Larry Walker	.60	.25	.07
□ 51	Vinny Castilla	.30	.14	.04
□ 52	Dante Bichette	.60	.25	.07
□ 53	Jeff Conine	.60	.25	.07
□ 54	John Burkett	.30	.14	.04
□ 55	Gary Sheffield	.60	.25	.07
□ 56	Andre Dawson	.60	.25	.07
□ 57	Terry Pendleton	.30	.14	.04
□ 58	Charles Johnson	.30	.14	.04
□ 59	Brian L. Hunter	.60	.25	.07
□ 60	Jeff Bagwell	1.50	.70	.19
□ 61	Craig Biggio	.60	.25	.07
□ 62	Phil Nevin	.15	.07	.02
□ 63	Doug Drabek	.15	.07	.02
□ 64	Derek Bell	.30	.14	.04
□ 65	Raul Mondesi	.60	.25	.07
□ 66	Eric Karros	.30	.14	.04
□ 67	Roger Cedeno	.30	.14	.04
□ 68	Delino DeShields	.15	.07	.02
□ 69	Ramon Martinez	.30	.14	.04
□ 70	Mike Piazza	2.50	1.10	.30
□ 71	Billy Ashley	.15	.07	.02
□ 72	Jeff Fassero	.15	.07	.02
□ 73	Shane Andrews	.15	.07	.02
□ 74	Wil Cordero	.15	.07	.02
□ 75	Tony Tarasco	.15	.07	.02
□ 76	Rondell White	.60	.25	.07
□ 77	Pedro J. Martinez	.30	.14	.04
□ 78	Moises Alou	.30	.14	.04
□ 79	Rico Brogna	.15	.07	.02
□ 80	Bobby Bonilla	.30	.14	.04
□ 81	Jeff Kent	.15	.07	.02
□ 82	Brett Butler	.30	.14	.04
□ 83	Bobby Jones	.30	.14	.04
□ 84	Bill Pulsipher	.30	.14	.04
□ 85	Bret Saberhagen	.30	.14	.04
□ 86	Gregg Jefferies	.30	.14	.04
□ 87	Lenny Dykstra	.30	.14	.04
□ 88	Dave Hollins	.15	.07	.02
□ 89	Charlie Hayes	.15	.07	.02
□ 90	Darren Daulton	.30	.14	.04
□ 91	Curt Schilling	.15	.07	.02
□ 92	Heathcliff Slocumb	.15	.07	.02
□ 93	Carlos Garcia	.15	.07	.02
□ 94	Denny Neagle	.30	.14	.04
□ 95	Jay Bell	.30	.14	.04
□ 96	Orlando Merced	.15	.07	.02
□ 97	Dave Clark	.15	.07	.02
□ 98	Bernard Gilkey	.30	.14	.04
□ 99	Scott Cooper	.15	.07	.02
□ 100	Ozzie Smith	.75	.35	.09
□ 101	Tom Henke	.15	.07	.02
□ 102	Ken Hill	.15	.07	.02
□ 103	Brian Jordan	.60	.25	.07
□ 104	Ray Lankford	.60	.25	.07
□ 105	Tony Gwynn	1.50	.70	.19
□ 106	Andy Benes	.15	.07	.02
□ 107	Ken Caminiti	.60	.25	.07
□ 108	Steve Finley	.30	.14	.04
□ 109	Joey Hamilton	.30	.14	.04
□ 110	Bip Roberts	.15	.07	.02
□ 111	Eddie Williams	.15	.07	.02
□ 112	Rod Beck	.15	.07	.02
□ 113	Matt Williams	.60	.25	.07
□ 114	Glenallen Hill	.15	.07	.02
□ 115	Barry Bonds	1.00	.45	.12
□ 116	Robby Thompson	.15	.07	.02
□ 117	Mark Portugal	.15	.07	.02
□ 118	Brady Anderson	.60	.25	.07
□ 119	Mike Mussina	.75	.35	.09
□ 120	Rafael Palmeiro	.60	.25	.07
□ 121	Chris Hoiles	.15	.07	.02
□ 122	Harold Baines	.30	.14	.04
□ 123	Jeffrey Hammonds	.30	.14	.04
□ 124	Tim Naehring	.15	.07	.02
□ 125	Mo Vaughn	1.00	.45	.12
□ 126	Mike Macfarlane	.15	.07	.02
□ 127	Roger Clemens	.60	.25	.07
□ 128	John Valentin	.30	.14	.04
□ 129	Aaron Sele	.30	.14	.04
□ 130	Jose Canseco	.60	.25	.07
□ 131	J.T. Snow	.30	.14	.04
□ 132	Mark Langston	.15	.07	.02
□ 133	Chili Davis	.30	.14	.04
□ 134	Chuck Finley	.30	.14	.04
□ 135	Tim Salmon	.60	.25	.07
□ 136	Tony Phillips	.30	.14	.04
□ 137	Jason Bere	.15	.07	.02
□ 138	Robin Ventura	.30	.14	.04
□ 139	Tim Raines	.60	.25	.07
□ 140	Frank Thomas COR	4.00	1.80	.50
□ 140A	Frank Thomas ERR	8.00	3.60	1.00
□ 141	Alex Fernandez	.30	.14	.04
□ 142	Jim Abbott	.15	.07	.02
□ 143	Wilson Alvarez	.30	.14	.04
□ 144	Carlos Baerga	.60	.25	.07
□ 145	Albert Belle	2.00	.90	.25
□ 146	Jim Thome	.75	.35	.09
□ 147	Dennis Martinez	.30	.14	.04
□ 148	Eddie Murray	1.00	.45	.12
□ 149	Dave Winfield	.60	.25	.07
□ 150	Kenny Lofton	1.00	.45	.12
□ 151	Manny Ramirez	1.00	.45	.12
□ 152	Chad Curtis	.15	.07	.02
□ 153	Lou Whitaker	.60	.25	.07
□ 154	Alan Trammell	.60	.25	.07
□ 155	Cecil Fielder	.30	.14	.04
□ 156	Kirk Gibson	.30	.14	.04
□ 157	Michael Tucker	.30	.14	.04
□ 158	Jon Nunnally	.30	.14	.04
□ 159	Wally Joyner	.30	.14	.04
□ 160	Kevin Appier	.30	.14	.04
□ 161	Jeff Montgomery	.30	.14	.04
□ 162	Greg Gagne	.15	.07	.02
□ 163	Ricky Bones	.15	.07	.02
□ 164	Cal Eldred	.15	.07	.02
□ 165	Greg Vaughn	.30	.14	.04
□ 166	Kevin Seitzer	.15	.07	.02
□ 167	Jose Valentin	.30	.14	.04
□ 168	Joe Oliver	.15	.07	.02
□ 169	Rick Aguilera	.15	.07	.02
□ 170	Kirby Puckett	1.25	.55	.16
□ 171	Scott Stahoviak	.15	.07	.02
□ 172	Kevin Tapani	.15	.07	.02
□ 173	Chuck Knoblauch	.60	.25	.07
□ 174	Rich Becker	.15	.07	.02
□ 175	Don Mattingly	2.00	.90	.25
□ 176	Jack McDowell	.30	.14	.04
□ 177	Jimmy Key	.30	.14	.04
□ 178	Paul O'Neill	.30	.14	.04
□ 179	John Wetteland	.30	.14	.04
□ 180	Wade Boggs	.60	.25	.07
□ 181	Derek Jeter	2.50	1.10	.30
□ 182	Rickey Henderson	.60	.25	.07
□ 183	Terry Steinbach	.30	.14	.04
□ 184	Ruben Sierra	.30	.14	.04
□ 185	Mark McGwire	1.25	.55	.16
□ 186	Todd Stottlemyre	.15	.07	.02
□ 187	Dennis Eckersley	.30	.14	.04
□ 188	Alex Rodriguez	5.00	2.20	.60
□ 189	Randy Johnson	.60	.25	.07
□ 190	Ken Griffey Jr.	4.00	1.80	.50
□ 191	Tino Martinez UER Mike Blowers pictured on back	.30	.14	.04
□ 192	Jay Buhner	.60	.25	.07
□ 193	Edgar Martinez	.60	.25	.07
□ 194	Mickey Tettleton	.15	.07	.02
□ 195	Juan Gonzalez	2.00	.90	.25
□ 196	Benji Gil	.15	.07	.02

□ 197 Dean Palmer	.30	.14	.04
□ 198 Ivan Rodriguez	.75	.35	.09
□ 199 Kenny Rogers	.15	.07	.02
□ 200 Will Clark	.60	.25	.07
□ 201 Roberto Alomar	1.00	.45	.12
□ 202 David Cone	.30	.14	.04
□ 203 Paul Molitor	.75	.35	.09
□ 204 Shawn Green	.30	.14	.04
□ 205 Joe Carter	.60	.25	.07
□ 206 Alex Gonzalez	.15	.07	.02
□ 207 Pat Hentgen	.30	.14	.04

1995 SP Platinum Power

This 20-card set was randomly inserted in packs at a rate of one in five. This die-cut set is comprised of the top home run hitters in baseball. The fronts have an action photo with a bronze background and rays of light coming out of the "SP" emblem at bottom right. The backs have a player photo in a box at the middle of the card with player statistics at the bottom. The set is sequenced in alphabetical order.

	MINT	NRMT	EXC
COMPLETE SET (20)	20.00	9.00	2.50
COMMON CARD (PP1-PP20)	.50	.23	.06
RANDOM INSERTS IN PACKS			

□ PP1 Jeff Bagwell	2.00	.90	.25
□ PP2 Barry Bonds	1.25	.55	.16
□ PP3 Ron Gant	.50	.23	.06
□ PP4 Fred McGriff	.75	.35	.09
□ PP5 Raul Mondesi	.50	.23	.06
□ PP6 Mike Piazza	3.00	1.35	.35
□ PP7 Larry Walker	.50	.23	.06
□ PP8 Matt Williams	.75	.35	.09
□ PP9 Albert Belle	2.50	1.10	.30
□ PP10 Cecil Fielder	.75	.35	.09
□ PP11 Juan Gonzalez	2.50	1.10	.30
□ PP12 Ken Griffey Jr.	5.00	2.20	.60
□ PP13 Mark McGwire	1.50	.70	.19
□ PP14 Eddie Murray	1.25	.55	.16
□ PP15 Manny Ramirez	1.25	.55	.16
□ PP16 Cal Ripken	4.00	1.80	.50
□ PP17 Tim Salmon	.50	.23	.06
□ PP18 Frank Thomas	5.00	2.20	.60
□ PP19 Jim Thome	1.00	.45	.12
□ PP20 Mo Vaughn	1.25	.55	.16

1995 SP Special FX

This 48-card set was randomly inserted in packs at a rate of one in 75. The set is comprised of the top names in baseball. The fronts have an action photo on a sky-colored foil background. There is also a hologram of the player's face that allows you to see a 50-degree, 3-D image. The backs have a photo with player information and statistics. The cards are numbered on the back "X/48."

	MINT	NRMT	EXC
COMPLETE SET (48)	1300.00	575.00	160.00
COMMON CARD (1-48)	10.00	4.50	1.25
SEMISTARS	15.00	6.75	1.85
RANDOM INSERTS IN PACKS			

□ 1 Jose Canseco	20.00	9.00	2.50
□ 2 Roger Clemens	20.00	9.00	2.50
□ 3 Mo Vaughn	40.00	18.00	5.00
□ 4 Tim Salmon	20.00	9.00	2.50
□ 5 Chuck Finley	10.00	4.50	1.25
□ 6 Robin Ventura	15.00	6.75	1.85
□ 7 Jason Bere	10.00	4.50	1.25
□ 8 Carlos Baerga	15.00	6.75	1.85
□ 9 Albert Belle	75.00	34.00	9.50
□ 10 Kenny Lofton	40.00	18.00	5.00
□ 11 Manny Ramirez	40.00	18.00	5.00
□ 12 Jeff Montgomery	10.00	4.50	1.25
□ 13 Kirby Puckett	50.00	22.00	6.25
□ 14 Wade Boggs	15.00	6.75	1.85
□ 15 Don Mattingly	75.00	34.00	9.50
□ 16 Cal Ripken	125.00	55.00	15.50
□ 17 Ruben Sierra	10.00	4.50	1.25
□ 18 Ken Griffey Jr.	150.00	70.00	19.00
□ 19 Randy Johnson	25.00	11.00	3.10
□ 20 Alex Rodriguez	150.00	70.00	19.00
□ 21 Will Clark	20.00	9.00	2.50
□ 22 Juan Gonzalez	75.00	34.00	9.50
□ 23 Roberto Alomar	40.00	18.00	5.00
□ 24 Joe Carter	15.00	6.75	1.85
□ 25 Alex Gonzalez	10.00	4.50	1.25
□ 26 Paul Molitor	30.00	13.50	3.70
□ 27 Ryan Klesko	30.00	13.50	3.70
□ 28 Fred McGriff	20.00	9.00	2.50
□ 29 Greg Maddux	100.00	45.00	12.50
□ 30 Sammy Sosa	25.00	11.00	3.10
□ 31 Bret Boone	10.00	4.50	1.25
□ 32 Barry Larkin	20.00	9.00	2.50
□ 33 Reggie Sanders	15.00	6.75	1.85
□ 34 Dante Bichette	20.00	9.00	2.50
□ 35 Andres Galarraga	20.00	9.00	2.50
□ 36 Charles Johnson	15.00	6.75	1.85
□ 37 Gary Sheffield	25.00	11.00	3.10
□ 38 Jeff Bagwell	60.00	27.00	7.50
□ 39 Craig Biggio	15.00	6.75	1.85
□ 40 Eric Karros	15.00	6.75	1.85
□ 41 Billy Ashley	10.00	4.50	1.25
□ 42 Raul Mondesi	20.00	9.00	2.50
□ 43 Mike Piazza	100.00	45.00	12.50
□ 44 Rondell White	15.00	6.75	1.85
□ 45 Bret Saberhagen	10.00	4.50	1.25
□ 46 Tony Gwynn	60.00	27.00	7.50
□ 47 Melvin Nieves	10.00	4.50	1.25
□ 48 Matt Williams	20.00	9.00	2.50

1996 SP

The 1996 SP set was issued in one series totalling 188 cards. The eight-card packs retail for $4.19 each. Cards number 1-20 feature color action player photos with "Premier Prospects" printed in silver foil across the top and the player's name and team at the bottom in the border. The backs carry player information and statistics. Cards number 21-185 display unique player photos with an outer woodgrain border and inner thin platinum foil border as well as a small inset player shot. The backs carry another color player photo with unique player statistics depending on his position. Rookie Cards in this set include Darin Erstad.

	MINT	NRMT	EXC
COMPLETE SET (188)	40.00	18.00	5.00
COMMON CARDS (1-188)	.15	.07	.02

	SEMISTARS	.30	.14	.04
	STARS	.60	.25	.07
□ 1	Rey Ordonez	.75	.35	.09
□ 2	George Arias	.15	.07	.02
□ 3	Osvaldo Fernandez	.30	.14	.04
□ 4	Darin Erstad	5.00	2.20	.60
□ 5	Paul Wilson	.30	.14	.04
□ 6	Richard Hidalgo	.15	.07	.02
□ 7	Justin Thompson	.15	.07	.02
□ 8	Jimmy Haynes	.15	.07	.02
□ 9	Edgar Renteria	.60	.25	.07
□ 10	Ruben Rivera	.60	.25	.07
□ 11	Chris Snopek	.15	.07	.02
□ 12	Billy Wagner	.15	.07	.02
□ 13	Mike Grace	.15	.07	.02
□ 14	Todd Greene	.30	.14	.04
□ 15	Karim Garcia	.75	.35	.09
□ 16	John Wasdin	.15	.07	.02
□ 17	Jason Kendall	.60	.25	.07
□ 18	Bob Abreu	.60	.25	.07
□ 19	Jermaine Dye	1.00	.45	.12
□ 20	Jason Schmidt	.30	.14	.04
□ 21	Javy Lopez	.60	.25	.07
□ 22	Ryan Klesko	.75	.35	.09
□ 23	Tom Glavine	.60	.25	.07
□ 24	John Smoltz	.60	.25	.07
□ 25	Greg Maddux	2.50	1.10	.30
□ 26	Chipper Jones	2.50	1.10	.30
□ 27	Fred McGriff	.60	.25	.07
□ 28	David Justice	.30	.14	.04
□ 29	Roberto Alomar	1.00	.45	.12
□ 30	Cal Ripken	3.00	1.35	.35
□ 31	B.J. Surhoff	.15	.07	.02
□ 32	Bobby Bonilla	.60	.25	.07
□ 33	Mike Mussina	.75	.35	.09
□ 34	Randy Myers	.15	.07	.02
□ 35	Rafael Palmeiro	.60	.25	.07
□ 36	Brady Anderson	.60	.25	.07
□ 37	Tim Naehring	.15	.07	.02
□ 38	Jose Canseco	.60	.25	.07
□ 39	Roger Clemens	.60	.25	.07
□ 40	Mo Vaughn	1.00	.45	.12
□ 41	Jose Valentin	.15	.07	.02
□ 42	Kevin Mitchell	.15	.07	.02
□ 43	Chili Davis	.15	.07	.02
□ 44	Garret Anderson	.60	.25	.07
□ 45	Tim Salmon	.30	.14	.04
□ 46	Chuck Finley	.15	.07	.02
□ 47	Troy Percival	.15	.07	.02
□ 48	Jim Abbott	.60	.25	.07
□ 49	J.T. Snow	.15	.07	.02
□ 50	Jim Edmonds	.30	.14	.04
□ 51	Sammy Sosa	.60	.25	.07
□ 52	Brian McRae	.15	.07	.02
□ 53	Ryne Sandberg	1.00	.45	.12
□ 54	Jaime Navarro	.15	.07	.02
□ 55	Mark Grace	.60	.25	.07
□ 56	Harold Baines	.30	.14	.04
□ 57	Robin Ventura	.60	.25	.07
□ 58	Tony Phillips	.30	.14	.04
□ 59	Alex Fernandez	.60	.25	.07
□ 60	Frank Thomas	4.00	1.80	.50
□ 61	Ray Durham	.60	.25	.07
□ 62	Bret Boone	.15	.07	.02
□ 63	Reggie Sanders	.15	.07	.02
□ 64	Pete Schourek	.15	.07	.02
□ 65	Barry Larkin	.60	.25	.07
□ 66	John Smiley	.15	.07	.02
□ 67	Carlos Baerga	.60	.25	.07
□ 68	Jim Thome	.75	.35	.09
□ 69	Eddie Murray	1.00	.45	.12
□ 70	Albert Belle	2.00	.90	.25
□ 71	Dennis Martinez	.30	.14	.04
□ 72	Jack McDowell	.60	.25	.07
□ 73	Kenny Lofton	1.00	.45	.12
□ 74	Manny Ramirez	1.00	.45	.12
□ 75	Dante Bichette	.60	.25	.07
□ 76	Vinny Castilla	.60	.25	.07
□ 77	Andres Galarraga	.60	.25	.07
□ 78	Walt Weiss	.15	.07	.02
□ 79	Ellis Burks	.60	.25	.07
□ 80	Larry Walker	.60	.25	.07
□ 81	Cecil Fielder	.60	.25	.07
□ 82	Melvin Nieves	.30	.14	.04
□ 83	Travis Fryman	.60	.25	.07
□ 84	Chad Curtis	.15	.07	.02
□ 85	Alan Trammell	.60	.25	.07
□ 86	Gary Sheffield	.60	.25	.07
□ 87	Charles Johnson	.30	.14	.04
□ 88	Andre Dawson	.60	.25	.07
□ 89	Jeff Conine	.60	.25	.07
□ 90	Greg Colbrunn	.15	.07	.02
□ 91	Derek Bell	.30	.14	.04
□ 92	Brian L.Hunter	.15	.07	.02
□ 93	Doug Drabek	.15	.07	.02
□ 94	Craig Biggio	.60	.25	.07
□ 95	Jeff Bagwell	1.50	.70	.19
□ 96	Kevin Appier	.30	.14	.04
□ 97	Jeff Montgomery	.15	.07	.02
□ 98	Michael Tucker	.30	.14	.04
□ 99	Bip Roberts	.15	.07	.02
□ 100	Johnny Damon	.30	.14	.04
□ 101	Eric Karros	.60	.25	.07
□ 102	Raul Mondesi	.60	.25	.07
□ 103	Ramon Martinez	.60	.25	.07
□ 104	Ismael Valdes	.30	.14	.04
□ 105	Mike Piazza	2.50	1.10	.30
□ 106	Hideo Nomo	1.00	.45	.12
□ 107	Chan Ho Park	.60	.25	.07
□ 108	Ben McDonald	.15	.07	.02
□ 109	Kevin Seitzer	.15	.07	.02
□ 110	Greg Vaughn	.60	.25	.07
□ 111	Jose Valentin	.15	.07	.02
□ 112	Rick Aguilera	.15	.07	.02
□ 113	Marty Cordova	.60	.25	.07
□ 114	Brad Radke	.15	.07	.02
□ 115	Kirby Puckett	1.25	.55	.16
□ 116	Chuck Knoblauch	.60	.25	.07
□ 117	Paul Molitor	.75	.35	.09
□ 118	Pedro Martinez	.30	.14	.04
□ 119	Mike Lansing	.15	.07	.02
□ 120	Rondell White	.60	.25	.07
□ 121	Moises Alou	.60	.25	.07
□ 122	Mark Grudzielanek	.30	.14	.04
□ 123	Jeff Fassero	.15	.07	.02
□ 124	Rico Brogna	.15	.07	.02
□ 125	Jason Isringhausen	.15	.07	.02
□ 126	Jeff Kent	.15	.07	.02
□ 127	Bernard Gilkey	.30	.14	.04
□ 128	Todd Hundley	.60	.25	.07
□ 129	David Cone	.60	.25	.07
□ 130	Andy Pettitte	1.25	.55	.16
□ 131	Wade Boggs	.60	.25	.07
□ 132	Paul O'Neill	.15	.07	.02
□ 133	Ruben Sierra	.15	.07	.02
□ 134	John Wetteland	.30	.14	.04
□ 135	Derek Jeter	2.50	1.10	.30
□ 136	Geronimo Berroa	.30	.14	.04
□ 137	Terry Steinbach	.30	.14	.04
□ 138	Ariel Prieto	.15	.07	.02
□ 139	Scott Brosius	.15	.07	.02
□ 140	Mark McGwire	1.25	.55	.16
□ 141	Lenny Dykstra	.30	.14	.04
□ 142	Todd Zeile	.30	.14	.04
□ 143	Benito Santiago	.15	.07	.02
□ 144	Mickey Morandini	.15	.07	.02
□ 145	Gregg Jefferies	.60	.25	.07
□ 146	Denny Neagle	.30	.14	.04
□ 147	Orlando Merced	.30	.14	.04
□ 148	Charlie Hayes	.15	.07	.02
□ 149	Carlos Garcia	.15	.07	.02
□ 150	Jay Bell	.30	.14	.04
□ 151	Ray Lankford	.60	.25	.07
□ 152	Alan Benes Andy Benes	.30	.14	.04

□ 153 Dennis Eckersley	.60	.25	.07
□ 154 Gary Gaetti	.30	.14	.04
□ 155 Ozzie Smith	.75	.35	.09
□ 156 Ron Gant	.60	.25	.07
□ 157 Brian Jordan	.60	.25	.07
□ 158 Ken Caminiti	.60	.25	.07
□ 159 Rickey Henderson	.60	.25	.07
□ 160 Tony Gwynn	1.50	.70	.19
□ 161 Wally Joyner	.15	.07	.02
□ 162 Andy Ashby	.15	.07	.02
□ 163 Steve Finley	.60	.25	.07
□ 164 Glenallen Hill	.15	.07	.02
□ 165 Matt Williams	.60	.25	.07
□ 166 Barry Bonds	1.00	.45	.12
□ 167 William VanLandingham	.15	.07	.02
□ 168 Rod Beck	.30	.14	.04
□ 169 Randy Johnson	.60	.25	.07
□ 170 Ken Griffey Jr.	4.00	1.80	.50
□ 171 Alex Rodriguez	4.00	1.80	.50
□ 172 Edgar Martinez	.60	.25	.07
□ 173 Jay Buhner	.60	.25	.07
□ 174 Russ Davis	.15	.07	.02
□ 175 Juan Gonzalez	2.00	.90	.25
□ 176 Mickey Tettleton	.30	.14	.04
□ 177 Will Clark	.60	.25	.07
□ 178 Ken Hill	.30	.14	.04
□ 179 Dean Palmer	.60	.25	.07
□ 180 Ivan Rodriguez	.75	.35	.09
□ 181 Carlos Delgado	.60	.25	.07
□ 182 Alex Gonzalez	.15	.07	.02
□ 183 Shawn Green	.15	.07	.02
□ 184 Juan Guzman	.15	.07	.02
□ 185 Joe Carter	.60	.25	.07
□ 186 Hideo Nomo CL	.60	.25	.07
□ 187 Cal Ripken CL	1.50	.70	.19
□ 188 Ken Griffey Jr. CL	2.00	.90	.25

1996 SP Baseball Heroes

This 10-card set was randomly inserted at the rate of one in 96 packs. It continues the insert set that was started in 1990 featuring ten of the top players in baseball. The fronts feature color action player photos with the team logo on an embossed foil background. The backs carry another color player photo, player information and statistics.

	MINT	NRMT	EXC
COMPLETE SET (10)	400.00	180.00	50.00
COMMON CARD (82-90/HDR)	20.00	9.00	2.50
RANDOM INSERTS IN PACKS			

□ 82 Frank Thomas	75.00	34.00	9.50
□ 83 Albert Belle	40.00	18.00	5.00
□ 84 Barry Bonds	20.00	9.00	2.50
□ 85 Chipper Jones	50.00	22.00	6.25
□ 86 Hideo Nomo	20.00	9.00	2.50
□ 87 Mike Piazza	50.00	22.00	6.25
□ 88 Manny Ramirez	25.00	11.00	3.10
□ 89 Greg Maddux	50.00	22.00	6.25
□ 90 Ken Griffey Jr.	75.00	34.00	9.50
□ NNO Ken Griffey Jr. HDR	75.00	34.00	9.50

1996 SP Marquee Matchups

Randomly inserted at the rate of one in five packs, this 20-card set highlights two superstars' cards with a common matching stadium background photograph in a blue border. Each card features double foil stamping and embossed player images. The backs carry player information.

	MINT	NRMT	EXC
COMPLETE SET (20)	50.00	22.00	6.25
COMMON CARD (MM1-MM20)	1.00	.45	.12
*DIE-CUTS: 5X VALUE			
RANDOM INSERTS IN PACKS			

□ MM1 Ken Griffey Jr.	8.00	3.60	1.00
□ MM2 Hideo Nomo	2.00	.90	.25
□ MM3 Derek Jeter	4.00	1.80	.50
□ MM4 Rey Ordonez	1.50	.70	.19
□ MM5 Tim Salmon	1.00	.45	.12
□ MM6 Mike Piazza	5.00	2.20	.60
□ MM7 Mark McGwire	2.50	1.10	.30
□ MM8 Barry Bonds	2.00	.90	.25
□ MM9 Cal Ripken	6.00	2.70	.75
□ MM10 Greg Maddux	5.00	2.20	.60
□ MM11 Albert Belle	4.00	1.80	.50
□ MM12 Barry Larkin	1.00	.45	.12
□ MM13 Jeff Bagwell	3.00	1.35	.35
□ MM14 Juan Gonzalez	3.00	1.35	.35
□ MM15 Frank Thomas	8.00	3.60	1.00
□ MM16 Sammy Sosa	1.25	.55	.16
□ MM17 Mike Mussina	1.50	.70	.19
□ MM18 Chipper Jones	5.00	2.20	.60
□ MM19 Roger Clemens	1.00	.45	.12
□ MM20 Fred McGriff	1.00	.45	.12

1996 SP Special FX

Randomly inserted at the rate of one in 5 packs, this 48-card set features a color action player cutout on a gold foil background with a holoview diamond shaped insert containing a black-and-white player portrait. A wide blue border runs vertically down one side of the card. The backs carry player information and statistics at home and away in baseball field designs on a blue background.

	MINT	NRMT	EXC
COMPLETE SET (48)	175.00	80.00	22.00
COMMON CARD (1-48)	2.00	.90	.25
SEMISTARS	2.50	1.10	.30
*DIE-CUTS: 6X VALUE			
RANDOM INSERTS IN PACKS			

□ 1 Greg Maddux	12.00	5.50	1.50
□ 2 Eric Karros	2.00	.90	.25

□ 3 Mike Piazza	12.00	5.50	1.50
□ 4 Raul Mondesi	2.00	.90	.25
□ 5 Hideo Nomo	5.00	2.20	.60
□ 6 Jim Edmonds	2.00	.90	.25
□ 7 Jason Isringhausen	2.00	.90	.25
□ 8 Jay Buhner	2.50	1.10	.30
□ 9 Barry Larkin	2.50	1.10	.30
□ 10 Ken Griffey Jr.	20.00	9.00	2.50
□ 11 Gary Sheffield	3.00	1.35	.35
□ 12 Craig Biggio	2.50	1.10	.30
□ 13 Paul Wilson	2.00	.90	.25
□ 14 Rondell White	2.50	1.10	.30
□ 15 Chipper Jones	12.00	5.50	1.50
□ 16 Kirby Puckett	6.00	2.70	.75
□ 17 Ron Gant	2.50	1.10	.30
□ 18 Wade Boggs	2.50	1.10	.30
□ 19 Fred McGriff	2.50	1.10	.30
□ 20 Cal Ripken	15.00	6.75	1.85
□ 21 Jason Kendall	2.00	.90	.25
□ 22 Johnny Damon	2.00	.90	.25
□ 23 Kenny Lofton	5.00	2.20	.60
□ 24 Roberto Alomar	5.00	2.20	.60
□ 25 Barry Bonds	5.00	2.20	.60
□ 26 Dante Bichette	2.50	1.10	.30
□ 27 Mark McGwire	6.00	2.70	.75
□ 28 Rafael Palmeiro	2.50	1.10	.30
□ 29 Juan Gonzalez	10.00	4.50	1.25
□ 30 Albert Belle	10.00	4.50	1.25
□ 31 Randy Johnson	3.00	1.35	.35
□ 32 Jose Canseco	2.50	1.10	.30
□ 33 Sammy Sosa	3.00	1.35	.35
□ 34 Eddie Murray	5.00	2.20	.60
□ 35 Frank Thomas	20.00	9.00	2.50
□ 36 Tom Glavine	2.50	1.10	.30
□ 37 Matt Williams	2.50	1.10	.30
□ 38 Roger Clemens	2.50	1.10	.30
□ 39 Paul Molitor	4.00	1.80	.50
□ 40 Tony Gwynn	8.00	3.60	1.00
□ 41 Mo Vaughn	5.00	2.20	.60
□ 42 Tim Salmon	2.00	.90	.25
□ 43 Manny Ramirez	5.00	2.20	.60
□ 44 Jeff Bagwell	8.00	3.60	1.00
□ 45 Edgar Martinez	2.50	1.10	.30
□ 46 Rey Ordonez	3.00	1.35	.35
□ 47 Osvaldo Fernandez	2.00	.90	.25
□ 48 Derek Jeter	10.00	4.50	1.25

1995 SP Championship

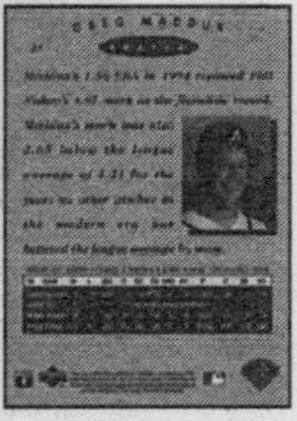

This set contains 200 cards that were sold in six-card retail packs for a suggested price of $2.99. The fronts have a full-bleed action photo with the words "SP Championship Series" in gold-foil in the bottom left-hand corner. In the bottom right-hand corner is the team's name in blue (National League) and red (American League) foil. The backs have a small head shot and player information. Statistics and team name are also on the back in blue or red just like on the front. Subsets featured are Diamonds in the Rough (1-20), October Legends (100-114) and Major League Profiles. Rookie Cards in this set include Hideo Nomo and Carlos Perez.

	MINT	NRMT	EXC
COMPLETE SET (200)	40.00	18.00	5.00
COMMON CARD (1-200)	.15	.07	.02
SEMISTARS	.30	.14	.04
STARS	.60	.25	.07
COMP.DIE CUT SET (200)	150.00	70.00	19.00
COMMON DIE CUT (1-200)	.25	.11	.03
DIE CUT SEMISTARS	.50	.23	.06
*DIE CUT STARS: 1.5X to 3X HI COLUMN...			
*DIE CUT YOUNG STARS: 1.25X to 2.5X HI			
ONE DIE CUT PER PACK			
□ 1 Hideo Nomo	4.00	1.80	.50
□ 2 Roger Cedeno	.30	.14	.04
□ 3 Curtis Goodwin	.30	.14	.04
□ 4 Jon Nunnally	.30	.14	.04
□ 5 Bill Pulsipher	.30	.14	.04
□ 6 Garret Anderson	.60	.25	.07
□ 7 Dustin Hermanson	.30	.14	.04
□ 8 Marty Cordova	.60	.25	.07
□ 9 Ruben Rivera	2.00	.90	.25
□ 10 Ariel Prieto	.30	.14	.04
□ 11 Edgardo Alfonzo	.30	.14	.04
□ 12 Ray Durham	.30	.14	.04
□ 13 Quilvio Veras	.15	.07	.02
□ 14 Ugueth Urbina	.15	.07	.02
□ 15 Carlos Perez	.30	.14	.04
□ 16 Glenn Dishman	.30	.14	.04
□ 17 Jeff Suppan	.60	.25	.07
□ 18 Jason Bates	.15	.07	.02
□ 19 Jason Isringhausen	1.00	.45	.12
□ 20 Derek Jeter	2.50	1.10	.30
□ 21 Fred McGriff MLP	.30	.14	.04
□ 22 Marquis Grissom	.60	.25	.07
□ 23 Fred McGriff	.60	.25	.07
□ 24 Tom Glavine	.60	.25	.07
□ 25 Greg Maddux	2.50	1.10	.30
□ 26 Chipper Jones	2.50	1.10	.30
□ 27 Sammy Sosa MLP	.30	.14	.04
□ 28 Randy Myers	.15	.07	.02
□ 29 Mark Grace	.60	.25	.07
□ 30 Sammy Sosa	.60	.25	.07
□ 31 Todd Zeile	.15	.07	.02
□ 32 Brian McRae	.30	.14	.04
□ 33 Ron Gant MLP	.30	.14	.04
□ 34 Reggie Sanders	.30	.14	.04
□ 35 Ron Gant	.30	.14	.04
□ 36 Barry Larkin	.60	.25	.07
□ 37 Bret Boone	.30	.14	.04
□ 38 John Smiley	.15	.07	.02
□ 39 Larry Walker MLP	.30	.14	.04
□ 40 Andres Galarraga	.60	.25	.07
□ 41 Bill Swift	.15	.07	.02
□ 42 Larry Walker	.60	.25	.07
□ 43 Vinny Castilla	.30	.14	.04
□ 44 Dante Bichette	.60	.25	.07
□ 45 Jeff Conine MLP	.30	.14	.04
□ 46 Charles Johnson	.30	.14	.04
□ 47 Gary Sheffield	.60	.25	.07
□ 48 Andre Dawson	.60	.25	.07
□ 49 Jeff Conine	.60	.25	.07
□ 50 Jeff Bagwell MLP	.75	.35	.09
□ 51 Phil Nevin	.15	.07	.02
□ 52 Craig Biggio	.60	.25	.07
□ 53 Brian L. Hunter	.60	.25	.07
□ 54 Doug Drabek	.15	.07	.02
□ 55 Jeff Bagwell	1.50	.70	.19
□ 56 Derek Bell	.30	.14	.04
□ 57 Mike Piazza MLP	1.25	.55	.16
□ 58 Raul Mondesi	.60	.25	.07
□ 59 Eric Karros	.30	.14	.04
□ 60 Mike Piazza	2.50	1.10	.30
□ 61 Ramon Martinez	.30	.14	.04
□ 62 Billy Ashley	.15	.07	.02
□ 63 Rondell White MLP	.30	.14	.04
□ 64 Jeff Fassero	.15	.07	.02
□ 65 Moises Alou	.30	.14	.04
□ 66 Tony Tarasco	.15	.07	.02
□ 67 Rondell White	.60	.25	.07
□ 68 Pedro J. Martinez	.30	.14	.04
□ 69 Bobby Jones MLP	.30	.14	.04
□ 70 Bobby Bonilla	.30	.14	.04
□ 71 Bobby Jones	.30	.14	.04
□ 72 Bret Saberhagen	.30	.14	.04
□ 73 Darren Daulton MLP	.15	.07	.02
□ 74 Darren Daulton	.30	.14	.04
□ 75 Gregg Jefferies	.30	.14	.04
□ 76 Tyler Green	.15	.07	.02
□ 77 Heathcliff Slocumb	.15	.07	.02
□ 78 Lenny Dykstra	.30	.14	.04

□ 79 Jay Bell MLP	.30	.14	.04
□ 80 Denny Neagle	.30	.14	.04
□ 81 Orlando Merced	.15	.07	.02
□ 82 Jay Bell	.30	.14	.04
□ 83 Ozzie Smith MLP	.60	.25	.07
□ 84 Ken Hill	.15	.07	.02
□ 85 Ozzie Smith	.75	.35	.09
□ 86 Bernard Gilkey	.30	.14	.04
□ 87 Ray Lankford	.60	.25	.07
□ 88 Tony Gwynn MLP	.75	.35	.09
□ 89 Ken Caminiti	.60	.25	.07
□ 90 Tony Gwynn	1.50	.70	.19
□ 91 Joey Hamilton	.30	.14	.04
□ 92 Bip Roberts	.15	.07	.02
□ 93 Deion Sanders MLP	.60	.25	.07
□ 94 Glenallen Hill	.15	.07	.02
□ 95 Matt Williams	.60	.25	.07
□ 96 Barry Bonds	1.00	.45	.12
□ 97 Rod Beck	.15	.07	.02
□ 98 Eddie Murray CL	.60	.25	.07
□ 99 Cal Ripken Jr. CL	1.50	.70	.19
□ 100 Roberto Alomar OL	.60	.25	.07
□ 101 George Brett OL	1.00	.45	.12
□ 102 Joe Carter OL	.30	.14	.04
□ 103 Will Clark OL	.30	.14	.04
□ 104 Dennis Eckersley OL	.30	.14	.04
□ 105 Whitey Ford OL	.60	.25	.07
□ 106 Steve Garvey OL	.30	.14	.04
□ 107 Kirk Gibson OL	.30	.14	.04
□ 108 Orel Hershiser OL	.30	.14	.04
□ 109 Reggie Jackson OL	.60	.25	.07
□ 110 Paul Molitor OL	.60	.25	.07
□ 111 Kirby Puckett OL	.60	.25	.07
□ 112 Mike Schmidt OL	.75	.35	.09
□ 113 Dave Stewart OL	.15	.07	.02
□ 114 Alan Trammell OL	.60	.25	.07
□ 115 Cal Ripken Jr. MLP	1.50	.70	.19
□ 116 Brady Anderson	.60	.25	.07
□ 117 Mike Mussina	.75	.35	.09
□ 118 Rafael Palmeiro	.60	.25	.07
□ 119 Chris Hoiles	.15	.07	.02
□ 120 Cal Ripken	3.00	1.35	.35
□ 121 Mo Vaughn MLP	.60	.25	.07
□ 122 Roger Clemens	.60	.25	.07
□ 123 Tim Naehring	.15	.07	.02
□ 124 John Valentin	.30	.14	.04
□ 125 Mo Vaughn	1.00	.45	.12
□ 126 Tim Wakefield	.15	.07	.02
□ 127 Jose Canseco	.60	.25	.07
□ 128 Rick Aguilera	.15	.07	.02
□ 129 Chili Davis MLP	.30	.14	.04
□ 130 Lee Smith	.30	.14	.04
□ 131 Jim Edmonds	.60	.25	.07
□ 132 Chuck Finley	.30	.14	.04
□ 133 Chili Davis	.30	.14	.04
□ 134 J.T. Snow	.30	.14	.04
□ 135 Tim Salmon	.60	.25	.07
□ 136 Frank Thomas MLP	2.00	.90	.25
□ 137 Jason Bere	.15	.07	.02
□ 138 Robin Ventura	.30	.14	.04
□ 139 Tim Raines	.60	.25	.07
□ 140 Frank Thomas	4.00	1.80	.50
□ 141 Alex Fernandez	.30	.14	.04
□ 142 Eddie Murray MLP	.60	.25	.07
□ 143 Carlos Baerga	.60	.25	.07
□ 144 Eddie Murray	1.00	.45	.12
□ 145 Albert Belle	2.00	.90	.25
□ 146 Jim Thome	.75	.35	.09
□ 147 Dennis Martinez	.30	.14	.04
□ 148 Dave Winfield	.60	.25	.07
□ 149 Kenny Lofton	1.00	.45	.12
□ 150 Manny Ramirez	1.00	.45	.12
□ 151 Cecil Fielder MLP	.30	.14	.04
□ 152 Lou Whitaker	.60	.25	.07
□ 153 Alan Trammell	.60	.25	.07
□ 154 Kirk Gibson	.30	.14	.04
□ 155 Cecil Fielder	.30	.14	.04
□ 156 Bobby Higginson	.60	.25	.07
□ 157 Kevin Appier MLP	.15	.07	.02
□ 158 Wally Joyner	.30	.14	.04
□ 159 Jeff Montgomery	.30	.14	.04
□ 160 Kevin Appier	.30	.14	.04
□ 161 Gary Gaetti	.30	.14	.04
□ 162 Greg Gagne	.15	.07	.02
□ 163 Ricky Bones MLP	.15	.07	.02
□ 164 Greg Vaughn	.30	.14	.04
□ 165 Kevin Seitzer	.15	.07	.02
□ 166 Ricky Bones	.15	.07	.02
□ 167 Kirby Puckett MLP	.60	.25	.07
□ 168 Pedro Munoz	.15	.07	.02
□ 169 Chuck Knoblauch	.60	.25	.07
□ 170 Kirby Puckett	1.25	.55	.16
□ 171 Don Mattingly MLP	1.00	.45	.12
□ 172 Wade Boggs	.60	.25	.07
□ 173 Paul O'Neill	.30	.14	.04
□ 174 John Wetteland	.30	.14	.04
□ 175 Don Mattingly	2.00	.90	.25
□ 176 Jack McDowell	.30	.14	.04
□ 177 Mark McGwire MLP	.60	.25	.07
□ 178 Rickey Henderson	.60	.25	.07
□ 179 Terry Steinbach	.30	.14	.04
□ 180 Ruben Sierra	.30	.14	.04
□ 181 Mark McGwire	1.25	.55	.16
□ 182 Dennis Eckersley	.30	.14	.04
□ 183 Ken Griffey Jr. MLP	2.00	.90	.25
□ 184 Alex Rodriguez	5.00	2.20	.60
□ 185 Ken Griffey Jr.	4.00	1.80	.50
□ 186 Randy Johnson	.60	.25	.07
□ 187 Jay Buhner	.60	.25	.07
□ 188 Edgar Martinez	.60	.25	.07
□ 189 Will Clark MLP	.30	.14	.04
□ 190 Juan Gonzalez	2.00	.90	.25
□ 191 Benji Gil	.15	.07	.02
□ 192 Ivan Rodriguez	.75	.35	.09
□ 193 Kenny Rogers	.15	.07	.02
□ 194 Will Clark	.60	.25	.07
□ 195 Paul Molitor MLP	.60	.25	.07
□ 196 Roberto Alomar	1.00	.45	.12
□ 197 David Cone	.30	.14	.04
□ 198 Paul Molitor	.75	.35	.09
□ 199 Shawn Green	.30	.14	.04
□ 200 Joe Carter	.60	.25	.07
□ CR1 Cal Ripken, Jr. Tribute	60.00	27.00	7.50
□ CR1 Cal Ripken 2131 Die-Cut	175.00	80.00	22.00

1995 SP Championship Classic Performances

This 10-card set was randomly inserted in packs at a rate of one in 15. The set consists of 10 of the most memorable highlights since the 1969 Miracle Mets. The fronts have a series action photo highlighted with the words "Classic Performances" at the top in gold-foil enclosed by red. The backs have a color head shot with information and statistics from the series. Diecut versions were inserted at a rate of 72 packs and are valued at three to six times the prices below.

	MINT	NRMT	EXC
COMPLETE SET (10)	40.00	18.00	5.00
COMMON CARD (CP1-CP10)	2.00	.90	.25
*DIE CUT: 2.5X TO 5X BASIC CARDS			
RANDOM INSERTS IN PACKS			
□ CP1 Reggie Jackson	4.00	1.80	.50
□ CP2 Nolan Ryan	20.00	9.00	2.50
□ CP3 Kirk Gibson	3.00	1.35	.35
□ CP4 Joe Carter	3.00	1.35	.35
□ CP5 George Brett	8.00	3.60	1.00
□ CP6 Roberto Alomar	5.00	2.20	.60
□ CP7 Ozzie Smith	4.00	1.80	.50
□ CP8 Kirby Puckett	6.00	2.70	.75

□ CP9 Bret Saberhagen	2.00	.90	.25
□ CP10 Steve Garvey	3.00	1.35	.35

1995 SP Championship Fall Classic

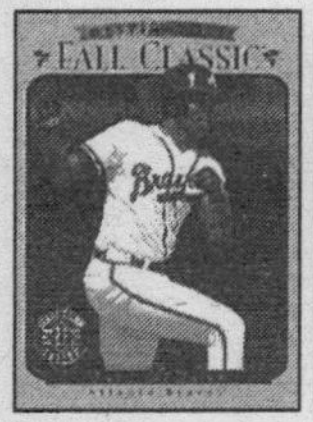

This nine-card set was randomly inserted in packs at a rate of one in 40. The set is comprised of players who had never been to the World Series prior to the 1995 Fall Classic. The fronts have a color-action photo with the game background in foil. There is a grain-colored border with the word "Destination" at the top in bronze-foil and "Fall Classic" underneath in black. The backs have a small, color picture inside a black box with player information underneath. Diecut versions were inserted at a rate of one in 72 packs and are valued at 1.5X to 3X the prices below.

	MINT	NRMT	EXC
COMPLETE SET (9)	125.00	55.00	15.50
COMMON CARD (1-9)	4.00	1.80	.50
*DIECUTS: 1X TO 2X BASIC CARDS			
RANDOM INSERTS IN PACKS			

□ 1 Ken Griffey Jr.	30.00	13.50	3.70
□ 2 Frank Thomas	30.00	13.50	3.70
□ 3 Albert Belle	15.00	6.75	1.85
□ 4 Mike Piazza	20.00	9.00	2.50
□ 5 Don Mattingly	15.00	6.75	1.85
□ 6 Hideo Nomo	15.00	6.75	1.85
□ 7 Greg Maddux	20.00	9.00	2.50
□ 8 Fred McGriff	4.00	1.80	.50
□ 9 Barry Bonds	6.00	2.70	.75

1994 Sportflics

Each of the 193 "Magic Motion" cards features two images, which alternate when the card is viewed from different angles and creates the illusion of movement. Cards 176-193 are Starflics featuring top stars. The two commemorative cards, featuring Cliff Floyd and Paul Molitor, were inserted at a rate of one in every 360 packs.

	MINT	NRMT	EXC
COMPLETE SET (193)	25.00	11.00	3.10
COMMON CARD (1-193)	.10	.05	.01
SEMISTARS	.25	.11	.03
STARS	.50	.23	.06

□ 1 Lenny Dykstra	.25	.11	.03
□ 2 Mike Stanley	.10	.05	.01
□ 3 Alex Fernandez	.50	.23	.06
□ 4 Mark McGwire UER (name spelled McGuire on front)	1.00	.45	.12
□ 5 Eric Karros	.25	.11	.03
□ 6 Dave Justice	.50	.23	.06
□ 7 Jeff Bagwell	1.25	.55	.16
□ 8 Darren Lewis	.10	.05	.01
□ 9 David McCarty	.10	.05	.01
□ 10 Albert Belle	1.50	.70	.19
□ 11 Ben McDonald	.10	.05	.01
□ 12 Joe Carter	.50	.23	.06
□ 13 Benito Santiago	.10	.05	.01
□ 14 Rob Dibble	.10	.05	.01
□ 15 Roger Clemens	.50	.23	.06
□ 16 Travis Fryman	.50	.23	.06
□ 17 Doug Drabek	.10	.05	.01
□ 18 Jay Buhner	.50	.23	.06
□ 19 Orlando Merced	.25	.11	.03
□ 20 Ryan Klesko	.75	.35	.09
□ 21 Chuck Finley	.10	.05	.01
□ 22 Dante Bichette	.50	.23	.06
□ 23 Wally Joyner	.25	.11	.03
□ 24 Robin Yount	.50	.23	.06
□ 25 Tony Gwynn	1.25	.55	.16
□ 26 Allen Watson	.10	.05	.01
□ 27 Rick Wilkins	.10	.05	.01
□ 28 Gary Sheffield	.50	.23	.06
□ 29 John Burkett	.10	.05	.01
□ 30 Randy Johnson	.50	.23	.06
□ 31 Roberto Alomar	.75	.35	.09
□ 32 Fred McGriff	.50	.23	.06
□ 33 Ozzie Guillen	.10	.05	.01
□ 34 Jimmy Key	.25	.11	.03
□ 35 Juan Gonzalez	1.50	.70	.19
□ 36 Wil Cordero	.25	.11	.03
□ 37 Aaron Sele	.25	.11	.03
□ 38 Mark Langston	.25	.11	.03
□ 39 David Cone	.50	.23	.06
□ 40 John Jaha	.25	.11	.03
□ 41 Ozzie Smith	.60	.25	.07
□ 42 Kirby Puckett	1.00	.45	.12
□ 43 Kenny Lofton	1.00	.45	.12
□ 44 Mike Mussina	.60	.25	.07
□ 45 Ryne Sandberg	.75	.35	.09
□ 46 Robby Thompson	.10	.05	.01
□ 47 Bryan Harvey	.10	.05	.01
□ 48 Marquis Grissom	.50	.23	.06
□ 49 Bobby Bonilla	.25	.11	.03
□ 50 Dennis Eckersley	.25	.11	.03
□ 51 Curt Schilling	.10	.05	.01
□ 52 Andy Benes	.25	.11	.03
□ 53 Greg Maddux	2.00	.90	.25
□ 54 Bill Swift	.10	.05	.01
□ 55 Andres Galarraga	.50	.23	.06
□ 56 Tony Phillips	.25	.11	.03
□ 57 Darryl Hamilton	.10	.05	.01
□ 58 Duane Ward	.10	.05	.01
□ 59 Bernie Williams	.50	.23	.06
□ 60 Steve Avery	.25	.11	.03
□ 61 Eduardo Perez	.10	.05	.01
□ 62 Jeff Conine	.50	.23	.06
□ 63 Dave Winfield	.50	.23	.06
□ 64 Phil Plantier	.10	.05	.01
□ 65 Ray Lankford	.50	.23	.06
□ 66 Robin Ventura	.25	.11	.03
□ 67 Mike Piazza	2.00	.90	.25
□ 68 Jason Bere	.25	.11	.03
□ 69 Cal Ripken	2.50	1.10	.30
□ 70 Frank Thomas	3.00	1.35	.35
□ 71 Carlos Baerga	.50	.23	.06
□ 72 Darryl Kile	.10	.05	.01
□ 73 Ruben Sierra	.25	.11	.03
□ 74 Gregg Jefferies UER Name spelled Jeffries on front	.50	.23	.06
□ 75 John Olerud	.10	.05	.01
□ 76 Andy Van Slyke	.25	.11	.03
□ 77 Larry Walker	.50	.23	.06
□ 78 Cecil Fielder	.25	.11	.03
□ 79 Andre Dawson	.50	.23	.06
□ 80 Tom Glavine	.50	.23	.06
□ 81 Sammy Sosa	.50	.23	.06

□ 82 Charlie Hayes	.10	.05	.01
□ 83 Chuck Knoblauch	.50	.23	.06
□ 84 Kevin Appier	.25	.11	.03
□ 85 Dean Palmer	.25	.11	.03
□ 86 Royce Clayton	.25	.11	.03
□ 87 Moises Alou	.25	.11	.03
□ 88 Ivan Rodriguez	.60	.25	.07
□ 89 Tim Salmon	.50	.23	.06
□ 90 Ron Gant	.25	.11	.03
□ 91 Barry Bonds	.75	.35	.09
□ 92 Jack McDowell	.25	.11	.03
□ 93 Alan Trammell	.50	.23	.06
□ 94 Doc Gooden	.25	.11	.03
□ 95 Jay Bell	.25	.11	.03
□ 96 Devon White	.10	.05	.01
□ 97 Wilson Alvarez	.25	.11	.03
□ 98 Jim Thome	.75	.35	.09
□ 99 Ramon Martinez	.25	.11	.03
□ 100 Kent Hrbek	.25	.11	.03
□ 101 John Kruk	.25	.11	.03
□ 102 Wade Boggs	.50	.23	.06
□ 103 Greg Vaughn	.50	.23	.06
□ 104 Tom Henke	.10	.05	.01
□ 105 Brian Jordan	.50	.23	.06
□ 106 Paul Molitor	.60	.25	.07
□ 107 Cal Eldred	.10	.05	.01
□ 108 Deion Sanders	.50	.23	.06
□ 109 Barry Larkin	.50	.23	.06
□ 110 Mike Greenwell	.10	.05	.01
□ 111 Jeff Blauser	.10	.05	.01
□ 112 Jose Rijo	.10	.05	.01
□ 113 Pete Harnisch	.10	.05	.01
□ 114 Chris Hoiles	.10	.05	.01
□ 115 Edgar Martinez	.50	.23	.06
□ 116 Juan Guzman	.25	.11	.03
□ 117 Todd Zeile	.10	.05	.01
□ 118 Danny Tartabull	.10	.05	.01
□ 119 Chad Curtis	.10	.05	.01
□ 120 Mark Grace	.50	.23	.06
□ 121 J.T. Snow	.25	.11	.03
□ 122 Mo Vaughn	.75	.35	.09
□ 123 Lance Johnson	.25	.11	.03
□ 124 Eric Davis	.25	.11	.03
□ 125 Orel Hershiser	.25	.11	.03
□ 126 Kevin Mitchell	.25	.11	.03
□ 127 Don Mattingly	1.50	.70	.19
□ 128 Darren Daulton	.25	.11	.03
□ 129 Rod Beck	.25	.11	.03
□ 130 Charles Nagy	.25	.11	.03
□ 131 Mickey Tettleton	.10	.05	.01
□ 132 Kevin Brown	.10	.05	.01
□ 133 Pat Hentgen	.50	.23	.06
□ 134 Terry Mulholland	.10	.05	.01
□ 135 Steve Finley	.50	.23	.06
□ 136 John Smoltz	.50	.23	.06
□ 137 Frank Viola	.10	.05	.01
□ 138 Jim Abbott	.10	.05	.01
□ 139 Matt Williams	.50	.23	.06
□ 140 Bernard Gilkey	.25	.11	.03
□ 141 Jose Canseco	.50	.23	.06
□ 142 Mark Whiten	.10	.05	.01
□ 143 Ken Griffey Jr.	3.00	1.35	.35
□ 144 Rafael Palmeiro	.50	.23	.06
□ 145 Dave Hollins	.10	.05	.01
□ 146 Will Clark	.50	.23	.06
□ 147 Paul O'Neill	.25	.11	.03
□ 148 Bobby Jones	.25	.11	.03
□ 149 Butch Huskey	.25	.11	.03
□ 150 Jeffrey Hammonds	.25	.11	.03
□ 151 Manny Ramirez	1.00	.45	.12
□ 152 Bob Hamelin	.10	.05	.01
□ 153 Kurt Abbott	.25	.11	.03
□ 154 Scott Stahoviak	.10	.05	.01
□ 155 Steve Hosey	.10	.05	.01
□ 156 Salomon Torres	.10	.05	.01
□ 157 Sterling Hitchcock	.25	.11	.03
□ 158 Nigel Wilson	.10	.05	.01
□ 159 Luis Lopez	.10	.05	.01
□ 160 Chipper Jones	2.50	1.10	.30
□ 161 Norberto Martin	.10	.05	.01
□ 162 Raul Mondesi	.50	.23	.06
□ 163 Steve Karsay	.10	.05	.01
□ 164 J.R. Phillips	.10	.05	.01
□ 165 Marc Newfield	.25	.11	.03
□ 166 Mark Hutton	.10	.05	.01
□ 167 Curtis Pride	.25	.11	.03
□ 168 Carl Everett	.10	.05	.01
□ 169 Scott Ruffcorn	.10	.05	.01
□ 170 Turk Wendell	.10	.05	.01
□ 171 Jeff McNeely	.10	.05	.01
□ 172 Javier Lopez	.50	.23	.06
□ 173 Cliff Floyd	.50	.23	.06
□ 174 Rondell White	.50	.23	.06
□ 175 Scott Lydy	.10	.05	.01
□ 176 Frank Thomas AS	1.50	.70	.19
□ 177 Roberto Alomar AS	.50	.23	.06
□ 178 Travis Fryman AS	.25	.11	.03
□ 179 Cal Ripken AS	1.25	.55	.16
□ 180 Chris Hoiles AS	.10	.05	.01
□ 181 Ken Griffey Jr. AS	1.50	.70	.19
□ 182 Juan Gonzalez AS	.50	.23	.06
□ 183 Joe Carter AS	.50	.23	.06
□ 184 Jack McDowell AS	.10	.05	.01
□ 185 Fred McGriff AS	.50	.23	.06
□ 186 Robby Thompson AS	.10	.05	.01
□ 187 Matt Williams AS	.50	.23	.06
□ 188 Jay Bell AS	.10	.05	.01
□ 189 Mike Piazza AS	1.00	.45	.12
□ 190 Barry Bonds AS	.50	.23	.06
□ 191 Lenny Dykstra AS	.10	.05	.01
□ 192 Dave Justice AS	.25	.11	.03
□ 193 Greg Maddux AS	1.00	.45	.12
□ NNO0 Cliff Floyd Special	5.00	2.20	.60
□ NNO0 Paul Molitor Special	15.00	6.75	1.85

1994 Sportflics Movers

These 12 standard-size chase cards were randomly inserted in retail foil packs and picture the game's top veterans. The insertion rate was one in every 24 packs. Fronts feature the dual image effect with the player's name appearing in dual image. The name "Movers" appears in a circular design off to the left of the player's name.

	MINT	NRMT	EXC
COMPLETE SET (12)	50.00	22.00	6.25
COMMON CARD (MM1-MM12)	1.50	.70	.19
SEMISTARS	3.00	1.35	.35
RANDOM INSERTS IN RETAIL PACKS			
□ MM1 Gregg Jefferies	3.00	1.35	.35
□ MM2 Ryne Sandberg	8.00	3.60	1.00
□ MM3 Cecil Fielder	3.00	1.35	.35
□ MM4 Kirby Puckett	8.00	3.60	1.00
□ MM5 Tony Gwynn	10.00	4.50	1.25
□ MM6 Andres Galarraga	3.00	1.35	.35
□ MM7 Sammy Sosa	4.00	1.80	.50
□ MM8 Rickey Henderson	3.00	1.35	.35
□ MM9 Don Mattingly	12.00	5.50	1.50
□ MM10 Joe Carter	3.00	1.35	.35
□ MM11 Carlos Baerga	3.00	1.35	.35
□ MM12 Lenny Dykstra	1.50	.70	.19

1994 Sportflics Shakers

These 12 standard-size chase cards were randomly inserted in hobby foil packs and picture baseball's elite young players. The insertion rate was one in every 24 packs. Fronts feature the dual image effect with the player's name also appearing as dual image. The name "Shakers" appears in a circular design off to the left of the player's name.

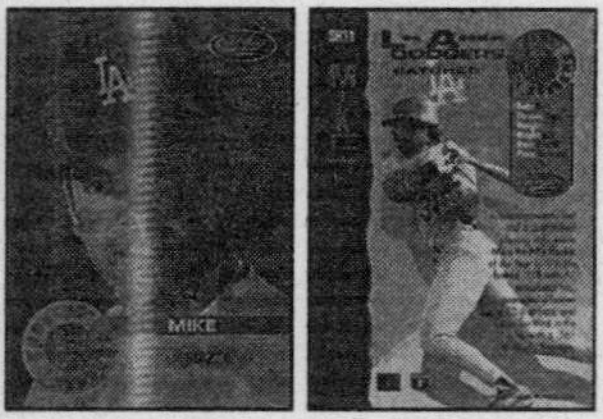

	MINT	NRMT	EXC
COMPLETE SET (12)	70.00	32.00	8.75
COMMON CARD (SH1-SH12)	2.00	.90	.25
RANDOM INSERTS IN HOBBY PACKS			

	MINT	NRMT	EXC
□ SH1 Kenny Lofton	12.00	5.50	1.50
□ SH2 Tim Salmon	5.00	2.20	.60
□ SH3 Jeff Bagwell	15.00	6.75	1.85
□ SH4 Jason Bere	2.00	.90	.25
□ SH5 Salomon Torres	2.00	.90	.25
□ SH6 Rondell White	4.00	1.80	.50
□ SH7 Javier Lopez	5.00	2.20	.60
□ SH8 Dean Palmer	3.00	1.35	.35
□ SH9 Jim Thome	8.00	3.60	1.00
□ SH10 J.T. Snow	2.00	.90	.25
□ SH11 Mike Piazza	20.00	9.00	2.50
□ SH12 Manny Ramirez	10.00	4.50	1.25

1994 Sportflics Rookie/Traded

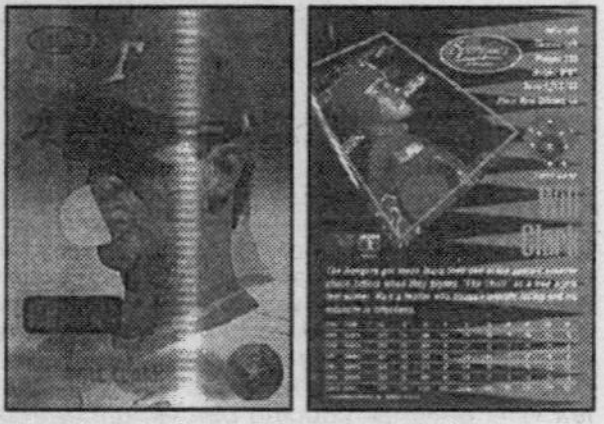

This set of 150 standard-size cards was distributed in five-card retail packs at a suggested price of $1.89. The set features top rookies and traded players. This set was released only through retail (non-hobby) outlets. The fronts feature the "Magic Motion" printing with two action views of the player which change with the tilting of the card. The playerís name is printed in red and expands and contracts with the tilting of the card. Numbered backs include a player biography and career stats and the 1994 performance of the rookie or how the player was acquired in a trade. A full-color photo of the player is framed at an angle with a red and black background. Rookie Cards in this set include Chan Ho Park, Alex Rodriguez and Julian Tavarez.

	MINT	NRMT	EXC
COMPLETE SET (150)	25.00	11.00	3.10
COMMON CARD (1-150)	.15	.07	.02
SEMISTARS	.30	.14	.04
STARS	.60	.25	.07

	MINT	NRMT	EXC
□ 1 Will Clark	.60	.25	.07
□ 2 Sid Fernandez	.15	.07	.02
□ 3 Joe Magrane	.15	.07	.02
□ 4 Pete Smith	.15	.07	.02
□ 5 Roberto Kelly	.15	.07	.02
□ 6 Delino DeShields	.15	.07	.02
□ 7 Brian Harper	.15	.07	.02
□ 8 Darrin Jackson	.15	.07	.02
□ 9 Omar Vizquel	.60	.25	.07
□ 10 Luis Polonia	.15	.07	.02
□ 11 Reggie Jefferson	.30	.14	.04
□ 12 Geronimo Berroa	.30	.14	.04
□ 13 Mike Harkey	.15	.07	.02
□ 14 Bret Boone	.30	.14	.04
□ 15 Dave Henderson	.15	.07	.02
□ 16 Pedro J.Martinez	.60	.25	.07
□ 17 Jose Vizcaino	.15	.07	.02
□ 18 Xavier Hernandez	.15	.07	.02
□ 19 Eddie Taubensee	.15	.07	.02
□ 20 Ellis Burks	.30	.14	.04
□ 21 Turner Ward	.15	.07	.02
□ 22 Terry Mulholland	.15	.07	.02
□ 23 Howard Johnson	.15	.07	.02
□ 24 Vince Coleman	.15	.07	.02
□ 25 Deion Sanders	.60	.25	.07
□ 26 Rafael Palmeiro	.60	.25	.07
□ 27 Dave Weathers	.15	.07	.02
□ 28 Kent Mercker	.15	.07	.02
□ 29 Gregg Olson	.15	.07	.02
□ 30 Cory Bailey	.15	.07	.02
□ 31 Brian L.Hunter	.60	.25	.07
□ 32 Garey Ingram	.15	.07	.02
□ 33 Daniel Smith	.15	.07	.02
□ 34 Denny Hocking	.15	.07	.02
□ 35 Charles Johnson	.60	.25	.07
□ 36 Otis Nixon	.15	.07	.02
□ 37 Hector Fajardo	.15	.07	.02
□ 38 Lee Smith	.30	.14	.04
□ 39 Phil Stidham	.15	.07	.02
□ 40 Melvin Nieves	.30	.14	.04
□ 41 Julio Franco	.30	.14	.04
□ 42 Greg Gohr	.15	.07	.02
□ 43 Steve Dunn	.15	.07	.02
□ 44 Tony Fernandez	.15	.07	.02
□ 45 Toby Borland	.15	.07	.02
□ 46 Paul Shuey	.15	.07	.02
□ 47 Shawn Hare	.15	.07	.02
□ 48 Shawn Green	.30	.14	.04
□ 49 Julian Tavarez	.30	.14	.04
□ 50 Ernie Young	.60	.25	.07
□ 51 Chris Sabo	.15	.07	.02
□ 52 Greg O'Halloran	.15	.07	.02
□ 53 Donnie Elliott	.15	.07	.02
□ 54 Jim Converse	.15	.07	.02
□ 55 Ray Holbert	.15	.07	.02
□ 56 Keith Lockhart	.15	.07	.02
□ 57 Tony Longmire	.15	.07	.02
□ 58 Jorge Fabregas	.15	.07	.02
□ 59 Ravelo Manzanillo	.15	.07	.02
□ 60 Marcus Moore	.15	.07	.02
□ 61 Carlos Rodriguez	.15	.07	.02
□ 62 Mark Portugal	.15	.07	.02
□ 63 Yorkis Perez	.15	.07	.02
□ 64 Dan Miceli	.15	.07	.02
□ 65 Chris Turner	.15	.07	.02
□ 66 Mike Oquist	.15	.07	.02
□ 67 Tom Quinlan	.15	.07	.02
□ 68 Matt Walbeck	.15	.07	.02
□ 69 Dave Staton	.15	.07	.02
□ 70 Wm.VanLandingham	.30	.14	.04
□ 71 Dave Stevens	.15	.07	.02
□ 72 Domingo Cedeno	.15	.07	.02
□ 73 Alex Diaz	.15	.07	.02
□ 74 Darren Bragg	.30	.14	.04
□ 75 James Hurst	.15	.07	.02
□ 76 Alex Gonzalez	.30	.14	.04
□ 77 Steve Dreyer	.15	.07	.02
□ 78 Robert Eenhoorn	.15	.07	.02
□ 79 Derek Parks	.15	.07	.02
□ 80 Jose Valentin	.30	.14	.04
□ 81 Wes Chamberlain	.15	.07	.02
□ 82 Tony Tarasco	.15	.07	.02
□ 83 Steve Traschel	.30	.14	.04
□ 84 Willie Banks	.15	.07	.02
□ 85 Rob Butler	.15	.07	.02
□ 86 Miguel Jimenez	.15	.07	.02
□ 87 Gerald Williams	.15	.07	.02
□ 88 Aaron Small	.15	.07	.02
□ 89 Matt Mieske	.15	.07	.02
□ 90 Tim Hyers	.15	.07	.02
□ 91 Eddie Murray	1.25	.55	.16
□ 92 Dennis Martinez	.30	.14	.04
□ 93 Tony Eusebio	.15	.07	.02

□ 94 Brian Anderson	.30	.14	.04
□ 95 Blaise Ilsley	.15	.07	.02
□ 96 Johnny Ruffin	.15	.07	.02
□ 97 Carlos Reyes	.15	.07	.02
□ 98 Greg Pirkl	.15	.07	.02
□ 99 Jack Morris	.30	.14	.04
□ 100 John Mabry	1.00	.45	.12
□ 101 Mike Kelly	.15	.07	.02
□ 102 Rich Becker	.30	.14	.04
□ 103 Chris Gomez	.15	.07	.02
□ 104 Jim Edmonds	1.00	.45	.12
□ 105 Rich Rowland	.15	.07	.02
□ 106 Damon Buford	.15	.07	.02
□ 107 Mark Kiefer	.15	.07	.02
□ 108 Matias Carrillo	.15	.07	.02
□ 109 James Mouton	.30	.14	.04
□ 110 Kelly Stinnett	.15	.07	.02
□ 111 Billy Ashley	.15	.07	.02
□ 112 Fausto Cruz	.15	.07	.02
□ 113 Roberto Petagine	.30	.14	.04
□ 114 Joe Hall	.15	.07	.02
□ 115 Brian Johnson	.15	.07	.02
□ 116 Kevin Jarvis	.15	.07	.02
□ 117 Tim Davis	.15	.07	.02
□ 118 John Patterson	.15	.07	.02
□ 119 Stan Royer	.15	.07	.02
□ 120 Jeff Juden	.15	.07	.02
□ 121 Bryan Eversgerd	.15	.07	.02
□ 122 Chan Ho Park	1.25	.55	.16
□ 123 Shane Reynolds	.30	.14	.04
□ 124 Danny Bautista	.15	.07	.02
□ 125 Rikkert Faneyte	.15	.07	.02
□ 126 Carlos Pulido	.15	.07	.02
□ 127 Mike Matheny	.15	.07	.02
□ 128 Hector Carrasco	.15	.07	.02
□ 129 Eddie Zambrano	.15	.07	.02
□ 130 Lee Tinsley	.30	.14	.04
□ 131 Roger Salkeld	.15	.07	.02
□ 132 Carlos Delgado	1.00	.45	.12
□ 133 Troy O'Leary	.15	.07	.02
□ 134 Keith Mitchell	.15	.07	.02
□ 135 Lance Painter	.15	.07	.02
□ 136 Nate Minchey	.15	.07	.02
□ 137 Eric Anthony	.15	.07	.02
□ 138 Rafael Bournigal	.15	.07	.02
□ 139 Joey Hamilton	1.00	.45	.12
□ 140 Bobby Munoz	.15	.07	.02
□ 141 Rex Hudler	.15	.07	.02
□ 142 Alex Cole	.15	.07	.02
□ 143 Stan Javier	.15	.07	.02
□ 144 Jose Oliva	.30	.14	.04
□ 145 Tom Brunansky	.15	.07	.02
□ 146 Greg Colbrunn	.15	.07	.02
□ 147 Luis S.Lopez	.15	.07	.02
□ 148 Alex Rodriguez	15.00	6.75	1.85
□ 149 Darryl Strawberry	.30	.14	.04
□ 150 Bo Jackson	.60	.25	.07
□ R01 R.Klesko ROY M.Ramirez	25.00	11.00	3.10

1994 Sportflics R/T Artist's Proofs

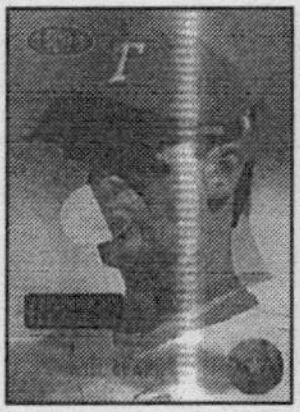

This set of cards mirrors the 150 regular issue rookie/traded cards and are embellished with the gold foil "Artist's Proof" stamp. They were randomly inserted in at a rate of one in 24.

	MINT	NRMT	EXC
COMPLETE SET (150)	2400.00	1100.00	300.00
COMMON CARD (1-150)	10.00	4.50	1.25
SEMISTARS	15.00	6.75	1.85
STARS	30.00	13.50	3.70
*VETERAN STARS: 40X TO 60X BASIC CARDS			
*YOUNG STARS: 25X TO 40X BASIC CARDS			
RANDOM INSERTS IN PACKS			
□ 1 Will Clark	50.00	22.00	6.25
□ 26 Rafael Palmeiro	50.00	22.00	6.25
□ 31 Brian L.Hunter	40.00	18.00	5.00
□ 91 Eddie Murray	100.00	45.00	12.50
□ 100 John Mabry	30.00	13.50	3.70
□ 104 Jim Edmonds	60.00	27.00	7.50
□ 122 Chan Ho Park	40.00	18.00	5.00
□ 132 Carlos Delgado	40.00	18.00	5.00
□ 139 Joey Hamilton	50.00	22.00	6.25
□ 148 Alex Rodriguez	600.00	275.00	75.00

1994 Sportflics R/T Going Going Gone

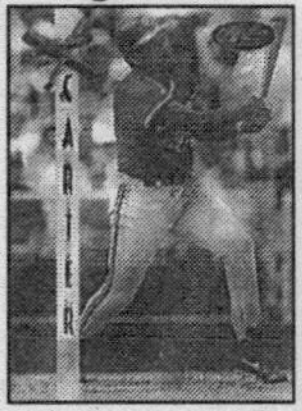

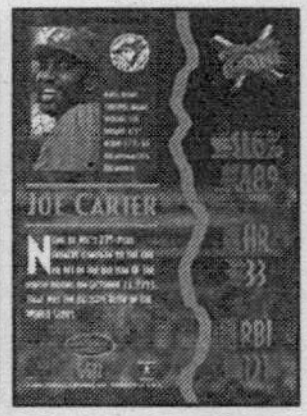

Randomly inserted in packs at a rate of one in 18, this 12-card set features big hitters. Sportflics used its "Magic Mirror" technology to produce two images when the card is tilted. The Going, Going, Gone logo is placed at the top left of the front and a gold strip runs vertically on the left side. The player's name is printed in black on top of the gold strip. It expands and contracts when the card is moved. Borderless backs are numbered with the prefix "GG" and have a dark background containing a blurred stadium. The player's close-up picture is bordered with a biography box and name on the left. The playerís slugging percentage, number of home runs and RBI totals are printed on the right side of the back with a shadow effect.

	MINT	NRMT	EXC
COMPLETE SET (12)	90.00	40.00	11.00
COMMON CARD (GG1-GG12)	3.00	1.35	.35
RANDOM INSERTS IN PACKS			
□ GG1 Gary Sheffield	4.00	1.80	.50
□ GG2 Matt Williams	5.00	2.20	.60
□ GG3 Juan Gonzalez	12.00	5.50	1.50
□ GG4 Ken Griffey Jr.	25.00	11.00	3.10
□ GG5 Mike Piazza	15.00	6.75	1.85
□ GG6 Frank Thomas	25.00	11.00	3.10
□ GG7 Tim Salmon	5.00	2.20	.60
□ GG8 Barry Bonds	6.00	2.70	.75
□ GG9 Fred McGriff	4.00	1.80	.50
□ GG10 Cecil Fielder	3.00	1.35	.35
□ GG11 Albert Belle	12.00	5.50	1.50
□ GG12 Joe Carter	3.00	1.35	.35

1994 Sportflics R/T Rookie Starflics

Randomly inserted in packs at a rate of one in 36, these 3-D cards highlight the rookie sensations of 1994. Horizontal fronts feature the player in a full-color action shot with a smaller, mirror image of the player set off in the blue back

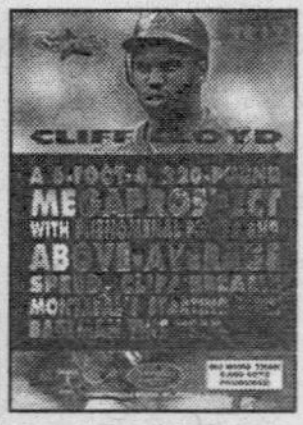

ground. The Starflics logo, player's name and team logo are printed on the left side of the front. Backs are borderless and carry full-color action shots of the player. The player's name is printed in gold foil and a player background is printed with reverse type on gold foil.

	MINT	NRMT	EXC
COMPLETE SET (18)	225.00	100.00	28.00
COMMON CARD (TR1-TR18)	5.00	2.20	.60
SEMISTARS	8.00	3.60	1.00
RANDOM INSERTS IN PACKS			
□ TR1 John Hudek	5.00	2.20	.60
□ TR2 Manny Ramirez	30.00	13.50	3.70
□ TR3 Jeffrey Hammonds	8.00	3.60	1.00
□ TR4 Carlos Delgado	12.00	5.50	1.50
□ TR5 Javier Lopez	12.00	5.50	1.50
□ TR6 Alex Gonzalez	8.00	3.60	1.00
□ TR7 Raul Mondesi	15.00	6.75	1.85
□ TR8 Bob Hamelin	5.00	2.20	.60
□ TR9 Ryan Klesko	25.00	11.00	3.10
□ TR10 Brian Anderson	5.00	2.20	.60
□ TR11 Alex Rodriguez	100.00	45.00	12.50
□ TR12 Cliff Floyd	8.00	3.60	1.00
□ TR13 Chan Ho Park	8.00	3.60	1.00
□ TR14 Steve Karsay	5.00	2.20	.60
□ TR15 Rondell White	10.00	4.50	1.25
□ TR16 Shawn Green	8.00	3.60	1.00
□ TR17 Rich Becker	5.00	2.20	.60
□ TR18 Charles Johnson	8.00	3.60	1.00

1995 Sportflix

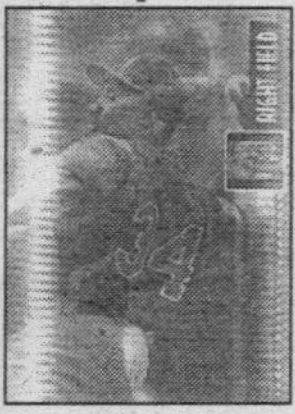

This 170 card standard-size set was released by Pinnacle brands. The set was issued in 5 card packs that had a suggested retail price of $1.89 per pack. Thirty-six of these packs are contained in a full box. Jumbo packs were also issued: these packs contained 8 cards per pack and had 36 packs in a box. These cards feature Pinnacle's "Magic Motion" printing which shows the player in two different action shots when the card is tilted. The player's position is printed diagonally on the top right with the team logo underneath. Horizontal backs feature a full-color player photo on the right. The cards are numbered in the upper right corner. Subsets include a rookies section (141-165) and a checklist grouping (166-170). There are no key Rookie Cards in this set.

	MINT	NRMT	EXC
COMPLETE SET (170)	20.00	9.00	2.50
COMMON CARD (1-170)	.10	.05	.01
SEMISTARS	.25	.11	.03
STARS	.50	.23	.06
COMPLETE AP SET (170)	1000.00	450.00	125.00
COMMON AP (1-170)	3.00	1.35	.35
AP SEMISTARS	6.00	2.70	.75
*AP VETERAN STARS: 18X TO 30X HI			
*AP YOUNG STARS: 15X TO 25X HI			
AP: RANDOM INSERTS IN PACKS			
□ 1 Ken Griffey Jr.	3.00	1.35	.35
□ 2 Jeffrey Hammonds	.25	.11	.03
□ 3 Fred McGriff	.50	.23	.06
□ 4 Rickey Henderson	.50	.23	.06
□ 5 Derrick May	.10	.05	.01
□ 6 Robin Ventura	.25	.11	.03
□ 7 Royce Clayton	.10	.05	.01
□ 8 Paul Molitor	.60	.25	.07
□ 9 Charlie Hayes	.10	.05	.01
□ 10 David Nied	.10	.05	.01
□ 11 Ellis Burks	.50	.23	.06
□ 12 Bernard Gilkey	.25	.11	.03
□ 13 Don Mattingly	1.50	.70	.19
□ 14 Albert Belle	1.50	.70	.19
□ 15 Doug Drabek	.10	.05	.01
□ 16 Tony Gwynn	1.25	.55	.16
□ 17 Delino DeShields	.10	.05	.01
□ 18 Bobby Bonilla	.25	.11	.03
□ 19 Cliff Floyd	.25	.11	.03
□ 20 Frank Thomas	3.00	1.35	.35
□ 21 Raul Mondesi	.50	.23	.06
□ 22 Dave Nilsson	.25	.11	.03
□ 23 Todd Zeile	.10	.05	.01
□ 24 Bernie Williams	.50	.23	.06
□ 25 Kirby Puckett	1.00	.45	.12
□ 26 David Cone	.25	.11	.03
□ 27 Darren Daulton	.25	.11	.03
□ 28 Marquis Grissom	.50	.23	.06
□ 29 Randy Johnson	.50	.23	.06
□ 30 Jeff Kent	.10	.05	.01
□ 31 Orlando Merced	.10	.05	.01
□ 32 Dave Justice	.50	.23	.06
□ 33 Ivan Rodriguez	.60	.25	.07
□ 34 Kirk Gibson	.25	.11	.03
□ 35 Alex Fernandez	.25	.11	.03
□ 36 Rick Wilkins	.10	.05	.01
□ 37 Andy Benes	.10	.05	.01
□ 38 Bret Saberhagen	.25	.11	.03
□ 39 Billy Ashley	.10	.05	.01
□ 40 Jose Rijo	.10	.05	.01
□ 41 Matt Williams	.50	.23	.06
□ 42 Lenny Dykstra	.25	.11	.03
□ 43 Jay Bell	.25	.11	.03
□ 44 Reggie Jefferson	.25	.11	.03
□ 45 Greg Maddux	2.00	.90	.25
□ 46 Gary Sheffield	.50	.23	.06
□ 47 Bret Boone	.25	.11	.03
□ 48 Jeff Bagwell	1.25	.55	.16
□ 49 Ben McDonald	.10	.05	.01
□ 50 Eric Karros	.25	.11	.03
□ 51 Roger Clemens	.50	.23	.06
□ 52 Sammy Sosa	.50	.23	.06
□ 53 Barry Bonds	.75	.35	.09
□ 54 Joey Hamilton	.25	.11	.03
□ 55 Brian Jordan	.50	.23	.06
□ 56 Wil Cordero	.10	.05	.01
□ 57 Aaron Sele	.25	.11	.03
□ 58 Paul O'Neill	.25	.11	.03
□ 59 Carlos Garcia	.10	.05	.01
□ 60 Mike Mussina	.60	.25	.07
□ 61 John Olerud	.10	.05	.01
□ 62 Kevin Appier	.25	.11	.03
□ 63 Matt Mieske	.25	.11	.03
□ 64 Carlos Baerga	.50	.23	.06
□ 65 Ryan Klesko	.60	.25	.07
□ 66 Jimmy Key	.25	.11	.03
□ 67 James Mouton	.10	.05	.01
□ 68 Tim Salmon	.50	.23	.06
□ 69 Hal Morris	.10	.05	.01
□ 70 Albie Lopez	.10	.05	.01
□ 71 Dave Hollins	.10	.05	.01
□ 72 Greg Colbrunn	.10	.05	.01
□ 73 Juan Gonzalez	1.50	.70	.19
□ 74 Wally Joyner	.25	.11	.03
□ 75 Bob Hamelin	.10	.05	.01
□ 76 Brady Anderson	.50	.23	.06
□ 77 Deion Sanders	.50	.23	.06

□ 78	Javier Lopez	.50	.23	.06
□ 79	Brian McRae	.25	.11	.03
□ 80	Craig Biggio	.50	.23	.06
□ 81	Kenny Lofton	.75	.35	.09
□ 82	Cecil Fielder	.25	.11	.03
□ 83	Mike Piazza	2.00	.90	.25
□ 84	Rafael Palmeiro	.50	.23	.06
□ 85	Jim Thome	.60	.25	.07
□ 86	Ruben Sierra	.25	.11	.03
□ 87	Mark Langston	.10	.05	.01
□ 88	John Valentin	.25	.11	.03
□ 89	Shawon Dunston	.10	.05	.01
□ 90	Travis Fryman	.25	.11	.03
□ 91	Chuck Knoblauch	.50	.23	.06
□ 92	Dean Palmer	.25	.11	.03
□ 93	Robby Thompson	.10	.05	.01
□ 94	Barry Larkin	.50	.23	.06
□ 95	Darren Lewis	.10	.05	.01
□ 96	Andres Galarraga	.50	.23	.06
□ 97	Tony Phillips	.25	.11	.03
□ 98	Mo Vaughn	.75	.35	.09
□ 99	Pedro Martinez	.25	.11	.03
□ 100	Chad Curtis	.10	.05	.01
□ 101	Brent Gates	.10	.05	.01
□ 102	Pat Hentgen	.25	.11	.03
□ 103	Rico Brogna	.10	.05	.01
□ 104	Carlos Delgado	.50	.23	.06
□ 105	Manny Ramirez	.75	.35	.09
□ 106	Mike Greenwell	.10	.05	.01
□ 107	Wade Boggs	.50	.23	.06
□ 108	Ozzie Smith	.60	.25	.07
□ 109	Rusty Greer	.50	.23	.06
□ 110	Willie Greene	.10	.05	.01
□ 111	Chili Davis	.25	.11	.03
□ 112	Reggie Sanders	.25	.11	.03
□ 113	Roberto Kelly	.10	.05	.01
□ 114	Tom Glavine	.50	.23	.06
□ 115	Moises Alou	.25	.11	.03
□ 116	Dennis Eckersley	.25	.11	.03
□ 117	Danny Tartabull	.10	.05	.01
□ 118	Jeff Conine	.50	.23	.06
□ 119	Will Clark	.50	.23	.06
□ 120	Joe Carter	.50	.23	.06
□ 121	Mark McGwire	1.00	.45	.12
□ 122	Cal Ripken Jr.	2.50	1.10	.30
□ 123	Danny Jackson	.10	.05	.01
□ 124	Phil Plantier	.10	.05	.01
□ 125	Dante Bichette	.50	.23	.06
□ 126	Jack McDowell	.25	.11	.03
□ 127	Jose Canseco	.50	.23	.06
□ 128	Roberto Alomar	.75	.35	.09
□ 129	Rondell White	.50	.23	.06
□ 130	Ray Lankford	.50	.23	.06
□ 131	Ryan Thompson	.10	.05	.01
□ 132	Ken Caminiti	.50	.23	.06
□ 133	Gregg Jefferies	.25	.11	.03
□ 134	Omar Vizquel	.50	.23	.06
□ 135	Mark Grace	.50	.23	.06
□ 136	Derek Bell	.25	.11	.03
□ 137	Mickey Tettleton	.10	.05	.01
□ 138	Wilson Alvarez	.25	.11	.03
□ 139	Larry Walker	.50	.23	.06
□ 140	Bo Jackson	.50	.23	.06
□ 141	Alex Rodriguez	4.00	1.80	.50
□ 142	Orlando Miller	.10	.05	.01
□ 143	Shawn Green	.25	.11	.03
□ 144	Steve Dunn	.10	.05	.01
□ 145	Midre Cummings	.10	.05	.01
□ 146	Chan Ho Park	.50	.23	.06
□ 147	Jose Oliva	.10	.05	.01
□ 148	Armando Benitez	.10	.05	.01
□ 149	J.R. Phillips	.10	.05	.01
□ 150	Charles Johnson	.25	.11	.03
□ 151	Garret Anderson	.50	.23	.06
□ 152	Russ Davis	.10	.05	.01
□ 153	Brian L.Hunter	.50	.23	.06
□ 154	Ernie Young	.25	.11	.03
□ 155	Marc Newfield	.25	.11	.03
□ 156	Greg Pirkl	.10	.05	.01
□ 157	Scott Ruffcorn	.10	.05	.01
□ 158	Rikkert Faneyte	.10	.05	.01
□ 159	Duane Singleton	.10	.05	.01
□ 160	Gabe White	.10	.05	.01
□ 161	Alex Gonzalez	.10	.05	.01
□ 162	Chipper Jones	2.00	.90	.25
□ 163	Mike Kelly	.10	.05	.01
□ 164	Kurt Miller	.10	.05	.01
□ 165	Roberto Petagine	.10	.05	.01
□ 166	Jeff Bagwell CL	.60	.25	.07
□ 167	Mike Piazza CL	1.00	.45	.12
□ 168	Ken Griffey Jr. CL	1.50	.70	.19
□ 169	Frank Thomas CL	1.50	.70	.19
□ 170	Barry Bonds CL Cal Ripken	1.25	.55	.16

1995 Sportflix Detonators

Randomly inserted in packs at a rate of one in 16, this nine-card set highlights power hitters. The player is featured in a full-color cutout action shot atop a gold column with his name inscribed. The background is set back and is lit up with fireworks. The player's team logo and a rocket with the word "Detonators" is printed along the bottom of the card. A blue-sky with a Greek column serves as a backdrop for the borderless backs. A full-color shot of the player is pictured in the column and a short synopsis of the playerís '94 performance is printed in black type on the right side of the back. Backs are numbered with the prefix "DE".

		MINT	NRMT	EXC
COMPLETE SET (9)		30.00	13.50	3.70
COMMON CARD (1-9)		1.00	.45	.12
RANDOM INSERTS IN PACKS				
□ DE1	Jeff Bagwell	4.00	1.80	.50
□ DE2	Matt Williams	1.50	.70	.19
□ DE3	Ken Griffey Jr.	10.00	4.50	1.25
□ DE4	Frank Thomas	10.00	4.50	1.25
□ DE5	Mike Piazza	6.00	2.70	.75
□ DE6	Barry Bonds	2.50	1.10	.30
□ DE7	Albert Belle	5.00	2.20	.60
□ DE8	Cliff Floyd	1.00	.45	.12
□ DE9	Juan Gonzalez	5.00	2.20	.60

1995 Sportflix Double Take

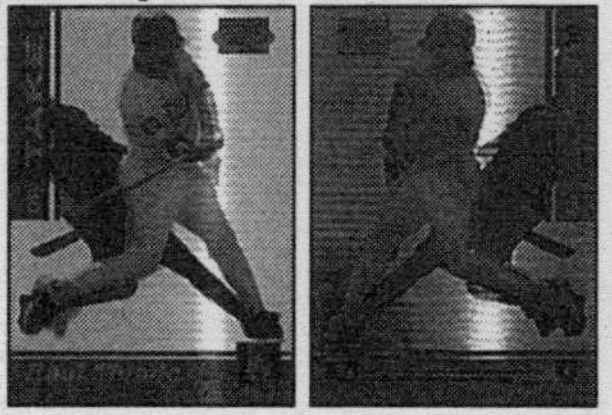

Randomly inserted in packs at a rate of one in 48, this 12-card set features two stars in one see-through 3-D card. Fronts feature the Sportflix "Magic Motion" process that allows the viewer to see two different images when the card is tilted. The players' names are reverse-printed across a red bar with the corresponding team logo on the bottom right. When the card is titled, the player's picture, name and team logo appear. "Double Take" is printed vertically on

the left side of the card. Backs are see through and contain only the card number.

	MINT	NRMT	EXC
COMPLETE SET (12)	150.00	70.00	19.00
COMMON CARD (1-12)	5.00	2.20	.60
RANDOM INSERTS IN PACKS			

	MINT	NRMT	EXC
□ 1 Jeff Bagwell / Frank Thomas	30.00	13.50	3.70
□ 2 Will Clark / Fred McGriff	5.00	2.20	.60
□ 3 Roberto Alomar / Jeff Kent	5.00	2.20	.60
□ 4 Matt Williams / Wade Boggs	5.00	2.20	.60
□ 5 Cal Ripken Jr. / Ozzie Smith	20.00	9.00	2.50
□ 6 Alex Rodriguez / Wil Cordero	20.00	9.00	2.50
□ 7 Mike Piazza / Carlos Delgado	15.00	6.75	1.85
□ 8 Kenny Lofton / Dave Justice	6.00	2.70	.75
□ 9 Barry Bonds / Ken Griffey Jr.	25.00	11.00	3.10
□ 10 Albert Belle / Raul Mondesi	12.00	5.50	1.50
□ 11 Tony Gwynn / Kirby Puckett	15.00	6.75	1.85
□ 12 Jimmy Key / Greg Maddux	12.00	5.50	1.50

1995 Sportflix Hammer Team

This 18-card set was inserted randomly in packs at a rate of one in 48 and looks at the league's top hitters. The 3-D fronts feature a full-color cutout of the player in action set against a backdrop of blue sky and basepaths. Sledgehammers are placed in the foreground and background of the fronts, while the player's name is printed at the bottom of the card against a green grass background. Full-bleed, horizontal backs are numbered with the prefix "HT" and picture the player in full color. A swinging sledgehammer is in motion against a backdrop of green grass while a 1994 player synopsis is printed in white type underneath the hammer.

	MINT	NRMT	EXC
COMPLETE SET (18)	25.00	11.00	3.10
COMMON CARD (1-18)	.50	.23	.06
RANDOM INSERTS IN PACKS			

	MINT	NRMT	EXC
□ HT1 Ken Griffey Jr.	5.00	2.20	.60
□ HT2 Frank Thomas	5.00	2.20	.60
□ HT3 Jeff Bagwell	2.00	.90	.25
□ HT4 Mike Piazza	3.00	1.35	.35
□ HT5 Cal Ripken Jr.	4.00	1.80	.50
□ HT6 Albert Belle	2.50	1.10	.30
□ HT7 Barry Bonds	1.25	.55	.16
□ HT8 Don Mattingly	2.50	1.10	.30
□ HT9 Will Clark	.75	.35	.09
□ HT10 Tony Gwynn	2.00	.90	.25
□ HT11 Matt Williams	.75	.35	.09
□ HT12 Kirby Puckett	1.50	.70	.19
□ HT13 Manny Ramirez	1.25	.55	.16
□ HT14 Fred McGriff	.75	.35	.09
□ HT15 Juan Gonzalez	2.50	1.10	.30
□ HT16 Kenny Lofton	1.25	.55	.16
□ HT17 Raul Mondesi	.50	.23	.06
□ HT18 Tim Salmon	.50	.23	.06

1995 Sportflix ProMotion

Randomly inserted in jumbo packs at a rate of one in 18, this 12-card set features top stars in the "Magic Motion" technology. Card fronts are coordinated in team colors and depict the player in a full-color action photo. The player's team logo is displayed when tilted. The horizontal backs feature the player in an action shot and are numbered with the prefix "PM". The player's name appears in white type across the top while the "Pro-Motion" logo is printed in black across the bottom of the back.

	MINT	NRMT	EXC
COMPLETE SET (12)	150.00	70.00	19.00
COMMPN CARD (PM1-PM12)	5.00	2.20	.60
RANDOM INSERTS IN JUMBOS			

	MINT	NRMT	EXC
□ PM1 Ken Griffey Jr.	40.00	18.00	5.00
□ PM2 Frank Thomas	40.00	18.00	5.00
□ PM3 Cal Ripken Jr.	30.00	13.50	3.70
□ PM4 Jeff Bagwell	15.00	6.75	1.85
□ PM5 Mike Piazza	25.00	11.00	3.10
□ PM6 Matt Williams	5.00	2.20	.60
□ PM7 Albert Belle	20.00	9.00	2.50
□ PM8 Jose Canseco	5.00	2.20	.60
□ PM9 Don Mattingly	20.00	9.00	2.50
□ PM10 Barry Bonds	10.00	4.50	1.25
□ PM11 Will Clark	5.00	2.20	.60
□ PM12 Kirby Puckett	12.00	5.50	1.50

1996 Sportflix

With retail only distribution, this 144 card set comes in five card packs that retail for $1.99. The set contains the UC3 Subset (97-120), Rookies Subset (121-141), and Checklists (142-144). Regular cards picture two different pieces of photography. By flicking the wrist, one image disappears and another appears. Some cards use two different photos, and others use sequence action photography to create the illusion of animation. The wording in the bottom border also changes with movement. The UC3 Subset features veteran superstars in 3-D ani-

mation. The 21-card Rookie subset carries color player photos on a background of part of a baseball that changes into a wooden baseball bat section when moved. The backs carry player information.

	MINT	NRMT	EXC
COMPLETE SET (144)	30.00	13.50	3.70
COMMON CARD (1-144)	.10	.05	.01
SEMISTARS	.25	.11	.03
STARS	.50	.23	.06

□ 1 Wade Boggs	.50	.23	.06
□ 2 Tim Salmon	.50	.23	.06
□ 3 Will Clark	.50	.23	.06
□ 4 Dante Bichette	.50	.23	.06
□ 5 Barry Bonds	.75	.35	.09
□ 6 Kirby Puckett	1.00	.45	.12
□ 7 Albert Belle	1.50	.70	.19
□ 8 Greg Maddux	2.00	.90	.25
□ 9 Tony Gwynn	1.25	.55	.16
□ 10 Mike Piazza	2.00	.90	.25
□ 11 Ivan Rodriguez	.60	.25	.07
□ 12 Marty Cordova	.50	.23	.06
□ 13 Frank Thomas	3.00	1.35	.35
□ 14 Raul Mondesi	.50	.23	.06
□ 15 Johnny Damon	.25	.11	.03
□ 16 Mark McGwire	1.00	.45	.12
□ 17 Len Dykstra	.25	.11	.03
□ 18 Ken Griffey Jr.	3.00	1.35	.35
□ 19 Chipper Jones	2.00	.90	.25
□ 20 Alex Rodriguez	3.00	1.35	.35
□ 21 Jeff Bagwell	1.25	.55	.16
□ 22 Jim Edmonds	.50	.23	.06
□ 23 Edgar Martinez	.50	.23	.06
□ 24 David Cone	.50	.23	.06
□ 25 Tom Glavine	.50	.23	.06
□ 26 Eddie Murray	.75	.35	.09
□ 27 Paul Molitor	.60	.25	.07
□ 28 Ryan Klesko	.60	.25	.07
□ 29 Rafael Palmeiro	.50	.23	.06
□ 30 Manny Ramirez	.75	.35	.09
□ 31 Mo Vaughn	.75	.35	.09
□ 32 Rico Brogna	.10	.05	.01
□ 33 Marc Newfield	.25	.11	.03
□ 34 J.T. Snow	.25	.11	.03
□ 35 Reggie Sanders	.50	.23	.06
□ 36 Fred McGriff	.50	.23	.06
□ 37 Craig Biggio	.50	.23	.06
□ 38 Jeff King	.25	.11	.03
□ 39 Kenny Lofton	.75	.35	.09
□ 40 Gary Gaetti	.25	.11	.03
□ 41 Eric Karros	.10	.05	.01
□ 42 Jason Isringhausen	.10	.05	.01
□ 43 B.J. Surhoff	.10	.05	.01
□ 44 Michael Tucker	.10	.05	.01
□ 45 Gary Sheffield	.50	.23	.06
□ 46 Chili Davis	.10	.05	.01
□ 47 Bobby Bonilla	.50	.23	.06
□ 48 Hideo Nomo	.75	.35	.09
□ 49 Ray Durham	.50	.23	.06
□ 50 Phil Nevin	.10	.05	.01
□ 51 Randy Johnson	.50	.23	.06
□ 52 Bill Pulsipher	.10	.05	.01
□ 53 Ozzie Smith	.60	.25	.07
□ 54 Cal Ripken	2.50	1.10	.30
□ 55 Cecil Fielder	.50	.23	.06
□ 56 Matt Williams	.50	.23	.06
□ 57 Sammy Sosa	.50	.23	.06
□ 58 Roger Clemens	.50	.23	.06
□ 59 Brian L.Hunter	.10	.05	.01
□ 60 Barry Larkin	.50	.23	.06
□ 61 Charles Johnson	.10	.05	.01
□ 62 David Justice	.25	.11	.03
□ 63 Garret Anderson	.50	.23	.06
□ 64 Rondell White	.50	.23	.06
□ 65 Derek Bell	.25	.11	.03
□ 66 Andres Galarraga	.50	.23	.06
□ 67 Moises Alou	.25	.11	.03
□ 68 Travis Fryman	.50	.23	.06
□ 69 Pedro J. Martinez	.25	.11	.03
□ 70 Carlos Baerga	.50	.23	.06
□ 71 John Valentin	.25	.11	.03
□ 72 Larry Walker	.50	.23	.06
□ 73 Roberto Alomar	.75	.35	.09
□ 74 Mike Mussina	.60	.25	.07
□ 75 Kevin Appier	.25	.11	.03
□ 76 Bernie Williams	.50	.23	.06
□ 77 Ray Lankford	.50	.23	.06
□ 78 Gregg Jefferies	.50	.23	.06
□ 79 Robin Ventura	.50	.23	.06
□ 80 Kenny Rogers	.10	.05	.01
□ 81 Paul O'Neill	.10	.05	.01
□ 82 Mark Grace	.50	.23	.06
□ 83 Deion Sanders	.50	.23	.06
□ 84 Tino Martinez	.50	.23	.06
□ 85 Joe Carter	.50	.23	.06
□ 86 Pete Schourek	.10	.05	.01
□ 87 Jack McDowell	.50	.23	.06
□ 88 John Mabry	.50	.23	.06
□ 89 Darren Daulton	.25	.11	.03
□ 90 Jim Thome	.60	.25	.07
□ 91 Jay Buhner	.50	.23	.06
□ 92 Jay Bell	.10	.05	.01
□ 93 Kevin Seitzer	.10	.05	.01
□ 94 Jose Canseco	.50	.23	.06
□ 95 Juan Gonzalez	1.50	.70	.19
□ 96 Jeff Conine	.50	.23	.06
□ 97 Chipper Jones UC3	1.00	.45	.12
□ 98 Ken Griffey Jr. UC3	1.50	.70	.19
□ 99 Frank Thomas UC3	1.50	.70	.19
□ 100 Cal Ripken UC3	1.25	.55	.16
□ 101 Albert Belle UC3	.75	.35	.09
□ 102 Mike Piazza UC3	1.00	.45	.12
□ 103 Dante Bichette UC3	.25	.11	.03
□ 104 Sammy Sosa UC3	.50	.23	.06
□ 105 Mo Vaughn UC3	.50	.23	.06
□ 106 Tim Salmon UC3	.25	.11	.03
□ 107 Reggie Sanders UC3	.10	.05	.01
□ 108 Gary Sheffield UC3	.50	.23	.06
□ 109 Ruben Rivera UC3	.25	.11	.03
□ 110 Rafael Palmeiro UC3	.50	.23	.06
□ 111 Edgar Martinez UC3	.50	.23	.06
□ 112 Barry Bonds UC3	.50	.23	.06
□ 113 Manny Ramirez UC3	.25	.11	.03
□ 114 Larry Walker UC3	.25	.11	.03
□ 115 Jeff Bagwell UC3	.60	.25	.07
□ 116 Matt Williams UC3	.50	.23	.06
□ 117 Mark McGwire UC3	.50	.23	.06
□ 118 Johnny Damon UC3	.10	.05	.01
□ 119 Eddie Murray UC3	.50	.23	.06
□ 120 Jay Buhner UC3	.25	.11	.03
□ 121 Tim Unroe	.10	.05	.01
□ 122 Todd Hollandsworth	.50	.23	.06
□ 123 Tony Clark	.50	.23	.06
□ 124 Roger Cedeno	.25	.11	.03
□ 125 Jim Pittsley	.10	.05	.01
□ 126 Ruben Rivera	.60	.25	.07
□ 127 Bob Wolcott	.10	.05	.01
□ 128 Chan Ho Park	.50	.23	.06
□ 129 Chris Snopek	.10	.05	.01
□ 130 Alex Ochoa	.25	.11	.03
□ 131 Yamil Benitez	.10	.05	.01
□ 132 Jimmy Haynes	.10	.05	.01
□ 133 Dustin Hermanson	.25	.11	.03
□ 134 Shawn Estes	.25	.11	.03
□ 135 Howard Battle	.10	.05	.01
□ 136 Matt Lawton	.10	.05	.01
□ 137 Terrell Wade	.50	.23	.06
□ 138 Jason Schmidt	.25	.11	.03
□ 139 Derek Jeter	2.00	.90	.25
□ 140 Shannon Stewart	.10	.05	.01
□ 141 Chris Stynes	.10	.05	.01
□ 142 Ken Griffey Jr. CL	1.50	.70	.19
□ 143 Greg Maddux CL	1.00	.45	.12
□ 144 Cal Ripken CL	1.25	.55	.16

1996 Sportflix Artist's Proofs

Inserted at the rate of one in 30, this 144-card set is parallel to the regular set. A gold-foil stamped Artist's Proof logo distinguishes it.

	MINT	NRMT	EXC
COMPLETE SET (144)	1200.00	550.00	150.00
COMMON CARD (1-144)	3.00	1.35	.35
SEMISTARS	10.00	4.50	1.25
STARS	20.00	9.00	2.50
*STARS: 25X TO 40X HI COLUMN			

*YOUNG STARS: 18X TO 30X HI
RANDOM INSERTS IN PACKS

□ 7 Albert Belle	60.00	27.00	7.50
□ 8 Greg Maddux	80.00	36.00	10.00
□ 10 Mike Piazza	80.00	36.00	10.00
□ 13 Frank Thomas	120.00	55.00	15.00
□ 18 Ken Griffey Jr.	120.00	55.00	15.00
□ 19 Chipper Jones	80.00	36.00	10.00
□ 20 Alex Rodriguez	120.00	55.00	15.00
□ 54 Cal Ripken	100.00	45.00	12.50
□ 95 Juan Gonzalez	60.00	27.00	7.50
□ 98 Ken Griffey Jr. UC3	60.00	27.00	7.50
□ 99 Frank Thomas UC3	60.00	27.00	7.50
□ 139 Derek Jeter	80.00	36.00	10.00
□ 142 Ken Griffey Jr. CL	60.00	27.00	7.50

1996 Sportflix Double Take

Randomly inserted in jumbo packs, this 12-card set features color player photos of 2 players per card that play the same position.

	MINT	NRMT	EXC
COMPLETE SET (12)	125.00	55.00	15.50
COMMON CARD (1-12)	5.00	2.20	.60
RANDOM INSERTS IN JUMBO PACKS			

□ 1 Barry Larkin Cal Ripken	15.00	6.75	1.85
□ 2 Roberto Alomar Craig Biggio	5.00	2.20	.60
□ 3 Chipper Jones Matt Williams	12.00	5.50	1.50
□ 4 Ken Griffey Ruben Rivera	20.00	9.00	2.50
□ 5 Greg Maddux Hideo Nomo	12.00	5.50	1.50
□ 6 Frank Thomas Mo Vaughn	20.00	9.00	2.50
□ 7 Ivan Rodriguez Mike Piazza	12.00	5.50	1.50
□ 8 Albert Belle Barry Bonds	12.00	5.50	1.50
□ 9 Alex Rodriguez Derek Jeter	25.00	11.00	3.10
□ 10 Kirby Puckett Tony Gwynn	12.00	5.50	1.50
□ 11 Manny Ramirez Sammy Sosa	6.00	2.70	.75
□ 12 Jeff Bagwell Rico Brogna	6.00	2.70	.75

1996 Sportflix Hit Parade

With an insertion rate of one in 35, this 16-card set features color player photos of hitters in 3D with a background scene in full-motion animation.

	MINT	NRMT	EXC
COMPLETE SET (16)	125.00	55.00	15.50
COMMON CARD (1-16)	2.50	1.10	.30
RANDOM INSERTS IN PACKS			

□ 1 Ken Griffey Jr.	20.00	9.00	2.50
□ 2 Cal Ripken	15.00	6.75	1.85
□ 3 Frank Thomas	20.00	9.00	2.50
□ 4 Mike Piazza	12.00	5.50	1.50
□ 5 Mo Vaughn	5.00	2.20	.60
□ 6 Albert Belle	10.00	4.50	1.25
□ 7 Jeff Bagwell	8.00	3.60	1.00
□ 8 Matt Williams	2.50	1.10	.30
□ 9 Sammy Sosa	3.00	1.35	.35
□ 10 Kirby Puckett	6.00	2.70	.75
□ 11 Dante Bichette	2.50	1.10	.30
□ 12 Gary Sheffield	3.00	1.35	.35
□ 13 Tony Gwynn	8.00	3.60	1.00
□ 14 Wade Boggs	2.50	1.10	.30
□ 15 Chipper Jones	12.00	5.50	1.50
□ 16 Barry Bonds	5.00	2.20	.60

1996 Sportflix Power Surge

With an insertion rate of one in 35, this retail only 25-card set is pinted on clear plastic and is a 3-D parallel rendition of the UC3 subset found in the regular Sportflix set.

	MINT	NRMT	EXC
COMPLETE SET (25)	225.00	100.00	28.00
COMMON CARD (1-25)	3.00	1.35	.35
SEMISTARS	5.00	2.20	.60
RANDOM INSERTS IN RETAIL PACKS			

□ 1 Chipper Jones	25.00	11.00	3.10
□ 2 Ken Griffey Jr.	40.00	18.00	5.00
□ 3 Frank Thomas	40.00	18.00	5.00
□ 4 Cal Ripken	30.00	13.50	3.70
□ 5 Albert Belle	20.00	9.00	2.50
□ 6 Mike Piazza	25.00	11.00	3.10
□ 7 Dante Bichette	5.00	2.20	.60
□ 8 Sammy Sosa	6.00	2.70	.75
□ 9 Mo Vaughn	10.00	4.50	1.25
□ 10 Tim Salmon	5.00	2.20	.60
□ 11 Reggie Sanders	3.00	1.35	.35
□ 12 Gary Sheffield	6.00	2.70	.75
□ 13 Ruben Rivera	8.00	3.60	1.00
□ 14 Rafael Palmeiro	5.00	2.20	.60
□ 15 Edgar Martinez	5.00	2.20	.60
□ 16 Barry Bonds	10.00	4.50	1.25
□ 17 Manny Ramirez	10.00	4.50	1.25
□ 18 Larry Walker	3.00	1.35	.35
□ 19 Jeff Bagwell	15.00	6.75	1.85
□ 20 Matt Williams	5.00	2.20	.60
□ 21 Mark McGwire	12.00	5.50	1.50
□ 22 Johnny Damon	3.00	1.35	.35
□ 23 Eddie Murray	10.00	4.50	1.25
□ 24 Jay Buhner	5.00	2.20	.60
□ 25 Kirby Puckett	12.00	5.50	1.50

1996 Sportflix ProMotion

Inserted at the rate of one in 17, this 20-card set uses morphing technology and multi-phase animation to turn a player's photo into a bat, a ball, a glove, or a catcher's mask.

	MINT	NRMT	EXC
COMPLETE SET (20)	100.00	45.00	12.50
COMMON CARD (1-20)	1.00	.45	.12
SEMISTARS	2.00	.90	.25
RANDOM INSERTS IN PACKS			

□ 1 Cal Ripken	12.00	5.50	1.50
□ 2 Greg Maddux	10.00	4.50	1.25
□ 3 Mo Vaughn	4.00	1.80	.50
□ 4 Albert Belle	8.00	3.60	1.00
□ 5 Mike Piazza	10.00	4.50	1.25
□ 6 Ken Griffey Jr.	15.00	6.75	1.85
□ 7 Frank Thomas	15.00	6.75	1.85
□ 8 Jeff Bagwell	6.00	2.70	.75
□ 9 Hideo Nomo	4.00	1.80	.50
□ 10 Chipper Jones	10.00	4.50	1.25
□ 11 Tony Gwynn	6.00	2.70	.75
□ 12 Don Mattingly	8.00	3.60	1.00
□ 13 Dante Bichette	1.00	.45	.12
□ 14 Matt Williams	2.00	.90	.25
□ 15 Manny Ramirez	4.00	1.80	.50
□ 16 Barry Bonds	4.00	1.80	.50
□ 17 Reggie Sanders	1.00	.45	.12
□ 18 Tim Salmon	2.00	.90	.25
□ 19 Ruben Rivera	3.00	1.35	.35
□ 20 Garret Anderson	1.00	.45	.12

1996 SPx

This 1996 SPx set was issued in one series totalling 60 cards. The one-card packs sell for $3.49. Printed on 32 pt. card stock with Holoview technology and a perimeter diecut design, the set features color player photos with a Holography background on the fronts and decorative foil stamping on the back. Two special cards are included in the set: a Ken Griffey

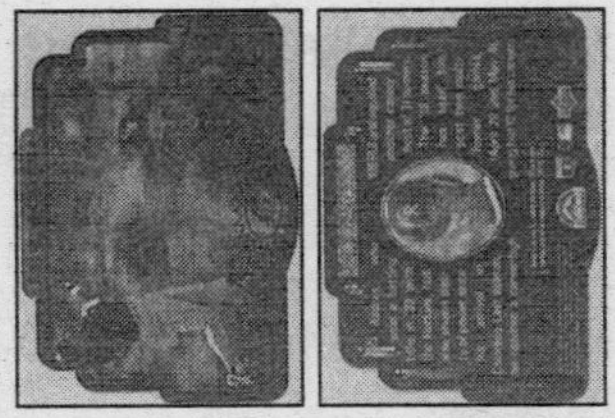

Jr. Commemorative card was inserted one in every 75 packs and a Mike Piazza Tribute card inserted one in every 95 packs. An autographed version of each of these cards was inserted at the rate of one in 2,000.

	MINT	NRMT	EXC
COMPLETE SET (60)	100.00	45.00	12.50
COMMON CARD (1-60)	1.00	.45	.12
SEMISTARS	1.50	.70	.19
COMP.GOLD SET (60)	300.00	135.00	38.00
COMMON GOLD (1-60)	4.00	1.80	.50
*GOLD STARS: 4X BASIC CARDS			
GOLD: RANDOM INSERTS IN PACKS			

□ 1 Greg Maddux	6.00	2.70	.75
□ 2 Chipper Jones	6.00	2.70	.75
□ 3 Fred McGriff	1.50	.70	.19
□ 4 Tom Glavine	1.50	.70	.19
□ 5 Cal Ripken	8.00	3.60	1.00
□ 6 Roberto Alomar	2.50	1.10	.30
□ 7 Rafael Palmeiro	1.50	.70	.19
□ 8 Jose Canseco	1.50	.70	.19
□ 9 Roger Clemens	1.50	.70	.19
□ 10 Mo Vaughn	2.50	1.10	.30
□ 11 Jim Edmonds	1.00	.45	.12
□ 12 Tim Salmon	1.50	.70	.19
□ 13 Sammy Sosa	1.50	.70	.19
□ 14 Ryne Sandberg	2.50	1.10	.30
□ 15 Mark Grace	1.50	.70	.19
□ 16 Frank Thomas	10.00	4.50	1.25
□ 17 Barry Larkin	1.50	.70	.19
□ 18 Kenny Lofton	2.50	1.10	.30
□ 19 Albert Belle	5.00	2.20	.60
□ 20 Eddie Murray	2.50	1.10	.30
□ 21 Manny Ramirez	2.50	1.10	.30
□ 22 Dante Bichette	1.50	.70	.19
□ 23 Larry Walker	1.00	.45	.12
□ 24 Vinny Castilla	1.00	.45	.12
□ 25 Andres Galarraga	1.50	.70	.19
□ 26 Cecil Fielder	1.50	.70	.19
□ 27 Gary Sheffield	1.50	.70	.19
□ 28 Craig Biggio	1.50	.70	.19
□ 29 Jeff Bagwell	4.00	1.80	.50
□ 30 Derek Bell	1.00	.45	.12
□ 31 Johnny Damon	1.00	.45	.12
□ 32 Eric Karros	1.50	.70	.19
□ 33 Mike Piazza	6.00	2.70	.75
□ 34 Raul Mondesi	1.50	.70	.19
□ 35 Hideo Nomo	2.50	1.10	.30
□ 36 Kirby Puckett	3.00	1.35	.35
□ 37 Paul Molitor	1.50	.70	.19
□ 38 Marty Cordova	1.00	.45	.12
□ 39 Rondell White	1.00	.45	.12
□ 40 Jason Isringhausen	1.00	.45	.12
□ 41 Paul Wilson	1.00	.45	.12
□ 42 Rey Ordonez	2.00	.90	.25
□ 43 Derek Jeter	6.00	2.70	.75
□ 44 Wade Boggs	1.50	.70	.19
□ 45 Mark McGwire	3.00	1.35	.35
□ 46 Jason Kendall	1.50	.70	.19
□ 47 Ron Gant	1.50	.70	.19
□ 48 Ozzie Smith	2.00	.90	.25
□ 49 Tony Gwynn	4.00	1.80	.50
□ 50 Ken Caminiti	1.50	.70	.19
□ 51 Barry Bonds	2.50	1.10	.30
□ 52 Matt Williams	1.50	.70	.19
□ 53 Osvaldo Fernandez	1.50	.70	.19
□ 54 Jay Buhner	1.50	.70	.19
□ 55 Ken Griffey Jr.	10.00	4.50	1.25
□ 56 Randy Johnson	1.50	.70	.19
□ 57 Alex Rodriguez	10.00	4.50	1.25
□ 58 Juan Gonzalez	5.00	2.20	.60
□ 59 Joe Carter	1.50	.70	.19
□ 60 Carlos Delgado	1.50	.70	.19
□ KG1 Ken Griffey Jr. Comm.	16.00	7.25	2.00
□ MP1 Mike Piazza Trib.	12.00	5.50	1.50
□ KGAU Ken Griffey Jr. Auto.	300.00	135.00	38.00
□ MPAU Mike Piazza Auto.	200.00	90.00	25.00

1996 SPx Bound for Glory

Randomly inserted in packs at a rate of one in 24, this 10-card set features players with a chance to be long remembered. The fronts display color player photos with a diecut perimeter design and a Holography background. The words, "Bound for Glory" are printed at the top. The backs carry decorative foil stamping.

	MINT	NRMT	EXC
COMPLETE SET (10)	150.00	70.00	19.00
COMMON CARD (1-10)	8.00	3.60	1.00
RANDOM INSERTS IN PACKS			

□ 1 Ken Griffey Jr.	30.00	13.50	3.70
□ 2 Frank Thomas	30.00	13.50	3.70
□ 3 Barry Bonds	8.00	3.60	1.00
□ 4 Cal Ripken	25.00	11.00	3.10
□ 5 Greg Maddux	20.00	9.00	2.50
□ 6 Chipper Jones	20.00	9.00	2.50
□ 7 Roberto Alomar	8.00	3.60	1.00
□ 8 Manny Ramirez	8.00	3.60	1.00
□ 9 Tony Gwynn	12.00	5.50	1.50
□ 10 Mike Piazza	20.00	9.00	2.50

1991 Stadium Club

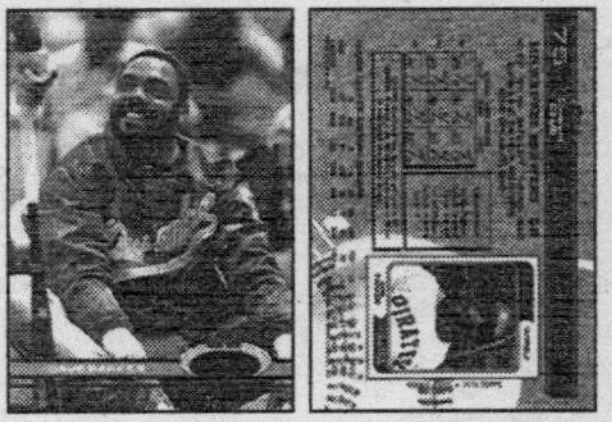

This 600-card standard size set marked Topps first premium quality set. The set was issued in two separate series of 300 cards each. Cards were distributed in plastic wrapped packs. Series II cards were also available at McDonald's restaurants in the Northeast at three cards per pack. The set created a stir in the hobby upon release with dazzling full-color borderless photos and slick, glossy card stock. The back of each card has the basic biographical information as well as making use of the Fastball BARS system and an inset photo of the player's Topps rookie card. Rookie Cards include Jeff Bagwell, Jeff Conine and Brian McRae.

	MINT	NRMT	EXC
COMPLETE SET (600)	90.00	40.00	11.00
COMPLETE SERIES 1 (300)	55.00	25.00	7.00
COMPLETE SERIES 2 (300)	35.00	16.00	4.40
COMMON CARD (1-600)	.15	.07	.02
SEMISTARS	.30	.14	.04
STARS	.60	.25	.07

□ 1 Dave Stewart TUX	.60	.25	.07
□ 2 Wally Joyner	.30	.14	.04
□ 3 Shawon Dunston	.15	.07	.02
□ 4 Darren Daulton	.30	.14	.04
□ 5 Will Clark	.60	.25	.07
□ 6 Sammy Sosa	1.25	.55	.16
□ 7 Dan Plesac	.15	.07	.02
□ 8 Marquis Grissom	.75	.35	.09
□ 9 Erik Hanson	.15	.07	.02
□ 10 Geno Petralli	.15	.07	.02
□ 11 Jose Rijo	.15	.07	.02
□ 12 Carlos Quintana	.15	.07	.02
□ 13 Junior Ortiz	.15	.07	.02
□ 14 Bob Walk	.15	.07	.02
□ 15 Mike Macfarlane	.15	.07	.02
□ 16 Eric Yelding	.15	.07	.02
□ 17 Bryn Smith	.15	.07	.02
□ 18 Bip Roberts	.15	.07	.02
□ 19 Mike Scioscia	.15	.07	.02
□ 20 Mark Williamson	.15	.07	.02
□ 21 Don Mattingly	2.50	1.10	.30
□ 22 John Franco	.15	.07	.02
□ 23 Chet Lemon	.15	.07	.02
□ 24 Tom Henke	.15	.07	.02
□ 25 Jerry Browne	.15	.07	.02
□ 26 Dave Justice	.75	.35	.09
□ 27 Mark Langston	.30	.14	.04
□ 28 Damon Berryhill	.15	.07	.02
□ 29 Kevin Bass	.15	.07	.02
□ 30 Scott Fletcher	.15	.07	.02
□ 31 Moises Alou	.60	.25	.07
□ 32 Dave Valle	.15	.07	.02
□ 33 Jody Reed	.15	.07	.02
□ 34 Dave West	.15	.07	.02
□ 35 Kevin McReynolds	.15	.07	.02
□ 36 Pat Combs	.15	.07	.02
□ 37 Eric Davis	.30	.14	.04
□ 38 Bret Saberhagen	.30	.14	.04
□ 39 Stan Javier	.15	.07	.02
□ 40 Chuck Cary	.15	.07	.02
□ 41 Tony Phillips	.30	.14	.04
□ 42 Lee Smith	.30	.14	.04
□ 43 Tim Teufel	.15	.07	.02
□ 44 Lance Dickson	.15	.07	.02
□ 45 Greg Litton	.15	.07	.02
□ 46 Teddy Higuera	.15	.07	.02
□ 47 Edgar Martinez	.60	.25	.07
□ 48 Steve Avery	.60	.25	.07
□ 49 Walt Weiss	.15	.07	.02
□ 50 David Segui	.30	.14	.04
□ 51 Andy Benes	.15	.07	.02
□ 52 Karl Rhodes	.15	.07	.02
□ 53 Neal Heaton	.15	.07	.02
□ 54 Danny Gladden	.15	.07	.02
□ 55 Luis Rivera	.15	.07	.02
□ 56 Kevin Brown	.30	.14	.04
□ 57 Frank Thomas	10.00	4.50	1.25
□ 58 Terry Mulholland	.15	.07	.02
□ 59 Dick Schofield	.15	.07	.02
□ 60 Ron Darling	.15	.07	.02
□ 61 Sandy Alomar Jr.	.30	.14	.04
□ 62 Dave Stieb	.15	.07	.02
□ 63 Alan Trammell	.60	.25	.07
□ 64 Matt Nokes	.15	.07	.02
□ 65 Lenny Harris	.15	.07	.02
□ 66 Milt Thompson	.15	.07	.02
□ 67 Storm Davis	.15	.07	.02
□ 68 Joe Oliver	.15	.07	.02
□ 69 Andres Galarraga	.60	.25	.07
□ 70 Ozzie Guillen	.15	.07	.02
□ 71 Ken Howell	.15	.07	.02
□ 72 Garry Templeton	.15	.07	.02
□ 73 Derrick May	.15	.07	.02
□ 74 Xavier Hernandez	.15	.07	.02
□ 75 Dave Parker	.30	.14	.04
□ 76 Rick Aguilera	.30	.14	.04
□ 77 Robby Thompson	.15	.07	.02
□ 78 Pete Incaviglia	.15	.07	.02

□ 79 Bob Welch	.15	.07	.02
□ 80 Randy Milligan	.15	.07	.02
□ 81 Chuck Finley	.30	.14	.04
□ 82 Alvin Davis	.15	.07	.02
□ 83 Tim Naehring	.30	.14	.04
□ 84 Jay Bell	.30	.14	.04
□ 85 Joe Magrane	.15	.07	.02
□ 86 Howard Johnson	.15	.07	.02
□ 87 Jack McDowell	.30	.14	.04
□ 88 Kevin Seitzer	.15	.07	.02
□ 89 Bruce Ruffin	.15	.07	.02
□ 90 Fernando Valenzuela	.30	.14	.04
□ 91 Terry Kennedy	.15	.07	.02
□ 92 Barry Larkin	.60	.25	.07
□ 93 Larry Walker	.75	.35	.09
□ 94 Luis Salazar	.15	.07	.02
□ 95 Gary Sheffield	1.00	.45	.12
□ 96 Bobby Witt	.15	.07	.02
□ 97 Lonnie Smith	.15	.07	.02
□ 98 Bryan Harvey	.15	.07	.02
□ 99 Mookie Wilson	.15	.07	.02
□ 100 Dwight Gooden	.30	.14	.04
□ 101 Lou Whitaker	.60	.25	.07
□ 102 Ron Karkovice	.15	.07	.02
□ 103 Jesse Barfield	.15	.07	.02
□ 104 Jose DeJesus	.15	.07	.02
□ 105 Benito Santiago	.15	.07	.02
□ 106 Brian Holman	.15	.07	.02
□ 107 Rafael Ramirez	.15	.07	.02
□ 108 Ellis Burks	.60	.25	.07
□ 109 Mike Bielecki	.15	.07	.02
□ 110 Kirby Puckett	1.50	.70	.19
□ 111 Terry Shumpert	.15	.07	.02
□ 112 Chuck Crim	.15	.07	.02
□ 113 Todd Benzinger	.15	.07	.02
□ 114 Brian Barnes	.15	.07	.02
□ 115 Carlos Baerga	.75	.35	.09
□ 116 Kal Daniels	.15	.07	.02
□ 117 Dave Johnson	.15	.07	.02
□ 118 Andy Van Slyke	.30	.14	.04
□ 119 John Burkett	.30	.14	.04
□ 120 Rickey Henderson	.60	.25	.07
□ 121 Tim Jones	.15	.07	.02
□ 122 Daryl Irvine	.15	.07	.02
□ 123 Ruben Sierra	.30	.14	.04
□ 124 Jim Abbott	.30	.14	.04
□ 125 Daryl Boston	.15	.07	.02
□ 126 Greg Maddux	3.00	1.35	.35
□ 127 Von Hayes	.15	.07	.02
□ 128 Mike Fitzgerald	.15	.07	.02
□ 129 Wayne Edwards	.15	.07	.02
□ 130 Greg Briley	.15	.07	.02
□ 131 Rob Dibble	.15	.07	.02
□ 132 Gene Larkin	.15	.07	.02
□ 133 David Wells	.15	.07	.02
□ 134 Steve Balboni	.15	.07	.02
□ 135 Greg Vaughn	.60	.25	.07
□ 136 Mark Davis	.15	.07	.02
□ 137 Dave Rhode	.15	.07	.02
□ 138 Eric Show	.15	.07	.02
□ 139 Bobby Bonilla	.30	.14	.04
□ 140 Dana Kiecker	.15	.07	.02
□ 141 Gary Pettis	.15	.07	.02
□ 142 Dennis Boyd	.15	.07	.02
□ 143 Mike Benjamin	.15	.07	.02
□ 144 Luis Polonia	.15	.07	.02
□ 145 Doug Jones	.15	.07	.02
□ 146 Al Newman	.15	.07	.02
□ 147 Alex Fernandez	1.00	.45	.12
□ 148 Bill Doran	.15	.07	.02
□ 149 Kevin Elster	.15	.07	.02
□ 150 Len Dykstra	.30	.14	.04
□ 151 Mike Gallego	.15	.07	.02
□ 152 Tim Belcher	.15	.07	.02
□ 153 Jay Buhner	.60	.25	.07
□ 154 Ozzie Smith UER (Rookie card is 1979, but card back says '78)	1.00	.45	.12
□ 155 Jose Canseco	.60	.25	.07
□ 156 Gregg Olson	.15	.07	.02
□ 157 Charlie O'Brien	.15	.07	.02
□ 158 Frank Tanana	.15	.07	.02
□ 159 George Brett	2.00	.90	.25
□ 160 Jeff Huson	.15	.07	.02
□ 161 Kevin Tapani	.15	.07	.02
□ 162 Jerome Walton	.15	.07	.02

□ 163	Charlie Hayes	.15	.07	.02
□ 164	Chris Bosio	.15	.07	.02
□ 165	Chris Sabo	.15	.07	.02
□ 166	Lance Parrish	.15	.07	.02
□ 167	Don Robinson	.15	.07	.02
□ 168	Manny Lee	.15	.07	.02
□ 169	Dennis Rasmussen	.15	.07	.02
□ 170	Wade Boggs	.60	.25	.07
□ 171	Bob Geren	.15	.07	.02
□ 172	Mackey Sasser	.15	.07	.02
□ 173	Julio Franco	.30	.14	.04
□ 174	Otis Nixon	.15	.07	.02
□ 175	Bert Blyleven	.30	.14	.04
□ 176	Craig Biggio	.60	.25	.07
□ 177	Eddie Murray	1.25	.55	.16
□ 178	Randy Tomlin	.15	.07	.02
□ 179	Tino Martinez	.60	.25	.07
□ 180	Carlton Fisk	.60	.25	.07
□ 181	Dwight Smith	.15	.07	.02
□ 182	Scott Garrelts	.15	.07	.02
□ 183	Jim Gantner	.15	.07	.02
□ 184	Dickie Thon	.15	.07	.02
□ 185	John Farrell	.15	.07	.02
□ 186	Cecil Fielder	.30	.14	.04
□ 187	Glenn Braggs	.15	.07	.02
□ 188	Allan Anderson	.15	.07	.02
□ 189	Kurt Stillwell	.15	.07	.02
□ 190	Jose Oquendo	.15	.07	.02
□ 191	Joe Orsulak	.15	.07	.02
□ 192	Ricky Jordan	.15	.07	.02
□ 193	Kelly Downs	.15	.07	.02
□ 194	Delino DeShields	.15	.07	.02
□ 195	Omar Vizquel	.60	.25	.07
□ 196	Mark Carreon	.15	.07	.02
□ 197	Mike Harkey	.15	.07	.02
□ 198	Jack Howell	.15	.07	.02
□ 199	Lance Johnson	.30	.14	.04
□ 200	Nolan Ryan TUX	5.00	2.20	.60
□ 201	John Marzano	.15	.07	.02
□ 202	Doug Drabek	.15	.07	.02
□ 203	Mark Lemke	.15	.07	.02
□ 204	Steve Sax	.15	.07	.02
□ 205	Greg Harris	.15	.07	.02
□ 206	B.J. Surhoff	.30	.14	.04
□ 207	Todd Burns	.15	.07	.02
□ 208	Jose Gonzalez	.15	.07	.02
□ 209	Mike Scott	.15	.07	.02
□ 210	Dave Magadan	.15	.07	.02
□ 211	Dante Bichette	.75	.35	.09
□ 212	Trevor Wilson	.15	.07	.02
□ 213	Hector Villanueva	.15	.07	.02
□ 214	Dan Pasqua	.15	.07	.02
□ 215	Greg Colbrunn	.30	.14	.04
□ 216	Mike Jeffcoat	.15	.07	.02
□ 217	Harold Reynolds	.15	.07	.02
□ 218	Paul O'Neill	.30	.14	.04
□ 219	Mark Guthrie	.15	.07	.02
□ 220	Barry Bonds	1.25	.55	.16
□ 221	Jimmy Key	.30	.14	.04
□ 222	Billy Ripken	.15	.07	.02
□ 223	Tom Pagnozzi	.15	.07	.02
□ 224	Bo Jackson	.60	.25	.07
□ 225	Sid Fernandez	.15	.07	.02
□ 226	Mike Marshall	.15	.07	.02
□ 227	John Kruk	.30	.14	.04
□ 228	Mike Fetters	.15	.07	.02
□ 229	Eric Anthony	.15	.07	.02
□ 230	Ryne Sandberg	1.25	.55	.16
□ 231	Carney Lansford	.30	.14	.04
□ 232	Melido Perez	.15	.07	.02
□ 233	Jose Lind	.15	.07	.02
□ 234	Darryl Hamilton	.30	.14	.04
□ 235	Tom Browning	.15	.07	.02
□ 236	Spike Owen	.15	.07	.02
□ 237	Juan Gonzalez	6.00	2.70	.75
□ 238	Felix Fermin	.15	.07	.02
□ 239	Keith Miller	.15	.07	.02
□ 240	Mark Gubicza	.15	.07	.02
□ 241	Kent Anderson	.15	.07	.02
□ 242	Alvaro Espinoza	.15	.07	.02
□ 243	Dale Murphy	.60	.25	.07
□ 244	Orel Hershiser	.30	.14	.04
□ 245	Paul Molitor	1.00	.45	.12
□ 246	Eddie Whitson	.15	.07	.02
□ 247	Joe Girardi	.30	.14	.04
□ 248	Kent Hrbek	.30	.14	.04
□ 249	Bill Sampen	.15	.07	.02
□ 250	Kevin Mitchell	.30	.14	.04
□ 251	Mariano Duncan	.15	.07	.02
□ 252	Scott Bradley	.15	.07	.02
□ 253	Mike Greenwell	.15	.07	.02
□ 254	Tom Gordon	.15	.07	.02
□ 255	Todd Zeile	.30	.14	.04
□ 256	Bobby Thigpen	.15	.07	.02
□ 257	Gregg Jefferies	.60	.25	.07
□ 258	Kenny Rogers	.15	.07	.02
□ 259	Shane Mack	.15	.07	.02
□ 260	Zane Smith	.15	.07	.02
□ 261	Mitch Williams	.15	.07	.02
□ 262	Jim Deshaies	.15	.07	.02
□ 263	Dave Winfield	.60	.25	.07
□ 264	Ben McDonald	.30	.14	.04
□ 265	Randy Ready	.15	.07	.02
□ 266	Pat Borders	.15	.07	.02
□ 267	Jose Uribe	.15	.07	.02
□ 268	Derek Lilliquist	.15	.07	.02
□ 269	Greg Brock	.15	.07	.02
□ 270	Ken Griffey Jr.	10.00	4.50	1.25
□ 271	Jeff Gray	.15	.07	.02
□ 272	Danny Tartabull	.15	.07	.02
□ 273	Denny Martinez	.30	.14	.04
□ 274	Robin Ventura	.60	.25	.07
□ 275	Randy Myers	.30	.14	.04
□ 276	Jack Daugherty	.15	.07	.02
□ 277	Greg Gagne	.15	.07	.02
□ 278	Jay Howell	.15	.07	.02
□ 279	Mike LaValliere	.15	.07	.02
□ 280	Rex Hudler	.15	.07	.02
□ 281	Mike Simms	.15	.07	.02
□ 282	Kevin Maas	.15	.07	.02
□ 283	Jeff Ballard	.15	.07	.02
□ 284	Dave Henderson	.15	.07	.02
□ 285	Pete O'Brien	.15	.07	.02
□ 286	Brook Jacoby	.15	.07	.02
□ 287	Mike Henneman	.15	.07	.02
□ 288	Greg Olson	.15	.07	.02
□ 289	Greg Myers	.15	.07	.02
□ 290	Mark Grace	.60	.25	.07
□ 291	Shawn Abner	.15	.07	.02
□ 292	Frank Viola	.15	.07	.02
□ 293	Lee Stevens	.15	.07	.02
□ 294	Jason Grimsley	.15	.07	.02
□ 295	Matt Williams	.60	.25	.07
□ 296	Ron Robinson	.15	.07	.02
□ 297	Tom Brunansky	.15	.07	.02
□ 298	Checklist 1-100	.15	.07	.02
□ 299	Checklist 101-200	.15	.07	.02
□ 300	Checklist 201-300	.15	.07	.02
□ 301	Darryl Strawberry	.30	.14	.04
□ 302	Bud Black	.15	.07	.02
□ 303	Harold Baines	.30	.14	.04
□ 304	Roberto Alomar	1.25	.55	.16
□ 305	Norm Charlton	.15	.07	.02
□ 306	Gary Thurman	.15	.07	.02
□ 307	Mike Felder	.15	.07	.02
□ 308	Tony Gwynn	2.00	.90	.25
□ 309	Roger Clemens	.60	.25	.07
□ 310	Andre Dawson	.60	.25	.07
□ 311	Scott Radinsky	.15	.07	.02
□ 312	Bob Melvin	.15	.07	.02
□ 313	Kirk McCaskill	.15	.07	.02
□ 314	Pedro Guerrero	.15	.07	.02
□ 315	Walt Terrell	.15	.07	.02
□ 316	Sam Horn	.15	.07	.02
□ 317	Wes Chamberlain UER (Card listed as 1989 Debut card, should be 1990)	.15	.07	.02
□ 318	Pedro Munoz	.30	.14	.04
□ 319	Roberto Kelly	.15	.07	.02
□ 320	Mark Portugal	.15	.07	.02
□ 321	Tim McIntosh	.15	.07	.02
□ 322	Jesse Orosco	.15	.07	.02
□ 323	Gary Green	.15	.07	.02
□ 324	Greg Harris	.15	.07	.02
□ 325	Hubie Brooks	.15	.07	.02
□ 326	Chris Nabholz	.15	.07	.02
□ 327	Terry Pendleton	.30	.14	.04
□ 328	Eric King	.15	.07	.02
□ 329	Chili Davis	.30	.14	.04
□ 330	Anthony Telford	.15	.07	.02
□ 331	Kelly Gruber	.15	.07	.02
□ 332	Dennis Eckersley	.30	.14	.04

□ 333	Mel Hall	.15	.07	.02
□ 334	Bob Kipper	.15	.07	.02
□ 335	Willie McGee	.15	.07	.02
□ 336	Steve Olin	.15	.07	.02
□ 337	Steve Buechele	.15	.07	.02
□ 338	Scott Leius	.15	.07	.02
□ 339	Hal Morris	.15	.07	.02
□ 340	Jose Offerman	.15	.07	.02
□ 341	Kent Mercker	.15	.07	.02
□ 342	Ken Griffey Sr.	.15	.07	.02
□ 343	Pete Harnisch	.15	.07	.02
□ 344	Kirk Gibson	.30	.14	.04
□ 345	Dave Smith	.15	.07	.02
□ 346	Dave Martinez	.15	.07	.02
□ 347	Atlee Hammaker	.15	.07	.02
□ 348	Brian Downing	.15	.07	.02
□ 349	Todd Hundley	2.00	.90	.25
□ 350	Candy Maldonado	.15	.07	.02
□ 351	Dwight Evans	.30	.14	.04
□ 352	Steve Searcy	.15	.07	.02
□ 353	Gary Gaetti	.30	.14	.04
□ 354	Jeff Reardon	.30	.14	.04
□ 355	Travis Fryman	1.50	.70	.19
□ 356	Dave Righetti	.15	.07	.02
□ 357	Fred McGriff	.60	.25	.07
□ 358	Don Slaught	.15	.07	.02
□ 359	Gene Nelson	.15	.07	.02
□ 360	Billy Spiers	.15	.07	.02
□ 361	Lee Guetterman	.15	.07	.02
□ 362	Darren Lewis	.30	.14	.04
□ 363	Duane Ward	.15	.07	.02
□ 364	Lloyd Moseby	.15	.07	.02
□ 365	John Smoltz	1.00	.45	.12
□ 366	Felix Jose	.15	.07	.02
□ 367	David Cone	.60	.25	.07
□ 368	Wally Backman	.15	.07	.02
□ 369	Jeff Montgomery	.30	.14	.04
□ 370	Rich Garces	.15	.07	.02
□ 371	Billy Hatcher	.15	.07	.02
□ 372	Bill Swift	.15	.07	.02
□ 373	Jim Eisenreich	.30	.14	.04
□ 374	Rob Ducey	.15	.07	.02
□ 375	Tim Crews	.15	.07	.02
□ 376	Steve Finley	.60	.25	.07
□ 377	Jeff Blauser	.15	.07	.02
□ 378	Willie Wilson	.15	.07	.02
□ 379	Gerald Perry	.15	.07	.02
□ 380	Jose Mesa	.30	.14	.04
□ 381	Pat Kelly	.30	.14	.04
□ 382	Matt Merullo	.15	.07	.02
□ 383	Ivan Calderon	.15	.07	.02
□ 384	Scott Chiamparino	.15	.07	.02
□ 385	Lloyd McClendon	.15	.07	.02
□ 386	Dave Bergman	.15	.07	.02
□ 387	Ed Sprague	.30	.14	.04
□ 388	Jeff Bagwell	6.00	2.70	.75
□ 389	Brett Butler	.30	.14	.04
□ 390	Larry Andersen	.15	.07	.02
□ 391	Glenn Davis	.15	.07	.02
□ 392	Alex Cole UER (Front photo actually Otis Nixon)	.15	.07	.02
□ 393	Mike Heath	.15	.07	.02
□ 394	Danny Darwin	.15	.07	.02
□ 395	Steve Lake	.15	.07	.02
□ 396	Tim Layana	.15	.07	.02
□ 397	Terry Leach	.15	.07	.02
□ 398	Bill Wegman	.15	.07	.02
□ 399	Mark McGwire	1.50	.70	.19
□ 400	Mike Boddicker	.15	.07	.02
□ 401	Steve Howe	.15	.07	.02
□ 402	Bernard Gilkey	.60	.25	.07
□ 403	Thomas Howard	.15	.07	.02
□ 404	Rafael Belliard	.15	.07	.02
□ 405	Tom Candiotti	.15	.07	.02
□ 406	Rene Gonzales	.15	.07	.02
□ 407	Chuck McElroy	.15	.07	.02
□ 408	Paul Sorrento	.30	.14	.04
□ 409	Randy Johnson	1.00	.45	.12
□ 410	Brady Anderson	.60	.25	.07
□ 411	Dennis Cook	.15	.07	.02
□ 412	Mickey Tettleton	.30	.14	.04
□ 413	Mike Stanton	.15	.07	.02
□ 414	Ken Oberkfell	.15	.07	.02
□ 415	Rick Honeycutt	.15	.07	.02
□ 416	Nelson Santovenia	.15	.07	.02

□ 417	Bob Tewksbury	.15	.07	.02
□ 418	Brent Mayne	.15	.07	.02
□ 419	Steve Farr	.15	.07	.02
□ 420	Phil Stephenson	.15	.07	.02
□ 421	Jeff Russell	.15	.07	.02
□ 422	Chris James	.15	.07	.02
□ 423	Tim Leary	.15	.07	.02
□ 424	Gary Carter	.60	.25	.07
□ 425	Glenallen Hill	.15	.07	.02
□ 426	Matt Young UER (Card mentions 83T/Tr as RC, but 84T shown)	.15	.07	.02
□ 427	Sid Bream	.15	.07	.02
□ 428	Greg Swindell	.15	.07	.02
□ 429	Scott Aldred	.15	.07	.02
□ 430	Cal Ripken	4.00	1.80	.50
□ 431	Bill Landrum	.15	.07	.02
□ 432	Earnest Riles	.15	.07	.02
□ 433	Danny Jackson	.15	.07	.02
□ 434	Casey Candaele	.15	.07	.02
□ 435	Ken Hill	.60	.25	.07
□ 436	Jaime Navarro	.15	.07	.02
□ 437	Lance Blankenship	.15	.07	.02
□ 438	Randy Velarde	.15	.07	.02
□ 439	Frank DiPino	.15	.07	.02
□ 440	Carl Nichols	.15	.07	.02
□ 441	Jeff M. Robinson	.15	.07	.02
□ 442	Deion Sanders	.75	.35	.09
□ 443	Vicente Palacios	.15	.07	.02
□ 444	Devon White	.30	.14	.04
□ 445	John Cerutti	.15	.07	.02
□ 446	Tracy Jones	.15	.07	.02
□ 447	Jack Morris	.30	.14	.04
□ 448	Mitch Webster	.15	.07	.02
□ 449	Bob Ojeda	.15	.07	.02
□ 450	Oscar Azocar	.15	.07	.02
□ 451	Luis Aquino	.15	.07	.02
□ 452	Mark Whiten	.30	.14	.04
□ 453	Stan Belinda	.15	.07	.02
□ 454	Ron Gant	.60	.25	.07
□ 455	Jose DeLeon	.15	.07	.02
□ 456	Mark Salas UER (Back has 85T photo, but calls it 86T)	.15	.07	.02
□ 457	Junior Felix	.15	.07	.02
□ 458	Wally Whitehurst	.15	.07	.02
□ 459	Phil Plantier	.30	.14	.04
□ 460	Juan Berenguer	.15	.07	.02
□ 461	Franklin Stubbs	.15	.07	.02
□ 462	Joe Boever	.15	.07	.02
□ 463	Tim Wallach	.15	.07	.02
□ 464	Mike Moore	.15	.07	.02
□ 465	Albert Belle	4.00	1.80	.50
□ 466	Mike Witt	.15	.07	.02
□ 467	Craig Worthington	.15	.07	.02
□ 468	Jerald Clark	.15	.07	.02
□ 469	Scott Terry	.15	.07	.02
□ 470	Milt Cuyler	.15	.07	.02
□ 471	John Smiley	.15	.07	.02
□ 472	Charles Nagy	1.00	.45	.12
□ 473	Alan Mills	.15	.07	.02
□ 474	John Russell	.15	.07	.02
□ 475	Bruce Hurst	.15	.07	.02
□ 476	Andujar Cedeno	.15	.07	.02
□ 477	Dave Eiland	.15	.07	.02
□ 478	Brian McRae	.75	.35	.09
□ 479	Mike LaCoss	.15	.07	.02
□ 480	Chris Gwynn	.15	.07	.02
□ 481	Jamie Moyer	.15	.07	.02
□ 482	John Olerud	.30	.14	.04
□ 483	Efrain Valdez	.15	.07	.02
□ 484	Sil Campusano	.15	.07	.02
□ 485	Pascual Perez	.15	.07	.02
□ 486	Gary Redus	.15	.07	.02
□ 487	Andy Hawkins	.15	.07	.02
□ 488	Cory Snyder	.15	.07	.02
□ 489	Chris Hoiles	.15	.07	.02
□ 490	Ron Hassey	.15	.07	.02
□ 491	Gary Wayne	.15	.07	.02
□ 492	Mark Lewis	.15	.07	.02
□ 493	Scott Coolbaugh	.15	.07	.02
□ 494	Gerald Young	.15	.07	.02
□ 495	Juan Samuel	.15	.07	.02
□ 496	Willie Fraser	.15	.07	.02
□ 497	Jeff Treadway	.15	.07	.02
□ 498	Vince Coleman	.15	.07	.02

□ 499	Cris Carpenter	.15	.07	.02
□ 500	Jack Clark	.30	.14	.04
□ 501	Kevin Appier	.75	.35	.09
□ 502	Rafael Palmeiro	.60	.25	.07
□ 503	Hensley Meulens	.15	.07	.02
□ 504	George Bell	.15	.07	.02
□ 505	Tony Pena	.15	.07	.02
□ 506	Roger McDowell	.15	.07	.02
□ 507	Luis Sojo	.15	.07	.02
□ 508	Mike Schooler	.15	.07	.02
□ 509	Robin Yount	.60	.25	.07
□ 510	Jack Armstrong	.15	.07	.02
□ 511	Rick Cerone	.15	.07	.02
□ 512	Curt Wilkerson	.15	.07	.02
□ 513	Joe Carter	.60	.25	.07
□ 514	Tim Burke	.15	.07	.02
□ 515	Tony Fernandez	.15	.07	.02
□ 516	Ramon Martinez	.30	.14	.04
□ 517	Tim Hulett	.15	.07	.02
□ 518	Terry Steinbach	.30	.14	.04
□ 519	Pete Smith	.15	.07	.02
□ 520	Ken Caminiti	.60	.25	.07
□ 521	Shawn Boskie	.15	.07	.02
□ 522	Mike Pagliarulo	.15	.07	.02
□ 523	Tim Raines	.60	.25	.07
□ 524	Alfredo Griffin	.15	.07	.02
□ 525	Henry Cotto	.15	.07	.02
□ 526	Mike Stanley	.15	.07	.02
□ 527	Charlie Leibrandt	.15	.07	.02
□ 528	Jeff King	.30	.14	.04
□ 529	Eric Plunk	.15	.07	.02
□ 530	Tom Lampkin	.15	.07	.02
□ 531	Steve Bedrosian	.15	.07	.02
□ 532	Tom Herr	.15	.07	.02
□ 533	Craig Lefferts	.15	.07	.02
□ 534	Jeff Reed	.15	.07	.02
□ 535	Mickey Morandini	.15	.07	.02
□ 536	Greg Cadaret	.15	.07	.02
□ 537	Ray Lankford	1.50	.70	.19
□ 538	John Candelaria	.15	.07	.02
□ 539	Rob Deer	.15	.07	.02
□ 540	Brad Arnsberg	.15	.07	.02
□ 541	Mike Sharperson	.15	.07	.02
□ 542	Jeff D. Robinson	.15	.07	.02
□ 543	Mo Vaughn	5.00	2.20	.60
□ 544	Jeff Parrett	.15	.07	.02
□ 545	Willie Randolph	.30	.14	.04
□ 546	Herm Winningham	.15	.07	.02
□ 547	Jeff Innis	.15	.07	.02
□ 548	Chuck Knoblauch	2.50	1.10	.30
□ 549	Tommy Greene UER (Born in North Carolina, not South Carolina)	.15	.07	.02
□ 550	Jeff Hamilton	.15	.07	.02
□ 551	Barry Jones	.15	.07	.02
□ 552	Ken Dayley	.15	.07	.02
□ 553	Rick Dempsey	.15	.07	.02
□ 554	Greg Smith	.15	.07	.02
□ 555	Mike Devereaux	.15	.07	.02
□ 556	Keith Comstock	.15	.07	.02
□ 557	Paul Faries	.15	.07	.02
□ 558	Tom Glavine	.60	.25	.07
□ 559	Craig Grebeck	.15	.07	.02
□ 560	Scott Erickson	.30	.14	.04
□ 561	Joel Skinner	.15	.07	.02
□ 562	Mike Morgan	.15	.07	.02
□ 563	Dave Gallagher	.15	.07	.02
□ 564	Todd Stottlemyre	.15	.07	.02
□ 565	Rich Rodriguez	.15	.07	.02
□ 566	Craig Wilson	.15	.07	.02
□ 567	Jeff Brantley	.15	.07	.02
□ 568	Scott Kamieniecki	.15	.07	.02
□ 569	Steve Decker	.15	.07	.02
□ 570	Juan Agosto	.15	.07	.02
□ 571	Tommy Gregg	.15	.07	.02
□ 572	Kevin Wickander	.15	.07	.02
□ 573	Jamie Quirk UER (Rookie card is 1976, but card back is 1990)	.15	.07	.02
□ 574	Jerry Don Gleaton	.15	.07	.02
□ 575	Chris Hammond	.15	.07	.02
□ 576	Luis Gonzalez	.60	.25	.07
□ 577	Russ Swan	.15	.07	.02
□ 578	Jeff Conine	1.50	.70	.19
□ 579	Charlie Hough	.15	.07	.02
□ 580	Jeff Kunkel	.15	.07	.02
□ 581	Darrel Akerfelds	.15	.07	.02
□ 582	Jeff Manto	.15	.07	.02
□ 583	Alejandro Pena	.15	.07	.02
□ 584	Mark Davidson	.15	.07	.02
□ 585	Bob MacDonald	.15	.07	.02
□ 586	Paul Assenmacher	.15	.07	.02
□ 587	Dan Wilson	.75	.35	.09
□ 588	Tom Bolton	.15	.07	.02
□ 589	Brian Harper	.15	.07	.02
□ 590	John Habyan	.15	.07	.02
□ 591	John Orton	.15	.07	.02
□ 592	Mark Gardner	.15	.07	.02
□ 593	Turner Ward	.15	.07	.02
□ 594	Bob Patterson	.15	.07	.02
□ 595	Ed Nunez	.15	.07	.02
□ 596	Gary Scott UER (Major League Batting Record should be Minor League)	.15	.07	.02
□ 597	Scott Bankhead	.15	.07	.02
□ 598	Checklist 301-400	.15	.07	.02
□ 599	Checklist 401-500	.15	.07	.02
□ 600	Checklist 501-600	.15	.07	.02

1992 Stadium Club Dome

The 1992 Stadium Club Dome set (issued by Topps) features 100 top draft picks, 56 1991 All-Star Game cards, 25 1991 Team U.S.A. cards, and 19 1991 Championship and World Series cards, all packaged in a factory set box inside a molded-plastic SkyDome display. Topps actually references this set as a 1991 set and the copyright lines on the card backs say 1991, but the set was released well into 1992. The standard-size cards display full-bleed glossy player photos on the fronts. The player's name appears in an sky-blue stripe that is accented by parallel gold stripes. Rookie Cards in this set include Shawn Green, Todd Hollandsworth, Alex Ochoa and Manny Ramirez.

	MINT	NRMT	EXC
COMPLETE FACT.SET (200)	12.00	5.50	1.50
COMMON CARD (1-200)	.10	.05	.01
SEMISTARS	.30	.14	.04

□ 1	Terry Adams	.20	.09	.03
□ 2	Tommy Adams	.10	.05	.01
□ 3	Rick Aguilera	.10	.05	.01
□ 4	Ron Allen	.10	.05	.01
□ 5	Roberto Alomar	.50	.23	.06
□ 6	Sandy Alomar	.20	.09	.03
□ 7	Greg Anthony	.10	.05	.01
□ 8	James Austin	.10	.05	.01
□ 9	Steve Avery	.20	.09	.03
□ 10	Harold Baines	.20	.09	.03
□ 11	Brian Barber	.20	.09	.03
□ 12	Jon Barnes	.10	.05	.01
□ 13	George Bell	.10	.05	.01
□ 14	Doug Bennett	.10	.05	.01
□ 15	Sean Bergman	.20	.09	.03
□ 16	Craig Biggio	.30	.14	.04
□ 17	Bill Bliss	.10	.05	.01
□ 18	Wade Boggs	.30	.14	.04
□ 19	Bobby Bonilla	.20	.09	.03
□ 20	Russell Brock	.10	.05	.01
□ 21	Tarrik Brock	.10	.05	.01

□ 22 Tom Browning	.10	.05	.01
□ 23 Brett Butler	.20	.09	.03
□ 24 Ivan Calderon	.10	.05	.01
□ 25 Joe Carter	.30	.14	.04
□ 26 Joe Caruso	.10	.05	.01
□ 27 Dan Cholowsky	.10	.05	.01
□ 28 Will Clark	.30	.14	.04
□ 29 Roger Clemens	.30	.14	.04
□ 30 Shawn Curran	.10	.05	.01
□ 31 Chris Curtis	.10	.05	.01
□ 32 Chili Davis	.20	.09	.03
□ 33 Andre Dawson	.30	.14	.04
□ 34 Joe DeBerry	.10	.05	.01
□ 35 John Dettmer	.10	.05	.01
□ 36 Rob Dibble	.10	.05	.01
□ 37 John Donati	.10	.05	.01
□ 38 Dave Doorneweerd	.10	.05	.01
□ 39 Darren Dreifort	.20	.09	.03
□ 40 Mike Durant	.10	.05	.01
□ 41 Chris Durkin	.10	.05	.01
□ 42 Dennis Eckersley	.20	.09	.03
□ 43 Brian Edmondson	.10	.05	.01
□ 44 Vaughn Eshelman	.20	.09	.03
□ 45 Shawn Estes	.30	.14	.04
□ 46 Jorge Fabregas	.20	.09	.03
□ 47 Jon Farrell	.10	.05	.01
□ 48 Cecil Fielder	.30	.14	.04
□ 49 Carlton Fisk	.30	.14	.04
□ 50 Tim Flannelly	.10	.05	.01
□ 51 Cliff Floyd	.40	.18	.05
□ 52 Julio Franco	.20	.09	.03
□ 53 Greg Gagne	.10	.05	.01
□ 54 Chris Gambs	.10	.05	.01
□ 55 Ron Gant	.30	.14	.04
□ 56 Brent Gates	.20	.09	.03
□ 57 Dwayne Gerald	.10	.05	.01
□ 58 Jason Giambi	1.50	.70	.19
□ 59 Benji Gil	.30	.14	.04
□ 60 Mark Gipner	.10	.05	.01
□ 61 Danny Gladden	.10	.05	.01
□ 62 Tom Glavine	.30	.14	.04
□ 63 Jimmy Gonzalez	.10	.05	.01
□ 64 Jeff Granger	.20	.09	.03
□ 65 Dan Grapenthien	.10	.05	.01
□ 66 Dennis Gray	.10	.05	.01
□ 67 Shawn Green	1.00	.45	.12
□ 68 Tyler Green	.20	.09	.03
□ 69 Todd Greene	.75	.35	.09
□ 70 Ken Griffey Jr.	2.50	1.10	.30
□ 71 Kelly Gruber	.10	.05	.01
□ 72 Ozzie Guillen	.10	.05	.01
□ 73 Tony Gwynn	.75	.35	.09
□ 74 Shane Halter	.10	.05	.01
□ 75 Jeffrey Hammonds	.30	.14	.04
□ 76 Larry Hanlon	.10	.05	.01
□ 77 Pete Harnisch	.10	.05	.01
□ 78 Mike Harrison	.10	.05	.01
□ 79 Bryan Harvey	.10	.05	.01
□ 80 Scott Hatteberg	.10	.05	.01
□ 81 Rick Helling	.10	.05	.01
□ 82 Dave Henderson	.10	.05	.01
□ 83 Rickey Henderson	.30	.14	.04
□ 84 Tyrone Hill	.10	.05	.01
□ 85 Todd Hollandsworth	1.50	.70	.19
□ 86 Brian Holliday	.10	.05	.01
□ 87 Terry Horn	.10	.05	.01
□ 88 Jeff Hostetler	.10	.05	.01
□ 89 Kent Hrbek	.20	.09	.03
□ 90 Mark Hubbard	.10	.05	.01
□ 91 Charles Johnson	.75	.35	.09
□ 92 Howard Johnson	.10	.05	.01
□ 93 Todd Johnson	.10	.05	.01
□ 94 Bobby Jones	.40	.18	.05
□ 95 Dan Jones	.10	.05	.01
□ 96 Felix Jose	.10	.05	.01
□ 97 David Justice	.30	.14	.04
□ 98 Jimmy Key	.20	.09	.03
□ 99 Marc Kroon	.20	.09	.03
□ 100 John Kruk	.20	.09	.03
□ 101 Mark Langston	.20	.09	.03
□ 102 Barry Larkin	.30	.14	.04
□ 103 Mike LaValliere	.10	.05	.01
□ 104 Scott Leius	.10	.05	.01
□ 105 Mark Lemke	.10	.05	.01
□ 106 Donnie Leshnock	.10	.05	.01
□ 107 Jimmy Lewis	.10	.05	.01
□ 108 Shane Livesy	.10	.05	.01
□ 109 Ryan Long	.10	.05	.01
□ 110 Trevor Mallory	.10	.05	.01
□ 111 Denny Martinez	.20	.09	.03
□ 112 Justin Mashore	.10	.05	.01
□ 113 Jason McDonald	.20	.09	.03
□ 114 Jack McDowell	.20	.09	.03
□ 115 Tom McKinnon	.10	.05	.01
□ 116 Billy McMillon	.20	.09	.03
□ 117 Buck McNabb	.20	.09	.03
□ 118 Jim Mecir	.10	.05	.01
□ 119 Dan Melendez	.10	.05	.01
□ 120 Shawn Miller	.20	.09	.03
□ 121 Trever Miller	.10	.05	.01
□ 122 Paul Molitor	.40	.18	.05
□ 123 Vincent Moore	.10	.05	.01
□ 124 Mike Morgan	.10	.05	.01
□ 125 Jack Morris WS	.20	.09	.03
□ 126 Jack Morris AS	.10	.05	.01
□ 127 Sean Mulligan	.10	.05	.01
□ 128 Eddie Murray AS	.50	.23	.06
□ 129 Mike Neill	.10	.05	.01
□ 130 Phil Nevin	.20	.09	.03
□ 131 Mark O'Brien	.10	.05	.01
□ 132 Alex Ochoa	1.25	.55	.16
□ 133 Chad Ogea	.50	.23	.06
□ 134 Greg Olson	.10	.05	.01
□ 135 Paul O'Neill	.20	.09	.03
□ 136 Jared Osentowski	.10	.05	.01
□ 137 Mike Pagliarulo	.10	.05	.01
□ 138 Rafael Palmeiro	.30	.14	.04
□ 139 Rodney Pedraza	.10	.05	.01
□ 140 Tony Phillips (P)	.10	.05	.01
□ 141 Scott Pisciotta	.20	.09	.03
□ 142 Christopher Pritchett	.10	.05	.01
□ 143 Jason Pruitt	.10	.05	.01
□ 144 Kirby Puckett WS UER (Championship series AB and BA is wrong)	.60	.25	.07
□ 145 Kirby Puckett AS	.60	.25	.07
□ 146 Manny Ramirez	4.00	1.80	.50
□ 147 Eddie Ramos	.10	.05	.01
□ 148 Mark Ratekin	.10	.05	.01
□ 149 Jeff Reardon	.20	.09	.03
□ 150 Sean Rees	.10	.05	.01
□ 151 Calvin Reese	.30	.14	.04
□ 152 Desmond Relaford	.20	.09	.03
□ 153 Eric Richardson	.10	.05	.01
□ 154 Cal Ripken	2.00	.90	.25
□ 155 Chris Roberts	.20	.09	.03
□ 156 Mike Robertson	.10	.05	.01
□ 157 Steve Rodriguez	.10	.05	.01
□ 158 Mike Rossiter	.10	.05	.01
□ 159 Scott Ruffcorn	.20	.09	.03
□ 160 Chris Sabo	.10	.05	.01
□ 161 Juan Samuel	.10	.05	.01
□ 162 Ryne Sandberg UER (On 5th line, prior misspelled as prilor)	.50	.23	.06
□ 163 Scott Sanderson	.10	.05	.01
□ 164 Benny Santiago	.10	.05	.01
□ 165 Gene Schall	.10	.05	.01
□ 166 Chad Schoenvogel	.10	.05	.01
□ 167 Chris Seelbach	.20	.09	.03
□ 168 Aaron Sele	.30	.14	.04
□ 169 Basil Shabazz	.10	.05	.01
□ 170 Al Shirley	.20	.09	.03
□ 171 Paul Shuey	.10	.05	.01
□ 172 Ruben Sierra	.30	.14	.04
□ 173 John Smiley	.10	.05	.01
□ 174 Lee Smith	.20	.09	.03
□ 175 Ozzie Smith	.40	.18	.05
□ 176 Tim Smith	.10	.05	.01
□ 177 Zane Smith	.10	.05	.01
□ 178 John Smoltz	.30	.14	.04
□ 179 Scott Stahoviak	.30	.14	.04
□ 180 Kennie Steenstra	.10	.05	.01
□ 181 Kevin Stocker	.10	.05	.01
□ 182 Chris Stynes	.20	.09	.03
□ 183 Danny Tartabull	.10	.05	.01
□ 184 Brien Taylor	.20	.09	.03
□ 185 Todd Taylor	.10	.05	.01
□ 186 Larry Thomas	.10	.05	.01
□ 187 Ozzie Timmons (See also 188)	.20	.09	.03
□ 188 David Tuttle UER	.10	.05	.01

(Mistakenly numbered as 187 on card)			
□ 189 Andy Van Slyke	.20	.09	.03
□ 190 Frank Viola	.10	.05	.01
□ 191 Michael Walkden	.10	.05	.01
□ 192 Jeff Ware	.10	.05	.01
□ 193 Allen Watson	.20	.09	.03
□ 194 Steve Whitaker	.10	.05	.01
□ 195 Jerry Willard	.10	.05	.01
□ 196 Craig Wilson	.10	.05	.01
□ 197 Chris Wimmer	.10	.05	.01
□ 198 Steve Wojciechowski	.10	.05	.01
□ 199 Joel Wolfe	.10	.05	.01
□ 200 Ivan Zweig	.10	.05	.01

1992 Stadium Club

The 1992 Stadium Club baseball card set consists of 900 standard-size cards issued in three series of 300 cards each. Cards were issued in plastic wrapped packs. A card-like application form for membership in Topps Stadium Club was inserted in each pack. The glossy color player photos on the fronts are full-bleed. The "Topps Stadium Club" logo is superimposed at the bottom of the card face, with the player's name appearing immediately below the logo. Some cards in the set have the Stadium Club logo printed upside down. The backs display a mini reprint of the player's rookie card and "BARS" (Baseball Analysis and Reporting System) statistics. Card numbers 591-610 form a "Members Choice" subset. The only notable Rookie Card in this set features Bill Pulsipher.

	MINT	NRMT	EXC
COMPLETE SET (900)	60.00	27.00	7.50
COMPLETE SERIES 1 (300)	20.00	9.00	2.50
COMPLETE SERIES 2 (300)	20.00	9.00	2.50
COMPLETE SERIES 3 (300)	20.00	9.00	2.50
COMMON CARD (1-900)	.10	.05	.01
SEMISTARS	.15	.07	.02
STARS	.30	.14	.04

□ 1 Cal Ripken UER	2.00	.90	.25
(Misspelled Ripkin on card back)			
□ 2 Eric Yelding	.10	.05	.01
□ 3 Geno Petralli	.10	.05	.01
□ 4 Wally Backman	.10	.05	.01
□ 5 Milt Cuyler	.10	.05	.01
□ 6 Kevin Bass	.10	.05	.01
□ 7 Dante Bichette	.30	.14	.04
□ 8 Ray Lankford	.30	.14	.04
□ 9 Mel Hall	.10	.05	.01
□ 10 Joe Carter	.30	.14	.04
□ 11 Juan Samuel	.10	.05	.01
□ 12 Jeff Montgomery	.15	.07	.02
□ 13 Glenn Braggs	.10	.05	.01
□ 14 Henry Cotto	.10	.05	.01
□ 15 Deion Sanders	.30	.14	.04
□ 16 Dick Schofield	.10	.05	.01
□ 17 David Cone	.30	.14	.04
□ 18 Chili Davis	.15	.07	.02
□ 19 Tom Foley	.10	.05	.01
□ 20 Ozzie Guillen	.10	.05	.01
□ 21 Luis Salazar	.10	.05	.01
□ 22 Terry Steinbach	.15	.07	.02
□ 23 Chris James	.10	.05	.01
□ 24 Jeff King	.15	.07	.02
□ 25 Carlos Quintana	.10	.05	.01
□ 26 Mike Maddux	.10	.05	.01
□ 27 Tommy Greene	.10	.05	.01
□ 28 Jeff Russell	.10	.05	.01
□ 29 Steve Finley	.30	.14	.04
□ 30 Mike Flanagan	.10	.05	.01
□ 31 Darren Lewis	.10	.05	.01
□ 32 Mark Lee	.10	.05	.01
□ 33 Willie Fraser	.10	.05	.01
□ 34 Mike Henneman	.10	.05	.01
□ 35 Kevin Maas	.10	.05	.01
□ 36 Dave Hansen	.10	.05	.01
□ 37 Erik Hanson	.10	.05	.01
□ 38 Bill Doran	.10	.05	.01
□ 39 Mike Boddicker	.10	.05	.01
□ 40 Vince Coleman	.10	.05	.01
□ 41 Devon White	.15	.07	.02
□ 42 Mark Gardner	.10	.05	.01
□ 43 Scott Lewis	.10	.05	.01
□ 44 Juan Berenguer	.10	.05	.01
□ 45 Carney Lansford	.15	.07	.02
□ 46 Curt Wilkerson	.10	.05	.01
□ 47 Shane Mack	.10	.05	.01
□ 48 Bip Roberts	.10	.05	.01
□ 49 Greg A. Harris	.10	.05	.01
□ 50 Ryne Sandberg	.50	.23	.06
□ 51 Mark Whiten	.15	.07	.02
□ 52 Jack McDowell	.15	.07	.02
□ 53 Jimmy Jones	.10	.05	.01
□ 54 Steve Lake	.10	.05	.01
□ 55 Bud Black	.10	.05	.01
□ 56 Dave Valle	.10	.05	.01
□ 57 Kevin Reimer	.10	.05	.01
□ 58 Rich Gedman UER	.10	.05	.01
(Wrong BARS chart used)			
□ 59 Travis Fryman	.30	.14	.04
□ 60 Steve Avery	.15	.07	.02
□ 61 Francisco de la Rosa	.10	.05	.01
□ 62 Scott Hemond	.10	.05	.01
□ 63 Hal Morris	.10	.05	.01
□ 64 Hensley Meulens	.10	.05	.01
□ 65 Frank Castillo	.15	.07	.02
□ 66 Gene Larkin	.10	.05	.01
□ 67 Jose DeLeon	.10	.05	.01
□ 68 Al Osuna	.10	.05	.01
□ 69 Dave Cochrane	.10	.05	.01
□ 70 Robin Ventura	.30	.14	.04
□ 71 John Cerutti	.10	.05	.01
□ 72 Kevin Gross	.10	.05	.01
□ 73 Ivan Calderon	.10	.05	.01
□ 74 Mike Macfarlane	.10	.05	.01
□ 75 Stan Belinda	.10	.05	.01
□ 76 Shawn Hillegas	.10	.05	.01
□ 77 Pat Borders	.10	.05	.01
□ 78 Jim Vatcher	.10	.05	.01
□ 79 Bobby Rose	.10	.05	.01
□ 80 Roger Clemens	.30	.14	.04
□ 81 Craig Worthington	.10	.05	.01
□ 82 Jeff Treadway	.10	.05	.01
□ 83 Jamie Quirk	.10	.05	.01
□ 84 Randy Bush	.10	.05	.01
□ 85 Anthony Young	.10	.05	.01
□ 86 Trevor Wilson	.10	.05	.01
□ 87 Jaime Navarro	.10	.05	.01
□ 88 Les Lancaster	.10	.05	.01
□ 89 Pat Kelly	.10	.05	.01
□ 90 Alvin Davis	.10	.05	.01
□ 91 Larry Andersen	.10	.05	.01
□ 92 Rob Deer	.10	.05	.01
□ 93 Mike Sharperson	.10	.05	.01
□ 94 Lance Parrish	.10	.05	.01
□ 95 Cecil Espy	.10	.05	.01
□ 96 Tim Spehr	.10	.05	.01
□ 97 Dave Stieb	.10	.05	.01
□ 98 Terry Mulholland	.10	.05	.01
□ 99 Dennis Boyd	.10	.05	.01
□ 100 Barry Larkin	.30	.14	.04
□ 101 Ryan Bowen	.10	.05	.01
□ 102 Felix Fermin	.10	.05	.01
□ 103 Luis Alicea	.10	.05	.01
□ 104 Tim Hulett	.10	.05	.01
□ 105 Rafael Belliard	.10	.05	.01
□ 106 Mike Gallego	.10	.05	.01
□ 107 Dave Righetti	.10	.05	.01
□ 108 Jeff Schaefer	.10	.05	.01

□ 109 Ricky Bones	.10	.05	.01
□ 110 Scott Erickson	.15	.07	.02
□ 111 Matt Nokes	.10	.05	.01
□ 112 Bob Scanlan	.10	.05	.01
□ 113 Tom Candiotti	.10	.05	.01
□ 114 Sean Berry	.15	.07	.02
□ 115 Kevin Morton	.10	.05	.01
□ 116 Scott Fletcher	.10	.05	.01
□ 117 B.J. Surhoff	.15	.07	.02
□ 118 Dave Magadan UER	.10	.05	.01
(Born Tampa, not Tamps)			
□ 119 Bill Gullickson	.10	.05	.01
□ 120 Marquis Grissom	.30	.14	.04
□ 121 Lenny Harris	.10	.05	.01
□ 122 Wally Joyner	.15	.07	.02
□ 123 Kevin Brown	.15	.07	.02
□ 124 Braulio Castillo	.10	.05	.01
□ 125 Eric King	.10	.05	.01
□ 126 Mark Portugal	.10	.05	.01
□ 127 Calvin Jones	.10	.05	.01
□ 128 Mike Heath	.10	.05	.01
□ 129 Todd Van Poppel	.10	.05	.01
□ 130 Benny Santiago	.10	.05	.01
□ 131 Gary Thurman	.10	.05	.01
□ 132 Joe Girardi	.10	.05	.01
□ 133 Dave Eiland	.10	.05	.01
□ 134 Orlando Merced	.15	.07	.02
□ 135 Joe Orsulak	.10	.05	.01
□ 136 John Burkett	.15	.07	.02
□ 137 Ken Dayley	.10	.05	.01
□ 138 Ken Hill	.30	.14	.04
□ 139 Walt Terrell	.10	.05	.01
□ 140 Mike Scioscia	.10	.05	.01
□ 141 Junior Felix	.10	.05	.01
□ 142 Ken Caminiti	.30	.14	.04
□ 143 Carlos Baerga	.30	.14	.04
□ 144 Tony Fossas	.10	.05	.01
□ 145 Craig Grebeck	.10	.05	.01
□ 146 Scott Bradley	.10	.05	.01
□ 147 Kent Mercker	.10	.05	.01
□ 148 Derrick May	.10	.05	.01
□ 149 Jerald Clark	.10	.05	.01
□ 150 George Brett	.75	.35	.09
□ 151 Luis Quinones	.10	.05	.01
□ 152 Mike Pagliarulo	.10	.05	.01
□ 153 Jose Guzman	.10	.05	.01
□ 154 Charlie O'Brien	.10	.05	.01
□ 155 Darren Holmes	.10	.05	.01
□ 156 Joe Boever	.10	.05	.01
□ 157 Rich Monteleone	.10	.05	.01
□ 158 Reggie Harris	.10	.05	.01
□ 159 Roberto Alomar	.50	.23	.06
□ 160 Robby Thompson	.10	.05	.01
□ 161 Chris Hoiles	.10	.05	.01
□ 162 Tom Pagnozzi	.10	.05	.01
□ 163 Omar Vizquel	.30	.14	.04
□ 164 John Candelaria	.10	.05	.01
□ 165 Terry Shumpert	.10	.05	.01
□ 166 Andy Mota	.10	.05	.01
□ 167 Scott Bailes	.10	.05	.01
□ 168 Jeff Blauser	.10	.05	.01
□ 169 Steve Olin	.10	.05	.01
□ 170 Doug Drabek	.10	.05	.01
□ 171 Dave Bergman	.10	.05	.01
□ 172 Eddie Whitson	.10	.05	.01
□ 173 Gilberto Reyes	.10	.05	.01
□ 174 Mark Grace	.30	.14	.04
□ 175 Paul O'Neill	.15	.07	.02
□ 176 Greg Cadaret	.10	.05	.01
□ 177 Mark Williamson	.10	.05	.01
□ 178 Casey Candaele	.10	.05	.01
□ 179 Candy Maldonado	.10	.05	.01
□ 180 Lee Smith	.15	.07	.02
□ 181 Harold Reynolds	.10	.05	.01
□ 182 David Justice	.30	.14	.04
□ 183 Lenny Webster	.10	.05	.01
□ 184 Donn Pall	.10	.05	.01
□ 185 Gerald Alexander	.10	.05	.01
□ 186 Jack Clark	.15	.07	.02
□ 187 Stan Javier	.10	.05	.01
□ 188 Ricky Jordan	.10	.05	.01
□ 189 Franklin Stubbs	.10	.05	.01
□ 190 Dennis Eckersley	.15	.07	.02
□ 191 Danny Tartabull	.10	.05	.01
□ 192 Pete O'Brien	.10	.05	.01
□ 193 Mark Lewis	.10	.05	.01
□ 194 Mike Felder	.10	.05	.01
□ 195 Mickey Tettleton	.10	.05	.01
□ 196 Dwight Smith	.10	.05	.01
□ 197 Shawn Abner	.10	.05	.01
□ 198 Jim Leyritz UER	.10	.05	.01
(Career totals less than 1991 totals)			
□ 199 Mike Devereaux	.10	.05	.01
□ 200 Craig Biggio	.30	.14	.04
□ 201 Kevin Elster	.10	.05	.01
□ 202 Rance Mulliniks	.10	.05	.01
□ 203 Tony Fernandez	.10	.05	.01
□ 204 Allan Anderson	.10	.05	.01
□ 205 Herm Winningham	.10	.05	.01
□ 206 Tim Jones	.10	.05	.01
□ 207 Ramon Martinez	.15	.07	.02
□ 208 Teddy Higuera	.10	.05	.01
□ 209 John Kruk	.15	.07	.02
□ 210 Jim Abbott	.10	.05	.01
□ 211 Dean Palmer	.15	.07	.02
□ 212 Mark Davis	.10	.05	.01
□ 213 Jay Buhner	.30	.14	.04
□ 214 Jesse Barfield	.10	.05	.01
□ 215 Kevin Mitchell	.15	.07	.02
□ 216 Mike LaValliere	.10	.05	.01
□ 217 Mark Wohlers	.30	.14	.04
□ 218 Dave Henderson	.10	.05	.01
□ 219 Dave Smith	.10	.05	.01
□ 220 Albert Belle	1.25	.55	.16
□ 221 Spike Owen	.10	.05	.01
□ 222 Jeff Gray	.10	.05	.01
□ 223 Paul Gibson	.10	.05	.01
□ 224 Bobby Thigpen	.10	.05	.01
□ 225 Mike Mussina	.60	.25	.07
□ 226 Darrin Jackson	.10	.05	.01
□ 227 Luis Gonzalez	.15	.07	.02
□ 228 Greg Briley	.10	.05	.01
□ 229 Brent Mayne	.10	.05	.01
□ 230 Paul Molitor	.40	.18	.05
□ 231 Al Leiter	.15	.07	.02
□ 232 Andy Van Slyke	.15	.07	.02
□ 233 Ron Tingley	.10	.05	.01
□ 234 Bernard Gilkey	.15	.07	.02
□ 235 Kent Hrbek	.15	.07	.02
□ 236 Eric Karros	.30	.14	.04
□ 237 Randy Velarde	.10	.05	.01
□ 238 Andy Allanson	.10	.05	.01
□ 239 Willie McGee	.10	.05	.01
□ 240 Juan Gonzalez	1.25	.55	.16
□ 241 Karl Rhodes	.10	.05	.01
□ 242 Luis Mercedes	.10	.05	.01
□ 243 Billy Swift	.10	.05	.01
□ 244 Tommy Gregg	.10	.05	.01
□ 245 David Howard	.10	.05	.01
□ 246 Dave Hollins	.10	.05	.01
□ 247 Kip Gross	.10	.05	.01
□ 248 Walt Weiss	.10	.05	.01
□ 249 Mackey Sasser	.10	.05	.01
□ 250 Cecil Fielder	.15	.07	.02
□ 251 Jerry Browne	.10	.05	.01
□ 252 Doug Dascenzo	.10	.05	.01
□ 253 Darryl Hamilton	.10	.05	.01
□ 254 Dann Bilardello	.10	.05	.01
□ 255 Luis Rivera	.10	.05	.01
□ 256 Larry Walker	.30	.14	.04
□ 257 Ron Karkovice	.10	.05	.01
□ 258 Bob Tewksbury	.10	.05	.01
□ 259 Jimmy Key	.15	.07	.02
□ 260 Bernie Williams	.50	.23	.06
□ 261 Gary Wayne	.10	.05	.01
□ 262 Mike Simms UER	.10	.05	.01
(Reversed negative)			
□ 263 John Orton	.10	.05	.01
□ 264 Marvin Freeman	.10	.05	.01
□ 265 Mike Jeffcoat	.10	.05	.01
□ 266 Roger Mason	.10	.05	.01
□ 267 Edgar Martinez	.30	.14	.04
□ 268 Henry Rodriguez	.30	.14	.04
□ 269 Sam Horn	.10	.05	.01
□ 270 Brian McRae	.30	.14	.04
□ 271 Kirt Manwaring	.10	.05	.01
□ 272 Mike Bordick	.15	.07	.02
□ 273 Chris Sabo	.10	.05	.01
□ 274 Jim Olander	.10	.05	.01
□ 275 Greg W. Harris	.10	.05	.01
□ 276 Dan Gakeler	.10	.05	.01

□ 277	Bill Sampen	.10	.05	.01
□ 278	Joel Skinner	.10	.05	.01
□ 279	Curt Schilling	.10	.05	.01
□ 280	Dale Murphy	.30	.14	.04
□ 281	Lee Stevens	.10	.05	.01
□ 282	Lonnie Smith	.10	.05	.01
□ 283	Manuel Lee	.10	.05	.01
□ 284	Shawn Boskie	.10	.05	.01
□ 285	Kevin Seitzer	.10	.05	.01
□ 286	Stan Royer	.10	.05	.01
□ 287	John Dopson	.10	.05	.01
□ 288	Scott Bullett	.10	.05	.01
□ 289	Ken Patterson	.10	.05	.01
□ 290	Todd Hundley	.30	.14	.04
□ 291	Tim Leary	.10	.05	.01
□ 292	Brett Butler	.15	.07	.02
□ 293	Gregg Olson	.10	.05	.01
□ 294	Jeff Brantley	.15	.07	.02
□ 295	Brian Holman	.10	.05	.01
□ 296	Brian Harper	.10	.05	.01
□ 297	Brian Bohanon	.10	.05	.01
□ 298	Checklist 1-100	.10	.05	.01
□ 299	Checklist 101-200	.10	.05	.01
□ 300	Checklist 201-300	.10	.05	.01
□ 301	Frank Thomas	3.00	1.35	.35
□ 302	Lloyd McClendon	.10	.05	.01
□ 303	Brady Anderson	.30	.14	.04
□ 304	Julio Valera	.10	.05	.01
□ 305	Mike Aldrete	.10	.05	.01
□ 306	Joe Oliver	.10	.05	.01
□ 307	Todd Stottlemyre	.15	.07	.02
□ 308	Rey Sanchez	.10	.05	.01
□ 309	Gary Sheffield UER (Listed as 5'1", should be 5'11")	.30	.14	.04
□ 310	Andujar Cedeno	.10	.05	.01
□ 311	Kenny Rogers	.10	.05	.01
□ 312	Bruce Hurst	.10	.05	.01
□ 313	Mike Schooler	.10	.05	.01
□ 314	Mike Benjamin	.10	.05	.01
□ 315	Chuck Finley	.10	.05	.01
□ 316	Mark Lemke	.10	.05	.01
□ 317	Scott Livingstone	.10	.05	.01
□ 318	Chris Nabholz	.10	.05	.01
□ 319	Mike Humphreys	.10	.05	.01
□ 320	Pedro Guerrero	.10	.05	.01
□ 321	Willie Banks	.10	.05	.01
□ 322	Tom Goodwin	.15	.07	.02
□ 323	Hector Wagner	.10	.05	.01
□ 324	Wally Ritchie	.10	.05	.01
□ 325	Mo Vaughn	.75	.35	.09
□ 326	Joe Klink	.10	.05	.01
□ 327	Cal Eldred	.10	.05	.01
□ 328	Daryl Boston	.10	.05	.01
□ 329	Mike Huff	.10	.05	.01
□ 330	Jeff Bagwell	1.25	.55	.16
□ 331	Bob Milacki	.10	.05	.01
□ 332	Tom Prince	.10	.05	.01
□ 333	Pat Tabler	.10	.05	.01
□ 334	Ced Landrum	.10	.05	.01
□ 335	Reggie Jefferson	.15	.07	.02
□ 336	Mo Sanford	.10	.05	.01
□ 337	Kevin Ritz	.10	.05	.01
□ 338	Gerald Perry	.10	.05	.01
□ 339	Jeff Hamilton	.10	.05	.01
□ 340	Tim Wallach	.10	.05	.01
□ 341	Jeff Huson	.10	.05	.01
□ 342	Jose Melendez	.10	.05	.01
□ 343	Willie Wilson	.10	.05	.01
□ 344	Mike Stanton	.10	.05	.01
□ 345	Joel Johnston	.10	.05	.01
□ 346	Lee Guetterman	.10	.05	.01
□ 347	Francisco Oliveras	.10	.05	.01
□ 348	Dave Burba	.10	.05	.01
□ 349	Tim Crews	.10	.05	.01
□ 350	Scott Leius	.10	.05	.01
□ 351	Danny Cox	.10	.05	.01
□ 352	Wayne Housie	.10	.05	.01
□ 353	Chris Donnels	.10	.05	.01
□ 354	Chris George	.10	.05	.01
□ 355	Gerald Young	.10	.05	.01
□ 356	Roberto Hernandez	.30	.14	.04
□ 357	Neal Heaton	.10	.05	.01
□ 358	Todd Frohwirth	.10	.05	.01
□ 359	Jose Vizcaino	.10	.05	.01
□ 360	Jim Thome	1.50	.70	.19
□ 361	Craig Wilson	.10	.05	.01
□ 362	Dave Haas	.10	.05	.01
□ 363	Billy Hatcher	.10	.05	.01
□ 364	John Barfield	.10	.05	.01
□ 365	Luis Aquino	.10	.05	.01
□ 366	Charlie Leibrandt	.10	.05	.01
□ 367	Howard Farmer	.10	.05	.01
□ 368	Bryn Smith	.10	.05	.01
□ 369	Mickey Morandini	.10	.05	.01
□ 370	Jose Canseco (See also 597)	.30	.14	.04
□ 371	Jose Uribe	.10	.05	.01
□ 372	Bob MacDonald	.10	.05	.01
□ 373	Luis Sojo	.10	.05	.01
□ 374	Craig Shipley	.10	.05	.01
□ 375	Scott Bankhead	.10	.05	.01
□ 376	Greg Gagne	.10	.05	.01
□ 377	Scott Cooper	.10	.05	.01
□ 378	Jose Offerman	.10	.05	.01
□ 379	Billy Spiers	.10	.05	.01
□ 380	John Smiley	.10	.05	.01
□ 381	Jeff Carter	.10	.05	.01
□ 382	Heathcliff Slocumb	.10	.05	.01
□ 383	Jeff Tackett	.10	.05	.01
□ 384	John Kiely	.10	.05	.01
□ 385	John Vander Wal	.10	.05	.01
□ 386	Omar Olivares	.10	.05	.01
□ 387	Ruben Sierra	.15	.07	.02
□ 388	Tom Gordon	.10	.05	.01
□ 389	Charles Nagy	.15	.07	.02
□ 390	Dave Stewart	.15	.07	.02
□ 391	Pete Harnisch	.10	.05	.01
□ 392	Tim Burke	.10	.05	.01
□ 393	Roberto Kelly	.10	.05	.01
□ 394	Freddie Benavides	.10	.05	.01
□ 395	Tom Glavine	.30	.14	.04
□ 396	Wes Chamberlain	.10	.05	.01
□ 397	Eric Gunderson	.10	.05	.01
□ 398	Dave West	.10	.05	.01
□ 399	Ellis Burks	.30	.14	.04
□ 400	Ken Griffey Jr.	3.00	1.35	.35
□ 401	Thomas Howard	.10	.05	.01
□ 402	Juan Guzman	.15	.07	.02
□ 403	Mitch Webster	.10	.05	.01
□ 404	Matt Merullo	.10	.05	.01
□ 405	Steve Buechele	.10	.05	.01
□ 406	Danny Jackson	.10	.05	.01
□ 407	Felix Jose	.10	.05	.01
□ 408	Doug Piatt	.10	.05	.01
□ 409	Jim Eisenreich	.10	.05	.01
□ 410	Bryan Harvey	.10	.05	.01
□ 411	Jim Austin	.10	.05	.01
□ 412	Jim Poole	.10	.05	.01
□ 413	Glenallen Hill	.10	.05	.01
□ 414	Gene Nelson	.10	.05	.01
□ 415	Ivan Rodriguez	.60	.25	.07
□ 416	Frank Tanana	.10	.05	.01
□ 417	Steve Decker	.10	.05	.01
□ 418	Jason Grimsley	.10	.05	.01
□ 419	Tim Layana	.10	.05	.01
□ 420	Don Mattingly	1.00	.45	.12
□ 421	Jerome Walton	.10	.05	.01
□ 422	Rob Ducey	.10	.05	.01
□ 423	Andy Benes	.10	.05	.01
□ 424	John Marzano	.10	.05	.01
□ 425	Gene Harris	.10	.05	.01
□ 426	Tim Raines	.30	.14	.04
□ 427	Bret Barberie	.10	.05	.01
□ 428	Harvey Pulliam	.10	.05	.01
□ 429	Cris Carpenter	.10	.05	.01
□ 430	Howard Johnson	.10	.05	.01
□ 431	Orel Hershiser	.15	.07	.02
□ 432	Brian Hunter	.10	.05	.01
□ 433	Kevin Tapani	.10	.05	.01
□ 434	Rick Reed	.10	.05	.01
□ 435	Ron Witmeyer	.15	.07	.02
□ 436	Gary Gaetti	.15	.07	.02
□ 437	Alex Cole	.10	.05	.01
□ 438	Chito Martinez	.10	.05	.01
□ 439	Greg Litton	.10	.05	.01
□ 440	Julio Franco	.15	.07	.02
□ 441	Mike Munoz	.10	.05	.01
□ 442	Erik Pappas	.10	.05	.01
□ 443	Pat Combs	.10	.05	.01
□ 444	Lance Johnson	.15	.07	.02
□ 445	Ed Sprague	.15	.07	.02

□ 446	Mike Greenwell	.10	.05	.01
□ 447	Milt Thompson	.10	.05	.01
□ 448	Mike Magnante	.10	.05	.01
□ 449	Chris Haney	.10	.05	.01
□ 450	Robin Yount	.30	.14	.04
□ 451	Rafael Ramirez	.10	.05	.01
□ 452	Gino Minutelli	.10	.05	.01
□ 453	Tom Lampkin	.10	.05	.01
□ 454	Tony Perezchica	.10	.05	.01
□ 455	Dwight Gooden	.15	.07	.02
□ 456	Mark Guthrie	.10	.05	.01
□ 457	Jay Howell	.10	.05	.01
□ 458	Gary DiSarcina	.10	.05	.01
□ 459	John Smoltz	.30	.14	.04
□ 460	Will Clark	.30	.14	.04
□ 461	Dave Otto	.10	.05	.01
□ 462	Rob Maurer	.10	.05	.01
□ 463	Dwight Evans	.15	.07	.02
□ 464	Tom Brunansky	.10	.05	.01
□ 465	Shawn Hare	.10	.05	.01
□ 466	Geronimo Pena	.10	.05	.01
□ 467	Alex Fernandez	.30	.14	.04
□ 468	Greg Myers	.10	.05	.01
□ 469	Jeff Fassero	.15	.07	.02
□ 470	Len Dykstra	.15	.07	.02
□ 471	Jeff Johnson	.10	.05	.01
□ 472	Russ Swan	.10	.05	.01
□ 473	Archie Corbin	.10	.05	.01
□ 474	Chuck McElroy	.10	.05	.01
□ 475	Mark McGwire	.60	.25	.07
□ 476	Wally Whitehurst	.10	.05	.01
□ 477	Tim McIntosh	.10	.05	.01
□ 478	Sid Bream	.10	.05	.01
□ 479	Jeff Juden	.10	.05	.01
□ 480	Carlton Fisk	.30	.14	.04
□ 481	Jeff Plympton	.10	.05	.01
□ 482	Carlos Martinez	.10	.05	.01
□ 483	Jim Gott	.10	.05	.01
□ 484	Bob McClure	.10	.05	.01
□ 485	Tim Teufel	.10	.05	.01
□ 486	Vicente Palacios	.10	.05	.01
□ 487	Jeff Reed	.10	.05	.01
□ 488	Tony Phillips	.15	.07	.02
□ 489	Mel Rojas	.15	.07	.02
□ 490	Ben McDonald	.10	.05	.01
□ 491	Andres Santana	.10	.05	.01
□ 492	Chris Beasley	.10	.05	.01
□ 493	Mike Timlin	.10	.05	.01
□ 494	Brian Downing	.10	.05	.01
□ 495	Kirk Gibson	.15	.07	.02
□ 496	Scott Sanderson	.10	.05	.01
□ 497	Nick Esasky	.10	.05	.01
□ 498	Johnny Guzman	.10	.05	.01
□ 499	Mitch Williams	.10	.05	.01
□ 500	Kirby Puckett	.60	.25	.07
□ 501	Mike Harkey	.10	.05	.01
□ 502	Jim Gantner	.10	.05	.01
□ 503	Bruce Egloff	.10	.05	.01
□ 504	Josias Manzanillo	.10	.05	.01
□ 505	Delino DeShields	.10	.05	.01
□ 506	Rheal Cormier	.10	.05	.01
□ 507	Jay Bell	.15	.07	.02
□ 508	Rich Rowland	.10	.05	.01
□ 509	Scott Servais	.10	.05	.01
□ 510	Terry Pendleton	.15	.07	.02
□ 511	Rich DeLucia	.10	.05	.01
□ 512	Warren Newson	.10	.05	.01
□ 513	Paul Faries	.10	.05	.01
□ 514	Kal Daniels	.10	.05	.01
□ 515	Jarvis Brown	.10	.05	.01
□ 516	Rafael Palmeiro	.30	.14	.04
□ 517	Kelly Downs	.10	.05	.01
□ 518	Steve Chitren	.10	.05	.01
□ 519	Moises Alou	.30	.14	.04
□ 520	Wade Boggs	.30	.14	.04
□ 521	Pete Schourek	.15	.07	.02
□ 522	Scott Terry	.10	.05	.01
□ 523	Kevin Appier	.15	.07	.02
□ 524	Gary Redus	.10	.05	.01
□ 525	George Bell	.10	.05	.01
□ 526	Jeff Kaiser	.10	.05	.01
□ 527	Alvaro Espinoza	.10	.05	.01
□ 528	Luis Polonia	.10	.05	.01
□ 529	Darren Daulton	.15	.07	.02
□ 530	Norm Charlton	.10	.05	.01
□ 531	John Olerud	.15	.07	.02
□ 532	Dan Plesac	.10	.05	.01
□ 533	Billy Ripken	.10	.05	.01
□ 534	Rod Nichols	.10	.05	.01
□ 535	Joey Cora	.10	.05	.01
□ 536	Harold Baines	.15	.07	.02
□ 537	Bob Ojeda	.10	.05	.01
□ 538	Mark Leonard	.10	.05	.01
□ 539	Danny Darwin	.10	.05	.01
□ 540	Shawon Dunston	.10	.05	.01
□ 541	Pedro Munoz	.10	.05	.01
□ 542	Mark Gubicza	.10	.05	.01
□ 543	Kevin Baez	.10	.05	.01
□ 544	Todd Zeile	.10	.05	.01
□ 545	Don Slaught	.10	.05	.01
□ 546	Tony Eusebio	.10	.05	.01
□ 547	Alonzo Powell	.10	.05	.01
□ 548	Gary Pettis	.10	.05	.01
□ 549	Brian Barnes	.10	.05	.01
□ 550	Lou Whitaker	.30	.14	.04
□ 551	Keith Mitchell	.10	.05	.01
□ 552	Oscar Azocar	.10	.05	.01
□ 553	Stu Cole	.10	.05	.01
□ 554	Steve Wapnick	.10	.05	.01
□ 555	Derek Bell	.15	.07	.02
□ 556	Luis Lopez	.10	.05	.01
□ 557	Anthony Telford	.10	.05	.01
□ 558	Tim Mauser	.10	.05	.01
□ 559	Glen Sutko	.10	.05	.01
□ 560	Darryl Strawberry	.15	.07	.02
□ 561	Tom Bolton	.10	.05	.01
□ 562	Cliff Young	.10	.05	.01
□ 563	Bruce Walton	.10	.05	.01
□ 564	Chico Walker	.10	.05	.01
□ 565	John Franco	.10	.05	.01
□ 566	Paul McClellan	.10	.05	.01
□ 567	Paul Abbott	.10	.05	.01
□ 568	Gary Varsho	.10	.05	.01
□ 569	Carlos Maldonado	.10	.05	.01
□ 570	Kelly Gruber	.10	.05	.01
□ 571	Jose Oquendo	.10	.05	.01
□ 572	Steve Frey	.10	.05	.01
□ 573	Tino Martinez	.30	.14	.04
□ 574	Bill Haselman	.10	.05	.01
□ 575	Eric Anthony	.10	.05	.01
□ 576	John Habyan	.10	.05	.01
□ 577	Jeff McNeely	.10	.05	.01
□ 578	Chris Bosio	.10	.05	.01
□ 579	Joe Grahe	.10	.05	.01
□ 580	Fred McGriff	.30	.14	.04
□ 581	Rick Honeycutt	.10	.05	.01
□ 582	Matt Williams	.30	.14	.04
□ 583	Cliff Brantley	.10	.05	.01
□ 584	Rob Dibble	.10	.05	.01
□ 585	Skeeter Barnes	.10	.05	.01
□ 586	Greg Hibbard	.10	.05	.01
□ 587	Randy Milligan	.10	.05	.01
□ 588	Checklist 301-400	.10	.05	.01
□ 589	Checklist 401-500	.10	.05	.01
□ 590	Checklist 501-600	.10	.05	.01
□ 591	Frank Thomas MC	1.50	.70	.19
□ 592	David Justice MC	.15	.07	.02
□ 593	Roger Clemens MC	.30	.14	.04
□ 594	Steve Avery MC	.15	.07	.02
□ 595	Cal Ripken MC	1.00	.45	.12
□ 596	Barry Larkin MC UER (Ranked in AL, should be NL)	.30	.14	.04
□ 597	Jose Canseco MC UER (Mistakenly numbered 370 on card back)	.15	.07	.02
□ 598	Will Clark MC	.15	.07	.02
□ 599	Cecil Fielder MC	.10	.05	.01
□ 600	Ryne Sandberg MC	.30	.14	.04
□ 601	Chuck Knoblauch MC	.30	.14	.04
□ 602	Dwight Gooden MC	.10	.05	.01
□ 603	Ken Griffey Jr. MC	1.50	.70	.19
□ 604	Barry Bonds MC	.30	.14	.04
□ 605	Nolan Ryan MC	1.00	.45	.12
□ 606	Jeff Bagwell MC	.60	.25	.07
□ 607	Robin Yount MC	.30	.14	.04
□ 608	Bobby Bonilla MC	.10	.05	.01
□ 609	George Brett MC	.40	.18	.05
□ 610	Howard Johnson MC	.10	.05	.01
□ 611	Esteban Beltre	.10	.05	.01
□ 612	Mike Christopher	.10	.05	.01
□ 613	Troy Afenir	.10	.05	.01

☐ 614	Mariano Duncan	.10	.05	.01
☐ 615	Doug Henry	.10	.05	.01
☐ 616	Doug Jones	.10	.05	.01
☐ 617	Alvin Davis	.10	.05	.01
☐ 618	Craig Lefferts	.10	.05	.01
☐ 619	Kevin McReynolds	.10	.05	.01
☐ 620	Barry Bonds	.50	.23	.06
☐ 621	Turner Ward	.10	.05	.01
☐ 622	Joe Magrane	.10	.05	.01
☐ 623	Mark Parent	.10	.05	.01
☐ 624	Tom Browning	.10	.05	.01
☐ 625	John Smiley	.10	.05	.01
☐ 626	Steve Wilson	.10	.05	.01
☐ 627	Mike Gallego	.10	.05	.01
☐ 628	Sammy Sosa	.50	.23	.06
☐ 629	Rico Rossy	.10	.05	.01
☐ 630	Royce Clayton	.15	.07	.02
☐ 631	Clay Parker	.10	.05	.01
☐ 632	Pete Smith	.10	.05	.01
☐ 633	Jeff McKnight	.10	.05	.01
☐ 634	Jack Daugherty	.10	.05	.01
☐ 635	Steve Sax	.10	.05	.01
☐ 636	Joe Hesketh	.10	.05	.01
☐ 637	Vince Horsman	.10	.05	.01
☐ 638	Eric King	.10	.05	.01
☐ 639	Joe Boever	.10	.05	.01
☐ 640	Jack Morris	.15	.07	.02
☐ 641	Arthur Rhodes	.10	.05	.01
☐ 642	Bob Melvin	.10	.05	.01
☐ 643	Rick Wilkins	.10	.05	.01
☐ 644	Scott Scudder	.10	.05	.01
☐ 645	Bip Roberts	.10	.05	.01
☐ 646	Julio Valera	.10	.05	.01
☐ 647	Kevin Campbell	.10	.05	.01
☐ 648	Steve Searcy	.10	.05	.01
☐ 649	Scott Kamieniecki	.10	.05	.01
☐ 650	Kurt Stillwell	.10	.05	.01
☐ 651	Bob Welch	.10	.05	.01
☐ 652	Andres Galarraga	.30	.14	.04
☐ 653	Mike Jackson	.10	.05	.01
☐ 654	Bo Jackson	.30	.14	.04
☐ 655	Sid Fernandez	.10	.05	.01
☐ 656	Mike Bielecki	.10	.05	.01
☐ 657	Jeff Reardon	.15	.07	.02
☐ 658	Wayne Rosenthal	.10	.05	.01
☐ 659	Eric Bullock	.10	.05	.01
☐ 660	Eric Davis	.15	.07	.02
☐ 661	Randy Tomlin	.10	.05	.01
☐ 662	Tom Edens	.10	.05	.01
☐ 663	Rob Murphy	.10	.05	.01
☐ 664	Leo Gomez	.10	.05	.01
☐ 665	Greg Maddux	1.50	.70	.19
☐ 666	Greg Vaughn	.30	.14	.04
☐ 667	Wade Taylor	.10	.05	.01
☐ 668	Brad Arnsberg	.10	.05	.01
☐ 669	Mike Moore	.10	.05	.01
☐ 670	Mark Langston	.15	.07	.02
☐ 671	Barry Jones	.10	.05	.01
☐ 672	Bill Landrum	.10	.05	.01
☐ 673	Greg Swindell	.10	.05	.01
☐ 674	Wayne Edwards	.10	.05	.01
☐ 675	Greg Olson	.10	.05	.01
☐ 676	Bill Pulsipher	1.00	.45	.12
☐ 677	Bobby Witt	.10	.05	.01
☐ 678	Mark Carreon	.10	.05	.01
☐ 679	Patrick Lennon	.10	.05	.01
☐ 680	Ozzie Smith	.40	.18	.05
☐ 681	John Briscoe	.10	.05	.01
☐ 682	Matt Young	.10	.05	.01
☐ 683	Jeff Conine	.30	.14	.04
☐ 684	Phil Stephenson	.10	.05	.01
☐ 685	Ron Darling	.10	.05	.01
☐ 686	Bryan Hickerson	.10	.05	.01
☐ 687	Dale Sveum	.10	.05	.01
☐ 688	Kirk McCaskill	.10	.05	.01
☐ 689	Rich Amaral	.10	.05	.01
☐ 690	Danny Tartabull	.10	.05	.01
☐ 691	Donald Harris	.10	.05	.01
☐ 692	Doug Davis	.10	.05	.01
☐ 693	John Farrell	.10	.05	.01
☐ 694	Paul Gibson	.10	.05	.01
☐ 695	Kenny Lofton	2.50	1.10	.30
☐ 696	Mike Fetters	.10	.05	.01
☐ 697	Rosario Rodriguez	.10	.05	.01
☐ 698	Chris Jones	.10	.05	.01
☐ 699	Jeff Manto	.10	.05	.01
☐ 700	Rick Sutcliffe	.10	.05	.01
☐ 701	Scott Bankhead	.10	.05	.01
☐ 702	Donnie Hill	.10	.05	.01
☐ 703	Todd Worrell	.10	.05	.01
☐ 704	Rene Gonzales	.10	.05	.01
☐ 705	Rick Cerone	.10	.05	.01
☐ 706	Tony Pena	.10	.05	.01
☐ 707	Paul Sorrento	.10	.05	.01
☐ 708	Gary Scott	.10	.05	.01
☐ 709	Junior Noboa	.10	.05	.01
☐ 710	Wally Joyner	.15	.07	.02
☐ 711	Charlie Hayes	.10	.05	.01
☐ 712	Rich Rodriguez	.10	.05	.01
☐ 713	Rudy Seanez	.10	.05	.01
☐ 714	Jim Bullinger	.10	.05	.01
☐ 715	Jeff M. Robinson	.10	.05	.01
☐ 716	Jeff Branson	.10	.05	.01
☐ 717	Andy Ashby	.15	.07	.02
☐ 718	Dave Burba	.10	.05	.01
☐ 719	Rich Gossage	.15	.07	.02
☐ 720	Randy Johnson	.30	.14	.04
☐ 721	David Wells	.10	.05	.01
☐ 722	Paul Kilgus	.10	.05	.01
☐ 723	Dave Martinez	.10	.05	.01
☐ 724	Denny Neagle	.15	.07	.02
☐ 725	Andy Stankiewicz	.10	.05	.01
☐ 726	Rick Aguilera	.10	.05	.01
☐ 727	Junior Ortiz	.10	.05	.01
☐ 728	Storm Davis	.10	.05	.01
☐ 729	Don Robinson	.10	.05	.01
☐ 730	Ron Gant	.30	.14	.04
☐ 731	Paul Assenmacher	.10	.05	.01
☐ 732	Mike Gardiner	.10	.05	.01
☐ 733	Milt Hill	.10	.05	.01
☐ 734	Jeremy Hernandez	.10	.05	.01
☐ 735	Ken Hill	.30	.14	.04
☐ 736	Xavier Hernandez	.10	.05	.01
☐ 737	Gregg Jefferies	.30	.14	.04
☐ 738	Dick Schofield	.10	.05	.01
☐ 739	Ron Robinson	.10	.05	.01
☐ 740	Sandy Alomar	.15	.07	.02
☐ 741	Mike Stanley	.10	.05	.01
☐ 742	Butch Henry	.10	.05	.01
☐ 743	Floyd Bannister	.10	.05	.01
☐ 744	Brian Drahman	.10	.05	.01
☐ 745	Dave Winfield	.30	.14	.04
☐ 746	Bob Walk	.10	.05	.01
☐ 747	Chris James	.10	.05	.01
☐ 748	Don Prybylinski	.10	.05	.01
☐ 749	Dennis Rasmussen	.10	.05	.01
☐ 750	Rickey Henderson	.30	.14	.04
☐ 751	Chris Hammond	.10	.05	.01
☐ 752	Bob Kipper	.10	.05	.01
☐ 753	Dave Rohde	.10	.05	.01
☐ 754	Hubie Brooks	.10	.05	.01
☐ 755	Bret Saberhagen	.15	.07	.02
☐ 756	Jeff D. Robinson	.10	.05	.01
☐ 757	Pat Listach	.15	.07	.02
☐ 758	Bill Wegman	.10	.05	.01
☐ 759	John Wetteland	.15	.07	.02
☐ 760	Phil Plantier	.15	.07	.02
☐ 761	Wilson Alvarez	.30	.14	.04
☐ 762	Scott Aldred	.10	.05	.01
☐ 763	Armando Reynoso	.10	.05	.01
☐ 764	Todd Benzinger	.10	.05	.01
☐ 765	Kevin Mitchell	.15	.07	.02
☐ 766	Gary Sheffield	.30	.14	.04
☐ 767	Allan Anderson	.10	.05	.01
☐ 768	Rusty Meacham	.10	.05	.01
☐ 769	Rick Parker	.10	.05	.01
☐ 770	Nolan Ryan	2.00	.90	.25
☐ 771	Jeff Ballard	.10	.05	.01
☐ 772	Cory Snyder	.10	.05	.01
☐ 773	Denis Boucher	.10	.05	.01
☐ 774	Jose Gonzalez	.10	.05	.01
☐ 775	Juan Guerrero	.10	.05	.01
☐ 776	Ed Nunez	.10	.05	.01
☐ 777	Scott Ruskin	.10	.05	.01
☐ 778	Terry Leach	.10	.05	.01
☐ 779	Carl Willis	.10	.05	.01
☐ 780	Bobby Bonilla	.15	.07	.02
☐ 781	Duane Ward	.10	.05	.01
☐ 782	Joe Slusarski	.10	.05	.01
☐ 783	David Segui	.10	.05	.01
☐ 784	Kirk Gibson	.15	.07	.02
☐ 785	Frank Viola	.10	.05	.01

□ 786 Keith Miller	.10	.05	.01
□ 787 Mike Morgan	.10	.05	.01
□ 788 Kim Batiste	.10	.05	.01
□ 789 Sergio Valdez	.10	.05	.01
□ 790 Eddie Taubensee	.10	.05	.01
□ 791 Jack Armstrong	.10	.05	.01
□ 792 Scott Fletcher	.10	.05	.01
□ 793 Steve Farr	.10	.05	.01
□ 794 Dan Pasqua	.10	.05	.01
□ 795 Eddie Murray	.50	.23	.06
□ 796 John Morris	.10	.05	.01
□ 797 Francisco Cabrera	.10	.05	.01
□ 798 Mike Perez	.10	.05	.01
□ 799 Ted Wood	.10	.05	.01
□ 800 Jose Rijo	.10	.05	.01
□ 801 Danny Gladden	.10	.05	.01
□ 802 Archi Cianfrocco	.10	.05	.01
□ 803 Monty Fariss	.10	.05	.01
□ 804 Roger McDowell	.10	.05	.01
□ 805 Randy Myers	.15	.07	.02
□ 806 Kirk Dressendorfer	.10	.05	.01
□ 807 Zane Smith	.10	.05	.01
□ 808 Glenn Davis	.10	.05	.01
□ 809 Torey Lovullo	.10	.05	.01
□ 810 Andre Dawson	.30	.14	.04
□ 811 Bill Pecota	.10	.05	.01
□ 812 Ted Power	.10	.05	.01
□ 813 Willie Blair	.10	.05	.01
□ 814 Dave Fleming	.10	.05	.01
□ 815 Chris Gwynn	.10	.05	.01
□ 816 Jody Reed	.10	.05	.01
□ 817 Mark Dewey	.10	.05	.01
□ 818 Kyle Abbott	.10	.05	.01
□ 819 Tom Henke	.10	.05	.01
□ 820 Kevin Seitzer	.10	.05	.01
□ 821 Al Newman	.10	.05	.01
□ 822 Tim Sherrill	.10	.05	.01
□ 823 Chuck Crim	.10	.05	.01
□ 824 Darren Reed	.10	.05	.01
□ 825 Tony Gwynn	.75	.35	.09
□ 826 Steve Foster	.10	.05	.01
□ 827 Steve Howe	.10	.05	.01
□ 828 Brook Jacoby	.10	.05	.01
□ 829 Rodney McCray	.10	.05	.01
□ 830 Chuck Knoblauch	.30	.14	.04
□ 831 John Wehner	.10	.05	.01
□ 832 Scott Garrelts	.10	.05	.01
□ 833 Alejandro Pena	.10	.05	.01
□ 834 Jeff Parrett UER (Kentucky)	.10	.05	.01
□ 835 Juan Bell	.10	.05	.01
□ 836 Lance Dickson	.10	.05	.01
□ 837 Darryl Kile	.10	.05	.01
□ 838 Efrain Valdez	.10	.05	.01
□ 839 Bob Zupcic	.10	.05	.01
□ 840 George Bell	.10	.05	.01
□ 841 Dave Gallagher	.10	.05	.01
□ 842 Tim Belcher	.10	.05	.01
□ 843 Jeff Shaw	.10	.05	.01
□ 844 Mike Fitzgerald	.10	.05	.01
□ 845 Gary Carter	.30	.14	.04
□ 846 John Russell	.10	.05	.01
□ 847 Eric Hillman	.10	.05	.01
□ 848 Mike Witt	.10	.05	.01
□ 849 Curt Wilkerson	.10	.05	.01
□ 850 Alan Trammell	.30	.14	.04
□ 851 Rex Hudler	.10	.05	.01
□ 852 Mike Walkden	.10	.05	.01
□ 853 Kevin Ward	.10	.05	.01
□ 854 Tim Naehring	.15	.07	.02
□ 855 Bill Swift	.10	.05	.01
□ 856 Damon Berryhill	.10	.05	.01
□ 857 Mark Eichhorn	.10	.05	.01
□ 858 Hector Villanueva	.10	.05	.01
□ 859 Jose Lind	.10	.05	.01
□ 860 Denny Martinez	.15	.07	.02
□ 861 Bill Krueger	.10	.05	.01
□ 862 Mike Kingery	.10	.05	.01
□ 863 Jeff Innis	.10	.05	.01
□ 864 Derek Lilliquist	.10	.05	.01
□ 865 Reggie Sanders	.30	.14	.04
□ 866 Ramon Garcia	.10	.05	.01
□ 867 Bruce Ruffin	.10	.05	.01
□ 868 Dickie Thon	.10	.05	.01
□ 869 Melido Perez	.10	.05	.01
□ 870 Ruben Amaro	.10	.05	.01
□ 871 Alan Mills	.10	.05	.01
□ 872 Matt Sinatro	.10	.05	.01
□ 873 Eddie Zosky	.10	.05	.01
□ 874 Pete Incaviglia	.10	.05	.01
□ 875 Tom Candiotti	.10	.05	.01
□ 876 Bob Patterson	.10	.05	.01
□ 877 Neal Heaton	.10	.05	.01
□ 878 Terrel Hansen	.10	.05	.01
□ 879 Dave Eiland	.10	.05	.01
□ 880 Von Hayes	.10	.05	.01
□ 881 Tim Scott	.10	.05	.01
□ 882 Otis Nixon	.10	.05	.01
□ 883 Herm Winningham	.10	.05	.01
□ 884 Dion James	.10	.05	.01
□ 885 Dave Wainhouse	.10	.05	.01
□ 886 Frank DiPino	.10	.05	.01
□ 887 Dennis Cook	.10	.05	.01
□ 888 Jose Mesa	.15	.07	.02
□ 889 Mark Leiter	.10	.05	.01
□ 890 Willie Randolph	.15	.07	.02
□ 891 Craig Colbert	.10	.05	.01
□ 892 Dwayne Henry	.10	.05	.01
□ 893 Jim Lindeman	.10	.05	.01
□ 894 Charlie Hough	.10	.05	.01
□ 895 Gil Heredia	.10	.05	.01
□ 896 Scott Chiamparino	.10	.05	.01
□ 897 Lance Blankenship	.10	.05	.01
□ 898 Checklist 601-700	.10	.05	.01
□ 899 Checklist 701-800	.10	.05	.01
□ 900 Checklist 801-900	.10	.05	.01

1992 Stadium Club First Draft Picks

This three-card standard-size set, featuring Major League Baseball's Number 1 draft pick for 1990, 1991, and 1992, was randomly inserted into 1992 Stadium Club Series III packs at an approximate rate of 1:72. One card also was mailed to each member of Topps Stadium Club. The cards feature on the fronts full-bleed posed color player photos. The player's draft year is printed on an orange circle in the upper right corner and is accented by gold foil stripes of varying lengths that run vertically down the right edge of the card. The player's name appears on the Stadium Club logo at the bottom. The number "1" is gold-foil stamped in a black diamond at the lower left and is followed by a red stripe gold-foil stamped with the words "Draft Pick of the '90s". The back design features color photos on a black and red background with the player's signature gold-foil stamped across the bottom of the photo and gold foil bars running down the right edge of the picture. The team name and biographical information is included in a yellow and white box.

	MINT	NRMT	EXC
COMPLETE SET (3)	20.00	9.00	2.50
COMMON CARD (1-3)	1.00	.45	.12
ONE CARD SENT TO EACH CLUB MEMBER.			
RANDOM INSERTS IN SER.3 PACKS			

□ 1 Chipper Jones	18.00	8.00	2.20
□ 2 Brien Taylor	1.00	.45	.12
□ 3 Phil Nevin	2.00	.90	.25

1993 Stadium Club Murphy

This 200-card boxed set features 1992 All-Star Game cards, 1992 Team USA cards, and 1992 Championship and World Series cards. Topps actually refers to this set as a 1992 issue, but the set was released in 1993. The standard-size cards display full-bleed posed and action color player shots on the fronts. The player's name appears below the Topps Stadium Club logo in the lower right with parallel gold foil stripes intersecting the logo. The horizontal back presents the player's biography, statistics, and highlights on a ghosted photo. This set is housed in a replica of San Diego's Jack Murphy Stadium, site of the 1992 All-Star Game. Production was limited to 8,000 cases, with 16 boxes per case. The set includes 100 Draft Pick cards, 56 All-Star cards, 25 Team USA cards, and 19 cards commemorating the 1992 National and American League Championship Series and the World Series. Rookie Cards in this set include Trey Beamon, Damon Hollins, Derek Jeter, Jason Kendall, Jon Lieber, Michael Moore, Chad Mottola, Benji Simonton and Preston Wilson.

	MINT	NRMT	EXC
COMPLETE FACT.SET (212)	30.00	13.50	3.70
COMPLETE SET (200)	25.00	11.00	3.10
COMMON CARD (1-200)	.10	.05	.01
SEMISTARS	.25	.11	.03
STARS	.50	.23	.06
MASTER PHOTO SET (12)	5.00	2.20	.60
MASTER PHOTOS: 1X BASIC CARDS			
ONE MP SET PER FACTORY SET			

□ 1 Dave Winfield	.50	.23	.06
□ 2 Juan Guzman	.25	.11	.03
□ 3 Tony Gwynn	1.25	.55	.16
□ 4 Chris Roberts	.25	.11	.03
□ 5 Benny Santiago	.10	.05	.01
□ 6 Sherard Clinkscales	.10	.05	.01
□ 7 Jon Nunnally	.25	.11	.03
□ 8 Chuck Knoblauch	.50	.23	.06
□ 9 Bob Wolcott	.50	.23	.06
□ 10 Steve Rodriguez	.10	.05	.01
□ 11 Mark Williams	.10	.05	.01
□ 12 Danny Clyburn	1.00	.45	.12
□ 13 Darren Dreifort	.10	.05	.01
□ 14 Andy Van Slyke	.25	.11	.03
□ 15 Wade Boggs	.50	.23	.06
□ 16 Scott Patton	.10	.05	.01
□ 17 Gary Sheffield	.50	.23	.06
□ 18 Ron Villone	.25	.11	.03
□ 19 Roberto Alomar	.75	.35	.09
□ 20 Marc Valdes	.10	.05	.01
□ 21 Daron Kirkreit	.10	.05	.01
□ 22 Jeff Granger	.10	.05	.01
□ 23 Levon Largusa	.10	.05	.01
□ 24 Jimmy Key	.25	.11	.03
□ 25 Kevin Pearson	.10	.05	.01
□ 26 Michael Moore	.10	.05	.01
□ 27 Preston Wilson	.50	.23	.06
□ 28 Kirby Puckett	1.00	.45	.12
□ 29 Tim Crabtree	.10	.05	.01
□ 30 Bip Roberts	.10	.05	.01
□ 31 Kelly Gruber	.10	.05	.01
□ 32 Tony Fernandez	.10	.05	.01
□ 33 Jason Angel	.10	.05	.01
□ 34 Calvin Murray	.10	.05	.01
□ 35 Chad McConnell	.10	.05	.01
□ 36 Jason Moler	.10	.05	.01
□ 37 Mark Lemke	.10	.05	.01
□ 38 Tom Knauss	.10	.05	.01
□ 39 Larry Mitchell	.10	.05	.01
□ 40 Doug Mirabelli	.10	.05	.01
□ 41 Everett Stull II	.30	.14	.04
□ 42 Chris Wimmer	.10	.05	.01
□ 43 Dan Serafini	.50	.23	.06
□ 44 Ryne Sandberg	.75	.35	.09
□ 45 Steve Lyons	25.00	11.00	3.10
□ 46 Ryan Freeburg	.10	.05	.01
□ 47 Ruben Sierra	.25	.11	.03
□ 48 David Mysel	.10	.05	.01
□ 49 Joe Hamilton	.10	.05	.01
□ 50 Steve Rodriguez	.10	.05	.01
□ 51 Tim Wakefield	.25	.11	.03
□ 52 Scott Gentile	.10	.05	.01
□ 53 Doug Jones	.10	.05	.01
□ 54 Willie Brown	.10	.05	.01
□ 55 Chad Mottola	.25	.11	.03
□ 56 Ken Griffey Jr.	3.00	1.35	.35
□ 57 Jon Lieber	.25	.11	.03
□ 58 Denny Martinez	.25	.11	.03
□ 59 Joe Petcka	.10	.05	.01
□ 60 Benji Simonton	.10	.05	.01
□ 61 Brett Backlund	.10	.05	.01
□ 62 Damon Berryhill	.10	.05	.01
□ 63 Juan Guzman	.25	.11	.03
□ 64 Doug Hecker	.10	.05	.01
□ 65 Jamie Arnold	.25	.11	.03
□ 66 Bob Tewksbury	.10	.05	.01
□ 67 Tim Leger	.10	.05	.01
□ 68 Todd Etler	.25	.11	.03
□ 69 Lloyd McClendon	.10	.05	.01
□ 70 Kurt Ehmann	.10	.05	.01
□ 71 Rick Magdaleno	.25	.11	.03
□ 72 Tom Pagnozzi	.10	.05	.01
□ 73 Jeffrey Hammonds	.25	.11	.03
□ 74 Joe Carter	.50	.23	.06
□ 75 Chris Holt	.10	.05	.01
□ 76 Charles Johnson	.50	.23	.06
□ 77 Bob Walk	.10	.05	.01
□ 78 Fred McGriff	.50	.23	.06
□ 79 Tom Evans	.25	.11	.03
□ 80 Scott Klingenbeck	.10	.05	.01
□ 81 Chad McConnell	.10	.05	.01
□ 82 Chris Eddy	.10	.05	.01
□ 83 Phil Nevin	.10	.05	.01
□ 84 John Kruk	.25	.11	.03
□ 85 Tony Sheffield	.10	.05	.01
□ 86 John Smoltz	.50	.23	.06
□ 87 Trevor Humphry	.10	.05	.01
□ 88 Charles Nagy	.25	.11	.03
□ 89 Sean Runyan	.10	.05	.01
□ 90 Mike Gulan	.10	.05	.01
□ 91 Darren Daulton	.25	.11	.03
□ 92 Otis Nixon	.10	.05	.01
□ 93 Nomar Garciaparra	2.00	.90	.25
□ 94 Larry Walker	.50	.23	.06
□ 95 Hut Smith	.10	.05	.01
□ 96 Rick Helling	.25	.11	.03
□ 97 Roger Clemens	.50	.23	.06
□ 98 Ron Gant	.50	.23	.06
□ 99 Kenny Felder	.10	.05	.01
□ 100 Steve Murphy	.10	.05	.01
□ 101 Mike Smith	.25	.11	.03
□ 102 Terry Pendleton	.25	.11	.03
□ 103 Tim Davis	.10	.05	.01
□ 104 Jeff Patzke	.50	.23	.06
□ 105 Craig Wilson	.10	.05	.01
□ 106 Tom Glavine	.50	.23	.06
□ 107 Mark Langston	.25	.11	.03
□ 108 Mark Thompson	.10	.05	.01
□ 109 Eric Owens	.25	.11	.03
□ 110 Keith Johnson	.10	.05	.01
□ 111 Robin Ventura	.25	.11	.03
□ 112 Ed Sprague	.25	.11	.03
□ 113 Jeff Schmidt	.10	.05	.01
□ 114 Don Wengert	.10	.05	.01
□ 115 Craig Biggio	.50	.23	.06
□ 116 Kenny Carlyle	.10	.05	.01
□ 117 Derek Jeter	6.00	2.70	.75
□ 118 Manuel Lee	.10	.05	.01
□ 119 Jeff Haas	.10	.05	.01

□ 120	Roger Bailey	.10	.05	.01
□ 121	Sean Lowe	.25	.11	.03
□ 122	Rick Aguilera	25.00	11.00	3.10
□ 123	Sandy Alomar	.25	.11	.03
□ 124	Derek Wallace	.10	.05	.01
□ 125	B.J. Wallace	.10	.05	.01
□ 126	Greg Maddux	2.00	.90	.25
□ 127	Tim Moore	.10	.05	.01
□ 128	Lee Smith	.25	.11	.03
□ 129	Todd Steverson	.10	.05	.01
□ 130	Chris Widger	.10	.05	.01
□ 131	Paul Molitor	.60	.25	.07
□ 132	Chris Smith	.10	.05	.01
□ 133	Chris Gomez	.25	.11	.03
□ 134	Jimmy Baron	.10	.05	.01
□ 135	John Smoltz	.50	.23	.06
□ 136	Pat Borders	.10	.05	.01
□ 137	Donnie Leshnock	.10	.05	.01
□ 138	Gus Gandarillos	.10	.05	.01
□ 139	Will Clark	.50	.23	.06
□ 140	Ryan Luzinski	.25	.11	.03
□ 141	Cal Ripken	2.50	1.10	.30
□ 142	B.J. Wallace	.10	.05	.01
□ 143	Trey Beamon	1.25	.55	.16
□ 144	Norm Charlton	.10	.05	.01
□ 145	Mike Mussina	.60	.25	.07
□ 146	Billy Owens	.10	.05	.01
□ 147	Ozzie Smith	.60	.25	.07
□ 148	Jason Kendall	2.00	.90	.25
□ 149	Mike Matthews	.25	.11	.03
□ 150	David Spykstra	.10	.05	.01
□ 151	Benji Grigsby	.10	.05	.01
□ 152	Sean Smith	.25	.11	.03
□ 153	Mark McGwire	1.00	.45	.12
□ 154	David Cone	.50	.23	.06
□ 155	Shon Walker	.25	.11	.03
□ 156	Jason Giambi	1.00	.45	.12
□ 157	Jack McDowell	.25	.11	.03
□ 158	Paxton Briley	.10	.05	.01
□ 159	Edgar Martinez	.50	.23	.06
□ 160	Brian Sackinsky	.10	.05	.01
□ 161	Barry Bonds	.75	.35	.09
□ 162	Roberto Kelly	25.00	11.00	3.10
□ 163	Jeff Alkire	.10	.05	.01
□ 164	Mike Sharperson	.10	.05	.01
□ 165	Jamie Taylor	.10	.05	.01
□ 166	John Saffer	.10	.05	.01
□ 167	Jerry Browne	.10	.05	.01
□ 168	Travis Fryman	.50	.23	.06
□ 169	Brady Anderson	.50	.23	.06
□ 170	Chris Roberts	.25	.11	.03
□ 171	Lloyd Peever	.10	.05	.01
□ 172	Francisco Cabrera	.10	.05	.01
□ 173	Ramiro Martinez	.10	.05	.01
□ 174	Jeff Alkire	.10	.05	.01
□ 175	Ivan Rodriguez	.60	.25	.07
□ 176	Kevin Brown	.10	.05	.01
□ 177	Chad Roper	.25	.11	.03
□ 178	Rod Henderson	.10	.05	.01
□ 179	Dennis Eckersley	.25	.11	.03
□ 180	Shannon Stewart	.50	.23	.06
□ 181	DeShawn Warren	.25	.11	.03
□ 182	Lonnie Smith	25.00	11.00	3.10
□ 183	Willie Adams	.10	.05	.01
□ 184	Jeff Montgomery	.25	.11	.03
□ 185	Damon Hollins	.50	.23	.06
□ 186	Byron Mathews	.10	.05	.01
□ 187	Harold Baines	.25	.11	.03
□ 188	Rick Greene	.10	.05	.01
□ 189	Carlos Baerga	.50	.23	.06
□ 190	Brandon Cromer	.25	.11	.03
□ 191	Roberto Alomar	.75	.35	.09
□ 192	Rich Ireland	.10	.05	.01
□ 193	Steve Montgomery	.10	.05	.01
□ 194	Brant Brown	.10	.05	.01
□ 195	Ritchie Moody	.10	.05	.01
□ 196	Michael Tucker	.50	.23	.06
□ 197	Jason Varitek	.50	.23	.06
□ 198	David Manning	.10	.05	.01
□ 199	Marquis Riley	.10	.05	.01
□ 200	Jason Giambi	1.00	.45	.12

1993 Stadium Club

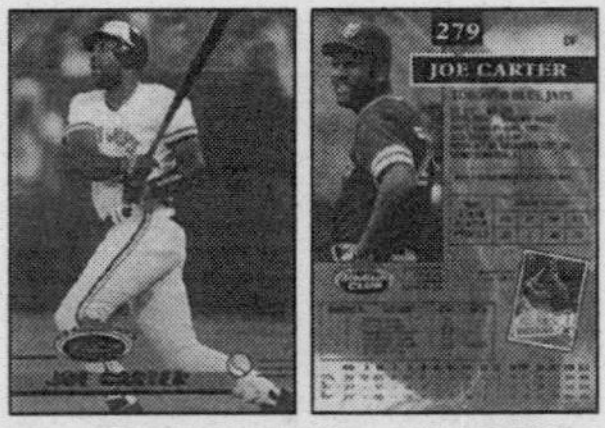

The 1993 Stadium Club baseball set consists of 750 standard-size cards issued in three series of 300, 300, and 150 cards respectively. Randomly inserted throughout first series packs were a Stadium Club Master Photo winner card (redeemable for three master photos), a 1st Day Production card, and four special bonus cards featuring the newest members of the 3,000 Hit Club (Robin Yount and George Brett) and the Number One Expansion Draft Picks of the Florida Marlins and Colorado Rockies (Nigel Wilson and David Nied). Fewer than 2,000 of each card were imprinted with a special foil First Day Production logo. According to Topps, one of these insert cards were to be found in approximately one in every 24 packs. Also every hobby box contained a Stadium Club Master Photo. The fronts display full-bleed glossy color player photos. A red stripe carrying the player's name and edged on the bottom by a gold stripe cuts across the bottom of the picture. A white baseball icon with gold motion streaks rounds out the front. Award Winner and League Leader cards are studded with gold foil stars. On a background consisting of an artistic drawing of a baseball player's arm extended with ball in glove, the backs carry a second color action photo, biographical information, 1992 Stats Player Profile, the player's ranking (either on his team and/or the AL or NL), statistics, and a miniature reproduction of his Topps rookie card. Each series closes with a Members Choice subset (291-300, 591-600, and 746-750. Rookie Cards in this set include Roberto Mejia, J.T. Snow, and Tony Tarasco. A 1993 Stadium Club "Members Only" set was also issued as a direct-mail offer to members of Topps Stadium Club. Also issued in three series, this set is identical to the regular 750-set, except that each card has in its upper corner a gold foil "Members Only" seal. With the third and final shipment, the collector received a certificate of authenticity registering the set serial number out of a production run of 12,000 sets.

	MINT	NRMT	EXC
COMPLETE SET (750)	60.00	27.00	7.50
COMPLETE SERIES 1 (300)	20.00	9.00	2.50
COMPLETE SERIES 2 (300)	25.00	11.00	3.10
COMPLETE SERIES 3 (150)	15.00	6.75	1.85
COMMON CARD (1-750)	.10	.05	.01
SEMISTARS	.25	.11	.03
STARS	.50	.23	.06
COMPLETE FDI SET (750)	2000.00	900.00	250.00
COMP.FDI SERIES 1 (300)	700.00	325.00	90.00
COMP.FDI SERIES 2 (300)	800.00	350.00	100.00
COMP.FDI SERIES 3 (150)	500.00	220.00	60.00
COMMON FDI (1-750)	1.00	.45	.12
FDI SEMISTARS	2.50	1.10	.30
*FDI VETERAN STARS: 15X TO 30X HI			
*FDI YOUNG STARS: 10X TO 20X HI			
FDI: RANDOM INSERTS IN PACKS			

□ 1	Pat Borders	.10	.05	.01
□ 2	Greg Maddux	2.00	.90	.25
□ 3	Daryl Boston	.10	.05	.01
□ 4	Bob Ayrault	.10	.05	.01
□ 5	Tony Phillips IF	.10	.05	.01
□ 6	Damion Easley	.10	.05	.01
□ 7	Kip Gross	.10	.05	.01
□ 8	Jim Thome	1.50	.70	.19

□ 9 Tim Belcher	.10	.05	.01
□ 10 Gary Wayne	.10	.05	.01
□ 11 Sam Militello	.10	.05	.01
□ 12 Mike Magnante	.10	.05	.01
□ 13 Tim Wakefield	.25	.11	.03
□ 14 Tim Hulett	.10	.05	.01
□ 15 Rheal Cormier	.10	.05	.01
□ 16 Juan Guerrero	.10	.05	.01
□ 17 Rich Gossage	.25	.11	.03
□ 18 Tim Laker	.10	.05	.01
□ 19 Darrin Jackson	.10	.05	.01
□ 20 Jack Clark	.10	.05	.01
□ 21 Roberto Hernandez	.25	.11	.03
□ 22 Dean Palmer	.25	.11	.03
□ 23 Harold Reynolds	.10	.05	.01
□ 24 Dan Plesac	.10	.05	.01
□ 25 Brent Mayne	.10	.05	.01
□ 26 Pat Hentgen	.50	.23	.06
□ 27 Luis Sojo	.10	.05	.01
□ 28 Ron Gant	.50	.23	.06
□ 29 Paul Gibson	.10	.05	.01
□ 30 Bip Roberts	.10	.05	.01
□ 31 Mickey Tettleton	.10	.05	.01
□ 32 Randy Velarde	.10	.05	.01
□ 33 Brian McRae	.25	.11	.03
□ 34 Wes Chamberlain	.10	.05	.01
□ 35 Wayne Kirby	.10	.05	.01
□ 36 Rey Sanchez	.10	.05	.01
□ 37 Jesse Orosco	.10	.05	.01
□ 38 Mike Stanton	.10	.05	.01
□ 39 Royce Clayton	.25	.11	.03
□ 40 Cal Ripken UER	2.50	1.10	.30
(Place of birth Havre de Grave; should be Havre de Grace)			
□ 41 John Dopson	.10	.05	.01
□ 42 Gene Larkin	.10	.05	.01
□ 43 Tim Raines	.50	.23	.06
□ 44 Randy Myers	.25	.11	.03
□ 45 Clay Parker	.10	.05	.01
□ 46 Mike Scioscia	.10	.05	.01
□ 47 Pete Incaviglia	.10	.05	.01
□ 48 Todd Van Poppel	.10	.05	.01
□ 49 Ray Lankford	.50	.23	.06
□ 50 Eddie Murray	.75	.35	.09
□ 51 Barry Bonds COR	.75	.35	.09
□ 51A Barry Bonds ERR	.75	.35	.09
(Missing four stars over name to indicate NL MVP)			
□ 52 Gary Thurman	.10	.05	.01
□ 53 Bob Wickman	.10	.05	.01
□ 54 Joey Cora	.10	.05	.01
□ 55 Kenny Rogers	.10	.05	.01
□ 56 Mike Devereaux	.10	.05	.01
□ 57 Kevin Seitzer	.10	.05	.01
□ 58 Rafael Belliard	.10	.05	.01
□ 59 David Wells	.10	.05	.01
□ 60 Mark Clark	.10	.05	.01
□ 61 Carlos Baerga	.50	.23	.06
□ 62 Scott Brosius	.10	.05	.01
□ 63 Jeff Grotewold	.10	.05	.01
□ 64 Rick Wrona	.10	.05	.01
□ 65 Kurt Knudsen	.10	.05	.01
□ 66 Lloyd McClendon	.10	.05	.01
□ 67 Omar Vizquel	.50	.23	.06
□ 68 Jose Vizcaino	.10	.05	.01
□ 69 Rob Ducey	.10	.05	.01
□ 70 Casey Candaele	.10	.05	.01
□ 71 Ramon Martinez	.25	.11	.03
□ 72 Todd Hundley	.50	.23	.06
□ 73 John Marzano	.10	.05	.01
□ 74 Derek Parks	.10	.05	.01
□ 75 Jack McDowell	.25	.11	.03
□ 76 Tim Scott	.10	.05	.01
□ 77 Mike Mussina	.60	.25	.07
□ 78 Delino DeShields	.10	.05	.01
□ 79 Chris Bosio	.10	.05	.01
□ 80 Mike Bordick	.10	.05	.01
□ 81 Rod Beck	.25	.11	.03
□ 82 Ted Power	.10	.05	.01
□ 83 John Kruk	.25	.11	.03
□ 84 Steve Shifflett	.10	.05	.01
□ 85 Danny Tartabull	.10	.05	.01
□ 86 Mike Greenwell	.10	.05	.01
□ 87 Jose Melendez	.10	.05	.01
□ 88 Craig Wilson	.10	.05	.01
□ 89 Melvin Nieves	.50	.23	.06
□ 90 Ed Sprague	.25	.11	.03
□ 91 Willie McGee	.10	.05	.01
□ 92 Joe Orsulak	.10	.05	.01
□ 93 Jeff King	.25	.11	.03
□ 94 Dan Pasqua	.10	.05	.01
□ 95 Brian Harper	.10	.05	.01
□ 96 Joe Oliver	.10	.05	.01
□ 97 Shane Turner	.10	.05	.01
□ 98 Lenny Harris	.10	.05	.01
□ 99 Jeff Parrett	.10	.05	.01
□ 100 Luis Polonia	.10	.05	.01
□ 101 Kent Bottenfield	.10	.05	.01
□ 102 Albert Belle	1.50	.70	.19
□ 103 Mike Maddux	.10	.05	.01
□ 104 Randy Tomlin	.10	.05	.01
□ 105 Andy Stankiewicz	.10	.05	.01
□ 106 Rico Rossy	.10	.05	.01
□ 107 Joe Hesketh	.10	.05	.01
□ 108 Dennis Powell	.10	.05	.01
□ 109 Derrick May	.10	.05	.01
□ 110 Pete Harnisch	.10	.05	.01
□ 111 Kent Mercker	.10	.05	.01
□ 112 Scott Fletcher	.10	.05	.01
□ 113 Rex Hudler	.10	.05	.01
□ 114 Chico Walker	.10	.05	.01
□ 115 Rafael Palmeiro	.50	.23	.06
□ 116 Mark Leiter	.10	.05	.01
□ 117 Pedro Munoz	.10	.05	.01
□ 118 Jim Bullinger	.10	.05	.01
□ 119 Ivan Calderon	.10	.05	.01
□ 120 Mike Timlin	.10	.05	.01
□ 121 Rene Gonzales	.10	.05	.01
□ 122 Greg Vaughn	.50	.23	.06
□ 123 Mike Flanagan	.10	.05	.01
□ 124 Mike Hartley	.10	.05	.01
□ 125 Jeff Montgomery	.25	.11	.03
□ 126 Mike Gallego	.10	.05	.01
□ 127 Don Slaught	.10	.05	.01
□ 128 Charlie O'Brien	.10	.05	.01
□ 129 Jose Offerman	.10	.05	.01
(Can be found with home town missing on back)			
□ 130 Mark Wohlers	.25	.11	.03
□ 131 Eric Fox	.10	.05	.01
□ 132 Doug Strange	.10	.05	.01
□ 133 Jeff Frye	.10	.05	.01
□ 134 Wade Boggs UER	.50	.23	.06
(Redundantly lists lefty breakdown)			
□ 135 Lou Whitaker	.50	.23	.06
□ 136 Craig Grebeck	.10	.05	.01
□ 137 Rich Rodriguez	.10	.05	.01
□ 138 Jay Bell	.25	.11	.03
□ 139 Felix Fermin	.10	.05	.01
□ 140 Denny Martinez	.25	.11	.03
□ 141 Eric Anthony	.10	.05	.01
□ 142 Roberto Alomar	.75	.35	.09
□ 143 Darren Lewis	.10	.05	.01
□ 144 Mike Blowers	.10	.05	.01
□ 145 Scott Bankhead	.10	.05	.01
□ 146 Jeff Reboulet	.10	.05	.01
□ 147 Frank Viola	.10	.05	.01
□ 148 Bill Pecota	.10	.05	.01
□ 149 Carlos Hernandez	.10	.05	.01
□ 150 Bobby Witt	.10	.05	.01
□ 151 Sid Bream	.10	.05	.01
□ 152 Todd Zeile	.10	.05	.01
□ 153 Dennis Cook	.10	.05	.01
□ 154 Brian Bohanon	.10	.05	.01
□ 155 Pat Kelly	.10	.05	.01
□ 156 Milt Cuyler	.10	.05	.01
□ 157 Juan Bell	.10	.05	.01
□ 158 Randy Milligan	.10	.05	.01
□ 159 Mark Gardner	.10	.05	.01
□ 160 Pat Tabler	.10	.05	.01
□ 161 Jeff Reardon	.25	.11	.03
□ 162 Ken Patterson	.10	.05	.01
□ 163 Bobby Bonilla	.25	.11	.03
□ 164 Tony Pena	.10	.05	.01
□ 165 Greg Swindell	.10	.05	.01
□ 166 Kirk McCaskill	.10	.05	.01
□ 167 Doug Drabek	.10	.05	.01
□ 168 Franklin Stubbs	.10	.05	.01
□ 169 Ron Tingley	.10	.05	.01
□ 170 Willie Banks	.10	.05	.01
□ 171 Sergio Valdez	.10	.05	.01

□ 172	Mark Lemke	.10	.05	.01
□ 173	Robin Yount	.50	.23	.06
□ 174	Storm Davis	.10	.05	.01
□ 175	Dan Walters	.10	.05	.01
□ 176	Steve Farr	.10	.05	.01
□ 177	Curt Wilkerson	.10	.05	.01
□ 178	Luis Alicea	.10	.05	.01
□ 179	Russ Swan	.10	.05	.01
□ 180	Mitch Williams	.10	.05	.01
□ 181	Wilson Alvarez	.25	.11	.03
□ 182	Carl Willis	.10	.05	.01
□ 183	Craig Biggio	.50	.23	.06
□ 184	Sean Berry	.10	.05	.01
□ 185	Trevor Wilson	.10	.05	.01
□ 186	Jeff Tackett	.10	.05	.01
□ 187	Ellis Burks	.50	.23	.06
□ 188	Jeff Branson	.10	.05	.01
□ 189	Matt Nokes	.10	.05	.01
□ 190	John Smiley	.10	.05	.01
□ 191	Danny Gladden	.10	.05	.01
□ 192	Mike Boddicker	.10	.05	.01
□ 193	Roger Pavlik	.25	.11	.03
□ 194	Paul Sorrento	.10	.05	.01
□ 195	Vince Coleman	.10	.05	.01
□ 196	Gary DiSarcina	.10	.05	.01
□ 197	Rafael Bournigal	.10	.05	.01
□ 198	Mike Schooler	.10	.05	.01
□ 199	Scott Ruskin	.10	.05	.01
□ 200	Frank Thomas	3.00	1.35	.35
□ 201	Kyle Abbott	.10	.05	.01
□ 202	Mike Perez	.10	.05	.01
□ 203	Andre Dawson	.50	.23	.06
□ 204	Bill Swift	.10	.05	.01
□ 205	Alejandro Pena	.10	.05	.01
□ 206	Dave Winfield	.50	.23	.06
□ 207	Andujar Cedeno	.10	.05	.01
□ 208	Terry Steinbach	.25	.11	.03
□ 209	Chris Hammond	.10	.05	.01
□ 210	Todd Burns	.10	.05	.01
□ 211	Hipolito Pichardo	.10	.05	.01
□ 212	John Kiely	.10	.05	.01
□ 213	Tim Teufel	.10	.05	.01
□ 214	Lee Guetterman	.10	.05	.01
□ 215	Geronimo Pena	.10	.05	.01
□ 216	Brett Butler	.25	.11	.03
□ 217	Bryan Hickerson	.10	.05	.01
□ 218	Rick Trlicek	.10	.05	.01
□ 219	Lee Stevens	.10	.05	.01
□ 220	Roger Clemens	.50	.23	.06
□ 221	Carlton Fisk	.50	.23	.06
□ 222	Chili Davis	.25	.11	.03
□ 223	Walt Terrell	.10	.05	.01
□ 224	Jim Eisenreich	.25	.11	.03
□ 225	Ricky Bones	.10	.05	.01
□ 226	Henry Rodriguez	.50	.23	.06
□ 227	Ken Hill	.25	.11	.03
□ 228	Rick Wilkins	.10	.05	.01
□ 229	Ricky Jordan	.10	.05	.01
□ 230	Bernard Gilkey	.50	.23	.06
□ 231	Tim Fortugno	.10	.05	.01
□ 232	Geno Petralli	.10	.05	.01
□ 233	Jose Rijo	.10	.05	.01
□ 234	Jim Leyritz	.10	.05	.01
□ 235	Kevin Campbell	.10	.05	.01
□ 236	Al Osuna	.10	.05	.01
□ 237	Pete Smith	.10	.05	.01
□ 238	Pete Schourek	.25	.11	.03
□ 239	Moises Alou	.50	.23	.06
□ 240	Donn Pall	.10	.05	.01
□ 241	Denny Neagle	.25	.11	.03
□ 242	Dan Peltier	.10	.05	.01
□ 243	Scott Scudder	.10	.05	.01
□ 244	Juan Guzman	.25	.11	.03
□ 245	Dave Burba	.10	.05	.01
□ 246	Rick Sutcliffe	.10	.05	.01
□ 247	Tony Fossas	.10	.05	.01
□ 248	Mike Munoz	.10	.05	.01
□ 249	Tim Salmon	.75	.35	.09
□ 250	Rob Murphy	.10	.05	.01
□ 251	Roger McDowell	.10	.05	.01
□ 252	Lance Parrish	.10	.05	.01
□ 253	Cliff Brantley	.10	.05	.01
□ 254	Scott Leius	.10	.05	.01
□ 255	Carlos Martinez	.10	.05	.01
□ 256	Vince Horsman	.10	.05	.01
□ 257	Oscar Azocar	.10	.05	.01
□ 258	Craig Shipley	.10	.05	.01
□ 259	Ben McDonald	.10	.05	.01
□ 260	Jeff Brantley	.10	.05	.01
□ 261	Damon Berryhill	.10	.05	.01
□ 262	Joe Grahe	.10	.05	.01
□ 263	Dave Hansen	.10	.05	.01
□ 264	Rich Amaral	.10	.05	.01
□ 265	Tim Pugh	.10	.05	.01
□ 266	Dion James	.10	.05	.01
□ 267	Frank Tanana	.10	.05	.01
□ 268	Stan Belinda	.10	.05	.01
□ 269	Jeff Kent	.25	.11	.03
□ 270	Bruce Ruffin	.10	.05	.01
□ 271	Xavier Hernandez	.10	.05	.01
□ 272	Darrin Fletcher	.10	.05	.01
□ 273	Tino Martinez	.25	.11	.03
□ 274	Benny Santiago	.10	.05	.01
□ 275	Scott Radinsky	.10	.05	.01
□ 276	Mariano Duncan	.10	.05	.01
□ 277	Kenny Lofton	1.25	.55	.16
□ 278	Dwight Smith	.10	.05	.01
□ 279	Joe Carter	.50	.23	.06
□ 280	Tim Jones	.10	.05	.01
□ 281	Jeff Huson	.10	.05	.01
□ 282	Phil Plantier	.10	.05	.01
□ 283	Kirby Puckett	1.00	.45	.12
□ 284	Johnny Guzman	.10	.05	.01
□ 285	Mike Morgan	.10	.05	.01
□ 286	Chris Sabo	.10	.05	.01
□ 287	Matt Williams	.50	.23	.06
□ 288	Checklist 1-100	.10	.05	.01
□ 289	Checklist 101-200	.10	.05	.01
□ 290	Checklist 201-300	.10	.05	.01
□ 291	Dennis Eckersley MC	.10	.05	.01
□ 292	Eric Karros MC	.25	.11	.03
□ 293	Pat Listach MC	.10	.05	.01
□ 294	Andy Van Slyke MC	.10	.05	.01
□ 295	Robin Ventura MC	.10	.05	.01
□ 296	Tom Glavine MC	.25	.11	.03
□ 297	Juan Gonzalez MC UER (Misspelled Gonzales)	.75	.35	.09
□ 298	Travis Fryman MC	.25	.11	.03
□ 299	Larry Walker MC	.25	.11	.03
□ 300	Gary Sheffield MC	.50	.23	.06
□ 301	Chuck Finley	.10	.05	.01
□ 302	Luis Gonzalez	.10	.05	.01
□ 303	Darryl Hamilton	.10	.05	.01
□ 304	Bien Figueroa	.10	.05	.01
□ 305	Ron Darling	.10	.05	.01
□ 306	Jonathan Hurst	.10	.05	.01
□ 307	Mike Sharperson	.10	.05	.01
□ 308	Mike Christopher	.10	.05	.01
□ 309	Marvin Freeman	.10	.05	.01
□ 310	Jay Buhner	.50	.23	.06
□ 311	Butch Henry	.10	.05	.01
□ 312	Greg W. Harris	.10	.05	.01
□ 313	Darren Daulton	.25	.11	.03
□ 314	Chuck Knoblauch	.50	.23	.06
□ 315	Greg A. Harris	.10	.05	.01
□ 316	John Franco	.10	.05	.01
□ 317	John Wehner	.10	.05	.01
□ 318	Donald Harris	.10	.05	.01
□ 319	Benny Santiago	.10	.05	.01
□ 320	Larry Walker	.50	.23	.06
□ 321	Randy Knorr	.10	.05	.01
□ 322	Ramon Martinez	.25	.11	.03
□ 323	Mike Stanley	.10	.05	.01
□ 324	Bill Wegman	.10	.05	.01
□ 325	Tom Candiotti	.10	.05	.01
□ 326	Glenn Davis	.10	.05	.01
□ 327	Chuck Crim	.10	.05	.01
□ 328	Scott Livingstone	.10	.05	.01
□ 329	Eddie Taubensee	.10	.05	.01
□ 330	George Bell	.10	.05	.01
□ 331	Edgar Martinez	.50	.23	.06
□ 332	Paul Assenmacher	.10	.05	.01
□ 333	Steve Hosey	.10	.05	.01
□ 334	Mo Vaughn	.75	.35	.09
□ 335	Bret Saberhagen	.25	.11	.03
□ 336	Mike Trombley	.10	.05	.01
□ 337	Mark Lewis	.10	.05	.01
□ 338	Terry Pendleton	.25	.11	.03
□ 339	Dave Hollins	.10	.05	.01
□ 340	Jeff Conine	.50	.23	.06
□ 341	Bob Tewksbury	.10	.05	.01
□ 342	Billy Ashley	.10	.05	.01

□ 343 Zane Smith	.10	.05	.01
□ 344 John Wetteland	.25	.11	.03
□ 345 Chris Hoiles	.10	.05	.01
□ 346 Frank Castillo	.10	.05	.01
□ 347 Bruce Hurst	.10	.05	.01
□ 348 Kevin McReynolds	.10	.05	.01
□ 349 Dave Henderson	.10	.05	.01
□ 350 Ryan Bowen	.10	.05	.01
□ 351 Sid Fernandez	.10	.05	.01
□ 352 Mark Whiten	.10	.05	.01
□ 353 Nolan Ryan	2.50	1.10	.30
□ 354 Rick Aguilera	.10	.05	.01
□ 355 Mark Langston	.25	.11	.03
□ 356 Jack Morris	.25	.11	.03
□ 357 Rob Deer	.10	.05	.01
□ 358 Dave Fleming	.10	.05	.01
□ 359 Lance Johnson	.25	.11	.03
□ 360 Joe Millette	.10	.05	.01
□ 361 Wil Cordero	.25	.11	.03
□ 362 Chito Martinez	.10	.05	.01
□ 363 Scott Servais	.10	.05	.01
□ 364 Bernie Williams	.50	.23	.06
□ 365 Pedro Martinez	.50	.23	.06
□ 366 Ryne Sandberg	.75	.35	.09
□ 367 Brad Ausmus	.10	.05	.01
□ 368 Scott Cooper	.10	.05	.01
□ 369 Rob Dibble	.10	.05	.01
□ 370 Walt Weiss	.10	.05	.01
□ 371 Mark Davis	.10	.05	.01
□ 372 Orlando Merced	.25	.11	.03
□ 373 Mike Jackson	.10	.05	.01
□ 374 Kevin Appier	.25	.11	.03
□ 375 Esteban Beltre	.10	.05	.01
□ 376 Joe Slusarski	.10	.05	.01
□ 377 William Suero	.10	.05	.01
□ 378 Pete O'Brien	.10	.05	.01
□ 379 Alan Embree	.10	.05	.01
□ 380 Lenny Webster	.10	.05	.01
□ 381 Eric Davis	.25	.11	.03
□ 382 Duane Ward	.10	.05	.01
□ 383 John Habyan	.10	.05	.01
□ 384 Jeff Bagwell	1.25	.55	.16
□ 385 Ruben Amaro	.10	.05	.01
□ 386 Julio Valera	.10	.05	.01
□ 387 Robin Ventura	.25	.11	.03
□ 388 Archi Cianfrocco	.10	.05	.01
□ 389 Skeeter Barnes	.10	.05	.01
□ 390 Tim Costo	.10	.05	.01
□ 391 Luis Mercedes	.10	.05	.01
□ 392 Jeremy Hernandez	.10	.05	.01
□ 393 Shawon Dunston	.10	.05	.01
□ 394 Andy Van Slyke	.25	.11	.03
□ 395 Kevin Maas	.10	.05	.01
□ 396 Kevin Brown	.10	.05	.01
□ 397 J.T. Bruett	.10	.05	.01
□ 398 Darryl Strawberry	.25	.11	.03
□ 399 Tom Pagnozzi	.10	.05	.01
□ 400 Sandy Alomar Jr.	.25	.11	.03
□ 401 Keith Miller	.10	.05	.01
□ 402 Rich DeLucia	.10	.05	.01
□ 403 Shawn Abner	.10	.05	.01
□ 404 Howard Johnson	.10	.05	.01
□ 405 Mike Benjamin	.10	.05	.01
□ 406 Roberto Mejia	.10	.05	.01
□ 407 Mike Butcher	.10	.05	.01
□ 408 Deion Sanders UER (Braves on front and Yankees on back)	.50	.23	.06
□ 409 Todd Stottlemyre	.25	.11	.03
□ 410 Scott Kamieniecki	.10	.05	.01
□ 411 Doug Jones	.10	.05	.01
□ 412 John Burkett	.10	.05	.01
□ 413 Lance Blankenship	.10	.05	.01
□ 414 Jeff Parrett	.10	.05	.01
□ 415 Barry Larkin	.50	.23	.06
□ 416 Alan Trammell	.50	.23	.06
□ 417 Mark Kiefer	.10	.05	.01
□ 418 Gregg Olson	.10	.05	.01
□ 419 Mark Grace	.50	.23	.06
□ 420 Shane Mack	.10	.05	.01
□ 421 Bob Walk	.10	.05	.01
□ 422 Curt Schilling	.10	.05	.01
□ 423 Erik Hanson	.10	.05	.01
□ 424 George Brett	1.25	.55	.16
□ 425 Reggie Jefferson	.25	.11	.03
□ 426 Mark Portugal	.10	.05	.01
□ 427 Ron Karkovice	.10	.05	.01
□ 428 Matt Young	.10	.05	.01
□ 429 Troy Neel	.10	.05	.01
□ 430 Hector Fajardo	.10	.05	.01
□ 431 Dave Righetti	.10	.05	.01
□ 432 Pat Listach	.10	.05	.01
□ 433 Jeff Innis	.10	.05	.01
□ 434 Bob MacDonald	.10	.05	.01
□ 435 Brian Jordan	.50	.23	.06
□ 436 Jeff Blauser	.10	.05	.01
□ 437 Mike Myers	.10	.05	.01
□ 438 Frank Seminara	.10	.05	.01
□ 439 Rusty Meacham	.10	.05	.01
□ 440 Greg Briley	.10	.05	.01
□ 441 Derek Lilliquist	.10	.05	.01
□ 442 John Vander Wal	.10	.05	.01
□ 443 Scott Erickson	.10	.05	.01
□ 444 Bob Scanlan	.10	.05	.01
□ 445 Todd Frohwirth	.10	.05	.01
□ 446 Tom Goodwin	.10	.05	.01
□ 447 William Pennyfeather	.10	.05	.01
□ 448 Travis Fryman	.50	.23	.06
□ 449 Mickey Morandini	.10	.05	.01
□ 450 Greg Olson	.10	.05	.01
□ 451 Trevor Hoffman	.25	.11	.03
□ 452 Dave Magadan	.10	.05	.01
□ 453 Shawn Jeter	.10	.05	.01
□ 454 Andres Galarraga	.50	.23	.06
□ 455 Ted Wood	.10	.05	.01
□ 456 Freddie Benavides	.10	.05	.01
□ 457 Junior Felix	.10	.05	.01
□ 458 Alex Cole	.10	.05	.01
□ 459 John Orton	.10	.05	.01
□ 460 Eddie Zosky	.10	.05	.01
□ 461 Dennis Eckersley	.25	.11	.03
□ 462 Lee Smith	.25	.11	.03
□ 463 John Smoltz	.50	.23	.06
□ 464 Ken Caminiti	.50	.23	.06
□ 465 Melido Perez	.10	.05	.01
□ 466 Tom Marsh	.10	.05	.01
□ 467 Jeff Nelson	.10	.05	.01
□ 468 Jesse Levis	.10	.05	.01
□ 469 Chris Nabholz	.10	.05	.01
□ 470 Mike Macfarlane	.10	.05	.01
□ 471 Reggie Sanders	.50	.23	.06
□ 472 Chuck McElroy	.10	.05	.01
□ 473 Kevin Gross	.10	.05	.01
□ 474 Matt Whiteside	.10	.05	.01
□ 475 Cal Eldred	.10	.05	.01
□ 476 Dave Gallagher	.10	.05	.01
□ 477 Len Dykstra	.25	.11	.03
□ 478 Mark McGwire	1.00	.45	.12
□ 479 David Segui	.10	.05	.01
□ 480 Mike Henneman	.10	.05	.01
□ 481 Bret Barberie	.10	.05	.01
□ 482 Steve Sax	.10	.05	.01
□ 483 Dave Valle	.10	.05	.01
□ 484 Danny Darwin	.10	.05	.01
□ 485 Devon White	.10	.05	.01
□ 486 Eric Plunk	.10	.05	.01
□ 487 Jim Gott	.10	.05	.01
□ 488 Scooter Tucker	.10	.05	.01
□ 489 Omar Olivares	.10	.05	.01
□ 490 Greg Myers	.10	.05	.01
□ 491 Brian Hunter	.10	.05	.01
□ 492 Kevin Tapani	.10	.05	.01
□ 493 Rich Monteleone	.10	.05	.01
□ 494 Steve Buechele	.10	.05	.01
□ 495 Bo Jackson	.50	.23	.06
□ 496 Mike LaValliere	.10	.05	.01
□ 497 Mark Leonard	.10	.05	.01
□ 498 Daryl Boston	.10	.05	.01
□ 499 Jose Canseco	.50	.23	.06
□ 500 Brian Barnes	.10	.05	.01
□ 501 Randy Johnson	.50	.23	.06
□ 502 Tim McIntosh	.10	.05	.01
□ 503 Cecil Fielder	.25	.11	.03
□ 504 Derek Bell	.50	.23	.06
□ 505 Kevin Koslofski	.10	.05	.01
□ 506 Darren Holmes	.10	.05	.01
□ 507 Brady Anderson	.50	.23	.06
□ 508 John Valentin	.50	.23	.06
□ 509 Jerry Browne	.10	.05	.01
□ 510 Fred McGriff	.50	.23	.06
□ 511 Pedro Astacio	.10	.05	.01
□ 512 Gary Gaetti	.25	.11	.03
□ 513 John Burke	.10	.05	.01

□ 514	Dwight Gooden	.25	.11	.03
□ 515	Thomas Howard	.10	.05	.01
□ 516	Darrell Whitmore UER (11 games played in 1992; should be 121)	.10	.05	.01
□ 517	Ozzie Guillen	.10	.05	.01
□ 518	Darryl Kile	.10	.05	.01
□ 519	Rich Rowland	.10	.05	.01
□ 520	Carlos Delgado	.75	.35	.09
□ 521	Doug Henry	.10	.05	.01
□ 522	Greg Colbrunn	.10	.05	.01
□ 523	Tom Gordon	.10	.05	.01
□ 524	Ivan Rodriguez	.60	.25	.07
□ 525	Kent Hrbek	.25	.11	.03
□ 526	Eric Young	.50	.23	.06
□ 527	Rod Brewer	.10	.05	.01
□ 528	Eric Karros	.50	.23	.06
□ 529	Marquis Grissom	.50	.23	.06
□ 530	Rico Brogna	.25	.11	.03
□ 531	Sammy Sosa	.50	.23	.06
□ 532	Bret Boone	.25	.11	.03
□ 533	Luis Rivera	.10	.05	.01
□ 534	Hal Morris	.10	.05	.01
□ 535	Monty Fariss	.10	.05	.01
□ 536	Leo Gomez	.10	.05	.01
□ 537	Wally Joyner	.25	.11	.03
□ 538	Tony Gwynn	1.25	.55	.16
□ 539	Mike Williams	.10	.05	.01
□ 540	Juan Gonzalez	1.50	.70	.19
□ 541	Ryan Klesko	1.50	.70	.19
□ 542	Ryan Thompson	.10	.05	.01
□ 543	Chad Curtis	.25	.11	.03
□ 544	Orel Hershiser	.25	.11	.03
□ 545	Carlos Garcia	.10	.05	.01
□ 546	Bob Welch	.10	.05	.01
□ 547	Vinny Castilla	.50	.23	.06
□ 548	Ozzie Smith	.60	.25	.07
□ 549	Luis Salazar	.10	.05	.01
□ 550	Mark Guthrie	.10	.05	.01
□ 551	Charles Nagy	.25	.11	.03
□ 552	Alex Fernandez	.50	.23	.06
□ 553	Mel Rojas	.25	.11	.03
□ 554	Orestes Destrade	.10	.05	.01
□ 555	Mark Gubicza	.10	.05	.01
□ 556	Steve Finley	.50	.23	.06
□ 557	Don Mattingly	1.50	.70	.19
□ 558	Rickey Henderson	.50	.23	.06
□ 559	Tommy Greene	.10	.05	.01
□ 560	Arthur Rhodes	.10	.05	.01
□ 561	Alfredo Griffin	.10	.05	.01
□ 562	Will Clark	.50	.23	.06
□ 563	Bob Zupcic	.10	.05	.01
□ 564	Chuck Carr	.10	.05	.01
□ 565	Henry Cotto	.10	.05	.01
□ 566	Billy Spiers	.10	.05	.01
□ 567	Jack Armstrong	.10	.05	.01
□ 568	Kurt Stillwell	.10	.05	.01
□ 569	David McCarty	.10	.05	.01
□ 570	Joe Vitiello	.25	.11	.03
□ 571	Gerald Williams	.10	.05	.01
□ 572	Dale Murphy	.50	.23	.06
□ 573	Scott Aldred	.10	.05	.01
□ 574	Bill Gullickson	.10	.05	.01
□ 575	Bobby Thigpen	.10	.05	.01
□ 576	Glenallen Hill	.10	.05	.01
□ 577	Dwayne Henry	.10	.05	.01
□ 578	Calvin Jones	.10	.05	.01
□ 579	Al Martin	.25	.11	.03
□ 580	Ruben Sierra	.25	.11	.03
□ 581	Andy Benes	.10	.05	.01
□ 582	Anthony Young	.10	.05	.01
□ 583	Shawn Boskie	.10	.05	.01
□ 584	Scott Pose	.10	.05	.01
□ 585	Mike Piazza	3.00	1.35	.35
□ 586	Donovan Osborne	.10	.05	.01
□ 587	James Austin	.10	.05	.01
□ 588	Checklist 301-400	.10	.05	.01
□ 589	Checklist 401-500	.10	.05	.01
□ 590	Checklist 501-600	.10	.05	.01
□ 591	Ken Griffey Jr. MC	1.50	.70	.19
□ 592	Ivan Rodriguez MC	.50	.23	.06
□ 593	Carlos Baerga MC	.25	.11	.03
□ 594	Fred McGriff MC	.50	.23	.06
□ 595	Mark McGwire MC	.50	.23	.06
□ 596	Roberto Alomar MC	.50	.23	.06
□ 597	Kirby Puckett MC	.50	.23	.06
□ 598	Marquis Grissom MC	.25	.11	.03
□ 599	John Smoltz MC	.25	.11	.03
□ 600	Ryne Sandberg MC	.50	.23	.06
□ 601	Wade Boggs	.50	.23	.06
□ 602	Jeff Reardon	.25	.11	.03
□ 603	Billy Ripken	.10	.05	.01
□ 604	Bryan Harvey	.10	.05	.01
□ 605	Carlos Quintana	.10	.05	.01
□ 606	Greg Hibbard	.10	.05	.01
□ 607	Ellis Burks	.50	.23	.06
□ 608	Greg Swindell	.10	.05	.01
□ 609	Dave Winfield	.50	.23	.06
□ 610	Charlie Hough	.10	.05	.01
□ 611	Chili Davis	.25	.11	.03
□ 612	Jody Reed	.10	.05	.01
□ 613	Mark Williamson	.10	.05	.01
□ 614	Phil Plantier	.10	.05	.01
□ 615	Jim Abbott	.10	.05	.01
□ 616	Dante Bichette	.50	.23	.06
□ 617	Mark Eichhorn	.10	.05	.01
□ 618	Gary Sheffield	.50	.23	.06
□ 619	Richie Lewis	.10	.05	.01
□ 620	Joe Girardi	.10	.05	.01
□ 621	Jaime Navarro	.10	.05	.01
□ 622	Willie Wilson	.10	.05	.01
□ 623	Scott Fletcher	.10	.05	.01
□ 624	Bud Black	.10	.05	.01
□ 625	Tom Brunansky	.10	.05	.01
□ 626	Steve Avery	.25	.11	.03
□ 627	Paul Molitor	.60	.25	.07
□ 628	Gregg Jefferies	.50	.23	.06
□ 629	Dave Stewart	.25	.11	.03
□ 630	Javier Lopez	.75	.35	.09
□ 631	Greg Gagne	.10	.05	.01
□ 632	Roberto Kelly	.10	.05	.01
□ 633	Mike Fetters	.10	.05	.01
□ 634	Ozzie Canseco	.10	.05	.01
□ 635	Jeff Russell	.10	.05	.01
□ 636	Pete Incaviglia	.10	.05	.01
□ 637	Tom Henke	.10	.05	.01
□ 638	Chipper Jones	4.00	1.80	.50
□ 639	Jimmy Key	.25	.11	.03
□ 640	Dave Martinez	.10	.05	.01
□ 641	Dave Stieb	.10	.05	.01
□ 642	Milt Thompson	.10	.05	.01
□ 643	Alan Mills	.10	.05	.01
□ 644	Tony Fernandez	.10	.05	.01
□ 645	Randy Bush	.10	.05	.01
□ 646	Joe Magrane	.10	.05	.01
□ 647	Ivan Calderon	.10	.05	.01
□ 648	Jose Guzman	.10	.05	.01
□ 649	John Olerud	.10	.05	.01
□ 650	Tom Glavine	.50	.23	.06
□ 651	Julio Franco	.25	.11	.03
□ 652	Armando Reynoso	.10	.05	.01
□ 653	Felix Jose	.10	.05	.01
□ 654	Ben Rivera	.10	.05	.01
□ 655	Andre Dawson	.50	.23	.06
□ 656	Mike Harkey	.10	.05	.01
□ 657	Kevin Seitzer	.10	.05	.01
□ 658	Lonnie Smith	.10	.05	.01
□ 659	Norm Charlton	.10	.05	.01
□ 660	David Justice	.50	.23	.06
□ 661	Fernando Valenzuela	.25	.11	.03
□ 662	Dan Wilson	.25	.11	.03
□ 663	Mark Gardner	.10	.05	.01
□ 664	Doug Dascenzo	.10	.05	.01
□ 665	Greg Maddux	2.00	.90	.25
□ 666	Harold Baines	.25	.11	.03
□ 667	Randy Myers	.25	.11	.03
□ 668	Harold Reynolds	.10	.05	.01
□ 669	Candy Maldonado	.10	.05	.01
□ 670	Al Leiter	.25	.11	.03
□ 671	Jerald Clark	.10	.05	.01
□ 672	Doug Drabek	.10	.05	.01
□ 673	Kirk Gibson	.25	.11	.03
□ 674	Steve Reed	.10	.05	.01
□ 675	Mike Felder	.10	.05	.01
□ 676	Ricky Gutierrez	.10	.05	.01
□ 677	Spike Owen	.10	.05	.01
□ 678	Otis Nixon	.10	.05	.01
□ 679	Scott Sanderson	.10	.05	.01
□ 680	Mark Carreon	.10	.05	.01
□ 681	Troy Percival	.25	.11	.03
□ 682	Kevin Stocker	.25	.11	.03
□ 683	Jim Converse	.10	.05	.01

□ 684 Barry Bonds	.75	.35	.09
□ 685 Greg Gohr	.10	.05	.01
□ 686 Tim Wallach	.10	.05	.01
□ 687 Matt Mieske	.25	.11	.03
□ 688 Robby Thompson	.10	.05	.01
□ 689 Brien Taylor	.10	.05	.01
□ 690 Kirt Manwaring	.10	.05	.01
□ 691 Mike Lansing	.25	.11	.03
□ 692 Steve Decker	.10	.05	.01
□ 693 Mike Moore	.10	.05	.01
□ 694 Kevin Mitchell	.25	.11	.03
□ 695 Phil Hiatt	.10	.05	.01
□ 696 Tony Tarasco	.25	.11	.03
□ 697 Benji Gil	.25	.11	.03
□ 698 Jeff Juden	.10	.05	.01
□ 699 Kevin Reimer	.10	.05	.01
□ 700 Andy Ashby	.25	.11	.03
□ 701 John Jaha	.25	.11	.03
□ 702 Tim Bogar	.10	.05	.01
□ 703 David Cone	.50	.23	.06
□ 704 Willie Greene	.25	.11	.03
□ 705 David Hulse	.10	.05	.01
□ 706 Cris Carpenter	.10	.05	.01
□ 707 Ken Griffey Jr.	3.00	1.35	.35
□ 708 Steve Bedrosian	.10	.05	.01
□ 709 Dave Nilsson	.25	.11	.03
□ 710 Paul Wagner	.10	.05	.01
□ 711 B.J. Surhoff	.25	.11	.03
□ 712 Rene Arocha	.10	.05	.01
□ 713 Manuel Lee	.10	.05	.01
□ 714 Brian Williams	.10	.05	.01
□ 715 Sherman Obando	.10	.05	.01
□ 716 Terry Mulholland	.10	.05	.01
□ 717 Paul O'Neill	.25	.11	.03
□ 718 David Nied	.10	.05	.01
□ 719 J.T. Snow	.50	.23	.06
□ 720 Nigel Wilson	.10	.05	.01
□ 721 Mike Bielecki	.10	.05	.01
□ 722 Kevin Young	.10	.05	.01
□ 723 Charlie Leibrandt	.10	.05	.01
□ 724 Frank Bolick	.10	.05	.01
□ 725 Jon Shave	.10	.05	.01
□ 726 Steve Cooke	.10	.05	.01
□ 727 Domingo Martinez	.10	.05	.01
□ 728 Todd Worrell	.10	.05	.01
□ 729 Jose Lind	.10	.05	.01
□ 730 Jim Tatum	.10	.05	.01
□ 731 Mike Hampton	.10	.05	.01
□ 732 Mike Draper	.10	.05	.01
□ 733 Henry Mercedes	.10	.05	.01
□ 734 John Johnstone	.10	.05	.01
□ 735 Mitch Webster	.10	.05	.01
□ 736 Russ Springer	.10	.05	.01
□ 737 Rob Natal	.10	.05	.01
□ 738 Steve Howe	.10	.05	.01
□ 739 Darrell Sherman	.10	.05	.01
□ 740 Pat Mahomes	.10	.05	.01
□ 741 Alex Arias	.10	.05	.01
□ 742 Damon Buford	.10	.05	.01
□ 743 Charlie Hayes	.10	.05	.01
□ 744 Guillermo Velasquez	.10	.05	.01
□ 745 Checklist 601-750 UER (650 Tom Glavine)	.10	.05	.01
□ 746 Frank Thomas MC	1.50	.70	.19
□ 747 Barry Bonds MC	.50	.23	.06
□ 748 Roger Clemens MC	.50	.23	.06
□ 749 Joe Carter MC	.25	.11	.03
□ 750 Greg Maddux MC	1.00	.45	.12

1993 Stadium Club Inserts

This 10-card set was randomly inserted in all series of Stadium Club packs, the first four in series 1, the second four in series 2 and the last two in series 3. The themes of the standard-size cards differ from series to series, but the basic design -- borderless color action shots on the fronts -- remains the same throughout. The series 1 and 3 cards are numbered on the back, the series 2 cards are unnumbered.

	MINT	NRMT	EXC
COMPLETE SET (10)	16.00	7.25	2.00
COMPLETE SERIES 1 (4)	5.00	2.20	.60
COMPLETE SERIES 2 (4)	10.00	4.50	1.25
COMPLETE SERIES 3 (2)	2.00	.90	.25
COMMON SER.1 CARD (A1-A4)	.50	.23	.06
COMMON SER.2 CARD (B1-B4)	1.25	.55	.16
COMMON SER.3 CARD (C1-C2)	.50	.23	.06
A1-A4 INSERTS IN SER.1 PACKS			
B1-B4 INSERTS IN SER.2 PACKS			
C1-C2 INSERTS IN SER.3 PACKS			

□ A1 Robin Yount 3000 Hit Club	1.00	.45	.12
□ A2 George Brett 3000 Hit Club	4.00	1.80	.50
□ A3 David Nied First Draft Pick of the Rockies	.50	.23	.06
□ A4 Nigel Wilson 1st DP Marlins	.50	.23	.06
□ B1 Will Clark Mark McGwire Pacific Terrific	1.25	.55	.16
□ B2 Dwight Gooden Don Mattingly Broadway Stars NY	1.50	.70	.19
□ B3 Ryne Sandberg Frank Thomas Second City Sluggers	5.00	2.20	.60
□ B4 Darryl Strawberry Ken Griffey Jr. Pacific Terrific	4.00	1.80	.50
□ C1 David Nied UER Colorado Rockies Firsts (Misspelled pitch-hitter on back)	.50	.23	.06
□ C2 Charlie Hough Florida Marlins Firsts	.50	.23	.06

1993 Stadium Club Master Photos

Each of the three Stadium Club series features Master Photos, uncropped versions of the regular Stadium Club cards. Each Master Photo is inlaid in a 5" by 7" white frame and bordered with a prismatic foil trim. The Master Photos were made available to the public in two ways. First, one in every 24 packs included a Master Photo winner card redeemable for a group of three Master Photos until Jan. 31, 1994. Second, each hobby dealer box contained one Master Photo. The cards are unnumbered and

checklisted below in alphabetical order within series I (1-12), II (13-24), and III (25-30). Two different versions of these master photos were issued, one with and one without the "Members Only" gold foil seal at the upper right corner. The "Members Only" Master Photos were only available with the direct-mail solicited 750-card Stadium Club Members Only set.

	MINT	NRMT	EXC
COMPLETE SET (30)	24.00	11.00	3.00
COMPLETE SERIES 1 (12)	6.00	2.70	.75
COMPLETE SERIES 2 (12)	8.00	3.60	1.00
COMPLETE SERIES 3 (6)	10.00	4.50	1.25
COMMON MASTER PHOTO	.25	.11	.03
SEMISTARS	.50	.23	.06
UNNUMBERED LARGE CARDS			
*WINNER CARDS SAME VALUE			
ONE PER HOBBY BOX			
THREE REDEEMED PER WINNER CARD			

	MINT	NRMT	EXC
□ 1 Carlos Baerga	.25	.11	.03
□ 2 Delino DeShields	.50	.23	.06
□ 3 Brian McRae	.50	.23	.06
□ 4 Sam Militello	.25	.11	.03
□ 5 Joe Oliver	.25	.11	.03
□ 6 Kirby Puckett	1.50	.70	.19
□ 7 Cal Ripken	4.00	1.80	.50
□ 8 Bip Roberts	.25	.11	.03
□ 9 Mike Scioscia	.25	.11	.03
□ 10 Rick Sutcliffe	.25	.11	.03
□ 11 Danny Tartabull	.50	.23	.06
□ 12 Tim Wakefield	.25	.11	.03
□ 13 George Brett	2.00	.90	.25
□ 14 Jose Canseco	.50	.23	.06
□ 15 Will Clark	.50	.23	.06
□ 16 Travis Fryman	.50	.23	.06
□ 17 Dwight Gooden	.50	.23	.06
□ 18 Mark Grace	.50	.23	.06
□ 19 Rickey Henderson	.50	.23	.06
□ 20 Mark McGwire MC	1.50	.70	.19
□ 21 Nolan Ryan	4.00	1.80	.50
□ 22 Ruben Sierra	.25	.11	.03
□ 23 Darryl Strawberry	.50	.23	.06
□ 24 Larry Walker	.50	.23	.06
□ 25 Barry Bonds	1.25	.55	.16
□ 26 Ken Griffey Jr.	5.00	2.20	.60
□ 27 Greg Maddux	3.00	1.35	.35
□ 28 David Nied	.25	.11	.03
□ 29 J.T. Snow	.50	.23	.06
□ 30 Brien Taylor	.25	.11	.03

1994 Stadium Club

The 720 standard-size cards comprising this set were issued two series of 270 and a third series of 180. Card fronts feature borderless color player action photos. The player's last name appears in white lettering within a red-foil-stamped rectangle at the bottom. His first name appears alongside in black "typewritten" lettering within a division color-coded "tear-away." The red-foil-stamped Stadium Club logo appears in an upper corner. The back carries a color player action cutout superimposed upon a blue and black background. The player's name, team, biography, career highlights and statistics appear in lettering of several different colors and typefaces. There are a number of subsets including Home Run Club (258-268), Tale of Two Players (525/526), Division Leaders (527-532), Quick Starts (533-538), Career Contributors (541-543), Rookie Rocker (626-630), Rookie Rocket (631-634) and Fantastic Finishes (714-719). Rookie Cards include Brian Anderson, Chan Ho Park and Julian Tavarez.

	MINT	NRMT	EXC
COMPLETE SET (720)	55.00	25.00	7.00
COMPLETE SERIES 1 (270)	20.00	9.00	2.50
COMPLETE SERIES 2 (270)	20.00	9.00	2.50
COMPLETE SERIES 3 (180)	15.00	6.75	1.85
COMMON CARD (1-720)	.10	.05	.01
SEMISTARS	.25	.11	.03
STARS	.50	.23	.06
COMP. RAINBOW SET (720)	170.00	75.00	21.00
COMP.RAINBOW SER.1 (270)	65.00	29.00	8.00
COMP.RAINBOW SER.2 (270)	65.00	29.00	8.00
COMP.RAINBOW SER.3 (180)	40.00	18.00	5.00
COMMON RAINBOW (1-720)	.25	.11	.03
GOLDEN RAINBOW SEMISTARS	.50	.23	.06
*G.RAINBOW STARS: 2X to 4X HI COLUMN			
*G.RAINBOW YOUNG STARS: 1.5X to 3X BASIC CARDS			
ONE GOLDEN RAINBOW PER PACK			
COMPLETE FDI SET (720)	2700.00	1200.00	350.00
COMP.FDI SERIES 1 (270)	1200.00	550.00	150.00
COMP.FDI SERIES 2 (270)	1000.00	450.00	125.00
COMP.FDI SERIES 3 (180)	500.00	220.00	60.00
COMMON FDI (1-720)	2.00	.90	.25
FDI SEMISTARS	4.00	1.80	.50
*FDI VETERAN STARS: 15X TO 30X HI			
*FDI YOUNG STARS/RCs: 10X TO 20X HI			
FDI: RANDOM INSERTS IN PACKS			

	MINT	NRMT	EXC
□ 1 Robin Yount	.40	.18	.05
□ 2 Rick Wilkins	.10	.05	.01
□ 3 Steve Scarsone	.10	.05	.01
□ 4 Gary Sheffield	.40	.18	.05
□ 5 George Brett UER (birthdate listed as 1963; should be 1953)	1.25	.55	.16
□ 6 Al Martin	.10	.05	.01
□ 7 Joe Oliver	.10	.05	.01
□ 8 Stan Belinda	.10	.05	.01
□ 9 Denny Hocking	.10	.05	.01
□ 10 Roberto Alomar	.75	.35	.09
□ 11 Luis Polonia	.10	.05	.01
□ 12 Scott Hemond	.10	.05	.01
□ 13 Jody Reed	.10	.05	.01
□ 14 Mel Rojas	.10	.05	.01
□ 15 Junior Ortiz	.10	.05	.01
□ 16 Harold Baines	.25	.11	.03
□ 17 Brad Pennington	.10	.05	.01
□ 18 Jay Bell	.25	.11	.03
□ 19 Tom Henke	.10	.05	.01
□ 20 Jeff Branson	.10	.05	.01
□ 21 Roberto Mejia	.10	.05	.01
□ 22 Pedro Munoz	.10	.05	.01
□ 23 Matt Nokes	.10	.05	.01
□ 24 Jack McDowell	.25	.11	.03
□ 25 Cecil Fielder	.25	.11	.03
□ 26 Tony Fossas	.10	.05	.01
□ 27 Jim Eisenreich	.10	.05	.01
□ 28 Anthony Young	.10	.05	.01
□ 29 Chuck Carr	.10	.05	.01
□ 30 Jeff Treadway	.10	.05	.01
□ 31 Chris Nabholz	.10	.05	.01
□ 32 Tom Candiotti	.10	.05	.01
□ 33 Mike Maddux	.10	.05	.01
□ 34 Nolan Ryan	2.50	1.10	.30
□ 35 Luis Gonzalez	.10	.05	.01
□ 36 Tim Salmon	.40	.18	.05
□ 37 Mark Whiten	.10	.05	.01
□ 38 Roger McDowell	.10	.05	.01
□ 39 Royce Clayton	.25	.11	.03
□ 40 Troy Neel	.10	.05	.01
□ 41 Mike Harkey	.10	.05	.01
□ 42 Darrin Fletcher	.10	.05	.01
□ 43 Wayne Kirby	.10	.05	.01
□ 44 Rich Amaral	.10	.05	.01
□ 45 Robb Nen UER (Nenn on back)	.25	.11	.03
□ 46 Tim Teufel	.10	.05	.01

□ 47	Steve Cooke	.10	.05	.01
□ 48	Jeff McNeely	.10	.05	.01
□ 49	Jeff Montgomery	.25	.11	.03
□ 50	Skeeter Barnes	.10	.05	.01
□ 51	Scott Stahoviak	.10	.05	.01
□ 52	Pat Kelly	.10	.05	.01
□ 53	Brady Anderson	.40	.18	.05
□ 54	Mariano Duncan	.10	.05	.01
□ 55	Brian Bohanon	.10	.05	.01
□ 56	Jerry Spradlin	.10	.05	.01
□ 57	Ron Karkovice	.10	.05	.01
□ 58	Jeff Gardner	.10	.05	.01
□ 59	Bobby Bonilla	.25	.11	.03
□ 60	Tino Martinez	.25	.11	.03
□ 61	Todd Benzinger	.10	.05	.01
□ 62	Steve Trachsel	.25	.11	.03
□ 63	Brian Jordan	.40	.18	.05
□ 64	Steve Bedrosian	.10	.05	.01
□ 65	Brent Gates	.10	.05	.01
□ 66	Shawn Green	.25	.11	.03
□ 67	Sean Berry	.10	.05	.01
□ 68	Joe Klink	.10	.05	.01
□ 69	Fernando Valenzuela	.25	.11	.03
□ 70	Andy Tomberlin	.10	.05	.01
□ 71	Tony Pena	.10	.05	.01
□ 72	Eric Young	.25	.11	.03
□ 73	Chris Gomez	.10	.05	.01
□ 74	Paul O'Neill	.25	.11	.03
□ 75	Ricky Gutierrez	.10	.05	.01
□ 76	Brad Holman	.10	.05	.01
□ 77	Lance Painter	.10	.05	.01
□ 78	Mike Butcher	.10	.05	.01
□ 79	Sid Bream	.10	.05	.01
□ 80	Sammy Sosa	.40	.18	.05
□ 81	Felix Fermin	.10	.05	.01
□ 82	Todd Hundley	.40	.18	.05
□ 83	Kevin Higgins	.10	.05	.01
□ 84	Todd Pratt	.10	.05	.01
□ 85	Ken Griffey Jr.	3.00	1.35	.35
□ 86	John O'Donoghue	.10	.05	.01
□ 87	Rick Renteria	.10	.05	.01
□ 88	John Burkett	.10	.05	.01
□ 89	Jose Vizcaino	.10	.05	.01
□ 90	Kevin Seitzer	.10	.05	.01
□ 91	Bobby Witt	.10	.05	.01
□ 92	Chris Turner	.10	.05	.01
□ 93	Omar Vizquel	.40	.18	.05
□ 94	David Justice	.40	.18	.05
□ 95	David Segui	.10	.05	.01
□ 96	Dave Hollins	.10	.05	.01
□ 97	Doug Strange	.10	.05	.01
□ 98	Jerald Clark	.10	.05	.01
□ 99	Mike Moore	.10	.05	.01
□ 100	Joey Cora	.10	.05	.01
□ 101	Scott Kamieniecki	.10	.05	.01
□ 102	Andy Benes	.25	.11	.03
□ 103	Chris Bosio	.10	.05	.01
□ 104	Rey Sanchez	.10	.05	.01
□ 105	John Jaha	.25	.11	.03
□ 106	Otis Nixon	.10	.05	.01
□ 107	Rickey Henderson	.40	.18	.05
□ 108	Jeff Bagwell	1.25	.55	.16
□ 109	Gregg Jefferies	.40	.18	.05
□ 110	Roberto Alomar	.40	.18	.05
	Paul Molitor			
	John Olerud			
□ 111	Ron Gant	.40	.18	.05
	David Justice			
	Fred McGriff			
□ 112	Juan Gonzalez	.40	.18	.05
	Rafael Palmeiro			
	Dean Palmer			
□ 113	Greg Swindell	.10	.05	.01
□ 114	Bill Haselman	.10	.05	.01
□ 115	Phil Plantier	.10	.05	.01
□ 116	Ivan Rodriguez	.60	.25	.07
□ 117	Kevin Tapani	.10	.05	.01
□ 118	Mike LaValliere	.10	.05	.01
□ 119	Tim Costo	.10	.05	.01
□ 120	Mickey Morandini	.10	.05	.01
□ 121	Brett Butler	.25	.11	.03
□ 122	Tom Pagnozzi	.10	.05	.01
□ 123	Ron Gant	.25	.11	.03
□ 124	Damion Easley	.10	.05	.01
□ 125	Dennis Eckersley	.25	.11	.03
□ 126	Matt Mieske	.10	.05	.01
□ 127	Cliff Floyd	.40	.18	.05
□ 128	Julian Tavarez	.25	.11	.03
□ 129	Arthur Rhodes	.10	.05	.01
□ 130	Dave West	.10	.05	.01
□ 131	Tim Naehring	.10	.05	.01
□ 132	Freddie Benavides	.10	.05	.01
□ 133	Paul Assenmacher	.10	.05	.01
□ 134	David McCarty	.10	.05	.01
□ 135	Jose Lind	.10	.05	.01
□ 136	Reggie Sanders	.40	.18	.05
□ 137	Don Slaught	.10	.05	.01
□ 138	Andujar Cedeno	.10	.05	.01
□ 139	Rob Deer	.10	.05	.01
□ 140	Mike Piazza UER	2.00	.90	.25
	(listed as outfielder)			
□ 141	Moises Alou	.25	.11	.03
□ 142	Tom Foley	.10	.05	.01
□ 143	Benito Santiago	.10	.05	.01
□ 144	Sandy Alomar	.25	.11	.03
□ 145	Carlos Hernandez	.10	.05	.01
□ 146	Luis Alicea	.10	.05	.01
□ 147	Tom Lampkin	.10	.05	.01
□ 148	Ryan Klesko	.75	.35	.09
□ 149	Juan Guzman	.25	.11	.03
□ 150	Scott Servais	.10	.05	.01
□ 151	Tony Gwynn	1.25	.55	.16
□ 152	Tim Wakefield	.10	.05	.01
□ 153	David Nied	.10	.05	.01
□ 154	Chris Haney	.10	.05	.01
□ 155	Danny Bautista	.10	.05	.01
□ 156	Randy Velarde	.10	.05	.01
□ 157	Darrin Jackson	.10	.05	.01
□ 158	J.R. Phillips	.10	.05	.01
□ 159	Greg Gagne	.10	.05	.01
□ 160	Luis Aquino	.10	.05	.01
□ 161	John Vander Wal	.10	.05	.01
□ 162	Randy Myers	.10	.05	.01
□ 163	Ted Power	.10	.05	.01
□ 164	Scott Brosius	.10	.05	.01
□ 165	Len Dykstra	.25	.11	.03
□ 166	Jacob Brumfield	.10	.05	.01
□ 167	Bo Jackson	.40	.18	.05
□ 168	Eddie Taubensee	.10	.05	.01
□ 169	Carlos Baerga	.40	.18	.05
□ 170	Tim Bogar	.10	.05	.01
□ 171	Jose Canseco	.40	.18	.05
□ 172	Greg Blosser UER	.10	.05	.01
	(Gregg on front)			
□ 173	Chili Davis	.25	.11	.03
□ 174	Randy Knorr	.10	.05	.01
□ 175	Mike Perez	.10	.05	.01
□ 176	Henry Rodriguez	.40	.18	.05
□ 177	Brian Turang	.10	.05	.01
□ 178	Roger Pavlik	.10	.05	.01
□ 179	Aaron Sele	.25	.11	.03
□ 180	Fred McGriff	.40	.18	.05
	Gary Sheffield			
□ 181	J.T. Snow	.25	.11	.03
	Tim Salmon			
□ 182	Roberto Hernandez	.25	.11	.03
□ 183	Jeff Reboulet	.10	.05	.01
□ 184	John Doherty	.10	.05	.01
□ 185	Danny Sheaffer	.10	.05	.01
□ 186	Bip Roberts	.10	.05	.01
□ 187	Denny Martinez	.25	.11	.03
□ 188	Darryl Hamilton	.10	.05	.01
□ 189	Eduardo Perez	.10	.05	.01
□ 190	Pete Harnisch	.10	.05	.01
□ 191	Rich Gossage	.25	.11	.03
□ 192	Mickey Tettleton	.10	.05	.01
□ 193	Lenny Webster	.10	.05	.01
□ 194	Lance Johnson	.25	.11	.03
□ 195	Don Mattingly	1.50	.70	.19
□ 196	Gregg Olson	.10	.05	.01
□ 197	Mark Gubicza	.10	.05	.01
□ 198	Scott Fletcher	.10	.05	.01
□ 199	Jon Shave	.10	.05	.01
□ 200	Tim Mauser	.10	.05	.01
□ 201	Jeromy Burnitz	.10	.05	.01
□ 202	Rob Dibble	.10	.05	.01
□ 203	Will Clark	.40	.18	.05
□ 204	Steve Buechele	.10	.05	.01
□ 205	Brian Williams	.10	.05	.01
□ 206	Carlos Garcia	.10	.05	.01
□ 207	Mark Clark	.10	.05	.01
□ 208	Rafael Palmeiro	.40	.18	.05

□ 209 Eric Davis	.25	.11	.03
□ 210 Pat Meares	.10	.05	.01
□ 211 Chuck Finley	.10	.05	.01
□ 212 Jason Bere	.25	.11	.03
□ 213 Gary DiSarcina	.10	.05	.01
□ 214 Tony Fernandez	.10	.05	.01
□ 215 B.J. Surhoff	.10	.05	.01
□ 216 Lee Guetterman	.10	.05	.01
□ 217 Tim Wallach	.10	.05	.01
□ 218 Kirt Manwaring	.10	.05	.01
□ 219 Albert Belle	1.50	.70	.19
□ 220 Doc Gooden	.25	.11	.03
□ 221 Archi Cianfrocco	.10	.05	.01
□ 222 Terry Mulholland	.10	.05	.01
□ 223 Hipolito Pichardo	.10	.05	.01
□ 224 Kent Hrbek	.25	.11	.03
□ 225 Craig Grebeck	.10	.05	.01
□ 226 Todd Jones	.10	.05	.01
□ 227 Mike Bordick	.10	.05	.01
□ 228 John Olerud	.10	.05	.01
□ 229 Jeff Blauser	.10	.05	.01
□ 230 Alex Arias	.10	.05	.01
□ 231 Bernard Gilkey	.25	.11	.03
□ 232 Denny Neagle	.25	.11	.03
□ 233 Pedro Borbon	.10	.05	.01
□ 234 Dick Schofield	.10	.05	.01
□ 235 Matias Carrillo	.10	.05	.01
□ 236 Juan Bell	.10	.05	.01
□ 237 Mike Hampton	.10	.05	.01
□ 238 Barry Bonds	.75	.35	.09
□ 239 Cris Carpenter	.10	.05	.01
□ 240 Eric Karros	.25	.11	.03
□ 241 Greg McMichael	.10	.05	.01
□ 242 Pat Hentgen	.40	.18	.05
□ 243 Tim Pugh	.10	.05	.01
□ 244 Vinny Castilla	.40	.18	.05
□ 245 Charlie Hough	.10	.05	.01
□ 246 Bobby Munoz	.10	.05	.01
□ 247 Kevin Baez	.10	.05	.01
□ 248 Todd Frohwirth	.10	.05	.01
□ 249 Charlie Hayes	.10	.05	.01
□ 250 Mike Macfarlane	.10	.05	.01
□ 251 Danny Darwin	.10	.05	.01
□ 252 Ben Rivera	.10	.05	.01
□ 253 Dave Henderson	.10	.05	.01
□ 254 Steve Avery	.25	.11	.03
□ 255 Tim Belcher	.10	.05	.01
□ 256 Dan Plesac	.10	.05	.01
□ 257 Jim Thome	.75	.35	.09
□ 258 Albert Belle 35	.75	.35	.09
□ 259 Barry Bonds 35	.40	.18	.05
□ 260 Ron Gant 35	.10	.05	.01
□ 261 Juan Gonzalez 35	.75	.35	.09
□ 262 Ken Griffey Jr. 35	1.50	.70	.19
□ 263 David Justice 35	.25	.11	.03
□ 264 Fred McGriff 35	.40	.18	.05
□ 265 Rafael Palmeiro 35	.40	.18	.05
□ 266 Mike Piazza 35	1.00	.45	.12
□ 267 Frank Thomas 35	1.50	.70	.19
□ 268 Matt Williams 35	.40	.18	.05
□ 269 Checklist 1-135	.10	.05	.01
□ 270 Checklist 136-270	.10	.05	.01
□ 271 Mike Stanley	.10	.05	.01
□ 272 Tony Tarasco	.10	.05	.01
□ 273 Teddy Higuera	.10	.05	.01
□ 274 Ryan Thompson	.10	.05	.01
□ 275 Rick Aguilera	.10	.05	.01
□ 276 Ramon Martinez	.25	.11	.03
□ 277 Orlando Merced	.25	.11	.03
□ 278 Guillermo Velasquez	.10	.05	.01
□ 279 Mark Hutton	.10	.05	.01
□ 280 Larry Walker	.40	.18	.05
□ 281 Kevin Gross	.10	.05	.01
□ 282 Jose Offerman	.10	.05	.01
□ 283 Jim Leyritz	.10	.05	.01
□ 284 Jamie Moyer	.10	.05	.01
□ 285 Frank Thomas	3.00	1.35	.35
□ 286 Derek Bell	.25	.11	.03
□ 287 Derrick May	.10	.05	.01
□ 288 Dave Winfield	.40	.18	.05
□ 289 Curt Schilling	.10	.05	.01
□ 290 Carlos Quintana	.10	.05	.01
□ 291 Bob Natal	.10	.05	.01
□ 292 David Cone	.40	.18	.05
□ 293 Al Osuna	.10	.05	.01
□ 294 Bob Hamelin	.10	.05	.01
□ 295 Chad Curtis	.10	.05	.01
□ 296 Danny Jackson	.10	.05	.01
□ 297 Bob Welch	.10	.05	.01
□ 298 Felix Jose	.10	.05	.01
□ 299 Jay Buhner	.40	.18	.05
□ 300 Joe Carter	.40	.18	.05
□ 301 Kenny Lofton	1.00	.45	.12
□ 302 Kirk Rueter	.10	.05	.01
□ 303 Kim Batiste	.10	.05	.01
□ 304 Mike Morgan	.10	.05	.01
□ 305 Pat Borders	.10	.05	.01
□ 306 Rene Arocha	.10	.05	.01
□ 307 Ruben Sierra	.25	.11	.03
□ 308 Steve Finley	.40	.18	.05
□ 309 Travis Fryman	.40	.18	.05
□ 310 Zane Smith	.10	.05	.01
□ 311 Willie Wilson	.10	.05	.01
□ 312 Trevor Hoffman	.25	.11	.03
□ 313 Terry Pendleton	.25	.11	.03
□ 314 Salomon Torres	.10	.05	.01
□ 315 Robin Ventura	.25	.11	.03
□ 316 Randy Tomlin	.10	.05	.01
□ 317 Dave Stewart	.25	.11	.03
□ 318 Mike Benjamin	.10	.05	.01
□ 319 Matt Turner	.10	.05	.01
□ 320 Manny Ramirez	1.00	.45	.12
□ 321 Kevin Young	.10	.05	.01
□ 322 Ken Caminiti	.40	.18	.05
□ 323 Joe Girardi	.10	.05	.01
□ 324 Jeff McKnight	.10	.05	.01
□ 325 Gene Harris	.10	.05	.01
□ 326 Devon White	.10	.05	.01
□ 327 Darryl Kile	.10	.05	.01
□ 328 Craig Paquette	.10	.05	.01
□ 329 Cal Eldred	.10	.05	.01
□ 330 Bill Swift	.10	.05	.01
□ 331 Alan Trammell	.40	.18	.05
□ 332 Armando Reynoso	.10	.05	.01
□ 333 Brent Mayne	.10	.05	.01
□ 334 Chris Donnels	.10	.05	.01
□ 335 Darryl Strawberry	.25	.11	.03
□ 336 Dean Palmer	.25	.11	.03
□ 337 Frank Castillo	.10	.05	.01
□ 338 Jeff King	.25	.11	.03
□ 339 John Franco	.10	.05	.01
□ 340 Kevin Appier	.25	.11	.03
□ 341 Lance Blankenship	.10	.05	.01
□ 342 Mark McLemore	.10	.05	.01
□ 343 Pedro Astacio	.10	.05	.01
□ 344 Rich Batchelor	.10	.05	.01
□ 345 Ryan Bowen	.10	.05	.01
□ 346 Terry Steinbach	.25	.11	.03
□ 347 Troy O'Leary	.10	.05	.01
□ 348 Willie Blair	.10	.05	.01
□ 349 Wade Boggs	.40	.18	.05
□ 350 Tim Raines	.40	.18	.05
□ 351 Scott Livingstone	.10	.05	.01
□ 352 Rod Correia	.10	.05	.01
□ 353 Ray Lankford	.40	.18	.05
□ 354 Pat Listach	.10	.05	.01
□ 355 Milt Thompson	.10	.05	.01
□ 356 Miguel Jimenez	.10	.05	.01
□ 357 Marc Newfield	.25	.11	.03
□ 358 Mark McGwire	1.00	.45	.12
□ 359 Kirby Puckett	1.00	.45	.12
□ 360 Kent Mercker	.10	.05	.01
□ 361 John Kruk	.25	.11	.03
□ 362 Jeff Kent	.10	.05	.01
□ 363 Hal Morris	.10	.05	.01
□ 364 Edgar Martinez	.40	.18	.05
□ 365 Dave Magadan	.10	.05	.01
□ 366 Dante Bichette	.40	.18	.05
□ 367 Chris Hammond	.10	.05	.01
□ 368 Bret Saberhagen	.25	.11	.03
□ 369 Billy Ripken	.10	.05	.01
□ 370 Bill Gullickson	.10	.05	.01
□ 371 Andre Dawson	.40	.18	.05
□ 372 Roberto Kelly	.10	.05	.01
□ 373 Cal Ripken	2.50	1.10	.30
□ 374 Craig Biggio	.40	.18	.05
□ 375 Dan Pasqua	.10	.05	.01
□ 376 Dave Nilsson	.25	.11	.03
□ 377 Duane Ward	.10	.05	.01
□ 378 Greg Vaughn	.40	.18	.05
□ 379 Jeff Fassero	.10	.05	.01
□ 380 Jerry DiPoto	.10	.05	.01

□ 381 John Patterson	.10	.05	.01
□ 382 Kevin Brown	.10	.05	.01
□ 383 Kevin Roberson	.10	.05	.01
□ 384 Joe Orsulak	.10	.05	.01
□ 385 Hilly Hathaway	.10	.05	.01
□ 386 Mike Greenwell	.10	.05	.01
□ 387 Orestes Destrade	.10	.05	.01
□ 388 Mike Gallego	.10	.05	.01
□ 389 Ozzie Guillen	.10	.05	.01
□ 390 Raul Mondesi	.40	.18	.05
□ 391 Scott Lydy	.10	.05	.01
□ 392 Tom Urbani	.10	.05	.01
□ 393 Wil Cordero	.25	.11	.03
□ 394 Tony Longmire	.10	.05	.01
□ 395 Todd Zeile	.10	.05	.01
□ 396 Scott Cooper	.10	.05	.01
□ 397 Ryne Sandberg	.75	.35	.09
□ 398 Ricky Bones	.10	.05	.01
□ 399 Phil Clark	.10	.05	.01
□ 400 Orel Hershiser	.25	.11	.03
□ 401 Mike Henneman	.10	.05	.01
□ 402 Mark Lemke	.10	.05	.01
□ 403 Mark Grace	.40	.18	.05
□ 404 Ken Ryan	.10	.05	.01
□ 405 John Smoltz	.40	.18	.05
□ 406 Jeff Conine	.40	.18	.05
□ 407 Greg Harris	.10	.05	.01
□ 408 Doug Drabek	.10	.05	.01
□ 409 Dave Fleming	.10	.05	.01
□ 410 Danny Tartabull	.10	.05	.01
□ 411 Chad Kreuter	.10	.05	.01
□ 412 Brad Ausmus	.10	.05	.01
□ 413 Ben McDonald	.10	.05	.01
□ 414 Barry Larkin	.40	.18	.05
□ 415 Bret Barberie	.10	.05	.01
□ 416 Chuck Knoblauch	.40	.18	.05
□ 417 Ozzie Smith	.60	.25	.07
□ 418 Ed Sprague	.25	.11	.03
□ 419 Matt Williams	.40	.18	.05
□ 420 Jeremy Hernandez	.10	.05	.01
□ 421 Jose Bautista	.10	.05	.01
□ 422 Kevin Mitchell	.25	.11	.03
□ 423 Manuel Lee	.10	.05	.01
□ 424 Mike Devereaux	.10	.05	.01
□ 425 Omar Olivares	.10	.05	.01
□ 426 Rafael Belliard	.10	.05	.01
□ 427 Richie Lewis	.10	.05	.01
□ 428 Ron Darling	.10	.05	.01
□ 429 Shane Mack	.10	.05	.01
□ 430 Tim Hulett	.10	.05	.01
□ 431 Wally Joyner	.25	.11	.03
□ 432 Wes Chamberlain	.10	.05	.01
□ 433 Tom Browning	.10	.05	.01
□ 434 Scott Radinsky	.10	.05	.01
□ 435 Rondell White	.40	.18	.05
□ 436 Rod Beck	.25	.11	.03
□ 437 Rheal Cormier	.10	.05	.01
□ 438 Randy Johnson	.40	.18	.05
□ 439 Pete Schourek	.25	.11	.03
□ 440 Mo Vaughn	.75	.35	.09
□ 441 Mike Timlin	.10	.05	.01
□ 442 Mark Langston	.25	.11	.03
□ 443 Lou Whitaker	.40	.18	.05
□ 444 Kevin Stocker	.10	.05	.01
□ 445 Ken Hill	.10	.05	.01
□ 446 John Wetteland	.25	.11	.03
□ 447 J.T. Snow	.25	.11	.03
□ 448 Erik Pappas	.10	.05	.01
□ 449 David Hulse	.10	.05	.01
□ 450 Darren Daulton	.25	.11	.03
□ 451 Chris Hoiles	.10	.05	.01
□ 452 Bryan Harvey	.10	.05	.01
□ 453 Darren Lewis	.10	.05	.01
□ 454 Andres Galarraga	.40	.18	.05
□ 455 Joe Hesketh	.10	.05	.01
□ 456 Jose Valentin	.25	.11	.03
□ 457 Dan Peltier	.10	.05	.01
□ 458 Joe Boever	.10	.05	.01
□ 459 Kevin Rogers	.10	.05	.01
□ 460 Craig Shipley	.10	.05	.01
□ 461 Alvaro Espinoza	.10	.05	.01
□ 462 Wilson Alvarez	.25	.11	.03
□ 463 Cory Snyder	.10	.05	.01
□ 464 Candy Maldonado	.10	.05	.01
□ 465 Blas Minor	.10	.05	.01
□ 466 Rod Bolton	.10	.05	.01
□ 467 Kenny Rogers	.10	.05	.01
□ 468 Greg Myers	.10	.05	.01
□ 469 Jimmy Key	.25	.11	.03
□ 470 Tony Castillo	.10	.05	.01
□ 471 Mike Stanton	.10	.05	.01
□ 472 Deion Sanders	.40	.18	.05
□ 473 Tito Navarro	.10	.05	.01
□ 474 Mike Gardiner	.10	.05	.01
□ 475 Steve Reed	.10	.05	.01
□ 476 John Roper	.10	.05	.01
□ 477 Mike Trombley	.10	.05	.01
□ 478 Charles Nagy	.25	.11	.03
□ 479 Larry Casian	.10	.05	.01
□ 480 Eric Hillman	.10	.05	.01
□ 481 Bill Wertz	.10	.05	.01
□ 482 Jeff Schwarz	.10	.05	.01
□ 483 John Valentin	.25	.11	.03
□ 484 Carl Willis	.10	.05	.01
□ 485 Gary Gaetti	.25	.11	.03
□ 486 Bill Pecota	.10	.05	.01
□ 487 John Smiley	.10	.05	.01
□ 488 Mike Mussina	.60	.25	.07
□ 489 Mike Ignasiak	.10	.05	.01
□ 490 Billy Brewer	.10	.05	.01
□ 491 Jack Voigt	.10	.05	.01
□ 492 Mike Munoz	.10	.05	.01
□ 493 Lee Tinsley	.25	.11	.03
□ 494 Bob Wickman	.10	.05	.01
□ 495 Roger Salkeld	.10	.05	.01
□ 496 Thomas Howard	.10	.05	.01
□ 497 Mark Davis	.10	.05	.01
□ 498 Dave Clark	.10	.05	.01
□ 499 Turk Wendell	.10	.05	.01
□ 500 Rafael Bournigal	.10	.05	.01
□ 501 Chip Hale	.10	.05	.01
□ 502 Matt Whiteside	.10	.05	.01
□ 503 Brian Koelling	.10	.05	.01
□ 504 Jeff Reed	.10	.05	.01
□ 505 Paul Wagner	.10	.05	.01
□ 506 Torey Lovullo	.10	.05	.01
□ 507 Curtis Leskanic	.25	.11	.03
□ 508 Derek Lilliquist	.10	.05	.01
□ 509 Joe Magrane	.10	.05	.01
□ 510 Mackey Sasser	.10	.05	.01
□ 511 Lloyd McClendon	.10	.05	.01
□ 512 Jayhawk Owens	.10	.05	.01
□ 513 Woody Williams	.10	.05	.01
□ 514 Gary Redus	.10	.05	.01
□ 515 Tim Spehr	.10	.05	.01
□ 516 Jim Abbott	.10	.05	.01
□ 517 Lou Frazier	.10	.05	.01
□ 518 Erik Plantenberg	.10	.05	.01
□ 519 Tim Worrell	.10	.05	.01
□ 520 Brian McRae	.25	.11	.03
□ 521 Chan Ho Park	.75	.35	.09
□ 522 Mark Wohlers	.25	.11	.03
□ 523 Geronimo Pena	.10	.05	.01
□ 524 Andy Ashby	.25	.11	.03
□ 525 Tim Raines TA	.25	.11	.03
□ 526 Paul Molitor TA	.40	.18	.05
□ 527 Joe Carter DL	.40	.18	.05
□ 528 Frank Thomas DL UER (listed as third in RBI in 1993; was actually second)	1.50	.70	.19
□ 529 Ken Griffey Jr. DL	1.50	.70	.19
□ 530 David Justice DL	.25	.11	.03
□ 531 Gregg Jefferies DL	.25	.11	.03
□ 532 Barry Bonds DL	.40	.18	.05
□ 533 John Kruk QS	.10	.05	.01
□ 534 Roger Clemens QS	.40	.18	.05
□ 535 Cecil Fielder QS	.10	.05	.01
□ 536 Ruben Sierra QS	.25	.11	.03
□ 537 Tony Gwynn QS	.60	.25	.07
□ 538 Tom Glavine QS	.25	.11	.03
□ 539 Checklist 271-405 UER (number on back is 269)	.10	.05	.01
□ 540 Checklist 406-540 UER (numbered 270 on back)	.10	.05	.01
□ 541 Ozzie Smith	.40	.18	.05
□ 542 Eddie Murray	.75	.35	.09
□ 543 Lee Smith	.25	.11	.03
□ 544 Greg Maddux	2.00	.90	.25
□ 545 Denis Boucher	.10	.05	.01
□ 546 Mark Gardner	.10	.05	.01
□ 547 Bo Jackson	.40	.18	.05
□ 548 Eric Anthony	.10	.05	.01

☐	549	Delino DeShields	.10	.05	.01
☐	550	Turner Ward	.10	.05	.01
☐	551	Scott Sanderson	.10	.05	.01
☐	552	Hector Carrasco	.10	.05	.01
☐	553	Tony Phillips	.25	.11	.03
☐	554	Melido Perez	.10	.05	.01
☐	555	Mike Felder	.10	.05	.01
☐	556	Jack Morris	.25	.11	.03
☐	557	Rafael Palmeiro	.40	.18	.05
☐	558	Shane Reynolds	.25	.11	.03
☐	559	Pete Incaviglia	.10	.05	.01
☐	560	Greg Harris	.10	.05	.01
☐	561	Matt Walbeck	.10	.05	.01
☐	562	Todd Van Poppel	.10	.05	.01
☐	563	Todd Stottlemyre	.10	.05	.01
☐	564	Ricky Bones	.10	.05	.01
☐	565	Mike Jackson	.10	.05	.01
☐	566	Kevin McReynolds	.10	.05	.01
☐	567	Melvin Nieves	.25	.11	.03
☐	568	Juan Gonzalez	1.50	.70	.19
☐	569	Frank Viola	.10	.05	.01
☐	570	Vince Coleman	.10	.05	.01
☐	571	Brian Anderson	.25	.11	.03
☐	572	Omar Vizquel	.40	.18	.05
☐	573	Bernie Williams	.40	.18	.05
☐	574	Tom Glavine	.40	.18	.05
☐	575	Mitch Williams	.10	.05	.01
☐	576	Shawon Dunston	.10	.05	.01
☐	577	Mike Lansing	.25	.11	.03
☐	578	Greg Pirkl	.10	.05	.01
☐	579	Sid Fernandez	.10	.05	.01
☐	580	Doug Jones	.10	.05	.01
☐	581	Walt Weiss	.10	.05	.01
☐	582	Tim Belcher	.10	.05	.01
☐	583	Alex Fernandez	.40	.18	.05
☐	584	Alex Cole	.10	.05	.01
☐	585	Greg Cadaret	.10	.05	.01
☐	586	Bob Tewksbury	.10	.05	.01
☐	587	Dave Hansen	.10	.05	.01
☐	588	Kurt Abbott	.25	.11	.03
☐	589	Rick White	.10	.05	.01
☐	590	Kevin Bass	.10	.05	.01
☐	591	Geronimo Berroa	.25	.11	.03
☐	592	Jaime Navarro	.10	.05	.01
☐	593	Steve Farr	.10	.05	.01
☐	594	Jack Armstrong	.10	.05	.01
☐	595	Steve Howe	.10	.05	.01
☐	596	Jose Rijo	.10	.05	.01
☐	597	Otis Nixon	.10	.05	.01
☐	598	Robby Thompson	.10	.05	.01
☐	599	Kelly Stinnett	.10	.05	.01
☐	600	Carlos Delgado	.40	.18	.05
☐	601	Brian Johnson	.10	.05	.01
☐	602	Gregg Olson	.10	.05	.01
☐	603	Jim Edmonds	.60	.25	.07
☐	604	Mike Blowers	.10	.05	.01
☐	605	Lee Smith	.25	.11	.03
☐	606	Pat Rapp	.10	.05	.01
☐	607	Mike Magnante	.10	.05	.01
☐	608	Karl Rhodes	.10	.05	.01
☐	609	Jeff Juden	.10	.05	.01
☐	610	Rusty Meacham	.10	.05	.01
☐	611	Pedro Martinez	.40	.18	.05
☐	612	Todd Worrell	.10	.05	.01
☐	613	Stan Javier	.10	.05	.01
☐	614	Mike Hampton	.10	.05	.01
☐	615	Jose Guzman	.10	.05	.01
☐	616	Xavier Hernandez	.10	.05	.01
☐	617	David Wells	.10	.05	.01
☐	618	John Habyan	.10	.05	.01
☐	619	Chris Nabholz	.10	.05	.01
☐	620	Bobby Jones	.25	.11	.03
☐	621	Chris James	.10	.05	.01
☐	622	Ellis Burks	.25	.11	.03
☐	623	Erik Hanson	.10	.05	.01
☐	624	Pat Meares	.10	.05	.01
☐	625	Harold Reynolds	.10	.05	.01
☐	626	Bob Hamelin	.10	.05	.01
☐	627	Manny Ramirez	.40	.18	.05
☐	628	Ryan Klesko	.40	.18	.05
☐	629	Carlos Delgado	.40	.18	.05
☐	630	Javier Lopez	.40	.18	.05
☐	631	Steve Karsay	.10	.05	.01
☐	632	Rick Helling	.10	.05	.01
☐	633	Steve Trachsel	.25	.11	.03
☐	634	Hector Carrasco	.10	.05	.01
☐	635	Andy Stankiewicz	.10	.05	.01
☐	636	Paul Sorrento	.10	.05	.01
☐	637	Scott Erickson	.10	.05	.01
☐	638	Chipper Jones	2.50	1.10	.30
☐	639	Luis Polonia	.10	.05	.01
☐	640	Howard Johnson	.10	.05	.01
☐	641	John Dopson	.10	.05	.01
☐	642	Jody Reed	.10	.05	.01
☐	643	Lonnie Smith	.10	.05	.01
☐	644	Mark Portugal	.10	.05	.01
☐	645	Paul Molitor	.60	.25	.07
☐	646	Paul Assenmacher	.10	.05	.01
☐	647	Hubie Brooks	.10	.05	.01
☐	648	Gary Wayne	.10	.05	.01
☐	649	Sean Berry	.10	.05	.01
☐	650	Roger Clemens	.40	.18	.05
☐	651	Brian L.Hunter	.40	.18	.05
☐	652	Wally Whitehurst	.10	.05	.01
☐	653	Allen Watson	.10	.05	.01
☐	654	Rickey Henderson	.40	.18	.05
☐	655	Sid Bream	.10	.05	.01
☐	656	Dan Wilson	.25	.11	.03
☐	657	Ricky Jordan	.10	.05	.01
☐	658	Sterling Hitchcock	.25	.11	.03
☐	659	Darrin Jackson	.10	.05	.01
☐	660	Junior Felix	.10	.05	.01
☐	661	Tom Brunansky	.10	.05	.01
☐	662	Jose Vizcaino	.10	.05	.01
☐	663	Mark Leiter	.10	.05	.01
☐	664	Gil Heredia	.10	.05	.01
☐	665	Fred McGriff	.40	.18	.05
☐	666	Will Clark	.40	.18	.05
☐	667	Al Leiter	.25	.11	.03
☐	668	James Mouton	.25	.11	.03
☐	669	Billy Bean	.10	.05	.01
☐	670	Scott Leius	.10	.05	.01
☐	671	Bret Boone	.25	.11	.03
☐	672	Darren Holmes	.10	.05	.01
☐	673	Dave Weathers	.10	.05	.01
☐	674	Eddie Murray	.75	.35	.09
☐	675	Felix Fermin	.10	.05	.01
☐	676	Chris Sabo	.10	.05	.01
☐	677	Billy Spiers	.10	.05	.01
☐	678	Aaron Sele	.25	.11	.03
☐	679	Juan Samuel	.10	.05	.01
☐	680	Julio Franco	.25	.11	.03
☐	681	Heathcliff Slocumb	.25	.11	.03
☐	682	Denny Martinez	.25	.11	.03
☐	683	Jerry Browne	.10	.05	.01
☐	684	Pedro Martinez	.10	.05	.01
☐	685	Rex Hudler	.10	.05	.01
☐	686	Willie McGee	.10	.05	.01
☐	687	Andy Van Slyke	.25	.11	.03
☐	688	Pat Mahomes	.10	.05	.01
☐	689	Dave Henderson	.10	.05	.01
☐	690	Tony Eusebio	.10	.05	.01
☐	691	Rick Sutcliffe	.10	.05	.01
☐	692	Willie Banks	.10	.05	.01
☐	693	Alan Mills	.10	.05	.01
☐	694	Jeff Treadway	.10	.05	.01
☐	695	Alex Gonzalez	.25	.11	.03
☐	696	David Segui	.10	.05	.01
☐	697	Rick Helling	.10	.05	.01
☐	698	Bip Roberts	.10	.05	.01
☐	699	Jeff Cirillo	.40	.18	.05
☐	700	Terry Mulholland	.10	.05	.01
☐	701	Marvin Freeman	.10	.05	.01
☐	702	Jason Bere	.25	.11	.03
☐	703	Javier Lopez	.40	.18	.05
☐	704	Greg Hibbard	.10	.05	.01
☐	705	Tommy Greene	.10	.05	.01
☐	706	Marquis Grissom	.40	.18	.05
☐	707	Brian Harper	.10	.05	.01
☐	708	Steve Karsay	.10	.05	.01
☐	709	Jeff Brantley	.10	.05	.01
☐	710	Jeff Russell	.10	.05	.01
☐	711	Bryan Hickerson	.10	.05	.01
☐	712	Jim Pittsley	.40	.18	.05
☐	713	Bobby Ayala	.10	.05	.01
☐	714	John Smoltz	.40	.18	.05
☐	715	Jose Rijo	.10	.05	.01
☐	716	Greg Maddux	1.00	.45	.12
☐	717	Matt Williams	.40	.18	.05
☐	718	Frank Thomas	1.50	.70	.19
☐	719	Ryne Sandberg	.40	.18	.05
☐	720	Checklist	.10	.05	.01

1994 Stadium Club Dugout Dirt

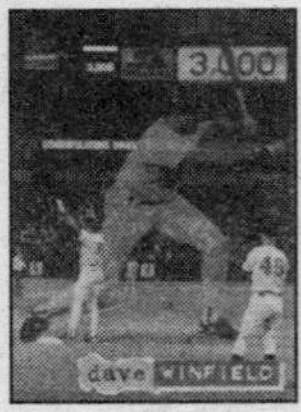

Randomly inserted at a rate of one per six packs, these standard-size cards feature some of baseball's most popular and colorful players by sports cartoonists Daniel Guidera and Steve Benson. The cards resemble basic Stadium Club cards except for a Dugout Dirt logo at the bottom. Backs contain a cartoon. Cards 1-4 were found in first series packs with cards 5-8 and 9-12 were inserted in second series and third series packs respectively.

	MINT	NRMT	EXC
COMPLETE SET (12)	10.00	4.50	1.25
COMPLETE SERIES 1 (4)	5.00	2.20	.60
COMPLETE SERIES 2 (4)	3.00	1.35	.35
COMPLETE SERIES 3 (4)	3.00	1.35	.35
COMMON CARD (DD1-DD12)	.25	.11	.03
RANDOM INSERTS IN PACKS			

□ DD1 Mike Piazza	2.00	.90	.25
□ DD2 Dave Winfield	.50	.23	.06
□ DD3 John Kruk	.25	.11	.03
□ DD4 Cal Ripken	2.50	1.10	.30
□ DD5 Kirby Puckett	1.00	.45	.12
□ DD6 Barry Bonds	.75	.35	.09
□ DD7 Ken Griffey Jr.	3.00	1.35	.35
□ DD8 Tim Salmon	.50	.23	.06
□ DD9 Frank Thomas	3.00	1.35	.35
□ DD10 Jeff Kent	.25	.11	.03
□ DD11 Randy Johnson	.50	.23	.06
□ DD12 Darren Daulton	.25	.11	.03

1994 Stadium Club Finest

This set contains 10 standard-size metallic cards of top players. They were randomly inserted one in 24 third series packs. The fronts feature a color player photo with a red and yellow background. Backs contain a color player photo with 1993 and career statistics. Jumbo versions measuring approximately five inches by seven inches were issued for retail repacks and are valued approximately 1.5X the regular versions.

	MINT	NRMT	EXC
COMPLETE SET (10)	30.00	13.50	3.70
COMMON CARD (F1-F10)	1.00	.45	.12
RANDOM INSERTS IN SER.3 PACKS			

□ F1 Jeff Bagwell	4.00	1.80	.50
□ F2 Albert Belle	5.00	2.20	.60
□ F3 Barry Bonds	2.50	1.10	.30
□ F4 Juan Gonzalez	5.00	2.20	.60
□ F5 Ken Griffey Jr.	10.00	4.50	1.25
□ F6 Marquis Grissom	1.00	.45	.12
□ F7 David Justice	1.00	.45	.12
□ F8 Mike Piazza	6.00	2.70	.75
□ F9 Tim Salmon	1.50	.70	.19
□ F10 Frank Thomas	10.00	4.50	1.25

1994 Stadium Club Super Teams

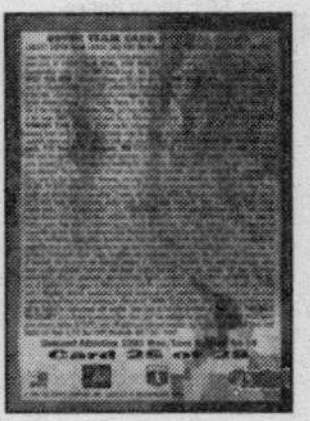

Randomly inserted at a rate of one per 24 first series packs only, this 28-card standard-size features one card for each of the 28 MLB teams. Collectors holding team cards could redeem them for special prizes if those teams won a division title, a league championship, or the World Series. But, since the strike affected the 1994 season, Topps postponed the promotion until the 1995 season. The expiration was pushed back to January 31, 1996.

	MINT	NRMT	EXC
COMPLETE SET (28)	60.00	27.00	7.50
COMMON TEAM (1-28)	1.50	.70	.19
RANDOM INSERTS IN SER.1 PACKS			
CONTEST APPLIED TO 1995 SEASON			
WINNERS LISTED UNDER 1995 STAD.CLUB			

□ ST1 Atlanta Braves (Jeff Blauser Terry Pendleton)	15.00	6.75	1.85
□ ST2 Chicago Cubs (Sammy Sosa Derrick May)	1.50	.70	.19
□ ST3 Cincinnati Reds (Reggie Sanders Barry Larkin)	4.00	1.80	.50
□ ST4 Colorado Rockies (Vinny Castilla Eric Young)	1.50	.70	.19
□ ST5 Florida Marlins (Alex Arias)	1.50	.70	.19
□ ST6 Houston Astros (Eric Anthony Steve Finley)	1.50	.70	.19
□ ST7 Los Angeles Dodgers (Mike Piazza)	4.00	1.80	.50
□ ST8 Montreal Expos (Marquis Grissom)	1.50	.70	.19
□ ST9 New York Mets (Bobby Bonilla)	1.50	.70	.19
□ ST10 Philadelphia Phillies (Mickey Morandini)	1.50	.70	.19
□ ST11 Pittsburgh Pirates (Andy Van Slyke Jay Bell)	1.50	.70	.19
□ ST12 St. Louis Cardinals (Todd Zeile Gregg Jefferies)	1.50	.70	.19
□ ST13 San Diego Padres (Ricky Gutierrez)	1.50	.70	.19
□ ST14 San Francisco Giants (Matt Williams Kirt Manwaring)	2.00	.90	.25

□ ST15 Baltimore Orioles (Cal Ripken)	8.00	3.60	1.00
□ ST16 Boston Red Sox (Luis Rivera John Valentin)	4.00	1.80	.50
□ ST17 California Angels (Tim Salmon)	1.50	.70	.19
□ ST18 Chicago White Sox (Joey Cora)	1.50	.70	.19
□ ST19 Cleveland Indians (Kenny Lofton Carlos Baerga Albert Belle)	8.00	3.60	1.00
□ ST20 Detroit Tigers (Alan Trammell Tony Phillips)	1.50	.70	.19
□ ST21 Kansas City Royals Jose Lind Curt Wilkerson)	1.50	.70	.19
□ ST22 Milwaukee Brewers (Julio Navarro John Jaha Cal Eldred)	1.50	.70	.19
□ ST23 Minnesota Twins (Kirby Puckett Kent Hrbek)	3.00	1.35	.35
□ ST24 New York Yankees Don Mattingly Bernie Williams)	4.00	1.80	.50
□ ST25 Oakland Athletics (Mike Bordick Brent Gates)	1.50	.70	.19
□ ST26 Seattle Mariners (Jay Buhner Mike Blowers)	4.00	1.80	.50
□ ST27 Texas Rangers (Ivan Rodriguez Dean Palmer Jose Canseco Juan Gonzalez)	2.00	.90	.25
□ ST28 Toronto Blue Jays (John Olerud)	1.50	.70	.19

1995 Stadium Club

The 1995 Stadium Club baseball card collection was issued in three series of 270, 225 and 135 standard-size cards for a total of 630. The cards were distributed in 14-card packs at a suggested retail price of $2.50 and contained 24 packs per box. Cards feature players in full-bleed action photos with team logo and player's name in gold foil at the bottom of the card. Backs feature statistical bar graphs and action photos of players. Rookie Cards include Scott Elarton, Hideo Nomo and Carlos Perez. Topps Stadium Club members received the Members Only set; just 4,000 sets were produced. These cards are identical to their regular issue counterparts except for the distinctive "Members Only" logo. A certificate of authenicity carrying the serial number accompanied each set.

	MINT	NRMT	EXC
COMPLETE SET (630)	60.00	27.00	7.50
COMPLETE SERIES 1 (270)	25.00	11.00	3.10
COMPLETE SERIES 2 (225)	20.00	9.00	2.50
COMPLETE SERIES 3 (135)	15.00	6.75	1.85
COMMON CARD (1-630)	.10	.05	.01
SEMISTARS	.25	.11	.03
STARS	.50	.23	.06
COMP.1ST DAY SET (270)	275.00	125.00	34.00
COMMON 1ST DAY (1-270)	1.00	.45	.12
1ST DAY SEMISTARS	1.50	.70	.19
*1ST DAY STARS: 15X BASIC CARDS			
*1ST DAY YOUNG STARS: 12X BASIC CARDS			
*1ST DAY DP STARS: 4X BASIC CARDS			
RANDOM INSERTS IN TOPPS SER.2 PACKS			
DP'S ALSO INSERTED IN TOPPS SER.1 PACKS			
TEN PER TOPPS FACTORY SET			
COMP.SUP.TEAM SET (585)	100.00	45.00	12.50
COMP.SUP.TM.EC/TA SET (45)	15.00	6.75	1.85
*STARS: 2X BASIC CARDS			
*YOUNG STARS: 1.5X BASIC CARDS			
ONE SET VIA MAIL PER 1994 BRAVES SUP.TEAM			
SER.3 EC AND TA SUBSETS SHIPPED LATER			
COMP.VIRT.REAL.SET (270)	90.00	40.00	11.00
COMP.VIRT.REAL.SER.1 (135)	45.00	20.00	5.50
COMP.VIRT.REAL.SER.2 (135)	45.00	20.00	5.50
*VIRT.REAL.STARS: 2X BASIC CARDS			
*VIRT.REAL.YOUNG STARS: 1.5X BASIC CARDS			
ONE VIRTUAL REALITY PER PACK			

□ 1 Cal Ripken	2.50	1.10	.30
□ 2 Bo Jackson	.50	.23	.06
□ 3 Bryan Harvey	.10	.05	.01
□ 4 Curt Schilling	.10	.05	.01
□ 5 Bruce Ruffin	.10	.05	.01
□ 6 Travis Fryman	.25	.11	.03
□ 7 Jim Abbott	.10	.05	.01
□ 8 David McCarty	.10	.05	.01
□ 9 Gary Gaetti	.25	.11	.03
□ 10 Roger Clemens	.50	.23	.06
□ 11 Carlos Garcia	.10	.05	.01
□ 12 Lee Smith	.25	.11	.03
□ 13 Bobby Ayala	.10	.05	.01
□ 14 Charles Nagy	.25	.11	.03
□ 15 Lou Frazier	.10	.05	.01
□ 16 Rene Arocha	.10	.05	.01
□ 17 Carlos Delgado	.50	.23	.06
□ 18 Steve Finley	.25	.11	.03
□ 19 Ryan Klesko	.60	.25	.07
□ 20 Cal Eldred	.10	.05	.01
□ 21 Rey Sanchez	.10	.05	.01
□ 22 Ken Hill	.10	.05	.01
□ 23 Benito Santiago	.10	.05	.01
□ 24 Julian Tavarez	.10	.05	.01
□ 25 Jose Vizcaino	.10	.05	.01
□ 26 Andy Benes	.10	.05	.01
□ 27 Mariano Duncan	.10	.05	.01
□ 28 Checklist A	.10	.05	.01
□ 29 Shawon Dunston	.10	.05	.01
□ 30 Rafael Palmeiro	.50	.23	.06
□ 31 Dean Palmer	.25	.11	.03
□ 32 Andres Galarraga	.50	.23	.06
□ 33 Joey Cora	.10	.05	.01
□ 34 Mickey Tettleton	.10	.05	.01
□ 35 Barry Larkin	.50	.23	.06
□ 36 Carlos Baerga	.50	.23	.06
□ 37 Orel Hershiser	.25	.11	.03
□ 38 Jody Reed	.10	.05	.01
□ 39 Paul Molitor	.60	.25	.07
□ 40 Jim Edmonds	.50	.23	.06
□ 41 Bob Tewksbury	.10	.05	.01
□ 42 John Patterson	.10	.05	.01
□ 43 Ray McDavid	.25	.11	.03
□ 44 Zane Smith	.10	.05	.01
□ 45 Bret Saberhagen SE	.10	.05	.01
□ 46 Greg Maddux SE	1.00	.45	.12
□ 47 Frank Thomas SE	1.50	.70	.19
□ 48 Carlos Baerga SE	.25	.11	.03
□ 49 Billy Spiers	.10	.05	.01
□ 50 Stan Javier	.10	.05	.01
□ 51 Rex Hudler	.10	.05	.01
□ 52 Denny Hocking	.10	.05	.01
□ 53 Todd Worrell	.10	.05	.01
□ 54 Mark Clark	.10	.05	.01
□ 55 Hipolito Pichardo	.10	.05	.01
□ 56 Bob Wickman	.10	.05	.01
□ 57 Raul Mondesi	.50	.23	.06
□ 58 Steve Cooke	.10	.05	.01
□ 59 Rod Beck	.10	.05	.01
□ 60 Tim Davis	.10	.05	.01
□ 61 Jeff Kent	.10	.05	.01
□ 62 John Valentin	.25	.11	.03

□ 63 Alex Arias	.10	.05	.01
□ 64 Steve Reed	.10	.05	.01
□ 65 Ozzie Smith	.60	.25	.07
□ 66 Terry Pendleton	.25	.11	.03
□ 67 Kenny Rogers	.10	.05	.01
□ 68 Vince Coleman	.10	.05	.01
□ 69 Tom Pagnozzi	.10	.05	.01
□ 70 Roberto Alomar	.75	.35	.09
□ 71 Darrin Jackson	.10	.05	.01
□ 72 Dennis Eckersley	.25	.11	.03
□ 73 Jay Buhner	.50	.23	.06
□ 74 Darren Lewis	.10	.05	.01
□ 75 Dave Weathers	.10	.05	.01
□ 76 Matt Walbeck	.10	.05	.01
□ 77 Brad Ausmus	.10	.05	.01
□ 78 Danny Bautista	.10	.05	.01
□ 79 Bob Hamelin	.10	.05	.01
□ 80 Steve Trachsel	.10	.05	.01
□ 81 Ken Ryan	.10	.05	.01
□ 82 Chris Turner	.10	.05	.01
□ 83 David Segui	.10	.05	.01
□ 84 Ben McDonald	.10	.05	.01
□ 85 Wade Boggs	.50	.23	.06
□ 86 John VanderWal	.10	.05	.01
□ 87 Sandy Alomar Jr.	.10	.05	.01
□ 88 Ron Karkovice	.10	.05	.01
□ 89 Doug Jones	.10	.05	.01
□ 90 Gary Sheffield	.50	.23	.06
□ 91 Ken Caminiti	.50	.23	.06
□ 92 Chris Bosio	.10	.05	.01
□ 93 Kevin Tapani	.10	.05	.01
□ 94 Walt Weiss	.10	.05	.01
□ 95 Erik Hanson	.10	.05	.01
□ 96 Ruben Sierra	.25	.11	.03
□ 97 Nomar Garciaparra	1.50	.70	.19
□ 98 Terrence Long	.25	.11	.03
□ 99 Jacob Shumate	.25	.11	.03
□ 100 Paul Wilson	.60	.25	.07
□ 101 Kevin Witt	.25	.11	.03
□ 102 Paul Konerko	2.50	1.10	.30
□ 103 Ben Grieve	1.25	.55	.16
□ 104 Mark Johnson	.25	.11	.03
□ 105 Cade Gaspar	.25	.11	.03
□ 106 Mark Farris	.25	.11	.03
□ 107 Dustin Hermanson	.25	.11	.03
□ 108 Scott Elarton	.50	.23	.06
□ 109 Doug Million	.25	.11	.03
□ 110 Matt Smith	.25	.11	.03
□ 111 Brian Buchanan	.25	.11	.03
□ 112 Jayson Peterson	.25	.11	.03
□ 113 Bret Wagner	.25	.11	.03
□ 114 C.J. Nitkowski	.25	.11	.03
□ 115 Ramon Castro	.25	.11	.03
□ 116 Rafael Bournigal	.10	.05	.01
□ 117 Jeff Fassero	.10	.05	.01
□ 118 Bobby Bonilla	.25	.11	.03
□ 119 Ricky Gutierrez	.10	.05	.01
□ 120 Roger Pavlik	.10	.05	.01
□ 121 Mike Greenwell	.10	.05	.01
□ 122 Deion Sanders	.50	.23	.06
□ 123 Charlie Hayes	.10	.05	.01
□ 124 Paul O'Neill	.25	.11	.03
□ 125 Jay Bell	.25	.11	.03
□ 126 Royce Clayton	.10	.05	.01
□ 127 Willie Banks	.10	.05	.01
□ 128 Mark Wohlers	.25	.11	.03
□ 129 Todd Jones	.10	.05	.01
□ 130 Todd Stottlemyre	.10	.05	.01
□ 131 Will Clark	.50	.23	.06
□ 132 Wilson Alvarez	.25	.11	.03
□ 133 Chili Davis	.25	.11	.03
□ 134 Dave Burba	.10	.05	.01
□ 135 Chris Hoiles	.10	.05	.01
□ 136 Jeff Blauser	.10	.05	.01
□ 137 Jeff Reboulet	.10	.05	.01
□ 138 Bret Saberhagen	.25	.11	.03
□ 139 Kirk Rueter	.10	.05	.01
□ 140 Dave Nilsson	.25	.11	.03
□ 141 Pat Borders	.10	.05	.01
□ 142 Ron Darling	.10	.05	.01
□ 143 Derek Bell	.25	.11	.03
□ 144 Dave Hollins	.10	.05	.01
□ 145 Juan Gonzalez	1.50	.70	.19
□ 146 Andre Dawson	.50	.23	.06
□ 147 Jim Thome	.60	.25	.07
□ 148 Larry Walker	.50	.23	.06
□ 149 Mike Piazza	2.00	.90	.25
□ 150 Mike Perez	.10	.05	.01
□ 151 Steve Avery	.25	.11	.03
□ 152 Dan Wilson	.25	.11	.03
□ 153 Andy Van Slyke	.25	.11	.03
□ 154 Junior Felix	.10	.05	.01
□ 155 Jack McDowell	.25	.11	.03
□ 156 Danny Tartabull	.10	.05	.01
□ 157 Willie Blair	.10	.05	.01
□ 158 Wm.VanLandingham	.10	.05	.01
□ 159 Robb Nen	.10	.05	.01
□ 160 Lee Tinsley	.10	.05	.01
□ 161 Ismael Valdes	.25	.11	.03
□ 162 Juan Guzman	.25	.11	.03
□ 163 Scott Servais	.10	.05	.01
□ 164 Cliff Floyd	.25	.11	.03
□ 165 Allen Watson	.10	.05	.01
□ 166 Eddie Taubensee	.10	.05	.01
□ 167 Scott Hemond	.10	.05	.01
□ 168 Jeff Tackett	.10	.05	.01
□ 169 Chad Curtis	.10	.05	.01
□ 170 Rico Brogna	.10	.05	.01
□ 171 Luis Polonia	.10	.05	.01
□ 172 Checklist B	.10	.05	.01
□ 173 Lance Johnson	.25	.11	.03
□ 174 Sammy Sosa	.50	.23	.06
□ 175 Mike Macfarlane	.10	.05	.01
□ 176 Darryl Hamilton	.10	.05	.01
□ 177 Rick Aguilera	.10	.05	.01
□ 178 Dave West	.10	.05	.01
□ 179 Mike Gallego	.10	.05	.01
□ 180 Marc Newfield	.25	.11	.03
□ 181 Steve Buechele	.10	.05	.01
□ 182 David Wells	.10	.05	.01
□ 183 Tom Glavine	.50	.23	.06
□ 184 Joe Girardi	.10	.05	.01
□ 185 Craig Biggio	.50	.23	.06
□ 186 Eddie Murray	.75	.35	.09
□ 187 Kevin Gross	.10	.05	.01
□ 188 Sid Fernandez	.10	.05	.01
□ 189 John Franco	.10	.05	.01
□ 190 Bernard Gilkey	.25	.11	.03
□ 191 Matt Williams	.50	.23	.06
□ 192 Darrin Fletcher	.10	.05	.01
□ 193 Jeff Conine	.50	.23	.06
□ 194 Ed Sprague	.25	.11	.03
□ 195 Eduardo Perez	.10	.05	.01
□ 196 Scott Livingstone	.10	.05	.01
□ 197 Ivan Rodriguez	.60	.25	.07
□ 198 Orlando Merced	.10	.05	.01
□ 199 Ricky Bones	.10	.05	.01
□ 200 Javier Lopez	.50	.23	.06
□ 201 Miguel Jimenez	.10	.05	.01
□ 202 Terry McGriff	.10	.05	.01
□ 203 Mike Lieberthal	.10	.05	.01
□ 204 David Cone	.25	.11	.03
□ 205 Todd Hundley	.25	.11	.03
□ 206 Ozzie Guillen	.10	.05	.01
□ 207 Alex Cole	.10	.05	.01
□ 208 Tony Phillips	.25	.11	.03
□ 209 Jim Eisenreich	.10	.05	.01
□ 210 Greg Vaughn BES	.10	.05	.01
□ 211 Barry Larkin BES	.50	.23	.06
□ 212 Don Mattingly BES	.75	.35	.09
□ 213 Mark Grace BES	.25	.11	.03
□ 214 Jose Canseco BES	.25	.11	.03
□ 215 Joe Carter BES	.25	.11	.03
□ 216 David Cone BES	.10	.05	.01
□ 217 Sandy Alomar Jr. BES	.10	.05	.01
□ 218 Al Martin BES	.10	.05	.01
□ 219 Roberto Kelly BES	.10	.05	.01
□ 220 Paul Sorrento	.10	.05	.01
□ 221 Tony Fernandez	.10	.05	.01
□ 222 Stan Belinda	.10	.05	.01
□ 223 Mike Stanley	.10	.05	.01
□ 224 Doug Drabek	.10	.05	.01
□ 225 Todd Van Poppel	.10	.05	.01
□ 226 Matt Mieske	.25	.11	.03
□ 227 Tino Martinez	.25	.11	.03
□ 228 Andy Ashby	.25	.11	.03
□ 229 Midre Cummings	.10	.05	.01
□ 230 Jeff Frye	.10	.05	.01
□ 231 Hal Morris	.10	.05	.01
□ 232 Jose Lind	.10	.05	.01
□ 233 Shawn Green	.25	.11	.03
□ 234 Rafael Belliard	.10	.05	.01

☐ 235	Randy Myers	.10	.05	.01
☐ 236	Frank Thomas CE	1.50	.70	.19
☐ 237	Darren Daulton CE	.10	.05	.01
☐ 238	Sammy Sosa CE	.25	.11	.03
☐ 239	Cal Ripken CE	1.25	.55	.16
☐ 240	Jeff Bagwell CE	.60	.25	.07
☐ 241	Ken Griffey Jr.	3.00	1.35	.35
☐ 242	Brett Butler	.25	.11	.03
☐ 243	Derrick May	.10	.05	.01
☐ 244	Pat Listach	.10	.05	.01
☐ 245	Mike Bordick	.10	.05	.01
☐ 246	Mark Langston	.10	.05	.01
☐ 247	Randy Velarde	.10	.05	.01
☐ 248	Julio Franco	.25	.11	.03
☐ 249	Chuck Knoblauch	.50	.23	.06
☐ 250	Bill Gullickson	.10	.05	.01
☐ 251	Dave Henderson	.10	.05	.01
☐ 252	Bret Boone	.25	.11	.03
☐ 253	Al Martin	.25	.11	.03
☐ 254	Armando Benitez	.10	.05	.01
☐ 255	Wil Cordero	.10	.05	.01
☐ 256	Al Leiter	.25	.11	.03
☐ 257	Luis Gonzalez	.10	.05	.01
☐ 258	Charlie O'Brien	.10	.05	.01
☐ 259	Tim Wallach	.10	.05	.01
☐ 260	Scott Sanders	.10	.05	.01
☐ 261	Tom Henke	.10	.05	.01
☐ 262	Otis Nixon	.10	.05	.01
☐ 263	Darren Daulton	.25	.11	.03
☐ 264	Manny Ramirez	.75	.35	.09
☐ 265	Bret Barberie	.10	.05	.01
☐ 266	Mel Rojas	.10	.05	.01
☐ 267	John Burkett	.25	.11	.03
☐ 268	Brady Anderson	.50	.23	.06
☐ 269	John Roper	.10	.05	.01
☐ 270	Shane Reynolds	.10	.05	.01
☐ 271	Barry Bonds	.75	.35	.09
☐ 272	Alex Fernandez	.25	.11	.03
☐ 273	Brian McRae	.25	.11	.03
☐ 274	Todd Zeile	.10	.05	.01
☐ 275	Greg Swindell	.10	.05	.01
☐ 276	Johnny Ruffin	.10	.05	.01
☐ 277	Troy Neel	.10	.05	.01
☐ 278	Eric Karros	.25	.11	.03
☐ 279	John Hudek	.10	.05	.01
☐ 280	Thomas Howard	.10	.05	.01
☐ 281	Joe Carter	.50	.23	.06
☐ 282	Mike Devereaux	.10	.05	.01
☐ 283	Butch Henry	.10	.05	.01
☐ 284	Reggie Jefferson	.25	.11	.03
☐ 285	Mark Lemke	.10	.05	.01
☐ 286	Jeff Montgomery	.25	.11	.03
☐ 287	Ryan Thompson	.10	.05	.01
☐ 288	Paul Shuey	.10	.05	.01
☐ 289	Mark McGwire	1.00	.45	.12
☐ 290	Bernie Williams	.50	.23	.06
☐ 291	Mickey Morandini	.10	.05	.01
☐ 292	Scott Leius	.10	.05	.01
☐ 293	David Hulse	.10	.05	.01
☐ 294	Greg Gagne	.10	.05	.01
☐ 295	Moises Alou	.25	.11	.03
☐ 296	Geronimo Berroa	.10	.05	.01
☐ 297	Eddie Zambrano	.10	.05	.01
☐ 298	Alan Trammell	.50	.23	.06
☐ 299	Don Slaught	.10	.05	.01
☐ 300	Jose Rijo	.10	.05	.01
☐ 301	Joe Ausanio	.10	.05	.01
☐ 302	Tim Raines	.50	.23	.06
☐ 303	Melido Perez	.10	.05	.01
☐ 304	Kent Mercker	.10	.05	.01
☐ 305	James Mouton	.10	.05	.01
☐ 306	Luis Lopez	.10	.05	.01
☐ 307	Mike Kingery	.10	.05	.01
☐ 308	Willie Greene	.10	.05	.01
☐ 309	Cecil Fielder	.25	.11	.03
☐ 310	Scott Kamieniecki	.10	.05	.01
☐ 311	Mike Greenwell BES	.10	.05	.01
☐ 312	Bobby Bonilla BES	.10	.05	.01
☐ 313	Andres Galarraga BES	.50	.23	.06
☐ 314	Cal Ripken BES	1.25	.55	.16
☐ 315	Matt Williams BES	.25	.11	.03
☐ 316	Tom Pagnozzi BES	.10	.05	.01
☐ 317	Len Dykstra BES	.10	.05	.01
☐ 318	Frank Thomas BES	1.50	.70	.19
☐ 319	Kirby Puckett BES	.50	.23	.06
☐ 320	Mike Piazza BES	1.00	.45	.12
☐ 321	Jason Jacome	.10	.05	.01
☐ 322	Brian Hunter	.10	.05	.01
☐ 323	Brent Gates	.10	.05	.01
☐ 324	Jim Converse	.10	.05	.01
☐ 325	Damion Easley	.10	.05	.01
☐ 326	Dante Bichette	.50	.23	.06
☐ 327	Kurt Abbott	.10	.05	.01
☐ 328	Scott Cooper	.10	.05	.01
☐ 329	Mike Henneman	.10	.05	.01
☐ 330	Orlando Miller	.10	.05	.01
☐ 331	John Kruk	.25	.11	.03
☐ 332	Jose Oliva	.10	.05	.01
☐ 333	Reggie Sanders	.25	.11	.03
☐ 334	Omar Vizquel	.50	.23	.06
☐ 335	Devon White	.25	.11	.03
☐ 336	Mike Morgan	.10	.05	.01
☐ 337	J.R. Phillips	.10	.05	.01
☐ 338	Gary DiSarcina	.10	.05	.01
☐ 339	Joey Hamilton	.25	.11	.03
☐ 340	Randy Johnson	.50	.23	.06
☐ 341	Jim Leyritz	.10	.05	.01
☐ 342	Bobby Jones	.25	.11	.03
☐ 343	Jaime Navarro	.10	.05	.01
☐ 344	Bip Roberts	.10	.05	.01
☐ 345	Steve Karsay	.10	.05	.01
☐ 346	Kevin Stocker	.10	.05	.01
☐ 347	Jose Canseco	.50	.23	.06
☐ 348	Bill Wegman	.10	.05	.01
☐ 349	Rondell White	.50	.23	.06
☐ 350	Mo Vaughn	.75	.35	.09
☐ 351	Joe Orsulak	.10	.05	.01
☐ 352	Pat Meares	.10	.05	.01
☐ 353	Albie Lopez	.10	.05	.01
☐ 354	Edgar Martinez	.50	.23	.06
☐ 355	Brian Jordan	.50	.23	.06
☐ 356	Tommy Greene	.10	.05	.01
☐ 357	Chuck Carr	.10	.05	.01
☐ 358	Pedro Astacio	.10	.05	.01
☐ 359	Russ Davis	.10	.05	.01
☐ 360	Chris Hammond	.10	.05	.01
☐ 361	Gregg Jefferies	.25	.11	.03
☐ 362	Shane Mack	.10	.05	.01
☐ 363	Fred McGriff	.50	.23	.06
☐ 364	Pat Rapp	.10	.05	.01
☐ 365	Bill Swift	.10	.05	.01
☐ 366	Checklist	.10	.05	.01
☐ 367	Robin Ventura	.25	.11	.03
☐ 368	Bobby Witt	.10	.05	.01
☐ 369	Karl Rhodes	.10	.05	.01
☐ 370	Eddie Williams	.10	.05	.01
☐ 371	John Jaha	.25	.11	.03
☐ 372	Steve Howe	.10	.05	.01
☐ 373	Leo Gomez	.10	.05	.01
☐ 374	Hector Fajardo	.10	.05	.01
☐ 375	Jeff Bagwell	1.25	.55	.16
☐ 376	Mark Acre	.10	.05	.01
☐ 377	Wayne Kirby	.10	.05	.01
☐ 378	Mark Portugal	.10	.05	.01
☐ 379	Jesus Tavarez	.10	.05	.01
☐ 380	Jim Lindeman	.10	.05	.01
☐ 381	Don Mattingly	1.50	.70	.19
☐ 382	Trevor Hoffman	.10	.05	.01
☐ 383	Chris Gomez	.10	.05	.01
☐ 384	Garret Anderson	.50	.23	.06
☐ 385	Bobby Munoz	.10	.05	.01
☐ 386	Jon Lieber	.10	.05	.01
☐ 387	Rick Helling	.10	.05	.01
☐ 388	Marvin Freeman	.10	.05	.01
☐ 389	Juan Castillo	.10	.05	.01
☐ 390	Jeff Cirillo	.25	.11	.03
☐ 391	Sean Berry	.10	.05	.01
☐ 392	Hector Carrasco	.10	.05	.01
☐ 393	Mark Grace	.50	.23	.06
☐ 394	Pat Kelly	.10	.05	.01
☐ 395	Tim Naehring	.10	.05	.01
☐ 396	Greg Pirkl	.10	.05	.01
☐ 397	John Smoltz	.50	.23	.06
☐ 398	Robby Thompson	.10	.05	.01
☐ 399	Rick White	.10	.05	.01
☐ 400	Frank Thomas	3.00	1.35	.35
☐ 401	Jeff Conine CS	.25	.11	.03
☐ 402	Jose Valentin CS	.10	.05	.01
☐ 403	Carlos Baerga CS	.25	.11	.03
☐ 404	Rick Aguilera CS	.10	.05	.01
☐ 405	Wilson Alvarez CS	.10	.05	.01
☐ 406	Juan Gonzalez CS	.75	.35	.09

☐ 407	Barry Larkin CS	.50	.23	.06
☐ 408	Ken Hill CS	.10	.05	.01
☐ 409	Chuck Carr CS	.10	.05	.01
☐ 410	Tim Raines CS	.25	.11	.03
☐ 411	Bryan Eversgerd	.10	.05	.01
☐ 412	Phil Plantier	.10	.05	.01
☐ 413	Josias Manzanillo	.10	.05	.01
☐ 414	Roberto Kelly	.10	.05	.01
☐ 415	Rickey Henderson	.50	.23	.06
☐ 416	John Smiley	.10	.05	.01
☐ 417	Kevin Brown	.25	.11	.03
☐ 418	Jimmy Key	.25	.11	.03
☐ 419	Wally Joyner	.25	.11	.03
☐ 420	Roberto Hernandez	.10	.05	.01
☐ 421	Felix Fermin	.10	.05	.01
☐ 422	Checklist	.10	.05	.01
☐ 423	Greg Vaughn	.25	.11	.03
☐ 424	Ray Lankford	.50	.23	.06
☐ 425	Greg Maddux	2.00	.90	.25
☐ 426	Mike Mussina	.60	.25	.07
☐ 427	Geronimo Pena	.10	.05	.01
☐ 428	David Nied	.10	.05	.01
☐ 429	Scott Erickson	.10	.05	.01
☐ 430	Kevin Mitchell	.25	.11	.03
☐ 431	Mike Lansing	.10	.05	.01
☐ 432	Brian Anderson	.10	.05	.01
☐ 433	Jeff King	.25	.11	.03
☐ 434	Ramon Martinez	.25	.11	.03
☐ 435	Kevin Seitzer	.10	.05	.01
☐ 436	Salomon Torres	.10	.05	.01
☐ 437	Brian L.Hunter	.50	.23	.06
☐ 438	Melvin Nieves	.25	.11	.03
☐ 439	Mike Kelly	.10	.05	.01
☐ 440	Marquis Grissom	.50	.23	.06
☐ 441	Chuck Finley	.25	.11	.03
☐ 442	Len Dykstra	.25	.11	.03
☐ 443	Ellis Burks	.50	.23	.06
☐ 444	Harold Baines	.25	.11	.03
☐ 445	Kevin Appier	.25	.11	.03
☐ 446	David Justice	.50	.23	.06
☐ 447	Darryl Kile	.10	.05	.01
☐ 448	John Olerud	.10	.05	.01
☐ 449	Greg McMichael	.10	.05	.01
☐ 450	Kirby Puckett	1.00	.45	.12
☐ 451	Jose Valentin	.25	.11	.03
☐ 452	Rick Wilkins	.10	.05	.01
☐ 453	Arthur Rhodes	.10	.05	.01
☐ 454	Pat Hentgen	.25	.11	.03
☐ 455	Tom Gordon	.10	.05	.01
☐ 456	Tom Candiotti	.10	.05	.01
☐ 457	Jason Bere	.10	.05	.01
☐ 458	Wes Chamberlain	.10	.05	.01
☐ 459	Greg Colbrunn	.10	.05	.01
☐ 460	John Doherty	.10	.05	.01
☐ 461	Kevin Foster	.10	.05	.01
☐ 462	Mark Whiten	.10	.05	.01
☐ 463	Terry Steinbach	.25	.11	.03
☐ 464	Aaron Sele	.25	.11	.03
☐ 465	Kirt Manwaring	.10	.05	.01
☐ 466	Darren Hall	.10	.05	.01
☐ 467	Delino DeShields	.10	.05	.01
☐ 468	Andujar Cedeno	.10	.05	.01
☐ 469	Billy Ashley	.10	.05	.01
☐ 470	Kenny Lofton	.75	.35	.09
☐ 471	Pedro Munoz	.10	.05	.01
☐ 472	John Wetteland	.25	.11	.03
☐ 473	Tim Salmon	.50	.23	.06
☐ 474	Denny Neagle	.25	.11	.03
☐ 475	Tony Gwynn	1.25	.55	.16
☐ 476	Vinny Castilla	.25	.11	.03
☐ 477	Steve Dreyer	.10	.05	.01
☐ 478	Jeff Shaw	.10	.05	.01
☐ 479	Chad Ogea	.10	.05	.01
☐ 480	Scott Ruffcorn	.10	.05	.01
☐ 481	Lou Whitaker	.50	.23	.06
☐ 482	J.T. Snow	.25	.11	.03
☐ 483	Rich Rowland	.10	.05	.01
☐ 484	Denny Martinez	.25	.11	.03
☐ 485	Pedro Martinez	.25	.11	.03
☐ 486	Rusty Greer	.50	.23	.06
☐ 487	Dave Fleming	.10	.05	.01
☐ 488	John Dettmer	.10	.05	.01
☐ 489	Albert Belle	1.50	.70	.19
☐ 490	Ravelo Manzanillo	.10	.05	.01
☐ 491	Henry Rodriguez	.50	.23	.06
☐ 492	Andrew Lorraine	.25	.11	.03
☐ 493	Dwayne Hosey	.10	.05	.01
☐ 494	Mike Blowers	.10	.05	.01
☐ 495	Turner Ward	.10	.05	.01
☐ 496	Fred McGriff EC	.25	.11	.03
☐ 497	Sammy Sosa EC	.50	.23	.06
☐ 498	Barry Larkin EC	.50	.23	.06
☐ 499	Andres Galarraga EC	.50	.23	.06
☐ 500	Gary Sheffield EC	.50	.23	.06
☐ 501	Jeff Bagwell EC	.60	.25	.07
☐ 502	Mike Piazza EC	1.00	.45	.12
☐ 503	Moises Alou EC	.10	.05	.01
☐ 504	Bobby Bonilla EC	.10	.05	.01
☐ 505	Darren Daulton EC	.10	.05	.01
☐ 506	Jeff King EC	.25	.11	.03
☐ 507	Ray Lankford EC	.25	.11	.03
☐ 508	Tony Gwynn EC	.60	.25	.07
☐ 509	Barry Bonds EC	.50	.23	.06
☐ 510	Cal Ripken EC	1.25	.55	.16
☐ 511	Mo Vaughn EC	.50	.23	.06
☐ 512	Tim Salmon EC	.50	.23	.06
☐ 513	Frank Thomas EC	1.50	.70	.19
☐ 514	Albert Belle EC	.75	.35	.09
☐ 515	Cecil Fielder EC	.25	.11	.03
☐ 516	Kevin Appier EC	.10	.05	.01
☐ 517	Greg Vaughn EC	.25	.11	.03
☐ 518	Kirby Puckett EC	.50	.23	.06
☐ 519	Paul O'Neill EC	.10	.05	.01
☐ 520	Ruben Sierra EC	.10	.05	.01
☐ 521	Ken Griffey Jr. EC	1.50	.70	.19
☐ 522	Will Clark EC	.50	.23	.06
☐ 523	Joe Carter EC	.50	.23	.06
☐ 524	Antonio Osuna	.10	.05	.01
☐ 525	Glenallen Hill	.10	.05	.01
☐ 526	Alex Gonzalez	.10	.05	.01
☐ 527	Dave Stewart	.25	.11	.03
☐ 528	Ron Gant	.25	.11	.03
☐ 529	Jason Bates	.10	.05	.01
☐ 530	Mike Macfarlane	.10	.05	.01
☐ 531	Esteban Loaiza	.10	.05	.01
☐ 532	Joe Randa	.10	.05	.01
☐ 533	Dave Winfield	.50	.23	.06
☐ 534	Danny Darwin	.10	.05	.01
☐ 535	Pete Harnisch	.10	.05	.01
☐ 536	Joey Cora	.10	.05	.01
☐ 537	Jaime Navarro	.10	.05	.01
☐ 538	Marty Cordova	.50	.23	.06
☐ 539	Andujar Cedeno	.10	.05	.01
☐ 540	Mickey Tettleton	.10	.05	.01
☐ 541	Andy Van Slyke	.25	.11	.03
☐ 542	Carlos Perez	.25	.11	.03
☐ 543	Chipper Jones	2.00	.90	.25
☐ 544	Tony Fernandez	.10	.05	.01
☐ 545	Tom Henke	.10	.05	.01
☐ 546	Pat Borders	.10	.05	.01
☐ 547	Chad Curtis	.10	.05	.01
☐ 548	Ray Durham	.25	.11	.03
☐ 549	Joe Oliver	.10	.05	.01
☐ 550	Jose Mesa	.10	.05	.01
☐ 551	Steve Finley	.25	.11	.03
☐ 552	Otis Nixon	.10	.05	.01
☐ 553	Jacob Brumfield	.10	.05	.01
☐ 554	Bill Swift	.10	.05	.01
☐ 555	Quilvio Veras	.10	.05	.01
☐ 556	Hideo Nomo UER	3.00	1.35	.35
	Wins and IP totals reversed			
☐ 557	Joe Vitiello	.10	.05	.01
☐ 558	Mike Perez	.10	.05	.01
☐ 559	Charlie Hayes	.10	.05	.01
☐ 560	Brad Radke	.25	.11	.03
☐ 561	Darren Bragg	.25	.11	.03
☐ 562	Orel Hershiser	.25	.11	.03
☐ 563	Edgardo Alfonzo	.25	.11	.03
☐ 564	Doug Jones	.10	.05	.01
☐ 565	Andy Pettitte	1.25	.55	.16
☐ 566	Benito Santiago	.10	.05	.01
☐ 567	John Burkett	.25	.11	.03
☐ 568	Brad Clontz	.10	.05	.01
☐ 569	Jim Abbott	.10	.05	.01
☐ 570	Joe Rosselli	.10	.05	.01
☐ 571	Mark Grudzielanek	.75	.35	.09
☐ 572	Dustin Hermanson	.25	.11	.03
☐ 573	Benji Gil	.10	.05	.01
☐ 574	Mark Whiten	.10	.05	.01
☐ 575	Mike Ignasiak	.10	.05	.01
☐ 576	Kevin Ritz	.10	.05	.01
☐ 577	Paul Quantrill	.10	.05	.01

□ 578 Andre Dawson	.50	.23	.06
□ 579 Jerald Clark	.10	.05	.01
□ 580 Frank Rodriguez	.25	.11	.03
□ 581 Mark Kiefer	.10	.05	.01
□ 582 Trevor Wilson	.10	.05	.01
□ 583 Gary Wilson	.10	.05	.01
□ 584 Andy Stankiewicz	.10	.05	.01
□ 585 Felipe Lira	.10	.05	.01
□ 586 Mike Mimbs	.25	.11	.03
□ 587 Jon Nunnally	.25	.11	.03
□ 588 Tomas Perez	.25	.11	.03
□ 589 Checklist	.10	.05	.01
□ 590 Todd Hollandsworth	.50	.23	.06
□ 591 Roberto Petagine	.10	.05	.01
□ 592 Mariano Rivera	.50	.23	.06
□ 593 Mark McLemore	.10	.05	.01
□ 594 Bobby Witt	.10	.05	.01
□ 595 Jose Offerman	.10	.05	.01
□ 596 Jason Christiansen	.10	.05	.01
□ 597 Jeff Manto	.10	.05	.01
□ 598 Jim Dougherty	.10	.05	.01
□ 599 Juan Acevedo	.10	.05	.01
□ 600 Troy O'Leary	.10	.05	.01
□ 601 Ron Villone	.10	.05	.01
□ 602 Tripp Cromer	.10	.05	.01
□ 603 Steve Scarsone	.10	.05	.01
□ 604 Lance Parrish	.10	.05	.01
□ 605 Ozzie Timmons	.10	.05	.01
□ 606 Ray Holbert	.10	.05	.01
□ 607 Tony Phillips	.25	.11	.03
□ 608 Phil Plantier	.10	.05	.01
□ 609 Shane Andrews	.10	.05	.01
□ 610 Heathcliff Slocumb	.10	.05	.01
□ 611 Bobby Higginson	.50	.23	.06
□ 612 Bob Tewksbury	.10	.05	.01
□ 613 Terry Pendleton	.25	.11	.03
□ 614 Scott Cooper TA	.10	.05	.01
□ 615 John Wetteland TA	.10	.05	.01
□ 616 Ken Hill TA	.10	.05	.01
□ 617 Marquis Grissom TA	.25	.11	.03
□ 618 Larry Walker TA	.25	.11	.03
□ 619 Derek Bell TA	.10	.05	.01
□ 620 David Cone TA	.10	.05	.01
□ 621 Ken Caminiti TA	.25	.11	.03
□ 622 Jack McDowell TA	.10	.05	.01
□ 623 Vaughn Eshelman TA	.10	.05	.01
□ 624 Brian McRae TA	.10	.05	.01
□ 625 Gregg Jefferies TA	.10	.05	.01
□ 626 Kevin Brown TA	.10	.05	.01
□ 627 Lee Smith TA	.10	.05	.01
□ 628 Tony Tarasco TA	.10	.05	.01
□ 629 Brett Butler TA	.10	.05	.01
□ 630 Jose Canseco TA	.25	.11	.03

1995 Stadium Club Clear Cut

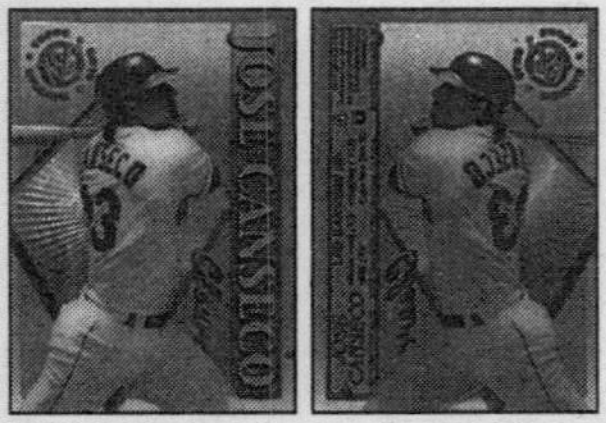

Randomly inserted at a rate of one in 16 packs, this 28-card set features a full color action photo of the player against a clear acetate background with the player's name printed vertically. Backs highlight the season achievement of the player on a thin horizontal strip.

	MINT	NRMT	EXC
COMPLETE SET (28)	100.00	45.00	12.50
COMPLETE SET (14)	50.00	22.00	6.25
COMPLETE SERIES 2 (14)	50.00	22.00	6.25
COMMON CARD (CC1-CC28)	1.50	.70	.19
SEMISTARS	3.00	1.35	.35
RANDOM INSERTS IN PACKS			

□ CC1 Mike Piazza	15.00	6.75	1.85
□ CC2 Ruben Sierra	3.00	1.35	.35
□ CC3 Tony Gwynn	10.00	4.50	1.25
□ CC4 Frank Thomas	25.00	11.00	3.10
□ CC5 Fred McGriff	3.00	1.35	.35
□ CC6 Rafael Palmeiro	3.00	1.35	.35
□ CC7 Bobby Bonilla	3.00	1.35	.35
□ CC8 Chili Davis	3.00	1.35	.35
□ CC9 Hal Morris	1.50	.70	.19
□ CC10 Jose Canseco	3.00	1.35	.35
□ CC11 Jay Bell	1.50	.70	.19
□ CC12 Kirby Puckett	8.00	3.60	1.00
□ CC13 Gary Sheffield	4.00	1.80	.50
□ CC14 Bob Hamelin	1.50	.70	.19
□ CC15 Jeff Bagwell	10.00	4.50	1.25
□ CC16 Albert Belle	12.00	5.50	1.50
□ CC17 Sammy Sosa	4.00	1.80	.50
□ CC18 Ken Griffey Jr.	25.00	11.00	3.10
□ CC19 Todd Zeile	1.50	.70	.19
□ CC20 Mo Vaughn	6.00	2.70	.75
□ CC21 Moises Alou	1.50	.70	.19
□ CC22 Paul O'Neill	3.00	1.35	.35
□ CC23 Andres Galarraga	3.00	1.35	.35
□ CC24 Greg Vaughn	3.00	1.35	.35
□ CC25 Len Dykstra	1.50	.70	.19
□ CC26 Joe Carter	3.00	1.35	.35
□ CC27 Barry Bonds	6.00	2.70	.75
□ CC28 Cecil Fielder	3.00	1.35	.35

1995 Stadium Club Crunch Time

This 20-card standard-size set features home run hitters and was randomly inserted in first series rack packs. Fronts are action illustrations of players on gold foil paper with the Crunch Time logo and player's name printed in gold foil at the bottom of the card. The horizontal backs include a pie chart and statistics of player offensive output and player action photos. The cards are numbered as "X" of 20 in the upper right corner.

	MINT	NRMT	EXC
COMPLETE SET (20)	40.00	18.00	5.00
COMMON CARD (1-20)	.75	.35	.09
SEMISTARS	1.25	.55	.16
ONE PER RACK PACK			

□ 1 Jeff Bagwell	4.00	1.80	.50
□ 2 Kirby Puckett	3.00	1.35	.35
□ 3 Frank Thomas	10.00	4.50	1.25
□ 4 Albert Belle	5.00	2.20	.60
□ 5 Julio Franco	.75	.35	.09
□ 6 Jose Canseco	1.25	.55	.16
□ 7 Paul Molitor	2.00	.90	.25
□ 8 Joe Carter	1.25	.55	.16
□ 9 Ken Griffey Jr.	10.00	4.50	1.25
□ 10 Larry Walker	.75	.35	.09
□ 11 Dante Bichette	1.25	.55	.16
□ 12 Carlos Baerga	1.25	.55	.16
□ 13 Fred McGriff	1.25	.55	.16
□ 14 Ruben Sierra	.75	.35	.09
□ 15 Will Clark	1.25	.55	.16

□ 16 Moises Alou	.75	.35	.09
□ 17 Rafael Palmeiro	1.25	.55	.16
□ 18 Travis Fryman	1.25	.55	.16
□ 19 Barry Bonds	2.50	1.10	.30
□ 20 Cal Ripken	8.00	3.60	1.00

1995 Stadium Club Crystal Ball

This 15-card standard-size set was inserted into series three packs at a rate of one in 24. Fifteen leading 1995 rookies and prospects were featured in this set. The fronts feature a player photo in the middle with the words "Crystal Ball" on the top with the player's name on the bottom. The backs have season-by-season stats with a sentence about the player's accomplishments during that season. A player photo in the upper right is set in a crystal ball. The player is identified on the top and the cards are numbered with a "CB" prefix in the upper left corner.

	MINT	NRMT	EXC
COMPLETE SET (15)	75.00	34.00	9.50
COMMON CARD (CB1-CB15)	2.00	.90	.25
SEMISTARS	4.00	1.80	.50
RANDOM INSERTS IN SER.3 PACKS			

□ CB1 Chipper Jones	25.00	11.00	3.10
□ CB2 Dustin Hermanson	2.00	.90	.25
□ CB3 Ray Durham	4.00	1.80	.50
□ CB4 Phil Nevin	2.00	.90	.25
□ CB5 Billy Ashley	2.00	.90	.25
□ CB6 Shawn Green	2.00	.90	.25
□ CB7 Jason Bates	2.00	.90	.25
□ CB8 Benji Gil	2.00	.90	.25
□ CB9 Marty Cordova	8.00	3.60	1.00
□ CB10 Quilvio Veras	2.00	.90	.25
□ CB11 Mark Grudzielanek	6.00	2.70	.75
□ CB12 Ruben Rivera	15.00	6.75	1.85
□ CB13 Bill Pulsipher	2.00	.90	.25
□ CB14 Derek Jeter	25.00	11.00	3.10
□ CB15 LaTroy Hawkins	2.00	.90	.25

1995 Stadium Club Power Zone

This 12-card standard-size set was inserted into series three packs at a rate of one in 24. The fronts feature a player photo and his name on the right. The left side of the card has the bat powering through an explosion. The words "Power Zone" are on the bottom. The horizontal backs feature a close-up photo, some vital information as well as some seasonal highlights. The cards are numbered in the upper right corner with a "PZ" prefix. The set is sequenced in alphabetical order.

	MINT	NRMT	EXC
COMPLETE SET (12)	90.00	40.00	11.00
COMMON CARD (PZ1-PZ12)	2.00	.90	.25
SEMISTARS	4.00	1.80	.50
RANDOM INSERTS IN SER.3 PACKS			

□ PZ1 Jeff Bagwell	12.00	5.50	1.50
□ PZ2 Albert Belle	15.00	6.75	1.85
□ PZ3 Barry Bonds	8.00	3.60	1.00
□ PZ4 Joe Carter	4.00	1.80	.50
□ PZ5 Cecil Fielder	4.00	1.80	.50
□ PZ6 Andres Galarraga	2.00	.90	.25
□ PZ7 Ken Griffey Jr.	30.00	13.50	3.70
□ PZ8 Paul Molitor	6.00	2.70	.75
□ PZ9 Fred McGriff	4.00	1.80	.50
□ PZ10 Rafael Palmeiro	4.00	1.80	.50
□ PZ11 Frank Thomas	30.00	13.50	3.70
□ PZ12 Matt Williams	4.00	1.80	.50

1995 Stadium Club Ring Leaders

Randomly inserted in packs, this set features players who have won various awards or titles. This set was also redeemable as a prize with winning regular phone cards. This set features Stadium Club's "Power Matrix Technology," which makes the cards shine and glow. The horizontal fronts feature a player photo, rings in both upper corners as well as other designs that make for a very busy front. The backs have information on how the player earned his rings, along with a player photo and some other pertinent information.

	MINT	NRMT	EXC
COMPLETE SET (40)	175.00	80.00	22.00
COMPLETE SERIES 1 (20)	65.00	29.00	8.00
COMPLETE SERIES 2 (20)	110.00	50.00	14.00
COMMON CARD (RL1-RL40)	2.00	.90	.25
SEMISTARS	4.00	1.80	.50
RANDOM INSERTS IN PACKS			
SET REDEEMABLE WITH WINNING PHONE CARD			

□ RL1 Jeff Bagwell	12.00	5.50	1.50
□ RL2 Mark McGwire	10.00	4.50	1.25
□ RL3 Ozzie Smith	6.00	2.70	.75
□ RL4 Paul Molitor	6.00	2.70	.75
□ RL5 Darryl Strawberry	4.00	1.80	.50
□ RL6 Eddie Murray	8.00	3.60	1.00
□ RL7 Tony Gwynn	12.00	5.50	1.50
□ RL8 Jose Canseco	4.00	1.80	.50
□ RL9 Howard Johnson	2.00	.90	.25
□ RL10 Andre Dawson	4.00	1.80	.50
□ RL11 Matt Williams	4.00	1.80	.50
□ RL12 Tim Raines	4.00	1.80	.50
□ RL13 Fred McGriff	4.00	1.80	.50
□ RL14 Ken Griffey Jr.	30.00	13.50	3.70
□ RL15 Gary Sheffield	5.00	2.20	.60

□ RL16	Dennis Eckersley	4.00	1.80	.50
□ RL17	Kevin Mitchell	2.00	.90	.25
□ RL18	Will Clark	4.00	1.80	.50
□ RL19	Darren Daulton	2.00	.90	.25
□ RL20	Paul O'Neill	2.00	.90	.25
□ RL21	Julio Franco	2.00	.90	.25
□ RL22	Albert Belle	15.00	6.75	1.85
□ RL23	Juan Gonzalez	15.00	6.75	1.85
□ RL24	Kirby Puckett	10.00	4.50	1.25
□ RL25	Joe Carter	4.00	1.80	.50
□ RL26	Frank Thomas	30.00	13.50	3.70
□ RL27	Cal Ripken	25.00	11.00	3.10
□ RL28	John Olerud	2.00	.90	.25
□ RL29	Ruben Sierra	2.00	.90	.25
□ RL30	Barry Bonds	8.00	3.60	1.00
□ RL31	Cecil Fielder	4.00	1.80	.50
□ RL32	Roger Clemens	4.00	1.80	.50
□ RL33	Don Mattingly	15.00	6.75	1.85
□ RL34	Terry Pendleton	2.00	.90	.25
□ RL35	Rickey Henderson	4.00	1.80	.50
□ RL36	Dave Winfield	4.00	1.80	.50
□ RL37	Edgar Martinez	4.00	1.80	.50
□ RL38	Wade Boggs	4.00	1.80	.50
□ RL39	Willie McGee	2.00	.90	.25
□ RL40	Andres Galarraga	4.00	1.80	.50

1995 Stadium Club Super Skills

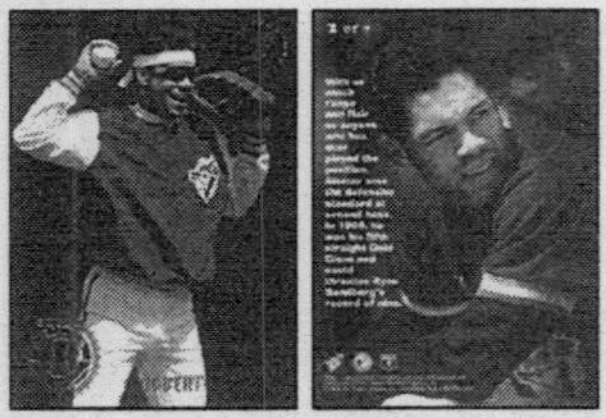

This 20-card set was randomly inserted into hobby packs. The full-bleed front features a player photo against a multi-colored background. The background was enhanced using Stadium Club's "Power Matrix" Technology. The "Super Skills" logo is in the lower left corner. The backs have a full-bleed photo with a description of the player's special skill. The cards are numbered in the upper left as "X" of 9.

	MINT	NRMT	EXC
COMPLETE SET (20)	80.00	36.00	10.00
COMPLETE SERIES 1 (9)	35.00	16.00	4.40
COMPLETE SERIES 2 (11)	45.00	20.00	5.50
COMMON CARD (SS1-SS20)	1.50	.70	.19
SEMISTARS	3.00	1.35	.35
RANDOM INSERTS IN PACKS			

□ SS1	Roberto Alomar	6.00	2.70	.75
□ SS2	Barry Bonds	6.00	2.70	.75
□ SS3	Jay Buhner	3.00	1.35	.35
□ SS4	Chuck Carr	1.50	.70	.19
□ SS5	Don Mattingly	12.00	5.50	1.50
□ SS6	Raul Mondesi	3.00	1.35	.35
□ SS7	Tim Salmon	3.00	1.35	.35
□ SS8	Deion Sanders	3.00	1.35	.35
□ SS9	Devon White	1.50	.70	.19
□ SS10	Mark Whiten	1.50	.70	.19
□ SS11	Ken Griffey Jr.	25.00	11.00	3.10
□ SS12	Marquis Grissom	3.00	1.35	.35
□ SS13	Paul O'Neill	3.00	1.35	.35
□ SS14	Kenny Lofton	6.00	2.70	.75
□ SS15	Larry Walker	3.00	1.35	.35
□ SS16	Scott Cooper	1.50	.70	.19
□ SS17	Barry Larkin	3.00	1.35	.35
□ SS18	Matt Williams	3.00	1.35	.35
□ SS19	John Wetteland	3.00	1.35	.35
□ SS20	Randy Johnson	4.00	1.80	.50

1995 Stadium Club Virtual Extremists

This 10-card set was inserted randomly into second series rack packs. The fronts feature a player photo against a baseball backdrop. The words "VR Extremist" are spelled vertically down the right side while the player name is in silver foil on the bottom. All of this is surrounded by blue and purple borders. The horizontal backs feature projected full-season 1994 stats. The cards are numbered with a "VRE" prefix in the upper right corner.

	MINT	NRMT	EXC
COMPLETE SET (10)	120.00	55.00	15.00
COMMON CARD (VRE1-VRE10)	2.50	1.10	.30
SEMISTARS	5.00	2.20	.60
RANDOM INSERTS IN SER.2 RACK PACKS.			

□ VRE1	Barry Bonds	10.00	4.50	1.25
□ VRE2	Ken Griffey Jr.	40.00	18.00	5.00
□ VRE3	Jeff Bagwell	15.00	6.75	1.85
□ VRE4	Albert Belle	20.00	9.00	2.50
□ VRE5	Frank Thomas	40.00	18.00	5.00
□ VRE6	Tony Gwynn	15.00	6.75	1.85
□ VRE7	Kenny Lofton	10.00	4.50	1.25
□ VRE8	Deion Sanders	5.00	2.20	.60
□ VRE9	Ken Hill	2.50	1.10	.30
□ VRE10	Jimmy Key	2.50	1.10	.30

1996 Stadium Club

The 1996 Stadium Club set consists of 450 cards. The fronts feature glossy, full-bleed color action photos. At the bottom, the player's name is gold foil stamped on a team color-coded nameplate that is highlighted by gold foil stamping. The colorful backs carry biography, highlights, and the TSC Skills Matrix. The set includes a Team TSC subset (181-270). These 90 cards were shortprinted compared to the other cards in the set. There was also a factory set packaged in cereal box type cartons available through retail outlets. These sets included four Mantle cards, issued one per carton.

	MINT	NRMT	EXC
COMP.CEREAL FACT.SET (454)	80.00	36.00	10.00
COMPLETE SET (450)	60.00	27.00	7.50

COMPLETE SERIES 1 (225)	30.00	13.50	3.70
COMPLETE SERIES 2 (225)	30.00	13.50	3.70
COMMON CARD (1-180/271-450)	.10	.05	.01
COMMON TSC SP (181-270)	.25	.11	.03
SEMISTARS	.25	.11	.03
STARS	.50	.23	.06
SILVER FOIL: ONLY IN CEREAL SETS			
*SILVER FOIL: SAME VALUE			
COMP.MANTLE SET (19)	170.00	75.00	21.00
COMP.MANTLE SER.1 (9)	110.00	50.00	14.00
COMP.MANTLE SER.2 (10)	60.00	27.00	7.50
COMMON MANTLE (1-9)	14.00	6.25	1.75
COMMON MANTLE (10-19)	8.00	3.60	1.00
MANTLE GOLD FOIL (1-19)	5.00	2.20	.60
MANTLE: RANDOM INSERTS IN ALL PACKS			
MANTLE GOLD FOIL: 1 PER CEREAL CARTON			

□ 1 Hideo Nomo EP	.75	.35	.09
□ 2 Paul Molitor	.60	.25	.07
□ 3 Garret Anderson	.50	.23	.06
□ 4 Jose Mesa	.25	.11	.03
□ 5 Vinny Castilla	.25	.11	.03
□ 6 Mike Mussina	.60	.25	.07
□ 7 Ray Durham	.50	.23	.06
□ 8 Jack McDowell	.50	.23	.06
□ 9 Juan Gonzalez	1.50	.70	.19
□ 10 Chipper Jones	2.00	.90	.25
□ 11 Deion Sanders	.50	.23	.06
□ 12 Rondell White	.50	.23	.06
□ 13 Tom Henke	.25	.11	.03
□ 14 Derek Bell	.25	.11	.03
□ 15 Randy Myers	.10	.05	.01
□ 16 Randy Johnson	.50	.23	.06
□ 17 Len Dykstra	.25	.11	.03
□ 18 Bill Pulsipher	.25	.11	.03
□ 19 Greg Colbrunn	.10	.05	.01
□ 20 David Wells	.10	.05	.01
□ 21 Chad Curtis	.10	.05	.01
□ 22 Roberto Hernandez	.25	.11	.03
□ 23 Kirby Puckett	1.00	.45	.12
□ 24 Joe Vitiello	.10	.05	.01
□ 25 Roger Clemens	.50	.23	.06
□ 26 Al Martin	.10	.05	.01
□ 27 Chad Ogea	.10	.05	.01
□ 28 David Segui	.10	.05	.01
□ 29 Joey Hamilton	.10	.05	.01
□ 30 Dan Wilson	.10	.05	.01
□ 31 Chad Fonville	.10	.05	.01
□ 32 Bernard Gilkey	.25	.11	.03
□ 33 Kevin Seitzer	.10	.05	.01
□ 34 Shawn Green	.25	.11	.03
□ 35 Rick Aguilera	.10	.05	.01
□ 36 Gary DiSarcina	.10	.05	.01
□ 37 Jaime Navarro	.10	.05	.01
□ 38 Doug Jones	.10	.05	.01
□ 39 Brent Gates	.10	.05	.01
□ 40 Dean Palmer	.50	.23	.06
□ 41 Pat Rapp	.10	.05	.01
□ 42 Tony Clark	.50	.23	.06
□ 43 Bill Swift	.10	.05	.01
□ 44 Randy Velarde	.10	.05	.01
□ 45 Matt Williams	.50	.23	.06
□ 46 John Mabry	.50	.23	.06
□ 47 Mike Fetters	.10	.05	.01
□ 48 Orlando Miller	.10	.05	.01
□ 49 Tom Glavine	.50	.23	.06
□ 50 Delino DeShields	.10	.05	.01
□ 51 Scott Erickson	.10	.05	.01
□ 52 Andy Van Slyke	.25	.11	.03
□ 53 Jim Bullinger	.10	.05	.01
□ 54 Lyle Mouton	.10	.05	.01
□ 55 Bret Saberhagen	.10	.05	.01
□ 56 Benito Santiago	.10	.05	.01
□ 57 Dan Miceli	.10	.05	.01
□ 58 Carl Everett	.10	.05	.01
□ 59 Rod Beck	.10	.05	.01
□ 60 Phil Nevin	.10	.05	.01
□ 61 Jason Giambi	.50	.23	.06
□ 62 Paul Menhart	.10	.05	.01
□ 63 Eric Karros	.50	.23	.06
□ 64 Allen Watson	.10	.05	.01
□ 65 Jeff Cirillo	.10	.05	.01
□ 66 Lee Smith	.50	.23	.06
□ 67 Sean Berry	.10	.05	.01
□ 68 Luis Sojo	.10	.05	.01
□ 69 Jeff Montgomery	.10	.05	.01
□ 70 Todd Hundley	.50	.23	.06
□ 71 John Burkett	.10	.05	.01
□ 72 Mark Gubicza	.10	.05	.01
□ 73 Don Mattingly	1.50	.70	.19
□ 74 Jeff Brantley	.10	.05	.01
□ 75 Matt Walbeck	.10	.05	.01
□ 76 Steve Parris	.10	.05	.01
□ 77 Ken Caminiti	.50	.23	.06
□ 78 Kirt Manwaring	.10	.05	.01
□ 79 Greg Vaughn	.50	.23	.06
□ 80 Pedro Martinez	.10	.05	.01
□ 81 Benji Gil	.10	.05	.01
□ 82 Heathcliff Slocumb	.10	.05	.01
□ 83 Joe Girardi	.10	.05	.01
□ 84 Sean Bergman	.10	.05	.01
□ 85 Matt Karchner	.10	.05	.01
□ 86 Butch Huskey	.25	.11	.03
□ 87 Mike Morgan	.10	.05	.01
□ 88 Todd Worrell	.25	.11	.03
□ 89 Mike Bordick	.10	.05	.01
□ 90 Bip Roberts	.10	.05	.01
□ 91 Mike Hampton	.10	.05	.01
□ 92 Troy O'Leary	.10	.05	.01
□ 93 Wally Joyner	.10	.05	.01
□ 94 Dave Stevens	.10	.05	.01
□ 95 Cecil Fielder	.50	.23	.06
□ 96 Wade Boggs	.50	.23	.06
□ 97 Hal Morris	.10	.05	.01
□ 98 Mickey Tettleton	.25	.11	.03
□ 99 Jeff Kent	.10	.05	.01
□ 100 Denny Martinez	.25	.11	.03
□ 101 Luis Gonzalez	.10	.05	.01
□ 102 John Jaha	.10	.05	.01
□ 103 Javier Lopez	.50	.23	.06
□ 104 Mark McGwire	1.00	.45	.12
□ 105 Ken Griffey Jr.	3.00	1.35	.35
□ 106 Darren Daulton	.25	.11	.03
□ 107 Bryan Rekar	.10	.05	.01
□ 108 Mike Macfarlane	.10	.05	.01
□ 109 Gary Gaetti	.25	.11	.03
□ 110 Shane Reynolds	.10	.05	.01
□ 111 Pat Meares	.10	.05	.01
□ 112 Jason Schmidt	.25	.11	.03
□ 113 Otis Nixon	.10	.05	.01
□ 114 John Franco	.10	.05	.01
□ 115 Marc Newfield	.25	.11	.03
□ 116 Andy Benes	.10	.05	.01
□ 117 Ozzie Guillen	.10	.05	.01
□ 118 Brian Jordan	.50	.23	.06
□ 119 Terry Pendleton	.10	.05	.01
□ 120 Chuck Finley	.10	.05	.01
□ 121 Scott Stahoviak	.10	.05	.01
□ 122 Sid Fernandez	.10	.05	.01
□ 123 Derek Jeter	2.00	.90	.25
□ 124 John Smiley	.10	.05	.01
□ 125 David Bell	.10	.05	.01
□ 126 Brett Butler	.10	.05	.01
□ 127 Doug Drabek	.10	.05	.01
□ 128 J.T. Snow	.25	.11	.03
□ 129 Joe Carter	.50	.23	.06
□ 130 Dennis Eckersley	.50	.23	.06
□ 131 Marty Cordova	.50	.23	.06
□ 132 Greg Maddux	2.00	.90	.25
□ 133 Tom Goodwin	.25	.11	.03
□ 134 Andy Ashby	.10	.05	.01
□ 135 Paul Sorrento	.10	.05	.01
□ 136 Ricky Bones	.10	.05	.01
□ 137 Shawon Dunston	.10	.05	.01
□ 138 Moises Alou	.10	.05	.01
□ 139 Mickey Morandini	.10	.05	.01
□ 140 Ramon Martinez	.50	.23	.06
□ 141 Royce Clayton	.10	.05	.01
□ 142 Brad Ausmus	.10	.05	.01
□ 143 Kenny Rogers	.10	.05	.01
□ 144 Tim Naehring	.10	.05	.01
□ 145 Chris Gomez	.10	.05	.01
□ 146 Bobby Bonilla	.50	.23	.06
□ 147 Wilson Alvarez	.50	.23	.06
□ 148 Johnny Damon	.25	.11	.03
□ 149 Pat Hentgen	.50	.23	.06
□ 150 Andres Galarraga	.50	.23	.06
□ 151 David Cone	.50	.23	.06
□ 152 Lance Johnson	.25	.11	.03
□ 153 Carlos Garcia	.10	.05	.01
□ 154 Doug Johns	.10	.05	.01
□ 155 Midre Cummings	.10	.05	.01

□ 156 Steve Sparks	.10	.05	.01
□ 157 Sandy Martinez	.10	.05	.01
□ 158 Wm. Van Landingham	.10	.05	.01
□ 159 David Justice	.50	.23	.06
□ 160 Mark Grace	.50	.23	.06
□ 161 Robb Nen	.10	.05	.01
□ 162 Mike Greenwell	.10	.05	.01
□ 163 Brad Radke	.10	.05	.01
□ 164 Edgardo Alfonzo	.25	.11	.03
□ 165 Mark Leiter	.10	.05	.01
□ 166 Walt Weiss	.10	.05	.01
□ 167 Mel Rojas	.25	.11	.03
□ 168 Bret Boone	.10	.05	.01
□ 169 Ricky Bottalico	.10	.05	.01
□ 170 Bobby Higginson	.50	.23	.06
□ 171 Trevor Hoffman	.25	.11	.03
□ 172 Jay Bell	.10	.05	.01
□ 173 Gabe White	.10	.05	.01
□ 174 Curtis Goodwin	.10	.05	.01
□ 175 Tyler Green	.10	.05	.01
□ 176 Roberto Alomar	.75	.35	.09
□ 177 Sterling Hitchcock	.10	.05	.01
□ 178 Ryan Klesko	.60	.25	.07
□ 179 Donne Wall	.10	.05	.01
□ 180 Brian McRae	.10	.05	.01
□ 181 Will Clark TSC SP	.50	.23	.06
□ 182 Frank Thomas TSC SP	4.00	1.80	.50
□ 183 Jeff Bagwell TSC SP	1.50	.70	.19
□ 184 Mo Vaughn TSC SP	1.00	.45	.12
□ 185 Tino Martinez TSC SP	.50	.23	.06
□ 186 Craig Biggio TSC SP	.50	.23	.06
□ 187 Chuck Knoblauch TSC SP	.50	.23	.06
□ 188 Carlos Baerga TSC SP	.50	.23	.06
□ 189 Quilvio Veras TSC SP	.25	.11	.03
□ 190 Luis Alicea TSC SP	.25	.11	.03
□ 191 Jim Thome TSC SP	.75	.35	.09
□ 192 Mike Blowers TSC SP	.25	.11	.03
□ 193 Robin Ventura TSC SP	.50	.23	.06
□ 194 Jeff King TSC SP	.25	.11	.03
□ 195 Tony Phillips TSC SP	.25	.11	.03
□ 196 John Valentin TSC SP	.50	.23	.06
□ 197 Barry Larkin TSC SP	.50	.23	.06
□ 198 Cal Ripken TSC SP	3.00	1.35	.35
□ 199 Omar Vizquel TSC SP	.25	.11	.03
□ 200 Kurt Abbott TSC SP	.25	.11	.03
□ 201 Albert Belle TSC SP	2.00	.90	.25
□ 202 Barry Bonds TSC SP	1.00	.45	.12
□ 203 Ron Gant TSC SP	.50	.23	.06
□ 204 Dante Bichette TSC SP	.50	.23	.06
□ 205 Jeff Conine TSC SP	.50	.23	.06
□ 206 Jim Edmonds TSC SP UER	.50	.23	.06
Greg Myers pictured on front			
□ 207 Stan Javier TSC SP	.25	.11	.03
□ 208 Kenny Lofton TSC SP	1.00	.45	.12
□ 209 Ray Lankford TSC SP	.50	.23	.06
□ 210 Bernie Williams TSC SP	.25	.11	.03
□ 211 Jay Buhner TSC SP	.50	.23	.06
□ 212 Paul O'Neill TSC SP	.10	.05	.01
□ 213 Tim Salmon TSC SP	.50	.23	.06
□ 214 Reggie Sanders TSC SP	.50	.23	.06
□ 215 Manny Ramirez TSC SP	1.00	.45	.12
□ 216 Mike Piazza TSC SP	2.50	1.10	.30
□ 217 Mike Stanley TSC SP	.25	.11	.03
□ 218 Tony Eusebio TSC SP	.25	.11	.03
□ 219 Chris Hoiles TSC SP	.25	.11	.03
□ 220 Ron Karkovice TSC SP	.25	.11	.03
□ 221 Edgar Martinez TSC SP	.50	.23	.06
□ 222 Chili Davis TSC SP	.50	.23	.06
□ 223 Jose Canseco TSC SP	.50	.23	.06
□ 224 Eddie Murray TSC SP	1.00	.45	.12
□ 225 Geronimo Berroa TSC SP	.25	.11	.03
□ 226 Chipper Jones TSC SP	2.50	1.10	.30
□ 227 Garret Anderson TSC SP	.50	.23	.06
□ 228 Marty Cordova TSC SP	.50	.23	.06
□ 229 Jon Nunnally TSC SP	.25	.11	.03
□ 230 Brian L.Hunter TSC SP	.25	.11	.03
□ 231 Shawn Green TSC SP	.25	.11	.03
□ 232 Ray Durham TSC SP	.50	.23	.06
□ 233 Alex Gonzalez TSC SP	.25	.11	.03
□ 234 Bobby Higginson TSC SP	.50	.23	.06
□ 235 Randy Johnson TSC SP	.50	.23	.06
□ 236 Al Leiter TSC SP	.25	.11	.03
□ 237 Tom Glavine TSC SP	.50	.23	.06
□ 238 Kenny Rogers TSC SP	.25	.11	.03
□ 239 Mike Hampton TSC SP	.25	.11	.03
□ 240 David Wells TSC SP	.25	.11	.03
□ 241 Jim Abbott TSC SP	.50	.23	.06
□ 242 Denny Neagle TSC SP	.25	.11	.03
□ 243 Wilson Alvarez TSC SP	.50	.23	.06
□ 244 John Smiley TSC SP	.25	.11	.03
□ 245 Greg Maddux TSC SP	2.50	1.10	.30
□ 246 Andy Ashby TSC SP	.25	.11	.03
□ 247 Hideo Nomo TSC SP	1.00	.45	.12
□ 248 Pat Rapp TSC SP	.25	.11	.03
□ 249 Tim Wakefield TSC SP	.25	.11	.03
□ 250 John Smoltz TSC SP	.60	.25	.07
□ 251 Joey Hamilton TSC SP	.25	.11	.03
□ 252 Frank Castillo TSC SP	.25	.11	.03
□ 253 Denny Martinez TSC SP	.25	.11	.03
□ 254 Jaime Navarro TSC SP	.25	.11	.03
□ 255 Karim Garcia TSC SP	.75	.35	.09
□ 256 Bob Abreu TSC SP	.50	.23	.06
□ 257 Butch Huskey TSC SP	.50	.23	.06
□ 258 Ruben Rivera TSC SP	.75	.35	.09
□ 259 Johnny Damon TSC SP	.25	.11	.03
□ 260 Derek Jeter TSC SP	2.50	1.10	.30
□ 261 Dennis Eckersley TSC SP	.50	.23	.06
□ 262 Jose Mesa TSC SP	.25	.11	.03
□ 263 Tom Henke TSC SP	.25	.11	.03
□ 264 Rick Aguilera TSC SP	.25	.11	.03
□ 265 Randy Myers TSC SP	.25	.11	.03
□ 266 John Franco TSC SP	.10	.05	.01
□ 267 Jeff Brantley TSC SP	.25	.11	.03
□ 268 John Wetteland TSC SP	.25	.11	.03
□ 269 Mark Wohlers TSC SP	.25	.11	.03
□ 270 Rod Beck TSC SP	.25	.11	.03
□ 271 Barry Larkin	.50	.23	.06
□ 272 Paul O'Neill	.10	.05	.01
□ 273 Bobby Jones	.10	.05	.01
□ 274 Will Clark	.50	.23	.06
□ 275 Steve Avery	.25	.11	.03
□ 276 Jim Edmonds	.50	.23	.06
□ 277 John Olerud	.10	.05	.01
□ 278 Carlos Perez	.10	.05	.01
□ 279 Chris Hoiles	.10	.05	.01
□ 280 Jeff Conine	.50	.23	.06
□ 281 Jim Eisenreich	.10	.05	.01
□ 282 Jason Jacome	.10	.05	.01
□ 283 Ray Lankford	.50	.23	.06
□ 284 John Wasdin	.10	.05	.01
□ 285 Frank Thomas	3.00	1.35	.35
□ 286 Jason Isringhausen	.25	.11	.03
□ 287 Glenallen Hill	.25	.11	.03
□ 288 Esteban Loaiza	.10	.05	.01
□ 289 Bernie Williams	.50	.23	.06
□ 290 Curtis Leskanic	.10	.05	.01
□ 291 Scott Cooper	.10	.05	.01
□ 292 Curt Schilling	.10	.05	.01
□ 293 Eddie Murray	.75	.35	.09
□ 294 Rick Krivda	.10	.05	.01
□ 295 Domingo Cedeno	.10	.05	.01
□ 296 Jeff Fassero	.10	.05	.01
□ 297 Albert Belle	1.50	.70	.19
□ 298 Craig Biggio	.50	.23	.06
□ 299 Fernando Vina	.10	.05	.01
□ 300 Edgar Martinez	.50	.23	.06
□ 301 Tony Gwynn	1.25	.55	.16
□ 302 Felipe Lira	.10	.05	.01
□ 303 Mo Vaughn	.75	.35	.09
□ 304 Alex Fernandez	.50	.23	.06
□ 305 Keith Lockhart	.10	.05	.01
□ 306 Roger Pavlik	.10	.05	.01
□ 307 Lee Tinsley	.10	.05	.01
□ 308 Omar Vizquel	.10	.05	.01
□ 309 Scott Servais	.10	.05	.01
□ 310 Danny Tartabull	.10	.05	.01
□ 311 Chili Davis	.10	.05	.01
□ 312 Cal Eldred	.10	.05	.01
□ 313 Roger Cedeno	.10	.05	.01
□ 314 Chris Hammond	.10	.05	.01
□ 315 Rusty Greer	.50	.23	.06
□ 316 Brady Anderson	.10	.05	.01
□ 317 Ron Villone	.10	.05	.01
□ 318 Mark Carreon	.10	.05	.01
□ 319 Larry Walker	.50	.23	.06
□ 320 Pete Harnisch	.10	.05	.01
□ 321 Robin Ventura	.50	.23	.06
□ 322 Tim Belcher	.10	.05	.01
□ 323 Tony Tarasco	.10	.05	.01
□ 324 Juan Guzman	.10	.05	.01
□ 325 Kenny Lofton	.75	.35	.09
□ 326 Kevin Foster	.10	.05	.01

□ 327 Wil Cordero .10 .05 .01
□ 328 Troy Percival .25 .11 .03
□ 329 Turk Wendell .25 .11 .03
□ 330 Thomas Howard .10 .05 .01
□ 331 Carlos Baerga .50 .23 .06
□ 332 B.J. Surhoff .10 .05 .01
□ 333 Jay Buhner .50 .23 .06
□ 334 Andujar Cedeno .10 .05 .01
□ 335 Jeff King .25 .11 .03
□ 336 Dante Bichette .50 .23 .06
□ 337 Alan Trammell .50 .23 .06
□ 338 Scott Leius .10 .05 .01
□ 339 Chris Snopek .10 .05 .01
□ 340 Roger Bailey .10 .05 .01
□ 341 Jacob Brumfield .10 .05 .01
□ 342 Jose Canseco .50 .23 .06
□ 343 Rafael Palmeiro .50 .23 .06
□ 344 Quilvio Veras .10 .05 .01
□ 345 Darrin Fletcher .10 .05 .01
□ 346 Carlos Delgado .50 .23 .06
□ 347 Tony Eusebio .10 .05 .01
□ 348 Ismael Valdes .25 .11 .03
□ 349 Terry Steinbach .25 .11 .03
□ 350 Orel Hershiser .25 .11 .03
□ 351 Kurt Abbott .10 .05 .01
□ 352 Jody Reed .10 .05 .01
□ 353 David Howard .10 .05 .01
□ 354 Ruben Sierra .10 .05 .01
□ 355 John Ericks .10 .05 .01
□ 356 Buck Showalter MG .10 .05 .01
□ 357 Jim Thome .60 .25 .07
□ 358 Geronimo Berroa .25 .11 .03
□ 359 Robby Thompson .10 .05 .01
□ 360 Jose Vizcaino .10 .05 .01
□ 361 Jeff Frye .10 .05 .01
□ 362 Kevin Appier .25 .11 .03
□ 363 Pat Kelly .10 .05 .01
□ 364 Ron Gant .50 .23 .06
□ 365 Luis Alicea .10 .05 .01
□ 366 Armando Benitez .10 .05 .01
□ 367 Rico Brogna .10 .05 .01
□ 368 Manny Ramirez .75 .35 .09
□ 369 Mike Lansing .10 .05 .01
□ 370 Sammy Sosa .50 .23 .06
□ 371 Don Wengert .10 .05 .01
□ 372 Dave Nilsson .25 .11 .03
□ 373 Sandy Alomar .10 .05 .01
□ 374 Joey Cora .10 .05 .01
□ 375 Larry Thomas .10 .05 .01
□ 376 John Valentin .25 .11 .03
□ 377 Kevin Ritz .10 .05 .01
□ 378 Steve Finley .50 .23 .06
□ 379 Frank Rodriguez .25 .11 .03
□ 380 Ivan Rodriguez .60 .25 .07
□ 381 Alex Ochoa .25 .11 .03
□ 382 Mark Lemke .10 .05 .01
□ 383 Scott Brosius .25 .11 .03
□ 384 James Mouton .10 .05 .01
□ 385 Mark Langston .10 .05 .01
□ 386 Ed Sprague .25 .11 .03
□ 387 Joe Oliver .10 .05 .01
□ 388 Steve Ontiveros .10 .05 .01
□ 389 Rey Sanchez .10 .05 .01
□ 390 Mike Henneman .10 .05 .01
□ 391 Jose Valentin .10 .05 .01
□ 392 Tom Candiotti .10 .05 .01
□ 393 Damon Buford .10 .05 .01
□ 394 Erik Hanson .10 .05 .01
□ 395 Mark Smith .10 .05 .01
□ 396 Pete Schourek .10 .05 .01
□ 397 John Flaherty .10 .05 .01
□ 398 Dave Martinez .10 .05 .01
□ 399 Tommy Greene .10 .05 .01
□ 400 Gary Sheffield .50 .23 .06
□ 401 Glenn Dishman .10 .05 .01
□ 402 Barry Bonds .75 .35 .09
□ 403 Tom Pagnozzi .10 .05 .01
□ 404 Todd Stottlemyre .10 .05 .01
□ 405 Tim Salmon .25 .11 .03
□ 406 John Hudek .10 .05 .01
□ 407 Fred McGriff .50 .23 .06
□ 408 Orlando Merced .10 .05 .01
□ 409 Brian Barber .10 .05 .01
□ 410 Ryan Thompson .10 .05 .01
□ 411 Mariano Rivera .50 .23 .06
□ 412 Eric Young .10 .05 .01
□ 413 Chris Bosio .10 .05 .01
□ 414 Chuck Knoblauch .50 .23 .06
□ 415 Jamie Moyer .10 .05 .01
□ 416 Chan Ho Park .50 .23 .06
□ 417 Mark Portugal .10 .05 .01
□ 418 Tim Raines .50 .23 .06
□ 419 Antonio Osuna .10 .05 .01
□ 420 Todd Zeile .25 .11 .03
□ 421 Steve Wojciechowski .10 .05 .01
□ 422 Marquis Grissom .50 .23 .06
□ 423 Norm Charlton .10 .05 .01
□ 424 Cal Ripken 2.50 1.10 .30
□ 425 Gregg Jefferies .50 .23 .06
□ 426 Mike Stanton .10 .05 .01
□ 427 Tony Fernandez .25 .11 .03
□ 428 Jose Rijo .10 .05 .01
□ 429 Jeff Bagwell 1.25 .55 .16
□ 430 Raul Mondesi .50 .23 .06
□ 431 Travis Fryman .50 .23 .06
□ 432 Ron Karkovice .10 .05 .01
□ 433 Alan Benes .50 .23 .06
□ 434 Tony Phillips .10 .05 .01
□ 435 Reggie Sanders .50 .23 .06
□ 436 Andy Pettitte 1.00 .45 .12
□ 437 Matt Lawton .10 .05 .01
□ 438 Jeff Blauser .10 .05 .01
□ 439 Michael Tucker .25 .11 .03
□ 440 Mark Loretta .10 .05 .01
□ 441 Charlie Hayes .10 .05 .01
□ 442 Mike Piazza 2.00 .90 .25
□ 443 Shane Andrews .10 .05 .01
□ 444 Jeff Suppan .10 .05 .01
□ 445 Steve Rodriguez .10 .05 .01
□ 446 Mike Matheny .10 .05 .01
□ 447 Trenidad Hubbard .10 .05 .01
□ 448 Denny Hocking .25 .11 .03
□ 449 Mark Grudzielanek .10 .05 .01
□ 450 Joe Randa .10 .05 .01

1996 Stadium Club Bash & Burn

Randomly inserted in packs at a rate of one in 29 (retail) and one in 48 (hobby), this ten card set features power/speed players. The fronts carry photos of the players hitting with a baseball background. The backs display photos of the same players running down the baseline on a background of flames.

	MINT	NRMT	EXC
COMPLETE SET (10)	30.00	13.50	3.70
COMMON CARD (B,B1-B,B10)	2.00	.90	.25
SEMISTARS	4.00	1.80	.50
RANDOM INSERTS IN SER.2 PACKS			
□ BB1 Sammy Sosa	8.00	3.60	1.00
□ BB2 Barry Bonds	12.00	5.50	1.50
□ BB3 Reggie Sanders	2.00	.90	.25
□ BB4 Craig Biggio	4.00	1.80	.50
□ BB5 Raul Mondesi	6.00	2.70	.75
□ BB6 Ron Gant	4.00	1.80	.50
□ BB7 Ray Lankford	4.00	1.80	.50
□ BB8 Glenallen Hill	2.00	.90	.25
□ BB9 Chad Curtis	2.00	.90	.25
□ BB10 John Valentin	4.00	1.80	.50

1996 Stadium Club Extreme Players

One hundred and seventy nine Extreme Player game cards were issued in 1996 Stadium Club, and each card has three versions with the following insertion rates: Bronze (1:12 packs); Silver (1:24 packs); and Gold (1:48 packs). At the conclusion of the 1996 regular season, an Extreme Player from each of ten positions were identified as winners based on scores calculated from their actual playing statistics. The Bronze EP winner cards were redeemable for a special 10-card set of diffraction foil stamped cards. The Silver EP winner cards were redeemable for a 10-card set of Finest Refractors. Finally, the Gold EP winner cards were redeemable for a Finest Refractor Gold card. The cards parallel the regular series except for the "EP" suffix on the number.

	MINT	NRMT	EXC
COMP.BRONZE SET (179)	250.00	110.00	31.00
COMP.BRONZE SER.1 (90)	125.00	55.00	15.50
COMP.BRONZE SER.2 (89)	125.00	55.00	15.50
COMMON BRONZE	1.00	.45	.12
BRONZE SEMISTARS	2.00	.90	.25

*SILVER: 2X BRONZE
*GOLD: 4X BRONZE
SET PARALLELS REG.CARDS W/EP SUFFIX
BEST EXTREME STATS PER POSITION WINS
BRONZE W: DIFFRACTION SET OF 10 WINNERS
SILVER W: REFRACTOR SET OF 10 WINNERS
GOLD W: BRONZE CARD OF CARD SUBMITTED
WINNER EXPIRATION: 12/31/96
UNNUMBERED INSERTS IN PACKS
LISTED PRICES ARE FOR BRONZE VERSIONS

□ 1	Hideo Nomo	4.00	1.80	.50
□ 3	Garret Anderson	1.00	.45	.12
□ 4	Jose Mesa	1.00	.45	.12
□ 5	Vinny Castilla	1.50	.70	.19
□ 6	Mike Mussina	3.00	1.35	.35
□ 7	Ray Durham	1.00	.45	.12
□ 8	Jack McDowell	1.50	.70	.19
□ 9	Juan Gonzalez	8.00	3.60	1.00
□ 10	Chipper Jones	10.00	4.50	1.25
□ 11	Deion Sanders	1.50	.70	.19
□ 12	Rondell White	1.50	.70	.19
□ 13	Tom Henke	1.00	.45	.12
□ 14	Derek Bell	1.50	.70	.19
□ 15	Randy Myers	1.00	.45	.12
□ 16	Randy Johnson	2.50	1.10	.30
□ 17	Len Dykstra	1.50	.70	.19
□ 18	Bill Pulsipher	1.00	.45	.12
□ 21	Chad Curtis	1.00	.45	.12
□ 22	Roberto Hernandez	1.00	.45	.12
□ 23	Kirby Puckett	5.00	2.20	.60
□ 25	Roger Clemens	2.00	.90	.25
□ 31	Chad Fonville	1.00	.45	.12
□ 32	Bernard Gilkey	1.50	.70	.19
□ 34	Shawn Green	1.00	.45	.12
□ 35	Rick Aguilera	1.00	.45	.12
□ 40	Dean Palmer	1.50	.70	.19
□ 45	Matt Williams	2.00	.90	.25
□ 49	Tom Glavine	2.00	.90	.25
□ 50	Delino DeShields	1.00	.45	.12
□ 56	Benito Santiago	1.00	.45	.12
□ 59	Rod Beck	1.00	.45	.12
□ 63	Eric Karros	1.50	.70	.19
□ 66	Lee Smith	1.50	.70	.19
□ 69	Jeff Montgomery	1.00	.45	.12
□ 70	Todd Hundley	1.50	.70	.19
□ 73	Don Mattingly	8.00	3.60	1.00
□ 77	Ken Caminiti W	6.00	2.70	.75
□ 80	Pedro Martinez	1.50	.70	.19
□ 82	Heathcliff Slocumb	1.00	.45	.12
□ 83	Joe Girardi	1.00	.45	.12
□ 88	Todd Worrell W	4.00	1.80	.50
□ 90	Bip Roberts	1.00	.45	.12
□ 95	Cecil Fielder	1.50	.70	.19
□ 96	Wade Boggs	2.00	.90	.25
□ 98	Mickey Tettleton	1.00	.45	.12
□ 99	Jeff Kent	1.00	.45	.12
□ 100	Denny Martinez	1.50	.70	.19
□ 101	Luis Gonzalez	1.00	.45	.12
□ 103	Javy Lopez	1.50	.70	.19
□ 104	Mark McGwire	5.00	2.20	.60
□ 105	Ken Griffey Jr. W	40.00	18.00	5.00
□ 106	Darren Daulton	1.50	.70	.19
□ 108	Mike Macfarlane	1.00	.45	.12
□ 110	Shane Reynolds	1.00	.45	.12
□ 114	John Franco	1.00	.45	.12
□ 116	Andy Benes	1.00	.45	.12
□ 118	Brian Jordan	1.50	.70	.19
□ 119	Terry Pendleton	1.50	.70	.19
□ 120	Chuck Finley	1.00	.45	.12
□ 123	Derek Jeter	10.00	4.50	1.25
□ 124	John Smiley	1.00	.45	.12
□ 126	Brett Butler	1.00	.45	.12
□ 127	Doug Drabek	1.00	.45	.12
□ 128	J.T. Snow	1.00	.45	.12
□ 129	Joe Carter	1.50	.70	.19
□ 130	Dennis Eckersley	1.50	.70	.19
□ 131	Marty Cordova	1.50	.70	.19
□ 132	Greg Maddux W	25.00	11.00	3.10
□ 135	Paul Sorrento	1.00	.45	.12
□ 137	Shawon Dunston	1.00	.45	.12
□ 138	Moises Alou	1.50	.70	.19
□ 140	Ramon Martinez	1.50	.70	.19
□ 141	Royce Clayton	1.00	.45	.12
□ 143	Kenny Rogers	1.00	.45	.12
□ 144	Tim Naehring	1.00	.45	.12
□ 145	Chris Gomez	1.00	.45	.12
□ 146	Bobby Bonilla	1.50	.70	.19
□ 148	Johnny Damon	1.50	.70	.19
□ 150	Andres Galarraga W	6.00	2.70	.75
□ 151	David Cone	1.50	.70	.19
□ 152	Lance Johnson	1.50	.70	.19
□ 159	David Justice	1.50	.70	.19
□ 160	Mark Grace	2.00	.90	.25
□ 161	Robb Nen	1.00	.45	.12
□ 162	Mike Greenwell	1.00	.45	.12
□ 167	Mel Rojas	1.00	.45	.12
□ 168	Bret Boone	1.00	.45	.12
□ 172	Jay Bell	1.00	.45	.12
□ 176	Roberto Alomar	4.00	1.80	.50
□ 178	Ryan Klesko	3.00	1.35	.35
□ 271	Barry Larkin W	6.00	2.70	.75
□ 272	Paul O'Neill	1.00	.45	.12
□ 274	Will Clark	2.00	.90	.25
□ 275	Steve Avery	1.00	.45	.12
□ 276	Jim Edmonds	1.50	.70	.19
□ 277	John Olerud	1.00	.45	.12
□ 279	Chris Hoiles	1.00	.45	.12
□ 280	Jeff Conine	1.50	.70	.19
□ 283	Ray Lankford	1.50	.70	.19
□ 285	Frank Thomas	15.00	6.75	1.85
□ 286	Jason Isringhausen	1.50	.70	.19
□ 287	Glenallen Hill	1.00	.45	.12
□ 289	Bernie Williams	2.50	1.10	.30
□ 290	Eddie Murray	4.00	1.80	.50
□ 296	Jeff Fassero	1.00	.45	.12
□ 297	Albert Belle	8.00	3.60	1.00
□ 298	Craig Biggio	1.50	.70	.19
□ 300	Edgar Martinez	2.00	.90	.25
□ 301	Tony Gwynn	6.00	2.70	.75
□ 303	Mo Vaughn	4.00	1.80	.50
□ 304	Alex Fernandez	2.00	.90	.25
□ 308	Omar Vizquel	1.00	.45	.12
□ 310	Danny Tartabull	1.00	.45	.12
□ 316	Brady Anderson	2.00	.90	.25
□ 319	Larry Walker	1.50	.70	.19
□ 321	Robin Ventura	1.50	.70	.19
□ 325	Kenny Lofton	4.00	1.80	.50
□ 327	Wil Cordero	1.00	.45	.12
□ 328	Troy Percival	1.00	.45	.12
□ 331	Carlos Baerga	1.50	.70	.19
□ 333	Jay Buhner	2.00	.90	.25
□ 335	Jeff King	1.00	.45	.12
□ 336	Dante Bichette	2.00	.90	.25
□ 337	Alan Trammell	2.00	.90	.25
□ 342	Jose Canseco	2.00	.90	.25
□ 343	Rafael Palmeiro	2.00	.90	.25
□ 344	Quilvio Veras	1.00	.45	.12
□ 345	Darrin Fletcher	1.00	.45	.12
□ 347	Tony Eusebio	1.00	.45	.12
□ 348	Ismael Valdes	1.50	.70	.19
□ 349	Terry Steinbach	1.50	.70	.19
□ 350	Orel Hershiser	1.50	.70	.19

□ 351	Kurt Abbott	1.00	.45	.12
□ 354	Ruben Sierra	1.00	.45	.12
□ 357	Jim Thome	3.00	1.35	.35
□ 358	Geronimo Berroa	1.00	.45	.12
□ 359	Robby Thompson	1.00	.45	.12
□ 360	Jose Vizcaino	1.00	.45	.12
□ 362	Kevin Appier	1.50	.70	.19
□ 364	Ron Gant	1.50	.70	.19
□ 367	Rico Brogna	1.00	.45	.12
□ 368	Manny Ramirez	4.00	1.80	.50
□ 370	Sammy Sosa	2.50	1.10	.30
□ 373	Sandy Alomar	1.00	.45	.12
□ 378	Steve Finley	1.50	.70	.19
□ 380	Ivan Rodriguez	3.00	1.35	.35
□ 382	Mark Lemke	1.00	.45	.12
□ 385	Mark Langston	1.00	.45	.12
□ 386	Ed Sprague	1.00	.45	.12
□ 388	Steve Ontiveros	1.00	.45	.12
□ 392	Tom Candiotti	1.00	.45	.12
□ 394	Erik Hanson	1.00	.45	.12
□ 396	Pete Schourek	1.00	.45	.12
□ 400	Gary Sheffield W	8.00	3.60	1.00
□ 402	Barry Bonds W	10.00	4.50	1.25
□ 403	Tom Pagnozzi	1.00	.45	.12
□ 404	Todd Stottlemyre	1.00	.45	.12
□ 405	Tim Salmon	2.00	.90	.25
□ 407	Fred McGriff	2.00	.90	.25
□ 408	Orlando Merced	1.00	.45	.12
□ 412	Eric Young	1.00	.45	.12
□ 414	Chuck Knoblauch W	6.00	2.70	.75
□ 417	Mark Portugal	1.00	.45	.12
□ 418	Tim Raines	1.50	.70	.19
□ 420	Todd Zeile	1.00	.45	.12
□ 422	Marquis Grissom	1.50	.70	.19
□ 423	Norm Charlton	1.00	.45	.12
□ 424	Cal Ripken	12.00	5.50	1.50
□ 425	Gregg Jefferies	1.50	.70	.19
□ 428	Jose Rijo	1.00	.45	.12
□ 429	Jeff Bagwell	6.00	2.70	.75
□ 430	Raul Mondesi	1.50	.70	.19
□ 431	Travis Fryman	1.50	.70	.19
□ 434	Tony Phillips	1.00	.45	.12
□ 435	Reggie Sanders	1.50	.70	.19
□ 436	Andy Pettitte	5.00	2.20	.60
□ 438	Jeff Blauser	1.00	.45	.12
□ 441	Charlie Hayes	1.00	.45	.12
□ 442	Mike Piazza W	25.00	11.00	3.10

1996 Stadium Club Megaheroes

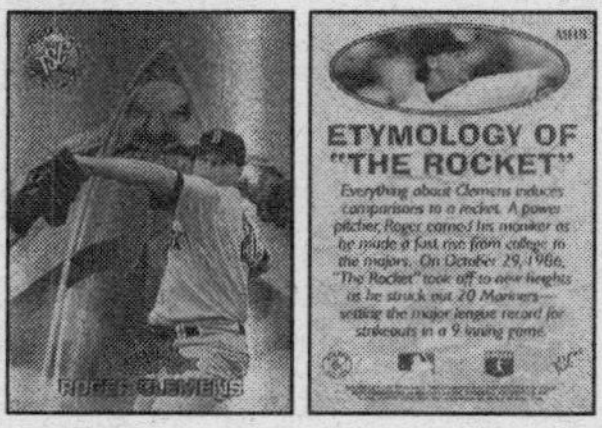

Randomly inserted at a rate of one in every 48 hobby and 24 retail packs, this 10-card set features super-heroic players matched with a comic book-style illustration depicting their nicknames. The fronts display a color player cutout superposed on diffraction foilboard illustrating the player's nickname. On a textured background, the backs present a closeup photo (in an oval format) and a career highlight in the form of an etymology of his nickname.

	MINT	NRMT	EXC
COMPLETE SET (10)	50.00	22.00	6.25
COMMON CARD (MH1-MH10)	1.50	.70	.19
SEMISTARS	2.50	1.10	.30
RANDOM INSERTS IN SER.1 PACKS			

□ MH1	Frank Thomas	20.00	9.00	2.50
□ MH2	Ken Griffey Jr.	20.00	9.00	2.50
□ MH3	Hideo Nomo	5.00	2.20	.60
□ MH4	Ozzie Smith	4.00	1.80	.50
□ MH5	Will Clark	2.50	1.10	.30
□ MH6	Jack McDowell	1.50	.70	.19
□ MH7	Andres Galarraga	2.50	1.10	.30
□ MH8	Roger Clemens	2.50	1.10	.30
□ MH9	Deion Sanders	2.50	1.10	.30
□ MH10	Mo Vaughn	5.00	2.20	.60

1996 Stadium Club Metalists

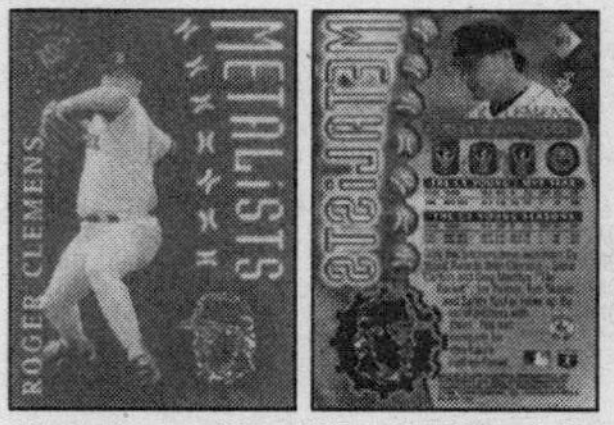

Randomly inserted in packs at a rate of one in 96 (retail) and one in 48 (hobby), this eight-card set features players with two or more MLB awards and is printed on laser-cut foil board.

	MINT	NRMT	EXC
COMPLETE SET (8)	50.00	22.00	6.25
COMMON CARD (M1-M8)	2.00	.90	.25
SEMISTARS	3.00	1.35	.35
RANDOM INSERTS IN SER.2 PACKS			

□ M1	Jeff Bagwell	8.00	3.60	1.00
□ M2	Barry Bonds	5.00	2.20	.60
□ M3	Jose Canseco	3.00	1.35	.35
□ M4	Roger Clemens	3.00	1.35	.35
□ M5	Dennis Eckersley	2.00	.90	.25
□ M6	Greg Maddux	12.00	5.50	1.50
□ M7	Cal Ripken	15.00	6.75	1.85
□ M8	Frank Thomas	20.00	9.00	2.50

1996 Stadium Club Midsummer Matchups

Randomly inserted at a rate of one in every 48 hobby and 24 retail packs, this 10-card set salutes 1995 National League and American League All-Stars as they are matched back-to-back by position on these two-sided etched foil cards. Each side features a color player cutout on a screened background of 1995 All-Star game emblems. On each side, the lower right corner is peeled back to reveal space for the American or National League logo.

	MINT	NRMT	EXC
COMPLETE SET (10)	100.00	45.00	12.50
COMMON CARD (M1-M10)	2.50	1.10	.30
RANDOM INSERTS IN SER.1 PACKS			

□ M1	Hideo Nomo Randy Johnson	8.00	3.60	1.00
□ M2	Mike Piazza Ivan Rodriguez	15.00	6.75	1.85
□ M3	Fred McGriff Frank Thomas	25.00	11.00	3.10
□ M4	Craig Biggio Carlos Baerga	2.50	1.10	.30
□ M5	Vinny Castilla Wade Boggs	2.50	1.10	.30
□ M6	Barry Larkin Cal Ripken	20.00	9.00	2.50
□ M7	Barry Bonds Albert Belle	15.00	6.75	1.85
□ M8	Len Dykstra Kenny Lofton	6.00	2.70	.75
□ M9	Tony Gwynn Kirby Puckett	15.00	6.75	1.85
□ M10	Ron Gant Edgar Martinez	2.50	1.10	.30

1996 Stadium Club Power Packed

Randomly inserted in packs at a rate of one in 48, this 15-card set features the biggest, most powerful hitters in the League. Printed on Power Matrix, the cards carry diagrams showing where the players hit the ball over the fence and how far.

	MINT	NRMT	EXC
COMPLETE SET (15)	80.00	36.00	10.00
COMMON CARD (PP1-PP15)	2.00	.90	.25
SEMISTARS	3.00	1.35	.35
RANDOM INSERTS IN SER.2 PACKS			

□ PP1	Albert Belle	12.00	5.50	1.50
□ PP2	Mark McGwire	8.00	3.60	1.00
□ PP3	Jose Canseco	3.00	1.35	.35
□ PP4	Mike Piazza	15.00	6.75	1.85
□ PP5	Ron Gant	2.00	.90	.25
□ PP6	Ken Griffey Jr.	25.00	11.00	3.10
□ PP7	Mo Vaughn	6.00	2.70	.75
□ PP8	Cecil Fielder	3.00	1.35	.35
□ PP9	Tim Salmon	3.00	1.35	.35
□ PP10	Frank Thomas	25.00	11.00	3.10
□ PP11	Juan Gonzalez	12.00	5.50	1.50
□ PP12	Andres Galarraga	3.00	1.35	.35
□ PP13	Fred McGriff	3.00	1.35	.35
□ PP14	Jay Buhner	3.00	1.35	.35
□ PP15	Dante Bichette	2.00	.90	.25

1996 Stadium Club Power Streak

Randomly inserted at a rate of one in every 24 hobby packs and 48 retail packs, this 15-card set spotlights baseball's most awesome power hitters and strikeout artists. The cards feature Topps' Power Matrix technology. The fronts display a color player cutout on a silver metallic and holographic background featuring a baseball. The backs carry a small color photo and biography; in addition, the player's batting prowess is presented under three topics: 1995 Power Profile, Power Stroke, and Power Zone.

	MINT	NRMT	EXC
COMPLETE SET (15)	70.00	32.00	8.75
COMMON CARD (PS1-PS15)	1.50	.70	.19
SEMISTARS	3.00	1.35	.35
RANDOM INSERTS IN SER.1 PACKS			

□ PS1	Randy Johnson	4.00	1.80	.50
□ PS2	Hideo Nomo	6.00	2.70	.75
□ PS3	Albert Belle	12.00	5.50	1.50
□ PS4	Dante Bichette	3.00	1.35	.35
□ PS5	Jay Buhner	3.00	1.35	.35
□ PS6	Frank Thomas	25.00	11.00	3.10
□ PS7	Mark McGwire	8.00	3.60	1.00
□ PS8	Rafael Palmeiro	3.00	1.35	.35
□ PS9	Mo Vaughn	6.00	2.70	.75
□ PS10	Sammy Sosa	4.00	1.80	.50
□ PS11	Larry Walker	3.00	1.35	.35
□ PS12	Gary Gaetti	1.50	.70	.19
□ PS13	Tim Salmon	3.00	1.35	.35
□ PS14	Barry Bonds	6.00	2.70	.75
□ PS15	Jim Edmonds	1.50	.70	.19

1996 Stadium Club Prime Cuts

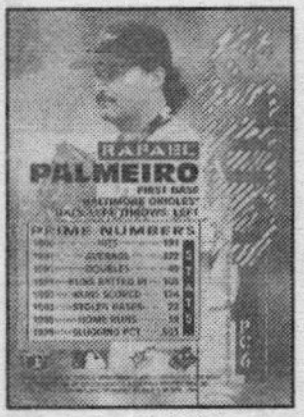

Randomly inserted at a rate of one in every 36 hobby and 72 retail packs, this 8-card set this set highlights eight hitters with the purest swings. These laser-cut cards feature diffraction gold foil. The cards are numbered on the back with a "PC" prefix.

	MINT	NRMT	EXC
COMPLETE SET (8)	60.00	27.00	7.50
COMMON CARD (PC1-PC8)	2.00	.90	.25
RANDOM INSERTS IN SER.1 PACKS			

□ PC1	Albert Belle	10.00	4.50	1.25
□ PC2	Barry Bonds	5.00	2.20	.60
□ PC3	Ken Griffey Jr.	20.00	9.00	2.50
□ PC4	Tony Gwynn	8.00	3.60	1.00
□ PC5	Edgar Martinez	2.00	.90	.25
□ PC6	Rafael Palmeiro	3.00	1.35	.35
□ PC7	Mike Piazza	12.00	5.50	1.50
□ PC8	Frank Thomas	20.00	9.00	2.50

1996 Stadium Club TSC Awards

Randomly inserted in packs at a rate of one in 24 (retail) and one in 48 (hobby), this ten-card

set features players whom TSC baseball experts voted to win various awards and is printed on diffraction foil.

	MINT	NRMT	EXC
COMPLETE SET (10)	40.00	18.00	5.00
COMMON CARD (1-10)	1.50	.70	.19
SEMISTARS	2.50	1.10	.30
RANDOM INSERTS IN SER.2 PACKS			
□ 1 Cal Ripken	12.00	5.50	1.50
□ 2 Albert Belle	8.00	3.60	1.00
□ 3 Tom Glavine	2.50	1.10	.30
□ 4 Jeff Conine	1.50	.70	.19
□ 5 Ken Griffey Jr.	15.00	6.75	1.85
□ 6 Hideo Nomo	4.00	1.80	.50
□ 7 Greg Maddux	10.00	4.50	1.25
□ 8 Chipper Jones	10.00	4.50	1.25
□ 9 Randy Johnson	2.50	1.10	.30
□ 10 Jose Mesa	1.50	.70	.19

1991 Studio Previews

This 18-card preview set was issued four at a time within 1991 Donruss retail factory sets in order to show dealers and collectors the look of their new Studio cards. The standard-size cards are exactly the same style as those in the Studio series, with black and white player photos bordered in mauve and player information on the backs.

	MINT	NRMT	EXC
COMPLETE SET (18)	20.00	9.00	2.50
COMMON CARD (1-17)	1.00	.45	.12
TITLE CARD (NNO)	1.00	.45	.12
SEMISTARS	1.50	.70	.19
FOUR PER DONRUSS RETAIL FACTORY SET			
□ 1 Juan Bell	1.00	.45	.12
□ 2 Roger Clemens	4.00	1.80	.50
□ 3 Dave Parker	1.50	.70	.19
□ 4 Tim Raines	1.50	.70	.19
□ 5 Kevin Seitzer	1.00	.45	.12
□ 6 Ted Higuera	1.00	.45	.12
□ 7 Bernie Williams	8.00	3.60	1.00
□ 8 Harold Baines	1.50	.70	.19
□ 9 Gary Pettis	1.00	.45	.12
□ 10 Dave Justice	4.00	1.80	.50
□ 11 Eric Davis	1.50	.70	.19
□ 12 Andujar Cedeno	1.00	.45	.12
□ 13 Tom Foley	1.00	.45	.12
□ 14 Dwight Gooden	1.50	.70	.19
□ 15 Doug Drabek	1.00	.45	.12
□ 16 Steve Decker	1.00	.45	.12
□ 17 Joe Torre MG	1.50	.70	.19
□ NNO Title card	1.00	.45	.12

1991 Studio

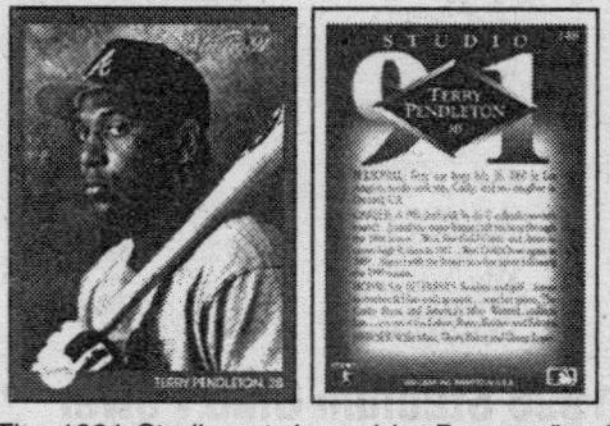

The 1991 Studio set, issued by Donruss/Leaf, contains 264 standard-size cards issued in one series. Cards were distributed in foil packs each of which contained one of 21 different Rod Carew puzzle panels. The Studio card fronts feature posed black and white head-and-shoulders player photos with mauve borders. The team logo, player's name, and position appear along the bottom of the card face. The cards are ordered alphabetically within and according to teams for each league with American League teams preceding National League. Rookie Cards in the set include Jeff Bagwell, Jeff Conine and Brian McRae.

	MINT	NRMT	EXC
COMPLETE SET (264)	15.00	6.75	1.85
COMMON CARD (1-263)	.05	.02	.01
COVER CARD (NNO)	.05	.02	.01
SEMISTARS	.15	.07	.02
STARS	.30	.14	.04
□ 1 Glenn Davis	.05	.02	.01
□ 2 Dwight Evans	.15	.07	.02
□ 3 Leo Gomez	.05	.02	.01
□ 4 Chris Hoiles	.05	.02	.01
□ 5 Sam Horn	.05	.02	.01
□ 6 Ben McDonald	.15	.07	.02
□ 7 Randy Milligan	.05	.02	.01
□ 8 Gregg Olson	.05	.02	.01
□ 9 Cal Ripken	1.50	.70	.19
□ 10 David Segui	.15	.07	.02
□ 11 Wade Boggs	.30	.14	.04
□ 12 Ellis Burks	.30	.14	.04
□ 13 Jack Clark	.15	.07	.02
□ 14 Roger Clemens	.30	.14	.04
□ 15 Mike Greenwell	.05	.02	.01
□ 16 Tim Naehring	.15	.07	.02
□ 17 Tony Pena	.05	.02	.01
□ 18 Phil Plantier	.15	.07	.02
□ 19 Jeff Reardon	.15	.07	.02
□ 20 Mo Vaughn	1.25	.55	.16
□ 21 Jimmy Reese CO	.15	.07	.02
□ 22 Jim Abbott UER (Born in 1967, not 1969)	.15	.07	.02
□ 23 Bert Blyleven	.15	.07	.02
□ 24 Chuck Finley	.15	.07	.02
□ 25 Gary Gaetti	.15	.07	.02
□ 26 Wally Joyner	.15	.07	.02
□ 27 Mark Langston	.15	.07	.02
□ 28 Kirk McCaskill	.05	.02	.01
□ 29 Lance Parrish	.05	.02	.01
□ 30 Dave Winfield	.30	.14	.04
□ 31 Alex Fernandez	.30	.14	.04
□ 32 Carlton Fisk	.30	.14	.04
□ 33 Scott Fletcher	.05	.02	.01
□ 34 Greg Hibbard	.05	.02	.01
□ 35 Charlie Hough	.05	.02	.01
□ 36 Jack McDowell	.15	.07	.02
□ 37 Tim Raines	.30	.14	.04
□ 38 Sammy Sosa	.60	.25	.07
□ 39 Bobby Thigpen	.05	.02	.01
□ 40 Frank Thomas	4.00	1.80	.50

□ 41 Sandy Alomar Jr.	.15	.07	.02
□ 42 John Farrell	.05	.02	.01
□ 43 Glenallen Hill	.05	.02	.01
□ 44 Brook Jacoby	.05	.02	.01
□ 45 Chris James	.05	.02	.01
□ 46 Doug Jones	.05	.02	.01
□ 47 Eric King	.05	.02	.01
□ 48 Mark Lewis	.05	.02	.01
□ 49 Greg Swindell UER (Photo actually Turner Ward)	.05	.02	.01
□ 50 Mark Whiten	.15	.07	.02
□ 51 Milt Cuyler	.05	.02	.01
□ 52 Rob Deer	.05	.02	.01
□ 53 Cecil Fielder	.15	.07	.02
□ 54 Travis Fryman	.30	.14	.04
□ 55 Bill Gullickson	.05	.02	.01
□ 56 Lloyd Moseby	.05	.02	.01
□ 57 Frank Tanana	.05	.02	.01
□ 58 Mickey Tettleton	.15	.07	.02
□ 59 Alan Trammell	.30	.14	.04
□ 60 Lou Whitaker	.30	.14	.04
□ 61 Mike Boddicker	.05	.02	.01
□ 62 George Brett	.75	.35	.09
□ 63 Jeff Conine	.75	.35	.09
□ 64 Warren Cromartie	.05	.02	.01
□ 65 Storm Davis	.05	.02	.01
□ 66 Kirk Gibson	.15	.07	.02
□ 67 Mark Gubicza	.05	.02	.01
□ 68 Brian McRae	.40	.18	.05
□ 69 Bret Saberhagen	.15	.07	.02
□ 70 Kurt Stillwell	.05	.02	.01
□ 71 Tim McIntosh	.05	.02	.01
□ 72 Candy Maldonado	.05	.02	.01
□ 73 Paul Molitor	.40	.18	.05
□ 74 Willie Randolph	.15	.07	.02
□ 75 Ron Robinson	.05	.02	.01
□ 76 Gary Sheffield	.30	.14	.04
□ 77 Franklin Stubbs	.05	.02	.01
□ 78 B.J. Surhoff	.15	.07	.02
□ 79 Greg Vaughn	.30	.14	.04
□ 80 Robin Yount	.30	.14	.04
□ 81 Rick Aguilera	.15	.07	.02
□ 82 Steve Bedrosian	.05	.02	.01
□ 83 Scott Erickson	.15	.07	.02
□ 84 Greg Gagne	.05	.02	.01
□ 85 Dan Gladden	.05	.02	.01
□ 86 Brian Harper	.05	.02	.01
□ 87 Kent Hrbek	.15	.07	.02
□ 88 Shane Mack	.05	.02	.01
□ 89 Jack Morris	.15	.07	.02
□ 90 Kirby Puckett	.60	.25	.07
□ 91 Jesse Barfield	.05	.02	.01
□ 92 Steve Farr	.05	.02	.01
□ 93 Steve Howe	.05	.02	.01
□ 94 Roberto Kelly	.05	.02	.01
□ 95 Tim Leary	.05	.02	.01
□ 96 Kevin Maas	.05	.02	.01
□ 97 Don Mattingly	1.00	.45	.12
□ 98 Hensley Meulens	.05	.02	.01
□ 99 Scott Sanderson	.05	.02	.01
□ 100 Steve Sax	.05	.02	.01
□ 101 Jose Canseco	.30	.14	.04
□ 102 Dennis Eckersley	.15	.07	.02
□ 103 Dave Henderson	.05	.02	.01
□ 104 Rickey Henderson	.30	.14	.04
□ 105 Rick Honeycutt	.05	.02	.01
□ 106 Mark McGwire	.60	.25	.07
□ 107 Dave Stewart UER (No-hitter against Toronto, not Texas)	.15	.07	.02
□ 108 Eric Show	.05	.02	.01
□ 109 Todd Van Poppel	.15	.07	.02
□ 110 Bob Welch	.05	.02	.01
□ 111 Alvin Davis	.05	.02	.01
□ 112 Ken Griffey Jr.	3.00	1.35	.35
□ 113 Ken Griffey Sr.	.05	.02	.01
□ 114 Erik Hanson UER (Misspelled Eric)	.05	.02	.01
□ 115 Brian Holman	.05	.02	.01
□ 116 Randy Johnson	.30	.14	.04
□ 117 Edgar Martinez	.30	.14	.04
□ 118 Tino Martinez	.30	.14	.04
□ 119 Harold Reynolds	.05	.02	.01
□ 120 David Valle	.05	.02	.01
□ 121 Kevin Belcher	.05	.02	.01
□ 122 Scott Chiamparino	.05	.02	.01
□ 123 Julio Franco	.15	.07	.02
□ 124 Juan Gonzalez	1.50	.70	.19
□ 125 Rich Gossage	.15	.07	.02
□ 126 Jeff Kunkel	.05	.02	.01
□ 127 Rafael Palmeiro	.30	.14	.04
□ 128 Nolan Ryan	1.50	.70	.19
□ 129 Ruben Sierra	.15	.07	.02
□ 130 Bobby Witt	.05	.02	.01
□ 131 Roberto Alomar	.50	.23	.06
□ 132 Tom Candiotti	.05	.02	.01
□ 133 Joe Carter	.30	.14	.04
□ 134 Ken Dayley	.05	.02	.01
□ 135 Kelly Gruber	.05	.02	.01
□ 136 John Olerud	.15	.07	.02
□ 137 Dave Stieb	.05	.02	.01
□ 138 Turner Ward	.05	.02	.01
□ 139 Devon White	.15	.07	.02
□ 140 Mookie Wilson	.05	.02	.01
□ 141 Steve Avery	.30	.14	.04
□ 142 Sid Bream	.05	.02	.01
□ 143 Nick Esasky UER (Homers abbreviated RH)	.05	.02	.01
□ 144 Ron Gant	.30	.14	.04
□ 145 Tom Glavine	.30	.14	.04
□ 146 David Justice	.30	.14	.04
□ 147 Kelly Mann	.05	.02	.01
□ 148 Terry Pendleton	.15	.07	.02
□ 149 John Smoltz	.30	.14	.04
□ 150 Jeff Treadway	.05	.02	.01
□ 151 George Bell	.05	.02	.01
□ 152 Shawn Boskie	.05	.02	.01
□ 153 Andre Dawson	.30	.14	.04
□ 154 Lance Dickson	.05	.02	.01
□ 155 Shawon Dunston	.05	.02	.01
□ 156 Joe Girardi	.15	.07	.02
□ 157 Mark Grace	.30	.14	.04
□ 158 Ryne Sandberg	.50	.23	.06
□ 159 Gary Scott	.05	.02	.01
□ 160 Dave Smith	.05	.02	.01
□ 161 Tom Browning	.05	.02	.01
□ 162 Eric Davis	.15	.07	.02
□ 163 Rob Dibble	.05	.02	.01
□ 164 Mariano Duncan	.05	.02	.01
□ 165 Chris Hammond	.05	.02	.01
□ 166 Billy Hatcher	.05	.02	.01
□ 167 Barry Larkin	.30	.14	.04
□ 168 Hal Morris	.05	.02	.01
□ 169 Paul O'Neill	.15	.07	.02
□ 170 Chris Sabo	.05	.02	.01
□ 171 Eric Anthony	.05	.02	.01
□ 172 Jeff Bagwell	3.00	1.35	.35
□ 173 Craig Biggio	.30	.14	.04
□ 174 Ken Caminiti	.30	.14	.04
□ 175 Jim Deshaies	.05	.02	.01
□ 176 Steve Finley	.30	.14	.04
□ 177 Pete Harnisch	.05	.02	.01
□ 178 Darryl Kile	.05	.02	.01
□ 179 Curt Schilling	.05	.02	.01
□ 180 Mike Scott	.05	.02	.01
□ 181 Brett Butler	.15	.07	.02
□ 182 Gary Carter	.30	.14	.04
□ 183 Orel Hershiser	.15	.07	.02
□ 184 Ramon Martinez	.15	.07	.02
□ 185 Eddie Murray	.50	.23	.06
□ 186 Jose Offerman	.05	.02	.01
□ 187 Bob Ojeda	.05	.02	.01
□ 188 Juan Samuel	.05	.02	.01
□ 189 Mike Scioscia	.05	.02	.01
□ 190 Darryl Strawberry	.15	.07	.02
□ 191 Moises Alou	.30	.14	.04
□ 192 Brian Barnes	.05	.02	.01
□ 193 Oil Can Boyd	.05	.02	.01
□ 194 Ivan Calderon	.05	.02	.01
□ 195 Delino DeShields	.05	.02	.01
□ 196 Mike Fitzgerald	.05	.02	.01
□ 197 Andres Galarraga	.30	.14	.04
□ 198 Marquis Grissom	.30	.14	.04
□ 199 Bill Sampen	.05	.02	.01
□ 200 Tim Wallach	.05	.02	.01
□ 201 Daryl Boston	.05	.02	.01
□ 202 Vince Coleman	.05	.02	.01
□ 203 John Franco	.05	.02	.01
□ 204 Dwight Gooden	.15	.07	.02
□ 205 Tom Herr	.05	.02	.01
□ 206 Gregg Jefferies	.30	.14	.04

□ 207 Howard Johnson	.05	.02	.01
□ 208 Dave Magadan UER (Born 1862, should be 1962)	.05	.02	.01
□ 209 Kevin McReynolds	.05	.02	.01
□ 210 Frank Viola	.05	.02	.01
□ 211 Wes Chamberlain	.05	.02	.01
□ 212 Darren Daulton	.15	.07	.02
□ 213 Len Dykstra	.15	.07	.02
□ 214 Charlie Hayes	.05	.02	.01
□ 215 Ricky Jordan	.05	.02	.01
□ 216 Steve Lake (Pictured with parrot on his shoulder)	.05	.02	.01
□ 217 Roger McDowell	.05	.02	.01
□ 218 Mickey Morandini	.05	.02	.01
□ 219 Terry Mulholland	.05	.02	.01
□ 220 Dale Murphy	.30	.14	.04
□ 221 Jay Bell	.15	.07	.02
□ 222 Barry Bonds	.50	.23	.06
□ 223 Bobby Bonilla	.15	.07	.02
□ 224 Doug Drabek	.05	.02	.01
□ 225 Bill Landrum	.05	.02	.01
□ 226 Mike LaValliere	.05	.02	.01
□ 227 Jose Lind	.05	.02	.01
□ 228 Don Slaught	.05	.02	.01
□ 229 John Smiley	.05	.02	.01
□ 230 Andy Van Slyke	.15	.07	.02
□ 231 Bernard Gilkey	.30	.14	.04
□ 232 Pedro Guerrero	.05	.02	.01
□ 233 Rex Hudler	.05	.02	.01
□ 234 Ray Lankford	.30	.14	.04
□ 235 Joe Magrane	.05	.02	.01
□ 236 Jose Oquendo	.05	.02	.01
□ 237 Lee Smith	.15	.07	.02
□ 238 Ozzie Smith	.40	.18	.05
□ 239 Milt Thompson	.05	.02	.01
□ 240 Todd Zeile	.15	.07	.02
□ 241 Larry Andersen	.05	.02	.01
□ 242 Andy Benes	.05	.02	.01
□ 243 Paul Faries	.05	.02	.01
□ 244 Tony Fernandez	.05	.02	.01
□ 245 Tony Gwynn	.75	.35	.09
□ 246 Atlee Hammaker	.05	.02	.01
□ 247 Fred McGriff	.30	.14	.04
□ 248 Bip Roberts	.05	.02	.01
□ 249 Bentio Santiago	.05	.02	.01
□ 250 Ed Whitson	.05	.02	.01
□ 251 Dave Anderson	.05	.02	.01
□ 252 Mike Benjamin	.05	.02	.01
□ 253 John Burkett UER (Front photo actually Trevor Wilson)	.15	.07	.02
□ 254 Will Clark	.30	.14	.04
□ 255 Scott Garrelts	.05	.02	.01
□ 256 Willie McGee	.05	.02	.01
□ 257 Kevin Mitchell	.15	.07	.02
□ 258 Dave Righetti	.05	.02	.01
□ 259 Matt Williams	.30	.14	.04
□ 260 Bud Black Steve Decker	.05	.02	.01
□ 261 Sparky Anderson MG CL	.15	.07	.02
□ 262 Tom Lasorda MG CL	.15	.07	.02
□ 263 Tony LaRussa MG CL	.15	.07	.02
□ NNO Title Card	.05	.02	.01

1992 Studio

The 1992 Studio set consists of ten players from each of the 26 major league teams, three checklists, and an introduction card for a total of 264 standard-size cards. Inside champagne color metallic borders, the fronts carry a color close-up shot superimposed on a black and white action player photo. The backs focus on the personal side of each player by providing an up-close look, and unusual statistics show the batter or pitcher each player "Loves to Face" or "Hates to Face". The key Rookie Cards in this set are Chad Curtis and Brian Jordan.

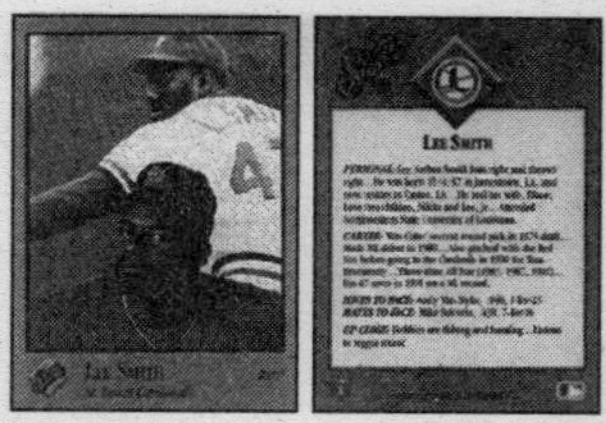

	MINT	NRMT	EXC
COMPLETE SET (264)	15.00	6.75	1.85
COMMON CARD (1-264)	.05	.02	.01
SEMISTARS	.10	.05	.01
STARS	.25	.11	.03

□ 1 Steve Avery	.10	.05	.01
□ 2 Sid Bream	.05	.02	.01
□ 3 Ron Gant	.25	.11	.03
□ 4 Tom Glavine	.25	.11	.03
□ 5 David Justice	.25	.11	.03
□ 6 Mark Lemke	.05	.02	.01
□ 7 Greg Olson	.05	.02	.01
□ 8 Terry Pendleton	.10	.05	.01
□ 9 Deion Sanders	.25	.11	.03
□ 10 John Smoltz	.25	.11	.03
□ 11 Doug Dascenzo	.05	.02	.01
□ 12 Andre Dawson	.25	.11	.03
□ 13 Joe Girardi	.05	.02	.01
□ 14 Mark Grace	.25	.11	.03
□ 15 Greg Maddux	1.25	.55	.16
□ 16 Chuck McElroy	.05	.02	.01
□ 17 Mike Morgan	.05	.02	.01
□ 18 Ryne Sandberg	.40	.18	.05
□ 19 Gary Scott	.05	.02	.01
□ 20 Sammy Sosa	.40	.18	.05
□ 21 Norm Charlton	.05	.02	.01
□ 22 Rob Dibble	.05	.02	.01
□ 23 Barry Larkin	.25	.11	.03
□ 24 Hal Morris	.05	.02	.01
□ 25 Paul O'Neill	.10	.05	.01
□ 26 Jose Rijo	.05	.02	.01
□ 27 Bip Roberts	.05	.02	.01
□ 28 Chris Sabo	.05	.02	.01
□ 29 Reggie Sanders	.25	.11	.03
□ 30 Greg Swindell	.05	.02	.01
□ 31 Jeff Bagwell	1.00	.45	.12
□ 32 Craig Biggio	.25	.11	.03
□ 33 Ken Caminiti	.25	.11	.03
□ 34 Andujar Cedeno	.05	.02	.01
□ 35 Steve Finley	.25	.11	.03
□ 36 Pete Harnisch	.05	.02	.01
□ 37 Butch Henry	.05	.02	.01
□ 38 Doug Jones	.05	.02	.01
□ 39 Darryl Kile	.05	.02	.01
□ 40 Eddie Taubensee	.05	.02	.01
□ 41 Brett Butler	.10	.05	.01
□ 42 Tom Candiotti	.05	.02	.01
□ 43 Eric Davis	.10	.05	.01
□ 44 Orel Hershiser	.10	.05	.01
□ 45 Eric Karros	.25	.11	.03
□ 46 Ramon Martinez	.10	.05	.01
□ 47 Jose Offerman	.05	.02	.01
□ 48 Mike Scioscia	.05	.02	.01
□ 49 Mike Sharperson	.05	.02	.01
□ 50 Darryl Strawberry	.10	.05	.01
□ 51 Bret Barberie	.05	.02	.01
□ 52 Ivan Calderon	.05	.02	.01
□ 53 Gary Carter	.25	.11	.03
□ 54 Delino DeShields	.05	.02	.01
□ 55 Marquis Grissom	.25	.11	.03
□ 56 Ken Hill	.25	.11	.03
□ 57 Dennis Martinez	.10	.05	.01
□ 58 Spike Owen	.05	.02	.01
□ 59 Larry Walker	.25	.11	.03
□ 60 Tim Wallach	.05	.02	.01
□ 61 Bobby Bonilla	.10	.05	.01
□ 62 Tim Burke	.05	.02	.01
□ 63 Vince Coleman	.05	.02	.01
□ 64 John Franco	.05	.02	.01
□ 65 Dwight Gooden	.10	.05	.01
□ 66 Todd Hundley	.25	.11	.03
□ 67 Howard Johnson	.05	.02	.01

□ 68 Eddie Murray UER (He's not all-time switch homer leader, but he has most games with homers from both sides)	.40	.18	.05
□ 69 Bret Saberhagen	.10	.05	.01
□ 70 Anthony Young	.05	.02	.01
□ 71 Kim Batiste	.05	.02	.01
□ 72 Wes Chamberlain	.05	.02	.01
□ 73 Darren Daulton	.10	.05	.01
□ 74 Mariano Duncan	.05	.02	.01
□ 75 Len Dykstra	.10	.05	.01
□ 76 John Kruk	.10	.05	.01
□ 77 Mickey Morandini	.05	.02	.01
□ 78 Terry Mulholland	.05	.02	.01
□ 79 Dale Murphy	.25	.11	.03
□ 80 Mitch Williams	.05	.02	.01
□ 81 Jay Bell	.10	.05	.01
□ 82 Barry Bonds	.40	.18	.05
□ 83 Steve Buechele	.05	.02	.01
□ 84 Doug Drabek	.05	.02	.01
□ 85 Mike LaValliere	.05	.02	.01
□ 86 Jose Lind	.05	.02	.01
□ 87 Denny Neagle	.10	.05	.01
□ 88 Randy Tomlin	.05	.02	.01
□ 89 Andy Van Slyke	.10	.05	.01
□ 90 Gary Varsho	.05	.02	.01
□ 91 Pedro Guerrero	.05	.02	.01
□ 92 Rex Hudler	.05	.02	.01
□ 93 Brian Jordan	.50	.23	.06
□ 94 Felix Jose	.05	.02	.01
□ 95 Donovan Osborne	.10	.05	.01
□ 96 Tom Pagnozzi	.05	.02	.01
□ 97 Lee Smith	.10	.05	.01
□ 98 Ozzie Smith	.30	.14	.04
□ 99 Todd Worrell	.05	.02	.01
□ 100 Todd Zeile	.05	.02	.01
□ 101 Andy Benes	.05	.02	.01
□ 102 Jerald Clark	.05	.02	.01
□ 103 Tony Fernandez	.05	.02	.01
□ 104 Tony Gwynn	.60	.25	.07
□ 105 Greg W. Harris	.05	.02	.01
□ 106 Fred McGriff	.25	.11	.03
□ 107 Benito Santiago	.05	.02	.01
□ 108 Gary Sheffield	.25	.11	.03
□ 109 Kurt Stillwell	.05	.02	.01
□ 110 Tim Teufel	.05	.02	.01
□ 111 Kevin Bass	.05	.02	.01
□ 112 Jeff Brantley	.10	.05	.01
□ 113 John Burkett	.10	.05	.01
□ 114 Will Clark	.25	.11	.03
□ 115 Royce Clayton	.10	.05	.01
□ 116 Mike Jackson	.05	.02	.01
□ 117 Darren Lewis	.05	.02	.01
□ 118 Bill Swift	.05	.02	.01
□ 119 Robby Thompson	.05	.02	.01
□ 120 Matt Williams	.25	.11	.03
□ 121 Brady Anderson	.25	.11	.03
□ 122 Glenn Davis	.05	.02	.01
□ 123 Mike Devereaux	.05	.02	.01
□ 124 Chris Hoiles	.05	.02	.01
□ 125 Sam Horn	.05	.02	.01
□ 126 Ben McDonald	.05	.02	.01
□ 127 Mike Mussina	.50	.23	.06
□ 128 Gregg Olson	.05	.02	.01
□ 129 Cal Ripken Jr.	1.25	.55	.16
□ 130 Rick Sutcliffe	.05	.02	.01
□ 131 Wade Boggs	.25	.11	.03
□ 132 Roger Clemens	.25	.11	.03
□ 133 Greg A. Harris	.05	.02	.01
□ 134 Tim Naehring	.10	.05	.01
□ 135 Tony Pena	.05	.02	.01
□ 136 Phil Plantier	.10	.05	.01
□ 137 Jeff Reardon	.10	.05	.01
□ 138 Jody Reed	.05	.02	.01
□ 139 Mo Vaughn	.60	.25	.07
□ 140 Frank Viola	.05	.02	.01
□ 141 Jim Abbott	.05	.02	.01
□ 142 Hubie Brooks	.05	.02	.01
□ 143 Chad Curtis	.25	.11	.03
□ 144 Gary DiSarcina	.05	.02	.01
□ 145 Chuck Finley	.05	.02	.01
□ 146 Bryan Harvey	.05	.02	.01
□ 147 Von Hayes	.05	.02	.01
□ 148 Mark Langston	.10	.05	.01
□ 149 Lance Parrish	.05	.02	.01
□ 150 Lee Stevens	.05	.02	.01
□ 151 George Bell	.05	.02	.01
□ 152 Alex Fernandez	.25	.11	.03
□ 153 Greg Hibbard	.05	.02	.01
□ 154 Lance Johnson	.10	.05	.01
□ 155 Kirk McCaskill	.05	.02	.01
□ 156 Tim Raines	.25	.11	.03
□ 157 Steve Sax	.05	.02	.01
□ 158 Bobby Thigpen	.05	.02	.01
□ 159 Frank Thomas	2.50	1.10	.30
□ 160 Robin Ventura	.25	.11	.03
□ 161 Sandy Alomar Jr.	.10	.05	.01
□ 162 Jack Armstrong	.05	.02	.01
□ 163 Carlos Baerga	.25	.11	.03
□ 164 Albert Belle	1.00	.45	.12
□ 165 Alex Cole	.05	.02	.01
□ 166 Glenallen Hill	.05	.02	.01
□ 167 Mark Lewis	.05	.02	.01
□ 168 Kenny Lofton	2.00	.90	.25
□ 169 Paul Sorrento	.05	.02	.01
□ 170 Mark Whiten	.10	.05	.01
□ 171 Milt Cuyler	.05	.02	.01
□ 172 Rob Deer	.05	.02	.01
□ 173 Cecil Fielder	.10	.05	.01
□ 174 Travis Fryman	.25	.11	.03
□ 175 Mike Henneman	.05	.02	.01
□ 176 Tony Phillips	.10	.05	.01
□ 177 Frank Tanana	.05	.02	.01
□ 178 Mickey Tettleton	.05	.02	.01
□ 179 Alan Trammell	.25	.11	.03
□ 180 Lou Whitaker	.25	.11	.03
□ 181 George Brett	.60	.25	.07
□ 182 Tom Gordon	.05	.02	.01
□ 183 Mark Gubicza	.05	.02	.01
□ 184 Gregg Jefferies	.25	.11	.03
□ 185 Wally Joyner	.10	.05	.01
□ 186 Brent Mayne	.05	.02	.01
□ 187 Brian McRae	.25	.11	.03
□ 188 Kevin McReynolds	.05	.02	.01
□ 189 Keith Miller	.05	.02	.01
□ 190 Jeff Montgomery	.10	.05	.01
□ 191 Dante Bichette	.25	.11	.03
□ 192 Ricky Bones	.05	.02	.01
□ 193 Scott Fletcher	.05	.02	.01
□ 194 Paul Molitor	.30	.14	.04
□ 195 Jaime Navarro	.05	.02	.01
□ 196 Franklin Stubbs	.05	.02	.01
□ 197 B.J. Surhoff	.10	.05	.01
□ 198 Greg Vaughn	.25	.11	.03
□ 199 Bill Wegman	.05	.02	.01
□ 200 Robin Yount	.25	.11	.03
□ 201 Rick Aguilera	.05	.02	.01
□ 202 Scott Erickson	.10	.05	.01
□ 203 Greg Gagne	.05	.02	.01
□ 204 Brian Harper	.05	.02	.01
□ 205 Kent Hrbek	.10	.05	.01
□ 206 Scott Leius	.05	.02	.01
□ 207 Shane Mack	.05	.02	.01
□ 208 Pat Mahomes	.05	.02	.01
□ 209 Kirby Puckett	.50	.23	.06
□ 210 John Smiley	.05	.02	.01
□ 211 Mike Gallego	.05	.02	.01
□ 212 Charlie Hayes	.05	.02	.01
□ 213 Pat Kelly	.05	.02	.01
□ 214 Roberto Kelly	.05	.02	.01
□ 215 Kevin Maas	.05	.02	.01
□ 216 Don Mattingly	.75	.35	.09
□ 217 Matt Nokes	.05	.02	.01
□ 218 Melido Perez	.05	.02	.01
□ 219 Scott Sanderson	.05	.02	.01
□ 220 Danny Tartabull	.05	.02	.01
□ 221 Harold Baines	.10	.05	.01
□ 222 Jose Canseco	.25	.11	.03
□ 223 Dennis Eckersley	.10	.05	.01
□ 224 Dave Henderson	.05	.02	.01
□ 225 Carney Lansford	.10	.05	.01
□ 226 Mark McGwire	.50	.23	.06
□ 227 Mike Moore	.05	.02	.01
□ 228 Randy Ready	.05	.02	.01
□ 229 Terry Steinbach	.10	.05	.01
□ 230 Dave Stewart	.10	.05	.01
□ 231 Jay Buhner	.25	.11	.03
□ 232 Ken Griffey Jr.	2.50	1.10	.30
□ 233 Erik Hanson	.05	.02	.01
□ 234 Randy Johnson	.25	.11	.03
□ 235 Edgar Martinez	.25	.11	.03

□ 236 Tino Martinez	.25	.11	.03
□ 237 Kevin Mitchell	.10	.05	.01
□ 238 Pete O'Brien	.05	.02	.01
□ 239 Harold Reynolds	.05	.02	.01
□ 240 David Valle	.05	.02	.01
□ 241 Julio Franco	.10	.05	.01
□ 242 Juan Gonzalez	1.00	.45	.12
□ 243 Jose Guzman	.05	.02	.01
□ 244 Rafael Palmeiro	.25	.11	.03
□ 245 Dean Palmer	.10	.05	.01
□ 246 Ivan Rodriguez	.50	.23	.06
□ 247 Jeff Russell	.05	.02	.01
□ 248 Nolan Ryan	1.25	.55	.16
□ 249 Ruben Sierra	.10	.05	.01
□ 250 Dickie Thon	.05	.02	.01
□ 251 Roberto Alomar	.40	.18	.05
□ 252 Derek Bell	.10	.05	.01
□ 253 Pat Borders	.05	.02	.01
□ 254 Joe Carter	.25	.11	.03
□ 255 Kelly Gruber	.05	.02	.01
□ 256 Juan Guzman	.10	.05	.01
□ 257 Jack Morris	.10	.05	.01
□ 258 John Olerud	.10	.05	.01
□ 259 Devon White	.10	.05	.01
□ 260 Dave Winfield	.25	.11	.03
□ 261 Checklist	.05	.02	.01
□ 262 Checklist	.05	.02	.01
□ 263 Checklist	.05	.02	.01
□ 264 History Card	.05	.02	.01

1992 Studio Heritage

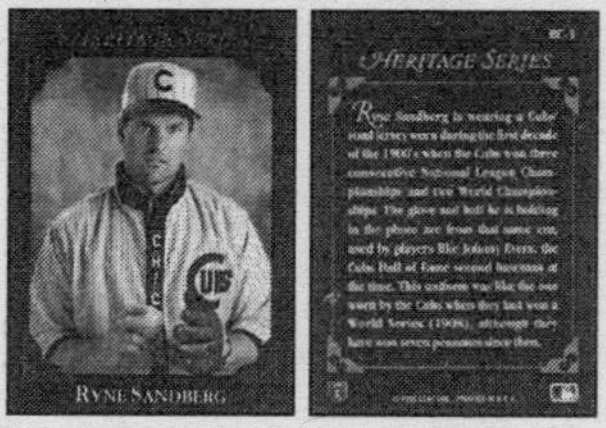

The 1992 Studio Heritage standard-size insert set presents today's star players dressed in vintage uniforms. Cards numbered 1-8 were randomly inserted in 12-card foil packs while cards numbered 9-14 were inserted one per pack in 28-card jumbo packs. The fronts display sepia-toned portraits of the players dressed in vintage uniforms of their current teams. The pictures are bordered by dark turquoise and have bronze foil picture holders at each corner. The set title "Heritage Series" also appears in bronze foil lettering above the pictures. Within a bronze picture frame design on dark turquoise, the backs give a brief history of the team with special reference to the year of the vintage uniform. The cards are numbered on the back with a "BC" prefix.

	MINT	NRMT	EXC
COMPLETE SET (14)	25.00	11.00	3.10
COMPLETE FOIL SET (8)	15.00	6.75	1.85
COMPLETE JUMBO SET (6)	10.00	4.50	1.25
COMMON CARD (BC1-BC8)	.75	.35	.09
RANDOM INSERTS IN FOIL PACKS			
COMMON CARD (BC9-BC14)	.75	.35	.09
ONE PER JUMBO PACK			
SEMISTARS	1.25	.55	.16

□ BC1 Ryne Sandberg	2.00	.90	.25
□ BC2 Carlton Fisk	1.25	.55	.16
□ BC3 Wade Boggs	1.25	.55	.16
□ BC4 Jose Canseco	1.25	.55	.16
□ BC5 Don Mattingly	4.00	1.80	.50
□ BC6 Darryl Strawberry	1.25	.55	.16
□ BC7 Cal Ripken	8.00	3.60	1.00
□ BC8 Will Clark	1.25	.55	.16
□ BC9 Andre Dawson	1.25	.55	.16
□ BC10 Andy Van Slyke	.75	.35	.09
□ BC11 Paul Molitor	1.25	.55	.16
□ BC12 Jeff Bagwell	5.00	2.20	.60
□ BC13 Darren Daulton	.75	.35	.09
□ BC14 Kirby Puckett	2.50	1.10	.30

1993 Studio

The 220 standard-size cards comprising this set feature borderless fronts with posed color player photos that are cut out and superposed upon a closeup of an embroidered team logo. A facsimile player autograph appears in prismatic gold foil across the lower portion of the photo. The borderless black backs carry another posed color player photo shunted to the right side, with the player's name, position, team, biography, and personal profile appearing in white lettering on the left side. The key Rookie Card in this set is J.T. Snow.

	MINT	NRMT	EXC
COMPLETE SET (220)	20.00	9.00	2.50
COMMON CARD (1-220)	.10	.05	.01
SEMISTARS	.20	.09	.03
STARS	.40	.18	.05
COMP.F.THOMAS SET (5)	30.00	13.50	3.70
COMMON THOMAS (1-5)	7.00	3.10	.85
THOMAS: RANDOM INSERTS IN ALL PACKS			

□ 1 Dennis Eckersley	.20	.09	.03
□ 2 Chad Curtis	.20	.09	.03
□ 3 Eric Anthony	.10	.05	.01
□ 4 Roberto Alomar	.60	.25	.07
□ 5 Steve Avery	.20	.09	.03
□ 6 Cal Eldred	.10	.05	.01
□ 7 Bernard Gilkey	.40	.18	.05
□ 8 Steve Buechele	.10	.05	.01
□ 9 Brett Butler	.20	.09	.03
□ 10 Terry Mulholland	.10	.05	.01
□ 11 Moises Alou	.40	.18	.05
□ 12 Barry Bonds	.60	.25	.07
□ 13 Sandy Alomar Jr.	.20	.09	.03
□ 14 Chris Bosio	.10	.05	.01
□ 15 Scott Sanderson	.10	.05	.01
□ 16 Bobby Bonilla	.20	.09	.03
□ 17 Brady Anderson	.40	.18	.05
□ 18 Derek Bell	.40	.18	.05
□ 19 Wes Chamberlain	.10	.05	.01
□ 20 Jay Bell	.20	.09	.03
□ 21 Kevin Brown	.10	.05	.01
□ 22 Roger Clemens	.40	.18	.05
□ 23 Roberto Kelly	.10	.05	.01
□ 24 Dante Bichette	.40	.18	.05
□ 25 George Brett	1.00	.45	.12
□ 26 Rob Deer	.10	.05	.01
□ 27 Brian Harper	.10	.05	.01
□ 28 George Bell	.10	.05	.01
□ 29 Jim Abbott	.10	.05	.01
□ 30 Dave Henderson	.10	.05	.01
□ 31 Wade Boggs	.40	.18	.05
□ 32 Chili Davis	.20	.09	.03
□ 33 Ellis Burks	.40	.18	.05
□ 34 Jeff Bagwell	1.00	.45	.12
□ 35 Kent Hrbek	.20	.09	.03
□ 36 Pat Borders	.10	.05	.01
□ 37 Cecil Fielder	.20	.09	.03
□ 38 Sid Bream	.10	.05	.01
□ 39 Greg Gagne	.10	.05	.01

□	40 Darryl Hamilton	.10	.05	.01
□	41 Jerald Clark	.10	.05	.01
□	42 Mark Grace	.40	.18	.05
□	43 Barry Larkin	.40	.18	.05
□	44 John Burkett	.10	.05	.01
□	45 Scott Cooper	.10	.05	.01
□	46 Mike Lansing	.20	.09	.03
□	47 Jose Canseco	.40	.18	.05
□	48 Will Clark	.40	.18	.05
□	49 Carlos Garcia	.10	.05	.01
□	50 Carlos Baerga	.40	.18	.05
□	51 Darren Daulton	.20	.09	.03
□	52 Jay Buhner	.40	.18	.05
□	53 Andy Benes	.10	.05	.01
□	54 Jeff Conine	.40	.18	.05
□	55 Mike Devereaux	.10	.05	.01
□	56 Vince Coleman	.10	.05	.01
□	57 Terry Steinbach	.20	.09	.03
□	58 J.T. Snow	.40	.18	.05
□	59 Greg Swindell	.10	.05	.01
□	60 Devon White	.10	.05	.01
□	61 John Smoltz	.40	.18	.05
□	62 Todd Zeile	.10	.05	.01
□	63 Rick Wilkins	.10	.05	.01
□	64 Tim Wallach	.10	.05	.01
□	65 John Wetteland	.20	.09	.03
□	66 Matt Williams	.40	.18	.05
□	67 Paul Sorrento	.10	.05	.01
□	68 David Valle	.10	.05	.01
□	69 Walt Weiss	.10	.05	.01
□	70 John Franco	.10	.05	.01
□	71 Nolan Ryan	2.00	.90	.25
□	72 Frank Viola	.10	.05	.01
□	73 Chris Sabo	.10	.05	.01
□	74 David Nied	.10	.05	.01
□	75 Kevin McReynolds	.10	.05	.01
□	76 Lou Whitaker	.40	.18	.05
□	77 Dave Winfield	.40	.18	.05
□	78 Robin Ventura	.20	.09	.03
□	79 Spike Owen	.10	.05	.01
□	80 Cal Ripken Jr.	2.00	.90	.25
□	81 Dan Walters	.10	.05	.01
□	82 Mitch Williams	.10	.05	.01
□	83 Tim Wakefield	.20	.09	.03
□	84 Rickey Henderson	.40	.18	.05
□	85 Gary DiSarcina	.10	.05	.01
□	86 Craig Biggio	.40	.18	.05
□	87 Joe Carter	.40	.18	.05
□	88 Ron Gant	.40	.18	.05
□	89 John Jaha	.20	.09	.03
□	90 Gregg Jefferies	.40	.18	.05
□	91 Jose Guzman	.10	.05	.01
□	92 Eric Karros	.40	.18	.05
□	93 Wil Cordero	.20	.09	.03
□	94 Royce Clayton	.20	.09	.03
□	95 Albert Belle	1.25	.55	.16
□	96 Ken Griffey Jr.	2.50	1.10	.30
□	97 Orestes Destrade	.10	.05	.01
□	98 Tony Fernandez	.10	.05	.01
□	99 Leo Gomez	.10	.05	.01
□	100 Tony Gwynn	1.00	.45	.12
□	101 Len Dykstra	.20	.09	.03
□	102 Jeff King	.20	.09	.03
□	103 Julio Franco	.20	.09	.03
□	104 Andre Dawson	.40	.18	.05
□	105 Randy Milligan	.10	.05	.01
□	106 Alex Cole	.10	.05	.01
□	107 Phil Hiatt	.10	.05	.01
□	108 Travis Fryman	.40	.18	.05
□	109 Chuck Knoblauch	.40	.18	.05
□	110 Bo Jackson	.40	.18	.05
□	111 Pat Kelly	.10	.05	.01
□	112 Bret Saberhagen	.20	.09	.03
□	113 Ruben Sierra	.20	.09	.03
□	114 Tim Salmon	.60	.25	.07
□	115 Doug Jones	.10	.05	.01
□	116 Ed Sprague	.20	.09	.03
□	117 Terry Pendleton	.20	.09	.03
□	118 Robin Yount	.40	.18	.05
□	119 Mark Whiten	.10	.05	.01
□	120 Checklist 1-110	.10	.05	.01
□	121 Sammy Sosa	.40	.18	.05
□	122 Darryl Strawberry	.20	.09	.03
□	123 Larry Walker	.40	.18	.05
□	124 Robby Thompson	.10	.05	.01
□	125 Carlos Martinez	.10	.05	.01
□	126 Edgar Martinez	.40	.18	.05
□	127 Benito Santiago	.10	.05	.01
□	128 Howard Johnson	.10	.05	.01
□	129 Harold Reynolds	.10	.05	.01
□	130 Craig Shipley	.10	.05	.01
□	131 Curt Schilling	.10	.05	.01
□	132 Andy Van Slyke	.20	.09	.03
□	133 Ivan Rodriguez	.50	.23	.06
□	134 Mo Vaughn	.60	.25	.07
□	135 Bip Roberts	.10	.05	.01
□	136 Charlie Hayes	.10	.05	.01
□	137 Brian McRae	.20	.09	.03
□	138 Mickey Tettleton	.10	.05	.01
□	139 Frank Thomas	2.50	1.10	.30
□	140 Paul O'Neill	.20	.09	.03
□	141 Mark McGwire	.75	.35	.09
□	142 Damion Easley	.10	.05	.01
□	143 Ken Caminiti	.40	.18	.05
□	144 Juan Guzman	.20	.09	.03
□	145 Tom Glavine	.40	.18	.05
□	146 Pat Listach	.10	.05	.01
□	147 Lee Smith	.20	.09	.03
□	148 Derrick May	.10	.05	.01
□	149 Ramon Martinez	.20	.09	.03
□	150 Delino DeShields	.10	.05	.01
□	151 Kirt Manwaring	.10	.05	.01
□	152 Reggie Jefferson	.20	.09	.03
□	153 Randy Johnson	.40	.18	.05
□	154 Dave Magadan	.10	.05	.01
□	155 Dwight Gooden	.20	.09	.03
□	156 Chris Hoiles	.10	.05	.01
□	157 Fred McGriff	.40	.18	.05
□	158 Dave Hollins	.10	.05	.01
□	159 Al Martin	.20	.09	.03
□	160 Juan Gonzalez	1.25	.55	.16
□	161 Mike Greenwell	.10	.05	.01
□	162 Kevin Mitchell	.20	.09	.03
□	163 Andres Galarraga	.40	.18	.05
□	164 Wally Joyner	.20	.09	.03
□	165 Kirk Gibson	.20	.09	.03
□	166 Pedro Munoz	.10	.05	.01
□	167 Ozzie Guillen	.10	.05	.01
□	168 Jimmy Key	.20	.09	.03
□	169 Kevin Seitzer	.10	.05	.01
□	170 Luis Polonia	.10	.05	.01
□	171 Luis Gonzalez	.10	.05	.01
□	172 Paul Molitor	.50	.23	.06
□	173 David Justice	.40	.18	.05
□	174 B.J. Surhoff	.20	.09	.03
□	175 Ray Lankford	.40	.18	.05
□	176 Ryne Sandberg	.60	.25	.07
□	177 Jody Reed	.10	.05	.01
□	178 Marquis Grissom	.40	.18	.05
□	179 Willie McGee	.10	.05	.01
□	180 Kenny Lofton	1.00	.45	.12
□	181 Junior Felix	.10	.05	.01
□	182 Jose Offerman	.10	.05	.01
□	183 John Kruk	.20	.09	.03
□	184 Orlando Merced	.20	.09	.03
□	185 Rafael Palmeiro	.40	.18	.05
□	186 Billy Hatcher	.10	.05	.01
□	187 Joe Oliver	.10	.05	.01
□	188 Joe Girardi	.10	.05	.01
□	189 Jose Lind	.10	.05	.01
□	190 Harold Baines	.20	.09	.03
□	191 Mike Pagliarulo	.10	.05	.01
□	192 Lance Johnson	.20	.09	.03
□	193 Don Mattingly	1.25	.55	.16
□	194 Doug Drabek	.10	.05	.01
□	195 John Olerud	.10	.05	.01
□	196 Greg Maddux	1.50	.70	.19
□	197 Greg Vaughn	.40	.18	.05
□	198 Tom Pagnozzi	.10	.05	.01
□	199 Willie Wilson	.10	.05	.01
□	200 Jack McDowell	.20	.09	.03
□	201 Mike Piazza	2.50	1.10	.30
□	202 Mike Mussina	.50	.23	.06
□	203 Charles Nagy	.20	.09	.03
□	204 Tino Martinez	.20	.09	.03
□	205 Charlie Hough	.10	.05	.01
□	206 Todd Hundley	.40	.18	.05
□	207 Gary Sheffield	.40	.18	.05
□	208 Mickey Morandini	.10	.05	.01
□	209 Don Slaught	.10	.05	.01
□	210 Dean Palmer	.20	.09	.03
□	211 Jose Rijo	.10	.05	.01

□ 212 Vinny Castilla	.40	.18	.05
□ 213 Tony Phillips	.20	.09	.03
□ 214 Kirby Puckett	.75	.35	.09
□ 215 Tim Raines	.40	.18	.05
□ 216 Otis Nixon	.10	.05	.01
□ 217 Ozzie Smith	.50	.23	.06
□ 218 Jose Vizcaino	.10	.05	.01
□ 219 Randy Tomlin	.10	.05	.01
□ 220 Checklist 111-220	.10	.05	.01

1993 Studio Heritage

This 12-card standard-size set was randomly inserted in all 1993 Leaf Studio foil packs, and features sepia-toned portraits of current players in vintage team uniforms. The pictures are bordered in turquoise blue and have bronze-foil simulated picture holders at each corner. The set title appears in white lettering above the picture, and the player's name is printed in white below. The horizontal and turquoise-blue-bordered back shades from beige to red from top to bottom, and carries a posed sepia-toned player picture on the right within an oval set off by red and black lines. His name appears in white lettering at the top within a black arc. A brief story of the team represented by the player's vintage uniform follows below.

	MINT	NRMT	EXC
COMPLETE SET (12)	30.00	13.50	3.70
COMMON CARD (1-12)	1.00	.45	.12
SEMISTARS	2.00	.90	.25
RANDOM INSERTS IN ALL PACKS			

□ 1 George Brett	6.00	2.70	.75
□ 2 Juan Gonzalez	8.00	3.60	1.00
□ 3 Roger Clemens	2.00	.90	.25
□ 4 Mark McGwire	5.00	2.20	.60
□ 5 Mark Grace	2.00	.90	.25
□ 6 Ozzie Smith	3.00	1.35	.35
□ 7 Barry Larkin	2.00	.90	.25
□ 8 Frank Thomas	15.00	6.75	1.85
□ 9 Carlos Baerga	2.00	.90	.25
□ 10 Eric Karros	2.00	.90	.25
□ 11 J.T. Snow	2.00	.90	.25
□ 12 John Kruk	1.00	.45	.12

1993 Studio Silhouettes

The 1993 Studio Silhouettes 10-card standard-size set was inserted one per 20-card Studio jumbo pack. Full-bleed grayish fronts display posed color photos of star players against action silhouettes. The set's title is printed across the top and the player's name appears along the bottom in copper foil within a darker gray area. The borderless and grayish back features a color player action photo on one side and a personal profile on the other.

	MINT	NRMT	EXC
COMPLETE SET (10)	25.00	11.00	3.10
COMMON CARD (1-10)	.50	.23	.06
ONE PER JUMBO PACK			

□ 1 Frank Thomas	8.00	3.60	1.00
□ 2 Barry Bonds	2.00	.90	.25
□ 3 Jeff Bagwell	3.00	1.35	.35
□ 4 Juan Gonzalez	4.00	1.80	.50
□ 5 Travis Fryman	1.00	.45	.12
□ 6 J.T. Snow	1.00	.45	.12
□ 7 John Kruk	1.00	.45	.12
□ 8 Jeff Blauser	.50	.23	.06
□ 9 Mike Piazza	5.00	2.20	.60
□ 10 Nolan Ryan	8.00	3.60	1.00

1993 Studio Superstars on Canvas

This ten-card standard-size set was randomly inserted in 1993 Studio hobby and retail foil packs. The set features players in gray-bordered portraits that blend photography and artwork. The design of each front simulates a canvas painting of a player displayed on an artist's easel. The player's name appears in copper foil across the easel's base near the bottom. The set's title appears in white lettering beneath. The horizontal back carries a cutout color action player photo on one side and the player's name and career highlights within a black rectangle on the other, all superposed upon an abstract team color-coded design.

	MINT	NRMT	EXC
COMPLETE SET (10)	35.00	16.00	4.40
COMMON CARD (1-10)	1.00	.45	.12
RANDOM INSERTS IN HOBBY/RETAIL PACKS			

□ 1 Ken Griffey Jr.	15.00	6.75	1.85
□ 2 Jose Canseco	2.00	.90	.25
□ 3 Mark McGwire	5.00	2.20	.60
□ 4 Mike Mussina	3.00	1.35	.35
□ 5 Joe Carter	2.00	.90	.25
□ 6 Frank Thomas	15.00	6.75	1.85
□ 7 Darren Daulton	1.00	.45	.12
□ 8 Mark Grace	2.00	.90	.25
□ 9 Andres Galarraga	2.00	.90	.25
□ 10 Barry Bonds	4.00	1.80	.50

1994 Studio

The 1994 Studio set consists of 220 full-bleed, standard-size cards. Card fronts offer a player photo with his jersey hanging in a locker room setting in the background. Backs contain statistics and a small photo. The set is grouped by team as follows: Oakland Athletics (1-7), California Angels (8-15), Houston Astros (16-

23), Toronto Blue Jays (24-32), Atlanta Braves (33-41), Milwaukee Brewers (42-49), St. Louis Cardinals (50-57), Chicago Cubs (58-65), Los Angeles Dodgers (66-73), Montreal Expos (74-81), San Francisco Giants (82-89), Cleveland Indians (90-97), Seattle Mariners (98-104), Florida Marlins (105-112), New York Mets (113-120), Baltimore Orioles (121-128), San Diego Padres (129-135), Philadelphia Phillies (136-143), Pittsburgh Pirates (144-150), Texas Rangers (151-158), Boston Red Sox (159-166), Cincinnati Reds (167-174), Colorado Rockies (175-181), Kansas City Royals (182-188), Detroit Tigers (189-195), Minnesota Twins (196-202), Chicago White Sox (203-210), and New York Yankees (211-218). Rookie Cards in this set include Kurt Abbott.

	MINT	NRMT	EXC
COMPLETE SET (220)	15.00	6.75	1.85
COMMON CARD (1-220)	.10	.05	.01
SEMISTARS	.25	.11	.03
STARS	.50	.23	.06
□ 1 Dennis Eckersley	.25	.11	.03
□ 2 Brent Gates	.10	.05	.01
□ 3 Rickey Henderson	.50	.23	.06
□ 4 Mark McGwire	1.00	.45	.12
□ 5 Troy Neel	.10	.05	.01
□ 6 Ruben Sierra	.25	.11	.03
□ 7 Terry Steinbach	.25	.11	.03
□ 8 Chad Curtis	.10	.05	.01
□ 9 Chili Davis	.25	.11	.03
□ 10 Gary DiSarcina	.10	.05	.01
□ 11 Damion Easley	.10	.05	.01
□ 12 Bo Jackson	.50	.23	.06
□ 13 Mark Langston	.25	.11	.03
□ 14 Eduardo Perez	.10	.05	.01
□ 15 Tim Salmon	.50	.23	.06
□ 16 Jeff Bagwell	1.25	.55	.16
□ 17 Craig Biggio	.50	.23	.06
□ 18 Ken Caminiti	.50	.23	.06
□ 19 Andujar Cedeno	.10	.05	.01
□ 20 Doug Drabek	.10	.05	.01
□ 21 Steve Finley	.50	.23	.06
□ 22 Luis Gonzalez	.10	.05	.01
□ 23 Darryl Kile	.10	.05	.01
□ 24 Roberto Alomar	.75	.35	.09
□ 25 Pat Borders	.10	.05	.01
□ 26 Joe Carter	.50	.23	.06
□ 27 Carlos Delgado	.50	.23	.06
□ 28 Pat Hentgen	.50	.23	.06
□ 29 Paul Molitor	.60	.25	.07
□ 30 John Olerud	.10	.05	.01
□ 31 Ed Sprague	.25	.11	.03
□ 32 Devon White	.10	.05	.01
□ 33 Steve Avery	.25	.11	.03
□ 34 Tom Glavine	.50	.23	.06
□ 35 David Justice	.50	.23	.06
□ 36 Roberto Kelly	.10	.05	.01
□ 37 Ryan Klesko	.75	.35	.09
□ 38 Javier Lopez	.50	.23	.06
□ 39 Greg Maddux	2.00	.90	.25
□ 40 Fred McGriff	.50	.23	.06
□ 41 Terry Pendleton	.25	.11	.03
□ 42 Ricky Bones	.10	.05	.01
□ 43 Darryl Hamilton	.10	.05	.01
□ 44 Brian Harper	.10	.05	.01
□ 45 John Jaha	.25	.11	.03
□ 46 Dave Nilsson	.25	.11	.03
□ 47 Kevin Seitzer	.10	.05	.01
□ 48 Greg Vaughn	.50	.23	.06
□ 49 Turner Ward	.10	.05	.01
□ 50 Bernard Gilkey	.25	.11	.03
□ 51 Gregg Jefferies	.50	.23	.06
□ 52 Ray Lankford	.50	.23	.06
□ 53 Tom Pagnozzi	.10	.05	.01
□ 54 Ozzie Smith	.60	.25	.07
□ 55 Bob Tewksbury	.10	.05	.01
□ 56 Mark Whiten	.10	.05	.01
□ 57 Todd Zeile	.10	.05	.01
□ 58 Steve Buechele	.10	.05	.01
□ 59 Shawon Dunston	.10	.05	.01
□ 60 Mark Grace	.50	.23	.06
□ 61 Derrick May	.10	.05	.01
□ 62 Karl Rhodes	.10	.05	.01
□ 63 Ryne Sandberg	.75	.35	.09
□ 64 Sammy Sosa	.50	.23	.06
□ 65 Rick Wilkins	.10	.05	.01
□ 66 Brett Butler	.25	.11	.03
□ 67 Delino DeShields	.10	.05	.01
□ 68 Orel Hershiser	.25	.11	.03
□ 69 Eric Karros	.25	.11	.03
□ 70 Raul Mondesi	.50	.23	.06
□ 71 Jose Offerman	.10	.05	.01
□ 72 Mike Piazza	2.00	.90	.25
□ 73 Tim Wallach	.10	.05	.01
□ 74 Moises Alou	.25	.11	.03
□ 75 Sean Berry	.10	.05	.01
□ 76 Wil Cordero	.25	.11	.03
□ 77 Cliff Floyd	.50	.23	.06
□ 78 Marquis Grissom	.50	.23	.06
□ 79 Ken Hill	.10	.05	.01
□ 80 Larry Walker	.50	.23	.06
□ 81 John Wetteland	.25	.11	.03
□ 82 Rod Beck	.25	.11	.03
□ 83 Barry Bonds	.75	.35	.09
□ 84 Royce Clayton	.25	.11	.03
□ 85 Darren Lewis	.10	.05	.01
□ 86 Willie McGee	.10	.05	.01
□ 87 Bill Swift	.10	.05	.01
□ 88 Robby Thompson	.10	.05	.01
□ 89 Matt Williams	.50	.23	.06
□ 90 Sandy Alomar Jr.	.25	.11	.03
□ 91 Carlos Baerga	.50	.23	.06
□ 92 Albert Belle	1.50	.70	.19
□ 93 Kenny Lofton	1.00	.45	.12
□ 94 Eddie Murray	.75	.35	.09
□ 95 Manny Ramirez	1.00	.45	.12
□ 96 Paul Sorrento	.10	.05	.01
□ 97 Jim Thome	.75	.35	.09
□ 98 Rich Amaral	.10	.05	.01
□ 99 Eric Anthony	.10	.05	.01
□ 100 Jay Buhner	.50	.23	.06
□ 101 Ken Griffey Jr.	3.00	1.35	.35
□ 102 Randy Johnson	.50	.23	.06
□ 103 Edgar Martinez	.50	.23	.06
□ 104 Tino Martinez	.25	.11	.03
□ 105 Kurt Abbott	.25	.11	.03
□ 106 Bret Barberie	.10	.05	.01
□ 107 Chuck Carr	.10	.05	.01
□ 108 Jeff Conine	.50	.23	.06
□ 109 Chris Hammond	.10	.05	.01
□ 110 Bryan Harvey	.10	.05	.01
□ 111 Benito Santiago	.10	.05	.01
□ 112 Gary Sheffield	.50	.23	.06
□ 113 Bobby Bonilla	.25	.11	.03
□ 114 Dwight Gooden	.25	.11	.03
□ 115 Todd Hundley	.50	.23	.06
□ 116 Bobby Jones	.25	.11	.03
□ 117 Jeff Kent	.10	.05	.01
□ 118 Kevin McReynolds	.10	.05	.01
□ 119 Bret Saberhagen	.25	.11	.03
□ 120 Ryan Thompson	.10	.05	.01
□ 121 Harold Baines	.25	.11	.03
□ 122 Mike Devereaux	.10	.05	.01
□ 123 Jeffrey Hammonds	.25	.11	.03
□ 124 Ben McDonald	.10	.05	.01
□ 125 Mike Mussina	.60	.25	.07
□ 126 Rafael Palmeiro	.50	.23	.06
□ 127 Cal Ripken Jr.	2.50	1.10	.30
□ 128 Lee Smith	.25	.11	.03
□ 129 Brad Ausmus	.10	.05	.01
□ 130 Derek Bell	.25	.11	.03
□ 131 Andy Benes	.25	.11	.03
□ 132 Tony Gwynn	1.25	.55	.16

□ 133 Trevor Hoffman	.25	.11	.03
□ 134 Scott Livingstone	.10	.05	.01
□ 135 Phil Plantier	.10	.05	.01
□ 136 Darren Daulton	.25	.11	.03
□ 137 Mariano Duncan	.10	.05	.01
□ 138 Lenny Dykstra	.25	.11	.03
□ 139 Dave Hollins	.10	.05	.01
□ 140 Pete Incaviglia	.10	.05	.01
□ 141 Danny Jackson	.10	.05	.01
□ 142 John Kruk	.25	.11	.03
□ 143 Kevin Stocker	.10	.05	.01
□ 144 Jay Bell	.25	.11	.03
□ 145 Carlos Garcia	.10	.05	.01
□ 146 Jeff King	.25	.11	.03
□ 147 Al Martin	.10	.05	.01
□ 148 Orlando Merced	.25	.11	.03
□ 149 Don Slaught	.10	.05	.01
□ 150 Andy Van Slyke	.25	.11	.03
□ 151 Kevin Brown	.10	.05	.01
□ 152 Jose Canseco	.50	.23	.06
□ 153 Will Clark	.50	.23	.06
□ 154 Juan Gonzalez	1.50	.70	.19
□ 155 David Hulse	.10	.05	.01
□ 156 Dean Palmer	.25	.11	.03
□ 157 Ivan Rodriguez	.60	.25	.07
□ 158 Kenny Rogers	.10	.05	.01
□ 159 Roger Clemens	.50	.23	.06
□ 160 Scott Cooper	.10	.05	.01
□ 161 Andre Dawson	.50	.23	.06
□ 162 Mike Greenwell	.10	.05	.01
□ 163 Otis Nixon	.10	.05	.01
□ 164 Aaron Sele	.25	.11	.03
□ 165 John Valentin	.25	.11	.03
□ 166 Mo Vaughn	.75	.35	.09
□ 167 Bret Boone	.25	.11	.03
□ 168 Barry Larkin	.50	.23	.06
□ 169 Kevin Mitchell	.25	.11	.03
□ 170 Hal Morris	.10	.05	.01
□ 171 Jose Rijo	.10	.05	.01
□ 172 Deion Sanders	.50	.23	.06
□ 173 Reggie Sanders	.50	.23	.06
□ 174 John Smiley	.10	.05	.01
□ 175 Dante Bichette	.50	.23	.06
□ 176 Ellis Burks	.25	.11	.03
□ 177 Andres Galarraga	.50	.23	.06
□ 178 Joe Girardi	.10	.05	.01
□ 179 Charlie Hayes	.10	.05	.01
□ 180 Roberto Mejia	.10	.05	.01
□ 181 Walt Weiss	.10	.05	.01
□ 182 David Cone	.50	.23	.06
□ 183 Gary Gaetti	.25	.11	.03
□ 184 Greg Gagne	.10	.05	.01
□ 185 Felix Jose	.10	.05	.01
□ 186 Wally Joyner	.25	.11	.03
□ 187 Mike Macfarlane	.10	.05	.01
□ 188 Brian McRae	.25	.11	.03
□ 189 Eric Davis	.25	.11	.03
□ 190 Cecil Fielder	.25	.11	.03
□ 191 Travis Fryman	.50	.23	.06
□ 192 Tony Phillips	.25	.11	.03
□ 193 Mickey Tettleton	.10	.05	.01
□ 194 Alan Trammell	.50	.23	.06
□ 195 Lou Whitaker	.50	.23	.06
□ 196 Kent Hrbek	.25	.11	.03
□ 197 Chuck Knoblauch	.50	.23	.06
□ 198 Shane Mack	.10	.05	.01
□ 199 Pat Meares	.10	.05	.01
□ 200 Kirby Puckett	1.00	.45	.12
□ 201 Matt Walbeck	.10	.05	.01
□ 202 Dave Winfield	.50	.23	.06
□ 203 Wilson Alvarez	.25	.11	.03
□ 204 Alex Fernandez	.50	.23	.06
□ 205 Julio Franco	.25	.11	.03
□ 206 Ozzie Guillen	.10	.05	.01
□ 207 Jack McDowell	.25	.11	.03
□ 208 Tim Raines	.50	.23	.06
□ 209 Frank Thomas	3.00	1.35	.35
□ 210 Robin Ventura	.25	.11	.03
□ 211 Jim Abbott	.10	.05	.01
□ 212 Wade Boggs	.50	.23	.06
□ 213 Pat Kelly	.10	.05	.01
□ 214 Jimmy Key	.25	.11	.03
□ 215 Don Mattingly	1.50	.70	.19
□ 216 Paul O'Neill	.25	.11	.03
□ 217 Mike Stanley	.10	.05	.01
□ 218 Danny Tartabull	.10	.05	.01
□ 219 Checklist	.10	.05	.01
□ 220 Checklist	.10	.05	.01

1994 Studio Editor's Choice

This eight-card standard-sized set was randomly inserted in foil packs at a rate of one in 36. These cards are acetate and were designed much like a film strip with black borders. The fronts have various stop-action shots of the player and no back.

	MINT	NRMT	EXC
COMPLETE SET (8)	40.00	18.00	5.00
COMMON CARD (1-8)	1.50	.70	.19
RANDOM INSERTS IN PACKS			

□ 1 Barry Bonds	4.00	1.80	.50
□ 2 Frank Thomas	15.00	6.75	1.85
□ 3 Ken Griffey Jr.	15.00	6.75	1.85
□ 4 Andres Galarraga	2.00	.90	.25
□ 5 Juan Gonzalez	8.00	3.60	1.00
□ 6 Tim Salmon	2.50	1.10	.30
□ 7 Paul O'Neill	1.50	.70	.19
□ 8 Mike Piazza	10.00	4.50	1.25

1994 Studio Heritage

Each player in this eight-card insert set (randomly inserted in foil packs at a rate of one in nine) is modelling a vintage uniform of his team. The year of the uniform is noted in gold lettering at the top with a gold Heritage Collection logo at the bottom. A black and white photo of the stadium that the team used from the era of the depicted uniform serves as background. The back has a small photo and a team highlight from that year.

	MINT	NRMT	EXC
COMPLETE SET (8)	15.00	6.75	1.85
COMMON CARD (1-8)	.50	.23	.06
RANDOM INSERTS IN PACKS			

□ 1 Barry Bonds	2.00	.90	.25
□ 2 Frank Thomas	8.00	3.60	1.00
□ 3 Joe Carter	.75	.35	.09
□ 4 Don Mattingly	4.00	1.80	.50
□ 5 Ryne Sandberg	2.00	.90	.25
□ 6 Javier Lopez	1.00	.45	.12
□ 7 Gregg Jefferies	.50	.23	.06
□ 8 Mike Mussina	1.50	.70	.19

1994 Studio Series Stars

This 10-card acetate set showcases top stars and was limited to 10,000 of each card. They were randomly inserted in foil packs at a rate of one in 60. The player cutout is surrounded by a small circle of stars with the player's name at the top. The team name, limited edition notation and the Series Stars logo are at the bottom. The back of the cutout contains a photo. Gold versions of this set were more difficult to obtain in packs (one in 120, 5,000 total) and are valued at twice the prices below.

	MINT	NRMT	EXC
COMPLETE SILVER SET (10)	150.00	70.00	19.00
COMMON SILVER (1-10)	4.00	1.80	.50
*GOLD VERSIONS: 2X VALUE			
RANDOM INSERTS IN PACKS			

□ 1 Tony Gwynn	12.00	5.50	1.50
□ 2 Barry Bonds	8.00	3.60	1.00
□ 3 Frank Thomas	30.00	13.50	3.70
□ 4 Ken Griffey Jr.	30.00	13.50	3.70
□ 5 Joe Carter	4.00	1.80	.50
□ 6 Mike Piazza	20.00	9.00	2.50
□ 7 Cal Ripken Jr.	25.00	11.00	3.10
□ 8 Greg Maddux	20.00	9.00	2.50
□ 9 Juan Gonzalez	15.00	6.75	1.85
□ 10 Don Mattingly	15.00	6.75	1.85

1995 Studio

This 200-card horizontal set was issued by Donruss for the fifth consecutive year. Using a different design than past Studio issues, these cards were designed similarly to credit cards. The cards were issued in five-card packs with a suggested retail price of $1.49. The fronts have a player photo on the right with holographic team logo in the right corner. The rest of the card has the player identified in the upper left. Underneath that information are 1994 stats as well as various vital statistics. There is also the "Studio" logo in the upper left corner. The horizontal backs have an action photo on the left. The right has the player's signature along with a pertinent fact and his career statistics. There are no Rookie Cards in this set.

	MINT	NRMT	EXC
COMPLETE SET (200)	50.00	22.00	6.25
COMMON CARD (1-200)	.15	.07	.02
SEMISTARS	.30	.14	.04
STARS	.60	.25	.07
COMPLETE GOLD SET (50)	40.00	18.00	5.00
COMMON GOLD (1-50)	.50	.23	.06
*GOLD STARS: 1.5X BASIC CARDS			
ONE GOLD PER PACK			
COMP.PLATINUM SET (25)	150.00	70.00	19.00
COMMON PLATINUM (1-25)	2.00	.90	.25
*PLATINUM: 6X BASIC CARDS			
PLATINUM: RANDOM INSERTS IN PACKS			

□ 1 Frank Thomas	4.00	1.80	.50
□ 2 Jeff Bagwell	1.50	.70	.19
□ 3 Don Mattingly	2.00	.90	.25
□ 4 Mike Piazza	2.50	1.10	.30
□ 5 Ken Griffey Jr.	4.00	1.80	.50
□ 6 Greg Maddux	2.50	1.10	.30
□ 7 Barry Bonds	1.00	.45	.12
□ 8 Cal Ripken Jr.	3.00	1.35	.35
□ 9 Jose Canseco	.60	.25	.07
□ 10 Paul Molitor	.75	.35	.09
□ 11 Kenny Lofton	1.00	.45	.12
□ 12 Will Clark	.60	.25	.07
□ 13 Tim Salmon	.60	.25	.07
□ 14 Joe Carter	.60	.25	.07
□ 15 Albert Belle	2.00	.90	.25
□ 16 Roger Clemens	.60	.25	.07
□ 17 Roberto Alomar	1.00	.45	.12
□ 18 Alex Rodriguez	5.00	2.20	.60
□ 19 Raul Mondesi	.60	.25	.07
□ 20 Deion Sanders	.60	.25	.07
□ 21 Juan Gonzalez	2.00	.90	.25
□ 22 Kirby Puckett	1.25	.55	.16
□ 23 Fred McGriff	.60	.25	.07
□ 24 Matt Williams	.60	.25	.07
□ 25 Tony Gwynn	1.50	.70	.19
□ 26 Cliff Floyd	.30	.14	.04
□ 27 Travis Fryman	.30	.14	.04
□ 28 Shawn Green	.30	.14	.04
□ 29 Mike Mussina	.75	.35	.09
□ 30 Bob Hamelin	.15	.07	.02
□ 31 David Justice	.60	.25	.07
□ 32 Manny Ramirez	1.00	.45	.12
□ 33 David Cone	.30	.14	.04
□ 34 Marquis Grissom	.60	.25	.07
□ 35 Moises Alou	.30	.14	.04
□ 36 Carlos Baerga	.60	.25	.07
□ 37 Barry Larkin	.60	.25	.07
□ 38 Robin Ventura	.30	.14	.04
□ 39 Mo Vaughn	1.00	.45	.12
□ 40 Jeffrey Hammonds	.30	.14	.04
□ 41 Ozzie Smith	.75	.35	.09
□ 42 Andres Galarraga	.60	.25	.07
□ 43 Carlos Delgado	.60	.25	.07
□ 44 Lenny Dykstra	.30	.14	.04
□ 45 Cecil Fielder	.30	.14	.04
□ 46 Wade Boggs	.60	.25	.07
□ 47 Gregg Jefferies	.30	.14	.04
□ 48 Randy Johnson	.60	.25	.07
□ 49 Rafael Palmeiro	.60	.25	.07
□ 50 Craig Biggio	.60	.25	.07
□ 51 Steve Avery	.30	.14	.04
□ 52 Ricky Bottalico	.30	.14	.04
□ 53 Chris Gomez	.15	.07	.02
□ 54 Carlos Garcia	.15	.07	.02
□ 55 Brian Anderson	.15	.07	.02
□ 56 Wilson Alvarez	.30	.14	.04
□ 57 Roberto Kelly	.15	.07	.02
□ 58 Larry Walker	.60	.25	.07
□ 59 Dean Palmer	.30	.14	.04
□ 60 Rick Aguilera	.15	.07	.02
□ 61 Javier Lopez	.60	.25	.07
□ 62 Shawon Dunston	.15	.07	.02
□ 63 Wm. VanLandingham	.15	.07	.02
□ 64 Jeff Kent	.15	.07	.02
□ 65 David McCarty	.15	.07	.02
□ 66 Armando Benitez	.15	.07	.02
□ 67 Brett Butler	.30	.14	.04
□ 68 Bernard Gilkey	.30	.14	.04
□ 69 Joey Hamilton	.30	.14	.04
□ 70 Chad Curtis	.15	.07	.02
□ 71 Dante Bichette	.60	.25	.07
□ 72 Chuck Carr	.15	.07	.02
□ 73 Pedro Martinez	.30	.14	.04
□ 74 Ramon Martinez	.30	.14	.04
□ 75 Rondell White	.60	.25	.07

□ 76 Alex Fernandez	.30	.14	.04
□ 77 Dennis Martinez	.30	.14	.04
□ 78 Sammy Sosa	.60	.25	.07
□ 79 Bernie Williams	.60	.25	.07
□ 80 Lou Whitaker	.60	.25	.07
□ 81 Kurt Abbott	.15	.07	.02
□ 82 Tino Martinez	.30	.14	.04
□ 83 Willie Greene	.15	.07	.02
□ 84 Garret Anderson	.60	.25	.07
□ 85 Jose Rijo	.15	.07	.02
□ 86 Jeff Montgomery	.30	.14	.04
□ 87 Mark Langston	.15	.07	.02
□ 88 Reggie Sanders	.30	.14	.04
□ 89 Rusty Greer	.60	.25	.07
□ 90 Delino DeShields	.15	.07	.02
□ 91 Jason Bere	.15	.07	.02
□ 92 Lee Smith	.30	.14	.04
□ 93 Devon White	.30	.14	.04
□ 94 John Wetteland	.30	.14	.04
□ 95 Luis Gonzalez	.15	.07	.02
□ 96 Greg Vaughn	.30	.14	.04
□ 97 Lance Johnson	.30	.14	.04
□ 98 Alan Trammell	.60	.25	.07
□ 99 Bret Saberhagen	.30	.14	.04
□ 100 Jack McDowell	.30	.14	.04
□ 101 Trevor Hoffman	.15	.07	.02
□ 102 Dave Nilsson	.30	.14	.04
□ 103 Bryan Harvey	.15	.07	.02
□ 104 Chuck Knoblauch	.60	.25	.07
□ 105 Bobby Bonilla	.30	.14	.04
□ 106 Hal Morris	.15	.07	.02
□ 107 Mark Whiten	.15	.07	.02
□ 108 Phil Plantier	.15	.07	.02
□ 109 Ryan Klesko	.75	.35	.09
□ 110 Greg Gagne	.15	.07	.02
□ 111 Ruben Sierra	.30	.14	.04
□ 112 J.R. Phillips	.15	.07	.02
□ 113 Terry Steinbach	.30	.14	.04
□ 114 Jay Buhner	.60	.25	.07
□ 115 Ken Caminiti	.60	.25	.07
□ 116 Gary DiSarcina	.15	.07	.02
□ 117 Ivan Rodriguez	.75	.35	.09
□ 118 Bip Roberts	.15	.07	.02
□ 119 Jay Bell	.30	.14	.04
□ 120 Ken Hill	.15	.07	.02
□ 121 Mike Greenwell	.15	.07	.02
□ 122 Rick Wilkins	.15	.07	.02
□ 123 Rickey Henderson	.60	.25	.07
□ 124 Dave Hollins	.15	.07	.02
□ 125 Terry Pendleton	.30	.14	.04
□ 126 Rich Becker	.15	.07	.02
□ 127 Billy Ashley	.15	.07	.02
□ 128 Derek Bell	.30	.14	.04
□ 129 Dennis Eckersley	.30	.14	.04
□ 130 Andujar Cedeno	.15	.07	.02
□ 131 John Jaha	.30	.14	.04
□ 132 Chuck Finley	.30	.14	.04
□ 133 Steve Finley	.30	.14	.04
□ 134 Danny Tartabull	.15	.07	.02
□ 135 Jeff Conine	.60	.25	.07
□ 136 Jon Lieber	.15	.07	.02
□ 137 Jim Abbott	.15	.07	.02
□ 138 Steve Trachsel	.15	.07	.02
□ 139 Bret Boone	.30	.14	.04
□ 140 Charles Johnson	.30	.14	.04
□ 141 Mark McGwire	1.25	.55	.16
□ 142 Eddie Murray	1.00	.45	.12
□ 143 Doug Drabek	.15	.07	.02
□ 144 Steve Cooke	.15	.07	.02
□ 145 Kevin Seitzer	.15	.07	.02
□ 146 Rod Beck	.15	.07	.02
□ 147 Eric Karros	.30	.14	.04
□ 148 Tim Raines	.60	.25	.07
□ 149 Joe Girardi	.15	.07	.02
□ 150 Aaron Sele	.30	.14	.04
□ 151 Robby Thompson	.15	.07	.02
□ 152 Chan Ho Park	.60	.25	.07
□ 153 Ellis Burks	.60	.25	.07
□ 154 Brian McRae	.30	.14	.04
□ 155 Jimmy Key	.30	.14	.04
□ 156 Rico Brogna	.15	.07	.02
□ 157 Ozzie Guillen	.15	.07	.02
□ 158 Chili Davis	.30	.14	.04
□ 159 Darren Daulton	.30	.14	.04
□ 160 Chipper Jones	2.50	1.10	.30
□ 161 Walt Weiss	.15	.07	.02
□ 162 Paul O'Neill	.30	.14	.04
□ 163 Al Martin	.30	.14	.04
□ 164 John Valentin	.30	.14	.04
□ 165 Tim Wallach	.15	.07	.02
□ 166 Scott Erickson	.15	.07	.02
□ 167 Ryan Thompson	.15	.07	.02
□ 168 Todd Zeile	.15	.07	.02
□ 169 Scott Cooper	.15	.07	.02
□ 170 Matt Mieske	.30	.14	.04
□ 171 Allen Watson	.15	.07	.02
□ 172 Brian L.Hunter	.60	.25	.07
□ 173 Kevin Stocker	.15	.07	.02
□ 174 Cal Eldred	.15	.07	.02
□ 175 Tony Phillips	.30	.14	.04
□ 176 Ben McDonald	.15	.07	.02
□ 177 Mark Grace	.60	.25	.07
□ 178 Midre Cummings	.15	.07	.02
□ 179 Orlando Merced	.15	.07	.02
□ 180 Jeff King	.30	.14	.04
□ 181 Gary Sheffield	.60	.25	.07
□ 182 Tom Glavine	.60	.25	.07
□ 183 Edgar Martinez	.60	.25	.07
□ 184 Steve Karsay	.15	.07	.02
□ 185 Pat Listach	.15	.07	.02
□ 186 Wil Cordero	.15	.07	.02
□ 187 Brady Anderson	.60	.25	.07
□ 188 Bobby Jones	.30	.14	.04
□ 189 Andy Benes	.15	.07	.02
□ 190 Ray Lankford	.60	.25	.07
□ 191 John Doherty	.15	.07	.02
□ 192 Wally Joyner	.30	.14	.04
□ 193 Jim Thome	.75	.35	.09
□ 194 Royce Clayton	.15	.07	.02
□ 195 John Olerud	.15	.07	.02
□ 196 Steve Buechele	.15	.07	.02
□ 197 Harold Baines	.30	.14	.04
□ 198 Geronimo Berroa	.15	.07	.02
□ 199 Checklist	.15	.07	.02
□ 200 Checklist	.15	.07	.02

1996 Studio

The 1996 Studio set was issued in one series totalling 150 cards. and distributed in seven-card packs. The fronts feature color action player photos with a player portrait in the background. The backs carry another player photo, biographical information, with a head photo and vital statistics printed on the letters of the card's name.

	MINT	NRMT	EXC
COMPLETE SET (150)	20.00	9.00	2.50
COMMON CARD (1-150)	.10	.05	.01
SEMISTARS	.25	.11	.03
STARS	.50	.23	.06
□ 1 Cal Ripken	2.50	1.10	.30
□ 2 Alex Gonzalez	.10	.05	.01
□ 3 Roger Cedeno	.25	.11	.03
□ 4 Todd Hollandsworth	.50	.23	.06
□ 5 Gregg Jefferies	.50	.23	.06
□ 6 Ryne Sandberg	.75	.35	.09
□ 7 Eric Karros	.50	.23	.06
□ 8 Jeff Conine	.50	.23	.06
□ 9 Rafael Palmeiro	.50	.23	.06
□ 10 Bip Roberts	.10	.05	.01
□ 11 Roger Clemens	.50	.23	.06
□ 12 Tom Glavine	.50	.23	.06

☐	13 Jason Giambi	.50	.23	.06
☐	14 Rey Ordonez	.60	.25	.07
☐	15 Chan Ho Park	.50	.23	.06
☐	16 Vinny Castilla	.50	.23	.06
☐	17 Butch Huskey	.25	.11	.03
☐	18 Greg Maddux	2.00	.90	.25
☐	19 Bernard Gilkey	.25	.11	.03
☐	20 Marquis Grissom	.50	.23	.06
☐	21 Chuck Knoblauch	.50	.23	.06
☐	22 Ozzie Smith	.60	.25	.07
☐	23 Garret Anderson	.50	.23	.06
☐	24 J.T. Snow	.25	.11	.03
☐	25 John Valentin	.25	.11	.03
☐	26 Barry Larkin	.50	.23	.06
☐	27 Bobby Bonilla	.50	.23	.06
☐	28 Todd Zeile	.25	.11	.03
☐	29 Roberto Alomar	.75	.35	.09
☐	30 Ramon Martinez	.50	.23	.06
☐	31 Jeff King	.25	.11	.03
☐	32 Dennis Eckersley	.50	.23	.06
☐	33 Derek Jeter	2.00	.90	.25
☐	34 Edgar Martinez	.50	.23	.06
☐	35 Geronimo Berroa	.25	.11	.03
☐	36 Hal Morris	.10	.05	.01
☐	37 Troy Percival	.25	.11	.03
☐	38 Jason Isringhausen	.25	.11	.03
☐	39 Greg Vaughn	.50	.23	.06
☐	40 Robin Ventura	.50	.23	.06
☐	41 Craig Biggio	.50	.23	.06
☐	42 Will Clark	.50	.23	.06
☐	43 Sammy Sosa	.50	.23	.06
☐	44 Bernie Williams	.50	.23	.06
☐	45 Kenny Lofton	.75	.35	.09
☐	46 Wade Boggs	.50	.23	.06
☐	47 Javy Lopez	.50	.23	.06
☐	48 Reggie Sanders	.50	.23	.06
☐	49 Jeff Bagwell	1.25	.55	.16
☐	50 Fred McGriff	.50	.23	.06
☐	51 Charles Johnson	.25	.11	.03
☐	52 Darren Daulton	.25	.11	.03
☐	53 Jose Canseco	.50	.23	.06
☐	54 Cecil Fielder	.50	.23	.06
☐	55 Hideo Nomo	.75	.35	.09
☐	56 Tim Salmon	.50	.23	.06
☐	57 Carlos Delgado	.50	.23	.06
☐	58 David Cone	.50	.23	.06
☐	59 Tim Raines	.50	.23	.06
☐	60 Lyle Mouton	.10	.05	.01
☐	61 Wally Joyner	.10	.05	.01
☐	62 Bret Boone	.10	.05	.01
☐	63 Raul Mondesi	.50	.23	.06
☐	64 Gary Sheffield	.50	.23	.06
☐	65 Alex Rodriguez	3.00	1.35	.35
☐	66 Russ Davis	.10	.05	.01
☐	67 Checklist	.10	.05	.01
☐	68 Marty Cordova	.50	.23	.06
☐	69 Ruben Sierra	.10	.05	.01
☐	70 Jose Mesa	.25	.11	.03
☐	71 Matt Williams	.50	.23	.06
☐	72 Chipper Jones	2.00	.90	.25
☐	73 Randy Johnson	.50	.23	.06
☐	74 Kirby Puckett	1.00	.45	.12
☐	75 Jim Edmonds	.50	.23	.06
☐	76 Barry Bonds	.75	.35	.09
☐	77 David Segui	.10	.05	.01
☐	78 Larry Walker	.50	.23	.06
☐	79 Jason Kendall	.50	.23	.06
☐	80 Mike Piazza	2.00	.90	.25
☐	81 Brian L.Hunter	.10	.05	.01
☐	82 Julio Franco	.25	.11	.03
☐	83 Jay Bell	.25	.11	.03
☐	84 Kevin Seitzer	.10	.05	.01
☐	85 John Smoltz	.50	.23	.06
☐	86 Joe Carter	.50	.23	.06
☐	87 Ray Durham	.50	.23	.06
☐	88 Carlos Baerga	.50	.23	.06
☐	89 Ron Gant	.50	.23	.06
☐	90 Orlando Merced	.10	.05	.01
☐	91 Lee Smith	.50	.23	.06
☐	92 Pedro Martinez	.25	.11	.03
☐	93 Frank Thomas	3.00	1.35	.35
☐	94 Al Martin	.10	.05	.01
☐	95 Chad Curtis	.10	.05	.01
☐	96 Eddie Murray	.75	.35	.09
☐	97 Rusty Greer	.50	.23	.06
☐	98 Jay Buhner	.50	.23	.06
☐	99 Rico Brogna	.10	.05	.01
☐	100 Todd Hundley	.50	.23	.06
☐	101 Moises Alou	.25	.11	.03
☐	102 Chili Davis	.10	.05	.01
☐	103 Ismael Valdes	.10	.05	.01
☐	104 Mo Vaughn	.75	.35	.09
☐	105 Juan Gonzalez	1.50	.70	.19
☐	106 Mark Grudzielanek	.25	.11	.03
☐	107 Derek Bell	.10	.05	.01
☐	108 Shawn Green	.10	.05	.01
☐	109 David Justice	.25	.11	.03
☐	110 Paul O'Neill	.10	.05	.01
☐	111 Kevin Appier	.10	.05	.01
☐	112 Ray Lankford	.25	.11	.03
☐	113 Travis Fryman	.50	.23	.06
☐	114 Manny Ramirez	.75	.35	.09
☐	115 Brooks Kieschnick	.10	.05	.01
☐	116 Ken Griffey Jr.	3.00	1.35	.35
☐	117 Jeffrey Hammonds	.10	.05	.01
☐	118 Mark McGwire	1.00	.45	.12
☐	119 Denny Neagle	.25	.11	.03
☐	120 Quilvio Veras	.10	.05	.01
☐	121 Alan Benes	.50	.23	.06
☐	122 Rondell White	.50	.23	.06
☐	123 Osvaldo Fernandez	.25	.11	.03
☐	124 Andres Galarraga	.50	.23	.06
☐	125 Johnny Damon	.10	.05	.01
☐	126 Lenny Dykstra	.25	.11	.03
☐	127 Jason Schmidt	.25	.11	.03
☐	128 Mike Mussina	.60	.25	.07
☐	129 Ken Caminiti	.50	.23	.06
☐	130 Michael Tucker	.25	.11	.03
☐	131 LaTroy Hawkins	.10	.05	.01
☐	132 Checklist	.10	.05	.01
☐	133 Delino DeShields	.10	.05	.01
☐	134 Dave Nilsson	.25	.11	.03
☐	135 Jack McDowell	.50	.23	.06
☐	136 Joey Hamilton	.10	.05	.01
☐	137 Dante Bichette	.50	.23	.06
☐	138 Paul Molitor	.60	.25	.07
☐	139 Ivan Rodriguez	.60	.25	.07
☐	140 Mark Grace	.50	.23	.06
☐	141 Paul Wilson	.10	.05	.01
☐	142 Orel Hershiser	.25	.11	.03
☐	143 Albert Belle	1.50	.70	.19
☐	144 Tino Martinez	.10	.05	.01
☐	145 Tony Gwynn	1.25	.55	.16
☐	146 George Arias	.10	.05	.01
☐	147 Brian Jordan	.50	.23	.06
☐	148 Brian McRae	.10	.05	.01
☐	149 Rickey Henderson	.50	.23	.06
☐	150 Ryan Klesko	.60	.25	.07

1996 Studio Press Proofs

Randomly inserted in packs, this 150-card set is parallel to the regular set and is similar in design with bronze foil stamping. Only 2,000 of this set were produced.

	MINT	NRMT	EXC
COMP.BRONZE SET (150)	500.00	220.00	60.00
COMMON BRONZE (1-150)	1.00	.45	.12
BRONZE SEMISTARS	2.00	.90	.25
BRONZE STARS	4.00	1.80	.50

*SILVER: 20X BRONZE CARDS
*GOLD: 5X BRONZE CARDS
BRONZE: RANDOM INS.IN HOBBY AND RETAIL
SILVER: RANDOM INSERTS IN MAGAZINE.
BRONZE CARDS LISTED BELOW

☐	1 Cal Ripken	25.00	11.00	3.10
☐	6 Ryne Sandberg	8.00	3.60	1.00
☐	14 Rey Ordonez	5.00	2.20	.60
☐	18 Greg Maddux	20.00	9.00	2.50
☐	22 Ozzie Smith	6.00	2.70	.75
☐	29 Roberto Alomar	8.00	3.60	1.00
☐	33 Derek Jeter	20.00	9.00	2.50
☐	43 Sammy Sosa	5.00	2.20	.60
☐	44 Bernie Williams	5.00	2.20	.60
☐	45 Kenny Lofton	8.00	3.60	1.00
☐	49 Jeff Bagwell	12.00	5.50	1.50
☐	63 Hideo Nomo	8.00	3.60	1.00
☐	64 Gary Sheffield	5.00	2.20	.60
☐	65 Alex Rodriguez	30.00	13.50	3.70

□ 72 Chipper Jones	20.00	9.00	2.50
□ 73 Randy Johnson	5.00	2.20	.60
□ 74 Kirby Puckett	10.00	4.50	1.25
□ 76 Barry Bonds	8.00	3.60	1.00
□ 80 Mike Piazza	20.00	9.00	2.50
□ 85 John Smoltz	5.00	2.20	.60
□ 93 Frank Thomas	30.00	13.50	3.70
□ 96 Eddie Murray	8.00	3.60	1.00
□ 104 Mo Vaughn	8.00	3.60	1.00
□ 105 Juan Gonzalez	15.00	6.75	1.85
□ 114 Manny Ramirez	8.00	3.60	1.00
□ 116 Ken Griffey Jr.	30.00	13.50	3.70
□ 118 Mark McGwire	10.00	4.50	1.25
□ 128 Mike Mussina	6.00	2.70	.75
□ 138 Paul Molitor	6.00	2.70	.75
□ 139 Ivan Rodriguez	6.00	2.70	.75
□ 143 Albert Belle	15.00	6.75	1.85
□ 145 Tony Gwynn	12.00	5.50	1.50
□ 150 Ryan Klesko	6.00	2.70	.75

1996 Studio Hit Parade

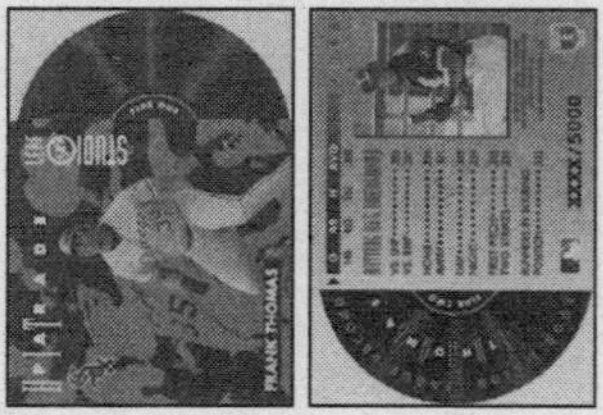

Randomly inserted in packs, this ten-card set features some of the Leagues's top long'ball hitters. The fronts feature color action player photos on a die-cut record design in the background. The backs carry the player's batting average breakdown.

	MINT	NRMT	EXC
COMPLETE SET (10)	100.00	45.00	12.50
COMMON CARD (1-10)	3.00	1.35	.35
RANDOM INSERTS IN PACKS			
□ 1 Tony Gwynn	10.00	4.50	1.25
□ 2 Ken Griffey Jr.	25.00	11.00	3.10
□ 3 Frank Thomas	25.00	11.00	3.10
□ 4 Jeff Bagwell	10.00	4.50	1.25
□ 5 Kirby Puckett	8.00	3.60	1.00
□ 6 Mike Piazza	15.00	6.75	1.85
□ 7 Barry Bonds	6.00	2.70	.75
□ 8 Albert Belle	12.00	5.50	1.50
□ 9 Tim Salmon	3.00	1.35	.35
□ 10 Mo Vaughn	6.00	2.70	.75

1996 Studio Masterstrokes

Randomly inserted in packs, this eight-card set features some of the League's most popular stars. Printed with brushed embossed technologies, the cards display color action player images in simulated oil painting detail. Each card from this set was also produced in a promo form.

	MINT	NRMT	EXC
COMPLETE SET (8)	150.00	70.00	19.00
COMMON CARD (1-8)	10.00	4.50	1.25
RANDOM INSERTS IN PACKS			
□ 1 Tony Gwynn	15.00	6.75	1.85
□ 2 Mike Piazza	25.00	11.00	3.10
□ 3 Jeff Bagwell	15.00	6.75	1.85
□ 4 Manny Ramirez	10.00	4.50	1.25
□ 5 Cal Ripken	30.00	13.50	3.70
□ 6 Frank Thomas	40.00	18.00	5.00
□ 7 Ken Griffey Jr.	40.00	18.00	5.00
□ 8 Greg Maddux	25.00	11.00	3.10

1996 Studio Stained Glass Stars

Randomly inserted in packs, this 12-card set honors some of the league's hottest superstars. The cards feature color player images on a genuine-look stained glass background and were printed with a clear plastic, die-cut technology.

	MINT	NRMT	EXC
COMPLETE SET (12)	100.00	45.00	12.50
COMMON CARD (1-12)	4.00	1.80	.50
RANDOM INSERTS IN PACKS			
□ 1 Cal Ripken	12.00	5.50	1.50
□ 2 Ken Griffey Jr.	15.00	6.75	1.85
□ 3 Frank Thomas	15.00	6.75	1.85
□ 4 Greg Maddux	10.00	4.50	1.25
□ 5 Chipper Jones	10.00	4.50	1.25
□ 6 Mike Piazza	10.00	4.50	1.25
□ 7 Albert Belle	8.00	3.60	1.00
□ 8 Jeff Bagwell	6.00	2.70	.75
□ 9 Hideo Nomo	4.00	1.80	.50
□ 10 Barry Bonds	4.00	1.80	.50
□ 11 Manny Ramirez	4.00	1.80	.50
□ 12 Kenny Lofton	4.00	1.80	.50

1995 Summit

This set contains 200 standard-size cards and was sold in seven-card retail packs for a suggested price of $1.99. This set is a premium product issued by Pinnacle Brands and produced on thicker paper than the regular set. The fronts have an action photo on a white background with the player's name and team emblem at the bottom in gold-foil. The backs

have a player color photo on the left side with a baseball diamond on the right that gives the player's statistics month by month for the season. Subsets featured are Rookies (112-173), Bat Speed (174-188) and Special Delivery (189-193). Rookie Cards in this set include Hideo Nomo and Carlos Perez.

	MINT	NRMT	EXC
COMPLETE SET (200)	25.00	11.00	3.10
COMMON CARD (1-200)	.10	.05	.01
SEMISTARS	.25	.11	.03
STARS	.50	.23	.06
COMP.NTH DEG.SET (200)	400.00	180.00	50.00
COMMON NTH DEGREE (1-200)	1.50	.70	.19
NTH DEGREE SEMISTARS	2.50	1.10	.30
NTH DEGREE STARS	6.00	2.70	.75

*NTH DEGREE STARS: 6X to 12X BASIC CARDS
*NTH DEGREE YOUNG STARS: 5X to 10X BASIC CARDS
NTH DEGREE: RANDOM INSERTS IN PACKS

□ 1 Ken Griffey Jr.	3.00	1.35	.35
□ 2 Alex Fernandez	.25	.11	.03
□ 3 Fred McGriff	.50	.23	.06
□ 4 Ben McDonald	.10	.05	.01
□ 5 Rafael Palmeiro	.50	.23	.06
□ 6 Tony Gwynn	1.25	.55	.16
□ 7 Jim Thome	.60	.25	.07
□ 8 Ken Hill	.10	.05	.01
□ 9 Barry Bonds	.75	.35	.09
□ 10 Barry Larkin	.50	.23	.06
□ 11 Albert Belle	1.50	.70	.19
□ 12 Billy Ashley	.10	.05	.01
□ 13 Matt Williams	.50	.23	.06
□ 14 Andy Benes	.10	.05	.01
□ 15 Midre Cummings	.10	.05	.01
□ 16 J.R. Phillips	.10	.05	.01
□ 17 Edgar Martinez	.50	.23	.06
□ 18 Manny Ramirez	.75	.35	.09
□ 19 Jose Canseco	.50	.23	.06
□ 20 Chili Davis	.25	.11	.03
□ 21 Don Mattingly	1.50	.70	.19
□ 22 Bernie Williams	.50	.23	.06
□ 23 Tom Glavine	.50	.23	.06
□ 24 Robin Ventura	.25	.11	.03
□ 25 Jeff Conine	.50	.23	.06
□ 26 Mark Grace	.50	.23	.06
□ 27 Mark McGwire	1.00	.45	.12
□ 28 Carlos Delgado	.50	.23	.06
□ 29 Greg Colbrunn	.10	.05	.01
□ 30 Greg Maddux	2.00	.90	.25
□ 31 Craig Biggio	.50	.23	.06
□ 32 Kirby Puckett	1.00	.45	.12
□ 33 Derek Bell	.25	.11	.03
□ 34 Lenny Dykstra	.25	.11	.03
□ 35 Tim Salmon	.50	.23	.06
□ 36 Deion Sanders	.50	.23	.06
□ 37 Moises Alou	.25	.11	.03
□ 38 Ray Lankford	.50	.23	.06
□ 39 Willie Greene	.10	.05	.01
□ 40 Ozzie Smith	.60	.25	.07
□ 41 Roger Clemens	.50	.23	.06
□ 42 Andres Galarraga	.50	.23	.06
□ 43 Gary Sheffield	.50	.23	.06
□ 44 Sammy Sosa	.50	.23	.06
□ 45 Larry Walker	.50	.23	.06
□ 46 Kevin Appier	.25	.11	.03
□ 47 Raul Mondesi	.50	.23	.06
□ 48 Kenny Lofton	.75	.35	.09
□ 49 Darryl Hamilton	.10	.05	.01
□ 50 Roberto Alomar	.75	.35	.09
□ 51 Hal Morris	.10	.05	.01
□ 52 Cliff Floyd	.25	.11	.03
□ 53 Brent Gates	.10	.05	.01
□ 54 Rickey Henderson	.50	.23	.06
□ 55 John Olerud	.10	.05	.01
□ 56 Gregg Jefferies	.25	.11	.03
□ 57 Cecil Fielder	.25	.11	.03
□ 58 Paul Molitor	.60	.25	.07
□ 59 Bret Boone	.25	.11	.03
□ 60 Greg Vaughn	.25	.11	.03
□ 61 Wally Joyner	.25	.11	.03
□ 62 Jeffrey Hammonds	.25	.11	.03
□ 63 James Mouton	.10	.05	.01
□ 64 Omar Vizquel	.50	.23	.06
□ 65 Wade Boggs	.50	.23	.06
□ 66 Terry Steinbach	.25	.11	.03
□ 67 Wil Cordero	.10	.05	.01
□ 68 Joey Hamilton	.25	.11	.03
□ 69 Rico Brogna	.10	.05	.01
□ 70 Darren Daulton	.25	.11	.03
□ 71 Chuck Knoblauch	.50	.23	.06
□ 72 Bob Hamelin	.10	.05	.01
□ 73 Carl Everett	.10	.05	.01
□ 74 Joe Carter	.50	.23	.06
□ 75 Dave Winfield	.50	.23	.06
□ 76 Bobby Bonilla	.25	.11	.03
□ 77 Paul O'Neill	.25	.11	.03
□ 78 Javier Lopez	.50	.23	.06
□ 79 Cal Ripken	2.50	1.10	.30
□ 80 David Cone	.25	.11	.03
□ 81 Bernard Gilkey	.25	.11	.03
□ 82 Ivan Rodriguez	.60	.25	.07
□ 83 Dean Palmer	.25	.11	.03
□ 84 Jason Bere	.10	.05	.01
□ 85 Will Clark	.50	.23	.06
□ 86 Scott Cooper	.10	.05	.01
□ 87 Royce Clayton	.10	.05	.01
□ 88 Mike Piazza	2.00	.90	.25
□ 89 Ryan Klesko	.60	.25	.07
□ 90 Juan Gonzalez	1.50	.70	.19
□ 91 Travis Fryman	.25	.11	.03
□ 92 Frank Thomas	3.00	1.35	.35
□ 93 Eduardo Perez	.10	.05	.01
□ 94 Mo Vaughn	.75	.35	.09
□ 95 Jay Bell	.25	.11	.03
□ 96 Jeff Bagwell	1.25	.55	.16
□ 97 Randy Johnson	.50	.23	.06
□ 98 Jimmy Key	.25	.11	.03
□ 99 Dennis Eckersley	.25	.11	.03
□ 100 Carlos Baerga	.50	.23	.06
□ 101 Eddie Murray	.75	.35	.09
□ 102 Mike Mussina	.60	.25	.07
□ 103 Brian Anderson	.10	.05	.01
□ 104 Jeff Cirillo	.25	.11	.03
□ 105 Dante Bichette	.50	.23	.06
□ 106 Bret Saberhagen	.25	.11	.03
□ 107 Jeff Kent	.10	.05	.01
□ 108 Ruben Sierra	.25	.11	.03
□ 109 Kirk Gibson	.25	.11	.03
□ 110 Steve Karsay	.10	.05	.01
□ 111 David Justice	.50	.23	.06
□ 112 Benji Gil	.10	.05	.01
□ 113 Vaughn Eshelman	.10	.05	.01
□ 114 Carlos Perez	.25	.11	.03
□ 115 Chipper Jones	2.00	.90	.25
□ 116 Shane Andrews	.10	.05	.01
□ 117 Orlando Miller	.10	.05	.01
□ 118 Scott Ruffcorn	.10	.05	.01
□ 119 Jose Oliva	.10	.05	.01
□ 120 Joe Vitiello	.10	.05	.01
□ 121 Jon Nunnally	.25	.11	.03
□ 122 Garret Anderson	.50	.23	.06
□ 123 Curtis Goodwin	.25	.11	.03
□ 124 Mark Grudzielanek	.75	.35	.09
□ 125 Alex Gonzalez	.10	.05	.01
□ 126 David Bell	.10	.05	.01
□ 127 Dustin Hermanson	.25	.11	.03
□ 128 Dave Nilsson	.25	.11	.03
□ 129 Wilson Heredia	.10	.05	.01
□ 130 Charles Johnson	.25	.11	.03
□ 131 Frank Rodriguez	.25	.11	.03
□ 132 Alex Ochoa	.50	.23	.06
□ 133 Alex Rodriguez	4.00	1.80	.50
□ 134 Bobby Higginson	.50	.23	.06
□ 135 Edgardo Alfonzo	.25	.11	.03
□ 136 Armando Benitez	.10	.05	.01
□ 137 Rich Aude	.10	.05	.01
□ 138 Tim Naehring	.10	.05	.01
□ 139 Joe Randa	.10	.05	.01
□ 140 Quilvio Veras	.10	.05	.01
□ 141 Hideo Nomo	3.00	1.35	.35
□ 142 Ray Holbert	.10	.05	.01
□ 143 Michael Tucker	.25	.11	.03
□ 144 Chad Mottola	.25	.11	.03
□ 145 John Valentin	.25	.11	.03
□ 146 James Baldwin	.50	.23	.06
□ 147 Esteban Loaiza	.10	.05	.01
□ 148 Marty Cordova	.50	.23	.06
□ 149 Juan Acevedo	.10	.05	.01
□ 150 Tim Unroe UER Cardinals logo	.25	.11	.03

□ 151	Brad Clontz UER	.10	.05	.01
	A's logo			
□ 152	Steve Rodriguez UER	.10	.05	.01
	Yankees logo			
□ 153	Rudy Pemberton UER	.10	.05	.01
	Dodgers logo			
□ 154	Ozzie Timmons UER	.10	.05	.01
	Tigers logo			
□ 155	Ricky Otero	.10	.05	.01
□ 156	Allen Battle	.10	.05	.01
□ 157	Joe Rosselli	.10	.05	.01
□ 158	Roberto Petagine	.10	.05	.01
□ 159	Todd Hollandsworth	.50	.23	.06
□ 160	Shannon Penn UER	.10	.05	.01
	Cubs logo			
□ 161	Antonio Osuna UER	.10	.05	.01
	Tigers logo			
□ 162	Russ Davis UER	.10	.05	.01
	Red Sox logo			
□ 163	Jason Giambi UER	.60	.25	.07
	two errors: front photo actually Brent Gates; also Braves logo			
□ 164	Terry Bradshaw UER	.10	.05	.01
	Brewers logo			
□ 165	Ray Durham	.25	.11	.03
□ 166	Todd Steverson	.10	.05	.01
□ 167	Tim Belk	.10	.05	.01
□ 168	Andy Pettitte	1.25	.55	.16
□ 169	Roger Cedeno	.25	.11	.03
□ 170	Jose Parra	.25	.11	.03
□ 171	Scott Sullivan	.10	.05	.01
□ 172	LaTroy Hawkins	.10	.05	.01
□ 173	Jeff McCurry	.10	.05	.01
□ 174	Ken Griffey Jr. BS	1.50	.70	.19
□ 175	Frank Thomas BS	1.50	.70	.19
□ 176	Cal Ripken Jr. BS	1.25	.55	.16
□ 177	Jeff Bagwell BS	.60	.25	.07
□ 178	Mike Piazza BS	1.00	.45	.12
□ 179	Barry Bonds BS	.50	.23	.06
□ 180	Matt Williams BS	.25	.11	.03
□ 181	Don Mattingly BS	.75	.35	.09
□ 182	Will Clark BS	.25	.11	.03
□ 183	Tony Gwynn BS	.60	.25	.07
□ 184	Kirby Puckett BS	.50	.23	.06
□ 185	Jose Canseco BS	.25	.11	.03
□ 186	Paul Molitor BS	.50	.23	.06
□ 187	Albert Belle BS	.75	.35	.09
□ 188	Joe Carter BS	.25	.11	.03
□ 189	Greg Maddux SD	1.00	.45	.12
□ 190	Roger Clemens SD	.50	.23	.06
□ 191	David Cone SD	.10	.05	.01
□ 192	Mike Mussina SD	.25	.11	.03
□ 193	Randy Johnson SD	.50	.23	.06
□ 194	Frank Thomas CL	1.50	.70	.19
□ 195	Ken Griffey Jr. CL	1.50	.70	.19
□ 196	Cal Ripken CL	1.25	.55	.16
□ 197	Jeff Bagwell CL	.60	.25	.07
□ 198	Mike Piazza CL	1.00	.45	.12
□ 199	Barry Bonds CL	.50	.23	.06
□ 200	Mo Vaughn CL	.50	.23	.06
	Matt Williams			

1995 Summit 21 Club

This nine-card set was randomly inserted in packs at a rate of one in 36. The set is comprised of young players with bright futures. Both sides of the card are done in foil with the front having a color photo with a gold background with "21 Club" in gray and red in the bottom right hand corner. The backs are laid out horizontally with a player head shot and information done in foil.

	MINT	NRMT	EXC
COMPLETE SET (9)	40.00	18.00	5.00
COMMON CARD (TC1-TC9)	4.00	1.80	.50
RANDOM INSERTS IN PACKS			

□ TC1	Bob Abreu	6.00	2.70	.75
□ TC2	Pokey Reese	4.00	1.80	.50
□ TC3	Edgardo Alfonzo	4.00	1.80	.50
□ TC4	Jim Pittsley	4.00	1.80	.50
□ TC5	Ruben Rivera	15.00	6.75	1.85
□ TC6	Chan Ho Park	4.00	1.80	.50
□ TC7	Julian Tavarez	4.00	1.80	.50
□ TC8	Ismael Valdes	10.00	4.50	1.25
□ TC9	Dmitri Young	6.00	2.70	.75

1995 Summit Big Bang

This 20-card set was randomly inserted in packs at a rate of one in 72. The set is comprised of the best home run hitters in the game. The set uses a process called "Spectrotech" which allows the card to be made of foil and have a holographic image. The fronts have an action photo with a game background which also shows the player. The backs have a player photo and information on his power exploits.

	MINT	NRMT	EXC
COMPLETE SET (20)	400.00	180.00	50.00
COMMON CARD (BB1-BB20)	6.00	2.70	.75
RANDOM INSERTS IN PACKS			

□ BB1	Ken Griffey Jr.	60.00	27.00	7.50
□ BB2	Frank Thomas	60.00	27.00	7.50
□ BB3	Cal Ripken	50.00	22.00	6.25
□ BB4	Jeff Bagwell	25.00	11.00	3.10
□ BB5	Mike Piazza	40.00	18.00	5.00
□ BB6	Barry Bonds	15.00	6.75	1.85
□ BB7	Matt Williams	8.00	3.60	1.00
□ BB8	Don Mattingly	30.00	13.50	3.70
□ BB9	Will Clark	8.00	3.60	1.00
□ BB10	Tony Gwynn	25.00	11.00	3.10
□ BB11	Kirby Puckett	20.00	9.00	2.50
□ BB12	Jose Canseco	8.00	3.60	1.00
□ BB13	Paul Molitor	12.00	5.50	1.50
□ BB14	Albert Belle	30.00	13.50	3.70
□ BB15	Joe Carter	6.00	2.70	.75
□ BB16	Rafael Palmeiro	8.00	3.60	1.00
□ BB17	Fred McGriff	8.00	3.60	1.00
□ BB18	David Justice	6.00	2.70	.75
□ BB19	Tim Salmon	8.00	3.60	1.00
□ BB20	Mo Vaughn	15.00	6.75	1.85

1995 Summit New Age

This 15-card set was randomly inserted in packs at a rate of one in 18. The set is comprised 15 of the best young players in baseball. The fronts are horizontally designed and have a color-action photo with a background of a baseball stadium with a red and gray background. The backs have a photo with player information and the words "New Age" at the bottom in red and white.

	MINT	NRMT	EXC
COMPLETE SET (15)	60.00	27.00	7.50
COMMON CARD (NA1-NA15)	1.50	.70	.19
SEMISTARS	3.00	1.35	.35
RANDOM INSERTS IN PACKS			

□ NA1 Cliff Floyd	3.00	1.35	.35
□ NA2 Manny Ramirez	8.00	3.60	1.00
□ NA3 Raul Mondesi	4.00	1.80	.50
□ NA4 Alex Rodriguez	30.00	13.50	3.70
□ NA5 Billy Ashley	1.50	.70	.19
□ NA6 Alex Gonzalez	1.50	.70	.19
□ NA7 Michael Tucker	1.50	.70	.19
□ NA8 Charles Johnson	3.00	1.35	.35
□ NA9 Carlos Delgado	4.00	1.80	.50
□ NA10 Benji Gil	1.50	.70	.19
□ NA11 Chipper Jones	20.00	9.00	2.50
□ NA12 Todd Hollandsworth	4.00	1.80	.50
□ NA13 Frankie Rodriguez	1.50	.70	.19
□ NA14 Shawn Green	1.50	.70	.19
□ NA15 Ray Durham	3.00	1.35	.35

1996 Summit

The 1996 Summit set was issued in one series totalling 200 cards. The seven-card packs had a suggested retail of $2.99 each. The fronts feature color player photos on a gold striped black background. The backs carry another player photo with player information and statistics.

	MINT	NRMT	EXC
COMPLETE SET (200)	30.00	13.50	3.70
COMMON CARD (1-200)	.10	.05	.01
SEMISTARS	.25	.11	.03
STARS	.50	.23	.06
*FOIL: 1.5X BASIC CARDS			
COMP.ABV/BYND.SET (200)	400.00	180.00	50.00
COMMON ABV/BYND (1-200)	1.50	.70	.19
ABV/BYND.SEMISTARS	3.00	1.35	.35
ABV/BYND.STARS	6.00	2.70	.75
*ABV/BYND.STARS: 6X to 12X BASIC CARDS			
*ABV/BYND.YOUNG STARS: 5X to 10X BASIC CARDS			
ABV/BYND: RANDOM INSERTS IN PACKS			

□ 1 Mike Piazza	2.00	.90	.25
□ 2 Matt Williams	.50	.23	.06
□ 3 Tino Martinez	.25	.11	.03
□ 4 Reggie Sanders	.50	.23	.06
□ 5 Ray Durham	.50	.23	.06
□ 6 Brad Radke	.10	.05	.01
□ 7 Jeff Bagwell	1.25	.55	.16
□ 8 Ron Gant	.50	.23	.06
□ 9 Lance Johnson	.25	.11	.03
□ 10 Kevin Seitzer	.10	.05	.01
□ 11 Dante Bichette	.50	.23	.06
□ 12 Ivan Rodriguez	.60	.25	.07
□ 13 Jim Abbott	.50	.23	.06
□ 14 Greg Colbrunn	.10	.05	.01
□ 15 Rondell White	.50	.23	.06
□ 16 Shawn Green	.10	.05	.01
□ 17 Gregg Jefferies	.25	.11	.03
□ 18 Omar Vizquel	.10	.05	.01
□ 19 Cal Ripken	2.50	1.10	.30
□ 20 Mark McGwire	1.00	.45	.12
□ 21 Wally Joyner	.10	.05	.01
□ 22 Chili Davis	.10	.05	.01
□ 23 Jose Canseco	.50	.23	.06
□ 24 Royce Clayton	.10	.05	.01
□ 25 Jay Bell	.10	.05	.01
□ 26 Travis Fryman	.50	.23	.06
□ 27 Jeff King	.10	.05	.01
□ 28 Todd Hundley	.50	.23	.06
□ 29 Joe Vitiello	.10	.05	.01
□ 30 Russ Davis	.10	.05	.01
□ 31 Mo Vaughn	.75	.35	.09
□ 32 Raul Mondesi	.50	.23	.06
□ 33 Ray Lankford	.50	.23	.06
□ 34 Mike Stanley	.10	.05	.01
□ 35 B.J. Surhoff	.10	.05	.01
□ 36 Greg Vaughn	.50	.23	.06
□ 37 Todd Stottleymyre	.10	.05	.01
□ 38 Carlos Delgado	.50	.23	.06
□ 39 Kenny Lofton	.75	.35	.09
□ 40 Hideo Nomo	.75	.35	.09
□ 41 Sterling Hitchcock	.10	.05	.01
□ 42 Pete Schourek	.10	.05	.01
□ 43 Edgardo Alfonzo	.25	.11	.03
□ 44 Ken Hill	.25	.11	.03
□ 45 Ken Caminiti	.50	.23	.06
□ 46 Bobby Higginson	.50	.23	.06
□ 47 Michael Tucker	.25	.11	.03
□ 48 David Cone	.50	.23	.06
□ 49 Cecil Fielder	.50	.23	.06
□ 50 Brian L. Hunter	.10	.05	.01
□ 51 Charles Johnson	.25	.11	.03
□ 52 Bobby Bonilla	.50	.23	.06
□ 53 Eddie Murray	.75	.35	.09
□ 54 Kenny Rogers	.10	.05	.01
□ 55 Jim Edmonds	.50	.23	.06
□ 56 Trevor Hoffman	.25	.11	.03
□ 57 Kevin Mtchell UER	.10	.05	.01
□ 58 Ruben Sierra	.10	.05	.01
□ 59 Benji Gil	.10	.05	.01
□ 60 Juan Gonzalez	1.50	.70	.19
□ 61 Larry Walker	.50	.23	.06
□ 62 Jack McDowell	.50	.23	.06
□ 63 Shawon Dunston	.10	.05	.01
□ 64 Andy Benes	.10	.05	.01
□ 65 Jay Buhner	.50	.23	.06
□ 66 Rickey Henderson	.50	.23	.06
□ 67 Alex Gonzalez	.10	.05	.01
□ 68 Mike Kelly	.10	.05	.01
□ 69 Fred McGriff	.50	.23	.06
□ 70 Ryne Sandberg	.75	.35	.09
□ 71 Ernie Young	.10	.05	.01
□ 72 Kevin Appier	.10	.05	.01
□ 73 Moises Alou	.10	.05	.01
□ 74 John Jaha	.10	.05	.01
□ 75 J.T. Snow	.10	.05	.01
□ 76 Jim Thome	.60	.25	.07
□ 77 Kirby Puckett	1.00	.45	.12
□ 78 Hal Morris	.10	.05	.01
□ 79 Robin Ventura	.50	.23	.06
□ 80 Ben McDonald	.10	.05	.01
□ 81 Tim Salmon	.50	.23	.06
□ 82 Albert Belle	1.50	.70	.19
□ 83 Marquis Grissom	.50	.23	.06
□ 84 Alex Rodriguez	3.00	1.35	.35
□ 85 Manny Ramirez	.75	.35	.09
□ 86 Ken Griffey Jr.	3.00	1.35	.35
□ 87 Sammy Sosa	.50	.23	.06
□ 88 Frank Thomas	3.00	1.35	.35
□ 89 Lee Smith	.50	.23	.06
□ 90 Marty Cordova	.50	.23	.06
□ 91 Greg Maddux	2.00	.90	.25
□ 92 Lenny Dykstra	.25	.11	.03
□ 93 Butch Huskey	.25	.11	.03

☐ 94 Garret Anderson	.50	.23	.06
☐ 95 Mike Bordick	.25	.11	.03
☐ 96 Dave Justice	.50	.23	.06
☐ 97 Chad Curtis	.10	.05	.01
☐ 98 Carlos Baerga	.50	.23	.06
☐ 99 Jason Isringhausen	.10	.05	.01
☐ 100 Gary Sheffield	.50	.23	.06
☐ 101 Roger Clemens	.50	.23	.06
☐ 102 Ozzie Smith	.60	.25	.07
☐ 103 Ramon Martinez	.50	.23	.06
☐ 104 Paul O'Neill	.10	.05	.01
☐ 105 Will Clark	.50	.23	.06
☐ 106 Tom Glavine	.50	.23	.06
☐ 107 Barry Bonds	.75	.35	.09
☐ 108 Barry Larkin	.50	.23	.06
☐ 109 Derek Bell	.10	.05	.01
☐ 110 Randy Johnson	.50	.23	.06
☐ 111 Jeff Conine	.25	.11	.03
☐ 112 John Mabry	.50	.23	.06
☐ 113 Julian Tavarez	.10	.05	.01
☐ 114 Gary DiSarcina	.10	.05	.01
☐ 115 Andres Galarraga	.50	.23	.06
☐ 116 Marc Newfield	.25	.11	.03
☐ 117 Frank Rodriguez	.25	.11	.03
☐ 118 Brady Anderson	.50	.23	.06
☐ 119 Mike Mussina	.60	.25	.07
☐ 120 Orlando Merced	.25	.11	.03
☐ 121 Melvin Nieves	.25	.11	.03
☐ 122 Brian Jordan	.50	.23	.06
☐ 123 Rafael Palmeiro	.50	.23	.06
☐ 124 Johnny Damon	.10	.05	.01
☐ 125 Wil Cordero	.10	.05	.01
☐ 126 Chipper Jones	2.00	.90	.25
☐ 127 Eric Karros	.50	.23	.06
☐ 128 Darren Daulton	.25	.11	.03
☐ 129 Vinny Castilla	.50	.23	.06
☐ 130 Joe Carter	.50	.23	.06
☐ 131 Bernie Williams	.50	.23	.06
☐ 132 Bernard Gilkey	.25	.11	.03
☐ 133 Bret Boone	.10	.05	.01
☐ 134 Tony Gwynn	1.25	.55	.16
☐ 135 Dave Nilsson	.25	.11	.03
☐ 136 Ryan Klesko	.60	.25	.07
☐ 137 Paul Molitor	.60	.25	.07
☐ 138 John Olerud	.10	.05	.01
☐ 139 Craig Biggio	.50	.23	.06
☐ 140 John Valentin	.25	.11	.03
☐ 141 Chuck Knoblauch	.50	.23	.06
☐ 142 Edgar Martinez	.50	.23	.06
☐ 143 Rico Brogna	.10	.05	.01
☐ 144 Dean Palmer	.50	.23	.06
☐ 145 Mark Grace	.50	.23	.06
☐ 146 Roberto Alomar	.75	.35	.09
☐ 147 Alex Fernandez	.50	.23	.06
☐ 148 Andre Dawson	.50	.23	.06
☐ 149 Wade Boggs	.50	.23	.06
☐ 150 Mark Lewis	.10	.05	.01
☐ 151 Gary Gaetti	.25	.11	.03
☐ 152 Paul Wilson Roger Clemens	.25	.11	.03
☐ 153 Rey Ordonez Ozzie Smith	.25	.11	.03
☐ 154 Derek Jeter Cal Ripken	1.50	.70	.19
☐ 155 Andy Benes Alan Benes	.10	.05	.01
☐ 156 Jason Kendall Mike Piazza	.75	.35	.09
☐ 157 Ryan Klesko Frank Thomas	1.00	.45	.12
☐ 158 Johnny Damon Ken Griffey Jr.	1.00	.45	.12
☐ 159 Karim Garcia Sammy Sosa	.10	.05	.01
☐ 160 Raul Mondesi Tim Salmon	.10	.05	.01
☐ 161 Chipper Jones Matt Williams	.75	.35	.09
☐ 162 Rey Ordonez	.60	.25	.07
☐ 163 Bob Wolcott	.10	.05	.01
☐ 164 Brooks Kieschnick	.10	.05	.01
☐ 165 Steve Gibralter	.10	.05	.01
☐ 166 Bob Abreu	.50	.23	.06
☐ 167 Greg Zaun	.10	.05	.01
☐ 168 Tavo Alvarez	.10	.05	.01
☐ 169 Sal Fasano	.10	.05	.01
☐ 170 George Arias	.10	.05	.01
☐ 171 Derek Jeter	2.00	.90	.25
☐ 172 Livan Hernandez	.50	.23	.06
☐ 173 Alan Benes	.50	.23	.06
☐ 174 George Williams	.10	.05	.01
☐ 175 John Wasdin	.10	.05	.01
☐ 176 Chan Ho Park	.50	.23	.06
☐ 177 Paul Wilson	.10	.05	.01
☐ 178 Jeff Suppan	.25	.11	.03
☐ 179 Quinton McCracken	.10	.05	.01
☐ 180 Wilton Guerrero	.60	.25	.07
☐ 181 Eric Owens	.10	.05	.01
☐ 182 Felipe Crespo	.10	.05	.01
☐ 183 LaTroy Hawkins	.10	.05	.01
☐ 184 Jason Schmidt	.25	.11	.03
☐ 185 Terrell Wade	.50	.23	.06
☐ 186 Mike Grace	.10	.05	.01
☐ 187 Chris Snopek	.10	.05	.01
☐ 188 Jason Kendall	.50	.23	.06
☐ 189 Todd Hollandsworth	.50	.23	.06
☐ 190 Jim Pittsley	.10	.05	.01
☐ 191 Jermaine Dye	.75	.35	.09
☐ 192 Mike Busby	.10	.05	.01
☐ 193 Richard Hidalgo	.10	.05	.01
☐ 194 Tyler Houston	.10	.05	.01
☐ 195 Jimmy Haynes	.10	.05	.01
☐ 196 Karim Garcia	.60	.25	.07
☐ 197 Ken Griffey Jr. CL	1.50	.70	.19
☐ 198 Frank Thomas CL	1.50	.70	.19
☐ 199 Greg Maddux CL	1.00	.45	.12
☐ 200 Cal Ripken CL	1.25	.55	.16

1996 Summit Artist's Proofs

Randomly inserted in packs at a rate of one in 36, this 200-card set is parallel to the regular set and is similar in design with the foil stamped Artist's Proof logo on the front.

	MINT	NRMT	EXC
COMPLETE SET (200)	2500.00	1100.00	300.00
COMMON CARD (1-200)	5.00	2.20	.60
SEMISTARS	12.00	5.50	1.50
STARS	25.00	11.00	3.10
*STARS: 25X to 50X BASIC CARDS			
*YOUNG STARS: 20X to 40X BASIC CARDS			
RANDOM INSERTS IN PACKS			
☐ 1 Mike Piazza	100.00	45.00	12.50
☐ 19 Cal Ripken	125.00	55.00	15.50
☐ 60 Juan Gonzalez	75.00	34.00	9.50
☐ 82 Albert Belle	75.00	34.00	9.50
☐ 84 Alex Rodriguez	150.00	70.00	19.00
☐ 86 Ken Griffey Jr.	150.00	70.00	19.00
☐ 88 Frank Thomas	150.00	70.00	19.00
☐ 91 Greg Maddux	100.00	45.00	12.50
☐ 126 Chipper Jones	100.00	45.00	12.50
☐ 171 Derek Jeter	80.00	36.00	10.00
☐ 197 Ken Griffey Jr. CL	75.00	34.00	9.50
☐ 198 Frank Thomas CL	75.00	34.00	9.50

1996 Summit Ballparks

Randomly inserted in packs at a rate of one in seven, this 18-card set features color action player photos on picture backgrounds of their home ballparks. The backs carry the name of the ballparks and players statistics.

	MINT	NRMT	EXC
COMPLETE SET (18)	150.00	70.00	19.00
COMMON CARD (1-18)	3.00	1.35	.35
RANDOM INSERTS IN PACKS			
□ 1 Cal Ripken	20.00	9.00	2.50
□ 2 Albert Belle	12.00	5.50	1.50
□ 3 Dante Bichette	5.00	2.20	.60
□ 4 Mo Vaughn	6.00	2.70	.75
□ 5 Ken Griffey Jr.	25.00	11.00	3.10
□ 6 Derek Jeter	12.00	5.50	1.50
□ 7 Juan Gonzalez	12.00	5.50	1.50
□ 8 Greg Maddux	15.00	6.75	1.85
□ 9 Frank Thomas	25.00	11.00	3.10
□ 10 Ryne Sandberg	6.00	2.70	.75
□ 11 Mike Piazza	15.00	6.75	1.85
□ 12 Johnny Damon	3.00	1.35	.35
□ 13 Barry Bonds	6.00	2.70	.75
□ 14 Jeff Bagwell	10.00	4.50	1.25
□ 15 Paul Wilson	3.00	1.35	.35
□ 16 Tim Salmon	5.00	2.20	.60
□ 17 Kirby Puckett	8.00	3.60	1.00
□ 18 Tony Gwynn	10.00	4.50	1.25

1996 Summit Big Bang

Randomly inserted in packs at a rate of one in 72, this 16-card set features the League's big hitters on Spectroetched backgrounds with etched foil highlights. The backs carry a player portrait in a diamond with a faded version of the front as a background and information about the player.

	MINT	NRMT	EXC
COMPLETE SET (16)	750.00	350.00	95.00
COMMON CARD (1-16)	10.00	4.50	1.25
*MIRAGE: 1.5X VALUE			
MIRAGE: SET REDEEMABLE FOR 1 BOX OF ALL 1997 PINNACLE BASEBALL PRODUCTS			
MIRAGE: SET w/MATCHING #S REDEEMABLE FOR 1 BOX OF ALL '97 PINNACLE PRODUCTS			
MIRAGE EXPIRATION: 12/31/96 POSTMARK			
RANDOM INSERTS IN PACKS			
□ 1 Frank Thomas	125.00	55.00	15.50
□ 2 Ken Griffey Jr.	125.00	55.00	15.50
□ 3 Albert Belle	60.00	27.00	7.50
□ 4 Mo Vaughn	30.00	13.50	3.70
□ 5 Barry Bonds	30.00	13.50	3.70
□ 6 Cal Ripken	100.00	45.00	12.50
□ 7 Jeff Bagwell	50.00	22.00	6.25
□ 8 Mike Piazza	80.00	36.00	10.00
□ 9 Ryan Klesko	25.00	11.00	3.10
□ 10 Manny Ramirez	30.00	13.50	3.70
□ 11 Tim Salmon	15.00	6.75	1.85
□ 12 Dante Bichette	15.00	6.75	1.85
□ 13 Sammy Sosa	20.00	9.00	2.50
□ 14 Raul Mondesi	15.00	6.75	1.85
□ 15 Chipper Jones	80.00	36.00	10.00
□ 16 Garret Anderson	10.00	4.50	1.25

1996 Summit Hitters Inc.

Randomly inserted in packs at a rate of one in 36, this 16-card set features color action player images with embossed highlights on an enlarged photo of the player's eyes for back-

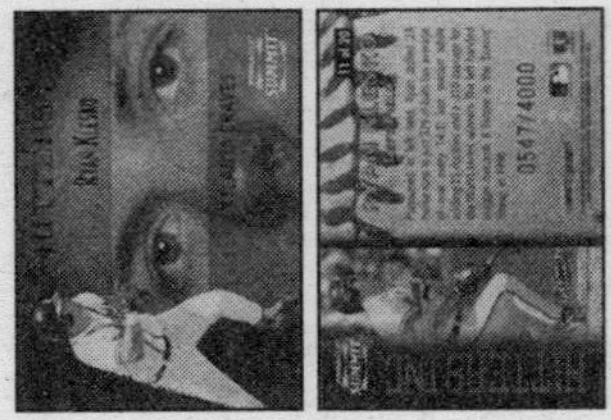

ground. The backs carry information about the player's batting ability.

	MINT	NRMT	EXC
COMPLETE SET (16)	250.00	110.00	31.00
COMMON CARD (1-16)	5.00	2.20	.60
RANDOM INSERTS IN PACKS			
□ 1 Tony Gwynn	15.00	6.75	1.85
□ 2 Mo Vaughn	10.00	4.50	1.25
□ 3 Tim Salmon	5.00	2.20	.60
□ 4 Ken Griffey Jr.	40.00	18.00	5.00
□ 5 Sammy Sosa	6.00	2.70	.75
□ 6 Frank Thomas	40.00	18.00	5.00
□ 7 Wade Boggs	5.00	2.20	.60
□ 8 Albert Belle	20.00	9.00	2.50
□ 9 Cal Ripken	30.00	13.50	3.70
□ 10 Manny Ramirez	10.00	4.50	1.25
□ 11 Ryan Klesko	8.00	3.60	1.00
□ 12 Dante Bichette	5.00	2.20	.60
□ 13 Mike Piazza	25.00	11.00	3.10
□ 14 Chipper Jones	25.00	11.00	3.10
□ 15 Ryne Sandberg	10.00	4.50	1.25
□ 16 Matt Williams	5.00	2.20	.60

1996 Summit Positions

Randomly inserted in Magazine packs only at the rate of one in 50, this nine-card set honors the best players at each playing position. The fronts feature color action player images on a baseball diamond background with head photos of the players at the bottom. The backs carry information about how well the players perform at their position.

	MINT	NRMT	EXC
COMPLETE SET (9)	325.00	145.00	40.00
COMMON CARD (1-9)	20.00	9.00	2.50
RANDOM INSERTS IN PACKS			
□ 1 Jeff Bagwell Mo Vaughn Frank Thomas	60.00	27.00	7.50
□ 2 Roberto Alomar Craig Biggio Chuck Knoblauch	20.00	9.00	2.50
□ 3 Matt Williams Jim Thome Chipper Jones	40.00	18.00	5.00
□ 4 Barry Larkin Cal Ripken Alex Rodriguez	75.00	34.00	9.50

□ 5 Mike Piazza	40.00	18.00	5.00
Ivan Rodriguez			
Charles Johnson			
□ 6 Hideo Nomo	40.00	18.00	5.00
Greg Maddux			
Randy Johnson			
□ 7 Barry Bonds	30.00	13.50	3.70
Albert Belle			
Ryan Klesko			
□ 8 Johnny Damon	50.00	22.00	6.25
Jim Edmonds			
Ken Griffey Jr.			
□ 9 Manny Ramirez	20.00	9.00	2.50
Gary Sheffield			
Sammy Sosa			

1952 Topps

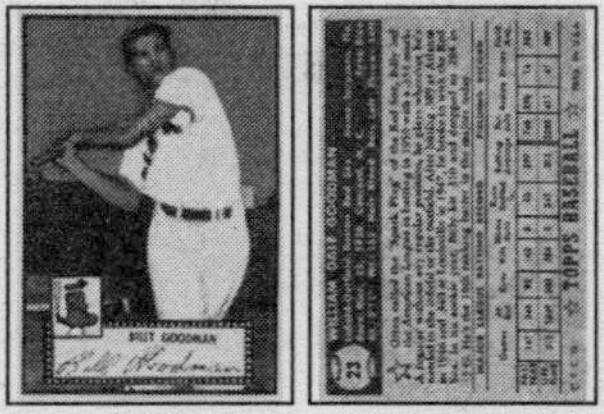

The cards in this 407-card set measure approximately 2 5/8" by 3 3/4". The 1952 Topps set is Topps' first truly major set. Card numbers 1 to 80 were issued with red or black backs, both of which are less plentiful than card numbers 81 to 250. In fact, the first series is considered the most difficult with respect to finding perfect condition cards. Card number 48 (Joe Page) and number 49 (Johnny Sain) can be found with each other's write-up on their back. Card numbers 251 to 310 are somewhat scarce and numbers 311 to 407 are quite scarce. Cards 281-300 were single printed compared to the other cards in the next to last series. Cards 311-313 were double printed on the last high number printing sheet. The key card in the set is obviously Mickey Mantle, number 311, Mickey's first of many Topps cards. A really obscure variation on cards from 311 through 313 is that they exist with the stitching on the number circle in the back either clockwise or counter clockwise. There is no price differential for either variation. In the early 1980's, Topps issued a standard-size reprint set of the 52 Topps set. These cards were issued only as a factory set and have a current market value of between two and three hundred dollars. Five people portrayed in the regular set: Billy Loes (#20), Dom DiMaggio (#22), Saul Rogovin (#159), Solly Hemus (#196) and Tommy Holmes (#289) are not in the reprint set. Although rarely seen, there exist salesman sample panels of three cards containing the fronts of regular cards with ad information on the back. Two such panels seen are Bob Mahoney/Robin Roberts/Sid Hudson and Wally Westlake/Dizzy Trout/Irv Noren. The cards were issued in one-card penny packs and six-card nickle packs. The key Rookie Cards in this set are Billy Martin, Eddie Mathews (the last card in the set), and Hoyt Wilhelm.

	NRMT	VG-E	GOOD
COMPLETE SET (407)	65000.00	29200.00	8100.00
COMMON CARD (1-80)	50.00	22.00	6.25
COMMON CARD (81-250)	35.00	16.00	4.40
COMMON CARD (251-310)	50.00	22.00	6.25
COMMON CARD (311-407)	250.00	110.00	31.00
COMMON DODGERS: 1.5X COM. VALUE	275.00	125.00	34.00
COMMON YANKEES: 1.5X COM. VALUE			

*RED/BLACK BACKS 1-80 SAME VALUE.....
CARDS PRICED IN NM CONDITION !...........

□ 1 Andy Pafko	1200.00	120.00	40.00
□ 2 Pete Runnels	90.00	40.00	11.00
□ 11 Phil Rizzuto	200.00	90.00	25.00
□ 20 Billy Loes	100.00	45.00	12.50
□ 22 Dom DiMaggio	90.00	40.00	11.00
□ 26 Monte Irvin	90.00	40.00	11.00
□ 29 Ted Kluszewski	90.00	40.00	11.00
□ 31 Gus Zernial	80.00	36.00	10.00
□ 33 Warren Spahn	200.00	90.00	25.00
□ 36 Gil Hodges	160.00	70.00	20.00
□ 37 Duke Snider	250.00	110.00	31.00
□ 48A Joe Page COR	75.00	34.00	9.50
□ 48B Joe Page ERR	275.00	125.00	34.00
(Bio for Sain)			
□ 49A Johnny Sain COR	75.00	34.00	9.50
□ 49B Johnny Sain ERR	275.00	125.00	34.00
(Bio for Page)			
□ 57 Ed Lopat	90.00	40.00	11.00
□ 59 Robin Roberts	150.00	70.00	19.00
□ 65 Enos Slaughter	150.00	70.00	19.00
□ 66 Preacher Roe	90.00	40.00	11.00
□ 67 Allie Reynolds	90.00	40.00	11.00
□ 88 Bob Feller	200.00	90.00	25.00
□ 91 Red Schoendienst	75.00	34.00	9.50
□ 122 Jackie Jensen	70.00	32.00	8.75
□ 129 Johnny Mize	90.00	40.00	11.00
□ 175 Billy Martin	300.00	135.00	38.00
□ 191 Yogi Berra	350.00	160.00	45.00
□ 195 Minnie Minoso	150.00	70.00	19.00
□ 200 Ralph Houk	70.00	32.00	8.75
□ 215 Hank Bauer	50.00	22.00	6.25
□ 216 Richie Ashburn	175.00	80.00	22.00
□ 227 Joe Garagiola	80.00	36.00	10.00
□ 233 Bob Friend	50.00	22.00	6.25
□ 243 Larry Doby	65.00	29.00	8.00
□ 246 George Kell	75.00	34.00	9.50
□ 250 Carl Erskine	80.00	36.00	10.00
□ 261 Willie Mays	2500.00	1100.00	300.00
□ 268 Bob Lemon	150.00	70.00	19.00
□ 274 Ralph Branca	100.00	45.00	12.50
□ 277 Early Wynn	150.00	70.00	19.00
□ 311 Mickey Mantle	24000.00	10800.00	3000.00
□ 312 Jackie Robinson DP	1400.00	650.00	180.00
□ 313 Bobby Thomson DP	300.00	135.00	38.00
□ 314 Roy Campanella	2000.00	900.00	250.00
□ 315 Leo Durocher MG	375.00	170.00	47.50
□ 321 Joe Black	350.00	160.00	45.00
□ 326 George Shuba	400.00	180.00	50.00
□ 333 Pee Wee Reese	1300.00	575.00	160.00
□ 334 Wilmer Mizell	300.00	135.00	38.00
□ 342 Clem Labine	400.00	180.00	50.00
□ 344 Ewell Blackwell	300.00	135.00	38.00
□ 347 Joe Adcock	300.00	135.00	38.00
□ 351 Alvin Dark	300.00	135.00	38.00
□ 357 Smoky Burgess	300.00	135.00	38.00
□ 369 Dick Groat	350.00	160.00	45.00
□ 372 Gil McDougald	350.00	160.00	45.00
□ 373 Jim Turner CO	400.00	180.00	50.00
□ 382 Sam Jones	300.00	135.00	38.00
□ 384 Frank Crosetti CO	400.00	180.00	50.00
□ 392 Hoyt Wilhelm	700.00	325.00	90.00
□ 394 Billy Herman CO	400.00	180.00	50.00
□ 396 Dick Williams	400.00	180.00	50.00
□ 400 Bill Dickey CO	800.00	350.00	100.00
□ 406 Joe Nuxhall	300.00	135.00	38.00
□ 407 Eddie Mathews	3400.00	850.00	350.00

1953 Topps

The cards in this 274-card set measure 2 5/8" by 3 3/4". Although the last card is numbered 280, there are only 274 cards in the set since numbers 253, 261, 267, 268, 271, and 275 were never issued. The 1953 Topps series contains line drawings of players in full color. The name and team panel at the card base is easily damaged, making it very difficult to complete a mint set. The high number series, 221 to 280, was produced in shorter supply late in the year and hence is more difficult to complete than the lower numbers. The key cards in the set are Mickey Mantle (82) and Willie Mays (244). The

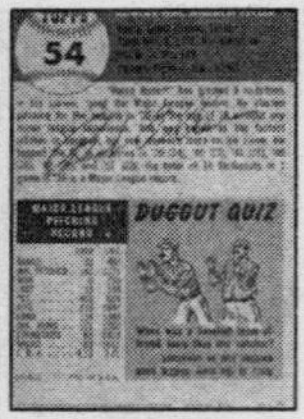

key Rookie Cards in this set are Roy Face, Jim Gilliam, and Johnny Podres, all from the last series. There are a number of double-printed cards (actually not double but 50 percent more of each of these numbers were printed compared to the other cards in the series) indicated by DP in the checklist below. There were five players (10 Smoky Burgess, 44 Ellis Kinder, 61 Early Wynn, 72 Fred Hutchinson, and 81 Joe Black) held out of the first run of 1-85 (but printed in with numbers 86-165), who are each marked by SP in the checklist below. In addition, there are five numbers which were printed with the more plentiful series 166-220; these cards (94, 107, 131, 145, and 156) are also indicated by DP in the checklist below. The cards were issued in one-card penny packs or six-card nickle packs. There were some three-card advertising panels produced by Topps; the players include Johnny Mize/Clem Koshorek/Toby Atwell and Mickey Mantle/Johnny Wyrostek/Sal Yvars. When cut apart, these advertising cards are distinguished by the non-standard card back, i.e., part of an advertisement for the 1953 Topps set instead of the typical statistics and biographical information about the player pictured.

	NRMT	VG-E	GOOD
COMPLETE SET (274)	13500.00	6100.00	1700.00
COMMON CARD (1-165)	30.00	13.50	3.70
COMMON CARD (166-220)	25.00	11.00	3.10
COMMON CARD (221-280)	100.00	45.00	12.50
DP (7/8/12/13/16/18/19)	15.00	6.75	1.85
DP (23/33/35/36/38)	15.00	6.75	1.85
DP (42/45-49/51-53/55)	15.00	6.75	1.85
DP (56/59/60/63/67/84)	15.00	6.75	1.85
DP (85/88-95/97/98/102)	15.00	6.75	1.85
DP (103/105/107/108)	15.00	6.75	1.85
DP (110-112/116/117)	15.00	6.75	1.85
DP (123/124/126/127)	15.00	6.75	1.85
DP (130/131/135/136/137)	15.00	6.75	1.85
DP (144/145/150/152)	15.00	6.75	1.85
DP (153/156/157/159)	15.00	6.75	1.85
DP (161/163/164)	15.00	6.75	1.85
DP (223/224/230/231)	50.00	22.00	6.25
DP (234-238/241/243)	50.00	22.00	6.25
DP (247/248/259/264/279)	50.00	22.00	6.25
COMMON DODGERS: 1.5X COM. VALUE			
COMMON YANKEES: 1.5X COM. VALUE			
NOT ISSUED (253/261/267)			
NOT ISSUED (268/271/275)			
CARDS PRICED IN NM CONDITION !			

□ 1 Jackie Robinson DP	450.00	125.00	45.00
□ 10 Smoky Burgess SP	70.00	32.00	8.75
□ 27 Roy Campanella DP	175.00	80.00	22.00
□ 31 Ewell Blackwell	50.00	22.00	6.25
□ 37 Eddie Mathews DP	100.00	45.00	12.50
□ 41 Enos Slaughter	80.00	36.00	10.00
□ 43 Gil McDougald	50.00	22.00	6.25
□ 44 Ellis Kinder SP	35.00	16.00	4.40
□ 54 Bob Feller DP	100.00	45.00	12.50
□ 61 Early Wynn SP	90.00	40.00	11.00
□ 62 Monte Irvin DP	35.00	16.00	4.40
□ 66 Minnie Minoso	50.00	22.00	6.25
□ 72 Fred Hutchinson MG SP	50.00	22.00	6.25
□ 76 Pee Wee Reese	150.00	70.00	19.00
□ 77 Johnny Mize DP	50.00	22.00	6.25
□ 78 Red Schoendienst	60.00	27.00	7.50
□ 81 Joe Black SP	70.00	32.00	8.75
□ 82 Mickey Mantle	3000.00	1350.00	375.00
□ 86 Billy Martin	120.00	55.00	15.00
□ 87 Ed Lopat	50.00	22.00	6.25
□ 104 Yogi Berra	200.00	90.00	25.00
□ 114 Phil Rizzuto	150.00	70.00	19.00
□ 119 Johnny Sain SP	50.00	22.00	6.25
□ 138 George Kell	60.00	27.00	7.50
□ 147 Warren Spahn	150.00	70.00	19.00
□ 149 Dom DiMaggio DP	35.00	16.00	4.40
□ 151 Hoyt Wilhelm	80.00	36.00	10.00
□ 158 Johnny Logan	35.00	16.00	4.40
□ 162 Ted Kluszewski	50.00	22.00	6.25
□ 188 Andy Carey	40.00	18.00	5.00
□ 191 Ralph Kiner	80.00	36.00	10.00
□ 207 Whitey Ford	150.00	70.00	19.00
□ 210 Bob Cerv	35.00	16.00	4.40
□ 220 Satchel Paige UER (Misspelled Satchell on card front)	450.00	200.00	55.00
□ 222 Vic Janowicz DP	60.00	27.00	7.50
□ 228 Hal Newhouser	150.00	70.00	19.00
□ 244 Willie Mays	2700.00	1200.00	350.00
□ 246 Roy Face DP	80.00	36.00	10.00
□ 254 Preacher Roe DP	80.00	36.00	10.00
□ 258 Jim Gilliam	300.00	135.00	38.00
□ 263 Johnny Podres	275.00	125.00	34.00
□ 265 Jackie Jensen	120.00	55.00	15.00
□ 273 Harvey Haddix	120.00	55.00	15.00
□ 280 Milt Bolling	300.00	50.00	20.00

1954 Topps

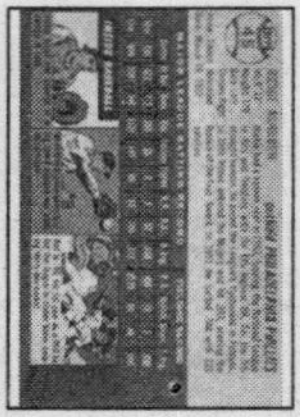

The cards in this 250-card set measure approximately 2 5/8" by 3 3/4". Each of the cards in the 1954 Topps set contains a large "head" shot of the player in color plus a smaller full-length photo in black and white set against a color background. The cards were issued in one-card penny packs or five-card nickle packs. This set contains the Rookie Cards of Hank Aaron, Ernie Banks, and Al Kaline and two separate cards of Ted Williams (number 1 and number 250). Conspicuous by his absence is Mickey Mantle who apparently was the exclusive property of Bowman during 1954 (and 1955). The first two issues of Sports Illustrated magazine contained "card" inserts on regular paper stock. The first issue showed actual cards in the set in color, while the second issue showed some created cards of New York Yankees players in black and white, including Mickey Mantle.

	NRMT	VG-E	GOOD
COMPLETE SET (250)	7500.00	3400.00	950.00
COMMON CARD (1-50)	15.00	6.75	1.85
COMMON CARD (51-75)	25.00	11.00	3.10
COMMON CARD (76-250)	15.00	6.75	1.85
SEMISTARS 1-50/76-250	20.00	9.00	2.50
SEMISTARS 51-75	30.00	13.50	3.70
COMMON DODGERS: 1.5X COM. VALUE			
COMMON YANKEES: 1.5X COM. VALUE			
CARDS PRICED IN NM CONDITION !			

□ 1 Ted Williams	650.00	230.00	65.00
□ 3 Monte Irvin	40.00	18.00	5.00
□ 7 Ted Kluszewski	40.00	18.00	5.00
□ 10 Jackie Robinson	275.00	125.00	34.00

☐	13 Billy Martin	50.00	22.00	6.25
☐	17 Phil Rizzuto	75.00	34.00	9.50
☐	20 Warren Spahn	75.00	34.00	9.50
☐	25 Harvey Kuenn	40.00	18.00	5.00
☐	30 Eddie Mathews	75.00	34.00	9.50
☐	32 Duke Snider	125.00	55.00	15.50
☐	35 Jim Gilliam	30.00	13.50	3.70
☐	36 Hoyt Wilhelm	50.00	22.00	6.25
☐	37 Whitey Ford	100.00	45.00	12.50
☐	45 Richie Ashburn	70.00	32.00	8.75
☐	50 Yogi Berra	150.00	70.00	19.00
☐	70 Larry Doby	50.00	22.00	6.25
☐	85 Bob Turley	30.00	13.50	3.70
☐	86 Billy Herman CO	25.00	11.00	3.10
☐	90 Willie Mays	500.00	220.00	60.00
☐	94 Ernie Banks	750.00	350.00	95.00
☐	98 Joe Black	25.00	11.00	3.10
☐	101 Gene Woodling	25.00	11.00	3.10
☐	102 Gil Hodges	70.00	32.00	8.75
☐	128 Hank Aaron	1500.00	700.00	190.00
☐	130 Hank Bauer	25.00	11.00	3.10
☐	132 Tom Lasorda	125.00	55.00	15.50
☐	137 Wally Moon	30.00	13.50	3.70
☐	139 The O'Briens Johnny O'Brien Eddie O'Brien	40.00	18.00	5.00
☐	166 Johnny Podres	30.00	13.50	3.70
☐	183 Earle Combs CO	25.00	11.00	3.10
☐	187 Heinie Manush CO	25.00	11.00	3.10
☐	201 Al Kaline	750.00	350.00	95.00
☐	205 Johnny Sain	30.00	13.50	3.70
☐	239 Bill Skowron	100.00	45.00	12.50
☐	250 Ted Williams	750.00	300.00	75.00

1955 Topps

The cards in this 206-card set measure approximately 2 5/8" by 3 3/4". Both the large "head" shot and the smaller full-length photos used on each card of the 1955 Topps set are in color. The card fronts were designed horizontally for the first time in Topps' history. The first card features Dusty Rhodes, hitting star and MVP in the New York Giants' 1954 World Series sweep over the Cleveland Indians. A "high" series, 161 to 210, is more difficult to find than cards 1 to 160. Numbers 175, 186, 203, and 209 were never issued. To fill in for the four cards not issued in the high number series, Topps double printed four players, those appearing on cards 170, 172, 184, and 188. Cards were issued in one-card penny packs or six-card nickle packs. Although rarely seen, there exist salesman sample panels of three cards containing the fronts of regular cards with ad information for the 1955 Topps regular and the 1955 Topps Doubleheaders on the back. One such ad panel depicts (from top to bottom) Danny Schell, Jake Thies, and Howie Pollet. The key Rookie Cards in this set are Ken Boyer, Roberto Clemente, Harmon Killebrew, and Sandy Koufax.

	NRMT	VG-E	GOOD
COMPLETE SET (206)	7200.00	3200.00	900.00
COMMON CARD (1-150)	12.00	5.50	1.50
COMMON CARD (151-160)	20.00	9.00	2.50
COMMON CARD (161-210)	30.00	13.50	3.70
DP (170/172/184/188)	15.00	6.75	1.85
LO SEMISTARS	18.00	8.00	2.20
HI SEMISTARS	35.00	16.00	4.40
COMMON DODGERS: 1.5X COM. VALUE			
COMMON YANKEES: 1.5X COM. VALUE			
NOT ISSUED (175/186/203/209)			
CARDS PRICED IN NM CONDITION !			

☐	1 Dusty Rhodes	50.00	10.00	3.30
☐	2 Ted Williams	450.00	200.00	55.00
☐	4 Al Kaline	175.00	80.00	22.00
☐	5 Jim Gilliam	25.00	11.00	3.10
☐	22 Bill Skowron	20.00	9.00	2.50
☐	25 Johnny Podres	20.00	9.00	2.50
☐	28 Ernie Banks	175.00	80.00	22.00
☐	31 Warren Spahn	90.00	40.00	11.00
☐	47 Hank Aaron UER (Birth incorrectly listed as 2/10)	350.00	160.00	45.00
☐	50 Jackie Robinson	275.00	125.00	34.00
☐	75 Sandy Amoros	30.00	13.50	3.70
☐	92 Don Zimmer	30.00	13.50	3.70
☐	100 Monte Irvin	35.00	16.00	4.40
☐	120 Ted Kluszewski	40.00	18.00	5.00
☐	123 Sandy Koufax	1000.00	450.00	125.00
☐	124 Harmon Killebrew	250.00	110.00	31.00
☐	125 Ken Boyer	60.00	27.00	7.50
☐	152 Harry Agganis	70.00	32.00	8.75
☐	155 Eddie Mathews	90.00	40.00	11.00
☐	156 Joe Black	35.00	16.00	4.40
☐	164 Roberto Clemente	2200.00	1000.00	275.00
☐	187 Gil Hodges	125.00	55.00	15.50
☐	189 Phil Rizzuto	125.00	55.00	15.50
☐	194 Willie Mays	400.00	180.00	50.00
☐	198 Yogi Berra	200.00	90.00	25.00
☐	210 Duke Snider	450.00	135.00	45.00

1956 Topps

The cards in this 340-card set measure approximately 2 5/8" by 3 3/4". Following up with another horizontally oriented card in 1956, Topps improved the format by layering the color "head" shot onto an actual action sequence involving the player. Cards 1 to 180 come with either white or gray backs: in the 1 to 100 sequence, gray backs are less common (worth about 10 percent more) and in the 101 to 180 sequence, white backs are less common (worth 30 percent more). The team cards, used for the first time in a regular set by Topps, are found dated 1955, or undated, with the team name appearing on either side. The dated team cards in the first series were not printed on the gray stock. The two unnumbered checklist cards are highly prized (must be unmarked to qualify as excellent or mint). The complete set price below does not include the unnumbered checklist cards or any of the variations. The set was issued in one-card penny packs or six-card nickle packs. Both types of packs included a piece of bubble gum. The key Rookie Cards in this set are Walt Alston, Luis Aparicio, and Roger Craig. There are ten double-printed cards in the first series as evidenced by the discovery of an uncut sheet of 110 cards (10 by 11); these DP's are listed below.

	NRMT	VG-E	GOOD
COMPLETE SET (340)	7000.00	3200.00	900.00
COMMON CARD (1-100)	10.00	4.50	1.25

COMMON CARD (101-180)	12.00	5.50	1.50
COMMON CARD (181-260)	15.00	6.75	1.85
COMMON CARD (261-340)	12.00	5.50	1.50
DP (9/21/46/60/75/80/86)	9.00	4.00	1.10
TEAMS (11A/72A/85A/90A)	30.00	13.50	3.70
TEAMS (11B/72B/85B/90B)	75.00	34.00	9.50
TEAMS (11C/72C/85C/90C)	30.00	13.50	3.70
TEAMS (111/121/134)	35.00	16.00	4.40
TEAMS (146/236)	35.00	16.00	4.40
SEMISTARS 1-180/261-340	16.00	7.25	2.00
SEMISTARS 181-260	20.00	9.00	2.50
COMMON DODGERS: 1.5X COM. VALUE			
COMMON YANKEES: 1.5X COM. VALUE			
CARDS PRICED IN NM CONDITION !			

□ 1 William Harridge	90.00	25.00	9.00
(AL President)			
□ 2 Warren Giles	24.00	11.00	3.00
(NL President)			
□ 5 Ted Williams	325.00	145.00	40.00
□ 8 Walter Alston MG	40.00	18.00	5.00
□ 10 Warren Spahn	70.00	32.00	8.75
□ 15 Ernie Banks DP	80.00	36.00	10.00
□ 20 Al Kaline	90.00	40.00	11.00
□ 25 Ted Kluszewski	30.00	13.50	3.70
□ 30 Jackie Robinson DP	160.00	70.00	20.00
□ 31 Hank Aaron UER	275.00	125.00	34.00
(Small photo actually Willie Mays)			
□ 33 Roberto Clemente	450.00	200.00	55.00
□ 79 Sandy Koufax	350.00	160.00	45.00
□ 95A Milwaukee Braves	42.00	19.00	5.25
Team (Centered)			
□ 95B Braves Team	75.00	34.00	9.50
(Dated 1955)			
□ 95C Braves Team	42.00	19.00	5.25
(Name at far left)			
□ 100A Baltimore Orioles	35.00	16.00	4.40
Team (centered)			
□ 100B Orioles Team	75.00	34.00	9.50
(Dated 1955)			
□ 100C Orioles Team	35.00	16.00	4.40
(Name at far left)			
□ 101 Roy Campanella	150.00	70.00	19.00
□ 107 Eddie Mathews	60.00	27.00	7.50
□ 109 Enos Slaughter	35.00	16.00	4.40
□ 110 Yogi Berra	125.00	55.00	15.50
□ 113 Phil Rizzuto	90.00	40.00	11.00
□ 118 Nellie Fox	40.00	18.00	5.00
□ 120 Richie Ashburn	50.00	22.00	6.25
□ 125 Minnie Minoso	25.00	11.00	3.10
□ 130 Willie Mays	300.00	135.00	38.00
□ 135 Mickey Mantle	1400.00	650.00	180.00
□ 140 Herb Score	60.00	27.00	7.50
□ 145 Gil Hodges	50.00	22.00	6.25
□ 150 Duke Snider	90.00	40.00	11.00
□ 164 Harmon Killebrew	100.00	45.00	12.50
□ 165 Red Schoendienst	35.00	16.00	4.40
□ 166 Brooklyn Dodgers	250.00	110.00	31.00
Team Card			
□ 180 Robin Roberts	40.00	18.00	5.00
□ 181 Billy Martin	50.00	22.00	6.25
□ 187 Early Wynn	40.00	18.00	5.00
□ 188 Chicago White Sox	40.00	18.00	5.00
Team Card			
□ 190 Carl Furillo	30.00	13.50	3.70
□ 194 Monte Irvin	35.00	16.00	4.40
□ 195 George Kell	35.00	16.00	4.40
□ 200 Bob Feller	100.00	45.00	12.50
□ 208 Elston Howard	50.00	22.00	6.25
□ 213 Detroit Tigers	55.00	25.00	7.00
Team Card			
□ 225 Gil McDougald	30.00	13.50	3.70
□ 226 New York Giants	75.00	34.00	9.50
Team Card			
□ 233 Carl Erskine	30.00	13.50	3.70
□ 235 Don Newcombe	50.00	22.00	6.25
□ 240 Whitey Ford	100.00	45.00	12.50
□ 250 Larry Doby	30.00	13.50	3.70
□ 251 New York Yankees	275.00	125.00	34.00
Team Card UER (Don Larsen misspelled as Larson on front)			
□ 255 Bob Lemon	35.00	16.00	4.40
□ 257 Bobby Thomson	35.00	16.00	4.40
□ 260 Pee Wee Reese	120.00	55.00	15.00
□ 280 Jim Gilliam	25.00	11.00	3.10
□ 288 Bob Cerv	40.00	18.00	5.00
□ 292 Luis Aparicio	125.00	55.00	15.50
□ 299 Charlie Neal	35.00	16.00	4.40
□ 307 Hoyt Wilhelm	35.00	16.00	4.40
□ 332 Don Larsen	60.00	27.00	7.50
□ 340 Mickey McDermott	60.00	12.00	3.60
□ NNO Checklist 1/3	300.00	95.00	45.00
□ NNO Checklist 2/4	300.00	95.00	45.00

1957 Topps

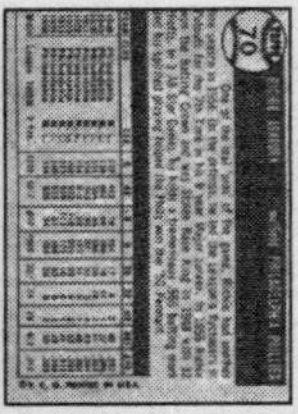

The cards in this 407-card set measure 2 1/2" by 3 1/2". In 1957, Topps returned to the vertical obverse, adopted what we now call the standard card size, and used a large, uncluttered color photo for the first time since 1952. Cards in the series 265 to 352 and the unnumbered checklist cards are scarcer than other cards in the set. However within this scarce series (265-352) there are 22 cards which were printed in double the quantity of the other cards in the series; these 22 double prints are indicated by DP in the checklist below. The first star combination cards, cards 400 and 407, are quite popular with collectors. They feature the big stars of the previous season's World Series teams, the Dodgers (Furillo, Hodges, Campanella, and Snider) and Yankees (Berra and Mantle). The complete set price below does not include the unnumbered checklist cards. Confirmed packaging includes one-cent penny packs and six-card nickle packs. Cello packs are definately known to exist and some collectors remember buyikng rack packs of 57's as well. The key Rookie Cards in this set are Jim Bunning, Rocky Colavito, Don Drysdale, Whitey Herzog, Tony Kubek, Bill Mazeroski, Bobby Richardson, Brooks Robinson, and Frank Robinson.

	NRMT	VG-E	GOOD
COMPLETE SET (407)	7000.00	3200.00	900.00
COMMON CARD (1-88)	10.00	4.50	1.25
COMMON CARD (89-176)	8.00	3.60	1.00
COMMON CARD (177-264)	8.00	3.60	1.00
COMMON CARD (265-352)	20.00	9.00	2.50
COMMON CARD (353-407)	8.00	3.60	1.00
TEAMS (161/171/183/198)	18.00	8.00	2.20
TEAMS (204/214/243/251)	18.00	8.00	2.20
TEAMS (270/275/329)	60.00	27.00	7.50
TEAMS (317/322)	70.00	32.00	8.75
ERR BAKEP (176A)	350.00	160.00	45.00
DP (266/271/278/282)	14.00	6.25	1.75
DP (283/289/290/294/295)	14.00	6.25	1.75
DP (298/301/306/307/309)	14.00	6.25	1.75
DP (310/311/314/315)	14.00	6.25	1.75
SEMISTARS 1-264/353-407	12.00	5.50	1.50
COMMON DODGERS: 1.5X COM. VALUE			
COMMON YANKEES: 1.5X COM. VALUE			
CARDS PRICED IN NM CONDITION			

□ 1 Ted Williams	500.00	150.00	50.00
□ 2 Yogi Berra	125.00	55.00	15.50
□ 7 Luis Aparicio	35.00	16.00	4.40
□ 10 Willie Mays	225.00	100.00	28.00
□ 15 Robin Roberts	35.00	16.00	4.40
□ 18 Don Drysdale	180.00	80.00	22.00
□ 20 Hank Aaron UER	200.00	90.00	25.00

	(Reverse negative photo on front)			
□ 24	Bill Mazeroski	75.00	34.00	9.50
□ 25	Whitey Ford	70.00	32.00	8.75
□ 29	Whitey Herzog	25.00	11.00	3.10
□ 30	Pee Wee Reese	65.00	29.00	8.00
□ 35	Frank Robinson	180.00	80.00	22.00
□ 38	Nellie Fox	30.00	13.50	3.70
□ 40	Early Wynn	30.00	13.50	3.70
□ 45	Carl Furillo	20.00	9.00	2.50
□ 50	Herb Score	20.00	9.00	2.50
□ 55	Ernie Banks	120.00	55.00	15.00
□ 62	Billy Martin	35.00	16.00	4.40
□ 70	Richie Ashburn	45.00	20.00	5.50
□ 76	Roberto Clemente	300.00	135.00	38.00
□ 80	Gil Hodges	45.00	20.00	5.50
□ 82	Elston Howard	20.00	9.00	2.50
□ 90	Warren Spahn	70.00	32.00	8.75
□ 95	Mickey Mantle	1000.00	450.00	125.00
□ 97	New York Yankees Team Card	80.00	36.00	10.00
□ 114	Milwaukee Braves Team Card	22.00	10.00	2.70
□ 120	Bob Lemon	25.00	11.00	3.10
□ 121	Clete Boyer	25.00	11.00	3.10
□ 122	Ken Boyer	15.00	6.75	1.85
□ 125	Al Kaline	100.00	45.00	12.50
□ 130	Don Newcombe	18.00	8.00	2.20
□ 135	Bill Skowron	15.00	6.75	1.85
□ 138	Minnie Minoso	15.00	6.75	1.85
□ 154	Red Schoendienst	25.00	11.00	3.10
□ 165	Ted Kluszewski	50.00	22.00	6.25
□ 170	Duke Snider	100.00	45.00	12.50
□ 175	Don Larsen	25.00	11.00	3.10
□ 200	Gil McDougald	15.00	6.75	1.85
□ 203	Hoyt Wilhelm	25.00	11.00	3.10
□ 210	Roy Campanella	125.00	55.00	15.50
□ 212	Rocky Colavito	160.00	70.00	20.00
□ 215	Enos Slaughter	25.00	11.00	3.10
□ 230	George Kell	25.00	11.00	3.10
□ 250	Eddie Mathews	45.00	20.00	5.50
□ 272	Bobby Shantz	25.00	11.00	3.10
□ 277	Johnny Podres DP	45.00	20.00	5.50
□ 284	Don Zimmer	35.00	16.00	4.40
□ 286	Bobby Richardson	120.00	55.00	15.00
□ 302	Sandy Koufax DP	250.00	110.00	31.00
□ 312	Tony Kubek DP	65.00	29.00	8.00
□ 324	Brooklyn Dodgers Team Card	125.00	55.00	15.50
□ 328	Brooks Robinson	400.00	180.00	50.00
□ 338	Jim Bunning	130.00	57.50	16.00
□ 400	Dodgers' Sluggers Carl Furillo Gil Hodges Roy Campanella Duke Snider	250.00	110.00	31.00
□ 407	Yankee Power Hitters Mickey Mantle Yogi Berra	500.00	150.00	50.00
□ NNO1	Checklist 1/2	250.00	75.00	25.00
□ NNO2	Checklist 2/3	400.00	100.00	40.00
□ NNO3	Checklist 3/4	750.00	170.00	75.00
□ NNO4	Checklist 4/5	900.00	200.00	90.00
□ NNO5	Saturday, May 4th Boston Red Sox vs. Cleveland Indians Cincinnati Redlegs vs. New York Giants	80.00	36.00	10.00
□ NNO6	Saturday, May 25th Detroit Tigers vs. Kansas City Athletics Pittsburgh Pirates vs. Philadelphia Phillies	80.00	36.00	10.00
□ NNO7	Saturday, June 22nd Brooklyn Dodgers vs. St. Louis Cardinals Chicago White Sox vs. New York Yankees	100.00	45.00	12.50
□ NNO8	Saturday, July 19th Milwaukee Braves vs. New York Giants Baltimore Orioles vs. Kansas City Athletics	100.00	45.00	12.50
□ NNO9	Lucky Penny Charm and Key Chain offer card	65.00	29.00	8.00

1958 Topps

This is a 494-card standard-size set. Card number 145, which was supposedly to be Ed Bouchee, was not issued. The 1958 Topps set contains the first Sport Magazine All-Star Selection series (475-495) and expanded use of combination cards. For the first time team cards carried series checklists on back (Milwaukee, Detroit, Baltimore, and Cincinnati are also found with players listed alphabetically). In the first series some cards were issued with yellow name (YL) or team (YT) lettering, as opposed to the common white lettering. They are explicity noted below. Cards were issued in one-card penny packs or six-card nickle packs. In the last series, All-Star cards of Stan Musial and Mickey Mantle were triple printed; the cards they replaced (443, 446, 450, and 462) on the printing sheet were hence printed in shorter supply than other cards in the last series and are marked with an SP in the list below. The All-Star card of Musial marked his first appearence on a Topps card. Technically the New York Giants team card (19) is an error as the Giants had already moved to San Francisco. The key Rookie Cards in this set are Orlando Cepeda, Curt Flood, Roger Maris, and Vada Pinson.

	NRMT	VG-E	GOOD
COMPLETE SET (494)	4800.00	2200.00	600.00
COMMON CARD (1-110)	12.00	5.50	1.50
COMMON CARD (111-198)	7.00	3.10	.85
COMMON CARD (199-352)	7.00	3.10	.85
COMMON CARD (353-440)	7.00	3.10	.85
COMMON CARD (441-474)	7.00	3.10	.85
COMMON AS (475-495)	7.00	3.10	.85
YL (8B/13B/23B/24B/32B)	45.00	20.00	5.50
YL (46B/53B/57B/60B/61B)	45.00	20.00	5.50
YL (65B/78B/92B/97B/98B)	45.00	20.00	5.50
YT (11B/33B/35B/50B/58B)	45.00	20.00	5.50
YT (76B/77B/79B/81B/108B)	45.00	20.00	5.50
ERR HERRER (433A)	650.00	300.00	80.00
TEAMS ! (44)	20.00	9.00	2.50
TEAMS ! (134/158/174)	15.00	6.75	1.85
TEAMS ! (216/256)	15.00	6.75	1.85
TEAMS ! (312/327/341/377A)	15.00	6.75	1.85
TEAMS ! (397A/408A/428A)	15.00	6.75	1.85
TEAMS ! (377B/397B)	100.00	45.00	12.50
TEAMS ! (408B/428B)	100.00	45.00	12.50
SP (443/446/450/462)	18.00	8.00	2.20
COMMON DODGERS: 1.25X COM. VALUE			
COMMON YANKEES: 1.25X COM. VALUE			
NOT ISSUED (145)			
CARDS PRICED IN NM CONDITION			

□ 1	Ted Williams	425.00	150.00	42.50
□ 2A	Bob Lemon	35.00	16.00	4.40
□ 2B	Bob Lemon YT	60.00	27.00	7.50
□ 5	Willie Mays	225.00	100.00	28.00
□ 19	New York Giants Team Card (Checklist on back)	40.00	8.00	4.00
□ 20A	Gil McDougald	18.00	8.00	2.20
□ 20B	Gil McDougald YL	60.00	27.00	7.50
□ 25	Don Drysdale	85.00	38.00	10.50
□ 30A	Hank Aaron	200.00	90.00	25.00
□ 30B	Hank Aaron YL	425.00	190.00	52.50

□ 37 Mike McCormick UER	15.00	6.75	1.85
(Photo actually			
Ray Monzant)			
□ 40 George Kell	18.00	8.00	2.20
□ 42 John Roseboro	24.00	11.00	3.00
□ 47 Roger Maris	400.00	180.00	50.00
□ 52A Bob Clemente	275.00	125.00	34.00
□ 52B Bob Clemente YT	450.00	200.00	55.00
□ 70A Al Kaline	100.00	45.00	12.50
□ 70B Al Kaline YL	180.00	80.00	22.00
□ 71 Dodgers Team	60.00	12.00	6.00
(Checklist on back)			
□ 85A Luis Aparicio	30.00	13.50	3.70
□ 85B Luis Aparicio YT	70.00	32.00	8.75
□ 88 Duke Snider	75.00	34.00	9.50
□ 90 Robin Roberts	30.00	13.50	3.70
□ 100A Early Wynn	25.00	11.00	3.10
□ 100B Early Wynn YT	60.00	27.00	7.50
□ 101A Bobby Richardson	24.00	11.00	3.00
□ 101B Bobby Richardson YL	55.00	25.00	7.00
□ 115 Jim Bunning	25.00	11.00	3.10
□ 120 Johnny Podres	10.00	4.50	1.25
□ 142 Enos Slaughter	25.00	11.00	3.10
□ 150 Mickey Mantle	800.00	350.00	100.00
□ 161 Don Larsen	14.00	6.25	1.75
□ 162 Gil Hodges	25.00	11.00	3.10
□ 175 Marv Throneberry	16.00	7.25	2.00
□ 178 Ted Kluszewski	16.00	7.25	2.00
□ 187 Sandy Koufax	225.00	100.00	28.00
□ 190 Red Schoendienst	18.00	8.00	2.20
□ 215 Jim Gilliam	12.00	5.50	1.50
□ 230 Richie Ashburn	35.00	16.00	4.40
□ 238 Bill Mazeroski	24.00	11.00	3.00
□ 240 Bill Skowron	16.00	7.25	2.00
□ 246 New York Yankees	80.00	16.00	8.00
Team Card			
(Checklist on back)			
□ 258 Carl Erskine	10.00	4.50	1.25
□ 270 Warren Spahn	50.00	22.00	6.25
□ 271 Billy Martin	20.00	9.00	2.50
□ 275 Elston Howard	16.00	7.25	2.00
□ 285 Frank Robinson	100.00	45.00	12.50
□ 288 Harmon Killebrew	85.00	38.00	10.50
□ 295 Minnie Minoso	10.00	4.50	1.25
□ 296 Ryne Duren	16.00	7.25	2.00
□ 300 League Presidents	10.00	4.50	1.25
Will Harridge			
Warren Giles			
□ 304 Tigers' Big Bats	20.00	9.00	2.50
Harvey Kuenn			
Al Kaline			
□ 307 Brooks Robinson	100.00	45.00	12.50
□ 310 Ernie Banks	100.00	45.00	12.50
□ 314 Dodgers' Boss and	25.00	11.00	3.10
Power: Duke Snider			
Walt Alston MG			
□ 320 Whitey Ford	50.00	22.00	6.25
□ 321 Sluggers Supreme	70.00	32.00	8.75
Ted Kluszewski			
Ted Williams			
□ 324 Hoyt Wilhelm	18.00	8.00	2.20
□ 340 Don Newcombe	12.00	5.50	1.50
□ 343 Orlando Cepeda	90.00	40.00	11.00
□ 350 Ken Boyer	16.00	7.25	2.00
□ 351 Braves Fence Busters	35.00	16.00	4.40
Del Crandall			
Eddie Mathews			
Hank Aaron			
Joe Adcock			
□ 352 Herb Score	14.00	6.25	1.75
□ 368 Rocky Colavito	50.00	22.00	6.25
□ 370 Yogi Berra	90.00	40.00	11.00
□ 375 Pee Wee Reese	50.00	22.00	6.25
□ 386 Birdie's Sluggers	14.00	6.25	1.75
Ed Bailey			
Birdie Tebbetts MG			
Frank Robinson			
□ 393 Tony Kubek	18.00	8.00	2.20
□ 400 Nellie Fox	18.00	8.00	2.20
□ 417 Carl Furillo	10.00	4.50	1.25
□ 418 World Series Batting	275.00	125.00	34.00
Foes: Mickey Mantle			
Hank Aaron			
□ 420 Vada Pinson	40.00	18.00	5.00
□ 424 Larry Doby	10.00	4.50	1.25
□ 436 Rival Fence Busters	75.00	34.00	9.50
Willie Mays			
Duke Snider			
□ 440 Eddie Mathews	40.00	18.00	5.00
□ 464 Curt Flood	25.00	11.00	3.10
□ 475 Fred Haney AS MG and	20.00	9.00	2.50
Casey Stengel AS MG			
(Checklist back)			
□ 476 Stan Musial AS TP	40.00	18.00	5.00
□ 479 Nellie Fox AS	12.00	5.50	1.50
□ 480 Eddie Mathews AS	20.00	9.00	2.50
□ 482 Ernie Banks AS	35.00	16.00	4.40
□ 483 Luis Aparicio AS	18.00	8.00	2.20
□ 484 Frank Robinson AS	24.00	11.00	3.00
□ 485 Ted Williams AS	125.00	55.00	15.50
□ 486 Willie Mays AS	50.00	22.00	6.25
□ 487 Mickey Mantle AS TP	200.00	90.00	25.00
□ 488 Hank Aaron AS	50.00	22.00	6.25
□ 494 Warren Spahn AS	24.00	11.00	3.00
□ 495 Herb Score AS	15.00	3.00	1.00
□ xx Contest Cards	40.00	18.00	5.00

1959 Topps

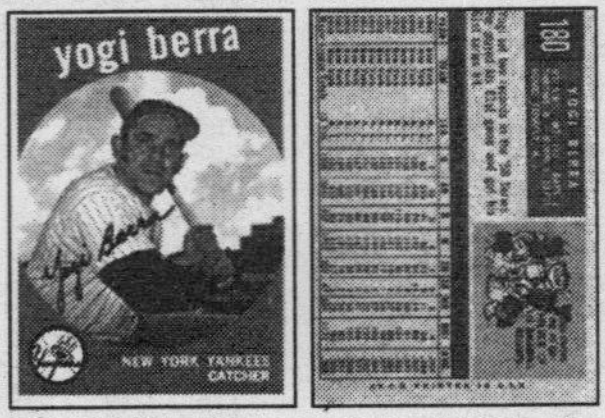

The cards in this 572-card set measure 2 1/2" by 3 1/2". The 1959 Topps set contains bust pictures of the players in a colored circle. Card numbers 551 to 572 are Sporting News All-Star Selections. High numbers 507 to 572 have the card number in a black background on the reverse rather than a green background as in the lower numbers. The high numbers are more difficult to obtain. Several cards in the 300s exist with or without an extra traded or option line on the back of the card. Cards 199 to 286 exist with either white or gray backs. There is no price differential for either colored back. Cards 461 to 470 contain "Highlights" while cards 116 to 146 give an alphabetically ordered listing of "Rookie Prospects." These Rookie Prospects (RP) were Topps' first organized inclusion of untested "Rookie" cards. Card 440 features Lew Burdette erroneously posing as a left-handed pitcher. Cards were issued in one-card penny packs or six-card nickle packs. There were some three-card advertising panels produced by Topps; the players included are from the first series. One advertising panel shows Don McMahon, Red Wilson and Bob Boyd on the front with Ted Kluszewski's card back on the back of the panel. Other panels are: Joe Pignatano, Sam Jones and Jack Urban also with Kluszewski's card back on back, Billy Hunter, Chuck Stobbs and Carl Sawatski on the front with the back of Nellie Fox's card on the back, Vito Valentinetti, Ken Lehman and Ed Bouchee on the front with Fox's card back on back and Mel Roach, Brooks Lawrence and Warren Spahn also with Fox on back. When separated, these advertising cards are distinguished by the non-standard card back, i.e., part of an advertisement for the 1959 Topps set instead of the typical statistics and biographical information about the player pictured. The key Rookie Cards in this set are Felipe Alou, Sparky Anderson (called George on the card), Norm Cash, Bob Gibson, and Bill White.

	NRMT	VG-E	GOOD
COMPLETE SET (572)	4500.00	2000.00	550.00
COMMON CARD (1-110)	6.00	2.70	.75
COMMON CARD (111-506)	4.00	1.80	.50
COMMON CARD (507-550)	16.00	7.25	2.00
COMMON AS (551-572)	16.00	7.25	2.00
TEAMS ! (48/69)	24.00	11.00	3.00
TEAMS ! (111/172/223)	15.00	6.75	1.85
TEAMS ! (248/304/329)	15.00	6.75	1.85
TEAMS ! (397/419/476)	15.00	6.75	1.85
ROOKIE PROSPECTS (116-146)	5.00	2.20	.60
VAR (316B/321B/322B)	80.00	36.00	10.00
VAR (336B/362B)	80.00	36.00	10.00
HL (461-470)	5.00	2.20	.60
COMMON DODGERS: 1.25X COM. VALUE			
COMMON YANKEES: 1.25X COM. VALUE			
CARDS PRICED IN NM CONDITION			
□ 1 Ford Frick COMM	50.00	13.50	4.50
□ 8 Phillies Team (Checklist on back)	65.00	13.00	6.50
□ 10 Mickey Mantle	600.00	275.00	75.00
□ 20 Duke Snider	50.00	22.00	6.25
□ 30 Nellie Fox	20.00	9.00	2.50
□ 34 Pitchers Beware Al Kaline Charley Maxwell	20.00	9.00	2.50
□ 35 Ted Kluszewski	16.00	7.25	2.00
□ 40A Warren Spahn ERR (Born 1931)	75.00	34.00	9.50
□ 40B Warren Spahn ERR (Born 1931, but three is partially obscured)	100.00	45.00	12.50
□ 40C Warren Spahn COR (Born 1921)	50.00	22.00	6.25
□ 50 Willie Mays	125.00	55.00	15.50
□ 70 Harvey Kuenn	8.00	3.60	1.00
□ 76 Bobby Richardson	20.00	9.00	2.50
□ 80 Minnie Minoso	10.00	4.50	1.25
□ 88 Herb Score	10.00	4.50	1.25
□ 90 Bill Skowron	16.00	7.25	2.00
□ 94 White Sox Team (Checklist on back)	40.00	8.00	4.00
□ 102 Felipe Alou	30.00	13.50	3.70
□ 116 Bob Allison RP	10.00	4.50	1.25
□ 119 John Callison RP	12.00	5.50	1.50
□ 147 Cubs Clubbers Dale Long Ernie Banks Walt Moryn	25.00	11.00	3.10
□ 149 Jim Bunning	20.00	9.00	2.50
□ 150 Stan Musial	125.00	55.00	15.50
□ 155 Enos Slaughter	20.00	9.00	2.50
□ 156 Ace Hurlers Billy Pierce Robin Roberts	10.00	4.50	1.25
□ 163 Sandy Koufax	150.00	70.00	19.00
□ 166 Destruction Crew Minnie Minoso Rocky Colavito (Misspelled Colovito on card back) Larry Doby	16.00	7.25	2.00
□ 180 Yogi Berra	75.00	34.00	9.50
□ 200 Warren Giles (NL President)	8.00	3.60	1.00
□ 202 Roger Maris	90.00	40.00	11.00
□ 205 Don Larsen	8.00	3.60	1.00
□ 212 Fence Busters Hank Aaron Eddie Mathews	75.00	34.00	9.50
□ 237 Run Preventers Gil McDougald Bob Turley Bobby Richardson	12.00	5.50	1.50
□ 260 Early Wynn UER (1957 Cleevland)	16.00	7.25	2.00
□ 262 Hitters' Foes Johnny Podres Clem Labine Don Drysdale	16.00	7.25	2.00
□ 270 Gil Hodges	25.00	11.00	3.10
□ 295 Billy Martin	20.00	9.00	2.50
□ 300 Richie Ashburn	25.00	11.00	3.10
□ 310 Luis Aparicio	20.00	9.00	2.50
□ 317 Hitting Kings Willie Mays Richie Ashburn	65.00	29.00	8.00
□ 325 Ken Boyer	10.00	4.50	1.25
□ 338 Sparky Anderson	75.00	34.00	9.50
□ 345 Gil McDougald	8.00	3.60	1.00
□ 349 Hoyt Wilhelm	16.00	7.25	2.00
□ 350 Ernie Banks	75.00	34.00	9.50
□ 352 Robin Roberts	20.00	9.00	2.50
□ 359 Bill White	25.00	11.00	3.10
□ 360 Al Kaline	65.00	29.00	8.00
□ 380 Hank Aaron	125.00	55.00	15.50
□ 383 Words of Wisdom Don Larsen Casey Stengel MG	14.00	6.25	1.75
□ 387 Don Drysdale	35.00	16.00	4.40
□ 390 Orlando Cepeda	16.00	7.25	2.00
□ 395 Elston Howard	10.00	4.50	1.25
□ 408 Keystone Combo Nellie Fox Luis Aparicio	20.00	9.00	2.50
□ 415 Bill Mazeroski	12.00	5.50	1.50
□ 420 Rocky Colavito	30.00	13.50	3.70
□ 430 Whitey Ford	50.00	22.00	6.25
□ 435 Frank Robinson	50.00	22.00	6.25
□ 439 Brooks Robinson	50.00	22.00	6.25
□ 440 Lou Burdette (Posing as if lefthanded)	8.00	3.60	1.00
□ 448 Vada Pinson UER (Born: 8/8/38, should be 8/11/38)	10.00	4.50	1.25
□ 450 Eddie Mathews	35.00	16.00	4.40
□ 457 Dodgers Team (Checklist on back)	30.00	6.00	3.00
□ 461 Mickey Mantle HL	130.00	57.50	16.00
□ 462 Rocky Colavito HL	16.00	7.25	2.00
□ 463 Al Kaline HL	20.00	9.00	2.50
□ 464 Willie Mays HL 54 World Series Catch	40.00	18.00	5.00
□ 467 Hank Aaron HL	30.00	13.50	3.70
□ 468 Duke Snider HL	18.00	8.00	2.20
□ 469 Ernie Banks HL	18.00	8.00	2.20
□ 470 Stan Musial HL 3,000 Hits	25.00	11.00	3.10
□ 478 Bob Clemente	225.00	100.00	28.00
□ 480 Red Schoendienst	16.00	7.25	2.00
□ 485 Ryne Duren	8.00	3.60	1.00
□ 505 Tony Kubek	10.00	4.50	1.25
□ 509 Norm Cash	65.00	29.00	8.00
□ 510 Yankees Team (Checklist on back)	125.00	25.00	12.50
□ 514 Bob Gibson	250.00	110.00	31.00
□ 515 Harmon Killebrew	125.00	55.00	15.50
□ 518 Mike Cueller UER (Sic, Cuellar)	30.00	13.50	3.70
□ 528 Pirates Team (Checklist on back)	65.00	13.00	6.50
□ 542 Jim Perry	30.00	13.50	3.70
□ 543 Corsair Trio Bob Skinner Bill Virdon Roberto Clemente	175.00	80.00	22.00
□ 550 Roy Campanella (Symbol of Courage)	160.00	70.00	20.00
□ 552 Casey Stengel AS MG	35.00	16.00	4.40
□ 553 Orlando Cepeda AS	25.00	11.00	3.10
□ 554 Bill Skowron AS	25.00	11.00	3.10
□ 555 Bill Mazeroski AS	25.00	11.00	3.10
□ 556 Nellie Fox AS	30.00	13.50	3.70
□ 557 Ken Boyer AS	25.00	11.00	3.10
□ 559 Ernie Banks AS	65.00	29.00	8.00
□ 560 Luis Aparicio AS	30.00	13.50	3.70
□ 561 Hank Aaron AS	125.00	55.00	15.50
□ 562 Al Kaline AS	65.00	29.00	8.00
□ 563 Willie Mays AS	125.00	55.00	15.50
□ 564 Mickey Mantle AS	300.00	135.00	38.00
□ 571 Warren Spahn AS	40.00	18.00	5.00
□ 572 Billy Pierce AS	25.00	8.00	2.50

1960 Topps

The cards in this 572-card set measure 2 1/2" by 3 1/2". The 1960 Topps set is the only Topps standard size issue to use a horizontally orient-

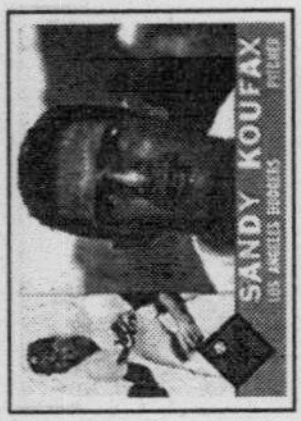

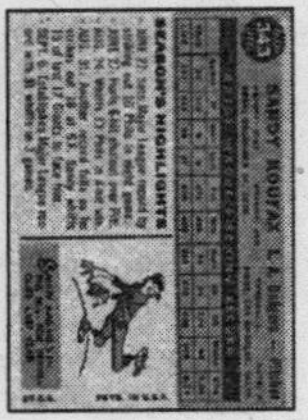

ed front. World Series cards appeared for the first time (385 to 391), and there is a Rookie Prospect (RP) series (117-148), the most famous of which is Carl Yastrzemski, and a Sport Magazine All-Star Selection (AS) series (553-572). There are 16 manager cards listed alphabetically from 212 through 227. The 1959 Topps All-Rookie team is featured on cards 316-325. The coaching staff of each team was also afforded their own card in a 16-card subset (455-470). Cards 375 to 440 come with either gray or white backs. There is no price differential for either color back. The high series (507-572) were printed on a more limited basis than the rest of the set. The team cards have series checklists on the reverse. Cards were issued in one-card penny packs and six-card nickle packs. The key Rookie Cards in this set are Jim Kaat, Willie McCovey and Carl Yastrzemski.

	NRMT	VG-E	GOOD
COMPLETE SET (572)	3500.00	1600.00	450.00
COMMON CARD (1-440)	4.00	1.80	.50
COMMON CARD (441-506)	7.00	3.10	.85
COMMON CARD (507-552)	16.00	7.25	2.00
COMMON AS (553-572)	16.00	7.25	2.00
TEAMS ! (43/151/164/174)	10.00	4.50	1.25
TEAMS ! (208/242/302/381/413)	10.00	4.50	1.25
TEAMS ! (513/537)	30.00	13.50	3.70
ROOKIE TROPHIES (316-325)	5.00	2.20	.60
WS (385-391)	7.00	3.10	.85
CO (455-470)	7.00	3.10	.85
SEMISTARS 1-440	5.00	2.20	.60
COMMON DODGERS: 1.25X COM. VALUE			
COMMON YANKEES: 1.25X COM. VALUE			
CARDS PRICED IN NM CONDITION			

	NRMT	VG-E	GOOD
□ 1 Early Wynn	30.00	7.50	3.00
□ 7 Master and Mentor	25.00	11.00	3.10
Willie Mays			
Bill Rigney MG			
□ 10 Ernie Banks	50.00	22.00	6.25
□ 18 Dodgers Team	50.00	10.00	5.00
(Checklist on back)			
□ 28 Brooks Robinson	50.00	22.00	6.25
□ 34 Sparky Anderson	14.00	6.25	1.75
□ 35 Whitey Ford	50.00	22.00	6.25
□ 50 Al Kaline	50.00	22.00	6.25
□ 55 Bill Mazeroski	10.00	4.50	1.25
□ 65 Elston Howard	6.00	2.70	.75
□ 72 Tigers Team	20.00	4.00	2.00
(Checklist on back)			
□ 73 Bob Gibson	50.00	22.00	6.25
□ 83 Tony Kubek	6.00	2.70	.75
□ 100 Nellie Fox	12.00	5.50	1.50
□ 115 Fork and Knuckler	6.00	2.70	.75
Roy Face			
Hoyt Wilhelm			
□ 132 Frank Howard RP	20.00	9.00	2.50
□ 136 Jim Kaat RP	40.00	18.00	5.00
□ 148 Carl Yastrzemski RP	125.00	55.00	15.50
□ 160 Rival All-Stars	140.00	65.00	17.50
Mickey Mantle			
Ken Boyer			
□ 173 Billy Martin	14.00	6.25	1.75
□ 200 Willie Mays	90.00	40.00	11.00
□ 210 Harmon Killebrew	25.00	11.00	3.10
□ 212 Walt Alston MG	12.00	5.50	1.50
□ 227 Casey Stengel MG	16.00	7.25	2.00
□ 230 Mound Magicians	12.00	5.50	1.50
Lou Burdette			
Warren Spahn			
Bob Buhl			
□ 240 Luis Aparicio	14.00	6.25	1.75
□ 250 Stan Musial	80.00	36.00	10.00
□ 260 Power Plus	14.00	6.25	1.75
Rocky Colavito			
Tito Francona			
□ 264 Robin Roberts	14.00	6.25	1.75
□ 295 Gil Hodges	20.00	9.00	2.50
□ 300 Hank Aaron	80.00	36.00	10.00
□ 305 Richie Ashburn	20.00	9.00	2.50
□ 316 Willie McCovey	115.00	52.50	14.50
□ 326 Bob Clemente	225.00	100.00	28.00
□ 332 Yankees Team	80.00	16.00	8.00
(Checklist on back)			
□ 335 Red Schoendienst	12.00	5.50	1.50
□ 343 Sandy Koufax	160.00	70.00	20.00
□ 350 Mickey Mantle	475.00	210.00	60.00
□ 352 Cincy Clouters	8.00	3.60	1.00
Gus Bell			
Frank Robinson			
Jerry Lynch			
□ 365 Minnie Minoso	6.00	2.70	.75
□ 366 Dallas Green	8.00	3.60	1.00
□ 370 Bill Skowron	6.00	2.70	.75
□ 377 Roger Maris	80.00	36.00	10.00
□ 388 Gil Hodges WS	10.00	4.50	1.25
□ 389 Luis Aparicio WS	12.00	5.50	1.50
Maury Wills			
□ 395 Hoyt Wilhelm	14.00	6.25	1.75
□ 400 Rocky Colavito	20.00	9.00	2.50
□ 405 Bobby Richardson	14.00	6.25	1.75
□ 420 Eddie Mathews	30.00	13.50	3.70
□ 429 AL Kings	8.00	3.60	1.00
Nellie Fox			
Harvey Kuenn			
□ 445 Warren Spahn	50.00	22.00	6.25
□ 448 Jim Gentile	20.00	9.00	2.50
□ 450 Orlando Cepeda	18.00	8.00	2.20
□ 456 Red Sox Coaches	8.00	3.60	1.00
Rudy York			
Billy Herman			
Sal Maglie			
Del Baker			
□ 460 Indians Coaches	8.00	3.60	1.00
Mel Harder			
Jo-Jo White			
Bob Lemon			
Ralph(Red) Kress			
□ 461 Tigers Coaches	8.00	3.60	1.00
Tom Ferrick			
Luke Appling			
Billy Hitchcock			
□ 465 Yankees Coaches	12.00	5.50	1.50
Bill Dickey			
Ralph Houk			
Frank Crosetti			
Ed Lopat			
□ 475 Don Drysdale	35.00	16.00	4.40
□ 480 Yogi Berra	70.00	32.00	8.75
□ 484 Pirates Team	50.00	10.00	5.00
(Checklist on back)			
□ 485 Ken Boyer	14.00	6.25	1.75
□ 488 Norm Cash	18.00	8.00	2.20
□ 490 Frank Robinson	50.00	22.00	6.25
□ 493 Duke Snider	50.00	22.00	6.25
□ 494 Orioles Team	25.00	5.00	2.50
(Checklist on back)			
□ 496 Bill Virdon	8.00	3.60	1.00
□ 502 Jim Bunning	20.00	9.00	2.50
□ 505 Ted Kluszewski	18.00	8.00	2.20
□ 509 Tommy Davis	25.00	11.00	3.10
□ 554 Willie McCovey AS	40.00	18.00	5.00
□ 555 Nellie Fox AS	25.00	11.00	3.10
□ 558 Eddie Mathews AS	30.00	13.50	3.70
□ 559 Luis Aparicio AS	25.00	11.00	3.10
□ 560 Ernie Banks AS	60.00	27.00	7.50
□ 561 Al Kaline AS	60.00	27.00	7.50
□ 563 Mickey Mantle AS	325.00	145.00	40.00
□ 564 Willie Mays AS	125.00	55.00	15.50
□ 565 Roger Maris AS	80.00	36.00	10.00
□ 566 Hank Aaron AS	115.00	52.50	14.50
□ 570 Don Drysdale AS	30.00	13.50	3.70
□ 572 Johnny Antonelli AS	25.00	7.50	2.50

1961 Topps

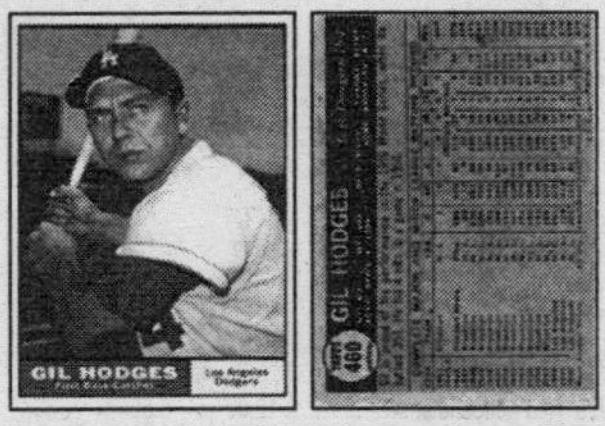

The cards in this 587-card set measure 2 1/2" by 3 1/2". In 1961, Topps returned to the vertical obverse format. Introduced for the first time were "League Leaders" (41-50) and separate, numbered checklist cards. Two number 463s exist: the Braves team card carrying that number was meant to be number 426. There are three versions of the second series checklist card number 98; the variations are distinguished by the color of the "CHECKLIST" headline on the front of the card, the color of the printing of the card number on the bottom of the reverse, and the presence of the copyright notice running vertically on the card back. There are two groups of managers (131-139/219-226) as well as separate subsets of World Series cards (306-313), Baseball Thrills (401-410), MVP's of the 1950's (AL 471-478/NL 479-486) and Sporting News All-Stars (566-589). The usual last series scarcity (523-589) exists. Some collectors believe that 61 high numbers are the toughest of all the Topps hi numbers. The set actually totals 587 cards since numbers 587 and 588 were never issued. Cards were issued in one-card penny packs as well as five-card nickle packs. The key Rookie Cards in this set are Juan Marichal, Ron Santo and Billy Williams.

	NRMT	VG-E	GOOD
COMPLETE SET (587)	4800.00	2200.00	600.00
COMMON CARD (1-370)	3.00	1.35	.35
COMMON CARD (371-446)	4.00	1.80	.50
COMMON CARD (447-522)	7.00	3.10	.85
COMMON CARD (523-565)	30.00	13.50	3.70
COMMON AS (566-589)	30.00	13.50	3.70
LL (41-50)	7.00	3.10	.85
WS (306-313)	8.00	3.60	1.00
THRILLS (401-410)	6.00	2.70	.75
TEAMS (7/51/86/122/159/167)	9.00	4.00	1.10
TEAMS (249/297/347)	9.00	4.00	1.10
TEAMS (373)	10.00	4.50	1.25
TEAMS (467/491)	12.00	5.50	1.50
TEAMS (542/554)	70.00	32.00	8.75
SP (421/423/428)	18.00	8.00	2.20
CL (17/98A/98B/98C/189A)	10.00	4.50	1.25
CL (189B/273B/361A)	10.00	4.50	1.25
CL (273A/361B/437A/437B/516)	15.00	6.75	1.85
NOT ISSUED (587/588)	30.00		
COMMON DODGERS: 1.25X COM. VALUE			
COMMON YANKEES: 1.25X COM. VALUE			
CARDS PRICED IN NM CONDITION			

□ 1 Dick Groat	30.00	6.00	3.00
□ 2 Roger Maris	140.00	65.00	17.50
□ 10 Brooks Robinson	40.00	18.00	5.00
□ 20 Robin Roberts	14.00	6.25	1.75
□ 25 Reds' Heavy Artillery	8.00	3.60	1.00
Vada Pinson			
Gus Bell			
Frank Robinson			
□ 30 Nellie Fox	14.00	6.25	1.75
□ 35 Ron Santo	45.00	20.00	5.50
□ 41 NL Batting Leaders	35.00	16.00	4.40
Dick Groat			
Norm Larker			
Willie Mays			
Roberto Clemente			
□ 43 NL Home Run Leaders	30.00	13.50	3.70
Ernie Banks			
Hank Aaron			
Ed Mathews			
Ken Boyer			
□ 44 AL Home Run Leaders	120.00	55.00	15.00
Mickey Mantle			
Roger Maris			
Jim Lemon			
Rocky Colavito			
□ 49 NL Strikeout Leaders	20.00	9.00	2.50
Don Drysdale			
Sandy Koufax			
Sam Jones			
Ernie Broglio			
□ 63 Jim Kaat	8.00	3.60	1.00
□ 65 Ted Kluszewski	7.00	3.10	.85
□ 80 Harmon Killebrew	20.00	9.00	2.50
□ 88 Richie Ashburn	16.00	7.25	2.00
□ 89 Billy Martin	14.00	6.25	1.75
□ 120 Eddie Mathews	30.00	13.50	3.70
□ 136 Walt Alston MG	6.00	2.70	.75
□ 141 Billy Williams	60.00	27.00	7.50
□ 150 Willie Mays	100.00	45.00	12.50
□ 160 Whitey Ford UER	40.00	18.00	5.00
(Incorrectly listed			
as 5'0" tall)			
□ 180 Bobby Richardson	12.00	5.50	1.50
□ 200 Warren Spahn	30.00	13.50	3.70
□ 207 Dodger Southpaws	30.00	13.50	3.70
Sandy Koufax			
Johnny Podres			
□ 211 Bob Gibson	40.00	18.00	5.00
□ 228 New York Yankees	70.00	32.00	8.75
Team Card			
□ 260 Don Drysdale	30.00	13.50	3.70
□ 265 Tony Kubek	8.00	3.60	1.00
□ 280 Frank Howard	8.00	3.60	1.00
□ 287 Carl Yastrzemski	50.00	22.00	6.25
□ 290 Stan Musial	100.00	45.00	12.50
□ 300 Mickey Mantle	475.00	210.00	60.00
□ 307 Mickey Mantle WS	100.00	45.00	12.50
□ 311 Whitey Ford WS	16.00	7.25	2.00
□ 312 Bill Mazeroski WS	20.00	9.00	2.50
Mazeroski Homer Wins it			
□ 313 World Series Summary	16.00	7.25	2.00
Pirates Celebrate			
□ 330 Rocky Colavito	20.00	9.00	2.50
□ 337 Al's Aces	6.00	2.70	.75
Early Wynn			
Al Lopez			
Herb Score			
□ 344 Sandy Koufax	120.00	55.00	15.00
□ 350 Ernie Banks	45.00	20.00	5.50
□ 360 Frank Robinson	40.00	18.00	5.00
□ 371 Bill Skowron SP	60.00	27.00	7.50
□ 375 Ken Boyer	10.00	4.50	1.25
□ 380 Minnie Minoso	7.00	3.10	.85
□ 388 Bob Clemente	160.00	70.00	20.00
□ 401 Babe Ruth HL	50.00	22.00	6.25
60th HR			
□ 402 Don Larsen HL SP	30.00	13.50	3.70
WS Perfect Game			
□ 404 Rogers Hornsby HL	10.00	4.50	1.25
.424 Season BA			
□ 405 Lou Gehrig HL	80.00	36.00	10.00
Consecutive Game Streak			
□ 406 Mickey Mantle HL	100.00	45.00	12.50
565 foot HR			
□ 408 Christy Mathewson HL SP	20.00	9.00	2.50
267 Strikeouts			
□ 409 Walter Johnson SL	12.00	5.50	1.50
3 Shutouts in 4 days			
□ 415 Hank Aaron	90.00	40.00	11.00
□ 416 Dick Howser	10.00	4.50	1.25
□ 417 Juan Marichal SP	125.00	55.00	15.50
□ 425 Yogi Berra	70.00	32.00	8.75
□ 426 Milwaukee Braves	12.00	5.50	1.50
Team Card			
(Back numbered 463)			
□ 429 Al Kaline	45.00	20.00	5.50
□ 430 Bill Mazeroski SP	60.00	27.00	7.50
□ 435 Orlando Cepeda UER	14.00	6.25	1.75
(San Francis on			
card front)			

□ 436 Jim Maloney SP	20.00	9.00	2.50
□ 440 Luis Aparicio	16.00	7.25	2.00
□ 443 Duke Snider	40.00	18.00	5.00
□ 455 Early Wynn	15.00	6.75	1.85
□ 460 Gil Hodges	16.00	7.25	2.00
□ 471 Phil Rizzuto MVP	20.00	9.00	2.50
□ 472 Yogi Berra MVP	60.00	27.00	7.50
□ 475 Mickey Mantle MVP	200.00	90.00	25.00
□ 477 Nellie Fox MVP	16.00	7.25	2.00
□ 478 Roger Maris MVP	45.00	20.00	5.50
□ 480 Roy Campanella MVP	35.00	16.00	4.40
□ 482 Willie Mays MVP	50.00	22.00	6.25
□ 484 Hank Aaron MVP	50.00	22.00	6.25
□ 485 Ernie Banks MVP	35.00	16.00	4.40
□ 490 Jim Bunning	16.00	7.25	2.00
□ 495 Elston Howard	12.00	5.50	1.50
□ 505 Red Schoendienst	14.00	6.25	1.75
□ 506 Willie Davis	16.00	7.25	2.00
□ 517 Willie McCovey	50.00	22.00	6.25
□ 525 Ron Perranoski	35.00	16.00	4.40
□ 540 Jackie Jensen	35.00	16.00	4.40
□ 541 Roland Sheldon	40.00	18.00	5.00
□ 545 Hoyt Wilhelm	50.00	22.00	6.25
□ 559 Jim Gentile	55.00	25.00	7.00
□ 563 Bob Cerv	45.00	20.00	5.50
□ 568 Bill Skowron AS	40.00	18.00	5.00
□ 570 Nellie Fox AS	40.00	18.00	5.00
□ 571 Bill Mazeroski AS	40.00	18.00	5.00
□ 572 Brooks Robinson AS	90.00	40.00	11.00
□ 573 Ken Boyer AS	40.00	18.00	5.00
□ 574 Luis Aparicio AS	45.00	20.00	5.50
□ 575 Ernie Banks AS	90.00	40.00	11.00
□ 576 Roger Maris AS	160.00	70.00	20.00
□ 577 Hank Aaron AS	160.00	70.00	20.00
□ 578 Mickey Mantle AS	425.00	190.00	52.50
□ 579 Willie Mays AS	160.00	70.00	20.00
□ 580 Al Kaline AS	90.00	40.00	11.00
□ 581 Frank Robinson AS	90.00	40.00	11.00
□ 586 Whitey Ford AS	90.00	40.00	11.00
□ 589 Warren Spahn AS	100.00	30.00	10.00

1962 Topps

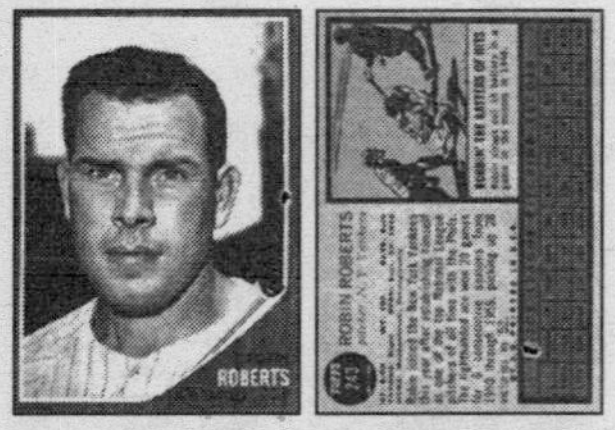

The cards in this 598-card set measure 2 1/2" by 3 1/2". The 1962 Topps set contains a mini-series spotlighting Babe Ruth (135-144). Other subsets in the set include League Leaders (51-60), World Series cards (232-237), In Action cards (311-319), NL All Stars (390-399), AL All Stars (466-475), and Rookie Prospects (591-598). The All-Star selections were again provided by Sport Magazine, as in 1958 and 1960. The second series had two distinct printings which are distinguishable by numerous color and pose variations. Those cards with a distinctive "green tint" are valued at a slight premuim as they are basically the result of a flawed printing process occurring early in the second series run. Card number 139 exists as A: Babe Ruth Special card, B: Hal Reniff with arms over head, or C: Hal Reniff in the same pose as card number 159. In addition, two poses exist for these cards: 129, 132, 134, 147, 174, 176, and 190. The high number series, 523 to 598, is somewhat more difficult to obtain than other cards in the set. Within the last series (523-598) there are 43 cards which were printed in lesser quantities; these are marked SP in the checklist below. In particular, the Rookie Parade subset (591-598) of this last series is even more difficult. This was the first year Topps produced multi-player Rookie Cards. The set price listed does not include the pose variations (see checklist below for individual values). Cards were issued in one-card penny packs as well as five-card nickle packs. The key Rookie Cards in this set are Lou Brock, Tim McCarver, Gaylord Perry, and Bob Uecker.

	NRMT	VG-E	GOOD
COMPLETE SET (598)	4600.00	2100.00	575.00
COMMON CARD (1-370)	5.00	2.20	.60
COMMON CARD (371-446)	6.00	2.70	.75
COMMON CARD (447-522)	12.00	5.50	1.50
COMMON CARD (523-590)	20.00	9.00	2.50
COMMON ROOKIES (591-598)	45.00	20.00	5.50
SP (523/524/526/529/533)	32.00	14.50	4.00
SP (534/540/541/543/546)	32.00	14.50	4.00
SP (549/550/554/555/557)	32.00	14.50	4.00
SP (560/561/566/567/569)	32.00	14.50	4.00
SP (570/571/576/577)	32.00	14.50	4.00
SP (579/585/586/587)	32.00	14.50	4.00
LL (51-60)	7.00	3.10	.85
GREEN TINT (110-196)	6.00	2.70	.75
POSE VAR (129B/132B/134B)	25.00	11.00	3.10
POSE VAR (147B/174B/176B)	25.00	11.00	3.10
POSE VAR (190B)	25.00	11.00	3.10
BABE RUTH STORY (135-144)	20.00	9.00	2.50
WS (232-237)	7.00	3.10	.85
AS (390-399)	6.00	2.70	.75
AS (466-475)	14.00	6.25	1.75
NO EMBLEM (458B/462B)	50.00	22.00	6.25
TEAMS (24/43/61/113/132A)	8.00	3.60	1.00
TEAMS (158/206/226)	8.00	3.60	1.00
TEAMS (294/334)	9.00	4.00	1.10
TEAMS (384/409)	12.00	5.50	1.50
TEAMS (465/476)	16.00	7.25	2.00
TEAMS (537)	50.00	22.00	6.25
TEAMS SP (552/584)	55.00	25.00	7.00
CL (22A/22B/98/192A)	12.00	5.50	1.50
CL (192B/277/367)	12.00	5.50	1.50
CL (441/516)	16.00	7.25	2.00
COMMON DODGERS: 1.25X COM. VALUE			
COMMON METS: 1.25X COM. VALUE			
COMMON YANKEES: 1.25X COM. VALUE			
CARDS PRICED IN NM CONDITION !			

□ 1 Roger Maris	200.00	50.00	20.00
□ 5 Sandy Koufax UER (Struck ou 18)	175.00	80.00	22.00
□ 10 Bob Clemente	225.00	100.00	28.00
□ 18 Managers' Dream Mickey Mantle Willie Mays	200.00	90.00	25.00
□ 20 Rocky Colavito	15.00	6.75	1.85
□ 21 Jim Kaat	8.00	3.60	1.00
□ 25 Ernie Banks	45.00	20.00	5.50
□ 28 Minnie Minoso	6.00	2.70	.75
□ 29 Casey Stengel MG	20.00	9.00	2.50
□ 30 Eddie Mathews	25.00	11.00	3.10
□ 31 Tom Tresh	20.00	9.00	2.50
□ 40 Orlando Cepeda	14.00	6.25	1.75
□ 45 Brooks Robinson	45.00	20.00	5.50
□ 50 Stan Musial	100.00	45.00	12.50
□ 51 AL Batting Leaders Norm Cash Jim Piersall Al Kaline Elston Howard	8.00	3.60	1.00
□ 52 NL Batting Leaders Bob Clemente Vada Pinson Ken Boyer Wally Moon	15.00	6.75	1.85
□ 53 AL Home Run Leaders Roger Maris Mickey Mantle Jim Gentile Harmon Killebrew	110.00	50.00	14.00
□ 54 NL Home Run Leaders Orlando Cepeda Willie Mays Frank Robinson	14.00	6.25	1.75
□ 56 NL ERA Leaders Warren Spahn	8.00	3.60	1.00

Jim O'Toole			
Curt Simmons			
Mike McCormick			
□ 57 AL Wins Leaders	8.00	3.60	1.00
Whitey Ford			
Frank Lary			
Steve Barber			
Jim Bunning			
□ 58 NL Wins Leaders	8.00	3.60	1.00
Warren Spahn			
Joe Jay			
Jim O'Toole			
□ 59 AL Strikeout Leaders	8.00	3.60	1.00
Camilo Pascual			
Whitey Ford			
Jim Bunning			
Juan Pizzaro			
□ 60 NL Strikeout Leaders	12.00	5.50	1.50
Sandy Koufax			
Stan Williams			
Don Drysdale			
Jim O'Toole			
□ 65 Bobby Richardson	12.00	5.50	1.50
□ 70 Harmon Killebrew	25.00	11.00	3.10
□ 73 Nellie Fox	10.00	4.50	1.25
□ 85 Gil Hodges	15.00	6.75	1.85
□ 99 John (Boog) Powell	30.00	13.50	3.70
□ 100 Warren Spahn	30.00	13.50	3.70
□ 110 Bill Skowron	7.00	3.10	.85
□ 139A Babe Ruth Special 5	30.00	13.50	3.70
Babe Hits 60			
□ 139B Hal Reniff PORT	12.00	5.50	1.50
□ 139C Hal Reniff	65.00	29.00	8.00
(Pitching)			
□ 140 Babe Ruth Special 6	50.00	22.00	6.25
With Lou Gehrig			
□ 150 Al Kaline	45.00	20.00	5.50
□ 167 Tim McCarver	30.00	13.50	3.70
□ 170 Ron Santo	14.00	6.25	1.75
□ 175 Frank Howard	6.00	2.70	.75
□ 199 Gaylord Perry	80.00	36.00	10.00
□ 200 Mickey Mantle	450.00	200.00	55.00
□ 208 Billy Martin	14.00	6.25	1.75
□ 209 Jim Fregosi	14.00	6.25	1.75
□ 213 Richie Ashburn	20.00	9.00	2.50
□ 217 Walt Alston MG	7.00	3.10	.85
□ 218 Joe Torre	35.00	16.00	4.40
□ 234 Roger Maris WS	20.00	9.00	2.50
□ 235 Whitey Ford WS	10.00	4.50	1.25
sets new mark			
□ 243 Robin Roberts	16.00	7.25	2.00
□ 250 Norm Cash	8.00	3.60	1.00
□ 251 New York Yankees	60.00	27.00	7.50
Team Card			
□ 286 Al Lopez MG	6.00	2.70	.75
□ 288 Billy Williams	30.00	13.50	3.70
□ 300 Willie Mays	150.00	70.00	19.00
□ 310 Whitey Ford	45.00	20.00	5.50
□ 311 Tony Kubek IA	7.00	3.10	.85
□ 312 Warren Spahn IA	14.00	6.25	1.75
□ 313 Roger Maris IA	35.00	16.00	4.40
Blasts 61th			
□ 314 Rocky Colavito IA	12.00	5.50	1.50
□ 315 Whitey Ford IA	15.00	6.75	1.85
□ 316 Harmon Killebrew IA	15.00	6.75	1.85
□ 317 Stan Musial IA	20.00	9.00	2.50
□ 318 Mickey Mantle IA	175.00	80.00	22.00
□ 320 Hank Aaron	140.00	65.00	17.50
□ 325 Luis Aparicio	16.00	7.25	2.00
□ 340 Don Drysdale	35.00	16.00	4.40
□ 350 Frank Robinson	45.00	20.00	5.50
□ 351 Braves' Backstops	8.00	3.60	1.00
Joe Torre			
Del Crandall			
□ 353 Bill Mazeroski	10.00	4.50	1.25
□ 360 Yogi Berra	75.00	34.00	9.50
□ 385 Early Wynn	18.00	8.00	2.20
□ 387 Lou Brock	125.00	55.00	15.50
□ 390 Orlando Cepeda AS	10.00	4.50	1.25
□ 391 Bill Mazeroski AS	10.00	4.50	1.25
□ 394 Hank Aaron AS	45.00	20.00	5.50
□ 395 Willie Mays AS	50.00	22.00	6.25
□ 396 Frank Robinson AS	16.00	7.25	2.00
□ 398 Don Drysdale AS	16.00	7.25	2.00
□ 399 Warren Spahn AS	16.00	7.25	2.00
□ 400 Elston Howard	10.00	4.50	1.25
□ 401 AL/NL Homer Kings	60.00	27.00	7.50
Roger Maris			
Orlando Cepeda			
□ 423 Rival League	8.00	3.60	1.00
Relief Aces:			
Roy Face			
Hoyt Wilhelm			
□ 425 Carl Yastrzemski	125.00	55.00	15.50
□ 430 Tony Kubek	10.00	4.50	1.25
□ 460 Jim Bunning	18.00	8.00	2.20
□ 461 Ken Hubbs	35.00	16.00	4.40
□ 468 Brooks Robinson AS	25.00	11.00	3.10
□ 469 Luis Aparicio AS	16.00	7.25	2.00
□ 470 Al Kaline AS	25.00	11.00	3.10
□ 471 Mickey Mantle AS	200.00	90.00	25.00
□ 472 Rocky Colavito AS	16.00	7.25	2.00
□ 475 Whitey Ford AS	16.00	7.25	2.00
□ 500 Duke Snider	50.00	22.00	6.25
□ 505 Juan Marichal	45.00	20.00	5.50
□ 527 Dick McAuliffe	25.00	11.00	3.10
□ 530 Bob Gibson SP	150.00	70.00	19.00
□ 544 Willie McCovey SP	115.00	52.50	14.50
□ 545 Hoyt Wilhelm SP	50.00	22.00	6.25
□ 572 Bob G. Miller SP	35.00	16.00	4.40
□ 575 Red Schoendienst SP	45.00	20.00	5.50
□ 590 Curt Flood	25.00	11.00	3.10
□ 591 Rookie Pitchers SP	70.00	32.00	8.75
Sam McDowell			
Ron Taylor			
Ron Nischwitz			
Art Quirk			
Dick Radatz			
□ 592 Rookie Pitchers SP	70.00	32.00	8.75
Dan Pfister			
Bo Belinsky			
Dave Stenhouse			
Jim Bouton			
Joe Bonikowski			
□ 594 Rookie Catchers SP	75.00	34.00	9.50
Doc Edwards			
Ken Retzer			
Bob Uecker			
Doug Camilli			
Don Pavletich			
□ 596 Rookie Infielders SP	70.00	32.00	8.75
Bernie Allen			
Joe Pepitone			
Phil Linz			
Rich Rollins			
□ 598 Rookie Outfielders SP	70.00	20.00	7.00
Al Luplow			
Manny Jimenez			
Howie Goss			
Jim Hickman			
Ed Olivares			

1963 Topps

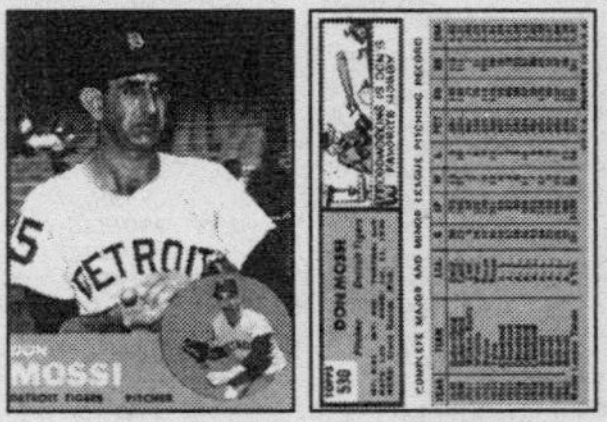

The cards in this 576-card set measure 2 1/2" by 3 1/2". The sharp color photographs of the 1963 set are a vivid contrast to the drab pictures of 1962. In addition to the "League Leaders" series (1-10) and World Series cards (142-148), the seventh and last series of cards (523-576) contains seven rookie cards (each depicting four players). Cards were issued, among other ways, in one-card penny packs and five-card nickle packs. There were some three-card advertising panels produced by

Topps; the players included are from the first series; one panel shows Hoyt Wilhelm, Don Lock, and Bob Duliba on the front with a Stan Musial ad/endorsement on one of the backs. Key Rookie Cards in this set are Bill Freehan, Tony Oliva, Pete Rose, Willie Stargell and Rusty Staub.

	NRMT	VG-E	GOOD
COMPLETE SET (576)	5000.00	2200.00	600.00
COMMON CARD (1-196)	4.00	1.80	.50
COMMON CARD (197-283)	5.00	2.20	.60
COMMON CARD (284-370)	5.00	2.20	.60
COMMON CARD (371-446)	5.00	2.20	.60
COMMON CARD (447-522)	20.00	9.00	2.50
COMMON CARD (523-576)	15.00	6.75	1.85
LL (1-10)	6.00	2.70	.75
WS (142-148)	6.00	2.70	.75
TEAMS (13/39/63/131)	6.00	2.70	.75
TEAMS (151/162)	6.00	2.70	.75
TEAMS (202/222)	7.00	3.10	.85
TEAMS (288/377/397/417)	10.00	4.50	1.25
TEAMS (451/503)	40.00	18.00	5.00
SP (484)	25.00	11.00	3.10
VAR (454B)	30.00	13.50	3.70
CL (79/102A/102B/191/274)	12.00	5.50	1.50
CL (362/431A)	12.00	5.50	1.50
CL (431B/509A/509B)	30.00	13.50	3.70
COMMON DODGERS: 1.25X COM. VALUE			
COMMON YANKEES: 1.25X COM. VALUE			
CARDS PRICED IN NM CONDITION !			

	NRMT	VG-E	GOOD
□ 1 NL Batting Leaders	40.00	8.00	4.00
Tommy Davis			
Frank Robinson			
Stan Musial			
Hank Aaron			
Bill White			
□ 2 AL Batting Leaders	50.00	22.00	6.25
Pete Runnels			
Mickey Mantle			
Floyd Robinson			
Norm Siebern			
Chuck Hinton			
□ 3 NL Home Run Leaders	30.00	13.50	3.70
Willie Mays			
Hank Aaron			
Frank Robinson			
Orlando Cepeda			
Ernie Banks			
□ 4 AL Home Run Leaders	16.00	7.25	2.00
Harmon Killebrew			
Norm Cash			
Rocky Colavito			
Roger Maris			
Jim Gentile			
Leon Wagner			
□ 5 NL ERA Leaders	20.00	9.00	2.50
Sandy Koufax			
Bob Shaw			
Bob Purkey			
Bob Gibson			
Don Drysdale			
□ 6 AL ERA Leaders	8.00	3.60	1.00
Hank Aguirre			
Robin Roberts			
Whitey Ford			
Eddie Fisher			
Dean Chance			
□ 7 NL Pitching Leaders	8.00	3.60	1.00
Don Drysdale			
Jack Sanford			
Bob Purkey			
Billy O'Dell			
Art Mahaffey			
Joe Jay			
□ 9 NL Strikeout Leaders	16.00	7.25	2.00
Don Drysdale			
Sandy Koufax			
Bob Gibson			
Billy O'Dell			
Dick Farrell			
□ 15 Ken Hubbs UER	6.00	2.70	.75
(No position listed on front of card)			
□ 18 Buc Blasters	70.00	32.00	8.75
Smoky Burgess			
Dick Stuart			
Bob Clemente			
Bob Skinner			
□ 20 Tony Kubek	6.00	2.70	.75
□ 25 Al Kaline	45.00	20.00	5.50
□ 29A 1962 Rookie Stars	7.00	3.10	.85
Sammy Ellis			
Ray Culp			
John Boozer			
Jesse Gonder			
□ 54A 1962 Rookie Stars	16.00	7.25	2.00
Nelson Mathews			
Harry Fanok			
Jack Cullen			
Dave DeBusschere			
□ 54B 1963 Rookie Stars	8.00	3.60	1.00
Nelson Mathews			
Harry Fanok			
Jack Cullen			
Dave DeBusschere			
□ 60 Elston Howard	6.00	2.70	.75
□ 68 Friendly Foes	25.00	11.00	3.10
Duke Snider			
Gil Hodges			
□ 108 Hoyt Wilhelm	10.00	4.50	1.25
□ 115 Carl Yastrzemski	40.00	18.00	5.00
□ 120 Roger Maris	45.00	20.00	5.50
□ 123 Frank Howard	6.00	2.70	.75
□ 125 Robin Roberts	14.00	6.25	1.75
□ 126 Bob Uecker	14.00	6.25	1.75
□ 135 Richie Ashburn	20.00	9.00	2.50
□ 138 Pride of NL	70.00	32.00	8.75
Willie Mays			
Stan Musial			
□ 141 Manny Mota	7.00	3.10	.85
□ 142 Whitey Ford WS	8.00	3.60	1.00
□ 144 Roger Maris WS	12.00	5.50	1.50
□ 154 Walt Alston MG	6.00	2.70	.75
□ 165 Jim Kaat	6.00	2.70	.75
□ 169 Rookie Stars	25.00	11.00	3.10
Dick Egan			
Julio Navarro			
Tommie Sisk			
Gaylord Perry			
□ 173 Bombers' Best	200.00	90.00	25.00
Tom Tresh			
Mickey Mantle			
Bobby Richardson			
□ 183 Joe Pepitone	6.00	2.70	.75
□ 190 Minnie Minoso	6.00	2.70	.75
□ 200 Mickey Mantle	550.00	250.00	70.00
□ 205 Luis Aparicio	16.00	7.25	2.00
□ 210 Sandy Koufax	175.00	80.00	22.00
□ 228 Rookie Stars	40.00	18.00	5.00
Max Alvis			
Bob Bailey			
Tony Oliva			
(Listed as Pedro)			
Ed Kranepool			
□ 233 Casey Stengel MG	20.00	9.00	2.50
□ 240 Rocky Colavito	16.00	7.25	2.00
□ 242 Power Plus	60.00	27.00	7.50
Ernie Banks			
Hank Aaron			
□ 245 Gil Hodges	20.00	9.00	2.50
□ 247 Yankees Team	40.00	18.00	5.00
□ 250 Stan Musial	125.00	55.00	15.50
□ 252 Ron Santo	10.00	4.50	1.25
□ 275 Eddie Mathews	20.00	9.00	2.50
□ 300 Willie Mays	135.00	60.00	17.00
□ 306 Star Receivers	7.00	3.10	.85
Earl Battey			
Elston Howard			
□ 312 Houston Colts	25.00	11.00	3.10
Team Card			
□ 317 Sam McDowell	8.00	3.60	1.00
□ 320 Warren Spahn	40.00	18.00	5.00
□ 323 Bill Mazeroski	8.00	3.60	1.00
□ 337 Dodgers Team	25.00	11.00	3.10
□ 340 Yogi Berra P/CO	70.00	32.00	8.75
□ 345 Brooks Robinson	60.00	27.00	7.50
□ 347 Joe Torre	12.00	5.50	1.50
□ 353 Billy Williams	30.00	13.50	3.70
□ 360 Don Drysdale	40.00	18.00	5.00
□ 365 Jim Bunning	16.00	7.25	2.00

□ 375	Ken Boyer	8.00	3.60	1.00
□ 380	Ernie Banks UER	75.00	34.00	9.50
	(Back has career Major and Minor, but he never played in Minors)			
□ 390	Hank Aaron	125.00	55.00	15.50
□ 394	Tim McCarver	14.00	6.25	1.75
□ 398	Boog Powell	25.00	11.00	3.10
□ 400	Frank Robinson	60.00	27.00	7.50
□ 401	Jim Bouton	14.00	6.25	1.75
□ 412	Dodger Big Three	40.00	18.00	5.00
	Johnny Podres			
	Don Drysdale			
	Sandy Koufax			
□ 415	Bob Gibson	60.00	27.00	7.50
□ 420	Bobby Richardson	14.00	6.25	1.75
□ 440	Juan Marichal	30.00	13.50	3.70
□ 445	Norm Cash	7.00	3.10	.85
□ 446	Whitey Ford	40.00	18.00	5.00
□ 466	Rookie Stars SP	60.00	27.00	7.50
	Nate Oliver			
	Tony Martinez			
	Bill Freehan			
	Jerry Robinson			
□ 470	Tom Tresh SP	60.00	27.00	7.50
□ 472	Lou Brock	100.00	45.00	12.50
□ 473	New York Mets	100.00	45.00	12.50
	Team Card			
□ 490	Willie McCovey	125.00	55.00	15.50
□ 495	Frank Thomas SP	30.00	13.50	3.70
□ 500	Harmon Killebrew SP	150.00	70.00	19.00
□ 520	Orlando Cepeda	30.00	13.50	3.70
□ 524	Cardinals Team	30.00	13.50	3.70
□ 525	Nellie Fox	30.00	13.50	3.70
□ 537	Rookie Stars	1000.00	450.00	125.00
	Pedro Gonzalez			
	Ken McMullen			
	Al Weis			
	Pete Rose			
□ 540	Bob Clemente	375.00	170.00	47.50
□ 544	Rookie Stars	40.00	18.00	5.00
	Duke Carmel			
	Bill Haas			
	Rusty Staub			
	Dick Phillips			
□ 550	Duke Snider	75.00	34.00	9.50
□ 552	Detroit Tigers	45.00	20.00	5.50
	Team Card			
□ 553	Rookie Stars	125.00	55.00	15.50
	Brock Davis			
	Jim Gosger			
	Willie Stargell			
	John Herrnstein			
□ 562	Rookie Stars	25.00	11.00	3.10
	Randy Cardinal			
	Dave McNally			
	Ken Rowe			
	Don Rowe			
□ 576	Johnny Temple	20.00	7.50	2.10

1964 Topps

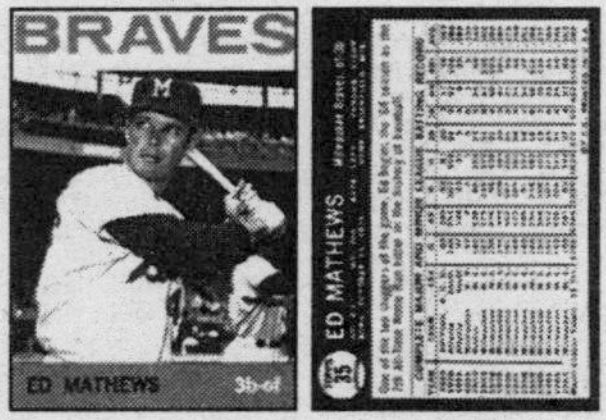

The cards in this 587-card set measure 2 1/2" by 3 1/2". Players in the 1964 Topps baseball series were easy to sort by team due to the giant block lettering found at the top of each card. The name and position of the player are found underneath the picture, and the card is numbered in a ball design on the orange-colored back. The usual last series scarcity holds for this set (523 to 587). Subsets within this set include League Leaders (1-12) and World Series cards (136-140). Among other vehicles, cards were issued in one-card penny packs as well as five-card nickle packs. There were some three-card advertising panels produced by Topps; the players included are from the first series; one panel shows Walt Alston, Bill Henry, and Vada Pinson on the front with a Mickey Mantle card back on one of the backs. Another panel shows Carl Willey, White Sox Rookies, and Bob Friend on the front with a Mickey Mantle card back on one of the backs. The key Rookie Cards in this set are Richie Allen, Tony Conigliaro, Tommy John, Tony LaRussa, Phil Niekro and Lou Piniella.

		NRMT	VG-E	GOOD
COMPLETE SET (587)		3000.00	1350.00	375.00
COMMON CARD (1-196)		3.00	1.35	.35
COMMON CARD (197-370)		4.00	1.80	.50
COMMON CARD (371-522)		7.00	3.10	.85
COMMON CARD (523-587)		16.00	7.25	2.00
LL (1-12)		6.00	2.70	.75
WS (136-140)		6.00	2.70	.75
TEAMS (67/87/132/151/172)		6.00	2.70	.75
TEAMS (213/237/257)		7.00	3.10	.85
TEAMS (293/318/343)		7.00	3.10	.85
TEAMS (373/403/473/496)		12.00	5.50	1.50
CL (76/102/188/274/362)		10.00	4.50	1.25
CL (438/517B)		16.00	7.25	2.00
CL (517A)		25.00	11.00	3.10
SEMISTARS 1-370		4.50	2.00	.55
COMMON DODGERS: 1.25X COM. VALUE...				
COMMON YANKEES: 1.25X COM. VALUE....				
CARDS PRICED IN NM CONDITION				
□ 1	NL ERA Leaders	30.00	9.00	3.00
	Sandy Koufax			
	Dick Ellsworth			
	Bob Friend			
□ 3	NL Pitching Leaders	18.00	8.00	2.20
	Sandy Koufax			
	Juan Marichal			
	Warren Spahn			
	Jim Maloney			
□ 4	AL Pitching Leaders	10.00	4.50	1.25
	Whitey Ford			
	Camilo Pascual			
	Jim Bouton			
□ 5	NL Strikeout Leaders	14.00	6.25	1.75
	Sandy Koufax			
	Jim Maloney			
	Don Drysdale			
□ 7	NL Batting Leaders	20.00	9.00	2.50
	Tommy Davis			
	Bob Clemente			
	Dick Groat			
	Hank Aaron			
□ 8	AL Batting Leaders	12.00	5.50	1.50
	Carl Yastrzemski			
	Al Kaline			
	Rich Rollins			
□ 9	NL Home Run Leaders	30.00	13.50	3.70
	Hank Aaron			
	Willie McCovey			
	Willie Mays			
	Orlando Cepeda			
□ 10	AL Home Run Leaders	10.00	4.50	1.25
	Harmon Killebrew			
	Dick Stuart			
	Bob Allison			
□ 11	NL RBI Leaders	12.00	5.50	1.50
	Hank Aaron			
	Ken Boyer			
	Bill White			
□ 12	AL RBI Leaders	10.00	4.50	1.25
	Dick Stuart			
	Al Kaline			
	Harmon Killebrew			
□ 13	Hoyt Wilhelm	10.00	4.50	1.25
□ 21	Yogi Berra MG	30.00	13.50	3.70
□ 27	New York Mets	8.00	3.60	1.00
	Team Card			
□ 29	Lou Brock	35.00	16.00	4.40

□ 35 Eddie Mathews	20.00	9.00	2.50
□ 38 Jim Wynn	7.00	3.10	.85
□ 41 Friendly Foes	8.00	3.60	1.00
Willie McCovey			
Leon Wagner			
□ 47 Giants Rookies	5.00	2.20	.60
Jesus Alou			
Ron Herbel			
□ 50 Mickey Mantle	300.00	135.00	38.00
□ 55 Ernie Banks	35.00	16.00	4.40
□ 70 Joe Torre	6.00	2.70	.75
□ 81 All-Star Vets	8.00	3.60	1.00
Nellie Fox			
Harmon Killebrew			
□ 89 Boog Powell	6.00	2.70	.75
□ 109 Rusty Staub	5.00	2.20	.60
□ 116 Twins Rookies	12.00	5.50	1.50
Jay Ward			
Tony Oliva			
□ 120 Don Drysdale	20.00	9.00	2.50
□ 125 Pete Rose	150.00	70.00	19.00
□ 128 Mickey Lolich	20.00	9.00	2.50
□ 136 Sandy Koufax WS	16.00	7.25	2.00
strikes out 15			
□ 146 Indians Rookies	30.00	13.50	3.70
Tommy John			
Bob Chance			
□ 150 Willie Mays	100.00	45.00	12.50
□ 155 Duke Snider	30.00	13.50	3.70
□ 167 Senators Rookies	30.00	13.50	3.70
Mike Brumley			
Lou Piniella			
□ 175 Billy Williams	14.00	6.25	1.75
□ 177 Harmon Killebrew	20.00	9.00	2.50
□ 182 Sox Sockers	14.00	6.25	1.75
Carl Yastrzemski			
Chuck Schilling			
□ 190 Bobby Richardson	8.00	3.60	1.00
□ 200 Sandy Koufax	100.00	45.00	12.50
□ 205 Nellie Fox	10.00	4.50	1.25
□ 210 Carl Yastrzemski	35.00	16.00	4.40
□ 225 Roger Maris	50.00	22.00	6.25
□ 226 Colts Rookies	7.00	3.10	.85
Jerry Grote			
Larry Yellen			
□ 230 Brooks Robinson	35.00	16.00	4.40
□ 243 Phillies Rookies	30.00	13.50	3.70
Richie Allen			
John Herrnstein			
□ 244 Tony LaRussa	30.00	13.50	3.70
□ 247 Dave DeBusschere	6.00	2.70	.75
□ 250 Al Kaline	40.00	18.00	5.00
□ 260 Frank Robinson	35.00	16.00	4.40
□ 265 Jim Bunning	14.00	6.25	1.75
□ 267 Wilbur Wood	7.00	3.10	.85
□ 280 Juan Marichal	14.00	6.25	1.75
□ 285 Robin Roberts	14.00	6.25	1.75
□ 287 Red Sox Rookies	50.00	22.00	6.25
Tony Conigliaro			
Bill Spanswick			
□ 300 Hank Aaron	90.00	40.00	11.00
□ 306 Giant Gunners	35.00	16.00	4.40
Willie Mays			
Orlando Cepeda			
□ 320 Rocky Colavito	14.00	6.25	1.75
□ 324 Casey Stengel MG	16.00	7.25	2.00
□ 331 AL Bombers	175.00	80.00	22.00
Roger Maris			
Norm Cash			
Mickey Mantle			
Al Kaline			
□ 342 Willie Stargell	30.00	13.50	3.70
□ 350 Willie McCovey	20.00	9.00	2.50
□ 360 Joe Pepitone	7.00	3.10	.85
□ 375 Ron Santo	10.00	4.50	1.25
□ 380 Whitey Ford	35.00	16.00	4.40
□ 390 Orlando Cepeda	8.00	3.60	1.00
□ 393 Casey Teaches	10.00	4.50	1.25
Casey Stengel MG			
Ed Kranepool			
□ 400 Warren Spahn	40.00	18.00	5.00
□ 415 Tony Kubek	10.00	4.50	1.25
□ 419 Ken Harrelson	14.00	6.25	1.75
□ 423 Tops in NL	125.00	55.00	15.50
Hank Aaron			
Willie Mays			
□ 429 Tim McCarver	10.00	4.50	1.25
□ 433 Yankees Team	35.00	16.00	4.40
□ 440 Bob Clemente UER	250.00	110.00	31.00
(1960 Pittsburfh)			
□ 456 Dodgers Rookies	10.00	4.50	1.25
Wes Parker			
John Werhas			
□ 460 Bob Gibson	35.00	16.00	4.40
□ 468 Gaylord Perry	40.00	18.00	5.00
□ 470 Jim Bouton	10.00	4.50	1.25
□ 471 Gates Brown	10.00	4.50	1.25
□ 476 Braves Rookies	14.00	6.25	1.75
Rico Carty			
Dick Kelley			
□ 512 Tigers Rookies	14.00	6.25	1.75
Willie Horton			
Joe Sparma			
□ 531 Los Angeles Dodgers	25.00	11.00	3.10
Team Card			
□ 540 Luis Aparicio	20.00	9.00	2.50
□ 541 Braves Rookies	90.00	40.00	11.00
Phil Roof			
Phil Niekro			
□ 543 Bob Uecker	40.00	18.00	5.00
□ 547 Gil Hodges MG	20.00	9.00	2.50
□ 550 Ken Hubbs MEM	35.00	16.00	4.40
□ 561 Phillies Rookies UER	20.00	9.00	2.50
Dave Bennett			
(19 ... is 18)			
Rick Wise			
□ 567 Jim Kaat	18.00	8.00	2.20
□ 570 Bill Mazeroski	18.00	8.00	2.20
□ 579 Red Sox Team	25.00	11.00	3.10
□ 587 Bennie Daniels	18.00	7.25	2.00

1965 Topps

The cards in this 598-card set measure 2 1/2" by 3 1/2". The cards comprising the 1965 Topps set have team names located within a distinctive pennant design below the picture. The cards have blue borders on the reverse and were issued by series. Within this last series (523-598) there are 44 cards that were printed in lesser quantities than the other cards in that series; these shorter-printed cards are marked by SP in the checklist below. Featured subsets within this set include League Leaders (1-12) and World Series cards (132-139). This was the last year Topps issued one-card penny packs. Card were also issued in five-card nickle packs. The key Rookie Cards in this set are Steve Carlton, Jim "Catfish" Hunter, Joe Morgan, Mansori Murakami and Tony Perez.

	NRMT	VG-E	GOOD
COMPLETE SET (598)	3500.00	1600.00	450.00
COMMON CARD (1-196)	2.00	.90	.25
COMMON CARD (197-283)	2.50	1.10	.30
COMMON CARD (284-370)	4.00	1.80	.50
COMMON CARD (371-598)	7.00	3.10	.85
SP (523/524/529/535)	12.00	5.50	1.50
SP (536/538/543/547)	12.00	5.50	1.50
SP (554/555/559/565/566)	12.00	5.50	1.50
SP (568/569/570/571/576)	12.00	5.50	1.50
SP (577/578/579/580)	12.00	5.50	1.50
SP (582/583/586/589)	12.00	5.50	1.50
SP (591/592/593/596)	12.00	5.50	1.50

LL (1-12)	4.00	1.80	.50
WS (132-139)	4.00	1.80	.50
TEAMS (24/57/91/151/173)	5.00	2.20	.60
TEAMS (209/234/267)	6.00	2.70	.75
TEAMS (293/316/338)	7.00	3.10	.85
TEAMS (379/403/426)	10.00	4.50	1.25
TEAMS (481)	12.00	5.50	1.50
CL (79A/79B/104/189/273)	10.00	4.50	1.25
CL (361/443/508)	12.00	5.50	1.50
COMMON DODGERS: 1.25X COM. VALUE			
COMMON YANKEES: 1.25X COM. VALUE			
CARDS PRICED IN NM CONDITION			
□ 1 AL Batting Leaders	20.00	6.00	2.00
Tony Oliva			
Elston Howard			
Brooks Robinson			
□ 2 NL Batting Leaders	24.00	11.00	3.00
Bob Clemente			
Hank Aaron			
Rico Carty			
□ 3 AL Home Run Leaders	40.00	18.00	5.00
Harmon Killebrew			
Mickey Mantle			
Boog Powell			
□ 4 NL Home Run Leaders	14.00	6.25	1.75
Willie Mays			
Billy Williams			
Jim Ray Hart			
Orlando Cepeda			
Johnny Callison			
□ 5 AL RBI Leaders	40.00	18.00	5.00
Brooks Robinson			
Harmon Killebrew			
Mickey Mantle			
Dick Stuart			
□ 6 NL RBI Leaders	8.00	3.60	1.00
Ken Boyer			
Willie Mays			
Ron Santo			
□ 8 NL ERA Leaders	20.00	9.00	2.50
Sandy Koufax			
Don Drysdale			
□ 12 NL Strikeout Leaders	8.00	3.60	1.00
Bob Veale			
Don Drysdale			
Bob Gibson			
□ 15 Robin Roberts	10.00	4.50	1.25
□ 16 Houston Rookies	70.00	32.00	8.75
Joe Morgan			
Sonny Jackson			
□ 20 Jim Bunning	10.00	4.50	1.25
□ 30 Jim Bouton	5.00	2.20	.60
□ 50 Juan Marichal	10.00	4.50	1.25
□ 55 Tony Conigliaro	15.00	6.75	1.85
□ 62 Jim Kaat UER	5.00	2.20	.60
(Misspelled Katt)			
□ 65 Tony Kubek	4.00	1.80	.50
□ 74 Red Sox Rookies	12.00	5.50	1.50
Rico Petrocelli			
Jerry Stephenson			
□ 82 Braves Rookies	6.00	2.70	.75
Santos Alomar			
John Braun			
□ 95 Bill Mazeroski	4.00	1.80	.50
□ 99 Gil Hodges MG	7.00	3.10	.85
□ 110 Ron Santo	5.00	2.20	.60
□ 115 Bobby Richardson	5.00	2.20	.60
□ 120 Frank Robinson	35.00	16.00	4.40
□ 126 Dodgers Team	5.00	2.20	.60
□ 130 Al Kaline	35.00	16.00	4.40
□ 134 Mickey Mantle WS	75.00	34.00	9.50
Mantle's Clutch HR			
□ 138 Bob Gibson WS	12.00	5.50	1.50
□ 145 Luis Tiant	18.00	8.00	2.20
□ 150 Brooks Robinson	35.00	16.00	4.40
□ 155 Roger Maris	40.00	18.00	5.00
□ 160 Bob Clemente UER	150.00	70.00	19.00
(1960 Pittsburfh)			
□ 170 Hank Aaron	90.00	40.00	11.00
□ 176 Willie McCovey	20.00	9.00	2.50
□ 187 Casey Stengel MG	15.00	6.75	1.85
□ 193 Gaylord Perry	18.00	8.00	2.20
□ 200 Joe Torre	5.00	2.20	.60
□ 205 Warren Spahn	30.00	13.50	3.70
□ 207 Pete Rose	150.00	70.00	19.00

□ 208 Tommy John	8.00	3.60	1.00
□ 217 Walt Alston MG	4.00	1.80	.50
□ 220 Billy Williams	10.00	4.50	1.25
□ 236 Denny McLain	30.00	13.50	3.70
□ 250 Willie Mays	100.00	45.00	12.50
□ 251 Billy Herman MG	4.00	1.80	.50
□ 259 Tigers Rookies	7.00	3.10	.85
Jim Northrup			
Ray Oyler			
□ 260 Don Drysdale	20.00	9.00	2.50
□ 266 Bert Campaneris	10.00	4.50	1.25
□ 276 Hoyt Wilhelm	10.00	4.50	1.25
□ 282 Giants Rookies	35.00	16.00	4.40
Dick Estelle			
Masanori Murakami			
□ 294 Tim McCarver	7.00	3.10	.85
□ 297 Dave DeBusschere	6.00	2.70	.75
□ 300 Sandy Koufax	120.00	55.00	15.00
□ 320 Bob Gibson	40.00	18.00	5.00
□ 321 Rusty Staub	5.00	2.20	.60
□ 330 Whitey Ford	35.00	16.00	4.40
□ 335 Mickey Lolich	8.00	3.60	1.00
□ 340 Tony Oliva	18.00	8.00	2.20
□ 350 Mickey Mantle	550.00	250.00	70.00
□ 360 Orlando Cepeda	8.00	3.60	1.00
□ 377 Willie Stargell	30.00	13.50	3.70
□ 380 Rocky Colavito	16.00	7.25	2.00
□ 385 Carl Yastrzemski	70.00	32.00	8.75
□ 400 Harmon Killebrew	40.00	18.00	5.00
□ 410 Luis Aparicio	10.00	4.50	1.25
□ 414 Al Lopez MG	8.00	3.60	1.00
□ 415 Curt Flood	10.00	4.50	1.25
□ 450 Elston Howard	10.00	4.50	1.25
□ 460 Richie Allen	40.00	18.00	5.00
□ 461 Braves Rookies	50.00	22.00	6.25
Clay Carroll			
Phil Niekro			
□ 470 Yogi Berra P/CO	50.00	22.00	6.25
□ 473 Orioles Rookies	16.00	7.25	2.00
Paul Blair			
Dave Johnson			
□ 477 Cards Rookies	250.00	110.00	31.00
Fritz Ackley			
Steve Carlton			
□ 485 Nellie Fox P/CO	16.00	7.25	2.00
□ 500 Eddie Mathews	35.00	16.00	4.40
□ 510 Ernie Banks	80.00	36.00	10.00
□ 513 New York Yankees	40.00	18.00	5.00
Team Card			
□ 519 Bob Uecker UER	30.00	13.50	3.70
(Posing as a left-handed batter)			
□ 526 Athletics Rookies SP	90.00	40.00	11.00
Rene Lachemann			
Johnny Odom			
Jim Hunter UER			
(Tim on back)			
Skip Lockwood			
□ 527 Jeff Torborg SP	16.00	7.25	2.00
□ 533 Mets Rookies SP	25.00	11.00	3.10
Dan Napoleon			
Ron Swoboda			
Tug McGraw			
Jim Bethke			
□ 540 Lou Brock SP	50.00	22.00	6.25
□ 549 Cubs Rookies SP	20.00	9.00	2.50
Roberto Pena			
Glenn Beckert			
□ 550 Mel Stottlemyre SP	30.00	13.50	3.70
□ 551 New York Mets SP	30.00	13.50	3.70
Team Card			
□ 556 Red Schoendienst	24.00	11.00	3.00
SP MG			
□ 560 Boog Powell SP	24.00	11.00	3.00
□ 572 Baltimore Orioles SP	30.00	13.50	3.70
Team Card			
□ 573 Red Sox Rookies SP	24.00	11.00	3.00
Jim Lonborg			
Gerry Moses			
Bill Schlesinger			
Mike Ryan			
□ 581 NL Rookie Stars SP	90.00	40.00	11.00
Tony Perez			
Dave Ricketts			
Kevin Collins			
□ 598 Al Downing SP	20.00	6.00	2.00

1966 Topps

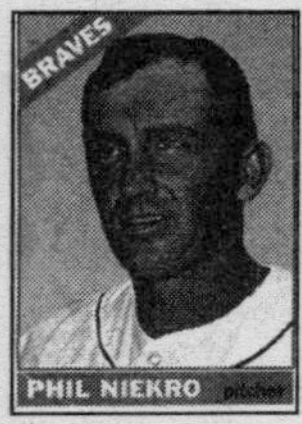

The cards in this 598-card set measure 2 1/2" by 3 1/2". There are the same number of cards as in the 1965 set. Once again, the seventh series cards (523 to 598) are considered more difficult to obtain than the cards of any other series in the set. Within this last series there are 43 cards that were printed in lesser quantities than the other cards in that series; these shorter-printed cards are marked by SP in the checklist below. Among other ways, cards were issued in five-card nickle packs. The only featured subset within this set is League Leaders (215-226). Noteworthy Rookie Cards in the set include Jim Palmer (126), Ferguson Jenkins (254), and Don Sutton (288). Jim Palmer is described in the bio (on his card back) as a left-hander.

	NRMT	VG-E	GOOD
COMPLETE SET (598)	4000.00	1800.00	500.00
COMMON CARD (1-109)	1.50	.70	.19
COMMON CARD (110-283)	2.00	.90	.25
COMMON CARD (284-370)	3.00	1.35	.35
COMMON CARD (371-446)	5.00	2.20	.60
COMMON CARD (447-522)	9.00	4.00	1.10
COMMON CARD (523-598)	15.00	6.75	1.85
SP (524/525/528/532/533)	30.00	13.50	3.70
SP (538/541/543-545/548)	30.00	13.50	3.70
SP (551/552/554/555/556)	30.00	13.50	3.70
SP (557/559/564)	30.00	13.50	3.70
SP (569/570/571/576/577)	30.00	13.50	3.70
SP (578/586/589/593)	30.00	13.50	3.70
VAR (43A/43B/43C)	2.00	.90	.25
VAR (62B/103B/104B)	40.00	18.00	5.00
LL (215-226)	5.00	2.20	.60
TEAMS (19/59)	4.00	1.80	.50
TEAMS (131/172/194)	5.00	2.20	.60
TEAMS (204/238/259)	5.00	2.20	.60
TEAMS (303/326)	5.00	2.20	.60
TEAMS (379/404/426)	10.00	4.50	1.25
TEAMS (463/492)	14.00	6.25	1.75
CL (34/183A/183B/279A/279B)	8.00	3.60	1.00
CL (101B/363/444)	10.00	4.50	1.25
CL (101A/517A/517B)	16.00	7.25	2.00
COMMON DODGERS: 1.25X COM. VALUE			
COMMON YANKEES: 1.25X COM. VALUE			
CARDS PRICED IN NM CONDITION			
LAST SERIES CONDITION SENSITIVE			

□ 1 Willie Mays	135.00	42.50	16.00
□ 24 Don Kessinger	5.00	2.20	.60
□ 28 Phil Niekro	20.00	9.00	2.50
□ 30 Pete Rose DP	35.00	16.00	4.40
□ 36 Jim Hunter UER	20.00	9.00	2.50
(Stats say 1963 and 1964, should be 1963 and 1964)			
□ 50 Mickey Mantle DP	200.00	90.00	25.00
□ 70 Carl Yastrzemski	25.00	11.00	3.10
□ 72 Tony Perez	25.00	11.00	3.10
□ 76 Red Schoendienst MG	4.00	1.80	.50
□ 80 Richie Allen	5.00	2.20	.60
□ 90 Luis Aparicio	7.00	3.10	.85
□ 91A Bob Uecker TR	12.00	5.50	1.50
□ 91B Bob Uecker NTR	40.00	18.00	5.00
□ 92 Yankees Team	14.00	6.25	1.75
□ 99 Buc Belters	6.00	2.70	.75
Willie Stargell			
Donn Clendenon			
□ 100 Sandy Koufax	75.00	34.00	9.50
□ 106 Rusty Staub	4.00	1.80	.50
□ 110 Ernie Banks	30.00	13.50	3.70
□ 116 Walt Alston MG	4.00	1.80	.50
□ 120 Harmon Killebrew	16.00	7.25	2.00
□ 124 Tug McGraw	4.00	1.80	.50
□ 125 Lou Brock	20.00	9.00	2.50
□ 126 Jim Palmer UER	100.00	45.00	12.50
(Described as a lefthander on card back)			
□ 130 Joe Torre	4.00	1.80	.50
□ 132 Orlando Cepeda	5.00	2.20	.60
□ 150 Rocky Colavito	8.00	3.60	1.00
□ 160 Whitey Ford	25.00	11.00	3.10
□ 167 Boog Powell	5.00	2.20	.60
□ 195 Joe Morgan	14.00	6.25	1.75
□ 200 Eddie Mathews	14.00	6.25	1.75
□ 210 Bill Mazeroski	5.00	2.20	.60
□ 215 NL Batting Leaders	50.00	22.00	6.25
Bob Clemente			
Hank Aaron			
Willie Mays			
□ 216 AL Batting Leaders	6.00	2.70	.75
Tony Oliva			
Carl Yastrzemski			
Vic Davalillo			
□ 217 NL Home Run Leaders	20.00	9.00	2.50
Willie Mays			
Willie McCovey			
Billy Williams			
□ 219 NL RBI Leaders	12.00	5.50	1.50
Deron Johnson			
Frank Robinson			
Willie Mays			
□ 221 NL ERA Leaders	12.00	5.50	1.50
Sandy Koufax			
Juan Marichal			
Vern Law			
□ 223 NL Pitching Leaders	12.00	5.50	1.50
Sandy Koufax			
Tony Cloninger			
Don Drysdale			
□ 225 NL Strikeout Leaders	12.00	5.50	1.50
Sandy Koufax			
Bob Veale			
Bob Gibson			
□ 234 Yankees Rookies	8.00	3.60	1.00
Rich Beck			
Roy White			
□ 254 Phillies Rookies	80.00	36.00	10.00
Ferguson Jenkins			
Bill Sorrell			
□ 255 Willie Stargell	20.00	9.00	2.50
□ 275 Tim McCarver	4.00	1.80	.50
□ 276 Jim Bouton	4.00	1.80	.50
□ 288 Dodgers Rookies	45.00	20.00	5.50
Bill Singer			
Don Sutton			
□ 290 Ron Santo	5.00	2.20	.60
□ 300 Bob Clemente	150.00	70.00	19.00
□ 310 Frank Robinson	30.00	13.50	3.70
□ 320 Bob Gibson	25.00	11.00	3.10
□ 348 Orioles Team	7.00	3.10	.85
□ 350 Mel Stottlemyre	5.00	2.20	.60
□ 365 Roger Maris	35.00	16.00	4.40
□ 380 Tony Conigliaro	10.00	4.50	1.25
□ 386 Gil Hodges MG	8.00	3.60	1.00
□ 390 Brooks Robinson	45.00	20.00	5.50
□ 392 Cubs Rookies	7.00	3.10	.85
Bill Hands			
Randy Hundley			
□ 405 Elston Howard	6.00	2.70	.75
□ 410 Al Kaline	35.00	16.00	4.40
□ 420 Juan Marichal	14.00	6.25	1.75
□ 424 Reds Rookies	10.00	4.50	1.25
Lee May			
Darrell Osteen			
□ 430 Don Drysdale	20.00	9.00	2.50
□ 435 Jim Bunning	14.00	6.25	1.75
□ 445 Jim Kaat	10.00	4.50	1.25
□ 447 Dick Ellsworth UER	12.00	5.50	1.50
(Photo actually Ken Hubbs)			

□ 450 Tony Oliva	10.00	4.50	1.25
□ 455 Mickey Lolich	10.00	4.50	1.25
□ 469 Yankees Rookies Bobby Murcer Dooley Womack	25.00	11.00	3.10
□ 486 Tommy John	10.00	4.50	1.25
□ 490 Bobby Richardson	12.00	5.50	1.50
□ 500 Hank Aaron	125.00	55.00	15.50
□ 510 Hoyt Wilhelm	16.00	7.25	2.00
□ 515 Frank Howard	14.00	6.25	1.75
□ 526 Twins Team SP	100.00	45.00	12.50
□ 530 Robin Roberts	60.00	27.00	7.50
□ 535 Willie Davis SP	40.00	18.00	5.00
□ 540 Denny McLain SP	80.00	36.00	10.00
□ 547 Horace Clarke SP	40.00	18.00	5.00
□ 550 Willie McCovey SP	90.00	40.00	11.00
□ 558 Red Sox Rookies Guido Grilli Pete Magrini George Scott	20.00	9.00	2.50
□ 565 Jim Piersall SP	40.00	18.00	5.00
□ 567 Dick Howser SP	40.00	18.00	5.00
□ 579 Orioles Rookies Frank Bertaina Gene Brabender Dave Johnson	20.00	9.00	2.50
□ 580 Billy Williams SP	70.00	32.00	8.75
□ 583 Tigers Team SP UER (Text on back states Tigers finished third in 1966 instead of fourth.)	125.00	55.00	15.50
□ 590 Bill Skowron SP	40.00	18.00	5.00
□ 591 NL Rookies SP Bart Shirley Grant Jackson	40.00	18.00	5.00
□ 598 Gaylord Perry SP	175.00	50.00	15.00

1967 Topps

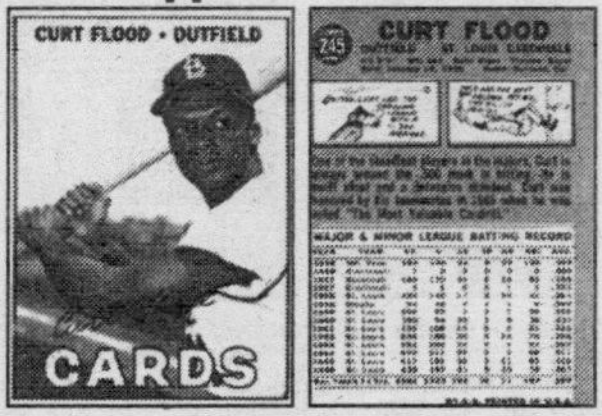

The cards in this 609-card set measure 2 1/2" by 3 1/2". The 1967 Topps series is considered by some collectors to be one of the company's finest accomplishments in baseball card production. Excellent color photographs are combined with easy-to-read backs. Cards 458 to 533 are slightly harder to find than numbers 1 to 457, and the inevitable high series (534 to 609) exists. Each checklist card features a small circular picture of a popular player included in that series. Printing discrepancies resulted in some high series cards being in shorter supply. The checklist below identifies (by DP) 22 double-printed high numbers; of the 76 cards in the last series, 54 cards were short printed and the other 22 cards are much more plentiful. Featured subsets within this set include World Series cards (151-155) and League Leaders (233-244). A limited number of "proof" Roger Maris cards were produced. These cards are blank backed and Maris is listed as a New York Yankee on it. The Maris card is currently valued between $500 and $1000. The key Rookie Cards in the set are high number cards of Rod Carew and Tom Seaver. Confirmed methods of selling these cards include five-card nickle wax packs. Although rarely seen, there exists a salesman's sample panel of three cards that pictures Earl Battey, Manny Mota, and Gene Brabender with ad information on the back about the "new" Topps cards.

	NRMT	VG-E	GOOD
COMPLETE SET (609)	4600.00	2100.00	575.00
COMMON CARD (1-109)	1.50	.70	.19
COMMON CARD (110-283)	2.00	.90	.25
COMMON CARD (284-370)	2.50	1.10	.30
COMMON CARD (371-457)	4.00	1.80	.50
COMMON CARD (458-533)	6.00	2.70	.75
COMMON CARD (534-609)	16.00	7.25	2.00
WS (151-155)	4.00	1.80	.50
LL (233-244)	4.00	1.80	.50
TEAMS (102)	3.00	1.35	.35
TEAMS (173/211/262)	4.00	1.80	.50
TEAMS (302/327/354)	6.00	2.70	.75
TEAMS (378/407/437)	8.00	3.60	1.00
TEAMS (477/492/503/516)	15.00	6.75	1.85
TEAMS (544/573)	30.00	13.50	3.70
VAR (26A/86A/417A)	30.00	13.50	3.70
CL (62/278)	7.00	3.10	.85
CL DP (454A/454B)	8.00	3.60	1.00
DP (534/537/539/547/548)	9.00	4.00	1.10
DP (551/554/556/559/562)	9.00	4.00	1.10
DP (564/566/582/588/589)	9.00	4.00	1.10
DP (596/599/601/608)	9.00	4.00	1.10
COMMON DODGERS: 1.25X COM. VALUE			
COMMON RED SOX: 1.25 COM. VALUE			
COMMON YANKEES: 1.25X COM. VALUE			
CARDS PRICED IN NM CONDITION			

□ 1 The Champs DP Frank Robinson Hank Bauer MG Brooks Robinson	20.00	6.00	2.00
□ 5 Whitey Ford UER (1953 listed as 1933 in stats on back)	20.00	9.00	2.50
□ 20 Orlando Cepeda	6.00	2.70	.75
□ 25 Elston Howard	4.00	1.80	.50
□ 30 Al Kaline DP	16.00	7.25	2.00
□ 33 Athletic Rookies Sal Bando Randy Schwartz	5.00	2.20	.60
□ 42 Mets Team	8.00	3.60	1.00
□ 45 Roger Maris	30.00	13.50	3.70
□ 50 Tony Oliva	6.00	2.70	.75
□ 55 Don Drysdale	16.00	7.25	2.00
□ 60 Luis Aparicio	6.00	2.70	.75
□ 63 Cards' Clubbers Lou Brock Curt Flood	9.00	4.00	1.10
□ 70 Ron Santo	4.00	1.80	.50
□ 73 Rusty Staub	4.00	1.80	.50
□ 88 Mickey Lolich	4.00	1.80	.50
□ 93 Yankees Rookies Stan Bahnsen Bobby Murcer	4.00	1.80	.50
□ 100 Frank Robinson DP	14.00	6.25	1.75
□ 103 Checklist 2 Mickey Mantle	16.00	3.20	1.60
□ 109 Tribe Thumpers Rocky Colavito Leon Wagner	5.00	2.20	.60
□ 131 Yankees Team	8.00	3.60	1.00
□ 140 Willie Stargell	20.00	9.00	2.50
□ 146 Steve Carlton	70.00	32.00	8.75
□ 150 Mickey Mantle	300.00	135.00	38.00
□ 152 Jim Palmer WS	8.00	3.60	1.00
□ 166 Eddie Mathews	16.00	7.25	2.00
□ 191A Checklist 3 (214 Tom Kelley) (Willie Mays)	8.00	1.60	.80
□ 191B Checklist 3 (214 Dick Kelley) (Willie Mays)	12.00	2.40	1.20
□ 200 Willie Mays UER ('63 Sna Francisco on card back stats)	85.00	38.00	10.50
□ 210 Bob Gibson	20.00	9.00	2.50
□ 215 Ernie Banks	20.00	9.00	2.50
□ 216 Bengal Belters Norm Cash Al Kaline	10.00	4.50	1.25
□ 228 Gil Hodges MG	5.00	2.20	.60
□ 230 Boog Powell	6.00	2.70	.75

□ 234 NL ERA Leaders	15.00	6.75	1.85
Sandy Koufax			
Mike Cuellar			
Juan Marichal			
□ 236 NL Pitching Leaders	25.00	11.00	3.10
Sandy Koufax			
Juan Marichal			
Bob Gibson			
Gaylord Perry			
□ 238 NL Strikeout Leaders	12.00	5.50	1.50
Sandy Koufax			
Jim Bunning			
Bob Veale			
□ 239 AL Batting Leaders	9.00	4.00	1.10
Frank Robinson			
Tony Oliva			
Al Kaline			
□ 241 AL RBI Leaders	9.00	4.00	1.10
Frank Robinson			
Harmon Killebrew			
Boog Powell			
□ 242 NL RBI Leaders	24.00	11.00	3.00
Hank Aaron			
Bob Clemente			
Richie Allen			
□ 243 AL Home Run Leaders	9.00	4.00	1.10
Frank Robinson			
Harmon Killebrew			
Boog Powell			
□ 244 NL Home Run Leaders	20.00	9.00	2.50
Hank Aaron			
Richie Allen			
Willie Mays			
□ 250 Hank Aaron UER	80.00	36.00	10.00
(Second 1961 in stats should be 1962)			
□ 255 Frank Howard	4.00	1.80	.50
□ 266 Pitt Power	5.00	2.20	.60
Willie Stargell			
Donn Clendenon			
□ 280 Tony Conigliaro	10.00	4.50	1.25
□ 285 Lou Brock	20.00	9.00	2.50
□ 294 Walt Alston MG	4.00	1.80	.50
□ 300 Jim Kaat	6.00	2.70	.75
□ 306 Bud Harrelson	6.00	2.70	.75
□ 314 Red Sox Rookies	8.00	3.60	1.00
Mike Andrews			
Reggie Smith			
□ 315 Billy Williams	10.00	4.50	1.25
□ 320 Gaylord Perry	14.00	6.25	1.75
□ 326 Bob Uecker	10.00	4.50	1.25
□ 333 Fergie Jenkins	18.00	8.00	2.20
□ 334 Twin Terrors	6.00	2.70	.75
Bob Allison			
Harmon Killebrew			
□ 337 Joe Morgan	14.00	6.25	1.75
□ 350 Joe Torre	4.00	1.80	.50
□ 355 Carl Yastrzemski	50.00	22.00	6.25
□ 361 Checklist 5	14.00	2.80	1.40
Roberto Clemente			
□ 369 Jim Hunter	18.00	8.00	2.20
□ 371 Jim Lonborg	6.00	2.70	.75
□ 400 Bob Clemente DP	90.00	40.00	11.00
□ 420 Denny McLain	6.00	2.70	.75
□ 422 Hoyt Wilhelm	8.00	3.60	1.00
□ 423 Fence Busters DP	25.00	11.00	3.10
Willie Mays			
Willie McCovey			
□ 430 Pete Rose	80.00	36.00	10.00
□ 445 Don Sutton	25.00	11.00	3.10
□ 450 Richie Allen	9.00	4.00	1.10
□ 456 Phil Niekro	14.00	6.25	1.75
□ 460 Harmon Killebrew	60.00	27.00	7.50
□ 475 Jim Palmer	85.00	38.00	10.50
□ 476 Tony Perez SP	70.00	32.00	8.75
□ 480 Willie McCovey	35.00	16.00	4.40
□ 481 Leo Durocher MG	15.00	6.75	1.85
□ 485 Tim McCarver	20.00	9.00	2.50
□ 500 Juan Marichal	25.00	11.00	3.10
□ 510 Bill Mazeroski	15.00	6.75	1.85
□ 512 Red Schoendienst MG	15.00	6.75	1.85
□ 515 Bert Campaneris	9.00	4.00	1.10
□ 528 Rico Petrocelli	10.00	4.50	1.25
□ 531 Checklist 7	14.00	2.80	1.40
Brooks Robinson			
□ 536 Cubs Rookies	35.00	16.00	4.40
Joe Niekro			
Paul Popovich			
□ 540 Norm Cash	35.00	16.00	4.40
□ 542 Athletics Rookies DP	15.00	6.75	1.85
Rick Monday			
Tony Pierce			
□ 553 Yankees Rookies	25.00	11.00	3.10
Mike Hegan			
Thad Tillotson			
□ 558 Orioles Rookies	50.00	22.00	6.25
Mark Belanger			
Bill Dillman			
□ 560 Jim Bunning	70.00	32.00	8.75
□ 563 Joe Adcock	20.00	9.00	2.50
□ 569 AL Rookies DP	250.00	110.00	31.00
Rod Carew			
Hank Allen			
□ 570 Maury Wills	85.00	38.00	10.50
□ 580 Rocky Colavito	85.00	38.00	10.50
□ 581 Mets Rookies	850.00	375.00	105.00
Bill Denehy			
Tom Seaver			
□ 584 Jim Piersall	25.00	11.00	3.10
□ 587 NL Rookies	25.00	11.00	3.10
Don Shaw			
Gary Sutherland			
□ 600 Brooks Robinson	275.00	125.00	34.00
□ 604 Red Sox Team	125.00	55.00	15.50
□ 605 Mike Shannon	50.00	22.00	6.25
□ 607 Mickey Stanley	35.00	16.00	4.40
□ 609 Tommy John	70.00	23.00	8.25

1968 Topps

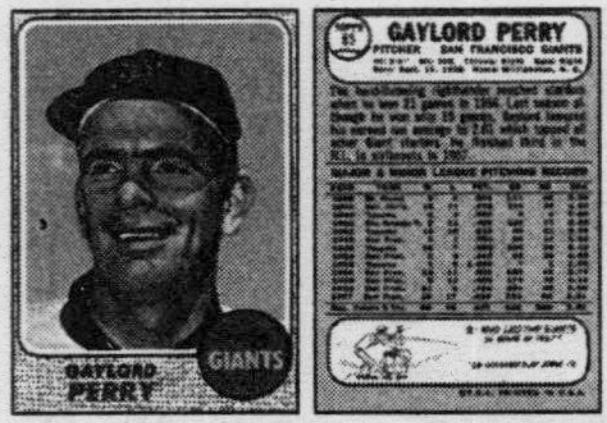

The cards in this 598-card set measure 2 1/2" by 3 1/2". The 1968 Topps set includes Sporting News All-Star Selections as card numbers 361 to 380. Other subsets in the set include League Leaders (1-12) and World Series cards (151-158). The front of each checklist card features a picture of a popular player inside a circle. Higher numbers 458 to 598 are slightly more difficult to obtain. The first series looks different from the other series, as it has a lighter, wider mesh background on the card front. The later series all had a much darker, finer mesh pattern. Among other fashions, cards were issued in five-card nickle packs. The key Rookie Cards in the set are Johnny Bench and Nolan Ryan.

	NRMT	VG-E	GOOD
COMPLETE SET (598)	3000.00	1350.00	375.00
COMMON CARD (1-457)	1.75	.80	.22
COMMON CARD (458-598)	3.50	1.55	.45
LL (1-12)	3.50	1.55	.45
WS (151-158)	4.50	2.00	.55
AS (361-380)	2.50	1.10	.30
VAR (49B)	50.00	22.00	6.25
VAR (66B)	100.00	45.00	12.50
VAR (400B)	150.00	70.00	19.00
TEAMS (137/168/221/252)	3.50	1.55	.45
TEAMS (308/334/401/424)	3.50	1.55	.45
TEAMS (477/497)	7.00	3.10	.85
TEAMS (554/574)	8.00	3.60	1.00
CL (67/107A/107B)	6.00	2.70	.75
CL (278/356A/356B)	6.00	2.70	.75
CL (192A/192B/454A/454B)	7.50	3.40	.95
CL (518A/518B)	12.00	5.50	1.50

LO SEMISTARS	3.00	1.35	.35
HI SEMISTARS	5.00	2.20	.60
COMMON DODGERS: 1.25X COM. VALUE			
COMMON TIGERS: 1.25X COM. VALUE			
COMMON YANKEES: 1.25X COM. VALUE			
CARDS PRICED IN NM CONDITION			
□ 1 NL Batting Leaders	30.00	12.00	6.00
Bob Clemente			
Tony Gonzalez			
Matty Alou			
□ 2 AL Batting Leaders	14.00	6.25	1.75
Carl Yastrzemski			
Frank Robinson			
Al Kaline			
□ 3 NL RBI Leaders	20.00	9.00	2.50
Orlando Cepeda			
Bob Clemente			
Hank Aaron			
□ 4 AL RBI Leaders	12.00	5.50	1.50
Carl Yastrzemski			
Harmon Killebrew			
Frank Robinson			
□ 5 NL Home Run Leaders	8.00	3.60	1.00
Hank Aaron			
Jim Wynn			
Ron Santo			
Willie McCovey			
□ 6 AL Home Run Leaders	8.00	3.60	1.00
Carl Yastrzemski			
Harmon Killebrew			
Frank Howard			
□ 9 NL Pitching Leaders	4.00	1.80	.50
Mike McCormick			
Ferguson Jenkins			
Jim Bunning			
Claude Osteen			
□ 10A AL Pitching Leaders	4.00	1.80	.50
Jim Lonborg ERR			
(Misspelled Lonberg			
on card back)			
Earl Wilson			
Dean Chance			
□ 10B AL Pitching Leaders	4.00	1.80	.50
Jim Lonborg COR			
Earl Wilson			
Dean Chance			
□ 11 NL Strikeout Leaders	5.00	2.20	.60
Jim Bunning			
Ferguson Jenkins			
Gaylord Perry			
□ 16 Indians Rookies	4.00	1.80	.50
Lou Piniella			
Richie Scheinblum			
□ 20 Brooks Robinson	25.00	11.00	3.10
□ 27 Gil Hodges MG	8.00	3.60	1.00
□ 30 Joe Torre	4.00	1.80	.50
□ 37 Billy Williams	10.00	4.50	1.25
□ 40 Denny McLain	10.00	4.50	1.25
□ 45 Tom Seaver	50.00	22.00	6.25
□ 50 Willie Mays	65.00	29.00	8.00
□ 58 Eddie Mathews	16.00	7.25	2.00
□ 72 Tommy John	5.00	2.20	.60
□ 80 Rod Carew	50.00	22.00	6.25
□ 85 Gaylord Perry	8.00	3.60	1.00
□ 86 Willie Stargell	8.00	3.60	1.00
□ 99 Rocky Colavito	7.00	3.10	.85
□ 100 Bob Gibson	25.00	11.00	3.10
□ 103 Don Sutton	6.00	2.70	.75
□ 110 Hank Aaron	60.00	27.00	7.50
□ 130 Tony Perez	8.00	3.60	1.00
□ 140 Tony Conigliaro	8.00	3.60	1.00
□ 144 Joe Morgan	12.00	5.50	1.50
□ 145 Don Drysdale	12.00	5.50	1.50
□ 150 Bob Clemente	70.00	32.00	8.75
□ 151 Lou Brock WS	10.00	4.50	1.25
□ 152 Carl Yastrzemski WS	10.00	4.50	1.25
□ 154 Bob Gibson WS	8.00	3.60	1.00
□ 175 Maury Wills	5.00	2.20	.60
□ 177 Mets Rookies	900.00	400.00	110.00
Jerry Koosman			
Nolan Ryan			
□ 200 Orlando Cepeda	5.00	2.20	.60
□ 205 Juan Marichal	8.00	3.60	1.00
□ 215 Jim Bunning	7.00	3.10	.85
□ 220 Harmon Killebrew	14.00	6.25	1.75
□ 225 Richie Allen	5.00	2.20	.60
□ 230 Pete Rose	40.00	18.00	5.00
□ 235 Ron Santo	5.00	2.20	.60
□ 240 Al Kaline	25.00	11.00	3.10
□ 247 Reds Rookies	125.00	55.00	15.50
Johnny Bench			
Ron Tompkins			
□ 250 Carl Yastrzemski	25.00	11.00	3.10
□ 251 Manny Sanguillen	6.00	2.70	.75
□ 256 Norm Cash	6.00	2.70	.75
□ 257 Phil Niekro	8.00	3.60	1.00
□ 275 Tim McCarver	4.00	1.80	.50
□ 280 Mickey Mantle	250.00	110.00	31.00
□ 290 Willie McCovey	12.00	5.50	1.50
□ 294 Red Schoendienst MG	4.00	1.80	.50
□ 310 Luis Aparicio	7.00	3.10	.85
□ 321 Leo Durocher MG	4.00	1.80	.50
□ 330 Roger Maris	30.00	13.50	3.70
□ 350 Hoyt Wilhelm	6.00	2.70	.75
□ 355 Ernie Banks	25.00	11.00	3.10
□ 361 Harmon Killebrew AS	8.00	3.60	1.00
□ 362 Orlando Cepeda AS	4.00	1.80	.50
□ 363 Rod Carew AS	8.00	3.60	1.00
□ 364 Joe Morgan AS	8.00	3.60	1.00
□ 365 Brooks Robinson AS	8.00	3.60	1.00
□ 369 Carl Yastrzemski AS	10.00	4.50	1.25
□ 370 Hank Aaron AS	20.00	9.00	2.50
□ 372 Lou Brock AS	8.00	3.60	1.00
□ 373 Frank Robinson AS	8.00	3.60	1.00
□ 374 Bob Clemente AS	30.00	13.50	3.70
□ 378 Bob Gibson AS	8.00	3.60	1.00
□ 381 Boog Powell	4.00	1.80	.50
□ 384 Reds Rookies	6.00	2.70	.75
Bill Henry			
Hal McRae			
□ 385 Jim Hunter	12.00	5.50	1.50
□ 390 Bill Mazeroski	4.00	1.80	.50
□ 408 Steve Carlton	30.00	13.50	3.70
□ 410 Fergie Jenkins	12.00	5.50	1.50
□ 414 Mickey Lolich	8.00	3.60	1.00
□ 450 Jim Kaat	5.00	2.20	.60
□ 480 Manager's Dream	80.00	36.00	10.00
Tony Oliva			
Chico Cardenas			
Bob Clemente			
□ 490 Super Stars	175.00	80.00	22.00
Harmon Killebrew			
Willie Mays			
Mickey Mantle			
□ 500 Frank Robinson	30.00	13.50	3.70
□ 505 Joe Sparma	10.00	4.50	1.25
□ 520 Lou Brock	25.00	11.00	3.10
□ 528 Tigers Team	70.00	32.00	8.75
□ 530 Bird Belters	40.00	18.00	5.00
Brooks Robinson			
Frank Robinson			
□ 544 Mayo Smith MG	8.00	3.60	1.00
□ 571 Tony LaRussa	12.00	5.50	1.50
□ 575 Jim Palmer	35.00	16.00	4.40
□ 583 Gates Brown	8.00	3.60	1.00
□ 598 Jerry May	5.00	1.55	.45

1969 Topps

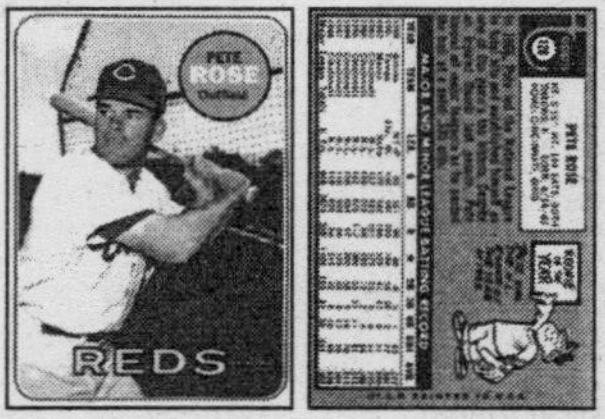

The cards in this 664-card set measure 2 1/2" by 3 1/2". The 1969 Topps set includes Sporting News All-Star Selections as card numbers 416 to 435. Other popular subsets within this set include League Leaders (1-12) and

World Series cards (162-169). The fifth series contains several variations; the more difficult variety consists of cards with the player's first name, last name, and/or position in white letters instead of lettering in some other color. These are designated in the checklist below by WL (white letters). Each checklist card features a different popular player's picture inside a circle on the front of the checklist card. Two different team identifications of Clay Dalrymple and Donn Clendenon exist, as indicated in the checklist. The key Rookie Cards in this set are Rollie Fingers, Reggie Jackson, and Graig Nettles. This was the last year that Topps issued multi-player special star cards, ending a 13-year tradition, which they had begun in 1957. There were cropping differences in checklist cards 57, 214, and 412, due to their each being printed with two different series. The differences are difficult to explain and have not been greatly sought by collectors; hence they are not listed explicitly in the list below. The All-Star cards 426-435, when turned over and placed together, form a puzzle back of Pete Rose. This would turn out to be the final year that Topps issued cards in five-card nickle wax packs.

	NRMT	VG-E	GOOD
COMPLETE SET (664)	2200.00	1000.00	275.00
COMMON CARD (1-218)	1.50	.70	.19
COMMON CARD (219-327)	2.50	1.10	.30
COMMON CARD (328-512)	1.50	.70	.19
COMMON CARD (513-588)	2.00	.90	.25
COMMON CARD (589-664)	3.00	1.35	.35
LL (1-12)	3.50	1.55	.45
WS (162-169)	5.00	2.20	.60
AS (416-425/426-435)	2.50	1.10	.30
WL (441B/444B/447B/451B)	20.00	9.00	2.50
WL (452B/454B/461B/464B)	20.00	9.00	2.50
WL (468B/471B/473B/482B)	20.00	9.00	2.50
WL (486B/491B/493B/501B)	20.00	9.00	2.50
WL (505B/511B)	20.00	9.00	2.50
VAR (47B/49B/77B)	25.00	11.00	3.10
VAR (151B/208B)	16.00	7.25	2.00
CL (57/107A/214/314/582A)	6.00	2.70	.75
CL (107B/582B)	7.50	3.40	.95

*COMMON DODGERS: 1.25X COMMON VALUE
*COMMON YANKEES: 1.25X COMMON VALUE
CARDS PRICED IN NM CONDITION

□ 1 AL Batting Leaders Carl Yastrzemski Danny Cater Tony Oliva	14.00	5.00	2.00
□ 2 NL Batting Leaders Pete Rose Matty Alou Felipe Alou	7.00	3.10	.85
□ 4 NL RBI Leaders Willie McCovey Ron Santo Billy Williams	6.00	2.70	.75
□ 6 NL Home Run Leaders Willie McCovey Richie Allen Ernie Banks	6.00	2.70	.75
□ 8 NL ERA Leaders Bob Gibson Bobby Bolin Bob Veale	5.00	2.20	.60
□ 10 NL Pitching Leaders Juan Marichal Bob Gibson Fergie Jenkins	7.00	3.10	.85
□ 12 NL Strikeout Leaders Bob Gibson Fergie Jenkins Bill Singer	4.00	1.80	.50
□ 15 Boog Powell	3.50	1.55	.45
□ 20 Ernie Banks	18.00	8.00	2.20
□ 35 Joe Morgan	10.00	4.50	1.25
□ 45 Maury Wills	3.00	1.35	.35
□ 50 Bob Clemente UER (Bats Right listed twice)	50.00	22.00	6.25
□ 75 Luis Aparicio	5.00	2.20	.60
□ 82 Pirates Rookies Rich Hebner Al Oliver	10.00	4.50	1.25
□ 85 Lou Brock	18.00	8.00	2.20
□ 95 Johnny Bench	45.00	20.00	5.50
□ 99A Twins Rookies Danny Morris Graig Nettles (No loop)	16.00	7.25	2.00
□ 99B Twins Rookies Danny Morris Graig Nettles (Errant loop in upper left corner of obverse)	16.00	7.25	2.00
□ 100 Hank Aaron	35.00	16.00	4.40
□ 120 Pete Rose	25.00	11.00	3.10
□ 130 Carl Yastrzemski	18.00	8.00	2.20
□ 147 Leo Durocher MG	4.00	1.80	.50
□ 150 Denny McLain	4.00	1.80	.50
□ 162 Bob Gibson WS Fans 17	8.00	3.60	1.00
□ 164 Tim McCarver WS	7.00	3.10	.85
□ 165 Lou Brock WS	8.00	3.60	1.00
□ 166 Al Kaline WS	8.00	3.60	1.00
□ 168 Mickey Lolich WS Bob Gibson	8.00	3.60	1.00
□ 170 Frank Howard	3.00	1.35	.35
□ 175 Jim Bunning	7.00	3.10	.85
□ 190 Willie Mays	45.00	20.00	5.50
□ 200 Bob Gibson	12.00	5.50	1.50
□ 216 Don Sutton	6.00	2.70	.75
□ 230 Rusty Staub UER For 1966 stats, Houston spelled Huoston	4.00	1.80	.50
□ 235 Jim Hunter	10.00	4.50	1.25
□ 237 Bobby Cox	10.00	4.50	1.25
□ 250 Frank Robinson	20.00	9.00	2.50
□ 255 Steve Carlton	30.00	13.50	3.70
□ 260 Reggie Jackson	350.00	160.00	45.00
□ 290 Jim Kaat	4.00	1.80	.50
□ 295 Tony Perez	12.00	5.50	1.50
□ 296 Andy Messersmith	4.00	1.80	.50
□ 304 Padres Rookies Bill Davis Clarence Gaston	8.00	3.60	1.00
□ 311 Sparky Lyle	8.00	3.60	1.00
□ 324 Tiger Rookies Les Cain Dave Campbell	4.00	1.80	.50
□ 330 Tony Conigliaro	5.00	2.20	.60
□ 335 Bill Mazeroski	3.00	1.35	.35
□ 350 Richie Allen	4.00	1.80	.50
□ 355 Phil Niekro	7.00	3.10	.85
□ 370 Juan Marichal	8.00	3.60	1.00
□ 375 Harmon Killebrew	16.00	7.25	2.00
□ 385 Orlando Cepeda	3.50	1.55	.45
□ 394 Pilots Rookies Lou Piniella Marv Staehle	5.00	2.20	.60
□ 400 Don Drysdale	15.00	6.75	1.85
□ 410 Al Kaline	25.00	11.00	3.10
□ 412 Checklist 5 DP Mickey Mantle	12.00	2.40	1.20
□ 416 Willie McCovey AS	7.00	3.10	.85
□ 419 Rod Carew AS	10.00	4.50	1.25
□ 421 Brooks Robinson AS	7.00	3.10	.85
□ 424 Pete Rose AS	15.00	6.75	1.85
□ 425 Carl Yastrzemski AS	10.00	4.50	1.25
□ 428 Lou Brock AS	6.00	2.70	.75
□ 430 Johnny Bench AS	10.00	4.50	1.25
□ 432 Bob Gibson AS	6.00	2.70	.75
□ 440A Willie McCovey	18.00	8.00	2.20
□ 440B Willie McCovey WL (McCovey white)	100.00	45.00	12.50
□ 450 Billy Williams	7.00	3.10	.85
□ 460 Joe Torre	3.50	1.55	.45
□ 462 Red Schoendienst MG	2.50	1.10	.30
□ 465 Tommy John	4.00	1.80	.50
□ 470A Mel Stottlemyre	2.50	1.10	.30
□ 470B Mel Stottlemyre WL (Stottlemyre white)	30.00	13.50	3.70
□ 475 Tim McCarver	3.00	1.35	.35
□ 476A Boston Rookies Ken Brett	3.00	1.35	.35

Gerry Moses			
□ 476B Boston Rookies WL	30.00	13.50	3.70
Ken Brett			
Gerry Moses			
(Names in white)			
□ 480 Tom Seaver	80.00	36.00	10.00
□ 485A Gaylord Perry	10.00	4.50	1.25
□ 485B Gaylord Perry WL	85.00	38.00	10.50
(Perry white)			
□ 500A Mickey Mantle UER	350.00	160.00	45.00
(No Topps copy-right on card back)			
□ 500B Mickey Mantle WL	1000.00	450.00	125.00
(Mantle in white; no Topps copyright on card back) UER			
□ 504 Checklist 6	7.00	1.40	.70
Brooks Robinson			
□ 510 Rod Carew	35.00	16.00	4.40
□ 516 Earl Weaver MG	18.00	8.00	2.20
□ 527 Al Lopez MG	4.00	1.80	.50
□ 533 Nolan Ryan	425.00	190.00	52.50
□ 539 Ted Shows How	8.00	3.60	1.00
Mike Epstein			
Ted Williams MG			
□ 545 Willie Stargell	12.00	5.50	1.50
□ 547 Billy Martin MG	6.00	2.70	.75
□ 550 Brooks Robinson	30.00	13.50	3.70
□ 562 Bob Watson	7.00	3.10	.85
□ 564 Gil Hodges MG	10.00	4.50	1.25
□ 565 Hoyt Wilhelm	7.00	3.10	.85
□ 570 Ron Santo	7.00	3.10	.85
□ 572 Giants Heroes	16.00	7.25	2.00
Willie McCovey			
Juan Marichal			
□ 573 Jim Palmer	35.00	16.00	4.40
□ 587 Joe Rudi	7.00	3.10	.85
□ 597 A.L. Rookies	45.00	20.00	5.50
Bob Floyd			
Larry Burchart			
Rollie Fingers			
□ 600 Tony Oliva	6.00	2.70	.75
□ 601 Tug McGraw	7.00	3.10	.85
□ 630 Bobby Bonds	35.00	16.00	4.40
□ 640 Fergie Jenkins	20.00	9.00	2.50
□ 650 Ted Williams MG	16.00	7.25	2.00
□ 653 Aurelio Rodriguez UER	5.00	2.20	.60
(Photo actually Angels' batboy)			
□ 657 Bobby Murcer	6.00	2.70	.75
□ 660 Reggie Smith	6.00	2.70	.75
□ 664 Ron Hunt	5.00	1.35	.40

1970 Topps

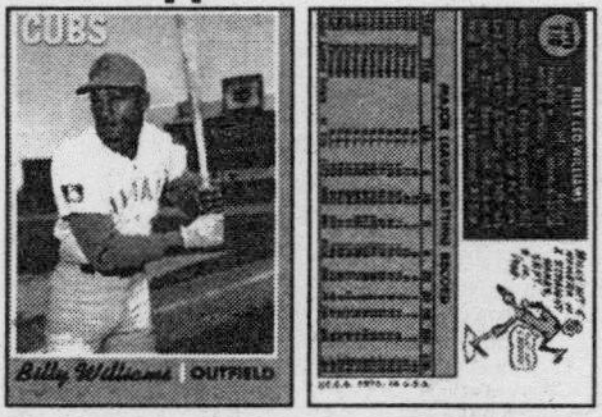

The cards in this 720-card set measure 2 1/2" by 3 1/2". The Topps set for 1970 has color photos surrounded by white frame lines and gray borders. The backs have a blue biographical section and a yellow record section. All-Star selections are featured on cards 450 to 469. Other topical subsets within this set include League Leaders (61-72), Playoffs cards (195-202), and World Series cards (305-310). There are graduations of scarcity, terminating in the high series (634-720), which are outlined in the value summary. Cards were issued in ten-card dime packs as well as thirty-three card cello packs encased in a small Topps box. The key Rookie Card in this set is Thurman Munson.

	NRMT	VG-E	GOOD
COMPLETE SET (720)	1800.00	800.00	220.00
COMMON CARD (1-372)	1.00	.45	.12
COMMON CARD (373-459)	1.50	.70	.19
COMMON CARD (460-546)	2.00	.90	.25
COMMON CARD (547-633)	4.00	1.80	.50
COMMON CARD (634-720)	10.00	4.50	1.25
LL (61-72)	2.00	.90	.25
PLAYOFFS (195-202)	2.50	1.10	.30
WS (305-310)	3.00	1.35	.35
AS (450-459)	2.00	.90	.25
AS (460-469)	2.50	1.10	.30
TEAMS (387/399/411)	3.00	1.35	.35
TEAMS (422/436/448)	3.00	1.35	.35
TEAMS (472/501/509)	3.50	1.55	.45
TEAMS (522/534/544)	3.50	1.55	.45
TEAMS (549/563/579/593)	6.00	2.70	.75
TEAMS (608/631)	6.00	2.70	.75
TEAMS (637/657/676/696)	12.00	5.50	1.50
CL (9)	12.00	5.50	1.50
CL (128A/128B/244A/244B)	6.00	2.70	.75
CL (343A/432A/542/588B)	6.00	2.70	.75
CL (343B/432B)	6.00	2.70	.75
CL (588A)	8.00	3.60	1.00
CARDS PRICED IN NM CONDITION !			

□ 1 New York Mets	16.00	5.00	1.50
Team Card			
□ 10 Carl Yastrzemski	14.00	6.25	1.75
□ 17 Hoyt Wilhelm	5.00	2.20	.60
□ 21 A's Rookies	6.00	2.70	.75
Vida Blue			
Gene Tenace			
□ 61 NL Batting Leaders	12.00	5.50	1.50
Pete Rose			
Bob Clemente			
Cleon Jones			
□ 62 AL Batting Leaders	3.50	1.55	.45
Rod Carew			
Reggie Smith			
Tony Oliva			
□ 63 NL RBI Leaders	4.00	1.80	.50
Willie McCovey			
Ron Santo			
Tony Perez			
□ 64 AL RBI Leaders	6.00	2.70	.75
Harmon Killebrew			
Boog Powell			
Reggie Jackson			
□ 65 NL Home Run Leaders	6.00	2.70	.75
Willie McCovey			
Hank Aaron			
Lee May			
□ 66 AL Home Run Leaders	6.00	2.70	.75
Harmon Killebrew			
Frank Howard			
Reggie Jackson			
□ 67 NL ERA Leaders	7.00	3.10	.85
Juan Marichal			
Steve Carlton			
Bob Gibson			
□ 68 AL ERA Leaders	3.00	1.35	.35
Dick Bosman			
Jim Palmer			
Mike Cuellar			
□ 69 NL Pitching Leaders	7.00	3.10	.85
Tom Seaver			
Phil Niekro			
Fergie Jenkins			
Juan Marichal			
□ 71 NL Strikeout Leaders	4.00	1.80	.50
Fergie Jenkins			
Bob Gibson			
Bill Singer			
□ 140 Reggie Jackson	50.00	22.00	6.25
□ 150 Harmon Killebrew	8.00	3.60	1.00
□ 160 Phil Niekro	5.00	2.20	.60
□ 170 Billy Williams	7.00	3.10	.85
□ 181 Sparky Anderson MG	5.00	2.20	.60
□ 189 Yankees Rookies	50.00	22.00	6.25
Thurman Munson			
Dave McDonald			
□ 195 Tom Seaver NLCS	15.00	6.75	1.85
□ 197 Nolan Ryan NLCS	30.00	13.50	3.70
□ 198 NL Playoff Summary	15.00	6.75	1.85
Mets celebrate			

	(Nolan Ryan)			
□ 210	Juan Marichal	7.00	3.10	.85
□ 211	Ted Williams MG	12.00	5.50	1.50
□ 220	Steve Carlton	15.00	6.75	1.85
□ 230	Brooks Robinson	14.00	6.25	1.75
□ 240	Fergie Jenkins	7.00	3.10	.85
□ 250	Willie McCovey UER	10.00	4.50	1.25
	(1963 San Francisci)			
□ 286	Dodgers Rookies	6.00	2.70	.75
	Jack Jenkins			
	Bill Buckner			
□ 290	Rod Carew	18.00	8.00	2.20
□ 291	Leo Durocher MG	3.00	1.35	.35
□ 300	Tom Seaver	40.00	18.00	5.00
□ 304	Bill Russell	6.00	2.70	.75
□ 310	World Series Summary	5.00	2.20	.60
	Mets whoop it up			
□ 315	Luis Aparicio	5.00	2.20	.60
□ 330	Lou Brock	10.00	4.50	1.25
□ 340	Tony Conigliaro	3.00	1.35	.35
□ 350	Roberto Clemente	70.00	32.00	8.75
□ 380	Tony Perez	7.00	3.10	.85
□ 394	Gil Hodges MG	5.00	2.20	.60
□ 403	Jim Bunning	5.00	2.20	.60
□ 425	Bobby Bonds	6.00	2.70	.75
□ 440	Bill Mazeroski	3.00	1.35	.35
□ 449	Jim Palmer	12.00	5.50	1.50
□ 450	Willie McCovey AS	7.00	3.10	.85
□ 453	Rod Carew AS	7.00	3.10	.85
□ 455	Brooks Robinson AS	7.00	3.10	.85
□ 458	Pete Rose AS	14.00	6.25	1.75
□ 459	Reggie Jackson AS	14.00	6.25	1.75
□ 461	Carl Yastrzemski AS	10.00	4.50	1.25
□ 462	Hank Aaron AS	15.00	6.75	1.85
□ 463	Frank Robinson AS	7.00	3.10	.85
□ 464	Johnny Bench AS	14.00	6.25	1.75
□ 466	Juan Marichal AS	4.00	1.80	.50
□ 470	Willie Stargell	10.00	4.50	1.25
□ 491	Graig Nettles	6.00	2.70	.75
□ 500	Hank Aaron	50.00	22.00	6.25
□ 502	Rollie Fingers	10.00	4.50	1.25
□ 530	Bob Gibson	14.00	6.25	1.75
□ 537	Joe Morgan	10.00	4.50	1.25
□ 539	Phillies Rookies	6.00	2.70	.75
	Denny Doyle			
	Larry Bowa			
□ 555	Orlando Cepeda	6.00	2.70	.75
□ 560	Gaylord Perry	10.00	4.50	1.25
□ 565	Jim Hunter	10.00	4.50	1.25
□ 580	Pete Rose	50.00	22.00	6.25
□ 600	Willie Mays	70.00	32.00	8.75
□ 621	Braves Rookies	10.00	4.50	1.25
	Mike McQueen			
	Darrell Evans			
	Rick Kester			
□ 622	Don Sutton	10.00	4.50	1.25
□ 630	Ernie Banks	50.00	22.00	6.25
□ 640	Al Kaline	50.00	22.00	6.25
□ 654	NL Rookies	12.00	5.50	1.50
	Oscar Gamble			
	Boots Day			
	Angel Mangual			
□ 660	Johnny Bench	100.00	45.00	12.50
□ 670	Ron Santo	12.00	5.50	1.50
□ 700	Frank Robinson	50.00	22.00	6.25
□ 712	Nolan Ryan	375.00	170.00	47.50
□ 713	Seattle Pilots	25.00	11.00	3.10
	Team Card			
□ 720	Rick Reichardt	14.00	4.70	1.35

1971 Topps

The cards in this 752-card set measure 2 1/2" by 3 1/2". The 1971 Topps set is a challenge to complete in strict mint condition because the black obverse border is easily scratched and damaged. An unusual feature of this set is that the player is also pictured in black and white on the back of the card. Featured subsets within this set include League Leaders (61-72), Playoffs cards (195-202), and World Series cards (327-332). Cards 524-643 and the last series (644-752) are somewhat scarce. The last series was printed in two sheets of 132. On the printing sheets 44 cards were printed in 50 percent greater quantity than the other 66 cards. These 66 (slightly) shorter-printed numbers are identified in the checklist below by SP. The key Rookie Cards in this set are the multi-player Rookie Card of Dusty Baker and Don Baylor and the individual cards of Bert Blyleven, Dave Concepcion, Steve Garvey, and Ted Simmons.

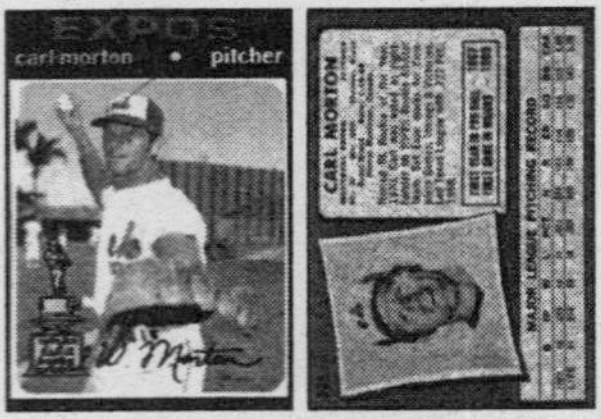

	NRMT	VG-E	GOOD
COMPLETE SET (752)	2000.00	900.00	250.00
COMMON CARD (1-393)	1.75	.80	.22
COMMON CARD (394-523)	2.50	1.10	.30
COMMON CARD (524-643)	4.00	1.80	.50
COMMON CARD (644-752)	8.00	3.60	1.00
LL (61-72)	2.50	1.10	.30
PLAYOFFS (195-202)	2.50	1.10	.30
WS (327-332)	2.50	1.10	.30
TEAMS (268/289/308/336)	3.00	1.35	.35
TEAMS (357/386)	3.00	1.35	.35
TEAMS (402/442/462/482)	5.00	2.20	.60
TEAMS (502/522)	5.00	2.20	.60
TEAMS (543/563/584/603/624)	8.00	3.60	1.00
TEAMS (652/674/742)	12.00	5.50	1.50
TEAMS SP (698/722)	20.00	9.00	2.50
SP (644-646/651)	12.00	5.50	1.50
SP (653-656/658/659)	12.00	5.50	1.50
SP (661/662/664/666/669)	12.00	5.50	1.50
SP (671-673/677/680)	12.00	5.50	1.50
SP (683/686/687/692-694)	12.00	5.50	1.50
SP (697/704-706)	12.00	5.50	1.50
SP (708/711/713-715/717)	12.00	5.50	1.50
SP (719/723-725/727/731)	12.00	5.50	1.50
SP (733-739/743-745/748)	12.00	5.50	1.50
CL (54/123A/123B/161/206)	6.00	2.70	.75
CL (369/499/619A)	6.00	2.70	.75
CL (619B)	10.00	4.50	1.25
CARDS PRICED IN NM CONDITION !			

□ 1	Baltimore Orioles	15.00	5.00	2.00
	Team Card			
□ 5	Thurman Munson	18.00	8.00	2.20
□ 14	Dave Concepcion	18.00	8.00	2.20
□ 16	Ken Singleton	4.00	1.80	.50
□ 20	Reggie Jackson	30.00	13.50	3.70
□ 26	Bert Blyleven	6.00	2.70	.75
□ 30	Phil Niekro	5.00	2.20	.60
□ 45	Jim Hunter	7.00	3.10	.85
□ 50	Willie McCovey	8.00	3.60	1.00
□ 55	Steve Carlton	15.00	6.75	1.85
□ 61	AL Batting Leaders	3.50	1.55	.45
	Alex Johnson			
	Carl Yastrzemski			
	Tony Oliva			
□ 64	NL RBI Leaders	5.00	2.20	.60
	Johnny Bench			
	Tony Perez			
	Billy Williams			
□ 65	AL HR Leaders	4.00	1.80	.50
	Frank Howard			
	Harmon Killebrew			
	Carl Yastrzemski			
□ 66	NL HR Leaders	6.00	2.70	.75
	Johnny Bench			
	Billy Williams			
	Tony Perez			
□ 67	AL ERA Leaders	3.50	1.55	.45
	Diego Segui			
	Jim Palmer			
	Clyde Wright			

□ 68 NL ERA Leaders	3.50	1.55	.45
Tom Seaver			
Wayne Simpson			
Luke Walker			
□ 70 NL Pitching Leaders	6.00	2.70	.75
Bob Gibson			
Gaylord Perry			
Fergie Jenkins			
□ 72 NL Strikeout Leaders	7.00	3.10	.85
Tom Seaver			
Bob Gibson			
Fergie Jenkins			
□ 100 Pete Rose	35.00	16.00	4.40
□ 117 Ted Simmons	12.00	5.50	1.50
□ 140 Gaylord Perry	7.00	3.10	.85
□ 160 Tom Seaver	18.00	8.00	2.20
□ 180 Al Kaline UER	18.00	8.00	2.20
(Home instead of Birth)			
□ 183 Gil Hodges MG	4.00	1.80	.50
□ 188 Dodgers Rookies	3.00	1.35	.35
Bob Valentine			
Mike Strahler			
□ 193 Bob Grich	4.00	1.80	.50
□ 197 Jim Palmer ALCS	5.00	2.20	.60
□ 208 Billy Martin MG	4.00	1.80	.50
□ 210 Rod Carew	18.00	8.00	2.20
□ 230 Willie Stargell	8.00	3.60	1.00
□ 237 Cesar Cedeno	3.00	1.35	.35
□ 248 Hoyt Wilhelm	4.00	1.80	.50
□ 250 Johnny Bench	18.00	8.00	2.20
□ 264 Joe Morgan	7.00	3.10	.85
□ 276 Giants Rookies	8.00	3.60	1.00
Mike Davison			
George Foster			
□ 280 Fergie Jenkins	7.00	3.10	.85
□ 295 Bobby Bonds	5.00	2.20	.60
□ 300 Brooks Robinson	18.00	8.00	2.20
□ 325 Juan Marichal	7.00	3.10	.85
□ 329 Frank Robinson WS	5.00	2.20	.60
□ 331 Brooks Robinson WS	6.00	2.70	.75
commits robbery			
□ 341 Steve Garvey	25.00	11.00	3.10
□ 350 Billy Williams	7.00	3.10	.85
□ 355 Bud Harrelson	3.50	1.55	.45
(Nolan Ryan in photo)			
□ 361 Don Sutton	7.00	3.10	.85
□ 380 Ted Williams MG	10.00	4.50	1.25
□ 384 Rollie Fingers	6.00	2.70	.75
□ 400 Hank Aaron	50.00	22.00	6.25
□ 439 Phillies Rookies	6.00	2.70	.75
Greg Luzinski			
Scott Reid			
□ 450 Bob Gibson	18.00	8.00	2.20
□ 513 Nolan Ryan	250.00	110.00	31.00
□ 520 Tommy John	5.00	2.20	.60
□ 525 Ernie Banks	50.00	22.00	6.25
□ 530 Carl Yastrzemski	40.00	18.00	5.00
□ 543 New York Yankees	8.00	3.60	1.00
Team Card			
□ 544 Vida Blue	6.00	2.70	.75
□ 550 Harmon Killebrew	25.00	11.00	3.10
□ 567 Walt Alston MG	6.00	2.70	.75
□ 570 Jim Palmer	30.00	13.50	3.70
□ 574 Jim Bunning	7.00	3.10	.85
□ 580 Tony Perez	18.00	8.00	2.20
□ 600 Willie Mays	90.00	40.00	11.00
□ 605 Orlando Cepeda	6.00	2.70	.75
□ 609 Leo Durocher MG	7.00	3.10	.85
□ 625 Lou Brock	30.00	13.50	3.70
□ 630 Roberto Clemente	110.00	50.00	14.00
□ 640 Frank Robinson	40.00	18.00	5.00
□ 641 New York Mets	14.00	6.25	1.75
Team Card			
□ 648 Mets Rookies SP	25.00	11.00	3.10
Rich Folkers			
Ted Martinez			
John Matlack			
□ 649 Sparky Lyle SP	18.00	8.00	2.20
□ 650 Rich Allen SP	40.00	18.00	5.00
□ 665 Ron Swoboda SP	18.00	8.00	2.20
□ 688 Sparky Anderson MG SP	40.00	18.00	5.00
□ 700 Boog Powell SP	30.00	13.50	3.70
□ 709 Rookie Outfielders SP	90.00	40.00	11.00
Dusty Baker			
Don Baylor			
Tom Paciorek			
□ 740 Luis Aparicio SP UER	30.00	13.50	3.70
(Led AL in steals from 1965 to 1964, should be 1956 to 1964)			
□ 750 Denny McLain SP	25.00	11.00	3.10
□ 751 Al Weis SP	15.00	6.75	1.85
□ 752 Dick Drago	12.00	2.90	.95

1972 Topps

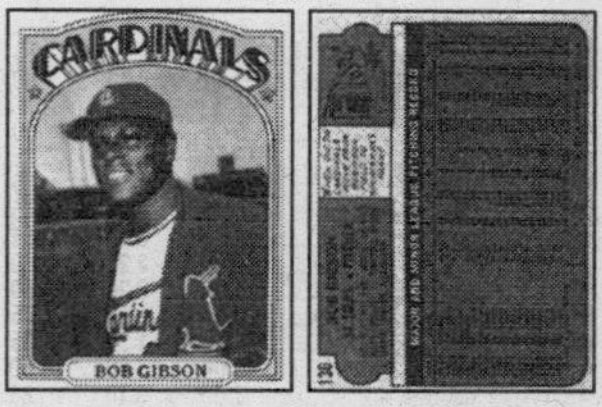

The cards in this 787-card set measure 2 1/2" by 3 1/2". The 1972 Topps set contained the most cards ever for a Topps set to that point in time. Features appearing for the first time were "Boyhood Photos" (341-348/491-498), Awards and Trophy cards (621-626), "In Action" (distributed throughout the set), and "Traded Cards" (751-757). Other subsets included League Leaders (85-96), Playoffs cards (221-222), and World Series cards (223-230). The curved lines of the color picture are a departure from the rectangular designs of other years. There is a series of intermediate scarcity (526-656) and the usual high numbers (657-787). The backs of cards 692, 694, 696, 700, 706 and 710 form a picture back of Tom Seaver. The backs of cards 698, 702, 704, 708, 712, 714 form a picture back of Tony Oliva. As in previous years, cards were issued in a variety of ways including ten-card dime wax packs. The key Rookie Card in this set is Carlton Fisk.

	NRMT	VG-E	GOOD
COMPLETE SET (787)	1700.00	750.00	210.00
COMMON CARD (1-132)	.60	.25	.07
COMMON CARD (133-263)	1.00	.45	.12
COMMON CARD (264-394)	1.25	.55	.16
COMMON CARD (395-525)	1.50	.70	.19
COMMON CARD (526-656)	4.00	1.80	.50
COMMON CARD (657-787)	12.00	5.50	1.50
LL (85-96)	1.75	.80	.22
CUBS VAR (18B/29B/45B/117B)	5.00	2.20	.60
PLAYOFFS (221-222)	1.50	.70	.19
WS (223-230)	1.75	.80	.22
KP (341-348)	1.25	.55	.16
KP (491-498)	1.75	.80	.22
AWARDS (621-626)	5.00	2.20	.60
TRADED CARDS (751-757)	12.00	5.50	1.50
TEAMS (21/71/106)	1.50	.70	.19
TEAMS (156/192/237/262)	1.50	.70	.19
TEAMS (282/328/362/381)	2.00	.90	.25
TEAMS (397/454/487/522)	3.00	1.35	.35
TEAMS (547/582/617/651)	7.00	3.10	.85
TEAMS (688/731/771)	20.00	9.00	2.50
CL (4/103/251/378/478)	4.00	1.80	.50
CL (604A/604B)	10.00	4.50	1.25
CARDS PRICED IN NM CONDITION			
LAST SERIES CONDITION SENSITIVE			

□ 1 Pittsburgh Pirates	7.00	2.50	1.00
Team Card			
□ 33 Billy Martin MG	4.00	1.80	.50
□ 34 Billy Martin IA	2.00	.90	.25
□ 37 Carl Yastrzemski	10.00	4.50	1.25
□ 38 Carl Yastrzemski IA	6.00	2.70	.75
□ 49 Willie Mays	25.00	11.00	3.10
□ 50 Willie Mays IA	12.00	5.50	1.50
□ 51 Harmon Killebrew	7.00	3.10	.85

□ 52 Harmon Killebrew IA	3.50	1.55	.45
□ 79 Red Sox Rookies	60.00	27.00	7.50
Mike Garman			
Cecil Cooper			
Carlton Fisk			
□ 80 Tony Perez	4.00	1.80	.50
□ 87 NL RBI Leaders	3.50	1.55	.45
Joe Torre			
Willie Stargell			
Hank Aaron			
□ 88 AL RBI Leaders	3.00	1.35	.35
Harmon Killebrew			
Frank Robinson			
Reggie Smith			
□ 89 NL Home Run Leaders	3.00	1.35	.35
Willie Stargell			
Hank Aaron			
Lee May			
□ 90 AL Home Run Leaders	2.50	1.10	.30
Bill Melton			
Norm Cash			
Reggie Jackson			
□ 91 NL ERA Leaders	2.50	1.10	.30
Tom Seaver			
Dave Roberts UER			
(Photo actually			
Danny Coombs)			
Don Wilson			
□ 92 AL ERA Leaders	2.50	1.10	.30
Vida Blue			
Wilbur Wood			
Jim Palmer			
□ 93 NL Pitching Leaders	4.00	1.80	.50
Fergie Jenkins			
Steve Carlton			
Al Downing			
Tom Seaver			
□ 95 NL Strikeout Leaders	3.00	1.35	.35
Tom Seaver			
Fergie Jenkins			
Bill Stoneman			
□ 100 Frank Robinson	8.00	3.60	1.00
□ 130 Bob Gibson	8.00	3.60	1.00
□ 132 Joe Morgan	6.00	2.70	.75
□ 142 Chris Chambliss	4.00	1.80	.50
□ 147 Dave Kingman	5.00	2.20	.60
□ 154 Ted Simmons	3.00	1.35	.35
□ 198 Dodgers Rookies	4.00	1.80	.50
Charlie Hough			
Bob O'Brien			
Mike Strahler			
□ 200 Lou Brock	7.00	3.10	.85
□ 222 Brooks Robinson ALCS	3.00	1.35	.35
□ 226 Roberto Clemente WS	6.00	2.70	.75
□ 241 Rollie Fingers	5.00	2.20	.60
□ 256 George Foster	2.50	1.10	.30
□ 267 Dave Concepcion	3.00	1.35	.35
□ 270 Jim Palmer	8.00	3.60	1.00
□ 280 Willie McCovey	7.00	3.10	.85
□ 285 Gaylord Perry	6.00	2.70	.75
□ 299 Hank Aaron	40.00	18.00	5.00
□ 300 Hank Aaron IA	20.00	9.00	2.50
□ 309 Roberto Clemente	50.00	22.00	6.25
□ 310 Roberto Clemente IA	25.00	11.00	3.10
□ 313 Luis Aparicio	4.00	1.80	.50
□ 314 Luis Aparicio IA	1.75	.80	.22
□ 330 Jim Hunter	4.00	1.80	.50
□ 343 Willie Stargell KP	1.50	.70	.19
□ 347 Tom Seaver KP	3.00	1.35	.35
□ 358 Sparky Anderson MG	3.00	1.35	.35
□ 410 Fergie Jenkins	6.00	2.70	.75
□ 420 Steve Carlton	18.00	8.00	2.20
□ 433 Johnny Bench	25.00	11.00	3.10
□ 434 Johnny Bench IA	14.00	6.25	1.75
□ 435 Reggie Jackson	25.00	11.00	3.10
□ 436 Reggie Jackson IA	14.00	6.25	1.75
□ 439 Billy Williams	6.00	2.70	.75
□ 440 Billy Williams IA	3.00	1.35	.35
□ 441 Thurman Munson	14.00	6.25	1.75
□ 442 Thurman Munson IA	7.00	3.10	.85
□ 445 Tom Seaver	30.00	13.50	3.70
□ 446 Tom Seaver IA	15.00	6.75	1.85
□ 447 Willie Stargell	6.00	2.70	.75
□ 448 Willie Stargell IA	3.00	1.35	.35
□ 449 Bob Lemon MG	1.75	.80	.22
□ 451 Tony LaRussa	3.00	1.35	.35
□ 465 Gil Hodges MG	4.00	1.80	.50
□ 474 Orioles Rookies	15.00	6.75	1.85
Don Baylor			
Roric Harrison			
Johnny Oates			
□ 498 Brooks Robinson KP	3.00	1.35	.35
□ 510 Ted Williams MG	10.00	4.50	1.25
□ 515 Bert Blyleven	3.00	1.35	.35
□ 530 Don Sutton	7.00	3.10	.85
□ 550 Brooks Robinson	25.00	11.00	3.10
□ 559 Pete Rose	40.00	18.00	5.00
□ 560 Pete Rose IA	20.00	9.00	2.50
□ 567 Juan Marichal	12.00	5.50	1.50
□ 568 Juan Marichal IA	6.00	2.70	.75
□ 576 Leo Durocher MG	5.00	2.20	.60
□ 580 Lou Piniella	5.00	2.20	.60
□ 595 Nolan Ryan	225.00	100.00	28.00
□ 600 Al Kaline	25.00	11.00	3.10
□ 620 Phil Niekro	10.00	4.50	1.25
□ 668 Texas Rangers	30.00	13.50	3.70
Team Card			
□ 686 Steve Garvey	40.00	18.00	5.00
□ 695 Rod Carew	75.00	34.00	9.50
□ 696 Rod Carew IA	35.00	16.00	4.40
□ 709 Jim Kaat	16.00	7.25	2.00
□ 710 Jim Kaat IA	14.00	6.25	1.75
□ 711 Bobby Bonds	20.00	9.00	2.50
□ 712 Bobby Bonds IA	14.00	6.25	1.75
□ 749 Walter Alston MG	14.00	6.25	1.75
□ 751 Steve Carlton TR	50.00	22.00	6.25
□ 752 Joe Morgan TR	45.00	20.00	5.50
□ 753 Denny McLain TR	20.00	9.00	2.50
□ 754 Frank Robinson TR	45.00	20.00	5.50
□ 760 Bill Mazeroski	18.00	8.00	2.20
□ 761 Rookie Outfielders	25.00	11.00	3.10
Ben Oglivie			
Ron Cey			
Bernie Williams			
□ 764 Dusty Baker	20.00	9.00	2.50
□ 777 Hoyt Wilhelm	25.00	11.00	3.10
□ 778 Twins Rookies	18.00	8.00	2.20
Vic Albury			
Rick Dempsey			
Jim Strickland			
□ 787 Ron Reed	16.00	5.50	1.50

1973 Topps

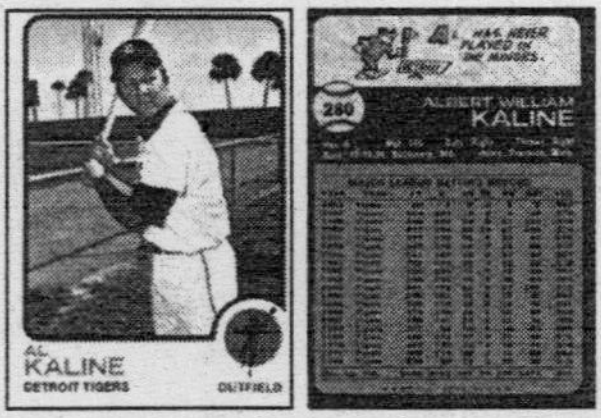

The cards in this 660-card set measure 2 1/2" by 3 1/2". The 1973 Topps set marked the last year in which Topps marketed baseball cards in consecutive series. The last series (529-660) is more difficult to obtain. In some parts of the country, however, all five series were distributed together. Beginning in 1974, all Topps cards were printed at the same time, thus eliminating the "high number" factor. The set features team leader cards with small individual pictures of the coaching staff members and a larger picture of the manager. The "background" variations below with respect to these leader cards are subtle and are best understood after a side-by-side comparison of the two varieties. An "All-Time Leaders" series (471-478) appeared for the first time in this set. Kid Pictures appeared again for the second year in a row (341-346). Other topical subsets within the set included League Leaders (61-68), Playoffs cards (201-202), World Series cards

(203-210), and Rookie Prospects (601-616). For the fourth and final time, cards were issued in ten-card dime packs, cards were also released in 54-card rack packs. The key Rookie Cards in this set are all in the Rookie Prospect series: Bob Boone, Dwight Evans, and Mike Schmidt.

	NRMT	VG-E	GOOD
COMPLETE SET (660)	750.00	350.00	95.00
COMMON CARD (1-264)	.50	.23	.06
COMMON CARD (265-396)	.75	.35	.09
COMMON CARD (397-528)	1.25	.55	.16
COMMON CARD (529-660)	3.50	1.55	.45
PLAYOFFS (201-202)	1.00	.45	.12
WS (203-210)	1.00	.45	.12
ATL (471-478)	3.00	1.35	.35
ROOKIE PROSPECTS (601-616)	4.00	1.80	.50
MG/CO (12A/49A/116A/131A)	.75	.35	.09
MG/CO (179A/252A/356/377)	.75	.35	.09
MG/CO (12B/49B/116B)	1.50	.70	.19
MG/CO (131B/179B/252B)	1.50	.70	.19
MG/CO (421A/486A/517A)	1.50	.70	.19
MG/CO (421B/486B/517B)	3.00	1.35	.35
MG/CO (593/646)	3.50	1.55	.45
TEAMS (7/26/91/127/158)	1.25	.55	.16
TEAMS (191/219/243)	1.25	.55	.16
TEAMS (278/316/347)	1.50	.70	.19
TEAMS (434/464/481/500/521)	2.50	1.10	.30
TEAMS (536/576/596/629)	6.00	2.70	.75
TEAMS (641/654)	6.00	2.70	.75
CL (54/264/338/453)	3.00	1.35	.35
CL (588)	24.00	11.00	3.00
BLUE TEAM CHECKLISTS	8.00	2.40	.80
CARDS PRICED IN NM CONDITION !			

□ 1 All-Time HR Leaders	40.00	11.50	4.00
Babe Ruth 714			
Hank Aaron 673			
Willie Mays 654			
□ 31 Buddy Bell	3.00	1.35	.35
□ 50 Roberto Clemente	60.00	27.00	7.50
□ 61 Batting Leaders	3.00	1.35	.35
Billy Williams			
Rod Carew			
□ 62 Home Run Leaders	2.50	1.10	.30
Johnny Bench			
Dick Allen			
□ 63 RBI Leaders	2.50	1.10	.30
Johnny Bench			
Dick Allen			
□ 64 Stolen Base Leaders	2.00	.90	.25
Lou Brock			
Bert Campaneris			
□ 65 ERA Leaders	2.00	.90	.25
Steve Carlton			
Luis Tiant			
□ 66 Victory Leaders	2.00	.90	.25
Steve Carlton			
Gaylord Perry			
Wilbur Wood			
□ 67 Strikeout Leaders	30.00	13.50	3.70
Steve Carlton			
Nolan Ryan			
□ 81A Cubs Leaders	1.50	.70	.19
Whitey Lockman MG			
Hank Aguirre CO			
Ernie Banks CO			
Larry Jansen CO			
Pete Reiser CO			
(Solid backgrounds)			
□ 81B Cubs Leaders	2.00	.90	.25
(Natural backgrounds)			
□ 84 Rollie Fingers	5.00	2.20	.60
□ 90 Brooks Robinson	7.00	3.10	.85
□ 100 Hank Aaron	30.00	13.50	3.70
□ 130 Pete Rose	18.00	8.00	2.20
□ 142 Thurman Munson	6.00	2.70	.75
□ 160 Jim Palmer	7.00	3.10	.85
□ 165 Luis Aparicio	3.00	1.35	.35
□ 170 Harmon Killebrew	5.00	2.20	.60
□ 174 Rich Gossage	8.00	3.60	1.00
□ 175 Frank Robinson	7.00	3.10	.85
□ 180 Fergie Jenkins	5.00	2.20	.60
□ 190 Bob Gibson	7.00	3.10	.85
□ 193 Carlton Fisk	10.00	4.50	1.25
□ 200 Billy Williams	5.00	2.20	.60
□ 208 Johnny Bench WS6	4.00	1.80	.50
□ 213 Steve Garvey	6.00	2.70	.75
□ 220 Nolan Ryan	100.00	45.00	12.50
□ 230 Joe Morgan	6.00	2.70	.75
□ 235 Jim Hunter	4.00	1.80	.50
□ 237A Braves Leaders	1.50	.70	.19
Eddie Mathews MG			
Lew Burdette CO			
Jim Busby CO			
Roy Hartsfield CO			
Ken Silvestri CO			
(Burdette right ear showing)			
□ 237B Braves Leaders	3.00	1.35	.35
(Burdette right ear not showing)			
□ 245 Carl Yastrzemski	10.00	4.50	1.25
□ 255 Reggie Jackson	16.00	7.25	2.00
□ 257A Mets Leaders	2.50	1.10	.30
Yogi Berra MG			
Roy McMillan CO			
Joe Pignatano CO			
Rube Walker CO			
Eddie Yost CO			
(Orange backgrounds)			
□ 257B Mets Leaders	5.00	2.20	.60
(Dark pale backgrounds)			
□ 275 Tony Perez	4.00	1.80	.50
□ 280 Al Kaline	7.00	3.10	.85
□ 296 Reds Leaders	2.50	1.10	.30
Sparky Anderson MG			
Alex Grammas CO			
Ted Kluszewski CO			
George Scherger CO			
Larry Shepard CO			
□ 300 Steve Carlton	10.00	4.50	1.25
□ 305 Willie Mays	40.00	18.00	5.00
□ 310 Dick Allen	1.50	.70	.19
□ 320 Lou Brock	6.00	2.70	.75
□ 323 Tigers Leaders	1.50	.70	.19
Billy Martin MG			
Art Fowler CO			
Charlie Silvera CO			
Dick Tracewski CO			
□ 330 Rod Carew	7.00	3.10	.85
□ 341 Jim Palmer KP	1.50	.70	.19
□ 344 Jim Hunter KP	1.50	.70	.19
□ 346 Gaylord Perry KP	1.50	.70	.19
□ 350 Tom Seaver	14.00	6.25	1.75
□ 370 Willie Stargell	5.00	2.20	.60
□ 380 Johnny Bench	8.00	3.60	1.00
□ 384 Don Baylor	4.00	1.80	.50
□ 389 New York Mets Team Card	3.00	1.35	.35
□ 400 Gaylord Perry	5.00	2.20	.60
□ 410 Willie McCovey	6.00	2.70	.75
(Bench behind plate)			
□ 449A Indians Leaders	4.00	1.80	.50
Ken Aspromonte MG			
Rocky Colavito CO			
Joe Lutz CO			
Warren Spahn CO			
(Spahn's right ear pointed)			
□ 449B Indians Leaders	4.00	1.80	.50
(Spahn's right ear round)			
□ 471 Ty Cobb ATL	8.00	3.60	1.00
4191 Hits			
□ 472 Lou Gehrig ATL	14.00	6.25	1.75
23 Grand Slams			
□ 473 Hank Aaron ATL	10.00	4.50	1.25
6172 Total Bases			
□ 474 Babe Ruth ATL	16.00	7.25	2.00
2209 RBI			
□ 475 Ty Cobb ATL	8.00	3.60	1.00
.367 Batting Average			
□ 480 Juan Marichal	5.00	2.20	.60
□ 503 Phil Niekro	5.00	2.20	.60
□ 530 Jim Kaat	5.00	2.20	.60
□ 545 Orlando Cepeda	5.00	2.20	.60
□ 549 Rangers Leaders	5.00	2.20	.60
Whitey Herzog MG			
Chuck Estrada CO			

Chuck Hiller CO			
Jackie Moore CO			
□ 554 Dave Concepcion	5.00	2.20	.60
□ 556 New York Yankees	8.00	3.60	1.00
Team Card			
□ 569 Dodgers Leaders	5.00	2.20	.60
Walt Alston MG			
Red Adams CO			
Monty Basgall CO			
Jim Gilliam CO			
Tom Lasorda CO			
□ 609 Rookie 2nd Basemen	6.00	2.70	.75
Larvell Blanks			
Pedro Garcia			
Dave Lopes			
□ 613 Rookie Catchers	25.00	11.00	3.10
Bob Boone			
Skip Jutze			
Mike Ivie			
□ 614 Rookie Outfielders	25.00	11.00	3.10
Al Bumbry			
Dwight Evans			
Charlie Spikes			
□ 615 Rookie 3rd Basemen	300.00	135.00	38.00
Ron Cey			
John Hilton			
Mike Schmidt			
□ 624 Astros Leaders	6.00	2.70	.75
Leo Durocher MG			
Preston Gomez CO			
Grady Hatton CO			
Hub Kittle CO			
Jim Owens CO			
□ 630 Denny McLain	5.00	2.20	.60
□ 660 Fred Scherman	4.00	1.55	.45

1974 Topps

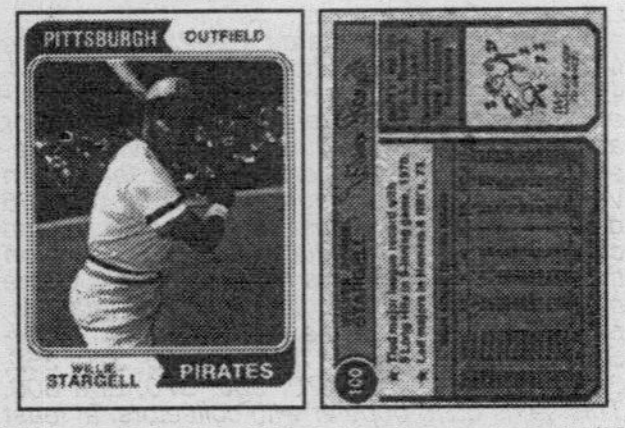

The cards in this 660-card set measure 2 1/2" by 3 1/2". This year marked the first time Topps issued all the cards of its baseball set at the same time rather than in series. Among other methods, cards were issued in eight-card dime wax packs and 42 card rack packs. For the first time, factory sets were issued through the JC Penny's catalog. Sales were probably disappointing for it would be several years before factory sets were issued again. Some interesting variations were created by the rumored move of the San Diego Padres to Washington. Fifteen cards (13 players, the team card, and the rookie card (599) of the Padres were printed either as "San Diego" (SD) or "Washington." The latter are the scarcer variety and are denoted in the checklist below by WAS. Each team's manager and his coaches again have a combined card with small pictures of each coach below the larger photo of the team's manager. The first six cards in the set (1-6) feature Hank Aaron and his illustrious career. Other topical subsets included in the set are League Leaders (201-208), All-Star selections (331-339), Playoffs cards (470-471), World Series cards (472-479), and Rookie Prospects (596-608). The card backs for the All-Stars (331-339) have no statistics, but form a picture puzzle of Bobby Bonds, the 1973 All-Star Game MVP. The key Rookie Cards in this set are Ken Griffey Sr., Dave Parker, and Dave Winfield.

	NRMT	VG-E	GOOD
COMPLETE SET (660)	600.00	275.00	75.00
COMPLETE FACT.SET (660)	625.00	275.00	80.00
COMMON CARD (1-660)	.50	.23	.06
AARON SPECIALS (2-6) !	7.00	3.10	.85
TEAM CARDS	1.50	.70	.19
WASH (32B/53B/77B/102B)	7.00	3.10	.85
WASH (125B/148B/197B/241B)	7.00	3.10	.85
WASH (226B/309B/387B)	9.00	4.00	1.10
CL (126/263/273/414/637)	2.50	1.10	.30
RED TEAM CHECKLISTS	1.00	.30	.10
SEMISTARS	.75	.35	.09
STARS	1.00	.45	.12
1974-85 PRICED IN NM-MT CONDITION			
□ 1 Hank Aaron	40.00	12.00	5.00
All-Time Home Run King			
(Complete ML record)			
□ 7 Jim Hunter	3.00	1.35	.35
□ 10 Johnny Bench	12.00	5.50	1.50
□ 20 Nolan Ryan	75.00	34.00	9.50
□ 29 Phil Niekro	2.50	1.10	.30
□ 35 Gaylord Perry	3.00	1.35	.35
□ 40 Jim Palmer	5.00	2.20	.60
□ 50 Rod Carew	5.00	2.20	.60
□ 55 Frank Robinson	7.00	3.10	.85
□ 60 Lou Brock	5.00	2.20	.60
□ 61 Luis Aparicio	3.00	1.35	.35
□ 80 Tom Seaver	14.00	6.25	1.75
□ 85 Joe Morgan	5.00	2.20	.60
□ 87 Fergie Jenkins	3.00	1.35	.35
□ 95 Steve Carlton	7.00	3.10	.85
□ 100 Willie Stargell	4.00	1.80	.50
□ 105 Carlton Fisk	14.00	6.25	1.75
□ 110 Billy Williams	4.00	1.80	.50
□ 130 Reggie Jackson	18.00	8.00	2.20
□ 160 Brooks Robinson	7.00	3.10	.85
□ 173B Randy Jones WAS	10.00	4.50	1.25
□ 179 Mets Leaders	2.00	.90	.25
Yogi Berra MG			
Rube Walker CO			
Eddie Yost CO			
Roy McMillan CO			
Joe Pignatano CO			
□ 201 Batting Leaders	5.00	2.20	.60
Rod Carew			
Pete Rose			
□ 202 Home Run Leaders	5.00	2.20	.60
Reggie Jackson			
Willie Stargell			
□ 203 RBI Leaders	5.00	2.20	.60
Reggie Jackson			
Willie Stargell			
□ 206 ERA Leaders	5.00	2.20	.60
Jim Palmer			
Tom Seaver			
□ 207 Strikeout Leaders	20.00	9.00	2.50
Nolan Ryan			
Tom Seaver			
□ 212 Rollie Fingers	3.00	1.35	.35
□ 215 Al Kaline UER	5.00	2.20	.60
(No copyright on back)			
□ 230 Tony Perez	3.00	1.35	.35
□ 250A Willie McCovey SD	6.00	2.70	.75
□ 250B Willie McCovey WAS	30.00	13.50	3.70
□ 252 Dave Parker	10.00	4.50	1.25
□ 280 Carl Yastrzemski	6.00	2.70	.75
□ 283 Mike Schmidt	50.00	22.00	6.25
□ 300 Pete Rose	16.00	7.25	2.00
□ 326 Reds Leaders	2.50	1.10	.30
Sparky Anderson MG			
Larry Shepard CO			
George Scherger CO			
Alex Grammas CO			
Ted Kluszewski CO			
□ 330 Juan Marichal	3.00	1.35	.35
□ 331 All-Star Catchers	5.00	2.20	.60
Carlton Fisk			
Johnny Bench			
□ 332 All-Star 1B	5.00	2.20	.60
Dick Allen			
Hank Aaron			
□ 333 All-Star 2B	2.50	1.10	.30
Rod Carew			

Joe Morgan			
□ 334 All-Star 3B	2.50	1.10	.30
Brooks Robinson			
Ron Santo			
□ 336 All-Star LF	3.00	1.35	.35
Bobby Murcer			
Pete Rose			
□ 338 All-Star RF	5.00	2.20	.60
Reggie Jackson			
Billy Williams			
□ 340 Thurman Munson	6.00	2.70	.75
□ 350 Bob Gibson	5.00	2.20	.60
□ 351 Dwight Evans	3.00	1.35	.35
□ 364B Cito Gaston WAS	10.00	4.50	1.25
□ 400 Harmon Killebrew	5.00	2.20	.60
□ 456 Dave Winfield	125.00	55.00	15.50
□ 470 Reggie Jackson ALCS	6.00	2.70	.75
□ 473 Willie Mays WS	7.00	3.10	.85
□ 477 Reggie Jackson WS	6.00	2.70	.75
□ 575 Steve Garvey	4.00	1.80	.50
□ 582 Bucky Dent	2.00	.90	.25
□ 598 Rookie Outfielders	14.00	6.25	1.75
Dave Augustine			
Ken Griffey			
Steve Ontiveros			
Jim Tyrone			
□ 599B Rookie Pitchers SD	4.00	1.80	.50
(SD in large print)			
□ 599C Rookie Pitchers SD	6.00	2.70	.75
(SD in small print)			
□ 600 Rookie Infielders	5.00	2.20	.60
Ron Cash			
Jim Cox			
Bill Madlock			
Reggie Sanders			
□ 601 Rookie Outfielders	3.00	1.35	.35
Ed Armbrister			
Rich Bladt			
Brian Downing			
Bake McBride			
□ 604 Rookie Infielders	5.00	2.20	.60
Terry Hughes			
John Knox			
Andre Thornton			
Frank White			
□ 605 Rookie Pitchers	4.00	1.80	.50
Vic Albury			
Ken Frailing			
Kevin Kobel			
Frank Tanana			
□ 654B Jesus Alou COR	7.00	3.10	.85
(Outfield)			

1974 Topps Traded

The cards in this 44-card set measure 2 1/2" by 3 1/2". The 1974 Topps Traded set contains 43 player cards and one unnumbered checklist card. The fronts have the word "traded" in block letters and the backs are designed in newspaper style. Card numbers are the same as in the regular set except they are followed by a "T." No known scarcities exist for this set. The cards were inserted in all packs toward the end of the production run. They were produced in large enough quantity that they are no scarcer than the regular Topps cards.

	NRMT	VG-E	GOOD
COMPLETE SET (44)	15.00	6.75	1.85
COMMON CARD	.50	.23	.06
CL ! (NNO)	1.50	.70	.19
SEMISTARS	.75	.35	.09
STARS	1.00	.45	.12
INCLUDED IN ALL LATE PACKS			
□ 330T Juan Marichal	2.00	.90	.25

1975 Topps

The cards in the 1975 Topps set were issued in two different sizes: a regular standard size (2 1/2" by 3 1/2") and a mini size (2 1/2" by 3 1/8") which was issued as a test in certain areas of the country. The 660-card Topps baseball set for 1975 was radically different in appearance from sets of the preceding years. The most prominent change was the use of a two-color frame surrounding the picture area rather than a single, subdued color. A facsimile autograph appears on the picture, and the backs are printed in red and green on gray. Cards were released in ten-card wax packs as well as in 42-card rack packs. Cards 189-212 depict the MVP's of both leagues from 1951 through 1974. The first seven cards (1-7) feature players (listed in alphabetical order) breaking records or achieving milestones during the previous season. Cards 306-313 picture league leaders in various statistical categories. Cards 459-466 depict the results of post-season action. Team cards feature a checklist back for players on that team and show a small inset photo of the manager on the front. The following players' regular issue cards are explicitly denoted as All-Stars, 1, 50, 80, 140, 170, 180, 260, 320, 350, 390, 400, 420, 440, 470, 530, 570, and 600. This set is quite popular with collectors, at least in part due to the fact that the Rookie Cards of George Brett, Gary Carter, Keith Hernandez, Fred Lynn, Jim Rice and Robin Yount are all in the set. Topps minis have the same checklist and are valued approximately 1.5 times the prices listed below.

	NRMT	VG-E	GOOD
COMPLETE SET (660)	800.00	350.00	100.00
COMMON CARD (1-660)	.50	.23	.06
TEAM CARDS !	2.00	.90	.25
CL (126/257/386/517/646)	2.00	.90	.25
MVP (189-212)	1.50	.70	.19
LL (306/308/309/310/311)	1.50	.70	.19
SEMISTARS	.75	.35	.09
STARS	1.00	.45	.12
*MINI: 1.5X VALUE			
CONDITION SENSITIVE SET			
□ 1 Hank Aaron RB	30.00	10.00	5.00
Sets Homer Mark			
□ 2 Lou Brock RB	3.50	1.55	.45
118 Stolen Bases			
□ 3 Bob Gibson RB	3.50	1.55	.45
3000th Strikeout			
□ 4 Al Kaline RB	4.00	1.80	.50
3000 Hit Club			
□ 5 Nolan Ryan RB	30.00	13.50	3.70
Fans 300 for			
3rd Year in a Row			
□ 7 Steve Busby HL	12.00	5.50	1.50

Dick Bosman			
Nolan Ryan			
□ 20 Thurman Munson	6.00	2.70	.75
□ 21 Rollie Fingers	3.00	1.35	.35
□ 29 Dave Parker	4.00	1.80	.50
□ 50 Brooks Robinson	6.00	2.70	.75
□ 60 Fergie Jenkins	3.00	1.35	.35
□ 61 Dave Winfield	50.00	22.00	6.25
□ 70 Mike Schmidt	50.00	22.00	6.25
□ 80 Carlton Fisk	12.00	5.50	1.50
□ 100 Willie Stargell	4.00	1.80	.50
□ 106 Mike Hargrove	3.00	1.35	.35
□ 130 Phil Niekro	2.50	1.10	.30
□ 140 Steve Garvey	5.00	2.20	.60
□ 150 Bob Gibson	5.00	2.20	.60
□ 180 Joe Morgan	5.00	2.20	.60
□ 185 Steve Carlton	6.00	2.70	.75
□ 189 1951 MVP's	3.50	1.55	.45
Larry (Yogi) Berra			
Roy Campanella			
(Campy never issued)			
□ 192 1954 MVP's	4.00	1.80	.50
Yogi Berra			
Willie Mays			
□ 193 1955 MVP's UER	3.50	1.55	.45
Yogi Berra			
Roy Campanella			
(Campy card never issued, pictured with LA cap, sic)			
□ 194 1956 MVP's	14.00	6.25	1.75
Mickey Mantle			
Don Newcombe			
□ 195 1957 MVP's	25.00	11.00	3.10
Mickey Mantle			
Hank Aaron			
□ 199 1961 MVP's	3.00	1.35	.35
Roger Maris			
Frank Robinson			
□ 200 1962 MVP's	14.00	6.25	1.75
Mickey Mantle			
Maury Wills			
(Wills never issued)			
□ 204 1966 MVP's	6.00	2.70	.75
Frank Robinson			
Bob Clemente			
□ 211 1973 MVP's	6.00	2.70	.75
Reggie Jackson			
Pete Rose			
□ 223 Robin Yount	110.00	50.00	14.00
□ 228 George Brett	200.00	90.00	25.00
□ 230 Jim Hunter	3.00	1.35	.35
□ 260 Johnny Bench	12.00	5.50	1.50
□ 280 Carl Yastrzemski	6.00	2.70	.75
□ 284 Ken Griffey	5.00	2.20	.60
□ 300 Reggie Jackson	20.00	9.00	2.50
□ 307 Home Run Leaders	3.50	1.55	.45
Dick Allen			
Mike Schmidt			
□ 312 Strikeout Leaders	20.00	9.00	2.50
Nolan Ryan			
Steve Carlton			
□ 320 Pete Rose	20.00	9.00	2.50
□ 335 Jim Palmer	5.00	2.20	.60
□ 370 Tom Seaver	14.00	6.25	1.75
□ 450 Willie McCovey	5.00	2.20	.60
□ 461 Reggie Jackson WS	4.00	1.80	.50
□ 500 Nolan Ryan	75.00	34.00	9.50
□ 530 Gaylord Perry	3.00	1.35	.35
□ 531 Reds: Team/Mgr.	4.00	.80	.40
Sparky Anderson			
(Checklist back)			
□ 540 Lou Brock	5.00	2.20	.60
□ 545 Billy Williams	3.50	1.55	.45
□ 560 Tony Perez	3.00	1.35	.35
□ 580 Frank Robinson	6.00	2.70	.75
□ 600 Rod Carew	5.00	2.20	.60
□ 616 Rookie Outfielders	14.00	6.25	1.75
Dave Augustine			
Pepe Mangual			
Jim Rice			
John Scott			
□ 620 Rookie Catcher/OF	25.00	11.00	3.10
Gary Carter			
Marc Hill			
Danny Meyer			
Leon Roberts			
□ 622 Rookie Outfielders	6.00	2.70	.75
Ed Armbrister			
Fred Lynn			
Tom Poquette			
Terry Whitfield UER			
(Listed as Ney York)			
□ 623 Rookie Infielders	6.00	2.70	.75
Phil Garner			
Keith Hernandez UER			
(Sic, bats right)			
Bob Sheldon			
Tom Veryzer			
□ 640 Harmon Killebrew	5.00	2.20	.60
□ 660 Hank Aaron	35.00	10.50	7.00

1976 Topps

The 1976 Topps set of 660 standard-size cards is known for its sharp color photographs and interesting presentation of subjects. Team cards feature a checklist back for players on that team and show a small inset photo of the manager on the front. A "Father and Son" series (66-70) spotlights five Major Leaguers whose fathers also made the "Big Show." Other subseries include "All Time All Stars" (341-350), "Record Breakers" from the previous season (1-6), League Leaders (191-205), Post-season cards (461-462), and Rookie Prospects (589-599). The following players' regular issue cards are explicitly denoted as All-Stars, 10, 48, 60, 140, 150, 165, 169, 240, 300, 370, 380, 395, 400, 420, 475, 500, 580, and 650. Cards were issued in ten-card wax packs, 42-card rack packs as well as cello packs and other options. The key Rookie Cards in this set are Dennis Eckersley, Ron Guidry, and Willie Randolph.

	NRMT	VG-E	GOOD
COMPLETE SET (660)	400.00	180.00	50.00
COMMON CARD (1-660)	.25	.11	.03
TEAM CARDS !	1.50	.70	.19
CL (119/262/392/526/643)	1.50	.70	.19
LL (195/197/199)	1.50	.70	.19
LL (200/201/203)	1.50	.70	.19
SEMISTARS	.50	.23	.06
STARS	1.00	.45	.12
□ 1 Hank Aaron RB	16.00	5.00	2.00
2262 Career RBIs			
□ 5 Tom Seaver RB	4.00	1.80	.50
Most Consecutive seasons with 200 Strikeouts			
□ 10 Lou Brock	4.00	1.80	.50
□ 19 George Brett	60.00	27.00	7.50
□ 55 Gaylord Perry	2.50	1.10	.30
□ 95 Brooks Robinson	6.00	2.70	.75
□ 98 Dennis Eckersley	40.00	18.00	5.00
□ 100 Jim Hunter	2.50	1.10	.30
□ 104 Cincinnati Reds	3.00	.60	.30
Team Card;			
Sparky Anderson MG			
(Checklist back)			
□ 128 Ken Griffey	2.50	1.10	.30
□ 150 Steve Garvey	4.00	1.80	.50
□ 160 Dave Winfield	25.00	11.00	3.10
□ 185 Dave Parker	2.00	.90	.25
□ 192 AL Batting Leaders	2.00	.90	.25

Rod Carew			
Fred Lynn			
Thurman Munson			
□ 193 NL Home Run Leaders	3.00	1.35	.35
Mike Schmidt			
Dave Kingman			
Greg Luzinski			
□ 194 AL Home Run Leaders	2.50	1.10	.30
Reggie Jackson			
George Scott			
John Mayberry			
□ 202 AL ERA Leaders	5.00	2.20	.60
Jim Palmer			
Jim Hunter			
Dennis Eckersley			
□ 230 Carl Yastrzemski	5.00	2.20	.60
□ 240 Pete Rose	12.00	5.50	1.50
□ 250 Fergie Jenkins	2.50	1.10	.30
□ 270 Willie Stargell	3.00	1.35	.35
□ 300 Johnny Bench	7.00	3.10	.85
□ 316 Robin Yount	30.00	13.50	3.70
□ 325 Tony Perez	2.00	.90	.25
□ 330 Nolan Ryan	65.00	29.00	8.00
□ 340 Jim Rice	5.00	2.20	.60
□ 341 Lou Gehrig ATG	12.00	5.50	1.50
□ 342 Rogers Hornsby ATG	3.00	1.35	.35
□ 344 Honus Wagner ATG	5.00	2.20	.60
□ 345 Babe Ruth ATG	15.00	6.75	1.85
□ 346 Ty Cobb ATG	8.00	3.60	1.00
□ 347 Ted Williams ATG	10.00	4.50	1.25
□ 349 Walter Johnson ATG	3.00	1.35	.35
□ 355 Steve Carlton	6.00	2.70	.75
□ 365 Carlton Fisk	7.00	3.10	.85
□ 400 Rod Carew	4.00	1.80	.50
□ 405 Rollie Fingers	2.50	1.10	.30
□ 420 Joe Morgan	4.00	1.80	.50
□ 435 Phil Niekro	2.00	.90	.25
□ 441 Gary Carter	7.00	3.10	.85
□ 450 Jim Palmer	4.00	1.80	.50
□ 480 Mike Schmidt	25.00	11.00	3.10
□ 500 Reggie Jackson	14.00	6.25	1.75
□ 520 Willie McCovey	4.00	1.80	.50
□ 525 Billy Williams	2.50	1.10	.30
□ 550 Hank Aaron	25.00	11.00	3.10
□ 592 Rookie Infielders	6.00	2.70	.75
Willie Randolph			
Dave McKay			
Jerry Royster			
Roy Staiger			
□ 599 Rookie Pitchers	6.00	2.70	.75
Rob Dressler			
Ron Guidry			
Bob McClure			
Pat Zachry			
□ 600 Tom Seaver	7.00	3.10	.85
□ 650 Thurman Munson	4.00	1.80	.50

1976 Topps Traded

The cards in this 44-card set measure 2 1/2" by 3 1/2". The 1976 Topps Traded set contains 43 players and one unnumbered checklist card. The individuals pictured were traded after the Topps regular set was printed. A "Sports Extra" heading design is found on each picture and is also used to introduce the biographical section of the reverse. Each card is numbered according to the player's regular 1976 card with the addition of "T" to indicate his new status. As in 1974, the cards were inserted in all packs toward the end of the production run. Because they were produced in large quantities, they are no scarcer than the basic cards.

	NRMT	VG-E	GOOD
COMPLETE SET (44)	15.00	6.75	1.85
COMMON CARD	.25	.11	.03
CL ! (NNO)	1.25	.55	.16
SEMISTARS	.50	.23	.06
STARS	1.00	.45	.12
INCLUDED IN ALL LATE PACKS			
□ 250T Fergie Jenkins	2.50	1.10	.30
□ 592T Willie Randolph	4.00	1.80	.50

1977 Topps

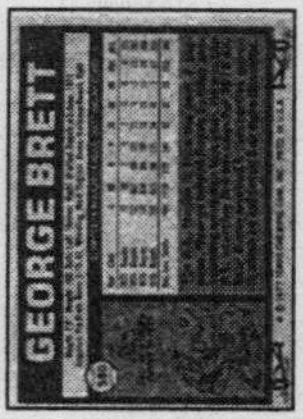

In 1977 for the fifth consecutive year, Topps produced a 660-card standard-size baseball set. Among other fashions, this set was released in 10-card wax packs as well as thirty-nine card rack packs. The player's name, team affiliation, and his position are compactly arranged over the picture area and a facsimile autograph appears on the photo. Team cards feature a checklist of that team's players in the set and a small picture of the manager on the front of the card. Appearing for the first time are the series "Brothers" (631-634) and "Turn Back the Clock" (433-437). Other subseries in the set are League Leaders (1-8), Record Breakers (231-234), Playoffs cards (276-277), World Series cards (411-413), and Rookie Prospects (472-479/487-494). The following players' regular issue cards are explicitly denoted as All-Stars, 30, 70, 100, 120, 170, 210, 240, 265, 301, 347, 400, 420, 450, 500, 521, 550, 560, and 580. The key Rookie Cards in the set are Jack Clark, Andre Dawson, Mark "The Bird" Fidrych, Dennis Martinez and Dale Murphy. Cards numbered 23 or lower, that feature Yankees and do not follow the numbering checklisted below, are not necessarily error cards. They are undoubtedly Burger King cards, a separate set with its own pricing and mass distribution. Burger King cards are indistinguishable from the corresponding Topps cards except for the card numbering difference and the fact that Burger King cards do not have a printing sheet designation (such as A through F like the regular Topps) anywhere on the card back in very small print. There was an aluminum version of the Dale Murphy rookie card number 476 produced (legally) in the early '80s; proceeds from the sales originally priced at 10.00) of this "card" went to the Huntington's Disease Foundation.

	NRMT	VG-E	GOOD
COMPLETE SET (660)	375.00	170.00	47.50
COMMON CARD (1-660)	.25	.11	.03
TEAM CARDS !	1.25	.55	.16
CL (32/208/356/451/562)	1.25	.55	.16
SEMISTARS	.40	.18	.05
STARS	.75	.35	.09
□ 1 Batting Leaders	7.00	2.00	.75
George Brett			

Bill Madlock			
□ 2 Home Run Leaders	1.75	.80	.22
Graig Nettles			
Mike Schmidt			
□ 6 Strikeout Leaders	15.00	6.75	1.85
Nolan Ryan			
Tom Seaver			
□ 10 Reggie Jackson	10.00	4.50	1.25
□ 70 Johnny Bench	6.00	2.70	.75
□ 100 Joe Morgan	3.00	1.35	.35
□ 110 Steve Carlton	5.00	2.20	.60
□ 120 Rod Carew	3.00	1.35	.35
□ 140 Mike Schmidt	16.00	7.25	2.00
□ 144 Bruce Sutter	2.50	1.10	.30
□ 150 Tom Seaver	5.00	2.20	.60
□ 152 Gaylord Perry	2.00	.90	.25
□ 170 Thurman Munson	4.00	1.80	.50
□ 231 George Brett RB	12.00	5.50	1.50
Most consecutive games			
3 or more hits			
□ 234 Nolan Ryan RB	18.00	8.00	2.20
Most seasons, 300 strikeouts			
□ 265 Mark Fidrych	5.00	2.20	.60
□ 277 Pete Rose NLCS	2.00	.90	.25
□ 280 Jim Hunter	2.00	.90	.25
□ 285 Brooks Robinson	4.00	1.80	.50
□ 295 Gary Carter	4.00	1.80	.50
□ 355 Lou Brock	3.00	1.35	.35
□ 387 Yankees Team/Mgr.	1.75	.35	.17
Billy Martin			
(Checklist back)			
□ 390 Dave Winfield	16.00	7.25	2.00
□ 400 Steve Garvey	2.50	1.10	.30
□ 411 Joe Morgan WS	1.75	.80	.22
Johnny Bench			
□ 412 Johnny Bench WS	1.75	.80	.22
□ 430 Fergie Jenkins	2.00	.90	.25
□ 434 Carl Yastrzemski TBC	1.50	.70	.19
'67 Triple Crown			
□ 450 Pete Rose	10.00	4.50	1.25
□ 460 Willie Stargell	2.50	1.10	.30
□ 473 Rookie Outfielders	60.00	27.00	7.50
Andre Dawson			
Gene Richards			
John Scott			
Denny Walling			
□ 476 Rookie Catchers	20.00	9.00	2.50
Gary Alexander			
Rick Cerone			
Dale Murphy			
Kevin Pasley			
□ 480 Carl Yastrzemski	4.00	1.80	.50
□ 488 Rookie Outfielders	5.00	2.20	.60
Jack Clark			
Ruppert Jones			
Lee Mazzilli			
Dan Thomas			
□ 491 Rookie Pitchers	6.00	2.70	.75
Mike Dupree			
Dennis Martinez			
Craig Mitchell			
Bob Sykes			
□ 523 Rollie Fingers	2.00	.90	.25
□ 525 Dennis Eckersley	6.00	2.70	.75
□ 547 Willie McCovey	3.00	1.35	.35
□ 580 George Brett	35.00	16.00	4.40
□ 600 Jim Palmer	3.00	1.35	.35
□ 615 Phil Niekro	1.50	.70	.19
□ 631 George Brett	8.00	3.60	1.00
Ken Brett			
□ 635 Robin Yount	20.00	9.00	2.50
□ 640 Carlton Fisk	5.00	2.20	.60
□ 650 Nolan Ryan	45.00	20.00	5.50
□ 655 Tony Perez	1.50	.70	.19

1978 Topps

The cards in this 726-card set measure 2 1/2" by 3 1/2". The 1978 Topps set experienced an increase in number of cards from the previous five regular issue sets of 660. Card numbers 1 through 7 feature Record Breakers (RB) of the 1977 season. Other subsets within this set

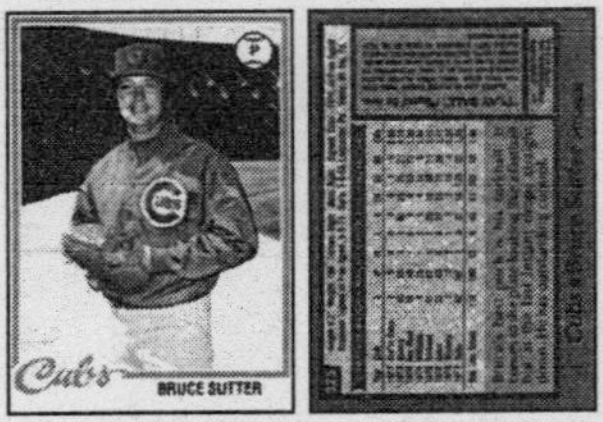

include League Leaders (201-208), Post-season cards (411-413), and Rookie Prospects (701-711). The key Rookie Cards in this set are the multi-player Rookie Card of Paul Molitor and Alan Trammell, Jack Morris, Eddie Murray, Lance Parrish, and Lou Whitaker. Almost all of the Molitor/Trammell cards are found with black printing smudges. The manager cards in the set feature a "then and now" format on the card front showing the manager as he looked during his playing days. While no scarcities exist, 66 of the cards are more abundant in supply, as they were "double printed." These 66 double-printed cards are noted in the checklist by DP. Team cards again feature a checklist of that team's players in the set on the back. As in previous years, this set was issued in many different ways: some of them include 14-card wax packs and 39-card rack packs. Cards numbered 23 or lower, that feature Astros, Rangers, Tigers, or Yankees and do not follow the numbering checklisted below, are not necessarily error cards. They are undoubtedly Burger King cards, a separate set with its own pricing and mass distribution. Burger King cards are indistinguishable from the corresponding Topps cards except for the card numbering difference and the fact that Burger King cards do not have a printing sheet designation (such as A through F like the regular Topps) anywhere on the card back in very small print.

	NRMT	VG-E	GOOD
COMPLETE SET (726)	275.00	125.00	34.00
COMMON CARD (1-726)	.25	.11	.03
COMMON CARD DP	.15	.07	.02
TEAM CARDS !	1.25	.55	.16
TEAM CARDS DP !	.50	.23	.06
CL (74/184/289/435/535/652)	1.25	.55	.16
SEMISTARS	.40	.18	.05
STARS	.75	.35	.09
□ 1 Lou Brock RB	2.50	.75	.25
Most lifetime steals			
□ 3 Willie McCovey RB	1.50	.70	.19
Most times 2 HR's in inning			
□ 4 Brooks Robinson RB	2.00	.90	.25
Most consecutive			
seasons with one club			
□ 5 Pete Rose RB	3.50	1.55	.45
Most lifetime switch-hitter hits			
□ 6 Nolan Ryan RB	15.00	6.75	1.85
Most games 10 or more strikeouts			
□ 7 Reggie Jackson RB	3.50	1.55	.45
Most homers,			
one World Series			
□ 10 Phil Niekro	1.00	.45	.12
□ 20 Pete Rose DP	5.00	2.20	.60
□ 34 Willie McCovey	2.50	1.10	.30
□ 36 Eddie Murray	125.00	55.00	15.50
□ 40 Carl Yastrzemski	3.00	1.35	.35
□ 60 Thurman Munson	3.00	1.35	.35
□ 72 Andre Dawson	15.00	6.75	1.85
□ 100 George Brett	22.00	10.00	2.70
□ 119 Dennis Martinez	2.00	.90	.25
□ 122 Dennis Eckersley	4.00	1.80	.50
□ 140 Rollie Fingers	1.50	.70	.19
□ 160 Jim Palmer	2.50	1.10	.30
□ 170 Lou Brock	2.50	1.10	.30
□ 173 Robin Yount UER	14.00	6.25	1.75

(Played for Newark in 1973, not 1971)			
□ 189 Tom Lasorda MG	1.00	.45	.12
□ 200 Reggie Jackson	8.00	3.60	1.00
□ 201 Batting Leaders	1.00	.45	.12
Dave Parker			
Rod Carew			
□ 205 Victory Leaders	1.50	.70	.19
Steve Carlton			
Dave Goltz			
Dennis Leonard			
Jim Palmer			
□ 206 Strikeout Leaders DP	5.00	2.20	.60
Phil Niekro			
Nolan Ryan			
□ 270 Carlton Fisk	3.00	1.35	.35
□ 282 New York Yankees	1.50	.30	.15
Team Card			
(Checklist back)			
□ 300 Joe Morgan	2.50	1.10	.30
□ 360 Mike Schmidt	12.00	5.50	1.50
□ 400 Nolan Ryan	35.00	16.00	4.40
□ 413 Reggie Jackson WS	3.00	1.35	.35
□ 450 Tom Seaver	4.00	1.80	.50
□ 460 Jim Hunter	1.50	.70	.19
□ 510 Willie Stargell	2.00	.90	.25
□ 530 Dave Winfield	12.00	5.50	1.50
□ 540 Steve Carlton	3.00	1.35	.35
□ 580 Rod Carew	2.50	1.10	.30
□ 674 Ray Knight	2.50	1.10	.30
□ 686 Gaylord Perry	1.50	.70	.19
□ 700 Johnny Bench	3.00	1.35	.35
□ 703 Rookie Pitchers DP	5.00	2.20	.60
Larry Andersen			
Tim Jones			
Mickey Mahler			
Jack Morris			
□ 704 Rookie 2nd Basemen	24.00	11.00	3.00
Garth Iorg			
Dave Oliver			
Sam Perlozzo			
Lou Whitaker			
□ 707 Rookie Shortstops	100.00	45.00	12.50
Mickey Klutts			
Paul Molitor			
Alan Trammell			
U.L. Washington			
□ 708 Rookie Catchers	10.00	4.50	1.25
Bo Diaz			
Dale Murphy			
Lance Parrish			
Ernie Whitt			
□ 720 Fergie Jenkins	1.50	.70	.19

1979 Topps

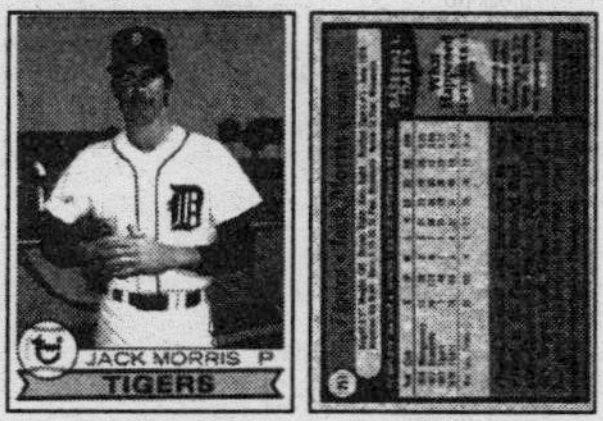

The cards in this 726-card set measure 2 1/2" by 3 1/2". Topps continued with the same number of cards as in 1978. Various series spotlight League Leaders (1-8), "Season and Career Record Holders" (411-418), "Record Breakers" (201-206), and one "Prospects" card for each team (701-726). Team cards feature a checklist on back of that team's players in the set and a small picture of the manager on the front of the card. There are 66 cards that were double printed and these are noted in the checklist by the abbreviation DP. Bump Wills (369) was initially depicted in a Ranger uniform but with a Blue Jays affiliation; later printings correctly labeled him with Texas. The set price includes either Wills card. The key Rookie Cards in this set are Pedro Guerrero, Carney Lansford, Ozzie Smith, Bob Welch and Willie Wilson. As in previous years, this set was released in many different formats, among them are 12-card wax packs and 39-card rack packs. Cards numbered 23 or lower, which feature Phillies or Yankees and do not follow the numbering checklisted below, are not necessarily error cards. They are undoubtedly Burger King cards, separate sets for each team each with its own pricing and mass distribution. Burger King cards are indistinguishable from the corresponding Topps cards except for the card numbering difference and the fact that Burger King cards do not have a printing sheet designation (such as A through F like the regular Topps) anywhere on the card back in very small print.

	NRMT	VG-E	GOOD
COMPLETE SET (726)	200.00	90.00	25.00
COMMON CARD (1-726)	.20	.09	.03
COMMON CARD DP	.10	.05	.01
TEAM CARDS !	1.00	.45	.12
VAR (369A/369B)	3.00	1.35	.35
CL ! (353/602/669)	1.00	.45	.12
CL DP ! (121/241/483)	.60	.25	.07
SEMISTARS	.35	.16	.04
STARS	.50	.23	.06
□ 1 Batting Leaders	2.50	.50	.25
Rod Carew			
Dave Parker			
□ 6 Strikeout Leaders	6.00	2.70	.75
Nolan Ryan			
J.R. Richard			
□ 20 Joe Morgan DP	1.00	.45	.12
□ 24 Paul Molitor	20.00	9.00	2.50
□ 25 Steve Carlton	2.50	1.10	.30
□ 30 Dave Winfield	8.00	3.60	1.00
□ 39 Dale Murphy	5.00	2.20	.60
□ 40 Dennis Eckersley	2.00	.90	.25
□ 55 Willie Stargell	1.50	.70	.19
□ 95 Robin Yount	10.00	4.50	1.25
□ 100 Tom Seaver DP	2.00	.90	.25
□ 115 Nolan Ryan	30.00	13.50	3.70
□ 116 Ozzie Smith	90.00	40.00	11.00
□ 123 Lou Whitaker	10.00	4.50	1.25
□ 200 Johnny Bench DP	2.00	.90	.25
□ 204 Pete Rose RB	2.00	.90	.25
□ 211 Denny Martinez	1.50	.70	.19
□ 212 Carney Lansford	2.00	.90	.25
□ 215 Willie McCovey	2.00	.90	.25
□ 251 Jack Morris	2.00	.90	.25
□ 300 Rod Carew	2.00	.90	.25
□ 310 Thurman Munson	2.00	.90	.25
□ 318 Bob Welch	2.00	.90	.25
□ 320 Carl Yastrzemski	2.50	1.10	.30
□ 321 Gaylord Perry	1.00	.45	.12
□ 330 George Brett	18.00	8.00	2.20
□ 340 Jim Palmer	2.00	.90	.25
□ 348 Andre Dawson	8.00	3.60	1.00
□ 358 Alan Trammell	12.00	5.50	1.50
□ 390 Rollie Fingers	1.00	.45	.12
□ 409 Willie Wilson	2.00	.90	.25
□ 411 George Sisler ATL	1.00	.45	.12
Ty Cobb			
□ 412 Hack Wilson ATL	1.00	.45	.12
Hank Aaron			
□ 413 Roger Maris ATL	1.50	.70	.19
Hank Aaron			
□ 414 Rogers Hornsby ATL	1.00	.45	.12
Ty Cobb			
□ 417 Nolan Ryan ATL DP	4.00	1.80	.50
Walter Johnson			
□ 495 Tony Perez	1.00	.45	.12
□ 544 Fergie Jenkins	1.00	.45	.12
□ 610 Mike Schmidt	8.00	3.60	1.00
□ 640 Eddie Murray	30.00	13.50	3.70
□ 650 Pete Rose	5.00	2.20	.60
□ 665 Lou Brock	2.00	.90	.25
□ 670 Jim Hunter DP	.75	.35	.09
□ 680 Carlton Fisk	2.50	1.10	.30

	MINT	NRMT	EXC
☐ 700 Reggie Jackson DP	2.00	.90	.25
☐ 719 Dodgers Prospects Pedro Guerrero Rudy Law Joe Simpson	2.00	.90	.25

1980 Topps

The cards in this 726-card set measure the standard size. In 1980 Topps released another set of the same size and number of cards as the previous two years. As with those sets, Topps again produced 66 double-printed cards in the set; they are noted by DP in the checklist below. The player's name appears over the picture and his position and team are found in pennant design. Every card carries a facsimile autograph. Team cards feature a team checklist of players in the set on the back and the manager's name on the front. Cards 1-6 show Highlights (HL) of the 1979 season, cards 201-207 are League Leaders, and cards 661-686 feature American and National League rookie "Future Stars," one card for each team showing three young prospects. Ways this set was released include 15-card wax packs as well as 42-card rack packs. A special experiment in 1980 was the issuance of a 28-card cello pack with a three-pack of gum at the bottom so no cards would be damaged. The key Rookie Card in this set is Rickey Henderson; other Rookie Cards included in this set are Dan Quisenberry, Dave Stieb and Rick Sutcliffe.

	MINT	NRMT	EXC
COMPLETE SET (726)	150.00	70.00	19.00
COMMON CARD (1-726)	.20	.09	.03
COMMON CARD DP	.10	.05	.01
TEAM CARDS	.75	.35	.09
CL (121/241/348/484/533/646)	.75	.35	.09
SEMISTARS	.35	.16	.04
STARS	.50	.23	.06

	MINT	NRMT	EXC
☐ 1 Lou Brock HL Carl Yastrzemski Enter 3000 hit circle	3.00	.60	.30
☐ 2 Willie McCovey HL 512th homer sets new mark for NL lefties	.75	.35	.09
☐ 4 Pete Rose HL Career Record 10th season with 200 or more hits	2.00	.90	.25
☐ 40 Carlton Fisk	2.00	.90	.25
☐ 77 Dave Stieb	1.50	.70	.19
☐ 100 Johnny Bench	3.00	1.35	.35
☐ 160 Eddie Murray	16.00	7.25	2.00
☐ 203 RBI Leaders Dave Winfield Don Baylor	1.00	.45	.12
☐ 206 Strikeout Leaders J.R. Richard Nolan Ryan	4.00	1.80	.50
☐ 210 Steve Carlton	2.00	.90	.25
☐ 230 Dave Winfield	6.00	2.70	.75
☐ 232 Alan Trammell	6.00	2.70	.75
☐ 235 Andre Dawson	5.00	2.20	.60
☐ 265 Robin Yount	8.00	3.60	1.00
☐ 270 Mike Schmidt DP	3.00	1.35	.35
☐ 274 Dale Murphy	2.50	1.10	.30
☐ 280 Gaylord Perry	.75	.35	.09
☐ 320 Dennis Eckersley	1.50	.70	.19
☐ 335 Willie McCovey	1.50	.70	.19
☐ 358 Lou Whitaker	5.00	2.20	.60
☐ 387A Fred Stanley YL	2.00	.90	.25
☐ 390 Fergie Jenkins	.75	.35	.09
☐ 393 Ozzie Smith	18.00	8.00	2.20
☐ 406 Paul Molitor	14.00	6.25	1.75
☐ 450 George Brett	16.00	7.25	2.00
☐ 482 Rickey Henderson UER (7 steals at Modesto, should be at Fresno)	40.00	18.00	5.00
☐ 500 Tom Seaver	3.00	1.35	.35
☐ 540 Pete Rose	4.00	1.80	.50
☐ 544 Rick Sutcliffe	2.00	.90	.25
☐ 580 Nolan Ryan	20.00	9.00	2.50
☐ 590 Jim Palmer	1.50	.70	.19
☐ 600 Reggie Jackson	4.00	1.80	.50
☐ 610 Willie Stargell	1.25	.55	.16
☐ 650 Joe Morgan	1.50	.70	.19
☐ 651 Rollie Fingers	.75	.35	.09
☐ 667 Royals Rookies Renie Martin Bill Paschall Dan Quisenberry	2.00	.90	.25
☐ 700 Rod Carew DP	1.00	.45	.12
☐ 720 Carl Yastrzemski DP	1.50	.70	.19

1981 Topps

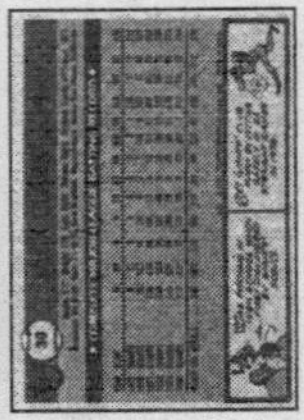

The cards in this 726-card set measure the standard size. League Leaders (1-8), Record Breakers (201-208), and Post-season cards (401-404) are the topical subsets. The team cards are all grouped together (661-686) and feature team checklist backs and a very small photo of the team's manager in the upper right corner of the obverse. The obverses carry the player's position and team in a baseball cap design, and the company name is printed in a small baseball. The backs are red and gray. The 66 double-printed cards are noted in the checklist by DP. This set was issued primarily in 15-card wax packs and 50-card rack packs. Notable Rookie Cards in the set include Harold Baines, Kirk Gibson, Tim Raines, Jeff Reardon, and Fernando Valenzuela.

	MINT	NRMT	EXC
COMPLETE SET (726)	50.00	22.00	6.25
COMMON CARD (1-726)	.15	.07	.02
COMMON CARD DP	.07	.03	.01
SEMISTARS	.40	.18	.05
STARS	.75	.35	.09

	MINT	NRMT	EXC
☐ 1 Batting Leaders George Brett Bill Buckner	2.50	1.10	.30
☐ 2 Home Run Leaders Reggie Jackson Ben Oglivie Mike Schmidt	1.00	.45	.12
☐ 3 RBI Leaders Cecil Cooper Mike Schmidt	.75	.35	.09
☐ 4 Stolen Base Leaders Rickey Henderson Ron LeFlore	1.50	.70	.19
☐ 5 Victory Leaders	.75	.35	.09

Steve Stone			
Steve Carlton			
□ 6 Strikeout Leaders	.75	.35	.09
Len Barker			
Steve Carlton			
□ 7 ERA Leaders	.40	.18	.05
Rudy May			
Don Sutton			
□ 8 Leading Firemen	.40	.18	.05
Dan Quisenberry			
Rollie Fingers			
Tom Hume			
□ 9 Pete LaCock DP	.07	.03	.01
□ 10 Mike Flanagan	.25	.11	.03
□ 11 Jim Wohlford DP	.07	.03	.01
□ 12 Mark Clear	.15	.07	.02
□ 13 Joe Charboneau	.25	.11	.03
□ 14 John Tudor	.25	.11	.03
□ 15 Larry Parrish	.15	.07	.02
□ 16 Ron Davis	.15	.07	.02
□ 17 Cliff Johnson	.15	.07	.02
□ 18 Glenn Adams	.15	.07	.02
□ 19 Jim Clancy	.15	.07	.02
□ 20 Jeff Burroughs	.15	.07	.02
□ 21 Ron Oester	.15	.07	.02
□ 22 Danny Darwin	.25	.11	.03
□ 23 Alex Trevino	.15	.07	.02
□ 24 Don Stanhouse	.15	.07	.02
□ 25 Sixto Lezcano	.15	.07	.02
□ 26 U.L. Washington	.15	.07	.02
□ 27 Champ Summers DP	.07	.03	.01
□ 28 Enrique Romo	.15	.07	.02
□ 29 Gene Tenace	.25	.11	.03
□ 30 Jack Clark	.25	.11	.03
□ 31 Checklist 1-121 DP	.15	.07	.02
□ 32 Ken Oberkfell	.15	.07	.02
□ 33 Rick Honeycutt	.15	.07	.02
□ 34 Aurelio Rodriguez	.15	.07	.02
□ 35 Mitchell Page	.15	.07	.02
□ 36 Ed Farmer	.15	.07	.02
□ 37 Gary Roenicke	.15	.07	.02
□ 38 Win Remmerswaal	.15	.07	.02
□ 39 Tom Veryzer	.15	.07	.02
□ 40 Tug McGraw	.25	.11	.03
□ 41 Ranger Rookies	.15	.07	.02
Bob Babcock			
John Butcher			
Jerry Don Gleaton			
□ 42 Jerry White DP	.07	.03	.01
□ 43 Jose Morales	.15	.07	.02
□ 44 Larry McWilliams	.15	.07	.02
□ 45 Enos Cabell	.15	.07	.02
□ 46 Rick Bosetti	.15	.07	.02
□ 47 Ken Brett	.15	.07	.02
□ 48 Dave Skaggs	.15	.07	.02
□ 49 Bob Shirley	.15	.07	.02
□ 50 Dave Lopes	.25	.11	.03
□ 51 Bill Robinson DP	.15	.07	.02
□ 52 Hector Cruz	.15	.07	.02
□ 53 Kevin Saucier	.15	.07	.02
□ 54 Ivan DeJesus	.15	.07	.02
□ 55 Mike Norris	.15	.07	.02
□ 56 Buck Martinez	.15	.07	.02
□ 57 Dave Roberts	.15	.07	.02
□ 58 Joel Youngblood	.15	.07	.02
□ 59 Dan Petry	.25	.11	.03
□ 60 Willie Randolph	.25	.11	.03
□ 61 Butch Wynegar	.15	.07	.02
□ 62 Joe Pettini	.15	.07	.02
□ 63 Steve Renko DP	.07	.03	.01
□ 64 Brian Asselstine	.15	.07	.02
□ 65 Scott McGregor	.15	.07	.02
□ 66 Royals Rookies	.15	.07	.02
Manny Castillo			
Tim Ireland			
Mike Jones			
□ 67 Ken Kravec	.15	.07	.02
□ 68 Matt Alexander DP	.07	.03	.01
□ 69 Ed Halicki	.15	.07	.02
□ 70 Al Oliver DP	.25	.11	.03
□ 71 Hal Dues	.15	.07	.02
□ 72 Barry Evans DP	.07	.03	.01
□ 73 Doug Bair	.15	.07	.02
□ 74 Mike Hargrove	.25	.11	.03
□ 75 Reggie Smith	.25	.11	.03
□ 76 Mario Mendoza	.15	.07	.02
□ 77 Mike Barlow	.15	.07	.02
□ 78 Steve Dillard	.15	.07	.02
□ 79 Bruce Robbins	.15	.07	.02
□ 80 Rusty Staub	.25	.11	.03
□ 81 Dave Stapleton	.15	.07	.02
□ 82 Astros Rookies DP	.15	.07	.02
Danny Heep			
Alan Knicely			
Bobby Sprowl			
□ 83 Mike Proly	.15	.07	.02
□ 84 Johnnie LeMaster	.15	.07	.02
□ 85 Mike Caldwell	.15	.07	.02
□ 86 Wayne Gross	.15	.07	.02
□ 87 Rick Camp	.15	.07	.02
□ 88 Joe Lefebvre	.15	.07	.02
□ 89 Darrell Jackson	.15	.07	.02
□ 90 Bake McBride	.15	.07	.02
□ 91 Tim Stoddard DP	.07	.03	.01
□ 92 Mike Easler	.15	.07	.02
□ 93 Ed Glynn DP	.15	.07	.02
□ 94 Harry Spilman DP	.07	.03	.01
□ 95 Jim Sundberg	.25	.11	.03
□ 96 A's Rookies	.15	.07	.02
Dave Beard			
Ernie Camacho			
Pat Dempsey			
□ 97 Chris Speier	.15	.07	.02
□ 98 Clint Hurdle	.15	.07	.02
□ 99 Eric Wilkins	.15	.07	.02
□ 100 Rod Carew	1.25	.55	.16
□ 101 Benny Ayala	.15	.07	.02
□ 102 Dave Tobik	.15	.07	.02
□ 103 Jerry Martin	.15	.07	.02
□ 104 Terry Forster	.15	.07	.02
□ 105 Jose Cruz	.25	.11	.03
□ 106 Don Money	.15	.07	.02
□ 107 Rich Wortham	.15	.07	.02
□ 108 Bruce Benedict	.15	.07	.02
□ 109 Mike Scott	.25	.11	.03
□ 110 Carl Yastrzemski	1.50	.70	.19
□ 111 Greg Minton	.15	.07	.02
□ 112 White Sox Rookies	.15	.07	.02
Rusty Kuntz			
Fran Mullins			
Leo Sutherland			
□ 113 Mike Phillips	.15	.07	.02
□ 114 Tom Underwood	.15	.07	.02
□ 115 Roy Smalley	.15	.07	.02
□ 116 Joe Simpson	.15	.07	.02
□ 117 Pete Falcone	.15	.07	.02
□ 118 Kurt Bevacqua	.15	.07	.02
□ 119 Tippy Martinez	.15	.07	.02
□ 120 Larry Bowa	.25	.11	.03
□ 121 Larry Harlow	.15	.07	.02
□ 122 John Denny	.15	.07	.02
□ 123 Al Cowens	.15	.07	.02
□ 124 Jerry Garvin	.15	.07	.02
□ 125 Andre Dawson	2.00	.90	.25
□ 126 Charlie Leibrandt	.40	.18	.05
□ 127 Rudy Law	.15	.07	.02
□ 128 Gary Allenson DP	.07	.03	.01
□ 129 Art Howe	.15	.07	.02
□ 130 Larry Gura	.15	.07	.02
□ 131 Keith Moreland	.25	.11	.03
□ 132 Tommy Boggs	.15	.07	.02
□ 133 Jeff Cox	.15	.07	.02
□ 134 Steve Mura	.15	.07	.02
□ 135 Gorman Thomas	.25	.11	.03
□ 136 Doug Capilla	.15	.07	.02
□ 137 Hosken Powell	.15	.07	.02
□ 138 Rich Dotson DP	.15	.07	.02
□ 139 Oscar Gamble	.15	.07	.02
□ 140 Bob Forsch	.15	.07	.02
□ 141 Miguel Dilone	.15	.07	.02
□ 142 Jackson Todd	.15	.07	.02
□ 143 Dan Meyer	.15	.07	.02
□ 144 Allen Ripley	.15	.07	.02
□ 145 Mickey Rivers	.25	.11	.03
□ 146 Bobby Castillo	.15	.07	.02
□ 147 Dale Berra	.15	.07	.02
□ 148 Randy Niemann	.15	.07	.02
□ 149 Joe Nolan	.15	.07	.02
□ 150 Mark Fidrych	.40	.18	.05
□ 151 Claudell Washington	.15	.07	.02
□ 152 John Urrea	.15	.07	.02
□ 153 Tom Poquette	.15	.07	.02

□ 154 Rick Langford	.15	.07	.02
□ 155 Chris Chambliss	.25	.11	.03
□ 156 Bob McClure	.15	.07	.02
□ 157 John Wathan	.15	.07	.02
□ 158 Fergie Jenkins	.75	.35	.09
□ 159 Brian Doyle	.15	.07	.02
□ 160 Garry Maddox	.15	.07	.02
□ 161 Dan Graham	.15	.07	.02
□ 162 Doug Corbett	.15	.07	.02
□ 163 Bill Almon	.15	.07	.02
□ 164 LaMarr Hoyt	.25	.11	.03
□ 165 Tony Scott	.15	.07	.02
□ 166 Floyd Bannister	.15	.07	.02
□ 167 Terry Whitfield	.15	.07	.02
□ 168 Don Robinson DP	.07	.03	.01
□ 169 John Mayberry	.15	.07	.02
□ 170 Ross Grimsley	.15	.07	.02
□ 171 Gene Richards	.15	.07	.02
□ 172 Gary Woods	.15	.07	.02
□ 173 Bump Wills	.15	.07	.02
□ 174 Doug Rau	.15	.07	.02
□ 175 Dave Collins	.15	.07	.02
□ 176 Mike Krukow	.15	.07	.02
□ 177 Rick Peters	.15	.07	.02
□ 178 Jim Essian DP	.07	.03	.01
□ 179 Rudy May	.15	.07	.02
□ 180 Pete Rose	2.50	1.10	.30
□ 181 Elias Sosa	.15	.07	.02
□ 182 Bob Grich	.25	.11	.03
□ 183 Dick Davis DP	.07	.03	.01
□ 184 Jim Dwyer	.15	.07	.02
□ 185 Dennis Leonard	.15	.07	.02
□ 186 Wayne Nordhagen	.15	.07	.02
□ 187 Mike Parrott	.15	.07	.02
□ 188 Doug DeCinces	.25	.11	.03
□ 189 Craig Swan	.15	.07	.02
□ 190 Cesar Cedeno	.25	.11	.03
□ 191 Rick Sutcliffe	.40	.18	.05
□ 192 Braves Rookies Terry Harper Ed Miller Rafael Ramirez	.25	.11	.03
□ 193 Pete Vuckovich	.25	.11	.03
□ 194 Rod Scurry	.15	.07	.02
□ 195 Rich Murray	.15	.07	.02
□ 196 Duffy Dyer	.15	.07	.02
□ 197 Jim Kern	.15	.07	.02
□ 198 Jerry Dybzinski	.15	.07	.02
□ 199 Chuck Rainey	.15	.07	.02
□ 200 George Foster	.25	.11	.03
□ 201 Johnny Bench RB Most homers catchers	.75	.35	.09
□ 202 Steve Carlton RB Most strikeouts, lefthander, lifetime	.75	.35	.09
□ 203 Bill Gullickson RB Most SO's, game, rookie	.40	.18	.05
□ 204 Ron LeFlore RB Rodney Scott RB Most stolen bases teammates, season	.25	.11	.03
□ 205 Pete Rose RB Most cons. seasons 600 or more at-bats	1.50	.70	.19
□ 206 Mike Schmidt RB Most homers, 3rd baseman, season	1.50	.70	.19
□ 207 Ozzie Smith RB Most assists, season, shortstop	2.00	.90	.25
□ 208 Willie Wilson RB Most AB's season	.25	.11	.03
□ 209 Dickie Thon DP	.25	.11	.03
□ 210 Jim Palmer	1.00	.45	.12
□ 211 Derrel Thomas	.15	.07	.02
□ 212 Steve Nicosia	.15	.07	.02
□ 213 Al Holland	.15	.07	.02
□ 214 Angels Rookies Ralph Botting Jim Dorsey John Harris	.15	.07	.02
□ 215 Larry Hisle	.15	.07	.02
□ 216 John Henry Johnson	.15	.07	.02
□ 217 Rich Hebner	.15	.07	.02
□ 218 Paul Splittorff	.15	.07	.02
□ 219 Ken Landreaux	.15	.07	.02
□ 220 Tom Seaver	2.00	.90	.25
□ 221 Bob Davis	.15	.07	.02
□ 222 Jorge Orta	.15	.07	.02
□ 223 Roy Lee Jackson	.15	.07	.02
□ 224 Pat Zachry	.15	.07	.02
□ 225 Ruppert Jones	.15	.07	.02
□ 226 Manny Sanguillen DP	.07	.03	.01
□ 227 Fred Martinez	.15	.07	.02
□ 228 Tom Paciorek	.15	.07	.02
□ 229 Rollie Fingers	.40	.18	.05
□ 230 George Hendrick	.15	.07	.02
□ 231 Joe Beckwith	.15	.07	.02
□ 232 Mickey Klutts	.15	.07	.02
□ 233 Skip Lockwood	.15	.07	.02
□ 234 Lou Whitaker	1.50	.70	.19
□ 235 Scott Sanderson	.15	.07	.02
□ 236 Mike Ivie	.15	.07	.02
□ 237 Charlie Moore	.15	.07	.02
□ 238 Willie Hernandez	.25	.11	.03
□ 239 Rick Miller DP	.07	.03	.01
□ 240 Nolan Ryan	8.00	3.60	1.00
□ 241 Checklist 122-242 DP	.15	.07	.02
□ 242 Chet Lemon	.15	.07	.02
□ 243 Sal Butera	.15	.07	.02
□ 244 Cardinals Rookies Tito Landrum Al Olmsted Andy Rincon	.15	.07	.02
□ 245 Ed Figueroa	.15	.07	.02
□ 246 Ed Ott DP	.07	.03	.01
□ 247 Glenn Hubbard DP	.07	.03	.01
□ 248 Joey McLaughlin	.15	.07	.02
□ 249 Larry Cox	.15	.07	.02
□ 250 Ron Guidry	.25	.11	.03
□ 251 Tom Brookens	.15	.07	.02
□ 252 Victor Cruz	.15	.07	.02
□ 253 Dave Bergman	.15	.07	.02
□ 254 Ozzie Smith	6.00	2.70	.75
□ 255 Mark Littell	.15	.07	.02
□ 256 Bombo Rivera	.15	.07	.02
□ 257 Rennie Stennett	.15	.07	.02
□ 258 Joe Price	.15	.07	.02
□ 259 Mets Rookies Juan Berenguer Hubie Brooks Mookie Wilson	.75	.35	.09
□ 260 Ron Cey	.25	.11	.03
□ 261 Rickey Henderson	5.00	2.20	.60
□ 262 Sammy Stewart	.15	.07	.02
□ 263 Brian Downing	.15	.07	.02
□ 264 Jim Norris	.15	.07	.02
□ 265 John Candelaria	.25	.11	.03
□ 266 Tom Herr	.25	.11	.03
□ 267 Stan Bahnsen	.15	.07	.02
□ 268 Jerry Royster	.15	.07	.02
□ 269 Ken Forsch	.15	.07	.02
□ 270 Greg Luzinski	.25	.11	.03
□ 271 Bill Castro	.15	.07	.02
□ 272 Bruce Kimm	.15	.07	.02
□ 273 Stan Papi	.15	.07	.02
□ 274 Craig Chamberlain	.15	.07	.02
□ 275 Dwight Evans	.40	.18	.05
□ 276 Dan Spillner	.15	.07	.02
□ 277 Alfredo Griffin	.15	.07	.02
□ 278 Rick Sofield	.15	.07	.02
□ 279 Bob Knepper	.15	.07	.02
□ 280 Ken Griffey	.25	.11	.03
□ 281 Fred Stanley	.15	.07	.02
□ 282 Mariners Rookies Rick Anderson Greg Biercevicz Rodney Craig	.15	.07	.02
□ 283 Billy Sample	.15	.07	.02
□ 284 Brian Kingman	.15	.07	.02
□ 285 Jerry Turner	.15	.07	.02
□ 286 Dave Frost	.15	.07	.02
□ 287 Lenn Sakata	.15	.07	.02
□ 288 Bob Clark	.15	.07	.02
□ 289 Mickey Hatcher	.25	.11	.03
□ 290 Bob Boone DP	.25	.11	.03
□ 291 Aurelio Lopez	.15	.07	.02
□ 292 Mike Squires	.15	.07	.02
□ 293 Charlie Lea	.15	.07	.02
□ 294 Mike Tyson DP	.07	.03	.01
□ 295 Hal McRae	.40	.18	.05
□ 296 Bill Nahorodny DP	.07	.03	.01
□ 297 Bob Bailor	.15	.07	.02

☐ 298	Buddy Solomon	.15	.07	.02
☐ 299	Elliott Maddox	.15	.07	.02
☐ 300	Paul Molitor	2.50	1.10	.30
☐ 301	Matt Keough	.15	.07	.02
☐ 302	Dodgers Rookies	3.00	1.35	.35
	Jack Perconte			
	Mike Scioscia			
	Fernando Valenzuela			
☐ 303	Johnny Oates	.25	.11	.03
☐ 304	John Castino	.15	.07	.02
☐ 305	Ken Clay	.15	.07	.02
☐ 306	Juan Beniquez DP	.07	.03	.01
☐ 307	Gene Garber	.15	.07	.02
☐ 308	Rick Manning	.15	.07	.02
☐ 309	Luis Salazar	.15	.07	.02
☐ 310	Vida Blue DP	.15	.07	.02
☐ 311	Freddie Patek	.15	.07	.02
☐ 312	Rick Rhoden	.15	.07	.02
☐ 313	Luis Pujols	.15	.07	.02
☐ 314	Rich Dauer	.15	.07	.02
☐ 315	Kirk Gibson	4.00	1.80	.50
☐ 316	Craig Minetto	.15	.07	.02
☐ 317	Lonnie Smith	.25	.11	.03
☐ 318	Steve Yeager	.15	.07	.02
☐ 319	Rowland Office	.15	.07	.02
☐ 320	Tom Burgmeier	.15	.07	.02
☐ 321	Leon Durham	.25	.11	.03
☐ 322	Neil Allen	.15	.07	.02
☐ 323	Jim Morrison DP	.07	.03	.01
☐ 324	Mike Willis	.15	.07	.02
☐ 325	Ray Knight	.25	.11	.03
☐ 326	Biff Pocoroba	.15	.07	.02
☐ 327	Moose Haas	.15	.07	.02
☐ 328	Twins Rookies	.15	.07	.02
	Dave Engle			
	Greg Johnston			
	Gary Ward			
☐ 329	Joaquin Andujar	.25	.11	.03
☐ 330	Frank White	.25	.11	.03
☐ 331	Dennis Lamp	.15	.07	.02
☐ 332	Lee Lacy DP	.07	.03	.01
☐ 333	Sid Monge	.15	.07	.02
☐ 334	Dane Iorg	.15	.07	.02
☐ 335	Rick Cerone	.15	.07	.02
☐ 336	Eddie Whitson	.15	.07	.02
☐ 337	Lynn Jones	.15	.07	.02
☐ 338	Checklist 243-363	.40	.18	.05
☐ 339	John Ellis	.15	.07	.02
☐ 340	Bruce Kison	.15	.07	.02
☐ 341	Dwayne Murphy	.15	.07	.02
☐ 342	Eric Rasmussen DP	.07	.03	.01
☐ 343	Frank Taveras	.15	.07	.02
☐ 344	Byron McLaughlin	.15	.07	.02
☐ 345	Warren Cromartie	.15	.07	.02
☐ 346	Larry Christenson DP	.07	.03	.01
☐ 347	Harold Baines	4.00	1.80	.50
☐ 348	Bob Sykes	.15	.07	.02
☐ 349	Glenn Hoffman	.15	.07	.02
☐ 350	J.R. Richard	.25	.11	.03
☐ 351	Otto Velez	.15	.07	.02
☐ 352	Dick Tidrow DP	.07	.03	.01
☐ 353	Terry Kennedy	.15	.07	.02
☐ 354	Mario Soto	.15	.07	.02
☐ 355	Bob Horner	.25	.11	.03
☐ 356	Padres Rookies	.15	.07	.02
	George Stablein			
	Craig Stimac			
	Tom Tellmann			
☐ 357	Jim Slaton	.15	.07	.02
☐ 358	Mark Wagner	.15	.07	.02
☐ 359	Tom Hausman	.15	.07	.02
☐ 360	Willie Wilson	.25	.11	.03
☐ 361	Joe Strain	.15	.07	.02
☐ 362	Bo Diaz	.15	.07	.02
☐ 363	Geoff Zahn	.15	.07	.02
☐ 364	Mike Davis	.15	.07	.02
☐ 365	Graig Nettles DP	.25	.11	.03
☐ 366	Mike Ramsey	.15	.07	.02
☐ 367	Dennis Martinez	.25	.11	.03
☐ 368	Leon Roberts	.15	.07	.02
☐ 369	Frank Tanana	.25	.11	.03
☐ 370	Dave Winfield	2.50	1.10	.30
☐ 371	Charlie Hough	.25	.11	.03
☐ 372	Jay Johnstone	.25	.11	.03
☐ 373	Pat Underwood	.15	.07	.02
☐ 374	Tommy Hutton	.15	.07	.02
☐ 375	Dave Concepcion	.25	.11	.03
☐ 376	Ron Reed	.15	.07	.02
☐ 377	Jerry Morales	.15	.07	.02
☐ 378	Dave Rader	.15	.07	.02
☐ 379	Lary Sorensen	.15	.07	.02
☐ 380	Willie Stargell	1.00	.45	.12
☐ 381	Cubs Rookies	.15	.07	.02
	Carlos Lezcano			
	Steve Macko			
	Randy Martz			
☐ 382	Paul Mirabella	.15	.07	.02
☐ 383	Eric Soderholm DP	.07	.03	.01
☐ 384	Mike Sadek	.15	.07	.02
☐ 385	Joe Sambito	.15	.07	.02
☐ 386	Dave Edwards	.15	.07	.02
☐ 387	Phil Niekro	.60	.25	.07
☐ 388	Andre Thornton	.25	.11	.03
☐ 389	Marty Pattin	.15	.07	.02
☐ 390	Cesar Geronimo	.15	.07	.02
☐ 391	Dave Lemanczyk DP	.07	.03	.01
☐ 392	Lance Parrish	.40	.18	.05
☐ 393	Broderick Perkins	.15	.07	.02
☐ 394	Woodie Fryman	.15	.07	.02
☐ 395	Scot Thompson	.15	.07	.02
☐ 396	Bill Campbell	.15	.07	.02
☐ 397	Julio Cruz	.15	.07	.02
☐ 398	Ross Baumgarten	.15	.07	.02
☐ 399	Orioles Rookies	.40	.18	.05
	Mike Boddicker			
	Mark Corey			
	Floyd Rayford			
☐ 400	Reggie Jackson	2.00	.90	.25
☐ 401	George Brett ALCS	2.00	.90	.25
☐ 402	NL Champs	.40	.18	.05
	Phillies squeak			
	past Astros			
	(Phillies celebrating)			
☐ 403	Larry Bowa WS	.40	.18	.05
☐ 404	Tug McGraw WS	.40	.18	.05
☐ 405	Nino Espinosa	.15	.07	.02
☐ 406	Dickie Noles	.15	.07	.02
☐ 407	Ernie Whitt	.15	.07	.02
☐ 408	Fernando Arroyo	.15	.07	.02
☐ 409	Larry Herndon	.15	.07	.02
☐ 410	Bert Campaneris	.25	.11	.03
☐ 411	Terry Puhl	.15	.07	.02
☐ 412	Britt Burns	.15	.07	.02
☐ 413	Tony Bernazard	.15	.07	.02
☐ 414	John Pacella DP	.07	.03	.01
☐ 415	Ben Oglivie	.25	.11	.03
☐ 416	Gary Alexander	.15	.07	.02
☐ 417	Dan Schatzeder	.15	.07	.02
☐ 418	Bobby Brown	.15	.07	.02
☐ 419	Tom Hume	.15	.07	.02
☐ 420	Keith Hernandez	.40	.18	.05
☐ 421	Bob Stanley	.15	.07	.02
☐ 422	Dan Ford	.15	.07	.02
☐ 423	Shane Rawley	.15	.07	.02
☐ 424	Yankees Rookies	.15	.07	.02
	Tim Lollar			
	Bruce Robinson			
	Dennis Werth			
☐ 425	Al Bumbry	.25	.11	.03
☐ 426	Warren Brusstar	.15	.07	.02
☐ 427	John D'Acquisto	.15	.07	.02
☐ 428	John Stearns	.15	.07	.02
☐ 429	Mick Kelleher	.15	.07	.02
☐ 430	Jim Bibby	.15	.07	.02
☐ 431	Dave Roberts	.15	.07	.02
☐ 432	Len Barker	.15	.07	.02
☐ 433	Rance Mulliniks	.15	.07	.02
☐ 434	Roger Erickson	.15	.07	.02
☐ 435	Jim Spencer	.15	.07	.02
☐ 436	Gary Lucas	.15	.07	.02
☐ 437	Mike Heath DP	.07	.03	.01
☐ 438	John Montefusco	.15	.07	.02
☐ 439	Denny Walling	.15	.07	.02
☐ 440	Jerry Reuss	.25	.11	.03
☐ 441	Ken Reitz	.15	.07	.02
☐ 442	Ron Pruitt	.15	.07	.02
☐ 443	Jim Beattie DP	.15	.07	.02
☐ 444	Garth Iorg	.15	.07	.02
☐ 445	Ellis Valentine	.15	.07	.02
☐ 446	Checklist 364-484	.40	.18	.05
☐ 447	Junior Kennedy DP	.07	.03	.01
☐ 448	Tim Corcoran	.15	.07	.02

□ 449 Paul Mitchell .15 .07 .02
□ 450 Dave Kingman DP .25 .11 .03
□ 451 Indians Rookies .15 .07 .02
Chris Bando
Tom Brennan
Sandy Wihtol
□ 452 Renie Martin .15 .07 .02
□ 453 Rob Wilfong DP .07 .03 .01
□ 454 Andy Hassler .15 .07 .02
□ 455 Rick Burleson .15 .07 .02
□ 456 Jeff Reardon 2.00 .90 .25
□ 457 Mike Lum .15 .07 .02
□ 458 Randy Jones .15 .07 .02
□ 459 Greg Gross .15 .07 .02
□ 460 Rich Gossage .40 .18 .05
□ 461 Dave McKay .15 .07 .02
□ 462 Jack Brohamer .15 .07 .02
□ 463 Milt May .15 .07 .02
□ 464 Adrian Devine .15 .07 .02
□ 465 Bill Russell .25 .11 .03
□ 466 Bob Molinaro .15 .07 .02
□ 467 Dave Stieb .25 .11 .03
□ 468 John Wockenfuss .15 .07 .02
□ 469 Jeff Leonard .25 .11 .03
□ 470 Manny Trillo .15 .07 .02
□ 471 Mike Vail .15 .07 .02
□ 472 Dyar Miller DP .07 .03 .01
□ 473 Jose Cardenal .15 .07 .02
□ 474 Mike LaCoss .15 .07 .02
□ 475 Buddy Bell .25 .11 .03
□ 476 Jerry Koosman .25 .11 .03
□ 477 Luis Gomez .15 .07 .02
□ 478 Juan Eichelberger .15 .07 .02
□ 479 Expos Rookies 6.00 2.70 .75
Tim Raines
Roberto Ramos
Bobby Pate
□ 480 Carlton Fisk 2.00 .90 .25
□ 481 Bob Lacey DP .07 .03 .01
□ 482 Jim Gantner .25 .11 .03
□ 483 Mike Griffin .15 .07 .02
□ 484 Max Venable DP .07 .03 .01
□ 485 Garry Templeton .15 .07 .02
□ 486 Marc Hill .15 .07 .02
□ 487 Dewey Robinson .15 .07 .02
□ 488 Damaso Garcia .15 .07 .02
□ 489 John Littlefield .15 .07 .02
□ 490 Eddie Murray 6.00 2.70 .75
□ 491 Gordy Pladson .15 .07 .02
□ 492 Barry Foote .15 .07 .02
□ 493 Dan Quisenberry .25 .11 .03
□ 494 Bob Walk .25 .11 .03
□ 495 Dusty Baker .40 .18 .05
□ 496 Paul Dade .15 .07 .02
□ 497 Fred Norman .15 .07 .02
□ 498 Pat Putnam .15 .07 .02
□ 499 Frank Pastore .15 .07 .02
□ 500 Jim Rice .40 .18 .05
□ 501 Tim Foli DP .07 .03 .01
□ 502 Giants Rookies .15 .07 .02
Chris Bourjos
Al Hargesheimer
Mike Rowland
□ 503 Steve McCatty .15 .07 .02
□ 504 Dale Murphy 1.25 .55 .16
□ 505 Jason Thompson .15 .07 .02
□ 506 Phil Huffman .15 .07 .02
□ 507 Jamie Quirk .15 .07 .02
□ 508 Rob Dressler .15 .07 .02
□ 509 Pete Mackanin .15 .07 .02
□ 510 Lee Mazzilli .15 .07 .02
□ 511 Wayne Garland .15 .07 .02
□ 512 Gary Thomasson .15 .07 .02
□ 513 Frank LaCorte .15 .07 .02
□ 514 George Riley .15 .07 .02
□ 515 Robin Yount 2.50 1.10 .30
□ 516 Doug Bird .15 .07 .02
□ 517 Richie Zisk .15 .07 .02
□ 518 Grant Jackson .15 .07 .02
□ 519 John Tamargo DP .07 .03 .01
□ 520 Steve Stone .25 .11 .03
□ 521 Sam Mejias .15 .07 .02
□ 522 Mike Colbern .15 .07 .02
□ 523 John Fulgham .15 .07 .02
□ 524 Willie Aikens .15 .07 .02
□ 525 Mike Torrez .15 .07 .02
□ 526 Phillies Rookies .15 .07 .02
Marty Bystrom
Jay Loviglio
Jim Wright
□ 527 Danny Goodwin .15 .07 .02
□ 528 Gary Matthews .25 .11 .03
□ 529 Dave LaRoche .15 .07 .02
□ 530 Steve Garvey .40 .18 .05
□ 531 John Curtis .15 .07 .02
□ 532 Bill Stein .15 .07 .02
□ 533 Jesus Figueroa .15 .07 .02
□ 534 Dave Smith .25 .11 .03
□ 535 Omar Moreno .15 .07 .02
□ 536 Bob Owchinko DP .07 .03 .01
□ 537 Ron Hodges .15 .07 .02
□ 538 Tom Griffin .15 .07 .02
□ 539 Rodney Scott .15 .07 .02
□ 540 Mike Schmidt DP 2.00 .90 .25
□ 541 Steve Swisher .15 .07 .02
□ 542 Larry Bradford DP .07 .03 .01
□ 543 Terry Crowley .15 .07 .02
□ 544 Rich Gale .15 .07 .02
□ 545 Johnny Grubb .15 .07 .02
□ 546 Paul Moskau .15 .07 .02
□ 547 Mario Guerrero .15 .07 .02
□ 548 Dave Goltz .15 .07 .02
□ 549 Jerry Remy .15 .07 .02
□ 550 Tommy John .40 .18 .05
□ 551 Pirates Rookies .75 .35 .09
Vance Law
Tony Pena
Pascual Perez
□ 552 Steve Trout .15 .07 .02
□ 553 Tim Blackwell .15 .07 .02
□ 554 Bert Blyleven UER .40 .18 .05
(1 is missing from
1980 on card back)
□ 555 Cecil Cooper .25 .11 .03
□ 556 Jerry Mumphrey .15 .07 .02
□ 557 Chris Knapp .15 .07 .02
□ 558 Barry Bonnell .15 .07 .02
□ 559 Willie Montanez .15 .07 .02
□ 560 Joe Morgan 1.00 .45 .12
□ 561 Dennis Littlejohn .15 .07 .02
□ 562 Checklist 485-605 .40 .18 .05
□ 563 Jim Kaat .25 .11 .03
□ 564 Ron Hassey DP .07 .03 .01
□ 565 Burt Hooton .15 .07 .02
□ 566 Del Unser .15 .07 .02
□ 567 Mark Bomback .15 .07 .02
□ 568 Dave Revering .15 .07 .02
□ 569 Al Williams DP .07 .03 .01
□ 570 Ken Singleton .25 .11 .03
□ 571 Todd Cruz .15 .07 .02
□ 572 Jack Morris .40 .18 .05
□ 573 Phil Garner .25 .11 .03
□ 574 Bill Caudill .15 .07 .02
□ 575 Tony Perez .75 .35 .09
□ 576 Reggie Cleveland .15 .07 .02
□ 577 Blue Jays Rookies .15 .07 .02
Luis Leal
Brian Milner
Ken Schrom
□ 578 Bill Gullickson .40 .18 .05
□ 579 Tim Flannery .15 .07 .02
□ 580 Don Baylor .40 .18 .05
□ 581 Roy Howell .15 .07 .02
□ 582 Gaylord Perry .75 .35 .09
□ 583 Larry Milbourne .15 .07 .02
□ 584 Randy Lerch .15 .07 .02
□ 585 Amos Otis .25 .11 .03
□ 586 Silvio Martinez .15 .07 .02
□ 587 Jeff Newman .15 .07 .02
□ 588 Gary Lavelle .15 .07 .02
□ 589 Lamar Johnson .15 .07 .02
□ 590 Bruce Sutter .25 .11 .03
□ 591 John Lowenstein .15 .07 .02
□ 592 Steve Comer .15 .07 .02
□ 593 Steve Kemp .15 .07 .02
□ 594 Preston Hanna DP .07 .03 .01
□ 595 Butch Hobson .15 .07 .02
□ 596 Jerry Augustine .15 .07 .02
□ 597 Rafael Landestoy .15 .07 .02
□ 598 George Vukovich DP .07 .03 .01
□ 599 Dennis Kinney .15 .07 .02
□ 600 Johnny Bench 2.00 .90 .25

□ 601 Don Aase	.15	.07	.02
□ 602 Bobby Murcer	.25	.11	.03
□ 603 John Verhoeven	.15	.07	.02
□ 604 Rob Picciolo	.15	.07	.02
□ 605 Don Sutton	.75	.35	.09
□ 606 Reds Rookies DP	.15	.07	.02
Bruce Berenyi			
Geoff Combe			
Paul Householder			
□ 607 David Palmer	.15	.07	.02
□ 608 Greg Pryor	.15	.07	.02
□ 609 Lynn McGlothen	.15	.07	.02
□ 610 Darrell Porter	.15	.07	.02
□ 611 Rick Matula DP	.07	.03	.01
□ 612 Duane Kuiper	.15	.07	.02
□ 613 Jim Anderson	.15	.07	.02
□ 614 Dave Rozema	.15	.07	.02
□ 615 Rick Dempsey	.25	.11	.03
□ 616 Rick Wise	.15	.07	.02
□ 617 Craig Reynolds	.15	.07	.02
□ 618 John Milner	.15	.07	.02
□ 619 Steve Henderson	.15	.07	.02
□ 620 Dennis Eckersley	1.25	.55	.16
□ 621 Tom Donohue	.15	.07	.02
□ 622 Randy Moffitt	.15	.07	.02
□ 623 Sal Bando	.25	.11	.03
□ 624 Bob Welch	.25	.11	.03
□ 625 Bill Buckner	.25	.11	.03
□ 626 Tigers Rookies	.15	.07	.02
Dave Steffen			
Jerry Ujdur			
Roger Weaver			
□ 627 Luis Tiant	.25	.11	.03
□ 628 Vic Correll	.15	.07	.02
□ 629 Tony Armas	.25	.11	.03
□ 630 Steve Carlton	1.50	.70	.19
□ 631 Ron Jackson	.15	.07	.02
□ 632 Alan Bannister	.15	.07	.02
□ 633 Bill Lee	.25	.11	.03
□ 634 Doug Flynn	.15	.07	.02
□ 635 Bobby Bonds	.25	.11	.03
□ 636 Al Hrabosky	.15	.07	.02
□ 637 Jerry Narron	.15	.07	.02
□ 638 Checklist 606-726	.40	.18	.05
□ 639 Carney Lansford	.25	.11	.03
□ 640 Dave Parker	.40	.18	.05
□ 641 Mark Belanger	.25	.11	.03
□ 642 Vern Ruhle	.15	.07	.02
□ 643 Lloyd Moseby	.25	.11	.03
□ 644 Ramon Aviles DP	.07	.03	.01
□ 645 Rick Reuschel	.25	.11	.03
□ 646 Marvis Foley	.15	.07	.02
□ 647 Dick Drago	.15	.07	.02
□ 648 Darrell Evans	.25	.11	.03
□ 649 Manny Sarmiento	.15	.07	.02
□ 650 Bucky Dent	.25	.11	.03
□ 651 Pedro Guerrero	.40	.18	.05
□ 652 John Montague	.15	.07	.02
□ 653 Bill Fahey	.15	.07	.02
□ 654 Ray Burris	.15	.07	.02
□ 655 Dan Driessen	.15	.07	.02
□ 656 Jon Matlack	.15	.07	.02
□ 657 Mike Cubbage DP	.07	.03	.01
□ 658 Milt Wilcox	.15	.07	.02
□ 659 Brewers Rookies	.15	.07	.02
John Flinn			
Ed Romero			
Ned Yost			
□ 660 Gary Carter	.75	.35	.09
□ 661 Orioles Team/Mgr.	.40	.18	.05
Earl Weaver			
(Checklist back)			
□ 662 Red Sox Team/Mgr.	.40	.18	.05
Ralph Houk			
(Checklist back)			
□ 663 Angels Team/Mgr.	.40	.18	.05
Jim Fregosi			
(Checklist back)			
□ 664 White Sox Team/Mgr.	.40	.18	.05
Tony LaRussa			
(Checklist back)			
□ 665 Indians Team/Mgr.	.40	.18	.05
Dave Garcia			
(Checklist back)			
□ 666 Tigers Team/Mgr.	.40	.18	.05
Sparky Anderson			
(Checklist back)			
□ 667 Royals Team/Mgr.	.40	.18	.05
Jim Frey			
(Checklist back)			
□ 668 Brewers Team/Mgr.	.40	.18	.05
Bob Rodgers			
(Checklist back)			
□ 669 Twins Team/Mgr.	.40	.18	.05
John Goryl			
(Checklist back)			
□ 670 Yankees Team/Mgr.	.40	.18	.05
Gene Michael			
(Checklist back)			
□ 671 A's Team/Mgr.	.40	.18	.05
Billy Martin			
(Checklist back)			
□ 672 Mariners Team/Mgr.	.40	.18	.05
Maury Wills			
(Checklist back)			
□ 673 Rangers Team/Mgr.	.40	.18	.05
Don Zimmer			
(Checklist back)			
□ 674 Blue Jays Team/Mgr.	.40	.18	.05
Bobby Mattick			
(Checklist back)			
□ 675 Braves Team/Mgr.	.40	.18	.05
Bobby Cox			
(Checklist back)			
□ 676 Cubs Team/Mgr.	.40	.18	.05
Joe Amalfitano			
(Checklist back)			
□ 677 Reds Team/Mgr.	.40	.18	.05
John McNamara			
(Checklist back)			
□ 678 Astros Team/Mgr.	.40	.18	.05
Bill Virdon			
(Checklist back)			
□ 679 Dodgers Team/Mgr.	.40	.18	.05
Tom Lasorda			
(Checklist back)			
□ 680 Expos Team/Mgr.	.40	.18	.05
Dick Williams			
(Checklist back)			
□ 681 Mets Team/Mgr.	.40	.18	.05
Joe Torre			
(Checklist back)			
□ 682 Phillies Team/Mgr.	.40	.18	.05
Dallas Green			
(Checklist back)			
□ 683 Pirates Team/Mgr.	.40	.18	.05
Chuck Tanner			
(Checklist back)			
□ 684 Cardinals Team/Mgr.	.40	.18	.05
Whitey Herzog			
(Checklist back)			
□ 685 Padres Team/Mgr.	.40	.18	.05
Frank Howard			
(Checklist back)			
□ 686 Giants Team/Mgr.	.40	.18	.05
Dave Bristol			
(Checklist back)			
□ 687 Jeff Jones	.15	.07	.02
□ 688 Kiko Garcia	.15	.07	.02
□ 689 Red Sox Rookies	.75	.35	.09
Bruce Hurst			
Keith MacWhorter			
Reid Nichols			
□ 690 Bob Watson	.25	.11	.03
□ 691 Dick Ruthven	.15	.07	.02
□ 692 Lenny Randle	.15	.07	.02
□ 693 Steve Howe	.15	.07	.02
□ 694 Bud Harrelson DP	.07	.03	.01
□ 695 Kent Tekulve	.25	.11	.03
□ 696 Alan Ashby	.15	.07	.02
□ 697 Rick Waits	.15	.07	.02
□ 698 Mike Jorgensen	.15	.07	.02
□ 699 Glenn Abbott	.15	.07	.02
□ 700 George Brett	6.00	2.70	.75
□ 701 Joe Rudi	.25	.11	.03
□ 702 George Medich	.15	.07	.02
□ 703 Alvis Woods	.15	.07	.02
□ 704 Bill Travers DP	.07	.03	.01
□ 705 Ted Simmons	.25	.11	.03
□ 706 Dave Ford	.15	.07	.02
□ 707 Dave Cash	.15	.07	.02
□ 708 Doyle Alexander	.15	.07	.02

□ 709 Alan Trammell DP	1.50	.70	.19
□ 710 Ron LeFlore DP	.07	.03	.01
□ 711 Joe Ferguson	.15	.07	.02
□ 712 Bill Bonham	.15	.07	.02
□ 713 Bill North	.15	.07	.02
□ 714 Pete Redfern	.15	.07	.02
□ 715 Bill Madlock	.25	.11	.03
□ 716 Glenn Borgmann	.15	.07	.02
□ 717 Jim Barr DP	.07	.03	.01
□ 718 Larry Biittner	.15	.07	.02
□ 719 Sparky Lyle	.25	.11	.03
□ 720 Fred Lynn	.25	.11	.03
□ 721 Toby Harrah	.25	.11	.03
□ 722 Joe Niekro	.25	.11	.03
□ 723 Bruce Bochte	.15	.07	.02
□ 724 Lou Piniella	.25	.11	.03
□ 725 Steve Rogers	.15	.07	.02
□ 726 Rick Monday	.25	.11	.03

1981 Topps Traded

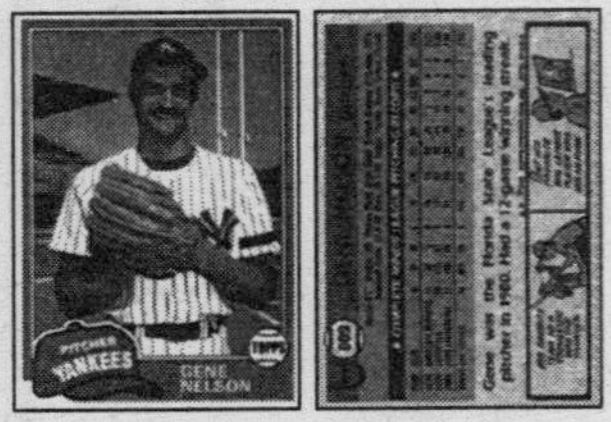

For the first time since 1976, Topps issued a 132-card factory boxed "traded" set in 1981, issued exclusively through hobby dealers. This set was sequentially numbered, alphabetically, from 727 to 858 and carries the same design as the regular issue 1981 Topps set. There are no key Rookie Cards in this set although Tim Raines, Jeff Reardon, and Fernando Valenzuela are depicted in their rookie year for cards. The key extended Rookie Card in the set is Danny Ainge.

	MINT	NRMT	EXC
COMPLETE SET (132)	30.00	13.50	3.70
COMPLETE FACT.SET (132)	32.00	14.50	4.00
COMMON CARD (727-858)	.25	.11	.03
SEMISTARS	.50	.23	.06
STARS	1.00	.45	.12

□ 727 Danny Ainge	5.00	2.20	.60
□ 728 Doyle Alexander	.25	.11	.03
□ 729 Gary Alexander	.25	.11	.03
□ 730 Bill Almon	.25	.11	.03
□ 731 Joaquin Andujar	.50	.23	.06
□ 732 Bob Bailor	.25	.11	.03
□ 733 Juan Beniquez	.25	.11	.03
□ 734 Dave Bergman	.25	.11	.03
□ 735 Tony Bernazard	.25	.11	.03
□ 736 Larry Biittner	.25	.11	.03
□ 737 Doug Bird	.25	.11	.03
□ 738 Bert Blyleven	1.00	.45	.12
□ 739 Mark Bomback	.25	.11	.03
□ 740 Bobby Bonds	.50	.23	.06
□ 741 Rick Bosetti	.25	.11	.03
□ 742 Hubie Brooks	.50	.23	.06
□ 743 Rick Burleson	.25	.11	.03
□ 744 Ray Burris	.25	.11	.03
□ 745 Jeff Burroughs	.25	.11	.03
□ 746 Enos Cabell	.25	.11	.03
□ 747 Ken Clay	.25	.11	.03
□ 748 Mark Clear	.25	.11	.03
□ 749 Larry Cox	.25	.11	.03
□ 750 Hector Cruz	.25	.11	.03
□ 751 Victor Cruz	.25	.11	.03
□ 752 Mike Cubbage	.25	.11	.03
□ 753 Dick Davis	.25	.11	.03
□ 754 Brian Doyle	.25	.11	.03
□ 755 Dick Drago	.25	.11	.03
□ 756 Leon Durham	.50	.23	.06
□ 757 Jim Dwyer	.25	.11	.03
□ 758 Dave Edwards UER	.25	.11	.03
No birthdate on card			
□ 759 Jim Essian	.25	.11	.03
□ 760 Bill Fahey	.25	.11	.03
□ 761 Rollie Fingers	1.00	.45	.12
□ 762 Carlton Fisk	4.00	1.80	.50
□ 763 Barry Foote	.25	.11	.03
□ 764 Ken Forsch	.25	.11	.03
□ 765 Kiko Garcia	.25	.11	.03
□ 766 Cesar Geronimo	.25	.11	.03
□ 767 Gary Gray	.25	.11	.03
□ 768 Mickey Hatcher	.50	.23	.06
□ 769 Steve Henderson	.25	.11	.03
□ 770 Marc Hill	.25	.11	.03
□ 771 Butch Hobson	.25	.11	.03
□ 772 Rick Honeycutt	.25	.11	.03
□ 773 Roy Howell	.25	.11	.03
□ 774 Mike Ivie	.25	.11	.03
□ 775 Roy Lee Jackson	.25	.11	.03
□ 776 Cliff Johnson	.25	.11	.03
□ 777 Randy Jones	.25	.11	.03
□ 778 Ruppert Jones	.25	.11	.03
□ 779 Mick Kelleher	.25	.11	.03
□ 780 Terry Kennedy	.25	.11	.03
□ 781 Dave Kingman	.50	.23	.06
□ 782 Bob Knepper	.25	.11	.03
□ 783 Ken Kravec	.25	.11	.03
□ 784 Bob Lacey	.25	.11	.03
□ 785 Dennis Lamp	.25	.11	.03
□ 786 Rafael Landestoy	.25	.11	.03
□ 787 Ken Landreaux	.25	.11	.03
□ 788 Carney Lansford	.50	.23	.06
□ 789 Dave LaRoche	.25	.11	.03
□ 790 Joe Lefebvre	.25	.11	.03
□ 791 Ron LeFlore	.50	.23	.06
□ 792 Randy Lerch	.25	.11	.03
□ 793 Sixto Lezcano	.25	.11	.03
□ 794 John Littlefield	.25	.11	.03
□ 795 Mike Lum	.25	.11	.03
□ 796 Greg Luzinski	.50	.23	.06
□ 797 Fred Lynn	.50	.23	.06
□ 798 Jerry Martin	.25	.11	.03
□ 799 Buck Martinez	.25	.11	.03
□ 800 Gary Matthews	.50	.23	.06
□ 801 Mario Mendoza	.25	.11	.03
□ 802 Larry Milbourne	.25	.11	.03
□ 803 Rick Miller	.25	.11	.03
□ 804 John Montefusco	.25	.11	.03
□ 805 Jerry Morales	.25	.11	.03
□ 806 Jose Morales	.25	.11	.03
□ 807 Joe Morgan	3.00	1.35	.35
□ 808 Jerry Mumphrey	.25	.11	.03
□ 809 Gene Nelson	.25	.11	.03
□ 810 Ed Ott	.25	.11	.03
□ 811 Bob Owchinko	.25	.11	.03
□ 812 Gaylord Perry	1.00	.45	.12
□ 813 Mike Phillips	.25	.11	.03
□ 814 Darrell Porter	.25	.11	.03
□ 815 Mike Proly	.25	.11	.03
□ 816 Tim Raines	10.00	4.50	1.25
□ 817 Lenny Randle	.25	.11	.03
□ 818 Doug Rau	.25	.11	.03
□ 819 Jeff Reardon	3.00	1.35	.35
□ 820 Ken Reitz	.25	.11	.03
□ 821 Steve Renko	.25	.11	.03
□ 822 Rick Reuschel	.50	.23	.06
□ 823 Dave Revering	.25	.11	.03
□ 824 Dave Roberts	.25	.11	.03
□ 825 Leon Roberts	.25	.11	.03
□ 826 Joe Rudi	.50	.23	.06
□ 827 Kevin Saucier	.25	.11	.03
□ 828 Tony Scott	.25	.11	.03
□ 829 Bob Shirley	.25	.11	.03
□ 830 Ted Simmons	.50	.23	.06
□ 831 Lary Sorensen	.25	.11	.03
□ 832 Jim Spencer	.25	.11	.03
□ 833 Harry Spilman	.25	.11	.03
□ 834 Fred Stanley	.25	.11	.03
□ 835 Rusty Staub	.50	.23	.06
□ 836 Bill Stein	.25	.11	.03
□ 837 Joe Strain	.25	.11	.03
□ 838 Bruce Sutter	.50	.23	.06
□ 839 Don Sutton	1.00	.45	.12
□ 840 Steve Swisher	.25	.11	.03

□ 841 Frank Tanana	.50	.23	.06
□ 842 Gene Tenace	.50	.23	.06
□ 843 Jason Thompson	.25	.11	.03
□ 844 Dickie Thon	.50	.23	.06
□ 845 Bill Travers	.25	.11	.03
□ 846 Tom Underwood	.25	.11	.03
□ 847 John Urrea	.25	.11	.03
□ 848 Mike Vail	.25	.11	.03
□ 849 Ellis Valentine	.25	.11	.03
□ 850 Fernando Valenzuela	2.50	1.10	.30
□ 851 Pete Vuckovich	.50	.23	.06
□ 852 Mark Wagner	.25	.11	.03
□ 853 Bob Walk	.50	.23	.06
□ 854 Claudell Washington	.25	.11	.03
□ 855 Dave Winfield	8.00	3.60	1.00
□ 856 Geoff Zahn	.25	.11	.03
□ 857 Richie Zisk	.25	.11	.03
□ 858 Checklist 727-858	.25	.11	.03

1982 Topps

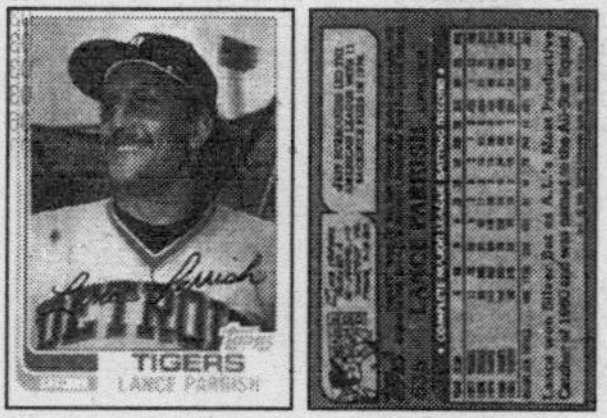

The cards in this 792-card set measure the standard size. The 1982 baseball series was the first of the largest sets Topps issued at one printing. The 66-card increase from the previous year's total eliminated the "double print" practice, that had occurred in every regular issue since 1978. Cards 1-6 depict Highlights of the strike-shortened 1981 season, cards 161-168 picture League Leaders, and there are subsets of AL (547-557) and NL (337-347) All-Stars (AS). The abbreviation "SA" in the checklist is given for the 40 "Super Action" cards introduced in this set. The team cards are actually Team Leader (TL) cards picturing the batting average and ERA leader for that team with a checklist back. All 26 of these cards were available from Topps on a perforated sheet through an offer on wax pack wrappers. Cards were primarily distributed in 15-card wax packs and 51-card rack packs. Notable Rookie Cards include Brett Butler, Chili Davis, Cal Ripken Jr., Lee Smith, and Dave Stewart. Be careful when purchasing blank-back Cal Ripken Jr. Rookie Cards. Those cards are undoubtedly counterfeit.

	MINT	NRMT	EXC
COMPLETE SET (792)	125.00	55.00	15.50
COMMON CARD (1-792)	.10	.05	.01
SEMISTARS	.25	.11	.03
STARS	.50	.23	.06
BEWARE RIPKEN BLANK-BACK FAKES	.20	.09	.03

□ 1 Steve Carlton HL	1.00	.45	.12
Sets new NL strikeout record			
□ 2 Ron Davis HL	.25	.11	.03
Fans 8 straight in relief			
□ 3 Tim Raines HL	.50	.23	.06
71 steals as rookie			
□ 4 Pete Rose HL	1.00	.45	.12
Sets NL hit mark			
□ 5 Nolan Ryan HL	3.00	1.35	.35
Pitches fifth no-hitter			
□ 6 Fernando Valenzuela HL	.25	.11	.03
8 shutouts as rookie			
□ 7 Scott Sanderson	.10	.05	.01
□ 8 Rich Dauer	.10	.05	.01
□ 9 Ron Guidry	.25	.11	.03
□ 10 Ron Guidry SA	.10	.05	.01
□ 11 Gary Alexander	.10	.05	.01
□ 12 Moose Haas	.10	.05	.01
□ 13 Lamar Johnson	.10	.05	.01
□ 14 Steve Howe	.10	.05	.01
□ 15 Ellis Valentine	.10	.05	.01
□ 16 Steve Comer	.10	.05	.01
□ 17 Darrell Evans	.25	.11	.03
□ 18 Fernando Arroyo	.10	.05	.01
□ 19 Ernie Whitt	.10	.05	.01
□ 20 Garry Maddox	.10	.05	.01
□ 21 Orioles Rookies	75.00	34.00	9.50
Bob Bonner			
Cal Ripken			
Jeff Schneider			
□ 22 Jim Beattie	.10	.05	.01
□ 23 Willie Hernandez	.25	.11	.03
□ 24 Dave Frost	.10	.05	.01
□ 25 Jerry Remy	.10	.05	.01
□ 26 Jorge Orta	.10	.05	.01
□ 27 Tom Herr	.25	.11	.03
□ 28 John Urrea	.10	.05	.01
□ 29 Dwayne Murphy	.10	.05	.01
□ 30 Tom Seaver	1.25	.55	.16
□ 31 Tom Seaver SA	.60	.25	.07
□ 32 Gene Garber	.10	.05	.01
□ 33 Jerry Morales	.10	.05	.01
□ 34 Joe Sambito	.10	.05	.01
□ 35 Willie Aikens	.10	.05	.01
□ 36 Rangers TL	.50	.23	.06
BA: Al Oliver			
Pitching: Doc Medich			
(Checklist on back)			
□ 37 Dan Graham	.10	.05	.01
□ 38 Charlie Lea	.10	.05	.01
□ 39 Lou Whitaker	.50	.23	.06
□ 40 Dave Parker	.50	.23	.06
□ 41 Dave Parker SA	.25	.11	.03
□ 42 Rick Sofield	.10	.05	.01
□ 43 Mike Cubbage	.10	.05	.01
□ 44 Britt Burns	.10	.05	.01
□ 45 Rick Cerone	.10	.05	.01
□ 46 Jerry Augustine	.10	.05	.01
□ 47 Jeff Leonard	.10	.05	.01
□ 48 Bobby Castillo	.10	.05	.01
□ 49 Alvis Woods	.10	.05	.01
□ 50 Buddy Bell	.25	.11	.03
□ 51 Cubs Rookies	.50	.23	.06
Jay Howell			
Carlos Lezcano			
Ty Waller			
□ 52 Larry Andersen	.10	.05	.01
□ 53 Greg Gross	.10	.05	.01
□ 54 Ron Hassey	.10	.05	.01
□ 55 Rick Burleson	.10	.05	.01
□ 56 Mark Littell	.10	.05	.01
□ 57 Craig Reynolds	.10	.05	.01
□ 58 John D'Acquisto	.10	.05	.01
□ 59 Rich Gedman	.25	.11	.03
□ 60 Tony Armas	.10	.05	.01
□ 61 Tommy Boggs	.10	.05	.01
□ 62 Mike Tyson	.10	.05	.01
□ 63 Mario Soto	.10	.05	.01
□ 64 Lynn Jones	.10	.05	.01
□ 65 Terry Kennedy	.10	.05	.01
□ 66 Astros TL	2.00	.90	.25
BA: Art Howe			
Pitching: Nolan Ryan			
(Checklist on back)			
□ 67 Rich Gale	.10	.05	.01
□ 68 Roy Howell	.10	.05	.01
□ 69 Al Williams	.10	.05	.01
□ 70 Tim Raines	2.00	.90	.25
□ 71 Roy Lee Jackson	.10	.05	.01
□ 72 Rick Auerbach	.10	.05	.01
□ 73 Buddy Solomon	.10	.05	.01
□ 74 Bob Clark	.10	.05	.01
□ 75 Tommy John	.50	.23	.06
□ 76 Greg Pryor	.10	.05	.01
□ 77 Miguel Dilone	.10	.05	.01
□ 78 George Medich	.10	.05	.01
□ 79 Bob Bailor	.10	.05	.01
□ 80 Jim Palmer	.75	.35	.09
□ 81 Jim Palmer SA	.50	.23	.06
□ 82 Bob Welch	.25	.11	.03
□ 83 Yankees Rookies	.50	.23	.06

Steve Balboni			
Andy McGaffigan			
Andre Robertson			
□ 84 Rennie Stennett	.10	.05	.01
□ 85 Lynn McGlothen	.10	.05	.01
□ 86 Dane Iorg	.10	.05	.01
□ 87 Matt Keough	.10	.05	.01
□ 88 Biff Pocoroba	.10	.05	.01
□ 89 Steve Henderson	.10	.05	.01
□ 90 Nolan Ryan	6.00	2.70	.75
□ 91 Carney Lansford	.25	.11	.03
□ 92 Brad Havens	.10	.05	.01
□ 93 Larry Hisle	.10	.05	.01
□ 94 Andy Hassler	.10	.05	.01
□ 95 Ozzie Smith	4.00	1.80	.50
□ 96 Royals TL	.75	.35	.09
BA: George Brett			
Pitching: Larry Gura			
(Checklist on back)			
□ 97 Paul Moskau	.10	.05	.01
□ 98 Terry Bulling	.10	.05	.01
□ 99 Barry Bonnell	.10	.05	.01
□ 100 Mike Schmidt	2.50	1.10	.30
□ 101 Mike Schmidt SA	1.50	.70	.19
□ 102 Dan Briggs	.10	.05	.01
□ 103 Bob Lacey	.10	.05	.01
□ 104 Rance Mulliniks	.10	.05	.01
□ 105 Kirk Gibson	1.00	.45	.12
□ 106 Enrique Romo	.10	.05	.01
□ 107 Wayne Krenchicki	.10	.05	.01
□ 108 Bob Sykes	.10	.05	.01
□ 109 Dave Revering	.10	.05	.01
□ 110 Carlton Fisk	1.50	.70	.19
□ 111 Carlton Fisk SA	.75	.35	.09
□ 112 Billy Sample	.10	.05	.01
□ 113 Steve McCatty	.10	.05	.01
□ 114 Ken Landreaux	.10	.05	.01
□ 115 Gaylord Perry	.50	.23	.06
□ 116 Jim Wohlford	.10	.05	.01
□ 117 Rawly Eastwick	.10	.05	.01
□ 118 Expos Rookies	.25	.11	.03
Terry Francona			
Brad Mills			
Bryn Smith			
□ 119 Joe Pittman	.10	.05	.01
□ 120 Gary Lucas	.10	.05	.01
□ 121 Ed Lynch	.10	.05	.01
□ 122 Jamie Easterly UER	.10	.05	.01
(Photo actually			
Reggie Cleveland)			
□ 123 Danny Goodwin	.10	.05	.01
□ 124 Reid Nichols	.10	.05	.01
□ 125 Danny Ainge	2.00	.90	.25
□ 126 Braves TL	.50	.23	.06
BA: Claudell Washington			
Pitching: Rick Mahler			
(Checklist on back)			
□ 127 Lonnie Smith	.25	.11	.03
□ 128 Frank Pastore	.10	.05	.01
□ 129 Checklist 1-132	.50	.23	.06
□ 130 Julio Cruz	.10	.05	.01
□ 131 Stan Bahnsen	.10	.05	.01
□ 132 Lee May	.25	.11	.03
□ 133 Pat Underwood	.10	.05	.01
□ 134 Dan Ford	.10	.05	.01
□ 135 Andy Rincon	.10	.05	.01
□ 136 Lenn Sakata	.10	.05	.01
□ 137 George Cappuzzello	.10	.05	.01
□ 138 Tony Pena	.25	.11	.03
□ 139 Jeff Jones	.10	.05	.01
□ 140 Ron LeFlore	.25	.11	.03
□ 141 Indians Rookies	.25	.11	.03
Chris Bando			
Tom Brennan			
Von Hayes			
□ 142 Dave LaRoche	.10	.05	.01
□ 143 Mookie Wilson	.25	.11	.03
□ 144 Fred Breining	.10	.05	.01
□ 145 Bob Horner	.25	.11	.03
□ 146 Mike Griffin	.10	.05	.01
□ 147 Denny Walling	.10	.05	.01
□ 148 Mickey Klutts	.10	.05	.01
□ 149 Pat Putnam	.10	.05	.01
□ 150 Ted Simmons	.25	.11	.03
□ 151 Dave Edwards	.10	.05	.01
□ 152 Ramon Aviles	.10	.05	.01
□ 153 Roger Erickson	.10	.05	.01
□ 154 Dennis Werth	.10	.05	.01
□ 155 Otto Velez	.10	.05	.01
□ 156 Oakland A's TL	.75	.35	.09
BA: Rickey Henderson			
Pitching: Steve McCatty			
(Checklist on back)			
□ 157 Steve Crawford	.10	.05	.01
□ 158 Brian Downing	.10	.05	.01
□ 159 Larry Biittner	.10	.05	.01
□ 160 Luis Tiant	.25	.11	.03
□ 161 Batting Leaders	.25	.11	.03
Bill Madlock			
Carney Lansford			
□ 162 Home Run Leaders	.75	.35	.09
Mike Schmidt			
Tony Armas			
Dwight Evans			
Bobby Grich			
Eddie Murray			
□ 163 RBI Leaders	.75	.35	.09
Mike Schmidt			
Eddie Murray			
□ 164 Stolen Base Leaders	1.00	.45	.12
Tim Raines			
Rickey Henderson			
□ 165 Victory Leaders	.50	.23	.06
Tom Seaver			
Denny Martinez			
Steve McCatty			
Jack Morris			
Pete Vuckovich			
□ 166 Strikeout Leaders	.25	.11	.03
Fernando Valenzuela			
Len Barker			
□ 167 ERA Leaders	2.00	.90	.25
Nolan Ryan			
Steve McCatty			
□ 168 Leading Firemen	.50	.23	.06
Bruce Sutter			
Rollie Fingers			
□ 169 Charlie Leibrandt	.10	.05	.01
□ 170 Jim Bibby	.10	.05	.01
□ 171 Giants Rookies	2.50	1.10	.30
Bob Brenly			
Chili Davis			
Bob Tufts			
□ 172 Bill Gullickson	.10	.05	.01
□ 173 Jamie Quirk	.10	.05	.01
□ 174 Dave Ford	.10	.05	.01
□ 175 Jerry Mumphrey	.10	.05	.01
□ 176 Dewey Robinson	.10	.05	.01
□ 177 John Ellis	.10	.05	.01
□ 178 Dyar Miller	.10	.05	.01
□ 179 Steve Garvey	.50	.23	.06
□ 180 Steve Garvey SA	.25	.11	.03
□ 181 Silvio Martinez	.10	.05	.01
□ 182 Larry Herndon	.10	.05	.01
□ 183 Mike Proly	.10	.05	.01
□ 184 Mick Kelleher	.10	.05	.01
□ 185 Phil Niekro	.50	.23	.06
□ 186 Cardinals TL	.50	.23	.06
BA: Keith Hernandez			
Pitching: Bob Forsch			
(Checklist on back)			
□ 187 Jeff Newman	.10	.05	.01
□ 188 Randy Martz	.10	.05	.01
□ 189 Glenn Hoffman	.10	.05	.01
□ 190 J.R. Richard	.25	.11	.03
□ 191 Tim Wallach	1.00	.45	.12
□ 192 Broderick Perkins	.10	.05	.01
□ 193 Darrell Jackson	.10	.05	.01
□ 194 Mike Vail	.10	.05	.01
□ 195 Paul Molitor	1.50	.70	.19
□ 196 Willie Upshaw	.10	.05	.01
□ 197 Shane Rawley	.10	.05	.01
□ 198 Chris Speier	.10	.05	.01
□ 199 Don Aase	.10	.05	.01
□ 200 George Brett	5.00	2.20	.60
□ 201 George Brett SA	2.50	1.10	.30
□ 202 Rick Manning	.10	.05	.01
□ 203 Blue Jays Rookies	.50	.23	.06
Jesse Barfield			
Brian Milner			
Boomer Wells			
□ 204 Gary Roenicke	.10	.05	.01

□ 205 Neil Allen .10 .05 .01
□ 206 Tony Bernazard .10 .05 .01
□ 207 Rod Scurry .10 .05 .01
□ 208 Bobby Murcer .25 .11 .03
□ 209 Gary Lavelle .10 .05 .01
□ 210 Keith Hernandez .50 .23 .06
□ 211 Dan Petry .10 .05 .01
□ 212 Mario Mendoza .10 .05 .01
□ 213 Dave Stewart 2.50 1.10 .30
□ 214 Brian Asselstine .10 .05 .01
□ 215 Mike Krukow .10 .05 .01
□ 216 White Sox TL .50 .23 .06
BA: Chet Lemon
Pitching: Dennis Lamp
(Checklist on back)
□ 217 Bo McLaughlin .10 .05 .01
□ 218 Dave Roberts .10 .05 .01
□ 219 John Curtis .10 .05 .01
□ 220 Manny Trillo .10 .05 .01
□ 221 Jim Slaton .10 .05 .01
□ 222 Butch Wynegar .10 .05 .01
□ 223 Lloyd Moseby .10 .05 .01
□ 224 Bruce Bochte .10 .05 .01
□ 225 Mike Torrez .10 .05 .01
□ 226 Checklist 133-264 .50 .23 .06
□ 227 Ray Burris .10 .05 .01
□ 228 Sam Mejias .10 .05 .01
□ 229 Geoff Zahn .10 .05 .01
□ 230 Willie Wilson .25 .11 .03
□ 231 Phillies Rookies .50 .23 .06
Mark Davis
Bob Dernier
Ozzie Virgil
□ 232 Terry Crowley .10 .05 .01
□ 233 Duane Kuiper .10 .05 .01
□ 234 Ron Hodges .10 .05 .01
□ 235 Mike Easler .10 .05 .01
□ 236 John Martin .10 .05 .01
□ 237 Rusty Kuntz .10 .05 .01
□ 238 Kevin Saucier .10 .05 .01
□ 239 Jon Matlack .10 .05 .01
□ 240 Bucky Dent .25 .11 .03
□ 241 Bucky Dent SA .10 .05 .01
□ 242 Milt May .10 .05 .01
□ 243 Bob Owchinko .10 .05 .01
□ 244 Rufino Linares .10 .05 .01
□ 245 Ken Reitz .10 .05 .01
□ 246 New York Mets TL .50 .23 .06
BA: Hubie Brooks
Pitching: Mike Scott
(Checklist on back)
□ 247 Pedro Guerrero .25 .11 .03
□ 248 Frank LaCorte .10 .05 .01
□ 249 Tim Flannery .10 .05 .01
□ 250 Tug McGraw .25 .11 .03
□ 251 Fred Lynn .25 .11 .03
□ 252 Fred Lynn SA .10 .05 .01
□ 253 Chuck Baker .10 .05 .01
□ 254 Jorge Bell 1.00 .45 .12
□ 255 Tony Perez .50 .23 .06
□ 256 Tony Perez SA .25 .11 .03
□ 257 Larry Harlow .10 .05 .01
□ 258 Bo Diaz .10 .05 .01
□ 259 Rodney Scott .10 .05 .01
□ 260 Bruce Sutter .25 .11 .03
□ 261 Tigers Rookies UER .10 .05 .01
Howard Bailey
Marty Castillo
Dave Rucker
(Rucker photo act-
ally Roger Weaver)
□ 262 Doug Bair .10 .05 .01
□ 263 Victor Cruz .10 .05 .01
□ 264 Dan Quisenberry .25 .11 .03
□ 265 Al Bumbry .25 .11 .03
□ 266 Rick Leach .10 .05 .01
□ 267 Kurt Bevacqua .10 .05 .01
□ 268 Rickey Keeton .10 .05 .01
□ 269 Jim Essian .10 .05 .01
□ 270 Rusty Staub .25 .11 .03
□ 271 Larry Bradford .10 .05 .01
□ 272 Bump Wills .10 .05 .01
□ 273 Doug Bird .10 .05 .01
□ 274 Bob Ojeda .50 .23 .06
□ 275 Bob Watson .25 .11 .03
□ 276 Angels TL .50 .23 .06
BA: Rod Carew
Pitching: Ken Forsch
(Checklist on back)
□ 277 Terry Puhl .10 .05 .01
□ 278 John Littlefield .10 .05 .01
□ 279 Bill Russell .25 .11 .03
□ 280 Ben Oglivie .25 .11 .03
□ 281 John Verhoeven .10 .05 .01
□ 282 Ken Macha .10 .05 .01
□ 283 Brian Allard .10 .05 .01
□ 284 Bob Grich .25 .11 .03
□ 285 Sparky Lyle .25 .11 .03
□ 286 Bill Fahey .10 .05 .01
□ 287 Alan Bannister .10 .05 .01
□ 288 Garry Templeton .10 .05 .01
□ 289 Bob Stanley .10 .05 .01
□ 290 Ken Singleton .25 .11 .03
□ 291 Pirates Rookies .25 .11 .03
Vance Law
Bob Long
Johnny Ray
□ 292 David Palmer .10 .05 .01
□ 293 Rob Picciolo .10 .05 .01
□ 294 Mike LaCoss .10 .05 .01
□ 295 Jason Thompson .10 .05 .01
□ 296 Bob Walk .10 .05 .01
□ 297 Clint Hurdle .10 .05 .01
□ 298 Danny Darwin .10 .05 .01
□ 299 Steve Trout .10 .05 .01
□ 300 Reggie Jackson 1.50 .70 .19
□ 301 Reggie Jackson SA .75 .35 .09
□ 302 Doug Flynn .10 .05 .01
□ 303 Bill Caudill .10 .05 .01
□ 304 Johnnie LeMaster .10 .05 .01
□ 305 Don Sutton .50 .23 .06
□ 306 Don Sutton SA .25 .11 .03
□ 307 Randy Bass .25 .11 .03
□ 308 Charlie Moore .10 .05 .01
□ 309 Pete Redfern .10 .05 .01
□ 310 Mike Hargrove .25 .11 .03
□ 311 Dodgers TL .50 .23 .06
BA: Dusty Baker
Pitching: Burt Hooton
(Checklist on back)
□ 312 Lenny Randle .10 .05 .01
□ 313 John Harris .10 .05 .01
□ 314 Buck Martinez .10 .05 .01
□ 315 Burt Hooton .10 .05 .01
□ 316 Steve Braun .10 .05 .01
□ 317 Dick Ruthven .10 .05 .01
□ 318 Mike Heath .10 .05 .01
□ 319 Dave Rozema .10 .05 .01
□ 320 Chris Chambliss .25 .11 .03
□ 321 Chris Chambliss SA .10 .05 .01
□ 322 Garry Hancock .10 .05 .01
□ 323 Bill Lee .25 .11 .03
□ 324 Steve Dillard .10 .05 .01
□ 325 Jose Cruz .25 .11 .03
□ 326 Pete Falcone .10 .05 .01
□ 327 Joe Nolan .10 .05 .01
□ 328 Ed Farmer .10 .05 .01
□ 329 U.L. Washington .10 .05 .01
□ 330 Rick Wise .10 .05 .01
□ 331 Benny Ayala .10 .05 .01
□ 332 Don Robinson .10 .05 .01
□ 333 Brewers Rookies .10 .05 .01
Frank DiPino
Marshall Edwards
Chuck Porter
□ 334 Aurelio Rodriguez .10 .05 .01
□ 335 Jim Sundberg .25 .11 .03
□ 336 Mariners TL .50 .23 .06
BA: Tom Paciorek
Pitching: Glenn Abbott
(Checklist on back)
□ 337 Pete Rose AS 1.00 .45 .12
□ 338 Dave Lopes AS .25 .11 .03
□ 339 Mike Schmidt AS .75 .35 .09
□ 340 Dave Concepcion AS .25 .11 .03
□ 341 Andre Dawson AS .50 .23 .06
□ 342A George Foster AS .25 .11 .03
(With autograph)
□ 342B George Foster AS 1.00 .45 .12
(W/o autograph)
□ 343 Dave Parker AS .25 .11 .03
□ 344 Gary Carter AS .50 .23 .06

□ 345 Fernando Valenzuela AS	.25	.11	.03
□ 346 Tom Seaver AS ERR	1.25	.55	.16
("t ed")			
□ 346B Tom Seaver AS COR	1.25	.55	.16
("tied")			
□ 347 Bruce Sutter AS	.25	.11	.03
□ 348 Derrel Thomas	.10	.05	.01
□ 349 George Frazier	.10	.05	.01
□ 350 Thad Bosley	.10	.05	.01
□ 351 Reds Rookies	.10	.05	.01
Scott Brown			
Geoff Combe			
Paul Householder			
□ 352 Dick Davis	.10	.05	.01
□ 353 Jack O'Connor	.10	.05	.01
□ 354 Roberto Ramos	.10	.05	.01
□ 355 Dwight Evans	.50	.23	.06
□ 356 Denny Lewallyn	.10	.05	.01
□ 357 Butch Hobson	.10	.05	.01
□ 358 Mike Parrott	.10	.05	.01
□ 359 Jim Dwyer	.10	.05	.01
□ 360 Len Barker	.10	.05	.01
□ 361 Rafael Landestoy	.10	.05	.01
□ 362 Jim Wright UER	.10	.05	.01
(Wrong Jim Wright pictured)			
□ 363 Bob Molinaro	.10	.05	.01
□ 364 Doyle Alexander	.10	.05	.01
□ 365 Bill Madlock	.25	.11	.03
□ 366 Padres TL	.50	.23	.06
BA: Luis Salazar			
Pitching: Juan Eichelberger			
(Checklist on back)			
□ 367 Jim Kaat	.25	.11	.03
□ 368 Alex Trevino	.10	.05	.01
□ 369 Champ Summers	.10	.05	.01
□ 370 Mike Norris	.10	.05	.01
□ 371 Jerry Don Gleaton	.10	.05	.01
□ 372 Luis Gomez	.10	.05	.01
□ 373 Gene Nelson	.10	.05	.01
□ 374 Tim Blackwell	.10	.05	.01
□ 375 Dusty Baker	.50	.23	.06
□ 376 Chris Welsh	.10	.05	.01
□ 377 Kiko Garcia	.10	.05	.01
□ 378 Mike Caldwell	.10	.05	.01
□ 379 Rob Wilfong	.10	.05	.01
□ 380 Dave Stieb	.25	.11	.03
□ 381 Red Sox Rookies	.25	.11	.03
Bruce Hurst			
Dave Schmidt			
Julio Valdez			
□ 382 Joe Simpson	.10	.05	.01
□ 383A Pascual Perez ERR	10.00	4.50	1.25
(No position on front)			
□ 383B Pascual Perez COR	.25	.11	.03
□ 384 Keith Moreland	.10	.05	.01
□ 385 Ken Forsch	.10	.05	.01
□ 386 Jerry White	.10	.05	.01
□ 387 Tom Veryzer	.10	.05	.01
□ 388 Joe Rudi	.10	.05	.01
□ 389 George Vukovich	.10	.05	.01
□ 390 Eddie Murray	5.00	2.20	.60
□ 391 Dave Tobik	.10	.05	.01
□ 392 Rick Bosetti	.10	.05	.01
□ 393 Al Hrabosky	.10	.05	.01
□ 394 Checklist 265-396	.50	.23	.06
□ 395 Omar Moreno	.10	.05	.01
□ 396 Twins TL	.50	.23	.06
BA: John Castino			
Pitching: Fernando Arroyo			
(Checklist on back)			
□ 397 Ken Brett	.10	.05	.01
□ 398 Mike Squires	.10	.05	.01
□ 399 Pat Zachry	.10	.05	.01
□ 400 Johnny Bench	1.25	.55	.16
□ 401 Johnny Bench SA	.60	.25	.07
□ 402 Bill Stein	.10	.05	.01
□ 403 Jim Tracy	.10	.05	.01
□ 404 Dickie Thon	.10	.05	.01
□ 405 Rick Reuschel	.25	.11	.03
□ 406 Al Holland	.10	.05	.01
□ 407 Danny Boone	.10	.05	.01
□ 408 Ed Romero	.10	.05	.01
□ 409 Don Cooper	.10	.05	.01
□ 410 Ron Cey	.25	.11	.03
□ 411 Ron Cey SA	.10	.05	.01
□ 412 Luis Leal	.10	.05	.01
□ 413 Dan Meyer	.10	.05	.01
□ 414 Elias Sosa	.10	.05	.01
□ 415 Don Baylor	.50	.23	.06
□ 416 Marty Bystrom	.10	.05	.01
□ 417 Pat Kelly	.10	.05	.01
□ 418 Rangers Rookies	.10	.05	.01
John Butcher			
Bobby Johnson			
Dave Schmidt			
□ 419 Steve Stone	.25	.11	.03
□ 420 George Hendrick	.10	.05	.01
□ 421 Mark Clear	.10	.05	.01
□ 422 Cliff Johnson	.10	.05	.01
□ 423 Stan Papi	.10	.05	.01
□ 424 Bruce Benedict	.10	.05	.01
□ 425 John Candelaria	.10	.05	.01
□ 426 Orioles TL	.50	.23	.06
BA: Eddie Murray			
Pitching: Sammy Stewart			
(Checklist on back)			
□ 427 Ron Oester	.10	.05	.01
□ 428 LaMarr Hoyt	.10	.05	.01
□ 429 John Wathan	.10	.05	.01
□ 430 Vida Blue	.25	.11	.03
□ 431 Vida Blue SA	.10	.05	.01
□ 432 Mike Scott	.25	.11	.03
□ 433 Alan Ashby	.10	.05	.01
□ 434 Joe Lefebvre	.10	.05	.01
□ 435 Robin Yount	2.00	.90	.25
□ 436 Joe Strain	.10	.05	.01
□ 437 Juan Berenguer	.10	.05	.01
□ 438 Pete Mackanin	.10	.05	.01
□ 439 Dave Righetti	.50	.23	.06
□ 440 Jeff Burroughs	.10	.05	.01
□ 441 Astros Rookies	.10	.05	.01
Danny Heep			
Billy Smith			
Bobby Sprowl			
□ 442 Bruce Kison	.10	.05	.01
□ 443 Mark Wagner	.10	.05	.01
□ 444 Terry Forster	.10	.05	.01
□ 445 Larry Parrish	.10	.05	.01
□ 446 Wayne Garland	.10	.05	.01
□ 447 Darrell Porter	.25	.11	.03
□ 448 Darrell Porter SA	.10	.05	.01
□ 449 Luis Aguayo	.10	.05	.01
□ 450 Jack Morris	.50	.23	.06
□ 451 Ed Miller	.10	.05	.01
□ 452 Lee Smith	8.00	3.60	1.00
□ 453 Art Howe	.10	.05	.01
□ 454 Rick Langford	.10	.05	.01
□ 455 Tom Burgmeier	.10	.05	.01
□ 456 Chicago Cubs TL	.50	.23	.06
BA: Bill Buckner			
Pitching: Randy Martz			
(Checklist on back)			
□ 457 Tim Stoddard	.10	.05	.01
□ 458 Willie Montanez	.10	.05	.01
□ 459 Bruce Berenyi	.10	.05	.01
□ 460 Jack Clark	.25	.11	.03
□ 461 Rich Dotson	.10	.05	.01
□ 462 Dave Chalk	.10	.05	.01
□ 463 Jim Kern	.10	.05	.01
□ 464 Juan Bonilla	.10	.05	.01
□ 465 Lee Mazzilli	.10	.05	.01
□ 466 Randy Lerch	.10	.05	.01
□ 467 Mickey Hatcher	.10	.05	.01
□ 468 Floyd Bannister	.10	.05	.01
□ 469 Ed Ott	.10	.05	.01
□ 470 John Mayberry	.10	.05	.01
□ 471 Royals Rookies	.10	.05	.01
Atlee Hammaker			
Mike Jones			
Darryl Motley			
□ 472 Oscar Gamble	.10	.05	.01
□ 473 Mike Stanton	.10	.05	.01
□ 474 Ken Oberkfell	.10	.05	.01
□ 475 Alan Trammell	1.25	.55	.16
□ 476 Brian Kingman	.10	.05	.01
□ 477 Steve Yeager	.10	.05	.01
□ 478 Ray Searage	.10	.05	.01
□ 479 Rowland Office	.10	.05	.01

□ 480	Steve Carlton	1.25	.55	.16
□ 481	Steve Carlton SA	.50	.23	.06
□ 482	Glenn Hubbard	.10	.05	.01
□ 483	Gary Woods	.10	.05	.01
□ 484	Ivan DeJesus	.10	.05	.01
□ 485	Kent Tekulve	.25	.11	.03
□ 486	Yankees TL	.25	.11	.03
	BA: Jerry Mumphrey			
	Pitching: Tommy John			
	(Checklist on back)			
□ 487	Bob McClure	.10	.05	.01
□ 488	Ron Jackson	.10	.05	.01
□ 489	Rick Dempsey	.25	.11	.03
□ 490	Dennis Eckersley	.50	.23	.06
□ 491	Checklist 397-528	.50	.23	.06
□ 492	Joe Price	.10	.05	.01
□ 493	Chet Lemon	.10	.05	.01
□ 494	Hubie Brooks	.25	.11	.03
□ 495	Dennis Leonard	.10	.05	.01
□ 496	Johnny Grubb	.10	.05	.01
□ 497	Jim Anderson	.10	.05	.01
□ 498	Dave Bergman	.10	.05	.01
□ 499	Paul Mirabella	.10	.05	.01
□ 500	Rod Carew	1.00	.45	.12
□ 501	Rod Carew SA	.50	.23	.06
□ 502	Braves Rookies	3.00	1.35	.35
	Steve Bedrosian UER			
	(Photo actually			
	Larry Owen)			
	Brett Butler			
	Larry Owen			
□ 503	Julio Gonzalez	.10	.05	.01
□ 504	Rick Peters	.10	.05	.01
□ 505	Graig Nettles	.25	.11	.03
□ 506	Graig Nettles SA	.10	.05	.01
□ 507	Terry Harper	.10	.05	.01
□ 508	Jody Davis	.10	.05	.01
□ 509	Harry Spilman	.10	.05	.01
□ 510	Fernando Valenzuela	.50	.23	.06
□ 511	Ruppert Jones	.10	.05	.01
□ 512	Jerry Dybzinski	.10	.05	.01
□ 513	Rick Rhoden	.10	.05	.01
□ 514	Joe Ferguson	.10	.05	.01
□ 515	Larry Bowa	.25	.11	.03
□ 516	Larry Bowa SA	.10	.05	.01
□ 517	Mark Brouhard	.10	.05	.01
□ 518	Garth Iorg	.10	.05	.01
□ 519	Glenn Adams	.10	.05	.01
□ 520	Mike Flanagan	.25	.11	.03
□ 521	Bill Almon	.10	.05	.01
□ 522	Chuck Rainey	.10	.05	.01
□ 523	Gary Gray	.10	.05	.01
□ 524	Tom Hausman	.10	.05	.01
□ 525	Ray Knight	.25	.11	.03
□ 526	Expos TL	.50	.23	.06
	BA: Warren Cromartie			
	Pitching: Bill Gullickson			
	(Checklist on back)			
□ 527	John Henry Johnson	.10	.05	.01
□ 528	Matt Alexander	.10	.05	.01
□ 529	Allen Ripley	.10	.05	.01
□ 530	Dickie Noles	.10	.05	.01
□ 531	A's Rookies	.10	.05	.01
	Rich Bordi			
	Mark Budaska			
	Kelvin Moore			
□ 532	Toby Harrah	.25	.11	.03
□ 533	Joaquin Andujar	.25	.11	.03
□ 534	Dave McKay	.10	.05	.01
□ 535	Lance Parrish	.50	.23	.06
□ 536	Rafael Ramirez	.10	.05	.01
□ 537	Doug Capilla	.10	.05	.01
□ 538	Lou Piniella	.25	.11	.03
□ 539	Vern Ruhle	.10	.05	.01
□ 540	Andre Dawson	1.50	.70	.19
□ 541	Barry Evans	.10	.05	.01
□ 542	Ned Yost	.10	.05	.01
□ 543	Bill Robinson	.10	.05	.01
□ 544	Larry Christenson	.10	.05	.01
□ 545	Reggie Smith	.25	.11	.03
□ 546	Reggie Smith SA	.10	.05	.01
□ 547	Rod Carew AS	.50	.23	.06
□ 548	Willie Randolph AS	.25	.11	.03
□ 549	George Brett AS	2.50	1.10	.30
□ 550	Bucky Dent AS	.25	.11	.03
□ 551	Reggie Jackson AS	.75	.35	.09

□ 552	Ken Singleton AS	.25	.11	.03
□ 553	Dave Winfield AS	1.25	.55	.16
□ 554	Carlton Fisk AS	.50	.23	.06
□ 555	Scott McGregor AS	.10	.05	.01
□ 556	Jack Morris AS	.50	.23	.06
□ 557	Rich Gossage AS	.25	.11	.03
□ 558	John Tudor	.25	.11	.03
□ 559	Indians TL	.25	.11	.03
	BA: Mike Hargrove			
	Pitching: Bert Blyleven			
	(Checklist on back)			
□ 560	Doug Corbett	.10	.05	.01
□ 561	Cardinals Rookies	.10	.05	.01
	Glenn Brummer			
	Luis DeLeon			
	Gene Roof			
□ 562	Mike O'Berry	.10	.05	.01
□ 563	Ross Baumgarten	.10	.05	.01
□ 564	Doug DeCinces	.25	.11	.03
□ 565	Jackson Todd	.10	.05	.01
□ 566	Mike Jorgensen	.10	.05	.01
□ 567	Bob Babcock	.10	.05	.01
□ 568	Joe Pettini	.10	.05	.01
□ 569	Willie Randolph	.25	.11	.03
□ 570	Willie Randolph SA	.10	.05	.01
□ 571	Glenn Abbott	.10	.05	.01
□ 572	Juan Beniquez	.10	.05	.01
□ 573	Rick Waits	.10	.05	.01
□ 574	Mike Ramsey	.10	.05	.01
□ 575	Al Cowens	.10	.05	.01
□ 576	Giants TL	.50	.23	.06
	BA: Milt May			
	Pitching: Vida Blue			
	(Checklist on back)			
□ 577	Rick Monday	.10	.05	.01
□ 578	Shooty Babitt	.10	.05	.01
□ 579	Rick Mahler	.10	.05	.01
□ 580	Bobby Bonds	.25	.11	.03
□ 581	Ron Reed	.10	.05	.01
□ 582	Luis Pujols	.10	.05	.01
□ 583	Tippy Martinez	.10	.05	.01
□ 584	Hosken Powell	.10	.05	.01
□ 585	Rollie Fingers	.50	.23	.06
□ 586	Rollie Fingers SA	.25	.11	.03
□ 587	Tim Lollar	.10	.05	.01
□ 588	Dale Berra	.10	.05	.01
□ 589	Dave Stapleton	.10	.05	.01
□ 590	Al Oliver	.25	.11	.03
□ 591	Al Oliver SA	.10	.05	.01
□ 592	Craig Swan	.10	.05	.01
□ 593	Billy Smith	.10	.05	.01
□ 594	Renie Martin	.10	.05	.01
□ 595	Dave Collins	.10	.05	.01
□ 596	Damaso Garcia	.10	.05	.01
□ 597	Wayne Nordhagen	.10	.05	.01
□ 598	Bob Galasso	.10	.05	.01
□ 599	White Sox Rookies	.10	.05	.01
	Jay Loviglio			
	Reggie Patterson			
	Leo Sutherland			
□ 600	Dave Winfield	2.00	.90	.25
□ 601	Sid Monge	.10	.05	.01
□ 602	Freddie Patek	.10	.05	.01
□ 603	Rich Hebner	.25	.11	.03
□ 604	Orlando Sanchez	.10	.05	.01
□ 605	Steve Rogers	.10	.05	.01
□ 606	Blue Jays TL	.50	.23	.06
	BA: John Mayberry			
	Pitching: Dave Stieb			
	(Checklist on back)			
□ 607	Leon Durham	.25	.11	.03
□ 608	Jerry Royster	.10	.05	.01
□ 609	Rick Sutcliffe	.25	.11	.03
□ 610	Rickey Henderson	3.00	1.35	.35
□ 611	Joe Niekro	.25	.11	.03
□ 612	Gary Ward	.10	.05	.01
□ 613	Jim Gantner	.25	.11	.03
□ 614	Juan Eichelberger	.10	.05	.01
□ 615	Bob Boone	.25	.11	.03
□ 616	Bob Boone SA	.10	.05	.01
□ 617	Scott McGregor	.10	.05	.01
□ 618	Tim Foli	.10	.05	.01
□ 619	Bill Campbell	.10	.05	.01
□ 620	Ken Griffey	.25	.11	.03
□ 621	Ken Griffey SA	.10	.05	.01
□ 622	Dennis Lamp	.10	.05	.01

□ 623	Mets Rookies	.50	.23	.06
	Ron Gardenhire			
	Terry Leach			
	Tim Leary			
□ 624	Fergie Jenkins	.50	.23	.06
□ 625	Hal McRae	.25	.11	.03
□ 626	Randy Jones	.10	.05	.01
□ 627	Enos Cabell	.10	.05	.01
□ 628	Bill Travers	.10	.05	.01
□ 629	John Wockenfuss	.10	.05	.01
□ 630	Joe Charboneau	.10	.05	.01
□ 631	Gene Tenace	.25	.11	.03
□ 632	Bryan Clark	.10	.05	.01
□ 633	Mitchell Page	.10	.05	.01
□ 634	Checklist 529-660	.50	.23	.06
□ 635	Ron Davis	.10	.05	.01
□ 636	Phillies TL	.50	.23	.06
	BA: Pete Rose			
	Pitching: Steve Carlton			
	(Checklist on back)			
□ 637	Rick Camp	.10	.05	.01
□ 638	John Milner	.10	.05	.01
□ 639	Ken Kravec	.10	.05	.01
□ 640	Cesar Cedeno	.25	.11	.03
□ 641	Steve Mura	.10	.05	.01
□ 642	Mike Scioscia	.25	.11	.03
□ 643	Pete Vuckovich	.10	.05	.01
□ 644	John Castino	.10	.05	.01
□ 645	Frank White	.25	.11	.03
□ 646	Frank White SA	.10	.05	.01
□ 647	Warren Brusstar	.10	.05	.01
□ 648	Jose Morales	.10	.05	.01
□ 649	Ken Clay	.10	.05	.01
□ 650	Carl Yastrzemski	1.25	.55	.16
□ 651	Carl Yastrzemski SA	.50	.23	.06
□ 652	Steve Nicosia	.10	.05	.01
□ 653	Angels Rookies	.50	.23	.06
	Tom Brunansky			
	Luis Sanchez			
	Daryl Sconiers			
□ 654	Jim Morrison	.10	.05	.01
□ 655	Joel Youngblood	.10	.05	.01
□ 656	Eddie Whitson	.10	.05	.01
□ 657	Tom Poquette	.10	.05	.01
□ 658	Tito Landrum	.10	.05	.01
□ 659	Fred Martinez	.10	.05	.01
□ 660	Dave Concepcion	.25	.11	.03
□ 661	Dave Concepcion SA	.10	.05	.01
□ 662	Luis Salazar	.10	.05	.01
□ 663	Hector Cruz	.10	.05	.01
□ 664	Dan Spillner	.10	.05	.01
□ 665	Jim Clancy	.10	.05	.01
□ 666	Tigers TL	.50	.23	.06
	BA: Steve Kemp			
	Pitching: Dan Petry			
	(Checklist on back)			
□ 667	Jeff Reardon	.50	.23	.06
□ 668	Dale Murphy	.50	.23	.06
□ 669	Larry Milbourne	.10	.05	.01
□ 670	Steve Kemp	.10	.05	.01
□ 671	Mike Davis	.10	.05	.01
□ 672	Bob Knepper	.10	.05	.01
□ 673	Keith Drumwright	.10	.05	.01
□ 674	Dave Goltz	.10	.05	.01
□ 675	Cecil Cooper	.25	.11	.03
□ 676	Sal Butera	.10	.05	.01
□ 677	Alfredo Griffin	.10	.05	.01
□ 678	Tom Paciorek	.10	.05	.01
□ 679	Sammy Stewart	.10	.05	.01
□ 680	Gary Matthews	.25	.11	.03
□ 681	Dodgers Rookies	.50	.23	.06
	Mike Marshall			
	Ron Roenicke			
	Steve Sax			
□ 682	Jesse Jefferson	.10	.05	.01
□ 683	Phil Garner	.25	.11	.03
□ 684	Harold Baines	.50	.23	.06
□ 685	Bert Blyleven	.50	.23	.06
□ 686	Gary Allenson	.10	.05	.01
□ 687	Greg Minton	.10	.05	.01
□ 688	Leon Roberts	.10	.05	.01
□ 689	Lary Sorensen	.10	.05	.01
□ 690	Dave Kingman	.25	.11	.03
□ 691	Dan Schatzeder	.10	.05	.01
□ 692	Wayne Gross	.10	.05	.01
□ 693	Cesar Geronimo	.10	.05	.01
□ 694	Dave Wehrmeister	.10	.05	.01
□ 695	Warren Cromartie	.10	.05	.01
□ 696	Pirates TL	.50	.23	.06
	BA: Bill Madlock			
	Pitching: Eddie Solomon			
	(Checklist on back)			
□ 697	John Montefusco	.10	.05	.01
□ 698	Tony Scott	.10	.05	.01
□ 699	Dick Tidrow	.10	.05	.01
□ 700	George Foster	.25	.11	.03
□ 701	George Foster SA	.10	.05	.01
□ 702	Steve Renko	.10	.05	.01
□ 703	Brewers TL	.50	.23	.06
	BA: Cecil Cooper			
	Pitching: Pete Vuckovich			
	(Checklist on back)			
□ 704	Mickey Rivers	.10	.05	.01
□ 705	Mickey Rivers SA	.10	.05	.01
□ 706	Barry Foote	.10	.05	.01
□ 707	Mark Bomback	.10	.05	.01
□ 708	Gene Richards	.10	.05	.01
□ 709	Don Money	.10	.05	.01
□ 710	Jerry Reuss	.25	.11	.03
□ 711	Mariners Rookies	.50	.23	.06
	Dave Edler			
	Dave Henderson			
	Reggie Walton			
□ 712	Dennis Martinez	.25	.11	.03
□ 713	Del Unser	.10	.05	.01
□ 714	Jerry Koosman	.25	.11	.03
□ 715	Willie Stargell	.50	.23	.06
□ 716	Willie Stargell SA	.25	.11	.03
□ 717	Rick Miller	.10	.05	.01
□ 718	Charlie Hough	.25	.11	.03
□ 719	Jerry Narron	.10	.05	.01
□ 720	Greg Luzinski	.25	.11	.03
□ 721	Greg Luzinski SA	.10	.05	.01
□ 722	Jerry Martin	.10	.05	.01
□ 723	Junior Kennedy	.10	.05	.01
□ 724	Dave Rosello	.10	.05	.01
□ 725	Amos Otis	.25	.11	.03
□ 726	Amos Otis SA	.10	.05	.01
□ 727	Sixto Lezcano	.10	.05	.01
□ 728	Aurelio Lopez	.10	.05	.01
□ 729	Jim Spencer	.10	.05	.01
□ 730	Gary Carter	.50	.23	.06
□ 731	Padres Rookies	.10	.05	.01
	Mike Armstrong			
	Doug Gwosdz			
	Fred Kuhaulua			
□ 732	Mike Lum	.10	.05	.01
□ 733	Larry McWilliams	.10	.05	.01
□ 734	Mike Ivie	.10	.05	.01
□ 735	Rudy May	.10	.05	.01
□ 736	Jerry Turner	.10	.05	.01
□ 737	Reggie Cleveland	.10	.05	.01
□ 738	Dave Engle	.10	.05	.01
□ 739	Joey McLaughlin	.10	.05	.01
□ 740	Dave Lopes	.25	.11	.03
□ 741	Dave Lopes SA	.10	.05	.01
□ 742	Dick Drago	.10	.05	.01
□ 743	John Stearns	.10	.05	.01
□ 744	Mike Witt	.25	.11	.03
□ 745	Bake McBride	.10	.05	.01
□ 746	Andre Thornton	.10	.05	.01
□ 747	John Lowenstein	.10	.05	.01
□ 748	Marc Hill	.10	.05	.01
□ 749	Bob Shirley	.10	.05	.01
□ 750	Jim Rice	.50	.23	.06
□ 751	Rick Honeycutt	.10	.05	.01
□ 752	Lee Lacy	.10	.05	.01
□ 753	Tom Brookens	.10	.05	.01
□ 754	Joe Morgan	.75	.35	.09
□ 755	Joe Morgan SA	.25	.11	.03
□ 756	Reds TL	.50	.23	.06
	BA: Ken Griffey			
	Pitching: Tom Seaver			
	(Checklist on back)			
□ 757	Tom Underwood	.10	.05	.01
□ 758	Claudell Washington	.10	.05	.01
□ 759	Paul Splittorff	.10	.05	.01
□ 760	Bill Buckner	.25	.11	.03
□ 761	Dave Smith	.10	.05	.01
□ 762	Mike Phillips	.10	.05	.01
□ 763	Tom Hume	.10	.05	.01
□ 764	Steve Swisher	.10	.05	.01

□ 765	Gorman Thomas	.25	.11	.03
□ 766	Twins Rookies Lenny Faedo Kent Hrbek Tim Laudner	3.00	1.35	.35
□ 767	Roy Smalley	.10	.05	.01
□ 768	Jerry Garvin	.10	.05	.01
□ 769	Richie Zisk	.10	.05	.01
□ 770	Rich Gossage	.50	.23	.06
□ 771	Rich Gossage SA	.25	.11	.03
□ 772	Bert Campaneris	.25	.11	.03
□ 773	John Denny	.10	.05	.01
□ 774	Jay Johnstone	.25	.11	.03
□ 775	Bob Forsch	.10	.05	.01
□ 776	Mark Belanger	.25	.11	.03
□ 777	Tom Griffin	.10	.05	.01
□ 778	Kevin Hickey	.10	.05	.01
□ 779	Grant Jackson	.10	.05	.01
□ 780	Pete Rose	2.00	.90	.25
□ 781	Pete Rose SA	1.00	.45	.12
□ 782	Frank Taveras	.10	.05	.01
□ 783	Greg Harris	.10	.05	.01
□ 784	Milt Wilcox	.10	.05	.01
□ 785	Dan Driessen	.10	.05	.01
□ 786	Red Sox TL BA: Carney Lansford Pitching: Mike Torrez (Checklist on back)	.50	.23	.06
□ 787	Fred Stanley	.10	.05	.01
□ 788	Woodie Fryman	.10	.05	.01
□ 789	Checklist 661-792	.50	.23	.06
□ 790	Larry Gura	.10	.05	.01
□ 791	Bobby Brown	.10	.05	.01
□ 792	Frank Tanana	.25	.11	.03

1982 Topps Traded

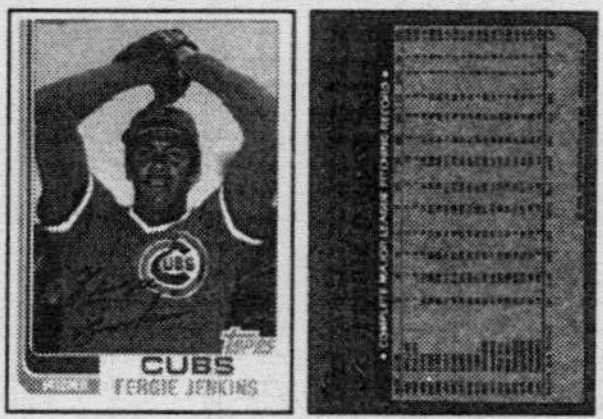

The cards in this 132-card set measure the standard size. The 1982 Topps Traded or extended series is distinguished by a "T" printed after the number (located on the reverse). This was the first time Topps began a tradition of newly numbering (and alphabetizing) their traded series from 1T to 132T. All 131 player photos used in the set are completely new. Of this total, 112 individuals are seen in the uniform of their new team, 11 youngsters have been elevated to single card status from multi-player "Future Stars" cards, and eight more are entirely new to the 1982 Topps lineup. The backs are almost completely red in color with black print. There are no key Rookie Cards in this set. Although the Cal Ripken card is this set's most valuable card, it is not his Rookie Card since he had already been included in the 1982 regular set, albeit on a multi-player card.

	MINT	NRMT	EXC
COMPLETE FACT.SET (132)	300.00	135.00	38.00
COMMON CARD (1T-132T)	.25	.11	.03
SEMISTARS	.50	.23	.06
STARS	1.00	.45	.12

□ 1T	Doyle Alexander	.25	.11	.03
□ 2T	Jesse Barfield	.50	.23	.06
□ 3T	Ross Baumgarten	.25	.11	.03
□ 4T	Steve Bedrosian	.50	.23	.06
□ 5T	Mark Belanger	.50	.23	.06
□ 6T	Kurt Bevacqua	.25	.11	.03
□ 7T	Tim Blackwell	.25	.11	.03
□ 8T	Vida Blue	.50	.23	.06
□ 9T	Bob Boone	.50	.23	.06
□ 10T	Larry Bowa	.50	.23	.06
□ 11T	Dan Briggs	.25	.11	.03
□ 12T	Bobby Brown	.25	.11	.03
□ 13T	Tom Brunansky	.50	.23	.06
□ 14T	Jeff Burroughs	.25	.11	.03
□ 15T	Enos Cabell	.25	.11	.03
□ 16T	Bill Campbell	.25	.11	.03
□ 17T	Bobby Castillo	.25	.11	.03
□ 18T	Bill Caudill	.25	.11	.03
□ 19T	Cesar Cedeno	.50	.23	.06
□ 20T	Dave Collins	.25	.11	.03
□ 21T	Doug Corbett	.25	.11	.03
□ 22T	Al Cowens	.25	.11	.03
□ 23T	Chili Davis	3.00	1.35	.35
□ 24T	Dick Davis	.25	.11	.03
□ 25T	Ron Davis	.25	.11	.03
□ 26T	Doug DeCinces	.50	.23	.06
□ 27T	Ivan DeJesus	.25	.11	.03
□ 28T	Bob Dernier	.25	.11	.03
□ 29T	Bo Diaz	.25	.11	.03
□ 30T	Roger Erickson	.25	.11	.03
□ 31T	Jim Essian	.25	.11	.03
□ 32T	Ed Farmer	.25	.11	.03
□ 33T	Doug Flynn	.25	.11	.03
□ 34T	Tim Foli	.25	.11	.03
□ 35T	Dan Ford	.25	.11	.03
□ 36T	George Foster	.50	.23	.06
□ 37T	Dave Frost	.25	.11	.03
□ 38T	Rich Gale	.25	.11	.03
□ 39T	Ron Gardenhire	.25	.11	.03
□ 40T	Ken Griffey	.50	.23	.06
□ 41T	Greg Harris	.25	.11	.03
□ 42T	Von Hayes	.50	.23	.06
□ 43T	Larry Herndon	.25	.11	.03
□ 44T	Kent Hrbek	2.00	.90	.25
□ 45T	Mike Ivie	.25	.11	.03
□ 46T	Grant Jackson	.25	.11	.03
□ 47T	Reggie Jackson	10.00	4.50	1.25
□ 48T	Ron Jackson	.25	.11	.03
□ 49T	Fergie Jenkins	1.00	.45	.12
□ 50T	Lamar Johnson	.25	.11	.03
□ 51T	Randy Johnson	.25	.11	.03
□ 52T	Jay Johnstone	.50	.23	.06
□ 53T	Mick Kelleher	.25	.11	.03
□ 54T	Steve Kemp	.25	.11	.03
□ 55T	Junior Kennedy	.25	.11	.03
□ 56T	Jim Kern	.25	.11	.03
□ 57T	Ray Knight	.50	.23	.06
□ 58T	Wayne Krenchicki	.25	.11	.03
□ 59T	Mike Krukow	.25	.11	.03
□ 60T	Duane Kuiper	.25	.11	.03
□ 61T	Mike LaCoss	.25	.11	.03
□ 62T	Chet Lemon	.25	.11	.03
□ 63T	Sixto Lezcano	.25	.11	.03
□ 64T	Dave Lopes	.50	.23	.06
□ 65T	Jerry Martin	.25	.11	.03
□ 66T	Renie Martin	.25	.11	.03
□ 67T	John Mayberry	.25	.11	.03
□ 68T	Lee Mazzilli	.25	.11	.03
□ 69T	Bake McBride	.25	.11	.03
□ 70T	Dan Meyer	.25	.11	.03
□ 71T	Larry Milbourne	.25	.11	.03
□ 72T	Eddie Milner	.25	.11	.03
□ 73T	Sid Monge	.25	.11	.03
□ 74T	John Montefusco	.25	.11	.03
□ 75T	Jose Morales	.25	.11	.03
□ 76T	Keith Moreland	.25	.11	.03
□ 77T	Jim Morrison	.25	.11	.03
□ 78T	Rance Mulliniks	.25	.11	.03
□ 79T	Steve Mura	.25	.11	.03
□ 80T	Gene Nelson	.25	.11	.03
□ 81T	Joe Nolan	.25	.11	.03
□ 82T	Dickie Noles	.25	.11	.03
□ 83T	Al Oliver	.50	.23	.06
□ 84T	Jorge Orta	.25	.11	.03
□ 85T	Tom Paciorek	.25	.11	.03
□ 86T	Larry Parrish	.25	.11	.03
□ 87T	Jack Perconte	.25	.11	.03
□ 88T	Gaylord Perry	1.00	.45	.12
□ 89T	Rob Picciolo	.25	.11	.03
□ 90T	Joe Pittman	.25	.11	.03
□ 91T	Hosken Powell	.25	.11	.03
□ 92T	Mike Proly	.25	.11	.03

□ 93T Greg Pryor	.25	.11	.03
□ 94T Charlie Puleo	.25	.11	.03
□ 95T Shane Rawley	.25	.11	.03
□ 96T Johnny Ray	.50	.23	.06
□ 97T Dave Revering	.25	.11	.03
□ 98T Cal Ripken	275.00	125.00	34.00
□ 99T Allen Ripley	.25	.11	.03
□ 100T Bill Robinson	.25	.11	.03
□ 101T Aurelio Rodriguez	.25	.11	.03
□ 102T Joe Rudi	.25	.11	.03
□ 103T Steve Sax	1.00	.45	.12
□ 104T Dan Schatzeder	.25	.11	.03
□ 105T Bob Shirley	.25	.11	.03
□ 106T Eric Show	.50	.23	.06
□ 107T Roy Smalley	.25	.11	.03
□ 108T Lonnie Smith	.50	.23	.06
□ 109T Ozzie Smith	25.00	11.00	3.10
□ 110T Reggie Smith	.50	.23	.06
□ 111T Lary Sorensen	.25	.11	.03
□ 112T Elias Sosa	.25	.11	.03
□ 113T Mike Stanton	.25	.11	.03
□ 114T Steve Stroughter	.25	.11	.03
□ 115T Champ Summers	.25	.11	.03
□ 116T Rick Sutcliffe	.50	.23	.06
□ 117T Frank Tanana	.50	.23	.06
□ 118T Frank Taveras	.25	.11	.03
□ 119T Garry Templeton	.25	.11	.03
□ 120T Alex Trevino	.25	.11	.03
□ 121T Jerry Turner	.25	.11	.03
□ 122T Ed VandeBerg	.25	.11	.03
□ 123T Tom Veryzer	.25	.11	.03
□ 124T Ron Washington	.25	.11	.03
□ 125T Bob Watson	.50	.23	.06
□ 126T Dennis Werth	.25	.11	.03
□ 127T Eddie Whitson	.25	.11	.03
□ 128T Rob Wilfong	.25	.11	.03
□ 129T Bump Wills	.25	.11	.03
□ 130T Gary Woods	.25	.11	.03
□ 131T Butch Wynegar	.25	.11	.03
□ 132T Checklist: 1-132	.25	.11	.03

1983 Topps

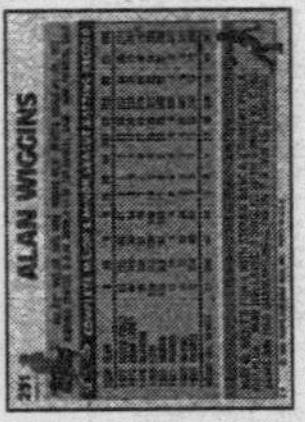

The cards in this 792-card set measure the standard size. Each player card front features a large action shot with a small cameo portrait at bottom right. There are special series for AL and NL All Stars (386-407), League Leaders (701-708), and Record Breakers (1-6). In addition, there are 34 "Super Veteran" (SV) cards and six numbered checklist cards. The Super Veteran cards are oriented horizontally and show two pictures of the featured player, a recent picture and a picture showing the player as a rookie. The team cards are actually Team Leader (TL) cards picturing the batting and pitching leader for that team with a checklist back. Cards were primarily issued in 15-card wax packs and 51-card rack packs. Notable Rookie Cards include Wade Boggs, Tony Gwynn and Ryne Sandberg.

	MINT	NRMT	EXC
COMPLETE SET (792)	125.00	55.00	15.50
COMMON CARD (1-792)	.10	.05	.01
SEMISTARS	.25	.11	.03
STARS	.50	.23	.06

□ 1 Tony Armas RB	.50	.23	.06
□ 2 Rickey Henderson RB Sets modern SB record	1.00	.45	.12
□ 3 Greg Minton RB 269 1/3 homerless innings streak	.10	.05	.01
□ 4 Lance Parrish RB	.25	.11	.03
□ 5 Manny Trillo RB 479 consecutive errorless chances, second baseman	.25	.11	.03
□ 6 John Wathan RB ML catcher steals, season	.10	.05	.01
□ 7 Gene Richards	.10	.05	.01
□ 8 Steve Balboni	.10	.05	.01
□ 9 Joey McLaughlin	.10	.05	.01
□ 10 Gorman Thomas	.10	.05	.01
□ 11 Billy Gardner MG	.10	.05	.01
□ 12 Paul Mirabella	.10	.05	.01
□ 13 Larry Herndon	.10	.05	.01
□ 14 Frank LaCorte	.10	.05	.01
□ 15 Ron Cey	.25	.11	.03
□ 16 George Vukovich	.10	.05	.01
□ 17 Kent Tekulve	.25	.11	.03
□ 18 Kent Tekulve SV	.10	.05	.01
□ 19 Oscar Gamble	.10	.05	.01
□ 20 Carlton Fisk	1.00	.45	.12
□ 21 Baltimore Orioles TL BA: Eddie Murray ERA: Jim Palmer (Checklist on back)	.50	.23	.06
□ 22 Randy Martz	.10	.05	.01
□ 23 Mike Heath	.10	.05	.01
□ 24 Steve Mura	.10	.05	.01
□ 25 Hal McRae	.25	.11	.03
□ 26 Jerry Royster	.10	.05	.01
□ 27 Doug Corbett	.10	.05	.01
□ 28 Bruce Bochte	.10	.05	.01
□ 29 Randy Jones	.10	.05	.01
□ 30 Jim Rice	.50	.23	.06
□ 31 Bill Gullickson	.25	.11	.03
□ 32 Dave Bergman	.10	.05	.01
□ 33 Jack O'Connor	.10	.05	.01
□ 34 Paul Householder	.10	.05	.01
□ 35 Rollie Fingers	.50	.23	.06
□ 36 Rollie Fingers SV	.25	.11	.03
□ 37 Darrell Johnson MG	.10	.05	.01
□ 38 Tim Flannery	.10	.05	.01
□ 39 Terry Puhl	.10	.05	.01
□ 40 Fernando Valenzuela	.25	.11	.03
□ 41 Jerry Turner	.10	.05	.01
□ 42 Dale Murray	.10	.05	.01
□ 43 Bob Dernier	.10	.05	.01
□ 44 Don Robinson	.10	.05	.01
□ 45 John Mayberry	.10	.05	.01
□ 46 Richard Dotson	.10	.05	.01
□ 47 Dave McKay	.10	.05	.01
□ 48 Lary Sorensen	.10	.05	.01
□ 49 Willie McGee	.50	.23	.06
□ 50 Bob Horner UER ('82 RBI total 7)	.10	.05	.01
□ 51 Chicago Cubs TL BA: Leon Durham ERA: Fergie Jenkins (Checklist on back)	.25	.11	.03
□ 52 Onix Concepcion	.10	.05	.01
□ 53 Mike Witt	.10	.05	.01
□ 54 Jim Maler	.10	.05	.01
□ 55 Mookie Wilson	.25	.11	.03
□ 56 Chuck Rainey	.10	.05	.01
□ 57 Tim Blackwell	.10	.05	.01
□ 58 Al Holland	.10	.05	.01
□ 59 Benny Ayala	.10	.05	.01
□ 60 Johnny Bench	1.00	.45	.12
□ 61 Johnny Bench SV	.50	.23	.06
□ 62 Bob McClure	.10	.05	.01
□ 63 Rick Monday	.10	.05	.01
□ 64 Bill Stein	.10	.05	.01
□ 65 Jack Morris	.50	.23	.06
□ 66 Bob Lillis MG	.10	.05	.01
□ 67 Sal Butera	.10	.05	.01
□ 68 Eric Show	.10	.05	.01
□ 69 Lee Lacy	.10	.05	.01
□ 70 Steve Carlton	1.00	.45	.12
□ 71 Steve Carlton SV	.50	.23	.06
□ 72 Tom Paciorek	.10	.05	.01
□ 73 Allen Ripley	.10	.05	.01
□ 74 Julio Gonzalez	.10	.05	.01

□ 75 Amos Otis	.25	.11	.03
□ 76 Rick Mahler	.10	.05	.01
□ 77 Hosken Powell	.10	.05	.01
□ 78 Bill Caudill	.10	.05	.01
□ 79 Mick Kelleher	.10	.05	.01
□ 80 George Foster	.25	.11	.03
□ 81 Yankees TL	.25	.11	.03
BA: Jerry Mumphrey			
ERA: Dave Righetti			
(Checklist on back)			
□ 82 Bruce Hurst	.25	.11	.03
□ 83 Ryne Sandberg	25.00	11.00	3.10
□ 84 Milt May	.10	.05	.01
□ 85 Ken Singleton	.25	.11	.03
□ 86 Tom Hume	.10	.05	.01
□ 87 Joe Rudi	.10	.05	.01
□ 88 Jim Gantner	.25	.11	.03
□ 89 Leon Roberts	.10	.05	.01
□ 90 Jerry Reuss	.25	.11	.03
□ 91 Larry Milbourne	.10	.05	.01
□ 92 Mike LaCoss	.10	.05	.01
□ 93 John Castino	.10	.05	.01
□ 94 Dave Edwards	.10	.05	.01
□ 95 Alan Trammell	.50	.23	.06
□ 96 Dick Howser MG	.25	.11	.03
□ 97 Ross Baumgarten	.10	.05	.01
□ 98 Vance Law	.10	.05	.01
□ 99 Dickie Noles	.10	.05	.01
□ 100 Pete Rose	2.00	.90	.25
□ 101 Pete Rose SV	1.00	.45	.12
□ 102 Dave Beard	.10	.05	.01
□ 103 Darrell Porter	.10	.05	.01
□ 104 Bob Walk	.10	.05	.01
□ 105 Don Baylor	.50	.23	.06
□ 106 Gene Nelson	.10	.05	.01
□ 107 Mike Jorgensen	.10	.05	.01
□ 108 Glenn Hoffman	.10	.05	.01
□ 109 Luis Leal	.10	.05	.01
□ 110 Ken Griffey	.10	.05	.01
□ 111 Montreal Expos TL	.25	.11	.03
BA: Al Oliver			
ERA: Steve Rogers			
(Checklist on back)			
□ 112 Bob Shirley	.10	.05	.01
□ 113 Ron Roenicke	.10	.05	.01
□ 114 Jim Slaton	.10	.05	.01
□ 115 Chili Davis	.50	.23	.06
□ 116 Dave Schmidt	.10	.05	.01
□ 117 Alan Knicely	.10	.05	.01
□ 118 Chris Welsh	.10	.05	.01
□ 119 Tom Brookens	.10	.05	.01
□ 120 Len Barker	.10	.05	.01
□ 121 Mickey Hatcher	.10	.05	.01
□ 122 Jimmy Smith	.10	.05	.01
□ 123 George Frazier	.10	.05	.01
□ 124 Marc Hill	.10	.05	.01
□ 125 Leon Durham	.10	.05	.01
□ 126 Joe Torre MG	.25	.11	.03
□ 127 Preston Hanna	.10	.05	.01
□ 128 Mike Ramsey	.10	.05	.01
□ 129 Checklist: 1-132	.25	.11	.03
□ 130 Dave Stieb	.25	.11	.03
□ 131 Ed Ott	.10	.05	.01
□ 132 Todd Cruz	.10	.05	.01
□ 133 Jim Barr	.10	.05	.01
□ 134 Hubie Brooks	.25	.11	.03
□ 135 Dwight Evans	.25	.11	.03
□ 136 Willie Aikens	.10	.05	.01
□ 137 Woodie Fryman	.10	.05	.01
□ 138 Rick Dempsey	.25	.11	.03
□ 139 Bruce Berenyi	.10	.05	.01
□ 140 Willie Randolph	.25	.11	.03
□ 141 Indians TL	.25	.11	.03
BA: Toby Harrah			
ERA: Rick Sutcliffe			
(Checklist on back)			
□ 142 Mike Caldwell	.10	.05	.01
□ 143 Joe Pettini	.10	.05	.01
□ 144 Mark Wagner	.10	.05	.01
□ 145 Don Sutton	.50	.23	.06
□ 146 Don Sutton SV	.25	.11	.03
□ 147 Rick Leach	.10	.05	.01
□ 148 Dave Roberts	.10	.05	.01
□ 149 Johnny Ray	.10	.05	.01
□ 150 Bruce Sutter	.25	.11	.03
□ 151 Bruce Sutter SV	.10	.05	.01
□ 152 Jay Johnstone	.25	.11	.03
□ 153 Jerry Koosman	.25	.11	.03
□ 154 Johnnie LeMaster	.10	.05	.01
□ 155 Dan Quisenberry	.25	.11	.03
□ 156 Billy Martin MG	.25	.11	.03
□ 157 Steve Bedrosian	.25	.11	.03
□ 158 Rob Wilfong	.10	.05	.01
□ 159 Mike Stanton	.10	.05	.01
□ 160 Dave Kingman	.25	.11	.03
□ 161 Dave Kingman SV	.10	.05	.01
□ 162 Mark Clear	.10	.05	.01
□ 163 Cal Ripken	20.00	9.00	2.50
□ 164 David Palmer	.10	.05	.01
□ 165 Dan Driessen	.10	.05	.01
□ 166 John Pacella	.10	.05	.01
□ 167 Mark Brouhard	.10	.05	.01
□ 168 Juan Eichelberger	.10	.05	.01
□ 169 Doug Flynn	.10	.05	.01
□ 170 Steve Howe	.10	.05	.01
□ 171 Giants TL	.50	.23	.06
BA: Joe Morgan			
ERA: Bill Laskey			
(Checklist on back)			
□ 172 Vern Ruhle	.10	.05	.01
□ 173 Jim Morrison	.10	.05	.01
□ 174 Jerry Ujdur	.10	.05	.01
□ 175 Bo Diaz	.10	.05	.01
□ 176 Dave Righetti	.25	.11	.03
□ 177 Harold Baines	.50	.23	.06
□ 178 Luis Tiant	.25	.11	.03
□ 179 Luis Tiant SV	.10	.05	.01
□ 180 Rickey Henderson	2.00	.90	.25
□ 181 Terry Felton	.10	.05	.01
□ 182 Mike Fischlin	.10	.05	.01
□ 183 Ed VandeBerg	.10	.05	.01
□ 184 Bob Clark	.10	.05	.01
□ 185 Tim Lollar	.10	.05	.01
□ 186 Whitey Herzog MG	.25	.11	.03
□ 187 Terry Leach	.10	.05	.01
□ 188 Rick Miller	.10	.05	.01
□ 189 Dan Schatzeder	.10	.05	.01
□ 190 Cecil Cooper	.25	.11	.03
□ 191 Joe Price	.10	.05	.01
□ 192 Floyd Rayford	.10	.05	.01
□ 193 Harry Spilman	.10	.05	.01
□ 194 Cesar Geronimo	.10	.05	.01
□ 195 Bob Stoddard	.10	.05	.01
□ 196 Bill Fahey	.10	.05	.01
□ 197 Jim Eisenreich	1.00	.45	.12
□ 198 Kiko Garcia	.10	.05	.01
□ 199 Marty Bystrom	.10	.05	.01
□ 200 Rod Carew	.75	.35	.09
□ 201 Rod Carew SV	.50	.23	.06
□ 202 Blue Jays TL	.25	.11	.03
BA: Damaso Garcia			
ERA: Dave Stieb			
(Checklist on back)			
□ 203 Mike Morgan	.10	.05	.01
□ 204 Junior Kennedy	.10	.05	.01
□ 205 Dave Parker	.50	.23	.06
□ 206 Ken Oberkfell	.10	.05	.01
□ 207 Rick Camp	.10	.05	.01
□ 208 Dan Meyer	.10	.05	.01
□ 209 Mike Moore	.25	.11	.03
□ 210 Jack Clark	.25	.11	.03
□ 211 John Denny	.10	.05	.01
□ 212 John Stearns	.10	.05	.01
□ 213 Tom Burgmeier	.10	.05	.01
□ 214 Jerry White	.10	.05	.01
□ 215 Mario Soto	.10	.05	.01
□ 216 Tony LaRussa MG	.25	.11	.03
□ 217 Tim Stoddard	.10	.05	.01
□ 218 Roy Howell	.10	.05	.01
□ 219 Mike Armstrong	.10	.05	.01
□ 220 Dusty Baker	.25	.11	.03
□ 221 Joe Niekro	.25	.11	.03
□ 222 Damaso Garcia	.10	.05	.01
□ 223 John Montefusco	.10	.05	.01
□ 224 Mickey Rivers	.10	.05	.01
□ 225 Enos Cabell	.10	.05	.01
□ 226 Enrique Romo	.10	.05	.01
□ 227 Chris Bando	.10	.05	.01
□ 228 Joaquin Andujar	.10	.05	.01
□ 229 Phillies TL	.50	.23	.06
BA: Bo Diaz			
ERA: Steve Carlton			

	(Checklist on back)			
□ 230	Fergie Jenkins	.50	.23	.06
□ 231	Fergie Jenkins SV	.25	.11	.03
□ 232	Tom Brunansky	.25	.11	.03
□ 233	Wayne Gross	.10	.05	.01
□ 234	Larry Andersen	.10	.05	.01
□ 235	Claudell Washington	.10	.05	.01
□ 236	Steve Renko	.10	.05	.01
□ 237	Dan Norman	.10	.05	.01
□ 238	Bud Black	.25	.11	.03
□ 239	Dave Stapleton	.10	.05	.01
□ 240	Rich Gossage	.50	.23	.06
□ 241	Rich Gossage SV	.25	.11	.03
□ 242	Joe Nolan	.10	.05	.01
□ 243	Duane Walker	.10	.05	.01
□ 244	Dwight Bernard	.10	.05	.01
□ 245	Steve Sax	.25	.11	.03
□ 246	George Bamberger MG	.10	.05	.01
□ 247	Dave Smith	.10	.05	.01
□ 248	Bake McBride	.10	.05	.01
□ 249	Checklist: 133-264	.25	.11	.03
□ 250	Bill Buckner	.25	.11	.03
□ 251	Alan Wiggins	.10	.05	.01
□ 252	Luis Aguayo	.10	.05	.01
□ 253	Larry McWilliams	.10	.05	.01
□ 254	Rick Cerone	.10	.05	.01
□ 255	Gene Garber	.10	.05	.01
□ 256	Gene Garber SV	.10	.05	.01
□ 257	Jesse Barfield	.25	.11	.03
□ 258	Manny Castillo	.10	.05	.01
□ 259	Jeff Jones	.10	.05	.01
□ 260	Steve Kemp	.10	.05	.01
□ 261	Tigers TL	.25	.11	.03
	BA: Larry Herndon			
	ERA: Dan Petry			
	(Checklist on back)			
□ 262	Ron Jackson	.10	.05	.01
□ 263	Renie Martin	.10	.05	.01
□ 264	Jamie Quirk	.10	.05	.01
□ 265	Joel Youngblood	.10	.05	.01
□ 266	Paul Boris	.10	.05	.01
□ 267	Terry Francona	.10	.05	.01
□ 268	Storm Davis	.10	.05	.01
□ 269	Ron Oester	.10	.05	.01
□ 270	Dennis Eckersley	.50	.23	.06
□ 271	Ed Romero	.10	.05	.01
□ 272	Frank Tanana	.25	.11	.03
□ 273	Mark Belanger	.10	.05	.01
□ 274	Terry Kennedy	.10	.05	.01
□ 275	Ray Knight	.25	.11	.03
□ 276	Gene Mauch MG	.10	.05	.01
□ 277	Rance Mulliniks	.10	.05	.01
□ 278	Kevin Hickey	.10	.05	.01
□ 279	Greg Gross	.10	.05	.01
□ 280	Bert Blyleven	.50	.23	.06
□ 281	Andre Robertson	.10	.05	.01
□ 282	Reggie Smith	.50	.23	.06
	(Ryne Sandberg			
	ducking back)			
□ 283	Reggie Smith SV	.10	.05	.01
□ 284	Jeff Lahti	.10	.05	.01
□ 285	Lance Parrish	.25	.11	.03
□ 286	Rick Langford	.10	.05	.01
□ 287	Bobby Brown	.10	.05	.01
□ 288	Joe Cowley	.10	.05	.01
□ 289	Jerry Dybzinski	.10	.05	.01
□ 290	Jeff Reardon	.50	.23	.06
□ 291	Pirates TL	.25	.11	.03
	BA: Bill Madlock			
	ERA: John Candelaria			
	(Checklist on back)			
□ 292	Craig Swan	.10	.05	.01
□ 293	Glenn Gulliver	.10	.05	.01
□ 294	Dave Engle	.10	.05	.01
□ 295	Jerry Remy	.10	.05	.01
□ 296	Greg Harris	.10	.05	.01
□ 297	Ned Yost	.10	.05	.01
□ 298	Floyd Chiffer	.10	.05	.01
□ 299	George Wright	.10	.05	.01
□ 300	Mike Schmidt	2.00	.90	.25
□ 301	Mike Schmidt SV	1.00	.45	.12
□ 302	Ernie Whitt	.10	.05	.01
□ 303	Miguel Dilone	.10	.05	.01
□ 304	Dave Rucker	.10	.05	.01
□ 305	Larry Bowa	.25	.11	.03
□ 306	Tom Lasorda MG	.25	.11	.03
□ 307	Lou Piniella	.25	.11	.03
□ 308	Jesus Vega	.10	.05	.01
□ 309	Jeff Leonard	.10	.05	.01
□ 310	Greg Luzinski	.25	.11	.03
□ 311	Glenn Brummer	.10	.05	.01
□ 312	Brian Kingman	.10	.05	.01
□ 313	Gary Gray	.10	.05	.01
□ 314	Ken Dayley	.10	.05	.01
□ 315	Rick Burleson	.10	.05	.01
□ 316	Paul Splittorff	.10	.05	.01
□ 317	Gary Rajsich	.10	.05	.01
□ 318	John Tudor	.10	.05	.01
□ 319	Lenn Sakata	.10	.05	.01
□ 320	Steve Rogers	.10	.05	.01
□ 321	Brewers TL	.50	.23	.06
	BA: Robin Yount			
	ERA: Pete Vuckovich			
	(Checklist on back)			
□ 322	Dave Van Gorder	.10	.05	.01
□ 323	Luis DeLeon	.10	.05	.01
□ 324	Mike Marshall	.10	.05	.01
□ 325	Von Hayes	.25	.11	.03
□ 326	Garth Iorg	.10	.05	.01
□ 327	Bobby Castillo	.10	.05	.01
□ 328	Craig Reynolds	.10	.05	.01
□ 329	Randy Niemann	.10	.05	.01
□ 330	Buddy Bell	.25	.11	.03
□ 331	Mike Krukow	.10	.05	.01
□ 332	Glenn Wilson	.25	.11	.03
□ 333	Dave LaRoche	.10	.05	.01
□ 334	Dave LaRoche SV	.10	.05	.01
□ 335	Steve Henderson	.10	.05	.01
□ 336	Rene Lachemann MG	.10	.05	.01
□ 337	Tito Landrum	.10	.05	.01
□ 338	Bob Owchinko	.10	.05	.01
□ 339	Terry Harper	.10	.05	.01
□ 340	Larry Gura	.10	.05	.01
□ 341	Doug DeCinces	.25	.11	.03
□ 342	Atlee Hammaker	.10	.05	.01
□ 343	Bob Bailor	.10	.05	.01
□ 344	Roger LaFrancois	.10	.05	.01
□ 345	Jim Clancy	.10	.05	.01
□ 346	Joe Pittman	.10	.05	.01
□ 347	Sammy Stewart	.10	.05	.01
□ 348	Alan Bannister	.10	.05	.01
□ 349	Checklist: 265-396	.25	.11	.03
□ 350	Robin Yount	2.00	.90	.25
□ 351	Reds TL	.25	.11	.03
	BA: Cesar Cedeno			
	ERA: Mario Soto			
	(Checklist on back)			
□ 352	Mike Scioscia	.25	.11	.03
□ 353	Steve Comer	.10	.05	.01
□ 354	Randy Johnson	.10	.05	.01
□ 355	Jim Bibby	.10	.05	.01
□ 356	Gary Woods	.10	.05	.01
□ 357	Len Matuszek	.10	.05	.01
□ 358	Jerry Garvin	.10	.05	.01
□ 359	Dave Collins	.10	.05	.01
□ 360	Nolan Ryan	6.00	2.70	.75
□ 361	Nolan Ryan SV	4.00	1.80	.50
□ 362	Bill Almon	.10	.05	.01
□ 363	John Stuper	.10	.05	.01
□ 364	Brett Butler	.50	.23	.06
□ 365	Dave Lopes	.25	.11	.03
□ 366	Dick Williams MG	.10	.05	.01
□ 367	Bud Anderson	.10	.05	.01
□ 368	Richie Zisk	.10	.05	.01
□ 369	Jesse Orosco	.10	.05	.01
□ 370	Gary Carter	.50	.23	.06
□ 371	Mike Richardt	.10	.05	.01
□ 372	Terry Crowley	.10	.05	.01
□ 373	Kevin Saucier	.10	.05	.01
□ 374	Wayne Krenchicki	.10	.05	.01
□ 375	Pete Vuckovich	.10	.05	.01
□ 376	Ken Landreaux	.10	.05	.01
□ 377	Lee May	.25	.11	.03
□ 378	Lee May SV	.10	.05	.01
□ 379	Guy Sularz	.10	.05	.01
□ 380	Ron Davis	.10	.05	.01
□ 381	Red Sox TL	.25	.11	.03
	BA: Jim Rice			
	ERA: Bob Stanley			
	(Checklist on back)			
□ 382	Bob Knepper	.10	.05	.01
□ 383	Ozzie Virgil	.10	.05	.01

□ 384	Dave Dravecky	.50	.23	.06
□ 385	Mike Easler	.10	.05	.01
□ 386	Rod Carew AS	.50	.23	.06
□ 387	Bob Grich AS	.25	.11	.03
□ 388	George Brett AS	2.00	.90	.25
□ 389	Robin Yount AS	1.25	.55	.16
□ 390	Reggie Jackson AS	.75	.35	.09
□ 391	Rickey Henderson AS	1.00	.45	.12
□ 392	Fred Lynn AS	.25	.11	.03
□ 393	Carlton Fisk AS	.50	.23	.06
□ 394	Pete Vuckovich AS	.10	.05	.01
□ 395	Larry Gura AS	.10	.05	.01
□ 396	Dan Quisenberry AS	.25	.11	.03
□ 397	Pete Rose AS	1.00	.45	.12
□ 398	Manny Trillo AS	.10	.05	.01
□ 399	Mike Schmidt AS	1.00	.45	.12
□ 400	Dave Concepcion AS	.25	.11	.03
□ 401	Dale Murphy AS	.50	.23	.06
□ 402	Andre Dawson AS	.50	.23	.06
□ 403	Tim Raines AS	.50	.23	.06
□ 404	Gary Carter AS	.50	.23	.06
□ 405	Steve Rogers AS	.10	.05	.01
□ 406	Steve Carlton AS	.50	.23	.06
□ 407	Bruce Sutter AS	.25	.11	.03
□ 408	Rudy May	.10	.05	.01
□ 409	Marvis Foley	.10	.05	.01
□ 410	Phil Niekro	.50	.23	.06
□ 411	Phil Niekro SV	.25	.11	.03
□ 412	Rangers TL	.25	.11	.03
	BA: Buddy Bell			
	ERA: Charlie Hough			
	(Checklist on back)			
□ 413	Matt Keough	.10	.05	.01
□ 414	Julio Cruz	.10	.05	.01
□ 415	Bob Forsch	.10	.05	.01
□ 416	Joe Ferguson	.10	.05	.01
□ 417	Tom Hausman	.10	.05	.01
□ 418	Greg Pryor	.10	.05	.01
□ 419	Steve Crawford	.10	.05	.01
□ 420	Al Oliver	.25	.11	.03
□ 421	Al Oliver SV	.10	.05	.01
□ 422	George Cappuzzello	.10	.05	.01
□ 423	Tom Lawless	.10	.05	.01
□ 424	Jerry Augustine	.10	.05	.01
□ 425	Pedro Guerrero	.25	.11	.03
□ 426	Earl Weaver MG	.50	.23	.06
□ 427	Roy Lee Jackson	.10	.05	.01
□ 428	Champ Summers	.10	.05	.01
□ 429	Eddie Whitson	.10	.05	.01
□ 430	Kirk Gibson	.50	.23	.06
□ 431	Gary Gaetti	1.00	.45	.12
□ 432	Porfirio Altamirano	.10	.05	.01
□ 433	Dale Berra	.10	.05	.01
□ 434	Dennis Lamp	.10	.05	.01
□ 435	Tony Armas	.10	.05	.01
□ 436	Bill Campbell	.10	.05	.01
□ 437	Rick Sweet	.10	.05	.01
□ 438	Dave LaPoint	.10	.05	.01
□ 439	Rafael Ramirez	.10	.05	.01
□ 440	Ron Guidry	.25	.11	.03
□ 441	Astros TL	.25	.11	.03
	BA: Ray Knight			
	ERA: Joe Niekro			
	(Checklist on back)			
□ 442	Brian Downing	.10	.05	.01
□ 443	Don Hood	.10	.05	.01
□ 444	Wally Backman	.10	.05	.01
□ 445	Mike Flanagan	.25	.11	.03
□ 446	Reid Nichols	.10	.05	.01
□ 447	Bryn Smith	.10	.05	.01
□ 448	Darrell Evans	.25	.11	.03
□ 449	Eddie Milner	.10	.05	.01
□ 450	Ted Simmons	.25	.11	.03
□ 451	Ted Simmons SV	.10	.05	.01
□ 452	Lloyd Moseby	.10	.05	.01
□ 453	Lamar Johnson	.10	.05	.01
□ 454	Bob Welch	.25	.11	.03
□ 455	Sixto Lezcano	.10	.05	.01
□ 456	Lee Elia MG	.10	.05	.01
□ 457	Milt Wilcox	.10	.05	.01
□ 458	Ron Washington	.10	.05	.01
□ 459	Ed Farmer	.10	.05	.01
□ 460	Roy Smalley	.10	.05	.01
□ 461	Steve Trout	.10	.05	.01
□ 462	Steve Nicosia	.10	.05	.01
□ 463	Gaylord Perry	.50	.23	.06

□ 464	Gaylord Perry SV	.25	.11	.03
□ 465	Lonnie Smith	.10	.05	.01
□ 466	Tom Underwood	.10	.05	.01
□ 467	Rufino Linares	.10	.05	.01
□ 468	Dave Goltz	.10	.05	.01
□ 469	Ron Gardenhire	.10	.05	.01
□ 470	Greg Minton	.10	.05	.01
□ 471	Kansas City Royals TL	.25	.11	.03
	BA: Willie Wilson			
	ERA: Vida Blue			
	(Checklist on back)			
□ 472	Gary Allenson	.10	.05	.01
□ 473	John Lowenstein	.10	.05	.01
□ 474	Ray Burris	.10	.05	.01
□ 475	Cesar Cedeno	.25	.11	.03
□ 476	Rob Picciolo	.10	.05	.01
□ 477	Tom Niedenfuer	.10	.05	.01
□ 478	Phil Garner	.25	.11	.03
□ 479	Charlie Hough	.25	.11	.03
□ 480	Toby Harrah	.10	.05	.01
□ 481	Scot Thompson	.10	.05	.01
□ 482	Tony Gwynn UER	35.00	16.00	4.40
	(No Topps logo under			
	card number on back)			
□ 483	Lynn Jones	.10	.05	.01
□ 484	Dick Ruthven	.10	.05	.01
□ 485	Omar Moreno	.10	.05	.01
□ 486	Clyde King MG	.10	.05	.01
□ 487	Jerry Hairston	.10	.05	.01
□ 488	Alfredo Griffin	.10	.05	.01
□ 489	Tom Herr	.25	.11	.03
□ 490	Jim Palmer	.60	.25	.07
□ 491	Jim Palmer SV	.50	.23	.06
□ 492	Paul Serna	.10	.05	.01
□ 493	Steve McCatty	.10	.05	.01
□ 494	Bob Brenly	.10	.05	.01
□ 495	Warren Cromartie	.10	.05	.01
□ 496	Tom Veryzer	.10	.05	.01
□ 497	Rick Sutcliffe	.25	.11	.03
□ 498	Wade Boggs	16.00	7.25	2.00
□ 499	Jeff Little	.10	.05	.01
□ 500	Reggie Jackson	1.25	.55	.16
□ 501	Reggie Jackson SV	.75	.35	.09
□ 502	Atlanta Braves TL	.25	.11	.03
	BA: Dale Murphy			
	ERA: Phil Niekro			
	(Checklist on back)			
□ 503	Moose Haas	.10	.05	.01
□ 504	Don Werner	.10	.05	.01
□ 505	Garry Templeton	.10	.05	.01
□ 506	Jim Gott	.10	.05	.01
□ 507	Tony Scott	.10	.05	.01
□ 508	Tom Filer	.10	.05	.01
□ 509	Lou Whitaker	.50	.23	.06
□ 510	Tug McGraw	.25	.11	.03
□ 511	Tug McGraw SV	.10	.05	.01
□ 512	Doyle Alexander	.10	.05	.01
□ 513	Fred Stanley	.10	.05	.01
□ 514	Rudy Law	.10	.05	.01
□ 515	Gene Tenace	.25	.11	.03
□ 516	Bill Virdon MG	.10	.05	.01
□ 517	Gary Ward	.10	.05	.01
□ 518	Bill Laskey	.10	.05	.01
□ 519	Terry Bulling	.10	.05	.01
□ 520	Fred Lynn	.25	.11	.03
□ 521	Bruce Benedict	.10	.05	.01
□ 522	Pat Zachry	.10	.05	.01
□ 523	Carney Lansford	.25	.11	.03
□ 524	Tom Brennan	.10	.05	.01
□ 525	Frank White	.25	.11	.03
□ 526	Checklist: 397-528	.25	.11	.03
□ 527	Larry Biittner	.10	.05	.01
□ 528	Jamie Easterly	.10	.05	.01
□ 529	Tim Laudner	.10	.05	.01
□ 530	Eddie Murray	3.50	1.55	.45
□ 531	Oakland A's TL	.50	.23	.06
	BA: Rickey Henderson			
	ERA: Rick Langford			
	(Checklist on back)			
□ 532	Dave Stewart	.50	.23	.06
□ 533	Luis Salazar	.10	.05	.01
□ 534	John Butcher	.10	.05	.01
□ 535	Manny Trillo	.10	.05	.01
□ 536	John Wockenfuss	.10	.05	.01
□ 537	Rod Scurry	.10	.05	.01
□ 538	Danny Heep	.10	.05	.01

□ 539	Roger Erickson	.10	.05	.01
□ 540	Ozzie Smith	3.00	1.35	.35
□ 541	Britt Burns	.10	.05	.01
□ 542	Jody Davis	.10	.05	.01
□ 543	Alan Fowlkes	.10	.05	.01
□ 544	Larry Whisenton	.10	.05	.01
□ 545	Floyd Bannister	.10	.05	.01
□ 546	Dave Garcia MG	.10	.05	.01
□ 547	Geoff Zahn	.10	.05	.01
□ 548	Brian Giles	.10	.05	.01
□ 549	Charlie Puleo	.10	.05	.01
□ 550	Carl Yastrzemski	1.00	.45	.12
□ 551	Carl Yastrzemski SV	.50	.23	.06
□ 552	Tim Wallach	.25	.11	.03
□ 553	Dennis Martinez	.25	.11	.03
□ 554	Mike Vail	.10	.05	.01
□ 555	Steve Yeager	.10	.05	.01
□ 556	Willie Upshaw	.10	.05	.01
□ 557	Rick Honeycutt	.10	.05	.01
□ 558	Dickie Thon	.10	.05	.01
□ 559	Pete Redfern	.10	.05	.01
□ 560	Ron LeFlore	.25	.11	.03
□ 561	Cardinals TL	.25	.11	.03
	BA: Lonnie Smith			
	ERA: Joaquin Andujar			
	(Checklist on back)			
□ 562	Dave Rozema	.10	.05	.01
□ 563	Juan Bonilla	.10	.05	.01
□ 564	Sid Monge	.10	.05	.01
□ 565	Bucky Dent	.25	.11	.03
□ 566	Manny Sarmiento	.10	.05	.01
□ 567	Joe Simpson	.10	.05	.01
□ 568	Willie Hernandez	.25	.11	.03
□ 569	Jack Perconte	.10	.05	.01
□ 570	Vida Blue	.25	.11	.03
□ 571	Mickey Klutts	.10	.05	.01
□ 572	Bob Watson	.25	.11	.03
□ 573	Andy Hassler	.10	.05	.01
□ 574	Glenn Adams	.10	.05	.01
□ 575	Neil Allen	.10	.05	.01
□ 576	Frank Robinson MG	.50	.23	.06
□ 577	Luis Aponte	.10	.05	.01
□ 578	David Green	.10	.05	.01
□ 579	Rich Dauer	.10	.05	.01
□ 580	Tom Seaver	1.00	.45	.12
□ 581	Tom Seaver SV	.50	.23	.06
□ 582	Marshall Edwards	.10	.05	.01
□ 583	Terry Forster	.10	.05	.01
□ 584	Dave Hostetler	.10	.05	.01
□ 585	Jose Cruz	.25	.11	.03
□ 586	Frank Viola	1.00	.45	.12
□ 587	Ivan DeJesus	.10	.05	.01
□ 588	Pat Underwood	.10	.05	.01
□ 589	Alvis Woods	.10	.05	.01
□ 590	Tony Pena	.25	.11	.03
□ 591	White Sox TL	.25	.11	.03
	BA: Greg Luzinski			
	ERA: LaMarr Hoyt			
	(Checklist on back)			
□ 592	Shane Rawley	.10	.05	.01
□ 593	Broderick Perkins	.10	.05	.01
□ 594	Eric Rasmussen	.10	.05	.01
□ 595	Tim Raines	.75	.35	.09
□ 596	Randy Johnson	.10	.05	.01
□ 597	Mike Proly	.10	.05	.01
□ 598	Dwayne Murphy	.10	.05	.01
□ 599	Don Aase	.10	.05	.01
□ 600	George Brett	4.00	1.80	.50
□ 601	Ed Lynch	.10	.05	.01
□ 602	Rich Gedman	.10	.05	.01
□ 603	Joe Morgan	.50	.23	.06
□ 604	Joe Morgan SV	.50	.23	.06
□ 605	Gary Roenicke	.10	.05	.01
□ 606	Bobby Cox MG	.25	.11	.03
□ 607	Charlie Leibrandt	.10	.05	.01
□ 608	Don Money	.10	.05	.01
□ 609	Danny Darwin	.10	.05	.01
□ 610	Steve Garvey	.50	.23	.06
□ 611	Bert Roberge	.10	.05	.01
□ 612	Steve Swisher	.10	.05	.01
□ 613	Mike Ivie	.10	.05	.01
□ 614	Ed Glynn	.10	.05	.01
□ 615	Garry Maddox	.10	.05	.01
□ 616	Bill Nahorodny	.10	.05	.01
□ 617	Butch Wynegar	.10	.05	.01
□ 618	LaMarr Hoyt	.25	.11	.03
□ 619	Keith Moreland	.10	.05	.01
□ 620	Mike Norris	.10	.05	.01
□ 621	New York Mets TL	.25	.11	.03
	BA: Mookie Wilson			
	ERA: Craig Swan			
	(Checklist on back)			
□ 622	Dave Edler	.10	.05	.01
□ 623	Luis Sanchez	.10	.05	.01
□ 624	Glenn Hubbard	.10	.05	.01
□ 625	Ken Forsch	.10	.05	.01
□ 626	Jerry Martin	.10	.05	.01
□ 627	Doug Bair	.10	.05	.01
□ 628	Julio Valdez	.10	.05	.01
□ 629	Charlie Lea	.10	.05	.01
□ 630	Paul Molitor	1.25	.55	.16
□ 631	Tippy Martinez	.10	.05	.01
□ 632	Alex Trevino	.10	.05	.01
□ 633	Vicente Romo	.10	.05	.01
□ 634	Max Venable	.10	.05	.01
□ 635	Graig Nettles	.25	.11	.03
□ 636	Graig Nettles SV	.10	.05	.01
□ 637	Pat Corrales MG	.10	.05	.01
□ 638	Dan Petry	.10	.05	.01
□ 639	Art Howe	.10	.05	.01
□ 640	Andre Thornton	.10	.05	.01
□ 641	Billy Sample	.10	.05	.01
□ 642	Checklist: 529-660	.25	.11	.03
□ 643	Bump Wills	.10	.05	.01
□ 644	Joe Lefebvre	.10	.05	.01
□ 645	Bill Madlock	.25	.11	.03
□ 646	Jim Essian	.10	.05	.01
□ 647	Bobby Mitchell	.10	.05	.01
□ 648	Jeff Burroughs	.10	.05	.01
□ 649	Tommy Boggs	.10	.05	.01
□ 650	George Hendrick	.10	.05	.01
□ 651	Angels TL	.50	.23	.06
	BA: Rod Carew			
	ERA: Mike Witt			
	(Checklist on back)			
□ 652	Butch Hobson	.10	.05	.01
□ 653	Ellis Valentine	.10	.05	.01
□ 654	Bob Ojeda	.10	.05	.01
□ 655	Al Bumbry	.25	.11	.03
□ 656	Dave Frost	.10	.05	.01
□ 657	Mike Gates	.10	.05	.01
□ 658	Frank Pastore	.10	.05	.01
□ 659	Charlie Moore	.10	.05	.01
□ 660	Mike Hargrove	.25	.11	.03
□ 661	Bill Russell	.25	.11	.03
□ 662	Joe Sambito	.10	.05	.01
□ 663	Tom O'Malley	.10	.05	.01
□ 664	Bob Molinaro	.10	.05	.01
□ 665	Jim Sundberg	.25	.11	.03
□ 666	Sparky Anderson MG	.25	.11	.03
□ 667	Dick Davis	.10	.05	.01
□ 668	Larry Christenson	.10	.05	.01
□ 669	Mike Squires	.10	.05	.01
□ 670	Jerry Mumphrey	.10	.05	.01
□ 671	Lenny Faedo	.10	.05	.01
□ 672	Jim Kaat	.25	.11	.03
□ 673	Jim Kaat SV	.10	.05	.01
□ 674	Kurt Bevacqua	.10	.05	.01
□ 675	Jim Beattie	.10	.05	.01
□ 676	Biff Pocoroba	.10	.05	.01
□ 677	Dave Revering	.10	.05	.01
□ 678	Juan Beniquez	.10	.05	.01
□ 679	Mike Scott	.25	.11	.03
□ 680	Andre Dawson	1.00	.45	.12
□ 681	Dodgers Leaders	.25	.11	.03
	BA: Pedro Guerrero			
	ERA: Fernando Valenzuela			
	(Checklist on back)			
□ 682	Bob Stanley	.10	.05	.01
□ 683	Dan Ford	.10	.05	.01
□ 684	Rafael Landestoy	.10	.05	.01
□ 685	Lee Mazzilli	.10	.05	.01
□ 686	Randy Lerch	.10	.05	.01
□ 687	U.L. Washington	.10	.05	.01
□ 688	Jim Wohlford	.10	.05	.01
□ 689	Ron Hassey	.10	.05	.01
□ 690	Kent Hrbek	.50	.23	.06
□ 691	Dave Tobik	.10	.05	.01
□ 692	Denny Walling	.10	.05	.01
□ 693	Sparky Lyle	.25	.11	.03
□ 694	Sparky Lyle SV	.10	.05	.01
□ 695	Ruppert Jones	.10	.05	.01

□ 696 Chuck Tanner MG	.25	.11	.03
□ 697 Barry Foote	.10	.05	.01
□ 698 Tony Bernazard	.10	.05	.01
□ 699 Lee Smith	2.50	1.10	.30
□ 700 Keith Hernandez	.50	.23	.06
□ 701 Batting Leaders AL: Willie Wilson NL: Al Oliver	.25	.11	.03
□ 702 Home Run Leaders AL: Reggie Jackson AL: Gorman Thomas NL: Dave Kingman	.50	.23	.06
□ 703 RBI Leaders AL: Hal McRae NL: Dale Murphy NL: Al Oliver	.25	.11	.03
□ 704 SB Leaders AL: Rickey Henderson NL: Tim Raines	1.00	.45	.12
□ 705 Victory Leaders AL: LaMarr Hoyt NL: Steve Carlton	.50	.23	.06
□ 706 Strikeout Leaders AL: Floyd Bannister NL: Steve Carlton	.50	.23	.06
□ 707 ERA Leaders AL: Rick Sutcliffe NL: Steve Rogers	.25	.11	.03
□ 708 Leading Firemen AL: Dan Quisenberry NL: Bruce Sutter	.25	.11	.03
□ 709 Jimmy Sexton	.10	.05	.01
□ 710 Willie Wilson	.25	.11	.03
□ 711 Mariners TL BA: Bruce Bochte ERA: Jim Beattie (Checklist on back)	.25	.11	.03
□ 712 Bruce Kison	.10	.05	.01
□ 713 Ron Hodges	.10	.05	.01
□ 714 Wayne Nordhagen	.10	.05	.01
□ 715 Tony Perez	.50	.23	.06
□ 716 Tony Perez SV	.25	.11	.03
□ 717 Scott Sanderson	.10	.05	.01
□ 718 Jim Dwyer	.10	.05	.01
□ 719 Rich Gale	.10	.05	.01
□ 720 Dave Concepcion	.25	.11	.03
□ 721 John Martin	.10	.05	.01
□ 722 Jorge Orta	.10	.05	.01
□ 723 Randy Moffitt	.10	.05	.01
□ 724 Johnny Grubb	.10	.05	.01
□ 725 Dan Spillner	.10	.05	.01
□ 726 Harvey Kuenn MG	.25	.11	.03
□ 727 Chet Lemon	.10	.05	.01
□ 728 Ron Reed	.10	.05	.01
□ 729 Jerry Morales	.10	.05	.01
□ 730 Jason Thompson	.10	.05	.01
□ 731 Al Williams	.10	.05	.01
□ 732 Dave Henderson	.25	.11	.03
□ 733 Buck Martinez	.10	.05	.01
□ 734 Steve Braun	.10	.05	.01
□ 735 Tommy John	.50	.23	.06
□ 736 Tommy John SV	.25	.11	.03
□ 737 Mitchell Page	.10	.05	.01
□ 738 Tim Foli	.10	.05	.01
□ 739 Rick Ownbey	.10	.05	.01
□ 740 Rusty Staub	.25	.11	.03
□ 741 Rusty Staub SV	.10	.05	.01
□ 742 Padres TL BA: Terry Kennedy ERA: Tim Lollar (Checklist on back)	.25	.11	.03
□ 743 Mike Torrez	.10	.05	.01
□ 744 Brad Mills	.10	.05	.01
□ 745 Scott McGregor	.10	.05	.01
□ 746 John Wathan	.10	.05	.01
□ 747 Fred Breining	.10	.05	.01
□ 748 Derrel Thomas	.10	.05	.01
□ 749 Jon Matlack	.10	.05	.01
□ 750 Ben Oglivie	.10	.05	.01
□ 751 Brad Havens	.10	.05	.01
□ 752 Luis Pujols	.10	.05	.01
□ 753 Elias Sosa	.10	.05	.01
□ 754 Bill Robinson	.10	.05	.01
□ 755 John Candelaria	.10	.05	.01
□ 756 Russ Nixon MG	.10	.05	.01
□ 757 Rick Manning	.10	.05	.01
□ 758 Aurelio Rodriguez	.10	.05	.01
□ 759 Doug Bird	.10	.05	.01
□ 760 Dale Murphy	.50	.23	.06
□ 761 Gary Lucas	.10	.05	.01
□ 762 Cliff Johnson	.10	.05	.01
□ 763 Al Cowens	.10	.05	.01
□ 764 Pete Falcone	.10	.05	.01
□ 765 Bob Boone	.25	.11	.03
□ 766 Barry Bonnell	.10	.05	.01
□ 767 Duane Kuiper	.10	.05	.01
□ 768 Chris Speier	.10	.05	.01
□ 769 Checklist: 661-792	.25	.11	.03
□ 770 Dave Winfield	2.00	.90	.25
□ 771 Twins TL BA: Kent Hrbek ERA: Bobby Castillo (Checklist on back)	.25	.11	.03
□ 772 Jim Kern	.10	.05	.01
□ 773 Larry Hisle	.10	.05	.01
□ 774 Alan Ashby	.10	.05	.01
□ 775 Burt Hooton	.10	.05	.01
□ 776 Larry Parrish	.10	.05	.01
□ 777 John Curtis	.10	.05	.01
□ 778 Rich Hebner	.25	.11	.03
□ 779 Rick Waits	.10	.05	.01
□ 780 Gary Matthews	.25	.11	.03
□ 781 Rick Rhoden	.10	.05	.01
□ 782 Bobby Murcer	.25	.11	.03
□ 783 Bobby Murcer SV	.10	.05	.01
□ 784 Jeff Newman	.10	.05	.01
□ 785 Dennis Leonard	.10	.05	.01
□ 786 Ralph Houk MG	.10	.05	.01
□ 787 Dick Tidrow	.10	.05	.01
□ 788 Dane Iorg	.10	.05	.01
□ 789 Bryan Clark	.10	.05	.01
□ 790 Bob Grich	.25	.11	.03
□ 791 Gary Lavelle	.10	.05	.01
□ 792 Chris Chambliss	.25	.11	.03

1983 Topps Traded

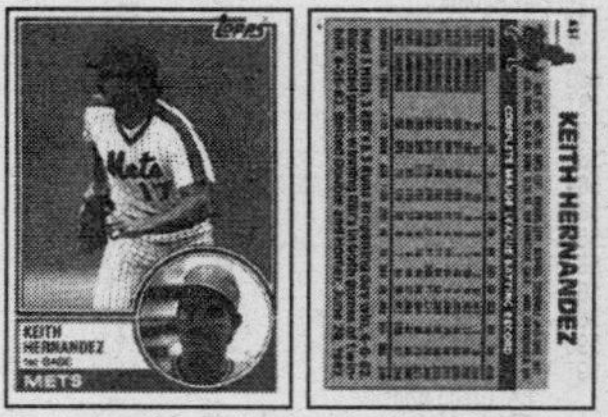

For the third year in a row, Topps issued a 132-card standard-size Traded (or extended) set featuring some of the year's top rookies and players who had changed teams during the year. The cards were available through hobby dealers only in factory set form and were printed in Ireland by the Topps affiliate in that country. The set is numbered alphabetically by player. The Darryl Strawberry card number 108 can be found with either one or two asterisks (in the lower left corner of the reverse). There is no difference in value for either version. The key (extended) Rookie Cards in this set include Julio Franco, Tony Phillips and Darryl Strawberry.

	MINT	NRMT	EXC
COMPLETE FACT.SET (132)	40.00	18.00	5.00
COMMON CARD (1T-132T)	.25	.11	.03
SEMISTARS	.50	.23	.06
STARS	1.00	.45	.12

□ 1T Neil Allen	.25	.11	.03
□ 2T Bill Almon	.25	.11	.03
□ 3T Joe Altobelli MG	.25	.11	.03
□ 4T Tony Armas	.25	.11	.03
□ 5T Doug Bair	.25	.11	.03

□	6T Steve Baker	.25	.11	.03
□	7T Floyd Bannister	.25	.11	.03
□	8T Don Baylor	1.00	.45	.12
□	9T Tony Bernazard	.25	.11	.03
□	10T Larry Biittner	.25	.11	.03
□	11T Dann Bilardello	.25	.11	.03
□	12T Doug Bird	.25	.11	.03
□	13T Steve Boros MG	.25	.11	.03
□	14T Greg Brock	.25	.11	.03
□	15T Mike C. Brown	.25	.11	.03
□	16T Tom Burgmeier	.25	.11	.03
□	17T Randy Bush	.25	.11	.03
□	18T Bert Campaneris	.50	.23	.06
□	19T Ron Cey	.50	.23	.06
□	20T Chris Codiroli	.25	.11	.03
□	21T Dave Collins	.25	.11	.03
□	22T Terry Crowley	.25	.11	.03
□	23T Julio Cruz	.25	.11	.03
□	24T Mike Davis	.25	.11	.03
□	25T Frank DiPino	.25	.11	.03
□	26T Bill Doran	.50	.23	.06
□	27T Jerry Dybzinski	.25	.11	.03
□	28T Jamie Easterly	.25	.11	.03
□	29T Juan Eichelberger	.25	.11	.03
□	30T Jim Essian	.25	.11	.03
□	31T Pete Falcone	.25	.11	.03
□	32T Mike Ferraro MG	.25	.11	.03
□	33T Terry Forster	.25	.11	.03
□	34T Julio Franco	3.00	1.35	.35
□	35T Rich Gale	.25	.11	.03
□	36T Kiko Garcia	.25	.11	.03
□	37T Steve Garvey	1.00	.45	.12
□	38T Johnny Grubb	.25	.11	.03
□	39T Mel Hall	.50	.23	.06
□	40T Von Hayes	.50	.23	.06
□	41T Danny Heep	.25	.11	.03
□	42T Steve Henderson	.25	.11	.03
□	43T Keith Hernandez	1.00	.45	.12
□	44T Leo Hernandez	.25	.11	.03
□	45T Willie Hernandez	.50	.23	.06
□	46T Al Holland	.25	.11	.03
□	47T Frank Howard MG	.50	.23	.06
□	48T Bobby Johnson	.25	.11	.03
□	49T Cliff Johnson	.25	.11	.03
□	50T Odell Jones	.25	.11	.03
□	51T Mike Jorgensen	.25	.11	.03
□	52T Bob Kearney	.25	.11	.03
□	53T Steve Kemp	.25	.11	.03
□	54T Matt Keough	.25	.11	.03
□	55T Ron Kittle	.50	.23	.06
□	56T Mickey Klutts	.25	.11	.03
□	57T Alan Knicely	.25	.11	.03
□	58T Mike Krukow	.25	.11	.03
□	59T Rafael Landestoy	.25	.11	.03
□	60T Carney Lansford	.50	.23	.06
□	61T Joe Lefebvre	.25	.11	.03
□	62T Bryan Little	.25	.11	.03
□	63T Aurelio Lopez	.25	.11	.03
□	64T Mike Madden	.25	.11	.03
□	65T Rick Manning	.25	.11	.03
□	66T Billy Martin MG	.50	.23	.06
□	67T Lee Mazzilli	.25	.11	.03
□	68T Andy McGaffigan	.25	.11	.03
□	69T Craig McMurtry	.25	.11	.03
□	70T John McNamara MG	.25	.11	.03
□	71T Orlando Mercado	.25	.11	.03
□	72T Larry Milbourne	.25	.11	.03
□	73T Randy Moffitt	.25	.11	.03
□	74T Sid Monge	.25	.11	.03
□	75T Jose Morales	.25	.11	.03
□	76T Omar Moreno	.25	.11	.03
□	77T Joe Morgan	2.00	.90	.25
□	78T Mike Morgan	.25	.11	.03
□	79T Dale Murray	.25	.11	.03
□	80T Jeff Newman	.25	.11	.03
□	81T Pete O'Brien	.50	.23	.06
□	82T Jorge Orta	.25	.11	.03
□	83T Alejandro Pena	.50	.23	.06
□	84T Pascual Perez	.25	.11	.03
□	85T Tony Perez	1.00	.45	.12
□	86T Broderick Perkins	.25	.11	.03
□	87T Tony Phillips	6.00	2.70	.75
□	88T Charlie Puleo	.25	.11	.03
□	89T Pat Putnam	.25	.11	.03
□	90T Jamie Quirk	.25	.11	.03
□	91T Doug Rader MG	.25	.11	.03
□	92T Chuck Rainey	.25	.11	.03
□	93T Bobby Ramos	.25	.11	.03
□	94T Gary Redus	.50	.23	.06
□	95T Steve Renko	.25	.11	.03
□	96T Leon Roberts	.25	.11	.03
□	97T Aurelio Rodriguez	.25	.11	.03
□	98T Dick Ruthven	.25	.11	.03
□	99T Daryl Sconiers	.25	.11	.03
□	100T Mike Scott	.50	.23	.06
□	101T Tom Seaver	5.00	2.20	.60
□	102T John Shelby	.25	.11	.03
□	103T Bob Shirley	.25	.11	.03
□	104T Joe Simpson	.25	.11	.03
□	105T Doug Sisk	.25	.11	.03
□	106T Mike Smithson	.25	.11	.03
□	107T Elias Sosa	.25	.11	.03
□	108T Darryl Strawberry	20.00	9.00	2.50
□	109T Tom Tellmann	.25	.11	.03
□	110T Gene Tenace	.50	.23	.06
□	111T Gorman Thomas	.25	.11	.03
□	112T Dick Tidrow	.25	.11	.03
□	113T Dave Tobik	.25	.11	.03
□	114T Wayne Tolleson	.25	.11	.03
□	115T Mike Torrez	.25	.11	.03
□	116T Manny Trillo	.25	.11	.03
□	117T Steve Trout	.25	.11	.03
□	118T Lee Tunnell	.25	.11	.03
□	119T Mike Vail	.25	.11	.03
□	120T Ellis Valentine	.25	.11	.03
□	121T Tom Veryzer	.25	.11	.03
□	122T George Vukovich	.25	.11	.03
□	123T Rick Waits	.25	.11	.03
□	124T Greg Walker	.50	.23	.06
□	125T Chris Welsh	.25	.11	.03
□	126T Len Whitehouse	.25	.11	.03
□	127T Eddie Whitson	.25	.11	.03
□	128T Jim Wohlford	.25	.11	.03
□	129T Matt Young	.25	.11	.03
□	130T Joel Youngblood	.25	.11	.03
□	131T Pat Zachry	.25	.11	.03
□	132T Checklist 1T-132T	.25	.11	.03

1984 Topps

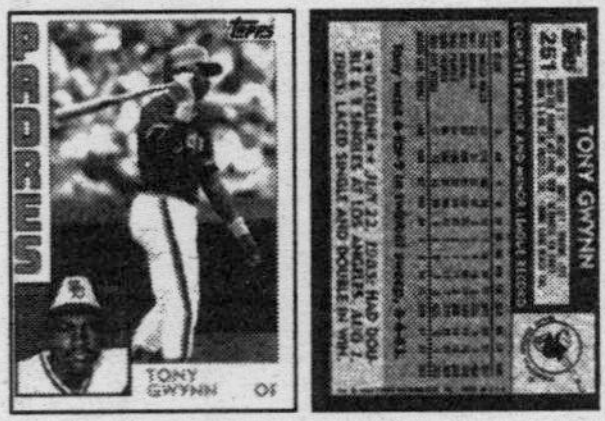

The cards in this 792-card set measure the standard size. For the second year in a row, Topps utilized a dual picture on the front of the card. A portrait is shown in a square insert and an action shot is featured in the main photo. Card numbers 1-6 feature 1983 Highlights (HL), cards 131-138 depict League Leaders, card numbers 386-407 feature All-Stars, and card numbers 701-718 feature active Major League career leaders in various statistical categories. Each team leader (TL) card features the team's leading hitter and pitcher pictured on the front with a team checklist back. There are six numerical checklist cards in the set. The player cards feature team logos in the upper right corner of the reverse. Cards were primarily distributed in 15-card wax packs and 54-card rack packs. The key Rookie Cards in this set are Don Mattingly and Darryl Strawberry. Topps tested a special send-in offer in Michigan and a few other states whereby collectors could obtain direct from Topps ten cards of their choice. Needless to say most people ordered the key (most valuable) players necessitating the printing of a special sheet to keep up with

the demand. The special sheet had five cards of Darryl Strawberry, three cards of Don Mattingly, etc. The test was apparently a failure in Topps' eyes as they have never tried it again.

	MINT	NRMT	EXC
COMPLETE SET (792)	50.00	22.00	6.25
COMMON CARD (1-792)	.08	.04	.01
SEMISTARS	.15	.07	.02
STARS	.40	.18	.05
□ 1 Steve Carlton HL	.50	.23	.06
300th win and			
all-time SO king			
□ 2 Rickey Henderson HL	.75	.35	.09
100 stolen bases,			
three times			
□ 3 Dan Quisenberry HL	.08	.04	.01
Sets save record			
□ 4 Nolan Ryan HL	1.00	.45	.12
Steve Carlton			
Gaylord Perry			
All surpass Johnson			
□ 5 Dave Righetti HL	.15	.07	.02
Bob Forsch			
Mike Warren			
All pitch no-hitters			
□ 6 Johnny Bench HL	.40	.18	.05
Gaylord Perry			
Carl Yastrzemski			
Superstars retire			
□ 7 Gary Lucas	.08	.04	.01
□ 8 Don Mattingly	12.00	5.50	1.50
□ 9 Jim Gott	.08	.04	.01
□ 10 Robin Yount	1.00	.45	.12
□ 11 Minnesota Twins TL	.15	.07	.02
Kent Hrbek			
Ken Schrom			
(Checklist on back)			
□ 12 Billy Sample	.08	.04	.01
□ 13 Scott Holman	.08	.04	.01
□ 14 Tom Brookens	.15	.07	.02
□ 15 Burt Hooton	.08	.04	.01
□ 16 Omar Moreno	.08	.04	.01
□ 17 John Denny	.08	.04	.01
□ 18 Dale Berra	.08	.04	.01
□ 19 Ray Fontenot	.08	.04	.01
□ 20 Greg Luzinski	.15	.07	.02
□ 21 Joe Altobelli MG	.08	.04	.01
□ 22 Bryan Clark	.08	.04	.01
□ 23 Keith Moreland	.08	.04	.01
□ 24 John Martin	.08	.04	.01
□ 25 Glenn Hubbard	.08	.04	.01
□ 26 Bud Black	.08	.04	.01
□ 27 Daryl Sconiers	.08	.04	.01
□ 28 Frank Viola	.15	.07	.02
□ 29 Danny Heep	.08	.04	.01
□ 30 Wade Boggs	1.25	.55	.16
□ 31 Andy McGaffigan	.08	.04	.01
□ 32 Bobby Ramos	.08	.04	.01
□ 33 Tom Burgmeier	.08	.04	.01
□ 34 Eddie Milner	.08	.04	.01
□ 35 Don Sutton	.40	.18	.05
□ 36 Denny Walling	.08	.04	.01
□ 37 Texas Rangers TL	.15	.07	.02
Buddy Bell			
Rick Honeycutt			
(Checklist on back)			
□ 38 Luis DeLeon	.08	.04	.01
□ 39 Garth Iorg	.08	.04	.01
□ 40 Dusty Baker	.40	.18	.05
□ 41 Tony Bernazard	.08	.04	.01
□ 42 Johnny Grubb	.08	.04	.01
□ 43 Ron Reed	.08	.04	.01
□ 44 Jim Morrison	.08	.04	.01
□ 45 Jerry Mumphrey	.08	.04	.01
□ 46 Ray Smith	.08	.04	.01
□ 47 Rudy Law	.08	.04	.01
□ 48 Julio Franco	.40	.18	.05
□ 49 John Stuper	.08	.04	.01
□ 50 Chris Chambliss	.08	.04	.01
□ 51 Jim Frey MG	.08	.04	.01
□ 52 Paul Splittorff	.08	.04	.01
□ 53 Juan Beniquez	.08	.04	.01
□ 54 Jesse Orosco	.08	.04	.01
□ 55 Dave Concepcion	.15	.07	.02
□ 56 Gary Allenson	.08	.04	.01
□ 57 Dan Schatzeder	.08	.04	.01
□ 58 Max Venable	.08	.04	.01
□ 59 Sammy Stewart	.08	.04	.01
□ 60 Paul Molitor UER	1.00	.45	.12
('83 stats .272, 613,			
167; should be .270,			
608, 164)			
□ 61 Chris Codiroli	.08	.04	.01
□ 62 Dave Hostetler	.08	.04	.01
□ 63 Ed VandeBerg	.08	.04	.01
□ 64 Mike Scioscia	.08	.04	.01
□ 65 Kirk Gibson	.40	.18	.05
□ 66 Houston Astros TL	.75	.35	.09
Jose Cruz			
Nolan Ryan			
(Checklist on back)			
□ 67 Gary Ward	.08	.04	.01
□ 68 Luis Salazar	.08	.04	.01
□ 69 Rod Scurry	.08	.04	.01
□ 70 Gary Matthews	.08	.04	.01
□ 71 Leo Hernandez	.08	.04	.01
□ 72 Mike Squires	.08	.04	.01
□ 73 Jody Davis	.08	.04	.01
□ 74 Jerry Martin	.08	.04	.01
□ 75 Bob Forsch	.08	.04	.01
□ 76 Alfredo Griffin	.08	.04	.01
□ 77 Brett Butler	.40	.18	.05
□ 78 Mike Torrez	.08	.04	.01
□ 79 Rob Wilfong	.08	.04	.01
□ 80 Steve Rogers	.08	.04	.01
□ 81 Billy Martin MG	.15	.07	.02
□ 82 Doug Bird	.08	.04	.01
□ 83 Richie Zisk	.08	.04	.01
□ 84 Lenny Faedo	.08	.04	.01
□ 85 Atlee Hammaker	.08	.04	.01
□ 86 John Shelby	.08	.04	.01
□ 87 Frank Pastore	.08	.04	.01
□ 88 Rob Picciolo	.08	.04	.01
□ 89 Mike Smithson	.08	.04	.01
□ 90 Pedro Guerrero	.15	.07	.02
□ 91 Dan Spillner	.08	.04	.01
□ 92 Lloyd Moseby	.08	.04	.01
□ 93 Bob Knepper	.08	.04	.01
□ 94 Mario Ramirez	.08	.04	.01
□ 95 Aurelio Lopez	.15	.07	.02
□ 96 Kansas City Royals TL	.40	.18	.05
Hal McRae			
Larry Gura			
(Checklist on back)			
□ 97 LaMarr Hoyt	.08	.04	.01
□ 98 Steve Nicosia	.08	.04	.01
□ 99 Craig Lefferts	.08	.04	.01
□ 100 Reggie Jackson	.75	.35	.09
□ 101 Porfirio Altamirano	.08	.04	.01
□ 102 Ken Oberkfell	.08	.04	.01
□ 103 Dwayne Murphy	.08	.04	.01
□ 104 Ken Dayley	.08	.04	.01
□ 105 Tony Armas	.08	.04	.01
□ 106 Tim Stoddard	.08	.04	.01
□ 107 Ned Yost	.08	.04	.01
□ 108 Randy Moffitt	.08	.04	.01
□ 109 Brad Wellman	.08	.04	.01
□ 110 Ron Guidry	.15	.07	.02
□ 111 Bill Virdon MG	.08	.04	.01
□ 112 Tom Niedenfuer	.08	.04	.01
□ 113 Kelly Paris	.08	.04	.01
□ 114 Checklist 1-132	.15	.07	.02
□ 115 Andre Thornton	.08	.04	.01
□ 116 George Bjorkman	.08	.04	.01
□ 117 Tom Veryzer	.08	.04	.01
□ 118 Charlie Hough	.15	.07	.02
□ 119 John Wockenfuss	.08	.04	.01
□ 120 Keith Hernandez	.40	.18	.05
□ 121 Pat Sheridan	.08	.04	.01
□ 122 Cecilio Guante	.08	.04	.01
□ 123 Butch Wynegar	.08	.04	.01
□ 124 Damaso Garcia	.08	.04	.01
□ 125 Britt Burns	.08	.04	.01
□ 126 Atlanta Braves TL	.40	.18	.05
Dale Murphy			
Craig McMurtry			
(Checklist on back)			
□ 127 Mike Madden	.08	.04	.01
□ 128 Rick Manning	.08	.04	.01
□ 129 Bill Laskey	.08	.04	.01

☐ 130	Ozzie Smith	1.25	.55	.16
☐ 131	Batting Leaders	.50	.23	.06
	Bill Madlock			
	Wade Boggs			
☐ 132	Home Run Leaders	.40	.18	.05
	Mike Schmidt			
	Jim Rice			
☐ 133	RBI Leaders	.40	.18	.05
	Dale Murphy			
	Cecil Cooper			
	Jim Rice			
☐ 134	Stolen Base Leaders	.75	.35	.09
	Tim Raines			
	Rickey Henderson			
☐ 135	Victory Leaders	.40	.18	.05
	John Denny			
	LaMarr Hoyt			
☐ 136	Strikeout Leaders	.40	.18	.05
	Steve Carlton			
	Jack Morris			
☐ 137	ERA Leaders	.40	.18	.05
	Atlee Hammaker			
	Rick Honeycutt			
☐ 138	Leading Firemen	.40	.18	.05
	Al Holland			
	Dan Quisenberry			
☐ 139	Bert Campaneris	.15	.07	.02
☐ 140	Storm Davis	.08	.04	.01
☐ 141	Pat Corrales MG	.08	.04	.01
☐ 142	Rich Gale	.08	.04	.01
☐ 143	Jose Morales	.08	.04	.01
☐ 144	Brian Harper	.40	.18	.05
☐ 145	Gary Lavelle	.08	.04	.01
☐ 146	Ed Romero	.08	.04	.01
☐ 147	Dan Petry	.15	.07	.02
☐ 148	Joe Lefebvre	.08	.04	.01
☐ 149	Jon Matlack	.08	.04	.01
☐ 150	Dale Murphy	.40	.18	.05
☐ 151	Steve Trout	.08	.04	.01
☐ 152	Glenn Brummer	.08	.04	.01
☐ 153	Dick Tidrow	.08	.04	.01
☐ 154	Dave Henderson	.15	.07	.02
☐ 155	Frank White	.15	.07	.02
☐ 156	Oakland A's TL	.40	.18	.05
	Rickey Henderson			
	Tim Conroy			
	(Checklist on back)			
☐ 157	Gary Gaetti	.40	.18	.05
☐ 158	John Curtis	.08	.04	.01
☐ 159	Darryl Cias	.08	.04	.01
☐ 160	Mario Soto	.08	.04	.01
☐ 161	Junior Ortiz	.08	.04	.01
☐ 162	Bob Ojeda	.08	.04	.01
☐ 163	Lorenzo Gray	.08	.04	.01
☐ 164	Scott Sanderson	.08	.04	.01
☐ 165	Ken Singleton	.08	.04	.01
☐ 166	Jamie Nelson	.08	.04	.01
☐ 167	Marshall Edwards	.08	.04	.01
☐ 168	Juan Bonilla	.08	.04	.01
☐ 169	Larry Parrish	.08	.04	.01
☐ 170	Jerry Reuss	.08	.04	.01
☐ 171	Frank Robinson MG	.40	.18	.05
☐ 172	Frank DiPino	.08	.04	.01
☐ 173	Marvell Wynne	.08	.04	.01
☐ 174	Juan Berenguer	.08	.04	.01
☐ 175	Graig Nettles	.15	.07	.02
☐ 176	Lee Smith	.75	.35	.09
☐ 177	Jerry Hairston	.08	.04	.01
☐ 178	Bill Krueger	.08	.04	.01
☐ 179	Buck Martinez	.08	.04	.01
☐ 180	Manny Trillo	.08	.04	.01
☐ 181	Roy Thomas	.08	.04	.01
☐ 182	Darryl Strawberry	3.00	1.35	.35
☐ 183	Al Williams	.08	.04	.01
☐ 184	Mike O'Berry	.08	.04	.01
☐ 185	Sixto Lezcano	.08	.04	.01
☐ 186	Cardinal TL	.15	.07	.02
	Lonnie Smith			
	John Stuper			
	(Checklist on back)			
☐ 187	Luis Aponte	.08	.04	.01
☐ 188	Bryan Little	.08	.04	.01
☐ 189	Tim Conroy	.08	.04	.01
☐ 190	Ben Oglivie	.08	.04	.01
☐ 191	Mike Boddicker	.08	.04	.01
☐ 192	Nick Esasky	.08	.04	.01
☐ 193	Darrell Brown	.08	.04	.01
☐ 194	Domingo Ramos	.08	.04	.01
☐ 195	Jack Morris	.40	.18	.05
☐ 196	Don Slaught	.15	.07	.02
☐ 197	Garry Hancock	.08	.04	.01
☐ 198	Bill Doran	.15	.07	.02
☐ 199	Willie Hernandez	.15	.07	.02
☐ 200	Andre Dawson	.75	.35	.09
☐ 201	Bruce Kison	.08	.04	.01
☐ 202	Bobby Cox MG	.15	.07	.02
☐ 203	Matt Keough	.08	.04	.01
☐ 204	Bobby Meacham	.08	.04	.01
☐ 205	Greg Minton	.08	.04	.01
☐ 206	Andy Van Slyke	.60	.25	.07
☐ 207	Donnie Moore	.08	.04	.01
☐ 208	Jose Oquendo	.15	.07	.02
☐ 209	Manny Sarmiento	.08	.04	.01
☐ 210	Joe Morgan	.40	.18	.05
☐ 211	Rick Sweet	.08	.04	.01
☐ 212	Broderick Perkins	.08	.04	.01
☐ 213	Bruce Hurst	.08	.04	.01
☐ 214	Paul Householder	.08	.04	.01
☐ 215	Tippy Martinez	.08	.04	.01
☐ 216	White Sox TL	.40	.18	.05
	Carlton Fisk			
	Richard Dotson			
	(Checklist on back)			
☐ 217	Alan Ashby	.08	.04	.01
☐ 218	Rick Waits	.08	.04	.01
☐ 219	Joe Simpson	.08	.04	.01
☐ 220	Fernando Valenzuela	.15	.07	.02
☐ 221	Cliff Johnson	.08	.04	.01
☐ 222	Rick Honeycutt	.08	.04	.01
☐ 223	Wayne Krenchicki	.08	.04	.01
☐ 224	Sid Monge	.08	.04	.01
☐ 225	Lee Mazzilli	.08	.04	.01
☐ 226	Juan Eichelberger	.08	.04	.01
☐ 227	Steve Braun	.08	.04	.01
☐ 228	John Rabb	.08	.04	.01
☐ 229	Paul Owens MG	.08	.04	.01
☐ 230	Rickey Henderson	1.00	.45	.12
☐ 231	Gary Woods	.08	.04	.01
☐ 232	Tim Wallach	.15	.07	.02
☐ 233	Checklist 133-264	.15	.07	.02
☐ 234	Rafael Ramirez	.08	.04	.01
☐ 235	Matt Young	.08	.04	.01
☐ 236	Ellis Valentine	.08	.04	.01
☐ 237	John Castino	.08	.04	.01
☐ 238	Reid Nichols	.08	.04	.01
☐ 239	Jay Howell	.08	.04	.01
☐ 240	Eddie Murray	1.50	.70	.19
☐ 241	Bill Almon	.08	.04	.01
☐ 242	Alex Trevino	.08	.04	.01
☐ 243	Pete Ladd	.08	.04	.01
☐ 244	Candy Maldonado	.08	.04	.01
☐ 245	Rick Sutcliffe	.15	.07	.02
☐ 246	New York Mets TL	.40	.18	.05
	Mookie Wilson			
	Tom Seaver			
	(Checklist on back)			
☐ 247	Onix Concepcion	.08	.04	.01
☐ 248	Bill Dawley	.08	.04	.01
☐ 249	Jay Johnstone	.15	.07	.02
☐ 250	Bill Madlock	.08	.04	.01
☐ 251	Tony Gwynn	5.00	2.20	.60
☐ 252	Larry Christenson	.08	.04	.01
☐ 253	Jim Wohlford	.08	.04	.01
☐ 254	Shane Rawley	.08	.04	.01
☐ 255	Bruce Benedict	.08	.04	.01
☐ 256	Dave Geisel	.08	.04	.01
☐ 257	Julio Cruz	.08	.04	.01
☐ 258	Luis Sanchez	.08	.04	.01
☐ 259	Sparky Anderson MG	.15	.07	.02
☐ 260	Scott McGregor	.08	.04	.01
☐ 261	Bobby Brown	.08	.04	.01
☐ 262	Tom Candiotti	.40	.18	.05
☐ 263	Jack Fimple	.08	.04	.01
☐ 264	Doug Frobel	.08	.04	.01
☐ 265	Donnie Hill	.08	.04	.01
☐ 266	Steve Lubratich	.08	.04	.01
☐ 267	Carmelo Martinez	.08	.04	.01
☐ 268	Jack O'Connor	.08	.04	.01
☐ 269	Aurelio Rodriguez	.08	.04	.01
☐ 270	Jeff Russell	.40	.18	.05
☐ 271	Moose Haas	.08	.04	.01
☐ 272	Rick Dempsey	.08	.04	.01

□ 273 Charlie Puleo	.08	.04	.01
□ 274 Rick Monday	.08	.04	.01
□ 275 Len Matuszek	.08	.04	.01
□ 276 Angels TL Rod Carew Geoff Zahn (Checklist on back)	.40	.18	.05
□ 277 Eddie Whitson	.08	.04	.01
□ 278 Jorge Bell	.15	.07	.02
□ 279 Ivan DeJesus	.08	.04	.01
□ 280 Floyd Bannister	.08	.04	.01
□ 281 Larry Milbourne	.08	.04	.01
□ 282 Jim Barr	.08	.04	.01
□ 283 Larry Biittner	.08	.04	.01
□ 284 Howard Bailey	.08	.04	.01
□ 285 Darrell Porter	.08	.04	.01
□ 286 Lary Sorensen	.08	.04	.01
□ 287 Warren Cromartie	.08	.04	.01
□ 288 Jim Beattie	.08	.04	.01
□ 289 Randy Johnson	.08	.04	.01
□ 290 Dave Dravecky	.15	.07	.02
□ 291 Chuck Tanner MG	.08	.04	.01
□ 292 Tony Scott	.08	.04	.01
□ 293 Ed Lynch	.08	.04	.01
□ 294 U.L. Washington	.08	.04	.01
□ 295 Mike Flanagan	.08	.04	.01
□ 296 Jeff Newman	.08	.04	.01
□ 297 Bruce Berenyi	.08	.04	.01
□ 298 Jim Gantner	.15	.07	.02
□ 299 John Butcher	.08	.04	.01
□ 300 Pete Rose	1.00	.45	.12
□ 301 Frank LaCorte	.08	.04	.01
□ 302 Barry Bonnell	.08	.04	.01
□ 303 Marty Castillo	.08	.04	.01
□ 304 Warren Brusstar	.08	.04	.01
□ 305 Roy Smalley	.08	.04	.01
□ 306 Dodgers TL Pedro Guerrero Bob Welch (Checklist on back)	.15	.07	.02
□ 307 Bobby Mitchell	.08	.04	.01
□ 308 Ron Hassey	.08	.04	.01
□ 309 Tony Phillips	1.00	.45	.12
□ 310 Willie McGee	.15	.07	.02
□ 311 Jerry Koosman	.15	.07	.02
□ 312 Jorge Orta	.08	.04	.01
□ 313 Mike Jorgensen	.08	.04	.01
□ 314 Orlando Mercado	.08	.04	.01
□ 315 Bob Grich	.15	.07	.02
□ 316 Mark Bradley	.08	.04	.01
□ 317 Greg Pryor	.08	.04	.01
□ 318 Bill Gullickson	.08	.04	.01
□ 319 Al Bumbry	.15	.07	.02
□ 320 Bob Stanley	.08	.04	.01
□ 321 Harvey Kuenn MG	.15	.07	.02
□ 322 Ken Schrom	.08	.04	.01
□ 323 Alan Knicely	.08	.04	.01
□ 324 Alejandro Pena	.15	.07	.02
□ 325 Darrell Evans	.15	.07	.02
□ 326 Bob Kearney	.08	.04	.01
□ 327 Ruppert Jones	.08	.04	.01
□ 328 Vern Ruhle	.08	.04	.01
□ 329 Pat Tabler	.08	.04	.01
□ 330 John Candelaria	.08	.04	.01
□ 331 Bucky Dent	.15	.07	.02
□ 332 Kevin Gross	.15	.07	.02
□ 333 Larry Herndon	.15	.07	.02
□ 334 Chuck Rainey	.08	.04	.01
□ 335 Don Baylor	.40	.18	.05
□ 336 Seattle Mariners TL Pat Putnam Matt Young (Checklist on back)	.15	.07	.02
□ 337 Kevin Hagen	.08	.04	.01
□ 338 Mike Warren	.08	.04	.01
□ 339 Roy Lee Jackson	.08	.04	.01
□ 340 Hal McRae	.15	.07	.02
□ 341 Dave Tobik	.08	.04	.01
□ 342 Tim Foli	.08	.04	.01
□ 343 Mark Davis	.08	.04	.01
□ 344 Rick Miller	.08	.04	.01
□ 345 Kent Hrbek	.40	.18	.05
□ 346 Kurt Bevacqua	.08	.04	.01
□ 347 Allan Ramirez	.08	.04	.01
□ 348 Toby Harrah	.15	.07	.02
□ 349 Bob L. Gibson	.08	.04	.01

□ 350 George Foster	.15	.07	.02
□ 351 Russ Nixon MG	.08	.04	.01
□ 352 Dave Stewart	.40	.18	.05
□ 353 Jim Anderson	.08	.04	.01
□ 354 Jeff Burroughs	.08	.04	.01
□ 355 Jason Thompson	.08	.04	.01
□ 356 Glenn Abbott	.08	.04	.01
□ 357 Ron Cey	.15	.07	.02
□ 358 Bob Dernier	.08	.04	.01
□ 359 Jim Acker	.08	.04	.01
□ 360 Willie Randolph	.15	.07	.02
□ 361 Dave Smith	.08	.04	.01
□ 362 David Green	.08	.04	.01
□ 363 Tim Laudner	.08	.04	.01
□ 364 Scott Fletcher	.08	.04	.01
□ 365 Steve Bedrosian	.08	.04	.01
□ 366 Padres TL Terry Kennedy Dave Dravecky (Checklist on back)	.15	.07	.02
□ 367 Jamie Easterly	.08	.04	.01
□ 368 Hubie Brooks	.08	.04	.01
□ 369 Steve McCatty	.08	.04	.01
□ 370 Tim Raines	.40	.18	.05
□ 371 Dave Gumpert	.08	.04	.01
□ 372 Gary Roenicke	.08	.04	.01
□ 373 Bill Scherrer	.08	.04	.01
□ 374 Don Money	.08	.04	.01
□ 375 Dennis Leonard	.08	.04	.01
□ 376 Dave Anderson	.08	.04	.01
□ 377 Danny Darwin	.08	.04	.01
□ 378 Bob Brenly	.08	.04	.01
□ 379 Checklist 265-396	.15	.07	.02
□ 380 Steve Garvey	.40	.18	.05
□ 381 Ralph Houk MG	.15	.07	.02
□ 382 Chris Nyman	.08	.04	.01
□ 383 Terry Puhl	.08	.04	.01
□ 384 Lee Tunnell	.08	.04	.01
□ 385 Tony Perez	.40	.18	.05
□ 386 George Hendrick AS	.08	.04	.01
□ 387 Johnny Ray AS	.08	.04	.01
□ 388 Mike Schmidt AS	.50	.23	.06
□ 389 Ozzie Smith AS	.60	.25	.07
□ 390 Tim Raines AS	.40	.18	.05
□ 391 Dale Murphy AS	.40	.18	.05
□ 392 Andre Dawson AS	.40	.18	.05
□ 393 Gary Carter AS	.15	.07	.02
□ 394 Steve Rogers AS	.08	.04	.01
□ 395 Steve Carlton AS	.40	.18	.05
□ 396 Jesse Orosco AS	.08	.04	.01
□ 397 Eddie Murray AS	.75	.35	.09
□ 398 Lou Whitaker AS	.40	.18	.05
□ 399 George Brett AS	1.00	.45	.12
□ 400 Cal Ripken AS	2.00	.90	.25
□ 401 Jim Rice AS	.15	.07	.02
□ 402 Dave Winfield AS	.60	.25	.07
□ 403 Lloyd Moseby AS	.08	.04	.01
□ 404 Ted Simmons AS	.15	.07	.02
□ 405 LaMarr Hoyt AS	.08	.04	.01
□ 406 Ron Guidry AS	.15	.07	.02
□ 407 Dan Quisenberry AS	.08	.04	.01
□ 408 Lou Piniella	.15	.07	.02
□ 409 Juan Agosto	.08	.04	.01
□ 410 Claudell Washington	.08	.04	.01
□ 411 Houston Jimenez	.08	.04	.01
□ 412 Doug Rader MG	.08	.04	.01
□ 413 Spike Owen	.15	.07	.02
□ 414 Mitchell Page	.08	.04	.01
□ 415 Tommy John	.40	.18	.05
□ 416 Dane Iorg	.08	.04	.01
□ 417 Mike Armstrong	.08	.04	.01
□ 418 Ron Hodges	.08	.04	.01
□ 419 John Henry Johnson	.08	.04	.01
□ 420 Cecil Cooper	.15	.07	.02
□ 421 Charlie Lea	.08	.04	.01
□ 422 Jose Cruz	.15	.07	.02
□ 423 Mike Morgan	.15	.07	.02
□ 424 Dann Bilardello	.08	.04	.01
□ 425 Steve Howe	.08	.04	.01
□ 426 Orioles TL Cal Ripken Mike Boddicker (Checklist on back)	1.50	.70	.19
□ 427 Rick Leach	.08	.04	.01
□ 428 Fred Breining	.08	.04	.01
□ 429 Randy Bush	.08	.04	.01

□ 430	Rusty Staub	.15	.07	.02
□ 431	Chris Bando	.08	.04	.01
□ 432	Charles Hudson	.08	.04	.01
□ 433	Rich Hebner	.08	.04	.01
□ 434	Harold Baines	.40	.18	.05
□ 435	Neil Allen	.08	.04	.01
□ 436	Rick Peters	.08	.04	.01
□ 437	Mike Proly	.08	.04	.01
□ 438	Biff Pocoroba	.08	.04	.01
□ 439	Bob Stoddard	.08	.04	.01
□ 440	Steve Kemp	.08	.04	.01
□ 441	Bob Lillis MG	.08	.04	.01
□ 442	Byron McLaughlin	.08	.04	.01
□ 443	Benny Ayala	.08	.04	.01
□ 444	Steve Renko	.08	.04	.01
□ 445	Jerry Remy	.08	.04	.01
□ 446	Luis Pujols	.08	.04	.01
□ 447	Tom Brunansky	.15	.07	.02
□ 448	Ben Hayes	.08	.04	.01
□ 449	Joe Pettini	.08	.04	.01
□ 450	Gary Carter	.40	.18	.05
□ 451	Bob Jones	.08	.04	.01
□ 452	Chuck Porter	.08	.04	.01
□ 453	Willie Upshaw	.08	.04	.01
□ 454	Joe Beckwith	.08	.04	.01
□ 455	Terry Kennedy	.08	.04	.01
□ 456	Chicago Cubs TL	.40	.18	.05
	Keith Moreland			
	Fergie Jenkins			
	(Checklist on back)			
□ 457	Dave Rozema	.08	.04	.01
□ 458	Kiko Garcia	.08	.04	.01
□ 459	Kevin Hickey	.08	.04	.01
□ 460	Dave Winfield	1.00	.45	.12
□ 461	Jim Maler	.08	.04	.01
□ 462	Lee Lacy	.08	.04	.01
□ 463	Dave Engle	.08	.04	.01
□ 464	Jeff A. Jones	.08	.04	.01
□ 465	Mookie Wilson	.15	.07	.02
□ 466	Gene Garber	.08	.04	.01
□ 467	Mike Ramsey	.08	.04	.01
□ 468	Geoff Zahn	.08	.04	.01
□ 469	Tom O'Malley	.08	.04	.01
□ 470	Nolan Ryan	4.00	1.80	.50
□ 471	Dick Howser MG	.08	.04	.01
□ 472	Mike G. Brown	.08	.04	.01
□ 473	Jim Dwyer	.08	.04	.01
□ 474	Greg Bargar	.08	.04	.01
□ 475	Gary Redus	.08	.04	.01
□ 476	Tom Tellmann	.08	.04	.01
□ 477	Rafael Landestoy	.08	.04	.01
□ 478	Alan Bannister	.08	.04	.01
□ 479	Frank Tanana	.15	.07	.02
□ 480	Ron Kittle	.08	.04	.01
□ 481	Mark Thurmond	.08	.04	.01
□ 482	Enos Cabell	.08	.04	.01
□ 483	Fergie Jenkins	.40	.18	.05
□ 484	Ozzie Virgil	.08	.04	.01
□ 485	Rick Rhoden	.08	.04	.01
□ 486	N.Y. Yankees TL	.40	.18	.05
	Don Baylor			
	Ron Guidry			
	(Checklist on back)			
□ 487	Ricky Adams	.08	.04	.01
□ 488	Jesse Barfield	.15	.07	.02
□ 489	Dave Von Ohlen	.08	.04	.01
□ 490	Cal Ripken	6.00	2.70	.75
□ 491	Bobby Castillo	.08	.04	.01
□ 492	Tucker Ashford	.08	.04	.01
□ 493	Mike Norris	.08	.04	.01
□ 494	Chili Davis	.40	.18	.05
□ 495	Rollie Fingers	.40	.18	.05
□ 496	Terry Francona	.08	.04	.01
□ 497	Bud Anderson	.08	.04	.01
□ 498	Rich Gedman	.08	.04	.01
□ 499	Mike Witt	.08	.04	.01
□ 500	George Brett	2.00	.90	.25
□ 501	Steve Henderson	.08	.04	.01
□ 502	Joe Torre MG	.15	.07	.02
□ 503	Elias Sosa	.08	.04	.01
□ 504	Mickey Rivers	.08	.04	.01
□ 505	Pete Vuckovich	.08	.04	.01
□ 506	Ernie Whitt	.08	.04	.01
□ 507	Mike LaCoss	.08	.04	.01
□ 508	Mel Hall	.15	.07	.02
□ 509	Brad Havens	.08	.04	.01
□ 510	Alan Trammell	.40	.18	.05
□ 511	Marty Bystrom	.08	.04	.01
□ 512	Oscar Gamble	.08	.04	.01
□ 513	Dave Beard	.08	.04	.01
□ 514	Floyd Rayford	.08	.04	.01
□ 515	Gorman Thomas	.08	.04	.01
□ 516	Montreal Expos TL	.15	.07	.02
	Al Oliver			
	Charlie Lea			
	(Checklist on back)			
□ 517	John Moses	.08	.04	.01
□ 518	Greg Walker	.15	.07	.02
□ 519	Ron Davis	.08	.04	.01
□ 520	Bob Boone	.15	.07	.02
□ 521	Pete Falcone	.08	.04	.01
□ 522	Dave Bergman	.08	.04	.01
□ 523	Glenn Hoffman	.08	.04	.01
□ 524	Carlos Diaz	.08	.04	.01
□ 525	Willie Wilson	.08	.04	.01
□ 526	Ron Oester	.08	.04	.01
□ 527	Checklist 397-528	.15	.07	.02
□ 528	Mark Brouhard	.08	.04	.01
□ 529	Keith Atherton	.08	.04	.01
□ 530	Dan Ford	.08	.04	.01
□ 531	Steve Boros MG	.08	.04	.01
□ 532	Eric Show	.08	.04	.01
□ 533	Ken Landreaux	.08	.04	.01
□ 534	Pete O'Brien	.40	.18	.05
□ 535	Bo Diaz	.08	.04	.01
□ 536	Doug Bair	.08	.04	.01
□ 537	Johnny Ray	.08	.04	.01
□ 538	Kevin Bass	.08	.04	.01
□ 539	George Frazier	.08	.04	.01
□ 540	George Hendrick	.08	.04	.01
□ 541	Dennis Lamp	.08	.04	.01
□ 542	Duane Kuiper	.08	.04	.01
□ 543	Craig McMurtry	.08	.04	.01
□ 544	Cesar Geronimo	.08	.04	.01
□ 545	Bill Buckner	.15	.07	.02
□ 546	Indians TL	.15	.07	.02
	Mike Hargrove			
	Lary Sorensen			
	(Checklist on back)			
□ 547	Mike Moore	.15	.07	.02
□ 548	Ron Jackson	.08	.04	.01
□ 549	Walt Terrell	.08	.04	.01
□ 550	Jim Rice	.40	.18	.05
□ 551	Scott Ullger	.08	.04	.01
□ 552	Ray Burris	.08	.04	.01
□ 553	Joe Nolan	.08	.04	.01
□ 554	Ted Power	.08	.04	.01
□ 555	Greg Brock	.08	.04	.01
□ 556	Joey McLaughlin	.08	.04	.01
□ 557	Wayne Tolleson	.08	.04	.01
□ 558	Mike Davis	.08	.04	.01
□ 559	Mike Scott	.15	.07	.02
□ 560	Carlton Fisk	.75	.35	.09
□ 561	Whitey Herzog MG	.15	.07	.02
□ 562	Manny Castillo	.08	.04	.01
□ 563	Glenn Wilson	.15	.07	.02
□ 564	Al Holland	.08	.04	.01
□ 565	Leon Durham	.08	.04	.01
□ 566	Jim Bibby	.08	.04	.01
□ 567	Mike Heath	.08	.04	.01
□ 568	Pete Filson	.08	.04	.01
□ 569	Bake McBride	.08	.04	.01
□ 570	Dan Quisenberry	.08	.04	.01
□ 571	Bruce Bochy	.08	.04	.01
□ 572	Jerry Royster	.08	.04	.01
□ 573	Dave Kingman	.15	.07	.02
□ 574	Brian Downing	.08	.04	.01
□ 575	Jim Clancy	.08	.04	.01
□ 576	Giants TL	.15	.07	.02
	Jeff Leonard			
	Atlee Hammaker			
	(Checklist on back)			
□ 577	Mark Clear	.08	.04	.01
□ 578	Lenn Sakata	.08	.04	.01
□ 579	Bob James	.08	.04	.01
□ 580	Lonnie Smith	.08	.04	.01
□ 581	Jose DeLeon	.08	.04	.01
□ 582	Bob McClure	.08	.04	.01
□ 583	Derrel Thomas	.08	.04	.01
□ 584	Dave Schmidt	.08	.04	.01
□ 585	Dan Driessen	.08	.04	.01
□ 586	Joe Niekro	.15	.07	.02

□ 587	Von Hayes	.08	.04	.01
□ 588	Milt Wilcox	.08	.04	.01
□ 589	Mike Easler	.08	.04	.01
□ 590	Dave Stieb	.08	.04	.01
□ 591	Tony LaRussa MG	.15	.07	.02
□ 592	Andre Robertson	.08	.04	.01
□ 593	Jeff Lahti	.08	.04	.01
□ 594	Gene Richards	.08	.04	.01
□ 595	Jeff Reardon	.40	.18	.05
□ 596	Ryne Sandberg	4.00	1.80	.50
□ 597	Rick Camp	.08	.04	.01
□ 598	Rusty Kuntz	.08	.04	.01
□ 599	Doug Sisk	.08	.04	.01
□ 600	Rod Carew	.60	.25	.07
□ 601	John Tudor	.08	.04	.01
□ 602	John Wathan	.08	.04	.01
□ 603	Renie Martin	.08	.04	.01
□ 604	John Lowenstein	.08	.04	.01
□ 605	Mike Caldwell	.08	.04	.01
□ 606	Blue Jays TL	.15	.07	.02
	Lloyd Moseby			
	Dave Stieb			
	(Checklist on back)			
□ 607	Tom Hume	.08	.04	.01
□ 608	Bobby Johnson	.08	.04	.01
□ 609	Dan Meyer	.08	.04	.01
□ 610	Steve Sax	.15	.07	.02
□ 611	Chet Lemon	.15	.07	.02
□ 612	Harry Spilman	.08	.04	.01
□ 613	Greg Gross	.08	.04	.01
□ 614	Len Barker	.08	.04	.01
□ 615	Garry Templeton	.08	.04	.01
□ 616	Don Robinson	.08	.04	.01
□ 617	Rick Cerone	.08	.04	.01
□ 618	Dickie Noles	.08	.04	.01
□ 619	Jerry Dybzinski	.08	.04	.01
□ 620	Al Oliver	.15	.07	.02
□ 621	Frank Howard MG	.15	.07	.02
□ 622	Al Cowens	.08	.04	.01
□ 623	Ron Washington	.08	.04	.01
□ 624	Terry Harper	.08	.04	.01
□ 625	Larry Gura	.08	.04	.01
□ 626	Bob Clark	.08	.04	.01
□ 627	Dave LaPoint	.08	.04	.01
□ 628	Ed Jurak	.08	.04	.01
□ 629	Rick Langford	.08	.04	.01
□ 630	Ted Simmons	.15	.07	.02
□ 631	Dennis Martinez	.15	.07	.02
□ 632	Tom Foley	.08	.04	.01
□ 633	Mike Krukow	.08	.04	.01
□ 634	Mike Marshall	.08	.04	.01
□ 635	Dave Righetti	.15	.07	.02
□ 636	Pat Putnam	.08	.04	.01
□ 637	Phillies TL	.15	.07	.02
	Gary Matthews			
	John Denny			
	(Checklist on back)			
□ 638	George Vukovich	.08	.04	.01
□ 639	Rick Lysander	.08	.04	.01
□ 640	Lance Parrish	.15	.07	.02
□ 641	Mike Richardt	.08	.04	.01
□ 642	Tom Underwood	.08	.04	.01
□ 643	Mike C. Brown	.08	.04	.01
□ 644	Tim Lollar	.08	.04	.01
□ 645	Tony Pena	.08	.04	.01
□ 646	Checklist 529-660	.15	.07	.02
□ 647	Ron Roenicke	.08	.04	.01
□ 648	Len Whitehouse	.08	.04	.01
□ 649	Tom Herr	.15	.07	.02
□ 650	Phil Niekro	.40	.18	.05
□ 651	John McNamara MG	.08	.04	.01
□ 652	Rudy May	.08	.04	.01
□ 653	Dave Stapleton	.08	.04	.01
□ 654	Bob Bailor	.08	.04	.01
□ 655	Amos Otis	.15	.07	.02
□ 656	Bryn Smith	.08	.04	.01
□ 657	Thad Bosley	.08	.04	.01
□ 658	Jerry Augustine	.08	.04	.01
□ 659	Duane Walker	.08	.04	.01
□ 660	Ray Knight	.15	.07	.02
□ 661	Steve Yeager	.08	.04	.01
□ 662	Tom Brennan	.08	.04	.01
□ 663	Johnnie LeMaster	.08	.04	.01
□ 664	Dave Stegman	.08	.04	.01
□ 665	Buddy Bell	.15	.07	.02
□ 666	Detroit Tigers TL	.40	.18	.05
	Lou Whitaker			
	Jack Morris			
	(Checklist on back)			
□ 667	Vance Law	.08	.04	.01
□ 668	Larry McWilliams	.08	.04	.01
□ 669	Dave Lopes	.15	.07	.02
□ 670	Rich Gossage	.40	.18	.05
□ 671	Jamie Quirk	.08	.04	.01
□ 672	Ricky Nelson	.08	.04	.01
□ 673	Mike Walters	.08	.04	.01
□ 674	Tim Flannery	.08	.04	.01
□ 675	Pascual Perez	.08	.04	.01
□ 676	Brian Giles	.08	.04	.01
□ 677	Doyle Alexander	.08	.04	.01
□ 678	Chris Speier	.08	.04	.01
□ 679	Art Howe	.08	.04	.01
□ 680	Fred Lynn	.15	.07	.02
□ 681	Tom Lasorda MG	.15	.07	.02
□ 682	Dan Morogiello	.08	.04	.01
□ 683	Marty Barrett	.15	.07	.02
□ 684	Bob Shirley	.08	.04	.01
□ 685	Willie Aikens	.08	.04	.01
□ 686	Joe Price	.08	.04	.01
□ 687	Roy Howell	.08	.04	.01
□ 688	George Wright	.08	.04	.01
□ 689	Mike Fischlin	.08	.04	.01
□ 690	Jack Clark	.15	.07	.02
□ 691	Steve Lake	.08	.04	.01
□ 692	Dickie Thon	.08	.04	.01
□ 693	Alan Wiggins	.08	.04	.01
□ 694	Mike Stanton	.08	.04	.01
□ 695	Lou Whitaker	.40	.18	.05
□ 696	Pirates TL	.15	.07	.02
	Bill Madlock			
	Rick Rhoden			
	(Checklist on back)			
□ 697	Dale Murray	.08	.04	.01
□ 698	Marc Hill	.08	.04	.01
□ 699	Dave Rucker	.08	.04	.01
□ 700	Mike Schmidt	1.50	.70	.19
□ 701	NL Active Batting	.40	.18	.05
	Bill Madlock			
	Pete Rose			
	Dave Parker			
□ 702	NL Active Hits	.40	.18	.05
	Pete Rose			
	Rusty Staub			
	Tony Perez			
□ 703	NL Active Home Run	.40	.18	.05
	Mike Schmidt			
	Tony Perez			
	Dave Kingman			
□ 704	NL Active RBI	.40	.18	.05
	Tony Perez			
	Rusty Staub			
	Al Oliver			
□ 705	NL Active Steals	.40	.18	.05
	Joe Morgan			
	Cesar Cedeno			
	Larry Bowa			
□ 706	NL Active Victory	.40	.18	.05
	Steve Carlton			
	Fergie Jenkins			
	Tom Seaver			
□ 707	NL Active Strikeout	1.50	.70	.19
	Steve Carlton			
	Nolan Ryan			
	Tom Seaver			
□ 708	NL Active ERA	.40	.18	.05
	Tom Seaver			
	Steve Carlton			
	Steve Rogers			
□ 709	NL Active Save	.15	.07	.02
	Bruce Sutter			
	Tug McGraw			
	Gene Garber			
□ 710	AL Active Batting	.40	.18	.05
	Rod Carew			
	George Brett			
	Cecil Cooper			
□ 711	AL Active Hits	.40	.18	.05
	Rod Carew			
	Bert Campaneris			
	Reggie Jackson			
□ 712	AL Active Home Run	.40	.18	.05
	Reggie Jackson			

Graig Nettles			
Greg Luzinski			
□ 713 AL Active RBI	.40	.18	.05
Reggie Jackson			
Ted Simmons			
Graig Nettles			
□ 714 AL Active Steals	.15	.07	.02
Bert Campaneris			
Dave Lopes			
Omar Moreno			
□ 715 AL Active Victory	.40	.18	.05
Jim Palmer			
Don Sutton			
Tommy John			
□ 716 AL Active Strikeout	.40	.18	.05
Don Sutton			
Bert Blyleven			
Jerry Koosman			
□ 717 AL Active ERA	.40	.18	.05
Jim Palmer			
Rollie Fingers			
Ron Guidry			
□ 718 AL Active Save	.40	.18	.05
Rollie Fingers			
Rich Gossage			
Dan Quisenberry			
□ 719 Andy Hassler	.08	.04	.01
□ 720 Dwight Evans	.15	.07	.02
□ 721 Del Crandall MG	.08	.04	.01
□ 722 Bob Welch	.08	.04	.01
□ 723 Rich Dauer	.08	.04	.01
□ 724 Eric Rasmussen	.08	.04	.01
□ 725 Cesar Cedeno	.15	.07	.02
□ 726 Brewers TL	.15	.07	.02
Ted Simmons			
Moose Haas			
(Checklist on back)			
□ 727 Joel Youngblood	.08	.04	.01
□ 728 Tug McGraw	.15	.07	.02
□ 729 Gene Tenace	.15	.07	.02
□ 730 Bruce Sutter	.15	.07	.02
□ 731 Lynn Jones	.08	.04	.01
□ 732 Terry Crowley	.08	.04	.01
□ 733 Dave Collins	.08	.04	.01
□ 734 Odell Jones	.08	.04	.01
□ 735 Rick Burleson	.08	.04	.01
□ 736 Dick Ruthven	.08	.04	.01
□ 737 Jim Essian	.08	.04	.01
□ 738 Bill Schroeder	.08	.04	.01
□ 739 Bob Watson	.15	.07	.02
□ 740 Tom Seaver	.75	.35	.09
□ 741 Wayne Gross	.08	.04	.01
□ 742 Dick Williams MG	.15	.07	.02
□ 743 Don Hood	.08	.04	.01
□ 744 Jamie Allen	.08	.04	.01
□ 745 Dennis Eckersley	.50	.23	.06
□ 746 Mickey Hatcher	.08	.04	.01
□ 747 Pat Zachry	.08	.04	.01
□ 748 Jeff Leonard	.08	.04	.01
□ 749 Doug Flynn	.08	.04	.01
□ 750 Jim Palmer	.60	.25	.07
□ 751 Charlie Moore	.08	.04	.01
□ 752 Phil Garner	.15	.07	.02
□ 753 Doug Gwosdz	.08	.04	.01
□ 754 Kent Tekulve	.15	.07	.02
□ 755 Garry Maddox	.08	.04	.01
□ 756 Reds TL	.15	.07	.02
Ron Oester			
Mario Soto			
(Checklist on back)			
□ 757 Larry Bowa	.15	.07	.02
□ 758 Bill Stein	.08	.04	.01
□ 759 Richard Dotson	.08	.04	.01
□ 760 Bob Horner	.08	.04	.01
□ 761 John Montefusco	.08	.04	.01
□ 762 Rance Mulliniks	.08	.04	.01
□ 763 Craig Swan	.08	.04	.01
□ 764 Mike Hargrove	.15	.07	.02
□ 765 Ken Forsch	.08	.04	.01
□ 766 Mike Vail	.08	.04	.01
□ 767 Carney Lansford	.15	.07	.02
□ 768 Champ Summers	.08	.04	.01
□ 769 Bill Caudill	.08	.04	.01
□ 770 Ken Griffey	.15	.07	.02
□ 771 Billy Gardner MG	.08	.04	.01
□ 772 Jim Slaton	.08	.04	.01
□ 773 Todd Cruz	.08	.04	.01
□ 774 Tom Gorman	.08	.04	.01
□ 775 Dave Parker	.40	.18	.05
□ 776 Craig Reynolds	.08	.04	.01
□ 777 Tom Paciorek	.08	.04	.01
□ 778 Andy Hawkins	.08	.04	.01
□ 779 Jim Sundberg	.15	.07	.02
□ 780 Steve Carlton	.75	.35	.09
□ 781 Checklist 661-792	.15	.07	.02
□ 782 Steve Balboni	.08	.04	.01
□ 783 Luis Leal	.08	.04	.01
□ 784 Leon Roberts	.08	.04	.01
□ 785 Joaquin Andujar	.08	.04	.01
□ 786 Red Sox TL	.40	.18	.05
Wade Boggs			
Bob Ojeda			
(Checklist on back)			
□ 787 Bill Campbell	.08	.04	.01
□ 788 Milt May	.08	.04	.01
□ 789 Bert Blyleven	.15	.07	.02
□ 790 Doug DeCinces	.08	.04	.01
□ 791 Terry Forster	.08	.04	.01
□ 792 Bill Russell	.08	.04	.01

1984 Topps Traded

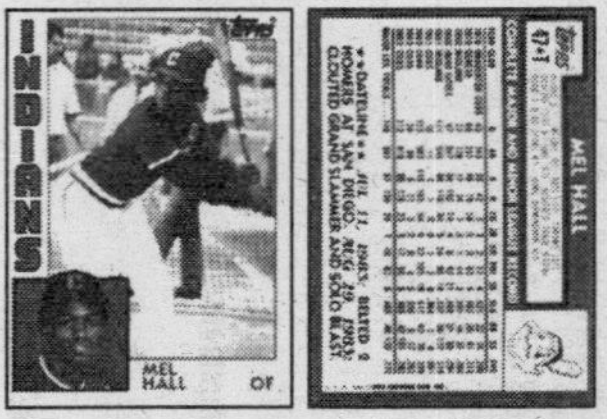

In now standard procedure, Topps issued its standard-size Traded (or extended) set for the fourth year in a row. Several of 1984's top rookies not contained in the regular set are pictured in the Traded set. Extended Rookie Cards in this set include Dwight Gooden, Jimmy Key, Mark Langston, Jose Rijo, and Bret Saberhagen. Again this year, the Topps affiliate in Ireland printed the cards, and the cards were available through hobby channels only in factory set form. The set numbering is in alphabetical order by player's name.

	MINT	NRMT	EXC
COMPLETE FACT.SET (132)	50.00	22.00	6.25
COMMON CARD (1T-132T)	.25	.11	.03
SEMISTARS	.40	.18	.05
STARS	.75	.35	.09
□ 1T Willie Aikens	.25	.11	.03
□ 2T Luis Aponte	.25	.11	.03
□ 3T Mike Armstrong	.25	.11	.03
□ 4T Bob Bailor	.25	.11	.03
□ 5T Dusty Baker	.75	.35	.09
□ 6T Steve Balboni	.25	.11	.03
□ 7T Alan Bannister	.25	.11	.03
□ 8T Dave Beard	.25	.11	.03
□ 9T Joe Beckwith	.25	.11	.03
□ 10T Bruce Berenyi	.25	.11	.03
□ 11T Dave Bergman	.25	.11	.03
□ 12T Tony Bernazard	.25	.11	.03
□ 13T Yogi Berra MG	1.00	.45	.12
□ 14T Barry Bonnell	.25	.11	.03
□ 15T Phil Bradley	.40	.18	.05
□ 16T Fred Breining	.25	.11	.03
□ 17T Bill Buckner	.40	.18	.05
□ 18T Ray Burris	.25	.11	.03
□ 19T John Butcher	.25	.11	.03
□ 20T Brett Butler	.75	.35	.09
□ 21T Enos Cabell	.25	.11	.03
□ 22T Bill Campbell	.25	.11	.03
□ 23T Bill Caudill	.25	.11	.03
□ 24T Bob Clark	.25	.11	.03

□ 25T	Bryan Clark	.25	.11	.03
□ 26T	Jaime Cocanower	.25	.11	.03
□ 27T	Ron Darling	.75	.35	.09
□ 28T	Alvin Davis	.40	.18	.05
□ 29T	Ken Dayley	.25	.11	.03
□ 30T	Jeff Dedmon	.25	.11	.03
□ 31T	Bob Dernier	.25	.11	.03
□ 32T	Carlos Diaz	.25	.11	.03
□ 33T	Mike Easler	.25	.11	.03
□ 34T	Dennis Eckersley	3.00	1.35	.35
□ 35T	Jim Essian	.25	.11	.03
□ 36T	Darrell Evans	.40	.18	.05
□ 37T	Mike Fitzgerald	.25	.11	.03
□ 38T	Tim Foli	.25	.11	.03
□ 39T	George Frazier	.25	.11	.03
□ 40T	Rich Gale	.25	.11	.03
□ 41T	Barbaro Garbey	.25	.11	.03
□ 42T	Dwight Gooden	10.00	4.50	1.25
□ 43T	Rich Gossage	.75	.35	.09
□ 44T	Wayne Gross	.25	.11	.03
□ 45T	Mark Gubicza	.75	.35	.09
□ 46T	Jackie Gutierrez	.25	.11	.03
□ 47T	Mel Hall	.40	.18	.05
□ 48T	Toby Harrah	.40	.18	.05
□ 49T	Ron Hassey	.25	.11	.03
□ 50T	Rich Hebner	.25	.11	.03
□ 51T	Willie Hernandez	.40	.18	.05
□ 52T	Ricky Horton	.25	.11	.03
□ 53T	Art Howe	.25	.11	.03
□ 54T	Dane Iorg	.25	.11	.03
□ 55T	Brook Jacoby	.40	.18	.05
□ 56T	Mike Jeffcoat	.25	.11	.03
□ 57T	Dave Johnson MG	.40	.18	.05
□ 58T	Lynn Jones	.25	.11	.03
□ 59T	Ruppert Jones	.25	.11	.03
□ 60T	Mike Jorgensen	.25	.11	.03
□ 61T	Bob Kearney	.25	.11	.03
□ 62T	Jimmy Key	2.50	1.10	.30
□ 63T	Dave Kingman	.40	.18	.05
□ 64T	Jerry Koosman	.40	.18	.05
□ 65T	Wayne Krenchicki	.25	.11	.03
□ 66T	Rusty Kuntz	.25	.11	.03
□ 67T	Rene Lachemann MG	.25	.11	.03
□ 68T	Frank LaCorte	.25	.11	.03
□ 69T	Dennis Lamp	.25	.11	.03
□ 70T	Mark Langston	3.00	1.35	.35
□ 71T	Rick Leach	.25	.11	.03
□ 72T	Craig Lefferts	.40	.18	.05
□ 73T	Gary Lucas	.25	.11	.03
□ 74T	Jerry Martin	.25	.11	.03
□ 75T	Carmelo Martinez	.25	.11	.03
□ 76T	Mike Mason	.25	.11	.03
□ 77T	Gary Matthews	.25	.11	.03
□ 78T	Andy McGaffigan	.25	.11	.03
□ 79T	Larry Milbourne	.25	.11	.03
□ 80T	Sid Monge	.25	.11	.03
□ 81T	Jackie Moore MG	.25	.11	.03
□ 82T	Joe Morgan	2.00	.90	.25
□ 83T	Graig Nettles	.40	.18	.05
□ 84T	Phil Niekro	.75	.35	.09
□ 85T	Ken Oberkfell	.25	.11	.03
□ 86T	Mike O'Berry	.25	.11	.03
□ 87T	Al Oliver	.40	.18	.05
□ 88T	Jorge Orta	.25	.11	.03
□ 89T	Amos Otis	.40	.18	.05
□ 90T	Dave Parker	.75	.35	.09
□ 91T	Tony Perez	.75	.35	.09
□ 92T	Gerald Perry	.40	.18	.05
□ 93T	Gary Pettis	.25	.11	.03
□ 94T	Rob Picciolo	.25	.11	.03
□ 95T	Vern Rapp MG	.25	.11	.03
□ 96T	Floyd Rayford	.25	.11	.03
□ 97T	Randy Ready	.40	.18	.05
□ 98T	Ron Reed	.25	.11	.03
□ 99T	Gene Richards	.25	.11	.03
□ 100T	Jose Rijo	3.00	1.35	.35
□ 101T	Jeff D. Robinson	.25	.11	.03
□ 102T	Ron Romanick	.25	.11	.03
□ 103T	Pete Rose	8.00	3.60	1.00
□ 104T	Bret Saberhagen	3.00	1.35	.35
□ 105T	Juan Samuel	.75	.35	.09
□ 106T	Scott Sanderson	.25	.11	.03
□ 107T	Dick Schofield	.40	.18	.05
□ 108T	Tom Seaver	4.00	1.80	.50
□ 109T	Jim Slaton	.25	.11	.03
□ 110T	Mike Smithson	.25	.11	.03
□ 111T	Lary Sorensen	.25	.11	.03
□ 112T	Tim Stoddard	.25	.11	.03
□ 113T	Champ Summers	.25	.11	.03
□ 114T	Jim Sundberg	.40	.18	.05
□ 115T	Rick Sutcliffe	.40	.18	.05
□ 116T	Craig Swan	.25	.11	.03
□ 117T	Tim Teufel	.25	.11	.03
□ 118T	Derrel Thomas	.25	.11	.03
□ 119T	Gorman Thomas	.25	.11	.03
□ 120T	Alex Trevino	.25	.11	.03
□ 121T	Manny Trillo	.25	.11	.03
□ 122T	John Tudor	.25	.11	.03
□ 123T	Tom Underwood	.25	.11	.03
□ 124T	Mike Vail	.25	.11	.03
□ 125T	Tom Waddell	.25	.11	.03
□ 126T	Gary Ward	.25	.11	.03
□ 127T	Curt Wilkerson	.25	.11	.03
□ 128T	Frank Williams	.25	.11	.03
□ 129T	Glenn Wilson	.40	.18	.05
□ 130T	John Wockenfuss	.25	.11	.03
□ 131T	Ned Yost	.25	.11	.03
□ 132T	Checklist 1T-132T	.25	.11	.03

1985 Topps

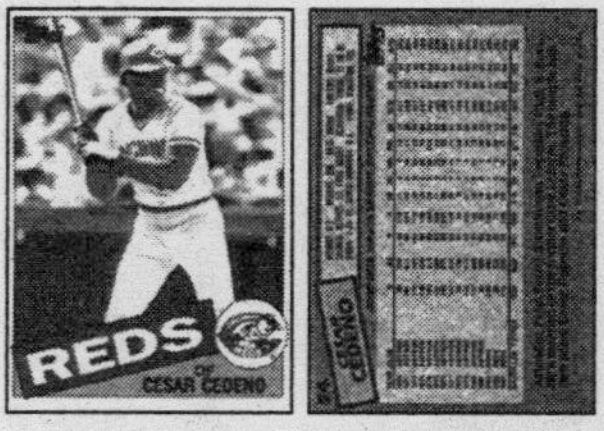

The 1985 Topps set contains 792 standard-size full-color cards. Cards were primarily distributed in 15-card wax packs and 51-card rack packs. Full color card fronts feature both the Topps and team logos along with the team name, player's name, and his position. The first ten cards (1-10) are Record Breakers, cards 131-143 are Father and Sons, and cards 701 to 722 portray All-Star selections. Cards 271-282 represent "First Draft Picks" still active in professional baseball and cards 389-404 feature selected members of the 1984 U.S. Olympic Baseball Team. Rookie Cards include Roger Clemens, Eric Davis, Shawon Dunston, Dwight Gooden, Orel Hershiser, Jimmy Key, Mark Langston, Mark McGwire, Terry Pendleton, Kirby Puckett, Jose Rijo and Bret Saberhagen.

	MINT	NRMT	EXC
COMPLETE SET (792)	50.00	22.00	6.25
COMMON CARD (1-792)	.08	.04	.01
SEMISTARS	.15	.07	.02
STARS	.30	.14	.04

□ 1	Carlton Fisk RB Longest game by catcher	.30	.14	.04
□ 2	Steve Garvey RB Consecutive error- less games, 1B	.30	.14	.04
□ 3	Dwight Gooden RB Most rookie strikeouts	.50	.23	.06
□ 4	Cliff Johnson RB Most pinch-hit homers	.08	.04	.01
□ 5	Joe Morgan RB Most homers 2B, lifetime	.30	.14	.04
□ 6	Pete Rose RB Most career singles	.40	.18	.05
□ 7	Nolan Ryan RB Most career strikeouts	1.50	.70	.19
□ 8	Juan Samuel RB Most SB's, rookie season	.08	.04	.01
□ 9	Bruce Sutter RB Most NL season saves	.15	.07	.02

☐ 10 Don Sutton RB	.15	.07	.02
Most seasons 100 or more K's			
☐ 11 Ralph Houk MG	.08	.04	.01
(Checklist back)			
☐ 12 Dave Lopes	.15	.07	.02
(Now with Cubs on card front)			
☐ 13 Tim Lollar	.08	.04	.01
☐ 14 Chris Bando	.08	.04	.01
☐ 15 Jerry Koosman	.08	.04	.01
☐ 16 Bobby Meacham	.08	.04	.01
☐ 17 Mike Scott	.08	.04	.01
☐ 18 Mickey Hatcher	.08	.04	.01
☐ 19 George Frazier	.08	.04	.01
☐ 20 Chet Lemon	.08	.04	.01
☐ 21 Lee Tunnell	.08	.04	.01
☐ 22 Duane Kuiper	.08	.04	.01
☐ 23 Bret Saberhagen	.60	.25	.07
☐ 24 Jesse Barfield	.08	.04	.01
☐ 25 Steve Bedrosian	.08	.04	.01
☐ 26 Roy Smalley	.08	.04	.01
☐ 27 Bruce Berenyi	.08	.04	.01
☐ 28 Dann Bilardello	.08	.04	.01
☐ 29 Odell Jones	.08	.04	.01
☐ 30 Cal Ripken	3.00	1.35	.35
☐ 31 Terry Whitfield	.08	.04	.01
☐ 32 Chuck Porter	.08	.04	.01
☐ 33 Tito Landrum	.08	.04	.01
☐ 34 Ed Nunez	.08	.04	.01
☐ 35 Graig Nettles	.15	.07	.02
☐ 36 Fred Breining	.08	.04	.01
☐ 37 Reid Nichols	.08	.04	.01
☐ 38 Jackie Moore MG	.08	.04	.01
(Checklist back)			
☐ 39 John Wockenfuss	.08	.04	.01
☐ 40 Phil Niekro	.30	.14	.04
☐ 41 Mike Fischlin	.08	.04	.01
☐ 42 Luis Sanchez	.08	.04	.01
☐ 43 Andre David	.08	.04	.01
☐ 44 Dickie Thon	.08	.04	.01
☐ 45 Greg Minton	.08	.04	.01
☐ 46 Gary Woods	.08	.04	.01
☐ 47 Dave Rozema	.08	.04	.01
☐ 48 Tony Fernandez	.15	.07	.02
☐ 49 Butch Davis	.08	.04	.01
☐ 50 John Candelaria	.08	.04	.01
☐ 51 Bob Watson	.15	.07	.02
☐ 52 Jerry Dybzinski	.08	.04	.01
☐ 53 Tom Gorman	.08	.04	.01
☐ 54 Cesar Cedeno	.15	.07	.02
☐ 55 Frank Tanana	.08	.04	.01
☐ 56 Jim Dwyer	.08	.04	.01
☐ 57 Pat Zachry	.08	.04	.01
☐ 58 Orlando Mercado	.08	.04	.01
☐ 59 Rick Waits	.08	.04	.01
☐ 60 George Hendrick	.08	.04	.01
☐ 61 Curt Kaufman	.08	.04	.01
☐ 62 Mike Ramsey	.08	.04	.01
☐ 63 Steve McCatty	.08	.04	.01
☐ 64 Mark Bailey	.08	.04	.01
☐ 65 Bill Buckner	.15	.07	.02
☐ 66 Dick Williams MG	.15	.07	.02
(Checklist back)			
☐ 67 Rafael Santana	.08	.04	.01
☐ 68 Von Hayes	.08	.04	.01
☐ 69 Jim Winn	.08	.04	.01
☐ 70 Don Baylor	.30	.14	.04
☐ 71 Tim Laudner	.08	.04	.01
☐ 72 Rick Sutcliffe	.08	.04	.01
☐ 73 Rusty Kuntz	.08	.04	.01
☐ 74 Mike Krukow	.08	.04	.01
☐ 75 Willie Upshaw	.08	.04	.01
☐ 76 Alan Bannister	.08	.04	.01
☐ 77 Joe Beckwith	.08	.04	.01
☐ 78 Scott Fletcher	.08	.04	.01
☐ 79 Rick Mahler	.08	.04	.01
☐ 80 Keith Hernandez	.15	.07	.02
☐ 81 Lenn Sakata	.08	.04	.01
☐ 82 Joe Price	.08	.04	.01
☐ 83 Charlie Moore	.08	.04	.01
☐ 84 Spike Owen	.08	.04	.01
☐ 85 Mike Marshall	.08	.04	.01
☐ 86 Don Aase	.08	.04	.01
☐ 87 David Green	.08	.04	.01
☐ 88 Bryn Smith	.08	.04	.01
☐ 89 Jackie Gutierrez	.08	.04	.01

☐ 90 Rich Gossage	.30	.14	.04
☐ 91 Jeff Burroughs	.08	.04	.01
☐ 92 Paul Owens MG	.08	.04	.01
(Checklist back)			
☐ 93 Don Schulze	.08	.04	.01
☐ 94 Toby Harrah	.08	.04	.01
☐ 95 Jose Cruz	.15	.07	.02
☐ 96 Johnny Ray	.08	.04	.01
☐ 97 Pete Filson	.08	.04	.01
☐ 98 Steve Lake	.08	.04	.01
☐ 99 Milt Wilcox	.08	.04	.01
☐ 100 George Brett	1.50	.70	.19
☐ 101 Jim Acker	.08	.04	.01
☐ 102 Tommy Dunbar	.08	.04	.01
☐ 103 Randy Lerch	.08	.04	.01
☐ 104 Mike Fitzgerald	.08	.04	.01
☐ 105 Ron Kittle	.08	.04	.01
☐ 106 Pascual Perez	.08	.04	.01
☐ 107 Tom Foley	.08	.04	.01
☐ 108 Darnell Coles	.08	.04	.01
☐ 109 Gary Roenicke	.08	.04	.01
☐ 110 Alejandro Pena	.08	.04	.01
☐ 111 Doug DeCinces	.08	.04	.01
☐ 112 Tom Tellmann	.08	.04	.01
☐ 113 Tom Herr	.15	.07	.02
☐ 114 Bob James	.08	.04	.01
☐ 115 Rickey Henderson	.60	.25	.07
☐ 116 Dennis Boyd	.08	.04	.01
☐ 117 Greg Gross	.08	.04	.01
☐ 118 Eric Show	.08	.04	.01
☐ 119 Pat Corrales MG	.08	.04	.01
(Checklist back)			
☐ 120 Steve Kemp	.08	.04	.01
☐ 121 Checklist: 1-132	.15	.07	.02
☐ 122 Tom Brunansky	.15	.07	.02
☐ 123 Dave Smith	.08	.04	.01
☐ 124 Rich Hebner	.08	.04	.01
☐ 125 Kent Tekulve	.08	.04	.01
☐ 126 Ruppert Jones	.08	.04	.01
☐ 127 Mark Gubicza	.30	.14	.04
☐ 128 Ernie Whitt	.08	.04	.01
☐ 129 Gene Garber	.08	.04	.01
☐ 130 Al Oliver	.15	.07	.02
☐ 131 Buddy Bell FS	.15	.07	.02
Gus Bell			
☐ 132 Dale Berra FS	.15	.07	.02
Yogi Berra			
☐ 133 Bob Boone FS	.15	.07	.02
Ray Boone			
☐ 134 Terry Francona FS	.15	.07	.02
Tito Francona			
☐ 135 Terry Kennedy FS	.15	.07	.02
Bob Kennedy			
☐ 136 Jeff Kunkel FS	.08	.04	.01
Bill Kunkel			
☐ 137 Vance Law FS	.15	.07	.02
Vern Law			
☐ 138 Dick Schofield FS	.08	.04	.01
Dick Schofield			
☐ 139 Joel Skinner FS	.08	.04	.01
Bob Skinner			
☐ 140 Roy Smalley Jr. FS	.15	.07	.02
Roy Smalley			
☐ 141 Mike Stenhouse FS	.08	.04	.01
Dave Stenhouse			
☐ 142 Steve Trout FS	.15	.07	.02
Dizzy Trout			
☐ 143 Ozzie Virgil FS	.08	.04	.01
Ossie Virgil			
☐ 144 Ron Gardenhire	.08	.04	.01
☐ 145 Alvin Davis	.15	.07	.02
☐ 146 Gary Redus	.08	.04	.01
☐ 147 Bill Swaggerty	.08	.04	.01
☐ 148 Steve Yeager	.08	.04	.01
☐ 149 Dickie Noles	.08	.04	.01
☐ 150 Jim Rice	.30	.14	.04
☐ 151 Moose Haas	.08	.04	.01
☐ 152 Steve Braun	.08	.04	.01
☐ 153 Frank LaCorte	.08	.04	.01
☐ 154 Argenis Salazar	.08	.04	.01
☐ 155 Yogi Berra MG	.30	.14	.04
(Checklist back)			
☐ 156 Craig Reynolds	.08	.04	.01
☐ 157 Tug McGraw	.15	.07	.02
☐ 158 Pat Tabler	.08	.04	.01
☐ 159 Carlos Diaz	.08	.04	.01

□ 160	Lance Parrish	.15	.07	.02
□ 161	Ken Schrom	.08	.04	.01
□ 162	Benny Distefano	.08	.04	.01
□ 163	Dennis Eckersley	.30	.14	.04
□ 164	Jorge Orta	.08	.04	.01
□ 165	Dusty Baker	.15	.07	.02
□ 166	Keith Atherton	.08	.04	.01
□ 167	Rufino Linares	.08	.04	.01
□ 168	Garth Iorg	.08	.04	.01
□ 169	Dan Spillner	.08	.04	.01
□ 170	George Foster	.15	.07	.02
□ 171	Bill Stein	.08	.04	.01
□ 172	Jack Perconte	.08	.04	.01
□ 173	Mike Young	.08	.04	.01
□ 174	Rick Honeycutt	.08	.04	.01
□ 175	Dave Parker	.30	.14	.04
□ 176	Bill Schroeder	.08	.04	.01
□ 177	Dave Von Ohlen	.08	.04	.01
□ 178	Miguel Dilone	.08	.04	.01
□ 179	Tommy John	.30	.14	.04
□ 180	Dave Winfield	.60	.25	.07
□ 181	Roger Clemens	7.00	3.10	.85
□ 182	Tim Flannery	.08	.04	.01
□ 183	Larry McWilliams	.08	.04	.01
□ 184	Carmen Castillo	.08	.04	.01
□ 185	Al Holland	.08	.04	.01
□ 186	Bob Lillis MG (Checklist back)	.08	.04	.01
□ 187	Mike Walters	.08	.04	.01
□ 188	Greg Pryor	.08	.04	.01
□ 189	Warren Brusstar	.08	.04	.01
□ 190	Rusty Staub	.15	.07	.02
□ 191	Steve Nicosia	.08	.04	.01
□ 192	Howard Johnson	.15	.07	.02
□ 193	Jimmy Key	.40	.18	.05
□ 194	Dave Stegman	.08	.04	.01
□ 195	Glenn Hubbard	.08	.04	.01
□ 196	Pete O'Brien	.08	.04	.01
□ 197	Mike Warren	.08	.04	.01
□ 198	Eddie Milner	.08	.04	.01
□ 199	Dennis Martinez	.15	.07	.02
□ 200	Reggie Jackson	.60	.25	.07
□ 201	Burt Hooton	.08	.04	.01
□ 202	Gorman Thomas	.08	.04	.01
□ 203	Bob McClure	.08	.04	.01
□ 204	Art Howe	.08	.04	.01
□ 205	Steve Rogers	.08	.04	.01
□ 206	Phil Garner	.08	.04	.01
□ 207	Mark Clear	.08	.04	.01
□ 208	Champ Summers	.08	.04	.01
□ 209	Bill Campbell	.08	.04	.01
□ 210	Gary Matthews	.08	.04	.01
□ 211	Clay Christiansen	.08	.04	.01
□ 212	George Vukovich	.08	.04	.01
□ 213	Billy Gardner MG (Checklist back)	.15	.07	.02
□ 214	John Tudor	.08	.04	.01
□ 215	Bob Brenly	.08	.04	.01
□ 216	Jerry Don Gleaton	.08	.04	.01
□ 217	Leon Roberts	.08	.04	.01
□ 218	Doyle Alexander	.08	.04	.01
□ 219	Gerald Perry	.08	.04	.01
□ 220	Fred Lynn	.15	.07	.02
□ 221	Ron Reed	.08	.04	.01
□ 222	Hubie Brooks	.08	.04	.01
□ 223	Tom Hume	.08	.04	.01
□ 224	Al Cowens	.08	.04	.01
□ 225	Mike Boddicker	.08	.04	.01
□ 226	Juan Beniquez	.08	.04	.01
□ 227	Danny Darwin	.08	.04	.01
□ 228	Dion James	.08	.04	.01
□ 229	Dave LaPoint	.08	.04	.01
□ 230	Gary Carter	.30	.14	.04
□ 231	Dwayne Murphy	.08	.04	.01
□ 232	Dave Beard	.08	.04	.01
□ 233	Ed Jurak	.08	.04	.01
□ 234	Jerry Narron	.08	.04	.01
□ 235	Garry Maddox	.08	.04	.01
□ 236	Mark Thurmond	.08	.04	.01
□ 237	Julio Franco	.30	.14	.04
□ 238	Jose Rijo	.40	.18	.05
□ 239	Tim Teufel	.08	.04	.01
□ 240	Dave Stieb	.15	.07	.02
□ 241	Jim Frey MG (Checklist back)	.08	.04	.01
□ 242	Greg Harris	.08	.04	.01

□ 243	Barbaro Garbey	.08	.04	.01
□ 244	Mike Jones	.08	.04	.01
□ 245	Chili Davis	.15	.07	.02
□ 246	Mike Norris	.08	.04	.01
□ 247	Wayne Tolleson	.08	.04	.01
□ 248	Terry Forster	.08	.04	.01
□ 249	Harold Baines	.15	.07	.02
□ 250	Jesse Orosco	.08	.04	.01
□ 251	Brad Gulden	.08	.04	.01
□ 252	Dan Ford	.08	.04	.01
□ 253	Sid Bream	.30	.14	.04
□ 254	Pete Vuckovich	.08	.04	.01
□ 255	Lonnie Smith	.08	.04	.01
□ 256	Mike Stanton	.08	.04	.01
□ 257	Bryan Little UER (Name spelled Brian on front)	.08	.04	.01
□ 258	Mike C. Brown	.08	.04	.01
□ 259	Gary Allenson	.08	.04	.01
□ 260	Dave Righetti	.15	.07	.02
□ 261	Checklist: 133-264	.15	.07	.02
□ 262	Greg Booker	.08	.04	.01
□ 263	Mel Hall	.08	.04	.01
□ 264	Joe Sambito	.08	.04	.01
□ 265	Juan Samuel	.08	.04	.01
□ 266	Frank Viola	.15	.07	.02
□ 267	Henry Cotto	.08	.04	.01
□ 268	Chuck Tanner MG (Checklist back)	.15	.07	.02
□ 269	Doug Baker	.08	.04	.01
□ 270	Dan Quisenberry	.15	.07	.02
□ 271	Tim Foli FDP68	.08	.04	.01
□ 272	Jeff Burroughs FDP69	.08	.04	.01
□ 273	Bill Almon FDP74	.08	.04	.01
□ 274	Floyd Bannister FDP76	.08	.04	.01
□ 275	Harold Baines FDP77	.15	.07	.02
□ 276	Bob Horner FDP78	.08	.04	.01
□ 277	Al Chambers FDP79	.08	.04	.01
□ 278	Darryl Strawberry FDP80	.30	.14	.04
□ 279	Mike Moore FDP81	.08	.04	.01
□ 280	Shawon Dunston FDP82	.40	.18	.05
□ 281	Tim Belcher FDP83	.30	.14	.04
□ 282	Shawn Abner FDP84	.08	.04	.01
□ 283	Fran Mullins	.08	.04	.01
□ 284	Marty Bystrom	.08	.04	.01
□ 285	Dan Driessen	.08	.04	.01
□ 286	Rudy Law	.08	.04	.01
□ 287	Walt Terrell	.08	.04	.01
□ 288	Jeff Kunkel	.08	.04	.01
□ 289	Tom Underwood	.08	.04	.01
□ 290	Cecil Cooper	.15	.07	.02
□ 291	Bob Welch	.08	.04	.01
□ 292	Brad Komminsk	.08	.04	.01
□ 293	Curt Young	.08	.04	.01
□ 294	Tom Nieto	.08	.04	.01
□ 295	Joe Niekro	.08	.04	.01
□ 296	Ricky Nelson	.08	.04	.01
□ 297	Gary Lucas	.08	.04	.01
□ 298	Marty Barrett	.08	.04	.01
□ 299	Andy Hawkins	.08	.04	.01
□ 300	Rod Carew	.50	.23	.06
□ 301	John Montefusco	.08	.04	.01
□ 302	Tim Corcoran	.08	.04	.01
□ 303	Mike Jeffcoat	.08	.04	.01
□ 304	Gary Gaetti	.15	.07	.02
□ 305	Dale Berra	.08	.04	.01
□ 306	Rick Reuschel	.08	.04	.01
□ 307	Sparky Anderson MG (Checklist back)	.15	.07	.02
□ 308	John Wathan	.08	.04	.01
□ 309	Mike Witt	.08	.04	.01
□ 310	Manny Trillo	.08	.04	.01
□ 311	Jim Gott	.08	.04	.01
□ 312	Marc Hill	.08	.04	.01
□ 313	Dave Schmidt	.08	.04	.01
□ 314	Ron Oester	.08	.04	.01
□ 315	Doug Sisk	.08	.04	.01
□ 316	John Lowenstein	.08	.04	.01
□ 317	Jack Lazorko	.08	.04	.01
□ 318	Ted Simmons	.15	.07	.02
□ 319	Jeff Jones	.08	.04	.01
□ 320	Dale Murphy	.30	.14	.04
□ 321	Ricky Horton	.08	.04	.01
□ 322	Dave Stapleton	.08	.04	.01
□ 323	Andy McGaffigan	.08	.04	.01
□ 324	Bruce Bochy	.08	.04	.01

□ 325	John Denny	.08	.04	.01
□ 326	Kevin Bass	.08	.04	.01
□ 327	Brook Jacoby	.08	.04	.01
□ 328	Bob Shirley	.08	.04	.01
□ 329	Ron Washington	.08	.04	.01
□ 330	Leon Durham	.08	.04	.01
□ 331	Bill Laskey	.08	.04	.01
□ 332	Brian Harper	.15	.07	.02
□ 333	Willie Hernandez	.08	.04	.01
□ 334	Dick Howser MG (Checklist back)	.15	.07	.02
□ 335	Bruce Benedict	.08	.04	.01
□ 336	Rance Mulliniks	.08	.04	.01
□ 337	Billy Sample	.08	.04	.01
□ 338	Britt Burns	.08	.04	.01
□ 339	Danny Heep	.08	.04	.01
□ 340	Robin Yount	.75	.35	.09
□ 341	Floyd Rayford	.08	.04	.01
□ 342	Ted Power	.08	.04	.01
□ 343	Bill Russell	.08	.04	.01
□ 344	Dave Henderson	.15	.07	.02
□ 345	Charlie Lea	.08	.04	.01
□ 346	Terry Pendleton	.60	.25	.07
□ 347	Rick Langford	.08	.04	.01
□ 348	Bob Boone	.15	.07	.02
□ 349	Domingo Ramos	.08	.04	.01
□ 350	Wade Boggs	1.00	.45	.12
□ 351	Juan Agosto	.08	.04	.01
□ 352	Joe Morgan	.30	.14	.04
□ 353	Julio Solano	.08	.04	.01
□ 354	Andre Robertson	.08	.04	.01
□ 355	Bert Blyleven	.30	.14	.04
□ 356	Dave Meier	.08	.04	.01
□ 357	Rich Bordi	.08	.04	.01
□ 358	Tony Pena	.08	.04	.01
□ 359	Pat Sheridan	.08	.04	.01
□ 360	Steve Carlton	.40	.18	.05
□ 361	Alfredo Griffin	.08	.04	.01
□ 362	Craig McMurtry	.08	.04	.01
□ 363	Ron Hodges	.08	.04	.01
□ 364	Richard Dotson	.08	.04	.01
□ 365	Danny Ozark MG (Checklist back)	.08	.04	.01
□ 366	Todd Cruz	.08	.04	.01
□ 367	Keefe Cato	.08	.04	.01
□ 368	Dave Bergman	.08	.04	.01
□ 369	R.J. Reynolds	.08	.04	.01
□ 370	Bruce Sutter	.15	.07	.02
□ 371	Mickey Rivers	.08	.04	.01
□ 372	Roy Howell	.08	.04	.01
□ 373	Mike Moore	.08	.04	.01
□ 374	Brian Downing	.08	.04	.01
□ 375	Jeff Reardon	.15	.07	.02
□ 376	Jeff Newman	.08	.04	.01
□ 377	Checklist: 265-396	.15	.07	.02
□ 378	Alan Wiggins	.08	.04	.01
□ 379	Charles Hudson	.08	.04	.01
□ 380	Ken Griffey	.15	.07	.02
□ 381	Roy Smith	.08	.04	.01
□ 382	Denny Walling	.08	.04	.01
□ 383	Rick Lysander	.08	.04	.01
□ 384	Jody Davis	.08	.04	.01
□ 385	Jose DeLeon	.08	.04	.01
□ 386	Dan Gladden	.15	.07	.02
□ 387	Buddy Biancalana	.08	.04	.01
□ 388	Bert Roberge	.08	.04	.01
□ 389	Rod Dedeaux OLY CO	.15	.07	.02
□ 390	Sid Akins OLY	.15	.07	.02
□ 391	Flavio Alfaro OLY	.15	.07	.02
□ 392	Don August OLY	.15	.07	.02
□ 393	Scott Bankhead OLY	.15	.07	.02
□ 394	Bob Caffrey OLY	.08	.04	.01
□ 395	Mike Dunne OLY	.15	.07	.02
□ 396	Gary Green OLY	.15	.07	.02
□ 397	John Hoover OLY	.08	.04	.01
□ 398	Shane Mack OLY	.30	.14	.04
□ 399	John Marzano OLY	.15	.07	.02
□ 400	Oddibe McDowell OLY	.15	.07	.02
□ 401	Mark McGwire OLY	18.00	8.00	2.20
□ 402	Pat Pacillo OLY	.15	.07	.02
□ 403	Cory Snyder OLY	.15	.07	.02
□ 404	Billy Swift OLY	.50	.23	.06
□ 405	Tom Veryzer	.08	.04	.01
□ 406	Len Whitehouse	.08	.04	.01
□ 407	Bobby Ramos	.08	.04	.01
□ 408	Sid Monge	.08	.04	.01
□ 409	Brad Wellman	.08	.04	.01
□ 410	Bob Horner	.08	.04	.01
□ 411	Bobby Cox MG (Checklist back)	.15	.07	.02
□ 412	Bud Black	.08	.04	.01
□ 413	Vance Law	.08	.04	.01
□ 414	Gary Ward	.08	.04	.01
□ 415	Ron Darling UER (No trivia answer)	.15	.07	.02
□ 416	Wayne Gross	.08	.04	.01
□ 417	John Franco	.40	.18	.05
□ 418	Ken Landreaux	.08	.04	.01
□ 419	Mike Caldwell	.08	.04	.01
□ 420	Andre Dawson	.30	.14	.04
□ 421	Dave Rucker	.08	.04	.01
□ 422	Carney Lansford	.15	.07	.02
□ 423	Barry Bonnell	.08	.04	.01
□ 424	Al Nipper	.08	.04	.01
□ 425	Mike Hargrove	.15	.07	.02
□ 426	Vern Ruhle	.08	.04	.01
□ 427	Mario Ramirez	.08	.04	.01
□ 428	Larry Andersen	.08	.04	.01
□ 429	Rick Cerone	.08	.04	.01
□ 430	Ron Davis	.08	.04	.01
□ 431	U.L. Washington	.08	.04	.01
□ 432	Thad Bosley	.08	.04	.01
□ 433	Jim Morrison	.08	.04	.01
□ 434	Gene Richards	.08	.04	.01
□ 435	Dan Petry	.08	.04	.01
□ 436	Willie Aikens	.08	.04	.01
□ 437	Al Jones	.08	.04	.01
□ 438	Joe Torre MG (Checklist back)	.30	.14	.04
□ 439	Junior Ortiz	.08	.04	.01
□ 440	Fernando Valenzuela	.15	.07	.02
□ 441	Duane Walker	.08	.04	.01
□ 442	Ken Forsch	.08	.04	.01
□ 443	George Wright	.08	.04	.01
□ 444	Tony Phillips	.30	.14	.04
□ 445	Tippy Martinez	.08	.04	.01
□ 446	Jim Sundberg	.08	.04	.01
□ 447	Jeff Lahti	.08	.04	.01
□ 448	Derrel Thomas	.08	.04	.01
□ 449	Phil Bradley	.15	.07	.02
□ 450	Steve Garvey	.30	.14	.04
□ 451	Bruce Hurst	.08	.04	.01
□ 452	John Castino	.08	.04	.01
□ 453	Tom Waddell	.08	.04	.01
□ 454	Glenn Wilson	.08	.04	.01
□ 455	Bob Knepper	.08	.04	.01
□ 456	Tim Foli	.08	.04	.01
□ 457	Cecilio Guante	.08	.04	.01
□ 458	Randy Johnson	.08	.04	.01
□ 459	Charlie Leibrandt	.08	.04	.01
□ 460	Ryne Sandberg	1.50	.70	.19
□ 461	Marty Castillo	.08	.04	.01
□ 462	Gary Lavelle	.08	.04	.01
□ 463	Dave Collins	.08	.04	.01
□ 464	Mike Mason	.08	.04	.01
□ 465	Bob Grich	.15	.07	.02
□ 466	Tony LaRussa MG (Checklist back)	.15	.07	.02
□ 467	Ed Lynch	.08	.04	.01
□ 468	Wayne Krenchicki	.08	.04	.01
□ 469	Sammy Stewart	.08	.04	.01
□ 470	Steve Sax	.15	.07	.02
□ 471	Pete Ladd	.08	.04	.01
□ 472	Jim Essian	.08	.04	.01
□ 473	Tim Wallach	.15	.07	.02
□ 474	Kurt Kepshire	.08	.04	.01
□ 475	Andre Thornton	.08	.04	.01
□ 476	Jeff Stone	.08	.04	.01
□ 477	Bob Ojeda	.08	.04	.01
□ 478	Kurt Bevacqua	.08	.04	.01
□ 479	Mike Madden	.08	.04	.01
□ 480	Lou Whitaker	.30	.14	.04
□ 481	Dale Murray	.08	.04	.01
□ 482	Harry Spilman	.08	.04	.01
□ 483	Mike Smithson	.08	.04	.01
□ 484	Larry Bowa	.15	.07	.02
□ 485	Matt Young	.08	.04	.01
□ 486	Steve Balboni	.08	.04	.01
□ 487	Frank Williams	.08	.04	.01
□ 488	Joel Skinner	.08	.04	.01
□ 489	Bryan Clark	.08	.04	.01
□ 490	Jason Thompson	.08	.04	.01

□ 491	Rick Camp	.08	.04	.01
□ 492	Dave Johnson MG	.15	.07	.02
	(Checklist back)			
□ 493	Orel Hershiser	1.00	.45	.12
□ 494	Rich Dauer	.08	.04	.01
□ 495	Mario Soto	.08	.04	.01
□ 496	Donnie Scott	.08	.04	.01
□ 497	Gary Pettis UER	.08	.04	.01
	(Photo actually			
	Gary's little			
	brother, Lynn)			
□ 498	Ed Romero	.08	.04	.01
□ 499	Danny Cox	.08	.04	.01
□ 500	Mike Schmidt	1.00	.45	.12
□ 501	Dan Schatzeder	.08	.04	.01
□ 502	Rick Miller	.08	.04	.01
□ 503	Tim Conroy	.08	.04	.01
□ 504	Jerry Willard	.08	.04	.01
□ 505	Jim Beattie	.08	.04	.01
□ 506	Franklin Stubbs	.08	.04	.01
□ 507	Ray Fontenot	.08	.04	.01
□ 508	John Shelby	.08	.04	.01
□ 509	Milt May	.08	.04	.01
□ 510	Kent Hrbek	.30	.14	.04
□ 511	Lee Smith	.30	.14	.04
□ 512	Tom Brookens	.08	.04	.01
□ 513	Lynn Jones	.08	.04	.01
□ 514	Jeff Cornell	.08	.04	.01
□ 515	Dave Concepcion	.15	.07	.02
□ 516	Roy Lee Jackson	.08	.04	.01
□ 517	Jerry Martin	.08	.04	.01
□ 518	Chris Chambliss	.08	.04	.01
□ 519	Doug Rader MG	.08	.04	.01
	(Checklist back)			
□ 520	LaMarr Hoyt	.08	.04	.01
□ 521	Rick Dempsey	.08	.04	.01
□ 522	Paul Molitor	.75	.35	.09
□ 523	Candy Maldonado	.08	.04	.01
□ 524	Rob Wilfong	.08	.04	.01
□ 525	Darrell Porter	.08	.04	.01
□ 526	David Palmer	.08	.04	.01
□ 527	Checklist: 397-528	.15	.07	.02
□ 528	Bill Krueger	.08	.04	.01
□ 529	Rich Gedman	.08	.04	.01
□ 530	Dave Dravecky	.15	.07	.02
□ 531	Joe Lefebvre	.08	.04	.01
□ 532	Frank DiPino	.08	.04	.01
□ 533	Tony Bernazard	.08	.04	.01
□ 534	Brian Dayett	.08	.04	.01
□ 535	Pat Putnam	.08	.04	.01
□ 536	Kirby Puckett	12.00	5.50	1.50
□ 537	Don Robinson	.08	.04	.01
□ 538	Keith Moreland	.08	.04	.01
□ 539	Aurelio Lopez	.08	.04	.01
□ 540	Claudell Washington	.08	.04	.01
□ 541	Mark Davis	.08	.04	.01
□ 542	Don Slaught	.08	.04	.01
□ 543	Mike Squires	.08	.04	.01
□ 544	Bruce Kison	.08	.04	.01
□ 545	Lloyd Moseby	.08	.04	.01
□ 546	Brent Gaff	.08	.04	.01
□ 547	Pete Rose MG	.50	.23	.06
	(Checklist back)			
□ 548	Larry Parrish	.08	.04	.01
□ 549	Mike Scioscia	.08	.04	.01
□ 550	Scott McGregor	.08	.04	.01
□ 551	Andy Van Slyke	.15	.07	.02
□ 552	Chris Codiroli	.08	.04	.01
□ 553	Bob Clark	.08	.04	.01
□ 554	Doug Flynn	.08	.04	.01
□ 555	Bob Stanley	.08	.04	.01
□ 556	Sixto Lezcano	.08	.04	.01
□ 557	Len Barker	.08	.04	.01
□ 558	Carmelo Martinez	.08	.04	.01
□ 559	Jay Howell	.08	.04	.01
□ 560	Bill Madlock	.08	.04	.01
□ 561	Darryl Motley	.08	.04	.01
□ 562	Houston Jimenez	.08	.04	.01
□ 563	Dick Ruthven	.08	.04	.01
□ 564	Alan Ashby	.08	.04	.01
□ 565	Kirk Gibson	.30	.14	.04
□ 566	Ed VandeBerg	.08	.04	.01
□ 567	Joel Youngblood	.08	.04	.01
□ 568	Cliff Johnson	.08	.04	.01
□ 569	Ken Oberkfell	.08	.04	.01
□ 570	Darryl Strawberry	.30	.14	.04
□ 571	Charlie Hough	.15	.07	.02
□ 572	Tom Paciorek	.08	.04	.01
□ 573	Jay Tibbs	.08	.04	.01
□ 574	Joe Altobelli MG	.08	.04	.01
	(Checklist back)			
□ 575	Pedro Guerrero	.15	.07	.02
□ 576	Jaime Cocanower	.08	.04	.01
□ 577	Chris Speier	.08	.04	.01
□ 578	Terry Francona	.08	.04	.01
□ 579	Ron Romanick	.08	.04	.01
□ 580	Dwight Evans	.15	.07	.02
□ 581	Mark Wagner	.08	.04	.01
□ 582	Ken Phelps	.08	.04	.01
□ 583	Bobby Brown	.08	.04	.01
□ 584	Kevin Gross	.08	.04	.01
□ 585	Butch Wynegar	.08	.04	.01
□ 586	Bill Scherrer	.08	.04	.01
□ 587	Doug Frobel	.08	.04	.01
□ 588	Bobby Castillo	.08	.04	.01
□ 589	Bob Dernier	.08	.04	.01
□ 590	Ray Knight	.15	.07	.02
□ 591	Larry Herndon	.08	.04	.01
□ 592	Jeff D. Robinson	.08	.04	.01
□ 593	Rick Leach	.08	.04	.01
□ 594	Curt Wilkerson	.08	.04	.01
□ 595	Larry Gura	.08	.04	.01
□ 596	Jerry Hairston	.08	.04	.01
□ 597	Brad Lesley	.08	.04	.01
□ 598	Jose Oquendo	.08	.04	.01
□ 599	Storm Davis	.08	.04	.01
□ 600	Pete Rose	.75	.35	.09
□ 601	Tom Lasorda MG	.30	.14	.04
	(Checklist back)			
□ 602	Jeff Dedmon	.08	.04	.01
□ 603	Rick Manning	.08	.04	.01
□ 604	Daryl Sconiers	.08	.04	.01
□ 605	Ozzie Smith	1.00	.45	.12
□ 606	Rich Gale	.08	.04	.01
□ 607	Bill Almon	.08	.04	.01
□ 608	Craig Lefferts	.08	.04	.01
□ 609	Broderick Perkins	.08	.04	.01
□ 610	Jack Morris	.30	.14	.04
□ 611	Ozzie Virgil	.08	.04	.01
□ 612	Mike Armstrong	.08	.04	.01
□ 613	Terry Puhl	.08	.04	.01
□ 614	Al Williams	.08	.04	.01
□ 615	Marvell Wynne	.08	.04	.01
□ 616	Scott Sanderson	.08	.04	.01
□ 617	Willie Wilson	.08	.04	.01
□ 618	Pete Falcone	.08	.04	.01
□ 619	Jeff Leonard	.08	.04	.01
□ 620	Dwight Gooden	2.00	.90	.25
□ 621	Marvis Foley	.08	.04	.01
□ 622	Luis Leal	.08	.04	.01
□ 623	Greg Walker	.08	.04	.01
□ 624	Benny Ayala	.08	.04	.01
□ 625	Mark Langston	.50	.23	.06
□ 626	German Rivera	.08	.04	.01
□ 627	Eric Davis	.60	.25	.07
□ 628	Rene Lachemann MG	.08	.04	.01
	(Checklist back)			
□ 629	Dick Schofield	.08	.04	.01
□ 630	Tim Raines	.30	.14	.04
□ 631	Bob Forsch	.08	.04	.01
□ 632	Bruce Bochte	.08	.04	.01
□ 633	Glenn Hoffman	.08	.04	.01
□ 634	Bill Dawley	.08	.04	.01
□ 635	Terry Kennedy	.08	.04	.01
□ 636	Shane Rawley	.08	.04	.01
□ 637	Brett Butler	.30	.14	.04
□ 638	Mike Pagliarulo	.08	.04	.01
□ 639	Ed Hodge	.08	.04	.01
□ 640	Steve Henderson	.08	.04	.01
□ 641	Rod Scurry	.08	.04	.01
□ 642	Dave Owen	.08	.04	.01
□ 643	Johnny Grubb	.08	.04	.01
□ 644	Mark Huismann	.08	.04	.01
□ 645	Damaso Garcia	.08	.04	.01
□ 646	Scot Thompson	.08	.04	.01
□ 647	Rafael Ramirez	.08	.04	.01
□ 648	Bob Jones	.08	.04	.01
□ 649	Sid Fernandez	.30	.14	.04
□ 650	Greg Luzinski	.15	.07	.02
□ 651	Jeff Russell	.15	.07	.02
□ 652	Joe Nolan	.08	.04	.01
□ 653	Mark Brouhard	.08	.04	.01

□ 654 Dave Anderson	.08	.04	.01
□ 655 Joaquin Andujar	.08	.04	.01
□ 656 Chuck Cottier MG (Checklist back)	.08	.04	.01
□ 657 Jim Slaton	.08	.04	.01
□ 658 Mike Stenhouse	.08	.04	.01
□ 659 Checklist: 529-660	.15	.07	.02
□ 660 Tony Gwynn	2.00	.90	.25
□ 661 Steve Crawford	.08	.04	.01
□ 662 Mike Heath	.08	.04	.01
□ 663 Luis Aguayo	.08	.04	.01
□ 664 Steve Farr	.15	.07	.02
□ 665 Don Mattingly	3.00	1.35	.35
□ 666 Mike LaCoss	.08	.04	.01
□ 667 Dave Engle	.08	.04	.01
□ 668 Steve Trout	.08	.04	.01
□ 669 Lee Lacy	.08	.04	.01
□ 670 Tom Seaver	.40	.18	.05
□ 671 Dane Iorg	.08	.04	.01
□ 672 Juan Berenguer	.08	.04	.01
□ 673 Buck Martinez	.08	.04	.01
□ 674 Atlee Hammaker	.08	.04	.01
□ 675 Tony Perez	.30	.14	.04
□ 676 Albert Hall	.08	.04	.01
□ 677 Wally Backman	.08	.04	.01
□ 678 Joey McLaughlin	.08	.04	.01
□ 679 Bob Kearney	.08	.04	.01
□ 680 Jerry Reuss	.08	.04	.01
□ 681 Ben Oglivie	.08	.04	.01
□ 682 Doug Corbett	.08	.04	.01
□ 683 Whitey Herzog MG (Checklist back)	.15	.07	.02
□ 684 Bill Doran	.08	.04	.01
□ 685 Bill Caudill	.08	.04	.01
□ 686 Mike Easler	.08	.04	.01
□ 687 Bill Gullickson	.08	.04	.01
□ 688 Len Matuszek	.08	.04	.01
□ 689 Luis DeLeon	.08	.04	.01
□ 690 Alan Trammell	.30	.14	.04
□ 691 Dennis Rasmussen	.08	.04	.01
□ 692 Randy Bush	.08	.04	.01
□ 693 Tim Stoddard	.08	.04	.01
□ 694 Joe Carter	2.50	1.10	.30
□ 695 Rick Rhoden	.08	.04	.01
□ 696 John Rabb	.08	.04	.01
□ 697 Onix Concepcion	.08	.04	.01
□ 698 Jorge Bell	.15	.07	.02
□ 699 Donnie Moore	.08	.04	.01
□ 700 Eddie Murray	1.25	.55	.16
□ 701 Eddie Murray AS	.30	.14	.04
□ 702 Damaso Garcia AS	.08	.04	.01
□ 703 George Brett AS	.75	.35	.09
□ 704 Cal Ripken AS	1.50	.70	.19
□ 705 Dave Winfield AS	.30	.14	.04
□ 706 Rickey Henderson AS	.30	.14	.04
□ 707 Tony Armas AS	.08	.04	.01
□ 708 Lance Parrish AS	.15	.07	.02
□ 709 Mike Boddicker AS	.08	.04	.01
□ 710 Frank Viola AS	.15	.07	.02
□ 711 Dan Quisenberry AS	.08	.04	.01
□ 712 Keith Hernandez AS	.15	.07	.02
□ 713 Ryne Sandberg AS	.60	.25	.07
□ 714 Mike Schmidt AS	.40	.18	.05
□ 715 Ozzie Smith AS	.50	.23	.06
□ 716 Dale Murphy AS	.15	.07	.02
□ 717 Tony Gwynn AS	.75	.35	.09
□ 718 Jeff Leonard AS	.08	.04	.01
□ 719 Gary Carter AS	.15	.07	.02
□ 720 Rick Sutcliffe AS	.08	.04	.01
□ 721 Bob Knepper AS	.08	.04	.01
□ 722 Bruce Sutter AS	.15	.07	.02
□ 723 Dave Stewart	.15	.07	.02
□ 724 Oscar Gamble	.08	.04	.01
□ 725 Floyd Bannister	.08	.04	.01
□ 726 Al Bumbry	.08	.04	.01
□ 727 Frank Pastore	.08	.04	.01
□ 728 Bob Bailor	.08	.04	.01
□ 729 Don Sutton	.30	.14	.04
□ 730 Dave Kingman	.15	.07	.02
□ 731 Neil Allen	.08	.04	.01
□ 732 John McNamara MG (Checklist back)	.08	.04	.01
□ 733 Tony Scott	.08	.04	.01
□ 734 John Henry Johnson	.08	.04	.01
□ 735 Garry Templeton	.08	.04	.01
□ 736 Jerry Mumphrey	.08	.04	.01
□ 737 Bo Diaz	.08	.04	.01
□ 738 Omar Moreno	.08	.04	.01
□ 739 Ernie Camacho	.08	.04	.01
□ 740 Jack Clark	.15	.07	.02
□ 741 John Butcher	.08	.04	.01
□ 742 Ron Hassey	.08	.04	.01
□ 743 Frank White	.15	.07	.02
□ 744 Doug Bair	.08	.04	.01
□ 745 Buddy Bell	.15	.07	.02
□ 746 Jim Clancy	.08	.04	.01
□ 747 Alex Trevino	.08	.04	.01
□ 748 Lee Mazzilli	.08	.04	.01
□ 749 Julio Cruz	.08	.04	.01
□ 750 Rollie Fingers	.30	.14	.04
□ 751 Kelvin Chapman	.08	.04	.01
□ 752 Bob Owchinko	.08	.04	.01
□ 753 Greg Brock	.08	.04	.01
□ 754 Larry Milbourne	.08	.04	.01
□ 755 Ken Singleton	.08	.04	.01
□ 756 Rob Picciolo	.08	.04	.01
□ 757 Willie McGee	.15	.07	.02
□ 758 Ray Burris	.08	.04	.01
□ 759 Jim Fanning MG (Checklist back)	.08	.04	.01
□ 760 Nolan Ryan	3.00	1.35	.35
□ 761 Jerry Remy	.08	.04	.01
□ 762 Eddie Whitson	.08	.04	.01
□ 763 Kiko Garcia	.08	.04	.01
□ 764 Jamie Easterly	.08	.04	.01
□ 765 Willie Randolph	.15	.07	.02
□ 766 Paul Mirabella	.08	.04	.01
□ 767 Darrell Brown	.08	.04	.01
□ 768 Ron Cey	.15	.07	.02
□ 769 Joe Cowley	.08	.04	.01
□ 770 Carlton Fisk	.40	.18	.05
□ 771 Geoff Zahn	.08	.04	.01
□ 772 Johnnie LeMaster	.08	.04	.01
□ 773 Hal McRae	.15	.07	.02
□ 774 Dennis Lamp	.08	.04	.01
□ 775 Mookie Wilson	.15	.07	.02
□ 776 Jerry Royster	.08	.04	.01
□ 777 Ned Yost	.08	.04	.01
□ 778 Mike Davis	.08	.04	.01
□ 779 Nick Esasky	.08	.04	.01
□ 780 Mike Flanagan	.08	.04	.01
□ 781 Jim Gantner	.08	.04	.01
□ 782 Tom Niedenfuer	.08	.04	.01
□ 783 Mike Jorgensen	.08	.04	.01
□ 784 Checklist: 661-792	.15	.07	.02
□ 785 Tony Armas	.08	.04	.01
□ 786 Enos Cabell	.08	.04	.01
□ 787 Jim Wohlford	.08	.04	.01
□ 788 Steve Comer	.08	.04	.01
□ 789 Luis Salazar	.08	.04	.01
□ 790 Ron Guidry	.15	.07	.02
□ 791 Ivan DeJesus	.08	.04	.01
□ 792 Darrell Evans	.15	.07	.02

1985 Topps Traded

In its now standard procedure, Topps issued its standard-size Traded (or extended) set for the fifth year in a row. In addition to the typical factory set hobby distribution, Topps tested the limited issuance of these Traded cards in wax packs. Card design is identical to the regular-issue 1985 Topps set except for whiter card stock and T-suffixed numbering on back. The set numbering is in alphabetical order by play-

er's name. The key extended Rookie Cards in this set include Vince Coleman, Mariano Duncan, Ozzie Guillen, and Mickey Tettleton.

	MINT	NRMT	EXC
COMPLETE FACT.SET (132)	15.00	6.75	1.85
COMMON CARD (1T-132T)	.15	.07	.02
SEMISTARS	.40	.18	.05
STARS	.75	.35	.09

□ 1T Don Aase	.15	.07	.02
□ 2T Bill Almon	.15	.07	.02
□ 3T Benny Ayala	.15	.07	.02
□ 4T Dusty Baker	.40	.18	.05
□ 5T George Bamberger MG	.15	.07	.02
□ 6T Dale Berra	.15	.07	.02
□ 7T Rich Bordi	.15	.07	.02
□ 8T Daryl Boston	.15	.07	.02
□ 9T Hubie Brooks	.15	.07	.02
□ 10T Chris Brown	.15	.07	.02
□ 11T Tom Browning	.75	.35	.09
□ 12T Al Bumbry	.15	.07	.02
□ 13T Ray Burris	.15	.07	.02
□ 14T Jeff Burroughs	.15	.07	.02
□ 15T Bill Campbell	.15	.07	.02
□ 16T Don Carman	.15	.07	.02
□ 17T Gary Carter	.75	.35	.09
□ 18T Bobby Castillo	.15	.07	.02
□ 19T Bill Caudill	.15	.07	.02
□ 20T Rick Cerone	.15	.07	.02
□ 21T Bryan Clark	.15	.07	.02
□ 22T Jack Clark	.40	.18	.05
□ 23T Pat Clements	.15	.07	.02
□ 24T Vince Coleman	1.00	.45	.12
□ 25T Dave Collins	.15	.07	.02
□ 26T Danny Darwin	.15	.07	.02
□ 27T Jim Davenport MG	.15	.07	.02
□ 28T Jerry Davis	.15	.07	.02
□ 29T Brian Dayett	.15	.07	.02
□ 30T Ivan DeJesus	.15	.07	.02
□ 31T Ken Dixon	.15	.07	.02
□ 32T Mariano Duncan	.75	.35	.09
□ 33T John Felske MG	.15	.07	.02
□ 34T Mike Fitzgerald	.15	.07	.02
□ 35T Ray Fontenot	.15	.07	.02
□ 36T Greg Gagne	.40	.18	.05
□ 37T Oscar Gamble	.15	.07	.02
□ 38T Scott Garrelts	.15	.07	.02
□ 39T Bob L. Gibson	.15	.07	.02
□ 40T Jim Gott	.15	.07	.02
□ 41T David Green	.15	.07	.02
□ 42T Alfredo Griffin	.15	.07	.02
□ 43T Ozzie Guillen	1.50	.70	.19
□ 44T Eddie Haas MG	.15	.07	.02
□ 45T Terry Harper	.15	.07	.02
□ 46T Toby Harrah	.15	.07	.02
□ 47T Greg Harris	.15	.07	.02
□ 48T Ron Hassey	.15	.07	.02
□ 49T Rickey Henderson	1.50	.70	.19
□ 50T Steve Henderson	.15	.07	.02
□ 51T George Hendrick	.15	.07	.02
□ 52T Joe Hesketh	.15	.07	.02
□ 53T Teddy Higuera	.40	.18	.05
□ 54T Donnie Hill	.15	.07	.02
□ 55T Al Holland	.15	.07	.02
□ 56T Burt Hooton	.15	.07	.02
□ 57T Jay Howell	.15	.07	.02
□ 58T Ken Howell	.15	.07	.02
□ 59T LaMarr Hoyt	.15	.07	.02
□ 60T Tim Hulett	.15	.07	.02
□ 61T Bob James	.15	.07	.02
□ 62T Steve Jeltz	.15	.07	.02
□ 63T Cliff Johnson	.15	.07	.02
□ 64T Howard Johnson	.40	.18	.05
□ 65T Ruppert Jones	.15	.07	.02
□ 66T Steve Kemp	.15	.07	.02
□ 67T Bruce Kison	.15	.07	.02
□ 68T Alan Knicely	.15	.07	.02
□ 69T Mike LaCoss	.15	.07	.02
□ 70T Lee Lacy	.15	.07	.02
□ 71T Dave LaPoint	.15	.07	.02
□ 72T Gary Lavelle	.15	.07	.02
□ 73T Vance Law	.15	.07	.02
□ 74T Johnnie LeMaster	.15	.07	.02
□ 75T Sixto Lezcano	.15	.07	.02
□ 76T Tim Lollar	.15	.07	.02
□ 77T Fred Lynn	.40	.18	.05
□ 78T Billy Martin MG	.40	.18	.05
□ 79T Ron Mathis	.15	.07	.02
□ 80T Len Matuszek	.15	.07	.02
□ 81T Gene Mauch MG	.40	.18	.05
□ 82T Oddibe McDowell	.40	.18	.05
□ 83T Roger McDowell	.40	.18	.05
□ 84T John McNamara MG	.15	.07	.02
□ 85T Donnie Moore	.15	.07	.02
□ 86T Gene Nelson	.15	.07	.02
□ 87T Steve Nicosia	.15	.07	.02
□ 88T Al Oliver	.40	.18	.05
□ 89T Joe Orsulak	.40	.18	.05
□ 90T Rob Picciolo	.15	.07	.02
□ 91T Chris Pittaro	.15	.07	.02
□ 92T Jim Presley	.40	.18	.05
□ 93T Rick Reuschel	.15	.07	.02
□ 94T Bert Roberge	.15	.07	.02
□ 95T Bob Rodgers MG	.15	.07	.02
□ 96T Jerry Royster	.15	.07	.02
□ 97T Dave Rozema	.15	.07	.02
□ 98T Dave Rucker	.15	.07	.02
□ 99T Vern Ruhle	.15	.07	.02
□ 100T Paul Runge	.15	.07	.02
□ 101T Mark Salas	.15	.07	.02
□ 102T Luis Salazar	.15	.07	.02
□ 103T Joe Sambito	.15	.07	.02
□ 104T Rick Schu	.15	.07	.02
□ 105T Donnie Scott	.15	.07	.02
□ 106T Larry Sheets	.15	.07	.02
□ 107T Don Slaught	.15	.07	.02
□ 108T Roy Smalley	.15	.07	.02
□ 109T Lonnie Smith	.15	.07	.02
□ 110T Nate Snell UER (Headings on back for a batter)	.15	.07	.02
□ 111T Chris Speier	.15	.07	.02
□ 112T Mike Stenhouse	.15	.07	.02
□ 113T Tim Stoddard	.15	.07	.02
□ 114T Jim Sundberg	.15	.07	.02
□ 115T Bruce Sutter	.40	.18	.05
□ 116T Don Sutton	.75	.35	.09
□ 117T Kent Tekulve	.15	.07	.02
□ 118T Tom Tellmann	.15	.07	.02
□ 119T Walt Terrell	.15	.07	.02
□ 120T Mickey Tettleton	4.00	1.80	.50
□ 121T Derrel Thomas	.15	.07	.02
□ 122T Rich Thompson	.15	.07	.02
□ 123T Alex Trevino	.15	.07	.02
□ 124T John Tudor	.15	.07	.02
□ 125T Jose Uribe	.15	.07	.02
□ 126T Bobby Valentine MG	.15	.07	.02
□ 127T Dave Von Ohlen	.15	.07	.02
□ 128T U.L. Washington	.15	.07	.02
□ 129T Earl Weaver MG	.75	.35	.09
□ 130T Eddie Whitson	.15	.07	.02
□ 131T Herm Winningham	.15	.07	.02
□ 132T Checklist 1-132	.15	.07	.02

1986 Topps

This set consists of 792 standard-size cards. Cards were primarily distributed in 15-card wax packs and 48-card rack packs. This was also the first year Topps offered a factory set to hobby dealers. Standard card fronts feature a black and white split border framing a color photo with team name on top and player name on bottom. Subsets include Pete Rose tribute (1-7), Record Breakers (201-207), Turn Back

the Clock (401-405), All-Stars (701-722) and Team Leaders (seeded throughout the set). Manager cards feature the team checklist on the reverse. There are two uncorrected errors involving misnumbered cards; see card numbers 51, 57, 141, and 171 in the checklist below. The key Rookie Cards in this set are Darren Daulton, Len Dykstra, Cecil Fielder, and Mickey Tettleton.

	MINT	NRMT	EXC
COMPLETE SET (792)	25.00	11.00	3.10
COMPLETE FACT.SET (792)	30.00	13.50	3.70
COMMON CARD (1-792)	.05	.02	.01
PETE ROSE SPECIALS (2-7)	.30	.14	.04
SEMISTARS	.10	.05	.01
STARS	.15	.07	.02

□ 1 Pete Rose	.75	.35	.09
□ 2 Rose Special: '63-'66	.30	.14	.04
□ 3 Rose Special: '67-'70	.30	.14	.04
□ 4 Rose Special: '71-'74	.30	.14	.04
□ 5 Rose Special: '75-'78	.30	.14	.04
□ 6 Rose Special: '79-'82	.30	.14	.04
□ 7 Rose Special: '83-'85	.30	.14	.04
□ 8 Dwayne Murphy	.05	.02	.01
□ 9 Roy Smith	.05	.02	.01
□ 10 Tony Gwynn	1.00	.45	.12
□ 11 Bob Ojeda	.05	.02	.01
□ 12 Jose Uribe	.05	.02	.01
□ 13 Bob Kearney	.05	.02	.01
□ 14 Julio Cruz	.05	.02	.01
□ 15 Eddie Whitson	.05	.02	.01
□ 16 Rick Schu	.05	.02	.01
□ 17 Mike Stenhouse	.05	.02	.01
□ 18 Brent Gaff	.05	.02	.01
□ 19 Rich Hebner	.05	.02	.01
□ 20 Lou Whitaker	.15	.07	.02
□ 21 George Bamberger MG	.05	.02	.01
(Checklist back)			
□ 22 Duane Walker	.05	.02	.01
□ 23 Manny Lee	.05	.02	.01
□ 24 Len Barker	.05	.02	.01
□ 25 Willie Wilson	.05	.02	.01
□ 26 Frank DiPino	.05	.02	.01
□ 27 Ray Knight	.10	.05	.01
□ 28 Eric Davis	.15	.07	.02
□ 29 Tony Phillips	.15	.07	.02
□ 30 Eddie Murray	.50	.23	.06
□ 31 Jamie Easterly	.05	.02	.01
□ 32 Steve Yeager	.05	.02	.01
□ 33 Jeff Lahti	.05	.02	.01
□ 34 Ken Phelps	.05	.02	.01
□ 35 Jeff Reardon	.10	.05	.01
□ 36 Lance Parrish TL	.05	.02	.01
□ 37 Mark Thurmond	.05	.02	.01
□ 38 Glenn Hoffman	.05	.02	.01
□ 39 Dave Rucker	.05	.02	.01
□ 40 Ken Griffey	.05	.02	.01
□ 41 Brad Wellman	.05	.02	.01
□ 42 Geoff Zahn	.05	.02	.01
□ 43 Dave Engle	.05	.02	.01
□ 44 Lance McCullers	.05	.02	.01
□ 45 Damaso Garcia	.05	.02	.01
□ 46 Billy Hatcher	.10	.05	.01
□ 47 Juan Berenguer	.05	.02	.01
□ 48 Bill Almon	.05	.02	.01
□ 49 Rick Manning	.05	.02	.01
□ 50 Dan Quisenberry	.05	.02	.01
□ 51 Bobby Wine MG ERR	.10	.05	.01
(Checklist back)			
(Number of card on			
back is actually 57)			
□ 52 Chris Welsh	.05	.02	.01
□ 53 Len Dykstra	.75	.35	.09
□ 54 John Franco	.10	.05	.01
□ 55 Fred Lynn	.10	.05	.01
□ 56 Tom Niedenfuer	.05	.02	.01
□ 57 Bill Doran	.05	.02	.01
(See also 51)			
□ 58 Bill Krueger	.05	.02	.01
□ 59 Andre Thornton	.05	.02	.01
□ 60 Dwight Evans	.10	.05	.01
□ 61 Karl Best	.05	.02	.01
□ 62 Bob Boone	.10	.05	.01
□ 63 Ron Roenicke	.05	.02	.01
□ 64 Floyd Bannister	.05	.02	.01
□ 65 Dan Driessen	.05	.02	.01
□ 66 Bob Forsch TL	.10	.05	.01
□ 67 Carmelo Martinez	.05	.02	.01
□ 68 Ed Lynch	.05	.02	.01
□ 69 Luis Aguayo	.05	.02	.01
□ 70 Dave Winfield	.25	.11	.03
□ 71 Ken Schrom	.05	.02	.01
□ 72 Shawon Dunston	.10	.05	.01
□ 73 Randy O'Neal	.05	.02	.01
□ 74 Rance Mulliniks	.05	.02	.01
□ 75 Jose DeLeon	.05	.02	.01
□ 76 Dion James	.05	.02	.01
□ 77 Charlie Leibrandt	.05	.02	.01
□ 78 Bruce Benedict	.05	.02	.01
□ 79 Dave Schmidt	.05	.02	.01
□ 80 Darryl Strawberry	.15	.07	.02
□ 81 Gene Mauch MG	.10	.05	.01
(Checklist back)			
□ 82 Tippy Martinez	.05	.02	.01
□ 83 Phil Garner	.05	.02	.01
□ 84 Curt Young	.05	.02	.01
□ 85 Tony Perez	.15	.07	.02
(Eric Davis also			
shown on card)			
□ 86 Tom Waddell	.05	.02	.01
□ 87 Candy Maldonado	.05	.02	.01
□ 88 Tom Nieto	.05	.02	.01
□ 89 Randy St.Claire	.05	.02	.01
□ 90 Garry Templeton	.05	.02	.01
□ 91 Steve Crawford	.05	.02	.01
□ 92 Al Cowens	.05	.02	.01
□ 93 Scot Thompson	.05	.02	.01
□ 94 Rich Bordi	.05	.02	.01
□ 95 Ozzie Virgil	.05	.02	.01
□ 96 Jim Clancy TL	.10	.05	.01
□ 97 Gary Gaetti	.15	.07	.02
□ 98 Dick Ruthven	.05	.02	.01
□ 99 Buddy Biancalana	.05	.02	.01
□ 100 Nolan Ryan	1.50	.70	.19
□ 101 Dave Bergman	.05	.02	.01
□ 102 Joe Orsulak	.05	.02	.01
□ 103 Luis Salazar	.05	.02	.01
□ 104 Sid Fernandez	.10	.05	.01
□ 105 Gary Ward	.05	.02	.01
□ 106 Ray Burris	.05	.02	.01
□ 107 Rafael Ramirez	.05	.02	.01
□ 108 Ted Power	.05	.02	.01
□ 109 Len Matuszek	.05	.02	.01
□ 110 Scott McGregor	.05	.02	.01
□ 111 Roger Craig MG	.10	.05	.01
(Checklist back)			
□ 112 Bill Campbell	.05	.02	.01
□ 113 U.L. Washington	.05	.02	.01
□ 114 Mike C. Brown	.05	.02	.01
□ 115 Jay Howell	.05	.02	.01
□ 116 Brook Jacoby	.05	.02	.01
□ 117 Bruce Kison	.05	.02	.01
□ 118 Jerry Royster	.05	.02	.01
□ 119 Barry Bonnell	.05	.02	.01
□ 120 Steve Carlton	.20	.09	.03
□ 121 Nelson Simmons	.05	.02	.01
□ 122 Pete Filson	.05	.02	.01
□ 123 Greg Walker	.05	.02	.01
□ 124 Luis Sanchez	.05	.02	.01
□ 125 Dave Lopes	.10	.05	.01
□ 126 Mookie Wilson TL	.10	.05	.01
□ 127 Jack Howell	.05	.02	.01
□ 128 John Wathan	.05	.02	.01
□ 129 Jeff Dedmon	.05	.02	.01
□ 130 Alan Trammell	.15	.07	.02
□ 131 Checklist: 1-132	.10	.05	.01
□ 132 Razor Shines	.05	.02	.01
□ 133 Andy McGaffigan	.05	.02	.01
□ 134 Carney Lansford	.10	.05	.01
□ 135 Joe Niekro	.05	.02	.01
□ 136 Mike Hargrove	.10	.05	.01
□ 137 Charlie Moore	.05	.02	.01
□ 138 Mark Davis	.05	.02	.01
□ 139 Daryl Boston	.05	.02	.01
□ 140 John Candelaria	.05	.02	.01
□ 141 Chuck Cottier MG	.05	.02	.01
(Checklist back)			
(See also 171)			
□ 142 Bob Jones	.05	.02	.01
□ 143 Dave Van Gorder	.05	.02	.01

□ 144	Doug Sisk	.05	.02	.01
□ 145	Pedro Guerrero	.10	.05	.01
□ 146	Jack Perconte	.05	.02	.01
□ 147	Larry Sheets	.05	.02	.01
□ 148	Mike Heath	.05	.02	.01
□ 149	Brett Butler	.15	.07	.02
□ 150	Joaquin Andujar	.05	.02	.01
□ 151	Dave Stapleton	.05	.02	.01
□ 152	Mike Morgan	.05	.02	.01
□ 153	Ricky Adams	.05	.02	.01
□ 154	Bert Roberge	.05	.02	.01
□ 155	Bob Grich	.10	.05	.01
□ 156	Richard Dotson TL	.05	.02	.01
□ 157	Ron Hassey	.05	.02	.01
□ 158	Derrel Thomas	.05	.02	.01
□ 159	Orel Hershiser UER (82 Alburquerque)	.15	.07	.02
□ 160	Chet Lemon	.05	.02	.01
□ 161	Lee Tunnell	.05	.02	.01
□ 162	Greg Gagne	.10	.05	.01
□ 163	Pete Ladd	.05	.02	.01
□ 164	Steve Balboni	.05	.02	.01
□ 165	Mike Davis	.05	.02	.01
□ 166	Dickie Thon	.05	.02	.01
□ 167	Zane Smith	.05	.02	.01
□ 168	Jeff Burroughs	.05	.02	.01
□ 169	George Wright	.05	.02	.01
□ 170	Gary Carter	.15	.07	.02
□ 171	Bob Rodgers MG ERR (Checklist back) (Number of card on back actually 141)	.05	.02	.01
□ 172	Jerry Reed	.05	.02	.01
□ 173	Wayne Gross	.05	.02	.01
□ 174	Brian Snyder	.05	.02	.01
□ 175	Steve Sax	.05	.02	.01
□ 176	Jay Tibbs	.05	.02	.01
□ 177	Joel Youngblood	.05	.02	.01
□ 178	Ivan DeJesus	.05	.02	.01
□ 179	Stu Cliburn	.05	.02	.01
□ 180	Don Mattingly	1.25	.55	.16
□ 181	Al Nipper	.05	.02	.01
□ 182	Bobby Brown	.05	.02	.01
□ 183	Larry Andersen	.05	.02	.01
□ 184	Tim Laudner	.05	.02	.01
□ 185	Rollie Fingers	.15	.07	.02
□ 186	Jose Cruz TL	.10	.05	.01
□ 187	Scott Fletcher	.05	.02	.01
□ 188	Bob Dernier	.05	.02	.01
□ 189	Mike Mason	.05	.02	.01
□ 190	George Hendrick	.05	.02	.01
□ 191	Wally Backman	.05	.02	.01
□ 192	Milt Wilcox	.05	.02	.01
□ 193	Daryl Sconiers	.05	.02	.01
□ 194	Craig McMurtry	.05	.02	.01
□ 195	Dave Concepcion	.10	.05	.01
□ 196	Doyle Alexander	.05	.02	.01
□ 197	Enos Cabell	.05	.02	.01
□ 198	Ken Dixon	.05	.02	.01
□ 199	Dick Howser MG (Checklist back)	.10	.05	.01
□ 200	Mike Schmidt	.40	.18	.05
□ 201	Vince Coleman RB Most SB's rookie season	.10	.05	.01
□ 202	Dwight Gooden RB Youngest 20 game winner	.15	.07	.02
□ 203	Keith Hernandez RB Most game-winning RBI's	.10	.05	.01
□ 204	Phil Niekro RB Oldest shutout pitcher	.15	.07	.02
□ 205	Tony Perez RB Oldest grand slammer	.10	.05	.01
□ 206	Pete Rose RB Most lifetime hits	.30	.14	.04
□ 207	Fernando Valenzuela RB Most cons. innings, start of season, no earned runs	.10	.05	.01
□ 208	Ramon Romero	.05	.02	.01
□ 209	Randy Ready	.05	.02	.01
□ 210	Calvin Schiraldi	.05	.02	.01
□ 211	Ed Wojna	.05	.02	.01
□ 212	Chris Speier	.05	.02	.01
□ 213	Bob Shirley	.05	.02	.01
□ 214	Randy Bush	.05	.02	.01
□ 215	Frank White	.10	.05	.01
□ 216	Dwayne Murphy TL	.10	.05	.01
□ 217	Bill Scherrer	.05	.02	.01
□ 218	Randy Hunt	.05	.02	.01
□ 219	Dennis Lamp	.05	.02	.01
□ 220	Bob Horner	.05	.02	.01
□ 221	Dave Henderson	.05	.02	.01
□ 222	Craig Gerber	.05	.02	.01
□ 223	Atlee Hammaker	.05	.02	.01
□ 224	Cesar Cedeno	.10	.05	.01
□ 225	Ron Darling	.05	.02	.01
□ 226	Lee Lacy	.05	.02	.01
□ 227	Al Jones	.05	.02	.01
□ 228	Tom Lawless	.05	.02	.01
□ 229	Bill Gullickson	.05	.02	.01
□ 230	Terry Kennedy	.05	.02	.01
□ 231	Jim Frey MG (Checklist back)	.10	.05	.01
□ 232	Rick Rhoden	.05	.02	.01
□ 233	Steve Lyons	.05	.02	.01
□ 234	Doug Corbett	.05	.02	.01
□ 235	Butch Wynegar	.05	.02	.01
□ 236	Frank Eufemia	.05	.02	.01
□ 237	Ted Simmons	.10	.05	.01
□ 238	Larry Parrish	.05	.02	.01
□ 239	Joel Skinner	.05	.02	.01
□ 240	Tommy John	.15	.07	.02
□ 241	Tony Fernandez	.05	.02	.01
□ 242	Rich Thompson	.05	.02	.01
□ 243	Johnny Grubb	.05	.02	.01
□ 244	Craig Lefferts	.05	.02	.01
□ 245	Jim Sundberg	.05	.02	.01
□ 246	Steve Carlton TL	.10	.05	.01
□ 247	Terry Harper	.05	.02	.01
□ 248	Spike Owen	.05	.02	.01
□ 249	Rob Deer	.10	.05	.01
□ 250	Dwight Gooden	.20	.09	.03
□ 251	Rich Dauer	.05	.02	.01
□ 252	Bobby Castillo	.05	.02	.01
□ 253	Dann Bilardello	.05	.02	.01
□ 254	Ozzie Guillen	.15	.07	.02
□ 255	Tony Armas	.05	.02	.01
□ 256	Kurt Kepshire	.05	.02	.01
□ 257	Doug DeCinces	.05	.02	.01
□ 258	Tim Burke	.05	.02	.01
□ 259	Dan Pasqua	.05	.02	.01
□ 260	Tony Pena	.05	.02	.01
□ 261	Bobby Valentine MG (Checklist back)	.10	.05	.01
□ 262	Mario Ramirez	.05	.02	.01
□ 263	Checklist: 133-264	.10	.05	.01
□ 264	Darren Daulton	.75	.35	.09
□ 265	Ron Davis	.05	.02	.01
□ 266	Keith Moreland	.05	.02	.01
□ 267	Paul Molitor	.40	.18	.05
□ 268	Mike Scott	.05	.02	.01
□ 269	Dane Iorg	.05	.02	.01
□ 270	Jack Morris	.10	.05	.01
□ 271	Dave Collins	.05	.02	.01
□ 272	Tim Tolman	.05	.02	.01
□ 273	Jerry Willard	.05	.02	.01
□ 274	Ron Gardenhire	.05	.02	.01
□ 275	Charlie Hough	.10	.05	.01
□ 276	Willie Randolph TL	.10	.05	.01
□ 277	Jaime Cocanower	.05	.02	.01
□ 278	Sixto Lezcano	.05	.02	.01
□ 279	Al Pardo	.05	.02	.01
□ 280	Tim Raines	.15	.07	.02
□ 281	Steve Mura	.05	.02	.01
□ 282	Jerry Mumphrey	.05	.02	.01
□ 283	Mike Fischlin	.05	.02	.01
□ 284	Brian Dayett	.05	.02	.01
□ 285	Buddy Bell	.10	.05	.01
□ 286	Luis DeLeon	.05	.02	.01
□ 287	John Christensen	.05	.02	.01
□ 288	Don Aase	.05	.02	.01
□ 289	Johnnie LeMaster	.05	.02	.01
□ 290	Carlton Fisk	.15	.07	.02
□ 291	Tom Lasorda MG (Checklist back)	.10	.05	.01
□ 292	Chuck Porter	.05	.02	.01
□ 293	Chris Chambliss	.10	.05	.01
□ 294	Danny Cox	.05	.02	.01
□ 295	Kirk Gibson	.10	.05	.01
□ 296	Geno Petralli	.05	.02	.01
□ 297	Tim Lollar	.05	.02	.01

□ 298	Craig Reynolds	.05	.02	.01
□ 299	Bryn Smith	.05	.02	.01
□ 300	George Brett	.75	.35	.09
□ 301	Dennis Rasmussen	.05	.02	.01
□ 302	Greg Gross	.05	.02	.01
□ 303	Curt Wardle	.05	.02	.01
□ 304	Mike Gallego	.10	.05	.01
□ 305	Phil Bradley	.05	.02	.01
□ 306	Terry Kennedy TL	.05	.02	.01
□ 307	Dave Sax	.05	.02	.01
□ 308	Ray Fontenot	.05	.02	.01
□ 309	John Shelby	.05	.02	.01
□ 310	Greg Minton	.05	.02	.01
□ 311	Dick Schofield	.05	.02	.01
□ 312	Tom Filer	.05	.02	.01
□ 313	Joe DeSa	.05	.02	.01
□ 314	Frank Pastore	.05	.02	.01
□ 315	Mookie Wilson	.10	.05	.01
□ 316	Sammy Khalifa	.05	.02	.01
□ 317	Ed Romero	.05	.02	.01
□ 318	Terry Whitfield	.05	.02	.01
□ 319	Rick Camp	.05	.02	.01
□ 320	Jim Rice	.15	.07	.02
□ 321	Earl Weaver MG (Checklist back)	.15	.07	.02
□ 322	Bob Forsch	.05	.02	.01
□ 323	Jerry Davis	.05	.02	.01
□ 324	Dan Schatzeder	.05	.02	.01
□ 325	Juan Beniquez	.05	.02	.01
□ 326	Kent Tekulve	.05	.02	.01
□ 327	Mike Pagliarulo	.05	.02	.01
□ 328	Pete O'Brien	.05	.02	.01
□ 329	Kirby Puckett	2.00	.90	.25
□ 330	Rick Sutcliffe	.05	.02	.01
□ 331	Alan Ashby	.05	.02	.01
□ 332	Darryl Motley	.05	.02	.01
□ 333	Tom Henke	.10	.05	.01
□ 334	Ken Oberkfell	.05	.02	.01
□ 335	Don Sutton	.15	.07	.02
□ 336	Andre Thornton TL	.05	.02	.01
□ 337	Darnell Coles	.05	.02	.01
□ 338	Jorge Bell	.10	.05	.01
□ 339	Bruce Berenyi	.05	.02	.01
□ 340	Cal Ripken	1.50	.70	.19
□ 341	Frank Williams	.05	.02	.01
□ 342	Gary Redus	.05	.02	.01
□ 343	Carlos Diaz	.05	.02	.01
□ 344	Jim Wohlford	.05	.02	.01
□ 345	Donnie Moore	.05	.02	.01
□ 346	Bryan Little	.05	.02	.01
□ 347	Teddy Higuera	.10	.05	.01
□ 348	Cliff Johnson	.05	.02	.01
□ 349	Mark Clear	.05	.02	.01
□ 350	Jack Clark	.10	.05	.01
□ 351	Chuck Tanner MG (Checklist back)	.10	.05	.01
□ 352	Harry Spilman	.05	.02	.01
□ 353	Keith Atherton	.05	.02	.01
□ 354	Tony Bernazard	.05	.02	.01
□ 355	Lee Smith	.15	.07	.02
□ 356	Mickey Hatcher	.05	.02	.01
□ 357	Ed VandeBerg	.05	.02	.01
□ 358	Rick Dempsey	.05	.02	.01
□ 359	Mike LaCoss	.05	.02	.01
□ 360	Lloyd Moseby	.05	.02	.01
□ 361	Shane Rawley	.05	.02	.01
□ 362	Tom Paciorek	.05	.02	.01
□ 363	Terry Forster	.05	.02	.01
□ 364	Reid Nichols	.05	.02	.01
□ 365	Mike Flanagan	.05	.02	.01
□ 366	Dave Concepcion TL	.10	.05	.01
□ 367	Aurelio Lopez	.05	.02	.01
□ 368	Greg Brock	.05	.02	.01
□ 369	Al Holland	.05	.02	.01
□ 370	Vince Coleman	.15	.07	.02
□ 371	Bill Stein	.05	.02	.01
□ 372	Ben Oglivie	.05	.02	.01
□ 373	Urbano Lugo	.05	.02	.01
□ 374	Terry Francona	.05	.02	.01
□ 375	Rich Gedman	.05	.02	.01
□ 376	Bill Dawley	.05	.02	.01
□ 377	Joe Carter	1.00	.45	.12
□ 378	Bruce Bochte	.05	.02	.01
□ 379	Bobby Meacham	.05	.02	.01
□ 380	LaMarr Hoyt	.05	.02	.01
□ 381	Ray Miller MG	.05	.02	.01

(Checklist back)

□ 382	Ivan Calderon	.10	.05	.01
□ 383	Chris Brown	.05	.02	.01
□ 384	Steve Trout	.05	.02	.01
□ 385	Cecil Cooper	.10	.05	.01
□ 386	Cecil Fielder	1.50	.70	.19
□ 387	Steve Kemp	.05	.02	.01
□ 388	Dickie Noles	.05	.02	.01
□ 389	Glenn Davis	.10	.05	.01
□ 390	Tom Seaver	.20	.09	.03
□ 391	Julio Franco	.15	.07	.02
□ 392	John Russell	.05	.02	.01
□ 393	Chris Pittaro	.05	.02	.01
□ 394	Checklist: 265-396	.10	.05	.01
□ 395	Scott Garrelts	.05	.02	.01
□ 396	Dwight Evans TL	.10	.05	.01
□ 397	Steve Buechele	.10	.05	.01
□ 398	Earnie Riles	.05	.02	.01
□ 399	Bill Swift	.10	.05	.01
□ 400	Rod Carew	.20	.09	.03
□ 401	Fernando Valenzuela TBC '81	.10	.05	.01
□ 402	Tom Seaver TBC '76	.15	.07	.02
□ 403	Willie Mays TBC '71	.15	.07	.02
□ 404	Frank Robinson TBC '66	.15	.07	.02
□ 405	Roger Maris TBC '61	.15	.07	.02
□ 406	Scott Sanderson	.05	.02	.01
□ 407	Sal Butera	.05	.02	.01
□ 408	Dave Smith	.05	.02	.01
□ 409	Paul Runge	.05	.02	.01
□ 410	Dave Kingman	.10	.05	.01
□ 411	Sparky Anderson MG (Checklist back)	.10	.05	.01
□ 412	Jim Clancy	.05	.02	.01
□ 413	Tim Flannery	.05	.02	.01
□ 414	Tom Gorman	.05	.02	.01
□ 415	Hal McRae	.10	.05	.01
□ 416	Dennis Martinez	.10	.05	.01
□ 417	R.J. Reynolds	.05	.02	.01
□ 418	Alan Knicely	.05	.02	.01
□ 419	Frank Wills	.05	.02	.01
□ 420	Von Hayes	.05	.02	.01
□ 421	David Palmer	.05	.02	.01
□ 422	Mike Jorgensen	.05	.02	.01
□ 423	Dan Spillner	.05	.02	.01
□ 424	Rick Miller	.05	.02	.01
□ 425	Larry McWilliams	.05	.02	.01
□ 426	Charlie Moore TL	.10	.05	.01
□ 427	Joe Cowley	.05	.02	.01
□ 428	Max Venable	.05	.02	.01
□ 429	Greg Booker	.05	.02	.01
□ 430	Kent Hrbek	.10	.05	.01
□ 431	George Frazier	.05	.02	.01
□ 432	Mark Bailey	.05	.02	.01
□ 433	Chris Codiroli	.05	.02	.01
□ 434	Curt Wilkerson	.05	.02	.01
□ 435	Bill Caudill	.05	.02	.01
□ 436	Doug Flynn	.05	.02	.01
□ 437	Rick Mahler	.05	.02	.01
□ 438	Clint Hurdle	.05	.02	.01
□ 439	Rick Honeycutt	.05	.02	.01
□ 440	Alvin Davis	.05	.02	.01
□ 441	Whitey Herzog MG (Checklist back)	.10	.05	.01
□ 442	Ron Robinson	.05	.02	.01
□ 443	Bill Buckner	.10	.05	.01
□ 444	Alex Trevino	.05	.02	.01
□ 445	Bert Blyleven	.15	.07	.02
□ 446	Lenn Sakata	.05	.02	.01
□ 447	Jerry Don Gleaton	.05	.02	.01
□ 448	Herm Winningham	.05	.02	.01
□ 449	Rod Scurry	.05	.02	.01
□ 450	Graig Nettles	.10	.05	.01
□ 451	Mark Brown	.05	.02	.01
□ 452	Bob Clark	.05	.02	.01
□ 453	Steve Jeltz	.05	.02	.01
□ 454	Burt Hooton	.05	.02	.01
□ 455	Willie Randolph	.10	.05	.01
□ 456	Dale Murphy TL	.10	.05	.01
□ 457	Mickey Tettleton	.60	.25	.07
□ 458	Kevin Bass	.05	.02	.01
□ 459	Luis Leal	.05	.02	.01
□ 460	Leon Durham	.05	.02	.01
□ 461	Walt Terrell	.05	.02	.01
□ 462	Domingo Ramos	.05	.02	.01

□ 463 Jim Gott	.05	.02	.01
□ 464 Ruppert Jones	.05	.02	.01
□ 465 Jesse Orosco	.05	.02	.01
□ 466 Tom Foley	.05	.02	.01
□ 467 Bob James	.05	.02	.01
□ 468 Mike Scioscia	.05	.02	.01
□ 469 Storm Davis	.05	.02	.01
□ 470 Bill Madlock	.05	.02	.01
□ 471 Bobby Cox MG (Checklist back)	.10	.05	.01
□ 472 Joe Hesketh	.05	.02	.01
□ 473 Mark Brouhard	.05	.02	.01
□ 474 John Tudor	.05	.02	.01
□ 475 Juan Samuel	.05	.02	.01
□ 476 Ron Mathis	.05	.02	.01
□ 477 Mike Easler	.05	.02	.01
□ 478 Andy Hawkins	.05	.02	.01
□ 479 Bob Melvin	.05	.02	.01
□ 480 Oddibe McDowell	.05	.02	.01
□ 481 Scott Bradley	.05	.02	.01
□ 482 Rick Lysander	.05	.02	.01
□ 483 George Vukovich	.05	.02	.01
□ 484 Donnie Hill	.05	.02	.01
□ 485 Gary Matthews	.05	.02	.01
□ 486 Bobby Grich TL	.10	.05	.01
□ 487 Bret Saberhagen	.15	.07	.02
□ 488 Lou Thornton	.05	.02	.01
□ 489 Jim Winn	.05	.02	.01
□ 490 Jeff Leonard	.05	.02	.01
□ 491 Pascual Perez	.05	.02	.01
□ 492 Kelvin Chapman	.05	.02	.01
□ 493 Gene Nelson	.05	.02	.01
□ 494 Gary Roenicke	.05	.02	.01
□ 495 Mark Langston	.15	.07	.02
□ 496 Jay Johnstone	.10	.05	.01
□ 497 John Stuper	.05	.02	.01
□ 498 Tito Landrum	.05	.02	.01
□ 499 Bob L. Gibson	.05	.02	.01
□ 500 Rickey Henderson	.30	.14	.04
□ 501 Dave Johnson MG (Checklist back)	.10	.05	.01
□ 502 Glen Cook	.05	.02	.01
□ 503 Mike Fitzgerald	.05	.02	.01
□ 504 Denny Walling	.05	.02	.01
□ 505 Jerry Koosman	.10	.05	.01
□ 506 Bill Russell	.05	.02	.01
□ 507 Steve Ontiveros	.10	.05	.01
□ 508 Alan Wiggins	.05	.02	.01
□ 509 Ernie Camacho	.05	.02	.01
□ 510 Wade Boggs	.40	.18	.05
□ 511 Ed Nunez	.05	.02	.01
□ 512 Thad Bosley	.05	.02	.01
□ 513 Ron Washington	.05	.02	.01
□ 514 Mike Jones	.05	.02	.01
□ 515 Darrell Evans	.10	.05	.01
□ 516 Greg Minton TL	.05	.02	.01
□ 517 Milt Thompson	.10	.05	.01
□ 518 Buck Martinez	.05	.02	.01
□ 519 Danny Darwin	.05	.02	.01
□ 520 Keith Hernandez	.10	.05	.01
□ 521 Nate Snell	.05	.02	.01
□ 522 Bob Bailor	.05	.02	.01
□ 523 Joe Price	.05	.02	.01
□ 524 Darrell Miller	.05	.02	.01
□ 525 Marvell Wynne	.05	.02	.01
□ 526 Charlie Lea	.05	.02	.01
□ 527 Checklist: 397-528	.10	.05	.01
□ 528 Terry Pendleton	.15	.07	.02
□ 529 Marc Sullivan	.05	.02	.01
□ 530 Rich Gossage	.15	.07	.02
□ 531 Tony LaRussa MG (Checklist back)	.10	.05	.01
□ 532 Don Carman	.05	.02	.01
□ 533 Billy Sample	.05	.02	.01
□ 534 Jeff Calhoun	.05	.02	.01
□ 535 Toby Harrah	.05	.02	.01
□ 536 Jose Rijo	.15	.07	.02
□ 537 Mark Salas	.05	.02	.01
□ 538 Dennis Eckersley	.10	.05	.01
□ 539 Glenn Hubbard	.05	.02	.01
□ 540 Dan Petry	.05	.02	.01
□ 541 Jorge Orta	.05	.02	.01
□ 542 Don Schulze	.05	.02	.01
□ 543 Jerry Narron	.05	.02	.01
□ 544 Eddie Milner	.05	.02	.01
□ 545 Jimmy Key	.15	.07	.02
□ 546 Dave Henderson TL	.10	.05	.01
□ 547 Roger McDowell	.10	.05	.01
□ 548 Mike Young	.05	.02	.01
□ 549 Bob Welch	.05	.02	.01
□ 550 Tom Herr	.05	.02	.01
□ 551 Dave LaPoint	.05	.02	.01
□ 552 Marc Hill	.05	.02	.01
□ 553 Jim Morrison	.05	.02	.01
□ 554 Paul Householder	.05	.02	.01
□ 555 Hubie Brooks	.05	.02	.01
□ 556 John Denny	.05	.02	.01
□ 557 Gerald Perry	.05	.02	.01
□ 558 Tim Stoddard	.05	.02	.01
□ 559 Tommy Dunbar	.05	.02	.01
□ 560 Dave Righetti	.05	.02	.01
□ 561 Bob Lillis MG (Checklist back)	.05	.02	.01
□ 562 Joe Beckwith	.05	.02	.01
□ 563 Alejandro Sanchez	.05	.02	.01
□ 564 Warren Brusstar	.05	.02	.01
□ 565 Tom Brunansky	.05	.02	.01
□ 566 Alfredo Griffin	.05	.02	.01
□ 567 Jeff Barkley	.05	.02	.01
□ 568 Donnie Scott	.05	.02	.01
□ 569 Jim Acker	.05	.02	.01
□ 570 Rusty Staub	.10	.05	.01
□ 571 Mike Jeffcoat	.05	.02	.01
□ 572 Paul Zuvella	.05	.02	.01
□ 573 Tom Hume	.05	.02	.01
□ 574 Ron Kittle	.05	.02	.01
□ 575 Mike Boddicker	.05	.02	.01
□ 576 Andre Dawson TL	.10	.05	.01
□ 577 Jerry Reuss	.05	.02	.01
□ 578 Lee Mazzilli	.05	.02	.01
□ 579 Jim Slaton	.05	.02	.01
□ 580 Willie McGee	.05	.02	.01
□ 581 Bruce Hurst	.05	.02	.01
□ 582 Jim Gantner	.05	.02	.01
□ 583 Al Bumbry	.05	.02	.01
□ 584 Brian Fisher	.05	.02	.01
□ 585 Garry Maddox	.05	.02	.01
□ 586 Greg Harris	.05	.02	.01
□ 587 Rafael Santana	.05	.02	.01
□ 588 Steve Lake	.05	.02	.01
□ 589 Sid Bream	.05	.02	.01
□ 590 Bob Knepper	.05	.02	.01
□ 591 Jackie Moore MG (Checklist back)	.05	.02	.01
□ 592 Frank Tanana	.05	.02	.01
□ 593 Jesse Barfield	.05	.02	.01
□ 594 Chris Bando	.05	.02	.01
□ 595 Dave Parker	.15	.07	.02
□ 596 Onix Concepcion	.05	.02	.01
□ 597 Sammy Stewart	.05	.02	.01
□ 598 Jim Presley	.05	.02	.01
□ 599 Rick Aguilera	.15	.07	.02
□ 600 Dale Murphy	.15	.07	.02
□ 601 Gary Lucas	.05	.02	.01
□ 602 Mariano Duncan	.15	.07	.02
□ 603 Bill Laskey	.05	.02	.01
□ 604 Gary Pettis	.05	.02	.01
□ 605 Dennis Boyd	.05	.02	.01
□ 606 Hal McRae TL	.05	.02	.01
□ 607 Ken Dayley	.05	.02	.01
□ 608 Bruce Bochy	.05	.02	.01
□ 609 Barbaro Garbey	.05	.02	.01
□ 610 Ron Guidry	.05	.02	.01
□ 611 Gary Woods	.05	.02	.01
□ 612 Richard Dotson	.05	.02	.01
□ 613 Roy Smalley	.05	.02	.01
□ 614 Rick Waits	.05	.02	.01
□ 615 Johnny Ray	.05	.02	.01
□ 616 Glenn Brummer	.05	.02	.01
□ 617 Lonnie Smith	.05	.02	.01
□ 618 Jim Pankovits	.05	.02	.01
□ 619 Danny Heep	.05	.02	.01
□ 620 Bruce Sutter	.10	.05	.01
□ 621 John Felske MG (Checklist back)	.05	.02	.01
□ 622 Gary Lavelle	.05	.02	.01
□ 623 Floyd Rayford	.05	.02	.01
□ 624 Steve McCatty	.05	.02	.01
□ 625 Bob Brenly	.05	.02	.01
□ 626 Roy Thomas	.05	.02	.01
□ 627 Ron Oester	.05	.02	.01
□ 628 Kirk McCaskill	.10	.05	.01

□ 629	Mitch Webster	.05	.02	.01
□ 630	Fernando Valenzuela	.10	.05	.01
□ 631	Steve Braun	.05	.02	.01
□ 632	Dave Von Ohlen	.05	.02	.01
□ 633	Jackie Gutierrez	.05	.02	.01
□ 634	Roy Lee Jackson	.05	.02	.01
□ 635	Jason Thompson	.05	.02	.01
□ 636	Lee Smith TL	.10	.05	.01
□ 637	Rudy Law	.05	.02	.01
□ 638	John Butcher	.05	.02	.01
□ 639	Bo Diaz	.05	.02	.01
□ 640	Jose Cruz	.05	.02	.01
□ 641	Wayne Tolleson	.05	.02	.01
□ 642	Ray Searage	.05	.02	.01
□ 643	Tom Brookens	.05	.02	.01
□ 644	Mark Gubicza	.10	.05	.01
□ 645	Dusty Baker	.10	.05	.01
□ 646	Mike Moore	.05	.02	.01
□ 647	Mel Hall	.05	.02	.01
□ 648	Steve Bedrosian	.05	.02	.01
□ 649	Ronn Reynolds	.05	.02	.01
□ 650	Dave Stieb	.05	.02	.01
□ 651	Billy Martin MG (Checklist back)	.10	.05	.01
□ 652	Tom Browning	.05	.02	.01
□ 653	Jim Dwyer	.05	.02	.01
□ 654	Ken Howell	.05	.02	.01
□ 655	Manny Trillo	.05	.02	.01
□ 656	Brian Harper	.05	.02	.01
□ 657	Juan Agosto	.05	.02	.01
□ 658	Rob Wilfong	.05	.02	.01
□ 659	Checklist: 529-660	.10	.05	.01
□ 660	Steve Garvey	.15	.07	.02
□ 661	Roger Clemens	1.00	.45	.12
□ 662	Bill Schroeder	.05	.02	.01
□ 663	Neil Allen	.05	.02	.01
□ 664	Tim Corcoran	.05	.02	.01
□ 665	Alejandro Pena	.05	.02	.01
□ 666	Rangers Leaders Charlie Hough	.10	.05	.01
□ 667	Tim Teufel	.05	.02	.01
□ 668	Cecilio Guante	.05	.02	.01
□ 669	Ron Cey	.10	.05	.01
□ 670	Willie Hernandez	.05	.02	.01
□ 671	Lynn Jones	.05	.02	.01
□ 672	Rob Picciolo	.05	.02	.01
□ 673	Ernie Whitt	.05	.02	.01
□ 674	Pat Tabler	.05	.02	.01
□ 675	Claudell Washington	.05	.02	.01
□ 676	Matt Young	.05	.02	.01
□ 677	Nick Esasky	.05	.02	.01
□ 678	Dan Gladden	.05	.02	.01
□ 679	Britt Burns	.05	.02	.01
□ 680	George Foster	.10	.05	.01
□ 681	Dick Williams MG (Checklist back)	.10	.05	.01
□ 682	Junior Ortiz	.05	.02	.01
□ 683	Andy Van Slyke	.10	.05	.01
□ 684	Bob McClure	.05	.02	.01
□ 685	Tim Wallach	.05	.02	.01
□ 686	Jeff Stone	.05	.02	.01
□ 687	Mike Trujillo	.05	.02	.01
□ 688	Larry Herndon	.05	.02	.01
□ 689	Dave Stewart	.10	.05	.01
□ 690	Ryne Sandberg UER (No Topps logo on front)	.75	.35	.09
□ 691	Mike Madden	.05	.02	.01
□ 692	Dale Berra	.05	.02	.01
□ 693	Tom Tellmann	.05	.02	.01
□ 694	Garth Iorg	.05	.02	.01
□ 695	Mike Smithson	.05	.02	.01
□ 696	Bill Russell TL	.10	.05	.01
□ 697	Bud Black	.05	.02	.01
□ 698	Brad Komminsk	.05	.02	.01
□ 699	Pat Corrales MG (Checklist back)	.05	.02	.01
□ 700	Reggie Jackson	.30	.14	.04
□ 701	Keith Hernandez AS	.10	.05	.01
□ 702	Tom Herr AS	.05	.02	.01
□ 703	Tim Wallach AS	.05	.02	.01
□ 704	Ozzie Smith AS	.15	.07	.02
□ 705	Dale Murphy AS	.10	.05	.01
□ 706	Pedro Guerrero AS	.10	.05	.01
□ 707	Willie McGee AS	.05	.02	.01
□ 708	Gary Carter AS	.10	.05	.01

□ 709	Dwight Gooden AS	.10	.05	.01
□ 710	John Tudor AS	.05	.02	.01
□ 711	Jeff Reardon AS	.10	.05	.01
□ 712	Don Mattingly AS	.50	.23	.06
□ 713	Damaso Garcia AS	.05	.02	.01
□ 714	George Brett AS	.50	.23	.06
□ 715	Cal Ripken AS	1.00	.45	.12
□ 716	Rickey Henderson AS	.15	.07	.02
□ 717	Dave Winfield AS	.15	.07	.02
□ 718	George Bell AS	.05	.02	.01
□ 719	Carlton Fisk AS	.10	.05	.01
□ 720	Bret Saberhagen AS	.10	.05	.01
□ 721	Ron Guidry AS	.05	.02	.01
□ 722	Dan Quisenberry AS	.05	.02	.01
□ 723	Marty Bystrom	.05	.02	.01
□ 724	Tim Hulett	.05	.02	.01
□ 725	Mario Soto	.05	.02	.01
□ 726	Rick Dempsey TL	.10	.05	.01
□ 727	David Green	.05	.02	.01
□ 728	Mike Marshall	.05	.02	.01
□ 729	Jim Beattie	.05	.02	.01
□ 730	Ozzie Smith	.40	.18	.05
□ 731	Don Robinson	.05	.02	.01
□ 732	Floyd Youmans	.05	.02	.01
□ 733	Ron Romanick	.05	.02	.01
□ 734	Marty Barrett	.05	.02	.01
□ 735	Dave Dravecky	.10	.05	.01
□ 736	Glenn Wilson	.05	.02	.01
□ 737	Pete Vuckovich	.05	.02	.01
□ 738	Andre Robertson	.05	.02	.01
□ 739	Dave Rozema	.05	.02	.01
□ 740	Lance Parrish	.10	.05	.01
□ 741	Pete Rose MG (Checklist back)	.20	.09	.03
□ 742	Frank Viola	.05	.02	.01
□ 743	Pat Sheridan	.05	.02	.01
□ 744	Lary Sorensen	.05	.02	.01
□ 745	Willie Upshaw	.05	.02	.01
□ 746	Denny Gonzalez	.05	.02	.01
□ 747	Rick Cerone	.05	.02	.01
□ 748	Steve Henderson	.05	.02	.01
□ 749	Ed Jurak	.05	.02	.01
□ 750	Gorman Thomas	.05	.02	.01
□ 751	Howard Johnson	.10	.05	.01
□ 752	Mike Krukow	.05	.02	.01
□ 753	Dan Ford	.05	.02	.01
□ 754	Pat Clements	.05	.02	.01
□ 755	Harold Baines	.15	.07	.02
□ 756	Rick Rhoden TL	.05	.02	.01
□ 757	Darrell Porter	.05	.02	.01
□ 758	Dave Anderson	.05	.02	.01
□ 759	Moose Haas	.05	.02	.01
□ 760	Andre Dawson	.15	.07	.02
□ 761	Don Slaught	.05	.02	.01
□ 762	Eric Show	.05	.02	.01
□ 763	Terry Puhl	.05	.02	.01
□ 764	Kevin Gross	.05	.02	.01
□ 765	Don Baylor	.15	.07	.02
□ 766	Rick Langford	.05	.02	.01
□ 767	Jody Davis	.05	.02	.01
□ 768	Vern Ruhle	.05	.02	.01
□ 769	Harold Reynolds	.20	.09	.03
□ 770	Vida Blue	.10	.05	.01
□ 771	John McNamara MG (Checklist back)	.05	.02	.01
□ 772	Brian Downing	.05	.02	.01
□ 773	Greg Pryor	.05	.02	.01
□ 774	Terry Leach	.05	.02	.01
□ 775	Al Oliver	.10	.05	.01
□ 776	Gene Garber	.05	.02	.01
□ 777	Wayne Krenchicki	.05	.02	.01
□ 778	Jerry Hairston	.05	.02	.01
□ 779	Rick Reuschel	.05	.02	.01
□ 780	Robin Yount	.30	.14	.04
□ 781	Joe Nolan	.05	.02	.01
□ 782	Ken Landreaux	.05	.02	.01
□ 783	Ricky Horton	.05	.02	.01
□ 784	Alan Bannister	.05	.02	.01
□ 785	Bob Stanley	.05	.02	.01
□ 786	Mickey Hatcher TL	.05	.02	.01
□ 787	Vance Law	.05	.02	.01
□ 788	Marty Castillo	.05	.02	.01
□ 789	Kurt Bevacqua	.05	.02	.01
□ 790	Phil Niekro	.15	.07	.02
□ 791	Checklist: 661-792	.10	.05	.01
□ 792	Charles Hudson	.05	.02	.01

1986 Topps Traded

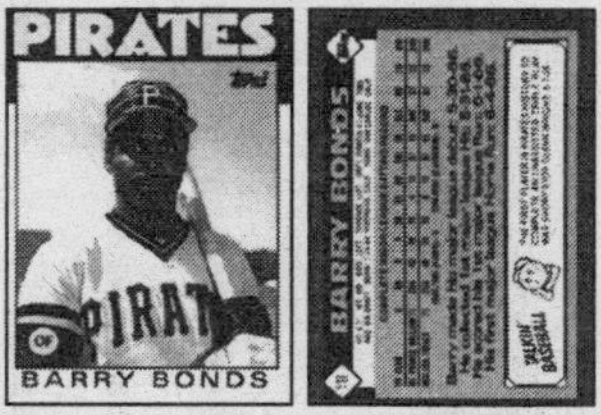

This 132-card standard-size Traded set was distributed in factory set form in a red and white box through hobby dealers. The cards are identical in style to regular-issue 1986 Topps cards except for whiter stock and t-suffixed numbering. The key extended Rookie Cards in this set are Barry Bonds, Bobby Bonilla, Jose Canseco, Will Clark, Andres Galarraga, Bo Jackson, Wally Joyner, John Kruk, and Kevin Mitchell.

	MINT	NRMT	EXC
COMPLETE FACT.SET (132)	12.00	5.50	1.50
COMMON CARD (1T-132T)	.05	.02	.01
SEMISTARS	.10	.05	.01

□ 1T Andy Allanson	.05	.02	.01
□ 2T Neil Allen	.05	.02	.01
□ 3T Joaquin Andujar	.05	.02	.01
□ 4T Paul Assenmacher	.05	.02	.01
□ 5T Scott Bailes	.05	.02	.01
□ 6T Don Baylor	.15	.07	.02
□ 7T Steve Bedrosian	.05	.02	.01
□ 8T Juan Beniquez	.05	.02	.01
□ 9T Juan Berenguer	.05	.02	.01
□ 10T Mike Bielecki	.05	.02	.01
□ 11T Barry Bonds	3.00	1.35	.35
□ 12T Bobby Bonilla	.50	.23	.06
□ 13T Juan Bonilla	.05	.02	.01
□ 14T Rich Bordi	.05	.02	.01
□ 15T Steve Boros MG	.05	.02	.01
□ 16T Rick Burleson	.05	.02	.01
□ 17T Bill Campbell	.05	.02	.01
□ 18T Tom Candiotti	.05	.02	.01
□ 19T John Cangelosi	.05	.02	.01
□ 20T Jose Canseco	2.00	.90	.25
□ 21T Carmen Castillo	.05	.02	.01
□ 22T Rick Cerone	.05	.02	.01
□ 23T John Cerutti	.05	.02	.01
□ 24T Will Clark	1.50	.70	.19
□ 25T Mark Clear	.05	.02	.01
□ 26T Darnell Coles	.05	.02	.01
□ 27T Dave Collins	.05	.02	.01
□ 28T Tim Conroy	.05	.02	.01
□ 29T Joe Cowley	.05	.02	.01
□ 30T Joel Davis	.05	.02	.01
□ 31T Rob Deer	.10	.05	.01
□ 32T John Denny	.05	.02	.01
□ 33T Mike Easler	.05	.02	.01
□ 34T Mark Eichhorn	.05	.02	.01
□ 35T Steve Farr	.05	.02	.01
□ 36T Scott Fletcher	.05	.02	.01
□ 37T Terry Forster	.05	.02	.01
□ 38T Terry Francona	.05	.02	.01
□ 39T Jim Fregosi MG	.05	.02	.01
□ 40T Andres Galarraga	1.25	.55	.16
□ 41T Ken Griffey	.05	.02	.01
□ 42T Bill Gullickson	.05	.02	.01
□ 43T Jose Guzman	.05	.02	.01
□ 44T Moose Haas	.05	.02	.01
□ 45T Billy Hatcher	.10	.05	.01
□ 46T Mike Heath	.05	.02	.01
□ 47T Tom Hume	.05	.02	.01
□ 48T Pete Incaviglia	.15	.07	.02
□ 49T Dane Iorg	.05	.02	.01
□ 50T Bo Jackson	.75	.35	.09
□ 51T Wally Joyner	.40	.18	.05
□ 52T Charlie Kerfeld	.05	.02	.01
□ 53T Eric King	.05	.02	.01
□ 54T Bob Kipper	.05	.02	.01
□ 55T Wayne Krenchicki	.05	.02	.01
□ 56T John Kruk	.15	.07	.02
□ 57T Mike LaCoss	.05	.02	.01
□ 58T Pete Ladd	.05	.02	.01
□ 59T Mike Laga	.05	.02	.01
□ 60T Hal Lanier MG	.05	.02	.01
□ 61T Dave LaPoint	.05	.02	.01
□ 62T Rudy Law	.05	.02	.01
□ 63T Rick Leach	.05	.02	.01
□ 64T Tim Leary	.05	.02	.01
□ 65T Dennis Leonard	.05	.02	.01
□ 66T Jim Leyland MG	.05	.02	.01
□ 67T Steve Lyons	.05	.02	.01
□ 68T Mickey Mahler	.05	.02	.01
□ 69T Candy Maldonado	.05	.02	.01
□ 70T Roger Mason	.05	.02	.01
□ 71T Bob McClure	.05	.02	.01
□ 72T Andy McGaffigan	.05	.02	.01
□ 73T Gene Michael MG	.05	.02	.01
□ 74T Kevin Mitchell	.15	.07	.02
□ 75T Omar Moreno	.05	.02	.01
□ 76T Jerry Mumphrey	.05	.02	.01
□ 77T Phil Niekro	.15	.07	.02
□ 78T Randy Niemann	.05	.02	.01
□ 79T Juan Nieves	.05	.02	.01
□ 80T Otis Nixon	.15	.07	.02
□ 81T Bob Ojeda	.05	.02	.01
□ 82T Jose Oquendo	.05	.02	.01
□ 83T Tom Paciorek	.05	.02	.01
□ 84T David Palmer	.05	.02	.01
□ 85T Frank Pastore	.05	.02	.01
□ 86T Lou Piniella MG	.10	.05	.01
□ 87T Dan Plesac	.05	.02	.01
□ 88T Darrell Porter	.05	.02	.01
□ 89T Rey Quinones	.05	.02	.01
□ 90T Gary Redus	.05	.02	.01
□ 91T Bip Roberts	.15	.07	.02
□ 92T Billy Joe Robidoux	.05	.02	.01
□ 93T Jeff D. Robinson	.05	.02	.01
□ 94T Gary Roenicke	.05	.02	.01
□ 95T Ed Romero	.05	.02	.01
□ 96T Argenis Salazar	.05	.02	.01
□ 97T Joe Sambito	.05	.02	.01
□ 98T Billy Sample	.05	.02	.01
□ 99T Dave Schmidt	.05	.02	.01
□ 100T Ken Schrom	.05	.02	.01
□ 101T Tom Seaver	.20	.09	.03
□ 102T Ted Simmons	.10	.05	.01
□ 103T Sammy Stewart	.05	.02	.01
□ 104T Kurt Stillwell	.05	.02	.01
□ 105T Franklin Stubbs	.05	.02	.01
□ 106T Dale Sveum	.05	.02	.01
□ 107T Chuck Tanner MG	.10	.05	.01
□ 108T Danny Tartabull	.10	.05	.01
□ 109T Tim Teufel	.05	.02	.01
□ 110T Bob Tewksbury	.10	.05	.01
□ 111T Andres Thomas	.05	.02	.01
□ 112T Milt Thompson	.05	.02	.01
□ 113T Robby Thompson	.10	.05	.01
□ 114T Jay Tibbs	.05	.02	.01
□ 115T Wayne Tolleson	.05	.02	.01
□ 116T Alex Trevino	.05	.02	.01
□ 117T Manny Trillo	.05	.02	.01
□ 118T Ed VandeBerg	.05	.02	.01
□ 119T Ozzie Virgil	.05	.02	.01
□ 120T Bob Walk	.05	.02	.01
□ 121T Gene Walter	.05	.02	.01
□ 122T Claudell Washington	.05	.02	.01
□ 123T Bill Wegman	.05	.02	.01
□ 124T Dick Williams MG	.10	.05	.01
□ 125T Mitch Williams	.10	.05	.01
□ 126T Bobby Witt	.10	.05	.01
□ 127T Todd Worrell	.15	.07	.02
□ 128T George Wright	.05	.02	.01
□ 129T Ricky Wright	.05	.02	.01
□ 130T Steve Yeager	.05	.02	.01
□ 131T Paul Zuvella	.05	.02	.01
□ 132T Checklist 1T-132T	.05	.02	.01

1987 Topps

This set consists of 792 standard-size cards. Cards were primarily issued in 17-card wax

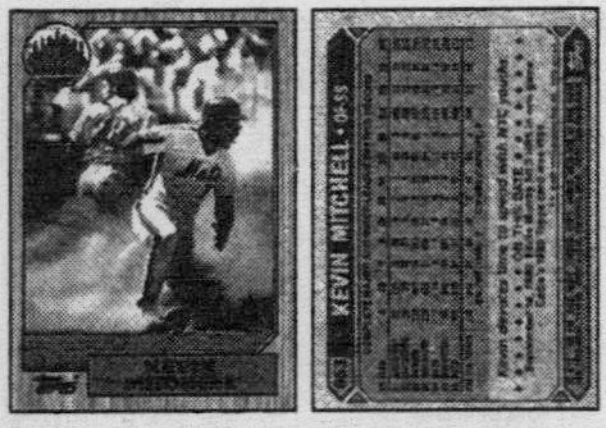

packs, 50-card rack packs and factory sets. Card fronts feature wood grain borders encasing a color photo (reminiscent of Topps' classic 1962 baseball set). Subsets include Record Breakers (1-7), Turn Back the Clock (311-315), All-Star selections (595-616) and Team Leaders (scattered throughout the set). The manager cards contain a team checklist on back. The key Rookie Cards in this set are Barry Bonds, Bobby Bonilla, Will Clark, Mike Greenwell, Bo Jackson, Wally Joyner, John Kruk, Barry Larkin, Kevin Mitchell, Rafael Palmiero, Ruben Sierra, and Devon White.

	MINT	NRMT	EXC
COMPLETE SET (792)	12.00	5.50	1.50
COMPLETE FACT.SET (792)	12.00	5.50	1.50
COMMON CARD (1-792)	.05	.02	.01
SEMISTARS	.10	.05	.01
STARS	.15	.07	.02

□ 1 Roger Clemens RB	.15	.07	.02
Most K's 9-inning game			
□ 2 Jim Deshaies RB	.05	.02	.01
Most cons. K's, start of game			
□ 3 Dwight Evans RB	.10	.05	.01
Earliest home run			
□ 4 Davey Lopes RB	.05	.02	.01
Most steals season, 40-year-old			
□ 5 Dave Righetti RB	.05	.02	.01
Most saves season			
□ 6 Ruben Sierra RB	.15	.07	.02
Youngest player to switch hit HR's, game			
□ 7 Todd Worrell RB	.10	.05	.01
Most saves rookie season			
□ 8 Terry Pendleton	.10	.05	.01
□ 9 Jay Tibbs	.05	.02	.01
□ 10 Cecil Cooper	.10	.05	.01
□ 11 Indians Team	.05	.02	.01
(Mound conference)			
□ 12 Jeff Sellers	.05	.02	.01
□ 13 Nick Esasky	.05	.02	.01
□ 14 Dave Stewart	.10	.05	.01
□ 15 Claudell Washington	.05	.02	.01
□ 16 Pat Clements	.05	.02	.01
□ 17 Pete O'Brien	.05	.02	.01
□ 18 Dick Howser MG	.10	.05	.01
(Checklist back)			
□ 19 Matt Young	.05	.02	.01
□ 20 Gary Carter	.15	.07	.02
□ 21 Mark Davis	.05	.02	.01
□ 22 Doug DeCinces	.05	.02	.01
□ 23 Lee Smith	.15	.07	.02
□ 24 Tony Walker	.05	.02	.01
□ 25 Bert Blyleven	.10	.05	.01
□ 26 Greg Brock	.05	.02	.01
□ 27 Joe Cowley	.05	.02	.01
□ 28 Rick Dempsey	.10	.05	.01
□ 29 Jimmy Key	.10	.05	.01
□ 30 Tim Raines	.10	.05	.01
□ 31 Braves Team	.05	.02	.01
(Glenn Hubbard and Rafael Ramirez)			
□ 32 Tim Leary	.05	.02	.01
□ 33 Andy Van Slyke	.10	.05	.01
□ 34 Jose Rijo	.05	.02	.01
□ 35 Sid Bream	.05	.02	.01
□ 36 Eric King	.05	.02	.01
□ 37 Marvell Wynne	.05	.02	.01
□ 38 Dennis Leonard	.05	.02	.01
□ 39 Marty Barrett	.05	.02	.01
□ 40 Dave Righetti	.05	.02	.01
□ 41 Bo Diaz	.05	.02	.01
□ 42 Gary Redus	.05	.02	.01
□ 43 Gene Michael MG	.05	.02	.01
(Checklist back)			
□ 44 Greg Harris	.05	.02	.01
□ 45 Jim Presley	.05	.02	.01
□ 46 Dan Gladden	.05	.02	.01
□ 47 Dennis Powell	.05	.02	.01
□ 48 Wally Backman	.05	.02	.01
□ 49 Terry Harper	.05	.02	.01
□ 50 Dave Smith	.05	.02	.01
□ 51 Mel Hall	.05	.02	.01
□ 52 Keith Atherton	.05	.02	.01
□ 53 Ruppert Jones	.05	.02	.01
□ 54 Bill Dawley	.05	.02	.01
□ 55 Tim Wallach	.05	.02	.01
□ 56 Brewers Team	.05	.02	.01
(Mound conference)			
□ 57 Scott Nielsen	.05	.02	.01
□ 58 Thad Bosley	.05	.02	.01
□ 59 Ken Dayley	.05	.02	.01
□ 60 Tony Pena	.05	.02	.01
□ 61 Bobby Thigpen	.10	.05	.01
□ 62 Bobby Meacham	.05	.02	.01
□ 63 Fred Toliver	.05	.02	.01
□ 64 Harry Spilman	.05	.02	.01
□ 65 Tom Browning	.05	.02	.01
□ 66 Marc Sullivan	.05	.02	.01
□ 67 Bill Swift	.05	.02	.01
□ 68 Tony LaRussa MG	.10	.05	.01
(Checklist back)			
□ 69 Lonnie Smith	.05	.02	.01
□ 70 Charlie Hough	.05	.02	.01
□ 71 Mike Aldrete	.10	.05	.01
□ 72 Walt Terrell	.05	.02	.01
□ 73 Dave Anderson	.05	.02	.01
□ 74 Dan Pasqua	.05	.02	.01
□ 75 Ron Darling	.05	.02	.01
□ 76 Rafael Ramirez	.05	.02	.01
□ 77 Bryan Oelkers	.05	.02	.01
□ 78 Tom Foley	.05	.02	.01
□ 79 Juan Nieves	.05	.02	.01
□ 80 Wally Joyner	.25	.11	.03
□ 81 Padres Team	.05	.02	.01
(Andy Hawkins and Terry Kennedy)			
□ 82 Rob Murphy	.05	.02	.01
□ 83 Mike Davis	.05	.02	.01
□ 84 Steve Lake	.05	.02	.01
□ 85 Kevin Bass	.05	.02	.01
□ 86 Nate Snell	.05	.02	.01
□ 87 Mark Salas	.05	.02	.01
□ 88 Ed Wojna	.05	.02	.01
□ 89 Ozzie Guillen	.10	.05	.01
□ 90 Dave Stieb	.05	.02	.01
□ 91 Harold Reynolds	.05	.02	.01
□ 92A Urbano Lugo	.15	.07	.02
ERR (no trademark)			
□ 92B Urbano Lugo COR	.05	.02	.01
□ 93 Jim Leyland MG	.10	.05	.01
(Checklist back)			
□ 94 Calvin Schiraldi	.05	.02	.01
□ 95 Oddibe McDowell	.05	.02	.01
□ 96 Frank Williams	.05	.02	.01
□ 97 Glenn Wilson	.05	.02	.01
□ 98 Bill Scherrer	.05	.02	.01
□ 99 Darryl Motley	.05	.02	.01
(Now with Braves on card front)			
□ 100 Steve Garvey	.15	.07	.02
□ 101 Carl Willis	.05	.02	.01
□ 102 Paul Zuvella	.05	.02	.01
□ 103 Rick Aguilera	.10	.05	.01
□ 104 Billy Sample	.05	.02	.01
□ 105 Floyd Youmans	.05	.02	.01
□ 106 Blue Jays Team	.05	.02	.01
(George Bell and Jesse Barfield)			
□ 107 John Butcher	.05	.02	.01
□ 108 Jim Gantner UER	.05	.02	.01
(Brewers logo			

	reversed)			
□ 109	R.J. Reynolds	.05	.02	.01
□ 110	John Tudor	.05	.02	.01
□ 111	Alfredo Griffin	.05	.02	.01
□ 112	Alan Ashby	.05	.02	.01
□ 113	Neil Allen	.05	.02	.01
□ 114	Billy Beane	.05	.02	.01
□ 115	Donnie Moore	.05	.02	.01
□ 116	Bill Russell	.05	.02	.01
□ 117	Jim Beattie	.05	.02	.01
□ 118	Bobby Valentine MG	.05	.02	.01
	(Checklist back)			
□ 119	Ron Robinson	.05	.02	.01
□ 120	Eddie Murray	.25	.11	.03
□ 121	Kevin Romine	.05	.02	.01
□ 122	Jim Clancy	.05	.02	.01
□ 123	John Kruk	.15	.07	.02
□ 124	Ray Fontenot	.05	.02	.01
□ 125	Bob Brenly	.05	.02	.01
□ 126	Mike Loynd	.05	.02	.01
□ 127	Vance Law	.05	.02	.01
□ 128	Checklist 1-132	.10	.05	.01
□ 129	Rick Cerone	.05	.02	.01
□ 130	Dwight Gooden	.15	.07	.02
□ 131	Pirates Team	.05	.02	.01
	(Sid Bream and			
	Tony Pena)			
□ 132	Paul Assenmacher	.05	.02	.01
□ 133	Jose Oquendo	.05	.02	.01
□ 134	Rich Yett	.05	.02	.01
□ 135	Mike Easler	.05	.02	.01
□ 136	Ron Romanick	.05	.02	.01
□ 137	Jerry Willard	.05	.02	.01
□ 138	Roy Lee Jackson	.05	.02	.01
□ 139	Devon White	.20	.09	.03
□ 140	Bret Saberhagen	.10	.05	.01
□ 141	Herm Winningham	.05	.02	.01
□ 142	Rick Sutcliffe	.05	.02	.01
□ 143	Steve Boros MG	.05	.02	.01
	(Checklist back)			
□ 144	Mike Scioscia	.05	.02	.01
□ 145	Charlie Kerfeld	.05	.02	.01
□ 146	Tracy Jones	.05	.02	.01
□ 147	Randy Niemann	.05	.02	.01
□ 148	Dave Collins	.05	.02	.01
□ 149	Ray Searage	.05	.02	.01
□ 150	Wade Boggs	.15	.07	.02
□ 151	Mike LaCoss	.05	.02	.01
□ 152	Toby Harrah	.05	.02	.01
□ 153	Duane Ward	.10	.05	.01
□ 154	Tom O'Malley	.05	.02	.01
□ 155	Eddie Whitson	.05	.02	.01
□ 156	Mariners Team	.05	.02	.01
	(Mound conference)			
□ 157	Danny Darwin	.05	.02	.01
□ 158	Tim Teufel	.05	.02	.01
□ 159	Ed Olwine	.05	.02	.01
□ 160	Julio Franco	.10	.05	.01
□ 161	Steve Ontiveros	.05	.02	.01
□ 162	Mike LaValliere	.05	.02	.01
□ 163	Kevin Gross	.05	.02	.01
□ 164	Sammy Khalifa	.05	.02	.01
□ 165	Jeff Reardon	.10	.05	.01
□ 166	Bob Boone	.10	.05	.01
□ 167	Jim Deshaies	.05	.02	.01
□ 168	Lou Piniella MG	.10	.05	.01
	(Checklist back)			
□ 169	Ron Washington	.05	.02	.01
□ 170	Bo Jackson	.50	.23	.06
□ 171	Chuck Cary	.05	.02	.01
□ 172	Ron Oester	.05	.02	.01
□ 173	Alex Trevino	.05	.02	.01
□ 174	Henry Cotto	.05	.02	.01
□ 175	Bob Stanley	.05	.02	.01
□ 176	Steve Buechele	.05	.02	.01
□ 177	Keith Moreland	.05	.02	.01
□ 178	Cecil Fielder	.30	.14	.04
□ 179	Bill Wegman	.05	.02	.01
□ 180	Chris Brown	.05	.02	.01
□ 181	Cardinals Team	.05	.02	.01
	(Mound conference)			
□ 182	Lee Lacy	.05	.02	.01
□ 183	Andy Hawkins	.05	.02	.01
□ 184	Bobby Bonilla	.30	.14	.04
□ 185	Roger McDowell	.05	.02	.01
□ 186	Bruce Benedict	.05	.02	.01
□ 187	Mark Huismann	.05	.02	.01
□ 188	Tony Phillips	.15	.07	.02
□ 189	Joe Hesketh	.05	.02	.01
□ 190	Jim Sundberg	.05	.02	.01
□ 191	Charles Hudson	.05	.02	.01
□ 192	Cory Snyder	.05	.02	.01
□ 193	Roger Craig MG	.10	.05	.01
	(Checklist back)			
□ 194	Kirk McCaskill	.05	.02	.01
□ 195	Mike Pagliarulo	.05	.02	.01
□ 196	Randy O'Neal UER	.05	.02	.01
	(Wrong ML career			
	W-L totals)			
□ 197	Mark Bailey	.05	.02	.01
□ 198	Lee Mazzilli	.05	.02	.01
□ 199	Mariano Duncan	.05	.02	.01
□ 200	Pete Rose	.20	.09	.03
□ 201	John Cangelosi	.05	.02	.01
□ 202	Ricky Wright	.05	.02	.01
□ 203	Mike Kingery	.10	.05	.01
□ 204	Sammy Stewart	.05	.02	.01
□ 205	Graig Nettles	.10	.05	.01
□ 206	Twins Team	.05	.02	.01
	(Frank Viola and			
	Tim Laudner)			
□ 207	George Frazier	.05	.02	.01
□ 208	John Shelby	.05	.02	.01
□ 209	Rick Schu	.05	.02	.01
□ 210	Lloyd Moseby	.05	.02	.01
□ 211	John Morris	.05	.02	.01
□ 212	Mike Fitzgerald	.05	.02	.01
□ 213	Randy Myers	.20	.09	.03
□ 214	Omar Moreno	.05	.02	.01
□ 215	Mark Langston	.10	.05	.01
□ 216	B.J. Surhoff	.15	.07	.02
□ 217	Chris Codiroli	.05	.02	.01
□ 218	Sparky Anderson MG	.10	.05	.01
	(Checklist back)			
□ 219	Cecilio Guante	.05	.02	.01
□ 220	Joe Carter	.20	.09	.03
□ 221	Vern Ruhle	.05	.02	.01
□ 222	Denny Walling	.05	.02	.01
□ 223	Charlie Leibrandt	.05	.02	.01
□ 224	Wayne Tolleson	.05	.02	.01
□ 225	Mike Smithson	.05	.02	.01
□ 226	Max Venable	.05	.02	.01
□ 227	Jamie Moyer	.10	.05	.01
□ 228	Curt Wilkerson	.05	.02	.01
□ 229	Mike Birkbeck	.05	.02	.01
□ 230	Don Baylor	.15	.07	.02
□ 231	Giants Team	.05	.02	.01
	(Bob Brenly and			
	Jim Gott)			
□ 232	Reggie Williams	.05	.02	.01
□ 233	Russ Morman	.05	.02	.01
□ 234	Pat Sheridan	.05	.02	.01
□ 235	Alvin Davis	.05	.02	.01
□ 236	Tommy John	.10	.05	.01
□ 237	Jim Morrison	.05	.02	.01
□ 238	Bill Krueger	.05	.02	.01
□ 239	Juan Espino	.05	.02	.01
□ 240	Steve Balboni	.05	.02	.01
□ 241	Danny Heep	.05	.02	.01
□ 242	Rick Mahler	.05	.02	.01
□ 243	Whitey Herzog MG	.10	.05	.01
	(Checklist back)			
□ 244	Dickie Noles	.05	.02	.01
□ 245	Willie Upshaw	.05	.02	.01
□ 246	Jim Dwyer	.05	.02	.01
□ 247	Jeff Reed	.05	.02	.01
□ 248	Gene Walter	.05	.02	.01
□ 249	Jim Pankovits	.05	.02	.01
□ 250	Teddy Higuera	.05	.02	.01
□ 251	Rob Wilfong	.05	.02	.01
□ 252	Dennis Martinez	.10	.05	.01
□ 253	Eddie Milner	.05	.02	.01
□ 254	Bob Tewksbury	.10	.05	.01
□ 255	Juan Samuel	.05	.02	.01
□ 256	Royals Team	.15	.07	.02
	(George Brett and			
	Frank White)			
□ 257	Bob Forsch	.05	.02	.01
□ 258	Steve Yeager	.05	.02	.01
□ 259	Mike Greenwell	.15	.07	.02
□ 260	Vida Blue	.10	.05	.01
□ 261	Ruben Sierra	.50	.23	.06

□ 262 Jim Winn	.05	.02	.01
□ 263 Stan Javier	.05	.02	.01
□ 264 Checklist 133-264	.10	.05	.01
□ 265 Darrell Evans	.10	.05	.01
□ 266 Jeff Hamilton	.05	.02	.01
□ 267 Howard Johnson	.05	.02	.01
□ 268 Pat Corrales MG (Checklist back)	.10	.05	.01
□ 269 Cliff Speck	.05	.02	.01
□ 270 Jody Davis	.05	.02	.01
□ 271 Mike G. Brown	.05	.02	.01
□ 272 Andres Galarraga	.30	.14	.04
□ 273 Gene Nelson	.05	.02	.01
□ 274 Jeff Hearron UER (Duplicate 1986 stat line on back)	.05	.02	.01
□ 275 LaMarr Hoyt	.05	.02	.01
□ 276 Jackie Gutierrez	.05	.02	.01
□ 277 Juan Agosto	.05	.02	.01
□ 278 Gary Pettis	.05	.02	.01
□ 279 Dan Plesac	.05	.02	.01
□ 280 Jeff Leonard	.05	.02	.01
□ 281 Reds Team (Pete Rose, Bo Diaz, and Bill Gullickson)	.15	.07	.02
□ 282 Jeff Calhoun	.05	.02	.01
□ 283 Doug Drabek	.15	.07	.02
□ 284 John Moses	.05	.02	.01
□ 285 Dennis Boyd	.05	.02	.01
□ 286 Mike Woodard	.05	.02	.01
□ 287 Dave Von Ohlen	.05	.02	.01
□ 288 Tito Landrum	.05	.02	.01
□ 289 Bob Kipper	.05	.02	.01
□ 290 Leon Durham	.05	.02	.01
□ 291 Mitch Williams	.10	.05	.01
□ 292 Franklin Stubbs	.05	.02	.01
□ 293 Bob Rodgers MG (Checklist back, inconsistent design on card back)	.05	.02	.01
□ 294 Steve Jeltz	.05	.02	.01
□ 295 Len Dykstra	.10	.05	.01
□ 296 Andres Thomas	.05	.02	.01
□ 297 Don Schulze	.05	.02	.01
□ 298 Larry Herndon	.05	.02	.01
□ 299 Joel Davis	.05	.02	.01
□ 300 Reggie Jackson	.20	.09	.03
□ 301 Luis Aquino UER (No trademark, never corrected)	.05	.02	.01
□ 302 Bill Schroeder	.05	.02	.01
□ 303 Juan Berenguer	.05	.02	.01
□ 304 Phil Garner	.05	.02	.01
□ 305 John Franco	.05	.02	.01
□ 306 Red Sox Team (Tom Seaver, John McNamara MG, and Rich Gedman)	.15	.07	.02
□ 307 Lee Guetterman	.05	.02	.01
□ 308 Don Slaught	.05	.02	.01
□ 309 Mike Young	.05	.02	.01
□ 310 Frank Viola	.05	.02	.01
□ 311 Rickey Henderson TBC '82	.15	.07	.02
□ 312 Reggie Jackson TBC '77	.15	.07	.02
□ 313 Roberto Clemente TBC '72	.20	.09	.03
□ 314 Carl Yastrzemski UER TBC '67 (Sic, 112 RBI's on back)	.15	.07	.02
□ 315 Maury Wills TBC '62	.10	.05	.01
□ 316 Brian Fisher	.05	.02	.01
□ 317 Clint Hurdle	.05	.02	.01
□ 318 Jim Fregosi MG (Checklist back)	.10	.05	.01
□ 319 Greg Swindell	.15	.07	.02
□ 320 Barry Bonds	1.25	.55	.16
□ 321 Mike Laga	.05	.02	.01
□ 322 Chris Bando	.05	.02	.01
□ 323 Al Newman	.05	.02	.01
□ 324 David Palmer	.05	.02	.01
□ 325 Garry Templeton	.05	.02	.01
□ 326 Mark Gubicza	.05	.02	.01
□ 327 Dale Sveum	.05	.02	.01
□ 328 Bob Welch	.05	.02	.01
□ 329 Ron Roenicke	.05	.02	.01
□ 330 Mike Scott	.05	.02	.01
□ 331 Mets Team (Gary Carter and Darryl Strawberry)	.10	.05	.01
□ 332 Joe Price	.05	.02	.01
□ 333 Ken Phelps	.05	.02	.01
□ 334 Ed Correa	.05	.02	.01
□ 335 Candy Maldonado	.05	.02	.01
□ 336 Allan Anderson	.05	.02	.01
□ 337 Darrell Miller	.05	.02	.01
□ 338 Tim Conroy	.05	.02	.01
□ 339 Donnie Hill	.05	.02	.01
□ 340 Roger Clemens	.40	.18	.05
□ 341 Mike C. Brown	.05	.02	.01
□ 342 Bob James	.05	.02	.01
□ 343 Hal Lanier MG (Checklist back)	.10	.05	.01
□ 344A Joe Niekro (Copyright inside righthand border)	.05	.02	.01
□ 344B Joe Niekro (Copyright outside righthand border)	.05	.02	.01
□ 345 Andre Dawson	.15	.07	.02
□ 346 Shawon Dunston	.10	.05	.01
□ 347 Mickey Brantley	.05	.02	.01
□ 348 Carmelo Martinez	.05	.02	.01
□ 349 Storm Davis	.05	.02	.01
□ 350 Keith Hernandez	.10	.05	.01
□ 351 Gene Garber	.05	.02	.01
□ 352 Mike Felder	.05	.02	.01
□ 353 Ernie Camacho	.05	.02	.01
□ 354 Jamie Quirk	.05	.02	.01
□ 355 Don Carman	.05	.02	.01
□ 356 White Sox Team (Mound conference)	.05	.02	.01
□ 357 Steve Fireovid	.05	.02	.01
□ 358 Sal Butera	.05	.02	.01
□ 359 Doug Corbett	.05	.02	.01
□ 360 Pedro Guerrero	.10	.05	.01
□ 361 Mark Thurmond	.05	.02	.01
□ 362 Luis Quinones	.05	.02	.01
□ 363 Jose Guzman	.05	.02	.01
□ 364 Randy Bush	.05	.02	.01
□ 365 Rick Rhoden	.05	.02	.01
□ 366 Mark McGwire	1.25	.55	.16
□ 367 Jeff Lahti	.05	.02	.01
□ 368 John McNamara MG (Checklist back)	.05	.02	.01
□ 369 Brian Dayett	.05	.02	.01
□ 370 Fred Lynn	.05	.02	.01
□ 371 Mark Eichhorn	.05	.02	.01
□ 372 Jerry Mumphrey	.05	.02	.01
□ 373 Jeff Dedmon	.05	.02	.01
□ 374 Glenn Hoffman	.05	.02	.01
□ 375 Ron Guidry	.05	.02	.01
□ 376 Scott Bradley	.05	.02	.01
□ 377 John Henry Johnson	.05	.02	.01
□ 378 Rafael Santana	.05	.02	.01
□ 379 John Russell	.05	.02	.01
□ 380 Rich Gossage	.10	.05	.01
□ 381 Expos Team (Mound conference)	.05	.02	.01
□ 382 Rudy Law	.05	.02	.01
□ 383 Ron Davis	.05	.02	.01
□ 384 Johnny Grubb	.05	.02	.01
□ 385 Orel Hershiser	.15	.07	.02
□ 386 Dickie Thon	.05	.02	.01
□ 387 T.R. Bryden	.05	.02	.01
□ 388 Geno Petralli	.05	.02	.01
□ 389 Jeff D. Robinson	.05	.02	.01
□ 390 Gary Matthews	.05	.02	.01
□ 391 Jay Howell	.05	.02	.01
□ 392 Checklist 265-396	.05	.02	.01
□ 393 Pete Rose MG (Checklist back)	.25	.11	.03
□ 394 Mike Bielecki	.05	.02	.01
□ 395 Damaso Garcia	.05	.02	.01
□ 396 Tim Lollar	.05	.02	.01
□ 397 Greg Walker	.05	.02	.01
□ 398 Brad Havens	.05	.02	.01
□ 399 Curt Ford	.05	.02	.01
□ 400 George Brett	.40	.18	.05
□ 401 Billy Joe Robidoux	.05	.02	.01
□ 402 Mike Trujillo	.05	.02	.01

□ 403	Jerry Royster	.05	.02	.01
□ 404	Doug Sisk	.05	.02	.01
□ 405	Brook Jacoby	.05	.02	.01
□ 406	Yankees Team (Rickey Henderson and Don Mattingly)	.15	.07	.02
□ 407	Jim Acker	.05	.02	.01
□ 408	John Mizerock	.05	.02	.01
□ 409	Milt Thompson	.05	.02	.01
□ 410	Fernando Valenzuela	.10	.05	.01
□ 411	Darnell Coles	.05	.02	.01
□ 412	Eric Davis	.15	.07	.02
□ 413	Moose Haas	.05	.02	.01
□ 414	Joe Orsulak	.05	.02	.01
□ 415	Bobby Witt	.10	.05	.01
□ 416	Tom Nieto	.05	.02	.01
□ 417	Pat Perry	.05	.02	.01
□ 418	Dick Williams MG (Checklist back)	.10	.05	.01
□ 419	Mark Portugal	.10	.05	.01
□ 420	Will Clark	.60	.25	.07
□ 421	Jose DeLeon	.05	.02	.01
□ 422	Jack Howell	.05	.02	.01
□ 423	Jaime Cocanower	.05	.02	.01
□ 424	Chris Speier	.05	.02	.01
□ 425	Tom Seaver UER Earned Runs amount is wrong For 86 Red Sox and Career Also the ERA is wrong for 86 and career	.15	.07	.02
□ 426	Floyd Rayford	.05	.02	.01
□ 427	Edwin Nunez	.05	.02	.01
□ 428	Bruce Bochy	.05	.02	.01
□ 429	Tim Pyznarski	.05	.02	.01
□ 430	Mike Schmidt	.20	.09	.03
□ 431	Dodgers Team (Mound conference)	.05	.02	.01
□ 432	Jim Slaton	.05	.02	.01
□ 433	Ed Hearn	.05	.02	.01
□ 434	Mike Fischlin	.05	.02	.01
□ 435	Bruce Sutter	.05	.02	.01
□ 436	Andy Allanson	.05	.02	.01
□ 437	Ted Power	.05	.02	.01
□ 438	Kelly Downs	.05	.02	.01
□ 439	Karl Best	.05	.02	.01
□ 440	Willie McGee	.05	.02	.01
□ 441	Dave Leiper	.05	.02	.01
□ 442	Mitch Webster	.05	.02	.01
□ 443	John Felske MG (Checklist back)	.05	.02	.01
□ 444	Jeff Russell	.05	.02	.01
□ 445	Dave Lopes	.10	.05	.01
□ 446	Chuck Finley	.25	.11	.03
□ 447	Bill Almon	.05	.02	.01
□ 448	Chris Bosio	.10	.05	.01
□ 449	Pat Dodson	.05	.02	.01
□ 450	Kirby Puckett	.75	.35	.09
□ 451	Joe Sambito	.05	.02	.01
□ 452	Dave Henderson	.05	.02	.01
□ 453	Scott Terry	.05	.02	.01
□ 454	Luis Salazar	.05	.02	.01
□ 455	Mike Boddicker	.05	.02	.01
□ 456	A's Team (Mound conference)	.05	.02	.01
□ 457	Len Matuszek	.05	.02	.01
□ 458	Kelly Gruber	.05	.02	.01
□ 459	Dennis Eckersley	.10	.05	.01
□ 460	Darryl Strawberry	.15	.07	.02
□ 461	Craig McMurtry	.05	.02	.01
□ 462	Scott Fletcher	.05	.02	.01
□ 463	Tom Candiotti	.05	.02	.01
□ 464	Butch Wynegar	.05	.02	.01
□ 465	Todd Worrell	.10	.05	.01
□ 466	Kal Daniels	.05	.02	.01
□ 467	Randy St.Claire	.05	.02	.01
□ 468	George Bamberger MG (Checklist back)	.10	.05	.01
□ 469	Mike Diaz	.05	.02	.01
□ 470	Dave Dravecky	.10	.05	.01
□ 471	Ronn Reynolds	.05	.02	.01
□ 472	Bill Doran	.05	.02	.01
□ 473	Steve Farr	.05	.02	.01
□ 474	Jerry Narron	.05	.02	.01
□ 475	Scott Garrelts	.05	.02	.01
□ 476	Danny Tartabull	.10	.05	.01
□ 477	Ken Howell	.05	.02	.01
□ 478	Tim Laudner	.05	.02	.01
□ 479	Bob Sebra	.05	.02	.01
□ 480	Jim Rice	.15	.07	.02
□ 481	Phillies Team (Glenn Wilson, Juan Samuel, and Von Hayes)	.05	.02	.01
□ 482	Daryl Boston	.05	.02	.01
□ 483	Dwight Lowry	.05	.02	.01
□ 484	Jim Traber	.05	.02	.01
□ 485	Tony Fernandez	.05	.02	.01
□ 486	Otis Nixon	.10	.05	.01
□ 487	Dave Gumpert	.05	.02	.01
□ 488	Ray Knight	.10	.05	.01
□ 489	Bill Gullickson	.05	.02	.01
□ 490	Dale Murphy	.15	.07	.02
□ 491	Ron Karkovice	.10	.05	.01
□ 492	Mike Heath	.05	.02	.01
□ 493	Tom Lasorda MG (Checklist back)	.10	.05	.01
□ 494	Barry Jones	.05	.02	.01
□ 495	Gorman Thomas	.05	.02	.01
□ 496	Bruce Bochte	.05	.02	.01
□ 497	Dale Mohorcic	.05	.02	.01
□ 498	Bob Kearney	.05	.02	.01
□ 499	Bruce Ruffin	.05	.02	.01
□ 500	Don Mattingly	.50	.23	.06
□ 501	Craig Lefferts	.05	.02	.01
□ 502	Dick Schofield	.05	.02	.01
□ 503	Larry Andersen	.05	.02	.01
□ 504	Mickey Hatcher	.05	.02	.01
□ 505	Bryn Smith	.05	.02	.01
□ 506	Orioles Team (Mound conference)	.05	.02	.01
□ 507	Dave L. Stapleton	.05	.02	.01
□ 508	Scott Bankhead	.05	.02	.01
□ 509	Enos Cabell	.05	.02	.01
□ 510	Tom Henke	.05	.02	.01
□ 511	Steve Lyons	.05	.02	.01
□ 512	Dave Magadan	.10	.05	.01
□ 513	Carmen Castillo	.05	.02	.01
□ 514	Orlando Mercado	.05	.02	.01
□ 515	Willie Hernandez	.05	.02	.01
□ 516	Ted Simmons	.10	.05	.01
□ 517	Mario Soto	.05	.02	.01
□ 518	Gene Mauch MG (Checklist back)	.10	.05	.01
□ 519	Curt Young	.05	.02	.01
□ 520	Jack Clark	.10	.05	.01
□ 521	Rick Reuschel	.05	.02	.01
□ 522	Checklist 397-528	.05	.02	.01
□ 523	Earnie Riles	.05	.02	.01
□ 524	Bob Shirley	.05	.02	.01
□ 525	Phil Bradley	.05	.02	.01
□ 526	Roger Mason	.05	.02	.01
□ 527	Jim Wohlford	.05	.02	.01
□ 528	Ken Dixon	.05	.02	.01
□ 529	Alvaro Espinoza	.05	.02	.01
□ 530	Tony Gwynn	.40	.18	.05
□ 531	Astros Team (Yogi Berra conference)	.10	.05	.01
□ 532	Jeff Stone	.05	.02	.01
□ 533	Argenis Salazar	.05	.02	.01
□ 534	Scott Sanderson	.05	.02	.01
□ 535	Tony Armas	.05	.02	.01
□ 536	Terry Mulholland	.10	.05	.01
□ 537	Rance Mulliniks	.05	.02	.01
□ 538	Tom Niedenfuer	.05	.02	.01
□ 539	Reid Nichols	.05	.02	.01
□ 540	Terry Kennedy	.05	.02	.01
□ 541	Rafael Belliard	.05	.02	.01
□ 542	Ricky Horton	.05	.02	.01
□ 543	Dave Johnson MG (Checklist back)	.10	.05	.01
□ 544	Zane Smith	.05	.02	.01
□ 545	Buddy Bell	.10	.05	.01
□ 546	Mike Morgan	.05	.02	.01
□ 547	Rob Deer	.05	.02	.01
□ 548	Bill Mooneyham	.05	.02	.01
□ 549	Bob Melvin	.05	.02	.01
□ 550	Pete Incaviglia	.10	.05	.01
□ 551	Frank Wills	.05	.02	.01
□ 552	Larry Sheets	.05	.02	.01
□ 553	Mike Maddux	.05	.02	.01
□ 554	Buddy Biancalana	.05	.02	.01
□ 555	Dennis Rasmussen	.05	.02	.01
□ 556	Angels Team	.05	.02	.01

	(Rene Lachemann CO, Mike Witt, and Bob Boone)			
□ 557	John Cerutti	.05	.02	.01
□ 558	Greg Gagne	.05	.02	.01
□ 559	Lance McCullers	.05	.02	.01
□ 560	Glenn Davis	.05	.02	.01
□ 561	Rey Quinones	.05	.02	.01
□ 562	Bryan Clutterbuck	.05	.02	.01
□ 563	John Stefero	.05	.02	.01
□ 564	Larry McWilliams	.05	.02	.01
□ 565	Dusty Baker	.10	.05	.01
□ 566	Tim Hulett	.05	.02	.01
□ 567	Greg Mathews	.05	.02	.01
□ 568	Earl Weaver MG (Checklist back)	.15	.07	.02
□ 569	Wade Rowdon	.05	.02	.01
□ 570	Sid Fernandez	.05	.02	.01
□ 571	Ozzie Virgil	.05	.02	.01
□ 572	Pete Ladd	.05	.02	.01
□ 573	Hal McRae	.10	.05	.01
□ 574	Manny Lee	.05	.02	.01
□ 575	Pat Tabler	.05	.02	.01
□ 576	Frank Pastore	.05	.02	.01
□ 577	Dann Bilardello	.05	.02	.01
□ 578	Billy Hatcher	.05	.02	.01
□ 579	Rick Burleson	.05	.02	.01
□ 580	Mike Krukow	.05	.02	.01
□ 581	Cubs Team (Ron Cey and Steve Trout)	.05	.02	.01
□ 582	Bruce Berenyi	.05	.02	.01
□ 583	Junior Ortiz	.05	.02	.01
□ 584	Ron Kittle	.05	.02	.01
□ 585	Scott Bailes	.05	.02	.01
□ 586	Ben Oglivie	.05	.02	.01
□ 587	Eric Plunk	.05	.02	.01
□ 588	Wallace Johnson	.05	.02	.01
□ 589	Steve Crawford	.05	.02	.01
□ 590	Vince Coleman	.05	.02	.01
□ 591	Spike Owen	.05	.02	.01
□ 592	Chris Welsh	.05	.02	.01
□ 593	Chuck Tanner MG (Checklist back)	.10	.05	.01
□ 594	Rick Anderson	.05	.02	.01
□ 595	Keith Hernandez AS	.10	.05	.01
□ 596	Steve Sax AS	.05	.02	.01
□ 597	Mike Schmidt AS	.15	.07	.02
□ 598	Ozzie Smith AS	.15	.07	.02
□ 599	Tony Gwynn AS	.20	.09	.03
□ 600	Dave Parker AS	.10	.05	.01
□ 601	Darryl Strawberry AS	.15	.07	.02
□ 602	Gary Carter AS	.10	.05	.01
□ 603A	Dwight Gooden AS ERR (no trademark)	.10	.05	.01
□ 603B	Dwight Gooden AS COR	.15	.07	.02
□ 604	Fernando Valenzuela AS	.10	.05	.01
□ 605	Todd Worrell AS	.10	.05	.01
□ 606	Don Mattingly AS COR	.25	.11	.03
□ 606A	Don Mattingly AS ERR (no trademark)	.75	.35	.09
□ 607	Tony Bernazard AS	.05	.02	.01
□ 608	Wade Boggs AS	.15	.07	.02
□ 609	Cal Ripken AS	.50	.23	.06
□ 610	Jim Rice AS	.10	.05	.01
□ 611	Kirby Puckett AS	.40	.18	.05
□ 612	George Bell AS	.05	.02	.01
□ 613	Lance Parrish AS UER (Pitcher heading on back)	.10	.05	.01
□ 614	Roger Clemens AS	.15	.07	.02
□ 615	Teddy Higuera AS	.05	.02	.01
□ 616	Dave Righetti AS	.05	.02	.01
□ 617	Al Nipper	.05	.02	.01
□ 618	Tom Kelly MG (Checklist back)	.10	.05	.01
□ 619	Jerry Reed	.05	.02	.01
□ 620	Jose Canseco	.60	.25	.07
□ 621	Danny Cox	.05	.02	.01
□ 622	Glenn Braggs	.05	.02	.01
□ 623	Kurt Stillwell	.05	.02	.01
□ 624	Tim Burke	.05	.02	.01
□ 625	Mookie Wilson	.10	.05	.01
□ 626	Joel Skinner	.05	.02	.01
□ 627	Ken Oberkfell	.05	.02	.01
□ 628	Bob Walk	.05	.02	.01
□ 629	Larry Parrish	.05	.02	.01
□ 630	John Candelaria	.05	.02	.01
□ 631	Tigers Team (Mound conference)	.05	.02	.01
□ 632	Rob Woodward	.05	.02	.01
□ 633	Jose Uribe	.05	.02	.01
□ 634	Rafael Palmeiro	1.00	.45	.12
□ 635	Ken Schrom	.05	.02	.01
□ 636	Darren Daulton	.10	.05	.01
□ 637	Bip Roberts	.15	.07	.02
□ 638	Rich Bordi	.05	.02	.01
□ 639	Gerald Perry	.05	.02	.01
□ 640	Mark Clear	.05	.02	.01
□ 641	Domingo Ramos	.05	.02	.01
□ 642	Al Pulido	.05	.02	.01
□ 643	Ron Shepherd	.05	.02	.01
□ 644	John Denny	.05	.02	.01
□ 645	Dwight Evans	.10	.05	.01
□ 646	Mike Mason	.05	.02	.01
□ 647	Tom Lawless	.05	.02	.01
□ 648	Barry Larkin	1.00	.45	.12
□ 649	Mickey Tettleton	.10	.05	.01
□ 650	Hubie Brooks	.05	.02	.01
□ 651	Benny Distefano	.05	.02	.01
□ 652	Terry Forster	.05	.02	.01
□ 653	Kevin Mitchell	.15	.07	.02
□ 654	Checklist 529-660	.10	.05	.01
□ 655	Jesse Barfield	.05	.02	.01
□ 656	Rangers Team (Bobby Valentine MG and Ricky Wright)	.05	.02	.01
□ 657	Tom Waddell	.05	.02	.01
□ 658	Robby Thompson	.10	.05	.01
□ 659	Aurelio Lopez	.05	.02	.01
□ 660	Bob Horner	.05	.02	.01
□ 661	Lou Whitaker	.15	.07	.02
□ 662	Frank DiPino	.05	.02	.01
□ 663	Cliff Johnson	.05	.02	.01
□ 664	Mike Marshall	.05	.02	.01
□ 665	Rod Scurry	.05	.02	.01
□ 666	Von Hayes	.05	.02	.01
□ 667	Ron Hassey	.05	.02	.01
□ 668	Juan Bonilla	.05	.02	.01
□ 669	Bud Black	.05	.02	.01
□ 670	Jose Cruz	.05	.02	.01
□ 671A	Ray Soff ERR (No D* before copyright line)	.05	.02	.01
□ 671B	Ray Soff COR (D* before copyright line)	.05	.02	.01
□ 672	Chili Davis	.10	.05	.01
□ 673	Don Sutton	.15	.07	.02
□ 674	Bill Campbell	.05	.02	.01
□ 675	Ed Romero	.05	.02	.01
□ 676	Charlie Moore	.05	.02	.01
□ 677	Bob Grich	.10	.05	.01
□ 678	Carney Lansford	.10	.05	.01
□ 679	Kent Hrbek	.15	.07	.02
□ 680	Ryne Sandberg	.25	.11	.03
□ 681	George Bell	.05	.02	.01
□ 682	Jerry Reuss	.05	.02	.01
□ 683	Gary Roenicke	.05	.02	.01
□ 684	Kent Tekulve	.05	.02	.01
□ 685	Jerry Hairston	.05	.02	.01
□ 686	Doyle Alexander	.05	.02	.01
□ 687	Alan Trammell	.15	.07	.02
□ 688	Juan Beniquez	.05	.02	.01
□ 689	Darrell Porter	.05	.02	.01
□ 690	Dane Iorg	.05	.02	.01
□ 691	Dave Parker	.15	.07	.02
□ 692	Frank White	.10	.05	.01
□ 693	Terry Puhl	.05	.02	.01
□ 694	Phil Niekro	.15	.07	.02
□ 695	Chico Walker	.05	.02	.01
□ 696	Gary Lucas	.05	.02	.01
□ 697	Ed Lynch	.05	.02	.01
□ 698	Ernie Whitt	.05	.02	.01
□ 699	Ken Landreaux	.05	.02	.01
□ 700	Dave Bergman	.05	.02	.01
□ 701	Willie Randolph	.10	.05	.01
□ 702	Greg Gross	.05	.02	.01
□ 703	Dave Schmidt	.05	.02	.01
□ 704	Jesse Orosco	.05	.02	.01
□ 705	Bruce Hurst	.05	.02	.01
□ 706	Rick Manning	.05	.02	.01

□ 707 Bob McClure	.05	.02	.01
□ 708 Scott McGregor	.05	.02	.01
□ 709 Dave Kingman	.10	.05	.01
□ 710 Gary Gaetti	.05	.02	.01
□ 711 Ken Griffey	.05	.02	.01
□ 712 Don Robinson	.05	.02	.01
□ 713 Tom Brookens	.05	.02	.01
□ 714 Dan Quisenberry	.05	.02	.01
□ 715 Bob Dernier	.05	.02	.01
□ 716 Rick Leach	.05	.02	.01
□ 717 Ed VandeBerg	.05	.02	.01
□ 718 Steve Carlton	.15	.07	.02
□ 719 Tom Hume	.05	.02	.01
□ 720 Richard Dotson	.05	.02	.01
□ 721 Tom Herr	.05	.02	.01
□ 722 Bob Knepper	.05	.02	.01
□ 723 Brett Butler	.10	.05	.01
□ 724 Greg Minton	.05	.02	.01
□ 725 George Hendrick	.05	.02	.01
□ 726 Frank Tanana	.05	.02	.01
□ 727 Mike Moore	.05	.02	.01
□ 728 Tippy Martinez	.05	.02	.01
□ 729 Tom Paciorek	.05	.02	.01
□ 730 Eric Show	.05	.02	.01
□ 731 Dave Concepcion	.10	.05	.01
□ 732 Manny Trillo	.05	.02	.01
□ 733 Bill Caudill	.05	.02	.01
□ 734 Bill Madlock	.05	.02	.01
□ 735 Rickey Henderson	.15	.07	.02
□ 736 Steve Bedrosian	.05	.02	.01
□ 737 Floyd Bannister	.05	.02	.01
□ 738 Jorge Orta	.05	.02	.01
□ 739 Chet Lemon	.05	.02	.01
□ 740 Rich Gedman	.05	.02	.01
□ 741 Paul Molitor	.20	.09	.03
□ 742 Andy McGaffigan	.05	.02	.01
□ 743 Dwayne Murphy	.05	.02	.01
□ 744 Roy Smalley	.05	.02	.01
□ 745 Glenn Hubbard	.05	.02	.01
□ 746 Bob Ojeda	.05	.02	.01
□ 747 Johnny Ray	.05	.02	.01
□ 748 Mike Flanagan	.05	.02	.01
□ 749 Ozzie Smith	.20	.09	.03
□ 750 Steve Trout	.05	.02	.01
□ 751 Garth Iorg	.05	.02	.01
□ 752 Dan Petry	.05	.02	.01
□ 753 Rick Honeycutt	.05	.02	.01
□ 754 Dave LaPoint	.05	.02	.01
□ 755 Luis Aguayo	.05	.02	.01
□ 756 Carlton Fisk	.15	.07	.02
□ 757 Nolan Ryan	.75	.35	.09
□ 758 Tony Bernazard	.05	.02	.01
□ 759 Joel Youngblood	.05	.02	.01
□ 760 Mike Witt	.05	.02	.01
□ 761 Greg Pryor	.05	.02	.01
□ 762 Gary Ward	.05	.02	.01
□ 763 Tim Flannery	.05	.02	.01
□ 764 Bill Buckner	.10	.05	.01
□ 765 Kirk Gibson	.15	.07	.02
□ 766 Don Aase	.05	.02	.01
□ 767 Ron Cey	.10	.05	.01
□ 768 Dennis Lamp	.05	.02	.01
□ 769 Steve Sax	.05	.02	.01
□ 770 Dave Winfield	.15	.07	.02
□ 771 Shane Rawley	.05	.02	.01
□ 772 Harold Baines	.10	.05	.01
□ 773 Robin Yount	.15	.07	.02
□ 774 Wayne Krenchicki	.05	.02	.01
□ 775 Joaquin Andujar	.05	.02	.01
□ 776 Tom Brunansky	.05	.02	.01
□ 777 Chris Chambliss	.05	.02	.01
□ 778 Jack Morris	.10	.05	.01
□ 779 Craig Reynolds	.05	.02	.01
□ 780 Andre Thornton	.05	.02	.01
□ 781 Atlee Hammaker	.05	.02	.01
□ 782 Brian Downing	.05	.02	.01
□ 783 Willie Wilson	.05	.02	.01
□ 784 Cal Ripken	.75	.35	.09
□ 785 Terry Francona	.05	.02	.01
□ 786 Jimy Williams MG (Checklist back)	.10	.05	.01
□ 787 Alejandro Pena	.05	.02	.01
□ 788 Tim Stoddard	.05	.02	.01
□ 789 Dan Schatzeder	.05	.02	.01
□ 790 Julio Cruz	.05	.02	.01
□ 791 Lance Parrish UER (No trademark, never corrected)	.10	.05	.01
□ 792 Checklist 661-792	.10	.05	.01

1987 Topps Traded

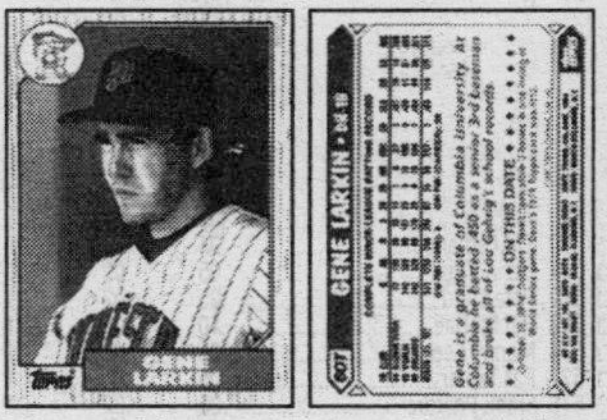

This 132-card standard-size Traded set was distributed exclusively in factory set form in a special green and white box through hobby dealers. The card fronts are identical in style to the Topps regular issue except for whiter stock and t-suffixed numbering on back. The cards are ordered alphabetically by player's last name. The key extended Rookie Cards in this set are Ellis Burks, David Cone, Greg Maddux, Fred McGriff and Matt Williams.

	MINT	NRMT	EXC
COMPLETE FACT.SET (132)	8.00	3.60	1.00
COMMON CARD (1T-132T)	.05	.02	.01
SEMISTARS	.10	.05	.01
□ 1T Bill Almon	.05	.02	.01
□ 2T Scott Bankhead	.05	.02	.01
□ 3T Eric Bell	.05	.02	.01
□ 4T Juan Beniquez	.05	.02	.01
□ 5T Juan Berenguer	.05	.02	.01
□ 6T Greg Booker	.05	.02	.01
□ 7T Thad Bosley	.05	.02	.01
□ 8T Larry Bowa MG	.10	.05	.01
□ 9T Greg Brock	.05	.02	.01
□ 10T Bob Brower	.05	.02	.01
□ 11T Jerry Browne	.05	.02	.01
□ 12T Ralph Bryant	.05	.02	.01
□ 13T DeWayne Buice	.05	.02	.01
□ 14T Ellis Burks	.50	.23	.06
□ 15T Ivan Calderon	.05	.02	.01
□ 16T Jeff Calhoun	.05	.02	.01
□ 17T Casey Candaele	.05	.02	.01
□ 18T John Cangelosi	.05	.02	.01
□ 19T Steve Carlton	.15	.07	.02
□ 20T Juan Castillo	.05	.02	.01
□ 21T Rick Cerone	.05	.02	.01
□ 22T Ron Cey	.10	.05	.01
□ 23T John Christensen	.05	.02	.01
□ 24T David Cone	.50	.23	.06
□ 25T Chuck Crim	.05	.02	.01
□ 26T Storm Davis	.05	.02	.01
□ 27T Andre Dawson	.15	.07	.02
□ 28T Rick Dempsey	.10	.05	.01
□ 29T Doug Drabek	.15	.07	.02
□ 30T Mike Dunne	.05	.02	.01
□ 31T Dennis Eckersley	.10	.05	.01
□ 32T Lee Elia MG	.05	.02	.01
□ 33T Brian Fisher	.05	.02	.01
□ 34T Terry Francona	.05	.02	.01
□ 35T Willie Fraser	.05	.02	.01
□ 36T Billy Gardner MG	.05	.02	.01
□ 37T Ken Gerhart	.05	.02	.01
□ 38T Dan Gladden	.05	.02	.01
□ 39T Jim Gott	.05	.02	.01
□ 40T Cecilio Guante	.05	.02	.01
□ 41T Albert Hall	.05	.02	.01
□ 42T Terry Harper	.05	.02	.01
□ 43T Mickey Hatcher	.05	.02	.01
□ 44T Brad Havens	.05	.02	.01
□ 45T Neal Heaton	.05	.02	.01
□ 46T Mike Henneman	.15	.07	.02

□ 47T Donnie Hill	.05	.02	.01
□ 48T Guy Hoffman	.05	.02	.01
□ 49T Brian Holton	.05	.02	.01
□ 50T Charles Hudson	.05	.02	.01
□ 51T Danny Jackson	.05	.02	.01
□ 52T Reggie Jackson	.20	.09	.03
□ 53T Chris James	.05	.02	.01
□ 54T Dion James	.05	.02	.01
□ 55T Stan Jefferson	.05	.02	.01
□ 56T Joe Johnson	.05	.02	.01
□ 57T Terry Kennedy	.05	.02	.01
□ 58T Mike Kingery	.10	.05	.01
□ 59T Ray Knight	.10	.05	.01
□ 60T Gene Larkin	.05	.02	.01
□ 61T Mike LaValliere	.05	.02	.01
□ 62T Jack Lazorko	.05	.02	.01
□ 63T Terry Leach	.05	.02	.01
□ 64T Tim Leary	.05	.02	.01
□ 65T Jim Lindeman	.05	.02	.01
□ 66T Steve Lombardozzi	.05	.02	.01
□ 67T Bill Long	.05	.02	.01
□ 68T Barry Lyons	.05	.02	.01
□ 69T Shane Mack	.10	.05	.01
□ 70T Greg Maddux	5.00	2.20	.60
□ 71T Bill Madlock	.05	.02	.01
□ 72T Joe Magrane	.05	.02	.01
□ 73T Dave Martinez	.10	.05	.01
□ 74T Fred McGriff	1.00	.45	.12
□ 75T Mark McLemore	.05	.02	.01
□ 76T Kevin McReynolds	.05	.02	.01
□ 77T Dave Meads	.05	.02	.01
□ 78T Eddie Milner	.05	.02	.01
□ 79T Greg Minton	.05	.02	.01
□ 80T John Mitchell	.05	.02	.01
□ 81T Kevin Mitchell	.15	.07	.02
□ 82T Charlie Moore	.05	.02	.01
□ 83T Jeff Musselman	.05	.02	.01
□ 84T Gene Nelson	.05	.02	.01
□ 85T Graig Nettles	.10	.05	.01
□ 86T Al Newman	.05	.02	.01
□ 87T Reid Nichols	.05	.02	.01
□ 88T Tom Niedenfuer	.05	.02	.01
□ 89T Joe Niekro	.05	.02	.01
□ 90T Tom Nieto	.05	.02	.01
□ 91T Matt Nokes	.10	.05	.01
□ 92T Dickie Noles	.05	.02	.01
□ 93T Pat Pacillo	.05	.02	.01
□ 94T Lance Parrish	.10	.05	.01
□ 95T Tony Pena	.05	.02	.01
□ 96T Luis Polonia	.15	.07	.02
□ 97T Randy Ready	.05	.02	.01
□ 98T Jeff Reardon	.10	.05	.01
□ 99T Gary Redus	.05	.02	.01
□ 100T Jeff Reed	.05	.02	.01
□ 101T Rick Rhoden	.05	.02	.01
□ 102T Cal Ripken Sr. MG	.10	.05	.01
□ 103T Wally Ritchie	.05	.02	.01
□ 104T Jeff M. Robinson	.05	.02	.01
□ 105T Gary Roenicke	.05	.02	.01
□ 106T Jerry Royster	.05	.02	.01
□ 107T Mark Salas	.05	.02	.01
□ 108T Luis Salazar	.05	.02	.01
□ 109T Benny Santiago	.10	.05	.01
□ 110T Dave Schmidt	.05	.02	.01
□ 111T Kevin Seitzer	.10	.05	.01
□ 112T John Shelby	.05	.02	.01
□ 113T Steve Shields	.05	.02	.01
□ 114T John Smiley	.10	.05	.01
□ 115T Chris Speier	.05	.02	.01
□ 116T Mike Stanley	.15	.07	.02
□ 117T Terry Steinbach	.25	.11	.03
□ 118T Les Straker	.05	.02	.01
□ 119T Jim Sundberg	.05	.02	.01
□ 120T Danny Tartabull	.10	.05	.01
□ 121T Tom Trebelhorn MG	.05	.02	.01
□ 122T Dave Valle	.05	.02	.01
□ 123T Ed VandeBerg	.05	.02	.01
□ 124T Andy Van Slyke	.10	.05	.01
□ 125T Gary Ward	.05	.02	.01
□ 126T Alan Wiggins	.05	.02	.01
□ 127T Bill Wilkinson	.05	.02	.01
□ 128T Frank Williams	.05	.02	.01
□ 129T Matt Williams	2.00	.90	.25
□ 130T Jim Winn	.05	.02	.01
□ 131T Matt Young	.05	.02	.01
□ 132T Checklist 1T-132T	.05	.02	.01

1988 Topps

This set consists of 792 standard-size cards. The cards were primarily issued in 15-card wax packs, 42-card rack packs and factory sets. Card fronts feature white borders encasing a color photo with team name running across the top and player name diagonally across the bottom. Subsets include Record Breakers (1-7), All-Stars (386-407), Turn Back the Clock (661-665), and Team Leaders (scattered throughout the set). The manager cards contain a team checklist on back. The key Rookie Cards in this set are Ellis Burks, Ken Caminiti, Tom Glavine, Jeff Montgomery, and Matt Williams.

	MINT	NRMT	EXC
COMPLETE SET (792)	10.00	4.50	1.25
COMPLETE FACT.SET (792)	12.00	5.50	1.50
COMMON CARD (1-792)	.05	.02	.01
SEMISTARS	.10	.05	.01
STARS	.15	.07	.02

□ 1 Vince Coleman RB 100 Steals for Third Cons. Season	.05	.02	.01
□ 2 Don Mattingly RB Six Grand Slams	.15	.07	.02
□ 3 Mark McGwire RB Rookie Homer Record (No white spot)	.30	.14	.04
□ 3A Mark McGwire RB Rookie Homer Record (White spot behind left foot)	.15	.07	.02
□ 4 Eddie Murray RB Switch Home Runs, Two Straight Games (No caption on front)	.20	.09	.03
□ 4A Eddie Murray RB Switch Home Runs, Two Straight Games (Caption in box on card front)	.40	.18	.05
□ 5 Phil Niekro Joe Niekro RB Brothers Win Record	.10	.05	.01
□ 6 Nolan Ryan RB 11th 200 K's Season	.40	.18	.05
□ 7 Benito Santiago RB 34-Game Hitting Streak, Rookie Record	.05	.02	.01
□ 8 Kevin Elster	.15	.07	.02
□ 9 Andy Hawkins	.05	.02	.01
□ 10 Ryne Sandberg	.25	.11	.03
□ 11 Mike Young	.05	.02	.01
□ 12 Bill Schroeder	.05	.02	.01
□ 13 Andres Thomas	.05	.02	.01
□ 14 Sparky Anderson MG (Checklist back)	.10	.05	.01
□ 15 Chili Davis	.15	.07	.02
□ 16 Kirk McCaskill	.05	.02	.01
□ 17 Ron Oester	.05	.02	.01
□ 18A Al Leiter ERR (Photo actually Steve George, right ear visible)	.15	.07	.02
□ 18B Al Leiter COR (Left ear visible)	.10	.05	.01

□ 19 Mark Davidson	.05	.02	.01
□ 20 Kevin Gross	.05	.02	.01
□ 21 Red Sox TL	.10	.05	.01
Wade Boggs and			
Spike Owen			
□ 22 Greg Swindell	.05	.02	.01
□ 23 Ken Landreaux	.05	.02	.01
□ 24 Jim Deshaies	.05	.02	.01
□ 25 Andres Galarraga	.15	.07	.02
□ 26 Mitch Williams	.10	.05	.01
□ 27 R.J. Reynolds	.05	.02	.01
□ 28 Jose Nunez	.05	.02	.01
□ 29 Argenis Salazar	.05	.02	.01
□ 30 Sid Fernandez	.05	.02	.01
□ 31 Bruce Bochy	.05	.02	.01
□ 32 Mike Morgan	.05	.02	.01
□ 33 Rob Deer	.05	.02	.01
□ 34 Ricky Horton	.05	.02	.01
□ 35 Harold Baines	.10	.05	.01
□ 36 Jamie Moyer	.05	.02	.01
□ 37 Ed Romero	.05	.02	.01
□ 38 Jeff Calhoun	.05	.02	.01
□ 39 Gerald Perry	.05	.02	.01
□ 40 Orel Hershiser	.15	.07	.02
□ 41 Bob Melvin	.05	.02	.01
□ 42 Bill Landrum	.05	.02	.01
□ 43 Dick Schofield	.05	.02	.01
□ 44 Lou Piniella MG	.10	.05	.01
(Checklist back)			
□ 45 Kent Hrbek	.10	.05	.01
□ 46 Darnell Coles	.05	.02	.01
□ 47 Joaquin Andujar	.05	.02	.01
□ 48 Alan Ashby	.05	.02	.01
□ 49 Dave Clark	.05	.02	.01
□ 50 Hubie Brooks	.05	.02	.01
□ 51 Orioles TL	.40	.18	.05
Eddie Murray and			
Cal Ripken			
□ 52 Don Robinson	.05	.02	.01
□ 53 Curt Wilkerson	.05	.02	.01
□ 54 Jim Clancy	.05	.02	.01
□ 55 Phil Bradley	.05	.02	.01
□ 56 Ed Hearn	.05	.02	.01
□ 57 Tim Crews	.10	.05	.01
□ 58 Dave Magadan	.05	.02	.01
□ 59 Danny Cox	.05	.02	.01
□ 60 Rickey Henderson	.15	.07	.02
□ 61 Mark Knudson	.05	.02	.01
□ 62 Jeff Hamilton	.05	.02	.01
□ 63 Jimmy Jones	.05	.02	.01
□ 64 Ken Caminiti	.75	.35	.09
□ 65 Leon Durham	.05	.02	.01
□ 66 Shane Rawley	.05	.02	.01
□ 67 Ken Oberkfell	.05	.02	.01
□ 68 Dave Dravecky	.10	.05	.01
□ 69 Mike Hart	.05	.02	.01
□ 70 Roger Clemens	.15	.07	.02
□ 71 Gary Pettis	.05	.02	.01
□ 72 Dennis Eckersley	.15	.07	.02
□ 73 Randy Bush	.05	.02	.01
□ 74 Tom Lasorda MG	.10	.05	.01
(Checklist back)			
□ 75 Joe Carter	.15	.07	.02
□ 76 Dennis Martinez	.10	.05	.01
□ 77 Tom O'Malley	.05	.02	.01
□ 78 Dan Petry	.05	.02	.01
□ 79 Ernie Whitt	.05	.02	.01
□ 80 Mark Langston	.10	.05	.01
□ 81 Reds TL	.05	.02	.01
Ron Robinson			
and John Franco			
□ 82 Darrel Akerfelds	.05	.02	.01
□ 83 Jose Oquendo	.05	.02	.01
□ 84 Cecilio Guante	.05	.02	.01
□ 85 Howard Johnson	.05	.02	.01
□ 86 Ron Karkovice	.05	.02	.01
□ 87 Mike Mason	.05	.02	.01
□ 88 Earnie Riles	.05	.02	.01
□ 89 Gary Thurman	.05	.02	.01
□ 90 Dale Murphy	.15	.07	.02
□ 91 Joey Cora	.15	.07	.02
□ 92 Len Matuszek	.05	.02	.01
□ 93 Bob Sebra	.05	.02	.01
□ 94 Chuck Jackson	.05	.02	.01
□ 95 Lance Parrish	.05	.02	.01
□ 96 Todd Benzinger	.10	.05	.01
□ 97 Scott Garrelts	.05	.02	.01
□ 98 Rene Gonzales	.05	.02	.01
□ 99 Chuck Finley	.10	.05	.01
□ 100 Jack Clark	.10	.05	.01
□ 101 Allan Anderson	.05	.02	.01
□ 102 Barry Larkin	.30	.14	.04
□ 103 Curt Young	.05	.02	.01
□ 104 Dick Williams MG	.10	.05	.01
(Checklist back)			
□ 105 Jesse Orosco	.05	.02	.01
□ 106 Jim Walewander	.05	.02	.01
□ 107 Scott Bailes	.05	.02	.01
□ 108 Steve Lyons	.05	.02	.01
□ 109 Joel Skinner	.05	.02	.01
□ 110 Teddy Higuera	.05	.02	.01
□ 111 Expos TL	.05	.02	.01
Hubie Brooks and			
Vance Law			
□ 112 Les Lancaster	.05	.02	.01
□ 113 Kelly Gruber	.05	.02	.01
□ 114 Jeff Russell	.05	.02	.01
□ 115 Johnny Ray	.05	.02	.01
□ 116 Jerry Don Gleaton	.05	.02	.01
□ 117 James Steels	.05	.02	.01
□ 118 Bob Welch	.05	.02	.01
□ 119 Robbie Wine	.05	.02	.01
□ 120 Kirby Puckett	.30	.14	.04
□ 121 Checklist 1-132	.10	.05	.01
□ 122 Tony Bernazard	.05	.02	.01
□ 123 Tom Candiotti	.05	.02	.01
□ 124 Ray Knight	.10	.05	.01
□ 125 Bruce Hurst	.05	.02	.01
□ 126 Steve Jeltz	.05	.02	.01
□ 127 Jim Gott	.05	.02	.01
□ 128 Johnny Grubb	.05	.02	.01
□ 129 Greg Minton	.05	.02	.01
□ 130 Buddy Bell	.10	.05	.01
□ 131 Don Schulze	.05	.02	.01
□ 132 Donnie Hill	.05	.02	.01
□ 133 Greg Mathews	.05	.02	.01
□ 134 Chuck Tanner MG	.10	.05	.01
(Checklist back)			
□ 135 Dennis Rasmussen	.05	.02	.01
□ 136 Brian Dayett	.05	.02	.01
□ 137 Chris Bosio	.05	.02	.01
□ 138 Mitch Webster	.05	.02	.01
□ 139 Jerry Browne	.05	.02	.01
□ 140 Jesse Barfield	.05	.02	.01
□ 141 Royals TL	.15	.07	.02
George Brett and			
Bret Saberhagen			
□ 142 Andy Van Slyke	.10	.05	.01
□ 143 Mickey Tettleton	.10	.05	.01
□ 144 Don Gordon	.05	.02	.01
□ 145 Bill Madlock	.05	.02	.01
□ 146 Donell Nixon	.05	.02	.01
□ 147 Bill Buckner	.10	.05	.01
□ 148 Carmelo Martinez	.05	.02	.01
□ 149 Ken Howell	.05	.02	.01
□ 150 Eric Davis	.10	.05	.01
□ 151 Bob Knepper	.05	.02	.01
□ 152 Jody Reed	.10	.05	.01
□ 153 John Habyan	.05	.02	.01
□ 154 Jeff Stone	.05	.02	.01
□ 155 Bruce Sutter	.10	.05	.01
□ 156 Gary Matthews	.05	.02	.01
□ 157 Atlee Hammaker	.05	.02	.01
□ 158 Tim Hulett	.05	.02	.01
□ 159 Brad Arnsberg	.05	.02	.01
□ 160 Willie McGee	.05	.02	.01
□ 161 Bryn Smith	.05	.02	.01
□ 162 Mark McLemore	.05	.02	.01
□ 163 Dale Mohorcic	.05	.02	.01
□ 164 Dave Johnson MG	.10	.05	.01
(Checklist back)			
□ 165 Robin Yount	.15	.07	.02
□ 166 Rick Rodriquez	.05	.02	.01
□ 167 Rance Mulliniks	.05	.02	.01
□ 168 Barry Jones	.05	.02	.01
□ 169 Ross Jones	.05	.02	.01
□ 170 Rich Gossage	.15	.07	.02
□ 171 Cubs TL	.05	.02	.01
Shawon Dunston			
and Manny Trillo			
□ 172 Lloyd McClendon	.05	.02	.01
□ 173 Eric Plunk	.05	.02	.01

□ 174	Phil Garner	.05	.02	.01
□ 175	Kevin Bass	.05	.02	.01
□ 176	Jeff Reed	.05	.02	.01
□ 177	Frank Tanana	.05	.02	.01
□ 178	Dwayne Henry	.05	.02	.01
□ 179	Charlie Puleo	.05	.02	.01
□ 180	Terry Kennedy	.05	.02	.01
□ 181	David Cone	.15	.07	.02
□ 182	Ken Phelps	.05	.02	.01
□ 183	Tom Lawless	.05	.02	.01
□ 184	Ivan Calderon	.05	.02	.01
□ 185	Rick Rhoden	.05	.02	.01
□ 186	Rafael Palmeiro	.25	.11	.03
□ 187	Steve Kiefer	.05	.02	.01
□ 188	John Russell	.05	.02	.01
□ 189	Wes Gardner	.05	.02	.01
□ 190	Candy Maldonado	.05	.02	.01
□ 191	John Cerutti	.05	.02	.01
□ 192	Devon White	.15	.07	.02
□ 193	Brian Fisher	.05	.02	.01
□ 194	Tom Kelly MG (Checklist back)	.10	.05	.01
□ 195	Dan Quisenberry	.05	.02	.01
□ 196	Dave Engle	.05	.02	.01
□ 197	Lance McCullers	.05	.02	.01
□ 198	Franklin Stubbs	.05	.02	.01
□ 199	Dave Meads	.05	.02	.01
□ 200	Wade Boggs	.15	.07	.02
□ 201	Rangers TL Bobby Valentine MG, Pete O'Brien, Pete Incaviglia, and Steve Buechele	.05	.02	.01
□ 202	Glenn Hoffman	.05	.02	.01
□ 203	Fred Toliver	.05	.02	.01
□ 204	Paul O'Neill	.15	.07	.02
□ 205	Nelson Liriano	.05	.02	.01
□ 206	Domingo Ramos	.05	.02	.01
□ 207	John Mitchell	.05	.02	.01
□ 208	Steve Lake	.05	.02	.01
□ 209	Richard Dotson	.05	.02	.01
□ 210	Willie Randolph	.10	.05	.01
□ 211	Frank DiPino	.05	.02	.01
□ 212	Greg Brock	.05	.02	.01
□ 213	Albert Hall	.05	.02	.01
□ 214	Dave Schmidt	.05	.02	.01
□ 215	Von Hayes	.05	.02	.01
□ 216	Jerry Reuss	.05	.02	.01
□ 217	Harry Spilman	.05	.02	.01
□ 218	Dan Schatzeder	.05	.02	.01
□ 219	Mike Stanley	.10	.05	.01
□ 220	Tom Henke	.05	.02	.01
□ 221	Rafael Belliard	.05	.02	.01
□ 222	Steve Farr	.05	.02	.01
□ 223	Stan Jefferson	.05	.02	.01
□ 224	Tom Trebelhorn MG (Checklist back)	.05	.02	.01
□ 225	Mike Scioscia	.05	.02	.01
□ 226	Dave Lopes	.10	.05	.01
□ 227	Ed Correa	.05	.02	.01
□ 228	Wallace Johnson	.05	.02	.01
□ 229	Jeff Musselman	.05	.02	.01
□ 230	Pat Tabler	.05	.02	.01
□ 231	Pirates TL Barry Bonds and Bobby Bonilla	.15	.07	.02
□ 232	Bob James	.05	.02	.01
□ 233	Rafael Santana	.05	.02	.01
□ 234	Ken Dayley	.05	.02	.01
□ 235	Gary Ward	.05	.02	.01
□ 236	Ted Power	.05	.02	.01
□ 237	Mike Heath	.05	.02	.01
□ 238	Luis Polonia	.15	.07	.02
□ 239	Roy Smalley	.05	.02	.01
□ 240	Lee Smith	.15	.07	.02
□ 241	Damaso Garcia	.05	.02	.01
□ 242	Tom Niedenfuer	.05	.02	.01
□ 243	Mark Ryal	.05	.02	.01
□ 244	Jeff D. Robinson	.05	.02	.01
□ 245	Rich Gedman	.05	.02	.01
□ 246	Mike Campbell	.05	.02	.01
□ 247	Thad Bosley	.05	.02	.01
□ 248	Storm Davis	.05	.02	.01
□ 249	Mike Marshall	.05	.02	.01
□ 250	Nolan Ryan	.75	.35	.09
□ 251	Tom Foley	.05	.02	.01
□ 252	Bob Brower	.05	.02	.01
□ 253	Checklist 133-264	.10	.05	.01
□ 254	Lee Elia MG (Checklist back)	.05	.02	.01
□ 255	Mookie Wilson	.10	.05	.01
□ 256	Ken Schrom	.05	.02	.01
□ 257	Jerry Royster	.05	.02	.01
□ 258	Ed Nunez	.05	.02	.01
□ 259	Ron Kittle	.05	.02	.01
□ 260	Vince Coleman	.05	.02	.01
□ 261	Giants TL (Five players)	.05	.02	.01
□ 262	Drew Hall	.05	.02	.01
□ 263	Glenn Braggs	.05	.02	.01
□ 264	Les Straker	.05	.02	.01
□ 265	Bo Diaz	.05	.02	.01
□ 266	Paul Assenmacher	.05	.02	.01
□ 267	Billy Bean	.05	.02	.01
□ 268	Bruce Ruffin	.05	.02	.01
□ 269	Ellis Burks	.40	.18	.05
□ 270	Mike Witt	.05	.02	.01
□ 271	Ken Gerhart	.05	.02	.01
□ 272	Steve Ontiveros	.05	.02	.01
□ 273	Garth Iorg	.05	.02	.01
□ 274	Junior Ortiz	.05	.02	.01
□ 275	Kevin Seitzer	.10	.05	.01
□ 276	Luis Salazar	.05	.02	.01
□ 277	Alejandro Pena	.05	.02	.01
□ 278	Jose Cruz	.05	.02	.01
□ 279	Randy St.Claire	.05	.02	.01
□ 280	Pete Incaviglia	.05	.02	.01
□ 281	Jerry Hairston	.05	.02	.01
□ 282	Pat Perry	.05	.02	.01
□ 283	Phil Lombardi	.05	.02	.01
□ 284	Larry Bowa MG (Checklist back)	.10	.05	.01
□ 285	Jim Presley	.05	.02	.01
□ 286	Chuck Crim	.05	.02	.01
□ 287	Manny Trillo	.05	.02	.01
□ 288	Pat Pacillo (Chris Sabo in background of photo)	.05	.02	.01
□ 289	Dave Bergman	.05	.02	.01
□ 290	Tony Fernandez	.05	.02	.01
□ 291	Astros TL Billy Hatcher and Kevin Bass	.05	.02	.01
□ 292	Carney Lansford	.10	.05	.01
□ 293	Doug Jones	.10	.05	.01
□ 294	Al Pedrique	.05	.02	.01
□ 295	Bert Blyleven	.10	.05	.01
□ 296	Floyd Rayford	.05	.02	.01
□ 297	Zane Smith	.05	.02	.01
□ 298	Milt Thompson	.05	.02	.01
□ 299	Steve Crawford	.05	.02	.01
□ 300	Don Mattingly	.50	.23	.06
□ 301	Bud Black	.05	.02	.01
□ 302	Jose Uribe	.05	.02	.01
□ 303	Eric Show	.05	.02	.01
□ 304	George Hendrick	.05	.02	.01
□ 305	Steve Sax	.05	.02	.01
□ 306	Billy Hatcher	.05	.02	.01
□ 307	Mike Trujillo	.05	.02	.01
□ 308	Lee Mazzilli	.05	.02	.01
□ 309	Bill Long	.05	.02	.01
□ 310	Tom Herr	.05	.02	.01
□ 311	Scott Sanderson	.05	.02	.01
□ 312	Joey Meyer	.05	.02	.01
□ 313	Bob McClure	.05	.02	.01
□ 314	Jimy Williams MG (Checklist back)	.05	.02	.01
□ 315	Dave Parker	.15	.07	.02
□ 316	Jose Rijo	.05	.02	.01
□ 317	Tom Nieto	.05	.02	.01
□ 318	Mel Hall	.05	.02	.01
□ 319	Mike Loynd	.05	.02	.01
□ 320	Alan Trammell	.15	.07	.02
□ 321	White Sox TL Harold Baines and Carlton Fisk	.10	.05	.01
□ 322	Vicente Palacios	.05	.02	.01
□ 323	Rick Leach	.05	.02	.01
□ 324	Danny Jackson	.05	.02	.01
□ 325	Glenn Hubbard	.05	.02	.01
□ 326	Al Nipper	.05	.02	.01
□ 327	Larry Sheets	.05	.02	.01

☐ 328	Greg Cadaret	.05	.02	.01
☐ 329	Chris Speier	.05	.02	.01
☐ 330	Eddie Whitson	.05	.02	.01
☐ 331	Brian Downing	.05	.02	.01
☐ 332	Jerry Reed	.05	.02	.01
☐ 333	Wally Backman	.05	.02	.01
☐ 334	Dave LaPoint	.05	.02	.01
☐ 335	Claudell Washington	.05	.02	.01
☐ 336	Ed Lynch	.05	.02	.01
☐ 337	Jim Gantner	.05	.02	.01
☐ 338	Brian Holton UER	.05	.02	.01
	(1987 ERA .389,			
	should be 3.89)			
☐ 339	Kurt Stillwell	.05	.02	.01
☐ 340	Jack Morris	.15	.07	.02
☐ 341	Carmen Castillo	.05	.02	.01
☐ 342	Larry Andersen	.05	.02	.01
☐ 343	Greg Gagne	.05	.02	.01
☐ 344	Tony LaRussa MG	.10	.05	.01
	(Checklist back)			
☐ 345	Scott Fletcher	.05	.02	.01
☐ 346	Vance Law	.05	.02	.01
☐ 347	Joe Johnson	.05	.02	.01
☐ 348	Jim Eisenreich	.10	.05	.01
☐ 349	Bob Walk	.05	.02	.01
☐ 350	Will Clark	.25	.11	.03
☐ 351	Cardinals TL	.10	.05	.01
	Red Schoendienst CO			
	and Tony Pena			
☐ 352	Billy Ripken	.10	.05	.01
☐ 353	Ed Olwine	.05	.02	.01
☐ 354	Marc Sullivan	.05	.02	.01
☐ 355	Roger McDowell	.05	.02	.01
☐ 356	Luis Aguayo	.05	.02	.01
☐ 357	Floyd Bannister	.05	.02	.01
☐ 358	Rey Quinones	.05	.02	.01
☐ 359	Tim Stoddard	.05	.02	.01
☐ 360	Tony Gwynn	.40	.18	.05
☐ 361	Greg Maddux	1.25	.55	.16
☐ 362	Juan Castillo	.05	.02	.01
☐ 363	Willie Fraser	.05	.02	.01
☐ 364	Nick Esasky	.05	.02	.01
☐ 365	Floyd Youmans	.05	.02	.01
☐ 366	Chet Lemon	.05	.02	.01
☐ 367	Tim Leary	.05	.02	.01
☐ 368	Gerald Young	.05	.02	.01
☐ 369	Greg Harris	.05	.02	.01
☐ 370	Jose Canseco	.25	.11	.03
☐ 371	Joe Hesketh	.05	.02	.01
☐ 372	Matt Williams	1.00	.45	.12
☐ 373	Checklist 265-396	.10	.05	.01
☐ 374	Doc Edwards MG	.05	.02	.01
	(Checklist back)			
☐ 375	Tom Brunansky	.05	.02	.01
☐ 376	Bill Wilkinson	.05	.02	.01
☐ 377	Sam Horn	.05	.02	.01
☐ 378	Todd Frohwirth	.05	.02	.01
☐ 379	Rafael Ramirez	.05	.02	.01
☐ 380	Joe Magrane	.05	.02	.01
☐ 381	Angels TL	.10	.05	.01
	Wally Joyner and			
	Jack Howell			
☐ 382	Keith A. Miller	.05	.02	.01
☐ 383	Eric Bell	.05	.02	.01
☐ 384	Neil Allen	.05	.02	.01
☐ 385	Carlton Fisk	.15	.07	.02
☐ 386	Don Mattingly AS	.20	.09	.03
☐ 387	Willie Randolph AS	.05	.02	.01
☐ 388	Wade Boggs AS	.15	.07	.02
☐ 389	Alan Trammell AS	.10	.05	.01
☐ 390	George Bell AS	.05	.02	.01
☐ 391	Kirby Puckett AS	.15	.07	.02
☐ 392	Dave Winfield AS	.15	.07	.02
☐ 393	Matt Nokes AS	.05	.02	.01
☐ 394	Roger Clemens AS	.15	.07	.02
☐ 395	Jimmy Key AS	.05	.02	.01
☐ 396	Tom Henke AS	.05	.02	.01
☐ 397	Jack Clark AS	.05	.02	.01
☐ 398	Juan Samuel AS	.05	.02	.01
☐ 399	Tim Wallach AS	.05	.02	.01
☐ 400	Ozzie Smith AS	.15	.07	.02
☐ 401	Andre Dawson AS	.10	.05	.01
☐ 402	Tony Gwynn AS	.20	.09	.03
☐ 403	Tim Raines AS	.10	.05	.01
☐ 404	Benny Santiago AS	.05	.02	.01
☐ 405	Dwight Gooden AS	.15	.07	.02
☐ 406	Shane Rawley AS	.05	.02	.01
☐ 407	Steve Bedrosian AS	.05	.02	.01
☐ 408	Dion James	.05	.02	.01
☐ 409	Joel McKeon	.05	.02	.01
☐ 410	Tony Pena	.05	.02	.01
☐ 411	Wayne Tolleson	.05	.02	.01
☐ 412	Randy Myers	.15	.07	.02
☐ 413	John Christensen	.05	.02	.01
☐ 414	John McNamara MG	.05	.02	.01
	(Checklist back)			
☐ 415	Don Carman	.05	.02	.01
☐ 416	Keith Moreland	.05	.02	.01
☐ 417	Mark Ciardi	.05	.02	.01
☐ 418	Joel Youngblood	.05	.02	.01
☐ 419	Scott McGregor	.05	.02	.01
☐ 420	Wally Joyner	.10	.05	.01
☐ 421	Ed VandeBerg	.05	.02	.01
☐ 422	Dave Concepcion	.10	.05	.01
☐ 423	John Smiley	.15	.07	.02
☐ 424	Dwayne Murphy	.05	.02	.01
☐ 425	Jeff Reardon	.10	.05	.01
☐ 426	Randy Ready	.05	.02	.01
☐ 427	Paul Kilgus	.05	.02	.01
☐ 428	John Shelby	.05	.02	.01
☐ 429	Tigers TL	.10	.05	.01
	Alan Trammell and			
	Kirk Gibson			
☐ 430	Glenn Davis	.05	.02	.01
☐ 431	Casey Candaele	.05	.02	.01
☐ 432	Mike Moore	.05	.02	.01
☐ 433	Bill Pecota	.05	.02	.01
☐ 434	Rick Aguilera	.15	.07	.02
☐ 435	Mike Pagliarulo	.05	.02	.01
☐ 436	Mike Bielecki	.05	.02	.01
☐ 437	Fred Manrique	.05	.02	.01
☐ 438	Rob Ducey	.05	.02	.01
☐ 439	Dave Martinez	.05	.02	.01
☐ 440	Steve Bedrosian	.05	.02	.01
☐ 441	Rick Manning	.05	.02	.01
☐ 442	Tom Bolton	.05	.02	.01
☐ 443	Ken Griffey	.05	.02	.01
☐ 444	Cal Ripken, Sr. MG	.10	.05	.01
	(Checklist back)			
	UER (two copyrights)			
☐ 445	Mike Krukow	.05	.02	.01
☐ 446	Doug DeCinces	.05	.02	.01
	(Now with Cardinals			
	on card front)			
☐ 447	Jeff Montgomery	.20	.09	.03
☐ 448	Mike Davis	.05	.02	.01
☐ 449	Jeff M. Robinson	.05	.02	.01
☐ 450	Barry Bonds	.60	.25	.07
☐ 451	Keith Atherton	.05	.02	.01
☐ 452	Willie Wilson	.05	.02	.01
☐ 453	Dennis Powell	.05	.02	.01
☐ 454	Marvell Wynne	.05	.02	.01
☐ 455	Shawn Hillegas	.05	.02	.01
☐ 456	Dave Anderson	.05	.02	.01
☐ 457	Terry Leach	.05	.02	.01
☐ 458	Ron Hassey	.05	.02	.01
☐ 459	Yankees TL	.15	.07	.02
	Dave Winfield and			
	Willie Randolph			
☐ 460	Ozzie Smith	.20	.09	.03
☐ 461	Danny Darwin	.05	.02	.01
☐ 462	Don Slaught	.05	.02	.01
☐ 463	Fred McGriff	.40	.18	.05
☐ 464	Jay Tibbs	.05	.02	.01
☐ 465	Paul Molitor	.20	.09	.03
☐ 466	Jerry Mumphrey	.05	.02	.01
☐ 467	Don Aase	.05	.02	.01
☐ 468	Darren Daulton	.10	.05	.01
☐ 469	Jeff Dedmon	.05	.02	.01
☐ 470	Dwight Evans	.10	.05	.01
☐ 471	Donnie Moore	.05	.02	.01
☐ 472	Robby Thompson	.05	.02	.01
☐ 473	Joe Niekro	.05	.02	.01
☐ 474	Tom Brookens	.05	.02	.01
☐ 475	Pete Rose MG	.20	.09	.03
	(Checklist back)			
☐ 476	Dave Stewart	.15	.07	.02
☐ 477	Jamie Quirk	.05	.02	.01
☐ 478	Sid Bream	.05	.02	.01
☐ 479	Brett Butler	.10	.05	.01
☐ 480	Dwight Gooden	.15	.07	.02
☐ 481	Mariano Duncan	.05	.02	.01

□ 482 Mark Davis	.05	.02	.01
□ 483 Rod Booker	.05	.02	.01
□ 484 Pat Clements	.05	.02	.01
□ 485 Harold Reynolds	.05	.02	.01
□ 486 Pat Keedy	.05	.02	.01
□ 487 Jim Pankovits	.05	.02	.01
□ 488 Andy McGaffigan	.05	.02	.01
□ 489 Dodgers TL	.05	.02	.01
Pedro Guerrero and Fernando Valenzuela			
□ 490 Larry Parrish	.05	.02	.01
□ 491 B.J. Surhoff	.10	.05	.01
□ 492 Doyle Alexander	.05	.02	.01
□ 493 Mike Greenwell	.15	.07	.02
□ 494 Wally Ritchie	.05	.02	.01
□ 495 Eddie Murray	.25	.11	.03
□ 496 Guy Hoffman	.05	.02	.01
□ 497 Kevin Mitchell	.10	.05	.01
□ 498 Bob Boone	.10	.05	.01
□ 499 Eric King	.05	.02	.01
□ 500 Andre Dawson	.15	.07	.02
□ 501 Tim Birtsas	.05	.02	.01
□ 502 Dan Gladden	.05	.02	.01
□ 503 Junior Noboa	.05	.02	.01
□ 504 Bob Rodgers MG	.05	.02	.01
(Checklist back)			
□ 505 Willie Upshaw	.05	.02	.01
□ 506 John Cangelosi	.05	.02	.01
□ 507 Mark Gubicza	.05	.02	.01
□ 508 Tim Teufel	.05	.02	.01
□ 509 Bill Dawley	.05	.02	.01
□ 510 Dave Winfield	.15	.07	.02
□ 511 Joel Davis	.05	.02	.01
□ 512 Alex Trevino	.05	.02	.01
□ 513 Tim Flannery	.05	.02	.01
□ 514 Pat Sheridan	.05	.02	.01
□ 515 Juan Nieves	.05	.02	.01
□ 516 Jim Sundberg	.05	.02	.01
□ 517 Ron Robinson	.05	.02	.01
□ 518 Greg Gross	.05	.02	.01
□ 519 Mariners TL	.05	.02	.01
Harold Reynolds and Phil Bradley			
□ 520 Dave Smith	.05	.02	.01
□ 521 Jim Dwyer	.05	.02	.01
□ 522 Bob Patterson	.05	.02	.01
□ 523 Gary Roenicke	.05	.02	.01
□ 524 Gary Lucas	.05	.02	.01
□ 525 Marty Barrett	.05	.02	.01
□ 526 Juan Berenguer	.05	.02	.01
□ 527 Steve Henderson	.05	.02	.01
□ 528A Checklist 397-528	.15	.07	.02
ERR (455 S. Carlton)			
□ 528B Checklist 397-528	.10	.05	.01
COR (455 S. Hillegas)			
□ 529 Tim Burke	.05	.02	.01
□ 530 Gary Carter	.15	.07	.02
□ 531 Rich Yett	.05	.02	.01
□ 532 Mike Kingery	.05	.02	.01
□ 533 John Farrell	.05	.02	.01
□ 534 John Wathan MG	.05	.02	.01
(Checklist back)			
□ 535 Ron Guidry	.05	.02	.01
□ 536 John Morris	.05	.02	.01
□ 537 Steve Buechele	.05	.02	.01
□ 538 Bill Wegman	.05	.02	.01
□ 539 Mike LaValliere	.05	.02	.01
□ 540 Bret Saberhagen	.10	.05	.01
□ 541 Juan Beniquez	.05	.02	.01
□ 542 Paul Noce	.05	.02	.01
□ 543 Kent Tekulve	.05	.02	.01
□ 544 Jim Traber	.05	.02	.01
□ 545 Don Baylor	.15	.07	.02
□ 546 John Candelaria	.05	.02	.01
□ 547 Felix Fermin	.05	.02	.01
□ 548 Shane Mack	.05	.02	.01
□ 549 Braves TL	.05	.02	.01
Albert Hall, Dale Murphy, Ken Griffey, and Dion James			
□ 550 Pedro Guerrero	.10	.05	.01
□ 551 Terry Steinbach	.10	.05	.01
□ 552 Mark Thurmond	.05	.02	.01
□ 553 Tracy Jones	.05	.02	.01
□ 554 Mike Smithson	.05	.02	.01
□ 555 Brook Jacoby	.05	.02	.01
□ 556 Stan Clarke	.05	.02	.01
□ 557 Craig Reynolds	.05	.02	.01
□ 558 Bob Ojeda	.05	.02	.01
□ 559 Ken Williams	.05	.02	.01
□ 560 Tim Wallach	.05	.02	.01
□ 561 Rick Cerone	.05	.02	.01
□ 562 Jim Lindeman	.05	.02	.01
□ 563 Jose Guzman	.05	.02	.01
□ 564 Frank Lucchesi MG	.05	.02	.01
(Checklist back)			
□ 565 Lloyd Moseby	.05	.02	.01
□ 566 Charlie O'Brien	.05	.02	.01
□ 567 Mike Diaz	.05	.02	.01
□ 568 Chris Brown	.05	.02	.01
□ 569 Charlie Leibrandt	.05	.02	.01
□ 570 Jeffrey Leonard	.05	.02	.01
□ 571 Mark Williamson	.05	.02	.01
□ 572 Chris James	.05	.02	.01
□ 573 Bob Stanley	.05	.02	.01
□ 574 Graig Nettles	.10	.05	.01
□ 575 Don Sutton	.15	.07	.02
□ 576 Tommy Hinzo	.05	.02	.01
□ 577 Tom Browning	.05	.02	.01
□ 578 Gary Gaetti	.05	.02	.01
□ 579 Mets TL	.10	.05	.01
Gary Carter and Kevin McReynolds			
□ 580 Mark McGwire	.60	.25	.07
□ 581 Tito Landrum	.05	.02	.01
□ 582 Mike Henneman	.10	.05	.01
□ 583 Dave Valle	.05	.02	.01
□ 584 Steve Trout	.05	.02	.01
□ 585 Ozzie Guillen	.10	.05	.01
□ 586 Bob Forsch	.05	.02	.01
□ 587 Terry Puhl	.05	.02	.01
□ 588 Jeff Parrett	.05	.02	.01
□ 589 Geno Petralli	.05	.02	.01
□ 590 George Bell	.05	.02	.01
□ 591 Doug Drabek	.10	.05	.01
□ 592 Dale Sveum	.05	.02	.01
□ 593 Bob Tewksbury	.05	.02	.01
□ 594 Bobby Valentine MG	.10	.05	.01
(Checklist back)			
□ 595 Frank White	.10	.05	.01
□ 596 John Kruk	.15	.07	.02
□ 597 Gene Garber	.05	.02	.01
□ 598 Lee Lacy	.05	.02	.01
□ 599 Calvin Schiraldi	.05	.02	.01
□ 600 Mike Schmidt	.20	.09	.03
□ 601 Jack Lazorko	.05	.02	.01
□ 602 Mike Aldrete	.05	.02	.01
□ 603 Rob Murphy	.05	.02	.01
□ 604 Chris Bando	.05	.02	.01
□ 605 Kirk Gibson	.10	.05	.01
□ 606 Moose Haas	.05	.02	.01
□ 607 Mickey Hatcher	.05	.02	.01
□ 608 Charlie Kerfeld	.05	.02	.01
□ 609 Twins TL	.10	.05	.01
Gary Gaetti and Kent Hrbek			
□ 610 Keith Hernandez	.10	.05	.01
□ 611 Tommy John	.10	.05	.01
□ 612 Curt Ford	.05	.02	.01
□ 613 Bobby Thigpen	.05	.02	.01
□ 614 Herm Winningham	.05	.02	.01
□ 615 Jody Davis	.05	.02	.01
□ 616 Jay Aldrich	.05	.02	.01
□ 617 Oddibe McDowell	.05	.02	.01
□ 618 Cecil Fielder	.15	.07	.02
□ 619 Mike Dunne	.05	.02	.01
(Inconsistent design, black name on front)			
□ 620 Cory Snyder	.05	.02	.01
□ 621 Gene Nelson	.05	.02	.01
□ 622 Kal Daniels	.05	.02	.01
□ 623 Mike Flanagan	.05	.02	.01
□ 624 Jim Leyland MG	.10	.05	.01
(Checklist back)			
□ 625 Frank Viola	.05	.02	.01
□ 626 Glenn Wilson	.05	.02	.01
□ 627 Joe Boever	.05	.02	.01
□ 628 Dave Henderson	.05	.02	.01
□ 629 Kelly Downs	.05	.02	.01
□ 630 Darrell Evans	.10	.05	.01
□ 631 Jack Howell	.05	.02	.01

□ 632	Steve Shields	.05	.02	.01
□ 633	Barry Lyons	.05	.02	.01
□ 634	Jose DeLeon	.05	.02	.01
□ 635	Terry Pendleton	.10	.05	.01
□ 636	Charles Hudson	.05	.02	.01
□ 637	Jay Bell	.20	.09	.03
□ 638	Steve Balboni	.05	.02	.01
□ 639	Brewers TL	.05	.02	.01
	Glenn Braggs			
	and Tony Muser CO			
□ 640	Garry Templeton	.05	.02	.01
	(Inconsistent design,			
	green border)			
□ 641	Rick Honeycutt	.05	.02	.01
□ 642	Bob Dernier	.05	.02	.01
□ 643	Rocky Childress	.05	.02	.01
□ 644	Terry McGriff	.05	.02	.01
□ 645	Matt Nokes	.05	.02	.01
□ 646	Checklist 529-660	.10	.05	.01
□ 647	Pascual Perez	.05	.02	.01
□ 648	Al Newman	.05	.02	.01
□ 649	DeWayne Buice	.05	.02	.01
□ 650	Cal Ripken	.75	.35	.09
□ 651	Mike Jackson	.10	.05	.01
□ 652	Bruce Benedict	.05	.02	.01
□ 653	Jeff Sellers	.05	.02	.01
□ 654	Roger Craig MG	.10	.05	.01
	(Checklist back)			
□ 655	Len Dykstra	.10	.05	.01
□ 656	Lee Guetterman	.05	.02	.01
□ 657	Gary Redus	.05	.02	.01
□ 658	Tim Conroy	.05	.02	.01
	(Inconsistent design,			
	name in white)			
□ 659	Bobby Meacham	.05	.02	.01
□ 660	Rick Reuschel	.05	.02	.01
□ 661	Nolan Ryan TBC '83	.35	.16	.04
□ 662	Jim Rice TBC '78	.10	.05	.01
□ 663	Ron Blomberg TBC '73	.05	.02	.01
□ 664	Bob Gibson TBC '68	.15	.07	.02
□ 665	Stan Musial TBC '63	.15	.07	.02
□ 666	Mario Soto	.05	.02	.01
□ 667	Luis Quinones	.05	.02	.01
□ 668	Walt Terrell	.05	.02	.01
□ 669	Phillies TL	.05	.02	.01
	Lance Parrish			
	and Mike Ryan CO			
□ 670	Dan Plesac	.05	.02	.01
□ 671	Tim Laudner	.05	.02	.01
□ 672	John Davis	.05	.02	.01
□ 673	Tony Phillips	.15	.07	.02
□ 674	Mike Fitzgerald	.05	.02	.01
□ 675	Jim Rice	.15	.07	.02
□ 676	Ken Dixon	.05	.02	.01
□ 677	Eddie Milner	.05	.02	.01
□ 678	Jim Acker	.05	.02	.01
□ 679	Darrell Miller	.05	.02	.01
□ 680	Charlie Hough	.10	.05	.01
□ 681	Bobby Bonilla	.10	.05	.01
□ 682	Jimmy Key	.10	.05	.01
□ 683	Julio Franco	.10	.05	.01
□ 684	Hal Lanier MG	.05	.02	.01
	(Checklist back)			
□ 685	Ron Darling	.05	.02	.01
□ 686	Terry Francona	.05	.02	.01
□ 687	Mickey Brantley	.05	.02	.01
□ 688	Jim Winn	.05	.02	.01
□ 689	Tom Pagnozzi	.10	.05	.01
□ 690	Jay Howell	.05	.02	.01
□ 691	Dan Pasqua	.05	.02	.01
□ 692	Mike Birkbeck	.05	.02	.01
□ 693	Benito Santiago	.10	.05	.01
□ 694	Eric Nolte	.05	.02	.01
□ 695	Shawon Dunston	.05	.02	.01
□ 696	Duane Ward	.10	.05	.01
□ 697	Steve Lombardozzi	.05	.02	.01
□ 698	Brad Havens	.05	.02	.01
□ 699	Padres TL	.10	.05	.01
	Benito Santiago			
	and Tony Gwynn			
□ 700	George Brett	.40	.18	.05
□ 701	Sammy Stewart	.05	.02	.01
□ 702	Mike Gallego	.05	.02	.01
□ 703	Bob Brenly	.05	.02	.01
□ 704	Dennis Boyd	.05	.02	.01
□ 705	Juan Samuel	.05	.02	.01
□ 706	Rick Mahler	.05	.02	.01
□ 707	Fred Lynn	.05	.02	.01
□ 708	Gus Polidor	.05	.02	.01
□ 709	George Frazier	.05	.02	.01
□ 710	Darryl Strawberry	.15	.07	.02
□ 711	Bill Gullickson	.05	.02	.01
□ 712	John Moses	.05	.02	.01
□ 713	Willie Hernandez	.05	.02	.01
□ 714	Jim Fregosi MG	.10	.05	.01
	(Checklist back)			
□ 715	Todd Worrell	.05	.02	.01
□ 716	Lenn Sakata	.05	.02	.01
□ 717	Jay Baller	.05	.02	.01
□ 718	Mike Felder	.05	.02	.01
□ 719	Denny Walling	.05	.02	.01
□ 720	Tim Raines	.15	.07	.02
□ 721	Pete O'Brien	.05	.02	.01
□ 722	Manny Lee	.05	.02	.01
□ 723	Bob Kipper	.05	.02	.01
□ 724	Danny Tartabull	.05	.02	.01
□ 725	Mike Boddicker	.05	.02	.01
□ 726	Alfredo Griffin	.05	.02	.01
□ 727	Greg Booker	.05	.02	.01
□ 728	Andy Allanson	.05	.02	.01
□ 729	Blue Jays TL	.10	.05	.01
	George Bell and			
	Fred McGriff			
□ 730	John Franco	.05	.02	.01
□ 731	Rick Schu	.05	.02	.01
□ 732	David Palmer	.05	.02	.01
□ 733	Spike Owen	.05	.02	.01
□ 734	Craig Lefferts	.05	.02	.01
□ 735	Kevin McReynolds	.05	.02	.01
□ 736	Matt Young	.05	.02	.01
□ 737	Butch Wynegar	.05	.02	.01
□ 738	Scott Bankhead	.05	.02	.01
□ 739	Daryl Boston	.05	.02	.01
□ 740	Rick Sutcliffe	.05	.02	.01
□ 741	Mike Easler	.05	.02	.01
□ 742	Mark Clear	.05	.02	.01
□ 743	Larry Herndon	.05	.02	.01
□ 744	Whitey Herzog MG	.10	.05	.01
	(Checklist back)			
□ 745	Bill Doran	.05	.02	.01
□ 746	Gene Larkin	.05	.02	.01
□ 747	Bobby Witt	.05	.02	.01
□ 748	Reid Nichols	.05	.02	.01
□ 749	Mark Eichhorn	.05	.02	.01
□ 750	Bo Jackson	.15	.07	.02
□ 751	Jim Morrison	.05	.02	.01
□ 752	Mark Grant	.05	.02	.01
□ 753	Danny Heep	.05	.02	.01
□ 754	Mike LaCoss	.05	.02	.01
□ 755	Ozzie Virgil	.05	.02	.01
□ 756	Mike Maddux	.05	.02	.01
□ 757	John Marzano	.05	.02	.01
□ 758	Eddie Williams	.10	.05	.01
□ 759	A's TL UER	.30	.14	.04
	Mark McGwire			
	and Jose Canseco			
	(two copyrights)			
□ 760	Mike Scott	.05	.02	.01
□ 761	Tony Armas	.05	.02	.01
□ 762	Scott Bradley	.05	.02	.01
□ 763	Doug Sisk	.05	.02	.01
□ 764	Greg Walker	.05	.02	.01
□ 765	Neal Heaton	.05	.02	.01
□ 766	Henry Cotto	.05	.02	.01
□ 767	Jose Lind	.10	.05	.01
□ 768	Dickie Noles	.05	.02	.01
	(Now with Tigers			
	on card front)			
□ 769	Cecil Cooper	.10	.05	.01
□ 770	Lou Whitaker	.15	.07	.02
□ 771	Ruben Sierra	.15	.07	.02
□ 772	Sal Butera	.05	.02	.01
□ 773	Frank Williams	.05	.02	.01
□ 774	Gene Mauch MG	.10	.05	.01
	(Checklist back)			
□ 775	Dave Stieb	.10	.05	.01
□ 776	Checklist 661-792	.10	.05	.01
□ 777	Lonnie Smith	.05	.02	.01
□ 778A	Keith Comstock ERR	2.00	.90	.25
	(White "Padres")			
□ 778B	Keith Comstock COR	.05	.02	.01
	(Blue "Padres")			

□ 779 Tom Glavine	1.00	.45	.12
□ 780 Fernando Valenzuela	.10	.05	.01
□ 781 Keith Hughes	.05	.02	.01
□ 782 Jeff Ballard	.05	.02	.01
□ 783 Ron Roenicke	.05	.02	.01
□ 784 Joe Sambito	.05	.02	.01
□ 785 Alvin Davis	.05	.02	.01
□ 786 Joe Price (Inconsistent design, orange team name)	.05	.02	.01
□ 787 Bill Almon	.05	.02	.01
□ 788 Ray Searage	.05	.02	.01
□ 789 Indians' TL Joe Carter and Cory Snyder	.10	.05	.01
□ 790 Dave Righetti	.10	.05	.01
□ 791 Ted Simmons	.10	.05	.01
□ 792 John Tudor	.05	.02	.01

1988 Topps Traded

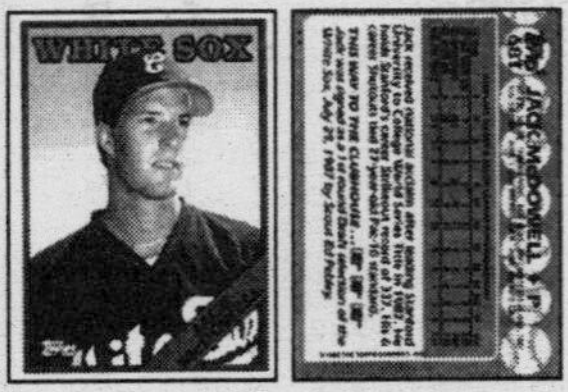

This standard-size 132-card Traded set was distributed exclusively in factory set form in blue and white taped boxes through hobby dealers. The cards are identical in style to the Topps regular issue except for whiter stock and t-suffixed numbering on back. Cards are ordered alphabetically by player's last name. This set generated additional interest upon release due to the inclusion of members of the 1988 U.S. Olympic baseball team. These Olympians are indicated in the checklist below by OLY. The key extended Rookie Cards in this set are Jim Abbott, Roberto Alomar, Brady Anderson, Andy Benes, Jay Buhner, Ron Gant, Mark Grace, Tino Martinez, Jack McDowell, Charles Nagy, Robin Ventura and Walt Weiss.

	MINT	NRMT	EXC
COMPLETE FACT.SET (132)	12.00	5.50	1.50
COMMON CARD (1T-132T)	.05	.02	.01
SEMISTARS	.10	.05	.01

□ 1T Jim Abbott OLY	.30	.14	.04
□ 2T Juan Agosto	.05	.02	.01
□ 3T Luis Alicea	.10	.05	.01
□ 4T Roberto Alomar	4.00	1.80	.50
□ 5T Brady Anderson	2.00	.90	.25
□ 6T Jack Armstrong	.05	.02	.01
□ 7T Don August	.05	.02	.01
□ 8T Floyd Bannister	.05	.02	.01
□ 9T Bret Barberie OLY	.10	.05	.01
□ 10T Jose Bautista	.05	.02	.01
□ 11T Don Baylor	.15	.07	.02
□ 12T Tim Belcher	.10	.05	.01
□ 13T Buddy Bell	.10	.05	.01
□ 14T Andy Benes OLY	.75	.35	.09
□ 15T Damon Berryhill	.05	.02	.01
□ 16T Bud Black	.05	.02	.01
□ 17T Pat Borders	.10	.05	.01
□ 18T Phil Bradley	.05	.02	.01
□ 19T Jeff Branson OLY	.10	.05	.01
□ 20T Tom Brunansky	.05	.02	.01
□ 21T Jay Buhner	2.00	.90	.25
□ 22T Brett Butler	.10	.05	.01
□ 23T Jim Campanis OLY	.05	.02	.01
□ 24T Sil Campusano	.05	.02	.01
□ 25T John Candelaria	.05	.02	.01
□ 26T Jose Cecena	.05	.02	.01
□ 27T Rick Cerone	.05	.02	.01
□ 28T Jack Clark	.10	.05	.01
□ 29T Kevin Coffman	.05	.02	.01
□ 30T Pat Combs OLY	.05	.02	.01
□ 31T Henry Cotto	.05	.02	.01
□ 32T Chili Davis	.15	.07	.02
□ 33T Mike Davis	.05	.02	.01
□ 34T Jose DeLeon	.05	.02	.01
□ 35T Richard Dotson	.05	.02	.01
□ 36T Cecil Espy	.05	.02	.01
□ 37T Tom Filer	.05	.02	.01
□ 38T Mike Fiore OLY	.05	.02	.01
□ 39T Ron Gant	1.00	.45	.12
□ 40T Kirk Gibson	.10	.05	.01
□ 41T Rich Gossage	.15	.07	.02
□ 42T Mark Grace	1.00	.45	.12
□ 43T Alfredo Griffin	.05	.02	.01
□ 44T Ty Griffin OLY	.05	.02	.01
□ 45T Bryan Harvey	.10	.05	.01
□ 46T Ron Hassey	.05	.02	.01
□ 47T Ray Hayward	.05	.02	.01
□ 48T Dave Henderson	.05	.02	.01
□ 49T Tom Herr	.05	.02	.01
□ 50T Bob Horner	.05	.02	.01
□ 51T Ricky Horton	.05	.02	.01
□ 52T Jay Howell	.05	.02	.01
□ 53T Glenn Hubbard	.05	.02	.01
□ 54T Jeff Innis	.05	.02	.01
□ 55T Danny Jackson	.05	.02	.01
□ 56T Darrin Jackson	.10	.05	.01
□ 57T Roberto Kelly	.15	.07	.02
□ 58T Ron Kittle	.05	.02	.01
□ 59T Ray Knight	.10	.05	.01
□ 60T Vance Law	.05	.02	.01
□ 61T Jeffrey Leonard	.05	.02	.01
□ 62T Mike Macfarlane	.15	.07	.02
□ 63T Scotti Madison	.05	.02	.01
□ 64T Kirt Manwaring	.10	.05	.01
□ 65T Mark Marquess OLY CO	.05	.02	.01
□ 66T Tino Martinez OLY	1.50	.70	.19
□ 67T Billy Masse OLY	.05	.02	.01
□ 68T Jack McDowell	.75	.35	.09
□ 69T Jack McKeon MG	.05	.02	.01
□ 70T Larry McWilliams	.05	.02	.01
□ 71T Mickey Morandini OLY	.15	.07	.02
□ 72T Keith Moreland	.05	.02	.01
□ 73T Mike Morgan	.05	.02	.01
□ 74T Charles Nagy OLY	1.50	.70	.19
□ 75T Al Nipper	.05	.02	.01
□ 76T Russ Nixon MG	.05	.02	.01
□ 77T Jesse Orosco	.05	.02	.01
□ 78T Joe Orsulak	.05	.02	.01
□ 79T Dave Palmer	.05	.02	.01
□ 80T Mark Parent	.05	.02	.01
□ 81T Dave Parker	.15	.07	.02
□ 82T Dan Pasqua	.05	.02	.01
□ 83T Melido Perez	.10	.05	.01
□ 84T Steve Peters	.05	.02	.01
□ 85T Dan Petry	.05	.02	.01
□ 86T Gary Pettis	.05	.02	.01
□ 87T Jeff Pico	.05	.02	.01
□ 88T Jim Poole OLY	.10	.05	.01
□ 89T Ted Power	.05	.02	.01
□ 90T Rafael Ramirez	.05	.02	.01
□ 91T Dennis Rasmussen	.05	.02	.01
□ 92T Jose Rijo	.05	.02	.01
□ 93T Ernie Riles	.05	.02	.01
□ 94T Luis Rivera	.05	.02	.01
□ 95T Doug Robbins OLY	.05	.02	.01
□ 96T Frank Robinson MG	.15	.07	.02
□ 97T Cookie Rojas MG	.05	.02	.01
□ 98T Chris Sabo	.10	.05	.01
□ 99T Mark Salas	.05	.02	.01
□ 100T Luis Salazar	.05	.02	.01
□ 101T Rafael Santana	.05	.02	.01
□ 102T Nelson Santovenia	.05	.02	.01
□ 103T Mackey Sasser	.05	.02	.01
□ 104T Calvin Schiraldi	.05	.02	.01
□ 105T Mike Schooler	.05	.02	.01
□ 106T Scott Servais OLY	.10	.05	.01
□ 107T Dave Silvestri OLY	.05	.02	.01
□ 108T Don Slaught	.05	.02	.01
□ 109T Joe Slusarski OLY	.05	.02	.01
□ 110T Lee Smith	.15	.07	.02
□ 111T Pete Smith	.05	.02	.01
□ 112T Jim Snyder MG	.05	.02	.01

□ 113T Ed Sprague OLY	.75	.35	.09
□ 114T Pete Stanicek	.05	.02	.01
□ 115T Kurt Stillwell	.05	.02	.01
□ 116T Todd Stottlemyre	.50	.23	.06
□ 117T Bill Swift	.05	.02	.01
□ 118T Pat Tabler	.05	.02	.01
□ 119T Scott Terry	.05	.02	.01
□ 120T Mickey Tettleton	.10	.05	.01
□ 121T Dickie Thon	.05	.02	.01
□ 122T Jeff Treadway	.05	.02	.01
□ 123T Willie Upshaw	.05	.02	.01
□ 124T Robin Ventura OLY	1.50	.70	.19
□ 125T Ron Washington	.05	.02	.01
□ 126T Walt Weiss	.10	.05	.01
□ 127T Bob Welch	.05	.02	.01
□ 128T David Wells	.15	.07	.02
□ 129T Glenn Wilson	.05	.02	.01
□ 130T Ted Wood OLY	.10	.05	.01
□ 131T Don Zimmer MG	.10	.05	.01
□ 132T Checklist 1T-132T	.05	.02	.01

1989 Topps

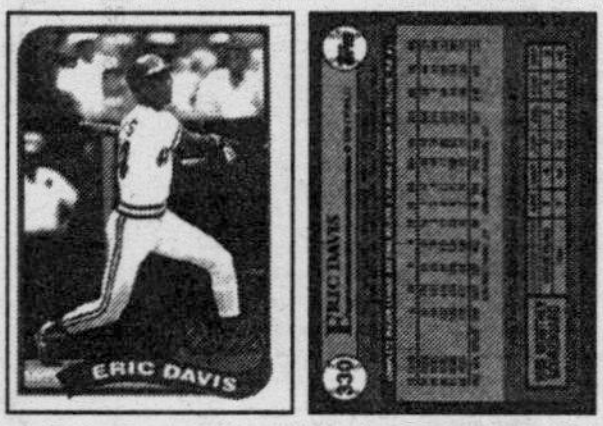

This set consists of 792 standard-size cards. Cards were primarily issued in 15-card wax packs, 42-card rack packs and factory sets. Subsets in the set include Record Breakers (1-7), Turn Back the Clock (661-665), All-Star selections (386-407) and First Draft Picks, Future Stars and Team Leaders (all scattered throughout the set). The manager cards contain a team checklist on back. The key Rookie Cards in this set are Jim Abbott, Sandy Alomar Jr., Brady Anderson, Steve Avery, Andy Benes, Dante Bichette, Craig Biggio, Randy Johnson, Ramon Martinez, Gary Sheffield, John Smoltz, and Robin Ventura.

	MINT	NRMT	EXC
COMPLETE SET (792)	10.00	4.50	1.25
COMPLETE FACT.SET (792)	10.00	4.50	1.25
COMMON CARD (1-792)	.05	.02	.01
SEMISTARS	.10	.05	.01
STARS	.15	.07	.02

□ 1 George Bell RB	.05	.02	.01
Slams 3 Opening Day HR's			
□ 2 Wade Boggs RB	.15	.07	.02
200 Hits 6th Straight Season			
□ 3 Gary Carter RB	.10	.05	.01
Career Putouts Record			
□ 4 Andre Dawson RB	.10	.05	.01
Logs Double Figures in HR and SB			
□ 5 Orel Hershiser RB	.10	.05	.01
59 Scoreless Innings			
□ 6 Doug Jones RB UER	.05	.02	.01
Earns His 15th Straight Save (Photo actually Chris Codiroli)			
□ 7 Kevin McReynolds RB	.05	.02	.01
Steals 21 Without Being Caught			
□ 8 Dave Eiland	.05	.02	.01
□ 9 Tim Teufel	.05	.02	.01
□ 10 Andre Dawson	.15	.07	.02
□ 11 Bruce Sutter	.05	.02	.01
□ 12 Dale Sveum	.05	.02	.01
□ 13 Doug Sisk	.05	.02	.01
□ 14 Tom Kelly MG	.05	.02	.01
(Team checklist back)			
□ 15 Robby Thompson	.05	.02	.01
□ 16 Ron Robinson	.05	.02	.01
□ 17 Brian Downing	.05	.02	.01
□ 18 Rick Rhoden	.05	.02	.01
□ 19 Greg Gagne	.05	.02	.01
□ 20 Steve Bedrosian	.05	.02	.01
□ 21 Chicago White Sox TL	.05	.02	.01
Greg Walker			
□ 22 Tim Crews	.05	.02	.01
□ 23 Mike Fitzgerald	.05	.02	.01
□ 24 Larry Andersen	.05	.02	.01
□ 25 Frank White	.10	.05	.01
□ 26 Dale Mohorcic	.05	.02	.01
□ 27A Orestes Destrade	.05	.02	.01
(F* next to copyright)			
□ 27B Orestes Destrade	.05	.02	.01
(E*F* next to copyright)			
□ 28 Mike Moore	.05	.02	.01
□ 29 Kelly Gruber	.05	.02	.01
□ 30 Dwight Gooden	.10	.05	.01
□ 31 Terry Francona	.05	.02	.01
□ 32 Dennis Rasmussen	.05	.02	.01
□ 33 B.J. Surhoff	.15	.07	.02
□ 34 Ken Williams	.05	.02	.01
□ 35 John Tudor UER	.05	.02	.01
(With Red Sox in '84,should be Pirates)			
□ 36 Mitch Webster	.05	.02	.01
□ 37 Bob Stanley	.05	.02	.01
□ 38 Paul Runge	.05	.02	.01
□ 39 Mike Maddux	.05	.02	.01
□ 40 Steve Sax	.05	.02	.01
□ 41 Terry Mulholland	.05	.02	.01
□ 42 Jim Eppard	.05	.02	.01
□ 43 Guillermo Hernandez	.05	.02	.01
□ 44 Jim Snyder MG	.05	.02	.01
(Team checklist back)			
□ 45 Kal Daniels	.05	.02	.01
□ 46 Mark Portugal	.05	.02	.01
□ 47 Carney Lansford	.10	.05	.01
□ 48 Tim Burke	.05	.02	.01
□ 49 Craig Biggio	.40	.18	.05
□ 50 George Bell	.05	.02	.01
□ 51 California Angels TL	.05	.02	.01
Mark McLemore			
□ 52 Bob Brenly	.05	.02	.01
□ 53 Ruben Sierra	.10	.05	.01
□ 54 Steve Trout	.05	.02	.01
□ 55 Julio Franco	.10	.05	.01
□ 56 Pat Tabler	.05	.02	.01
□ 57 Alejandro Pena	.05	.02	.01
□ 58 Lee Mazzilli	.05	.02	.01
□ 59 Mark Davis	.05	.02	.01
□ 60 Tom Brunansky	.05	.02	.01
□ 61 Neil Allen	.05	.02	.01
□ 62 Alfredo Griffin	.05	.02	.01
□ 63 Mark Clear	.05	.02	.01
□ 64 Alex Trevino	.05	.02	.01
□ 65 Rick Reuschel	.05	.02	.01
□ 66 Manny Trillo	.05	.02	.01
□ 67 Dave Palmer	.05	.02	.01
□ 68 Darrell Miller	.05	.02	.01
□ 69 Jeff Ballard	.05	.02	.01
□ 70 Mark McGwire	.30	.14	.04
□ 71 Mike Boddicker	.05	.02	.01
□ 72 John Moses	.05	.02	.01
□ 73 Pascual Perez	.05	.02	.01
□ 74 Nick Leyva MG	.05	.02	.01
(Team checklist back)			
□ 75 Tom Henke	.05	.02	.01
□ 76 Terry Blocker	.05	.02	.01
□ 77 Doyle Alexander	.05	.02	.01
□ 78 Jim Sundberg	.05	.02	.01
□ 79 Scott Bankhead	.05	.02	.01
□ 80 Cory Snyder	.05	.02	.01
□ 81 Montreal Expos TL	.10	.05	.01
Tim Raines			
□ 82 Dave Leiper	.05	.02	.01
□ 83 Jeff Blauser	.10	.05	.01
□ 84 Bill Bene FDP	.05	.02	.01
□ 85 Kevin McReynolds	.05	.02	.01
□ 86 Al Nipper	.05	.02	.01
□ 87 Larry Owen	.05	.02	.01

□ 88 Darryl Hamilton	.10	.05	.01
□ 89 Dave LaPoint	.05	.02	.01
□ 90 Vince Coleman UER	.05	.02	.01
(Wrong birth year)			
□ 91 Floyd Youmans	.05	.02	.01
□ 92 Jeff Kunkel	.05	.02	.01
□ 93 Ken Howell	.05	.02	.01
□ 94 Chris Speier	.05	.02	.01
□ 95 Gerald Young	.05	.02	.01
□ 96 Rick Cerone	.05	.02	.01
□ 97 Greg Mathews	.05	.02	.01
□ 98 Larry Sheets	.05	.02	.01
□ 99 Sherman Corbett	.05	.02	.01
□ 100 Mike Schmidt	.20	.09	.03
□ 101 Les Straker	.05	.02	.01
□ 102 Mike Gallego	.05	.02	.01
□ 103 Tim Birtsas	.05	.02	.01
□ 104 Dallas Green MG	.05	.02	.01
(Team checklist back)			
□ 105 Ron Darling	.05	.02	.01
□ 106 Willie Upshaw	.05	.02	.01
□ 107 Jose DeLeon	.05	.02	.01
□ 108 Fred Manrique	.05	.02	.01
□ 109 Hipolito Pena	.05	.02	.01
□ 110 Paul Molitor	.20	.09	.03
□ 111 Cincinnati Reds TL	.05	.02	.01
Eric Davis			
(Swinging bat)			
□ 112 Jim Presley	.05	.02	.01
□ 113 Lloyd Moseby	.05	.02	.01
□ 114 Bob Kipper	.05	.02	.01
□ 115 Jody Davis	.05	.02	.01
□ 116 Jeff Montgomery	.10	.05	.01
□ 117 Dave Anderson	.05	.02	.01
□ 118 Checklist 1-132	.05	.02	.01
□ 119 Terry Puhl	.05	.02	.01
□ 120 Frank Viola	.05	.02	.01
□ 121 Garry Templeton	.05	.02	.01
□ 122 Lance Johnson	.15	.07	.02
□ 123 Spike Owen	.05	.02	.01
□ 124 Jim Traber	.05	.02	.01
□ 125 Mike Krukow	.05	.02	.01
□ 126 Sid Bream	.05	.02	.01
□ 127 Walt Terrell	.05	.02	.01
□ 128 Milt Thompson	.05	.02	.01
□ 129 Terry Clark	.05	.02	.01
□ 130 Gerald Perry	.05	.02	.01
□ 131 Dave Otto	.05	.02	.01
□ 132 Curt Ford	.05	.02	.01
□ 133 Bill Long	.05	.02	.01
□ 134 Don Zimmer MG	.05	.02	.01
(Team checklist back)			
□ 135 Jose Rijo	.05	.02	.01
□ 136 Joey Meyer	.05	.02	.01
□ 137 Geno Petralli	.05	.02	.01
□ 138 Wallace Johnson	.05	.02	.01
□ 139 Mike Flanagan	.05	.02	.01
□ 140 Shawon Dunston	.05	.02	.01
□ 141 Cleveland Indians TL	.05	.02	.01
Brook Jacoby			
□ 142 Mike Diaz	.05	.02	.01
□ 143 Mike Campbell	.05	.02	.01
□ 144 Jay Bell	.15	.07	.02
□ 145 Dave Stewart	.10	.05	.01
□ 146 Gary Pettis	.05	.02	.01
□ 147 DeWayne Buice	.05	.02	.01
□ 148 Bill Pecota	.05	.02	.01
□ 149 Doug Dascenzo	.05	.02	.01
□ 150 Fernando Valenzuela	.10	.05	.01
□ 151 Terry McGriff	.05	.02	.01
□ 152 Mark Thurmond	.05	.02	.01
□ 153 Jim Pankovits	.05	.02	.01
□ 154 Don Carman	.05	.02	.01
□ 155 Marty Barrett	.05	.02	.01
□ 156 Dave Gallagher	.05	.02	.01
□ 157 Tom Glavine	.25	.11	.03
□ 158 Mike Aldrete	.05	.02	.01
□ 159 Pat Clements	.05	.02	.01
□ 160 Jeffrey Leonard	.05	.02	.01
□ 161 Gregg Olson FDP UER	.15	.07	.02
(Born Scribner, NE,			
should be Omaha, NE)			
□ 162 John Davis	.05	.02	.01
□ 163 Bob Forsch	.05	.02	.01
□ 164 Hal Lanier MG	.05	.02	.01
(Team checklist back)			

□ 165 Mike Dunne	.05	.02	.01
□ 166 Doug Jennings	.05	.02	.01
□ 167 Steve Searcy FS	.05	.02	.01
□ 168 Willie Wilson	.05	.02	.01
□ 169 Mike Jackson	.05	.02	.01
□ 170 Tony Fernandez	.05	.02	.01
□ 171 Atlanta Braves TL	.05	.02	.01
Andres Thomas			
□ 172 Frank Williams	.05	.02	.01
□ 173 Mel Hall	.05	.02	.01
□ 174 Todd Burns	.05	.02	.01
□ 175 John Shelby	.05	.02	.01
□ 176 Jeff Parrett	.05	.02	.01
□ 177 Monty Fariss FDP	.05	.02	.01
□ 178 Mark Grant	.05	.02	.01
□ 179 Ozzie Virgil	.05	.02	.01
□ 180 Mike Scott	.05	.02	.01
□ 181 Craig Worthington	.05	.02	.01
□ 182 Bob McClure	.05	.02	.01
□ 183 Oddibe McDowell	.05	.02	.01
□ 184 John Costello	.05	.02	.01
□ 185 Claudell Washington	.05	.02	.01
□ 186 Pat Perry	.05	.02	.01
□ 187 Darren Daulton	.10	.05	.01
□ 188 Dennis Lamp	.05	.02	.01
□ 189 Kevin Mitchell	.10	.05	.01
□ 190 Mike Witt	.05	.02	.01
□ 191 Sil Campusano	.05	.02	.01
□ 192 Paul Mirabella	.05	.02	.01
□ 193 Sparky Anderson MG	.10	.05	.01
(Team checklist back)			
UER (553 Salazer)			
□ 194 Greg W. Harris	.05	.02	.01
□ 195 Ozzie Guillen	.05	.02	.01
□ 196 Denny Walling	.05	.02	.01
□ 197 Neal Heaton	.05	.02	.01
□ 198 Danny Heep	.05	.02	.01
□ 199 Mike Schooler	.05	.02	.01
□ 200 George Brett	.40	.18	.05
□ 201 Blue Jays TL	.05	.02	.01
Kelly Gruber			
□ 202 Brad Moore	.05	.02	.01
□ 203 Rob Ducey	.05	.02	.01
□ 204 Brad Havens	.05	.02	.01
□ 205 Dwight Evans	.10	.05	.01
□ 206 Roberto Alomar	.50	.23	.06
□ 207 Terry Leach	.05	.02	.01
□ 208 Tom Pagnozzi	.05	.02	.01
□ 209 Jeff Bittiger	.05	.02	.01
□ 210 Dale Murphy	.15	.07	.02
□ 211 Mike Pagliarulo	.05	.02	.01
□ 212 Scott Sanderson	.05	.02	.01
□ 213 Rene Gonzales	.05	.02	.01
□ 214 Charlie O'Brien	.05	.02	.01
□ 215 Kevin Gross	.05	.02	.01
□ 216 Jack Howell	.05	.02	.01
□ 217 Joe Price	.05	.02	.01
□ 218 Mike LaValliere	.05	.02	.01
□ 219 Jim Clancy	.05	.02	.01
□ 220 Gary Gaetti	.05	.02	.01
□ 221 Cecil Espy	.05	.02	.01
□ 222 Mark Lewis FDP	.15	.07	.02
□ 223 Jay Buhner	.25	.11	.03
□ 224 Tony LaRussa MG	.10	.05	.01
(Team checklist back)			
□ 225 Ramon Martinez	.25	.11	.03
□ 226 Bill Doran	.05	.02	.01
□ 227 John Farrell	.05	.02	.01
□ 228 Nelson Santovenia	.05	.02	.01
□ 229 Jimmy Key	.10	.05	.01
□ 230 Ozzie Smith	.20	.09	.03
□ 231 San Diego Padres TL	.15	.07	.02
Roberto Alomar			
(Gary Carter at plate)			
□ 232 Ricky Horton	.05	.02	.01
□ 233 Gregg Jefferies FS	.15	.07	.02
□ 234 Tom Browning	.05	.02	.01
□ 235 John Kruk	.10	.05	.01
□ 236 Charles Hudson	.05	.02	.01
□ 237 Glenn Hubbard	.05	.02	.01
□ 238 Eric King	.05	.02	.01
□ 239 Tim Laudner	.05	.02	.01
□ 240 Greg Maddux	.75	.35	.09
□ 241 Brett Butler	.10	.05	.01
□ 242 Ed VandeBerg	.05	.02	.01
□ 243 Bob Boone	.10	.05	.01

□ 244 Jim Acker	.05	.02	.01
□ 245 Jim Rice	.15	.07	.02
□ 246 Rey Quinones	.05	.02	.01
□ 247 Shawn Hillegas	.05	.02	.01
□ 248 Tony Phillips	.15	.07	.02
□ 249 Tim Leary	.05	.02	.01
□ 250 Cal Ripken	.75	.35	.09
□ 251 John Dopson	.05	.02	.01
□ 252 Billy Hatcher	.05	.02	.01
□ 253 Jose Alvarez	.05	.02	.01
□ 254 Tom Lasorda MG (Team checklist back)	.10	.05	.01
□ 255 Ron Guidry	.05	.02	.01
□ 256 Benny Santiago	.10	.05	.01
□ 257 Rick Aguilera	.10	.05	.01
□ 258 Checklist 133-264	.05	.02	.01
□ 259 Larry McWilliams	.05	.02	.01
□ 260 Dave Winfield	.15	.07	.02
□ 261 St.Louis Cardinals TL Tom Brunansky (With Luis Alicea)	.05	.02	.01
□ 262 Jeff Pico	.05	.02	.01
□ 263 Mike Felder	.05	.02	.01
□ 264 Rob Dibble	.10	.05	.01
□ 265 Kent Hrbek	.10	.05	.01
□ 266 Luis Aquino	.05	.02	.01
□ 267 Jeff M. Robinson	.05	.02	.01
□ 268 N. Keith Miller	.05	.02	.01
□ 269 Tom Bolton	.05	.02	.01
□ 270 Wally Joyner	.10	.05	.01
□ 271 Jay Tibbs	.05	.02	.01
□ 272 Ron Hassey	.05	.02	.01
□ 273 Jose Lind	.05	.02	.01
□ 274 Mark Eichhorn	.05	.02	.01
□ 275 Danny Tartabull UER (Born San Juan, PR should be Miami, FL)	.05	.02	.01
□ 276 Paul Kilgus	.05	.02	.01
□ 277 Mike Davis	.05	.02	.01
□ 278 Andy McGaffigan	.05	.02	.01
□ 279 Scott Bradley	.05	.02	.01
□ 280 Bob Knepper	.05	.02	.01
□ 281 Gary Redus	.05	.02	.01
□ 282 Cris Carpenter	.05	.02	.01
□ 283 Andy Allanson	.05	.02	.01
□ 284 Jim Leyland MG (Team checklist back)	.05	.02	.01
□ 285 John Candelaria	.05	.02	.01
□ 286 Darrin Jackson	.05	.02	.01
□ 287 Juan Nieves	.05	.02	.01
□ 288 Pat Sheridan	.05	.02	.01
□ 289 Ernie Whitt	.05	.02	.01
□ 290 John Franco	.05	.02	.01
□ 291 New York Mets TL Darryl Strawberry (With Keith Hernandez and Kevin McReynolds)	.10	.05	.01
□ 292 Jim Corsi	.05	.02	.01
□ 293 Glenn Wilson	.05	.02	.01
□ 294 Juan Berenguer	.05	.02	.01
□ 295 Scott Fletcher	.05	.02	.01
□ 296 Ron Gant	.15	.07	.02
□ 297 Oswald Peraza	.05	.02	.01
□ 298 Chris James	.05	.02	.01
□ 299 Steve Ellsworth	.05	.02	.01
□ 300 Darryl Strawberry	.10	.05	.01
□ 301 Charlie Leibrandt	.05	.02	.01
□ 302 Gary Ward	.05	.02	.01
□ 303 Felix Fermin	.05	.02	.01
□ 304 Joel Youngblood	.05	.02	.01
□ 305 Dave Smith	.05	.02	.01
□ 306 Tracy Woodson	.05	.02	.01
□ 307 Lance McCullers	.05	.02	.01
□ 308 Ron Karkovice	.05	.02	.01
□ 309 Mario Diaz	.05	.02	.01
□ 310 Rafael Palmeiro	.15	.07	.02
□ 311 Chris Bosio	.05	.02	.01
□ 312 Tom Lawless	.05	.02	.01
□ 313 Dennis Martinez	.10	.05	.01
□ 314 Bobby Valentine MG (Team checklist back)	.05	.02	.01
□ 315 Greg Swindell	.05	.02	.01
□ 316 Walt Weiss	.05	.02	.01
□ 317 Jack Armstrong	.05	.02	.01
□ 318 Gene Larkin	.05	.02	.01
□ 319 Greg Booker	.05	.02	.01
□ 320 Lou Whitaker	.15	.07	.02
□ 321 Boston Red Sox TL Jody Reed	.05	.02	.01
□ 322 John Smiley	.05	.02	.01
□ 323 Gary Thurman	.05	.02	.01
□ 324 Bob Milacki	.05	.02	.01
□ 325 Jesse Barfield	.05	.02	.01
□ 326 Dennis Boyd	.05	.02	.01
□ 327 Mark Lemke	.10	.05	.01
□ 328 Rick Honeycutt	.05	.02	.01
□ 329 Bob Melvin	.05	.02	.01
□ 330 Eric Davis	.10	.05	.01
□ 331 Curt Wilkerson	.05	.02	.01
□ 332 Tony Armas	.05	.02	.01
□ 333 Bob Ojeda	.05	.02	.01
□ 334 Steve Lyons	.05	.02	.01
□ 335 Dave Righetti	.05	.02	.01
□ 336 Steve Balboni	.05	.02	.01
□ 337 Calvin Schiraldi	.05	.02	.01
□ 338 Jim Adduci	.05	.02	.01
□ 339 Scott Bailes	.05	.02	.01
□ 340 Kirk Gibson	.10	.05	.01
□ 341 Jim Deshaies	.05	.02	.01
□ 342 Tom Brookens	.05	.02	.01
□ 343 Gary Sheffield FS	.75	.35	.09
□ 344 Tom Trebelhorn MG (Team checklist back)	.05	.02	.01
□ 345 Charlie Hough	.10	.05	.01
□ 346 Rex Hudler	.05	.02	.01
□ 347 John Cerutti	.05	.02	.01
□ 348 Ed Hearn	.05	.02	.01
□ 349 Ron Jones	.05	.02	.01
□ 350 Andy Van Slyke	.10	.05	.01
□ 351 San Fran. Giants TL Bob Melvin (With Bill Fahey CO)	.05	.02	.01
□ 352 Rick Schu	.05	.02	.01
□ 353 Marvell Wynne	.05	.02	.01
□ 354 Larry Parrish	.05	.02	.01
□ 355 Mark Langston	.10	.05	.01
□ 356 Kevin Elster	.10	.05	.01
□ 357 Jerry Reuss	.05	.02	.01
□ 358 Ricky Jordan	.10	.05	.01
□ 359 Tommy John	.10	.05	.01
□ 360 Ryne Sandberg	.25	.11	.03
□ 361 Kelly Downs	.05	.02	.01
□ 362 Jack Lazorko	.05	.02	.01
□ 363 Rich Yett	.05	.02	.01
□ 364 Rob Deer	.05	.02	.01
□ 365 Mike Henneman	.05	.02	.01
□ 366 Herm Winningham	.05	.02	.01
□ 367 Johnny Paredes	.05	.02	.01
□ 368 Brian Holton	.05	.02	.01
□ 369 Ken Caminiti	.15	.07	.02
□ 370 Dennis Eckersley	.10	.05	.01
□ 371 Manny Lee	.05	.02	.01
□ 372 Craig Lefferts	.05	.02	.01
□ 373 Tracy Jones	.05	.02	.01
□ 374 John Wathan MG (Team checklist back)	.05	.02	.01
□ 375 Terry Pendleton	.10	.05	.01
□ 376 Steve Lombardozzi	.05	.02	.01
□ 377 Mike Smithson	.05	.02	.01
□ 378 Checklist 265-396	.05	.02	.01
□ 379 Tim Flannery	.05	.02	.01
□ 380 Rickey Henderson	.15	.07	.02
□ 381 Baltimore Orioles TL Larry Sheets	.05	.02	.01
□ 382 John Smoltz	.75	.35	.09
□ 383 Howard Johnson	.05	.02	.01
□ 384 Mark Salas	.05	.02	.01
□ 385 Von Hayes	.05	.02	.01
□ 386 Andres Galarraga AS	.15	.07	.02
□ 387 Ryne Sandberg AS	.15	.07	.02
□ 388 Bobby Bonilla AS	.10	.05	.01
□ 389 Ozzie Smith AS	.15	.07	.02
□ 390 Darryl Strawberry AS	.10	.05	.01
□ 391 Andre Dawson AS	.15	.07	.02
□ 392 Andy Van Slyke AS	.05	.02	.01
□ 393 Gary Carter AS	.10	.05	.01
□ 394 Orel Hershiser AS	.10	.05	.01
□ 395 Danny Jackson AS	.05	.02	.01
□ 396 Kirk Gibson AS	.10	.05	.01
□ 397 Don Mattingly AS	.25	.11	.03
□ 398 Julio Franco AS	.05	.02	.01
□ 399 Wade Boggs AS	.15	.07	.02

□ 400 Alan Trammell AS	.10	.05	.01
□ 401 Jose Canseco AS	.15	.07	.02
□ 402 Mike Greenwell AS	.05	.02	.01
□ 403 Kirby Puckett AS	.15	.07	.02
□ 404 Bob Boone AS	.05	.02	.01
□ 405 Roger Clemens AS	.15	.07	.02
□ 406 Frank Viola AS	.05	.02	.01
□ 407 Dave Winfield AS	.15	.07	.02
□ 408 Greg Walker	.05	.02	.01
□ 409 Ken Dayley	.05	.02	.01
□ 410 Jack Clark	.10	.05	.01
□ 411 Mitch Williams	.05	.02	.01
□ 412 Barry Lyons	.05	.02	.01
□ 413 Mike Kingery	.05	.02	.01
□ 414 Jim Fregosi MG	.05	.02	.01
(Team checklist back)			
□ 415 Rich Gossage	.15	.07	.02
□ 416 Fred Lynn	.05	.02	.01
□ 417 Mike LaCoss	.05	.02	.01
□ 418 Bob Dernier	.05	.02	.01
□ 419 Tom Filer	.05	.02	.01
□ 420 Joe Carter	.15	.07	.02
□ 421 Kirk McCaskill	.05	.02	.01
□ 422 Bo Diaz	.05	.02	.01
□ 423 Brian Fisher	.05	.02	.01
□ 424 Luis Polonia UER	.10	.05	.01
(Wrong birthdate)			
□ 425 Jay Howell	.05	.02	.01
□ 426 Dan Gladden	.05	.02	.01
□ 427 Eric Show	.05	.02	.01
□ 428 Craig Reynolds	.05	.02	.01
□ 429 Minnesota Twins TL	.05	.02	.01
Greg Gagne			
(Taking throw at 2nd)			
□ 430 Mark Gubicza	.05	.02	.01
□ 431 Luis Rivera	.05	.02	.01
□ 432 Chad Kreuter	.05	.02	.01
□ 433 Albert Hall	.05	.02	.01
□ 434 Ken Patterson	.05	.02	.01
□ 435 Len Dykstra	.10	.05	.01
□ 436 Bobby Meacham	.05	.02	.01
□ 437 Andy Benes FDP	.25	.11	.03
□ 438 Greg Gross	.05	.02	.01
□ 439 Frank DiPino	.05	.02	.01
□ 440 Bobby Bonilla	.10	.05	.01
□ 441 Jerry Reed	.05	.02	.01
□ 442 Jose Oquendo	.05	.02	.01
□ 443 Rod Nichols	.05	.02	.01
□ 444 Moose Stubing MG	.05	.02	.01
(Team checklist back)			
□ 445 Matt Nokes	.05	.02	.01
□ 446 Rob Murphy	.05	.02	.01
□ 447 Donell Nixon	.05	.02	.01
□ 448 Eric Plunk	.05	.02	.01
□ 449 Carmelo Martinez	.05	.02	.01
□ 450 Roger Clemens	.15	.07	.02
□ 451 Mark Davidson	.05	.02	.01
□ 452 Israel Sanchez	.05	.02	.01
□ 453 Tom Prince	.05	.02	.01
□ 454 Paul Assenmacher	.05	.02	.01
□ 455 Johnny Ray	.05	.02	.01
□ 456 Tim Belcher	.05	.02	.01
□ 457 Mackey Sasser	.05	.02	.01
□ 458 Donn Pall	.05	.02	.01
□ 459 Seattle Mariners TL	.05	.02	.01
Dave Valle			
□ 460 Dave Stieb	.05	.02	.01
□ 461 Buddy Bell	.10	.05	.01
□ 462 Jose Guzman	.05	.02	.01
□ 463 Steve Lake	.05	.02	.01
□ 464 Bryn Smith	.05	.02	.01
□ 465 Mark Grace	.20	.09	.03
□ 466 Chuck Crim	.05	.02	.01
□ 467 Jim Walewander	.05	.02	.01
□ 468 Henry Cotto	.05	.02	.01
□ 469 Jose Bautista	.05	.02	.01
□ 470 Lance Parrish	.05	.02	.01
□ 471 Steve Curry	.05	.02	.01
□ 472 Brian Harper	.05	.02	.01
□ 473 Don Robinson	.05	.02	.01
□ 474 Bob Rodgers MG	.05	.02	.01
(Team checklist back)			
□ 475 Dave Parker	.10	.05	.01
□ 476 Jon Perlman	.05	.02	.01
□ 477 Dick Schofield	.05	.02	.01
□ 478 Doug Drabek	.10	.05	.01
□ 479 Mike Macfarlane	.10	.05	.01
□ 480 Keith Hernandez	.10	.05	.01
□ 481 Chris Brown	.05	.02	.01
□ 482 Steve Peters	.05	.02	.01
□ 483 Mickey Hatcher	.05	.02	.01
□ 484 Steve Shields	.05	.02	.01
□ 485 Hubie Brooks	.05	.02	.01
□ 486 Jack McDowell	.15	.07	.02
□ 487 Scott Lusader	.05	.02	.01
□ 488 Kevin Coffman	.05	.02	.01
Now with Cubs			
□ 489 Phila. Phillies TL	.10	.05	.01
Mike Schmidt			
□ 490 Chris Sabo	.05	.02	.01
□ 491 Mike Birkbeck	.05	.02	.01
□ 492 Alan Ashby	.05	.02	.01
□ 493 Todd Benzinger	.05	.02	.01
□ 494 Shane Rawley	.05	.02	.01
□ 495 Candy Maldonado	.05	.02	.01
□ 496 Dwayne Henry	.05	.02	.01
□ 497 Pete Stanicek	.05	.02	.01
□ 498 Dave Valle	.05	.02	.01
□ 499 Don Heinkel	.05	.02	.01
□ 500 Jose Canseco	.15	.07	.02
□ 501 Vance Law	.05	.02	.01
□ 502 Duane Ward	.05	.02	.01
□ 503 Al Newman	.05	.02	.01
□ 504 Bob Walk	.05	.02	.01
□ 505 Pete Rose MG	.20	.09	.03
(Team checklist back)			
□ 506 Kirt Manwaring	.05	.02	.01
□ 507 Steve Farr	.05	.02	.01
□ 508 Wally Backman	.05	.02	.01
□ 509 Bud Black	.05	.02	.01
□ 510 Bob Horner	.05	.02	.01
□ 511 Richard Dotson	.05	.02	.01
□ 512 Donnie Hill	.05	.02	.01
□ 513 Jesse Orosco	.05	.02	.01
□ 514 Chet Lemon	.05	.02	.01
□ 515 Barry Larkin	.20	.09	.03
□ 516 Eddie Whitson	.05	.02	.01
□ 517 Greg Brock	.05	.02	.01
□ 518 Bruce Ruffin	.05	.02	.01
□ 519 New York Yankees TL	.05	.02	.01
Willie Randolph			
□ 520 Rick Sutcliffe	.05	.02	.01
□ 521 Mickey Tettleton	.10	.05	.01
□ 522 Randy Kramer	.05	.02	.01
□ 523 Andres Thomas	.05	.02	.01
□ 524 Checklist 397-528	.05	.02	.01
□ 525 Chili Davis	.10	.05	.01
□ 526 Wes Gardner	.05	.02	.01
□ 527 Dave Henderson	.05	.02	.01
□ 528 Luis Medina	.05	.02	.01
(Lower left front			
has white triangle)			
□ 529 Tom Foley	.05	.02	.01
□ 530 Nolan Ryan	.75	.35	.09
□ 531 Dave Hengel	.05	.02	.01
□ 532 Jerry Browne	.05	.02	.01
□ 533 Andy Hawkins	.05	.02	.01
□ 534 Doc Edwards MG	.05	.02	.01
(Team checklist back)			
□ 535 Todd Worrell UER	.05	.02	.01
(4 wins in '88,			
should be 5)			
□ 536 Joel Skinner	.05	.02	.01
□ 537 Pete Smith	.05	.02	.01
□ 538 Juan Castillo	.05	.02	.01
□ 539 Barry Jones	.05	.02	.01
□ 540 Bo Jackson	.15	.07	.02
□ 541 Cecil Fielder	.10	.05	.01
□ 542 Todd Frohwirth	.05	.02	.01
□ 543 Damon Berryhill	.05	.02	.01
□ 544 Jeff Sellers	.05	.02	.01
□ 545 Mookie Wilson	.10	.05	.01
□ 546 Mark Williamson	.05	.02	.01
□ 547 Mark McLemore	.05	.02	.01
□ 548 Bobby Witt	.05	.02	.01
□ 549 Chicago Cubs TL	.05	.02	.01
Jamie Moyer			
(Pitching)			
□ 550 Orel Hershiser	.15	.07	.02
□ 551 Randy Ready	.05	.02	.01
□ 552 Greg Cadaret	.05	.02	.01
□ 553 Luis Salazar	.05	.02	.01

☐ 554	Nick Esasky	.05	.02	.01
☐ 555	Bert Blyleven	.10	.05	.01
☐ 556	Bruce Fields	.05	.02	.01
☐ 557	Keith A. Miller	.05	.02	.01
☐ 558	Dan Pasqua	.05	.02	.01
☐ 559	Juan Agosto	.05	.02	.01
☐ 560	Tim Raines	.15	.07	.02
☐ 561	Luis Aguayo	.05	.02	.01
☐ 562	Danny Cox	.05	.02	.01
☐ 563	Bill Schroeder	.05	.02	.01
☐ 564	Russ Nixon MG	.05	.02	.01
	(Team checklist back)			
☐ 565	Jeff Russell	.05	.02	.01
☐ 566	Al Pedrique	.05	.02	.01
☐ 567	David Wells UER	.05	.02	.01
	(Complete Pitching Recor)			
☐ 568	Mickey Brantley	.05	.02	.01
☐ 569	German Jimenez	.05	.02	.01
☐ 570	Tony Gwynn UER	.40	.18	.05
	('88 average should be italicized as league leader)			
☐ 571	Billy Ripken	.05	.02	.01
☐ 572	Atlee Hammaker	.05	.02	.01
☐ 573	Jim Abbott FDP	.15	.07	.02
☐ 574	Dave Clark	.05	.02	.01
☐ 575	Juan Samuel	.05	.02	.01
☐ 576	Greg Minton	.05	.02	.01
☐ 577	Randy Bush	.05	.02	.01
☐ 578	John Morris	.05	.02	.01
☐ 579	Houston Astros TL	.05	.02	.01
	Glenn Davis (Batting stance)			
☐ 580	Harold Reynolds	.05	.02	.01
☐ 581	Gene Nelson	.05	.02	.01
☐ 582	Mike Marshall	.05	.02	.01
☐ 583	Paul Gibson	.05	.02	.01
☐ 584	Randy Velarde UER	.05	.02	.01
	(Signed 1935, should be 1985)			
☐ 585	Harold Baines	.10	.05	.01
☐ 586	Joe Boever	.05	.02	.01
☐ 587	Mike Stanley	.05	.02	.01
☐ 588	Luis Alicea	.05	.02	.01
☐ 589	Dave Meads	.05	.02	.01
☐ 590	Andres Galarraga	.15	.07	.02
☐ 591	Jeff Musselman	.05	.02	.01
☐ 592	John Cangelosi	.05	.02	.01
☐ 593	Drew Hall	.05	.02	.01
☐ 594	Jimy Williams MG	.05	.02	.01
	(Team checklist back)			
☐ 595	Teddy Higuera	.05	.02	.01
☐ 596	Kurt Stillwell	.05	.02	.01
☐ 597	Terry Taylor	.05	.02	.01
☐ 598	Ken Gerhart	.05	.02	.01
☐ 599	Tom Candiotti	.05	.02	.01
☐ 600	Wade Boggs	.15	.07	.02
☐ 601	Dave Dravecky	.10	.05	.01
☐ 602	Devon White	.10	.05	.01
☐ 603	Frank Tanana	.05	.02	.01
☐ 604	Paul O'Neill	.15	.07	.02
☐ 605A	Bob Welch ERR	2.00	.90	.25
	(Missing line on back, "Complete M.L. Pitching Record")			
☐ 605B	Bob Welch COR	.05	.02	.01
☐ 606	Rick Dempsey	.05	.02	.01
☐ 607	Willie Ansley FDP	.05	.02	.01
☐ 608	Phil Bradley	.05	.02	.01
☐ 609	Detroit Tigers TL	.05	.02	.01
	Frank Tanana (With Alan Trammell and Mike Heath)			
☐ 610	Randy Myers	.10	.05	.01
☐ 611	Don Slaught	.05	.02	.01
☐ 612	Dan Quisenberry	.05	.02	.01
☐ 613	Gary Varsho	.05	.02	.01
☐ 614	Joe Hesketh	.05	.02	.01
☐ 615	Robin Yount	.20	.09	.03
☐ 616	Steve Rosenberg	.05	.02	.01
☐ 617	Mark Parent	.05	.02	.01
☐ 618	Rance Mulliniks	.05	.02	.01
☐ 619	Checklist 529-660	.05	.02	.01
☐ 620	Barry Bonds	.40	.18	.05
☐ 621	Rick Mahler	.05	.02	.01
☐ 622	Stan Javier	.05	.02	.01
☐ 623	Fred Toliver	.05	.02	.01
☐ 624	Jack McKeon MG	.05	.02	.01
	(Team checklist back)			
☐ 625	Eddie Murray	.25	.11	.03
☐ 626	Jeff Reed	.05	.02	.01
☐ 627	Greg A. Harris	.05	.02	.01
☐ 628	Matt Williams	.25	.11	.03
☐ 629	Pete O'Brien	.05	.02	.01
☐ 630	Mike Greenwell	.05	.02	.01
☐ 631	Dave Bergman	.05	.02	.01
☐ 632	Bryan Harvey	.10	.05	.01
☐ 633	Daryl Boston	.05	.02	.01
☐ 634	Marvin Freeman	.05	.02	.01
☐ 635	Willie Randolph	.10	.05	.01
☐ 636	Bill Wilkinson	.05	.02	.01
☐ 637	Carmen Castillo	.05	.02	.01
☐ 638	Floyd Bannister	.05	.02	.01
☐ 639	Oakland A's TL	.05	.02	.01
	Walt Weiss			
☐ 640	Willie McGee	.05	.02	.01
☐ 641	Curt Young	.05	.02	.01
☐ 642	Argenis Salazar	.05	.02	.01
☐ 643	Louie Meadows	.05	.02	.01
☐ 644	Lloyd McClendon	.05	.02	.01
☐ 645	Jack Morris	.10	.05	.01
☐ 646	Kevin Bass	.05	.02	.01
☐ 647	Randy Johnson	.75	.35	.09
☐ 648	Sandy Alomar FS	.20	.09	.03
☐ 649	Stewart Cliburn	.05	.02	.01
☐ 650	Kirby Puckett	.30	.14	.04
☐ 651	Tom Niedenfuer	.05	.02	.01
☐ 652	Rich Gedman	.05	.02	.01
☐ 653	Tommy Barrett	.05	.02	.01
☐ 654	Whitey Herzog MG	.10	.05	.01
	(Team checklist back)			
☐ 655	Dave Magadan	.05	.02	.01
☐ 656	Ivan Calderon	.05	.02	.01
☐ 657	Joe Magrane	.05	.02	.01
☐ 658	R.J. Reynolds	.05	.02	.01
☐ 659	Al Leiter	.10	.05	.01
☐ 660	Will Clark	.20	.09	.03
☐ 661	Dwight Gooden TBC84	.10	.05	.01
☐ 662	Lou Brock TBC79	.15	.07	.02
☐ 663	Hank Aaron TBC74	.20	.09	.03
☐ 664	Gil Hodges TBC69	.15	.07	.02
☐ 665A	Tony Oliva TBC64	2.00	.90	.25
	ERR (fabricated card is enlarged version of Oliva's 64T card; Topps copyright missing)			
☐ 665B	Tony Oliva TBC64	.10	.05	.01
	COR (fabricated card)			
☐ 666	Randy St.Claire	.05	.02	.01
☐ 667	Dwayne Murphy	.05	.02	.01
☐ 668	Mike Bielecki	.05	.02	.01
☐ 669	L.A. Dodgers TL	.10	.05	.01
	Orel Hershiser (Mound conference with Mike Scioscia)			
☐ 670	Kevin Seitzer	.05	.02	.01
☐ 671	Jim Gantner	.05	.02	.01
☐ 672	Allan Anderson	.05	.02	.01
☐ 673	Don Baylor	.15	.07	.02
☐ 674	Otis Nixon	.05	.02	.01
☐ 675	Bruce Hurst	.05	.02	.01
☐ 676	Ernie Riles	.05	.02	.01
☐ 677	Dave Schmidt	.05	.02	.01
☐ 678	Dion James	.05	.02	.01
☐ 679	Willie Fraser	.05	.02	.01
☐ 680	Gary Carter	.15	.07	.02
☐ 681	Jeff D. Robinson	.05	.02	.01
☐ 682	Rick Leach	.05	.02	.01
☐ 683	Jose Cecena	.05	.02	.01
☐ 684	Dave Johnson MG	.05	.02	.01
	(Team checklist back)			
☐ 685	Jeff Treadway	.05	.02	.01
☐ 686	Scott Terry	.05	.02	.01
☐ 687	Alvin Davis	.05	.02	.01
☐ 688	Zane Smith	.05	.02	.01
☐ 689A	Stan Jefferson	.05	.02	.01
	(Pink triangle on front bottom left)			
☐ 689B	Stan Jefferson	.05	.02	.01

	(Violet triangle on front bottom left)			
□ 690	Doug Jones	.05	.02	.01
□ 691	Roberto Kelly UER	.10	.05	.01
	(83 Oneonita)			
□ 692	Steve Ontiveros	.05	.02	.01
□ 693	Pat Borders	.10	.05	.01
□ 694	Les Lancaster	.05	.02	.01
□ 695	Carlton Fisk	.15	.07	.02
□ 696	Don August	.05	.02	.01
□ 697A	Franklin Stubbs	.05	.02	.01
	(Team name on front in white)			
□ 697B	Franklin Stubbs	.05	.02	.01
	(Team name on front in gray)			
□ 698	Keith Atherton	.05	.02	.01
□ 699	Pittsburgh Pirates TL	.05	.02	.01
	Al Pedrique			
	(Tony Gwynn sliding)			
□ 700	Don Mattingly	.50	.23	.06
□ 701	Storm Davis	.05	.02	.01
□ 702	Jamie Quirk	.05	.02	.01
□ 703	Scott Garrelts	.05	.02	.01
□ 704	Carlos Quintana	.05	.02	.01
□ 705	Terry Kennedy	.05	.02	.01
□ 706	Pete Incaviglia	.10	.05	.01
□ 707	Steve Jeltz	.05	.02	.01
□ 708	Chuck Finley	.10	.05	.01
□ 709	Tom Herr	.05	.02	.01
□ 710	David Cone	.15	.07	.02
□ 711	Candy Sierra	.05	.02	.01
□ 712	Bill Swift	.05	.02	.01
□ 713	Ty Griffin FDP	.05	.02	.01
□ 714	Joe Morgan MG	.05	.02	.01
	(Team checklist back)			
□ 715	Tony Pena	.05	.02	.01
□ 716	Wayne Tolleson	.05	.02	.01
□ 717	Jamie Moyer	.05	.02	.01
□ 718	Glenn Braggs	.05	.02	.01
□ 719	Danny Darwin	.05	.02	.01
□ 720	Tim Wallach	.05	.02	.01
□ 721	Ron Tingley	.05	.02	.01
□ 722	Todd Stottlemyre	.10	.05	.01
□ 723	Rafael Belliard	.05	.02	.01
□ 724	Jerry Don Gleaton	.05	.02	.01
□ 725	Terry Steinbach	.10	.05	.01
□ 726	Dickie Thon	.05	.02	.01
□ 727	Joe Orsulak	.05	.02	.01
□ 728	Charlie Puleo	.05	.02	.01
□ 729	Texas Rangers TL	.05	.02	.01
	Steve Buechele			
	(Inconsistent design, team name on front surrounded by black, should be white)			
□ 730	Danny Jackson	.05	.02	.01
□ 731	Mike Young	.05	.02	.01
□ 732	Steve Buechele	.05	.02	.01
□ 733	Randy Bockus	.05	.02	.01
□ 734	Jody Reed	.05	.02	.01
□ 735	Roger McDowell	.05	.02	.01
□ 736	Jeff Hamilton	.05	.02	.01
□ 737	Norm Charlton	.10	.05	.01
□ 738	Darnell Coles	.05	.02	.01
□ 739	Brook Jacoby	.05	.02	.01
□ 740	Dan Plesac	.05	.02	.01
□ 741	Ken Phelps	.05	.02	.01
□ 742	Mike Harkey FS	.05	.02	.01
□ 743	Mike Heath	.05	.02	.01
□ 744	Roger Craig MG	.05	.02	.01
	(Team checklist back)			
□ 745	Fred McGriff	.20	.09	.03
□ 746	German Gonzalez UER	.05	.02	.01
	(Wrong birthdate)			
□ 747	Wil Tejada	.05	.02	.01
□ 748	Jimmy Jones	.05	.02	.01
□ 749	Rafael Ramirez	.05	.02	.01
□ 750	Bret Saberhagen	.10	.05	.01
□ 751	Ken Oberkfell	.05	.02	.01
□ 752	Jim Gott	.05	.02	.01
□ 753	Jose Uribe	.05	.02	.01
□ 754	Bob Brower	.05	.02	.01
□ 755	Mike Scioscia	.05	.02	.01
□ 756	Scott Medvin	.05	.02	.01
□ 757	Brady Anderson	.60	.25	.07
□ 758	Gene Walter	.05	.02	.01
□ 759	Milwaukee Brewers TL	.05	.02	.01
	Rob Deer			
□ 760	Lee Smith	.15	.07	.02
□ 761	Dante Bichette	.60	.25	.07
□ 762	Bobby Thigpen	.05	.02	.01
□ 763	Dave Martinez	.05	.02	.01
□ 764	Robin Ventura FDP	.40	.18	.05
□ 765	Glenn Davis	.05	.02	.01
□ 766	Cecilio Guante	.05	.02	.01
□ 767	Mike Capel	.05	.02	.01
□ 768	Bill Wegman	.05	.02	.01
□ 769	Junior Ortiz	.05	.02	.01
□ 770	Alan Trammell	.15	.07	.02
□ 771	Ron Kittle	.05	.02	.01
□ 772	Ron Oester	.05	.02	.01
□ 773	Keith Moreland	.05	.02	.01
□ 774	Frank Robinson MG	.15	.07	.02
	(Team checklist back)			
□ 775	Jeff Reardon	.10	.05	.01
□ 776	Nelson Liriano	.05	.02	.01
□ 777	Ted Power	.05	.02	.01
□ 778	Bruce Benedict	.05	.02	.01
□ 779	Craig McMurtry	.05	.02	.01
□ 780	Pedro Guerrero	.10	.05	.01
□ 781	Greg Briley	.05	.02	.01
□ 782	Checklist 661-792	.05	.02	.01
□ 783	Trevor Wilson	.05	.02	.01
□ 784	Steve Avery FDP	.40	.18	.05
□ 785	Ellis Burks	.15	.07	.02
□ 786	Melido Perez	.05	.02	.01
□ 787	Dave West	.05	.02	.01
□ 788	Mike Morgan	.05	.02	.01
□ 789	Kansas City Royals TL	.15	.07	.02
	Bo Jackson			
	(Throwing)			
□ 790	Sid Fernandez	.05	.02	.01
□ 791	Jim Lindeman	.05	.02	.01
□ 792	Rafael Santana	.05	.02	.01

1989 Topps Traded

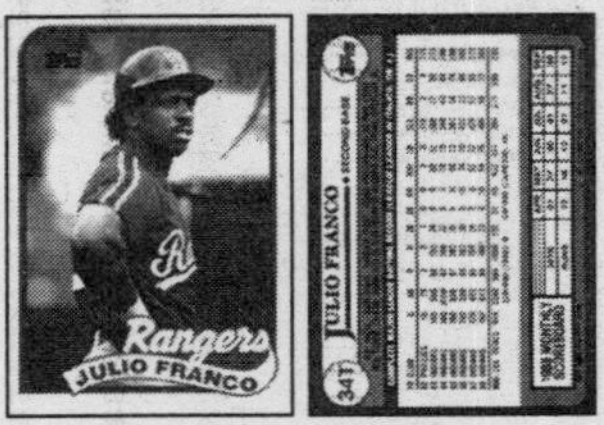

The 1989 Topps Traded set contains 132 standard-size cards. The cards were distributed exclusively in factory set form in red and white taped boxes through hobby dealers. The cards are identical to the 1989 Topps regular issue cards except for whiter stock and t-suffixed numbering on back. Rookie Cards in this set include Ken Griffey Jr., Ken Hill and Deion Sanders.

		MINT	NRMT	EXC
COMPLETE FACT.SET (132)		6.00	2.70	.75
COMMON CARD (1T-132T)		.05	.02	.01
SEMISTARS		.10	.05	.01
□ 1T	Don Aase	.05	.02	.01
□ 2T	Jim Abbott	.15	.07	.02
□ 3T	Kent Anderson	.05	.02	.01
□ 4T	Keith Atherton	.05	.02	.01
□ 5T	Wally Backman	.05	.02	.01
□ 6T	Steve Balboni	.05	.02	.01
□ 7T	Jesse Barfield	.05	.02	.01
□ 8T	Steve Bedrosian	.05	.02	.01
□ 9T	Todd Benzinger	.05	.02	.01
□ 10T	Geronimo Berroa	.10	.05	.01
□ 11T	Bert Blyleven	.10	.05	.01
□ 12T	Bob Boone	.10	.05	.01

□ 13T	Phil Bradley	.05	.02	.01
□ 14T	Jeff Brantley	.05	.02	.01
□ 15T	Kevin Brown	.15	.07	.02
□ 16T	Jerry Browne	.05	.02	.01
□ 17T	Chuck Cary	.05	.02	.01
□ 18T	Carmen Castillo	.05	.02	.01
□ 19T	Jim Clancy	.05	.02	.01
□ 20T	Jack Clark	.10	.05	.01
□ 21T	Bryan Clutterbuck	.05	.02	.01
□ 22T	Jody Davis	.05	.02	.01
□ 23T	Mike Devereaux	.05	.02	.01
□ 24T	Frank DiPino	.05	.02	.01
□ 25T	Benny Distefano	.05	.02	.01
□ 26T	John Dopson	.05	.02	.01
□ 27T	Len Dykstra	.10	.05	.01
□ 28T	Jim Eisenreich	.10	.05	.01
□ 29T	Nick Esasky	.05	.02	.01
□ 30T	Alvaro Espinoza	.05	.02	.01
□ 31T	Darrell Evans UER (Stat headings on back are for a pitcher)	.10	.05	.01
□ 32T	Junior Felix	.05	.02	.01
□ 33T	Felix Fermin	.05	.02	.01
□ 34T	Julio Franco	.10	.05	.01
□ 35T	Terry Francona	.05	.02	.01
□ 36T	Cito Gaston MG	.10	.05	.01
□ 37T	Bob Geren UER (Photo actually Mike Fennell)	.05	.02	.01
□ 38T	Tom Gordon	.10	.05	.01
□ 39T	Tommy Gregg	.05	.02	.01
□ 40T	Ken Griffey Sr.	.05	.02	.01
□ 41T	Ken Griffey Jr.	4.00	1.80	.50
□ 42T	Kevin Gross	.05	.02	.01
□ 43T	Lee Guetterman	.05	.02	.01
□ 44T	Mel Hall	.05	.02	.01
□ 45T	Erik Hanson	.15	.07	.02
□ 46T	Gene Harris	.05	.02	.01
□ 47T	Andy Hawkins	.05	.02	.01
□ 48T	Rickey Henderson	.15	.07	.02
□ 49T	Tom Herr	.05	.02	.01
□ 50T	Ken Hill	.40	.18	.05
□ 51T	Brian Holman	.05	.02	.01
□ 52T	Brian Holton	.05	.02	.01
□ 53T	Art Howe MG	.05	.02	.01
□ 54T	Ken Howell	.05	.02	.01
□ 55T	Bruce Hurst	.05	.02	.01
□ 56T	Chris James	.05	.02	.01
□ 57T	Randy Johnson	.60	.25	.07
□ 58T	Jimmy Jones	.05	.02	.01
□ 59T	Terry Kennedy	.05	.02	.01
□ 60T	Paul Kilgus	.05	.02	.01
□ 61T	Eric King	.05	.02	.01
□ 62T	Ron Kittle	.05	.02	.01
□ 63T	John Kruk	.10	.05	.01
□ 64T	Randy Kutcher	.05	.02	.01
□ 65T	Steve Lake	.05	.02	.01
□ 66T	Mark Langston	.10	.05	.01
□ 67T	Dave LaPoint	.05	.02	.01
□ 68T	Rick Leach	.05	.02	.01
□ 69T	Terry Leach	.05	.02	.01
□ 70T	Jim Lefebvre MG	.05	.02	.01
□ 71T	Al Leiter	.10	.05	.01
□ 72T	Jeffrey Leonard	.05	.02	.01
□ 73T	Derek Lilliquist	.05	.02	.01
□ 74T	Rick Mahler	.05	.02	.01
□ 75T	Tom McCarthy	.05	.02	.01
□ 76T	Lloyd McClendon	.05	.02	.01
□ 77T	Lance McCullers	.05	.02	.01
□ 78T	Oddibe McDowell	.05	.02	.01
□ 79T	Roger McDowell	.05	.02	.01
□ 80T	Larry McWilliams	.05	.02	.01
□ 81T	Randy Milligan	.05	.02	.01
□ 82T	Mike Moore	.05	.02	.01
□ 83T	Keith Moreland	.05	.02	.01
□ 84T	Mike Morgan	.05	.02	.01
□ 85T	Jamie Moyer	.05	.02	.01
□ 86T	Rob Murphy	.05	.02	.01
□ 87T	Eddie Murray	.25	.11	.03
□ 88T	Pete O'Brien	.05	.02	.01
□ 89T	Gregg Olson	.10	.05	.01
□ 90T	Steve Ontiveros	.05	.02	.01
□ 91T	Jesse Orosco	.05	.02	.01
□ 92T	Spike Owen	.05	.02	.01
□ 93T	Rafael Palmeiro	.15	.07	.02
□ 94T	Clay Parker	.05	.02	.01
□ 95T	Jeff Parrett	.05	.02	.01
□ 96T	Lance Parrish	.05	.02	.01
□ 97T	Dennis Powell	.05	.02	.01
□ 98T	Rey Quinones	.05	.02	.01
□ 99T	Doug Rader MG	.05	.02	.01
□ 100T	Willie Randolph	.10	.05	.01
□ 101T	Shane Rawley	.05	.02	.01
□ 102T	Randy Ready	.05	.02	.01
□ 103T	Bip Roberts	.10	.05	.01
□ 104T	Kenny Rogers	.10	.05	.01
□ 105T	Ed Romero	.05	.02	.01
□ 106T	Nolan Ryan	1.25	.55	.16
□ 107T	Luis Salazar	.05	.02	.01
□ 108T	Juan Samuel	.05	.02	.01
□ 109T	Alex Sanchez	.05	.02	.01
□ 110T	Deion Sanders	.75	.35	.09
□ 111T	Steve Sax	.05	.02	.01
□ 112T	Rick Schu	.05	.02	.01
□ 113T	Dwight Smith	.10	.05	.01
□ 114T	Lonnie Smith	.05	.02	.01
□ 115T	Billy Spiers	.05	.02	.01
□ 116T	Kent Tekulve	.05	.02	.01
□ 117T	Walt Terrell	.05	.02	.01
□ 118T	Milt Thompson	.05	.02	.01
□ 119T	Dickie Thon	.05	.02	.01
□ 120T	Jeff Torborg MG	.05	.02	.01
□ 121T	Jeff Treadway	.05	.02	.01
□ 122T	Omar Vizquel	.40	.18	.05
□ 123T	Jerome Walton	.10	.05	.01
□ 124T	Gary Ward	.05	.02	.01
□ 125T	Claudell Washington	.05	.02	.01
□ 126T	Curt Wilkerson	.05	.02	.01
□ 127T	Eddie Williams	.05	.02	.01
□ 128T	Frank Williams	.05	.02	.01
□ 129T	Ken Williams	.05	.02	.01
□ 130T	Mitch Williams	.05	.02	.01
□ 131T	Steve Wilson	.05	.02	.01
□ 132T	Checklist 1T-132T	.05	.02	.01

1990 Topps

The 1990 Topps set contains 792 standard-size cards. Cards were issued primarily in wax packs, rack packs and hobby and retail factory sets. Card fronts feature various colored borders with the player's name at the bottom and team name at top. Subsets include All-Stars (385-407), Turn Back the Clock (661-665) and Draft Picks (scattered throughout the set). The key Rookie Cards in this set are Juan Gonzalez, Marquis Grissom, Ben McDonald, Sammy Sosa, Frank Thomas, Larry Walker and Bernie Williams. The Thomas card (414A) was printed without his name on front creating a scarce variation. The card is rarely seen and, for a newer issue, has experienced unprecedented growth as far as value. Be careful when purchasing this card as counterfeits have been produced.

	MINT	NRMT	EXC
COMPLETE SET (792)	12.00	5.50	1.50
COMPLETE FACT.SET (792)	12.00	5.50	1.50
COMMON CARD (1-792)	.05	.02	.01
RYAN SALUTE (2-5)	.40	.18	.05
SEMISTARS	.10	.05	.01
STARS	.15	.07	.02
BEWARE COUNTERFEIT THOMAS NNOF			

□ 1 Nolan Ryan	.75	.35	.09
□ 2 Nolan Ryan Salute New York Mets	.40	.18	.05
□ 3 Nolan Ryan Salute California Angels	.40	.18	.05
□ 4 Nolan Ryan Salute Houston Astros	.40	.18	.05
□ 5 Nolan Ryan Salute Texas Rangers UER (Says Texas Stadium rather than Arlington Stadium)	.40	.18	.05
□ 6 Vince Coleman RB (50 consecutive SB's	.05	.02	.01
□ 7 Rickey Henderson RB (40 career leadoff HR's	.15	.07	.02
□ 8 Cal Ripken RB (20 or more homers for 8 consecutive years, record for shortstops)	.40	.18	.05
□ 9 Eric Plunk	.05	.02	.01
□ 10 Barry Larkin	.15	.07	.02
□ 11 Paul Gibson	.05	.02	.01
□ 12 Joe Girardi	.10	.05	.01
□ 13 Mark Williamson	.05	.02	.01
□ 14 Mike Fetters	.10	.05	.01
□ 15 Teddy Higuera	.05	.02	.01
□ 16 Kent Anderson	.05	.02	.01
□ 17 Kelly Downs	.05	.02	.01
□ 18 Carlos Quintana	.05	.02	.01
□ 19 Al Newman	.05	.02	.01
□ 20 Mark Gubicza	.05	.02	.01
□ 21 Jeff Torborg MG	.05	.02	.01
□ 22 Bruce Ruffin	.05	.02	.01
□ 23 Randy Velarde	.05	.02	.01
□ 24 Joe Hesketh	.05	.02	.01
□ 25 Willie Randolph	.10	.05	.01
□ 26 Don Slaught	.05	.02	.01
□ 27 Rick Leach	.05	.02	.01
□ 28 Duane Ward	.05	.02	.01
□ 29 John Cangelosi	.05	.02	.01
□ 30 David Cone	.15	.07	.02
□ 31 Henry Cotto	.05	.02	.01
□ 32 John Farrell	.05	.02	.01
□ 33 Greg Walker	.05	.02	.01
□ 34 Tony Fossas	.05	.02	.01
□ 35 Benito Santiago	.05	.02	.01
□ 36 John Costello	.05	.02	.01
□ 37 Domingo Ramos	.05	.02	.01
□ 38 Wes Gardner	.05	.02	.01
□ 39 Curt Ford	.05	.02	.01
□ 40 Jay Howell	.05	.02	.01
□ 41 Matt Williams	.15	.07	.02
□ 42 Jeff M. Robinson	.05	.02	.01
□ 43 Dante Bichette	.15	.07	.02
□ 44 Roger Salkeld FDP	.05	.02	.01
□ 45 Dave Parker UER (Born in Jackson, not Calhoun)	.10	.05	.01
□ 46 Rob Dibble	.05	.02	.01
□ 47 Brian Harper	.05	.02	.01
□ 48 Zane Smith	.05	.02	.01
□ 49 Tom Lawless	.05	.02	.01
□ 50 Glenn Davis	.05	.02	.01
□ 51 Doug Rader MG	.05	.02	.01
□ 52 Jack Daugherty	.05	.02	.01
□ 53 Mike LaCoss	.05	.02	.01
□ 54 Joel Skinner	.05	.02	.01
□ 55 Darrell Evans UER (HR total should be 414, not 424)	.10	.05	.01
□ 56 Franklin Stubbs	.05	.02	.01
□ 57 Greg Vaughn	.15	.07	.02
□ 58 Keith Miller	.05	.02	.01
□ 59 Ted Power	.05	.02	.01
□ 60 George Brett	.40	.18	.05
□ 61 Deion Sanders	.20	.09	.03
□ 62 Ramon Martinez	.15	.07	.02
□ 63 Mike Pagliarulo	.05	.02	.01
□ 64 Danny Darwin	.05	.02	.01
□ 65 Devon White	.10	.05	.01
□ 66 Greg Litton	.05	.02	.01
□ 67 Scott Sanderson	.05	.02	.01
□ 68 Dave Henderson	.05	.02	.01
□ 69 Todd Frohwirth	.05	.02	.01
□ 70 Mike Greenwell	.05	.02	.01
□ 71 Allan Anderson	.05	.02	.01
□ 72 Jeff Huson	.05	.02	.01
□ 73 Bob Milacki	.05	.02	.01
□ 74 Jeff Jackson FDP	.05	.02	.01
□ 75 Doug Jones	.05	.02	.01
□ 76 Dave Valle	.05	.02	.01
□ 77 Dave Bergman	.05	.02	.01
□ 78 Mike Flanagan	.05	.02	.01
□ 79 Ron Kittle	.05	.02	.01
□ 80 Jeff Russell	.05	.02	.01
□ 81 Bob Rodgers MG	.05	.02	.01
□ 82 Scott Terry	.05	.02	.01
□ 83 Hensley Meulens	.05	.02	.01
□ 84 Ray Searage	.05	.02	.01
□ 85 Juan Samuel	.05	.02	.01
□ 86 Paul Kilgus	.05	.02	.01
□ 87 Rick Luecken	.05	.02	.01
□ 88 Glenn Braggs	.05	.02	.01
□ 89 Clint Zavaras	.05	.02	.01
□ 90 Jack Clark	.10	.05	.01
□ 91 Steve Frey	.05	.02	.01
□ 92 Mike Stanley	.05	.02	.01
□ 93 Shawn Hillegas	.05	.02	.01
□ 94 Herm Winningham	.05	.02	.01
□ 95 Todd Worrell	.05	.02	.01
□ 96 Jody Reed	.05	.02	.01
□ 97 Curt Schilling	.05	.02	.01
□ 98 Jose Gonzalez	.05	.02	.01
□ 99 Rich Monteleone	.05	.02	.01
□ 100 Will Clark	.15	.07	.02
□ 101 Shane Rawley	.05	.02	.01
□ 102 Stan Javier	.05	.02	.01
□ 103 Marvin Freeman	.05	.02	.01
□ 104 Bob Knepper	.05	.02	.01
□ 105 Randy Myers	.10	.05	.01
□ 106 Charlie O'Brien	.05	.02	.01
□ 107 Fred Lynn	.05	.02	.01
□ 108 Rod Nichols	.05	.02	.01
□ 109 Roberto Kelly	.10	.05	.01
□ 110 Tommy Helms MG	.05	.02	.01
□ 111 Ed Whited	.05	.02	.01
□ 112 Glenn Wilson	.05	.02	.01
□ 113 Manny Lee	.05	.02	.01
□ 114 Mike Bielecki	.05	.02	.01
□ 115 Tony Pena	.05	.02	.01
□ 116 Floyd Bannister	.05	.02	.01
□ 117 Mike Sharperson	.05	.02	.01
□ 118 Erik Hanson	.10	.05	.01
□ 119 Billy Hatcher	.05	.02	.01
□ 120 John Franco	.05	.02	.01
□ 121 Robin Ventura	.15	.07	.02
□ 122 Shawn Abner	.05	.02	.01
□ 123 Rich Gedman	.05	.02	.01
□ 124 Dave Dravecky	.10	.05	.01
□ 125 Kent Hrbek	.10	.05	.01
□ 126 Randy Kramer	.05	.02	.01
□ 127 Mike Devereaux	.05	.02	.01
□ 128 Checklist 1	.05	.02	.01
□ 129 Ron Jones	.05	.02	.01
□ 130 Bert Blyleven	.10	.05	.01
□ 131 Matt Nokes	.05	.02	.01
□ 132 Lance Blankenship	.05	.02	.01
□ 133 Ricky Horton	.05	.02	.01
□ 134 Earl Cunningham FDP	.05	.02	.01
□ 135 Dave Magadan	.05	.02	.01
□ 136 Kevin Brown	.10	.05	.01
□ 137 Marty Pevey	.05	.02	.01
□ 138 Al Leiter	.10	.05	.01
□ 139 Greg Brock	.05	.02	.01
□ 140 Andre Dawson	.15	.07	.02
□ 141 John Hart MG	.05	.02	.01
□ 142 Jeff Wetherby	.05	.02	.01
□ 143 Rafael Belliard	.05	.02	.01
□ 144 Bud Black	.05	.02	.01
□ 145 Terry Steinbach	.10	.05	.01
□ 146 Rob Richie	.05	.02	.01
□ 147 Chuck Finley	.10	.05	.01
□ 148 Edgar Martinez	.15	.07	.02
□ 149 Steve Farr	.05	.02	.01
□ 150 Kirk Gibson	.10	.05	.01
□ 151 Rick Mahler	.05	.02	.01
□ 152 Lonnie Smith	.05	.02	.01
□ 153 Randy Milligan	.05	.02	.01
□ 154 Mike Maddux	.05	.02	.01
□ 155 Ellis Burks	.15	.07	.02
□ 156 Ken Patterson	.05	.02	.01

☐ 157 Craig Biggio	.15	.07	.02
☐ 158 Craig Lefferts	.05	.02	.01
☐ 159 Mike Felder	.05	.02	.01
☐ 160 Dave Righetti	.05	.02	.01
☐ 161 Harold Reynolds	.05	.02	.01
☐ 162 Todd Zeile	.10	.05	.01
☐ 163 Phil Bradley	.05	.02	.01
☐ 164 Jeff Juden FDP	.05	.02	.01
☐ 165 Walt Weiss	.05	.02	.01
☐ 166 Bobby Witt	.05	.02	.01
☐ 167 Kevin Appier	.15	.07	.02
☐ 168 Jose Lind	.05	.02	.01
☐ 169 Richard Dotson	.05	.02	.01
☐ 170 George Bell	.05	.02	.01
☐ 171 Russ Nixon MG	.05	.02	.01
☐ 172 Tom Lampkin	.05	.02	.01
☐ 173 Tim Belcher	.05	.02	.01
☐ 174 Jeff Kunkel	.05	.02	.01
☐ 175 Mike Moore	.05	.02	.01
☐ 176 Luis Quinones	.05	.02	.01
☐ 177 Mike Henneman	.05	.02	.01
☐ 178 Chris James	.05	.02	.01
☐ 179 Brian Holton	.05	.02	.01
☐ 180 Tim Raines	.15	.07	.02
☐ 181 Juan Agosto	.05	.02	.01
☐ 182 Mookie Wilson	.05	.02	.01
☐ 183 Steve Lake	.05	.02	.01
☐ 184 Danny Cox	.05	.02	.01
☐ 185 Ruben Sierra	.10	.05	.01
☐ 186 Dave LaPoint	.05	.02	.01
☐ 187 Rick Wrona	.05	.02	.01
☐ 188 Mike Smithson	.05	.02	.01
☐ 189 Dick Schofield	.05	.02	.01
☐ 190 Rick Reuschel	.05	.02	.01
☐ 191 Pat Borders	.05	.02	.01
☐ 192 Don August	.05	.02	.01
☐ 193 Andy Benes	.15	.07	.02
☐ 194 Glenallen Hill	.10	.05	.01
☐ 195 Tim Burke	.05	.02	.01
☐ 196 Gerald Young	.05	.02	.01
☐ 197 Doug Drabek	.05	.02	.01
☐ 198 Mike Marshall	.05	.02	.01
☐ 199 Sergio Valdez	.05	.02	.01
☐ 200 Don Mattingly	.50	.23	.06
☐ 201 Cito Gaston MG	.05	.02	.01
☐ 202 Mike Macfarlane	.05	.02	.01
☐ 203 Mike Roesler	.05	.02	.01
☐ 204 Bob Dernier	.05	.02	.01
☐ 205 Mark Davis	.05	.02	.01
☐ 206 Nick Esasky	.05	.02	.01
☐ 207 Bob Ojeda	.05	.02	.01
☐ 208 Brook Jacoby	.05	.02	.01
☐ 209 Greg Mathews	.05	.02	.01
☐ 210 Ryne Sandberg	.25	.11	.03
☐ 211 John Cerutti	.05	.02	.01
☐ 212 Joe Orsulak	.05	.02	.01
☐ 213 Scott Bankhead	.05	.02	.01
☐ 214 Terry Francona	.05	.02	.01
☐ 215 Kirk McCaskill	.05	.02	.01
☐ 216 Ricky Jordan	.05	.02	.01
☐ 217 Don Robinson	.05	.02	.01
☐ 218 Wally Backman	.05	.02	.01
☐ 219 Donn Pall	.05	.02	.01
☐ 220 Barry Bonds	.25	.11	.03
☐ 221 Gary Mielke	.05	.02	.01
☐ 222 Kurt Stillwell UER (Graduate misspelled as gradute)	.05	.02	.01
☐ 223 Tommy Gregg	.05	.02	.01
☐ 224 Delino DeShields	.10	.05	.01
☐ 225 Jim Deshaies	.05	.02	.01
☐ 226 Mickey Hatcher	.05	.02	.01
☐ 227 Kevin Tapani	.10	.05	.01
☐ 228 Dave Martinez	.05	.02	.01
☐ 229 David Wells	.05	.02	.01
☐ 230 Keith Hernandez	.10	.05	.01
☐ 231 Jack McKeon MG	.05	.02	.01
☐ 232 Darnell Coles	.05	.02	.01
☐ 233 Ken Hill	.15	.07	.02
☐ 234 Mariano Duncan	.05	.02	.01
☐ 235 Jeff Reardon	.10	.05	.01
☐ 236 Hal Morris	.10	.05	.01
☐ 237 Kevin Ritz	.05	.02	.01
☐ 238 Felix Jose	.05	.02	.01
☐ 239 Eric Show	.05	.02	.01
☐ 240 Mark Grace	.15	.07	.02
☐ 241 Mike Krukow	.05	.02	.01
☐ 242 Fred Manrique	.05	.02	.01
☐ 243 Barry Jones	.05	.02	.01
☐ 244 Bill Schroeder	.05	.02	.01
☐ 245 Roger Clemens	.15	.07	.02
☐ 246 Jim Eisenreich	.05	.02	.01
☐ 247 Jerry Reed	.05	.02	.01
☐ 248 Dave Anderson	.05	.02	.01
☐ 249 Mike(Texas) Smith	.05	.02	.01
☐ 250 Jose Canseco	.15	.07	.02
☐ 251 Jeff Blauser	.10	.05	.01
☐ 252 Otis Nixon	.05	.02	.01
☐ 253 Mark Portugal	.05	.02	.01
☐ 254 Francisco Cabrera	.05	.02	.01
☐ 255 Bobby Thigpen	.05	.02	.01
☐ 256 Marvell Wynne	.05	.02	.01
☐ 257 Jose DeLeon	.05	.02	.01
☐ 258 Barry Lyons	.05	.02	.01
☐ 259 Lance McCullers	.05	.02	.01
☐ 260 Eric Davis	.10	.05	.01
☐ 261 Whitey Herzog MG	.10	.05	.01
☐ 262 Checklist 2	.05	.02	.01
☐ 263 Mel Stottlemyre Jr.	.05	.02	.01
☐ 264 Bryan Clutterbuck	.05	.02	.01
☐ 265 Pete O'Brien	.05	.02	.01
☐ 266 German Gonzalez	.05	.02	.01
☐ 267 Mark Davidson	.05	.02	.01
☐ 268 Rob Murphy	.05	.02	.01
☐ 269 Dickie Thon	.05	.02	.01
☐ 270 Dave Stewart	.10	.05	.01
☐ 271 Chet Lemon	.05	.02	.01
☐ 272 Bryan Harvey	.05	.02	.01
☐ 273 Bobby Bonilla	.10	.05	.01
☐ 274 Mauro Gozzo	.05	.02	.01
☐ 275 Mickey Tettleton	.10	.05	.01
☐ 276 Gary Thurman	.05	.02	.01
☐ 277 Lenny Harris	.05	.02	.01
☐ 278 Pascual Perez	.05	.02	.01
☐ 279 Steve Buechele	.05	.02	.01
☐ 280 Lou Whitaker	.15	.07	.02
☐ 281 Kevin Bass	.05	.02	.01
☐ 282 Derek Lilliquist	.05	.02	.01
☐ 283 Joey Belle	1.00	.45	.12
☐ 284 Mark Gardner	.05	.02	.01
☐ 285 Willie McGee	.05	.02	.01
☐ 286 Lee Guetterman	.05	.02	.01
☐ 287 Vance Law	.05	.02	.01
☐ 288 Greg Briley	.05	.02	.01
☐ 289 Norm Charlton	.05	.02	.01
☐ 290 Robin Yount	.15	.07	.02
☐ 291 Dave Johnson MG	.10	.05	.01
☐ 292 Jim Gott	.05	.02	.01
☐ 293 Mike Gallego	.05	.02	.01
☐ 294 Craig McMurtry	.05	.02	.01
☐ 295 Fred McGriff	.15	.07	.02
☐ 296 Jeff Ballard	.05	.02	.01
☐ 297 Tommy Herr	.05	.02	.01
☐ 298 Dan Gladden	.05	.02	.01
☐ 299 Adam Peterson	.05	.02	.01
☐ 300 Bo Jackson	.15	.07	.02
☐ 301 Don Aase	.05	.02	.01
☐ 302 Marcus Lawton	.05	.02	.01
☐ 303 Rick Cerone	.05	.02	.01
☐ 304 Marty Clary	.05	.02	.01
☐ 305 Eddie Murray	.25	.11	.03
☐ 306 Tom Niedenfuer	.05	.02	.01
☐ 307 Bip Roberts	.05	.02	.01
☐ 308 Jose Guzman	.05	.02	.01
☐ 309 Eric Yelding	.05	.02	.01
☐ 310 Steve Bedrosian	.05	.02	.01
☐ 311 Dwight Smith	.05	.02	.01
☐ 312 Dan Quisenberry	.05	.02	.01
☐ 313 Gus Polidor	.05	.02	.01
☐ 314 Donald Harris FDP	.05	.02	.01
☐ 315 Bruce Hurst	.05	.02	.01
☐ 316 Carney Lansford	.10	.05	.01
☐ 317 Mark Guthrie	.05	.02	.01
☐ 318 Wallace Johnson	.05	.02	.01
☐ 319 Dion James	.05	.02	.01
☐ 320 Dave Stieb	.05	.02	.01
☐ 321 Joe Morgan MG	.05	.02	.01
☐ 322 Junior Ortiz	.05	.02	.01
☐ 323 Willie Wilson	.05	.02	.01
☐ 324 Pete Harnisch	.05	.02	.01
☐ 325 Robby Thompson	.05	.02	.01
☐ 326 Tom McCarthy	.05	.02	.01

□ 327	Ken Williams	.05	.02	.01
□ 328	Curt Young	.05	.02	.01
□ 329	Oddibe McDowell	.05	.02	.01
□ 330	Ron Darling	.05	.02	.01
□ 331	Juan Gonzalez	2.00	.90	.25
□ 332	Paul O'Neill	.10	.05	.01
□ 333	Bill Wegman	.05	.02	.01
□ 334	Johnny Ray	.05	.02	.01
□ 335	Andy Hawkins	.05	.02	.01
□ 336	Ken Griffey Jr.	1.50	.70	.19
□ 337	Lloyd McClendon	.05	.02	.01
□ 338	Dennis Lamp	.05	.02	.01
□ 339	Dave Clark	.05	.02	.01
□ 340	Fernando Valenzuela	.10	.05	.01
□ 341	Tom Foley	.05	.02	.01
□ 342	Alex Trevino	.05	.02	.01
□ 343	Frank Tanana	.05	.02	.01
□ 344	George Canale	.05	.02	.01
□ 345	Harold Baines	.10	.05	.01
□ 346	Jim Presley	.05	.02	.01
□ 347	Junior Felix	.05	.02	.01
□ 348	Gary Wayne	.05	.02	.01
□ 349	Steve Finley	.15	.07	.02
□ 350	Bret Saberhagen	.10	.05	.01
□ 351	Roger Craig MG	.05	.02	.01
□ 352	Bryn Smith	.05	.02	.01
□ 353	Sandy Alomar Jr. (Not listed as Jr. on card front)	.10	.05	.01
□ 354	Stan Belinda	.05	.02	.01
□ 355	Marty Barrett	.05	.02	.01
□ 356	Randy Ready	.05	.02	.01
□ 357	Dave West	.05	.02	.01
□ 358	Andres Thomas	.05	.02	.01
□ 359	Jimmy Jones	.05	.02	.01
□ 360	Paul Molitor	.20	.09	.03
□ 361	Randy McCament	.05	.02	.01
□ 362	Damon Berryhill	.05	.02	.01
□ 363	Dan Petry	.05	.02	.01
□ 364	Rolando Roomes	.05	.02	.01
□ 365	Ozzie Guillen	.05	.02	.01
□ 366	Mike Heath	.05	.02	.01
□ 367	Mike Morgan	.05	.02	.01
□ 368	Bill Doran	.05	.02	.01
□ 369	Todd Burns	.05	.02	.01
□ 370	Tim Wallach	.05	.02	.01
□ 371	Jimmy Key	.10	.05	.01
□ 372	Terry Kennedy	.05	.02	.01
□ 373	Alvin Davis	.05	.02	.01
□ 374	Steve Cummings	.05	.02	.01
□ 375	Dwight Evans	.10	.05	.01
□ 376	Checklist 3 UER (Higuera misalphabet-ized in Brewer list)	.05	.02	.01
□ 377	Mickey Weston	.05	.02	.01
□ 378	Luis Salazar	.05	.02	.01
□ 379	Steve Rosenberg	.05	.02	.01
□ 380	Dave Winfield	.15	.07	.02
□ 381	Frank Robinson MG	.15	.07	.02
□ 382	Jeff Musselman	.05	.02	.01
□ 383	John Morris	.05	.02	.01
□ 384	Pat Combs	.05	.02	.01
□ 385	Fred McGriff AS	.15	.07	.02
□ 386	Julio Franco AS	.05	.02	.01
□ 387	Wade Boggs AS	.15	.07	.02
□ 388	Cal Ripken AS	.40	.18	.05
□ 389	Robin Yount AS	.10	.05	.01
□ 390	Ruben Sierra AS	.05	.02	.01
□ 391	Kirby Puckett AS	.15	.07	.02
□ 392	Carlton Fisk AS	.15	.07	.02
□ 393	Bret Saberhagen AS	.10	.05	.01
□ 394	Jeff Ballard AS	.05	.02	.01
□ 395	Jeff Russell AS	.05	.02	.01
□ 396	A.Bartlett Giamatti COMM MEM	.15	.07	.02
□ 397	Will Clark AS	.15	.07	.02
□ 398	Ryne Sandberg AS	.15	.07	.02
□ 399	Howard Johnson AS	.05	.02	.01
□ 400	Ozzie Smith AS	.15	.07	.02
□ 401	Kevin Mitchell AS	.05	.02	.01
□ 402	Eric Davis AS	.10	.05	.01
□ 403	Tony Gwynn AS	.20	.09	.03
□ 404	Craig Biggio AS	.15	.07	.02
□ 405	Mike Scott AS	.05	.02	.01
□ 406	Joe Magrane AS	.05	.02	.01
□ 407	Mark Davis AS	.05	.02	.01

□ 408	Trevor Wilson	.05	.02	.01
□ 409	Tom Brunansky	.05	.02	.01
□ 410	Joe Boever	.05	.02	.01
□ 411	Ken Phelps	.05	.02	.01
□ 412	Jamie Moyer	.05	.02	.01
□ 413	Brian DuBois	.05	.02	.01
□ 414A	Frank Thomas FDP ERR (Name missing on card front)	2000.00	900.00	250.00
□ 414B	Frank Thomas FDP COR	4.00	1.80	.50
□ 415	Shawon Dunston	.05	.02	.01
□ 416	Dave Johnson (P)	.05	.02	.01
□ 417	Jim Gantner	.05	.02	.01
□ 418	Tom Browning	.05	.02	.01
□ 419	Beau Allred	.05	.02	.01
□ 420	Carlton Fisk	.15	.07	.02
□ 421	Greg Minton	.05	.02	.01
□ 422	Pat Sheridan	.05	.02	.01
□ 423	Fred Toliver	.05	.02	.01
□ 424	Jerry Reuss	.05	.02	.01
□ 425	Bill Landrum	.05	.02	.01
□ 426	Jeff Hamilton UER (Stats say he fanned 197 times in 1987, but he only had 147 at bats)	.05	.02	.01
□ 427	Carmen Castillo	.05	.02	.01
□ 428	Steve Davis	.05	.02	.01
□ 429	Tom Kelly MG	.05	.02	.01
□ 430	Pete Incaviglia	.05	.02	.01
□ 431	Randy Johnson	.25	.11	.03
□ 432	Damaso Garcia	.05	.02	.01
□ 433	Steve Olin	.10	.05	.01
□ 434	Mark Carreon	.05	.02	.01
□ 435	Kevin Seitzer	.05	.02	.01
□ 436	Mel Hall	.05	.02	.01
□ 437	Les Lancaster	.05	.02	.01
□ 438	Greg Myers	.05	.02	.01
□ 439	Jeff Parrett	.05	.02	.01
□ 440	Alan Trammell	.15	.07	.02
□ 441	Bob Kipper	.05	.02	.01
□ 442	Jerry Browne	.05	.02	.01
□ 443	Cris Carpenter	.05	.02	.01
□ 444	Kyle Abbott FDP	.05	.02	.01
□ 445	Danny Jackson	.05	.02	.01
□ 446	Dan Pasqua	.05	.02	.01
□ 447	Atlee Hammaker	.05	.02	.01
□ 448	Greg Gagne	.05	.02	.01
□ 449	Dennis Rasmussen	.05	.02	.01
□ 450	Rickey Henderson	.15	.07	.02
□ 451	Mark Lemke	.10	.05	.01
□ 452	Luis DeLosSantos	.05	.02	.01
□ 453	Jody Davis	.05	.02	.01
□ 454	Jeff King	.10	.05	.01
□ 455	Jeffrey Leonard	.05	.02	.01
□ 456	Chris Gwynn	.05	.02	.01
□ 457	Gregg Jefferies	.15	.07	.02
□ 458	Bob McClure	.05	.02	.01
□ 459	Jim Lefebvre MG	.05	.02	.01
□ 460	Mike Scott	.05	.02	.01
□ 461	Carlos Martinez	.05	.02	.01
□ 462	Denny Walling	.05	.02	.01
□ 463	Drew Hall	.05	.02	.01
□ 464	Jerome Walton	.05	.02	.01
□ 465	Kevin Gross	.05	.02	.01
□ 466	Rance Mulliniks	.05	.02	.01
□ 467	Juan Nieves	.05	.02	.01
□ 468	Bill Ripken	.05	.02	.01
□ 469	John Kruk	.10	.05	.01
□ 470	Frank Viola	.05	.02	.01
□ 471	Mike Brumley	.05	.02	.01
□ 472	Jose Uribe	.05	.02	.01
□ 473	Joe Price	.05	.02	.01
□ 474	Rich Thompson	.05	.02	.01
□ 475	Bob Welch	.05	.02	.01
□ 476	Brad Komminsk	.05	.02	.01
□ 477	Willie Fraser	.05	.02	.01
□ 478	Mike LaValliere	.05	.02	.01
□ 479	Frank White	.10	.05	.01
□ 480	Sid Fernandez	.05	.02	.01
□ 481	Garry Templeton	.05	.02	.01
□ 482	Steve Carter	.05	.02	.01
□ 483	Alejandro Pena	.05	.02	.01
□ 484	Mike Fitzgerald	.05	.02	.01
□ 485	John Candelaria	.05	.02	.01
□ 486	Jeff Treadway	.05	.02	.01
□ 487	Steve Searcy	.05	.02	.01

□ 488 Ken Oberkfell	.05	.02	.01
□ 489 Nick Leyva MG	.05	.02	.01
□ 490 Dan Plesac	.05	.02	.01
□ 491 Dave Cochrane	.05	.02	.01
□ 492 Ron Oester	.05	.02	.01
□ 493 Jason Grimsley	.05	.02	.01
□ 494 Terry Puhl	.05	.02	.01
□ 495 Lee Smith	.10	.05	.01
□ 496 Cecil Espy UER ('88 stats have 3 SB's, should be 33)	.05	.02	.01
□ 497 Dave Schmidt	.05	.02	.01
□ 498 Rick Schu	.05	.02	.01
□ 499 Bill Long	.05	.02	.01
□ 500 Kevin Mitchell	.10	.05	.01
□ 501 Matt Young	.05	.02	.01
□ 502 Mitch Webster	.05	.02	.01
□ 503 Randy St.Claire	.05	.02	.01
□ 504 Tom O'Malley	.05	.02	.01
□ 505 Kelly Gruber	.05	.02	.01
□ 506 Tom Glavine	.15	.07	.02
□ 507 Gary Redus	.05	.02	.01
□ 508 Terry Leach	.05	.02	.01
□ 509 Tom Pagnozzi	.05	.02	.01
□ 510 Dwight Gooden	.10	.05	.01
□ 511 Clay Parker	.05	.02	.01
□ 512 Gary Pettis	.05	.02	.01
□ 513 Mark Eichhorn	.05	.02	.01
□ 514 Andy Allanson	.05	.02	.01
□ 515 Len Dykstra	.10	.05	.01
□ 516 Tim Leary	.05	.02	.01
□ 517 Roberto Alomar	.30	.14	.04
□ 518 Bill Krueger	.05	.02	.01
□ 519 Bucky Dent MG	.05	.02	.01
□ 520 Mitch Williams	.05	.02	.01
□ 521 Craig Worthington	.05	.02	.01
□ 522 Mike Dunne	.05	.02	.01
□ 523 Jay Bell	.10	.05	.01
□ 524 Daryl Boston	.05	.02	.01
□ 525 Wally Joyner	.10	.05	.01
□ 526 Checklist 4	.05	.02	.01
□ 527 Ron Hassey	.05	.02	.01
□ 528 Kevin Wickander UER (Monthly scoreboard strikeout total was 2.2, that was his innings pitched total)	.05	.02	.01
□ 529 Greg A. Harris	.05	.02	.01
□ 530 Mark Langston	.10	.05	.01
□ 531 Ken Caminiti	.15	.07	.02
□ 532 Cecilio Guante	.05	.02	.01
□ 533 Tim Jones	.05	.02	.01
□ 534 Louie Meadows	.05	.02	.01
□ 535 John Smoltz	.25	.11	.03
□ 536 Bob Geren	.05	.02	.01
□ 537 Mark Grant	.05	.02	.01
□ 538 Bill Spiers UER (Photo actually George Canale)	.05	.02	.01
□ 539 Neal Heaton	.05	.02	.01
□ 540 Danny Tartabull	.05	.02	.01
□ 541 Pat Perry	.05	.02	.01
□ 542 Darren Daulton	.10	.05	.01
□ 543 Nelson Liriano	.05	.02	.01
□ 544 Dennis Boyd	.05	.02	.01
□ 545 Kevin McReynolds	.05	.02	.01
□ 546 Kevin Hickey	.05	.02	.01
□ 547 Jack Howell	.05	.02	.01
□ 548 Pat Clements	.05	.02	.01
□ 549 Don Zimmer MG	.05	.02	.01
□ 550 Julio Franco	.10	.05	.01
□ 551 Tim Crews	.05	.02	.01
□ 552 Mike(Miss.) Smith	.05	.02	.01
□ 553 Scott Scudder UER (Cedar Rap1ds)	.05	.02	.01
□ 554 Jay Buhner	.15	.07	.02
□ 555 Jack Morris	.10	.05	.01
□ 556 Gene Larkin	.05	.02	.01
□ 557 Jeff Innis	.05	.02	.01
□ 558 Rafael Ramirez	.05	.02	.01
□ 559 Andy McGaffigan	.05	.02	.01
□ 560 Steve Sax	.05	.02	.01
□ 561 Ken Dayley	.05	.02	.01
□ 562 Chad Kreuter	.05	.02	.01
□ 563 Alex Sanchez	.05	.02	.01
□ 564 Tyler Houston FDP	.15	.07	.02

□ 565 Scott Fletcher	.05	.02	.01
□ 566 Mark Knudson	.05	.02	.01
□ 567 Ron Gant	.15	.07	.02
□ 568 John Smiley	.10	.05	.01
□ 569 Ivan Calderon	.05	.02	.01
□ 570 Cal Ripken	.75	.35	.09
□ 571 Brett Butler	.10	.05	.01
□ 572 Greg W. Harris	.05	.02	.01
□ 573 Danny Heep	.05	.02	.01
□ 574 Bill Swift	.05	.02	.01
□ 575 Lance Parrish	.05	.02	.01
□ 576 Mike Dyer	.05	.02	.01
□ 577 Charlie Hayes	.10	.05	.01
□ 578 Joe Magrane	.05	.02	.01
□ 579 Art Howe MG	.05	.02	.01
□ 580 Joe Carter	.15	.07	.02
□ 581 Ken Griffey Sr.	.05	.02	.01
□ 582 Rick Honeycutt	.05	.02	.01
□ 583 Bruce Benedict	.05	.02	.01
□ 584 Phil Stephenson	.05	.02	.01
□ 585 Kal Daniels	.05	.02	.01
□ 586 Edwin Nunez	.05	.02	.01
□ 587 Lance Johnson	.15	.07	.02
□ 588 Rick Rhoden	.05	.02	.01
□ 589 Mike Aldrete	.05	.02	.01
□ 590 Ozzie Smith	.20	.09	.03
□ 591 Todd Stottlemyre	.10	.05	.01
□ 592 R.J. Reynolds	.05	.02	.01
□ 593 Scott Bradley	.05	.02	.01
□ 594 Luis Sojo	.05	.02	.01
□ 595 Greg Swindell	.05	.02	.01
□ 596 Jose DeJesus	.05	.02	.01
□ 597 Chris Bosio	.05	.02	.01
□ 598 Brady Anderson	.15	.07	.02
□ 599 Frank Williams	.05	.02	.01
□ 600 Darryl Strawberry	.10	.05	.01
□ 601 Luis Rivera	.05	.02	.01
□ 602 Scott Garrelts	.05	.02	.01
□ 603 Tony Armas	.05	.02	.01
□ 604 Ron Robinson	.05	.02	.01
□ 605 Mike Scioscia	.05	.02	.01
□ 606 Storm Davis	.05	.02	.01
□ 607 Steve Jeltz	.05	.02	.01
□ 608 Eric Anthony	.10	.05	.01
□ 609 Sparky Anderson MG	.10	.05	.01
□ 610 Pedro Guerrero	.05	.02	.01
□ 611 Walt Terrell	.05	.02	.01
□ 612 Dave Gallagher	.05	.02	.01
□ 613 Jeff Pico	.05	.02	.01
□ 614 Nelson Santovenia	.05	.02	.01
□ 615 Rob Deer	.05	.02	.01
□ 616 Brian Holman	.05	.02	.01
□ 617 Geronimo Berroa	.10	.05	.01
□ 618 Ed Whitson	.05	.02	.01
□ 619 Rob Ducey	.05	.02	.01
□ 620 Tony Castillo	.05	.02	.01
□ 621 Melido Perez	.05	.02	.01
□ 622 Sid Bream	.05	.02	.01
□ 623 Jim Corsi	.05	.02	.01
□ 624 Darrin Jackson	.05	.02	.01
□ 625 Roger McDowell	.05	.02	.01
□ 626 Bob Melvin	.05	.02	.01
□ 627 Jose Rijo	.05	.02	.01
□ 628 Candy Maldonado	.05	.02	.01
□ 629 Eric Hetzel	.05	.02	.01
□ 630 Gary Gaetti	.10	.05	.01
□ 631 John Wetteland	.10	.05	.01
□ 632 Scott Lusader	.05	.02	.01
□ 633 Dennis Cook	.05	.02	.01
□ 634 Luis Polonia	.05	.02	.01
□ 635 Brian Downing	.05	.02	.01
□ 636 Jesse Orosco	.05	.02	.01
□ 637 Craig Reynolds	.05	.02	.01
□ 638 Jeff Montgomery	.10	.05	.01
□ 639 Tony LaRussa MG	.10	.05	.01
□ 640 Rick Sutcliffe	.05	.02	.01
□ 641 Doug Strange	.05	.02	.01
□ 642 Jack Armstrong	.05	.02	.01
□ 643 Alfredo Griffin	.05	.02	.01
□ 644 Paul Assenmacher	.05	.02	.01
□ 645 Jose Oquendo	.05	.02	.01
□ 646 Checklist 5	.05	.02	.01
□ 647 Rex Hudler	.05	.02	.01
□ 648 Jim Clancy	.05	.02	.01
□ 649 Dan Murphy	.05	.02	.01
□ 650 Mike Witt	.05	.02	.01

□ 651 Rafael Santana	.05	.02	.01
□ 652 Mike Boddicker	.05	.02	.01
□ 653 John Moses	.05	.02	.01
□ 654 Paul Coleman FDP	.05	.02	.01
□ 655 Gregg Olson	.05	.02	.01
□ 656 Mackey Sasser	.05	.02	.01
□ 657 Terry Mulholland	.05	.02	.01
□ 658 Donell Nixon	.05	.02	.01
□ 659 Greg Cadaret	.05	.02	.01
□ 660 Vince Coleman	.05	.02	.01
□ 661 Dick Howser TBC'85 UER (Seaver's 300th on 7/11/85, should be 8/4/85)	.05	.02	.01
□ 662 Mike Schmidt TBC'80	.15	.07	.02
□ 663 Fred Lynn TBC'75	.05	.02	.01
□ 664 Johnny Bench TBC'70	.15	.07	.02
□ 665 Sandy Koufax TBC'65	.25	.11	.03
□ 666 Brian Fisher	.05	.02	.01
□ 667 Curt Wilkerson	.05	.02	.01
□ 668 Joe Oliver	.05	.02	.01
□ 669 Tom Lasorda MG	.10	.05	.01
□ 670 Dennis Eckersley	.10	.05	.01
□ 671 Bob Boone	.10	.05	.01
□ 672 Roy Smith	.05	.02	.01
□ 673 Joey Meyer	.05	.02	.01
□ 674 Spike Owen	.05	.02	.01
□ 675 Jim Abbott	.10	.05	.01
□ 676 Randy Kutcher	.05	.02	.01
□ 677 Jay Tibbs	.05	.02	.01
□ 678 Kirt Manwaring UER ('88 Phoenix stats repeated)	.05	.02	.01
□ 679 Gary Ward	.05	.02	.01
□ 680 Howard Johnson	.05	.02	.01
□ 681 Mike Schooler	.05	.02	.01
□ 682 Dann Bilardello	.05	.02	.01
□ 683 Kenny Rogers	.10	.05	.01
□ 684 Julio Machado	.05	.02	.01
□ 685 Tony Fernandez	.05	.02	.01
□ 686 Carmelo Martinez	.05	.02	.01
□ 687 Tim Birtsas	.05	.02	.01
□ 688 Milt Thompson	.05	.02	.01
□ 689 Rich Yett	.05	.02	.01
□ 690 Mark McGwire	.30	.14	.04
□ 691 Chuck Cary	.05	.02	.01
□ 692 Sammy Sosa	.75	.35	.09
□ 693 Calvin Schiraldi	.05	.02	.01
□ 694 Mike Stanton	.10	.05	.01
□ 695 Tom Henke	.05	.02	.01
□ 696 B.J. Surhoff	.10	.05	.01
□ 697 Mike Davis	.05	.02	.01
□ 698 Omar Vizquel	.10	.05	.01
□ 699 Jim Leyland MG	.05	.02	.01
□ 700 Kirby Puckett	.30	.14	.04
□ 701 Bernie Williams	.75	.35	.09
□ 702 Tony Phillips	.15	.07	.02
□ 703 Jeff Brantley	.10	.05	.01
□ 704 Chip Hale	.05	.02	.01
□ 705 Claudell Washington	.05	.02	.01
□ 706 Geno Petralli	.05	.02	.01
□ 707 Luis Aquino	.05	.02	.01
□ 708 Larry Sheets	.05	.02	.01
□ 709 Juan Berenguer	.05	.02	.01
□ 710 Von Hayes	.05	.02	.01
□ 711 Rick Aguilera	.10	.05	.01
□ 712 Todd Benzinger	.05	.02	.01
□ 713 Tim Drummond	.05	.02	.01
□ 714 Marquis Grissom	.60	.25	.07
□ 715 Greg Maddux	.60	.25	.07
□ 716 Steve Balboni	.05	.02	.01
□ 717 Ron Karkovice	.05	.02	.01
□ 718 Gary Sheffield	.25	.11	.03
□ 719 Wally Whitehurst	.05	.02	.01
□ 720 Andres Galarraga	.15	.07	.02
□ 721 Lee Mazzilli	.05	.02	.01
□ 722 Felix Fermin	.05	.02	.01
□ 723 Jeff D. Robinson	.05	.02	.01
□ 724 Juan Bell	.05	.02	.01
□ 725 Terry Pendleton	.10	.05	.01
□ 726 Gene Nelson	.05	.02	.01
□ 727 Pat Tabler	.05	.02	.01
□ 728 Jim Acker	.05	.02	.01
□ 729 Bobby Valentine MG	.05	.02	.01
□ 730 Tony Gwynn	.40	.18	.05
□ 731 Don Carman	.05	.02	.01
□ 732 Ernest Riles	.05	.02	.01
□ 733 John Dopson	.05	.02	.01
□ 734 Kevin Elster	.05	.02	.01
□ 735 Charlie Hough	.05	.02	.01
□ 736 Rick Dempsey	.05	.02	.01
□ 737 Chris Sabo	.05	.02	.01
□ 738 Gene Harris	.05	.02	.01
□ 739 Dale Sveum	.05	.02	.01
□ 740 Jesse Barfield	.05	.02	.01
□ 741 Steve Wilson	.05	.02	.01
□ 742 Ernie Whitt	.05	.02	.01
□ 743 Tom Candiotti	.05	.02	.01
□ 744 Kelly Mann	.05	.02	.01
□ 745 Hubie Brooks	.05	.02	.01
□ 746 Dave Smith	.05	.02	.01
□ 747 Randy Bush	.05	.02	.01
□ 748 Doyle Alexander	.05	.02	.01
□ 749 Mark Parent UER ('87 BA .80, should be .080)	.05	.02	.01
□ 750 Dale Murphy	.15	.07	.02
□ 751 Steve Lyons	.05	.02	.01
□ 752 Tom Gordon	.05	.02	.01
□ 753 Chris Speier	.05	.02	.01
□ 754 Bob Walk	.05	.02	.01
□ 755 Rafael Palmeiro	.15	.07	.02
□ 756 Ken Howell	.05	.02	.01
□ 757 Larry Walker	.50	.23	.06
□ 758 Mark Thurmond	.05	.02	.01
□ 759 Tom Trebelhorn MG	.05	.02	.01
□ 760 Wade Boggs	.15	.07	.02
□ 761 Mike Jackson	.05	.02	.01
□ 762 Doug Dascenzo	.05	.02	.01
□ 763 Dennis Martinez	.10	.05	.01
□ 764 Tim Teufel	.05	.02	.01
□ 765 Chili Davis	.10	.05	.01
□ 766 Brian Meyer	.05	.02	.01
□ 767 Tracy Jones	.05	.02	.01
□ 768 Chuck Crim	.05	.02	.01
□ 769 Greg Hibbard	.05	.02	.01
□ 770 Cory Snyder	.05	.02	.01
□ 771 Pete Smith	.05	.02	.01
□ 772 Jeff Reed	.05	.02	.01
□ 773 Dave Leiper	.05	.02	.01
□ 774 Ben McDonald	.15	.07	.02
□ 775 Andy Van Slyke	.10	.05	.01
□ 776 Charlie Leibrandt	.05	.02	.01
□ 777 Tim Laudner	.05	.02	.01
□ 778 Mike Jeffcoat	.05	.02	.01
□ 779 Lloyd Moseby	.05	.02	.01
□ 780 Orel Hershiser	.10	.05	.01
□ 781 Mario Diaz	.05	.02	.01
□ 782 Jose Alvarez	.05	.02	.01
□ 783 Checklist 6	.05	.02	.01
□ 784 Scott Bailes	.05	.02	.01
□ 785 Jim Rice	.15	.07	.02
□ 786 Eric King	.05	.02	.01
□ 787 Rene Gonzales	.05	.02	.01
□ 788 Frank DiPino	.05	.02	.01
□ 789 John Wathan MG	.05	.02	.01
□ 790 Gary Carter	.15	.07	.02
□ 791 Alvaro Espinoza	.05	.02	.01
□ 792 Gerald Perry	.05	.02	.01

1990 Topps Traded

The 1990 Topps Traded Set was the tenth consecutive year Topps issued a 132-card standard-size set at the end of the year. For the first time, Topps not only issued the set in factory set form but also distributed (on a significant basis) the set via 7-card wax packs. Unlike the factory set cards (which feature the whiter paper stock typical of the previous years Traded sets), the wax pack cards feature gray paper stock. This set was arranged alphabetically by player and includes a mix of traded players and rookies for whom Topps did not include a card in the regular set. The key Rookie Cards in this set are Carlos Baerga, Travis Fryman, Todd Hundley and Dave Justice.

	MINT	NRMT	EXC
COMPLETE SET (132)	3.00	1.35	.35

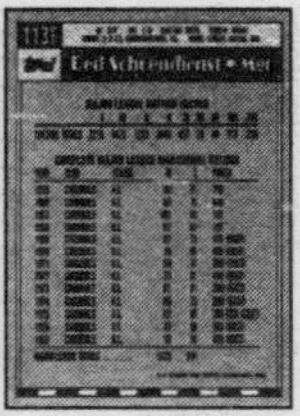

COMPLETE FACT.SET (132)	3.00	1.35	.35
COMMON CARD (1T-132T)	.05	.02	.01
SEMISTARS	.10	.05	.01

*GRAY AND WHITE BACKS: SAME VALUE..

□ 1T Darrel Akerfelds	.05	.02	.01
□ 2T Sandy Alomar Jr.	.10	.05	.01
□ 3T Brad Arnsberg	.05	.02	.01
□ 4T Steve Avery	.15	.07	.02
□ 5T Wally Backman	.05	.02	.01
□ 6T Carlos Baerga	.50	.23	.06
□ 7T Kevin Bass	.05	.02	.01
□ 8T Willie Blair	.05	.02	.01
□ 9T Mike Blowers	.15	.07	.02
□ 10T Shawn Boskie	.05	.02	.01
□ 11T Daryl Boston	.05	.02	.01
□ 12T Dennis Boyd	.05	.02	.01
□ 13T Glenn Braggs	.05	.02	.01
□ 14T Hubie Brooks	.05	.02	.01
□ 15T Tom Brunansky	.05	.02	.01
□ 16T John Burkett	.10	.05	.01
□ 17T Casey Candaele	.05	.02	.01
□ 18T John Candelaria	.05	.02	.01
□ 19T Gary Carter	.15	.07	.02
□ 20T Joe Carter	.15	.07	.02
□ 21T Rick Cerone	.05	.02	.01
□ 22T Scott Coolbaugh	.05	.02	.01
□ 23T Bobby Cox MG	.05	.02	.01
□ 24T Mark Davis	.05	.02	.01
□ 25T Storm Davis	.05	.02	.01
□ 26T Edgar Diaz	.05	.02	.01
□ 27T Wayne Edwards	.05	.02	.01
□ 28T Mark Eichhorn	.05	.02	.01
□ 29T Scott Erickson	.15	.07	.02
□ 30T Nick Esasky	.05	.02	.01
□ 31T Cecil Fielder	.10	.05	.01
□ 32T John Franco	.05	.02	.01
□ 33T Travis Fryman	.50	.23	.06
□ 34T Bill Gullickson	.05	.02	.01
□ 35T Darryl Hamilton	.10	.05	.01
□ 36T Mike Harkey	.05	.02	.01
□ 37T Bud Harrelson MG	.05	.02	.01
□ 38T Billy Hatcher	.05	.02	.01
□ 39T Keith Hernandez	.10	.05	.01
□ 40T Joe Hesketh	.05	.02	.01
□ 41T Dave Hollins	.15	.07	.02
□ 42T Sam Horn	.05	.02	.01
□ 43T Steve Howard	.05	.02	.01
□ 44T Todd Hundley	.60	.25	.07
□ 45T Jeff Huson	.05	.02	.01
□ 46T Chris James	.05	.02	.01
□ 47T Stan Javier	.05	.02	.01
□ 48T Dave Justice	.50	.23	.06
□ 49T Jeff Kaiser	.05	.02	.01
□ 50T Dana Kiecker	.05	.02	.01
□ 51T Joe Klink	.05	.02	.01
□ 52T Brent Knackert	.05	.02	.01
□ 53T Brad Komminsk	.05	.02	.01
□ 54T Mark Langston	.10	.05	.01
□ 55T Tim Layana	.05	.02	.01
□ 56T Rick Leach	.05	.02	.01
□ 57T Terry Leach	.05	.02	.01
□ 58T Tim Leary	.05	.02	.01
□ 59T Craig Lefferts	.05	.02	.01
□ 60T Charlie Leibrandt	.05	.02	.01
□ 61T Jim Leyritz	.15	.07	.02
□ 62T Fred Lynn	.05	.02	.01
□ 63T Kevin Maas	.10	.05	.01
□ 64T Shane Mack	.05	.02	.01
□ 65T Candy Maldonado	.05	.02	.01
□ 66T Fred Manrique	.05	.02	.01
□ 67T Mike Marshall	.05	.02	.01
□ 68T Carmelo Martinez	.05	.02	.01
□ 69T John Marzano	.05	.02	.01
□ 70T Ben McDonald	.10	.05	.01
□ 71T Jack McDowell	.15	.07	.02
□ 72T John McNamara MG	.05	.02	.01
□ 73T Orlando Mercado	.05	.02	.01
□ 74T Stump Merrill MG	.05	.02	.01
□ 75T Alan Mills	.05	.02	.01
□ 76T Hal Morris	.10	.05	.01
□ 77T Lloyd Moseby	.05	.02	.01
□ 78T Randy Myers	.10	.05	.01
□ 79T Tim Naehring	.15	.07	.02
□ 80T Junior Noboa	.05	.02	.01
□ 81T Matt Nokes	.05	.02	.01
□ 82T Pete O'Brien	.05	.02	.01
□ 83T John Olerud	.15	.07	.02
□ 84T Greg Olson	.05	.02	.01
□ 85T Junior Ortiz	.05	.02	.01
□ 86T Dave Parker	.10	.05	.01
□ 87T Rick Parker	.05	.02	.01
□ 88T Bob Patterson	.05	.02	.01
□ 89T Alejandro Pena	.05	.02	.01
□ 90T Tony Pena	.05	.02	.01
□ 91T Pascual Perez	.05	.02	.01
□ 92T Gerald Perry	.05	.02	.01
□ 93T Dan Petry	.05	.02	.01
□ 94T Gary Pettis	.05	.02	.01
□ 95T Tony Phillips	.15	.07	.02
□ 96T Lou Piniella MG	.10	.05	.01
□ 97T Luis Polonia	.05	.02	.01
□ 98T Jim Presley	.05	.02	.01
□ 99T Scott Radinsky	.05	.02	.01
□ 100T Willie Randolph	.10	.05	.01
□ 101T Jeff Reardon	.10	.05	.01
□ 102T Greg Riddoch MG	.05	.02	.01
□ 103T Jeff Robinson	.05	.02	.01
□ 104T Ron Robinson	.05	.02	.01
□ 105T Kevin Romine	.05	.02	.01
□ 106T Scott Ruskin	.05	.02	.01
□ 107T John Russell	.05	.02	.01
□ 108T Bill Sampen	.05	.02	.01
□ 109T Juan Samuel	.05	.02	.01
□ 110T Scott Sanderson	.05	.02	.01
□ 111T Jack Savage	.05	.02	.01
□ 112T Dave Schmidt	.05	.02	.01
□ 113T Red Schoendienst MG	.15	.07	.02
□ 114T Terry Shumpert	.05	.02	.01
□ 115T Matt Sinatro	.05	.02	.01
□ 116T Don Slaught	.05	.02	.01
□ 117T Bryn Smith	.05	.02	.01
□ 118T Lee Smith	.10	.05	.01
□ 119T Paul Sorrento	.15	.07	.02
□ 120T Franklin Stubbs UER ('84 says '99 and has the same stats as '89, '83 stats are missing)	.05	.02	.01
□ 121T Russ Swan	.05	.02	.01
□ 122T Bob Tewksbury	.05	.02	.01
□ 123T Wayne Tolleson	.05	.02	.01
□ 124T John Tudor	.05	.02	.01
□ 125T Randy Veres	.05	.02	.01
□ 126T Hector Villanueva	.05	.02	.01
□ 127T Mitch Webster	.05	.02	.01
□ 128T Ernie Whitt	.05	.02	.01
□ 129T Frank Wills	.05	.02	.01
□ 130T Dave Winfield	.15	.07	.02
□ 131T Matt Young	.05	.02	.01
□ 132T Checklist 1T-132T	.05	.02	.01

1991 Topps

This set marks Topps tenth consecutive year of issuing a 792-card standard-size set. Cards were primarily issued in wax packs, rack packs and factory sets. The fronts feature a full color player photo with a white border. Topps also commemorated their fortieth anniversary by including a "Topps 40" logo on the front and back of each card. Virtually all of the cards have been discovered without the 40th logo on the back. Subsets include Record Breakers (2-8) and All-Stars (386-407). In addition, First Draft Picks and Future Stars subset cards are

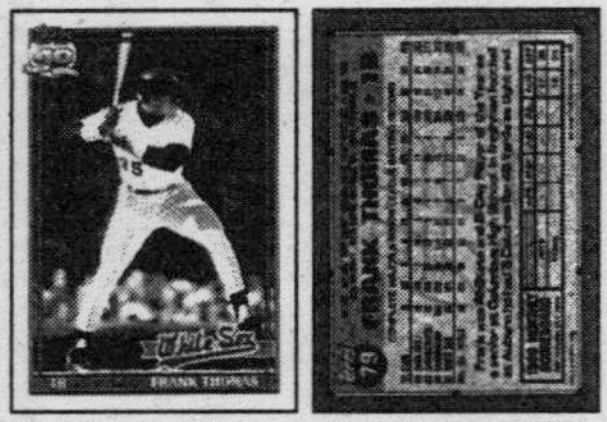

scattered throughout the set. The key Rookie Cards include Chipper Jones and Brian McRae. As a special promotion Topps inserted (randomly) into their wax packs one of every previous card they ever issued.

	MINT	NRMT	EXC
COMPLETE SET (792)	12.00	5.50	1.50
COMPLETE FACT.SET (792)	15.00	6.75	1.85
COMMON CARD (1-792)	.05	.02	.01
SEMISTARS	.10	.05	.01
STARS	.15	.07	.02

	MINT	NRMT	EXC
□ 1 Nolan Ryan	.75	.35	.09
□ 2 George Brett RB	.20	.09	.03
Batting Title, 3 decades			
□ 3 Carlton Fisk RB	.15	.07	.02
Catcher HR Record			
□ 4 Kevin Maas RB	.05	.02	.01
Quickest to 10 HR's			
□ 5 Cal Ripken RB	.40	.18	.05
Most cons. errorless games			
□ 6 Nolan Ryan RB	.40	.18	.05
Oldest pitcher, no-hitter			
□ 7 Ryne Sandberg RB	.15	.07	.02
Most cons. errorless games			
□ 8 Bobby Thigpen RB	.05	.02	.01
Most saves, season			
□ 9 Darrin Fletcher	.05	.02	.01
□ 10 Gregg Olson	.05	.02	.01
□ 11 Roberto Kelly	.05	.02	.01
□ 12 Paul Assenmacher	.05	.02	.01
□ 13 Mariano Duncan	.05	.02	.01
□ 14 Dennis Lamp	.05	.02	.01
□ 15 Von Hayes	.05	.02	.01
□ 16 Mike Heath	.05	.02	.01
□ 17 Jeff Brantley	.05	.02	.01
□ 18 Nelson Liriano	.05	.02	.01
□ 19 Jeff D. Robinson	.05	.02	.01
□ 20 Pedro Guerrero	.05	.02	.01
□ 21 Joe Morgan MG	.05	.02	.01
□ 22 Storm Davis	.05	.02	.01
□ 23 Jim Gantner	.05	.02	.01
□ 24 Dave Martinez	.05	.02	.01
□ 25 Tim Belcher	.05	.02	.01
□ 26 Luis Sojo UER	.05	.02	.01
(Born in Barquisimento, not Carquis)			
□ 27 Bobby Witt	.05	.02	.01
□ 28 Alvaro Espinoza	.05	.02	.01
□ 29 Bob Walk	.05	.02	.01
□ 30 Gregg Jefferies	.15	.07	.02
□ 31 Colby Ward	.05	.02	.01
□ 32 Mike Simms	.05	.02	.01
□ 33 Barry Jones	.05	.02	.01
□ 34 Atlee Hammaker	.05	.02	.01
□ 35 Greg Maddux	.60	.25	.07
□ 36 Donnie Hill	.05	.02	.01
□ 37 Tom Bolton	.05	.02	.01
□ 38 Scott Bradley	.05	.02	.01
□ 39 Jim Neidlinger	.05	.02	.01
□ 40 Kevin Mitchell	.10	.05	.01
□ 41 Ken Dayley	.05	.02	.01
□ 42 Chris Hoiles	.05	.02	.01
□ 43 Roger McDowell	.05	.02	.01
□ 44 Mike Felder	.05	.02	.01
□ 45 Chris Sabo	.05	.02	.01
□ 46 Tim Drummond	.05	.02	.01
□ 47 Brook Jacoby	.05	.02	.01
□ 48 Dennis Boyd	.05	.02	.01
□ 49A Pat Borders ERR	.15	.07	.02
(40 steals at Kinston in '86)			
□ 49B Pat Borders COR	.05	.02	.01
(0 steals at Kinston in '86)			
□ 50 Bob Welch	.05	.02	.01
□ 51 Art Howe MG	.05	.02	.01
□ 52 Francisco Oliveras	.05	.02	.01
□ 53 Mike Sharperson UER	.05	.02	.01
(Born in 1961, not 1960)			
□ 54 Gary Mielke	.05	.02	.01
□ 55 Jeffrey Leonard	.05	.02	.01
□ 56 Jeff Parrett	.05	.02	.01
□ 57 Jack Howell	.05	.02	.01
□ 58 Mel Stottlemyre Jr.	.05	.02	.01
□ 59 Eric Yelding	.05	.02	.01
□ 60 Frank Viola	.05	.02	.01
□ 61 Stan Javier	.05	.02	.01
□ 62 Lee Guetterman	.05	.02	.01
□ 63 Milt Thompson	.05	.02	.01
□ 64 Tom Herr	.05	.02	.01
□ 65 Bruce Hurst	.05	.02	.01
□ 66 Terry Kennedy	.05	.02	.01
□ 67 Rick Honeycutt	.05	.02	.01
□ 68 Gary Sheffield	.15	.07	.02
□ 69 Steve Wilson	.05	.02	.01
□ 70 Ellis Burks	.15	.07	.02
□ 71 Jim Acker	.05	.02	.01
□ 72 Junior Ortiz	.05	.02	.01
□ 73 Craig Worthington	.05	.02	.01
□ 74 Shane Andrews	.10	.05	.01
□ 75 Jack Morris	.10	.05	.01
□ 76 Jerry Browne	.05	.02	.01
□ 77 Drew Hall	.05	.02	.01
□ 78 Geno Petralli	.05	.02	.01
□ 79 Frank Thomas	2.00	.90	.25
□ 80A Fernando Valenzuela	.10	.05	.01
ERR (104 earned runs in '90 tied for league lead)			
□ 80B Fernando Valenzuela	.10	.05	.01
COR (104 earned runs in '90 led league, 20 CG's in 1986 now italicized)			
□ 81 Cito Gaston MG	.05	.02	.01
□ 82 Tom Glavine	.15	.07	.02
□ 83 Daryl Boston	.05	.02	.01
□ 84 Bob McClure	.05	.02	.01
□ 85 Jesse Barfield	.05	.02	.01
□ 86 Les Lancaster	.05	.02	.01
□ 87 Tracy Jones	.05	.02	.01
□ 88 Bob Tewksbury	.05	.02	.01
□ 89 Darren Daulton	.10	.05	.01
□ 90 Danny Tartabull	.05	.02	.01
□ 91 Greg Colbrunn	.10	.05	.01
□ 92 Danny Jackson	.05	.02	.01
□ 93 Ivan Calderon	.05	.02	.01
□ 94 John Dopson	.05	.02	.01
□ 95 Paul Molitor	.20	.09	.03
□ 96 Trevor Wilson	.05	.02	.01
□ 97A Brady Anderson ERR	.25	.11	.03
(September, 2 RBI and 3 hits, should be 3 RBI and 14 hits			
□ 97B Brady Anderson COR	.15	.07	.02
□ 98 Sergio Valdez	.05	.02	.01
□ 99 Chris Gwynn	.05	.02	.01
□ 100 Don Mattingly COR	.50	.23	.06
(101 hits in 1990)			
□ 100A Don Mattingly ERR	1.00	.45	.12
(10 hits in 1990)			
□ 101 Rob Ducey	.05	.02	.01
□ 102 Gene Larkin	.05	.02	.01
□ 103 Tim Costo	.05	.02	.01
□ 104 Don Robinson	.05	.02	.01
□ 105 Kevin McReynolds	.05	.02	.01
□ 106 Ed Nunez	.05	.02	.01
□ 107 Luis Polonia	.05	.02	.01
□ 108 Matt Young	.05	.02	.01
□ 109 Greg Riddoch MG	.05	.02	.01
□ 110 Tom Henke	.05	.02	.01
□ 111 Andres Thomas	.05	.02	.01
□ 112 Frank DiPino	.05	.02	.01
□ 113 Carl Everett	.15	.07	.02

□ 114 Lance Dickson	.05	.02	.01
□ 115 Hubie Brooks	.05	.02	.01
□ 116 Mark Davis	.05	.02	.01
□ 117 Dion James	.05	.02	.01
□ 118 Tom Edens	.05	.02	.01
□ 119 Carl Nichols	.05	.02	.01
□ 120 Joe Carter	.15	.07	.02
□ 121 Eric King	.05	.02	.01
□ 122 Paul O'Neill	.10	.05	.01
□ 123 Greg A. Harris	.05	.02	.01
□ 124 Randy Bush	.05	.02	.01
□ 125 Steve Bedrosian	.05	.02	.01
□ 126 Bernard Gilkey	.15	.07	.02
□ 127 Joe Price	.05	.02	.01
□ 128 Travis Fryman (Front has SS, back has SS-3B)	.15	.07	.02
□ 129 Mark Eichhorn	.05	.02	.01
□ 130 Ozzie Smith	.20	.09	.03
□ 131A Checklist 1 ERR 727 Phil Bradley	.15	.07	.02
□ 131B Checklist 1 COR 717 Phil Bradley	.05	.02	.01
□ 132 Jamie Quirk	.05	.02	.01
□ 133 Greg Briley	.05	.02	.01
□ 134 Kevin Elster	.05	.02	.01
□ 135 Jerome Walton	.05	.02	.01
□ 136 Dave Schmidt	.05	.02	.01
□ 137 Randy Ready	.05	.02	.01
□ 138 Jamie Moyer	.05	.02	.01
□ 139 Jeff Treadway	.05	.02	.01
□ 140 Fred McGriff	.15	.07	.02
□ 141 Nick Leyva MG	.05	.02	.01
□ 142 Curt Wilkerson	.05	.02	.01
□ 143 John Smiley	.05	.02	.01
□ 144 Dave Henderson	.05	.02	.01
□ 145 Lou Whitaker	.15	.07	.02
□ 146 Dan Plesac	.05	.02	.01
□ 147 Carlos Baerga	.15	.07	.02
□ 148 Rey Palacios	.05	.02	.01
□ 149 Al Osuna UER (Shown throwing right, but bio says lefty)	.05	.02	.01
□ 150 Cal Ripken	.75	.35	.09
□ 151 Tom Browning	.05	.02	.01
□ 152 Mickey Hatcher	.05	.02	.01
□ 153 Bryan Harvey	.05	.02	.01
□ 154 Jay Buhner	.15	.07	.02
□ 155A Dwight Evans ERR (Led league with 162 games in '82)	.15	.07	.02
□ 155B Dwight Evans COR (Tied for lead with 162 games in '82)	.10	.05	.01
□ 156 Carlos Martinez	.05	.02	.01
□ 157 John Smoltz	.15	.07	.02
□ 158 Jose Uribe	.05	.02	.01
□ 159 Joe Boever	.05	.02	.01
□ 160 Vince Coleman UER (Wrong birth year, born 9/22/60)	.05	.02	.01
□ 161 Tim Leary	.05	.02	.01
□ 162 Ozzie Canseco	.05	.02	.01
□ 163 Dave Johnson	.05	.02	.01
□ 164 Edgar Diaz	.05	.02	.01
□ 165 Sandy Alomar Jr.	.10	.05	.01
□ 166 Harold Baines	.10	.05	.01
□ 167A Randy Tomlin ERR (Harriburg)	.15	.07	.02
□ 167B Randy Tomlin COR (Harrisburg)	.05	.02	.01
□ 168 John Olerud	.10	.05	.01
□ 169 Luis Aquino	.05	.02	.01
□ 170 Carlton Fisk	.15	.07	.02
□ 171 Tony LaRussa MG	.10	.05	.01
□ 172 Pete Incaviglia	.05	.02	.01
□ 173 Jason Grimsley	.05	.02	.01
□ 174 Ken Caminiti	.15	.07	.02
□ 175 Jack Armstrong	.05	.02	.01
□ 176 John Orton	.05	.02	.01
□ 177 Reggie Harris	.05	.02	.01
□ 178 Dave Valle	.05	.02	.01
□ 179 Pete Harnisch	.05	.02	.01
□ 180 Tony Gwynn	.40	.18	.05
□ 181 Duane Ward	.05	.02	.01
□ 182 Junior Noboa	.05	.02	.01
□ 183 Clay Parker	.05	.02	.01
□ 184 Gary Green	.05	.02	.01
□ 185 Joe Magrane	.05	.02	.01
□ 186 Rod Booker	.05	.02	.01
□ 187 Greg Cadaret	.05	.02	.01
□ 188 Damon Berryhill	.05	.02	.01
□ 189 Daryl Irvine	.05	.02	.01
□ 190 Matt Williams	.15	.07	.02
□ 191 Willie Blair	.05	.02	.01
□ 192 Rob Deer	.05	.02	.01
□ 193 Felix Fermin	.05	.02	.01
□ 194 Xavier Hernandez	.05	.02	.01
□ 195 Wally Joyner	.10	.05	.01
□ 196 Jim Vatcher	.05	.02	.01
□ 197 Chris Nabholz	.05	.02	.01
□ 198 R.J. Reynolds	.05	.02	.01
□ 199 Mike Hartley	.05	.02	.01
□ 200 Darryl Strawberry	.10	.05	.01
□ 201 Tom Kelly MG	.05	.02	.01
□ 202 Jim Leyritz	.10	.05	.01
□ 203 Gene Harris	.05	.02	.01
□ 204 Herm Winningham	.05	.02	.01
□ 205 Mike Perez	.05	.02	.01
□ 206 Carlos Quintana	.05	.02	.01
□ 207 Gary Wayne	.05	.02	.01
□ 208 Willie Wilson	.05	.02	.01
□ 209 Ken Howell	.05	.02	.01
□ 210 Lance Parrish	.05	.02	.01
□ 211 Brian Barnes	.05	.02	.01
□ 212 Steve Finley	.15	.07	.02
□ 213 Frank Wills	.05	.02	.01
□ 214 Joe Girardi	.10	.05	.01
□ 215 Dave Smith	.05	.02	.01
□ 216 Greg Gagne	.05	.02	.01
□ 217 Chris Bosio	.05	.02	.01
□ 218 Rick Parker	.05	.02	.01
□ 219 Jack McDowell	.10	.05	.01
□ 220 Tim Wallach	.05	.02	.01
□ 221 Don Slaught	.05	.02	.01
□ 222 Brian McRae	.25	.11	.03
□ 223 Allan Anderson	.05	.02	.01
□ 224 Juan Gonzalez	.75	.35	.09
□ 225 Randy Johnson	.15	.07	.02
□ 226 Alfredo Griffin	.05	.02	.01
□ 227 Steve Avery UER (Pitched 13 games for Durham in 1989, not 2)	.15	.07	.02
□ 228 Rex Hudler	.05	.02	.01
□ 229 Rance Mulliniks	.05	.02	.01
□ 230 Sid Fernandez	.05	.02	.01
□ 231 Doug Rader MG	.05	.02	.01
□ 232 Jose DeJesus	.05	.02	.01
□ 233 Al Leiter	.10	.05	.01
□ 234 Scott Erickson	.10	.05	.01
□ 235 Dave Parker	.10	.05	.01
□ 236A Frank Tanana ERR (Tied for lead with 269 K's in '75)	.10	.05	.01
□ 236B Frank Tanana COR (Led league with 269 K's in '75)	.05	.02	.01
□ 237 Rick Cerone	.05	.02	.01
□ 238 Mike Dunne	.05	.02	.01
□ 239 Darren Lewis	.10	.05	.01
□ 240 Mike Scott	.05	.02	.01
□ 241 Dave Clark UER (Career totals 19 HR and 5 3B, should be 22 and 3)	.05	.02	.01
□ 242 Mike LaCoss	.05	.02	.01
□ 243 Lance Johnson	.10	.05	.01
□ 244 Mike Jeffcoat	.05	.02	.01
□ 245 Kal Daniels	.05	.02	.01
□ 246 Kevin Wickander	.05	.02	.01
□ 247 Jody Reed	.05	.02	.01
□ 248 Tom Gordon	.05	.02	.01
□ 249 Bob Melvin	.05	.02	.01
□ 250 Dennis Eckersley	.10	.05	.01
□ 251 Mark Lemke	.05	.02	.01
□ 252 Mel Rojas	.10	.05	.01
□ 253 Garry Templeton	.05	.02	.01
□ 254 Shawn Boskie	.05	.02	.01
□ 255 Brian Downing	.05	.02	.01
□ 256 Greg Hibbard	.05	.02	.01
□ 257 Tom O'Malley	.05	.02	.01
□ 258 Chris Hammond	.05	.02	.01

□ 259	Hensley Meulens	.05	.02	.01
□ 260	Harold Reynolds	.05	.02	.01
□ 261	Bud Harrelson MG	.05	.02	.01
□ 262	Tim Jones	.05	.02	.01
□ 263	Checklist 2	.05	.02	.01
□ 264	Dave Hollins	.05	.02	.01
□ 265	Mark Gubicza	.05	.02	.01
□ 266	Carmelo Castillo	.05	.02	.01
□ 267	Mark Knudson	.05	.02	.01
□ 268	Tom Brookens	.05	.02	.01
□ 269	Joe Hesketh	.05	.02	.01
□ 270	Mark McGwire COR (1987 Slugging Pctg. listed as .618)	.30	.14	.04
□ 270A	Mark McGwire ERR (1987 Slugging Pctg. listed as 618)	.50	.23	.06
□ 271	Omar Olivares	.05	.02	.01
□ 272	Jeff King	.10	.05	.01
□ 273	Johnny Ray	.05	.02	.01
□ 274	Ken Williams	.05	.02	.01
□ 275	Alan Trammell	.15	.07	.02
□ 276	Bill Swift	.05	.02	.01
□ 277	Scott Coolbaugh	.05	.02	.01
□ 278	Alex Fernandez UER (No '90 White Sox stats)	.15	.07	.02
□ 279A	Jose Gonzalez ERR (Photo actually Billy Bean)	.05	.02	.01
□ 279B	Jose Gonzalez COR	.05	.02	.01
□ 280	Bret Saberhagen	.10	.05	.01
□ 281	Larry Sheets	.05	.02	.01
□ 282	Don Carman	.05	.02	.01
□ 283	Marquis Grissom	.15	.07	.02
□ 284	Billy Spiers	.05	.02	.01
□ 285	Jim Abbott	.10	.05	.01
□ 286	Ken Oberkfell	.05	.02	.01
□ 287	Mark Grant	.05	.02	.01
□ 288	Derrick May	.05	.02	.01
□ 289	Tim Birtsas	.05	.02	.01
□ 290	Steve Sax	.05	.02	.01
□ 291	John Wathan MG	.05	.02	.01
□ 292	Bud Black	.05	.02	.01
□ 293	Jay Bell	.10	.05	.01
□ 294	Mike Moore	.05	.02	.01
□ 295	Rafael Palmeiro	.15	.07	.02
□ 296	Mark Williamson	.05	.02	.01
□ 297	Manny Lee	.05	.02	.01
□ 298	Omar Vizquel	.15	.07	.02
□ 299	Scott Radinsky	.05	.02	.01
□ 300	Kirby Puckett	.30	.14	.04
□ 301	Steve Farr	.05	.02	.01
□ 302	Tim Teufel	.05	.02	.01
□ 303	Mike Boddicker	.05	.02	.01
□ 304	Kevin Reimer	.05	.02	.01
□ 305	Mike Scioscia	.05	.02	.01
□ 306A	Lonnie Smith ERR (136 games in '90)	.15	.07	.02
□ 306B	Lonnie Smith COR (135 games in '90)	.05	.02	.01
□ 307	Andy Benes	.05	.02	.01
□ 308	Tom Pagnozzi	.05	.02	.01
□ 309	Norm Charlton	.05	.02	.01
□ 310	Gary Carter	.15	.07	.02
□ 311	Jeff Pico	.05	.02	.01
□ 312	Charlie Hayes	.05	.02	.01
□ 313	Ron Robinson	.05	.02	.01
□ 314	Gary Pettis	.05	.02	.01
□ 315	Roberto Alomar	.25	.11	.03
□ 316	Gene Nelson	.05	.02	.01
□ 317	Mike Fitzgerald	.05	.02	.01
□ 318	Rick Aguilera	.10	.05	.01
□ 319	Jeff McKnight	.05	.02	.01
□ 320	Tony Fernandez	.05	.02	.01
□ 321	Bob Rodgers MG	.05	.02	.01
□ 322	Terry Shumpert	.05	.02	.01
□ 323	Cory Snyder	.05	.02	.01
□ 324A	Ron Kittle ERR (Set another standard ...)	.15	.07	.02
□ 324B	Ron Kittle COR (Tied another standard ...)	.05	.02	.01
□ 325	Brett Butler	.10	.05	.01
□ 326	Ken Patterson	.05	.02	.01
□ 327	Ron Hassey	.05	.02	.01
□ 328	Walt Terrell	.05	.02	.01
□ 329	Dave Justice UER (Drafted third round on card, should say fourth pick)	.15	.07	.02
□ 330	Dwight Gooden	.10	.05	.01
□ 331	Eric Anthony	.05	.02	.01
□ 332	Kenny Rogers	.05	.02	.01
□ 333	Chipper Jones FDP	3.00	1.35	.35
□ 334	Todd Benzinger	.05	.02	.01
□ 335	Mitch Williams	.05	.02	.01
□ 336	Matt Nokes	.05	.02	.01
□ 337A	Keith Comstock ERR (Cubs logo on front)	.15	.07	.02
□ 337B	Keith Comstock COR (Mariners logo on front)	.05	.02	.01
□ 338	Luis Rivera	.05	.02	.01
□ 339	Larry Walker	.15	.07	.02
□ 340	Ramon Martinez	.10	.05	.01
□ 341	John Moses	.05	.02	.01
□ 342	Mickey Morandini	.05	.02	.01
□ 343	Jose Oquendo	.05	.02	.01
□ 344	Jeff Russell	.05	.02	.01
□ 345	Len Dykstra	.10	.05	.01
□ 346	Jesse Orosco	.05	.02	.01
□ 347	Greg Vaughn	.15	.07	.02
□ 348	Todd Stottlemyre	.05	.02	.01
□ 349	Dave Gallagher	.05	.02	.01
□ 350	Glenn Davis	.05	.02	.01
□ 351	Joe Torre MG	.10	.05	.01
□ 352	Frank White	.10	.05	.01
□ 353	Tony Castillo	.05	.02	.01
□ 354	Sid Bream	.05	.02	.01
□ 355	Chili Davis	.10	.05	.01
□ 356	Mike Marshall	.05	.02	.01
□ 357	Jack Savage	.05	.02	.01
□ 358	Mark Parent	.05	.02	.01
□ 359	Chuck Cary	.05	.02	.01
□ 360	Tim Raines	.15	.07	.02
□ 361	Scott Garrelts	.05	.02	.01
□ 362	Hector Villenueva	.05	.02	.01
□ 363	Rick Mahler	.05	.02	.01
□ 364	Dan Pasqua	.05	.02	.01
□ 365	Mike Schooler	.05	.02	.01
□ 366A	Checklist 3 ERR 19 Carl Nichols	.15	.07	.02
□ 366B	Checklist 3 COR 119 Carl Nichols	.05	.02	.01
□ 367	Dave Walsh	.05	.02	.01
□ 368	Felix Jose	.05	.02	.01
□ 369	Steve Searcy	.05	.02	.01
□ 370	Kelly Gruber	.05	.02	.01
□ 371	Jeff Montgomery	.10	.05	.01
□ 372	Spike Owen	.05	.02	.01
□ 373	Darrin Jackson	.05	.02	.01
□ 374	Larry Casian	.05	.02	.01
□ 375	Tony Pena	.05	.02	.01
□ 376	Mike Harkey	.05	.02	.01
□ 377	Rene Gonzales	.05	.02	.01
□ 378A	Wilson Alvarez ERR ('89 Port Charlotte and '90 Birmingham stat lines omitted)	.50	.23	.06
□ 378B	Wilson Alvarez COR (Text still says 143 K's in 1988, whereas stats say 134)	.15	.07	.02
□ 379	Randy Velarde	.05	.02	.01
□ 380	Willie McGee	.05	.02	.01
□ 381	Jim Leyland MG	.05	.02	.01
□ 382	Mackey Sasser	.05	.02	.01
□ 383	Pete Smith	.05	.02	.01
□ 384	Gerald Perry	.05	.02	.01
□ 385	Mickey Tettleton	.10	.05	.01
□ 386	Cecil Fielder AS	.10	.05	.01
□ 387	Julio Franco AS	.05	.02	.01
□ 388	Kelly Gruber AS	.05	.02	.01
□ 389	Alan Trammell AS	.15	.07	.02
□ 390	Jose Canseco AS	.15	.07	.02
□ 391	Rickey Henderson AS	.15	.07	.02
□ 392	Ken Griffey Jr. AS	.75	.35	.09
□ 393	Carlton Fisk AS	.15	.07	.02
□ 394	Bob Welch AS	.05	.02	.01
□ 395	Chuck Finley AS	.05	.02	.01
□ 396	Bobby Thigpen AS	.05	.02	.01
□ 397	Eddie Murray AS	.15	.07	.02

☐ 398	Ryne Sandberg AS	.15	.07	.02
☐ 399	Matt Williams AS	.15	.07	.02
☐ 400	Barry Larkin AS	.15	.07	.02
☐ 401	Barry Bonds AS	.15	.07	.02
☐ 402	Darryl Strawbery AS	.10	.05	.01
☐ 403	Bobby Bonilla AS	.10	.05	.01
☐ 404	Mike Scioscia AS	.05	.02	.01
☐ 405	Doug Drabek AS	.05	.02	.01
☐ 406	Frank Viola AS	.05	.02	.01
☐ 407	John Franco AS	.05	.02	.01
☐ 408	Earnie Riles	.05	.02	.01
☐ 409	Mike Stanley	.05	.02	.01
☐ 410	Dave Righetti	.05	.02	.01
☐ 411	Lance Blankenship	.05	.02	.01
☐ 412	Dave Bergman	.05	.02	.01
☐ 413	Terry Mulholland	.05	.02	.01
☐ 414	Sammy Sosa	.25	.11	.03
☐ 415	Rick Sutcliffe	.05	.02	.01
☐ 416	Randy Milligan	.05	.02	.01
☐ 417	Bill Krueger	.05	.02	.01
☐ 418	Nick Esasky	.05	.02	.01
☐ 419	Jeff Reed	.05	.02	.01
☐ 420	Bobby Thigpen	.05	.02	.01
☐ 421	Alex Cole	.05	.02	.01
☐ 422	Rick Reuschel	.05	.02	.01
☐ 423	Rafael Ramirez UER	.05	.02	.01
	(Born 1959, not 1958)			
☐ 424	Calvin Schiraldi	.05	.02	.01
☐ 425	Andy Van Slyke	.10	.05	.01
☐ 426	Joe Grahe	.05	.02	.01
☐ 427	Rick Dempsey	.05	.02	.01
☐ 428	John Barfield	.05	.02	.01
☐ 429	Stump Merrill MG	.05	.02	.01
☐ 430	Gary Gaetti	.10	.05	.01
☐ 431	Paul Gibson	.05	.02	.01
☐ 432	Delino DeShields	.05	.02	.01
☐ 433	Pat Tabler	.05	.02	.01
☐ 434	Julio Machado	.05	.02	.01
☐ 435	Kevin Maas	.05	.02	.01
☐ 436	Scott Bankhead	.05	.02	.01
☐ 437	Doug Dascenzo	.05	.02	.01
☐ 438	Vicente Palacios	.05	.02	.01
☐ 439	Dickie Thon	.05	.02	.01
☐ 440	George Bell	.05	.02	.01
☐ 441	Zane Smith	.05	.02	.01
☐ 442	Charlie O'Brien	.05	.02	.01
☐ 443	Jeff Innis	.05	.02	.01
☐ 444	Glenn Braggs	.05	.02	.01
☐ 445	Greg Swindell	.05	.02	.01
☐ 446	Craig Grebeck	.05	.02	.01
☐ 447	John Burkett	.10	.05	.01
☐ 448	Craig Lefferts	.05	.02	.01
☐ 449	Juan Berenguer	.05	.02	.01
☐ 450	Wade Boggs	.15	.07	.02
☐ 451	Neal Heaton	.05	.02	.01
☐ 452	Bill Schroeder	.05	.02	.01
☐ 453	Lenny Harris	.05	.02	.01
☐ 454A	Kevin Appier ERR	.15	.07	.02
	('90 Omaha stat line omitted)			
☐ 454B	Kevin Appier COR	.10	.05	.01
☐ 455	Walt Weiss	.05	.02	.01
☐ 456	Charlie Leibrandt	.05	.02	.01
☐ 457	Todd Hundley	.15	.07	.02
☐ 458	Brian Holman	.05	.02	.01
☐ 459	Tom Trebelhorn MG UER	.05	.02	.01
	(Pitching and batting columns switched)			
☐ 460	Dave Stieb	.05	.02	.01
☐ 461	Robin Ventura	.15	.07	.02
☐ 462	Steve Frey	.05	.02	.01
☐ 463	Dwight Smith	.05	.02	.01
☐ 464	Steve Buechele	.05	.02	.01
☐ 465	Ken Griffey Sr.	.05	.02	.01
☐ 466	Charles Nagy	.10	.05	.01
☐ 467	Dennis Cook	.05	.02	.01
☐ 468	Tim Hulett	.05	.02	.01
☐ 469	Chet Lemon	.05	.02	.01
☐ 470	Howard Johnson	.05	.02	.01
☐ 471	Mike Lieberthal	.10	.05	.01
☐ 472	Kirt Manwaring	.05	.02	.01
☐ 473	Curt Young	.05	.02	.01
☐ 474	Phil Plantier	.10	.05	.01
☐ 475	Teddy Higuera	.05	.02	.01
☐ 476	Glenn Wilson	.05	.02	.01
☐ 477	Mike Fetters	.05	.02	.01
☐ 478	Kurt Stillwell	.05	.02	.01
☐ 479	Bob Patterson UER	.05	.02	.01
	(Has a decimal point between 7 and 9)			
☐ 480	Dave Magadan	.05	.02	.01
☐ 481	Eddie Whitson	.05	.02	.01
☐ 482	Tino Martinez	.15	.07	.02
☐ 483	Mike Aldrete	.05	.02	.01
☐ 484	Dave LaPoint	.05	.02	.01
☐ 485	Terry Pendleton	.10	.05	.01
☐ 486	Tommy Greene	.05	.02	.01
☐ 487	Rafael Belliard	.05	.02	.01
☐ 488	Jeff Manto	.05	.02	.01
☐ 489	Bobby Valentine MG	.05	.02	.01
☐ 490	Kirk Gibson	.10	.05	.01
☐ 491	Kurt Miller	.05	.02	.01
☐ 492	Ernie Whitt	.05	.02	.01
☐ 493	Jose Rijo	.05	.02	.01
☐ 494	Chris James	.05	.02	.01
☐ 495	Charlie Hough	.05	.02	.01
☐ 496	Marty Barrett	.05	.02	.01
☐ 497	Ben McDonald	.10	.05	.01
☐ 498	Mark Salas	.05	.02	.01
☐ 499	Melido Perez	.05	.02	.01
☐ 500	Will Clark	.15	.07	.02
☐ 501	Mike Bielecki	.05	.02	.01
☐ 502	Carney Lansford	.10	.05	.01
☐ 503	Roy Smith	.05	.02	.01
☐ 504	Julio Valera	.05	.02	.01
☐ 505	Chuck Finley	.10	.05	.01
☐ 506	Darnell Coles	.05	.02	.01
☐ 507	Steve Jeltz	.05	.02	.01
☐ 508	Mike York	.05	.02	.01
☐ 509	Glenallen Hill	.05	.02	.01
☐ 510	John Franco	.05	.02	.01
☐ 511	Steve Balboni	.05	.02	.01
☐ 512	Jose Mesa	.10	.05	.01
☐ 513	Jerald Clark	.05	.02	.01
☐ 514	Mike Stanton	.05	.02	.01
☐ 515	Alvin Davis	.05	.02	.01
☐ 516	Karl Rhodes	.05	.02	.01
☐ 517	Joe Oliver	.05	.02	.01
☐ 518	Cris Carpenter	.05	.02	.01
☐ 519	Sparky Anderson MG	.10	.05	.01
☐ 520	Mark Grace	.15	.07	.02
☐ 521	Joe Orsulak	.05	.02	.01
☐ 522	Stan Belinda	.05	.02	.01
☐ 523	Rodney McCray	.05	.02	.01
☐ 524	Darrel Akerfelds	.05	.02	.01
☐ 525	Willie Randolph	.10	.05	.01
☐ 526A	Moises Alou ERR	.50	.23	.06
	(37 runs in 2 games for '90 Pirates)			
☐ 526B	Moises Alou COR	.15	.07	.02
	(0 runs in 2 games for '90 Pirates)			
☐ 527A	Checklist 4 ERR	.15	.07	.02
	105 Keith Miller 719 Kevin McReynolds			
☐ 527B	Checklist 4 COR	.05	.02	.01
	105 Kevin McReynolds 719 Keith Miller			
☐ 528	Denny Martinez	.10	.05	.01
☐ 529	Marc Newfield	.15	.07	.02
☐ 530	Roger Clemens	.15	.07	.02
☐ 531	Dave Rohde	.05	.02	.01
☐ 532	Kirk McCaskill	.05	.02	.01
☐ 533	Oddibe McDowell	.05	.02	.01
☐ 534	Mike Jackson	.05	.02	.01
☐ 535	Ruben Sierra UER	.10	.05	.01
	(Back reads 100 Runs amd 100 RBI's)			
☐ 536	Mike Witt	.05	.02	.01
☐ 537	Jose Lind	.05	.02	.01
☐ 538	Bip Roberts	.05	.02	.01
☐ 539	Scott Terry	.05	.02	.01
☐ 540	George Brett	.40	.18	.05
☐ 541	Domingo Ramos	.05	.02	.01
☐ 542	Rob Murphy	.05	.02	.01
☐ 543	Junior Felix	.05	.02	.01
☐ 544	Alejandro Pena	.05	.02	.01
☐ 545	Dale Murphy	.15	.07	.02
☐ 546	Jeff Ballard	.05	.02	.01
☐ 547	Mike Pagliarulo	.05	.02	.01
☐ 548	Jaime Navarro	.05	.02	.01
☐ 549	John McNamara MG	.05	.02	.01

□ 550 Eric Davis	.10	.05	.01
□ 551 Bob Kipper	.05	.02	.01
□ 552 Jeff Hamilton	.05	.02	.01
□ 553 Joe Klink	.05	.02	.01
□ 554 Brian Harper	.05	.02	.01
□ 555 Turner Ward	.05	.02	.01
□ 556 Gary Ward	.05	.02	.01
□ 557 Wally Whitehurst	.05	.02	.01
□ 558 Otis Nixon	.05	.02	.01
□ 559 Adam Peterson	.05	.02	.01
□ 560 Greg Smith	.05	.02	.01
□ 561 Tim McIntosh	.05	.02	.01
□ 562 Jeff Kunkel	.05	.02	.01
□ 563 Brent Knackert	.05	.02	.01
□ 564 Dante Bichette	.15	.07	.02
□ 565 Craig Biggio	.15	.07	.02
□ 566 Craig Wilson	.05	.02	.01
□ 567 Dwayne Henry	.05	.02	.01
□ 568 Ron Karkovice	.05	.02	.01
□ 569 Curt Schilling	.05	.02	.01
□ 570 Barry Bonds	.25	.11	.03
□ 571 Pat Combs	.05	.02	.01
□ 572 Dave Anderson	.05	.02	.01
□ 573 Rich Rodriguez UER (Stats say drafted 4th, but bio says 9th round)	.05	.02	.01
□ 574 John Marzano	.05	.02	.01
□ 575 Robin Yount	.15	.07	.02
□ 576 Jeff Kaiser	.05	.02	.01
□ 577 Bill Doran	.05	.02	.01
□ 578 Dave West	.05	.02	.01
□ 579 Roger Craig MG	.05	.02	.01
□ 580 Dave Stewart	.10	.05	.01
□ 581 Luis Quinones	.05	.02	.01
□ 582 Marty Clary	.05	.02	.01
□ 583 Tony Phillips	.10	.05	.01
□ 584 Kevin Brown	.10	.05	.01
□ 585 Pete O'Brien	.05	.02	.01
□ 586 Fred Lynn	.05	.02	.01
□ 587 Jose Offerman UER (Text says he signed 7/24/86, but bio says 1988)	.05	.02	.01
□ 588 Mark Whiten	.10	.05	.01
□ 589 Scott Ruskin	.05	.02	.01
□ 590 Eddie Murray	.25	.11	.03
□ 591 Ken Hill	.15	.07	.02
□ 592 B.J. Surhoff	.10	.05	.01
□ 593A Mike Walker ERR ('90 Canton-Akron stat line omitted)	.15	.07	.02
□ 593B Mike Walker COR	.05	.02	.01
□ 594 Rich Garces	.05	.02	.01
□ 595 Bill Landrum	.05	.02	.01
□ 596 Ronnie Walden	.05	.02	.01
□ 597 Jerry Don Gleaton	.05	.02	.01
□ 598 Sam Horn	.05	.02	.01
□ 599A Greg Myers ERR ('90 Syracuse stat line omitted)	.15	.07	.02
□ 599B Greg Myers COR	.05	.02	.01
□ 600 Bo Jackson	.15	.07	.02
□ 601 Bob Ojeda	.05	.02	.01
□ 602 Casey Candaele	.05	.02	.01
□ 603A Wes Chamberlain ERR (Photo actually Louie Meadows)	.15	.07	.02
□ 603B Wes Chamberlain COR	.05	.02	.01
□ 604 Billy Hatcher	.05	.02	.01
□ 605 Jeff Reardon	.10	.05	.01
□ 606 Jim Gott	.05	.02	.01
□ 607 Edgar Martinez	.15	.07	.02
□ 608 Todd Burns	.05	.02	.01
□ 609 Jeff Torborg MG	.05	.02	.01
□ 610 Andres Galarraga	.15	.07	.02
□ 611 Dave Eiland	.05	.02	.01
□ 612 Steve Lyons	.05	.02	.01
□ 613 Eric Show	.05	.02	.01
□ 614 Luis Salazar	.05	.02	.01
□ 615 Bert Blyleven	.10	.05	.01
□ 616 Todd Zeile	.10	.05	.01
□ 617 Bill Wegman	.05	.02	.01
□ 618 Sil Campusano	.05	.02	.01
□ 619 David Wells	.05	.02	.01
□ 620 Ozzie Guillen	.05	.02	.01
□ 621 Ted Power	.05	.02	.01
□ 622 Jack Daugherty	.05	.02	.01
□ 623 Jeff Blauser	.05	.02	.01
□ 624 Tom Candiotti	.05	.02	.01
□ 625 Terry Steinbach	.10	.05	.01
□ 626 Gerald Young	.05	.02	.01
□ 627 Tim Layana	.05	.02	.01
□ 628 Greg Litton	.05	.02	.01
□ 629 Wes Gardner	.05	.02	.01
□ 630 Dave Winfield	.15	.07	.02
□ 631 Mike Morgan	.05	.02	.01
□ 632 Lloyd Moseby	.05	.02	.01
□ 633 Kevin Tapani	.05	.02	.01
□ 634 Henry Cotto	.05	.02	.01
□ 635 Andy Hawkins	.05	.02	.01
□ 636 Geronimo Pena	.05	.02	.01
□ 637 Bruce Ruffin	.05	.02	.01
□ 638 Mike Macfarlane	.05	.02	.01
□ 639 Frank Robinson MG	.15	.07	.02
□ 640 Andre Dawson	.15	.07	.02
□ 641 Mike Henneman	.05	.02	.01
□ 642 Hal Morris	.05	.02	.01
□ 643 Jim Presley	.05	.02	.01
□ 644 Chuck Crim	.05	.02	.01
□ 645 Juan Samuel	.05	.02	.01
□ 646 Andujar Cedeno	.05	.02	.01
□ 647 Mark Portugal	.05	.02	.01
□ 648 Lee Stevens	.05	.02	.01
□ 649 Bill Sampen	.05	.02	.01
□ 650 Jack Clark	.10	.05	.01
□ 651 Alan Mills	.05	.02	.01
□ 652 Kevin Romine	.05	.02	.01
□ 653 Anthony Telford	.05	.02	.01
□ 654 Paul Sorrento	.10	.05	.01
□ 655 Erik Hanson	.05	.02	.01
□ 656A Checklist 5 ERR 348 Vicente Palacios 381 Jose Lind 537 Mike LaValliere 665 Jim Leyland	.15	.07	.02
□ 656B Checklist 5 ERR 433 Vicente Palacios (Palacios should be 438) 537 Jose Lind 665 Mike LaValliere 381 Jim Leyland	.15	.07	.02
□ 656C Checklist 5 COR 438 Vicente Palacios 537 Jose Lind 665 Mike LaValliere 381 Jim Leyland	.15	.07	.02
□ 657 Mike Kingery	.05	.02	.01
□ 658 Scott Aldred	.05	.02	.01
□ 659 Oscar Azocar	.05	.02	.01
□ 660 Lee Smith	.10	.05	.01
□ 661 Steve Lake	.05	.02	.01
□ 662 Ron Dibble	.05	.02	.01
□ 663 Greg Brock	.05	.02	.01
□ 664 John Farrell	.05	.02	.01
□ 665 Mike LaValliere	.05	.02	.01
□ 666 Danny Darwin	.05	.02	.01
□ 667 Kent Anderson	.05	.02	.01
□ 668 Bill Long	.05	.02	.01
□ 669 Lou Piniella MG	.10	.05	.01
□ 670 Rickey Henderson	.15	.07	.02
□ 671 Andy McGaffigan	.05	.02	.01
□ 672 Shane Mack	.05	.02	.01
□ 673 Greg Olson UER (6 RBI in '88 at Tidewater and 2 RBI in '87, should be 48 and 15)	.05	.02	.01
□ 674A Kevin Gross ERR (89 BB with Phillies in '88 tied for league lead)	.15	.07	.02
□ 674B Kevin Gross COR (89 BB with Phillies in '88 led league)	.05	.02	.01
□ 675 Tom Brunansky	.05	.02	.01
□ 676 Scott Chiamparino	.05	.02	.01
□ 677 Billy Ripken	.05	.02	.01
□ 678 Mark Davidson	.05	.02	.01
□ 679 Bill Bathe	.05	.02	.01
□ 680 David Cone	.15	.07	.02
□ 681 Jeff Schaefer	.05	.02	.01
□ 682 Ray Lankford	.15	.07	.02
□ 683 Derek Lilliquist	.05	.02	.01

□ 684 Milt Cuyler	.05	.02	.01
□ 685 Doug Drabek	.05	.02	.01
□ 686 Mike Gallego	.05	.02	.01
□ 687A John Cerutti ERR (4.46 ERA in '90)	.15	.07	.02
□ 687B John Cerutti COR (4.76 ERA in '90)	.05	.02	.01
□ 688 Rosario Rodriguez	.05	.02	.01
□ 689 John Kruk	.10	.05	.01
□ 690 Orel Hershiser	.10	.05	.01
□ 691 Mike Blowers	.05	.02	.01
□ 692A Efrain Valdez ERR (Born 6/11/66)	.15	.07	.02
□ 692B Efrain Valdez COR (Born 7/11/66 and two lines of text added)	.05	.02	.01
□ 693 Francisco Cabrera	.05	.02	.01
□ 694 Randy Veres	.05	.02	.01
□ 695 Kevin Seitzer	.05	.02	.01
□ 696 Steve Olin	.05	.02	.01
□ 697 Shawn Abner	.05	.02	.01
□ 698 Mark Guthrie	.05	.02	.01
□ 699 Jim Lefebvre MG	.05	.02	.01
□ 700 Jose Canseco	.15	.07	.02
□ 701 Pascual Perez	.05	.02	.01
□ 702 Tim Naehring	.10	.05	.01
□ 703 Juan Agosto	.05	.02	.01
□ 704 Devon White	.10	.05	.01
□ 705 Robby Thompson	.05	.02	.01
□ 706A Brad Arnsberg ERR (68.2 IP in '90)	.15	.07	.02
□ 706B Brad Arnsberg COR (62.2 IP in '90)	.05	.02	.01
□ 707 Jim Eisenreich	.10	.05	.01
□ 708 John Mitchell	.05	.02	.01
□ 709 Matt Sinatro	.05	.02	.01
□ 710 Kent Hrbek	.10	.05	.01
□ 711 Jose DeLeon	.05	.02	.01
□ 712 Ricky Jordan	.05	.02	.01
□ 713 Scott Scudder	.05	.02	.01
□ 714 Marvell Wynne	.05	.02	.01
□ 715 Tim Burke	.05	.02	.01
□ 716 Bob Geren	.05	.02	.01
□ 717 Phil Bradley	.05	.02	.01
□ 718 Steve Crawford	.05	.02	.01
□ 719 Keith Miller	.05	.02	.01
□ 720 Cecil Fielder	.10	.05	.01
□ 721 Mark Lee	.05	.02	.01
□ 722 Wally Backman	.05	.02	.01
□ 723 Candy Maldonado	.05	.02	.01
□ 724 David Segui	.10	.05	.01
□ 725 Ron Gant	.15	.07	.02
□ 726 Phil Stephenson	.05	.02	.01
□ 727 Mookie Wilson	.05	.02	.01
□ 728 Scott Sanderson	.05	.02	.01
□ 729 Don Zimmer MG	.05	.02	.01
□ 730 Barry Larkin	.15	.07	.02
□ 731 Jeff Gray	.05	.02	.01
□ 732 Franklin Stubbs	.05	.02	.01
□ 733 Kelly Downs	.05	.02	.01
□ 734 John Russell	.05	.02	.01
□ 735 Ron Darling	.05	.02	.01
□ 736 Dick Schofield	.05	.02	.01
□ 737 Tim Crews	.05	.02	.01
□ 738 Mel Hall	.05	.02	.01
□ 739 Russ Swan	.05	.02	.01
□ 740 Ryne Sandberg	.25	.11	.03
□ 741 Jimmy Key	.10	.05	.01
□ 742 Tommy Gregg	.05	.02	.01
□ 743 Bryn Smith	.05	.02	.01
□ 744 Nelson Santovenia	.05	.02	.01
□ 745 Doug Jones	.05	.02	.01
□ 746 John Shelby	.05	.02	.01
□ 747 Tony Fossas	.05	.02	.01
□ 748 Al Newman	.05	.02	.01
□ 749 Greg W. Harris	.05	.02	.01
□ 750 Bobby Bonilla	.10	.05	.01
□ 751 Wayne Edwards	.05	.02	.01
□ 752 Kevin Bass	.05	.02	.01
□ 753 Paul Marak UER (Stats say drafted in Jan., but bio says May)	.05	.02	.01
□ 754 Bill Pecota	.05	.02	.01
□ 755 Mark Langston	.10	.05	.01
□ 756 Jeff Huson	.05	.02	.01
□ 757 Mark Gardner	.05	.02	.01
□ 758 Mike Devereaux	.05	.02	.01
□ 759 Bobby Cox MG	.05	.02	.01
□ 760 Benny Santiago	.05	.02	.01
□ 761 Larry Andersen	.05	.02	.01
□ 762 Mitch Webster	.05	.02	.01
□ 763 Dana Kiecker	.05	.02	.01
□ 764 Mark Carreon	.05	.02	.01
□ 765 Shawon Dunston	.05	.02	.01
□ 766 Jeff Robinson	.05	.02	.01
□ 767 Dan Wilson	.25	.11	.03
□ 768 Don Pall	.05	.02	.01
□ 769 Tim Sherrill	.05	.02	.01
□ 770 Jay Howell	.05	.02	.01
□ 771 Gary Redus UER (Born in Tanner, should say Athens)	.05	.02	.01
□ 772 Kent Mercker UER (Born in Indianapolis, should say Dublin, Ohio)	.05	.02	.01
□ 773 Tom Foley	.05	.02	.01
□ 774 Dennis Rasmussen	.05	.02	.01
□ 775 Julio Franco	.10	.05	.01
□ 776 Brent Mayne	.05	.02	.01
□ 777 John Candelaria	.05	.02	.01
□ 778 Dan Gladden	.05	.02	.01
□ 779 Carmelo Martinez	.05	.02	.01
□ 780A Randy Myers ERR (15 career losses)	.15	.07	.02
□ 780B Randy Myers COR (19 career losses)	.10	.05	.01
□ 781 Darryl Hamilton	.10	.05	.01
□ 782 Jim Deshaies	.05	.02	.01
□ 783 Joel Skinner	.05	.02	.01
□ 784 Willie Fraser	.05	.02	.01
□ 785 Scott Fletcher	.05	.02	.01
□ 786 Eric Plunk	.05	.02	.01
□ 787 Checklist 6	.05	.02	.01
□ 788 Bob Milacki	.05	.02	.01
□ 789 Tom Lasorda MG	.10	.05	.01
□ 790 Ken Griffey Jr.	1.50	.70	.19
□ 791 Mike Benjamin	.05	.02	.01
□ 792 Mike Greenwell	.05	.02	.01

1991 Topps Traded

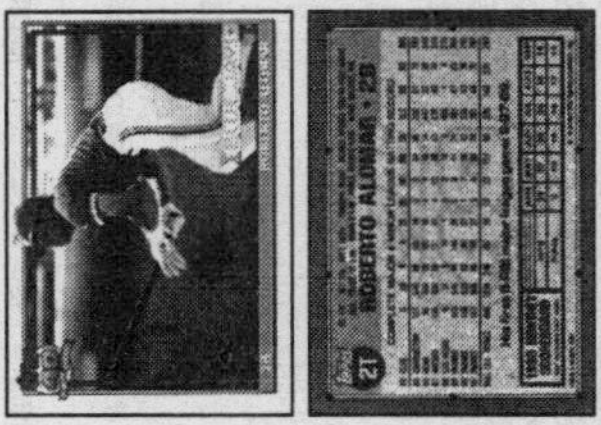

The 1991 Topps Traded set contains 132 standard-size cards. The cards were issued primarily in factory set form through hobby dealers but were also made available on a limited basis in wax packs. The cards in the wax packs (gray backs) and collated factory sets (white backs) are from different card stock. Both versions are valued equally. The card design is identical to the regular issue 1991 Topps cards except for the whiter stock (for factory set cards) and T-suffixed numbering. The set is numbered in alphabetical order. The set includes a Team U.S.A. subset, featuring 25 of America's top collegiate players. The key Rookie Cards in this set are Jeff Bagwell, Jason Giambi, Todd Greene, Charles Johnson and Ivan Rodriguez.

	MINT	NRMT	EXC
COMPLETE SET (132)	5.00	2.20	.60
COMPLETE FACT.SET (132)	5.00	2.20	.60
COMMON CARD (1T-132T)	.05	.02	.01
SEMISTARS	.10	.05	.01

*GRAY AND WHITE BACKS: SAME VALUE

□ 1T Juan Agosto	.05	.02	.01
□ 2T Roberto Alomar	.25	.11	.03
□ 3T Wally Backman	.05	.02	.01
□ 4T Jeff Bagwell	2.50	1.10	.30
□ 5T Skeeter Barnes	.05	.02	.01
□ 6T Steve Bedrosian	.05	.02	.01
□ 7T Derek Bell	.15	.07	.02
□ 8T George Bell	.05	.02	.01
□ 9T Rafael Belliard	.05	.02	.01
□ 10T Dante Bichette	.15	.07	.02
□ 11T Bud Black	.05	.02	.01
□ 12T Mike Boddicker	.05	.02	.01
□ 13T Sid Bream	.05	.02	.01
□ 14T Hubie Brooks	.05	.02	.01
□ 15T Brett Butler	.10	.05	.01
□ 16T Ivan Calderon	.05	.02	.01
□ 17T John Candelaria	.05	.02	.01
□ 18T Tom Candiotti	.05	.02	.01
□ 19T Gary Carter	.15	.07	.02
□ 20T Joe Carter	.15	.07	.02
□ 21T Rick Cerone	.05	.02	.01
□ 22T Jack Clark	.10	.05	.01
□ 23T Vince Coleman	.05	.02	.01
□ 24T Scott Coolbaugh	.05	.02	.01
□ 25T Danny Cox	.05	.02	.01
□ 26T Danny Darwin	.05	.02	.01
□ 27T Chili Davis	.10	.05	.01
□ 28T Glenn Davis	.05	.02	.01
□ 29T Steve Decker	.05	.02	.01
□ 30T Rob Deer	.05	.02	.01
□ 31T Rich DeLucia	.05	.02	.01
□ 32T John Dettmer USA	.10	.05	.01
□ 33T Brian Downing	.05	.02	.01
□ 34T Darren Dreifort USA	.15	.07	.02
□ 35T Kirk Dressendorfer	.05	.02	.01
□ 36T Jim Essian MG	.05	.02	.01
□ 37T Dwight Evans	.10	.05	.01
□ 38T Steve Farr	.05	.02	.01
□ 39T Jeff Fassero	.10	.05	.01
□ 40T Junior Felix	.05	.02	.01
□ 41T Tony Fernandez	.05	.02	.01
□ 42T Steve Finley	.15	.07	.02
□ 43T Jim Fregosi MG	.05	.02	.01
□ 44T Gary Gaetti	.10	.05	.01
□ 45T Jason Giambi USA	1.00	.45	.12
□ 46T Kirk Gibson	.10	.05	.01
□ 47T Leo Gomez	.05	.02	.01
□ 48T Luis Gonzalez	.15	.07	.02
□ 49T Jeff Granger USA	.15	.07	.02
□ 50T Todd Greene USA	.50	.23	.06
□ 51T Jeffrey Hammonds USA	.25	.11	.03
□ 52T Mike Hargrove MG	.05	.02	.01
□ 53T Pete Harnisch	.05	.02	.01
□ 54T Rick Helling USA UER (Misspelled Hellings on card back)	.10	.05	.01
□ 55T Glenallen Hill	.05	.02	.01
□ 56T Charlie Hough	.05	.02	.01
□ 57T Pete Incaviglia	.05	.02	.01
□ 58T Bo Jackson	.15	.07	.02
□ 59T Danny Jackson	.05	.02	.01
□ 60T Reggie Jefferson	.10	.05	.01
□ 61T Charles Johnson USA	.75	.35	.09
□ 62T Jeff Johnson	.05	.02	.01
□ 63T Todd Johnson USA	.05	.02	.01
□ 64T Barry Jones	.05	.02	.01
□ 65T Chris Jones	.05	.02	.01
□ 66T Scott Kamieniecki	.05	.02	.01
□ 67T Pat Kelly	.10	.05	.01
□ 68T Darryl Kile	.05	.02	.01
□ 69T Chuck Knoblauch	.25	.11	.03
□ 70T Bill Krueger	.05	.02	.01
□ 71T Scott Leius	.05	.02	.01
□ 72T Donnie Leshnock USA	.05	.02	.01
□ 73T Mark Lewis	.05	.02	.01
□ 74T Candy Maldonado	.05	.02	.01
□ 75T Jason McDonald USA	.15	.07	.02
□ 76T Willie McGee	.05	.02	.01
□ 77T Fred McGriff	.15	.07	.02
□ 78T Billy McMillon USA	.15	.07	.02
□ 79T Hal McRae MG	.05	.02	.01
□ 80T Dan Melendez USA	.05	.02	.01
□ 81T Orlando Merced	.15	.07	.02
□ 82T Jack Morris	.10	.05	.01
□ 83T Phil Nevin USA	.15	.07	.02
□ 84T Otis Nixon	.05	.02	.01
□ 85T Johnny Oates MG	.05	.02	.01
□ 86T Bob Ojeda	.05	.02	.01
□ 87T Mike Pagliarulo	.05	.02	.01
□ 88T Dean Palmer	.10	.05	.01
□ 89T Dave Parker	.10	.05	.01
□ 90T Terry Pendleton	.10	.05	.01
□ 91T Tony Phillips (P) USA	.05	.02	.01
□ 92T Doug Piatt	.05	.02	.01
□ 93T Ron Polk USA CO	.10	.05	.01
□ 94T Tim Raines	.15	.07	.02
□ 95T Willie Randolph	.10	.05	.01
□ 96T Dave Righetti	.05	.02	.01
□ 97T Ernie Riles	.05	.02	.01
□ 98T Chris Roberts USA	.15	.07	.02
□ 99T Jeff D. Robinson	.05	.02	.01
□ 100T Jeff M. Robinson	.05	.02	.01
□ 101T Ivan Rodriguez	1.00	.45	.12
□ 102T Steve Rodriguez USA	.05	.02	.01
□ 103T Tom Runnells MG	.05	.02	.01
□ 104T Scott Sanderson	.05	.02	.01
□ 105T Bob Scanlan	.05	.02	.01
□ 106T Pete Schourek	.15	.07	.02
□ 107T Gary Scott	.05	.02	.01
□ 108T Paul Shuey USA	.15	.07	.02
□ 109T Doug Simons	.05	.02	.01
□ 110T Dave Smith	.05	.02	.01
□ 111T Cory Snyder	.05	.02	.01
□ 112T Luis Sojo	.05	.02	.01
□ 113T Kennie Steenstra USA	.05	.02	.01
□ 114T Darryl Strawberry	.10	.05	.01
□ 115T Franklin Stubbs	.05	.02	.01
□ 116T Todd Taylor USA	.05	.02	.01
□ 117T Wade Taylor	.05	.02	.01
□ 118T Garry Templeton	.05	.02	.01
□ 119T Mickey Tettleton	.10	.05	.01
□ 120T Tim Teufel	.05	.02	.01
□ 121T Mike Timlin	.05	.02	.01
□ 122T David Tuttle USA	.05	.02	.01
□ 123T Mo Vaughn	.50	.23	.06
□ 124T Jeff Ware USA	.10	.05	.01
□ 125T Devon White	.10	.05	.01
□ 126T Mark Whiten	.10	.05	.01
□ 127T Mitch Williams	.05	.02	.01
□ 128T Craig Wilson USA	.05	.02	.01
□ 129T Willie Wilson	.05	.02	.01
□ 130T Chris Wimmer USA	.05	.02	.01
□ 131T Ivan Zweig USA	.05	.02	.01
□ 132T Checklist 1T-132T	.05	.02	.01

1992 Topps

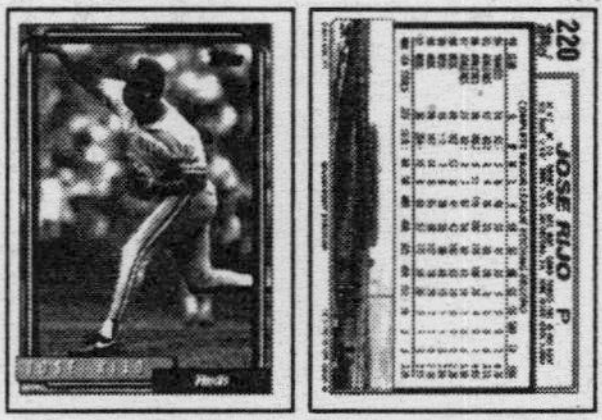

The 1992 Topps set contains 792 standard-size cards. Cards were distributed in plastic wrap packs, jumbo packs, rack packs and factory sets. The fronts have either posed or action color player photos on a white card face. Different color stripes frame the pictures, and the player's name and team name appear in two short color stripes respectively at the bottom. Special subsets included are Record Breakers (2-5), Prospects (58, 126, 179, 473, 551, 591, 618, 656, 676), and All-Stars (386-407). The key Rookie Cards in this set are Shawn Green, John Jaha and Manny Ramirez.

	MINT	NRMT	EXC
COMPLETE SET (792)	25.00	11.00	3.10
COMPLETE FACT.SET (802)	30.00	13.50	3.70
COMP. HOLIDAY SET (811)	35.00	16.00	4.40

1993 PREPROD. SET (9)	6.00	2.70	.75
COMMON CARD (1-792)	.05	.02	.01
SEMISTARS	.10	.05	.01
STARS	.15	.07	.02
COMPLETE GOLD SET (792)	125.00	55.00	15.50
COMP.GOLD FACT.SET (793)	130.00	57.50	16.00
COMMON GOLD (1-792)	.25	.11	.03
GOLD SEMISTARS	.50	.23	.06
*GOLD STARS: 9X to 15X HI COLUMN			
*GOLD YOUNG STARS: 6X to 12X HI			
GOLD: RANDOM INSERTS IN WAX PACKS .			
COMP.GOLD WIN.SET (792)	60.00	27.00	7.50
COMMON GOLD WIN. (1-792)	.10	.05	.01
GOLD WINNER SEMISTARS	.10	.05	.01
*GOLD WIN.STARS: 2.5X to 5X HI COLUMN			
*GOLD WIN.YOUNG STARS: 2X to 4X HI			
GOLD WIN. DISTRIB. W/GAME CARDS			

□ 1 Nolan Ryan	.75	.35	.09
□ 2 Ricky Henderson RB	.15	.07	.02
Most career SB's (Some cards have print marks that show 1.991 on the front)			
□ 3 Jeff Reardon RB	.05	.02	.01
10 seasons, 20 or more saves			
□ 4 Nolan Ryan RB	.40	.18	.05
22 cons. 100 K seasons			
□ 5 Dave Winfield RB	.10	.05	.01
Oldest player, cycle			
□ 6 Brien Taylor	.10	.05	.01
□ 7 Jim Olander	.05	.02	.01
□ 8 Bryan Hickerson	.05	.02	.01
□ 9 Jon Farrell	.05	.02	.01
□ 10 Wade Boggs	.15	.07	.02
□ 11 Jack McDowell	.10	.05	.01
□ 12 Luis Gonzalez	.10	.05	.01
□ 13 Mike Scioscia	.05	.02	.01
□ 14 Wes Chamberlain	.05	.02	.01
□ 15 Dennis Martinez	.10	.05	.01
□ 16 Jeff Montgomery	.10	.05	.01
□ 17 Randy Milligan	.05	.02	.01
□ 18 Greg Cadaret	.05	.02	.01
□ 19 Jamie Quirk	.05	.02	.01
□ 20 Bip Roberts	.05	.02	.01
□ 21 Buck Rogers MG	.05	.02	.01
□ 22 Bill Wegman	.05	.02	.01
□ 23 Chuck Knoblauch	.15	.07	.02
□ 24 Randy Myers	.10	.05	.01
□ 25 Ron Gant	.15	.07	.02
□ 26 Mike Bielecki	.05	.02	.01
□ 27 Juan Gonzalez	.60	.25	.07
□ 28 Mike Schooler	.05	.02	.01
□ 29 Mickey Tettleton	.05	.02	.01
□ 30 John Kruk	.10	.05	.01
□ 31 Bryn Smith	.05	.02	.01
□ 32 Chris Nabholz	.05	.02	.01
□ 33 Carlos Baerga	.15	.07	.02
□ 34 Jeff Juden	.05	.02	.01
□ 35 Dave Righetti	.05	.02	.01
□ 36 Scott Ruffcorn	.10	.05	.01
□ 37 Luis Polonia	.05	.02	.01
□ 38 Tom Candiotti	.05	.02	.01
□ 39 Greg Olson	.05	.02	.01
□ 40 Cal Ripken	2.50	1.10	.30
□ 41 Craig Lefferts	.05	.02	.01
□ 42 Mike Macfarlane	.05	.02	.01
□ 43 Jose Lind	.05	.02	.01
□ 44 Rick Aguilera	.05	.02	.01
□ 45 Gary Carter	.15	.07	.02
□ 46 Steve Farr	.05	.02	.01
□ 47 Rex Hudler	.05	.02	.01
□ 48 Scott Scudder	.05	.02	.01
□ 49 Damon Berryhill	.05	.02	.01
□ 50 Ken Griffey Jr.	1.50	.70	.19
□ 51 Tom Runnells MG	.05	.02	.01
□ 52 Juan Bell	.05	.02	.01
□ 53 Tommy Gregg	.05	.02	.01
□ 54 David Wells	.05	.02	.01
□ 55 Rafael Palmeiro	.15	.07	.02
□ 56 Charlie O'Brien	.05	.02	.01
□ 57 Donn Pall	.05	.02	.01
□ 58 1992 Prospects C	.15	.07	.02
Brad Ausmus			
Jim Campanis Jr.			
Dave Nilsson			
Doug Robbins			
□ 59 Mo Vaughn	.40	.18	.05
□ 60 Tony Fernandez	.05	.02	.01
□ 61 Paul O'Neill	.10	.05	.01
□ 62 Gene Nelson	.05	.02	.01
□ 63 Randy Ready	.05	.02	.01
□ 64 Bob Kipper	.05	.02	.01
□ 65 Willie McGee	.05	.02	.01
□ 66 Scott Stahoviak	.15	.07	.02
□ 67 Luis Salazar	.05	.02	.01
□ 68 Marvin Freeman	.05	.02	.01
□ 69 Kenny Lofton	1.00	.45	.12
□ 70 Gary Gaetti	.10	.05	.01
□ 71 Erik Hanson	.05	.02	.01
□ 72 Eddie Zosky	.05	.02	.01
□ 73 Brian Barnes	.05	.02	.01
□ 74 Scott Leius	.05	.02	.01
□ 75 Bret Saberhagen	.10	.05	.01
□ 76 Mike Gallego	.05	.02	.01
□ 77 Jack Armstrong	.05	.02	.01
□ 78 Ivan Rodriguez	.30	.14	.04
□ 79 Jesse Orosco	.05	.02	.01
□ 80 David Justice	.15	.07	.02
□ 81 Ced Landrum	.05	.02	.01
□ 82 Doug Simons	.05	.02	.01
□ 83 Tommy Greene	.05	.02	.01
□ 84 Leo Gomez	.05	.02	.01
□ 85 Jose DeLeon	.05	.02	.01
□ 86 Steve Finley	.15	.07	.02
□ 87 Bob MacDonald	.05	.02	.01
□ 88 Darrin Jackson	.05	.02	.01
□ 89 Neal Heaton	.05	.02	.01
□ 90 Robin Yount	.15	.07	.02
□ 91 Jeff Reed	.05	.02	.01
□ 92 Lenny Harris	.05	.02	.01
□ 93 Reggie Jefferson	.10	.05	.01
□ 94 Sammy Sosa	.25	.11	.03
□ 95 Scott Bailes	.05	.02	.01
□ 96 Tom McKinnon	.05	.02	.01
□ 97 Luis Rivera	.05	.02	.01
□ 98 Mike Harkey	.05	.02	.01
□ 99 Jeff Treadway	.05	.02	.01
□ 100 Jose Canseco	.15	.07	.02
□ 101 Omar Vizquel	.15	.07	.02
□ 102 Scott Kamieniecki	.05	.02	.01
□ 103 Ricky Jordan	.05	.02	.01
□ 104 Jeff Ballard	.05	.02	.01
□ 105 Felix Jose	.05	.02	.01
□ 106 Mike Boddicker	.05	.02	.01
□ 107 Dan Pasqua	.05	.02	.01
□ 108 Mike Timlin	.05	.02	.01
□ 109 Roger Craig MG	.05	.02	.01
□ 110 Ryne Sandberg	.25	.11	.03
□ 111 Mark Carreon	.05	.02	.01
□ 112 Oscar Azocar	.05	.02	.01
□ 113 Mike Greenwell	.05	.02	.01
□ 114 Mark Portugal	.05	.02	.01
□ 115 Terry Pendleton	.10	.05	.01
□ 116 Willie Randolph	.10	.05	.01
□ 117 Scott Terry	.05	.02	.01
□ 118 Chili Davis	.10	.05	.01
□ 119 Mark Gardner	.05	.02	.01
□ 120 Alan Trammell	.15	.07	.02
□ 121 Derek Bell	.10	.05	.01
□ 122 Gary Varsho	.05	.02	.01
□ 123 Bob Ojeda	.05	.02	.01
□ 124 Shawn Livsey	.05	.02	.01
□ 125 Chris Hoiles	.05	.02	.01
□ 126 1992 Prospects 1B	1.00	.45	.12
Ryan Klesko			
John Jaha			
Rico Brogna			
Dave Staton			
□ 127 Carlos Quintana	.05	.02	.01
□ 128 Kurt Stillwell	.05	.02	.01
□ 129 Melido Perez	.05	.02	.01
□ 130 Alvin Davis	.05	.02	.01
□ 131 Checklist 1-132	.05	.02	.01
□ 132 Eric Show	.05	.02	.01
□ 133 Rance Mulliniks	.05	.02	.01
□ 134 Darryl Kile	.05	.02	.01
□ 135 Von Hayes	.05	.02	.01
□ 136 Bill Doran	.05	.02	.01
□ 137 Jeff D. Robinson	.05	.02	.01
□ 138 Monty Fariss	.05	.02	.01
□ 139 Jeff Innis	.05	.02	.01

□ 140 Mark Grace UER .15 .07 .02
(Home Calie., should be Calif.)
□ 141 Jim Leyland MG UER .05 .02 .01
(No closed parenthesis after East in 1991)
□ 142 Todd Van Poppel .05 .02 .01
□ 143 Paul Gibson .05 .02 .01
□ 144 Bill Swift .05 .02 .01
□ 145 Danny Tartabull .05 .02 .01
□ 146 Al Newman .05 .02 .01
□ 147 Cris Carpenter .05 .02 .01
□ 148 Anthony Young .05 .02 .01
□ 149 Brian Bohanon .05 .02 .01
□ 150 Roger Clemens UER .15 .07 .02
(League leading ERA in 1990 not italicized)
□ 151 Jeff Hamilton .05 .02 .01
□ 152 Charlie Leibrandt .05 .02 .01
□ 153 Ron Karkovice .05 .02 .01
□ 154 Hensley Meulens .05 .02 .01
□ 155 Scott Bankhead .05 .02 .01
□ 156 Manny Ramirez 2.00 .90 .25
□ 157 Keith Miller .05 .02 .01
□ 158 Todd Frohwirth .05 .02 .01
□ 159 Darrin Fletcher .05 .02 .01
□ 160 Bobby Bonilla .10 .05 .01
□ 161 Casey Candaele .05 .02 .01
□ 162 Paul Faries .05 .02 .01
□ 163 Dana Kiecker .05 .02 .01
□ 164 Shane Mack .05 .02 .01
□ 165 Mark Langston .10 .05 .01
□ 166 Geronimo Pena .05 .02 .01
□ 167 Andy Allanson .05 .02 .01
□ 168 Dwight Smith .05 .02 .01
□ 169 Chuck Crim .05 .02 .01
□ 170 Alex Cole .05 .02 .01
□ 171 Bill Plummer MG .05 .02 .01
□ 172 Juan Berenguer .05 .02 .01
□ 173 Brian Downing .05 .02 .01
□ 174 Steve Frey .05 .02 .01
□ 175 Orel Hershiser .10 .05 .01
□ 176 Ramon Garcia .05 .02 .01
□ 177 Dan Gladden .05 .02 .01
□ 178 Jim Acker .05 .02 .01
□ 179 1992 Prospects 2B .05 .02 .01
Bobby DeJardin
Cesar Bernhardt
Armando Moreno
Andy Stankiewicz
□ 180 Kevin Mitchell .10 .05 .01
□ 181 Hector Villanueva .05 .02 .01
□ 182 Jeff Reardon .10 .05 .01
□ 183 Brent Mayne .05 .02 .01
□ 184 Jimmy Jones .05 .02 .01
□ 185 Benito Santiago .05 .02 .01
□ 186 Cliff Floyd .20 .09 .03
□ 187 Ernie Riles .05 .02 .01
□ 188 Jose Guzman .05 .02 .01
□ 189 Junior Felix .05 .02 .01
□ 190 Glenn Davis .05 .02 .01
□ 191 Charlie Hough .05 .02 .01
□ 192 Dave Fleming .05 .02 .01
□ 193 Omar Olivares .05 .02 .01
□ 194 Eric Karros .15 .07 .02
□ 195 David Cone .15 .07 .02
□ 196 Frank Castillo .10 .05 .01
□ 197 Glenn Braggs .05 .02 .01
□ 198 Scott Aldred .05 .02 .01
□ 199 Jeff Blauser .05 .02 .01
□ 200 Len Dykstra .10 .05 .01
□ 201 Buck Showalter MG .10 .05 .01
□ 202 Rick Honeycutt .05 .02 .01
□ 203 Greg Myers .05 .02 .01
□ 204 Trevor Wilson .05 .02 .01
□ 205 Jay Howell .05 .02 .01
□ 206 Luis Sojo .05 .02 .01
□ 207 Jack Clark .10 .05 .01
□ 208 Julio Machado .05 .02 .01
□ 209 Lloyd McClendon .05 .02 .01
□ 210 Ozzie Guillen .05 .02 .01
□ 211 Jeremy Hernandez .05 .02 .01
□ 212 Randy Velarde .05 .02 .01
□ 213 Les Lancaster .05 .02 .01
□ 214 Andy Mota .05 .02 .01
□ 215 Rich Gossage .10 .05 .01
□ 216 Brent Gates .10 .05 .01
□ 217 Brian Harper .05 .02 .01
□ 218 Mike Flanagan .05 .02 .01
□ 219 Jerry Browne .05 .02 .01
□ 220 Jose Rijo .05 .02 .01
□ 221 Skeeter Barnes .05 .02 .01
□ 222 Jaime Navarro .05 .02 .01
□ 223 Mel Hall .05 .02 .01
□ 224 Bret Barberie .05 .02 .01
□ 225 Roberto Alomar .25 .11 .03
□ 226 Pete Smith .05 .02 .01
□ 227 Daryl Boston .05 .02 .01
□ 228 Eddie Whitson .05 .02 .01
□ 229 Shawn Boskie .05 .02 .01
□ 230 Dick Schofield .05 .02 .01
□ 231 Brian Drahman .05 .02 .01
□ 232 John Smiley .05 .02 .01
□ 233 Mitch Webster .05 .02 .01
□ 234 Terry Steinbach .10 .05 .01
□ 235 Jack Morris .10 .05 .01
□ 236 Bill Pecota .05 .02 .01
□ 237 Jose Hernandez .05 .02 .01
□ 238 Greg Litton .05 .02 .01
□ 239 Brian Holman .05 .02 .01
□ 240 Andres Galarraga .15 .07 .02
□ 241 Gerald Young .05 .02 .01
□ 242 Mike Mussina .30 .14 .04
□ 243 Alvaro Espinoza .05 .02 .01
□ 244 Darren Daulton .10 .05 .01
□ 245 John Smoltz .15 .07 .02
□ 246 Jason Pruitt .05 .02 .01
□ 247 Chuck Finley .05 .02 .01
□ 248 Jim Gantner .05 .02 .01
□ 249 Tony Fossas .05 .02 .01
□ 250 Ken Griffey Sr. .05 .02 .01
□ 251 Kevin Elster .05 .02 .01
□ 252 Dennis Rasmussen .05 .02 .01
□ 253 Terry Kennedy .05 .02 .01
□ 254 Ryan Bowen .05 .02 .01
□ 255 Robin Ventura .15 .07 .02
□ 256 Mike Aldrete .05 .02 .01
□ 257 Jeff Russell .05 .02 .01
□ 258 Jim Lindeman .05 .02 .01
□ 259 Ron Darling .05 .02 .01
□ 260 Devon White .10 .05 .01
□ 261 Tom Lasorda MG .10 .05 .01
□ 262 Terry Lee .05 .02 .01
□ 263 Bob Patterson .05 .02 .01
□ 264 Checklist 133-264 .05 .02 .01
□ 265 Teddy Higuera .05 .02 .01
□ 266 Roberto Kelly .05 .02 .01
□ 267 Steve Bedrosian .05 .02 .01
□ 268 Brady Anderson .15 .07 .02
□ 269 Ruben Amaro Jr. .05 .02 .01
□ 270 Tony Gwynn .40 .18 .05
□ 271 Tracy Jones .05 .02 .01
□ 272 Jerry Don Gleaton .05 .02 .01
□ 273 Craig Grebeck .05 .02 .01
□ 274 Bob Scanlan .05 .02 .01
□ 275 Todd Zeile .05 .02 .01
□ 276 Shawn Green .50 .23 .06
□ 277 Scott Chiamparino .05 .02 .01
□ 278 Darryl Hamilton .05 .02 .01
□ 279 Jim Clancy .05 .02 .01
□ 280 Carlos Martinez .05 .02 .01
□ 281 Kevin Appier .10 .05 .01
□ 282 John Wehner .05 .02 .01
□ 283 Reggie Sanders .15 .07 .02
□ 284 Gene Larkin .05 .02 .01
□ 285 Bob Welch .05 .02 .01
□ 286 Gilberto Reyes .05 .02 .01
□ 287 Pete Schourek .10 .05 .01
□ 288 Andujar Cedeno .05 .02 .01
□ 289 Mike Morgan .05 .02 .01
□ 290 Bo Jackson .15 .07 .02
□ 291 Phil Garner MG .05 .02 .01
□ 292 Ray Lankford .15 .07 .02
□ 293 Mike Henneman .05 .02 .01
□ 294 Dave Valle .05 .02 .01
□ 295 Alonzo Powell .05 .02 .01
□ 296 Tom Brunansky .05 .02 .01
□ 297 Kevin Brown .10 .05 .01
□ 298 Kelly Gruber .05 .02 .01
□ 299 Charles Nagy .10 .05 .01
□ 300 Don Mattingly .50 .23 .06
□ 301 Kirk McCaskill .05 .02 .01

□ 302	Joey Cora	.05	.02	.01
□ 303	Dan Plesac	.05	.02	.01
□ 304	Joe Oliver	.05	.02	.01
□ 305	Tom Glavine	.15	.07	.02
□ 306	Al Shirley	.10	.05	.01
□ 307	Bruce Ruffin	.05	.02	.01
□ 308	Craig Shipley	.05	.02	.01
□ 309	Dave Martinez	.05	.02	.01
□ 310	Jose Mesa	.10	.05	.01
□ 311	Henry Cotto	.05	.02	.01
□ 312	Mike LaValliere	.05	.02	.01
□ 313	Kevin Tapani	.05	.02	.01
□ 314	Jeff Huson (Shows Jose Canseco sliding into second)	.10	.05	.01
□ 315	Juan Samuel	.05	.02	.01
□ 316	Curt Schilling	.05	.02	.01
□ 317	Mike Bordick	.10	.05	.01
□ 318	Steve Howe	.05	.02	.01
□ 319	Tony Phillips	.10	.05	.01
□ 320	George Bell	.05	.02	.01
□ 321	Lou Piniella MG	.10	.05	.01
□ 322	Tim Burke	.05	.02	.01
□ 323	Milt Thompson	.05	.02	.01
□ 324	Danny Darwin	.05	.02	.01
□ 325	Joe Orsulak	.05	.02	.01
□ 326	Eric King	.05	.02	.01
□ 327	Jay Buhner	.15	.07	.02
□ 328	Joel Johnston	.05	.02	.01
□ 329	Franklin Stubbs	.05	.02	.01
□ 330	Will Clark	.15	.07	.02
□ 331	Steve Lake	.05	.02	.01
□ 332	Chris Jones	.05	.02	.01
□ 333	Pat Tabler	.05	.02	.01
□ 334	Kevin Gross	.05	.02	.01
□ 335	Dave Henderson	.05	.02	.01
□ 336	Greg Anthony	.05	.02	.01
□ 337	Alejandro Pena	.05	.02	.01
□ 338	Shawn Abner	.05	.02	.01
□ 339	Tom Browning	.05	.02	.01
□ 340	Otis Nixon	.05	.02	.01
□ 341	Bob Geren	.05	.02	.01
□ 342	Tim Spehr	.05	.02	.01
□ 343	John Vander Wal	.05	.02	.01
□ 344	Jack Daugherty	.05	.02	.01
□ 345	Zane Smith	.05	.02	.01
□ 346	Rheal Cormier	.05	.02	.01
□ 347	Kent Hrbek	.10	.05	.01
□ 348	Rick Wilkins	.05	.02	.01
□ 349	Steve Lyons	.05	.02	.01
□ 350	Gregg Olson	.05	.02	.01
□ 351	Greg Riddoch MG	.05	.02	.01
□ 352	Ed Nunez	.05	.02	.01
□ 353	Braulio Castillo	.05	.02	.01
□ 354	Dave Bergman	.05	.02	.01
□ 355	Warren Newson	.05	.02	.01
□ 356	Luis Quinones	.05	.02	.01
□ 357	Mike Witt	.05	.02	.01
□ 358	Ted Wood	.05	.02	.01
□ 359	Mike Moore	.05	.02	.01
□ 360	Lance Parrish	.05	.02	.01
□ 361	Barry Jones	.05	.02	.01
□ 362	Javier Ortiz	.05	.02	.01
□ 363	John Candelaria	.05	.02	.01
□ 364	Glenallen Hill	.05	.02	.01
□ 365	Duane Ward	.05	.02	.01
□ 366	Checklist 265-396	.05	.02	.01
□ 367	Rafael Belliard	.05	.02	.01
□ 368	Bill Krueger	.05	.02	.01
□ 369	Steve Whitaker	.05	.02	.01
□ 370	Shawon Dunston	.05	.02	.01
□ 371	Dante Bichette	.15	.07	.02
□ 372	Kip Gross	.05	.02	.01
□ 373	Don Robinson	.05	.02	.01
□ 374	Bernie Williams	.40	.18	.05
□ 375	Bert Blyleven	.10	.05	.01
□ 376	Chris Donnels	.05	.02	.01
□ 377	Bob Zupcic	.05	.02	.01
□ 378	Joel Skinner	.05	.02	.01
□ 379	Steve Chitren	.05	.02	.01
□ 380	Barry Bonds	.25	.11	.03
□ 381	Sparky Anderson MG	.10	.05	.01
□ 382	Sid Fernandez	.05	.02	.01
□ 383	Dave Hollins	.05	.02	.01
□ 384	Mark Lee	.05	.02	.01
□ 385	Tim Wallach	.05	.02	.01
□ 386	Will Clark AS	.10	.05	.01
□ 387	Ryne Sandberg AS	.15	.07	.02
□ 388	Howard Johnson AS	.05	.02	.01
□ 389	Barry Larkin AS	.10	.05	.01
□ 390	Barry Bonds AS	.15	.07	.02
□ 391	Ron Gant AS	.10	.05	.01
□ 392	Bobby Bonilla AS	.05	.02	.01
□ 393	Craig Biggio AS	.10	.05	.01
□ 394	Dennis Martinez AS	.05	.02	.01
□ 395	Tom Glavine AS	.10	.05	.01
□ 396	Lee Smith AS	.05	.02	.01
□ 397	Cecil Fielder AS	.05	.02	.01
□ 398	Julio Franco AS	.05	.02	.01
□ 399	Wade Boggs AS	.10	.05	.01
□ 400	Cal Ripken AS	.40	.18	.05
□ 401	Jose Canseco AS	.10	.05	.01
□ 402	Joe Carter AS	.15	.07	.02
□ 403	Ruben Sierra AS	.05	.02	.01
□ 404	Matt Nokes AS	.05	.02	.01
□ 405	Roger Clemens AS	.15	.07	.02
□ 406	Jim Abbott AS	.05	.02	.01
□ 407	Bryan Harvey AS	.05	.02	.01
□ 408	Bob Milacki	.05	.02	.01
□ 409	Geno Petralli	.05	.02	.01
□ 410	Dave Stewart	.10	.05	.01
□ 411	Mike Jackson	.05	.02	.01
□ 412	Luis Aquino	.05	.02	.01
□ 413	Tim Teufel	.05	.02	.01
□ 414	Jeff Ware	.05	.02	.01
□ 415	Jim Deshaies	.05	.02	.01
□ 416	Ellis Burks	.15	.07	.02
□ 417	Allan Anderson	.05	.02	.01
□ 418	Alfredo Griffin	.05	.02	.01
□ 419	Wally Whitehurst	.05	.02	.01
□ 420	Sandy Alomar Jr.	.10	.05	.01
□ 421	Juan Agosto	.05	.02	.01
□ 422	Sam Horn	.05	.02	.01
□ 423	Jeff Fassero	.10	.05	.01
□ 424	Paul McClellan	.05	.02	.01
□ 425	Cecil Fielder	.10	.05	.01
□ 426	Tim Raines	.15	.07	.02
□ 427	Eddie Taubensee	.05	.02	.01
□ 428	Dennis Boyd	.05	.02	.01
□ 429	Tony LaRussa MG	.10	.05	.01
□ 430	Steve Sax	.05	.02	.01
□ 431	Tom Gordon	.05	.02	.01
□ 432	Billy Hatcher	.05	.02	.01
□ 433	Cal Eldred	.05	.02	.01
□ 434	Wally Backman	.05	.02	.01
□ 435	Mark Eichhorn	.05	.02	.01
□ 436	Mookie Wilson	.05	.02	.01
□ 437	Scott Servais	.05	.02	.01
□ 438	Mike Maddux	.05	.02	.01
□ 439	Chico Walker	.05	.02	.01
□ 440	Doug Drabek	.05	.02	.01
□ 441	Rob Deer	.05	.02	.01
□ 442	Dave West	.05	.02	.01
□ 443	Spike Owen	.05	.02	.01
□ 444	Tyrone Hill	.05	.02	.01
□ 445	Matt Williams	.15	.07	.02
□ 446	Mark Lewis	.05	.02	.01
□ 447	David Segui	.05	.02	.01
□ 448	Tom Pagnozzi	.05	.02	.01
□ 449	Jeff Johnson	.05	.02	.01
□ 450	Mark McGwire	.30	.14	.04
□ 451	Tom Henke	.05	.02	.01
□ 452	Wilson Alvarez	.15	.07	.02
□ 453	Gary Redus	.05	.02	.01
□ 454	Darren Holmes	.05	.02	.01
□ 455	Pete O'Brien	.05	.02	.01
□ 456	Pat Combs	.05	.02	.01
□ 457	Hubie Brooks	.05	.02	.01
□ 458	Frank Tanana	.05	.02	.01
□ 459	Tom Kelly MG	.05	.02	.01
□ 460	Andre Dawson	.15	.07	.02
□ 461	Doug Jones	.05	.02	.01
□ 462	Rich Rodriguez	.05	.02	.01
□ 463	Mike Simms	.05	.02	.01
□ 464	Mike Jeffcoat	.05	.02	.01
□ 465	Barry Larkin	.15	.07	.02
□ 466	Stan Belinda	.05	.02	.01
□ 467	Lonnie Smith	.05	.02	.01
□ 468	Greg Harris	.05	.02	.01
□ 469	Jim Eisenreich	.05	.02	.01
□ 470	Pedro Guerrero	.05	.02	.01
□ 471	Jose DeJesus	.05	.02	.01

☐ 472	Rich Rowland	.05	.02	.01
☐ 473	1992 Prospects 3B UER	.15	.07	.02
	Frank Bolick			
	Craig Paquette			
	Tom Redington			
	Paul Russo			
	(Line around top border)			
☐ 474	Mike Rossiter	.05	.02	.01
☐ 475	Robby Thompson	.05	.02	.01
☐ 476	Randy Bush	.05	.02	.01
☐ 477	Greg Hibbard	.05	.02	.01
☐ 478	Dale Sveum	.05	.02	.01
☐ 479	Chito Martinez	.05	.02	.01
☐ 480	Scott Sanderson	.05	.02	.01
☐ 481	Tino Martinez	.15	.07	.02
☐ 482	Jimmy Key	.10	.05	.01
☐ 483	Terry Shumpert	.05	.02	.01
☐ 484	Mike Hartley	.05	.02	.01
☐ 485	Chris Sabo	.05	.02	.01
☐ 486	Bob Walk	.05	.02	.01
☐ 487	John Cerutti	.05	.02	.01
☐ 488	Scott Cooper	.05	.02	.01
☐ 489	Bobby Cox MG	.05	.02	.01
☐ 490	Julio Franco	.10	.05	.01
☐ 491	Jeff Brantley	.10	.05	.01
☐ 492	Mike Devereaux	.05	.02	.01
☐ 493	Jose Offerman	.05	.02	.01
☐ 494	Gary Thurman	.05	.02	.01
☐ 495	Carney Lansford	.10	.05	.01
☐ 496	Joe Grahe	.05	.02	.01
☐ 497	Andy Ashby	.10	.05	.01
☐ 498	Gerald Perry	.05	.02	.01
☐ 499	Dave Otto	.05	.02	.01
☐ 500	Vince Coleman	.05	.02	.01
☐ 501	Rob Mallicoat	.05	.02	.01
☐ 502	Greg Briley	.05	.02	.01
☐ 503	Pascual Perez	.05	.02	.01
☐ 504	Aaron Sele	.15	.07	.02
☐ 505	Bobby Thigpen	.05	.02	.01
☐ 506	Todd Benzinger	.05	.02	.01
☐ 507	Candy Maldonado	.05	.02	.01
☐ 508	Bill Gullickson	.05	.02	.01
☐ 509	Doug Dascenzo	.05	.02	.01
☐ 510	Frank Viola	.05	.02	.01
☐ 511	Kenny Rogers	.05	.02	.01
☐ 512	Mike Heath	.05	.02	.01
☐ 513	Kevin Bass	.05	.02	.01
☐ 514	Kim Batiste	.05	.02	.01
☐ 515	Delino DeShields	.05	.02	.01
☐ 516	Ed Sprague Jr.	.10	.05	.01
☐ 517	Jim Gott	.05	.02	.01
☐ 518	Jose Melendez	.05	.02	.01
☐ 519	Hal McRae MG	.05	.02	.01
☐ 520	Jeff Bagwell	.60	.25	.07
☐ 521	Joe Hesketh	.05	.02	.01
☐ 522	Milt Cuyler	.05	.02	.01
☐ 523	Shawn Hillegas	.05	.02	.01
☐ 524	Don Slaught	.05	.02	.01
☐ 525	Randy Johnson	.15	.07	.02
☐ 526	Doug Piatt	.05	.02	.01
☐ 527	Checklist 397-528	.05	.02	.01
☐ 528	Steve Foster	.05	.02	.01
☐ 529	Joe Girardi	.05	.02	.01
☐ 530	Jim Abbott	.05	.02	.01
☐ 531	Larry Walker	.15	.07	.02
☐ 532	Mike Huff	.05	.02	.01
☐ 533	Mackey Sasser	.05	.02	.01
☐ 534	Benji Gil	.15	.07	.02
☐ 535	Dave Stieb	.05	.02	.01
☐ 536	Willie Wilson	.05	.02	.01
☐ 537	Mark Leiter	.05	.02	.01
☐ 538	Jose Uribe	.05	.02	.01
☐ 539	Thomas Howard	.05	.02	.01
☐ 540	Ben McDonald	.05	.02	.01
☐ 541	Jose Tolentino	.05	.02	.01
☐ 542	Keith Mitchell	.05	.02	.01
☐ 543	Jerome Walton	.05	.02	.01
☐ 544	Cliff Brantley	.05	.02	.01
☐ 545	Andy Van Slyke	.10	.05	.01
☐ 546	Paul Sorrento	.05	.02	.01
☐ 547	Herm Winningham	.05	.02	.01
☐ 548	Mark Guthrie	.05	.02	.01
☐ 549	Joe Torre MG	.10	.05	.01
☐ 550	Darryl Strawberry	.10	.05	.01
☐ 551	1992 Prospects SS UER	2.00	.90	.25
	Wilfredo Cordero			
	Chipper Jones			
	Manny Alexander			
	Alex Arias			
	(No line around			
	top border)			
☐ 552	Dave Gallagher	.05	.02	.01
☐ 553	Edgar Martinez	.15	.07	.02
☐ 554	Donald Harris	.05	.02	.01
☐ 555	Frank Thomas	1.50	.70	.19
☐ 556	Storm Davis	.05	.02	.01
☐ 557	Dickie Thon	.05	.02	.01
☐ 558	Scott Garrelts	.05	.02	.01
☐ 559	Steve Olin	.05	.02	.01
☐ 560	Rickey Henderson	.15	.07	.02
☐ 561	Jose Vizcaino	.05	.02	.01
☐ 562	Wade Taylor	.05	.02	.01
☐ 563	Pat Borders	.05	.02	.01
☐ 564	Jimmy Gonzalez	.05	.02	.01
☐ 565	Lee Smith	.10	.05	.01
☐ 566	Bill Sampen	.05	.02	.01
☐ 567	Dean Palmer	.10	.05	.01
☐ 568	Bryan Harvey	.05	.02	.01
☐ 569	Tony Pena	.05	.02	.01
☐ 570	Lou Whitaker	.15	.07	.02
☐ 571	Randy Tomlin	.05	.02	.01
☐ 572	Greg Vaughn	.15	.07	.02
☐ 573	Kelly Downs	.05	.02	.01
☐ 574	Steve Avery UER	.10	.05	.01
	(Should be 13 games			
	for Durham in 1989)			
☐ 575	Kirby Puckett	.30	.14	.04
☐ 576	Heathcliff Slocumb	.05	.02	.01
☐ 577	Kevin Seitzer	.05	.02	.01
☐ 578	Lee Guetterman	.05	.02	.01
☐ 579	Johnny Oates MG	.05	.02	.01
☐ 580	Greg Maddux	.75	.35	.09
☐ 581	Stan Javier	.05	.02	.01
☐ 582	Vicente Palacios	.05	.02	.01
☐ 583	Mel Rojas	.10	.05	.01
☐ 584	Wayne Rosenthal	.05	.02	.01
☐ 585	Lenny Webster	.05	.02	.01
☐ 586	Rod Nichols	.05	.02	.01
☐ 587	Mickey Morandini	.05	.02	.01
☐ 588	Russ Swan	.05	.02	.01
☐ 589	Mariano Duncan	.05	.02	.01
☐ 590	Howard Johnson	.05	.02	.01
☐ 591	1992 Prospects OF	.10	.05	.01
	Jeromy Burnitz			
	Jacob Brumfield			
	Alan Cockrell			
	D.J. Dozier			
☐ 592	Denny Neagle	.10	.05	.01
☐ 593	Steve Decker	.05	.02	.01
☐ 594	Brian Barber	.10	.05	.01
☐ 595	Bruce Hurst	.05	.02	.01
☐ 596	Kent Mercker	.05	.02	.01
☐ 597	Mike Magnante	.05	.02	.01
☐ 598	Jody Reed	.05	.02	.01
☐ 599	Steve Searcy	.05	.02	.01
☐ 600	Paul Molitor	.20	.09	.03
☐ 601	Dave Smith	.05	.02	.01
☐ 602	Mike Fetters	.05	.02	.01
☐ 603	Luis Mercedes	.05	.02	.01
☐ 604	Chris Gwynn	.05	.02	.01
☐ 605	Scott Erickson	.10	.05	.01
☐ 606	Brook Jacoby	.05	.02	.01
☐ 607	Todd Stottlemyre	.10	.05	.01
☐ 608	Scott Bradley	.05	.02	.01
☐ 609	Mike Hargrove MG	.05	.02	.01
☐ 610	Eric Davis	.10	.05	.01
☐ 611	Brian Hunter	.05	.02	.01
☐ 612	Pat Kelly	.05	.02	.01
☐ 613	Pedro Munoz	.05	.02	.01
☐ 614	Al Osuna	.05	.02	.01
☐ 615	Matt Merullo	.05	.02	.01
☐ 616	Larry Andersen	.05	.02	.01
☐ 617	Junior Ortiz	.05	.02	.01
☐ 618	1992 Prospects OF	.05	.02	.01
	Cesar Hernandez			
	Steve Hosey			
	Jeff McNeely			
	Dan Peltier			
☐ 619	Danny Jackson	.05	.02	.01
☐ 620	George Brett	.40	.18	.05
☐ 621	Dan Gakeler	.05	.02	.01
☐ 622	Steve Buechele	.05	.02	.01

☐ 623 Bob Tewksbury	.05	.02	.01
☐ 624 Shawn Estes	.15	.07	.02
☐ 625 Kevin McReynolds	.05	.02	.01
☐ 626 Chris Haney	.05	.02	.01
☐ 627 Mike Sharperson	.05	.02	.01
☐ 628 Mark Williamson	.05	.02	.01
☐ 629 Wally Joyner	.10	.05	.01
☐ 630 Carlton Fisk	.15	.07	.02
☐ 631 Armando Reynoso	.05	.02	.01
☐ 632 Felix Fermin	.05	.02	.01
☐ 633 Mitch Williams	.05	.02	.01
☐ 634 Manuel Lee	.05	.02	.01
☐ 635 Harold Baines	.10	.05	.01
☐ 636 Greg Harris	.05	.02	.01
☐ 637 Orlando Merced	.05	.02	.01
☐ 638 Chris Bosio	.05	.02	.01
☐ 639 Wayne Housie	.05	.02	.01
☐ 640 Xavier Hernandez	.05	.02	.01
☐ 641 David Howard	.05	.02	.01
☐ 642 Tim Crews	.05	.02	.01
☐ 643 Rick Cerone	.05	.02	.01
☐ 644 Terry Leach	.05	.02	.01
☐ 645 Deion Sanders	.15	.07	.02
☐ 646 Craig Wilson	.05	.02	.01
☐ 647 Marquis Grissom	.15	.07	.02
☐ 648 Scott Fletcher	.05	.02	.01
☐ 649 Norm Charlton	.05	.02	.01
☐ 650 Jesse Barfield	.05	.02	.01
☐ 651 Joe Slusarski	.05	.02	.01
☐ 652 Bobby Rose	.05	.02	.01
☐ 653 Dennis Lamp	.05	.02	.01
☐ 654 Allen Watson	.10	.05	.01
☐ 655 Brett Butler	.10	.05	.01
☐ 656 1992 Prospects OF	.15	.07	.02
Rudy Pemberton			
Henry Rodriguez			
Lee Tinsley			
Gerald Williams			
☐ 657 Dave Johnson	.05	.02	.01
☐ 658 Checklist 529-660	.05	.02	.01
☐ 659 Brian McRae	.15	.07	.02
☐ 660 Fred McGriff	.15	.07	.02
☐ 661 Bill Landrum	.05	.02	.01
☐ 662 Juan Guzman	.10	.05	.01
☐ 663 Greg Gagne	.05	.02	.01
☐ 664 Ken Hill	.15	.07	.02
☐ 665 Dave Haas	.05	.02	.01
☐ 666 Tom Foley	.05	.02	.01
☐ 667 Roberto Hernandez	.15	.07	.02
☐ 668 Dwayne Henry	.05	.02	.01
☐ 669 Jim Fregosi MG	.05	.02	.01
☐ 670 Harold Reynolds	.05	.02	.01
☐ 671 Mark Whiten	.10	.05	.01
☐ 672 Eric Plunk	.05	.02	.01
☐ 673 Todd Hundley	.15	.07	.02
☐ 674 Mo Sanford	.05	.02	.01
☐ 675 Bobby Witt	.05	.02	.01
☐ 676 1992 Prospects P	.05	.02	.01
Sam Militello			
Pat Mahomes			
Turk Wendell			
Roger Salkeld			
☐ 677 John Marzano	.05	.02	.01
☐ 678 Joe Klink	.05	.02	.01
☐ 679 Pete Incaviglia	.05	.02	.01
☐ 680 Dale Murphy	.15	.07	.02
☐ 681 Rene Gonzales	.05	.02	.01
☐ 682 Andy Benes	.05	.02	.01
☐ 683 Jim Poole	.05	.02	.01
☐ 684 Trever Miller	.05	.02	.01
☐ 685 Scott Livingstone	.05	.02	.01
☐ 686 Rich DeLucia	.05	.02	.01
☐ 687 Harvey Pulliam	.05	.02	.01
☐ 688 Tim Belcher	.05	.02	.01
☐ 689 Mark Lemke	.05	.02	.01
☐ 690 John Franco	.05	.02	.01
☐ 691 Walt Weiss	.05	.02	.01
☐ 692 Scott Ruskin	.05	.02	.01
☐ 693 Jeff King	.10	.05	.01
☐ 694 Mike Gardiner	.05	.02	.01
☐ 695 Gary Sheffield	.15	.07	.02
☐ 696 Joe Boever	.05	.02	.01
☐ 697 Mike Felder	.05	.02	.01
☐ 698 John Habyan	.05	.02	.01
☐ 699 Cito Gaston MG	.05	.02	.01
☐ 700 Ruben Sierra	.10	.05	.01
☐ 701 Scott Radinsky	.05	.02	.01
☐ 702 Lee Stevens	.05	.02	.01
☐ 703 Mark Wohlers	.15	.07	.02
☐ 704 Curt Young	.05	.02	.01
☐ 705 Dwight Evans	.10	.05	.01
☐ 706 Rob Murphy	.05	.02	.01
☐ 707 Gregg Jefferies	.15	.07	.02
☐ 708 Tom Bolton	.05	.02	.01
☐ 709 Chris James	.05	.02	.01
☐ 710 Kevin Maas	.05	.02	.01
☐ 711 Ricky Bones	.05	.02	.01
☐ 712 Curt Wilkerson	.05	.02	.01
☐ 713 Roger McDowell	.05	.02	.01
☐ 714 Calvin Reese	.15	.07	.02
☐ 715 Craig Biggio	.15	.07	.02
☐ 716 Kirk Dressendorfer	.05	.02	.01
☐ 717 Ken Dayley	.05	.02	.01
☐ 718 B.J. Surhoff	.10	.05	.01
☐ 719 Terry Mulholland	.05	.02	.01
☐ 720 Kirk Gibson	.10	.05	.01
☐ 721 Mike Pagliarulo	.05	.02	.01
☐ 722 Walt Terrell	.05	.02	.01
☐ 723 Jose Oquendo	.05	.02	.01
☐ 724 Kevin Morton	.05	.02	.01
☐ 725 Dwight Gooden	.10	.05	.01
☐ 726 Kirt Manwaring	.05	.02	.01
☐ 727 Chuck McElroy	.05	.02	.01
☐ 728 Dave Burba	.05	.02	.01
☐ 729 Art Howe MG	.05	.02	.01
☐ 730 Ramon Martinez	.10	.05	.01
☐ 731 Donnie Hill	.05	.02	.01
☐ 732 Nelson Santovenia	.05	.02	.01
☐ 733 Bob Melvin	.05	.02	.01
☐ 734 Scott Hatteberg	.05	.02	.01
☐ 735 Greg Swindell	.05	.02	.01
☐ 736 Lance Johnson	.10	.05	.01
☐ 737 Kevin Reimer	.05	.02	.01
☐ 738 Dennis Eckersley	.10	.05	.01
☐ 739 Rob Ducey	.05	.02	.01
☐ 740 Ken Caminiti	.15	.07	.02
☐ 741 Mark Gubicza	.05	.02	.01
☐ 742 Billy Spiers	.05	.02	.01
☐ 743 Darren Lewis	.05	.02	.01
☐ 744 Chris Hammond	.05	.02	.01
☐ 745 Dave Magadan	.05	.02	.01
☐ 746 Bernard Gilkey	.10	.05	.01
☐ 747 Willie Banks	.05	.02	.01
☐ 748 Matt Nokes	.05	.02	.01
☐ 749 Jerald Clark	.05	.02	.01
☐ 750 Travis Fryman	.15	.07	.02
☐ 751 Steve Wilson	.05	.02	.01
☐ 752 Billy Ripken	.05	.02	.01
☐ 753 Paul Assenmacher	.05	.02	.01
☐ 754 Charlie Hayes	.05	.02	.01
☐ 755 Alex Fernandez	.15	.07	.02
☐ 756 Gary Pettis	.05	.02	.01
☐ 757 Rob Dibble	.05	.02	.01
☐ 758 Tim Naehring	.10	.05	.01
☐ 759 Jeff Torborg MG	.05	.02	.01
☐ 760 Ozzie Smith	.20	.09	.03
☐ 761 Mike Fitzgerald	.05	.02	.01
☐ 762 John Burkett	.10	.05	.01
☐ 763 Kyle Abbott	.05	.02	.01
☐ 764 Tyler Green	.10	.05	.01
☐ 765 Pete Harnisch	.05	.02	.01
☐ 766 Mark Davis	.05	.02	.01
☐ 767 Kal Daniels	.05	.02	.01
☐ 768 Jim Thome	.75	.35	.09
☐ 769 Jack Howell	.05	.02	.01
☐ 770 Sid Bream	.05	.02	.01
☐ 771 Arthur Rhodes	.05	.02	.01
☐ 772 Garry Templeton UER	.05	.02	.01
(Stat heading in for pitchers)			
☐ 773 Hal Morris	.05	.02	.01
☐ 774 Bud Black	.05	.02	.01
☐ 775 Ivan Calderon	.05	.02	.01
☐ 776 Doug Henry	.05	.02	.01
☐ 777 John Olerud	.10	.05	.01
☐ 778 Tim Leary	.05	.02	.01
☐ 779 Jay Bell	.10	.05	.01
☐ 780 Eddie Murray	.25	.11	.03
☐ 781 Paul Abbott	.05	.02	.01
☐ 782 Phil Plantier	.10	.05	.01
☐ 783 Joe Magrane	.05	.02	.01
☐ 784 Ken Patterson	.05	.02	.01
☐ 785 Albert Belle	.60	.25	.07

□ 786 Royce Clayton	.10	.05	.01
□ 787 Checklist 661-792	.05	.02	.01
□ 788 Mike Stanton	.05	.02	.01
□ 789 Bobby Valentine MG	.05	.02	.01
□ 790 Joe Carter	.15	.07	.02
□ 791 Danny Cox	.05	.02	.01
□ 792 Dave Winfield	.15	.07	.02
□ 793G Brien Taylor Gold AU	10.00	4.50	1.25

1992 Topps Traded

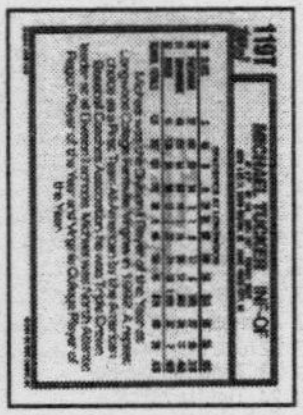

The 1992 Topps Traded set comprises 132 standard-size cards. The set was distributed exclusively in factory set form through hobby dealers. As in past editions, the set focuses on promising rookies, new managers, and players who changed teams. The set also includes a Team U.S.A. subset, featuring 25 of America's top college players and the Team U.S.A. coach. Card design is identical to the regular issue 1992 Topps cards except for the T-suffixed numbering. The cards are arranged in alphabetical order by player's last name. The key Rookie Cards in this set are Nomar Garciaparra, Brian Jordan and Michael Tucker.

	MINT	NRMT	EXC
COMPLETE FACT.SET (132)	12.00	5.50	1.50
COMMON CARD (1T-132T)	.05	.02	.01
SEMISTARS	.15	.07	.02
STARS	.30	.14	.04
COMP.GOLD.FACT.SET (132)	24.00	11.00	3.00
*GOLD: 2X BASIC CARDS			

□ 1T Willie Adams USA	.05	.02	.01
□ 2T Jeff Alkire USA	.05	.02	.01
□ 3T Felipe Alou MG	.05	.02	.01
□ 4T Moises Alou	.30	.14	.04
□ 5T Ruben Amaro	.05	.02	.01
□ 6T Jack Armstrong	.05	.02	.01
□ 7T Scott Bankhead	.05	.02	.01
□ 8T Tim Belcher	.05	.02	.01
□ 9T George Bell	.05	.02	.01
□ 10T Freddie Benavides	.05	.02	.01
□ 11T Todd Benzinger	.05	.02	.01
□ 12T Joe Boever	.05	.02	.01
□ 13T Ricky Bones	.05	.02	.01
□ 14T Bobby Bonilla	.15	.07	.02
□ 15T Hubie Brooks	.05	.02	.01
□ 16T Jerry Browne	.05	.02	.01
□ 17T Jim Bullinger	.05	.02	.01
□ 18T Dave Burba	.05	.02	.01
□ 19T Kevin Campbell	.05	.02	.01
□ 20T Tom Candiotti	.05	.02	.01
□ 21T Mark Carreon	.05	.02	.01
□ 22T Gary Carter	.30	.14	.04
□ 23T Archi Cianfrocco	.05	.02	.01
□ 24T Phil Clark	.05	.02	.01
□ 25T Chad Curtis	.30	.14	.04
□ 26T Eric Davis	.15	.07	.02
□ 27T Tim Davis USA	.05	.02	.01
□ 28T Gary DiSarcina	.05	.02	.01
□ 29T Darren Dreifort USA	.15	.07	.02
□ 30T Mariano Duncan	.05	.02	.01
□ 31T Mike Fitzgerald	.05	.02	.01
□ 32T John Flaherty	.05	.02	.01
□ 33T Darrin Fletcher	.05	.02	.01
□ 34T Scott Fletcher	.05	.02	.01
□ 35T Ron Fraser CO USA	.15	.07	.02
□ 36T Andres Galarraga	.30	.14	.04
□ 37T Dave Gallagher	.05	.02	.01
□ 38T Mike Gallego	.05	.02	.01
□ 39T Nomar Garciaparra USA	2.00	.90	.25
□ 40T Jason Giambi USA	1.00	.45	.12
□ 41T Danny Gladden	.05	.02	.01
□ 42T Rene Gonzales	.05	.02	.01
□ 43T Jeff Granger USA	.15	.07	.02
□ 44T Rick Greene USA	.05	.02	.01
□ 45T Jeffrey Hammonds USA	.30	.14	.04
□ 46T Charlie Hayes	.05	.02	.01
□ 47T Von Hayes	.05	.02	.01
□ 48T Rick Helling USA	.05	.02	.01
□ 49T Butch Henry	.05	.02	.01
□ 50T Carlos Hernandez	.05	.02	.01
□ 51T Ken Hill	.30	.14	.04
□ 52T Butch Hobson	.05	.02	.01
□ 53T Vince Horsman	.05	.02	.01
□ 54T Pete Incaviglia	.05	.02	.01
□ 55T Gregg Jefferies	.30	.14	.04
□ 56T Charles Johnson USA	.75	.35	.09
□ 57T Doug Jones	.05	.02	.01
□ 58T Brian Jordan	.75	.35	.09
□ 59T Wally Joyner	.15	.07	.02
□ 60T Daron Kirkreit USA	.15	.07	.02
□ 61T Bill Krueger	.05	.02	.01
□ 62T Gene Lamont MG	.05	.02	.01
□ 63T Jim Lefebvre MG	.05	.02	.01
□ 64T Danny Leon	.05	.02	.01
□ 65T Pat Listach	.15	.07	.02
□ 66T Kenny Lofton	2.00	.90	.25
□ 67T Dave Martinez	.05	.02	.01
□ 68T Derrick May	.05	.02	.01
□ 69T Kirk McCaskill	.05	.02	.01
□ 70T Chad McConnell USA	.15	.07	.02
□ 71T Kevin McReynolds	.05	.02	.01
□ 72T Rusty Meacham	.05	.02	.01
□ 73T Keith Miller	.05	.02	.01
□ 74T Kevin Mitchell	.15	.07	.02
□ 75T Jason Moler USA	.05	.02	.01
□ 76T Mike Morgan	.05	.02	.01
□ 77T Jack Morris	.15	.07	.02
□ 78T Calvin Murray USA	.15	.07	.02
□ 79T Eddie Murray	.40	.18	.05
□ 80T Randy Myers	.15	.07	.02
□ 81T Denny Neagle	.15	.07	.02
□ 82T Phil Nevin USA	.15	.07	.02
□ 83T Dave Nilsson	.30	.14	.04
□ 84T Junior Ortiz	.05	.02	.01
□ 85T Donovan Osborne	.15	.07	.02
□ 86T Bill Pecota	.05	.02	.01
□ 87T Melido Perez	.05	.02	.01
□ 88T Mike Perez	.05	.02	.01
□ 89T Hipolito Pichardo	.05	.02	.01
□ 90T Willie Randolph	.15	.07	.02
□ 91T Darren Reed	.05	.02	.01
□ 92T Bip Roberts	.05	.02	.01
□ 93T Chris Roberts USA	.15	.07	.02
□ 94T Steve Rodriguez USA	.05	.02	.01
□ 95T Bruce Ruffin	.05	.02	.01
□ 96T Scott Ruskin	.05	.02	.01
□ 97T Bret Saberhagen	.15	.07	.02
□ 98T Rey Sanchez	.05	.02	.01
□ 99T Steve Sax	.05	.02	.01
□ 100T Curt Schilling	.05	.02	.01
□ 101T Dick Schofield	.05	.02	.01
□ 102T Gary Scott	.05	.02	.01
□ 103T Kevin Seitzer	.05	.02	.01
□ 104T Frank Seminara	.05	.02	.01
□ 105T Gary Sheffield	.30	.14	.04
□ 106T John Smiley	.05	.02	.01
□ 107T Cory Snyder	.05	.02	.01
□ 108T Paul Sorrento	.05	.02	.01
□ 109T Sammy Sosa	.40	.18	.05
□ 110T Matt Stairs	.05	.02	.01
□ 111T Andy Stankiewicz	.05	.02	.01
□ 112T Kurt Stillwell	.05	.02	.01
□ 113T Rick Sutcliffe	.05	.02	.01
□ 114T Bill Swift	.05	.02	.01
□ 115T Jeff Tackett	.05	.02	.01
□ 116T Danny Tartabull	.05	.02	.01
□ 117T Eddie Taubensee	.05	.02	.01
□ 118T Dickie Thon	.05	.02	.01
□ 119T Michael Tucker USA	.40	.18	.05
□ 120T Scooter Tucker	.05	.02	.01
□ 121T Marc Valdes USA	.05	.02	.01

□ 122T	Julio Valera	.05	.02	.01
□ 123T	Jason Varitek USA	.40	.18	.05
□ 124T	Ron Villone USA	.15	.07	.02
□ 125T	Frank Viola	.05	.02	.01
□ 126T	B.J. Wallace USA	.15	.07	.02
□ 127T	Dan Walters	.05	.02	.01
□ 128T	Craig Wilson USA	.05	.02	.01
□ 129T	Chris Wimmer USA	.05	.02	.01
□ 130T	Dave Winfield	.30	.14	.04
□ 131T	Herm Winningham	.05	.02	.01
□ 132T	Checklist 1T-132T	.05	.02	.01

1993 Topps

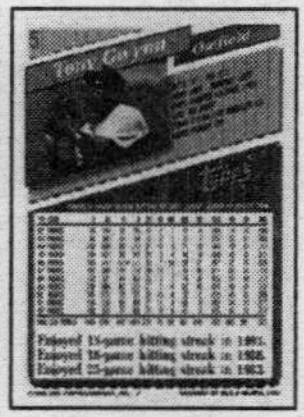

The 1993 Topps baseball set consists of two series, respectively, of 396 and 429 standard-size cards. A Topps Gold card was inserted in every 15-card pack, and Topps Black Gold cards were randomly inserted throughout the packs. The fronts feature color action player photos with white borders. The player's name appears in a stripe at the bottom of the picture, and this stripe and two short diagonal stripes at the bottom corners of the picture are team color-coded. The backs are colorful and carry a color head shot, biography, complete statistical information, with a career highlight if space permitted. Cards 401-411 comprise an All-Star subset. Rookie Cards in this set include Jim Edmonds, Derek Jeter, Jason Kendall, Chad Mottola, J.T. Snow, and Preston Wilson. For the Colorado Rockies and the Florida Marlins, Topps also produced cards gold-foil stamped factory complete sets on the front with the inaugural team's logo. Five thousand complete factory sets with the Rockies' logo and four thousand complete factory sets with the Marlins' logo were initially printed, and each team has the option of having a maximum of 10,000 special sets produced. The Rockies' sets were distributed through the four team-owned stores and at Mile High Stadium. The Marlins' sets were distributed through FMI and Joe Robbie Stadium. The complete 1993 Topps set was also issued as a factory set of micro baseball cards with cards measuring approximately one-fourth the size of the regular size cards but identical in other respects. The micro set and its cards are valued at approximately half the values listed below for the regular size cards.

	MINT	NRMT	EXC
COMPLETE SET (825)	30.00	13.50	3.70
COMPLETE RETAIL SET (838)	40.00	18.00	5.00
COMPLETE HOBBY SET (847)	45.00	20.00	5.50
COMP.1994 PREPROD. (9)	7.00	3.10	.85
COMPLETE SERIES 1 (396)	15.00	6.75	1.85
COMPLETE SERIES 2 (429)	15.00	6.75	1.85
COMMON CARD (1-825)	.05	.02	.01
SEMISTARS	.15	.07	.02
STARS	.30	.14	.04
COMPLETE GOLD SET (825)	70.00	32.00	8.75
COMP.GOLD SER.1 (396)	40.00	18.00	5.00
COMP.GOLD SER.2 (429)	30.00	13.50	3.70
COMMON GOLD (1-825)	.10	.05	.01
GOLD SEMISTARS	.20	.09	.03
GOLD STARS	.30	.14	.04
*GOLD STARS: 2X to 4X HI COLUMN			
*GOLD YOUNG STARS: 1.5X to 3X HI			
ONE GOLD PER SER.1 , SER.2 PACK			
10 GOLD CARDS PER FACTORY SET			

□ 1	Robin Yount	.15	.07	.02
□ 2	Barry Bonds	.50	.23	.06
□ 3	Ryne Sandberg	.50	.23	.06
□ 4	Roger Clemens	.15	.07	.02
□ 5	Tony Gwynn	.75	.35	.09
□ 6	Jeff Tackett	.05	.02	.01
□ 7	Pete Incaviglia	.05	.02	.01
□ 8	Mark Wohlers	.10	.05	.01
□ 9	Kent Hrbek	.10	.05	.01
□ 10	Will Clark	.15	.07	.02
□ 11	Eric Karros	.15	.07	.02
□ 12	Lee Smith	.10	.05	.01
□ 13	Esteban Beltre	.05	.02	.01
□ 14	Greg Briley	.05	.02	.01
□ 15	Marquis Grissom	.15	.07	.02
□ 16	Dan Plesac	.05	.02	.01
□ 17	Dave Hollins	.05	.02	.01
□ 18	Terry Steinbach	.10	.05	.01
□ 19	Ed Nunez	.05	.02	.01
□ 20	Tim Salmon	.50	.23	.06
□ 21	Luis Salazar	.05	.02	.01
□ 22	Jim Eisenreich	.10	.05	.01
□ 23	Todd Stottlemyre	.10	.05	.01
□ 24	Tim Naehring	.05	.02	.01
□ 25	John Franco	.05	.02	.01
□ 26	Skeeter Barnes	.05	.02	.01
□ 27	Carlos Garcia	.05	.02	.01
□ 28	Joe Orsulak	.05	.02	.01
□ 29	Dwayne Henry	.05	.02	.01
□ 30	Fred McGriff	.15	.07	.02
□ 31	Derek Lilliquist	.05	.02	.01
□ 32	Don Mattingly	1.00	.45	.12
□ 33	B.J. Wallace	.05	.02	.01
□ 34	Juan Gonzalez	1.00	.45	.12
□ 35	John Smoltz	.15	.07	.02
□ 36	Scott Servais	.05	.02	.01
□ 37	Lenny Webster	.05	.02	.01
□ 38	Chris James	.05	.02	.01
□ 39	Roger McDowell	.05	.02	.01
□ 40	Ozzie Smith	.40	.18	.05
□ 41	Alex Fernandez	.15	.07	.02
□ 42	Spike Owen	.05	.02	.01
□ 43	Ruben Amaro	.05	.02	.01
□ 44	Kevin Seitzer	.05	.02	.01
□ 45	Dave Fleming	.05	.02	.01
□ 46	Eric Fox	.05	.02	.01
□ 47	Bob Scanlan	.05	.02	.01
□ 48	Bert Blyleven	.10	.05	.01
□ 49	Brian McRae	.10	.05	.01
□ 50	Roberto Alomar	.50	.23	.06
□ 51	Mo Vaughn	.50	.23	.06
□ 52	Bobby Bonilla	.10	.05	.01
□ 53	Frank Tanana	.05	.02	.01
□ 54	Mike LaValliere	.05	.02	.01
□ 55	Mark McLemore	.05	.02	.01
□ 56	Chad Mottola	.10	.05	.01
□ 57	Norm Charlton	.05	.02	.01
□ 58	Jose Melendez	.05	.02	.01
□ 59	Carlos Martinez	.05	.02	.01
□ 60	Roberto Kelly	.05	.02	.01
□ 61	Gene Larkin	.05	.02	.01
□ 62	Rafael Belliard	.05	.02	.01
□ 63	Al Osuna	.05	.02	.01
□ 64	Scott Chiamparino	.05	.02	.01
□ 65	Brett Butler	.10	.05	.01
□ 66	John Burkett	.05	.02	.01
□ 67	Felix Jose	.05	.02	.01
□ 68	Omar Vizquel	.15	.07	.02
□ 69	John Vander Wal	.05	.02	.01
□ 70	Roberto Hernandez	.10	.05	.01
□ 71	Ricky Bones	.05	.02	.01
□ 72	Jeff Grotewold	.05	.02	.01
□ 73	Mike Moore	.05	.02	.01
□ 74	Steve Buechele	.05	.02	.01
□ 75	Juan Guzman	.10	.05	.01
□ 76	Kevin Appier	.10	.05	.01
□ 77	Junior Felix	.05	.02	.01
□ 78	Greg W. Harris	.05	.02	.01
□ 79	Dick Schofield	.05	.02	.01
□ 80	Cecil Fielder	.10	.05	.01
□ 81	Lloyd McClendon	.05	.02	.01
□ 82	David Segui	.05	.02	.01
□ 83	Reggie Sanders	.15	.07	.02

□ 84 Kurt Stillwell	.05	.02	.01
□ 85 Sandy Alomar	.10	.05	.01
□ 86 John Habyan	.05	.02	.01
□ 87 Kevin Reimer	.05	.02	.01
□ 88 Mike Stanton	.05	.02	.01
□ 89 Eric Anthony	.05	.02	.01
□ 90 Scott Erickson	.05	.02	.01
□ 91 Craig Colbert	.05	.02	.01
□ 92 Tom Pagnozzi	.05	.02	.01
□ 93 Pedro Astacio	.05	.02	.01
□ 94 Lance Johnson	.10	.05	.01
□ 95 Larry Walker	.15	.07	.02
□ 96 Russ Swan	.05	.02	.01
□ 97 Scott Fletcher	.05	.02	.01
□ 98 Derek Jeter	4.00	1.80	.50
□ 99 Mike Williams	.05	.02	.01
□ 100 Mark McGwire	.60	.25	.07
□ 101 Jim Bullinger	.05	.02	.01
□ 102 Brian Hunter	.05	.02	.01
□ 103 Jody Reed	.05	.02	.01
□ 104 Mike Butcher	.05	.02	.01
□ 105 Gregg Jefferies	.15	.07	.02
□ 106 Howard Johnson	.05	.02	.01
□ 107 John Kiely	.05	.02	.01
□ 108 Jose Lind	.05	.02	.01
□ 109 Sam Horn	.05	.02	.01
□ 110 Barry Larkin	.15	.07	.02
□ 111 Bruce Hurst	.05	.02	.01
□ 112 Brian Barnes	.05	.02	.01
□ 113 Thomas Howard	.05	.02	.01
□ 114 Mel Hall	.05	.02	.01
□ 115 Robby Thompson	.05	.02	.01
□ 116 Mark Lemke	.05	.02	.01
□ 117 Eddie Taubensee	.05	.02	.01
□ 118 David Hulse	.05	.02	.01
□ 119 Pedro Munoz	.05	.02	.01
□ 120 Ramon Martinez	.10	.05	.01
□ 121 Todd Worrell	.05	.02	.01
□ 122 Joey Cora	.05	.02	.01
□ 123 Moises Alou	.15	.07	.02
□ 124 Franklin Stubbs	.05	.02	.01
□ 125 Pete O'Brien	.05	.02	.01
□ 126 Bob Ayrault	.05	.02	.01
□ 127 Carney Lansford	.10	.05	.01
□ 128 Kal Daniels	.05	.02	.01
□ 129 Joe Grahe	.05	.02	.01
□ 130 Jeff Montgomery	.10	.05	.01
□ 131 Dave Winfield	.15	.07	.02
□ 132 Preston Wilson	.30	.14	.04
□ 133 Steve Wilson	.05	.02	.01
□ 134 Lee Guetterman	.05	.02	.01
□ 135 Mickey Tettleton	.05	.02	.01
□ 136 Jeff King	.10	.05	.01
□ 137 Alan Mills	.05	.02	.01
□ 138 Joe Oliver	.05	.02	.01
□ 139 Gary Gaetti	.10	.05	.01
□ 140 Gary Sheffield	.15	.07	.02
□ 141 Dennis Cook	.05	.02	.01
□ 142 Charlie Hayes	.05	.02	.01
□ 143 Jeff Huson	.05	.02	.01
□ 144 Kent Mercker	.05	.02	.01
□ 145 Eric Young	.15	.07	.02
□ 146 Scott Leius	.05	.02	.01
□ 147 Bryan Hickerson	.05	.02	.01
□ 148 Steve Finley	.15	.07	.02
□ 149 Rheal Cormier	.05	.02	.01
□ 150 Frank Thomas UER (Categories leading league are italicized but not printed in red)	2.00	.90	.25
□ 151 Archi Cianfrocco	.05	.02	.01
□ 152 Rich DeLucia	.05	.02	.01
□ 153 Greg Vaughn	.15	.07	.02
□ 154 Wes Chamberlain	.05	.02	.01
□ 155 Dennis Eckersley	.10	.05	.01
□ 156 Sammy Sosa	.15	.07	.02
□ 157 Gary DiSarcina	.05	.02	.01
□ 158 Kevin Koslofski	.05	.02	.01
□ 159 Doug Linton	.05	.02	.01
□ 160 Lou Whitaker	.15	.07	.02
□ 161 Chad McConnell	.05	.02	.01
□ 162 Joe Hesketh	.05	.02	.01
□ 163 Tim Wakefield	.10	.05	.01
□ 164 Leo Gomez	.05	.02	.01
□ 165 Jose Rijo	.05	.02	.01
□ 166 Tim Scott	.05	.02	.01
□ 167 Steve Olin UER (Born 10/4/65, should say 10/10/65)	.05	.02	.01
□ 168 Kevin Maas	.05	.02	.01
□ 169 Kenny Rogers	.05	.02	.01
□ 170 David Justice	.15	.07	.02
□ 171 Doug Jones	.05	.02	.01
□ 172 Jeff Reboulet	.05	.02	.01
□ 173 Andres Galarraga	.15	.07	.02
□ 174 Randy Velarde	.05	.02	.01
□ 175 Kirk McCaskill	.05	.02	.01
□ 176 Darren Lewis	.05	.02	.01
□ 177 Lenny Harris	.05	.02	.01
□ 178 Jeff Fassero	.10	.05	.01
□ 179 Ken Griffey Jr.	2.00	.90	.25
□ 180 Darren Daulton	.10	.05	.01
□ 181 John Jaha	.10	.05	.01
□ 182 Ron Darling	.05	.02	.01
□ 183 Greg Maddux	1.25	.55	.16
□ 184 Damion Easley	.05	.02	.01
□ 185 Jack Morris	.10	.05	.01
□ 186 Mike Magnante	.05	.02	.01
□ 187 John Dopson	.05	.02	.01
□ 188 Sid Fernandez	.05	.02	.01
□ 189 Tony Phillips	.10	.05	.01
□ 190 Doug Drabek	.05	.02	.01
□ 191 Sean Lowe	.10	.05	.01
□ 192 Bob Milacki	.05	.02	.01
□ 193 Steve Foster	.05	.02	.01
□ 194 Jerald Clark	.05	.02	.01
□ 195 Pete Harnisch	.05	.02	.01
□ 196 Pat Kelly	.05	.02	.01
□ 197 Jeff Frye	.05	.02	.01
□ 198 Alejandro Pena	.05	.02	.01
□ 199 Junior Ortiz	.05	.02	.01
□ 200 Kirby Puckett	.60	.25	.07
□ 201 Jose Uribe	.05	.02	.01
□ 202 Mike Scioscia	.05	.02	.01
□ 203 Bernard Gilkey	.15	.07	.02
□ 204 Dan Pasqua	.05	.02	.01
□ 205 Gary Carter	.15	.07	.02
□ 206 Henry Cotto	.05	.02	.01
□ 207 Paul Molitor	.40	.18	.05
□ 208 Mike Hartley	.05	.02	.01
□ 209 Jeff Parrett	.05	.02	.01
□ 210 Mark Langston	.10	.05	.01
□ 211 Doug Dascenzo	.05	.02	.01
□ 212 Rick Reed	.05	.02	.01
□ 213 Candy Maldonado	.05	.02	.01
□ 214 Danny Darwin	.05	.02	.01
□ 215 Pat Howell	.05	.02	.01
□ 216 Mark Leiter	.05	.02	.01
□ 217 Kevin Mitchell	.10	.05	.01
□ 218 Ben McDonald	.05	.02	.01
□ 219 Bip Roberts	.05	.02	.01
□ 220 Benny Santiago	.05	.02	.01
□ 221 Carlos Baerga	.15	.07	.02
□ 222 Bernie Williams	.15	.07	.02
□ 223 Roger Pavlik	.10	.05	.01
□ 224 Sid Bream	.05	.02	.01
□ 225 Matt Williams	.15	.07	.02
□ 226 Willie Banks	.05	.02	.01
□ 227 Jeff Bagwell	.75	.35	.09
□ 228 Tom Goodwin	.05	.02	.01
□ 229 Mike Perez	.05	.02	.01
□ 230 Carlton Fisk	.15	.07	.02
□ 231 John Wetteland	.10	.05	.01
□ 232 Tino Martinez	.10	.05	.01
□ 233 Rick Greene	.05	.02	.01
□ 234 Tim McIntosh	.05	.02	.01
□ 235 Mitch Williams	.05	.02	.01
□ 236 Kevin Campbell	.05	.02	.01
□ 237 Jose Vizcaino	.05	.02	.01
□ 238 Chris Donnels	.05	.02	.01
□ 239 Mike Boddicker	.05	.02	.01
□ 240 John Olerud	.05	.02	.01
□ 241 Mike Gardiner	.05	.02	.01
□ 242 Charlie O'Brien	.05	.02	.01
□ 243 Rob Deer	.05	.02	.01
□ 244 Denny Neagle	.10	.05	.01
□ 245 Chris Sabo	.05	.02	.01
□ 246 Gregg Olson	.05	.02	.01
□ 247 Frank Seminara UER (Acquired 12/3/98)	.05	.02	.01
□ 248 Scott Scudder	.05	.02	.01
□ 249 Tim Burke	.05	.02	.01

□ 250 Chuck Knoblauch	.15	.07	.02
□ 251 Mike Bielecki	.05	.02	.01
□ 252 Xavier Hernandez	.05	.02	.01
□ 253 Jose Guzman	.05	.02	.01
□ 254 Cory Snyder	.05	.02	.01
□ 255 Orel Hershiser	.10	.05	.01
□ 256 Wil Cordero	.10	.05	.01
□ 257 Luis Alicea	.05	.02	.01
□ 258 Mike Schooler	.05	.02	.01
□ 259 Craig Grebeck	.05	.02	.01
□ 260 Duane Ward	.05	.02	.01
□ 261 Bill Wegman	.05	.02	.01
□ 262 Mickey Morandini	.05	.02	.01
□ 263 Vince Horsman	.05	.02	.01
□ 264 Paul Sorrento	.05	.02	.01
□ 265 Andre Dawson	.15	.07	.02
□ 266 Rene Gonzales	.05	.02	.01
□ 267 Keith Miller	.05	.02	.01
□ 268 Derek Bell	.15	.07	.02
□ 269 Todd Steverson	.05	.02	.01
□ 270 Frank Viola	.05	.02	.01
□ 271 Wally Whitehurst	.05	.02	.01
□ 272 Kurt Knudsen	.05	.02	.01
□ 273 Dan Walters	.05	.02	.01
□ 274 Rick Sutcliffe	.05	.02	.01
□ 275 Andy Van Slyke	.10	.05	.01
□ 276 Paul O'Neill	.10	.05	.01
□ 277 Mark Whiten	.05	.02	.01
□ 278 Chris Nabholz	.05	.02	.01
□ 279 Todd Burns	.05	.02	.01
□ 280 Tom Glavine	.15	.07	.02
□ 281 Butch Henry	.05	.02	.01
□ 282 Shane Mack	.05	.02	.01
□ 283 Mike Jackson	.05	.02	.01
□ 284 Henry Rodriguez	.15	.07	.02
□ 285 Bob Tewksbury	.05	.02	.01
□ 286 Ron Karkovice	.05	.02	.01
□ 287 Mike Gallego	.05	.02	.01
□ 288 Dave Cochrane	.05	.02	.01
□ 289 Jesse Orosco	.05	.02	.01
□ 290 Dave Stewart	.10	.05	.01
□ 291 Tommy Greene	.05	.02	.01
□ 292 Rey Sanchez	.05	.02	.01
□ 293 Rob Ducey	.05	.02	.01
□ 294 Brent Mayne	.05	.02	.01
□ 295 Dave Stieb	.05	.02	.01
□ 296 Luis Rivera	.05	.02	.01
□ 297 Jeff Innis	.05	.02	.01
□ 298 Scott Livingstone	.05	.02	.01
□ 299 Bob Patterson	.05	.02	.01
□ 300 Cal Ripken	1.50	.70	.19
□ 301 Cesar Hernandez	.05	.02	.01
□ 302 Randy Myers	.10	.05	.01
□ 303 Brook Jacoby	.05	.02	.01
□ 304 Melido Perez	.05	.02	.01
□ 305 Rafael Palmeiro	.15	.07	.02
□ 306 Damon Berryhill	.05	.02	.01
□ 307 Dan Serafini	.30	.14	.04
□ 308 Darryl Kile	.05	.02	.01
□ 309 J.T. Bruett	.05	.02	.01
□ 310 Dave Righetti	.05	.02	.01
□ 311 Jay Howell	.05	.02	.01
□ 312 Geronimo Pena	.05	.02	.01
□ 313 Greg Hibbard	.05	.02	.01
□ 314 Mark Gardner	.05	.02	.01
□ 315 Edgar Martinez	.15	.07	.02
□ 316 Dave Nilsson	.10	.05	.01
□ 317 Kyle Abbott	.05	.02	.01
□ 318 Willie Wilson	.05	.02	.01
□ 319 Paul Assenmacher	.05	.02	.01
□ 320 Tim Fortugno	.05	.02	.01
□ 321 Rusty Meacham	.05	.02	.01
□ 322 Pat Borders	.05	.02	.01
□ 323 Mike Greenwell	.05	.02	.01
□ 324 Willie Randolph	.10	.05	.01
□ 325 Bill Gullickson	.05	.02	.01
□ 326 Gary Varsho	.05	.02	.01
□ 327 Tim Hulett	.05	.02	.01
□ 328 Scott Ruskin	.05	.02	.01
□ 329 Mike Maddux	.05	.02	.01
□ 330 Danny Tartabull	.05	.02	.01
□ 331 Kenny Lofton	.75	.35	.09
□ 332 Geno Petralli	.05	.02	.01
□ 333 Otis Nixon	.05	.02	.01
□ 334 Jason Kendall	1.00	.45	.12
□ 335 Mark Portugal	.05	.02	.01
□ 336 Mike Pagliarulo	.05	.02	.01
□ 337 Kirt Manwaring	.05	.02	.01
□ 338 Bob Ojeda	.05	.02	.01
□ 339 Mark Clark	.05	.02	.01
□ 340 John Kruk	.10	.05	.01
□ 341 Mel Rojas	.10	.05	.01
□ 342 Erik Hanson	.05	.02	.01
□ 343 Doug Henry	.05	.02	.01
□ 344 Jack McDowell	.10	.05	.01
□ 345 Harold Baines	.10	.05	.01
□ 346 Chuck McElroy	.05	.02	.01
□ 347 Luis Sojo	.05	.02	.01
□ 348 Andy Stankiewicz	.05	.02	.01
□ 349 Hipolito Pichardo	.05	.02	.01
□ 350 Joe Carter	.15	.07	.02
□ 351 Ellis Burks	.15	.07	.02
□ 352 Pete Schourek	.10	.05	.01
□ 353 Bubby Groom	.05	.02	.01
□ 354 Jay Bell	.10	.05	.01
□ 355 Brady Anderson	.15	.07	.02
□ 356 Freddie Benavides	.05	.02	.01
□ 357 Phil Stephenson	.05	.02	.01
□ 358 Kevin Wickander	.05	.02	.01
□ 359 Mike Stanley	.05	.02	.01
□ 360 Ivan Rodriguez	.40	.18	.05
□ 361 Scott Bankhead	.05	.02	.01
□ 362 Luis Gonzalez	.05	.02	.01
□ 363 John Smiley	.05	.02	.01
□ 364 Trevor Wilson	.05	.02	.01
□ 365 Tom Candiotti	.05	.02	.01
□ 366 Craig Wilson	.05	.02	.01
□ 367 Steve Sax	.05	.02	.01
□ 368 Delino DeShields	.05	.02	.01
□ 369 Jaime Navarro	.05	.02	.01
□ 370 Dave Valle	.05	.02	.01
□ 371 Mariano Duncan	.05	.02	.01
□ 372 Rod Nichols	.05	.02	.01
□ 373 Mike Morgan	.05	.02	.01
□ 374 Julio Valera	.05	.02	.01
□ 375 Wally Joyner	.10	.05	.01
□ 376 Tom Henke	.05	.02	.01
□ 377 Herm Winningham	.05	.02	.01
□ 378 Orlando Merced	.10	.05	.01
□ 379 Mike Munoz	.05	.02	.01
□ 380 Todd Hundley	.15	.07	.02
□ 381 Mike Flanagan	.05	.02	.01
□ 382 Tim Belcher	.05	.02	.01
□ 383 Jerry Browne	.05	.02	.01
□ 384 Mike Benjamin	.05	.02	.01
□ 385 Jim Leyritz	.05	.02	.01
□ 386 Ray Lankford	.15	.07	.02
□ 387 Devon White	.05	.02	.01
□ 388 Jeremy Hernandez	.05	.02	.01
□ 389 Brian Harper	.05	.02	.01
□ 390 Wade Boggs	.15	.07	.02
□ 391 Derrick May	.05	.02	.01
□ 392 Travis Fryman	.15	.07	.02
□ 393 Ron Gant	.15	.07	.02
□ 394 Checklist 1-132	.05	.02	.01
□ 395 Checklist 133-264 UER (Eckerlsey)	.05	.02	.01
□ 396 Checklist 265-396	.05	.02	.01
□ 397 George Brett	.75	.35	.09
□ 398 Bobby Witt	.05	.02	.01
□ 399 Daryl Boston	.05	.02	.01
□ 400 Bo Jackson	.15	.07	.02
□ 401 Fred McGriff / Frank Thomas	.50	.23	.06
□ 402 Ryne Sandberg / Carlos Baerga	.10	.05	.01
□ 403 Gary Sheffield / Edgar Martinez	.10	.05	.01
□ 404 Barry Larkin / Travis Fryman	.10	.05	.01
□ 405 Andy Van Slyke / Ken Griffey Jr.	.50	.23	.06
□ 406 Larry Walker / Kirby Puckett	.10	.05	.01
□ 407 Barry Bonds / Joe Carter	.10	.05	.01
□ 408 Darren Daulton / Brian Harper	.05	.02	.01
□ 409 Greg Maddux / Roger Clemens	.40	.18	.05
□ 410 Tom Glavine / Dave Fleming	.10	.05	.01

☐ 411 Lee Smith	.05	.02	.01
Dennis Eckersley			
☐ 412 Jamie McAndrew	.05	.02	.01
☐ 413 Pete Smith	.05	.02	.01
☐ 414 Juan Guerrero	.05	.02	.01
☐ 415 Todd Frohwirth	.05	.02	.01
☐ 416 Randy Tomlin	.05	.02	.01
☐ 417 B.J. Surhoff	.10	.05	.01
☐ 418 Jim Gott	.05	.02	.01
☐ 419 Mark Thompson	.05	.02	.01
☐ 420 Kevin Tapani	.05	.02	.01
☐ 421 Curt Schilling	.05	.02	.01
☐ 422 J.T. Snow	.15	.07	.02
☐ 423 1993 Prospects	1.00	.45	.12
Ryan Klesko			
Ivan Cruz			
Bubba Smith			
Larry Sutton			
☐ 424 John Valentin	.15	.07	.02
☐ 425 Joe Girardi	.05	.02	.01
☐ 426 Nigel Wilson	.05	.02	.01
☐ 427 Bob MacDonald	.05	.02	.01
☐ 428 Todd Zeile	.05	.02	.01
☐ 429 Milt Cuyler	.05	.02	.01
☐ 430 Eddie Murray	.50	.23	.06
☐ 431 Rich Amaral	.05	.02	.01
☐ 432 Pete Young	.05	.02	.01
☐ 433 Roger Bailey and	.10	.05	.01
Tom Schmidt			
☐ 434 Jack Armstrong	.05	.02	.01
☐ 435 Willie McGee	.05	.02	.01
☐ 436 Greg W. Harris	.05	.02	.01
☐ 437 Chris Hammond	.05	.02	.01
☐ 438 Ritchie Moody	.05	.02	.01
☐ 439 Bryan Harvey	.05	.02	.01
☐ 440 Ruben Sierra	.10	.05	.01
☐ 441 Don Lemon and	.10	.05	.01
Todd Pridy			
☐ 442 Kevin McReynolds	.05	.02	.01
☐ 443 Terry Leach	.05	.02	.01
☐ 444 David Nied	.05	.02	.01
☐ 445 Dale Murphy	.15	.07	.02
☐ 446 Luis Mercedes	.05	.02	.01
☐ 447 Keith Shepherd	.05	.02	.01
☐ 448 Ken Caminiti	.15	.07	.02
☐ 449 James Austin	.05	.02	.01
☐ 450 Darryl Strawberry	.10	.05	.01
☐ 451 1993 Prospects	.10	.05	.01
Ramon Caraballo			
Jon Shave			
Brent Gates			
Quinton McCracken			
☐ 452 Bob Wickman	.05	.02	.01
☐ 453 Victor Cole	.05	.02	.01
☐ 454 John Johnstone	.05	.02	.01
☐ 455 Chili Davis	.10	.05	.01
☐ 456 Scott Taylor	.05	.02	.01
☐ 457 Tracy Woodson	.05	.02	.01
☐ 458 David Wells	.05	.02	.01
☐ 459 Derek Wallace	.05	.02	.01
☐ 460 Randy Johnson	.15	.07	.02
☐ 461 Steve Reed	.05	.02	.01
☐ 462 Felix Fermin	.05	.02	.01
☐ 463 Scott Aldred	.05	.02	.01
☐ 464 Greg Colbrunn	.05	.02	.01
☐ 465 Tony Fernandez	.05	.02	.01
☐ 466 Mike Felder	.05	.02	.01
☐ 467 Lee Stevens	.05	.02	.01
☐ 468 Matt Whiteside	.05	.02	.01
☐ 469 Dave Hansen	.05	.02	.01
☐ 470 Rob Dibble	.05	.02	.01
☐ 471 Dave Gallagher	.05	.02	.01
☐ 472 Chris Gwynn	.05	.02	.01
☐ 473 Dave Henderson	.05	.02	.01
☐ 474 Ozzie Guillen	.05	.02	.01
☐ 475 Jeff Reardon	.10	.05	.01
☐ 476 Mark Voisard and	.10	.05	.01
Will Scalzitti			
☐ 477 Jimmy Jones	.05	.02	.01
☐ 478 Greg Cadaret	.05	.02	.01
☐ 479 Todd Pratt	.05	.02	.01
☐ 480 Pat Listach	.05	.02	.01
☐ 481 Ryan Luzinski	.10	.05	.01
☐ 482 Darren Reed	.05	.02	.01
☐ 483 Brian Griffiths	.05	.02	.01
☐ 484 John Wehner	.05	.02	.01

☐ 485 Glenn Davis	.05	.02	.01
☐ 486 Eric Wedge	.05	.02	.01
☐ 487 Jesse Hollins	.05	.02	.01
☐ 488 Manuel Lee	.05	.02	.01
☐ 489 Scott Fredrickson	.05	.02	.01
☐ 490 Omar Olivares	.05	.02	.01
☐ 491 Shawn Hare	.05	.02	.01
☐ 492 Tom Lampkin	.05	.02	.01
☐ 493 Jeff Nelson	.05	.02	.01
☐ 494 1993 Prospects	.10	.05	.01
Kevin Young			
Adell Davenport			
Eduardo Perez			
Lou Lucca			
☐ 495 Ken Hill	.10	.05	.01
☐ 496 Reggie Jefferson	.10	.05	.01
☐ 497 Matt Petersen and	.10	.05	.01
Willie Brown			
☐ 498 Bud Black	.05	.02	.01
☐ 499 Chuck Crim	.05	.02	.01
☐ 500 Jose Canseco	.15	.07	.02
☐ 501 Johnny Oates MG	.10	.05	.01
Bobby Cox MG			
☐ 502 Butch Hobson MG	.05	.02	.01
Jim Lefebvre MG			
☐ 503 Buck Rodgers MG	.10	.05	.01
Tony Perez MG			
☐ 504 Gene Lamont MG	.10	.05	.01
Don Baylor MG			
☐ 505 Mike Hargrove MG	.10	.05	.01
Rene Lachemann MG			
☐ 506 Sparky Anderson MG	.10	.05	.01
Art Howe MG			
☐ 507 Hal McRae MG	.10	.05	.01
Tom Lasorda MG			
☐ 508 Phil Garner MG	.05	.02	.01
Felipe Alou MG			
☐ 509 Tom Kelly MG	.05	.02	.01
Jeff Torborg MG			
☐ 510 Buck Showalter MG	.05	.02	.01
Jim Fregosi MG			
☐ 511 Tony LaRussa MG	.10	.05	.01
Jim Leyland MG			
☐ 512 Lou Piniella MG	.10	.05	.01
Joe Torre MG			
☐ 513 Kevin Kennedy MG	.05	.02	.01
Jim Riggleman MG			
☐ 514 Cito Gaston MG	.10	.05	.01
Dusty Baker MG			
☐ 515 Greg Swindell	.05	.02	.01
☐ 516 Alex Arias	.05	.02	.01
☐ 517 Bill Pecota	.05	.02	.01
☐ 518 Benji Grigsby UER	.05	.02	.01
(Misspelled Bengi			
on card front)			
☐ 519 David Howard	.05	.02	.01
☐ 520 Charlie Hough	.05	.02	.01
☐ 521 Kevin Flora	.05	.02	.01
☐ 522 Shane Reynolds	.10	.05	.01
☐ 523 Doug Bochtler	.05	.02	.01
☐ 524 Chris Hoiles	.05	.02	.01
☐ 525 Scott Sanderson	.05	.02	.01
☐ 526 Mike Sharperson	.05	.02	.01
☐ 527 Mike Fetters	.05	.02	.01
☐ 528 Paul Quantrill	.05	.02	.01
☐ 529 1993 Prospects	2.50	1.10	.30
Dave Silvestri			
Chipper Jones			
Benji Gil			
Jeff Patzke			
☐ 530 Sterling Hitchcock	.10	.05	.01
☐ 531 Joe Millette	.05	.02	.01
☐ 532 Tom Brunansky	.05	.02	.01
☐ 533 Frank Castillo	.05	.02	.01
☐ 534 Randy Knorr	.05	.02	.01
☐ 535 Jose Oquendo	.05	.02	.01
☐ 536 Dave Haas	.05	.02	.01
☐ 537 Jason Hutchins and	.10	.05	.01
Ryan Turner			
☐ 538 Jimmy Baron	.05	.02	.01
☐ 539 Kerry Woodson	.05	.02	.01
☐ 540 Ivan Calderon	.05	.02	.01
☐ 541 Denis Boucher	.05	.02	.01
☐ 542 Royce Clayton	.10	.05	.01
☐ 543 Reggie Williams	.05	.02	.01
☐ 544 Steve Decker	.05	.02	.01

□ 545 Dean Palmer	.10	.05	.01
□ 546 Hal Morris	.05	.02	.01
□ 547 Ryan Thompson	.05	.02	.01
□ 548 Lance Blankenship	.05	.02	.01
□ 549 Hensley Meulens	.05	.02	.01
□ 550 Scott Radinsky	.05	.02	.01
□ 551 Eric Young	.15	.07	.02
□ 552 Jeff Blauser	.05	.02	.01
□ 553 Andujar Cedeno	.05	.02	.01
□ 554 Arthur Rhodes	.05	.02	.01
□ 555 Terry Mulholland	.05	.02	.01
□ 556 Darryl Hamilton	.05	.02	.01
□ 557 Pedro Martinez	.15	.07	.02
□ 558 Ryan Whitman and	.10	.05	.01
Mark Skeels			
□ 559 Jamie Arnold	.10	.05	.01
□ 560 Zane Smith	.05	.02	.01
□ 561 Matt Nokes	.05	.02	.01
□ 562 Bob Zupcic	.05	.02	.01
□ 563 Shawn Boskie	.05	.02	.01
□ 564 Mike Timlin	.05	.02	.01
□ 565 Jerald Clark	.05	.02	.01
□ 566 Rod Brewer	.05	.02	.01
□ 567 Mark Carreon	.05	.02	.01
□ 568 Andy Benes	.05	.02	.01
□ 569 Shawn Barton	.05	.02	.01
□ 570 Tim Wallach	.05	.02	.01
□ 571 Dave Mlicki	.05	.02	.01
□ 572 Trevor Hoffman	.10	.05	.01
□ 573 John Patterson	.05	.02	.01
□ 574 De Shawn Warren	.10	.05	.01
□ 575 Monty Fariss	.05	.02	.01
□ 576 1993 Prospects	.10	.05	.01
Darrell Sherman			
Damon Buford			
Cliff Floyd			
Michael Moore			
□ 577 Tim Costo	.05	.02	.01
□ 578 Dave Magadan	.05	.02	.01
□ 579 Neil Garret and	.10	.05	.01
Jason Bates			
□ 580 Walt Weiss	.05	.02	.01
□ 581 Chris Haney	.05	.02	.01
□ 582 Shawn Abner	.05	.02	.01
□ 583 Marvin Freeman	.05	.02	.01
□ 584 Casey Candaele	.05	.02	.01
□ 585 Ricky Jordan	.05	.02	.01
□ 586 Jeff Tabaka	.05	.02	.01
□ 587 Manny Alexander	.05	.02	.01
□ 588 Mike Trombley	.05	.02	.01
□ 589 Carlos Hernandez	.05	.02	.01
□ 590 Cal Eldred	.05	.02	.01
□ 591 Alex Cole	.05	.02	.01
□ 592 Phil Plantier	.05	.02	.01
□ 593 Brett Merriman	.05	.02	.01
□ 594 Jerry Nielsen	.05	.02	.01
□ 595 Shawon Dunston	.05	.02	.01
□ 596 Jimmy Key	.10	.05	.01
□ 597 Gerald Perry	.05	.02	.01
□ 598 Rico Brogna	.10	.05	.01
□ 599 Clemente Nunez and	.10	.05	.01
Daniel Robinson			
□ 600 Bret Saberhagen	.10	.05	.01
□ 601 Craig Shipley	.05	.02	.01
□ 602 Henry Mercedes	.05	.02	.01
□ 603 Jim Thome	1.00	.45	.12
□ 604 Rod Beck	.10	.05	.01
□ 605 Chuck Finley	.05	.02	.01
□ 606 J. Owens	.10	.05	.01
□ 607 Dan Smith	.05	.02	.01
□ 608 Bill Doran	.05	.02	.01
□ 609 Lance Parrish	.05	.02	.01
□ 610 Denny Martinez	.10	.05	.01
□ 611 Tom Gordon	.05	.02	.01
□ 612 Byron Mathews	.05	.02	.01
□ 613 Joel Adamson	.05	.02	.01
□ 614 Brian Williams	.05	.02	.01
□ 615 Steve Avery	.10	.05	.01
□ 616 1993 Prospects	.15	.07	.02
Matt Mieske			
Tracy Sanders			
Midre Cummings			
Ryan Freeburg			
□ 617 Craig Lefferts	.05	.02	.01
□ 618 Tony Pena	.05	.02	.01
□ 619 Billy Spiers	.05	.02	.01

□ 620 Todd Benzinger	.05	.02	.01
□ 621 Mike Kotarski and	.10	.05	.01
Greg Boyd			
□ 622 Ben Rivera	.05	.02	.01
□ 623 Al Martin	.10	.05	.01
□ 624 Sam Militello UER	.05	.02	.01
(Profile says drafted			
in 1988, bio says			
drafted in 1990)			
□ 625 Rick Aguilera	.05	.02	.01
□ 626 Dan Gladden	.05	.02	.01
□ 627 Andres Berumen	.05	.02	.01
□ 628 Kelly Gruber	.05	.02	.01
□ 629 Cris Carpenter	.05	.02	.01
□ 630 Mark Grace	.15	.07	.02
□ 631 Jeff Brantley	.05	.02	.01
□ 632 Chris Widger	.05	.02	.01
□ 633 Three Russians UER	.10	.05	.01
Rudolf Razjigaev			
Eugneyi Puchkov			
Ilya Bogatyrev			
Bogatyrev is a shortstop,			
card has pitching header			
□ 634 Mo Sanford	.05	.02	.01
□ 635 Albert Belle	1.00	.45	.12
□ 636 Tim Teufel	.05	.02	.01
□ 637 Greg Myers	.05	.02	.01
□ 638 Brian Bohanon	.05	.02	.01
□ 639 Mike Bordick	.05	.02	.01
□ 640 Dwight Gooden	.10	.05	.01
□ 641 Pat Leahy and	.10	.05	.01
Gavin Baugh			
□ 642 Milt Hill	.05	.02	.01
□ 643 Luis Aquino	.05	.02	.01
□ 644 Dante Bichette	.15	.07	.02
□ 645 Bobby Thigpen	.05	.02	.01
□ 646 Rich Scheid	.05	.02	.01
□ 647 Brian Sackinsky	.05	.02	.01
□ 648 Ryan Hawblitzel	.05	.02	.01
□ 649 Tom Marsh	.05	.02	.01
□ 650 Terry Pendleton	.10	.05	.01
□ 651 Rafael Bournigal	.05	.02	.01
□ 652 Dave West	.05	.02	.01
□ 653 Steve Hosey	.05	.02	.01
□ 654 Gerald Williams	.05	.02	.01
□ 655 Scott Cooper	.05	.02	.01
□ 656 Gary Scott	.05	.02	.01
□ 657 Mike Harkey	.05	.02	.01
□ 658 1993 Prospects	.10	.05	.01
Jeromy Burnitz			
Melvin Nieves			
Rich Becker			
Shon Walker			
□ 659 Ed Sprague	.10	.05	.01
□ 660 Alan Trammell	.15	.07	.02
□ 661 Garvin Alston and	.10	.05	.01
Michael Case			
□ 662 Donovan Osborne	.05	.02	.01
□ 663 Jeff Gardner	.05	.02	.01
□ 664 Calvin Jones	.05	.02	.01
□ 665 Darrin Fletcher	.05	.02	.01
□ 666 Glenallen Hill	.05	.02	.01
□ 667 Jim Rosenbohm	.05	.02	.01
□ 668 Scott Lewis	.05	.02	.01
□ 669 Kip Yaughn	.05	.02	.01
□ 670 Julio Franco	.10	.05	.01
□ 671 Dave Martinez	.05	.02	.01
□ 672 Kevin Bass	.05	.02	.01
□ 673 Todd Van Poppel	.05	.02	.01
□ 674 Mark Gubicza	.05	.02	.01
□ 675 Tim Raines	.15	.07	.02
□ 676 Rudy Seanez	.05	.02	.01
□ 677 Charlie Leibrandt	.05	.02	.01
□ 678 Randy Milligan	.05	.02	.01
□ 679 Kim Batiste	.05	.02	.01
□ 680 Craig Biggio	.15	.07	.02
□ 681 Darren Holmes	.05	.02	.01
□ 682 John Candelaria	.05	.02	.01
□ 683 Jerry Stafford and	.10	.05	.01
Eddie Christian			
□ 684 Pat Mahomes	.05	.02	.01
□ 685 Bob Walk	.05	.02	.01
□ 686 Russ Springer	.05	.02	.01
□ 687 Tony Sheffield	.05	.02	.01
□ 688 Dwight Smith	.05	.02	.01
□ 689 Eddie Zosky	.05	.02	.01

□ 690 Bien Figueroa	.05	.02	.01
□ 691 Jim Tatum	.05	.02	.01
□ 692 Chad Kreuter	.05	.02	.01
□ 693 Rich Rodriguez	.05	.02	.01
□ 694 Shane Turner	.05	.02	.01
□ 695 Kent Bottenfield	.05	.02	.01
□ 696 Jose Mesa	.10	.05	.01
□ 697 Darrell Whitmore	.05	.02	.01
□ 698 Ted Wood	.05	.02	.01
□ 699 Chad Curtis	.10	.05	.01
□ 700 Nolan Ryan	1.50	.70	.19
□ 701 1993 Prospects	2.00	.90	.25
Mike Piazza			
Brook Fordyce			
Carlos Delgado			
Donnie Leshnock			
□ 702 Tim Pugh	.05	.02	.01
□ 703 Jeff Kent	.10	.05	.01
□ 704 Jon Goodrich and	.10	.05	.01
Danny Figueroa			
□ 705 Bob Welch	.05	.02	.01
□ 706 Sherard Clinkscales	.05	.02	.01
□ 707 Donn Pall	.05	.02	.01
□ 708 Greg Olson	.05	.02	.01
□ 709 Jeff Juden	.05	.02	.01
□ 710 Mike Mussina	.40	.18	.05
□ 711 Scott Chiamparino	.05	.02	.01
□ 712 Stan Javier	.05	.02	.01
□ 713 John Doherty	.05	.02	.01
□ 714 Kevin Gross	.05	.02	.01
□ 715 Greg Gagne	.05	.02	.01
□ 716 Steve Cooke	.05	.02	.01
□ 717 Steve Farr	.05	.02	.01
□ 718 Jay Buhner	.15	.07	.02
□ 719 Butch Henry	.05	.02	.01
□ 720 David Cone	.15	.07	.02
□ 721 Rick Wilkins	.05	.02	.01
□ 722 Chuck Carr	.05	.02	.01
□ 723 Kenny Felder	.05	.02	.01
□ 724 Guillermo Velasquez	.05	.02	.01
□ 725 Billy Hatcher	.05	.02	.01
□ 726 Mike Veneziale and	.10	.05	.01
Ken Kendrena			
□ 727 Jonathan Hurst	.05	.02	.01
□ 728 Steve Frey	.05	.02	.01
□ 729 Mark Leonard	.05	.02	.01
□ 730 Charles Nagy	.10	.05	.01
□ 731 Donald Harris	.05	.02	.01
□ 732 Travis Buckley	.05	.02	.01
□ 733 Tom Browning	.05	.02	.01
□ 734 Anthony Young	.05	.02	.01
□ 735 Steve Shifflett	.05	.02	.01
□ 736 Jeff Russell	.05	.02	.01
□ 737 Wilson Alvarez	.10	.05	.01
□ 738 Lance Painter	.05	.02	.01
□ 739 Dave Weathers	.05	.02	.01
□ 740 Len Dykstra	.10	.05	.01
□ 741 Mike Devereaux	.05	.02	.01
□ 742 1993 Prospects	.10	.05	.01
Rene Arocha			
Alan Embree			
Brien Taylor			
Tim Crabtree			
□ 743 Dave Landaker	.05	.02	.01
□ 744 Chris George	.05	.02	.01
□ 745 Eric Davis	.10	.05	.01
□ 746 Mark Strittmatter and	.10	.05	.01
Lamarr Rogers			
□ 747 Carl Willis	.05	.02	.01
□ 748 Stan Belinda	.05	.02	.01
□ 749 Scott Kamieniecki	.05	.02	.01
□ 750 Rickey Henderson	.15	.07	.02
□ 751 Eric Hillman	.05	.02	.01
□ 752 Pat Hentgen	.15	.07	.02
□ 753 Jim Corsi	.05	.02	.01
□ 754 Brian Jordan	.15	.07	.02
□ 755 Bill Swift	.05	.02	.01
□ 756 Mike Henneman	.05	.02	.01
□ 757 Harold Reynolds	.05	.02	.01
□ 758 Sean Berry	.05	.02	.01
□ 759 Charlie Hayes	.05	.02	.01
□ 760 Luis Polonia	.05	.02	.01
□ 761 Darrin Jackson	.05	.02	.01
□ 762 Mark Lewis	.05	.02	.01
□ 763 Rob Maurer	.05	.02	.01
□ 764 Willie Greene	.10	.05	.01
□ 765 Vince Coleman	.05	.02	.01
□ 766 Todd Revenig	.05	.02	.01
□ 767 Rich Ireland	.05	.02	.01
□ 768 Mike Macfarlane	.05	.02	.01
□ 769 Francisco Cabrera	.05	.02	.01
□ 770 Robin Ventura	.10	.05	.01
□ 771 Kevin Ritz	.05	.02	.01
□ 772 Chito Martinez	.05	.02	.01
□ 773 Cliff Brantley	.05	.02	.01
□ 774 Curtis Leskanic	.05	.02	.01
□ 775 Chris Bosio	.05	.02	.01
□ 776 Jose Offerman	.05	.02	.01
□ 777 Mark Guthrie	.05	.02	.01
□ 778 Don Slaught	.05	.02	.01
□ 779 Rich Monteleone	.05	.02	.01
□ 780 Jim Abbott	.05	.02	.01
□ 781 Jack Clark	.05	.02	.01
□ 782 Reynol Mendoza and	.10	.05	.01
Dan Roman			
□ 783 Heathcliff Slocumb	.05	.02	.01
□ 784 Jeff Branson	.05	.02	.01
□ 785 Kevin Brown	.05	.02	.01
□ 786 1993 Prospects	.10	.05	.01
Mike Christopher			
Ken Ryan			
Aaron Taylor			
Gus Gandarillas			
□ 787 Mike Matthews	.10	.05	.01
□ 788 Mackey Sasser	.05	.02	.01
□ 789 Jeff Conine UER	.15	.07	.02
(No inclusion of 1990 stats in career total)			
□ 790 George Bell	.05	.02	.01
□ 791 Pat Rapp	.10	.05	.01
□ 792 Joe Boever	.05	.02	.01
□ 793 Jim Poole	.05	.02	.01
□ 794 Andy Ashby	.10	.05	.01
□ 795 Deion Sanders	.15	.07	.02
□ 796 Scott Brosius	.05	.02	.01
□ 797 Brad Pennington	.05	.02	.01
□ 798 Greg Blosser	.05	.02	.01
□ 799 Jim Edmonds	1.50	.70	.19
□ 800 Shawn Jeter	.05	.02	.01
□ 801 Jesse Levis	.05	.02	.01
□ 802 Phil Clark UER	.05	.02	.01
(Word "a" is missing in sentence beginning with "In 1992 ...)			
□ 803 Ed Pierce	.05	.02	.01
□ 804 Jose Valentin	.50	.23	.06
□ 805 Terry Jorgensen	.05	.02	.01
□ 806 Mark Hutton	.05	.02	.01
□ 807 Troy Neel	.05	.02	.01
□ 808 Bret Boone	.10	.05	.01
□ 809 Cris Colon	.05	.02	.01
□ 810 Domingo Martinez	.05	.02	.01
□ 811 Javier Lopez	.50	.23	.06
□ 812 Matt Walbeck	.05	.02	.01
□ 813 Dan Wilson	.10	.05	.01
□ 814 Scooter Tucker	.05	.02	.01
□ 815 Billy Ashley	.05	.02	.01
□ 816 Tim Laker	.05	.02	.01
□ 817 Bobby Jones	.10	.05	.01
□ 818 Brad Brink	.05	.02	.01
□ 819 William Pennyfeather	.05	.02	.01
□ 820 Stan Royer	.05	.02	.01
□ 821 Doug Brocail	.05	.02	.01
□ 822 Kevin Rogers	.05	.02	.01
□ 823 Checklist 397-540	.05	.02	.01
□ 824 Checklist 541-691	.05	.02	.01
□ 825 Checklist 692-825	.05	.02	.01

1993 Topps Black Gold

Topps Black Gold cards 1-22 were randomly inserted in series I wax packs while card numbers 23-44 were featured in series II packs. They were also inserted three per factory set. Hobbyists could obtain the set by collecting individual random insert cards or receive 11, 22, or 44 Black Gold cards by mail when they sent in special "You've Just Won" cards, which were randomly inserted in packs. Series I packs featured three different "You've Just Won" cards, entitling the holder to receive Group A

(cards 1-11), Group B (cards 12-22), or Groups A and B (Cards 1-22). In a similar fashion, four "You've Just Won" cards were inserted in series II packs and entitled the holder to receive Group C (23-33), Group D (34-44), Groups C and D (23-44), or Groups A-D (1-44). By returning the "You've Just Won" card with 1.50 for postage and handling, the collector received not only the Black Gold cards won but also a special "You've Just Won" card and a congratulatory letter informing the collector that his/her name has been entered into a drawing for one of 500 uncut sheets of all 44 Topps Black Gold cards in a leatherette frame. These standard-size cards feature different color player photos than either the 1993 Topps regular issue or the Topps Gold issue. The player pictures are cut out and superimposed on a black gloss background. Inside white borders, gold refractory foil edges the top and bottom of the card face. On a black-and-gray pinstripe pattern inside white borders, the horizontal backs have a a second cut out player photo and a player profile on a blue panel. The player's name appears in gold foil lettering on a blue-and-gray geometric shape. The first 22 cards are National Leaguers while the second 22 cards are American Leaguers. Winner cards C and D were both originally produced erroneously and later corrected; the error versions show the players from Winner A and B on the respective fronts of Winner cards Cand D. There is no value difference in the variations at this time. The winner cards were redeemable until January 31, 1994.

	MINT	NRMT	EXC
COMPLETE SET (44)	12.00	5.50	1.50
COMPLETE SERIES 1 (22)	5.00	2.20	.60
COMPLETE SERIES 2 (22)	7.00	3.10	.85
COMMON CARD (1-44)	.10	.05	.01
SEMISTARS	.25	.11	.03
STARS	.50	.23	.06
RANDOM INSERTS IN PACKS			
THREE PER FACTORY SET			

□ 1 Barry Bonds	.75	.35	.09
□ 2 Will Clark	.50	.23	.06
□ 3 Darren Daulton	.25	.11	.03
□ 4 Andre Dawson	.50	.23	.06
□ 5 Delino DeShields	.25	.11	.03
□ 6 Tom Glavine	.50	.23	.06
□ 7 Marquis Grissom	.50	.23	.06
□ 8 Tony Gwynn	1.25	.55	.16
□ 9 Eric Karros	.25	.11	.03
□ 10 Ray Lankford	.25	.11	.03
□ 11 Barry Larkin	.50	.23	.06
□ 12 Greg Maddux	2.00	.90	.25
□ 13 Fred McGriff	.50	.23	.06
□ 14 Joe Oliver	.10	.05	.01
□ 15 Terry Pendleton	.25	.11	.03
□ 16 Bip Roberts	.25	.11	.03
□ 17 Ryne Sandberg	.75	.35	.09
□ 18 Gary Sheffield	.50	.23	.06
□ 19 Lee Smith	.50	.23	.06
□ 20 Ozzie Smith	.60	.25	.07
□ 21 Andy Van Slyke	.10	.05	.01
□ 22 Larry Walker	.50	.23	.06
□ 23 Roberto Alomar	.75	.35	.09
□ 24 Brady Anderson	.50	.23	.06
□ 25 Carlos Baerga	.50	.23	.06
□ 26 Joe Carter	.50	.23	.06
□ 27 Roger Clemens	.50	.23	.06
□ 28 Mike Devereaux	.10	.05	.01
□ 29 Dennis Eckersley	.50	.23	.06
□ 30 Cecil Fielder	.50	.23	.06
□ 31 Travis Fryman	.50	.23	.06
□ 32 Juan Gonzalez UER (No copyright or licensing on card)	1.50	.70	.19
□ 33 Ken Griffey Jr.	3.00	1.35	.35
□ 34 Brian Harper	.10	.05	.01
□ 35 Pat Listach	.10	.05	.01
□ 36 Kenny Lofton	1.25	.55	.16
□ 37 Edgar Martinez	.50	.23	.06
□ 38 Jack McDowell	.50	.23	.06
□ 39 Mark McGwire	1.00	.45	.12
□ 40 Kirby Puckett	1.00	.45	.12
□ 41 Mickey Tettleton	.25	.11	.03
□ 42 Frank Thomas UER (No copyright or licensing on card)	3.00	1.35	.35
□ 43 Robin Ventura	.50	.23	.06
□ 44 Dave Winfield	.50	.23	.06
□ A Winner A 1-11	.50	.23	.06
□ B Winner B 12-22	.50	.23	.06
□ C Winner C 23-33	.75	.35	.09
□ D Winner D 34-44	.75	.35	.09
□ AB Winner AB 1-22 UER (Numbers 10 and 11 have the 1 missing)	1.00	.45	.12
□ CD Winner C/D 23-44	1.50	.70	.19
□ ABCD Winner ABCD 1-44	2.50	1.10	.30

1993 Topps Traded

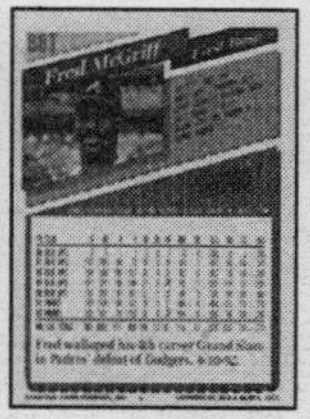

This 132-card standard-size set focuses on promising rookies, new managers, free agents, and players who changed teams. The set also includes 22 members of Team USA. The set has the same design on the front as the regular 1993 Topps issue. The backs are also the same design and carry a head shot, biography, stats, and career highlights. Rookie Cards in this set include Matt Beaumont, Todd Helton, Dante Powell, Todd Walker and Paul Wilson.

	MINT	NRMT	EXC
COMPLETE FACT.SET (132)	12.00	5.50	1.50
COMMON CARD (1T-132T)	.05	.02	.01
SEMISTARS	.15	.07	.02
STARS	.30	.14	.04

□ 1T Barry Bonds	.50	.23	.06
□ 2T Rich Renteria	.05	.02	.01
□ 3T Aaron Sele	.15	.07	.02
□ 4T Carlton Loewer USA	.15	.07	.02
□ 5T Erik Pappas	.05	.02	.01
□ 6T Greg McMichael	.15	.07	.02
□ 7T Freddie Benavides	.05	.02	.01
□ 8T Kirk Gibson	.15	.07	.02
□ 9T Tony Fernandez	.05	.02	.01
□ 10T Jay Gainer	.05	.02	.01
□ 11T Orestes Destrade	.05	.02	.01
□ 12T A.J. Hinch USA	.50	.23	.06
□ 13T Bobby Munoz	.05	.02	.01
□ 14T Tom Henke	.05	.02	.01
□ 15T Rob Butler	.05	.02	.01
□ 16T Gary Wayne	.05	.02	.01
□ 17T David McCarty	.05	.02	.01

☐ 18T	Walt Weiss	.05	.02	.01
☐ 19T	Todd Helton USA	2.50	1.10	.30
☐ 20T	Mark Whiten	.05	.02	.01
☐ 21T	Ricky Gutierrez	.05	.02	.01
☐ 22T	Dustin Hermanson USA	.40	.18	.05
☐ 23T	Sherman Obando	.05	.02	.01
☐ 24T	Mike Piazza	2.00	.90	.25
☐ 25T	Jeff Russell	.05	.02	.01
☐ 26T	Jason Bere	.15	.07	.02
☐ 27T	Jack Voigt	.05	.02	.01
☐ 28T	Chris Bosio	.05	.02	.01
☐ 29T	Phil Hiatt	.05	.02	.01
☐ 30T	Matt Beaumont USA	.40	.18	.05
☐ 31T	Andres Galarraga	.30	.14	.04
☐ 32T	Greg Swindell	.05	.02	.01
☐ 33T	Vinny Castilla	.30	.14	.04
☐ 34T	Pat Clougherty USA	.05	.02	.01
☐ 35T	Greg Briley	.05	.02	.01
☐ 36T	Dallas Green MG Davey Johnson MG	.05	.02	.01
☐ 37T	Tyler Green	.05	.02	.01
☐ 38T	Craig Paquette	.05	.02	.01
☐ 39T	Danny Sheaffer	.05	.02	.01
☐ 40T	Jim Converse	.05	.02	.01
☐ 41T	Terry Harvey USA	.05	.02	.01
☐ 42T	Phil Plantier	.05	.02	.01
☐ 43T	Doug Saunders	.05	.02	.01
☐ 44T	Benny Santiago	.05	.02	.01
☐ 45T	Dante Powell USA	1.50	.70	.19
☐ 46T	Jeff Parrett	.05	.02	.01
☐ 47T	Wade Boggs	.30	.14	.04
☐ 48T	Paul Molitor	.40	.18	.05
☐ 49T	Turk Wendell	.05	.02	.01
☐ 50T	David Wells	.05	.02	.01
☐ 51T	Gary Sheffield	.30	.14	.04
☐ 52T	Kevin Young	.05	.02	.01
☐ 53T	Nelson Liriano	.05	.02	.01
☐ 54T	Greg Maddux	1.25	.55	.16
☐ 55T	Derek Bell	.30	.14	.04
☐ 56T	Matt Turner	.05	.02	.01
☐ 57T	Charlie Nelson USA	.05	.02	.01
☐ 58T	Mike Hampton	.05	.02	.01
☐ 59T	Troy O'Leary	.30	.14	.04
☐ 60T	Benji Gil	.15	.07	.02
☐ 61T	Mitch Lyden	.05	.02	.01
☐ 62T	J.T. Snow	.30	.14	.04
☐ 63T	Damon Buford	.05	.02	.01
☐ 64T	Gene Harris	.05	.02	.01
☐ 65T	Randy Myers	.15	.07	.02
☐ 66T	Felix Jose	.05	.02	.01
☐ 67T	Todd Dunn USA	.15	.07	.02
☐ 68T	Jimmy Key	.15	.07	.02
☐ 69T	Pedro Castellano	.05	.02	.01
☐ 70T	Mark Merila USA	.15	.07	.02
☐ 71T	Rich Rodriguez	.05	.02	.01
☐ 72T	Matt Mieske	.15	.07	.02
☐ 73T	Pete Incaviglia	.05	.02	.01
☐ 74T	Carl Everett	.15	.07	.02
☐ 75T	Jim Abbott	.05	.02	.01
☐ 76T	Luis Aquino	.05	.02	.01
☐ 77T	Rene Arocha	.05	.02	.01
☐ 78T	Jon Shave	.05	.02	.01
☐ 79T	Todd Walker USA	2.50	1.10	.30
☐ 80T	Jack Armstrong	.05	.02	.01
☐ 81T	Jeff Richardson	.05	.02	.01
☐ 82T	Blas Minor	.05	.02	.01
☐ 83T	Dave Winfield	.30	.14	.04
☐ 84T	Paul O'Neill	.15	.07	.02
☐ 85T	Steve Reich USA	.05	.02	.01
☐ 86T	Chris Hammond	.05	.02	.01
☐ 87T	Hilly Hathaway	.05	.02	.01
☐ 88T	Fred McGriff	.30	.14	.04
☐ 89T	Dave Telgheder	.05	.02	.01
☐ 90T	Richie Lewis	.05	.02	.01
☐ 91T	Brent Gates	.15	.07	.02
☐ 92T	Andre Dawson	.30	.14	.04
☐ 93T	Andy Barkett USA	.15	.07	.02
☐ 94T	Doug Drabek	.05	.02	.01
☐ 95T	Joe Klink	.05	.02	.01
☐ 96T	Willie Blair	.05	.02	.01
☐ 97T	Danny Graves USA	.30	.14	.04
☐ 98T	Pat Meares	.15	.07	.02
☐ 99T	Mike Lansing	.15	.07	.02
☐ 100T	Marcos Armas	.05	.02	.01
☐ 101T	Darren Grass USA	.05	.02	.01
☐ 102T	Chris Jones	.05	.02	.01
☐ 103T	Ken Ryan	.05	.02	.01
☐ 104T	Ellis Burks	.30	.14	.04
☐ 105T	Roberto Kelly	.05	.02	.01
☐ 106T	Dave Magadan	.05	.02	.01
☐ 107T	Paul Wilson USA	1.25	.55	.16
☐ 108T	Rob Natal	.05	.02	.01
☐ 109T	Paul Wagner	.05	.02	.01
☐ 110T	Jeromy Burnitz	.05	.02	.01
☐ 111T	Monty Fariss	.05	.02	.01
☐ 112T	Kevin Mitchell	.15	.07	.02
☐ 113T	Scott Pose	.05	.02	.01
☐ 114T	Dave Stewart	.15	.07	.02
☐ 115T	Russ Johnson USA	.75	.35	.09
☐ 116T	Armando Reynoso	.05	.02	.01
☐ 117T	Geronimo Berroa	.15	.07	.02
☐ 118T	Woody Williams	.05	.02	.01
☐ 119T	Tim Bogar	.05	.02	.01
☐ 120T	Bob Scafa USA	.05	.02	.01
☐ 121T	Henry Cotto	.05	.02	.01
☐ 122T	Gregg Jefferies	.30	.14	.04
☐ 123T	Norm Charlton	.05	.02	.01
☐ 124T	Bret Wagner USA	.40	.18	.05
☐ 125T	David Cone	.30	.14	.04
☐ 126T	Daryl Boston	.05	.02	.01
☐ 127T	Tim Wallach	.05	.02	.01
☐ 128T	Mike Martin USA	.15	.07	.02
☐ 129T	John Cummings	.05	.02	.01
☐ 130T	Ryan Bowen	.05	.02	.01
☐ 131T	John Powell USA	.15	.07	.02
☐ 132T	Checklist 1-132	.05	.02	.01

1994 Topps

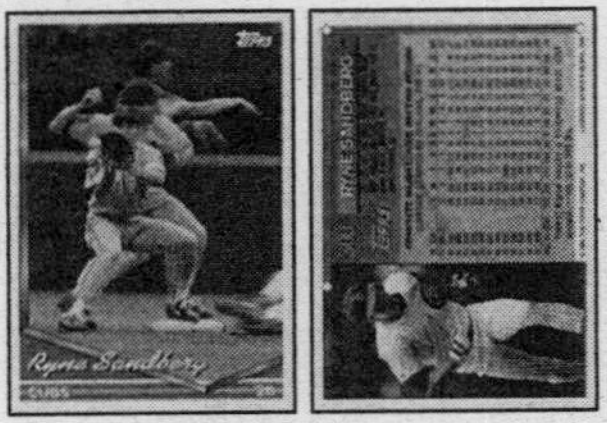

These 792 standard-size cards were issued in two series of 396. Two types of factory sets were also issued. One features the 792 basic cards, ten Topps Gold, three Black Gold and three Finest Pre-Production cards for a total of 808. The other factory set (Bakers Dozen) includes the 792 basic cards, ten Topps Gold, three Black Gold, ten 1995 Topps Pre-Production cards and a sample pack of three special Topps cards for a total of 818. In each case, one of the Pre-Production cards is a Spectralite version of one of the nine players included among the sample. The sample pack consists of three different Topps brand cards (Bowman, Finest, Stadium Club) of the same player. Including those featured in the special packs are Mo Vaughn, Larry Walker, Cliff Floyd, Rafael Palmeiro, David Justice and Ken Griffey Jr. The standard cards feature glossy color player photos with white borders on the fronts. The player's name is in white cursive lettering at the bottom left, with the team name and player's position printed on a team color-coded bar. There is an inner multicolored border along the left side that extends obliquely across the bottom. The horizontal backs carry an action shot of the player with biography, statistics and highlights. Subsets include Draft Picks (201-210/739-762), All-Stars (384-394) and Stat Twins (601-609). Rookie Cards include Alan Benes, Jeff D'Amico, Brooks Kieschnick, Kirk Presley and Pat Watkins.

	MINT	NRMT	EXC
COMPLETE SET (792)	30.00	13.50	3.70
COMPLETE FACT.SET (808)	50.00	22.00	6.25

COMP.BAKERS DOZEN (818)	50.00	22.00	6.25
COMPLETE SERIES 1 (396)	15.00	6.75	1.85
COMPLETE SERIES 2 (396)	15.00	6.75	1.85
COMMON CARD (1-792)	.05	.02	.01
SEMISTARS	.15	.07	.02
STARS	.30	.14	.04
COMPLETE GOLD SET (792)	80.00	36.00	10.00
COMP.GOLD SERIES 1 (396)	40.00	18.00	5.00
COMP.GOLD SERIES 2 (396)	40.00	18.00	5.00
COMMON GOLD (1-792)	.10	.05	.01
GOLD SEMISTARS	.25	.11	.03
*GOLD VETERAN STARS: 2X X BASIC CARDS			
*GOLD YOUNG STARS: 1.5X to 3X HI			
ONE GOLD PER PACK			
TEN GOLD PER FACTORY SET			

□ 1 Mike Piazza	1.25	.55	.16
□ 2 Bernie Williams	.30	.14	.04
□ 3 Kevin Rogers	.05	.02	.01
□ 4 Paul Carey	.05	.02	.01
□ 5 Ozzie Guillen	.05	.02	.01
□ 6 Derrick May	.05	.02	.01
□ 7 Jose Mesa	.15	.07	.02
□ 8 Todd Hundley	.30	.14	.04
□ 9 Chris Haney	.05	.02	.01
□ 10 John Olerud	.05	.02	.01
□ 11 Andujar Cedeno	.05	.02	.01
□ 12 John Smiley	.05	.02	.01
□ 13 Phil Plantier	.05	.02	.01
□ 14 Willie Banks	.05	.02	.01
□ 15 Jay Bell	.15	.07	.02
□ 16 Doug Henry	.05	.02	.01
□ 17 Lance Blankenship	.05	.02	.01
□ 18 Greg W. Harris	.05	.02	.01
□ 19 Scott Livingstone	.05	.02	.01
□ 20 Bryan Harvey	.05	.02	.01
□ 21 Wil Cordero	.15	.07	.02
□ 22 Roger Pavlik	.05	.02	.01
□ 23 Mark Lemke	.05	.02	.01
□ 24 Jeff Nelson	.05	.02	.01
□ 25 Todd Zeile	.05	.02	.01
□ 26 Billy Hatcher	.05	.02	.01
□ 27 Joe Magrane	.05	.02	.01
□ 28 Tony Longmire	.05	.02	.01
□ 29 Omar Daal	.05	.02	.01
□ 30 Kirt Manwaring	.05	.02	.01
□ 31 Melido Perez	.05	.02	.01
□ 32 Tim Hulett	.05	.02	.01
□ 33 Jeff Schwartz	.05	.02	.01
□ 34 Nolan Ryan	1.50	.70	.19
□ 35 Jose Guzman	.05	.02	.01
□ 36 Felix Fermin	.05	.02	.01
□ 37 Jeff Innis	.05	.02	.01
□ 38 Brett Mayne	.05	.02	.01
□ 39 Huck Flener	.05	.02	.01
□ 40 Jeff Bagwell	.75	.35	.09
□ 41 Kevin Wickander	.05	.02	.01
□ 42 Ricky Gutierrez	.05	.02	.01
□ 43 Pat Mahomes	.05	.02	.01
□ 44 Jeff King	.15	.07	.02
□ 45 Cal Eldred	.05	.02	.01
□ 46 Craig Paquette	.05	.02	.01
□ 47 Richie Lewis	.05	.02	.01
□ 48 Tony Phillips	.15	.07	.02
□ 49 Armando Reynoso	.05	.02	.01
□ 50 Moises Alou	.15	.07	.02
□ 51 Manuel Lee	.05	.02	.01
□ 52 Otis Nixon	.05	.02	.01
□ 53 Billy Ashley	.05	.02	.01
□ 54 Mark Whiten	.05	.02	.01
□ 55 Jeff Russell	.05	.02	.01
□ 56 Chad Curtis	.05	.02	.01
□ 57 Kevin Stocker	.05	.02	.01
□ 58 Mike Jackson	.05	.02	.01
□ 59 Matt Nokes	.05	.02	.01
□ 60 Chris Bosio	.05	.02	.01
□ 61 Damon Buford	.05	.02	.01
□ 62 Tim Belcher	.05	.02	.01
□ 63 Glenallen Hill	.05	.02	.01
□ 64 Bill Wertz	.05	.02	.01
□ 65 Eddie Murray	.50	.23	.06
□ 66 Tom Gordon	.05	.02	.01
□ 67 Alex Gonzalez	.15	.07	.02
□ 68 Eddie Taubensee	.05	.02	.01
□ 69 Jacob Brumfield	.05	.02	.01
□ 70 Andy Benes	.15	.07	.02
□ 71 Rich Becker	.15	.07	.02
□ 72 Steve Cooke	.05	.02	.01
□ 73 Billy Spiers	.05	.02	.01
□ 74 Scott Brosius	.05	.02	.01
□ 75 Alan Trammell	.30	.14	.04
□ 76 Luis Aquino	.05	.02	.01
□ 77 Jerald Clark	.05	.02	.01
□ 78 Mel Rojas	.05	.02	.01
□ 79 Outfield Prospects	.30	.14	.04
Billy Masse			
Stanton Cameron			
Tim Clark			
Craig McClure			
□ 80 Jose Canseco	.30	.14	.04
□ 81 Greg McMichael	.05	.02	.01
□ 82 Brian Turang	.05	.02	.01
□ 83 Tom Urbani	.05	.02	.01
□ 84 Garret Anderson	.30	.14	.04
□ 85 Tony Pena	.05	.02	.01
□ 86 Ricky Jordan	.05	.02	.01
□ 87 Jim Gott	.05	.02	.01
□ 88 Pat Kelly	.05	.02	.01
□ 89 Bud Black	.05	.02	.01
□ 90 Robin Ventura	.15	.07	.02
□ 91 Rick Sutcliffe	.05	.02	.01
□ 92 Jose Bautista	.05	.02	.01
□ 93 Bob Ojeda	.05	.02	.01
□ 94 Phil Hiatt	.05	.02	.01
□ 95 Tim Pugh	.05	.02	.01
□ 96 Randy Knorr	.05	.02	.01
□ 97 Todd Jones	.05	.02	.01
□ 98 Ryan Thompson	.05	.02	.01
□ 99 Tim Mauser	.05	.02	.01
□ 100 Kirby Puckett	.60	.25	.07
□ 101 Mark Dewey	.05	.02	.01
□ 102 B.J. Surhoff	.05	.02	.01
□ 103 Sterling Hitchcock	.15	.07	.02
□ 104 Alex Arias	.05	.02	.01
□ 105 David Wells	.05	.02	.01
□ 106 Daryl Boston	.05	.02	.01
□ 107 Mike Stanton	.05	.02	.01
□ 108 Gary Redus	.05	.02	.01
□ 109 Delino DeShields	.05	.02	.01
□ 110 Lee Smith	.15	.07	.02
□ 111 Greg Litton	.05	.02	.01
□ 112 Frankie Rodriguez	.15	.07	.02
□ 113 Russ Springer	.05	.02	.01
□ 114 Mitch Williams	.05	.02	.01
□ 115 Eric Karros	.15	.07	.02
□ 116 Jeff Brantley	.05	.02	.01
□ 117 Jack Voigt	.05	.02	.01
□ 118 Jason Bere	.15	.07	.02
□ 119 Kevin Roberson	.05	.02	.01
□ 120 Jimmy Key	.15	.07	.02
□ 121 Reggie Jefferson	.15	.07	.02
□ 122 Jeromy Burnitz	.05	.02	.01
□ 123 Billy Brewer	.05	.02	.01
□ 124 Willie Canate	.05	.02	.01
□ 125 Greg Swindell	.05	.02	.01
□ 126 Hal Morris	.05	.02	.01
□ 127 Brad Ausmus	.05	.02	.01
□ 128 George Tsamis	.05	.02	.01
□ 129 Denny Neagle	.15	.07	.02
□ 130 Pat Listach	.05	.02	.01
□ 131 Steve Karsay	.05	.02	.01
□ 132 Bret Barberie	.05	.02	.01
□ 133 Mark Leiter	.05	.02	.01
□ 134 Greg Colbrunn	.05	.02	.01
□ 135 David Nied	.05	.02	.01
□ 136 Dean Palmer	.15	.07	.02
□ 137 Steve Avery	.15	.07	.02
□ 138 Bill Haselman	.05	.02	.01
□ 139 Tripp Cromer	.05	.02	.01
□ 140 Frank Viola	.05	.02	.01
□ 141 Rene Gonzales	.05	.02	.01
□ 142 Curt Schilling	.05	.02	.01
□ 143 Tim Wallach	.05	.02	.01
□ 144 Bobby Munoz	.05	.02	.01
□ 145 Brady Anderson	.30	.14	.04
□ 146 Rod Beck	.15	.07	.02
□ 147 Mike LaValliere	.05	.02	.01
□ 148 Greg Hibbard	.05	.02	.01
□ 149 Kenny Lofton	.60	.25	.07
□ 150 Doc Gooden	.15	.07	.02
□ 151 Greg Gagne	.05	.02	.01
□ 152 Ray McDavid	.15	.07	.02

□ 153	Chris Donnels	.05	.02	.01
□ 154	Dan Wilson	.15	.07	.02
□ 155	Todd Stottlemyre	.05	.02	.01
□ 156	David McCarty	.05	.02	.01
□ 157	Paul Wagner	.05	.02	.01
□ 158	Shortstop Prospects	1.50	.70	.19
	Orlando Miller			
	Brandon Wilson			
	Derek Jeter			
	Mike Neal			
□ 159	Mike Fetters	.05	.02	.01
□ 160	Scott Lydy	.05	.02	.01
□ 161	Darrell Whitmore	.05	.02	.01
□ 162	Bob MacDonald	.05	.02	.01
□ 163	Vinny Castilla	.30	.14	.04
□ 164	Denis Boucher	.05	.02	.01
□ 165	Ivan Rodriguez	.40	.18	.05
□ 166	Ron Gant	.15	.07	.02
□ 167	Tim Davis	.05	.02	.01
□ 168	Steve Dixon	.05	.02	.01
□ 169	Scott Fletcher	.05	.02	.01
□ 170	Terry Mulholland	.05	.02	.01
□ 171	Greg Myers	.05	.02	.01
□ 172	Brett Butler	.15	.07	.02
□ 173	Bob Wickman	.05	.02	.01
□ 174	Dave Martinez	.05	.02	.01
□ 175	Fernando Valenzuela	.15	.07	.02
□ 176	Craig Grebeck	.05	.02	.01
□ 177	Shawn Boskie	.05	.02	.01
□ 178	Albie Lopez	.15	.07	.02
□ 179	Butch Huskey	.15	.07	.02
□ 180	George Brett	.75	.35	.09
□ 181	Juan Guzman	.15	.07	.02
□ 182	Eric Anthony	.05	.02	.01
□ 183	Rob Dibble	.05	.02	.01
□ 184	Craig Shipley	.05	.02	.01
□ 185	Kevin Tapani	.05	.02	.01
□ 186	Marcus Moore	.05	.02	.01
□ 187	Graeme Lloyd	.05	.02	.01
□ 188	Mike Bordick	.05	.02	.01
□ 189	Chris Hammond	.05	.02	.01
□ 190	Cecil Fielder	.15	.07	.02
□ 191	Curtis Leskanic	.15	.07	.02
□ 192	Lou Frazier	.05	.02	.01
□ 193	Steve Dreyer	.05	.02	.01
□ 194	Javier Lopez	.30	.14	.04
□ 195	Edgar Martinez	.30	.14	.04
□ 196	Allen Watson	.05	.02	.01
□ 197	John Flaherty	.05	.02	.01
□ 198	Kurt Stillwell	.05	.02	.01
□ 199	Danny Jackson	.05	.02	.01
□ 200	Cal Ripken	1.50	.70	.19
□ 201	Mike Bell FDP	.40	.18	.05
□ 202	Alan Benes FDP	.75	.35	.09
□ 203	Matt Farner FDP	.15	.07	.02
□ 204	Jeff Granger FDP	.15	.07	.02
□ 205	Brooks Kieschnick FDP	.40	.18	.05
□ 206	Jeremy Lee FDP	.25	.11	.03
□ 207	Charles Peterson FDP	.30	.14	.04
□ 208	Alan Rice FDP	.15	.07	.02
□ 209	Billy Wagner FDP	.50	.23	.06
□ 210	Kelly Wunsch FDP	.15	.07	.02
□ 211	Tom Candiotti	.05	.02	.01
□ 212	Domingo Jean	.05	.02	.01
□ 213	John Burkett	.05	.02	.01
□ 214	George Bell	.05	.02	.01
□ 215	Dan Plesac	.05	.02	.01
□ 216	Manny Ramirez	.60	.25	.07
□ 217	Mike Maddux	.05	.02	.01
□ 218	Kevin McReynolds	.05	.02	.01
□ 219	Pat Borders	.05	.02	.01
□ 220	Doug Drabek	.05	.02	.01
□ 221	Larry Luebbers	.05	.02	.01
□ 222	Trevor Hoffman	.15	.07	.02
□ 223	Pat Meares	.05	.02	.01
□ 224	Danny Miceli	.05	.02	.01
□ 225	Greg Vaughn	.30	.14	.04
□ 226	Scott Hemond	.05	.02	.01
□ 227	Pat Rapp	.05	.02	.01
□ 228	Kirk Gibson	.15	.07	.02
□ 229	Lance Painter	.05	.02	.01
□ 230	Larry Walker	.30	.14	.04
□ 231	Benji Gil	.05	.02	.01
□ 232	Mark Wohlers	.15	.07	.02
□ 233	Rich Amaral	.05	.02	.01
□ 234	Eric Pappas	.05	.02	.01
□ 235	Scott Cooper	.05	.02	.01
□ 236	Mike Butcher	.05	.02	.01
□ 237	Outfield Prospects	.30	.14	.04
	Curtis Pride			
	Shawn Green			
	Mark Sweeney			
	Eddie Davis			
□ 238	Kim Batiste	.05	.02	.01
□ 239	Paul Assenmacher	.05	.02	.01
□ 240	Will Clark	.30	.14	.04
□ 241	Jose Offerman	.05	.02	.01
□ 242	Todd Frohwirth	.05	.02	.01
□ 243	Tim Raines	.30	.14	.04
□ 244	Rick Wilkins	.05	.02	.01
□ 245	Bret Saberhagen	.15	.07	.02
□ 246	Thomas Howard	.05	.02	.01
□ 247	Stan Belinda	.05	.02	.01
□ 248	Rickey Henderson	.30	.14	.04
□ 249	Brian Williams	.05	.02	.01
□ 250	Barry Larkin	.30	.14	.04
□ 251	Jose Valentin	.15	.07	.02
□ 252	Lenny Webster	.05	.02	.01
□ 253	Blas Minor	.05	.02	.01
□ 254	Tim Teufel	.05	.02	.01
□ 255	Bobby Witt	.05	.02	.01
□ 256	Walt Weiss	.05	.02	.01
□ 257	Chad Kreuter	.05	.02	.01
□ 258	Roberto Mejia	.05	.02	.01
□ 259	Cliff Floyd	.30	.14	.04
□ 260	Julio Franco	.15	.07	.02
□ 261	Rafael Belliard	.05	.02	.01
□ 262	Marc Newfield	.15	.07	.02
□ 263	Gerald Perry	.05	.02	.01
□ 264	Ken Ryan	.05	.02	.01
□ 265	Chili Davis	.15	.07	.02
□ 266	Dave West	.05	.02	.01
□ 267	Royce Clayton	.15	.07	.02
□ 268	Pedro Martinez	.30	.14	.04
□ 269	Mark Hutton	.05	.02	.01
□ 270	Frank Thomas	2.00	.90	.25
□ 271	Brad Pennington	.05	.02	.01
□ 272	Mike Harkey	.05	.02	.01
□ 273	Sandy Alomar	.15	.07	.02
□ 274	Dave Gallagher	.05	.02	.01
□ 275	Wally Joyner	.15	.07	.02
□ 276	Ricky Trlicek	.05	.02	.01
□ 277	Al Osuna	.05	.02	.01
□ 278	Calvin Reese	.15	.07	.02
□ 279	Kevin Higgins	.05	.02	.01
□ 280	Rick Aguilera	.05	.02	.01
□ 281	Orlando Merced	.15	.07	.02
□ 282	Mike Mohler	.05	.02	.01
□ 283	John Jaha	.15	.07	.02
□ 284	Robb Nen	.15	.07	.02
□ 285	Travis Fryman	.30	.14	.04
□ 286	Mark Thompson	.15	.07	.02
□ 287	Mike Lansing	.15	.07	.02
□ 288	Craig Lefferts	.05	.02	.01
□ 289	Damon Berryhill	.05	.02	.01
□ 290	Randy Johnson	.30	.14	.04
□ 291	Jeff Reed	.05	.02	.01
□ 292	Danny Darwin	.05	.02	.01
□ 293	J.T. Snow	.15	.07	.02
□ 294	Tyler Green	.05	.02	.01
□ 295	Chris Hoiles	.05	.02	.01
□ 296	Roger McDowell	.05	.02	.01
□ 297	Spike Owen	.05	.02	.01
□ 298	Salomon Torres	.05	.02	.01
□ 299	Wilson Alvarez	.15	.07	.02
□ 300	Ryne Sandberg	.50	.23	.06
□ 301	Derek Lilliquist	.05	.02	.01
□ 302	Howard Johnson	.05	.02	.01
□ 303	Greg Cadaret	.05	.02	.01
□ 304	Pat Hentgen	.30	.14	.04
□ 305	Craig Biggio	.30	.14	.04
□ 306	Scott Service	.05	.02	.01
□ 307	Melvin Nieves	.15	.07	.02
□ 308	Mike Trombley	.05	.02	.01
□ 309	Carlos Garcia	.05	.02	.01
□ 310	Robin Yount UER	.30	.14	.04
	(listed with 111 triples in 1988; should be 11)			
□ 311	Marcos Armas	.05	.02	.01
□ 312	Rich Rodriguez	.05	.02	.01
□ 313	Justin Thompson	.15	.07	.02
□ 314	Danny Sheaffer	.05	.02	.01

□ 315 Ken Hill	.05	.02	.01
□ 316 Pitching Prospects	.40	.18	.05
Chad Ogea			
Duff Brumley			
Terrell Wade			
Chris Michalak			
□ 317 Cris Carpenter	.05	.02	.01
□ 318 Jeff Blauser	.05	.02	.01
□ 319 Ted Power	.05	.02	.01
□ 320 Ozzie Smith	.40	.18	.05
□ 321 John Dopson	.05	.02	.01
□ 322 Chris Turner	.05	.02	.01
□ 323 Pete Incaviglia	.05	.02	.01
□ 324 Alan Mills	.05	.02	.01
□ 325 Jody Reed	.05	.02	.01
□ 326 Rich Monteleone	.05	.02	.01
□ 327 Mark Carreon	.05	.02	.01
□ 328 Donn Pall	.05	.02	.01
□ 329 Matt Walbeck	.05	.02	.01
□ 330 Charles Nagy	.15	.07	.02
□ 331 Jeff McKnight	.05	.02	.01
□ 332 Jose Lind	.05	.02	.01
□ 333 Mike Timlin	.05	.02	.01
□ 334 Doug Jones	.05	.02	.01
□ 335 Kevin Mitchell	.15	.07	.02
□ 336 Luis Lopez	.05	.02	.01
□ 337 Shane Mack	.05	.02	.01
□ 338 Randy Tomlin	.05	.02	.01
□ 339 Matt Mieske	.05	.02	.01
□ 340 Mark McGwire	.60	.25	.07
□ 341 Nigel Wilson	.05	.02	.01
□ 342 Danny Gladden	.05	.02	.01
□ 343 Mo Sanford	.05	.02	.01
□ 344 Sean Berry	.05	.02	.01
□ 345 Kevin Brown	.05	.02	.01
□ 346 Greg Olson	.05	.02	.01
□ 347 Dave Magadan	.05	.02	.01
□ 348 Rene Arocha	.05	.02	.01
□ 349 Carlos Quintana	.05	.02	.01
□ 350 Jim Abbott	.05	.02	.01
□ 351 Gary DiSarcina	.05	.02	.01
□ 352 Ben Rivera	.05	.02	.01
□ 353 Carlos Hernandez	.05	.02	.01
□ 354 Darren Lewis	.05	.02	.01
□ 355 Harold Reynolds	.05	.02	.01
□ 356 Scott Ruffcorn	.05	.02	.01
□ 357 Mark Gubicza	.05	.02	.01
□ 358 Paul Sorrento	.05	.02	.01
□ 359 Anthony Young	.05	.02	.01
□ 360 Mark Grace	.30	.14	.04
□ 361 Rob Butler	.05	.02	.01
□ 362 Kevin Bass	.05	.02	.01
□ 363 Eric Helfand	.05	.02	.01
□ 364 Derek Bell	.15	.07	.02
□ 365 Scott Erickson	.05	.02	.01
□ 366 Al Martin	.05	.02	.01
□ 367 Ricky Bones	.05	.02	.01
□ 368 Jeff Branson	.05	.02	.01
□ 369 Third Base Prospects	1.00	.45	.12
Luis Ortiz			
David Bell			
Jason Giambi			
George Arias			
□ 370 Benito Santiago	.05	.02	.01
(See also 379)			
□ 371 John Doherty	.05	.02	.01
□ 372 Joe Girardi	.05	.02	.01
□ 373 Tim Scott	.05	.02	.01
□ 374 Marvin Freeman	.05	.02	.01
□ 375 Deion Sanders	.30	.14	.04
□ 376 Roger Salkeld	.05	.02	.01
□ 377 Bernard Gilkey	.15	.07	.02
□ 378 Tony Fossas	.05	.02	.01
□ 379 Mark McLemore UER	.05	.02	.01
(Card number is 370)			
□ 380 Darren Daulton	.15	.07	.02
□ 381 Chuck Finley	.05	.02	.01
□ 382 Mitch Webster	.05	.02	.01
□ 383 Gerald Williams	.15	.07	.02
□ 384 Frank Thomas AS	.60	.25	.07
Fred McGriff AS			
□ 385 Roberto Alomar AS	.15	.07	.02
Robby Thompson AS			
□ 386 Wade Boggs AS	.30	.14	.04
Matt Williams AS			
□ 387 Cal Ripken AS	.50	.23	.06
Jeff Blauser AS			
□ 388 Ken Griffey Jr. AS	.50	.23	.06
Len Dykstra AS			
□ 389 Juan Gonzalez AS	.30	.14	.04
David Justice AS			
□ 390 George Belle AS	.15	.07	.02
Bobby Bonds AS			
□ 391 Mike Stanley AS	.40	.18	.05
Mike Piazza AS			
□ 392 Jack McDowell AS	.40	.18	.05
Greg Maddux AS			
□ 393 Jimmy Key AS	.15	.07	.02
Tom Glavine AS			
□ 394 Jeff Montgomery AS	.05	.02	.01
Randy Myers AS			
□ 395 Checklist 1-198	.05	.02	.01
□ 396 Checklist 199-396	.05	.02	.01
□ 397 Tim Salmon	.30	.14	.04
□ 398 Todd Benzinger	.05	.02	.01
□ 399 Frank Castillo	.05	.02	.01
□ 400 Ken Griffey Jr.	2.00	.90	.25
□ 401 John Kruk	.15	.07	.02
□ 402 Dave Telgheder	.05	.02	.01
□ 403 Gary Gaetti	.15	.07	.02
□ 404 Jim Edmonds	.40	.18	.05
□ 405 Don Slaught	.05	.02	.01
□ 406 Jose Oquendo	.05	.02	.01
□ 407 Bruce Ruffin	.05	.02	.01
□ 408 Phil Clark	.05	.02	.01
□ 409 Joe Klink	.05	.02	.01
□ 410 Lou Whitaker	.30	.14	.04
□ 411 Kevin Seitzer	.05	.02	.01
□ 412 Darrin Fletcher	.05	.02	.01
□ 413 Kenny Rogers	.05	.02	.01
□ 414 Bill Pecota	.05	.02	.01
□ 415 Dave Fleming	.05	.02	.01
□ 416 Luis Alicea	.05	.02	.01
□ 417 Paul Quantrill	.05	.02	.01
□ 418 Damion Easley	.05	.02	.01
□ 419 Wes Chamberlain	.05	.02	.01
□ 420 Harold Baines	.15	.07	.02
□ 421 Scott Radinsky	.05	.02	.01
□ 422 Rey Sanchez	.05	.02	.01
□ 423 Junior Ortiz	.05	.02	.01
□ 424 Jeff Kent	.05	.02	.01
□ 425 Brian McRae	.15	.07	.02
□ 426 Ed Sprague	.15	.07	.02
□ 427 Tom Edens	.05	.02	.01
□ 428 Willie Greene	.15	.07	.02
□ 429 Bryan Hickerson	.05	.02	.01
□ 430 Dave Winfield	.30	.14	.04
□ 431 Pedro Astacio	.05	.02	.01
□ 432 Mike Gallego	.05	.02	.01
□ 433 Dave Burba	.05	.02	.01
□ 434 Bob Walk	.05	.02	.01
□ 435 Darryl Hamilton	.05	.02	.01
□ 436 Vince Horsman	.05	.02	.01
□ 437 Bob Natal	.05	.02	.01
□ 438 Mike Henneman	.05	.02	.01
□ 439 Willie Blair	.05	.02	.01
□ 440 Denny Martinez	.15	.07	.02
□ 441 Dan Peltier	.05	.02	.01
□ 442 Tony Tarasco	.05	.02	.01
□ 443 John Cummings	.05	.02	.01
□ 444 Geronimo Pena	.05	.02	.01
□ 445 Aaron Sele	.15	.07	.02
□ 446 Stan Javier	.05	.02	.01
□ 447 Mike Williams	.05	.02	.01
□ 448 First Basmen	.30	.14	.04
Prospects			
Greg Pirkl			
Roberto Petagine			
D.J.Boston			
Shawn Wooten			
□ 449 Jim Poole	.05	.02	.01
□ 450 Carlos Baerga	.30	.14	.04
□ 451 Bob Scanlan	.05	.02	.01
□ 452 Lance Johnson	.15	.07	.02
□ 453 Eric Hillman	.05	.02	.01
□ 454 Keith Miller	.05	.02	.01
□ 455 Dave Stewart	.15	.07	.02
□ 456 Pete Harnisch	.05	.02	.01
□ 457 Roberto Kelly	.05	.02	.01
□ 458 Tim Worrell	.05	.02	.01
□ 459 Pedro Munoz	.05	.02	.01
□ 460 Orel Hershiser	.15	.07	.02

☐	461	Randy Velarde	.05	.02	.01
☐	462	Trevor Wilson	.05	.02	.01
☐	463	Jerry Goff	.05	.02	.01
☐	464	Bill Wegman	.05	.02	.01
☐	465	Dennis Eckersley	.15	.07	.02
☐	466	Jeff Conine	.30	.14	.04
☐	467	Joe Boever	.05	.02	.01
☐	468	Dante Bichette	.30	.14	.04
☐	469	Jeff Shaw	.05	.02	.01
☐	470	Rafael Palmeiro	.30	.14	.04
☐	471	Phil Leftwich	.05	.02	.01
☐	472	Jay Buhner	.30	.14	.04
☐	473	Bob Tewksbury	.05	.02	.01
☐	474	Tim Naehring	.05	.02	.01
☐	475	Tom Glavine	.30	.14	.04
☐	476	Dave Hollins	.05	.02	.01
☐	477	Arthur Rhodes	.05	.02	.01
☐	478	Joey Cora	.05	.02	.01
☐	479	Mike Morgan	.05	.02	.01
☐	480	Albert Belle	1.00	.45	.12
☐	481	John Franco	.05	.02	.01
☐	482	Hipolito Pichardo	.05	.02	.01
☐	483	Duane Ward	.05	.02	.01
☐	484	Luis Gonzalez	.05	.02	.01
☐	485	Joe Oliver	.05	.02	.01
☐	486	Wally Whitehurst	.05	.02	.01
☐	487	Mike Benjamin	.05	.02	.01
☐	488	Eric Davis	.15	.07	.02
☐	489	Scott Kamieniecki	.05	.02	.01
☐	490	Kent Hrbek	.15	.07	.02
☐	491	John Hope	.05	.02	.01
☐	492	Jesse Orosco	.05	.02	.01
☐	493	Troy Neel	.05	.02	.01
☐	494	Ryan Bowen	.05	.02	.01
☐	495	Mickey Tettleton	.05	.02	.01
☐	496	Chris Jones	.05	.02	.01
☐	497	John Wetteland	.15	.07	.02
☐	498	David Hulse	.05	.02	.01
☐	499	Greg Maddux	1.25	.55	.16
☐	500	Bo Jackson	.30	.14	.04
☐	501	Donovan Osborne	.05	.02	.01
☐	502	Mike Greenwell	.05	.02	.01
☐	503	Steve Frey	.05	.02	.01
☐	504	Jim Eisenreich	.05	.02	.01
☐	505	Robby Thompson	.05	.02	.01
☐	506	Leo Gomez	.05	.02	.01
☐	507	Dave Staton	.05	.02	.01
☐	508	Wayne Kirby	.05	.02	.01
☐	509	Tim Bogar	.05	.02	.01
☐	510	David Cone	.30	.14	.04
☐	511	Devon White	.05	.02	.01
☐	512	Xavier Hernandez	.05	.02	.01
☐	513	Tim Costo	.05	.02	.01
☐	514	Gene Harris	.05	.02	.01
☐	515	Jack McDowell	.15	.07	.02
☐	516	Kevin Gross	.05	.02	.01
☐	517	Scott Leius	.05	.02	.01
☐	518	Lloyd McClendon	.05	.02	.01
☐	519	Alex Diaz	.05	.02	.01
☐	520	Wade Boggs	.30	.14	.04
☐	521	Bob Welch	.05	.02	.01
☐	522	Henry Cotto	.05	.02	.01
☐	523	Mike Moore	.05	.02	.01
☐	524	Tim Laker	.05	.02	.01
☐	525	Andres Galarraga	.30	.14	.04
☐	526	Jamie Moyer	.05	.02	.01
☐	527	Second Baseman Prospects Norberto Martin Ruben Santana Jason Hardtke Chris Sexton	.15	.07	.02
☐	528	Sid Bream	.05	.02	.01
☐	529	Erik Hanson	.05	.02	.01
☐	530	Ray Lankford	.30	.14	.04
☐	531	Rob Deer	.05	.02	.01
☐	532	Rod Correia	.05	.02	.01
☐	533	Roger Mason	.05	.02	.01
☐	534	Mike Devereaux	.05	.02	.01
☐	535	Jeff Montgomery	.15	.07	.02
☐	536	Dwight Smith	.05	.02	.01
☐	537	Jeremy Hernandez	.05	.02	.01
☐	538	Ellis Burks	.15	.07	.02
☐	539	Bobby Jones	.15	.07	.02
☐	540	Paul Molitor	.40	.18	.05
☐	541	Jeff Juden	.05	.02	.01
☐	542	Chris Sabo	.05	.02	.01
☐	543	Larry Casian	.05	.02	.01
☐	544	Jeff Gardner	.05	.02	.01
☐	545	Ramon Martinez	.15	.07	.02
☐	546	Paul O'Neill	.15	.07	.02
☐	547	Steve Hosey	.05	.02	.01
☐	548	Dave Nilsson	.15	.07	.02
☐	549	Ron Darling	.05	.02	.01
☐	550	Matt Williams	.30	.14	.04
☐	551	Jack Armstrong	.05	.02	.01
☐	552	Bill Krueger	.05	.02	.01
☐	553	Freddie Benavides	.05	.02	.01
☐	554	Jeff Fassero	.05	.02	.01
☐	555	Chuck Knoblauch	.30	.14	.04
☐	556	Guillermo Velasquez	.05	.02	.01
☐	557	Joel Johnston	.05	.02	.01
☐	558	Tom Lampkin	.05	.02	.01
☐	559	Todd Van Poppel	.05	.02	.01
☐	560	Gary Sheffield	.30	.14	.04
☐	561	Skeeter Barnes	.05	.02	.01
☐	562	Darren Holmes	.05	.02	.01
☐	563	John Vander Wal	.05	.02	.01
☐	564	Mike Ignasiak	.05	.02	.01
☐	565	Fred McGriff	.30	.14	.04
☐	566	Luis Polonia	.05	.02	.01
☐	567	Mike Perez	.05	.02	.01
☐	568	John Valentin	.15	.07	.02
☐	569	Mike Felder	.05	.02	.01
☐	570	Tommy Greene	.05	.02	.01
☐	571	David Segui	.05	.02	.01
☐	572	Roberto Hernandez	.15	.07	.02
☐	573	Steve Wilson	.05	.02	.01
☐	574	Willie McGee	.05	.02	.01
☐	575	Randy Myers	.05	.02	.01
☐	576	Darrin Jackson	.05	.02	.01
☐	577	Eric Plunk	.05	.02	.01
☐	578	Mike Macfarlane	.05	.02	.01
☐	579	Doug Brocail	.05	.02	.01
☐	580	Steve Finley	.30	.14	.04
☐	581	John Roper	.05	.02	.01
☐	582	Danny Cox	.05	.02	.01
☐	583	Chip Hale	.05	.02	.01
☐	584	Scott Bullett	.05	.02	.01
☐	585	Kevin Reimer	.05	.02	.01
☐	586	Brent Gates	.05	.02	.01
☐	587	Matt Turner	.05	.02	.01
☐	588	Rich Rowland	.05	.02	.01
☐	589	Kent Bottenfield	.05	.02	.01
☐	590	Marquis Grissom	.30	.14	.04
☐	591	Doug Strange	.05	.02	.01
☐	592	Jay Howell	.05	.02	.01
☐	593	Omar Vizquel	.30	.14	.04
☐	594	Rheal Cormier	.05	.02	.01
☐	595	Andre Dawson	.30	.14	.04
☐	596	Hilly Hathaway	.05	.02	.01
☐	597	Todd Pratt	.05	.02	.01
☐	598	Mike Mussina	.40	.18	.05
☐	599	Alex Fernandez	.30	.14	.04
☐	600	Don Mattingly	1.00	.45	.12
☐	601	Frank Thomas ST	1.00	.45	.12
☐	602	Ryne Sandberg ST	.30	.14	.04
☐	603	Wade Boggs ST	.15	.07	.02
☐	604	Cal Ripken ST	.75	.35	.09
☐	605	Barry Bonds ST	.30	.14	.04
☐	606	Ken Griffey Jr. ST	1.00	.45	.12
☐	607	Kirby Puckett ST	.30	.14	.04
☐	608	Darren Daulton ST	.15	.07	.02
☐	609	Paul Molitor ST	.30	.14	.04
☐	610	Terry Steinbach	.15	.07	.02
☐	611	Todd Worrell	.05	.02	.01
☐	612	Jim Thome	.50	.23	.06
☐	613	Chuck McElroy	.05	.02	.01
☐	614	John Habyan	.05	.02	.01
☐	615	Sid Fernandez	.05	.02	.01
☐	616	Outfield Prospects Eddie Zambrano Glenn Murray Chad Mottola Jermaine Allensworth	.15	.07	.02
☐	617	Steve Bedrosian	.05	.02	.01
☐	618	Rob Ducey	.05	.02	.01
☐	619	Tom Browning	.05	.02	.01
☐	620	Tony Gwynn	.75	.35	.09
☐	621	Carl Willis	.05	.02	.01
☐	622	Kevin Young	.05	.02	.01

□ 623	Rafael Novoa	.05	.02	.01
□ 624	Jerry Browne	.05	.02	.01
□ 625	Charlie Hough	.05	.02	.01
□ 626	Chris Gomez	.05	.02	.01
□ 627	Steve Reed	.05	.02	.01
□ 628	Kirk Rueter	.05	.02	.01
□ 629	Matt Whiteside	.05	.02	.01
□ 630	David Justice	.30	.14	.04
□ 631	Brad Holman	.05	.02	.01
□ 632	Brian Jordan	.30	.14	.04
□ 633	Scott Bankhead	.05	.02	.01
□ 634	Torey Lovullo	.05	.02	.01
□ 635	Len Dykstra	.15	.07	.02
□ 636	Ben McDonald	.05	.02	.01
□ 637	Steve Howe	.05	.02	.01
□ 638	Jose Vizcaino	.05	.02	.01
□ 639	Bill Swift	.05	.02	.01
□ 640	Darryl Strawberry	.15	.07	.02
□ 641	Steve Farr	.05	.02	.01
□ 642	Tom Kramer	.05	.02	.01
□ 643	Joe Orsulak	.05	.02	.01
□ 644	Tom Henke	.05	.02	.01
□ 645	Joe Carter	.30	.14	.04
□ 646	Ken Caminiti	.30	.14	.04
□ 647	Reggie Sanders	.30	.14	.04
□ 648	Andy Ashby	.15	.07	.02
□ 649	Derek Parks	.05	.02	.01
□ 650	Andy Van Slyke	.15	.07	.02
□ 651	Juan Bell	.05	.02	.01
□ 652	Roger Smithberg	.05	.02	.01
□ 653	Chuck Carr	.05	.02	.01
□ 654	Bill Gullickson	.05	.02	.01
□ 655	Charlie Hayes	.05	.02	.01
□ 656	Chris Nabholz	.05	.02	.01
□ 657	Karl Rhodes	.05	.02	.01
□ 658	Pete Smith	.05	.02	.01
□ 659	Bret Boone	.15	.07	.02
□ 660	Gregg Jefferies	.30	.14	.04
□ 661	Bob Zupcic	.05	.02	.01
□ 662	Steve Sax	.05	.02	.01
□ 663	Mariano Duncan	.05	.02	.01
□ 664	Jeff Tackett	.05	.02	.01
□ 665	Mark Langston	.15	.07	.02
□ 666	Steve Buechele	.05	.02	.01
□ 667	Candy Maldonado	.05	.02	.01
□ 668	Woody Williams	.05	.02	.01
□ 669	Tim Wakefield	.05	.02	.01
□ 670	Danny Tartabull	.05	.02	.01
□ 671	Charlie O'Brien	.05	.02	.01
□ 672	Felix Jose	.05	.02	.01
□ 673	Bobby Ayala	.05	.02	.01
□ 674	Scott Servais	.05	.02	.01
□ 675	Roberto Alomar	.50	.23	.06
□ 676	Pedro Martinez	.30	.14	.04
□ 677	Eddie Guardado	.05	.02	.01
□ 678	Mark Lewis	.05	.02	.01
□ 679	Jaime Navarro	.05	.02	.01
□ 680	Ruben Sierrra	.15	.07	.02
□ 681	Rick Renteria	.05	.02	.01
□ 682	Storm Davis	.05	.02	.01
□ 683	Cory Snyder	.05	.02	.01
□ 684	Ron Karkovice	.05	.02	.01
□ 685	Juan Gonzalez	1.00	.45	.12
□ 686	Catchers	.40	.18	.05
	Prospects			
	Chris Howard			
	Carlos Delgado			
	Jason Kendall			
	Paul Bako			
□ 687	John Smoltz	.30	.14	.04
□ 688	Brian Dorsett	.05	.02	.01
□ 689	Omar Olivares	.05	.02	.01
□ 690	Mo Vaughn	.50	.23	.06
□ 691	Joe Grahe	.05	.02	.01
□ 692	Mickey Morandini	.05	.02	.01
□ 693	Tino Martinez	.15	.07	.02
□ 694	Brian Barnes	.05	.02	.01
□ 695	Mike Stanley	.05	.02	.01
□ 696	Mark Clark	.05	.02	.01
□ 697	Dave Hansen	.05	.02	.01
□ 698	Willie Wilson	.05	.02	.01
□ 699	Pete Schourek	.15	.07	.02
□ 700	Barry Bonds	.50	.23	.06
□ 701	Kevin Appier	.15	.07	.02
□ 702	Tony Fernandez	.05	.02	.01
□ 703	Darryl Kile	.05	.02	.01
□ 704	Archi Cianfrocco	.05	.02	.01
□ 705	Jose Rijo	.05	.02	.01
□ 706	Brian Harper	.05	.02	.01
□ 707	Zane Smith	.05	.02	.01
□ 708	Dave Henderson	.05	.02	.01
□ 709	Angel Miranda UER	.05	.02	.01
	(no Topps logo on back)			
□ 710	Orestes Destrade	.05	.02	.01
□ 711	Greg Gohr	.05	.02	.01
□ 712	Eric Young	.15	.07	.02
□ 713	Relief Pitchers	.15	.07	.02
	Prospects			
	Todd Williams			
	Ron Watson			
	Kirk Bullinger			
	Mike Welch			
□ 714	Tim Spehr	.05	.02	.01
□ 715	Hank Aaron	.50	.23	.06
□ 716	Nate Minchey	.05	.02	.01
□ 717	Mike Blowers	.05	.02	.01
□ 718	Kent Mercker	.05	.02	.01
□ 719	Tom Pagnozzi	.05	.02	.01
□ 720	Roger Clemens	.30	.14	.04
□ 721	Eduardo Perez	.05	.02	.01
□ 722	Milt Thompson	.05	.02	.01
□ 723	Gregg Olson	.05	.02	.01
□ 724	Kirk McCaskill	.05	.02	.01
□ 725	Sammy Sosa	.30	.14	.04
□ 726	Alvaro Espinoza	.05	.02	.01
□ 727	Henry Rodriguez	.30	.14	.04
□ 728	Jim Leyritz	.05	.02	.01
□ 729	Steve Scarsone	.05	.02	.01
□ 730	Bobby Bonilla	.15	.07	.02
□ 731	Chris Gwynn	.05	.02	.01
□ 732	Al Leiter	.15	.07	.02
□ 733	Bip Roberts	.05	.02	.01
□ 734	Mark Portugal	.05	.02	.01
□ 735	Terry Pendleton	.15	.07	.02
□ 736	Dave Valle	.05	.02	.01
□ 737	Paul Kilgus	.05	.02	.01
□ 738	Greg A. Harris	.05	.02	.01
□ 739	Jon Ratliff DP	.15	.07	.02
□ 740	Kirk Presley DP	.30	.14	.04
□ 741	Josue Estrada DP	.15	.07	.02
□ 742	Wayne Gomes DP	.15	.07	.02
□ 743	Pat Watkins DP	.30	.14	.04
□ 744	Jamey Wright DP	.50	.23	.06
□ 745	Jay Powell DP	.15	.07	.02
□ 746	Ryan McGuire DP	.15	.07	.02
□ 747	Marc Barcelo DP	.15	.07	.02
□ 748	Sloan Smith DP	.15	.07	.02
□ 749	John Wasdin DP	.25	.11	.03
□ 750	Marc Vlades DP	.15	.07	.02
□ 751	Dan Ehler DP	.15	.07	.02
□ 752	Andre King DP	.15	.07	.02
□ 753	Greg Keagle DP	.05	.02	.01
□ 754	Jason Myers DP	.15	.07	.02
□ 755	Dax Winslett DP	.15	.07	.02
□ 756	Casey Whitten DP	.15	.07	.02
□ 757	Tony Fuduric DP	.15	.07	.02
□ 758	Greg Norton DP	.15	.07	.02
□ 759	Jeff D'Amico DP	.50	.23	.06
□ 760	Ryan Hancock DP	.15	.07	.02
□ 761	David Cooper DP	.15	.07	.02
□ 762	Kevin Orie DP	.30	.14	.04
□ 763	John O'Donoghue	.05	.02	.01
	Mike Oquist			
□ 764	Cory Bailey	.05	.02	.01
	Scott Hatteberg			
□ 765	Mark Holzemer	.05	.02	.01
	Paul Swingle			
□ 766	James Baldwin	.30	.14	.04
	Rod Bolton			
□ 767	Jerry Di Poto	.15	.07	.02
	Julian Tavarez			
□ 768	Danny Bautista	.15	.07	.02
	Sean Bergman			
□ 769	Bob Hamelin	.05	.02	.01
	Joe Vitiello			
□ 770	Mark Kiefer	.15	.07	.02
	Troy O'Leary			
□ 771	Denny Hocking	.15	.07	.02
	Oscar Munoz			
□ 772	Russ Davis	.15	.07	.02
	Brien Taylor			
□ 773	Kyle Abbott	.15	.07	.02

Miguel Jimenez			
□ 774 Kevin King	.05	.02	.01
Eric Plantenberg			
□ 775 Jon Shave	.05	.02	.01
Desi Wilson			
□ 776 Domingo Cedeno	.05	.02	.01
Paul Spoljaric			
□ 777 Chipper Jones	2.50	1.10	.30
Ryan Klesko			
□ 778 Steve Trachsel	.15	.07	.02
Turk Wendell			
□ 779 Johnny Ruffin	.05	.02	.01
Jerry Spradlin			
□ 780 Jason Bates	.15	.07	.02
John Burke			
□ 781 Carl Everett	.15	.07	.02
Dave Weathers			
□ 782 Gary Mota	.15	.07	.02
James Mouton			
□ 783 Raul Mondesi	.30	.14	.04
Ben Van Ryn			
□ 784 Gabe White	.30	.14	.04
Rondell White			
□ 785 Brook Fordyce	.15	.07	.02
Bill Pulsipher			
□ 786 Kevin Foster	.15	.07	.02
Gene Schall			
□ 787 Rich Aude	.05	.02	.01
Midre Cummings			
□ 788 Brian Barber	.15	.07	.02
Rich Batchelor			
□ 789 Brian Johnson	.05	.02	.01
Scott Sanders			
□ 790 Ricky Faneyte	.05	.02	.01
J.R. Phillips			
□ 791 Checklist 3	.05	.02	.01
□ 792 Checklist 4	.05	.02	.01

1994 Topps Black Gold

Randomly inserted one in every 72 packs, this 44-card standard-size set was issued in two series of 22. Cards were also issued three per 1994 Topps factory set. Collectors had a chance, through redemption cards to receive all or part of the set. There are seven Winner redemption cards for a total 51 cards associated with this set. The set is considered complete with the 44 player cards. Card fronts feature color player action photos. The player's name at bottom and the team name at top are screened in gold foil. The backs contain a player photo and statistical rankings. The winner cards were redeemable until January 31, 1995

	MINT	NRMT	EXC
COMPLETE SET (44)	25.00	11.00	3.10
COMPLETE SERIES 1 (22)	15.00	6.75	1.85
COMPLETE SERIES 2 (22)	10.00	4.50	1.25
COMMON CARD (1-44)	.25	.11	.03
SEMISTARS	.60	.25	.07
RANDOM INSERTS IN PACKS			
THREE PER FACTORY SET			

□ 1 Roberto Alomar	1.00	.45	.12
□ 2 Carlos Baerga	.60	.25	.07
□ 3 Albert Belle	2.00	.90	.25
□ 4 Joe Carter	.60	.25	.07
□ 5 Cecil Fielder	.60	.25	.07
□ 6 Travis Fryman	.60	.25	.07
□ 7 Juan Gonzalez	2.00	.90	.25
□ 8 Ken Griffey Jr.	4.00	1.80	.50
□ 9 Chris Hoiles	.25	.11	.03
□ 10 Randy Johnson	.60	.25	.07
□ 11 Kenny Lofton	1.25	.55	.16
□ 12 Jack McDowell	.60	.25	.07
□ 13 Paul Molitor	.60	.25	.07
□ 14 Jeff Montgomery	.25	.11	.03
□ 15 John Olerud	.60	.25	.07
□ 16 Rafael Palmeiro	.60	.25	.07
□ 17 Kirby Puckett	1.25	.55	.16
□ 18 Cal Ripken	3.00	1.35	.35
□ 19 Tim Salmon	.60	.25	.07
□ 20 Mike Stanley	.25	.11	.03
□ 21 Frank Thomas	4.00	1.80	.50
□ 22 Robin Ventura	.60	.25	.07
□ 23 Jeff Bagwell	1.50	.70	.19
□ 24 Jay Bell	.25	.11	.03
□ 25 Craig Biggio	.60	.25	.07
□ 26 Jeff Blauser	.25	.11	.03
□ 27 Barry Bonds	1.00	.45	.12
□ 28 Darren Daulton	.60	.25	.07
□ 29 Len Dykstra	.60	.25	.07
□ 30 Andres Galarraga	.60	.25	.07
□ 31 Ron Gant	.60	.25	.07
□ 32 Tom Glavine	.60	.25	.07
□ 33 Mark Grace	.60	.25	.07
□ 34 Marquis Grissom	.60	.25	.07
□ 35 Gregg Jefferies	.60	.25	.07
□ 36 David Justice	.60	.25	.07
□ 37 John Kruk	.25	.11	.03
□ 38 Greg Maddux	2.50	1.10	.30
□ 39 Fred McGriff	.60	.25	.07
□ 40 Randy Myers	.25	.11	.03
□ 41 Mike Piazza	2.50	1.10	.30
□ 42 Sammy Sosa	.60	.25	.07
□ 43 Robby Thompson	.25	.11	.03
□ 44 Matt Williams	.60	.25	.07
□ A Winner A 1-11	1.00	.45	.12
□ B Winner B 12-22	1.00	.45	.12
□ C Winner C 23-33	1.00	.45	.12
□ D Winner D 34-44	1.00	.45	.12
□ AB Winner AB 1-22	2.00	.90	.25
□ CD Winner CD 23-44	2.00	.90	.25
□ ABCD Winner ABCD 1-44	4.00	1.80	.50

1994 Topps Traded

This set consists of 132 standard-size cards featuring traded players in their new uniforms, rookies and draft choices. Factory sets consisted of 140 cards including a set of eight Topps Finest cards. Card fronts feature a player photo with the player's name, team and position at the bottom. The horizontal backs have a player photo to the left with complete career statisics and highlights. The cards are numbered with a "T" suffix. Rookie Cards include Brian Anderson, Ben Grieve, Paul Konerko, Terrance Long, Doug Million, Chan Ho Park, Reid Ryan, Mac Suzuki, Terrell Wade and Kevin Witt.

	MINT	NRMT	EXC
COMPLETE FACT.SET (140)	40.00	18.00	5.00
COMPLETE SET (132)	10.00	4.50	1.25
COMMON CARD (1T-132T)	.05	.02	.01
SEMISTARS	.15	.07	.02
STARS	.30	.14	.04

	COMPLETE FINEST SET (8)	30.00	13.50	3.70
	ONE FINEST SET PER FACTORY SET			
□ 1T	Paul Wilson	.50	.23	.06
□ 2T	Bill Taylor	.05	.02	.01
□ 3T	Dan Wilson	.15	.07	.02
□ 4T	Mark Smith	.05	.02	.01
□ 5T	Toby Borland	.05	.02	.01
□ 6T	Dave Clark	.05	.02	.01
□ 7T	Denny Martinez	.15	.07	.02
□ 8T	Dave Gallagher	.05	.02	.01
□ 9T	Josias Manzanillo	.05	.02	.01
□ 10T	Brian Anderson	.15	.07	.02
□ 11T	Damon Berryhill	.05	.02	.01
□ 12T	Alex Cole	.05	.02	.01
□ 13T	Jacob Shumate	.15	.07	.02
□ 14T	Oddibe McDowell	.05	.02	.01
□ 15T	Willie Banks	.05	.02	.01
□ 16T	Jerry Browne	.05	.02	.01
□ 17T	Donnie Elliott	.05	.02	.01
□ 18T	Ellis Burks	.15	.07	.02
□ 19T	Chuck McElroy	.05	.02	.01
□ 20T	Luis Polonia	.05	.02	.01
□ 21T	Brian Harper	.05	.02	.01
□ 22T	Mark Portugal	.05	.02	.01
□ 23T	Dave Henderson	.05	.02	.01
□ 24T	Mark Acre	.05	.02	.01
□ 25T	Julio Franco	.15	.07	.02
□ 26T	Darren Hall	.05	.02	.01
□ 27T	Eric Anthony	.05	.02	.01
□ 28T	Sid Fernandez	.05	.02	.01
□ 29T	Rusty Greer	.75	.35	.09
□ 30T	Riccardo Ingram	.05	.02	.01
□ 31T	Gabe White	.05	.02	.01
□ 32T	Tim Belcher	.05	.02	.01
□ 33T	Terrence Long	.75	.35	.09
□ 34T	Mark Dalesandro	.05	.02	.01
□ 35T	Mike Kelly	.05	.02	.01
□ 36T	Jack Morris	.15	.07	.02
□ 37T	Jeff Brantley	.05	.02	.01
□ 38T	Larry Barnes	.15	.07	.02
□ 39T	Brian R. Hunter	.05	.02	.01
□ 40T	Otis Nixon	.05	.02	.01
□ 41T	Bret Wagner	.30	.14	.04
□ 42T	Pedro Martinez TR Delino Deshields	.15	.07	.02
□ 43T	Heathcliff Slocumb	.15	.07	.02
□ 44T	Ben Grieve	2.00	.90	.25
□ 45T	John Hudek	10.00	4.50	1.25
□ 46T	Shawon Dunston	.05	.02	.01
□ 47T	Greg Colbrunn	.05	.02	.01
□ 48T	Joey Hamilton	.40	.18	.05
□ 49T	Marvin Freeman	.05	.02	.01
□ 50T	Terry Mulholland	.05	.02	.01
□ 51T	Keith Mitchell	.05	.02	.01
□ 52T	Dwight Smith	.05	.02	.01
□ 53T	Shawn Boskie	.05	.02	.01
□ 54T	Kevin Witt	.50	.23	.06
□ 55T	Ron Gant	.15	.07	.02
□ 56T	1994 Prospects Trenidad Hubbard Jason Schmidt Larry Sutton Stephen Larkin	.75	.35	.09
□ 57T	Jody Reed	.05	.02	.01
□ 58T	Rick Helling	.05	.02	.01
□ 59T	John Powell	.15	.07	.02
□ 60T	Eddie Murray	.50	.23	.06
□ 61T	Joe Hall	.05	.02	.01
□ 62T	Jorge Fabregas	.05	.02	.01
□ 63T	Mike Mordecai	.05	.02	.01
□ 64T	Ed Vosberg	.05	.02	.01
□ 65T	Rickey Henderson	.30	.14	.04
□ 66T	Tim Grieve	.05	.02	.01
□ 67T	Jon Lieber	.05	.02	.01
□ 68T	Chris Howard	.05	.02	.01
□ 69T	Matt Walbeck	.05	.02	.01
□ 70T	Chan Ho Park	.50	.23	.06
□ 71T	Bryan Eversgerd	.05	.02	.01
□ 72T	John Dettmer	.05	.02	.01
□ 73T	Erik Hanson	.05	.02	.01
□ 74T	Mike Thurman	.05	.02	.01
□ 75T	Bobby Ayala	.05	.02	.01
□ 76T	Rafael Palmeiro	.30	.14	.04
□ 77T	Bret Boone	.15	.07	.02
□ 78T	Paul Shuey	10.00	4.50	1.25
□ 79T	Kevin Foster	.05	.02	.01
□ 80T	Dave Magadan	.05	.02	.01
□ 81T	Bip Roberts	.05	.02	.01
□ 82T	Howard Johnson	.05	.02	.01
□ 83T	Xavier Hernandez	.05	.02	.01
□ 84T	Ross Powell	.05	.02	.01
□ 85T	Doug Million	.75	.35	.09
□ 86T	Geronimo Berroa	.15	.07	.02
□ 87T	Mark Farris	.15	.07	.02
□ 88T	Butch Henry	.05	.02	.01
□ 89T	Junior Felix	.05	.02	.01
□ 90T	Bo Jackson	.30	.14	.04
□ 91T	Hector Carrasco	.05	.02	.01
□ 92T	Charlie O'Brien	.05	.02	.01
□ 93T	Omar Vizquel	.30	.14	.04
□ 94T	David Segui	10.00	4.50	1.25
□ 95T	Dustin Hermanson	.15	.07	.02
□ 96T	Gar Finnvold	.05	.02	.01
□ 97T	Dave Stevens	.05	.02	.01
□ 98T	Corey Pointer	.25	.11	.03
□ 99T	Felix Fermin	.05	.02	.01
□ 100T	Lee Smith	.15	.07	.02
□ 101T	Reid Ryan	.15	.07	.02
□ 102T	Bobby Munoz	.05	.02	.01
□ 103T	Deion Sanders TR Roberto Kelly	.15	.07	.02
□ 104T	Turner Ward	.05	.02	.01
□ 105T	W.VanLandingham	.15	.07	.02
□ 106T	Vince Coleman	.05	.02	.01
□ 107T	Stan Javier	.05	.02	.01
□ 108T	Darrin Jackson	.05	.02	.01
□ 109T	C.J. Nitkowski	.15	.07	.02
□ 110T	Anthony Young	.05	.02	.01
□ 111T	Kurt Miller	.05	.02	.01
□ 112T	Paul Konerko	4.00	1.80	.50
□ 113T	Walt Weiss	10.00	4.50	1.25
□ 114T	Daryl Boston	.05	.02	.01
□ 115T	Will Clark	.30	.14	.04
□ 116T	Matt Smith	.15	.07	.02
□ 117T	Mark Leiter	.05	.02	.01
□ 118T	Gregg Olson	.05	.02	.01
□ 119T	Tony Pena	.05	.02	.01
□ 120T	Jose Vizcaino	.05	.02	.01
□ 121T	Rick White	.05	.02	.01
□ 122T	Rich Rowland	.05	.02	.01
□ 123T	Jeff Reboulet	.05	.02	.01
□ 124T	Greg Hibbard	.05	.02	.01
□ 125T	Chris Sabo	.05	.02	.01
□ 126T	Doug Jones	.05	.02	.01
□ 127T	Tony Fernandez	.05	.02	.01
□ 128T	Carlos Reyes	.05	.02	.01
□ 129T	Kevin Brown	.75	.35	.09
□ 130T	Ryne Sandberg Farewell	1.25	.55	.16
□ 131T	Ryne Sandberg Farewell	1.25	.55	.16
□ 132T	Checklist 1-132	.05	.02	.01
□ F1	Greg Maddux	6.00	2.70	.75
□ F2	Mike Piazza	6.00	2.70	.75
□ F3	Matt Williams	1.25	.55	.16
□ F4	Raul Mondesi	1.50	.70	.19
□ F5	Ken Griffey Jr.	10.00	4.50	1.25
□ F6	Kenny Lofton	3.00	1.35	.35
□ F7	Frank Thomas	10.00	4.50	1.25
□ F8	Manny Ramirez	2.50	1.10	.30

1995 Topps

These 660 standard-size cards feature color action player photos with white borders on the fronts. This set was released in two series. The first series contained 396 cards while the second series had 264 cards. The player's name in gold-foil appears below the photo, with his position and team name underneath. The horizontal backs carry a color player close-up with a color player cut-out superimposed over it. Player biography, statistics and career highlights complete the backs. One "Own The Game" instant winner card has been inserted in every 120 packs. Rookie cards in this set include Jeff Abbott, Jacob Cruz, Tommy Davis, Scott Elarton, Jay Payton and Carlos Perez.

	MINT	NRMT	EXC
COMP.HOB.FACT.SET (677)	60.00	27.00	7.50
COMP.RET.FACT.SET (677)	50.00	22.00	6.25
COMPLETE SET (660)	45.00	20.00	5.50
COMPLETE SERIES 1 (396)	25.00	11.00	3.10
COMPLETE SERIES 2 (264)	20.00	9.00	2.50
COMMON CARD (1-660)	.10	.05	.01
SEMISTARS	.25	.11	.03
STARS	.50	.23	.06
COMP.CYBERSTATS SET (396)	80.00	36.00	10.00
COMP.CYBER.SER.1 (198)	40.00	18.00	5.00
COMP.CYBER.SER.2 (198)	40.00	18.00	5.00
COMMON CYBER. (1-396)	.25	.11	.03
CYBERSTATS SEMISTARS	.50	.23	.06

*CYBER.STARS: 1.25X to 2.5X BASIC CARDS
*CYBER.YOUNG STARS: 1X to 2X BASIC CARDS
ONE CYBERSTATS PER PACK

□ 1	Frank Thomas	3.00	1.35	.35
□ 2	Mickey Morandini	.10	.05	.01
□ 3	Babe Ruth	2.00	.90	.25
□ 4	Scott Cooper	.10	.05	.01
□ 5	David Cone	.25	.11	.03
□ 6	Jacob Shumate	.25	.11	.03
□ 7	Trevor Hoffman	.10	.05	.01
□ 8	Shane Mack	.10	.05	.01
□ 9	Delino DeShields	.10	.05	.01
□ 10	Matt Williams	.50	.23	.06
□ 11	Sammy Sosa	.50	.23	.06
□ 12	Gary DiSarcina	.10	.05	.01
□ 13	Kenny Rogers	.10	.05	.01
□ 14	Jose Vizcaino	.10	.05	.01
□ 15	Lou Whitaker	.50	.23	.06
□ 16	Ron Darling	.10	.05	.01
□ 17	Dave Nilsson	.25	.11	.03
□ 18	Chris Hammond	.10	.05	.01
□ 19	Sid Bream	.10	.05	.01
□ 20	Denny Martinez	.25	.11	.03
□ 21	Orlando Merced	.10	.05	.01
□ 22	John Wetteland	.25	.11	.03
□ 23	Mike Devereaux	.10	.05	.01
□ 24	Rene Arocha	.10	.05	.01
□ 25	Jay Buhner	.50	.23	.06
□ 26	Darren Holmes	.10	.05	.01
□ 27	Hal Morris	.10	.05	.01
□ 28	Brian Buchanan	.25	.11	.03
□ 29	Keith Miller	.10	.05	.01
□ 30	Paul Molitor	.60	.25	.07
□ 31	Dave West	.10	.05	.01
□ 32	Tony Tarasco	.10	.05	.01
□ 33	Scott Sanders	.10	.05	.01
□ 34	Eddie Zambrano	.10	.05	.01
□ 35	Ricky Bones	.10	.05	.01
□ 36	John Valentin	.25	.11	.03
□ 37	Kevin Tapani	.10	.05	.01
□ 38	Tim Wallach	.10	.05	.01
□ 39	Darren Lewis	.10	.05	.01
□ 40	Travis Fryman	.25	.11	.03
□ 41	Mark Leiter	.10	.05	.01
□ 42	Jose Bautista	.10	.05	.01
□ 43	Pete Smith	.10	.05	.01
□ 44	Bret Barberie	.10	.05	.01
□ 45	Dennis Eckersley	.25	.11	.03
□ 46	Ken Hill	.10	.05	.01
□ 47	Chad Ogea	.10	.05	.01
□ 48	Pete Harnisch	.10	.05	.01
□ 49	James Baldwin	.50	.23	.06
□ 50	Mike Mussina	.60	.25	.07
□ 51	Al Martin	.25	.11	.03
□ 52	Mark Thompson	.10	.05	.01
□ 53	Matt Smith	.25	.11	.03
□ 54	Joey Hamilton	.25	.11	.03
□ 55	Edgar Martinez	.50	.23	.06
□ 56	John Smiley	.10	.05	.01
□ 57	Rey Sanchez	.10	.05	.01
□ 58	Mike Timlin	.10	.05	.01
□ 59	Ricky Bottalico	.25	.11	.03
□ 60	Jim Abbott	.10	.05	.01
□ 61	Mike Kelly	.10	.05	.01
□ 62	Brian Jordan	.50	.23	.06
□ 63	Ken Ryan	.10	.05	.01
□ 64	Matt Mieske	.25	.11	.03
□ 65	Rick Aguilera	.10	.05	.01
□ 66	Ismael Valdes	.25	.11	.03
□ 67	Royce Clayton	.10	.05	.01
□ 68	Junior Felix	.10	.05	.01
□ 69	Harold Reynolds	.10	.05	.01
□ 70	Juan Gonzalez	1.50	.70	.19
□ 71	Kelly Stinnett	.10	.05	.01
□ 72	Carlos Reyes	.10	.05	.01
□ 73	Dave Weathers	.10	.05	.01
□ 74	Mel Rojas	.10	.05	.01
□ 75	Doug Drabek	.10	.05	.01
□ 76	Charles Nagy	.25	.11	.03
□ 77	Tim Raines	.50	.23	.06
□ 78	Midre Cummings	.10	.05	.01
□ 79	First Base Prospects	.50	.23	.06
	Gene Schall			
	Scott Talanoa			
	Harold Williams			
	Ray Brown			
□ 80	Rafael Palmeiro	.50	.23	.06
□ 81	Charlie Hayes	.10	.05	.01
□ 82	Ray Lankford	.50	.23	.06
□ 83	Tim Davis	.10	.05	.01
□ 84	C.J. Nitkowski	.25	.11	.03
□ 85	Andy Ashby	.25	.11	.03
□ 86	Gerald Williams	.10	.05	.01
□ 87	Terry Shumpert	.10	.05	.01
□ 88	Heathcliff Slocumb	.10	.05	.01
□ 89	Domingo Cedeno	.10	.05	.01
□ 90	Mark Grace	.50	.23	.06
□ 91	Brad Woodall	.10	.05	.01
□ 92	Gar Finnvold	.10	.05	.01
□ 93	Jaime Navarro	.10	.05	.01
□ 94	Carlos Hernandez	.10	.05	.01
□ 95	Mark Langston	.10	.05	.01
□ 96	Chuck Carr	.10	.05	.01
□ 97	Mike Gardiner	.10	.05	.01
□ 98	Dave McCarty	.10	.05	.01
□ 99	Cris Carpenter	.10	.05	.01
□ 100	Barry Bonds	.75	.35	.09
□ 101	David Segui	.10	.05	.01
□ 102	Scott Brosius	.10	.05	.01
□ 103	Mariano Duncan	.10	.05	.01
□ 104	Kenny Lofton	.75	.35	.09
□ 105	Ken Caminiti	.50	.23	.06
□ 106	Darrin Jackson	.10	.05	.01
□ 107	Jim Poole	.10	.05	.01
□ 108	Wil Cordero	.10	.05	.01
□ 109	Danny Miceli	.10	.05	.01
□ 110	Walt Weiss	.10	.05	.01
□ 111	Tom Pagnozzi	.10	.05	.01
□ 112	Terrence Long	.25	.11	.03
□ 113	Bret Boone	.25	.11	.03
□ 114	Daryl Boston	.10	.05	.01
□ 115	Wally Joyner	.25	.11	.03
□ 116	Rob Butler	.10	.05	.01
□ 117	Rafael Belliard	.10	.05	.01
□ 118	Luis Lopez	.10	.05	.01
□ 119	Tony Fossas	.10	.05	.01
□ 120	Len Dykstra	.25	.11	.03
□ 121	Mike Morgan	.10	.05	.01
□ 122	Denny Hocking	.10	.05	.01
□ 123	Kevin Gross	.10	.05	.01
□ 124	Todd Benzinger	.10	.05	.01
□ 125	John Doherty	.10	.05	.01
□ 126	Eduardo Perez	.10	.05	.01
□ 127	Dan Smith	.10	.05	.01
□ 128	Joe Orsulak	.10	.05	.01
□ 129	Brent Gates	.10	.05	.01
□ 130	Jeff Conine	.50	.23	.06
□ 131	Doug Henry	.10	.05	.01
□ 132	Paul Sorrento	.10	.05	.01
□ 133	Mike Hampton	.10	.05	.01

□ 134	Tim Spehr	.10	.05	.01
□ 135	Julio Franco	.25	.11	.03
□ 136	Mike Dyer	.10	.05	.01
□ 137	Chris Sabo	.10	.05	.01
□ 138	Rheal Cormier	.10	.05	.01
□ 139	Paul Konerko	2.50	1.10	.30
□ 140	Dante Bichette	.50	.23	.06
□ 141	Chuck McElroy	.10	.05	.01
□ 142	Mike Stanley	.10	.05	.01
□ 143	Bob Hamelin	.10	.05	.01
□ 144	Tommy Greene	.10	.05	.01
□ 145	John Smoltz	.50	.23	.06
□ 146	Ed Sprague	.25	.11	.03
□ 147	Ray McDavid	.25	.11	.03
□ 148	Otis Nixon	.10	.05	.01
□ 149	Turk Wendell	.10	.05	.01
□ 150	Chris James	.10	.05	.01
□ 151	Derek Parks	.10	.05	.01
□ 152	Jose Offerman	.10	.05	.01
□ 153	Tony Clark	.50	.23	.06
□ 154	Chad Curtis	.10	.05	.01
□ 155	Mark Portugal	.10	.05	.01
□ 156	Bill Pulsipher	.25	.11	.03
□ 157	Troy Neel	.10	.05	.01
□ 158	Dave Winfield	.50	.23	.06
□ 159	Bill Wegman	.10	.05	.01
□ 160	Benito Santiago	.10	.05	.01
□ 161	Jose Mesa	.10	.05	.01
□ 162	Luis Gonzalez	.10	.05	.01
□ 163	Alex Fernandez	.25	.11	.03
□ 164	Freddie Benavides	.10	.05	.01
□ 165	Ben McDonald	.10	.05	.01
□ 166	Blas Minor	.10	.05	.01
□ 167	Bret Wagner	.25	.11	.03
□ 168	Mac Suzuki	.25	.11	.03
□ 169	Roberto Mejia	.10	.05	.01
□ 170	Wade Boggs	.50	.23	.06
□ 171	Calvin Reese	.10	.05	.01
□ 172	Hipolito Pichardo	.10	.05	.01
□ 173	Kim Batiste	.10	.05	.01
□ 174	Darren Hall	.10	.05	.01
□ 175	Tom Glavine	.50	.23	.06
□ 176	Phil Plantier	.10	.05	.01
□ 177	Chris Howard	.10	.05	.01
□ 178	Karl Rhodes	.10	.05	.01
□ 179	LaTroy Hawkins	.10	.05	.01
□ 180	Raul Mondesi	.50	.23	.06
□ 181	Jeff Reed	.10	.05	.01
□ 182	Milt Cuyler	.10	.05	.01
□ 183	Jim Edmonds	.50	.23	.06
□ 184	Hector Fajardo	.10	.05	.01
□ 185	Jeff Kent	.10	.05	.01
□ 186	Wilson Alvarez	.25	.11	.03
□ 187	Geronimo Berroa	.10	.05	.01
□ 188	Billy Spiers	.10	.05	.01
□ 189	Derek Lilliquist	.10	.05	.01
□ 190	Craig Biggio	.50	.23	.06
□ 191	Roberto Hernandez	.10	.05	.01
□ 192	Bob Natal	.10	.05	.01
□ 193	Bobby Ayala	.10	.05	.01
□ 194	Travis Miller	.25	.11	.03
□ 195	Bob Tewksbury	.10	.05	.01
□ 196	Rondell White	.50	.23	.06
□ 197	Steve Cooke	.10	.05	.01
□ 198	Jeff Branson	.10	.05	.01
□ 199	Derek Jeter	2.00	.90	.25
□ 200	Tim Salmon	.50	.23	.06
□ 201	Steve Frey	.10	.05	.01
□ 202	Kent Mercker	.10	.05	.01
□ 203	Randy Johnson	.50	.23	.06
□ 204	Todd Worrell	.10	.05	.01
□ 205	Mo Vaughn	.75	.35	.09
□ 206	Howard Johnson	.10	.05	.01
□ 207	John Wasdin	.10	.05	.01
□ 208	Eddie Williams	.10	.05	.01
□ 209	Tim Belcher	.25	.11	.03
□ 210	Jeff Montgomery	.25	.11	.03
□ 211	Kirt Manwaring	.10	.05	.01
□ 212	Ben Grieve	1.25	.55	.16
□ 213	Pat Hentgen	.25	.11	.03
□ 214	Shawon Dunston	.10	.05	.01
□ 215	Mike Greenwell	.10	.05	.01
□ 216	Alex Diaz	.10	.05	.01
□ 217	Pat Mahomes	.10	.05	.01
□ 218	Dave Hansen	.10	.05	.01
□ 219	Kevin Rogers	.10	.05	.01

□ 220	Cecil Fielder	.25	.11	.03
□ 221	Andrew Lorraine	.25	.11	.03
□ 222	Jack Armstrong	.10	.05	.01
□ 223	Todd Hundley	.25	.11	.03
□ 224	Mark Acre	.10	.05	.01
□ 225	Darrell Whitmore	.10	.05	.01
□ 226	Randy Milligan	.10	.05	.01
□ 227	Wayne Kirby	.10	.05	.01
□ 228	Darryl Kile	.10	.05	.01
□ 229	Bob Zupcic	.10	.05	.01
□ 230	Jay Bell	.25	.11	.03
□ 231	Dustin Hermanson	.25	.11	.03
□ 232	Harold Baines	.25	.11	.03
□ 233	Alan Benes	.50	.23	.06
□ 234	Felix Fermin	.10	.05	.01
□ 235	Ellis Burks	.50	.23	.06
□ 236	Jeff Brantley	.10	.05	.01
□ 237	Outfield Prospects	3.00	1.35	.35
	Brian Hunter			
	Jose Malave			
	Karim Garcia			
	Shane Pullen			
□ 238	Matt Nokes	.10	.05	.01
□ 239	Ben Rivera	.10	.05	.01
□ 240	Joe Carter	.50	.23	.06
□ 241	Jeff Granger	.10	.05	.01
□ 242	Terry Pendelton	.25	.11	.03
□ 243	Melvin Nieves	.25	.11	.03
□ 244	Frankie Rodriguez	.25	.11	.03
□ 245	Darryl Hamilton	.10	.05	.01
□ 246	Brooks Kieschnick	.25	.11	.03
□ 247	Todd Hollandsworth	.50	.23	.06
□ 248	Joe Rosselli	.10	.05	.01
□ 249	Bill Gullickson	.10	.05	.01
□ 250	Chuck Knoblauch	.50	.23	.06
□ 251	Kurt Miller	.10	.05	.01
□ 252	Bobby Jones	.25	.11	.03
□ 253	Lance Blankenship	.10	.05	.01
□ 254	Matt Whiteside	.10	.05	.01
□ 255	Darrin Fletcher	.10	.05	.01
□ 256	Eric Plunk	.10	.05	.01
□ 257	Shane Reynolds	.10	.05	.01
□ 258	Norberto Martin	.10	.05	.01
□ 259	Mike Thurman	.10	.05	.01
□ 260	Andy Van Slyke	.25	.11	.03
□ 261	Dwight Smith	.10	.05	.01
□ 262	Allen Watson	.10	.05	.01
□ 263	Dan Wilson	.25	.11	.03
□ 264	Brent Mayne	.10	.05	.01
□ 265	Bip Roberts	.10	.05	.01
□ 266	Sterling Hitchcock	.25	.11	.03
□ 267	Alex Gonzalez	.10	.05	.01
□ 268	Greg Harris	.10	.05	.01
□ 269	Ricky Jordan	.10	.05	.01
□ 270	Johnny Ruffin	.10	.05	.01
□ 271	Mike Stanton	.10	.05	.01
□ 272	Rich Rowland	.10	.05	.01
□ 273	Steve Trachsel	.10	.05	.01
□ 274	Pedro Munoz	.10	.05	.01
□ 275	Ramon Martinez	.25	.11	.03
□ 276	Dave Henderson	.10	.05	.01
□ 277	Chris Gomez	.10	.05	.01
□ 278	Joe Grahe	.10	.05	.01
□ 279	Rusty Greer	.50	.23	.06
□ 280	John Franco	.10	.05	.01
□ 281	Mike Bordick	.10	.05	.01
□ 282	Jeff D'Amico	.25	.11	.03
□ 283	Dave Magadan	.10	.05	.01
□ 284	Tony Pena	.10	.05	.01
□ 285	Greg Swindell	.10	.05	.01
□ 286	Doug Million	.25	.11	.03
□ 287	Gabe White	.10	.05	.01
□ 288	Trey Beamon	.25	.11	.03
□ 289	Arthur Rhodes	.10	.05	.01
□ 290	Juan Guzman	.25	.11	.03
□ 291	Jose Oquendo	.10	.05	.01
□ 292	Willie Blair	.10	.05	.01
□ 293	Eddie Taubensee	.10	.05	.01
□ 294	Steve Howe	.10	.05	.01
□ 295	Greg Maddux	2.00	.90	.25
□ 296	Mike Macfarlane	.10	.05	.01
□ 297	Curt Schilling	.10	.05	.01
□ 298	Phil Clark	.10	.05	.01
□ 299	Woody Williams	.10	.05	.01
□ 300	Jose Canseco	.50	.23	.06
□ 301	Aaron Sele	.25	.11	.03

□ 302	Carl Willis	.10	.05	.01
□ 303	Steve Buechele	.10	.05	.01
□ 304	Dave Burba	.10	.05	.01
□ 305	Orel Hershiser	.25	.11	.03
□ 306	Damion Easley	.10	.05	.01
□ 307	Mike Henneman	.10	.05	.01
□ 308	Josias Manzanillo	.10	.05	.01
□ 309	Kevin Seitzer	.10	.05	.01
□ 310	Ruben Sierra	.25	.11	.03
□ 311	Bryan Harvey	.10	.05	.01
□ 312	Jim Thome	.60	.25	.07
□ 313	Ramon Castro	.25	.11	.03
□ 314	Lance Johnson	.25	.11	.03
□ 315	Marquis Grissom	.50	.23	.06
□ 316	Starting Pitcher	.50	.23	.06
	Prospects			
	Terrell Wade			
	Juan Acevedo			
	Matt Arrandale			
	Eddie Priest			
□ 317	Paul Wagner	.10	.05	.01
□ 318	Jamie Moyer	.10	.05	.01
□ 319	Todd Zeile	.10	.05	.01
□ 320	Chris Bosio	.10	.05	.01
□ 321	Steve Reed	.10	.05	.01
□ 322	Erik Hanson	.10	.05	.01
□ 323	Luis Polonia	.10	.05	.01
□ 324	Ryan Klesko	.60	.25	.07
□ 325	Kevin Appier	.25	.11	.03
□ 326	Jim Eisenreich	.10	.05	.01
□ 327	Randy Knorr	.10	.05	.01
□ 328	Craig Shipley	.10	.05	.01
□ 329	Tim Naehring	.10	.05	.01
□ 330	Randy Myers	.10	.05	.01
□ 331	Alex Cole	.10	.05	.01
□ 332	Jim Gott	.10	.05	.01
□ 333	Mike Jackson	.10	.05	.01
□ 334	John Flaherty	.10	.05	.01
□ 335	Chili Davis	.25	.11	.03
□ 336	Benji Gil	.10	.05	.01
□ 337	Jason Jacome	.10	.05	.01
□ 338	Stan Javier	.10	.05	.01
□ 339	Mike Fetters	.10	.05	.01
□ 340	Rich Renteria	.10	.05	.01
□ 341	Kevin Witt	.25	.11	.03
□ 342	Scott Servais	.10	.05	.01
□ 343	Craig Grebeck	.10	.05	.01
□ 344	Kirk Rueter	.10	.05	.01
□ 345	Don Slaught	.10	.05	.01
□ 346	Armando Benitez	.10	.05	.01
□ 347	Ozzie Smith	.60	.25	.07
□ 348	Mike Blowers	.10	.05	.01
□ 349	Armando Reynoso	.10	.05	.01
□ 350	Barry Larkin	.50	.23	.06
□ 351	Mike Williams	.10	.05	.01
□ 352	Scott Kamieniecki	.10	.05	.01
□ 353	Gary Gaetti	.25	.11	.03
□ 354	Todd Stottlemyre	.10	.05	.01
□ 355	Fred McGriff	.50	.23	.06
□ 356	Tim Mauser	.10	.05	.01
□ 357	Chris Gwynn	.10	.05	.01
□ 358	Frank Castillo	.10	.05	.01
□ 359	Jeff Reboulet	.10	.05	.01
□ 360	Roger Clemens	.50	.23	.06
□ 361	Mark Carreon	.10	.05	.01
□ 362	Chad Kreuter	.10	.05	.01
□ 363	Mark Farris	.25	.11	.03
□ 364	Bob Welch	.10	.05	.01
□ 365	Dean Palmer	.25	.11	.03
□ 366	Jeromy Burnitz	.10	.05	.01
□ 367	B.J. Surhoff	.25	.11	.03
□ 368	Mike Butcher	.10	.05	.01
□ 369	Relief Pitcher	.25	.11	.03
	Prospects			
	Brad Clontz			
	Steve Phoenix			
	Scott Gentile			
	Bucky Buckles			
□ 370	Eddie Murray	.75	.35	.09
□ 371	Orlando Miller	.10	.05	.01
□ 372	Ron Karkovice	.10	.05	.01
□ 373	Richie Lewis	.10	.05	.01
□ 374	Lenny Webster	.10	.05	.01
□ 375	Jeff Tackett	.10	.05	.01
□ 376	Tom Urbani	.10	.05	.01
□ 377	Tino Martinez	.25	.11	.03
□ 378	Mark Dewey	.10	.05	.01
□ 379	Charles O'Brien	.10	.05	.01
□ 380	Terry Mulholland	.10	.05	.01
□ 381	Thomas Howard	.10	.05	.01
□ 382	Chris Haney	.10	.05	.01
□ 383	Billy Hatcher	.10	.05	.01
□ 384	Jeff Bagwell AS	.75	.35	.09
	Frank Thomas AS			
□ 385	Bret Boone AS	.25	.11	.03
	Carlos Baerga AS			
□ 386	Matt Williams AS	.25	.11	.03
	Wade Boggs AS			
□ 387	Wil Cordero AS	.50	.23	.06
	Cal Ripken AS			
□ 388	Barry Bonds AS	.75	.35	.09
	Ken Griffey AS			
□ 389	Tony Gwynn AS	.60	.25	.07
	Albert Belle AS			
□ 390	Dante Bichette AS	.25	.11	.03
	Kirby Puckett AS			
□ 391	Mike Piazza AS	.50	.23	.06
	Mike Stanley AS			
□ 392	Greg Maddux AS	.50	.23	.06
	David Cone AS			
□ 393	Danny Jackson AS	.10	.05	.01
	Jimmy Key AS			
□ 394	John Franco AS	.10	.05	.01
	Lee Smith AS			
□ 395	Checklist 1-198	.10	.05	.01
□ 396	Checklist 199-396	.10	.05	.01
□ 397	Ken Griffey Jr.	3.00	1.35	.35
□ 398	Rick Heiserman	.25	.11	.03
□ 399	Don Mattingly	1.50	.70	.19
□ 400	Henry Rodriguez	.50	.23	.06
□ 401	Lenny Harris	.10	.05	.01
□ 402	Ryan Thompson	.10	.05	.01
□ 403	Darren Oliver	.25	.11	.03
□ 404	Omar Vizquel	.50	.23	.06
□ 405	Jeff Bagwell	1.25	.55	.16
□ 406	Doug Webb	.10	.05	.01
□ 407	Todd Van Poppel	.10	.05	.01
□ 408	Leo Gomez	.10	.05	.01
□ 409	Mark Whiten	.10	.05	.01
□ 410	Pedro Martinez	.10	.05	.01
□ 411	Reggie Sanders	.25	.11	.03
□ 412	Kevin Foster	.10	.05	.01
□ 413	Danny Tartabull	.10	.05	.01
□ 414	Jeff Blauser	.10	.05	.01
□ 415	Mike Magnante	.10	.05	.01
□ 416	Tom Candiotti	.10	.05	.01
□ 417	Rod Beck	.10	.05	.01
□ 418	Jody Reed	.10	.05	.01
□ 419	Vince Coleman	.10	.05	.01
□ 420	Danny Jackson	.10	.05	.01
□ 421	Ryan Nye	.25	.11	.03
□ 422	Larry Walker	.50	.23	.06
□ 423	Russ Johnson DP	.25	.11	.03
□ 424	Pat Borders	.10	.05	.01
□ 425	Lee Smith	.25	.11	.03
□ 426	Paul O'Neill	.25	.11	.03
□ 427	Devon White	.25	.11	.03
□ 428	Jim Bullinger	.10	.05	.01
□ 429	Starting Pitchers	.25	.11	.03
	Prospects			
	Greg Hansell			
	Brian Sackinsky			
	Carey Paige			
	Rob Welch			
□ 430	Steve Avery	.25	.11	.03
□ 431	Tony Gwynn	1.25	.55	.16
□ 432	Pat Meares	.10	.05	.01
□ 433	Bill Swift	.10	.05	.01
□ 434	David Wells	.10	.05	.01
□ 435	John Briscoe	.10	.05	.01
□ 436	Roger Pavlik	.10	.05	.01
□ 437	Jayson Peterson	.25	.11	.03
□ 438	Roberto Alomar	.75	.35	.09
□ 439	Billy Brewer	.10	.05	.01
□ 440	Gary Sheffield	.50	.23	.06
□ 441	Lou Frazier	.10	.05	.01
□ 442	Terry Steinbach	.25	.11	.03
□ 443	Jay Payton	2.00	.90	.25
□ 444	Jason Bere	.10	.05	.01
□ 445	Denny Neagle	.25	.11	.03
□ 446	Andres Galarraga	.50	.23	.06
□ 447	Hector Carrasco	.10	.05	.01

□ 448	Bill Risley	.10	.05	.01
□ 449	Andy Benes	.10	.05	.01
□ 450	Jim Leyritz	.10	.05	.01
□ 451	Jose Oliva	.10	.05	.01
□ 452	Greg Vaughn	.25	.11	.03
□ 453	Rich Monteleone	.10	.05	.01
□ 454	Tony Eusebio	.10	.05	.01
□ 455	Chuck Finley	.25	.11	.03
□ 456	Kevin Brown	.25	.11	.03
□ 457	Joe Boever	.10	.05	.01
□ 458	Bobby Munoz	.10	.05	.01
□ 459	Bret Saberhagen	.25	.11	.03
□ 460	Kurt Abbott	.10	.05	.01
□ 461	Bobby Witt	.10	.05	.01
□ 462	Cliff Floyd	.25	.11	.03
□ 463	Mark Clark	.10	.05	.01
□ 464	Andujar Cedeno	.10	.05	.01
□ 465	Marvin Freeman	.10	.05	.01
□ 466	Mike Piazza	2.00	.90	.25
□ 467	Willie Greene	.10	.05	.01
□ 468	Pat Kelly	.10	.05	.01
□ 469	Carlos Delgado	.50	.23	.06
□ 470	Willie Banks	.10	.05	.01
□ 471	Matt Walbeck	.10	.05	.01
□ 472	Mark McGwire	1.00	.45	.12
□ 473	McKay Christensen	.25	.11	.03
□ 474	Alan Trammell	.50	.23	.06
□ 475	Tom Gordon	.10	.05	.01
□ 476	Greg Colbrunn	.10	.05	.01
□ 477	Darren Daulton	.25	.11	.03
□ 478	Albie Lopez	.10	.05	.01
□ 479	Robin Ventura	.25	.11	.03
□ 480	Catcher Prospects	.25	.11	.03
	Eddie Perez			
	Jason Kendall			
	Einar Diaz			
	Bret Hemphill			
□ 481	Bryan Eversgerd	.10	.05	.01
□ 482	Dave Fleming	.10	.05	.01
□ 483	Scott Livingstone	.10	.05	.01
□ 484	Pete Schourek	.25	.11	.03
□ 485	Bernie Williams	.50	.23	.06
□ 486	Mark Lemke	.10	.05	.01
□ 487	Eric Karros	.25	.11	.03
□ 488	Scott Ruffcorn	.10	.05	.01
□ 489	Billy Ashley	.10	.05	.01
□ 490	Rico Brogna	.10	.05	.01
□ 491	John Burkett	.25	.11	.03
□ 492	Cade Gaspar	.25	.11	.03
□ 493	Jorge Fabregas	.10	.05	.01
□ 494	Greg Gagne	.10	.05	.01
□ 495	Doug Jones	.10	.05	.01
□ 496	Troy O'Leary	.10	.05	.01
□ 497	Pat Rapp	.10	.05	.01
□ 498	Butch Henry	.10	.05	.01
□ 499	John Olerud	.10	.05	.01
□ 500	John Hudek	.10	.05	.01
□ 501	Jeff King	.25	.11	.03
□ 502	Bobby Bonilla	.25	.11	.03
□ 503	Albert Belle	1.50	.70	.19
□ 504	Rick Wilkins	.10	.05	.01
□ 505	John Jaha	.25	.11	.03
□ 506	Nigel Wilson	.10	.05	.01
□ 507	Sid Fernandez	.10	.05	.01
□ 508	Deion Sanders	.50	.23	.06
□ 509	Gil Heredia	.10	.05	.01
□ 510	Scott Elarton	.50	.23	.06
□ 511	Melido Perez	.10	.05	.01
□ 512	Greg McMichael	.10	.05	.01
□ 513	Rusty Meacham	.10	.05	.01
□ 514	Shawn Green	.25	.11	.03
□ 515	Carlos Garcia	.10	.05	.01
□ 516	Dave Stevens	.10	.05	.01
□ 517	Eric Young	.25	.11	.03
□ 518	Omar Daal	.10	.05	.01
□ 519	Kirk Gibson	.25	.11	.03
□ 520	Spike Owen	.10	.05	.01
□ 521	Jacob Cruz	.75	.35	.09
□ 522	Sandy Alomar Jr.	.10	.05	.01
□ 523	Steve Bedrosian	.10	.05	.01
□ 524	Ricky Gutierrez	.10	.05	.01
□ 525	Dave Veres	.10	.05	.01
□ 526	Gregg Jefferies	.25	.11	.03
□ 527	Jose Valentin	.25	.11	.03
□ 528	Robb Nen	.10	.05	.01
□ 529	Jose Rijo	.10	.05	.01
□ 530	Sean Berry	.10	.05	.01
□ 531	Mike Gallego	.10	.05	.01
□ 532	Roberto Kelly	.10	.05	.01
□ 533	Kevin Stocker	.10	.05	.01
□ 534	Kirby Puckett	1.00	.45	.12
□ 535	Chipper Jones	2.00	.90	.25
□ 536	Russ Davis	.10	.05	.01
□ 537	Jon Lieber	.10	.05	.01
□ 538	Trey Moore	.25	.11	.03
□ 539	Joe Girardi	.10	.05	.01
□ 540	Second Baseman	.25	.11	.03
	Prospects			
	Quilvio Veras			
	Arquimedez Pozo			
	Miguel Cairo			
	Jason Camilli			
□ 541	Tony Phillips	.25	.11	.03
□ 542	Brian Anderson	.10	.05	.01
□ 543	Ivan Rodriguez	.60	.25	.07
□ 544	Jeff Cirillo	.25	.11	.03
□ 545	Joey Cora	.10	.05	.01
□ 546	Chris Hoiles	.10	.05	.01
□ 547	Bernard Gilkey	.25	.11	.03
□ 548	Mike Lansing	.10	.05	.01
□ 549	Jimmy Key	.25	.11	.03
□ 550	Mark Wohlers	.25	.11	.03
□ 551	Chris Clemons	.25	.11	.03
□ 552	Vinny Castilla	.25	.11	.03
□ 553	Mark Guthrie	.10	.05	.01
□ 554	Mike Lieberthal	.10	.05	.01
□ 555	Tommy Davis	.25	.11	.03
□ 556	Robby Thompson	.10	.05	.01
□ 557	Danny Bautista	.10	.05	.01
□ 558	Will Clark	.50	.23	.06
□ 559	Rickey Henderson	.50	.23	.06
□ 560	Todd Jones	.10	.05	.01
□ 561	Jack McDowell	.25	.11	.03
□ 562	Carlos Rodriguez	.10	.05	.01
□ 563	Mark Eichhorn	.10	.05	.01
□ 564	Jeff Nelson	.10	.05	.01
□ 565	Eric Anthony	.10	.05	.01
□ 566	Randy Velarde	.10	.05	.01
□ 567	Javier Lopez	.50	.23	.06
□ 568	Kevin Mitchell	.25	.11	.03
□ 569	Steve Karsay	.10	.05	.01
□ 570	Brian Meadows	.30	.14	.04
□ 571	Rey Ordonez	2.00	.90	.25
	Mike Metcalfe			
□ 572	John Kruk	.25	.11	.03
□ 573	Scott Leius	.10	.05	.01
□ 574	John Patterson	.10	.05	.01
□ 575	Kevin Brown	.25	.11	.03
□ 576	Mike Moore	.10	.05	.01
□ 577	Manny Ramirez	.75	.35	.09
□ 578	Jose Lind	.10	.05	.01
□ 579	Derrick May	.10	.05	.01
□ 580	Cal Eldred	.10	.05	.01
□ 581	Third Baseman	.40	.18	.05
	Prospects			
	David Bell			
	Joel Chelmis			
	Lino Diaz			
	Aaron Boone			
□ 582	J.T. Snow	.25	.11	.03
□ 583	Luis Sojo	.10	.05	.01
□ 584	Moises Alou	.25	.11	.03
□ 585	Dave Clark	.10	.05	.01
□ 586	Dave Hollins	.10	.05	.01
□ 587	Nomar Garciaparra	1.50	.70	.19
□ 588	Cal Ripken	2.50	1.10	.30
□ 589	Pedro Astacio	.10	.05	.01
□ 590	J.R. Phillips	.10	.05	.01
□ 591	Jeff Frye	.10	.05	.01
□ 592	Bo Jackson	.50	.23	.06
□ 593	Steve Ontiveros	.10	.05	.01
□ 594	David Nied	.10	.05	.01
□ 595	Brad Ausmus	.10	.05	.01
□ 596	Carlos Baerga	.50	.23	.06
□ 597	James Mouton	.10	.05	.01
□ 598	Ozzie Guillen	.10	.05	.01
□ 599	Outfielders	.50	.23	.06
	Prospects			
	Ozzie Timmons			
	Curtis Goodwin			
	Johnny Damon			
	Jeff Abbott			

□ 600	Yorkis Perez	.10	.05	.01
□ 601	Rich Rodriguez	.10	.05	.01
□ 602	Mark McLemore	.10	.05	.01
□ 603	Jeff Fassero	.10	.05	.01
□ 604	John Roper	.10	.05	.01
□ 605	Mark Johnson	.25	.11	.03
□ 606	Wes Chamberlain	.10	.05	.01
□ 607	Felix Jose	.10	.05	.01
□ 608	Tony Longmire	.10	.05	.01
□ 609	Duane Ward	.10	.05	.01
□ 610	Brett Butler	.25	.11	.03
□ 611	William VanLandingham	.10	.05	.01
□ 612	Mickey Tettleton	.10	.05	.01
□ 613	Brady Anderson	.50	.23	.06
□ 614	Reggie Jefferson	.25	.11	.03
□ 615	Mike Kingery	.10	.05	.01
□ 616	Derek Bell	.25	.11	.03
□ 617	Scott Erickson	.10	.05	.01
□ 618	Bob Wickman	.10	.05	.01
□ 619	Phil Leftwich	.10	.05	.01
□ 620	David Justice	.50	.23	.06
□ 621	Paul Wilson	.60	.25	.07
□ 622	Pedro Martinez	.10	.05	.01
□ 623	Terry Mathews	.10	.05	.01
□ 624	Brian McRae	.25	.11	.03
□ 625	Bruce Ruffin	.10	.05	.01
□ 626	Steve Finley	.25	.11	.03
□ 627	Ron Gant	.25	.11	.03
□ 628	Rafael Bournigal	.10	.05	.01
□ 629	Darryl Strawberry	.25	.11	.03
□ 630	Luis Alicea	.10	.05	.01
□ 631	Orioles Prospects Mark Smith Scott Klingenbeck	.25	.11	.03
□ 632	Red Sox Prospects Cory Bailey Scott Hatteberg	.25	.11	.03
□ 633	Angels Prospects Todd Greene Troy Percival	.50	.23	.06
□ 634	White Sox Prospects Rod Bolton Olmedo Saenz	.10	.05	.01
□ 635	Indians Prospects Steve Kline Herb Perry	.25	.11	.03
□ 636	Tigers Prospects Sean Bergman Shannon Penn	.25	.11	.03
□ 637	Royals Prospects Joe Randa Joe Vitiello	.25	.11	.03
□ 638	Brewers Prospects Jose Mercedes Duane Singleton	.25	.11	.03
□ 639	Twins Prospects Marc Barcelo Marty Cordova	.50	.23	.06
□ 640	Yankees Prospects Andy Pettitte Ruben Rivera	2.50	1.10	.30
□ 641	Athletics Prospects Willie Adams Scott Spiezio	.25	.11	.03
□ 642	Mariners Prospects Eddy Diaz Desi Relaford	.25	.11	.03
□ 643	Rangers Prospects Terrell Lowery Jon Shave	.10	.05	.01
□ 644	Blue Jays Prospects Angel Martinez Paul Spoljaric	.25	.11	.03
□ 645	Braves Prospects Tony Graffanino Damon Hollins	.50	.23	.06
□ 646	Cubs Prospects Darron Cox Doug Glanville	.25	.11	.03
□ 647	Reds Prospects Tim Belk Pat Watkins	.25	.11	.03
□ 648	Rockies Propsects Rod Pedraza Phil Schneider	.10	.05	.01
□ 649	Marlins Prospects Vic Darensbourg Marc Valdes	.25	.11	.03
□ 650	Astros Prospects Rick Huisman Roberto Petagine	.25	.11	.03
□ 651	Dodgers Prospects Roger Cedeno Ron Coomer	.50	.23	.06
□ 652	Expos Prospects Shane Andrews Carlos Perez	.25	.11	.03
□ 653	Mets Prospects Jason Isringhausen Chris Roberts	.75	.35	.09
□ 654	Phillies Prospects Wayne Gomes Kevin Jordan	.25	.11	.03
□ 655	Pirates Prospects Esteban Loiaza Steve Pegues	.25	.11	.03
□ 656	Cardinals Prospects Terry Bradshaw John Frascatore	.25	.11	.03
□ 657	Padres Prospects Andres Berumen Bryce Florie	.25	.11	.03
□ 658	Giants Prospects Dan Carlson Keith Williams	.25	.11	.03
□ 659	Checklist	.10	.05	.01
□ 660	Checklist	.10	.05	.01

1995 Topps Finest

This 15-card standard-size set was inserted one every 36 Topps series two packs. This set featured the top 15 players in total bases from the 1994 season. The fronts feature a player photo, with his team identification and name on the bottom of the card. The horizontal backs feature another player photo along with a breakdown of how many of each type of hit each player got on the way to their season total. The set is sequenced in order of how they finished in the majors for the 1994 season.

	MINT	NRMT	EXC
COMPLETE SET (15)	70.00	32.00	8.75
COMMON CARD (1-15)	1.50	.70	.19
SEMISTARS	2.50	1.10	.30
RANDOM INSERTS IN SER .2 PACKS			

□ 1	Jeff Bagwell	8.00	3.60	1.00
□ 2	Albert Belle	10.00	4.50	1.25
□ 3	Ken Griffey Jr.	20.00	9.00	2.50
□ 4	Frank Thomas	20.00	9.00	2.50
□ 5	Matt Williams	2.50	1.10	.30
□ 6	Dante Bichette	2.50	1.10	.30
□ 7	Barry Bonds	5.00	2.20	.60
□ 8	Moises Alou	1.50	.70	.19
□ 9	Andres Galarraga	2.50	1.10	.30
□ 10	Kenny Lofton	5.00	2.20	.60
□ 11	Rafael Palmeiro	2.50	1.10	.30
□ 12	Tony Gwynn	8.00	3.60	1.00
□ 13	Kirby Puckett	6.00	2.70	.75
□ 14	Jose Canseco	2.50	1.10	.30
□ 15	Jeff Conine	1.50	.70	.19

1995 Topps League Leaders

Randomly inserted in jumbo packs at a rate of one in three, this 50-card standard-size set showcases those that were among league leaders in various categories. Card fronts feature a player photo with a black background. The player's name appears in gold foil at the bottom and the category with which he led the league or was among the leaders is in yellow letters up the right side. The backs contain various graphs and where the player placed among the leaders.

	MINT	NRMT	EXC
COMPLETE SET (50)	50.00	22.00	6.25
COMPLETE SERIES 1 (25)	20.00	9.00	2.50
COMPLETE SERIES 2 (25)	30.00	13.50	3.70
COMMON CARD (LL1-LL50)	.25	.11	.03
SEMISTARS	.50	.23	.06
STARS	.75	.35	.09
RANDOM INSERTS IN JUMBO AND RETAIL PACKS			

	MINT	NRMT	EXC
□ LL1 Albert Belle	3.00	1.35	.35
□ LL2 Kevin Mitchell	.50	.23	.06
□ LL3 Wade Boggs	.75	.35	.09
□ LL4 Tony Gwynn	2.50	1.10	.30
□ LL5 Moises Alou	.25	.11	.03
□ LL6 Andres Galarraga	.75	.35	.09
□ LL7 Matt Williams	.75	.35	.09
□ LL8 Barry Bonds	1.50	.70	.19
□ LL9 Frank Thomas	6.00	2.70	.75
□ LL10 Jose Canseco	.75	.35	.09
□ LL11 Jeff Bagwell	2.50	1.10	.30
□ LL12 Kirby Puckett	2.00	.90	.25
□ LL13 Julio Franco	.50	.23	.06
□ LL14 Albert Belle	3.00	1.35	.35
□ LL15 Fred McGriff	.75	.35	.09
□ LL16 Kenny Lofton	1.50	.70	.19
□ LL17 Otis Nixon	.25	.11	.03
□ LL18 Brady Anderson	.75	.35	.09
□ LL19 Deion Sanders	.75	.35	.09
□ LL20 Chuck Carr	.25	.11	.03
□ LL21 Pat Hentgen	.75	.35	.09
□ LL22 Andy Benes	.50	.23	.06
□ LL23 Roger Clemens	.75	.35	.09
□ LL24 Greg Maddux	4.00	1.80	.50
□ LL25 Pedro Martinez	.50	.23	.06
□ LL26 Paul O'Neill	.50	.23	.06
□ LL27 Jeff Bagwell	2.50	1.10	.30
□ LL28 Frank Thomas	6.00	2.70	.75
□ LL29 Hal Morris	.25	.11	.03
□ LL30 Kenny Lofton	1.50	.70	.19
□ LL31 Ken Griffey Jr.	6.00	2.70	.75
□ LL32 Jeff Bagwell	2.50	1.10	.30
□ LL33 Albert Belle	3.00	1.35	.35
□ LL34 Fred McGriff	.75	.35	.09
□ LL35 Cecil Fielder	.75	.35	.09
□ LL36 Matt Williams	.75	.35	.09
□ LL37 Joe Carter	.75	.35	.09
□ LL38 Dante Bichette	.75	.35	.09
□ LL39 Frank Thomas	6.00	2.70	.75
□ LL40 Mike Piazza	4.00	1.80	.50
□ LL41 Craig Biggio	.75	.35	.09
□ LL42 Vince Coleman	.25	.11	.03
□ LL43 Marquis Grissom	.75	.35	.09
□ LL44 Chuck Knoblauch	.75	.35	.09
□ LL45 Darren Lewis	.25	.11	.03
□ LL46 Randy Johnson	.75	.35	.09
□ LL47 Jose Rijo	.25	.11	.03
□ LL48 Chuck Finley	.50	.23	.06
□ LL49 Bret Saberhagen	.25	.11	.03
□ LL50 Kevin Appier	.50	.23	.06

1995 Topps Traded

This set contains 165 standard-size cards and was sold in 11-card packs for $1.29. The set features rookies, draft picks and players who had been traded. The fronts contain a photo with a white border. The backs have a player picture in a scoreboard and his statistics and information. All cards are numbered with a "T" prefix. Subsets featured are: At the Break (1T-10T) and All-Stars (156T-164T). Rookie Cards in this set include Ben Davis, Corey Jenkins, Hideo Nomo and Carlos Perez.

	MINT	NRMT	EXC
COMPLETE SET (165)	20.00	9.00	2.50
COMMON CARD (1-165)	.10	.05	.01
SEMISTARS	.25	.11	.03
STARS	.50	.23	.06
T PREFIX ON CARD NUMBERS			

	MINT	NRMT	EXC
□ 1 Frank Thomas ATB	1.50	.70	.19
□ 2 Ken Griffey Jr. ATB	1.50	.70	.19
□ 3 Barry Bonds ATB	.50	.23	.06
□ 4 Albert Belle ATB	.75	.35	.09
□ 5 Cal Ripken ATB	1.25	.55	.16
□ 6 Mike Piazza ATB	1.00	.45	.12
□ 7 Tony Gwynn ATB	.60	.25	.07
□ 8 Jeff Bagwell ATB	.60	.25	.07
□ 9 Mo Vaughn ATB	.50	.23	.06
□ 10 Matt Williams ATB	.25	.11	.03
□ 11 Ray Durham	.25	.11	.03
□ 12 Juan LeBron	.40	.18	.05
□ 13 Shawn Green	.25	.11	.03
□ 14 Kevin Gross	.10	.05	.01
□ 15 Jon Nunnally	.25	.11	.03
□ 16 Brian Maxcy	.10	.05	.01
□ 17 Mark Kiefer	.10	.05	.01
□ 18 Carlos Beltran	.50	.23	.06
□ 19 Mike Mimbs	.25	.11	.03
□ 20 Larry Walker	.50	.23	.06
□ 21 Chad Curtis	.10	.05	.01
□ 22 Jeff Barry	.10	.05	.01
□ 23 Joe Oliver	.10	.05	.01
□ 24 Tomas Perez	.25	.11	.03
□ 25 Michael Barrett	.25	.11	.03
□ 26 Brian McRae	.25	.11	.03
□ 27 Derek Bell	.25	.11	.03
□ 28 Ray Durham	.25	.11	.03
□ 29 Todd Williams	.10	.05	.01
□ 30 Ryan Jaroncyk	.40	.18	.05
□ 31 Todd Steverson	.10	.05	.01
□ 32 Mike Devereaux	.10	.05	.01
□ 33 Rheal Cormier	.10	.05	.01
□ 34 Benny Santiago	.10	.05	.01
□ 35 Bobby Higginson	.50	.23	.06
□ 36 Jack McDowell	.25	.11	.03
□ 37 Mike Macfarlane	.10	.05	.01
□ 38 Tony McKnight	.25	.11	.03
□ 39 Brian Hunter	.50	.23	.06
□ 40 Hideo Nomo	3.00	1.35	.35
□ 41 Brett Butler	.25	.11	.03
□ 42 Donovan Osborne	.10	.05	.01
□ 43 Scott Karl	.10	.05	.01

☐ 44	Tony Phillips	.25	.11	.03
☐ 45	Marty Cordova	.50	.23	.06
☐ 46	Dave Mlicki	.10	.05	.01
☐ 47	Bronson Arroyo	.40	.18	.05
☐ 48	John Burkett	.25	.11	.03
☐ 49	J.D. Smart	.10	.05	.01
☐ 50	Mickey Tettleton	.10	.05	.01
☐ 51	Todd Stottlemyre	.10	.05	.01
☐ 52	Mike Perez	.10	.05	.01
☐ 53	Terry Mulholland	.10	.05	.01
☐ 54	Edgardo Alfonzo	.25	.11	.03
☐ 55	Zane Smith	.10	.05	.01
☐ 56	Jacob Brumfield	.10	.05	.01
☐ 57	Andujar Cedeno	.10	.05	.01
☐ 58	Jose Parra	.25	.11	.03
☐ 59	Manny Alexander	.10	.05	.01
☐ 60	Tony Tarasco	.10	.05	.01
☐ 61	Orel Hershiser	.25	.11	.03
☐ 62	Tim Scott	.10	.05	.01
☐ 63	Felix Rodriguez	.25	.11	.03
☐ 64	Ken Hill	.10	.05	.01
☐ 65	Marquis Grissom	.50	.23	.06
☐ 66	Lee Smith	.25	.11	.03
☐ 67	Jason Bates	.10	.05	.01
☐ 68	Felipe Lira	.10	.05	.01
☐ 69	Alex Hernandez	.30	.14	.04
☐ 70	Tony Fernandez	.10	.05	.01
☐ 71	Scott Radinsky	.10	.05	.01
☐ 72	Jose Canseco	.50	.23	.06
☐ 73	Mark Grudzielanek	.75	.35	.09
☐ 74	Ben Davis	.60	.25	.07
☐ 75	Jim Abbott	.10	.05	.01
☐ 76	Roger Bailey	.10	.05	.01
☐ 77	Gregg Jefferies	.25	.11	.03
☐ 78	Erik Hanson	.10	.05	.01
☐ 79	Brad Radke	.25	.11	.03
☐ 80	Jaime Navarro	.10	.05	.01
☐ 81	John Wetteland	.25	.11	.03
☐ 82	Chad Fonville	.25	.11	.03
☐ 83	John Mabry	.50	.23	.06
☐ 84	Glenallen Hill	.10	.05	.01
☐ 85	Ken Caminiti	.50	.23	.06
☐ 86	Tom Goodwin	.10	.05	.01
☐ 87	Darren Bragg	.25	.11	.03
☐ 88	Pitching Prospects Pat Ahearne Gary Rath Larry Wimberly Robbie Bell	.40	.18	.05
☐ 89	Jeff Russell	.10	.05	.01
☐ 90	Dave Gallagher	.10	.05	.01
☐ 91	Steve Finley	.25	.11	.03
☐ 92	Vaughn Eshelman	.10	.05	.01
☐ 93	Kevin Jarvis	.10	.05	.01
☐ 94	Mark Gubicza	.10	.05	.01
☐ 95	Tim Wakefield	.10	.05	.01
☐ 96	Bob Tewksbury	.10	.05	.01
☐ 97	Sid Roberson	.10	.05	.01
☐ 98	Tom Henke	.10	.05	.01
☐ 99	Michael Tucker	.25	.11	.03
☐ 100	Jason Bates	.10	.05	.01
☐ 101	Otis Nixon	.10	.05	.01
☐ 102	Mark Whiten	.10	.05	.01
☐ 103	Dilson Torres	.10	.05	.01
☐ 104	Melvin Bunch	.10	.05	.01
☐ 105	Terry Pendleton	.25	.11	.03
☐ 106	Corey Jenkins	.50	.23	.06
☐ 107	Glenn Dishman Rob Grable	.25	.11	.03
☐ 108	Reggie Taylor	.50	.23	.06
☐ 109	Curtis Goodwin	.25	.11	.03
☐ 110	David Cone	.25	.11	.03
☐ 111	Antonio Osuna	.10	.05	.01
☐ 112	Paul Shuey	.10	.05	.01
☐ 113	Doug Jones	.10	.05	.01
☐ 114	Mark McLemore	.10	.05	.01
☐ 115	Kevin Ritz	.10	.05	.01
☐ 116	John Kruk	.25	.11	.03
☐ 117	Trevor Wilson	.10	.05	.01
☐ 118	Jerald Clark	.10	.05	.01
☐ 119	Julian Tavarez	.10	.05	.01
☐ 120	Tim Pugh	.10	.05	.01
☐ 121	Todd Zeile	.10	.05	.01
☐ 122	Prospects Mark Sweeney UER George Arias Richie Sexson Brian Schneider	1.00	.45	.12
☐ 123	Bobby Witt	.10	.05	.01
☐ 124	Hideo Nomo	1.25	.55	.16
☐ 125	Joey Cora	.10	.05	.01
☐ 126	Jim Scharrer	.30	.14	.04
☐ 127	Paul Quantrill	.10	.05	.01
☐ 128	Chipper Jones ROY	1.50	.70	.19
☐ 129	Kenny James	.10	.05	.01
☐ 130	Lyle Mouton Mariano Rivera	.25	.11	.03
☐ 131	Tyler Green	.10	.05	.01
☐ 132	Brad Clontz	.10	.05	.01
☐ 133	Jon Nunnally	.25	.11	.03
☐ 134	Dave Magadan	.10	.05	.01
☐ 135	Al Leiter	.25	.11	.03
☐ 136	Bret Barberie	.10	.05	.01
☐ 137	Bill Swift	.10	.05	.01
☐ 138	Scott Cooper	.10	.05	.01
☐ 139	Roberto Kelly	.10	.05	.01
☐ 140	Charlie Hayes	.10	.05	.01
☐ 141	Pete Harnisch	.10	.05	.01
☐ 142	Rich Amaral	.10	.05	.01
☐ 143	Rudy Seanez	.10	.05	.01
☐ 144	Pat Listach	.10	.05	.01
☐ 145	Quilvio Veras	.10	.05	.01
☐ 146	Jose Olmeda	.10	.05	.01
☐ 147	Roberto Petagine	.10	.05	.01
☐ 148	Kevin Brown	.25	.11	.03
☐ 149	Phil Plantier	.10	.05	.01
☐ 150	Carlos Perez	.25	.11	.03
☐ 151	Pat Borders	.10	.05	.01
☐ 152	Tyler Green	.10	.05	.01
☐ 153	Stan Belinda	.10	.05	.01
☐ 154	Dave Stewart	.25	.11	.03
☐ 155	Andre Dawson	.10	.05	.01
☐ 156	Frank Thomas AS Fred McGriff UER (McGriff's team shown as Blue Jays)	.75	.35	.09
☐ 157	Carlos Baerga AS Craig Biggio	.25	.11	.03
☐ 158	Wade Boggs AS Matt Williams	.25	.11	.03
☐ 159	Cal Ripken AS Ozzie Smith	.60	.25	.07
☐ 160	Ken Griffey Jr. AS Tony Gwynn	.75	.35	.09
☐ 161	Albert Belle AS Barry Bonds	.25	.11	.03
☐ 162	Kirby Puckett Len Dykstra	.25	.11	.03
☐ 163	Ivan Rodriguez AS Mike Piazza	.25	.11	.03
☐ 164	Randy Johnson AS Hideo Nomo	.25	.11	.03
☐ 165	Checklist	.10	.05	.01

1995 Topps Traded Power Boosters

This 10-card standard-size set was inserted in packs at a rate of one in 36. The set is comprised of parallel cards for the first 10 cards of the regular Topps Traded set which was the "At the Break" subset. The cards are done on extra-thick stock. The fronts have an action photo on a "Power Boosted" background, which is similar to diffraction technology, with the

words "at the break" on the left side. The backs have a head shot and player information including his mid-season statistics for 1995 and previous years.

	MINT	NRMT	EXC
COMPLETE SET (10)	120.00	55.00	15.00
COMMON CARD (1-10)	4.00	1.80	.50
RANDOM INSERTS IN PACKS			

□ 1 Frank Thomas	30.00	13.50	3.70
□ 2 Ken Griffey Jr.	30.00	13.50	3.70
□ 3 Barry Bonds	8.00	3.60	1.00
□ 4 Albert Belle	15.00	6.75	1.85
□ 5 Cal Ripken	25.00	11.00	3.10
□ 6 Mike Piazza	20.00	9.00	2.50
□ 7 Tony Gwynn	12.00	5.50	1.50
□ 8 Jeff Bagwell	12.00	5.50	1.50
□ 9 Mo Vaughn	8.00	3.60	1.00
□ 10 Matt Williams	4.00	1.80	.50

1996 Topps

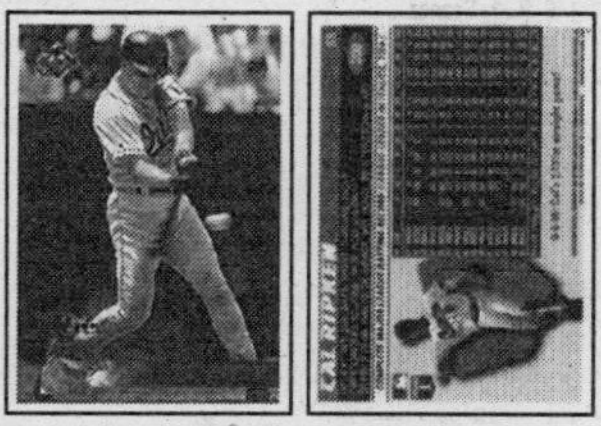

This set consists of 440 standard-size cards. These cards were issued in 12-card foil packs with a suggested retail price of $1.29. The fronts feature full-color photos surrounded by a white background. Information on the backs includes a player photo, season and career stats and text. First series subsets include Star Power (1-6, 8-12), Draft Picks (13-26), AAA Stars (101-104), and Future Stars (210-219). A special Mickey Mantle card was issued as card #7 (his uniform number) and became the last card to be issued as card #7 in the Topps brand set. Rookie Cards in this set include Sean Casey and Geoff Jenkins.

	MINT	NRMT	EXC
COMPLETE SET (440)	35.00	16.00	4.40
COMP.HOBBY FACT.SET (449)	50.00	22.00	6.25
COMP.CEREAL FACT.SET (444)	50.00	22.00	6.25
COMPLETE SERIES 1 (220)	25.00	11.00	3.10
COMPLETE SERIES 2 (220)	10.00	4.50	1.25
COMMON CARD (1-220)	.10	.05	.01
COMMON CARD (221-440)	.05	.02	.01
SERIES 1 SEMISTARS	.25	.11	.03
SERIES 2 SEMISTARS	.15	.07	.02
SERIES 1 STARS	.50	.23	.06
SERIES 2 STARS	.30	.14	.04
ONE LAST DAY MANTLE PER FACT.SET			

□ 1 Tony Gwynn STP	.60	.25	.07
□ 2 Mike Piazza STP	1.00	.45	.12
□ 3 Greg Maddux STP	1.00	.45	.12
□ 4 Jeff Bagwell STP	.60	.25	.07
□ 5 Larry Walker STP	.25	.11	.03
□ 6 Barry Larkin STP	.50	.23	.06
□ 7 Mickey Mantle	4.00	1.80	.50
□ 8 Tom Glavine STP UER Won 21 games in June 95	.50	.23	.06
□ 9 Craig Biggio STP	.50	.23	.06
□ 10 Barry Bonds STP	.50	.23	.06
□ 11 Heathcliff Slocumb STP	.10	.05	.01
□ 12 Matt Williams STP	.50	.23	.06
□ 13 Todd Helton	1.25	.55	.16
□ 14 Mark Redman	.25	.11	.03
□ 15 Michael Barrett	.10	.05	.01
□ 16 Ben Davis	.40	.18	.05
□ 17 Juan LeBron	.10	.05	.01
□ 18 Tony McKnight	.10	.05	.01
□ 19 Ryan Jaroncyk	.10	.05	.01
□ 20 Corey Jenkins	.25	.11	.03
□ 21 Jim Scharrer	.10	.05	.01
□ 22 Mark Bellhorn	.30	.14	.04
□ 23 Jarrod Washburn	.25	.11	.03
□ 24 Geoff Jenkins	.50	.23	.06
□ 25 Sean Casey	.75	.35	.09
□ 26 Brett Tomko	.10	.05	.01
□ 27 Tony Fernandez	.10	.05	.01
□ 28 Rich Becker	.25	.11	.03
□ 29 Andujar Cedeno	.10	.05	.01
□ 30 Paul Molitor	.60	.25	.07
□ 31 Brent Gates	.10	.05	.01
□ 32 Glenallen Hill	.25	.11	.03
□ 33 Mike Macfarlane	.10	.05	.01
□ 34 Manny Alexander	.10	.05	.01
□ 35 Todd Zeile	.10	.05	.01
□ 36 Joe Girardi	.10	.05	.01
□ 37 Tony Tarasco	.10	.05	.01
□ 38 Tim Belcher	.10	.05	.01
□ 39 Tom Goodwin	.25	.11	.03
□ 40 Orel Hershiser	.25	.11	.03
□ 41 Tripp Cromer	.10	.05	.01
□ 42 Sean Bergman	.10	.05	.01
□ 43 Troy Percival	.25	.11	.03
□ 44 Kevin Stocker	.10	.05	.01
□ 45 Albert Belle	1.50	.70	.19
□ 46 Tony Eusebio	.10	.05	.01
□ 47 Sid Roberson	.10	.05	.01
□ 48 Todd Hollandsworth	.50	.23	.06
□ 49 Mark Wohlers	.25	.11	.03
□ 50 Kirby Puckett	1.00	.45	.12
□ 51 Darren Holmes	.10	.05	.01
□ 52 Ron Karkovice	.10	.05	.01
□ 53 Al Martin	.10	.05	.01
□ 54 Pat Rapp	.10	.05	.01
□ 55 Mark Grace	.50	.23	.06
□ 56 Greg Gagne	.10	.05	.01
□ 57 Stan Javier	.10	.05	.01
□ 58 Scott Sanders	.10	.05	.01
□ 59 J.T. Snow	.50	.23	.06
□ 60 David Justice	.25	.11	.03
□ 61 Royce Clayton	.10	.05	.01
□ 62 Kevin Foster	.10	.05	.01
□ 63 Tim Naehring	.10	.05	.01
□ 64 Orlando Miller	.10	.05	.01
□ 65 Mike Mussina	.60	.25	.07
□ 66 Jim Eisenreich	.10	.05	.01
□ 67 Felix Fermin	.10	.05	.01
□ 68 Bernie Williams	.50	.23	.06
□ 69 Robb Nen	.10	.05	.01
□ 70 Ron Gant	.50	.23	.06
□ 71 Felipe Lira	.10	.05	.01
□ 72 Jacob Brumfield	.10	.05	.01
□ 73 John Mabry	.50	.23	.06
□ 74 Mark Carreon	.10	.05	.01
□ 75 Carlos Baerga	.50	.23	.06
□ 76 Jim Dougherty	.10	.05	.01
□ 77 Ryan Thompson	.10	.05	.01
□ 78 Scott Leius	.10	.05	.01
□ 79 Roger Pavlik	.10	.05	.01
□ 80 Gary Sheffield	.50	.23	.06
□ 81 Julian Tavarez	.10	.05	.01
□ 82 Andy Ashby	.10	.05	.01
□ 83 Mark Lemke	.10	.05	.01
□ 84 Omar Vizquel	.10	.05	.01
□ 85 Darren Daulton	.25	.11	.03
□ 86 Mike Lansing	.10	.05	.01
□ 87 Rusty Greer	.50	.23	.06
□ 88 Dave Stevens	.10	.05	.01
□ 89 Jose Offerman	.10	.05	.01
□ 90 Tom Henke	.25	.11	.03
□ 91 Troy O'Leary	.10	.05	.01
□ 92 Michael Tucker	.25	.11	.03
□ 93 Marvin Freeman	.10	.05	.01
□ 94 Alex Diaz	.10	.05	.01
□ 95 John Wetteland	.25	.11	.03
□ 96 Cal Ripken 2131	3.00	1.35	.35
□ 97 Mike Mimbs	.10	.05	.01
□ 98 Bobby Higginson	.50	.23	.06
□ 99 Edgardo Alfonzo	.25	.11	.03
□ 100 Frank Thomas	3.00	1.35	.35
□ 101 Steve Gibralter Bob Abreu	.25	.11	.03

☐ 102 Brian Givens T.J. Mathews	.10	.05	.01
☐ 103 Chris Pritchett Trenidad Hubbard	.10	.05	.01
☐ 104 Eric Owens Butch Huskey	.25	.11	.03
☐ 105 Doug Drabek	.10	.05	.01
☐ 106 Tomas Perez	.10	.05	.01
☐ 107 Mark Leiter	.10	.05	.01
☐ 108 Joe Oliver	.10	.05	.01
☐ 109 Tony Castillo	.10	.05	.01
☐ 110 Checklist (1-110)	.10	.05	.01
☐ 111 Kevin Seitzer	.10	.05	.01
☐ 112 Pete Schourek	.25	.11	.03
☐ 113 Sean Berry	.10	.05	.01
☐ 114 Todd Stottlemyre	.10	.05	.01
☐ 115 Joe Carter	.50	.23	.06
☐ 116 Jeff King	.25	.11	.03
☐ 117 Dan Wilson	.10	.05	.01
☐ 118 Kurt Abbott	.10	.05	.01
☐ 119 Lyle Mouton	.10	.05	.01
☐ 120 Jose Rijo	.10	.05	.01
☐ 121 Curtis Goodwin	.10	.05	.01
☐ 122 Jose Valentin	.10	.05	.01
☐ 123 Ellis Burks	.50	.23	.06
☐ 124 David Cone	.50	.23	.06
☐ 125 Eddie Murray	.75	.35	.09
☐ 126 Brian Jordan	.50	.23	.06
☐ 127 Darrin Fletcher	.10	.05	.01
☐ 128 Curt Schilling	.10	.05	.01
☐ 129 Ozzie Guillen	.10	.05	.01
☐ 130 Kenny Rogers	.10	.05	.01
☐ 131 Tom Pagnozzi	.10	.05	.01
☐ 132 Garret Anderson	.50	.23	.06
☐ 133 Bobby Jones	.10	.05	.01
☐ 134 Chris Gomez	.10	.05	.01
☐ 135 Mike Stanley	.10	.05	.01
☐ 136 Hideo Nomo	.75	.35	.09
☐ 137 Jon Nunnally	.10	.05	.01
☐ 138 Tim Wakefield	.10	.05	.01
☐ 139 Steve Finley	.50	.23	.06
☐ 140 Ivan Rodriguez	.60	.25	.07
☐ 141 Quilvio Veras	.10	.05	.01
☐ 142 Mike Fetters	.10	.05	.01
☐ 143 Mike Greenwell	.10	.05	.01
☐ 144 Bill Pulsipher	.25	.11	.03
☐ 145 Mark McGwire	1.00	.45	.12
☐ 146 Frank Castillo	.10	.05	.01
☐ 147 Greg Vaughn	.50	.23	.06
☐ 148 Pat Hentgen	.50	.23	.06
☐ 149 Walt Weiss	.10	.05	.01
☐ 150 Randy Johnson	.50	.23	.06
☐ 151 David Segui	.10	.05	.01
☐ 152 Benji Gil	.10	.05	.01
☐ 153 Tom Candiotti	.10	.05	.01
☐ 154 Geronimo Berroa	.25	.11	.03
☐ 155 John Franco	.10	.05	.01
☐ 156 Jay Bell	.25	.11	.03
☐ 157 Mark Gubicza	.10	.05	.01
☐ 158 Hal Morris	.10	.05	.01
☐ 159 Wilson Alvarez	.50	.23	.06
☐ 160 Derek Bell	.50	.23	.06
☐ 161 Ricky Bottalico	.10	.05	.01
☐ 162 Bret Boone	.10	.05	.01
☐ 163 Brad Radke	.10	.05	.01
☐ 164 John Valentin	.50	.23	.06
☐ 165 Steve Avery	.25	.11	.03
☐ 166 Mark McLemore	.10	.05	.01
☐ 167 Danny Jackson	.10	.05	.01
☐ 168 Tino Martinez	.50	.23	.06
☐ 169 Shane Reynolds	.10	.05	.01
☐ 170 Terry Pendleton	.25	.11	.03
☐ 171 Jim Edmonds	.50	.23	.06
☐ 172 Esteban Loaiza	.10	.05	.01
☐ 173 Ray Durham	.50	.23	.06
☐ 174 Carlos Perez	.10	.05	.01
☐ 175 Raul Mondesi	.50	.23	.06
☐ 176 Steve Ontiveros	.10	.05	.01
☐ 177 Chipper Jones	2.00	.90	.25
☐ 178 Otis Nixon	.10	.05	.01
☐ 179 John Burkett	.10	.05	.01
☐ 180 Gregg Jefferies	.50	.23	.06
☐ 181 Denny Martinez	.25	.11	.03
☐ 182 Ken Caminiti	.50	.23	.06
☐ 183 Doug Jones	.10	.05	.01
☐ 184 Brian McRae	.10	.05	.01
☐ 185 Don Mattingly	1.50	.70	.19
☐ 186 Mel Rojas	.25	.11	.03
☐ 187 Marty Cordova	.50	.23	.06
☐ 188 Vinny Castilla	.50	.23	.06
☐ 189 John Smoltz	.50	.23	.06
☐ 190 Travis Fryman	.50	.23	.06
☐ 191 Chris Hoiles	.10	.05	.01
☐ 192 Chuck Finley	.10	.05	.01
☐ 193 Ryan Klesko	.60	.25	.07
☐ 194 Alex Fernandez	.50	.23	.06
☐ 195 Dante Bichette	.50	.23	.06
☐ 196 Eric Karros	.50	.23	.06
☐ 197 Roger Clemens	.50	.23	.06
☐ 198 Randy Myers	.10	.05	.01
☐ 199 Tony Phillips	.25	.11	.03
☐ 200 Cal Ripken	2.50	1.10	.30
☐ 201 Rod Beck	.25	.11	.03
☐ 202 Chad Curtis	.10	.05	.01
☐ 203 Jack McDowell	.50	.23	.06
☐ 204 Gary Gaetti	.25	.11	.03
☐ 205 Ken Griffey Jr.	3.00	1.35	.35
☐ 206 Ramon Martinez	.25	.11	.03
☐ 207 Jeff Kent	.10	.05	.01
☐ 208 Brad Ausmus	.10	.05	.01
☐ 209 Devon White	.10	.05	.01
☐ 210 Jason Giambi	.50	.23	.06
☐ 211 Nomar Garciaparra	.75	.35	.09
☐ 212 Billy Wagner	.10	.05	.01
☐ 213 Todd Greene	.25	.11	.03
☐ 214 Paul Wilson	.25	.11	.03
☐ 215 Johnny Damon	.25	.11	.03
☐ 216 Alan Benes	.50	.23	.06
☐ 217 Karim Garcia	.60	.25	.07
☐ 218 Dustin Hermanson	.25	.11	.03
☐ 219 Derek Jeter	2.00	.90	.25
☐ 220 Checklist (111-220)	.10	.05	.01
☐ 221 Kirby Puckett STP	.30	.14	.04
☐ 222 Cal Ripken STP	.75	.35	.09
☐ 223 Albert Belle STP	.50	.23	.06
☐ 224 Randy Johnson STP	.30	.14	.04
☐ 225 Wade Boggs STP	.30	.14	.04
☐ 226 Carlos Baerga STP	.30	.14	.04
☐ 227 Ivan Rodriguez STP	.30	.14	.04
☐ 228 Mike Mussina STP	.30	.14	.04
☐ 229 Frank Thomas STP	1.00	.45	.12
☐ 230 Ken Griffey Jr. STP	1.00	.45	.12
☐ 231 Jose Mesa STP	.05	.02	.01
☐ 232 Matt Morris	.40	.18	.05
☐ 233 Craig Wilson	.30	.14	.04
☐ 234 Alvie Shepherd	.20	.09	.03
☐ 235 Randy Winn	.15	.07	.02
☐ 236 David Yocum	.15	.07	.02
☐ 237 Jason Brester	.15	.07	.02
☐ 238 Shane Monahan	.50	.23	.06
☐ 239 Brian McNichol	.15	.07	.02
☐ 240 Reggie Taylor	.15	.07	.02
☐ 241 Garrett Long	.15	.07	.02
☐ 242 Jonathan Johnson	.30	.14	.04
☐ 243 Jeff Liefer	.50	.23	.06
☐ 244 Brian Powell	.15	.07	.02
☐ 245 Brian Buchanan	.15	.07	.02
☐ 246 Mike Piazza	1.25	.55	.16
☐ 247 Edgar Martinez	.30	.14	.04
☐ 248 Chuck Knoblauch	.30	.14	.04
☐ 249 Andres Galarraga	.30	.14	.04
☐ 250 Tony Gwynn	.75	.35	.09
☐ 251 Lee Smith	.30	.14	.04
☐ 252 Sammy Sosa	.30	.14	.04
☐ 253 Jim Thome	.40	.18	.05
☐ 254 Frank Rodriguez	.15	.07	.02
☐ 255 Charlie Hayes	.15	.07	.02
☐ 256 Bernard Gilkey	.30	.14	.04
☐ 257 John Smiley	.10	.05	.01
☐ 258 Brady Anderson	.30	.14	.04
☐ 259 Rico Brogna	.15	.07	.02
☐ 260 Kirt Manwaring	.05	.02	.01
☐ 261 Len Dykstra	.15	.07	.02
☐ 262 Tom Glavine	.30	.14	.04
☐ 263 Vince Coleman	.15	.07	.02
☐ 264 John Olerud	.10	.05	.01
☐ 265 Orlando Merced	.15	.07	.02
☐ 266 Kent Mercker	.05	.02	.01
☐ 267 Terry Steinbach	.15	.07	.02
☐ 268 Brian L. Hunter	.15	.07	.02
☐ 269 Jeff Fassero	.05	.02	.01
☐ 270 Jay Buhner	.30	.14	.04

□ 271 Jeff Brantley	.10	.05	.01
□ 272 Tim Raines	.30	.14	.04
□ 273 Jimmy Key	.15	.07	.02
□ 274 Mo Vaughn	.50	.23	.06
□ 275 Andre Dawson	.30	.14	.04
□ 276 Jose Mesa	.15	.07	.02
□ 277 Brett Butler	.10	.05	.01
□ 278 Luis Gonzalez	.15	.07	.02
□ 279 Steve Sparks	.05	.02	.01
□ 280 Chili Davis	.15	.07	.02
□ 281 Carl Everett	.15	.07	.02
□ 282 Jeff Cirillo	.15	.07	.02
□ 283 Thomas Howard	.05	.02	.01
□ 284 Paul O'Neill	.15	.07	.02
□ 285 Pat Meares	.15	.07	.02
□ 286 Mickey Tettleton	.15	.07	.02
□ 287 Rey Sanchez	.05	.02	.01
□ 288 Bip Roberts	.15	.07	.02
□ 289 Roberto Alomar	.50	.23	.06
□ 290 Ruben Sierra	.15	.07	.02
□ 291 John Flaherty	.05	.02	.01
□ 292 Bret Saberhagen	.15	.07	.02
□ 293 Barry Larkin	.30	.14	.04
□ 294 Sandy Alomar	.15	.07	.02
□ 295 Ed Sprague	.15	.07	.02
□ 296 Gary DiSarcina	.05	.02	.01
□ 297 Marquis Grissom	.30	.14	.04
□ 298 John Frascatore	.10	.05	.01
□ 299 Will Clark	.30	.14	.04
□ 300 Barry Bonds	.50	.23	.06
□ 301 Ozzie Smith	.40	.18	.05
□ 302 Dave Nilsson	.15	.07	.02
□ 303 Pedro Martinez	.15	.07	.02
□ 304 Joey Cora	.05	.02	.01
□ 305 Rick Aguilera	.15	.07	.02
□ 306 Craig Biggio	.30	.14	.04
□ 307 Jose Vizcaino	.15	.07	.02
□ 308 Jeff Montgomery	.10	.05	.01
□ 309 Moises Alou	.15	.07	.02
□ 310 Robin Ventura	.30	.14	.04
□ 311 David Wells	.15	.07	.02
□ 312 Delino DeShields	.15	.07	.02
□ 313 Trevor Hoffman	.15	.07	.02
□ 314 Andy Benes	.15	.07	.02
□ 315 Deion Sanders	.30	.14	.04
□ 316 Jim Bullinger	.05	.02	.01
□ 317 John Jaha	.15	.07	.02
□ 318 Greg Maddux	1.25	.55	.16
□ 319 Tim Salmon	.30	.14	.04
□ 320 Ben McDonald	.15	.07	.02
□ 321 Sandy Martinez	.05	.02	.01
□ 322 Dan Miceli	.05	.02	.01
□ 323 Wade Boggs	.30	.14	.04
□ 324 Ismael Valdes	.15	.07	.02
□ 325 Juan Gonzalez	1.00	.45	.12
□ 326 Charles Nagy	.15	.07	.02
□ 327 Ray Lankford	.30	.14	.04
□ 328 Mark Portugal	.05	.02	.01
□ 329 Bobby Bonilla	.30	.14	.04
□ 330 Reggie Sanders	.30	.14	.04
□ 331 Jamie Brewington	.05	.02	.01
□ 332 Aaron Sele	.05	.02	.01
□ 333 Pete Harnisch	.05	.02	.01
□ 334 Cliff Floyd	.15	.07	.02
□ 335 Cal Eldred	.05	.02	.01
□ 336 Jason Bates	.05	.02	.01
□ 337 Tony Clark	.30	.14	.04
□ 338 Jose Herrera	.05	.02	.01
□ 339 Alex Ochoa	.15	.07	.02
□ 340 Mark Loretta	.05	.02	.01
□ 341 Donne Wall	.05	.02	.01
□ 342 Jason Kendall	.30	.14	.04
□ 343 Shannon Stewart	.05	.02	.01
□ 344 Brooks Kieschnick	.05	.02	.01
□ 345 Chris Snopek	.05	.02	.01
□ 346 Ruben Rivera	.40	.18	.05
□ 347 Jeff Suppan	.05	.02	.01
□ 348 Phil Nevin	.15	.07	.02
□ 349 John Wasdin	.05	.02	.01
□ 350 Jay Payton	.30	.14	.04
□ 351 Tim Crabtree	.05	.02	.01
□ 352 Rick Krivda	.05	.02	.01
□ 353 Bob Wolcott	.05	.02	.01
□ 354 Jimmy Haynes	.05	.02	.01
□ 355 Herb Perry	.05	.02	.01
□ 356 Ryne Sandberg	.50	.23	.06
□ 357 Harold Baines	.15	.07	.02
□ 358 Chad Ogea	.05	.02	.01
□ 359 Lee Tinsley	.05	.02	.01
□ 360 Matt Williams	.30	.14	.04
□ 361 Randy Velarde	.05	.02	.01
□ 362 Jose Canseco	.30	.14	.04
□ 363 Larry Walker	.30	.14	.04
□ 364 Kevin Appier	.15	.07	.02
□ 365 Darryl Hamilton	.05	.02	.01
□ 366 Jose Lima	.05	.02	.01
□ 367 Javy Lopez	.30	.14	.04
□ 368 Dennis Eckersley	.30	.14	.04
□ 369 Jason Isringhausen	.15	.07	.02
□ 370 Mickey Morandini	.05	.02	.01
□ 371 Scott Cooper	.05	.02	.01
□ 372 Jim Abbott	.30	.14	.04
□ 373 Paul Sorrento	.15	.07	.02
□ 374 Chris Hammond	.05	.02	.01
□ 375 Lance Johnson	.15	.07	.02
□ 376 Kevin Brown	.15	.07	.02
□ 377 Luis Alicea	.05	.02	.01
□ 378 Andy Pettitte	.60	.25	.07
□ 379 Dean Palmer	.30	.14	.04
□ 380 Jeff Bagwell	.75	.35	.09
□ 381 Jaime Navarro	.05	.02	.01
□ 382 Rondell White	.30	.14	.04
□ 383 Erik Hanson	.05	.02	.01
□ 384 Pedro Munoz	.15	.07	.02
□ 385 Heathcliff Slocumb	.15	.07	.02
□ 386 Wally Joyner	.15	.07	.02
□ 387 Bob Tewksbury	.05	.02	.01
□ 388 David Bell	.05	.02	.01
□ 389 Fred McGriff	.30	.14	.04
□ 390 Mike Henneman	.15	.07	.02
□ 391 Robby Thompson	.05	.02	.01
□ 392 Norm Charlton	.05	.02	.01
□ 393 Cecil Fielder	.30	.14	.04
□ 394 Benito Santiago	.15	.07	.02
□ 395 Rafael Palmeiro	.30	.14	.04
□ 396 Ricky Bones	.05	.02	.01
□ 397 Rickey Henderson	.30	.14	.04
□ 398 C.J. Nitkowski	.05	.02	.01
□ 399 Shawon Dunston	.05	.02	.01
□ 400 Manny Ramirez	.50	.23	.06
□ 401 Bill Swift	.05	.02	.01
□ 402 Chad Fonville	.05	.02	.01
□ 403 Joey Hamilton	.15	.07	.02
□ 404 Alex Gonzalez	.05	.02	.01
□ 405 Roberto Hernandez	.15	.07	.02
□ 406 Jeff Blauser	.05	.02	.01
□ 407 LaTroy Hawkins	.05	.02	.01
□ 408 Greg Colbrunn	.05	.02	.01
□ 409 Todd Hundley	.30	.14	.04
□ 410 Glenn Dishman	.05	.02	.01
□ 411 Joe Vitiello	.05	.02	.01
□ 412 Todd Worrell	.15	.07	.02
□ 413 Wil Cordero	.05	.02	.01
□ 414 Ken Hill	.15	.07	.02
□ 415 Carlos Garcia	.15	.07	.02
□ 416 Bryan Rekar	.05	.02	.01
□ 417 Shawn Green	.05	.02	.01
□ 418 Tyler Green	.05	.02	.01
□ 419 Mike Blowers	.05	.02	.01
□ 420 Kenny Lofton	.50	.23	.06
□ 421 Denny Neagle	.15	.07	.02
□ 422 Jeff Conine	.15	.07	.02
□ 423 Mark Langston	.15	.07	.02
□ 424 Steve Cox Jesse Ibarra Derrek Lee Ron Wright	1.50	.70	.19
□ 425 Jim Bonnici Billy Owens Richie Sexson Daryle Ward	.50	.23	.06
□ 426 Kevin Jordan Bobby Morris Desi Relaford Adam Riggs	.15	.07	.02
□ 427 Tim Harkrider Rey Ordonez Neifi Perez Enrique Wilson	.15	.07	.02
□ 428 Bartolo Colon Doug Million Rafael Orellano	.15	.07	.02

Ray Ricken			
□ 429 Jeff D'Amico	.15	.07	.02
Marty Janzen			
Gary Rath			
Clint Sodowsky			
□ 430 Matt Drews	.15	.07	.02
Rich Hunter			
Matt Ruebel			
Bret Wagner			
□ 431 Jaime Bluma	.30	.14	.04
David Coggin			
Steve Montgomery			
Brandon Reed			
□ 432 Mike Figga	.15	.07	.02
Raul Ibanez			
Paul Konerko			
Julio Mosquera			
□ 433 Brian Barber	.15	.07	.02
Marc Kroon			
Marc Valdes			
Don Wengert			
□ 434 George Arias	1.25	.55	.16
Chris Haas			
Scott Rolen			
Scott Spiezio			
□ 435 Brian Banks	5.00	2.20	.60
Vladimir Guerrero			
Andruw Jones			
Billy McMillon			
□ 436 Roger Cedeno	.75	.35	.09
Derrick Gibson			
Ben Grieve			
Shane Spencer			
□ 437 Anton French	.30	.14	.04
Demond Smith			
Darond Stovall			
Keith Williams			
□ 438 Michael Coleman	.30	.14	.04
Jacob Cruz			
Richard Hidalgo			
Charles Peterson			
□ 439 Trey Beamon	.50	.23	.06
Yamil Benitez			
Jermaine Dye			
Angel Echevarria			
□ 440 Checklist	.05	.02	.01
□ F7 Sealed Mantle Last Day	8.00	3.60	1.00

1996 Topps Classic Confrontations

These cards were inserted at a rate of one in every 5-card retail pack sold at Walmart. The first ten cards showcase hitters, while the last five cards feature pitchers. Inside white borders, the fronts show player cutouts on a brownish rock background featuring a shadow image of the player. The player's name is gold foil stamped across the bottom. The horizontal backs of the hitters' cards are aqua and present headshots and statistics. The backs of the pitchers cards are purple and present the same information.

	MINT	NRMT	EXC
COMPLETE SET (15)	6.00	2.70	.75
COMMON CARD (CC1-CC15)	.15	.07	.02
SEMISTARS	.30	.14	.04
ONE PER SPECIAL SER.1 RETAIL PACK			

□ CC1 Ken Griffey Jr.	1.50	.70	.19
□ CC2 Cal Ripken	1.25	.55	.16
□ CC3 Edgar Martinez	.30	.14	.04
□ CC4 Kirby Puckett	.50	.23	.06
□ CC5 Frank Thomas	1.50	.70	.19
□ CC6 Barry Bonds	.40	.18	.05
□ CC7 Reggie Sanders	.15	.07	.02
□ CC8 Andres Galarraga	.30	.14	.04
□ CC9 Tony Gwynn	.60	.25	.07
□ CC10 Mike Piazza	1.00	.45	.12
□ CC11 Randy Johnson	.30	.14	.04
□ CC12 Mike Mussina	.30	.14	.04
□ CC13 Roger Clemens	.30	.14	.04
□ CC14 Tom Glavine	.30	.14	.04
□ CC15 Greg Maddux	1.00	.45	.12

1996 Topps Mantle

Randomly inserted in packs, these cards are reprints of the original Mickey Mantle cards issued from 1951 through 1969. The fronts look the same except for a commemorative stamp, while the backs clearly state that they are "Mickey Mantle Commemorative" cards and have a 1996 copyright date. These cards honor Yankee great Mickey Mantle, who passed away in August 1995 after a gallant battle against cancer. Based on evidence from an uncut sheet auctioned off at the 1996 Kit Young Hawaii Trade Show, some collectors/dealers believe that cards 15 through 19 were slightly shorter printed in relation to the other 14 cards.

	MINT	NRMT	EXC
COMPLETE SET (19)	150.00	70.00	19.00
COMMON MANTLE (1-14)	8.00	3.60	1.00
COMMON MANTLE SP (15-19)	12.00	5.50	1.50
CARDS 15-19 SHORTPRINTED BY 20%			
RANDOM INSERTS IN SER.1 PACKS			
FOUR PER CEREAL FACT.SET			

□ 1 1951 Bowman	15.00	6.75	1.85
□ 2 1952 Topps	18.00	8.00	2.20
□ 3 1953 Topps	10.00	4.50	1.25

1996 Topps Mantle Case

These 19 cards were inserted as one per case chiptoppers in second series Hobby, Jumbo or Vending Case. Similar to the regular issue, the last five cards were printed in less quantities than the other 14 cards.

	MINT	NRMT	EXC
COMPLETE SET (19)	1000.00	450.00	125.00
COMMON MANTLE (1-14)	50.00	22.00	6.25
COMMON MANTLE SP (15-19)	60.00	27.00	7.50
CARDS 15-19 SHORTPRINTED BY 20%			
ONE PER SER.2 HOBBY/JUMBO/VEND CASE			

□ 1 1951 Bowman	75.00	34.00	9.50
□ 2 1952 Topps	125.00	55.00	15.50
□ 3 1953 Topps	60.00	27.00	7.50

1996 Topps Mantle Finest

Randomly inserted in packs at a rate of one in 18, this 19-card set is a reprint of the regular insert set using Finest technology. Each card front is covered with the exclusive Topps Finest Protector to guarantee its brilliant uncirculated condition.

	MINT	NRMT	EXC
COMPLETE SET (19)	150.00	70.00	19.00
COMMON MANTLE (1-14)	8.00	3.60	1.00
COMMON MANTLE SP (15-19)	12.00	5.50	1.50
CARDS 15-19 SHORTPRINTED BY 20%			
RANDOM INSERTS IN SER.2 PACKS			
□ 1 1951 Bowman	15.00	6.75	1.85
□ 2 1952 Topps	20.00	9.00	2.50
□ 3 1953 Topps	10.00	4.50	1.25

1996 Topps Mantle Finest Refractors

Randomly inserted at the rate of one in 144 packs, this 19-card set is parallel to the regular set and is similar in design. It is distinguished from the regular set by the refractive quality of the cards.

	MINT	NRMT	EXC
COMPLETE SET (19)	900.00	400.00	110.00
COMMON MANTLE (1-14)	50.00	22.00	6.25
COMMON MANTLE SP (15-19)	60.00	27.00	7.50
CARDS 15-19 SHORTPRINTED BY 20%			
RANDOM INSERTS IN SER.2 PACKS			
□ 1 1951 Bowman	100.00	45.00	12.50
□ 2 1952 Topps	150.00	70.00	19.00
□ 3 1953 Topps	60.00	27.00	7.50

1996 Topps Mantle Redemption

Randomly inserted at the rate of one in 108 packs, this 19-card set features redemption cards that made the collector eligible to win the original card whose reprinted design is portrayed on that redemption card front. Only 76 original Mantle cards were to be given away.

	MINT	NRMT	EXC
COMPLETE SET (19)	350.00	160.00	45.00
COMMON MANTLE (1-19)	20.00	9.00	2.50
RANDOM INSERTS IN SER.2 PACKS			
NNO CARDS LISTED BELOW IN YR ORDER			
REDEMPTION DEADLINE: 10/15/96			
□ 1 1951 Bowman (2)	30.00	13.50	3.70
□ 2 1952 Topps (1)	50.00	22.00	6.25
□ 3 1953 Topps (4)	30.00	13.50	3.70

1996 Topps Masters of the Game

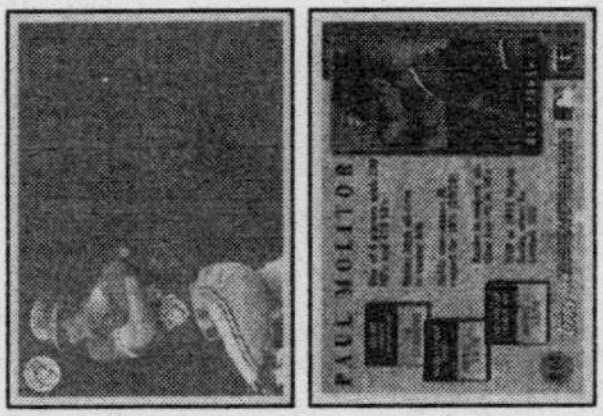

This 20-card standard-size set was randomly inserted into hobby packs. The horizontal fronts comprise of silver foil set against white borders. The left side of the card has a player photo. The words "Master of the Game" and the player's name are printed on the right. The horizontal backs have a player photo, a brief write-up and some quick important dates in the player's career. The cards are numbered with a "MG" prefix in the lower left corner.

	MINT	NRMT	EXC
COMPLETE SET (20)	40.00	18.00	5.00
COMMON CARD (1-20)	.75	.35	.09
SEMISTARS	1.25	.55	.16
RANDOM INSERTS IN SER.1 HOBBY PACKS			
TWO PER HOBBY FACTORY SET			
□ 1 Dennis Eckersley	1.25	.55	.16
□ 2 Denny Martinez	.75	.35	.09
□ 3 Eddie Murray	2.50	1.10	.30
□ 4 Paul Molitor	2.00	.90	.25
□ 5 Ozzie Smith	2.00	.90	.25
□ 6 Rickey Henderson	1.25	.55	.16
□ 7 Tim Raines	.75	.35	.09
□ 8 Lee Smith	1.25	.55	.16
□ 9 Cal Ripken	8.00	3.60	1.00
□ 10 Chili Davis	.75	.35	.09
□ 11 Wade Boggs	1.25	.55	.16
□ 12 Tony Gwynn	4.00	1.80	.50
□ 13 Don Mattingly	5.00	2.20	.60
□ 14 Bret Saberhagen	.75	.35	.09
□ 15 Kirby Puckett	3.00	1.35	.35
□ 16 Joe Carter	1.25	.55	.16
□ 17 Roger Clemens	1.25	.55	.16
□ 18 Barry Bonds	2.50	1.10	.30
□ 19 Greg Maddux	6.00	2.70	.75
□ 20 Frank Thomas	10.00	4.50	1.25

1996 Topps Mystery Finest

Randomly inserted in packs, this 26-card standard-size set features a bit of a mystery. The fronts have opaque coating that must be removed before the player can be identified. After the opaque coating is removed, the fronts feature a player photo surrounded by silver borders. The backs feature a choice of players along with a corresponding mystery finest trivia fact. Some of these cards were also issued with refractor fronts. These cards are more difficult to find and sell for a multiple of the listed prices below.

	MINT	NRMT	EXC
COMPLETE SET (26)	150.00	70.00	19.00
COMMON CARD (M1-M26)	1.50	.70	.19
SEMISTARS	2.50	1.10	.30
REFRACTORS: 3X BASIC CARDS			
RANDOM INSERTS IN SER.1 PACKS			
□ M1 Hideo Nomo	5.00	2.20	.60
□ M2 Greg Maddux	12.00	5.50	1.50
□ M3 Randy Johnson	3.00	1.35	.35
□ M4 Chipper Jones	12.00	5.50	1.50
□ M5 Marty Cordova	1.50	.70	.19
□ M6 Garret Anderson	1.50	.70	.19
□ M7 Cal Ripken	15.00	6.75	1.85
□ M8 Kirby Puckett	6.00	2.70	.75
□ M9 Tony Gwynn	8.00	3.60	1.00

□ M10 Manny Ramirez	5.00	2.20	.60
□ M11 Jim Edmonds	1.50	.70	.19
□ M12 Mike Piazza	12.00	5.50	1.50
□ M13 Barry Bonds	5.00	2.20	.60
□ M14 Raul Mondesi	2.50	1.10	.30
□ M15 Sammy Sosa	3.00	1.35	.35
□ M16 Ken Griffey Jr.	20.00	9.00	2.50
□ M17 Albert Belle	10.00	4.50	1.25
□ M18 Dante Bichette	2.50	1.10	.30
□ M19 Mo Vaughn	5.00	2.20	.60
□ M20 Jeff Bagwell	8.00	3.60	1.00
□ M21 Frank Thomas	20.00	9.00	2.50
□ M22 Hideo Nomo	5.00	2.20	.60
□ M23 Cal Ripken	15.00	6.75	1.85
□ M24 Mike Piazza	12.00	5.50	1.50
□ M25 Ken Griffey Jr.	20.00	9.00	2.50
□ M26 Frank Thomas	20.00	9.00	2.50

1996 Topps Power Boosters

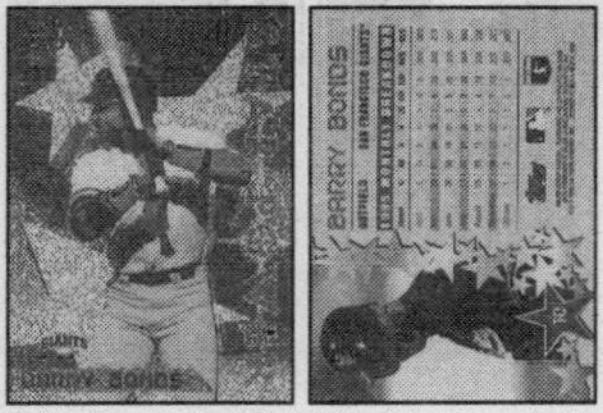

Randomly inserted into packs, these cards are a metallic version of 25 of the first 26 cards from the basic Topps set. Card numbers 1-6 and 8-12 were issued in retail packs, while numbers 13-26 were issued in hobby packs. Inserted in place of two basic cards, they are printed on 28 point stock and the fronts have prismatic foil printing. Card number 7, which is Mickey Mantle in the regular set, was not issued in a Power Booster form.

	MINT	NRMT	EXC
COMPLETE SET (25)	90.00	40.00	11.00
COMP. STAR POWER SET (11)	50.00	22.00	6.25
COMP. DRAFT PICKS SET (14)	40.00	18.00	5.00
COMMON STAR POWER (1-6/8-12)	1.50	.70	.19
COMMON DRAFT PICK (12-26)	2.50	1.10	.30
STAR POWER SEMISTARS	2.50	1.10	.30
DRAFT PICK SEMISTARS	4.00	1.80	.50
CARD #7 DOES NOT EXIST			
1-6/8-12 RANDOM INS.IN SER.1 RETAIL PACKS			
13-26 RANDOM INS.IN SER.1 HOBBY PACKS			

□ 1 Tony Gwynn	8.00	3.60	1.00
□ 2 Mike Piazza	12.00	5.50	1.50
□ 3 Greg Maddux	12.00	5.50	1.50
□ 4 Jeff Bagwell	8.00	3.60	1.00
□ 5 Larry Walker	1.50	.70	.19
□ 6 Barry Larkin	2.50	1.10	.30
□ 8 Tom Glavine	2.50	1.10	.30
□ 9 Craig Biggio	2.50	1.10	.30
□ 10 Barry Bonds	5.00	2.20	.60
□ 11 Heathcliff Slocumb	1.50	.70	.19
□ 12 Matt Williams	2.50	1.10	.30
□ 13 Todd Helton	15.00	6.75	1.85
□ 14 Mark Redman	2.50	1.10	.30
□ 15 Michael Barrett	2.50	1.10	.30
□ 16 Ben Davis	5.00	2.20	.60
□ 17 Juan LeBron	4.00	1.80	.50
□ 18 Tony McKnight	2.50	1.10	.30
□ 19 Ryan Jaroncyk	2.50	1.10	.30
□ 20 Corey Jenkins	4.00	1.80	.50
□ 21 Jim Scharrer	2.50	1.10	.30
□ 22 Mark Bellhorn	2.50	1.10	.30
□ 23 Jarrod Washburn	2.50	1.10	.30
□ 24 Geoff Jenkins	5.00	2.20	.60
□ 25 Sean Casey	8.00	3.60	1.00
□ 26 Brett Tomko	2.50	1.10	.30

1996 Topps Profiles

Randomly inserted into packs, this 20-card standard-size set features 10 players from each league. Topps spokesmen Kirby Puckett (AL) and Tony Gwynn (NL) give opinions on players within their league. The fronts feature a player photo set against a silver-foil background. The playerís name is on the bottom. A photo of either Gwynn or Puckett as well as the words "Profiles by ..." is on the right. The backs feature a player photo, some career data as well as Gwynn's or Puckett's opinion about the featured player. The cards are numbered with either an "AL or NL" prefix on the back depending on the player's league. The cards are sequenced in alphabetical order within league.

	MINT	NRMT	EXC
COMPLETE SET (40)	40.00	18.00	5.00
COMPLETE SERIES 1 (20)	30.00	13.50	3.70
COMPLETE SERIES 2 (20)	10.00	4.50	1.25
COMMON SER.1 (AL1-AL10)	.50	.23	.06
COMMON SER.1 (NL1-NL10)	.50	.23	.06
COMMON SER.2 (AL11-AL20)	.50	.23	.06
COMMON SER.2 (NL11-NL20)	.50	.23	.06
SEMISTARS	.75	.35	.09
RANDOM INSERTS IN PACKS			
1 SER.1 AND 2 SER.2 PER HOB.FACT.SET			

□ AL1 Roberto Alomar	1.25	.55	.16
□ AL2 Carlos Baerga	.50	.23	.06
□ AL3 Albert Belle	2.50	1.10	.30
□ AL4 Cecil Fielder	.75	.35	.09
□ AL5 Ken Griffey Jr.	5.00	2.20	.60
□ AL6 Randy Johnson	.75	.35	.09
□ AL7 Paul O'Neill	.50	.23	.06
□ AL8 Cal Ripken	4.00	1.80	.50
□ AL9 Frank Thomas	5.00	2.20	.60
□ AL10 Mo Vaughn	1.25	.55	.16
□ AL11 Jay Buhner	.75	.35	.09
□ AL12 Marty Cordova	.50	.23	.06
□ AL13 Jim Edmonds	.50	.23	.06
□ AL14 Juan Gonzalez	2.50	1.10	.30
□ AL15 Kenny Lofton	1.25	.55	.16
□ AL16 Edgar Martinez	.75	.35	.09
□ AL17 Don Mattingly	2.50	1.10	.30
□ AL18 Mark McGwire	1.50	.70	.19
□ AL19 Rafael Palmeiro	.75	.35	.09
□ AL20 Tim Salmon	.50	.23	.06
□ NL1 Jeff Bagwell	2.00	.90	.25
□ NL2 Derek Bell	.50	.23	.06
□ NL3 Barry Bonds	1.25	.55	.16
□ NL4 Greg Maddux	3.00	1.35	.35
□ NL5 Fred McGriff	.75	.35	.09
□ NL6 Raul Mondesi	.75	.35	.09
□ NL7 Mike Piazza	3.00	1.35	.35
□ NL8 Reggie Sanders	.50	.23	.06
□ NL9 Sammy Sosa	.75	.35	.09
□ NL10 Larry Walker	.50	.23	.06
□ NL11 Dante Bichette	.75	.35	.09
□ NL12 Andres Galarraga	.75	.35	.09
□ NL13 Ron Gant	.75	.35	.09
□ NL14 Tom Glavine	.75	.35	.09
□ NL15 Chipper Jones	3.00	1.35	.35
□ NL16 David Justice	.50	.23	.06
□ NL17 Barry Larkin	.75	.35	.09
□ NL18 Hideo Nomo	1.25	.55	.16
□ NL19 Gary Sheffield	.75	.35	.09
□ NL20 Matt Williams	.75	.35	.09

1996 Topps Road Warriors

This 20-card set was inserted only into Wal-mart packs and featured leading hitters of the majors. The set is sequenced in alphabetical order.

	MINT	NRMT	EXC
COMPLETE SET (20)	12.00	5.50	1.50
COMMON CARD (RW1-RW20)	.25	.11	.03
SEMISTARS	.50	.23	.06
ONE PER SPECIAL SER.2 RETAIL PACK			

□ RW1 Derek Bell	.25	.11	.03
□ RW2 Albert Belle	2.00	.90	.25
□ RW3 Craig Biggio	.50	.23	.06
□ RW4 Barry Bonds	1.00	.45	.12
□ RW5 Jay Buhner	.50	.23	.06
□ RW6 Jim Edmonds	.25	.11	.03
□ RW7 Gary Gaetti	.50	.23	.06
□ RW8 Ron Gant	.50	.23	.06
□ RW9 Edgar Martinez	.50	.23	.06
□ RW10 Tino Martinez	.25	.11	.03
□ RW11 Mark McGwire	1.25	.55	.16
□ RW12 Mike Piazza	2.50	1.10	.30
□ RW13 Manny Ramirez	1.00	.45	.12
□ RW14 Tim Salmon	.25	.11	.03
□ RW15 Reggie Sanders	.25	.11	.03
□ RW16 Frank Thomas	4.00	1.80	.50
□ RW17 John Valentin	.25	.11	.03
□ RW18 Mo Vaughn	1.00	.45	.12
□ RW19 Robin Ventura	.50	.23	.06
□ RW20 Matt Williams	.50	.23	.06

1996 Topps Wrecking Crew

Randomly inserted in Hobby only packs, this 15-card set honors some of the hottest home run producers in the League. The cards feature color action player photos with foil stamping.

	MINT	NRMT	EXC
COMPLETE SET (15)	70.00	32.00	8.75
COMMON CARD (1-15)	1.50	.70	.19
SEMISTARS	2.50	1.10	.30
RANDOM INSERTS IN SER.2 HOBBY PACKS			
ONE PER HOBBY FACTORY SET			

□ WC1 Jeff Bagwell	8.00	3.60	1.00
□ WC2 Albert Belle	10.00	4.50	1.25
□ WC3 Barry Bonds	5.00	2.20	.60
□ WC4 Jose Canseco	2.50	1.10	.30
□ WC5 Joe Carter	2.50	1.10	.30
□ WC6 Cecil Fielder	2.50	1.10	.30
□ WC7 Ron Gant	1.50	.70	.19
□ WC8 Juan Gonzalez	10.00	4.50	1.25
□ WC9 Ken Griffey Jr.	20.00	9.00	2.50
□ WC10 Fred McGriff	2.50	1.10	.30
□ WC11 Mark McGwire	6.00	2.70	.75
□ WC12 Mike Piazza	12.00	5.50	1.50
□ WC13 Frank Thomas	20.00	9.00	2.50
□ WC14 Mo Vaughn	5.00	2.20	.60
□ WC15 Matt Williams	2.50	1.10	.30

1997 Topps

This 276-card Topps Series I set was distributed in 11-card packs with a suggested retail price of $1.29. The fronts feature a color action player photo with a gloss coating and a spot matte finish on the outside border with gold foil stamping. The backs carry another player photo, player information and statistics. The set includes the following subsets: Season Highlights (#100-104), Prospects (#200-207 with three players on each card), the first ever expansion team cards of the Arizona Diamondbacks (#249-251 with two players on each) and the Tampa Bay Devil Rays (#252-253), and Draft Picks (#269-274 with two players on each card). Card #42 is a special Jackie Robinson tribute card commemorating the 50th anniversary of his contribution to Baseball history and numbered for his Dodgers uniform number.

	MINT	NRMT	EXC
COMPLETE SERIES 1 (276)	20.00	9.00	2.50
COMMON CARD (1-276)	.10	.05	.01
SEMISTARS	.25	.11	.03
STARS	.50	.23	.06
CARDS 7 AND 84 DON'T EXIST			
ELSTER/FETTERS BOTH #61			

□ 1 Barry Bonds	.75	.35	.09
□ 2 Tom Pagnozzi	.10	.05	.01
□ 3 Terrell Wade	.10	.05	.01
□ 4 Jose Valentin	.10	.05	.01
□ 5 Mark Clark	.10	.05	.01
□ 6 Brady Anderson	.50	.23	.06
□ 8 Wade Boggs	.50	.23	.06
□ 9 Scott Stahoviak	.10	.05	.01
□ 10 Andres Galarraga	.50	.23	.06
□ 11 Steve Avery	.10	.05	.01
□ 12 Rusty Greer	.25	.11	.03
□ 13 Derek Jeter	2.00	.90	.25
□ 14 Ricky Bottalico	.25	.11	.03
□ 15 Andy Ashby	.10	.05	.01
□ 16 Paul Shuey	.10	.05	.01
□ 17 F.P. Santangelo	.10	.05	.01
□ 18 Royce Clayton	.10	.05	.01
□ 19 Mike Mohler	.10	.05	.01
□ 20 Mike Piazza	2.00	.90	.25
□ 21 Jaime Navarro	.10	.05	.01
□ 22 Billy Wagner	.25	.11	.03
□ 23 Mike Timlin	.10	.05	.01
□ 24 Garret Anderson	.25	.11	.03
□ 25 Ben McDonald	.10	.05	.01
□ 26 Mel Rojas	.10	.05	.01
□ 27 John Burkett	.10	.05	.01
□ 28 Jeff King	.10	.05	.01

□ 29 Reggie Jefferson	.10	.05	.01
□ 30 Kevin Appier	.25	.11	.03
□ 31 Felipe Lira	.10	.05	.01
□ 32 Kevin Tapani	.10	.05	.01
□ 33 Mark Portugal	.10	.05	.01
□ 34 Carlos Garcia	.10	.05	.01
□ 35 Joey Cora	.10	.05	.01
□ 36 David Segui	.10	.05	.01
□ 37 Mark Grace	.50	.23	.06
□ 38 Erik Hanson	.10	.05	.01
□ 39 Jeff D'Amico	.25	.11	.03
□ 40 Jay Buhner	.50	.23	.06
□ 41 B.J. Surhoff	.10	.05	.01
□ 42 Jackie Robinson TRIB	2.50	1.10	.30
□ 43 Roger Pavlik	.10	.05	.01
□ 44 Hal Morris	.10	.05	.01
□ 45 Mariano Duncan	.10	.05	.01
□ 46 Harold Baines	.25	.11	.03
□ 47 Jorge Fabregas	.10	.05	.01
□ 48 Jose Herrera	.10	.05	.01
□ 49 Jeff Cirillo	.10	.05	.01
□ 50 Tom Glavine	.50	.23	.06
□ 51 Pedro Astacio	.10	.05	.01
□ 52 Mark Gardner	.10	.05	.01
□ 53 Arthur Rhodes	.10	.05	.01
□ 54 Troy O'Leary	.10	.05	.01
□ 55 Bip Roberts	.10	.05	.01
□ 56 Mike Lieberthal	.10	.05	.01
□ 57 Shane Andrews	.10	.05	.01
□ 58 Scott Karl	.10	.05	.01
□ 59 Gary DiSarcina	.10	.05	.01
□ 60 Andy Pettitte	.75	.35	.09
□ 61 Kevin Elster	.10	.05	.01
□ 62 Mark McGwire	1.00	.45	.12
□ 63 Dan Wilson	.10	.05	.01
□ 64 Mickey Morandini	.10	.05	.01
□ 65 Chuck Knoblauch	.50	.23	.06
□ 66 Tim Wakefield	.10	.05	.01
□ 67 Raul Mondesi	.25	.11	.03
□ 68 Todd Jones	.10	.05	.01
□ 69 Albert Belle	1.50	.70	.19
□ 70 Trevor Hoffman	.10	.05	.01
□ 71 Eric Young	.25	.11	.03
□ 72 Robert Perez	.10	.05	.01
□ 73 Butch Huskey	.10	.05	.01
□ 74 Brian McRae	.25	.11	.03
□ 75 Jim Edmonds	.25	.11	.03
□ 76 Mike Henneman	.10	.05	.01
□ 77 Frank Rodriguez	.10	.05	.01
□ 78 Danny Tartabull	.10	.05	.01
□ 79 Robb Nen	.10	.05	.01
□ 80 Reggie Sanders	.25	.11	.03
□ 81 Ron Karkovice	.10	.05	.01
□ 82 Benito Santiago	.10	.05	.01
□ 83 Mike Lansing	.10	.05	.01
□ 84 Mike Fetters UER Card numbered 61	.10	.05	.01
□ 85 Craig Biggio	.25	.11	.03
□ 86 Mike Bordick	.10	.05	.01
□ 87 Ray Lankford	.25	.11	.03
□ 88 Charles Nagy	.25	.11	.03
□ 89 Paul Wilson	.25	.11	.03
□ 90 John Wetteland	.25	.11	.03
□ 91 Tom Candiotti	.10	.05	.01
□ 92 Carlos Delgado	.25	.11	.03
□ 93 Derek Bell	.25	.11	.03
□ 94 Mark Lemke	.10	.05	.01
□ 95 Edgar Martinez	.50	.23	.06
□ 96 Rickey Henderson	.25	.11	.03
□ 97 Greg Myers	.10	.05	.01
□ 98 Jim Leyritz	.10	.05	.01
□ 99 Mark Johnson	.10	.05	.01
□ 100 Dwight Gooden HL	.25	.11	.03
□ 101 Al Leiter HL	.10	.05	.01
□ 102 John Mabry HL	.10	.05	.01
□ 103 Alex Ochoa HL	.25	.11	.03
□ 104 Mike Piazza HL	1.00	.45	.12
□ 105 Jim Thome	.50	.23	.06
□ 106 Ricky Otero	.10	.05	.01
□ 107 Jamey Wright	.10	.05	.01
□ 108 Frank Thomas	3.00	1.35	.35
□ 109 Jody Reed	.10	.05	.01
□ 110 Orel Hershiser	.25	.11	.03
□ 111 Terry Steinbach	.25	.11	.03
□ 112 Mark Loretta	.10	.05	.01
□ 113 Turk Wendell	.10	.05	.01

□ 114 Marvin Benard	.10	.05	.01
□ 115 Kevin Brown	.25	.11	.03
□ 116 Robert Person	.10	.05	.01
□ 117 Joey Hamilton	.25	.11	.03
□ 118 Francisco Cordova	.10	.05	.01
□ 119 John Smiley	.10	.05	.01
□ 120 Travis Fryman	.25	.11	.03
□ 121 Jimmy Key	.25	.11	.03
□ 122 Tom Goodwin	.10	.05	.01
□ 123 Mike Greenwell	.10	.05	.01
□ 124 Juan Gonzalez	1.50	.70	.19
□ 125 Pete Harnisch	.10	.05	.01
□ 126 Roger Cedeno	.10	.05	.01
□ 127 Ron Gant	.25	.11	.03
□ 128 Mark Langston	.10	.05	.01
□ 129 Tim Crabtree	.10	.05	.01
□ 130 Greg Maddux	2.00	.90	.25
□ 131 William VanLandingham	.10	.05	.01
□ 132 Wally Joyner	.25	.11	.03
□ 133 Randy Myers	.10	.05	.01
□ 134 John Valentin	.10	.05	.01
□ 135 Bret Boone	.10	.05	.01
□ 136 Bruce Ruffin	.10	.05	.01
□ 137 Chris Snopek	.10	.05	.01
□ 138 Paul Molitor	.60	.25	.07
□ 139 Mark McLemore	.10	.05	.01
□ 140 Rafael Palmeiro	.50	.23	.06
□ 141 Herb Perry	.10	.05	.01
□ 142 Luis Gonzalez	.10	.05	.01
□ 143 Doug Drabek	.10	.05	.01
□ 144 Ken Ryan	.10	.05	.01
□ 145 Todd Hundley	.25	.11	.03
□ 146 Ellis Burks	.25	.11	.03
□ 147 Ozzie Guillen	.10	.05	.01
□ 148 Rich Becker	.10	.05	.01
□ 149 Sterling Hitchcock	.10	.05	.01
□ 150 Bernie Williams	.50	.23	.06
□ 151 Mike Stanley	.10	.05	.01
□ 152 Roberto Alomar	.75	.35	.09
□ 153 Jose Mesa	.25	.11	.03
□ 154 Steve Trachsel	.10	.05	.01
□ 155 Alex Gonzalez	.10	.05	.01
□ 156 Troy Percival	.25	.11	.03
□ 157 John Smoltz	.50	.23	.06
□ 158 Pedro Martinez	.25	.11	.03
□ 159 Jeff Conine	.25	.11	.03
□ 160 Bernard Gilkey	.25	.11	.03
□ 161 Jim Eisenreich	.10	.05	.01
□ 162 Mickey Tettleton	.10	.05	.01
□ 163 Justin Thompson	.10	.05	.01
□ 164 Jose Offerman	.10	.05	.01
□ 165 Tony Phillips	.25	.11	.03
□ 166 Ismael Valdes	.25	.11	.03
□ 167 Ryne Sandberg	.75	.35	.09
□ 168 Matt Mieske	.10	.05	.01
□ 169 Geronimo Berroa	.10	.05	.01
□ 170 Otis Nixon	.10	.05	.01
□ 171 John Mabry	.10	.05	.01
□ 172 Shawon Dunston	.10	.05	.01
□ 173 Omar Vizquel	.25	.11	.03
□ 174 Chris Hoiles	.10	.05	.01
□ 175 Dwight Gooden	.25	.11	.03
□ 176 Wilson Alvarez	.10	.05	.01
□ 177 Todd Hollandsworth	.25	.11	.03
□ 178 Roger Salkeld	.10	.05	.01
□ 179 Rey Sanchez	.10	.05	.01
□ 180 Rey Ordonez	.50	.23	.06
□ 181 Denny Martinez	.25	.11	.03
□ 182 Ramon Martinez	.25	.11	.03
□ 183 Dave Nilsson	.10	.05	.01
□ 184 Marquis Grissom	.25	.11	.03
□ 185 Randy Velarde	.10	.05	.01
□ 186 Ron Coomer	.10	.05	.01
□ 187 Tino Martinez	.25	.11	.03
□ 188 Jeff Brantley	.10	.05	.01
□ 189 Steve Finley	.25	.11	.03
□ 190 Andy Benes	.25	.11	.03
□ 191 Terry Adams	.10	.05	.01
□ 192 Mike Blowers	.10	.05	.01
□ 193 Russ Davis	.10	.05	.01
□ 194 Darryl Hamilton	.10	.05	.01
□ 195 Jason Kendall	.25	.11	.03
□ 196 Johnny Damon	.25	.11	.03
□ 197 Dave Martinez	.10	.05	.01
□ 198 Mike Macfarlane	.10	.05	.01
□ 199 Norm Charlton	.10	.05	.01

□ 200	Doug Million	.25	.11	.03
	Damian Moss			
	Bobby Rodgers			
□ 201	Geoff Jenkins	.25	.11	.03
	Raul Ibanez			
	Mike Cameron			
□ 202	Sean Casey	.25	.11	.03
	Jim Bonnici#[Dmitri Young			
□ 203	Jed Hansen	.25	.11	.03
	Homer Bush			
	Feilipe Crespo			
□ 204	Kevin Orie	.25	.11	.03
	Gabe Alvarez			
	Aaron Boone			
□ 205	Ben Davis	.25	.11	.03
	Kevin Brown			
	Bobby Estalella			
□ 206	Billy McMillon	.50	.23	.06
	Bubba Trammell			
	Dante Powell			
□ 207	Jarrod Washburn	.25	.11	.03
	Marc Wilkins			
	Glendon Rusch			
□ 208	Brian Hunter	.25	.11	.03
□ 209	Jason Giambi	.25	.11	.03
□ 210	Henry Rodriguez	.25	.11	.03
□ 211	Edgar Renteria	.50	.23	.06
□ 212	Edgardo Alfonzo	.10	.05	.01
□ 213	Fernando Vina	.10	.05	.01
□ 214	Shawn Green	.10	.05	.01
□ 215	Ray Durham	.10	.05	.01
□ 216	Joe Randa	.10	.05	.01
□ 217	Armando Reynoso	.10	.05	.01
□ 218	Eric Davis	.10	.05	.01
□ 219	Bob Tewksbury	.10	.05	.01
□ 220	Jacob Cruz	.10	.05	.01
□ 221	Glenallen Hill	.10	.05	.01
□ 222	Gary Gaetti	.10	.05	.01
□ 223	Donne Wall	.10	.05	.01
□ 224	Brad Clontz	.10	.05	.01
□ 225	Marty Janzen	.10	.05	.01
□ 226	Todd Worrell	.10	.05	.01
□ 227	John Franco	.10	.05	.01
□ 228	David Wells	.10	.05	.01
□ 229	Gregg Jefferies	.25	.11	.03
□ 230	Tim Naehring	.10	.05	.01
□ 231	Thomas Howard	.10	.05	.01
□ 232	Roberto Hernandez	.10	.05	.01
□ 233	Kevin Ritz	.10	.05	.01
□ 234	Julian Tavarez	.10	.05	.01
□ 235	Ken Hill	.10	.05	.01
□ 236	Greg Gagne	.10	.05	.01
□ 237	Bobby Chouinard	.10	.05	.01
□ 238	Joe Carter	.25	.11	.03
□ 239	Jermaine Dye	.50	.23	.06
□ 240	Antonio Osuna	.10	.05	.01
□ 241	Julio Franco	.25	.11	.03
□ 242	Mike Grace	.10	.05	.01
□ 243	Aaron Sele	.10	.05	.01
□ 244	David Justice	.25	.11	.03
□ 245	Sandy Alomar	.10	.05	.01
□ 246	Jose Canseco	.50	.23	.06
□ 247	Paul O'Neill	.25	.11	.03
□ 248	Sean Berry	.10	.05	.01
□ 249	Nick Bierbrodt	.75	.35	.09
	Kevin Sweeney			
□ 250	Larry Rodriguez	.50	.23	.06
	Vladimir Nunez			
□ 251	Ron Hartman	.75	.35	.09
	David Hayman			
□ 252	Alex Sanchez	.50	.23	.06
	Matthew Quatraro			
□ 253	Ronni Seberino	.40	.18	.05
	Pablo Ortego			
□ 254	Rex Hudler	.10	.05	.01
□ 255	Orlando Miller	.10	.05	.01
□ 256	Mariano Rivera	.25	.11	.03
□ 257	Brad Radke	.10	.05	.01
□ 258	Bobby Higginson	.25	.11	.03
□ 259	Jay Bell	.10	.05	.01
□ 260	Mark Grudzielanek	.10	.05	.01
□ 261	Lance Johnson	.25	.11	.03
□ 262	Ken Caminiti	.50	.23	.06
□ 263	J.T. Snow	.10	.05	.01
□ 264	Gary Sheffield	.50	.23	.06
□ 265	Darrin Fletcher	.10	.05	.01
□ 266	Eric Owens	.10	.05	.01
□ 267	Luis Castillo	.25	.11	.03
□ 268	Scott Rolen			
□ 269	Todd Noel	.25	.11	.03
	John Oliver			
□ 270	Robert Stratton	.25	.11	.03
	Corey Lee			
□ 271	Gil Meche	.40	.18	.05
	Matt Halloran			
□ 272	Eric Milton	.40	.18	.05
	Dermal Brown			
□ 273	Josh Garrett	.50	.23	.06
	Chris Reitsma			
□ 274	A.J.Zapp	.50	.23	.06
	Jason Marquis			
□ 275	Checklist	.10	.05	.01
□ 276	Checklist	.10	.05	.01

1997 Topps All-Stars

Randomly inserted in packs at a rate of one in 18, this 22-card set printed on rainbow foilboard features the top 11 players from each league and from each position as voted by the Topps Sports Department. The fronts carry a photo of a "first team" all-star player while the backs carry a different photo of that player alongside the "second team" and "third team" selections. Only the "first team" players are checklisted below.

	MINT	NRMT	EXC
COMPLETE SET (22)	70.00	32.00	8.75
COMMON CARD (AS1-AS22)	1.50	.70	.19
SEMISTARS	2.50	1.10	.30
RANDOM INSERTS IN PACKS			

□ AS1	Ivan Rodriguez	3.00	1.35	.35
□ AS2	Todd Hundley	2.00	.90	.25
□ AS3	Frank Thomas	15.00	6.75	1.85
□ AS4	Andres Galarraga	2.50	1.10	.30
□ AS5	Chuck Knoblauch	2.50	1.10	.30
□ AS6	Eric Young	2.00	.90	.25
□ AS7	Jim Thome	3.00	1.35	.35
□ AS8	Chipper Jones	10.00	4.50	1.25
□ AS9	Cal Ripken	12.00	5.50	1.50
□ AS10	Barry Larkin	2.50	1.10	.30
□ AS11	Albert Belle	8.00	3.60	1.00
□ AS12	Barry Bonds	4.00	1.80	.50
□ AS13	Ken Griffey Jr.	15.00	6.75	1.85
□ AS14	Ellis Burks	2.00	.90	.25
□ AS15	Juan Gonzalez	8.00	3.60	1.00
□ AS16	Gary Sheffield	2.50	1.10	.30
□ AS17	Andy Pettitte	4.00	1.80	.50
□ AS18	Tom Glavine	2.50	1.10	.30
□ AS19	Pat Hentgen	2.00	.90	.25
□ AS20	John Smoltz	2.50	1.10	.30
□ AS21	Roberto Hernandez	1.50	.70	.19
□ AS22	Mark Wohlers	2.00	.90	.25

1997 Topps Hobby Masters

Randomly inserted in packs at a rate of one in 36, this 10-card hobby only set honors ten players picked by top hobby dealers from across the country as their all-time favorites. Printed on 28-point diffraction foilboard, one card replaces two regular cards when inserted in packs. The

fronts feature borderless color player photos on a background of the player's profile. The backs carry player information.

	MINT	NRMT	EXC
COMPLETE SET (10)	60.00	27.00	7.50
COMMON CARD (HM1-HM10)	2.00	.90	.25
RANDOM INSERTS IN PACKS			
□ HM1 Ken Griffey Jr.	15.00	6.75	1.85
□ HM2 Cal Ripken	12.00	5.50	1.50
□ HM3 Greg Maddux	10.00	4.50	1.25
□ HM4 Albert Belle	8.00	3.60	1.00
□ HM5 Tony Gwynn	6.00	2.70	.75
□ HM6 Jeff Bagwell	6.00	2.70	.75
□ HM7 Randy Johnson	2.50	1.10	.30
□ HM8 Raul Mondesi	2.00	.90	.25
□ HM9 Juan Gonzalez	8.00	3.60	1.00
□ HM10 Kenny Lofton	4.00	1.80	.50

1997 Topps Inter-League Finest

Randomly inserted in packs at a rate of one in 36, this 14-card set features top individual match-ups from inter-league rivalries. One player from each major league team is represented on each side of this double-sided set with a color photo and is covered with the patented Finest clear protector.

	MINT	NRMT	EXC
COMPLETE SET (14)	75.00	34.00	9.50
COMMON CARD (ILM1-ILM14)	3.00	1.35	.35
SEMISTARS	4.00	1.80	.50
*REFRACTORS:6X VALUE			
RANDOM INSERTS IN PACKS			
□ ILM1 Mark McGwire Barry Bonds	6.00	2.70	.75
□ ILM2 Tim Salmon Mike Piazza	10.00	4.50	1.25
□ ILM3 Ken Griffey Jr. Dante Bichette	15.00	6.75	1.85
□ ILM4 Juan Gonzalez Tony Gwynn	10.00	4.50	1.25
□ ILM5 Frank Thomas Sammy Sosa	15.00	6.75	1.85
□ ILM6 Albert Belle Barry Larkin	8.00	3.60	1.00
□ ILM7 Johnny Damon Brian Jordan	3.00	1.35	.35
□ ILM8 Paul Molitor Jeff King	4.00	1.80	.50
□ ILM9 John Jaha Jeff Bagwell	5.00	2.20	.60
□ ILM10 Bernie Williams Todd Hundley	4.00	1.80	.50
□ ILM11 Joe Carter Henry Rodriguez	3.00	1.35	.35
□ ILM12 Cal Ripken Graig Jefferies	10.00	4.50	1.25
□ ILM13 Mo Vaughn Chipper Jones	10.00	4.50	1.25
□ ILM14 Travis Fryman Gary Sheffield	4.00	1.80	.50

1997 Topps Mantle Reprints

Randomly inserted at the rate of one in 12, this 16-card set features authentic reprints of Topps Mickey Mantle cards that were not reprinted last year. Each card is stamped with the commemorative gold foil logo.

	MINT	NRMT	EXC
COMPLETE SET (16)	90.00	40.00	11.00
COMMON CARD (21-36)	6.00	2.70	.75
RANDOM INSERTS IN SER.1 PACKS			

1997 Topps Mays Reprints

Randomly inserted at the rate of one in eight first series packs, cards from this 27-card set feature reprints of both the Topps and Bowman vintage Mays cards . Each card front is highlighted by a special commemorative gold foil stamp. Randomly inserted in first series hobby packs only (at the rate of one in 2,400) are personally signed cards. According to Topps, Mays signed about 65 each of the following cards: 51B, 52T, 53T, 55T, 57T, 58T, 60T, 60T AS, 61T, 61T AS, 63T, 64T, 65T, 66T, 69T, 70T, 72T, 73T.

	MINT	NRMT	EXC
COMPLETE SET (27)	65.00	29.00	8.00
COMMON CARD (1-27)	4.00	1.80	.50
RANDOM INSERTS IN SER.1 PACKS			
□ 1 1951 Bowman	8.00	3.60	1.00
□ 2 1952 Topps	6.00	2.70	.75

1997 Topps Sweet Strokes

This 15-card retail only set was randomly inserted in series one packs at a rate of one in 12. Printed on Rainbow foilboard, the set features color photos of some of Baseball's top hitters.

	MINT	NRMT	EXC
COMPLETE SET (15)	40.00	18.00	5.00
COMMON CARD (SS1-SS15)	1.50	.70	.19
RANDOM INSERTS IN SER.1 RETAIL PACKS			
□ SS1 Roberto Alomar	2.50	1.10	.30
□ SS2 Jeff Bagwell	4.00	1.80	.50
□ SS3 Albert Belle	5.00	2.20	.60
□ SS4 Barry Bonds	2.50	1.10	.30
□ SS5 Mark Grace	1.50	.70	.19
□ SS6 Ken Griffey Jr.	10.00	4.50	1.25
□ SS7 Tony Gwynn	4.00	1.80	.50
□ SS8 Chipper Jones	6.00	2.70	.75
□ SS9 Edgar Martinez	1.50	.70	.19
□ SS10 Mark McGwire	3.00	1.35	.35
□ SS11 Rafael Palmeiro	1.50	.70	.19
□ SS12 Mike Piazza	6.00	2.70	.75
□ SS13 Gary Sheffield	1.50	.70	.19
□ SS14 Frank Thomas	10.00	4.50	1.25
□ SS15 Mo Vaughn	2.50	1.10	.30

1996 Topps Chrome

The 1996 Topps Chrome set was issued in one series totalling 165 cards and features the best old and new players from the 1996 Topps regular Baseball Series 1 , 2. Each chromium card is a replica of its regular version with the exception of the Topps Chrome logo replacing the traditional logo. Inclued in the set is a Mickey Mantle #7 Commemorative card and a Cal Ripken Tribute card. The four-card packs retail for $3.00 each.

	MINT	NRMT	EXC
COMPLETE SET (165)	75.00	34.00	9.50
COMMON CARD (1-165)	.25	.11	.03
SEMISTARS	.50	.23	.06
STARS	1.00	.45	.12

□ 1 Tony Gwynn STA	1.50	.70	.19
□ 2 Mike Piazza STA	2.50	1.10	.30
□ 3 Greg Maddux STA	2.50	1.10	.30
□ 4 Jeff Bagwell STA	1.50	.70	.19
□ 5 Larry Walker STA	.50	.23	.06
□ 6 Barry Larkin STA	1.00	.45	.12
□ 7 Mickey Mantle COMM	10.00	4.50	1.25
□ 8 Tom Glavine STA	1.00	.45	.12
□ 9 Craig Biggio STA	1.00	.45	.12
□ 10 Barry Bonds STA	1.00	.45	.12
□ 11 Heathcliff Slocumb STA	.25	.11	.03
□ 12 Matt Williams STA	1.00	.45	.12
□ 13 Todd Helton DP	2.00	.90	.25
□ 14 Paul Molitor	1.50	.70	.19
□ 15 Glenallen Hill	.25	.11	.03
□ 16 Troy Percival	.25	.11	.03
□ 17 Albert Belle	4.00	1.80	.50
□ 18 Mark Wohlers	.50	.23	.06
□ 19 Kirby Puckett	2.50	1.10	.30
□ 20 Mark Grace	1.00	.45	.12
□ 21 J.T. Snow	.50	.23	.06
□ 22 David Justice	.50	.23	.06
□ 23 Mike Mussina	1.50	.70	.19
□ 24 Bernie Williams	1.25	.55	.16
□ 25 Ron Gant	1.00	.45	.12
□ 26 Carlos Baerga	1.00	.45	.12
□ 27 Gary Sheffield	1.25	.55	.16
□ 28 Cal Ripken 2131	6.00	2.70	.75
□ 29 Frank Thomas	8.00	3.60	1.00
□ 30 Kevin Seitzer	.25	.11	.03
□ 31 Joe Carter	1.00	.45	.12
□ 32 Jeff King	.50	.23	.06
□ 33 David Cone	1.00	.45	.12
□ 34 Eddie Murray	2.00	.90	.25
□ 35 Brian Jordan	1.00	.45	.12
□ 36 Garret Anderson	1.00	.45	.12
□ 37 Hideo Nomo	2.00	.90	.25
□ 38 Steve Finley	1.00	.45	.12
□ 39 Ivan Rodriguez	1.50	.70	.19
□ 40 Quilvio Veras	.25	.11	.03
□ 41 Mark McGwire	2.50	1.10	.30
□ 42 Greg Vaughn	1.00	.45	.12
□ 43 Randy Johnson	1.25	.55	.16
□ 44 David Segui	.25	.11	.03
□ 45 Derek Bell	1.00	.45	.12
□ 46 John Valentin	.50	.23	.06
□ 47 Steve Avery	.50	.23	.06
□ 48 Tino Martinez	.50	.23	.06
□ 49 Shane Reynolds	.25	.11	.03
□ 50 Jim Edmonds	1.00	.45	.12
□ 51 Raul Mondesi	1.00	.45	.12
□ 52 Chipper Jones	5.00	2.20	.60
□ 53 Gregg Jefferies	1.00	.45	.12
□ 54 Ken Caminiti	1.00	.45	.12
□ 55 Brian McRae	.25	.11	.03
□ 56 Don Mattingly	4.00	1.80	.50
□ 57 Marty Cordova	1.00	.45	.12
□ 58 Vinny Castilla	1.00	.45	.12
□ 59 John Smoltz	1.25	.55	.16
□ 60 Travis Fryman	1.00	.45	.12
□ 61 Ryan Klesko	1.50	.70	.19
□ 62 Alex Fernandez	1.00	.45	.12
□ 63 Dante Bichette	1.00	.45	.12
□ 64 Eric Karros	1.00	.45	.12
□ 65 Roger Clemens	1.00	.45	.12
□ 66 Randy Myers	.25	.11	.03
□ 67 Cal Ripken	6.00	2.70	.75
□ 68 Rod Beck	.50	.23	.06
□ 69 Jack McDowell	1.00	.45	.12
□ 70 Ken Griffey Jr.	8.00	3.60	1.00
□ 71 Ramon Martinez	1.00	.45	.12
□ 72 Jason Giambi FS	1.00	.45	.12
□ 73 Nomar Garciaparra FS	1.50	.70	.19
□ 74 Billy Wagner FS	.25	.11	.03
□ 75 Todd Greene FS	.50	.23	.06
□ 76 Paul Wilson FS	.50	.23	.06
□ 77 Johnny Damon FS	.50	.23	.06
□ 78 Alan Benes FS	1.00	.45	.12
□ 79 Karim Garcia FS	1.50	.70	.19
□ 80 Derek Jeter FS	5.00	2.20	.60
□ 81 Kirby Puckett STA	1.00	.45	.12
□ 82 Cal Ripken STA	3.00	1.35	.35
□ 83 Albert Belle STA	2.00	.90	.25
□ 84 Randy Johnson STA	1.00	.45	.12
□ 85 Wade Boggs STA	1.00	.45	.12
□ 86 Carlos Baerga STA	1.00	.45	.12
□ 87 Ivan Rodriguez STA	1.00	.45	.12
□ 88 Mike Mussina STA	1.00	.45	.12
□ 89 Frank Thomas STA	4.00	1.80	.50
□ 90 Ken Griffey Jr. STA	4.00	1.80	.50
□ 91 Jose Mesa STA	.25	.11	.03
□ 92 Matt Morris DP	1.00	.45	.12
□ 93 Mike Piazza	5.00	2.20	.60
□ 94 Edgar Martinez	1.00	.45	.12
□ 95 Chuck Knoblauch	1.00	.45	.12
□ 96 Andres Galarraga	1.00	.45	.12
□ 97 Tony Gwynn	3.00	1.35	.35
□ 98 Lee Smith	1.00	.45	.12
□ 99 Sammy Sosa	1.25	.55	.16
□ 100 Jim Thome	1.50	.70	.19
□ 101 Bernard Gilkey	.50	.23	.06
□ 102 Brady Anderson	1.00	.45	.12
□ 103 Rico Brogna	.25	.11	.03
□ 104 Len Dykstra	.50	.23	.06
□ 105 Tom Glavine	1.00	.45	.12
□ 106 John Olerud	.25	.11	.03
□ 107 Terry Steinbach	.50	.23	.06
□ 108 Brian Hunter	.25	.11	.03
□ 109 Jay Buhner	1.00	.45	.12
□ 110 Mo Vaughn	2.00	.90	.25
□ 111 Jose Mesa	.50	.23	.06
□ 112 Brett Butler	.25	.11	.03
□ 113 Chili Davis	.25	.11	.03
□ 114 Paul O'Neill	.25	.11	.03
□ 115 Roberto Alomar	2.00	.90	.25
□ 116 Barry Larkin	1.00	.45	.12
□ 117 Marquis Grissom	1.00	.45	.12
□ 118 Will Clark	1.00	.45	.12
□ 119 Barry Bonds	2.00	.90	.25
□ 120 Ozzie Smith	1.50	.70	.19
□ 121 Pedro Martinez	.50	.23	.06
□ 122 Craig Biggio	1.00	.45	.12
□ 123 Moises Alou	.50	.23	.06
□ 124 Robin Ventura	.50	.23	.06
□ 125 Greg Maddux	5.00	2.20	.60
□ 126 Tim Salmon	1.00	.45	.12
□ 127 Wade Boggs	1.00	.45	.12
□ 128 Ismael Valdes	.50	.23	.06
□ 129 Juan Gonzalez	4.00	1.80	.50
□ 130 Ray Lankford	1.00	.45	.12
□ 131 Bobby Bonilla	1.00	.45	.12
□ 132 Reggie Sanders	1.00	.45	.12
□ 133 Alex Ochoa NOW	.50	.23	.06
□ 134 Mark Loretta NOW	.25	.11	.03
□ 135 Jason Kendall NOW	1.00	.45	.12
□ 136 Brooks Kieschnick NOW	.25	.11	.03
□ 137 Chris Snopek NOW	.25	.11	.03
□ 138 Ruben Rivera NOW	1.50	.70	.19
□ 139 Jeff Suppan NOW	.25	.11	.03
□ 140 John Wasdin NOW	.25	.11	.03
□ 141 Jay Payton NOW	1.00	.45	.12
□ 142 Rick Krivda NOW	.25	.11	.03
□ 143 Jimmy Haynes NOW	.25	.11	.03
□ 144 Ryne Sandberg	2.00	.90	.25
□ 145 Matt Williams	1.00	.45	.12
□ 146 Jose Canseco	1.00	.45	.12
□ 147 Larry Walker	.50	.23	.06
□ 148 Kevin Appier	.25	.11	.03
□ 149 Javy Lopez	1.00	.45	.12
□ 150 Dennis Eckersley	1.00	.45	.12
□ 151 Jason Isringhausen	.50	.23	.06
□ 152 Dean Palmer	1.00	.45	.12
□ 153 Jeff Bagwell	3.00	1.35	.35
□ 154 Rondell White	1.00	.45	.12
□ 155 Wally Joyner	.25	.11	.03
□ 156 Fred McGriff	1.00	.45	.12

	MINT	NRMT	EXC
□ 157 Cecil Fielder	1.00	.45	.12
□ 158 Rafael Palmeiro	1.00	.45	.12
□ 159 Rickey Henderson	1.00	.45	.12
□ 160 Shawon Dunston	.25	.11	.03
□ 161 Manny Ramirez	2.00	.90	.25
□ 162 Alex Gonzalez	.25	.11	.03
□ 163 Shawn Green	.25	.11	.03
□ 164 Kenny Lofton	2.00	.90	.25
□ 165 Jeff Conine	.25	.11	.03

1996 Topps Chrome Refractors

Randomly inserted at the rate of one in every 12 packs, this 165-card set is parallel to the regular Chrome set. The difference in design is the refractive quality of the cards.

	MINT	NRMT	EXC
COMPLETE SET (165)	1500.00	700.00	190.00
COMMON CARD (1-165)	3.00	1.35	.35
SEMISTARS	6.00	2.70	.75
STARS	12.00	5.50	1.50
*VETERAN STARS: 12X VALUE			
*YOUNG STARS: 10X VALUE			
RANDOM INSERTS IN PACKS			

□ 7 Mickey Mantle COMM	120.00	55.00	15.00
□ 17 Albert Belle	50.00	22.00	6.25
□ 19 Kirby Puckett	30.00	13.50	3.70
□ 28 Cal Ripken TRIB	80.00	36.00	10.00
□ 29 Frank Thomas	100.00	45.00	12.50
□ 41 Mark McGwire	30.00	13.50	3.70
□ 52 Chipper Jones	60.00	27.00	7.50
□ 56 Don Mattingly	50.00	22.00	6.25
□ 67 Cal Ripken	80.00	36.00	10.00
□ 70 Ken Griffey Jr.	100.00	45.00	12.50
□ 80 Derek Jeter FS	60.00	27.00	7.50
□ 82 Cal Ripken STA	40.00	18.00	5.00
□ 89 Frank Thomas STA	50.00	22.00	6.25
□ 90 Ken Griffey Jr. STA	50.00	22.00	6.25
□ 93 Mike Piazza	60.00	27.00	7.50
□ 97 Tony Gwynn	40.00	18.00	5.00
□ 125 Greg Maddux	60.00	27.00	7.50
□ 129 Juan Gonzalez	50.00	22.00	6.25
□ 153 Jeff Bagwell	40.00	18.00	5.00

1996 Topps Chrome Masters of the Game

Randomly inserted in packs at a rate of one in 12, this 20-card set honors players who are masters of their playing positions. The fronts feature color action photography with brilliant color metallization.

	MINT	NRMT	EXC
COMPLETE SET (20)	80.00	36.00	10.00
COMMON CARD (1-20)	1.50	.70	.19
COMP.REFRACTOR SET (20)	250.00	110.00	31.00
*REFRACTORS: 3X VALUE			
RANDOM INSERTS IN PACKS			

□ 1 Dennis Eckersley	3.00	1.35	.35
□ 2 Denny Martinez	1.50	.70	.19
□ 3 Eddie Murray	5.00	2.20	.60
□ 4 Paul Molitor	4.00	1.80	.50
□ 5 Ozzie Smith	4.00	1.80	.50
□ 6 Rickey Henderson	3.00	1.35	.35
□ 7 Tim Raines	1.50	.70	.19
□ 8 Lee Smith	1.50	.70	.19
□ 9 Cal Ripken	15.00	6.75	1.85
□ 10 Chili Davis	1.50	.70	.19
□ 11 Wade Boggs	3.00	1.35	.35
□ 12 Tony Gwynn	8.00	3.60	1.00
□ 13 Don Mattingly	10.00	4.50	1.25
□ 14 Bret Saberhagen	1.50	.70	.19
□ 15 Kirby Puckett	6.00	2.70	.75
□ 16 Joe Carter	3.00	1.35	.35
□ 17 Roger Clemens	3.00	1.35	.35
□ 18 Barry Bonds	5.00	2.20	.60
□ 19 Greg Maddux	12.00	5.50	1.50
□ 20 Frank Thomas	20.00	9.00	2.50

1996 Topps Chrome Wrecking Crew

Randomly inserted in packs at a rate of one in 24, this 15-card set features baseball's top hitters and is printed in color action photography with brilliant color metallization.

	MINT	NRMT	EXC
COMPLETE SET (15)	80.00	36.00	10.00
COMMON CARD (WC1-WC15)	2.00	.90	.25
COMP.REFRACTOR SET (15)	250.00	110.00	31.00
*REFRACTORS: 3X VALUE			
RANDOM INSERTS IN PACKS			

□ WC1 Jeff Bagwell	10.00	4.50	1.25
□ WC2 Albert Belle	12.00	5.50	1.50
□ WC3 Barry Bonds	6.00	2.70	.75
□ WC4 Jose Canseco	4.00	1.80	.50
□ WC5 Joe Carter	4.00	1.80	.50
□ WC6 Cecil Fielder	4.00	1.80	.50
□ WC7 Ron Gant	2.00	.90	.25
□ WC8 Juan Gonzalez	12.00	5.50	1.50
□ WC9 Ken Griffey Jr.	25.00	11.00	3.10
□ WC10 Fred McGriff	4.00	1.80	.50
□ WC11 Mark McGwire	8.00	3.60	1.00
□ WC12 Mike Piazza	15.00	6.75	1.85
□ WC13 Frank Thomas	25.00	11.00	3.10
□ WC14 Mo Vaughn	6.00	2.70	.75
□ WC15 Matt Williams	4.00	1.80	.50

1996 Topps Gallery

The 1996 Topps Gallery set was issued in one series totalling 180 cards. The 8-card packs retail for $3.00 each. The set is divided into 5 themes: Classics (1-90), New Editions (91-108), Modernists (109-126), Futurists (127-144) and Masters (145-180). Scheduled release date is June 24, 1996.

	MINT	NRMT	EXC
COMPLETE SET (180)	40.00	18.00	5.00
COMMON CARD (1-180)	.15	.07	.02
SEMISTARS	.40	.18	.05
STARS	.75	.35	.09

□ 1 Tom Glavine	.75	.35	.09
□ 2 Carlos Baerga	.75	.35	.09
□ 3 Dante Bichette	.75	.35	.09
□ 4 Mark Langston	.15	.07	.02
□ 5 Ray Lankford	.75	.35	.09
□ 6 Moises Alou	.40	.18	.05
□ 7 Marquis Grissom	.75	.35	.09
□ 8 Ramon Martinez	.40	.18	.05
□ 9 Steve Finley	.40	.18	.05
□ 10 Todd Hundley	.75	.35	.09
□ 11 Brady Anderson	.75	.35	.09
□ 12 John Valentin	.40	.18	.05
□ 13 Heathcliff Slocumb	.15	.07	.02
□ 14 Ruben Sierra	.15	.07	.02
□ 15 Jeff Conine	.40	.18	.05
□ 16 Jay Buhner	.75	.35	.09
□ 17 Sammy Sosa	.75	.35	.09

□ 18 Doug Drabek	.15	.07	.02
□ 19 Jose Mesa	.40	.18	.05
□ 20 Jeff King	.40	.18	.05
□ 21 Mickey Tettleton	.40	.18	.05
□ 22 Jeff Montgomery	.15	.07	.02
□ 23 Alex Fernandez	.75	.35	.09
□ 24 Greg Vaughn	.75	.35	.09
□ 25 Chuck Finley	.15	.07	.02
□ 26 Terry Steinbach	.40	.18	.05
□ 27 Rod Beck	.40	.18	.05
□ 28 Jack McDowell	.75	.35	.09
□ 29 Mark Wohlers	.75	.35	.09
□ 30 Len Dykstra	.40	.18	.05
□ 31 Bernie Williams	.75	.35	.09
□ 32 Travis Fryman	.75	.35	.09
□ 33 Jose Canseco	.75	.35	.09
□ 34 Ken Caminiti	.75	.35	.09
□ 35 Devon White	.15	.07	.02
□ 36 Bobby Bonilla	.75	.35	.09
□ 37 Paul Sorrento	.15	.07	.02
□ 38 Ryne Sandberg	1.25	.55	.16
□ 39 Derek Bell	.40	.18	.05
□ 40 Bobby Jones	.15	.07	.02
□ 41 J.T. Snow	.15	.07	.02
□ 42 Denny Neagle	.40	.18	.05
□ 43 Tim Wakefield	.15	.07	.02
□ 44 Andres Galarraga	.75	.35	.09
□ 45 David Segui	.15	.07	.02
□ 46 Lee Smith	.75	.35	.09
□ 47 Mel Rojas	.40	.18	.05
□ 48 John Franco	.15	.07	.02
□ 49 Pete Schourek	.15	.07	.02
□ 50 John Wetteland	.40	.18	.05
□ 51 Paul Molitor	1.00	.45	.12
□ 52 Ivan Rodriguez	1.00	.45	.12
□ 53 Chris Hoiles	.15	.07	.02
□ 54 Mike Greenwell	.15	.07	.02
□ 55 Orel Hershiser	.40	.18	.05
□ 56 Brian McRae	.15	.07	.02
□ 57 Geronimo Berroa	.40	.18	.05
□ 58 Craig Biggio	.75	.35	.09
□ 59 David Justice	.40	.18	.05
□ 60 Lance Johnson	.40	.18	.05
□ 61 Andy Ashby	.15	.07	.02
□ 62 Randy Myers	.15	.07	.02
□ 63 Gregg Jefferies	.75	.35	.09
□ 64 Kevin Appier	.40	.18	.05
□ 65 Rick Aguilera	.15	.07	.02
□ 66 Shane Reynolds	.15	.07	.02
□ 67 John Smoltz	.75	.35	.09
□ 68 Ron Gant	.75	.35	.09
□ 69 Eric Karros	.75	.35	.09
□ 70 Jim Thome	1.00	.45	.12
□ 71 Terry Pendleton	.40	.18	.05
□ 72 Kenny Rogers	.15	.07	.02
□ 73 Robin Ventura	.75	.35	.09
□ 74 Dave Nilsson	.40	.18	.05
□ 75 Brian Jordan	.75	.35	.09
□ 76 Glenallen Hill	.15	.07	.02
□ 77 Greg Colbrunn	.15	.07	.02
□ 78 Roberto Alomar	1.25	.55	.16
□ 79 Rickey Henderson	.75	.35	.09
□ 80 Carlos Garcia	.15	.07	.02
□ 81 Dean Palmer	.75	.35	.09
□ 82 Mike Stanley	.15	.07	.02
□ 83 Hal Morris	.15	.07	.02
□ 84 Wade Boggs	.75	.35	.09
□ 85 Chad Curtis	.15	.07	.02
□ 86 Roberto Hernandez	.40	.18	.05
□ 87 John Olerud	.15	.07	.02
□ 88 Frank Castillo	.15	.07	.02
□ 89 Rafael Palmeiro	.75	.35	.09
□ 90 Trevor Hoffman	.40	.18	.05
□ 91 Marty Cordova	.75	.35	.09
□ 92 Hideo Nomo	1.25	.55	.16
□ 93 Johnny Damon	.40	.18	.05
□ 94 Bill Pulsipher	.15	.07	.02
□ 95 Garret Anderson	.75	.35	.09
□ 96 Ray Durham	.75	.35	.09
□ 97 Ricky Bottalico	.15	.07	.02
□ 98 Carlos Perez	.15	.07	.02
□ 99 Troy Percival	.15	.07	.02
□ 100 Chipper Jones	3.00	1.35	.35
□ 101 Esteban Loaiza	.15	.07	.02
□ 102 John Mabry	.75	.35	.09
□ 103 Jon Nunnally	.15	.07	.02
□ 104 Andy Pettitte	1.50	.70	.19
□ 105 Lyle Mouton	.15	.07	.02
□ 106 Jason Isringhausen	.15	.07	.02
□ 107 Brian L.Hunter	.15	.07	.02
□ 108 Quilvio Veras	.15	.07	.02
□ 109 Jim Edmonds	.75	.35	.09
□ 110 Ryan Klesko	1.00	.45	.12
□ 111 Pedro Martinez	.15	.07	.02
□ 112 Joey Hamilton	.40	.18	.05
□ 113 Vinny Castilla	.75	.35	.09
□ 114 Alex Gonzalez	.15	.07	.02
□ 115 Raul Mondesi	.40	.18	.05
□ 116 Rondell White	.75	.35	.09
□ 117 Dan Miceli	.15	.07	.02
□ 118 Tom Goodwin	.40	.18	.05
□ 119 Bret Boone	.15	.07	.02
□ 120 Shawn Green	.15	.07	.02
□ 121 Jeff Cirillo	.15	.07	.02
□ 122 Rico Brogna	.15	.07	.02
□ 123 Chris Gomez	.15	.07	.02
□ 124 Ismael Valdes	.40	.18	.05
□ 125 Javy Lopez	.75	.35	.09
□ 126 Manny Ramirez	1.25	.55	.16
□ 127 Paul Wilson	.15	.07	.02
□ 128 Billy Wagner	.15	.07	.02
□ 129 Eric Owens	.15	.07	.02
□ 130 Todd Greene	.40	.18	.05
□ 131 Karim Garcia	1.00	.45	.12
□ 132 Jimmy Haynes	.15	.07	.02
□ 133 Michael Tucker	.40	.18	.05
□ 134 John Wasdin	.15	.07	.02
□ 135 Brooks Kieschnick	.15	.07	.02
□ 136 Alex Ochoa	.40	.18	.05
□ 137 Ariel Prieto	.15	.07	.02
□ 138 Tony Clark	.75	.35	.09
□ 139 Mark Loretta	.15	.07	.02
□ 140 Rey Ordonez	1.00	.45	.12
□ 141 Chris Snopek	.15	.07	.02
□ 142 Roger Cedeno	.15	.07	.02
□ 143 Derek Jeter	3.00	1.35	.35
□ 144 Jeff Suppan	.15	.07	.02
□ 145 Greg Maddux	3.00	1.35	.35
□ 146 Ken Griffey Jr.	5.00	2.20	.60
□ 147 Tony Gwynn	2.00	.90	.25
□ 148 Darren Daulton	.40	.18	.05
□ 149 Will Clark	.75	.35	.09
□ 150 Mo Vaughn	1.25	.55	.16
□ 151 Reggie Sanders	.40	.18	.05
□ 152 Kirby Puckett	1.50	.70	.19
□ 153 Paul O'Neill	.15	.07	.02
□ 154 Tim Salmon	.75	.35	.09
□ 155 Mark McGwire	1.50	.70	.19
□ 156 Barry Bonds	1.25	.55	.16
□ 157 Albert Belle	2.50	1.10	.30
□ 158 Edgar Martinez	.75	.35	.09
□ 159 Mike Mussina	1.00	.45	.12
□ 160 Cecil Fielder	.40	.18	.05
□ 161 Kenny Lofton	1.25	.55	.16
□ 162 Randy Johnson	.75	.35	.09
□ 163 Juan Gonzalez	2.50	1.10	.30
□ 164 Jeff Bagwell	2.00	.90	.25
□ 165 Joe Carter	.75	.35	.09
□ 166 Mike Piazza	3.00	1.35	.35
□ 167 Eddie Murray	1.25	.55	.16
□ 168 Cal Ripken	4.00	1.80	.50
□ 169 Barry Larkin	.75	.35	.09
□ 170 Chuck Knoblauch	.75	.35	.09
□ 171 Chili Davis	.15	.07	.02
□ 172 Fred McGriff	.75	.35	.09
□ 173 Matt Williams	.75	.35	.09
□ 174 Roger Clemens	.75	.35	.09
□ 175 Frank Thomas	5.00	2.20	.60
□ 176 Dennis Eckersley	.75	.35	.09
□ 177 Gary Sheffield	.75	.35	.09
□ 178 David Cone	.75	.35	.09
□ 179 Larry Walker	.75	.35	.09
□ 180 Mark Grace	.75	.35	.09
□ NNO Mantle Masterpiece	20.00	9.00	2.50

1996 Topps Gallery Players Private Issue

Randomly inserted in packs at a rate of one in 12, this 180-card parallel is foil stamped. The backs are sequentially numbered 0-999, with the first 100 (#s0-99) cards sent to the players and the balance inserted in packs. The backs are UV-coated to allow for autographs.

	MINT	NRMT	EXC
COMPLETE SET (180)	800.00	350.00	100.00
COMMON CARD (1-180)	2.00	.90	.25
SEMISTARS	5.00	2.20	.60
STARS	12.00	5.50	1.50
*STARS: 7.5X to 15X HI COLUMN			
*YOUNG STARS: 6X to 12X HI			
RANDOM INSERTS IN PACKS			
□ 100 Chipper Jones	50.00	22.00	6.25
□ 143 Derek Jeter	50.00	22.00	6.25
□ 145 Greg Maddux	50.00	22.00	6.25
□ 146 Ken Griffey Jr.	80.00	36.00	10.00
□ 157 Albert Belle	40.00	18.00	5.00
□ 163 Juan Gonzalez	40.00	18.00	5.00
□ 166 Mike Piazza	50.00	22.00	6.25
□ 168 Cal Ripken	60.00	27.00	7.50
□ 175 Frank Thomas	80.00	36.00	10.00

1996 Topps Gallery Expressionists

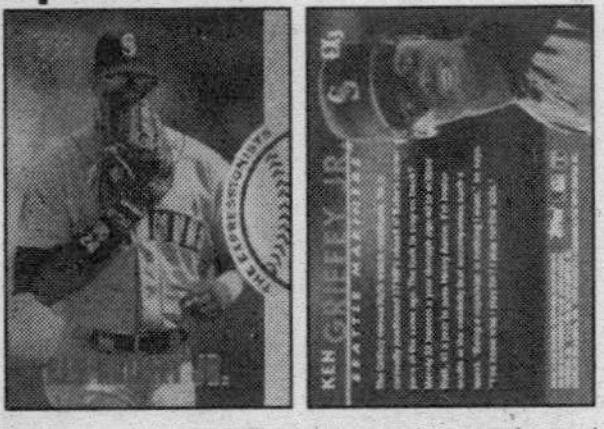

Randomly inserted in packs at a rate of one in 24, this 20-card set features 20 spiritual leaders printed on triple foil stamped and texture embossed cards. Card backs contain a second photo and narrative about the player.

	MINT	NRMT	EXC
COMPLETE SET (20)	120.00	55.00	15.00
COMMON CARD (1-20)	2.00	.90	.25
SEMISTARS	4.00	1.80	.50
RANDOM INSERTS IN PACKS			
□ 1 Mike Piazza	20.00	9.00	2.50
□ 2 J.T. Snow	2.00	.90	.25
□ 3 Ken Griffey Jr.	30.00	13.50	3.70
□ 4 Kirby Puckett	10.00	4.50	1.25
□ 5 Carlos Baerga	4.00	1.80	.50
□ 6 Chipper Jones	20.00	9.00	2.50
□ 7 Hideo Nomo	8.00	3.60	1.00
□ 8 Mark McGwire	10.00	4.50	1.25
□ 9 Gary Sheffield	5.00	2.20	.60
□ 10 Randy Johnson	5.00	2.20	.60
□ 11 Ray Lankford	4.00	1.80	.50
□ 12 Sammy Sosa	5.00	2.20	.60
□ 13 Denny Martinez	2.00	.90	.25
□ 14 Jose Canseco	4.00	1.80	.50
□ 15 Tony Gwynn	12.00	5.50	1.50
□ 16 Edgar Martinez	4.00	1.80	.50
□ 17 Reggie Sanders	2.00	.90	.25
□ 18 Andres Galarraga	4.00	1.80	.50
□ 19 Albert Belle	15.00	6.75	1.85
□ 20 Barry Larkin	4.00	1.80	.50

1996 Topps Gallery Photo Gallery

Randomly inserted in packs at a rate of one in 30, this 15-card set features top photography chronicling baseball's biggest stars and greatest moments from last year. Each double foil stamped card is printed on 24 pt. stock with customized designs to accentuate the photography.

	MINT	NRMT	EXC
COMPLETE SET (15)	100.00	45.00	12.50
COMMON CARD (PG1-PG15)	1.50	.70	.19
SEMISTARS	3.00	1.35	.35
RANDOM INSERTS IN PACKS			
□ PG1 Eddie Murray	6.00	2.70	.75
□ PG2 Randy Johnson	4.00	1.80	.50
□ PG3 Cal Ripken	20.00	9.00	2.50
□ PG4 Bret Boone	1.50	.70	.19
□ PG5 Frank Thomas	25.00	11.00	3.10
□ PG6 Jeff Conine	1.50	.70	.19
□ PG7 Johnny Damon	1.50	.70	.19
□ PG8 Roger Clemens	3.00	1.35	.35
□ PG9 Albert Belle	12.00	5.50	1.50
□ PG10 Ken Griffey Jr.	25.00	11.00	3.10
□ PG11 Kirby Puckett	8.00	3.60	1.00
□ PG12 David Justice	1.50	.70	.19
□ PG13 Bobby Bonilla	3.00	1.35	.35
□ PG14 Colorado Rockies	4.00	1.80	.50
□ PG15 Atlanta Braves	4.00	1.80	.50

1996 Topps Laser

The 1996 Topps Laser contains 128 regular cards that are found on one of four perfected designs. Every card is etch foil-stamped and laser-cut. The four-card packs retail for $5.00 each.

	MINT	NRMT	EXC
COMPLETE SET (128)	120.00	55.00	15.00
COMPLETE SERIES 1 (64)	60.00	27.00	7.50
COMPLETE SERIES 2 (64)	60.00	27.00	7.50
COMMON CARD (1-128)	.50	.23	.06
SEMISTARS	1.00	.45	.12
□ 1 Moises Alou	.50	.23	.06
□ 2 Derek Bell	.50	.23	.06
□ 3 Joe Carter	1.00	.45	.12
□ 4 Jeff Conine	.75	.35	.09
□ 5 Darren Daulton	.75	.35	.09
□ 6 Jim Edmonds	.50	.23	.06
□ 7 Ron Gant	1.00	.45	.12
□ 8 Juan Gonzalez	5.00	2.20	.60
□ 9 Brian Jordan	1.00	.45	.12

□ 10	Ryan Klesko	2.00	.90	.25
□ 11	Paul Molitor	2.00	.90	.25
□ 12	Tony Phillips	.50	.23	.06
□ 13	Manny Ramirez	2.50	1.10	.30
□ 14	Sammy Sosa	1.50	.70	.19
□ 15	Devon White	.50	.23	.06
□ 16	Bernie Williams	1.50	.70	.19
□ 17	Garrett Anderson	1.00	.45	.12
□ 18	Jay Bell	.50	.23	.06
□ 19	Craig Biggio	1.00	.45	.12
□ 20	Bobby Bonilla	1.00	.45	.12
□ 21	Ken Caminiti	1.00	.45	.12
□ 22	Shawon Dunston	.50	.23	.06
□ 23	Mark Grace	1.00	.45	.12
□ 24	Gregg Jefferies	.75	.35	.09
□ 25	Jeff King	.75	.35	.09
□ 26	Javy Lopez	1.00	.45	.12
□ 27	Edgar Martinez	1.00	.45	.12
□ 28	Dean Palmer	1.00	.45	.12
□ 29	J.T. Snow	.75	.35	.09
□ 30	Mike Stanley	.50	.23	.06
□ 31	Terry Steinbach	.75	.35	.09
□ 32	Robin Ventura	1.00	.45	.12
□ 33	Roberto Alomar	2.50	1.10	.30
□ 34	Jeff Bagwell	4.00	1.80	.50
□ 35	Dante Bichette	1.00	.45	.12
□ 36	Wade Boggs	1.00	.45	.12
□ 37	Barry Bonds	2.50	1.10	.30
□ 38	Jose Canseco	1.00	.45	.12
□ 39	Vinny Castilla	1.00	.45	.12
□ 40	Will Clark	1.00	.45	.12
□ 41	Marty Cordova	.75	.35	.09
□ 42	Ken Griffey Jr.	10.00	4.50	1.25
□ 43	Tony Gwynn	4.00	1.80	.50
□ 44	Rickey Henderson	1.00	.45	.12
□ 45	Chipper Jones	6.00	2.70	.75
□ 46	Mark McGwire	3.00	1.35	.35
□ 47	Brian McRae	.50	.23	.06
□ 48	Ryne Sandberg	2.50	1.10	.30
□ 49	Andy Ashby	.50	.23	.06
□ 50	Alan Benes	1.00	.45	.12
□ 51	Andy Benes	.50	.23	.06
□ 52	Roger Clemens	1.00	.45	.12
□ 53	Doug Drabek	.50	.23	.06
□ 54	Dennis Eckersley	1.00	.45	.12
□ 55	Tom Glavine	1.00	.45	.12
□ 56	Randy Johnson	1.50	.70	.19
□ 57	Mark Langston	.50	.23	.06
□ 58	Denny Martinez	.75	.35	.09
□ 59	Jack McDowell	1.00	.45	.12
□ 60	Hideo Nomo	2.50	1.10	.30
□ 61	Shane Reynolds	.50	.23	.06
□ 62	John Smoltz	1.50	.70	.19
□ 63	Paul Wilson	1.25	.55	.16
□ 64	Mark Wohlers	.75	.35	.09
□ 65	Shawn Green	.50	.23	.06
□ 66	Marquis Grissom	1.00	.45	.12
□ 67	Dave Hollins	.50	.23	.06
□ 68	Todd Hundley	1.00	.45	.12
□ 69	David Justice	.75	.35	.09
□ 70	Eric Karros	1.00	.45	.12
□ 71	Ray Lankford	1.00	.45	.12
□ 72	Fred McGriff	1.00	.45	.12
□ 73	Hal Morris	.50	.23	.06
□ 74	Eddie Murray	2.00	.90	.25
□ 75	Paul O'Neill	.50	.23	.06
□ 76	Rey Ordonez	1.00	.45	.12
□ 77	Reggie Sanders	.75	.35	.09
□ 78	Gary Sheffield	1.50	.70	.19
□ 79	Jim Thome	1.00	.45	.12
□ 80	Rondell White	1.00	.45	.12
□ 81	Travis Fryman	1.00	.45	.12
□ 82	Derek Jeter	6.00	2.70	.75
□ 83	Chuck Knoblauch	1.00	.45	.12
□ 84	Barry Larkin	1.00	.45	.12
□ 85	Tino Martinez	.75	.35	.09
□ 86	Raul Mondesi	1.00	.45	.12
□ 87	John Olerud	.50	.23	.06
□ 88	Rafael Palmeiro	1.00	.45	.12
□ 89	Mike Piazza	6.00	2.70	.75
□ 90	Cal Ripken	8.00	3.60	1.00
□ 91	Ivan Rodriguez	2.00	.90	.25
□ 92	Frank Thomas	10.00	4.50	1.25
□ 93	John Valentin	.75	.35	.09
□ 94	Mo Vaughn	2.00	.90	.25
□ 95	Quilvio Veras	.50	.23	.06
□ 96	Matt Williams	1.00	.45	.12
□ 97	Brady Anderson	1.00	.45	.12
□ 98	Carlos Baerga	1.00	.45	.12
□ 99	Albert Belle	5.00	2.20	.60
□ 100	Jay Buhner	1.00	.45	.12
□ 101	Johnny Damon	.50	.23	.06
□ 102	Chili Davis	.50	.23	.06
□ 103	Ray Durham	1.00	.45	.12
□ 104	Len Dykstra	.75	.35	.09
□ 105	Cecil Fielder	1.00	.45	.12
□ 106	Andres Galarraga	1.00	.45	.12
□ 107	Brian L.Hunter	.50	.23	.06
□ 108	Kenny Lofton	2.50	1.10	.30
□ 109	Kirby Puckett	3.00	1.35	.35
□ 110	Tim Salmon	1.00	.45	.12
□ 111	Greg Vaughn	1.00	.45	.12
□ 112	Larry Walker	.50	.23	.06
□ 113	Rick Aguilera	.50	.23	.06
□ 114	Kevin Appier	.50	.23	.06
□ 115	Kevin Brown	.75	.35	.09
□ 116	David Cone	.50	.23	.06
□ 117	Alex Fernandez	1.00	.45	.12
□ 118	Chuck Finley	.50	.23	.06
□ 119	Joey Hamilton	.75	.35	.09
□ 120	Jason Isringhausen	.50	.23	.06
□ 121	Greg Maddux	6.00	2.70	.75
□ 122	Pedro Martinez	.50	.23	.06
□ 123	Jose Mesa	.75	.35	.09
□ 124	Jeff Montgomery	.50	.23	.06
□ 125	Mike Mussina	1.00	.45	.12
□ 126	Randy Myers	.50	.23	.06
□ 127	Kenny Rogers	.50	.23	.06
□ 128	Ismael Valdes	.75	.35	.09

1996 Topps Laser Bright Spots

Randomly inserted in packs at a rate of one in 20, this 16-card set highlights top young star players. The cards are printed on etched silver and gold diffraction foil.

	MINT	NRMT	EXC
COMPLETE SET (16)	150.00	70.00	19.00
COMPLETE SERIES 1 (8)	60.00	27.00	7.50
COMPLETE SERIES 2 (8)	100.00	45.00	12.50
COMMON CARD (1-16)	5.00	2.20	.60
SEMISTARS	6.00	2.70	.75

RANDOM INSERTS IN BOTH SERIES PACKS

□ 1	Brian L.Hunter	5.00	2.20	.60
□ 2	Derek Jeter	30.00	13.50	3.70
□ 3	Jason Kendall	8.00	3.60	1.00
□ 4	Brooks Kieschnick	5.00	2.20	.60
□ 5	Rey Ordonez	12.00	5.50	1.50
□ 6	Jason Schmidt	5.00	2.20	.60
□ 7	Chris Snopek	5.00	2.20	.60
□ 8	Bob Wolcott	5.00	2.20	.60
□ 9	Alan Benes	6.00	2.70	.75
□ 10	Marty Cordova	8.00	3.60	1.00
□ 11	Jimmy Haynes	5.00	2.20	.60
□ 12	Todd Hollandsworth	8.00	3.60	1.00
□ 13	Derek Jeter	30.00	13.50	3.70
□ 14	Chipper Jones	40.00	18.00	5.00
□ 15	Hideo Nomo	15.00	6.75	1.85
□ 16	Paul Wilson	8.00	3.60	1.00

1996 Topps Laser Power Cuts

Randomly inserted in packs at a rate of one in 40, this 16-card set features baseball's biggest bats on laser-cut stock polished off with etched silver and gold diffraction foil.

	MINT	NRMT	EXC
COMPLETE SET (16)	250.00	110.00	31.00
COMPLETE SERIES 1 (8)	125.00	55.00	15.50
COMPLETE SERIES 2 (8)	125.00	55.00	15.50
COMMON CARD (1-16)	6.00	2.70	.75
RANDOM INSERTS IN BOTH SERIES PACKS			

□ 1 Albert Belle	30.00	13.50	3.70
□ 2 Jay Buhner	8.00	3.60	1.00
□ 3 Fred McGriff	8.00	3.60	1.00
□ 4 Mike Piazza	40.00	18.00	5.00
□ 5 Tim Salmon	8.00	3.60	1.00
□ 6 Frank Thomas	60.00	27.00	7.50
□ 7 Mo Vaughn	15.00	6.75	1.85
□ 8 Matt Williams	8.00	3.60	1.00
□ 9 Jeff Bagwell	25.00	11.00	3.10
□ 10 Barry Bonds	15.00	6.75	1.85
□ 11 Jose Canseco	8.00	3.60	1.00
□ 12 Cecil Fielder	6.00	2.70	.75
□ 13 Juan Gonzalez	30.00	13.50	3.70
□ 14 Ken Griffey Jr.	60.00	27.00	7.50
□ 15 Sammy Sosa	10.00	4.50	1.25
□ 16 Larry Walker	6.00	2.70	.75

1996 Topps Laser Stadium Stars

Randomly inserted in packs at a rate of one in 60, this 16-card set features the best and the brightest stars of the baseball diamond. Each highly detailed, laser-sculpted cover folds back to reveal striated silver and gold etched diffraction foil on every card.

	MINT	NRMT	EXC
COMPLETE SET (16)	300.00	135.00	38.00
COMPLETE SERIES 1 (8)	150.00	70.00	19.00
COMPLETE SERIES 2 (8)	150.00	70.00	19.00
COMMON CARD (1-16)	8.00	3.60	1.00
RANDOM INSERTS IN BOTH SERIES PACKS			

□ 1 Carlos Baerga	8.00	3.60	1.00
□ 2 Barry Bonds	20.00	9.00	2.50
□ 3 Andres Galarraga	10.00	4.50	1.25
□ 4 Ken Griffey Jr.	80.00	36.00	10.00
□ 5 Barry Larkin	10.00	4.50	1.25
□ 6 Raul Mondesi	10.00	4.50	1.25
□ 7 Kirby Puckett	25.00	11.00	3.10
□ 8 Cal Ripken	60.00	27.00	7.50
□ 9 Will Clark	10.00	4.50	1.25
□ 10 Roger Clemens	10.00	4.50	1.25
□ 11 Tony Gwynn	30.00	13.50	3.70
□ 12 Randy Johnson	12.00	5.50	1.50
□ 13 Kenny Lofton	20.00	9.00	2.50
□ 14 Edgar Martinez	10.00	4.50	1.25
□ 15 Ryne Sandberg	20.00	9.00	2.50
□ 16 Frank Thomas	80.00	36.00	10.00

1992 Triple Play

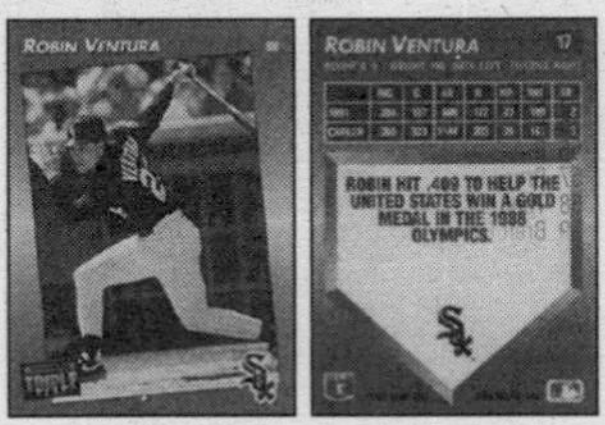

The 1992 Triple Play set contains 264 standard-size cards. Cards were distributed in 15-card foil packs and jumbo packs. Each 15-card foil pack came with one rub off game card. The Triple Play set was created especially for children ages 5-12, featuring bright color borders, player quotes, fun facts.The color action player photos on the fronts are slightly tilted to the left, and the border alternates shades from red to yellow and back to red again as one moves down the card face. Subsets include Little Hotshots (picturing some players when they were kids) and Awesome Action.

	MINT	NRMT	EXC
COMPLETE SET (264)	10.00	4.50	1.25
COMMON CARD (1-264)	.05	.02	.01
SEMISTARS	.10	.05	.01
STARS	.15	.07	.02

□ 1 SkyDome	.10	.05	.01
□ 2 Tom Foley	.05	.02	.01
□ 3 Scott Erickson	.10	.05	.01
□ 4 Matt Williams	.15	.07	.02
□ 5 David Valle	.05	.02	.01
□ 6 Andy Van Slyke LH	.05	.02	.01
□ 7 Tom Glavine	.15	.07	.02
□ 8 Kevin Appier	.10	.05	.01
□ 9 Pedro Guerrero	.05	.02	.01
□ 10 Terry Steinbach	.10	.05	.01
□ 11 Terry Mulholland	.05	.02	.01
□ 12 Mike Boddicker	.05	.02	.01
□ 13 Gregg Olson	.05	.02	.01
□ 14 Tim Burke	.05	.02	.01
□ 15 Candy Maldonado	.05	.02	.01
□ 16 Orlando Merced	.05	.02	.01
□ 17 Robin Ventura	.15	.07	.02
□ 18 Eric Anthony	.05	.02	.01
□ 19 Greg Maddux	.75	.35	.09
□ 20 Erik Hanson	.05	.02	.01
□ 21 Bobby Ojeda	.05	.02	.01
□ 22 Nolan Ryan	.75	.35	.09
□ 23 Dave Righetti	.05	.02	.01
□ 24 Reggie Jefferson	.10	.05	.01
□ 25 Jody Reed	.05	.02	.01
□ 26 Steve Finley and Gary Carter AA	.15	.07	.02
□ 27 Chili Davis	.10	.05	.01
□ 28 Hector Villanueva	.05	.02	.01
□ 29 Cecil Fielder	.10	.05	.01
□ 30 Hal Morris	.05	.02	.01
□ 31 Barry Larkin	.15	.07	.02

□	32 Bobby Thigpen	.05	.02	.01
□	33 Andy Benes	.05	.02	.01
□	34 Harold Baines	.10	.05	.01
□	35 David Cone	.15	.07	.02
□	36 Mark Langston	.10	.05	.01
□	37 Bryan Harvey	.05	.02	.01
□	38 John Kruk	.10	.05	.01
□	39 Scott Sanderson	.05	.02	.01
□	40 Lonnie Smith	.05	.02	.01
□	41 Rex Hudler AA	.05	.02	.01
□	42 George Bell	.05	.02	.01
□	43 Steve Finley	.15	.07	.02
□	44 Mickey Tettleton	.05	.02	.01
□	45 Robby Thompson	.05	.02	.01
□	46 Pat Kelly	.05	.02	.01
□	47 Marquis Grissom	.15	.07	.02
□	48 Tony Pena	.05	.02	.01
□	49 Alex Cole	.05	.02	.01
□	50 Steve Buechele	.05	.02	.01
□	51 Ivan Rodriguez	.30	.14	.04
□	52 John Smiley	.05	.02	.01
□	53 Gary Sheffield	.15	.07	.02
□	54 Greg Olson	.05	.02	.01
□	55 Ramon Martinez	.10	.05	.01
□	56 B.J. Surhoff	.10	.05	.01
□	57 Bruce Hurst	.05	.02	.01
□	58 Todd Stottlemyre	.10	.05	.01
□	59 Brett Butler	.10	.05	.01
□	60 Glenn Davis	.05	.02	.01
□	61 Glenn Braggs and Kirt Manwaring AA	.05	.02	.01
□	62 Lee Smith	.10	.05	.01
□	63 Rickey Henderson	.15	.07	.02
□	64 Fun at the Ballpark Dave Cone Jeff Innis John Franco	.10	.05	.01
□	65 Rick Aguilera	.05	.02	.01
□	66 Kevin Elster	.05	.02	.01
□	67 Dwight Evans	.10	.05	.01
□	68 Andujar Cedeno	.05	.02	.01
□	69 Brian McRae	.15	.07	.02
□	70 Benito Santiago	.05	.02	.01
□	71 Randy Johnson	.15	.07	.02
□	72 Roberto Kelly	.05	.02	.01
□	73 Juan Samuel AA	.05	.02	.01
□	74 Alex Fernandez	.15	.07	.02
□	75 Felix Jose	.05	.02	.01
□	76 Brian Harper	.05	.02	.01
□	77 Scott Sanderson LH	.05	.02	.01
□	78 Ken Caminiti	.15	.07	.02
□	79 Mo Vaughn	.40	.18	.05
□	80 Roger McDowell	.05	.02	.01
□	81 Robin Yount	.15	.07	.02
□	82 Dave Magadan	.05	.02	.01
□	83 Julio Franco	.10	.05	.01
□	84 Roberto Alomar	.25	.11	.03
□	85 Steve Avery	.10	.05	.01
□	86 Travis Fryman	.15	.07	.02
□	87 Fred McGriff	.15	.07	.02
□	88 Dave Stewart	.10	.05	.01
□	89 Larry Walker	.15	.07	.02
□	90 Chris Sabo	.05	.02	.01
□	91 Chuck Finley	.05	.02	.01
□	92 Dennis Martinez	.10	.05	.01
□	93 Jeff Johnson	.05	.02	.01
□	94 Len Dykstra	.10	.05	.01
□	95 Mark Whiten	.10	.05	.01
□	96 Wade Taylor	.05	.02	.01
□	97 Lance Dickson	.05	.02	.01
□	98 Kevin Tapani	.05	.02	.01
□	99 Luis Polonia and Tony Phillips AA	.05	.02	.01
□	100 Milt Cuyler	.05	.02	.01
□	101 Willie McGee	.05	.02	.01
□	102 Tony Fernandez AA	.05	.02	.01
□	103 Albert Belle	.60	.25	.07
□	104 Todd Hundley	.15	.07	.02
□	105 Ben McDonald	.05	.02	.01
□	106 Doug Drabek	.05	.02	.01
□	107 Tim Raines	.15	.07	.02
□	108 Joe Carter	.15	.07	.02
□	109 Reggie Sanders	.15	.07	.02
□	110 John Olerud	.10	.05	.01
□	111 Darren Lewis	.05	.02	.01
□	112 Juan Gonzalez	.60	.25	.07
□	113 Andre Dawson AA	.15	.07	.02
□	114 Mark Grace	.15	.07	.02
□	115 George Brett	.40	.18	.05
□	116 Barry Bonds	.25	.11	.03
□	117 Lou Whitaker	.15	.07	.02
□	118 Jose Oquendo	.05	.02	.01
□	119 Lee Stevens	.05	.02	.01
□	120 Phil Plantier	.10	.05	.01
□	121 Matt Merullo AA	.05	.02	.01
□	122 Greg Vaughn	.15	.07	.02
□	123 Royce Clayton	.10	.05	.01
□	124 Bob Welch	.05	.02	.01
□	125 Juan Samuel	.05	.02	.01
□	126 Ron Gant	.15	.07	.02
□	127 Edgar Martinez	.15	.07	.02
□	128 Andy Ashby	.10	.05	.01
□	129 Jack McDowell	.10	.05	.01
□	130 Dave Henderson and Jerry Browne AA	.05	.02	.01
□	131 Leo Gomez	.05	.02	.01
□	132 Checklist 1-88	.05	.02	.01
□	133 Phillie Phanatic	.15	.07	.02
□	134 Bret Barberie	.05	.02	.01
□	135 Kent Hrbek	.10	.05	.01
□	136 Hall of Fame	.10	.05	.01
□	137 Omar Vizquel	.15	.07	.02
□	138 The Famous Chicken	.15	.07	.02
□	139 Terry Pendleton	.10	.05	.01
□	140 Jim Eisenreich	.05	.02	.01
□	141 Todd Zeile	.05	.02	.01
□	142 Todd Van Poppel	.05	.02	.01
□	143 Darren Daulton	.10	.05	.01
□	144 Mike Macfarlane	.05	.02	.01
□	145 Luis Mercedes	.05	.02	.01
□	146 Trevor Wilson	.05	.02	.01
□	147 Dave Stieb	.05	.02	.01
□	148 Andy Van Slyke	.10	.05	.01
□	149 Carlton Fisk	.15	.07	.02
□	150 Craig Biggio	.15	.07	.02
□	151 Joe Girardi	.05	.02	.01
□	152 Ken Griffey Jr.	1.50	.70	.19
□	153 Jose Offerman	.05	.02	.01
□	154 Bobby Witt	.05	.02	.01
□	155 Will Clark	.15	.07	.02
□	156 Steve Olin	.05	.02	.01
□	157 Greg W. Harris	.05	.02	.01
□	158 Dale Murphy LH	.10	.05	.01
□	159 Don Mattingly	.50	.23	.06
□	160 Shawon Dunston	.05	.02	.01
□	161 Bill Gullickson	.05	.02	.01
□	162 Paul O'Neill	.10	.05	.01
□	163 Norm Charlton	.05	.02	.01
□	164 Bo Jackson	.15	.07	.02
□	165 Tony Fernandez	.05	.02	.01
□	166 Dave Henderson	.05	.02	.01
□	167 Dwight Gooden	.10	.05	.01
□	168 Junior Felix	.05	.02	.01
□	169 Lance Parrish	.05	.02	.01
□	170 Pat Combs	.05	.02	.01
□	171 Chuck Knoblauch	.15	.07	.02
□	172 John Smoltz	.15	.07	.02
□	173 Wrigley Field	.10	.05	.01
□	174 Andre Dawson	.15	.07	.02
□	175 Pete Harnisch	.05	.02	.01
□	176 Alan Trammell	.15	.07	.02
□	177 Kirk Dressendorfer	.05	.02	.01
□	178 Matt Nokes	.05	.02	.01
□	179 Wil Cordero	.10	.05	.01
□	180 Scott Cooper	.05	.02	.01
□	181 Glenallen Hill	.05	.02	.01
□	182 John Franco	.05	.02	.01
□	183 Rafael Palmeiro	.15	.07	.02
□	184 Jay Bell	.10	.05	.01
□	185 Bill Wegman	.05	.02	.01
□	186 Deion Sanders	.15	.07	.02
□	187 Darryl Strawberry	.10	.05	.01
□	188 Jaime Navarro	.05	.02	.01
□	189 Darrin Jackson	.05	.02	.01
□	190 Eddie Zosky	.05	.02	.01
□	191 Mike Scioscia	.05	.02	.01
□	192 Chito Martinez	.05	.02	.01
□	193 Pat Kelly and Ron Tingley AA	.05	.02	.01
□	194 Ray Lankford	.15	.07	.02
□	195 Dennis Eckersley	.10	.05	.01
□	196 Ivan Calderon and	.05	.02	.01

Mike Maddux AA			
□ 197 Shane Mack	.05	.02	.01
□ 198 Checklist 89-176	.05	.02	.01
□ 199 Cal Ripken	.75	.35	.09
□ 200 Jeff Bagwell	.60	.25	.07
□ 201 Dave Howard	.05	.02	.01
□ 202 Kirby Puckett	.30	.14	.04
□ 203 Harold Reynolds	.05	.02	.01
□ 204 Jim Abbott	.05	.02	.01
□ 205 Mark Lewis	.05	.02	.01
□ 206 Frank Thomas	1.50	.70	.19
□ 207 Rex Hudler	.05	.02	.01
□ 208 Vince Coleman	.05	.02	.01
□ 209 Delino DeShields	.05	.02	.01
□ 210 Luis Gonzalez	.10	.05	.01
□ 211 Wade Boggs	.15	.07	.02
□ 212 Orel Hershiser	.10	.05	.01
□ 213 Cal Eldred	.05	.02	.01
□ 214 Jose Canseco	.15	.07	.02
□ 215 Jose Guzman	.05	.02	.01
□ 216 Roger Clemens	.15	.07	.02
□ 217 David Justice	.15	.07	.02
□ 218 Tony Phillips	.10	.05	.01
□ 219 Tony Gwynn	.40	.18	.05
□ 220 Mitch Williams	.05	.02	.01
□ 221 Bill Sampen	.05	.02	.01
□ 222 Billy Hatcher	.05	.02	.01
□ 223 Gary Gaetti	.10	.05	.01
□ 224 Tim Wallach	.05	.02	.01
□ 225 Kevin Maas	.05	.02	.01
□ 226 Kevin Brown	.10	.05	.01
□ 227 Sandy Alomar Jr.	.10	.05	.01
□ 228 John Habyan	.05	.02	.01
□ 229 Ryne Sandberg	.25	.11	.03
□ 230 Greg Gagne	.05	.02	.01
□ 231 Autographs (Mark McGwire)	.15	.07	.02
□ 232 Mike LaValliere	.05	.02	.01
□ 233 Mark Gubicza	.05	.02	.01
□ 234 Lance Parrish LH	.05	.02	.01
□ 235 Carlos Baerga	.15	.07	.02
□ 236 Howard Johnson	.05	.02	.01
□ 237 Mike Mussina	.30	.14	.04
□ 238 Ruben Sierra	.10	.05	.01
□ 239 Lance Johnson	.10	.05	.01
□ 240 Devon White	.10	.05	.01
□ 241 Dan Wilson	.15	.07	.02
□ 242 Kelly Gruber	.05	.02	.01
□ 243 Brett Butler LH	.05	.02	.01
□ 244 Ozzie Smith	.20	.09	.03
□ 245 Chuck McElroy	.05	.02	.01
□ 246 Shawn Boskie	.05	.02	.01
□ 247 Mark Davis	.05	.02	.01
□ 248 Bill Landrum	.05	.02	.01
□ 249 Frank Tanana	.05	.02	.01
□ 250 Darryl Hamilton	.05	.02	.01
□ 251 Gary DiSarcina	.05	.02	.01
□ 252 Mike Greenwell	.05	.02	.01
□ 253 Cal Ripken LH	.40	.18	.05
□ 254 Paul Molitor	.20	.09	.03
□ 255 Tim Teufel	.05	.02	.01
□ 256 Chris Hoiles	.05	.02	.01
□ 257 Rob Dibble	.05	.02	.01
□ 258 Sid Bream	.05	.02	.01
□ 259 Tino Martinez	.15	.07	.02
□ 260 Dale Murphy	.15	.07	.02
□ 261 Greg Hibbard	.05	.02	.01
□ 262 Mark McGwire	.30	.14	.04
□ 263 Oriole Park	.10	.05	.01
□ 264 Checklist 177-264	.05	.02	.01

1992 Triple Play Gallery

The 1992 Triple Play Gallery of Stars was an insert to the 1992 Triple Play baseball set. Randomly inserted into foil packs, the first six cards feature top players who changed teams in 1992 in their new uniforms. The second six cards were inserted one per jumbo pack. Each group of six cards is sequenced in alphabetical order. On bright-colored backgrounds, the fronts display color player portraits by noted sports artist Dick Perez. The words "Gallery of Stars" appear in a red and silver-foil stamped banner above the portrait, while the player's

name appears in a similarly colored bar between two silver foil stars at the card bottom.

	MINT	NRMT	EXC
COMPLETE SET (12)	20.00	9.00	2.50
COMPLETE FOIL SET (6)	2.50	1.10	.30
COMPLETE JUMBO SET (6)	18.00	8.00	2.20
COMMON CARD (GS1-GS6)	.50	.23	.06
RANDOM INSERTS IN FOIL PACKS			
COMMON CARD (GS7-GS12)	1.00	.45	.12
ONE PER JUMBO PACK			

□ GS1 Bobby Bonilla	.50	.23	.06
□ GS2 Wally Joyner	.50	.23	.06
□ GS3 Jack Morris	.50	.23	.06
□ GS4 Steve Sax	.50	.23	.06
□ GS5 Danny Tartabull	.50	.23	.06
□ GS6 Frank Viola	.50	.23	.06
□ GS7 Jeff Bagwell	4.00	1.80	.50
□ GS8 Ken Griffey Jr.	6.00	2.70	.75
□ GS9 Dave Justice	1.00	.45	.12
□ GS10 Ryan Klesko	4.00	1.80	.50
□ GS11 Cal Ripken	5.00	2.20	.60
□ GS12 Frank Thomas	6.00	2.70	.75

1993 Triple Play

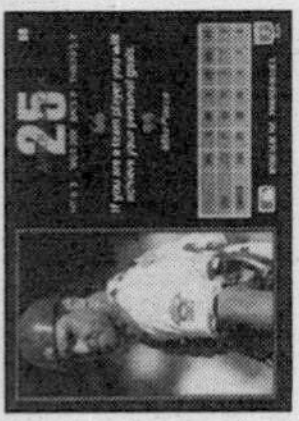

The 1993 Donruss Triple Play baseball set consists of 264 standard-size cards. Approximately eight players from each of the 28 teams is represented in the set. Each pack also included one of thirty Triple Play Action Baseball game cards. The fronts display color action player photos inside a red frame on a black card face. The player's last name appears in silver block lettering across the top of the picture. The team logo is placed at the lower right corner. The horizontal backs feature a color close-up photo, biography, and either trivia questions, fun facts, or player quotes. Scattered throughout the set are seven Little Hotshot (11, 77, 97, 143, 209, 229, 245) and eight Awesome Action (12, 61, 64, 68, 144, 193, 196, 200) cards. There are no key Rookie Cards in this set, however the set does feature the first card of President Bill Clinton.

	MINT	NRMT	EXC
COMPLETE SET (264)	10.00	4.50	1.25
COMMON CARD (1-264)	.05	.02	.01
SEMISTARS	.15	.07	.02
STARS	.30	.14	.04

□ 1	Ken Griffey Jr.	2.00	.90	.25
□ 2	Roberto Alomar	.50	.23	.06
□ 3	Cal Ripken	1.50	.70	.19
□ 4	Eric Karros	.30	.14	.04
□ 5	Cecil Fielder	.15	.07	.02
□ 6	Gary Sheffield	.30	.14	.04
□ 7	Darren Daulton	.15	.07	.02
□ 8	Andy Van Slyke	.15	.07	.02
□ 9	Dennis Eckersley	.15	.07	.02
□ 10	Ryne Sandberg	.50	.23	.06
□ 11	Mark Grace LH	.15	.07	.02
□ 12	David Segui and	.05	.02	.01
	Luis Polonia AA			
□ 13	Mike Mussina	.40	.18	.05
□ 14	Vince Coleman	.05	.02	.01
□ 15	Rafael Belliard	.05	.02	.01
□ 16	Ivan Rodriguez	.40	.18	.05
□ 17	Eddie Taubensee	.05	.02	.01
□ 18	Cal Eldred	.05	.02	.01
□ 19	Rick Wilkins	.05	.02	.01
□ 20	Edgar Martinez	.30	.14	.04
□ 21	Brian McRae	.15	.07	.02
□ 22	Darren Holmes	.05	.02	.01
□ 23	Mark Whiten	.05	.02	.01
□ 24	Todd Zeile	.05	.02	.01
□ 25	Scott Cooper	.05	.02	.01
□ 26	Frank Thomas	2.00	.90	.25
□ 27	Wil Cordero	.15	.07	.02
□ 28	Juan Guzman	.15	.07	.02
□ 29	Pedro Astacio	.05	.02	.01
□ 30	Steve Avery	.15	.07	.02
□ 31	Barry Larkin	.30	.14	.04
□ 32	Bill Clinton	1.00	.45	.12
□ 33	Scott Erickson	.05	.02	.01
□ 34	Mike Devereaux	.05	.02	.01
□ 35	Tino Martinez	.15	.07	.02
□ 36	Brent Mayne	.05	.02	.01
□ 37	Tim Salmon	.50	.23	.06
□ 38	Dave Hollins	.05	.02	.01
□ 39	Royce Clayton	.15	.07	.02
□ 40	Shawon Dunston	.05	.02	.01
□ 41	Eddie Murray	.50	.23	.06
□ 42	Larry Walker	.30	.14	.04
□ 43	Jeff Bagwell	.75	.35	.09
□ 44	Milt Cuyler	.05	.02	.01
□ 45	Mike Bordick	.05	.02	.01
□ 46	Mike Greenwell	.05	.02	.01
□ 47	Steve Sax	.05	.02	.01
□ 48	Chuck Knoblauch	.30	.14	.04
□ 49	Charles Nagy	.15	.07	.02
□ 50	Tim Wakefield	.15	.07	.02
□ 51	Tony Gwynn	.75	.35	.09
□ 52	Rob Dibble	.05	.02	.01
□ 53	Mickey Morandini	.05	.02	.01
□ 54	Steve Hosey	.05	.02	.01
□ 55	Mike Piazza	2.00	.90	.25
□ 56	Bill Wegman	.05	.02	.01
□ 57	Kevin Maas	.05	.02	.01
□ 58	Gary DiSarcina	.05	.02	.01
□ 59	Travis Fryman	.30	.14	.04
□ 60	Ruben Sierra	.15	.07	.02
□ 61	Ken Caminiti AA	.15	.07	.02
□ 62	Brian Jordan	.30	.14	.04
□ 63	Scott Chiamparino	.05	.02	.01
□ 64	George Brett and	.40	.18	.05
	Mike Bordick AA			
□ 65	Carlos Garcia	.05	.02	.01
□ 66	Checklist	.05	.02	.01
□ 67	John Smoltz	.30	.14	.04
□ 68	Mark McGwire and	.30	.14	.04
	Brian Harper AA			
□ 69	Kurt Stillwell	.05	.02	.01
□ 70	Chad Curtis	.15	.07	.02
□ 71	Rafael Palmeiro	.30	.14	.04
□ 72	Kevin Young	.05	.02	.01
□ 73	Glenn Davis	.05	.02	.01
□ 74	Dennis Martinez	.15	.07	.02
□ 75	Sam Militello	.05	.02	.01
□ 76	Mike Morgan	.05	.02	.01
□ 77	Frank Thomas LH	1.00	.45	.12
□ 78	Staying Fit	.05	.02	.01
□ 79	Steve Buechele	.05	.02	.01
□ 80	Carlos Baerga	.30	.14	.04
□ 81	Robby Thompson	.05	.02	.01
□ 82	Kirk McCaskill	.05	.02	.01
□ 83	Lee Smith	.15	.07	.02
□ 84	Gary Scott	.05	.02	.01
□ 85	Tony Pena	.05	.02	.01
□ 86	Howard Johnson	.05	.02	.01
□ 87	Mark McGwire	.60	.25	.07
□ 88	Bip Roberts	.05	.02	.01
□ 89	Devon White	.05	.02	.01
□ 90	John Franco	.05	.02	.01
□ 91	Tom Browning	.05	.02	.01
□ 92	Mickey Tettleton	.05	.02	.01
□ 93	Jeff Conine	.30	.14	.04
□ 94	Albert Belle	1.00	.45	.12
□ 95	Fred McGriff	.30	.14	.04
□ 96	Nolan Ryan	1.50	.70	.19
□ 97	Paul Molitor LH	.15	.07	.02
□ 98	Juan Bell	.05	.02	.01
□ 99	Dave Fleming	.05	.02	.01
□ 100	Craig Biggio	.30	.14	.04
□ 101A	Andy Stankiewicz ERR	.15	.07	.02
	(Name on front in white)			
□ 101B	Andy Stankiewicz ERR	.15	.07	.02
	(Name on front in red)			
□ 102	Delino DeShields	.05	.02	.01
□ 103	Damion Easley	.05	.02	.01
□ 104	Kevin McReynolds	.05	.02	.01
□ 105	David Nied	.05	.02	.01
□ 106	Rick Sutcliffe	.05	.02	.01
□ 107	Will Clark	.30	.14	.04
□ 108	Tim Raines	.30	.14	.04
□ 109	Eric Anthony	.05	.02	.01
□ 110	Mike LaValliere	.05	.02	.01
□ 111	Dean Palmer	.15	.07	.02
□ 112	Eric Davis	.15	.07	.02
□ 113	Damon Berryhill	.05	.02	.01
□ 114	Felix Jose	.05	.02	.01
□ 115	Ozzie Guillen	.05	.02	.01
□ 116	Pat Listach	.05	.02	.01
□ 117	Tom Glavine	.30	.14	.04
□ 118	Roger Clemens	.30	.14	.04
□ 119	Dave Henderson	.05	.02	.01
□ 120	Don Mattingly	1.00	.45	.12
□ 121	Orel Hershiser	.15	.07	.02
□ 122	Ozzie Smith	.40	.18	.05
□ 123	Joe Carter	.30	.14	.04
□ 124	Bret Saberhagen	.15	.07	.02
□ 125	Mitch Williams	.05	.02	.01
□ 126	Jerald Clark	.05	.02	.01
□ 127	Mile High Stadium	.15	.07	.02
□ 128	Kent Hrbek	.15	.07	.02
□ 129	Equipment	.05	.02	.01
	Curt Schilling			
□ 130	Gregg Jefferies	.30	.14	.04
□ 131	John Orton	.05	.02	.01
□ 132	Checklist	.05	.02	.01
□ 133	Bret Boone	.15	.07	.02
□ 134	Pat Borders	.05	.02	.01
□ 135	Gregg Olson	.05	.02	.01
□ 136	Brett Butler	.15	.07	.02
□ 137	Rob Deer	.05	.02	.01
□ 138	Darrin Jackson	.05	.02	.01
□ 139	John Kruk	.15	.07	.02
□ 140	Jay Bell	.15	.07	.02
□ 141	Bobby Witt	.05	.02	.01
□ 142	Dan Plesac	.05	.02	.01
	Randy Myers			
	Jose Guzman			
	New Cubs			
□ 143	Wade Boggs LH	.30	.14	.04
□ 144	Ken Lofton AA	.40	.18	.05
□ 145	Ben McDonald	.05	.02	.01
□ 146	Dwight Gooden	.15	.07	.02
□ 147	Terry Pendleton	.15	.07	.02
□ 148	Julio Franco	.15	.07	.02
□ 149	Ken Caminiti	.30	.14	.04
□ 150	Greg Vaughn	.30	.14	.04
□ 151	Sammy Sosa	.30	.14	.04
□ 152	David Valle	.05	.02	.01
□ 153	Wally Joyner	.15	.07	.02
□ 154	Dante Bichette	.30	.14	.04
□ 155	Mark Lewis	.05	.02	.01
□ 156	Bob Tewksbury	.05	.02	.01
□ 157	Billy Hatcher	.05	.02	.01
□ 158	Jack McDowell	.15	.07	.02
□ 159	Marquis Grissom	.30	.14	.04
□ 160	Jack Morris	.15	.07	.02
□ 161	Ramon Martinez	.15	.07	.02
□ 162	Deion Sanders	.30	.14	.04

□ 163 Tim Belcher	.05	.02	.01
□ 164 Mascots	.05	.02	.01
Pirate Parrot			
□ 165 Scott Leius	.05	.02	.01
□ 166 Brady Anderson	.30	.14	.04
□ 167 Randy Johnson	.30	.14	.04
□ 168 Mark Gubicza	.05	.02	.01
□ 169 Chuck Finley	.05	.02	.01
□ 170 Terry Mulholland	.05	.02	.01
□ 171 Matt Williams	.30	.14	.04
□ 172 Dwight Smith	.05	.02	.01
□ 173 Bobby Bonilla	.15	.07	.02
□ 174 Ken Hill	.15	.07	.02
□ 175 Doug Jones	.05	.02	.01
□ 176 Tony Phillips	.15	.07	.02
□ 177 Terry Steinbach	.15	.07	.02
□ 178 Frank Viola	.05	.02	.01
□ 179 Robin Ventura	.15	.07	.02
□ 180 Shane Mack	.05	.02	.01
□ 181 Kenny Lofton	.75	.35	.09
□ 182 Jeff King	.15	.07	.02
□ 183 Tim Teufel	.05	.02	.01
□ 184 Chris Sabo	.05	.02	.01
□ 185 Len Dykstra	.15	.07	.02
□ 186 Trevor Wilson	.05	.02	.01
□ 187 Darryl Strawberry	.15	.07	.02
□ 188 Robin Yount	.30	.14	.04
□ 189 Bob Wickman	.05	.02	.01
□ 190 Luis Polonia	.05	.02	.01
□ 191 Alan Trammell	.30	.14	.04
□ 192 Bob Welch	.05	.02	.01
□ 193 Omar Vizquel AA	.15	.07	.02
□ 194 Tom Pagnozzi	.05	.02	.01
□ 195 Bret Barberie	.05	.02	.01
□ 196 Mike Scioscia AA	.05	.02	.01
□ 197 Randy Tomlin	.05	.02	.01
□ 198 Checklist	.05	.02	.01
□ 199 Ron Gant	.30	.14	.04
□ 200 Roberto Alomar AA	.30	.14	.04
□ 201 Andy Benes	.05	.02	.01
□ 202 Six Pirates Playing	.05	.02	.01
Pepper			
□ 203 Steve Finley	.30	.14	.04
□ 204 Steve Olin	.05	.02	.01
□ 205 Chris Hoiles	.05	.02	.01
□ 206 John Wetteland	.15	.07	.02
□ 207 Danny Tartabull	.05	.02	.01
□ 208 Bernard Gilkey	.30	.14	.04
□ 209 Tom Glavine LH	.15	.07	.02
□ 210 Benito Santiago	.05	.02	.01
□ 211 Mark Grace	.30	.14	.04
□ 212 Glenallen Hill	.05	.02	.01
□ 213 Jeff Brantley	.05	.02	.01
□ 214 George Brett	.75	.35	.09
□ 215 Mark Lemke	.05	.02	.01
□ 216 Ron Karkovice	.05	.02	.01
□ 217 Tom Brunansky	.05	.02	.01
□ 218 Todd Hundley	.30	.14	.04
□ 219 Rickey Henderson	.30	.14	.04
□ 220 Joe Oliver	.05	.02	.01
□ 221 Juan Gonzalez	1.00	.45	.12
□ 222 John Olerud	.05	.02	.01
□ 223 Hal Morris	.05	.02	.01
□ 224 Lou Whitaker	.30	.14	.04
□ 225 Bryan Harvey	.05	.02	.01
□ 226 Mike Gallego	.05	.02	.01
□ 227 Willie McGee	.05	.02	.01
□ 228 Jose Oquendo	.05	.02	.01
□ 229 Darren Daulton LH	.05	.02	.01
□ 230 Curt Schilling	.05	.02	.01
□ 231 Jay Buhner	.30	.14	.04
□ 232 Doug Drabek	.05	.02	.01
Greg Swindell			
New Astros			
□ 233 Jaime Navarro	.05	.02	.01
□ 234 Kevin Appier	.15	.07	.02
□ 235 Mark Langston	.15	.07	.02
□ 236 Jeff Montgomery	.15	.07	.02
□ 237 Joe Girardi	.05	.02	.01
□ 238 Ed Sprague	.15	.07	.02
□ 239 Dan Walters	.05	.02	.01
□ 240 Kevin Tapani	.05	.02	.01
□ 241 Pete Harnisch	.05	.02	.01
□ 242 Al Martin	.15	.07	.02
□ 243 Jose Canseco	.30	.14	.04
□ 244 Moises Alou	.30	.14	.04
□ 245 Mark McGwire LH	.30	.14	.04
□ 246 Luis Rivera	.05	.02	.01
□ 247 George Bell	.05	.02	.01
□ 248 B.J. Surhoff	.15	.07	.02
□ 249 David Justice	.30	.14	.04
□ 250 Brian Harper	.05	.02	.01
□ 251 Sandy Alomar Jr.	.15	.07	.02
□ 252 Kevin Brown	.05	.02	.01
□ 253 Tim Wallach	.05	.02	.01
Todd Worrell			
Jody Reed			
New Dodgers			
□ 254 Ray Lankford	.30	.14	.04
□ 255 Derek Bell	.30	.14	.04
□ 256 Joe Grahe	.05	.02	.01
□ 257 Charlie Hayes	.05	.02	.01
□ 258 Wade Boggs	.30	.14	.04
Jim Abbott			
New Yankees			
□ 259A Joe Robbie Stadium	.15	.07	.02
ERR (Misnumbered 129)			
□ 259B Joe Robbie Stadium	.15	.07	.02
COR			
□ 260 Kirby Puckett	.60	.25	.07
□ 261 Jay Bell	.05	.02	.01
Fun at the Ballpark			
□ 262 Bill Swift	.05	.02	.01
□ 263 Roger McDowell	.05	.02	.01
Fun at the Ballpark			
□ 264 Checklist	.05	.02	.01

1993 Triple Play Action

The 1993 Triple Play Action set was inserted one per pack of Triple Play. The cards were designed to serve as a game card with a scratch-off section inside beside a baseball diamond design. The cards are printed on a lighter weight card stock. When unfolded the cards measure approximately 5" by 3 1/2", however when folded they measure the standard size. The front of the folded card features a color action player shot with a wide vertical gray border across the top. Within the upper border are the set title and the words "Action Baseball" printed in black. The player pictured on the card front is not named. Two team logos are superimposed across the photo at the bottom indicating which teams are paired up to play the scratch-off game inside. The inner portion of the card has six game rules printed on the upper left side followed by 32 scratch-off boxes. On the inner right side is a scoreboard printed above a green background baseball diamond. The backs are silver with the Leaf logo printed at the bottom.

	MINT	NRMT	EXC
COMPLETE SET (30)	10.00	4.50	1.25
COMMON CARD (1-30)	.10	.05	.01
SEMISTARS	.30	.14	.04
ONE PER PACK			
□ 1 Andy Van Slyke	.10	.05	.01
□ 2 Bobby Bonilla	.30	.14	.04
□ 3 Ozzie Smith	.40	.18	.05
□ 4 Ryne Sandberg	.50	.23	.06
□ 5 Darren Daulton	.30	.14	.04
□ 6 Larry Walker	.30	.14	.04

□ 7 Eric Karros	.30	.14	.04
□ 8 Barry Larkin	.30	.14	.04
□ 9 Deion Sanders	.30	.14	.04
□ 10 Gary Sheffield	.30	.14	.04
□ 11 Will Clark	.30	.14	.04
□ 12 Jeff Bagwell	.75	.35	.09
□ 13 Roberto Alomar	.50	.23	.06
□ 14 Roger Clemens	.30	.14	.04
□ 15 Cecil Fielder	.30	.14	.04
□ 16 Robin Yount	.30	.14	.04
□ 17 Cal Ripken	1.50	.70	.19
□ 18 Carlos Baerga	.30	.14	.04
□ 19 Don Mattingly	1.00	.45	.12
□ 20 Kirby Puckett	.60	.25	.07
□ 21 Frank Thomas	2.00	.90	.25
□ 22 Juan Gonzalez	1.00	.45	.12
□ 23 Mark McGwire	.60	.25	.07
□ 24 Ken Griffey Jr.	2.00	.90	.25
□ 25 Wally Joyner	.10	.05	.01
□ 26 Chad Curtis	.10	.05	.01
□ 27 Rockies Vs. Marlins	.10	.05	.01
□ 28 Juan Guzman	.10	.05	.01
□ 29 David Justice	.10	.05	.01
□ 30 Joe Carter	.30	.14	.04

1993 Triple Play Gallery

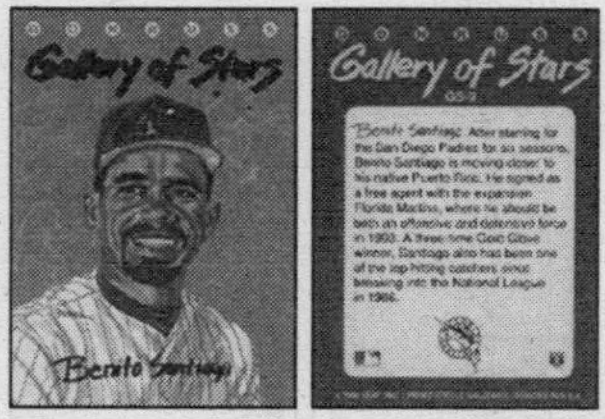

A one per pack insert in 1993 Donruss Triple Play jumbo packs, these ten standard-size cards have fronts that feature color player portraits by noted sports artist Dick Perez. The words "Gallery of Stars" printed in gold foil appear near the top, and the player's name, also in gold foil, rests at the bottom. The backs have a gray-bordered, white rectangle with rounded corners that carries the player's career highlights and team logo. The set name appears above in yellow lettering. The cards are numbered on the back with a "GS" prefix.

	MINT	NRMT	EXC
COMPLETE SET (10)	20.00	9.00	2.50
COMMON CARD (GS1-GS10)	1.50	.70	.19
ONE PER JUMBO PACK			

□ GS1 Barry Bonds	5.00	2.20	.60
□ GS2 Andre Dawson	2.50	1.10	.30
□ GS3 Wade Boggs	2.50	1.10	.30
□ GS4 Greg Maddux	12.00	5.50	1.50
□ GS5 Dave Winfield	2.50	1.10	.30
□ GS6 Paul Molitor	4.00	1.80	.50
□ GS7 Jim Abbott	2.50	1.10	.30
□ GS8 J.T. Snow	2.50	1.10	.30
□ GS9 Benito Santiago	1.50	.70	.19
□ GS10 David Nied	1.50	.70	.19

1993 Triple Play League Leaders

Randomly inserted in magazine distributor packs only, the six standard-size cards comprising this set feature borderless color action player shots on both sides. A National League leader appears on one side, an American League leader is on the other. The player's league appears in gold-foil lettering across the top. The player's name in white cursive lettering

is displayed near the bottom within the set logo, which has a simulated black marble plaque design. The cards are numbered on the American League side with an "L" prefix.

	MINT	NRMT	EXC
COMPLETE SET (6)	35.00	16.00	4.40
COMMON PAIR (L1-L6)	3.00	1.35	.35
RANDOM INSERTS IN RETAIL PACKS			

□ L1 Barry Bonds Dennis Eckersley	6.00	2.70	.75
□ L2 Greg Maddux Dennis Eckersley	15.00	6.75	1.85
□ L3 Eric Karros Pat Listach	3.00	1.35	.35
□ L4 Fred McGriff Juan Gonzalez	15.00	6.75	1.85
□ L5 Darren Daulton Cecil Fielder	4.00	1.80	.50
□ L6 Gary Sheffield Edgar Martinez	5.00	2.20	.60

1993 Triple Play Nicknames

Randomly inserted in foil packs only, this ten-card standard-size set is a new insert set featuring popular player's nicknames. The borderless fronts feature color player action shots. The player's name appears at the bottom, within an irregular red stripe that simulates a stroke of a paintbrush. His nickname appears in large prismatic-foil lettering at the top of the photo. The white back shades to red near the bottom and carries the player's last name in large purplish letters at the top. His first name appears in smaller white cursive lettering superposed upon his last name. The player's biography, set off by thin black lines, is shown below. A color player action shot appears beneath on the left side, and his career highlights are shown alongside on the right. The player's team logo at the bottom rounds out the card.

	MINT	NRMT	EXC
COMPLETE SET (10)	35.00	16.00	4.40
COMMON CARD (1-10)	1.00	.45	.12
SEMISTARS	1.25	.55	.16
RANDOM INSERTS IN HOBBY PACKS			

□ 1 Frank Thomas Big Hurt	10.00	4.50	1.25
□ 2 Roger Clemens	1.50	.70	.19

Rocket			
□ 3 Ryne Sandberg	3.00	1.35	.35
Ryno			
□ 4 Will Clark	1.50	.70	.19
Thrill			
□ 5 Ken Griffey Jr.	10.00	4.50	1.25
Junior			
□ 6 Dwight Gooden	1.00	.45	.12
□ 7 Nolan Ryan	10.00	4.50	1.25
Express			
□ 8 Deion Sanders	1.50	.70	.19
Prime Time			
□ 9 Ozzie Smith	2.50	1.10	.30
Wizard			
□ 10 Fred McGriff	1.50	.70	.19
Crime Dog			

1994 Triple Play

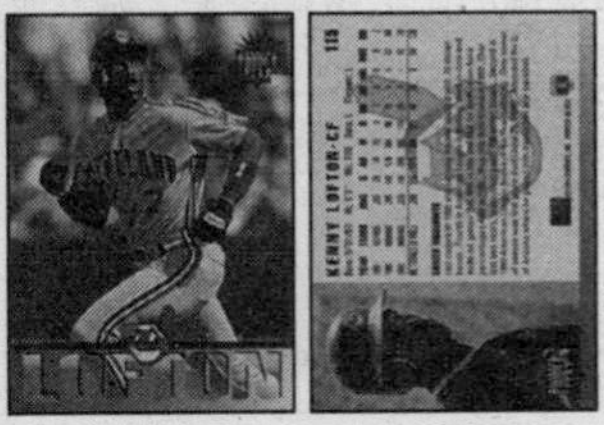

The 1994 Triple Play set consists of 300 standard-size cards, featuring ten players from each team along with a 17-card Rookie Review set. The fronts have color player action shots that are borderless, except at the bottom, where the player's name appears within a colored stripe. The horizontal back carries a posed color player photo on the left side. On the right, beneath the player's name and position, appear biography, statistics, and career highlights on a white background highlighted by his team's ghosted logo. Triple Play game cards, redeemable for various prizes, were inserted one per pack.

	MINT	NRMT	EXC
COMPLETE SET (300)	15.00	6.75	1.85
COMMON CARD (1-300)	.05	.02	.01
SEMISTARS	.15	.07	.02
STARS	.30	.14	.04

□ 1 Mike Bordick	.05	.02	.01
□ 2 Dennis Eckersley	.15	.07	.02
□ 3 Brent Gates	.05	.02	.01
□ 4 Rickey Henderson	.30	.14	.04
□ 5 Mark McGwire	.60	.25	.07
□ 6 Troy Neel	.05	.02	.01
□ 7 Craig Paquette	.05	.02	.01
□ 8 Ruben Sierra	.15	.07	.02
□ 9 Terry Steinbach	.15	.07	.02
□ 10 Bobby Witt	.05	.02	.01
□ 11 Chad Curtis	.05	.02	.01
□ 12 Chili Davis	.15	.07	.02
□ 13 Gary DiSarcina	.05	.02	.01
□ 14 Damion Easley	.05	.02	.01
□ 15 Chuck Finley	.05	.02	.01
□ 16 Joe Grahe	.05	.02	.01
□ 17 Mark Langston	.15	.07	.02
□ 18 Eduardo Perez	.05	.02	.01
□ 19 Tim Salmon	.30	.14	.04
□ 20 J.T. Snow	.15	.07	.02
□ 21 Jeff Bagwell	.75	.35	.09
□ 22 Craig Biggio	.30	.14	.04
□ 23 Ken Caminiti	.30	.14	.04
□ 24 Andujar Cedeno	.05	.02	.01
□ 25 Doug Drabek	.05	.02	.01
□ 26 Steve Finley	.30	.14	.04
□ 27 Luis Gonzalez	.05	.02	.01
□ 28 Pete Harnisch	.05	.02	.01
□ 29 Darryl Kile	.05	.02	.01
□ 30 Mitch Williams	.05	.02	.01
□ 31 Roberto Alomar	.50	.23	.06
□ 32 Joe Carter	.30	.14	.04
□ 33 Juan Guzman	.15	.07	.02
□ 34 Pat Hentgen	.30	.14	.04
□ 35 Paul Molitor	.40	.18	.05
□ 36 John Olerud	.05	.02	.01
□ 37 Ed Sprague	.15	.07	.02
□ 38 Dave Stewart	.15	.07	.02
□ 39 Duane Ward	.05	.02	.01
□ 40 Devon White	.05	.02	.01
□ 41 Steve Avery	.15	.07	.02
□ 42 Jeff Blauser	.05	.02	.01
□ 43 Ron Gant	.15	.07	.02
□ 44 Tom Glavine	.30	.14	.04
□ 45 David Justice	.30	.14	.04
□ 46 Greg Maddux	1.25	.55	.16
□ 47 Fred McGriff	.30	.14	.04
□ 48 Terry Pendleton	.15	.07	.02
□ 49 Deion Sanders	.30	.14	.04
□ 50 John Smoltz	.30	.14	.04
□ 51 Ricky Bones	.05	.02	.01
□ 52 Cal Eldred	.05	.02	.01
□ 53 Darryl Hamilton	.05	.02	.01
□ 54 John Jaha	.15	.07	.02
□ 55 Pat Listach	.05	.02	.01
□ 56 Jaime Navarro	.05	.02	.01
□ 57 Dave Nilsson	.15	.07	.02
□ 58 B.J. Surhoff	.05	.02	.01
□ 59 Greg Vaughn	.30	.14	.04
□ 60 Robin Yount	.30	.14	.04
□ 61 Bernard Gilkey	.15	.07	.02
□ 62 Gregg Jefferies	.30	.14	.04
□ 63 Brian Jordan	.30	.14	.04
□ 64 Ray Lankford	.30	.14	.04
□ 65 Tom Pagnozzi	.05	.02	.01
□ 66 Ozzie Smith	.40	.18	.05
□ 67 Bob Tewksbury	.05	.02	.01
□ 68 Allen Watson	.05	.02	.01
□ 69 Mark Whiten	.05	.02	.01
□ 70 Todd Zeile	.05	.02	.01
□ 71 Steve Buechele	.05	.02	.01
□ 72 Mark Grace	.30	.14	.04
□ 73 Jose Guzman	.05	.02	.01
□ 74 Derrick May	.05	.02	.01
□ 75 Mike Morgan	.05	.02	.01
□ 76 Randy Myers	.05	.02	.01
□ 77 Ryne Sandberg	.50	.23	.06
□ 78 Sammy Sosa	.30	.14	.04
□ 79 Jose Vizcaino	.05	.02	.01
□ 80 Rick Wilkins	.05	.02	.01
□ 81 Pedro Astacio	.05	.02	.01
□ 82 Brett Butler	.15	.07	.02
□ 83 Delino DeShields	.05	.02	.01
□ 84 Orel Hershiser	.15	.07	.02
□ 85 Eric Karros	.15	.07	.02
□ 86 Ramon Martinez	.15	.07	.02
□ 87 Jose Offerman	.05	.02	.01
□ 88 Mike Piazza	1.25	.55	.16
□ 89 Darryl Strawberry	.15	.07	.02
□ 90 Tim Wallach	.05	.02	.01
□ 91 Moises Alou	.15	.07	.02
□ 92 Wil Cordero	.15	.07	.02
□ 93 Jeff Fassero	.05	.02	.01
□ 94 Darrin Fletcher	.05	.02	.01
□ 95 Marquis Grissom	.30	.14	.04
□ 96 Ken Hill	.05	.02	.01
□ 97 Mike Lansing	.15	.07	.02
□ 98 Kirk Rueter	.05	.02	.01
□ 99 Larry Walker	.30	.14	.04
□ 100 John Wetteland	.15	.07	.02
□ 101 Rod Beck	.15	.07	.02
□ 102 Barry Bonds	.50	.23	.06
□ 103 John Burkett	.05	.02	.01
□ 104 Royce Clayton	.15	.07	.02
□ 105 Darren Lewis	.05	.02	.01
□ 106 Kirt Manwaring	.05	.02	.01
□ 107 Willie McGee	.05	.02	.01
□ 108 Bill Swift	.05	.02	.01
□ 109 Robby Thompson	.05	.02	.01
□ 110 Matt Williams	.30	.14	.04
□ 111 Sandy Alomar Jr.	.15	.07	.02
□ 112 Carlos Baerga	.30	.14	.04
□ 113 Albert Belle	1.00	.45	.12
□ 114 Wayne Kirby	.05	.02	.01
□ 115 Kenny Lofton	.60	.25	.07
□ 116 Jose Mesa	.15	.07	.02

□	117 Eddie Murray	.50	.23	.06
□	118 Charles Nagy	.15	.07	.02
□	119 Paul Sorrento	.05	.02	.01
□	120 Jim Thome	.50	.23	.06
□	121 Rich Amaral	.05	.02	.01
□	122 Eric Anthony	.05	.02	.01
□	123 Mike Blowers	.05	.02	.01
□	124 Chris Bosio	.05	.02	.01
□	125 Jay Buhner	.30	.14	.04
□	126 Dave Fleming	.05	.02	.01
□	127 Ken Griffey Jr.	2.00	.90	.25
□	128 Randy Johnson	.30	.14	.04
□	129 Edgar Martinez	.30	.14	.04
□	130 Tino Martinez	.15	.07	.02
□	131 Bret Barberie	.05	.02	.01
□	132 Ryan Bowen	.05	.02	.01
□	133 Chuck Carr	.05	.02	.01
□	134 Jeff Conine	.30	.14	.04
□	135 Orestes Destrade	.05	.02	.01
□	136 Chris Hammond	.05	.02	.01
□	137 Bryan Harvey	.05	.02	.01
□	138 Dave Magadan	.05	.02	.01
□	139 Benito Santiago	.05	.02	.01
□	140 Gary Sheffield	.30	.14	.04
□	141 Bobby Bonilla	.15	.07	.02
□	142 Jeromy Burnitz	.05	.02	.01
□	143 Dwight Gooden	.15	.07	.02
□	144 Todd Hundley	.30	.14	.04
□	145 Bobby Jones	.15	.07	.02
□	146 Jeff Kent	.05	.02	.01
□	147 Joe Orsulak	.05	.02	.01
□	148 Bret Saberhagen	.15	.07	.02
□	149 Pete Schourek	.15	.07	.02
□	150 Ryan Thompson	.05	.02	.01
□	151 Brady Anderson	.30	.14	.04
□	152 Harold Baines	.15	.07	.02
□	153 Mike Devereaux	.05	.02	.01
□	154 Chris Hoiles	.05	.02	.01
□	155 Ben McDonald	.05	.02	.01
□	156 Mark McLemore	.05	.02	.01
□	157 Mike Mussina	.40	.18	.05
□	158 Rafael Palmeiro	.30	.14	.04
□	159 Cal Ripken	1.50	.70	.19
□	160 Chris Sabo	.05	.02	.01
□	161 Brad Ausmus	.05	.02	.01
□	162 Derek Bell	.15	.07	.02
□	163 Andy Benes	.15	.07	.02
□	164 Doug Brocail	.05	.02	.01
□	165 Archi Cianfrocco	.05	.02	.01
□	166 Ricky Gutierrez	.05	.02	.01
□	167 Tony Gwynn	.75	.35	.09
□	168 Gene Harris	.05	.02	.01
□	169 Pedro Martinez	.05	.02	.01
□	170 Phil Plantier	.05	.02	.01
□	171 Darren Daulton	.15	.07	.02
□	172 Mariano Duncan	.05	.02	.01
□	173 Lenny Dykstra	.15	.07	.02
□	174 Tommy Greene	.05	.02	.01
□	175 Dave Hollins	.05	.02	.01
□	176 Danny Jackson	.05	.02	.01
□	177 John Kruk	.15	.07	.02
□	178 Terry Mulholland	.05	.02	.01
□	179 Curt Schilling	.05	.02	.01
□	180 Kevin Stocker	.05	.02	.01
□	181 Jay Bell	.15	.07	.02
□	182 Steve Cooke	.05	.02	.01
□	183 Carlos Garcia	.05	.02	.01
□	184 Joel Johnston	.05	.02	.01
□	185 Jeff King	.15	.07	.02
□	186 Al Martin	.05	.02	.01
□	187 Orlando Merced	.15	.07	.02
□	188 Don Slaught	.05	.02	.01
□	189 Andy Van Slyke	.15	.07	.02
□	190 Kevin Young	.05	.02	.01
□	191 Kevin Brown	.05	.02	.01
□	192 Jose Canseco	.30	.14	.04
□	193 Will Clark	.30	.14	.04
□	194 Juan Gonzalez	1.00	.45	.12
□	195 Tom Henke	.05	.02	.01
□	196 David Hulse	.05	.02	.01
□	197 Dean Palmer	.15	.07	.02
□	198 Roger Pavlik	.05	.02	.01
□	199 Ivan Rodriguez	.40	.18	.05
□	200 Kenny Rogers	.05	.02	.01
□	201 Roger Clemens	.30	.14	.04
□	202 Scott Cooper	.05	.02	.01
□	203 Andre Dawson	.30	.14	.04
□	204 Mike Greenwell	.05	.02	.01
□	205 Billy Hatcher	.05	.02	.01
□	206 Jeff Russell	.05	.02	.01
□	207 Aaron Sele	.15	.07	.02
□	208 John Valentin	.15	.07	.02
□	209 Mo Vaughn	.50	.23	.06
□	210 Frank Viola	.05	.02	.01
□	211 Rob Dibble	.05	.02	.01
□	212 Willie Greene	.15	.07	.02
□	213 Roberto Kelly	.05	.02	.01
□	214 Barry Larkin	.30	.14	.04
□	215 Kevin Mitchell	.15	.07	.02
□	216 Hal Morris	.05	.02	.01
□	217 Joe Oliver	.05	.02	.01
□	218 Jose Rijo	.05	.02	.01
□	219 Reggie Sanders	.30	.14	.04
□	220 John Smiley	.05	.02	.01
□	221 Dante Bichette	.30	.14	.04
□	222 Ellis Burks	.15	.07	.02
□	223 Andres Galarraga	.30	.14	.04
□	224 Joe Girardi	.05	.02	.01
□	225 Charlie Hayes	.05	.02	.01
□	226 Darren Holmes	.05	.02	.01
□	227 Howard Johnson	.05	.02	.01
□	228 Roberto Mejia	.05	.02	.01
□	229 David Nied	.05	.02	.01
□	230 Armando Reynoso	.05	.02	.01
□	231 Kevin Appier	.15	.07	.02
□	232 David Cone	.30	.14	.04
□	233 Greg Gagne	.05	.02	.01
□	234 Tom Gordon	.05	.02	.01
□	235 Felix Jose	.05	.02	.01
□	236 Wally Joyner	.15	.07	.02
□	237 Jose Lind	.05	.02	.01
□	238 Brian McRae	.15	.07	.02
□	239 Mike Macfarliane	.05	.02	.01
□	240 Jeff Montgomery	.15	.07	.02
□	241 Eric Davis	.15	.07	.02
□	242 John Doherty	.05	.02	.01
□	243 Cecil Fielder	.15	.07	.02
□	244 Travis Fryman	.30	.14	.04
□	245 Bill Gullickson	.05	.02	.01
□	246 Mike Henneman	.05	.02	.01
□	247 Tony Phillips	.15	.07	.02
□	248 Mickey Tettleton	.05	.02	.01
□	249 Alan Trammell	.30	.14	.04
□	250 Lou Whitaker	.30	.14	.04
□	251 Rick Aguilera	.05	.02	.01
□	252 Scott Erickson	.05	.02	.01
□	253 Kent Hrbek	.15	.07	.02
□	254 Chuck Knoblauch	.30	.14	.04
□	255 Shane Mack	.05	.02	.01
□	256 Dave McCarty	.05	.02	.01
□	257 Pat Meares	.05	.02	.01
□	258 Kirby Puckett	.60	.25	.07
□	259 Kevin Tapani	.05	.02	.01
□	260 Dave Winfield	.30	.14	.04
□	261 Wilson Alvarez	.15	.07	.02
□	262 Jason Bere	.15	.07	.02
□	263 Alex Fernandez	.30	.14	.04
□	264 Ozzie Guillen	.05	.02	.01
□	265 Roberto Hernandez	.15	.07	.02
□	266 Lance Johnson	.15	.07	.02
□	267 Jack McDowell	.15	.07	.02
□	268 Tim Raines	.30	.14	.04
□	269 Frank Thomas	2.00	.90	.25
□	270 Robin Ventura	.15	.07	.02
□	271 Jim Abbott	.05	.02	.01
□	272 Wade Boggs	.30	.14	.04
□	273 Mike Gallego	.05	.02	.01
□	274 Pat Kelly	.05	.02	.01
□	275 Jimmy Key	.15	.07	.02
□	276 Don Mattingly	1.00	.45	.12
□	277 Paul O'Neill	.15	.07	.02
□	278 Mike Stanley	.05	.02	.01
□	279 Danny Tartabull	.05	.02	.01
□	280 Bernie Williams	.30	.14	.04
□	281 Chipper Jones	1.50	.70	.19
□	282 Ryan Klesko	.50	.23	.06
□	283 Javier Lopez	.30	.14	.04
□	284 Jeffrey Hammonds	.15	.07	.02
□	285 Jeff McNeely	.05	.02	.01
□	286 Manny Ramirez	.60	.25	.07
□	287 Billy Ashley	.05	.02	.01
□	288 Raul Mondesi	.30	.14	.04

		MINT	NRMT	EXC
☐ 289	Cliff Floyd	.30	.14	.04
☐ 290	Rondell White	.30	.14	.04
☐ 291	Steve Karsay	.05	.02	.01
☐ 292	Midre Cummings	.05	.02	.01
☐ 293	Salomon Torres	.05	.02	.01
☐ 294	J.R. Phillips	.05	.02	.01
☐ 295	Marc Newfield	.15	.07	.02
☐ 296	Carlos Delgado	.30	.14	.04
☐ 297	Butch Huskey	.15	.07	.02
☐ 298	Checklist	.05	.02	.01
☐ 299	Checklist	.05	.02	.01
☐ 300	Checklist	.05	.02	.01

1994 Triple Play Bomb Squad

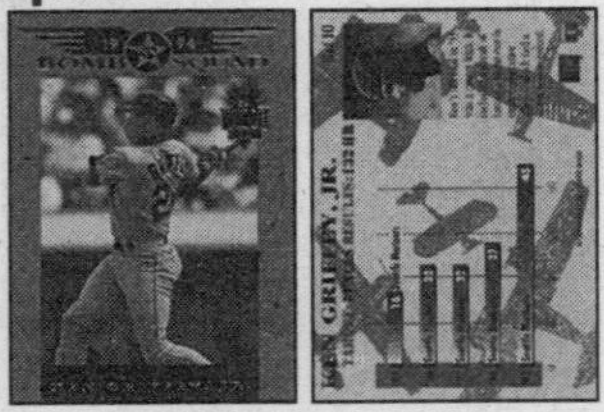

Randomly inserted in regular (one in 18) and jumbo (one in 8) packs, this ten-card standard-size set focuses on the top home run hitters in the majors. Card fronts feature a brown border surrounding a black and white photo. The Bomb Squad logo which includes a pair of wings is at the top. The player's name is at the bottom. Horizontal backs offer more color including a bar graph on yearly home run production with drawings of fighter planes serving as a background.

	MINT	NRMT	EXC
COMPLETE SET (10)	40.00	18.00	5.00
COMMON CARD (1-10)	1.00	.45	.12
SEMISTARS	1.50	.70	.19
RANDOM INSERTS IN PACKS			

		MINT	NRMT	EXC
☐ 1	Frank Thomas	12.00	5.50	1.50
☐ 2	Cecil Fielder	1.50	.70	.19
☐ 3	Juan Gonzalez	6.00	2.70	.75
☐ 4	Barry Bonds	3.00	1.35	.35
☐ 5	David Justice	1.00	.45	.12
☐ 6	Fred McGriff	1.50	.70	.19
☐ 7	Ron Gant	1.00	.45	.12
☐ 8	Ken Griffey Jr.	12.00	5.50	1.50
☐ 9	Albert Belle	6.00	2.70	.75
☐ 10	Matt Williams	1.50	.70	.19

1994 Triple Play Medalists

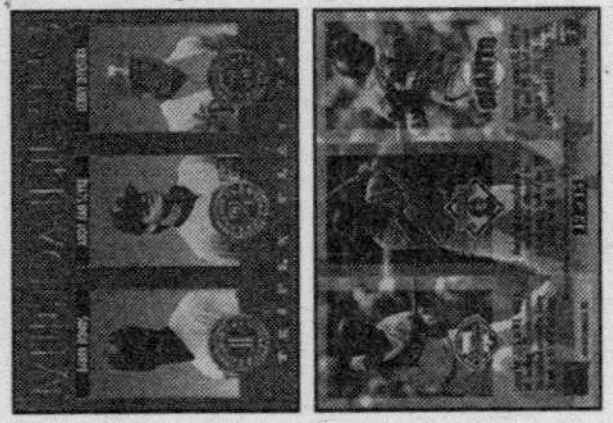

Randomly inserted in regular (one in 12) and jumbo packs (one in six), this 15-card standard-size set features the top three players in each league at their position. The players included were determined by statistical rankings over the past two seasons. Each card is horizontally designed with gold, silver and bronze foil on front with three player photos. There are also three player photos and brief highlights on back.

	MINT	NRMT	EXC
COMPLETE SET (15)	35.00	16.00	4.40
COMMON CARD (1-15)	1.00	.45	.12
SEMISTARS	1.50	.70	.19
RANDOM INSERTS IN PACKS			

		MINT	NRMT	EXC
☐ 1	Chris Hoiles Mickey Tettleton Brian Harper	1.00	.45	.12
☐ 2	Darren Daulton Rick Wilkins Kirt Manwaring	1.00	.45	.12
☐ 3	Frank Thomas Rafael Palmeiro John Olerud	8.00	3.60	1.00
☐ 4	Mark Grace Fred McGriff Jeff Bagwell	3.00	1.35	.35
☐ 5	Roberto Alomar Carlos Baerga Lou Whitaker	2.00	.90	.25
☐ 6	Ryne Sandberg Craig Biggio Roggie Thompson	2.50	1.10	.30
☐ 7	Tony Fernandez Cal Ripken Alan Trammel	6.00	2.70	.75
☐ 8	Barry Larkin Jay Bell Jeff Blauser	1.50	.70	.19
☐ 9	Robin Ventura Travis Fryman Wade Boggs	1.50	.70	.19
☐ 10	Terry Pendleton Dave Hollins Gary Sheffield	1.00	.45	.12
☐ 11	Ken Griffey Jr. Kirby Puckett Albert Belle	12.00	5.50	1.50
☐ 12	Barry Bonds Andy Van Slyke Len Dykstra	2.00	.90	.25
☐ 13	Jack McDowell Kevin Brown Randy Johnson	1.00	.45	.12
☐ 14	Greg Maddux Jose Rijo Bill Swift	5.00	2.20	.60
☐ 15	Paul Molitor Dave Winfield Harold Baines	1.50	.70	.19

1994 Triple Play Nicknames

Randomly inserted in regular (one in 36) and jumbo packs (one in 12), this eight-card standard-size set features players with a photo depicting the team name and mascot in the background. The back of each card describes how the team got its nickname as well as a player photo.

	MINT	NRMT	EXC
COMPLETE SET (8)	40.00	18.00	5.00
COMMON CARD (1-8)	2.00	.90	.25

SEMISTARS	4.00	1.80	.50
RANDOM INSERTS IN PACKS			

□ 1 Cecil Fielder	4.00	1.80	.50
□ 2 Ryne Sandberg	8.00	3.60	1.00
□ 3 Gary Sheffield	5.00	2.20	.60
□ 4 Joe Carter	4.00	1.80	.50
□ 5 John Olerud	2.00	.90	.25
□ 6 Cal Ripken	25.00	11.00	3.10
□ 7 Mark McGwire	10.00	4.50	1.25
□ 8 Gregg Jefferies	4.00	1.80	.50

1995 UC3

This 147-card standard-size set was issued by Pinnacle Brands. The cards were issued in 16-box cases with 36 packs per box and five cards per pack. The cases cost hobby dealers $1076.40. The fronts feature a mix of horizontal and vertical designs. The player's photo is shown against a computer generated background. According to Pinnacle, this is the first set issued as an all-3D product. The key Rookie Card in this set is Hideo Nomo. In 1996, Pinnacle used their UC3 technology as a subset in their Sportsflic issue.

	MINT	NRMT	EXC
COMPLETE SET (147)	20.00	9.00	2.50
COMMON CARD (1-147)	.10	.05	.01
SEMISTARS	.25	.11	.03
STARS	.50	.23	.06
COMPLETE AP SET (147)	800.00	350.00	100.00
COMMON AP (1-147)	2.50	1.10	.30
AP SEMISTARS	5.00	2.20	.60
AP STARS	10.00	4.50	1.25
*AP VETERAN STARS: 15X TO 25X HI			
*AP YOUNG STARS: 10X TO 20X HI			
AP: RANDOM INSERTS IN PACKS			

□ 1 Frank Thomas	3.00	1.35	.35
□ 2 Wil Cordero	.10	.05	.01
□ 3 John Olerud	.10	.05	.01
□ 4 Deion Sanders	.50	.23	.06
□ 5 Mike Mussina	.60	.25	.07
□ 6 Mo Vaughn	.75	.35	.09
□ 7 Will Clark	.50	.23	.06
□ 8 Chili Davis	.25	.11	.03
□ 9 Jimmy Key	.25	.11	.03
□ 10 John Valentin	.25	.11	.03
□ 11 Tony Tarasco	.10	.05	.01
□ 12 Alan Trammell	.50	.23	.06
□ 13 David Cone	.25	.11	.03
□ 14 Tim Salmon	.50	.23	.06
□ 15 Danny Tartabull	.10	.05	.01
□ 16 Aaron Sele	.25	.11	.03
□ 17 Alex Fernandez	.25	.11	.03
□ 18 Barry Bonds	.75	.35	.09
□ 19 Andres Galarraga	.50	.23	.06
□ 20 Don Mattingly	1.50	.70	.19
□ 21 Kevin Appier	.25	.11	.03
□ 22 Paul Molitor	.60	.25	.07
□ 23 Omar Vizquel	.50	.23	.06
□ 24 Andy Benes	.10	.05	.01
□ 25 Rafael Palmeiro	.50	.23	.06
□ 26 Barry Larkin	.50	.23	.06
□ 27 Bernie Williams	.50	.23	.06
□ 28 Gary Sheffield	.50	.23	.06
□ 29 Wally Joyner	.25	.11	.03
□ 30 Wade Boggs	.50	.23	.06
□ 31 Rico Brogna	.10	.05	.01
□ 32 Ken Caminiti	.50	.23	.06
□ 33 Kirby Puckett	1.00	.45	.12
□ 34 Bobby Bonilla	.25	.11	.03
□ 35 Hal Morris	.10	.05	.01
□ 36 Moises Alou	.25	.11	.03
□ 37 Jim Thome	.60	.25	.07
□ 38 Chuck Knoblauch	.50	.23	.06
□ 39 Mike Piazza	2.00	.90	.25
□ 40 Travis Fryman	.25	.11	.03
□ 41 Rickey Henderson	.50	.23	.06
□ 42 Jack McDowell	.25	.11	.03
□ 43 Carlos Baerga	.50	.23	.06
□ 44 Gregg Jefferies	.25	.11	.03
□ 45 Kirk Gibson	.25	.11	.03
□ 46 Bret Saberhagen	.25	.11	.03
□ 47 Cecil Fielder	.25	.11	.03
□ 48 Manny Ramirez	.75	.35	.09
□ 49 Marquis Grissom	.50	.23	.06
□ 50 Dave Winfield	.50	.23	.06
□ 51 Mark McGwire	1.00	.45	.12
□ 52 Dennis Eckersley	.25	.11	.03
□ 53 Robin Ventura	.25	.11	.03
□ 54 Ryan Klesko	.60	.25	.07
□ 55 Jeff Bagwell	1.25	.55	.16
□ 56 Ozzie Smith	.60	.25	.07
□ 57 Brian McRae	.25	.11	.03
□ 58 Albert Belle	1.50	.70	.19
□ 59 Darren Daulton	.25	.11	.03
□ 60 Jose Canseco	.50	.23	.06
□ 61 Greg Maddux	2.00	.90	.25
□ 62 Ben McDonald	.10	.05	.01
□ 63 Lenny Dykstra	.25	.11	.03
□ 64 Randy Johnson	.50	.23	.06
□ 65 Fred McGriff	.50	.23	.06
□ 66 Ray Lankford	.50	.23	.06
□ 67 Dave Justice	.50	.23	.06
□ 68 Paul O'Neill	.25	.11	.03
□ 69 Tony Gwynn	1.25	.55	.16
□ 70 Matt Williams	.50	.23	.06
□ 71 Dante Bichette	.50	.23	.06
□ 72 Craig Biggio	.50	.23	.06
□ 73 Ken Griffey Jr.	3.00	1.35	.35
□ 74 Juan Gonzalez	1.50	.70	.19
□ 75 Cal Ripken	2.50	1.10	.30
□ 76 Jay Bell	.25	.11	.03
□ 77 Joe Carter	.50	.23	.06
□ 78 Roberto Alomar	.75	.35	.09
□ 79 Mark Langston	.10	.05	.01
□ 80 Dave Hollins	.10	.05	.01
□ 81 Tom Glavine	.50	.23	.06
□ 82 Ivan Rodriguez	.60	.25	.07
□ 83 Mark Whiten	.10	.05	.01
□ 84 Raul Mondesi	.50	.23	.06
□ 85 Kenny Lofton	.75	.35	.09
□ 86 Ruben Sierra	.25	.11	.03
□ 87 Mark Grace	.50	.23	.06
□ 88 Royce Clayton	.10	.05	.01
□ 89 Billy Ashley	.10	.05	.01
□ 90 Larry Walker	.50	.23	.06
□ 91 Sammy Sosa	.50	.23	.06
□ 92 Jason Bere	.10	.05	.01
□ 93 Bob Hamelin	.10	.05	.01
□ 94 Greg Vaughn	.25	.11	.03
□ 95 Roger Clemens	.50	.23	.06
□ 96 Scott Ruffcorn	.10	.05	.01
□ 97 Hideo Nomo	3.00	1.35	.35
□ 98 Michael Tucker	.25	.11	.03
□ 99 J.R. Phillips	.10	.05	.01
□ 100 Roberto Petagine	.10	.05	.01
□ 101 Chipper Jones	2.00	.90	.25
□ 102 Armando Benitez	.10	.05	.01
□ 103 Orlando Miller	.10	.05	.01
□ 104 Carlos Delgado	.50	.23	.06
□ 105 Jeff Cirillo	.25	.11	.03
□ 106 Shawn Green	.25	.11	.03
□ 107 Joe Randa	.10	.05	.01
□ 108 Vaughn Eshelman	.10	.05	.01
□ 109 Frank Rodriguez	.25	.11	.03
□ 110 Russ Davis	.10	.05	.01
□ 111 Todd Hollandsworth	.50	.23	.06
□ 112 Mark Grudzielanek	.75	.35	.09
□ 113 Jose Oliva	.10	.05	.01
□ 114 Ray Durham	.25	.11	.03
□ 115 Alex Rodriguez	4.00	1.80	.50
□ 116 Alex Gonzalez	.10	.05	.01

□ 117 Midre Cummings	.10	.05	.01
□ 118 Marty Cordova	.50	.23	.06
□ 119 John Mabry	.50	.23	.06
□ 120 Jason Jacome	.10	.05	.01
□ 121 Joe Vitiello	.10	.05	.01
□ 122 Charles Johnson	.25	.11	.03
□ 123 Cal Ripken ID	1.25	.55	.16
□ 124 Ken Griffey Jr. ID	1.50	.70	.19
□ 125 Frank Thomas ID	1.50	.70	.19
□ 126 Mike Piazza ID	1.00	.45	.12
□ 127 Matt Williams ID	.25	.11	.03
□ 128 Barry Bonds ID	.50	.23	.06
□ 129 Greg Maddux ID	1.00	.45	.12
□ 130 Randy Johnson ID	.50	.23	.06
□ 131 Albert Belle ID	.75	.35	.09
□ 132 Will Clark ID	.25	.11	.03
□ 133 Tony Gwynn ID	.60	.25	.07
□ 134 Manny Ramirez ID	.50	.23	.06
□ 135 Raul Mondesi ID	.25	.11	.03
□ 136 Mo Vaughn ID	.50	.23	.06
□ 137 Mark McGwire ID	.50	.23	.06
□ 138 Kirby Puckett ID	.50	.23	.06
□ 139 Don Mattingly ID	.75	.35	.09
□ 140 Carlos Baerga ID	.25	.11	.03
□ 141 Roger Clemens ID	.50	.23	.06
□ 142 Fred McGriff ID	.25	.11	.03
□ 143 Kenny Lofton ID	.50	.23	.06
□ 144 Jeff Bagwell ID	.60	.25	.07
□ 145 Larry Walker ID	.25	.11	.03
□ 146 Joe Carter ID	.25	.11	.03
□ 147 Rafael Palmeiro ID	.25	.11	.03

1995 UC3 Clear Shots

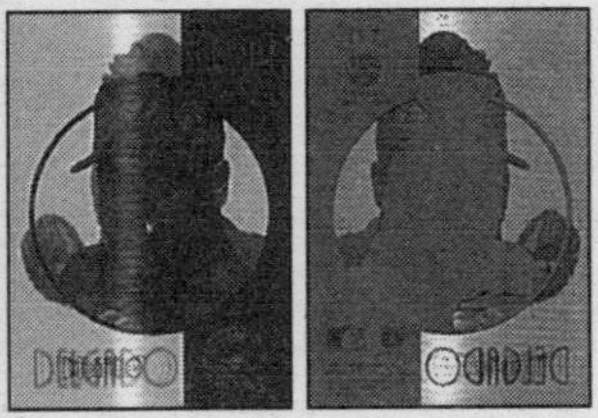

This 12-card standard-size set was inserted approximately one in every 24 packs. The fronts have two photos that alternate when the card is tilted slightly. One photo is a portrait while the other is an action shot. Along with the two photos changing are the words "Clear Shots," and a "UC3 1995" logo which changes with the player's team logo. The backs are opaque, but do have the card number in the upper left corner with a "CS" prefix.

	MINT	NRMT	EXC
COMPLETE SET (12)	70.00	32.00	8.75
COMMON CARD (CS1-CS12)	2.00	.90	.25
RANDOM INSERTS IN PACKS			
□ CS1 Alex Rodriguez	30.00	13.50	3.70
□ CS2 Shawn Green	2.00	.90	.25
□ CS3 Hideo Nomo	15.00	6.75	1.85
□ CS4 Charles Johnson	2.00	.90	.25
□ CS5 Orlando Miller	2.00	.90	.25
□ CS6 Billy Ashley	2.00	.90	.25
□ CS7 Carlos Delgado	4.00	1.80	.50
□ CS8 Cliff Floyd	2.00	.90	.25
□ CS9 Chipper Jones	20.00	9.00	2.50
□ CS10 Alex Gonzalez	2.00	.90	.25
□ CS11 J.R. Phillips	2.00	.90	.25
□ CS12 Michael Tucker	2.00	.90	.25
□ PCS8 Cliff Floyd Promo	2.00	.90	.25

1995 UC3 Cyclone Squad

This 20-card standard-size set was inserted approximately one in every four packs. The

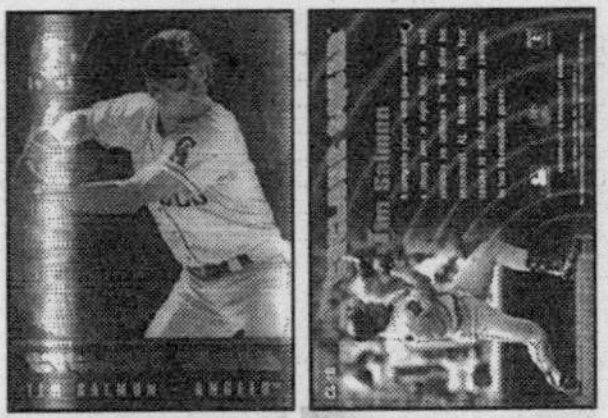

front features a player photo against a background of two circular objects. The "UC3" logo is in the upper left. The bottom has the words "Cyclone Squad" and the player's name and team. The horizontal backs contain a black and white player photo along with some information. The cards are numbered in the upper left with a "CS" prefix.

	MINT	NRMT	EXC
COMPLETE SET (20)	20.00	9.00	2.50
COMMON CARD (CS1-CS20)	.50	.23	.06
RANDOM INSERTS IN PACKS			
□ CS1 Frank Thomas	4.00	1.80	.50
□ CS2 Ken Griffey Jr.	4.00	1.80	.50
□ CS3 Jeff Bagwell	1.50	.70	.19
□ CS4 Cal Ripken	3.00	1.35	.35
□ CS5 Barry Bonds	1.00	.45	.12
□ CS6 Mike Piazza	2.50	1.10	.30
□ CS7 Matt Williams	.75	.35	.09
□ CS8 Kirby Puckett	1.25	.55	.16
□ CS9 Jose Canseco	.75	.35	.09
□ CS10 Will Clark	.75	.35	.09
□ CS11 Don Mattingly	2.00	.90	.25
□ CS12 Albert Belle	2.00	.90	.25
□ CS13 Tony Gwynn	1.50	.70	.19
□ CS14 Raul Mondesi	.50	.23	.06
□ CS15 Bobby Bonilla	.50	.23	.06
□ CS16 Rafael Palmeiro	.75	.35	.09
□ CS17 Fred McGriff	.75	.35	.09
□ CS18 Tim Salmon	.50	.23	.06
□ CS19 Kenny Lofton	1.00	.45	.12
□ CS20 Joe Carter	.75	.35	.09

1995 UC3 In Motion

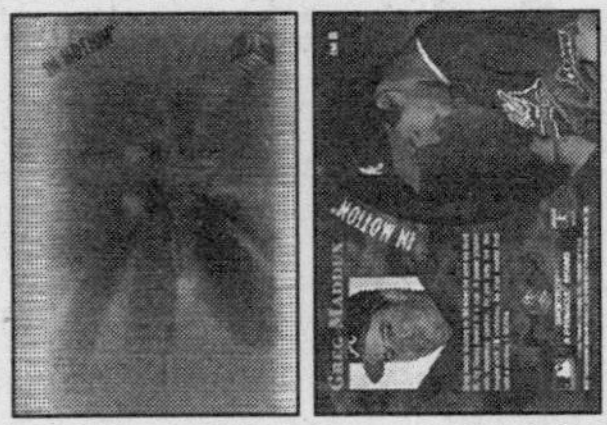

This 10-card standard-size set was inserted approximately one in every 18 packs. The fronts feature a player photo that compresses into many pieces when the card is tilted slightly. The upper left features the words "In Motion 95" with the UC3 logo in the upper right and the player's name in the lower left. The horizontal back features two color photos along with a short informational blurb. The cards are numbered with an "IM" prefix in the upper right corner.

	MINT	NRMT	EXC
COMPLETE SET (10)	40.00	18.00	5.00
COMMON CARD (IM1-IM10)	.75	.35	.09
RANDOM INSERTS IN PACKS			

□ IM1 Cal Ripken	6.00	2.70	.75
□ IM2 Ken Griffey Jr.	8.00	3.60	1.00
□ IM3 Frank Thomas	8.00	3.60	1.00
□ IM4 Mike Piazza	5.00	2.20	.60
□ IM5 Barry Bonds	2.00	.90	.25
□ IM6 Matt Williams	.75	.35	.09
□ IM7 Kirby Puckett	2.50	1.10	.30
□ IM8 Greg Maddux	5.00	2.20	.60
□ IM9 Don Mattingly	4.00	1.80	.50
□ IM10 Will Clark	.75	.35	.09

1991 Ultra

This 400-card standard-size set marked Fleer's first entry into the premium card market. The cards were distributed exclusively in foil-wrapped packs. Fleer claimed in their original press release that there would only be 15 percent the amount of Ultra issued as there was of the regular issue. The cards feature full color action photography on the fronts and three full-color photos on the backs. Fleer also issued the sets in their now traditional alphabetical order as well as the teams in alphabetical order. Subsets include Major League Prospects (373-390), Elite Performance (391-396), and Checklists (397-400). The key Rookie Cards in this set are Jeff Conine, Eric Karros and Brian McRae, Denny Neagle and Henry Rodriguez.

	MINT	NRMT	EXC
COMPLETE SET (400)	20.00	9.00	2.50
COMMON CARD (1-400)	.05	.02	.01
SEMISTARS	.15	.07	.02
STARS	.30	.14	.04

□ 1 Steve Avery	.30	.14	.04
□ 2 Jeff Blauser	.05	.02	.01
□ 3 Francisco Cabrera	.05	.02	.01
□ 4 Ron Gant	.30	.14	.04
□ 5 Tom Glavine	.30	.14	.04
□ 6 Tommy Gregg	.05	.02	.01
□ 7 Dave Justice	.30	.14	.04
□ 8 Oddibe McDowell	.05	.02	.01
□ 9 Greg Olson	.05	.02	.01
□ 10 Terry Pendleton	.15	.07	.02
□ 11 Lonnie Smith	.05	.02	.01
□ 12 John Smoltz	.30	.14	.04
□ 13 Jeff Treadway	.05	.02	.01
□ 14 Glenn Davis	.05	.02	.01
□ 15 Mike Devereaux	.05	.02	.01
□ 16 Leo Gomez	.05	.02	.01
□ 17 Chris Hoiles	.05	.02	.01
□ 18 Dave Johnson	.05	.02	.01
□ 19 Ben McDonald	.15	.07	.02
□ 20 Randy Milligan	.05	.02	.01
□ 21 Gregg Olson	.05	.02	.01
□ 22 Joe Orsulak	.05	.02	.01
□ 23 Bill Ripken	.05	.02	.01
□ 24 Cal Ripken	1.50	.70	.19
□ 25 David Segui	.15	.07	.02
□ 26 Craig Worthington	.05	.02	.01
□ 27 Wade Boggs	.30	.14	.04
□ 28 Tom Bolton	.05	.02	.01
□ 29 Tom Brunansky	.05	.02	.01
□ 30 Ellis Burks	.30	.14	.04
□ 31 Roger Clemens	.30	.14	.04
□ 32 Mike Greenwell	.05	.02	.01
□ 33 Greg A. Harris	.05	.02	.01
□ 34 Daryl Irvine	.05	.02	.01
□ 35 Mike Marshall UER (1990 in stats is shown as 990)	.05	.02	.01
□ 36 Tim Naehring	.15	.07	.02
□ 37 Tony Pena	.05	.02	.01
□ 38 Phil Plantier	.15	.07	.02
□ 39 Carlos Quintana	.05	.02	.01
□ 40 Jeff Reardon	.15	.07	.02
□ 41 Jody Reed	.05	.02	.01
□ 42 Luis Rivera	.05	.02	.01
□ 43 Jim Abbott	.15	.07	.02
□ 44 Chuck Finley	.15	.07	.02
□ 45 Bryan Harvey	.05	.02	.01
□ 46 Donnie Hill	.05	.02	.01
□ 47 Jack Howell	.05	.02	.01
□ 48 Wally Joyner	.15	.07	.02
□ 49 Mark Langston	.15	.07	.02
□ 50 Kirk McCaskill	.05	.02	.01
□ 51 Lance Parrish	.05	.02	.01
□ 52 Dick Schofield	.05	.02	.01
□ 53 Lee Stevens	.05	.02	.01
□ 54 Dave Winfield	.30	.14	.04
□ 55 George Bell	.05	.02	.01
□ 56 Damon Berryhill	.05	.02	.01
□ 57 Mike Bielecki	.05	.02	.01
□ 58 Andre Dawson	.30	.14	.04
□ 59 Shawon Dunston	.05	.02	.01
□ 60 Joe Girardi UER (Bats right, LH hitter shown is Doug Dascenzo)	.15	.07	.02
□ 61 Mark Grace	.30	.14	.04
□ 62 Mike Harkey	.05	.02	.01
□ 63 Les Lancaster	.05	.02	.01
□ 64 Greg Maddux	1.25	.55	.16
□ 65 Derrick May	.05	.02	.01
□ 66 Ryne Sandberg	.50	.23	.06
□ 67 Luis Salazar	.05	.02	.01
□ 68 Dwight Smith	.05	.02	.01
□ 69 Hector Villanueva	.05	.02	.01
□ 70 Jerome Walton	.05	.02	.01
□ 71 Mitch Williams	.05	.02	.01
□ 72 Carlton Fisk	.30	.14	.04
□ 73 Scott Fletcher	.05	.02	.01
□ 74 Ozzie Guillen	.05	.02	.01
□ 75 Greg Hibbard	.05	.02	.01
□ 76 Lance Johnson	.15	.07	.02
□ 77 Steve Lyons	.05	.02	.01
□ 78 Jack McDowell	.15	.07	.02
□ 79 Dan Pasqua	.05	.02	.01
□ 80 Melido Perez	.05	.02	.01
□ 81 Tim Raines	.30	.14	.04
□ 82 Sammy Sosa	.60	.25	.07
□ 83 Cory Snyder	.05	.02	.01
□ 84 Bobby Thigpen	.05	.02	.01
□ 85 Frank Thomas (Card says he is an outfielder)	4.00	1.80	.50
□ 86 Robin Ventura	.30	.14	.04
□ 87 Todd Benzinger	.05	.02	.01
□ 88 Glenn Braggs	.05	.02	.01
□ 89 Tom Browning UER (Front photo actually Norm Charlton)	.05	.02	.01
□ 90 Norm Charlton	.05	.02	.01
□ 91 Eric Davis	.15	.07	.02
□ 92 Rob Dibble	.05	.02	.01
□ 93 Bill Doran	.05	.02	.01
□ 94 Mariano Duncan UER (Right back photo is Billy Hatcher)	.05	.02	.01
□ 95 Billy Hatcher	.05	.02	.01
□ 96 Barry Larkin	.30	.14	.04
□ 97 Randy Myers	.15	.07	.02
□ 98 Hal Morris	.05	.02	.01
□ 99 Joe Oliver	.05	.02	.01
□ 100 Paul O'Neill	.15	.07	.02
□ 101 Jeff Reed (See also 104)	.05	.02	.01
□ 102 Jose Rijo	.05	.02	.01
□ 103 Chris Sabo (See also 106)	.05	.02	.01
□ 104 Beau Allred UER (Card number is 101)	.05	.02	.01
□ 105 Sandy Alomar Jr.	.15	.07	.02
□ 106 Carlos Baerga UER	.30	.14	.04

(Card number is 103)			
□ 107 Albert Belle	1.25	.55	.16
□ 108 Jerry Browne	.05	.02	.01
□ 109 Tom Candiotti	.05	.02	.01
□ 110 Alex Cole	.05	.02	.01
□ 111 John Farrell	.05	.02	.01
(See also 114)			
□ 112 Felix Fermin	.05	.02	.01
□ 113 Brook Jacoby	.05	.02	.01
□ 114 Chris James UER	.05	.02	.01
(Card number is 111)			
□ 115 Doug Jones	.05	.02	.01
□ 116 Steve Olin	.05	.02	.01
(See also 119)			
□ 117 Greg Swindell	.05	.02	.01
□ 118 Turner Ward	.05	.02	.01
□ 119 Mitch Webster UER	.05	.02	.01
(Card number is 116)			
□ 120 Dave Bergman	.05	.02	.01
□ 121 Cecil Fielder	.15	.07	.02
□ 122 Travis Fryman	.30	.14	.04
□ 123 Mike Henneman	.05	.02	.01
□ 124 Lloyd Moseby	.05	.02	.01
□ 125 Dan Petry	.05	.02	.01
□ 126 Tony Phillips	.15	.07	.02
□ 127 Mark Salas	.05	.02	.01
□ 128 Frank Tanana	.05	.02	.01
□ 129 Alan Trammell	.30	.14	.04
□ 130 Lou Whitaker	.30	.14	.04
□ 131 Eric Anthony	.05	.02	.01
□ 132 Craig Biggio	.30	.14	.04
□ 133 Ken Caminiti	.30	.14	.04
□ 134 Casey Candaele	.05	.02	.01
□ 135 Andujar Cedeno	.05	.02	.01
□ 136 Mark Davidson	.05	.02	.01
□ 137 Jim Deshaies	.05	.02	.01
□ 138 Mark Portugal	.05	.02	.01
□ 139 Rafael Ramirez	.05	.02	.01
□ 140 Mike Scott	.05	.02	.01
□ 141 Eric Yelding	.05	.02	.01
□ 142 Gerald Young	.05	.02	.01
□ 143 Kevin Appier	.15	.07	.02
□ 144 George Brett	.75	.35	.09
□ 145 Jeff Conine	.75	.35	.09
□ 146 Jim Eisenreich	.15	.07	.02
□ 147 Tom Gordon	.05	.02	.01
□ 148 Mark Gubicza	.05	.02	.01
□ 149 Bo Jackson	.30	.14	.04
□ 150 Brent Mayne	.05	.02	.01
□ 151 Mike Macfarlane	.05	.02	.01
□ 152 Brian McRae	.40	.18	.05
□ 153 Jeff Montgomery	.15	.07	.02
□ 154 Bret Saberhagen	.15	.07	.02
□ 155 Kevin Seitzer	.05	.02	.01
□ 156 Terry Shumpert	.05	.02	.01
□ 157 Kurt Stillwell	.05	.02	.01
□ 158 Danny Tartabull	.05	.02	.01
□ 159 Tim Belcher	.05	.02	.01
□ 160 Kal Daniels	.05	.02	.01
□ 161 Alfredo Griffin	.05	.02	.01
□ 162 Lenny Harris	.05	.02	.01
□ 163 Jay Howell	.05	.02	.01
□ 164 Ramon Martinez	.15	.07	.02
□ 165 Mike Morgan	.05	.02	.01
□ 166 Eddie Murray	.50	.23	.06
□ 167 Jose Offerman	.05	.02	.01
□ 168 Juan Samuel	.05	.02	.01
□ 169 Mike Scioscia	.05	.02	.01
□ 170 Mike Sharperson	.05	.02	.01
□ 171 Darryl Strawberry	.15	.07	.02
□ 172 Greg Brock	.05	.02	.01
□ 173 Chuck Crim	.05	.02	.01
□ 174 Jim Gantner	.05	.02	.01
□ 175 Ted Higuera	.05	.02	.01
□ 176 Mark Knudson	.05	.02	.01
□ 177 Tim McIntosh	.05	.02	.01
□ 178 Paul Molitor	.40	.18	.05
□ 179 Dan Plesac	.05	.02	.01
□ 180 Gary Sheffield	.30	.14	.04
□ 181 Bill Spiers	.05	.02	.01
□ 182 B.J. Surhoff	.15	.07	.02
□ 183 Greg Vaughn	.30	.14	.04
□ 184 Robin Yount	.30	.14	.04
□ 185 Rick Aguilera	.15	.07	.02
□ 186 Greg Gagne	.05	.02	.01
□ 187 Dan Gladden	.05	.02	.01
□ 188 Brian Harper	.05	.02	.01
□ 189 Kent Hrbek	.15	.07	.02
□ 190 Gene Larkin	.05	.02	.01
□ 191 Shane Mack	.05	.02	.01
□ 192 Pedro Munoz	.15	.07	.02
□ 193 Al Newman	.05	.02	.01
□ 194 Junior Ortiz	.05	.02	.01
□ 195 Kirby Puckett	.60	.25	.07
□ 196 Kevin Tapani	.05	.02	.01
□ 197 Dennis Boyd	.05	.02	.01
□ 198 Tim Burke	.05	.02	.01
□ 199 Ivan Calderon	.05	.02	.01
□ 200 Delino DeShields	.05	.02	.01
□ 201 Mike Fitzgerald	.05	.02	.01
□ 202 Steve Frey	.05	.02	.01
□ 203 Andres Galarraga	.30	.14	.04
□ 204 Marquis Grissom	.30	.14	.04
□ 205 Dave Martinez	.05	.02	.01
□ 206 Dennis Martinez	.15	.07	.02
□ 207 Junior Noboa	.05	.02	.01
□ 208 Spike Owen	.05	.02	.01
□ 209 Scott Ruskin	.05	.02	.01
□ 210 Tim Wallach	.05	.02	.01
□ 211 Daryl Boston	.05	.02	.01
□ 212 Vince Coleman	.05	.02	.01
□ 213 David Cone	.30	.14	.04
□ 214 Ron Darling	.05	.02	.01
□ 215 Kevin Elster	.05	.02	.01
□ 216 Sid Fernandez	.05	.02	.01
□ 217 John Franco	.05	.02	.01
□ 218 Dwight Gooden	.15	.07	.02
□ 219 Tom Herr	.05	.02	.01
□ 220 Todd Hundley	.30	.14	.04
□ 221 Gregg Jefferies	.30	.14	.04
□ 222 Howard Johnson	.05	.02	.01
□ 223 Dave Magadan	.05	.02	.01
□ 224 Kevin McReynolds	.05	.02	.01
□ 225 Keith Miller	.05	.02	.01
□ 226 Mackey Sasser	.05	.02	.01
□ 227 Frank Viola	.05	.02	.01
□ 228 Jesse Barfield	.05	.02	.01
□ 229 Greg Cadaret	.05	.02	.01
□ 230 Alvaro Espinoza	.05	.02	.01
□ 231 Bob Geren	.05	.02	.01
□ 232 Lee Guetterman	.05	.02	.01
□ 233 Mel Hall	.05	.02	.01
□ 234 Andy Hawkins UER	.05	.02	.01
(Back center photo is not him)			
□ 235 Roberto Kelly	.05	.02	.01
□ 236 Tim Leary	.05	.02	.01
□ 237 Jim Leyritz	.15	.07	.02
□ 238 Kevin Maas	.05	.02	.01
□ 239 Don Mattingly	1.00	.45	.12
□ 240 Hensley Meulens	.05	.02	.01
□ 241 Eric Plunk	.05	.02	.01
□ 242 Steve Sax	.05	.02	.01
□ 243 Todd Burns	.05	.02	.01
□ 244 Jose Canseco	.30	.14	.04
□ 245 Dennis Eckersley	.15	.07	.02
□ 246 Mike Gallego	.05	.02	.01
□ 247 Dave Henderson	.05	.02	.01
□ 248 Rickey Henderson	.30	.14	.04
□ 249 Rick Honeycutt	.05	.02	.01
□ 250 Carney Lansford	.15	.07	.02
□ 251 Mark McGwire	.60	.25	.07
□ 252 Mike Moore	.05	.02	.01
□ 253 Terry Steinbach	.15	.07	.02
□ 254 Dave Stewart	.15	.07	.02
□ 255 Walt Weiss	.05	.02	.01
□ 256 Bob Welch	.05	.02	.01
□ 257 Curt Young	.05	.02	.01
□ 258 Wes Chamberlain	.05	.02	.01
□ 259 Pat Combs	.05	.02	.01
□ 260 Darren Daulton	.15	.07	.02
□ 261 Jose DeJesus	.05	.02	.01
□ 262 Len Dykstra	.15	.07	.02
□ 263 Charlie Hayes	.05	.02	.01
□ 264 Von Hayes	.05	.02	.01
□ 265 Ken Howell	.05	.02	.01
□ 266 John Kruk	.15	.07	.02
□ 267 Roger McDowell	.05	.02	.01
□ 268 Mickey Morandini	.05	.02	.01
□ 269 Terry Mulholland	.05	.02	.01
□ 270 Dale Murphy	.30	.14	.04
□ 271 Randy Ready	.05	.02	.01

□ 272 Dickie Thon	.05	.02	.01
□ 273 Stan Belinda	.05	.02	.01
□ 274 Jay Bell	.15	.07	.02
□ 275 Barry Bonds	.50	.23	.06
□ 276 Bobby Bonilla	.15	.07	.02
□ 277 Doug Drabek	.05	.02	.01
□ 278 Carlos Garcia	.30	.14	.04
□ 279 Neal Heaton	.05	.02	.01
□ 280 Jeff King	.15	.07	.02
□ 281 Bill Landrum	.05	.02	.01
□ 282 Mike LaValliere	.05	.02	.01
□ 283 Jose Lind	.05	.02	.01
□ 284 Orlando Merced	.30	.14	.04
□ 285 Gary Redus	.05	.02	.01
□ 286 Don Slaught	.05	.02	.01
□ 287 Andy Van Slyke	.15	.07	.02
□ 288 Jose DeLeon	.05	.02	.01
□ 289 Pedro Guerrero	.05	.02	.01
□ 290 Ray Lankford	.30	.14	.04
□ 291 Joe Magrane	.05	.02	.01
□ 292 Jose Oquendo	.05	.02	.01
□ 293 Tom Pagnozzi	.05	.02	.01
□ 294 Bryn Smith	.05	.02	.01
□ 295 Lee Smith	.15	.07	.02
□ 296 Ozzie Smith UER (Born 12-26, 54, should have hyphen)	.40	.18	.05
□ 297 Milt Thompson	.05	.02	.01
□ 298 Craig Wilson	.05	.02	.01
□ 299 Todd Zeile	.15	.07	.02
□ 300 Shawn Abner	.05	.02	.01
□ 301 Andy Benes	.05	.02	.01
□ 302 Paul Faries	.05	.02	.01
□ 303 Tony Gwynn	.75	.35	.09
□ 304 Greg W. Harris	.05	.02	.01
□ 305 Thomas Howard	.05	.02	.01
□ 306 Bruce Hurst	.05	.02	.01
□ 307 Craig Lefferts	.05	.02	.01
□ 308 Fred McGriff	.30	.14	.04
□ 309 Dennis Rasmussen	.05	.02	.01
□ 310 Bip Roberts	.05	.02	.01
□ 311 Benito Santiago	.05	.02	.01
□ 312 Garry Templeton	.05	.02	.01
□ 313 Ed Whitson	.05	.02	.01
□ 314 Dave Anderson	.05	.02	.01
□ 315 Kevin Bass	.05	.02	.01
□ 316 Jeff Brantley	.05	.02	.01
□ 317 John Burkett	.15	.07	.02
□ 318 Will Clark	.30	.14	.04
□ 319 Steve Decker	.05	.02	.01
□ 320 Scott Garrelts	.05	.02	.01
□ 321 Terry Kennedy	.05	.02	.01
□ 322 Mark Leonard	.05	.02	.01
□ 323 Darren Lewis	.15	.07	.02
□ 324 Greg Litton	.05	.02	.01
□ 325 Willie McGee	.05	.02	.01
□ 326 Kevin Mitchell	.15	.07	.02
□ 327 Don Robinson	.05	.02	.01
□ 328 Andres Santana	.05	.02	.01
□ 329 Robby Thompson	.05	.02	.01
□ 330 Jose Uribe	.05	.02	.01
□ 331 Matt Williams	.30	.14	.04
□ 332 Scott Bradley	.05	.02	.01
□ 333 Henry Cotto	.05	.02	.01
□ 334 Alvin Davis	.05	.02	.01
□ 335 Ken Griffey Sr.	.05	.02	.01
□ 336 Ken Griffey Jr.	3.00	1.35	.35
□ 337 Erik Hanson	.05	.02	.01
□ 338 Brian Holman	.05	.02	.01
□ 339 Randy Johnson	.30	.14	.04
□ 340 Edgar Martinez UER (Listed as playing SS)	.30	.14	.04
□ 341 Tino Martinez	.30	.14	.04
□ 342 Pete O'Brien	.05	.02	.01
□ 343 Harold Reynolds	.05	.02	.01
□ 344 Dave Valle	.05	.02	.01
□ 345 Omar Vizquel	.30	.14	.04
□ 346 Brad Arnsberg	.05	.02	.01
□ 347 Kevin Brown	.15	.07	.02
□ 348 Julio Franco	.15	.07	.02
□ 349 Jeff Huson	.05	.02	.01
□ 350 Rafael Palmeiro	.30	.14	.04
□ 351 Geno Petralli	.05	.02	.01
□ 352 Gary Pettis	.05	.02	.01
□ 353 Kenny Rogers	.05	.02	.01
□ 354 Jeff Russell	.05	.02	.01
□ 355 Nolan Ryan	1.50	.70	.19
□ 356 Ruben Sierra	.15	.07	.02
□ 357 Bobby Witt	.05	.02	.01
□ 358 Roberto Alomar	.50	.23	.06
□ 359 Pat Borders	.05	.02	.01
□ 360 Joe Carter UER (Reverse negative on back photo)	.30	.14	.04
□ 361 Kelly Gruber	.05	.02	.01
□ 362 Tom Henke	.05	.02	.01
□ 363 Glenallen Hill	.05	.02	.01
□ 364 Jimmy Key	.15	.07	.02
□ 365 Manny Lee	.05	.02	.01
□ 366 Rance Mulliniks	.05	.02	.01
□ 367 John Olerud UER (Throwing left on card; back has throws right; he does throw lefty)	.15	.07	.02
□ 368 Dave Stieb	.05	.02	.01
□ 369 Duane Ward	.05	.02	.01
□ 370 David Wells	.05	.02	.01
□ 371 Mark Whiten	.15	.07	.02
□ 372 Mookie Wilson	.05	.02	.01
□ 373 Willie Banks MLP	.05	.02	.01
□ 374 Steve Carter MLP	.05	.02	.01
□ 375 Scott Chiamparino MLP	.05	.02	.01
□ 376 Steve Chitren MLP	.05	.02	.01
□ 377 Darrin Fletcher MLP	.05	.02	.01
□ 378 Rich Garces MLP	.05	.02	.01
□ 379 Reggie Jefferson MLP	.15	.07	.02
□ 380 Eric Karros MLP	1.00	.45	.12
□ 381 Pat Kelly MLP	.15	.07	.02
□ 382 Chuck Knoblauch MLP	.50	.23	.06
□ 383 Denny Neagle MLP	.60	.25	.07
□ 384 Dan Opperman MLP	.05	.02	.01
□ 385 John Ramos MLP	.05	.02	.01
□ 386 Henry Rodriguez MLP	.75	.35	.09
□ 387 Mo Vaughn MLP	1.25	.55	.16
□ 388 Gerald Williams MLP	.05	.02	.01
□ 389 Mike York MLP	.05	.02	.01
□ 390 Eddie Zosky MLP	.05	.02	.01
□ 391 Barry Bonds EP	.30	.14	.04
□ 392 Cecil Fielder EP	.15	.07	.02
□ 393 Rickey Henderson EP	.30	.14	.04
□ 394 Dave Justice EP	.30	.14	.04
□ 395 Nolan Ryan EP	.75	.35	.09
□ 396 Bobby Thigpen EP	.05	.02	.01
□ 397 Gregg Jefferies CL	.15	.07	.02
□ 398 Von Hayes CL	.05	.02	.01
□ 399 Terry Kennedy CL	.05	.02	.01
□ 400 Nolan Ryan CL	.30	.14	.04

1991 Ultra Gold

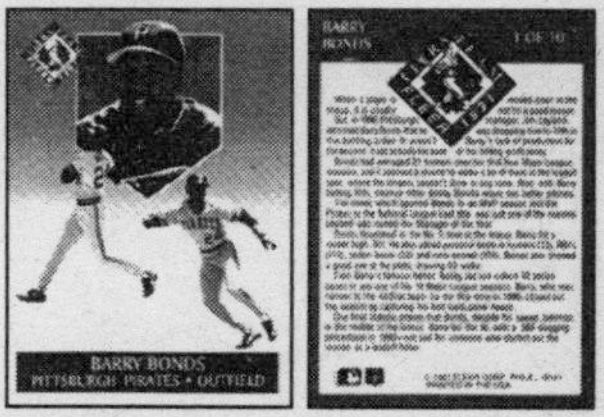

This ten-card standard-size set presents Fleer's 1991 Ultra Team. These cards were randomly inserted into Ultra packs. On a gold background that fades as one moves toward the bottom of the card, the front design has a color head shot, with two cut-out action shots below. Player information is given in a dark blue strip at the bottom of the card face. In blue print on white background with gold borders, the back highlights the player's outstanding achievements. The set is sequenced in alphabetical order.

	MINT	NRMT	EXC
COMPLETE SET (10)	10.00	4.50	1.25
COMMON CARD (1-10)	.25	.11	.03

SEMISTARS	.50	.23	.06
RANDOM INSERTS IN FOIL PACKS			

□ 1 Barry Bonds	1.00	.45	.12
□ 2 Will Clark	.50	.23	.06
□ 3 Doug Drabek	.25	.11	.03
□ 4 Ken Griffey Jr.	6.00	2.70	.75
□ 5 Rickey Henderson	.50	.23	.06
□ 6 Bo Jackson	.25	.11	.03
□ 7 Ramon Martinez	.25	.11	.03
□ 8 Kirby Puckett UER (Boggs won 1988 batting title, so Puckett didn't win consecutive titles)	1.25	.55	.16
□ 9 Chris Sabo	.25	.11	.03
□ 10 Ryne Sandberg UER (Johnson and Hornsby didn't hit 40 homers in 1990, Fielder did hit 51 in '90)	1.00	.45	.12

1991 Ultra Update

The 120-card set was distributed exclusively in factory set form along with 20 team logo stickers through hobby dealers. The set includes the year's hottest rookies and important veteran players traded after the original Ultra series was produced. Card design is identical to regular issue 1991 cards except for the U-prefixed numbering on back. Cards are ordered alphabetically within and according to teams for each league. Rookie Cards in this set include Jeff Bagwell, Juan Guzman, Mike Mussina, and Ivan Rodriguez.

	MINT	NRMT	EXC
COMPLETE FACT.SET (120)	32.00	14.50	4.00
COMMON CARD (1-120)	.10	.05	.01
SEMISTARS	.25	.11	.03
STARS	.50	.23	.06
U PREFIX ON CARD NUMBER			

□ 1 Dwight Evans	.25	.11	.03
□ 2 Chito Martinez	.10	.05	.01
□ 3 Bob Melvin	.10	.05	.01
□ 4 Mike Mussina	6.00	2.70	.75
□ 5 Jack Clark	.25	.11	.03
□ 6 Dana Kiecker	.10	.05	.01
□ 7 Steve Lyons	.10	.05	.01
□ 8 Gary Gaetti	.25	.11	.03
□ 9 Dave Gallagher	.10	.05	.01
□ 10 Dave Parker	.25	.11	.03
□ 11 Luis Polonia	.10	.05	.01
□ 12 Luis Sojo	.10	.05	.01
□ 13 Wilson Alvarez	1.00	.45	.12
□ 14 Alex Fernandez	1.50	.70	.19
□ 15 Craig Grebeck	.10	.05	.01
□ 16 Ron Karkovice	.10	.05	.01
□ 17 Warren Newson	.10	.05	.01
□ 18 Scott Radinsky	.10	.05	.01
□ 19 Glenallen Hill	.10	.05	.01
□ 20 Charles Nagy	1.25	.55	.16
□ 21 Mark Whiten	.25	.11	.03
□ 22 Milt Cuyler	.10	.05	.01
□ 23 Paul Gibson	.10	.05	.01
□ 24 Mickey Tettleton	.25	.11	.03
□ 25 Todd Benzinger	.10	.05	.01
□ 26 Storm Davis	.10	.05	.01
□ 27 Kirk Gibson	.25	.11	.03
□ 28 Bill Pecota	.10	.05	.01
□ 29 Gary Thurman	.10	.05	.01
□ 30 Darryl Hamilton	.25	.11	.03
□ 31 Jaime Navarro	.10	.05	.01
□ 32 Willie Randolph	.25	.11	.03
□ 33 Bill Wegman	.10	.05	.01
□ 34 Randy Bush	.10	.05	.01
□ 35 Chili Davis	.25	.11	.03
□ 36 Scott Erickson	.25	.11	.03
□ 37 Chuck Knoblauch	3.00	1.35	.35
□ 38 Scott Leius	.10	.05	.01
□ 39 Jack Morris	.25	.11	.03
□ 40 John Habyan	.10	.05	.01
□ 41 Pat Kelly	.25	.11	.03
□ 42 Matt Nokes	.10	.05	.01
□ 43 Scott Sanderson	.10	.05	.01
□ 44 Bernie Williams	5.00	2.20	.60
□ 45 Harold Baines	.25	.11	.03
□ 46 Brook Jacoby	.10	.05	.01
□ 47 Earnest Riles	.10	.05	.01
□ 48 Willie Wilson	.10	.05	.01
□ 49 Jay Buhner	.75	.35	.09
□ 50 Rich DeLucia	.10	.05	.01
□ 51 Mike Jackson	.10	.05	.01
□ 52 Bill Krueger	.10	.05	.01
□ 53 Bill Swift	.10	.05	.01
□ 54 Brian Downing	.10	.05	.01
□ 55 Juan Gonzalez	15.00	6.75	1.85
□ 56 Dean Palmer	1.50	.70	.19
□ 57 Kevin Reimer	.10	.05	.01
□ 58 Ivan Rodriguez	8.00	3.60	1.00
□ 59 Tom Candiotti	.10	.05	.01
□ 60 Juan Guzman	.75	.35	.09
□ 61 Bob MacDonald	.10	.05	.01
□ 62 Greg Myers	.10	.05	.01
□ 63 Ed Sprague	.25	.11	.03
□ 64 Devon White	.25	.11	.03
□ 65 Rafael Belliard	.10	.05	.01
□ 66 Juan Berenguer	.10	.05	.01
□ 67 Brian R. Hunter	.10	.05	.01
□ 68 Kent Mercker	.10	.05	.01
□ 69 Otis Nixon	.10	.05	.01
□ 70 Danny Jackson	.10	.05	.01
□ 71 Chuck McElroy	.10	.05	.01
□ 72 Gary Scott	.10	.05	.01
□ 73 Heathcliff Slocumb	.50	.23	.06
□ 74 Chico Walker	.10	.05	.01
□ 75 Rick Wilkins	.10	.05	.01
□ 76 Chris Hammond	.10	.05	.01
□ 77 Luis Quinones	.10	.05	.01
□ 78 Herm Winningham	.10	.05	.01
□ 79 Jeff Bagwell	15.00	6.75	1.85
□ 80 Jim Corsi	.10	.05	.01
□ 81 Steve Finley	.50	.23	.06
□ 82 Luis Gonzalez	.50	.23	.06
□ 83 Pete Harnisch	.10	.05	.01
□ 84 Darryl Kile	.25	.11	.03
□ 85 Brett Butler	.25	.11	.03
□ 86 Gary Carter	.50	.23	.06
□ 87 Tim Crews	.10	.05	.01
□ 88 Orel Hershiser	.25	.11	.03
□ 89 Bob Ojeda	.10	.05	.01
□ 90 Bret Barberie	.10	.05	.01
□ 91 Barry Jones	.10	.05	.01
□ 92 Gilberto Reyes	.10	.05	.01
□ 93 Larry Walker	1.00	.45	.12
□ 94 Hubie Brooks	.10	.05	.01
□ 95 Tim Burke	.10	.05	.01
□ 96 Rick Cerone	.10	.05	.01
□ 97 Jeff Innis	.10	.05	.01
□ 98 Wally Backman	.10	.05	.01
□ 99 Tommy Greene	.10	.05	.01
□ 100 Ricky Jordan	.10	.05	.01
□ 101 Mitch Williams	.10	.05	.01
□ 102 John Smiley	.10	.05	.01
□ 103 Randy Tomlin	.10	.05	.01
□ 104 Gary Varsho	.10	.05	.01
□ 105 Cris Carpenter	.10	.05	.01
□ 106 Ken Hill	1.25	.55	.16
□ 107 Felix Jose	.10	.05	.01
□ 108 Omar Olivares	.10	.05	.01
□ 109 Gerald Perry	.10	.05	.01
□ 110 Jerald Clark	.10	.05	.01
□ 111 Tony Fernandez	.10	.05	.01

□ 112 Darrin Jackson	.10	.05	.01
□ 113 Mike Maddux	.10	.05	.01
□ 114 Tim Teufel	.10	.05	.01
□ 115 Bud Black	.10	.05	.01
□ 116 Kelly Downs	.10	.05	.01
□ 117 Mike Felder	.10	.05	.01
□ 118 Willie McGee	.10	.05	.01
□ 119 Trevor Wilson	.10	.05	.01
□ 120 Checklist 1-120	.10	.05	.01

1992 Ultra

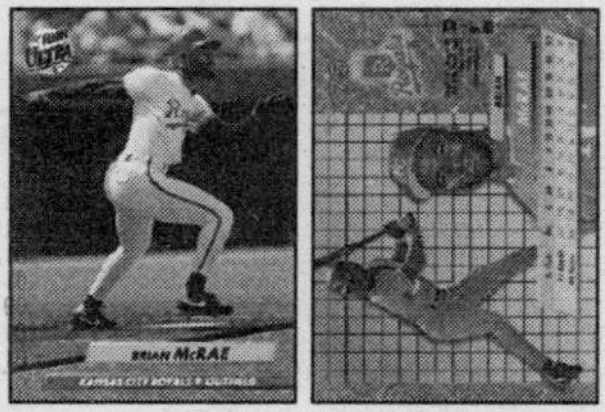

Consisting of 600 standard-size cards, the 1992 Fleer Ultra set was issued in two series of 300 cards each. Cards were distributed exclusively in foil packs. The glossy color action player photos on the fronts are full-bleed except at the bottom where a diagonal gold-foil stripe edges a green marbleized border. The player's name and team appear on the marble-colored area in bars that are color-coded by team. The cards are numbered on the back and ordered below alphabetically within and according to teams for each league with AL preceding NL. There are no notable Rookie Cards in the set. Some cards have been found without the word Fleer on the front.

	MINT	NRMT	EXC
COMPLETE SET (600)	40.00	18.00	5.00
COMPLETE SERIES 1 (300)	25.00	11.00	3.10
COMPLETE SERIES 2 (300)	15.00	6.75	1.85
COMMON CARD (1-600)	.10	.05	.01
SEMISTARS	.15	.07	.02
STARS	.30	.14	.04
COMP.GWYNN SET (10)	10.00	4.50	1.25
COMMON GWYNN (1-10)	1.00	.45	.12
CERTIFIED GWYNN AUTO	175.00	80.00	22.00
RANDOM INSERTS IN SER.1 PACKS			
COMMON GWYNN MAIL (S1-S2)	1.00	.45	.12
GWYNN MAIL-IN AVAIL.VIA WRAPPER EXCH.			

□ 1 Glenn Davis	.10	.05	.01
□ 2 Mike Devereaux	.10	.05	.01
□ 3 Dwight Evans	.15	.07	.02
□ 4 Leo Gomez	.10	.05	.01
□ 5 Chris Hoiles	.10	.05	.01
□ 6 Sam Horn	.10	.05	.01
□ 7 Chito Martinez	.10	.05	.01
□ 8 Randy Milligan	.10	.05	.01
□ 9 Mike Mussina	.60	.25	.07
□ 10 Billy Ripken	.10	.05	.01
□ 11 Cal Ripken	1.50	.70	.19
□ 12 Tom Brunansky	.10	.05	.01
□ 13 Ellis Burks	.30	.14	.04
□ 14 Jack Clark	.15	.07	.02
□ 15 Roger Clemens	.30	.14	.04
□ 16 Mike Greenwell	.10	.05	.01
□ 17 Joe Hesketh	.10	.05	.01
□ 18 Tony Pena	.10	.05	.01
□ 19 Carlos Quintana	.10	.05	.01
□ 20 Jeff Reardon	.15	.07	.02
□ 21 Jody Reed	.10	.05	.01
□ 22 Luis Rivera	.10	.05	.01
□ 23 Mo Vaughn	.75	.35	.09
□ 24 Gary DiSarcina	.10	.05	.01
□ 25 Chuck Finley	.10	.05	.01
□ 26 Gary Gaetti	.15	.07	.02
□ 27 Bryan Harvey	.10	.05	.01
□ 28 Lance Parrish	.10	.05	.01
□ 29 Luis Polonia	.10	.05	.01
□ 30 Dick Schofield	.10	.05	.01
□ 31 Luis Sojo	.10	.05	.01
□ 32 Wilson Alvarez	.30	.14	.04
□ 33 Carlton Fisk	.30	.14	.04
□ 34 Craig Grebeck	.10	.05	.01
□ 35 Ozzie Guillen	.10	.05	.01
□ 36 Greg Hibbard	.10	.05	.01
□ 37 Charlie Hough	.10	.05	.01
□ 38 Lance Johnson	.15	.07	.02
□ 39 Ron Karkovice	.10	.05	.01
□ 40 Jack McDowell	.15	.07	.02
□ 41 Donn Pall	.10	.05	.01
□ 42 Melido Perez	.10	.05	.01
□ 43 Tim Raines	.30	.14	.04
□ 44 Frank Thomas	3.00	1.35	.35
□ 45 Sandy Alomar Jr.	.15	.07	.02
□ 46 Carlos Baerga	.30	.14	.04
□ 47 Albert Belle	1.25	.55	.16
□ 48 Jerry Browne UER (Reversed negative on card back)	.10	.05	.01
□ 49 Felix Fermin	.10	.05	.01
□ 50 Reggie Jefferson UER (Born 1968, not 1966)	.15	.07	.02
□ 51 Mark Lewis	.10	.05	.01
□ 52 Carlos Martinez	.10	.05	.01
□ 53 Steve Olin	.10	.05	.01
□ 54 Jim Thome	1.50	.70	.19
□ 55 Mark Whiten	.15	.07	.02
□ 56 Dave Bergman	.10	.05	.01
□ 57 Milt Cuyler	.10	.05	.01
□ 58 Rob Deer	.10	.05	.01
□ 59 Cecil Fielder	.15	.07	.02
□ 60 Travis Fryman	.30	.14	.04
□ 61 Scott Livingstone	.10	.05	.01
□ 62 Tony Phillips	.15	.07	.02
□ 63 Mickey Tettleton	.10	.05	.01
□ 64 Alan Trammell	.30	.14	.04
□ 65 Lou Whitaker	.30	.14	.04
□ 66 Kevin Appier	.15	.07	.02
□ 67 Mike Boddicker	.10	.05	.01
□ 68 George Brett	.75	.35	.09
□ 69 Jim Eisenreich	.10	.05	.01
□ 70 Mark Gubicza	.10	.05	.01
□ 71 David Howard	.10	.05	.01
□ 72 Joel Johnson	.10	.05	.01
□ 73 Mike Macfarlane	.10	.05	.01
□ 74 Brent Mayne	.10	.05	.01
□ 75 Brian McRae	.30	.14	.04
□ 76 Jeff Montgomery	.15	.07	.02
□ 77 Danny Tartabull	.10	.05	.01
□ 78 Don August	.10	.05	.01
□ 79 Dante Bichette	.30	.14	.04
□ 80 Ted Higuera	.10	.05	.01
□ 81 Paul Molitor	.40	.18	.05
□ 82 Jaime Navarro	.10	.05	.01
□ 83 Gary Sheffield	.30	.14	.04
□ 84 Bill Spiers	.10	.05	.01
□ 85 B.J. Surhoff	.15	.07	.02
□ 86 Greg Vaughn	.30	.14	.04
□ 87 Robin Yount	.30	.14	.04
□ 88 Rick Aguilera	.10	.05	.01
□ 89 Chili Davis	.15	.07	.02
□ 90 Scott Erickson	.15	.07	.02
□ 91 Brian Harper	.10	.05	.01
□ 92 Kent Hrbek	.15	.07	.02
□ 93 Chuck Knoblauch	.30	.14	.04
□ 94 Scott Leius	.10	.05	.01
□ 95 Shane Mack	.10	.05	.01
□ 96 Mike Pagliarulo	.10	.05	.01
□ 97 Kirby Puckett	.60	.25	.07
□ 98 Kevin Tapani	.10	.05	.01
□ 99 Jesse Barfield	.10	.05	.01
□ 100 Alvaro Espinoza	.10	.05	.01
□ 101 Mel Hall	.10	.05	.01
□ 102 Pat Kelly	.10	.05	.01
□ 103 Roberto Kelly	.10	.05	.01
□ 104 Kevin Maas	.10	.05	.01
□ 105 Don Mattingly	1.00	.45	.12
□ 106 Hensley Meulens	.10	.05	.01
□ 107 Matt Nokes	.10	.05	.01
□ 108 Steve Sax	.10	.05	.01
□ 109 Harold Baines	.15	.07	.02
□ 110 Jose Canseco	.30	.14	.04

□ 111 Ron Darling	.10	.05	.01
□ 112 Mike Gallego	.10	.05	.01
□ 113 Dave Henderson	.10	.05	.01
□ 114 Rickey Henderson	.30	.14	.04
□ 115 Mark McGwire	.60	.25	.07
□ 116 Terry Steinbach	.15	.07	.02
□ 117 Dave Stewart	.15	.07	.02
□ 118 Todd Van Poppel	.10	.05	.01
□ 119 Bob Welch	.10	.05	.01
□ 120 Greg Briley	.10	.05	.01
□ 121 Jay Buhner	.30	.14	.04
□ 122 Rick DeLucia	.10	.05	.01
□ 123 Ken Griffey Jr.	3.00	1.35	.35
□ 124 Erik Hanson	.10	.05	.01
□ 125 Randy Johnson	.30	.14	.04
□ 126 Edgar Martinez	.30	.14	.04
□ 127 Tino Martinez	.30	.14	.04
□ 128 Pete O'Brien	.10	.05	.01
□ 129 Harold Reynolds	.10	.05	.01
□ 130 Dave Valle	.10	.05	.01
□ 131 Julio Franco	.15	.07	.02
□ 132 Juan Gonzalez	1.25	.55	.16
□ 133 Jeff Huson	.15	.07	.02
(Shows Jose Canseco sliding into second)			
□ 134 Mike Jeffcoat	.10	.05	.01
□ 135 Terry Mathews	.10	.05	.01
□ 136 Rafael Palmeiro	.30	.14	.04
□ 137 Dean Palmer	.15	.07	.02
□ 138 Geno Petralli	.10	.05	.01
□ 139 Ivan Rodriguez	.60	.25	.07
□ 140 Jeff Russell	.10	.05	.01
□ 141 Nolan Ryan	1.50	.70	.19
□ 142 Ruben Sierra	.15	.07	.02
□ 143 Roberto Alomar	.50	.23	.06
□ 144 Pat Borders	.10	.05	.01
□ 145 Joe Carter	.30	.14	.04
□ 146 Kelly Gruber	.10	.05	.01
□ 147 Jimmy Key	.15	.07	.02
□ 148 Manny Lee	.10	.05	.01
□ 149 Rance Mulliniks	.10	.05	.01
□ 150 Greg Myers	.10	.05	.01
□ 151 John Olerud	.15	.07	.02
□ 152 Dave Stieb	.10	.05	.01
□ 153 Todd Stottlemyre	.15	.07	.02
□ 154 Duane Ward	.10	.05	.01
□ 155 Devon White	.15	.07	.02
□ 156 Eddie Zosky	.10	.05	.01
□ 157 Steve Avery	.15	.07	.02
□ 158 Rafael Belliard	.10	.05	.01
□ 159 Jeff Blauser	.10	.05	.01
□ 160 Sid Bream	.10	.05	.01
□ 161 Ron Gant	.30	.14	.04
□ 162 Tom Glavine	.30	.14	.04
□ 163 Brian Hunter	.10	.05	.01
□ 164 Dave Justice	.30	.14	.04
□ 165 Mark Lemke	.10	.05	.01
□ 166 Greg Olson	.10	.05	.01
□ 167 Terry Pendleton	.15	.07	.02
□ 168 Lonnie Smith	.10	.05	.01
□ 169 John Smoltz	.30	.14	.04
□ 170 Mike Stanton	.10	.05	.01
□ 171 Jeff Treadway	.10	.05	.01
□ 172 Paul Assenmacher	.10	.05	.01
□ 173 George Bell	.10	.05	.01
□ 174 Shawon Dunston	.10	.05	.01
□ 175 Mark Grace	.30	.14	.04
□ 176 Danny Jackson	.10	.05	.01
□ 177 Les Lancaster	.10	.05	.01
□ 178 Greg Maddux	1.50	.70	.19
□ 179 Luis Salazar	.10	.05	.01
□ 180 Rey Sanchez	.10	.05	.01
□ 181 Ryne Sandberg	.50	.23	.06
□ 182 Jose Vizcaino	.10	.05	.01
□ 183 Chico Walker	.10	.05	.01
□ 184 Jerome Walton	.10	.05	.01
□ 185 Glenn Braggs	.10	.05	.01
□ 186 Tom Browning	.10	.05	.01
□ 187 Rob Dibble	.10	.05	.01
□ 188 Bill Doran	.10	.05	.01
□ 189 Chris Hammond	.10	.05	.01
□ 190 Billy Hatcher	.10	.05	.01
□ 191 Barry Larkin	.30	.14	.04
□ 192 Hal Morris	.10	.05	.01
□ 193 Joe Oliver	.10	.05	.01
□ 194 Paul O'Neill	.15	.07	.02
□ 195 Jeff Reed	.10	.05	.01
□ 196 Jose Rijo	.10	.05	.01
□ 197 Chris Sabo	.10	.05	.01
□ 198 Jeff Bagwell	1.25	.55	.16
□ 199 Craig Biggio	.30	.14	.04
□ 200 Ken Caminiti	.30	.14	.04
□ 201 Andujar Cedeno	.10	.05	.01
□ 202 Steve Finley	.30	.14	.04
□ 203 Luis Gonzalez	.15	.07	.02
□ 204 Pete Harnisch	.10	.05	.01
□ 205 Xavier Hernandez	.10	.05	.01
□ 206 Darryl Kile	.10	.05	.01
□ 207 Al Osuna	.10	.05	.01
□ 208 Curt Schilling	.10	.05	.01
□ 209 Brett Butler	.15	.07	.02
□ 210 Kal Daniels	.10	.05	.01
□ 211 Lenny Harris	.10	.05	.01
□ 212 Stan Javier	.10	.05	.01
□ 213 Ramon Martinez	.15	.07	.02
□ 214 Roger McDowell	.10	.05	.01
□ 215 Jose Offerman	.10	.05	.01
□ 216 Juan Samuel	.10	.05	.01
□ 217 Mike Scioscia	.10	.05	.01
□ 218 Mike Sharperson	.10	.05	.01
□ 219 Darryl Strawberry	.15	.07	.02
□ 220 Delino DeShields	.10	.05	.01
□ 221 Tom Foley	.10	.05	.01
□ 222 Steve Frey	.10	.05	.01
□ 223 Dennis Martinez	.15	.07	.02
□ 224 Spike Owen	.10	.05	.01
□ 225 Gilberto Reyes	.10	.05	.01
□ 226 Tim Wallach	.10	.05	.01
□ 227 Daryl Boston	.10	.05	.01
□ 228 Tim Burke	.10	.05	.01
□ 229 Vince Coleman	.10	.05	.01
□ 230 David Cone	.30	.14	.04
□ 231 Kevin Elster	.10	.05	.01
□ 232 Dwight Gooden	.15	.07	.02
□ 233 Todd Hundley	.30	.14	.04
□ 234 Jeff Innis	.10	.05	.01
□ 235 Howard Johnson	.10	.05	.01
□ 236 Dave Magadan	.10	.05	.01
□ 237 Mackey Sasser	.10	.05	.01
□ 238 Anthony Young	.10	.05	.01
□ 239 Wes Chamberlain	.10	.05	.01
□ 240 Darren Daulton	.15	.07	.02
□ 241 Len Dykstra	.15	.07	.02
□ 242 Tommy Greene	.10	.05	.01
□ 243 Charlie Hayes	.10	.05	.01
□ 244 Dave Hollins	.10	.05	.01
□ 245 Ricky Jordan	.10	.05	.01
□ 246 John Kruk	.15	.07	.02
□ 247 Mickey Morandini	.10	.05	.01
□ 248 Terry Mulholland	.10	.05	.01
□ 249 Dale Murphy	.30	.14	.04
□ 250 Jay Bell	.15	.07	.02
□ 251 Barry Bonds	.50	.23	.06
□ 252 Steve Buechele	.10	.05	.01
□ 253 Doug Drabek	.10	.05	.01
□ 254 Mike LaValliere	.10	.05	.01
□ 255 Jose Lind	.10	.05	.01
□ 256 Lloyd McClendon	.10	.05	.01
□ 257 Orlando Merced	.15	.07	.02
□ 258 Don Slaught	.10	.05	.01
□ 259 John Smiley	.10	.05	.01
□ 260 Zane Smith	.10	.05	.01
□ 261 Randy Tomlin	.10	.05	.01
□ 262 Andy Van Slyke	.15	.07	.02
□ 263 Pedro Guerrero	.10	.05	.01
□ 264 Felix Jose	.10	.05	.01
□ 265 Ray Lankford	.30	.14	.04
□ 266 Omar Olivares	.10	.05	.01
□ 267 Jose Oquendo	.10	.05	.01
□ 268 Tom Pagnozzi	.10	.05	.01
□ 269 Bryn Smith	.10	.05	.01
□ 270 Lee Smith UER	.15	.07	.02
(1991 record listed as 61-61)			
□ 271 Ozzie Smith UER	.40	.18	.05
(Comma before year of birth on card back)			
□ 272 Milt Thompson	.10	.05	.01
□ 273 Todd Zeile	.10	.05	.01
□ 274 Andy Benes	.10	.05	.01
□ 275 Jerald Clark	.10	.05	.01
□ 276 Tony Fernandez	.10	.05	.01

□ 277	Tony Gwynn	.75	.35	.09
□ 278	Greg W. Harris	.10	.05	.01
□ 279	Thomas Howard	.10	.05	.01
□ 280	Bruce Hurst	.10	.05	.01
□ 281	Mike Maddux	.10	.05	.01
□ 282	Fred McGriff	.30	.14	.04
□ 283	Benito Santiago	.10	.05	.01
□ 284	Kevin Bass	.10	.05	.01
□ 285	Jeff Brantley	.15	.07	.02
□ 286	John Burkett	.15	.07	.02
□ 287	Will Clark	.30	.14	.04
□ 288	Royce Clayton	.15	.07	.02
□ 289	Steve Decker	.10	.05	.01
□ 290	Kelly Downs	.10	.05	.01
□ 291	Mike Felder	.10	.05	.01
□ 292	Darren Lewis	.10	.05	.01
□ 293	Kirt Manwaring	.10	.05	.01
□ 294	Willie McGee	.10	.05	.01
□ 295	Robby Thompson	.10	.05	.01
□ 296	Matt Williams	.30	.14	.04
□ 297	Trevor Wilson	.10	.05	.01
□ 298	Checklist 1-100	.10	.05	.01
□ 299	Checklist 101-200	.10	.05	.01
□ 300	Checklist 201-300	.10	.05	.01
□ 301	Brady Anderson	.30	.14	.04
□ 302	Todd Frohwirth	.10	.05	.01
□ 303	Ben McDonald	.10	.05	.01
□ 304	Mark McLemore	.10	.05	.01
□ 305	Jose Mesa	.15	.07	.02
□ 306	Bob Milacki	.10	.05	.01
□ 307	Gregg Olson	.10	.05	.01
□ 308	David Segui	.10	.05	.01
□ 309	Rick Sutcliffe	.10	.05	.01
□ 310	Jeff Tackett	.10	.05	.01
□ 311	Wade Boggs	.30	.14	.04
□ 312	Scott Cooper	.10	.05	.01
□ 313	John Flaherty	.10	.05	.01
□ 314	Wayne Housie	.10	.05	.01
□ 315	Peter Hoy	.10	.05	.01
□ 316	John Marzano	.10	.05	.01
□ 317	Tim Naehring	.15	.07	.02
□ 318	Phil Plantier	.15	.07	.02
□ 319	Frank Viola	.10	.05	.01
□ 320	Matt Young	.10	.05	.01
□ 321	Jim Abbott	.10	.05	.01
□ 322	Hubie Brooks	.10	.05	.01
□ 323	Chad Curtis	.30	.14	.04
□ 324	Alvin Davis	.10	.05	.01
□ 325	Junior Felix	.10	.05	.01
□ 326	Von Hayes	.10	.05	.01
□ 327	Mark Langston	.15	.07	.02
□ 328	Scott Lewis	.10	.05	.01
□ 329	Don Robinson	.10	.05	.01
□ 330	Bobby Rose	.10	.05	.01
□ 331	Lee Stevens	.10	.05	.01
□ 332	George Bell	.10	.05	.01
□ 333	Esteban Beltre	.10	.05	.01
□ 334	Joey Cora	.10	.05	.01
□ 335	Alex Fernandez	.30	.14	.04
□ 336	Roberto Hernandez	.30	.14	.04
□ 337	Mike Huff	.10	.05	.01
□ 338	Kirk McCaskill	.10	.05	.01
□ 339	Dan Pasqua	.10	.05	.01
□ 340	Scott Radinsky	.10	.05	.01
□ 341	Steve Sax	.10	.05	.01
□ 342	Bobby Thigpen	.10	.05	.01
□ 343	Robin Ventura	.30	.14	.04
□ 344	Jack Armstrong	.10	.05	.01
□ 345	Alex Cole	.10	.05	.01
□ 346	Dennis Cook	.10	.05	.01
□ 347	Glenallen Hill	.10	.05	.01
□ 348	Thomas Howard	.10	.05	.01
□ 349	Brook Jacoby	.10	.05	.01
□ 350	Kenny Lofton	2.50	1.10	.30
□ 351	Charles Nagy	.15	.07	.02
□ 352	Rod Nichols	.10	.05	.01
□ 353	Junior Ortiz	.10	.05	.01
□ 354	Dave Otto	.10	.05	.01
□ 355	Tony Perezchica	.10	.05	.01
□ 356	Scott Scudder	.10	.05	.01
□ 357	Paul Sorrento	.10	.05	.01
□ 358	Skeeter Barnes	.10	.05	.01
□ 359	Mark Carreon	.10	.05	.01
□ 360	John Doherty	.10	.05	.01
□ 361	Dan Gladden	.10	.05	.01
□ 362	Bill Gullickson	.10	.05	.01
□ 363	Shawn Hare	.10	.05	.01
□ 364	Mike Henneman	.10	.05	.01
□ 365	Chad Kreuter	.10	.05	.01
□ 366	Mark Leiter	.10	.05	.01
□ 367	Mike Munoz	.10	.05	.01
□ 368	Kevin Ritz	.10	.05	.01
□ 369	Mark Davis	.10	.05	.01
□ 370	Tom Gordon	.10	.05	.01
□ 371	Chris Gwynn	.10	.05	.01
□ 372	Gregg Jefferies	.30	.14	.04
□ 373	Wally Joyner	.15	.07	.02
□ 374	Kevin McReynolds	.10	.05	.01
□ 375	Keith Miller	.10	.05	.01
□ 376	Rico Rossy	.10	.05	.01
□ 377	Curtis Wilkerson	.10	.05	.01
□ 378	Ricky Bones	.10	.05	.01
□ 379	Chris Bosio	.10	.05	.01
□ 380	Cal Eldred	.10	.05	.01
□ 381	Scott Fletcher	.10	.05	.01
□ 382	Jim Gantner	.10	.05	.01
□ 383	Darryl Hamilton	.10	.05	.01
□ 384	Doug Henry	.10	.05	.01
□ 385	Pat Listach	.15	.07	.02
□ 386	Tim McIntosh	.10	.05	.01
□ 387	Edwin Nunez	.10	.05	.01
□ 388	Dan Plesac	.10	.05	.01
□ 389	Kevin Seitzer	.10	.05	.01
□ 390	Franklin Stubbs	.10	.05	.01
□ 391	William Suero	.10	.05	.01
□ 392	Bill Wegman	.10	.05	.01
□ 393	Willie Banks	.10	.05	.01
□ 394	Jarvis Brown	.10	.05	.01
□ 395	Greg Gagne	.10	.05	.01
□ 396	Mark Guthrie	.10	.05	.01
□ 397	Bill Krueger	.10	.05	.01
□ 398	Pat Mahomes	.10	.05	.01
□ 399	Pedro Munoz	.10	.05	.01
□ 400	John Smiley	.10	.05	.01
□ 401	Gary Wayne	.10	.05	.01
□ 402	Lenny Webster	.10	.05	.01
□ 403	Carl Willis	.10	.05	.01
□ 404	Greg Cadaret	.10	.05	.01
□ 405	Steve Farr	.10	.05	.01
□ 406	Mike Gallego	.10	.05	.01
□ 407	Charlie Hayes	.10	.05	.01
□ 408	Steve Howe	.10	.05	.01
□ 409	Dion James	.10	.05	.01
□ 410	Jeff Johnson	.10	.05	.01
□ 411	Tim Leary	.10	.05	.01
□ 412	Jim Leyritz	.10	.05	.01
□ 413	Melido Perez	.10	.05	.01
□ 414	Scott Sanderson	.10	.05	.01
□ 415	Andy Stankiewicz	.10	.05	.01
□ 416	Mike Stanley	.10	.05	.01
□ 417	Danny Tartabull	.10	.05	.01
□ 418	Lance Blankenship	.10	.05	.01
□ 419	Mike Bordick	.15	.07	.02
□ 420	Scott Brosius	.30	.14	.04
□ 421	Dennis Eckersley	.15	.07	.02
□ 422	Scott Hemond	.10	.05	.01
□ 423	Carney Lansford	.15	.07	.02
□ 424	Henry Mercedes	.10	.05	.01
□ 425	Mike Moore	.10	.05	.01
□ 426	Gene Nelson	.10	.05	.01
□ 427	Randy Ready	.10	.05	.01
□ 428	Bruce Walton	.10	.05	.01
□ 429	Willie Wilson	.10	.05	.01
□ 430	Rich Amaral	.10	.05	.01
□ 431	Dave Cochrane	.10	.05	.01
□ 432	Henry Cotto	.10	.05	.01
□ 433	Calvin Jones	.10	.05	.01
□ 434	Kevin Mitchell	.15	.07	.02
□ 435	Clay Parker	.10	.05	.01
□ 436	Omar Vizquel	.30	.14	.04
□ 437	Floyd Bannister	.10	.05	.01
□ 438	Kevin Brown	.15	.07	.02
□ 439	John Cangelosi	.10	.05	.01
□ 440	Brian Downing	.10	.05	.01
□ 441	Monty Fariss	.10	.05	.01
□ 442	Jose Guzman	.10	.05	.01
□ 443	Donald Harris	.10	.05	.01
□ 444	Kevin Reimer	.10	.05	.01
□ 445	Kenny Rogers	.10	.05	.01
□ 446	Wayne Rosenthal	.10	.05	.01
□ 447	Dickie Thon	.10	.05	.01
□ 448	Derek Bell	.15	.07	.02

□ 449 Juan Guzman	.15	.07	.02
□ 450 Tom Henke	.10	.05	.01
□ 451 Candy Maldonado	.10	.05	.01
□ 452 Jack Morris	.15	.07	.02
□ 453 David Wells	.10	.05	.01
□ 454 Dave Winfield	.30	.14	.04
□ 455 Juan Berenguer	.10	.05	.01
□ 456 Damon Berryhill	.10	.05	.01
□ 457 Mike Bielecki	.10	.05	.01
□ 458 Marvin Freeman	.10	.05	.01
□ 459 Charlie Leibrandt	.10	.05	.01
□ 460 Kent Mercker	.10	.05	.01
□ 461 Otis Nixon	.10	.05	.01
□ 462 Alejandro Pena	.10	.05	.01
□ 463 Ben Rivera	.10	.05	.01
□ 464 Deion Sanders	.30	.14	.04
□ 465 Mark Wohlers	.30	.14	.04
□ 466 Shawn Boskie	.10	.05	.01
□ 467 Frank Castillo	.15	.07	.02
□ 468 Andre Dawson	.30	.14	.04
□ 469 Joe Girardi	.10	.05	.01
□ 470 Chuck McElroy	.10	.05	.01
□ 471 Mike Morgan	.10	.05	.01
□ 472 Ken Patterson	.10	.05	.01
□ 473 Bob Scanlan	.10	.05	.01
□ 474 Gary Scott	.10	.05	.01
□ 475 Dave Smith	.10	.05	.01
□ 476 Sammy Sosa	.50	.23	.06
□ 477 Hector Villanueva	.10	.05	.01
□ 478 Scott Bankhead	.10	.05	.01
□ 479 Tim Belcher	.10	.05	.01
□ 480 Freddie Benavides	.10	.05	.01
□ 481 Jacob Brumfield	.10	.05	.01
□ 482 Norm Charlton	.10	.05	.01
□ 483 Dwayne Henry	.10	.05	.01
□ 484 Dave Martinez	.10	.05	.01
□ 485 Bip Roberts	.10	.05	.01
□ 486 Reggie Sanders	.30	.14	.04
□ 487 Greg Swindell	.10	.05	.01
□ 488 Ryan Bowen	.10	.05	.01
□ 489 Casey Candaele	.10	.05	.01
□ 490 Juan Guerrero UER (photo on front is Andujar Cedeno	.10	.05	.01
□ 491 Pete Incaviglia	.10	.05	.01
□ 492 Jeff Juden	.10	.05	.01
□ 493 Rob Murphy	.10	.05	.01
□ 494 Mark Portugal	.10	.05	.01
□ 495 Rafael Ramirez	.10	.05	.01
□ 496 Scott Servais	.10	.05	.01
□ 497 Ed Taubensee	.10	.05	.01
□ 498 Brian Williams	.10	.05	.01
□ 499 Todd Benzinger	.10	.05	.01
□ 500 John Candelaria	.10	.05	.01
□ 501 Tom Candiotti	.10	.05	.01
□ 502 Tim Crews	.10	.05	.01
□ 503 Eric Davis	.15	.07	.02
□ 504 Jim Gott	.10	.05	.01
□ 505 Dave Hansen	.10	.05	.01
□ 506 Carlos Hernandez	.10	.05	.01
□ 507 Orel Hershiser	.15	.07	.02
□ 508 Eric Karros	.30	.14	.04
□ 509 Bob Ojeda	.10	.05	.01
□ 510 Steve Wilson	.10	.05	.01
□ 511 Moises Alou	.30	.14	.04
□ 512 Bret Barberie	.10	.05	.01
□ 513 Ivan Calderon	.10	.05	.01
□ 514 Gary Carter	.30	.14	.04
□ 515 Archi Cianfrocco	.10	.05	.01
□ 516 Jeff Fassero	.15	.07	.02
□ 517 Darrin Fletcher	.10	.05	.01
□ 518 Marquis Grissom	.30	.14	.04
□ 519 Chris Haney	.10	.05	.01
□ 520 Ken Hill	.30	.14	.04
□ 521 Chris Nabholz	.10	.05	.01
□ 522 Bill Sampen	.10	.05	.01
□ 523 John Vander Wal	.10	.05	.01
□ 524 Dave Wainhouse	.10	.05	.01
□ 525 Larry Walker	.30	.14	.04
□ 526 John Wetteland	.15	.07	.02
□ 527 Bobby Bonilla	.15	.07	.02
□ 528 Sid Fernandez	.10	.05	.01
□ 529 John Franco	.10	.05	.01
□ 530 Dave Gallagher	.10	.05	.01
□ 531 Paul Gibson	.10	.05	.01
□ 532 Eddie Murray	.50	.23	.06
□ 533 Junior Noboa	.10	.05	.01
□ 534 Charlie O'Brien	.10	.05	.01
□ 535 Bill Pecota	.10	.05	.01
□ 536 Willie Randolph	.15	.07	.02
□ 537 Bret Saberhagen	.15	.07	.02
□ 538 Dick Schofield	.10	.05	.01
□ 539 Pete Schourek	.15	.07	.02
□ 540 Ruben Amaro	.10	.05	.01
□ 541 Andy Ashby	.15	.07	.02
□ 542 Kim Batiste	.10	.05	.01
□ 543 Cliff Brantley	.10	.05	.01
□ 544 Mariano Duncan	.10	.05	.01
□ 545 Jeff Grotewold	.10	.05	.01
□ 546 Barry Jones	.10	.05	.01
□ 547 Julio Peguero	.10	.05	.01
□ 548 Curt Schilling	.10	.05	.01
□ 549 Mitch Williams	.10	.05	.01
□ 550 Stan Belinda	.10	.05	.01
□ 551 Scott Bullett	.10	.05	.01
□ 552 Cecil Espy	.10	.05	.01
□ 553 Jeff King	.15	.07	.02
□ 554 Roger Mason	.10	.05	.01
□ 555 Paul Miller	.10	.05	.01
□ 556 Denny Neagle	.15	.07	.02
□ 557 Vicente Palacios	.10	.05	.01
□ 558 Bob Patterson	.10	.05	.01
□ 559 Tom Prince	.10	.05	.01
□ 560 Gary Redus	.10	.05	.01
□ 561 Gary Varsho	.10	.05	.01
□ 562 Juan Agosto	.10	.05	.01
□ 563 Cris Carpenter	.10	.05	.01
□ 564 Mark Clark	.15	.07	.02
□ 565 Jose DeLeon	.10	.05	.01
□ 566 Rich Gedman	.10	.05	.01
□ 567 Bernard Gilkey	.15	.07	.02
□ 568 Rex Hudler	.10	.05	.01
□ 569 Tim Jones	.10	.05	.01
□ 570 Donovan Osborne	.15	.07	.02
□ 571 Mike Perez	.10	.05	.01
□ 572 Gerald Perry	.10	.05	.01
□ 573 Bob Tewksbury	.10	.05	.01
□ 574 Todd Worrell	.10	.05	.01
□ 575 Dave Eiland	.10	.05	.01
□ 576 Jeremy Hernandez	.10	.05	.01
□ 577 Craig Lefferts	.10	.05	.01
□ 578 Jose Melendez	.10	.05	.01
□ 579 Randy Myers	.15	.07	.02
□ 580 Gary Pettis	.10	.05	.01
□ 581 Rich Rodriguez	.10	.05	.01
□ 582 Gary Sheffield	.30	.14	.04
□ 583 Craig Shipley	.10	.05	.01
□ 584 Kurt Stillwell	.10	.05	.01
□ 585 Tim Teufel	.10	.05	.01
□ 586 Rod Beck	.40	.18	.05
□ 587 Dave Burba	.10	.05	.01
□ 588 Craig Colbert	.10	.05	.01
□ 589 Bryan Hickerson	.10	.05	.01
□ 590 Mike Jackson	.10	.05	.01
□ 591 Mark Leonard	.10	.05	.01
□ 592 Jim McNamara	.10	.05	.01
□ 593 John Patterson	.10	.05	.01
□ 594 Dave Righetti	.10	.05	.01
□ 595 Cory Snyder	.10	.05	.01
□ 596 Bill Swift	.10	.05	.01
□ 597 Ted Wood	.10	.05	.01
□ 598 Checklist 301-400	.10	.05	.01
□ 599 Checklist 401-500	.10	.05	.01
□ 600 Checklist 501-600	.10	.05	.01

1992 Ultra All-Rookies

Cards from this ten-card standard-size set highlighting a selection of top rookies were randomly inserted in 1992 Ultra II foil packs. The fronts feature borderless color action player photos except at the bottom where they are edged by a marbleized black wedge. The words "All-Rookie Team" in gold foil lettering appear in a black marbleized inverted triangle at the lower right corner, with the player's name on a color banner.

	MINT	NRMT	EXC
COMPLETE SET (10)	14.00	6.25	1.75
COMMON CARD (1-10)	.50	.23	.06
RANDOM INSERTS IN SER.2 PACKS			

□ 1 Eric Karros	2.00	.90	.25
□ 2 Andy Stankiewicz	.50	.23	.06
□ 3 Gary DiSarcina	.50	.23	.06
□ 4 Archi Cianfrocco	.50	.23	.06
□ 5 Jim McNamara	.50	.23	.06
□ 6 Chad Curtis	1.00	.45	.12
□ 7 Kenny Lofton	10.00	4.50	1.25
□ 8 Reggie Sanders	2.00	.90	.25
□ 9 Pat Mahomes	.50	.23	.06
□ 10 Donovan Osborne	1.00	.45	.12

1992 Ultra All-Stars

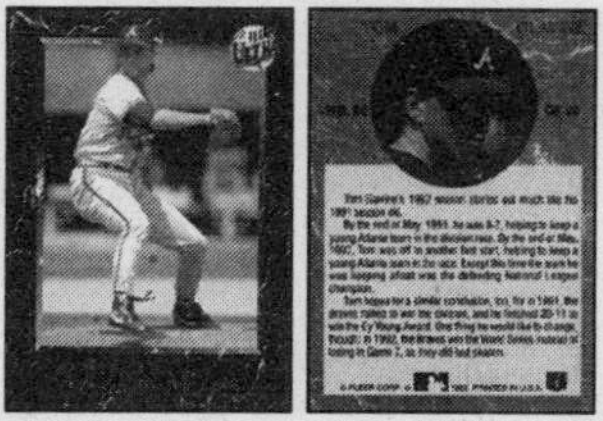

Featuring many of the 1992 season's stars, cards from this 20-card standard-size set were randomly inserted in 1992 Ultra II foil packs. The front design displays color action player photos enclosed by black marbleized borders. The word "All-Star" and the player's name are printed in gold foil lettering in the bottom border.

	MINT	NRMT	EXC
COMPLETE SET (20)	25.00	11.00	3.10
COMMON CARD (1-20)	.50	.23	.06
SEMISTARS	.75	.35	.09
RANDOM INSERTS IN SER.2 PACKS			
□ 1 Mark McGwire	2.00	.90	.25
□ 2 Roberto Alomar	1.50	.70	.19
□ 3 Cal Ripken Jr.	6.00	2.70	.75
□ 4 Wade Boggs	.75	.35	.09
□ 5 Mickey Tettleton	.50	.23	.06
□ 6 Ken Griffey Jr.	8.00	3.60	1.00
□ 7 Roberto Kelly	.50	.23	.06
□ 8 Kirby Puckett	2.00	.90	.25
□ 9 Frank Thomas	8.00	3.60	1.00
□ 10 Jack McDowell	.75	.35	.09
□ 11 Will Clark	.75	.35	.09
□ 12 Ryne Sandberg	1.50	.70	.19
□ 13 Barry Larkin	.75	.35	.09
□ 14 Gary Sheffield	1.00	.45	.12
□ 15 Tom Pagnozzi	.50	.23	.06
□ 16 Barry Bonds	1.50	.70	.19
□ 17 Deion Sanders	.75	.35	.09
□ 18 Darryl Strawberry	.75	.35	.09
□ 19 David Cone	.75	.35	.09
□ 20 Tom Glavine	.75	.35	.09

1992 Ultra Award Winners

This 25-card standard-size set features 18 Gold Glove winners, both Cy Young Award winners, both Rookies of the Year, both league MVP's, and the World Series MVP. The cards were randomly inserted in 1992 Fleer Ultra I packs. The fronts carry full-bleed color player photos that have a diagonal blue marbleized border at the bottom. The player's name appears in this bottom border, and a diamond-shaped gold foil seal signifying the award the player won is superimposed at the lower right corner.

	MINT	NRMT	EXC
COMPLETE SET (25)	50.00	22.00	6.25
COMMON CARD (1-25)	.75	.35	.09
SEMISTARS	1.25	.55	.16
RANDOM INSERTS IN SER.1 PACKS			
□ 1 Jack Morris	1.25	.55	.16
□ 2 Chuck Knoblauch	1.50	.70	.19
□ 3 Jeff Bagwell	8.00	3.60	1.00
□ 4 Terry Pendleton	1.25	.55	.16
□ 5 Cal Ripken	10.00	4.50	1.25
□ 6 Roger Clemens	1.25	.55	.16
□ 7 Tom Glavine	1.25	.55	.16
□ 8 Tom Pagnozzi	.75	.35	.09
□ 9 Ozzie Smith	2.00	.90	.25
□ 10 Andy Van Slyke	1.25	.55	.16
□ 11 Barry Bonds	2.50	1.10	.30
□ 12 Tony Gwynn	4.00	1.80	.50
□ 13 Matt Williams	1.25	.55	.16
□ 14 Will Clark	1.25	.55	.16
□ 15 Robin Ventura	1.25	.55	.16
□ 16 Mark Langston	1.25	.55	.16
□ 17 Tony Pena	.75	.35	.09
□ 18 Devon White	1.25	.55	.16
□ 19 Don Mattingly	5.00	2.20	.60
□ 20 Roberto Alomar	2.50	1.10	.30
□ 21A Cal Ripken ERR (Reversed negative on card back)	15.00	6.75	1.85
□ 21B Cal Ripken COR	10.00	4.50	1.25
□ 22 Ken Griffey Jr.	12.00	5.50	1.50
□ 23 Kirby Puckett	3.00	1.35	.35
□ 24 Greg Maddux	8.00	3.60	1.00
□ 25 Ryne Sandberg	2.50	1.10	.30

1993 Ultra

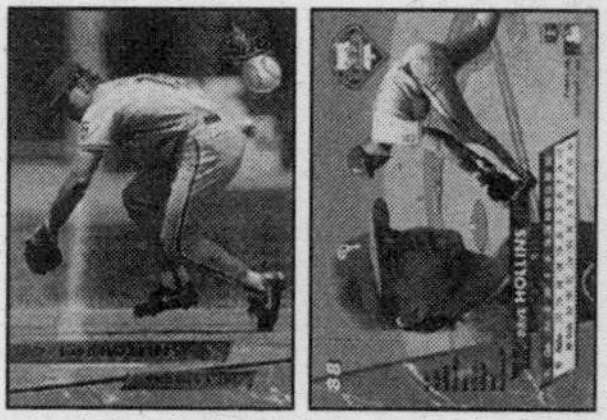

The 1993 Ultra baseball set was issued in two series and totaled 650 standard-size cards. The full-bleed color-enhanced action photos are edged at the bottom by a gold foil stripe and a fawn-colored border that is streaked with white for a marbleized effect. On a dimensionalized ball park background, the horizontal backs have an action shot, a portrait, last season statistics, and the player's entire professional career totals. The cards are numbered on the back, grouped alphabetically within teams, and checklisted below alphabetically according to teams for the National and American Leagues as follows: Atlanta Braves (1-13), Chicago Cubs (14-25), Cincinnati Reds (26-36), Houston Astros (37-48), Los Angeles Dodgers (49-60), Montreal Expos (61-71), New York Mets (72-81), Philadelphia Phillies (82-94), Pittsburgh Pirates (95-105), St. Louis Cardinals (106-115), San Diego Padres (116-125), and San Francisco Giants (126-137), Baltimore Orioles (138-147), Boston Red Sox (148-158), California Angels (159-169), Chicago White

Sox (170-181), Cleveland Indians (182-193), Detroit Tigers (194-204), Kansas City Royals (205-216), Milwaukee Brewers (217-227), Minnesota Twins (228-239), New York Yankees (240-252), Oakland Athletics (253-264), Seattle Mariners (265-275), Texas Rangers (276-285), and Toronto Blue Jays (286-297). The first series closes with checklist cards (298-300). The second series features 83 Ultra Rookies, 51 Rockies and Marlins, traded veteran players, and other major league veterans not included in the first series. The Rookie cards show a gold foil stamped Rookie "flag" as part of the card design. Rookie Cards in this set include Rene Arocha, Russ Davis, Jim Edmonds, and J.T. Snow.

	MINT	NRMT	EXC
COMPLETE SET (650)	40.00	18.00	5.00
COMPLETE SERIES 1 (300)	20.00	9.00	2.50
COMPLETE SERIES 2 (350)	20.00	9.00	2.50
COMMON CARD (1-650)	.10	.05	.01
SEMISTARS	.25	.11	.03
STARS	.50	.23	.06
COMP.ECKERSLEY SET (10)	5.00	2.20	.60
COMMON ECKERSLEY (1-10)	.50	.23	.06
CERTIFIED ECKERSLEY AUTO	50.00	22.00	6.25
ECKERSLEY:RANDOM INSERTS IN PACKS			
COMMON ECK.MAIL-IN (11-12)	1.00	.45	.12
ECK.MAIL-IN AVAIL.VIA WRAPPER EXCH.			

□ 1 Steve Avery	.25	.11	.03
□ 2 Rafael Belliard	.10	.05	.01
□ 3 Damon Berryhill	.10	.05	.01
□ 4 Sid Bream	.10	.05	.01
□ 5 Ron Gant	.40	.18	.05
□ 6 Tom Glavine	.40	.18	.05
□ 7 Ryan Klesko	1.50	.70	.19
□ 8 Mark Lemke	.10	.05	.01
□ 9 Javier Lopez	.75	.35	.09
□ 10 Greg Olson	.10	.05	.01
□ 11 Terry Pendleton	.25	.11	.03
□ 12 Deion Sanders	.40	.18	.05
□ 13 Mike Stanton	.10	.05	.01
□ 14 Paul Assenmacher	.10	.05	.01
□ 15 Steve Buechele	.10	.05	.01
□ 16 Frank Castillo	.10	.05	.01
□ 17 Shawon Dunston	.10	.05	.01
□ 18 Mark Grace	.40	.18	.05
□ 19 Derrick May	.10	.05	.01
□ 20 Chuck McElroy	.10	.05	.01
□ 21 Mike Morgan	.10	.05	.01
□ 22 Bob Scanlan	.10	.05	.01
□ 23 Dwight Smith	.10	.05	.01
□ 24 Sammy Sosa	.40	.18	.05
□ 25 Rick Wilkins	.10	.05	.01
□ 26 Tim Belcher	.10	.05	.01
□ 27 Jeff Branson	.10	.05	.01
□ 28 Bill Doran	.10	.05	.01
□ 29 Chris Hammond	.10	.05	.01
□ 30 Barry Larkin	.40	.18	.05
□ 31 Hal Morris	.10	.05	.01
□ 32 Joe Oliver	.10	.05	.01
□ 33 Jose Rijo	.10	.05	.01
□ 34 Bip Roberts	.10	.05	.01
□ 35 Chris Sabo	.10	.05	.01
□ 36 Reggie Sanders	.40	.18	.05
□ 37 Craig Biggio	.40	.18	.05
□ 38 Ken Caminiti	.40	.18	.05
□ 39 Steve Finley	.40	.18	.05
□ 40 Luis Gonzalez	.10	.05	.01
□ 41 Juan Guerrero	.10	.05	.01
□ 42 Pete Harnisch	.10	.05	.01
□ 43 Xavier Hernandez	.10	.05	.01
□ 44 Doug Jones	.10	.05	.01
□ 45 Al Osuna	.10	.05	.01
□ 46 Eddie Taubensee	.10	.05	.01
□ 47 Scooter Tucker	.10	.05	.01
□ 48 Brian Williams	.10	.05	.01
□ 49 Pedro Astacio	.10	.05	.01
□ 50 Rafael Bournigal	.10	.05	.01
□ 51 Brett Butler	.25	.11	.03
□ 52 Tom Candiotti	.10	.05	.01
□ 53 Eric Davis	.25	.11	.03
□ 54 Lenny Harris	.10	.05	.01
□ 55 Orel Hershiser	.25	.11	.03
□ 56 Eric Karros	.40	.18	.05
□ 57 Pedro Martinez	.40	.18	.05
□ 58 Roger McDowell	.10	.05	.01
□ 59 Jose Offerman	.10	.05	.01
□ 60 Mike Piazza	3.00	1.35	.35
□ 61 Moises Alou	.40	.18	.05
□ 62 Kent Bottenfield	.10	.05	.01
□ 63 Archi Cianfrocco	.10	.05	.01
□ 64 Greg Colbrunn	.10	.05	.01
□ 65 Wil Cordero	.25	.11	.03
□ 66 Delino DeShields	.10	.05	.01
□ 67 Darrin Fletcher	.10	.05	.01
□ 68 Ken Hill	.25	.11	.03
□ 69 Chris Nabholz	.10	.05	.01
□ 70 Mel Rojas	.25	.11	.03
□ 71 Larry Walker	.40	.18	.05
□ 72 Sid Fernandez	.10	.05	.01
□ 73 John Franco	.10	.05	.01
□ 74 Dave Gallagher	.10	.05	.01
□ 75 Todd Hundley	.40	.18	.05
□ 76 Howard Johnson	.10	.05	.01
□ 77 Jeff Kent	.25	.11	.03
□ 78 Eddie Murray	.75	.35	.09
□ 79 Bret Saberhagen	.25	.11	.03
□ 80 Chico Walker	.10	.05	.01
□ 81 Anthony Young	.10	.05	.01
□ 82 Kyle Abbott	.10	.05	.01
□ 83 Ruben Amaro	.10	.05	.01
□ 84 Juan Bell	.10	.05	.01
□ 85 Wes Chamberlain	.10	.05	.01
□ 86 Darren Daulton	.25	.11	.03
□ 87 Mariano Duncan	.10	.05	.01
□ 88 Dave Hollins	.10	.05	.01
□ 89 Ricky Jordan	.10	.05	.01
□ 90 John Kruk	.25	.11	.03
□ 91 Mickey Morandini	.10	.05	.01
□ 92 Terry Mulholland	.10	.05	.01
□ 93 Ben Rivera	.10	.05	.01
□ 94 Mike Williams	.10	.05	.01
□ 95 Stan Belinda	.10	.05	.01
□ 96 Jay Bell	.25	.11	.03
□ 97 Jeff King	.25	.11	.03
□ 98 Mike LaValliere	.10	.05	.01
□ 99 Lloyd McClendon	.10	.05	.01
□ 100 Orlando Merced	.25	.11	.03
□ 101 Zane Smith	.10	.05	.01
□ 102 Randy Tomlin	.10	.05	.01
□ 103 Andy Van Slyke	.25	.11	.03
□ 104 Tim Wakefield	.25	.11	.03
□ 105 John Wehner	.10	.05	.01
□ 106 Bernard Gilkey	.40	.18	.05
□ 107 Brian Jordan	.40	.18	.05
□ 108 Ray Lankford	.40	.18	.05
□ 109 Donovan Osborne	.10	.05	.01
□ 110 Tom Pagnozzi	.10	.05	.01
□ 111 Mike Perez	.10	.05	.01
□ 112 Lee Smith	.25	.11	.03
□ 113 Ozzie Smith	.60	.25	.07
□ 114 Bob Tewksbury	.10	.05	.01
□ 115 Todd Zeile	.10	.05	.01
□ 116 Andy Benes	.10	.05	.01
□ 117 Greg W. Harris	.10	.05	.01
□ 118 Darrin Jackson	.10	.05	.01
□ 119 Fred McGriff	.40	.18	.05
□ 120 Rich Rodriguez	.10	.05	.01
□ 121 Frank Seminara	.10	.05	.01
□ 122 Gary Sheffield	.40	.18	.05
□ 123 Craig Shipley	.10	.05	.01
□ 124 Kurt Stillwell	.10	.05	.01
□ 125 Dan Walters	.10	.05	.01
□ 126 Rod Beck	.25	.11	.03
□ 127 Mike Benjamin	.10	.05	.01
□ 128 Jeff Brantley	.10	.05	.01
□ 129 John Burkett	.10	.05	.01
□ 130 Will Clark	.40	.18	.05
□ 131 Royce Clayton	.25	.11	.03
□ 132 Steve Hosey	.10	.05	.01
□ 133 Mike Jackson	.10	.05	.01
□ 134 Darren Lewis	.10	.05	.01
□ 135 Kirt Manwaring	.10	.05	.01
□ 136 Bill Swift	.10	.05	.01
□ 137 Robby Thompson	.10	.05	.01
□ 138 Brady Anderson	.40	.18	.05
□ 139 Glenn Davis	.10	.05	.01
□ 140 Leo Gomez	.10	.05	.01
□ 141 Chito Martinez	.10	.05	.01

□ 142 Ben McDonald	.10	.05	.01
□ 143 Alan Mills	.10	.05	.01
□ 144 Mike Mussina	.60	.25	.07
□ 145 Gregg Olson	.10	.05	.01
□ 146 David Segui	.10	.05	.01
□ 147 Jeff Tackett	.10	.05	.01
□ 148 Jack Clark	.10	.05	.01
□ 149 Scott Cooper	.10	.05	.01
□ 150 Danny Darwin	.10	.05	.01
□ 151 John Dopson	.10	.05	.01
□ 152 Mike Greenwell	.10	.05	.01
□ 153 Tim Naehring	.10	.05	.01
□ 154 Tony Pena	.10	.05	.01
□ 155 Paul Quantrill	.10	.05	.01
□ 156 Mo Vaughn	.75	.35	.09
□ 157 Frank Viola	.10	.05	.01
□ 158 Bob Zupcic	.10	.05	.01
□ 159 Chad Curtis	.25	.11	.03
□ 160 Gary DiSarcina	.10	.05	.01
□ 161 Damion Easley	.10	.05	.01
□ 162 Chuck Finley	.10	.05	.01
□ 163 Tim Fortugno	.10	.05	.01
□ 164 Rene Gonzales	.10	.05	.01
□ 165 Joe Grahe	.10	.05	.01
□ 166 Mark Langston	.25	.11	.03
□ 167 John Orton	.10	.05	.01
□ 168 Luis Polonia	.10	.05	.01
□ 169 Julio Valera	.10	.05	.01
□ 170 Wilson Alvarez	.25	.11	.03
□ 171 George Bell	.10	.05	.01
□ 172 Joey Cora	.10	.05	.01
□ 173 Alex Fernandez	.40	.18	.05
□ 174 Lance Johnson	.25	.11	.03
□ 175 Ron Karkovice	.10	.05	.01
□ 176 Jack McDowell	.25	.11	.03
□ 177 Scott Radinsky	.10	.05	.01
□ 178 Tim Raines	.40	.18	.05
□ 179 Steve Sax	.10	.05	.01
□ 180 Bobby Thigpen	.10	.05	.01
□ 181 Frank Thomas	3.00	1.35	.35
□ 182 Sandy Alomar	.25	.11	.03
□ 183 Carlos Baerga	.40	.18	.05
□ 184 Felix Fermin	.10	.05	.01
□ 185 Thomas Howard	.10	.05	.01
□ 186 Mark Lewis	.10	.05	.01
□ 187 Derek Lilliquist	.10	.05	.01
□ 188 Carlos Martinez	.10	.05	.01
□ 189 Charles Nagy	.25	.11	.03
□ 190 Scott Scudder	.10	.05	.01
□ 191 Paul Sorrento	.10	.05	.01
□ 192 Jim Thome	1.50	.70	.19
□ 193 Mark Whiten	.10	.05	.01
□ 194 Milt Cuyler UER (Reversed negative on card front)	.10	.05	.01
□ 195 Rob Deer	.10	.05	.01
□ 196 John Doherty	.10	.05	.01
□ 197 Travis Fryman	.40	.18	.05
□ 198 Dan Gladden	.10	.05	.01
□ 199 Mike Henneman	.10	.05	.01
□ 200 John Kiely	.10	.05	.01
□ 201 Chad Kreuter	.10	.05	.01
□ 202 Scott Livingstone	.10	.05	.01
□ 203 Tony Phillips	.25	.11	.03
□ 204 Alan Trammell	.40	.18	.05
□ 205 Mike Boddicker	.10	.05	.01
□ 206 George Brett	1.25	.55	.16
□ 207 Tom Gordon	.10	.05	.01
□ 208 Mark Gubicza	.10	.05	.01
□ 209 Gregg Jefferies	.40	.18	.05
□ 210 Wally Joyner	.25	.11	.03
□ 211 Kevin Koslofski	.10	.05	.01
□ 212 Brent Mayne	.10	.05	.01
□ 213 Brian McRae	.25	.11	.03
□ 214 Kevin McReynolds	.10	.05	.01
□ 215 Rusty Meacham	.10	.05	.01
□ 216 Steve Shifflett	.10	.05	.01
□ 217 James Austin	.10	.05	.01
□ 218 Cal Eldred	.10	.05	.01
□ 219 Darryl Hamilton	.10	.05	.01
□ 220 Doug Henry	.10	.05	.01
□ 221 John Jaha	.25	.11	.03
□ 222 Dave Nilsson	.25	.11	.03
□ 223 Jesse Orosco	.10	.05	.01
□ 224 B.J. Surhoff	.25	.11	.03
□ 225 Greg Vaughn	.40	.18	.05
□ 226 Bill Wegman	.10	.05	.01
□ 227 Robin Yount UER (Born in Illinois, not in Virginia)	.40	.18	.05
□ 228 Rick Aguilera	.10	.05	.01
□ 229 J.T. Bruett	.10	.05	.01
□ 230 Scott Erickson	.10	.05	.01
□ 231 Kent Hrbek	.25	.11	.03
□ 232 Terry Jorgensen	.10	.05	.01
□ 233 Scott Leius	.10	.05	.01
□ 234 Pat Mahomes	.10	.05	.01
□ 235 Pedro Munoz	.10	.05	.01
□ 236 Kirby Puckett	1.00	.45	.12
□ 237 Kevin Tapani	.10	.05	.01
□ 238 Lenny Webster	.10	.05	.01
□ 239 Carl Willis	.10	.05	.01
□ 240 Mike Gallego	.10	.05	.01
□ 241 John Habyan	.10	.05	.01
□ 242 Pat Kelly	.10	.05	.01
□ 243 Kevin Maas	.10	.05	.01
□ 244 Don Mattingly	1.50	.70	.19
□ 245 Hensley Meulens	.10	.05	.01
□ 246 Sam Militello	.10	.05	.01
□ 247 Matt Nokes	.10	.05	.01
□ 248 Melido Perez	.10	.05	.01
□ 249 Andy Stankiewicz	.10	.05	.01
□ 250 Randy Velarde	.10	.05	.01
□ 251 Bob Wickman	.10	.05	.01
□ 252 Bernie Williams	.40	.18	.05
□ 253 Lance Blankenship	.10	.05	.01
□ 254 Mike Bordick	.10	.05	.01
□ 255 Jerry Browne	.10	.05	.01
□ 256 Ron Darling	.10	.05	.01
□ 257 Dennis Eckersley	.25	.11	.03
□ 258 Rickey Henderson	.40	.18	.05
□ 259 Vince Horsman	.10	.05	.01
□ 260 Troy Neel	.10	.05	.01
□ 261 Jeff Parrett	.10	.05	.01
□ 262 Terry Steinbach	.25	.11	.03
□ 263 Bob Welch	.10	.05	.01
□ 264 Bobby Witt	.10	.05	.01
□ 265 Rich Amaral	.10	.05	.01
□ 266 Bret Boone	.25	.11	.03
□ 267 Jay Buhner	.40	.18	.05
□ 268 Dave Fleming	.10	.05	.01
□ 269 Randy Johnson	.40	.18	.05
□ 270 Edgar Martinez	.40	.18	.05
□ 271 Mike Schooler	.10	.05	.01
□ 272 Russ Swan	.10	.05	.01
□ 273 Dave Valle	.10	.05	.01
□ 274 Omar Vizquel	.40	.18	.05
□ 275 Kerry Woodson	.10	.05	.01
□ 276 Kevin Brown	.10	.05	.01
□ 277 Julio Franco	.25	.11	.03
□ 278 Jeff Frye	.10	.05	.01
□ 279 Juan Gonzalez	1.50	.70	.19
□ 280 Jeff Huson	.10	.05	.01
□ 281 Rafael Palmeiro	.40	.18	.05
□ 282 Dean Palmer	.25	.11	.03
□ 283 Roger Pavlik	.25	.11	.03
□ 284 Ivan Rodriguez	.60	.25	.07
□ 285 Kenny Rogers	.10	.05	.01
□ 286 Derek Bell	.40	.18	.05
□ 287 Pat Borders	.10	.05	.01
□ 288 Joe Carter	.40	.18	.05
□ 289 Bob MacDonald	.10	.05	.01
□ 290 Jack Morris	.25	.11	.03
□ 291 John Olerud	.10	.05	.01
□ 292 Ed Sprague	.25	.11	.03
□ 293 Todd Stottlemyre	.25	.11	.03
□ 294 Mike Timlin	.10	.05	.01
□ 295 Duane Ward	.10	.05	.01
□ 296 David Wells	.10	.05	.01
□ 297 Devon White	.10	.05	.01
□ 298 Checklist 1-94 Ray Lankford	.25	.11	.03
□ 299 Checklist 95-193 Bobby Witt	.10	.05	.01
□ 300 Checklist 194-300 Mike Piazza	.40	.18	.05
□ 301 Steve Bedrosian	.10	.05	.01
□ 302 Jeff Blauser	.10	.05	.01
□ 303 Francisco Cabrera	.10	.05	.01
□ 304 Marvin Freeman	.10	.05	.01
□ 305 Brian Hunter	.10	.05	.01
□ 306 David Justice	.40	.18	.05

□	307	Greg Maddux	2.00	.90	.25
□	308	Greg McMichael	.25	.11	.03
□	309	Kent Mercker	.10	.05	.01
□	310	Otis Nixon	.10	.05	.01
□	311	Pete Smith	.10	.05	.01
□	312	John Smoltz	.40	.18	.05
□	313	Jose Guzman	.10	.05	.01
□	314	Mike Harkey	.10	.05	.01
□	315	Greg Hibbard	.10	.05	.01
□	316	Candy Maldonado	.10	.05	.01
□	317	Randy Myers	.25	.11	.03
□	318	Dan Plesac	.10	.05	.01
□	319	Rey Sanchez	.10	.05	.01
□	320	Ryne Sandberg	.75	.35	.09
□	321	Tommy Shields	.10	.05	.01
□	322	Jose Vizcaino	.10	.05	.01
□	323	Matt Walbeck	.10	.05	.01
□	324	Willie Wilson	.10	.05	.01
□	325	Tom Browning	.10	.05	.01
□	326	Tim Costo	.10	.05	.01
□	327	Rob Dibble	.10	.05	.01
□	328	Steve Foster	.10	.05	.01
□	329	Roberto Kelly	.10	.05	.01
□	330	Randy Milligan	.10	.05	.01
□	331	Kevin Mitchell	.25	.11	.03
□	332	Tim Pugh	.10	.05	.01
□	333	Jeff Reardon	.25	.11	.03
□	334	John Roper	.10	.05	.01
□	335	Juan Samuel	.10	.05	.01
□	336	John Smiley	.10	.05	.01
□	337	Dan Wilson	.25	.11	.03
□	338	Scott Aldred	.10	.05	.01
□	339	Andy Ashby	.25	.11	.03
□	340	Freddie Benavides	.10	.05	.01
□	341	Dante Bichette	.40	.18	.05
□	342	Willie Blair	.10	.05	.01
□	343	Daryl Boston	.10	.05	.01
□	344	Vinny Castilla	.40	.18	.05
□	345	Jerald Clark	.10	.05	.01
□	346	Alex Cole	.10	.05	.01
□	347	Andres Galarraga	.40	.18	.05
□	348	Joe Girardi	.10	.05	.01
□	349	Ryan Hawblitzel	.10	.05	.01
□	350	Charlie Hayes	.10	.05	.01
□	351	Butch Henry	.10	.05	.01
□	352	Darren Holmes	.10	.05	.01
□	353	Dale Murphy	.40	.18	.05
□	354	David Nied	.10	.05	.01
□	355	Jeff Parrett	.10	.05	.01
□	356	Steve Reed	.10	.05	.01
□	357	Bruce Ruffin	.10	.05	.01
□	358	Danny Sheaffer	.10	.05	.01
□	359	Bryn Smith	.10	.05	.01
□	360	Jim Tatum	.10	.05	.01
□	361	Eric Young	.40	.18	.05
□	362	Gerald Young	.10	.05	.01
□	363	Luis Aquino	.10	.05	.01
□	364	Alex Arias	.10	.05	.01
□	365	Jack Armstrong	.10	.05	.01
□	366	Bret Barberie	.10	.05	.01
□	367	Ryan Bowen	.10	.05	.01
□	368	Greg Briley	.10	.05	.01
□	369	Cris Carpenter	.10	.05	.01
□	370	Chuck Carr	.10	.05	.01
□	371	Jeff Conine	.40	.18	.05
□	372	Steve Decker	.10	.05	.01
□	373	Orestes Destrade	.10	.05	.01
□	374	Monty Fariss	.10	.05	.01
□	375	Junior Felix	.10	.05	.01
□	376	Chris Hammond	.10	.05	.01
□	377	Bryan Harvey	.10	.05	.01
□	378	Trevor Hoffman	.25	.11	.03
□	379	Charlie Hough	.10	.05	.01
□	380	Joe Klink	.10	.05	.01
□	381	Richie Lewis	.10	.05	.01
□	382	Dave Magadan	.10	.05	.01
□	383	Bob McClure	.10	.05	.01
□	384	Scott Pose	.10	.05	.01
□	385	Rich Renteria	.10	.05	.01
□	386	Benito Santiago	.10	.05	.01
□	387	Walt Weiss	.10	.05	.01
□	388	Nigel Wilson	.10	.05	.01
□	389	Eric Anthony	.10	.05	.01
□	390	Jeff Bagwell	1.25	.55	.16
□	391	Andujar Cedeno	.10	.05	.01
□	392	Doug Drabek	.10	.05	.01
□	393	Darryl Kile	.10	.05	.01
□	394	Mark Portugal	.10	.05	.01
□	395	Karl Rhodes	.10	.05	.01
□	396	Scott Servais	.10	.05	.01
□	397	Greg Swindell	.10	.05	.01
□	398	Tom Goodwin	.10	.05	.01
□	399	Kevin Gross	.10	.05	.01
□	400	Carlos Hernandez	.10	.05	.01
□	401	Ramon Martinez	.25	.11	.03
□	402	Raul Mondesi	1.00	.45	.12
□	403	Jody Reed	.10	.05	.01
□	404	Mike Sharperson	.10	.05	.01
□	405	Cory Snyder	.10	.05	.01
□	406	Darryl Strawberry	.25	.11	.03
□	407	Rick Trlicek	.10	.05	.01
□	408	Tim Wallach	.10	.05	.01
□	409	Todd Worrell	.10	.05	.01
□	410	Tavo Alvarez	.10	.05	.01
□	411	Sean Berry	.10	.05	.01
□	412	Frank Bolick	.10	.05	.01
□	413	Cliff Floyd	.40	.18	.05
□	414	Mike Gardiner	.10	.05	.01
□	415	Marquis Grissom	.40	.18	.05
□	416	Tim Laker	.10	.05	.01
□	417	Mike Lansing	.25	.11	.03
□	418	Dennis Martinez	.25	.11	.03
□	419	John Vander Wal	.10	.05	.01
□	420	John Wetteland	.25	.11	.03
□	421	Rondell White	.60	.25	.07
□	422	Bobby Bonilla	.25	.11	.03
□	423	Jeromy Burnitz	.10	.05	.01
□	424	Vince Coleman	.10	.05	.01
□	425	Mike Draper	.10	.05	.01
□	426	Tony Fernandez	.10	.05	.01
□	427	Dwight Gooden	.25	.11	.03
□	428	Jeff Innis	.10	.05	.01
□	429	Bobby Jones	.25	.11	.03
□	430	Mike Maddux	.10	.05	.01
□	431	Charlie O'Brien	.10	.05	.01
□	432	Joe Orsulak	.10	.05	.01
□	433	Pete Schourek	.25	.11	.03
□	434	Frank Tanana	.10	.05	.01
□	435	Ryan Thompson	.10	.05	.01
□	436	Kim Batiste	.10	.05	.01
□	437	Mark Davis	.10	.05	.01
□	438	Jose DeLeon	.10	.05	.01
□	439	Len Dykstra	.25	.11	.03
□	440	Jim Eisenreich	.25	.11	.03
□	441	Tommy Greene	.10	.05	.01
□	442	Pete Incaviglia	.10	.05	.01
□	443	Danny Jackson	.10	.05	.01
□	444	Todd Pratt	.10	.05	.01
□	445	Curt Schilling	.10	.05	.01
□	446	Milt Thompson	.10	.05	.01
□	447	David West	.10	.05	.01
□	448	Mitch Williams	.10	.05	.01
□	449	Steve Cooke	.10	.05	.01
□	450	Carlos Garcia	.10	.05	.01
□	451	Al Martin	.25	.11	.03
□	452	Blas Minor	.10	.05	.01
□	453	Dennis Moeller	.10	.05	.01
□	454	Denny Neagle	.25	.11	.03
□	455	Don Slaught	.10	.05	.01
□	456	Lonnie Smith	.10	.05	.01
□	457	Paul Wagner	.10	.05	.01
□	458	Bob Walk	.10	.05	.01
□	459	Kevin Young	.10	.05	.01
□	460	Rene Arocha	.10	.05	.01
□	461	Brian Barber	.10	.05	.01
□	462	Rheal Cormier	.10	.05	.01
□	463	Gregg Jefferies	.40	.18	.05
□	464	Joe Magrane	.10	.05	.01
□	465	Omar Olivares	.10	.05	.01
□	466	Geronimo Pena	.10	.05	.01
□	467	Allen Watson	.10	.05	.01
□	468	Mark Whiten	.10	.05	.01
□	469	Derek Bell	.40	.18	.05
□	470	Phil Clark	.10	.05	.01
□	471	Pat Gomez	.10	.05	.01
□	472	Tony Gwynn	1.25	.55	.16
□	473	Jeremy Hernandez	.10	.05	.01
□	474	Bruce Hurst	.10	.05	.01
□	475	Phil Plantier	.10	.05	.01
□	476	Scott Sanders	.10	.05	.01
□	477	Tim Scott	.10	.05	.01
□	478	Darrell Sherman	.10	.05	.01

□ 479 Guillermo Velasquez	.10	.05	.01
□ 480 Tim Worrell	.10	.05	.01
□ 481 Todd Benzinger	.10	.05	.01
□ 482 Bud Black	.10	.05	.01
□ 483 Barry Bonds	.75	.35	.09
□ 484 Dave Burba	.10	.05	.01
□ 485 Bryan Hickerson	.10	.05	.01
□ 486 Dave Martinez	.10	.05	.01
□ 487 Willie McGee	.10	.05	.01
□ 488 Jeff Reed	.10	.05	.01
□ 489 Kevin Rogers	.10	.05	.01
□ 490 Matt Williams	.40	.18	.05
□ 491 Trevor Wilson	.10	.05	.01
□ 492 Harold Baines	.25	.11	.03
□ 493 Mike Devereaux	.10	.05	.01
□ 494 Todd Frohwirth	.10	.05	.01
□ 495 Chris Hoiles	.10	.05	.01
□ 496 Luis Mercedes	.10	.05	.01
□ 497 Sherman Obando	.10	.05	.01
□ 498 Brad Pennington	.10	.05	.01
□ 499 Harold Reynolds	.10	.05	.01
□ 500 Arthur Rhodes	.10	.05	.01
□ 501 Cal Ripken	2.50	1.10	.30
□ 502 Rick Sutcliffe	.10	.05	.01
□ 503 Fernando Valenzuela	.25	.11	.03
□ 504 Mark Williamson	.10	.05	.01
□ 505 Scott Bankhead	.10	.05	.01
□ 506 Greg Blosser	.10	.05	.01
□ 507 Ivan Calderon	.10	.05	.01
□ 508 Roger Clemens	.40	.18	.05
□ 509 Andre Dawson	.40	.18	.05
□ 510 Scott Fletcher	.10	.05	.01
□ 511 Greg A. Harris	.10	.05	.01
□ 512 Billy Hatcher	.10	.05	.01
□ 513 Bob Melvin	.10	.05	.01
□ 514 Carlos Quintana	.10	.05	.01
□ 515 Luis Rivera	.10	.05	.01
□ 516 Jeff Russell	.10	.05	.01
□ 517 Ken Ryan	.10	.05	.01
□ 518 Chili Davis	.25	.11	.03
□ 519 Jim Edmonds	2.50	1.10	.30
□ 520 Gary Gaetti	.25	.11	.03
□ 521 Torey Lovullo	.10	.05	.01
□ 522 Troy Percival	.25	.11	.03
□ 523 Tim Salmon	.75	.35	.09
□ 524 Scott Sanderson	.10	.05	.01
□ 525 J.T. Snow	.40	.18	.05
□ 526 Jerome Walton	.10	.05	.01
□ 527 Jason Bere	.25	.11	.03
□ 528 Rod Bolton	.10	.05	.01
□ 529 Ellis Burks	.40	.18	.05
□ 530 Carlton Fisk	.40	.18	.05
□ 531 Craig Grebeck	.10	.05	.01
□ 532 Ozzie Guillen	.10	.05	.01
□ 533 Roberto Hernandez	.25	.11	.03
□ 534 Bo Jackson	.40	.18	.05
□ 535 Kirk McCaskill	.10	.05	.01
□ 536 Dave Stieb	.10	.05	.01
□ 537 Robin Ventura	.25	.11	.03
□ 538 Albert Belle	1.50	.70	.19
□ 539 Mike Bielecki	.10	.05	.01
□ 540 Glenallen Hill	.10	.05	.01
□ 541 Reggie Jefferson	.25	.11	.03
□ 542 Kenny Lofton	1.25	.55	.16
□ 543 Jeff Mutis	.10	.05	.01
□ 544 Junior Ortiz	.10	.05	.01
□ 545 Manny Ramirez	2.00	.90	.25
□ 546 Jeff Treadway	.10	.05	.01
□ 547 Kevin Wickander	.10	.05	.01
□ 548 Cecil Fielder	.25	.11	.03
□ 549 Kirk Gibson	.25	.11	.03
□ 550 Greg Gohr	.10	.05	.01
□ 551 David Haas	.10	.05	.01
□ 552 Bill Krueger	.10	.05	.01
□ 553 Mike Moore	.10	.05	.01
□ 554 Mickey Tettleton	.10	.05	.01
□ 555 Lou Whitaker	.40	.18	.05
□ 556 Kevin Appier	.25	.11	.03
□ 557 Billy Brewer	.10	.05	.01
□ 558 David Cone	.40	.18	.05
□ 559 Greg Gagne	.10	.05	.01
□ 560 Mark Gardner	.10	.05	.01
□ 561 Phil Hiatt	.10	.05	.01
□ 562 Felix Jose	.10	.05	.01
□ 563 Jose Lind	.10	.05	.01
□ 564 Mike Macfarlane	.10	.05	.01
□ 565 Keith Miller	.10	.05	.01
□ 566 Jeff Montgomery	.25	.11	.03
□ 567 Hipolito Pichardo	.10	.05	.01
□ 568 Ricky Bones	.10	.05	.01
□ 569 Tom Brunansky	.10	.05	.01
□ 570 Joe Kmak	.10	.05	.01
□ 571 Pat Listach	.10	.05	.01
□ 572 Graeme Lloyd	.10	.05	.01
□ 573 Carlos Maldonado	.10	.05	.01
□ 574 Josias Manzanillo	.10	.05	.01
□ 575 Matt Mieske	.25	.11	.03
□ 576 Kevin Reimer	.10	.05	.01
□ 577 Bill Spiers	.10	.05	.01
□ 578 Dickie Thon	.10	.05	.01
□ 579 Willie Banks	.10	.05	.01
□ 580 Jim Deshaies	.10	.05	.01
□ 581 Mark Guthrie	.10	.05	.01
□ 582 Brian Harper	.10	.05	.01
□ 583 Chuck Knoblauch	.40	.18	.05
□ 584 Gene Larkin	.10	.05	.01
□ 585 Shane Mack	.10	.05	.01
□ 586 David McCarty	.10	.05	.01
□ 587 Mike Pagliarulo	.10	.05	.01
□ 588 Mike Trombley	.10	.05	.01
□ 589 Dave Winfield	.40	.18	.05
□ 590 Jim Abbott	.10	.05	.01
□ 591 Wade Boggs	.40	.18	.05
□ 592 Russ Davis	.25	.11	.03
□ 593 Steve Farr	.10	.05	.01
□ 594 Steve Howe	.10	.05	.01
□ 595 Mike Humphreys	.10	.05	.01
□ 596 Jimmy Key	.25	.11	.03
□ 597 Jim Leyritz	.10	.05	.01
□ 598 Bobby Munoz	.10	.05	.01
□ 599 Paul O'Neill	.25	.11	.03
□ 600 Spike Owen	.10	.05	.01
□ 601 Mike Stanley	.10	.05	.01
□ 602 Danny Tartabull	.10	.05	.01
□ 603 Scott Brosius	.10	.05	.01
□ 604 Storm Davis	.10	.05	.01
□ 605 Eric Fox	.10	.05	.01
□ 606 Rich Gossage	.25	.11	.03
□ 607 Scott Hemond	.10	.05	.01
□ 608 Dave Henderson	.10	.05	.01
□ 609 Mark McGwire	1.00	.45	.12
□ 610 Mike Mohler	.10	.05	.01
□ 611 Edwin Nunez	.10	.05	.01
□ 612 Kevin Seitzer	.10	.05	.01
□ 613 Ruben Sierra	.25	.11	.03
□ 614 Chris Bosio	.10	.05	.01
□ 615 Norm Charlton	.10	.05	.01
□ 616 Jim Converse	.10	.05	.01
□ 617 John Cummings	.10	.05	.01
□ 618 Mike Felder	.10	.05	.01
□ 619 Ken Griffey Jr.	3.00	1.35	.35
□ 620 Mike Hampton	.10	.05	.01
□ 621 Erik Hanson	.10	.05	.01
□ 622 Bill Haselman	.10	.05	.01
□ 623 Tino Martinez	.25	.11	.03
□ 624 Lee Tinsley	.25	.11	.03
□ 625 Fernando Vina	.10	.05	.01
□ 626 David Wainhouse	.10	.05	.01
□ 627 Jose Canseco	.40	.18	.05
□ 628 Benji Gil	.25	.11	.03
□ 629 Tom Henke	.10	.05	.01
□ 630 David Hulse	.10	.05	.01
□ 631 Manuel Lee	.10	.05	.01
□ 632 Craig Lefferts	.10	.05	.01
□ 633 Robb Nen	.25	.11	.03
□ 634 Gary Redus	.10	.05	.01
□ 635 Bill Ripken	.10	.05	.01
□ 636 Nolan Ryan	2.50	1.10	.30
□ 637 Dan Smith	.10	.05	.01
□ 638 Matt Whiteside	.10	.05	.01
□ 639 Roberto Alomar	.75	.35	.09
□ 640 Juan Guzman	.25	.11	.03
□ 641 Pat Hentgen	.40	.18	.05
□ 642 Darrin Jackson	.10	.05	.01
□ 643 Randy Knorr	.10	.05	.01
□ 644 Domingo Martinez	.10	.05	.01
□ 645 Paul Molitor	.60	.25	.07
□ 646 Dick Schofield	.10	.05	.01
□ 647 Dave Stewart	.25	.11	.03
□ 648 Checklist 301-421 Rey Sanchez	.10	.05	.01
□ 649 Checklist 422-537	.10	.05	.01

Jeremy Hernandez			
□ 650 Checklist 538-650	.10	.05	.01
Junior Ortiz			

1993 Ultra All-Rookies

Randomly inserted into series II packs, this ten-card standard-size set features cutout color player action shots that are superposed upon a black background, which carries the player's uniform number, position, team name, and the set's title in multicolored lettering. The player's name appears in gold foil at the bottom. A posed color cutout player shot adorns the back, and is also projected upon a black background. The set's title appears at the top printed in gold foil and red lettering, and the player's name in gold foil precedes his career highlights, printed in white. The set is sequenced in alphabetical order. The key cards in this set are Mike Piazza and Tim Salmon.

	MINT	NRMT	EXC
COMPLETE SET (10)	15.00	6.75	1.85
COMMON CARD (1-10)	.50	.23	.06
SEMISTARS	1.00	.45	.12
RANDOM INSERTS IN SER.2 PACKS			
□ 1 Rene Arocha	.50	.23	.06
□ 2 Jeff Conine	1.50	.70	.19
□ 3 Phil Hiatt	.50	.23	.06
□ 4 Mike Lansing	1.00	.45	.12
□ 5 Al Martin	1.00	.45	.12
□ 6 David Nied	1.00	.45	.12
□ 7 Mike Piazza	12.00	5.50	1.50
□ 8 Tim Salmon	4.00	1.80	.50
□ 9 J.T. Snow	1.00	.45	.12
□ 10 Kevin Young	.50	.23	.06

1993 Ultra All-Stars

Randomly inserted into series II packs, this 20-card standard-size set features National League (1-10) and American League (11-20) All-Stars. The gray-bordered fronts carry color player action shots that are cutout and superposed upon their original, but faded and shifted, backgrounds. The player's name and the set's title are printed in gold foil upon simulated flames that issue from a baseball icon in the lower right. That same design of the player's name, the set's title, and flaming baseball icon appears again at the top of the gray-bordered back. The player's career highlights follow below.

	MINT	NRMT	EXC
COMPLETE SET (20)	40.00	18.00	5.00
COMMON CARD (1-20)	.75	.35	.09
SEMISTARS	1.50	.70	.19
RANDOM INSERTS IN SER.2 PACKS			
□ 1 Darren Daulton	.75	.35	.09
□ 2 Will Clark	1.50	.70	.19
□ 3 Ryne Sandberg	3.00	1.35	.35
□ 4 Barry Larkin	1.50	.70	.19
□ 5 Gary Sheffield	2.00	.90	.25
□ 6 Barry Bonds	3.00	1.35	.35
□ 7 Ray Lankford	.75	.35	.09
□ 8 Larry Walker	1.50	.70	.19
□ 9 Greg Maddux	8.00	3.60	1.00
□ 10 Lee Smith	1.50	.70	.19
□ 11 Ivan Rodriguez	2.50	1.10	.30
□ 12 Mark McGwire	4.00	1.80	.50
□ 13 Carlos Baerga	1.50	.70	.19
□ 14 Cal Ripken	10.00	4.50	1.25
□ 15 Edgar Martinez	1.50	.70	.19
□ 16 Juan Gonzalez	6.00	2.70	.75
□ 17 Ken Griffey Jr.	12.00	5.50	1.50
□ 18 Kirby Puckett	4.00	1.80	.50
□ 19 Frank Thomas	12.00	5.50	1.50
□ 20 Mike Mussina	2.50	1.10	.30

1993 Ultra Award Winners

Randomly inserted in first series packs, this first series of 1993 Ultra Award Winners presents the Top Glove for the National (1-9) and American (10-18) Leagues and other major award winners (19-25). The 25 standard-size cards comprising this set feature horizontal black-marbleized card designs and carry two color player photos: an action shot on the left and a posed photo on the right. The player's name appears in gold-foil cursive lettering near the bottom left. The category of award is shown in gold foil below. A gold-foil line highlights the card's lower edge. The horizontal and black-marbleized design continues on the back. A color player head shot appears on the left side. The player's name reappears in gold-foil cursive lettering near the top. Below is the player's award category in gold foil above a gold-foil underline. The player's career highlights are shown in white lettering below.

	MINT	NRMT	EXC
COMPLETE SET (25)	40.00	18.00	5.00
COMMON CARD (1-25)	.75	.35	.09
SEMISTARS	1.50	.70	.19
RANDOM INSERTS IN SER.1 PACKS			
□ 1 Greg Maddux	8.00	3.60	1.00
□ 2 Tom Pagnozzi	.75	.35	.09
□ 3 Mark Grace	1.50	.70	.19
□ 4 Jose Lind	.75	.35	.09
□ 5 Terry Pendleton	1.50	.70	.19
□ 6 Ozzie Smith	2.50	1.10	.30
□ 7 Barry Bonds	3.00	1.35	.35
□ 8 Andy Van Slyke	.75	.35	.09
□ 9 Larry Walker	1.50	.70	.19

☐ 10 Mark Langston	.75	.35	.09
☐ 11 Ivan Rodriguez	2.50	1.10	.30
☐ 12 Don Mattingly	6.00	2.70	.75
☐ 13 Roberto Alomar	3.00	1.35	.35
☐ 14 Robin Ventura	1.50	.70	.19
☐ 15 Cal Ripken	10.00	4.50	1.25
☐ 16 Ken Griffey	12.00	5.50	1.50
☐ 17 Kirby Puckett	4.00	1.80	.50
☐ 18 Devon White	.75	.35	.09
☐ 19 Pat Listach	.75	.35	.09
☐ 20 Eric Karros	1.50	.70	.19
☐ 21 Pat Borders	.75	.35	.09
☐ 22 Greg Maddux	8.00	3.60	1.00
☐ 23 Dennis Eckersley	1.50	.70	.19
☐ 24 Barry Bonds	3.00	1.35	.35
☐ 25 Gary Sheffield	2.00	.90	.25

1993 Ultra Home Run Kings

Randomly inserted into all 1993 Ultra packs, this ten-card standard-size set features the best long ball hitters in baseball. The borderless cards carry cutout color action player photos that are superposed upon an outer space scene, which includes a baseball "planet" and background stars. The player's name and team, along with the set's logo, are printed in gold foil and rest at the bottom. The horizontal black-and-stellar back carries a color player close-up on the left side, and the player's name, nickname, and career highlights in white lettering on the right side. The set's logo, printed in gold foil at the upper right, rounds out the card.

	MINT	NRMT	EXC
COMPLETE SET (10)	15.00	6.75	1.85
COMMON CARD (1-10)	1.00	.45	.12
SEMISTARS	2.00	.90	.25
RANDOM INSERTS IN PACKS			
☐ 1 Juan Gonzalez	8.00	3.60	1.00
☐ 2 Mark McGwire	5.00	2.20	.60
☐ 3 Cecil Fielder	2.00	.90	.25
☐ 4 Fred McGriff	2.00	.90	.25
☐ 5 Albert Belle	8.00	3.60	1.00
☐ 6 Barry Bonds	4.00	1.80	.50
☐ 7 Joe Carter	2.00	.90	.25
☐ 8 Gary Sheffield	2.50	1.10	.30
☐ 9 Darren Daulton	1.00	.45	.12
☐ 10 Dave Hollins	1.00	.45	.12

1993 Ultra Performers

This ten-card standard-size set could only be ordered directly from Fleer by sending in 9.95, five Fleer/Fleer Ultra baseball wrappers, and an order blank found in hobby and sports periodicals. Each borderless front features a color player action shot superposed upon four other player photos, which are ghosted and color-screened. The player's name and the set name, both stamped in gold foil, appear at the bottom. The Ultra Performers set logo, a gold-foil-rimmed baseball icon with a blue trail, lies just above. The gold-foil Fleer Ultra logo appears in an upper corner. The back features a borderless color player action photo that is ghosted and color-screened on one side, where the

player's name and career highlights appear. The set logo and gold-foil-stamped name appear below. The set's production number (out of 150,000 produced) rests within a ghosted rectangle at the bottom. The set is sequenced in alphabetical order.

	MINT	NRMT	EXC
COMPLETE SET (10)	25.00	11.00	3.10
COMMON CARD (1-10)	.50	.23	.06
SEMISTARS	1.00	.45	.12
SETS DISTRIBUTED VIA MAIL-IN OFFER			
☐ 1 Barry Bonds	2.00	.90	.25
☐ 2 Juan Gonzalez	3.00	1.35	.35
☐ 3 Ken Griffey Jr.	8.00	3.60	1.00
☐ 4 Eric Karros	1.00	.45	.12
☐ 5 Pat Listach	.50	.23	.06
☐ 6 Greg Maddux	5.00	2.20	.60
☐ 7 David Nied	.50	.23	.06
☐ 8 Gary Sheffield	1.25	.55	.16
☐ 9 J.T. Snow	1.00	.45	.12
☐ 10 Frank Thomas	8.00	3.60	1.00

1993 Ultra Strikeout Kings

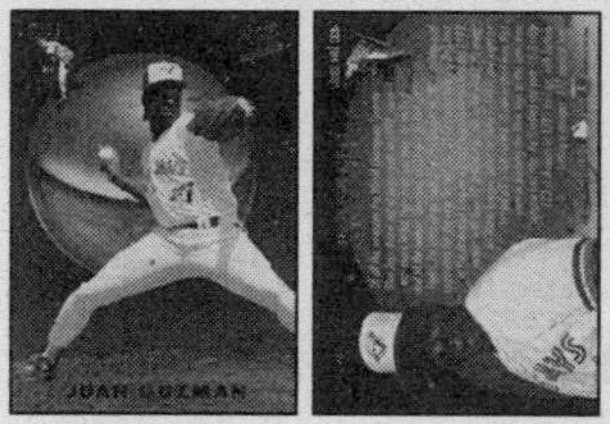

Randomly inserted into series II packs, this five-card standard-size showcases outstanding pitchers from both leagues. The color cutout action player photo on the front of each card shows a pitcher on the mound superimposed upon a background of stars and and metallic baseball. The player's name appears in gold foil at the bottom. The gold foil-stamped set logo also appears on the front. Upon a metallic-baseball-and-stellar background, the horizontal back carries a posed color player photo on the left side, and the player's career highlights in yellow lettering on the right side. The player's name and team, as well as the set's logo, appear in gold foil at the top. The set is sequenced in alphabetical order.

	MINT	NRMT	EXC
COMPLETE SET (5)	20.00	9.00	2.50
COMMON CARD (1-5)	1.00	.45	.12
RANDOM INSERTS IN SER.2 PACKS			
☐ 1 Roger Clemens	2.00	.90	.25
☐ 2 Juan Guzman	1.00	.45	.12
☐ 3 Randy Johnson	2.50	1.10	.30
☐ 4 Nolan Ryan	15.00	6.75	1.85
☐ 5 John Smoltz	2.50	1.10	.30

1994 Ultra

The 1994 Ultra baseball set consists of 600 standard-size cards that were issued in two series of 300. Each pack contains at least one insert card, while "Hot Packs" have nothing but insert cards in them. The front features a full-bleed color action player photo except at the bottom, where a gold foil strip edges the picture. The player's name, his position, team name, and company logo are gold foil stamped across the bottom of the front. The horizontal back has a montage of three different player cutouts on a action scene with a team color-coded border. Biography and statistics on a thin panel toward the bottom round out the back. The cards are numbered on the back, grouped alphabetically within teams, and checklisted below alphabetically according to teams for each league as follows: Baltimore Orioles (1-10/301-311), Boston Red Sox (11-19/312-319), California Angels (20-29/320-331), Chicago White Sox (30-39/332-341), Cleveland Indians (40-50/342-351), Detroit Tigers (51-60/352-358), Kansas City Royals (61-71/359-368), Milwaukee Brewers (72-82/369-381), Minnesota Twins (83-92/382-393), New York Yankees (93-103/394-401), Oakland Athletics (104-115/402-412), Seattle Mariners (116-125/413-424), Texas Rangers (126-134/425-433), Toronto Blue Jays (135-146/434-442), Atlanta Braves (147-158/443-453), Chicago Cubs (159-169/454-466), Cincinnati Reds (170-179/467-476), Colorado Rockies (180-190/477-488), Florida Marlins (191-201/489-498), Houston Astros (202-211/499-512), Los Angeles Dodgers (212-221/513-522), Montreal Expos (222-233/523-528), New York Mets (234-241/529-540), Philadelphia Phillies (242-253/541-554), Pittsburgh Pirates (254-263/555-560), St. Louis Cardinals (264-274/561-570), San Diego Padres (275-284/571-585) and San Francisco Giants (285-296/586-595). Rookie Cards include Brian Anderson, Ray Durham, LaTroy Hawkins, Brooks Kieschnick, Chan Ho Park, Mac Suzuki and Terrell Wade.

	MINT	NRMT	EXC
COMPLETE SET (600)	50.00	22.00	6.25
COMPLETE SERIES 1 (300)	25.00	11.00	3.10
COMPLETE SERIES 2 (300)	25.00	11.00	3.10
COMMON CARD (1-600)	.10	.05	.01
SEMISTARS	.25	.11	.03
STARS	.50	.23	.06
COMP.FIREMAN SET (10)	8.00	3.60	1.00
COMP.PHILLIES SET (20)	10.00	4.50	1.25
COMP.PHILLIES SER.1 (10)	5.00	2.20	.60
COMP.PHILLIES SER.2 (10)	5.00	2.20	.60
COMMON DAULTON (1-5/11/15)	.50	.23	.06
COMMON KRUK (6-10/16-20)	.50	.23	.06
CERT.DAULTON AUTO (AU1)	50.00	22.00	6.25
CERT.KRUK AUTO (AU2)	50.00	22.00	6.25
PHILLIES: RANDOM INSERTS IN ALL PACKS			
COMMON PHIL.MAIL (M1-M4)	1.00	.45	.12
PHILLIES MAIL-IN DIST.VIA WRAPPER EXCH.			

□ 1 Jeffrey Hammonds	.25	.11	.03
□ 2 Chris Hoiles	.10	.05	.01
□ 3 Ben McDonald	.10	.05	.01
□ 4 Mark McLemore	.10	.05	.01
□ 5 Alan Mills	.10	.05	.01
□ 6 Jamie Moyer	.10	.05	.01
□ 7 Brad Pennington	.10	.05	.01
□ 8 Jim Poole	.10	.05	.01
□ 9 Cal Ripken Jr.	2.50	1.10	.30
□ 10 Jack Voigt	.10	.05	.01
□ 11 Roger Clemens	.50	.23	.06
□ 12 Danny Darwin	.10	.05	.01
□ 13 Andre Dawson	.50	.23	.06
□ 14 Scott Fletcher	.10	.05	.01
□ 15 Greg A Harris	.10	.05	.01
□ 16 Billy Hatcher	.10	.05	.01
□ 17 Jeff Russell	.10	.05	.01
□ 18 Aaron Sele	.25	.11	.03
□ 19 Mo Vaughn	.75	.35	.09
□ 20 Mike Butcher	.10	.05	.01
□ 21 Rod Correia	.10	.05	.01
□ 22 Steve Frey	.10	.05	.01
□ 23 Phil Leftwich	.10	.05	.01
□ 24 Torey Lovullo	.10	.05	.01
□ 25 Ken Patterson	.10	.05	.01
□ 26 Eduardo Perez UER (listed as a Twin instead of Angel)	.10	.05	.01
□ 27 Tim Salmon	.50	.23	.06
□ 28 J.T. Snow	.25	.11	.03
□ 29 Chris Turner	.10	.05	.01
□ 30 Wilson Alvarez	.25	.11	.03
□ 31 Jason Bere	.25	.11	.03
□ 32 Joey Cora	.10	.05	.01
□ 33 Alex Fernandez	.50	.23	.06
□ 34 Roberto Hernandez	.25	.11	.03
□ 35 Lance Johnson	.25	.11	.03
□ 36 Ron Karkovice	.10	.05	.01
□ 37 Kirk McCaskill	.10	.05	.01
□ 38 Jeff Schwarz	.10	.05	.01
□ 39 Frank Thomas	3.00	1.35	.35
□ 40 Sandy Alomar Jr.	.25	.11	.03
□ 41 Albert Belle	1.50	.70	.19
□ 42 Felix Fermin	.10	.05	.01
□ 43 Wayne Kirby	.10	.05	.01
□ 44 Tom Kramer	.10	.05	.01
□ 45 Kenny Lofton	1.00	.45	.12
□ 46 Jose Mesa	.25	.11	.03
□ 47 Eric Plunk	.10	.05	.01
□ 48 Paul Sorrento	.10	.05	.01
□ 49 Jim Thome	.75	.35	.09
□ 50 Bill Wertz	.10	.05	.01
□ 51 John Doherty	.10	.05	.01
□ 52 Cecil Fielder	.25	.11	.03
□ 53 Travis Fryman	.50	.23	.06
□ 54 Chris Gomez	.10	.05	.01
□ 55 Mike Henneman	.10	.05	.01
□ 56 Chad Kreuter	.10	.05	.01
□ 57 Bob MacDonald	.10	.05	.01
□ 58 Mike Moore	.10	.05	.01
□ 59 Tony Phillips	.25	.11	.03
□ 60 Lou Whitaker	.50	.23	.06
□ 61 Kevin Appier	.25	.11	.03
□ 62 Greg Gagne	.10	.05	.01
□ 63 Chris Gwynn	.10	.05	.01
□ 64 Bob Hamelin	.10	.05	.01
□ 65 Chris Haney	.10	.05	.01
□ 66 Phil Hiatt	.10	.05	.01
□ 67 Felix Jose	.10	.05	.01
□ 68 Jose Lind	.10	.05	.01
□ 69 Mike Macfarlane	.10	.05	.01
□ 70 Jeff Montgomery	.25	.11	.03
□ 71 Hipolito Pichardo	.10	.05	.01
□ 72 Juan Bell	.10	.05	.01
□ 73 Cal Eldred	.10	.05	.01
□ 74 Darryl Hamilton	.10	.05	.01
□ 75 Doug Henry	.10	.05	.01
□ 76 Mike Ignasiak	.10	.05	.01
□ 77 John Jaha	.25	.11	.03
□ 78 Graeme Lloyd	.10	.05	.01
□ 79 Angel Miranda	.10	.05	.01
□ 80 Dave Nilsson	.25	.11	.03
□ 81 Troy O'Leary	.10	.05	.01
□ 82 Kevin Reimer	.10	.05	.01
□ 83 Willie Banks	.10	.05	.01
□ 84 Larry Casian	.10	.05	.01
□ 85 Scott Erickson	.10	.05	.01
□ 86 Eddie Guardado	.10	.05	.01
□ 87 Kent Hrbek	.25	.11	.03

□ 88	Terry Jorgensen	.10	.05	.01
□ 89	Chuck Knoblauch	.50	.23	.06
□ 90	Pat Meares	.10	.05	.01
□ 91	Mike Trombley	.10	.05	.01
□ 92	Dave Winfield	.50	.23	.06
□ 93	Wade Boggs	.50	.23	.06
□ 94	Scott Kamieniecki	.10	.05	.01
□ 95	Pat Kelly	.10	.05	.01
□ 96	Jimmy Key	.25	.11	.03
□ 97	Jim Leyritz	.10	.05	.01
□ 98	Bobby Munoz	.10	.05	.01
□ 99	Paul O'Neill	.25	.11	.03
□ 100	Melido Perez	.10	.05	.01
□ 101	Mike Stanley	.10	.05	.01
□ 102	Danny Tartabull	.10	.05	.01
□ 103	Bernie Williams	.50	.23	.06
□ 104	Kurt Abbott	.25	.11	.03
□ 105	Mike Bordick	.10	.05	.01
□ 106	Ron Darling	.10	.05	.01
□ 107	Brent Gates	.10	.05	.01
□ 108	Miguel Jimenez	.10	.05	.01
□ 109	Steve Karsay	.10	.05	.01
□ 110	Scott Lydy	.10	.05	.01
□ 111	Mark McGwire	1.00	.45	.12
□ 112	Troy Neel	.10	.05	.01
□ 113	Craig Paquette	.10	.05	.01
□ 114	Bob Welch	.10	.05	.01
□ 115	Bobby Witt	.10	.05	.01
□ 116	Rich Amaral	.10	.05	.01
□ 117	Mike Blowers	.10	.05	.01
□ 118	Jay Buhner	.50	.23	.06
□ 119	Dave Fleming	.10	.05	.01
□ 120	Ken Griffey Jr.	3.00	1.35	.35
□ 121	Tino Martinez	.25	.11	.03
□ 122	Marc Newfield	.25	.11	.03
□ 123	Ted Power	.10	.05	.01
□ 124	Mackey Sasser	.10	.05	.01
□ 125	Omar Vizquel	.50	.23	.06
□ 126	Kevin Brown	.10	.05	.01
□ 127	Juan Gonzalez	1.50	.70	.19
□ 128	Tom Henke	.10	.05	.01
□ 129	David Hulse	.10	.05	.01
□ 130	Dean Palmer	.25	.11	.03
□ 131	Roger Pavlik	.10	.05	.01
□ 132	Ivan Rodriguez	.60	.25	.07
□ 133	Kenny Rogers	.10	.05	.01
□ 134	Doug Strange	.10	.05	.01
□ 135	Pat Borders	.10	.05	.01
□ 136	Joe Carter	.50	.23	.06
□ 137	Darnell Coles	.10	.05	.01
□ 138	Pat Hentgen	.50	.23	.06
□ 139	Al Leiter	.25	.11	.03
□ 140	Paul Molitor	.60	.25	.07
□ 141	John Olerud	.10	.05	.01
□ 142	Ed Sprague	.25	.11	.03
□ 143	Dave Stewart	.25	.11	.03
□ 144	Mike Timlin	.10	.05	.01
□ 145	Duane Ward	.10	.05	.01
□ 146	Devon White	.10	.05	.01
□ 147	Steve Avery	.25	.11	.03
□ 148	Steve Bedrosian	.10	.05	.01
□ 149	Damon Berryhill	.10	.05	.01
□ 150	Jeff Blauser	.10	.05	.01
□ 151	Tom Glavine	.50	.23	.06
□ 152	Chipper Jones	2.50	1.10	.30
□ 153	Mark Lemke	.10	.05	.01
□ 154	Fred McGriff	.50	.23	.06
□ 155	Greg McMichael	.10	.05	.01
□ 156	Deion Sanders	.50	.23	.06
□ 157	John Smoltz	.50	.23	.06
□ 158	Mark Wohlers	.25	.11	.03
□ 159	Jose Bautista	.10	.05	.01
□ 160	Steve Buechele	.10	.05	.01
□ 161	Mike Harkey	.10	.05	.01
□ 162	Greg Hibbard	.10	.05	.01
□ 163	Chuck McElroy	.10	.05	.01
□ 164	Mike Morgan	.10	.05	.01
□ 165	Kevin Roberson	.10	.05	.01
□ 166	Ryne Sandberg	.75	.35	.09
□ 167	Jose Vizcaino	.10	.05	.01
□ 168	Rick Wilkins	.10	.05	.01
□ 169	Willie Wilson	.10	.05	.01
□ 170	Willie Greene	.25	.11	.03
□ 171	Roberto Kelly	.10	.05	.01
□ 172	Larry Luebbers	.10	.05	.01
□ 173	Kevin Mitchell	.25	.11	.03
□ 174	Joe Oliver	.10	.05	.01
□ 175	John Roper	.10	.05	.01
□ 176	Johnny Ruffin	.10	.05	.01
□ 177	Reggie Sanders	.50	.23	.06
□ 178	John Smiley	.10	.05	.01
□ 179	Jerry Spradlin	.10	.05	.01
□ 180	Freddie Benavides	.10	.05	.01
□ 181	Dante Bichette	.50	.23	.06
□ 182	Willie Blair	.10	.05	.01
□ 183	Kent Bottenfield	.10	.05	.01
□ 184	Jerald Clark	.10	.05	.01
□ 185	Joe Girardi	.10	.05	.01
□ 186	Roberto Mejia	.10	.05	.01
□ 187	Steve Reed	.10	.05	.01
□ 188	Armando Reynoso	.10	.05	.01
□ 189	Bruce Ruffin	.10	.05	.01
□ 190	Eric Young	.25	.11	.03
□ 191	Luis Aquino	.10	.05	.01
□ 192	Bret Barberie	.10	.05	.01
□ 193	Ryan Bowen	.10	.05	.01
□ 194	Chuck Carr	.10	.05	.01
□ 195	Orestes Destrade	.10	.05	.01
□ 196	Richie Lewis	.10	.05	.01
□ 197	Dave Magadan	.10	.05	.01
□ 198	Bob Natal	.10	.05	.01
□ 199	Gary Sheffield	.50	.23	.06
□ 200	Matt Turner	.10	.05	.01
□ 201	Darrell Whitmore	.10	.05	.01
□ 202	Eric Anthony	.10	.05	.01
□ 203	Jeff Bagwell	1.25	.55	.16
□ 204	Andujar Cedeno	.10	.05	.01
□ 205	Luis Gonzalez	.10	.05	.01
□ 206	Xavier Hernandez	.10	.05	.01
□ 207	Doug Jones	.10	.05	.01
□ 208	Darryl Kile	.10	.05	.01
□ 209	Scott Servais	.10	.05	.01
□ 210	Greg Swindell	.10	.05	.01
□ 211	Brian Williams	.10	.05	.01
□ 212	Pedro Astacio	.10	.05	.01
□ 213	Brett Butler	.25	.11	.03
□ 214	Omar Daal	.10	.05	.01
□ 215	Jim Gott	.10	.05	.01
□ 216	Raul Mondesi	.50	.23	.06
□ 217	Jose Offerman	.10	.05	.01
□ 218	Mike Piazza	2.00	.90	.25
□ 219	Cory Snyder	.10	.05	.01
□ 220	Tim Wallach	.10	.05	.01
□ 221	Todd Worrell	.10	.05	.01
□ 222	Moises Alou	.25	.11	.03
□ 223	Sean Berry	.10	.05	.01
□ 224	Wil Cordero	.25	.11	.03
□ 225	Jeff Fassero	.10	.05	.01
□ 226	Darrin Fletcher	.10	.05	.01
□ 227	Cliff Floyd	.50	.23	.06
□ 228	Marquis Grissom	.50	.23	.06
□ 229	Ken Hill	.10	.05	.01
□ 230	Mike Lansing	.25	.11	.03
□ 231	Kirk Rueter	.10	.05	.01
□ 232	John Wetteland	.25	.11	.03
□ 233	Rondell White	.50	.23	.06
□ 234	Tim Bogar	.10	.05	.01
□ 235	Jeromy Burnitz	.10	.05	.01
□ 236	Dwight Gooden	.25	.11	.03
□ 237	Todd Hundley	.50	.23	.06
□ 238	Jeff Kent	.10	.05	.01
□ 239	Josias Manzanillo	.10	.05	.01
□ 240	Joe Orsulak	.10	.05	.01
□ 241	Ryan Thompson	.10	.05	.01
□ 242	Kim Batiste	.10	.05	.01
□ 243	Darren Daulton	.25	.11	.03
□ 244	Tommy Greene	.10	.05	.01
□ 245	Dave Hollins	.10	.05	.01
□ 246	Pete Incaviglia	.10	.05	.01
□ 247	Danny Jackson	.10	.05	.01
□ 248	Ricky Jordan	.10	.05	.01
□ 249	John Kruk	.25	.11	.03
□ 250	Mickey Morandini	.10	.05	.01
□ 251	Terry Mulholland	.10	.05	.01
□ 252	Ben Rivera	.10	.05	.01
□ 253	Kevin Stocker	.10	.05	.01
□ 254	Jay Bell	.25	.11	.03
□ 255	Steve Cooke	.10	.05	.01
□ 256	Jeff King	.25	.11	.03
□ 257	Al Martin	.10	.05	.01
□ 258	Danny Miceli	.10	.05	.01
□ 259	Blas Minor	.10	.05	.01

260	Don Slaught	.10	.05	.01
261	Paul Wagner	.10	.05	.01
262	Tim Wakefield	.10	.05	.01
263	Kevin Young	.10	.05	.01
264	Rene Arocha	.10	.05	.01
265	Richard Batchelor	.10	.05	.01
266	Gregg Jefferies	.50	.23	.06
267	Brian Jordan	.50	.23	.06
268	Jose Oquendo	.10	.05	.01
269	Donovan Osborne	.10	.05	.01
270	Erik Pappas	.10	.05	.01
271	Mike Perez	.10	.05	.01
272	Bob Tewksbury	.10	.05	.01
273	Mark Whiten	.10	.05	.01
274	Todd Zeile	.10	.05	.01
275	Andy Ashby	.25	.11	.03
276	Brad Ausmus	.10	.05	.01
277	Phil Clark	.10	.05	.01
278	Jeff Gardner	.10	.05	.01
279	Ricky Gutierrez	.10	.05	.01
280	Tony Gwynn	1.25	.55	.16
281	Tim Mauser	.10	.05	.01
282	Scott Sanders	.10	.05	.01
283	Frank Seminara	.10	.05	.01
284	Wally Whitehurst	.10	.05	.01
285	Rod Beck	.25	.11	.03
286	Barry Bonds	.75	.35	.09
287	Dave Burba	.10	.05	.01
288	Mark Carreon	.10	.05	.01
289	Royce Clayton	.25	.11	.03
290	Mike Jackson	.10	.05	.01
291	Darren Lewis	.10	.05	.01
292	Kirt Manwaring	.10	.05	.01
293	Dave Martinez	.10	.05	.01
294	Billy Swift	.10	.05	.01
295	Salomon Torres	.10	.05	.01
296	Matt Williams	.50	.23	.06
297	Checklist 1-75	.10	.05	.01
298	Checklist 76-150	.10	.05	.01
299	Checklist 151-225	.10	.05	.01
300	Checklist 226-300	.10	.05	.01
301	Brady Anderson	.50	.23	.06
302	Harold Baines	.25	.11	.03
303	Damon Buford	.10	.05	.01
304	Mike Devereaux	.10	.05	.01
305	Sid Fernandez	.10	.05	.01
306	Rick Krivda	.10	.05	.01
307	Mike Mussina	.60	.25	.07
308	Rafael Palmeiro	.50	.23	.06
309	Arthur Rhodes	.10	.05	.01
310	Chris Sabo	.10	.05	.01
311	Lee Smith	.25	.11	.03
312	Gregg Zaun	.25	.11	.03
313	Scott Cooper	.10	.05	.01
314	Mike Greenwell	.10	.05	.01
315	Tim Naehring	.10	.05	.01
316	Otis Nixon	.10	.05	.01
317	Paul Quantrill	.10	.05	.01
318	John Valentin	.25	.11	.03
319	Dave Valle	.10	.05	.01
320	Frank Viola	.10	.05	.01
321	Brian Anderson	.25	.11	.03
322	Garret Anderson	.50	.23	.06
323	Chad Curtis	.10	.05	.01
324	Chili Davis	.25	.11	.03
325	Gary DiSarcina	.10	.05	.01
326	Damion Easley	.10	.05	.01
327	Jim Edmonds	.60	.25	.07
328	Chuck Finley	.10	.05	.01
329	Joe Grahe	.10	.05	.01
330	Bo Jackson	.50	.23	.06
331	Mark Langston	.25	.11	.03
332	Harold Reynolds	.10	.05	.01
333	James Baldwin	.50	.23	.06
334	Ray Durham	.75	.35	.09
335	Julio Franco	.25	.11	.03
336	Craig Grebeck	.10	.05	.01
337	Ozzie Guillen	.10	.05	.01
338	Joe Hall	.10	.05	.01
339	Darrin Jackson	.10	.05	.01
340	Jack McDowell	.25	.11	.03
341	Tim Raines	.50	.23	.06
342	Robin Ventura	.25	.11	.03
343	Carlos Baerga	.50	.23	.06
344	Derek Lilliquist	.10	.05	.01
345	Dennis Martinez	.25	.11	.03

346	Jack Morris	.25	.11	.03
347	Eddie Murray	.75	.35	.09
348	Chris Nabholz	.10	.05	.01
349	Charles Nagy	.25	.11	.03
350	Chad Ogea	.25	.11	.03
351	Manny Ramirez	1.00	.45	.12
352	Omar Vizquel	.50	.23	.06
353	Tim Belcher	.10	.05	.01
354	Eric Davis	.25	.11	.03
355	Kirk Gibson	.25	.11	.03
356	Rick Greene	.10	.05	.01
357	Mickey Tettleton	.10	.05	.01
358	Alan Trammell	.50	.23	.06
359	David Wells	.10	.05	.01
360	Stan Belinda	.10	.05	.01
361	Vince Coleman	.10	.05	.01
362	David Cone	.50	.23	.06
363	Gary Gaetti	.25	.11	.03
364	Tom Gordon	.10	.05	.01
365	Dave Henderson	.10	.05	.01
366	Wally Joyner	.25	.11	.03
367	Brent Mayne	.10	.05	.01
368	Brian McRae	.25	.11	.03
369	Michael Tucker	.50	.23	.06
370	Ricky Bones	.10	.05	.01
371	Brian Harper	.10	.05	.01
372	Tyrone Hill	.10	.05	.01
373	Mark Kiefer	.10	.05	.01
374	Pat Listach	.10	.05	.01
375	Mike Matheny	.10	.05	.01
376	Jose Mercedes	.10	.05	.01
377	Jody Reed	.10	.05	.01
378	Kevin Seitzer	.10	.05	.01
379	B.J. Surhoff	.10	.05	.01
380	Greg Vaughn	.50	.23	.06
381	Turner Ward	.10	.05	.01
382	Wes Weger	.10	.05	.01
383	Bill Wegman	.10	.05	.01
384	Rick Aguilera	.10	.05	.01
385	Rich Becker	.25	.11	.03
386	Alex Cole	.10	.05	.01
387	Steve Dunn	.10	.05	.01
388	Keith Garagozzo	.10	.05	.01
389	LaTroy Hawkins	.25	.11	.03
390	Shane Mack	.10	.05	.01
391	David McCarty	.10	.05	.01
392	Pedro Munoz	.10	.05	.01
393	Derek Parks	.10	.05	.01
394	Kirby Puckett	1.00	.45	.12
395	Kevin Tapani	.10	.05	.01
396	Matt Walbeck	.10	.05	.01
397	Jim Abbott	.10	.05	.01
398	Mike Gallego	.10	.05	.01
399	Xavier Hernandez	.10	.05	.01
400	Don Mattingly	1.50	.70	.19
401	Terry Mulholland	.10	.05	.01
402	Matt Nokes	.10	.05	.01
403	Luis Polonia	.10	.05	.01
404	Bob Wickman	.10	.05	.01
405	Mark Acre	.10	.05	.01
406	Fausto Cruz	.10	.05	.01
407	Dennis Eckersley	.25	.11	.03
408	Rickey Henderson	.50	.23	.06
409	Stan Javier	.10	.05	.01
410	Carlos Reyes	.10	.05	.01
411	Ruben Sierra	.25	.11	.03
412	Terry Steinbach	.25	.11	.03
413	Bill Taylor	.10	.05	.01
414	Todd Van Poppel	.10	.05	.01
415	Eric Anthony	.10	.05	.01
416	Bobby Ayala	.10	.05	.01
417	Chris Bosio	.10	.05	.01
418	Tim Davis	.10	.05	.01
419	Randy Johnson	.50	.23	.06
420	Kevin King	.10	.05	.01
421	Anthony Manahan	.10	.05	.01
422	Edgar Martinez	.50	.23	.06
423	Keith Mitchell	.10	.05	.01
424	Roger Salkeld	.10	.05	.01
425	Mac Suzuki	.25	.11	.03
426	Dan Wilson	.25	.11	.03
427	Duff Brumley	.10	.05	.01
428	Jose Canseco	.50	.23	.06
429	Will Clark	.50	.23	.06
430	Steve Dreyer	.10	.05	.01
431	Rick Helling	.10	.05	.01

□ 432 Chris James	.10	.05	.01
□ 433 Matt Whiteside	.10	.05	.01
□ 434 Roberto Alomar	.75	.35	.09
□ 435 Scott Brow	.10	.05	.01
□ 436 Domingo Cedeno	.10	.05	.01
□ 437 Carlos Delgado	.50	.23	.06
□ 438 Juan Guzman	.25	.11	.03
□ 439 Paul Spoljaric	.10	.05	.01
□ 440 Todd Stottlemyre	.10	.05	.01
□ 441 Woody Williams	.10	.05	.01
□ 442 David Justice	.50	.23	.06
□ 443 Mike Kelly	.10	.05	.01
□ 444 Ryan Klesko	.75	.35	.09
□ 445 Javier Lopez	.50	.23	.06
□ 446 Greg Maddux	2.00	.90	.25
□ 447 Kent Mercker	.10	.05	.01
□ 448 Charlie O'Brien	.10	.05	.01
□ 449 Terry Pendleton	.25	.11	.03
□ 450 Mike Stanton	.10	.05	.01
□ 451 Tony Tarasco	.10	.05	.01
□ 452 Terrell Wade	.60	.25	.07
□ 453 Willie Banks	.10	.05	.01
□ 454 Shawon Dunston	.10	.05	.01
□ 455 Mark Grace	.50	.23	.06
□ 456 Jose Guzman	.10	.05	.01
□ 457 Jose Hernandez	.10	.05	.01
□ 458 Glenallen Hill	.10	.05	.01
□ 459 Blaise Ilsley	.10	.05	.01
□ 460 Brooks Kieschnick	.60	.25	.07
□ 461 Derrick May	.10	.05	.01
□ 462 Randy Myers	.10	.05	.01
□ 463 Karl Rhodes	.10	.05	.01
□ 464 Sammy Sosa	.50	.23	.06
□ 465 Steve Trachsel	.25	.11	.03
□ 466 Anthony Young	.10	.05	.01
□ 467 Eddie Zambrano	.10	.05	.01
□ 468 Bret Boone	.25	.11	.03
□ 469 Tom Browning	.10	.05	.01
□ 470 Hector Carrasco	.10	.05	.01
□ 471 Rob Dibble	.10	.05	.01
□ 472 Erik Hanson	.10	.05	.01
□ 473 Thomas Howard	.10	.05	.01
□ 474 Barry Larkin	.50	.23	.06
□ 475 Hal Morris	.10	.05	.01
□ 476 Jose Rijo	.10	.05	.01
□ 477 John Burke	.10	.05	.01
□ 478 Ellis Burks	.25	.11	.03
□ 479 Marvin Freeman	.10	.05	.01
□ 480 Andres Galarraga	.50	.23	.06
□ 481 Greg W. Harris	.10	.05	.01
□ 482 Charlie Hayes	.10	.05	.01
□ 483 Darren Holmes	.10	.05	.01
□ 484 Howard Johnson	.10	.05	.01
□ 485 Marcus Moore	.10	.05	.01
□ 486 David Nied	.10	.05	.01
□ 487 Mark Thompson	.25	.11	.03
□ 488 Walt Weiss	.10	.05	.01
□ 489 Kurt Abbott	.25	.11	.03
□ 490 Matias Carrillo	.10	.05	.01
□ 491 Jeff Conine	.50	.23	.06
□ 492 Chris Hammond	.10	.05	.01
□ 493 Bryan Harvey	.10	.05	.01
□ 494 Charlie Hough	.10	.05	.01
□ 495 Yorkis Perez	.10	.05	.01
□ 496 Pat Rapp	.10	.05	.01
□ 497 Benito Santiago	.10	.05	.01
□ 498 David Weathers	.10	.05	.01
□ 499 Craig Biggio	.50	.23	.06
□ 500 Ken Caminiti	.50	.23	.06
□ 501 Doug Drabek	.10	.05	.01
□ 502 Tony Eusebio	.10	.05	.01
□ 503 Steve Finley	.50	.23	.06
□ 504 Pete Harnisch	.10	.05	.01
□ 505 Brian Hunter	.50	.23	.06
□ 506 Domingo Jean	.10	.05	.01
□ 507 Todd Jones	.10	.05	.01
□ 508 Orlando Miller	.10	.05	.01
□ 509 James Mouton	.25	.11	.03
□ 510 Roberto Petagine	.25	.11	.03
□ 511 Shane Reynolds	.25	.11	.03
□ 512 Mitch Williams	.10	.05	.01
□ 513 Billy Ashley	.10	.05	.01
□ 514 Tom Candiotti	.10	.05	.01
□ 515 Delino DeShields	.10	.05	.01
□ 516 Kevin Gross	.10	.05	.01
□ 517 Orel Hershiser	.25	.11	.03

□ 518 Eric Karros	.25	.11	.03
□ 519 Ramon Martinez	.25	.11	.03
□ 520 Chan Ho Park	.75	.35	.09
□ 521 Henry Rodriguez	.50	.23	.06
□ 522 Joey Eischen	.10	.05	.01
□ 523 Rod Henderson	.10	.05	.01
□ 524 Pedro J. Martinez	.50	.23	.06
□ 525 Mel Rojas	.10	.05	.01
□ 526 Larry Walker	.50	.23	.06
□ 527 Gabe White	.10	.05	.01
□ 528 Bobby Bonilla	.25	.11	.03
□ 529 Jonathan Hurst	.10	.05	.01
□ 530 Bobby Jones	.25	.11	.03
□ 531 Kevin McReynolds	.10	.05	.01
□ 532 Bill Pulsipher	.25	.11	.03
□ 533 Bret Saberhagen	.25	.11	.03
□ 534 David Segui	.10	.05	.01
□ 535 Pete Smith	.10	.05	.01
□ 536 Kelly Stinnett	.10	.05	.01
□ 537 Dave Telgheder	.10	.05	.01
□ 538 Quilvio Veras	.25	.11	.03
□ 539 Jose Vizcaino	.10	.05	.01
□ 540 Pete Walker	.10	.05	.01
□ 541 Ricky Bottalico	.40	.18	.05
□ 542 Wes Chamberlain	.10	.05	.01
□ 543 Mariano Duncan	.10	.05	.01
□ 544 Lenny Dykstra	.25	.11	.03
□ 545 Jim Eisenreich	.10	.05	.01
□ 546 Phil Geisler	.10	.05	.01
□ 547 Wayne Gomes	.25	.11	.03
□ 548 Doug Jones	.10	.05	.01
□ 549 Jeff Juden	.10	.05	.01
□ 550 Mike Lieberthal	.10	.05	.01
□ 551 Tony Longmire	.10	.05	.01
□ 552 Tom Marsh	.10	.05	.01
□ 553 Bobby Munoz	.10	.05	.01
□ 554 Curt Schilling	.10	.05	.01
□ 555 Carlos Garcia	.10	.05	.01
□ 556 Ravelo Manzanillo	.10	.05	.01
□ 557 Orlando Merced	.25	.11	.03
□ 558 Will Pennyfeather	.10	.05	.01
□ 559 Zane Smith	.10	.05	.01
□ 560 Andy Van Slyke	.25	.11	.03
□ 561 Rick White	.10	.05	.01
□ 562 Luis Alicea	.10	.05	.01
□ 563 Brian Barber	.10	.05	.01
□ 564 Clint Davis	.10	.05	.01
□ 565 Bernard Gilkey	.25	.11	.03
□ 566 Ray Lankford	.50	.23	.06
□ 567 Tom Pagnozzi	.10	.05	.01
□ 568 Ozzie Smith	.60	.25	.07
□ 569 Rick Sutcliffe	.10	.05	.01
□ 570 Allen Watson	.10	.05	.01
□ 571 Dmitri Young	.60	.25	.07
□ 572 Derek Bell	.25	.11	.03
□ 573 Andy Benes	.25	.11	.03
□ 574 Archi Cianfrocco	.10	.05	.01
□ 575 Joey Hamilton	.60	.25	.07
□ 576 Gene Harris	.10	.05	.01
□ 577 Trevor Hoffman	.25	.11	.03
□ 578 Tim Hyers	.10	.05	.01
□ 579 Brian Johnson	.10	.05	.01
□ 580 Keith Lockhart	.10	.05	.01
□ 581 Pedro A. Martinez	.10	.05	.01
□ 582 Ray McDavid	.25	.11	.03
□ 583 Phil Plantier	.10	.05	.01
□ 584 Bip Roberts	.10	.05	.01
□ 585 Dave Staton	.10	.05	.01
□ 586 Todd Benzinger	.10	.05	.01
□ 587 John Burkett	.10	.05	.01
□ 588 Bryan Hickerson	.10	.05	.01
□ 589 Willie McGee	.10	.05	.01
□ 590 John Patterson	.10	.05	.01
□ 591 Mark Portugal	.10	.05	.01
□ 592 Kevin Rogers	.10	.05	.01
□ 593 Joe Rosselli	.10	.05	.01
□ 594 Steve Soderstrom	.25	.11	.03
□ 595 Robby Thompson	.10	.05	.01
□ 596 125th Anniversary Card	.10	.05	.01
□ 597 Checklist	.10	.05	.01
□ 598 Checklist	.10	.05	.01
□ 599 Checklist	.10	.05	.01
□ 600 Checklist	.10	.05	.01
□ P243 Darren Daulton Promo	2.00	.90	.25
□ P249 John Kruk Promo	2.00	.90	.25

1994 Ultra All-Rookies

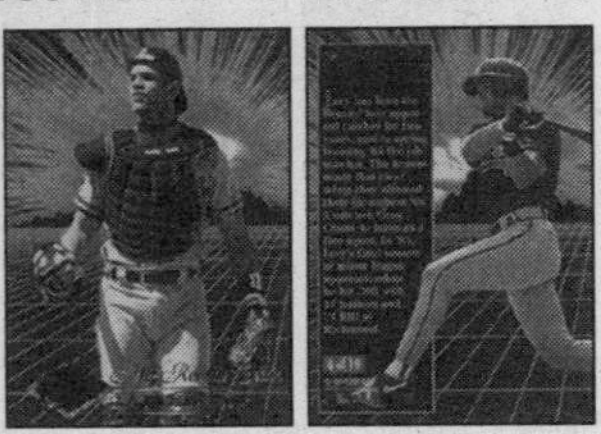

This 10-card standard-size set features top rookies of 1994 and were randomly inserted in second series jumbo and foil packs at a rate of one in 10. Card fronts have a color player photo cut-out over a computer generated background that resembles volcanic activity. The player's name and All-Rookie Team logo appear in gold foil at the bottom. On the backs, the player cut-out appears toward the right with text on the left. The background is much the same as the front. The set is sequenced in alphabetical order. Every second series Ultra hobby case included this set in jumbo (3 1/2" by 5") form. These jumbo versions are priced up to twice the values below.

	MINT	NRMT	EXC
COMPLETE SET (10)	10.00	4.50	1.25
COMMON CARD (1-10)	.50	.23	.06
RANDOM INSERTS IN ALL SER.2 PACKS			
*JUMBO ART's: 1X to 2X BASIC CARDS			
ONE JUMBO SET PER HOBBY CASE			
□ 1 Kurt Abbott	.50	.23	.06
□ 2 Carlos Delgado	1.50	.70	.19
□ 3 Cliff Floyd	1.00	.45	.12
□ 4 Jeffrey Hammonds	1.00	.45	.12
□ 5 Ryan Klesko	3.00	1.35	.35
□ 6 Javier Lopez	1.50	.70	.19
□ 7 Raul Mondesi	2.00	.90	.25
□ 8 James Mouton	1.00	.45	.12
□ 9 Chan Ho Park	1.00	.45	.12
□ 10 Dave Staton	.50	.23	.06

1994 Ultra All-Stars

Randomly inserted in second series foil and jumbo packs at a rate of one in three, this 20-card standard-size set contains top major league stars. The fronts have a color player photo superimposed over a bright red (American League players) or dark blue (National League) background. The backs are much the same except they include highlights from 1993.

	MINT	NRMT	EXC
COMPLETE SET (20)	18.00	8.00	2.20
COMMON CARD (1-20)	.25	.11	.03
SEMISTARS	.60	.25	.07
RANDOM INSERTS IN ALL SER.2 PACKS			
□ 1 Chris Hoiles	.25	.11	.03
□ 2 Frank Thomas	5.00	2.20	.60
□ 3 Roberto Alomar	1.25	.55	.16
□ 4 Cal Ripken Jr.	4.00	1.80	.50
□ 5 Robin Ventura	.60	.25	.07
□ 6 Albert Belle	2.50	1.10	.30
□ 7 Juan Gonzalez	2.50	1.10	.30
□ 8 Ken Griffey Jr.	5.00	2.20	.60
□ 9 John Olerud	.25	.11	.03
□ 10 Jack McDowell	.60	.25	.07
□ 11 Mike Piazza	3.00	1.35	.35
□ 12 Fred McGriff	.60	.25	.07
□ 13 Ryne Sandberg	1.25	.55	.16
□ 14 Jay Bell	.25	.11	.03
□ 15 Matt Williams	.60	.25	.07
□ 16 Barry Bonds	1.25	.55	.16
□ 17 Lenny Dykstra	.60	.25	.07
□ 18 David Justice	.25	.11	.03
□ 19 Tom Glavine	.60	.25	.07
□ 20 Greg Maddux	3.00	1.35	.35

1994 Ultra Award Winners

Randomly inserted in all first series packs at a rate of one in three, this 25-card standard-size set features three MVP's, two Rookies of the Year, and 18 Top Glove defensive standouts. The set is divided into American League Top Gloves (1-9), National League Top Gloves (10-18), and Award Winners (19-25). A horizontal design includes a color player cut-out over a gold background on front. Also on front, is a gold foil logo that indicates the honor. The backs have a small photo and text.

	MINT	NRMT	EXC
COMPLETE SET (25)	18.00	8.00	2.20
COMMON CARD (1-25)	.25	.11	.03
SEMISTARS	.60	.25	.07
RANDOM INSERTS IN ALL SER.1 PACKS			
□ 1 Ivan Rodriguez	1.00	.45	.12
□ 2 Don Mattingly	2.50	1.10	.30
□ 3 Roberto Alomar	1.25	.55	.16
□ 4 Robin Ventura	.60	.25	.07
□ 5 Omar Vizquel	.25	.11	.03
□ 6 Ken Griffey Jr.	5.00	2.20	.60
□ 7 Kenny Lofton	1.50	.70	.19
□ 8 Devon White	.25	.11	.03
□ 9 Mark Langston	.25	.11	.03
□ 10 Kirt Manwaring	.25	.11	.03
□ 11 Mark Grace	.60	.25	.07
□ 12 Robby Thompson	.25	.11	.03
□ 13 Matt Williams	.60	.25	.07
□ 14 Jay Bell	.25	.11	.03
□ 15 Barry Bonds	1.25	.55	.16
□ 16 Marquis Grissom	.60	.25	.07
□ 17 Larry Walker	.60	.25	.07
□ 18 Greg Maddux	3.00	1.35	.35
□ 19 Frank Thomas	5.00	2.20	.60
□ 20 Barry Bonds	1.25	.55	.16
□ 21 Paul Molitor	1.00	.45	.12
□ 22 Jack McDowell	.60	.25	.07
□ 23 Greg Maddux	3.00	1.35	.35
□ 24 Tim Salmon	.75	.35	.09
□ 25 Mike Piazza	3.00	1.35	.35

1994 Ultra Career Achievement

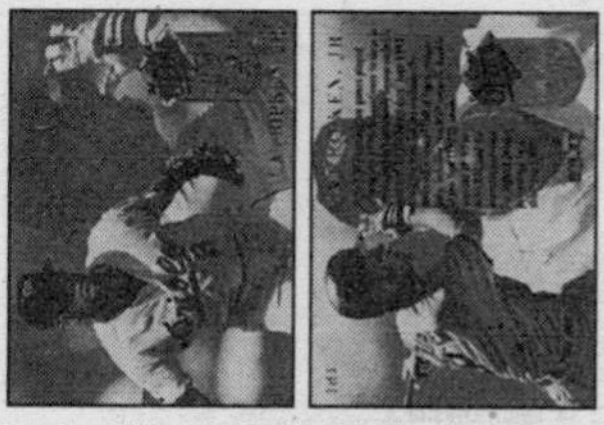

Randomly inserted in all second series packs at a rate of one in 21, this five card standard-size set highlights veteran stars and milestones they have reached during their brilliant careers. Horizontally designed cards have fronts that feature a color player photo superimposed over solid color background that contains another player photo. A photo of the player earlier in his career is on back along with text. The cards are sequenced in alphabetical order.

	MINT	NRMT	EXC
COMPLETE SET (5)	15.00	6.75	1.85
COMMON CARD (1-5)	1.00	.45	.12
RANDOM INSERTS IN ALL SER.2 PACKS....			

	MINT	NRMT	EXC
□ 1 Joe Carter	1.00	.45	.12
□ 2 Paul Molitor	2.00	.90	.25
□ 3 Cal Ripken Jr.	8.00	3.60	1.00
□ 4 Ryne Sandberg	2.50	1.10	.30
□ 5 Dave Winfield	1.50	.70	.19

1994 Ultra Hitting Machines

Randomly inserted in all second series packs at a rate of one in five, this 10-card horizontally designed standard-size set features top hitters from 1993. The fronts have a color player cut-out over a "Hitting Machines" background. The back has a smaller player cut-out and text. The set is sequenced in alphabetical order.

	MINT	NRMT	EXC
COMPLETE SET (10)	12.00	5.50	1.50
COMMON CARD (1-10)	.50	.23	.06
RANDOM INSERTS IN ALL SER.2 PACKS....			

	MINT	NRMT	EXC
□ 1 Roberto Alomar	1.25	.55	.16
□ 2 Carlos Baerga	1.00	.45	.12
□ 3 Barry Bonds	1.25	.55	.16
□ 4 Andres Galarraga	.75	.35	.09
□ 5 Juan Gonzalez	2.50	1.10	.30
□ 6 Tony Gwynn	2.00	.90	.25
□ 7 Paul Molitor	1.00	.45	.12
□ 8 John Olerud	.50	.23	.06
□ 9 Mike Piazza	3.00	1.35	.35
□ 10 Frank Thomas	5.00	2.20	.60

1994 Ultra Home Run Kings

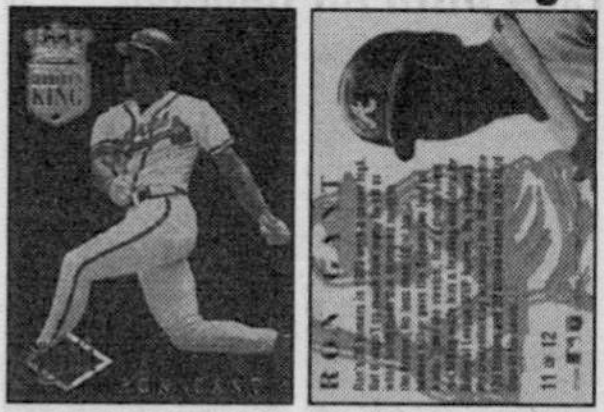

Randomly inserted exclusively in first series foil packs at a rate of one in 36, these 12 standard-size cards highlight home run hitters by an etched metallized look. Cards 1-6 feature American League Home Run Kings while cards 7-12 present National League Home Run Kings.

	MINT	NRMT	EXC
COMPLETE SET (12)	80.00	36.00	10.00
COMMON CARD (1-12)	2.00	.90	.25
SEMISTARS	3.00	1.35	.35
INSERTS IN SER.1 FOIL AND 20-CARD JUMBOS			

	MINT	NRMT	EXC
□ 1 Juan Gonzalez	12.00	5.50	1.50
□ 2 Ken Griffey Jr.	25.00	11.00	3.10
□ 3 Frank Thomas	25.00	11.00	3.10
□ 4 Albert Belle	12.00	5.50	1.50
□ 5 Rafael Palmeiro	3.00	1.35	.35
□ 6 Joe Carter	3.00	1.35	.35
□ 7 Barry Bonds	6.00	2.70	.75
□ 8 David Justice	2.00	.90	.25
□ 9 Matt Williams	3.00	1.35	.35
□ 10 Fred McGriff	3.00	1.35	.35
□ 11 Ron Gant	2.00	.90	.25
□ 12 Mike Piazza	15.00	6.75	1.85

1994 Ultra League Leaders

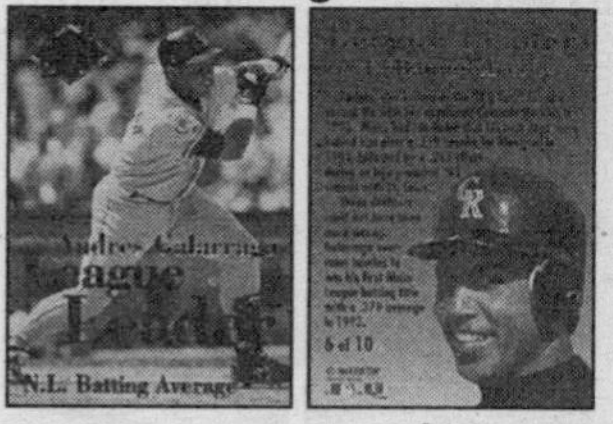

Randomly inserted in all first series packs at a rate of one in 11, this ten-card standard-size set features ten of 1993's leading players. The fronts feature borderless color player action shots, with a color-screening that shades from being imperceptible at the top to washing out the photos' true colors at the bottom. The player's name in gold foil appears across the card face. The borderless back carries a color player head shot in a lower corner with his career highlights appearing above, all on a monochrome background that shades from dark to light, from top to bottom. The set is arranged according to American League (1-5) and National League (6-10) players.

	MINT	NRMT	EXC
COMPLETE SET (10)	5.00	2.20	.60
COMMON CARD (1-10)	.25	.11	.03
RANDOM INSERTS IN ALL SER.1 PACKS....			

	MINT	NRMT	EXC
□ 1 John Olerud	.25	.11	.03
□ 2 Rafael Palmeiro	.50	.23	.06

□ 3 Kenny Lofton	2.00	.90	.25
□ 4 Jack McDowell	.50	.23	.06
□ 5 Randy Johnson	1.00	.45	.12
□ 6 Andres Galarraga	.50	.23	.06
□ 7 Lenny Dykstra	.50	.23	.06
□ 8 Chuck Carr	.25	.11	.03
□ 9 Tom Glavine	.50	.23	.06
□ 10 Jose Rijo	.25	.11	.03

1994 Ultra On-Base Leaders

Randomly inserted in second series jumbo packs at a rate of one in 36, this 12-card standard-size set features those that were among the Major League leaders in on-base percentage. Card fronts have the player superimposed over a metallic background that simulates statistics from a sports page. The backs have a player cut-out and text over a statistical background that is not metallic. The set is sequenced in alphabetical order.

	MINT	NRMT	EXC
COMPLETE SET (12)	150.00	70.00	19.00
COMMON CARD (1-12)	4.00	1.80	.50
SEMISTARS	6.00	2.70	.75
RANDOM INSERTS IN SER.2 17-CARD JUMBOS			
□ 1 Roberto Alomar	15.00	6.75	1.85
□ 2 Barry Bonds	15.00	6.75	1.85
□ 3 Lenny Dykstra	6.00	2.70	.75
□ 4 Andres Galarraga	6.00	2.70	.75
□ 5 Mark Grace	6.00	2.70	.75
□ 6 Ken Griffey Jr.	60.00	27.00	7.50
□ 7 Gregg Jefferies	6.00	2.70	.75
□ 8 Orlando Merced	4.00	1.80	.50
□ 9 Paul Molitor	12.00	5.50	1.50
□ 10 John Olerud	4.00	1.80	.50
□ 11 Tony Phillips	4.00	1.80	.50
□ 12 Frank Thomas	60.00	27.00	7.50

1994 Ultra RBI Kings

Randomly inserted in first series jumbo packs at a rate of one in 36, this 12-card standard-size set features RBI leaders. These horizontal, metallized cards have a color player photo on front that superimposes a player image.The backs have a write-up and a small color player photo. Cards 1-6 feature American League RBI Kings while cards 7-12 present National League RBI Kings.

	MINT	NRMT	EXC
COMPLETE SET (12)	150.00	70.00	19.00
COMMON CARD (1-12)	6.00	2.70	.75
RANDOM INSERTS IN SER.1 17-CARD JUMBOS			
□ 1 Albert Belle	30.00	13.50	3.70
□ 2 Frank Thomas	60.00	27.00	7.50
□ 3 Joe Carter	6.00	2.70	.75
□ 4 Juan Gonzalez	30.00	13.50	3.70
□ 5 Cecil Fielder	6.00	2.70	.75
□ 6 Carlos Baerga	6.00	2.70	.75
□ 7 Barry Bonds	15.00	6.75	1.85
□ 8 David Justice	6.00	2.70	.75
□ 9 Ron Gant	6.00	2.70	.75
□ 10 Mike Piazza	40.00	18.00	5.00
□ 11 Matt Williams	8.00	3.60	1.00
□ 12 Darren Daulton	6.00	2.70	.75

1994 Ultra Rising Stars

Randomly inserted in second series foil packs and jumbo packs at a rate of one in 36, this 12-card set spotlights top young major league stars. Metallic fronts have the player superimposed over icons resembling outer space. The backs feature the player in the same format along with text. The set is sequenced in alphabetical order.

	MINT	NRMT	EXC
COMPLETE SET (12)	125.00	55.00	15.50
COMMON CARD (1-12)	4.00	1.80	.50
SEMISTARS	6.00	2.70	.75
INSERTS IN SER.2 FOIL AND 20-CARD JUMBOS			
□ 1 Carlos Baerga	6.00	2.70	.75
□ 2 Jeff Bagwell	25.00	11.00	3.10
□ 3 Albert Belle	30.00	13.50	3.70
□ 4 Cliff Floyd	6.00	2.70	.75
□ 5 Travis Fryman	6.00	2.70	.75
□ 6 Marquis Grissom	6.00	2.70	.75
□ 7 Kenny Lofton	20.00	9.00	2.50
□ 8 John Olerud	4.00	1.80	.50
□ 9 Mike Piazza	40.00	18.00	5.00
□ 10 Kirk Rueter	4.00	1.80	.50
□ 11 Tim Salmon	10.00	4.50	1.25
□ 12 Aaron Sele	4.00	1.80	.50

1994 Ultra Second Year Standouts

Randomly inserted in all first series packs at a rate of one in 11, this 10-card standard-size set included 10 1993 outstanding rookies who are destined to become future stars. The fronts feature two color playe action cutouts superimposed upon borderless team-colored backgrounds. The player's name appears in gold foil at the bottom. The back carries a color player head shot in a lower corner with his career highlights appearing alongside, all on a borderless team color-coded background. The set is arranged in alphabetical order according to American League (1-5) and National League (6-10) players.

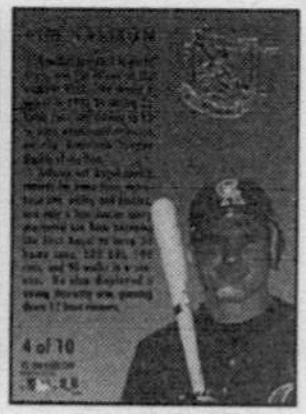

	MINT	NRMT	EXC
COMPLETE SET (10)	15.00	6.75	1.85
COMMON CARD (1-10)	.50	.23	.06
SEMISTARS	1.00	.45	.12
RANDOM INSERTS IN ALL SER.1 PACKS			

□ 1 Jason Bere	1.00	.45	.12
□ 2 Brent Gates	.50	.23	.06
□ 3 Jeffrey Hammonds	1.00	.45	.12
□ 4 Tim Salmon	3.00	1.35	.35
□ 5 Aaron Sele	1.00	.45	.12
□ 6 Chuck Carr	.50	.23	.06
□ 7 Jeff Conine	1.50	.70	.19
□ 8 Greg McMichael	.50	.23	.06
□ 9 Mike Piazza	12.00	5.50	1.50
□ 10 Kevin Stocker	.50	.23	.06

1994 Ultra Strikeout Kings

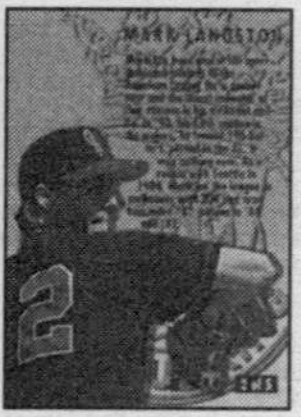

Randomly inserted in all second series packs at a rate of one in seven, this five-card standard-size set features top strikeout artists. Full-bleed fronts offer triple exposure photos and a gold foil Strikeout King logo. The backs contain a photo and write-up with the Strikeout King logo as background. The set is sequenced in alphabetical order.

	MINT	NRMT	EXC
COMPLETE SET (5)	5.00	2.20	.60
COMMON CARD (1-5)	.25	.11	.03
RANDOM INSERTS IN ALL SER.2 PACKS			

□ 1 Randy Johnson	.75	.35	.09
□ 2 Mark Langston	.50	.23	.06
□ 3 Greg Maddux	3.00	1.35	.35
□ 4 Jose Rijo	.25	.11	.03
□ 5 John Smoltz	.75	.35	.09

1995 Ultra

This 450-card standard-size set was issued in two series. The first series contained 250 cards while the second series consisted of 200 cards. They were issued in 12-card packs (either hobby or retail) with a suggested retail price of $1.99. Also, 15-card pre-priced packs with a suggested retail of $2.69. Each pack contained two inserts: one is a Gold Medallion parallel while the other is from one of Ultra's many insert sets. "Hot Packs" contain nothing but insert cards. The full-bleed fronts feature the player's photo with the team name and player's name at the bottom. The "95 Fleer Ultra" logo is in the upper right corner. The backs have a two-photo design; one of which is a full-size duotone shot with the other being a full-color action shot. Personal bio, seasonal and career information are also included on the back. In each series the cards were grouped alphabetically within teams and checklisted alphabetically according to teams for each league as follows: Baltimore Orioles (1-8/251-258), Boston Red Sox (9-17/259-264), California Angels (18-25/265-272), Chicago White Sox (26-34/273-277), Cleveland Indians (35-43/278-283), Detroit Tigers (44-52/284-287), Kansas City Royals (53-61/288-293), Milwaukee Brewers (62-70/294-300), Minnesota Twins (71-79/301-306), New York Yankees (80-88/307-314), Oakland Athletics (89-97/315-323), Seattle Mariners (98-106/324-331), Texas Rangers (107-115/332-336), Toronto Blue Jays (116-124/ 337-344), Atlanta Braves (125-133/345-356), Chicago Cubs (134-141/357-362), Cincinnati Reds (142-150/363-372), Colorado Rockies (151-159/373-377), Florida Marlins (160-168/378-383), Houston Astros (169-177/384-391), Los Angeles Dodgers (178-185/392-401), Montreal Expos (186-194/402-410), New York Mets (195-202/411-416), Philadelphia Phillies (203-211/417-422), Pittsburgh Pirates (212-220/423-428), St. Louis Cardinals (221-229/429-434), San Diego Padres (230-238/435-441) and San Francisco Giants (239-247/442-447). There are no key Rookie Cards in this set.

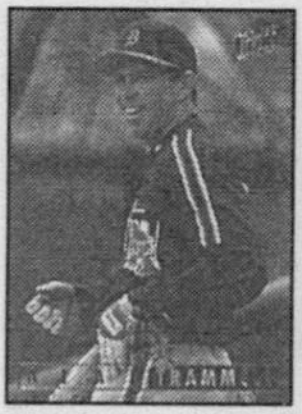

	MINT	NRMT	EXC
COMPLETE SET (450)	30.00	13.50	3.70
COMPLETE SERIES 1 (250)	18.00	8.00	2.20
COMPLETE SERIES 2 (200)	12.00	5.50	1.50
COMMON CARD (1-450)	.10	.05	.01
SEMISTARS	.25	.11	.03
STARS	.50	.23	.06
COMP.G.MED.SET (450)	110.00	50.00	14.00
COMP.G.MED.SER.1 (250)	60.00	27.00	7.50
COMP.G.MED.SER.2 (200)	50.00	22.00	6.25
COMMON G.MED. (1-450)	.25	.11	.03
G.MED.SEMISTARS	.50	.23	.06
*G.MED.STARS: 2X to 4X HI COLUMN			
*G.MED.YOUNG STARS: 1.5X to 3X HI			
ONE GOLD MEDALLION PER PACK			

□ 1 Brady Anderson	.50	.23	.06
□ 2 Sid Fernandez	.10	.05	.01
□ 3 Jeffrey Hammonds	.25	.11	.03
□ 4 Chris Hoiles	.10	.05	.01
□ 5 Ben McDonald	.10	.05	.01
□ 6 Mike Mussina	.60	.25	.07
□ 7 Rafael Palmeiro	.50	.23	.06
□ 8 Jack Voigt	.10	.05	.01
□ 9 Wes Chamberlain	.10	.05	.01
□ 10 Roger Clemens	.50	.23	.06
□ 11 Chris Howard	.10	.05	.01
□ 12 Tim Naehring	.10	.05	.01
□ 13 Otis Nixon	.10	.05	.01
□ 14 Rich Rowland	.10	.05	.01
□ 15 Ken Ryan	.10	.05	.01
□ 16 John Valentin	.25	.11	.03
□ 17 Mo Vaughn	.75	.35	.09
□ 18 Brian Anderson	.10	.05	.01

□ 19 Chili Davis	.25	.11	.03
□ 20 Damion Easley	.10	.05	.01
□ 21 Jim Edmonds	.50	.23	.06
□ 22 Mark Langston	.10	.05	.01
□ 23 Tim Salmon	.50	.23	.06
□ 24 J.T. Snow	.25	.11	.03
□ 25 Chris Turner	.10	.05	.01
□ 26 Wilson Alvarez	.25	.11	.03
□ 27 Joey Cora	.10	.05	.01
□ 28 Alex Fernandez	.25	.11	.03
□ 29 Roberto Hernandez	.10	.05	.01
□ 30 Lance Johnson	.25	.11	.03
□ 31 Ron Karkovice	.10	.05	.01
□ 32 Kirk McCaskill	.10	.05	.01
□ 33 Tim Raines	.50	.23	.06
□ 34 Frank Thomas	3.00	1.35	.35
□ 35 Sandy Alomar Jr.	.10	.05	.01
□ 36 Albert Belle	1.50	.70	.19
□ 37 Mark Clark	.10	.05	.01
□ 38 Kenny Lofton	.75	.35	.09
□ 39 Eddie Murray	.75	.35	.09
□ 40 Eric Plunk	.10	.05	.01
□ 41 Manny Ramirez	.75	.35	.09
□ 42 Jim Thome	.60	.25	.07
□ 43 Omar Vizquel	.50	.23	.06
□ 44 Danny Bautista	.10	.05	.01
□ 45 Junior Felix	.10	.05	.01
□ 46 Cecil Fielder	.25	.11	.03
□ 47 Chris Gomez	.10	.05	.01
□ 48 Chad Kreuter	.10	.05	.01
□ 49 Mike Moore	.10	.05	.01
□ 50 Tony Phillips	.25	.11	.03
□ 51 Alan Trammell	.50	.23	.06
□ 52 David Wells	.10	.05	.01
□ 53 Kevin Appier	.25	.11	.03
□ 54 Billy Brewer	.10	.05	.01
□ 55 David Cone	.25	.11	.03
□ 56 Greg Gagne	.10	.05	.01
□ 57 Bob Hamelin	.10	.05	.01
□ 58 Jose Lind	.10	.05	.01
□ 59 Brent Mayne	.10	.05	.01
□ 60 Brian McRae	.25	.11	.03
□ 61 Terry Shumpert	.10	.05	.01
□ 62 Ricky Bones	.10	.05	.01
□ 63 Mike Fetters	.10	.05	.01
□ 64 Darryl Hamilton	.10	.05	.01
□ 65 John Jaha	.25	.11	.03
□ 66 Graeme Lloyd	.10	.05	.01
□ 67 Matt Mieske	.25	.11	.03
□ 68 Kevin Seitzer	.10	.05	.01
□ 69 Jose Valentin	.25	.11	.03
□ 70 Turner Ward	.10	.05	.01
□ 71 Rick Aguilera	.10	.05	.01
□ 72 Rich Becker	.10	.05	.01
□ 73 Alex Cole	.10	.05	.01
□ 74 Scott Leius	.10	.05	.01
□ 75 Pat Meares	.10	.05	.01
□ 76 Kirby Puckett	1.00	.45	.12
□ 77 Dave Stevens	.10	.05	.01
□ 78 Kevin Tapani	.10	.05	.01
□ 79 Matt Walbeck	.10	.05	.01
□ 80 Wade Boggs	.50	.23	.06
□ 81 Scott Kamieniecki	.10	.05	.01
□ 82 Pat Kelly	.10	.05	.01
□ 83 Jimmy Key	.25	.11	.03
□ 84 Paul O'Neill	.25	.11	.03
□ 85 Luis Polonia	.10	.05	.01
□ 86 Mike Stanley	.10	.05	.01
□ 87 Danny Tartabull	.10	.05	.01
□ 88 Bob Wickman	.10	.05	.01
□ 89 Mark Acre	.10	.05	.01
□ 90 Geronimo Berroa	.10	.05	.01
□ 91 Mike Bordick	.10	.05	.01
□ 92 Ron Darling	.10	.05	.01
□ 93 Stan Javier	.10	.05	.01
□ 94 Mark McGwire	1.00	.45	.12
□ 95 Troy Neel	.10	.05	.01
□ 96 Ruben Sierra	.25	.11	.03
□ 97 Terry Steinbach	.25	.11	.03
□ 98 Eric Anthony	.10	.05	.01
□ 99 Chris Bosio	.10	.05	.01
□ 100 Dave Fleming	.10	.05	.01
□ 101 Ken Griffey Jr.	3.00	1.35	.35
□ 102 Reggie Jefferson	.25	.11	.03
□ 103 Randy Johnson	.50	.23	.06
□ 104 Edgar Martinez	.50	.23	.06
□ 105 Bill Risley	.10	.05	.01
□ 106 Dan Wilson	.25	.11	.03
□ 107 Cris Carpenter	.10	.05	.01
□ 108 Will Clark	.50	.23	.06
□ 109 Juan Gonzalez	1.50	.70	.19
□ 110 Rusty Greer	.50	.23	.06
□ 111 David Hulse	.10	.05	.01
□ 112 Roger Pavlik	.10	.05	.01
□ 113 Ivan Rodriguez	.60	.25	.07
□ 114 Doug Strange	.10	.05	.01
□ 115 Matt Whiteside	.10	.05	.01
□ 116 Roberto Alomar	.75	.35	.09
□ 117 Brad Cornett	.10	.05	.01
□ 118 Carlos Delgado	.50	.23	.06
□ 119 Alex Gonzalez	.10	.05	.01
□ 120 Darren Hall	.10	.05	.01
□ 121 Pat Hentgen	.25	.11	.03
□ 122 Paul Molitor	.60	.25	.07
□ 123 Ed Sprague	.25	.11	.03
□ 124 Devon White	.25	.11	.03
□ 125 Tom Glavine	.50	.23	.06
□ 126 David Justice	.50	.23	.06
□ 127 Roberto Kelly	.10	.05	.01
□ 128 Mark Lemke	.10	.05	.01
□ 129 Greg Maddux	2.00	.90	.25
□ 130 Greg McMichael	.10	.05	.01
□ 131 Kent Mercker	.10	.05	.01
□ 132 Charlie O'Brien	.10	.05	.01
□ 133 John Smoltz	.50	.23	.06
□ 134 Willie Banks	.10	.05	.01
□ 135 Steve Buechele	.10	.05	.01
□ 136 Kevin Foster	.10	.05	.01
□ 137 Glenallen Hill	.10	.05	.01
□ 138 Rey Sanchez	.10	.05	.01
□ 139 Sammy Sosa	.50	.23	.06
□ 140 Steve Trachsel	.10	.05	.01
□ 141 Rick Wilkins	.10	.05	.01
□ 142 Jeff Brantley	.10	.05	.01
□ 143 Hector Carrasco	.10	.05	.01
□ 144 Kevin Jarvis	.10	.05	.01
□ 145 Barry Larkin	.50	.23	.06
□ 146 Chuck McElroy	.10	.05	.01
□ 147 Jose Rijo	.10	.05	.01
□ 148 Johnny Ruffin	.10	.05	.01
□ 149 Deion Sanders	.50	.23	.06
□ 150 Eddie Taubensee	.10	.05	.01
□ 151 Dante Bichette	.50	.23	.06
□ 152 Ellis Burks	.50	.23	.06
□ 153 Joe Girardi	.10	.05	.01
□ 154 Charlie Hayes	.10	.05	.01
□ 155 Mike Kingery	.10	.05	.01
□ 156 Steve Reed	.10	.05	.01
□ 157 Kevin Ritz	.10	.05	.01
□ 158 Bruce Ruffin	.10	.05	.01
□ 159 Eric Young	.25	.11	.03
□ 160 Kurt Abbott	.10	.05	.01
□ 161 Chuck Carr	.10	.05	.01
□ 162 Chris Hammond	.10	.05	.01
□ 163 Bryan Harvey	.10	.05	.01
□ 164 Terry Mathews	.10	.05	.01
□ 165 Yorkis Perez	.10	.05	.01
□ 166 Pat Rapp	.10	.05	.01
□ 167 Gary Sheffield	.50	.23	.06
□ 168 Dave Weathers	.10	.05	.01
□ 169 Jeff Bagwell	1.25	.55	.16
□ 170 Ken Caminiti	.50	.23	.06
□ 171 Doug Drabek	.10	.05	.01
□ 172 Steve Finley	.25	.11	.03
□ 173 John Hudek	.10	.05	.01
□ 174 Todd Jones	.10	.05	.01
□ 175 James Mouton	.10	.05	.01
□ 176 Shane Reynolds	.10	.05	.01
□ 177 Scott Servais	.10	.05	.01
□ 178 Tom Candiotti	.10	.05	.01
□ 179 Omar Daal	.10	.05	.01
□ 180 Darren Dreifort	.10	.05	.01
□ 181 Eric Karros	.25	.11	.03
□ 182 Ramon J.Martinez	.25	.11	.03
□ 183 Raul Mondesi	.50	.23	.06
□ 184 Henry Rodriguez	.50	.23	.06
□ 185 Todd Worrell	.10	.05	.01
□ 186 Moises Alou	.25	.11	.03
□ 187 Sean Berry	.10	.05	.01
□ 188 Wil Cordero	.10	.05	.01
□ 189 Jeff Fassero	.10	.05	.01
□ 190 Darrin Fletcher	.10	.05	.01

☐ 191	Butch Henry	.10	.05	.01
☐ 192	Ken Hill	.10	.05	.01
☐ 193	Mel Rojas	.10	.05	.01
☐ 194	John Wetteland	.25	.11	.03
☐ 195	Bobby Bonilla	.25	.11	.03
☐ 196	Rico Brogna	.10	.05	.01
☐ 197	Bobby Jones	.25	.11	.03
☐ 198	Jeff Kent	.10	.05	.01
☐ 199	Josias Manzanillo	.10	.05	.01
☐ 200	Kelly Stinnett	.10	.05	.01
☐ 201	Ryan Thompson	.10	.05	.01
☐ 202	Jose Vizcaino	.10	.05	.01
☐ 203	Lenny Dykstra	.25	.11	.03
☐ 204	Jim Eisenreich	.10	.05	.01
☐ 205	Dave Hollins	.10	.05	.01
☐ 206	Mike Lieberthal	.10	.05	.01
☐ 207	Mickey Morandini	.10	.05	.01
☐ 208	Bobby Munoz	.10	.05	.01
☐ 209	Curt Schilling	.10	.05	.01
☐ 210	Heathcliff Slocumb	.10	.05	.01
☐ 211	David West	.10	.05	.01
☐ 212	Dave Clark	.10	.05	.01
☐ 213	Steve Cooke	.10	.05	.01
☐ 214	Midre Cummings	.10	.05	.01
☐ 215	Carlos Garcia	.10	.05	.01
☐ 216	Jeff King	.25	.11	.03
☐ 217	Jon Lieber	.10	.05	.01
☐ 218	Orlando Merced	.10	.05	.01
☐ 219	Don Slaught	.10	.05	.01
☐ 220	Rick White	.10	.05	.01
☐ 221	Rene Arocha	.10	.05	.01
☐ 222	Bernard Gilkey	.25	.11	.03
☐ 223	Brian Jordan	.50	.23	.06
☐ 224	Tom Pagnozzi	.10	.05	.01
☐ 225	Vicente Palacios	.10	.05	.01
☐ 226	Geronimo Pena	.10	.05	.01
☐ 227	Ozzie Smith	.60	.25	.07
☐ 228	Allen Watson	.10	.05	.01
☐ 229	Mark Whiten	.10	.05	.01
☐ 230	Brad Ausmus	.10	.05	.01
☐ 231	Derek Bell	.25	.11	.03
☐ 232	Andy Benes	.10	.05	.01
☐ 233	Tony Gwynn	1.25	.55	.16
☐ 234	Joey Hamilton	.25	.11	.03
☐ 235	Luis Lopez	.10	.05	.01
☐ 236	Pedro A.Martinez	.10	.05	.01
☐ 237	Scott Sanders	.10	.05	.01
☐ 238	Eddie Williams	.10	.05	.01
☐ 239	Rod Beck	.10	.05	.01
☐ 240	Dave Burba	.10	.05	.01
☐ 241	Darren Lewis	.10	.05	.01
☐ 242	Kirt Manwaring	.10	.05	.01
☐ 243	Mark Portugal	.10	.05	.01
☐ 244	Darryl Strawberry	.25	.11	.03
☐ 245	Robby Thompson	.10	.05	.01
☐ 246	Wm.VanLandingham	.10	.05	.01
☐ 247	Matt Williams	.50	.23	.06
☐ 248	Checklist	.10	.05	.01
☐ 249	Checklist	.10	.05	.01
☐ 250	Checklist	.10	.05	.01
☐ 251	Harold Baines	.25	.11	.03
☐ 252	Bret Barberie	.10	.05	.01
☐ 253	Armando Benitez	.10	.05	.01
☐ 254	Mike Devereaux	.10	.05	.01
☐ 255	Leo Gomez	.10	.05	.01
☐ 256	Jamie Moyer	.10	.05	.01
☐ 257	Arthur Rhodes	.10	.05	.01
☐ 258	Cal Ripken	2.50	1.10	.30
☐ 259	Luis Alicea	.10	.05	.01
☐ 260	Jose Canseco	.50	.23	.06
☐ 261	Scott Cooper	.10	.05	.01
☐ 262	Andre Dawson	.50	.23	.06
☐ 263	Mike Greenwell	.10	.05	.01
☐ 264	Aaron Sele	.25	.11	.03
☐ 265	Garret Anderson	.50	.23	.06
☐ 266	Chad Curtis	.10	.05	.01
☐ 267	Gary DiSarcina	.10	.05	.01
☐ 268	Chuck Finley	.25	.11	.03
☐ 269	Rex Hudler	.10	.05	.01
☐ 270	Andrew Lorraine	.25	.11	.03
☐ 271	Spike Owen	.10	.05	.01
☐ 272	Lee Smith	.25	.11	.03
☐ 273	Jason Bere	.10	.05	.01
☐ 274	Ozzie Guillen	.10	.05	.01
☐ 275	Norberto Martin	.10	.05	.01
☐ 276	Scott Ruffcorn	.10	.05	.01
☐ 277	Robin Ventura	.25	.11	.03
☐ 278	Carlos Baerga	.50	.23	.06
☐ 279	Jason Grimsley	.10	.05	.01
☐ 280	Dennis Martinez	.25	.11	.03
☐ 281	Charles Nagy	.25	.11	.03
☐ 282	Paul Sorrento	.10	.05	.01
☐ 283	Dave Winfield	.50	.23	.06
☐ 284	John Doherty	.10	.05	.01
☐ 285	Travis Fryman	.25	.11	.03
☐ 286	Kirk Gibson	.25	.11	.03
☐ 287	Lou Whitaker	.50	.23	.06
☐ 288	Gary Gaetti	.25	.11	.03
☐ 289	Tom Gordon	.10	.05	.01
☐ 290	Mark Gubicza	.10	.05	.01
☐ 291	Wally Joyner	.25	.11	.03
☐ 292	Mike Macfarlane	.10	.05	.01
☐ 293	Jeff Montgomery	.25	.11	.03
☐ 294	Jeff Cirillo	.25	.11	.03
☐ 295	Cal Eldred	.10	.05	.01
☐ 296	Pat Listach	.10	.05	.01
☐ 297	Jose Mercedes	.10	.05	.01
☐ 298	Dave Nilsson	.25	.11	.03
☐ 299	Duane Singleton	.10	.05	.01
☐ 300	Greg Vaughn	.25	.11	.03
☐ 301	Scott Erickson	.10	.05	.01
☐ 302	Denny Hocking	.10	.05	.01
☐ 303	Chuck Knoblauch	.50	.23	.06
☐ 304	Pat Mahomes	.10	.05	.01
☐ 305	Pedro Munoz	.10	.05	.01
☐ 306	Erik Schullstrom	.10	.05	.01
☐ 307	Jim Abbott	.10	.05	.01
☐ 308	Tony Fernandez	.10	.05	.01
☐ 309	Sterling Hitchcock	.25	.11	.03
☐ 310	Jim Leyritz	.10	.05	.01
☐ 311	Don Mattingly	1.50	.70	.19
☐ 312	Jack McDowell	.25	.11	.03
☐ 313	Melido Perez	.10	.05	.01
☐ 314	Bernie Williams	.50	.23	.06
☐ 315	Scott Brosius	.10	.05	.01
☐ 316	Dennis Eckersley	.25	.11	.03
☐ 317	Brent Gates	.10	.05	.01
☐ 318	Rickey Henderson	.50	.23	.06
☐ 319	Steve Karsay	.10	.05	.01
☐ 320	Steve Ontiveros	.10	.05	.01
☐ 321	Bill Taylor	.10	.05	.01
☐ 322	Todd Van Poppel	.10	.05	.01
☐ 323	Bob Welch	.10	.05	.01
☐ 324	Bobby Ayala	.10	.05	.01
☐ 325	Mike Blowers	.10	.05	.01
☐ 326	Jay Buhner	.50	.23	.06
☐ 327	Felix Fermin	.10	.05	.01
☐ 328	Tino Martinez	.25	.11	.03
☐ 329	Marc Newfield	.25	.11	.03
☐ 330	Greg Pirkl	.10	.05	.01
☐ 331	Alex Rodriguez	4.00	1.80	.50
☐ 332	Kevin Brown	.25	.11	.03
☐ 333	John Burkett	.25	.11	.03
☐ 334	Jeff Frye	.10	.05	.01
☐ 335	Kevin Gross	.10	.05	.01
☐ 336	Dean Palmer	.25	.11	.03
☐ 337	Joe Carter	.50	.23	.06
☐ 338	Shawn Green	.25	.11	.03
☐ 339	Juan Guzman	.25	.11	.03
☐ 340	Mike Huff	.10	.05	.01
☐ 341	Al Leiter	.25	.11	.03
☐ 342	John Olerud	.10	.05	.01
☐ 343	Dave Stewart	.25	.11	.03
☐ 344	Todd Stottlemyre	.10	.05	.01
☐ 345	Steve Avery	.25	.11	.03
☐ 346	Jeff Blauser	.10	.05	.01
☐ 347	Chipper Jones	2.00	.90	.25
☐ 348	Mike Kelly	.10	.05	.01
☐ 349	Ryan Klesko	.60	.25	.07
☐ 350	Javier Lopez	.50	.23	.06
☐ 351	Fred McGriff	.50	.23	.06
☐ 352	Jose Oliva	.10	.05	.01
☐ 353	Terry Pendleton	.25	.11	.03
☐ 354	Mike Stanton	.10	.05	.01
☐ 355	Tony Tarasco	.10	.05	.01
☐ 356	Mark Wohlers	.25	.11	.03
☐ 357	Jim Bullinger	.10	.05	.01
☐ 358	Shawon Dunston	.10	.05	.01
☐ 359	Mark Grace	.50	.23	.06
☐ 360	Derrick May	.10	.05	.01
☐ 361	Randy Myers	.10	.05	.01
☐ 362	Karl Rhodes	.10	.05	.01

□	363 Bret Boone	.25	.11	.03
□	364 Brian Dorsett	.10	.05	.01
□	365 Ron Gant	.25	.11	.03
□	366 Brian A.Hunter	.10	.05	.01
□	367 Hal Morris	.10	.05	.01
□	368 Jack Morris	.50	.23	.06
□	369 John Roper	.10	.05	.01
□	370 Reggie Sanders	.25	.11	.03
□	371 Pete Schourek	.25	.11	.03
□	372 John Smiley	.10	.05	.01
□	373 Marvin Freeman	.10	.05	.01
□	374 Andres Galarraga	.50	.23	.06
□	375 Mike Munoz	.10	.05	.01
□	376 David Nied	.10	.05	.01
□	377 Walt Weiss	.10	.05	.01
□	378 Greg Colbrunn	.10	.05	.01
□	379 Jeff Conine	.50	.23	.06
□	380 Charles Johnson	.25	.11	.03
□	381 Kurt Miller	.10	.05	.01
□	382 Robb Nen	.10	.05	.01
□	383 Benito Santiago	.10	.05	.01
□	384 Craig Biggio	.50	.23	.06
□	385 Tony Eusebio	.10	.05	.01
□	386 Luis Gonzalez	.10	.05	.01
□	387 Brian L.Hunter	.50	.23	.06
□	388 Darryl Kile	.10	.05	.01
□	389 Orlando Miller	.10	.05	.01
□	390 Phil Plantier	.10	.05	.01
□	391 Greg Swindell	.10	.05	.01
□	392 Billy Ashley	.10	.05	.01
□	393 Pedro Astacio	.10	.05	.01
□	394 Brett Butler	.25	.11	.03
□	395 Delino DeShields	.10	.05	.01
□	396 Orel Hershiser	.25	.11	.03
□	397 Garey Ingram	.10	.05	.01
□	398 Chan Ho Park	.50	.23	.06
□	399 Mike Piazza	2.00	.90	.25
□	400 Ismael Valdes	.25	.11	.03
□	401 Tim Wallach	.10	.05	.01
□	402 Cliff Floyd	.25	.11	.03
□	403 Marquis Grissom	.50	.23	.06
□	404 Mike Lansing	.10	.05	.01
□	405 Pedro J.Martinez	.25	.11	.03
□	406 Kirk Rueter	.10	.05	.01
□	407 Tim Scott	.10	.05	.01
□	408 Jeff Shaw	.10	.05	.01
□	409 Larry Walker	.50	.23	.06
□	410 Rondell White	.50	.23	.06
□	411 John Franco	.10	.05	.01
□	412 Todd Hundley	.25	.11	.03
□	413 Jason Jacome	.10	.05	.01
□	414 Joe Orsulak	.10	.05	.01
□	415 Bret Saberhagen	.25	.11	.03
□	416 David Segui	.10	.05	.01
□	417 Darren Daulton	.25	.11	.03
□	418 Mariano Duncan	.10	.05	.01
□	419 Tommy Greene	.10	.05	.01
□	420 Gregg Jefferies	.25	.11	.03
□	421 John Kruk	.25	.11	.03
□	422 Kevin Stocker	.10	.05	.01
□	423 Jay Bell	.25	.11	.03
□	424 Al Martin	.25	.11	.03
□	425 Denny Neagle	.25	.11	.03
□	426 Zane Smith	.10	.05	.01
□	427 Andy Van Slyke	.25	.11	.03
□	428 Paul Wagner	.10	.05	.01
□	429 Tom Henke	.10	.05	.01
□	430 Danny Jackson	.10	.05	.01
□	431 Ray Lankford	.50	.23	.06
□	432 John Mabry	.50	.23	.06
□	433 Bob Tewksbury	.10	.05	.01
□	434 Todd Zeile	.10	.05	.01
□	435 Andy Ashby	.25	.11	.03
□	436 Andujar Cedeno	.10	.05	.01
□	437 Donnie Elliott	.10	.05	.01
□	438 Bryce Florie	.10	.05	.01
□	439 Trevor Hoffman	.10	.05	.01
□	440 Melvin Nieves	.25	.11	.03
□	441 Bip Roberts	.10	.05	.01
□	442 Barry Bonds	.75	.35	.09
□	443 Royce Clayton	.10	.05	.01
□	444 Mike Jackson	.10	.05	.01
□	445 John Patterson	.10	.05	.01
□	446 J.R. Phillips	.10	.05	.01
□	447 Bill Swift	.10	.05	.01
□	448 Checklist	.10	.05	.01
□	449 Checklist	.10	.05	.01
□	450 Checklist	.10	.05	.01

1995 Ultra All-Rookies

This 10-card standard-size set features rookies who emerged with an impact in 1994. These cards were inserted one in every five second series packs. The fronts feature a player's photo in the middle of the card with each corner devoted to a close-up of part of that action shot. The horizontal backs feature some player information as well as a photo. That same photo is also included in the background as a duotone photo as well. The cards are numbered in the lower left as "X" of 10 and are sequenced in alphabetical order. The tougher to find Gold Medallion versions are valued at two to three times these prices.

	MINT	NRMT	EXC
COMPLETE SET (10)	6.00	2.70	.75
COMMON CARD (1-10)	.25	.11	.03
*GOLD MEDALLION: 1.5X TO 3X BASIC CARDS			
RANDOM INSERTS IN SER.2 PACKS			

□	1 Cliff Floyd	.50	.23	.06
□	2 Chris Gomez	.25	.11	.03
□	3 Rusty Greer	.50	.23	.06
□	4 Bob Hamelin	.25	.11	.03
□	5 Joey Hamilton	1.00	.45	.12
□	6 John Hudek	.25	.11	.03
□	7 Ryan Klesko	1.50	.70	.19
□	8 Raul Mondesi	1.00	.45	.12
□	9 Manny Ramirez	2.00	.90	.25
□	10 Steve Trachsel	.25	.11	.03

1995 Ultra All-Stars

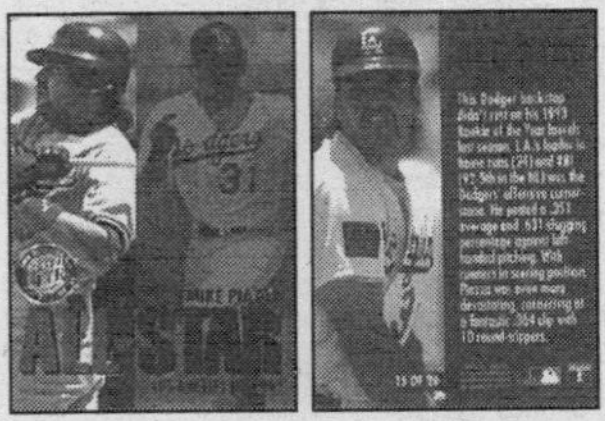

This 20-card standard-size set feature players who are considered to be the top players in the game. Cards were inserted one in every four second series packs. The fronts feature two photos. One photo is in full-color while the other is a shaded black and white shot. The player's name, "All-Star" and his team name are at the bottom. The back is split between a player photo and career highlights. The cards are numbered in the bottom left as "X" of 20 and are sequenced in alphabetical order. The tougher to find Gold Medallion versions are valued at two to three times these prices.

	MINT	NRMT	EXC
COMPLETE SET (20)	20.00	9.00	2.50
COMMON CARD (1-20)	.25	.11	.03
SEMISTARS	.60	.25	.07
*GOLD MEDALLION: 1.5X TO 3X BASIC CARDS			
RANDOM INSERTS IN SER.2 PACKS			

	MINT	NRMT	EXC
□ 1 Moises Alou	.25	.11	.03
□ 2 Albert Belle	2.50	1.10	.30
□ 3 Craig Biggio	.60	.25	.07
□ 4 Wade Boggs	.60	.25	.07
□ 5 Barry Bonds	1.25	.55	.16
□ 6 David Cone	.60	.25	.07
□ 7 Ken Griffey Jr.	5.00	2.20	.60
□ 8 Tony Gwynn	2.00	.90	.25
□ 9 Chuck Knoblauch	.60	.25	.07
□ 10 Barry Larkin	.60	.25	.07
□ 11 Kenny Lofton	1.25	.55	.16
□ 12 Greg Maddux	3.00	1.35	.35
□ 13 Fred McGriff	.60	.25	.07
□ 14 Paul O'Neill	.25	.11	.03
□ 15 Mike Piazza	3.00	1.35	.35
□ 16 Kirby Puckett	1.50	.70	.19
□ 17 Cal Ripken	4.00	1.80	.50
□ 18 Ivan Rodriguez	1.00	.45	.12
□ 19 Frank Thomas	5.00	2.20	.60
□ 20 Matt Williams	.60	.25	.07

1995 Ultra Award Winners

Featuring players who won major awards in 1994, this 25-card standard-size set was inserted one in every four first series packs. The horizontal fronts feature a full-color photo as well as a "stretched" duotone photo. The award the player won is indicated at the top while the player's name is on the bottom. The backs feature two more photos as well as reasons for the player winning the given award. The cards are numbered as "X" of 25. The tougher to find Gold Medallion versions are valued at two to three times these prices.

	MINT	NRMT	EXC
COMPLETE SET (25)	20.00	9.00	2.50
COMMON CARD (1-25)	.25	.11	.03
SEMISTARS	.60	.25	.07
*GOLD MEDALLION: 1.5X TO 3X BASIC CARDS			
RANDOM INSERTS IN PACKS			

	MINT	NRMT	EXC
□ 1 Ivan Rodriguez	1.00	.45	.12
□ 2 Don Mattingly	2.50	1.10	.30
□ 3 Roberto Alomar	1.25	.55	.16
□ 4 Wade Boggs	.60	.25	.07
□ 5 Omar Vizquel	.25	.11	.03
□ 6 Ken Griffey Jr.	5.00	2.20	.60
□ 7 Kenny Lofton	1.25	.55	.16
□ 8 Devon White	.25	.11	.03
□ 9 Mark Langston	.25	.11	.03
□ 10 Tom Pagnozzi	.25	.11	.03
□ 11 Jeff Bagwell	2.00	.90	.25
□ 12 Craig Biggio	.60	.25	.07
□ 13 Matt Williams	.60	.25	.07
□ 14 Barry Larkin	.60	.25	.07
□ 15 Barry Bonds	1.25	.55	.16
□ 16 Marquis Grissom	.60	.25	.07
□ 17 Darren Lewis	.25	.11	.03
□ 18 Greg Maddux	3.00	1.35	.35
□ 19 Frank Thomas	5.00	2.20	.60
□ 20 Jeff Bagwell	2.00	.90	.25
□ 21 David Cone	.60	.25	.07
□ 22 Greg Maddux	3.00	1.35	.35
□ 23 Bob Hamelin	.25	.11	.03
□ 24 Raul Mondesi	.60	.25	.07
□ 25 Moises Alou	.25	.11	.03

1995 Ultra Gold Medallion Rookies

This 20-card standard-size set was available through a mail-in wrapper offer that expired 9/30/95. These players featured were all rookies in 1995 and were not included in the regular Ultra set. The design is essentially the same as the corresponding basic cards save for the medallion in the upper left-hand corner. The cards are numbered with an "M" prefix. The set is sequenced in alphabetical order.

	MINT	NRMT	EXC
COMPLETE SET (20)	15.00	6.75	1.85
COMMON CARD (M1-M20)	.25	.11	.03
SEMISTARS	.50	.23	.06
SET DISTRIBUTED VIA MAIL-IN WRAPPER OFFER			

	MINT	NRMT	EXC
□ M1 Manny Alexander	.25	.11	.03
□ M2 Edgardo Alfonzo	.50	.23	.06
□ M3 Jason Bates	.25	.11	.03
□ M4 Andres Berumen	.25	.11	.03
□ M5 Darren Bragg	.25	.11	.03
□ M6 Jamie Brewington	.25	.11	.03
□ M7 Jason Christiansen	.25	.11	.03
□ M8 Brad Clontz	.25	.11	.03
□ M9 Marty Cordova	2.00	.90	.25
□ M10 Johnny Damon	1.50	.70	.19
□ M11 Vaughn Eshelman	.25	.11	.03
□ M12 Chad Fonville	.25	.11	.03
□ M13 Curtis Goodwin	.25	.11	.03
□ M14 Tyler Green	.25	.11	.03
□ M15 Bob Higginson	1.00	.45	.12
□ M16 Jason Isringhausen	2.00	.90	.25
□ M17 Hideo Nomo	6.00	2.70	.75
□ M18 Jon Nunnally	.25	.11	.03
□ M19 Carlos Perez	.25	.11	.03
□ M20 Julian Tavarez	.25	.11	.03

1995 Ultra Golden Prospects

Inserted one every eight first series hobby packs, this 10-card standard-size set features potential impact players. The horizontal fronts

feature the same photo with multiple viewpoints giving the impression the photo has been "cut up" into various parts. The words "Golden Prospect" as well as the player's name and team are across the bottom. The horizontal backs have information about his career as well as a normal full-color photo. The cards are numbered as "X" of 10 and are sequenced alphabetically. The tougher to find Gold Medallion versions are valued at two to three times these prices.

	MINT	NRMT	EXC
COMPLETE SET (10)	10.00	4.50	1.25
COMMON CARD (1-10)	.50	.23	.06
SEMISTARS	.75	.35	.09
*GOLD MEDALLION: 1.5X TO 3X BASIC CARDS			
RANDOM INSERTS IN HOBBY PACKS			

	MINT	NRMT	EXC
□ 1 James Baldwin	1.25	.55	.16
□ 2 Alan Benes	1.00	.45	.12
□ 3 Armando Benitez	.50	.23	.06
□ 4 Ray Durham	.75	.35	.09
□ 5 LaTroy Hawkins	.50	.23	.06
□ 6 Brian L.Hunter	1.00	.45	.12
□ 7 Derek Jeter	5.00	2.20	.60
□ 8 Charles Johnson	.75	.35	.09
□ 9 Alex Rodriguez	8.00	3.60	1.00
□ 10 Michael Tucker	.75	.35	.09

1995 Ultra Hitting Machines

This 10-card standard-size set features some of baseball's leading batters. Inserted one in every eight second-series retail packs, these horizontal cards have the player's photo against a background of the words "Hitting Machine." The player's name and team are identified on the bottom. The horizontal backs feature another player photo and reasons why they are great batters. The cards are numbered as "X" of 10 in the upper right and are sequenced in alphabetical order. The tougher to find Gold Medallion versions are valued at two to three times these prices.

	MINT	NRMT	EXC
COMPLETE SET (10)	15.00	6.75	1.85
COMMON CARD (1-10)	.50	.23	.06
*GOLD MEDALLION: 1.5X TO 3X BASIC CARDS			
RANDOM INSERTS IN SER.2 PACKS			

	MINT	NRMT	EXC
□ 1 Jeff Bagwell	2.00	.90	.25
□ 2 Albert Belle	2.50	1.10	.30
□ 3 Dante Bichette	.50	.23	.06
□ 4 Barry Bonds	1.25	.55	.16
□ 5 Jose Canseco	.75	.35	.09
□ 6 Ken Griffey Jr.	5.00	2.20	.60
□ 7 Tony Gwynn	2.00	.90	.25
□ 8 Fred McGriff	.75	.35	.09
□ 9 Mike Piazza	3.00	1.35	.35
□ 10 Frank Thomas	5.00	2.20	.60

1995 Ultra Home Run Kings

This 10-card standard-size set featured the five leading home run hitters in each league. These cards were issued one every eight first series retail packs. These cards have a player photo on one side with the letters HRK on the other side. The player is identified vertically in the middle. The backs have information about the playerís home run prowess as well as another action photo. The cards are numbered as "X" of 10 and are sequenced by league according to 1994's home rum standings. The tougher to find Gold Medallion versions are valued at two to three times these prices.

	MINT	NRMT	EXC
COMPLETE SET (10)	35.00	16.00	4.40
COMMON CARD (1-10)	1.00	.45	.12
SEMISTARS	1.50	.70	.19
*GOLD MEDALLION: 1.5X TO 3X BASIC CARDS			
RANDOM INSERTS IN RETAIL PACKS			

	MINT	NRMT	EXC
□ 1 Ken Griffey Jr.	12.00	5.50	1.50
□ 2 Frank Thomas	12.00	5.50	1.50
□ 3 Albert Belle	6.00	2.70	.75
□ 4 Jose Canseco	1.50	.70	.19
□ 5 Cecil Fielder	1.50	.70	.19
□ 6 Matt Williams	1.50	.70	.19
□ 7 Jeff Bagwell	5.00	2.20	.60
□ 8 Barry Bonds	3.00	1.35	.35
□ 9 Fred McGriff	1.50	.70	.19
□ 10 Andres Galarraga	1.00	.45	.12

1995 Ultra League Leaders

This 10-card standard-size set was inserted one in three first series packs. The horizontal fronts feature a player photo against a background of his league's logo. The player is identified in one corner and the category he led the league in is featured in the other corner. The horizontal backs have a player photo as well as explaining more about the stat with which he paced the field. The tougher to find Gold Medallion versions are valued at two to three times these prices.

	MINT	NRMT	EXC
COMPLETE SET (10)	8.00	3.60	1.00
COMMON CARD (1-10)	.25	.11	.03
*GOLD MEDALLION: 1.5X TO 3X BASIC CARDS			
RANDOM INSERTS IN PACKS			

	MINT	NRMT	EXC
□ 1 Paul O'Neill	.25	.11	.03
□ 2 Kenny Lofton	1.25	.55	.16
□ 3 Jimmy Key	.25	.11	.03
□ 4 Randy Johnson	.75	.35	.09

□ 5 Lee Smith	.50	.23	.06
□ 6 Tony Gwynn	2.00	.90	.25
□ 7 Craig Biggio	.50	.23	.06
□ 8 Greg Maddux	3.00	1.35	.35
□ 9 Andy Benes	.25	.11	.03
□ 10 John Franco	.25	.11	.03

1995 Ultra On-Base Leaders

This 10-card standard-size set features ten players who are constantly reaching base safely. These cards were inserted one in every eight pre-priced second series jumbo packs. The fronts have an action photo against a background of several smaller action photos. The words "On-Base Leaders" are featured in the upper right corner along with the player's name. The horizontal backs contain the player's team, some information on how often they get on base and a player photo. The cards are numbered in the upper right corner as "X" of 10 and are sequenced in alphabetical order. The tougher to find Gold Medallion versions are valued at two to three times these prices.

	MINT	NRMT	EXC
COMPLETE SET (10)	40.00	18.00	5.00
COMMON CARD (1-10)	2.50	1.10	.30
*GOLD MEDALLION: 1.5X TO 3X BASIC CARDS			
RANDOM INSERTS IN SER.2 JUMBOS			

□ 1 Jeff Bagwell	8.00	3.60	1.00
□ 2 Albert Belle	10.00	4.50	1.25
□ 3 Craig Biggio	4.00	1.80	.50
□ 4 Wade Boggs	4.00	1.80	.50
□ 5 Barry Bonds	5.00	2.20	.60
□ 6 Will Clark	4.00	1.80	.50
□ 7 Tony Gwynn	8.00	3.60	1.00
□ 8 David Justice	2.50	1.10	.30
□ 9 Paul O'Neill	2.50	1.10	.30
□ 10 Frank Thomas	20.00	9.00	2.50

1995 Ultra Power Plus

This six-card standard-size set was inserted one in every 37 first series packs. The six players portrayed are not only sluggers, but also excel at another part of the game. Unlike the 1995 Ultra cards and the other insert sets, these cards are 100 percent foil. The fronts have a player photo against a background that has the words "Power Plus" spelled in various size letters. The player and his team are identified on the bottom in gold foil. The backs have a player photo and some player information. The cards are numbered on the bottom right as "X" of 6 and are sequenced in alphabetical order by league. The tougher to find Gold Medallion versions are valued at two to three times these prices.

	MINT	NRMT	EXC
COMPLETE SET (6)	50.00	22.00	6.25
COMMON CARD (1-6)	2.50	1.10	.30
*GOLD MEDALLION: 1.5X TO 3X BASIC CARDS			
RANDOM INSERTS IN PACKS			

□ 1 Albert Belle	10.00	4.50	1.25
□ 2 Ken Griffey Jr.	20.00	9.00	2.50
□ 3 Frank Thomas	20.00	9.00	2.50
□ 4 Jeff Bagwell	8.00	3.60	1.00
□ 5 Barry Bonds	5.00	2.20	.60
□ 6 Matt Williams	2.50	1.10	.30

1995 Ultra RBI Kings

This 10-card standard-size set was inserted into series one jumbo packs at a rate of one every 11. The cards feature a player photo against a multi-colored background. The player's name, the words "RBI King" as well as his team identity are printed in gold foil in the middle. The backs have a player photo as well as some information about the players batting prowess. The cards are numbered in the upper left as "X" of 10 and are sequenced in order by league. The tougher to find Gold Medallion versions are valued at two to three times these prices.

	MINT	NRMT	EXC
COMPLETE SET (10)	50.00	22.00	6.25
COMMON CARD (1-10)	1.50	.70	.19
SEMISTARS	2.50	1.10	.30
*GOLD MEDALLION: 1.5X TO 3X BASIC CARDS			
RANDOM INSERTS IN JUMBO PACKS			

□ 1 Kirby Puckett	6.00	2.70	.75
□ 2 Joe Carter	2.50	1.10	.30
□ 3 Albert Belle	10.00	4.50	1.25
□ 4 Frank Thomas	20.00	9.00	2.50
□ 5 Julio Franco	1.50	.70	.19
□ 6 Jeff Bagwell	8.00	3.60	1.00
□ 7 Matt Williams	2.50	1.10	.30
□ 8 Dante Bichette	2.50	1.10	.30
□ 9 Fred McGriff	2.50	1.10	.30
□ 10 Mike Piazza	12.00	5.50	1.50

1995 Ultra Rising Stars

This nine-card standard-size set was inserted one every 37 second series packs. Horizontal fronts feature two photos with the words "Rising Stars" as well as the player's name and team on the bottom left. This front design is set against a shiny background. The backs contain player information as well as a player photo. The cards are numbered "X" of 9 and are sequenced in alphabetical order. The tougher to find Gold Medallion versions are valued at two to three times these prices.

	MINT	NRMT	EXC
COMPLETE SET (9)	80.00	36.00	10.00
COMMON CARD (1-9)	2.00	.90	.25
SEMISTARS	4.00	1.80	.50
*GOLD MEDALLION: 1.5X TO 3X BASIC CARDS			
RANDOM INSERTS IN SER.2 PACKS			

	MINT	NRMT	EXC
□ 1 Moises Alou	2.00	.90	.25
□ 2 Jeff Bagwell	12.00	5.50	1.50
□ 3 Albert Belle	15.00	6.75	1.85
□ 4 Juan Gonzalez	15.00	6.75	1.85
□ 5 Chuck Knoblauch	4.00	1.80	.50
□ 6 Kenny Lofton	8.00	3.60	1.00
□ 7 Raul Mondesi	4.00	1.80	.50
□ 8 Mike Piazza	20.00	9.00	2.50
□ 9 Frank Thomas	30.00	13.50	3.70

1995 Ultra Second Year Standouts

This 15-card standard-size set was inserted into first series packs at a rate of not greater than one in six packs. The players in this set were all rookies in 1994 whom big things were expected from in 1995. The horizontal fronts feature the player's photo against a yellowish background. The player, his team's identification as well as the team logo are all printed in gold foil in the middle. The horizontal backs have another player photo as well as information about the player's 1994 season. The cards are numbered in the lower right as "X" of 15 and are sequenced in alphabetical order. The tougher to find Gold Medallion versions are valued at two to three times these prices.

	MINT	NRMT	EXC
COMPLETE SET (15)	10.00	4.50	1.25
COMMON CARD (1-15)	.50	.23	.06
SEMISTARS	1.00	.45	.12
*GOLD MEDALLION: 1.5X TO 3X BASIC CARDS			
RANDOM INSERTS IN PACKS			

	MINT	NRMT	EXC
□ 1 Cliff Floyd	1.00	.45	.12
□ 2 Chris Gomez	.50	.23	.06
□ 3 Rusty Greer	1.00	.45	.12
□ 4 Darren Hall	.50	.23	.06
□ 5 Bob Hamelin	.50	.23	.06
□ 6 Joey Hamilton	1.50	.70	.19
□ 7 Jeffrey Hammonds	.50	.23	.06
□ 8 John Hudek	.50	.23	.06
□ 9 Ryan Klesko	2.50	1.10	.30
□ 10 Raul Mondesi	1.50	.70	.19
□ 11 Manny Ramirez	3.00	1.35	.35
□ 12 Bill Risley	.50	.23	.06
□ 13 Steve Trachsel	.50	.23	.06
□ 14 W.VanLandingham	.50	.23	.06
□ 15 Rondell White	1.00	.45	.12

1995 Ultra Strikeout Kings

This six-card standard-size set was inserted one every five second series packs. The fronts have a player photo as well as photos of grips for four major pitches. The player's name as well as the words "Strikeout King" is printed in a bottom corner. The horizontal backs feature a player photo, a brief blurb as well as a team logo. The cards are numbered as "X" of 6 and are sequenced in alphabetical order. The tougher to find Gold Medallion versions are valued at two to three times these prices.

	MINT	NRMT	EXC
COMPLETE SET (6)	5.00	2.20	.60
COMMON CARD (1-6)	.25	.11	.03
SEMISTARS	.50	.23	.06
*GOLD MEDALLION: 1.5X TO 3X BASIC CARDS			
RANDOM INSERTS IN SER.2 PACKS			

	MINT	NRMT	EXC
□ 1 Andy Benes	.25	.11	.03
□ 2 Roger Clemens	.50	.23	.06
□ 3 Randy Johnson	.75	.35	.09
□ 4 Greg Maddux	3.00	1.35	.35
□ 5 Pedro Martinez	.25	.11	.03
□ 6 Jose Rijo	.25	.11	.03

1996 Ultra

The 1996 Ultra set, produced by Fleer, contains 600 standard-size cards. The cards were distributed in packs that included two inserts. One insert is a Gold Medallion parallel while the other insert comes from one of the many Ultra insert sets. The cards are thicker than their 1995 counterparts and the fronts feature the player in an action shot in full-bleed color. Player's name and team are emblazoned across the bottom in silver foil. Backs show the players in two action shots and one pose. The backs are full-bleed color and include biography and player 1995 statistics in gold print across the bottom. The cards are sequenced in alphabetical order within league and team order.

	MINT	NRMT	EXC
COMPLETE SET (600)	60.00	27.00	7.50
COMPLETE SERIES 1 (300)	30.00	13.50	3.70
COMPLETE SERIES 2 (300)	30.00	13.50	3.70
COMMON CARD (1-600)	.10	.05	.01
SEMISTARS	.25	.11	.03
STARS	.50	.23	.06
COMP.G.MED.SET (600)	200.00	90.00	25.00
COMP.G.MED.SER.1 (300)	100.00	45.00	12.50
COMP.G.MED.SER.2 (300)	100.00	45.00	12.50
COMMON G.MED (1-600)	.25	.11	.03
G.MED.SEMISTARS	1.00	.45	.12
G.MED STARS	2.00	.90	.25

*G.MED.STARS: 2X TO 4X BASIC CARDS ...
*G.MED.YOUNG STARS: 1.5X TO 3X BASIC CARDS
ONE INSERT PER PACK ....
PRODUCED BY FLEER..............................

□ 1	Manny Alexander	.10	.05	.01
□ 2	Brady Anderson	.50	.23	.06
□ 3	Bobby Bonilla	.50	.23	.06
□ 4	Scott Erickson	.10	.05	.01
□ 5	Curtis Goodwin	.10	.05	.01
□ 6	Chris Hoiles	.10	.05	.01
□ 7	Doug Jones	.10	.05	.01
□ 8	Jeff Manto	.10	.05	.01
□ 9	Mike Mussina	.60	.25	.07
□ 10	Rafael Palmeiro	.50	.23	.06
□ 11	Cal Ripken	2.50	1.10	.30
□ 12	Rick Aguilera	.10	.05	.01
□ 13	Luis Alicea	.10	.05	.01
□ 14	Stan Belinda	.10	.05	.01
□ 15	Jose Canseco	.50	.23	.06
□ 16	Roger Clemens	.50	.23	.06
□ 17	Mike Greenwell	.10	.05	.01
□ 18	Mike Macfarlane	.10	.05	.01
□ 19	Tim Naehring	.25	.11	.03
□ 20	Troy O'Leary	.25	.11	.03
□ 21	John Valentin	.25	.11	.03
□ 22	Mo Vaughn	.75	.35	.09
□ 23	Tim Wakefield	.10	.05	.01
□ 24	Brian Anderson	.10	.05	.01
□ 25	Garret Anderson	.50	.23	.06
□ 26	Chili Davis	.10	.05	.01
□ 27	Gary DiSarcina	.10	.05	.01
□ 28	Jim Edmonds	.50	.23	.06
□ 29	Jorge Fabregas	.10	.05	.01
□ 30	Chuck Finley	.10	.05	.01
□ 31	Mark Langston	.10	.05	.01
□ 32	Troy Percival	.25	.11	.03
□ 33	Tim Salmon	.50	.23	.06
□ 34	Lee Smith	.50	.23	.06
□ 35	Wilson Alvarez	.50	.23	.06
□ 36	Ray Durham	.50	.23	.06
□ 37	Alex Fernandez	.50	.23	.06
□ 38	Ozzie Guillen	.10	.05	.01
□ 39	Roberto Hernandez	.25	.11	.03
□ 40	Lance Johnson	.25	.11	.03
□ 41	Ron Karkovice	.10	.05	.01
□ 42	Lyle Mouton	.10	.05	.01
□ 43	Tim Raines	.50	.23	.06
□ 44	Frank Thomas	3.00	1.35	.35
□ 45	Carlos Baerga	.50	.23	.06
□ 46	Albert Belle	1.50	.70	.19
□ 47	Orel Hershiser	.25	.11	.03
□ 48	Kenny Lofton	.75	.35	.09
□ 49	Dennis Martinez	.25	.11	.03
□ 50	Jose Mesa	.25	.11	.03
□ 51	Eddie Murray	.75	.35	.09
□ 52	Chad Ogea	.10	.05	.01
□ 53	Manny Ramirez	.75	.35	.09
□ 54	Jim Thome	.60	.25	.07
□ 55	Omar Vizquel	.10	.05	.01
□ 56	Dave Winfield	.50	.23	.06
□ 57	Chad Curtis	.10	.05	.01
□ 58	Cecil Fielder	.50	.23	.06
□ 59	John Flaherty	.10	.05	.01
□ 60	Travis Fryman	.50	.23	.06
□ 61	Chris Gomez	.10	.05	.01
□ 62	Bob Higginson	.50	.23	.06
□ 63	Felipe Lira	.10	.05	.01
□ 64	Brian Maxcy	.10	.05	.01
□ 65	Alan Trammell	.50	.23	.06
□ 66	Lou Whitaker	.50	.23	.06
□ 67	Kevin Appier	.25	.11	.03
□ 68	Gary Gaetti	.25	.11	.03
□ 69	Tom Goodwin	.25	.11	.03
□ 70	Tom Gordon	.10	.05	.01
□ 71	Jason Jacome	.10	.05	.01
□ 72	Wally Joyner	.10	.05	.01
□ 73	Brent Mayne	.10	.05	.01
□ 74	Jeff Montgomery	.10	.05	.01
□ 75	Jon Nunnally	.10	.05	.01
□ 76	Joe Vitiello	.10	.05	.01
□ 77	Ricky Bones	.10	.05	.01
□ 78	Jeff Cirillo	.10	.05	.01
□ 79	Mike Fetters	.10	.05	.01
□ 80	Darryl Hamilton	.10	.05	.01
□ 81	David Hulse	.10	.05	.01
□ 82	Dave Nilsson	.25	.11	.03
□ 83	Kevin Seitzer	.10	.05	.01
□ 84	Steve Sparks	.10	.05	.01
□ 85	B.J. Surhoff	.10	.05	.01
□ 86	Jose Valentin	.10	.05	.01
□ 87	Greg Vaughn	.50	.23	.06
□ 88	Marty Cordova	.25	.11	.03
□ 89	Chuck Knoblauch	.50	.23	.06
□ 90	Pat Meares	.10	.05	.01
□ 91	Pedro Munoz	.10	.05	.01
□ 92	Kirby Puckett	1.00	.45	.12
□ 93	Brad Radke	.10	.05	.01
□ 94	Scott Stahoviak	.10	.05	.01
□ 95	Dave Stevens	.10	.05	.01
□ 96	Mike Trombley	.10	.05	.01
□ 97	Matt Walbeck	.10	.05	.01
□ 98	Wade Boggs	.50	.23	.06
□ 99	Russ Davis	.10	.05	.01
□ 100	Jim Leyritz	.10	.05	.01
□ 101	Don Mattingly	1.50	.70	.19
□ 102	Jack McDowell	.50	.23	.06
□ 103	Paul O'Neill	.10	.05	.01
□ 104	Andy Pettitte	1.00	.45	.12
□ 105	Mariano Rivera	.50	.23	.06
□ 106	Ruben Sierra	.10	.05	.01
□ 107	Darryl Strawberry	.50	.23	.06
□ 108	John Wetteland	.25	.11	.03
□ 109	Bernie Williams	.50	.23	.06
□ 110	Geronimo Berroa	.25	.11	.03
□ 111	Scott Brosius	.25	.11	.03
□ 112	Dennis Eckersley	.50	.23	.06
□ 113	Brent Gates	.10	.05	.01
□ 114	Rickey Henderson	.50	.23	.06
□ 115	Mark McGwire	1.00	.45	.12
□ 116	Ariel Prieto	.10	.05	.01
□ 117	Terry Steinbach	.25	.11	.03
□ 118	Todd Stottlemyre	.10	.05	.01
□ 119	Todd Van Poppel	.10	.05	.01
□ 120	Steve Wojciechowski	.10	.05	.01
□ 121	Rich Amaral	.10	.05	.01
□ 122	Bobby Ayala	.10	.05	.01
□ 123	Mike Blowers	.10	.05	.01
□ 124	Chris Bosio	.10	.05	.01
□ 125	Joey Cora	.10	.05	.01
□ 126	Ken Griffey Jr.	3.00	1.35	.35
□ 127	Randy Johnson	.50	.23	.06
□ 128	Edgar Martinez	.50	.23	.06
□ 129	Tino Martinez	.50	.23	.06
□ 130	Alex Rodriguez	3.00	1.35	.35
□ 131	Dan Wilson	.10	.05	.01
□ 132	Will Clark	.50	.23	.06
□ 133	Jeff Frye	.10	.05	.01
□ 134	Benji Gil	.10	.05	.01
□ 135	Juan Gonzalez	1.50	.70	.19
□ 136	Rusty Greer	.50	.23	.06
□ 137	Mark McLemore	.10	.05	.01
□ 138	Roger Pavlik	.10	.05	.01
□ 139	Ivan Rodriguez	.60	.25	.07
□ 140	Kenny Rogers	.10	.05	.01
□ 141	Mickey Tettleton	.25	.11	.03
□ 142	Roberto Alomar	.75	.35	.09
□ 143	Joe Carter	.50	.23	.06
□ 144	Tony Castillo	.10	.05	.01
□ 145	Alex Gonzalez	.10	.05	.01
□ 146	Shawn Green	.25	.11	.03
□ 147	Pat Hentgen	.50	.23	.06
□ 148	Sandy Martinez	.10	.05	.01
□ 149	Paul Molitor	.60	.25	.07
□ 150	John Olerud	.10	.05	.01
□ 151	Ed Sprague	.25	.11	.03
□ 152	Jeff Blauser	.10	.05	.01
□ 153	Brad Clontz	.10	.05	.01
□ 154	Tom Glavine	.50	.23	.06
□ 155	Marquis Grissom	.50	.23	.06
□ 156	Chipper Jones	2.00	.90	.25
□ 157	David Justice	.25	.11	.03
□ 158	Ryan Klesko	.60	.25	.07
□ 159	Javier Lopez	.50	.23	.06
□ 160	Greg Maddux	2.00	.90	.25
□ 161	John Smoltz	.50	.23	.06
□ 162	Mark Wohlers	.25	.11	.03
□ 163	Jim Bullinger	.10	.05	.01
□ 164	Frank Castillo	.10	.05	.01
□ 165	Shawon Dunston	.10	.05	.01
□ 166	Kevin Foster	.10	.05	.01
□ 167	Luis Gonzalez	.10	.05	.01

☐ 168	Mark Grace	.50	.23	.06
☐ 169	Rey Sanchez	.10	.05	.01
☐ 170	Scott Servais	.10	.05	.01
☐ 171	Sammy Sosa	.50	.23	.06
☐ 172	Ozzie Timmons	.10	.05	.01
☐ 173	Steve Trachsel	.10	.05	.01
☐ 174	Bret Boone	.10	.05	.01
☐ 175	Jeff Branson	.10	.05	.01
☐ 176	Jeff Brantley	.10	.05	.01
☐ 177	Dave Burba	.10	.05	.01
☐ 178	Ron Gant	.50	.23	.06
☐ 179	Barry Larkin	.50	.23	.06
☐ 180	Darren Lewis	.10	.05	.01
☐ 181	Mark Portugal	.10	.05	.01
☐ 182	Reggie Sanders	.50	.23	.06
☐ 183	Pete Schourek	.25	.11	.03
☐ 184	John Smiley	.10	.05	.01
☐ 185	Jason Bates	.10	.05	.01
☐ 186	Dante Bichette	.50	.23	.06
☐ 187	Ellis Burks	.50	.23	.06
☐ 188	Vinny Castilla	.50	.23	.06
☐ 189	Andres Galarraga	.50	.23	.06
☐ 190	Darren Holmes	.10	.05	.01
☐ 191	Armando Reynoso	.10	.05	.01
☐ 192	Kevin Ritz	.10	.05	.01
☐ 193	Bill Swift	.10	.05	.01
☐ 194	Larry Walker	.50	.23	.06
☐ 195	Kurt Abbott	.10	.05	.01
☐ 196	John Burkett	.10	.05	.01
☐ 197	Greg Colbrunn	.50	.23	.06
☐ 198	Jeff Conine	.50	.23	.06
☐ 199	Andre Dawson	.50	.23	.06
☐ 200	Chris Hammond	.10	.05	.01
☐ 201	Charles Johnson	.25	.11	.03
☐ 202	Robb Nen	.10	.05	.01
☐ 203	Terry Pendleton	.25	.11	.03
☐ 204	Quilvio Veras	.10	.05	.01
☐ 205	Jeff Bagwell	1.25	.55	.16
☐ 206	Derek Bell	.25	.11	.03
☐ 207	Doug Drabek	.10	.05	.01
☐ 208	Tony Eusebio	.10	.05	.01
☐ 209	Mike Hampton	.10	.05	.01
☐ 210	Brian L. Hunter	.10	.05	.01
☐ 211	Todd Jones	.10	.05	.01
☐ 212	Orlando Miller	.10	.05	.01
☐ 213	James Mouton	.10	.05	.01
☐ 214	Shane Reynolds	.25	.11	.03
☐ 215	Dave Veres	.10	.05	.01
☐ 216	Billy Ashley	.10	.05	.01
☐ 217	Brett Butler	.10	.05	.01
☐ 218	Chad Fonville	.10	.05	.01
☐ 219	Todd Hollandsworth	.50	.23	.06
☐ 220	Eric Karros	.50	.23	.06
☐ 221	Ramon Martinez	.25	.11	.03
☐ 222	Raul Mondesi	.50	.23	.06
☐ 223	Hideo Nomo	.75	.35	.09
☐ 224	Mike Piazza	2.00	.90	.25
☐ 225	Kevin Tapani	.10	.05	.01
☐ 226	Ismael Valdes	.25	.11	.03
☐ 227	Todd Worrell	.25	.11	.03
☐ 228	Moises Alou	.25	.11	.03
☐ 229	Wil Cordero	.10	.05	.01
☐ 230	Jeff Fassero	.10	.05	.01
☐ 231	Darrin Fletcher	.10	.05	.01
☐ 232	Mike Lansing	.10	.05	.01
☐ 233	Pedro J.Martinez	.25	.11	.03
☐ 234	Carlos Perez	.10	.05	.01
☐ 235	Mel Rojas	.25	.11	.03
☐ 236	David Segui	.10	.05	.01
☐ 237	Tony Tarasco	.10	.05	.01
☐ 238	Rondell White	.50	.23	.06
☐ 239	Edgardo Alfonzo	.25	.11	.03
☐ 240	Rico Brogna	.10	.05	.01
☐ 241	Carl Everett	.10	.05	.01
☐ 242	Todd Hundley	.50	.23	.06
☐ 243	Butch Huskey	.25	.11	.03
☐ 244	Jason Isringhausen	.25	.11	.03
☐ 245	Bobby Jones	.10	.05	.01
☐ 246	Jeff Kent	.10	.05	.01
☐ 247	Bill Pulsipher	.25	.11	.03
☐ 248	Jose Vizcaino	.10	.05	.01
☐ 249	Ricky Bottalico	.10	.05	.01
☐ 250	Darren Daulton	.25	.11	.03
☐ 251	Jim Eisenreich	.10	.05	.01
☐ 252	Tyler Green	.10	.05	.01
☐ 253	Charlie Hayes	.10	.05	.01
☐ 254	Gregg Jefferies	.50	.23	.06
☐ 255	Tony Longmire	.10	.05	.01
☐ 256	Michael Mimbs	.10	.05	.01
☐ 257	Mickey Morandini	.10	.05	.01
☐ 258	Paul Quantrill	.10	.05	.01
☐ 259	Heathcliff Slocumb	.10	.05	.01
☐ 260	Jay Bell	.25	.11	.03
☐ 261	Jacob Brumfield	.10	.05	.01
☐ 262	Angelo Encarnacion	.10	.05	.01
☐ 263	John Ericks	.10	.05	.01
☐ 264	Mark Johnson	.10	.05	.01
☐ 265	Esteban Loaiza	.10	.05	.01
☐ 266	Al Martin	.10	.05	.01
☐ 267	Orlando Merced	.25	.11	.03
☐ 268	Dan Miceli	.10	.05	.01
☐ 269	Denny Neagle	.25	.11	.03
☐ 270	Brian Barber	.10	.05	.01
☐ 271	Scott Cooper	.10	.05	.01
☐ 272	Tripp Cromer	.10	.05	.01
☐ 273	Bernard Gilkey	.25	.11	.03
☐ 274	Tom Henke	.25	.11	.03
☐ 275	Brian Jordan	.50	.23	.06
☐ 276	John Mabry	.50	.23	.06
☐ 277	Tom Pagnozzi	.10	.05	.01
☐ 278	Mark Petkovsek	.10	.05	.01
☐ 279	Ozzie Smith	.60	.25	.07
☐ 280	Andy Ashby	.10	.05	.01
☐ 281	Brad Ausmus	.10	.05	.01
☐ 282	Ken Caminiti	.50	.23	.06
☐ 283	Glenn Dishman	.10	.05	.01
☐ 284	Tony Gwynn	1.25	.55	.16
☐ 285	Joey Hamilton	.25	.11	.03
☐ 286	Trevor Hoffman	.25	.11	.03
☐ 287	Phil Plantier	.10	.05	.01
☐ 288	Jody Reed	.10	.05	.01
☐ 289	Eddie Williams	.10	.05	.01
☐ 290	Barry Bonds	.75	.35	.09
☐ 291	Jamie Brewington	.10	.05	.01
☐ 292	Mark Carreon	.10	.05	.01
☐ 293	Royce Clayton	.10	.05	.01
☐ 294	Glenallen Hill	.25	.11	.03
☐ 295	Mark Leiter	.10	.05	.01
☐ 296	Kirt Manwaring	.10	.05	.01
☐ 297	J.R. Phillips	.10	.05	.01
☐ 298	Deion Sanders	.50	.23	.06
☐ 299	Wm. VanLandingham	.10	.05	.01
☐ 300	Matt Williams	.50	.23	.06
☐ 301	Roberto Alomar	.75	.35	.09
☐ 302	Armando Benitez	.10	.05	.01
☐ 303	Mike Devereaux	.10	.05	.01
☐ 304	Jeffrey Hammonds	.10	.05	.01
☐ 305	Jimmy Haynes	.10	.05	.01
☐ 306	Scott McClain	.10	.05	.01
☐ 307	Kent Mercker	.10	.05	.01
☐ 308	Randy Myers	.10	.05	.01
☐ 309	B.J. Surhoff	.10	.05	.01
☐ 310	Tony Tarasco	.10	.05	.01
☐ 311	David Wells	.10	.05	.01
☐ 312	Wil Cordero	.10	.05	.01
☐ 313	Alex Delgado	.10	.05	.01
☐ 314	Tom Gordon	.10	.05	.01
☐ 315	Dwayne Hosey	.10	.05	.01
☐ 316	Jose Malave	.10	.05	.01
☐ 317	Kevin Mitchell	.10	.05	.01
☐ 318	Jamie Moyer	.10	.05	.01
☐ 319	Aaron Sele	.10	.05	.01
☐ 320	Heathcliff Slocumb	.10	.05	.01
☐ 321	Mike Stanley	.10	.05	.01
☐ 322	Jeff Suppan	.10	.05	.01
☐ 323	Jim Abbott	.50	.23	.06
☐ 324	George Arias	.10	.05	.01
☐ 325	Todd Greene	.50	.23	.06
☐ 326	Bryan Harvey	.10	.05	.01
☐ 327	J.T. Snow	.25	.11	.03
☐ 328	Randy Velarde	.10	.05	.01
☐ 329	Tim Wallach	.10	.05	.01
☐ 330	Harold Baines	.25	.11	.03
☐ 331	Jason Bere	.10	.05	.01
☐ 332	Darren Lewis	.10	.05	.01
☐ 333	Norberto Martin	.10	.05	.01
☐ 334	Tony Phillips	.25	.11	.03
☐ 335	Bill Simas	.10	.05	.01
☐ 336	Chris Snopek	.10	.05	.01
☐ 337	Kevin Tapani	.10	.05	.01
☐ 338	Danny Tartabull	.10	.05	.01
☐ 339	Robin Ventura	.50	.23	.06

☐ 340	Sandy Alomar Jr.	.10	.05	.01
☐ 341	Julio Franco	.25	.11	.03
☐ 342	Jack McDowell	.50	.23	.06
☐ 343	Charles Nagy	.10	.05	.01
☐ 344	Julian Tavarez	.10	.05	.01
☐ 345	Kimera Bartee	.10	.05	.01
☐ 346	Greg Keagle	.10	.05	.01
☐ 347	Mark Lewis	.10	.05	.01
☐ 348	Jose Lima	.10	.05	.01
☐ 349	Melvin Nieves	.25	.11	.03
☐ 350	Mark Parent	.10	.05	.01
☐ 351	Eddie Williams	.10	.05	.01
☐ 352	Johnny Damon	.10	.05	.01
☐ 353	Sal Fasano	.10	.05	.01
☐ 354	Mark Gubicza	.10	.05	.01
☐ 355	Bob Hamelin	.10	.05	.01
☐ 356	Chris Haney	.10	.05	.01
☐ 357	Keith Lockhart	.10	.05	.01
☐ 358	Mike Macfarlane	.10	.05	.01
☐ 359	Jose Offerman	.10	.05	.01
☐ 360	Bip Roberts	.10	.05	.01
☐ 361	Michael Tucker	.25	.11	.03
☐ 362	Chuck Carr	.10	.05	.01
☐ 363	Bobby Hughes	.10	.05	.01
☐ 364	John Jaha	.10	.05	.01
☐ 365	Mark Loretta	.10	.05	.01
☐ 366	Mike Matheny	.10	.05	.01
☐ 367	Ben McDonald	.10	.05	.01
☐ 368	Matt Mieske	.10	.05	.01
☐ 369	Angel Miranda	.10	.05	.01
☐ 370	Fernando Vina	.10	.05	.01
☐ 371	Rick Aguilera	.10	.05	.01
☐ 372	Rich Becker	.10	.05	.01
☐ 373	LaTroy Hawkins	.10	.05	.01
☐ 374	Dave Hollins	.10	.05	.01
☐ 375	Roberto Kelly	.10	.05	.01
☐ 376	Matt Lawton	.10	.05	.01
☐ 377	Paul Molitor	.60	.25	.07
☐ 378	Dan Naulty	.10	.05	.01
☐ 379	Rich Robertson	.10	.05	.01
☐ 380	Frank Rodriguez	.10	.05	.01
☐ 381	David Cone	.50	.23	.06
☐ 382	Mariano Duncan	.10	.05	.01
☐ 383	Andy Fox	.10	.05	.01
☐ 384	Joe Girardi	.10	.05	.01
☐ 385	Dwight Gooden	.50	.23	.06
☐ 386	Derek Jeter	2.00	.90	.25
☐ 387	Pat Kelly	.10	.05	.01
☐ 388	Jimmy Key	.25	.11	.03
☐ 389	Matt Luke	.10	.05	.01
☐ 390	Tino Martinez	.50	.23	.06
☐ 391	Jeff Nelson	.10	.05	.01
☐ 392	Melido Perez	.10	.05	.01
☐ 393	Tim Raines	.50	.23	.06
☐ 394	Ruben Rivera	.60	.25	.07
☐ 395	Kenny Rogers	.10	.05	.01
☐ 396	Tony Batista	.10	.05	.01
☐ 397	Allen Battle	.10	.05	.01
☐ 398	Mike Bordick	.25	.11	.03
☐ 399	Steve Cox	.10	.05	.01
☐ 400	Jason Giambi	.50	.23	.06
☐ 401	Doug Johns	.10	.05	.01
☐ 402	Pedro Munoz	.10	.05	.01
☐ 403	Phil Plantier	.10	.05	.01
☐ 404	Scott Spiezio	.10	.05	.01
☐ 405	George Williams	.10	.05	.01
☐ 406	Ernie Young	.10	.05	.01
☐ 407	Darren Bragg	.10	.05	.01
☐ 408	Jay Buhner	.50	.23	.06
☐ 409	Norm Charlton	.10	.05	.01
☐ 410	Russ Davis	.10	.05	.01
☐ 411	Sterling Hitchcock	.10	.05	.01
☐ 412	Edwin Hurtado	.10	.05	.01
☐ 413	Raul Ibanez	.10	.05	.01
☐ 414	Mike Jackson	.10	.05	.01
☐ 415	Luis Sojo	.10	.05	.01
☐ 416	Paul Sorrento	.10	.05	.01
☐ 417	Bob Wolcott	.10	.05	.01
☐ 418	Damon Buford	.10	.05	.01
☐ 419	Kevin Gross	.10	.05	.01
☐ 420	Darryl Hamilton UER	.10	.05	.01
☐ 421	Mike Henneman	.10	.05	.01
☐ 422	Ken Hill	.25	.11	.03
☐ 423	Dean Palmer	.50	.23	.06
☐ 424	Bobby Witt	.10	.05	.01
☐ 425	Tilson Brito	.10	.05	.01
☐ 426	Giovanni Carrara	.10	.05	.01
☐ 427	Domingo Cedeno	.10	.05	.01
☐ 428	Felipe Crespo	.10	.05	.01
☐ 429	Carlos Delgado	.50	.23	.06
☐ 430	Juan Guzman	.10	.05	.01
☐ 431	Erik Hanson	.10	.05	.01
☐ 432	Marty Janzen	.10	.05	.01
☐ 433	Otis Nixon	.10	.05	.01
☐ 434	Robert Perez	.10	.05	.01
☐ 435	Paul Quantrill	.10	.05	.01
☐ 436	Bill Risley	.10	.05	.01
☐ 437	Steve Avery	.25	.11	.03
☐ 438	Jermaine Dye	.75	.35	.09
☐ 439	Mark Lemke	.10	.05	.01
☐ 440	Marty Malloy	.10	.05	.01
☐ 441	Fred McGriff	.50	.23	.06
☐ 442	Greg McMichael	.10	.05	.01
☐ 443	Wonderful Monds	.10	.05	.01
☐ 444	Eddie Perez	.10	.05	.01
☐ 445	Jason Schmidt	.25	.11	.03
☐ 446	Terrell Wade	.50	.23	.06
☐ 447	Terry Adams	.10	.05	.01
☐ 448	Scott Bullett	.10	.05	.01
☐ 449	Robin Jennings	.10	.05	.01
☐ 450	Doug Jones	.10	.05	.01
☐ 451	Brooks Kieschnick	.10	.05	.01
☐ 452	Dave Magadan	.10	.05	.01
☐ 453	Jason Maxwell	.10	.05	.01
☐ 454	Brian McRae	.10	.05	.01
☐ 455	Rodney Myers	.10	.05	.01
☐ 456	Jaime Navarro	.10	.05	.01
☐ 457	Ryne Sandberg	.50	.23	.06
☐ 458	Vince Coleman	.10	.05	.01
☐ 459	Eric Davis	.25	.11	.03
☐ 460	Steve Gibralter	.10	.05	.01
☐ 461	Thomas Howard	.10	.05	.01
☐ 462	Mike Kelly	.10	.05	.01
☐ 463	Hal Morris	.10	.05	.01
☐ 464	Eric Owens	.10	.05	.01
☐ 465	Jose Rijo	.10	.05	.01
☐ 466	Chris Sabo	.10	.05	.01
☐ 467	Eddie Taubensee	.10	.05	.01
☐ 468	Trenidad Hubbard	.10	.05	.01
☐ 469	Curt Leskanic	.10	.05	.01
☐ 470	Quinton McCracken	.10	.05	.01
☐ 471	Jayhawk Owens	.10	.05	.01
☐ 472	Steve Reed	.10	.05	.01
☐ 473	Bryan Rekar	.10	.05	.01
☐ 474	Bruce Ruffin	.10	.05	.01
☐ 475	Bret Saberhagen	.10	.05	.01
☐ 476	Walt Weiss	.10	.05	.01
☐ 477	Eric Young	.10	.05	.01
☐ 478	Kevin Brown	.10	.05	.01
☐ 479	Al Leiter	.10	.05	.01
☐ 480	Pat Rapp	.10	.05	.01
☐ 481	Gary Sheffield	.50	.23	.06
☐ 482	Devon White	.10	.05	.01
☐ 483	Bob Abreu	.50	.23	.06
☐ 484	Sean Berry	.10	.05	.01
☐ 485	Craig Biggio	.50	.23	.06
☐ 486	Jim Dougherty	.10	.05	.01
☐ 487	Richard Hidalgo	.10	.05	.01
☐ 488	Darryl Kile	.10	.05	.01
☐ 489	Derrick May	.10	.05	.01
☐ 490	Greg Swindell	.10	.05	.01
☐ 491	Rick Wilkins	.10	.05	.01
☐ 492	Mike Blowers	.10	.05	.01
☐ 493	Tom Candiotti	.10	.05	.01
☐ 494	Roger Cedeno	.25	.11	.03
☐ 495	Delino DeShields	.10	.05	.01
☐ 496	Greg Gagne	.10	.05	.01
☐ 497	Karim Garcia	.60	.25	.07
☐ 498	Wilton Guerrero	.60	.25	.07
☐ 499	Chan Ho Park	.50	.23	.06
☐ 500	Isreal Alcantara	.10	.05	.01
☐ 501	Shane Andrews	.10	.05	.01
☐ 502	Yamil Benitez	.10	.05	.01
☐ 503	Cliff Floyd	.10	.05	.01
☐ 504	Mark Grudzielanek	.10	.05	.01
☐ 505	Ryan McGuire	.10	.05	.01
☐ 506	Sherman Obando	.10	.05	.01
☐ 507	Jose Paniagua	.10	.05	.01
☐ 508	Henry Rodriguez	.50	.23	.06
☐ 509	Kirk Rueter	.10	.05	.01
☐ 510	Juan Acevedo	.10	.05	.01
☐ 511	John Franco	.10	.05	.01

□ 512 Bernard Gilkey	.25	.11	.03
□ 513 Lance Johnson	.25	.11	.03
□ 514 Rey Ordonez	.60	.25	.07
□ 515 Robert Person	.10	.05	.01
□ 516 Paul Wilson	.25	.11	.03
□ 517 Toby Borland	.10	.05	.01
□ 518 David Doster	.10	.05	.01
□ 519 Lenny Dykstra	.25	.11	.03
□ 520 Sid Fernandez	.10	.05	.01
□ 521 Mike Grace	.10	.05	.01
□ 522 Rich Hunter	.10	.05	.01
□ 523 Benito Santiago	.10	.05	.01
□ 524 Gene Schall	.10	.05	.01
□ 525 Curt Schilling	.10	.05	.01
□ 526 Kevin Sefcik	.10	.05	.01
□ 527 Lee Tinsley	.10	.05	.01
□ 528 David West	.10	.05	.01
□ 529 Mark Whiten	.10	.05	.01
□ 530 Todd Zeile	.25	.11	.03
□ 531 Carlos Garcia	.10	.05	.01
□ 532 Charlie Hayes	.10	.05	.01
□ 533 Jason Kendall	.50	.23	.06
□ 534 Jeff King	.25	.11	.03
□ 535 Mike Kingery	.10	.05	.01
□ 536 Nelson Liriano	.10	.05	.01
□ 537 Dan Plesac	.10	.05	.01
□ 538 Paul Wagner	.10	.05	.01
□ 539 Luis Alicea	.10	.05	.01
□ 540 David Bell	.10	.05	.01
□ 541 Alan Benes	.50	.23	.06
□ 542 Andy Benes	.10	.05	.01
□ 543 Mike Busby	.10	.05	.01
□ 544 Royce Clayton	.10	.05	.01
□ 545 Dennis Eckersley	.50	.23	.06
□ 546 Gary Gaetti	.25	.11	.03
□ 547 Ron Gant	.50	.23	.06
□ 548 Aaron Holbert	.10	.05	.01
□ 549 Ray Lankford	.50	.23	.06
□ 550 T.J. Mathews	.10	.05	.01
□ 551 Willie McGee	.10	.05	.01
□ 552 Miguel Mejia	.40	.18	.05
□ 553 Todd Stottlemyre	.10	.05	.01
□ 554 Sean Bergman	.10	.05	.01
□ 555 Willie Blair	.10	.05	.01
□ 556 Andujar Cedeno	.10	.05	.01
□ 557 Steve Finley	.50	.23	.06
□ 558 Rickey Henderson	.50	.23	.06
□ 559 Wally Joyner	.10	.05	.01
□ 560 Scott Livingstone	.10	.05	.01
□ 561 Marc Newfield	.25	.11	.03
□ 562 Bob Tewksbury	.10	.05	.01
□ 563 Fernando Valenzuela	.25	.11	.03
□ 564 Rod Beck	.10	.05	.01
□ 565 Doug Creek	.10	.05	.01
□ 566 Shawon Dunston	.10	.05	.01
□ 567 Osvaldo Fernandez	.25	.11	.03
□ 568 Stan Javier	.10	.05	.01
□ 569 Marcus Jensen	.10	.05	.01
□ 570 Steve Scarsone	.10	.05	.01
□ 571 Robby Thompson	.10	.05	.01
□ 572 Allen Watson	.10	.05	.01
□ 573 Roberto Alomar STA	.50	.23	.06
□ 574 Jeff Bagwell STA	.60	.25	.07
□ 575 Albert Belle STA	.75	.35	.09
□ 576 Wade Boggs STA	.50	.23	.06
□ 577 Barry Bonds STA	.50	.23	.06
□ 578 Juan Gonzalez STA	.75	.35	.09
□ 579 Ken Griffey Jr. STA	1.50	.70	.19
□ 580 Tony Gwynn STA	.60	.25	.07
□ 581 Randy Johnson STA	.50	.23	.06
□ 582 Chipper Jones STA	1.00	.45	.12
□ 583 Barry Larkin STA	.50	.23	.06
□ 584 Kenny Lofton STA	.50	.23	.06
□ 585 Greg Maddux STA	1.00	.45	.12
□ 586 Raul Mondesi STA	.25	.11	.03
□ 587 Mike Piazza STA	1.00	.45	.12
□ 588 Cal Ripken STA	1.25	.55	.16
□ 589 Tim Salmon STA	.25	.11	.03
□ 590 Frank Thomas STA	1.50	.70	.19
□ 591 Mo Vaughn STA	.50	.23	.06
□ 592 Matt Williams STA	.50	.23	.06
□ 593 Marty Cordova RAW	.25	.11	.03
□ 594 Jim Edmonds RAW	.25	.11	.03
□ 595 Cliff Floyd RAW	.10	.05	.01
□ 596 Chipper Jones RAW	1.00	.45	.12
□ 597 Ryan Klesko RAW	.25	.11	.03
□ 598 Raul Mondesi RAW	.25	.11	.03
□ 599 Manny Ramirez RAW	.25	.11	.03
□ 600 Ruben Rivera RAW	.25	.11	.03

1996 Ultra Call to the Hall

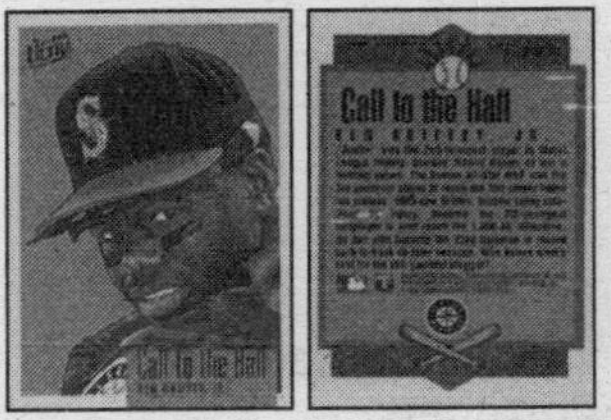

Randomly inserted in packs at a rate of one in 24, this ten-card set features original illustrations of possible future Hall of Famers. The backs state why the player is a possible HOF.

	MINT	NRMT	EXC
COMPLETE SET (10)	80.00	36.00	10.00
COMMON CARD (1-10)	2.00	.90	.25
*GOLD MEDALLION: 3X BASIC CARDS			
RANDOM INSERTS IN SER.2 PACKS			
□ 1 Barry Bonds	5.00	2.20	.60
□ 2 Ken Griffey Jr.	20.00	9.00	2.50
□ 3 Tony Gwynn	8.00	3.60	1.00
□ 4 Rickey Henderson	2.00	.90	.25
□ 5 Greg Maddux	12.00	5.50	1.50
□ 6 Eddie Murray	5.00	2.20	.60
□ 7 Cal Ripken	15.00	6.75	1.85
□ 8 Ryne Sandberg	5.00	2.20	.60
□ 9 Ozzie Smith	4.00	1.80	.50
□ 10 Frank Thomas	20.00	9.00	2.50

1996 Ultra Checklists

Randomly inserted in packs, this set of 10 standard-size cards features superstars of the game. Fronts are full-bleed color action photos of players with "Checklist" written in gold foil across the card. The horizontal backs are numbered and show the different card sets that are included in the Ultra line. The cards are sequenced in alphabetical order. A gold medallion parallel version of each card was issued. These cards are valued at two to three times regular cards.

	MINT	NRMT	EXC
COMPLETE SERIES 1 (10)	10.00	4.50	1.25
COMPLETE SERIES 2 (10)	10.00	4.50	1.25
COMMON SERIES 1 (A1-A10)	.50	.23	.06
COMMON SERIES 2 (B1-B10)	.50	.23	.06
*GOLD MEDALLION: 3X BASIC CARDS			
RANDOM INSERTS IN BOTH SERIES PACKS			
□ A1 Jeff Bagwell	1.50	.70	.19
□ A2 Barry Bonds	1.00	.45	.12

		MINT	NRMT	EXC
□ A3	Juan Gonzalez	2.00	.90	.25
□ A4	Ken Griffey Jr.	4.00	1.80	.50
□ A5	Chipper Jones	2.50	1.10	.30
□ A6	Mike Piazza	2.50	1.10	.30
□ A7	Manny Ramirez	.75	.35	.09
□ A8	Cal Ripken	3.00	1.35	.35
□ A9	Frank Thomas	4.00	1.80	.50
□ A10	Matt Williams	.50	.23	.06
□ B1	Albert Belle	2.00	.90	.25
□ B2	Cecil Fielder	.50	.23	.06
□ B3	Ken Griffey Jr.	4.00	1.80	.50
□ B4	Tony Gwynn	1.50	.70	.19
□ B5	Derek Jeter	2.50	1.10	.30
□ B6	Jason Kendall	.50	.23	.06
□ B7	Ryan Klesko	.75	.35	.09
□ B8	Greg Maddux	2.50	1.10	.30
□ B9	Cal Ripken	3.00	1.35	.35
□ B10	Frank Thomas	4.00	1.80	.50

1996 Ultra Diamond Producers

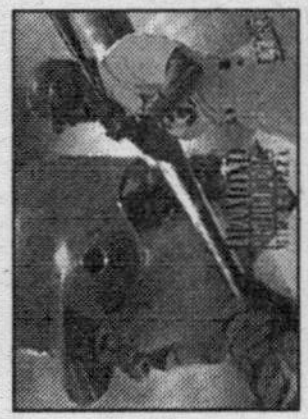

This 12-card standard-size set highlights the achievements of Major League stars. The cards were randomly inserted at a rate of one in 20. The horizontal fronts show the player close-up and an action photo on a metallic-silver paper. "Diamond Producers" and the player's name are printed in silver foil at the bottom of the card. The backs feature the player in an action shot on the left half and a white on black description of the player's career achievements. The cards are sequenced in alphabetical order and there are also gold medallion versions of these cards. The gold medallion versions are valued at two to three times the regular cards.

	MINT	NRMT	EXC
COMPLETE SET (12)	60.00	27.00	7.50
COMMON CARD (1-12)	2.00	.90	.25
*GOLD MEDALLION: 3X BASIC CARDS			
RANDOM INSERTS IN SER.1 PACKS			

		MINT	NRMT	EXC
□ 1	Albert Belle	8.00	3.60	1.00
□ 2	Barry Bonds	4.00	1.80	.50
□ 3	Ken Griffey Jr.	15.00	6.75	1.85
□ 4	Tony Gwynn	6.00	2.70	.75
□ 5	Greg Maddux	10.00	4.50	1.25
□ 6	Hideo Nomo	4.00	1.80	.50
□ 7	Mike Piazza	10.00	4.50	1.25
□ 8	Kirby Puckett	5.00	2.20	.60
□ 9	Cal Ripken	12.00	5.50	1.50
□ 10	Frank Thomas	15.00	6.75	1.85
□ 11	Mo Vaughn	4.00	1.80	.50
□ 12	Matt Williams	2.00	.90	.25

1996 Ultra Fresh Foundations

Randomly inserted one every three packs, this 10-card standard-size set highlights the play of hot young players. The fronts feature the player in a full-color action cut-out with a red prismatic background. The Ultra seal, card title, player name and team are printed in silver-foil down the left side of the card. Backs are full-bleed color action shots with player information. The cards are sequenced in alphabetical order and there are also gold medallion versions of these cards. The gold medallion versions are valued at two to three times the regular cards.

	MINT	NRMT	EXC
COMPLETE SET (10)	5.00	2.20	.60
COMMON CARD (1-10)	.15	.07	.02
SEMISTARS	.30	.14	.04
*GOLD MEDALLION: 3X BASIC CARDS			
RANDOM INSERTS IN SER.1 PACKS			

		MINT	NRMT	EXC
□ 1	Garret Anderson	.30	.14	.04
□ 2	Marty Cordova	.30	.14	.04
□ 3	Jim Edmonds	.30	.14	.04
□ 4	Brian L.Hunter	.15	.07	.02
□ 5	Chipper Jones	2.00	.90	.25
□ 6	Ryan Klesko	.60	.25	.07
□ 7	Raul Mondesi	.30	.14	.04
□ 8	Hideo Nomo	.75	.35	.09
□ 9	Manny Ramirez	.75	.35	.09
□ 10	Rondell White	.15	.07	.02

1996 Ultra Golden Prospects

Randomly inserted at a rate of one in five hobby packs, this 10-card standard-size set features players who are likely to make it as major leaguers. The full-bleed fronts have team color-coded tinting over a stadium background. The player is featured in a horizontal action shot with the player's name and team name printed in gold foil. The horizontal backs also feature the minor leaguer in action and player information printed in white type. The cards are sequenced in alphabetical order and there are also gold medallion versions of these cards. The gold medallion versions are valued at two to three times the regular cards.

	MINT	NRMT	EXC
COMPLETE SET (10)	5.00	2.20	.60
COMMON CARD (1-10)	.25	.11	.03
*GOLD MEDALLION: 3X BASIC CARDS			
RANDOM INSERTS IN SER.1 HOBBY PACKS			

		MINT	NRMT	EXC
□ 1	Yamil Benitez	.25	.11	.03
□ 2	Alberto Castillo	.25	.11	.03
□ 3	Roger Cedeno	.50	.23	.06
□ 4	Johnny Damon	1.25	.55	.16
□ 5	Micah Franklin	.25	.11	.03
□ 6	Jason Giambi	1.50	.70	.19
□ 7	Jose Herrera	.25	.11	.03
□ 8	Derek Jeter	5.00	2.20	.60
□ 9	Kevin Jordan	.25	.11	.03
□ 10	Ruben Rivera	2.00	.90	.25

1996 Ultra Golden Prospects Hobby

Randomly inserted in hobby packs only at a rate of one in 72, this 15-card set is printed on

crystal card stock and showcases players awaiting their Major League debut. The backs carry some of their accomplishments in the Minor League.

	MINT	NRMT	EXC
COMPLETE SET (15)	125.00	55.00	15.50
COMMON CARD (1-15)	8.00	3.60	1.00
*GOLD MEDALLION: 3X BASIC CARDS			
RANDOM INSERTS IN SER.2 HOBBY PACKS			
□ 1 Bob Abreu	10.00	4.50	1.25
□ 2 Israel Alcantara	8.00	3.60	1.00
□ 3 Tony Batista	8.00	3.60	1.00
□ 4 Mike Cameron	15.00	6.75	1.85
□ 5 Steve Cox	8.00	3.60	1.00
□ 6 Jermaine Dye	20.00	9.00	2.50
□ 7 Wilton Guerrero	10.00	4.50	1.25
□ 8 Richard Hidalgo	12.00	5.50	1.50
□ 9 Raul Ibanez	8.00	3.60	1.00
□ 10 Marty Janzen	10.00	4.50	1.25
□ 11 Robin Jennings	8.00	3.60	1.00
□ 12 Jason Maxwell	8.00	3.60	1.00
□ 13 Scott McClain	8.00	3.60	1.00
□ 14 Wonderful Monds	8.00	3.60	1.00
□ 15 Chris Singleton	8.00	3.60	1.00

1996 Ultra Hitting Machines

Randomly inserted in second series packs at a rate of one in 288, this 10-card set features players who hit the ball hard and often. The fronts display color action player photos on a die-cut machine gear background. The backs carry a color player portrait and player information.

	MINT	NRMT	EXC
COMPLETE SET (10)	550.00	250.00	70.00
COMMON CARD (1-10)	20.00	9.00	2.50
*GOLD MEDALLION: 3X BASIC CARDS			
RANDOM INSERTS IN SER.2 PACKS			
□ 1 Albert Belle	75.00	34.00	9.50
□ 2 Barry Bonds	40.00	18.00	5.00
□ 3 Juan Gonzalez	75.00	34.00	9.50
□ 4 Ken Griffey Jr.	150.00	70.00	19.00
□ 5 Edgar Martinez	20.00	9.00	2.50
□ 6 Rafael Palmeiro	20.00	9.00	2.50
□ 7 Mike Piazza	100.00	45.00	12.50
□ 8 Tim Salmon	20.00	9.00	2.50
□ 9 Frank Thomas	150.00	70.00	19.00
□ 10 Matt Williams	20.00	9.00	2.50

1996 Ultra Home Run Kings

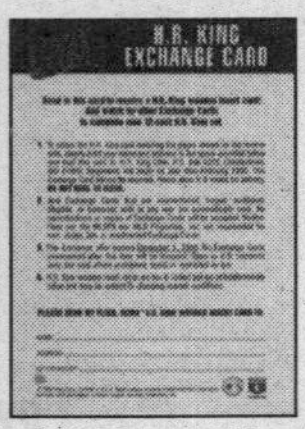

This 12-card standard-size set features leading power hitters. These cards were randomly inserted at a rate of one in 75 packs. The card fronts are thin wood with a color cut out of the player and HR KING printed diagonally in copper foil down the left side. The Fleer company was not happy with the final look of the card because of the transfer of the copper foil. Therefore all cards were made redemption cards. Backs of the cards have information about how to redeem the cards for replacement. The exchange offer expired on December 1, 1996. The cards are sequenced in alphabetical order. Gold medallion versions of these cards are valued as a multiple of the regular issue.

	MINT	NRMT	EXC
COMPLETE SET (12)	60.00	27.00	7.50
COMMON CARD (1-12)	2.50	1.10	.30
*GOLD MEDALLION: 6X TO 10X BASIC CARDS			
*REDEMPTION CARDS: 1X BASIC CARDS			
NNO RANDOM INSERTS IN SER.1 PACKS			
EXCHANGE DEADLINE: 12/1/96			
□ 1 Albert Belle	10.00	4.50	1.25
□ 2 Dante Bichette	2.50	1.10	.30
□ 3 Barry Bonds	5.00	2.20	.60
□ 4 Jose Canseco	4.00	1.80	.50
□ 5 Juan Gonzalez	10.00	4.50	1.25
□ 6 Ken Griffey Jr.	20.00	9.00	2.50
□ 7 Mark McGwire	6.00	2.70	.75
□ 8 Manny Ramirez	5.00	2.20	.60
□ 9 Tim Salmon	2.50	1.10	.30
□ 10 Frank Thomas	20.00	9.00	2.50
□ 11 Mo Vaughn	5.00	2.20	.60
□ 12 Matt Williams	4.00	1.80	.50

1996 Ultra On-Base Leaders

Randomly inserted in second series packs at a rate of one in four, this 10-card set features players with consistently high on-base percentage. The fronts display a color action player image on a black-and-white player background photo with images of bases along the side. The backs carry a color player portrait and player information.

	MINT	NRMT	EXC
COMPLETE SET (10)	6.00	2.70	.75
COMMON CARD (1-10)	.50	.23	.06
*GOLD MEDALLION: 3X BASIC CARDS			
RANDOM INSERTS IN SER.2 PACKS			
□ 1 Wade Boggs	.50	.23	.06
□ 2 Barry Bonds	1.00	.45	.12
□ 3 Tony Gwynn	1.50	.70	.19
□ 4 Rickey Henderson	.50	.23	.06
□ 5 Chuck Knoblauch	.50	.23	.06
□ 6 Edgar Martinez	.50	.23	.06
□ 7 Mike Piazza	2.50	1.10	.30
□ 8 Tim Salmon	.50	.23	.06
□ 9 Frank Thomas	4.00	1.80	.50
□ 10 Jim Thome	.75	.35	.09

1996 Ultra Power Plus

Randomly inserted at a rate of one in ten packs, this 12-card standard-size set features top all-around players. The horizontal fronts feature the player in two cut-out action photos against a multi-colored prismatic wheel background. The player's name and "Power Plus" are stamped in foil across the bottom. The backs are split between a full-color close-up shot of the player and player information printed in white type against a multi-colored circular background. The cards are sequenced in alphabetical order and gold medallion versions of these cards were also issued. The gold medallion versions are valued at two to three times the regular cards.

	MINT	NRMT	EXC
COMPLETE SET (12)	25.00	11.00	3.10
COMMON CARD (1-12)	1.00	.45	.12
*GOLD MEDALLION: 3X BASIC CARDS			
RANDOM INSERTS IN SER.1 PACKS			
□ 1 Jeff Bagwell	4.00	1.80	.50
□ 2 Barry Bonds	2.50	1.10	.30
□ 3 Ken Griffey Jr.	10.00	4.50	1.25
□ 4 Raul Mondesi	1.00	.45	.12
□ 5 Rafael Palmeiro	1.00	.45	.12
□ 6 Mike Piazza	6.00	2.70	.75
□ 7 Manny Ramirez	2.50	1.10	.30
□ 8 Tim Salmon	1.00	.45	.12
□ 9 Reggie Sanders	1.00	.45	.12
□ 10 Frank Thomas	10.00	4.50	1.25
□ 11 Larry Walker	1.00	.45	.12
□ 12 Matt Williams	1.00	.45	.12

1996 Ultra Prime Leather

Eighteen outstanding defensive players are featured in this standard-size set which is inserted approximately one in every eight packs. The horizontal fronts feature a color cut-out shot of the player against an embossed leather-like background. The player's name and team are embossed across the bottom with a black shadow effect. The backs have player's achievements noted in black type with a red outline against a glossy leather background. The other half of the back is a full color shot of the player.

The cards are sequenced in alphabetical order and gold medallion versions of these cards were also issued. The gold medallion versions are valued at two to three times the regular cards.

	MINT	NRMT	EXC
COMPLETE SET (18)	30.00	13.50	3.70
COMMON CARD (1-18)	1.00	.45	.12
SEMISTARS	1.50	.70	.19
*GOLD MEDALLION: 3X BASIC CARDS			
RANDOM INSERTS IN SER.1 PACKS			
□ 1 Ivan Rodriguez	2.00	.90	.25
□ 2 Will Clark	1.50	.70	.19
□ 3 Roberto Alomar	2.50	1.10	.30
□ 4 Cal Ripken	8.00	3.60	1.00
□ 5 Wade Boggs	1.50	.70	.19
□ 6 Ken Griffey Jr.	10.00	4.50	1.25
□ 7 Kenny Lofton	2.50	1.10	.30
□ 8 Kirby Puckett	3.00	1.35	.35
□ 9 Tim Salmon	1.00	.45	.12
□ 10 Mike Piazza	6.00	2.70	.75
□ 11 Mark Grace	1.50	.70	.19
□ 12 Craig Biggio	1.50	.70	.19
□ 13 Barry Larkin	1.50	.70	.19
□ 14 Matt Williams	1.50	.70	.19
□ 15 Barry Bonds	2.50	1.10	.30
□ 16 Tony Gwynn	4.00	1.80	.50
□ 17 Brian McRae	1.00	.45	.12
□ 18 Raul Mondesi	1.50	.70	.19

1996 Ultra Rawhide

Randomly inserted in second series packs at a rate of one in 8, this 10-card set features leading defensive players. The embossed cards feature the Ultra logo, the word "Rawhide" and the players name against a background of a glove. The back gives a description of the player's defensive abilities.

	MINT	NRMT	EXC
COMPLETE SET (10)	20.00	9.00	2.50
COMMON CARD (1-10)	1.00	.45	.12
*GOLD MEDALLION: 3X BASIC CARDS			
RANDOM INSERTS IN SER.2 PACKS			
□ 1 Roberto Alomar	1.50	.70	.19
□ 2 Barry Bonds	1.50	.70	.19
□ 3 Mark Grace	1.00	.45	.12
□ 4 Ken Griffey Jr.	6.00	2.70	.75
□ 5 Kenny Lofton	1.50	.70	.19

	MINT	NRMT	EXC
□ 6 Greg Maddux	4.00	1.80	.50
□ 7 Raul Mondesi	1.00	.45	.12
□ 8 Mike Piazza	4.00	1.80	.50
□ 9 Cal Ripken	5.00	2.20	.60
□ 10 Matt Williams	1.00	.45	.12

1996 Ultra RBI Kings

This 10-card standard-size set was randomly inserted at a rate of one in five retail packs. This set features top run producers. The full-color, full-bleed fronts feature player cutouts set against a background of baseballs. The player's name and team logo are printed in silver foil across the bottom. The backs show the players on a full-bleed surface with baseballs in the background and player name and accomplishments printed in white with a white box surrounding the type. The cards are sequenced in alphabetical order and gold medallion versions of these cards were also issued. The gold medallion versions are valued at two to three times the regular cards.

	MINT	NRMT	EXC
COMPLETE SET (10)	40.00	18.00	5.00
COMMON CARD (1-10)	2.50	1.10	.30
*GOLD MEDALLION: 3X BASIC CARDS			
RANDOM INSERTS IN SER.1 RETAIL PACKS			
□ 1 Derek Bell	2.50	1.10	.30
□ 2 Albert Belle	12.00	5.50	1.50
□ 3 Dante Bichette	2.50	1.10	.30
□ 4 Barry Bonds	6.00	2.70	.75
□ 5 Jim Edmonds	2.50	1.10	.30
□ 6 Manny Ramirez	6.00	2.70	.75
□ 7 Reggie Sanders	2.50	1.10	.30
□ 8 Sammy Sosa	4.00	1.80	.50
□ 9 Frank Thomas	25.00	11.00	3.10
□ 10 Mo Vaughn	6.00	2.70	.75

1996 Ultra Respect

Randomly inserted in second series packs at a rate of one in 18, this 10-card set features players who are well regarded by their peers for both on and off field activies. The fronts consist of a player photo with the word "Respect" as well as his name and the Ultra logo on the right. The back has another player photo as well as reasons why the player has earned his reputation.

	MINT	NRMT	EXC
COMPLETE SET (10)	60.00	27.00	7.50
COMMON CARD (1-10)	1.50	.70	.19
*GOLD MEDALLION: 3X BASIC CARDS			
RANDOM INSERTS IN SER.1 PACKS			
□ 1 Joe Carter	1.50	.70	.19
□ 2 Ken Griffey Jr.	15.00	6.75	1.85
□ 3 Tony Gwynn	6.00	2.70	.75
□ 4 Greg Maddux	10.00	4.50	1.25
□ 5 Eddie Murray	4.00	1.80	.50
□ 6 Kirby Puckett	5.00	2.20	.60
□ 7 Cal Ripken	12.00	5.50	1.50
□ 8 Ryne Sandberg	4.00	1.80	.50
□ 9 Frank Thomas	15.00	6.75	1.85
□ 10 Mo Vaughn	4.00	1.80	.50

1996 Ultra Rising Stars

Randomly inserted in second series packs at a rate of one in 4, this 10-card set features leadgin players of tomorrow. The fronts have a player photo superimposed on a stadium background. The words "Rising Star" as well as the player's name and the Ultra logo are in the middle of the front. The back has another player photo and informaton on the future of these young stars.

	MINT	NRMT	EXC
COMPLETE SET (10)	5.00	2.20	.60
COMMON CARD (1-10)	.25	.11	.03
SEMISTARS	.50	.23	.06
*GOLD MEDALLION: 3X BASIC CARDS			
RANDOM INSERTS IN SER.2 PACKS			
□ 1 Garret Anderson	.25	.11	.03
□ 2 Marty Cordova	.50	.23	.06
□ 3 Jim Edmonds	.50	.23	.06
□ 4 Cliff Floyd	.25	.11	.03
□ 5 Brian L.Hunter	.25	.11	.03
□ 6 Chipper Jones	2.50	1.10	.30
□ 7 Ryan Klesko	.75	.35	.09
□ 8 Hideo Nomo	1.00	.45	.12
□ 9 Manny Ramirez	1.00	.45	.12
□ 10 Rondell White	.25	.11	.03

1996 Ultra Season Crowns

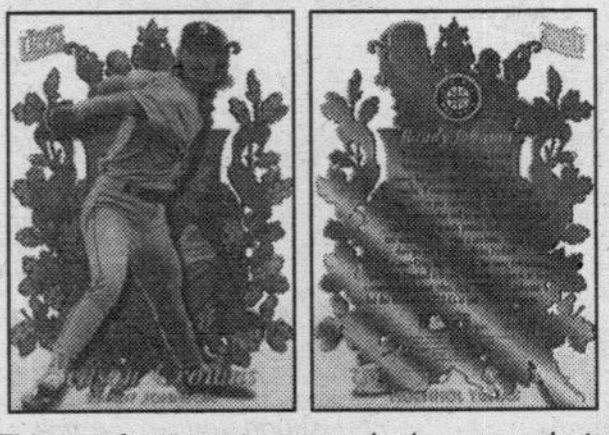

This set features ten award winners and stat leaders. The cards were randomly inserted at a rate of one in ten. The clear acetate cards fea-

ture a full-color player cutout against a background of colored foliage and laurels. Backs include the player's 1995 statistics and other facts on a multi-colored background. The cards are sequenced in alphabetical order and gold medallion versions of these cards were also issued. The gold medallion versions are valued at two to three times the regular cards.

	MINT	NRMT	EXC
COMPLETE SET (10)	35.00	16.00	4.40
COMMON CARD (1-10)	.50	.23	.06
*GOLD MEDALLION: 3X BASIC CARDS			
RANDOM INSERTS IN SER.1 PACKS			

	MINT	NRMT	EXC
□ 1 Barry Bonds	2.50	1.10	.30
□ 2 Tony Gwynn	4.00	1.80	.50
□ 3 Randy Johnson	1.50	.70	.19
□ 4 Kenny Lofton	2.50	1.10	.30
□ 5 Greg Maddux	6.00	2.70	.75
□ 6 Edgar Martinez	.75	.35	.09
□ 7 Hideo Nomo	2.50	1.10	.30
□ 8 Cal Ripken	8.00	3.60	1.00
□ 9 Frank Thomas	10.00	4.50	1.25
□ 10 Tim Wakefield	.50	.23	.06

1996 Ultra Thunderclap

Randomly inserted one in 72 retail packs, these cards feature the leading power hitters. The player's photo is against a background of thunder and lightning and the words "Thunder Clap" and the player's name are on the bottom. The back consists of another player photo as well as a biography as to the player's power skills.

	MINT	NRMT	EXC
COMPLETE SET (20)	300.00	135.00	38.00
COMMON CARD (1-20)	6.00	2.70	.75
*GOLD MEDALLION: 3X BASIC CARDS			
RANDOM INSERTS IN SER.2 RETAIL PACKS			

	MINT	NRMT	EXC
□ 1 Albert Belle	30.00	13.50	3.70
□ 2 Barry Bonds	15.00	6.75	1.85
□ 3 Bobby Bonilla	6.00	2.70	.75
□ 4 Jose Canseco	8.00	3.60	1.00
□ 5 Joe Carter	6.00	2.70	.75
□ 6 Will Clark	8.00	3.60	1.00
□ 7 Andre Dawson	6.00	2.70	.75
□ 8 Cecil Fielder	6.00	2.70	.75
□ 9 Andres Galarraga	8.00	3.60	1.00
□ 10 Juan Gonzalez	30.00	13.50	3.70
□ 11 Ken Griffey Jr.	60.00	27.00	7.50
□ 12 Fred McGriff	8.00	3.60	1.00
□ 13 Mark McGwire	20.00	9.00	2.50
□ 14 Eddie Murray	15.00	6.75	1.85
□ 15 Rafael Palmeiro	8.00	3.60	1.00
□ 16 Kirby Puckett	20.00	9.00	2.50
□ 17 Cal Ripken	50.00	22.00	6.25
□ 18 Ryne Sandberg	15.00	6.75	1.85
□ 19 Frank Thomas	60.00	27.00	7.50
□ 20 Matt Williams	8.00	3.60	1.00

1997 Ultra

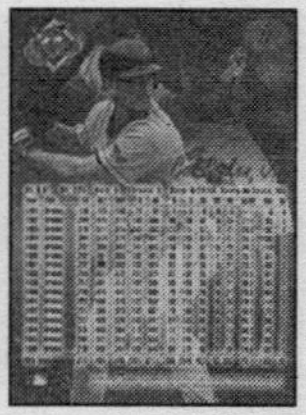

The 1997 Ultra first series totals 300 cards. The 10-card packs had a suggested retail price of 2.49 each. Each pack had two insert cards, with one insert being a gold medallion parallel and the other insert being from a group of nine different insert sets. As in most Fleer produced sets, the cards are arranged in alphabetical order by league, player and team.

	MINT	NRMT	EXC
COMPLETE SET (300)	30.00	13.50	3.70
COMMON CARD (1-300)	.10	.05	.01
SEMISTARS	.25	.11	.03
STARS	.50	.23	.06
COMP.G.MED.SER.1 (300)	150.00	70.00	19.00
COMMON G.MED. (1-300)	.25	.11	.03
*GOLD MEDALLION: 2X to 4X BASIC CARDS			
GOLD MEDALLION ONE PER PACK			
MEDALLIONS HAVE NEW PHOTOS			

	MINT	NRMT	EXC
□ 1 Roberto Alomar	.75	.35	.09
□ 2 Brady Anderson	.50	.23	.06
□ 3 Rocky Coppinger	.25	.11	.03
□ 4 Jeffrey Hammonds	.10	.05	.01
□ 5 Chris Hoiles	.10	.05	.01
□ 6 Eddie Murray	.75	.35	.09
□ 7 Mike Mussina	.60	.25	.07
□ 8 Jimmy Myers	.10	.05	.01
□ 9 Randy Myers	.10	.05	.01
□ 10 Arthur Rhodes	.10	.05	.01
□ 11 Cal Ripken Jr.	2.50	1.10	.30
□ 12 Jose Canseco	.50	.23	.06
□ 13 Roger Clemens	.50	.23	.06
□ 14 Tom Gordon	.10	.05	.01
□ 15 Jose Malave	.10	.05	.01
□ 16 Tim Naehring	.10	.05	.01
□ 17 Troy O'Leary	.10	.05	.01
□ 18 Bill Selby	.10	.05	.01
□ 19 Heathcliff Slocumb	.10	.05	.01
□ 20 Mike Stanley	.10	.05	.01
□ 21 Mo Vaughn	.75	.35	.09
□ 22 Garret Anderson	.25	.11	.03
□ 23 George Arias	.10	.05	.01
□ 24 Chili Davis	.25	.11	.03
□ 25 Jim Edmonds	.25	.11	.03
□ 26 Darin Erstad	1.50	.70	.19
□ 27 Chuck Finley	.10	.05	.01
□ 28 Todd Greene	.25	.11	.03
□ 29 Troy Percival	.25	.11	.03
□ 30 Tim Salmon	.50	.23	.06
□ 31 Jeff Schmidt	.10	.05	.01
□ 32 Randy Velarde	.10	.05	.01
□ 33 Shad Williams	.10	.05	.01
□ 34 Wilson Alvarez	.10	.05	.01
□ 35 Harold Baines	.25	.11	.03
□ 36 James Baldwin	.25	.11	.03
□ 37 Mike Cameron	.25	.11	.03
□ 38 Ray Durham	.10	.05	.01
□ 39 Ozzie Guillen	.10	.05	.01
□ 40 Roberto Hernandez	.10	.05	.01
□ 41 Darren Lewis	.10	.05	.01
□ 42 Jose Munoz	.10	.05	.01
□ 43 Tony Phillips	.25	.11	.03
□ 44 Frank Thomas	3.00	1.35	.35
□ 45 Sandy Alomar Jr.	.10	.05	.01
□ 46 Albert Belle	1.50	.70	.19
□ 47 Mark Carreon	.10	.05	.01
□ 48 Julio Franco	.25	.11	.03
□ 49 Orel Hershiser	.25	.11	.03
□ 50 Kenny Lofton	.75	.35	.09
□ 51 Jack McDowell	.25	.11	.03
□ 52 Jose Mesa	.25	.11	.03
□ 53 Charles Nagy	.25	.11	.03
□ 54 Manny Ramirez	.75	.35	.09

□	55 Julian Tavarez	.10	.05	.01
□	56 Omar Vizquel	.25	.11	.03
□	57 Raul Casanova	.10	.05	.01
□	58 Tony Clark	.25	.11	.03
□	59 Travis Fryman	.25	.11	.03
□	60 Bob Higginson	.25	.11	.03
□	61 Melvin Nieves	.10	.05	.01
□	62 Curtis Pride	.10	.05	.01
□	63 Justin Thompson	.10	.05	.01
□	64 Alan Trammell	.25	.11	.03
□	65 Kevin Appier	.25	.11	.03
□	66 Johnny Damon	.25	.11	.03
□	67 Keith Lockhart	.10	.05	.01
□	68 Jeff Montgomery	.10	.05	.01
□	69 Jose Offerman	.10	.05	.01
□	70 Bip Roberts	.10	.05	.01
□	71 Jose Rosado	.10	.05	.01
□	72 Chris Stynes	.10	.05	.01
□	73 Mike Sweeney	.10	.05	.01
□	74 Jeff Cirillo	.10	.05	.01
□	75 Jeff D'Amico	.25	.11	.03
□	76 John Jaha	.10	.05	.01
□	77 Scott Karl	.10	.05	.01
□	78 Mike Matheny	.10	.05	.01
□	79 Ben McDonald	.10	.05	.01
□	80 Matt Mieske	.10	.05	.01
□	81 Marc Newfield	.10	.05	.01
□	82 Dave Nilsson	.10	.05	.01
□	83 Jose Valentin	.10	.05	.01
□	84 Fernando Vina	.10	.05	.01
□	85 Rick Aguilera	.10	.05	.01
□	86 Marty Cordova	.25	.11	.03
□	87 Chuck Knoblauch	.50	.23	.06
□	88 Matt Lawton	.10	.05	.01
□	89 Pat Meares	.10	.05	.01
□	90 Paul Molitor	.60	.25	.07
□	91 Greg Myers	.10	.05	.01
□	92 Dan Naulty	.10	.05	.01
□	93 Kirby Puckett	1.00	.45	.12
□	94 Frank Rodriguez	.10	.05	.01
□	95 Wade Boggs	.50	.23	.06
□	96 Cecil Fielder	.25	.11	.03
□	97 Joe Girardi	.10	.05	.01
□	98 Dwight Gooden	.25	.11	.03
□	99 Derek Jeter	2.00	.90	.25
□	100 Tino Martinez	.25	.11	.03
□	101 Ramiro Mendoza	.10	.05	.01
□	102 Andy Pettitte	.75	.35	.09
□	103 Mariano Rivera	.25	.11	.03
□	104 Ruben Rivera	.50	.23	.06
□	105 Kenny Rogers	.10	.05	.01
□	106 Darryl Strawberry	.25	.11	.03
□	107 Bernie Williams	.50	.23	.06
□	108 Tony Batista	.10	.05	.01
□	109 Geronimo Berroa	.10	.05	.01
□	110 Bobby Chouinard	.10	.05	.01
□	111 Brent Gates	.10	.05	.01
□	112 Jason Giambi	.25	.11	.03
□	113 Damon Mashore	.10	.05	.01
□	114 Mark McGwire	1.00	.45	.12
□	115 Scott Spiezio	.10	.05	.01
□	116 John Wasdin	.10	.05	.01
□	117 Steve Wojciechowski	.10	.05	.01
□	118 Ernie Young	.10	.05	.01
□	119 Norm Charlton	.10	.05	.01
□	120 Joey Cora	.10	.05	.01
□	121 Ken Griffey Jr.	3.00	1.35	.35
□	122 Sterling Hitchcock	.10	.05	.01
□	123 Raul Ibanez	.10	.05	.01
□	124 Randy Johnson	.50	.23	.06
□	125 Edgar Martinez	.50	.23	.06
□	126 Alex Rodriguez	3.00	1.35	.35
□	127 Matt Wagner	.10	.05	.01
□	128 Bob Wells	.10	.05	.01
□	129 Dan Wilson	.10	.05	.01
□	130 Will Clark	.50	.23	.06
□	131 Kevin Elster	.10	.05	.01
□	132 Juan Gonzalez	1.50	.70	.19
□	133 Rusty Greer	.25	.11	.03
□	134 Darryl Hamilton	.10	.05	.01
□	135 Mike Henneman	.10	.05	.01
□	136 Ken Hill	.10	.05	.01
□	137 Mark McLemore	.10	.05	.01
□	138 Dean Palmer	.25	.11	.03
□	139 Roger Pavlik	.10	.05	.01
□	140 Ivan Rodriguez	.60	.25	.07
□	141 Joe Carter	.25	.11	.03
□	142 Carlos Delgado	.50	.23	.06
□	143 Alex Gonzalez	.10	.05	.01
□	144 Juan Guzman	.10	.05	.01
□	145 Pat Hentgen	.25	.11	.03
□	146 Marty Janzen	.10	.05	.01
□	147 Otis Nixon	.10	.05	.01
□	148 Charlie O'Brien	.10	.05	.01
□	149 John Olerud	.10	.05	.01
□	150 Robert Perez	.10	.05	.01
□	151 Jermaine Dye	.50	.23	.06
□	152 Tom Glavine	.50	.23	.06
□	153 Andruw Jones	3.00	1.35	.35
□	154 Chipper Jones	2.00	.90	.25
□	155 Ryan Klesko	.50	.23	.06
□	156 Javier Lopez	.25	.11	.03
□	157 Greg Maddux	2.00	.90	.25
□	158 Fred McGriff	.50	.23	.06
□	159 Wonderful Monds	.10	.05	.01
□	160 John Smoltz	.50	.23	.06
□	161 Terrell Wade	.10	.05	.01
□	162 Mark Wohlers	.25	.11	.03
□	163 Brant Brown	.10	.05	.01
□	164 Mark Grace	.50	.23	.06
□	165 Tyler Houston	.10	.05	.01
□	166 Robin Jennings	.10	.05	.01
□	167 Jason Maxwell	.10	.05	.01
□	168 Ryne Sandberg	.75	.35	.09
□	169 Sammy Sosa	.50	.23	.06
□	170 Amaury Telemaco	.10	.05	.01
□	171 Steve Trachsel	.10	.05	.01
□	172 Pedro Valdes	.10	.05	.01
□	173 Tim Belk	.10	.05	.01
□	174 Bret Boone	.10	.05	.01
□	175 Jeff Brantley	.10	.05	.01
□	176 Eric Davis	.10	.05	.01
□	177 Barry Larkin	.50	.23	.06
□	178 Chad Mottola	.10	.05	.01
□	179 Mark Portugal	.10	.05	.01
□	180 Reggie Sanders	.25	.11	.03
□	181 John Smiley	.10	.05	.01
□	182 Eddie Taubensee	.10	.05	.01
□	183 Dante Bichette	.50	.23	.06
□	184 Ellis Burks	.25	.11	.03
□	185 Andres Galarraga	.50	.23	.06
□	186 Curt Leskanic	.10	.05	.01
□	187 Quinton McCracken	.10	.05	.01
□	188 Jeff Reed	.10	.05	.01
□	189 Kevin Ritz	.10	.05	.01
□	190 Walt Weiss	.10	.05	.01
□	191 Jamey Wright	.10	.05	.01
□	192 Eric Young	.25	.11	.03
□	193 Kevin Brown	.25	.11	.03
□	194 Luis Castillo	.25	.11	.03
□	195 Jeff Conine	.25	.11	.03
□	196 Andre Dawson	.25	.11	.03
□	197 Charles Johnson	.25	.11	.03
□	198 Al Leiter	.10	.05	.01
□	199 Ralph Milliard	.10	.05	.01
□	200 Robb Nen	.10	.05	.01
□	201 Edgar Renteria	.50	.23	.06
□	202 Gary Sheffield	.50	.23	.06
□	203 Bob Abreu	.25	.11	.03
□	204 Jeff Bagwell	1.25	.55	.16
□	205 Derek Bell	.25	.11	.03
□	206 Sean Berry	.10	.05	.01
□	207 Richard Hidalgo	.25	.11	.03
□	208 Todd Jones	.10	.05	.01
□	209 Darryl Kile	.10	.05	.01
□	210 Orlando Miller	.10	.05	.01
□	211 Shane Reynolds	.10	.05	.01
□	212 Billy Wagner	.25	.11	.03
□	213 Donne Wall	.10	.05	.01
□	214 Roger Cedeno	.10	.05	.01
□	215 Greg Gagne	.10	.05	.01
□	216 Karim Garcia	.60	.25	.07
□	217 Wilton Guerrero	.25	.11	.03
□	218 Todd Hollandsworth	.25	.11	.03
□	219 Ramon Martinez	.25	.11	.03
□	220 Raul Mondesi	.25	.11	.03
□	221 Hideo Nomo	.75	.35	.09
□	222 Chan Ho Park	.25	.11	.03
□	223 Mike Piazza	2.00	.90	.25
□	224 Ismael Valdes	.25	.11	.03
□	225 Moises Alou	.25	.11	.03
□	226 Derek Aucoin	.10	.05	.01

□ 227 Yamil Benitez	.10	.05	.01
□ 228 Jeff Fassero	.10	.05	.01
□ 229 Darrin Fletcher	.10	.05	.01
□ 230 Mark Grudzielanek	.10	.05	.01
□ 231 Barry Manuel	.10	.05	.01
□ 232 Pedro Martinez	.25	.11	.03
□ 233 Henry Rodriguez	.25	.11	.03
□ 234 Ugueth Urbina	.10	.05	.01
□ 235 Rondell White	.25	.11	.03
□ 236 Carlos Baerga	.25	.11	.03
□ 237 John Franco	.10	.05	.01
□ 238 Bernard Gilkey	.25	.11	.03
□ 239 Todd Hundley	.25	.11	.03
□ 240 Butch Huskey	.10	.05	.01
□ 241 Jason Isringhausen	.10	.05	.01
□ 242 Lance Johnson	.25	.11	.03
□ 243 Bobby Jones	.10	.05	.01
□ 244 Alex Ochoa	.25	.11	.03
□ 245 Rey Ordonez	.50	.23	.06
□ 246 Paul Wilson	.25	.11	.03
□ 247 Ron Blazier	.10	.05	.01
□ 248 David Doster	.10	.05	.01
□ 249 Jim Eisenreich	.10	.05	.01
□ 250 Mike Grace	.10	.05	.01
□ 251 Mike Lieberthal	.10	.05	.01
□ 252 Wendell Magee	.10	.05	.01
□ 253 Mickey Morandini	.10	.05	.01
□ 254 Ricky Otero	.10	.05	.01
□ 255 Scott Rolen	1.00	.45	.12
□ 256 Curt Schilling	.10	.05	.01
□ 257 Todd Zeile	.10	.05	.01
□ 258 Jermaine Allensworth	.10	.05	.01
□ 259 Trey Beamon	.10	.05	.01
□ 260 Carlos Garcia	.10	.05	.01
□ 261 Mark Johnson	.10	.05	.01
□ 262 Jason Kendall	.25	.11	.03
□ 263 Jeff King	.10	.05	.01
□ 264 Al Martin	.10	.05	.01
□ 265 Denny Neagle	.25	.11	.03
□ 266 Matt Reubel	.10	.05	.01
□ 267 Marc Wilkins	.10	.05	.01
□ 268 Alan Benes	.25	.11	.03
□ 269 Dennis Eckersley	.25	.11	.03
□ 270 Ron Gant	.25	.11	.03
□ 271 Aaron Holbert	.10	.05	.01
□ 272 Brian Jordan	.25	.11	.03
□ 273 Ray Lankford	.25	.11	.03
□ 274 John Mabry	.10	.05	.01
□ 275 T.J. Mathews	.10	.05	.01
□ 276 Ozzie Smith	.60	.25	.07
□ 277 Todd Stottlemyre	.10	.05	.01
□ 278 Mark Sweeney	.10	.05	.01
□ 279 Andy Ashby	.10	.05	.01
□ 280 Steve Finley	.25	.11	.03
□ 281 John Flaherty	.10	.05	.01
□ 282 Chris Gomez	.10	.05	.01
□ 283 Tony Gwynn	1.25	.55	.16
□ 284 Joey Hamilton	.25	.11	.03
□ 285 Rickey Henderson	.25	.11	.03
□ 286 Trevor Hoffman	.10	.05	.01
□ 287 Jason Thompson	.10	.05	.01
□ 288 Fernando Valenzuela	.25	.11	.03
□ 289 Greg Vaughn	.25	.11	.03
□ 290 Barry Bonds	.75	.35	.09
□ 291 Jay Canizaro	.10	.05	.01
□ 292 Jacob Cruz	.10	.05	.01
□ 293 Shawon Dunston	.10	.05	.01
□ 294 Shawn Estes	.10	.05	.01
□ 295 Mark Gardner	.10	.05	.01
□ 296 Marcus Jensen	.10	.05	.01
□ 297 Bill Mueller	.10	.05	.01
□ 298 Chris Singleton	.10	.05	.01
□ 299 Allen Watson	.10	.05	.01
□ 300 Matt Williams	.50	.23	.06

1997 Ultra Platinum Medallion Edition

This 300 card first series set is a parallel to the regular Ultra first series and cards were inserted one per 100 packs. Sparkling platinum lettering on front differentiates these cards from their far more common regular issue brethren. No set price is provided due to scarcity.

	MINT	NRMT	EXC
COMMON CARD (1-300)	10.00	4.50	1.25
SEMISTARS	20.00	9.00	2.50
*VETERAN STARS: 35X TO 60X HI			
*YOUNG STARS: 25X TO 50X HI			
RANDOM INSERTS IN PACKS			

□ 11 Cal Ripken	160.00	70.00	20.00
□ 26 Darin Erstad	100.00	45.00	12.50
□ 44 Frank Thomas	200.00	90.00	25.00
□ 46 Albert Belle	100.00	45.00	12.50
□ 93 Kirby Puckett	60.00	27.00	7.50
□ 99 Derek Jeter	120.00	55.00	15.00
□ 114 Mark McGwire	60.00	27.00	7.50
□ 121 Ken Griffey Jr.	200.00	90.00	25.00
□ 126 Alex Rodriguez	200.00	90.00	25.00
□ 132 Juan Gonzalez	100.00	45.00	12.50
□ 153 Andruw Jones	200.00	90.00	25.00
□ 154 Chipper Jones	120.00	55.00	15.00
□ 157 Greg Maddux	120.00	55.00	15.00
□ 204 Jeff Bagwell	80.00	36.00	10.00
□ 223 Mike Piazza	120.00	55.00	15.00
□ 283 Tony Gwynn	80.00	36.00	10.00

1997 Ultra Checklists

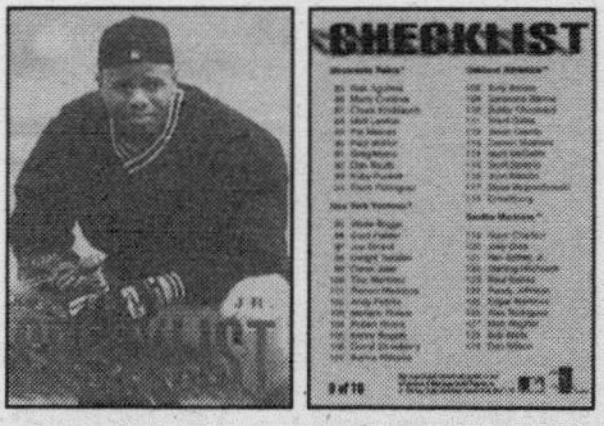

Randomly inserted in packs at a rate of one in four, this 10-card set features player photos on the front along with the word "Checklist", the player's name as well as the "ultra" logo on the bottom. The backs are checklists.

	MINT	NRMT	EXC
COMPLETE SET (10)	8.00	3.60	1.00
COMMON CARD (1-10)	.25	.11	.03
RANDOM INSERTS IN PACKS			

□ 1 Dante Bichette	.25	.11	.03
□ 2 Barry Bonds	.50	.23	.06
□ 3 Ken Griffey Jr.	2.00	.90	.25
□ 4 Greg Maddux	1.25	.55	.16
□ 5 Mark McGwire	.60	.25	.07
□ 6 Mike Piazza	1.25	.55	.16
□ 7 Cal Ripken	1.50	.70	.19
□ 8 John Smoltz	.25	.11	.03
□ 9 Sammy Sosa	.25	.11	.03
□ 10 Frank Thomas	2.00	.90	.25

1997 Ultra Diamond Producers

Randomly inserted in packs at a rate of one in 288, this 12-card set features "flannel" material mounted on card stock and attempt to look and feel like actual uniforms.

	MINT	NRMT	EXC
COMPLETE SET (12)	650.00	300.00	80.00
COMMON CARD (1-12)	20.00	9.00	2.50
RANDOM INSERTS IN PACKS			

□ 1 Jeff Bagwell	50.00	22.00	6.25
□ 2 Barry Bonds	30.00	13.50	3.70
□ 3 Ken Griffey Jr.	120.00	55.00	15.00
□ 4 Chipper Jones	80.00	36.00	10.00

□ 5 Kenny Lofton	30.00	13.50	3.70
□ 6 Greg Maddux	80.00	36.00	10.00
□ 7 Mark McGwire	40.00	18.00	5.00
□ 8 Mike Piazza	80.00	36.00	10.00
□ 9 Cal Ripken	100.00	45.00	12.50
□ 10 Alex Rodriguez	120.00	55.00	15.00
□ 11 Frank Thomas	120.00	55.00	15.00
□ 12 Matt Williams	20.00	9.00	2.50

1997 Ultra Double Trouble

Randomly inserted in packs at a rate of one in four, this 20-card set features two players from each team. The horizontal cards feature players photos with their names in silver foil on the bottom and the words "double trouble" on the top. The backs feature information on what the players contributed to their team in 1996.

	MINT	NRMT	EXC
COMPLETE SET (20)	25.00	11.00	3.10
COMMON CARD (1-20)	.50	.23	.06
SEMISTARS	.75	.35	.09
RANDOM INSERTS IN PACKS			

□ 1 Roberto Alomar	4.00	1.80	.50
Cal Ripken			
□ 2 Mo Vaughn	1.00	.45	.12
Jose Canseco			
□ 3 Jim Edmonds	.75	.35	.09
Jim Salmon			
□ 4 Harold Baines	3.00	1.35	.35
Frank Thomas			
□ 5 Albert Belle	3.00	1.35	.35
Kenny Lofton			
□ 6 Marty Cordova	.75	.35	.09
Chuck Knoblauch			
□ 7 Derek Jetter	3.00	1.35	.35
Andy Pettitte			
□ 8 Jason Giambi	1.50	.70	.19
Mark McGwire			
□ 9 Ken Griffey Jr.	8.00	3.60	1.00
Alex Rodriguez			
□ 10 Juan Gonzalez	2.50	1.10	.30
Will Clark			
□ 11 Greg Maddux	5.00	2.20	.60
Chipper Jones			
□ 12 Mark Grace	.75	.35	.09
Sammy Sosa			
□ 13 Dante Bichette	.75	.35	.09
Andres Galarraga			
□ 14 Jeff Bagwell	2.00	.90	.25
Derek Bell			
□ 15 Hideo Nomo	3.00	1.35	.35
Mike Piazza			
□ 16 Henry Rodriguez	.50	.23	.06
Moises Alou			
□ 17 Rey Ordonez	.50	.23	.06
Alex Ochoa			
□ 18 Ray Lankford	.50	.23	.06
Ron Gant			
□ 19 Tony Gwynn	2.00	.90	.25
Rickey Henderson			
□ 20 Barry Bonds	1.00	.45	.12
Matt Williams			

1997 Ultra Fielder's Choice

Randomly inserted in packs at a rate of one in 144, this 18-card set uses leather and gold foil to honor leading defensive players. The horizontal cards also include a player photo on the front as well as the big bold words "97 Fleer Ultra", "Fielder's Choice" and the player's name. The horizontal backs have another player photo as well as information about their defensive prowess.

	MINT	NRMT	EXC
COMPLETE SET (18)	300.00	135.00	38.00
COMMON CARD (1-18)	8.00	3.60	1.00
SEMISTARS	10.00	4.50	1.25
RANDOM INSERTS IN PACKS			

□ 1 Roberto Alomar	20.00	9.00	2.50
□ 2 Jeff Bagwell	30.00	13.50	3.70
□ 3 Wade Boggs	10.00	4.50	1.25
□ 4 Barry Bonds	20.00	9.00	2.50
□ 5 Mark Grace	10.00	4.50	1.25
□ 6 Ken Griffey Jr.	80.00	36.00	10.00
□ 7 Marquis Grissom	8.00	3.60	1.00
□ 8 Charles Johnson	8.00	3.60	1.00
□ 9 Chuck Knoblauch	10.00	4.50	1.25
□ 10 Barry Larkin	10.00	4.50	1.25
□ 11 Kenny Lofton	20.00	9.00	2.50
□ 12 Greg Maddux	50.00	22.00	6.25
□ 13 Raul Mondesi	8.00	3.60	1.00
□ 14 Rey Ordonez	10.00	4.50	1.25
□ 15 Cal Ripken	60.00	27.00	7.50
□ 16 Alex Rodriguez	80.00	36.00	10.00
□ 17 Ivan Rodriguez	15.00	6.75	1.85
□ 18 Matt Williams	10.00	4.50	1.25

1997 Ultra Home Run Kings

Randomly inserted only in hobby packs at a rate of one in 36, this 12-card set feaures ultra crystal cards with transparent refractive holo-foil technology. The players pictured are all leading power hitters.

	MINT	NRMT	EXC
COMPLETE SET (12)	100.00	45.00	12.50
COMMON CARD (1-12)	3.00	1.35	.35
RANDOM INSERTS IN PACKS			

□ 1 Albert Belle	12.00	5.50	1.50
□ 2 Barry Bonds	6.00	2.70	.75
□ 3 Juan Gonzalez	12.00	5.50	1.50
□ 4 Ken Griffey Jr.	25.00	11.00	3.10
□ 5 Todd Hundley	3.00	1.35	.35

□ 6 Ryan Klesko	5.00	2.20	.60
□ 7 Mark McGwire	8.00	3.60	1.00
□ 8 Mike Piazza	15.00	6.75	1.85
□ 9 Sammy Sosa	4.00	1.80	.50
□ 10 Frank Thomas	25.00	11.00	3.10
□ 11 Mo Vaughn	6.00	2.70	.75
□ 12 Matt Williams	3.00	1.35	.35

1997 Ultra Power Plus

Randomly inserted in packs at a rate of one in 24, this 12-card set utilizes silver rainbow holo-foil and features players who not only hit with power but also excel at other parts of the game.

	MINT	NRMT	EXC
COMPLETE SET (12)	100.00	45.00	12.50
COMMON CARD (1-12)	2.50	1.10	.30
RANDOM INSERTS IN PACKS			
□ 1 Jeff Bagwell	8.00	3.60	1.00
□ 2 Barry Bonds	5.00	2.20	.60
□ 3 Juan Gonzalez	10.00	4.50	1.25
□ 4 Ken Griffey Jr.	20.00	9.00	2.50
□ 5 Chipper Jones	12.00	5.50	1.50
□ 6 Mark McGwire	6.00	2.70	.75
□ 7 Mike Piazza	12.00	5.50	1.50
□ 8 Cal Ripken	15.00	6.75	1.85
□ 9 Alex Rodriguez	20.00	9.00	2.50
□ 10 Sammy Sosa	3.00	1.35	.35
□ 11 Frank Thomas	20.00	9.00	2.50
□ 12 Matt Williams	2.50	1.10	.30

1997 Ultra RBI Kings

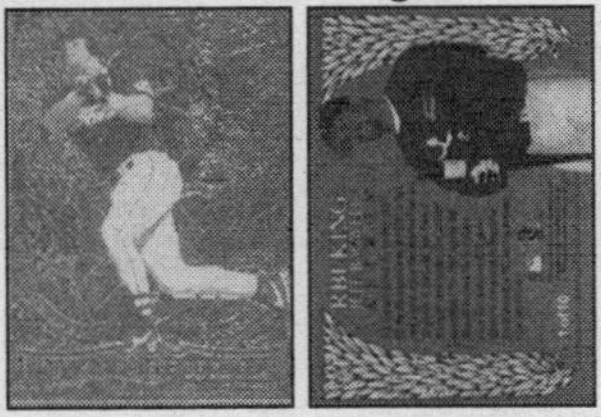

Randomly inserted in packs at a rate of one in 18, this 10-card set features 100 percent etched-foil cards. The cards feature players who drive in many runs. The horizontal backs contain player information and another player photo.

	MINT	NRMT	EXC
COMPLETE SET (10)	50.00	22.00	6.25
COMMON CARD (1-10)	2.50	1.10	.30
RANDOM INSERTS IN PACKS			
□ 1 Jeff Bagwell	6.00	2.70	.75
□ 2 Albert Belle	8.00	3.60	1.00
□ 3 Dante Bichette	2.50	1.10	.30
□ 4 Barry Bonds	4.00	1.80	.50
□ 5 Jay Buhner	2.50	1.10	.30
□ 6 Juan Gonzalez	8.00	3.60	1.00
□ 7 Ken Griffey Jr.	15.00	6.75	1.85
□ 8 Sammy Sosa	3.00	1.35	.35
□ 9 Frank Thomas	15.00	6.75	1.85
□ 10 Mo Vaughn	4.00	1.80	.50

1997 Ultra Rookie Reflections

Randomly inserted in packs at a rate of one in 4, this 10-card set uses a silver foil design to feature young players. The horizontal backs contain player information as well as another player photo.

	MINT	NRMT	EXC
COMPLETE SET (10)	10.00	4.50	1.25
COMMON CARD (1-10)	.25	.11	.03
RANDOM INSERTS IN PACKS			
□ 1 James Baldwin	.25	.11	.03
□ 2 Jermaine Dye	1.00	.45	.12
□ 3 Darin Erstad	4.00	1.80	.50
□ 4 Todd Hollandsworth	.25	.11	.03
□ 5 Derek Jeter	4.00	1.80	.50
□ 6 Jason Kendall	.25	.11	.03
□ 7 Alex Ochoa	.25	.11	.03
□ 8 Rey Ordonez	.25	.11	.03
□ 9 Edgar Renteria	.50	.23	.06
□ 10 Scott Rolen	2.00	.90	.25

1997 Ultra Season Crowns

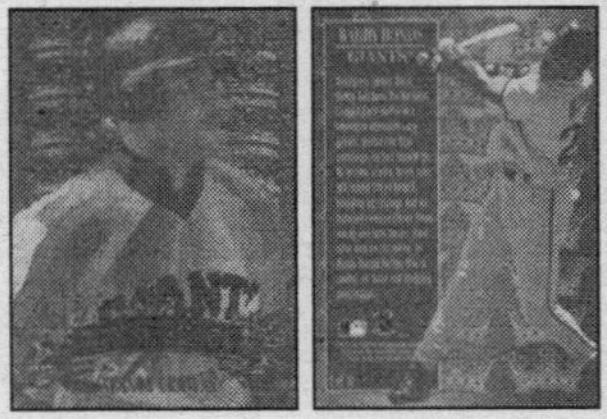

Randomly inserted in packs at a rate of one in 8, this 12-card set features long-standing stars with etched foil backgrounds.

	MINT	NRMT	EXC
COMPLETE SET (12)	30.00	13.50	3.70
COMMON CARD (1-12)	1.00	.45	.12
RANDOM INSERTS IN PACKS			
□ 1 Albert Belle	4.00	1.80	.50
□ 2 Dante Bichette	1.00	.45	.12
□ 3 Barry Bonds	2.00	.90	.25
□ 4 Kenny Lofton	2.00	.90	.25
□ 5 Edgar Martinez	1.00	.45	.12
□ 6 Mark McGwire	2.50	1.10	.30
□ 7 Andy Pettitte	2.00	.90	.25
□ 8 Mike Piazza	5.00	2.20	.60
□ 9 Alex Rodriguez	8.00	3.60	1.00
□ 10 John Smoltz	1.00	.45	.12
□ 11 Sammy Sosa	1.00	.45	.12
□ 12 Frank Thomas	8.00	3.60	1.00

1989 Upper Deck

This attractive 800-card standard-size set was introduced in 1989 as the premier issue by the then-fledgling Upper Deck company. Unlike other 1989 releases, this set was issued in two separate series - a low series numbered 1-700 and a high series numbered 701-800. Cards were primarily issued in fin-wrapped low and high series foil packs, complete 800-card factory sets and 100-card high series factory sets. High series packs contained a mixture of both

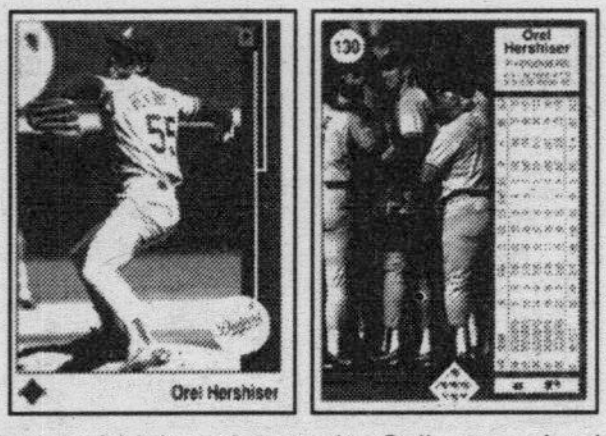

low and high series cards. Collectors should also note that many dealers consider that Upper Deck's "planned" production of 1,000,000 of each player was increased (perhaps even doubled) later in the year due to the explosion in popularity of the product. The cards feature slick paper stock, full color on both the front and the back and carry a hologram on the reverse to protect against counterfeiting. Subsets include Rookie Stars (1-26) and Collector's Choice art cards (668-693). The more significant variations involving changed photos or changed type are listed below. According to the company, the Murphy and Sheridan cards were corrected very early, after only two percent of the cards had been produced. Similarly, the Sheffield was corrected after 15 percent had been printed; Varsho, Gallego, and Schroeder were corrected after 20 percent; and Holton, Manrique, and Winningham were corrected 30 percent of the way through. Rookie Cards in the set include Jim Abbott, Sandy Alomar Jr., Dante Bichette, Craig Biggio, Steve Finley, Ken Griffey Jr., Erik Hanson, Charlie Hayes, Randy Johnson, Ramon Martinez, Gary Sheffield, John Smoltz and Todd Zeile. Cards with missing or duplicate holograms appear to be relatively common and are generally considered to be flawed copies that sell for substantial discounts.

	MINT	NRMT	EXC
COMPLETE SET (800)	100.00	45.00	12.50
COMPLETE FACT.SET (800)	100.00	45.00	12.50
COMPLETE LO SET (700)	90.00	40.00	11.00
COMPLETE HI SET (100)	10.00	4.50	1.25
COMPLETE HI FACT.SET (100)	8.00	3.60	1.00
COMMON CARD (1-800)	.10	.05	.01
SEMISTARS	.25	.11	.03
STARS	.50	.23	.06

□ 1	Ken Griffey Jr.	75.00	34.00	9.50
□ 2	Luis Medina	.10	.05	.01
□ 3	Tony Chance	.10	.05	.01
□ 4	Dave Otto	.10	.05	.01
□ 5	Sandy Alomar Jr. UER (Born 6/16/66, should be 6/18/66)	.75	.35	.09
□ 6	Rolando Roomes	.10	.05	.01
□ 7	Dave West	.10	.05	.01
□ 8	Cris Carpenter	.10	.05	.01
□ 9	Gregg Jefferies	.50	.23	.06
□ 10	Doug Dascenzo	.10	.05	.01
□ 11	Ron Jones	.10	.05	.01
□ 12	Luis DeLosSantos	.10	.05	.01
□ 13	Gary Sheffield COR	4.00	1.80	.50
□ 13A	Gary Sheffield ERR (SS upside down on card front)	4.00	1.80	.50
□ 14	Mike Harkey	.10	.05	.01
□ 15	Lance Blankenship	.10	.05	.01
□ 16	William Brennan	.10	.05	.01
□ 17	John Smoltz	4.00	1.80	.50
□ 18	Ramon Martinez	1.00	.45	.12
□ 19	Mark Lemke	.25	.11	.03
□ 20	Juan Bell	.10	.05	.01
□ 21	Rey Palacios	.10	.05	.01
□ 22	Felix Jose	.10	.05	.01
□ 23	Van Snider	.10	.05	.01
□ 24	Dante Bichette	3.00	1.35	.35
□ 25	Randy Johnson	4.00	1.80	.50
□ 26	Carlos Quintana	.10	.05	.01
□ 27	Star Rookie CL	.10	.05	.01
□ 28	Mike Schooler	.10	.05	.01
□ 29	Randy St.Claire	.10	.05	.01
□ 30	Jerald Clark	.10	.05	.01
□ 31	Kevin Gross	.10	.05	.01
□ 32	Dan Firova	.10	.05	.01
□ 33	Jeff Calhoun	.10	.05	.01
□ 34	Tommy Hinzo	.10	.05	.01
□ 35	Ricky Jordan	.25	.11	.03
□ 36	Larry Parrish	.10	.05	.01
□ 37	Bret Saberhagen UER (Hit total 931, should be 1031)	.25	.11	.03
□ 38	Mike Smithson	.10	.05	.01
□ 39	Dave Dravecky	.25	.11	.03
□ 40	Ed Romero	.10	.05	.01
□ 41	Jeff Musselman	.10	.05	.01
□ 42	Ed Hearn	.10	.05	.01
□ 43	Rance Mulliniks	.10	.05	.01
□ 44	Jim Eisenreich	.25	.11	.03
□ 45	Sil Campusano	.10	.05	.01
□ 46	Mike Krukow	.10	.05	.01
□ 47	Paul Gibson	.10	.05	.01
□ 48	Mike LaCoss	.10	.05	.01
□ 49	Larry Herndon	.10	.05	.01
□ 50	Scott Garrelts	.10	.05	.01
□ 51	Dwayne Henry	.10	.05	.01
□ 52	Jim Acker	.10	.05	.01
□ 53	Steve Sax	.10	.05	.01
□ 54	Pete O'Brien	.10	.05	.01
□ 55	Paul Runge	.10	.05	.01
□ 56	Rick Rhoden	.10	.05	.01
□ 57	John Dopson	.10	.05	.01
□ 58	Casey Candaele UER (No stats for Astros for '88 season)	.10	.05	.01
□ 59	Dave Righetti	.10	.05	.01
□ 60	Joe Hesketh	.10	.05	.01
□ 61	Frank DiPino	.10	.05	.01
□ 62	Tim Laudner	.10	.05	.01
□ 63	Jamie Moyer	.10	.05	.01
□ 64	Fred Toliver	.10	.05	.01
□ 65	Mitch Webster	.10	.05	.01
□ 66	John Tudor	.10	.05	.01
□ 67	John Cangelosi	.10	.05	.01
□ 68	Mike Devereaux	.10	.05	.01
□ 69	Brian Fisher	.10	.05	.01
□ 70	Mike Marshall	.10	.05	.01
□ 71	Zane Smith	.10	.05	.01
□ 72A	Brian Holton ERR (Photo actually Shawn Hillegas)	1.00	.45	.12
□ 72B	Brian Holton COR	.25	.11	.03
□ 73	Jose Guzman	.10	.05	.01
□ 74	Rick Mahler	.10	.05	.01
□ 75	John Shelby	.10	.05	.01
□ 76	Jim Deshaies	.10	.05	.01
□ 77	Bobby Meacham	.10	.05	.01
□ 78	Bryn Smith	.10	.05	.01
□ 79	Joaquin Andujar	.10	.05	.01
□ 80	Richard Dotson	.10	.05	.01
□ 81	Charlie Lea	.10	.05	.01
□ 82	Calvin Schiraldi	.10	.05	.01
□ 83	Les Straker	.10	.05	.01
□ 84	Les Lancaster	.10	.05	.01
□ 85	Allan Anderson	.10	.05	.01
□ 86	Junior Ortiz	.10	.05	.01
□ 87	Jesse Orosco	.10	.05	.01
□ 88	Felix Fermin	.10	.05	.01
□ 89	Dave Anderson	.10	.05	.01
□ 90	Rafael Belliard UER (Born '61, not '51)	.10	.05	.01
□ 91	Franklin Stubbs	.10	.05	.01
□ 92	Cecil Espy	.10	.05	.01
□ 93	Albert Hall	.10	.05	.01
□ 94	Tim Leary	.10	.05	.01
□ 95	Mitch Williams	.10	.05	.01
□ 96	Tracy Jones	.10	.05	.01
□ 97	Danny Darwin	.10	.05	.01
□ 98	Gary Ward	.10	.05	.01
□ 99	Neal Heaton	.10	.05	.01
□ 100	Jim Pankovits	.10	.05	.01
□ 101	Bill Doran	.10	.05	.01
□ 102	Tim Wallach	.10	.05	.01

□ 103 Joe Magrane	.10	.05	.01
□ 104 Ozzie Virgil	.10	.05	.01
□ 105 Alvin Davis	.10	.05	.01
□ 106 Tom Brookens	.10	.05	.01
□ 107 Shawon Dunston	.10	.05	.01
□ 108 Tracy Woodson	.10	.05	.01
□ 109 Nelson Liriano	.10	.05	.01
□ 110 Devon White UER (Doubles total 46, should be 56)	.25	.11	.03
□ 111 Steve Balboni	.10	.05	.01
□ 112 Buddy Bell	.25	.11	.03
□ 113 German Jimenez	.10	.05	.01
□ 114 Ken Dayley	.10	.05	.01
□ 115 Andres Galarraga	.60	.25	.07
□ 116 Mike Scioscia	.10	.05	.01
□ 117 Gary Pettis	.10	.05	.01
□ 118 Ernie Whitt	.10	.05	.01
□ 119 Bob Boone	.25	.11	.03
□ 120 Ryne Sandberg	1.00	.45	.12
□ 121 Bruce Benedict	.10	.05	.01
□ 122 Hubie Brooks	.10	.05	.01
□ 123 Mike Moore	.10	.05	.01
□ 124 Wallace Johnson	.10	.05	.01
□ 125 Bob Horner	.10	.05	.01
□ 126 Chili Davis	.25	.11	.03
□ 127 Manny Trillo	.10	.05	.01
□ 128 Chet Lemon	.10	.05	.01
□ 129 John Cerutti	.10	.05	.01
□ 130 Orel Hershiser	.50	.23	.06
□ 131 Terry Pendleton	.25	.11	.03
□ 132 Jeff Blauser	.25	.11	.03
□ 133 Mike Fitzgerald	.10	.05	.01
□ 134 Henry Cotto	.10	.05	.01
□ 135 Gerald Young	.10	.05	.01
□ 136 Luis Salazar	.10	.05	.01
□ 137 Alejandro Pena	.10	.05	.01
□ 138 Jack Howell	.10	.05	.01
□ 139 Tony Fernandez	.10	.05	.01
□ 140 Mark Grace	.75	.35	.09
□ 141 Ken Caminiti	.75	.35	.09
□ 142 Mike Jackson	.10	.05	.01
□ 143 Larry McWilliams	.10	.05	.01
□ 144 Andres Thomas	.10	.05	.01
□ 145 Nolan Ryan 3X	3.00	1.35	.35
□ 146 Mike Davis	.10	.05	.01
□ 147 DeWayne Buice	.10	.05	.01
□ 148 Jody Davis	.10	.05	.01
□ 149 Jesse Barfield	.10	.05	.01
□ 150 Matt Nokes	.10	.05	.01
□ 151 Jerry Reuss	.10	.05	.01
□ 152 Rick Cerone	.10	.05	.01
□ 153 Storm Davis	.10	.05	.01
□ 154 Marvell Wynne	.10	.05	.01
□ 155 Will Clark	.75	.35	.09
□ 156 Luis Aguayo	.10	.05	.01
□ 157 Willie Upshaw	.10	.05	.01
□ 158 Randy Bush	.10	.05	.01
□ 159 Ron Darling	.10	.05	.01
□ 160 Kal Daniels	.10	.05	.01
□ 161 Spike Owen	.10	.05	.01
□ 162 Luis Polonia	.25	.11	.03
□ 163 Kevin Mitchell UER ('88/total HR's 18/52, should be 19/53)	.25	.11	.03
□ 164 Dave Gallagher	.10	.05	.01
□ 165 Benito Santiago	.25	.11	.03
□ 166 Greg Gagne	.10	.05	.01
□ 167 Ken Phelps	.10	.05	.01
□ 168 Sid Fernandez	.10	.05	.01
□ 169 Bo Diaz	.10	.05	.01
□ 170 Cory Snyder	.10	.05	.01
□ 171 Eric Show	.10	.05	.01
□ 172 Robby Thompson	.10	.05	.01
□ 173 Marty Barrett	.10	.05	.01
□ 174 Dave Henderson	.10	.05	.01
□ 175 Ozzie Guillen	.10	.05	.01
□ 176 Barry Lyons	.10	.05	.01
□ 177 Kelvin Torve	.10	.05	.01
□ 178 Don Slaught	.10	.05	.01
□ 179 Steve Lombardozzi	.10	.05	.01
□ 180 Chris Sabo	.10	.05	.01
□ 181 Jose Uribe	.10	.05	.01
□ 182 Shane Mack	.10	.05	.01
□ 183 Ron Karkovice	.10	.05	.01
□ 184 Todd Benzinger	.10	.05	.01
□ 185 Dave Stewart	.25	.11	.03
□ 186 Julio Franco	.25	.11	.03
□ 187 Ron Robinson	.10	.05	.01
□ 188 Wally Backman	.10	.05	.01
□ 189 Randy Velarde	.10	.05	.01
□ 190 Joe Carter	.50	.23	.06
□ 191 Bob Welch	.10	.05	.01
□ 192 Kelly Paris	.10	.05	.01
□ 193 Chris Brown	.10	.05	.01
□ 194 Rick Reuschel	.10	.05	.01
□ 195 Roger Clemens	.50	.23	.06
□ 196 Dave Concepcion	.25	.11	.03
□ 197 Al Newman	.10	.05	.01
□ 198 Brook Jacoby	.10	.05	.01
□ 199 Mookie Wilson	.25	.11	.03
□ 200 Don Mattingly	2.00	.90	.25
□ 201 Dick Schofield	.10	.05	.01
□ 202 Mark Gubicza	.10	.05	.01
□ 203 Gary Gaetti	.10	.05	.01
□ 204 Dan Pasqua	.10	.05	.01
□ 205 Andre Dawson	.50	.23	.06
□ 206 Chris Speier	.10	.05	.01
□ 207 Kent Tekulve	.10	.05	.01
□ 208 Rod Scurry	.10	.05	.01
□ 209 Scott Bailes	.10	.05	.01
□ 210 Rickey Henderson UER (Throws Right)	.50	.23	.06
□ 211 Harold Baines	.25	.11	.03
□ 212 Tony Armas	.10	.05	.01
□ 213 Kent Hrbek	.25	.11	.03
□ 214 Darrin Jackson	.10	.05	.01
□ 215 George Brett	1.50	.70	.19
□ 216 Rafael Santana	.10	.05	.01
□ 217 Andy Allanson	.10	.05	.01
□ 218 Brett Butler	.25	.11	.03
□ 219 Steve Jeltz	.10	.05	.01
□ 220 Jay Buhner	1.00	.45	.12
□ 221 Bo Jackson	.50	.23	.06
□ 222 Angel Salazar	.10	.05	.01
□ 223 Kirk McCaskill	.10	.05	.01
□ 224 Steve Lyons	.10	.05	.01
□ 225 Bert Blyleven	.25	.11	.03
□ 226 Scott Bradley	.10	.05	.01
□ 227 Bob Melvin	.10	.05	.01
□ 228 Ron Kittle	.10	.05	.01
□ 229 Phil Bradley	.10	.05	.01
□ 230 Tommy John	.25	.11	.03
□ 231 Greg Walker	.10	.05	.01
□ 232 Juan Berenguer	.10	.05	.01
□ 233 Pat Tabler	.10	.05	.01
□ 234 Terry Clark	.10	.05	.01
□ 235 Rafael Palmeiro	1.00	.45	.12
□ 236 Paul Zuvella	.10	.05	.01
□ 237 Willie Randolph	.25	.11	.03
□ 238 Bruce Fields	.10	.05	.01
□ 239 Mike Aldrete	.10	.05	.01
□ 240 Lance Parrish	.10	.05	.01
□ 241 Greg Maddux	5.00	2.20	.60
□ 242 John Moses	.10	.05	.01
□ 243 Melido Perez	.10	.05	.01
□ 244 Willie Wilson	.10	.05	.01
□ 245 Mark McLemore	.10	.05	.01
□ 246 Von Hayes	.10	.05	.01
□ 247 Matt Williams	1.00	.45	.12
□ 248 John Candelaria UER (Listed as Yankee for part of '87, should be Mets)	.10	.05	.01
□ 249 Harold Reynolds	.10	.05	.01
□ 250 Greg Swindell	.10	.05	.01
□ 251 Juan Agosto	.10	.05	.01
□ 252 Mike Felder	.10	.05	.01
□ 253 Vince Coleman	.10	.05	.01
□ 254 Larry Sheets	.10	.05	.01
□ 255 George Bell	.10	.05	.01
□ 256 Terry Steinbach	.25	.11	.03
□ 257 Jack Armstrong	.10	.05	.01
□ 258 Dickie Thon	.10	.05	.01
□ 259 Ray Knight	.10	.05	.01
□ 260 Darryl Strawberry	.25	.11	.03
□ 261 Doug Sisk	.10	.05	.01
□ 262 Alex Trevino	.10	.05	.01
□ 263 Jeffrey Leonard	.10	.05	.01
□ 264 Tom Henke	.10	.05	.01
□ 265 Ozzie Smith	.75	.35	.09
□ 266 Dave Bergman	.10	.05	.01

267	Tony Phillips	.50	.23	.06
268	Mark Davis	.10	.05	.01
269	Kevin Elster	.25	.11	.03
270	Barry Larkin	.75	.35	.09
271	Manny Lee	.10	.05	.01
272	Tom Brunansky	.10	.05	.01
273	Craig Biggio	2.00	.90	.25
274	Jim Gantner	.10	.05	.01
275	Eddie Murray	1.00	.45	.12
276	Jeff Reed	.10	.05	.01
277	Tim Teufel	.10	.05	.01
278	Rick Honeycutt	.10	.05	.01
279	Guillermo Hernandez	.10	.05	.01
280	John Kruk	.25	.11	.03
281	Luis Alicea	.10	.05	.01
282	Jim Clancy	.10	.05	.01
283	Billy Ripken	.10	.05	.01
284	Craig Reynolds	.10	.05	.01
285	Robin Yount	.60	.25	.07
286	Jimmy Jones	.10	.05	.01
287	Ron Oester	.10	.05	.01
288	Terry Leach	.10	.05	.01
289	Dennis Eckersley	.25	.11	.03
290	Alan Trammell	.50	.23	.06
291	Jimmy Key	.25	.11	.03
292	Chris Bosio	.10	.05	.01
293	Jose DeLeon	.10	.05	.01
294	Jim Traber	.10	.05	.01
295	Mike Scott	.10	.05	.01
296	Roger McDowell	.10	.05	.01
297	Garry Templeton	.10	.05	.01
298	Doyle Alexander	.10	.05	.01
299	Nick Esasky	.10	.05	.01
300	Mark McGwire UER (Doubles total 52, should be 51)	1.25	.55	.16
301	Darryl Hamilton	.25	.11	.03
302	Dave Smith	.10	.05	.01
303	Rick Sutcliffe	.10	.05	.01
304	Dave Stapleton	.10	.05	.01
305	Alan Ashby	.10	.05	.01
306	Pedro Guerrero	.25	.11	.03
307	Ron Guidry	.10	.05	.01
308	Steve Farr	.10	.05	.01
309	Curt Ford	.10	.05	.01
310	Claudell Washington	.10	.05	.01
311	Tom Prince	.10	.05	.01
312	Chad Kreuter	.10	.05	.01
313	Ken Oberkfell	.10	.05	.01
314	Jerry Browne	.10	.05	.01
315	R.J. Reynolds	.10	.05	.01
316	Scott Bankhead	.10	.05	.01
317	Milt Thompson	.10	.05	.01
318	Mario Diaz	.10	.05	.01
319	Bruce Ruffin	.10	.05	.01
320	Dave Valle	.10	.05	.01
321A	Gary Varsho ERR (Back photo actually Mike Bielecki bunting)	2.00	.90	.25
321B	Gary Varsho COR (In road uniform)	.10	.05	.01
322	Paul Mirabella	.10	.05	.01
323	Chuck Jackson	.10	.05	.01
324	Drew Hall	.10	.05	.01
325	Don August	.10	.05	.01
326	Israel Sanchez	.10	.05	.01
327	Denny Walling	.10	.05	.01
328	Joel Skinner	.10	.05	.01
329	Danny Tartabull	.10	.05	.01
330	Tony Pena	.10	.05	.01
331	Jim Sundberg	.10	.05	.01
332	Jeff D. Robinson	.10	.05	.01
333	Oddibe McDowell	.10	.05	.01
334	Jose Lind	.10	.05	.01
335	Paul Kilgus	.10	.05	.01
336	Juan Samuel	.10	.05	.01
337	Mike Campbell	.10	.05	.01
338	Mike Maddux	.10	.05	.01
339	Darnell Coles	.10	.05	.01
340	Bob Dernier	.10	.05	.01
341	Rafael Ramirez	.10	.05	.01
342	Scott Sanderson	.10	.05	.01
343	B.J. Surhoff	.50	.23	.06
344	Billy Hatcher	.10	.05	.01
345	Pat Perry	.10	.05	.01
346	Jack Clark	.25	.11	.03
347	Gary Thurman	.10	.05	.01
348	Tim Jones	.10	.05	.01
349	Dave Winfield	.50	.23	.06
350	Frank White	.25	.11	.03
351	Dave Collins	.10	.05	.01
352	Jack Morris	.25	.11	.03
353	Eric Plunk	.10	.05	.01
354	Leon Durham	.10	.05	.01
355	Ivan DeJesus	.10	.05	.01
356	Brian Holman	.10	.05	.01
357A	Dale Murphy ERR (Front has reverse negative)	15.00	6.75	1.85
357B	Dale Murphy COR	.50	.23	.06
358	Mark Portugal	.10	.05	.01
359	Andy McGaffigan	.10	.05	.01
360	Tom Glavine	1.00	.45	.12
361	Keith Moreland	.10	.05	.01
362	Todd Stottlemyre	.25	.11	.03
363	Dave Leiper	.10	.05	.01
364	Cecil Fielder	.25	.11	.03
365	Carmelo Martinez	.10	.05	.01
366	Dwight Evans	.25	.11	.03
367	Kevin McReynolds	.10	.05	.01
368	Rich Gedman	.10	.05	.01
369	Len Dykstra	.25	.11	.03
370	Jody Reed	.10	.05	.01
371	Jose Canseco UER (Strikeout total 391, should be 491)	.60	.25	.07
372	Rob Murphy	.10	.05	.01
373	Mike Henneman	.10	.05	.01
374	Walt Weiss	.10	.05	.01
375	Rob Dibble	.25	.11	.03
376	Kirby Puckett (Mark McGwire in background)	1.25	.55	.16
377	Dennis Martinez	.25	.11	.03
378	Ron Gant	.50	.23	.06
379	Brian Harper	.10	.05	.01
380	Nelson Santovenia	.10	.05	.01
381	Lloyd Moseby	.10	.05	.01
382	Lance McCullers	.10	.05	.01
383	Dave Stieb	.10	.05	.01
384	Tony Gwynn	1.50	.70	.19
385	Mike Flanagan	.10	.05	.01
386	Bob Ojeda	.10	.05	.01
387	Bruce Hurst	.10	.05	.01
388	Dave Magadan	.10	.05	.01
389	Wade Boggs	.50	.23	.06
390	Gary Carter	.50	.23	.06
391	Frank Tanana	.10	.05	.01
392	Curt Young	.10	.05	.01
393	Jeff Treadway	.10	.05	.01
394	Darrell Evans	.25	.11	.03
395	Glenn Hubbard	.10	.05	.01
396	Chuck Cary	.10	.05	.01
397	Frank Viola	.10	.05	.01
398	Jeff Parrett	.10	.05	.01
399	Terry Blocker	.10	.05	.01
400	Dan Gladden	.10	.05	.01
401	Louie Meadows	.10	.05	.01
402	Tim Raines	.50	.23	.06
403	Joey Meyer	.10	.05	.01
404	Larry Andersen	.10	.05	.01
405	Rex Hudler	.10	.05	.01
406	Mike Schmidt	.75	.35	.09
407	John Franco	.10	.05	.01
408	Brady Anderson	3.00	1.35	.35
409	Don Carman	.10	.05	.01
410	Eric Davis	.25	.11	.03
411	Bob Stanley	.10	.05	.01
412	Pete Smith	.10	.05	.01
413	Jim Rice	.50	.23	.06
414	Bruce Sutter	.10	.05	.01
415	Oil Can Boyd	.10	.05	.01
416	Ruben Sierra	.25	.11	.03
417	Mike LaValliere	.10	.05	.01
418	Steve Buechele	.10	.05	.01
419	Gary Redus	.10	.05	.01
420	Scott Fletcher	.10	.05	.01
421	Dale Sveum	.10	.05	.01
422	Bob Knepper	.10	.05	.01
423	Luis Rivera	.10	.05	.01
424	Ted Higuera	.10	.05	.01
425	Kevin Bass	.10	.05	.01

□ 426 Ken Gerhart	.10	.05	.01
□ 427 Shane Rawley	.10	.05	.01
□ 428 Paul O'Neill	.25	.11	.03
□ 429 Joe Orsulak	.10	.05	.01
□ 430 Jackie Gutierrez	.10	.05	.01
□ 431 Gerald Perry	.10	.05	.01
□ 432 Mike Greenwell	.10	.05	.01
□ 433 Jerry Royster	.10	.05	.01
□ 434 Ellis Burks	.50	.23	.06
□ 435 Ed Olwine	.10	.05	.01
□ 436 Dave Rucker	.10	.05	.01
□ 437 Charlie Hough	.25	.11	.03
□ 438 Bob Walk	.10	.05	.01
□ 439 Bob Brower	.10	.05	.01
□ 440 Barry Bonds	1.50	.70	.19
□ 441 Tom Foley	.10	.05	.01
□ 442 Rob Deer	.10	.05	.01
□ 443 Glenn Davis	.10	.05	.01
□ 444 Dave Martinez	.10	.05	.01
□ 445 Bill Wegman	.10	.05	.01
□ 446 Lloyd McClendon	.10	.05	.01
□ 447 Dave Schmidt	.10	.05	.01
□ 448 Darren Daulton	.25	.11	.03
□ 449 Frank Williams	.10	.05	.01
□ 450 Don Aase	.10	.05	.01
□ 451 Lou Whitaker	.50	.23	.06
□ 452 Goose Gossage	.50	.23	.06
□ 453 Ed Whitson	.10	.05	.01
□ 454 Jim Walewander	.10	.05	.01
□ 455 Damon Berryhill	.10	.05	.01
□ 456 Tim Burke	.10	.05	.01
□ 457 Barry Jones	.10	.05	.01
□ 458 Joel Youngblood	.10	.05	.01
□ 459 Floyd Youmans	.10	.05	.01
□ 460 Mark Salas	.10	.05	.01
□ 461 Jeff Russell	.10	.05	.01
□ 462 Darrell Miller	.10	.05	.01
□ 463 Jeff Kunkel	.10	.05	.01
□ 464 Sherman Corbett	.10	.05	.01
□ 465 Curtis Wilkerson	.10	.05	.01
□ 466 Bud Black	.10	.05	.01
□ 467 Cal Ripken	3.00	1.35	.35
□ 468 John Farrell	.10	.05	.01
□ 469 Terry Kennedy	.10	.05	.01
□ 470 Tom Candiotti	.10	.05	.01
□ 471 Roberto Alomar	2.00	.90	.25
□ 472 Jeff M. Robinson	.10	.05	.01
□ 473 Vance Law	.10	.05	.01
□ 474 Randy Ready UER (Strikeout total 136, should be 115)	.10	.05	.01
□ 475 Walt Terrell	.10	.05	.01
□ 476 Kelly Downs	.10	.05	.01
□ 477 Johnny Paredes	.10	.05	.01
□ 478 Shawn Hillegas	.10	.05	.01
□ 479 Bob Brenly	.10	.05	.01
□ 480 Otis Nixon	.10	.05	.01
□ 481 Johnny Ray	.10	.05	.01
□ 482 Geno Petralli	.10	.05	.01
□ 483 Stu Cliburn	.10	.05	.01
□ 484 Pete Incaviglia	.25	.11	.03
□ 485 Brian Downing	.10	.05	.01
□ 486 Jeff Stone	.10	.05	.01
□ 487 Carmen Castillo	.10	.05	.01
□ 488 Tom Niedenfuer	.10	.05	.01
□ 489 Jay Bell	.50	.23	.06
□ 490 Rick Schu	.10	.05	.01
□ 491 Jeff Pico	.10	.05	.01
□ 492 Mark Parent	.10	.05	.01
□ 493 Eric King	.10	.05	.01
□ 494 Al Nipper	.10	.05	.01
□ 495 Andy Hawkins	.10	.05	.01
□ 496 Daryl Boston	.10	.05	.01
□ 497 Ernie Riles	.10	.05	.01
□ 498 Pascual Perez	.10	.05	.01
□ 499 Bill Long UER (Games started total 70, should be 44)	.10	.05	.01
□ 500 Kirt Manwaring	.10	.05	.01
□ 501 Chuck Crim	.10	.05	.01
□ 502 Candy Maldonado	.10	.05	.01
□ 503 Dennis Lamp	.10	.05	.01
□ 504 Glenn Braggs	.10	.05	.01
□ 505 Joe Price	.10	.05	.01
□ 506 Ken Williams	.10	.05	.01
□ 507 Bill Pecota	.10	.05	.01

□ 508 Rey Quinones	.10	.05	.01
□ 509 Jeff Bittiger	.10	.05	.01
□ 510 Kevin Seitzer	.10	.05	.01
□ 511 Steve Bedrosian	.10	.05	.01
□ 512 Todd Worrell	.10	.05	.01
□ 513 Chris James	.10	.05	.01
□ 514 Jose Oquendo	.10	.05	.01
□ 515 David Palmer	.10	.05	.01
□ 516 John Smiley	.10	.05	.01
□ 517 Dave Clark	.10	.05	.01
□ 518 Mike Dunne	.10	.05	.01
□ 519 Ron Washington	.10	.05	.01
□ 520 Bob Kipper	.10	.05	.01
□ 521 Lee Smith	.50	.23	.06
□ 522 Juan Castillo	.10	.05	.01
□ 523 Don Robinson	.10	.05	.01
□ 524 Kevin Romine	.10	.05	.01
□ 525 Paul Molitor	.75	.35	.09
□ 526 Mark Langston	.25	.11	.03
□ 527 Donnie Hill	.10	.05	.01
□ 528 Larry Owen	.10	.05	.01
□ 529 Jerry Reed	.10	.05	.01
□ 530 Jack McDowell	.50	.23	.06
□ 531 Greg Mathews	.10	.05	.01
□ 532 John Russell	.10	.05	.01
□ 533 Dan Quisenberry	.10	.05	.01
□ 534 Greg Gross	.10	.05	.01
□ 535 Danny Cox	.10	.05	.01
□ 536 Terry Francona	.10	.05	.01
□ 537 Andy Van Slyke	.25	.11	.03
□ 538 Mel Hall	.10	.05	.01
□ 539 Jim Gott	.10	.05	.01
□ 540 Doug Jones	.10	.05	.01
□ 541 Craig Lefferts	.10	.05	.01
□ 542 Mike Boddicker	.10	.05	.01
□ 543 Greg Brock	.10	.05	.01
□ 544 Atlee Hammaker	.10	.05	.01
□ 545 Tom Bolton	.10	.05	.01
□ 546 Mike Macfarlane	.25	.11	.03
□ 547 Rich Renteria	.10	.05	.01
□ 548 John Davis	.10	.05	.01
□ 549 Floyd Bannister	.10	.05	.01
□ 550 Mickey Brantley	.10	.05	.01
□ 551 Duane Ward	.10	.05	.01
□ 552 Dan Petry	.10	.05	.01
□ 553 Mickey Tettleton UER (Walks total 175, should be 136)	.25	.11	.03
□ 554 Rick Leach	.10	.05	.01
□ 555 Mike Witt	.10	.05	.01
□ 556 Sid Bream	.10	.05	.01
□ 557 Bobby Witt	.10	.05	.01
□ 558 Tommy Herr	.10	.05	.01
□ 559 Randy Milligan	.10	.05	.01
□ 560 Jose Cecena	.10	.05	.01
□ 561 Mackey Sasser	.10	.05	.01
□ 562 Carney Lansford	.25	.11	.03
□ 563 Rick Aguilera	.25	.11	.03
□ 564 Ron Hassey	.10	.05	.01
□ 565 Dwight Gooden	.25	.11	.03
□ 566 Paul Assenmacher	.10	.05	.01
□ 567 Neil Allen	.10	.05	.01
□ 568 Jim Morrison	.10	.05	.01
□ 569 Mike Pagliarulo	.10	.05	.01
□ 570 Ted Simmons	.25	.11	.03
□ 571 Mark Thurmond	.10	.05	.01
□ 572 Fred McGriff	.75	.35	.09
□ 573 Wally Joyner	.25	.11	.03
□ 574 Jose Bautista	.10	.05	.01
□ 575 Kelly Gruber	.10	.05	.01
□ 576 Cecilio Guante	.10	.05	.01
□ 577 Mark Davidson	.10	.05	.01
□ 578 Bobby Bonilla UER (Total steals 2 in '87, should be 3)	.25	.11	.03
□ 579 Mike Stanley	.10	.05	.01
□ 580 Gene Larkin	.10	.05	.01
□ 581 Stan Javier	.10	.05	.01
□ 582 Howard Johnson	.10	.05	.01
□ 583A Mike Gallego ERR (Front reversed negative)	1.00	.45	.12
□ 583B Mike Gallego COR	.50	.23	.06
□ 584 David Cone	.75	.35	.09
□ 585 Doug Jennings	.10	.05	.01
□ 586 Charles Hudson	.10	.05	.01

□	587 Dion James	.10	.05	.01
□	588 Al Leiter	.25	.11	.03
□	589 Charlie Puleo	.10	.05	.01
□	590 Roberto Kelly	.25	.11	.03
□	591 Thad Bosley	.10	.05	.01
□	592 Pete Stanicek	.10	.05	.01
□	593 Pat Borders	.25	.11	.03
□	594 Bryan Harvey	.25	.11	.03
□	595 Jeff Ballard	.10	.05	.01
□	596 Jeff Reardon	.25	.11	.03
□	597 Doug Drabek	.25	.11	.03
□	598 Edwin Correa	.10	.05	.01
□	599 Keith Atherton	.10	.05	.01
□	600 Dave LaPoint	.10	.05	.01
□	601 Don Baylor	.50	.23	.06
□	602 Tom Pagnozzi	.10	.05	.01
□	603 Tim Flannery	.10	.05	.01
□	604 Gene Walter	.10	.05	.01
□	605 Dave Parker	.25	.11	.03
□	606 Mike Diaz	.10	.05	.01
□	607 Chris Gwynn	.10	.05	.01
□	608 Odell Jones	.10	.05	.01
□	609 Carlton Fisk	.50	.23	.06
□	610 Jay Howell	.10	.05	.01
□	611 Tim Crews	.10	.05	.01
□	612 Keith Hernandez	.25	.11	.03
□	613 Willie Fraser	.10	.05	.01
□	614 Jim Eppard	.10	.05	.01
□	615 Jeff Hamilton	.10	.05	.01
□	616 Kurt Stillwell	.10	.05	.01
□	617 Tom Browning	.10	.05	.01
□	618 Jeff Montgomery	.25	.11	.03
□	619 Jose Rijo	.10	.05	.01
□	620 Jamie Quirk	.10	.05	.01
□	621 Willie McGee	.10	.05	.01
□	622 Mark Grant UER	.10	.05	.01
	(Glove on wrong hand)			
□	623 Bill Swift	.10	.05	.01
□	624 Orlando Mercado	.10	.05	.01
□	625 John Costello	.10	.05	.01
□	626 Jose Gonzalez	.10	.05	.01
□	627A Bill Schroeder ERR	1.00	.45	.12
	(Back photo actually Ronn Reynolds buckling shin guards)			
□	627B Bill Schroeder COR	.50	.23	.06
□	628A Fred Manrique ERR	.50	.23	.06
	(Back photo actually Ozzie Guillen throwing)			
□	628B Fred Manrique COR	.10	.05	.01
	(Swinging bat on back)			
□	629 Ricky Horton	.10	.05	.01
□	630 Dan Plesac	.10	.05	.01
□	631 Alfredo Griffin	.10	.05	.01
□	632 Chuck Finley	.25	.11	.03
□	633 Kirk Gibson	.25	.11	.03
□	634 Randy Myers	.25	.11	.03
□	635 Greg Minton	.10	.05	.01
□	636A Herm Winningham	.50	.23	.06
	ERR (W1nningham on back)			
□	636B Herm Winningham COR	.10	.05	.01
□	637 Charlie Leibrandt	.10	.05	.01
□	638 Tim Birtsas	.10	.05	.01
□	639 Bill Buckner	.25	.11	.03
□	640 Danny Jackson	.10	.05	.01
□	641 Greg Booker	.10	.05	.01
□	642 Jim Presley	.10	.05	.01
□	643 Gene Nelson	.10	.05	.01
□	644 Rod Booker	.10	.05	.01
□	645 Dennis Rasmussen	.10	.05	.01
□	646 Juan Nieves	.10	.05	.01
□	647 Bobby Thigpen	.10	.05	.01
□	648 Tim Belcher	.10	.05	.01
□	649 Mike Young	.10	.05	.01
□	650 Ivan Calderon	.10	.05	.01
□	651 Oswaldo Peraza	.10	.05	.01
□	652A Pat Sheridan ERR	8.00	3.60	1.00
	(No position on front)			
□	652B Pat Sheridan COR	.10	.05	.01
□	653 Mike Morgan	.10	.05	.01
□	654 Mike Heath	.10	.05	.01
□	655 Jay Tibbs	.10	.05	.01
□	656 Fernando Valenzuela	.25	.11	.03
□	657 Lee Mazzilli	.10	.05	.01
□	658 Frank Viola AL CY	.10	.05	.01

□	659A Jose Canseco AL MVP	.50	.23	.06
	(Eagle logo in black)			
□	659B Jose Canseco AL MVP	.50	.23	.06
	(Eagle logo in blue)			
□	660 Walt Weiss AL ROY	.10	.05	.01
□	661 Orel Hershiser NL CY	.25	.11	.03
□	662 Kirk Gibson NL MVP	.25	.11	.03
□	663 Chris Sabo NL ROY	.10	.05	.01
□	664 Dennis Eckersley	.25	.11	.03
	ALCS MVP			
□	665 Orel Hershiser	.25	.11	.03
	NLCS MVP			
□	666 Kirk Gibson WS	.50	.23	.06
□	667 Orel Hershiser WS MVP	.25	.11	.03
□	668 Wally Joyner TC	.25	.11	.03
□	669 Nolan Ryan TC	.75	.35	.09
□	670 Jose Canseco TC	.25	.11	.03
□	671 Fred McGriff TC	.25	.11	.03
□	672 Dale Murphy TC	.25	.11	.03
□	673 Paul Molitor TC	.50	.23	.06
□	674 Ozzie Smith TC	.50	.23	.06
□	675 Ryne Sandberg TC	.50	.23	.06
□	676 Kirk Gibson TC	.25	.11	.03
□	677 Andres Galarraga TC	.25	.11	.03
□	678 Will Clark TC	.25	.11	.03
□	679 Cory Snyder TC	.10	.05	.01
□	680 Alvin Davis TC	.10	.05	.01
□	681 Darryl Strawberry TC	.25	.11	.03
□	682 Cal Ripken TC	.75	.35	.09
□	683 Tony Gwynn TC	.50	.23	.06
□	684 Mike Schmidt TC	.50	.23	.06
□	685 Andy Van Slyke TC UER	.10	.05	.01
	(96 Junior Ortiz)			
□	686 Ruben Sierra TC	.50	.23	.06
□	687 Wade Boggs TC	.50	.23	.06
□	688 Eric Davis TC	.25	.11	.03
□	689 George Brett TC	.50	.23	.06
□	690 Alan Trammell TC	.25	.11	.03
□	691 Frank Viola TC	.10	.05	.01
□	692 Harold Baines TC	.25	.11	.03
□	693 Don Mattingly TC	.50	.23	.06
□	694 Checklist 1-100	.10	.05	.01
□	695 Checklist 101-200	.10	.05	.01
□	696 Checklist 201-300	.10	.05	.01
□	697 Checklist 301-400	.10	.05	.01
□	698 Checklist 401-500 UER	.10	.05	.01
	(467 Cal Ripkin Jr.)			
□	699 Checklist 501-600 UER	.10	.05	.01
	(543 Greg Booker)			
□	700 Checklist 601-700	.10	.05	.01
□	701 Checklist 701-800	.10	.05	.01
□	702 Jesse Barfield	.10	.05	.01
□	703 Walt Terrell	.10	.05	.01
□	704 Dickie Thon	.10	.05	.01
□	705 Al Leiter	.25	.11	.03
□	706 Dave LaPoint	.10	.05	.01
□	707 Charlie Hayes	.50	.23	.06
□	708 Andy Hawkins	.10	.05	.01
□	709 Mickey Hatcher	.10	.05	.01
□	710 Lance McCullers	.10	.05	.01
□	711 Ron Kittle	.10	.05	.01
□	712 Bert Blyleven	.25	.11	.03
□	713 Rick Dempsey	.10	.05	.01
□	714 Ken Williams	.10	.05	.01
□	715 Steve Rosenberg	.10	.05	.01
□	716 Joe Skalski	.10	.05	.01
□	717 Spike Owen	.10	.05	.01
□	718 Todd Burns	.10	.05	.01
□	719 Kevin Gross	.10	.05	.01
□	720 Tommy Herr	.10	.05	.01
□	721 Rob Ducey	.10	.05	.01
□	722 Gary Green	.10	.05	.01
□	723 Gregg Olson	.25	.11	.03
□	724 Greg W. Harris	.10	.05	.01
□	725 Craig Worthington	.10	.05	.01
□	726 Tom Howard	.10	.05	.01
□	727 Dale Mohorcic	.10	.05	.01
□	728 Rich Yett	.10	.05	.01
□	729 Mel Hall	.10	.05	.01
□	730 Floyd Youmans	.10	.05	.01
□	731 Lonnie Smith	.10	.05	.01
□	732 Wally Backman	.10	.05	.01
□	733 Trevor Wilson	.10	.05	.01
□	734 Jose Alvarez	.10	.05	.01
□	735 Bob Milacki	.10	.05	.01
□	736 Tom Gordon	.25	.11	.03

□ 737 Wally Whitehurst	.10	.05	.01
□ 738 Mike Aldrete	.10	.05	.01
□ 739 Keith Miller	.10	.05	.01
□ 740 Randy Milligan	.10	.05	.01
□ 741 Jeff Parrett	.10	.05	.01
□ 742 Steve Finley	1.00	.45	.12
□ 743 Junior Felix	.10	.05	.01
□ 744 Pete Harnisch	.25	.11	.03
□ 745 Bill Spiers	.10	.05	.01
□ 746 Hensley Meulens	.10	.05	.01
□ 747 Juan Bell	.10	.05	.01
□ 748 Steve Sax	.10	.05	.01
□ 749 Phil Bradley	.10	.05	.01
□ 750 Rey Quinones	.10	.05	.01
□ 751 Tommy Gregg	.10	.05	.01
□ 752 Kevin Brown	.50	.23	.06
□ 753 Derek Lilliquist	.10	.05	.01
□ 754 Todd Zeile	.50	.23	.06
□ 755 Jim Abbott (Triple exposure)	.50	.23	.06
□ 756 Ozzie Canseco	.10	.05	.01
□ 757 Nick Esasky	.10	.05	.01
□ 758 Mike Moore	.10	.05	.01
□ 759 Rob Murphy	.10	.05	.01
□ 760 Rick Mahler	.10	.05	.01
□ 761 Fred Lynn	.10	.05	.01
□ 762 Kevin Blankenship	.10	.05	.01
□ 763 Eddie Murray	1.00	.45	.12
□ 764 Steve Searcy	.10	.05	.01
□ 765 Jerome Walton	.25	.11	.03
□ 766 Erik Hanson	.50	.23	.06
□ 767 Bob Boone	.25	.11	.03
□ 768 Edgar Martinez	1.00	.45	.12
□ 769 Jose DeJesus	.10	.05	.01
□ 770 Greg Briley	.10	.05	.01
□ 771 Steve Peters	.10	.05	.01
□ 772 Rafael Palmeiro	1.00	.45	.12
□ 773 Jack Clark	.25	.11	.03
□ 774 Nolan Ryan (Throwing football)	3.00	1.35	.35
□ 775 Lance Parrish	.10	.05	.01
□ 776 Joe Girardi	.50	.23	.06
□ 777 Willie Randolph	.25	.11	.03
□ 778 Mitch Williams	.10	.05	.01
□ 779 Dennis Cook	.10	.05	.01
□ 780 Dwight Smith	.25	.11	.03
□ 781 Lenny Harris	.10	.05	.01
□ 782 Torey Lovullo	.10	.05	.01
□ 783 Norm Charlton	.25	.11	.03
□ 784 Chris Brown	.10	.05	.01
□ 785 Todd Benzinger	.10	.05	.01
□ 786 Shane Rawley	.10	.05	.01
□ 787 Omar Vizquel	2.00	.90	.25
□ 788 LaVel Freeman	.10	.05	.01
□ 789 Jeffrey Leonard	.10	.05	.01
□ 790 Eddie Williams	.10	.05	.01
□ 791 Jamie Moyer	.10	.05	.01
□ 792 Bruce Hurst UER (Workd Series)	.10	.05	.01
□ 793 Julio Franco	.25	.11	.03
□ 794 Claudell Washington	.10	.05	.01
□ 795 Jody Davis	.10	.05	.01
□ 796 Oddibe McDowell	.10	.05	.01
□ 797 Paul Kilgus	.10	.05	.01
□ 798 Tracy Jones	.10	.05	.01
□ 799 Steve Wilson	.10	.05	.01
□ 800 Pete O'Brien	.10	.05	.01

1990 Upper Deck

The 1990 Upper Deck set contains 800 standard-size cards issued in two series, low numbers (1-700) and high numbers (701-800). Cards were distributed in fin-wrapped low and high series foil packs, complete 800-card factory sets and 100-card high series factory sets. High series foil packs contained a mixture of low and high series cards. The front and back borders are white, and both sides feature full-color photos. The horizontally oriented backs have recent stats and anti-counterfeiting holograms. Team checklist cards are mixed in with the first 100 cards of the set. Rookie Cards in the set include Wilson Alvarez, Carlos Baerga, Juan Gonzalez, Marquis Grissom, Todd Hundley, David Justice, Ray Lankford, Ben McDonald, Dean Palmer, Sammy Sosa and Larry Walker. The high series contains a Nolan Ryan variation; all cards produced before August 12th only discuss Ryan's sixth no-hitter while the later-issue cards include a stripe honoring Ryan's 300th victory. Card 702 (Rookie Threats) was originally scheduled to be Mike Witt. A few Witt cards with 702 on back and checklist cards showing Witt as 702 escaped into early packs; they are characterized by a black rectangle covering much of the card's back.

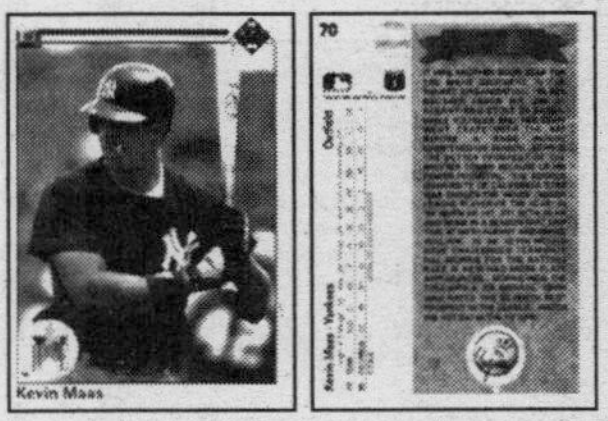

	MINT	NRMT	EXC
COMPLETE SET (800)	20.00	9.00	2.50
COMPLETE FACT.SET (800)	20.00	9.00	2.50
COMPLETE LO SET (700)	16.00	7.25	2.00
COMPLETE HI SET (100)	4.00	1.80	.50
COMPLETE HI FACT.SET (100)	4.00	1.80	.50
COMMON CARD (1-800)	.05	.02	.01
SEMISTARS	.15	.07	.02
STARS	.30	.14	.04
COMP.REGGIE SET (10)	20.00	9.00	2.50
COMMON REGGIE (1-9)	2.00	.90	.25
REGGIE HEADER (NNO)	4.00	1.80	.50
REGGIE AUTO/2500 (AU1)	300.00	135.00	38.00
REGGIE: RANDOM INSERTS IN HI SERIES..			

□ 1 Star Rookie Checklist	.05	.02	.01
□ 2 Randy Nosek	.05	.02	.01
□ 3 Tom Drees UER (11th line, hulred, should be hurled)	.05	.02	.01
□ 4 Curt Young	.05	.02	.01
□ 5 Devon White TC	.15	.07	.02
□ 6 Luis Salazar	.05	.02	.01
□ 7 Von Hayes TC	.05	.02	.01
□ 8 Jose Bautista	.05	.02	.01
□ 9 Marquis Grissom	1.25	.55	.16
□ 10 Orel Hershiser TC	.15	.07	.02
□ 11 Rick Aguilera	.15	.07	.02
□ 12 Benito Santiago TC	.05	.02	.01
□ 13 Deion Sanders	.40	.18	.05
□ 14 Marvell Wynne	.05	.02	.01
□ 15 Dave West	.05	.02	.01
□ 16 Bobby Bonilla TC	.15	.07	.02
□ 17 Sammy Sosa	1.60	.70	.19
□ 18 Steve Sax TC	.05	.02	.01
□ 19 Jack Howell	.05	.02	.01
□ 20 Mike Schmidt Special UER (Suprising, should be surprising)	.50	.23	.06
□ 21 Robin Ventura UER (Samta Maria)	.30	.14	.04
□ 22 Brian Meyer	.05	.02	.01
□ 23 Blaine Beatty	.05	.02	.01
□ 24 Ken Griffey Jr. TC	.75	.35	.09
□ 25 Greg Vaughn UER (Association misspelled as assiocation)	.30	.14	.04
□ 26 Xavier Hernandez	.05	.02	.01
□ 27 Jason Grimsley	.05	.02	.01
□ 28 Eric Anthony UER (Ashville, should be Asheville)	.15	.07	.02
□ 29 Tim Raines TC UER (Wallach listed before Walker)	.15	.07	.02
□ 30 David Wells	.05	.02	.01
□ 31 Hal Morris	.15	.07	.02

□ 32 Bo Jackson TC	.15	.07	.02
□ 33 Kelly Mann	.05	.02	.01
□ 34 Nolan Ryan Special	.75	.35	.09
□ 35 Scott Service UER	.05	.02	.01
(Born Cincinatti on 7/27/67, should be Cincinnati 2/27)			
□ 36 Mark McGwire TC	.30	.14	.04
□ 37 Tino Martinez	.30	.14	.04
□ 38 Chili Davis	.15	.07	.02
□ 39 Scott Sanderson	.05	.02	.01
□ 40 Kevin Mitchell TC	.05	.02	.01
□ 41 Lou Whitaker TC	.15	.07	.02
□ 42 Scott Coolbaugh UER	.05	.02	.01
(Definately)			
□ 43 Jose Cano UER	.05	.02	.01
(Born 9/7/62, should be 3/7/62)			
□ 44 Jose Vizcaino	.30	.14	.04
□ 45 Bob Hamelin	.15	.07	.02
□ 46 Jose Offerman UER	.15	.07	.02
(Posesses)			
□ 47 Kevin Blankenship	.05	.02	.01
□ 48 Kirby Puckett TC	.30	.14	.04
□ 49 Tommy Greene UER	.05	.02	.01
(Livest, should be liveliest)			
□ 50 Will Clark Special UER (Perenial, should be perennial)	.30	.14	.04
□ 51 Rob Nelson	.05	.02	.01
□ 52 Chris Hammond UER	.05	.02	.01
(Chatanooga)			
□ 53 Joe Carter TC	.15	.07	.02
□ 54A Ben McDonald ERR	8.00	3.60	1.00
(No Rookie designation on card front)			
□ 54B Ben McDonald COR	.30	.14	.04
□ 55 Andy Benes UER	.30	.14	.04
(Whichita)			
□ 56 John Olerud	.30	.14	.04
□ 57 Roger Clemens TC	.30	.14	.04
□ 58 Tony Armas	.05	.02	.01
□ 59 George Canale	.05	.02	.01
□ 60A Mickey Tettleton TC ERR (683 Jamie Weston)	2.00	.90	.25
□ 60B Mickey Tettleton TC COR (683 Mickey Weston)	.05	.02	.01
□ 61 Mike Stanton	.15	.07	.02
□ 62 Dwight Gooden TC	.15	.07	.02
□ 63 Kent Mercker UER	.15	.07	.02
(Albuguerque)			
□ 64 Francisco Cabrera	.05	.02	.01
□ 65 Steve Avery UER	.30	.14	.04
(Born NJ, should be MI, Merker should be Mercker)			
□ 66 Jose Canseco	.30	.14	.04
□ 67 Matt Merullo	.05	.02	.01
□ 68 Vince Coleman TC UER	.05	.02	.01
(Guererro)			
□ 69 Ron Karkovice	.05	.02	.01
□ 70 Kevin Maas	.15	.07	.02
□ 71 Dennis Cook UER	.05	.02	.01
(Shown with righty glove on card back)			
□ 72 Juan Gonzalez UER	4.00	1.80	.50
(135 games for Tulsa in '89, should be 133)			
□ 73 Andre Dawson TC	.30	.14	.04
□ 74 Dean Palmer UER	.75	.35	.09
(Permanent misspelled as perminant)			
□ 75 Bo Jackson Special UER (Monsterous, should be monstrous)	.30	.14	.04
□ 76 Rob Richie	.05	.02	.01
□ 77 Bobby Rose UER	.05	.02	.01
(Pickin, should be pick in)			
□ 78 Brian DuBois UER	.05	.02	.01
(Commiting)			
□ 79 Ozzie Guillen TC	.05	.02	.01
□ 80 Gene Nelson	.05	.02	.01
□ 81 Bob McClure	.05	.02	.01
□ 82 Julio Franco TC	.05	.02	.01
□ 83 Greg Minton	.05	.02	.01
□ 84 John Smoltz TC UER	.30	.14	.04
(Oddibe not Odibbe)			
□ 85 Willie Fraser	.05	.02	.01
□ 86 Neal Heaton	.05	.02	.01
□ 87 Kevin Tapani UER	.15	.07	.02
(24th line has excpet, should be except)			
□ 88 Mike Scott TC	.05	.02	.01
□ 89A Jim Gott ERR	2.50	1.10	.30
(Photo actually Rick Reed)			
□ 89B Jim Gott COR	.05	.02	.01
□ 90 Lance Johnson	.30	.14	.04
□ 91 Robin Yount TC UER	.30	.14	.04
(Checklist on back has 178 Rob Deer and 176 Mike Felder)			
□ 92 Jeff Parrett	.05	.02	.01
□ 93 Julio Machado UER	.05	.02	.01
(Valenzuelan, should be Venezuelan)			
□ 94 Ron Jones	.05	.02	.01
□ 95 George Bell TC	.05	.02	.01
□ 96 Jerry Reuss	.05	.02	.01
□ 97 Brian Fisher	.05	.02	.01
□ 98 Kevin Ritz UER	.05	.02	.01
(Amercian)			
□ 99 Barry Larkin TC	.30	.14	.04
□ 100 Checklist 1-100	.05	.02	.01
□ 101 Gerald Perry	.05	.02	.01
□ 102 Kevin Appier	.30	.14	.04
□ 103 Julio Franco	.15	.07	.02
□ 104 Craig Biggio	.30	.14	.04
□ 105 Bo Jackson UER	.30	.14	.04
('89 BA wrong, should be .256)			
□ 106 Junior Felix	.05	.02	.01
□ 107 Mike Harkey	.05	.02	.01
□ 108 Fred McGriff	.30	.14	.04
□ 109 Rick Sutcliffe	.05	.02	.01
□ 110 Pete O'Brien	.05	.02	.01
□ 111 Kelly Gruber	.05	.02	.01
□ 112 Dwight Evans	.15	.07	.02
□ 113 Pat Borders	.05	.02	.01
□ 114 Dwight Gooden	.15	.07	.02
□ 115 Kevin Batiste	.05	.02	.01
□ 116 Eric Davis	.15	.07	.02
□ 117 Kevin Mitchell UER	.15	.07	.02
(Career HR total 99, should be 100)			
□ 118 Ron Oester	.05	.02	.01
□ 119 Brett Butler	.15	.07	.02
□ 120 Danny Jackson	.05	.02	.01
□ 121 Tommy Gregg	.05	.02	.01
□ 122 Ken Caminiti	.30	.14	.04
□ 123 Kevin Brown	.15	.07	.02
□ 124 George Brett UER	.75	.35	.09
(133 runs, should be 1300)			
□ 125 Mike Scott	.05	.02	.01
□ 126 Cory Snyder	.05	.02	.01
□ 127 George Bell	.05	.02	.01
□ 128 Mark Grace	.30	.14	.04
□ 129 Devon White	.15	.07	.02
□ 130 Tony Fernandez	.05	.02	.01
□ 131 Don Aase	.05	.02	.01
□ 132 Rance Mulliniks	.05	.02	.01
□ 133 Marty Barrett	.05	.02	.01
□ 134 Nelson Liriano	.05	.02	.01
□ 135 Mark Carreon	.05	.02	.01
□ 136 Candy Maldonado	.05	.02	.01
□ 137 Tim Birtsas	.05	.02	.01
□ 138 Tom Brookens	.05	.02	.01
□ 139 John Franco	.05	.02	.01
□ 140 Mike LaCoss	.05	.02	.01
□ 141 Jeff Treadway	.05	.02	.01
□ 142 Pat Tabler	.05	.02	.01
□ 143 Darrell Evans	.15	.07	.02
□ 144 Rafael Ramirez	.05	.02	.01
□ 145 Oddibe McDowell UER	.05	.02	.01
(Misspelled Odibbe)			
□ 146 Brian Downing	.05	.02	.01
□ 147 Curt Wilkerson	.05	.02	.01
□ 148 Ernie Whitt	.05	.02	.01
□ 149 Bill Schroeder	.05	.02	.01
□ 150 Domingo Ramos UER	.05	.02	.01

	(Says throws right, but shows him throwing lefty)			
□ 151	Rick Honeycutt	.05	.02	.01
□ 152	Don Slaught	.05	.02	.01
□ 153	Mitch Webster	.05	.02	.01
□ 154	Tony Phillips	.30	.14	.04
□ 155	Paul Kilgus	.05	.02	.01
□ 156	Ken Griffey Jr. UER	3.00	1.35	.35
	(Simultaniously)			
□ 157	Gary Sheffield	.50	.23	.06
□ 158	Wally Backman	.05	.02	.01
□ 159	B.J. Surhoff	.15	.07	.02
□ 160	Louie Meadows	.05	.02	.01
□ 161	Paul O'Neill	.15	.07	.02
□ 162	Jeff McKnight	.05	.02	.01
□ 163	Alvaro Espinoza	.05	.02	.01
□ 164	Scott Scudder	.05	.02	.01
□ 165	Jeff Reed	.05	.02	.01
□ 166	Gregg Jefferies	.30	.14	.04
□ 167	Barry Larkin	.30	.14	.04
□ 168	Gary Carter	.30	.14	.04
□ 169	Robby Thompson	.05	.02	.01
□ 170	Rolando Roomes	.05	.02	.01
□ 171	Mark McGwire UER	.60	.25	.07
	(Total games 427 and hits 479, should be 467 and 427)			
□ 172	Steve Sax	.05	.02	.01
□ 173	Mark Williamson	.05	.02	.01
□ 174	Mitch Williams	.05	.02	.01
□ 175	Brian Holton	.05	.02	.01
□ 176	Rob Deer	.05	.02	.01
□ 177	Tim Raines	.30	.14	.04
□ 178	Mike Felder	.05	.02	.01
□ 179	Harold Reynolds	.05	.02	.01
□ 180	Terry Francona	.05	.02	.01
□ 181	Chris Sabo	.05	.02	.01
□ 182	Darryl Strawberry	.15	.07	.02
□ 183	Willie Randolph	.15	.07	.02
□ 184	Bill Ripken	.05	.02	.01
□ 185	Mackey Sasser	.05	.02	.01
□ 186	Todd Benzinger	.05	.02	.01
□ 187	Kevin Elster UER	.05	.02	.01
	(16 homers in 1989, should be 10)			
□ 188	Jose Uribe	.05	.02	.01
□ 189	Tom Browning	.05	.02	.01
□ 190	Keith Miller	.05	.02	.01
□ 191	Don Mattingly	1.00	.45	.12
□ 192	Dave Parker	.15	.07	.02
□ 193	Roberto Kelly UER	.15	.07	.02
	(96 RBI, should be 62)			
□ 194	Phil Bradley	.05	.02	.01
□ 195	Ron Hassey	.05	.02	.01
□ 196	Gerald Young	.05	.02	.01
□ 197	Hubie Brooks	.05	.02	.01
□ 198	Bill Doran	.05	.02	.01
□ 199	Al Newman	.05	.02	.01
□ 200	Checklist 101-200	.05	.02	.01
□ 201	Terry Puhl	.05	.02	.01
□ 202	Frank DiPino	.05	.02	.01
□ 203	Jim Clancy	.05	.02	.01
□ 204	Bob Ojeda	.05	.02	.01
□ 205	Alex Trevino	.05	.02	.01
□ 206	Dave Henderson	.05	.02	.01
□ 207	Henry Cotto	.05	.02	.01
□ 208	Rafael Belliard UER	.05	.02	.01
	(Born 1961, not 1951)			
□ 209	Stan Javier	.05	.02	.01
□ 210	Jerry Reed	.05	.02	.01
□ 211	Doug Dascenzo	.05	.02	.01
□ 212	Andres Thomas	.05	.02	.01
□ 213	Greg Maddux	1.25	.55	.16
□ 214	Mike Schooler	.05	.02	.01
□ 215	Lonnie Smith	.05	.02	.01
□ 216	Jose Rijo	.05	.02	.01
□ 217	Greg Gagne	.05	.02	.01
□ 218	Jim Gantner	.05	.02	.01
□ 219	Allan Anderson	.05	.02	.01
□ 220	Rick Mahler	.05	.02	.01
□ 221	Jim Deshaies	.05	.02	.01
□ 222	Keith Hernandez	.15	.07	.02
□ 223	Vince Coleman	.05	.02	.01
□ 224	David Cone	.30	.14	.04
□ 225	Ozzie Smith	.40	.18	.05
□ 226	Matt Nokes	.05	.02	.01
□ 227	Barry Bonds	.50	.23	.06
□ 228	Felix Jose	.05	.02	.01
□ 229	Dennis Powell	.05	.02	.01
□ 230	Mike Gallego	.05	.02	.01
□ 231	Shawon Dunston UER	.05	.02	.01
	('89 stats are Andre Dawson's)			
□ 232	Ron Gant	.30	.14	.04
□ 233	Omar Vizquel	.15	.07	.02
□ 234	Derek Lilliquist	.05	.02	.01
□ 235	Erik Hanson	.15	.07	.02
□ 236	Kirby Puckett UER	.60	.25	.07
	(824 games, should be 924)			
□ 237	Bill Spiers	.05	.02	.01
□ 238	Dan Gladden	.05	.02	.01
□ 239	Bryan Clutterbuck	.05	.02	.01
□ 240	John Moses	.05	.02	.01
□ 241	Ron Darling	.05	.02	.01
□ 242	Joe Magrane	.05	.02	.01
□ 243	Dave Magadan	.05	.02	.01
□ 244	Pedro Guerrero UER	.05	.02	.01
	(Misspelled Guererro)			
□ 245	Glenn Davis	.05	.02	.01
□ 246	Terry Steinbach	.15	.07	.02
□ 247	Fred Lynn	.05	.02	.01
□ 248	Gary Redus	.05	.02	.01
□ 249	Ken Williams	.05	.02	.01
□ 250	Sid Bream	.05	.02	.01
□ 251	Bob Welch UER	.05	.02	.01
	(2587 career strikeouts, should be 1587)			
□ 252	Bill Buckner	.05	.02	.01
□ 253	Carney Lansford	.15	.07	.02
□ 254	Paul Molitor	.40	.18	.05
□ 255	Jose DeJesus	.05	.02	.01
□ 256	Orel Hershiser	.15	.07	.02
□ 257	Tom Brunansky	.05	.02	.01
□ 258	Mike Davis	.05	.02	.01
□ 259	Jeff Ballard	.05	.02	.01
□ 260	Scott Terry	.05	.02	.01
□ 261	Sid Fernandez	.05	.02	.01
□ 262	Mike Marshall	.05	.02	.01
□ 263	Howard Johnson UER	.05	.02	.01
	(192 SO, should be 592)			
□ 264	Kirk Gibson UER	.15	.07	.02
	(659 runs, should be 669)			
□ 265	Kevin McReynolds	.05	.02	.01
□ 266	Cal Ripken	1.50	.70	.19
□ 267	Ozzie Guillen UER	.05	.02	.01
	(Career triples 27, should be 29)			
□ 268	Jim Traber	.05	.02	.01
□ 269	Bobby Thigpen UER	.05	.02	.01
	(31 saves in 1989, should be 34)			
□ 270	Joe Orsulak	.05	.02	.01
□ 271	Bob Boone	.15	.07	.02
□ 272	Dave Stewart UER	.15	.07	.02
	(Totals wrong due to omission of '86 stats)			
□ 273	Tim Wallach	.05	.02	.01
□ 274	Luis Aquino UER	.05	.02	.01
	(Says throws lefty, but shows him throwing righty)			
□ 275	Mike Moore	.05	.02	.01
□ 276	Tony Pena	.05	.02	.01
□ 277	Eddie Murray UER	.50	.23	.06
	(Several typos in career total stats)			
□ 278	Milt Thompson	.05	.02	.01
□ 279	Alejandro Pena	.05	.02	.01
□ 280	Ken Dayley	.05	.02	.01
□ 281	Carmen Castillo	.05	.02	.01
□ 282	Tom Henke	.05	.02	.01
□ 283	Mickey Hatcher	.05	.02	.01
□ 284	Roy Smith	.05	.02	.01
□ 285	Manny Lee	.05	.02	.01
□ 286	Dan Pasqua	.05	.02	.01
□ 287	Larry Sheets	.05	.02	.01
□ 288	Garry Templeton	.05	.02	.01
□ 289	Eddie Williams	.05	.02	.01
□ 290	Brady Anderson UER	.30	.14	.04

(Home: Silver Springs, not Siver Springs)			
□ 291 Spike Owen	.05	.02	.01
□ 292 Storm Davis	.05	.02	.01
□ 293 Chris Bosio	.05	.02	.01
□ 294 Jim Eisenreich	.05	.02	.01
□ 295 Don August	.05	.02	.01
□ 296 Jeff Hamilton	.05	.02	.01
□ 297 Mickey Tettleton	.15	.07	.02
□ 298 Mike Scioscia	.05	.02	.01
□ 299 Kevin Hickey	.05	.02	.01
□ 300 Checklist 201-300	.05	.02	.01
□ 301 Shawn Abner	.05	.02	.01
□ 302 Kevin Bass	.05	.02	.01
□ 303 Bip Roberts	.05	.02	.01
□ 304 Joe Girardi	.15	.07	.02
□ 305 Danny Darwin	.05	.02	.01
□ 306 Mike Heath	.05	.02	.01
□ 307 Mike Macfarlane	.05	.02	.01
□ 308 Ed Whitson	.05	.02	.01
□ 309 Tracy Jones	.05	.02	.01
□ 310 Scott Fletcher	.05	.02	.01
□ 311 Darnell Coles	.05	.02	.01
□ 312 Mike Brumley	.05	.02	.01
□ 313 Bill Swift	.05	.02	.01
□ 314 Charlie Hough	.05	.02	.01
□ 315 Jim Presley	.05	.02	.01
□ 316 Luis Polonia	.05	.02	.01
□ 317 Mike Morgan	.05	.02	.01
□ 318 Lee Guetterman	.05	.02	.01
□ 319 Jose Oquendo	.05	.02	.01
□ 320 Wayne Tolleson	.05	.02	.01
□ 321 Jody Reed	.05	.02	.01
□ 322 Damon Berryhill	.05	.02	.01
□ 323 Roger Clemens	.30	.14	.04
□ 324 Ryne Sandberg	.50	.23	.06
□ 325 Benito Santiago UER (Misspelled Santago on card back)	.05	.02	.01
□ 326 Bret Saberhagen UER (1140 hits, should be 1240; 56 CG, should be 52)	.15	.07	.02
□ 327 Lou Whitaker	.30	.14	.04
□ 328 Dave Gallagher	.05	.02	.01
□ 329 Mike Pagliarulo	.05	.02	.01
□ 330 Doyle Alexander	.05	.02	.01
□ 331 Jeffrey Leonard	.05	.02	.01
□ 332 Torey Lovullo	.05	.02	.01
□ 333 Pete Incaviglia	.05	.02	.01
□ 334 Rickey Henderson	.30	.14	.04
□ 335 Rafael Palmeiro	.30	.14	.04
□ 336 Ken Hill	.30	.14	.04
□ 337 Dave Winfield UER (1418 RBI, should be 1438)	.30	.14	.04
□ 338 Alfredo Griffin	.05	.02	.01
□ 339 Andy Hawkins	.05	.02	.01
□ 340 Ted Power	.05	.02	.01
□ 341 Steve Wilson	.05	.02	.01
□ 342 Jack Clark UER (916 BB, should be 1006; 1142 SO, should be 1130)	.15	.07	.02
□ 343 Ellis Burks	.30	.14	.04
□ 344 Tony Gwynn UER (Doubles stats on card back are wrong)	.75	.35	.09
□ 345 Jerome Walton UER (Total At Bats 476, should be 475)	.05	.02	.01
□ 346 Roberto Alomar UER (61 doubles, should be 51)	.60	.25	.07
□ 347 Carlos Martinez UER (Born 8/11/64, should be 8/11/65)	.05	.02	.01
□ 348 Chet Lemon	.05	.02	.01
□ 349 Willie Wilson	.05	.02	.01
□ 350 Greg Walker	.05	.02	.01
□ 351 Tom Bolton	.05	.02	.01
□ 352 German Gonzalez	.05	.02	.01
□ 353 Harold Baines	.15	.07	.02
□ 354 Mike Greenwell	.05	.02	.01
□ 355 Ruben Sierra	.15	.07	.02
□ 356 Andres Galarraga	.30	.14	.04
□ 357 Andre Dawson	.30	.14	.04
□ 358 Jeff Brantley	.15	.07	.02
□ 359 Mike Bielecki	.05	.02	.01
□ 360 Ken Oberkfell	.05	.02	.01
□ 361 Kurt Stillwell	.05	.02	.01
□ 362 Brian Holman	.05	.02	.01
□ 363 Kevin Seitzer UER (Career triples total does not add up)	.05	.02	.01
□ 364 Alvin Davis	.05	.02	.01
□ 365 Tom Gordon	.05	.02	.01
□ 366 Bobby Bonilla UER (Two steals in 1987, should be 3)	.15	.07	.02
□ 367 Carlton Fisk	.30	.14	.04
□ 368 Steve Carter UER (Charlotesville)	.05	.02	.01
□ 369 Joel Skinner	.05	.02	.01
□ 370 John Cangelosi	.05	.02	.01
□ 371 Cecil Espy	.05	.02	.01
□ 372 Gary Wayne	.05	.02	.01
□ 373 Jim Rice	.30	.14	.04
□ 374 Mike Dyer	.05	.02	.01
□ 375 Joe Carter	.30	.14	.04
□ 376 Dwight Smith	.05	.02	.01
□ 377 John Wetteland	.15	.07	.02
□ 378 Earnie Riles	.05	.02	.01
□ 379 Otis Nixon	.05	.02	.01
□ 380 Vance Law	.05	.02	.01
□ 381 Dave Bergman	.05	.02	.01
□ 382 Frank White	.15	.07	.02
□ 383 Scott Bradley	.05	.02	.01
□ 384 Israel Sanchez UER (Totals don't include '89 stats)	.05	.02	.01
□ 385 Gary Pettis	.05	.02	.01
□ 386 Donn Pall	.05	.02	.01
□ 387 John Smiley	.15	.07	.02
□ 388 Tom Candiotti	.05	.02	.01
□ 389 Junior Ortiz	.05	.02	.01
□ 390 Steve Lyons	.05	.02	.01
□ 391 Brian Harper	.05	.02	.01
□ 392 Fred Manrique	.05	.02	.01
□ 393 Lee Smith	.15	.07	.02
□ 394 Jeff Kunkel	.05	.02	.01
□ 395 Claudell Washington	.05	.02	.01
□ 396 John Tudor	.05	.02	.01
□ 397 Terry Kennedy UER (Career totals all wrong)	.05	.02	.01
□ 398 Lloyd McClendon	.05	.02	.01
□ 399 Craig Lefferts	.05	.02	.01
□ 400 Checklist 301-400	.05	.02	.01
□ 401 Keith Moreland	.05	.02	.01
□ 402 Rich Gedman	.05	.02	.01
□ 403 Jeff D. Robinson	.05	.02	.01
□ 404 Randy Ready	.05	.02	.01
□ 405 Rick Cerone	.05	.02	.01
□ 406 Jeff Blauser	.15	.07	.02
□ 407 Larry Andersen	.05	.02	.01
□ 408 Joe Boever	.05	.02	.01
□ 409 Felix Fermin	.05	.02	.01
□ 410 Glenn Wilson	.05	.02	.01
□ 411 Rex Hudler	.05	.02	.01
□ 412 Mark Grant	.05	.02	.01
□ 413 Dennis Martinez	.15	.07	.02
□ 414 Darrin Jackson	.05	.02	.01
□ 415 Mike Aldrete	.05	.02	.01
□ 416 Roger McDowell	.05	.02	.01
□ 417 Jeff Reardon	.15	.07	.02
□ 418 Darren Daulton	.15	.07	.02
□ 419 Tim Laudner	.05	.02	.01
□ 420 Don Carman	.05	.02	.01
□ 421 Lloyd Moseby	.05	.02	.01
□ 422 Doug Drabek	.05	.02	.01
□ 423 Lenny Harris UER (Walks 2 in '89, should be 20)	.05	.02	.01
□ 424 Jose Lind	.05	.02	.01
□ 425 Dave Johnson (P)	.05	.02	.01
□ 426 Jerry Browne	.05	.02	.01
□ 427 Eric Yelding	.05	.02	.01
□ 428 Brad Komminsk	.05	.02	.01
□ 429 Jody Davis	.05	.02	.01
□ 430 Mariano Duncan	.05	.02	.01
□ 431 Mark Davis	.05	.02	.01

□ 432	Nelson Santovenia	.05	.02	.01
□ 433	Bruce Hurst	.05	.02	.01
□ 434	Jeff Huson	.05	.02	.01
□ 435	Chris James	.05	.02	.01
□ 436	Mark Guthrie	.05	.02	.01
□ 437	Charlie Hayes	.15	.07	.02
□ 438	Shane Rawley	.05	.02	.01
□ 439	Dickie Thon	.05	.02	.01
□ 440	Juan Berenguer	.05	.02	.01
□ 441	Kevin Romine	.05	.02	.01
□ 442	Bill Landrum	.05	.02	.01
□ 443	Todd Frohwirth	.05	.02	.01
□ 444	Craig Worthington	.05	.02	.01
□ 445	Fernando Valenzuela	.15	.07	.02
□ 446	Joey Belle	2.00	.90	.25
□ 447	Ed Whited UER (Ashville, should be Asheville)	.05	.02	.01
□ 448	Dave Smith	.05	.02	.01
□ 449	Dave Clark	.05	.02	.01
□ 450	Juan Agosto	.05	.02	.01
□ 451	Dave Valle	.05	.02	.01
□ 452	Kent Hrbek	.15	.07	.02
□ 453	Von Hayes	.05	.02	.01
□ 454	Gary Gaetti	.15	.07	.02
□ 455	Greg Briley	.05	.02	.01
□ 456	Glenn Braggs	.05	.02	.01
□ 457	Kirt Manwaring	.05	.02	.01
□ 458	Mel Hall	.05	.02	.01
□ 459	Brook Jacoby	.05	.02	.01
□ 460	Pat Sheridan	.05	.02	.01
□ 461	Rob Murphy	.05	.02	.01
□ 462	Jimmy Key	.15	.07	.02
□ 463	Nick Esasky	.05	.02	.01
□ 464	Rob Ducey	.05	.02	.01
□ 465	Carlos Quintana UER (Internatinoal)	.05	.02	.01
□ 466	Larry Walker	1.00	.45	.12
□ 467	Todd Worrell	.05	.02	.01
□ 468	Kevin Gross	.05	.02	.01
□ 469	Terry Pendleton	.15	.07	.02
□ 470	Dave Martinez	.05	.02	.01
□ 471	Gene Larkin	.05	.02	.01
□ 472	Len Dykstra UER ('89 and total runs understated by 10)	.15	.07	.02
□ 473	Barry Lyons	.05	.02	.01
□ 474	Terry Mulholland	.05	.02	.01
□ 475	Chip Hale	.05	.02	.01
□ 476	Jesse Barfield	.05	.02	.01
□ 477	Dan Plesac	.05	.02	.01
□ 478A	Scott Garrelts ERR (Photo actually Bill Bathe)	2.00	.90	.25
□ 478B	Scott Garrelts COR	.05	.02	.01
□ 479	Dave Righetti	.05	.02	.01
□ 480	Gus Polidor UER (Wearing 14 on front, but 10 on back)	.05	.02	.01
□ 481	Mookie Wilson	.05	.02	.01
□ 482	Luis Rivera	.05	.02	.01
□ 483	Mike Flanagan	.05	.02	.01
□ 484	Dennis Boyd	.05	.02	.01
□ 485	John Cerutti	.05	.02	.01
□ 486	John Costello	.05	.02	.01
□ 487	Pascual Perez	.05	.02	.01
□ 488	Tommy Herr	.05	.02	.01
□ 489	Tom Foley	.05	.02	.01
□ 490	Curt Ford	.05	.02	.01
□ 491	Steve Lake	.05	.02	.01
□ 492	Tim Teufel	.05	.02	.01
□ 493	Randy Bush	.05	.02	.01
□ 494	Mike Jackson	.05	.02	.01
□ 495	Steve Jeltz	.05	.02	.01
□ 496	Paul Gibson	.05	.02	.01
□ 497	Steve Balboni	.05	.02	.01
□ 498	Bud Black	.05	.02	.01
□ 499	Dale Sveum	.05	.02	.01
□ 500	Checklist 401-500	.05	.02	.01
□ 501	Tim Jones	.05	.02	.01
□ 502	Mark Portugal	.05	.02	.01
□ 503	Ivan Calderon	.05	.02	.01
□ 504	Rick Rhoden	.05	.02	.01
□ 505	Willie McGee	.05	.02	.01
□ 506	Kirk McCaskill	.05	.02	.01
□ 507	Dave LaPoint	.05	.02	.01
□ 508	Jay Howell	.05	.02	.01
□ 509	Johnny Ray	.05	.02	.01
□ 510	Dave Anderson	.05	.02	.01
□ 511	Chuck Crim	.05	.02	.01
□ 512	Joe Hesketh	.05	.02	.01
□ 513	Dennis Eckersley	.15	.07	.02
□ 514	Greg Brock	.05	.02	.01
□ 515	Tim Burke	.05	.02	.01
□ 516	Frank Tanana	.05	.02	.01
□ 517	Jay Bell	.15	.07	.02
□ 518	Guillermo Hernandez	.05	.02	.01
□ 519	Randy Kramer UER (Codiroli misspelled as Codoroli)	.05	.02	.01
□ 520	Charles Hudson	.05	.02	.01
□ 521	Jim Corsi (Word "originally" is misspelled on back)	.05	.02	.01
□ 522	Steve Rosenberg	.05	.02	.01
□ 523	Cris Carpenter	.05	.02	.01
□ 524	Matt Winters	.05	.02	.01
□ 525	Melido Perez	.05	.02	.01
□ 526	Chris Gwynn UER (Albeguergue)	.05	.02	.01
□ 527	Bert Blyleven UER (Games career total is wrong, should be 644)	.15	.07	.02
□ 528	Chuck Cary	.05	.02	.01
□ 529	Daryl Boston	.05	.02	.01
□ 530	Dale Mohorcic	.05	.02	.01
□ 531	Geronimo Berroa	.15	.07	.02
□ 532	Edgar Martinez	.30	.14	.04
□ 533	Dale Murphy	.30	.14	.04
□ 534	Jay Buhner	.30	.14	.04
□ 535	John Smoltz UER (HEA Stadium)	.50	.23	.06
□ 536	Andy Van Slyke	.15	.07	.02
□ 537	Mike Henneman	.05	.02	.01
□ 538	Miguel Garcia	.05	.02	.01
□ 539	Frank Williams	.05	.02	.01
□ 540	R.J. Reynolds	.05	.02	.01
□ 541	Shawn Hillegas	.05	.02	.01
□ 542	Walt Weiss	.05	.02	.01
□ 543	Greg Hibbard	.05	.02	.01
□ 544	Nolan Ryan	1.50	.70	.19
□ 545	Todd Zeile	.15	.07	.02
□ 546	Hensley Meulens	.05	.02	.01
□ 547	Tim Belcher	.05	.02	.01
□ 548	Mike Witt	.05	.02	.01
□ 549	Greg Cadaret UER (Aquiring, should be Acquiring)	.05	.02	.01
□ 550	Franklin Stubbs	.05	.02	.01
□ 551	Tony Castillo	.05	.02	.01
□ 552	Jeff M. Robinson	.05	.02	.01
□ 553	Steve Olin	.15	.07	.02
□ 554	Alan Trammell	.30	.14	.04
□ 555	Wade Boggs 4X (Bo Jackson in background)	.30	.14	.04
□ 556	Will Clark	.30	.14	.04
□ 557	Jeff King	.15	.07	.02
□ 558	Mike Fitzgerald	.05	.02	.01
□ 559	Ken Howell	.05	.02	.01
□ 560	Bob Kipper	.05	.02	.01
□ 561	Scott Bankhead	.05	.02	.01
□ 562A	Jeff Innis ERR (Photo actually David West)	2.00	.90	.25
□ 562B	Jeff Innis COR	.05	.02	.01
□ 563	Randy Johnson	.50	.23	.06
□ 564	Wally Whitehurst	.05	.02	.01
□ 565	Gene Harris	.05	.02	.01
□ 566	Norm Charlton	.05	.02	.01
□ 567	Robin Yount UER (7602 career hits, should be 2606)	.30	.14	.04
□ 568	Joe Oliver UER (Fl.orida)	.05	.02	.01
□ 569	Mark Parent	.05	.02	.01
□ 570	John Farrell UER (Loss total added wrong)	.05	.02	.01
□ 571	Tom Glavine	.30	.14	.04
□ 572	Rod Nichols	.05	.02	.01
□ 573	Jack Morris	.15	.07	.02
□ 574	Greg Swindell	.05	.02	.01

□ 575	Steve Searcy	.05	.02	.01
□ 576	Ricky Jordan	.05	.02	.01
□ 577	Matt Williams	.30	.14	.04
□ 578	Mike LaValliere	.05	.02	.01
□ 579	Bryn Smith	.05	.02	.01
□ 580	Bruce Ruffin	.05	.02	.01
□ 581	Randy Myers	.15	.07	.02
□ 582	Rick Wrona	.05	.02	.01
□ 583	Juan Samuel	.05	.02	.01
□ 584	Les Lancaster	.05	.02	.01
□ 585	Jeff Musselman	.05	.02	.01
□ 586	Rob Dibble	.05	.02	.01
□ 587	Eric Show	.05	.02	.01
□ 588	Jesse Orosco	.05	.02	.01
□ 589	Herm Winningham	.05	.02	.01
□ 590	Andy Allanson	.05	.02	.01
□ 591	Dion James	.05	.02	.01
□ 592	Carmelo Martinez	.05	.02	.01
□ 593	Luis Quinones	.05	.02	.01
□ 594	Dennis Rasmussen	.05	.02	.01
□ 595	Rich Yett	.05	.02	.01
□ 596	Bob Walk	.05	.02	.01
□ 597A	Andy McGaffigan ERR (Photo actually Rich Thompson)	.15	.07	.02
□ 597B	Andy McGaffigan COR	.05	.02	.01
□ 598	Billy Hatcher	.05	.02	.01
□ 599	Bob Knepper	.05	.02	.01
□ 600	Checklist 501-600 UER (599 Bob Kneppers)	.05	.02	.01
□ 601	Joey Cora	.30	.14	.04
□ 602	Steve Finley	.30	.14	.04
□ 603	Kal Daniels UER (12 hits in '87, should be 123; 335 runs, should be 235)	.05	.02	.01
□ 604	Gregg Olson	.05	.02	.01
□ 605	Dave Stieb	.05	.02	.01
□ 606	Kenny Rogers (Shown catching football)	.15	.07	.02
□ 607	Zane Smith	.05	.02	.01
□ 608	Bob Geren UER (Origionally)	.05	.02	.01
□ 609	Chad Kreuter	.05	.02	.01
□ 610	Mike Smithson	.05	.02	.01
□ 611	Jeff Wetherby	.05	.02	.01
□ 612	Gary Mielke	.05	.02	.01
□ 613	Pete Smith	.05	.02	.01
□ 614	Jack Daugherty UER (Born 7/30/60, should be 7/3/60; origionally)	.05	.02	.01
□ 615	Lance McCullers	.05	.02	.01
□ 616	Don Robinson	.05	.02	.01
□ 617	Jose Guzman	.05	.02	.01
□ 618	Steve Bedrosian	.05	.02	.01
□ 619	Jamie Moyer	.05	.02	.01
□ 620	Atlee Hammaker	.05	.02	.01
□ 621	Rick Luecken UER (Innings pitched wrong)	.05	.02	.01
□ 622	Greg W. Harris	.05	.02	.01
□ 623	Pete Harnisch	.05	.02	.01
□ 624	Jerald Clark	.05	.02	.01
□ 625	Jack McDowell UER (Career totals for Games and GS don't include 1987 season)	.30	.14	.04
□ 626	Frank Viola	.05	.02	.01
□ 627	Teddy Higuera	.05	.02	.01
□ 628	Marty Pevey	.05	.02	.01
□ 629	Bill Wegman	.05	.02	.01
□ 630	Eric Plunk	.05	.02	.01
□ 631	Drew Hall	.05	.02	.01
□ 632	Doug Jones	.05	.02	.01
□ 633	Geno Petralli UER (Sacremento)	.05	.02	.01
□ 634	Jose Alvarez	.05	.02	.01
□ 635	Bob Milacki	.05	.02	.01
□ 636	Bobby Witt	.05	.02	.01
□ 637	Trevor Wilson	.05	.02	.01
□ 638	Jeff Russell UER (Shutout stats wrong)	.05	.02	.01
□ 639	Mike Krukow	.05	.02	.01
□ 640	Rick Leach	.05	.02	.01
□ 641	Dave Schmidt	.05	.02	.01
□ 642	Terry Leach	.05	.02	.01
□ 643	Calvin Schiraldi	.05	.02	.01
□ 644	Bob Melvin	.05	.02	.01
□ 645	Jim Abbott	.15	.07	.02
□ 646	Jaime Navarro	.05	.02	.01
□ 647	Mark Langston UER (Several errors in stats totals)	.15	.07	.02
□ 648	Juan Nieves	.05	.02	.01
□ 649	Damaso Garcia	.05	.02	.01
□ 650	Charlie O'Brien	.05	.02	.01
□ 651	Eric King	.05	.02	.01
□ 652	Mike Boddicker	.05	.02	.01
□ 653	Duane Ward	.05	.02	.01
□ 654	Bob Stanley	.05	.02	.01
□ 655	Sandy Alomar Jr.	.15	.07	.02
□ 656	Danny Tartabull UER (395 BB, should be 295)	.05	.02	.01
□ 657	Randy McCament	.05	.02	.01
□ 658	Charlie Leibrandt	.05	.02	.01
□ 659	Dan Quisenberry	.05	.02	.01
□ 660	Paul Assenmacher	.05	.02	.01
□ 661	Walt Terrell	.05	.02	.01
□ 662	Tim Leary	.05	.02	.01
□ 663	Randy Milligan	.05	.02	.01
□ 664	Bo Diaz	.05	.02	.01
□ 665	Mark Lemke UER (Richmond misspelled as Richomond)	.15	.07	.02
□ 666	Jose Gonzalez	.05	.02	.01
□ 667	Chuck Finley UER (Born 11/16/62, should be 11/26/62)	.15	.07	.02
□ 668	John Kruk	.15	.07	.02
□ 669	Dick Schofield	.05	.02	.01
□ 670	Tim Crews	.05	.02	.01
□ 671	John Dopson	.05	.02	.01
□ 672	John Orton	.05	.02	.01
□ 673	Eric Hetzel	.05	.02	.01
□ 674	Lance Parrish	.05	.02	.01
□ 675	Ramon Martinez	.30	.14	.04
□ 676	Mark Gubicza	.05	.02	.01
□ 677	Greg Litton	.05	.02	.01
□ 678	Greg Mathews	.05	.02	.01
□ 679	Dave Dravecky	.15	.07	.02
□ 680	Steve Farr	.05	.02	.01
□ 681	Mike Devereaux	.05	.02	.01
□ 682	Ken Griffey Sr.	.05	.02	.01
□ 683A	Mickey Weston ERR (Listed as Jamie on card)	2.00	.90	.25
□ 683B	Mickey Weston COR (Technically still an error as birthdate is listed as 3/26/81)	.05	.02	.01
□ 684	Jack Armstrong	.05	.02	.01
□ 685	Steve Buechele	.05	.02	.01
□ 686	Bryan Harvey	.05	.02	.01
□ 687	Lance Blankenship	.05	.02	.01
□ 688	Dante Bichette	.30	.14	.04
□ 689	Todd Burns	.05	.02	.01
□ 690	Dan Petry	.05	.02	.01
□ 691	Kent Anderson	.05	.02	.01
□ 692	Todd Stottlemyre	.15	.07	.02
□ 693	Wally Joyner UER (Several stats errors)	.15	.07	.02
□ 694	Mike Rochford	.05	.02	.01
□ 695	Floyd Bannister	.05	.02	.01
□ 696	Rick Reuschel	.05	.02	.01
□ 697	Jose DeLeon	.05	.02	.01
□ 698	Jeff Montgomery	.15	.07	.02
□ 699	Kelly Downs	.05	.02	.01
□ 700A	Checklist 601-700 (683 Jamie Weston)	2.00	.90	.25
□ 700B	Checklist 601-700 (683 Mickey Weston)	.05	.02	.01
□ 701	Jim Gott	.05	.02	.01
□ 702	Rookie Threats Delino DeShields Marquis Grissom Larry Walker	.50	.23	.06
□ 703	Alejandro Pena	.05	.02	.01
□ 704	Willie Randolph	.15	.07	.02
□ 705	Tim Leary	.05	.02	.01
□ 706	Chuck McElroy	.05	.02	.01
□ 707	Gerald Perry	.05	.02	.01
□ 708	Tom Brunansky	.05	.02	.01

□ 709 John Franco	.05	.02	.01
□ 710 Mark Davis	.05	.02	.01
□ 711 David Justice	1.00	.45	.12
□ 712 Storm Davis	.05	.02	.01
□ 713 Scott Ruskin	.05	.02	.01
□ 714 Glenn Braggs	.05	.02	.01
□ 715 Kevin Bearse	.05	.02	.01
□ 716 Jose Nunez	.05	.02	.01
□ 717 Tim Layana	.05	.02	.01
□ 718 Greg Myers	.05	.02	.01
□ 719 Pete O'Brien	.05	.02	.01
□ 720 John Candelaria	.05	.02	.01
□ 721 Craig Grebeck	.05	.02	.01
□ 722 Shawn Boskie	.05	.02	.01
□ 723 Jim Leyritz	.30	.14	.04
□ 724 Bill Sampen	.05	.02	.01
□ 725 Scott Radinsky	.05	.02	.01
□ 726 Todd Hundley	1.25	.55	.16
□ 727 Scott Hemond	.05	.02	.01
□ 728 Lenny Webster	.05	.02	.01
□ 729 Jeff Reardon	.15	.07	.02
□ 730 Mitch Webster	.05	.02	.01
□ 731 Brian Bohanon	.05	.02	.01
□ 732 Rick Parker	.05	.02	.01
□ 733 Terry Shumpert	.05	.02	.01
□ 734A Ryan's 6th No-Hitter (No stripe on front)	3.00	1.35	.35
□ 734B Ryan's 6th No-Hitter (stripe added on card front for 300th win)	.75	.35	.09
□ 735 John Burkett	.15	.07	.02
□ 736 Derrick May	.30	.14	.04
□ 737 Carlos Baerga	1.00	.45	.12
□ 738 Greg Smith	.05	.02	.01
□ 739 Scott Sanderson	.05	.02	.01
□ 740 Joe Kraemer	.05	.02	.01
□ 741 Hector Villanueva	.05	.02	.01
□ 742 Mike Fetters	.15	.07	.02
□ 743 Mark Gardner	.05	.02	.01
□ 744 Matt Nokes	.05	.02	.01
□ 745 Dave Winfield	.30	.14	.04
□ 746 Delino DeShields	.15	.07	.02
□ 747 Dann Howitt	.05	.02	.01
□ 748 Tony Pena	.05	.02	.01
□ 749 Oil Can Boyd	.05	.02	.01
□ 750 Mike Benjamin	.05	.02	.01
□ 751 Alex Cole	.15	.07	.02
□ 752 Eric Gunderson	.05	.02	.01
□ 753 Howard Farmer	.05	.02	.01
□ 754 Joe Carter	.30	.14	.04
□ 755 Ray Lankford	1.00	.45	.12
□ 756 Sandy Alomar Jr.	.15	.07	.02
□ 757 Alex Sanchez	.05	.02	.01
□ 758 Nick Esasky	.05	.02	.01
□ 759 Stan Belinda	.05	.02	.01
□ 760 Jim Presley	.05	.02	.01
□ 761 Gary DiSarcina	.30	.14	.04
□ 762 Wayne Edwards	.05	.02	.01
□ 763 Pat Combs	.05	.02	.01
□ 764 Mickey Pina	.05	.02	.01
□ 765 Wilson Alvarez	.50	.23	.06
□ 766 Dave Parker	.15	.07	.02
□ 767 Mike Blowers	.30	.14	.04
□ 768 Tony Phillips	.30	.14	.04
□ 769 Pascual Perez	.05	.02	.01
□ 770 Gary Pettis	.05	.02	.01
□ 771 Fred Lynn	.05	.02	.01
□ 772 Mel Rojas	.30	.14	.04
□ 773 David Segui	.30	.14	.04
□ 774 Gary Carter	.30	.14	.04
□ 775 Rafael Valdez	.05	.02	.01
□ 776 Glenallen Hill	.15	.07	.02
□ 777 Keith Hernandez	.15	.07	.02
□ 778 Billy Hatcher	.05	.02	.01
□ 779 Marty Clary	.05	.02	.01
□ 780 Candy Maldonado	.05	.02	.01
□ 781 Mike Marshall	.05	.02	.01
□ 782 Billy Joe Robidoux	.05	.02	.01
□ 783 Mark Langston	.15	.07	.02
□ 784 Paul Sorrento	.30	.14	.04
□ 785 Dave Hollins	.30	.14	.04
□ 786 Cecil Fielder	.15	.07	.02
□ 787 Matt Young	.05	.02	.01
□ 788 Jeff Huson	.05	.02	.01
□ 789 Lloyd Moseby	.05	.02	.01
□ 790 Ron Kittle	.05	.02	.01
□ 791 Hubie Brooks	.05	.02	.01
□ 792 Craig Lefferts	.05	.02	.01
□ 793 Kevin Bass	.05	.02	.01
□ 794 Bryn Smith	.05	.02	.01
□ 795 Juan Samuel	.05	.02	.01
□ 796 Sam Horn	.05	.02	.01
□ 797 Randy Myers	.15	.07	.02
□ 798 Chris James	.05	.02	.01
□ 799 Bill Gullickson	.05	.02	.01
□ 800 Checklist 701-800	.05	.02	.01

1991 Upper Deck

This set marked the third year Upper Deck issued a 800-card standard-size set in two separate series of 700 and 100 cards respectively. Cards were distributed in low and high series foil packs and factory sets. The 100-card extended or high-number series was issued by Upper Deck several months after the release of their first series. For the first time in Upper Deck's three-year history, they did not issue a factory Extended set. The basic cards are made on the typical Upper Deck slick, white card stock and features full-color photos on both the front and the back. Subsets include Star Rookies (1-26), Team Cards (28-34, 43-49, 77-82, 95-99) and Top Prospects (50-76). Several other special achievement cards are seeded throughout the set. The team checklist (TC) cards in the set feature an attractive Vernon Wells drawing of a featured player for that particular team. Rookie Cards in this set include Jeff Bagwell, Jeff Conine, Chipper Jones, Eric Karros, Brian McRae, Mike Mussina and Reggie Sanders. A special Michael Jordan card (numbered SP1) was randomly included in packs on a somewhat limited basis. The Hank Aaron hologram card was randomly inserted in the 1991 Upper Deck high number foil packs. Neither card is included in the price of the regular issue set.

	MINT	NRMT	EXC
COMPLETE SET (800)	20.00	9.00	2.50
COMPLETE FACT.SET (800)	20.00	9.00	2.50
COMPLETE LO SET (700)	16.00	7.25	2.00
COMPLETE HI SET (100)	4.00	1.80	.50
COMMON CARD (1-800)	.05	.02	.01
SEMISTARS	.10	.05	.01
STARS	.15	.07	.02
COMP.AARON SET (10)	6.00	2.70	.75
COMMON AARON (19-27)	.50	.23	.06
AARON HEADER SP (NNO)	3.00	1.35	.35
AARON AUTO/2500 (AU3)	300.00	135.00	38.00
AARON: RANDOM INSERTS IN HI SERIES ..			
COMP.RYAN SET (10)	6.00	2.70	.75
COMMON RYAN (10-18)	.50	.23	.06
RYAN HEADER SP (NNO)	3.00	1.35	.35
RYAN AUTO/2500 (AU2)	600.00	275.00	75.00
RYAN: RANDOM INSERTS IN LO SERIES....			

□ 1 Star Rookie Checklist	.05	.02	.01
□ 2 Phil Plantier	.10	.05	.01
□ 3 D.J. Dozier	.05	.02	.01
□ 4 Dave Hansen	.05	.02	.01
□ 5 Maurice Vaughn	.50	.23	.06
□ 6 Leo Gomez	.05	.02	.01
□ 7 Scott Aldred	.05	.02	.01

□ 8 Scott Chiamparino	.05	.02	.01
□ 9 Lance Dickson	.05	.02	.01
□ 10 Sean Berry	.10	.05	.01
□ 11 Bernie Williams	.25	.11	.03
□ 12 Brian Barnes UER (Photo either not him or in wrong jersey)	.05	.02	.01
□ 13 Narciso Elvira	.05	.02	.01
□ 14 Mike Gardiner	.05	.02	.01
□ 15 Greg Colbrunn	.10	.05	.01
□ 16 Bernard Gilkey	.15	.07	.02
□ 17 Mark Lewis	.05	.02	.01
□ 18 Mickey Morandini	.05	.02	.01
□ 19 Charles Nagy	.10	.05	.01
□ 20 Geronimo Pena	.05	.02	.01
□ 21 Henry Rodriguez	.50	.23	.06
□ 22 Scott Cooper	.05	.02	.01
□ 23 Andujar Cedeno UER (Shown batting left, back says right)	.05	.02	.01
□ 24 Eric Karros	.60	.25	.07
□ 25 Steve Decker UER (Lewis-Clark State College, not Lewis and Clark)	.05	.02	.01
□ 26 Kevin Belcher	.05	.02	.01
□ 27 Jeff Conine	.50	.23	.06
□ 28 Dave Stewart TC	.10	.05	.01
□ 29 Carlton Fisk TC	.15	.07	.02
□ 30 Rafael Palmeiro TC	.15	.07	.02
□ 31 Chuck Finley TC	.05	.02	.01
□ 32 Harold Reynolds TC	.05	.02	.01
□ 33 Bret Saberhagen TC	.10	.05	.01
□ 34 Gary Gaetti TC	.05	.02	.01
□ 35 Scott Leius	.05	.02	.01
□ 36 Neal Heaton	.05	.02	.01
□ 37 Terry Lee	.05	.02	.01
□ 38 Gary Redus	.05	.02	.01
□ 39 Barry Jones	.05	.02	.01
□ 40 Chuck Knoblauch	.25	.11	.03
□ 41 Larry Andersen	.05	.02	.01
□ 42 Darryl Hamilton	.10	.05	.01
□ 43 Mike Greenwell TC	.05	.02	.01
□ 44 Kelly Gruber TC	.05	.02	.01
□ 45 Jack Morris TC	.10	.05	.01
□ 46 Sandy Alomar Jr. TC	.05	.02	.01
□ 47 Gregg Olson TC	.05	.02	.01
□ 48 Dave Parker TC	.10	.05	.01
□ 49 Roberto Kelly TC	.05	.02	.01
□ 50 Top Prospect Checklist	.05	.02	.01
□ 51 Kyle Abbott	.05	.02	.01
□ 52 Jeff Juden	.05	.02	.01
□ 53 Todd Van Poppel UER (Born Arlington and attended John Martin HS, should say Hinsdale and James Martin HS)	.10	.05	.01
□ 54 Steve Karsay	.10	.05	.01
□ 55 Chipper Jones	4.00	1.80	.50
□ 56 Chris Johnson UER (Called Tim on back)	.05	.02	.01
□ 57 John Ericks	.05	.02	.01
□ 58 Gary Scott	.05	.02	.01
□ 59 Kiki Jones	.05	.02	.01
□ 60 Wil Cordero	.15	.07	.02
□ 61 Royce Clayton	.15	.07	.02
□ 62 Tim Costo	.05	.02	.01
□ 63 Roger Salkeld	.05	.02	.01
□ 64 Brook Fordyce	.05	.02	.01
□ 65 Mike Mussina	1.25	.55	.16
□ 66 Dave Staton	.05	.02	.01
□ 67 Mike Lieberthal	.10	.05	.01
□ 68 Kurt Miller	.05	.02	.01
□ 69 Dan Peltier	.05	.02	.01
□ 70 Greg Blosser	.05	.02	.01
□ 71 Reggie Sanders	.50	.23	.06
□ 72 Brent Mayne	.05	.02	.01
□ 73 Rico Brogna	.10	.05	.01
□ 74 Willie Banks	.05	.02	.01
□ 75 Len Brutcher	.05	.02	.01
□ 76 Pat Kelly	.10	.05	.01
□ 77 Chris Sabo TC	.05	.02	.01
□ 78 Ramon Martinez TC	.10	.05	.01
□ 79 Matt Williams TC	.15	.07	.02
□ 80 Roberto Alomar TC	.15	.07	.02
□ 81 Glenn Davis TC	.05	.02	.01
□ 82 Ron Gant TC	.10	.05	.01
□ 83 Cecil Fielder FEAT	.10	.05	.01
□ 84 Orlando Merced	.15	.07	.02
□ 85 Domingo Ramos	.05	.02	.01
□ 86 Tom Bolton	.05	.02	.01
□ 87 Andres Santana	.05	.02	.01
□ 88 John Dopson	.05	.02	.01
□ 89 Kenny Williams	.05	.02	.01
□ 90 Marty Barrett	.05	.02	.01
□ 91 Tom Pagnozzi	.05	.02	.01
□ 92 Carmelo Martinez	.05	.02	.01
□ 93 Bobby Thigpen SAVE	.05	.02	.01
□ 94 Barry Bonds TC	.15	.07	.02
□ 95 Gregg Jefferies TC	.10	.05	.01
□ 96 Tim Wallach TC	.05	.02	.01
□ 97 Len Dykstra TC	.10	.05	.01
□ 98 Pedro Guerrero TC	.05	.02	.01
□ 99 Mark Grace TC	.15	.07	.02
□ 100 Checklist 1-100	.05	.02	.01
□ 101 Kevin Elster	.05	.02	.01
□ 102 Tom Brookens	.05	.02	.01
□ 103 Mackey Sasser	.05	.02	.01
□ 104 Felix Fermin	.05	.02	.01
□ 105 Kevin McReynolds	.05	.02	.01
□ 106 Dave Stieb	.05	.02	.01
□ 107 Jeffrey Leonard	.05	.02	.01
□ 108 Dave Henderson	.05	.02	.01
□ 109 Sid Bream	.05	.02	.01
□ 110 Henry Cotto	.05	.02	.01
□ 111 Shawon Dunston	.05	.02	.01
□ 112 Mariano Duncan	.05	.02	.01
□ 113 Joe Girardi	.10	.05	.01
□ 114 Billy Hatcher	.05	.02	.01
□ 115 Greg Maddux	.60	.25	.07
□ 116 Jerry Browne	.05	.02	.01
□ 117 Juan Samuel	.05	.02	.01
□ 118 Steve Olin	.05	.02	.01
□ 119 Alfredo Griffin	.05	.02	.01
□ 120 Mitch Webster	.05	.02	.01
□ 121 Joel Skinner	.05	.02	.01
□ 122 Frank Viola	.05	.02	.01
□ 123 Cory Snyder	.05	.02	.01
□ 124 Howard Johnson	.05	.02	.01
□ 125 Carlos Baerga	.15	.07	.02
□ 126 Tony Fernandez	.05	.02	.01
□ 127 Dave Stewart	.10	.05	.01
□ 128 Jay Buhner	.15	.07	.02
□ 129 Mike LaValliere	.05	.02	.01
□ 130 Scott Bradley	.05	.02	.01
□ 131 Tony Phillips	.10	.05	.01
□ 132 Ryne Sandberg	.25	.11	.03
□ 133 Paul O'Neill	.10	.05	.01
□ 134 Mark Grace	.15	.07	.02
□ 135 Chris Sabo	.05	.02	.01
□ 136 Ramon Martinez	.10	.05	.01
□ 137 Brook Jacoby	.05	.02	.01
□ 138 Candy Maldonado	.05	.02	.01
□ 139 Mike Scioscia	.05	.02	.01
□ 140 Chris James	.05	.02	.01
□ 141 Craig Worthington	.05	.02	.01
□ 142 Manny Lee	.05	.02	.01
□ 143 Tim Raines	.15	.07	.02
□ 144 Sandy Alomar Jr.	.10	.05	.01
□ 145 John Olerud	.10	.05	.01
□ 146 Ozzie Canseco (With Jose)	.10	.05	.01
□ 147 Pat Borders	.05	.02	.01
□ 148 Harold Reynolds	.05	.02	.01
□ 149 Tom Henke	.05	.02	.01
□ 150 R.J. Reynolds	.05	.02	.01
□ 151 Mike Gallego	.05	.02	.01
□ 152 Bobby Bonilla	.10	.05	.01
□ 153 Terry Steinbach	.10	.05	.01
□ 154 Barry Bonds	.25	.11	.03
□ 155 Jose Canseco	.15	.07	.02
□ 156 Gregg Jefferies	.15	.07	.02
□ 157 Matt Williams	.15	.07	.02
□ 158 Craig Biggio	.15	.07	.02
□ 159 Daryl Boston	.05	.02	.01
□ 160 Ricky Jordan	.05	.02	.01
□ 161 Stan Belinda	.05	.02	.01
□ 162 Ozzie Smith	.20	.09	.03
□ 163 Tom Brunansky	.05	.02	.01
□ 164 Todd Zeile	.10	.05	.01
□ 165 Mike Greenwell	.05	.02	.01
□ 166 Kal Daniels	.05	.02	.01

□ 167 Kent Hrbek	.10	.05	.01
□ 168 Franklin Stubbs	.05	.02	.01
□ 169 Dick Schofield	.05	.02	.01
□ 170 Junior Ortiz	.05	.02	.01
□ 171 Hector Villanueva	.05	.02	.01
□ 172 Dennis Eckersley	.10	.05	.01
□ 173 Mitch Williams	.05	.02	.01
□ 174 Mark McGwire	.30	.14	.04
□ 175 Fernando Valenzuela 3X	.10	.05	.01
□ 176 Gary Carter	.15	.07	.02
□ 177 Dave Magadan	.05	.02	.01
□ 178 Robby Thompson	.05	.02	.01
□ 179 Bob Ojeda	.05	.02	.01
□ 180 Ken Caminiti	.15	.07	.02
□ 181 Don Slaught	.05	.02	.01
□ 182 Luis Rivera	.05	.02	.01
□ 183 Jay Bell	.10	.05	.01
□ 184 Jody Reed	.05	.02	.01
□ 185 Wally Backman	.05	.02	.01
□ 186 Dave Martinez	.05	.02	.01
□ 187 Luis Polonia	.05	.02	.01
□ 188 Shane Mack	.05	.02	.01
□ 189 Spike Owen	.05	.02	.01
□ 190 Scott Bailes	.05	.02	.01
□ 191 John Russell	.05	.02	.01
□ 192 Walt Weiss	.05	.02	.01
□ 193 Jose Oquendo	.05	.02	.01
□ 194 Carney Lansford	.10	.05	.01
□ 195 Jeff Huson	.05	.02	.01
□ 196 Keith Miller	.05	.02	.01
□ 197 Eric Yelding	.05	.02	.01
□ 198 Ron Darling	.05	.02	.01
□ 199 John Kruk	.10	.05	.01
□ 200 Checklist 101-200	.05	.02	.01
□ 201 John Shelby	.05	.02	.01
□ 202 Bob Geren	.05	.02	.01
□ 203 Lance McCullers	.05	.02	.01
□ 204 Alvaro Espinoza	.05	.02	.01
□ 205 Mark Salas	.05	.02	.01
□ 206 Mike Pagliarulo	.05	.02	.01
□ 207 Jose Uribe	.05	.02	.01
□ 208 Jim Deshaies	.05	.02	.01
□ 209 Ron Karkovice	.05	.02	.01
□ 210 Rafael Ramirez	.05	.02	.01
□ 211 Donnie Hill	.05	.02	.01
□ 212 Brian Harper	.05	.02	.01
□ 213 Jack Howell	.05	.02	.01
□ 214 Wes Gardner	.05	.02	.01
□ 215 Tim Burke	.05	.02	.01
□ 216 Doug Jones	.05	.02	.01
□ 217 Hubie Brooks	.05	.02	.01
□ 218 Tom Candiotti	.05	.02	.01
□ 219 Gerald Perry	.05	.02	.01
□ 220 Jose DeLeon	.05	.02	.01
□ 221 Wally Whitehurst	.05	.02	.01
□ 222 Alan Mills	.05	.02	.01
□ 223 Alan Trammell	.15	.07	.02
□ 224 Dwight Gooden	.10	.05	.01
□ 225 Travis Fryman	.15	.07	.02
□ 226 Joe Carter	.15	.07	.02
□ 227 Julio Franco	.10	.05	.01
□ 228 Craig Lefferts	.05	.02	.01
□ 229 Gary Pettis	.05	.02	.01
□ 230 Dennis Rasmussen	.05	.02	.01
□ 231A Brian Downing ERR (No position on front)	.05	.02	.01
□ 231B Brian Downing COR (DH on front)	.10	.05	.01
□ 232 Carlos Quintana	.05	.02	.01
□ 233 Gary Gaetti	.10	.05	.01
□ 234 Mark Langston	.10	.05	.01
□ 235 Tim Wallach	.05	.02	.01
□ 236 Greg Swindell	.05	.02	.01
□ 237 Eddie Murray	.25	.11	.03
□ 238 Jeff Manto	.05	.02	.01
□ 239 Lenny Harris	.05	.02	.01
□ 240 Jesse Orosco	.05	.02	.01
□ 241 Scott Lusader	.05	.02	.01
□ 242 Sid Fernandez	.05	.02	.01
□ 243 Jim Leyritz	.10	.05	.01
□ 244 Cecil Fielder	.10	.05	.01
□ 245 Darryl Strawberry	.10	.05	.01
□ 246 Frank Thomas UER (Comiskey Park misspelled Comisky)	2.00	.90	.25
□ 247 Kevin Mitchell	.10	.05	.01
□ 248 Lance Johnson	.10	.05	.01
□ 249 Rick Reuschel	.05	.02	.01
□ 250 Mark Portugal	.05	.02	.01
□ 251 Derek Lilliquist	.05	.02	.01
□ 252 Brian Holman	.05	.02	.01
□ 253 Rafael Valdez UER (Born 4/17/68, should be 12/17/67)	.05	.02	.01
□ 254 B.J. Surhoff	.10	.05	.01
□ 255 Tony Gwynn	.40	.18	.05
□ 256 Andy Van Slyke	.10	.05	.01
□ 257 Todd Stottlemyre	.05	.02	.01
□ 258 Jose Lind	.05	.02	.01
□ 259 Greg Myers	.05	.02	.01
□ 260 Jeff Ballard	.05	.02	.01
□ 261 Bobby Thigpen	.05	.02	.01
□ 262 Jimmy Kremers	.05	.02	.01
□ 263 Robin Ventura	.15	.07	.02
□ 264 John Smoltz	.15	.07	.02
□ 265 Sammy Sosa	.25	.11	.03
□ 266 Gary Sheffield	.15	.07	.02
□ 267 Len Dykstra	.10	.05	.01
□ 268 Bill Spiers	.05	.02	.01
□ 269 Charlie Hayes	.05	.02	.01
□ 270 Brett Butler	.10	.05	.01
□ 271 Bip Roberts	.05	.02	.01
□ 272 Rob Deer	.05	.02	.01
□ 273 Fred Lynn	.05	.02	.01
□ 274 Dave Parker	.10	.05	.01
□ 275 Andy Benes	.05	.02	.01
□ 276 Glenallen Hill	.05	.02	.01
□ 277 Steve Howard	.05	.02	.01
□ 278 Doug Drabek	.05	.02	.01
□ 279 Joe Oliver	.05	.02	.01
□ 280 Todd Benzinger	.05	.02	.01
□ 281 Eric King	.05	.02	.01
□ 282 Jim Presley	.05	.02	.01
□ 283 Ken Patterson	.05	.02	.01
□ 284 Jack Daugherty	.05	.02	.01
□ 285 Ivan Calderon	.05	.02	.01
□ 286 Edgar Diaz	.05	.02	.01
□ 287 Kevin Bass	.05	.02	.01
□ 288 Don Carman	.05	.02	.01
□ 289 Greg Brock	.05	.02	.01
□ 290 John Franco	.05	.02	.01
□ 291 Joey Cora	.10	.05	.01
□ 292 Bill Wegman	.05	.02	.01
□ 293 Eric Show	.05	.02	.01
□ 294 Scott Bankhead	.05	.02	.01
□ 295 Garry Templeton	.05	.02	.01
□ 296 Mickey Tettleton	.10	.05	.01
□ 297 Luis Sojo	.05	.02	.01
□ 298 Jose Rijo	.05	.02	.01
□ 299 Dave Johnson	.05	.02	.01
□ 300 Checklist 201-300	.05	.02	.01
□ 301 Mark Grant	.05	.02	.01
□ 302 Pete Harnisch	.05	.02	.01
□ 303 Greg Olson	.05	.02	.01
□ 304 Anthony Telford	.05	.02	.01
□ 305 Lonnie Smith	.05	.02	.01
□ 306 Chris Hoiles	.05	.02	.01
□ 307 Bryn Smith	.05	.02	.01
□ 308 Mike Devereaux	.05	.02	.01
□ 309A Milt Thompson ERR (Under yr information has print dot)	.15	.07	.02
□ 309B Milt Thompson COR (Under yr information says 86)	.05	.02	.01
□ 310 Bob Melvin	.05	.02	.01
□ 311 Luis Salazar	.05	.02	.01
□ 312 Ed Whitson	.05	.02	.01
□ 313 Charlie Hough	.05	.02	.01
□ 314 Dave Clark	.05	.02	.01
□ 315 Eric Gunderson	.05	.02	.01
□ 316 Dan Petry	.05	.02	.01
□ 317 Dante Bichette UER (Assists misspelled as assissts)	.15	.07	.02
□ 318 Mike Heath	.05	.02	.01
□ 319 Damon Berryhill	.05	.02	.01
□ 320 Walt Terrell	.05	.02	.01
□ 321 Scott Fletcher	.05	.02	.01
□ 322 Dan Plesac	.05	.02	.01
□ 323 Jack McDowell	.10	.05	.01
□ 324 Paul Molitor	.20	.09	.03

□ 325 Ozzie Guillen	.05	.02	.01
□ 326 Gregg Olson	.05	.02	.01
□ 327 Pedro Guerrero	.05	.02	.01
□ 328 Bob Milacki	.05	.02	.01
□ 329 John Tudor UER ('90 Cardinals, should be '90 Dodgers)	.05	.02	.01
□ 330 Steve Finley UER (Born 3/12/65, should be 5/12)	.15	.07	.02
□ 331 Jack Clark	.10	.05	.01
□ 332 Jerome Walton	.05	.02	.01
□ 333 Andy Hawkins	.05	.02	.01
□ 334 Derrick May	.05	.02	.01
□ 335 Roberto Alomar	.25	.11	.03
□ 336 Jack Morris	.10	.05	.01
□ 337 Dave Winfield	.15	.07	.02
□ 338 Steve Searcy	.05	.02	.01
□ 339 Chili Davis	.10	.05	.01
□ 340 Larry Sheets	.05	.02	.01
□ 341 Ted Higuera	.05	.02	.01
□ 342 David Segui	.10	.05	.01
□ 343 Greg Cadaret	.05	.02	.01
□ 344 Robin Yount	.15	.07	.02
□ 345 Nolan Ryan	.75	.35	.09
□ 346 Ray Lankford	.15	.07	.02
□ 347 Cal Ripken	.75	.35	.09
□ 348 Lee Smith	.10	.05	.01
□ 349 Brady Anderson	.15	.07	.02
□ 350 Frank DiPino	.05	.02	.01
□ 351 Hal Morris	.05	.02	.01
□ 352 Deion Sanders	.15	.07	.02
□ 353 Barry Larkin	.15	.07	.02
□ 354 Don Mattingly	.50	.23	.06
□ 355 Eric Davis	.10	.05	.01
□ 356 Jose Offerman	.05	.02	.01
□ 357 Mel Rojas	.10	.05	.01
□ 358 Rudy Seanez	.05	.02	.01
□ 359 Oil Can Boyd	.05	.02	.01
□ 360 Nelson Liriano	.05	.02	.01
□ 361 Ron Gant	.15	.07	.02
□ 362 Howard Farmer	.05	.02	.01
□ 363 David Justice	.15	.07	.02
□ 364 Delino DeShields	.05	.02	.01
□ 365 Steve Avery	.15	.07	.02
□ 366 David Cone	.15	.07	.02
□ 367 Lou Whitaker	.15	.07	.02
□ 368 Von Hayes	.05	.02	.01
□ 369 Frank Tanana	.05	.02	.01
□ 370 Tim Teufel	.05	.02	.01
□ 371 Randy Myers	.10	.05	.01
□ 372 Roberto Kelly	.05	.02	.01
□ 373 Jack Armstrong	.05	.02	.01
□ 374 Kelly Gruber	.05	.02	.01
□ 375 Kevin Maas	.05	.02	.01
□ 376 Randy Johnson	.15	.07	.02
□ 377 David West	.05	.02	.01
□ 378 Brent Knackert	.05	.02	.01
□ 379 Rick Honeycutt	.05	.02	.01
□ 380 Kevin Gross	.05	.02	.01
□ 381 Tom Foley	.05	.02	.01
□ 382 Jeff Blauser	.05	.02	.01
□ 383 Scott Ruskin	.05	.02	.01
□ 384 Andres Thomas	.05	.02	.01
□ 385 Dennis Martinez	.10	.05	.01
□ 386 Mike Henneman	.05	.02	.01
□ 387 Felix Jose	.05	.02	.01
□ 388 Alejandro Pena	.05	.02	.01
□ 389 Chet Lemon	.05	.02	.01
□ 390 Craig Wilson	.05	.02	.01
□ 391 Chuck Crim	.05	.02	.01
□ 392 Mel Hall	.05	.02	.01
□ 393 Mark Knudson	.05	.02	.01
□ 394 Norm Charlton	.05	.02	.01
□ 395 Mike Felder	.05	.02	.01
□ 396 Tim Layana	.05	.02	.01
□ 397 Steve Frey	.05	.02	.01
□ 398 Bill Doran	.05	.02	.01
□ 399 Dion James	.05	.02	.01
□ 400 Checklist 301-400	.05	.02	.01
□ 401 Ron Hassey	.05	.02	.01
□ 402 Don Robinson	.05	.02	.01
□ 403 Gene Nelson	.05	.02	.01
□ 404 Terry Kennedy	.05	.02	.01
□ 405 Todd Burns	.05	.02	.01
□ 406 Roger McDowell	.05	.02	.01
□ 407 Bob Kipper	.05	.02	.01
□ 408 Darren Daulton	.10	.05	.01
□ 409 Chuck Cary	.05	.02	.01
□ 410 Bruce Ruffin	.05	.02	.01
□ 411 Juan Berenguer	.05	.02	.01
□ 412 Gary Ward	.05	.02	.01
□ 413 Al Newman	.05	.02	.01
□ 414 Danny Jackson	.05	.02	.01
□ 415 Greg Gagne	.05	.02	.01
□ 416 Tom Herr	.05	.02	.01
□ 417 Jeff Parrett	.05	.02	.01
□ 418 Jeff Reardon	.10	.05	.01
□ 419 Mark Lemke	.05	.02	.01
□ 420 Charlie O'Brien	.05	.02	.01
□ 421 Willie Randolph	.10	.05	.01
□ 422 Steve Bedrosian	.05	.02	.01
□ 423 Mike Moore	.05	.02	.01
□ 424 Jeff Brantley	.05	.02	.01
□ 425 Bob Welch	.05	.02	.01
□ 426 Terry Mulholland	.05	.02	.01
□ 427 Willie Blair	.05	.02	.01
□ 428 Darrin Fletcher	.05	.02	.01
□ 429 Mike Witt	.05	.02	.01
□ 430 Joe Boever	.05	.02	.01
□ 431 Tom Gordon	.05	.02	.01
□ 432 Pedro Munoz	.10	.05	.01
□ 433 Kevin Seitzer	.05	.02	.01
□ 434 Kevin Tapani	.05	.02	.01
□ 435 Bret Saberhagen	.10	.05	.01
□ 436 Ellis Burks	.15	.07	.02
□ 437 Chuck Finley	.10	.05	.01
□ 438 Mike Boddicker	.05	.02	.01
□ 439 Francisco Cabrera	.05	.02	.01
□ 440 Todd Hundley	.15	.07	.02
□ 441 Kelly Downs	.05	.02	.01
□ 442 Dann Howitt	.05	.02	.01
□ 443 Scott Garrelts	.05	.02	.01
□ 444 Rickey Henderson 3X	.15	.07	.02
□ 445 Will Clark	.15	.07	.02
□ 446 Ben McDonald	.10	.05	.01
□ 447 Dale Murphy	.15	.07	.02
□ 448 Dave Righetti	.05	.02	.01
□ 449 Dickie Thon	.05	.02	.01
□ 450 Ted Power	.05	.02	.01
□ 451 Scott Coolbaugh	.05	.02	.01
□ 452 Dwight Smith	.05	.02	.01
□ 453 Pete Incaviglia	.05	.02	.01
□ 454 Andre Dawson	.15	.07	.02
□ 455 Ruben Sierra	.10	.05	.01
□ 456 Andres Galarraga	.15	.07	.02
□ 457 Alvin Davis	.05	.02	.01
□ 458 Tony Castillo	.05	.02	.01
□ 459 Pete O'Brien	.05	.02	.01
□ 460 Charlie Leibrandt	.05	.02	.01
□ 461 Vince Coleman	.05	.02	.01
□ 462 Steve Sax	.05	.02	.01
□ 463 Omar Olivares	.05	.02	.01
□ 464 Oscar Azocar	.05	.02	.01
□ 465 Joe Magrane	.05	.02	.01
□ 466 Karl Rhodes	.05	.02	.01
□ 467 Benito Santiago	.05	.02	.01
□ 468 Joe Klink	.05	.02	.01
□ 469 Sil Campusano	.05	.02	.01
□ 470 Mark Parent	.05	.02	.01
□ 471 Shawn Boskie UER (Depleted misspelled as depleated)	.05	.02	.01
□ 472 Kevin Brown	.10	.05	.01
□ 473 Rick Sutcliffe	.05	.02	.01
□ 474 Rafael Palmeiro	.15	.07	.02
□ 475 Mike Harkey	.05	.02	.01
□ 476 Jaime Navarro	.05	.02	.01
□ 477 Marquis Grissom UER (DeShields misspelled as DeSheilds)	.15	.07	.02
□ 478 Marty Clary	.05	.02	.01
□ 479 Greg Briley	.05	.02	.01
□ 480 Tom Glavine	.15	.07	.02
□ 481 Lee Guetterman	.05	.02	.01
□ 482 Rex Hudler	.05	.02	.01
□ 483 Dave LaPoint	.05	.02	.01
□ 484 Terry Pendleton	.10	.05	.01
□ 485 Jesse Barfield	.05	.02	.01
□ 486 Jose DeJesus	.05	.02	.01
□ 487 Paul Abbott	.05	.02	.01
□ 488 Ken Howell	.05	.02	.01

□ 489	Greg W. Harris	.05	.02	.01
□ 490	Roy Smith	.05	.02	.01
□ 491	Paul Assenmacher	.05	.02	.01
□ 492	Geno Petralli	.05	.02	.01
□ 493	Steve Wilson	.05	.02	.01
□ 494	Kevin Reimer	.05	.02	.01
□ 495	Bill Long	.05	.02	.01
□ 496	Mike Jackson	.05	.02	.01
□ 497	Oddibe McDowell	.05	.02	.01
□ 498	Bill Swift	.05	.02	.01
□ 499	Jeff Treadway	.05	.02	.01
□ 500	Checklist 401-500	.05	.02	.01
□ 501	Gene Larkin	.05	.02	.01
□ 502	Bob Boone	.10	.05	.01
□ 503	Allan Anderson	.05	.02	.01
□ 504	Luis Aquino	.05	.02	.01
□ 505	Mark Guthrie	.05	.02	.01
□ 506	Joe Orsulak	.05	.02	.01
□ 507	Dana Kiecker	.05	.02	.01
□ 508	Dave Gallagher	.05	.02	.01
□ 509	Greg A. Harris	.05	.02	.01
□ 510	Mark Williamson	.05	.02	.01
□ 511	Casey Candaele	.05	.02	.01
□ 512	Mookie Wilson	.05	.02	.01
□ 513	Dave Smith	.05	.02	.01
□ 514	Chuck Carr	.05	.02	.01
□ 515	Glenn Wilson	.05	.02	.01
□ 516	Mike Fitzgerald	.05	.02	.01
□ 517	Devon White	.10	.05	.01
□ 518	Dave Hollins	.05	.02	.01
□ 519	Mark Eichhorn	.05	.02	.01
□ 520	Otis Nixon	.05	.02	.01
□ 521	Terry Shumpert	.05	.02	.01
□ 522	Scott Erickson	.10	.05	.01
□ 523	Danny Tartabull	.05	.02	.01
□ 524	Orel Hershiser	.10	.05	.01
□ 525	George Brett	.40	.18	.05
□ 526	Greg Vaughn	.15	.07	.02
□ 527	Tim Naehring	.10	.05	.01
□ 528	Curt Schilling	.05	.02	.01
□ 529	Chris Bosio	.05	.02	.01
□ 530	Sam Horn	.05	.02	.01
□ 531	Mike Scott	.05	.02	.01
□ 532	George Bell	.05	.02	.01
□ 533	Eric Anthony	.05	.02	.01
□ 534	Julio Valera	.05	.02	.01
□ 535	Glenn Davis	.05	.02	.01
□ 536	Larry Walker UER (Should have comma after Expos in text)	.15	.07	.02
□ 537	Pat Combs	.05	.02	.01
□ 538	Chris Nabholz	.05	.02	.01
□ 539	Kirk McCaskill	.05	.02	.01
□ 540	Randy Ready	.05	.02	.01
□ 541	Mark Gubicza	.05	.02	.01
□ 542	Rick Aguilera	.10	.05	.01
□ 543	Brian McRae	.25	.11	.03
□ 544	Kirby Puckett	.30	.14	.04
□ 545	Bo Jackson	.15	.07	.02
□ 546	Wade Boggs	.15	.07	.02
□ 547	Tim McIntosh	.05	.02	.01
□ 548	Randy Milligan	.05	.02	.01
□ 549	Dwight Evans	.10	.05	.01
□ 550	Billy Ripken	.05	.02	.01
□ 551	Erik Hanson	.05	.02	.01
□ 552	Lance Parrish	.05	.02	.01
□ 553	Tino Martinez	.15	.07	.02
□ 554	Jim Abbott	.10	.05	.01
□ 555	Ken Griffey Jr. UER (Second most votes for 1991 All-Star Game)	1.50	.70	.19
□ 556	Milt Cuyler	.05	.02	.01
□ 557	Mark Leonard	.05	.02	.01
□ 558	Jay Howell	.05	.02	.01
□ 559	Lloyd Moseby	.05	.02	.01
□ 560	Chris Gwynn	.05	.02	.01
□ 561	Mark Whiten	.10	.05	.01
□ 562	Harold Baines	.10	.05	.01
□ 563	Junior Felix	.05	.02	.01
□ 564	Darren Lewis	.10	.05	.01
□ 565	Fred McGriff	.15	.07	.02
□ 566	Kevin Appier	.10	.05	.01
□ 567	Luis Gonzalez	.15	.07	.02
□ 568	Frank White	.10	.05	.01
□ 569	Juan Agosto	.05	.02	.01
□ 570	Mike Macfarlane	.05	.02	.01

□ 571	Bert Blyleven	.10	.05	.01
□ 572	Ken Griffey Sr. Ken Griffey Jr.	.50	.23	.06
□ 573	Lee Stevens	.05	.02	.01
□ 574	Edgar Martinez	.15	.07	.02
□ 575	Wally Joyner	.10	.05	.01
□ 576	Tim Belcher	.05	.02	.01
□ 577	John Burkett	.10	.05	.01
□ 578	Mike Morgan	.05	.02	.01
□ 579	Paul Gibson	.05	.02	.01
□ 580	Jose Vizcaino	.05	.02	.01
□ 581	Duane Ward	.05	.02	.01
□ 582	Scott Sanderson	.05	.02	.01
□ 583	David Wells	.05	.02	.01
□ 584	Willie McGee	.05	.02	.01
□ 585	John Cerutti	.05	.02	.01
□ 586	Danny Darwin	.05	.02	.01
□ 587	Kurt Stillwell	.05	.02	.01
□ 588	Rich Gedman	.05	.02	.01
□ 589	Mark Davis	.05	.02	.01
□ 590	Bill Gullickson	.05	.02	.01
□ 591	Matt Young	.05	.02	.01
□ 592	Bryan Harvey	.05	.02	.01
□ 593	Omar Vizquel	.15	.07	.02
□ 594	Scott Lewis	.05	.02	.01
□ 595	Dave Valle	.05	.02	.01
□ 596	Tim Crews	.05	.02	.01
□ 597	Mike Bielecki	.05	.02	.01
□ 598	Mike Sharperson	.05	.02	.01
□ 599	Dave Bergman	.05	.02	.01
□ 600	Checklist 501-600	.05	.02	.01
□ 601	Steve Lyons	.05	.02	.01
□ 602	Bruce Hurst	.05	.02	.01
□ 603	Donn Pall	.05	.02	.01
□ 604	Jim Vatcher	.05	.02	.01
□ 605	Dan Pasqua	.05	.02	.01
□ 606	Kenny Rogers	.05	.02	.01
□ 607	Jeff Schulz	.05	.02	.01
□ 608	Brad Arnsberg	.05	.02	.01
□ 609	Willie Wilson	.05	.02	.01
□ 610	Jamie Moyer	.05	.02	.01
□ 611	Ron Oester	.05	.02	.01
□ 612	Dennis Cook	.05	.02	.01
□ 613	Rick Mahler	.05	.02	.01
□ 614	Bill Landrum	.05	.02	.01
□ 615	Scott Scudder	.05	.02	.01
□ 616	Tom Edens	.05	.02	.01
□ 617	1917 Revisited (White Sox in vintage uniforms)	.10	.05	.01
□ 618	Jim Gantner	.05	.02	.01
□ 619	Darrel Akerfelds	.05	.02	.01
□ 620	Ron Robinson	.05	.02	.01
□ 621	Scott Radinsky	.05	.02	.01
□ 622	Pete Smith	.05	.02	.01
□ 623	Melido Perez	.05	.02	.01
□ 624	Jerald Clark	.05	.02	.01
□ 625	Carlos Martinez	.05	.02	.01
□ 626	Wes Chamberlain	.05	.02	.01
□ 627	Bobby Witt	.05	.02	.01
□ 628	Ken Dayley	.05	.02	.01
□ 629	John Barfield	.05	.02	.01
□ 630	Bob Tewksbury	.05	.02	.01
□ 631	Glenn Braggs	.05	.02	.01
□ 632	Jim Neidlinger	.05	.02	.01
□ 633	Tom Browning	.05	.02	.01
□ 634	Kirk Gibson	.10	.05	.01
□ 635	Rob Dibble	.05	.02	.01
□ 636	Rickey Henderson SB Lou Brock May 1, 1991 on front)	.30	.14	.04
□ 636A	Rickey Henderson SB Lou Brock no date on card)	.15	.07	.02
□ 637	Jeff Montgomery	.10	.05	.01
□ 638	Mike Schooler	.05	.02	.01
□ 639	Storm Davis	.05	.02	.01
□ 640	Rich Rodriguez	.05	.02	.01
□ 641	Phil Bradley	.05	.02	.01
□ 642	Kent Mercker	.05	.02	.01
□ 643	Carlton Fisk	.15	.07	.02
□ 644	Mike Bell	.05	.02	.01
□ 645	Alex Fernandez	.15	.07	.02
□ 646	Juan Gonzalez	.75	.35	.09
□ 647	Ken Hill	.15	.07	.02
□ 648	Jeff Russell	.05	.02	.01

□ 649	Chuck Malone	.05	.02	.01
□ 650	Steve Buechele	.05	.02	.01
□ 651	Mike Benjamin	.05	.02	.01
□ 652	Tony Pena	.05	.02	.01
□ 653	Trevor Wilson	.05	.02	.01
□ 654	Alex Cole	.05	.02	.01
□ 655	Roger Clemens	.15	.07	.02
□ 656	Mark McGwire BASH	.15	.07	.02
□ 657	Joe Grahe	.05	.02	.01
□ 658	Jim Eisenreich	.10	.05	.01
□ 659	Dan Gladden	.05	.02	.01
□ 660	Steve Farr	.05	.02	.01
□ 661	Bill Sampen	.05	.02	.01
□ 662	Dave Rohde	.05	.02	.01
□ 663	Mark Gardner	.05	.02	.01
□ 664	Mike Simms	.05	.02	.01
□ 665	Moises Alou	.15	.07	.02
□ 666	Mickey Hatcher	.05	.02	.01
□ 667	Jimmy Key	.10	.05	.01
□ 668	John Wetteland	.10	.05	.01
□ 669	John Smiley	.05	.02	.01
□ 670	Jim Acker	.05	.02	.01
□ 671	Pascual Perez	.05	.02	.01
□ 672	Reggie Harris UER	.05	.02	.01
	(Opportunity misspelled			
	as oppurtinty)			
□ 673	Matt Nokes	.05	.02	.01
□ 674	Rafael Novoa	.05	.02	.01
□ 675	Hensley Meulens	.05	.02	.01
□ 676	Jeff M. Robinson	.05	.02	.01
□ 677	Ground Breaking	.10	.05	.01
	(New Comiskey Park;			
	Carlton Fisk and			
	Robin Ventura)			
□ 678	Johnny Ray	.05	.02	.01
□ 679	Greg Hibbard	.05	.02	.01
□ 680	Paul Sorrento	.10	.05	.01
□ 681	Mike Marshall	.05	.02	.01
□ 682	Jim Clancy	.05	.02	.01
□ 683	Rob Murphy	.05	.02	.01
□ 684	Dave Schmidt	.05	.02	.01
□ 685	Jeff Gray	.05	.02	.01
□ 686	Mike Hartley	.05	.02	.01
□ 687	Jeff King	.10	.05	.01
□ 688	Stan Javier	.05	.02	.01
□ 689	Bob Walk	.05	.02	.01
□ 690	Jim Gott	.05	.02	.01
□ 691	Mike LaCoss	.05	.02	.01
□ 692	John Farrell	.05	.02	.01
□ 693	Tim Leary	.05	.02	.01
□ 694	Mike Walker	.05	.02	.01
□ 695	Eric Plunk	.05	.02	.01
□ 696	Mike Fetters	.05	.02	.01
□ 697	Wayne Edwards	.05	.02	.01
□ 698	Tim Drummond	.05	.02	.01
□ 699	Willie Fraser	.05	.02	.01
□ 700	Checklist 601-700	.05	.02	.01
□ 701	Mike Heath	.05	.02	.01
□ 702	Rookie Threats	.75	.35	.09
	Luis Gonzalez			
	Karl Rhodes			
	Jeff Bagwell			
□ 703	Jose Mesa	.10	.05	.01
□ 704	Dave Smith	.05	.02	.01
□ 705	Danny Darwin	.05	.02	.01
□ 706	Rafael Belliard	.05	.02	.01
□ 707	Rob Murphy	.05	.02	.01
□ 708	Terry Pendleton	.10	.05	.01
□ 709	Mike Pagliarulo	.05	.02	.01
□ 710	Sid Bream	.05	.02	.01
□ 711	Junior Felix	.05	.02	.01
□ 712	Dante Bichette	.15	.07	.02
□ 713	Kevin Gross	.05	.02	.01
□ 714	Luis Sojo	.05	.02	.01
□ 715	Bob Ojeda	.05	.02	.01
□ 716	Julio Machado	.05	.02	.01
□ 717	Steve Farr	.05	.02	.01
□ 718	Franklin Stubbs	.05	.02	.01
□ 719	Mike Boddicker	.05	.02	.01
□ 720	Willie Randolph	.10	.05	.01
□ 721	Willie McGee	.05	.02	.01
□ 722	Chili Davis	.10	.05	.01
□ 723	Danny Jackson	.05	.02	.01
□ 724	Cory Snyder	.05	.02	.01
□ 725	MVP Lineup	.15	.07	.02
	Andre Dawson			
	George Bell			
	Ryne Sandberg			
□ 726	Rob Deer	.05	.02	.01
□ 727	Rich DeLucia	.05	.02	.01
□ 728	Mike Perez	.05	.02	.01
□ 729	Mickey Tettleton	.10	.05	.01
□ 730	Mike Blowers	.05	.02	.01
□ 731	Gary Gaetti	.10	.05	.01
□ 732	Brett Butler	.10	.05	.01
□ 733	Dave Parker	.10	.05	.01
□ 734	Eddie Zosky	.05	.02	.01
□ 735	Jack Clark	.10	.05	.01
□ 736	Jack Morris	.10	.05	.01
□ 737	Kirk Gibson	.10	.05	.01
□ 738	Steve Bedrosian	.05	.02	.01
□ 739	Candy Maldonado	.05	.02	.01
□ 740	Matt Young	.05	.02	.01
□ 741	Rich Garces	.05	.02	.01
□ 742	George Bell	.05	.02	.01
□ 743	Deion Sanders	.15	.07	.02
□ 744	Bo Jackson	.15	.07	.02
□ 745	Luis Mercedes	.05	.02	.01
□ 746	Reggie Jefferson UER	.10	.05	.01
	(Throwing left on card;			
	back has throws right)			
□ 747	Pete Incaviglia	.05	.02	.01
□ 748	Chris Hammond	.05	.02	.01
□ 749	Mike Stanton	.05	.02	.01
□ 750	Scott Sanderson	.05	.02	.01
□ 751	Paul Faries	.05	.02	.01
□ 752	Al Osuna	.05	.02	.01
□ 753	Steve Chitren	.05	.02	.01
□ 754	Tony Fernandez	.05	.02	.01
□ 755	Jeff Bagwell UER	2.50	1.10	.30
	(Strikeout and walk			
	totals reversed)			
□ 756	Kirk Dressendorfer	.05	.02	.01
□ 757	Glenn Davis	.05	.02	.01
□ 758	Gary Carter	.15	.07	.02
□ 759	Zane Smith	.05	.02	.01
□ 760	Vance Law	.05	.02	.01
□ 761	Denis Boucher	.05	.02	.01
□ 762	Turner Ward	.05	.02	.01
□ 763	Roberto Alomar	.25	.11	.03
□ 764	Albert Belle	.60	.25	.07
□ 765	Joe Carter	.15	.07	.02
□ 766	Pete Schourek	.15	.07	.02
□ 767	Heathcliff Slocumb	.15	.07	.02
□ 768	Vince Coleman	.05	.02	.01
□ 769	Mitch Williams	.05	.02	.01
□ 770	Brian Downing	.05	.02	.01
□ 771	Dana Allison	.05	.02	.01
□ 772	Pete Harnisch	.05	.02	.01
□ 773	Tim Raines	.15	.07	.02
□ 774	Darryl Kile	.05	.02	.01
□ 775	Fred McGriff	.15	.07	.02
□ 776	Dwight Evans	.10	.05	.01
□ 777	Joe Slusarski	.05	.02	.01
□ 778	Dave Righetti	.05	.02	.01
□ 779	Jeff Hamilton	.05	.02	.01
□ 780	Ernest Riles	.05	.02	.01
□ 781	Ken Dayley	.05	.02	.01
□ 782	Eric King	.05	.02	.01
□ 783	Devon White	.10	.05	.01
□ 784	Beau Allred	.05	.02	.01
□ 785	Mike Timlin	.05	.02	.01
□ 786	Ivan Calderon	.05	.02	.01
□ 787	Hubie Brooks	.05	.02	.01
□ 788	Juan Agosto	.05	.02	.01
□ 789	Barry Jones	.05	.02	.01
□ 790	Wally Backman	.05	.02	.01
□ 791	Jim Presley	.05	.02	.01
□ 792	Charlie Hough	.05	.02	.01
□ 793	Larry Andersen	.05	.02	.01
□ 794	Steve Finley	.15	.07	.02
□ 795	Shawn Abner	.05	.02	.01
□ 796	Jeff M. Robinson	.05	.02	.01
□ 797	Joe Bitker	.05	.02	.01
□ 798	Eric Show	.05	.02	.01
□ 799	Bud Black	.05	.02	.01
□ 800	Checklist 701-800	.05	.02	.01
□ HH1	Hank Aaron Hologram	2.00	.90	.25
□ SP1	Michael Jordan SP	18.00	8.00	2.20
	(Shown batting in			
	White Sox uniform)			
□ SP2	Rickey Henderson	2.50	1.10	.30

Nolan Ryan
May 1, 1991 Records

1991 Upper Deck Heroes of Baseball

These standard-size cards were randomly inserted in Upper Deck Baseball Heroes wax packs. On a white card face, the fronts of the first three cards have sepia-toned player photos, with red, gold, and blue border stripes. The player's name appears in a gold border stripe beneath the picture, with the Upper Deck "Heroes of Baseball" logo in the lower right corner. The backs have a similar design to the fronts, except with a career summary and an advertisement for Upper Deck "Heroes of Baseball" games that will be played prior to regularly scheduled Major League games. The fourth card features a color portrait of the three players by noted sports artist Vernon Wells.

	MINT	NRMT	EXC
COMPLETE SET (4)	30.00	13.50	3.70
COMMON CARD (H1-H4)	8.00	3.60	1.00
RANDOM INSERTS IN HEROES FOIL			

	MINT	NRMT	EXC
□ H1 Harmon Killebrew	8.00	3.60	1.00
□ H2 Gaylord Perry	8.00	3.60	1.00
□ H3 Ferguson Jenkins	8.00	3.60	1.00
□ H4 Harmon Killebrew DRAW Ferguson Jenkins Gaylord Perry	8.00	3.60	1.00
□ AU1 Harmon Killebrew AU/3000	75.00	34.00	9.50
□ AU2 Gaylord Perry AU/3000	60.00	27.00	7.50
□ AU3 Ferguson Jenkins AU/3000	75.00	34.00	9.50

1991 Upper Deck Silver Sluggers

The Upper Deck Silver Slugger set features nine players from each league, representing the nine batting positions on the team. The cards were issued one per 1991 Upper Deck jumbo pack. The cards measure the standard size. The fronts have glossy color action player photos, with white borders on three sides and a "Silver Slugger" bat serving as the border on the left side. The player's name appears in a tan stripe below the picture, with the team logo superimposed at the lower right corner. The card back is dominated by another color action photo with career highlights in a horizontally oriented rectangle to the left of the picture. The cards are numbered on the back with an SS prefix.

	MINT	NRMT	EXC
COMPLETE SET (18)	15.00	6.75	1.85
COMMON CARD (SS1-SS18)	.50	.23	.06
SEMISTARS	1.25	.55	.16
ONE PER LO OR HI JUMBO PACK			

	MINT	NRMT	EXC
□ SS1 Julio Franco	.75	.35	.09
□ SS2 Alan Trammell	1.25	.55	.16
□ SS3 Rickey Henderson	1.25	.55	.16
□ SS4 Jose Canseco	1.25	.55	.16
□ SS5 Barry Bonds	2.00	.90	.25
□ SS6 Eddie Murray	1.25	.55	.16
□ SS7 Kelly Gruber	.50	.23	.06
□ SS8 Ryne Sandberg	2.00	.90	.25
□ SS9 Darryl Strawberry	.75	.35	.09
□ SS10 Ellis Burks	1.25	.55	.16
□ SS11 Lance Parrish	.50	.23	.06
□ SS12 Cecil Fielder	.75	.35	.09
□ SS13 Matt Williams	1.25	.55	.16
□ SS14 Dave Parker	.75	.35	.09
□ SS15 Bobby Bonilla	.75	.35	.09
□ SS16 Don Robinson	.50	.23	.06
□ SS17 Benito Santiago	.50	.23	.06
□ SS18 Barry Larkin	1.25	.55	.16

1991 Upper Deck Final Edition

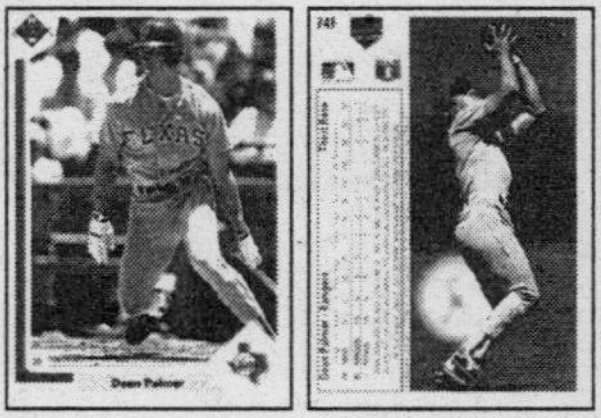

The 1991 Upper Deck Final Edition boxed set contains 100 standard-size cards and showcases players who made major contributions during their team's late-season pennant drive. In addition to the late season traded and impact rookie cards (22-78), the set includes two special subsets: Diamond Skills cards (1-21), depicting the best Minor League prospects, and All-Star cards (80-99). Six assorted team logo hologram cards were issued with each set. The basic card fronts feature posed or action color player photos on a white card face, with the upper left corner of the picture cut out to provide space for the Upper Deck logo. The pictures are bordered in green on the left, with the player's name in a tan border below the picture. The cards are numbered on the back with an F suffix. Among the outstanding Rookie Cards in this set are Ryan Klesko, Kenny Lofton, Pedro Martinez, Ivan Rodriguez, Jim Thome, Rondell White, and Dmitri Young.

	MINT	NRMT	EXC
COMPLETE FACT.SET (100)	4.00	1.80	.50
COMMON CARD (1F-100F)	.05	.02	.01
SEMISTARS	.10	.05	.01

	MINT	NRMT	EXC
□ 1F Ryan Klesko CL Reggie Sanders	.30	.14	.04
□ 2F Pedro Martinez	.40	.18	.05
□ 3F Lance Dickson	.05	.02	.01
□ 4F Royce Clayton	.10	.05	.01
□ 5F Scott Bryant	.05	.02	.01
□ 6F Dan Wilson	.25	.11	.03
□ 7F Dmitri Young	.50	.23	.06
□ 8F Ryan Klesko	1.25	.55	.16
□ 9F Tom Goodwin	.10	.05	.01
□ 10F Rondell White	.40	.18	.05
□ 11F Reggie Sanders	.25	.11	.03
□ 12F Todd Van Poppel	.10	.05	.01
□ 13F Arthur Rhodes	.10	.05	.01
□ 14F Eddie Zosky	.05	.02	.01
□ 15F Gerald Williams	.05	.02	.01
□ 16F Robert Eenhoorn	.05	.02	.01
□ 17F Jim Thome	1.25	.55	.16
□ 18F Marc Newfield	.15	.07	.02
□ 19F Kerwin Moore	.05	.02	.01
□ 20F Jeff McNeely	.05	.02	.01
□ 21F Frankie Rodriguez	.15	.07	.02
□ 22F Andy Mota	.05	.02	.01
□ 23F Chris Haney	.05	.02	.01
□ 24F Kenny Lofton	2.00	.90	.25

□ 25F Dave Nilsson	.15	.07	.02
□ 26F Derek Bell	.15	.07	.02
□ 27F Frank Castillo	.10	.05	.01
□ 28F Candy Maldonado	.05	.02	.01
□ 29F Chuck McElroy	.05	.02	.01
□ 30F Chito Martinez	.05	.02	.01
□ 31F Steve Howe	.05	.02	.01
□ 32F Freddie Benavides	.05	.02	.01
□ 33F Scott Kamieniecki	.05	.02	.01
□ 34F Denny Neagle	.40	.18	.05
□ 35F Mike Humphreys	.05	.02	.01
□ 36F Mike Remlinger	.05	.02	.01
□ 37F Scott Coolbaugh	.05	.02	.01
□ 38F Darren Lewis	.10	.05	.01
□ 39F Thomas Howard	.05	.02	.01
□ 40F John Candelaria	.05	.02	.01
□ 41F Todd Benzinger	.05	.02	.01
□ 42F Wilson Alvarez	.15	.07	.02
□ 43F Patrick Lennon	.05	.02	.01
□ 44F Rusty Meacham	.05	.02	.01
□ 45F Ryan Bowen	.05	.02	.01
□ 46F Rick Wilkins	.05	.02	.01
□ 47F Ed Sprague	.10	.05	.01
□ 48F Bob Scanlan	.05	.02	.01
□ 49F Tom Candiotti	.05	.02	.01
□ 50F Dennis Martinez (Perfecto)	.10	.05	.01
□ 51F Oil Can Boyd	.05	.02	.01
□ 52F Glenallen Hill	.05	.02	.01
□ 53F Scott Livingstone	.05	.02	.01
□ 54F Brian R. Hunter	.05	.02	.01
□ 55F Ivan Rodriguez	.75	.35	.09
□ 56F Keith Mitchell	.05	.02	.01
□ 57F Roger McDowell	.05	.02	.01
□ 58F Otis Nixon	.05	.02	.01
□ 59F Juan Bell	.05	.02	.01
□ 60F Bill Krueger	.05	.02	.01
□ 61F Chris Donnels	.05	.02	.01
□ 62F Tommy Greene	.05	.02	.01
□ 63F Doug Simons	.05	.02	.01
□ 64F Andy Ashby	.15	.07	.02
□ 65F Anthony Young	.05	.02	.01
□ 66F Kevin Morton	.05	.02	.01
□ 67F Bret Barberie	.05	.02	.01
□ 68F Scott Servais	.05	.02	.01
□ 69F Ron Darling	.05	.02	.01
□ 70F Tim Burke	.05	.02	.01
□ 71F Vicente Palacios	.05	.02	.01
□ 72F Gerald Alexander	.05	.02	.01
□ 73F Reggie Jefferson	.10	.05	.01
□ 74F Dean Palmer	.10	.05	.01
□ 75F Mark Whiten	.10	.05	.01
□ 76F Randy Tomlin	.05	.02	.01
□ 77F Mark Wohlers	.40	.18	.05
□ 78F Brook Jacoby	.05	.02	.01
□ 79F Ken Griffey Jr. CL Ryne Sandberg	.40	.18	.05
□ 80F Jack Morris AS	.10	.05	.01
□ 81F Sandy Alomar Jr. AS	.05	.02	.01
□ 82F Cecil Fielder AS	.10	.05	.01
□ 83F Roberto Alomar AS	.15	.07	.02
□ 84F Wade Boggs AS	.15	.07	.02
□ 85F Cal Ripken AS	.40	.18	.05
□ 86F Rickey Henderson AS	.15	.07	.02
□ 87F Ken Griffey Jr. AS	.75	.35	.09
□ 88F Dave Henderson AS	.05	.02	.01
□ 89F Danny Tartabull AS	.05	.02	.01
□ 90F Tom Glavine AS	.15	.07	.02
□ 91F Benito Santiago AS	.05	.02	.01
□ 92F Will Clark AS	.15	.07	.02
□ 93F Ryne Sandberg AS	.15	.07	.02
□ 94F Chris Sabo AS	.05	.02	.01
□ 95F Ozzie Smith AS	.10	.05	.01
□ 96F Ivan Calderon AS	.05	.02	.01
□ 97F Tony Gwynn AS	.20	.09	.03
□ 98F Andre Dawson AS	.15	.07	.02
□ 99F Bobby Bonilla AS	.10	.05	.01
□ 100F Checklist 1-100	.05	.02	.01

1992 Upper Deck

The 1992 Upper Deck set contains 800 standard-size cards issued in two separate series of 700 and 100 cards respectively. The cards were distributed in low and high series foil

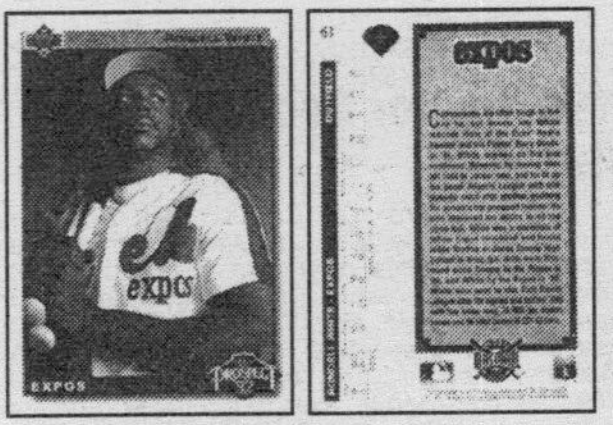

packs in addition to factory sets. Factory sets feature a unique gold-foil hologram on the card backs (in contrast to the silver hologram on foil pack cards). The basic issue card fronts features shadow-bordered action color player photos on a white card face. The player's name appears above the photo, with the team name superimposed at the lower right corner. Special subsets included in the set are Star Rookies (1-27), Team Checklists (29-40/86-99), with player portraits by Vernon Wells; Top Prospects (52-77); Bloodlines (79-85), Diamond Skills (640-650/711-721) and Diamond Debuts (771-780). Rookie Cards in the set include Shawn Green, Joey Hamilton, Brian Jordan and Manny Ramirez. A special card picturing Tom Selleck and Frank Thomas, commemorating the forgettable movie "Mr. Baseball", was randomly inserted into high series packs. A standard-size Ted Williams hologram card was randomly inserted into low series packs. By mailing in 15 low series foil wrappers, a completed order form, and a handling fee, the collector could receive an 8 1/2" by 11" numbered, black and white lithograph picturing Ted Williams in his batting swing.

	MINT	NRMT	EXC
COMPLETE SET (800)	15.00	6.75	1.85
COMPLETE FACT.SET (800)	20.00	9.00	2.50
COMPLETE LO SET (700)	12.00	5.50	1.50
COMPLETE HI SET (100)	3.00	1.35	.35
COMMON CARD (1-800)	.05	.02	.01
SEMISTARS	.10	.05	.01
STARS	.15	.07	.02
COMP.BENCH/MORG. (10)	12.00	5.50	1.50
COMMON BENCH/MORG. (37-45)	1.00	.45	.12
BENCH/MORG.HDR SP (NNO)	5.00	2.20	.60
BENCH/MORG.AU/2500 (AU5)	200.00	90.00	25.00
BENCH/MORG: INSERTS IN HI PACKS			
COMP.COLLEGE POY SET (3)	2.00	.90	.25
COLLEGE POY: INSERTS IN HI PACKS			
COMP.T.WILLIAMS SET (10)	7.00	3.10	.85
COMMON T.WILLIAMS (28-36)	.50	.23	.06
T.WILLIAMS HDR SP (NNO)	4.00	1.80	.50
T.WILLIAMS AU/2500 (AU4)	500.00	220.00	60.00
T.WILLIAMS: RANDOM INSERTS IN LO PACKS			

□ 1 Ryan Klesko CL Jim Thome	.75	.35	.09
□ 2 Royce Clayton SR	.10	.05	.01
□ 3 Brian Jordan SR	.40	.18	.05
□ 4 Dave Fleming SR	.05	.02	.01
□ 5 Jim Thome SR	.75	.35	.09
□ 6 Jeff Juden SR	.05	.02	.01
□ 7 Roberto Hernandez SR	.15	.07	.02
□ 8 Kyle Abbott SR	.05	.02	.01
□ 9 Chris George SR	.05	.02	.01
□ 10 Rob Maurer SR	.05	.02	.01
□ 11 Donald Harris SR	.05	.02	.01
□ 12 Ted Wood SR	.05	.02	.01
□ 13 Patrick Lennon SR	.05	.02	.01
□ 14 Willie Banks SR	.05	.02	.01
□ 15 Roger Salkeld SR UER (Bill was his grandfather, not his father)	.05	.02	.01
□ 16 Wil Cordero SR	.10	.05	.01
□ 17 Arthur Rhodes SR	.05	.02	.01
□ 18 Pedro Martinez SR	.25	.11	.03
□ 19 Andy Ashby SR	.10	.05	.01

□ 20 Tom Goodwin SR	.10	.05	.01
□ 21 Braulio Castillo SR	.05	.02	.01
□ 22 Todd Van Poppel SR	.05	.02	.01
□ 23 Brian Williams SR	.05	.02	.01
□ 24 Ryan Klesko SR	.75	.35	.09
□ 25 Kenny Lofton SR	1.00	.45	.12
□ 26 Derek Bell SR	.10	.05	.01
□ 27 Reggie Sanders SR	.15	.07	.02
□ 28 Dave Winfield's 400th	.15	.07	.02
□ 29 David Justice TC	.10	.05	.01
□ 30 Rob Dibble TC	.05	.02	.01
□ 31 Craig Biggio TC	.10	.05	.01
□ 32 Eddie Murray TC	.15	.07	.02
□ 33 Fred McGriff TC	.10	.05	.01
□ 34 Willie McGee TC	.05	.02	.01
□ 35 Shawon Dunston TC	.05	.02	.01
□ 36 Delino DeShields TC	.05	.02	.01
□ 37 Howard Johnson TC	.05	.02	.01
□ 38 John Kruk TC	.05	.02	.01
□ 39 Doug Drabek TC	.05	.02	.01
□ 40 Todd Zeile TC	.05	.02	.01
□ 41 Steve Avery	.10	.05	.01
Playoff Perfection			
□ 42 Jeremy Hernandez	.05	.02	.01
□ 43 Doug Henry	.05	.02	.01
□ 44 Chris Donnels	.05	.02	.01
□ 45 Mo Sanford	.05	.02	.01
□ 46 Scott Kamieniecki	.05	.02	.01
□ 47 Mark Lemke	.05	.02	.01
□ 48 Steve Farr	.05	.02	.01
□ 49 Francisco Oliveras	.05	.02	.01
□ 50 Ced Landrum	.05	.02	.01
□ 51 Rondell White CL	.15	.07	.02
Mark Newfield			
□ 52 Eduardo Perez TP	.10	.05	.01
□ 53 Tom Nevers TP	.05	.02	.01
□ 54 David Zancanaro TP	.05	.02	.01
□ 55 Shawn Green TP	.50	.23	.06
□ 56 Mark Wohlers TP	.15	.07	.02
□ 57 Dave Nilsson TP	.15	.07	.02
□ 58 Dmitri Young TP	.25	.11	.03
□ 59 Ryan Hawblitzel TP	.05	.02	.01
□ 60 Raul Mondesi TP	.60	.25	.07
□ 61 Rondell White TP	.30	.14	.04
□ 62 Steve Hosey TP	.05	.02	.01
□ 63 Manny Ramirez TP	2.00	.90	.25
□ 64 Marc Newfield TP	.10	.05	.01
□ 65 Jeromy Burnitz TP	.10	.05	.01
□ 66 Mark Smith TP	.10	.05	.01
□ 67 Joey Hamilton TP	.75	.35	.09
□ 68 Tyler Green TP	.10	.05	.01
□ 69 Jon Farrell TP	.05	.02	.01
□ 70 Kurt Miller TP	.05	.02	.01
□ 71 Jeff Plympton TP	.05	.02	.01
□ 72 Dan Wilson TP	.15	.07	.02
□ 73 Joe Vitiello TP	.10	.05	.01
□ 74 Rico Brogna TP	.10	.05	.01
□ 75 David McCarty TP	.05	.02	.01
□ 76 Bob Wickman TP	.05	.02	.01
□ 77 Carlos Rodriguez TP	.05	.02	.01
□ 78 Jim Abbott	.05	.02	.01
Stay In School			
□ 79 Ramon Martinez	.15	.07	.02
Pedro Martinez			
□ 80 Kevin Mitchell	.05	.02	.01
Keith Mitchell			
□ 81 Sandy Alomar Jr.	.15	.07	.02
Roberto Alomar			
□ 82 Cal Ripken	.50	.23	.06
Billy Ripken			
□ 83 Tony Gwynn	.15	.07	.02
Chris Gwynn			
□ 84 Dwight Gooden	.15	.07	.02
Gary Sheffield			
□ 85 Ken Griffey Sr.	.75	.35	.09
Ken Griffey Jr.			
Craig Griffey			
□ 86 Jim Abbott TC	.05	.02	.01
□ 87 Frank Thomas TC	.75	.35	.09
□ 88 Danny Tartabull TC	.05	.02	.01
□ 89 Scott Erickson TC	.05	.02	.01
□ 90 Rickey Henderson TC	.15	.07	.02
□ 91 Edgar Martinez TC	.10	.05	.01
□ 92 Nolan Ryan TC	.40	.18	.05
□ 93 Ben McDonald TC	.05	.02	.01
□ 94 Ellis Burks TC	.10	.05	.01

□ 95 Greg Swindell TC	.05	.02	.01
□ 96 Cecil Fielder TC	.05	.02	.01
□ 97 Greg Vaughn TC	.10	.05	.01
□ 98 Kevin Maas TC	.05	.02	.01
□ 99 Dave Stieb TC	.05	.02	.01
□ 100 Checklist 1-100	.05	.02	.01
□ 101 Joe Oliver	.05	.02	.01
□ 102 Hector Villanueva	.05	.02	.01
□ 103 Ed Whitson	.05	.02	.01
□ 104 Danny Jackson	.05	.02	.01
□ 105 Chris Hammond	.05	.02	.01
□ 106 Ricky Jordan	.05	.02	.01
□ 107 Kevin Bass	.05	.02	.01
□ 108 Darrin Fletcher	.05	.02	.01
□ 109 Junior Ortiz	.05	.02	.01
□ 110 Tom Bolton	.05	.02	.01
□ 111 Jeff King	.10	.05	.01
□ 112 Dave Magadan	.05	.02	.01
□ 113 Mike LaValliere	.05	.02	.01
□ 114 Hubie Brooks	.05	.02	.01
□ 115 Jay Bell	.10	.05	.01
□ 116 David Wells	.05	.02	.01
□ 117 Jim Leyritz	.05	.02	.01
□ 118 Manuel Lee	.05	.02	.01
□ 119 Alvaro Espinoza	.05	.02	.01
□ 120 B.J. Surhoff	.10	.05	.01
□ 121 Hal Morris	.05	.02	.01
□ 122 Shawon Dawson	.05	.02	.01
□ 123 Chris Sabo	.05	.02	.01
□ 124 Andre Dawson	.15	.07	.02
□ 125 Eric Davis	.10	.05	.01
□ 126 Chili Davis	.10	.05	.01
□ 127 Dale Murphy	.15	.07	.02
□ 128 Kirk McCaskill	.05	.02	.01
□ 129 Terry Mulholland	.05	.02	.01
□ 130 Rick Aguilera	.05	.02	.01
□ 131 Vince Coleman	.05	.02	.01
□ 132 Andy Van Slyke	.10	.05	.01
□ 133 Gregg Jefferies	.15	.07	.02
□ 134 Barry Bonds	.25	.11	.03
□ 135 Dwight Gooden	.10	.05	.01
□ 136 Dave Stieb	.05	.02	.01
□ 137 Albert Belle	.60	.25	.07
□ 138 Teddy Higuera	.05	.02	.01
□ 139 Jesse Barfield	.05	.02	.01
□ 140 Pat Borders	.05	.02	.01
□ 141 Bip Roberts	.05	.02	.01
□ 142 Rob Dibble	.05	.02	.01
□ 143 Mark Grace	.15	.07	.02
□ 144 Barry Larkin	.15	.07	.02
□ 145 Ryne Sandberg	.25	.11	.03
□ 146 Scott Erickson	.10	.05	.01
□ 147 Luis Polonia	.05	.02	.01
□ 148 John Burkett	.10	.05	.01
□ 149 Luis Sojo	.05	.02	.01
□ 150 Dickie Thon	.05	.02	.01
□ 151 Walt Weiss	.05	.02	.01
□ 152 Mike Scioscia	.05	.02	.01
□ 153 Mark McGwire	.30	.14	.04
□ 154 Matt Williams	.15	.07	.02
□ 155 Rickey Henderson	.15	.07	.02
□ 156 Sandy Alomar Jr.	.10	.05	.01
□ 157 Brian McRae	.15	.07	.02
□ 158 Harold Baines	.10	.05	.01
□ 159 Kevin Appier	.10	.05	.01
□ 160 Felix Fermin	.05	.02	.01
□ 161 Leo Gomez	.05	.02	.01
□ 162 Craig Biggio	.15	.07	.02
□ 163 Ben McDonald	.05	.02	.01
□ 164 Randy Johnson	.15	.07	.02
□ 165 Cal Ripken	.75	.35	.09
□ 166 Frank Thomas	1.50	.70	.19
□ 167 Delino DeShields	.05	.02	.01
□ 168 Greg Gagne	.05	.02	.01
□ 169 Ron Karkovice	.05	.02	.01
□ 170 Charlie Leibrandt	.05	.02	.01
□ 171 Dave Righetti	.05	.02	.01
□ 172 Dave Henderson	.05	.02	.01
□ 173 Steve Decker	.05	.02	.01
□ 174 Darryl Strawberry	.10	.05	.01
□ 175 Will Clark	.15	.07	.02
□ 176 Ruben Sierra	.10	.05	.01
□ 177 Ozzie Smith	.20	.09	.03
□ 178 Charles Nagy	.10	.05	.01
□ 179 Gary Pettis	.05	.02	.01
□ 180 Kirk Gibson	.10	.05	.01

☐ 181	Randy Milligan	.05	.02	.01
☐ 182	Dave Valle	.05	.02	.01
☐ 183	Chris Hoiles	.05	.02	.01
☐ 184	Tony Phillips	.10	.05	.01
☐ 185	Brady Anderson	.15	.07	.02
☐ 186	Scott Fletcher	.05	.02	.01
☐ 187	Gene Larkin	.05	.02	.01
☐ 188	Lance Johnson	.10	.05	.01
☐ 189	Greg Olson	.05	.02	.01
☐ 190	Melido Perez	.05	.02	.01
☐ 191	Lenny Harris	.05	.02	.01
☐ 192	Terry Kennedy	.05	.02	.01
☐ 193	Mike Gallego	.05	.02	.01
☐ 194	Willie McGee	.05	.02	.01
☐ 195	Juan Samuel	.05	.02	.01
☐ 196	Jeff Huson (Shows Jose Canseco sliding into second)	.10	.05	.01
☐ 197	Alex Cole	.05	.02	.01
☐ 198	Ron Robinson	.05	.02	.01
☐ 199	Joel Skinner	.05	.02	.01
☐ 200	Checklist 101-200	.05	.02	.01
☐ 201	Kevin Reimer	.05	.02	.01
☐ 202	Stan Belinda	.05	.02	.01
☐ 203	Pat Tabler	.05	.02	.01
☐ 204	Jose Guzman	.05	.02	.01
☐ 205	Jose Lind	.05	.02	.01
☐ 206	Spike Owen	.05	.02	.01
☐ 207	Joe Orsulak	.05	.02	.01
☐ 208	Charlie Hayes	.05	.02	.01
☐ 209	Mike Devereaux	.05	.02	.01
☐ 210	Mike Fitzgerald	.05	.02	.01
☐ 211	Willie Randolph	.10	.05	.01
☐ 212	Rod Nichols	.05	.02	.01
☐ 213	Mike Boddicker	.05	.02	.01
☐ 214	Bill Spiers	.05	.02	.01
☐ 215	Steve Olin	.05	.02	.01
☐ 216	David Howard	.05	.02	.01
☐ 217	Gary Varsho	.05	.02	.01
☐ 218	Mike Harkey	.05	.02	.01
☐ 219	Luis Aquino	.05	.02	.01
☐ 220	Chuck McElroy	.05	.02	.01
☐ 221	Doug Drabek	.05	.02	.01
☐ 222	Dave Winfield	.15	.07	.02
☐ 223	Rafael Palmeiro	.15	.07	.02
☐ 224	Joe Carter	.15	.07	.02
☐ 225	Bobby Bonilla	.10	.05	.01
☐ 226	Ivan Calderon	.05	.02	.01
☐ 227	Gregg Olson	.05	.02	.01
☐ 228	Tim Wallach	.05	.02	.01
☐ 229	Terry Pendleton	.10	.05	.01
☐ 230	Gilberto Reyes	.05	.02	.01
☐ 231	Carlos Baerga	.15	.07	.02
☐ 232	Greg Vaughn	.15	.07	.02
☐ 233	Bret Saberhagen	.10	.05	.01
☐ 234	Gary Sheffield	.15	.07	.02
☐ 235	Mark Lewis	.05	.02	.01
☐ 236	George Bell	.05	.02	.01
☐ 237	Danny Tartabull	.05	.02	.01
☐ 238	Willie Wilson	.05	.02	.01
☐ 239	Doug Dascenzo	.05	.02	.01
☐ 240	Bill Pecota	.05	.02	.01
☐ 241	Julio Franco	.10	.05	.01
☐ 242	Ed Sprague	.10	.05	.01
☐ 243	Juan Gonzalez	.60	.25	.07
☐ 244	Chuck Finley	.05	.02	.01
☐ 245	Ivan Rodriguez	.30	.14	.04
☐ 246	Len Dykstra	.10	.05	.01
☐ 247	Deion Sanders	.15	.07	.02
☐ 248	Dwight Evans	.10	.05	.01
☐ 249	Larry Walker	.15	.07	.02
☐ 250	Billy Ripken	.05	.02	.01
☐ 251	Mickey Tettleton	.05	.02	.01
☐ 252	Tony Pena	.05	.02	.01
☐ 253	Benito Santiago	.05	.02	.01
☐ 254	Kirby Puckett	.30	.14	.04
☐ 255	Cecil Fielder	.10	.05	.01
☐ 256	Howard Johnson	.05	.02	.01
☐ 257	Andujar Cedeno	.05	.02	.01
☐ 258	Jose Rijo	.05	.02	.01
☐ 259	Al Osuna	.05	.02	.01
☐ 260	Todd Hundley	.15	.07	.02
☐ 261	Orel Hershiser	.10	.05	.01
☐ 262	Ray Lankford	.15	.07	.02
☐ 263	Robin Ventura	.15	.07	.02
☐ 264	Felix Jose	.05	.02	.01
☐ 265	Eddie Murray	.25	.11	.03
☐ 266	Kevin Mitchell	.10	.05	.01
☐ 267	Gary Carter	.15	.07	.02
☐ 268	Mike Benjamin	.05	.02	.01
☐ 269	Dick Schofield	.05	.02	.01
☐ 270	Jose Uribe	.05	.02	.01
☐ 271	Pete Incaviglia	.05	.02	.01
☐ 272	Tony Fernandez	.05	.02	.01
☐ 273	Alan Trammell	.15	.07	.02
☐ 274	Tony Gwynn	.40	.18	.05
☐ 275	Mike Greenwell	.05	.02	.01
☐ 276	Jeff Bagwell	.60	.25	.07
☐ 277	Frank Viola	.05	.02	.01
☐ 278	Randy Myers	.10	.05	.01
☐ 279	Ken Caminiti	.15	.07	.02
☐ 280	Bill Doran	.05	.02	.01
☐ 281	Dan Pasqua	.05	.02	.01
☐ 282	Alfredo Griffin	.05	.02	.01
☐ 283	Jose Oquendo	.05	.02	.01
☐ 284	Kal Daniels	.05	.02	.01
☐ 285	Bobby Thigpen	.05	.02	.01
☐ 286	Robby Thompson	.05	.02	.01
☐ 287	Mark Eichhorn	.05	.02	.01
☐ 288	Mike Felder	.05	.02	.01
☐ 289	Dave Gallagher	.05	.02	.01
☐ 290	Dave Anderson	.05	.02	.01
☐ 291	Mel Hall	.05	.02	.01
☐ 292	Jerald Clark	.05	.02	.01
☐ 293	Al Newman	.05	.02	.01
☐ 294	Rob Deer	.05	.02	.01
☐ 295	Matt Nokes	.05	.02	.01
☐ 296	Jack Armstrong	.05	.02	.01
☐ 297	Jim Deshaies	.05	.02	.01
☐ 298	Jeff Innis	.05	.02	.01
☐ 299	Jeff Reed	.05	.02	.01
☐ 300	Checklist 201-300	.05	.02	.01
☐ 301	Lonnie Smith	.05	.02	.01
☐ 302	Jimmy Key	.10	.05	.01
☐ 303	Junior Felix	.05	.02	.01
☐ 304	Mike Heath	.05	.02	.01
☐ 305	Mark Langston	.10	.05	.01
☐ 306	Greg W. Harris	.05	.02	.01
☐ 307	Brett Butler	.10	.05	.01
☐ 308	Luis Rivera	.05	.02	.01
☐ 309	Bruce Ruffin	.05	.02	.01
☐ 310	Paul Faries	.05	.02	.01
☐ 311	Terry Leach	.05	.02	.01
☐ 312	Scott Brosius	.15	.07	.02
☐ 313	Scott Leius	.05	.02	.01
☐ 314	Harold Reynolds	.05	.02	.01
☐ 315	Jack Morris	.10	.05	.01
☐ 316	David Segui	.05	.02	.01
☐ 317	Bill Gullickson	.05	.02	.01
☐ 318	Todd Frohwirth	.05	.02	.01
☐ 319	Mark Leiter	.05	.02	.01
☐ 320	Jeff M. Robinson	.05	.02	.01
☐ 321	Gary Gaetti	.10	.05	.01
☐ 322	John Smoltz	.15	.07	.02
☐ 323	Andy Benes	.05	.02	.01
☐ 324	Kelly Gruber	.05	.02	.01
☐ 325	Jim Abbott	.05	.02	.01
☐ 326	John Kruk	.10	.05	.01
☐ 327	Kevin Seitzer	.05	.02	.01
☐ 328	Darrin Jackson	.05	.02	.01
☐ 329	Kurt Stillwell	.05	.02	.01
☐ 330	Mike Maddux	.05	.02	.01
☐ 331	Dennis Eckersley	.10	.05	.01
☐ 332	Dan Gladden	.05	.02	.01
☐ 333	Jose Canseco	.15	.07	.02
☐ 334	Kent Hrbek	.10	.05	.01
☐ 335	Ken Griffey Sr.	.05	.02	.01
☐ 336	Greg Swindell	.05	.02	.01
☐ 337	Trevor Wilson	.05	.02	.01
☐ 338	Sam Horn	.05	.02	.01
☐ 339	Mike Henneman	.05	.02	.01
☐ 340	Jerry Browne	.05	.02	.01
☐ 341	Glenn Braggs	.05	.02	.01
☐ 342	Tom Glavine	.15	.07	.02
☐ 343	Wally Joyner	.10	.05	.01
☐ 344	Fred McGriff	.15	.07	.02
☐ 345	Ron Gant	.15	.07	.02
☐ 346	Ramon Martinez	.10	.05	.01
☐ 347	Wes Chamberlain	.05	.02	.01
☐ 348	Terry Shumpert	.05	.02	.01
☐ 349	Tim Teufel	.05	.02	.01
☐ 350	Wally Backman	.05	.02	.01

□ 351	Joe Girardi	.05	.02	.01
□ 352	Devon White	.10	.05	.01
□ 353	Greg Maddux	.75	.35	.09
□ 354	Ryan Bowen	.05	.02	.01
□ 355	Roberto Alomar	.25	.11	.03
□ 356	Don Mattingly	.50	.23	.06
□ 357	Pedro Guerrero	.05	.02	.01
□ 358	Steve Sax	.05	.02	.01
□ 359	Joey Cora	.05	.02	.01
□ 360	Jim Gantner	.05	.02	.01
□ 361	Brian Barnes	.05	.02	.01
□ 362	Kevin McReynolds	.05	.02	.01
□ 363	Bret Barberie	.05	.02	.01
□ 364	David Cone	.15	.07	.02
□ 365	Dennis Martinez	.10	.05	.01
□ 366	Brian Hunter	.05	.02	.01
□ 367	Edgar Martinez	.15	.07	.02
□ 368	Steve Finley	.15	.07	.02
□ 369	Greg Briley	.05	.02	.01
□ 370	Jeff Blauser	.05	.02	.01
□ 371	Todd Stottlemyre	.10	.05	.01
□ 372	Luis Gonzalez	.10	.05	.01
□ 373	Rick Wilkins	.05	.02	.01
□ 374	Darryl Kile	.05	.02	.01
□ 375	John Olerud	.10	.05	.01
□ 376	Lee Smith	.10	.05	.01
□ 377	Kevin Maas	.05	.02	.01
□ 378	Dante Bichette	.15	.07	.02
□ 379	Tom Pagnozzi	.05	.02	.01
□ 380	Mike Flanagan	.05	.02	.01
□ 381	Charlie O'Brien	.05	.02	.01
□ 382	Dave Martinez	.05	.02	.01
□ 383	Keith Miller	.05	.02	.01
□ 384	Scott Ruskin	.05	.02	.01
□ 385	Kevin Elster	.05	.02	.01
□ 386	Alvin Davis	.05	.02	.01
□ 387	Casey Candaele	.05	.02	.01
□ 388	Pete O'Brien	.05	.02	.01
□ 389	Jeff Treadway	.05	.02	.01
□ 390	Scott Bradley	.05	.02	.01
□ 391	Mookie Wilson	.05	.02	.01
□ 392	Jimmy Jones	.05	.02	.01
□ 393	Candy Maldonado	.05	.02	.01
□ 394	Eric Yelding	.05	.02	.01
□ 395	Tom Henke	.05	.02	.01
□ 396	Franklin Stubbs	.05	.02	.01
□ 397	Milt Thompson	.05	.02	.01
□ 398	Mark Carreon	.05	.02	.01
□ 399	Randy Velarde	.05	.02	.01
□ 400	Checklist 301-400	.05	.02	.01
□ 401	Omar Vizquel	.15	.07	.02
□ 402	Joe Boever	.05	.02	.01
□ 403	Bill Krueger	.05	.02	.01
□ 404	Jody Reed	.05	.02	.01
□ 405	Mike Schooler	.05	.02	.01
□ 406	Jason Grimsley	.05	.02	.01
□ 407	Greg Myers	.05	.02	.01
□ 408	Randy Ready	.05	.02	.01
□ 409	Mike Timlin	.05	.02	.01
□ 410	Mitch Williams	.05	.02	.01
□ 411	Garry Templeton	.05	.02	.01
□ 412	Greg Cadaret	.05	.02	.01
□ 413	Donnie Hill	.05	.02	.01
□ 414	Wally Whitehurst	.05	.02	.01
□ 415	Scott Sanderson	.05	.02	.01
□ 416	Thomas Howard	.05	.02	.01
□ 417	Neal Heaton	.05	.02	.01
□ 418	Charlie Hough	.05	.02	.01
□ 419	Jack Howell	.05	.02	.01
□ 420	Greg Hibbard	.05	.02	.01
□ 421	Carlos Quintana	.05	.02	.01
□ 422	Kim Batiste	.05	.02	.01
□ 423	Paul Molitor	.20	.09	.03
□ 424	Ken Griffey Jr.	1.50	.70	.19
□ 425	Phil Plantier	.10	.05	.01
□ 426	Denny Neagle	.10	.05	.01
□ 427	Von Hayes	.05	.02	.01
□ 428	Shane Mack	.05	.02	.01
□ 429	Darren Daulton	.10	.05	.01
□ 430	Dwayne Henry	.05	.02	.01
□ 431	Lance Parrish	.05	.02	.01
□ 432	Mike Humphreys	.05	.02	.01
□ 433	Tim Burke	.05	.02	.01
□ 434	Bryan Harvey	.05	.02	.01
□ 435	Pat Kelly	.05	.02	.01
□ 436	Ozzie Guillen	.05	.02	.01
□ 437	Bruce Hurst	.05	.02	.01
□ 438	Sammy Sosa	.25	.11	.03
□ 439	Dennis Rasmussen	.05	.02	.01
□ 440	Ken Patterson	.05	.02	.01
□ 441	Jay Buhner	.15	.07	.02
□ 442	Pat Combs	.05	.02	.01
□ 443	Wade Boggs	.15	.07	.02
□ 444	George Brett	.40	.18	.05
□ 445	Mo Vaughn	.40	.18	.05
□ 446	Chuck Knoblauch	.15	.07	.02
□ 447	Tom Candiotti	.05	.02	.01
□ 448	Mark Portugal	.05	.02	.01
□ 449	Mickey Morandini	.05	.02	.01
□ 450	Duane Ward	.05	.02	.01
□ 451	Otis Nixon	.05	.02	.01
□ 452	Bob Welch	.05	.02	.01
□ 453	Rusty Meacham	.05	.02	.01
□ 454	Keith Mitchell	.05	.02	.01
□ 455	Marquis Grissom	.15	.07	.02
□ 456	Robin Yount	.15	.07	.02
□ 457	Harvey Pulliam	.05	.02	.01
□ 458	Jose DeLeon	.05	.02	.01
□ 459	Mark Gubicza	.05	.02	.01
□ 460	Darryl Hamilton	.05	.02	.01
□ 461	Tom Browning	.05	.02	.01
□ 462	Monty Fariss	.05	.02	.01
□ 463	Jerome Walton	.05	.02	.01
□ 464	Paul O'Neill	.10	.05	.01
□ 465	Dean Palmer	.10	.05	.01
□ 466	Travis Fryman	.15	.07	.02
□ 467	John Smiley	.05	.02	.01
□ 468	Lloyd Moseby	.05	.02	.01
□ 469	John Wehner	.05	.02	.01
□ 470	Skeeter Barnes	.05	.02	.01
□ 471	Steve Chitren	.05	.02	.01
□ 472	Kent Mercker	.05	.02	.01
□ 473	Terry Steinbach	.10	.05	.01
□ 474	Andres Galarraga	.15	.07	.02
□ 475	Steve Avery	.10	.05	.01
□ 476	Tom Gordon	.05	.02	.01
□ 477	Cal Eldred	.05	.02	.01
□ 478	Omar Olivares	.05	.02	.01
□ 479	Julio Machado	.05	.02	.01
□ 480	Bob Milacki	.05	.02	.01
□ 481	Les Lancaster	.05	.02	.01
□ 482	John Candelaria	.05	.02	.01
□ 483	Brian Downing	.05	.02	.01
□ 484	Roger McDowell	.05	.02	.01
□ 485	Scott Scudder	.05	.02	.01
□ 486	Zane Smith	.05	.02	.01
□ 487	John Cerutti	.05	.02	.01
□ 488	Steve Buechele	.05	.02	.01
□ 489	Paul Gibson	.05	.02	.01
□ 490	Curtis Wilkerson	.05	.02	.01
□ 491	Marvin Freeman	.05	.02	.01
□ 492	Tom Foley	.05	.02	.01
□ 493	Juan Berenguer	.05	.02	.01
□ 494	Ernest Riles	.05	.02	.01
□ 495	Sid Bream	.05	.02	.01
□ 496	Chuck Crim	.05	.02	.01
□ 497	Mike Macfarlane	.05	.02	.01
□ 498	Dale Sveum	.05	.02	.01
□ 499	Storm Davis	.05	.02	.01
□ 500	Checklist 401-500	.05	.02	.01
□ 501	Jeff Reardon	.10	.05	.01
□ 502	Shawn Abner	.05	.02	.01
□ 503	Tony Fossas	.05	.02	.01
□ 504	Cory Snyder	.05	.02	.01
□ 505	Matt Young	.05	.02	.01
□ 506	Allan Anderson	.05	.02	.01
□ 507	Mark Lee	.05	.02	.01
□ 508	Gene Nelson	.05	.02	.01
□ 509	Mike Pagliarulo	.05	.02	.01
□ 510	Rafael Belliard	.05	.02	.01
□ 511	Jay Howell	.05	.02	.01
□ 512	Bob Tewksbury	.05	.02	.01
□ 513	Mike Morgan	.05	.02	.01
□ 514	John Franco	.05	.02	.01
□ 515	Kevin Gross	.05	.02	.01
□ 516	Lou Whitaker	.15	.07	.02
□ 517	Orlando Merced	.05	.02	.01
□ 518	Todd Benzinger	.05	.02	.01
□ 519	Gary Redus	.05	.02	.01
□ 520	Walt Terrell	.05	.02	.01
□ 521	Jack Clark	.10	.05	.01
□ 522	Dave Parker	.10	.05	.01

□ 523	Tim Naehring	.10	.05	.01
□ 524	Mark Whiten	.10	.05	.01
□ 525	Ellis Burks	.15	.07	.02
□ 526	Frank Castillo	.10	.05	.01
□ 527	Brian Harper	.05	.02	.01
□ 528	Brook Jacoby	.05	.02	.01
□ 529	Rick Sutcliffe	.05	.02	.01
□ 530	Joe Klink	.05	.02	.01
□ 531	Terry Bross	.05	.02	.01
□ 532	Jose Offerman	.05	.02	.01
□ 533	Todd Zeile	.05	.02	.01
□ 534	Eric Karros	.15	.07	.02
□ 535	Anthony Young	.05	.02	.01
□ 536	Milt Cuyler	.05	.02	.01
□ 537	Randy Tomlin	.05	.02	.01
□ 538	Scott Livingstone	.05	.02	.01
□ 539	Jim Eisenreich	.05	.02	.01
□ 540	Don Slaught	.05	.02	.01
□ 541	Scott Cooper	.05	.02	.01
□ 542	Joe Grahe	.05	.02	.01
□ 543	Tom Brunansky	.05	.02	.01
□ 544	Eddie Zosky	.05	.02	.01
□ 545	Roger Clemens	.15	.07	.02
□ 546	David Justice	.15	.07	.02
□ 547	Dave Stewart	.10	.05	.01
□ 548	David West	.05	.02	.01
□ 549	Dave Smith	.05	.02	.01
□ 550	Dan Plesac	.05	.02	.01
□ 551	Alex Fernandez	.15	.07	.02
□ 552	Bernard Gilkey	.10	.05	.01
□ 553	Jack McDowell	.10	.05	.01
□ 554	Tino Martinez	.15	.07	.02
□ 555	Bo Jackson	.15	.07	.02
□ 556	Bernie Williams	.25	.11	.03
□ 557	Mark Gardner	.05	.02	.01
□ 558	Glenallen Hill	.05	.02	.01
□ 559	Oil Can Boyd	.05	.02	.01
□ 560	Chris James	.05	.02	.01
□ 561	Scott Servais	.05	.02	.01
□ 562	Rey Sanchez	.05	.02	.01
□ 563	Paul McClellan	.05	.02	.01
□ 564	Andy Mota	.05	.02	.01
□ 565	Darren Lewis	.05	.02	.01
□ 566	Jose Melendez	.05	.02	.01
□ 567	Tommy Greene	.05	.02	.01
□ 568	Rich Rodriguez	.05	.02	.01
□ 569	Heathcliff Slocumb	.05	.02	.01
□ 570	Joe Hesketh	.05	.02	.01
□ 571	Carlton Fisk	.15	.07	.02
□ 572	Erik Hanson	.05	.02	.01
□ 573	Wilson Alvarez	.15	.07	.02
□ 574	Rheal Cormier	.05	.02	.01
□ 575	Tim Raines	.15	.07	.02
□ 576	Bobby Witt	.05	.02	.01
□ 577	Roberto Kelly	.05	.02	.01
□ 578	Kevin Brown	.10	.05	.01
□ 579	Chris Nabholz	.05	.02	.01
□ 580	Jesse Orosco	.05	.02	.01
□ 581	Jeff Brantley	.10	.05	.01
□ 582	Rafael Ramirez	.05	.02	.01
□ 583	Kelly Downs	.05	.02	.01
□ 584	Mike Simms	.05	.02	.01
□ 585	Mike Remlinger	.05	.02	.01
□ 586	Dave Hollins	.05	.02	.01
□ 587	Larry Andersen	.05	.02	.01
□ 588	Mike Gardiner	.05	.02	.01
□ 589	Craig Lefferts	.05	.02	.01
□ 590	Paul Assenmacher	.05	.02	.01
□ 591	Bryn Smith	.05	.02	.01
□ 592	Donn Pall	.05	.02	.01
□ 593	Mike Jackson	.05	.02	.01
□ 594	Scott Radinsky	.05	.02	.01
□ 595	Brian Holman	.05	.02	.01
□ 596	Geronimo Pena	.05	.02	.01
□ 597	Mike Jeffcoat	.05	.02	.01
□ 598	Carlos Martinez	.05	.02	.01
□ 599	Geno Petralli	.05	.02	.01
□ 600	Checklist 501-600	.05	.02	.01
□ 601	Jerry Don Gleaton	.05	.02	.01
□ 602	Adam Peterson	.05	.02	.01
□ 603	Craig Grebeck	.05	.02	.01
□ 604	Mark Guthrie	.05	.02	.01
□ 605	Frank Tanana	.05	.02	.01
□ 606	Hensley Meulens	.05	.02	.01
□ 607	Mark Davis	.05	.02	.01
□ 608	Eric Plunk	.05	.02	.01

□ 609	Mark Williamson	.05	.02	.01
□ 610	Lee Guetterman	.05	.02	.01
□ 611	Bobby Rose	.05	.02	.01
□ 612	Bill Wegman	.05	.02	.01
□ 613	Mike Hartley	.05	.02	.01
□ 614	Chris Beasley	.05	.02	.01
□ 615	Chris Bosio	.05	.02	.01
□ 616	Henry Cotto	.05	.02	.01
□ 617	Chico Walker	.05	.02	.01
□ 618	Russ Swan	.05	.02	.01
□ 619	Bob Walk	.05	.02	.01
□ 620	Billy Swift	.05	.02	.01
□ 621	Warren Newson	.05	.02	.01
□ 622	Steve Bedrosian	.05	.02	.01
□ 623	Ricky Bones	.05	.02	.01
□ 624	Kevin Tapani	.05	.02	.01
□ 625	Juan Guzman	.10	.05	.01
□ 626	Jeff Johnson	.05	.02	.01
□ 627	Jeff Montgomery	.10	.05	.01
□ 628	Ken Hill	.15	.07	.02
□ 629	Gary Thurman	.05	.02	.01
□ 630	Steve Howe	.05	.02	.01
□ 631	Jose DeJesus	.05	.02	.01
□ 632	Kirk Dressendorfer	.05	.02	.01
□ 633	Jaime Navarro	.05	.02	.01
□ 634	Lee Stevens	.05	.02	.01
□ 635	Pete Harnisch	.05	.02	.01
□ 636	Bill Landrum	.05	.02	.01
□ 637	Rich DeLucia	.05	.02	.01
□ 638	Luis Salazar	.05	.02	.01
□ 639	Rob Murphy	.05	.02	.01
□ 640	Jose Canseco CL Rickey Henderson	.15	.07	.02
□ 641	Roger Clemens DS	.15	.07	.02
□ 642	Jim Abbott DS	.05	.02	.01
□ 643	Travis Fryman DS	.10	.05	.01
□ 644	Jesse Barfield DS	.05	.02	.01
□ 645	Cal Ripken DS	.40	.18	.05
□ 646	Wade Boggs DS	.10	.05	.01
□ 647	Cecil Fielder DS	.05	.02	.01
□ 648	Rickey Henderson DS	.15	.07	.02
□ 649	Jose Canseco DS	.10	.05	.01
□ 650	Ken Griffey Jr. DS	.75	.35	.09
□ 651	Kenny Rogers	.05	.02	.01
□ 652	Luis Mercedes	.05	.02	.01
□ 653	Mike Stanton	.05	.02	.01
□ 654	Glenn Davis	.05	.02	.01
□ 655	Nolan Ryan	.75	.35	.09
□ 656	Reggie Jefferson	.10	.05	.01
□ 657	Javier Ortiz	.05	.02	.01
□ 658	Greg A. Harris	.05	.02	.01
□ 659	Mariano Duncan	.05	.02	.01
□ 660	Jeff Shaw	.05	.02	.01
□ 661	Mike Moore	.05	.02	.01
□ 662	Chris Haney	.05	.02	.01
□ 663	Joe Slusarski	.05	.02	.01
□ 664	Wayne Housie	.05	.02	.01
□ 665	Carlos Garcia	.10	.05	.01
□ 666	Bob Ojeda	.05	.02	.01
□ 667	Bryan Hickerson	.05	.02	.01
□ 668	Tim Belcher	.05	.02	.01
□ 669	Ron Darling	.05	.02	.01
□ 670	Rex Hudler	.05	.02	.01
□ 671	Sid Fernandez	.05	.02	.01
□ 672	Chito Martinez	.05	.02	.01
□ 673	Pete Schourek	.10	.05	.01
□ 674	Armando Reynoso	.05	.02	.01
□ 675	Mike Mussina	.30	.14	.04
□ 676	Kevin Morton	.05	.02	.01
□ 677	Norm Charlton	.05	.02	.01
□ 678	Danny Darwin	.05	.02	.01
□ 679	Eric King	.05	.02	.01
□ 680	Ted Power	.05	.02	.01
□ 681	Barry Jones	.05	.02	.01
□ 682	Carney Lansford	.10	.05	.01
□ 683	Mel Rojas	.10	.05	.01
□ 684	Rick Honeycutt	.05	.02	.01
□ 685	Jeff Fassero	.10	.05	.01
□ 686	Cris Carpenter	.05	.02	.01
□ 687	Tim Crews	.05	.02	.01
□ 688	Scott Terry	.05	.02	.01
□ 689	Chris Gwynn	.05	.02	.01
□ 690	Gerald Perry	.05	.02	.01
□ 691	John Barfield	.05	.02	.01
□ 692	Bob Melvin	.05	.02	.01
□ 693	Juan Agosto	.05	.02	.01

□ 694	Alejandro Pena	.05	.02	.01
□ 695	Jeff Russell	.05	.02	.01
□ 696	Carmelo Martinez	.05	.02	.01
□ 697	Bud Black	.05	.02	.01
□ 698	Dave Otto	.05	.02	.01
□ 699	Billy Hatcher	.05	.02	.01
□ 700	Checklist 601-700	.05	.02	.01
□ 701	Clemente Nunez	.15	.07	.02
□ 702	Rookie Threats	.15	.07	.02
	Mark Clark			
	Donovan Osborne			
	Brian Jordan			
□ 703	Mike Morgan	.05	.02	.01
□ 704	Keith Miller	.05	.02	.01
□ 705	Kurt Stillwell	.05	.02	.01
□ 706	Damon Berryhill	.05	.02	.01
□ 707	Von Hayes	.05	.02	.01
□ 708	Rick Sutcliffe	.05	.02	.01
□ 709	Hubie Brooks	.05	.02	.01
□ 710	Ryan Turner	.05	.02	.01
□ 711	Barry Bonds CL	.10	.05	.01
	Andy Van Slyke			
□ 712	Jose Rijo DS	.05	.02	.01
□ 713	Tom Glavine DS	.10	.05	.01
□ 714	Shawon Dunston DS	.05	.02	.01
□ 715	Andy Van Slyke DS	.05	.02	.01
□ 716	Ozzie Smith DS	.15	.07	.02
□ 717	Tony Gwynn DS	.20	.09	.03
□ 718	Will Clark DS	.10	.05	.01
□ 719	Marquis Grissom DS	.10	.05	.01
□ 720	Howard Johnson DS	.05	.02	.01
□ 721	Barry Bonds DS	.15	.07	.02
□ 722	Kirk McCaskill	.05	.02	.01
□ 723	Sammy Sosa	.25	.11	.03
□ 724	George Bell	.05	.02	.01
□ 725	Gregg Jefferies	.15	.07	.02
□ 726	Gary DiSarcina	.05	.02	.01
□ 727	Mike Bordick	.10	.05	.01
□ 728	Eddie Murray	.15	.07	.02
	400 Home Run Club			
□ 729	Rene Gonzales	.05	.02	.01
□ 730	Mike Bielecki	.05	.02	.01
□ 731	Calvin Jones	.05	.02	.01
□ 732	Jack Morris	.10	.05	.01
□ 733	Frank Viola	.05	.02	.01
□ 734	Dave Winfield	.15	.07	.02
□ 735	Kevin Mitchell	.10	.05	.01
□ 736	Bill Swift	.05	.02	.01
□ 737	Dan Gladden	.05	.02	.01
□ 738	Mike Jackson	.05	.02	.01
□ 739	Mark Carreon	.05	.02	.01
□ 740	Kirt Manwaring	.05	.02	.01
□ 741	Randy Myers	.10	.05	.01
□ 742	Kevin McReynolds	.05	.02	.01
□ 743	Steve Sax	.05	.02	.01
□ 744	Wally Joyner	.10	.05	.01
□ 745	Gary Sheffield	.15	.07	.02
□ 746	Danny Tartabull	.05	.02	.01
□ 747	Julio Valera	.05	.02	.01
□ 748	Denny Neagle	.10	.05	.01
□ 749	Lance Blankenship	.05	.02	.01
□ 750	Mike Gallego	.05	.02	.01
□ 751	Bret Saberhagen	.10	.05	.01
□ 752	Ruben Amaro	.05	.02	.01
□ 753	Eddie Murray	.25	.11	.03
□ 754	Kyle Abbott	.05	.02	.01
□ 755	Bobby Bonilla	.10	.05	.01
□ 756	Eric Davis	.10	.05	.01
□ 757	Eddie Taubensee	.05	.02	.01
□ 758	Andres Galarraga	.15	.07	.02
□ 759	Pete Incaviglia	.05	.02	.01
□ 760	Tom Candiotti	.05	.02	.01
□ 761	Tim Belcher	.05	.02	.01
□ 762	Ricky Bones	.05	.02	.01
□ 763	Bip Roberts	.05	.02	.01
□ 764	Pedro Munoz	.05	.02	.01
□ 765	Greg Swindell	.05	.02	.01
□ 766	Kenny Lofton	1.00	.45	.12
□ 767	Gary Carter	.15	.07	.02
□ 768	Charlie Hayes	.05	.02	.01
□ 769	Dickie Thon	.05	.02	.01
□ 770	Donovan Osborne DD CL	.05	.02	.01
□ 771	Bret Boone DD	.15	.07	.02
□ 772	Archi Cianfrocco DD	.05	.02	.01
□ 773	Mark Clark DD	.10	.05	.01
□ 774	Chad Curtis DD	.10	.05	.01
□ 775	Pat Listach DD	.10	.05	.01
□ 776	Pat Mahomes DD	.05	.02	.01
□ 777	Donovan Osborne DD	.10	.05	.01
□ 778	John Patterson DD	.05	.02	.01
□ 779	Andy Stankiewicz DD	.05	.02	.01
□ 780	Turk Wendell DD	.10	.05	.01
□ 781	Bill Krueger	.05	.02	.01
□ 782	Rickey Henderson	.15	.07	.02
	Grand Theft			
□ 783	Kevin Seitzer	.05	.02	.01
□ 784	Dave Martinez	.05	.02	.01
□ 785	John Smiley	.05	.02	.01
□ 786	Matt Stairs	.05	.02	.01
□ 787	Scott Scudder	.05	.02	.01
□ 788	John Wetteland	.10	.05	.01
□ 789	Jack Armstrong	.05	.02	.01
□ 790	Ken Hill	.15	.07	.02
□ 791	Dick Schofield	.05	.02	.01
□ 792	Mariano Duncan	.05	.02	.01
□ 793	Bill Pecota	.05	.02	.01
□ 794	Mike Kelly	.05	.02	.01
□ 795	Willie Randolph	.10	.05	.01
□ 796	Butch Henry	.05	.02	.01
□ 797	Carlos Hernandez	.05	.02	.01
□ 798	Doug Jones	.05	.02	.01
□ 799	Melido Perez	.05	.02	.01
□ 800	Checklist 701-800	.05	.02	.01
□ HH2	Ted Williams Hologram	2.00	.90	.25
	(Top left corner says,			
	91 Upper Deck 92)			
□ SP3	Deion Sanders FB/BB	3.00	1.35	.35
□ SP4	Tom Selleck	5.00	2.20	.60
	Frank Thomas SP			
	(Mr. Baseball)			

1992 Upper Deck Heroes of Baseball

Continuing a popular insert set introduced the previous year, Upper Deck produced four new commemorative cards, including three player cards and one portrait card by sports artist Vernon Wells. These cards were randomly inserted in 1992 Upper Deck baseball low number foil packs. Three thousand of each card were personally numbered and autographed by each player. On a white card face, the fronts carry sepia-tone player photos with red, gold, and blue border stripes. The player's name appears in a gold border stripe beneath the picture, with the Upper Deck "Heroes of Baseball" logo in the lower right corner.

		MINT	NRMT	EXC
COMPLETE SET (4)		15.00	6.75	1.85
COMMON CARD (H5-H8)		3.00	1.35	.35
RANDOM INSERTS IN HEROES FOIL				
□ H5	Vida Blue	3.00	1.35	.35
□ H6	Lou Brock	5.00	2.20	.60
□ H7	Rollie Fingers	4.00	1.80	.50
□ H8	Vida Blue ART	4.00	1.80	.50
	Lou Brock			
	Rollie Fingers			
□ AU5	Vida Blue AU/3000	40.00	18.00	5.00
□ AU6	Lou Brock AU/3000	70.00	32.00	8.75
□ AU7	R.Fingers AU/3000	60.00	27.00	7.50

1992 Upper Deck Home Run Heroes

This 26-card standard-size set was inserted one per pack into 1992 Upper Deck low series jumbo packs. The set spotlights the 1991 home run leaders from each of the 26 Major League teams. The fronts display color action player photos with a shadow strip around the picture for a three-dimensional effect. A gold bat icon runs vertically down the left side and contains the words "Homerun Heroes" printed in white.

	MINT	NRMT	EXC
COMPLETE SET (26)	15.00	6.75	1.85
COMMON CARD (HR1-HR26)	.25	.11	.03
SEMISTARS	.60	.25	.07
ONE PER LO SERIES JUMBO			

	MINT	NRMT	EXC
□ HR1 Jose Canseco	.60	.25	.07
□ HR2 Cecil Fielder	.60	.25	.07
□ HR3 Howard Johnson	.25	.11	.03
□ HR4 Cal Ripken	4.00	1.80	.50
□ HR5 Matt Williams	.60	.25	.07
□ HR6 Joe Carter	.60	.25	.07
□ HR7 Ron Gant	.60	.25	.07
□ HR8 Frank Thomas	4.00	1.80	.50
□ HR9 Andre Dawson	.60	.25	.07
□ HR10 Fred McGriff	.60	.25	.07
□ HR11 Danny Tartabull	.25	.11	.03
□ HR12 Chili Davis	.60	.25	.07
□ HR13 Albert Belle	1.50	.70	.19
□ HR14 Jack Clark	.25	.11	.03
□ HR15 Paul O'Neill	.60	.25	.07
□ HR16 Darryl Strawberry	.60	.25	.07
□ HR17 Dave Winfield	.60	.25	.07
□ HR18 Jay Buhner	.60	.25	.07
□ HR19 Juan Gonzalez	1.50	.70	.19
□ HR20 Greg Vaughn	.60	.25	.07
□ HR21 Barry Bonds	.75	.35	.09
□ HR22 Matt Nokes	.25	.11	.03
□ HR23 John Kruk	.60	.25	.07
□ HR24 Ivan Calderon	.25	.11	.03
□ HR25 Jeff Bagwell	2.00	.90	.25
□ HR26 Todd Zeile	.25	.11	.03

1992 Upper Deck Scouting Report

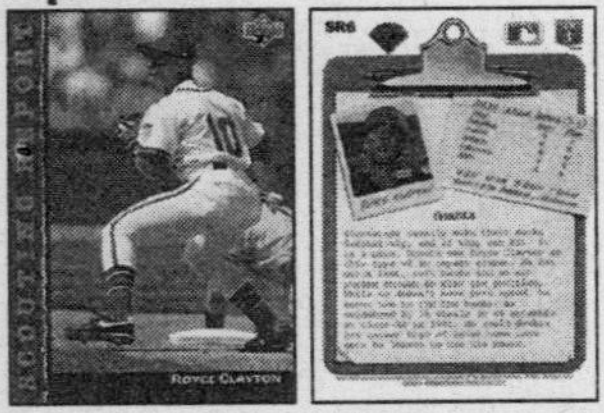

Inserted one per high series jumbo pack, cards from this 25-card standard-size set feature outstanding prospects in baseball. The fronts carry color action player photos that are full-bleed on the top and right, bordered below by a black stripe with the player's name, and by a black jagged left border that resembles torn paper. The words "Scouting Report" are printed vertically in silver lettering in the left border.

	MINT	NRMT	EXC
COMPLETE SET (25)	15.00	6.75	1.85
COMMON CARD (SR1-SR25)	.25	.11	.03
ONE PER HI SERIES JUMBO			

	MINT	NRMT	EXC
□ SR1 Andy Ashby	.35	.16	.04
□ SR2 Willie Banks	.25	.11	.03
□ SR3 Kim Batiste	.25	.11	.03
□ SR4 Derek Bell	1.25	.55	.16
□ SR5 Archi Cianfrocco	.25	.11	.03
□ SR6 Royce Clayton	.35	.16	.04
□ SR7 Gary DiSarcina	.25	.11	.03
□ SR8 Dave Fleming	.25	.11	.03
□ SR9 Butch Henry	.25	.11	.03
□ SR10 Todd Hundley	1.25	.55	.16
□ SR11 Brian Jordan	2.00	.90	.25
□ SR12 Eric Karros	1.50	.70	.19
□ SR13 Pat Listach	.35	.16	.04
□ SR14 Scott Livingstone	.25	.11	.03
□ SR15 Kenny Lofton	8.00	3.60	1.00
□ SR16 Pat Mahomes	.25	.11	.03
□ SR17 Denny Neagle	1.25	.55	.16
□ SR18 Dave Nilsson	.50	.23	.06
□ SR19 Donovan Osborne	.25	.11	.03
□ SR20 Reggie Sanders	1.50	.70	.19
□ SR21 Andy Stankiewicz	.25	.11	.03
□ SR22 Jim Thome	6.00	2.70	.75
□ SR23 Julio Valera	.25	.11	.03
□ SR24 Mark Wohlers	.75	.35	.09
□ SR25 Anthony Young	.25	.11	.03

1992 Upper Deck Williams Best

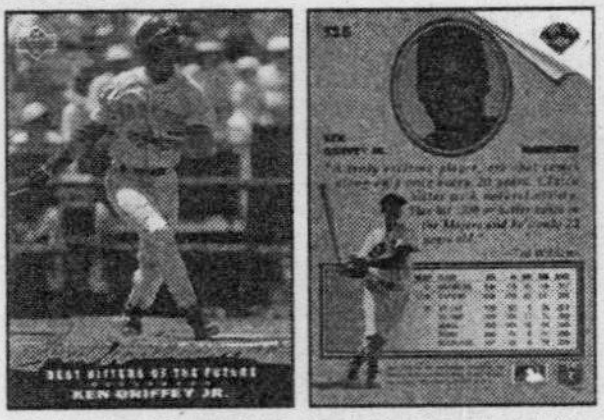

This 20-card standard-size set contains Ted Williams' choices of best current and future hitters in the game. The cards were randomly inserted in Upper Deck high number foil packs. The fronts feature full-bleed color action photos with the player's name in a black field separated from the picture by Ted Williams' gold-stamped signature.

	MINT	NRMT	EXC
COMPLETE SET (20)	30.00	13.50	3.70
COMMON CARD (T1-T20)	.50	.23	.06
SEMISTARS	.75	.35	.09
RANDOM INSERTS IN HI SERIES			

	MINT	NRMT	EXC
□ T1 Wade Boggs	.75	.35	.09
□ T2 Barry Bonds	1.25	.55	.16
□ T3 Jose Canseco	.75	.35	.09
□ T4 Will Clark	.75	.35	.09
□ T5 Cecil Fielder	.75	.35	.09
□ T6 Tony Gwynn	1.50	.70	.19
□ T7 Rickey Henderson	.75	.35	.09
□ T8 Fred McGriff	.75	.35	.09
□ T9 Kirby Puckett	1.50	.70	.19
□ T10 Ruben Sierra	.75	.35	.09
□ T11 Roberto Alomar	1.25	.55	.16
□ T12 Jeff Bagwell	3.00	1.35	.35
□ T13 Albert Belle	3.00	1.35	.35
□ T14 Juan Gonzalez	3.00	1.35	.35
□ T15 Ken Griffey Jr.	8.00	3.60	1.00
□ T16 Chris Hoiles	.50	.23	.06
□ T17 David Justice	.75	.35	.09
□ T18 Phil Plantier	.50	.23	.06
□ T19 Frank Thomas	8.00	3.60	1.00
□ T20 Robin Ventura	.75	.35	.09

1993 Upper Deck

The 1993 Upper Deck set consists of two series of 420 standard-size cards. A special card (SP5) was randomly inserted in first series

packs to commemorate the 3,000th hit of George Brett and Robin Yount. A special card (SP6) commemorating Nolan Ryan's last season was randomly inserted into second series packs. The front designs features color action player photos bordered in white. The company name is printed along the photo surface of the card top. The player's name appears in script in a color stripe cutting across the bottom of the picture while the team name and his position appear in another color stripe immediately below. The backs have a color close-up photo on the upper portion and biography, statistics, and career higlights on the lower portion. Special subsets featured include Star Rookies (1-29), Community Heroes (30-40), and American League Teammates (41-55), Top Prospects (421-449), Inside the Numbers (450-470), Team Stars (471-485), Award Winners (486-499), and Diamond Debuts (500-510). Rookie Cards in this set include Midre Cummings, Derek Jeter, Ray McDavid, Michael Moore, Chad Mottola, J.T. Snow, and Tony Tarasco.

	MINT	NRMT	EXC
COMPLETE SET (840)	40.00	18.00	5.00
COMPLETE FACT.SET (840)	45.00	20.00	5.50
COMPLETE SERIES 1 (420)	20.00	9.00	2.50
COMPLETE SERIES 2 (420)	20.00	9.00	2.50
COMMON CARD (1-840)	.05	.02	.01
SEMISTARS	.15	.07	.02
STARS	.30	.14	.04
*GOLD HOLOGRAM: 1.5X VALUE			
COMPLETE MAYS SET (10)	3.00	1.35	.35
COMMON MAYS (46-54/HDR)	.50	.23	.06
MAYS: RANDOM INSERTS IN SER.1 PACKS			

□ 1 Tim Salmon CL	.30	.14	.04
□ 2 Mike Piazza SR	2.00	.90	.25
□ 3 Rene Arocha SR	.05	.02	.01
□ 4 Willie Greene SR	.15	.07	.02
□ 5 Manny Alexander SR	.05	.02	.01
□ 6 Dan Wilson SR	.15	.07	.02
□ 7 Dan Smith SR	.05	.02	.01
□ 8 Kevin Rogers SR	.05	.02	.01
□ 9 Kurt Miller SR	.05	.02	.01
□ 10 Joe Vitko SR	.05	.02	.01
□ 11 Tim Costo SR	.05	.02	.01
□ 12 Alan Embree SR	.05	.02	.01
□ 13 Jim Tatum SR	.05	.02	.01
□ 14 Cris Colon SR	.05	.02	.01
□ 15 Steve Hosey SR	.05	.02	.01
□ 16 Sterling Hitchcock SR	.15	.07	.02
□ 17 Dave Mlicki SR	.05	.02	.01
□ 18 Jessie Hollins SR	.05	.02	.01
□ 19 Bobby Jones SR	.15	.07	.02
□ 20 Kurt Miller SR	.05	.02	.01
□ 21 Melvin Nieves SR	.30	.14	.04
□ 22 Billy Ashley SR	.05	.02	.01
□ 23 J.T. Snow SR	.30	.14	.04
□ 24 Chipper Jones SR	2.50	1.10	.30
□ 25 Tim Salmon SR	.50	.23	.06
□ 26 Tim Pugh SR	.05	.02	.01
□ 27 David Nied SR	.05	.02	.01
□ 28 Mike Trombley SR	.05	.02	.01
□ 29 Javier Lopez SR	.50	.23	.06
□ 30 Jim Abbott CL	.05	.02	.01
□ 31 Jim Abbott CH	.05	.02	.01
□ 32 Dale Murphy CH	.30	.14	.04
□ 33 Tony Pena CH	.05	.02	.01
□ 34 Kirby Puckett CH	.30	.14	.04
□ 35 Harold Reynolds CH	.05	.02	.01
□ 36 Cal Ripken CH	.75	.35	.09
□ 37 Nolan Ryan CH	.75	.35	.09
□ 38 Ryne Sandberg CH	.30	.14	.04
□ 39 Dave Stewart CH	.05	.02	.01
□ 40 Dave Winfield CH	.30	.14	.04
□ 41 Joe Carter CL	.30	.14	.04
Mark McGwire			
□ 42 Blockbuster Trade	.30	.14	.04
Joe Carter			
Roberto Alomar			
□ 43 Brew Crew	.30	.14	.04
Paul Molitor			
Pat Listach			
Robin Yount			
□ 44 Iron and Steel	.50	.23	.06
Cal Ripken			
Brady Anderson			
□ 45 Youthful Tribe	.50	.23	.06
Albert Belle			
Sandy Alomar Jr.			
Jim Thome			
Carlos Baerga			
Kenny Lofton			
□ 46 Motown Mashers	.15	.07	.02
Cecil Fielder			
Mickey Tettleton			
□ 47 Yankee Pride	.30	.14	.04
Roberto Kelly			
Don Mattingly			
□ 48 Boston Cy Sox	.15	.07	.02
Frank Viola			
Roger Clemens			
□ 49 Bash Brothers	.15	.07	.02
Ruben Sierra			
Mark McGwire			
□ 50 Twin Titles	.30	.14	.04
Kent Hrbek			
Kirby Puckett			
□ 51 Southside Sluggers	.50	.23	.06
Robin Ventura			
Frank Thomas			
□ 52 Latin Stars	.50	.23	.06
Juan Gonzalez			
Jose Canseco			
Ivan Rodriguez			
Rafael Palmeiro			
□ 53 Lethal Lefties	.15	.07	.02
Mark Langston			
Jim Abbott			
Chuck Finley			
□ 54 Royal Family	.15	.07	.02
Wally Joyner			
Gregg Jefferies			
George Brett			
□ 55 Pacific Sock Exchange	.50	.23	.06
Kevin Mitchell			
Ken Griffey Jr.			
Jay Buhner			
□ 56 George Brett	.75	.35	.09
□ 57 Scott Cooper	.05	.02	.01
□ 58 Mike Maddux	.05	.02	.01
□ 59 Rusty Meacham	.05	.02	.01
□ 60 Wil Cordero	.15	.07	.02
□ 61 Tim Teufel	.05	.02	.01
□ 62 Jeff Montgomery	.15	.07	.02
□ 63 Scott Livingstone	.05	.02	.01
□ 64 Doug Dascenzo	.05	.02	.01
□ 65 Bret Boone	.15	.07	.02
□ 66 Tim Wakefield	.15	.07	.02
□ 67 Curt Schilling	.05	.02	.01
□ 68 Frank Tanana	.05	.02	.01
□ 69 Len Dykstra	.15	.07	.02
□ 70 Derek Lilliquist	.05	.02	.01
□ 71 Anthony Young	.05	.02	.01
□ 72 Hipolito Pichardo	.05	.02	.01
□ 73 Rod Beck	.15	.07	.02
□ 74 Kent Hrbek	.15	.07	.02
□ 75 Tom Glavine	.30	.14	.04
□ 76 Kevin Brown	.05	.02	.01
□ 77 Chuck Finley	.05	.02	.01
□ 78 Bob Walk	.05	.02	.01
□ 79 Rheal Cormier UER	.05	.02	.01
(Born in New Brunswick,			

not British Columbia)

□ 80 Rick Sutcliffe	.05	.02	.01
□ 81 Harold Baines	.15	.07	.02
□ 82 Lee Smith	.15	.07	.02
□ 83 Geno Petralli	.05	.02	.01
□ 84 Jose Oquendo	.05	.02	.01
□ 85 Mark Gubicza	.05	.02	.01
□ 86 Mickey Tettleton	.05	.02	.01
□ 87 Bobby Witt	.05	.02	.01
□ 88 Mark Lewis	.05	.02	.01
□ 89 Kevin Appier	.15	.07	.02
□ 90 Mike Stanton	.05	.02	.01
□ 91 Rafael Belliard	.05	.02	.01
□ 92 Kenny Rogers	.05	.02	.01
□ 93 Randy Velarde	.05	.02	.01
□ 94 Luis Sojo	.05	.02	.01
□ 95 Mark Leiter	.05	.02	.01
□ 96 Jody Reed	.05	.02	.01
□ 97 Pete Harnisch	.05	.02	.01
□ 98 Tom Candiotti	.05	.02	.01
□ 99 Mark Portugal	.05	.02	.01
□ 100 Dave Valle	.05	.02	.01
□ 101 Shawon Dunston	.05	.02	.01
□ 102 B.J. Surhoff	.15	.07	.02
□ 103 Jay Bell	.15	.07	.02
□ 104 Sid Bream	.05	.02	.01
□ 105 Frank Thomas CL	.30	.14	.04
□ 106 Mike Morgan	.05	.02	.01
□ 107 Bill Doran	.05	.02	.01
□ 108 Lance Blankenship	.05	.02	.01
□ 109 Mark Lemke	.05	.02	.01
□ 110 Brian Harper	.05	.02	.01
□ 111 Brady Anderson	.30	.14	.04
□ 112 Bip Roberts	.05	.02	.01
□ 113 Mitch Williams	.05	.02	.01
□ 114 Craig Biggio	.30	.14	.04
□ 115 Eddie Murray	.50	.23	.06
□ 116 Matt Nokes	.05	.02	.01
□ 117 Lance Parrish	.05	.02	.01
□ 118 Bill Swift	.05	.02	.01
□ 119 Jeff Innis	.05	.02	.01
□ 120 Mike LaValliere	.05	.02	.01
□ 121 Hal Morris	.05	.02	.01
□ 122 Walt Weiss	.05	.02	.01
□ 123 Ivan Rodriguez	.40	.18	.05
□ 124 Andy Van Slyke	.15	.07	.02
□ 125 Roberto Alomar	.50	.23	.06
□ 126 Robby Thompson	.05	.02	.01
□ 127 Sammy Sosa	.30	.14	.04
□ 128 Mark Langston	.15	.07	.02
□ 129 Jerry Browne	.05	.02	.01
□ 130 Chuck McElroy	.05	.02	.01
□ 131 Frank Viola	.05	.02	.01
□ 132 Leo Gomez	.05	.02	.01
□ 133 Ramon Martinez	.15	.07	.02
□ 134 Don Mattingly	1.00	.45	.12
□ 135 Roger Clemens	.30	.14	.04
□ 136 Rickey Henderson	.30	.14	.04
□ 137 Darren Daulton	.15	.07	.02
□ 138 Ken Hill	.15	.07	.02
□ 139 Ozzie Guillen	.05	.02	.01
□ 140 Jerald Clark	.05	.02	.01
□ 141 Dave Fleming	.05	.02	.01
□ 142 Delino DeShields	.05	.02	.01
□ 143 Matt Williams	.30	.14	.04
□ 144 Larry Walker	.30	.14	.04
□ 145 Ruben Sierra	.15	.07	.02
□ 146 Ozzie Smith	.40	.18	.05
□ 147 Chris Sabo	.05	.02	.01
□ 148 Carlos Hernandez	.05	.02	.01
□ 149 Pat Borders	.05	.02	.01
□ 150 Orlando Merced	.15	.07	.02
□ 151 Royce Clayton	.15	.07	.02
□ 152 Kurt Stillwell	.05	.02	.01
□ 153 Dave Hollins	.05	.02	.01
□ 154 Mike Greenwell	.05	.02	.01
□ 155 Nolan Ryan	1.50	.70	.19
□ 156 Felix Jose	.05	.02	.01
□ 157 Junior Felix	.05	.02	.01
□ 158 Derek Bell	.30	.14	.04
□ 159 Steve Buechele	.05	.02	.01
□ 160 John Burkett	.05	.02	.01
□ 161 Pat Howell	.05	.02	.01
□ 162 Milt Cuyler	.05	.02	.01
□ 163 Terry Pendleton	.15	.07	.02
□ 164 Jack Morris	.15	.07	.02
□ 165 Tony Gwynn	.75	.35	.09
□ 166 Deion Sanders	.30	.14	.04
□ 167 Mike Devereaux	.05	.02	.01
□ 168 Ron Darling	.05	.02	.01
□ 169 Orel Hershiser	.15	.07	.02
□ 170 Mike Jackson	.05	.02	.01
□ 171 Doug Jones	.05	.02	.01
□ 172 Dan Walters	.05	.02	.01
□ 173 Darren Lewis	.05	.02	.01
□ 174 Carlos Baerga	.30	.14	.04
□ 175 Ryne Sandberg	.50	.23	.06
□ 176 Gregg Jefferies	.30	.14	.04
□ 177 John Jaha	.15	.07	.02
□ 178 Luis Polonia	.05	.02	.01
□ 179 Kirt Manwaring	.05	.02	.01
□ 180 Mike Magnante	.05	.02	.01
□ 181 Billy Ripken	.05	.02	.01
□ 182 Mike Moore	.05	.02	.01
□ 183 Eric Anthony	.05	.02	.01
□ 184 Lenny Harris	.05	.02	.01
□ 185 Tony Pena	.05	.02	.01
□ 186 Mike Felder	.05	.02	.01
□ 187 Greg Olson	.05	.02	.01
□ 188 Rene Gonzales	.05	.02	.01
□ 189 Mike Bordick	.05	.02	.01
□ 190 Mel Rojas	.15	.07	.02
□ 191 Todd Frohwirth	.05	.02	.01
□ 192 Darryl Hamilton	.05	.02	.01
□ 193 Mike Fetters	.05	.02	.01
□ 194 Omar Olivares	.05	.02	.01
□ 195 Tony Phillips	.15	.07	.02
□ 196 Paul Sorrento	.05	.02	.01
□ 197 Trevor Wilson	.05	.02	.01
□ 198 Kevin Gross	.05	.02	.01
□ 199 Ron Karkovice	.05	.02	.01
□ 200 Brook Jacoby	.05	.02	.01
□ 201 Mariano Duncan	.05	.02	.01
□ 202 Dennis Cook	.05	.02	.01
□ 203 Daryl Boston	.05	.02	.01
□ 204 Mike Perez	.05	.02	.01
□ 205 Manuel Lee	.05	.02	.01
□ 206 Steve Olin	.05	.02	.01
□ 207 Charlie Hough	.05	.02	.01
□ 208 Scott Scudder	.05	.02	.01
□ 209 Charlie O'Brien	.05	.02	.01
□ 210 Barry Bonds CL	.30	.14	.04
□ 211 Jose Vizcaino	.05	.02	.01
□ 212 Scott Leius	.05	.02	.01
□ 213 Kevin Mitchell	.15	.07	.02
□ 214 Brian Barnes	.05	.02	.01
□ 215 Pat Kelly	.05	.02	.01
□ 216 Chris Hammond	.05	.02	.01
□ 217 Rob Deer	.05	.02	.01
□ 218 Cory Snyder	.05	.02	.01
□ 219 Gary Carter	.30	.14	.04
□ 220 Danny Darwin	.05	.02	.01
□ 221 Tom Gordon	.05	.02	.01
□ 222 Gary Sheffield	.30	.14	.04
□ 223 Joe Carter	.30	.14	.04
□ 224 Jay Buhner	.30	.14	.04
□ 225 Jose Offerman	.05	.02	.01
□ 226 Jose Rijo	.05	.02	.01
□ 227 Mark Whiten	.05	.02	.01
□ 228 Randy Milligan	.05	.02	.01
□ 229 Bud Black	.05	.02	.01
□ 230 Gary DiSarcina	.05	.02	.01
□ 231 Steve Finley	.30	.14	.04
□ 232 Dennis Martinez	.15	.07	.02
□ 233 Mike Mussina	.30	.14	.04
□ 234 Joe Oliver	.05	.02	.01
□ 235 Chad Curtis	.15	.07	.02
□ 236 Shane Mack	.05	.02	.01
□ 237 Jaime Navarro	.05	.02	.01
□ 238 Brian McRae	.15	.07	.02
□ 239 Chili Davis	.15	.07	.02
□ 240 Jeff King	.15	.07	.02
□ 241 Dean Palmer	.15	.07	.02
□ 242 Danny Tartabull	.05	.02	.01
□ 243 Charles Nagy	.15	.07	.02
□ 244 Ray Lankford	.30	.14	.04
□ 245 Barry Larkin	.30	.14	.04
□ 246 Steve Avery	.15	.07	.02
□ 247 John Kruk	.15	.07	.02
□ 248 Derrick May	.05	.02	.01
□ 249 Stan Javier	.05	.02	.01
□ 250 Roger McDowell	.05	.02	.01

□ 251 Dan Gladden	.05	.02	.01
□ 252 Wally Joyner	.15	.07	.02
□ 253 Pat Listach	.05	.02	.01
□ 254 Chuck Knoblauch	.30	.14	.04
□ 255 Sandy Alomar Jr.	.15	.07	.02
□ 256 Jeff Bagwell	.75	.35	.09
□ 257 Andy Stankiewicz	.05	.02	.01
□ 258 Darrin Jackson	.05	.02	.01
□ 259 Brett Butler	.15	.07	.02
□ 260 Joe Orsulak	.05	.02	.01
□ 261 Andy Benes	.05	.02	.01
□ 262 Kenny Lofton	.75	.35	.09
□ 263 Robin Ventura	.15	.07	.02
□ 264 Ron Gant	.30	.14	.04
□ 265 Ellis Burks	.30	.14	.04
□ 266 Juan Guzman	.15	.07	.02
□ 267 Wes Chamberlain	.05	.02	.01
□ 268 John Smiley	.05	.02	.01
□ 269 Franklin Stubbs	.05	.02	.01
□ 270 Tom Browning	.05	.02	.01
□ 271 Dennis Eckersley	.15	.07	.02
□ 272 Carlton Fisk	.30	.14	.04
□ 273 Lou Whitaker	.30	.14	.04
□ 274 Phil Plantier	.05	.02	.01
□ 275 Bobby Bonilla	.15	.07	.02
□ 276 Ben McDonald	.05	.02	.01
□ 277 Bob Zupcic	.05	.02	.01
□ 278 Terry Steinbach	.15	.07	.02
□ 279 Terry Mulholland	.05	.02	.01
□ 280 Lance Johnson	.15	.07	.02
□ 281 Willie McGee	.05	.02	.01
□ 282 Bret Saberhagen	.15	.07	.02
□ 283 Randy Myers	.15	.07	.02
□ 284 Randy Tomlin	.05	.02	.01
□ 285 Mickey Morandini	.05	.02	.01
□ 286 Brian Williams	.05	.02	.01
□ 287 Tino Martinez	.15	.07	.02
□ 288 Jose Melendez	.05	.02	.01
□ 289 Jeff Huson	.05	.02	.01
□ 290 Joe Grahe	.05	.02	.01
□ 291 Mel Hall	.05	.02	.01
□ 292 Otis Nixon	.05	.02	.01
□ 293 Todd Hundley	.30	.14	.04
□ 294 Casey Candaele	.05	.02	.01
□ 295 Kevin Seitzer	.05	.02	.01
□ 296 Eddie Taubensee	.05	.02	.01
□ 297 Moises Alou	.30	.14	.04
□ 298 Scott Radinsky	.05	.02	.01
□ 299 Thomas Howard	.05	.02	.01
□ 300 Kyle Abbott	.05	.02	.01
□ 301 Omar Vizquel	.30	.14	.04
□ 302 Keith Miller	.05	.02	.01
□ 303 Rick Aguilera	.05	.02	.01
□ 304 Bruce Hurst	.05	.02	.01
□ 305 Ken Caminiti	.30	.14	.04
□ 306 Mike Pagliarulo	.05	.02	.01
□ 307 Frank Seminara	.05	.02	.01
□ 308 Andre Dawson	.30	.14	.04
□ 309 Jose Lind	.05	.02	.01
□ 310 Joe Boever	.05	.02	.01
□ 311 Jeff Parrett	.05	.02	.01
□ 312 Alan Mills	.05	.02	.01
□ 313 Kevin Tapani	.05	.02	.01
□ 314 Darryl Kile	.05	.02	.01
□ 315 Will Clark CL	.15	.07	.02
□ 316 Mike Sharperson	.05	.02	.01
□ 317 John Orton	.05	.02	.01
□ 318 Bob Tewksbury	.05	.02	.01
□ 319 Xavier Hernandez	.05	.02	.01
□ 320 Paul Assenmacher	.05	.02	.01
□ 321 John Franco	.05	.02	.01
□ 322 Mike Timlin	.05	.02	.01
□ 323 Jose Guzman	.05	.02	.01
□ 324 Pedro Martinez	.30	.14	.04
□ 325 Bill Spiers	.05	.02	.01
□ 326 Melido Perez	.05	.02	.01
□ 327 Mike Macfarlane	.05	.02	.01
□ 328 Ricky Bones	.05	.02	.01
□ 329 Scott Bankhead	.05	.02	.01
□ 330 Rich Rodriguez	.05	.02	.01
□ 331 Geronimo Pena	.05	.02	.01
□ 332 Bernie Williams	.30	.14	.04
□ 333 Paul Molitor	.40	.18	.05
□ 334 Carlos Garcia	.05	.02	.01
□ 335 David Cone	.30	.14	.04
□ 336 Randy Johnson	.30	.14	.04
□ 337 Pat Mahomes	.05	.02	.01
□ 338 Erik Hanson	.05	.02	.01
□ 339 Duane Ward	.05	.02	.01
□ 340 Al Martin	.15	.07	.02
□ 341 Pedro Munoz	.05	.02	.01
□ 342 Greg Colbrunn	.05	.02	.01
□ 343 Julio Valera	.05	.02	.01
□ 344 John Olerud	.05	.02	.01
□ 345 George Bell	.05	.02	.01
□ 346 Devon White	.05	.02	.01
□ 347 Donovan Osborne	.05	.02	.01
□ 348 Mark Gardner	.05	.02	.01
□ 349 Zane Smith	.05	.02	.01
□ 350 Wilson Alvarez	.15	.07	.02
□ 351 Kevin Koslofski	.05	.02	.01
□ 352 Roberto Hernandez	.15	.07	.02
□ 353 Glenn Davis	.05	.02	.01
□ 354 Reggie Sanders	.30	.14	.04
□ 355 Ken Griffey Jr.	2.00	.90	.25
□ 356 Marquis Grissom	.30	.14	.04
□ 357 Jack McDowell	.15	.07	.02
□ 358 Jimmy Key	.15	.07	.02
□ 359 Stan Belinda	.05	.02	.01
□ 360 Gerald Williams	.05	.02	.01
□ 361 Sid Fernandez	.05	.02	.01
□ 362 Alex Fernandez	.30	.14	.04
□ 363 John Smoltz	.30	.14	.04
□ 364 Travis Fryman	.30	.14	.04
□ 365 Jose Canseco	.30	.14	.04
□ 366 David Justice	.30	.14	.04
□ 367 Pedro Astacio	.05	.02	.01
□ 368 Tim Belcher	.05	.02	.01
□ 369 Steve Sax	.05	.02	.01
□ 370 Gary Gaetti	.15	.07	.02
□ 371 Jeff Frye	.05	.02	.01
□ 372 Bob Wickman	.05	.02	.01
□ 373 Ryan Thompson	.05	.02	.01
□ 374 David Hulse	.05	.02	.01
□ 375 Cal Eldred	.05	.02	.01
□ 376 Ryan Klesko	1.00	.45	.12
□ 377 Damion Easley	.05	.02	.01
□ 378 John Kiely	.05	.02	.01
□ 379 Jim Bullinger	.05	.02	.01
□ 380 Brian Bohanon	.05	.02	.01
□ 381 Rod Brewer	.05	.02	.01
□ 382 Fernando Ramsey	.05	.02	.01
□ 383 Sam Militello	.05	.02	.01
□ 384 Arthur Rhodes	.05	.02	.01
□ 385 Eric Karros	.30	.14	.04
□ 386 Rico Brogna	.15	.07	.02
□ 387 John Valentin	.30	.14	.04
□ 388 Kerry Woodson	.05	.02	.01
□ 389 Ben Rivera	.05	.02	.01
□ 390 Matt Whiteside	.05	.02	.01
□ 391 Henry Rodriguez	.30	.14	.04
□ 392 John Wetteland	.15	.07	.02
□ 393 Kent Mercker	.05	.02	.01
□ 394 Bernard Gilkey	.30	.14	.04
□ 395 Doug Henry	.05	.02	.01
□ 396 Mo Vaughn	.50	.23	.06
□ 397 Scott Erickson	.05	.02	.01
□ 398 Bill Gullickson	.05	.02	.01
□ 399 Mark Guthrie	.05	.02	.01
□ 400 Dave Martinez	.05	.02	.01
□ 401 Jeff Kent	.15	.07	.02
□ 402 Chris Hoiles	.05	.02	.01
□ 403 Mike Henneman	.05	.02	.01
□ 404 Chris Nabholz	.05	.02	.01
□ 405 Tom Pagnozzi	.05	.02	.01
□ 406 Kelly Gruber	.05	.02	.01
□ 407 Bob Welch	.05	.02	.01
□ 408 Frank Castillo	.05	.02	.01
□ 409 John Dopson	.05	.02	.01
□ 410 Steve Farr	.05	.02	.01
□ 411 Henry Cotto	.05	.02	.01
□ 412 Bob Patterson	.05	.02	.01
□ 413 Todd Stottlemyre	.15	.07	.02
□ 414 Greg A. Harris	.05	.02	.01
□ 415 Denny Neagle	.15	.07	.02
□ 416 Bill Wegman	.05	.02	.01
□ 417 Willie Wilson	.05	.02	.01
□ 418 Terry Leach	.05	.02	.01
□ 419 Willie Randolph	.15	.07	.02
□ 420 Mark McGwire CL	.30	.14	.04
□ 421 Calvin Murray CL	.05	.02	.01
□ 422 Pete Janicki TP	.05	.02	.01

□ 423 Todd Jones TP	.15	.07	.02
□ 424 Mike Neill TP	.05	.02	.01
□ 425 Carlos Delgado TP	.50	.23	.06
□ 426 Jose Oliva TP	.05	.02	.01
□ 427 Tyrone Hill TP	.05	.02	.01
□ 428 Dmitri Young TP	.50	.23	.06
□ 429 Derek Wallace TP	.05	.02	.01
□ 430 Michael Moore TP	.05	.02	.01
□ 431 Cliff Floyd TP	.30	.14	.04
□ 432 Calvin Murray TP	.05	.02	.01
□ 433 Manny Ramirez TP	1.25	.55	.16
□ 434 Marc Newfield TP	.15	.07	.02
□ 435 Charles Johnson TP	.40	.18	.05
□ 436 Butch Huskey TP	.15	.07	.02
□ 437 Brad Pennington TP	.05	.02	.01
□ 438 Ray McDavid TP	.15	.07	.02
□ 439 Chad McConnell TP	.05	.02	.01
□ 440 Midre Cummings TP	.15	.07	.02
□ 441 Benji Gil TP	.15	.07	.02
□ 442 Frankie Rodriguez TP	.15	.07	.02
□ 443 Chad Mottola TP	.15	.07	.02
□ 444 John Burke TP	.05	.02	.01
□ 445 Michael Tucker TP	.30	.14	.04
□ 446 Rick Greene TP	.05	.02	.01
□ 447 Rich Becker TP	.30	.14	.04
□ 448 Mike Robertson TP	.05	.02	.01
□ 449 Derek Jeter TP	4.00	1.80	.50
□ 450 Ivan Rodriguez CL David McCarty	.15	.07	.02
□ 451 Jim Abbott IN	.05	.02	.01
□ 452 Jeff Bagwell IN	.40	.18	.05
□ 453 Jason Bere IN	.15	.07	.02
□ 454 Delino DeShields IN	.05	.02	.01
□ 455 Travis Fryman IN	.15	.07	.02
□ 456 Alex Gonzalez IN	.30	.14	.04
□ 457 Phil Hiatt IN	.05	.02	.01
□ 458 Dave Hollins IN	.05	.02	.01
□ 459 Chipper Jones IN	1.25	.55	.16
□ 460 David Justice IN	.15	.07	.02
□ 461 Ray Lankford IN	.15	.07	.02
□ 462 David McCarty IN	.05	.02	.01
□ 463 Mike Mussina IN	.30	.14	.04
□ 464 Jose Offerman IN	.05	.02	.01
□ 465 Dean Palmer IN	.05	.02	.01
□ 466 Geronimo Pena IN	.05	.02	.01
□ 467 Eduardo Perez IN	.05	.02	.01
□ 468 Ivan Rodriguez IN	.30	.14	.04
□ 469 Reggie Sanders IN	.30	.14	.04
□ 470 Bernie Williams IN	.30	.14	.04
□ 471 Barry Bonds CL Matt Williams Will Clark	.30	.14	.04
□ 472 Strike Force Greg Maddux Steve Avery John Smoltz Tom Glavine	.50	.23	.06
□ 473 Red October Jose Rijo Rob Dibble Roberto Kelly Reggie Sanders Barry Larkin	.05	.02	.01
□ 474 Four Corners Gary Sheffield Phil Plantier Tony Gwynn Fred McGriff	.30	.14	.04
□ 475 Shooting Stars Doug Drabek Craig Biggio Jeff Bagwell	.15	.07	.02
□ 476 Giant Sticks Will Clark Barry Bonds Matt Williams	.30	.14	.04
□ 477 Boyhood Friends Eric Davis Darryl Strawberry	.15	.07	.02
□ 478 Rock Solid Foundation Dante Bichette David Nied Andres Galarraga	.30	.14	.04
□ 479 Inaugural Catch Dave Magadan Orestes Destrade Bret Barberie Jeff Conine	.05	.02	.01
□ 480 Steel City Champions Tim Wakefield Andy Van Slyke Jay Bell	.05	.02	.01
□ 481 Les Grandes Etoiles Marquis Grissom Delino DeShields Dennis Martinez Larry Walker	.15	.07	.02
□ 482 Runnin' Redbirds Geronimo Pena Ray Lankford Ozzie Smith Bernard Gilkey	.15	.07	.02
□ 483 Ivy Leaguers Randy Myers Ryne Sandberg Mark Grace	.15	.07	.02
□ 484 Big Apple Power Switch Eddie Murray Howard Johnson Bobby Bonilla	.15	.07	.02
□ 485 Hammers and Nails John Kruk Dave Hollins Darren Daulton Len Dykstra	.05	.02	.01
□ 486 Barry Bonds AW	.30	.14	.04
□ 487 Dennis Eckersley AW	.05	.02	.01
□ 488 Greg Maddux AW	.60	.25	.07
□ 489 Dennis Eckersley AW	.05	.02	.01
□ 490 Eric Karros AW	.15	.07	.02
□ 491 Pat Listach AW	.05	.02	.01
□ 492 Gary Sheffield AW	.30	.14	.04
□ 493 Mark McGwire AW	.30	.14	.04
□ 494 Gary Sheffield AW	.30	.14	.04
□ 495 Edgar Martinez AW	.30	.14	.04
□ 496 Fred McGriff AW	.30	.14	.04
□ 497 Juan Gonzalez AW	.50	.23	.06
□ 498 Darren Daulton AW	.05	.02	.01
□ 499 Cecil Fielder AW	.05	.02	.01
□ 500 Brent Gates CL	.05	.02	.01
□ 501 Tavo Alvarez DD	.05	.02	.01
□ 502 Rod Bolton DD	.05	.02	.01
□ 503 John Cummings DD	.05	.02	.01
□ 504 Brent Gates DD	.15	.07	.02
□ 505 Tyler Green DD	.05	.02	.01
□ 506 Jose Martinez DD	.05	.02	.01
□ 507 Troy Percival DD	.15	.07	.02
□ 508 Kevin Stocker DD	.15	.07	.02
□ 509 Matt Walbeck DD	.05	.02	.01
□ 510 Rondell White DD	.40	.18	.05
□ 511 Billy Ripken	.05	.02	.01
□ 512 Mike Moore	.05	.02	.01
□ 513 Jose Lind	.05	.02	.01
□ 514 Chito Martinez	.05	.02	.01
□ 515 Jose Guzman	.05	.02	.01
□ 516 Kim Batiste	.05	.02	.01
□ 517 Jeff Tackett	.05	.02	.01
□ 518 Charlie Hough	.05	.02	.01
□ 519 Marvin Freeman	.05	.02	.01
□ 520 Carlos Martinez	.05	.02	.01
□ 521 Eric Young	.30	.14	.04
□ 522 Pete Incaviglia	.05	.02	.01
□ 523 Scott Fletcher	.05	.02	.01
□ 524 Orestes Destrade	.05	.02	.01
□ 525 Ken Griffey Jr. CL	.30	.14	.04
□ 526 Ellis Burks	.30	.14	.04
□ 527 Juan Samuel	.05	.02	.01
□ 528 Dave Magadan	.05	.02	.01
□ 529 Jeff Parrett	.05	.02	.01
□ 530 Bill Krueger	.05	.02	.01
□ 531 Frank Bolick	.05	.02	.01
□ 532 Alan Trammell	.30	.14	.04
□ 533 Walt Weiss	.05	.02	.01
□ 534 David Cone	.30	.14	.04
□ 535 Greg Maddux	1.25	.55	.16
□ 536 Kevin Young	.05	.02	.01
□ 537 Dave Hansen	.05	.02	.01
□ 538 Alex Cole	.05	.02	.01
□ 539 Greg Hibbard	.05	.02	.01
□ 540 Gene Larkin	.05	.02	.01
□ 541 Jeff Reardon	.15	.07	.02
□ 542 Felix Jose	.05	.02	.01

□ 543 Jimmy Key	.15	.07	.02
□ 544 Reggie Jefferson	.15	.07	.02
□ 545 Gregg Jefferies	.30	.14	.04
□ 546 Dave Stewart	.15	.07	.02
□ 547 Tim Wallach	.05	.02	.01
□ 548 Spike Owen	.05	.02	.01
□ 549 Tommy Greene	.05	.02	.01
□ 550 Fernando Valenzuela	.15	.07	.02
□ 551 Rich Amaral	.05	.02	.01
□ 552 Bret Barberie	.05	.02	.01
□ 553 Edgar Martinez	.30	.14	.04
□ 554 Jim Abbott	.05	.02	.01
□ 555 Frank Thomas	2.00	.90	.25
□ 556 Wade Boggs	.30	.14	.04
□ 557 Tom Henke	.05	.02	.01
□ 558 Milt Thompson	.05	.02	.01
□ 559 Lloyd McClendon	.05	.02	.01
□ 560 Vinny Castilla	.30	.14	.04
□ 561 Ricky Jordan	.05	.02	.01
□ 562 Andujar Cedeno	.05	.02	.01
□ 563 Greg Vaughn	.30	.14	.04
□ 564 Cecil Fielder	.15	.07	.02
□ 565 Kirby Puckett	.60	.25	.07
□ 566 Mark McGwire	1.00	.45	.12
□ 567 Barry Bonds	.50	.23	.06
□ 568 Jody Reed	.05	.02	.01
□ 569 Todd Zeile	.05	.02	.01
□ 570 Mark Carreon	.05	.02	.01
□ 571 Joe Girardi	.05	.02	.01
□ 572 Luis Gonzalez	.05	.02	.01
□ 573 Mark Grace	.30	.14	.04
□ 574 Rafael Palmeiro	.30	.14	.04
□ 575 Darryl Strawberry	.15	.07	.02
□ 576 Will Clark	.30	.14	.04
□ 577 Fred McGriff	.30	.14	.04
□ 578 Kevin Reimer	.05	.02	.01
□ 579 Dave Righetti	.05	.02	.01
□ 580 Juan Bell	.05	.02	.01
□ 581 Jeff Brantley	.05	.02	.01
□ 582 Brian Hunter	.05	.02	.01
□ 583 Tim Naehring	.05	.02	.01
□ 584 Glenallen Hill	.05	.02	.01
□ 585 Cal Ripken	1.50	.70	.19
□ 586 Albert Belle	1.00	.45	.12
□ 587 Robin Yount	.30	.14	.04
□ 588 Chris Bosio	.05	.02	.01
□ 589 Pete Smith	.05	.02	.01
□ 590 Chuck Carr	.05	.02	.01
□ 591 Jeff Blauser	.05	.02	.01
□ 592 Kevin McReynolds	.05	.02	.01
□ 593 Andres Galarraga	.30	.14	.04
□ 594 Kevin Maas	.05	.02	.01
□ 595 Eric Davis	.15	.07	.02
□ 596 Brian Jordan	.30	.14	.04
□ 597 Tim Raines	.30	.14	.04
□ 598 Rick Wilkins	.05	.02	.01
□ 599 Steve Cooke	.05	.02	.01
□ 600 Mike Gallego	.05	.02	.01
□ 601 Mike Munoz	.05	.02	.01
□ 602 Luis Rivera	.05	.02	.01
□ 603 Junior Ortiz	.05	.02	.01
□ 604 Brent Mayne	.05	.02	.01
□ 605 Luis Alicea	.05	.02	.01
□ 606 Damon Berryhill	.05	.02	.01
□ 607 Dave Henderson	.05	.02	.01
□ 608 Kirk McCaskill	.05	.02	.01
□ 609 Jeff Fassero	.15	.07	.02
□ 610 Mike Harkey	.05	.02	.01
□ 611 Francisco Cabrera	.05	.02	.01
□ 612 Rey Sanchez	.05	.02	.01
□ 613 Scott Servais	.05	.02	.01
□ 614 Darrin Fletcher	.05	.02	.01
□ 615 Felix Fermin	.05	.02	.01
□ 616 Kevin Seitzer	.05	.02	.01
□ 617 Bob Scanlan	.05	.02	.01
□ 618 Billy Hatcher	.05	.02	.01
□ 619 John Vander Wal	.05	.02	.01
□ 620 Joe Hesketh	.05	.02	.01
□ 621 Hector Villanueva	.05	.02	.01
□ 622 Randy Milligan	.05	.02	.01
□ 623 Tony Tarasco	.15	.07	.02
□ 624 Russ Swan	.05	.02	.01
□ 625 Willie Wilson	.05	.02	.01
□ 626 Frank Tanana	.05	.02	.01
□ 627 Pete O'Brien	.05	.02	.01
□ 628 Lenny Webster	.05	.02	.01
□ 629 Mark Clark	.05	.02	.01
□ 630 Roger Clemens CL	.30	.14	.04
□ 631 Alex Arias	.05	.02	.01
□ 632 Chris Gwynn	.05	.02	.01
□ 633 Tom Bolton	.05	.02	.01
□ 634 Greg Briley	.05	.02	.01
□ 635 Kent Bottenfield	.05	.02	.01
□ 636 Kelly Downs	.05	.02	.01
□ 637 Manuel Lee	.05	.02	.01
□ 638 Al Leiter	.15	.07	.02
□ 639 Jeff Gardner	.05	.02	.01
□ 640 Mike Gardiner	.05	.02	.01
□ 641 Mark Gardner	.05	.02	.01
□ 642 Jeff Branson	.05	.02	.01
□ 643 Paul Wagner	.05	.02	.01
□ 644 Sean Berry	.05	.02	.01
□ 645 Phil Hiatt	.05	.02	.01
□ 646 Kevin Mitchell	.15	.07	.02
□ 647 Charlie Hayes	.05	.02	.01
□ 648 Jim Deshaies	.05	.02	.01
□ 649 Dan Pasqua	.05	.02	.01
□ 650 Mike Maddux	.05	.02	.01
□ 651 Domingo Martinez	.05	.02	.01
□ 652 Greg McMichael	.15	.07	.02
□ 653 Eric Wedge	.05	.02	.01
□ 654 Mark Whiten	.05	.02	.01
□ 655 Roberto Kelly	.05	.02	.01
□ 656 Julio Franco	.15	.07	.02
□ 657 Gene Harris	.05	.02	.01
□ 658 Pete Schourek	.15	.07	.02
□ 659 Mike Bielecki	.05	.02	.01
□ 660 Ricky Gutierrez	.05	.02	.01
□ 661 Chris Hammond	.05	.02	.01
□ 662 Tim Scott	.05	.02	.01
□ 663 Norm Charlton	.05	.02	.01
□ 664 Doug Drabek	.05	.02	.01
□ 665 Dwight Gooden	.15	.07	.02
□ 666 Jim Gott	.05	.02	.01
□ 667 Randy Myers	.15	.07	.02
□ 668 Darren Holmes	.05	.02	.01
□ 669 Tim Spehr	.05	.02	.01
□ 670 Bruce Ruffin	.05	.02	.01
□ 671 Bobby Thigpen	.05	.02	.01
□ 672 Tony Fernandez	.05	.02	.01
□ 673 Darrin Jackson	.05	.02	.01
□ 674 Gregg Olson	.05	.02	.01
□ 675 Rob Dibble	.05	.02	.01
□ 676 Howard Johnson	.05	.02	.01
□ 677 Mike Lansing	.15	.07	.02
□ 678 Charlie Leibrandt	.05	.02	.01
□ 679 Kevin Bass	.05	.02	.01
□ 680 Hubie Brooks	.05	.02	.01
□ 681 Scott Brosius	.05	.02	.01
□ 682 Randy Knorr	.05	.02	.01
□ 683 Dante Bichette	.30	.14	.04
□ 684 Bryan Harvey	.05	.02	.01
□ 685 Greg Gohr	.05	.02	.01
□ 686 Willie Banks	.05	.02	.01
□ 687 Robb Nen	.15	.07	.02
□ 688 Mike Sciosia	.05	.02	.01
□ 689 John Farrell	.05	.02	.01
□ 690 John Candelaria	.05	.02	.01
□ 691 Damon Buford	.05	.02	.01
□ 692 Todd Worrell	.05	.02	.01
□ 693 Pat Hentgen	.30	.14	.04
□ 694 John Smiley	.05	.02	.01
□ 695 Greg Swindell	.05	.02	.01
□ 696 Derek Bell	.30	.14	.04
□ 697 Terry Jorgensen	.05	.02	.01
□ 698 Jimmy Jones	.05	.02	.01
□ 699 David Wells	.05	.02	.01
□ 700 Dave Martinez	.05	.02	.01
□ 701 Steve Bedrosian	.05	.02	.01
□ 702 Jeff Russell	.05	.02	.01
□ 703 Joe Magrane	.05	.02	.01
□ 704 Matt Mieske	.15	.07	.02
□ 705 Paul Molitor	.40	.18	.05
□ 706 Dale Murphy	.30	.14	.04
□ 707 Steve Howe	.05	.02	.01
□ 708 Greg Gagne	.05	.02	.01
□ 709 Dave Eiland	.05	.02	.01
□ 710 David West	.05	.02	.01
□ 711 Luis Aquino	.05	.02	.01
□ 712 Joe Orsulak	.05	.02	.01
□ 713 Eric Plunk	.05	.02	.01
□ 714 Mike Felder	.05	.02	.01

□	715 Joe Klink	.05	.02	.01
□	716 Lonnie Smith	.05	.02	.01
□	717 Monty Fariss	.05	.02	.01
□	718 Craig Lefferts	.05	.02	.01
□	719 John Habyan	.05	.02	.01
□	720 Willie Blair	.05	.02	.01
□	721 Darnell Coles	.05	.02	.01
□	722 Mark Williamson	.05	.02	.01
□	723 Bryn Smith	.05	.02	.01
□	724 Greg W. Harris	.05	.02	.01
□	725 Graeme Lloyd	.05	.02	.01
□	726 Cris Carpenter	.05	.02	.01
□	727 Chico Walker	.05	.02	.01
□	728 Tracy Woodson	.05	.02	.01
□	729 Jose Uribe	.05	.02	.01
□	730 Stan Javier	.05	.02	.01
□	731 Jay Howell	.05	.02	.01
□	732 Freddie Benavides	.05	.02	.01
□	733 Jeff Reboulet	.05	.02	.01
□	734 Scott Sanderson	.05	.02	.01
□	735 Ryne Sandberg CL	.30	.14	.04
□	736 Archi Cianfrocco	.05	.02	.01
□	737 Daryl Boston	.05	.02	.01
□	738 Craig Grebeck	.05	.02	.01
□	739 Doug Dascenzo	.05	.02	.01
□	740 Gerald Young	.05	.02	.01
□	741 Candy Maldonado	.05	.02	.01
□	742 Joey Cora	.05	.02	.01
□	743 Don Slaught	.05	.02	.01
□	744 Steve Decker	.05	.02	.01
□	745 Blas Minor	.05	.02	.01
□	746 Storm Davis	.05	.02	.01
□	747 Carlos Quintana	.05	.02	.01
□	748 Vince Coleman	.05	.02	.01
□	749 Todd Burns	.05	.02	.01
□	750 Steve Frey	.05	.02	.01
□	751 Ivan Calderon	.05	.02	.01
□	752 Steve Reed	.05	.02	.01
□	753 Danny Jackson	.05	.02	.01
□	754 Jeff Conine	.30	.14	.04
□	755 Juan Gonzalez	1.00	.45	.12
□	756 Mike Kelly	.05	.02	.01
□	757 John Doherty	.05	.02	.01
□	758 Jack Armstrong	.05	.02	.01
□	759 John Wehner	.05	.02	.01
□	760 Scott Bankhead	.05	.02	.01
□	761 Jim Tatum	.05	.02	.01
□	762 Scott Pose	.05	.02	.01
□	763 Andy Ashby	.15	.07	.02
□	764 Ed Sprague	.15	.07	.02
□	765 Harold Baines	.15	.07	.02
□	766 Kirk Gibson	.15	.07	.02
□	767 Troy Neel	.05	.02	.01
□	768 Dick Schofield	.05	.02	.01
□	769 Dickie Thon	.05	.02	.01
□	770 Butch Henry	.05	.02	.01
□	771 Junior Felix	.05	.02	.01
□	772 Ken Ryan	.05	.02	.01
□	773 Trevor Hoffman	.15	.07	.02
□	774 Phil Plantier	.05	.02	.01
□	775 Bo Jackson	.30	.14	.04
□	776 Benito Santiago	.05	.02	.01
□	777 Andre Dawson	.30	.14	.04
□	778 Bryan Hickerson	.05	.02	.01
□	779 Dennis Moeller	.05	.02	.01
□	780 Ryan Bowen	.05	.02	.01
□	781 Eric Fox	.05	.02	.01
□	782 Joe Kmak	.05	.02	.01
□	783 Mike Hampton	.05	.02	.01
□	784 Darrell Sherman	.05	.02	.01
□	785 J.T. Snow	.30	.14	.04
□	786 Dave Winfield	.30	.14	.04
□	787 Jim Austin	.05	.02	.01
□	788 Craig Shipley	.05	.02	.01
□	789 Greg Myers	.05	.02	.01
□	790 Todd Benzinger	.05	.02	.01
□	791 Cory Snyder	.05	.02	.01
□	792 David Segui	.05	.02	.01
□	793 Armando Reynoso	.05	.02	.01
□	794 Chili Davis	.15	.07	.02
□	795 Dave Nilsson	.15	.07	.02
□	796 Paul O'Neill	.15	.07	.02
□	797 Jerald Clark	.05	.02	.01
□	798 Jose Mesa	.15	.07	.02
□	799 Brain Holman	.05	.02	.01
□	800 Jim Eisenreich	.15	.07	.02

□	801 Mark McLemore	.05	.02	.01
□	802 Luis Sojo	.05	.02	.01
□	803 Harold Reynolds	.05	.02	.01
□	804 Dan Plesac	.05	.02	.01
□	805 Dave Stieb	.05	.02	.01
□	806 Tom Brunansky	.05	.02	.01
□	807 Kelly Gruber	.05	.02	.01
□	808 Bob Ojeda	.05	.02	.01
□	809 Dave Burba	.05	.02	.01
□	810 Joe Boever	.05	.02	.01
□	811 Jeremy Hernandez	.05	.02	.01
□	812 Tim Salmon TC	.30	.14	.04
□	813 Jeff Bagwell TC	.40	.18	.05
□	814 Dennis Eckersley TC	.05	.02	.01
□	815 Roberto Alomar TC	.30	.14	.04
□	816 Steve Avery TC	.05	.02	.01
□	817 Pat Listach TC	.05	.02	.01
□	818 Gregg Jefferies TC	.15	.07	.02
□	819 Sammy Sosa TC	.30	.14	.04
□	820 Darryl Strawberry TC	.05	.02	.01
□	821 Dennis Martinez TC	.05	.02	.01
□	822 Robby Thompson TC	.05	.02	.01
□	823 Albert Belle TC	.50	.23	.06
□	824 Randy Johnson TC	.15	.07	.02
□	825 Nigel Wilson TC	.05	.02	.01
□	826 Bobby Bonilla TC	.05	.02	.01
□	827 Glenn Davis TC	.05	.02	.01
□	828 Gary Sheffield TC	.30	.14	.04
□	829 Darren Daulton TC	.05	.02	.01
□	830 Jay Bell TC	.05	.02	.01
□	831 Juan Gonzalez TC	.50	.23	.06
□	832 Andre Dawson TC	.30	.14	.04
□	833 Hal Morris TC	.05	.02	.01
□	834 David Nied TC	.05	.02	.01
□	835 Felix Jose TC	.05	.02	.01
□	836 Travis Fryman TC	.15	.07	.02
□	837 Shane Mack TC	.05	.02	.01
□	838 Robin Ventura TC	.05	.02	.01
□	839 Danny Tartabull TC	.05	.02	.01
□	840 Roberto Alomar CL	.30	.14	.04
□	SP5 George Brett Robin Yount 3,000th Hit	1.50	.70	.19
□	SP6 Nolan Ryan	4.00	1.80	.50

1993 Upper Deck Clutch Performers

These 20 standard-size cards were randomly inserted into series II retail foil packs, as well as inserted one per series II retail jumbo packs. The fronts feature color player action shots that are borderless, except at the bottom, where a black stripe is set off by a gold-foil line and carries the set's title and Reggie Jackson's gold-foil signature. The player's name printed in white lettering rests at the bottom of the photo. The back carries a color player action shot below a black bar at the top that carries the player's name in gold-colored lettering. Below the picture appears a small black-and-white head shot of Reggie Jackson alongside his comments on the player. A player stat table appears below. The cards are numbered on the back with an "R" prefix and appear in alphabetical order. These 20 cards represent Reggie

Jackson's selection of players who have come through under pressure.

	MINT	NRMT	EXC
COMPLETE SET (20)	20.00	9.00	2.50
COMMON CARD (R1-R20)	.25	.11	.03
SEMISTARS	.60	.25	.07
RANDOM INSERTS IN SER.2 RETAIL PACKS			
ONE PER SER.2 RED JUMBO PACK			

□ R1 Roberto Alomar	1.25	.55	.16
□ R2 Wade Boggs	.60	.25	.07
□ R3 Barry Bonds	1.25	.55	.16
□ R4 Jose Canseco	.60	.25	.07
□ R5 Joe Carter	.60	.25	.07
□ R6 Will Clark	.60	.25	.07
□ R7 Roger Clemens	.60	.25	.07
□ R8 Dennis Eckersley	.60	.25	.07
□ R9 Cecil Fielder	.60	.25	.07
□ R10 Juan Gonzalez	2.50	1.10	.30
□ R11 Ken Griffey Jr.	5.00	2.20	.60
□ R12 Rickey Henderson	.60	.25	.07
□ R13 Barry Larkin	.60	.25	.07
□ R14 Don Mattingly	2.50	1.10	.30
□ R15 Fred McGriff	.60	.25	.07
□ R16 Terry Pendleton	.25	.11	.03
□ R17 Kirby Puckett	1.50	.70	.19
□ R18 Ryne Sandberg	1.25	.55	.16
□ R19 John Smoltz	.75	.35	.09
□ R20 Frank Thomas	5.00	2.20	.60

1993 Upper Deck Fifth Anniversary

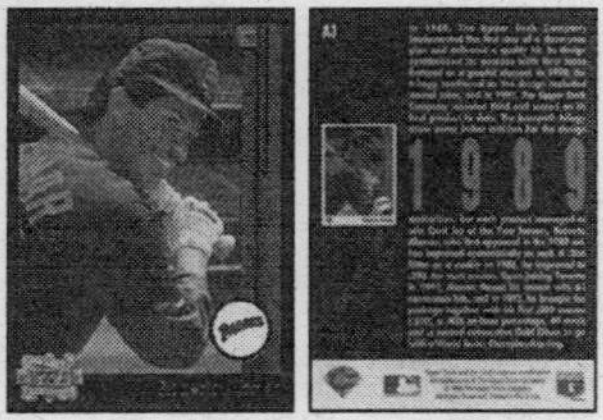

This 15-card standard-size set celebrates Upper Deck's five years in the sports card business.The cards are essentially reprinted versions of some of Upper Deck's most popular cards in the last five years. These cards were randomly inserted in second series hobby packs. The black-bordered fronts feature player photos that previously appeared on an Upper Deck card. The Five-Year Anniversary logo is located in one of the corners and the player's name is printed in gold-foil along the lower black border. The black backs carry a picture of the original card on the left side with narrative historical information on Upper Deck and a brief career summary of the player. The gold-colored year of issue of the original card is prominently displayed in the middle of the text. The cards are numbered on the back with an A prefix. One over-sized (3 1/2" by 5") version of each of these cards was initially inserted into retail blister repacks, which contained one foil pack each of 1993 Upper Deck Series I and II. These cards are individually numbered out of 10,000 and were later inserted into various forms of repackaging. These oversized cards are valued up to 2X the prices listed below.

	MINT	NRMT	EXC
COMPLETE SET (15)	20.00	9.00	2.50
COMMON CARD (A1-A15)	.25	.11	.03
SEMISTARS	.60	.25	.07
RANDOM INSERTS IN SER.2 HOBBY PACKS			

□ A1 Ken Griffey Jr.	8.00	3.60	1.00
□ A2 Gary Sheffield	.60	.25	.07
□ A3 Roberto Alomar	1.25	.55	.16
□ A4 Jim Abbott	.60	.25	.07
□ A5 Nolan Ryan	5.00	2.20	.60
□ A6 Juan Gonzalez	2.50	1.10	.30
□ A7 David Justice	.60	.25	.07
□ A8 Carlos Baerga	.60	.25	.07
□ A9 Reggie Jackson	.75	.35	.09
□ A10 Eric Karros	.60	.25	.07
□ A11 Chipper Jones	4.00	1.80	.50
□ A12 Ivan Rodriguez	1.00	.45	.12
□ A13 Pat Listach	.25	.11	.03
□ A14 Frank Thomas	5.00	2.20	.60
□ A15 Tim Salmon	1.00	.45	.12

1993 Upper Deck Future Heroes

Randomly inserted in second series foil packs and continuing the Heroes insert set begun in the 1990 Upper Deck high-number set, this ten-card standard-size set features eight different "Future Heroes" along with a checklist and header card. The fronts feature borderless color player action shots that bear the player's simulated autograph in gold foil in an upper corner. The player's name appears within a black stripe formed by the simulated tearing away of a piece of the photo. The player's team appears below. The back carries the player's name vertically within a black "tear-away" stripe along the right edge. Career highlights are displayed within a white, gray, and tan panel on the left.

	MINT	NRMT	EXC
COMPLETE SET (10)	12.00	5.50	1.50
COMMON CARD (55-63)	.50	.23	.06
HEROES HEADER SP (NNO)	.75	.35	.09
RANDOM INSERTS IN SER.2 PACKS			

□ 55 Roberto Alomar	1.25	.55	.16
□ 56 Barry Bonds	1.25	.55	.16
□ 57 Roger Clemens	.75	.35	.09
□ 58 Juan Gonzalez	2.50	1.10	.30
□ 59 Ken Griffey Jr.	5.00	2.20	.60
□ 60 Mark McGwire	1.50	.70	.19
□ 61 Kirby Puckett	1.50	.70	.19
□ 62 Frank Thomas	5.00	2.20	.60
□ 63 Checklist	.50	.23	.06
□ NNO Header Card SP	.75	.35	.09

1993 Upper Deck Home Run Heroes

This 28-card standard-size set features the home run leader from each Major League team. Each 1993 first series 27-card jumbo pack contained one of these cards. The cards feature action color player photos with a three-dimensional baseball bat design at the bottom. Featuring embossed printing, the bat looks and feels as if it stands off the card, and a shadow design below it adds to the effect. The words

"Homerun Heroes" are printed vertically down the left. The backs show a team color-coded photo as the background for player information. The player's name appears in a white border on the right. The baseball bat design is repeated at the bottom. The cards are numbered on the back with an "HR" prefix and the set is arranged in descending order according to the number of home runs.

	MINT	NRMT	EXC
COMPLETE SET (28)	15.00	6.75	1.85
COMMON CARD (HR1-HR28)	.25	.11	.03
SEMISTARS	.60	.25	.07
ONE PER SER.1 JUMBO PACK			

	MINT	NRMT	EXC
□ HR1 Juan Gonzalez	2.50	1.10	.30
□ HR2 Mark McGwire	1.50	.70	.19
□ HR3 Cecil Fielder	.60	.25	.07
□ HR4 Fred McGriff	.60	.25	.07
□ HR5 Albert Belle	2.50	1.10	.30
□ HR6 Barry Bonds	1.25	.55	.16
□ HR7 Joe Carter	.60	.25	.07
□ HR8 Darren Daulton	.25	.11	.03
□ HR9 Ken Griffey Jr.	5.00	2.20	.60
□ HR10 Dave Hollins	.25	.11	.03
□ HR11 Ryne Sandberg	1.25	.55	.16
□ HR12 George Bell	.25	.11	.03
□ HR13 Danny Tartabull	.60	.25	.07
□ HR14 Mike Devereaux	.25	.11	.03
□ HR15 Greg Vaughn	.60	.25	.07
□ HR16 Larry Walker	.60	.25	.07
□ HR17 David Justice	.25	.11	.03
□ HR18 Terry Pendleton	.25	.11	.03
□ HR19 Eric Karros	.60	.25	.07
□ HR20 Ray Lankford	.60	.25	.07
□ HR21 Matt Williams	.60	.25	.07
□ HR22 Eric Anthony	.25	.11	.03
□ HR23 Bobby Bonilla	.60	.25	.07
□ HR24 Kirby Puckett	1.50	.70	.19
□ HR25 Mike Macfarlane	.25	.11	.03
□ HR26 Tom Brunansky	.25	.11	.03
□ HR27 Paul O'Neill	.60	.25	.07
□ HR28 Gary Gaetti	.60	.25	.07

1993 Upper Deck Looss Collection

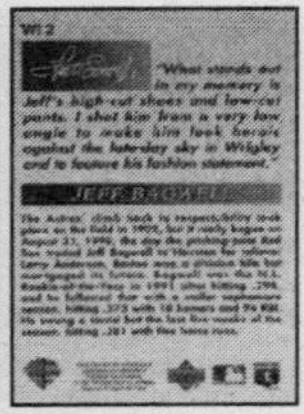

This 27-card standard-size set spotlights the work of famous sports photographer Walter Looss Jr. by presenting 26 of the game's current greats in a candid photo set. The cards were randomly inserted in series I foil packs purchased from major retail outlets only. The posed color player photos on the fronts are full-bleed and either horizontally or vertically oriented. The words "The Upper Deck Looss Collection" are printed in gold foil. The back carries a quote from looss about the shoot and the player's career Highlights. The text blocks on the card backs are separated by a gradated bars of varying colors. The cards are numbered on the back with a "WI" prefix. One over-sized version of each of these cards were initially inserted into retail blister repacks containing one foil pack each of 1993 Upper Deck Series I and II. These over-sized (3 1/2" by 5") cards are individually numbered out of 10,000 and were later inserted in various forms of repackaging. They are valued up to 2X the prices below.

	MINT	NRMT	EXC
COMPLETE SET (27)	25.00	11.00	3.10
COMMON CARD (WI1-WI26)	.30	.14	.04
SEMISTARS	.75	.35	.09
RANDOM INSERTS IN SER.1 RETAIL PACKS			

	MINT	NRMT	EXC
□ WI1 Tim Salmon	1.25	.55	.16
□ WI2 Jeff Bagwell	2.50	1.10	.30
□ WI3 Mark McGwire	2.00	.90	.25
□ WI4 Roberto Alomar	1.50	.70	.19
□ WI5 Steve Avery	.30	.14	.04
□ WI6 Paul Molitor	1.25	.55	.16
□ WI7 Ozzie Smith	1.25	.55	.16
□ WI8 Mark Grace	.75	.35	.09
□ WI9 Eric Karros	.75	.35	.09
□ WI10 Delino DeShields	.75	.35	.09
□ WI11 Will Clark	.75	.35	.09
□ WI12 Albert Belle	3.00	1.35	.35
□ WI13 Ken Griffey Jr.	6.00	2.70	.75
□ WI14 Howard Johnson	.30	.14	.04
□ WI15 Cal Ripken Jr.	5.00	2.20	.60
□ WI16 Fred McGriff	.75	.35	.09
□ WI17 Darren Daulton	.30	.14	.04
□ WI18 Andy Van Slyke	.30	.14	.04
□ WI19 Nolan Ryan	5.00	2.20	.60
□ WI20 Wade Boggs	.75	.35	.09
□ WI21 Barry Larkin	.75	.35	.09
□ WI22 George Brett	2.50	1.10	.30
□ WI23 Cecil Fielder	.75	.35	.09
□ WI24 Kirby Puckett	2.00	.90	.25
□ WI25 Frank Thomas	6.00	2.70	.75
□ WI26 Don Mattingly	3.00	1.35	.35
□ NNO Title Card Looss Header	.75	.35	.09

1993 Upper Deck On Deck

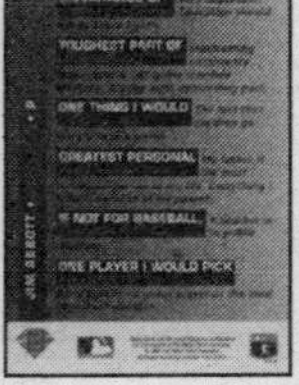

Inserted one per series II jumbo packs, these 25 standard-size cards profile baseball's top players. The fronts feature borderless color player photos, some action, others posed, and carry the player's simulated gold-foil signature within a team color-coded stripe that appears as part of the set's logo. The gradated-tan-colored back carries the player's name, position, and team vertically within a team color-coded stripe near the left edge. The player's answers

to personal questions rounds out the back. The cards are numbered on the back with a "D" prefix in alphabetical order by name.

	MINT	NRMT	EXC
COMPLETE SET (25)	20.00	9.00	2.50
COMMON CARD (D1-D25)	.25	.11	.03
SEMISTARS	.60	.25	.07
ONE PER SER.2 BLUE OR RED JUMBO PACK			

	MINT	NRMT	EXC
□ D1 Jim Abbott	.60	.25	.07
□ D2 Roberto Alomar	1.25	.55	.16
□ D3 Carlos Baerga	.25	.11	.03
□ D4 Albert Belle	2.50	1.10	.30
□ D5 Wade Boggs	.60	.25	.07
□ D6 George Brett	2.00	.90	.25
□ D7 Jose Canseco	.60	.25	.07
□ D8 Will Clark	.60	.25	.07
□ D9 Roger Clemens	.60	.25	.07
□ D10 Dennis Eckersley	.60	.25	.07
□ D11 Cecil Fielder	.60	.25	.07
□ D12 Juan Gonzalez	2.50	1.10	.30
□ D13 Ken Griffey Jr.	5.00	2.20	.60
□ D14 Tony Gwynn	2.00	.90	.25
□ D15 Bo Jackson	.60	.25	.07
□ D16 Chipper Jones	4.00	1.80	.50
□ D17 Eric Karros	.60	.25	.07
□ D18 Mark McGwire	1.50	.70	.19
□ D19 Kirby Puckett	1.50	.70	.19
□ D20 Nolan Ryan	5.00	2.20	.60
□ D21 Tim Salmon	1.00	.45	.12
□ D22 Ryne Sandberg	1.25	.55	.16
□ D23 Darryl Strawberry	.60	.25	.07
□ D24 Frank Thomas	5.00	2.20	.60
□ D25 Andy Van Slyke	.25	.11	.03

1993 Upper Deck Season Highlights

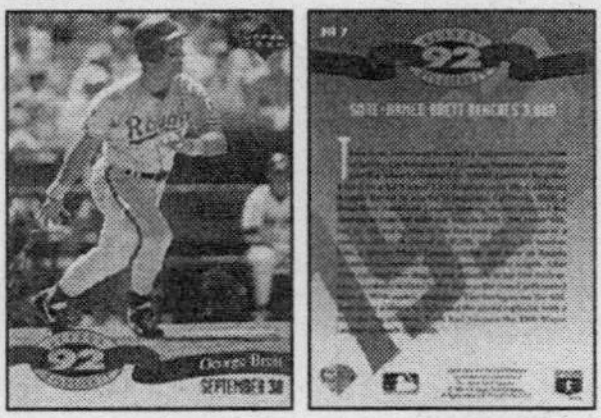

This 20-card standard-size insert set captures great moments of the 1992 Major League Baseball season. The set was randomly packed into specially marked cases that were available only at Upper Deck Heroes of Baseball Card Shows and through the purchase of a specified quantity of second series cases. The fronts display a full-bleed color action photo with a special "'92 Season Highlights" logo running across the bottom. The ribbon intersecting the logo is blue on the American League cards and red on the National League. The date of the player's outstanding achievement is gold-foil stamped at the lower right. On backs that fade from the league color to white, a description of the achievement is presented. The year 1992 is printed diagonally across the backs. The cards are numbered on the back with an "HI" prefix in alphabetical order by player's name.

	MINT	NRMT	EXC
COMPLETE SET (20)	160.00	70.00	20.00
COMMON CARD (HI1-HI20)	2.50	1.10	.30
SEMISTARS	5.00	2.20	.60
RANDOM INSERTS IN SER.1 AND 2 SH PACKS			

	MINT	NRMT	EXC
□ HI1 Roberto Alomar	12.00	5.50	1.50
□ HI2 Steve Avery	2.50	1.10	.30
□ HI3 Harold Baines	5.00	2.20	.60
□ HI4 Damon Berryhill	2.50	1.10	.30
□ HI5 Barry Bonds	12.00	5.50	1.50
□ HI6 Bret Boone	2.50	1.10	.30
□ HI7 George Brett	20.00	9.00	2.50
□ HI8 Francisco Cabrera	2.50	1.10	.30
□ HI9 Ken Griffey Jr.	50.00	22.00	6.25
□ HI10 Rickey Henderson	5.00	2.20	.60
□ HI11 Kenny Lofton	15.00	6.75	1.85
□ HI12 Mickey Morandini	2.50	1.10	.30
□ HI13 Eddie Murray	12.00	5.50	1.50
□ HI14 David Nied	2.50	1.10	.30
□ HI15 Jeff Reardon	5.00	2.20	.60
□ HI16 Bip Roberts	2.50	1.10	.30
□ HI17 Nolan Ryan	50.00	22.00	6.25
□ HI18 Ed Sprague	5.00	2.20	.60
□ HI19 Dave Winfield	5.00	2.20	.60
□ HI20 Robin Yount	5.00	2.20	.60

1993 Upper Deck Then And Now

This 18-card, standard-size hologram set highlights veteran stars in their rookie year and today, reflecting on how they and the game have changed. Cards 1-9 were randomly inserted in series I foil packs; cards 10-18 were randomly inserted in series II foil packs. The nine lithogram cards in the second series feature one card each of Hall of Famers Reggie Jackson, Mickey Mantle, and Willie Mays, as well as six active players. The horizontal fronts have a color close-up photo cutout and superimposed at the left corner of a full-bleed hologram portraying the player in an action scene. The skyline of the player's city serves as the background for the holograms. The player's name and the manufacturer's name form a right angle at the upper right corner. At the upper left corner, a "Then And Now" logo which includes the length of the player's career in years rounds out the front. On a sand-colored panel that resembles a postage stamp, the backs present career summary. The cards are numbered on the back with a "TN" prefix and arranged alphabetically within subgroup according to player's last name.

	MINT	NRMT	EXC
COMPLETE SET (18)	50.00	22.00	6.25
COMPLETE SERIES 1 (9)	20.00	9.00	2.50
COMPLETE SERIES 2 (9)	30.00	13.50	3.70
COMMON CARD (TN1-TN18)	.50	.23	.06
SEMISTARS	1.00	.45	.12
RANDOM INSERTS IN HOBBY FOIL PACKS.			

	MINT	NRMT	EXC
□ TN1 Wade Boggs	1.00	.45	.12
□ TN2 George Brett	4.00	1.80	.50
□ TN3 Rickey Henderson	1.00	.45	.12
□ TN4 Cal Ripken	8.00	3.60	1.00
□ TN5 Nolan Ryan	8.00	3.60	1.00
□ TN6 Ryne Sandberg	2.50	1.10	.30
□ TN7 Ozzie Smith	2.00	.90	.25
□ TN8 Darryl Strawberry	1.00	.45	.12
□ TN9 Dave Winfield	1.00	.45	.12
□ TN10 Dennis Eckersley	1.00	.45	.12
□ TN11 Tony Gwynn	4.00	1.80	.50
□ TN12 Howard Johnson	.50	.23	.06

□ TN13 Don Mattingly	5.00	2.20	.60
□ TN14 Eddie Murray	2.50	1.10	.30
□ TN15 Robin Yount	1.00	.45	.12
□ TN16 Reggie Jackson	2.50	1.10	.30
□ TN17 Mickey Mantle	15.00	6.75	1.85
□ TN18 Willie Mays	8.00	3.60	1.00

1993 Upper Deck Triple Crown

This ten-card, standard-size insert set highlights ten players who were selected by Upper Deck as having the best shot at winning Major League Baseball's Triple Crown. The cards were randomly inserted in series I foil packs sold by hobby dealers only. The fronts display glossy full-bleed color player photos. At the bottom, a purple ribbon edged in gold foil carries the words "Triple Crown Contenders," while the player's name appears in gold foil lettering immediately below on a gradated black background. A crown overlays the ribbon at the lower left corner and rounds out the front. On a gradated black background, the backs summarize the player's performance in home runs, RBIs, and batting average. The cards are numbered on the back with a "TC" prefix and arranged alphabetically by player's last name.

	MINT	NRMT	EXC
COMPLETE SET (10)	30.00	13.50	3.70
COMMON CARD (TC1-TC10)	1.00	.45	.12
SEMISTARS	1.25	.55	.16
RANDOM INSERTS IN HOBBY FOIL PACKS.			

□ TC1 Barry Bonds	2.50	1.10	.30
□ TC2 Jose Canseco	1.25	.55	.16
□ TC3 Will Clark	1.25	.55	.16
□ TC4 Ken Griffey Jr.	10.00	4.50	1.25
□ TC5 Fred McGriff	1.25	.55	.16
□ TC6 Kirby Puckett	3.00	1.35	.35
□ TC7 Cal Ripken Jr.	8.00	3.60	1.00
□ TC8 Gary Sheffield	1.50	.70	.19
□ TC9 Frank Thomas	10.00	4.50	1.25
□ TC10 Larry Walker	1.00	.45	.12

1994 Upper Deck

The 1994 Upper Deck set was issued in two series of 280 and 270 standard-size cards for a total of 550. Card fronts feature a color photo of the player with a smaller version of the same photo along the left-hand border. The player's name appears in a black box in the upper left-hand corner. There are a number of subsets including Star Rookies (1-30), Fantasy Team (31-40), The Future is Now (41-55), Home Field Advantage (267-294), Upper Deck Classic Alumni (295-299), Diamond Debuts (511-522) and Top Prospects (523-550). Three autograph cards were randomly inserted in first series retail packs. They are Ken Griffey, Jr. (KG), Mickey Mantle (MM) and Griffey/Mantle (GM). An Alex Rodriguez (298A) autograph card was randomly inserted in second series retail packs. Rookie Cards include Brian Anderson, Alan Benes, Michael Jordan, Brooks Kieschnick, Derrek Lee, Trot Nixon, Chan Ho Park, Alex Rodriguez, Will VanLandingham and Billy Wagner. Many cards have been found with a significant variation on the backs. The player's name, the horizontal bar containing the biographical information and the vertical bar containing the stats header are normally printed in a copper-gold color. On the variation cards these areas are printed in silver. It is not known exactly how many of the 550 cards have silver versions, nor has any premium been established for them.

	MINT	NRMT	EXC
COMPLETE SET (550)	50.00	22.00	6.25
COMPLETE SERIES 1 (280)	30.00	13.50	3.70
COMPLETE SERIES 2 (270)	20.00	9.00	2.50
COMMON CARD (1-550)	.10	.05	.01
SEMISTARS	.25	.11	.03
STARS	.50	.23	.06
COMP.ELEC.DIAM.SET (550)	125.00	55.00	15.50
COMP.ELEC.DIAM.SER.1 (280)	80.00	36.00	10.00
COMP.ELEC.DIAM.SER.2 (270)	50.00	22.00	6.25
COMMON ELEC.DIAM. (1-550)	.15	.07	.02
ELEC.DIAM.SEMISTARS	.30	.14	.04
*ELEC.DIAM.STARS: 2X to 4X HI COLUMN.			
*ELEC.DIAM.YOUNG STARS: 1.5X to 3X HI			
ONE ELECTRIC DIAMOND PER PACK			
COMP.MANTLE SET (10)	100.00	45.00	12.50
COMMON MANTLE (64-72/HDR)	12.00	5.50	1.50
MANTLE: INSERTS IN ALL SER.2 PACKS			
GRIFFEY/MANTLE AU INSERTS IN SER.1 RET.			
A.RODRIGUEZ AU INSERTS IN SER.2 RET..			

□ 1 Brian Anderson	.25	.11	.03
□ 2 Shane Andrews	.25	.11	.03
□ 3 James Baldwin	.50	.23	.06
□ 4 Rich Becker	.25	.11	.03
□ 5 Greg Blosser	.10	.05	.01
□ 6 Ricky Bottalico	.40	.18	.05
□ 7 Midre Cummings	.10	.05	.01
□ 8 Carlos Delgado	.50	.23	.06
□ 9 Steve Dreyer	.10	.05	.01
□ 10 Joey Eischen	.10	.05	.01
□ 11 Carl Everett	.10	.05	.01
□ 12 Cliff Floyd UER (text indicates he throws left; should be right)	.50	.23	.06
□ 13 Alex Gonzalez	.25	.11	.03
□ 14 Jeff Granger	.25	.11	.03
□ 15 Shawn Green	.25	.11	.03
□ 16 Brian Hunter	.50	.23	.06
□ 17 Butch Huskey	.25	.11	.03
□ 18 Mark Hutton	.10	.05	.01
□ 19 Michael Jordan	10.00	4.50	1.25
□ 20 Steve Karsay	.10	.05	.01
□ 21 Jeff McNeely	.10	.05	.01
□ 22 Marc Newfield	.25	.11	.03
□ 23 Manny Ramirez	1.00	.45	.12
□ 24 Alex Rodriguez	10.00	4.50	1.25
□ 25 Scott Ruffcorn UER (photo on back is Robert Ellis)	.10	.05	.01
□ 26 Paul Spoljaric UER (Expos logo on back)	.10	.05	.01
□ 27 Salomon Torres	.10	.05	.01
□ 28 Steve Trachsel	.25	.11	.03
□ 29 Chris Turner	.10	.05	.01
□ 30 Gabe White	.10	.05	.01
□ 31 Randy Johnson FT	.25	.11	.03
□ 32 John Wetteland FT	.10	.05	.01

□ 33 Mike Piazza FT	1.00	.45	.12
□ 34 Rafael Palmeiro FT	.50	.23	.06
□ 35 Roberto Alomar FT	.50	.23	.06
□ 36 Matt Williams FT	.50	.23	.06
□ 37 Travis Fryman FT	.25	.11	.03
□ 38 Barry Bonds FT	.50	.23	.06
□ 39 Marquis Grissom FT	.25	.11	.03
□ 40 Albert Belle FT	.75	.35	.09
□ 41 Steve Avery FUT	.10	.05	.01
□ 42 Jason Bere FUT	.10	.05	.01
□ 43 Alex Fernandez FUT	.25	.11	.03
□ 44 Mike Mussina FUT	.50	.23	.06
□ 45 Aaron Sele FUT	.10	.05	.01
□ 46 Rod Beck FUT	.10	.05	.01
□ 47 Mike Piazza FUT	1.00	.45	.12
□ 48 John Olerud FUT	.10	.05	.01
□ 49 Carlos Baerga FUT	.25	.11	.03
□ 50 Gary Sheffield FUT	.50	.23	.06
□ 51 Travis Fryman FUT	.25	.11	.03
□ 52 Juan Gonzalez FUT	.75	.35	.09
□ 53 Ken Griffey Jr. FUT	1.50	.70	.19
□ 54 Tim Salmon FUT	.25	.11	.03
□ 55 Frank Thomas FUT	1.50	.70	.19
□ 56 Tony Phillips	.25	.11	.03
□ 57 Julio Franco	.25	.11	.03
□ 58 Kevin Mitchell	.25	.11	.03
□ 59 Raul Mondesi	.50	.23	.06
□ 60 Rickey Henderson	.50	.23	.06
□ 61 Jay Buhner	.50	.23	.06
□ 62 Bill Swift	.10	.05	.01
□ 63 Brady Anderson	.50	.23	.06
□ 64 Ryan Klesko	.75	.35	.09
□ 65 Darren Daulton	.25	.11	.03
□ 66 Damion Easley	.10	.05	.01
□ 67 Mark McGwire	1.00	.45	.12
□ 68 John Roper	.10	.05	.01
□ 69 Dave Telgheder	.10	.05	.01
□ 70 Dave Nied	.10	.05	.01
□ 71 Mo Vaughn	.75	.35	.09
□ 72 Tyler Green	.10	.05	.01
□ 73 Dave Magadan	.10	.05	.01
□ 74 Chili Davis	.25	.11	.03
□ 75 Archi Cianfrocco	.10	.05	.01
□ 76 Joe Girardi	.10	.05	.01
□ 77 Chris Hoiles	.10	.05	.01
□ 78 Ryan Bowen	.10	.05	.01
□ 79 Greg Gagne	.10	.05	.01
□ 80 Aaron Sele	.25	.11	.03
□ 81 Dave Winfield	.50	.23	.06
□ 82 Chad Curtis	.10	.05	.01
□ 83 Andy Van Slyke	.25	.11	.03
□ 84 Kevin Stocker	.10	.05	.01
□ 85 Deion Sanders	.50	.23	.06
□ 86 Bernie Williams	.50	.23	.06
□ 87 John Smoltz	.50	.23	.06
□ 88 Ruben Santana	.10	.05	.01
□ 89 Dave Stewart	.25	.11	.03
□ 90 Don Mattingly	1.50	.70	.19
□ 91 Joe Carter	.50	.23	.06
□ 92 Ryne Sandberg	.75	.35	.09
□ 93 Chris Gomez	.10	.05	.01
□ 94 Tino Martinez	.25	.11	.03
□ 95 Terry Pendleton	.25	.11	.03
□ 96 Andre Dawson	.50	.23	.06
□ 97 Wil Cordero	.25	.11	.03
□ 98 Kent Hrbek	.25	.11	.03
□ 99 John Olerud	.10	.05	.01
□ 100 Kirt Manwaring	.10	.05	.01
□ 101 Tim Bogar	.10	.05	.01
□ 102 Mike Mussina	.60	.25	.07
□ 103 Nigel Wilson	.10	.05	.01
□ 104 Ricky Gutierrez	.10	.05	.01
□ 105 Roberto Mejia	.10	.05	.01
□ 106 Tom Pagnozzi	.10	.05	.01
□ 107 Mike Macfarlane	.10	.05	.01
□ 108 Jose Bautista	.10	.05	.01
□ 109 Luis Ortiz	.10	.05	.01
□ 110 Brent Gates	.10	.05	.01
□ 111 Tim Salmon	.50	.23	.06
□ 112 Wade Boggs	.50	.23	.06
□ 113 Tripp Cromer	.10	.05	.01
□ 114 Denny Hocking	.10	.05	.01
□ 115 Carlos Baerga	.50	.23	.06
□ 116 J.R. Phillips	.10	.05	.01
□ 117 Bo Jackson	.50	.23	.06
□ 118 Lance Johnson	.25	.11	.03
□ 119 Bobby Jones	.25	.11	.03
□ 120 Bobby Witt	.10	.05	.01
□ 121 Ron Karkovice	.10	.05	.01
□ 122 Jose Vizcaino	.10	.05	.01
□ 123 Danny Darwin	.10	.05	.01
□ 124 Eduardo Perez	.10	.05	.01
□ 125 Brian Looney	.10	.05	.01
□ 126 Pat Hentgen	.50	.23	.06
□ 127 Frank Viola	.10	.05	.01
□ 128 Darren Holmes	.10	.05	.01
□ 129 Wally Whitehurst	.10	.05	.01
□ 130 Matt Walbeck	.10	.05	.01
□ 131 Albert Belle	1.50	.70	.19
□ 132 Steve Cooke	.10	.05	.01
□ 133 Kevin Appier	.25	.11	.03
□ 134 Joe Oliver	.10	.05	.01
□ 135 Benji Gil	.10	.05	.01
□ 136 Steve Buechele	.10	.05	.01
□ 137 Devon White	.10	.05	.01
□ 138 Sterling Hitchcock UER (two losses for career; should be four)	.25	.11	.03
□ 139 Phil Leftwich	.10	.05	.01
□ 140 Jose Canseco	.50	.23	.06
□ 141 Rick Aguilera	.10	.05	.01
□ 142 Rod Beck	.25	.11	.03
□ 143 Jose Rijo	.10	.05	.01
□ 144 Tom Glavine	.50	.23	.06
□ 145 Phil Plantier	.10	.05	.01
□ 146 Jason Bere	.25	.11	.03
□ 147 Jamie Moyer	.10	.05	.01
□ 148 Wes Chamberlain	.10	.05	.01
□ 149 Glenallen Hill	.10	.05	.01
□ 150 Mark Whiten	.10	.05	.01
□ 151 Bret Barberie	.10	.05	.01
□ 152 Chuck Knoblauch	.50	.23	.06
□ 153 Trevor Hoffman	.25	.11	.03
□ 154 Rick Wilkins	.10	.05	.01
□ 155 Juan Gonzalez	1.50	.70	.19
□ 156 Ozzie Guillen	.10	.05	.01
□ 157 Jim Eisenreich	.10	.05	.01
□ 158 Pedro Astacio	.10	.05	.01
□ 159 Joe Magrane	.10	.05	.01
□ 160 Ryan Thompson	.10	.05	.01
□ 161 Jose Lind	.10	.05	.01
□ 162 Jeff Conine	.50	.23	.06
□ 163 Todd Benzinger	.10	.05	.01
□ 164 Roger Salkeld	.10	.05	.01
□ 165 Gary DiSarcina	.10	.05	.01
□ 166 Kevin Gross	.10	.05	.01
□ 167 Charlie Hayes	.10	.05	.01
□ 168 Tim Costo	.10	.05	.01
□ 169 Wally Joyner	.25	.11	.03
□ 170 Johnny Ruffin	.10	.05	.01
□ 171 Kirk Rueter	.10	.05	.01
□ 172 Lenny Dykstra	.25	.11	.03
□ 173 Ken Hill	.10	.05	.01
□ 174 Mike Bordick	.10	.05	.01
□ 175 Billy Hall	.10	.05	.01
□ 176 Rob Butler	.10	.05	.01
□ 177 Jay Bell	.25	.11	.03
□ 178 Jeff Kent	.10	.05	.01
□ 179 David Wells	.10	.05	.01
□ 180 Dean Palmer	.25	.11	.03
□ 181 Mariano Duncan	.10	.05	.01
□ 182 Orlando Merced	.25	.11	.03
□ 183 Brett Butler	.25	.11	.03
□ 184 Milt Thompson	.10	.05	.01
□ 185 Chipper Jones	2.50	1.10	.30
□ 186 Paul O'Neill	.25	.11	.03
□ 187 Mike Greenwell	.10	.05	.01
□ 188 Harold Baines	.25	.11	.03
□ 189 Todd Stottlemyre	.10	.05	.01
□ 190 Jeromy Burnitz	.10	.05	.01
□ 191 Rene Arocha	.10	.05	.01
□ 192 Jeff Fassero	.10	.05	.01
□ 193 Robby Thompson	.10	.05	.01
□ 194 Greg W. Harris	.10	.05	.01
□ 195 Todd Van Poppel	.10	.05	.01
□ 196 Jose Guzman	.10	.05	.01
□ 197 Shane Mack	.10	.05	.01
□ 198 Carlos Garcia	.10	.05	.01
□ 199 Kevin Roberson	.10	.05	.01
□ 200 David McCarty	.10	.05	.01
□ 201 Alan Trammell	.50	.23	.06
□ 202 Chuck Carr	.10	.05	.01

□ 203 Tommy Greene	.10	.05	.01
□ 204 Wilson Alvarez	.25	.11	.03
□ 205 Dwight Gooden	.25	.11	.03
□ 206 Tony Tarasco	.10	.05	.01
□ 207 Darren Lewis	.10	.05	.01
□ 208 Eric Karros	.25	.11	.03
□ 209 Chris Hammond	.10	.05	.01
□ 210 Jeffrey Hammonds	.25	.11	.03
□ 211 Rich Amaral	.10	.05	.01
□ 212 Danny Tartabull	.10	.05	.01
□ 213 Jeff Russell	.10	.05	.01
□ 214 Dave Staton	.10	.05	.01
□ 215 Kenny Lofton	1.00	.45	.12
□ 216 Manuel Lee	.10	.05	.01
□ 217 Brian Koelling	.10	.05	.01
□ 218 Scott Lydy	.10	.05	.01
□ 219 Tony Gwynn	1.25	.55	.16
□ 220 Cecil Fielder	.25	.11	.03
□ 221 Royce Clayton	.25	.11	.03
□ 222 Reggie Sanders	.50	.23	.06
□ 223 Brian Jordan	.50	.23	.06
□ 224 Ken Griffey Jr.	3.00	1.35	.35
□ 225 Fred McGriff	.50	.23	.06
□ 226 Felix Jose	.10	.05	.01
□ 227 Brad Pennington	.10	.05	.01
□ 228 Chris Bosio	.10	.05	.01
□ 229 Mike Stanley	.10	.05	.01
□ 230 Willie Greene	.25	.11	.03
□ 231 Alex Fernandez	.50	.23	.06
□ 232 Brad Ausmus	.10	.05	.01
□ 233 Darrell Whitmore	.10	.05	.01
□ 234 Marcus Moore	.10	.05	.01
□ 235 Allen Watson	.10	.05	.01
□ 236 Jose Offerman	.10	.05	.01
□ 237 Rondell White	.50	.23	.06
□ 238 Jeff King	.25	.11	.03
□ 239 Luis Alicea	.10	.05	.01
□ 240 Dan Wilson	.25	.11	.03
□ 241 Ed Sprague	.25	.11	.03
□ 242 Todd Hundley	.50	.23	.06
□ 243 Al Martin	.10	.05	.01
□ 244 Mike Lansing	.25	.11	.03
□ 245 Ivan Rodriguez	.60	.25	.07
□ 246 Dave Fleming	.10	.05	.01
□ 247 John Doherty	.10	.05	.01
□ 248 Mark McLemore	.10	.05	.01
□ 249 Bob Hamelin	.10	.05	.01
□ 250 Curtis Pride	.25	.11	.03
□ 251 Zane Smith	.10	.05	.01
□ 252 Eric Young	.25	.11	.03
□ 253 Brian McRae	.25	.11	.03
□ 254 Tim Raines	.50	.23	.06
□ 255 Javier Lopez	.50	.23	.06
□ 256 Melvin Nieves	.25	.11	.03
□ 257 Randy Myers	.10	.05	.01
□ 258 Willie McGee	.10	.05	.01
□ 259 Jimmy Key UER (birthdate missing on back)	.25	.11	.03
□ 260 Tom Candiotti	.10	.05	.01
□ 261 Eric Davis	.25	.11	.03
□ 262 Craig Paquette	.10	.05	.01
□ 263 Robin Ventura	.25	.11	.03
□ 264 Pat Kelly	.10	.05	.01
□ 265 Gregg Jefferies	.50	.23	.06
□ 266 Cory Snyder	.10	.05	.01
□ 267 David Justice HFA	.25	.11	.03
□ 268 Sammy Sosa HFA	.50	.23	.06
□ 269 Barry Larkin HFA	.50	.23	.06
□ 270 Andres Galarraga HFA	.50	.23	.06
□ 271 Gary Sheffield HFA	.50	.23	.06
□ 272 Jeff Bagwell HFA	.60	.25	.07
□ 273 Mike Piazza HFA	1.00	.45	.12
□ 274 Larry Walker HFA	.25	.11	.03
□ 275 Bobby Bonilla HFA	.10	.05	.01
□ 276 John Kruk HFA	.10	.05	.01
□ 277 Jay Bell HFA	.10	.05	.01
□ 278 Ozzie Smith HFA	.50	.23	.06
□ 279 Tony Gwynn HFA	.60	.25	.07
□ 280 Barry Bonds HFA	.50	.23	.06
□ 281 Cal Ripken Jr. HFA	1.25	.55	.16
□ 282 Mo Vaughn HFA	.50	.23	.06
□ 283 Tim Salmon HFA	.25	.11	.03
□ 284 Frank Thomas HFA	1.50	.70	.19
□ 285 Albert Belle HFA	.75	.35	.09
□ 286 Cecil Fielder HFA	.10	.05	.01
□ 287 Wally Joyner HFA	.10	.05	.01
□ 288 Greg Vaughn HFA	.25	.11	.03
□ 289 Kirby Puckett HFA	.50	.23	.06
□ 290 Don Mattingly HFA	.75	.35	.09
□ 291 Terry Steinbach HFA	.10	.05	.01
□ 292 Ken Griffey Jr. HFA	1.50	.70	.19
□ 293 Juan Gonzalez HFA	.75	.35	.09
□ 294 Paul Molitor HFA	.50	.23	.06
□ 295 Tavo Alvarez UDC	.10	.05	.01
□ 296 Matt Brunson UDC	.25	.11	.03
□ 297 Shawn Green UDC	.25	.11	.03
□ 298 Alex Rodriguez UDC	4.00	1.80	.50
□ 299 Shannon Stewart UDC	.25	.11	.03
□ 300 Frank Thomas	3.00	1.35	.35
□ 301 Mickey Tettleton	.10	.05	.01
□ 302 Pedro Munoz	.10	.05	.01
□ 303 Jose Valentin	.25	.11	.03
□ 304 Orestes Destrade	.10	.05	.01
□ 305 Pat Listach	.10	.05	.01
□ 306 Scott Brosius	.10	.05	.01
□ 307 Kurt Miller	.10	.05	.01
□ 308 Rob Dibble	.10	.05	.01
□ 309 Mike Blowers	.10	.05	.01
□ 310 Jim Abbott	.10	.05	.01
□ 311 Mike Jackson	.10	.05	.01
□ 312 Craig Biggio	.50	.23	.06
□ 313 Kurt Abbott	.25	.11	.03
□ 314 Chuck Finley	.10	.05	.01
□ 315 Andres Galarraga	.50	.23	.06
□ 316 Mike Moore	.10	.05	.01
□ 317 Doug Strange	.10	.05	.01
□ 318 Pedro J. Martinez	.50	.23	.06
□ 319 Kevin McReynolds	.10	.05	.01
□ 320 Greg Maddux	2.00	.90	.25
□ 321 Mike Henneman	.10	.05	.01
□ 322 Scott Leius	.10	.05	.01
□ 323 John Franco	.10	.05	.01
□ 324 Jeff Blauser	.10	.05	.01
□ 325 Kirby Puckett	1.00	.45	.12
□ 326 Darryl Hamilton	.10	.05	.01
□ 327 John Smiley	.10	.05	.01
□ 328 Derrick May	.10	.05	.01
□ 329 Jose Vizcaino	.10	.05	.01
□ 330 Randy Johnson	.50	.23	.06
□ 331 Jack Morris	.25	.11	.03
□ 332 Graeme Lloyd	.10	.05	.01
□ 333 Dave Valle	.10	.05	.01
□ 334 Greg Myers	.10	.05	.01
□ 335 John Wetteland	.25	.11	.03
□ 336 Jim Gott	.10	.05	.01
□ 337 Tim Naehring	.10	.05	.01
□ 338 Mike Kelly	.10	.05	.01
□ 339 Jeff Montgomery	.25	.11	.03
□ 340 Rafael Palmeiro	.50	.23	.06
□ 341 Eddie Murray	.50	.23	.06
□ 342 Xavier Hernandez	.10	.05	.01
□ 343 Bobby Munoz	.10	.05	.01
□ 344 Bobby Bonilla	.25	.11	.03
□ 345 Travis Fryman	.50	.23	.06
□ 346 Steve Finley	.50	.23	.06
□ 347 Chris Sabo	.10	.05	.01
□ 348 Armando Reynoso	.10	.05	.01
□ 349 Ramon Martinez	.25	.11	.03
□ 350 Will Clark	.50	.23	.06
□ 351 Moises Alou	.25	.11	.03
□ 352 Jim Thome	.75	.35	.09
□ 353 Bob Tewksbury	.10	.05	.01
□ 354 Andujar Cedeno	.10	.05	.01
□ 355 Orel Hershiser	.25	.11	.03
□ 356 Mike Devereaux	.10	.05	.01
□ 357 Mike Perez	.10	.05	.01
□ 358 Dennis Martinez	.25	.11	.03
□ 359 Dave Nilsson	.25	.11	.03
□ 360 Ozzie Smith	.60	.25	.07
□ 361 Eric Anthony	.10	.05	.01
□ 362 Scott Sanders	.10	.05	.01
□ 363 Paul Sorrento	.10	.05	.01
□ 364 Tim Belcher	.10	.05	.01
□ 365 Dennis Eckersley	.25	.11	.03
□ 366 Mel Rojas	.10	.05	.01
□ 367 Tom Henke	.10	.05	.01
□ 368 Randy Tomlin	.10	.05	.01
□ 369 B.J. Surhoff	.10	.05	.01
□ 370 Larry Walker	.50	.23	.06
□ 371 Joey Cora	.10	.05	.01
□ 372 Mike Harkey	.10	.05	.01
□ 373 John Valentin	.25	.11	.03

□ 374 Doug Jones	.10	.05	.01
□ 375 David Justice	.50	.23	.06
□ 376 Vince Coleman	.10	.05	.01
□ 377 David Hulse	.10	.05	.01
□ 378 Kevin Seitzer	.10	.05	.01
□ 379 Pete Harnisch	.10	.05	.01
□ 380 Ruben Sierra	.25	.11	.03
□ 381 Mark Lewis	.10	.05	.01
□ 382 Bip Roberts	.10	.05	.01
□ 383 Paul Wagner	.10	.05	.01
□ 384 Stan Javier	.10	.05	.01
□ 385 Barry Larkin	.50	.23	.06
□ 386 Mark Portugal	.10	.05	.01
□ 387 Roberto Kelly	.10	.05	.01
□ 388 Andy Benes	.25	.11	.03
□ 389 Felix Fermin	.10	.05	.01
□ 390 Marquis Grissom	.50	.23	.06
□ 391 Troy Neel	.10	.05	.01
□ 392 Chad Kreuter	.10	.05	.01
□ 393 Gregg Olson	.10	.05	.01
□ 394 Charles Nagy	.25	.11	.03
□ 395 Jack McDowell	.25	.11	.03
□ 396 Luis Gonzalez	.10	.05	.01
□ 397 Benito Santiago	.10	.05	.01
□ 398 Chris James	.10	.05	.01
□ 399 Terry Mulholland	.10	.05	.01
□ 400 Barry Bonds	.75	.35	.09
□ 401 Joe Grahe	.10	.05	.01
□ 402 Duane Ward	.10	.05	.01
□ 403 John Burkett	.10	.05	.01
□ 404 Scott Servais	.10	.05	.01
□ 405 Bryan Harvey	.10	.05	.01
□ 406 Bernard Gilkey	.25	.11	.03
□ 407 Greg McMichael	.10	.05	.01
□ 408 Tim Wallach	.10	.05	.01
□ 409 Ken Caminiti	.50	.23	.06
□ 410 John Kruk	.25	.11	.03
□ 411 Darrin Jackson	.10	.05	.01
□ 412 Mike Gallego	.10	.05	.01
□ 413 David Cone	.50	.23	.06
□ 414 Lou Whitaker	.50	.23	.06
□ 415 Sandy Alomar Jr.	.25	.11	.03
□ 416 Bill Wegman	.10	.05	.01
□ 417 Pat Borders	.10	.05	.01
□ 418 Roger Pavlik	.10	.05	.01
□ 419 Pete Smith	.10	.05	.01
□ 420 Steve Avery	.25	.11	.03
□ 421 David Segui	.10	.05	.01
□ 422 Rheal Cormier	.10	.05	.01
□ 423 Harold Reynolds	.10	.05	.01
□ 424 Edgar Martinez	.50	.23	.06
□ 425 Cal Ripken Jr.	2.50	1.10	.30
□ 426 Jaime Navarro	.10	.05	.01
□ 427 Sean Berry	.10	.05	.01
□ 428 Bret Saberhagen	.25	.11	.03
□ 429 Bob Welch	.10	.05	.01
□ 430 Juan Guzman	.25	.11	.03
□ 431 Cal Eldred	.10	.05	.01
□ 432 Dave Hollins	.10	.05	.01
□ 433 Sid Fernandez	.10	.05	.01
□ 434 Willie Banks	.10	.05	.01
□ 435 Darryl Kile	.10	.05	.01
□ 436 Henry Rodriguez	.50	.23	.06
□ 437 Tony Fernandez	.10	.05	.01
□ 438 Walt Weiss	.10	.05	.01
□ 439 Kevin Tapani	.10	.05	.01
□ 440 Mark Grace	.50	.23	.06
□ 441 Brian Harper	.10	.05	.01
□ 442 Kent Mercker	.10	.05	.01
□ 443 Anthony Young	.10	.05	.01
□ 444 Todd Zeile	.10	.05	.01
□ 445 Greg Vaughn	.50	.23	.06
□ 446 Ray Lankford	.50	.23	.06
□ 447 Dave Weathers	.10	.05	.01
□ 448 Bret Boone	.25	.11	.03
□ 449 Charlie Hough	.10	.05	.01
□ 450 Roger Clemens	.50	.23	.06
□ 451 Mike Morgan	.10	.05	.01
□ 452 Doug Drabek	.10	.05	.01
□ 453 Danny Jackson	.10	.05	.01
□ 454 Dante Bichette	.50	.23	.06
□ 455 Roberto Alomar	.75	.35	.09
□ 456 Ben McDonald	.10	.05	.01
□ 457 Kenny Rogers	.10	.05	.01
□ 458 Bill Gullickson	.10	.05	.01
□ 459 Darrin Fletcher	.10	.05	.01
□ 460 Curt Schilling	.10	.05	.01
□ 461 Billy Hatcher	.10	.05	.01
□ 462 Howard Johnson	.10	.05	.01
□ 463 Mickey Morandini	.10	.05	.01
□ 464 Frank Castillo	.10	.05	.01
□ 465 Delino DeShields	.10	.05	.01
□ 466 Gary Gaetti	.25	.11	.03
□ 467 Steve Farr	.10	.05	.01
□ 468 Roberto Hernandez	.25	.11	.03
□ 469 Jack Armstrong	.10	.05	.01
□ 470 Paul Molitor	.60	.25	.07
□ 471 Melido Perez	.10	.05	.01
□ 472 Greg Hibbard	.10	.05	.01
□ 473 Jody Reed	.10	.05	.01
□ 474 Tom Gordon	.10	.05	.01
□ 475 Gary Sheffield	.50	.23	.06
□ 476 John Jaha	.25	.11	.03
□ 477 Shawon Dunston	.10	.05	.01
□ 478 Reggie Jefferson	.25	.11	.03
□ 479 Don Slaught	.10	.05	.01
□ 480 Jeff Bagwell	1.25	.55	.16
□ 481 Tim Pugh	.10	.05	.01
□ 482 Kevin Young	.10	.05	.01
□ 483 Ellis Burks	.25	.11	.03
□ 484 Greg Swindell	.10	.05	.01
□ 485 Mark Langston	.25	.11	.03
□ 486 Omar Vizquel	.50	.23	.06
□ 487 Kevin Brown	.10	.05	.01
□ 488 Terry Steinbach	.25	.11	.03
□ 489 Mark Lemke	.10	.05	.01
□ 490 Matt Williams	.50	.23	.06
□ 491 Pete Incaviglia	.10	.05	.01
□ 492 Karl Rhodes	.10	.05	.01
□ 493 Shawn Green	.25	.11	.03
□ 494 Hal Morris	.10	.05	.01
□ 495 Derek Bell	.25	.11	.03
□ 496 Luis Polonia	.10	.05	.01
□ 497 Otis Nixon	.10	.05	.01
□ 498 Ron Darling	.10	.05	.01
□ 499 Mitch Williams	.10	.05	.01
□ 500 Mike Piazza	2.00	.90	.25
□ 501 Pat Meares	.10	.05	.01
□ 502 Scott Cooper	.10	.05	.01
□ 503 Scott Erickson	.10	.05	.01
□ 504 Jeff Juden	.10	.05	.01
□ 505 Lee Smith	.25	.11	.03
□ 506 Bobby Ayala	.10	.05	.01
□ 507 Dave Henderson	.10	.05	.01
□ 508 Erik Hanson	.10	.05	.01
□ 509 Bob Wickman	.10	.05	.01
□ 510 Sammy Sosa	.50	.23	.06
□ 511 Hector Carrasco DD	.10	.05	.01
□ 512 Tim Davis DD	.10	.05	.01
□ 513 Joey Hamilton DD	.60	.25	.07
□ 514 Robert Eenhoorn DD	.10	.05	.01
□ 515 Jorge Fabregas DD	.10	.05	.01
□ 516 Tim Hyers DD	.10	.05	.01
□ 517 John Hudek DD	.10	.05	.01
□ 518 James Mouton DD	.25	.11	.03
□ 519 Herbert Perry DD	.25	.11	.03
□ 520 Chan Ho Park DD	.75	.35	.09
□ 521 W.Van Landingham DD	.25	.11	.03
□ 522 Paul Shuey DD	.10	.05	.01
□ 523 Ryan Hancock TP	.25	.11	.03
□ 524 Billy Wagner TP	.75	.35	.09
□ 525 Jason Giambi	.75	.35	.09
□ 526 Jose Silva TP	.25	.11	.03
□ 527 Terrell Wade TP	.60	.25	.07
□ 528 Todd Dunn TP	.10	.05	.01
□ 529 Alan Benes TP	1.25	.55	.16
□ 530 Brooks Kieschnick TP	.60	.25	.07
□ 531 Todd Hollandsworth TP	.75	.35	.09
□ 532 Brad Fullmer TP	.60	.25	.07
□ 533 Steve Soderstrom TP	.25	.11	.03
□ 534 Daron Kirkreit TP	.25	.11	.03
□ 535 Arquimedez Pozo TP	.40	.18	.05
□ 536 Charles Johnson TP	.50	.23	.06
□ 537 Preston Wilson TP	.25	.11	.03
□ 538 Alex Ochoa TP	.25	.11	.03
□ 539 Derrek Lee TP	2.00	.90	.25
□ 540 Wayne Gomes TP	.25	.11	.03
□ 541 Jermaine Allensworth TP	.25	.11	.03
□ 542 Mike Bell TP	.60	.25	.07
□ 543 Trot Nixon TP	.50	.23	.06
□ 544 Pokey Reese TP	.25	.11	.03
□ 545 Neifi Perez TP	.75	.35	.09

□ 546 Johnny Damon TP	.50	.23	.06
□ 547 Matt Brunson TP	.25	.11	.03
□ 548 LaTroy Hawkins TP	.25	.11	.03
□ 549 Eddie Pearson TP	.40	.18	.05
□ 550 Derek Jeter TP	2.50	1.10	.30
□ A298 Alex Rodriguez AU	200.00	90.00	25.00
□ GMA1 Ken Griffey Jr. AU Mickey Mantle AU/1000	1200.00	550.00	150.00
□ KGA1 Ken Griffey AU/1000	250.00	110.00	31.00
□ MMA1 Mickey Mantle AU/1000	600.00	275.00	75.00

1994 Upper Deck Diamond Collection

This 30-card standard-size set was inserted regionally in first series hobby packs at a rate of one in 18. The three regions are Central (C1-C10), East (E1-E10) and West (W1-W10). While each card has the same horizontal format, the color scheme differs by region. The Central cards have a blue background, the East green and the West a deep shade of red. Color player photos are superimposed over the backgrounds. Each card has, "The Upper Deck Diamond Collection" as part of the background. The backs have a small photo and career highlights.

	MINT	NRMT	EXC
COMPLETE SET (30)	325.00	145.00	40.00
COMPLETE CENTRAL (10)	150.00	70.00	19.00
COMPLETE EAST (10)	75.00	34.00	9.50
COMPLETE WEST (10)	100.00	45.00	12.50
COMMON CARD	2.50	1.10	.30
SEMISTARS	5.00	2.20	.60
REGIONAL INSERTS IN SER.1 HOBBY PACKS			
□ C1 Jeff Bagwell	15.00	6.75	1.85
□ C2 Michael Jordan	50.00	22.00	6.25
□ C3 Barry Larkin	5.00	2.20	.60
□ C4 Kirby Puckett	12.00	5.50	1.50
□ C5 Manny Ramirez	12.00	5.50	1.50
□ C6 Ryne Sandberg	10.00	4.50	1.25
□ C7 Ozzie Smith	8.00	3.60	1.00
□ C8 Frank Thomas	40.00	18.00	5.00
□ C9 Andy Van Slyke	2.50	1.10	.30
□ C10 Robin Yount	5.00	2.20	.60
□ E1 Roberto Alomar	8.00	3.60	1.00
□ E2 Roger Clemens	5.00	2.20	.60
□ E3 Lenny Dykstra	5.00	2.20	.60
□ E4 Cecil Fielder	5.00	2.20	.60
□ E5 Cliff Floyd	2.50	1.10	.30
□ E6 Dwight Gooden	5.00	2.20	.60
□ E7 David Justice	2.50	1.10	.30
□ E8 Don Mattingly	15.00	6.75	1.85
□ E9 Cal Ripken Jr.	30.00	13.50	3.70
□ E10 Gary Sheffield	6.00	2.70	.75
□ W1 Barry Bonds	10.00	4.50	1.25
□ W2 Andres Galarraga	5.00	2.20	.60
□ W3 Juan Gonzalez	20.00	9.00	2.50
□ W4 Ken Griffey Jr.	40.00	18.00	5.00
□ W5 Tony Gwynn	15.00	6.75	1.85
□ W6 Rickey Henderson	5.00	2.20	.60
□ W7 Bo Jackson	5.00	2.20	.60
□ W8 Mark McGwire	12.00	5.50	1.50
□ W9 Mike Piazza	20.00	9.00	2.50
□ W10 Tim Salmon	6.00	2.70	.75

1994 Upper Deck Griffey Jumbos

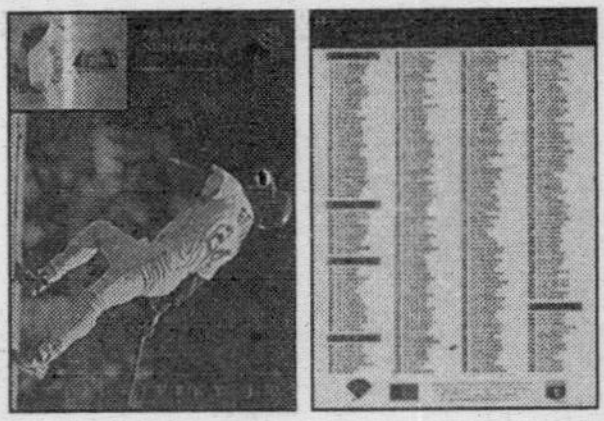

Measuring 4 7/8" by 6 13/16", these four Griffey cards serve as checklists for first series Upper Deck issues. They were issued one per first series hobby foil box. Card fronts have a full color photo with a small Griffey hologram. The first three cards provide a numerical, alphabetical and team organized checklist for the basic set. The fourth card is a checklist of inserts. Each card was printed in different quantities with CL1 the most plentiful and CL4 the more scarce. The backs are numbered with a CL prefix.

	MINT	NRMT	EXC
COMPLETE SET (4)	20.00	9.00	2.50
COMMON GRIFFEY (CL1-CL4)	4.00	1.80	.50
ONE PER SEALED SER.1 HOBBY FOIL BOX.			
□ CL1 Numerical CL TP	4.00	1.80	.50
□ CL2 Alphabetical CL DP	5.00	2.20	.60
□ CL3 Team CL	6.00	2.70	.75
□ CL4 Insert CL SP	8.00	3.60	1.00

1994 Upper Deck Mantle's Long Shots

Randomly inserted in first series retail packs at a rate of one in 18, this 21-card silver foil standard-size set features top longball hitters as selected by Mickey Mantle. Two trade cards, were also random inserts and were redeemable (expiration: December 31, 1994) for either the basic silver foil set version (Silver Trade card) or the Electric Diamond version (blue Trade card). The Electric Diamond set and singles command up to 1.25X the values below. The only way to obtain the Electric Diamond version was through the trade card. These cards differ in that they have an Electric Diamond logo on front. Card fronts are horizontal with a color player photo standing out from a dulled holographic image. The backs have a vertical format with a player photo at the top, a small photo of Mickey Mantle, a quote from The Mick and career power numbers. The cards are

numbered on the back with a "MM" prefix and sequenced in alphabetical order.

	MINT	NRMT	EXC
COMPLETE SET (21)	50.00	22.00	6.25
COMMON CARD (MM1-MM21)	.50	.23	.06
SEMISTARS	1.25	.55	.16

RANDOM INSERTS IN SER.1 RETAIL PACKS
SETS WERE REDEEMABLE w/TRADE CARDS
*ELEC. DIAMOND VERSIONS: 1.25X VALUE

□ MM1 Jeff Bagwell	4.00	1.80	.50
□ MM2 Albert Belle	5.00	2.20	.60
□ MM3 Barry Bonds	2.50	1.10	.30
□ MM4 Jose Canseco	1.25	.55	.16
□ MM5 Joe Carter	1.25	.55	.16
□ MM6 Carlos Delgado	1.50	.70	.19
□ MM7 Cecil Fielder	1.25	.55	.16
□ MM8 Cliff Floyd	.50	.23	.06
□ MM9 Juan Gonzalez	5.00	2.20	.60
□ MM10 Ken Griffey Jr.	10.00	4.50	1.25
□ MM11 David Justice	.50	.23	.06
□ MM12 Fred McGriff	1.25	.55	.16
□ MM13 Mark McGwire	3.00	1.35	.35
□ MM14 Dean Palmer	1.25	.55	.16
□ MM15 Mike Piazza	6.00	2.70	.75
□ MM16 Manny Ramirez	3.00	1.35	.35
□ MM17 Tim Salmon	1.50	.70	.19
□ MM18 Frank Thomas	10.00	4.50	1.25
□ MM19 Mo Vaughn	2.50	1.10	.30
□ MM20 Matt Williams	1.25	.55	.16
□ MM21 Mickey Mantle	15.00	6.75	1.85
□ NNO Mantle ED LS Tr. Blue	12.00	5.50	1.50
□ NNO Mantle LS Trade Silver	6.00	2.70	.75

1994 Upper Deck Next Generation

Randomly inserted in second series retail packs at a rate of one in 35, this 18-card standard-size set spotlights young established stars and promising prospects. The set is sequenced in alphabetical order. Metallic fronts feature a color player photo on solid background. A small player hologram is halfway up the card on the right and comes between the player's first and last name. The Next Generation logo is at bottom left. Horizontal backs contain statistical comparisons, where applicable, to Hall of Famers and brief write-up noting the comparisons. A Next Generation Electric Diamond Trade Card and a Next Generation Trade Card were randomly in second series hobby packs. Each card could be redeemed for that set. Expiration date for redemption was October 31, 1994. The Electric Diamond versions are priced at 1.25X the values below.

	MINT	NRMT	EXC
COMPLETE SET (18)	150.00	70.00	19.00
COMMON CARD (1-18)	1.50	.70	.19
SEMISTARS	2.50	1.10	.30

RANDOM INSERTS IN SER.2 RETAIL PACKS
TRADE CARDS INSERTS IN SER.2 HOBBY..
SETS WERE REDEEMABLE w/TRADE CARDS
*ELEC. DIAMOND VERSIONS: 1.25X VALUE

□ 1 Roberto Alomar	8.00	3.60	1.00
□ 2 Carlos Delgado	4.00	1.80	.50
□ 3 Cliff Floyd	2.50	1.10	.30
□ 4 Alex Gonzalez	1.50	.70	.19
□ 5 Juan Gonzalez	12.00	5.50	1.50
□ 6 Ken Griffey Jr.	30.00	13.50	3.70
□ 7 Jeffrey Hammonds	1.50	.70	.19
□ 8 Michael Jordan	40.00	18.00	5.00
□ 9 David Justice	2.50	1.10	.30
□ 10 Ryan Klesko	8.00	3.60	1.00
□ 11 Javier Lopez	4.00	1.80	.50
□ 12 Raul Mondesi	5.00	2.20	.60
□ 13 Mike Piazza	20.00	9.00	2.50
□ 14 Kirby Puckett	10.00	4.50	1.25
□ 15 Manny Ramirez	10.00	4.50	1.25
□ 16 Alex Rodriguez	40.00	18.00	5.00
□ 17 Tim Salmon	4.00	1.80	.50
□ 18 Gary Sheffield	5.00	2.20	.60
□ NNO Expired NG Trade Card	4.00	1.80	.50
□ NNO Expired NG Trade Card	4.00	1.80	.50

1995 Upper Deck

The 1995 Upper Deck baseball set was issued in two series of 225 cards for a total of 450. Five randomly inserted Trade Cards were each redeemable for nine updated cards of new rookies or players who changed teams, comprising a 45-card Trade Redemption set. The Trade cards expired Feb 1, 1996. Autographed jumbo cards (Roger Clemens for series one, Alex Rodriguez for either series) were available through a wrapper redemption offer. The cards were distributed in 12-card packs (36 per box) with a suggested retail price of $1.99. The fronts display full-bleed color action photos, with the player's name in copper foil across the bottom. The backs carry another photo, biography, and season and career statistics. Second series packs contained trade cards for autographed cards of these players: Roger Clemens, Reggie Jackson, Willie Mays, Raul Mondesi and Frank Robinson. Subsets include Top Prospect (1-15, 251-265), 90's Midpoint (101-110), Star Rookie (211-240), and Diamond Debuts (241-250). Rookie Cards in this set include Raul Casanova, Karim Garcia, Hideo Nomo and Carlos Perez.

	MINT	NRMT	EXC
COMPLETE SET (450)	60.00	27.00	7.50
COMPLETE SERIES 1 (225)	30.00	13.50	3.70
COMPLETE SET (225)	30.00	13.50	3.70
COMMON CARD (1-450)	.10	.05	.01
SEMISTARS	.25	.11	.03
STARS	.50	.23	.06
COMPLETE TRADE SET (45)	10.00	4.50	1.25
COMMON TRADE (451T-495T)	.20	.09	.03
NINE TRADE CARDS PER TRADE EXCH.CARD			
TRADE EXCH.SET (5)	4.00	1.80	.50
COMMON TRADE EXCH. (1-5)	1.00	.45	.12
COMP.ELEC.DIAM.SET (450)	110.00	50.00	14.00
COMP.ELEC.DIAM.SER.1 (225)	50.00	22.00	6.25
COMP.ELEC.DIAM.SER.2 (225)	60.00	27.00	7.50
COMMON ELEC.DIAM. (1-450)	.15	.07	.02
ELEC.DIAM.SEMISTARS	.30	.14	.04

*ELEC.DIAM.STARS: 2X to 4X HI COLUMN.
*ELEC.DIAM YOUNG STARS: 1.5X to 3X HI
ONE ELECTRIC DIAMOND PER RETAIL PACK

COMPLETE B.RUTH SET (10)	120.00	55.00	15.00
COMMON RUTH (73-81/HDR)	15.00	6.75	1.85

RUTH: RANDOM INSERTS IN SER.2 PACKS
CLEMENS JUMBO AU REDEEMABLE..........

□ 1 Ruben Rivera	1.50	.70	.19
□ 2 Bill Pulsipher	.25	.11	.03
□ 3 Ben Grieve	1.25	.55	.16
□ 4 Curtis Goodwin	.25	.11	.03
□ 5 Damon Hollins	.25	.11	.03
□ 6 Todd Greene	.50	.23	.06
□ 7 Glenn Williams	.50	.23	.06
□ 8 Bret Wagner	.25	.11	.03
□ 9 Karim Garcia	3.00	1.35	.35
□ 10 Nomar Garciaparra	1.50	.70	.19
□ 11 Raul Casanova	.50	.23	.06
□ 12 Matt Smith	.25	.11	.03
□ 13 Paul Wilson	.60	.25	.07
□ 14 Jason Isringhausen	.75	.35	.09
□ 15 Reid Ryan	.50	.23	.06
□ 16 Lee Smith	.25	.11	.03
□ 17 Chili Davis	.25	.11	.03
□ 18 Brian Anderson	.10	.05	.01
□ 19 Gary DiSarcina	.10	.05	.01
□ 20 Bo Jackson	.50	.23	.06
□ 21 Chuck Finley	.25	.11	.03
□ 22 Darryl Kile	.10	.05	.01
□ 23 Shane Reynolds	.10	.05	.01
□ 24 Tony Eusebio	.10	.05	.01
□ 25 Craig Biggio	.50	.23	.06
□ 26 Doug Drabek	.10	.05	.01
□ 27 Brian L. Hunter	.50	.23	.06
□ 28 James Mouton	.10	.05	.01
□ 29 Geronimo Berroa	.10	.05	.01
□ 30 Rickey Henderson	.50	.23	.06
□ 31 Steve Karsay	.10	.05	.01
□ 32 Steve Ontiveros	.10	.05	.01
□ 33 Ernie Young	.25	.11	.03
□ 34 Dennis Eckersley	.25	.11	.03
□ 35 Mark McGwire	1.00	.45	.12
□ 36 Dave Stewart	.25	.11	.03
□ 37 Pat Hentgen	.25	.11	.03
□ 38 Carlos Delgado	.50	.23	.06
□ 39 Joe Carter	.50	.23	.06
□ 40 Roberto Alomar	.75	.35	.09
□ 41 John Olerud	.10	.05	.01
□ 42 Devon White	.25	.11	.03
□ 43 Roberto Kelly	.10	.05	.01
□ 44 Jeff Blauser	.10	.05	.01
□ 45 Fred McGriff	.50	.23	.06
□ 46 Tom Glavine	.50	.23	.06
□ 47 Mike Kelly	.10	.05	.01
□ 48 Javier Lopez	.50	.23	.06
□ 49 Greg Maddux	2.00	.90	.25
□ 50 Matt Mieske	.25	.11	.03
□ 51 Troy O'Leary	.10	.05	.01
□ 52 Jeff Cirillo	.25	.11	.03
□ 53 Cal Eldred	.10	.05	.01
□ 54 Pat Listach	.10	.05	.01
□ 55 Jose Valentin	.25	.11	.03
□ 56 John Mabry	.50	.23	.06
□ 57 Bob Tewksbury	.10	.05	.01
□ 58 Brian Jordan	.50	.23	.06
□ 59 Gregg Jefferies	.25	.11	.03
□ 60 Ozzie Smith	.60	.25	.07
□ 61 Geronimo Pena	.10	.05	.01
□ 62 Mark Whiten	.10	.05	.01
□ 63 Rey Sanchez	.10	.05	.01
□ 64 Willie Banks	.10	.05	.01
□ 65 Mark Grace	.50	.23	.06
□ 66 Randy Myers	.10	.05	.01
□ 67 Steve Trachsel	.10	.05	.01
□ 68 Derrick May	.10	.05	.01
□ 69 Brett Butler	.25	.11	.03
□ 70 Eric Karros	.25	.11	.03
□ 71 Tim Wallach	.10	.05	.01
□ 72 Delino DeShields	.10	.05	.01
□ 73 Darren Dreifort	.10	.05	.01
□ 74 Orel Hershiser	.25	.11	.03
□ 75 Billy Ashley	.10	.05	.01
□ 76 Sean Berry	.10	.05	.01
□ 77 Ken Hill	.10	.05	.01
□ 78 John Wetteland	.25	.11	.03
□ 79 Moises Alou	.25	.11	.03
□ 80 Cliff Floyd	.25	.11	.03
□ 81 Marquis Grissom	.50	.23	.06
□ 82 Larry Walker	.50	.23	.06
□ 83 Rondell White	.50	.23	.06
□ 84 William VanLandingham	.10	.05	.01
□ 85 Matt Williams	.50	.23	.06
□ 86 Rod Beck	.10	.05	.01
□ 87 Darren Lewis	.10	.05	.01
□ 88 Robby Thompson	.10	.05	.01
□ 89 Darryl Strawberry	.25	.11	.03
□ 90 Kenny Lofton	.75	.35	.09
□ 91 Charles Nagy	.25	.11	.03
□ 92 Sandy Alomar Jr.	.10	.05	.01
□ 93 Mark Clark	.10	.05	.01
□ 94 Dennis Martinez	.25	.11	.03
□ 95 Dave Winfield	.50	.23	.06
□ 96 Jim Thome	.60	.25	.07
□ 97 Manny Ramirez	.75	.35	.09
□ 98 Goose Gossage	.25	.11	.03
□ 99 Tino Martinez	.25	.11	.03
□ 100 Ken Griffey Jr.	3.00	1.35	.35
□ 101 Greg Maddux ANA	1.00	.45	.12
□ 102 Randy Johnson ANA	.50	.23	.06
□ 103 Barry Bonds ANA	.50	.23	.06
□ 104 Juan Gonzalez ANA	.30	.14	.04
□ 105 Frank Thomas ANA	1.50	.70	.19
□ 106 Matt Williams ANA	.25	.11	.03
□ 107 Paul Molitor ANA	.50	.23	.06
□ 108 Fred McGriff ANA	.25	.11	.03
□ 109 Carlos Baerga ANA	.25	.11	.03
□ 110 Ken Griffey Jr. ANA	1.50	.70	.19
□ 111 Reggie Jefferson	.25	.11	.03
□ 112 Randy Johnson	.50	.23	.06
□ 113 Marc Newfield	.25	.11	.03
□ 114 Robb Nen	.10	.05	.01
□ 115 Jeff Conine	.50	.23	.06
□ 116 Kurt Abbott	.10	.05	.01
□ 117 Charlie Hough	.10	.05	.01
□ 118 Dave Weathers	.10	.05	.01
□ 119 Juan Castillo	.10	.05	.01
□ 120 Bret Saberhagen	.25	.11	.03
□ 121 Rico Brogna	.10	.05	.01
□ 122 John Franco	.10	.05	.01
□ 123 Todd Hundley	.25	.11	.03
□ 124 Jason Jacome	.10	.05	.01
□ 125 Bobby Jones	.25	.11	.03
□ 126 Bret Barberie	.10	.05	.01
□ 127 Ben McDonald	.10	.05	.01
□ 128 Harold Baines	.25	.11	.03
□ 129 Jeffrey Hammonds	.25	.11	.03
□ 130 Mike Mussina	.60	.25	.07
□ 131 Chris Hoiles	.10	.05	.01
□ 132 Brady Anderson	.50	.23	.06
□ 133 Eddie Williams	.10	.05	.01
□ 134 Andy Benes	.10	.05	.01
□ 135 Tony Gwynn	1.25	.55	.16
□ 136 Bip Roberts	.10	.05	.01
□ 137 Joey Hamilton	.25	.11	.03
□ 138 Luis Lopez	.10	.05	.01
□ 139 Ray McDavid	.25	.11	.03
□ 140 Lenny Dykstra	.25	.11	.03
□ 141 Mariano Duncan	.10	.05	.01
□ 142 Fernando Valenzuela	.25	.11	.03
□ 143 Bobby Munoz	.10	.05	.01
□ 144 Kevin Stocker	.10	.05	.01
□ 145 John Kruk	.25	.11	.03
□ 146 Jon Lieber	.10	.05	.01
□ 147 Zane Smith	.10	.05	.01
□ 148 Steve Cooke	.10	.05	.01
□ 149 Andy Van Slyke	.25	.11	.03
□ 150 Jay Bell	.25	.11	.03
□ 151 Carlos Garcia	.10	.05	.01
□ 152 John Dettmer	.10	.05	.01
□ 153 Darren Oliver	.25	.11	.03
□ 154 Dean Palmer	.25	.11	.03
□ 155 Otis Nixon	.10	.05	.01
□ 156 Rusty Greer	.50	.23	.06
□ 157 Rick Helling	.10	.05	.01
□ 158 Jose Canseco	.50	.23	.06
□ 159 Roger Clemens	.50	.23	.06
□ 160 Andre Dawson	.50	.23	.06
□ 161 Mo Vaughn	.75	.35	.09
□ 162 Aaron Sele	.25	.11	.03
□ 163 John Valentin	.25	.11	.03
□ 164 Brian R. Hunter	.10	.05	.01

□ 165 Bret Boone	.25	.11	.03
□ 166 Hector Carrasco	.10	.05	.01
□ 167 Pete Schourek	.25	.11	.03
□ 168 Willie Greene	.10	.05	.01
□ 169 Kevin Mitchell	.25	.11	.03
□ 170 Deion Sanders	.50	.23	.06
□ 171 John Roper	.10	.05	.01
□ 172 Charlie Hayes	.10	.05	.01
□ 173 David Nied	.10	.05	.01
□ 174 Ellis Burks	.50	.23	.06
□ 175 Dante Bichette	.50	.23	.06
□ 176 Marvin Freeman	.10	.05	.01
□ 177 Eric Young	.25	.11	.03
□ 178 David Cone	.25	.11	.03
□ 179 Greg Gagne	.10	.05	.01
□ 180 Bob Hamelin	.10	.05	.01
□ 181 Wally Joyner	.25	.11	.03
□ 182 Jeff Montgomery	.25	.11	.03
□ 183 Jose Lind	.10	.05	.01
□ 184 Chris Gomez	.10	.05	.01
□ 185 Travis Fryman	.25	.11	.03
□ 186 Kirk Gibson	.25	.11	.03
□ 187 Mike Moore	.10	.05	.01
□ 188 Lou Whitaker	.50	.23	.06
□ 189 Sean Bergman	.10	.05	.01
□ 190 Shane Mack	.10	.05	.01
□ 191 Rick Aguilera	.10	.05	.01
□ 192 Denny Hocking	.10	.05	.01
□ 193 Chuck Knoblauch	.50	.23	.06
□ 194 Kevin Tapani	.10	.05	.01
□ 195 Kent Hrbek	.25	.11	.03
□ 196 Ozzie Guillen	.10	.05	.01
□ 197 Wilson Alvarez	.25	.11	.03
□ 198 Tim Raines	.50	.23	.06
□ 199 Scott Ruffcorn	.10	.05	.01
□ 200 Michael Jordan	4.00	1.80	.50
□ 201 Robin Ventura	.25	.11	.03
□ 202 Jason Bere	.10	.05	.01
□ 203 Darrin Jackson	.10	.05	.01
□ 204 Russ Davis	.10	.05	.01
□ 205 Jimmy Key	.25	.11	.03
□ 206 Jack McDowell	.25	.11	.03
□ 207 Jim Abbott	.10	.05	.01
□ 208 Paul O'Neill	.25	.11	.03
□ 209 Bernie Williams	.50	.23	.06
□ 210 Don Mattingly	1.50	.70	.19
□ 211 Orlando Miller	.10	.05	.01
□ 212 Alex Gonzalez	.10	.05	.01
□ 213 Terrell Wade	.25	.11	.03
□ 214 Jose Oliva	.10	.05	.01
□ 215 Alex Rodriguez	4.00	1.80	.50
□ 216 Garret Anderson	.50	.23	.06
□ 217 Alan Benes	.50	.23	.06
□ 218 Armando Benitez	.10	.05	.01
□ 219 Dustin Hermanson	.25	.11	.03
□ 220 Charles Johnson	.25	.11	.03
□ 221 Julian Tavarez	.10	.05	.01
□ 222 Jason Giambi	.60	.25	.07
□ 223 LaTroy Hawkins	.10	.05	.01
□ 224 Todd Hollandsworth	.50	.23	.06
□ 225 Derek Jeter	2.00	.90	.25
□ 226 Hideo Nomo	3.00	1.35	.35
□ 227 Tony Clark	.50	.23	.06
□ 228 Roger Cedeno	.25	.11	.03
□ 229 Scott Stahoviak	.10	.05	.01
□ 230 Michael Tucker	.25	.11	.03
□ 231 Joe Rosselli	.10	.05	.01
□ 232 Antonio Osuna	.10	.05	.01
□ 233 Bobby Higginson	.50	.23	.06
□ 234 Mark Grudzielanek	.75	.35	.09
□ 235 Ray Durham	.25	.11	.03
□ 236 Frank Rodriguez	.25	.11	.03
□ 237 Quilvio Veras	.10	.05	.01
□ 238 Darren Bragg	.25	.11	.03
□ 239 Ugueth Urbina	.10	.05	.01
□ 240 Jason Bates	.10	.05	.01
□ 241 David Bell	.10	.05	.01
□ 242 Ron Villone	.10	.05	.01
□ 243 Joe Randa	.10	.05	.01
□ 244 Carlos Perez	.25	.11	.03
□ 245 Brad Clontz	.10	.05	.01
□ 246 Steve Rodriguez	.10	.05	.01
□ 247 Joe Vitiello	.10	.05	.01
□ 248 Ozzie Timmons	.10	.05	.01
□ 249 Rudy Pemberton	.10	.05	.01
□ 250 Marty Cordova	.50	.23	.06
□ 251 Tony Graffanino	.10	.05	.01
□ 252 Mark Johnson	.25	.11	.03
□ 253 Tomas Perez	.25	.11	.03
□ 254 Jimmy Hurst	.25	.11	.03
□ 255 Edgardo Alfonzo	.25	.11	.03
□ 256 Jose Malave	.10	.05	.01
□ 257 Brad Radke	.25	.11	.03
□ 258 Jon Nunnally	.25	.11	.03
□ 259 Dilson Torres	.10	.05	.01
□ 260 Esteban Loaiza	.10	.05	.01
□ 261 Freddy Garcia	.25	.11	.03
□ 262 Don Wengert	.10	.05	.01
□ 263 Robert Person	.10	.05	.01
□ 264 Tim Unroe	.25	.11	.03
□ 265 Juan Acevedo	.10	.05	.01
□ 266 Eduardo Perez	.10	.05	.01
□ 267 Tony Phillips	.25	.11	.03
□ 268 Jim Edmonds	.50	.23	.06
□ 269 Jorge Fabregas	.10	.05	.01
□ 270 Tim Salmon	.50	.23	.06
□ 271 Mark Langston	.10	.05	.01
□ 272 J.T. Snow	.25	.11	.03
□ 273 Phil Plantier	.10	.05	.01
□ 274 Derek Bell	.25	.11	.03
□ 275 Jeff Bagwell	1.25	.55	.16
□ 276 Luis Gonzalez	.10	.05	.01
□ 277 John Hudek	.10	.05	.01
□ 278 Todd Stottlemyre	.10	.05	.01
□ 279 Mark Acre	.10	.05	.01
□ 280 Ruben Sierra	.25	.11	.03
□ 281 Mike Bordick	.10	.05	.01
□ 282 Ron Darling	.10	.05	.01
□ 283 Brent Gates	.10	.05	.01
□ 284 Todd Van Poppel	.10	.05	.01
□ 285 Paul Molitor	.60	.25	.07
□ 286 Ed Sprague	.25	.11	.03
□ 287 Juan Guzman	.25	.11	.03
□ 288 David Cone	.25	.11	.03
□ 289 Shawn Green	.25	.11	.03
□ 290 Marquis Grissom	.50	.23	.06
□ 291 Kent Mercker	.10	.05	.01
□ 292 Steve Avery	.25	.11	.03
□ 293 Chipper Jones	2.00	.90	.25
□ 294 John Smoltz	.50	.23	.06
□ 295 David Justice	.50	.23	.06
□ 296 Ryan Klesko	.60	.25	.07
□ 297 Joe Oliver	.10	.05	.01
□ 298 Ricky Bones	.10	.05	.01
□ 299 John Jaha	.25	.11	.03
□ 300 Greg Vaughn	.25	.11	.03
□ 301 Dave Nilsson	.25	.11	.03
□ 302 Kevin Seitzer	.10	.05	.01
□ 303 Bernard Gilkey	.25	.11	.03
□ 304 Allen Battle	.10	.05	.01
□ 305 Ray Lankford	.50	.23	.06
□ 306 Tom Pagnozzi	.10	.05	.01
□ 307 Allen Watson	.10	.05	.01
□ 308 Danny Jackson	.10	.05	.01
□ 309 Ken Hill	.10	.05	.01
□ 310 Todd Zeile	.10	.05	.01
□ 311 Kevin Roberson	.10	.05	.01
□ 312 Steve Buechele	.10	.05	.01
□ 313 Rick Wilkins	.10	.05	.01
□ 314 Kevin Foster	.10	.05	.01
□ 315 Sammy Sosa	.50	.23	.06
□ 316 Howard Johnson	.10	.05	.01
□ 317 Greg Hansell	.10	.05	.01
□ 318 Pedro Astacio	.10	.05	.01
□ 319 Rafael Bournigal	.10	.05	.01
□ 320 Mike Piazza	2.00	.90	.25
□ 321 Ramon Martinez	.25	.11	.03
□ 322 Raul Mondesi	.50	.23	.06
□ 323 Ismael Valdes	.25	.11	.03
□ 324 Wil Cordero	.10	.05	.01
□ 325 Tony Tarasco	.10	.05	.01
□ 326 Roberto Kelly	.10	.05	.01
□ 327 Jeff Fassero	.10	.05	.01
□ 328 Mike Lansing	.10	.05	.01
□ 329 Pedro J. Martinez	.25	.11	.03
□ 330 Kirk Rueter	.10	.05	.01
□ 331 Glenallen Hill	.10	.05	.01
□ 332 Kirt Manwaring	.10	.05	.01
□ 333 Royce Clayton	.10	.05	.01
□ 334 J.R. Phillips	.10	.05	.01
□ 335 Barry Bonds	.75	.35	.09
□ 336 Mark Portugal	.10	.05	.01

□ 337	Terry Mulholland	.10	.05	.01
□ 338	Omar Vizquel	.50	.23	.06
□ 339	Carlos Baerga	.50	.23	.06
□ 340	Albert Belle	1.50	.70	.19
□ 341	Eddie Murray	.75	.35	.09
□ 342	Wayne Kirby	.10	.05	.01
□ 343	Chad Ogea	.10	.05	.01
□ 344	Tim Davis	.10	.05	.01
□ 345	Jay Buhner	.50	.23	.06
□ 346	Bobby Ayala	.10	.05	.01
□ 347	Mike Blowers	.10	.05	.01
□ 348	Dave Fleming	.10	.05	.01
□ 349	Edgar Martinez	.50	.23	.06
□ 350	Andre Dawson	.50	.23	.06
□ 351	Darrell Whitmore	.10	.05	.01
□ 352	Chuck Carr	.10	.05	.01
□ 353	John Burkett	.25	.11	.03
□ 354	Chris Hammond	.10	.05	.01
□ 355	Gary Sheffield	.50	.23	.06
□ 356	Pat Rapp	.10	.05	.01
□ 357	Greg Colbrunn	.10	.05	.01
□ 358	David Segui	.10	.05	.01
□ 359	Jeff Kent	.10	.05	.01
□ 360	Bobby Bonilla	.25	.11	.03
□ 361	Pete Harnisch	.10	.05	.01
□ 362	Ryan Thompson	.10	.05	.01
□ 363	Jose Vizcaino	.10	.05	.01
□ 364	Brett Butler	.25	.11	.03
□ 365	Cal Ripken Jr.	2.50	1.10	.30
□ 366	Rafael Palmeiro	.50	.23	.06
□ 367	Leo Gomez	.10	.05	.01
□ 368	Andy Van Slyke	.25	.11	.03
□ 369	Arthur Rhodes	.10	.05	.01
□ 370	Ken Caminiti	.50	.23	.06
□ 371	Steve Finley	.25	.11	.03
□ 372	Melvin Nieves	.25	.11	.03
□ 373	Andujar Cedeno	.10	.05	.01
□ 374	Trevor Hoffman	.10	.05	.01
□ 375	Fernando Valenzuela	.25	.11	.03
□ 376	Ricky Bottalico	.25	.11	.03
□ 377	Dave Hollins	.10	.05	.01
□ 378	Charlie Hayes	.10	.05	.01
□ 379	Tommy Greene	.10	.05	.01
□ 380	Darren Daulton	.25	.11	.03
□ 381	Curt Schilling	.10	.05	.01
□ 382	Midre Cummings	.10	.05	.01
□ 383	Al Martin	.25	.11	.03
□ 384	Jeff King	.25	.11	.03
□ 385	Orlando Merced	.10	.05	.01
□ 386	Denny Neagle	.25	.11	.03
□ 387	Don Slaught	.10	.05	.01
□ 388	Dave Clark	.10	.05	.01
□ 389	Kevin Gross	.10	.05	.01
□ 390	Will Clark	.50	.23	.06
□ 391	Ivan Rodriguez	.60	.25	.07
□ 392	Benji Gil	.10	.05	.01
□ 393	Jeff Frye	.10	.05	.01
□ 394	Kenny Rogers	.10	.05	.01
□ 395	Juan Gonzalez	1.50	.70	.19
□ 396	Mike Macfarlane	.10	.05	.01
□ 397	Lee Tinsley	.10	.05	.01
□ 398	Tim Naehring	.10	.05	.01
□ 399	Tim Vanegmond	.10	.05	.01
□ 400	Mike Greenwell	.10	.05	.01
□ 401	Ken Ryan	.10	.05	.01
□ 402	John Smiley	.10	.05	.01
□ 403	Tim Pugh	.10	.05	.01
□ 404	Reggie Sanders	.25	.11	.03
□ 405	Barry Larkin	.50	.23	.06
□ 406	Hal Morris	.10	.05	.01
□ 407	Jose Rijo	.10	.05	.01
□ 408	Lance Painter	.10	.05	.01
□ 409	Joe Girardi	.10	.05	.01
□ 410	Andres Galarraga	.50	.23	.06
□ 411	Mike Kingery	.10	.05	.01
□ 412	Roberto Mejia	.10	.05	.01
□ 413	Walt Weiss	.10	.05	.01
□ 414	Bill Swift	.10	.05	.01
□ 415	Larry Walker	.50	.23	.06
□ 416	Billy Brewer	.10	.05	.01
□ 417	Pat Borders	.10	.05	.01
□ 418	Tom Gordon	.10	.05	.01
□ 419	Kevin Appier	.25	.11	.03
□ 420	Gary Gaetti	.25	.11	.03
□ 421	Greg Gohr	.10	.05	.01
□ 422	Felipe Lira	.10	.05	.01
□ 423	John Doherty	.10	.05	.01
□ 424	Chad Curtis	.10	.05	.01
□ 425	Cecil Fielder	.25	.11	.03
□ 426	Alan Trammell	.50	.23	.06
□ 427	David McCarty	.10	.05	.01
□ 428	Scott Erickson	.10	.05	.01
□ 429	Pat Mahomes	.10	.05	.01
□ 430	Kirby Puckett	1.00	.45	.12
□ 431	Dave Stevens	.10	.05	.01
□ 432	Pedro Munoz	.10	.05	.01
□ 433	Chris Sabo	.10	.05	.01
□ 434	Alex Fernandez	.25	.11	.03
□ 435	Frank Thomas	3.00	1.35	.35
□ 436	Roberto Hernandez	.10	.05	.01
□ 437	Lance Johnson	.25	.11	.03
□ 438	Jim Abbott	.10	.05	.01
□ 439	John Wetteland	.25	.11	.03
□ 440	Melido Perez	.10	.05	.01
□ 441	Tony Fernandez	.10	.05	.01
□ 442	Pat Kelly	.10	.05	.01
□ 443	Mike Stanley	.10	.05	.01
□ 444	Danny Tartabull	.10	.05	.01
□ 445	Wade Boggs	.50	.23	.06
□ 446	Robin Yount	.50	.23	.06
□ 447	Ryne Sandberg	.60	.25	.07
□ 448	Nolan Ryan	2.50	1.10	.30
□ 449	George Brett	1.00	.45	.12
□ 450	Mike Schmidt	.60	.25	.07
□ 451T	Jim Abbott TRADE	.50	.23	.06
□ 452T	Danny Tartabull TRADE	.50	.23	.06
□ 453T	Ariel Prieto TRADE	.25	.11	.03
□ 454T	Scott Cooper TRADE	.10	.05	.01
□ 455T	Tom Henke TRADE	.25	.11	.03
□ 456T	Todd Zeile TRADE	.25	.11	.03
□ 457T	Brian McRae TRADE	.25	.11	.03
□ 458T	Luis Gonzalez TRADE	.25	.11	.03
□ 459T	Julio Navarro TRADE	.10	.05	.01
□ 460T	Todd Worrell TRADE	.25	.11	.03
□ 461T	Roberto Kelly TRADE	.10	.05	.01
□ 462T	Chad Fonville TRADE	.25	.11	.03
□ 463T	Shane Andrews TRADE	.25	.11	.03
□ 464T	David Segui TRADE	.25	.11	.03
□ 465T	Deion Sanders TRADE	.50	.23	.06
□ 466T	Orel Hershiser TRADE	.25	.11	.03
□ 467T	Ken Hill TRADE	.25	.11	.03
□ 468T	Andy Benes TRADE	.10	.05	.01
□ 469T	Terry Pendleton TRADE	.25	.11	.03
□ 470T	Bobby Bonilla TRADE	.50	.23	.06
□ 471T	Scott Erickson TRADE	.10	.05	.01
□ 472T	Kevin Brown TRADE	.25	.11	.03
□ 473T	Glenn Dishman TRADE	.25	.11	.03
□ 474T	Phil Plantier TRADE	.10	.05	.01
□ 475T	Gregg Jefferies TRADE	.50	.23	.06
□ 476T	Tyler Green TRADE	.10	.05	.01
□ 477T	Heathcliff Slocumb TRADE	.20	.09	.03
□ 478T	Mark Whiten TRADE	.25	.11	.03
□ 479T	Mickey Tettleton TRADE	.25	.11	.03
□ 480T	Tim Wakefield TRADE	.25	.11	.03
□ 481T	Vaughn Eshelman TRADE	.10	.05	.01
□ 482T	Rick Aguilera TRADE	.25	.11	.03
□ 483T	Erik Hanson TRADE	.10	.05	.01
□ 484T	Willie McGee TRADE	.25	.11	.03
□ 485T	Troy O'Leary TRADE	.25	.11	.03
□ 486T	Benito Santiago TRADE	.20	.09	.03
□ 487T	Darren Lewis TRADE	.10	.05	.01
□ 488T	Dave Burba TRADE	.10	.05	.01
□ 489T	Ron Gant TRADE	.50	.23	.06
□ 490T	Bret Saberhagen TRADE	.25	.11	.03
□ 491T	Vinny Castilla TRADE	.50	.23	.06
□ 492T	Frank Rodriguez TRADE	.25	.11	.03
□ 493T	Andy Pettitte TRADE	4.00	1.80	.50
□ 494T	Ruben Sierra TRADE	.25	.11	.03
□ 495T	David Cone TRADE	.50	.23	.06
□ J159	R. Clemens Jumbo AU	20.00	9.00	2.50
□ J215	A. Rodriguez Jumbo AU	75.00	34.00	9.50
□ TC1	Orel Hershiser	1.00	.45	.12
□ TC2	Terry Pendleton	1.00	.45	.12
□ TC3	Benito Santiago	1.00	.45	.12
□ TC4	Kevin Brown	1.00	.45	.12
□ TC5	Gregg Jefferies	1.00	.45	.12
□ NNO	Expired AU Trade	.10	.05	.01
□ NNO	R. Clemens AU Trade	30.00	13.50	3.70
□ NNO	R. Jackson AU Trade	30.00	13.50	3.70
□ NNO	W. Mays AU Trade	75.00	34.00	9.50
□ NNO	R. Mondesi AU Trade	40.00	18.00	5.00
□ NNO	F. Robinson AU Trade	40.00	18.00	5.00

1995 Upper Deck Electric Diamond Gold

This 450-card parallel standard-size set was randomly inserted in retail and mini-jumbo packs. These cards are identical to the Electric Diamond series except for the special gold foil treatment.

	MINT	NRMT	EXC
COMPLETE SET (450)	1500.00	700.00	190.00
COMPLETE SERIES 1 (225)	700.00	325.00	90.00
COMPLETE SERIES 2 (225)	800.00	350.00	100.00
COMMON CARD (1-450)	4.00	1.80	.50
SEMISTARS	8.00	3.60	1.00
STARS	12.00	5.50	1.50
*VETERAN STARS: 25X TO 40X BASIC CARDS			
*YOUNG STARS: 15X TO 25X BASIC CARDS			
INSERTS IN RETAIL AND MINI JUMBO PACKS			
□ 1 Ruben Rivera	40.00	18.00	5.00
□ 9 Karim Garcia	50.00	22.00	6.25
□ 10 Nomar Garciaparra	40.00	18.00	5.00
□ 40 Roberto Alomar	30.00	13.50	3.70
□ 49 Greg Maddux	75.00	34.00	9.50
□ 90 Kenny Lofton	30.00	13.50	3.70
□ 97 Manny Ramirez	30.00	13.50	3.70
□ 100 Ken Griffey Jr.	125.00	55.00	15.50
□ 101 Greg Maddux ANA	40.00	18.00	5.00
□ 105 Frank Thomas ANA	60.00	27.00	7.50
□ 110 Ken Griffey Jr. ANA	60.00	27.00	7.50
□ 135 Tony Gwynn	50.00	22.00	6.25
□ 200 Michael Jordan	125.00	55.00	15.50
□ 210 Don Mattingly	60.00	27.00	7.50
□ 215 Alex Rodriguez	125.00	55.00	15.50
□ 225 Derek Jeter	75.00	34.00	9.50
□ 226 Hideo Nomo	60.00	27.00	7.50
□ 275 Jeff Bagwell	50.00	22.00	6.25
□ 293 Chipper Jones	75.00	34.00	9.50
□ 320 Mike Piazza	75.00	34.00	9.50
□ 340 Albert Belle	60.00	27.00	7.50
□ 365 Cal Ripken	100.00	45.00	12.50
□ 395 Juan Gonzalez	60.00	27.00	7.50
□ 435 Frank Thomas	125.00	55.00	15.50
□ 448 Nolan Ryan TRIB	100.00	45.00	12.50
□ 449 George Brett TRIB	40.00	18.00	5.00

1995 Upper Deck Checklists

Each of these 10 cards features a star player(s) on the front and a checklist on the back. The cards were randomly inserted in hobby and retail packs at a rate of one in 17. The horizontal fronts feature a player photo along with a sentence about the 1994 highlight. The cards are numbered as "X" of 5 in the upper left.

	MINT	NRMT	EXC
COMPLETE SET (5)	25.00	11.00	3.10
COMPLETE SERIES 1 (5)	10.00	4.50	1.25
COMPLETE SERIES 2 (5)	15.00	6.75	1.85
COMMON CARD (1A-5A)	.75	.35	.09
COMMON CARD (1B-5B)	.75	.35	.09
SEMISTARS	1.25	.55	.16
RANDOM INSERTS IN PACKS			
□ 1A Montreal Expos	.75	.35	.09
□ 2A Fred McGriff	1.25	.55	.16
□ 3A John Valentin	.75	.35	.09
□ 4A Kenny Rogers	.75	.35	.09
□ 5A Greg Maddux	6.00	2.70	.75
□ 1B Cecil Fielder	1.25	.55	.16
□ 2B Tony Gwynn	4.00	1.80	.50
□ 3B Greg Maddux	6.00	2.70	.75
□ 4B Randy Johnson	1.25	.55	.16
□ 5B Mike Schmidt	2.50	1.10	.30

1995 Upper Deck Predictor Award Winners

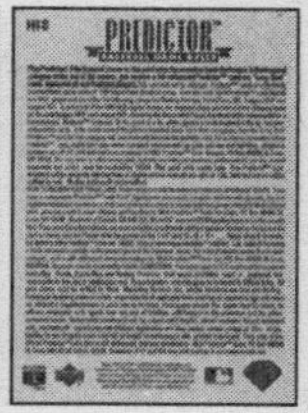

This set was inserted in hobby packs at a rate of approximately one in 30. This 40-card standard-size set features nine players and a Long Shot in each league for each of two categories -- MVP and Rookie of the Year. If the player pictured on the card won his category, the card was redeemable for a special foil version of all 20 Hobby Predictor cards. Fronts are full-color player action photos. Backs include the rules of the contest. These cards were redeemable until December 31, 1995. The cards are numbered in the upper left with an "H" prefix.

	MINT	NRMT	EXC
COMPLETE SET (40)	125.00	55.00	15.50
COMPLETE SERIES 1 (20)	60.00	27.00	7.50
COMPLETE SERIES 2 (20)	65.00	29.00	8.00
COMMON PREDICTOR	1.00	.45	.12
SEMISTARS	2.00	.90	.25
RANDOM INSERTS IN HOBBY PACKS			
□ H1 Albert Belle	8.00	3.60	1.00
□ H2 Juan Gonzalez	8.00	3.60	1.00
□ H3 Ken Griffey Jr.	15.00	6.75	1.85
□ H4 Kirby Puckett	5.00	2.20	.60
□ H5 Frank Thomas	15.00	6.75	1.85
□ H6 Jeff Bagwell	6.00	2.70	.75
□ H7 Barry Bonds	4.00	1.80	.50
□ H8 Mike Piazza	10.00	4.50	1.25
□ H9 Matt Williams	2.00	.90	.25
□ H10 MVP Wild Card	1.00	.45	.12
□ H11 Armando Benitez	1.00	.45	.12
□ H12 Alex Gonzalez	1.00	.45	.12
□ H13 Shawn Green	1.00	.45	.12
□ H14 Derek Jeter	10.00	4.50	1.25
□ H15 Alex Rodriguez	15.00	6.75	1.85
□ H16 Alan Benes	2.00	.90	.25
□ H17 Brian L.Hunter	2.00	.90	.25
□ H18 Charles Johnson	2.00	.90	.25
□ H19 Jose Oliva	1.00	.45	.12
□ H20 ROY Wild Card	1.00	.45	.12
□ H21 Cal Ripken Jr.	12.00	5.50	1.50
□ H22 Don Mattingly	8.00	3.60	1.00
□ H23 Roberto Alomar	4.00	1.80	.50
□ H24 Kenny Lofton	4.00	1.80	.50
□ H25 Will Clark	2.00	.90	.25
□ H26 Mark McGwire	5.00	2.20	.60
□ H27 Greg Maddux	10.00	4.50	1.25
□ H28 Fred McGriff	2.00	.90	.25
□ H29 Andres Galarraga	2.00	.90	.25
□ H30 Jose Canseco	2.00	.90	.25
□ H31 Ray Durham	2.00	.90	.25
□ H32 Mark Grudzielanek	2.00	.90	.25

□ H33 Scott Ruffcorn	1.00	.45	.12
□ H34 Michael Tucker	2.00	.90	.25
□ H35 Garret Anderson	2.00	.90	.25
□ H36 Darren Bragg	1.00	.45	.12
□ H37 Quilvio Veras	1.00	.45	.12
□ H38 Hideo Nomo	8.00	3.60	1.00
□ H39 Chipper Jones	10.00	4.50	1.25
□ H40 Marty Cordova	2.00	.90	.25

1995 Upper Deck Predictor League Leaders

This 60-card standard-size insert set was available only in retail packs. The set included nine players and a Long Shot in each league for each of three categories -- Batting Average Leader, Home Run Leader and Runs Batted In Leader. If the player pictured on the card won his category, the card was redeemable for a special foil version of all 30 Retail Predictor cards. These cards were redeemable until December 31, 1995. Card fronts are full-color action photos of the player emerging from a marble diamond. Backs list the rules of the game. The cards are numbered in the upper left with an "R" prefix.

	MINT	NRMT	EXC
COMPLETE SET (60)	175.00	80.00	22.00
COMPLETE SERIES 1 (30)	100.00	45.00	12.50
COMPLETE SERIES 2 (30)	75.00	34.00	9.50
COMMON PREDICTOR	1.00	.45	.12
SEMISTARS	2.00	.90	.25
RANDOM INSERTS IN RETAIL PACKS			

□ R1 Albert Belle	8.00	3.60	1.00
□ R2 Jose Canseco	2.00	.90	.25
□ R3 Matt Williams	8.00	3.60	1.00
□ R4 Ken Griffey Jr.	15.00	6.75	1.85
□ R5 Frank Thomas	15.00	6.75	1.85
□ R6 Jeff Bagwell	6.00	2.70	.75
□ R7 Barry Bonds	4.00	1.80	.50
□ R8 Fred McGriff	2.00	.90	.25
□ R9 Matt Williams	2.00	.90	.25
□ R10 Home Run Wild Card	1.00	.45	.12
□ R11 Albert Belle	8.00	3.60	1.00
□ R12 Joe Carter	2.00	.90	.25
□ R13 Cecil Fielder	2.00	.90	.25
□ R14 Kirby Puckett	5.00	2.20	.60
□ R15 Frank Thomas	15.00	6.75	1.85
□ R16 Jeff Bagwell	6.00	2.70	.75
□ R17 Barry Bonds	4.00	1.80	.50
□ R18 Mike Piazza	10.00	4.50	1.25
□ R19 Matt Williams	2.00	.90	.25
□ R20 RBI Wild Card	1.00	.45	.12
□ R21 Wade Boggs	2.00	.90	.25
□ R22 Kenny Lofton	4.00	1.80	.50
□ R23 Paul Molitor	2.00	.90	.25
□ R24 Paul O'Neill	2.00	.90	.25
□ R25 Frank Thomas	15.00	6.75	1.85
□ R26 Jeff Bagwell	6.00	2.70	.75
□ R27 Tony Gwynn	6.00	2.70	.75
□ R28 Gregg Jefferies	2.00	.90	.25
□ R29 Hal Morris	1.00	.45	.12
□ R30 Batting Wild Card	1.00	.45	.12
□ R31 Joe Carter	2.00	.90	.25
□ R32 Cecil Fielder	2.00	.90	.25
□ R33 Rafael Palmeiro	2.00	.90	.25
□ R34 Larry Walker	2.00	.90	.25
□ R35 Manny Ramirez	4.00	1.80	.50
□ R36 Tim Salmon	2.00	.90	.25
□ R37 Mike Piazza	10.00	4.50	1.25
□ R38 Andres Galarraga	2.00	.90	.25
□ R39 David Justice	1.00	.45	.12
□ R40 Gary Sheffield	2.00	.90	.25
□ R41 Juan Gonzalez	8.00	3.60	1.00
□ R42 Jose Canseco	2.00	.90	.25
□ R43 Will Clark	2.00	.90	.25
□ R44 Rafael Palmeiro	2.00	.90	.25
□ R45 Ken Griffey Jr.	15.00	6.75	1.85
□ R46 Ruben Sierra	1.00	.45	.12
□ R47 Larry Walker	2.00	.90	.25
□ R48 Fred McGriff	2.00	.90	.25
□ R49 Dante Bichette	2.00	.90	.25
□ R50 Darren Daulton	1.00	.45	.12
□ R51 Will Clark	2.00	.90	.25
□ R52 Ken Griffey Jr.	15.00	6.75	1.85
□ R53 Don Mattingly	8.00	3.60	1.00
□ R54 John Olerud	1.00	.45	.12
□ R55 Kirby Puckett	5.00	2.20	.60
□ R56 Raul Mondesi	2.00	.90	.25
□ R57 Moises Alou	1.00	.45	.12
□ R58 Bret Boone	1.00	.45	.12
□ R59 Albert Belle	8.00	3.60	1.00
□ R60 Mike Piazza	10.00	4.50	1.25

1995 Upper Deck Special Edition

Inserted at a rate of one per pack, this 270 standard-size card set features full color action shots of players on a silver foil background. The back highlights the player's previous perfor mance, including 1994 and career statistics. Another player photo is also featured on the back.

	MINT	NRMT	EXC
COMPLETE SET (270)	200.00	90.00	25.00
COMPLETE SERIES 1 (135)	90.00	40.00	11.00
COMPLETE SERIES 2 (135)	110.00	50.00	14.00
COMMON CARD (1-270)	.25	.11	.03
SEMISTARS	.50	.23	.06
STARS	1.25	.55	.16
ONE PER HOBBY PACK			

□ 1 Cliff Floyd	1.25	.55	.16
□ 2 Wil Cordero	.50	.23	.06
□ 3 Pedro J. Martinez	1.25	.55	.16
□ 4 Larry Walker	1.25	.55	.16
□ 5 Derek Jeter	6.00	2.70	.75
□ 6 Mike Stanley	.50	.23	.06
□ 7 Melido Perez	.25	.11	.03
□ 8 Jim Leyritz	.25	.11	.03
□ 9 Danny Tartabull	.50	.23	.06
□ 10 Wade Boggs	1.25	.55	.16
□ 11 Ryan Klesko	2.00	.90	.25
□ 12 Steve Avery	.50	.23	.06
□ 13 Damon Hollins	1.25	.55	.16
□ 14 Chipper Jones	6.00	2.70	.75
□ 15 David Justice	1.25	.55	.16
□ 16 Glenn Williams	.50	.23	.06

□ 17 Jose Oliva	.25	.11	.03
□ 18 Terrell Wade	1.25	.55	.16
□ 19 Alex Fernandez	1.25	.55	.16
□ 20 Frank Thomas	10.00	4.50	1.25
□ 21 Ozzie Guillen	.50	.23	.06
□ 22 Roberto Hernandez	.50	.23	.06
□ 23 Albie Lopez	.25	.11	.03
□ 24 Eddie Murray	2.50	1.10	.30
□ 25 Albert Belle	5.00	2.20	.60
□ 26 Omar Vizquel	.50	.23	.06
□ 27 Carlos Baerga	1.25	.55	.16
□ 28 Jose Rijo	.25	.11	.03
□ 29 Hal Morris	.25	.11	.03
□ 30 Reggie Sanders	1.25	.55	.16
□ 31 Jack Morris	1.25	.55	.16
□ 32 Raul Mondesi	1.25	.55	.16
□ 33 Karim Garcia	8.00	3.60	1.00
□ 34 Todd Hollandsworth	1.25	.55	.16
□ 35 Mike Piazza	6.00	2.70	.75
□ 36 Chan Ho Park	1.25	.55	.16
□ 37 Ramon Martinez	1.25	.55	.16
□ 38 Kenny Rogers	.25	.11	.03
□ 39 Will Clark	1.25	.55	.16
□ 40 Juan Gonzalez	5.00	2.20	.60
□ 41 Ivan Rodriguez	2.00	.90	.25
□ 42 Orlando Miller	.50	.23	.06
□ 43 John Hudek	.25	.11	.03
□ 44 Luis Gonzalez	.50	.23	.06
□ 45 Jeff Bagwell	4.00	1.80	.50
□ 46 Cal Ripken	8.00	3.60	1.00
□ 47 Mike Oquist	.25	.11	.03
□ 48 Armando Benitez	.25	.11	.03
□ 49 Ben McDonald	.50	.23	.06
□ 50 Rafael Palmeiro	1.25	.55	.16
□ 51 Curtis Goodwin	.25	.11	.03
□ 52 Vince Coleman	.50	.23	.06
□ 53 Tom Gordon	.25	.11	.03
□ 54 Mike Macfarlane	.25	.11	.03
□ 55 Brian McRae	.50	.23	.06
□ 56 Matt Smith	.25	.11	.03
□ 57 David Segui	.50	.23	.06
□ 58 Paul Wilson	2.00	.90	.25
□ 59 Bill Pulsipher	.50	.23	.06
□ 60 Bobby Bonilla	1.25	.55	.16
□ 61 Jeff Kent	.50	.23	.06
□ 62 Ryan Thompson	.25	.11	.03
□ 63 Jason Isringhausen	2.00	.90	.25
□ 64 Ed Sprague	.50	.23	.06
□ 65 Paul Molitor	2.00	.90	.25
□ 66 Juan Guzman	.50	.23	.06
□ 67 Alex Gonzalez	.50	.23	.06
□ 68 Shawn Green	.50	.23	.06
□ 69 Mark Portugal	.25	.11	.03
□ 70 Barry Bonds	2.50	1.10	.30
□ 71 Robby Thompson	.25	.11	.03
□ 72 Royce Clayton	.50	.23	.06
□ 73 Ricky Bottalico	.50	.23	.06
□ 74 Doug Jones	.25	.11	.03
□ 75 Darren Daulton	.50	.23	.06
□ 76 Gregg Jefferies	1.25	.55	.16
□ 77 Scott Cooper	.25	.11	.03
□ 78 Nomar Garciaparra	4.00	1.80	.50
□ 79 Ken Ryan	.25	.11	.03
□ 80 Mike Greenwell	.50	.23	.06
□ 81 LaTroy Hawkins	.25	.11	.03
□ 82 Rich Becker	.50	.23	.06
□ 83 Scott Erickson	.50	.23	.06
□ 84 Pedro Munoz	.50	.23	.06
□ 85 Kirby Puckett	3.00	1.35	.35
□ 86 Orlando Merced	.50	.23	.06
□ 87 Jeff King	.50	.23	.06
□ 88 Midre Cummings	.25	.11	.03
□ 89 Bernard Gilkey	1.25	.55	.16
□ 90 Ray Lankford	1.25	.55	.16
□ 91 Todd Zeile	.50	.23	.06
□ 92 Alan Benes	1.25	.55	.16
□ 93 Bret Wagner	.25	.11	.03
□ 94 Rene Arocha	.25	.11	.03
□ 95 Cecil Fielder	1.25	.55	.16
□ 96 Alan Trammell	1.25	.55	.16
□ 97 Tony Phillips	.50	.23	.06
□ 98 Junior Felix	.25	.11	.03
□ 99 Brian Harper	.25	.11	.03
□ 100 Greg Vaughn	1.25	.55	.16
□ 101 Ricky Bones	.25	.11	.03
□ 102 Walt Weiss	.25	.11	.03
□ 103 Lance Painter	.25	.11	.03
□ 104 Roberto Mejia	.25	.11	.03
□ 105 Andres Galarraga	1.25	.55	.16
□ 106 Todd Van Poppel	.25	.11	.03
□ 107 Ben Grieve	3.00	1.35	.35
□ 108 Brent Gates	.25	.11	.03
□ 109 Jason Giambi	2.00	.90	.25
□ 110 Ruben Sierra	.50	.23	.06
□ 111 Terry Steinbach	.50	.23	.06
□ 112 Chris Hammond	.25	.11	.03
□ 113 Charles Johnson	1.25	.55	.16
□ 114 Jesus Tavarez	.25	.11	.03
□ 115 Gary Sheffield	1.50	.70	.19
□ 116 Chuck Carr	.25	.11	.03
□ 117 Bobby Ayala	.25	.11	.03
□ 118 Randy Johnson	1.50	.70	.19
□ 119 Edgar Martinez	1.25	.55	.16
□ 120 Alex Rodriguez	10.00	4.50	1.25
□ 121 Kevin Foster	.25	.11	.03
□ 122 Kevin Roberson	.25	.11	.03
□ 123 Sammy Sosa	1.50	.70	.19
□ 124 Steve Trachsel	.25	.11	.03
□ 125 Eduardo Perez	.25	.11	.03
□ 126 Tim Salmon	1.25	.55	.16
□ 127 Todd Greene	1.25	.55	.16
□ 128 Jorge Fabregas	.25	.11	.03
□ 129 Mark Langston	.50	.23	.06
□ 130 Mitch Williams	.50	.23	.06
□ 131 Raul Casanova	1.50	.70	.19
□ 132 Mel Nieves	.50	.23	.06
□ 133 Andy Benes	.50	.23	.06
□ 134 Dustin Hermanson	.25	.11	.03
□ 135 Trevor Hoffman	.50	.23	.06
□ 136 Mark Grudzielanek	2.00	.90	.25
□ 137 Ugueth Urbina	.50	.23	.06
□ 138 Moises Alou	.50	.23	.06
□ 139 Roberto Kelly	.25	.11	.03
□ 140 Rondell White	1.25	.55	.16
□ 141 Paul O'Neill	.50	.23	.06
□ 142 Jimmy Key	.50	.23	.06
□ 143 Jack McDowell	1.25	.55	.16
□ 144 Ruben Rivera	4.00	1.80	.50
□ 145 Don Mattingly	5.00	2.20	.60
□ 146 John Wetteland	.50	.23	.06
□ 147 Tom Glavine	1.25	.55	.16
□ 148 Marquis Grissom	1.25	.55	.16
□ 149 Javier Lopez	1.25	.55	.16
□ 150 Fred McGriff	1.25	.55	.16
□ 151 Greg Maddux	6.00	2.70	.75
□ 152 Chris Sabo	.25	.11	.03
□ 153 Ray Durham	1.25	.55	.16
□ 154 Robin Ventura	1.25	.55	.16
□ 155 Jim Abbott	1.25	.55	.16
□ 156 Jimmy Hurst	.25	.11	.03
□ 157 Tim Raines	1.25	.55	.16
□ 158 Dennis Martinez	.50	.23	.06
□ 159 Kenny Lofton	2.50	1.10	.30
□ 160 Dave Winfield	1.25	.55	.16
□ 161 Manny Ramirez	2.50	1.10	.30
□ 162 Jim Thome	2.00	.90	.25
□ 163 Barry Larkin	1.25	.55	.16
□ 164 Bret Boone	.50	.23	.06
□ 165 Deion Sanders	1.25	.55	.16
□ 166 Ron Gant	1.25	.55	.16
□ 167 Benito Santiago	.50	.23	.06
□ 168 Hideo Nomo	8.00	3.60	1.00
□ 169 Billy Ashley	.25	.11	.03
□ 170 Roger Cedeno	.50	.23	.06
□ 171 Ismael Valdes	.50	.23	.06
□ 172 Eric Karros	1.25	.55	.16
□ 173 Rusty Greer	1.25	.55	.16
□ 174 Rick Helling	.25	.11	.03
□ 175 Nolan Ryan	8.00	3.60	1.00
□ 176 Dean Palmer	1.25	.55	.16
□ 177 Phil Plantier	.25	.11	.03
□ 178 Darryl Kile	.25	.11	.03
□ 179 Derek Bell	1.25	.55	.16
□ 180 Doug Drabek	.50	.23	.06
□ 181 Craig Biggio	1.25	.55	.16
□ 182 Kevin Brown	.50	.23	.06
□ 183 Harold Baines	.50	.23	.06
□ 184 Jeffrey Hammonds	.50	.23	.06
□ 185 Chris Hoiles	.50	.23	.06
□ 186 Mike Mussina	2.00	.90	.25
□ 187 Bob Hamelin	.25	.11	.03
□ 188 Jeff Montgomery	.50	.23	.06

□ 189 Michael Tucker	1.25	.55	.16
□ 190 George Brett	4.00	1.80	.50
□ 191 Edgardo Alfonzo	.50	.23	.06
□ 192 Brett Butler	.50	.23	.06
□ 193 Bobby Jones	.50	.23	.06
□ 194 Todd Hundley	1.25	.55	.16
□ 195 Bret Saberhagen	.50	.23	.06
□ 196 Pat Hentgen	1.25	.55	.16
□ 197 Roberto Alomar	2.50	1.10	.30
□ 198 David Cone	1.25	.55	.16
□ 199 Carlos Delgado	1.25	.55	.16
□ 200 Joe Carter	1.25	.55	.16
□ 201 Wm. VanLandingham	.25	.11	.03
□ 202 Rod Beck	.50	.23	.06
□ 203 J.R. Phillips	.25	.11	.03
□ 204 Darren Lewis	.25	.11	.03
□ 205 Matt Williams	1.25	.55	.16
□ 206 Lenny Dykstra	.50	.23	.06
□ 207 Dave Hollins	.25	.11	.03
□ 208 Mike Schmidt	2.50	1.10	.30
□ 209 Charlie Hayes	.50	.23	.06
□ 210 Mo Vaughn	2.50	1.10	.30
□ 211 Jose Malave	.25	.11	.03
□ 212 Roger Clemens	1.25	.55	.16
□ 213 Jose Canseco	1.25	.55	.16
□ 214 Mark Whiten	.50	.23	.06
□ 215 Marty Cordova	1.25	.55	.16
□ 216 Rick Aguilera	.50	.23	.06
□ 217 Kevin Tapani	.50	.23	.06
□ 218 Chuck Knoblauch	1.25	.55	.16
□ 219 Al Martin	.50	.23	.06
□ 220 Jay Bell	.50	.23	.06
□ 221 Carlos Garcia	.50	.23	.06
□ 222 Freddy Garcia	.50	.23	.06
□ 223 Jon Lieber	.25	.11	.03
□ 224 Danny Jackson	.25	.11	.03
□ 225 Ozzie Smith	2.00	.90	.25
□ 226 Brian Jordan	1.25	.55	.16
□ 227 Ken Hill	.25	.11	.03
□ 228 Scott Cooper	.25	.11	.03
□ 229 Chad Curtis	.50	.23	.06
□ 230 Lou Whitaker	1.25	.55	.16
□ 231 Kirk Gibson	1.25	.55	.16
□ 232 Travis Fryman	1.25	.55	.16
□ 233 Jose Valentin	.50	.23	.06
□ 234 Dave Nilsson	.50	.23	.06
□ 235 Cal Eldred	.25	.11	.03
□ 236 Matt Mieske	.50	.23	.06
□ 237 Bill Swift	.25	.11	.03
□ 238 Marvin Freeman	.25	.11	.03
□ 239 Jason Bates	.25	.11	.03
□ 240 Larry Walker	1.25	.55	.16
□ 241 Dave Nied	.25	.11	.03
□ 242 Dante Bichette	1.25	.55	.16
□ 243 Dennis Eckersley	1.25	.55	.16
□ 244 Todd Stottlemyre	.50	.23	.06
□ 245 Rickey Henderson	1.25	.55	.16
□ 246 Geronimo Berroa	.50	.23	.06
□ 247 Mark McGwire	3.00	1.35	.35
□ 248 Quilvio Veras	.25	.11	.03
□ 249 Terry Pendleton	.50	.23	.06
□ 250 Andre Dawson	1.25	.55	.16
□ 251 Jeff Conine	1.25	.55	.16
□ 252 Kurt Abbott	.25	.11	.03
□ 253 Jay Buhner	1.25	.55	.16
□ 254 Darren Bragg	.25	.11	.03
□ 255 Ken Griffey Jr.	10.00	4.50	1.25
□ 256 Tino Martinez	1.25	.55	.16
□ 257 Mark Grace	1.25	.55	.16
□ 258 Ryne Sandberg	2.50	1.10	.30
□ 259 Randy Myers	.50	.23	.06
□ 260 Howard Johnson	.50	.23	.06
□ 261 Lee Smith	1.25	.55	.16
□ 262 J.T. Snow	.25	.11	.03
□ 263 Chili Davis	.50	.23	.06
□ 264 Chuck Finley	.50	.23	.06
□ 265 Eddie Williams	.25	.11	.03
□ 266 Joey Hamilton	.50	.23	.06
□ 267 Ken Caminiti	1.25	.55	.16
□ 268 Andujar Cedeno	.25	.11	.03
□ 269 Steve Finley	1.25	.55	.16
□ 270 Tony Gwynn	4.00	1.80	.50

1995 Upper Deck Special Edition Gold

The Gold set parallels the basic Special Edition set and features the player in a full color photo on gold foil paper. Backs include the player's close-up photo and outstanding achievements. Season and career statistics are featured at the bottom of the cards.

	MINT	NRMT	EXC
COMPLETE SET (270)	2600.00	1150.00	325.00
COMPLETE SERIES 1 (135)	1200.00	550.00	150.00
COMPLETE SERIES 2 (135)	1400.00	650.00	180.00
COMMON CARD (1-270)	4.00	1.80	.50
SEMISTARS	8.00	3.60	1.00
STARS	12.00	5.50	1.50
*VETERAN STARS: 8X TO 12X BASIC CARDS			
*YOUNG STARS: 4X TO 8X BASIC CARDS			
RANDOM INSERTS IN HOBBY PACKS			

□ 5 Derek Jeter	75.00	34.00	9.50
□ 14 Chipper Jones	75.00	34.00	9.50
□ 20 Frank Thomas	125.00	55.00	15.50
□ 25 Albert Belle	60.00	27.00	7.50
□ 33 Karim Garcia	50.00	22.00	6.25
□ 35 Mike Piazza	75.00	34.00	9.50
□ 40 Juan Gonzalez	60.00	27.00	7.50
□ 45 Jeff Bagwell	50.00	22.00	6.25
□ 46 Cal Ripken	100.00	45.00	12.50
□ 78 Nomar Garciaparra	40.00	18.00	5.00
□ 120 Alex Rodriguez	125.00	55.00	15.50
□ 144 Ruben Rivera	40.00	18.00	5.00
□ 145 Don Mattingly	60.00	27.00	7.50
□ 151 Greg Maddux	75.00	34.00	9.50
□ 159 Kenny Lofton	30.00	13.50	3.70
□ 161 Manny Ramirez	30.00	13.50	3.70
□ 168 Hideo Nomo	60.00	27.00	7.50
□ 175 Nolan Ryan TRIB	100.00	45.00	12.50
□ 190 George Brett TRIB	40.00	18.00	5.00
□ 197 Roberto Alomar	30.00	13.50	3.70
□ 255 Ken Griffey Jr.	125.00	55.00	15.50
□ 270 Tony Gwynn	50.00	22.00	6.25

1995 Upper Deck Steal of a Deal

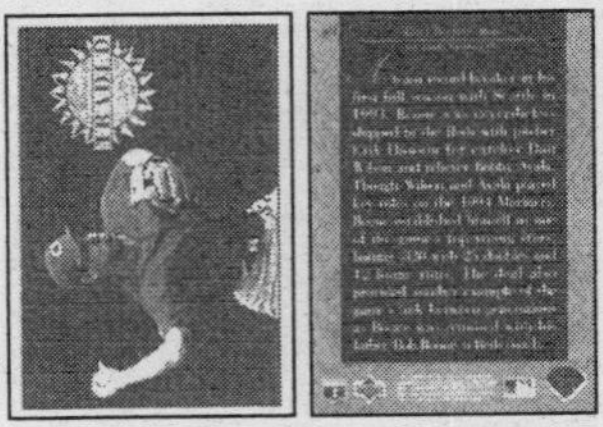

This set was inserted in hobby and retail packs at a rate of approximately one in 34. This 15-card standard-size set focuses on players who were acquired through, according to Upper Deck, "astute trades" or low round draft picks. The horizontal fronts feature a player cutout on a green background with a bronze seal. Backs feature information of how the player was acquired and past performance. The cards are numbered in the upper left with an "SD" prefix.

	MINT	NRMT	EXC
COMPLETE SET (15)	100.00	45.00	12.50
COMMON CARD (SD1-SD15)	2.00	.90	.25
SEMISTARS	4.00	1.80	.50
RANDOM INSERTS IN PACKS			

		MINT	NRMT	EXC
□ SD1	Mike Piazza	20.00	9.00	2.50
□ SD2	Fred McGriff	4.00	1.80	.50
□ SD3	Kenny Lofton	8.00	3.60	1.00
□ SD4	Jose Oliva	2.00	.90	.25
□ SD5	Jeff Bagwell	12.00	5.50	1.50
□ SD6	Roberto Alomar Joe Carter	8.00	3.60	1.00
□ SD7	Steve Karsay	2.00	.90	.25
□ SD8	Ozzie Smith	6.00	2.70	.75
□ SD9	Dennis Eckersley	4.00	1.80	.50
□ SD10	Jose Canseco	4.00	1.80	.50
□ SD11	Carlos Baerga	4.00	1.80	.50
□ SD12	Cecil Fielder	4.00	1.80	.50
□ SD13	Don Mattingly	15.00	6.75	1.85
□ SD14	Bret Boone	2.00	.90	.25
□ SD15	Michael Jordan	30.00	13.50	3.70

1996 Upper Deck

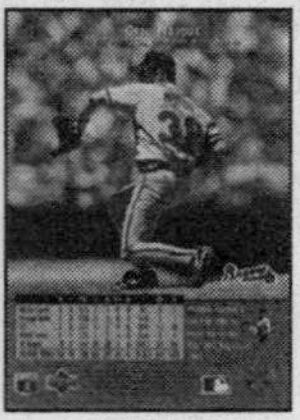

The 1996 Upper Deck set was issued in two series of 240 cards, and a 30 card update set, for a total of 510 cards. The cards were distributed in 10-card packs with a suggested retail price of $1.99, and 28 packs were contained in each box.

	MINT	NRMT	EXC
COMP.FACT.SET (510)	80.00	36.00	10.00
COMPLETE SET (480)	65.00	29.00	8.00
COMPLETE SERIES 1 (240)	35.00	16.00	4.40
COMPLETE SERIES 2 (240)	30.00	13.50	3.70
COMMON CARD (1-480)	.10	.05	.01
SEMISTARS	.25	.11	.03
STARS	.50	.23	.06
COMP.UPDATE SET (30)	8.00	3.60	1.00
COMMON UPDATE (481U-510U)	.25	.11	.03
UPDATE SEMISTARS	.50	.23	.06
ONE UPDATE SET PER FACTORY SET			
UPDATE SET VIA SER.2 WRAPPER OFFER TOO			
COMP.NOMO SET (5)	20.00	9.00	2.50
COMMON NOMO (1-5)	5.00	2.20	.60
NOMO: RANDOM INSERTS IN SER.2 PACKS			

		MINT	NRMT	EXC
□ 1	Cal Ripken 2131	4.00	1.80	.50
□ 2	Eddie Murray 3000 Hits	.75	.35	.09
□ 3	Mark Wohlers	.25	.11	.03
□ 4	David Justice	.25	.11	.03
□ 5	Chipper Jones	2.00	.90	.25
□ 6	Javier Lopez	.50	.23	.06
□ 7	Mark Lemke	.10	.05	.01
□ 8	Marquis Grissom	.50	.23	.06
□ 9	Tom Glavine	.50	.23	.06
□ 10	Greg Maddux	2.00	.90	.25
□ 11	Manny Alexander	.10	.05	.01
□ 12	Curtis Goodwin	.10	.05	.01
□ 13	Scott Erickson	.10	.05	.01
□ 14	Chris Hoiles	.10	.05	.01
□ 15	Rafael Palmeiro	.50	.23	.06
□ 16	Rick Krivda	.10	.05	.01
□ 17	Jeff Manto	.10	.05	.01
□ 18	Mo Vaughn	.75	.35	.09
□ 19	Tim Wakefield	.10	.05	.01
□ 20	Roger Clemens	.50	.23	.06
□ 21	Tim Naehring	.10	.05	.01
□ 22	Troy O'Leary	.10	.05	.01
□ 23	Mike Greenwell	.10	.05	.01
□ 24	Stan Belinda	.10	.05	.01
□ 25	John Valentin	.25	.11	.03
□ 26	J.T. Snow	.25	.11	.03
□ 27	Gary DiSarcina	.10	.05	.01
□ 28	Mark Langston	.10	.05	.01
□ 29	Brian Anderson	.10	.05	.01
□ 30	Jim Edmonds	.50	.23	.06
□ 31	Garret Anderson	.50	.23	.06
□ 32	Orlando Palmeiro	.10	.05	.01
□ 33	Brian McRae	.10	.05	.01
□ 34	Kevin Foster	.10	.05	.01
□ 35	Sammy Sosa	.50	.23	.06
□ 36	Todd Zeile	.25	.11	.03
□ 37	Jim Bullinger	.10	.05	.01
□ 38	Luis Gonzalez	.10	.05	.01
□ 39	Lyle Mouton	.10	.05	.01
□ 40	Ray Durham	.50	.23	.06
□ 41	Ozzie Guillen	.10	.05	.01
□ 42	Alex Fernandez	.50	.23	.06
□ 43	Brian Keyser	.10	.05	.01
□ 44	Robin Ventura	.25	.11	.03
□ 45	Reggie Sanders	.50	.23	.06
□ 46	Pete Schourek	.25	.11	.03
□ 47	John Smiley	.10	.05	.01
□ 48	Jeff Brantley	.10	.05	.01
□ 49	Thomas Howard	.10	.05	.01
□ 50	Bret Boone	.10	.05	.01
□ 51	Kevin Jarvis	.10	.05	.01
□ 52	Jeff Branson	.10	.05	.01
□ 53	Carlos Baerga	.50	.23	.06
□ 54	Jim Thome	.60	.25	.07
□ 55	Manny Ramirez	.75	.35	.09
□ 56	Omar Vizquel	.10	.05	.01
□ 57	Jose Mesa	.25	.11	.03
□ 58	Julian Tavarez UER	.10	.05	.01
□ 59	Orel Hershiser	.25	.11	.03
□ 60	Larry Walker	.50	.23	.06
□ 61	Bret Saberhagen	.10	.05	.01
□ 62	Vinny Castilla	.50	.23	.06
□ 63	Eric Young	.10	.05	.01
□ 64	Bryan Rekar	.10	.05	.01
□ 65	Andres Galarraga	.50	.23	.06
□ 66	Steve Reed	.10	.05	.01
□ 67	Chad Curtis	.10	.05	.01
□ 68	Bobby Higginson	.50	.23	.06
□ 69	Phil Nevin	.10	.05	.01
□ 70	Cecil Fielder	.50	.23	.06
□ 71	Felipe Lira	.10	.05	.01
□ 72	Chris Gomez	.10	.05	.01
□ 73	Charles Johnson	.10	.05	.01
□ 74	Quilvio Veras	.10	.05	.01
□ 75	Jeff Conine	.50	.23	.06
□ 76	John Burkett	.10	.05	.01
□ 77	Greg Colbrunn	.10	.05	.01
□ 78	Terry Pendleton	.10	.05	.01
□ 79	Shane Reynolds	.10	.05	.01
□ 80	Jeff Bagwell	1.25	.55	.16
□ 81	Orlando Miller	.10	.05	.01
□ 82	Mike Hampton	.10	.05	.01
□ 83	James Mouton	.10	.05	.01
□ 84	Brian L. Hunter	.10	.05	.01
□ 85	Derek Bell	.25	.11	.03
□ 86	Kevin Appier	.10	.05	.01
□ 87	Joe Vitiello	.10	.05	.01
□ 88	Wally Joyner	.10	.05	.01
□ 89	Michael Tucker	.25	.11	.03
□ 90	Johnny Damon	.25	.11	.03
□ 91	Jon Nunnally	.10	.05	.01
□ 92	Jason Jacome	.10	.05	.01
□ 93	Chad Fonville	.10	.05	.01
□ 94	Chan Ho Park	.50	.23	.06
□ 95	Hideo Nomo	.75	.35	.09
□ 96	Ismael Valdes	.25	.11	.03
□ 97	Greg Gagne	.10	.05	.01
□ 98	Diamondbacks-Devil Rays	.10	.05	.01
□ 99	Raul Mondesi	.50	.23	.06
□ 100	Dave Winfield	.50	.23	.06
□ 101	Dennis Eckersley	.50	.23	.06
□ 102	Andre Dawson	.50	.23	.06
□ 103	Dennis Martinez	.25	.11	.03
□ 104	Lance Parrish	.25	.11	.03
□ 105	Eddie Murray	.50	.23	.06
□ 106	Alan Trammell	.50	.23	.06
□ 107	Lou Whitaker	.50	.23	.06
□ 108	Ozzie Smith	.50	.23	.06
□ 109	Paul Molitor	.60	.25	.07
□ 110	Rickey Henderson	.50	.23	.06

□	111 Tim Raines	.25	.11	.03
□	112 Harold Baines	.25	.11	.03
□	113 Lee Smith	.25	.11	.03
□	114 Fernando Valenzuela	.25	.11	.03
□	115 Cal Ripken YH	1.25	.55	.16
□	116 Tony Gwynn YH	.60	.25	.07
□	117 Wade Boggs	.50	.23	.06
□	118 Todd Hollandsworth	.50	.23	.06
□	119 Dave Nilsson	.25	.11	.03
□	120 Jose Valentin	.10	.05	.01
□	121 Steve Sparks	.10	.05	.01
□	122 Chuck Carr	.10	.05	.01
□	123 John Jaha	.10	.05	.01
□	124 Scott Karl	.10	.05	.01
□	125 Chuck Knoblauch	.50	.23	.06
□	126 Brad Radke	.10	.05	.01
□	127 Pat Meares	.10	.05	.01
□	128 Ron Coomer	.10	.05	.01
□	129 Pedro Munoz	.10	.05	.01
□	130 Kirby Puckett	1.00	.45	.12
□	131 David Segui	.10	.05	.01
□	132 Mark Grudzielanek	.10	.05	.01
□	133 Mike Lansing	.10	.05	.01
□	134 Sean Berry	.10	.05	.01
□	135 Rondell White	.50	.23	.06
□	136 Pedro J. Martinez	.10	.05	.01
□	137 Carl Everett	.10	.05	.01
□	138 Dave Mlicki	.10	.05	.01
□	139 Bill Pulsipher	.10	.05	.01
□	140 Jason Isringhausen	.10	.05	.01
□	141 Rico Brogna	.10	.05	.01
□	142 Edgardo Alfonzo	.25	.11	.03
□	143 Jeff Kent	.10	.05	.01
□	144 Andy Pettitte	1.00	.45	.12
□	145 Mike Piazza BO	1.00	.45	.12
□	146 Cliff Floyd	.10	.05	.01
□	147 Jason Isringhausen BO	.10	.05	.01
□	148 Tim Wakefield	.10	.05	.01
□	149 Chipper Jones BO	1.00	.45	.12
□	150 Hideo Nomo BO	.50	.23	.06
□	151 Mark McGwire	1.00	.45	.12
□	152 Ron Gant	.50	.23	.06
□	153 Gary Gaetti	.25	.11	.03
□	154 Don Mattingly	1.50	.70	.19
□	155 Paul O'Neill	.10	.05	.01
□	156 Derek Jeter	2.00	.90	.25
□	157 Joe Girardi	.10	.05	.01
□	158 Ruben Sierra	.10	.05	.01
□	159 Jorge Posada	.10	.05	.01
□	160 Geronimo Berroa	.25	.11	.03
□	161 Steve Ontiveros	.10	.05	.01
□	162 George Williams	.10	.05	.01
□	163 Doug Johns	.10	.05	.01
□	164 Ariel Prieto	.10	.05	.01
□	165 Scott Brosius	.10	.05	.01
□	166 Mike Bordick	.10	.05	.01
□	167 Tyler Green	.10	.05	.01
□	168 Mickey Morandini	.10	.05	.01
□	169 Darren Daulton	.25	.11	.03
□	170 Gregg Jefferies	.25	.11	.03
□	171 Jim Eisenreich	.10	.05	.01
□	172 Heathcliff Slocumb	.10	.05	.01
□	173 Kevin Stocker	.10	.05	.01
□	174 Esteban Loaiza	.10	.05	.01
□	175 Jeff King	.25	.11	.03
□	176 Mark Johnson	.10	.05	.01
□	177 Denny Neagle	.25	.11	.03
□	178 Orlando Merced	.25	.11	.03
□	179 Carlos Garcia	.10	.05	.01
□	180 Brian Jordan	.50	.23	.06
□	181 Mike Morgan	.10	.05	.01
□	182 Mark Petkovsek	.10	.05	.01
□	183 Bernard Gilkey	.25	.11	.03
□	184 John Mabry	.50	.23	.06
□	185 Tom Henke	.25	.11	.03
□	186 Glenn Dishman	.10	.05	.01
□	187 Andy Ashby	.10	.05	.01
□	188 Bip Roberts	.10	.05	.01
□	189 Melvin Nieves	.10	.05	.01
□	190 Ken Caminiti	.50	.23	.06
□	191 Brad Ausmus	.10	.05	.01
□	192 Deion Sanders	.50	.23	.06
□	193 Jamie Brewington	.10	.05	.01
□	194 Glenallen Hill	.10	.05	.01
□	195 Barry Bonds	.75	.35	.09
□	196 Wm. Van Landingham	.10	.05	.01
□	197 Mark Carreon	.10	.05	.01
□	198 Royce Clayton	.10	.05	.01
□	199 Joey Cora	.10	.05	.01
□	200 Ken Griffey Jr.	3.00	1.35	.35
□	201 Jay Buhner	.50	.23	.06
□	202 Alex Rodriguez	3.00	1.35	.35
□	203 Norm Charlton	.10	.05	.01
□	204 Andy Benes	.10	.05	.01
□	205 Edgar Martinez	.50	.23	.06
□	206 Juan Gonzalez	1.50	.70	.19
□	207 Will Clark	.50	.23	.06
□	208 Kevin Gross	.10	.05	.01
□	209 Roger Pavlik	.10	.05	.01
□	210 Ivan Rodriguez	.60	.25	.07
□	211 Rusty Greer	.50	.23	.06
□	212 Angel Martinez	.10	.05	.01
□	213 Tomas Perez	.10	.05	.01
□	214 Alex Gonzalez	.10	.05	.01
□	215 Joe Carter	.50	.23	.06
□	216 Shawn Green	.10	.05	.01
□	217 Edwin Hurtado	.10	.05	.01
□	218 Edgar Martinez Tony Pena	.10	.05	.01
□	219 Chipper Jones Barry Larkin	.75	.35	.09
□	220 Orel Hershiser	.25	.11	.03
□	221 Mike Devereaux	.10	.05	.01
□	222 Tom Glavine	.50	.23	.06
□	223 Karim Garcia	.60	.25	.07
□	224 Arquimedez Pozo	.10	.05	.01
□	225 Billy Wagner	.10	.05	.01
□	226 John Wasdin	.10	.05	.01
□	227 Jeff Suppan	.25	.11	.03
□	228 Steve Gibralter	.10	.05	.01
□	229 Jimmy Haynes	.10	.05	.01
□	230 Ruben Rivera	.60	.25	.07
□	231 Chris Snopex	.10	.05	.01
□	232 Alex Ochoa	.25	.11	.03
□	233 Shannon Stewart	.10	.05	.01
□	234 Quinton McCracken	.10	.05	.01
□	235 Trey Beamon	.10	.05	.01
□	236 Billy McMillon	.10	.05	.01
□	237 Steve Cox	.10	.05	.01
□	238 George Arias	.10	.05	.01
□	239 Jose Herrera	.10	.05	.01
□	240 Todd Greene	.50	.23	.06
□	241 Jason Kendall	.10	.05	.01
□	242 Brooks Kieschnick	.10	.05	.01
□	243 Osvaldo Fernandez	.10	.05	.01
□	244 Livan Hernandez	.50	.23	.06
□	245 Rey Ordonez	.60	.25	.07
□	246 Mike Grace	.10	.05	.01
□	247 Jay Canizaro	.10	.05	.01
□	248 Bob Wolcott	.10	.05	.01
□	249 Jermaine Dye	.75	.35	.09
□	250 Jason Schmidt	.10	.05	.01
□	251 Mike Sweeney	.60	.25	.07
□	252 Marcus Jensen	.10	.05	.01
□	253 Mendy Lopez	.10	.05	.01
□	254 Wilton Guerrero	.60	.25	.07
□	255 Paul Wilson	.10	.05	.01
□	256 Edgar Renteria	.50	.23	.06
□	257 Richard Hidalgo	.10	.05	.01
□	258 Bob Abreu	.10	.05	.01
□	259 Robert Smith	.50	.23	.06
□	260 Sal Fasano	.10	.05	.01
□	261 Enrique Wilson	.10	.05	.01
□	262 Rich Hunter	.10	.05	.01
□	263 Sergio Nunez	.10	.05	.01
□	264 Dan Serafini	.10	.05	.01
□	265 David Doster	.10	.05	.01
□	266 Ryan McGuire	.10	.05	.01
□	267 Scott Spiezio	.10	.05	.01
□	268 Rafael Orellano	.10	.05	.01
□	269 Steve Avery	.25	.11	.03
□	270 Fred McGriff	.50	.23	.06
□	271 John Smoltz	.50	.23	.06
□	272 Ryan Klesko	.60	.25	.07
□	273 Jeff Blauser	.10	.05	.01
□	274 Brad Clontz	.10	.05	.01
□	275 Roberto Alomar	.75	.35	.09
□	276 B.J. Surhoff	.10	.05	.01
□	277 Jeffrey Hammonds	.10	.05	.01
□	278 Brady Anderson	.50	.23	.06
□	279 Bobby Bonilla	.50	.23	.06
□	280 Cal Ripken	2.50	1.10	.30

☐ 281 Mike Mussina .60 .25 .07
☐ 282 Wil Cordero .10 .05 .01
☐ 283 Mike Stanley .10 .05 .01
☐ 284 Aaron Sele .10 .05 .01
☐ 285 Jose Canseco .50 .23 .06
☐ 286 Tom Gordon .10 .05 .01
☐ 287 Heathcliff Slocumb .10 .05 .01
☐ 288 Lee Smith .50 .23 .06
☐ 289 Troy Percival .25 .11 .03
☐ 290 Tim Salmon .50 .23 .06
☐ 291 Chuck Finley .10 .05 .01
☐ 292 Jim Abbott .50 .23 .06
☐ 293 Chili Davis .10 .05 .01
☐ 294 Steve Trachsel .10 .05 .01
☐ 295 Mark Grace .50 .23 .06
☐ 296 Rey Sanchez .10 .05 .01
☐ 297 Scott Servais .10 .05 .01
☐ 298 Jaime Navarro .10 .05 .01
☐ 299 Frank Castillo .10 .05 .01
☐ 300 Frank Thomas 3.00 1.35 .35
☐ 301 Jason Bere .10 .05 .01
☐ 302 Danny Tartabull .10 .05 .01
☐ 303 Darren Lewis .10 .05 .01
☐ 304 Roberto Hernandez .25 .11 .03
☐ 305 Tony Phillips .25 .11 .03
☐ 306 Wilson Alvarez .50 .23 .06
☐ 307 Jose Rijo .10 .05 .01
☐ 308 Hal Morris .10 .05 .01
☐ 309 Mark Portugal .10 .05 .01
☐ 310 Barry Larkin .50 .23 .06
☐ 311 Dave Burba .10 .05 .01
☐ 312 Ed Taubensee .10 .05 .01
☐ 313 Sandy Alomar Jr. .10 .05 .01
☐ 314 Dennis Martinez .25 .11 .03
☐ 315 Albert Belle 1.50 .70 .19
☐ 316 Eddie Murray .75 .35 .09
☐ 317 Charles Nagy .10 .05 .01
☐ 318 Chad Ogea .10 .05 .01
☐ 319 Kenny Lofton .75 .35 .09
☐ 320 Dante Bichette .50 .23 .06
☐ 321 Armando Reynoso .10 .05 .01
☐ 322 Walt Weiss .10 .05 .01
☐ 323 Ellis Burks .50 .23 .06
☐ 324 Kevin Ritz .10 .05 .01
☐ 325 Bill Swift .10 .05 .01
☐ 326 Jason Bates .10 .05 .01
☐ 327 Tony Clark .50 .23 .06
☐ 328 Travis Fryman .50 .23 .06
☐ 329 Mark Parent .10 .05 .01
☐ 330 Alan Trammell .50 .23 .06
☐ 331 C.J. Nitkowski .10 .05 .01
☐ 332 Jose Lima .10 .05 .01
☐ 333 Phil Plantier .10 .05 .01
☐ 334 Kurt Abbott .10 .05 .01
☐ 335 Andre Dawson .50 .23 .06
☐ 336 Chris Hammond .10 .05 .01
☐ 337 Robb Nen .10 .05 .01
☐ 338 Pat Rapp .10 .05 .01
☐ 339 Al Leiter .10 .05 .01
☐ 340 Gary Sheffield UER .50 .23 .06
(HR total says 17
☐ 341 Todd Jones .10 .05 .01
☐ 342 Doug Drabek .10 .05 .01
☐ 343 Greg Swindell .10 .05 .01
☐ 344 Tony Eusebio .10 .05 .01
☐ 345 Craig Biggio .50 .23 .06
☐ 346 Darryl Kile .10 .05 .01
☐ 347 Mike Macfarlane .10 .05 .01
☐ 348 Jeff Montgomery .10 .05 .01
☐ 349 Chris Haney .10 .05 .01
☐ 350 Bip Roberts .10 .05 .01
☐ 351 Tom Goodwin .25 .11 .03
☐ 352 Mark Gubicza .10 .05 .01
☐ 353 Joe Randa .10 .05 .01
☐ 354 Ramon Martinez .50 .23 .06
☐ 355 Eric Karros .50 .23 .06
☐ 356 Delino DeShields .10 .05 .01
☐ 357 Brett Butler .10 .05 .01
☐ 358 Todd Worrell .50 .23 .06
☐ 359 Mike Blowers .10 .05 .01
☐ 360 Mike Piazza 2.00 .90 .25
☐ 361 Ben McDonald .10 .05 .01
☐ 362 Ricky Bones .10 .05 .01
☐ 363 Greg Vaughn .50 .23 .06
☐ 364 Matt Mieske .10 .05 .01
☐ 365 Kevin Seitzer .10 .05 .01
☐ 366 Jeff Cirillo .10 .05 .01
☐ 367 LaTroy Hawkins .10 .05 .01
☐ 368 Frank Rodriguez .10 .05 .01
☐ 369 Rick Aguilera .10 .05 .01
☐ 370 Roberto Alomar BG .50 .23 .06
☐ 371 Albert Belle BG .75 .35 .09
☐ 372 Wade Boggs BG .50 .23 .06
☐ 373 Barry Bonds BG .50 .23 .06
☐ 374 Roger Clemens BG .50 .23 .06
☐ 375 Dennis Eckersley BG .50 .23 .06
☐ 376 Ken Griffey Jr. BG 1.50 .70 .19
☐ 377 Tony Gwynn BG .60 .25 .07
☐ 378 Rickey Henderson BG .50 .23 .06
☐ 379 Greg Maddux BG 1.00 .45 .12
☐ 380 Fred McGriff BG .50 .23 .06
☐ 381 Paul Molitor BG .50 .23 .06
☐ 382 Eddie Murray BG .50 .23 .06
☐ 383 Mike Piazza BG 1.00 .45 .12
☐ 384 Kirby Puckett BG .50 .23 .06
☐ 385 Cal Ripken BG 1.25 .55 .16
☐ 386 Ozzie Smith BG .50 .23 .06
☐ 387 Frank Thomas BG 1.50 .70 .19
☐ 388 Matt Walbeck .10 .05 .01
☐ 389 Dave Stevens .10 .05 .01
☐ 390 Marty Cordova .50 .23 .06
☐ 391 Darrin Fletcher .10 .05 .01
☐ 392 Cliff Floyd .10 .05 .01
☐ 393 Mel Rojas .10 .05 .01
☐ 394 Shane Andrews .10 .05 .01
☐ 395 Moises Alou .25 .11 .03
☐ 396 Carlos Perez .10 .05 .01
☐ 397 Jeff Fassero .10 .05 .01
☐ 398 Bobby Jones .10 .05 .01
☐ 399 Todd Hundley .50 .23 .06
☐ 400 John Franco .10 .05 .01
☐ 401 Jose Vizcaino .10 .05 .01
☐ 402 Bernard Gilkey .25 .11 .03
☐ 403 Pete Harnisch .10 .05 .01
☐ 404 Pat Kelly .10 .05 .01
☐ 405 David Cone .50 .23 .06
☐ 406 Bernie Williams .50 .23 .06
☐ 407 John Wetteland .50 .23 .06
☐ 408 Scott Kamieniecki .10 .05 .01
☐ 409 Tim Raines .50 .23 .06
☐ 410 Wade Boggs .50 .23 .06
☐ 411 Terry Steinbach .25 .11 .03
☐ 412 Jason Giambi .50 .23 .06
☐ 413 Todd Van Poppel .10 .05 .01
☐ 414 Pedro Munoz .10 .05 .01
☐ 415 Eddie Murray 90SBT .50 .23 .06
☐ 416 Dennis Eckersley 90SBT .50 .23 .06
☐ 417 Bip Roberts 92SBT .10 .05 .01
☐ 418 Glenallen Hill 92SBT .10 .05 .01
☐ 419 John Hudek 94SBT .10 .05 .01
☐ 420 Derek Bell 95SBT .10 .05 .01
☐ 421 Larry Walker 95SBT .10 .05 .01
☐ 422 Greg Maddux 95SBT 1.00 .45 .12
☐ 423 Ken Caminiti 95SBT .50 .23 .06
☐ 424 Brent Gates .10 .05 .01
☐ 425 Mark McGwire 1.00 .45 .12
☐ 426 Mark Whiten .10 .05 .01
☐ 427 Sid Fernandez .10 .05 .01
☐ 428 Ricky Bottalico .10 .05 .01
☐ 429 Mike Mimbs .10 .05 .01
☐ 430 Lenny Dykstra .25 .11 .03
☐ 431 Todd Zeile .25 .11 .03
☐ 432 Benito Santiago .10 .05 .01
☐ 433 Danny Miceli .10 .05 .01
☐ 434 Al Martin .10 .05 .01
☐ 435 Jay Bell .25 .11 .03
☐ 436 Charlie Hayes .10 .05 .01
☐ 437 Mike Kingery .10 .05 .01
☐ 438 Paul Wagner .10 .05 .01
☐ 439 Tom Pagnozzi .10 .05 .01
☐ 440 Ozzie Smith .60 .25 .07
☐ 441 Ray Lankford .50 .23 .06
☐ 442 Dennis Eckersley .50 .23 .06
☐ 443 Ron Gant .50 .23 .06
☐ 444 Alan Benes .50 .23 .06
☐ 445 Rickey Henderson .50 .23 .06
☐ 446 Jody Reed .10 .05 .01
☐ 447 Trevor Hoffman .25 .11 .03
☐ 448 Andujar Cedeno .10 .05 .01
☐ 449 Steve Finley .50 .23 .06
☐ 450 Tony Gwynn 1.25 .55 .16
☐ 451 Joey Hamilton .25 .11 .03

☐ 452	Mark Leiter	.10	.05	.01
☐ 453	Rod Beck	.10	.05	.01
☐ 454	Kirt Manwaring	.10	.05	.01
☐ 455	Matt Williams	.50	.23	.06
☐ 456	Robby Thompson	.10	.05	.01
☐ 457	Shawon Dunston	.10	.05	.01
☐ 458	Russ Davis	.10	.05	.01
☐ 459	Paul Sorrento	.10	.05	.01
☐ 460	Randy Johnson	.50	.23	.06
☐ 461	Chris Bosio	.10	.05	.01
☐ 462	Luis Sojo	.10	.05	.01
☐ 463	Sterling Hitchcock	.10	.05	.01
☐ 464	Benji Gil	.10	.05	.01
☐ 465	Mickey Tettleton	.25	.11	.03
☐ 466	Mark McLemore	.10	.05	.01
☐ 467	Darryl Hamilton	.10	.05	.01
☐ 468	Ken Hill	.25	.11	.03
☐ 469	Dean Palmer	.50	.23	.06
☐ 470	Carlos Delgado	.50	.23	.06
☐ 471	Ed Sprague	.25	.11	.03
☐ 472	Otis Nixon	.10	.05	.01
☐ 473	Pat Hentgen	.50	.23	.06
☐ 474	Juan Guzman	.10	.05	.01
☐ 475	John Olerud	.10	.05	.01
☐ 476	Buck Showalter CL	.10	.05	.01
☐ 477	Bobby Cox CL	.10	.05	.01
☐ 478	Tommy Lasorda CL	.50	.23	.06
☐ 479	Buck Showalter CL	.10	.05	.01
☐ 480	Sparky Anderson CL	.25	.11	.03
☐ 481U	Randy Myers	.25	.11	.03
☐ 482U	Kent Mercker	.25	.11	.03
☐ 483U	David Wells	.25	.11	.03
☐ 484U	Kevin Mitchell	.25	.11	.03
☐ 485U	Randy Velarde	.25	.11	.03
☐ 486U	Ryne Sandberg	1.50	.70	.19
☐ 487U	Doug Jones	.25	.11	.03
☐ 488U	Terry Adams	.25	.11	.03
☐ 489U	Kevin Tapani	.25	.11	.03
☐ 490U	Harold Baines	.50	.23	.06
☐ 491U	Eric Davis	.25	.11	.03
☐ 492U	Julio Franco	.25	.11	.03
☐ 493U	Jack McDowell	.50	.23	.06
☐ 494U	Devon White	.25	.11	.03
☐ 495U	Kevin Brown	.25	.11	.03
☐ 496U	Rick Wilkins	.25	.11	.03
☐ 497U	Sean Berry	.25	.11	.03
☐ 498U	Keith Lockhart	.25	.11	.03
☐ 499U	Mark Loretta	.25	.11	.03
☐ 500U	Paul Molitor	1.25	.55	.16
☐ 501U	Roberto Kelly	.25	.11	.03
☐ 502U	Lance Johnson	.50	.23	.06
☐ 503U	Tino Martinez	.50	.23	.06
☐ 504U	Kenny Rogers	.25	.11	.03
☐ 505U	Todd Stottlemyre	.25	.11	.03
☐ 506U	Gary Gaetti	.25	.11	.03
☐ 507U	Royce Clayton	.25	.11	.03
☐ 508U	Andy Benes	.25	.11	.03
☐ 509U	Wally Joyner	.25	.11	.03
☐ 510U	Erik Hanson	.25	.11	.03

1996 Upper Deck Blue Chip Prospects

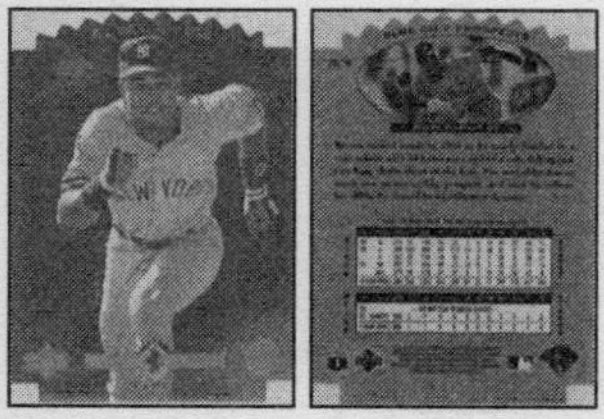

Randomly inserted in retail packs at a rate of one in 72, this 20-card die-cut set features some of the best young stars in the majors.

	MINT	NRMT	EXC
COMPLETE SET (20)	250.00	110.00	31.00
COMMON CARD (BC1-BC20)	6.00	2.70	.75
SEMISTARS	8.00	3.60	1.00
RANDOM INSERTS IN SER.1 PACKS			

☐ BC1	Hideo Nomo	20.00	9.00	2.50
☐ BC2	Johnny Damon	6.00	2.70	.75
☐ BC3	Jason Isringhausen	10.00	4.50	1.25
☐ BC4	Bill Pulsipher	6.00	2.70	.75
☐ BC5	Marty Cordova	10.00	4.50	1.25
☐ BC6	Michael Tucker	6.00	2.70	.75
☐ BC7	John Wasdin	6.00	2.70	.75
☐ BC8	Karim Garcia	15.00	6.75	1.85
☐ BC9	Ruben Rivera	15.00	6.75	1.85
☐ BC10	Chipper Jones	40.00	18.00	5.00
☐ BC11	Billy Wagner	6.00	2.70	.75
☐ BC12	Brooks Kieschnick	6.00	2.70	.75
☐ BC13	Alan Benes	8.00	3.60	1.00
☐ BC14	Roger Cedeno	6.00	2.70	.75
☐ BC15	Alex Rodriguez	75.00	34.00	9.50
☐ BC16	Jason Schmidt	6.00	2.70	.75
☐ BC17	Derek Jeter	40.00	18.00	5.00
☐ BC18	Brian L.Hunter	6.00	2.70	.75
☐ BC19	Garret Anderson	8.00	3.60	1.00
☐ BC20	Manny Ramirez	25.00	11.00	3.10

1996 Upper Deck Future Stock Prospects

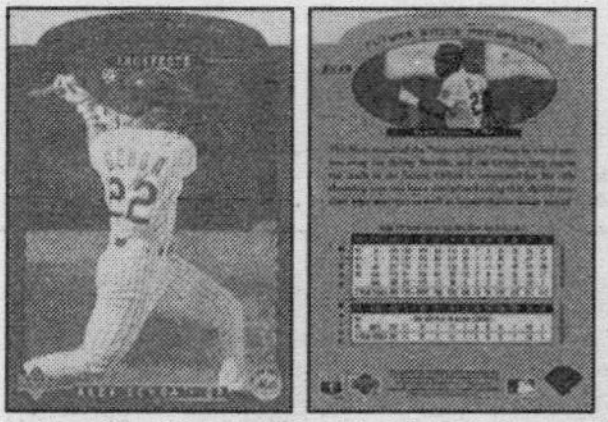

Randomly inserted in packs at a rate of one in 6, this 20-card die-cut set highlights the top prospects who made their major league debuts in 1995.

	MINT	NRMT	EXC
COMPLETE SET (20)	12.00	5.50	1.50
COMMON CARD (FS1-FS20)	1.00	.45	.12
RANDOM INSERTS IN SER.1 PACKS			

☐ FS1	George Arias	1.50	.70	.19
☐ FS2	Brian Barber	1.00	.45	.12
☐ FS3	Trey Beamon	1.00	.45	.12
☐ FS4	Yamil Benitez	1.00	.45	.12
☐ FS5	Jamie Brewington	1.00	.45	.12
☐ FS6	Tony Clark	1.25	.55	.16
☐ FS7	Steve Cox	1.00	.45	.12
☐ FS8	Carlos Delgado	2.50	1.10	.30
☐ FS9	Chad Fonville	1.00	.45	.12
☐ FS10	Alex Ochoa	2.50	1.10	.30
☐ FS11	Curtis Goodwin	1.00	.45	.12
☐ FS12	Todd Greene	2.00	.90	.25
☐ FS13	Jimmy Haynes	1.00	.45	.12
☐ FS14	Quinton McCracken	1.00	.45	.12
☐ FS15	Billy McMillon	1.00	.45	.12
☐ FS16	Chan Ho Park	1.50	.70	.19
☐ FS17	Arquimedez Pozo	1.00	.45	.12
☐ FS18	Chris Snopek	1.00	.45	.12
☐ FS19	Shannon Stewart	1.00	.45	.12
☐ FS20	Jeff Suppan	1.00	.45	.12

1996 Upper Deck Gameface

These Gameface cards were seeded at a rate of one per Upper Deck and Collector's Choice

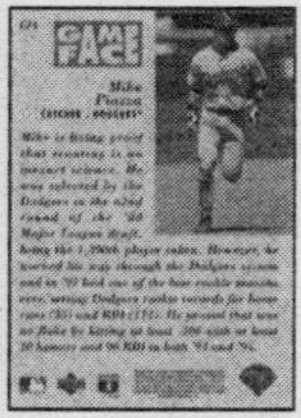

Wal Mart retail pack. The Upper Deck packs contained eight cards and the Collector's Choice packs contained sixteen cards. Both packs carried a suggested retail price of $1.50.

	MINT	NRMT	EXC
COMPLETE SET (10)	12.00	5.50	1.50
COMMON CARD (GF1-GF10)	.30	.14	.04
ONE PER SPECIAL RETAIL PACK			
□ GF1 Ken Griffey Jr.	2.50	1.10	.30
□ GF2 Frank Thomas	2.50	1.10	.30
□ GF3 Barry Bonds	.60	.25	.07
□ GF4 Albert Belle	1.25	.55	.16
□ GF5 Cal Ripken	2.00	.90	.25
□ GF6 Mike Piazza	1.50	.70	.19
□ GF7 Chipper Jones	1.50	.70	.19
□ GF8 Matt Williams	.30	.14	.04
□ GF9 Hideo Nomo	.60	.25	.07
□ GF10 Greg Maddux	1.50	.70	.19

1996 Upper Deck Hot Commodities

This 20 card set double die-cut set was randomly inserted into series two Upper Deck packs at a rate of one in 37. The set features some of baseball's most popular players.

	MINT	NRMT	EXC
COMPLETE SET (20)	200.00	90.00	25.00
COMMON CARD (HC1-HC20)	4.00	1.80	.50
RANDOM INSERTS IN SER.2 PACKS			
□ HC1 Ken Griffey Jr.	30.00	13.50	3.70
□ HC2 Hideo Nomo	8.00	3.60	1.00
□ HC3 Roberto Alomar	8.00	3.60	1.00
□ HC4 Paul Wilson	4.00	1.80	.50
□ HC5 Albert Belle	15.00	6.75	1.85
□ HC6 Manny Ramirez	8.00	3.60	1.00
□ HC7 Kirby Puckett	10.00	4.50	1.25
□ HC8 Johnny Damon	4.00	1.80	.50
□ HC9 Randy Johnson	5.00	2.20	.60
□ HC10 Greg Maddux	20.00	9.00	2.50
□ HC11 Chipper Jones	20.00	9.00	2.50
□ HC12 Barry Bonds	8.00	3.60	1.00
□ HC13 Mo Vaughn	8.00	3.60	1.00
□ HC14 Mike Piazza	20.00	9.00	2.50
□ HC15 Cal Ripken	25.00	11.00	3.10
□ HC16 Tim Salmon	4.00	1.80	.50
□ HC17 Sammy Sosa	5.00	2.20	.60
□ HC18 Kenny Lofton	8.00	3.60	1.00
□ HC19 Tony Gwynn	12.00	5.50	1.50
□ HC20 Frank Thomas	30.00	13.50	3.70

1996 Upper Deck V.J. Lovero Showcase

Upper Deck utilized photos from the files of V.J. Lovero to produce this set. The cards feature the photos along with a story of how Lovero took the photos. The cards are numbered with a "VJ" prefix.

	MINT	NRMT	EXC
COMPLETE SET (19)	25.00	11.00	3.10
COMMON CARD (VJ1-VJ19)	.50	.23	.06
SEMISTARS	1.00	.45	.12
RANDOM INSERTS IN SER.2 PACKS			
□ VJ1 Jim Abbott	.50	.23	.06
□ VJ2 Hideo Nomo	2.00	.90	.25
□ VJ3 Derek Jeter	4.00	1.80	.50
□ VJ4 Barry Bonds	2.00	.90	.25
□ VJ5 Greg Maddux	5.00	2.20	.60
□ VJ6 Mark McGwire	2.50	1.10	.30
□ VJ7 Jose Canseco	1.00	.45	.12
□ VJ8 Ken Caminiti	1.00	.45	.12
□ VJ9 Raul Mondesi	1.00	.45	.12
□ VJ10 Ken Griffey Jr.	8.00	3.60	1.00
□ VJ11 Jay Buhner	1.00	.45	.12
□ VJ12 Randy Johnson	1.25	.55	.16
□ VJ13 Roger Clemens	1.00	.45	.12
□ VJ14 Brady Anderson	1.00	.45	.12
□ VJ15 Frank Thomas	8.00	3.60	1.00
□ VJ16 Garret Anderson Jim Edmonds Tim Salmon	.50	.23	.06
□ VJ17 Mike Piazza	5.00	2.20	.60
□ VJ18 Dante Bichette	1.00	.45	.12
□ VJ19 Tony Gwynn	3.00	1.35	.35

1996 Upper Deck Power Driven

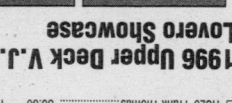

Randomly inserted in packs at a rate of one in 36, this 20-card set consists of embossed rainbow foil inserts of baseball's top power hitters.

	MINT	NRMT	EXC
COMPLETE SET (20)	125.00	55.00	15.50
COMMON CARD (PD1-PD20)	2.50	1.10	.30
SEMISTARS	4.00	1.80	.50
RANDOM INSERTS IN SER.1 PACKS			
□ PD1 Albert Belle	15.00	6.75	1.85
□ PD2 Barry Bonds	8.00	3.60	1.00
□ PD3 Jay Buhner	4.00	1.80	.50
□ PD4 Jose Canseco	4.00	1.80	.50
□ PD5 Cecil Fielder	4.00	1.80	.50
□ PD6 Juan Gonzalez	15.00	6.75	1.85
□ PD7 Ken Griffey Jr.	30.00	13.50	3.70
□ PD8 Eric Karros	2.50	1.10	.30
□ PD9 Fred McGriff	4.00	1.80	.50
□ PD10 Mark McGwire	10.00	4.50	1.25
□ PD11 Rafael Palmeiro	4.00	1.80	.50
□ PD12 Mike Piazza	20.00	9.00	2.50
□ PD13 Manny Ramirez	8.00	3.60	1.00
□ PD14 Tim Salmon	4.00	1.80	.50
□ PD15 Reggie Sanders	2.50	1.10	.30
□ PD16 Sammy Sosa	5.00	2.20	.60
□ PD17 Frank Thomas	30.00	13.50	3.70
□ PD18 Mo Vaughn	8.00	3.60	1.00
□ PD19 Larry Walker	2.50	1.10	.30
□ PD20 Matt Williams	4.00	1.80	.50

1996 Upper Deck Predictor Hobby

Randomly inserted in hobby packs at a rate of one in 12, this 60-card predictor set offers unique prizes as Major League Baseball players compete for "monthly milestones and awards".

	MINT	NRMT	EXC
COMPLETE SET (60)	150.00	70.00	19.00
COMPLETE SERIES 1 (30)	75.00	34.00	9.50
COMPLETE SERIES 2 (30)	75.00	34.00	9.50
COMMON CARD (H1-H60)	1.00	.45	.12
SEMISTARS	1.50	.70	.19
RANDOM INSERTS IN ALL HOBBY PACKS			
EXPIRATION DATE: 11/18/96			
□ H1 Albert Belle	5.00	2.20	.60
□ H2 Kenny Lofton	2.50	1.10	.30
□ H3 Rafael Palmeiro	1.50	.70	.19
□ H4 Ken Griffey Jr.	10.00	4.50	1.25
□ H5 Tim Salmon	1.50	.70	.19
□ H6 Cal Ripken	8.00	3.60	1.00
□ H7 Mark McGwire	6.00	2.70	.75
□ H8 Frank Thomas W	12.00	5.50	1.50
□ H9 Mo Vaughn W	6.00	2.70	.75
□ H10 Player of Month Longshot	5.00	2.20	.60
□ H11 Roger Clemens	1.50	.70	.19
□ H12 David Cone	1.50	.70	.19
□ H13 Jose Mesa	1.00	.45	.12
□ H14 Randy Johnson	1.50	.70	.19
□ H15 Chuck Finley	1.00	.45	.12
□ H16 Mike Mussina	2.00	.90	.25
□ H17 Kevin Appier	1.00	.45	.12
□ H18 Kenny Rogers	1.00	.45	.12
□ H19 Lee Smith	1.50	.70	.19
□ H20 Pitcher of Month Longshot W	5.00	2.20	.60
□ H21 George Arias	1.00	.45	.12
□ H22 Jose Herrera	1.00	.45	.12
□ H23 Tony Clark	1.50	.70	.19
□ H24 Todd Greene	1.50	.70	.19
□ H25 Derek Jeter W	8.00	3.60	1.00
□ H26 Arquimedez Pozo	1.00	.45	.12
□ H27 Matt Lawton	1.00	.45	.12
□ H28 Shannon Stewart	1.00	.45	.12
□ H29 Chris Snopek	1.00	.45	.12
□ H30 Most Rookie Hits Longshot	6.00	2.70	.75
□ H31 Jeff Bagwell	6.00	2.70	.75
□ H32 Dante Bichette	6.00	2.70	.75
□ H33 Barry Bonds	6.00	2.70	.75
□ H34 Tony Gwynn	4.00	1.80	.50
□ H35 Chipper Jones	6.00	2.70	.75
□ H36 Eric Karros	1.50	.70	.19
□ H37 Barry Larkin	1.50	.70	.19
□ H38 Mike Piazza	6.00	2.70	.75
□ H39 Matt Williams	1.50	.70	.19
□ H40 Long Shot Card	5.00	2.20	.60
□ H41 Osvaldo Fernandez	1.00	.45	.12
□ H42 Tom Glavine	1.50	.70	.19
□ H43 Jason Isringhausen	1.00	.45	.12
□ H44 Greg Maddux	6.00	2.70	.75
□ H45 Pedro Martinez	1.00	.45	.12
□ H46 Hideo Nomo	2.50	1.10	.30
□ H47 Pete Schourek	1.00	.45	.12
□ H48 Paul Wilson	1.00	.45	.12
□ H49 Mark Wohlers	1.50	.70	.19
□ H50 Long Shot Card	5.00	2.20	.60
□ H51 Bob Abreu	1.50	.70	.19
□ H52 Trey Beamon	1.00	.45	.12
□ H53 Yamil Benitez	1.00	.45	.12
□ H54 Roger Cedeno	6.00	2.70	.75
□ H55 Todd Hollandsworth	1.50	.70	.19
□ H56 Marvin Benard	1.00	.45	.12
□ H57 Jason Kendall	1.00	.45	.12
□ H58 Brooks Kieschnick	1.00	.45	.12
□ H59 Rey Ordonez	6.00	2.70	.75
□ H60 Long Shot Card	5.00	2.20	.60

1996 Upper Deck Predictor Retail

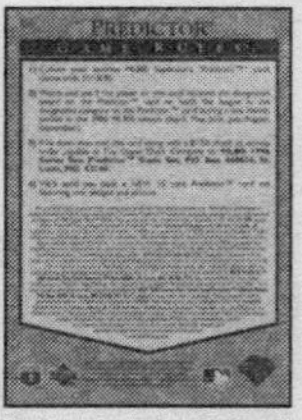

Randomly inserted in retail packs at a rate of one in 12, this 60-card predictor set offers unique prizes as Major League Baseball players compete for "monthly milestones and awards".

	MINT	NRMT	EXC
COMPLETE SET (60)	175.00	80.00	22.00
COMPLETE SERIES 1 (30)	100.00	45.00	12.50
COMPLETE SERIES 2 (30)	75.00	34.00	9.50
COMMON CARD (R1-R60)	1.00	.45	.12
SEMISTARS	1.50	.70	.19
RANDOM INSERTS IN ALL RETAIL PACKS			
EXPIRATION DATE: 11/18/96			
□ R1 Albert Belle W	6.00	2.70	.75
□ R2 Jay Buhner W	6.00	2.70	.75
□ R3 Juan Gonzalez	6.00	2.70	.75
□ R4 Ken Griffey Jr.	10.00	4.50	1.25
□ R5 Mark McGwire	6.00	2.70	.75
□ R6 Rafael Palmeiro	1.50	.70	.19
□ R7 Tim Salmon	1.50	.70	.19
□ R8 Frank Thomas	10.00	4.50	1.25
□ R9 Mo Vaughn W	6.00	2.70	.75
□ R10 Monthly HR Ldr Longshot W	5.00	2.20	.60
□ R11 Albert Belle W	6.00	2.70	.75
□ R12 Jay Buhner	1.50	.70	.19
□ R13 Jim Edmonds	1.50	.70	.19
□ R14 Cecil Fielder	1.50	.70	.19
□ R15 Ken Griffey Jr.	10.00	4.50	1.25
□ R16 Edgar Martinez	1.50	.70	.19
□ R17 Manny Ramirez	2.50	1.10	.30
□ R18 Frank Thomas	10.00	4.50	1.25
□ R19 Mo Vaughn W	6.00	2.70	.75
□ R20 Monthly RBI Ldr Longshot	5.00	2.20	.60
□ R21 Roberto Alomar W	6.00	2.70	.75
□ R22 Carlos Baerga	1.50	.70	.19

□ R23 Wade Boggs	1.50	.70	.19
□ R24 Ken Griffey Jr.	10.00	4.50	1.25
□ R25 Chuck Knoblauch	1.50	.70	.19
□ R26 Kenny Lofton	2.50	1.10	.30
□ R27 Edgar Martinez	1.50	.70	.19
□ R28 Tim Salmon	1.50	.70	.19
□ R29 Frank Thomas	10.00	4.50	1.25
□ R30 Monthly Hits Ldr Longshot W	5.00	2.20	.60
□ R31 Dante Bichette	1.50	.70	.19
□ R32 Barry Bonds	6.00	2.70	.75
□ R33 Ron Gant	1.50	.70	.19
□ R34 Chipper Jones	6.00	2.70	.75
□ R35 Fred McGriff	1.50	.70	.19
□ R36 Mike Piazza	6.00	2.70	.75
□ R37 Sammy Sosa	6.00	2.70	.75
□ R38 Larry Walker	1.50	.70	.19
□ R39 Matt Williams	1.50	.70	.19
□ R40 Long Shot Card	6.00	2.70	.75
□ R41 Jeff Bagwell	6.00	2.70	.75
□ R42 Dante Bichette	6.00	2.70	.75
□ R43 Barry Bonds	6.00	2.70	.75
□ R44 Jeff Conine	1.50	.70	.19
□ R45 Andres Galarraga	1.50	.70	.19
□ R46 Mike Piazza	6.00	2.70	.75
□ R47 Reggie Sanders	1.00	.45	.12
□ R48 Sammy Sosa	1.50	.70	.19
□ R49 Matt Williams	1.50	.70	.19
□ R50 Long Shot Card	5.00	2.20	.60
□ R51 Jeff Bagwell	4.00	1.80	.50
□ R52 Derek Bell	1.00	.45	.12
□ R53 Dante Bichette	1.50	.70	.19
□ R54 Craig Biggio	1.50	.70	.19
□ R55 Barry Bonds	2.50	1.10	.30
□ R56 Bret Boone	1.00	.45	.12
□ R57 Tony Gwynn	4.00	1.80	.50
□ R58 Barry Larkin	1.50	.70	.19
□ R59 Mike Piazza	8.00	3.60	1.00
□ R60 Long Shot Card	5.00	2.20	.60

1996 Upper Deck Ripken Collection

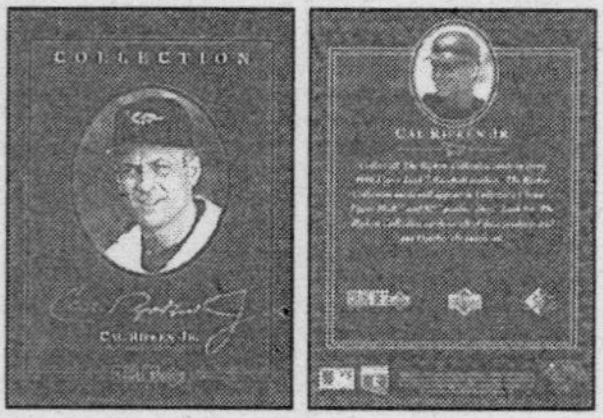

This 23 card set was issued across all the various Upper Deck brands. The cards were issued to commemorate Cal Ripken's career, which had been capped the previous season by the breaking of the consecutive game streak long held by Lou Gehrig.

	MINT	NRMT	EXC
COMPLETE SET (23)	125.00	55.00	15.50
COMP.COLC SER.1 (5)	15.00	6.75	1.85
COMP.UD SER.1 (4)	25.00	11.00	3.10
COMP.COLC SER.2 (4)	12.00	5.50	1.50
COMP.UD SER.2 (5)	25.00	11.00	3.10
COMPLETE SP SET (5)	50.00	22.00	6.25
COMMON COLC (1-4/9-12)	4.00	1.80	.50
COMMON UD (5-8/13-17)	6.00	2.70	.75
COMMON SP (18-22)	12.00	5.50	1.50
HEADER CARD (CCH)	4.00	1.80	.50

1-4 RANDOM INSERTS IN CC SER.1 PACKS
5-8 RANDOM INSERTS IN UD SER.1 PACKS
9-12 RANDOM INSERTS IN CC SER.2 PACKS
13-17 RANDOM INSERTS IN UD SER.2 PACKS
18-22 RANDOM INSERTS IN SP PACKS......

1996 Upper Deck Run Producers

This 20 card set was randomly inserted into series two packs at a rate of one every 71 packs. The cards are thermographically printed, which gives the card a rubber surface texture. The cards are double die-cut and are foil stamped. These cards are designed to show off the technology of the Upper Deck cards.

	MINT	NRMT	EXC
COMPLETE SET (20)	225.00	100.00	28.00
COMMON CARD (RP1-RP20)	5.00	2.20	.60

RANDOM INSERTS IN SER.2 PACKS..........
CONDITION SENSITIVE SET........................
CARDS PRICED BELOW IN NEAR MINT.......

□ RP1 Albert Belle	20.00	9.00	2.50
□ RP2 Dante Bichette	5.00	2.20	.60
□ RP3 Barry Bonds	10.00	4.50	1.25
□ RP4 Jay Buhner	5.00	2.20	.60
□ RP5 Jose Canseco	5.00	2.20	.60
□ RP6 Juan Gonzalez	20.00	9.00	2.50
□ RP7 Ken Griffey Jr.	40.00	18.00	5.00
□ RP8 Tony Gwynn	15.00	6.75	1.85
□ RP9 Kenny Lofton	10.00	4.50	1.25
□ RP10 Edgar Martinez	5.00	2.20	.60
□ RP11 Fred McGriff	5.00	2.20	.60
□ RP12 Mark McGwire	12.00	5.50	1.50
□ RP13 Rafael Palmeiro	5.00	2.20	.60
□ RP14 Mike Piazza	25.00	11.00	3.10
□ RP15 Manny Ramirez	10.00	4.50	1.25
□ RP16 Tim Salmon	5.00	2.20	.60
□ RP17 Sammy Sosa	6.00	2.70	.75
□ RP18 Frank Thomas	40.00	18.00	5.00
□ RP19 Mo Vaughn	10.00	4.50	1.25
□ RP20 Matt Williams	5.00	2.20	.60

1996 Upper Deck Tech Diamond Destiny

Issued one per WalMark pack, these 40 cards feature leading players of baseball. The cards have two photos on the front with the player's name listed on the bottom. The backs have another photo along with biographical information. The cards are numbered with a "DD" prefix.

	MINT	NRMT	EXC
COMPLETE SET (40)	125.00	55.00	15.50
COMMON CARD (DD1-DD40)	1.50	.70	.19
SEMISTARS	2.50	1.10	.30
ONE PER UD TECH PACK			

		MINT	NRMT	EXC
□ DD1	Chipper Jones	10.00	4.50	1.25
□ DD2	Fred McGriff	2.50	1.10	.30
□ DD3	John Smoltz	2.50	1.10	.30
□ DD4	Ryan Klesko	3.00	1.35	.35
□ DD5	Greg Maddux	10.00	4.50	1.25
□ DD6	Cal Ripken	12.00	5.50	1.50
□ DD7	Roberto Alomar	4.00	1.80	.50
□ DD8	Eddie Murray	4.00	1.80	.50
□ DD9	Brady Anderson	1.50	.70	.19
□ DD10	Mo Vaughn	4.00	1.80	.50
□ DD11	Roger Clemens	2.50	1.10	.30
□ DD12	Darin Erstad	8.00	3.60	1.00
□ DD13	Sammy Sosa	1.50	.70	.19
□ DD14	Frank Thomas	15.00	6.75	1.85
□ DD15	Barry Larkin	2.50	1.10	.30
□ DD16	Albert Belle	8.00	3.60	1.00
□ DD17	Manny Ramirez	4.00	1.80	.50
□ DD18	Kenny Lofton	4.00	1.80	.50
□ DD19	Dante Bichette	1.50	.70	.19
□ DD20	Gary Sheffield	2.50	1.10	.30
□ DD21	Jeff Bagwell	6.00	2.70	.75
□ DD22	Hideo Nomo	4.00	1.80	.50
□ DD23	Mike Piazza	10.00	4.50	1.25
□ DD24	Kirby Puckett	5.00	2.20	.60
□ DD25	Paul Molitor	3.00	1.35	.35
□ DD26	Chuck Knoblauch	2.50	1.10	.30
□ DD27	Wade Boggs	2.50	1.10	.30
□ DD28	Derek Jeter	10.00	4.50	1.25
□ DD29	Rey Ordonez	3.00	1.35	.35
□ DD30	Mark McGwire	5.00	2.20	.60
□ DD31	Ozzie Smith	3.00	1.35	.35
□ DD32	Tony Gwynn	6.00	2.70	.75
□ DD33	Barry Bonds	4.00	1.80	.50
□ DD34	Matt Williams	2.50	1.10	.30
□ DD35	Ken Griffey Jr.	15.00	6.75	1.85
□ DD36	Jay Buhner	2.50	1.10	.30
□ DD37	Randy Johnson	2.50	1.10	.30
□ DD38	Alex Rodriguez	15.00	6.75	1.85
□ DD39	Juan Gonzalez	8.00	3.60	1.00
□ DD40	Joe Carter	2.50	1.10	.30

1997 Upper Deck

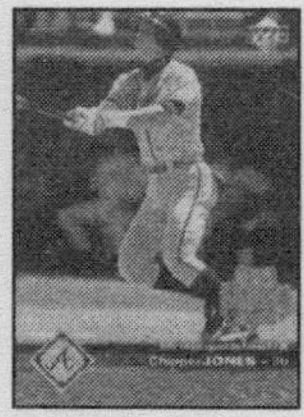

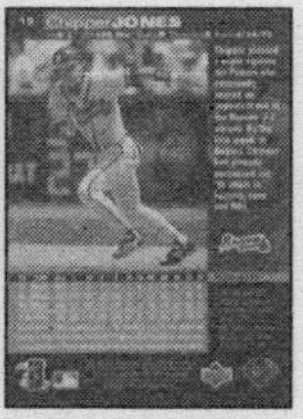

The 1997 Upper Deck first series totals 240 cards. The 12-card packs retail for $2.49 each. Among the susbets in the first series are Star Rookies, Global Impact, Defensive Gems, Strike Force, Season Highlights and a nine card Jackie Robinson 50th anniversary set to lead off the 97 issue. Many cards have dates on the front to identify when, and when possible, what significant event is pictured. The backs include a player photo, stats and a brief blurb to go with vital statistics.

	MINT	NRMT	EXC
COMPLETE SERIES 1 (240)	30.00	13.50	3.70
COMMON CARD (1-240)	.10	.05	.01
JACKIE ROBINSON (1-9)	.50	.23	.06
SEMISTARS	.25	.11	.03
STARS	.50	.23	.06

□ 1	Jackie Robinson	.50	.23	.06
□ 2	Jackie Robinson	.50	.23	.06
□ 3	Jackie Robinson	.50	.23	.06
□ 4	Jackie Robinson	.50	.23	.06
□ 5	Jackie Robinson	.50	.23	.06
□ 6	Jackie Robinson	.50	.23	.06
□ 7	Jackie Robinson	.50	.23	.06
□ 8	Jackie Robinson	.50	.23	.06
□ 9	Jackie Robinson	.50	.23	.06
□ 10	Chipper Jones	2.00	.90	.25
□ 11	Marquis Grissom	.25	.11	.03
□ 12	Jermaine Dye	.50	.23	.06
□ 13	Mark Lemke	.10	.05	.01
□ 14	Terrell Wade	.10	.05	.01
□ 15	Fred McGriff	.50	.23	.06
□ 16	Tom Glavine	.50	.23	.06
□ 17	Mark Wohlers	.25	.11	.03
□ 18	Randy Myers	.10	.05	.01
□ 19	Roberto Alomar	.75	.35	.09
□ 20	Cal Ripken	2.50	1.10	.30
□ 21	Rafael Palmeiro	.50	.23	.06
□ 22	Mike Mussina	.60	.25	.07
□ 23	Brady Anderson	.50	.23	.06
□ 24	Jose Canseco	.50	.23	.06
□ 25	Mo Vaughn	.75	.35	.09
□ 26	Roger Clemens	.50	.23	.06
□ 27	Tim Naehring	.10	.05	.01
□ 28	Jeff Suppan	.25	.11	.03
□ 29	Troy Percival	.25	.11	.03
□ 30	Sammy Sosa	.50	.23	.06
□ 31	Amaury Telemaco	.10	.05	.01
□ 32	Rey Sanchez	.10	.05	.01
□ 33	Scott Servais	.10	.05	.01
□ 34	Steve Trachsel	.10	.05	.01
□ 35	Mark Grace	.50	.23	.06
□ 36	Wilson Alvarez	.10	.05	.01
□ 37	Harold Baines	.25	.11	.03
□ 38	Tony Phillips	.25	.11	.03
□ 39	James Baldwin	.25	.11	.03
□ 40	Frank Thomas	3.00	1.35	.35
□ 41	Lyle Mouton	.10	.05	.01
□ 42	Chris Snopek	.10	.05	.01
□ 43	Hal Morris	.10	.05	.01
□ 44	Eric Davis	.10	.05	.01
□ 45	Barry Larkin	.50	.23	.06
□ 46	Reggie Sanders	.25	.11	.03
□ 47	Pete Schourek	.10	.05	.01
□ 48	Lee Smith	.25	.11	.03
□ 49	Charles Nagy	.25	.11	.03
□ 50	Albert Belle	1.50	.70	.19
□ 51	Julio Franco	.25	.11	.03
□ 52	Kenny Lofton	.75	.35	.09
□ 53	Orel Hershiser	.25	.11	.03
□ 54	Omar Vizquel	.25	.11	.03
□ 55	Eric Young	.25	.11	.03
□ 56	Curtis Leskanic	.10	.05	.01
□ 57	Quinton McCracken	.10	.05	.01
□ 58	Kevin Ritz	.10	.05	.01
□ 59	Walt Weiss	.10	.05	.01
□ 60	Dante Bichette	.50	.23	.06
□ 61	Mark Lewis	.10	.05	.01
□ 62	Tony Clark	.25	.11	.03
□ 63	Travis Fryman	.25	.11	.03
□ 64	John Smoltz SF	.50	.23	.06
□ 65	Greg Maddux SF	1.00	.45	.12
□ 66	Tom Glavine SF	.25	.11	.03
□ 67	Mike Mussina SF	.50	.23	.06
□ 68	Andy Pettitte SF	.50	.23	.06
□ 69	Mariano Rivera SF	.25	.11	.03
□ 70	Hideo Nomo SF	.50	.23	.06
□ 71	Kevin Brown SF	.25	.11	.03
□ 72	Randy Johnson SF	.50	.23	.06
□ 73	Felipe Lira	.10	.05	.01
□ 74	Kimera Bartee	.10	.05	.01
□ 75	Alan Trammell	.25	.11	.03
□ 76	Kevin Brown	.25	.11	.03
□ 77	Edgar Renteria	.50	.23	.06
□ 78	Al Leiter	.10	.05	.01
□ 79	Charles Johnson	.25	.11	.03
□ 80	Andre Dawson	.25	.11	.03
□ 81	Billy Wagner	.25	.11	.03
□ 82	Donne Wall	.10	.05	.01
□ 83	Jeff Bagwell	1.25	.55	.16
□ 84	Keith Lockhart	.10	.05	.01
□ 85	Jeff Montgomery	.10	.05	.01
□ 86	Tom Goodwin	.10	.05	.01

□ 87 Tim Belcher	.10	.05	.01
□ 88 Mike Macfarlane	.10	.05	.01
□ 89 Joe Randa	.10	.05	.01
□ 90 Brett Butler	.25	.11	.03
□ 91 Todd Worrell	.10	.05	.01
□ 92 Todd Hollandsworth	.25	.11	.03
□ 93 Ismael Valdes	.25	.11	.03
□ 94 Hideo Nomo	.75	.35	.09
□ 95 Mike Piazza	2.00	.90	.25
□ 96 Jeff Cirillo	.10	.05	.01
□ 97 Ricky Bones	.10	.05	.01
□ 98 Fernando Vina	.10	.05	.01
□ 99 Ben McDonald	.10	.05	.01
□ 100 John Jaha	.10	.05	.01
□ 101 Mark Loretta	.10	.05	.01
□ 102 Paul Molitor	.60	.25	.07
□ 103 Rick Aguilera	.10	.05	.01
□ 104 Marty Cordova	.25	.11	.03
□ 105 Kirby Puckett	.75	.35	.09
□ 106 Dan Naulty	.10	.05	.01
□ 107 Frank Rodriguez	.10	.05	.01
□ 108 Shane Andrews	.10	.05	.01
□ 109 Henry Rodriguez	.25	.11	.03
□ 110 Mark Grudzielanek	.10	.05	.01
□ 111 Pedro Martinez	.25	.11	.03
□ 112 Ugueth Urbina	.10	.05	.01
□ 113 David Segui	.10	.05	.01
□ 114 Rey Ordonez	.50	.23	.06
□ 115 Bernard Gilkey	.25	.11	.03
□ 116 Butch Huskey	.10	.05	.01
□ 117 Paul Wilson	.25	.11	.03
□ 118 Alex Ochoa	.25	.11	.03
□ 119 John Franco	.10	.05	.01
□ 120 Dwight Gooden	.25	.11	.03
□ 121 Ruben Rivera	.50	.23	.06
□ 122 Andy Pettitte	.75	.35	.09
□ 123 Tino Martinez	.25	.11	.03
□ 124 Bernie Williams	.50	.23	.06
□ 125 Wade Boggs	.50	.23	.06
□ 126 Paul O'Neill	.25	.11	.03
□ 127 Scott Brosius	.10	.05	.01
□ 128 Ernie Young	.10	.05	.01
□ 129 Doug Johns	.10	.05	.01
□ 130 Geronimo Berroa	.10	.05	.01
□ 131 Jason Giambi	.25	.11	.03
□ 132 John Wasdin	.10	.05	.01
□ 133 Jim Eisenreich	.10	.05	.01
□ 134 Ricky Otero	.10	.05	.01
□ 135 Ricky Bottalico	.10	.05	.01
□ 136 Mark Langston DG	.10	.05	.01
□ 137 Greg Maddux DG	1.00	.45	.12
□ 138 Ivan Rodriguez DG	.50	.23	.06
□ 139 Charles Johnson DG	.25	.11	.03
□ 140 J.T. Snow DG	.10	.05	.01
□ 141 Mark Grace DG	.25	.11	.03
□ 142 Roberto Alomar DG	.50	.23	.06
□ 143 Craig Biggio DG	.25	.11	.03
□ 144 Ken Caminiti DG	.25	.11	.03
□ 145 Matt Williams DG	.25	.11	.03
□ 146 Omar Vizquel DG	.25	.11	.03
□ 147 Cal Ripken DG	1.25	.55	.16
□ 148 Ozzie Smith DG	.50	.23	.06
□ 149 Rey Ordonez DG	.25	.11	.03
□ 150 Ken Griffey Jr. DG	1.50	.70	.19
□ 151 Devon White DG	.10	.05	.01
□ 152 Barry Bonds DG	.50	.23	.06
□ 153 Kenny Lofton DG	.50	.23	.06
□ 154 Mickey Morandini	.10	.05	.01
□ 155 Gregg Jefferies	.25	.11	.03
□ 156 Curt Schilling	.10	.05	.01
□ 157 Jason Kendall	.25	.11	.03
□ 158 Francisco Cordova	.10	.05	.01
□ 159 Dennis Eckersley	.25	.11	.03
□ 160 Ron Gant	.25	.11	.03
□ 161 Ozzie Smith	.40	.18	.05
□ 162 Brian Jordan	.25	.11	.03
□ 163 John Mabry	.10	.05	.01
□ 164 Andy Ashby	.10	.05	.01
□ 165 Steve Finley	.25	.11	.03
□ 166 Fernando Valenzuela	.25	.11	.03
□ 167 Archi Cianfrocco	.10	.05	.01
□ 168 Wally Joyner	.25	.11	.03
□ 169 Greg Vaughn	.25	.11	.03
□ 170 Barry Bonds	.75	.35	.09
□ 171 William VanLandingham	.10	.05	.01
□ 172 Marvin Benard	.10	.05	.01
□ 173 Rich Aurilia	.10	.05	.01
□ 174 Jay Canizaro	.10	.05	.01
□ 175 Ken Griffey Jr.	3.00	1.35	.35
□ 176 Bob Wells	.10	.05	.01
□ 177 Jay Buhner	.50	.23	.06
□ 178 Sterling Hitchcock	.10	.05	.01
□ 179 Edgar Martinez	.50	.23	.06
□ 180 Rusty Greer	.25	.11	.03
□ 181 Dave Nilsson GI	.10	.05	.01
□ 182 Larry Walker GI	.25	.11	.03
□ 183 Edgar Renteria GI	.25	.11	.03
□ 184 Rey Ordonez GI	.25	.11	.03
□ 185 Rafael Palmeiro GI	.25	.11	.03
□ 186 Osvaldo Fernandez GI	.10	.05	.01
□ 187 Raul Mondesi GI	.25	.11	.03
□ 188 Manny Ramirez GI	.50	.23	.06
□ 189 Sammy Sosa GI	.25	.11	.03
□ 190 Robert Eenhoorn GI	.10	.05	.01
□ 191 Devon White GI	.10	.05	.01
□ 192 Hideo Nomo GI	.50	.23	.06
□ 193 Mac Suzuki GI	.10	.05	.01
□ 194 Chan Ho Park GI	.25	.11	.03
□ 195 Fernando Valenzuela GI	.25	.11	.03
□ 196 Andruw Jones GI	1.50	.70	.19
□ 197 Vinny Castilla GI	.25	.11	.03
□ 198 Dennis Martinez GI	.25	.11	.03
□ 199 Ruben Rivera GI	.25	.11	.03
□ 200 Juan Gonzalez GI	.75	.35	.09
□ 201 Roberto Alomar GI	.50	.23	.06
□ 202 Edgar Martinez GI	.50	.23	.06
□ 203 Ivan Rodriguez GI	.50	.23	.06
□ 204 Carlos Delgado GI	.25	.11	.03
□ 205 Andres Galarraga GI	.50	.23	.06
□ 206 Ozzie Guillen GI	.10	.05	.01
□ 207 Midre Cummings GI	.10	.05	.01
□ 208 Roger Pavlik	.10	.05	.01
□ 209 Darren Oliver	.10	.05	.01
□ 210 Dean Palmer	.25	.11	.03
□ 211 Ivan Rodriguez	.60	.25	.07
□ 212 Otis Nixon	.10	.05	.01
□ 213 Pat Hentgen	.25	.11	.03
□ 214 Ozzie Smith Andre Dawson Kirby Puckett HL/CL (1-27)	.25	.11	.03
□ 215 Barry Bonds Gary Sheffield Brady Anderson HL/CL (28-54)	.25	.11	.03
□ 216 Ken Caminiti HL/CL (55-81)	.25	.11	.03
□ 217 John Smoltz HL/CL (82-108)	.50	.23	.06
□ 218 Eric Young HL/CL (109-135)	.25	.11	.03
□ 219 Juan Gonzalez HL/CL (136-162)	.50	.23	.06
□ 220 Eddie Murray HL/CL (163-189)	.50	.23	.06
□ 221 Tommy Lasorda HL/CL (190-216)	.25	.11	.03
□ 222 Paul Molitor HL/CL (217-240)	.50	.23	.06
□ 223 Luis Castillo	.25	.11	.03
□ 224 Justin Thompson	.10	.05	.01
□ 225 Rocky Coppinger	.25	.11	.03
□ 226 Jermaine Allensworth	.10	.05	.01
□ 227 Jeff D'Amico	.25	.11	.03
□ 228 Jamey Wright	.10	.05	.01
□ 229 Scott Rolen	1.00	.45	.12
□ 230 Darin Erstad	1.50	.70	.19
□ 231 Marty Janzen	.10	.05	.01
□ 232 Jacob Cruz	.10	.05	.01
□ 233 Raul Ibanez	.10	.05	.01
□ 234 Nomar Garciaparra	.50	.23	.06
□ 235 Todd Walker	.75	.35	.09
□ 236 Brian Giles	.10	.05	.01
□ 237 Matt Beech	.10	.05	.01
□ 238 Mike Cameron	.25	.11	.03
□ 239 Jose Paniagua	.10	.05	.01
□ 240 Andruw Jones	3.00	1.35	.35

1997 Upper Deck Amazing Greats

Randomly inserted in packs at a rate of one in 138, this 20-card set features a horizontal design along with two player photos on the

front. The cards feature translucent player images against a real wood grain stock. The cards are numbered with an "AG" prefix.

	MINT	NRMT	EXC
COMPLETE SET (20)	600.00	275.00	75.00
COMMON CARD (AG1-AG20)	12.00	5.50	1.50
RANDOM INSERTS IN PACKS			
☐ AG1 Ken Griffey Jr.	80.00	36.00	10.00
☐ AG2 Roberto Alomar	20.00	9.00	2.50
☐ AG3 Alex Rodriguez	80.00	36.00	10.00
☐ AG4 Paul Molitor	15.00	6.75	1.85
☐ AG5 Chipper Jones	50.00	22.00	6.25
☐ AG6 Tony Gwynn	30.00	13.50	3.70
☐ AG7 Kenny Lofton	20.00	9.00	2.50
☐ AG8 Albert Belle	40.00	18.00	5.00
☐ AG9 Matt Williams	12.00	5.50	1.50
☐ AG10 Frank Thomas	80.00	36.00	10.00
☐ AG11 Greg Maddux	50.00	22.00	6.25
☐ AG12 Sammy Sosa	12.00	5.50	1.50
☐ AG13 Kirby Puckett	25.00	11.00	3.10
☐ AG14 Jeff Bagwell	30.00	13.50	3.70
☐ AG15 Cal Ripken	60.00	27.00	7.50
☐ AG16 Manny Ramirez	20.00	9.00	2.50
☐ AG17 Barry Bonds	20.00	9.00	2.50
☐ AG18 Mo Vaughn	20.00	9.00	2.50
☐ AG19 Eddie Murray	20.00	9.00	2.50
☐ AG20 Mike Piazza	50.00	22.00	6.25

1997 Upper Deck Game Jersey

Randomly inserted in packs at a rate of one in 660, this 3-card set feaures swatches of real jerseys cut up and placed on the cards. The cards are numbered with a "GJ" prefix.

	MINT	NRMT	EXC
COMPLETE SET (3)	750.00	350.00	95.00
COMMON CARD (GJ1-GJ3)	125.00	55.00	15.50
RANDOM INSERTS IN PACKS			
☐ GJ1 Ken Griffey Jr.	450.00	200.00	55.00
☐ GJ2 Tony Gwynn	250.00	110.00	31.00
☐ GJ3 Rey Ordonez	125.00	55.00	15.50

1997 Upper Deck Power Package

Randomly inserted in packs at a rate of one in 23, this 20-card set feaures some of the best long hitters. The die cut cards feature some of baseball's leading power hitters. The backs have a player photo, some information and are numbered with a "PP" prefix.-

	MINT	NRMT	EXC
COMPLETE SET (20)	135.00	60.00	17.00
COMMON CARD (PP1-PP20)	4.00	1.80	.50
RANDOM INSERTS IN PACKS			
☐ PP1 Ken Griffey Jr.	30.00	13.50	3.70
☐ PP2 Joe Carter	4.00	1.80	.50
☐ PP3 Rafael Palmeiro	5.00	2.20	.60
☐ PP4 Jay Buhner	5.00	2.20	.60
☐ PP5 Sammy Sosa	5.00	2.20	.60
☐ PP6 Fred McGriff	5.00	2.20	.60
☐ PP7 Jeff Bagwell	12.00	5.50	1.50
☐ PP8 Albert Belle	15.00	6.75	1.85
☐ PP9 Matt Williams	5.00	2.20	.60
☐ PP10 Mark McGwire	10.00	4.50	1.25
☐ PP11 Gary Sheffield	5.00	2.20	.60
☐ PP12 Tim Salmon	5.00	2.20	.60
☐ PP13 Ryan Klesko	6.00	2.70	.75
☐ PP14 Manny Ramirez	8.00	3.60	1.00
☐ PP15 Mike Piazza	20.00	9.00	2.50
☐ PP16 Barry Bonds	8.00	3.60	1.00
☐ PP17 Mo Vaughn	8.00	3.60	1.00
☐ PP18 Jose Canseco	5.00	2.20	.60
☐ PP19 Juan Gonzalez	15.00	6.75	1.85
☐ PP20 Frank Thomas	30.00	13.50	3.70

1997 Upper Deck Rock Solid Foundation

Randomly inserted in packs at a rate of one in 34, this 20-card set features players 25 and under who have made an impact in the majors. The fronts feature a player photo against a "silver" type background. The backs give player information as well as another player photo and are numbered with a "RS" prefix.

	MINT	NRMT	EXC
COMPLETE SET (20)	50.00	22.00	6.25
COMMON CARD (RS1-RS20)	2.00	.90	.25
RANDOM INSERTS IN PACKS			
☐ RS1 Alex Rodriguez	15.00	6.75	1.85
☐ RS2 Rey Ordonez	2.50	1.10	.30
☐ RS3 Derek Jeter	10.00	4.50	1.25
☐ RS4 Darin Erstad	8.00	3.60	1.00
☐ RS5 Chipper Jones	10.00	4.50	1.25
☐ RS6 Johnny Damon	2.00	.90	.25
☐ RS7 Ryan Klesko	2.50	1.10	.30
☐ RS8 Charles Johnson	2.00	.90	.25
☐ RS9 Andy Pettitte	4.00	1.80	.50
☐ RS10 Manny Ramirez	4.00	1.80	.50
☐ RS11 Ivan Rodriguez	3.00	1.35	.35
☐ RS12 Jason Kendall	2.00	.90	.25
☐ RS13 Rondell White	2.00	.90	.25
☐ RS14 Alex Ochoa	2.00	.90	.25
☐ RS15 Javier Lopez	2.00	.90	.25
☐ RS16 Pedro Martinez	2.00	.90	.25
☐ RS17 Carlos Delgado	2.00	.90	.25
☐ RS18 Paul Wilson	2.00	.90	.25
☐ RS19 Alan Benes	2.00	.90	.25
☐ RS20 Raul Mondesi	2.00	.90	.25

1997 Upper Deck Ticket To Stardom

Randomly inserted in packs at a rate of one in 7, this 20-card set is designed in the form of a ticket and are designed to be matched. The horizontal fronts feature two player photos as well as using "light f/x technology and embossed player images.

	MINT	NRMT	EXC
COMPLETE SET (20)	150.00	70.00	19.00
COMMON CARD (TS1-TS20)	2.00	.90	.25
RANDOM INSERTS IN PACKS			
☐ TS1 Chipper Jones	25.00	11.00	3.10
☐ TS2 Jermaine Dye	5.00	2.20	.60
☐ TS3 Rey Ordonez	4.00	1.80	.50
☐ TS4 Alex Ochoa	3.00	1.35	.35
☐ TS5 Derek Jeter	25.00	11.00	3.10
☐ TS6 Ruben Rivera	4.00	1.80	.50
☐ TS7 Billy Wagner	3.00	1.35	.35
☐ TS8 Jason Kendall	3.00	1.35	.35
☐ TS9 Darin Erstad	20.00	9.00	2.50

□ TS10 Alex Rodriguez	40.00	18.00	5.00
□ TS11 Bob Abreu	3.00	1.35	.35
□ TS12 Richard Hidalgo	3.00	1.35	.35
□ TS13 Karim Garcia	4.00	1.80	.50
□ TS14 Andruw Jones	40.00	18.00	5.00
□ TS15 Carlos Delgado	3.00	1.35	.35
□ TS16 Rocky Coppinger	3.00	1.35	.35
□ TS17 Jeff D'Amico	3.00	1.35	.35
□ TS18 Johnny Damon	3.00	1.35	.35
□ TS19 John Wasdin	2.00	.90	.25
□ TS20 Manny Ramirez	10.00	4.50	1.25

1995 Zenith

The complete 1995 Zenith set consists of 150 standard-size cards. The cards are made of thick stock and are borderless. The fronts have an action photo with a pyramid design serving as background. The player's name appears vertically up the left side with the Pinnacle logo in the upper right corner. The backs have a head shot and statistical information such as pitcherís strike frequency and what part of the field batters have the tendency to go to most. Included is a subset of 50 Rookies (111-150). The regular issued cards are in alphabetical order by first name. Rookie Cards in this set include Hideo Nomo and Carlos Perez.

	MINT	NRMT	EXC
COMPLETE SET (150)	40.00	18.00	5.00
COMMON CARD (1-150)	.15	.07	.02
SEMISTARS	.30	.14	.04
STARS	.75	.35	.09
□ 1 Albert Belle	2.50	1.10	.30
□ 2 Alex Fernandez	.30	.14	.04
□ 3 Andy Benes	.15	.07	.02
□ 4 Barry Larkin	.75	.35	.09
□ 5 Barry Bonds	1.25	.55	.16
□ 6 Ben McDonald	.15	.07	.02
□ 7 Bernard Gilkey	.30	.14	.04
□ 8 Billy Ashley	.15	.07	.02
□ 9 Bobby Bonilla	.30	.14	.04
□ 10 Bret Saberhagen	.30	.14	.04
□ 11 Brian Jordan	.75	.35	.09
□ 12 Cal Ripken	4.00	1.80	.50
□ 13 Carlos Baerga	.75	.35	.09
□ 14 Carlos Delgado	.75	.35	.09
□ 15 Cecil Fielder	.30	.14	.04
□ 16 Chili Davis	.30	.14	.04
□ 17 Chuck Knoblauch	.75	.35	.09
□ 18 Craig Biggio	.75	.35	.09
□ 19 Danny Tartabull	.15	.07	.02
□ 20 Dante Bichette	.75	.35	.09
□ 21 Darren Daulton	.30	.14	.04
□ 22 David Justice	.75	.35	.09
□ 23 Dave Winfield	.75	.35	.09
□ 24 David Cone	.30	.14	.04
□ 25 Dean Palmer	.30	.14	.04
□ 26 Deion Sanders	.75	.35	.09
□ 27 Dennis Eckersley	.30	.14	.04
□ 28 Derek Bell	.30	.14	.04
□ 29 Don Mattingly	2.50	1.10	.30
□ 30 Edgar Martinez	.75	.35	.09
□ 31 Eric Karros	.30	.14	.04
□ 32 James Mouton	.15	.07	.02
□ 33 Frank Thomas	5.00	2.20	.60
□ 34 Fred McGriff	.75	.35	.09
□ 35 Gary Sheffield	.75	.35	.09
□ 36 Gary Gaetti	.30	.14	.04
□ 37 Greg Maddux	3.00	1.35	.35
□ 38 Gregg Jefferies	.30	.14	.04
□ 39 Ivan Rodriguez	1.00	.45	.12
□ 40 Kenny Rogers	.15	.07	.02
□ 41 J.T. Snow	.30	.14	.04
□ 42 Hal Morris	.15	.07	.02
□ 43 Eddie Murray 3000th Hit	1.25	.55	.16
□ 44 Javier Lopez	.75	.35	.09
□ 45 Jay Bell	.30	.14	.04
□ 46 Jeff Conine	.75	.35	.09
□ 47 Jeff Bagwell	2.00	.90	.25
□ 48 Hideo Nomo Japanese	5.00	2.20	.60
□ 49 Jeff Kent	.15	.07	.02
□ 50 Jeff King	.30	.14	.04
□ 51 Jim Thome	1.00	.45	.12
□ 52 Jimmy Key	.30	.14	.04
□ 53 Joe Carter	.75	.35	.09
□ 54 John Valentin	.30	.14	.04
□ 55 John Olerud	.15	.07	.02
□ 56 Jose Canseco	.75	.35	.09
□ 57 Jose Rijo	.15	.07	.02
□ 58 Jose Offerman	.15	.07	.02
□ 59 Juan Gonzalez	2.50	1.10	.30
□ 60 Ken Caminiti	.75	.35	.09
□ 61 Ken Griffey Jr.	5.00	2.20	.60
□ 62 Kenny Lofton	1.25	.55	.16
□ 63 Kevin Appier	.30	.14	.04
□ 64 Kevin Seitzer	.15	.07	.02
□ 65 Kirby Puckett	1.50	.70	.19
□ 66 Kirk Gibson	.30	.14	.04
□ 67 Larry Walker	.75	.35	.09
□ 68 Lenny Dykstra	.30	.14	.04
□ 69 Manny Ramirez	1.25	.55	.16
□ 70 Mark Grace	.75	.35	.09
□ 71 Mark McGwire	1.50	.70	.19
□ 72 Marquis Grissom	.75	.35	.09
□ 73 Jim Edmonds	.75	.35	.09
□ 74 Matt Williams	.75	.35	.09
□ 75 Mike Mussina	1.00	.45	.12
□ 76 Mike Piazza	3.00	1.35	.35
□ 77 Mo Vaughn	1.25	.55	.16
□ 78 Moises Alou	.30	.14	.04
□ 79 Ozzie Smith	1.00	.45	.12
□ 80 Paul O'Neill	.30	.14	.04
□ 81 Paul Molitor	1.00	.45	.12
□ 82 Rafael Palmeiro	.75	.35	.09
□ 83 Randy Johnson	.75	.35	.09
□ 84 Raul Mondesi	.75	.35	.09
□ 85 Ray Lankford	.75	.35	.09
□ 86 Reggie Sanders	.30	.14	.04
□ 87 Rickey Henderson	.75	.35	.09
□ 88 Rico Brogna	.15	.07	.02
□ 89 Roberto Alomar	1.25	.55	.16
□ 90 Robin Ventura	.30	.14	.04
□ 91 Roger Clemens	.75	.35	.09
□ 92 Ron Gant	.30	.14	.04
□ 93 Rondell White	.75	.35	.09
□ 94 Royce Clayton	.15	.07	.02
□ 95 Ruben Sierra	.30	.14	.04
□ 96 Rusty Greer	.75	.35	.09
□ 97 Ryan Klesko	1.00	.45	.12
□ 98 Sammy Sosa	.75	.35	.09
□ 99 Shawon Dunston	.15	.07	.02
□ 100 Steve Ontiveros	.15	.07	.02
□ 101 Tim Naehring	.15	.07	.02
□ 102 Tim Salmon	.75	.35	.09
□ 103 Tino Martinez	.30	.14	.04
□ 104 Tony Gwynn	2.00	.90	.25
□ 105 Travis Fryman	.30	.14	.04
□ 106 Vinny Castilla	.30	.14	.04
□ 107 Wade Boggs	.75	.35	.09
□ 108 Wally Joyner	.30	.14	.04
□ 109 Wil Cordero	.15	.07	.02
□ 110 Will Clark	.75	.35	.09
□ 111 Chipper Jones	3.00	1.35	.35
□ 112 Armando Benitez	.15	.07	.02
□ 113 Curtis Goodwin	.30	.14	.04
□ 114 Gabe White	.15	.07	.02
□ 115 Vaughn Eshelman	.15	.07	.02
□ 116 Marty Cordova	.75	.35	.09

□ 117 Dustin Hermanson	.30	.14	.04
□ 118 Rich Becker	.15	.07	.02
□ 119 Ray Durham	.30	.14	.04
□ 120 Shane Andrews	.15	.07	.02
□ 121 Scott Ruffcorn	.15	.07	.02
□ 122 Mark Grudzielanek	1.25	.55	.16
□ 123 James Baldwin	.75	.35	.09
□ 124 Carlos Perez	.30	.14	.04
□ 125 Julian Tavarez	.15	.07	.02
□ 126 Joe Vitiello	.15	.07	.02
□ 127 Jason Bates	.15	.07	.02
□ 128 Edgardo Alfonzo	.30	.14	.04
□ 129 Juan Acevedo	.15	.07	.02
□ 130 Bill Pulsipher	.30	.14	.04
□ 131 Bob Higginson	.75	.35	.09
□ 132 Russ Davis	.15	.07	.02
□ 133 Charles Johnson	.30	.14	.04
□ 134 Derek Jeter	3.00	1.35	.35
□ 135 Orlando Miller	.15	.07	.02
□ 136 LaTroy Hawkins	.15	.07	.02
□ 137 Brian L.Hunter	.75	.35	.09
□ 138 Roberto Petagine	.15	.07	.02
□ 139 Midre Cummings	.15	.07	.02
□ 140 Garret Anderson	.75	.35	.09
□ 141 Ugueth Urbina	.15	.07	.02
□ 142 Antonio Osuna	.15	.07	.02
□ 143 Michael Tucker	.30	.14	.04
□ 144 Benji Gil	.15	.07	.02
□ 145 Jon Nunnally	.30	.14	.04
□ 146 Alex Rodriguez	6.00	2.70	.75
□ 147 Todd Hollandsworth	.75	.35	.09
□ 148 Alex Gonzalez	.15	.07	.02
□ 149 Hideo Nomo	5.00	2.20	.60
□ 150 Shawn Green	.30	.14	.04

1995 Zenith All-Star Salute

This 18-card set was randomly inserted in packs at a rate of one in six. The set commemorates many of the memorable plays of the 1995 All-Star Game played in Arlington, TX. The fronts have an action photo set out against the background of the game giving it a 3D look. The words "All-Star Salute" are in gold on the left with the player's name at the bottom. The backs have a color photo with personal All-Star Game tidbits. The cards are numbered "X of 18."

	MINT	NRMT	EXC
COMPLETE SET (18)	60.00	27.00	7.50
COMMON CARD (1-18)	1.00	.45	.12
RANDOM INSERTS IN PACKS			
□ 1 Cal Ripken	8.00	3.60	1.00
□ 2 Frank Thomas	10.00	4.50	1.25
□ 3 Mike Piazza	6.00	2.70	.75
□ 4 Kirby Puckett	3.00	1.35	.35
□ 5 Manny Ramirez	2.50	1.10	.30
□ 6 Tony Gwynn	4.00	1.80	.50
□ 7 Hideo Nomo	6.00	2.70	.75
□ 8 Matt Williams	1.00	.45	.12
□ 9 Randy Johnson	1.50	.70	.19
□ 10 Raul Mondesi	1.00	.45	.12
□ 11 Albert Belle	5.00	2.20	.60
□ 12 Ivan Rodriguez	2.00	.90	.25
□ 13 Barry Bonds	2.50	1.10	.30
□ 14 Carlos Baerga	1.00	.45	.12
□ 15 Ken Griffey Jr.	10.00	4.50	1.25
□ 16 Jeff Conine	1.00	.45	.12
□ 17 Frank Thomas	10.00	4.50	1.25
□ 18 Cal Ripken Barry Bonds	6.00	2.70	.75

1995 Zenith Rookie Roll Call

This 18-card, Dufex-designed standard-size set was randomly inserted in packs at a rate of one in 24. The set is comprised of 18 top rookies from 1995. The fronts have two photos and a colorful star in the background with which rays of color emanate. The backs are laid out horizontally with a color photo on a multi-color foil background. Player information of previous accomplishments is also on the back and the cards are numbered "X of 18."

	MINT	NRMT	EXC
COMPLETE SET (18)	240.00	110.00	30.00
COMMON CARD (1-18)	8.00	3.60	1.00
RANDOM INSERTS IN PACKS			
□ 1 Alex Rodriguez	100.00	45.00	12.50
□ 2 Derek Jeter	60.00	27.00	7.50
□ 3 Chipper Jones	60.00	27.00	7.50
□ 4 Shawn Green	8.00	3.60	1.00
□ 5 Todd Hollandsworth	12.00	5.50	1.50
□ 6 Bill Pulsipher	8.00	3.60	1.00
□ 7 Hideo Nomo	40.00	18.00	5.00
□ 8 Ray Durham	8.00	3.60	1.00
□ 9 Curtis Goodwin	8.00	3.60	1.00
□ 10 Brian L.Hunter	12.00	5.50	1.50
□ 11 Julian Tavarez	8.00	3.60	1.00
□ 12 Marty Cordova UER Kevin Maas pictured	15.00	6.75	1.85
□ 13 Michael Tucker	8.00	3.60	1.00
□ 14 Edgardo Alfonzo	8.00	3.60	1.00
□ 15 LaTroy Hawkins	8.00	3.60	1.00
□ 16 Carlos Perez	8.00	3.60	1.00
□ 17 Charles Johnson	10.00	4.50	1.25
□ 18 Benji Gil	8.00	3.60	1.00

1995 Zenith Z-Team

This 18-card standard-size set was randomly inserted in packs at a rate of one in 72. The set is comprised of the best players in baseball and is done in 3-D Dufex. The fronts have a player action photo positioned on home plate which has the words "Z Team". There are multi-colored rays coming out of the card background. The back is laid out horizontally with a color head shot and a stadium crowd background. The back also has player information and a "Z Team" emblem.

	MINT	NRMT	EXC
COMPLETE SET (18)	500.00	220.00	60.00
COMMON CARD (1-18)	8.00	3.60	1.00
RANDOM INSERTS IN PACKS			

		MINT	NRMT	EXC
□	1 Cal Ripken	60.00	27.00	7.50
□	2 Ken Griffey Jr.	80.00	36.00	10.00
□	3 Frank Thomas	80.00	36.00	10.00
□	4 Matt Williams	10.00	4.50	1.25
□	5 Mike Piazza UER (Card says started at first base Piazza is a catcher)	50.00	22.00	6.25
□	6 Barry Bonds	20.00	9.00	2.50
□	7 Raul Mondesi	10.00	4.50	1.25
□	8 Greg Maddux	50.00	22.00	6.25
□	9 Jeff Bagwell	30.00	13.50	3.70
□	10 Manny Ramirez	20.00	9.00	2.50
□	11 Larry Walker	8.00	3.60	1.00
□	12 Tony Gwynn	30.00	13.50	3.70
□	13 Will Clark	10.00	4.50	1.25
□	14 Albert Belle	40.00	18.00	5.00
□	15 Kenny Lofton	20.00	9.00	2.50
□	16 Rafael Palmeiro	10.00	4.50	1.25
□	17 Don Mattingly	40.00	18.00	5.00
□	18 Carlos Baerga	8.00	3.60	1.00

1996 Zenith

This 1996 Zenith set was issued in one series totalling 150 cards. The six-card packs retail for $3.99 each. The set contains the subset: Honor Roll (131-150). The fronts feature a color player cutout over an arrangement of baseball bats on a black background. The backs carry a hit location chart and player statistics. The only notable Rookie Card is of Darin Erstad.

		MINT	NRMT	EXC
	COMPLETE SET (150)	40.00	18.00	5.00
	COMMON CARD (1-150)	.15	.07	.02
	SEMISTARS	.30	.14	.04
	STARS	.60	.25	.07
□	1 Ken Griffey Jr.	4.00	1.80	.50
□	2 Ozzie Smith	.75	.35	.09
□	3 Greg Maddux	2.50	1.10	.30
□	4 Rondell White	.30	.14	.04
□	5 Mark McGwire	1.25	.55	.16
□	6 Jim Thome	.75	.35	.09
□	7 Ivan Rodriguez	.75	.35	.09
□	8 Marc Newfield	.30	.14	.04
□	9 Travis Fryman	.60	.25	.07
□	10 Fred McGriff	.60	.25	.07
□	11 Shawn Green	.15	.07	.02
□	12 Mike Piazza	2.50	1.10	.30
□	13 Dante Bichette	.60	.25	.07
□	14 Tino Martinez	.60	.25	.07
□	15 Sterling Hitchcock	.15	.07	.02
□	16 Ryne Sandberg	1.00	.45	.12
□	17 Rico Brogna	.15	.07	.02
□	18 Roberto Alomar	1.00	.45	.12
□	19 Barry Larkin	.60	.25	.07
□	20 Bernie Williams	.60	.25	.07
□	21 Gary Sheffield	.60	.25	.07
□	22 Frank Thomas	4.00	1.80	.50
□	23 Gregg Jefferies	.60	.25	.07
□	24 Jeff Bagwell	1.50	.70	.19
□	25 Marty Cordova	.60	.25	.07
□	26 Jim Edmonds	.60	.25	.07
□	27 Jay Bell	.30	.14	.04
□	28 Ben McDonald	.15	.07	.02
□	29 Barry Bonds	1.00	.45	.12
□	30 Mo Vaughn	1.00	.45	.12
□	31 Johnny Damon	.15	.07	.02
□	32 Dean Palmer	.60	.25	.07
□	33 Ismael Valdes	.30	.14	.04
□	34 Manny Ramirez	1.00	.45	.12
□	35 Edgar Martinez	.60	.25	.07
□	36 Cecil Fielder	.60	.25	.07
□	37 Ryan Klesko	.75	.35	.09
□	38 Ray Lankford	.60	.25	.07
□	39 Tim Salmon	.30	.14	.04
□	40 Joe Carter	.60	.25	.07
□	41 Jason Isringhausen	.15	.07	.02
□	42 Rickey Henderson	.60	.25	.07
□	43 Lenny Dykstra	.30	.14	.04
□	44 Andre Dawson	.60	.25	.07
□	45 Paul O'Neill	.15	.07	.02
□	46 Ray Durham	.60	.25	.07
□	47 Raul Mondesi	.60	.25	.07
□	48 Jay Buhner	.60	.25	.07
□	49 Eddie Murray	1.00	.45	.12
□	50 Henry Rodriguez	.15	.07	.02
□	51 Hal Morris	.15	.07	.02
□	52 Mike Mussina	.75	.35	.09
□	53 Wally Joyner	.15	.07	.02
□	54 Will Clark	.60	.25	.07
□	55 Chipper Jones	2.50	1.10	.30
□	56 Brian Jordan	.60	.25	.07
□	57 Larry Walker	.60	.25	.07
□	58 Wade Boggs	.60	.25	.07
□	59 Melvin Nieves	.30	.14	.04
□	60 Charles Johnson	.30	.14	.04
□	61 Juan Gonzalez	2.00	.90	.25
□	62 Carlos Delgado	.60	.25	.07
□	63 Reggie Sanders	.30	.14	.04
□	64 Brian L.Hunter	.15	.07	.02
□	65 Edgardo Alfonzo	.15	.07	.02
□	66 Kenny Lofton	1.00	.45	.12
□	67 Paul Molitor	.75	.35	.09
□	68 Mike Bordick	.15	.07	.02
□	69 Garret Anderson	.60	.25	.07
□	70 Orlando Merced	.15	.07	.02
□	71 Craig Biggio	.60	.25	.07
□	72 Chuck Knoblauch	.60	.25	.07
□	73 Mark Grace	.60	.25	.07
□	74 Jack McDowell	.60	.25	.07
□	75 Randy Johnson	.60	.25	.07
□	76 Cal Ripken	3.00	1.35	.35
□	77 Matt Williams	.60	.25	.07
□	78 Benji Gil	.15	.07	.02
□	79 Moises Alou	.30	.14	.04
□	80 Robin Ventura	.60	.25	.07
□	81 Greg Vaughn	.60	.25	.07
□	82 Carlos Baerga	.60	.25	.07
□	83 Roger Clemens	.60	.25	.07
□	84 Hideo Nomo	1.00	.45	.12
□	85 Pedro Martinez	.30	.14	.04
□	86 John Valentin	.30	.14	.04
□	87 Andres Galarraga	.60	.25	.07
□	88 Andy Pettitte	1.25	.55	.16
□	89 Derek Bell	.15	.07	.02
□	90 Kirby Puckett	1.25	.55	.16
□	91 Tony Gwynn	1.50	.70	.19
□	92 Brady Anderson	.60	.25	.07
□	93 Derek Jeter	2.50	1.10	.30
□	94 Michael Tucker	.15	.07	.02
□	95 Albert Belle	2.00	.90	.25
□	96 David Cone	.60	.25	.07
□	97 J.T. Snow	.30	.14	.04
□	98 Tom Glavine	.60	.25	.07

□ 99 Alex Rodriguez	4.00	1.80	.50
□ 100 Sammy Sosa	.60	.25	.07
□ 101 Karim Garcia	.75	.35	.09
□ 102 Alan Benes	.60	.25	.07
□ 103 Chad Mottola	.15	.07	.02
□ 104 Robin Jennings	.15	.07	.02
□ 105 Bob Abreu	.60	.25	.07
□ 106 Tony Clark	.60	.25	.07
□ 107 George Arias	.15	.07	.02
□ 108 Jermaine Dye	.75	.35	.09
□ 109 Jeff Suppan	.30	.14	.04
□ 110 Ralph Milliard	.15	.07	.02
□ 111 Ruben Rivera	.75	.35	.09
□ 112 Billy Wagner	.15	.07	.02
□ 113 Jason Kendall	.60	.25	.07
□ 114 Mike Grace	.15	.07	.02
□ 115 Edgar Renteria	.60	.25	.07
□ 116 Jason Schmidt	.30	.14	.04
□ 117 Paul Wilson	.30	.14	.04
□ 118 Rey Ordonez	.75	.35	.09
□ 119 Rocky Coppinger	.75	.35	.09
□ 120 Wilton Guerrero	.75	.35	.09
□ 121 Brooks Kieschnick	.15	.07	.02
□ 122 Raul Casanova	.15	.07	.02
□ 123 Alex Ochoa	.30	.14	.04
□ 124 Chan Ho Park	.60	.25	.07
□ 125 John Wasdin	.15	.07	.02
□ 126 Eric Owens	.15	.07	.02
□ 127 Justin Thompson	.15	.07	.02
□ 128 Chris Snopek	.15	.07	.02
□ 129 Terrell Wade	.60	.25	.07
□ 130 Darin Erstad	4.00	1.80	.50
□ 131 Albert Belle HON	1.00	.45	.12
□ 132 Cal Ripken HON	1.50	.70	.19
□ 133 Frank Thomas HON	2.00	.90	.25
□ 134 Greg Maddux HON	1.25	.55	.16
□ 135 Ken Griffey Jr. HON	2.00	.90	.25
□ 136 Mo Vaughn HON	.60	.25	.07
□ 137 Chipper Jones HON	1.25	.55	.16
□ 138 Mike Piazza HON	1.25	.55	.16
□ 139 Ryan Klesko HON	.30	.14	.04
□ 140 Hideo Nomo HON	.60	.25	.07
□ 141 Roberto Alomar HON	.60	.25	.07
□ 142 Manny Ramirez HON	.30	.14	.04
□ 143 Gary Sheffield HON	.60	.25	.07
□ 144 Barry Bonds HON	.60	.25	.07
□ 145 Matt Williams HON	.60	.25	.07
□ 146 Jim Edmonds HON	.30	.14	.04
□ 147 Derek Jeter HON	1.25	.55	.16
□ 148 Sammy Sosa HON	.60	.25	.07
□ 149 Kirby Puckett HON	.60	.25	.07
□ 150 Tony Gwynn HON	.75	.35	.09

1996 Zenith Artist's Proofs

Randomly inserted in packs at a rate of one in 35, this 150-card set is parallel to the regular Zenith set. The cards are distinguished from the regular set by the "Artist's Proof" all-gold, rainbow holographic foil stamp on the front.

	MINT	NRMT	EXC
COMPLETE SET (150)	2500.00	1100.00	300.00
COMMON CARD (1-150)	4.00	1.80	.50
SEMISTARS	8.00	3.60	1.00
STARS	15.00	6.75	1.85
*STARS: 15X to 30X BASIC CARDS			
*YOUNG STARS: 12.5X to 25X BASIC CARDS			
RANDOM INSERTS IN PACKS			
□ 1 Ken Griffey Jr.	120.00	55.00	15.00
□ 3 Greg Maddux	75.00	34.00	9.50
□ 12 Mike Piazza	75.00	34.00	9.50
□ 22 Frank Thomas	120.00	55.00	15.00
□ 55 Chipper Jones	75.00	34.00	9.50
□ 61 Juan Gonzalez	60.00	27.00	7.50
□ 76 Cal Ripken	100.00	45.00	12.50
□ 93 Derek Jeter	75.00	34.00	9.50
□ 95 Albert Belle	60.00	27.00	7.50
□ 99 Alex Rodriguez	120.00	55.00	15.00
□ 130 Darin Erstad	60.00	27.00	7.50
□ 133 Frank Thomas HON	60.00	27.00	7.50
□ 135 Ken Griffey Jr. HON	60.00	27.00	7.50

1996 Zenith Diamond Club

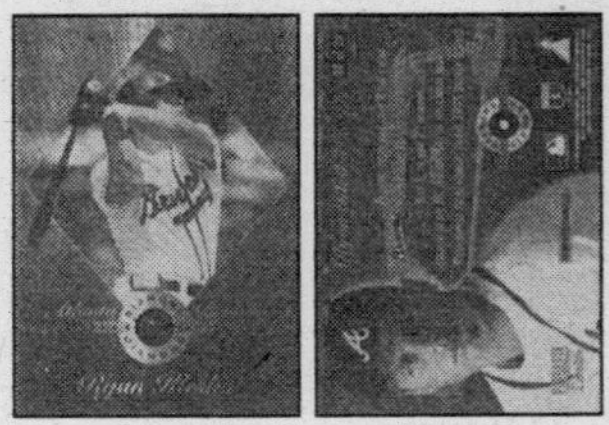

Randomly inserted in packs at a rate of one in 24, this 20-card set honors 20 top mega-performers on a spectacular Spectroetch card design printed on thick foil stock with etched highlights. The fronts feature an above-the-waist color action player cutout over a diamond-shaped opening on a grass-green background. The backs carry player information.

	MINT	NRMT	EXC
COMPLETE SET (20)	250.00	110.00	31.00
COMMON CARD (1-20)	4.00	1.80	.50
REAL DIAMOND: 8X VALUE			
RANDOM INSERTS IN PACKS			
□ 1 Albert Belle	15.00	6.75	1.85
□ 2 Mo Vaughn	8.00	3.60	1.00
□ 3 Ken Griffey Jr.	30.00	13.50	3.70
□ 4 Mike Piazza	20.00	9.00	2.50
□ 5 Cal Ripken	25.00	11.00	3.10
□ 6 Jermaine Dye	6.00	2.70	.75
□ 7 Jeff Bagwell	12.00	5.50	1.50
□ 8 Frank Thomas	30.00	13.50	3.70
□ 9 Alex Rodriguez	30.00	13.50	3.70
□ 10 Ryan Klesko	6.00	2.70	.75
□ 11 Roberto Alomar	8.00	3.60	1.00
□ 12 Sammy Sosa	5.00	2.20	.60
□ 13 Matt Williams	4.00	1.80	.50
□ 14 Gary Sheffield	5.00	2.20	.60
□ 15 Ruben Rivera	6.00	2.70	.75
□ 16 Darin Erstad	25.00	11.00	3.10
□ 17 Randy Johnson	5.00	2.20	.60
□ 18 Greg Maddux	20.00	9.00	2.50
□ 19 Karim Garcia	6.00	2.70	.75
□ 20 Chipper Jones	20.00	9.00	2.50

1996 Zenith Mozaics

Randomly inserted in packs at a rate of one in 10, this 25-card set features three-player image cards of the hottest superstars. The fronts display multiple player images representing the core of each of the 28 teams and are printed on rainbow holographic foil.

	MINT	NRMT	EXC
COMPLETE SET (25)	200.00	90.00	25.00
COMMON CARD (1-25)	4.00	1.80	.50
SEMISTARS	5.00	2.20	.60
RANDOM INSERTS IN PACKS			
□ 1 Greg Maddux Chipper Jones Ryan Klesko	30.00	13.50	3.70
□ 2 Juan Gonzalez Will Clark Ivan Rodriguez	12.00	5.50	1.50
□ 3 Frank Thomas Robin Ventura Ray Durham	25.00	11.00	3.10
□ 4 Matt Williams Barry Bonds Osvaldo Fernandez	6.00	2.70	.75
□ 5 Ken Griffey Jr. Randy Johnson Alex Rodriguez	35.00	16.00	4.40
□ 6 Sammy Sosa Ryne Sandberg Mark Grace	8.00	3.60	1.00
□ 7 Jim Edmonds Tim Salmon Garret Anderson	4.00	1.80	.50
□ 8 Cal Ripken Roberto Alomar Mike Mussina	25.00	11.00	3.10
□ 9 Mo Vaughn Roger Clemens John Valentin	10.00	4.50	1.25
□ 10 Barry Larkin Reggie Sanders Hal Morris	4.00	1.80	.50
□ 11 Ray Lankford Brian Jordan Ozzie Smith	6.00	2.70	.75
□ 12 Dante Bichette Larry Walker Andres Galarraga	6.00	2.70	.75
□ 13 Mike Piazza Hideo Nomo Raul Mondesi	20.00	9.00	2.50
□ 14 Ben McDonald Greg Vaughn Kevin Seitzer	4.00	1.80	.50
□ 15 Joe Carter Carlos Delgado Alex Gonzalez	4.00	1.80	.50
□ 16 Gary Sheffield Charles Johnson Jeff Conine	4.00	1.80	.50
□ 17 Rondell White Moises Alou Henry Rodriguez	4.00	1.80	.50
□ 18 Albert Belle Manny Ramirez Carlos Baerga	15.00	6.75	1.85
□ 19 Kirby Puckett Paul Molitor Chuck Knoblauch	10.00	4.50	1.25
□ 20 Tony Gwynn Rickey Henderson Wally Joyner	10.00	4.50	1.25
□ 21 Mark McGwire Mike Bordick Scott Brosius	8.00	3.60	1.00
□ 22 Paul O'Neill Bernie Williams Wade Boggs	8.00	3.60	1.00
□ 23 Jay Bell Orlando Merced Jason Kendall	4.00	1.80	.50
□ 24 Rico Brogna Paul Wilson Jason Isringhausen	4.00	1.80	.50
□ 25 Jeff Bagwell Craig Biggio Derek Bell	10.00	4.50	1.25

1996 Zenith Z-Team

Randomly inserted in packs at a rate of one in 72, this 18-card set features a color action player cutout on a clear micro-etched design with a gold foil Z-Team logo and a see-through green baseball field background. The backs carry player information printed on the back of the Z.

	MINT	NRMT	EXC
COMPLETE SET (18)	500.00	220.00	60.00
COMMON CARD (1-18)	10.00	4.50	1.25
RANDOM INSERTS IN PACKS			
□ 1 Ken Griffey Jr.	80.00	36.00	10.00
□ 2 Albert Belle	40.00	18.00	5.00
□ 3 Cal Ripken	60.00	27.00	7.50
□ 4 Frank Thomas	80.00	36.00	10.00
□ 5 Greg Maddux	50.00	22.00	6.25
□ 6 Mo Vaughn	20.00	9.00	2.50
□ 7 Chipper Jones	50.00	22.00	6.25
□ 8 Mike Piazza	50.00	22.00	6.25
□ 9 Ryan Klesko	15.00	6.75	1.85
□ 10 Hideo Nomo	20.00	9.00	2.50
□ 11 Roberto Alomar	20.00	9.00	2.50
□ 12 Manny Ramirez	20.00	9.00	2.50
□ 13 Gary Sheffield	12.00	5.50	1.50
□ 14 Barry Bonds	20.00	9.00	2.50
□ 15 Matt Williams	10.00	4.50	1.25
□ 16 Jim Edmonds	10.00	4.50	1.25
□ 17 Kirby Puckett	25.00	11.00	3.10
□ 18 Sammy Sosa	12.00	5.50	1.50

Acknowledgments

Each year we refine the process of developing the most accurate and up-to-date information for this book. I believe this year's Price Guide is our best yet. Thanks again to all the contributors nationwide (listed below) as well as our staff here in Dallas.

Those who have worked closely with us on this and many other books have again proven themselves invaluable: Levi Bleam and Jim Fleck (707 Sportscards), Peter Brennan, Ray Bright, Card Collectors Co., Cartophilium (Andrew Pywowarczuk), Barry Colla, Bill and Diane Dodge, Donruss/Leaf (Shawn Heilbron, Eric Tijerina), David Festberg, Fleer/SkyBox (Rich Bradley, Doug Drotman and Ted Taylor), Steve Freedman, Gervise Ford, Larry and Jeff Fritsch, Tony Galovich, Georgia Music and Sports (Dick DeCourcey), Dick Gilkeson, Steve Gold (AU Sports), Bill Goodwin (St. Louis Baseball Cards), Mike and Howard Gordon, George Grauer, John Greenwald, Greg's Cards, Wayne Grove, Bill Henderson, Jerry and Etta Hersh, Mike Hersh, Neil Hoppenworth, Jay and Mary Kasper, David Kohler (SportsCards Plus), Paul Lewicki, Lew Lipset, Mike Livingston (University Trading Cards), Mark Macrae, Bill Madden, Bill Mastro, Michael McDonald (The Sports Page), Mid-Atlantic Sports Cards (Bill Bossert), Gary Mills, Brian Morris, Mike Mosier (Columbia City Collectibles Co.), B.A. Murry, Ralph Nozaki, Mike O'Brien, Oldies and Goodies (Nigel Spill), Pacific Trading Cards (Mike Cramer and Mike Monson), Pinnacle (Laurie Goldberg, Kurt Iverson), Jack Pollard, Jeff Prillaman, Pat Quinn, Jerald Reichstein (Fabulous Cardboard), Gavin Riley, Clifton Rouse, John Rumierz, San Diego Sport Collectibles (Bill Goepner and Nacho Arredondo), Kevin Savage (Sports Gallery), Gary Sawatski, Mike Schechter, Scoreboard (Brian Cahill), Barry Sloate, John E. Spalding, Phil Spector, Frank Steele, Don Steinbach, Murvin Sterling, Lee Temanson, Topps (Marty Appel, Sy Berger and Melissa Rosen), Treat (Harold Anderson), Ed Twombly (New England Bullpen), Upper Deck (Steve Ryan, Marilyn Van Dyke), Wayne Varner, Bill Vizas, Bill Wesslund (Portland Sports Card Co.), Kit Young and Bob Ivanjack (Kit Young Cards), Rick Young, Ted Zanidakis, Robert Zanze (Z-Cards and Sports), and Bill Zimpleman. Finally we give a special acknowledgment to the late Dennis W. Eckes, "Mr. Sport Americana." The success of the Beckett Price Guides has always been the result of a team effort.

It is very difficult to be "accurate" -- one can only do one's best. But this job is especially difficult since we're shooting at a moving target: Prices are fluctuating all the time. Having several full-time pricing experts has definitely proven to be better than just one, and I thank all of them for working together to provide you, our readers, with the most accurate prices possible.

Many people have provided price input, illustrative material, checklist verifications, errata, and/or background information. We should like to individually thank AbD Cards (Dale Wesolewski), Action Card Sales, Jerry Adamic, Johnny and Sandy Adams, Alex's MVP Cards & Comics, Doug Allen (Round Tripper Sportscards), Will Allison, Dennis Anderson, Ed Anderson, Shane Anderson, Bruce W. Andrews, Ellis Anmuth, Tom Antonowicz, Alan Applegate, Ric Apter, Jason Arasate, Clyde Archer, Randy Archer, Matt Argento, Burl Armstrong, Neil Armstrong (World Series Cards), Todd Armstrong, Ara Arzoumanian, B and J Sportscards, Shawn Bailey, Ball Four Cards (Frank and Steve Pemper), Frank and Vivian Barning, Bob Bartosz, Nathan Basford, Carl Berg, David Berman, Beulah Sports (Jeff Blatt), Brian Bigelow, George Birsic, B.J. Sportscollectables, David Boedicker (The Wild Pitch Inc.), Bob Boffa, Louis Bollman, Tim Bond (Tim's Cards & Comics), Andrew Bosarge, Brian W. Bottles, Kenneth Braatz, Bill Brandt, Jeff Breitenfield, John Brigandi, John Broggi, Chuck Brooks, Dan Bruner, Lesha Bundrick, Michael Bunker, John E.

Burick, Ed Burkey Jr., Bubba Burnett, Virgil Burns, California Card Co., Capital Cards, Danny Cariseo, Carl Carlson (C.T.S.), Jim Carr, Patrick Carroll, Ira Cetron, Don Chaffee, Michael Chan, Sandy Chan, Ric Chandgie, Dwight Chapin, Ray Cherry, Bigg Wayne Christian, Josh Chidester, Dick Cianciotto, Michael and Abe Citron, Dr. Jeffrey Clair, Derrick F. Clark, Bill Cochran, Don Coe, Michael Cohen, Tom Cohoon (Cardboard Dreams), Collection de Sport AZ (Ronald Villaneuve), Gary Collett, Andrew T. Collier, Charles A. Collins, Curt Cooter, Steven Cooter, Pedro Cortes, Rick Cosmen (RC Card Co.), Lou Costanzo (Champion Sports), Mike Coyne, Paul and Ryan Crabb, Tony Craig (T.C. Card Co.), Kevin Crane, Taylor Crane, Chad Cripe, Brian Cunningham, Allen Custer, Donald L. Cutler, Eugene C. Dalager, Dave Dame, Brett Daniel, Tony Daniele III, Scott Dantio, Roy Datema, John Davidson, Travis Deaton, Dee's Baseball Cards (Dee Robinson), Joe Delgrippo, Tim DelVecchio, Steve Dempski, John Derossett, Mark Diamond, Gilberto Diaz Jr., Ken Dinerman (California Cruizers), Frank DiRoberto, Cliff Dolgins, Discount Dorothy, Walter J. Dodds Sr., Bill Dodson, Richard Dolloff (Dolloff Coin Center), Ron Dorsey, Double Play Baseball Cards, Richard Duglin (Baseball Cards-N-More), The Dugout, Kyle Dunbar, B.M. Dungan, Ken Edick (Home Plate of Utah), Randall Edwards, Rick Einhorn, Mark Ely, Todd Entenman, Doak Ewing, Bryan Failing, R.J. Faletti, Terry Falkner, Mike and Chris Fanning, John Fedak, Stephen A. Ferradino, Tom Ferrara, Dick Fields, Louis Fineberg, Jay Finglass, L.V. Fischer, Bob Flitter, Fremont Fong, Perry Fong, Craig Frank, Mark Franke, Walter Franklin, Tom Freeman, Bob Frye, Chris Gala, Richard Galasso, Ray Garner, David Garza, David Gaumer, Georgetown Card Exchange, Richard Gibson Jr., Glenn A. Giesey, David Giove, Dick Goddard, Alvin Goldblum, Brian Goldner, Jeff Goldstein, Ron Gomez, Rich Gove, Joseph Griffin, Mike Grimm, Neil Gubitz (What-A-Card), Hall's Nostalgia, Hershell Hanks, Gregg Hara, Zac Hargis, Floyd Haynes (H and H Baseball Cards), Ben Heckert, Kevin Heffner, Kevin Heimbigner, Dennis Heitland, Joel Hellman, Arthur W. Henkel, Kevin Hense, Hit and Run Cards (Jon, David, and Kirk Peterson), Gary Holcomb, Lyle Holcomb, Rich Hovorka, John Howard, Mark Hromalik, H.P. Hubert, Dennis Hughes, Harold Hull, Johnny Hustle Card Co., Tom Imboden, Chris Imbriaco, Vern Isenberg, Dale Jackson, Marshall Jackson, Mike Jardina, Hal Jarvis, Paul Jastrzembski, Jeff's Sports Cards, David Jenkins, Donn Jennings Cards, George Johnson, Robe Johnson, Stephen Jones, Al Julian, Chuck Juliana, Dave Jurgensmeier, John Just, Robert Just, Nick Kardoulias, Scott Kashner, Frank J. Katen, Jerry Katz (Bottom of the Ninth), Mark Kauffman, Allan Kaye, Rick Keplinger, Sam Kessler, Kevin's Kards, Larry B. Killian, Kingdom Collectibles, Inc., John Klassnik, Philip C. Klutts, Don Knutsen, Steven Koenigsberg, Bob & Bryan Kornfield, Blake Krier, Neil Krohn, Scott Ku, Thomas Kunnecke, Gary Lambert, Matthew Lancaster (MC's Card and Hobby), Jason Lassic, Allan Latawiec, Howard Lau, Gerald A. Lavelle, Dan Lavin, Richard S. Lawrence, William Lawrence, Brent Lee, W.H. Lee, Morley Leeking, Ronald Lenhardt, Brian Lentz, Tom Leon, Leo's Sports Collectibles, Irv Lerner, Larry and Sally Levine, Lisa Licitra, James Litopoulos, Larry Loeschen (A and J Sportscards), Neil Lopez, Allan Lowenberg, Kendall Loyd (Orlando Sportscards South), Robert Luce, David Macaray, Jim Macie, Joe Maddigan, David Madison, Rob Maerten, Frank Magaha, Pierre Marceau, Paul Marchant, Jim Marsh, Rich Markus, Bob Marquette, Brad L. Marten, Ronald L. Martin, Scott Martinez, Frank J. Masi, Duane Matthes, James S. Maxwell Jr., Dr. William McAvoy, Michael McCormick, Paul McCormick, McDag Productions Inc., Tony McLaughlin, Mendal Mearkle, Carlos Medina, Ken Melanson, William Mendel, Eric Meredith, Blake Meyer (Lone Star Sportscards), Tim Meyer, Joe Michalowicz, Lee Milazzo, Jimmy Milburn, Cary S. Miller, David (Otis) Miller, Eldon Miller, George Miller, Wayne Miller, Dick

Millerd, Mitchell's Baseball Cards, Perry Miyashita, Douglas Mo, John Morales, William Munn, Mark Murphy, John Musacchio, Robert Nappe, National Sportscard Exchange, Roger Neufeldt, Bud Obermeyer, Francisco Ochoa, John O'Hara, Glenn Olson, Mike Orth, Ron Oser, Luther Owen, Earle Parrish, Clay Pasternack, Mickey Payne, Michael Perrotta, Doug and Zachary Perry, Tom Pfirrmann, Bob Pirro, George Pollitt, Don Prestia, Coy Priest, Loran Pulver, Bob Ragonese, Richard H. Ranck, Bryan Rappaport, Robert M. Ray, R.W. Ray, Phil Regli, Tom Reid, Glenn Renick, Rob Resnick, John Revell, Carson Ritchey, Bill Rodman, Craig Roehrig, David H. Rogers, Michael H. Rosen, Martin Rotunno, Michael Runyan, Mark Rush, George Rusnak, Mark Russell, Terry Sack, Joe Sak, Jennifer Salems, Barry Sanders, Everett Sands, Jon Sands, Tony Scarpa, John Schad, Dave Schau (Baseball Cards), Bruce M. Schwartz, Keith A. Schwartz, Charlie Seaver, Tom Shanyfelt, Steven C. Sharek, Eddie Silard, Art Smith, Ben Smith, Michael Smith, Jerry Sorice, Don Spagnolo, Carl Specht, Sports Card Fan-Attic, The Sport Hobbyist, Dauer Stackpole, Norm Stapleton, Bill Steinberg, Bob Stern, Lisa Stellato, Jason Stern, Andy Stoltz, Bill Stone, Tim Strandberg (East Texas Sports Cards), Edward Strauss, Strike Three, Richard Strobino, Superior Sport Card, Dr. Richard Swales, Paul Taglione, George Tahinos, Ian Taylor, Lyle Telfer, The Thirdhand Shoppe, Scott A. Thomas, Paul Thornton, Carl N. Thrower, Jim Thurtell, John Tomko, Bud Tompkins (Minnesota Connection), Philip J. Tremont, Ralph Triplette, Mike Trotta, Umpire's Choice Inc., Eric Unglaub, Hoyt Vanderpool, Rob Veres, Nathan Voss, Steven Wagman, Jonathan Waldman, Terry Walker, T. Wall, Gary A. Walter, Mark Weber, Joe and John Weisenburger (The Wise Guys), Brian Wentz, Richard West, Mike Wheat, Richard Wiercinski, Don Williams (Robin's Nest of Dolls), Jeff Williams, John Williams, Kent Williams, Craig Williamson, Opry Winston, Brandon Witz, Rich Wojtasick, John Wolf Jr., Jay Wolt (Cavalcade of Sports), Carl Womack, Pete Wooten, Peter Yee, Wes Young, Dean Zindler, Mark Zubrensky and Tim Zwick.

Every year we make active solicitations for expert input. We are particularly appreciative of help (however extensive or cursory) provided for this volume. We receive many inquiries, comments and questions regarding material within this book. In fact, each and every one is read and digested. Time constraints, however, prevent us from personally replying. But keep sharing your knowledge. Your letters and input are part of the "big picture" of hobby information we can pass along to readers in our books and magazines. Even though we cannot respond to each letter, you are making significant contributions to the hobby through your interest and comments.

The effort to continually refine and improve this book also involves a growing number of people and types of expertise on our home team. Our company boasts a substantial Sports Data Publishing team, which strengthens our ability to provide comprehensive analysis of the marketplace. SDP capably handled numerous technical details and provided able assistance in the preparation of this edition.

Our baseball analysts played a major part in compiling this year's book, traveling thousands of miles during the past year to attend sports card shows and visit card shops around the United States and Canada. The Beckett baseball specialists are Randy Barning, Theo Chen (Assistant Manager, Hobby Information), Ben Ecklar, Mike Jaspersen, Rich Klein and Grant Sandground (Senior Price Guide Editor). Their pricing analysis and careful proofreading were key contributions to the accuracy of this annual.

Grant Sandground's coordination and reconciling of prices as Beckett Baseball Card Monthly Price Guide Editor helped immeasurably. Rich Klein, as

research analyst, contributed detailed pricing analysis and hours of proofing. They were ably assisted by Jeany Finch and Beverly Mills, who helped enter new sets and pricing information, and ably handled administration of our contributor Price Guide surveys. Card librarian Gabriel Rangel handled the ever-growing quantity of cards we need organized for efforts such as this.

The effort was led by SDP Senior Manager Pepper Hastings and Manager of Technical Services Dan Hitt. They were ably assisted by the rest of the Price Guide analysts: Pat Blandford, Steven Judd, Eddie Kelly, Allan Muir, Rob Springs and William Sutherland.

The price gathering and analytical talents of this fine group of hobbyists have helped make our Beckett team stronger, while making this guide and its companion monthly Price Guide more widely recognized as the hobby's most reliable and relied upon sources of pricing information.

The IS (Information Services) department, ably headed by Mark Harwell, played a critical role in technology. Working with software designed by assistant manager David Schneider and Eric Best, they spent countless hours programming, testing, and implementing it to simplify the handling of thousands of prices that must be checked and updated for each edition.

In the Production Department, Paul Kerutis and Marlon DePaula were responsible for the typesetting and for the card photos you see throughout the book.

Loretta Gibbs spent tireless hours on the phone attending to the wishes of our dealer advertisers. Once the ad specifications were delivered to our offices, Phaedra Strecher used her computer skills to turn raw copy into attractive display advertisements.

In the years since this guide debuted, Beckett Publications has grown beyond any rational expectation. A great many talented and hard working individuals have been instrumental in this growth and success. Our whole team is to be congratulated for what we together have accomplished. Our Beckett Publications team is led by President Jeff Amano, Vice Presidents Claire Backus and Joe Galindo, Directors Mark Harwell, Reed Poole and Dave Stock, and Senior Managers Jeff Anthony, Beth Harwell and Pepper Hastings. They are ably assisted by Pete Adauto, Dana Alecknavage, Kaye Ball, Airey Baringer, Rob Barry, Therese Bellar, Andrea Bergeron, Eric Best, Julie Binion, Louise Bird, Amy Brougher, Bob Brown, Chris Calandro, Randall Calvert, Emily Camp, Mary Campana, Cara Carmichael, Susan Catka, Jud Chappell, Albert Chavez, Marty Click, Andy Costilla, Belinda Cross, Randy Cummings, Aaron Derr, Shannon Drawe, Ryan Duckworth, Denise Ellison, Eric Evans, Barbara Faraldo, Craig Ferris, Gean Paul Figari, Carol Fowler, Mary Gonzalez-Davis, Rosanna Gonzalez-Oleachea, Duane Green, Jeff Greer, Mary Gregory, Robert Gregory, Jenifer Grellhesl, Julie Grove, Tracy Hackler, Patti Harris, Steve Harris, Mark Hartley, Joanna Hayden, Chris Hellem, Melissa Herzog, Julia Jernigan, Wendy Kizer, Gayle Klancnik, Rudy J. Klancnik, Brian Kosley, Tom Layberger, Jane Ann Layton, Sara Leeman, Benedito Leme, Lori Lindsey, Stanley Lira, Kirk Lockhart, Sara Maneval, Louis Marroquin, John Marshall, Mike McAllister, Teri McGahey, Matt McGuire, Omar Mediano, Lisa McQuilkin Monaghan, Sherry Monday, Mila Morante, Daniel Moscoso Jr., Mike Moss, Randy Mosty, Hugh Murphy, Shawn Murphy, Mike Obert, Stacy Olivieri, Lisa O'Neill, Clark Palomino, Mike Pagel, Wendy Pallugna, Laura Patterson, Mike Payne, Tim Polzer, Will Pry, Bob Richardson, Tina Riojas, Lisa Runyon, Susan Sainz, David Schneider, Christine Seibert, Brett Setter, Len Shelton, Dave Sliepka, Judi Smalling, Sheri Smith, Jeff Stanton, Margaret Steele, Marcia Stoesz, Dawn Sturgeon, Doree Tate, Jim Tereschuk, Doug Williams, Steve Wilson, Bryan Winstead and Mark Zeske. The whole Beckett Publications team has my thanks for jobs well done. Thank you, everyone.

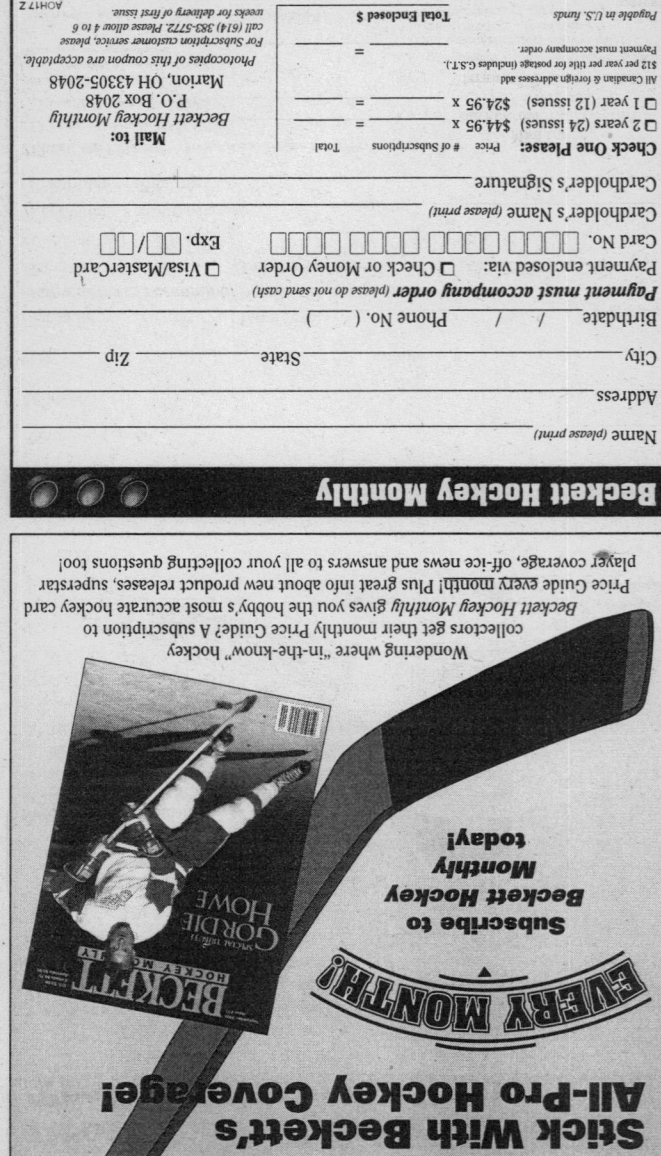

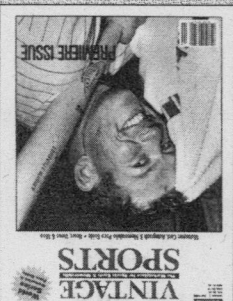

NOTES